KU-535-308

Longman Concise English Dictionary

Longman Concise English Dictionary

Longman Group Limited,
Longman House, Burnt Mill, Harlow,
Essex CM20 2JE, England
and Associated Companies throughout the world.

First published 1985

Longman concise English dictionary.
1. English language—Dictionaries
423 PE1625

ISBN 0-582-89244-9

Set in Videocomp Times and Univers

Printed in Great Britain
at The Bath Press, Avon

Contents

Foreword *page* ix
Preface x
Explanatory chart xiii
Explanatory chart – pronunciations xv
How to use this Dictionary xvi

The Dictionary 1–1623

Foreign Phrases 1624
Abbreviations 1630

Abbreviations used in this Dictionary 1649
Pronunciation symbols used in this Dictionary 1651

Editor-in-Chief

Paul Procter

Managing Editor

John Ayto

Senior Research Editor

Janet Whitcut

Text Processing Manager

Ken Moore

Etymology Editor

Brian O'Kill

Pronunciation Editor

Beverley Britton

Lexicographers

Timothy Burton
Faye Carney
Roger Cohen
Norman Gill
Anne Gilpin
Christine Hatt
Malcolm Jones
Robin Mann
Yvonne O'Leary
Sarah Overton
Katherine Seed
Penelope Stock
Paul Surzyn

Publishing

Sheila Dallas
Anna Hodson
Kathy Rooney

Clerical Staff

Melanie Ashurst
Ann Brown
Carol Buckley
Joyce Nairn
Elaine Roberts
Ursula Springham

Computer Systems

Christine Barnes
Kent Barnett
Thom Sewell

Keyboarders

Bob Cole
Jan Hulston
Barbara Mansergh
Robert Mansergh
Steven Parish

Picture Research

Carolyn Fisher
Sidney Johnson
Andrea Moore

Administration and Design

Catharine Freer
Pat Hill
Arthur Lockwood
Clive McKeough
Linda O'Donnell
Paul Price-Smith
Ruth Swan

Illustrators

Richard Bonson
Ray Burrows
Vincent Driver
Gordon Cramp Studios
Illustra Design Ltd
Kathleen King
Oxford Illustrators Ltd
Ken Stott
Carole Vincer
Robert Wheeler

The publishers are indebted to other past and present members of the Longman Lexicographic Unit for their contribution to the dictionary, including particularly Robert F. Ilson, James Clarke, James Coakley, David Fairlamb, Heather Gay, Sean O'Boyle, Ellayne Parker, and Margaret Penney. In addition, they wish to express their thanks to the following: for editorial assistance, Peter Adams, Barbara Burge, Jacky Billington, Valerie Dudley, Susan Engineer, Bonnie Hearn, Sylvia Mansfield; for assistance with pronunciations, Philip Brew, Gordon Walsh, Vera Grant, Cliff Waterman, and the BBC Pronunciation Unit; and for assistance with etymologies, John Clark, Peter Davies, Anthony Neale, Margaret Procter, Eva Wagner, and Hazel Wright.

We would like to acknowledge the services of the panel of eminent linguists who have provided invaluable guidance in the compilation of Longman dictionaries:

Chairman

Professor Sir Randolph Quirk

Louis Alexander
Professor Dwight Bolinger
Professor Christopher Candlin
Reg Close
Professor David Crystal
Professor A C Gimson
Denis Girard
Dr Philip Johnson-Laird
Professor Geoffrey Leech
Professor John Lyons
Philip J Scholefield
Professor Barbara Strang
Professor Jan Svartvik
Dr Walter Voigt
Owen Watson
David Wilkins
Professor Yorick Wilks

Our gratitude is due also to the members of the Longman Advisory Board, who have given generously of their advice, encouragement, and constructive criticism of various matters relating to the compilation and presentation of dictionaries that we have laid before them:

Chairman

Lord Briggs

Melvyn Bragg
Alan Brien
Ernestine Carter
Sir Frederick Dainton
Bernard Dixon
Derek Dougan
Clement Freud
Professor L C B Gower
Germaine Greer
John Gross
Professor S M Hall
Antony Hopkins
Clive Jenkins
Elizabeth Jennings
Professor Frank Kermode
Dr R D Laing
Professor Peter Lasko
Sir Jack Longland
George Melly
Mike Molloy
Dipak Nandy
Anne Nightingale
Michael O'Donnell
Professor Sir Randolph Quirk
Dr John Robinson
Audrey Slaughter
Janet Street-Porter
John Treasure
Jeff Wayne

Consultants

The compilers have made extensive use of consultants to ensure the accuracy of the dictionary's definitions and illustrations ◉, and would like to express their thanks to the following:

Aeronautics

Dr R Hiller,
Imperial College of Science and Technology, London

Agriculture

Dr E J Evans,
Department of Agriculture, University of Newcastle upon Tyne

Frank H Garner,
Formerly Lecturer in Agriculture, Cambridge, and Principal of the Royal Agricultural College, Cirencester

Dr Peter Rowlinson,
Department of Agriculture, University of Newcastle upon Tyne

Aircraft

◉ Mark Hewish

Alphabets

Geoffrey Sampson,
University of Lancaster

Anatomy

Dr Keith Thompson

Anthropology

R Angus Downie

Architecture

R H Franks, ARIBA,
Senior Lecturer, Polytechnic of North London

◉ Tony Aldous

Arts and Crafts

Frank Hilton

Astronomy

◉ Nigel Henbest

British History

◉ Sidney Johnson

Building

David Bringloe, MSc Dip Arch ARIBA

Building Science

C R Bassett, FCIOB,
Formerly Principal Lecturer, Guildford County College of Technology

Botany

Dr C J Humphries,
British Museum (Natural History)

Camera

◉ Trevor Clifford

Car

◉ Leonard Setwright

Commerce

Alison Farrow

Gordon Heald

Clothing

Ernestine Carter, OBE

Ann Thomas

Civil Engineering

Professor W Fisher Cassie,
University of Newcastle upon Tyne

Dancing

John Allen

Dentistry

Professor Malcolm Harris,
Institute of Dental Surgery, University of London

Domestic Science

Annette Thomas

Economics

Mr D Deadman,
University of Leicester

Education

Professor Roy Niblett,
Formerly Dean, University of London, Institute of Education

Electrical Engineering

Dr A R Bean

Energy

◉ Ian Breach,
Current Affairs, Tyne Tees Television

Entomology

Dr J D Bradley,
Commonwealth Institute of Entomology, London

Evolution

◉ Dr Brian Rosen,
British Museum (Natural History)

Firearms

Colin Hayes

Food and Drink

Elma McLean,
Essex Education Authority

Forestry

Professor F T Last,
Institute of Terrestrial Ecology, Penicuik, Midlothian

Geography

◉ Derek Weber,
The Geographical Magazine

◉ Iain Bain,
The Geographical Magazine

Glass and Ceramics

Geoffrey Payton

Horse-riding

Bridget Hamilton

Kate Reddick

Hunting and Fishing

Dr William B Currie,
Edinburgh Language Foundation

History

L E Snellgrove

Industrial Relations

Dr S R Hill,
London School of Economics

Insurance

A G Andrusier,
Director, Sheldon Monk & Co Ltd, Insurance Brokers

Journalism

Bob James,
Westminster Press, London

Law

◉ Professor Laurence Gower,
Formerly Vice-Chancellor, University of Southampton

Law, Scottish

◉ Dr Robert Burgess,
University of East Anglia

Linguistics

R Angus Downie

Mechanical Engineering

Rayner Joel,
BSc(Eng) CEng FIMechE FIMarE

Meats, cuts of

◉ Clement Freud, MP

◉ Robert Tyler,
Meat Industry Consultancy Associates

Metallurgy

Professor J G Ball,
Imperial College of Science and Technology, London

Meteorology

R P W Lewis,
Meteorological Office

Military Ranks

◉ David Bradley,
National Military Museum

◉ Nigel Der Lee,
Royal Military Academy,
Sandhurst

Mineralogy

M P Jones,
Mineral Resources Engineering Department, Imperial College of Science and Technology, London

Mining

Dr John Stocks,
Royal School of Mines, London

Motoring

Rayner Joel

Music

Peter Holman

◉ Rosalyn Asher

Nautical Terms

Gordon Fairley,
Royal Yachting Association

Numbers

David Walker,
Simon Balle School, Hertford

Pharmacy

V Osbourne, MPS,
The Boots Company Ltd,
Nottingham

Dr M A Simmonds,
The School of Pharmacy,
University of London

Political Science

D M Shapiro,
Reader in Government, Brunel University

Printing

Walter Partridge

Psychology

Dr H G Procter,
Senior Clinical Psychologist,
Southwood House, Bridgwater,
Somerset

Railways

D W Peacock, BSc CEng,
British Railways Research Dept (Retd)

Scouting

Anthony Eyre

Sports

Norman Barrett, MA

John Goodbody

Andrew F Wilson

Stamp and Coin Collecting

James A Mackay,
Numismatic and Philatelic Columnist of the *Financial Times*

Statistics

◉ Dr David Jones

Telecommunications

◉ Derek Wilson,
British Telecom

◉ Barry Fox

Television

◉ Michael Hallet,
IBA Broadcasting Galleries

◉ John Campbell McKeller,
Philips, Croydon

◉ Alan Kilkenny,
Sony (UK) Ltd

Textiles

Dr E Dyson,
Reader in Textile Engineering,
University of Bradford

Theatre

Professor John Allen OBE,
Visiting Professor of Drama,
Westfield College, University of London

Tobacco

J W Drummond,
British-American Tobacco Company Ltd, London

Transport

Peter Levy

Video

◉ Barry Fox

Weights and Measures

◉ David Walker,
Simon Balle School, Hertford

World History

◉ Sidney Johnson

Zoology

Dr Ian Bishop

Australian English

Dr J R L Bernard,
Macquarie University

Canadian English

Walter S Avis, BA MA PhD,
Professor of English and Dean,
Canadian Forces Military College, Royal Military College of Canada, Kingston, Ontario

New Zealand English

C C Bowley,
University of Auckland

Scottish English

Professor Tom McArthur,
Université du Québec

South African English

Pieter D Williams,
Department of English,
University of the Orange Free State

We are grateful also to the following organizations, who have provided us with information:

British Aerospace

British Telecom

Ford Motor Company

IBA Broadcasting Galleries

Olympus Optical Co Ltd

Philips, Croydon

Sony (UK) Ltd

Thorn EMI Video Programmes Ltd

Foreword

by Professor Sir Randolph Quirk

For me, the publication of any new dictionary provides interest and pleasure. This should indeed be true for *anyone* who loves the English language, who takes pride in the way it is used, and who takes pride also in the world leadership in the art of dictionary-making exerted by English-speaking lexicographers.

But the present occasion is one of special pleasure and excitement. The skilled team of lexicographers at Longman (the firm which published Johnson's Dictionary in 1755) have addressed themselves to the task of producing a dictionary specially designed for that most unspecialized readership, *the family*. There are of course many excellent dictionaries which seek to cater for this public. But the Longman team have given a great deal of original thought, and have conducted a good deal of original research, to ensure that they have the best technique of presentation, the best selection of words and meanings, the best and most informative modes of definition, explanation, and illustration.

To the arduous nature of such fundamental inquiry, I can personally testify, as the chairman of the linguistic advisory group that has been privileged to discuss these issues with the Longman team and to offer help, guidance, and criticism. But many of the admirable features of this dictionary have proceeded from advances in computational technology, to the potential of which the Longman Group have been quite exceptionally alert. In consequence, users will find, as they move from word to word, a far higher degree of consistency in treatment than they have been accustomed to; a solid defence against circularity of definition; a guarantee that all appropriate cross-references have indeed been provided.

The general introduction explains the special features in more detail. My happy task is merely to congratulate the team on a magnificent achievement.

Randolph Quirk
Vice-Chancellor, University of London, 1985 (formerly Quain Professor of English Language and Literature, University College London)

Preface

In 1755, Longman published Dr Johnson's *Dictionary of the English Language*. In the two hundred or so years since then, English has changed considerably, and branched off down some pathways Johnson could never have anticipated, but the underlying characteristics and processes of language that he attempted to classify and describe remain much the same today as in the eighteenth century: a continuing challenge to the art and science of the lexicographer.

With the rapid expansion of science and technology, the vocabulary of English is growing more quickly and exuberantly than at any time in its history. There are simply more words about nowadays than ever there were in the past, and in order to be able to cope with the complexities of late 20th-century life, and understand the messages that are streaming towards us from all sides, we need an up-to-date, reliable, and straightforward guidebook. That is what the editors of this dictionary have attempted to provide: a reference work that gathers together over 70000 current English words and expressions, from wherever in the world the language is spoken, gives a clear and concise account of their meanings, and offers guidance on the way in which they are used and pronounced.

How have we gone about ensuring that this dictionary is as comprehensive and as useful as possible? I spoke above of the art and science of lexicography: much of the science lies in the collection of evidence about the language, and much of the art in the interpretation of that evidence and in the use of it to create lucid dictionary definitions. No single person could carry in his or her head all the myriad new terms spawned every year in all the various fields of human endeavour, let alone recall them at will; so the lexicographer must collect data. In order to compile this dictionary, we set up an extensive reading programme of current books, periodicals, and newspapers, searching for new words and new meanings of old words. The file of examples of words in context that we have accumulated, which numbers in excess of half a million, enables us to make authoritative statements about the current state of the language over a broad spectrum of subject areas, from biochemistry and computing to the cinema and cricket. As the map on p xi indicates, we have gathered our evidence from all over the British Isles, and from wherever else in the world English is spoken as a first language.

Once the data has been gathered, it must be interpreted and put into a convenient form for you, the user of the dictionary. This is the art of the lexicographer: to condense and codify the confusing babble of words that fly about our heads every day into an understandable and easily used work of reference.

How is it all done? Well of course no dictionary-maker nowadays starts completely from scratch. In this sense all lexicographers are standing on giants' shoulders, using the basic common core of the language, which has been amply recorded in the past, as the starting-off point for their labours. And the information that has been accumulated about changes in the language is the cue to depart from that point.

For example, the lexicographer working on the word *acrobatic* for this dictionary, which in all other dictionaries is defined in very general terms simply as 'of or relating to an acrobat', found this example of its use by Tina Brown in *Punch* (February 1976):

> 'The hero still wields a low, mocking laugh and vertiginously acrobatic eyebrows.'

On the basis of this and other evidence, she was able to record a new meaning of *acrobatic*, 'very mobile', and illustrate it with the *Punch* quotation.

Another editor, working on the word *bottle*, had these examples available to her:

> 'Once I stole a jar of Brylcream [sic] from the tuck shop. But I didn't have the bottle to carry it through. In the end I took it back again.'
>
> Nik Cohn, *Rolling Stone* (July 1973)

> 'Soft, that's what they are. They pay them too much. Kids of 14 with money in their pocket instead of a steel comb. Stands to reason they ain't got no bottle . . . Know what I mean?'
>
> Llew Gardner, *The Listener* (June 1974)

> 'In its 150-year existence, the Metropolitan Police has developed its own group loyalties, inbred customs and language. With the helmet that passes from father to son, goes a demotic inheritance: "We were mobhanded in the nondescript and chummy's bottle went and we felt his collar" (A number of us were in the unmarked car together and the suspect lost his nerve and we arrested him).'
>
> Michael Cockerell, *The Listener* (February 1975)

> 'I simply was not born with the right amount of what is known in cockney circles as bottle. Downright nerve, in other words.'
>
> Christopher Matthew, *Punch* (October 1976)

> 'To their critics, their [West Ham's] failures have not been down to their refusal to kick their way to the top, but to lacking the character, the 'bottle' to make their skill count.'
>
> *Time Out* (May 1980)

Some sources used in compiling the dictionary

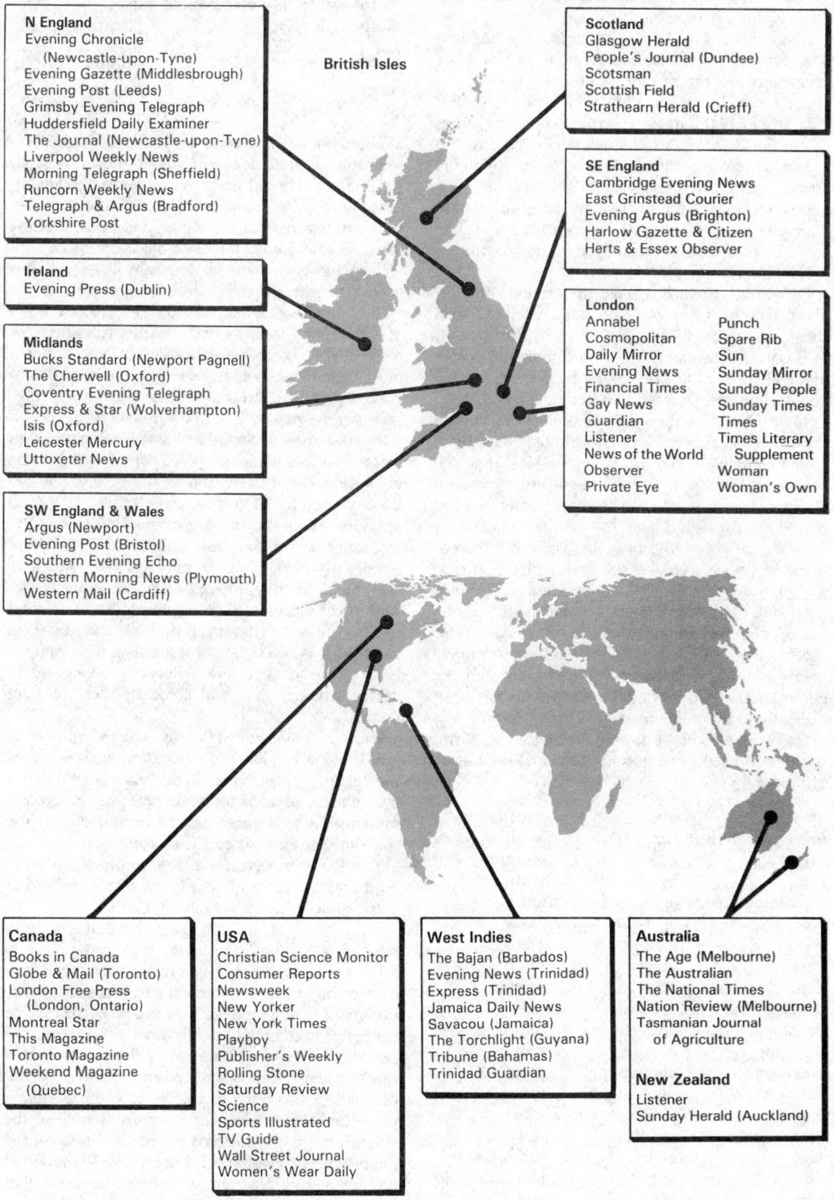

British Isles

N England
Evening Chronicle (Newcastle-upon-Tyne)
Evening Gazette (Middlesbrough)
Evening Post (Leeds)
Grimsby Evening Telegraph
Huddersfield Daily Examiner
The Journal (Newcastle-upon-Tyne)
Liverpool Weekly News
Morning Telegraph (Sheffield)
Runcorn Weekly News
Telegraph & Argus (Bradford)
Yorkshire Post

Ireland
Evening Press (Dublin)

Midlands
Bucks Standard (Newport Pagnell)
The Cherwell (Oxford)
Coventry Evening Telegraph
Express & Star (Wolverhampton)
Isis (Oxford)
Leicester Mercury
Uttoxeter News

SW England & Wales
Argus (Newport)
Evening Post (Bristol)
Southern Evening Echo
Western Morning News (Plymouth)
Western Mail (Cardiff)

Scotland
Glasgow Herald
People's Journal (Dundee)
Scotsman
Scottish Field
Strathearn Herald (Crieff)

SE England
Cambridge Evening News
East Grinstead Courier
Evening Argus (Brighton)
Harlow Gazette & Citizen
Herts & Essex Observer

London
Annabel
Cosmopolitan
Daily Mirror
Evening News
Financial Times
Gay News
Guardian
Listener
News of the World
Observer
Private Eye
Punch
Spare Rib
Sun
Sunday Mirror
Sunday People
Sunday Times
Times
Times Literary Supplement
Woman
Woman's Own

Canada
Books in Canada
Globe & Mail (Toronto)
London Free Press (London, Ontario)
Montreal Star
This Magazine
Toronto Magazine
Weekend Magazine (Quebec)

USA
Christian Science Monitor
Consumer Reports
Newsweek
New Yorker
New York Times
Playboy
Publisher's Weekly
Rolling Stone
Saturday Review
Science
Sports Illustrated
TV Guide
Wall Street Journal
Women's Wear Daily

West Indies
The Bajan (Barbados)
Evening News (Trinidad)
Express (Trinidad)
Jamaica Daily News
Savacou (Jamaica)
The Torchlight (Guyana)
Tribune (Bahamas)
Trinidad Guardian

Australia
The Age (Melbourne)
The Australian
The National Times
Nation Review (Melbourne)
Tasmanian Journal of Agriculture

New Zealand
Listener
Sunday Herald (Auckland)

These enabled her to enter the British slang meaning of *bottle*, 'nerve', which does not appear in any other dictionary of comparable size.

If one facet of the lexicographer's art is the identification of new meanings, another, and perhaps even more important one, is the writing of clear, understandable, and unambiguous definitions. We have striven in this dictionary to make the meanings of the 50000 words we define as accessible to the user as is possible within what is, in lexicographic terms, a fairly limited scope. We have avoided overly technical terms where we can, and where their use is unavoidable we have ensured that they are in their turn clearly defined at their own entry in the dictionary.

Of course, in such a huge undertaking few individual human beings could hope to apply such standards with absolute consistency throughout. This is where the technology of the computer comes to the aid of the art of lexicography. Longman have devised a unique processing system that has enabled us to perform a number of automated operations on the dictionary that previously could only have been done manually, with much labour and less than 100 per cent accuracy, or indeed might not have been attempted at all. Among the tasks the computer has performed for us has been the monitoring of every word we have used in definitions. This has involved, in the first place, a cross check against all the entries, to make sure that every word used in a definition is itself defined in the dictionary and in the second place, a careful examination of all vocabulary items used in definitions in over 180 different subject areas, ensuring consistency of treatment and the elimination of words that would present too great difficulty to the non-expert.

For example, the following 80 specialized terms have been used in definitions of words relating to photography:

aperture	iris	screen
black-and-white	lamp	sensitive
bright	lens	sensitivity
camera	light	sensitized
cinematographic	lightproof	setting
colour	light-sensitive	shade
contrast	mounted	shadow
dark	moving	sharp
darkroom	negative	shutter
develop	opaque	silver
development	optical	slides
diaphragm	paper	sodium
emulsion	photograph	spectrum
enlargement	photographic	speed
expose	photography	spool
exposure	picture	still
fast	plate	subject
filter	positive	take
film	print	television
fixing	projector	tones
flashbulb	radiation	transparency
flashlight	rays	transparent
f number	reflected	view
focus	reflection	viewfinder
ground glass	reproduce	wide-angle
hand-held	reproduction	zoom
image	safelight	

Of these, the most common are:

photographic	48	occurrences	light	12
photograph	29		picture	12
film	22		plate	12
camera	20		print	11
image	16		negative	10
lens	16		photography	9

Technology in the service of art. For although lexicography is fundamentally about the exercise of judgment, it should never be subjective judgment unsupported by evidence. The definition-writer's skill, of teasing out meanings and encapsulating them elegantly and concisely, must always be subject to the corrective of linguistic fact. And this holds true just as much in the area of usage as in the area of meaning. We do not see it as part of the job of a dictionary to propound arbitrary rules for 'correct English' based on yesterday's usage; rather it must be a dispassionate observer and recorder of current linguistic trends. This stance should not, however, be viewed as an abdication of the responsibility to inform: for opinions on the 'correctness' of certain words and meanings are part of the linguistic facts about those words and meanings, and this dictionary attempts to give an accurate record of such opinions where they are widespread. For example, we note that the meaning 'uninterested' for *disinterested* (which in fact predates the meaning 'unbiased') is 'disapproved of by some speakers'. This is not a prescriptive dictionary; but it does set out to describe the prescriptions that exist in English. It is and must always remain the responsibility of the speakers and writers of the language to decide whether they will abide by them or flout them.

Recognizing the need to give clear and up-to-date guidance on English pronunciation, we have, with the help of market research, devised a system that is a significant advance over previous ones in its comprehensibility. It relies almost exclusively on the spelling system of English, thus avoiding the unfamiliar symbols of the International Phonetic Alphabet and the confusing use of accents and other marks that change the value of a letter.

Language is always one jump ahead of lexicography; or, as Samuel Johnson more elegantly phrased it in the Preface to his Dictionary, 'there never can be wanting some . . . who will consider that no dictionary of a living tongue ever can be perfect, since while it is hastening to publication, some words are budding, and some falling away.' But it is our belief that the lexicographic and computational expertise devoted to this book enable us to claim a unique place for it as a mirror of the current state of the English language, and that the contributions of the many expert consultants listed on pp vii–viii, and of our own specialist editors, have ensured that another of Johnson's disclaimers, 'that he, whose design includes whatever language can express, must often speak of what he does not understand', need no longer be made.

John Ayto

Explanatory chart

Numbers in brackets refer to paragraphs in the guide to the dictionary (pp xvi–xxvi).

angle brackets enclosing an example of an entry used in context **(7)**

aah /ah *often prolonged*/ *vi* to exclaim in amazement, joy, or surprise [<*oohing and* ~ing>]

capitalization (5)

academy /əˈkadəmi/ *n* **1** [*cap*] **a** the school for advanced education founded by Plato **b** the philosophical doctrines associated with Plato's Academy

usage note indicating the phrase (**collocation**) in which a verb frequently appears **(8.5)**

acquiesce /ˌakweeˈes/ *vi* to submit or comply tacitly or passively [— often + *in*]

usage note indicating the phrase (**collocation**) in which an entry is frequently found **(8.5)**

adrift /əˈdrift/ *adv or adj* **1** afloat without motive power or mooring and at the mercy of winds and currents **2** in or into a state of being unstuck or unfastened [— esp in *come adrift*]

arrow indicating the part of speech formed when a **combining form** is added to a word or word part **(10)**

-agogue /-əgog/ *comb form* [(→*n*)] **1** substance that promotes the secretion or expulsion of <*emmen*agogue> **2** leader, guide <*peda*gogue> — sometimes derog <*dem*agogue>

cross-reference recommending the user to look up a related entry **(9)**

agranulocyte /ayˈgranyooləˌsiet/ *n* any of various white blood cells with cytoplasm that does not contain conspicuous granules [— compare GRANULOCYTE]

italicized **definite article** indicating that an entry is always preceded by *the* **(8.5)**

alternative society *n* [*the*] group of people who reject conventional social institutions, practices, and values in favour of a lifestyle based esp on communal ownership and self-sufficiency — compare COUNTERCULTURE

etymology showing history of an entry **(12)**

anabatic /ˌanəˈbatik/ *adj* moving upwards <*an* ~ *wind*> [[*Gk anabatos*, verbal of *anabainein* to go up or inland, fr *ana-* + *bainein* to go]]

example showing an entry used in a typical context **(7)**

antebellum /ˌantiˈbeləm/ *adj* existing before the war, esp the US Civil War [<*an* ~ *brick mansion*>]

example consisting of an illustrative quotation showing the use of an entry in an actual context **(7)**

assignation /ˌasigˈnaysh(ə)n/ *n* **1** the act of assigning; *also* the assignment made **2** a meeting, esp a secret one with a lover [<*returned from an* ~ *with his mistress* — W B Yeats>]

eye symbol indicating that the entry has an accompanying illustration or table **(9)**

astronomy /əˈstronəmi/ *n* a branch of science dealing with the celestial bodies [◉]

feminine form of an entry **(2)**

author /ˈawthə/, [*fem* **authoress**] /-res, -ris/ *n* **1a** the writer of a literary work...

usage note giving **grammatical information** about an entry **(4.1)**

ˈbagˌpipe /-ˌpiep/ *n* a wind instrument consisting of a leather bag, mouth tube, chanter, and drone pipes [— often pl with sing. meaning but sing. or pl in constr]

hand symbol recommending the user to look up an illustration or table **(9)**

[3]**bail** *n* **1** either of the 2 crosspieces that lie on the stumps to form the wicket in cricket [☞ SPORT] **2** *chiefly Br* a device for confining or separating animals

homograph number (1.1)

[1] **ban** /ban/ *vt* **-nn-** to prohibit, esp by legal means or social pressure

idiom (1.3)

ˈbandˌwagon /-ˌwagən/ *n* a party, faction, or cause that attracts adherents by its timeliness, momentum, etc [[3]*band* + *wagon*] [— **jump/climb on the bandwagon** to attach oneself to a successful cause or enterprise in the hope of personal gain]

inflection (4)

[2]**barrel** *vt* [**-ll-** (*NAm* **-l-**, **-ll-**)] to put or pack in a barrel

inflectional cross-reference giving an inflected form of an entry **(9)**

blew /blooh/ [*past of* BLOW]

irregular plural (4.1)

boletus /bəˈleetəs, boh-/ *n, pl* **boletuses**, [**boleti** /-tie/] any of a genus of fleshy fungi, some of which are edible

Explanatory chart

[1]**bolshie, bolshy** /'bolshi/ *n* a Bolshevik — infml — usage note indicating the style, attitude, or level of formality of an entry **(8.3)**

main entry (1.1) — 'bolt-,hole *n* **1** a hole into which an animal runs for safety **2** a means of rapid escape or place of refuge

object of a verb **(6.3)** — [2]**bond** *vt* **1** to overlap (eg bricks) for solidity of construction **2** to put (goods) in bond until duties and taxes are paid

part of speech (3) — [1]**bone** /bohn/ *n* **1a** (any of the hard body structures composed of) the largely calcium-containing connective tissue of which the adult skeleton of most vertebrate animals is chiefly composed ☞ ANATOMY . . .

two **parts of speech** shown in combination **(3)** — [1]**bop** /bop/ *vt or n* **-pp-** (to strike with) a blow (eg of the fist) — infml

bottom drawer *n, Br* (a drawer for storing) a young woman's collection of clothes and esp household articles, kept in anticipation of her marriage — **regional label,** in this case indicating that the entry is used only in British English **(8.2)**

undefined **run-on** entry **(1.2)** — **cacophony** /kə'kofəni/ *n* harsh or discordant sound; dissonance . . . — **cacophonous** *adj*

caff /kaf/ *n, Br* CAFE 1; *esp* a cheap plain one — **sense divider (6.1)**

sense number (6.1) — **caisson** /'kays(ə)n, kə'soohn/ *n* **1** a chest or wagon for artillery ammunition **2a** a watertight chamber used for construction work under water or as a foundation **b** a float for raising a sunken vessel . . . — **sense letter (6.1)**

note indicating whether an entry takes a **singular** or **plural** verb **(4.1)** — **calends, kalends** /'kalindz/ *n pl but sing or pl in constr* the first day of the ancient Roman month . . .

[1]**call** /kawl/ . . . *vi* **1** . . . **c** *of an animal* to utter a characteristic note or cry . . . — usual/only **subject** of a verb

arrow indicating the part of speech formed when a **suffix** is added to a word or word part **(10)** — [2]**-d** *suffix* (→*vb*) — used to form the past tense of regular weak verbs that end in *e*; compare [2]-ED

[1]**daring** /'deəring/ *adj* adventurously bold in action or thought <~ *acrobats*> <~ *crimes*> — **swung dash** replacing entry in an example **(7)**

'**date,line** /-,lien/ *n* **1** a line in a written document or publication giving the date and place of composition or issue **2** INTERNATIONAL DATE LINE — **dateline** *vt* — **synonymous cross-reference** to a compound entry **(9)**

'**day,break** /-,brayk/ *n* DAWN 1 — **synonymous cross-reference** to a particular sense **(9)**

temporal label showing that the use of a word or meaning is limited to special contexts **(8.1)** — **deer** /diə/ *n, pl* **deer** *also* **deers** **1** any of several ruminant mammals of which most of the males and some of the females bear antlers **2** *archaic* an animal; *esp* a small mammal

usage note applying to more than one sense **(8)** — **dependent** /di'pend(ə)nt/ *adj* **1** determined or conditioned by another; contingent **2** relying on another for support . . . *USE (1&2) + on* or *upon*

verb entry ending in **-ize** separated by a comma from **-ise,** indicating that the two forms are **equal variants (2)** — **depersonal·ize, -ise** /,dee'puhsənl·iez/ *vt* to deprive of the sense of personal identity . . .

dermat- /duhmət-/, **dermato-** *comb form* skin <dermat*itis*> <dermato*logy*> — two entries separated by a comma indicating that they are **equal variants (2)**

diaeresis, *chiefly NAm* **dieresis** /die'iərisis/ *n, pl* **diaereses** /-,seez/ **1** a mark ¨ placed over a vowel to indicate pronunciation as a separate syllable (eg in *naïve*) . . . — **regional variant,** in this case indicating that the second form is used chiefly in the USA and Canada **(2)**

two entries separated by *also* indicating that the latter is a **secondary variant (2)** — [1]**diagnostic** /,die·əg'nostik/ *also* **diagnostical** /-kl/ *adj* of or involving diagnosis

Explanatory chart – pronunciations

oblique lines enclosing a pronunciation (**11.1.2**)

hiss /his/ *vi* . . .

pronunciation containing a **centred dot** (**11.3.4**)

¹**hire** /hie·ə/ *n* . . .

Deutsche Mark /ˈdoych͵mahk (*Ger* dɔɪtʃə mark)/ *n* . . .

foreign pronunciations (**11.8.2**)

entente /onˈtont (*Fr* ɑ̃tɑ̃t)/ *n* . . .

pronunciation containing (ə) (**11.3.2**)

honorary /ˈon(ə)rəri/ *adj* . . .

specialist pronunciation, in this case indicating that the word is pronounced differently by sailors (**11.4.3**)

¹**leeward** /ˈleewood; *naut* ˈlooh·əd/ *adj or adv* . . .

stress mark showing primary stress (**11.2.1**)

stress mark showing secondary stress (**11.2.2**)

hoodwink /ˈhood͵wingk/ *vt* . . .

stress pattern shown in compound words and phrases (**11.2.3**)

ˈhoof͵beat /-͵beet/ *n* . . .

another **stress pattern** that can be used without otherwise changing the pronunciation (**11.2.4**)

impossible /imˈposəbl/ *adj* . . . — **impossibly** *adv*, **impossibility** /im͵posəˈbiləti, ͵---ˈ---/*n*

swung dash indicating that the plural is pronounced in the same way as the singular (**11.3.5**)

hors d'oeuvre /͵aw ˈduhv (*Fr* ɔːr dœvr)/ *n*, *pl* **hors d'oeuvres** *also* **hors d'oeuvre** /ˈduhv(z) (*Fr* ~)/ . . .

two pronunciations separated by *also*, indicating that they are **variants** but that the second is less common, or is considered less correct by some speakers (**11.4.1**)

controversy /ˈkontrə͵vuhsi; *also* kənˈtrovəsi/ *n* . . .

two pronunciations separated by *often*, indicating that they are **variants** but that the second is considered incorrect by many speakers (**11.4.1**)

gypsophila /jipˈsofilə; *often* ͵jipsəˈfili·ə/ *n* . . .

lieutenant /lef'tenənt; *Royal Navy* lə'tenənt; *NAm* looh'tenənt/ *n* . . .

pronunciation showing specialist and **regional variant** (**11.4.3**)

How to use this Dictionary

1 Order of entries

1.1 Main entries

Alphabetical order of entry, letter by letter, applies to all main entries, whether they are single words, hyphenated words, or compounds consisting of two or more individual words. This means that, for example, **give away** comes between **giveaway** and **give in**.

A compound written as a single word comes before the same compound written with a hyphen, which in turn comes before the same compound written as two or more separate words; hence **rundown** precedes **run-down** and **run down**.

A main entry with a number in it comes before a main entry with a letter in the same position; so **MI5** and **MI6** come between **mi-** and **miaow**.

But main entries that *begin* with a number (eg **2, 4, 5-T**) are listed as if the number were spelt out as a word.

Main entries beginning with **Mc-** are listed as if they were spelt **Mac-;** those beginning with **St** are shown with the abbreviation spelt out as **Saint**.

Many words that share the same spelling have a different pronunciation or a different history, or are different in grammar. Such words are shown separately in this dictionary, with small numbers in front to distinguish them; see, for example, the four entries at **lead**. These words are listed in historical order, according to when they first appeared in English.

1.2 Undefined words

Words whose meaning can easily be deduced, because they consist of a base form plus an added ending, are not given definitions. These words (run-ons) are shown at the end of the definition their base form, and after the etymology, if there is one:

> **charitable** ... *adj* ... – **charitableness** *n*, **charitably** *adv*

The meaning of **charitableness** can be guessed from the meaning of **charitable** plus the meaning of the ending **-ness,** which can be found at its own place in the dictionary. Sometimes the undefined entry has the same form as its base, but a different part of speech:

> [2]**chink** *n* a short sharp sound – **chink** *vb*

This means that the verb **chink** is obviously related to the noun **chink** – 'to make, or cause to make, a short sharp sound'.

Words whose meaning can be guessed because they consist of a base form plus something added at the beginning are shown at their own place in the dictionary, but with no definition; see, for example, **indecorous** and **unabridged**.

Some words formed with beginnings and endings have a specific meaning, but also a very general one that can be guessed. For these words, the general meaning is shown in the form of an etymology:

> **airer** ... *n* ... a freestanding, usu collapsible, framework for airing or drying clothes, linen, etc [[2]AIR+[2]-ER]

This means that the noun **airer** has also a very general meaning which is the sum of the meanings of the verb **air** and the ending **-er**: 'a person or thing that airs' (see 12.7).

1.3 Idiomatic phrases

An idiom is a fixed phrase whose meaning cannot be guessed from the meanings of the individual words from which it is made up. Idioms are shown at the end of an entry, after the etymology and any derived undefined words:

> [1]**call** *vi* ... – **call a spade a spade** to speak frankly and usu bluntly

Compound verbs that end in a preposition, such as **put up with**, are treated as idioms, although those that end in an adverb, such as **give away**, are main entries.

Idioms are entered at the first meaningful word they contain. Hence **live it up** is entered at **live, on the ball** appears at **ball**, and **in spite of** is shown at **spite**. When an idiom has more than one accepted form, it is entered at the first invariable meaningful word it contains. The alternative form is shown after an oblique (/):

> [1]**seed** ... *n* ... – **go/run to seed** ...

1.4 Other entries

Abbreviations, and foreign phrases that are commonly used in English, are mostly listed in separate appendixes on pp 1630 and 1624. However, some abbreviations that are used like ordinary words, such as the noun **IOU** and the verb **KO**, and the many foreign words and phrases that have become thoroughly anglicized, such as **ad hoc** and **coup de grace**, are entered in their alphabetical places in the main body of the text.

2 Alternative versions of words

Many words come in pairs, or even trios, that may differ only in spelling (e g **judgment, judgement**), or in their ending (e g **excellence, excellency**), or even in the presence or absence of a complete word in a compound (e g **silk screen, silk screen printing**). In this dictionary, variant forms of a word are shown immediately after the main entry. When the variant is preceded by a comma, it is about as common as the main entry in current standard usage; when the variant is preceded by *also,* it is rather less common. These alternative forms are shown separately as main entries only if they fall more than ten places away from their main form in the alphabetical list.

Variant spellings of the **-ize/-ise** type are shown in abbreviated form at the main entry:

computer·ize, -ise . . . *vt*

This means that **computerize** can also be spelt **computerise.**

Feminine forms of words are shown in the same way as other variants:

author. . . *fem* **authoress** . . . *n*

Individual meanings, as well as whole main entries, can have variant forms:

excellence *n* . . . **1** . . . **2** . . . **3 Excellency, Excellence** – used as a title for certain high dignitaries (eg ambassadors)

Variant forms that are entirely or partially restricted to British or American English are labelled *Br* or *NAm*:

jail, *Br also* **gaol** . . . *n* . . .
gaol . . . *vb or n, chiefly Br* (to) jail

This means that the spelling **jail** is used everywhere in the English-speaking world, but British English also uses **gaol** (See 8.2).

If the variable part of a pair of words is shown as a main entry in its own right, then this variation is *not* shown in the entry for the word formed from it. Hence **hemorrhage**, the American variant spelling of **haemorrhage**, is not shown because **hemo-** is already entered as the American variant of **haemo-**.

3 Parts of speech

These are the various word classes to which the entries in this dictionary belong:

adj	adjective:	**energetic, durable**
adv	adverb:	**very, happily**
comb form	combining form:	**Anglo-, mal-**
conj	conjunction:	**but, insofar as**
interj	interjection:	**hey, bravo**
n	noun:	**dynamite, bird of paradise**
prefix		**pre-, trans-**
prep	preposition:	**for, according to**
pron	pronoun:	**herself, ours**
suffix		**-ful, -ness**
trademark		**Hoover, Valium**
vb	verb (both transitive and intransitive):	**agglomerate, americanize**
vb impersonal	impersonal verb:	**methinks**
verbal auxiliary		**can, must**
vi	intransitive verb:	**arise, arrive**
vt	transitive verb:	**indicate, thank**

Sometimes two parts of speech are combined:

zilch . . . *adj or n, chiefly NAm* zero
yelp . . . *vi or n* (to utter) a sharp quick shrill cry

4 Inflections

The dictionary shows inflections only if they are irregular or may cause difficulty. They are written out in full, unless they involve merely the doubling of a consonant or the change of **-c-** to **-ck-**:

[1]**swat** . . . *vt* **-tt-**
picnic . . . *vi* **-ck-**

This means that the present participle and past of **swat** are **swatting** and **swatted**, and those of **picnic** are **picnicking** and **picnicked**.

4.1 Nouns

Regular plurals of nouns (e g **cats, matches, spies**) are not shown. All other plurals (e g **louse, lice; sheep, sheep; putto, putti**) are given. Sometimes alternative plurals are possible:

salmon . . . *n, pl* **salmon**, *esp for different types* **salmons**

or a plural may have an alternative pronunciation:

[1]**bath** /bahth/ *n, pl* **baths** /bahths; *sense 3 often* bahdhz/

Some plurals are regular but might have been expected to be irregular:

coleus . . . *n, pl* **coleuses** . . .

Nouns that are always plural are shown as follows:

environs . . . *n pl* . . .

Sometimes an individual sense of a noun is exclusively plural:

[1]**victual** . . . *n* . . . **2** *pl* supplies of food; provisions

Not all plural nouns always take a plural verb. This is shown as follows:

genetics *n but sing in constr* . . .
forty winks *n pl but sing or pl in constr* . . .

This means that one says 'Genetics is . . .' but one says either 'Forty winks is . . .' or 'Forty winks are . . .'

Some nouns have no recognizable plural form, but nevertheless can take a plural verb:

police *n* . . . **2a** . . . **b** *pl in constr* policemen
silent majority *n sing or pl in constr* . . .

This means that one says 'Several police are . . .' but one says either 'The silent majority is . . .' or '. . . are . . .'

Some nouns are used with the same meaning in the plural. They are shown like this:

latitude ... *n* ... a region as marked by its latitude – often pl with sing. meaning

This means that one can say 'It's very hot at this latitude' or '... at these latitudes.'

4.2 Verbs

Regular verb forms (e g **halted, cadged, carrying**) are not shown. All other verb inflections (e g **ring, rang, rung**) are shown, including those for verbs ending in a vowel other than *-e*, for verbs which keep a final *-e* before inflections, for verbs having alternative inflections, and where a pronunciation may be irregular.

Inflections are shown in the following order:

present: 1st, 2nd, and 3rd person singular; plural; present subjunctive; present participle; past: 1st, 2nd, and 3rd person singular; plural; past subjunctive; past participle.

Only the irregular inflections are shown. Certain forms (e g the entire past tense, or the past tense and the past participle) are combined if they are identical. Thus in

[1]**run** ... *vb* **-nn-; ran; run**

the present participle is **running**, the entire past tense is **ran**, and the past participle is **run**.

Irregular American and archaic inflections are listed as separate entries in the dictionary, but are not shown at the main form of the verb.

4.3 Adjectives and adverbs

Adjectives and adverbs whose comparative and superlative are formed with **more** and **most**, or by adding **-(e)r** and **-(e)st** (e g **nicer, fastest, happier**) are not shown.

All other inflections are shown:

[1]**good** ... *adj* **better** ... **best** ...

Inflections that involve a change of pronunciation are shown:

[1]**young** /yung/ *adj* **younger** /'yung·gə/; **youngest** /'yung·gist/

So are alternative inflections:

[1]**shy** ... *adj* **shier, shyer; shiest, shyest** ...

4.4 Pronouns

Inflections of pronouns are entered at their alphabetical place in the dictionary and cross-referred to their main form, where the definition is given:

[2]**her** *pron, objective case of* SHE

5 Capitalization

Some words, or meanings of words, can be used with or without a capital letter, and we show this with the notes *often cap* and *often not cap*. In the case of compound words, the note specifies which parts are capitalized:

pop art *n, often cap P&A* ...

6 Definitions

6.1 The numbering of meanings

The main meanings of a word are numbered (**1, 2**, etc). When a numbered main meaning of a word is divided into subsenses, they are introduced by letters (**1a, b, c**, etc). Divisions of a subsense are indicated by bracketed numbers.

When a definition is followed by a colon and two or more subsenses, this indicates that the meaning of the subsenses is covered by the introductory definition.

Sometimes an introductory definition is simply the common element shared by the following subsenses:

cheapen ... *vb* to make or become **a** cheap in price or value **b** lower in esteem **c** tawdry, vulgar, or inferior

This indicates that **cheapen** means 'to make or become cheap in price and value', 'to make or become lower in esteem', and 'to make or become tawdry, vulgar, or inferior'.

When two meanings of a word are very closely related, they are not separated off with numbers or letters, but run together, with the word *esp, specif, also,* or *broadly* between them to show the way in which they are related:

aggression ... *n* ... **2** attack, encroachment; *esp* unprovoked violation by one country of the territory of another

6.2 The order of senses

Those meanings that would be understood anywhere in the English-speaking world are shown first, in their historical order: the older senses before the newer. After these come the meanings whose usage is restricted in some way (e g because they are used in only one area, or have gone out of current use).

6.3 Brackets

Round brackets are used in four main ways in definitions in this dictionary:

They enclose the object of a verb:

[2]**contract** ... *vt* ... **2a** to catch (an illness)

They give extra information:

[3]**nap** *n* a hairy or downy surface (e g on a woven fabric)

They separate the parts of a combined definition that relate to different parts of speech:

cheep ... *vi or n* (to utter) a faint shrill sound characteristic of a young bird

They enclose optional wording:

afloat ... *adj or adv* **1a** borne (as if) on the water or air

This indicates that **afloat** means both 'borne on the water or air' and 'borne as if on the water or air'.

6.4 Descriptive accounts

Sometimes, instead of giving a definition, the dictionary describes how a word is used:

> [2]**after** *prep* ... **3** – used to indicate the goal or purpose of an action **<***go ~ gold***>**

Trademarked terms too are treated in this way

> **Hoover** ... *trademark* – used for a vacuum cleaner

7 Examples

Definitions, particularly of words with several senses, may be followed by a phrase or sentence illustrating a typical use of the word in context. Many of these are actual quotations from a written, or spoken, source; in such cases the author or source is named.

Examples are printed in italics between angle brackets (**< >**). Occasionally the word being illustrated is written out in full, but usually it is represented by a swung dash (~). When an inflected form of the main entry is being illustrated, it is usually shown by a swung dash followed by the inflection:

> [1]**dare** ... *vt* to confront boldly; defy **<**~ d *the anger of her family***>**

The complete example is therefore 'dared the anger of her family'.

8 Usage

There is more to a complete description of a word than a definition of its meaning; many words have peculiarities of usage that a dictionary must take account of. They may be restricted to a particular geographical area; they may be colloquial or slang, or felt to be 'incorrect'; they may have fallen out of use; and there may be limitations on the sort of context they can be used in.

This dictionary shows such restrictions in two different ways. Words, or meanings, that are limited to a particular period or area are identified by an italic label:

> **fain** *adv, archaic* **1** with pleasure ...
> **howff** ... *n, Scot* a haunt, resort; *esp* a pub

When an italic label comes between the main entry and the first definition it refers to all meanings of the word; otherwise, it applies to all subsenses of the number or letter it follows.

All other information on usage is given in a note at the end of a definition:

> **tootsy** ... *n* FOOT 1 – used chiefly to children

When such a note applies to all or several meanings of a word, it follows the last definition, and is introduced by the word ***USE***.

8.1 Words that are no longer in current use

The label *obs* for 'obsolete' means there is no evidence of use for a word or meaning since 1755 (the date of publication of Samuel Johnson's Dictionary); this label is a comment on the word being defined, not on the thing it designates.

The label *archaic* means that a word or meaning once in common use is found today only in special contexts, such as poetry or historical fiction, where it is used to introduce a flavour of the past.

Some of the more common archaisms that tend to linger on in poetic diction are treated more explicitly by means of a note:

> **e'en** ... *adv* even – chiefly poetic

The same treatment is given to comparatively modern terms which have become old-fashioned because they belong to rapidly changing areas of vocabulary such as science and technology, or casual everyday speech:

> **matron** ... *n* ... **3** a woman in charge of the nursing in a hospital – not now used technically
> **cripes** ... *interj, Br* – used to express surprise; no longer in vogue

8.2 Words that are not used throughout the English-speaking world

A word or sense limited in use to one or more of the countries of the English-speaking world is labelled accordingly:

> [3]**crook** *adj, Austr & NZ* **1** ill, sick ...

The label *Br* indicates that a word or meaning is used in Britain and also usually the Commonwealth countries of Australasia. The label *NAm* indicates the use of a word or meaning in both the USA and Canada.

A word or meaning whose use is limited to a particular part of Britain, or occasionally of the USA, is labelled accordingly:

> [2]**hinny** ... *n, Scot & N Eng* DEAR 1b
> **you-'all** *pron, chiefly S US* you

The label *dial* for 'dialect' indicates that a word or meaning belongs to the common local speech of several different places.

8.3 Words that suggest a particular style, attitude, or level of formality

Most English words can be generally used in both speech and writing, but some would be traditionally described as 'colloquial' or 'slang', and others, perhaps, as 'formal'.

Words of this sort are identified by notes at the end of definitions. It is always hard to apply such descriptions consistently, since the status of these words is constantly shifting with the passage of time, and they are also frequently used in an incongruous setting for stylistic effect.

The note '—infml' is used for words or senses that are characteristic of conversational speech and casual writing (e g between friends and contemporaries) rather than of official or 'serious' speech or writing.

The note '—slang' is used for words or meanings found in contexts of extreme informality. Such words may be, or may have been until recently, used by a particular social group such as criminals or drug users. They often refer to topics that are thought of as risqué or 'low'.

At the opposite end of the scale, the note '—fml', for 'formal', is used for words or meanings characteristic of written rather than spoken English, and particularly of official or academic writings.

Some notes describe the attitude or tone of the user of a word:

egghead . . . *n* an intellectual, highbrow – derog or humor

pass away *vi* . . . **2** to die – euph

8.4 Words that are not 'correct'

It is not the role of a responsible modern dictionary to dictate usage; it can only make statements, based on reference to a large stock of spoken and written data, about how a word is being used by the community at large. It can always warn the dictionary user that a use of a word is likely to arouse controversy or disapproval. Many people would disapprove of the use of some of the words we have described as 'slang' or 'informal', and there are of course many contexts in which their use would be quite inappropriate; but there is a further distinct class of words that are generally felt to be 'incorrect'.

The note '– nonstandard' is used for words or meanings that are quite commonly used in standard English but are considered incorrect by many speakers:

flaunt . . . *vt* . . . **2** to flout – nonstandard

Certain highly controversial words or meanings have the warning note '– disapproved of by some speakers':

disinterested *adj* **1** uninterested – disapproved of by some speakers

The note '– substandard' is used for words or meanings that are widely used but are not part of standard English:

learn . . . *vb* . . . **2** to teach – substandard

8.5 The context in which a word can appear

Many words or meanings can be used only in certain contexts within a sentence: some verbs are only used in the passive; some words can appear only in the negative, along with **not, never**, etc; others are always used with particular prepositions or adverbs, or in certain fixed phrases. Such restrictions are shown in a note following a definition:

abide . . . *vb* **1** to bear patiently; tolerate – used negatively

agree . . . *vi* . . . **2a** to be of one mind – often + *with set* <*I ~ with you*>

dumps . . . *n pl* a gloomy state of mind; despondency – esp in *in the dumps*

Sometimes a word that is commonly used with the main entry word in a sentence is printed in italic within the definition:

allude . . . *vi* to make indirect, casual, or implicit reference *to*

[2]**altogether** *n the* nude <*posed in the ~*> – infml

This means that **allude** is almost always used in the phrase **allude to**, and that the noun **altogether** is almost always used with **the**.

9 Cross-references

Cross-references draw attention to a related word in another part of the dictionary. Any word printed in SMALL CAPITAL letters is a cross-reference.

An entire definition may take the form of a cross-reference. This happens either when the word used in the definition has more than one meaning, and it is necessary to specify which meaning is referred to:

[2]**flash** *n* . . . **6a** . . . **c** FLASHLIGHT 2

or when the word used in the definition is a compound that is a main entry in the dictionary:

rubella . . . *n* GERMAN MEASLES

A cross-reference to a related entry, or one that may give additional information, is introduced by 'compare'.

Entries followed by an eye symbol ◉ cross-refer to an illustration or table on the facing page:

music . . . *n* . . . **3** the score of a musical composition set down on paper ***USE*** ◉

Entries followed by a hand symbol ☞ cross-refer to an illustration or table appearing at a main entry elsewhere in the dictionary:

air marshal *n* ☞ RANK

10 Prefixes, suffixes, and combining forms

Word elements that can be used to form new words in English are entered at their alphabetical place in the dictionary. These elements are prefixes (e g **pre-**, **un-**), suffixes (e g **-ous**, **-ly**), and combining forms (e g **Anglo-**, **-logy**).

Suffixes and combining forms added to the end of a word may alter the grammatical function as well as the meaning of the word. Where appropriate, this change of part of speech is indicated as follows:

-ful *suffix* (*n→adj*) full of <*event*ful> <*colour*ful>

This means that the suffix **-ful** is added to nouns to make adjectives.

11 Pronunciation

Most of us have at some time had a disagreement about the pronunciation of a word, or perhaps we have simply come across a new word when reading and have wanted to know how it is pronounced. Unfortunately, when we look the word up in a dictionary we are often confronted with a baffling series of symbols. The pronunciation entries in this dictionary are concise and easy to understand, since they are based almost entirely on English spelling, and special characters or marks have been avoided.

11.1.1 Type of pronunciation represented

The dictionary attempts to give all the most common variant pronunciations of each word. It is not, however, possible to include all the regional and social variants, and so the pronunciation represented here is what may be called a 'standard' or 'neutral British English' accent: the type of speech characteristic of those people often described as having 'no accent'. A better definition would be that it is an accent that betrays nothing of the region to which the speaker belongs.

Different age groups may also pronounce words differently. Some pronunciations that have become so old-fashioned as to be used only by the elderly have been excluded, as have certain others which have recently come into vogue amongst the young but which are not yet sufficiently established to be worthy of inclusion.

11.1.2 Choice of symbols
English spelling is often a poor guide to the pronunciation of a word. In **bough, cough, rough, thorough, though, thought**, and **through**, the sequence **ough** represents seven different sounds. There are in fact 23 vowel sounds in English (see the chart below) and only five letters (a, e, i, o, u) in the spelling to represent these sounds. Nevertheless, by choosing those combinations of letters which are regularly used in English spelling to represent a particular sound, it is possible to produce a pronunciation system that is quick and easy to learn.

Vowels			*Consonants*		
a	as in	b*a*d, f*a*t	b	as in	*b*ad
ah	,,	f*a*ther, oomp*ah*	ch	,,	*ch*eer
aw	,,	s*aw*, *aw*ful	d	,,	*d*ay
ay	,,	m*a*ke, h*ay*	dh	,,	*th*ey
e	,,	b*e*d, h*ea*d	f	,,	*f*ew
ee	,,	sh*ee*p, k*ey*	g	,,	*g*ay
eə	,,	th*ere*, h*air*	h	,,	*h*ot
i	,,	sh*i*p, l*i*ck	j	,,	*j*ump
ie	,,	b*i*te, l*ie*d	k	,,	*k*ing
ie·ə	,,	f*ire*, l*iar*	kh	,,	lo*ch*
iə	,,	h*ere*, f*ear*	l	,,	*l*ed
o	,,	p*o*t, cr*o*p	m	,,	*m*an
oh	,,	n*o*te, J*oa*n	n	,,	su*n*
oo	,,	p*u*t, c*oo*k	ng	,,	su*ng*
ooh	,,	b*oo*t, l*u*te	nh	,,	restaura*nt*
ooə	,,	j*u*ry, c*ure*	p	,,	*p*ot
ow	,,	n*ow*, b*ough*	r	,,	*r*ed
owə	,,	*our*, p*ower*	s	,,	*s*oon
oy	,,	b*oy*, l*oi*ter	sh	,,	fi*sh*
oyə	,,	l*awyer*, s*awyer*	t	,,	*t*ea
u	,,	c*u*t, l*u*ck	th	,,	*th*ing
uh	,,	b*ir*d, abs*ur*d	v	,,	*v*iew
ə	,,	moth*er*, *a*bout	w	,,	*w*et
			y	,,	*y*et
			z	,,	*z*ero
			zh	,,	plea*s*ure

All pronunciations are shown within slant lines (/ /): so for instance /ie/ is pronounced as it is spelt in *lied, spied, cried,* although this same sound may also be spelt in other ways (e g *cry, giant, right*), and /ee/ is pronounced as it is spelt in *meet, street, feet,* etc, although this same sound may also be spelt as in *stream, key, quay*, and *people*.

11.2 Stress

11.2.1 Primary stress
In all English words of 2 or more syllables, one syllable is more prominent than the others, and we say it has greater stress or *primary stress.* For instance, in the word **paper** the first syllable **pa-** has greater stress than the second syllable **-per**, and in **complete** the second syllable has greater stress than the first.

In the pronunciation entries the symbol /ˈ/ is placed *before* the syllable with primary stress:

paper /ˈpaypə/
complete /kəmˈpleet/

11.2.2 Secondary stress
Some longer words also have *secondary stress* on another syllable; that is, the syllable has some prominence but not so much as that syllable with primary stress. The symbol /ˌ/ is used before such syllables. For instance, in **university** the syllable **-ver-** has primary stress, but the first syllable also has some stress. This is secondary stress, and we show the pronunciation of **university** as /ˌyoohniˈvuhsəti/.

11.2.3 Stress on compounds
Some main entries in the dictionary consist of two or more words separated by a hyphen. If each of these words is listed and given a pronunciation at its own alphabetical place in the dictionary, the hyphenated word is not given a full pronunciation, but only a 'stress pattern':

ˌdry-ˈrot
ˈcover-ˌup

A main entry which consists of two or more words separated by spaces will be given a stress pattern only if this is not obvious, or if the stress pattern does not depend on the position of the phrase within a sentence.

Main entries consisting of two or more individual words are not normally given a full pronunciation. Since the pronunciation of **bookcase** may be partially guessed from that of **book**, only the pronunciation of the latter part of the compound is shown, together with a stress pattern:

book /book/
ˈbookˌcase /-ˌkays/

11.2.4 Alternative stress patterns
It is sometimes convenient to show alternative stress patterns by using a hyphen to represent each syllable. For example, **carrier bag** may be pronounced with the primary stress either on the **ca-** of **carrier**, or on **bag**. In such cases, the alternative stress patterns are shown like this:

carrier bag /ˈ---ˌ-, ˌ---ˈ-/

Similarly, if an undefined related word (run-on) has the same pronunciation as the main entry from which it is formed, but a different stress pattern, its stress pattern is shown with hyphens and stress marks:

ˌdry as ˈdust *adj* . . . – **dryasdust** /ˈ--ˌ-/ *n*

11.2.5 Stress shift
There are certain words for which the stress pattern changes according to the position of the word within a phrase or sentence. For example, **brigadier** has primary stress on the last syllable **-dier**, but when this word is used in the phrase **brigadier general**, the primary stress shifts to the first syllable of **general**, and there is now secondary stress on the first syllable of **brigadier**. For words like **brigadier**, the stress pattern shown is always that which would be used if the word were read out by itself.

11.3 Special symbols

11.3.1. The symbol /ə/
This is the only special phonetic character used in this dictionary. It represents the unstressed vowel sound in moth*er*, *a*bout, purp*o*se, and may correspond to many different vowels in ordinary spelling.

11.3.2 Bracketed (ə)
This symbol is used when the sound /ə/ may be either pronounced or missed out, or where its presence or absence is uncertain. Most syllables of English contain a vowel: **telephone** /'telifohn/ has three syllables and three vowels, /e/, /i/, and /oh/. But certain consonants can form a syllable by themselves: **cattle** /'katl/ has two syllables, /'kat/ and /l/. In a word such as **memory** /'mem(ə)ri/, a bracketed /(ə)/ is used, to show that the /r/ may or may not form a syllable: one can say /'memri/, /'meməri/, or /'memr·i/. Similarly, **sudden** /'sud(ə)n/ may be pronounced /'sudn/ or /'sudən/.

The bracketed symbol (ə) may also be used after the vowels /ie/ and /oo/:

giro /'jie(ə)roh/
neuralgia /nyoo(ə)'raljə/

This means that some people pronounce the vowels as /ie·ə/ or /ooə/ and others simply as /ie/ or /oo/.

11.3.3 Hyphens
A hyphen in the spelling of a word is not shown in its pronunciation. However, a hyphen is used in pronunciation entries in the following cases:
i to show that the pronunciation is not a full word and cannot stand alone (e g for prefixes or suffixes):

pre- /pri-/
-tion /-sh(ə)n/

ii to show that part of the pronunciation has not been repeated:

digest /di'jest, die-/

Since the syllable /-'jest/ is the same for both variants it is not written twice.

11.3.4 Centred dot
A centred dot (·) separates pairs of letters that might otherwise be wrongly read as one sound. It separates /n/ from /g/ where the sound /ng/ as in **sing** is not intended, or /t/ from /h/ where /th/ as in **through** is not intended:

knighthood /'niet·hood/

The centred dot may also occur within a single syllable:

fire /fie·ə/

This shows that the sequence /ieə/ should not be read /i·eə/ as in **Riviera**.

11.3.5 Swung dash
A swung dash (~) means that the plural is pronounced in the same way as the singular:

hors d'oeuvre ... *pl* **hors d'oeuvres** *also* **hors d'oeuvre** /'duhv(z) (*Fr* ~)/

11.4 Variant pronunciations

11.4.1 Alternative pronunciations
In general, the first variant shown is considered to be the most usual, although even if two or more pronunciations are genuinely equal in acceptability, it is inevitable because of the nature of print that one must be placed first on the page. All pronunciations shown may be safely used, with the following exceptions:
i A pronunciation preceded by *also* is not so usual as the other pronunciation(s) given, or, though widely used, is not considered correct by some speakers.

ii A pronunciation preceded by *often* is commonly used but is generally considered incorrect.

11.4.2 Common variants that are not shown
There are many words which some speakers pronounce slightly differently from other speakers. Where such differences are very slight, as in the cases below, it has been decided not to show both variants, although each may be quite usual.

i/ə

The two sounds /i/ and /ə/ are often variants within a word. Some people pronounce the final syllable of **bargain**, **painless**, **meanness** with an /i/ and others with /ə/. Because such words are so very numerous, normally either /i/ or /ə/ is shown but not both.

i/y

Words like **apiary**, **anaemia** may be pronounced with either /i/ or /y/:

apiary /'aypi·əri/ or /'aypyəri/

For such words only the /i/ variant is usually given, except after /l/, /m/, and /n/, where both variants are shown:

anaemia /ə'neemyə, -mi·ə/

n/ng

When a prefix such as **un-** is followed by a /k/ or a /g/ sound, the *n* may be pronounced either as /n/ or as /ng/:

ungainly /un'gaynli/ or /ung'gaynli/.

Only one variant is normally shown.

11.4.3 Specialized pronunciations
Pronunciations marked *naut* and *tech* are those used by experts within the field to which the word belongs:

leeward /'leewood; *naut* 'looh·əd/

Here, ordinary people say /'leewood/ but sailors would say /'looh·əd/.

11.5 Main entries which are abbreviations

If the main entry consists merely of a sequence of capital letters, such as **BA**, **ESP**, or **YMCA**, the pronunciation is obvious, and so need not be given. However, abbreviations which may be pronounced as a word do receive a pronunciation:

UFO /'yooh,foh, ,yooh ef 'oh/

11.6 Inflections

Regular inflections are not given a pronunciation unless they are a main entry, in which case the stress pattern alone is shown. Irregular inflections are given pronunciations throughout.

A pronunciation is sometimes shown for the present participle of a verb. The present participle of **travel** may be pronounced either /'travling/ or /'travl·ing/, but that of **tunnel** can be pronounced only /'tunl·ing/.

The Latin plurals **-ae** and **-i** are pronounced in a number of ways, but it is normally necessary to show only one pronunciation: the plural ending **-i** is shown as /-ie/ and the ending **-ae** as /-i/ or /-ee/.

11.7 Strong and weak forms

Many common words have both a *strong form* and a *weak form*. The strong form is used only when the word is stressed or carries emphasis. Otherwise the weak form is used.

For instance, if I say 'I am going out', **am** is pronounced in its unstressed or weak form /əm/. But if someone denies that I am going out, I may repeat the same sentence with a different emphasis and say 'I *am* going out.' Here I have stressed the verb **am**, and the *strong form* /am/ is used.

Since the weak form is the most usual form of the word, this is given first in pronunciation entries and the strong form follows the word *strong*:

am /əm, m; *strong* am/

11.8 Foreign words and phrases

11.8.1 American pronunciations

American pronunciation often differs from that of British English speakers, but a specifically American pronunciation is shown only when a word is pronounced in such a way that it might not be recognized by British speakers:

clerk /klahk; *NAm* kluhk/

Some American-influenced pronunciations are gaining popularity in Britain in such words as **temporary** /'tempəreri/, **temporarily** /ˌtempə'rerəli/, or **mandatory** /man'daytǝ)ri/ instead of the more conventionally British English /'temprəri/, /temprərəli/, and /'mandət(ə)ri/. Such pronunciations are shown only when they are considered to be sufficiently usual to have gained general acceptance.

11.8.2 Borrowed words and phrases

Where English has 'borrowed' a word or phrase from a foreign language it eventually acquires an anglicized pronunciation. All such words in this dictionary are given a pronunciation which may be easily used by native English speakers who know nothing of the language from which the word is borrowed. However, many of these words are normally pronounced in a manner that is closer to the original pronunciation, and in these cases the foreign pronunciation is also given within round brackets, using the International Phonetic Alphabet (IPA). This is because many foreign sounds cannot be adequately represented using the English alphabet. The IPA symbols used are as follows:

Symbol	*as in:*		*Nearest English Equivalent*
	French	*German*	
i	nid	Inhalt	heat
iː	—	riechen	feed
ɪə	—	Bier	beer
e	*été*	Medikament	day
eː	—	mehr	fair
ɛ	sept	Kette	pet
ɛː	mère	Rätsel	fair
eə	—	Wiedersehen	fair
a	patte	Album	cart
a	tard	—	card
aɪ	—	Fräulein	tie
aʊ	—	auf	cow
ɑ	bas	Ahnung	card
ɑː	sable	—	card
ɔ	tonne	Post	hot
ɔː	mors	—	sort
ɔɪ	—	Fräulein	toy
o	chaud	Tomate	coat
oː	rose	Kohle	code
ʊ	—	unter	put
u	coup	—	cool
uː	rouge	Uhr	cool
y	cru	Führer	crude
yː	buche	physisch	crude
ø	bleu	öffnen	early
øː	jeune	böse	early
œ	seul	—	early
œː	peur	—	early
ə	le	genug	ado
ɛ̃	vin	—	—
ɑ̃	blanc	—	restaurant
ɔ̃	non	—	—
œ̃	jeune	—	—
ɥ	nuit	—	wheat
ç	—	ich	—
x	—	nach	loch
ɲ	pagne	—	new
ŋ	—	ringen	pang
ʒ	journal	Genie	pleasure
ʃ	chat	Strasse	show
tʃ	(tcheque)	—	cheat
j	mieux	Jahr	you

12 Etymologies

12.1 Etymologies (histories of words) are shown in square brackets [ ] after the definition of a word, but before any derived undefined words or idioms (unless an idiom itself has been given an etymology).

12.2 Within the square brackets, words or word-elements in *italics* are the source from which the main entry is historically descended. An English word or phrase in ordinary type after such a source-word explains the meaning or function of that source-word:

eulogy ... [... Gk *eulogia* praise ...]
parturition ... [... L *parturitus*, pp of *parturire* ...]

If a source-word is an English word in use since 1501, but is not listed in this dictionary, its meaning is given in round brackets:

frump ... [prob fr *frumple* (to wrinkle), fr ME fromplen ...]

12.3 Special terminology

12.3.1 fr = from. This indicates various kinds of relationship between one word and another: e g borrowing, compounding, or grammatical change.

12.3.2 deriv = derivative. This means that at least one intermediate step has been left out in tracing the history of a word:

apricot ... [alter. of earlier *abrecock*, deriv of Ar *al-birqūq* the apricot]

Here, the Arabic word may have reached us through Catalan, Italian, French, Spanish, or Portuguese.

12.3.3 alter. = alteration. This means that there has been a change of form, within a single language, following no regular pattern of linguistic change, as with **apricot**.

12.3.4 modif = modification. This means that there has been the same kind of change in a word borrowed from another language:

boulevard ... [F, modif of MD *bolwerc* bulwark]

12.3.5 blend. This describes a word formed from two or more constituents which has at least one letter or sound in common with those constituents, or in which part of one constituent is inserted into the other:

smog ... [blend of *smoke* and *fog*]

Compounds which do not meet these special conditions are treated differently:

brunch ... [*br*eakfast + l*unch*]

12.4 Usually the etymology traces the origin and development of a main entry as far back as possible within the recorded history of language, describing (when applicable) the following chief features:
i *Earlier forms in English* Whenever an etymologized word is descendant of a word recorded in either or both of the earlier periods of English, its occurrence in the earlier period(s) is noted, and its form and meaning are stated if they differ from the present form of the main entry, or from the earliest sense defined:

[1]**clog** ... [ME *clogge* short thick piece of wood]
[1]**clot** ... [ME, fr OE *clott* ...]

ii *Loanwords* When a word has been borrowed into English at any period from another language, the source-language is identified, and the form and meaning of the source-word are stated if they differ from those shown for the English word:

[1]**join** ... [ME *joinen,* fr OF *joindre* ...]
polo ... [Balti, ball]

iii *Earlier history of loanwords* In the case of most words which belong to the general vocabulary of English, the earlier history of a foreign source-word is traced as far back as possible:

dine ... [ME *dinen,* fr OF *diner,* fr (assumed) VL *disjejunare* to break one's fast, fr L *dis-* + LL *jejunare* to fast, fr L *jejunus* fasting]

Specialized or 'exotic' words which have entered English, such as **hummus** and **sargasso**, are often treated rather less fully, and with few exceptions a word from a language outside the Indo-European family is not traced any further back.
iv *Pre-history and use of 'akin to'* When a word has been traced back to the earliest language in which it is recorded, then – if that language belongs to the Indo-European family – a selection is given of related forms from other languages of this family. Such a list of related forms is preceded by the phrase 'akin to':

hound ... [ME, fr OE *hund*; akin to OHG *hunt* dog, L *canis*, Gk *kyōn*]

A somewhat different use of 'akin to' occurs when a word is known to be derived from a word in a certain group of languages (e g Celtic or Scandinavian) but cannot be definitely traced to any recognized word in any particular language:

skulk ... [ME *skulken,* of Scand origin; akin to Dan *skulke to* shirk, play truant]

The Danish word shown here is related to the English **skulk**, which certainly derived from a Scandinavian language; but no more definite relationship between the two words can be established.

12.5 If a source-word had the same form as the English word that comes from it, but a different meaning, that meaning is given:

nimbus ... [L, rainstorm, cloud]

If a source-word had the same meaning as the English word but a different form, that form is given. (If there is no language-label before the first word in italics, it is English):

gracile ... [L *gracilis*]

If the source-word had the same form and meaning as the English word, it appears like this:

scabies ... [L]

The same principles can be applied throughout an etymology:

famous ... [ME, fr MF *fameux,* fr L *famosus,* fr *fama* fame]

If the form, meaning, and language had to be stated in every case, this would be written as:

famous ... [ME *famous* well-known, fr MF *fameux* well-known, fr L *famosus* well-known, fr L *fama* fame]

12.6 Cross-references

An explicit cross-reference such as 'more at SHILLING' directs you to another main entry where further information about etymology is to be found.

Any mention in italics of an English word listed in the dictionary may be taken as an implicit reference to the etymology (if any) at that word:

chortle ... [blend of *chuckle* and *snort*]

Etymological information about both **chuckle** and **snort** may be found at their own entries.

[1]a /ay/ *n, pl* **a's, as** *often cap* **1a** (a graphic representation of or device for reproducing) the 1st letter of the English alphabet **b** a speech counterpart of orthographic *a* **2** the 6th note of a C-major scale **3** one designated *a*, esp as the 1st in order or class **4** a grade rating a student's work as superior

[2]a /ə; *strong* ay/ *indefinite article* **1** one – used before singular nouns when the referent is unspecified ⟨*~ man overboard*⟩ and before number collectives and some numbers ⟨*~ great many*⟩ **2** the same ⟨*birds of ~ feather*⟩ ⟨*swords all of ~ length*⟩ **3a(1)** any ⟨*~ bicycle has 2 wheels*⟩ **(2)** one single ⟨*can't see ~ thing*⟩ **b** one particular ⟨*glucose is ~ simple sugar*⟩ **c** – used before the gerund or infinitive of a verb to denote a period or occurrence of the activity concerned ⟨*had ~ little weep*⟩ ⟨*heard ~ crashing of gears*⟩ **4** – used before a proper name to denote (1) membership of a class ⟨I *was ~ Burton before my marriage – SEU S*⟩ (2) resemblance ⟨*~ Daniel come to judgment*⟩ (3) one named but not otherwise known ⟨*~ Mrs Jones*⟩ **5** – used before a pair of items to be considered as a unit ⟨*~ cap and gown*⟩ ***USE*** used before words or letter sequences with an initial consonant sound; compare [1]AN 1 [ME, fr OE *ān* one – more at ONE]

[3]a /ə/ *prep* **1** PER 2 ⟨*twice ~ week*⟩ **2** *chiefly dial* on, in, at ***USE*** used before words or letter sequences with an initial consonant sound [ME, fr OE *a-, an, on*]

[4]a /ə/ *prep* of – often attached to the preceding word ⟨*kinda*⟩ ⟨*lotta*⟩ [ME, by contr]

A /ay/ *n or adj* (a film that is) certified in Britain as suitable for all ages but requiring parental guidance for children under 14 [*a*dult]

[1]a- /ə-/ *prefix* **1** on; in; at; to ⟨*abed*⟩ ⟨*ajar*⟩ **2** in (such) a state or condition ⟨*ablaze*⟩ **3** in (such) a manner ⟨*aloud*⟩ **4** in the act or process of ⟨*gone a-hunting*⟩ ⟨*atingle*⟩ ***USE*** in predicative adjectives and adverbs [ME, fr OE]

[2]a- /ay-, a-/, **an-** /an-/ *prefix* not; without ⟨*asexual*⟩ ⟨*amoral*⟩ – *a-* usu before consonants other than *h*, *an-* before vowels and usu before *h* ⟨*anaesthetic*⟩ ⟨*anhedral*⟩ [L & Gk; L, fr Gk – more at [1]UN-]

-a- *comb form* replacing carbon, esp in a ring ⟨*aza-*⟩ [ISV]

-a /-ə/ *suffix* (→ *n*) oxide ⟨*thoria*⟩ ⟨*alumina*⟩ [NL, fr *-a* (as in *magnesia*)]

A1 *adj* **1** *of a ship* having the highest possible classification of seaworthiness for insurance purposes **2** of the finest quality; first-rate

A4 *n* a size of paper usu 297 × 210mm (about 11¾ × 8¼in)

A5 *n* a size of paper usu 210 × 148mm (about 8¼ × 5⅞in)

AA *n or adj* (a film that is) certified in Britain as suitable for people over 14

aah /ah *often prolonged*/ *vi* to exclaim in amazement, joy, or surprise ⟨*oohing and ~ing*⟩ – **aah** *n*

aardvark /ˈahd,vahk/ *n* a large burrowing ant- and termite-eating nocturnal African mammal [obs Afrik, fr Afrik *aard* earth + *vark* pig]

aardwolf /ˈahd,woolf/ *n* a striped African mammal that resembles the hyenas and eats esp carrion and insects [Afrik, fr *aard* + *wolf*]

ab- /ab-, əb-/ *prefix* from; away; off ⟨*abaxial*⟩ ⟨*abduct*⟩ [ME, fr OF & L; OF, fr L *ab-, abs-, a-*, fr *ab, a* – more at OF]

aba /əˈbah, ahˈbah/ *n* a loose sleeveless outer garment worn by Arabs [Ar *ʽabā*]

abaca /,abəˈkah/ *n* (a fibre obtained from the leafstalk of) a banana native to the Philippines [Sp *abacá*, fr Tag *abaká*]

aback /əˈbak/ *adv* **1** unintentionally in a position to catch the wind on what is normally the leeward side – used with reference to a sail **2** by surprise – + *take* ⟨*was taken ~ by her sharp retort*⟩ [ME *abak* back, backwards, fr OE *on bæc*, fr *on* on + *bæc* back]

abacus /ˈabəkəs/ *n, pl* **abaci** /-kie, -sie/, **abacuses 1** a slab that forms the uppermost part of the capital of a column ☞ ARCHITECTURE **2** an instrument for performing calculations by sliding counters along rods or in grooves [L, fr Gk *abak-, abax*, lit., slab]

[1]abaft /əˈbahft/ *adv* towards or at the stern [[1]*a-* + *baft* (aft)]

[2]abaft *prep* towards the stern from

abalone /,abəˈlohni/ *n* any of several related edible rock-clinging gastropod molluscs with flattened slightly spiral shells [AmerSp *abulón*]

[1]abandon /əˈband(ə)n/ *vt* **1** to give up completely, esp with the intention of never resuming or reclaiming ⟨*~ed his studies*⟩ ⟨*slow to ~ their native language*⟩ **2** to leave, often in the face of danger ⟨*~ ship*⟩ **3** to forsake or desert, esp in spite of an allegiance, duty, or responsibility ⟨*endure the ignominy of his ~ing her* – D H Lawrence⟩ ⟨*~ed to a humble death*⟩ **4** to give (oneself) over unrestrainedly *to* an emotion or activity [ME *abandounen*, fr MF *abandoner*, fr *abandon*, n, surrender, fr *a bandon* in one's power] – **abandoner** *n*, **abandonment** *n*

[2]abandon *n* freedom from constraint or inhibitions ⟨*danced with gay ~*⟩

aˈbandoned *adj* wholly free from restraint ⟨*an ~ party*⟩

abase /əˈbays/ *vt* to bring lower in rank, office, prestige, or esteem [ME *abassen*, fr MF *abaisser*, fr *a-* (fr L *ad-*) + (assumed) VL *bassiare* to lower] – **abasement** *n*

abash /əˈbash/ *vt* to destroy the self-possession or self-confidence of; disconcert – usu pass [ME *abaishen*, fr (assumed) MF *abaiss-, abair* to astonish, alter. of MF *esbair*, fr *ex-* + *baer* to yawn, fr ML *batare*] – **abashment** *n*

abate /ə'bayt/ *vt* **1** to put an end to; abolish ⟨~ *a nuisance*⟩ **2** to reduce in amount, intensity, or degree; moderate ⟨~ *a tax*⟩ ~ *vi* to decrease in force or intensity ⟨*the wind has* ~d⟩ [ME *abaten*, fr OF *abattre* to beat down, slaughter – more at [1]REBATE] – **abatement** *n*, **abater** *n*

abatis, abattis /'abətee, -tis/ *n, pl* **abatis, abatises, abattis, abattises** a defensive obstacle made of felled trees with sharpened branches facing the enemy [F, fr *abattre*]

abattoir /'abə,twah/ *n* a slaughterhouse [F, fr *abattre*]

abaxial /ab'aksi·əl/ *adj* situated outside or directed away from the axis of an organ, plant part, or organism – compare ADAXIAL

abbacy /'abəsee/ *n* the office, jurisdiction, or tenure of an abbot or abbess [ME *abbatie*, fr LL *abbatia*]

abbé /'abay/ *n* a member of the French secular clergy in major or minor orders – used as a title [F, fr LL *abbat-, abbas*]

abbess /'abes/ *n* the female superior of a convent of nuns [ME *abbesse*, fr OF, fr LL *abbatissa*, fem of *abbat-, abbas*]

Abbevillian /,ab(ə)'vilyən/ *adj* of the earliest Palaeolithic culture in Europe [*Abbeville*, town in France]

abbey /'abi/ *n* **1** a religious community governed by an abbot or abbess **2** the buildings, esp the church, of a (former) monastery ⟨*Westminster* ~⟩ [ME, fr OF *abaïe*, fr LL *abbatia* abbey, fr *abbat-, abbas*]

abbot /'abət/ *n* the superior of an abbey of monks [ME *abbod*, fr OE, fr LL *abbat-, abbas*, fr LGk *abbas*, fr Aram *abbā* father]

abbreviate /ə'breeviayt/ *vt* to make briefer; *esp* to reduce to a shorter form intended to stand for the whole [ME *abbreviaten*, fr LL *abbreviatus*, pp of *abbreviare* – more at ABRIDGE] – **abbreviator** *n*

abbreviation /ə,breevi'aysh(ə)n/ *n* a shortened form of a written word or phrase ⟨amt *is an* ~ *for* amount⟩ [ABBREVIATE + -ION]

ABC *n, pl* **ABC's, ABCs 1** the alphabet **2** the rudiments of a subject – usu pl with sing. meaning in NAm

abdicate /'abdikayt/ *vt* to relinquish (e g sovereign power) formally ~ *vi* to renounce a throne, dignity, etc [L *abdicatus*, pp of *abdicare*, fr *ab-* + *dicare* to proclaim – more at DICTION] – **abdicator** *n*, **abdicable** /-kəbl/ *adj*, **abdication** /-'kaysh(ə)n/ *n*

abdomen /'abdəmən, əb'dohmən/ *n* **1** (the cavity of) the part of the body between the thorax and the pelvis that contains the liver, gut, etc **2** the rear part of the body behind the thorax in an insect or other arthropod [MF & L; MF, fr L] – **abdominal** /əb'dominl, ab-/ *adj*, **abdominally** *adv*

abducens nerve /əb'dyoohsənz, -kenz/ *n* either of the 6th pair of cranial nerves which are motor nerves supplying muscles of the eye [L *abducens*, prp of *abducere*]

abduct /əb'dukt/ *vt* **1** to carry off secretly or by force – compare KIDNAP **2** to draw away (e g a limb) from a position near or parallel to the main part of the body [L *abductus*, pp of *abducere*, lit., to lead away, fr *ab-* + *ducere* to lead – more at [1]TOW] – **abductor** *n*, **abduction** /əb'duksh(ə)n/ *n*

abeam /ə'beem/ *adv or adj* on a line at right angles to the length of a ship or aircraft [[1]*a-* + [1]*beam*]

abed /ə'bed/ *adv or adj* in bed

Aberdeen Angus /,abədeen 'ang·gəs/ *n* (any of) a breed of black hornless orig Scottish beef cattle [*Aberdeen & Angus*, counties in Scotland]

aberrant /ə'berənt/ *adj* **1** deviating from the right or normal way ⟨~ *behaviour*⟩ **2** diverging from the usual or natural type [L *aberrant-, aberrans*, prp of *aberrare* to go astray, fr *ab-* + *errare* to wander, err] – **aberrance** *n*, **aberrancy** *n*, **aberrantly** *adv*

aberration /,abə'raysh(ə)n/ *n* **1** being aberrant, esp with respect to a moral standard or normal state **2** the failure of a mirror, lens, etc to produce exact correspondence between an object and its image **3** (an instance of) unsoundness or disorder of the mind **4** a small periodic change of apparent position in celestial bodies due to the combined effect of the motion of light and the motion of the observer **5** an aberrant organ or individual; SPORT 5 [L *aberratus*, pp of *aberrare*] – **aberrational** *adj*

abet /ə'bet/ *vt* **-tt-** to give active encouragement or approval to ⟨*aided and* ~ted *in the crime by his wife*⟩ [ME *abetten*, fr MF *abeter*, fr OF, fr *a-* (fr L *ad-*) + *beter* to bait, of Gmc origin; akin to OE *bǣtan* to bait] – **abetment** *n*, **abettor, abetter** *n*

abeyance /ə'bayəns/ *n* temporary inactivity; suspension ⟨*a rule in* ~ *since 1935*⟩ [MF *abeance* expectation, fr *abaer* to desire, fr *a-* + *baer* to yawn, fr ML *batare*]

abhor /əb'(h)aw/ *vt* **-rr-** to regard with extreme repugnance; loathe [ME *abhorren*, fr L *abhorrēre*, fr *ab-* + *horrēre* to shudder – more at HORROR] – **abhorrer** *n*

abhorrent /əb'(h)orənt, əb'(h)awrənt/ *adj* **1** opposed, contrary *to* **2** causing horror; repugnant ⟨*acts* ~ *to every right-minded person*⟩ [L *abhorrent-, abhorrens*, prp of *abhorrēre*] – **abhorrence** *n*, **abhorrently** *adv*

abidance /ə'bied(ə)ns/ *n* compliance ⟨~ *by the rules*⟩ [ABIDE + -ANCE]

abide /ə'bied/ *vb* **abode** /ə'bohd/, **abided** *vt* to bear patiently; tolerate – used negatively ⟨*can't* ~ *such bigots*⟩ ~ *vi* **1** to remain stable or fixed in a state **2** *archaic* to dwell [ME *abiden*, fr OE *ābīdan*, fr *ā-*, perfective prefix + *bīdan* to bide] – **abider** *n* – **abide by** to remain true to; comply with ⟨abide by *the rules*⟩ ⟨abide by *one's word*⟩

abiding /ə'bieding/ *adj* enduring ⟨*an* ~ *interest in nature*⟩ – **abidingly** *adv*

ability /ə'biləti/ *n* **1a** being able; *esp* physical, mental, or legal power to perform ⟨*doubted her* ~ *to walk so far*⟩ **b** natural or acquired competence in doing; skill ⟨*a man of great* ~⟩ **2** a natural talent; aptitude – usu pl [ME *abilite*, fr MF *habilité*, fr L *habilitat-, habilitas*, fr *habilis* apt, skilful – more at ABLE]

-ability *also* **-ibility** /-ə'biləti/ *suffix* (*vb, adj* → *n*) capacity, suitability, or tendency to (so act or be acted on) ⟨*read*ability⟩ ⟨*excit*ability⟩ [ME *-abilite, -ibilite*, fr MF *-abilité, -ibilité*, fr L *-abilitas, -ibilitas*, fr *-abilis, -ibilis*, -able + *-tas* -ty]

ab initio /,ab i'nishioh/ *adv* from the beginning [L]

abiogenesis /,ay,bie·oh'jenəsis/ *n* the supposed spontaneous origination of living organisms directly from lifeless matter [NL, fr [2]*a-* + *bio-* + L *genesis*] – **abiogenetic** /-jə'netik/, **abiogenetical** *adj*, **abiogenetically** *adv*, **abiogenist** /,aybie'ojənist/ *n*

abiotic /,aybie'otik/ *adj* not involving or produced

by living organisms [[2]*a-* + *biotic*] – **abiotically** *adv*

abject /'abjekt/ *adj* **1** showing utter hopelessness; wretched, miserable ⟨~ *poverty*⟩ **2** despicable, degraded **3** very humble, esp to the point of servility ⟨*an* ~ *apology*⟩ [ME, fr L *abjectus*, fr pp of *abicere* to cast off, fr *ab-* + *jacere* to throw – more at [2]JET] – **abjection** /əb'jeksh(ə)n/ *n*, **abjectly** /'abjektli/ *adv*, **abjectness** *n*

abjure /əb'jooə/ *vt* to renounce on oath or reject formally (e g a claim, opinion, or allegiance) [ME *abjuren*, fr MF or L; MF *abjurer*, fr L *abjurare*, fr *ab-* + *jurare* to swear – more at JURY] – **abjurer** *n*, **abjuration** /,abjə'raysh(ə)n/ *n*

ablate /ə'blayt/ *vb* to remove or be removed by cutting, erosion, melting, evaporation, or vaporization [L *ablatus* (suppletive pp of *auferre* to remove, fr *au-* away + *ferre* to carry), fr *ab-* + *latus*, suppletive pp of *ferre* – more at UKASE, [2]BEAR, TOLERATE] – **ablative** /a'blaytiv/ *adj*, **ablation** /a'blaysh(ə)n/ *n*, **ablator** *n*

ablative /'ablətiv/ *n* (a form in) a grammatical case expressing typically separation, source, cause, or instrument [adj ME, fr MF or L; MF *ablatif*, fr L *ablativus*, fr *ablatus*; n fr adj] – **ablative** *adj*

,ablative 'absolute *n* a construction in Latin in which a noun or pronoun and its adjunct, both in the ablative case, together form an adverbial phrase

ablaut /'aplowt, 'ab-/ *n* a systematic variation of vowels in the same root, esp in the Indo-European languages, usu accompanied by differences in use or meaning (e g in *sing, sang, sung, song*) [G, fr *ab* away from + *laut* sound]

ablaze /ə'blayz/ *adj or adv* **1** on fire **2** radiant with light or bright colour

able /'aybl/ *adj* **1** having sufficient power, skill, resources, or qualifications *to* ⟨*with more money I was better* ~ *to help*⟩ **2** marked by intelligence, knowledge, skill, or competence ⟨*the* ~st *lawyer in London*⟩ [ME, fr MF, fr L *habilis* apt, fr *habēre* to have – more at GIVE] – **ably** /'aybli/ *adv*

-able *also* **-ible** /-əbl/ *suffix* **1** (*vb* → *adj*) fit for, able to, liable to, or worthy to (so act or be acted on) ⟨*break*able⟩ ⟨*reli*able⟩ ⟨*get-at*-able⟩ **2** (*n* → *adj*) marked by, providing, or possessing (a specified quality or attribute) ⟨*knowledge*able⟩ ⟨*comfort*able⟩ [ME, fr OF, fr L *-abilis, -ibilis*, fr *-a-*, *-i-*, verb stem vowels + *-bilis* capable or worthy of] – **-ably** *suffix* (*vb, n* → *adv*)

,able-'bodied *adj* physically strong and healthy; fit

,able 'seaman, ,able-bodied 'seaman *n* ☞ RANK

ablution /ə'bloohsh(ə)n/ *n* the washing of (a part of) one's body, esp in a ritual purification [ME, fr MF or L; MF, fr L *ablution-, ablutio*, fr *ablutus*, pp of *abluere* to wash away, fr *ab-* + *lavere* to wash – more at LYE] – **ablutionary** /-(ə)ri/ *adj*

ABM *n* ANTIBALLISTIC MISSILE

Abnaki /ab'nahki/ *n, pl* **Abnakis,** *esp collectively* **Abnaki** a member, or the Algonquin language, of an American Indian people of Maine and S Quebec

abnegation /,abni'gaysh(ə)n/ *n* renunciation, self-denial [LL *abnegation-, abnegatio*, fr L *abnegatus*, pp of *abnegare* to refute, fr *ab-* + *negare* to deny – more at NEGATE]

abnormal /,ab'nawməl, əb-/ *adj* deviating from the normal or average; *esp* markedly and disturbingly irregular ⟨~ *behaviour*⟩ [alter. of earlier *anormal*, fr F, fr ML *anormalis*, fr L *a-* + LL *normalis* normal] – **abnormally** *adv*, **abnormality** /,abnaw'maləti/ *n*

ab,normal psy'chology *n* the psychology of mental disorder

abo /'aboh/ *n, pl* **abos** *often cap, Austr* an Australian aborigine – chiefly derog [by shortening] – **abo** *adj*

aboard /ə'bawd/ *adv or prep* **1** on, onto, or within (a ship, aircraft, train, or road vehicle) ⟨*climb* ~⟩ ⟨*they were* ~ *a plane bound for Rome*⟩ **2** alongside [ME *abord*, fr [1]*a-* + *bord* board – more at BOARD]

abode /ə'bohd/ *n* a home, residence – fml [ME *abod*, fr *abiden* to abide]

abolish /ə'bolish/ *vt* to do away with (e g a law or custom) wholly; annul [ME *abolisshen*, fr MF *aboliss-*, stem of *abolir*, fr L *abolēre*, prob back-formation fr *abolescere* to disappear, fr *ab-* + *-olescere* (as in *adolescere* to grow up) – more at ADULT] – **abolishable** *adj*, **abolisher** *n*, **abolishment** *n*, **abolition** /,abə'lish(ə)n/ *n*, **abolitionary** *adj*

abolitionism /,abə'lishəniz(ə)m/ *n* principles or measures fostering abolition (e g of slavery in the USA) – **abolitionist** *n or adj*

abomasum /,abə'mays(ə)m/ *n, pl* **abomasa** /-sə/ the fourth or true digestive stomach of a ruminant mammal [NL, fr L *ab-* + *omasum* tripe of a bullock] – **abomasal** *adj*

'A-,bomb /ay/ *n* ATOM BOMB

abominable /ə'bominəbl/ *adj* **1** worthy of or causing disgust or hatred; detestable **2** very disagreeable or unpleasant – esp in colloquial exaggeration ⟨~ *weather*⟩ [ME, fr MF, fr L *abominabilis*, fr *abominari*, lit., to deprecate as an ill-omen, fr *ab-* + *omin-*, *omen* omen] – **abominably** *adv*

a,bominable 'snowman *n, often cap A&S* a large manlike animal reported as existing high in the Himalayas

abominate /ə'bominayt/ *vt* to hate or loathe intensely and unremittingly; abhor [L *abominatus*, pp of *abominari*] – **abominator** *n*

abomination /ə,bomi'naysh(ə)n/ *n* **1** sthg abominable; *esp* a detestable or shameful action **2** extreme disgust and hatred; loathing [ME *abominacioun*, fr MF *abomination*, fr LL *abomination-, abominatio*, fr L *abominatus*]

[1]aboriginal /,abə'rijin(ə)l/ *adj* **1** indigenous **2** of esp Australian aborigines – **aboriginally** *adv*

[2]aboriginal *n* an (Australian) aborigine

aborigine /,abə'rijinee/ *n* **1** an indigenous inhabitant, esp as contrasted with an invading or colonizing people; *specif, often cap* a member of the indigenous people of Australia **2** *pl* the original fauna and flora of an area [L *aborigines*, pl, prob fr *ab origine* from the beginning]

[1]abort /ə'bawt/ *vi* **1** to expel a premature nonviable foetus **2** to fail to develop completely; shrink away ~ *vt* **1** to induce the abortion of (a foetus) **2a** to end prematurely ⟨~ *a project*⟩ **b** to stop in the early stages ⟨~ *a disease*⟩ [L *abortare*, fr *abortus*, pp of *aboriri* to miscarry, fr *ab-* + *oriri* to rise, be born – more at RISE]

[2]abort *n* the premature termination of a mission or procedure involving a military aircraft or spacecraft

abortifacient /ə,bawti'fayshənt/ *n or adj* (a drug or other agent) inducing abortion

abortion /ə'bawsh(ə)n/ *n* **1** the spontaneous or induced expulsion of a foetus **2** a monstrosity ⟨*mon-*

strously carved ~s – *Country Life*⟩ **3** (the result of) an arresting of development of a part, process, etc – **abortionist** *n*

abortive /ə'bawtiv/ *adj* **1** fruitless, unsuccessful ⟨*an ~ attempt*⟩ **2** imperfectly formed or developed – **abortively** *adv*, **abortiveness** *n*

aboulia, abulia /ay'byoohli·ə/ *n* pathological loss of willpower [NL, fr [2]*a-* + Gk *boulē* will]

abound /ə'bownd/ *vi* **1** to be present in large numbers or in great quantity ⟨*wild animals* ~⟩ **2** to be amply supplied – + *in* ⟨*the old edition* ~*ed in coloured pictures – TLS*⟩ **3** to be crowded or infested *with* ⟨*the attics* ~ *with rats*⟩ [ME *abounden*, fr MF *abonder*, fr L *abundare*, fr *ab-* + *unda* wave – more at WATER]

[1]**about** /ə'bowt/ *adv* **1** ROUND 2, 3c **2** in succession or rotation; alternately ⟨*turn and turn* ~⟩ **3** approximately ⟨*cost* ~ *£5*⟩ **4** almost ⟨~ *starved*⟩ ⟨~ *as interesting as a wet Sunday*⟩ **5** in the vicinity ⟨*there was nobody* ~⟩ [ME, fr OE *abūtan*, fr [1]*a-* + *būtan* outside – more at BUT]

[2]**about** *prep* **1** on every side of; surrounding ⟨*the wall* ~ *the prison*⟩ **2a** in the vicinity of **b** on or near the person of ⟨*have you a match* ~ *you?*⟩ **c** in the make-up of ⟨*a mature wisdom* ~ *him*⟩ **d** at the command of ⟨*has his wits* ~ *him*⟩ **3a** engaged in ⟨*knows what she's* ~⟩ **b** on the verge of – + *to* ⟨~ *to join the army*⟩ **4a** with regard to, concerning ⟨*a story* ~ *rabbits*⟩ **b** intimately concerned with ⟨*politics is* ~ *capturing votes*⟩ **5** over or in different parts of ⟨*walked* ~ *the streets*⟩ **6** *chiefly NAm* – used with the negative to express intention or determination ⟨*is not* ~ *to quit*⟩

[3]**about** *adj* **1** moving from place to place; *specif* out of bed **2** in existence, evidence, or circulation ⟨*skateboards weren't* ~ *long*⟩

a,bout-'face *vi or n, chiefly NAm* (to) about-turn [fr the military command *about face*, fr [1]*about* + [2]*face*]

a,bout-'turn *n* **1** a 180° turn to the right, esp as a drill movement **2** *chiefly Br* a reversal of direction, policy, or opinion ⟨*a massive* ~ *on the Stock Exchange – Daily Mirror*⟩ [fr the military command *about turn*] – **about-turn** *vi*

[1]**above** /ə'buv/ *adv* **1a** in the sky overhead **b** in or to heaven **2a** in or to a higher place **b** higher on the same or an earlier page **c** upstairs ⟨*the flat* ~⟩ **3** in or to a higher rank or number ⟨*30 and* ~⟩ **4** upstage **5** *archaic* besides; IN ADDITION [ME, fr OE *abufan*, fr *a-* + *bufan* above, fr *be-* + *ufan* above; akin to OE *ofer* over]

[2]**above** *prep* **1** higher than the level of ⟨*rose* ~ *the clouds*⟩ ⟨*shout* ~ *the noise*⟩ **2** OVER 3 ⟨*values safety* ~ *excitement*⟩ ⟨*nothing* ~ *£5*⟩ **3** beyond, transcending ⟨~ *criticism*⟩ ⟨*the lecture was* ~ *me*⟩ **4a** superior to (e g in rank) **b** too proud or honourable to stoop to **5** upstream from – **above oneself** excessively self-satisfied

[3]**above** *n, pl* **above** **1a** sthg (written) above ⟨*the* ~ *are the main facts*⟩ **b** a person whose name is written above **2a** a higher authority **b** heaven

[4]**above** *adj* written higher on the same, or on a preceding, page

a,bove 'all *adv* before every other consideration; especially

a,bove'board /-'bawd/ *adj* free from all traces of deceit or dishonesty [fr the difficulty of cheating at cards when the hands are above the table] – **above board** *adv*

a'bove,ground /-grownd/ *adj* **1** located on or above the surface of the ground **2** not yet buried; alive – **above ground** /-,- '-/ *adv*

a'bove,mentioned /-,mensh(ə)nd/ *adj* aforementioned

abracadabra /,abrəkə'dabrə/ *n* a magical charm or incantation – used interjectionally as an accompaniment to conjuring tricks [LL]

abrade /ə'brayd/ *vt* to roughen, irritate, or wear away, esp by friction [L *abradere* to scrape off, fr *ab-* + *radere* to scrape – more at RAT] – **abradable** *adj*, **abrader** *n*

abrasion /ə'brayzh(ə)n/ *n* **1** a wearing, grinding, or rubbing away by friction **2** an abraded area of the skin or mucous membrane [ML *abrasion-*, *abrasio*, fr L *abrasus*, pp of *abradere*]

[1]**abrasive** /ə'braysiv, -ziv/ *adj* tending to abrade; causing irritation ⟨*an* ~ *personality*⟩ – **abrasively** *adv*, **abrasiveness** *n*

[2]**abrasive** *n* a substance (e g emery) that may be used for grinding away, smoothing, or polishing

abreaction /,abri'aksh(ə)n/ *n* the release of tension due to a repressed emotion by means of reliving the situation in which it orig occurred [part trans of G *abreagierung*, fr *ab* away from + *reagierung* reaction] – **abreact** /,abri'akt/ *vt*

abreast /ə'brest/ *adv or adj* **1** side by side and facing in the same direction ⟨*columns of men 5* ~⟩ **2** up-to-date in attainment or information ⟨*keeps* ~ *of the latest trends*⟩ [ME *abrest*, fr [1]*a-* + *brest* breast]

abridge /ə'brij/ *vt* **1** to reduce in scope; curtail ⟨*attempts to* ~ *the right of free speech*⟩ **2** to shorten by omission of words without sacrifice of sense; condense [ME *abregen*, fr MF *abregier*, fr LL *abbreviare*, fr L *ad-* + *brevis* short – more at BRIEF] – **abridger** *n*

a'bridgment, abridgement /-mənt/ *n* a shortened form of a work retaining the sense and unity of the original [ABRIDGE + -MENT]

abroad /ə'brawd/ *adv or adj* **1** over a wide area; widely **2** away from one's home; out of doors ⟨*few people* ~ *at this hour*⟩ **3** beyond the boundaries of one's country **4** in wide circulation; about ⟨*the idea has got* ~⟩ [ME *abrood*, fr [1]*a-* + *brood* broad]

abrogate /'abrəgayt/ *vt* to abolish by authoritative action; annul, repeal [L *abrogatus*, pp of *abrogare*, fr *ab-* + *rogare* to ask, propose a law – more at [1]RIGHT] – **abrogation** /-'gaysh(ə)n/ *n*

abrupt /ə'brupt/ *adj* **1** ending as if sharply cut off; truncated ⟨~ *plant filaments*⟩ **2a** occurring without warning; unexpected ⟨~ *weather changes*⟩ **b** unceremoniously curt ⟨*an* ~ *manner*⟩ **c** marked by sudden changes in subject matter **3** rising or dropping sharply; steep [L *abruptus*, fr pp of *abrumpere* to break off, fr *ab-* + *rumpere* to break – more at BEREAVE] – **abruptly** *adv*, **abruptness** *n*

abscess /'abses, -sis/ *n* a pocket of pus surrounded by inflamed tissue [L *abscessus*, lit., act of going away, fr *abscessus*, pp of *abscedere* to go away, fr *abs-*, *ab-* + *cedere* to go – more at CEDE] – **abscessed** *adj*

abscise /əb'siez/ *vb* to separate by abscission [L *abscisus*, pp of *abscidere*, fr *abs-* + *caedere* to cut – more at CONCISE]

ab,scisic 'acid /ab'sisik, -'siz-/ *n* a plant hormone

that typically promotes leaf abscission and dormancy [*abscision* (var of *abscission*) + *-ic*]

abscisin *also* **abscissin** /ab'sisin, əb'sisin/ *n* abscisic acid or a similar plant hormone tending to inhibit growth or promote leaf abscission [*abscision, abscission* + *-in*]

abscissa /əb'sisə, ab-/ *n, pl* **abscissas** *also* **abscissae** /-si/ the coordinate of a point in a plane Cartesian coordinate system obtained by measuring parallel to the x-axis – compare ORDINATE [NL, fr L, fem of *abscissus,* pp of *abscindere* to cut off, fr *ab-* + *scindere* to cut – more at [1]SHED]

abscission /ab'sish(ə)n, əb-/ *n* the natural separation of flowers, leaves, etc from plants [L *abscission-, abscissio,* fr *abscissus*]

abscond /əb'skond/ *vi* to depart secretly, esp so as to evade retribution ⟨~ed *with the funds*⟩ [L *abscondere* to hide away, fr *abs-* + *condere* to store up, conceal – more at CONDIMENT] – **absconder** *n*

abseil /'apsiel/ *vi* to descend a vertical surface by sliding down a rope secured from above and wound round the body [G *abseilen,* fr *ab-* down + *seil* rope]

absence /'absəns/ *n* **1** the state of being absent **2** the period of time that one is absent **3** a lack ⟨*an* ~ *of detail*⟩

,absence of 'mind *n* inattention to present surroundings or occurrences

[1]**absent** /'absənt/ *adj* **1** not present or attending; missing **2** not existing; lacking **3** preoccupied [ME, fr MF, fr L *absent-, absens,* prp of *abesse* to be absent, fr *ab-* + *esse* to be – more at IS] – **absently** *adv*

[2]**absent** /əb'sent/ *vt* to take or keep (oneself) away – usu + *from* ⟨~ed *himself from morning prayers*⟩

absentee /,abz(ə)n'tee/ *n* one who is absent or who absents him-/herself – **absentee** *adj*

absentee ballot *n* a ballot submitted (e g by post) before an election by a voter who is unable to attend

,absen'tee,ism /-,iz(ə)m/ *n* persistent and deliberate absence from work or duty

,absent'minded /-'miendid/ *adj* lost in thought and unaware of one's surroundings or actions; forgetful; *also* given to absence of mind – **absentmindedly** *adv,* **absentmindedness** *n*

absinthe, absinth /'absinth (*Fr* absɛ̃t)/ *n* **1** WORMWOOD 1 **2** a green liqueur flavoured with wormwood or a substitute, aniseed, and other aromatics [F *absinthe,* fr L *absinthium,* fr Gk *apsinthion*]

absolute /'absəlooht, -bz-, -ps-/ *adj* **1a** perfect ⟨~ *bliss*⟩ **b** (relatively) pure or unmixed ⟨~ *alcohol*⟩ **c** outright, unmitigated ⟨*an* ~ *lie*⟩ **2** completely free from constitutional or other restraint ⟨*an* ~ *monarch*⟩ **3** standing apart from a usual syntactic relation with other words or sentence elements **4** having no restriction, exception, or qualification ⟨~ *ownership*⟩ **5** positive, unquestionable ⟨~ *proof*⟩ **6** being self-sufficient and free of external references or relationships ⟨*an* ~ *term in logic*⟩ **7** relating to a temperature scale that has absolute zero as its lower reference point ⟨*10°* ~⟩ [ME *absolut,* fr L *absolutus,* fr pp of *absolvere* to set free, absolve] – **absolute** *n,* **absoluteness** *n*

,absolute 'discharge *n* a nominal penalty that consists of being set free and is imposed by a court where punishment is inappropriate – compare CONDITIONAL DISCHARGE

,absolute hu'midity *n* the concentration of a vapour (in the atmosphere)

,abso'lutely /-li/ *adv* totally, completely – often used to express emphatic agreement

,absolute 'magnitude *n* the intrinsic luminosity of a star or other celestial body when viewed from a distance of 10 parsecs

,absolute ma'jority *n* a number of votes greater than ½ the total cast; *also* the number by which this exceeds the total votes of other candidates

,absolute 'pitch *n* **1** the pitch of a note determined by its rate of vibration **2** the ability to sing or name a note asked for or heard

,absolute 'zero *n* the lowest temperature theoretically possible at which there is a complete absence of heat and which is equivalent to about –273.16°C or 0°K

absolution /,absə'loohsh(ə)n, -bz-, -ps-/ *n* the act of absolving; *specif* a declaration of forgiveness of sins pronounced by a priest

absolutism /,absə'loohtiz(ə)m, -bz-, -ps-, '---,--/ *n* (the theory favouring) government by an absolute ruler or authority – **absolutist** *n or adj,* **absolutistic** /-'tistik/ *adj*

absolve /əb'zolv/ *vt* **1** to set free *from* an obligation or the consequences of guilt **2** to declare (a sin) of (a person) forgiven by absolution [ME *absolven,* fr L *absolvere,* fr *ab-* + *solvere* to loosen – more at SOLVE] – **absolver** *n*

absorb /əb'zawb; *also* -bs-/ *vt* **1** to take in and make part of an existing whole; incorporate **2a** to suck up or take up ⟨*plant roots* ~ *water*⟩ **b** to assimilate; TAKE IN **3** to engage or occupy wholly ⟨~ed *in thought*⟩ **4** to receive and transform (sound, radiant energy, etc) without reflecting or transmitting ⟨*the earth* ~s *the sun's rays*⟩ ⟨*a sound*-absorbing *surface*⟩ [MF *absorber,* fr L *absorbēre,* fr *ab-* + *sorbēre* to suck up; akin to Gk *rhophein* to suck up] – **absorbable** *adj,* **absorber** *n,* **absorbability** /-bə'biləti/ *n*

ab'sorbed *adj* intensely engrossed or preoccupied

absorbent *also* **absorbant** /əb'zawb(ə)nt; *also* -bs-/ *n or adj* (sthg) able to absorb a liquid, gas, etc [L *absorbent-, absorbens,* prp of *absorbēre*] – **absorbency** *n*

absorbing /əb'zawbing; *also* -bs-/ *adj* engaging one's full attention; engrossing – **absorbingly** *adv*

absorption /əb'zawpsh(ə)n; *also* əb'sawpsh(ə)n/ *n* **1** absorbing or being absorbed – compare ADSORPTION **2** total involvement of the mind ⟨~ *in his work*⟩ [F & L; F, fr L *absorption-, absorptio,* fr *absorptus,* pp of *absorbēre*] – **absorptive** *adj*

abstain /əb'stayn/ *vi* **1** to refrain deliberately, and often with an effort of self-denial, *from* ⟨*resolved to* ~ *from intoxicating liquor*⟩ **2** to refrain from using one's vote [ME *absteinen,* fr MF *abstenir,* fr L *abstinēre,* fr *abs-, ab-* + *tenēre* to hold – more at THIN] – **abstainer** *n*

abstemious /əb'steemi·əs/ *adj* sparing, esp in eating or drinking; marked by abstinence [L *abstemius,* fr *abs-* + *temetum* mead, strong drink] – **abstemiously** *adv*

abstention /əb'stensh(ə)n/ *n* **1** abstaining – often + *from* **2** an instance of withholding a vote [LL *abstention-, abstentio,* fr L *abstentus,* pp of *abstinēre*] – **abstentious** /-shəs/ *adj*

abstinence /'abstinəns/ *also* **abstinency** /-si/ *n* **1** voluntary forbearance, esp from indulgence of appetite or from eating some foods – often + *from* **2** habitual abstaining from intoxicating beverages – esp in *total abstinence* [ME, fr OF, fr L *abstinentia*, fr *abstinent-*, *abstinens*, prp of *abstinēre*] – **abstinent** *adj*, **abstinently** *adv*

[1]**abstract** /ˈabstrakt/ *adj* **1a** detached from any specific instance or object ⟨~ *entity*⟩ **b** difficult to understand; abstruse ⟨~ *problems*⟩ **c** ideal ⟨~ *justice*⟩ **2** *of a noun* naming a quality, state, or action rather than a thing; not concrete ⟨*the word* poem *is concrete,* poetry *is* ~⟩ **3** theoretical rather than practical ⟨~ *science*⟩ **4** having little or no element of pictorial representation [ML *abstractus*, fr L, pp of *abstrahere* to draw away, fr *abs-*, *ab-* + *trahere* to draw – more at DRAW] – **abstractly** *adv*, **abstractness** *n*

[2]**abstract** *n* **1** a summary of points (e g of a piece of writing) **2** an abstract concept or state **3** an abstract composition or creation [ME, fr L *abstractus*]

[3]**abstract** /əbˈstrakt/ *vt* **1** to remove, separate **2** to consider in the abstract **3** to make an abstract of; summarize **4** to draw away the attention of **5** to steal, purloin – euph – **abstractor, abstracter** *n*

abˈstracted *adj* preoccupied, absentminded ⟨*the* ~ *look of a professor*⟩ – **abstractedly** *adv*, **abstractedness** *n*

ˌabstract exˈpressionism *n* art in which the artist attempts to express his/her attitudes and emotions through nonrepresentational means – **abstract expressionist** *n*

abstraction /əbˈstraksh(ə)n/ *n* **1** an abstract idea or term stripped of its concrete manifestations **2** absentmindedness **3** [2]ABSTRACT 3 [[3]ABSTRACT + -ION] – **abstractionism** *n*, **abstractionist** *n*, **abstractive** *adj*

abstruse /əbˈstroohs/ *adj* difficult to understand; recondite [L *abstrusus*, fr pp of *abstrudere* to conceal, fr *abs-*, *ab-* + *trudere* to push – more at THREAT] – **abstrusely** *adv*, **abstruseness** *n*

[1]**absurd** /əbˈsuhd, -bz-/ *adj* **1** ridiculously unreasonable or incongruous; silly **2** lacking order or value; meaningless [MF *absurde*, fr L *absurdus*, fr *ab-* + *surdus* deaf, stupid – more at SURD] – **absurdity** *n*, **absurdly** *adv*, **absurdness** *n*

[2]**absurd** *n* *the* state or condition in which human beings exist in an irrational and meaningless universe, and in which their life has no meaning outside their own existence – **absurdism** *n*, **absurdist** *n or adj*

abulia /ayˈbyoohli·ə/ *n* aboulia

abundance /əˈbund(ə)ns/ *n* **1** an ample quantity; a profusion **2** affluence, wealth **3** the relative degree of plentifulness of a living organism, substance, etc in an area

abundant /əˈbund(ə)nt/ *adj* **1a** marked by great plenty (e g of resources) ⟨*a fair and* ~ *land*⟩ **b** amply supplied *with*; abounding *in* **2** occurring in abundance ⟨~ *rainfall*⟩ [ME, fr MF, fr L *abundant-*, *abundans*, prp of *abundare* to abound] – **abundantly** *adv*

[1]**abuse** /əˈbyoohz/ *vt* **1** to attack in words; revile **2** to put to a wrong or improper use ⟨~ *a privilege*⟩ **3** to use so as to injure or damage; maltreat ⟨~ *a dog*⟩ [ME *abusen*, fr MF *abuser*, fr L *abusus*, pp of *abuti*, fr *ab-* + *uti* to use] – **abuser** *n*

[2]**abuse** /əˈbyoohs/ *n* **1** a corrupt practice or custom **2** improper use or treatment; misuse ⟨*drug* ~⟩ **3** vehemently expressed condemnation or disapproval ⟨*greeted them with a torrent of* ~⟩ **4** physical maltreatment – **abusive** *adj*, **abusively** *adv*, **abusiveness** *n*

abut /əˈbut/ *vb* **-tt-** *vi* **1** *of an area* to touch along a boundary; border – + *on* or *upon* ⟨*land* ~s *on the road*⟩ **2** *of a structure* **a** to terminate at a point of contact; be adjacent – + *on* or *against* ⟨*the town hall* ~s *on the church*⟩ **b** to lean for support – + *on* or *upon* ⟨*the neighbours' shed* ~s *on our wall*⟩ ~ *vt* to border on; touch [ME *abutten*; partly fr OF *aboter* to border on, fr *a-* (fr L *ad-*) + *bout* blow, end, fr *boter* to strike; partly fr OF *abuter* to come to an end, fr *a-* + *but* end, aim – more at [1]BUTT, [3]BUTT] – **abutter** *n*

abutment /əˈbutmənt/ *n* **1** the place at which abutting occurs **2** the part of a structure that directly receives thrust or pressure (e g of an arch)

abysmal /əˈbizməl/ *adj* **1** deplorably great ⟨~ *ignorance*⟩ **2** immeasurably bad ⟨*standard of writing was* ~ *– Punch*⟩ [*abysm* (abyss), fr ME *abime*, fr OF *abisme*, modif of LL *abyssus*] – **abysmally** *adv*

abyss /əˈbis/ *n* **1** the infernal regions or chaos of the old cosmogonies, thought of as a bottomless pit **2a** an immeasurably deep gulf **b** moral or emotional depths ⟨*an* ~ *of hopelessness*⟩ [ME *abissus*, fr LL *abyssus*, fr Gk *abyssos*, fr *abyssos* bottomless, fr *a-* + *byssos* depth; akin to Gk *bathys* deep – more at BATHY-]

abyssal /əˈbis(ə)l/ *adj* of the bottom waters of the ocean

[1]**-ac** /-ak, -ək/ *suffix* (→ *n*) one affected with ⟨*mani*ac⟩ ⟨*haemophili*ac⟩ [NL *-acus* of or relating to, fr Gk *-akos*]

[2]**-ac** *suffix* (→ *adj*) of or relating to ⟨*cardi*ac⟩ ⟨*ili*ac⟩

acacia /əˈkaysh(y)ə/ *n* **1** any of a genus of woody leguminous plants of warm regions with white or yellow flowers **2** GUM ARABIC [NL, genus name, fr L, acacia tree, fr Gk *akakia*, a tree]

academe /ˈakədeem/ *n*, *chiefly NAm* a college; *also* the university community [irreg fr NL *academia*, fr L, academy]

[1]**academic** /ˌakəˈdemik/ *also* **academical** /-kl/ *adj* **1a** of an institution of higher learning **b** scholarly **c** very learned but inexperienced in practical matters ⟨~ *thinkers*⟩ **2** conventional, formal ⟨*an* ~ *painting*⟩ **3** theoretical with no practical or useful bearing ⟨*an* ~ *question*⟩ **4** *chiefly NAm* of liberal rather than technical or vocational studies – **academically** *adv*, **academicize** /-misiez/ *vt*

[2]**academic** *n* a member (of the teaching staff) of an institution of higher learning

academicals /ˌakəˈdemiklz/ *n pl* the cap and gown worn as formal academic dress ☞ GARMENT

ˌacaˌdemic ˈfreedom *n* freedom to teach or learn without interference

academician /əˌkadəˈmish(ə)n/ *n* a member of an academy for the advancement of science, art, or literature

academicism /ˌakəˈdemisiz(ə)m/ *n* purely speculative thought and attitudes

academy /əˈkadəmi/ *n* **1** *cap* **a** the school for advanced education founded by Plato **b** the philosophical doctrines associated with Plato's Academy **2a** a secondary school; *esp* a private high school – now only in names **b** a college in which special subjects or skills are taught ⟨*an* ~ *of music*⟩ **3** a society of learned people organized to promote the arts or sciences [L *academia*, fr Gk *Akadēmeia*, fr *Akadēmeia*, gymnasium where Plato taught, fr *Akadēmos* Attic mythological hero; (2) and (3) largely fr F *académie* university, fr NL *academia*]

Acadian /ə'kaydi·ən/ *n* a native or inhabitant of Nova Scotia [*Acadia*, old name for F colony in N America, fr F *Acadie*] – **Acadian** *adj*

acanthus /ə'kanthəs/ *n, pl* **acanthuses** *also* **acanthi** /-,thie/ **1** any of a genus of usu large prickly plants, esp of the Mediterranean region **2** an ornamental device representing the leaves of the acanthus (e g on a Corinthian column) ☞ ARCHITECTURE [NL, genus name, fr Gk *akanthos*, a hellebore, fr *akantha* thorn]

a cappella *also* **a capella** /,ah kə'pelə/ *adv or adj* without instrumental accompaniment [It *a cappella* in chapel style]

acariasis /,akə'rie·əsis/ *n* infestation with or disease caused by mites

acarid /'akərid/ *n* a typical mite or other related arachnid [NL *Acarida*, fr *Acarus*, genus name, fr Gk *akari*, a mite] – **acarid** *adj*

acatalectic /ə,katə'lektik/ *adj* having the full number of syllables ⟨~ *verse*⟩ [LL *acatalecticus*, fr *acatalectus*, fr Gk *akatalēktos*, fr *a-* + *katalēgein* to leave off – more at CATALECTIC] – **acatalectic** *n*

accede /ək'seed/ *vi* **1** to become a party (e g to a treaty) **2** to express approval or give consent, often in response to urging **3** to enter on an office or position; *esp* to become monarch ⟨~ *to the throne*⟩ *USE* usu + *to* [ME *acceden* to approach, fr L *accedere* to go to, be added, fr *ad-* + *cedere* to go – more at CEDE]

accelerando /ək,selə'randoh/ *n, adv, or adj* (a musical passage that gets) gradually faster [It, lit., accelerating, fr L *accelerandum*, gerund of *accelerare*]

accelerate /ək'selərayt/ *vt* **1** to bring about at an earlier time **2** to increase the speed of **3** to hasten the progress, development, or growth of ~ *vi* **1** to move faster; gain speed **2** to increase more rapidly ⟨*believed inflation was* accelerating⟩ [L *acceleratus*, pp of *accelerare*, fr *ad-* + *celer* swift] – **accelerative** /-rətiv/ *adj*

acceleration /ək,selə'raysh(ə)n/ *n* (the rate of) change, specif increase, of velocity ⟨*this car has good* ~⟩ [ACCELERATE + -ION]

accelerator /ək'selərayta/ *n* **1** a pedal in a motor vehicle that controls the speed of the motor **2** a substance that speeds up a chemical reaction **3** an apparatus for giving high velocities to charged particles (e g electrons) [ACCELERATE + [1]-OR]

accelerometer /ək,selə'romitə/ *n* an instrument for measuring acceleration or vibrations [ISV *acceleration* + *-o-* + *-meter*]

[1]**accent** /'aksənt/ *n* **1** a distinctive manner of expression; *specif* a distinctive pattern in inflection, tone, or choice of words, esp as characteristic of a regional or national area **2a** prominence given to 1 syllable over others by stress or a change in pitch **b** greater stress given to 1 musical note **c** rhythmically significant stress on the syllables of a verse **3a accent, accent mark** a mark added to a letter (e g in à, ñ, ç) to indicate how it should be pronounced – compare DIACRITIC **b** a symbol used to indicate musical stress ☞ MUSIC **4** a sharply contrasting detail **5** special concern or attention; emphasis ⟨*an* ~ *on youth*⟩ [MF, fr L *accentus*, fr *ad-* + *cantus* song, fr *cantus*, pp of *canere* to sing – more at CHANT] – **accentless** *adj*

[2]**accent** /ək'sent/ *vt* **1a** to pronounce (a vowel, syllable, or word) with accent; stress **b** to mark with a written or printed accent **2** to make more prominent; emphasize

accentor /ək'sentaw, -tə/ *n* any of a genus of rather drab birds (e g the dunnock) resembling sparrows [NL, fr ML, one who sings with another, fr L *ad-* + *cantor* singer]

accentual /ak'sentyoo·əl, -choo·əl/ *adj* of or characterized by accent; *specif, of metre in poetry* based on the stress patterns of syllables rather than their length – compare QUANTITATIVE 3 [L *accentus*] – **accentually** *adv*

accentuate /ək'sentyoo·ayt, -choo·ayt/ *vt* to accent, emphasize [ML *accentuatus*, pp of *accentuare*, fr L *accentus*] – **accentuation** /-'aysh(ə)n/ *n*

accept /ək'sept/ *vt* **1a** to agree to receive ⟨~ *a gift*⟩ ⟨~ *a suitor*⟩; *also* to agree to ⟨~ *an invitation*⟩ **b** to be able or designed to take or hold (sthg applied or inserted) ⟨*machine* ~s *only pennies*⟩ **2** to give admittance or approval to ⟨~ *her as one of the group*⟩ **3a** to endure without protest; accommodate oneself to ⟨~ *poor living conditions*⟩ **b** to regard as proper, normal, or inevitable **c** to recognize as true, factual, or adequate ⟨*refused to* ~ *my explanation*⟩ **4** to undertake the responsibility of ⟨~ *a job*⟩ ~ *vi* to receive favourably sthg offered [ME *accepten*, fr MF *accepter*, fr L *acceptare*, fr *acceptus*, pp of *accipere* to receive, fr *ad-* + *capere* to take – more at HEAVE]

acceptable /ək'septəbl/ *adj* **1** capable or worthy of being accepted; satisfactory **2** welcome or pleasing to the receiver ⟨*compliments are always* ~⟩ **3** tolerable – **acceptableness** *n*, **acceptably** *adv*, **acceptability** /-tə'biləti/ *n*

acceptance /ək'sept(ə)ns/ *n* **1** accepting, approval **2** acceptability **3** agreement to the act or offer of another so that the parties become legally bound

acceptation /,aksep'taysh(ə)n/ *n* a generally accepted meaning of a word or concept

ac'cepted *adj* generally approved or used; customary – **acceptedly** *adv*

acceptor /ək'septaw, -tə/ *n* **1** a compound, atom, elementary particle, or radical capable of combining with another – compare DONOR 3a **2** a horse that has been entered for a race [ACCEPT + [1]-OR]

[1]**access** /'akses, -səs/ *n* **1** a fit *of* intense feeling; an outburst ⟨*an* ~ *of rage*⟩ **2a** freedom to approach, reach, or make use of sthg ⟨~ *to classified information*⟩ **b** a means (e g a doorway or channel) of access **c** the state of being readily reached or obtained ⟨*the building is not easy of* ~⟩ [ME, fr MF & L; MF *acces* arrival, fr L *accessus* approach, fr *accessus*, pp of *accedere* to approach – more at ACCEDE]

[2]**access** *vt* to get at; gain access to ⟨*accumulator and index registers can be* ~ed *by the programmer – Datamation*⟩

accessary /ək'ses(ə)ri/ *n or adj* (one) involved in or privy to a crime, but not present when it is committed

accessible /ək'sesəbl/ *adj* **1** capable of being reached ⟨~ *by rail*⟩ **2** of a form that can be readily grasped intellectually **3** able to be influenced ⟨~ *to persuasion*⟩ – **accessibly** *adv*, **accessibility** /-sə'biləti/ *n*

[1]**accession** /ək'sesh(ə)n/ *n* **1** sthg added; an acqui-

sition; *specif* a book added to a library **2** becoming joined **3** the act by which a nation becomes party to an agreement already in force **4a** an increase due to sthg added **b** acquisition of property by addition to existing property **5** the act of entering on a high office ⟨*his ~ to the Papacy*⟩ **6** assent, agreement – fml – **accessional** *adj*

[2]**accession** *vt* to record (e g books) in order of acquisition

[1]**accessory** /ək'sesəri/ *n* an inessential object or device that adds to the beauty, convenience, or effectiveness of sthg else ⟨*car* accessories⟩ ⟨*clothing* accessories⟩

[2]**accessory** *adj* aiding or contributing in a secondary way; supplementary, subordinate

accessory after the fact *n* one who knowingly aids or shelters an offender – no longer used technically

accessory before the fact *n* one who contributes to a crime but is not present when it is committed – no longer used technically

'access ,time *n* the time lag between the request and delivery of stored information (e g in a computer)

acciaccatura /ə,chakə'tooərə/ *n* a discordant note sounded with or before a principal note or chord and immediately released ☞ MUSIC [It, lit., crushing, fr *acciaccare* to crush]

accidence /'aksid(ə)ns/ *n* the part of grammar that deals with inflections [L *accidentia* inflections of words, nonessential qualities, pl of *accident-, accidens*, n]

accident /'aksid(ə)nt/ *n* **1a** an event occurring by chance or arising from unknown causes **b** lack of intention or necessity; chance ⟨*met by ~ rather than by design*⟩ **2** an unexpected happening causing loss or injury **3** a nonessential property or condition of sthg **4** an irregularity of a surface (e g of the moon) [ME, fr MF, fr L *accident-, accidens* nonessential quality, chance, fr prp of *accidere* to happen, fr *ad-* + *cadere* to fall – more at CHANCE]

[1]**accidental** /,aksi'dentl/ *adj* **1** arising incidentally; nonessential **2a** occurring unexpectedly or by chance **b** happening without intent or through carelessness and often with unfortunate results – **accidentally** *adv*, **accidentalness** *n*

[2]**accidental** *n* **1** ACCIDENT 3 **2** (a sign indicating) a note altered to sharp, flat, or natural and foreign to a key indicated by a key signature ☞ MUSIC

'accident-,prone *adj* having personality traits that predispose to accidents

accipiter /ək'sipitə/ *n* any of a genus of medium-sized short-winged long-legged hawks (e g the sparrow hawk) with low darting flight [NL, genus name, fr L, hawk] – **accipitrine** /-treen/ *adj or n*

[1]**acclaim** /ə'klaym/ *vt vt* **1** to applaud, praise **2** to hail or proclaim by acclamation ⟨~ed *her Queen*⟩ [L *acclamare*, lit., to shout at, fr *ad-* + *clamare* to shout – more at CLAIM] – **acclaimer** *n*

[2]**acclaim** *n* ACCLAMATION 1

acclamation /,aklə'maysh(ə)n/ *n* **1** a loud expression of praise, goodwill, or assent **2** an overwhelming affirmative vote by cheers or applause rather than by ballot ⟨*motion was carried by ~*⟩ [L *acclamation-, acclamatio*, fr *acclamatus*, pp of *acclamare*]

acclimate /'aklimayt, ə'kliemət/ *vb, NAm* to acclimatize [F *acclimater*, fr *a-* (fr L *ad-*) + *climat* climate] – **acclimation** /,akli'maysh(ə)n/ *n*

acclimat·ize, -ise /ə'kliemə,tiez/ *vb* to adapt to a new climate or situation – **acclimatizer** *n*, **acclimatization** /-tie'zaysh(ə)n/ *n*

acclivity /ə'klivəti/ *n* an ascending slope [L *acclivitas*, fr *acclivis* ascending, fr *ad-* + *clivus* slope – more at DECLIVITY]

accolade /'akəlayd/ *n* **1** a ceremony marking the conferral of knighthood, in which each of the candidate's shoulders is touched with a sword **2a** a mark of acknowledgment or honour; an award **b** an expression of strong praise [F, fr *accoler* to embrace, fr (assumed) VL *accollare*, fr L *ad-* + *collum* neck – more at COLLAR]

accommodate /ə'komədayt/ *vt* **1** to make fit, suitable, or congruous *to* **2** to bring into agreement or concord; reconcile **3a** to give help to; oblige *with* **b** to provide with lodgings; house **4** to have or make adequate room for **5** to give consideration to; allow for [L *accommodatus*, pp of *accommodare*, fr *ad-* + *commodare* to make fit, fr *commodus* suitable – more at COMMODE] – **accommodative** /-dətiv, -,daytiv/ *adj*, **accommodativeness** /-,daytivnis, -dətivnis/ *n*

accommodating /ə'komədayting/ *adj* helpful, obliging – **accommodatingly** *adv*

accommodation /ə,komə'daysh(ə)n/ *n* **1a** lodging, housing – usu pl with sing. meaning in NAm **b** space, premises ⟨*office ~*⟩ **2a** sthg needed or desired for convenience; a facility **b** an adaptation, adjustment **c** a settlement, agreement **d** a bank loan **e** the (range of) automatic adjustment of the eye, esp by changes in the amount by which the lens bends light, for seeing at different distances [ACCOMMODATE + -ION] – **accommodational** *adj*

ac,commo'dation ad,dress *n* an address to which letters may be sent to sby who does not have or wish to give a permanent address

ac,commo'dation ,ladder *n* a ladder hung over the side of a ship for ascending from or descending to small boats

accompaniment /ə'kump(ə)nimənt/ *n* **1** a subordinate instrumental or vocal part supporting or complementing a principal voice or instrument **2** an addition intended to give completeness; a complement

accompany /ə'kump(ə)ni/ *vt* **1** to go with as an escort or companion **2** to perform an accompaniment to or for **3a** to make an addition to; supplement *with* **b** *of a thing* to happen, exist, or be found with ⟨*the pictures that ~ the text*⟩ ~ *vi* to perform an accompaniment [ME *accompanien*, fr MF *acompaignier*, fr *a-* (fr L *ad-*) + *compaing* companion, fr LL *companio*] – **accompanist** *n*

accomplice /ə'kumplis, -'kom-/ *n* sby who collaborates with another, esp in wrongdoing [alter. (by incorrect division of *a complice*) of arch *complice* (associate), fr ME, fr MF, fr LL *complic-, complex*, fr L *com-* + *plicare* to fold – more at PLY]

accomplish /ə'kumplish, -'kom-/ *vt* **1** to bring to a successful conclusion; achieve **2** to complete, cover (a measure of time or distance) [ME *accomplisshen*, fr MF *acompliss-*, stem of *acomplir*, fr (assumed) VL *accomplēre*, fr L *ad-* + *complēre* to fill up – more at COMPLETE] – **accomplishable** *adj*, **accomplisher** *n*

ac'complished *adj* **1** fully effected; completed ⟨*an*

~ *fact*⟩ **2a** skilled, proficient ⟨*an* ~ *dancer*⟩ **b** having many social accomplishments

ac'complishment /-mənt/ *n* **1** completion, fulfilment **2** an achievement **3** an acquired ability or esp social skill [ACCOMPLISH + -MENT]

[1]**accord** /ə'kawd/ *vt* **1** to grant, concede ⟨~ed *them permission*⟩ **2** to give, award ⟨~ed *her a warm welcome*⟩ ~ *vi* to be consistent *with* [ME *accorden* to reconcile, agree, fr OF *acorder*, fr (assumed) VL *accordare*, fr L *ad-* + *cord-*, *cor* heart – more at HEART]

[2]**accord** *n* **1a** ACCORDANCE 1 **b** a formal treaty of agreement **2** balanced interrelationship (e g of colours or sounds); harmony [ME, fr OF *acort*, fr *acorder*] – **of one's own accord** of one's own volition; unbidden – **with one accord** with the consent or agreement of all

accordance /ə'kawd(ə)ns/ *n* **1** agreement, conformity ⟨*in* ~ *with a rule*⟩ **2** the act of granting

accordant /ə'kawd(ə)nt/ *adj* consonant *with* – **accordantly** *adv*

ac'cording as /ə'kawding/ *conj* **1** in accordance with the way in which **2** depending on how or whether

accordingly /ə'kawdingli/ *adv* **1** as suggested; appropriately **2** consequently, so

ac'cording to *prep* **1** in conformity with **2** as declared by **3** depending on

accordion /ə'kawdi·ən/ *n* a portable keyboard wind instrument in which the wind is forced past free reeds by means of a hand-operated bellows [G *akkordion*, fr *akkord* chord, fr F *accord*, fr OF *acort*] – **accordionist** *n*

accost /ə'kost/ *vt* **1** to approach and speak to, esp boldly or challengingly **2** *of a prostitute* to solicit [MF *accoster*, deriv of L *ad-* + *costa* rib, side – more at COAST]

accoucheur /ə,kooh'shuh (*Fr* akuʃœːr)/, *fem* **accoucheuse** /-'shuhz (*Fr* akuʃœːz)/ *n* sby who assists at a birth [F, fr *accoucher* to deliver a child]

[1]**account** /ə'kownt/ *n* **1** a record of debits and credits relating to a particular item, person, or concern **2** a list of items of expenditure to be balanced against income – usu pl ⟨*doing her monthly* ~s⟩ **3a** a periodically rendered calculation listing purchases and credits ⟨*a grocery* ~⟩ **b** business, patronage ⟨*glad to get that customer's* ~⟩ **4** a business arrangement whereby money is deposited in, and may be withdrawn from, a bank, building society, etc **5** a commission to carry out a particular business operation (e g an advertising campaign) given by one company to another **6** value, importance ⟨*a man of no* ~⟩ **7** profit, advantage ⟨*turned his wit to good* ~⟩ **8** careful thought; consideration ⟨*left nothing out of* ~⟩ **9a** a statement explaining one's conduct ⟨*render an* ~⟩ **b** a statement of facts or events; a relation ⟨*a newspaper* ~⟩ **10** hearsay, report – usu pl ⟨*by all* ~s *a rich man*⟩ **11** a version, rendering ⟨*the pianist's sensitive* ~ *of it*⟩ – **on account of** due to; BECAUSE OF – **on no account** *or* **not on any account** under no circumstances – **on one's own account** **1** on one's own behalf **2** at one's own risk – **on somebody's account** for sby's sake

[2]**account** *vt* to think of as; consider ⟨~s *himself lucky*⟩ [ME *accounten*, fr MF *acompter*, fr *a-* (fr L *ad-*) + *compter* to count] – **account for** **1** to give an explanation or reason for **2** to be the sole or primary explanation for **3** to bring about the defeat, death, or destruction of ⟨accounted for *3 of the attackers*⟩

accountable /ə'kowntəbl/ *adj* **1** responsible, answerable **2** explicable – **accountableness** *n*, **accountably** *adv*, **accountability** /-tə'biləti/ *n*

accountancy /ə'kownt(ə)nsi/ *n* the profession or practice of accounting

accountant /əkownt(ə)nt/ *n* one who practises and is usu qualified in accounting

accounting /ə'kownting/ *n* the recording, analysis, and verification of business and financial transactions

accoutrement /ə'koohtrəmənt/, *NAm also* **accouterment** /ə'koohtəmənt/ *n* equipment, trappings; *specif* a soldier's outfit excluding clothes and weapons – usu pl [MF, fr *accoutrer* to equip, fr *a-* + *costure* seam, fr (assumed) VL *consutura*, fr L *consutus*, pp of *consuere* to sew together, fr *com-* + *suere* to sew – more at SEW]

accredit /ə'kredit/ *vt* **1a** to give official authorization to or approval of **b** to send (esp an envoy) with credentials **c** to recognize or vouch for as conforming to a standard **2** to credit *with*, attribute *to* [F *accréditer*, fr *ad-* + *crédit* credit] – **accreditable** *adj*, **accreditation** /-di'taysh(ə)n/ *n*

accrete /ə'kreet/ *vb* to (cause to) grow together or become attached by accretion [back-formation fr *accretion*]

accretion /ə'kreesh(ə)n/ *n* **1a** an increase in size caused by natural growth or the external adhesion or addition of matter **b** sthg added or stuck extraneously **2a** an increase in area of land owned, caused esp by the action of natural forces **b** an increase in an inheritor's share of an estate caused by a co-inheritor not claiming his/her share **3** the growth of separate particles or parts (e g of a plant) into one; concretion [L *accretion-*, *accretio*, fr *accretus*, pp of *accrescere* to increase] – **accretionary** *adj*, **accretive** /ə'kreetiv/ *adj*

accrue /ə'krooh/ *vi* **1** to come as an increase or addition to sthg; arise as a growth or result **2** to be periodically accumulated ⟨*interest has* ~d *over the year*⟩ ~ *vt* to collect, accumulate [ME *acreuen*, prob fr MF *acreue* increase, fr *acreistre* to increase, fr L *accrescere*, fr *ad-* + *crescere* to grow – more at CRESCENT] – **accruable** *adj*, **accruement** *n*

acculturation /ə,kulchə'raysh(ə)n/ *n* the assimilation and adoption of the values of a different culture [*ad-* + *culture* + *-ation*] – **acculturate** *vt*

accumulate /ə'kyoohmyoo,layt/ *vt* to collect together gradually; amass ~ *vi* to increase in quantity or number [L *accumulatus*, pp of *accumulare*, fr *ad-* + *cumulare* to heap up – more at CUMULATE]

accumulation /ə,kyoohmyoo'laysh(ə)n/ *n* **1** increase or growth caused by esp repeated or continuous addition; *specif* increase in capital from interest payments **2** sthg that has accumulated [ACCUMULATE + -ION]

accumulative /ə'kyoohmyooləttiv/ *adj* **1** cumulative **2** tending or given to accumulation, esp of money – **accumulatively** *adv*, **accumulativeness** *n*

accumulator /ə'kyoohmyoo,laytə/ *n* **1** a part (e g in a computer) where numbers are added or stored **2** *Br* a rechargeable secondary electric cell; *also* a connected set of these **3** *Br* a bet whereby the winnings from one of a series of events are staked on the next event [ACCUMULATE + [1]-OR]

accurate /'akyoorət/ *adj* **1** free from error, esp as the result of care ⟨*an* ~ *estimate*⟩ **2** conforming precisely to truth or a measurable standard; exact ⟨~ *instruments*⟩ [L *accuratus*, fr pp of *accurare* to take care of, fr *ad-* + *cura* care – more at CURE] – **accurately** *adv*, **accurateness** *n*, **accuracy** /-rəsi/ *n*

accursed /ə'kuhst, ə'kuhsid/, **accurst** /ə'kuhst/ *adj* **1** under a curse; ill-fated **2** damnable, detestable [ME *acursed*, fr pp of *acursen* to consign to destruction with a curse, fr *a-* (fr OE *ā*, perfective prefix) + *cursen* to curse] – **accursedly** /-sidli/ *adv*, **accursedness** /-sidnis/ *n*

accusation /,akyoo'zaysh(ə)n/ *n* a charge of wrongdoing; an allegation [ACCUSE + -ATION]

[1]**accusative** /ə'kyoohzətiv/ *adj* of or being the grammatical accusative [ME, fr MF or L; MF *accusatif*, fr L *accusativus*, fr *accusatus*, pp of *accusare*]

[2]**accusative** *n* (a form (e g *me*) in) a grammatical case expressing the direct object of a verb or of some prepositions

accusatorial /ə,kyoohzə'tawri·əl/ *adj* **1** accusatory **2** of or involving (a) prosecution before a judge who is not himself the prosecutor – compare INQUISITORIAL

accusatory /ə'kyoohzət(ə)ri/ *adj* containing or expressing (an) accusation

accuse /ə'kyoohz/ *vt* to charge with a fault or crime; blame ⟨~d *him of murder*⟩ [ME *accusen*, fr OF *acuser*, fr L *accusare* to call to account, fr *ad-* + *causa* lawsuit, cause] – **accuser** *n*, **accusingly** *adv*

ac'cused *n, pl* **accused** *the* defendant in a criminal case

accustom /ə'kust(ə)m/ *vt* to make used *to* through use or experience; habituate [ME *accustomen*, fr MF *acostumer*, fr *a-* (fr L *ad-*) + *costume* custom] – **accustomation** /-'aysh(ə)n/ *n*

ac'customed *adj* **1** customary, habitual **2** in the habit of; used *to* ⟨~ *to making decisions*⟩ – **accustomedness** *n*

AC/DC /,-- '--/ *adj* BISEXUAL 1b – infml [*a*lternating *c*urrent, *d*irect *c*urrent]

[1]**ace** /ays/ *n* **1** a die face, playing card, or domino marked with 1 spot or pip; *also* the single spot or pip on any of these **2** (a point scored by) a shot, esp a service in tennis, that an opponent fails to touch **3** a combat pilot who has brought down at least 5 enemy aircraft **4** an expert or leading performer in a specified field ⟨*a soccer* ~⟩ [ME *as*, fr OF, fr L, unit, a copper coin] – **ace in the hole** an effective argument or resource held in reserve – **within an ace of** on the point of; very near to ⟨*came* within an ace of *winning*⟩

[2]**ace** *vt* to score an ace against (an opponent)

[3]**ace** *adj* great, excellent – infml ⟨*their new album's really* ~⟩

-aceae *suffix* (→ *n pl*) members of the plant family of ⟨*Ros*aceae⟩ [NL, fr L, fem pl of *-aceus* -aceous]

-aceous /-'aysi·əs, -'aysh(y)əs/ *suffix* (→ *adj*) **1a** having the characteristics of ⟨*herb*aceous⟩ ⟨*tuff*aceous⟩ **b** consisting of ⟨*car bon*aceous⟩ ⟨*set*aceous⟩; containing ⟨*farin*aceous⟩ ⟨*argill*aceous⟩ **2a** of a group of animals characterized by (a specified form or feature) ⟨*cet*aceous⟩ **b** of a (specified) plant family ⟨*ros*aceous⟩ [L *-aceus*]

acephalous /ə'sefələs, ,ay-/ *adj* lacking a head or having the head reduced [Gk *akephalos*, fr *a-* + *kephalē* head – more at CEPHALIC]

acerbic /ə'suhbik/ *adj* **1** bitter or sour in taste **2** sharp or vitriolic in speech, temper, or manner [*acerb* (sour), fr F or L; F *acerbe*, fr L *acerbus*, fr *acer* – more at EDGE] – **acerbically** *adv*, **acerbity** *n*

acescent /ə'kes(ə)nt, -'ses-/ *adj* (becoming) slightly sour [F, fr L *acescent-*, *acescens*, prp of *acescere* to turn sour, incho of *acēre*] – **acescence** *n*

acet-, **aceto-** *comb form* acetic acid; acetic ⟨acet*yl*⟩ [F & L; F *acét-*, fr L *acet-*, fr *acetum* vinegar, fr *acēre* to be sour, fr *acer* sharp – more at EDGE]

acetabularia /,asitəbyoo'leəri·ə, ,asi,tabyoo'leəri·ə/ *n* a large single-celled green alga that grows in warm seas and is shaped like a small mushroom [NL, genus name, fr L *acetabulum* vinegar cup]

acetabulum /,asi'tabyooləm/ *n, pl* **acetabulums**, **acetabula** /-lə/ **1a** the cup-shaped socket in the hipbone into which the head of the thighbone fits **b** the cavity in the body of an insect into which its leg fits **2** a round sucker of a leech or other invertebrate [L, lit., vinegar cup, fr *acetum* vinegar] – **acetabular** *adj*

acetal /'asitl/ *n* any of various compounds containing the grouping $C(OR)_2$ [G *azetal*, fr *azet-* acet- + *al*kohol alcohol]

acetaldehyde /,asi'taldihied/ *n* a volatile liquid aldehyde used chiefly in organic synthesis [ISV]

acetanilide /,asi'tanilied/, **acetanilid** /-lid/ *n* a derivative of aniline used in chemical synthesis [ISV]

acetate /'asitayt/ *n* **1** a salt or ester of acetic acid **2** (a textile fibre or gramophone record made from) cellulose acetate

acetic /ə'seetik, -'set-/ *adj* of or producing acetic acid or vinegar [prob fr F *acétique*, fr L *acetum* vinegar]

a,cetic 'acid *n* a pungent liquid acid that is the major acid in vinegar

acetify /ə'seetifie, -'set-/ *vt* to turn into acetic acid or vinegar – **acetifier** *n*, **acetification** /-tifi'kaysh(ə)n/ *n*

aceto- – see ACET-

acetone /'asitohn/ *n* a volatile fragrant inflammable liquid ketone used esp as a solvent and in organic chemical synthesis [G *azeton*, fr L *acetum*] – **acetonic** /-'tonik/ *adj*

acetous /'asitəs/ *adj* acetic; *also* sour, vinegary

acetyl /'asitil, ə'si-, ə'see-, -tiel/ *n* the radical of acetic acid

acetylcholine /,asitil'kohleen, -lin/ *n* a neurotransmitter released esp at autonomic nerve endings [ISV] – **acetylcholinic** /-'linik/ *adj*

acetyl-coA /-koh'ay/ *n* acetyl coenzyme A

acetyl coenzyme A *n* a compound formed as an essential intermediate in the metabolism of most living cells

acetylene /ə'setileen, -lin/ *n* a colourless unsaturated hydrocarbon gas used esp as a fuel (e g in oxyacetylene torches) – **acetylenic** /-'leenik, -'lenik/ *adj*

,acetylsali,cylic 'acid /,asitil,sali'silik/ *n* aspirin [ISV]

[1]**ache** /ayk/ *vi* **1a** to suffer a usu dull persistent pain **b** to feel anguish or distress ⟨*heart* ~d *for her*⟩ **2** to yearn, long ⟨aching *to see you*⟩ [ME *aken*, fr OE *acan*; akin to LG *äken* to hurt] – **achingly** *adv*

[2]**ache** *n* a usu dull persistent pain

achene /ə'keen/ *n* a small dry indehiscent 1-seeded fruit (e g that of the dandelion) [NL *achaenium*, fr a- + Gk *chainein* to yawn – more at YAWN] – **achenial** /əˈkeenyəl, -ni·əl/ *adj*

Acheulian, Acheulean /əˈshoohli·ən/ *adj* of a Lower Palaeolithic culture following the Abbevillian [F *Acheuléen*, fr St *Acheul*, near Amiens in France]

à cheval /ˌah shəˈval/ *adv* so as to be split evenly between 2 numbers, cards, events, etc ⟨*betting* ~⟩ [F, lit., on horseback]

achieve /əˈcheev/ *vt* **1** to carry out successfully; accomplish **2** to obtain by effort; win [ME *acheven*, fr MF *achever* to finish, fr *a-* (fr L *ad-*) + *chief* end, head – more at CHIEF] – **achievable** *adj*, **achiever** *n*

aˈchievement /-mənt/ *n* **1** successful completion; accomplishment **2** sthg accomplished, esp by resolve, persistence, or courage; a feat **3** performance in a test or academic course **4** a coat of arms with its formal accompaniments (e g helm, crest, and supporters) [ACHIEVE + -MENT]

Aˌchilles' ˈheel /əˈkileez, -liz/ *n* a person's only vulnerable point [*Achilles*, legendary Gk warrior, reputedly vulnerable only in the heel]

Aˌchilles ˈtendon *n* the strong tendon joining the muscles in the calf to the heelbone

achromatic /ˌakrohˈmatik, -krə-/ *adj* **1** transmitting light without dispersing it into its constituent colours **2** possessing no colour; neutral [F *achromatique*, fr Gk *achrōmatos*, fr *a* + *chromat-*, *chroma* colour – more at CHROMATIC] – **achromatically** *adv*, **achromaticity** /əˌkrohməˈtisəti/ *n*, **achromatism** /əˈkrohməˌtiz(ə)m/ *n*, **achromatize** /əˈkrohməˌtiez/ *vt*

achy /ˈayki/ *adj* afflicted with aches – **achiness** *n*

[1]**acid** /ˈasid/ *adj* **1a** sour or sharp to the taste **b** sharp, biting, or sour in speech, manner, or disposition; caustic ⟨*an* ~ *wit*⟩ **2** of, like, containing, or being an acid ⟨~ *soil*⟩; *specif* having a pH of less than 7 **3** of, being, or made by a steelmaking process in which the furnace is lined with acidic material **4** *of rock* rich in silica [F or L; F *acide*, fr L *acidus*, fr *acēre* to be sour, fr *acer* sharp – more at EDGE] – **acidly** *adv*, **acidness** *n*, **acidity** /əˈsidəti/ *n*

[2]**acid** *n* **1** a sour substance; *specif* any of various typically water-soluble and sour compounds having a pH of less than 7 that are capable of giving up a hydrogen ion to or accepting an unshared pair of electrons from a base to form a salt **2** LSD – infml

ˈacid ˌdrop *n* a hard tart sweet made with sugar and tartaric acid

acidic /əˈsidik/ *adj* **1** acid-forming **2** acid

acidify /əˈsidifie/ *vt* to make or convert into (an) acid – **acidifier** *n*, **acidification** /əˌsidifiˈkaysh(ə)n/ *n*

acidophil /əˈsidəfil, -doh-/, **acidophile** /-fiel/ *n* an acidophilic tissue, organism, etc; *esp* an eosinophilic white blood cell

acidophilic /ˌasidohˈfilik/, **acidophil** /əˈsidəfil, -doh-/ *adj* **1** staining readily with acid dyes **2** preferring or thriving in an acid environment

acidosis /ˌasiˈdohsis/ *n* a disorder in which the blood, tissues, etc are unusually acid – **acidotic** /-ˈdotik/ *adj*

ˌacid ˈrock *n* rock music marked by long passages of electronic musical effects intended to convey the atmosphere of drug-induced hallucinations

ˌacid ˈtest *n* a severe or crucial test (e g of value or suitability) [fr use of nitric acid to test for gold]

acidulate /əˈsidyoolayt/ *vt* to make (slightly) acid [L *acidulus*] – **acidulation** /-ˈlaysh(ə)n/ *n*

acidulous /əˈsidyooləs/ *adj* somewhat acid in taste or manner; caustic [L *acidulus* sourish, fr *acidus*] – **acidulosity** /əˌsidyooˈlosəti/ *n*

ack-ack /ˈakˌak/ *adj* antiaircraft [signallers' terms for *AA*, fr antiaircraft]

ackee /ˈakee, aˈkee/ *n* (a tropical tree bearing) a red fruit which is edible when cooked [Kru *ā-kee*]

acknowledge /əkˈnolij/ *vt* **1** to admit knowledge of; concede to be true or valid **2** to recognize the status or claims of **3a** to express gratitude or obligation for **b** to show recognition of (e g by smiling or nodding) **c** to confirm receipt of [*ac-* (as in *accord*) + *knowledge*] – **acknowledgeable** *adj*

acˈknowledged *adj* generally recognized, accepted, or admitted – **acknowledgedly** *adv*

acˈknowledgment *also* **acknowledgement** /-mənt/ *n* **1** recognition or favourable reception of an act or achievement **2** a thing done or given in recognition of sthg received **3** a declaration or avowal of a fact **4** an author's list of people to whom he/she is indebted, usu appearing at the front of a book – usu pl with sing. meaning [ACKNOWLEDGE + -MENT]

aˌclinic ˈline /əˈklinik/ *n* an imaginary line round the earth where a magnetic needle remains horizontal [[2]*a-* + *-clinic*]

acme /ˈakmi/ *n* the highest point or stage; *esp* a perfect representative of a specified class or thing ⟨*was the* ~ *of courtesy*⟩ [Gk *akmē* point, highest point – more at EDGE]

acne /ˈakni/ *n* a skin disorder found esp among adolescents, characterized by inflammation of the skin glands and hair follicles and causing red pustules, esp on the face and neck [Gk *aknē* eruption of the face, MS var of *akmē*, lit., point] – **acned** /ˈaknid/ *adj*

acoelomate /ˌayˈseeləmayt, -mət/ *adj, of an animal* having no coelom – **acoelomate** *n*

acolyte /ˈakəliet/ *n* **1** an assistant performing minor duties in a liturgical service **2** one who attends or assists; a follower [ME *acolite*, fr OF & ML; OF, fr ML *acoluthus*, fr MGk *akolouthos*, fr Gk, adj, following, fr *a-*, *ha-* (akin to Gk *homos* same) + *keleuthos* path]

aconite /ˈakəniet/ *n* (a drug obtained from) monkshood [MF or L; MF, fr L *aconitum*, fr Gk *akoniton*] – **aconitic** /-ˈnitik/ *adj*

acorn /ˈayˌkawn/ *n* the nut of the oak, usu seated in a hard woody cup [ME *akern*, fr OE *æcern*; akin to MHG *ackeran* acorns collectively, Russ *yagoda* berry]

ˌacorn ˈbarnacle *n* any of numerous barnacles that form an incrustation on coastal rocks

ˈacorn ˌworm *n* any of a group of burrowing wormlike marine animals usu classed with the chordates

[1]**acoustic** /əˈkoohstik/ *also* **acoustical** /-kl/ *adj* **1** of sound, the sense of hearing, or acoustics **2** of or being a musical instrument whose sound is not electronically modified [Gk *akoustikos* of hearing, fr *akouein* to hear – more at HEAR] – **acoustically** *adv*

[2]**acoustic** *n* **1** *pl but sing in constr* the science of sound **2** the properties of a room, hall, etc that govern the quality of sound heard – usu pl with sing. meaning – **acoustician** /ˌakoohˈstish(ə)n/ *n*

acquaint /əˈkwaynt/ *vt* to cause to know; make familiar *with* sthg ⟨~ *oneself with the law*⟩ [ME *aquainten*, fr OF *acointier*, fr ML *accognitare*, fr LL *accognitus*, pp of *accognoscere* to know perfectly, fr L *ad-* + *cognoscere* to know – more at COGNITION]

acquaintance /ə'kwaynt(ə)ns/ *n* **1** personal knowledge; familiarity **2a** *sing or pl in constr* the people with whom one is acquainted **b** a person whom one knows but who is not a particularly close friend – **acquaintanceship** *n* – **make the acquaintance of** to come to know; meet

ac'quainted *adj* having met (each other) socially; familiar *with* (each other) ⟨*we are not* ~⟩ ⟨*is* ~ *with the mayor*⟩

acquiesce /,akwee'es/ *vi* to submit or comply tacitly or passively – often + *in* [F *acquiescer*, fr L *acquiescere*, fr *ad-* + *quiescere* to be quiet, fr *quies*, n, quiet, rest] – **acquiescence** *n*, **acquiescent** *adj*, **acquiescently** *adv*

acquire /ə'kwie·ə/ *vt* **1a** to gain or come into possession of, often by unspecified means; *also* to steal – euph **b** to gain as a new characteristic or ability, esp as a result of skill or hard work **2** to locate and hold (an object) in a detector ⟨~ *a target by radar*⟩ [ME *aqueren*, fr MF *aquerre*, fr L *acquirere*, fr *ad-* + *quaerere* to seek, obtain] – **acquirable** *adj*, **acquirement** *n*

acquisition /,akwi'zish(ə)n/ *n* **1** acquiring, gaining **2** sby or sthg acquired or gained, esp to one's advantage [ME *acquisicioun*, fr MF or L; MF *acquisition*, fr L *acquisition-*, *acquisitio*, fr *acquisitus*, pp of *acquirere*] – **acquisitional** *adj*, **acquisitor** /ə'kwizitə/ *n*

acquisitive /ə'kwizətiv/ *adj* keen or tending to acquire and possess – **acquisitively** *adv*, **acquisitiveness** *n*

acquit /ə'kwit/ *vt* **-tt-** **1** to free from responsibility or obligation; *specif* to declare not guilty ⟨*the court* ~ted *him of the charge*⟩ **2** to conduct (oneself) in a specified, usu favourable, manner [ME *aquiten*, fr OF *aquiter*, fr *a-* (fr L *ad-*) + *quite* free of – more at ²QUIT] – **acquitter** *n*

acquittal /ə'kwitl/ *n* a judicial release from a criminal charge

acquittance /ə'kwit(ə)ns/ *n* (a document giving proof of) a discharge from an obligation

acr-, acro- *comb form* **1** beginning; end ⟨acr*onym*⟩ ⟨acr*ostic*⟩ **2a** top; peak; summit; apex ⟨acr*odont*⟩ ⟨acr*opolis*⟩ ⟨acr*opetal*⟩ **b** height ⟨acr*ophobia*⟩ ⟨acr*obat*⟩ **c** extremity ⟨acr*omegaly*⟩ [MF or Gk; MF *acro-*, fr Gk *akr-*, *akro-*, fr *akros* topmost, extreme; akin to Gk *akmē* point – more at EDGE]

acre /'aykə/ *n* **1** *pl* lands, fields **2** a unit of area equal to 4840yd² (4046.86m²) ☞ UNIT **3** *pl* great quantities – infml [ME, fr OE *æcer*; akin to OHG *ackar* field, L *ager*, Gk *agros*, L *agere* to drive – more at AGENT]

acreage /'ayk(ə)rij/ *n* area in acres

acrid /'akrid/ *adj* **1** unpleasantly pungent in taste or smell **2** violently bitter in manner or language; acrimonious [modif of L *acr-*, *acer* sharp – more at EDGE] – **acridly** *adv*, **acridness** *n*, **acridity** /ə'kridəti/ *n*

acridine /'akrideen, -dien, -din/ *n* a compound occurring in coal tar and important as the parent compound of dyes and antiseptics

acriflavine /,akri'flayveen, -vin/ *n* a red or orange dye used as a skin disinfectant [*acri*dine + *flavine*]

Acrilan /'akrilan/ *trademark* – used for an acrylic fibre

acrimony /'akriməni/ *n* caustic sharpness of manner or language resulting from anger or ill nature [MF or L; MF *acrimonie*, fr L *acrimonia*, fr *acr-*, *acer*] – **acrimonious** /,akri'mohnyəs/ *adj*, **acrimoniously** *adv*, **acrimoniousness** *n*

acrobat /'akrəbat/ *n* **1** one who performs gymnastic feats requiring skilful control of the body **2** one who nimbly and often too readily changes his position or viewpoint ⟨*a political* ~⟩ [F & Gk; F *acrobate*, fr Gk *akrobatēs*, fr *akrobatos* walking on tiptoe, fr *akros* + *bainein* to go – more at COME]

acrobatic /,akrə'batik/ *adj* **1** of or like an acrobat **2** very mobile ⟨~ *eyebrows* – *Punch*⟩ – **acrobatically** *adv*

,acro'batics *n pl* **1** *sing or pl in constr* the art, performance, or activity of an acrobat **2** a spectacular performance involving great agility ⟨*contralto's vocal* ~⟩

acromegaly /,akroh'megəli, ,akrə-/ *n* abnormal enlargement of the hands, feet, and face caused by excessive production of growth hormone by the pituitary gland [F *acromégalie*, fr *acr-* + Gk *megal-*, *megas* large – more at MUCH] – **acromegalic** /-mə'galik/ *adj or n*

acronychal, **acronycal,** *NAm* **acronical** /,akroh'niekl, ,akrə-/ *adj*, *esp of the setting or rising of a star* happening at sunset [Gk *akronychos*, fr *akr-* acr- + *nyx* night]

acronym /'akrənim/ *n* a word (e g *radar*) formed from the initial letters of other words [*acr-* + *-onym* (as in *homonym*)] – **acronymic** /-'nimik/ *adj*, **acronymically** *adv*

acrophobia /,akrə'fohbi·ə/ *n* abnormal dread of being at a great height [NL]

acropolis /ə'kropəlis/ *n* the citadel of an ancient Greek city [Gk *akropolis*, fr *akr-* acr- + *polis* city – more at POLICE]

¹across /ə'kros/ *adv* **1** from one side to the other crosswise **2** to or on the opposite side **3** so as to be understandable, acceptable, or successful – compare GET ACROSS [ME *acros*, fr AF *an crois*, fr *an* in (fr L *in*) + *crois* cross, fr L *crux* – more at IN, RIDGE]

²across *prep* **1a** from one side to the other of ⟨*walk* ~ *the lawn*⟩ **b** on the opposite side of ⟨*lives* ~ *the street*⟩ **2** so as to intersect at an angle ⟨*sawed* ~ *the grain of the wood*⟩ **3** into transitory contact with – compare RUN ACROSS

a,cross-the-'board *adj* blanket ⟨*an* ~ *pay rise*⟩ – **across the board** *adv*

acrostic /ə'krostik/ *n* **1** a composition, usu in verse, in which sets of letters (e g the first of each line) form a word or phrase **2** a series of words of equal length arranged to read the same horizontally or vertically [MF & Gk; MF *acrostiche*, fr Gk *akrostichis*, fr *akr-* acr- + *stichos* line of verse; akin to *steichein* to go – more at STAIR] – **acrostic** *also* **acrostical** *adj*, **acrostically** *adv*

acrylate /'akrilayt/ *n* **1** a salt or ester of acrylic acid **2** ACRYLIC RESIN

¹acrylic /ə'krilik/ *adj* of acrylic acid or its derivatives [ISV *acro*lein (a liquid aldehyde; fr L *acr-*, *acer* sharp + *olēre* to smell) + *-yl* + *-ic*]

²acrylic *n* **1a** ACRYLIC RESIN **b** (a painting done in) a paint containing an acrylic resin **2** ACRYLIC FIBRE

a,crylic 'acid *n* an unsaturated liquid acid that polymerizes readily to form plastics

a,crylic 'fibre *n* a synthetic textile fibre made by

polymerization of acrylonitrile usu with other polymers

a,crylic 'resin *n* a glasslike plastic made by polymerizing (a derivative of) acrylic acid

acrylonitrile /,akriloh'nietril/ *n* a liquid nitrile used chiefly in organic synthesis and for polymerization

[1]act /akt/ *n* **1** a thing done; a deed **2** STATUTE 1; *also* a decree, edict ☞ LAW **3** the process of doing ⟨*caught in the very* ~⟩ **4** *often cap* a formal record of sthg done or transacted **5a** any of the principal divisions of a play or opera **b** any of the successive parts or performances in an entertainment (e g a circus) **6** a display of affected behaviour; a pretence [ME; partly fr L *actus* doing, act, fr *actus*, pp of *agere* to drive, do; partly fr L *actum* thing done, record, fr neut of *actus*, pp – more at AGENT] – **be/get in on the act** to be or deliberately become involved in a situation or undertaking, esp for one's own advantage

[2]act *vt* **1** to represent by action, esp on the stage **2** to feign, simulate **3** to play the part of (as if) in a play ⟨~ *the fool*⟩ ⟨~ *Hamlet*⟩ **4** to behave in a manner suitable to ⟨~ *your age*⟩ ~ *vi* **1a** to perform on the stage; engage in acting **b** to behave insincerely **2** to function or behave in a specified manner ⟨~ed *generously*⟩ **3** to perform a specified function; serve *as* **4** to be a substitute or representative *for* **5** to produce an effect ⟨*wait for the medicine to* ~⟩ – **actable** *adj*, **actability** /,aktə'biləti/ *n*

-acter /-aktə/ *comb form* (→ *n*) sthg, esp a play, containing a specified number of acts ⟨*a one*-acter⟩

ACTH *n* ADRENOCORTICOTROPHIC HORMONE [*a*drenocorti*co*trophic *h*ormone]

actin /'aktin/ *n* a protein found in muscle and other cells that combines with myosin in producing muscular contraction [ISV, fr L *actus*]

actin-, actini-, actino- *comb form* having a radiate form ⟨Actino*myces*⟩ [NL, ray, fr Gk *aktin-, aktino-*, fr *aktin-, aktis*; akin to OE *ūhte* morning twilight, L *noct-, nox* night – more at NIGHT]

[1]acting /'akting/ *adj* holding a temporary rank or position ⟨~ *president*⟩

[2]acting *n* the art or practice of representing a character in a dramatic production

actinide /'aktinied/ *n* any of a series of 15 radioactive elements from actinium (atomic number 89) to lawrencium (atomic number 103) [ISV]

actinism /'aktiniz(ə)m/ *n* the property of esp visible radiant energy by which chemical changes are produced (e g in photography) – **actinic** /ak'tinik/ *adj*

actinium /ak'tini·əm/ *n* a radioactive trivalent metallic element found esp in pitchblende ☞ PERIODIC TABLE [NL]

actinometer /,akti'nomitə/ *n* an instrument for measuring the intensity of esp solar radiation – **actinometry** *n*, **actinometric** /,aktinoh'metrik/ *adj*

actinomorphic /,aktinoh'mawfik/ *also* **actinomorphous** /-fəs/ *adj, of an organism or part* radially symmetrical [ISV] – **actinomorphy** /'aktinə,mawfi/ *n*

actinomycete /,aktinoh'mieseet/ *n* any of an order of filamentous or rod-shaped bacteria [deriv of Gk *aktin-, aktis* + *mykēt-, mykēs* fungus; akin to Gk *myxa* mucus – more at MUCUS] – **actinomycetous** /-mie'seetəs/ *adj*

,actino'zoan /-'zoh·ən/ *n* an anthozoan [*actin-* + Gk *zōion* animal; akin to Gk *zōē* life – more at [1]QUICK] – **actinozoan** *adj*

[1]action /'aksh(ə)n/ *n* **1** a civil legal proceeding **2** the process of acting or working, esp to produce alteration by force or through a natural agency **3a** the mode of movement of the body **b** a function of (a part of) the body **4** a voluntary act; a deed ⟨*know him by his* ~s⟩ **5a** the state of functioning actively ⟨*machine is out of* ~⟩ **b** practical, often militant, activity, often directed towards a political end ⟨*an* ~ *group*⟩ **c** energetic activity; enterprise ⟨*a man of* ~⟩ **6a(1)** an engagement between troops or ships **(2)** [2]COMBAT 3 **b** (the unfolding of) the events in a play or work of fiction **7** an operating mechanism (e g of a gun or piano); *also* the manner in which it operates **8** (*the* most) lively or productive activity ⟨*go where the* ~ *is*⟩ – infml [ME *accioun*, fr MF *action*, fr L *action-, actio*, fr *actus*, pp of *agere* to drive, do– more at AGENT]

[2]action *vt* to take action on; implement

'actionable /-əbl/ *adj* giving grounds for an action at law – **actionably** *adv*

'action ,painting *n* abstract art in which spontaneous techniques (e g dribbling or smearing) are used to apply paint

,action po'tential *n* a momentary change in the electrical potential across the membrane of a (nerve) cell resulting from activation by a stimulus

,action 'replay *n* a videotape recording of a televised incident played back usu immediately after the event and often in slow motion

activate /'aktivayt/ *vt* **1** to make (more) active or reactive, esp in chemical or physical properties: e g **a** to make (a substance) radioactive **b** to aerate (sewage) so as to favour the growth of organisms that decompose organic matter **2** *NAm* to equip or put (troops) on active duty – **activator** *n*, **activation** /-'vaysh(ə)n/ *n*

,activated 'carbon *n* highly adsorbent powdered carbon used esp for purifying by adsorption

,acti'vation a,nalysis /,akti'vaysh(ə)n/ *n* the determination of chemical composition by bombardment with neutrons and detection of the resulting characteristic radioactive atoms

[1]active /'aktiv/ *adj* **1** characterized by practical action rather than by contemplation or speculation ⟨*take an* ~ *interest in*⟩ **2** quick in physical movement; lively **3a** marked by or requiring vigorous activity ⟨~ *sports*⟩ **b** full of activity; busy ⟨*an* ~ *life*⟩ **4** having practical operation or results; effective ⟨*an* ~ *law*⟩ **5** *of a volcano* liable to erupt; not extinct **6** *of a verb form or voice* having as the subject the person or thing doing the action **7** of, in, or being full-time service, esp in the armed forces ⟨*on* ~ *duty*⟩ **8** capable of acting or reacting; activated ⟨~ *nitrogen*⟩ **9** *of an electronic device* containing and sometimes directing a power source [ME, fr MF or L; MF *actif*, fr L *activus*, fr *actus*, pp] – **actively** *adv*, **activeness** *n*

[2]active *n* **1** an active verb form **2** the active voice of a language

,active 'transport *n* movement of a chemical substance across a (cell) membrane in living tissue by the expenditure of energy

activism /'aktiviz(ə)m/ *n* a doctrine or practice that emphasizes vigorous action (e g the use of mass demonstrations) in controversial, esp political, matters – **activist** *n or adj*, **activistic** /-'vistik/ *adj*

activity /ak'tivəti/ *n* **1** the quality or state of being active **2** vigorous or energetic action; liveliness **3** a pursuit in which a person is active – usu pl ⟨*social* activities⟩

ˌact of ˈfaith *n* an action demonstrating the strength of one's esp religious convictions

ˌact of ˈGod *n* a sudden event, esp a catastrophe, brought about by uncontrollable natural forces

actor /'aktə/, *fem* **actress** /'aktris/ *n* one who represents a character in a dramatic production; *esp* one whose profession is acting [[2]ACT + [1]-OR] – **actorish** *adj*

act out *vt* **1a** to represent in action ⟨*children* act out *what they read*⟩ **b** to translate into action ⟨*unwilling to* act out *what they believe*⟩ **2** to express (repressed or unconscious impulses) unwittingly in overt behaviour

Acts /akts/ *n pl but sing in constr* the fifth book of the New Testament narrating the beginnings of the Church

ˌActs of the Aˈpostles *n pl but sing in constr the* Acts

actual /'aktyoo(ə)l, -choo(ə)l/ *adj* **1** existing in fact or reality; real ⟨~ *and imagined conditions*⟩ **2** existing or occurring at the time; current ⟨*caught in the* ~ *commission of a crime*⟩ [ME *actuel,* fr MF, fr LL *actualis,* fr L *actus* act] – **actualize** *vt,* **actualization** /-lie'zaysh(ə)n/ *n*

actuality /ˌaktyoo'aləti, ˌakchoo-/ *n* an existing circumstance; a real fact – often pl ⟨*possible risks which have been seized upon as* actualities – T S Eliot⟩ [ACTUAL + -ITY]

'actually /-li/ *adv* **1** really; IN FACT ⟨*nominally but not* ~ *independent*⟩ **2** at the present moment ⟨*the party* ~ *in power*⟩ **3** strange as it may seem; even ⟨*she* ~ *spoke Latin*⟩

actuary /'aktyoo(ə)ri, 'akchoo-/ *n* a statistician who calculates insurance risks and premiums [L *actuarius* shorthand writer, accountant, fr *actum* record – more at ACT] – **actuarial** /ˌaktyoo'eəri·əl, -choo-/ *adj,* **actuarially** *adv*

actuate /'aktyooayt, -choo-/ *vt* **1** to put into action or motion **2** to incite to action ⟨~d *by greed*⟩ [ML *actuatus,* pp of *actuare,* fr L *actus* act] – **actuation** /-'aysh(ə)n/ *n,* **actuator** /-ˌaytə/ *n*

act up *vi* **1** to behave in an unruly manner; PLAY UP **2** to give pain or trouble ⟨*this typewriter is* acting up *again*⟩ *USE* infml

acuity /ə'kyooh·əti/ *n* keenness of mental or physical perception – fml [MF *acuité,* fr OF *agüeté,* fr *agu* sharp, fr L *acutus*]

aculeate /ə'kyoohli·ət/ *adj* having a sting ⟨*an* ~ *insect*⟩ [L *aculeatus* having stings, fr *aculeus,* dim. of *acus*]

acumen /'akyoomən/ *n* keenness and depth of discernment or discrimination, esp in practical matters [L *acumin-, acumen,* lit., point, fr *acuere*]

acuminate /ə'kyoohminayt/ *adj* tapering to a slender point ☞ PLANT

acupuncture /'ak(y)ooˌpungkchə/ *n* an orig Chinese practice of puncturing the body at particular points with needles to cure disease, relieve pain, produce anaesthesia, etc [L *acus* + E *puncture*] – **acupuncturist** /-'pungkchərist, -ˌpungkchərist/ *n*

acute /ə'kyooht/ *adj* **1a** *of an angle* measuring less than 90° **b** composed of acute angles ⟨~ *triangle*⟩ **2a** marked by keen discernment or intellectual perception, esp of subtle distinctions ⟨*an* ~ *thinker*⟩ **b** responsive to slight impressions or stimuli ⟨~ *eyesight*⟩ **3** intensely felt or perceived ⟨~ *pain*⟩ **4** *esp of an illness* having a sudden severe onset and short course – contrasted with *chronic* **5** demanding urgent attention; severe ⟨*an* ~ *housing shortage*⟩ **6** marked with, having the pronunciation indicated by, or being an accent mark written ´ ☞ SYMBOL [L *acutus,* pp of *acuere* to sharpen, fr *acus* needle; akin to L *acer* sharp – more at EDGE] – **acutely** *adv,* **acuteness** *n*

acyl /'as(i)l, 'asiel/ *n* a radical derived from a carboxylic acid by removal of the hydroxyl group [ISV, fr *acid*]

ad /ad/ *n* an advertisement – infml

ad-, ac-, af-, ag-, al-, ap-, as-, at- *prefix* **1** to; towards – usu *ac-* before *c, k,* or *q* ⟨acculturation⟩, *af-* before *f, ag-* before *g* ⟨aggrade⟩, *al-* before *l* ⟨alliteration⟩, *ap-* before *p* ⟨approximate⟩, *as-* before *s* ⟨assuage⟩, *at-* before *t* ⟨attune⟩, and *ad-* before other sounds, but sometimes *ad-* even before one of the listed consonants ⟨ad*sorb*⟩ **2** near; adjacent to – in this sense always in the form *ad-* ⟨ad*renal*⟩ [ME, fr MF, OF, & L; MF, fr OF, fr L, fr *ad* – more at [1]AT]

-ad /-əd, -ad/ *suffix* (→ *adv*) in the direction of; towards ⟨*cephal*ad⟩ [L *ad*]

adage /'adij/ *n* a maxim or proverb that embodies a commonly accepted observation [MF, fr L *adagium,* fr *ad-* + *-agium* (akin to *aio* I say); akin to Gk *ē* he spoke]

[1]adagio /ə'dahjioh/ *adv or adj* in an easy slow graceful manner – used in music [It, fr *ad* at, to + *agio* ease]

[2]adagio *n, pl* **adagios** **1** a musical composition or movement in adagio tempo **2** ballet dancing, esp a pas de deux, involving difficult feats of balance

Adam /'adəm/ *adj* of a decorative style of furniture and architecture that originated in the 18th c [Robert *Adam* †1792 & James *Adam* †1794 Sc architects & designers]

[1]adamant /'adəmənt/ *n* a stone formerly believed to be of impenetrable hardness and sometimes identified with the diamond; *broadly* any very hard unbreakable substance [ME, fr OF, fr L *adamant-, adamas* hardest metal, diamond, fr Gk]

[2]adamant *adj* unshakable in determination; unyielding – **adamancy** *n,* **adamantly** *adv*

adamantine /ˌadə'mantien/ *adj* **1** made of or like adamant **2** resembling the diamond in hardness or lustre [ME, fr L *adamantinus,* fr Gk *adamantinos,* fr *adamant-, adamas*]

Adamite /'adəmiet/ *n* **1** a human **2** a member of a nudist sect [*Adam,* the first man according to the Bible; (2) fr his nakedness before his fall from grace (Gen 2 & 3)]

ˌAdam's ˈapple *n* the projection in the front of the neck formed by the largest cartilage of the larynx

adapt /ə'dapt/ *vb* to make or become fit, often by modification [F or L; F *adapter,* fr L *adaptare,* fr *ad-* + *aptare* to fit, fr *aptus* apt, fit] – **adaptable** *adj,* **adaptability** /-tə'biləti/ *n,* **adaptedness** *n*

adaptation /ˌadap'taysh(ə)n/ *n* **1** adjustment to prevailing or changing conditions: e g **a** adjustment of a sense organ to the intensity or quality of stimulation **b** modification of (the parts of) an organism fitting it better for existence and successful breeding **2** a composition rewritten in a new form or for a different medium [ADAPT + -ATION] – **adaptational** *adj,* **adaptationally** *adv*

adapter *also* **adaptor** /ə'daptə/ *n* **1** a writer who adapts sthg **2** a device **a** for connecting 2 pieces of apparatus not orig intended to be joined **b** for converting a tool or piece of apparatus to some new use **c** for connecting several pieces of electrical apparatus to a single power point, or connecting a plug of one type to a socket of a different type [ADAPT + [2]-ER, [1]-OR]

adaptive /ə'daptiv/ *adj, of an organism* showing or having a capacity for or tendency towards adaptation – **adaptively** *adv*, **adaptiveness** *n*, **adaptivity** /-'tivəti/ *n*

adaxial /,ad'aksi·əl/ *adj* situated on the same side as or facing the axis of an organ, plant part, or organism – compare ABAXIAL

add /ad/ *vt* **1** to join so as to bring about an increase or improvement ⟨*wine* ~s *a creative touch to cooking*⟩ **2** to say or write further **3** to combine (numbers) into a single number – often + *up* ~ *vi* **1a** to perform addition **b** to come together or unite by addition **2** to make or serve as an addition *to* [ME, *adden*, fr L *addere*, fr *ad-* + *-dere* to put – more at [1]DO] – **addable, addible** *adj*

addend /'adend, ə'dend/ *n* a number to be added to another [short for *addendum*]

addendum /ə'dendəm/ *n, pl* **addenda** /-də/ a supplement to a book – often pl with sing. meaning but sing. in constr [L, neut of *addendus*, gerundive of *addere*]

[1]**adder** /'adə/ *n* the common European venomous viper or other ground-living viper [ME, alter. (by incorrect division of *a naddre*) of *naddre*, fr OE *nǣdre*; akin to OHG *nātara* adder, L *natrix* water snake]

[2]**adder** *n* a device (e g in a computer) that performs addition [ADD +[2]-ER]

'**adder's-,tongue** *n* a fern whose fruiting spike resembles a snake's tongue

[1]**addict** /ə'dikt/ *vt* **1** to devote or surrender (oneself) to sthg habitually or obsessively – usu pass **2** to cause (an animal or human) to become physiologically dependent upon a habit-forming drug [L *addictus*, pp of *addicere* to favour, fr *ad-* + *dicere* to say – more at DICTION] – **addictive** *adj*, **addiction** /ə'diksh(ə)n/ *n*

[2]**addict** /'adikt/ *n* **1** one who is addicted to a drug **2** DEVOTEE 2 ⟨*a detective-novel* ~⟩

'**Addison's di,sease** /'adis(ə)nz/ *n* a disease marked by deficient secretion of the steroid hormones of the cortex of the adrenal gland and characterized by extreme weakness, loss of weight, and brownish pigmentation of the skin [Thomas *Addison* †1860 E physician]

addition /ə'dish(ə)n/ *n* **1** sthg or sby added, esp as an improvement **2** the act or process of adding, esp adding numbers **3** direct chemical combination of substances to form a single product [ME, fr MF, fr L *addition-*, *additio*, fr *additus*, pp of *addere*] – **in addition** also, furthermore ⟨*a telephone in the kitchen* in addition *to the one in the hall*⟩

additional /ə'dish(ə)nl/ *adj* existing by way of addition; supplementary – **additionally** /ə'dish(ə)nəli/ *adv*

[1]**additive** /'adətiv/ *adj* of or characterized by addition – **additively** *adv*, **additivity** /,adə'tivəti/ *n*

[2]**additive** *n* a substance added to another in relatively small amounts to impart desirable properties or suppress undesirable ones ⟨*food* ~s⟩

addle /'adl/ *vb* **addling** /'adling, 'adl·ing/ *vt* to throw into confusion ~ *vi* **1** *of an egg* to become rotten **2** to become confused or muddled [*addle* (rotten, unsound), fr ME *adel* filth, fr OE *adela*; akin to MLG *adele* liquid manure]

[1]**address** /ə'dres/ *vt* **1** to direct the efforts or attention of (oneself) ⟨~ *himself to the problem*⟩ **2a** to communicate directly ⟨~es *his thanks to his host*⟩ **b** to speak or write directly to; *esp* to deliver a formal speech to **3** to mark directions for delivery on ⟨~ *a letter*⟩ **4** to greet by a prescribed form ⟨~ed *him as 'My Lord'*⟩ **5** to take one's stance and adjust the club before hitting (a golf ball) ~ *vi obs* to direct one's speech or attentions [ME *adressen*, fr MF *adresser*, fr *a-* (fr L *ad-*) + *dresser* to arrange – more at DRESS] – **addresser** *n*, **addressee** /,adre'see/ *n*

[2]**address** /ə'dres/ *n* **1** dutiful and courteous attention, esp in courtship – usu pl ⟨*paid his* ~es *to her*⟩ **2** readiness and capability for dealing (e g with a person or problem) skilfully and smoothly; adroitness **3** a formal communication; *esp* a prepared speech delivered to an audience **4** a place of residence (where a person or organization may be communicated with); *also* a detailed description of its location (e g on an envelope) **5** a location (e g in the memory of a computer) where particular information is stored; *also* the digits that identify such a location

addressable /ə'dresəbl/ *adj* accessible by an address ⟨~ *registers in a computer*⟩

Addressograph /ə'dresə,grahf, -,graf, -soh-/ *trademark* – used for a device that prints addresses on envelopes

adduce /ə'dyoohs/ *vt* to offer as example, reason, or proof in discussion or analysis – fml [L *adducere*, lit., to lead to, fr *ad-* + *ducere* to lead – more at [1]TOW] – **adducer** *n*, **adduction** /ə'duksh(ə)n/ *n*

adduct /ə'dukt/ *vt* to draw (e g a limb) towards the main part of the body; *also* to bring together (similar parts) ⟨~ *the fingers*⟩ [L *adductus*, pp of *adducere*] – **adductive** *adj*, **adductor** *n*, **adduction** /ə'duk sh(ə)n/ *n*

add up *vi* **1** to amount *to* in total or substance ⟨*the play* adds up *to a lot of laughs*⟩ **2** to come to the expected total ⟨*the bill doesn't* add up⟩ **3** to be internally consistent; make sense ~ *vt* SIZE UP

-ade /-ayd/ *suffix* (→*n*) **1a** act or action of ⟨*block*ade⟩ ⟨*escap*ade⟩ **b** individual or group of people involved in (a specified action) ⟨*caval*cade⟩ ⟨*reneg*ade⟩ **2** product; *esp* sweet drink made from (a specified fruit) ⟨*lime*ade⟩ [ME, fr MF, fr OProv *-ada*, fr LL *-ata*, fr L, fem of *-atus* -ate]

aden-, adeno- *comb form* gland ⟨aden*itis*⟩ [NL, fr Gk, fr *aden-*, *adēn*; akin to L *inguen* groin, Gk *nephros* kidney – more at NEPHRITIS]

adenine /'adəneen, -nin/ *n* a purine base that is 1 of the 4 bases whose order in a DNA or RNA chain codes genetic information – compare CYTOSINE, GUANINE, THYMINE, URACIL [ISV; fr its presence in glandular tissue]

adenoid /'adənoyd/ *adj or n* (of) an enlarged mass of lymphoid tissue at the back of the pharynx, often obstructing breathing – usu pl with sing. meaning [Gk *adenoeidēs* glandular, fr *adēn*]

adenoidal /,adə'noydl/ *adj* of (sby with enlarged) adenoids – **adenoidally** *adv*

adenoma /,adə'nohmə/ *n, pl* **adenomas, adenomata** /-noh'mahtə/ a benign tumour of a glandular structure or of glandular origin [NL *adenomat-, adenoma*] – **adenomatous** /-ˈnohmətəs; *also* -nohˈmahtəs/ *adj*

adenosine /əˈdenəseen, -sin/ *n* a nucleoside containing adenine [ISV, blend of *adenine* and *ribose*]

aˌdenosine diˈphosphate *n* ADP

aˌdenosine ˌmonoˈphosphate *n* **1** AMP **2** CYCLIC AMP

aˌdenosine ˌtriˈphosphate *n* ATP

adept /ˈadept, əˈdept/ *adj or n* (being) a highly skilled expert *at* [NL *adeptus* alchemist who has discovered how to change base metals into gold, fr L, pp of *adipisci* to attain, fr *ad-* + *apisci* to reach – more at APT] – **adeptly** /əˈdeptli/ *adv*, **adeptness** /əˈdeptnis/ *n*

adequate /ˈadikwət/ *adj* sufficient for a specific requirement ⟨~ *grounds for divorce*⟩; *esp* barely sufficient or satisfactory [L *adaequatus*, pp of *adaequare* to make equal, fr *ad-* + *aequare* to equal – more at EQUABLE] – **adequacy** /-kwəsi/ *n*, **adequately** *adv*, **adequateness** *n*

ad eundem /ˌad ayˈoondəm/, **ad eundem gradum** /ˈgrahdəm/ *adv or adj* to or of the same degree at another university [NL *ad eundem gradum*]

à deux /ah ˈduh (*Fr* a dø)/ *adj or adv* having only 2 (people) present ⟨*a cosy evening* ~⟩ [F]

adhere /ədˈ(h)iə/ *vi* **1** to give continued support, observance, or loyalty ⟨~ *to the treaty*⟩ **2** to hold or stick fast (as if) by gluing, suction, grasping, or fusing ~ *vt* to cause to stick fast [MF or L; MF *adhérer*, fr L *adhaerēre*, fr *ad-* + *haerēre* to stick – more at HESITATE] – **adherent** *adj*, **adherence** *n*

adherent /ədˈ(h)iərənt/ *n* a supporter of a leader, faction, etc [ME, fr MF or L; MF *adhérent*, adj, fr L *adhaerent-, adhaerens*, prp of *adhaerēre*]

adhesion /ədˈ(h)eezh(ə)n, adˈhee-/ *n* **1** the action or state of adhering **2** (the tissues united by) an abnormal union of tissues that are usu separated in the body [F or L; F *adhésion*, fr L *adhaesion-, adhaesio*, fr *adhaesus*, pp of *adhaerēre*] – **adhesional** *adj*

¹adhesive /ədˈ(h)eeziv, -siv/ *adj* causing or prepared for sticking; sticky – **adhesively** *adv*, **adhesiveness** *n*

²adhesive *n* an adhesive substance (e g glue or cement)

ad hoc /ˌad ˈhok/ *adj or adv* with respect to the particular purpose at hand and without consideration of wider application ⟨*an* ~ *investigation*⟩ [L, for this]

ad hominem /ˌad ˈhominem/ *adj or adv* appealing to or attacking on personal rather than intellectual grounds [NL, lit., to the man]

adiabatic /ˌadi·əˈbatik/ *adj* occurring without loss or gain of heat [Gk *adiabatos* impassable, fr *a-* + *diabatos* passable, fr *diabainein* to go across, fr *dia-* + *bainein* to go – more at COME] – **adiabatically** *adv*

adieu /əˈdyooh, əˈdyuh (*Fr* adjø)/ *n, pl* **adieus, adieux** /əˈdyooh(z), əˈdyuh(z) (*Fr* ~)/ a farewell – often used interjectionally; usu poetic [ME, fr MF, fr *a* (fr L *ad*) + *Dieu* God, fr L *Deus* – more at AT, DEITY]

ad infinitum /ˌad infiˈnietəm/ *adv or adj* without end or limit [L, to an infinite extent]

aˌdipic ˈacid /əˈdipik/ *n* an organic acid used esp in manufacturing plastics, esp nylon [deriv of L *adip-, adeps*]

adipose /ˈadipohs, -pohz/ *adj* of animal fat; fatty [NL *adiposus*, fr L *adip-, adeps* fat, fr Gk *aleipha*; akin to Gk *lipos* fat – more at LEAVE] – **adiposity** /-ˈposəti/ *n*

ˌadipose ˈtissue *n* connective tissue in which fat is stored

adit /ˈadit/ *n* a nearly horizontal passage from the surface into a mine [L *aditus* approach, fr *aditus*, pp of *adire* to go to, fr *ad-* + *ire* to go – more at ISSUE]

adjacent /əˈjays(ə)nt/ *adj* having a common border; *broadly* neighbouring, nearby [ME, fr MF or L; MF, fr L *adjacent-, adjacens*, prp of *adjacēre* to lie near, fr *ad-* + *jacēre* to lie; akin to L *jacere* to throw – more at ²JET] – **adjacency** *n*, **adjacently** *adv*

adjectival /ˌajikˈtievl/ *adj* relating to or characterized by the use of adjectives – **adjectivally** *adv*

¹adjective /ˈajiktiv/ *adj* **1** adjectival **2** *of a dye* requiring a mordant [ME, fr MF or LL; MF *adjectif*, fr LL *adjectivus*, fr L *adjectus*, pp of *adjicere* to throw to, fr *ad-* + *jacere* to throw – more at ²JET]

²adjective *n* a word that modifies a noun or pronoun by describing a particular characteristic of it

adjoin /əˈjoyn/ *vb* to be next to or in contact with (one another) [ME *adjoinen*, fr MF *adjoindre*, fr L *adjungere*, fr *ad-* + *jungere* to join – more at YOKE] – **adjoining** *adj*

adjourn /əˈjuhn/ *vb* to suspend (a session) until a later stated time [ME *ajournen*, fr MF *ajourner*, fr *a-* (fr L *ad-*) + *jour* day – more at JOURNEY]

adˈjournment /-mənt/ *n* the state or interval of being adjourned

adjudge /əˈjuj/ *vt* **1a** to adjudicate **b** to pronounce formally ⟨~ *him guilty*⟩ **2** to pronounce to be; deem ⟨~ *the book a success*⟩ [ME *ajugen*, fr MF *ajugier*, fr L *adjudicare*, fr *ad-* + *judicare* to judge – more at ¹JUDGE]

adjudicate /əˈjoohdikayt/ *vt* to make a judicial decision on ~ *vi* to act as judge (e g in a competition) [L *adjudicatus*, pp of *adjudicare*] – **adjudicative** /-kətiv/ *adj*, **adjudicator** /-ˌkaytə/ *n*

adjudication /əjoohdiˈkaysh(ə)n/ *n* a judicial decision; *specif* a decree in bankruptcy [ADJUDICATE + -ION] – **adjudicatory** /əˈjoohdikət(ə)ri/ *adj*

adjunct /ˈajungkt/ *n* **1** sthg joined to another thing as an incidental accompaniment but not essentially a part of it **2** a word or phrase (e g an adverb or prepositional phrase) that can be left out and still leave the sentence grammatically complete **3** a person, usu in a subordinate or temporary capacity, assisting another to perform some duty or service [L *adjunctum*, fr neut of *adjunctus*, pp of *adjungere*] – **adjunct** *adj*, **adjunctly** *adv*, **adjunctive** /əˈjungktiv/ *adj*, **adjunctively** *adv*

adjure /əˈjooə/ *vt* **1** to charge or command solemnly (as if) under oath or penalty of a curse **2** to entreat or advise earnestly ***USE*** fml [ME *adjuren*, fr MF & L; MF *ajurer*, fr L *adjurare*, fr *ad-* + *jurare* to swear – more at JURY] – **adjuration** /ˌajooˈraysh(ə)n/ *n*, **adjuratory** /əˈjooərət(ə)ri/ *adj*

adjust /əˈjust/ *vt* **1** to bring to a more satisfactory or conformable state by minor change or adaptation; regulate, correct, or modify **2** to determine the amount to be paid under an insurance policy in settlement of (a loss) ~ *vi* to adapt or conform oneself (e g to climate) [F *ajuster*, fr *a-* + *juste* exact, just] – **adjustable** *adj*, **adjustive** *adj*, **adjustability** /-stəˈbiləti/ *n*

adjusted *adj* having achieved a harmonious relationship with one's environment or with others – often used in combination

adjuster *also* **adjustor** /ə'justə/ *n* ASSESSOR 3 [ADJUST + ²-ER]

ad'justment /-mənt/ *n* **1** a correction or modification to reflect actual conditions **2** a means (e g a mechanism) by which things are adjusted one to another **3** a settlement of a disputed claim or debt [ADJUST + -MENT] – **adjustmental** /ˌajust'mentl/ *adj*

adjutant /'ajoot(ə)nt/ *n* an officer who assists the commanding officer and is responsible for correspondence and for ensuring that his orders are carried out [L *adjutant-, adjutans*, prp of *adjutare* to help – more at AID] – **adjutancy** /-t(ə)nsi/ *n*

ˌadjutant 'general *n, pl* **adjutants general** the chief administrative officer of an army, responsible for all the personnel and their welfare, training, records, etc

adjuvant /'ajoov(ə)nt/ *n* sthg that helps or makes esp medical treatment more effective [F or L; F, adj, auxiliary, fr L *adjuvant-, adjuvans*, prp of *adjuvare* to aid, fr *ad-* + *juvare* to help]

¹ad-lib /ˌad 'lib/ *adj* spoken, composed, or performed without preparation – infml [*ad lib*]

²ad-lib *vb* **-bb-** to say (e g lines or a speech) spontaneously and without preparation; improvise – **ad-lib** *n*

ad lib *adv* without restraint or limit [NL *ad libitum* in accordance with desire]

ad libitum /ˌad 'libitəm/ *adv* AD LIB

adman /'adˌman/ *n* a member of the advertising profession – infml [*ad* + *man*]

admass /'adˌmas/ *n, chiefly Br* a society in which the drive to consume material goods is promoted by mass-media advertising [*ad*vertising + ²*mass*] – **admass** *adj*

admin /'admin/ *n, chiefly Br* (work involving) administration –infml

administer /əd'ministə/ *vt* **1** to manage, supervise **2a** to mete out; dispense ⟨~ *punishment*⟩ **b** to give or perform ritually ⟨~ *the last rites*⟩ **c** to give remedially ~*vi* to perform the office of administrator; manage affairs [ME *administren*, fr MF *administrer*, fr L *administrare*, fr *ad-* + *ministrare* to serve, fr *minister* servant] – **administrable** /-strəbl/ *adj*, **administrant** *n*

administration /ədˌmini'straysh(ə)n/ *n* **1** the act or process of administering **2** performance of executive duties; management **3** the execution of public affairs as distinguished from the making of policy **4a** a body of people who administer **b** *cap* GOVERNMENT 5 [ME *administracioun*, fr MF or L; MF *administration*, fr L *administration-, administratio*, fr *administratus*, pp of *administrare*] – **administrate** /-strayt/ *vb*, **administrational** *adj*, **administrationist** *n*

administrative /əd'ministrətiv/ *adj* of (an) administration – **administratively** *adv*

administrator /əd'miniˌstraytə/ *n* sby who administers esp business, school, or governmental affairs [L, manager, fr *administratus*]

administratrix /əd'ministrətriks/ *n, pl* **administratrices** /əd ˌmini'straytrəseez/ a female administrator, esp of an estate [NL]

admirable /'admərəbl/ *adj* deserving the highest respect; excellent – **admirableness** *n*, **admirably** *adv*, **admirability** /ˌadmərə'biləti/ *n*

admiral /'admərəl/ *n.* the commander in chief of a navy ☞ RANK [ME, fr MF *amiral* admiral & ML *admiralis* emir, *admirallus* admiral, fr Ar *amīr-al-* commander of the (as in *amīr-al-baḥr* commander of the sea)]

ˌadmiral of the 'fleet *n* ☞ RANK

'admiralty /-ti/ *n* **1** *sing or pl in constr, cap* the executive department formerly having authority over naval affairs **2** the court having jurisdiction over maritime questions ☞ LAW

ˌAdmiralty 'Board *n* the department of the Ministry of Defence that administers the British navy

admiration /ˌadmə'raysh(ə)n/ *n* **1** a feeling of delighted or astonished approval **2** the object of admiring respect

admire /əd'mie·ə/ *vt* to think highly of; express admiration for – sometimes sarcastically ⟨*I* ~ *your cheek*⟩ [MF *admirer* to wonder at, fr L *admirari*, fr *ad-* + *mirari* to wonder – more at SMILE] – **admiringly** *adv*

admirer /əd'mie·ərə/ *n* a woman's suitor [ADMIRE + ²-ER]

admissible /əd'misəbl/ *adj, esp of legal evidence* capable of being allowed or conceded; permissible [F, fr ML *admissibilis*, fr L *admissus*, pp of *admittere*] – **admissibility** /-sə'biləti/ *n*

admission /əd'mish(ə)n/ *n* **1** acknowledgment that a fact or allegation is true **2a** allowing or being allowed to enter sthg (e g a secret society) **b** a fee paid at or for admission – **admissive** /-siv/ *adj*

admit /əd'mit/ *vb* **-tt-** *vt* **1a** to allow scope for; permit **b** to concede as true or valid **2** to allow to enter sthg (e g a place or fellowship) ~*vi* **1** to give entrance or access **2a** to allow, permit – often + *of* **b** to make acknowledgment – + *to* [ME *admitten*, fr L *admittere*, fr *ad-* + *mittere* to send – more at SMITE]

admittance /əd'mit(ə)ns/ *n* **1** permission to enter a place **2** access, entrance

admittedly /əd'mitidli/ *adv* as must reluctantly be admitted

admixture /əd'mikschə, 'admikschə/ *n* **1** mixing or being mixed **2** an ingredient added by mixing, or the resulting mixture [L *admixtus*, pp of *admiscēre* to mix with, fr *ad-* + *miscēre* to mix – more at MIX] – **admix** /ˌad'miks/ *vt*

admonish /əd'monish/ *vt* **1a** to indicate duties to **b** to warn about remissness or error, esp gently **2** to give friendly earnest advice or encouragement to [ME *admonesten*, fr MF *admonester*, fr (assumed) VL *admonestare*, alter. of L *admonēre* to warn, fr *ad-* + *monēre* to warn – more at MIND] – **admonisher** *n*, **admonishingly** *adv*, **admonishment** *n*

admonition /ˌadmə'nish(ə)n/ *n* (a) gentle friendly reproof, counsel, or warning [ME *amonicioun*, fr MF *amonition*, fr L *admonition-, admonitio*, fr *admonitus*, pp of *admonēre*]

admonitory /əd'monit(ə)ri/ *adj* expressing admonition; warning – **admonitorily** /-t(ə)rəli/ *adv*

ad nauseam /ˌad 'nawzi·əm, -si·əm/ *adv* in an extremely tedious manner; enough to make one sick [L, to sickness]

ado /ə'dooh/ *n* fussy bustling excitement, esp over trivia; to-do [ME, fr *at do*, fr *at* + *don, do* to do]

adobe /ə'dohbi/ *n* **1** a building brick of sun-dried earth and straw **2** a heavy clay used in making adobe bricks [Sp, fr Ar *aṭ-ṭub* the brick, fr Copt *tōbe* brick] – **adobe** *adj*

adolescent /ˌadə'les(ə)nt/ *n* sby in the period of life between puberty and maturity [F, fr L *adolescent-*, *adolescens,* prp of *adolescere* to grow up – more at ADULT] – **adolescent** *adj,* **adolescence** *n*

Adonai /ˌadəˈnie, ˌadəˈnay·ie/ *n* – used as the sacred title of the God of the Jews, only to be pronounced in solemn prayer and with the head covered [Heb *ădhōnāy*]

Adonis /əˈdohnis/ *n* a strikingly handsome young man [L, fr Gk *Adōnis,* a youth loved by Aphrodite in mythology] – **adonic** *adj*

adopt /əˈdopt/ *vt* **1** to take by choice into a new relationship; *specif* to bring up voluntarily (a child of other parents) as one's own child **2** to take up and practise; take to oneself **3** to vote to accept ⟨~ *a constitutional amendment*⟩ **4** *of a constituency* to nominate as a Parliamentary candidate **5** *Br, of a local authority* to assume responsibility for the maintenance of (e g a road) [MF or L; MF *adopter,* fr L *adoptare,* fr *ad-* + *optare* to choose – more at OPTION] – **adopter** *n,* **adoptable** *adj,* **adoptability** /-təˈbiləti/ *n,* **adoption** /əˈdopsh(ə)n/ *n,* **adoptee** /ˌadopˈtee/ *n*

adoptive /əˈdoptiv/ *adj* made or acquired by adoption ⟨*one's ~ country*⟩ ⟨*the ~ father*⟩ – **adoptively** *adv*

adorable /əˈdawrəbl/ *adj* sweetly lovable; charming [ADORE + -ABLE] – **adorableness** *n,* **adorably** *adv,* **adorability** /-rəˈbiləti/ *n*

adore /əˈdaw/ *vt* **1** to worship or honour as a deity **2** to regard with reverent admiration and devotion **3** to like very much – infml [MF *adorer,* fr L *adorare,* fr *ad-* + *orare* to speak, pray – more at ORATION] – **adorer** *n,* **adoration** /ˌadəˈraysh(ə)n/ *n*

adorn /əˈdawn/ *vt* **1** to decorate, esp with ornaments **2** to add to the pleasantness or attractiveness of [ME *adornen,* fr MF *adorner,* fr L *adornare,* fr *ad-* + *ornare* to furnish – more at ORNATE] – **adornment** *n*

ADP *n* a derivative of adenine that is reversibly converted to ATP for the storing of cellular energy [*a*denosine *d*i*p*hosphate]

ad rem /ˌad ˈrem/ *adv or adj* to the point or purpose [L, to the matter]

adren-, adreno- *comb form* **1** adrenal ⟨adreno*cortical*⟩ **2** adrenalin ⟨adren*ergic*⟩ [*adrenal*]

[1]**adrenal** /əˈdreenl/ *adj* **1** adjacent to the kidneys **2** of or derived from adrenal glands [*ad-* + *renal*] – **adrenally** *adv*

[2]**adrenal** *n* ADRENAL GLAND

aˈdrenal ˌgland *n* an endocrine gland near the front of each kidney with a cortex that secretes steroid hormones and a medulla that secretes adrenalin ☞ DIGESTION

adrenalin, adrenaline /əˈdrenəlin/ *n* a hormone produced by the adrenal gland that occurs as a neurotransmitter in the sympathetic nervous system and that stimulates the heart and causes constriction of blood vessels and relaxation of smooth muscle

adrenergic /ˌadriˈnuhjik/ *adj* **1** liberating or activated by (a substance like) adrenalin **2** *of a drug* resembling adrenalin [*adren-* + Gk *ergon* work – more at [1]WORK]

adrenocorticotrophic /əˌdreenohˌkawtikohˈtrohfik/, **adrenocorticotropic** /-ˈtrohpik, -ˈtropik/ *adj* acting on or stimulating the adrenal cortex

adrenocorticotrophic hormone *n* a hormone of the front lobe of the pituitary gland that stimulates the adrenal cortex

aˌdrenoˌcorticoˈtrophin /-ˈtrohfin/ *n* ADRENOCORTICOTROPHIC HORMONE

adrift /əˈdrift/ *adv or adj* **1** afloat without motive power or mooring and at the mercy of winds and currents **2** in or into a state of being unstuck or unfastened; loose – esp in *come adrift* **3** astray – infml ⟨*his reasoning's gone completely ~*⟩ [[1]*a-* + *drift*]

adroit /əˈdroyt/ *adj* **1** dexterous, nimble **2** marked by shrewdness, readiness, or resourcefulness in coping with difficulty or danger [F, fr *à droit* properly, fr *à* to, at + *droit* right] – **adroitly** *adv,* **adroitness** *n*

adsorb /ədˈzawb/ *vt* to take up and hold by adsorption ~ *vi* to become absorbed [*ad-* + *-sorb* (as in *absorb*)] – **adsorbable** *adj,* **adsorbent** *adj or n*

adsorption /ədˈzawpsh(ə)n/ *n* the adhesion in an extremely thin layer of molecules of gases, liquids, etc to the surface of solids or liquids – compare ABSORPTION [irreg fr *adsorb*] – **adsorptive** *adj*

adulate /ˈadyoolayt/ *vt* to flatter or admire excessively or slavishly [back-formation fr *adulation,* fr ME, fr MF, fr L *adulation-, adulatio,* fr *adulatus,* pp of *adulari* to flatter] – **adulator** *n,* **adulation** /-ˈlaysh(ə)n/ *n,* **adulatory** /ˈadyoolət(ə)ri/ *adj*

[1]**adult** /ˈadult, əˈdult/ *adj* **1** fully developed and mature; grown-up **2** of or befitting adults ⟨*an ~ approach to a problem*⟩ **3** suitable only for adults; *broadly* salacious, pornographic ⟨~ *magazines*⟩ [L *adultus,* pp of *adolescere* to grow up, fr *ad-* + *-olescere* (fr *alescere* to grow) – more at OLD] – **adulthood** /-hood/ *n,* **adultlike** *adj,* **adultness** *n*

[2]**adult** *n* a grown-up person or creature; *esp* a human being after an age specified by law (in Britain, 18)

ˌadult eduˈcation *n* mainly nonvocational part-time courses for adults

[1]**adulterate** /əˈdultərayt/ *vt* to corrupt or make impure by the addition of a foreign or inferior substance [L *adulteratus,* pp of *adulterare,* fr *ad-* + *alter* other – more at ELSE] – **adulterant** *n or adj,* **adulterator** *n,* **adulteration** /-ˈraysh(ə)n/ *n*

[2]**adulterate** /əˈdultərət/ *adj* being adulterated, debased, or impure

adulterer /əˈdultərə/, *fem* **adulteress** /-ris/ *n* sby who commits adultery

adultery /əˈdultəri/ *n* (an act of) voluntary sexual intercourse between a married person and sby other than his/her spouse [ME, alter. of *avoutrie,* fr MF, fr L *adulterium,* fr *adulter* adulterer, back-formation fr *adulterare*] – **adulterous** *adj,* **adulterously** *adv*

adumbrate /ˈadəmbrayt/ *vt* **1** to foreshadow (a future event) vaguely **2** to outline broadly without details ***USE*** fml [L *adumbratus,* pp of *adumbrare,* fr *ad-* + *umbra* shadow – more at UMBRAGE] – **adumbration** /-ˈbraysh(ə)n/ *n,* **adumbrative** /əˈdumbrətiv/ *adj,* **adumbratively** *adv*

ad valorem /ˌad vaˈlawrəm/ *adj or adv, of a tax* imposed at a rate proportional to the stated value – compare SPECIFIC 5b [L, according to the value]

[1]**advance** /ədˈvahns/ *vt* **1** to bring or move forwards in position or time ⟨~ *the date of the meeting*⟩ **2** to accelerate the growth or progress of; further **3** to raise in rank; promote **4** to supply (money or goods) ahead of time or as a loan **5** to bring (an opinion or argument) forward for notice; propose ~ *vi* **1** to go forwards; proceed **2** to make progress **3** to rise in rank, position, or importance [ME *advauncen,* fr OF *avancier,* fr (assumed) VL *abantiare,* fr L *abante*

before, fr *ab-* + *ante* before – more at ANTE-] – **advancer** *n*

[2]**advance** *n* **1a** a moving forward **b** (a signal for) forward movement (of troops) **2a** progress in development; an improvement ⟨*an ~ in medical technique*⟩ **b** ADVANCEMENT 1a **3** a friendly or esp an amorous approach – usu pl ⟨*her attitude discouraged all ~*s⟩ **4** (a provision of) money or goods supplied before a return is received **– in advance** beforehand

[3]**advance** *adj* **1** made, sent, or provided ahead of time **2** going or situated ahead of others ⟨*an ~ party of soldiers*⟩

advanced *adj* **1** far on in time or course ⟨*a man ~ in years*⟩ **2** beyond the elementary; more developed ⟨*~ chemistry*⟩

Ad'vanced ˌlevel *n, often cap L* an examination that is the second of the 3 levels of the British General Certificate of Education and is a partial qualification for university entrance

ad'vancement /-mənt/ *n* **1a** (a) promotion or elevation to a higher rank or position **b** furtherance towards perfection or completeness ⟨*the ~ of knowledge*⟩ **2** an advance of money or value [[1]ADVANCE + -MENT]

advantage /əd'vahntij/ *n* **1** superiority of position or condition ⟨*higher ground gave the enemy the ~*⟩ – often + *of* or *over* **2** a benefit, gain; *esp* one resulting from some course of action ⟨*a mistake which turned out to his ~*⟩ **3** (the score of) the first point won in tennis after deuce [ME *avantage*, fr MF, fr *avant* before, fr L *abante*] **– to advantage** so as to produce a favourable impression or effect

advantageous /ˌadv(ə)n'tayjəs/ *adj* furnishing an advantage; favourable – **advantageously** *adv*

advection /əd'veksh(ə)n/ *n* the horizontal movement of a mass of air causing changes esp in its temperature [L *advection-, advectio* act of bringing, fr *advectus*, pp of *advehere* to carry to, fr *ad-* + *vehere* to carry – more at WAY] – **advective** /-'vektiv/ *adj*

Advent /'advent, -vənt/ *n* **1** the 4-week period before Christmas, observed by some Christians as a season of prayer and fasting ⟨*the second Sunday in ~*⟩ **2** the coming of Christ to earth as a human being **3** *not cap* a coming into being; an arrival ⟨*the ~ of spring*⟩ [ME, fr ML *adventus*, fr L, arrival, fr *adventus*, pp]

Adventism /'adventiz(ə)m, -vən-/ *n* the doctrine that the second coming of Christ and the end of the world are near at hand – **Adventist** *adj or n*

adventitious /ˌadvən'tishəs, -ven-/ *adj* **1** coming accidentally or casually from another source; extraneous **2** occurring sporadically or in an unusual place ⟨*~ buds on a plant*⟩ [L *adventicius* coming from outside, fr *adventus*, pp] – **adventitiously** *adv*, **adventitiousness** *n*

[1]**adventure** /əd'venchə/ *n* **1** an undertaking involving danger, risks, and uncertainty of outcome; *broadly* (an) exciting or remarkable experience **2** an enterprise involving financial risk [ME *aventure*, fr OF, fr (assumed) VL *adventura*, fr L *adventus*, pp of *advenire* to arrive, fr *ad-* + *venire* to come – more at COME] – **adventuresome** /-s(ə)m/ *adj*, **adventurous** *adj*, **adventurously** *adv*, **adventurousness** *n*

[2]**adventure** *vt* to venture, risk *~ vi* **1** to hazard oneself; dare to go or enter **2** to take a risk

adˌventure 'playground *n* a children's playground equipped with large interesting often old or disused objects

adventurer /əd'venchərə/, *fem* **adventuress** /-ris/ *n* **1** sby who takes part in an adventure; *esp* SOLDIER OF FORTUNE **2** sby who seeks wealth or position by unscrupulous means

adventurism /əd'venchəˌriz(ə)m/ *n* risky improvisation, esp in politics – **adventurist** *n*, **adventuristic** /-'ristik/ *adj*

adverb /'advuhb/ *n* a word that modifies a verb, an adjective, another adverb, a preposition, a phrase, a clause, or a sentence, and that answers such questions as how?, when?, where?, etc [MF *adverbe*, fr L *adverbium*, fr *ad-* + *verbum* word – more at WORD]

adverbial /əd'vuhbi·əl/ *adj* of or functioning as an adverb – **adverbial** *n*, **adverbially** *adv*

adversary /'advəs(ə)ri/ *n* an enemy, opponent, or opposing faction

adversative /əd'vuhsətiv/ *adj* expressing contrast, opposition, or adverse circumstance ⟨*the ~ conjunction* but⟩ – **adversatively** *adv*

adverse /'advuhs, əd'vuhs/ *adj* **1** acting against or in a contrary direction ⟨*hindered by ~ winds*⟩ **2** unfavourable ⟨*~ criticism*⟩ [ME, fr MF *advers*, fr L *adversus*, pp of *advertere*] – **adversely** /'advuhsli/ *adv*, **adverseness** *n*

adversity /əd'vuhsəti/ *n* a condition of suffering, affliction, or hardship

[1]**advert** /əd'vuht/ *vi* to make a (glancing) reference or refer casually *to* – fml [ME *adverten*, fr MF & L; MF *advertir*, fr L *advertere*, fr *ad-* + *vertere* to turn – more at [1]WORTH]

[2]**advert** /'advuht/ *n, chiefly Br* an advertisement

advertise /'advətiez/ *vt* **1** to make publicly and generally known ⟨*~*d *her presence by sneezing*⟩ **2** to announce (e g an article for sale or a vacancy) publicly, esp in the press **3** to encourage sales or patronage of, esp by emphasizing desirable qualities *~ vi* **1** to encourage sales or patronage, esp by description in the mass media **2** to seek *for* by means of advertising [ME *advertisen*, fr MF *advertiss-*, stem of *advertir*] – **advertiser** *n*

advertisement /əd'vuhtismənt, -tiz-, 'advəˌtiezmənt/ *n* a public notice; *esp* one published, broadcast, or displayed publicly to advertise a product, service, etc [ADVERTISE + -MENT]

advertising /'advəˌtiezing/ *n* **1** the action of calling sthg to the attention of the public, esp by paid announcements **2** advertisements ⟨*the magazine contains much ~*⟩ **3** the profession of preparing advertisements for publication or broadcast

advice /əd'vies/ *n* **1** recommendation regarding a decision or course of conduct ⟨*my ~ to you is: don't do it*⟩ **2** communication, esp from a distance; intelligence – usu pl **3** an official notice concerning a business transaction ⟨*a remittance ~*⟩ [ME, fr OF *avis* opinion, prob fr the phrase *ce m'est a vis* that appears to me, part trans of L *mihi visum est* it seemed so to me, I decided]

advisable /əd'viezəbl/ *adj* fitting to be advised or done; prudent – **advisability** /-zə'biləti/ *n*, **advisably** *adv*

advise /əd'viez/ *vt* **1a** to give advice to ⟨*~ her to try a drier climate*⟩ **b** to caution, warn ⟨*~ him against going*⟩ **2** to give information or notice to; inform ⟨*~ his friends of his intentions*⟩ *~ vi* to give advice [MF *advisen*, fr OF *aviser*, fr *avis*] – **adviser, advisor** *n*

ad'vised *adj* **1** thought out; considered – chiefly in *ill-advised, well-advised* **2** informed – in *keep someone advised* – **advisedly** /-zidli/ *adv*

advisory /əd'viez(ə)ri/ *adj* **1** having or exercising power to advise **2** containing or giving advice

advocaat /'advəkah/ *n* a sweet liqueur consisting chiefly of brandy and eggs [D, short for *advocatenborrel*, fr *advocaat* lawyer + *borrel* drink, bubble, fr *borrelen* to bubble]

advocacy /'advəkəsi/ *n* **1** active support or pleading ⟨*her* ~ *of reform*⟩ **2** the function of an advocate [ADVOCATE + -CY]

[1]**advocate** /'advəkət/ *n* **1** a professional pleader before a tribunal or court **2** one who defends or supports a cause or proposal [ME *advocat*, fr MF, fr L *advocatus*, fr pp of *advocare* to summon, fr *ad-* + *vocare* to call – more at VOICE]

[2]**advocate** /'advəkayt/ *vt* to plead in favour of – **advocator** *n*, **advocatory** *adj*

advowson /əd'vowz(ə)n/ *n* the right of presenting a nominee to a vacant benefice in the Church of England [ME, fr OF *avoueson*, fr ML *advocation-, advocatio*, fr L, act of calling, fr *advocatus*, pp]

adytum /'aditəm/ *n, pl* **adyta** /-tə/ the innermost sanctuary in an ancient temple; the sanctum [L, fr Gk *adyton*, neut of *adytos* not to be entered, fr *a-* + *dyein* to enter; akin to Skt *upā-du* to put on]

adze, *NAm chiefly* **adz** /adz/ *n* a tool that has the blade at right angles to the handle for cutting or shaping wood [ME *adse*, fr OE *adese*]

ae /ay/ *adj, chiefly Scot* one [ME (northern) *a*, alter. of *an*]

-ae /-i, -ee, -ie/ *suffix* (→ *n pl*) members of the family or subfamily of ⟨*Compositae*⟩ – in names of animal and some plant families and plant subfamilies [NL, fr L, pl of *-a*, ending of fem nouns and adjectives]

aedile /'aydiel/ *n* an ancient Roman official in charge of public works, the grain supply, etc [L *aedilis*, fr *aedes* temple – more at EDIFY]

aegis /'eejis/ *n* auspices, sponsorship ⟨*under the* ~ *of the education department*⟩ [L, shield of Jupiter or Minerva, protection, fr Gk *aigis* goatskin, shield of Zeus, perh fr *aig-, aix* goat; akin to Arm *aic* goat]

aegrotat /'egrətat/ *n* an unclassified degree awarded in British universities to a student prevented by illness from taking his/her examinations [L, he is ill, fr *aegrotare* to be ill, fr *aegr-, aeger* ill]

-aemia, *chiefly NAm* **-emia** /-'eemyə, -'eemi·ə/ *comb form* **1** condition of having (such) usu abnormal blood ⟨*leukaemia*⟩ **2** condition of having (sthg specified) usu abnormally in the blood ⟨*uraemia*⟩ [NL, fr Gk *-aimia*, fr *haima* blood]

aeolian, *NAm chiefly* **eolian** /ee'ohli·ən/ *adj* borne, deposited, or produced by the wind [*Aeolus*, god of the winds, fr L, fr Gk *Aiolos*]

[1]**Aeolian, Ae'olic** /-lik/ *adj* of Aeolis or its inhabitants [*Aeolis, Aeolia*, ancient district of Asia Minor, fr L, fr Gk *Aiolis*]

[2]**Aeolian** *n* **1** a member of a group of Greek peoples of Thessaly and Boeotia that colonized Lesbos and the adjacent coast of Asia Minor **2 Aeolic, Aeolian** a group of ancient Greek dialects used by the Aeolians

ae,olian 'harp *n* a stringed musical instrument on which the wind produces varying harmonics over the same fundamental tone

aeolotropic /,ee·əloh'tropik/ *adj* anisotropic [Gk *aiolos* variegated] – **aeolotropy** /,ee·ə'lotrəpi/ *n*

aeon, eon /'ee·ən, 'ee,on/ *n* **1** an immeasurably or indefinitely long period of time **2** a unit of geological time equal to 1000 million years [L, fr Gk *aiōn* – more at [1]AYE]

aer- /eər-/, **aero-** *comb form* **1** air; atmosphere ⟨*aerate*⟩ ⟨*aerobiology*⟩ **2** gas ⟨*aerosol*⟩ **3** aircraft ⟨*aerodrome*⟩ [ME *aero-*, fr MF, fr L, fr Gk *aer-, aero-*, fr *aer*]

aerate /'eərayt, -'-/ *vt* **1** to combine, supply, charge, or impregnate with a gas, esp air, oxygen, or carbon dioxide **2** to make effervescent – **aerator** *n*, **aeration** /eə'raysh(ə)n/ *n*

[1]**aerial** /'eəri·əl/ *adj* **1a** of or occurring in the air or atmosphere **b** consisting of air ⟨~ *particles*⟩ **c** growing in the air rather than in the ground or water ⟨~ *roots*⟩ **d** operating overhead on elevated cables or rails ⟨*an* ~ *railway*⟩ **2** lacking substance; thin **3a** of aircraft ⟨~ *navigation*⟩ **b** by or from an aircraft ⟨~ *photo*⟩ **4** lofty ⟨~ *spires*⟩ – poetic **5** ethereal ⟨*visions of* ~ *joy* – P B Shelley⟩ – poetic [L *aerius*, fr Gk *aerios*, fr *aēr*] – **aerially** *adv*

[2]**aerial** *n* a conductor (e g a wire) or arrangement of conductors designed to radiate or receive radio waves ☞ TELEVISION

aerie /'eəri, 'iəri/ *n* an eyrie

aero /'eəroh/ *adj* of aircraft or aeronautics ⟨*an* ~ *engine*⟩ [*aer-, aero-*]

aerobatics /,eərə'batiks/ *n pl but sing or pl in constr* the performance of feats (e g rolls) in an aircraft [blend of *aer-* and *acrobatics*] – **aerobatic** *adj*

aerobe /'eərohb/ *n* an organism (e g a bacterium) that lives only in the presence of oxygen [F *aérobie*, fr *aér-* aer- + *-bie* (fr Gk *bios* life) – more at QUICK] – **aerobic** /eə'rohbik/ *adj*

aerobics /eə'rohbiks/ *n pl but sing or pl in constr* a system of physical exercises designed to improve respiration and circulation, usu executed to music and resembling a dance routine

aerodrome /'eərə,drohm/ *n, chiefly Br* an airfield

aerodynamics /,eərohdie'namiks, -di-/ *n pl but sing or pl in constr* the dynamics of the motion of (solid bodies moving through) gases (e g air) – **aerodynamic** *adj*, **aerodynamically** *adv*, **aerodynamicist** /-die'naməsist, -di-/ *n*

aerofoil /'eərə,foyl, -roh-/ *n, chiefly Br* a body (e g an aircraft wing) designed to provide an aerodynamic reaction ☞ FLIGHT [*aer-* + [3]*foil*]

aerogram, aerogramme /'eərə,gram/ *n* AIR LETTER 2

aerolite /'eərə,liet/ *also* **aerolith** /-,lith/ *n* a stony meteorite – **aerolitic** /-'litik/ *adj*

aerology /eə'roləji/ *n* meteorology – **aerological** /,eərə'lojikl/ *adj*, **aerologist** /eə'roləjist/ *n*

aeronaut /'eərənawt/ *n* one who operates or travels in an airship or balloon [F *aéronaute*, fr *aér-* aer- + Gk *nautēs* sailor – more at NAUTICAL]

aeronautics /,eərə'nawtiks/ *n pl but sing in constr* the art or science of flight – **aeronautical** *adj*, **aeronautically** *adv*

aeroplane /'eərəplayn/ *n, chiefly Br* an aircraft that is heavier than air, has nonrotating wings from which it derives its lift, and is mechanically propelled (e g by a propeller or jet engine) ☞ FLIGHT [F *aéroplane*, fr *aér-* aer- + *plan* [5]plane]

[1]**aerosol** /'eərəsol/ *n* **1** a suspension of fine solid or liquid particles in gas (e g fog or smoke) **2** a sub-

stance dispersed from a pressurized container as an aerosol **3** AEROSOL CONTAINER [*aer-* + [3]*sol*]

[2]**aerosol** *vt* **-ll-** to write with an aerosol ⟨*a slogan* ~led *on a wall*⟩

'**aerosol con,tainer** *n* a metal container for substances in aerosol form

'**aerosol ,pack** *n* AEROSOL CONTAINER

[1]**aerospace** /'eəroh,spays/ *n* **1** (a branch of physical science dealing with) the earth's atmosphere and the space beyond **2** the aerospace industry

[2]**aerospace** *adj* of or relating to aerospace, to vehicles used in aerospace or the manufacture of such vehicles, or to travel in aerospace ⟨~ *research*⟩ ⟨~ *medicine*⟩

Aertex /'eə,teks/ *trademark* – used for a cellular cotton fabric

Aesculapian /,eskyoo'laypi·ən/ *adj* of the healing art; medical [*Aesculapius*, Greco-Roman god of medicine, fr L, fr Gk *Asklēpios*]

aesthesia, *NAm* **esthesia** /ees'theezyə, -zh(y)ə/ *n* the capacity for sensation and feeling [NL, back-formation fr *anaesthesia*]

aesthesio-, *NAm chiefly* **esthesio-** *comb form* sensation ⟨aesthesio*logy*⟩ [Gk *aisthēsis*]

aesthete, *NAm also* **esthete** /'ees,theet/ *n* **1** one who has or professes a developed sensitivity to the beautiful in art or nature **2** one who affects concern for the arts and indifference to practical affairs [back-formation fr *aesthetic*]

aesthetic /ees'thetik, es-, əs-/ *also* **aesthetical** /-kl/, *NAm also* **esthetic** *also* **esthetical** *adj* **1a** of or dealing with aesthetics or the appreciation of the beautiful ⟨~ *theories*⟩ **b** artistic ⟨*a work of* ~ *value*⟩ **2** having a developed sense of beauty [G *ästhetisch*, fr NL *aestheticus*, fr Gk *aisthētikos* of sense perception, fr *aisthanesthai* to perceive – more at AUDIBLE] – **aesthetically** *adv*

aestheticism /ees'thetisiz(ə)m/, *NAm also* **estheticism** /ees-, es-/ *n* **1** the doctrine that the principles of beauty form a fundamental standard prior to other, esp moral, principles **2** devotion to or emphasis on beauty or the cultivation of the arts

aesthetics /ees'thetiks/, *NAm also* **esthetics** /ees-, es-/ *n pl but sing or pl in constr* a branch of philosophy dealing with the nature of the beautiful, with judgments concerning beauty and taste, and with theories of criticism in the arts – **aesthetician** /-thə'tish(ə)n/ *n*

aestivate, *NAm also* **estivate** /'eestivayt/ *vi, of animals, esp insects* to pass the summer in a state of torpor – compare HIBERNATE [L *aestivatus*, pp of *aestivare* to spend the summer, fr *aestivus* of summer, fr *aestas* summer – more at EDIFY]

aestivation /,eesti'vaysh(ə)n/ *n* the arrangement of floral parts in a bud – compare VERNATION [AESTIVATE + -ION]

aether /'eethə/ *n* ETHER 1, 2

aetiology, *chiefly NAm* **etiology** /,eeti'oləji/ *n* (the study of) the causes or origin, specif of a disease or abnormal condition [ML *aetiologia* statement of causes, fr Gk *aitiologia*, fr *aitia* cause; akin to L *aemulus* rivalling] – **aetiologic** /,eeti·ə'lojik/, **aetiological** *adj*, **aetiologically** *adv*

af- – see AD-

afar /ə'fah/ *adv or n* (from, to, or at) a great distance ⟨*saw her* ~ *off*⟩ ⟨*saw him from* ~⟩ [ME *afer*, fr *on fer* at a distance & *of fer* from a distance]

affable /'afəbl/ *adj* **1** being pleasant and relaxed in talking to others **2** characterized by ease and friendliness; benign [MF, fr L *affabilis*, fr *affari* to speak to, fr *ad-* + *fari* to speak – more at [1]BAN] – **affably** *adv*, **affability** /,afə'biləti/ *n*

affair /ə'feə/ *n* **1a** *pl* commercial, professional, or public business or matters ⟨*world* ~s⟩ **b** a particular or personal concern ⟨*that's my* ~, *not yours*⟩ **2a** a procedure, action, or occasion only vaguely specified **b** a social event; a party ⟨*a catered* ~⟩ **3** *also* **affaire, affaire de coeur** a romantic or passionate attachment between 2 people who are not married to each other, often of considerable but limited duration **4** a matter causing public anxiety, controversy, or scandal ⟨*the Dreyfus* ~⟩ **5** an object or collection of objects only vaguely specified – used with a descriptive or qualifying term; infml ⟨*the house was a 2-storey* ~⟩ [ME & MF; ME *affaire*, fr MF, fr *a faire* to do]

[1]**affect** /'afekt/ *n* the conscious subjective aspect of an emotion considered apart from bodily changes [G *affekt*, fr L *affectus* disposition, fr *affectus*, pp]

[2]**affect** /ə'fekt/ *vt* **1** to be given to ⟨~ *flashy clothes*⟩ **2** to put on a pretence of (being); feign ⟨~ *indifference*⟩ ⟨~ *the experienced traveller*⟩ [MF & L; MF *affecter* to aim at, fr L *affectare*, fr *affectus*, pp of *afficere* to influence, fr *ad-* + *facere* to do – more at [1]DO]

[3]**affect** *vt* to have a material effect on or produce an alteration in ⟨*paralysis* ~ed *his limbs*⟩ **2** to act on (e g a person or his/her mind or feelings) so as to effect a response ⟨*was deeply* ~ed *by the news*⟩

affectation /,afek'taysh(ə)n/ *n* **1** an insincere display (e g of a quality not really possessed) ⟨*the* ~ *of righteous indignation*⟩ **2** a deliberately assumed peculiarity of speech or conduct; an artificiality

affected /ə'fektid/ *adj* **1** inclined, disposed *towards* – chiefly in *well-affected, ill-affected* **2a** given to affectation **b** assumed artificially or falsely; pretended ⟨*an* ~ *interest in art*⟩ – **affectedly** *adv*, **affectedness** *n*

affecting /ə'fekting/ *adj* evoking a strong emotional response; moving – **affectingly** *adv*

[1]**affection** /ə'feksh(ə)n/ *n* **1** emotion as compared with reason – often pl with sing. meaning **2** tender and lasting attachment; fondness ⟨*she had a deep* ~ *for her parents*⟩ [ME, fr MF *affection*, fr L *affection-, affectio*, fr *affectus*, pp] – **affectional** *adj*, **affectionally** *adv*

[2]**affection** *n* a disease, malady, or other bodily condition

affectionate /ə'feksh(ə)nət/ *adj* **1** showing affection or warm regard; loving **2** proceeding from affection; tender ⟨~ *care*⟩ – **affectionately** *adv*

affective /ə'fektiv/ *adj* **1** of, arising from, or influencing affect; emotional ⟨~ *disorders*⟩ **2** expressing emotion ⟨~ *language*⟩ – **affectively** *adv*, **affectivity** /,afek'tivəti/ *n*

afferent /'afərənt/ *adj* bearing or conducting (nervous impulses) inwards (towards the brain) – compare EFFERENT [L *afferent-, afferens*, prp of *afferre* to bring to, fr *ad-* + *ferre* to bear – more at [2]BEAR] – **afferently** *adv*

affiance /ə'fie·əns/ *vt* to promise (oneself or another) solemnly in marriage; betroth [MF *afiancer*, fr *afiance* trust, fr *afier* to trust, fr ML *affidare*, fr L *ad-* + (assumed) VL *fidare* to trust – more at FIANCÉ]

affidavit /,afi'dayvit/ *n* a sworn written statement

for use as judicial proof [ML, he has made an oath, fr *affidare*]

[1]**affiliate** /ə'filiayt/ *vt* to attach as a member or branch – + *to* or *with* ⟨*the union is* ~d *to the TUC*⟩ ~ *vi* to connect or associate oneself *with* another, often in a dependent or subordinate position; combine [ML *affiliatus,* pp of *affiliare* to adopt as a son, fr L *ad-* + *filius* son – more at FEMININE] – **affiliation** /-'aysh(ə)n/ *n*

[2]**affiliate** /ə'filiayt, -ət/ *n* an affiliated person or organization

af,fili'ation ,order /ə,fili'aysh(ə)n/ *n* a legal order that the father of an illegitimate child must pay towards its maintenance

affinity /ə'finəti/ *n* **1** SYMPATHY 2a ⟨*this mysterious* ~ *between us*⟩ **2** an attraction, esp between substances, causing them to combine chemically **3** resemblance based on relationship or causal connection [ME *affinite,* fr MF or L; MF *afinité,* fr L *affinitas,* fr *affinis* bordering on, related by marriage, fr *ad-* + *finis* end, border]

affirm /ə'fuhm/ *vt* **1a** to validate, confirm **b** to state positively **2** to assert (e g a judgment of a lower court) as valid; ratify ~ *vi* **1** to testify by affirmation **2** to uphold a judgment or decree of a lower court [ME *affermen,* fr MF *afermer,* fr L *affirmare,* fr *ad-* + *firmare* to make firm, fr *firmus* firm – more at [1]FIRM] – **affirmable** *adj,* **affirmance** *n*

affirmation /,afə'maysh(ə)n/ *n* **1** sthg affirmed; a positive assertion **2** a solemn declaration made by sby who conscientiously declines taking an oath [AFFIRM + -ATION]

[1]**affirmative** /ə'fuhmətiv/ *adj* **1** asserting or answering that the fact is so ⟨*gave an* ~ *nod*⟩ **2** favouring or supporting a proposition or motion ⟨*an* ~ *vote*⟩ **3** *chiefly NAm* positive ⟨*an* ~ *responsibility*⟩ – **affirmatively** *adv*

[2]**affirmative** *n* **1** an expression (e g the word *yes*) of agreement or assent **2** an affirmative proposition

[1]**affix** /ə'fiks/ *vt* **1** to attach (physically) ⟨~ *a stamp to a letter*⟩; *esp* to add in writing ⟨~ *a signature*⟩ **2** to impress ⟨~ed *his seal*⟩ [ML *affixare,* fr L *affixus,* pp of *affigere* to fasten to, fr *ad-* + *figere* to fasten – more at DYKE] – **affixable** *adj,* **affixment, affixation** /,afik'saysh(ə)n/, **affixture** /'afikschə/ *n*

[2]**affix** /'afiks/ *n* **1** an addition to the beginning or end of or an insertion in a word or root to produce a derivative word or inflectional form **2** an appendage – **affixal** /'afiksəl/, **affixial** /a'fiksi·əl/ *adj*

afflatus /ə'flaytəs/ *n* divine imparting of knowledge or mental power; inspiration [L, act of blowing or breathing on, fr *afflatus,* pp of *afflare* to blow on, fr *ad-* + *flare* to blow – more at [1]BLOW]

afflict /ə'flikt/ *vt* **1** to distress so severely as to cause persistent suffering **2** to trouble ⟨~ed *with shyness*⟩ [ME *afflicten* to overthrow, fr L *afflictus,* pp of *affligere* to cast down, fr *ad-* + *fligere* to strike – more at PROFLIGATE]

affliction /ə'fliksh(ə)n/ *n* **1** great suffering **2** a cause of persistent pain or distress [AFFLICT + -ION]

affluent /'afloo·ənt/ *adj* **1** flowing in abundance **2** having a generously sufficient supply of material possessions; wealthy ⟨*our* ~ *society*⟩ [ME, fr MF, fr L *affluent-, affluens,* prp of *affluere* to flow to, flow abundantly, fr *ad-* + *fluere* to flow – more at FLUID] – **affluence** /-əns/, **affluency** /-ənsi/ *n,* **affluently** *adv*

afford /ə'fawd/ *vt* **1a** to be able to do or to bear without serious harm – esp + *can* ⟨*you can't* ~ *to neglect your health*⟩ **b** to be able to bear the cost of ⟨~ *a new coat*⟩ **2** to provide, supply ⟨*her letters* ~ *no clue to her intentions*⟩ [ME *aforthen,* fr OE *geforthian* to carry out, fr *ge-,* perfective prefix + *forthian* to carry out, fr *forth* – more at CO-, FORTH] – **affordable** *adj*

afforest /a'forist/ *vt* to establish or plant forest cover on [ML *afforestare,* fr L *ad-* + ML *forestis* forest – more at FOREST] – **afforestation** /ə,fori'staysh(ə)n/ *n*

affranchise /ə'franchiez/ *vt* to set free; enfranchise [modif of MF *afranchiss-,* stem of *afranchir,* fr *a-* (fr L *ad-*) + *franchir* to free – more at FRANCHISE]

affray /ə'fray/ *n* a (public) brawl [ME, fr MF, fr *affreer* to startle]

affricate /'afrikət/ *n* a composite speech sound consisting of a stop and an immediately following fricative (e g the /t/ and /sh/ that are the constituents of the /tsh/ in *why choose*) [prob fr G *affrikata,* fr L *affricata,* fem of *affricatus,* pp of *affricare* to rub against, fr *ad-* + *fricare* to rub – more at FRICTION] – **affrication** /,afri'kaysh(ə)n/ *n,* **affricative** /ə'frikətiv/ *n or adj*

affront /ə'frunt/ *vt* to insult by openly insolent or disrespectful behaviour or language; give offence to [ME *afronten,* fr MF *afronter* to defy, fr (assumed) VL *affrontare,* fr L *ad-* + *front-, frons* forehead – more at BRINK] – **affront** *n*

Afghan /'afgan/ *n* **1** a native or inhabitant of Afghanistan **2** Pashto **3** *not cap* a blanket or shawl of coloured wool knitted or crocheted in strips or squares **4 Afghan, Afghan hound** a tall hunting dog with a coat of silky thick hair [Pashto *afghānī*] – **Afghan** *adj*

afghani /af'gahni/ *n, pl* **afghanis** ☞ *Afghanistan* at NATIONALITY [Pashto *afghānī,* lit., Afghan]

aficionado /ə,fishyə'nahdoh/, *fem* **aficionada** /-'nahdə/ *n, pl* **aficionados,** *fem* **aficionadas** a devotee, fan ⟨~s *of the bullfight*⟩ [Sp, fr pp of *aficionar* to inspire affection, fr *afición* affection, fr L *affection-affectio* – more at AFFECTION]

afield /ə'feeld/ *adv* **1** to, in, or on the field **2** (far) away from home; abroad **3** out of the way; astray ⟨*irrelevant remarks that carried us far* ~⟩ [ME *afelde,* fr OE *on felda,* fr *on* + *felda,* dat of *feld* field]

afire /ə'fie·ə/ *adj or adv* on fire ⟨~ *with enthusiasm*⟩

aflame /ə'flaym/ *adj or adv* afire

aflatoxin /,aflə'toksin/ *n* any of several poisons that are produced by moulds (e g in badly stored peanuts) and cause (liver) cancers [NL *Aspergillus flavus,* species of mould + E *toxin*]

afloat /ə'floht/ *adj or adv* **1a** borne (as if) on the water or air **b** at sea or on ship **2** free of debt **3** circulating about; rumoured ⟨*nasty stories were* ~⟩ **4** flooded with or submerged under water [ME *aflot,* fr OE *on flot,* fr *on* + *flot,* fr *flot* deep water, sea; akin to OE *flēotan* to float – more at FLEET]

aflutter /ə'flutə/ *adj* fluttering

afoot /ə'foot/ *adv or adj* **1** on foot **2** (in the process of) happening; astir ⟨*there's trouble* ~⟩

afore /ə'faw/ *adv, conj, or prep, chiefly dial* before [ME, fr OE *onforan,* fr *on* + *foran* before – more at BEFORE]

aforementioned /ə'faw,menshənd/ *adj* mentioned previously

aforesaid /ə'faw,sed/ *adj* aforementioned

aforethought /ə'faw,thawt/ *adj* premeditated, deliberate – fml; esp in *with malice aforethought*

a fortiori /,ay fawti'awri/ *adv* with still greater reason or certainty – used in drawing a conclusion that is inferred to be even more certain than another ⟨*if he can afford a house, ~, he can afford a tent*⟩ [NL, lit., from the stronger (argument)]

Afr- – see AFRO-

afraid /ə'frayd/ *adj* **1** filled with fear or apprehension ⟨*~ of machines*⟩ ⟨*~ for his job*⟩ **2** regretfully of the opinion – in apology for an utterance ⟨*I'm ~ I won't be able to go*⟩ [ME *affraied*, fr pp of *affraien* to frighten, fr MF *affreer*]

afreet /'afreet, ə'freet/, **afrit** /ə'frit/ *n* a powerful evil spirit or monster in Arabic mythology [Ar *'ifrit*]

afresh /ə'fresh/ *adv* anew, again [ME, fr [1]*a-* + *fresh*]

African /'afrikən/ *n or adj* (a native or inhabitant) of Africa [ME, fr L *Africanus*, fr *Africa*] – **Africanness** /-nis/ *n*

Africander, Afrikander /,afri'kandə/ *n* (any of) a breed of tall red large-horned southern African cattle [Afrik *Afrikaner, Afrikaander*, lit., Afrikaner]

Africanism /'afrikə,niz(ə)m/ *n* **1** a characteristic feature of African culture or language **2** allegiance to the traditions, interests, or ideals of Africa

Africanist /'afrikənist/ *n* a specialist in African cultures or languages

African·ize, -ise /'afrikə,niez/ *vt* to make African; *esp* to bring under (Black) African control – **Africanization** /-nie'zaysh(ə)n/ *n*

African violet *n* any of several tropical African plants grown as houseplants for their velvety leaves and showy purple, pink, or white flowers

Afrikaans /,afri'kahnz/ *n* a language of S Africa developed from 17th-c Dutch [Afrik, fr *afrikaans*, adj, African, fr obs Afrik *afrikanisch*, fr L *africanus*]

Afrikaner /,afri'kahnə/ *n* an Afrikaans-speaking S African of European, esp Dutch, descent [Afrik, lit., African, fr L *africanus*]

,Afri'kanerdom /-dəm/ *n* the political and social supremacy of Afrikaners in S Africa

afrit /ə'frit/ *n* an afreet

Afro /'afroh/ *n or adj, pl* **Afros** (a hairstyle) shaped into a round curly bushy mass [prob fr *Afro-American*]

Afro- /afroh-/, **Afr-** *comb form* African ⟨Afro-*American*⟩; African and ⟨Afro-*Asiatic*⟩ [L *Afr-, Afer*]

,Afro-Asi'atic *adj* of or constituting a family of languages comprising Semitic, Egyptian, Berber, Cushitic, and Chad

[1]**aft** /ahft/ *adv* near, towards, or in the stern of a ship or the tail of an aircraft ☞ SHIP [ME *afte* back, fr OE *æftan* from behind, behind; akin to OE *æfter*]

[2]**aft** *adj* rearward; [4]AFTER 2 ⟨*the ~ decks*⟩ ☞ SHIP

[1]**after** /'ahftə/ *adv* **1** BEHIND 1b ⟨*mourners follow ~ – SEU S*⟩ **2** afterwards [ME, fr OE *æfter*, akin to OHG *aftar* after]

[2]**after** *prep* **1** behind in place or order ⟨*shut the door ~ you*⟩ – used in yielding precedence ⟨*~ you!*⟩ or in asking for the next turn ⟨*~ you with the pencil*⟩ **2a** following in time; later than ⟨*~ breakfast*⟩ **b** continuously succeeding ⟨*saw play ~ play*⟩ **c** in view or in spite of (sthg preceding) ⟨*~ all our advice*⟩ **3** – used to indicate the goal or purpose of an action ⟨*go ~ gold*⟩ **4** so as to resemble: e g **a** in accordance with **b** in allusion to the name of **c** in the characteristic manner of **d** in imitation of **5** about, concerning ⟨*ask ~ his health*⟩

[3]**after** *conj* later than the time when

[4]**after** *adj* **1** later, subsequent ⟨*in ~ years*⟩ **2** located towards the rear or stern of a ship, aircraft, etc

,after 'all *adv* **1** in spite of everything **2** it must be remembered ⟨*he can't swim but, ~, he's only 2*⟩

'after,birth /-,buhth/ *n* the placenta and foetal membranes expelled after delivery of a baby, young animal, etc

'after,burner /-,buhnə/ *n* a device in a jet engine for providing reheat

'after,care /-,keə/ *n* the care, treatment, etc given to people discharged from a hospital or other institution

'afteref,fect /-i,fekt/ *n* an effect that follows its cause after an interval of time

'after,glow /-,gloh/ *n* **1** a glow remaining (e g in the sky) where a light source has disappeared **2** a vestige of past splendour, success, or happy emotion

,after-'hours *adj or adv* (done or operating) after closing time

'after,image /-,imij/ *n* a usu visual sensation remaining after stimulation (e g of the retina) has ceased

'after,life /-,lief/ *n* **1** an existence after death **2** a later period in one's life

'after,math /-,mahth, -,math/ *n* **1** a second growth of forage after the harvest of an earlier crop **2** a consequence, result **3** the period immediately following a usu ruinous event ⟨*in the ~ of the war*⟩ [[4]*after* + *math* (mowing, crop)]

'after,most /-,mohst/ *adj* farthest aft

,after'noon /-'noohn/ *n* the time between noon and sunset – **afternoon** *adj*

,after'noons *adv, chiefly NAm* in the afternoon repeatedly; on any afternoon ⟨*~ he usually slept*⟩

afters /'ahftəz/ *n pl, Br* a dessert – infml

'after-,shave *n* (a) usu scented lotion for use on the face after shaving

'after,taste /-,tayst/ *n* persistence of a flavour or impression ⟨*the bitter ~ of a quarrel*⟩

'after,thought /-,thawt/ *n* **1** an idea occurring later **2** sthg added later

'afterwards /-woodz/ *adv* after that; subsequently, thereafter ⟨*for years ~*⟩

'after,word /-,wuhd/ *n* EPILOGUE 1

again /ə'gayn, ə'gen/ *adv* **1** so as to be as before ⟨*put it back ~*⟩ **2** another time; once more **3** on the other hand ⟨*he might go, and ~ he might not*⟩ **4** further; IN ADDITION ⟨*could eat as much ~*⟩ [ME, opposite, again, fr OE *ongēan* opposite, back, fr *on* + *gēn, gēan* still, again; akin to OE *gēan-* against, OHG *gegin* against, towards]

a,gain and a'gain *adv* often, repeatedly

[1]**against** /ə'gaynst, ə'genst/ *prep* **1a** in opposition or hostility to ⟨*the rule ~ smoking*⟩ **b** unfavourable to ⟨*his appearance is ~ him*⟩ **c** as a defence or protection from ⟨*warned them ~ opening the box*⟩ **2** compared or contrasted with ⟨*cost only £2, as ~ £3 at home*⟩ **3a** in preparation or provision for ⟨*saving ~ his retirement*⟩ **b** with respect to; towards ⟨*customs which had the force of law ~ both landlord and*

tenant⟩ **4** (in the direction of and) in contact with ⟨*rain beat* ~ *the windows*⟩ ⟨*leaning* ~ *the wall*⟩ **5** in a direction opposite to the motion or course of; counter to ⟨*swam* ~ *the tide*⟩ **6** in exchange for [ME, alter. of *againes*, fr *again*]

[2]**against** *adj* **1** opposed to a motion or measure **2** unfavourable to a specified degree; *esp* unfavourable to a win ⟨*the odds are 2 to 1* ~⟩

Aga Khan /ˌahgə 'kahn/ *n* the leader of a Shiite sect of Muslims [Turk *ağa* lord, master]

agamic /ay'gamik, ə-/ *adj* asexual, parthenogenetic [Gk *agamos* unmarried, fr *a-* + *gamos* marriage – more at BIGAMY] – **agamically** *adv*

agapanthus /ˌagə'panthəs/ *n* any of several African plants of the lily family with umbels of showy blue or purple flowers [NL, genus name, fr Gk *agapē* + *anthos* flower – more at ANTHOLOGY]

[1]**agape** /ə'gayp/ *adj* **1** wide open; gaping **2** in a state of wonder ⟨~ *with expectation*⟩ [[1]*a-* + [1]*gape*]

[2]**agape** /ə'gahpay, 'ahgəˌpay/ *n* LOVE FEAST [LL, fr Gk *agapē*, lit., love, fr *agapan* to welcome, love] – **agapeic** /ˌahgə'payik/ *adj*

agar, ˌagar 'jelly /'aygah/ *n* agar-agar

agar-agar /ˌaygahr 'aygah/ *n* a gelatinous extract from any of various red algae used esp in culture media or as a gelling agent in foods [Malay]

agaric /'agərik, ə'garik/ *n* any of a family of fungi (e g the common edible mushroom) with an umbrella-shaped cap [L *agaricum*, a fungus, fr Gk *agarikon*]

agate /'agət, 'agayt/ *n* **1** a mineral used as a gem composed of quartz of various colours, often arranged in bands **2** sthg made of or fitted with agate [MF, fr L *achates*, fr Gk *achatēs*]

agave /ə'gayvi/ *n* any of a N or S American genus of plants of the daffodil family with spiny leaves [NL *Agave*, genus name, fr L, a daughter of Cadmus in mythology, fr Gk *Agauē*]

[1]**age** /ayj/ *n* **1a** the length of time a person has lived or a thing existed ⟨*a boy 10 years of* ~⟩ **b** the time of life at which some particular qualification, power, or capacity arises ⟨*the voting* ~ *is 18*⟩ **c** a stage of life ⟨*the 7* ~s *of man*⟩ **2** a generation ⟨*the* ~s *to come*⟩ **3** a period of time dominated by a central figure or prominent feature ⟨*the* ~ *of Pericles*⟩: e g **a** a period in history ⟨*the steam* ~⟩ **b** a cultural period marked by the prominence of a specified item ⟨*the atomic* ~⟩ **c** a division of geological time, usu shorter than an epoch **4** an individual's development in terms of the years required by an average individual for similar development ⟨*a mental* ~ *of 6*⟩ **5** a long time – usu pl with sing. meaning; infml ⟨*haven't seen him for* ~s⟩ [ME, fr OF *aage*, fr (assumed) VL *aetaticum*, fr L *aetat-*, *aetas*, fr *aevum* lifetime – more at [1]AYE] – **of age** of legal adult status

[2]**age** *vb* **aging, ageing** /'ayjing/ *vi* **1** to become old; show the effects of increasing age ⟨*he's* ~d *terribly since you last saw him*⟩ **2** to become mellow or mature; ripen ⟨*this cheese has* ~d *for nearly 2 years*⟩ ~ *vt* **1** to cause to seem old, esp prematurely ⟨*illness has* ~d *him*⟩ **2** to bring to a state fit for use or to maturity

-age /-ij/ *suffix* (→ *n*) **1** aggregate or collection of ⟨*baggage*⟩ ⟨*acreage*⟩ **2a** action or process of ⟨*haulage*⟩ **b** cumulative result of ⟨*breakage*⟩ ⟨*spillage*⟩ **c** rate or amount of ⟨*dosage*⟩ **3** house or place of ⟨*orphanage*⟩ **4** condition or rank of ⟨*bondage*⟩ ⟨*peerage*⟩ **5** fee or charge for ⟨*postage*⟩ ⟨*wharfage*⟩ [ME, fr OF, fr L *-aticum*]

aged /'ayjid; *sense* '*b* ayjd/ *adj* **1** grown old: e g **a** of an advanced age **b** having attained a specified age ⟨*a man* ~ *40 years*⟩ **2** typical of old age ⟨*his* ~ *steps*⟩ – **agedness** *n*

ageless /'ayjlis/ *adj* **1** never growing old or showing the effects of age **2** timeless, eternal ⟨~ *truths*⟩ – **agelessly** *adv*, **agelessness** *n*

agency /'ayjənsi/ *n* **1** a power or force through which a result is achieved; instrumentality ⟨*communicated through the* ~ *of his ambassador*⟩ **2** the function or place of business of an agent or representative **3** an establishment that does business for another ⟨*an advertising* ~⟩

agenda /ə'jendə/ *n* **1** a list of items to be discussed or business to be transacted (e g at a meeting) **2 a** plan of procedure; a programme [L, pl of *agendum*, neut of *agendus*, gerundive of *agere*] – **agendaless** *adj*

agent /'ayjənt/ *n* **1a** sthg or sby that produces an effect or that acts or exerts power **b** a chemically, physically, or biologically active substance **2** a person who acts for or in the place of another by authority from him/her: e g **a** a business representative **b** one employed by or controlling an agency ⟨*my literary* ~⟩ **3a** a representative of a government **b** a spy [ME, fr ML *agent-*, *agens*, fr L, prp of *agere* to drive, lead, act, do; akin to ON *aka* to travel in a vehicle, Gk *agein* to drive, lead]

agentive /'ayjəntiv/ *adj or n* (of or being) a linguistic form indicating the doer of an action (e g the suffix *-er* in *singer*)

agent provocateur /ˌahzhonh provokə'tuh, ˌayjənt (*Fr* ajɑ̃ provokatœːr)/ *n, pl* **agents provocateurs** /~/ a person employed to incite suspected people to some open action that will make them liable to punishment [F, lit., provoking agent]

ˌage of con'sent *n* the age at which one is legally competent to give consent; *specif* that at which a person, esp a female, may consent to sexual intercourse

ˌage of 'reason *n* **1** *often cap A&R* a period characterized by the repudiation of religious, social, and philosophical beliefs not founded on reason; *esp* the 18th c in Europe – compare ENLIGHTENMENT **2** the time of life when one begins to be able to distinguish right from wrong

'age-ˌold *adj* having existed for ages; ancient

[1]**agglomerate** /ə'glomərayt/ *vb* to (cause to) gather into a cluster or disorderly mass [L *agglomeratus*, pp of *agglomerare* to heap up, join, fr *ad-* + *glomer-*, *glomus* ball]

[2]**ag'glomerate** /-rət/ *adj* gathered into a ball, mass, or cluster

[3]**ag'glomerate** /-rət/ *n* **1** a disorderly mass or collection **2** a rock composed of irregular volcanic fragments

agglomeration /əˌglomə'raysh(ə)n/ *n* a mass or cluster of disparate elements [AGGLOMERATE + -ION] – **agglomerative** /ə'glomərətiv/ *adj*

agglutinate /ə'gloohtiˌnayt/ *vt* **1** to cause to stick; fasten together (as if) with glue **2** to combine into a compound; attach to a base as an affix **3** to cause to undergo agglutination ~ *vi* to form words by agglutination [L *agglutinatus*, pp of *agglutinare* to glue to, fr *ad-* + *glutinare* to glue, fr *glutin-*, *gluten* glue –

more at GLUTEN] – **agglutinability** /ə,gloohtinə'biləti/ *n*

agglutination /ə,gloohti'naysh(ə)n/ *n* **1** the formation of compound words by combining (parts of) other words which already have a single definite meaning **2** the collection of red blood cells or other minute suspended particles into clumps, esp as a response to a specific antibody [AGGLUTINATE + -ION] – **agglutinative** /ə'gloohtinətiv/ *adj*

agglutinin /ə'gloohtinin/ *n* a substance producing biological agglutination [ISV *agglutin*ation + *-in*]

aggrand·ize, -ise /ə'grandiez, 'agrən-/ *vt* **1** to give a false air of greatness to; praise highly ⟨~d *the one and disparaged the other*⟩ **2** to enhance the power, wealth, position, or reputation of [F *agrandiss-*, stem of *agrandir*, fr *a-* (fr L *ad-*) + *grandir* to increase, fr L *grandire*, fr *grandis* great] – **aggrandizement** /ə'grandizmənt/ *n*

aggravate /'agrəvayt/ *vt* **1** to make worse or more severe **2** to annoy, irritate [L *aggravatus*, pp of *aggravare* to make heavier, fr *ad-* + *gravare* to burden, fr *gravis* heavy – more at [1]GRIEVE] – **aggravation** /-'vaysh(ə)n/ *n*

[1]**aggregate** /'agrigət/ *adj* formed by the collection of units or particles into a body, mass, or amount: e g **a** *of a flower* clustered in a dense mass or head **b** *of a fruit* formed from the several ovaries of a single flower **c** taking all units as a whole; total ⟨~ *earnings*⟩ ⟨~ *sales*⟩ [ME *aggregat*, fr L *aggregatus*, pp of *aggregare* to add to, fr *ad-* + *greg-*, *grex* flock – more at GREGARIOUS] – **aggregately** *adv*, **aggregateness** *n*

[2]**aggregate** /'agri,gayt/ *vt* **1** to bring together into a mass or whole **2** to amount to (a specified total) – **aggregative** *adj*, **aggregation** /-'gaysh(ə)n/ *n*, **aggregational** *adj*

[3]**aggregate** /'agrigət/ *n* **1** a mass of loosely associated parts; an assemblage **2** the whole amount; the sum total **3a** a rock composed of closely packed mineral crystals **b** sand, gravel, etc for mixing with cement to make concrete ☞ BUILDING **c** a clustered mass of individual particles of various shapes and sizes that is considered to be the basic structural unit of soil

aggression /ə'greshən/ *n* **1** a hostile attack; *esp* one made without just cause **2** attack, encroachment; *esp* unprovoked violation by one country of the territory of another **3** hostile, injurious, or destructive behaviour or outlook [L *aggression-*, *aggressio*, fr *aggressus*, pp of *aggredi* to attack, fr *ad-* + *gradi* to step, go – more at GRADE] – **aggressor** *n*

aggressive /ə'gresiv/ *adj* **1a** tending towards or practising aggression ⟨*an* ~ *foreign policy*⟩ **b** ready to attack ⟨*an* ~ *fighter*⟩ **2** forceful, dynamic ⟨*an* ~ *salesman*⟩ – **aggressively** *adv*, **aggressiveness** *n*

aggrieve /ə'greev/ *vt* **1** to give pain or trouble to; distress **2** to inflict injury on ***USE*** usu pass [ME *agreven*, fr MF *agrever*, fr L *aggravare* to make heavier]

ag'grieved *adj* showing or expressing resentment; hurt – **aggrievedly** /-vidli/ *adv*

aggro /'agroh/ *n*, *chiefly Br* **1** provocation, hostility **2** deliberate aggression or violence ***USE*** infml [by shortening & alter. fr *aggravation* or *aggression*]

aghast /ə'gahst/ *adj* suddenly struck with terror or amazement; shocked ⟨*stood by* ~ *as the building collapsed*⟩ [ME *agast*, fr pp of *agasten* to frighten, fr *a-* (perfective prefix) + *gasten* to frighten, fr *gast*, *gost* ghost]

agile /'ajiel/ *adj* **1** quick, easy, and graceful in movement **2** mentally quick and resourceful [MF, fr L *agilis*, fr *agere* to drive, act – more at AGENT] – **agilely** *adv*, **agility** /ə'jiləti/ *n*

agin /ə'gin/ *prep*, *dial Br* against

agio /'ajioh/ *n*, *pl* **agios** a premium or percentage paid for the exchange of one currency for another [It, alter. of It dial. *lajjë*, fr MGk *allagion* exchange, fr Gk *allagē* exchange, fr *allos* other – more at ELSE]

agiotage /'ajətij/ *n* **1** the business of money exchange **2** the speculative buying or selling of stocks [F, fr *agioter* to practise stockjobbing, fr *agio* stockjobbing, fr It]

agitate /'ajitayt/ *vt* **1** to move, shake **2** to excite and often trouble the mind or feelings of; disturb ~ *vi* to work to arouse public feeling for or against a cause ⟨~d *for better schools*⟩ [L *agitatus*, pp of *agitare*, freq of *agere* to drive – more at AGENT] – **agitatedly** /-,taytidli/ *adv*, **agitation** /,aji'taysh(ə)n/ *n*, **agitational** *adj*

agitator /'ajitaytə/ *n* **1** sby who stirs up public feeling on controversial issues ⟨*political* ~s⟩ **2** a device or apparatus for stirring or shaking [AGITATE + [1]-OR]

agitprop /'ajit,prop, ,--'-/ *n* (pro-communist) political propaganda, esp in the arts [Russ, office of agitation and propaganda, fr *agitatsiya* agitation + *prop*aganda] – **agitprop** *adj*

aglet /'aglət/ *n* a (metal) tag attached to the end of a lace, cord, or ribbon [ME *aglet*, fr MF *aguillette*, *aiguillette*, dim. of *aguille*, *aiguille* needle, fr LL *acicula*, *acucula* ornamental pin, dim. of L *acus* needle, pin – more at ACUTE]

agley /ə'glay, ə'glee/ *adv*, *chiefly Scot* awry, wrong ⟨*the best-laid schemes o' mice an' men gang aft* ~ – Robert Burns⟩ [Sc, lit., squintingly, fr [1]*a-* + *gley* to squint]

aglow /ə'gloh/ *adj* radiant with warmth or excitement

AGM *n* an annual general meeting (e g of a society or company)

agnail /'agnayl/ *n* a sore or inflammation about a fingernail or toenail; *also* a hangnail [ME, corn on the foot or toe, fr OE *angnægl*, fr *ang-* (akin to *enge* narrow, tight, painful) + *nægl* metal nail – more at ANGER, NAIL]

agnosia /ag'nozh(y)ə/ *n* a disturbance of perception caused esp by neurological dysfunction [NL, fr Gk *agnōsia* ignorance, fr *a-* + *gnōsis* knowledge]

[1]**agnostic** /ag'nostik, əg-/ *n* sby who holds the view that any ultimate reality is unknown and prob unknowable; *also* one who doubts the existence of God [modif of Gk *agnōstos* unknown, unknowable, fr *a-* + *gnōstos* known, fr *gignōskein* to know – more at KNOW] – **agnosticism** /ag'nostisiz(ə)m, əg-/ *n*

[2]**agnostic** *adj* of or being an agnostic or the beliefs of agnostics

Agnus Dei /,agnəs 'day·ee/ *n* a liturgical prayer addressed to Christ as Saviour, often set to music ⟨*the* ~ *from Bach's B Minor Mass*⟩ [ME, fr LL, lamb of God; fr its opening words]

ago /ə'goh/ *adj or adv* earlier than now ⟨*10 years* ~⟩ ⟨*how long* ~ *did they leave?*⟩ [ME *agon*, *ago*, fr pp of *agon* to pass away, fr OE *āgān*, fr *ā-* (perfective prefix) + *gān* to go – more at [1]GO]

agog /ə'gog/ *adj* full of intense anticipation or excitement; eager ⟨*the court was ~ with gossip, scandal and intrigue – TLS*⟩ [MF *en gogues* in mirth]

-agogue /-əgog/ *comb form* (→ *n*) **1** substance that promotes the secretion or expulsion of ⟨*emmen*agogue⟩ **2** leader; guide ⟨*ped*agogue⟩ – sometimes derog ⟨*dem*agogue⟩ [F & NL; F, fr LL *-agogus* inducing, leading, fr Gk *-agōgos*, fr *agein* to lead; NL *-agogon*, fr Gk, neut of *-agōgos* – more at AGENT]

agonic /ə'gonik/, **agonic line** *n* an imaginary line connecting points where there is no magnetic declination [Gk *agōnos* without angle, fr *a-* + *gōnia* angle – more at -GON]

agonist /'agənist/ *n* **1** a muscle that is restricted by the action of an antagonistic muscle with which it is paired **2** a substance capable of combining with a receptor on the surface of a (nerve) cell and initiating a reaction *USE* compare ANTAGONIST [LL *agonista* competitor, fr Gk *agōnistēs*, fr *agōnizesthai* to contend, fr *agōn*; in both these senses, prob back-formation fr *antagonist*]

agonistic /,agə'nistik/, **agonistical** /-kl/ *adj* argumentative – **agonistically** *adv*

agon·ize, -ise /'agəniez/ *vt* to cause to suffer agony ~ *vi* **1** to suffer agony or anguish **2** to make a great effort [MF *agoniser* to be in agony, fr LL *agonizare*, fr Gk *agōnizethai*, fr *agōnia*]

'agon·ized, -ised *adj* characterized by, suffering, or expressing agony

agonizing, -ising /'agəniezing/ *adj* causing agony; painful ⟨*an ~ reappraisal of his policies*⟩ – **agonizingly** *adv*

agony /'agəni/ *n* **1** intense and often prolonged pain or suffering of mind or body; anguish **2** the struggle that precedes death ⟨*his last ~*⟩ [ME *agonie*, fr LL *agonia*, fr Gk *agōnia* struggle, anguish, fr *agōn* gathering, contest for a prize, fr *agein* to lead, celebrate – more at AGENT]

[1]**agora** /'agərə/ *n, pl* **agoras, agorae** /-ri/ a gathering place for popular political assembly in ancient Greece [Gk – more at GREGARIOUS]

[2]**agora** /,agə'rah/ *n, pl* **agorot** /-'roht/ ☞ *Israel* at NATIONALITY [NHeb *ăgōrāh*, fr Heb, a small coin]

agoraphobia /,agrə'fohbi·ə/ *n* abnormal dread of being in open spaces [NL, fr Gk *agora* + NL *phobia*] – **agoraphobic** *n or adj*, **agoraphobe** /'agrə,fohb/ *n*

agouti /ə'goohti/ *n, pl* **agoutis,** *esp collectively* **agouti 1** a tropical American rodent about the size of a rabbit **2** a colour of fur resulting from the barring of each hair in alternate dark and light bands [F, fr Sp *agutí*, fr Guarani]

agranulocyte /ay'granyooləˌsiet/ *n* any of various white blood cells with cytoplasm that does not contain conspicuous granules – compare GRANULOCYTE – **agranulocytic** /-'sitik/ *adj*

[1]**agrarian** /ə'greəri·ən/ *adj* **1** of or relating to (the tenure of) fields **2** (characteristic) of farmers or agricultural life or interests [L *agrarius*, fr *agr-*, *ager* field – more at ACRE]

[2]**agrarian** *n* a member of an agrarian party or movement

agrarianism /ə'greəri·ə,niz(ə)m/ *n* a movement to bring about land reforms (e g by the redistribution of land)

agree /ə'gree/ *vt* **1** to admit, concede – usu + a clause ⟨*I ~ that you're right*⟩ **2** to bring into harmony **3** *chiefly Br* to come to terms on, usu after discussion; accept by mutual consent ⟨*the following articles were ~*d – Winston Churchill⟩ ~ *vi* **1** to give assent; accede – often + *to* ⟨*~ to your proposal*⟩ **2a** to be of one mind – often + *with* ⟨*I ~ with you*⟩ **b** to get along together **c** to decide together ⟨*~ on blue for the kitchen*⟩ **3a** to correspond **b** to be consistent **4** to suit the health – + *with* ⟨*onions don't ~ with me*⟩ **5** to correspond in grammatical gender, number, case, or person [ME *agreen*, fr MF *agreer*, fr *a-* (fr L *ad-*) + *gre* will, pleasure, fr L *gratum*, neut of *gratus* pleasing, agreeable – more at GRACE]

agreeable /ə'gree·əbl/ *adj* **1** to one's liking; pleasing **2** willing to agree or consent – **agreeableness** *n*, **agreeably** *adv*

agreed /ə'greed/ *adj* **1** arranged by consent ⟨*the ~ plan*⟩ **2** of the joint opinion ⟨*in this we are ~*⟩

a'greement /-mənt/ *n* **1a** harmony of opinion or feeling **b** correspondence ⟨*~ between the copy and the original*⟩ **2a** an arrangement laying down terms, conditions, etc **b** a treaty **3** (the language or document embodying) a legally binding contract [AGREE + -MENT]

agriculture /'agri,kulchə/ *n* the theory and practice of cultivating and producing crops from the soil and of raising livestock [F, fr L *agricultura*, fr *agr-*, *ager* field + *cultura* cultivation – more at ACRE, CULTURE] – **agricultural** /,agri'kulchərəl/ *adj*, **agriculturally** *adv*, **agriculturist** /-'kulchərist/, **agriculturalist** /-'kulchərəlist/ *n*

agrimony /'agriməni/ *n* any of a genus of plants of the rose family with spikes of yellow flowers; *also* a similar or related plant [ME, fr MF & L; MF *aigremoine*, fr L *agrimonia*, MS var of *argemonia*, fr Gk *argemōnē*]

agro- *comb form* **1** fields; soil; agriculture ⟨agro*logy*⟩ **2** agricultural and ⟨agro-*industrial*⟩ [F, fr Gk, fr *agros* field – more at ACRE]

agronomy /ə'gronəmi/ *n* a branch of agriculture dealing with field-crop production and soil management [prob fr F *agronomie*, fr *agro-* + *-nomie* -nomy] – **agronomic** /,agrə'nomik/ *adj*, **agronomically** *adv*, **agronomist** /ə'gronəmist/ *n*

aground /ə'grownd/ *adv or adj* on or onto the shore or the bottom of a body of water ⟨*the ship ran ~*⟩ [ME, fr [1]*a-* + *ground*]

ague /'aygyooh/ *n* a (malarial) fever with regularly recurring attacks of chills and sweating [ME, fr MF *ague*, fr ML (*febris*) *acuta*, lit., sharp fever, fr L, fem of *acutus* sharp – more at ACUTE] – **aguish** /'ay,gyooh·ish/ *adj*

ah /ah *often prolonged*/ *interj* – used to express delight, relief, regret, or contempt [ME]

aha /ah'hah/ *interj* – used to express surprise, triumph, derision, or amused discovery [ME]

ahead /ə'hed/ *adv or adj* **1a** in a forward direction **b** in front ⟨*the road ~*⟩ **2** in, into, or for the future ⟨*plan ~*⟩ **3** in or towards a better position ⟨*get ~ of the rest*⟩ [[1]*a-* + *head*]

a'head of *prep* **1** in front or advance of ⟨*~ his time*⟩ **2** better than

ahem /ə'hoom/ *interj* – used esp to attract attention or express mild disapproval [imit]

A-horizon /ay/ *n* mineral material mixed with humus forming the surface layer of soil

ahoy /ə'hoy/ *interj* – used chiefly by seamen as a greeting or warning ⟨*land ~*⟩ [*a-* (as in *aha*) + *hoy*, interj, a cry for attention]

Ahura Mazda /,ah·hoorə 'mazdə/ *n* the Supreme

Being represented as a deity of goodness and light in Zoroastrianism [Av *Ahuramazda,* lit., wise god]

ai /ie, ah'ee/ *n* a sloth with 3 claws on each front foot [Pg *ai* or Sp *aí,* fr Tupi *ai*]

[1]**aid** /ayd/ *vt vt* **1** to give assistance to; help **2** to bring about the accomplishment of; facilitate ⟨~ *his recovery*⟩ [ME *eyden,* fr MF *aider,* fr L *adjutare,* fr *adjutus,* pp of *adjuvare,* fr *ad-* + *juvare* to help] – **aider** *n*

[2]**aid** *n* **1** help; assistance; *specif* tangible means of assistance (e g money or supplies) **2a** a helper – compare AIDE **b** sthg that helps or supports ⟨*a visual* ~⟩; *specif* a hearing aid **3** a tribute paid by a vassal to his lord **– in aid of 1** in order to aid; for the use of ⟨*sold her jewels* in aid of *charity*⟩ **2** *Br* for the purpose of ⟨*what's this* in aid of*?*⟩ – infml

aide /ayd, ed/ *n* **1** an aide-de-camp **2** *chiefly NAm* an assistant [short for *aide-de-camp*]

,aide-de-'camp /də 'kamp/ *n, pl* **aides-de-camp** / ~ / an officer in the armed forces acting as a personal assistant to a senior officer [F *aide de camp,* lit., camp assistant]

,aide-mém'oire /mem'wah/ *n, pl* **aides-mémoire** / ~ / **1** an aid to the memory (e g a note or sketch) **2** a memorandum [F, fr *aider* to aid + *mémoire* memory]

AIDS /aydz/ *n* an acute infectious disease caused by a virus attacking cells that normally stimulate the production of antibodies to fight infection [*a*cquired *i*mmune *d*eficiency *s*yndrome]

aiguille /ay'gweel, '--/ *n* a sharp-pointed pinnacle of rock [F, lit., needle – more at AGLET]

aiguillette /,aygwi'let/ *n* an aglet; *specif* a shoulder cord on certain military uniforms [F – more at AGLET]

aikido /ay'keedoh, ie-/ *n* a martial art employing locks and holds and using nonresistance to cause an opponent's own momentum to work against him/her [Jap *aikidō,* fr *ai-* together, mutual + *ki* spirit + *dō* art]

ail /ayl/ *vt* to give pain, discomfort, or trouble to ~ *vi* to be unwell [ME *eilen,* fr OE *eglan;* akin to MLG *egelen* to annoy]

aileron /'aylərn, -rən/ *n* a movable control surface of an aircraft wing or a movable aerofoil external to the wing at the trailing edge for giving a rolling motion and providing lateral control ☞ FLIGHT [F, fr dim. of *aile* wing, fr L *ala*]

ailment /'aylmənt/ *n* a bodily disorder or chronic disease [AIL + -MENT]

[1]**aim** /aym/ *vi* **1** to direct a course; *specif* to point a weapon at an object **2** to channel one's efforts; aspire **3** to have the intention; mean ⟨~s *to marry a duke*⟩ ~ *vt* **1** to direct or point (e g a weapon) at a target **2** to direct at or towards a specified goal; intend ⟨*shows* ~ed *at children*⟩ [ME *aimen,* fr MF *aesmer* & *esmer;* MF *aesmer,* fr OF, fr *a-* (fr L *ad-*) + *esmer* to estimate, fr L *aestimare*]

[2]**aim** *n* **1a** the pointing of a weapon at a mark **b** the ability to hit a target **c** a weapon's accuracy or effectiveness **2** a clear intention or purpose – **aimless** *adj,* **aimlessly** *adv,* **aimlessness** *n*

ain /ayn/ *adj, Scot* own [prob fr ON *eiginn*]

ain't /aynt/ **1** are not **2** is not **3** am not **4** have not **5** has not *USE* chiefly nonstandard or humor in Br but acceptable in *ain't I* meaning 'am I not' in NAm [prob contr of *are not*]

[1]**air** /eə/ *n* **1a** the mixture of invisible odourless tasteless gases, containing esp nitrogen and oxygen, that surrounds the earth **b** a light breeze **2a** empty unconfined space – compare OPEN AIR **b** nothingness ⟨*vanished into thin* ~⟩ **3a(1)** aircraft ⟨*go by* ~⟩ **(2)** aviation ⟨~ *safety*⟩ **b** the supposed medium of transmission of radio waves; *also* radio, television ⟨*went on the* ~⟩ **4a** the appearance or bearing of a person; demeanour ⟨*an* ~ *of dignity*⟩ **b** *pl* an artificial or affected manner; haughtiness ⟨*to put on* ~s⟩ **c** outward appearance of a thing ⟨*an* ~ *of luxury*⟩ **d** a surrounding or pervading influence; an atmosphere ⟨*an* ~ *of mystery*⟩ **5** a tune, melody [ME, fr OF, fr L *aer,* fr Gk *aēr;* (4) F, fr OF; (5) prob trans of It *aria,* modif of L *aer*] **– in the air 1** not yet settled; uncertain **2** being generally spread round or hinted at ⟨*rumours* in the air *that he will be promoted*⟩

[2]**air** *vt* **1** to expose to the air for drying, freshening, etc; ventilate **2** to expose to public view or bring to public notice **3** *chiefly Br* to expose to heat so as to warm or finish drying ⟨~ *the sheets round the fire*⟩ ~ *vi* to become exposed to the open air

'air ,bed *n, chiefly Br* an inflatable mattress

'air,borne /-,bawn/ *adj* supported or transported by air

'air ,brake *n* **1** a brake operated by compressed air **2** a movable surface projected into the air for slowing an aircraft

'air ,brick *n* a building brick or brick-sized metal box perforated to allow ventilation

'air,brush /-,brush/ *n* an atomizer for spraying paint – **airbrush** *vt*

'air,bus /-,bus/ *n* a subsonic jet passenger aeroplane designed for short intercity flights

air chief marshal *n* ☞ RANK

air commodore *n* ☞ RANK

'air-con,dition *vt* to equip (e g a building) with an apparatus for cleaning air and controlling its humidity and temperature; *also* to subject (air) to these processes [back-formation fr *air conditioning*] – **air conditioner** *n,* **air conditioning** *n*

'air-,cool *vt* to cool the cylinders of (an internal-combustion engine) directly by air [back-formation fr *air-cooled* & *air cooling*]

'air,craft /-,krahft/ *n, pl* **aircraft** a weight-carrying structure that can travel through the air and is supported either by its own buoyancy or by the dynamic action of the air against its surfaces ☞ FLIGHT

'aircraft ,carrier *n* a warship designed so that aircraft can be operated from it

'air,craftman /-mən/ *n* ☞ RANK

air-cushion vehicle *n, chiefly NAm* a hovercraft

'air,drop /-,drop/ *n* a delivery of cargo or personnel by parachute from an aircraft – **air-drop** *vt,* **air-droppable** *adj*

Airedale /'eə,dayl/, **,Airedale 'terrier** *n* any of a breed of large terriers with a hard wiry coat that is dark on the back and sides and tan elsewhere [*Airedale,* district in Yorkshire, England]

airer /'eərə/ *n, chiefly Br* a freestanding, usu collapsible, framework for airing or drying clothes, linen, etc [[2]AIR + [2]-ER]

'air,fare /-,feə/ *n* a fare paid to enable one to travel on an aircraft

'air,field /-,feeld/ *n* an area of land maintained for the landing and takeoff of aircraft

'air,flow /-,floh/ *n* the motion of air round a moving or stationary object (e g in wind) ☞ FLIGHT
'air,foil /-,foyl/ *n, chiefly NAm* an aerofoil
'air ,force *n* the branch of a country's armed forces for air warfare ☞ RANK
'air,frame /-,fraym/ *n* the structure of an aircraft or missile, without the power plant [*air*craft + *frame*]
'air ,gun *n* **1** a gun from which a projectile is propelled by compressed air **2** any of various hand tools that work by compressed air
'air ,hole *n* a hole to admit or discharge air
'air ho,stess *n* a stewardess on an airliner
airily /'eərəli/ *adv* in an airy manner; jauntily, lightly
'airing ,cupboard *n* a heated cupboard in which esp household linen is aired and kept dry
'air ,lane *n* a path customarily followed by aeroplanes
'airless /-lis/ *adj* **1** still, windless **2** lacking fresh air; stuffy – **airlessness** *n*
'air ,letter *n* **1** an airmail letter **2** a sheet of airmail stationery that can be folded and sealed with the message inside and the address outside
'air,lift /-,lift/ *n* the transport of cargo or passengers by air, usu to an otherwise inaccessible area – **airlift** *vt*
'air,line /-,lien/ *n* an organization that provides regular public air transport
'air ,line *n, chiefly NAm* a beeline
'air,liner /-,lienə/ *n* a passenger aircraft operated by an airline ☞ FLIGHT
'air ,lock *n* **1** an airtight intermediate chamber (e g in a spacecraft or submerged caisson) which allows movement between 2 areas of different pressures or atmospheres **2** a stoppage of flow caused by air being in a part where liquid ought to circulate
'air,mail /-,mayl/ *n* (the postal system using) mail transported by aircraft – **airmail** *vt*
'airman /-mən/ *n, pl* **airmen** a civilian or military pilot, aircraft crew member, etc
airman basic *n* ☞ RANK
airman first class *n* ☞ RANK
,airman ,second 'class *n* ☞ RANK
,airman ,third 'class *n* ☞ RANK
air marshal *n* ☞ RANK
'air ,pistol *n* a small air gun
'air,plane /-,playn/ *n, chiefly NAm* an aeroplane
'air ,pocket *n* a region of down-flowing or rarefied air that causes an aircraft to drop suddenly
airport /'eə,pawt/ *n* a fully-equipped airfield that is used as a base for the transport of passengers and cargo by air
'air ,power *n* the military strength of an air force
'air ,pump *n* a pump for exhausting air from a closed space or for compressing air or forcing it through other apparatus
'air ,raid *n* an attack by armed aircraft on a surface target
'air ,rifle *n* an air gun with a rifled bore
'air,screw /-,skrooh/ *n* an aircraft propeller
'air,ship /-,ship/ *n* a gas-filled lighter-than-air self-propelled aircraft that has a steering system
'air,sick /-,sik/ *adj* suffering from the motion sickness associated with flying – **airsickness** *n*
'air,space /-,spays/ *n* the space lying above the earth or a certain area of land or water; *esp* the space lying above a nation and coming under its jurisdiction
'air,speed /-,speed/ *n* the speed (e g of an aircraft) relative to the air
'air,strip /-,strip/ *n* LANDING STRIP
'air,tight /-,tiet/ *adj* **1** impermeable to air **2** unassailable – **airtightness** *n*
,air-to-'air *adj* (launched) from one aircraft in flight at another
air vice-marshal *n* ☞ RANK
'air,wave /-,wayv/ *n* the supposed medium of radio and television transmission – usu pl with sing. meaning
'air,way /-,way/ *n* **1** a passage for air in a mine **2** a designated route along which aircraft fly
'air,worthy /-,wuhdhi/ *adj* fit for operation in the air – **airworthiness** *n*
airy /'eəri/ *adj* **1a** not having solid foundation; illusory ⟨~ *promises*⟩ **b** showing lack of concern; flippant **2** being light and graceful in movement or manner **3** delicately thin in texture **4** open to the free circulation of air; breezy **5** high in the air; lofty – poetic [ME, fr [2]*air* + *-y*] – **airiness** *n*
,airy-'fairy *adj, chiefly Br* whimsically unrealistic ⟨*too much* ~ *idealism*⟩
aisle /iel/ *n* **1** the side division of a church separated from the nave by columns or piers ☞ CHURCH **2** *chiefly NAm* a gangway [alter. of ME *ele, ile,* fr MF *ele, aile* wing, fr L *ala*; akin to OE *eaxl* shoulder, L *axilla* armpit – more at AXIS] – **aisleless** *adj*
ait /ayt/, **eyot** /~, 'ayət/ *n, Br* a little island in a river [ME *eyt, eit,* alter. of OE *īgeoth,* fr *īg* island – more at ISLAND]
aitch /aych/ *n* the letter *h* [F *hache,* fr (assumed) VL *hacca*]
'aitch,bone /-,bohn/ *n* (the cut of beef containing) the hipbone, esp of cattle [ME *hachbon,* alter. (by incorrect division of *a nachebon*) of (assumed) ME *nachebon,* fr ME *nache* buttock (fr MF, fr LL *natica,* fr L *natis*) + *bon* bone – more at NATES]
ajar /ə'jah/ *adj or adv, esp of a door* slightly open [earlier *on char,* fr *on* + *char* turn, piece of work, fr OE *cierr*]
Akan /'ahkahn/ *n, pl* **Akans,** *esp collectively* **Akan** **1** (a member of) a group of peoples who live in African countries of the Guinea Coast, esp Ghana **2** the Kwa language of these peoples ☞ LANGUAGE
akimbo /ə'kimboh/ *adj or adv* having the hands on the hips and the elbows turned outwards [ME *in kenebowe,* prob fr (assumed) ON *i keng boginn* bent in a curve]
akin /ə'kin/ *adj* **1** descended from a common ancestor **2** essentially similar, related, or compatible ***USE*** often + *to* ['*a* + *kin*]
Akkadian /ə'kaydi·ən/ *n or adj* (a member or the language) of a Semitic people inhabiting central Mesopotamia before 2000 BC [*Akkad,* northern region of ancient Babylonia]
al- – see AD-
[1]-al /-(ə)l/, **-ial** /-i·əl/ *suffix* (*n* → *adj*) (having the character) of ⟨*direction*al⟩ ⟨*fiction*al⟩ [ME, fr OF & L; OF, fr L *-alis*]
[2]-al *suffix* (*vb* → *n*) action or process of ⟨*rehears*al⟩ ⟨*withdraw*al⟩ [ME *-aille,* fr OF, fr L *-alia,* neut pl of *-alis*]
[3]-al /-al, -(ə)l/ *suffix* (→ *n*) **1** aldehyde ⟨*butan*al⟩ **2** acetal ⟨*butyr*al⟩ [F, fr *alcool* alcohol, fr ML *alcohol*]
à la /'ah lah (*Fr* a la)/ *prep* **1** in the manner of **2**

prepared, flavoured, or served with ⟨*spinach* ~ *crème*⟩ [F *à la*]

alabaster /ˈaləbastə, -bah-/ *n* a fine-textured usu white and translucent chalky stone often carved into ornaments [ME *alabastre*, fr MF, fr L *alabaster* vase of alabaster, fr Gk *alabastros*] – **alabaster, alabastrine** /-ˈbastrin/ *adj*

à la carte /ˌah lah ˈkaht/ *adv or adj* according to a menu that prices each item separately – compare TABLE D'HÔTE [F *à la carte* by the bill of fare]

alack /əˈlak/ *interj, archaic* – used to express sorrow or regret [ME, prob fr *a* ah + *lack* fault, loss]

alacrity /əˈlakrəti/ *n* promptness or cheerful readiness – fml [L *alacritas*, fr *alacr-, alacer* lively, eager; akin to OE & OHG *ellen* zeal]

à la mode /ˌah lah ˈmod, ˈmohd/ *adj* fashionable, stylish [F, according to the fashion]

alanine /ˈaləneen, -nien/ *n* an amino acid found in most proteins [G *alanin*, irreg fr *aldehyd* aldehyde]

alar /ˈaylə/ *adj* of or like a wing [L *alaris*, fr *ala* wing – more at AISLE]

[1]**alarm** /əˈlahm/ *n* **1** a signal (e g a loud noise or flashing light) that warns or alerts; *also* an automatic device that alerts or rouses **2** the fear resulting from the sudden sensing of danger [ME *alarme, alarom* call to arms, fr MF *alarme*, fr OIt *all'arme*, lit., to the weapon]

[2]**alarm** *vt* **1** to give warning to **2** to strike with fear – **alarmingly** *adv*

aˈlarm ˌclock *n* a clock that can be set to sound an alarm at a desired time

alarmism /əˈlahˌmiz(ə)m/ *n* the often unwarranted or excessive arousing of fears; scaremongering – **alarmist** *n or adj*

alarum /əˈlarəm/ *vt or n, archaic* (to) alarm

aˌlarums and exˈcursions *n pl* clamour and confusion

alas /əˈlas, əˈlahs/ *interj* – used to express unhappiness, pity, or disappointment [ME, fr OF, fr *a* ah + *las* weary, fr L *lassus* – more at [2]LET]

alb /alb/ *n* a full-length white linen vestment with long tight sleeves, held at the waist with a cincture and worn by a priest at Mass ☞ GARMENT [ME *albe*, fr OE, fr ML *alba*, fr L, fem of *albus* white]

Albanian /ˌalˈbaynyən, -ni·ən/ *n or adj* (the Indo-European language or a native or inhabitant) of Albania ☞ LANGUAGE [*Albania*, country in the Balkan peninsula]

albatross /ˈalbətros/ *n, pl* **albatrosses**, *esp collectively* **albatross** any of various (very) large web-footed seabirds related to the petrels [prob alter. of *alcatras* (water bird), fr Pg or Sp *alcatraz* pelican]

albedo /alˈbeedoh/ *n, pl* **albedos** the fraction of incident light or other electromagnetic radiation reflected by a surface or body (e g the moon or a cloud) [LL, whiteness, fr L *albus*]

albeit /awlˈbee·it/ *conj* even though – fml [ME, lit., all though it be]

albino /alˈbeenoh/ *n, pl* **albinos** an organism with (congenitally) deficient pigmentation; *esp* a human being or other animal with a (congenital) lack of pigment resulting in a white or translucent skin, white or colourless hair, and eyes with a pink pupil [Pg, fr Sp, fr *albo* white, fr L *albus*] – **albinic** /alˈbinik/ *adj*, **albinism** /ˈalbiniz(ə)m/ *n*

Albion /ˈalbi·ən/ *n* Britain – poetic [ME, fr OE, fr L, fr Gk *Alouiōn*, of Celt origin; akin to IrGael *Alba* Scotland]

album /ˈalbəm/ *n* **1** a book with blank pages used for making a collection (e g of stamps or photographs) **2** a recording or collection of recordings issued on 1 or more long-playing gramophone records or cassettes [L, a white tablet, fr neut of *albus*]

albumen /ˈalbyoomin, alˈbyoohmin/ *n* **1** the white of an egg **2** albumin [L, fr *albus*]

albumin /ˈalbyoomin, alˈbyoohmin/ *n* any of numerous proteins that occur in large quantities in blood plasma, milk, egg white, plant fluids, etc and are coagulated by heat [ISV *albumen* + *-in*]

albuminous /alˈbyoohminəs/ *adj* relating to, containing, or like albumen or albumin

albuminuria /alˌbyoohmiˈnyooəri·ə/ *n* the (abnormal) presence of albumin in the urine, usu symptomatic of kidney disease [NL] – **albuminuric** /-ˈyooərik/ *adj*

alburnum /alˈbuhnəm/ *n* sapwood [L, fr *albus* white]

alchemy /ˈalkəmi/ *n* **1** a medieval chemical science and philosophical doctrine aiming to achieve the transmutation of the base metals into gold, a cure for disease, and immortality **2** the transformation of sthg common into sthg precious [ME *alkamie, alquemie*, fr MF or ML; MF *alquemie*, fr ML *alchymia*, fr Ar *al-kīmiyā'*, fr *al* the + *kīmiyā'* alchemy, fr LGk *chēmeia*] – **alchemist** *n*, **alchemic** /alˈkemik/, **alchemical** *adj*

alcohol /ˈalkəhol/ *n* **1** a colourless volatile inflammable liquid that is the intoxicating agent in fermented and distilled drinks and is used also as a solvent **2** any of various organic compounds, specif derived from hydrocarbons, containing the hydroxyl group **3** intoxicating drink containing alcohol; *esp* spirits [NL, fr ML, powdered antimony, fr OSp, fr Ar *al-kuḥul* the powdered antimony]

[1]**alcoholic** /ˌalkəˈholik/ *adj* **1** of, containing, or caused by alcohol **2** affected with alcoholism – **alcoholically** *adv*

[2]**alcoholic** *n* sby affected with alcoholism

alcoholism /ˈalkəhoˌliz(ə)m/ *n* (a complex chronic psychological and nutritional disorder associated with) excessive and usu compulsive use of alcoholic drinks

alcove /ˈalkohv/ *n* **1a** a nook or recess off a larger room **b** a niche or arched opening (e g in a wall or hedge) **2** *archaic* a summerhouse [F *alcôve*, fr Sp *alcoba*, fr Ar *al-qubbah* the arch]

aldehyde /ˈaldiˌhied/ *n* any of various highly reactive compounds (e g acetaldehyde) characterized by the group CHO [G *aldehyd*, fr NL *al dehyd*, abbr of *alcohol dehydrogenatum* dehydrogenated alcohol] – **aldehydic** /-ˈhiedik/ *adj*

al dente /al ˈdenti/ *adj, esp of pasta and vegetables* cooked but firm when bitten [It, lit., to the tooth]

alder /ˈawldə/ *n* any of a genus of trees or shrubs of the birch family that grow in moist ground [ME, fr OE *alor*; akin to OHG *elira* alder, L *alnus*]

alderman /ˈawldəmən/ *n, pl* **aldermen** /-mən/ **1** a person governing a kingdom, district, or shire as viceroy for an Anglo-Saxon king **2** a senior member of a county or borough council elected by the other councillors – not used officially in Britain after 1974 [ME, fr OE *ealdorman*, fr *ealdor* parent (fr *eald* old) + *man* – more at OLD] – **aldermanic** /-ˈmanik/ *adj*

aldosterone /alˈdostərohn/ *n* a steroid hormone

produced by the adrenal cortex that affects the salt and water balance of the body [*ald*ehyde + *-o-* + *ster*ol + *-one*]

aldrin /'awldrin/ *n* a chlorinated insecticide that is very poisonous to human beings [Kurt *Alder* †1958 G chemist + E *-in*]

ale /ayl/ *n* **1** beer **2** a malted and hopped alcoholic drink that is usually more bitter, stronger, and heavier than beer [ME, fr OE *ealu*; akin to ON *öl* ale, L *alumen* alum]

aleatoric /,ali·ə'torik/ *adj* improvisatory or random in character ⟨~ *music*⟩ [L *aleatorius* of a gambler]

aleatory /'ali·ət(ə)ri/ *adj* **1** depending on chance **2** relating to or based on luck, esp bad luck [L *aleatorius* of a gambler, fr *aleator* gambler, fr *alea*, a dice game]

Alemannic /,alə'manik/ *n* the group of German dialects spoken in Alsace, Switzerland, and SW Germany [LL *alemanni* (pl), name of a Germanic people (of Gmc origin; akin to Goth *alamans* totality of people)]

alembic /ə'lembik/ *n* **1** an apparatus formerly used in distillation **2** a means of refining or transmuting [ME, fr MF & ML; MF *alambic* & ML *alembicum*, fr Ar *al-anbīq*, fr *al* the + *anbīq* still, fr LGk *ambik-*, *ambix* alembic, fr Gk, cap of a still]

[1]**alert** /ə'luht/ *adj* **1** watchful, aware **2** active, brisk [F *alerte*, fr It *all' erta*, lit., on the ascent] – **alertly** *adv*, **alertness** *n*

[2]**alert** *n* **1** an alarm or other signal that warns of danger (e g from hostile aircraft) **2** the danger period during which an alert is in effect – **on the alert** on the lookout, esp for danger or opportunity

[3]**alert** *vt* **1** to call to a state of readiness; warn **2** to cause to be aware (e g of a need or responsibility)

-ales /-'ayleez/ *suffix* (→ *n pl*) plants consisting of or related to – in the names of taxonomic orders [NL, fr L, pl of *-alis* -al]

aleurone /'alyoorohn/ *n* minute granules of protein in (the endosperm of) seeds [G *aleuron*, fr Gk, flour; akin to Arm ałam I grind] – **aleuronic** /-'ronik/ *adj*

Aleut /ə'l(y)ooht, 'al(y)ooht/ *n* (a member or the language of) a people of the Aleutian and Shumagin islands and W Alaska [Russ]

'A ,level /ay/ *n* ADVANCED LEVEL

alevin /'alivin/ *n* a young fish, esp a salmon [F, fr OF, fr *alever* to lift up, rear (offspring), fr L *allevare*, fr *ad-* + *levare* to raise – more at LEVER]

alexanders /,alig'zahndəz/ *n, pl* **alexanders** a biennial greenish-yellow-flowered European plant of the carrot family [ME *alexaundre*, fr OF & ML; OF *alexandre*, fr ML *alexandrum*, prob by folk etymology fr L *holus atrum* black vegetable]

Alexandrian /,alig'zahndri·ən/ *adj* Hellenistic [*Alexandria*, city in Egypt, centre of Hellenistic culture]

alexandrine /,alig'zahndrin/ *n, often cap* a 12-syllable verse line consisting of 6 iambics with a caesura after the third [MF *alexandrin*, adj, fr *Alexandre* Alexander the Great †323 BC king of Macedonia; fr its use in a poem on Alexander] – **alexandrine** *adj*

alexandrite /,alig'zahndriet/ *n* a green gemstone that appears red in artificial light [G *alexandrit*, fr *Alexander I* †1825 Russ emperor]

alexia /ə'leksi·ə/ *n* (partial) loss of the ability to read, owing to brain damage – compare APHASIA, DYSLEXIA [NL, fr *a-* + Gk *lexis* speech, fr *legein* to speak – more at LEGEND]

Alfa /'alfə/ Alpha

alfalfa /al'falfə/ *n, NAm* lucerne [Sp, modif of Ar. dial *al-faṣfaṣah* the alfalfa]

alfresco *also* **al fresco** /al'freskoh/ *adj or adv* taking place in the open air ⟨*an* ~ *lunch*⟩ [It]

alg-, **algo-** *comb form* pain ⟨algo*phobia*⟩ [NL, fr Gk *alg-*, fr *algos*]

alga /'algə/ *n, pl* **algae** /'alji, -gi/ *also* **algas** any of a group of chiefly aquatic nonvascular plants (e g seaweeds and pond scums); *also* BLUE-GREEN ALGA ☞ PLANT [L, seaweed] – **algal** /'algəl/ *adj*, **algoid** /'algoyd/ *adj*

algebra /'aljibrə/ *n* a branch of mathematics in which letters, symbols, etc representing various entities are combined according to special rules of operation [ML, fr Ar *al-jabr*, lit., the reduction] – **algebraist** /-,brayist/ *n*

algebraic /,alji'brayik/ *adj* **1** relating to, involving, or according to the laws of algebra **2** involving only a finite number of repetitions of addition, subtraction, multiplication, division, extraction of roots, and raising to a power ⟨~ *equation*⟩ – compare TRANSCENDENTAL 3b – **algebraically** *adv*

-algia /-'aljə/ *comb form* (→ *n*) pain ⟨*neur*algia⟩ [Gk, fr *algos*]

algin /'aljin/ *n* alginic acid, an alginate, or other colloidal substance obtained from seaweed or other marine brown algae [*alga* + *-in*]

alginate /'aljinayt/ *n* a salt of alginic acid used as a stabilizing, gelling, or thickening agent in the manufacture of ice cream, plastics, etc

al,ginic 'acid /al'jinik/ *n* an insoluble colloidal acid found in the cell walls of brown algae [ISV *algin* + *-ic*]

Algol, ALGOL /'algol/ *n* a high-level computer language designed primarily for mathematical and scientific use [*algo*rithmic *l*anguage]

algolagnia /,algoh'lagni·ə/ *n* the finding of sexual pleasure in inflicting or suffering pain [NL, fr *alg-* + Gk *lagneia* lust] – **algolagnic** /-'lagnik/ *adj*, **algolagnist** /-'lagnist/ *n*

Algonkian /al'gongki·ən/ *n* (an) Algonquian

Algonkin /al'gongkin/ *n* (an) Algonquian

Algonquian /al'gongkwi·ən/ *n* **1** a stock of American Indian languages spoken esp in the eastern parts of Canada and the USA ☞ LANGUAGE **2** a member of any of the N American Indian peoples speaking Algonquian languages **3** ALGONQUIN 1 [CanF *Algonquin*]

Algonquin /al'gongkwin/ *n* **1** a dialect of Ojibwa **2** ALGONQUIAN 1, 2

algorithm /'algə,ridhəm/ *n* a systematic procedure for solving a mathematical problem in a finite number of steps; *broadly* a step-by-step procedure for solving a problem or accomplishing some end [alter. of ME *algorisme*, fr OF & ML; OF, fr ML *algorismus*, fr Ar *al-khuwārizmi*, fr *al-Khuwārizmi fl* 825 Arab mathematician] – **algorithmic** /-'ridhmik/ *adj*

Alhambra /al'hambrə/ *n* the palace of the Moorish kings at Granada in Spain [Sp, fr Ar *al-ḥamrā'* the red house]

ali- *comb form* wing ⟨ali*form*⟩ [L, fr *ala* – more at AISLE]

[1]**alias** /'ayli·əs/ *adv* otherwise called or known as

⟨*Hancock ~ Jones*⟩ [L, otherwise, fr *alius* other – more at ELSE]

[2]**alias** *n* an assumed name

alibi /'aləbie/ *n* **1** (evidence supporting) the plea of having been elsewhere when a crime was committed **2** a plausible excuse, usu intended to avert blame or punishment [L, elsewhere, fr *alius*]

alicyclic /,ali'sieklik, -'siklik/ *adj* combining the properties of aliphatic and cyclic organic chemical compounds [ISV *ali*phatic + *cyclic*]

alidade /'alidayd/ *n* a rule equipped with sights used to determine direction in astronomy or surveying (e g as part of an astrolabe) [ME *allidatha,* fr ML *alhidada,* fr Ar *al-'iḍādah* the revolving radius of a circle]

[1]**alien** /'ayli·ən/ *adj* **1a** of or belonging to another person, place, or thing; strange **b** foreign ⟨*~ property*⟩ **2** differing in nature or character, esp to the extent of being opposed – + *to* ⟨*ideas quite ~ to ours*⟩ [ME, fr OF, fr L *alienus,* fr *alius*]

[2]**alien** *n* **1** a person from another family, race, or nation; *also* an extraterrestrial being **2** a foreign-born resident who has not been naturalized; *broadly* a foreign-born citizen – **alienage** *n*, **alienism** *n*

alienable /'ayli·ənəbl, 'aylyənəbl/ *adj* legally capable of being sold or transferred – **alienability** /-ə'biləti/ *n*

alienate /'ayli·ə,nayt, 'aylyə-/ *vt* **1** to convey or transfer (e g property or a right) to another, usu by a specific act **2** to make hostile or indifferent, esp in cases where attachment formerly existed ⟨~d *from their mothers*⟩ **3** to cause to be withdrawn or diverted [L *alienatus,* pp of *alienare* to estrange, fr *alienus*] – **alienator** *n*

alienation /,ayli·ə'naysh(ə)n, ,aylyə-/ *n* **1** a conveyance of property to another **2** (a feeling of) withdrawal from or apathy towards one's former attachments or whole social existence

alienist /'ayli·ənist, 'aylyə-/ *n* **1** *NAm* a specialist in legal aspects of psychiatry **2** *archaic* one who treats diseases of the mind [F *aliéniste,* fr *aliéné* insane, fr L *alienatus,* pp of *alienare*]

[1]**alight** /ə'liet/ *vi* **alighted** *also* **alit** /ə'lit/ **1** to come down from sthg: e g **a** to dismount **b** to disembark **2** to descend from the air and settle; land [ME *alighten,* fr OE *ālīhtan,* fr *ā-* (perfective prefix) + *līhtan* to alight – more at [6]LIGHT] – **alightment** *n*

[2]**alight** *adj* **1** animated, alive ⟨*see the place ~ with merriment – Punch*⟩ **2** *chiefly Br* on fire; ignited ⟨*paper caught ~*⟩ [prob fr [1]*a-* + [1]*light*]

align *also* **aline** /ə'lien/ *vt* **1** to bring into proper relative position or state of adjustment; *specif* to place (3 or more points) in a straight line **2** to array or position on the side of or against a party or cause ⟨*nations* ~ed *against fascism*⟩ ~ *vi* **1** to join with others in a common cause **2** to be in or come into alignment [F *aligner,* fr OF, fr *a-* (fr L *ad-*) + *ligne* line, fr L *linea*] – **alignment** *n*

[1]**alike** /ə'liek/ *adj* showing close resemblance without being identical ⟨*~ in their beliefs*⟩ [ME *ilik* (alter. of *ilich*) & *alik,* alter. of OE *onlīc,* fr *on* + *līc* body – more at [3]LIKE]

[2]**alike** *adv* in the same manner, form, or degree; equally ⟨*peasants and nobility ~ – SEU W*⟩

aliment /'alimənt/ *n* food, nutriment; *also* sustenance – fml [ME, fr L *alimentum,* fr *alere* to nourish – more at OLD]

alimentary /,ali'ment(ə)ri/ *adj* of nourishment or nutrition

ali,mentary ca'nal *n* the tubular passage that extends from the mouth to the anus and functions in the digestion and absorption of food

alimentation /,alimən'taysh(ə)n/ *n* nourishing or being nourished – fml – **alimentative** /-'mentətiv/ *adj*

alimony /'aliməni/ *n* **1** means of living; maintenance **2** *chiefly NAm* MAINTENANCE 3 [L *alimonia* sustenance, fr *alere*]

aliphatic /,ali'fatik/ *adj* of or derived from fat; *specif* being an organic compound with an open-chain rather than a cyclic structure [ISV, fr Gk *aleiphat-, aleiphar* oil, fr *aleiphein* to smear; akin to Gk *lipos* fat – more at [1]LEAVE]

aliquot /'alikwot/ *adj* **1** contained an exact number of times in another ⟨*5 is an ~ part of 15*⟩ ⟨*an ~ portion of a solution*⟩ **2** fractional ⟨*an ~ part of invested capital*⟩ [ML *aliquotus,* fr L *aliquot* some, several, fr *alius* other + *quot* how many – more at ELSE, QUOTE] – **aliquot** *n*

alive /ə'liev/ *adj* **1** having life **2a** still in existence, force, or operation; active **b** LIVE 3b **3** realizing the existence of sthg; aware of sthg ⟨*~ to the danger*⟩ **4** marked by alertness **5** showing much activity or animation; swarming ⟨*sea was ~ with large whales* – Herman Melville⟩ **6** of all those living – used as an intensive following the noun ⟨*the proudest mother ~*⟩ [ME, fr OE *on life,* fr *on* + *līf* life] – **aliveness** *n*

alizarin /ə'lizərin/ *n* an orange or red dye formerly obtained from madder [prob fr F *alizarine,* fr *alizari* madder, fr Sp, prob fr Ar *al-'aṣārah* the juice]

alkali /'alkəlie/ *n, pl* **alkalies, alkalis** any of various chemical bases, esp a hydroxide or carbonate of an alkali metal – compare ACID 1, BASE 7 [ME, fr ML, fr Ar *al-qili* the ashes of the plant saltwort]

alkalify /al'kalifie, 'alkəlifie/ *vb* to make or become alkaline

alkali metal *n* any of the univalent metals lithium, sodium, potassium, rubidium, caesium, and francium that comprise group IA of the periodic table

alkaline /'alkəlien/ *adj* (having the properties) of an alkali; *specif* having a pH of more than 7 – **alkalinity** /-'linəti/ *n*

,alkaline 'earth *n* **1** an oxide of any of the bivalent metals calcium, strontium, and barium and sometimes also magnesium, radium, or beryllium of group IIA of the periodic table **2** any of the metals whose oxides are alkaline earths

alkaline-earth metal *n* ALKALINE EARTH 2

alkaloid /'alkəloyd/ *n* any of numerous nitrogen-containing organic compounds (e g morphine) that are usu chemical bases, occur esp in flowering plants, and are extensively used as drugs – **alkaloidal** /-'loydl/ *adj*

alkalosis /,alkə'lohsis/ *n* a medical disorder in which the blood, tissues, etc are abnormally alkaline [NL]

alkane /'alkayn/ *n* any of a series of saturated open-chain hydrocarbons (e g methane, ethane, propane, or butane) [*alk*yl + *-ane*]

alkanet /'alkənet/ *n* a plant of the borage family that yields a strong red dye; *also* any of several related plants [ME, fr OSp *alcaneta,* dim. of *alcana* henna shrub, fr ML *alchanna,* fr Ar *al-ḥinnā'* the henna]

alkene /'alkeen/ *n* any of a series of unsaturated

hydrocarbons (e g ethylene or propylene) in which the carbon atoms are arranged in a straight line and there is a single double bond between 2 carbon atoms [*alk*yl + *-ene*]

alkyl /'alkil/ *n* (a compound with a metal of) a univalent radical C_nH_{2n+1} (e g methyl) derived from an alkane (e g methane) by removal of a hydrogen atom [prob fr G, fr *alkohol* alcohol, fr ML *alcohol*] – **alkylic** /-'kilik/ *adj*

alkylate /'alkilayt/ *vt* to introduce 1 or more alkyl groups into (a compound) – **alkylation** /-'laysh(ə)n/ *n*

alkyne /'alkien/ *n* any of a series of unsaturated hydrocarbons (e g acetylene) in which the carbon atoms are arranged in a straight line and there is a single triple bond between 2 carbon atoms [*alk*yl + *-yne*, var of [2]*-ine*]

[1]**all** /awl/ *adj* **1a** the whole amount or quantity of ⟨*sat up ~ night*⟩ ⟨*~ the year round*⟩ **b** as much as possible ⟨*spoke in ~ seriousness*⟩ **2a** every one of (more than 2) **b** – used in logic as a verbalized equivalent of the universal quantifier **3** the whole number or sum of ⟨*~ dogs love aniseed*⟩ **4** every ⟨*~ manner of hardship*⟩ **5** any whatever ⟨*beyond ~ doubt*⟩ **6a** given to or displaying only ⟨*was ~ attention*⟩ **b** having or seeming to have (some physical feature) conspicuously or excessively ⟨*~ thumbs*⟩ ⟨*~ ears*⟩ [ME *all, al*, fr OE *eall*; akin to OHG *al* all] – **all there** not mentally subnormal; *esp* shrewd – infml – **all very well** – used in rejection of advice or sympathy ⟨*it's* all very well *for you to talk*⟩

[2]**all** *adv* **1** wholly, altogether ⟨*sat ~ alone*⟩ ⟨*I'm ~ for it*⟩ **2** to a supreme degree – usu in combination ⟨all-*powerful*⟩ **3** for each side ⟨*the score is 2 ~*⟩

[3]**all** *pron, pl* **all** **1** the whole number, quantity, or amount ⟨*it was ~ I could do not to cry*⟩ **2** everybody, everything ⟨*sacrificed ~ for love*⟩ – **all in all** **1** generally; ON THE WHOLE 1 **2** supremely important ⟨*she was* all in all *to him*⟩ – **all of** fully; AT LEAST ⟨*lost* all of *£50*⟩ – **all the same** JUST THE SAME

[4]**all** *n* one's total resources ⟨*gave his ~ for the cause*⟩ – **in all** ALL TOLD

all-, allo- *comb form* **1** other; different; atypical ⟨allo*gamous*⟩ ⟨allo*pathy*⟩ **2** being one of a (specified) group whose members together constitute a structural unit, esp of a language ⟨allo*phone*⟩ [Gk, fr *allos* other – more at ELSE]

alla breve /,alə 'brevi/ *n, adv, or adj* (a sign marking a piece to be played) in duple or quadruple time with the beat represented by a minim ☞ MUSIC [It, lit., according to the breve]

Allah /'alah, 'alə/ *n* GOD 1 – used by Muslims or in reference to the Islamic religion [Ar *allāh*]

,all-A'merican *adj* representative of the ideals of the USA ⟨*an ~ boy*⟩

allantois /ə'lantoh·is/ *n, pl* **allantoides** /-'toh·ideez/ a vascular foetal membrane that in placental mammals is closely attached to the chorion in the formation of the placenta [NL, deriv of Gk *allantoeidēs* sausage-shaped, fr *allant-, allas* sausage] – **allantoic** /-'toh·ik/ *adj*

,all-a'round *adj, chiefly NAm* all-round

allay /ə'lay/ *vt* **1** to reduce the severity of; alleviate **2** to make quiet; pacify [ME *alayen*, fr OE *ālecgan*, fr *ā-* (perfective prefix) + *lecgan* to lay – more at [1]LAY]

'all but *adv* very nearly; almost

,all 'clear *n* a signal that a danger has passed or that it is safe to proceed

allegation /,ali'gaysh(ə)n/ *n* a statement of what one undertakes to prove [ALLEGE + -ATION]

allege /ə'lej/ *vt* to assert without proof or before proving [ME *alleggen*, fr OF *alleguer*, fr L *allegare* to dispatch, cite, fr *ad-* + *legare* to depute – more at LEGATE] – **alleged** /a'lejd, ə'lejid/ *adj*

allegedly /ə'lejidli/ *adv* according to allegation – used in reporting statements that have not been verified

allegiance /ə'leejəns/ *n* **1** the obligation of a subject or citizen to his/her sovereign or government **2** dedication to or dutiful support of a person, group, or cause [ME *allegeaunce*, modif of MF *ligeance*, fr OF, fr *lige* liege]

allegorical /,ali'gorikl/, **allegoric** /-'gorik/ *adj* **1** (having the characteristics) of allegory **2** having hidden spiritual meaning that transcends the literal sense of a sacred text – **allegorically** *adv*, **allegoricalness** *n*

allegorist /'aligərist/ *n* one who uses or writes allegory

allegor·ize, -ise /'aligəriez/ *vb* to compose, explain, or interpret (sthg) as allegory – **allegorizer** *n*, **allegorization** /-rie'zaysh(ə)n/ *n*

allegory /'alig(ə)ri/ *n* **1a** the expression by means of symbolic figures and actions of truths or generalizations about human existence **b** an instance (e g Spenser's *Faery Queene*) of such expression **2** a symbolic representation; an emblem [ME *allegorie*, fr L *allegoria*, fr Gk *allēgoria*, fr *allēgorein* to speak figuratively, fr *allos* other + *-agorein* to speak publicly, fr *agora* assembly – more at ELSE, GREGARIOUS]

allegretto /,ali'gretoh/ *adv or adj* faster than andante but not so fast as allegro – used in music [It, fr *allegro*]

allegro /ə'legroh/ *n, adv, or adj, pl* **allegros** (a musical composition or movement to be played) in a brisk lively manner [It, merry, fr (assumed) VL *alecrus* lively, alter. of L *alacr-, alacer* – more at ALACRITY]

allele /ə'leel/ *n* any of (the alternative hereditary characters determined by) 2 or more genes that occur as alternatives at a given place on a chromosome [G *allel*, short for *allelomorph*] – **allelic** /ə'le(e)lik/ *adj*, **allelism** /ə'le(e)lizəm/ *n*

allelomorph /ə'le(e)lə,mawf/ *n* an allele [Gk *allēlōn* of each other (fr *allos* allos one the other, fr *allos* other) + *morphē* form – more at ELSE] – **allelomorphism** /-,mawfiz(ə)m/ *n*, **allelomorphic** /-'mawfik/ *adj*

alleluia /,ali'looh·yə/ *interj* hallelujah [ME, fr LL, fr Gk *allēlouia*, fr Heb *hallālūyāh* praise ye Jehovah]

allemande /'aləmand/ *n, often cap* (music for) a 17th-c and 18th-c court or folk dance [F, fr fem of *allemand* German]

,all-em'bracing *adj* complete, sweeping

allergen /'aləjən, -jen/ *n* a substance that induces allergy – **allergenic** /-'jenik/ *adj*, **allergenicity** /-jə'nisəti/ *n*

allergic /ə'luhjik/ *adj* **1** of or inducing allergy **2** averse, antipathetic *to* – infml ⟨*~ to marriage*⟩

allergy /'aləji/ *n* **1** altered bodily reactivity to an antigen in response to a first exposure ⟨*his bee-venom ~ may make a second sting fatal*⟩ **2** exaggerated reaction by sneezing, itching, skin rashes, etc to substances that have no such effect on the average individual **3** a feeling of antipathy or aversion – infml [G *allergie*, fr *all-* + Gk *ergon* work – more at [1]WORK]

alleviate /ə'leevi,ayt/ *vt* to relieve (a troublesome situation, state of mind, etc) [LL *alleviatus*, pp of *alleviare*, fr L *ad-* + *levis* light – more at [4]LIGHT] – **alleviative** /-ətiv/, **alleviatory** /-ətri/ *adj*, **alleviation** /-'aysh(ə)n/ *n*

[1]**alley** /'ali/ *n* **1** a garden walk bordered by trees or a hedge **2** a bowling alley **3** a narrow back street or passageway between buildings [ME, fr MF *alee*, fr OF, fr *aler* to go, modif of L *ambulare* to walk] – **up/down one's alley** *chiefly NAm* UP ONE'S STREET

[2]**alley** *n* a playing marble (of superior quality) [by shortening & alter. fr *alabaster*]

'alley,way /-,way/ *n* ALLEY 3

,All 'Fools' ,Day *n* APRIL FOOLS' DAY

,all 'found *adv*, *chiefly Br* with free food and lodging provided in addition to wages ⟨*£30 a week and* ~⟩

,all 'fours *n pl* **1** all 4 legs of a quadruped **2** hands and knees ⟨*crawling on* ~⟩

,all 'hail *interj* – used as a formal greeting or acclamation

alliaceous /,ali'ayshəs/ *adj* resembling garlic or onion, esp in smell or taste [L *allium* garlic]

alliance /ə'lie·əns/ *n* **1** a union of families by marriage **2** a confederation of nations by formal treaty **3** a tie, connection ⟨*a closer* ~ *between government and industry*⟩ [ALLY + -ANCE]

allied /'alied, ə'lied/ *adj* **1** in close association; united **2** joined in alliance by agreement or treaty **3a** related by resemblance or common properties; associated ⟨*heraldry and* ~ *subjects*⟩ **b** related genetically **4** *cap* of the Allies

Allies /'aliez/ *n pl* the nations united against the Central European powers in WW I or against the Axis powers in WW II

alligator /'ali,gaytə/ *n* **1** either of 2 crocodilians with broad heads that do not taper towards the snout **2** leather made from alligator hide [Sp *el lagarto* the lizard, fr *el* the (fr L *ille* that) + *lagarto* lizard, fr (assumed) VL *lacartus*, fr L *lacertus, lacerta* – more at LIZARD]

alligator pear *n* an avocado [by folk etymology fr *avocado pear*]

,all-im'portant *adj* of very great or greatest importance ⟨*an* ~ *question*⟩

,all-'in *adj* **1** *chiefly Br* all-inclusive; *esp* including all costs ⟨*an* ~ *holiday in Greece*⟩ **2** *Br, of wrestling* having almost no holds barred

all in *adj* tired out; exhausted – infml

,all-in'clusive *adj* including everything ⟨*a broader and more* ~ *view*⟩ – **all-inclusiveness** *n*

alliterate /ə'litərayt/ *vi* to form an alliteration ~ *vt* to arrange or place so as to make alliteration [back-formation fr *alliteration*]

alliteration /ə,litə'raysh(ə)n/ *n* the repetition of usu initial consonant sounds in neighbouring words or syllables (e g *thr*eatening *thr*ongs of *thr*eshers) [*ad-* + L *littera* letter] – **alliterative** /-rətiv/ *adj*, **alliteratively** *adv*

allium /'ali·əm/ *n* any of a large genus of plants of the lily family including the onion, garlic, chives, leek, and shallot [NL, genus name, fr L, garlic]

allo- – see ALL-

allocable /'aləkəbl/ *adj* capable of being allocated

allocate /'aləkayt/ *vt* **1a** to apportion and distribute (e g money or responsibility) in shares **b** to assign (sthg limited in supply) to as a share ⟨*we've been* ~d *the top flat*⟩ **2** to earmark, designate ⟨~ *a section of the building for research purposes*⟩ [ML *allocatus*, pp of *allocare*, fr L *ad-* + *locare* to place, fr *locus* place – more at [1]STALL] – **allocatable** *adj*, **allocator** *n*, **allocation** /-'kaysh(ə)n/ *n*

allochthonous, allocthonous /ə'lokthənəs/ *adj*, *of a plant, animal, or substance* entering a particular ecological region from an outside source [*all-* + *-chthonous* (as in *autochthonous*)]

allocution /,alə'kyoohsh(ə)n/ *n* a (stirring) formal speech [L *allocution-, allocutio*, fr *allocutus*, pp of *alloqui* to speak to, fr *ad-* + *loqui* to speak]

allogamous /ə'logəməs/ *adj* reproducing by cross-fertilization [*all-* + *-gamous*] – **allogamy** /-mi/ *n*

allograft /'alə,grahft, -,graft/ *n* a graft between 2 genetically unlike members of the same species

[1]**allomorph** /'alə,mawf/ *n* any of 2 or more distinct crystalline forms of the same substance [ISV] – **allomorphic** /-'mawfik/ *adj*, **allomorphism** /-,mawfiz(ə)m/ *n*

[2]**allomorph** *n* any of 2 or more alternative forms of a morpheme (e g the *-es* of *dishes*, and the *-s* of *dreams*) [*allo-* + *morph*eme] – **allomorphic** /-'mawfik/ *adj*, **allomorphism** /-,mawfiz(ə)m/ *n*

allopathy /ə'lopəthi/ *n* conventional medical practice using all effective treatments, esp when producing effects different from those of the disease being treated [G *allopathie*, fr *all-* + *-pathie* -pathy] – **allopathic** /,alə'pathik/ *adj*, **allopathically** *adv*

allophone /'aləfohn/ *n* any of 2 or more alternative forms of a phoneme (e g the aspirated /*p*/ of *pin* and the nonaspirated /*p*/ of *spin*) [*allo-* + *phone*] – **allophonic** /-'fonik/ *adj*

allopurinol /,alə'pyooərinol/ *n* a drug used to promote excretion of uric acid (e g in the treatment of gout) [*all-* + *purine* + *-ol*]

allosteric /,alə'sterik, -loh-, -'stiərik/ *adj* of or being the inhibition, stimulation, etc of enzyme activity caused by a change (e g combining with a molecule) at a point on the enzyme other than its active site [*all-* + *steric*] – **allosterically** *adv*

allot /ə'lot/ *vt* **-tt-** to allocate [ME *alotten*, fr MF *aloter*, fr *a-* (fr L *ad-*) + *lot*, of Gmc origin; akin to OE *hlot* lot] – **allotter** *n*

allotment /ə'lotmənt/ *n*, *Br* a small plot of land let out to an individual (e g by a town council) for cultivation [ALLOT + -MENT]

allotrope /'alə,trohp/ *n* a form showing allotropy ⟨*graphite and diamond are* ~s *of carbon*⟩ [ISV, back-formation fr *allotropy*] – **allotropic** /-'tropik/ *adj*, **allotropically** *adv*

allotropy /ə'lotrəpi/ *n* the existence of a substance, esp an element, in 2 or more different forms with different properties [*all-* + *-tropy*]

,all-'out *adj* using maximum effort and resources ⟨*an* ~ *effort to win the contest*⟩

,all 'out *adv* with maximum determination and effort; FLAT OUT – chiefly in *go all out*

,all'over /-'ohvə/ *adj* covering the whole extent or surface ⟨*a sweater with an* ~ *pattern*⟩

,all 'over *adv* **1** over the whole extent or surface ⟨*decorated* ~ *with a flower pattern*⟩ **2** in every respect ⟨*that's Paul* ~⟩

allow /ə'low/ *vt* **1a(1)** to assign as a share or suitable amount (e g of time or money) ⟨~ *an hour for lunch*⟩ **(2)** to grant as an allowance ⟨~ed *him £500 a year*⟩ **b** to reckon as a deduction or an addition ⟨~ *a gallon for leakage*⟩ **2a** to admit as true or valid; acknowledge **b** to admit the possibility of ⟨*the facts ~ only one explanation*⟩ **3** to permit: e g **a** to make it possible for; enable ⟨*the gift will ~ me to buy a car*⟩ **b** to fail to prevent; let ⟨~ *herself to get fat*⟩ ~ *vi* **1** to admit the possibility *of* ⟨*evidence that* ~s *of only one conclusion*⟩ **2** to make allowance *for* ⟨~ *for expansion*⟩ [ME *allowen*, fr MF *alouer* to place (fr ML *allocare*) & *allouer* to approve, fr L *adlaudare* to extol, fr *ad-* + *laudare* to praise – more at ALLOCATE, LAUD]

allowable /əˈlowəbl/ *adj* **1** permissible **2** assigned as an allowance ⟨*expenses ~ against tax*⟩

[1]allowance /əˈlowəns/ *n* **1a** a (limited) share or portion allotted or granted; a ration **b** a sum granted as a reimbursement or bounty or for expenses **c** a reduction from a list price or stated price **2** a handicap (e g in a race) **3a** permission, sanction **b** acknowledgment ⟨~ *of your claim*⟩ **4** the taking into account of mitigating circumstances – often pl with sing. meaning ⟨*make* ~s *for his youth*⟩

[2]allowance *vt* **1** to put on a fixed allowance **2** to provide in a limited quantity

allowedly /əˈlowidli/ *adv* as is allowed; admittedly

[1]alloy /ˈaloy/ *n* **1** a solid substance composed of a mixture of metals or a metal and a nonmetal thoroughly intermixed **2** a metal mixed with a more valuable metal **3** an addition that impairs or debases [MF *aloi*, fr *aloier* to combine, fr L *alligare* to bind – more at ALLY]

[2]alloy /əˈloy/ *vt* **1** to reduce the purity or value of by adding sthg **2** to mix so as to form an alloy **3a** to impair or debase by addition **b** to temper, moderate

ˌall-ˈpowerful *adj* having complete or sole power; omnipotent

ˌall-ˈpurpose *adj* suited for many purposes or uses

[1]ˌall ˈright *adv* **1** well enough ⟨*does ~ in school*⟩ **2** beyond doubt; certainly ⟨*he has pneumonia ~*⟩ [ME *alriht* exactly, fr *al* all + *riht* right]

[2]ˌall ˈright *adj* **1** satisfactory, acceptable ⟨*the film is ~ for children*⟩ **2** safe, well ⟨*he was ill but he's ~ now*⟩ **3** agreeable, pleasing – used as a generalized term of approval

[3]ˌall ˈright *interj* **1** – used for giving assent ⟨~, *let's go*⟩ **2** – used in indignant or menacing response ⟨~*! Just you wait*⟩

ˌall-ˈround *adj* **1** competent in many fields ⟨*an ~ athlete*⟩ **2** having general utility **3** encompassing all aspects; comprehensive ⟨*an ~ reduction in price*⟩

ˌall ˈround *adv* **1** by, for, or to everyone present ⟨*ordered drinks ~*⟩ **2** in every respect

ˌall-ˈrounder *n* sby who is competent in many fields; *specif* a cricketer who bats and bowls to a relatively high standard

ˌAll ˈSaints' ˌDay *n* November 1 observed in Western churches as a festival in honour of all the saints

ˈallˌseed /-ˌseed/ *n* any of several many-seeded plants (e g knotgrass)

ˌAll ˈSouls' ˌDay *n* November 2 observed in Western churches as a day of prayer for the souls of the departed faithful

ˈallˌspice /-ˌspies/ *n* (a mildly pungent spice prepared from) the berry of a W Indian tree belonging to the myrtle family [*all* + *spice*; fr its supposed combination of the flavours of cinnamon, cloves, and nutmeg]

ˌall-ˈstar *adj* composed wholly or chiefly of stars of the theatre, cinema, etc ⟨*an ~ cast*⟩

ˌall ˈthat *adv* to a marked or unusual extent; very – chiefly in negatives and questions ⟨*didn't take his threats ~ seriously*⟩

ˌall the ˈbest *interj* – used as an expression of goodwill and usu farewell

ˌall the ˈsame *adv* nevertheless

ˈall-ˌtime *adj* exceeding all others yet known ⟨*an ~ best seller*⟩

ˌall ˈtold *adv* with everything taken into account

allude /əˈl(y)oohd/ *vi* to make indirect, casual, or implicit reference *to* [L *alludere*, lit., to play with, fr *ad-* + *ludere* to play – more at LUDICROUS]

ˌall-ˈup *adj* total inclusive of everything necessary for operation ⟨~ *weight of the aircraft*⟩

[1]allure /əˈl(y)ooə/ *vt* to entice by charm or attraction [ME *aluren*, fr MF *alurer*, fr OF, fr *a-* (fr L *ad-*) + *loire* lure – more at LURE] – **allurement** *n*

[2]allure *n* power of attraction or fascination; charm

allusion /əˈlyooh·zh(ə)n, -ˈlooh-/ *n* **1** alluding or hinting **2** (the use of) implied or indirect reference, esp in literature [LL *allusion-*, *allusio*, fr L *allusus*, pp of *alludere*] – **allusive** /-siv, -ziv/ *adj*, **allusively** *adv*, **allusiveness** *n*

alluvion /əˈl(y)oohvi·ən/ *n* **1** the wash of water against a shore **2** FLOOD 1 **3** alluvium **4** new land formed esp by water action [L *alluvion-*, *alluvio*, fr *alluere* to wash against, fr *ad-* + *lavere* to wash – more at LYE]

alˈluvium /-vi·əm/ *n, pl* **alluviums, alluvia** /-vi·ə/ clay, silt, or similar detrital material deposited by running water [LL, neut of *alluvius* alluvial, fr L *alluere*] – **alluvial** /-vi·əl/ *adj*

[1]ally /ˈalie; *also* əˈlie/ *vt* **1** to join, unite *with/to* ⟨*allied himself with a wealthy family by marriage*⟩ **2** to relate *to* by resemblance or common properties ⟨*its beak* allies *it to the finches*⟩ ~ *vi* to form or enter into an alliance *with* [ME *allien*, fr OF *alier*, fr L *alligare* to bind to, fr *ad-* + *ligare* to bind – more at LIGATURE]

[2]ally /ˈalie/ *n* **1** a sovereign or state associated with another by treaty or league **2** a helper, auxiliary

-ally /-(ə)li/ *suffix* (*adj* → *adv*) [2]-LY ⟨*terrific*ally⟩ [[1]*-al* + *-ly*]

allyl /ˈalil/ *n* an unsaturated univalent radical CH_2CHCH_2 [ISV, fr L *allium* garlic] – **allylic** /əˈlilik/ *adj*

alma mater /ˌalmə ˈmahtə, ˈmaytə/ *n* a school, college, or university which one has attended [L, fostering mother]

almanac, almanack /ˈawlmənak/ *n* **1** a usu annual publication containing statistical, tabular, and general information **2** *chiefly Br* a publication containing astronomical and meteorological data arranged according to the days, weeks, and months of a given year [ME *almenak*, fr ML *almanach*, perh fr Ar *al-manākh* the calendar]

almandine /ˈalmәndeen, -dien/ *n* a deep violet to red garnet used as a gemstone [ME *alabandine*, fr ML *alabandina*, fr *Alabanda*, ancient city in Asia Minor]

[1]almighty /awlˈmieti/ *adj* **1** *often cap* having absolute power over all ⟨Almighty *God*⟩ **2** having relatively unlimited power ⟨*the ~ dollar*⟩ **3** great in extent, seriousness, force, etc ⟨*an ~ crash*⟩ – infml [ME, fr OE *ealmihtig,* fr *eall* all + *mihtig* mighty] – **almightiness** *n, often cap,* **almightiest** *adj*

[2]**almighty** *adv* to a great degree; mighty – infml

Almighty *n* GOD 1 – + *the*

almond /'ahmənd; *also* 'awl-; *NAm* al-/ *n* (the edible oval nut of) a small tree of the rose family [ME *almande,* fr OF, fr LL *amandula,* alter. of L *amygdala,* fr Gk *amygdalē*]

,almond-'eyed *adj* having narrow slanting almond-shaped eyes

almoner /'ahmənə, 'al-/ *n* **1** one who distributes alms **2** a social worker attached to a British hospital – not now used technically [ME *almoiner,* fr OF *almosnier,* fr *almosne* alms, fr LL *eleemosyna*]

almost /'awlmohst/ *adv* very nearly but not exactly or entirely [ME, fr OE *ealmǣst,* fr *eall* + *mǣst* most]

alms /'ahmz/ *n sing or pl in constr* money, food, etc given to help the poor [ME *almesse, almes,* fr OE *ǣlmesse, ǣlms*; akin to OHG *alamuosan* alms; both fr a prehistoric WGmc word borrowed fr LL *eleemosyna* alms, fr Gk *eleēmosynē* pity, alms, fr *eleēmōn* merciful, fr *eleos* pity] – **almsgiver** /-,givə/ *n,* **almsgiving** *n*

'alms,house /-,hows/ *n, Br* a privately endowed house in which a poor person can live

alnico /'alnikoh/ *trademark* – used for an alloy containing iron, nickel, and aluminium, from which permanent magnets are made

aloe /'aloh/ *n* **1** any of a large genus of succulent plants of the lily family with tall spikes of flowers **2** the dried juice of the leaves of various aloes used esp as a purgative – usu pl but sing. in constr [ME, fr LL, fr L, dried juice of aloe leaves, fr Gk *aloē*]

aloft /ə'loft/ *adv* **1** at or to a great height **2** at, on, or to the masthead or the upper rigging of a ship – compare ALOW [ME, fr ON *ā lopt,* fr *ā* on, in + *lopt* air]

alone /ə'lohn/ *adj or adv* **1** considered without reference to any other; *esp* unassisted ⟨*the children ~ would eat that much*⟩ **2** separated from others; isolated ⟨*stands ~*⟩ **3** exclusive of other factors ⟨*time ~ will show*⟩ **4** free from interference ⟨*leave my bag ~*⟩ [ME, fr *al* all + *one* one] – **aloneness** *n*

[1]**along** /ə'long/ *prep* **1** in a line parallel with the length or direction of **2** in the course of (a route or journey) **3** in accordance with ⟨*something ~ these lines*⟩ [ME, fr OE *andlang,* fr *and-* against + *lang* long – more at ANTE-]

[2]**along** *adv* **1** forward, on ⟨*move ~*⟩ **2** as a necessary or pleasant addition; with one ⟨*take your flute ~*⟩ **3** in company and simultaneously *with* ⟨*pay a penny a week ~ with all the other village boys – SEU S*⟩ **4** also; IN ADDITION ⟨*a bill came ~ with the parcel*⟩ **5** on hand, there ⟨*I'll be ~ in 5 minutes*⟩ – **all along** all the time ⟨*knew the truth* all along⟩

a'long of *prep, dial* in company with [ME *ilong on,* fr OE *gelang on,* fr *ge-,* associative prefix + *lang* – more at CO-]

[1]**a,long'side** /-'sied/ *adv* along or at the side

[2]**alongside, alongside of** *prep* **1** side by side with; *specif* parallel to **2** concurrently with

[1]**aloof** /ə'loohf/ *adv* at a distance; out of involvement [obs *aloof* (to windward), fr [1]*a-* + *loof,* var of *luff*]

[2]**aloof** *adj* distant in interest or feeling; reserved, unsympathetic – **aloofly** *adv,* **aloofness** *n*

alopecia /,alə'peeshə/ *n* usu abnormal baldness in humans or loss of wool, feathers, etc in animals [ME *allopicia,* fr L *alopecia,* fr Gk *alōpekia,* fr *alōpek-, alōpēx* fox – more at VULPINE] – **alopecic** /-'peesik/ *adj*

aloud /ə'lowd/ *adv* with the speaking voice [ME, fr [1]*a-* + *loud*]

alow /ə'loh/ *adv* below, esp in a ship; *also* on or near the deck – compare ALOFT [ME, fr [1]*a-* + *low*]

alp /alp/ *n* a high mountain [back-formation fr *Alps,* mountain system of Europe]

alpaca /al'pakə/ *n* **1** (the fine long woolly hair of) a type of domesticated llama found in Peru **2** a thin cloth made of or containing this wool [Sp, fr Aymara *allpaca*]

alpenglow /'alpən,gloh/ *n* a reddish glow seen near sunset or sunrise on the summits of mountains [prob part trans of G *Alpenglühen,* fr *Alpen* Alps + *glühen* glow]

'alpen,horn /-,hawn/ *n* a long straight wooden horn used, esp formerly, by Swiss herdsmen to call sheep and cattle [G, fr *Alpen* + *horn* horn]

'alpen,stock /-,stok/ *n* a long iron-pointed staff, now superseded by the ice axe, for use in mountain climbing [G, fr *Alpen* + *stock* staff]

[1]**alpha** /'alfə/ *n* **1** the 1st letter of the Greek alphabet **2** sthg that is first; a beginning – compare OMEGA 2 **3** – used to designate the chief or brightest star of a constellation **4** [1]A 4 [ME, fr L, fr Gk, of Sem origin; akin to Heb *āleph,* 1st letter of the Heb alphabet]

[2]**alpha,** α**-** *adj* alphabetical ⟨*~ order*⟩

Alpha, Alfa – a communications code word for the letter *a*

,alpha and 'omega *n* the beginning and ending [fr the first and last letters of the Gk alphabet]

alphabet /'alfəbet/ *n* a set of characters, esp letters, used to represent 1 or more languages, esp when arranged in a conventional order; *also* a system of signs and signals that can be used in place of letters [ME *alphabete,* fr LL *alphabetum,* fr Gk *alphabētos,* fr *alpha* + *bēta* beta]

alphabetical /,alfə'betikl/, **alphabetic** /-'betik/ *adj* **1** of or employing an alphabet **2** in the order of the letters of the alphabet – **alphabetically** *adv*

alphabet·ize, -ise /'alfəbe,tiez/ *vt* to arrange alphabetically – **alphabetizer** *n,* **alphabetization** /-tie'zaysh(ə)n/ *n*

alphameric /,alfə'merik/, **alphamerical** /-kl/ *adj* alphanumeric [*alpha*bet + nu*meric,* nu*merical*]

alphanumeric /,alfənyooh'merik/ *also* **,alphanu'merical** *adj* **1** consisting of both letters and numbers and often symbols (e g punctuation marks and mathematical symbols) ⟨*RT756 is the ~ code*⟩; *also* being a character in an alphanumeric system **2** able to display alphanumeric characters [*alpha*bet + *numeric, numerical*] – **alphanumerically** *adv*

alpha particle *n* a positively charged nuclear particle identical with the nucleus of a helium atom ejected at high speed by some radioactive substances

alpha ray *n* a stream of alpha particles

'alpha-re,ceptor *n* a receptor for neurotransmitters (e g adrenalin) in the sympathetic nervous system whose stimulation is associated esp with the constriction of small blood vessels and an increase in blood pressure – compare BETA-RECEPTOR

The evolution of the alphabet

This diagram illustrates the history of the alphabet by showing how one of the original Semitic letters, *shin*, has evolved in some of the principal descendant scripts.

Proto-Semitic

The original 22-letter Semitic alphabet was invented in the Palestine/Syria area some time before 1500 BC, probably in imitation of Egyptian writing. Stylized pictures stood for the initial sounds of the things pictured; all Semitic words began with consonants, so the script had no vowels.

Western or Canaanite branch

Eastern or Aramaic branch

Early Greek and Etruscan

The Greeks borrowed the Semitic alphabet from the Phoenicians about 1000 BC. They adapted letters for non-Greek sounds to represent vowels; thus Semitic *alp* (glottal stop) became Greek *alpha (a)*. Greek was written right-to-left and left-to-right in alternate lines, but later settled on left-to-right order.

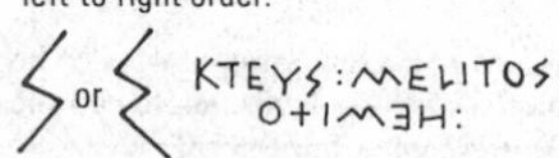

Mongolian

The Mongolian alphabet is one of several Central Asian scripts descended from the Semitic alphabet; it is written vertically, starting at the left.

Monumental Roman capitals

The Romans borrowed the alphabet from the Etruscans. These serifed capitals were used for inscriptions on stone; cursive forms developed for handwriting.

Later Greek

By about 350 BC the form of alphabet used in Ionia was standardized throughout the Greek world.

Arabic

Arabic script is always written cursively; there is no separate printed form. The letter-shapes are so simplified that some have become identical, and dots are added to distinguish them.

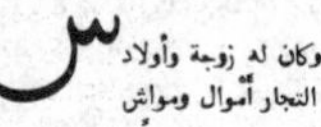

Hebrew

The 'Square Hebrew' alphabet used today was developed after 300 BC; previously the Hebrew language had been written in a script belonging to the Western Semitic branch. Like Arabic, Hebrew is written from right to left.

National cursive hands

After the Roman Empire broke up, divergent forms of script evolved in various parts of Europe.

Anglo-Irish

Black Letter or 'Gothic'

Carolingian

Cyrillic

Russian uses an alphabet invented in the 9th century by St Cyril; it derives from the Greek alphabet, supplemented by Hebrew letters for non-Greek sounds.

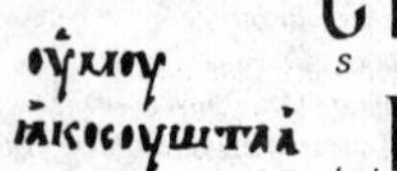

The modern 'Roman alphabet'

15-century Italian typographers combined Carolingian minuscules with Monumental capitals to create an alphabet with distinct upper and lower case shapes for most letters. Small s had two forms, 'short s' being used only at ends of words until it supplanted 'long s' in the 19th century.

S s ſ Poſt Habraam ſilius eius Iſaac in pietate ſucceſſit

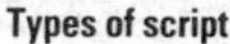

Types of script

The several hundred writing-systems of the world are based on many different principles. This diagram classifies and illustrates the various possibilities in terms of a sequence of choices.

1 Is the system an independent 'language' in its own right?
YES →

Many primitive tribes have evolved subtle systems for transmitting messages graphically without reference to spoken words. This letter from a girl of the Yukaghir tribe of Siberia to her errant lover expresses a complex message through stylized pictures:

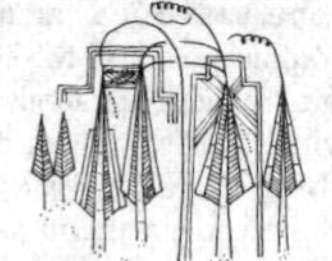

Western mathematics is another such system; a formula such as $\sqrt{100} > 3^2$ is understood in the same way by people who speak different languages. This kind of 'writing' is on the increase at present, to create internationally-recognizable signs in areas such as clothes care and traffic information.

Or is it a means of transcribing a spoken language?
YES ↓

2 Do the elements of the script stand for meaningful units? YES →

Chinese script has a separate written symbol for each word or 'morpheme' in the language. (Morphemes are the minimal meaningful elements out of which complex words are built.) Chinese words vary greatly in pronunciation in different regions, but their written form is constant.

筆 墨 相 副 曰 豐

brush ink co- operate is-called rich

'For brush and ink to co-operate is known as richness (in calligraphy).'

Or for units of pronunciation?
YES ↓

3 What size are the pronunciation units to which script elements correspond?
SYLLABLES →

Because there are fewer different symbols in the script than Greek has syllables, pairs of consonants were written by 'borrowing' a following vowel, and consonants at the end of syllables were ignored: thus *mnon* became *mo-no*.

a ga me mo no 'Agamemnon'

The Linear B script was used to write Greek before the fall of the Mycenean civilization about 1200 BC.

PHONETIC FEATURES ↓

In the Han'gul script of Korea, separate features of a sound are symbolized independently.

airstream interrupted
hissing between tongue and teeth
tongue-tip touches teeth-ridge

조 cho
선 son

Choson 'Morning Fresh' (ancient name of Korea)

Pitman's Shorthand uses a similar system to represent the sounds of English.

SEGMENTS ↓

4 'Segments' are individual consonant and vowel sounds. Does the script include signs for vowels as well as for consonants?

NO →

Semitic languages are mostly written in vowel-less scripts. In Hebrew writing, some vowels may be indicated by consonant-letters (*w* for long *u*, *h* for long *a*) but most vowels are ignored. The script reads from right to left:

ברוך אַתה

h t k w r b

barukh atta 'Blessed art Thou . . .'

A system for indicating vowels exactly by adding small marks to the consonant-letters has been invented, but is not normally used in practice.

YES . . . ↓

5 Are the vowel and consonant symbols grouped together into syllables?
YES →

In Indian scripts such as Devanagari (used for classical Sanskrit and modern Hindi), groups of consonants are indicated by amalgamating the symbols for single consonants, and vowels are shown by strokes above and below the consonant letters:

म ब म्ब म्बे म्बु जाम्बूनद

m b mb mbe mbu jambunada

Or written in a linear sequence?
YES . . . ↓

He vencido al ángel del sueño, el funesto alegórico

Spanish is a good example of a language with a 'phonemic' spelling system (one sound = one symbol).

Mixed systems

Many scripts involve more than one of the principles displayed here. For instance, Japanese writing uses both the morpheme-symbols of Chinese and syllabic script comparable to Linear B. English orthography can be regarded as a mixed system; it is approximately phonemic, but the many 'irregularities' tend to provide distinctive spellings for meaningful units, as in Chinese writing. (compare *sign* with *sign-ature*; or *right*, *write*, and *wright*.)

alpha wave *n* a variation in the electroencephalographic record of the electrical activity of the brain of a frequency of about 10Hz that is often associated with states of waking relaxation

alpine /'alpien/ *n* an (ornamental) plant native to alpine or northern parts of the northern hemisphere

Alpine *adj* **1** *often not cap* of, growing in, or resembling the Alps; *broadly* of or resembling any mountains **2** *often not cap* of or growing in the elevated slopes above the tree line **3** of or being competitive ski events comprising slalom and downhill racing – compare NORDIC

alpinism /'alpiniz(ə)m/ *n, often cap* the climbing of high, esp Alpine, mountains – **alpinist** *n*

already /awl'redi/ *adv* **1** no later than now or then; even by this or that time ⟨*he had ~ left*⟩ **2** before, previously ⟨*had seen the film ~*⟩ [ME *al redy*, fr *al redy*, adj, wholly ready, fr *al* all + *redy* ready]

alright /awl'riet/ *adv, adj, or interj* ALL RIGHT – nonstandard [ME, fr *al* + *right*]

Alsatian /al'saysh(ə)n/ *n* (any of) a breed of large intelligent dogs often used as guard dogs [ML *Alsatia* Alsace, region of France (formerly of Germany)]

'alsike ,clover /'alsiek, 'awl-, -sik/ *n* a European perennial clover used as a forage plant [*Alsike*, town in Sweden]

also /'awlsoh/ *adv* as an additional circumstance; besides [ME, fr OE *eallswā*, fr *eall* all + *swā* so – more at so]

'also-,ran *n* **1** an entrant, esp a horse, that finishes outside the first 3 places in a race **2** a person of little importance

Altaic /al'tayik/ *adj* of or constituting a language family comprising Turkic, Tungusic, and Mongolian [*Altai* mountains, range in central Asia]

altar /'awltə/ *n* **1** a usu raised structure or place on which sacrifices are offered or incense is burnt in worship **2** a table on which the bread and wine used at communion are consecrated or which serves as a centre of worship or ritual *USE* ☞ CHURCH [ME *alter*, fr OE *altar*, fr L *altare*; akin to L *adolēre* to burn up]

'altar,piece /-,pees/ *n* a work of art that decorates the space above and behind an altar

altazimuth /al'tazimәth/ *n* an instrument, specif a telescope, mounted so that it can swivel horizontally and vertically [ISV *alt*itude + *azimuth*]

alter /'awltə/ *vt* **1** to make different without changing into sthg else **2** *chiefly NAm* to castrate, spay – euph ~ *vi* to become different [ME *alteren*, fr MF *alterer*, fr ML *alterare*, fr L *alter* other (of two); akin to L *alius* other – more at ELSE] – **alterer** *n*, **alterable** *adj*, **alterably** *adv*, **alteration** /-'raysh(ə)n/ *n*, **alterability** /-rə'biləti/ *n*

altercation /,awltə'kaysh(ə)n/ *n* a heated quarrel; *also* quarrelling [ME *altercacioun*, fr MF *altercation*, fr L *altercation-, altercatio*, fr *altercatus*, pp of *altercari* to quarrel, dispute, fr (assumed) *altercus* contending, fr *alter* other]

,alter 'ego /'altә/ *n* a second self; *esp* a trusted friend [L, lit., another I]

¹alternate /awl'tuhnət/ *adj* **1** occurring or succeeding each other by turns ⟨*a day of ~ sunshine and rain*⟩ **2a** *of plant parts* arranged singly first on one side and then on the other of an axis – compare OPPOSITE 1b ☞ PLANT **b** arranged one above or alongside the other **3** every other; every second ⟨*he works on ~ days*⟩ **4** *of an angle* being either of a pair on opposite sides of a transverse line at its intersection with 2 other lines **5** *NAm* ¹ALTERNATIVE 2 [L *alternatus*, pp of *alternare* to alternate, fr *alternus* alternate, fr *alter*] – **alternately** *adv*

²alternate /'awltə,nayt/ *vt* to interchange with sthg else in turn ⟨*~ work with sleep*⟩ ~ *vi* **1** *of 2 things* to occur or succeed each other by turns ⟨*work and sleep ~*⟩ **2** to undergo or consist of repeated change from one thing to another ⟨*he ~s between work and sleep*⟩ – **alternation** /-'naysh(ə)n/ *n*

alternating current *n* an electric current that reverses its direction at regularly recurring intervals

alternation of generations *n* the occurrence of 2 or more usu alternating sexual and asexual forms differently produced in the life cycle of a plant or animal

¹alternative /awl'tuhnətiv/ *adj* **1** affording a choice, esp between 2 mutually exclusive options **2** constituting an alternative **3** of or catering for the alternative society ⟨*~ technology*⟩ – **alternatively** *adv*

²alternative *n* **1** an opportunity or need for deciding between 2 or more possibilities **2** either of 2 possibilities between which a choice is to be made; *also* any of more than 2 such possibilities

alternative society *n* *the* group of people who reject conventional social institutions, practices, and values in favour of a life-style based esp on communal ownership and self-sufficiency – compare COUNTERCULTURE

alternator /'awltə,naytə/ *n* an electric generator for producing alternating current ☞ CAR

although *also* **altho** /awl'dhoh/ *conj* in spite of the fact or possibility that; though [ME *although*, fr *al* all + *though*]

altimeter /'alti,meetə/ *n* an instrument for measuring altitude [L *altus* + E *-meter*] – **altimetry** /al'timətri/ *n*

altitude /'altityoohd/ *n* **1** the angular elevation of a celestial object above the horizon **2** the height of an object (e g an aircraft), esp above sea level **3** the perpendicular distance from the base of a geometrical figure to the vertex or the side parallel to the base ☞ MATHEMATICS [ME, fr L *altitudo* height, depth, fr *altus* high, deep – more at OLD] – **altitudinal** /,alti'tyoohdinl/ *adj*

alto /'altoh/ *n, pl* **altos 1a** a countertenor **b** a contralto **2** the second highest part in 4-part harmony **3** a member of a family of instruments having a range between the treble or soprano and the tenor [It, lit., high, fr L *altus*] – **alto** *adj*

alto clef *n* a C clef placing middle C on the 3rd line of the staff ☞ MUSIC

altocumulus /,altoh'kyoohmyooləs/ *n, pl* **altocumuli** /-lie/ a cloud formation consisting of large whitish globular cloudlets at a higher level than cumulus [NL, fr L *altus* + NL *-o-* + *cumulus*]

¹altogether /,awltə'gedhə/ *adv* **1** wholly, thoroughly ⟨*an ~ different problem*⟩ **2** ALL TOLD **3** in the main; ON THE WHOLE **4** in every way ⟨*more complicated ~*⟩ [ME *altogedere*, fr *al* all + *togedere* together]

²altogether *n* *the* nude ⟨*posed in the ~*⟩ – infml

altostratus /,altoh'strahtəs/ *n, pl* **altostrati** /-tie/ a cloud formation similar to cirrostratus but darker and at a lower level ☞ WEATHER [NL, fr L *altus* + NL *-o-* + *stratus*]

altricial /al'trish(ə)l/ *adj, of a bird* (having young) needing care for some time after birth – compare PRECOCIAL [L *altric-, altrix,* fem of *altor* one who nourishes, fr *altus,* pp of *alere* to nourish – more at OLD]

altruism /'altrooh,iz(ə)m/ *n* unselfish regard for or devotion to the welfare of others [F *altruisme,* fr *autrui* other people, fr OF, oblique case form of *autre* other, fr L *alter*] – **altruist** *n,* **altruistic** /-'istik/ *adj,* **altruistically** *adv*

alula /'alyoolə/ *n, pl* **alulae** /-li/ BASTARD WING [NL, fr L, dim. of *ala* wing – more at AISLE] – **alular** *adj*

alum /'aləm/ *n* (any of various double salts with a similar crystal structure to) a sulphate of aluminium with potassium or ammonium, used esp as an emetic and astringent [ME, fr MF *alum, alun,* fr L *alumen* – more at ALE]

alumina /ə'l(y)oohminə/ *n* aluminium oxide that occurs naturally as corundum [NL, fr L *alumin-, alumen* alum]

aluminate /ə'l(y)oohminayt/ *n* a compound of alumina with a metallic oxide

aluminium /,alyooh'mini·əm, -yoo-/ *n* a bluish silver-white malleable light trivalent metallic element with good electrical and thermal conductivity and resistance to oxidation ☞ PERIODIC TABLE [NL, fr *alumina*]

alumin·ize, -ise /ə'lyoohmi,niez/ *vt* to treat or coat with aluminium

aluminous /ə'l(y)oohminəs/ *adj* of or containing alum or aluminium

aluminum /ə'loohminəm/ *n, NAm* aluminium

alumnus /ə'lumnəs/, *fem* **alumna** /-nə/ *n, pl* **alumni** /-nie/, *fem* **alumnae** /-ni/ *chiefly NAm* a former student of a particular school, college, or university; *broadly* a former member of any organization [L, foster son, pupil, fr *alere* to nourish – more at OLD]

alveolar /,alvi'ohlə, al'vee·ələ/ *adj* **1** of, resembling, made up of, or having alveoli or an alveolus **2** articulated with the tip of the tongue touching or near the ridge of flesh behind the front teeth ⟨*an ~ consonant*⟩

alveolus /,alvi'ohləs, al'vee·ələs/ *n, pl* **alveoli** /-lie/ a small cavity or pit: e g **a** a socket for a tooth **b** an air cell of the lungs ☞ DIGESTION **c** a cell or compartment of a honeycomb [NL, fr L, dim. of *alveus* cavity, hollow, fr *alvus* belly; akin to ON hvann*jōli* stalk of angelica, Gk *aulos,* a reed instrument]

alway /'awlway/ *adv, archaic* always [ME]

always /'awlwayz, -wiz/ *adv* **1a** at all times ⟨*have ~ lived here*⟩ **b** in all cases ⟨*they ~ have long tails*⟩ **2** on every occasion; repeatedly ⟨*he's ~ complaining*⟩ **3** forever, perpetually ⟨*will ~ love you*⟩ **4** as a last resort; at any rate ⟨*they could ~ eat cake*⟩ [ME *alway, alwayes,* fr OE *ealne weg,* lit., all the way, fr *ealne* (acc of *eall* all) + *weg* (acc) way – more at WAY]

alyssum /'alisəm/ *n* **1** any of a genus of Old World yellow-flowered plants of the mustard family **2** an annual or perennial European plant of the mustard family that has clusters of small fragrant usu white flowers [NL, fr Gk *alysson,* plant believed to cure rabies, fr neut of *alyssos* curing rabies, fr *a-* + *lyssa* rabies]

am /əm, m; *strong* am/ *pres 1 sing of* BE [ME, fr OE *eom*; akin to ON *em* am, L *sum,* Gk *eimi,* OE *is* is]

AM /,ay 'em/ *adj* of or being a broadcasting or receiving system using amplitude modulation [*a*mplitude *m*odulation]

amah /'amə, 'ahmə/ *n* an Oriental female servant; *esp* a Chinese nurse [Pg *ama* wet nurse, fr ML *amma*]

amalgam /ə'malgəm/ *n* **1** an alloy of mercury with another metal (e g used in making dental fillings) **2** a mixture of different elements [ME *amalgame,* fr MF, fr ML *amalgama,* prob deriv of Gk *malagma* emollient, fr *malassein* to soften]

amalgamate /ə'malgəmayt/ *vt* to unite (as if) in an amalgam; *esp* to combine into a single body

amalgamation /ə,malgə'maysh(ə)n/ *n* **1** amalgamating or being amalgamated **2** a consolidation, merger ⟨*~ of 2 companies*⟩

amanuensis /ə,manyooh'ensis/ *n, pl* **amanuenses** /-seez/ sby employed to write from dictation or to copy manuscript [L, fr (*servus*) *a manu* slave with secretarial duties]

amaranth /'amərantn/ *n* **1** any of a large genus of coarse plants some of which are cultivated for their showy (purple) flowers **2** a dark reddish purple colour **3** an imaginary flower that never fades – chiefly poetic [L *amarantus,* a flower, fr Gk *amaranton,* fr neut of *amarantos* unfading, fr *a-* + *marainein* to waste away – more at SMART] – **amaranthine** /,amə'ranthin, -thien/ *adj*

amaryllis /,amə'rilis/ *n* any of a genus of bulbous African plants of the daffodil family with showy flowers in umbels [NL, genus name, prob fr L, name of a shepherdess in Vergil's *Eclogues*]

amass /ə'mas/ *vt* **1** to collect for oneself; accumulate ⟨*~ a great fortune*⟩ **2** to bring together into a mass; gather [MF *amasser,* fr OF, fr *a-* (fr L *ad-*) + *masser* to gather into a mass, fr *masse* mass]

amateur /'amətə, -chə/ *n* **1** one who engages in a pursuit as a pastime rather than as a profession; *esp* a sportsman who has never competed for money **2** one who practises an art or science unskilfully; a dabbler [F, fr L *amator* lover, fr *amatus,* pp of *amare* to love] – **amateur** *adj,* **amateurish** *adj,* **amateurishly** *adv,* **amateurishness** *n,* **amateurism** *n*

amative /'amətiv/ *adj* disposed to love; amorous – fml [ML *amativus,* fr L *amatus*]

amatory /'amət(ə)ri/ *adj* of or expressing sexual love

amaurosis /,amaw'rohsis/ *n, pl* **amauroses** /-seez/ decay of sight, esp due to neurological disease, without obvious change or damage to the eye [NL, fr Gk *amaurōsis,* lit., dimming, fr *amauroun* to dim, fr *amauros* dim] – **amaurotic** /-'rotik/ *adj*

amaze /ə'mayz/ *vt vt* to fill with wonder; astound [ME *amasen,* fr OE *āmasian,* fr *ā-* (perfective prefix) + (assumed) *masian* to confuse]

a'mazement /-mənt/ *n* great astonishment [AMAZE + -MENT]

amazing /ə'mayzing/ *adj* – used as a generalized term of approval ⟨*she has the most ~ vintage car*⟩

a'mazingly /-li/ *adv* **1** to an amazing degree **2** as is amazing ⟨*~, she believed his story*⟩

amazon /'aməz(ə)n/ *n, often cap* a tall strong athletic woman [ME, fr L, fr Gk *Amazōn,* one of a mythological race of female warriors]

Amazonian /ˌamə'zohnyən, -ni·ən/ *adj* **1** *not cap, esp of a woman* masculine, aggressive **2** of the Amazon river or its valley

ambassador /am'basədə/ *n* **1** an official envoy: e g **a** a top-ranking diplomat accredited to a foreign government or sovereign as a resident representative **b** one similarly appointed for a special and often temporary diplomatic assignment **2** a representative, messenger [ME *ambassadour,* fr MF *ambassadeur,* of Gmc origin; akin to OHG *ambaht* service] – **ambassadorship** *n,* **ambassadorial** /amˌbasə'dawri·əl/ *adj*

amˌbassador-at-'large *n, pl* **ambassadors-at-large** a diplomatic or ministerial representative of the highest rank not accredited to a particular foreign government or sovereign

ambassadress /am'basədris/ *n* **1** a female representative or authorized messenger **2** the wife of an ambassador

amber /'ambə/ *n* **1** a hard yellowish to brownish translucent fossil resin used chiefly for ornaments and jewellery **2** the colour of amber **3** a yellow traffic light meaning 'caution' [ME *ambre,* fr MF, fr ML *ambra,* fr Ar *'anbar* ambergris] – **amber** *adj*

'amberˌgris /-ˌgrees, -ˌgris/ *n* a waxy substance found floating in tropical waters, believed to originate in the intestines of the sperm whale, and used in perfumery as a fixative [ME *ambregris,* fr MF *ambre gris,* fr *ambre* + *gris* grey – more at GRIZZLED]

ambi- /ambi-/ *prefix* both; two ⟨ambi*valent*⟩ ⟨ambi*guous*⟩ [L *ambi-, amb-* both, around; akin to L *ambo* both, Gk *amphō* both, *amphi* around – more at BY]

ambidextrous /ˌambi'dekstrəs/ *adj* **1** able to use either hand with equal ease **2** unusually skilful; versatile **3** characterized by deceitfulness and double-dealing [LL *ambidexter,* fr L *ambi-* + *dexter* on the right, skilful] – **ambidextrously** *adv,* **ambidexterity** /-dek'sterəti/ *n*

ambience, ambiance /'ambi·əns (Fr ɑ̃biɑ̃s)/ *n* a surrounding or pervading atmosphere; an environment, milieu [F *ambiance,* fr *ambiant* surrounding, fr L *ambient-, ambiens*]

¹ambient /'ambi·ənt/ *adj* surrounding on all sides; encompassing – fml [L *ambient-, ambiens,* prp of *ambire* to go round, fr *ambi-* + *ire* to go – more at ISSUE]

²ambient *n* ambience – fml

ambiguity /ˌambi'gyooh·əti/ *n* **1** (a word or expression with) the quality of being ambiguous or imprecise in meaning **2** uncertainty of meaning or relative position ⟨*the basic* ~ *of her political stance*⟩

ambiguous /am'bigyoo·əs/ *adj* **1** vague, indistinct, or difficult to classify **2** capable of 2 or more interpretations [L *ambiguus,* fr *ambigere* to wander about, fr *ambi-* + *agere* to drive – more at AGENT] – **ambiguously** *adv,* **ambiguousness** *n*

ambit /'ambit/ *n* **1** a limiting circumference **2** the bounds or limits of a place; the precincts **3** a sphere of influence; a scope [ME, fr L *ambitus,* fr *ambitus,* pp of *ambire*]

ambition /am'bish(ə)n/ *n* **1a** a strong desire for status, wealth, or power **b** a desire to achieve a particular end **2** an object of ambition [ME, fr MF or L; MF, fr L *ambition-, ambitio,* lit., going round, fr *ambitus,* pp] – **ambitionless** *adj*

ambitious /am'bishəs/ *adj* **1a** having or controlled by ambition **b** desirous *of,* aspiring **2** resulting from or showing ambition ⟨*an* ~ *attempt*⟩ **3** elaborate ⟨*cooked nothing more* ~ *than boiled eggs*⟩ – **ambitiously** *adv,* **ambitiousness** *n*

ambivalence /am'bivələns/ *n* the state of having 2 opposing and contradictory attitudes or feelings towards an object, person, etc [ISV] – **ambivalent** *adj,* **ambivalently** *adv*

ambivert /'ambiˌvuht/ *n* a person with both extroverted and introverted characteristics [*ambi-* + *-vert* (as in *introvert*)] – ˌ**ambi'version** /-'vuhsh(ə)n/ *n*

¹amble /'ambl/ *vi* **ambling** /'ambling, 'ambl·ing/ to move at an amble [ME *amblen,* fr MF *ambler,* fr L *ambulare* to walk]

²amble *n* **1** an easy gait of a horse in which the legs on the same side of the body move together **2** an easy gait **3** a leisurely stroll

amblyopia /ˌambli'ohpi·ə/ *n* poor sight without obvious change or damage to the eye [NL, fr Gk *amblyōpia,* fr *amblys* blunt, dull + *-ōpia* -opia] – **amblyopic** /-'ohpik/ *adj*

ambo /'amboh/ *n, pl* **ambos, ambones** /am'bohneez/ a pulpit in an early Christian church [ML *ambon-, ambo,* fr LGK *ambōn,* fr Gk, rim]

ambrosia /am'brohzi·ə, -zh(y)ə/ *n* **1** the food of the Greek and Roman gods **2** sthg extremely pleasing to the taste or smell [L, fr Gk, lit., immortality, fr *ambrotos* immortal, fr *a-* + *-mbrotos* (akin to *brotos* mortal) – more at MURDER] – **ambrosial** *adj*

ambulance /'ambyooləns/ *n* a vehicle equipped to transport the injured or ill [F, field hospital, fr *ambulant* itinerant, fr L *ambulant-, ambulans,* prp of *ambulare*]

ambulant /'ambyoolənt/ *adj* **1** *of a patient* not confined to bed; able to walk **2** moving about [L *ambulant-, ambulans*]

¹ambulatory /'ambyoolət(ə)ri/ *adj* **1** of or adapted for walking; *also* occurring while walking **2** moving or movable from place to place; not fixed **3a** AMBULANT 1 **b** of or for sby who is able to walk about ⟨~ *treatment*⟩ [L *ambulatorius,* fr *ambulatus,* pp of *ambulare*]

²ambulatory *n* a sheltered place for walking; *specif* the apse aisle of a church

ambuscade /ˌamboo'skayd/ *n* an ambush [MF *embuscade,* modif of OIt *imboscata,* fr *imboscare* to place in ambush, fr *in* (fr L) + *bosco* forest, perh of Gmc origin; akin to OHG *busc* forest – more at IN]

¹ambush /'amboosh/ *vt* to attack from an ambush; waylay ~ *vi* to lie in wait; lurk [ME *embushen,* fr OF *embuschier,* fr *en* in (fr L *in*) + *busche* stick of firewood] – **ambushment** *n*

²ambush *n* **1** the concealment of soldiers, police, etc in order to carry out a surprise attack from a hidden position **2** people stationed in ambush; *also* their concealed position

ameba /ə'meebə/ *n, chiefly NAm* an amoeba – **amebic** *also* **ameban** *adj,* **ameboid** *adj*

ameer /ə'miə/ *n* an emir

ameliorate /ə'meelyərayt/ *vb* to make or become better or more tolerable [alter. of *meliorate*] – **ameliorative** /-rətiv/ *adj,* **amelioration** /-'raysh(ə)n/ *n*

amen /ˌah'men, ˌay-, '-ˌ-/ *interj* – used to express solemn ratification (e g of an expression of faith) or hearty approval (e g of an assertion) [ME, fr OE, fr LL, fr Gk *amēn,* fr Heb *āmēn*]

amenable /ə'meenəbl/ *adj* **1** liable to be brought to account; answerable **2a** capable of submission (e g to judgment or test) **b** readily persuaded to yield or agree; tractable [prob fr (assumed) AF, fr MF *amener* to lead up, fr OF, fr *a-* (fr L *ad-*) + *mener* to lead, fr L *minare* to drive, fr *minari* to threaten – more at [1]MOUNT] – **amenably** *adv*, **amenability** /-nə'biləti/ *n*

amend /ə'mend/ *vt* **1** to put right; *specif* to make emendations in (e g a text) **2a** to change or modify for the better; improve **b** to alter (e g a document) formally ⟨~ *the constitution*⟩ [ME *amenden*, fr OF *amender*, modif of L *emendare*, fr *e*, *ex* out + *menda* fault; akin to L *mendax* lying, *mendicus* beggar, Skt *mindā* physical defect]

a'mendment /-mənt/ *n* **1** the act of amending, esp for the better **2** an alteration proposed or effected by amending ⟨*several* ~s *to the Bill*⟩

a'mends *n pl but sing or pl in constr* compensation for a loss or injury; recompense ⟨*make* ~⟩ [ME *amendes*, fr OF, pl of *amende* reparation, fr *amender*]

amenity /ə'menəti, ə'mee-/ *n* **1** sthg (e g a public facility) conducive to material comfort – often pl ⟨*urban* amenities*: roads, water, sewerage, and power – National Times (Sydney)*⟩ **2** sthg (e g a conventional social gesture) conducive to ease of social intercourse – usu pl **3** pleasantness, esp of environment – fml [ME *amenite* pleasantness, fr L *amoenitat-*, *amoenitas*, fr *amoenus* pleasant]

amenorrhoea, *chiefly NAm* **amenorrhea** /ə,menə'riə, ay-/ *n* abnormal absence of the menstrual discharge [NL, fr *a-* + Gk *mēn* month + NL *-o-* + *-rrhoea* – more at MOON]

amentia /ə'menshə/ *n* (congenital) mental deficiency [NL, fr L, madness, fr *ament-*, *amens* mad, fr *a-* (fr *ab-*) + *ment-*, *mens* mind – more at MIND]

amerce /ə'muhs/ *vt* to punish, esp by a fine [ME *amercien*, fr AF *amercier*, fr OF *a merci* at (one's) mercy] – **amercement** *n*, **amerciable** /-shəbl/ *adj*

[1]**American** /ə'merikən/ *n* **1** a N or S American Indian **2** a native or inhabitant of N or S America **3** a citizen of the USA **4** English as typically spoken and written in the USA [*America*, western continent, fr NL, fr *Americus* Vespucius (Amerigo Vespucci) †1512 It navigator]

[2]**American** *adj* **1** (characteristic) of N or S America **2** (characteristic) of the USA **3** of the N and S American Indians

A,merican 'dream *n* a vision of freedom, equality, material prosperity, and glossy modernity as being realized or attainable in the USA – usu + *the*

American Indian *n* a member of any of the indigenous peoples of N, S, or central America excluding the Eskimos

Americanism /a'merikəniz(ə)m/ *n* **1** a characteristic feature (e g a custom or belief) of Americans or American culture **2a** adherence or attachment to America and its culture **b** the promotion of American policies

american·ize, -ise /ə'merikəniez/ *vb*, *often cap* to (cause to) have or acquire American customs, characteristics, etc – **americanization** /-nie'zaysh(ə)n/ *n*, *often cap*

americium /,amə'risi·əm/ *n* a radioactive metallic element produced by bombardment of uranium with alpha particles ☞ PERIODIC TABLE [NL, fr *America* + NL *-ium*]

Amerindian /,amə'rindi·ən/ *n*, *chiefly NAm* AMERICAN INDIAN [*American* + *Indian*] – **Amerind** /'amə,rind/ *n*, **Amerindian** *adj*, **Amerindic** /,amə'rindik/ *adj*

amethyst /'aməthist/ *n* a semiprecious gemstone of clear purple or violet quartz [ME *amatiste*, fr OF & L; OF, fr L *amethystus*, fr Gk *amethystos*, lit., remedy against drunkenness, fr *a-* + *methyein* to be drunk, fr *methy* wine – more at [1]MEAD] – **amethystine** /,amə'thistin/ *adj*

Amharic /am'harik/ *n* an Ethiopian Semitic language ☞ LANGUAGE – **Amharic** *adj*

amiable /'aymi·əbl/ *adj* **1** (seeming) agreeable and well-intentioned; inoffensive **2** friendly, congenial [ME, fr MF, fr LL *amicabilis* friendly, fr L *amicus* friend; akin to L *amare* to love] – **amiableness** *n*, **amiably** *adv*, **amiability** /-'biləti/ *n*

amianthus /,ami'anthəs/ *n* a fine silky asbestos [L *amiantus*, fr Gk *amiantos*, fr *amiantos* unpolluted, fr *a-* + *miainein* to pollute]

amiantus /,ami'antəs/ *n* amianthus

amicable /'amikəbl/ *adj* characterized by friendly goodwill; peaceable [ME, fr LL *amicabilis*] – **amicableness** *n*, **amicably** *adv*, **amicability** /-'biləti/ *n*

amice /'amis/ *n* a vestment made of an oblong piece of white cloth worn by a priest round the neck and shoulders and partly under the alb ☞ GARMENT [ME *amis*, prob fr MF, pl of *amit*, fr ML *amictus*, fr L, cloak, fr *amictus*, pp of *amicire* to wrap round, fr *am-*, *amb-* round + *jacere* to throw – more at AMBI-, [2]JET]

amid /ə'mid/ *prep* in or to the middle of – poetic [ME *amidde*, fr OE *onmiddan*, fr *on* + *middan*, dat of *midde* mid]

amid-, amido- *comb form* **1** containing an amido group ⟨amido*sulphuric*⟩ **2** amin- ⟨amido*pyrene*⟩ [ISV, fr *amide*]

amide /'amied, 'amid/ *n* any of various compounds resulting from replacement of an atom of hydrogen in ammonia by a metal atom or a (specif organic acid) radical [ISV, fr NL *ammonia*] – **amidic** /ə'midik/ *adj*

amido /'amidoh, ə'meedoh/ *adj* of, being, or containing (a derivative of) the chemical group NH_2– united to a radical derived from an acid – compare AMINO [*amid-*]

amidships /ə'mid,ships/ *adv* in or towards the middle part (of a ship) ☞ SHIP

amidst /ə'midst/ *prep* amid [ME *amiddes*, fr *amidde* + *-es* -s]

amin-, amino- *comb form* containing an amino group ⟨amino*methane*⟩ [ISV, fr *amine*]

amine /'ameen, ə'meen/ *n* any of various usu organic compounds that are chemical bases and contain 1 or more amino groups [ISV, fr NL *ammonia*] – **aminic** /ə'minik/ *adj*

amino /ə'meenoh/ *adj* of, being, or containing (a derivative of) the chemical group NH_2– united to a radical derived from a compound that is not an acid – compare AMIDO [*amin-*]

a,mino 'acid *n* any of various organic acids containing an amino group and occurring esp in linear chains as the chief components of proteins

amir /ə'miə/ *n* an emir

amiss /ə'mis/ *adv or adj* **1** astray **2** out of order; at fault **3** out of place in given circumstances – usu +

a negative ⟨*a few pertinent remarks may not come ~ here*⟩ [adv ME *amis*, fr [1]*a-* + *mis* (n) mistake, wrong; adj fr adv]

amitriptyline /,ami'triptəleen/ *n* a drug widely used to treat depression [origin unknown]

amity /'amiti/ *n* friendship [ME *amite*, fr MF *amité*, fr ML *amicitas*, fr L *amicus* friend – more at AMIABLE]

ammeter /'ameetə/ *n* an instrument for measuring electric current in amperes [*ampere* + *-meter*]

ammo /'amoh/ *n* ammunition – infml [by shortening & alter.]

ammonia /ə'mohnyə, -ni·ə/ *n* a pungent colourless gas that is a compound of nitrogen and hydrogen and is very soluble in water, forming an alkaline solution [NL, fr L *sal ammoniacus* sal ammoniac, lit., salt of Ammon, fr Gk *ammōniakos* of Ammon, fr *Ammōn* Ammon, Amen, an Egyptian god near one of whose temples it was prepared]

ammoniacal /,amə'nie·əkl/, **ammoniac** /ə'mohni,ak/ *adj* of, containing, or having the properties of ammonia

ammoniate /ə'mohni,ayt/ *vt* **1** to combine or impregnate with ammonia or an ammonium compound **2** to subject to ammonification – **ammoniation** /-'aysh(ə)n/ *n*

ammonification /ə,mohnifi'kaysh(ə)n/ *n* **1** ammoniating **2** decomposition, esp of nitrogenous organic matter by bacteria, with production of ammonia or ammonium compounds – **ammonify** /-,fie/ *vb*, **ammonifier** *n*

ammonite /'amәniet/ *n* a flat spiral fossil shell of a mollusc abundant esp in the Mesozoic age ☞ EVOLUTION [NL *ammonites*, fr L *cornu Ammonis*, lit., horn of Ammon] – **ammonitic** /-'nitik/ *adj*

ammonium /ə'mohnyəm, -ni·əm/ *n* an ion or radical derived from ammonia by combination with a hydrogen ion or atom [NL, fr *ammonia*]

ammonoid /'amənoyd/ *n* an ammonite

ammunition /,amyoo'nish(ə)n/ *n* **1** the projectiles, together with their propelling charges, used in the firing of guns; *also* bombs, grenades, etc containing explosives **2** material used to defend or attack a point of view ⟨*his indiscretions provided ~ for the press*⟩ [obs F *amunition*, fr MF, alter. of *munition*]

amnesia /am'neezyə, -zh(y)ə/ *n* a (pathological) loss of memory [NL, fr Gk *amnēsia* forgetfulness, prob alter. of *amnēstia*] – **amnesiac** /-zi,ak/, **amnesic** /-zik/ *adj or n*, **amnestic** /am'nestik/ *adj*

amnesty /'amnəsti/ *n* the act of pardoning a large group of individuals, esp for political offences [Gk *amnēstia* forgetfulness, fr *amnēstos* forgotten, fr *a-* + *mnasthai* to remember – more at MIND] – **amnesty** *vt*

amniocentesis /,amniohsen'teesis/ *n* the insertion of a hollow needle into the uterus of a pregnant female, esp to obtain amniotic fluid (e g for the detection of chromosomal abnormality) [NL, fr *amnion* + *centesis* puncture, fr Gk *kentesis*, fr *kentein* to prick – more at CENTRE]

amnion /'amni·ən/ *n, pl* **amnions, amnia** /'amni·ə/ a thin membrane forming a closed sac containing the watery fluid in which an embryo is immersed ☞ REPRODUCTION [NL, fr Gk, caul, prob fr dim. of *amnos* lamb] – **amniote** /'amni,oht/ *adj or n*, **amniotic** /-'otik/ *adj*

amoeba, *chiefly NAm* **ameba** /ə'meebə/ *n, pl* **amoebas, amoebae** /-bi/ any of various protozoans with lobed pseudopodia and without permanent organelles that are widely distributed in water and wet places [NL, genus name, fr Gk *amoibē* change, fr *ameibein* to change – more at MIGRATE] – **amoebic** *also* **amoeban** *adj*

amoeboid, *chiefly NAm* **ameboid** /ə'mee,boyd/ *adj* (moving by means of protoplasmic flow) like an amoeba

amok, amuck /ə'muk/ *adv* **1** in a murderous frenzy; raging violently **2** OUT OF HAND 2 *USE* chiefly in *run amok* [Malay *amok*]

among /ə'mung/ *prep* **1** in or through the midst of; surrounded by ⟨*living ~ artists*⟩ **2** by or through the whole group of ⟨*discontent ~ the poor*⟩ **3** in the number or class of ⟨*~ other things he was head boy*⟩ **4** between – used for more than 2 ⟨*divided ~ the heirs*⟩ ⟨*quarrel ~ themselves*⟩ **5** through the joint action of ⟨*made a fortune ~ themselves*⟩ [ME, fr OE *on gemonge*, fr *on* + *gemonge*, dat of *gemong* crowd, fr *ge-* (associative prefix) + *-mong* (akin to OE *mengan* to mix) – more at CO-, MINGLE]

amongst /ə'mungst/ *prep* among [alter. of ME *amonges*, fr *among* + *-es* -s]

amontillado /ə,monti'lahdoh/ *n, pl* **amontillados** a pale fairly dry sherry [Sp, fr *a* to + *montilla* wine from Montilla, town in Spain]

amoral /a(y)'morəl, ə-/ *adj* **1** being neither moral nor immoral; *specif* lying outside the sphere of ethical judgments **2** having no understanding of, or unconcerned with, morals – **amoralism** *n*, **amorally** *adv*, **amorality** /,a(y)mə'raləti/ *n*

amorist /'amərist/ *n* **1** a devotee of sexual love; a gallant **2** one who writes about romantic love – **amoristic** /-'ristik/ *adj*

amorous /'amərəs/ *adj* **1** of or relating to love **2** moved by or inclined to love or desire [ME, fr MF, fr ML *amorosus*, fr L *amor* love, fr *amare* to love] – **amorously** *adv*, **amorousness** *n*

amorphous /ə'mawfəs/ *adj* **1a** having no definite form; shapeless **b** without definite character; unclassifiable **2** not crystalline [Gk *amorphos*, fr *a-* + *morphē* form] – **amorphously** *adv*, **amorphousness** *n*

amort·ize, -ise /ə'mawtiez/ *vt* to provide for the gradual extinguishment of (e g a mortgage), usu by periodic contributions to a sinking fund [ME *amortisen* to deaden, alienate in mortmain, modif of MF *amortiss-*, stem of *amortir*, fr (assumed) VL *admortire* to deaden, fr L *ad-* + *mort-*, *mors* death – more at MURDER] – **amortizable** /ə'maw,tiezəbl/ *adj*, **amortization** /ə,mawtie'zaysh(ə)n, ,amaw-/ *n*

Amos /'aymos/ *n* (a prophetic book of the Old Testament attributed to) a Hebrew prophet of the 8th c BC [Heb *'Āmōs*]

[1]**amount** /ə'mownt/ *vi* to be equal in number, quantity, or significance *to* [ME *amounten*, fr OF *amonter*, fr *amont* upwards, fr *a-* (fr L *ad-*) + *mont* mountain – more at [1]MOUNT]

[2]**amount** *n* **1** the total quantity **2** the quantity at hand or under consideration ⟨*has an enormous ~ of energy*⟩

amour /ə'maw, ə'mooə (*Fr* amur)/ *n* a love affair, esp when illicit [ME, love, affection, fr OF, fr OProv *amor*, fr L]

a,mour 'propre /'proprə (*Fr* prɔpr)/ *n* self-esteem [F *amour-propre*, lit., love of oneself]

amp /amp/ *n* **1** an ampere **2** an amplifier *USE* infml

AMP *n* a mononucleotide of adenine that is reversibly converted in cells to ADP and ATP [*a*denosine *m*ono*p*hosphate]

amperage /'amp(ə)rij/ *n* the strength of a current of electricity expressed in amperes

ampere /'ampeə/ *n* the basic SI unit of electric current equal to a constant current that when maintained in 2 straight parallel conductors of infinite length and negligible circular cross-section 1 metre apart in a vacuum produces between the conductors a force equal to 2 x 10^{-7} newton per metre of length ☞ PHYSICS [André M *Ampère* †1836 F physicist]

,ampere-'hour *n* a unit quantity of electricity equal to the quantity carried past any point of a circuit by a steady current of 1 ampere flowing for 1 hour

ampersand /'ampə,sand/ *n* a sign, typically &, standing for the word *and* [alter. of *and* (&) *per se and*, lit., (the character) & by itself (is the word) *and*]

amphetamine /am'fetəmeen, -min/ *n* (any of several derivatives of) a synthetic stimulant of the brain which is a common drug of abuse [ISV *a*lpha + *m*ethyl + *ph*en- + *et*hyl + *amine*]

amphi- /amfi-/, **amph-** *prefix* **1** on both sides; round ⟨amphi*theatre*⟩ **2** of both kinds; both ⟨amphi*bian*⟩ [L *amphi-* round, on both sides, fr Gk *amphi-, amph-*, fr *amphi* – more at AMBI-]

amphibian /am'fibi·ən/ *n, pl* **amphibians,** (*I*) **amphibians,** *esp collectively* **amphibia** /-bi·ə/ **1** an amphibious organism; *esp* a frog, toad, newt, or other member of a class of cold-blooded vertebrates intermediate in many characteristics between fishes and reptiles **2** an aeroplane, tank, etc adapted to operate on or from both land and water [deriv of Gk *amphibion* amphibious being, fr neut of *amphibios*] – **amphibian** *adj*

amphibious /am'fibi·əs/ *adj* **1** able to live both on land and in water **2a** relating to or adapted for both land and water ⟨~ *vehicles*⟩ **b** involving or trained for coordinated action of land, sea, and air forces organized for invasion **3** combining 2 positions or qualities [Gk *amphibios*, lit., living a double life, fr *amphi-* + *bios* mode of life – more at [1]QUICK] – **amphibiously** *adv*, **amphibiousness** *n*

amphibole /'amfi,bohl/ *n* any of a group of silicate minerals (e g hornblende) that are important constituents of many rocks [F, fr LL *amphibolus*, fr Gk *amphibolos* ambiguous, fr *amphiballein* to throw round, doubt, fr *amphi-* + *ballein* to throw] – **amphibolitic** /-bə'litik/ *adj*

,amphi'mictic /-'miktik/ *adj* capable of (producing fertile offspring by) interbreeding [ISV *amphi-* + Gk *miktos* blended, fr *mignynai*] – **amphimictically** *adv*

,amphi'mixis /-'miksis/ *n, pl* **amphimixes** /-'mikseez/ (the union of germ cells in) sexual reproduction – compare APOMIXIS [NL, fr *amphi-* + Gk *mixis* mingling, fr *mignynai* to mix – more at MIX]

amphioxus /,amfi'oksəs/ *n, pl* **amphioxi** /-'oksie/, **amphioxuses** any of a genus of lancelets; *broadly* a lancelet [NL, fr *amphi-* + Gk *oxys* sharp]

'amphi,pod /-,pod/ *n* any of various small crustaceans (e g the sandhopper) with a body flattened sideways [deriv of Gk *amphi-* + *pod-, pous* foot – more at FOOT] – **amphipod** *adj*

amphisbaena /,amfis'beenə/ *n* a mythological serpent with a head at each end and capable of moving in either direction [L, fr Gk *amphisbaina*, fr *amphis* on both sides (fr *amphi* round) + *bainein* to walk, go – more at BY, COME]

'amphi,theatre /-,thiətə/ *n* **1** an oval or circular building with rising tiers of seats ranged about an open space **2a** a semicircular gallery in a theatre **b** a flat or gently sloping area surrounded by abrupt slopes **3** a place of public games or contests [L *amphitheatrum*, fr Gk *amphitheatron*, fr *amphi-* + *theatron* theatre]

amphora /'amfərə/ *n, pl* **amphorae** /-ri,-rie/, **amphoras** a 2-handled oval jar or vase with a narrow neck and base, orig used by the ancient Greeks and Romans for holding oil or wine [L, modif of Gk *amphoreus, amphiphoreus*, fr *amphi-* + *phoreus* bearer, fr *pherein* to bear – more at [2]BEAR]

amphoteric /,amfə'terik/ *adj* partly one and partly the other; *specif* capable of reacting chemically as both an acid and a base [ISV, fr Gk *amphoteros* each of two, fr *amphō* both – more at AMBI-]

ampicillin /,ampi'silin/ *n* a type of penicillin used esp to treat respiratory infections [ISV *amin-* + *penicillin*]

ample /'ampl/ *adj* **1** generous in size, scope, or capacity **2** abundant, plentiful ⟨*they had* ~ *money for the trip*⟩ **3** buxom, portly – chiefly euph [MF, fr L *amplus* large, spacious] – **ampleness** *n*, **amply** /'ampli/ *adv*

amplexus /am'pleksəs/ *n* the mating embrace of a frog or toad during which eggs are shed into the water and there fertilized [NL, fr L, embrace, fr *amplexus*, pp of *amplecti* to entwine, embrace, fr *ambi-* + *plectere* to plait]

amplifier /'ampli,fie·ə/ *n* a device usu employing valves or transistors to obtain amplification of voltage, current, or power [AMPLIFY + [2]-ER]

amplify /'ampli,fie/ *vt* **1** to expand (e g a statement) by the use of detail, illustration, etc **2** to make larger or greater; increase **3** to increase the magnitude of (a signal or other input of power) ~ *vi* to expand *on* one's remarks or ideas [ME *amplifien*, fr MF *amplifier*, fr L *amplificare*, fr *amplus*] – **amplification** /-fi'kaysh(ə)n/ *n*

amplitude /'amplityoohd, -choohd/ *n* **1** largeness of **a** dimensions **b** scope; abundance **2** the extent of a vibration or oscillation measured from the mean to a maximum [L *amplitudo*, fr *amplus* + *-tudo* -tude]

,amplitude modu'lation *n* a modulation of the amplitude of a wave, esp a radio carrier wave, so as to correspond with the instantaneous value of some signal waveform – compare FREQUENCY MODULATION

ampoule, *chiefly NAm* **ampul, ampule** /'ampoohl/ *n* a hermetically sealed small bulbous glass vessel used esp to hold a sterile solution for hypodermic injection [ME *ampulle* flask, fr OE *ampulle* & OF *ampoule*, both fr L *ampulla*]

ampulla /am'poolə/ *n, pl* **ampullae** /-li/ **1** a 2-handled globular flask used esp by the ancient Romans to hold ointment, perfume, or wine **2** a saclike anatomical swelling or pouch [ME, fr OE, fr L, dim. of *amphora*] – **ampullar** *adj*

amputate /'ampyootayt/ *vt* to cut or lop off; *esp* to cut (e g a damaged or diseased limb) from the body [L *amputatus*, pp of *amputare*, fr *am-, amb-* round

+ *putare* to cut, prune – more at AMBI-, PAVE] – **amputator** *n*, **amputation** /-'taysh(ə)n/ *n*

amputee /,ampyoo'tee/ *n* sby who has had a limb amputated

amuck /ə'muk/ *adv* amok

amulet /'amyoolit/ *n* a small object worn as a charm against evil [L *amuletum*]

amuse /ə'myoohz/ *vt* **1** to entertain or occupy in a light or pleasant manner ⟨~ *the child with a story*⟩ **2** to appeal to the sense of humour of ⟨*the joke doesn't* ~ *me*⟩ [MF *amuser*, fr OF, fr *a-* (fr L *ad-*) + *muser* to muse] – **amuser** *n*, **amusing** *adj*, **amusingly** *adv*, **amusingness** *n*, **amusedly** /-zidli/ *adv*

a'musement /-mənt/ *n* a means of entertaining or occupying; a pleasurable diversion [AMUSE + -MENT]

a'musement ar,cade *n, chiefly Br* a covered area containing coin-operated games machines for recreation

a'musement ,park *n* an enclosed park where various amusements (e g roundabouts, sideshows, etc) are permanently set up

amygdalin /ə'migdəlin/ *n* a glucoside found esp in the bitter almond [NL *Amygdalus*, genus name, fr LL, almond tree, fr Gk *amygdalos*; akin to Gk *amygdalē* almond]

amyl /'amil, 'amiel/ *n* a univalent hydrocarbon radical C_5H_{11} derived from pentane [blend of *amyl-* and *-yl*]

amyl-, amylo- *comb form* starch ⟨amylase⟩ [LL *amyl-*, fr L *amylum*, fr Gk *amylon*, fr neut of *amylos* not ground at the mill, fr *a-* + *mylē* mill – more at [2]MEAL]

amylase /'amilayz, -lays/ *n* an enzyme that accelerates the hydrolytic breakdown of starch and glycogen

amyloid /'amiloyd/ *n* a firm waxy substance deposited in animal organs under abnormal conditions

amyloidosis /,amiloy'dohsis/ *n* a pathological condition in which amyloid is deposited [NL]

amylopsin /,ami'lopsin/ *n* the amylase of the pancreatic juice [*amyl-* + *-psin* (as in *trypsin*)]

amylose /'amilohz, -lohs/ *n* (a component or hydrolysis product of) starch or a similar polysaccharide

[1]an /(ə)n; *strong* an/ *indefinite article* [2]A – used (1) before words with an initial vowel sound ⟨~ *oak*⟩ ⟨~ *honour*⟩ (2) frequently, esp formerly or in the USA, before words whose initial /h/ sound is often lost before the *an* ⟨~ *hotel*⟩ (3) sometimes, esp formerly in British writing, before words like *union* or *European* whose initial sound is /y/ [ME, fr OE *ān* one – more at ONE]

[2]an, an' *conj* **1** and – infml **2** *archaic* if [ME *an*, alter. of *and*]

[3]an *prep* [3]A – used under the same conditions as [1]AN

an- – see [2]A-

[1]-an /-ən/, **-ian** *also* **-ean** *suffix* (→ *n*) **1** one who is of or belonging to ⟨*Mancun*ian⟩ ⟨*republic*an⟩ **2** one skilled in or specializing in ⟨*phonetic*ian⟩ [*-an* & *-ian* fr ME, fr OF & L; OF *-ien*, fr L *-ianus*, fr *-i-* + *-anus*, fr *-anus*, adj suffix; *-ean* fr such words as *Mediterranean, European*]

[2]-an, -ian *also* **-ean** *suffix* (→ *adj*) **1** of or belonging to ⟨*Amer* ican⟩ ⟨*Christ*ian⟩ **2** characteristic of; resembling ⟨*Mozart*ean⟩ ⟨*Shav*ian⟩

[3]-an *suffix* (→ *n*) **1** unsaturated carbon compound ⟨*fur*an⟩ **2** polymeric anhydride of (a specified carbohydrate) ⟨*dextr*an⟩ [ISV *-an, -ane*, alter. of *-ene, -ine*, & *-one*]

ana- /anə-/, **an-** *prefix* **1** up; upwards ⟨ana*basis*⟩ **2** back; backwards ⟨ana*tropous*⟩ **3** again ⟨ana*baptism*⟩ [L, fr Gk, up, back, again, fr *ana* up – more at ON]

-ana /-'ahnə/, **-iana** /-i'ahnə/ *suffix* (→ *n pl*) collected objects or information relating to or characteristic of (a specified topic or individual) ⟨*Cricket*ana⟩ ⟨*Johnson*iana⟩ [NL, fr L, neut pl of *-anus* -an & *-ianus* -ian]

anabaptism /,anə'baptiz(ə)m/ *n* **1** *cap* the (doctrine or practices of the) Anabaptist movement **2** the baptism of one previously baptized [NL *anabaptismus*, fr LGk *anabaptismos* rebaptism, fr *anabaptizein* to rebaptize, fr *ana-* again + *baptizein* to baptize]

,Ana'baptist /-'baptist/ *n or adj* (a member) of a radical egalitarian Protestant movement arising orig in Zurich in 1524, whose chief distinguishing feature was its insistence on baptism or rebaptism of adult believers

anabatic /,anə'batik/ *adj* moving upwards ⟨*an* ~ *wind*⟩ [Gk *anabatos*, verbal of *anabainein* to go up or inland, fr *ana-* + *bainein* to go]

anabiosis /,anəbie'ohsis/ *n, pl* **anabioses** /-seez/ a state of suspended animation induced in some organisms by desiccation [NL, fr Gk *anabiōsis* return to life, fr *anabioun* to return to life, fr *ana-* + *bios* life – more at [1]QUICK] – **anabiotic** /-bie'otik/ *adj*

anabolic steroid /,anə'bolik/ *n* any of several synthetic steroid hormones that cause a rapid increase in the size and weight of skeletal muscle

anabolism /ə'nabə,liz(ə)m/ *n* constructive metabolism involving the use of energy by a living organism to make proteins, fats, etc from simpler materials – compare CATABOLISM [ISV *ana-* + *-bolism* (as in *metabolism*)] – **anabolic** /,anə'bolik/ *adj*

anabranch /'anə,brahnch/ *n* a diverging branch of a river which reenters the river or sinks into the ground

anachronism /ə'nakrə,niz(ə)m/ *n* **1** an error in chronology; *esp* a chronological misplacing of people, events, objects, or customs **2** sby who or sthg that seems chronologically out of place [prob fr MGk *anachronismos*, fr *anachronizesthai* to be an anachronism, fr LGk *anachronizein* to be late, fr Gk *ana-* + *chronos* time] – **anachronistic** /-'nistik/ *also* **anachronic** /,anə'kronik/, **anachronous** /ə'nakrənəs/ *adj*, **anachronistically** /ə,nakrə'nistikli/ *also* **anachronously** /ə'nakrənəsli/ *adv*

anacoluthon /,anəkə'looh,thon/ *n, pl* **anacolutha** /-thə/, **anacoluthons** syntactic inconsistency; *esp* the shift from one construction to another (e g in 'you really ought – well, do it your own way') [LL, fr LGk *anakolouthon* inconsistency in logic, fr Gk, neut of *anakolouthos* inconsistent, fr *an-* + *akolouthos* following] – **anacoluthic** *adj*, **anacoluthically** *adv*

anaconda /,anə'kondə/ *n* a large semiaquatic S American snake of the boa family that crushes its prey in its coils [prob modif of Sinhalese *henakandayā* a slender green snake]

anacrusis /,anə'kroohsis/ *n, pl* **anacruses** /-,seez/ **1** an unstressed syllable at the beginning of a line of poetry **2** 1 or more notes preceding the first downbeat of a musical phrase [NL, fr Gk *anakrousis* beginning of a song, fr *anakrouein* to begin a song, fr *ana-* + *krouein* to strike, beat; akin to Lith *krušti* to stamp]

anadromous /ə'nadrəməs/ *adj* ascending rivers from the sea for breeding ⟨*salmon are* ~⟩ [Gk *anadromos* running upwards, fr *anadramein* to run upwards, fr *ana-* + *dramein* to run – more at DROMEDARY]

anaemia, *chiefly NAm* **anemia** /ə'neemyə, -mi·ə/ *n* **1a** a condition in which the blood is deficient in red blood cells, haemoglobin, or total volume **b** ischaemia **2** lack of vitality [NL, fr Gk *anaimia* bloodlessness, fr *an-* + *haima* blood] – **anaemic** *adj*, **anaemically** *adv*

anaerobe /ə'neərohb, 'anə,rohb/ *n* an organism (e g a bacterium) that lives only in the absence of oxygen [ISV *an-* + *aerobe*] – **anaerobic** /,anə'rohbik/ *adj*, **anaerobically** *adv*

anaesthesia, *chiefly NAm* **anesthesia** /,anəs'theezh(y)ə, -zyə/ *n* loss of sensation, esp loss of sensation of pain, resulting either from injury or a disorder of the nerves or from the action of drugs [NL, fr Gk *anaisthēsia*, fr *an-* + *aisthēsis* sensation, fr *aisthanesthai* to perceive – more at AUDIBLE]

anaesthetic, *chiefly NAm* **anesthetic** /,anəs'thetik/ *n* a substance that produces anaesthesia, e g so that surgery can be carried out painlessly – **anaesthetic** *adj*, **anaesthetically** *adv*

anaesthet·ize, -ise, *chiefly NAm* **anesthetize** /ə'neesthə,tiez/ *vt* to subject to anaesthesia, esp for purposes of surgery – **anaesthetist** *n*

anaglyph /'anə,glif/ *n* an embossed ornament in low relief [LL *anaglyphus* embossed, fr Gk *anaglyphos*, fr *anaglyphein* to emboss, fr *ana-* + *glyphein* to carve – more at [2]CLEAVE] – **anaglyphic** /-'glifik/ *adj*

anagoge, anagogy /'anə,gohji/ *n* mystical or allegorical interpretation (e g of a text) [LL *anagoge*, fr LGk *anagōgē*, fr Gk, reference, fr *anagein* to refer, fr *ana-* + *agein* to lead – more at AGENT] – **anagogic** /-'gojik/, **anagogical** *adj*, **anagogically** *adv*

anagram /'anə,gram/ *n* a word or phrase made by rearranging the letters of another [prob fr MF *anagramme*, fr NL *anagrammat-*, *anagramma*, modif of Gk *anagrammatismos*, fr *anagrammatizein* to transpose letters, fr *ana-* + *grammat-*, *gramma* letter – more at [2]GRAM] – **anagrammatic** /-grə'matik/, **anagrammatical** *adj*, **anagrammatically** *adv*, **anagrammatize** /,anə'gramətiez/ *vt*

anal /'aynl/ *adj* **1** of or situated near the anus **2** of or characterized by (parsimony, meticulousness, or other personality traits typical of) the stage of sexual development during which the child is concerned esp with its faeces – compare ORAL, GENITAL – **anally** *adv*, **anality** /ay'naləti/ *n*

analecta /,anə'lektə/ *n pl* analects

analects /'anə,lekts/ *n pl* selected miscellaneous writings [NL *analecta*, fr Gk *analekta*, neut pl of *analektos*, verbal of *analegein* to collect, fr *ana-* + *legein* to gather – more at LEGEND]

analeptic /,anə'leptik/ *adj*, *esp of a medicine* stimulating the central nervous system; restorative [Gk *analēptikos*, fr *analambanein* to take up, restore] – **analeptic** *n*

analgesia /,anl'jeezh(y)ə, -zyə/ *n* insensibility to pain without loss of consciousness [NL, fr Gk *analgēsia*, fr *an-* + *algēsis* sense of pain, fr *algein* to suffer pain, fr *algos* pain] – **analgesic** /-'jeezik/ *adj or n*, **analgetic** /-'jetik/ *adj or n*

analogist /ə'naləjist/ *n* one who searches for or reasons from analogies

analog·ize, -ise /ə'naləjiez/ *vb* to compare by or use analogy

analogous /ə'naləgəs/ *adj* **1** corresponding by analogy **2** being or related to as an analogue [L *analogus*, fr Gk *analogos*, lit., proportionate, fr *ana-* + *logos* reason, ratio, fr *legein* to gather, speak – more at LEGEND] – **analogously** *adv*, **analogousness** *n*

[1]**analogue,** *NAm chiefly* **analog** /'anəlog/ *n* sthg analogous or parallel to sthg else [F *analogue*, fr *analogue* analogous, fr Gk *analogos*]

[2]**analogue,** *NAm chiefly* **analog** *adj* of an analogue computer

analogue computer *n* a computer that operates with numbers represented by directly measurable quantities (e g voltages or mechanical rotations) – compare DIGITAL COMPUTER

analogy /ə'naləji/ *n* **1** inference from a parallel case **2** resemblance in some particulars; similarity **3** the tendency for new words or linguistic forms to be created in imitation of existing patterns **4** correspondence in function between anatomical parts of different structure and origin [prob fr Gk *analogia* mathematical proportion, correspondence, fr *analogos*] – **analogic** /,anə'lojik/, **analogical** /,anə'lojikl/ *adj*, **analogically** *adv*

analysand /ə'nali,sand/ *n* sby undergoing psychoanalysis [*analyse* + *-and* (as in *multiplicand*)]

analyse, *NAm chiefly* **analyze** /'anəliez/ *vt* **1** to subject to analysis **2** to determine by analysis the constitution or structure of **3** to psychoanalyse [prob irreg fr *analysis*] – **analysable** *adj*

analysis /ə'naləsis/ *n*, *pl* **analyses** /-seez/ **1a** examination and identification of the components of a whole **b** a statement of such an analysis **2** the use of function words instead of inflectional forms as a characteristic device of a language **3** psychoanalysis [NL, fr Gk, fr *analyein* to break up, fr *ana-* + *lyein* to loosen – more at LOSE]

analyst /'anəlist/ *n* **1** a person who analyses or is skilled in analysis **2** a psychoanalyst [irreg fr *analyse* or *analysis*]

analytic /,anə'litik/, **analytical** /-kl/ *adj* **1** of analysis **2** skilled in or using analysis, esp in reasoning ⟨*a keenly* ~ *man*⟩ **3** asserting of a subject a predicate that is part of the meaning of that subject; *broadly* logically necessary; tautologous ⟨*'all women are female" is an* ~ *truth*⟩ – compare SYNTHETIC **4** characterized by analysis rather than inflection ⟨~ *languages*⟩ **5** psychoanalytic [LL *analyticus*, fr Gk *analytikos*, fr *analyein*] – **analytically** *adv*, **analyticity** /-li'tisəti/ *n*

analytical geometry /,anə'litikl/ *n* the study of geometric properties by means of algebraic operations on coordinates in a coordinate system

anamnesis /,anəm'neesis/ *n*, *pl* **anamneses** /-,seez/ **1** a recalling to mind; reminiscence **2** a patient's preliminary case history [NL, fr Gk *anamnēsis*, fr *anamimnēskesthai* to remember, fr *ana-* + *mimnēskesthai* to remember – more at MIND] – **anamnestic** /-'nestik/ *adj*

anamorphic /,anə'mawfik/ *adj*, *of (the image produced by) an optical instrument* producing or having a different image magnification in each of 2 perpendicular directions [NL *anamorphosis* distorted optical image, fr MGk *anamorphōsis*, fr LGk *ana-*

morphoun to transform, fr Gk *ana-* + *morphoun* to form, fr *morphē* shape]

ananas /ˈananəs, -nas/ *n* PINEAPPLE 1 [F or Sp; F, fr Sp *ananás*, fr Pg, modif of Guarani *naná*]

anapaest, *NAm chiefly* **anapest** /ˈanə,pest, -,peest/ *n* a metrical foot consisting of 2 short syllables followed by 1 long [L *anapaestus*, fr Gk *anapaistos*, lit., struck back (i e a dactyl reversed), fr (assumed) *anapaiein* to strike back, fr *ana-* + *paiein* to strike] – **anapaestic** /-ˈpestik, -ˈpeestik/ *adj or n*

anaphase /ˈanə,fayz/ *n* the stage of mitosis and meiosis in which the chromosomes move towards the poles of the spindle [ISV] – **anaphasic** /-ˈfayzik/ *adj*

anaphora /əˈnafərə/ *n* **1** repetition of a word or phrase at the beginning of successive clauses, esp for effect – compare EPISTROPHE **2** use of a grammatical substitute (e g a pronoun) to refer to a preceding word or phrase [LL, fr LGk, fr Gk, act of carrying back, reference, fr *anapherein* to carry back, refer, fr *ana-* + *pherein* to carry – more at ²BEAR] – **anaphoric** /,anəˈforik/ *adj,* **anaphorically** *adv*

anaphrodisiac /,anafrəˈdiziak/ *n or adj* (sthg) that impairs sexual desire [NL *anaphrodisia* lack of sexual desire, fr *a-* + Gk *aphrodisios* sexual – more at APHRODISIAC]

anaphylaxis /,anəfəˈlaksis/ *n, pl* **anaphylaxes** /-seez/ a sometimes fatal reaction to drugs, insect venom, etc due to hypersensitivity resulting from earlier contact [NL, fr *ana-* + *-phylaxis* (as in *prophylaxis*)] – **anaphylactic** *adj,* **anaphylactoid** *adj*

anarchism /ˈanə,kiz(ə)m/ *n* **1** a political theory holding all forms of governmental authority to be undesirable **2** the attacking of the established social order or laws; rebellion [*anarchy* + *-ism*]

anarchist /ˈanəkist/ *n* **1** one who attacks the established social order or laws; a rebel **2** a believer in or (violent) promoter of anarchism or anarchy – **anarchist, anarchistic** /-ˈkistik/ *adj*

anarchy /ˈanəki/ *n* **1a** absence of government **b** lawlessness; (political) disorder **c** a utopian society with complete freedom and no government **2** anarchism [ML *anarchia*, fr Gk, fr *anarchos* having no ruler, fr *an-* + *archos* ruler – more at ARCH-] – **anarchic** /əˈnahkik, a-/ *adj,* **anarchically** *adv*

anastigmat /əˈnastigmat, anəˈstigmat/ *n* a lens that is not astigmatic [G, back-formation fr *anastigmatisch* anastigmatic] – **anastigmatic** /-ˈmatik/ *adj*

anastomose /əˈnastə,mohz/ *vb* to interconnect or join by anastomosis [prob back-formation fr *anastomosis*]

anastomosis /ə,nastəˈmohsis/ *n, pl* **anastomoses** /-,seez/ **1** the interconnecting union of parts or branches of streams, leaf veins, blood vessels, etc **2** the surgical joining of 2 hollow organs (e g the rejoining of the gut after part has been removed) [LL, fr Gk *anastomōsis*, fr *anastomoun* to provide with an outlet, fr *ana-* + *stoma* mouth, opening – more at STOMACH] – **anastomotic** /-ˈmotik/ *adj*

anathema /əˈnathəmə/ *n* **1a** (the object of) a ban or curse solemnly pronounced by ecclesiastical authority and accompanied by excommunication **b** a vigorous denunciation; a curse **2** sby or sthg despised ⟨*his opinions are ~ to me*⟩ [LL *anathemat-, anathema*, fr Gk, thing devoted to evil, curse, fr *anatithenai* to set up, dedicate, fr *ana-* + *tithenai* to place, set – more at ¹DO] – **anathematize** /əˈnathəmə,tiez/ *vt*

Anatolian /,anəˈtohlyən/ *n* a branch of the Indo-European language family including a group of extinct languages of ancient Anatolia [*Anatolia*, Asia Minor] – **Anatolian** *adj*

anatomist /əˈnatəmist/ *n* **1** a student of anatomy (skilled in dissection) **2** one who analyses minutely and critically ⟨*an ~ of urban society*⟩

anatom·ize, -ise /əˈnatəmiez/ *vt* **1** to dissect **2** to analyse, esp critically

anatomy /əˈnatəmi/ *n* **1** (a treatise on) the biology of the structure of organisms **2** dissection **3** structural make-up, esp of (a part of) an organism **4** an analysis **5** the human body ***USE*** *(3&5)* 👁 [ME, prob fr MF *anatomie*, fr LL *anatomia* dissection, fr Gk *anatomē*, fr *anatemnein* to dissect, fr *ana-* + *temnein* to cut – more at TOME] – **anatomic** /,anəˈtomik/, **anatomical** *adj,* **anatomically** *adv*

-ance /-əns/ *suffix* (→ *n*) **1** action or process of ⟨*furtherance*⟩; *also* instance of (a specified action or process) ⟨*performance*⟩ **2** quality or state of ⟨*brilliance*⟩; *also* instance of (a specified quality or state) ⟨*protuberance*⟩ **3** amount or degree of ⟨*conductance*⟩ [ME, fr OF, fr L *-antia*, fr *-ant-*, *-ans* -ant + *-ia* -y]

ancestor /ˈansestə, -səs-/, *fem* **ancestress** /-tris/ *n* **1a** one from whom a person is descended, usu more distant than a grandparent **b** FOREFATHER 2 **2** a progenitor of a more recent (species of) organism [ME *ancestre*, fr OF, fr L *antecessor* sby or sthg that goes before, fr *antecessus*, pp of *antecedere* to go before, fr *ante-* + *cedere* to go – more at CEDE] – **ancestral** /anˈsestrəl/ *adj,* **ancestrally** *adv*

ancestry /ˈansestri, -səs-/ *n* a line of esp noble descent; a lineage

¹anchor /ˈangkə/ *n* **1** a usu metal device dropped to the bottom from a ship or boat to hold it in a particular place **2** sby or sthg providing support and security; a mainstay **3** sthg that serves to hold an object firmly [ME *ancre*, fr OE *ancor*, fr L *anchora*, fr Gk *ankyra*; akin to L *uncus* hook – more at ³ANGLE] – **anchorless** *adj*

²anchor *vt* **1** to hold in place in the water by an anchor **2** to secure firmly; fix ~ *vi* **1** to cast anchor **2** to become fixed; settle

anchorage /ˈangkərij/ *n* **1** a place (suitable) for vessels to anchor **2** a source of reassurance **3** sthg that provides a secure hold or attachment [²ANCHOR + -AGE]

anchoret /ˈangkərət/ *n* an anchorite

anchorite /ˈangkə,riet/, *fem* **anchoress** /ˈangk(ə)ris/, **anchress** /ˈangkris/ *n* one who lives in seclusion, usu for religious reasons [ME, fr ML *anchorita*, alter. of LL *anachoreta*, fr LGk *anachōrētēs*, fr Gk *anachōrein* to withdraw, fr *ana-* + *chōrein* to make room, fr *chōros* place; akin to Gk *chēros* left, bereaved – more at HEIR] – **anchoritic** /-ˈritik/ *adj*

anchorman /ˈangkəmən, -,man/ *n* **1** the member of a team who competes last ⟨*the ~ on a relay team*⟩ **2** a linkman

anchovy /ˈanchəvi/ *n, pl* **anchovies,** *esp collectively* **anchovy** a common small Mediterranean fish resembling a herring and used esp in appetizers and as a garnish; *also* any of various small fish related to this [Sp *anchova*, prob fr It dial. *ancioa*, fr (assumed) VL *apjua*, fr Gk *aphyē* small fry]

ancien régime /ˌahnsyen rayˈzheem (*Fr* ɑ̃sjɛ̃ reʒim)/ *n* **1** the political and social system of France before the Revolution of 1789 **2** a superseded system or arrangement [F, lit., old regime]

[1]**ancient** /ˈaynsh(ə)nt, -chənt/ *adj* **1** having existed for many years **2** of (those living in) a remote period, specif that from the earliest known civilizations to the fall of the western Roman Empire in AD 476 **3** old-fashioned, antique [ME *ancien*, fr MF, fr (assumed) VL *anteanus*, fr L *ante* before – more at ANTE-]

[2]**ancient** *n* **1a** sby who lived in ancient times **b** *pl the* members of a civilized, esp a classical, nation of antiquity **2** *archaic* an aged person

ˌ**ancient ˈhistory** *n* **1** the history of the classical civilizations of Greece and Rome **2** sthg which has been common knowledge for a long time

ˌ**ancient ˈlights** *n pl but sing in constr* a legally enforceable right to unobstructed daylight from an opening (e g a window) in a building

ˈ**anciently** /-li/ *adv* in ancient times; long ago

[1]**ancillary** /anˈsiləri; *NAm usu* ˈansəˌleri/ *adj* **1** subordinate, subsidiary **2** auxiliary, supplementary [L *ancillaris* of a maid-servant, fr *ancilla*, fem dim. of *anculus* servant, fr *an-* round + *-culus* circulating]

[2]**ancillary** *n, Br* one who assists; a helper

ancress /ˈangkris/ *n* a female anchorite [ME *ankeresse, ancresse*, fr *anker, ancre* hermit]

-ancy /-ənsi/ *suffix* (→ *n*) quality or state of ⟨*piquancy*⟩ ⟨*expectancy*⟩ [L *-antia* – more at -ANCE]

and /(ə)n, (ə)nd; *strong* and/ *conj* **1** – used to join coordinate sentence elements of the same class or function expressing addition or combination ⟨*cold ~ hungry*⟩ ⟨*John ~ I*⟩ **2** – used, esp in Br speech, before the numbers 1–99 after the number 100 ⟨*three hundred ~ seventeen*⟩; used also orig between tens and units ⟨*five ~ twenty blackbirds*⟩ **3** plus ⟨*three ~ three make six*⟩ **4** – used to introduce a second clause expressing temporal sequence ⟨*came to tea ~ stayed to dinner*⟩, consequence ⟨*water the seeds ~ they will grow*⟩, contrast ⟨*he's old ~ I'm young*⟩, or supplementary explanation ⟨*she's ill ~ can't travel*⟩ **5** – used to join repeated words expressing continuation or progression ⟨*ran ~ ran*⟩ ⟨*waited hours ~ hours*⟩ ⟨*came nearer ~ nearer*⟩ **6** – used to join words expressing contrast of type or quality ⟨*there are aunts ~ aunts*⟩ ⟨*gynaecology of one sort ~ another* – Jan Morris⟩ **7** – used instead of *to* to introduce an infinitive after *come, go, run, try, stop* ⟨*come ~ look*⟩ [ME, fr OE; akin to OHG *unti* and, ON *enn* and, but] – **and all that, and all** AND SO FORTH – **and how** – used to emphasize the preceding idea; infml – **and so forth, and so on 1** and others or more of the same kind **2** and further in the same manner **3** and the rest **4** and other things – **and that** *chiefly Br* AND SO FORTH – nonstandard

andante /anˈdanti/ *n, adv, or adj* (a musical composition or movement to be played) moderately slow [It, lit., going, prp of *andare* to go]

andiron /ˈandie·ən/ *n* either of a pair of metal stands used on a hearth to support burning wood [ME *aundiren*, modif of OF *andier*, fr (assumed) Gaulish *anderos* young bull; akin to W *anner* heifer, MIr *ainder* young woman]

ˌ**and/ˈor** *conj* – used to indicate that 2 words or expressions may be taken either together or individually

andr-, andro- *comb form* **1** man ⟨andro*gynous*⟩ **2** male ⟨andr*oecium*⟩ [MF, fr L, fr Gk, fr *andr-, anēr* man (male); akin to Oscan *ner* man, Skt *nr*, OIr *nert* strength]

androecium /ˌanˈdreesyəm, -sh(y)əm/ *n, pl* **androecia** /-syə, -sh(y)ə/ all the stamens collectively in the flower of a seed plant [NL, fr *andr-* + Gk *oikion*, dim. of *oikos* house – more at VICINITY]

androgen /ˈandrəjən/ *n* a male sex hormone (e g testosterone) [ISV] – **androgenic** /-ˈjenik/ *adj*

androgynous /anˈdrojənəs/ *adj* having characteristics of both the male and female forms [L *androgynus* hermaphrodite, fr Gk *androgynos*, fr *andr-* + *gynē* woman – more at QUEEN] – **androgyny** /-ni/ *n*

android /ˈandroyd/ *n* an automaton externally indistinguishable from a human [LGk *androeidēs* manlike, fr Gk *andr-* + *-oeides* -oid]

-androus /-andrəs/ *comb form* (→ *adj*) having (such or so many) stamens ⟨*mon*androus⟩ [NL *-andrus*, fr Gk *-andros* having (such or so many) men, fr *andr-, anēr*]

ane /ayn/ *adj, n, or pron, chiefly Scot* one [ME (northern) *an*, fr OE *ān* – more at ONE]

-ane /-ayn/ *suffix* (→ *n*) saturated carbon compound; *esp* hydrocarbon of the alkane series ⟨*meth*ane⟩ ⟨*alk*ane⟩ [ISV *-an, -ane*, alter. of *-ene, -ine, & -one*]

anecdotal /ˌanikˈdohtl/ *adj* consisting of or depicting an anecdote ⟨~ *art*⟩ – **anecdotally** *adv*

anecdote /ˈanikˌdoht/ *n* a usu short narrative about an interesting or amusing person or incident [F, fr Gk *anekdota* unpublished items, fr neut pl of *anekdotos* unpublished, fr *a-* + *ekdidonai* to publish, fr *ex* out + *didonai* to give – more at EX-, [2]DATE] – **anecdotist, anecdotalist** *n*, **anecdotic** /-ˈdotik/, **anecdotical** *adj*

anechoic /ˌaneˈkoh·ik, ˌanə-/ *adj* free from echoes and reverberations

anem-, anemo- *comb form* wind ⟨anemo*meter*⟩ [prob fr F *anémo-*, fr Gk *anem-, anemo-*, fr *anemos* – more at ANIMATE]

anemia /əˈneemyə, -mi·ə/ *n, chiefly NAm* anaemia – **anemic** /əˈneemik/ *adj*, **anemically** *adv*

anemograph /əˈneməˌgrahf, -ˌgraf/ *n* a recording anemometer – **anemographic** /-ˈgrafik/ *adj*

anemometer /ˌaniˈmomitə/ *n* an instrument for measuring the force or speed of the wind – **anemometry** *n*, **anemometric** /-mohˈmetrik/ *also* **anemometrical** *adj*

anemone /əˈneməni/ *n* **1** any of a large genus of plants of the buttercup family with lobed or divided leaves and showy flowers **2** SEA ANEMONE [L, fr Gk *anemōnē*, perh by folk etymology fr a word of Sem origin; akin to Heb *Na'ămān*, epithet of Adonis]

anemophilous /ˌaniˈmofələs/ *adj* (usually) wind-pollinated – **anemophily** /-li/ *n*

anent /əˈnent/ *prep* about, concerning – chiefly archaic or humor [ME *onevent, anent*, fr OE *on efen* alongside, fr *on* + *efen* even]

aneroid /ˈanəroyd/ *adj* containing no liquid or operated without the use of liquid ⟨*an ~ barometer*⟩ [F *anéroïde*, fr Gk *a-* + LGk *nēron* water, fr Gk, neut of *nearos, nēros* fresh; akin to Gk *neos* new – more at NEW]

anesthesia /ˌanəsˈtheezyə, -zh(y)ə/ *n, chiefly NAm* anaesthesia – **anesthetic** /ˌanəsˈthetik/ *n or adj*, **anesthetist** /əˈneesthətist/ *n*, **anesthetize** /-ˌtiez/ *vt*

The skeleton

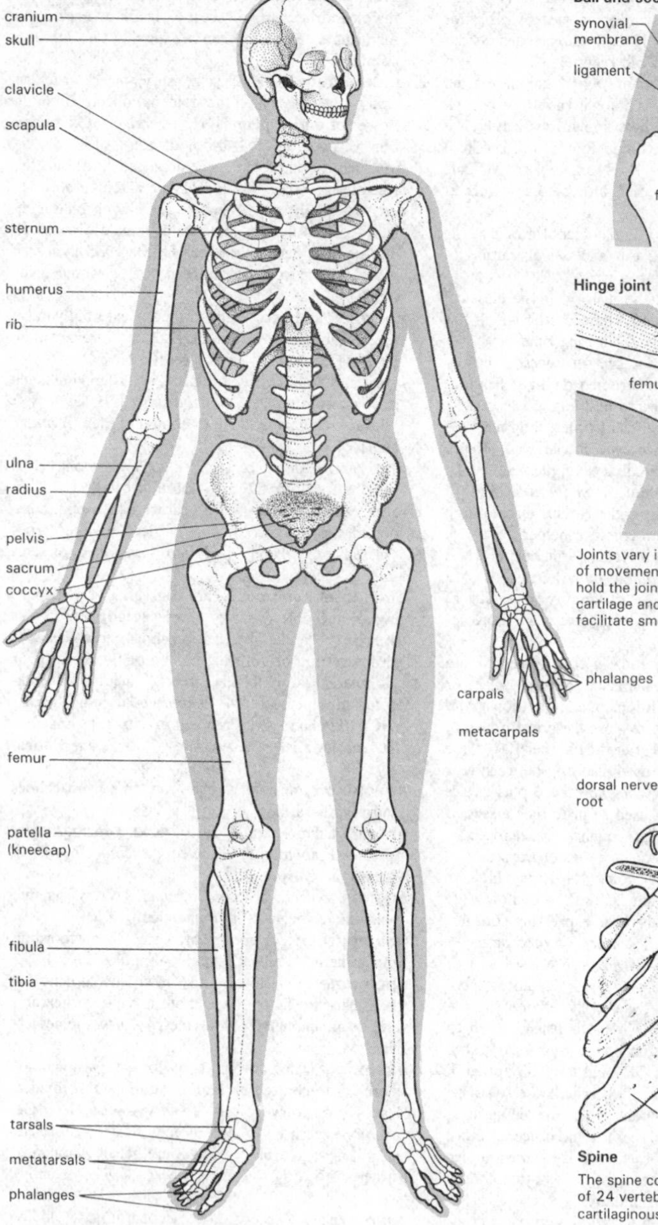

cranium
skull
clavicle
scapula
sternum
humerus
rib
ulna
radius
pelvis
sacrum
coccyx
carpals
metacarpals
phalanges
femur
patella (kneecap)
fibula
tibia
tarsals
metatarsals
phalanges

☞ DIGESTION, NERVE, REPRODUCTION

Ball and socket joint

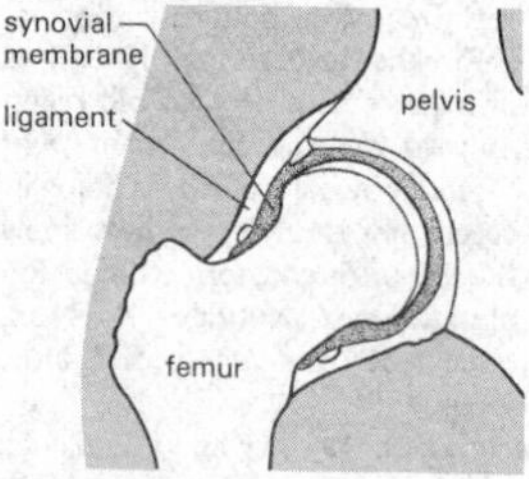

synovial membrane
ligament
pelvis
femur

Hinge joint

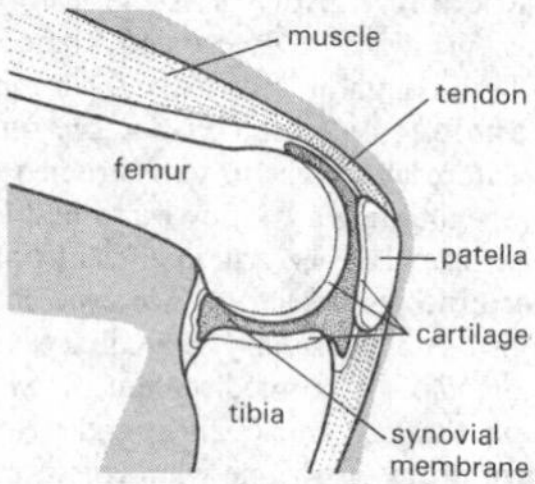

muscle
tendon
femur
patella
cartilage
tibia
synovial membrane

Joints vary in their strength and range of movement. Ligaments and muscles hold the joint in place, while the lining cartilage and synovial membrane facilitate smooth movement.

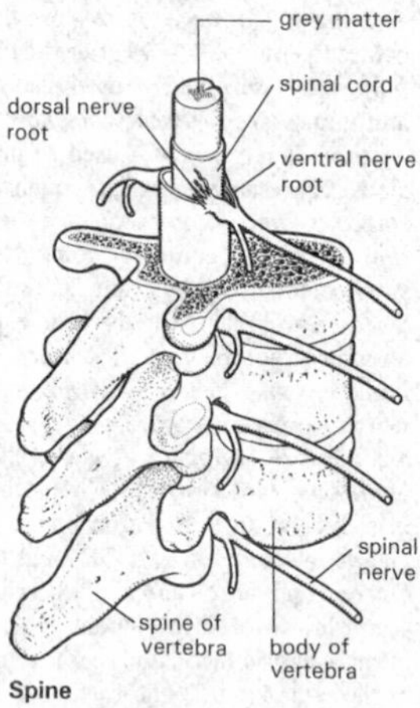

grey matter
spinal cord
dorsal nerve root
ventral nerve root
spinal nerve
spine of vertebra
body of vertebra

Spine

The spine consists of a curving column of 24 vertebrae, separated by cartilaginous discs.

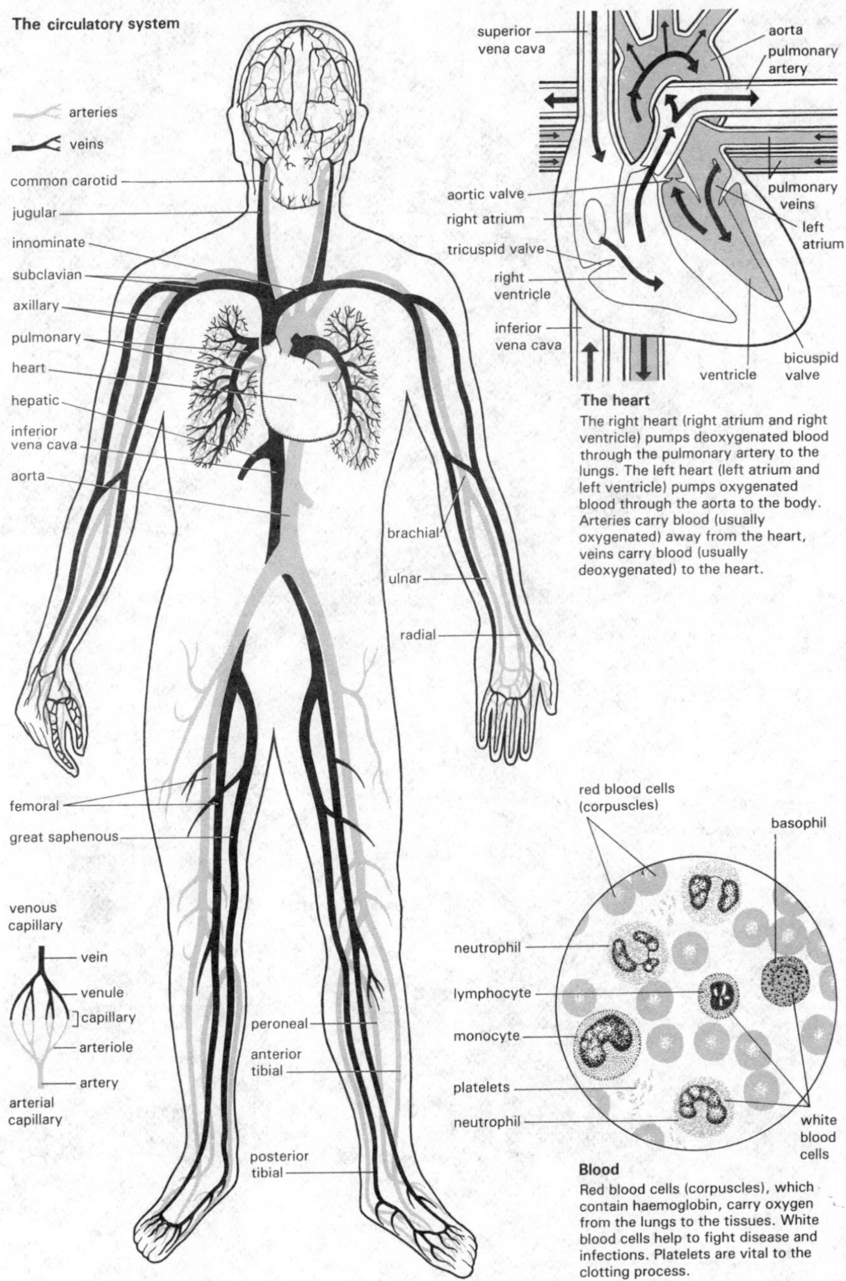

The heart

The right heart (right atrium and right ventricle) pumps deoxygenated blood through the pulmonary artery to the lungs. The left heart (left atrium and left ventricle) pumps oxygenated blood through the aorta to the body. Arteries carry blood (usually oxygenated) away from the heart, veins carry blood (usually deoxygenated) to the heart.

Blood

Red blood cells (corpuscles), which contain haemoglobin, carry oxygen from the lungs to the tissues. White blood cells help to fight disease and infections. Platelets are vital to the clotting process.

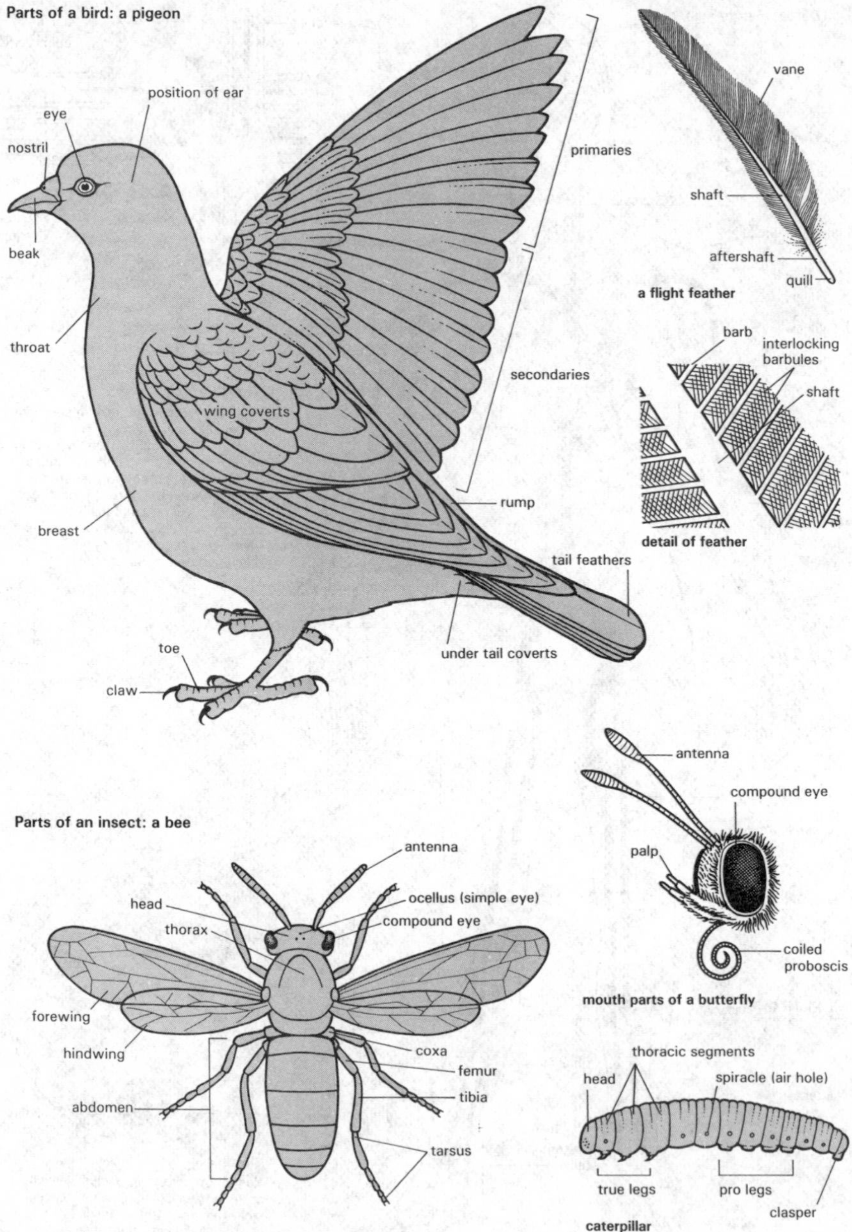
Parts of a bird: a pigeon
position of ear
eye
nostril
beak
throat
wing coverts
breast
toe
claw
primaries
secondaries
rump
tail feathers
under tail coverts
vane
shaft
aftershaft
quill
a flight feather
barb
interlocking barbules
shaft
detail of feather
Parts of an insect: a bee
antenna
head
ocellus (simple eye)
thorax
compound eye
forewing
hindwing
coxa
femur
abdomen
tibia
tarsus
antenna
compound eye
palp
coiled proboscis
mouth parts of a butterfly
thoracic segments
head
spiracle (air hole)
true legs
pro legs
clasper
caterpillar

Parts of a mammal: a horse

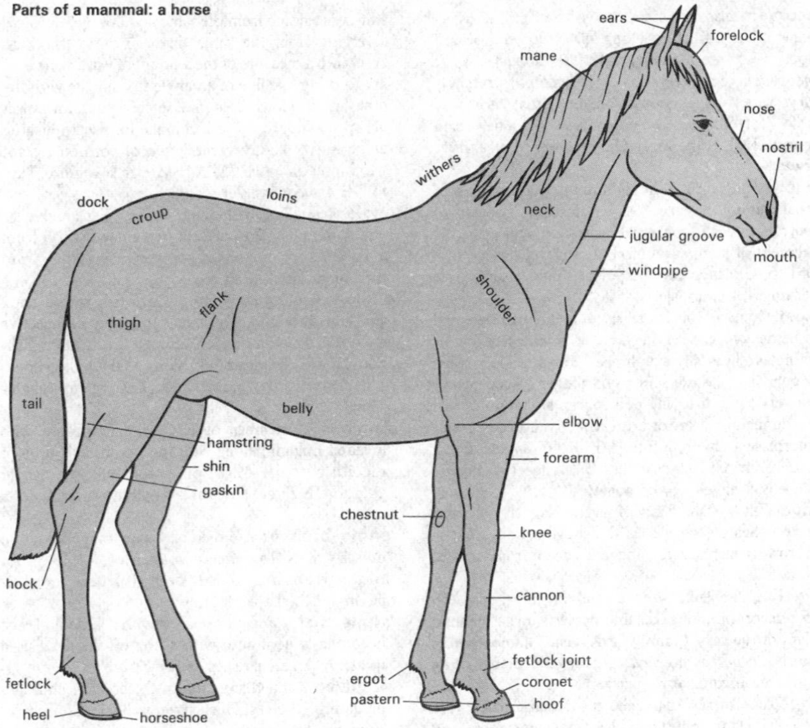

ears
forelock
mane
nose
nostril
withers
dock
loins
croup
neck
jugular groove
mouth
windpipe
shoulder
flank
thigh
tail
belly
elbow
hamstring
forearm
shin
gaskin
chestnut
knee
hock
cannon
fetlock joint
ergot
coronet
fetlock
pastern
hoof
heel
horseshoe

Parts of a fish: a minnow

dorsal fin
lateral line
caudal fin
eye
nostril
mouth
operculum (gill cover)
pectoral fin
overlapping scales
ventral fin
pelvic fin
annual rings
visible area of scale
detail of a scale

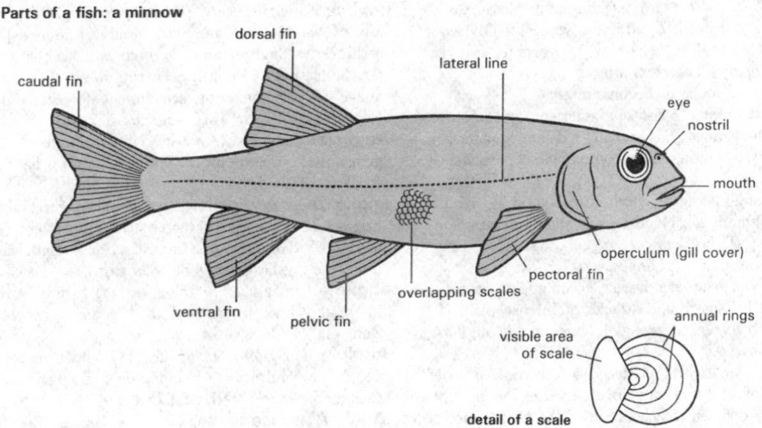

aneurysm *also* **aneurism** /ˈanyoo,riz(ə)m/ *n* a permanent blood-filled swelling of a (large) diseased blood vessel (e g the aorta) [Gk *aneurysma*, fr *aneurynein* to dilate, fr *ana-* + *eurynein* to stretch, fr *eurys* wide] – **aneurysmal** /,anyooˈrizməl/ *adj*

anew /əˈnyooh/ *adv* **1** again, afresh **2** in a new form or way [ME *of newe*, fr OE *of nīwe*, fr *of* + *nīwe* new]

angary /ˈang·gəri/ *n* the right in international law of a belligerent to seize, use, or destroy property of neutrals under military necessity and subject to the payment of compensation [LL *angaria* service to a lord, fr Gk *angareia* compulsory public service, fr Per *angaros* courier]

angel /ˈaynj(ə)l/ *n* **1** a spiritual being, usu depicted as being winged, serving as God's intermediary or acting as a heavenly worshipper **2** an attendant spirit or guardian **3** a messenger, harbinger ⟨~ *of death*⟩ **4** a very kind or loving person, esp a woman or girl **5** a financial backer of a theatrical venture or other enterprise – chiefly infml [ME, fr OF *angele*, fr LL *angelus*, fr Gk *angelos*, lit., messenger] – **angelic** /anˈjelik/, **angelical** *adj*, **angelically** *adv*

ˈangel,fish /-,fish/ *n* any of several brightly coloured bony fishes of warm seas that have a body that is narrow from side to side and deep from top to bottom

angelica /anˈjelikə/ *n* (the candied stalks, used esp as a decoration on cakes and desserts, of) a biennial plant of the carrot family [NL, genus name, fr ML, short for *herba angelica*, lit., angelic plant; fr its supposed medicinal properties]

Angelus /ˈanjələs/ *n* (a bell rung to mark) a devotion of the Western church said at morning, noon, and evening to commemorate the Incarnation [ML, fr LL, angel; fr the first word of the opening versicle]

[1]**anger** /ˈang·gə/ *n* a strong feeling of displeasure and usu antagonism [ME, affliction, anger, fr ON *angr* grief; akin to OE *enge* narrow, L *angere* to strangle, Gk *anchein*] – **angerless** *adj*

[2]**anger** *vb* to make or become angry

Angevin /ˈanjivin/ *adj* (characteristic) of Anjou or the Plantagenets [F, fr OF, fr ML *andegavinus*, fr *Andegavia* Anjou, former province of France] – **Angevin** *n*

angi- /anji-/, **angio-** *comb form* blood or lymph vessel ⟨angi*oma*⟩; blood vessels and ⟨angio*cardiography*⟩ [NL, fr Gk *angei-*, *angeio-*, fr *angeion* vessel, blood vessel, dim. of *angos* vessel]

angina /anˈjienə/ *n* a disease, specif angina pectoris, marked by spasmodic attacks of intense pain [L, quinsy, fr *angere* to strangle] – **anginal** *adj*, **anginose** /ˈanjinohs/ *adj*

angina pectoris /ˈpektəris, pekˈtawris/ *n* brief attacks of intense chest pain, esp on exertion, precipitated by deficient oxygenation of the heart muscles [NL, lit., angina of the chest]

angiosperm /ˈanji·ə,spuhm/ *n* any of a class of vascular plants that includes nearly all the seed plants (e g buttercups, orchids, roses, oaks, or grasses) – compare GYMNOSPERM ☞ PLANT [deriv of NL *angi-* + Gk *sperma* seed – more at SPERM] – **angiospermous** /-ˈspuhməs/ *adj*

angiotensin /,anji·əˈtensin/ *n* either of 2 related hormones that influence the fluid balance of the body – compare RENIN [*angi-* + hyper*tension* + *-in*]

[1]**angle** /ˈang·gl/ *n* **1** a corner **2a** the figure formed by 2 lines extending from the same point or by 2 surfaces diverging from the same line ☞ MATHEMATICS, SYMBOL **b** a measure of the amount of turning necessary to bring one line of an angle to coincide with the other at all points **3a** a precise viewpoint; an aspect **b** a special approach or technique for accomplishing an objective **4** a divergent course or position; a slant – esp in *at an angle* [ME, fr MF, fr L *angulus*; akin to OE *anclēow* ankle] – **angled** *adj*

[2]**angle** *vb* **angling** /ˈang·gling/ *vt* **1** to place, move, or direct obliquely **2** to present (e g a news story) from a particular or prejudiced point of view; slant ~ *vi* to turn or proceed at an angle

[3]**angle** *vi* **angling** /ˈang·gling/ **1** to fish with a hook and line **2** to use artful means to attain an objective ⟨~d *for an invitation*⟩ [ME *angelen*, fr *angel* fishhook, fr OE, fr *anga* hook; akin to OHG *ango* hook, L *uncus*, Gk *onkos* barbed hook, *ankos* glen] – **angler** /ˈang·glə/ *n*

Angle *n* a member of a Germanic people who invaded England along with the Saxons and Jutes in the 5th c AD [L *Angli*, pl, a word of Gmc origin; akin to OE *Engle* Angles] – **Anglian** /ˈang·gli·ən/ *n or adj*

ˈangle ,bracket *n* either of a pair of punctuation marks ⟨ ⟩ used to enclose matter

ˈangle ,iron *n* a rolled steel structural member having an L-shaped section

ˈangler ,fish /ˈang·glə/ *n* a fish with a large flattened head and wide mouth with a lure on the head used to attract smaller fishes as prey

Anglican /ˈang·glikən/ *adj* of the body of churches including the established episcopal Church of England and churches of similar faith in communion with it [ML *anglicanus*, fr *anglicus* English, fr LL *Angli* English people, fr L, Angles] – **Anglican** *n*, **Anglicanism** *n*

anglice /ˈang·glisi/ *adv, often cap* in English ⟨*the city of Napoli,* ~ *Naples*⟩ [ML, adv of *anglicus*]

anglicism /ˈangli,siz(ə)m/ *n, often cap* **1** a characteristic feature of English occurring in another language **2** adherence or attachment to England, English culture, etc [ML *anglicus* English]

Anglicist /ˈang·glisist/ *n* a specialist in English language, literature, or culture – not usu used for native speakers of English

anglic·ize, -ise /ˈang·gli,siez/ *vt, often cap* **1** to make English in tastes or characteristics **2** to adapt (a foreign word or phrase) to English usage – **anglicization** /-sieˈzaysh(ə)n, -si-/ *n, often cap*

angling /ˈang·gling/ *n* (the sport of) fishing with hook and line [fr gerund of [3] *angle*] – **angler** /ˈang·glə/ *n*

Anglo- /,ang·gloh-/ *comb form* English nation, people, or culture ⟨Anglo*phobia*⟩; English and ⟨Anglo-*Japanese*⟩ [NL, fr LL *Angli*]

,Anglo-Aˈmerican /,ang·gloh-/ *n or adj* (a) N American, esp of the USA, of English origin or descent

,Anglo-ˈCatholic *adj* of a High Church movement in Anglicanism fostering Catholic dogmatic and liturgical traditions – **Anglo-Catholic** *n*, **Anglo-Catholicism** *n*

,Anglo-ˈFrench *n* the French language used in medieval England

,Anglo-ˈIndian *n* **1** a British person domiciled for a long time in India **2** a Eurasian of mixed British and Indian birth or descent – **Anglo-Indian** *adj*

,Anglo-'Irish *n* *the* formerly dominant group of English Protestant settlers in Ireland – **Anglo-Irish** *adj*

,Anglo-'Norman *n* **1** a Norman living in England after the Conquest **2** the form of Anglo-French used by Anglo-Normans

anglophile /'ang·glәfiel, -fil/ *also* **anglophil** /-fil/ *n, often cap* a foreigner who is greatly interested in and admires England and things English [F, fr *anglo-* + *-phile*] – **anglophilia** /,ang·glә'fili·ә/ *n, often cap,* **anglophilic** *adj, often cap,* **anglophilism** /ang'glofi,liz(ә)m/ *n, often cap,* **anglophily** *n*

anglophobe /'ang·glә,fohb/ *n, often cap* a foreigner who is averse to England and things English [prob fr F, fr *anglo-* + *-phobe*] – **anglophobia** /-'fohbi·ә/ *n, often cap,* **anglophobic** *adj, often cap*

'anglo,phone /-,fohn/ *adj, often cap* consisting of or belonging to an English-speaking population – **Anglophone** *n*

,Anglo-'Saxon *n* **1** a member of the Germanic peoples who conquered England in the 5th c AD and formed the ruling group until the Norman conquest **2** sby of English, esp Anglo-Saxon, descent **3** OLD ENGLISH ☞ LANGUAGE [NL *Anglo-Saxones,* pl, alter. of ML *Angli Saxones,* fr L *Angli* Angles + LL *Saxones* Saxons] – **Anglo-Saxon** *adj*

angora /ang'gawrә/ *n* **1** the hair of the Angora rabbit or goat **2** a fabric or yarn made (in part) of Angora rabbit hair, used esp for knitting – compare MOHAIR **3** *cap* an Angora cat, goat, or rabbit [*Angora* (Ankara), capital city of Turkey]

An,gora 'cat *n* a long-haired domestic cat

An,gora 'goat *n* (any of) a breed of the domestic goat raised for its long silky hair which is the true mohair

An,gora 'rabbit *n* a long-haired usu white domestic rabbit

angostura bark /,ang·gә'stooәrә/ *n* the aromatic bitter bark of a S American tree of the rue family used as a bitter and formerly as a tonic [*Angostura* (now Ciudad Bolivar), town in Venezuela]

angry /'ang·gri/ *adj* **1** feeling or showing anger ⟨~ *with his brother*⟩ ⟨~ *at his rude remark*⟩ **2** seeming to show or typify anger ⟨*an* ~ *sky*⟩ **3** painfully inflamed ⟨*an* ~ *rash*⟩ – **angrily** *adv,* **angriness** *n*

angst /angst/ *n* anxiety and anguish, caused esp by considering the state of the world and the human condition [Dan & G; Dan, fr G; akin to L *angustus*]

angstrom /'angstrәm, -,strom/ *n* a unit of length equal to 10^{-10}m – not now recommended for technical use ☞ PHYSICS [Anders J *Ångström* †1874 Sw physicist]

anguish /'ang·gwish/ *n* extreme physical pain or mental distress [ME *angwisshe,* fr OF *angoisse,* fr L *angustiae,* pl, straits, distress, fr *angustus* narrow; akin to OE *enge* narrow – more at ANGER]

anguished *adj* suffering or expressing anguish

angular /'ang·gyoolә/ *adj* **1a** having 1 or more angles **b** forming an angle; sharp-cornered **2** measured by an angle ⟨~ *distance*⟩ ⟨~ *separation*⟩ **3a** stiff in character or manner; awkward **b** lean, bony [MF or L; MF *angulaire,* fr L *angularis,* fr *angulus* angle] – **angularly** *adv,* **angularity** /,ang·gyoo'larәti/ *n*

,angular mo'mentum *n* the product of the angular velocity of a rotating body or system and its moment of inertia with respect to the rotation axis

,angular ve'locity *n* the rate of change of angular position with time

Angus /'ang·gәs/ *n* ABERDEEN ANGUS [*Angus,* county in Scotland]

anhedral /an'heedrәl/ *n* the angle between a downwardly inclined wing of an aircraft and a horizontal line [*an-* + *-hedral*]

anhydride /an'hiedried/ *n* a compound derived from another, esp an acid, by removal of the elements of water

anhydrous /an'hiedrәs/ *adj* free from water (of crystallization) [Gk *anydros,* fr *a-* + *hydōr* water – more at WATER]

anilinctus /,ayni'lingktәs/ *n* anilingus [NL, fr *anus* + *-i-* + *-linctus* (as in *cunnilinctus*)]

aniline /'anilin, -leen/ *n* a liquid amine used chiefly in organic chemical synthesis (e g of dyes) [G *anilin,* fr *anil* indigo, fr F, fr Pg, fr Ar *an-nīl* the indigo plant, fr Skt *nīlī* indigo, fr fem of *nīla* dark blue]

,aniline 'dye *n* a synthetic organic dye; *specif* one made from or chemically related to aniline

anilingus /,ayni'ling·gәs/ *n* erotic oral stimulation of the anus [NL, fr *anus* + *-i-* + *-lingus* (as in *cunnilingus*)]

anima /'animә/ *n* an individual's true inner self reflecting archetypal ideals of conduct; *also* an inner feminine part of the male personality – used in Jungian psychology; compare ANIMUS 3, PERSONA 2 [NL, fr L, soul]

animadversion /,animad'vuhsh(ә)n/ *n* **1** a critical and usu censorious remark **2** hostile criticism *USE* fml [L *animadversion-, animadversio,* fr *animadversus,* pp of *animadvertere*]

animadvert /,animad'vuht/ *vi* to comment critically or adversely *on* – fml [L *animadvertere* to pay attention to, censure, fr *animum advertere,* lit., to turn the mind to]

¹animal /'animәl/ *n* **1** any of a kingdom of living things typically differing from plants in their capacity for spontaneous movement, esp in response to stimulation **2a** any of the lower animals as distinguished from human beings **b** a mammal – not in technical use **3** a person considered as a purely physical being; a creature [L, fr *animale,* neut of *animalis* animate, fr *anima* soul] – **animallike** *adj,* **animalness** *n*

²animal *adj* **1** of or derived from animals **2** of the body as opposed to the mind or spirit – chiefly derog – **animally** *adv*

animalcule /,ani'malkyoohl/ *n* a minute usu microscopic organism [NL *animalculum,* dim. of L *animal*] – **animalcular** /-kyoolә/ *adj*

animalculum /,ani'malkyoolәm/ *n, pl* **animalcula** /-lә/ an animalcule

animalism /'animә,liz(ә)m/ *n* **1a** the state of having qualities typical of animals; lack of spiritual feeling **b** preoccupation with the satisfaction of physical drives; sensuality **2** a theory that human beings are nothing more than animals – **animalist** *n,* **animalistic** /-'listik/ *adj*

animality /,ani'malәti/ *n* **1** ANIMALISM 1a **2a** the state of being an animal **b** animal nature **3** ANIMAL KINGDOM

animal·ize, -ise /'animә,liez/ *vt* **1** to brutalize ⟨*men* ~d *by the war*⟩ **2** to sensualize ⟨~d *by passion*⟩ – **animalization** /-lie'zaysh(ә)n, -li-/ *n*

animal kingdom *n* that one of the 3 basic groups of natural objects that includes all living and extinct animals – compare MINERAL KINGDOM, PLANT KINGDOM

,animal 'magnetism *n* **1** a force held to reside in some individuals by which a strong hypnotic influence can be exerted **2** physical charm

[1]**animate** /'animət/ *adj* **1** possessing life; alive **2** of animal life **3** lively [ME, fr L *animatus*, pp of *animare* to give life to, fr *anima* breath, soul; akin to OE *ōthian* to breathe, L *animus* spirit, mind, courage, Gk *anemos* wind, Skt *aniti* he breathes] – **animately** *adv*, **animateness** *n*

[2]**animate** /'animayt/ *vt* **1** to give spirit and support to; encourage **2** to give life or vigour to **3** to produce in the form of an animated cartoon – **animatedly** *adv*

,animated car'toon *n* a film that creates the illusion of movement by photographing successive positional changes (e g of drawings)

animation /,ani'maysh(ə)n/ *n* **1** vigorous liveliness **2** (the preparation of) an animated cartoon [[2]ANIMATE + -ION]

animato /,ani'mahtoh/ *adv or adj* with liveliness and vigour – used in music [It, fr L *animatus*]

animator /'animaytə/ *n* the artist responsible for the production of the illusion of movement in animated cartoons

animism /'animiz(ə)m/ *n* attribution of conscious life, spirits, or souls to nature or natural objects or phenomena [G *animismus*, fr L *anima* soul] – **animist** *n*, **animistic** /-'mistik/ *adj*

animosity /,ani'mosəti/ *n* powerful often active ill will or resentment [ME *animosite*, fr MF or LL; MF *animosité*, fr LL *animositat-, animositas*, fr L *animosus* spirited, fr *animus*]

animus /'animəs/ *n* **1** a pervading attitude or spirit **2** ill will, animosity **3** an inner masculine part of the female personality – used in Jungian psychology; compare ANIMA [L, spirit, mind, courage, anger]

anion /'an,ie·ən/ *n* a negatively charged ion (that moves towards the anode in an electrolysed solution) – compare CATION [Gk, neut of *aniōn*, prp of *anienai* to go up, fr *ana-* + *ienai* to go – more at ISSUE] – **anionic** /,anie'onik/ *adj*, **anionically** *adv*

anis- /an,ies-/, **aniso-** *comb form* unequal; unlike ⟨aniso*dactylous*⟩ ⟨aniso*metropia*⟩ [NL, fr Gk, fr *anisos*, fr *a-* + *isos* equal]

anise /'anis/ *n* a plant of the carrot family with aromatic seeds of a liquorice-like flavour; *also* aniseed [ME *anis*, fr OF, fr L *anisum*, fr Gk *annēson*, *anison*]

aniseed /'anəseed/ *n* the seed of anise used esp as a flavouring (e g in liqueurs) [ME *anis seed*, fr *anis* + *seed*]

anisotropic /,aniesoh'trohpik, -'tropik/ *adj* exhibiting properties with different values when measured in different directions ⟨*an ~ crystal*⟩ [ISV *an-* + *isotropic*] – **anisotropically** *adv*, **anisotropy** /,anie'sotrəpi/, **anisotropism** /-'sotrə,piz(ə)m/ *n*

ankh /angk/ *n* a cross having a loop for its upper vertical arm and serving, esp in ancient Egypt, as an emblem of life ☞ SYMBOL [Egypt *'nh*]

ankle /'angkl/ *n* **1** the (region of the) joint between the foot and the leg; the tarsus **2** the joint between the cannon bone and pastern of a horse or related animal [ME *ankel*, fr OE *anclēow*; akin to OHG *anchlāo* ankle, L *angulus* angle]

anklet /'angklit/ *n* an ornamental band or chain worn round the ankle

ankylose /'angkilohz, -lohs/ *vb* to unite by, stiffen by, or undergo ankylosis [back-formation fr *ankylosis*]

ankylosis /,angki'lohsis/ *n, pl* **ankyloses** /-,seez/ **1** abnormal or surgical union of the bones in a joint resulting in a stiff or immovable joint **2** union of separate bones or hard parts to form a single bone or part [NL, fr Gk *ankylōsis*, fr *ankyloun* to make crooked, fr *ankylos* crooked; akin to L *uncus* hooked – more at [3]ANGLE] – **ankylotic** /-'lotik/ *adj*

anlage /'an,lahgə/ *n, pl* **anlagen** /-gən/ *also* **anlages** /-gəz/ the foundation of a subsequent development; *specif* a primordium [G]

anna /'anə/ *n* (a coin representing) a former money unit of Burma, India, and Pakistan worth $^1/_{16}$ rupee [Hindi *ānā*]

annalist /'anl·ist/ *n* a writer of annals; a historian – **annalistic** /-'istik/ *adj*

annals /'anlz/ *n pl* **1** a record of events, activities, etc, arranged in yearly sequence **2** historical records; chronicles [L *annales*, fr pl of *annalis* yearly – more at ANNUAL]

Annamese /,anə'meez/ *n, pl* **Annamese** **1** a member of a Mongolian people inhabiting Vietnam **2** the language of the Annamese; Vietnamese [*Annam*, region of Vietnam] – **Annamese** *adj*, **Annamite** /'anəmiet/ *adj*

annatto /ə'natoh/ *n* a yellowish red dye made from the pulp round the seeds of a tropical tree [of Cariban origin; akin to Galibi *annoto* tree producing annatto]

anneal /ə'neel/ *vt* **1** to toughen or relieve internal stresses in (steel, glass, etc) by heating and usu gradually cooling **2** to temper, toughen [ME *anelen*, fr OE *onǣlan*, fr *on* + *ǣlan* to set on fire, burn, fr *āl* fire; akin to OE *ād* funeral pyre – more at EDIFY]

annelid /'anəlid/ *n* any of a phylum of usu elongated segmented invertebrates (e g earthworms and leeches) [deriv of L *anellus* little ring, dim. of *annulus* ring] – **annelid** *adj*, **annelidan** /ə'nelidən/ *adj or n*

[1]**annex** /ə'neks/ *vt* **1** to subjoin, append **2** to take possession of; *esp* to incorporate (a country or other territory) within the domain of a state [ME *annexen*, fr MF *annexer*, fr OF, fr *annexe* joined, fr L *annexus*, pp of *annectere* to bind to, fr *ad-* + *nectere* to bind] – **annexation** /,anek'saysh(ə)n/ *n*, **annexational** *adj*, **annexationist** *n*

[2]**annex**, *chiefly Br* **annexe** /'aneks/ *n* **1** sthg, esp an addition to a document, annexed or appended **2** a separate or attached extra structure; *esp* a building providing extra accommodation

annihilate /ə'nie·ə,layt/ *vt* **1** to destroy (almost) entirely **2** to defeat conclusively; rout ⟨*his team was ~d in the quarterfinals*⟩ [LL *annihilatus*, pp of *annihilare* to reduce to nothing, fr L *ad-* + *nihil* nothing – more at NIL] – **annihilator** /-,laytə/ *n*, **annihilative** /-lətiv/ *adj*, **annihilatory** /-lətri/ *adj*, **annihilation** /-'laysh(ə)n/ *n*

anni mirabiles /,ani mi'rahbilayz, -leez/ *pl of* ANNUS MIRABILIS

anniversary /,ani'vuhs(ə)ri/ *n* (the celebration of) a day marking the annual recurrence of the date of a notable event [ME *anniversarie*, fr ML *anniversarium*, fr L, neut of *anniversarius* returning annually, fr *annus* year + *versus*, pp of *vertere* to turn – more at ANNUAL, [1]WORTH]

anno Domini /,anoh 'dominie/ *adv, often cap A* –

used to indicate that a year or century comes within the Christian era [ML, lit., in the year of the Lord]

,anno he'girae /hi'jie·əri/ *adv, often cap A&H* – used to indicate that a year or century comes within the Muhammadan era; compare HEGIRA [NL, lit., in the year of the Hegira]

annotate /'anətayt, 'anoh-/ *vt* to provide (e g a literary work) with notes [L *annotatus*, pp of *annotare*, fr *ad-* + *notare* to mark – more at NOTE] – **annotative** *adj*, **annotator** *n*, **annotation** /-'taysh(ə)n/ *n*

announce /ə'nowns/ *vt* **1** to make known publicly; proclaim **2a** to give notice of the arrival, presence, or readiness of **b** to indicate in advance; foretell **3** to give evidence of; indicate by action or appearance ~ *vi NAm* to serve as an announcer [ME *announcen*, fr MF *annoncer*, fr L *annuntiare*, fr *ad-* + *nuntiare* to report, fr *nuntius* messenger] – **announcement** *n*

announcer /ə'nownsə/ *n* one who introduces television or radio programmes, makes commercial announcements, reads news summaries, or gives station identification [ANNOUNCE + [2]-ER]

annoy /ə'noy/ *vt* **1** to disturb or irritate, esp by repeated acts; vex – often pass + *with* or *at* **2** to harass ~ *vi* to be a source of annoyance [ME *anoien*, fr OF *enuier*, fr LL *inodiare* to make loathsome, fr L *in* + *odium* hatred – more at ODIUM] – **annoyance** *n*, **annoyer** *n*, **annoying** *adj*, **annoyingly** *adv*

[1]**annual** /'anyoo(ə)l/ *adj* **1** covering or lasting for the period of a year ⟨~ *rainfall*⟩ **2** occurring or performed once a year; yearly ⟨*an ~ reunion*⟩ **3** *of a plant* completing the life cycle in 1 growing season [ME, fr MF & LL; MF *annuel*, fr LL *annualis*, fr L *annuus* yearly & *annalis* yearly (both fr *annus* year); akin to Goth *athnam* (dat pl) years, Skt *atati* he walks, goes] – **annually** *adv*

[2]**annual** *n* **1** a publication appearing yearly **2** sthg lasting 1 year or season; *specif* an annual plant

,annual 'ring *n* the layer of wood produced by a single year's growth of a woody plant

annuitant /ə'nyooh·it(ə)nt/ *n* a beneficiary of an annuity

annuity /ə'nyooh·əti/ *n* **1** an amount payable at a regular (e g yearly) interval **2** (a contract embodying) the right to receive or the obligation to pay an annuity [ME *annuite*, fr MF *annuité*, fr ML *annuitat-*, *annuitas*, fr L *annuus* yearly]

annul /ə'nul/ *vt* **-ll-** **1** to reduce to nothing; obliterate, cancel **2** to declare (e g a marriage) legally invalid [ME *annullen*, fr MF *annuller*, fr LL *annullare*, fr L *ad-* + *nullus* not any – more at NULL] – **annulment** *n*

annular /'anyoolə/ *adj* of or forming a ring [MF or L; MF *annulaire*, fr L *annularis*, fr *annulus* ring] – **annularly** *adv*, **annularity** /-'larəti/ *n*

,annular e'clipse *n* an eclipse of the sun in which a thin outer ring of the sun's disc remains visible

annulate /'anyoolət/, **annulated** /-,laytid/ *adj* having or composed of rings – **annulately** *adv*

annulet /'anyoolət/ *n* a small ring or circle [modif of MF *annelet*, dim. of *anel*, fr L *anellus*, dim. of *annulus, anulus* ring]

annulus /'anyooləs/ *n, pl* **annuli** /-lie/ *also* **annuluses** a ring-shaped part, structure, or marking [L, dim. of *anus* ring, anus – more at ANUS]

annunciate /ə'nunsi·ayt/ *vt* to announce – fml – **annunciator** *n*, **annunciatory** /ə'nunsi·ət(ə)ri/ *adj*

Annunciation /ə,nunsi'aysh(ə)n/ *n* (March 25 observed as a church festival commemorating) the announcement of the Incarnation to the Virgin Mary related in Luke 1:26–28 [ME *annunciacioun*, fr MF *anunciation*, fr LL *annuntiation-*, *annuntiatio*, fr L *annuntiatus*, pp of *annuntiare* – more at ANNOUNCE]

annus mirabilis /,anəs mi'rahbilis/ *n, pl* **anni mirabiles** /,anie mi'rahbilayz, -leez/ a remarkably auspicious year [NL, lit., wonderful year]

anoa /ə'noh·ə/ *n* a small wild ox of Celebes [native name in Celebes in Indonesia]

anode /'anohd/ *n* **1** the electrode by which electrons leave a device and enter an external circuit; *specif* the negative terminal of a primary or secondary cell that is delivering current – compare CATHODE **2** a positive electrode used to accelerate electrons in an electron gun [Gk *anodos* way up, fr *ana-* + *hodos* way – more at CEDE] – **anodal** /a'nohdl/ *adj*, **anodally** *adv*, **anodic** /a'nodik/ *adj*, **anodically** *adv*

anod·ize, -ise /'anohdiez, 'anədiez/ *vt* to subject (a metal) to electrolytic action by making it the anode of a cell in order to coat it with a protective or decorative film – **anodization** /,anohdie'zaysh(ə)n/ *n*

[1]**anodyne** /'anədien/ *adj* **1** easing pain **2** mentally or emotionally soothing [L *anodynos*, fr Gk *anōdynos*, fr *a-* + *odynē* pain; akin to OE *etan* to eat – more at EAT]

[2]**anodyne** *n* **1** an analgesic drug **2** sthg that soothes or calms – **anodynic** /,anə'dinik/ *adj*

anoestrus /a'neestrəs/ *adj or n* (of) the period in which there is no sexual activity between 2 periods of sexual activity in cyclically breeding mammals (e g dogs) [NL, fr *a-* + *oestrus*]

anoint /ə'noynt/ *vt* **1** to smear or rub with oil or a similar substance **2a** to apply oil to as a sacred rite, esp for consecration **b** to designate (as if) through the rite of anointment; consecrate [ME *anointen*, fr MF *enoint*, pp of *enoindre*, fr L *inunguere*, fr *in-* + *unguere* to smear – more at OINTMENT] – **anointer** *n*, **anointment** *n*

anomalous /ə'noməlas/ *adj* **1** deviating from a general rule or standard; irregular, abnormal **2** incongruous [LL *anomalus*, fr Gk *anōmalos*, lit., uneven, fr *a-* + *homalos* even, fr *homos* same – more at SAME] – **anomalously** *adv*, **anomalousness** *n*

anomaly /ə'noməli/ *n* **1** the angular distance of **a** a planet from its last perihelion **b** a satellite from its last perigee **2** deviation from the common rule; an irregularity, incongruity **3** sthg anomalous [L *anomalia*, fr Gk *anōmalia*, fr *anōmalos*] – **anomalistic** /-'listik/ *adj*

anomie, anomy /'anomi/ *n* the lack, in a society or individual, of moral or social standards of conduct and belief [F *anomie*, fr Gk *anomia* lawlessness, fr *anomos* lawless, fr *a-* + *nomos* law, fr *nemein* to distribute – more at NIMBLE] – **anomic** /a'nomik/ *adj*

anon /ə'non/ *adv, archaic* **1** soon, presently **2** at another time [ME, fr OE *on ān*, fr *on* in + *ān* one – more at ON, ONE]

anonym /'anənim/ *n* **1** an anonymous person **2** a pseudonym

anonymous /ə'nonəməs/ *adj* **1** having or giving no name ⟨*an ~ author*⟩ **2** of unknown or unnamed origin or authorship ⟨~ *gifts*⟩ **3** nondescript [LL *anonymus*, fr Gk *anōnymos*, fr *a-* + *onyma* name – more at NAME] – **anonymously** *adv*, **anonymousness** *n*, **anonymity** /ˌanəˈniməti/ *n*

anopheles /əˈnofileez/ *n* any of the genus of mosquitoes that includes all those which transmit malaria to human beings [NL, genus name, fr Gk *anōphelēs* useless, fr *a-* + *ophelos* advantage, help; akin to Skt *phalam* fruit, profit] – **anopheline** /-lien/ *adj or n*

anorak /ˈanərak/ *n, chiefly Br* a short weatherproof coat with a hood ☞ GARMENT [Greenland Esk *ánorâq*]

anorexia /ˌanəˈreksi·ə/ *n* (prolonged) loss of appetite; *specif* ANOREXIA NERVOSA [NL, fr Gk, fr *a-* + *orexis* appetite, fr *oregein* to stretch out, reach after – more at 1RIGHT] – **anorectic** /ˌanəˈrektik/ *adj or n*, **anorexigenic** /ˌanəˌreksəˈjenik/ *adj*

anoˌrexia nerˈvosa / nuhˈvohzə/ *n* pathological aversion to food induced by emotional disturbance and typically accompanied by emaciation [NL, nervous anorexia]

anosmia /aˈnozmi·ə/ *n* (partial) loss of the sense of smell [NL, fr *a-* + Gk *osmē* smell – more at ODOUR] – **anosmic** *adj*

1another /əˈnudhə/ *adj* **1** being a different or distinct one ⟨*the same scene viewed from ~ angle*⟩ **2** some other ⟨*do it ~ time*⟩ **3** being one additional ⟨*have ~ piece of pie*⟩ **4** patterned after ⟨*~ Napoleon*⟩ [ME *an other*]

2another *pron, pl* **others** **1** an additional one; one more **2** a different one ⟨*he loved ~*⟩ ⟨*for one reason or ~*⟩

anovulant /əˈnovyoolənt/ *n or adj* (a drug) that suppresses ovulation [2*a-* + *ovulate* + *-ant*]

anovulatory /əˈnovyoolət(ə)ri/ *adj* without or suppressing ovulation [2*a-* + *ovulate* + *-ory*]

anoxia /əˈnoksi·ə/ *n* hypoxia, esp so severe that it causes permanent damage [NL] – **anoxic** *adj*

anschluss /ˈanshloos (or anʃlʊs)/ *n* political union; *specif, often cap* that between Germany and Austria in 1938 [G, lit., joining, fr *anschliessen* to join]

1answer /ˈahnsə/ *n* **1** a spoken or written reply to a question, remark, etc **2** an esp correct solution to a problem **3** a response or reaction ⟨*his only ~ was to walk out*⟩ **4** sby or sthg intended to be a close equivalent or rival of another ⟨*Scotland's ~ to Andy Williams*⟩ [ME, fr OE *andswaru*; akin to ON *andsvar* answer; both fr a prehistoric WGmc-NGmc compound whose first constituent is represented by OE *and-* against, and whose second is akin to OE *swerian* to swear – more at ANTE-]

2answer *vi* **1** to speak, write, or act in reply **2a** to be responsible or accountable *for* **b** to make amends; atone *for* **3** to correspond *to* **4** to be adequate or usable ~ *vt* **1a** to speak or write in reply to **b** to reply to in justification or explanation ⟨*~ a charge*⟩ **2a** to correspond to **b** to be adequate or usable for **3** to act in response to (a sound or other signal) ⟨*~ the telephone*⟩ **4** to offer a solution for; *esp* to solve ⟨*~ a riddle*⟩ – **answerer** /ˈahns(ə)rə/ *n*

answerable /ˈahns(ə)rəbl/ *adj* **1** responsible **2** capable of being answered or refuted – **answerability** /-ˈbiləti/ *n*

answer back *vb, esp of a child* to reply rudely (to)

ant /ant/ *n* any of a family of insects that live in large social groups having a complex organization and hierarchy ☞ FOOD [ME *ante, emete*, fr OE *æmette*; akin to OHG *āmeiza* ant]

ant- /ant-/ – see ANTI-

1-ant /-(ə)nt/ *suffix* (→ *n*) **1** sby or sthg that performs (a specified action) ⟨*claim*ant⟩ ⟨*deodor*ant⟩ **2** thing that causes (a specified action or process) ⟨*expector*ant⟩ **3** thing that is used or acted upon (in a specified manner) ⟨*inhal*ant⟩ [ME, fr OF, fr *-ant*, prp suffix, fr L *-ant, -ans*, prp suffix of 1st conjugation, fr *-a-* (stem vowel of 1st conjugation) + *-nt-, -ns*, prp suffix; akin to OE *-nde*, prp suffix, Gk *-nt-, -n*, participle suffix]

2-ant *suffix* (→ *adj*) **1** performing (a specified action) or being (in a specified condition) ⟨*repent*ant⟩ ⟨*somnambul*ant⟩ **2** causing (a specified action or process) ⟨*expector*ant⟩

antacid /antˈasid/ *adj* that corrects excessive acidity, esp in the stomach – **antacid** /-ˈ--, ˈ-ˌ--/ *n*

antagonism /anˈtaganiz(ə)m/ *n* **1** hostility or antipathy, esp when actively expressed **2** opposition in physiological or biochemical action, esp between an agonist and an antagonist

antagonist /anˈtagənist/ *n* **1** an opponent, adversary **2** a drug that opposes the action of another or of a substance (e g a neurotransmitter) that occurs naturally in the body

antagonistic /anˌtagəˈnistik, ˌ---ˈ--/ *adj* characterized by or resulting from antagonism; opposing – **antagonistically** *adv*

antagon·ize, -ise /anˈtaganiez/ *vt* **1** to oppose or counteract **2** to provoke the hostility of [Gk *antagōnizesthai*, fr *anti-* + *agōnizesthai* to struggle, fr *agōn* contest – more at AGONY]

antarctic /anˈtahktik/ *adj, often cap* of the South Pole or surrounding region [ME *antartik*, fr L *antarcticus*, fr Gk *antarktikos*, fr *anti-* + *arktikos* arctic – more at ARCTIC]

anˌtarctic ˈcircle *n, often cap A&C* the parallel of latitude approx 66½° south of the equator that circumscribes the south polar region

ˈant ˌbear *n* an aardvark

1ante /ˈanti/ *n* **1** a poker stake usu put up before the deal **2** an amount paid ⟨*these improvements would raise the ~*⟩ – infml [*ante-*]

2ante *vt* **anteing** to put up (an ante) – compare ANTE UP

ante- *prefix* **1a** prior; before ⟨ante*cedent*⟩ ⟨ante*date*⟩ **b** prior to; earlier than ⟨ante*diluvian*⟩ **2** anterior; situated before ⟨ante*room*⟩ [ME, fr L, fr *ante* before, in front of; akin to OE *and-* against, Gk *anti* before, against – more at END]

ˈantˌeater /-ˌeetə/ *n* any of several mammals that feed (chiefly) on ants and termites: e g **a** an edentate; *specif* GIANT ANTEATER **b** an echidna **c** an aardvark

antebellum /ˌantiˈbeləm/ *adj* existing before the war, esp the US Civil War ⟨*an ~ brick mansion*⟩ [L *ante bellum* before the war]

1antecedent /ˌantiˈseed(ə)nt/ *n* **1** a word, phrase, or clause functioning as a noun and referred to by a pronoun **2** the premise of a conditional proposition (e g *if A* in 'if A, then B") **3** the first term of a mathematical ratio **4** a preceding thing, event, or circumstance **5a** a model or stimulus for later developments ⟨*the boneshaker was the ~ of the modern bicycle*⟩ **b** *pl* family origins; parentage [ME, fr ML & L; ML *antecedent-, antecedens*, fr L, logical antecedent, lit., sthg that goes before, fr neut of *antecedent-, antecedens*, prp of *antecedere* to precede]

[2]**antecedent** *adj* **1** prior in time or order **2** causally or logically prior – **antecedently** *adv*

antechamber /'anti,chaymbə/ *n* an anteroom [F *antichambre*, fr MF, fr It *anti-* (fr L *ante-*) + MF *chambre* room – more at CHAMBER]

'ante,chapel /-,chapl/ *n* a porch or lobby at the west end of a chapel

'ante,date /-,dayt/ *vt* **1** to attach or assign a date earlier than the true one to (e g a document), esp with intent to deceive **2** to precede in time ⟨*his death* ~d *his brother's*⟩

,antedi'luvian /-di'loohvi·ən/ *adj* **1** of the period before the flood described in the Bible **2** completely out-of-date; antiquated ⟨*an* ~ *car*⟩ [*ante-* + L *diluvium* flood – more at DELUGE] – **antediluvian** *n*

antelope /'antilohp/ *n, pl* **antelopes,** *esp collectively* **antelope** **1** any of various Old World ruminant mammals that are lighter and more graceful than the true oxen **2** leather made from antelope hide [ME, fabulous heraldic beast, prob fr MF *antelop* savage animal with sawlike horns, fr ML *anthalopus*, fr LGk *antholop-, antholops*]

ante meridiem /,anti mə'ridi·əm/ *adj* being before noon – abbr *am* [L]

,ante'mortem /-'mawtəm/ *adj* preceding death [L *ante mortem*]

,ante'natal /-'naytl/ *adj* of or concerned with an unborn child, pregnancy, or a pregnant woman; prenatal ⟨*an* ~ *clinic*⟩

antenna /an'tenə/ *n, pl* **antennae** /-ni/, **antennas** **1** a movable segmented sense organ on the head of insects, myriapods, and crustaceans ☞ ANATOMY **2** an aerial – chiefly used in Br with reference to complex aerials [ML, fr L *antemna, antenna* sail yard] – **antennal** *adj*

ante-post /'anti ,pohst/ *adj* of, occurring in, or placed in the period before the day of a horse race [*ante-* + [1] *post*; fr the post on which are displayed the numbers of the horses to run]

anterior /an'tiəri·ə/ *adj* **1** before in time **2** situated before or towards the front: e g **a** *of an animal part* near the head; cephalic **b** *of the human body or its parts* ventral **3** *of a plant part* (on the side) facing away from the stem or axis; *also* INFERIOR 4a ***USE*** compare POSTERIOR [L, compar of *ante* before – more at ANTE-] – **anteriorly** *adv*

anteroom /'anti,roohm, -room/ *n* an outer room that leads to another usu more important one, often used as a waiting room

ante up /'anti/ *vb, chiefly NAm* PAY UP [[2]*ante*]

anth- – see ANTI-

anthelion /ant'heelyən, an'thee-/ *n, pl* **anthelia** /-lyə/, **anthelions** a luminous spot appearing on the parhelic circle opposite the sun [Gk *anthēlion*, fr neut of *anthēlios* opposite the sun, fr *anti-* + *hēlios* sun – more at [1]SOLAR]

anthelmintic /,ant·hel'mintik, ,anthel-/ *adj* expelling or destroying parasitic worms (e g tapeworms) [*anti-* + Gk *helminth-, helmis* worm – more at HELMINTH] – **anthelmintic** *n*

anthem /'anthəm/ *n* **1a** an antiphon **b** a piece of church music for voices usu set to a biblical text **2** a song or hymn of praise or gladness [ME *antem*, fr OE *antefn*, fr LL *antiphona*, fr LGk *antiphōna*, pl of *antiphōnon*, fr Gk, neut of *antiphōnos* responsive, fr *anti-* + *phōnē* sound – more at [1]BAN]

anther /'anthə/ *n* the part of a stamen that contains and releases pollen ☞ PLANT [NL *anthera*, fr L, medicine made of flowers, fr Gk *anthēra*, fr fem of *anthēros* flowery, fr *anthos* flower] – **antheral** *adj*

antheridium /,anthə'ridi·əm/ *n, pl* **antheridia** /-di·ə/ the male reproductive organ of a fern or related plant [NL, fr *anthera* + *-idium*] – **antheridial** *adj*

'ant,hill /-,hil/ *n* **1** a mound thrown up by ants or termites in digging their nest **2** a place (e g a city) that is overcrowded and constantly busy ⟨*the human* ~ – H G Wells⟩

anthocyanin /,anthoh'sie·ənin/ *also* **anthocyan** /-'sie,an/ *n* any of various blue to red plant pigments [Gk *anthos* + *kyanos* dark blue]

antholog·ize, -ise /an'tholəjiez/ *vt* to compile or publish in an anthology – **anthologizer** *n*

anthology /an'tholəji/ *n* **1** a collection of selected literary pieces or passages **2** a collection of selected non-literary works ⟨*a fine* ~ *of Byzantine icons*⟩ [NL *anthologia* collection of epigrams, fr MGk, fr Gk, flower gathering, fr *anthos* flower (akin to Skt *andha* herb) + *logia* collecting, fr *legein* to gather – more at LEGEND] – **anthologist** *n*

anthozoan /,anthə'zoh·ən/ *n* any of a class of marine coelenterates that includes the corals and sea anemones [deriv of Gk *anthos* + *zōion* animal; akin to Gk *zōē* life – more at [1]QUICK] – **anthozoan** *adj*

anthracene /'anthrə,seen/ *n* a cyclic hydrocarbon obtained from coal tar and used in the synthesis of dyestuffs

anthracite /'anthrə,siet/ *n* a hard slow-burning coal containing little volatile matter [Gk *anthrakitis*, fr *anthrak, anthrax* coal] – **anthracitic** /-'sitik/ *adj*

anthrax /'anthraks/ *n* an often fatal infectious disease of warm-blooded animals (e g cattle, sheep, or human beings) caused by a spore-forming bacterium [ME *antrax* carbuncle, fr L *anthrax*, fr Gk, coal, carbuncle]

anthrop-, anthropo- *comb form* human being ⟨anthrop*ology*⟩ [L *anthropo-*, fr Gk *anthrōp-, anthrōpo-*, fr *anthrōpos*]

anthropocentric /,anthrəpə'sentrik, -poh-/ *adj* considering human beings to be the most significant entities of the universe – **anthropocentrically** *adv*, **anthropocentricity** /-sen'trisəti/ *n*

anthropogenesis /,anthrəpoh'jenəsis/ *n* the study of the origin and development of human beings [NL, fr *anthrop-* + L *genesis*] – **anthropogenetic** /-jə'netik/ *adj*, **anthropogeny** /,anthrə'pojəni/ *n*

anthropography /,anthrə'pogrəfi/ *n* a branch of anthropology dealing with the geographical distribution of human beings

anthropoid /'anthrə,poyd/ *adj* **1** resembling human beings or the anthropoid apes (e g in form or behaviour); apelike **2** resembling an ape ⟨~ *gangsters*⟩ [Gk *anthrōpoeidēs*, fr *anthrōpos*]

,anthropoid 'ape *n* APE 1

anthropology /,anthrə'poləji/ *n* the scientific study of human beings, esp in relation to physical characteristics, social relations and culture, and the origin and distribution of races [NL *anthropologia*, fr *anthrop-* + *-logia* -logy] – **anthropologist** *n*, **anthropological** /,anthrəpə'lojikl/ *adj*, **anthropologically** *adv*

anthropometry /,anthrə'pomətri/ *n* the study of the measurement of the human body [F *anthro-*

pométrie, fr *anthrop-* + *-métrie* -metry] – **anthropometric** /ˌanthrəpəˈmetrik, -poh-/ *adj,* **anthropometrical** *adj,* **anthropometrically** *adv*

anthropomorphic /ˌanthrəpəˈmawfik/, **anthropomorphous** /-fəs/ *adj* **1** having a human form or human attributes ⟨~ *deities*⟩ **2** ascribing human characteristics to nonhuman things [LL *anthropomorphus* of human form, fr Gk *anthrōpomorphos,* fr *anthrōp-* + *-morphos* -morphous] – **anthropomorphically** *adv,* **anthropomorphously** *adv*

anthropomorphism /ˌanthrəpəˈmawfiz(ə)m/ *n* the ascribing of human behaviour, form, etc to what is not human (e g a god or animal); humanization – **anthropomorphist** *n,* **anthropomorphize** *vt*

anthropophagous /ˌanthrəˈpofəgəs/ *adj* feeding on human flesh – **anthropophagy** /-ji/ *n*

anthropophagus /ˌanthrəˈpofəgəs/ *n, pl* **anthropophagi** /-gie/ a man-eater, cannibal [L, fr Gk *anthrōpophagos,* fr *anthrōp-* + *-phagos* -phagous]

¹anti /ˈanti/ *n, pl* **antis** an opponent of a practice or policy [*anti-*]

²anti *prep* opposed or antagonistic to

anti-, ant-, anth- *prefix* **1a** of the same kind but situated opposite; in the opposite direction to ⟨anti*podes*⟩ ⟨anti*clockwise*⟩ **b** opposite in kind to ⟨anti*climax*⟩ ⟨anti-*hero*⟩ **2a** opposing or hostile to in opinion, sympathy, or practice ⟨anti-*Semite*⟩ ⟨anti*slavery*⟩ **b** opposing in effect or activity; preventing ⟨anti*septic*⟩ ⟨anti-*thief device*⟩ **3** being the antimatter counterpart of ⟨anti*neutrino*⟩ **4** combatting or defending against ⟨anti*aircraft*⟩ ⟨anti*tank*⟩ [*anti-* fr ME, fr OF & L; OF, fr L, against, fr Gk, fr *anti-; ant-* fr ME, fr L, against, fr Gk, fr *anti; anth-* fr L, against, fr Gk, fr *anti* – more at ANTE-]

antiballistic missile /ˌantibəˈlistik/ *n* a missile for intercepting and destroying ballistic missiles

ˌantibiˈosis /-bieˈohsis/ *n* antagonism between organisms, specif microorganisms, or between one organism and a metabolic product of another [NL, fr *anti-* + *-biosis*]

ˌantibiˈotic /-bieˈotik/ *n* a substance produced by a microorganism and able in dilute solution to inhibit the growth of or kill another microorganism – **antibiotic** *adj,* **antibiotically** *adv*

ˈantiˌbody /-ˌbodi/ *n* a protein (e g an immunoglobulin) that is produced by the body in response to a specific antigen and that counteracts its effects (e g by neutralizing toxins or grouping bacteria into clumps)

antic /ˈantik/ *n* a ludicrous act or action; a caper – usu pl ⟨*childish* ~s⟩ [It *antico,* lit., ancient, fr L *antiquus* – more at ANTIQUE]

ˈAntiˌchrist /-ˌkriest/ *n* an enemy of Christ; *specif* a great personal opponent of Christ expected to appear shortly before the end of the world – usu + *the* [ME *anticrist,* fr OF & LL; OF, fr LL *Antichristus,* fr Gk *Antichristos,* fr *anti-* + *Christos* Christ]

anticipate /anˈtisipayt/ *vt* **1** to give advance thought, discussion, or treatment to **2** to foresee and deal with in advance; forestall **3** to use, expend, or act on before the right or natural time **4** to act before (another) often so as to thwart **5** to look forward to as certain; expect ~ *vi* to speak or write in knowledge or expectation of sthg due to happen [L *anticipatus,* pp of *anticipare,* fr *ante-* + *-cipare* (fr *capere* to take) – more at HEAVE] – **anticipator** *n,* **anticipatable** /-ˌpaytəbl/ *adj,* **anticipative** /-pətiv/ *adj,* **anticipatively** *adv,* **anticipatory** /anˈtisipətri, -ˌpaytəri/ *adj*

anticipation /anˌtisiˈpaysh(ə)n/ *n* an act of looking forward; *specif* pleasurable expectation [ANTICIPATE + -ION]

ˌantiˈclerical /-ˈklerikl/ *adj* opposed to the influence of the clergy or church in secular affairs – **anticlerical** *n,* **anticlericalism** *n,* **anticlericalist** *n*

ˌantiˈclimax /-ˈkliemaks/ *n* **1** (an instance of) the usu sudden and ludicrous descent in writing or speaking from a significant to a trivial idea **2** an event (e g at the end of a series) that is strikingly less important or exciting than expected – **anticlimactic** /-klieˈmaktik/, **anticlimactical** *adj,* **anticlimactically** *adv*

ˈantiˌcline /-ˌklien/ *n* an arch of stratified rock in which the layers bend downwards in opposite directions from the crest – compare SYNCLINE ☞ GEOGRAPHY [back-formation fr *anticlinal,* fr *anti-* + Gk *klinein* to lean] – **anticlinal** /-ˈklienl/ *adj*

ˌantiˈclockwise /-ˈklokwiez/ *adj or adv* in a direction opposite to that in which the hands of a clock rotate when viewed from the front

ˌanticoˈagulant /-kohˈagyoolənt/ *n or adj* (a substance) that inhibits the clotting of blood

ˌantiˈcodon /-ˈkohdon/ *n* a group of 3 nucleotide bases in a transfer RNA molecule that identifies the amino acid carried and that binds to a complementary codon in messenger RNA during protein synthesis at a ribosome [*anti-* + *codon*]

ˌanticonˈvulsant /-kənˈvuls(ə)nt/, **anticonvulsive** /-siv/ *adj* used in treating, controlling, or preventing esp epileptic convulsions – **anticonvulsant** *n*

ˌantiˈcyclone /-ˈsieklohn/ *n* **1** a system of winds that rotates about a centre of high atmospheric pressure **2** ³HIGH 1 [*anti-* + *cyclone*] – **anticyclonic** /-sieˈklonik/ *adj*

ˌantideˈpressant /-diˈpres(ə)nt/, **antidepressive** /-siv/ *adj, esp of a drug* used to relieve mental depression – **antidepressant** *n*

antidiuretic hormone /-dieyooˈretik/ *n* vasopressin

antidote /ˈantiˌdoht/ *n* **1** a remedy that counteracts the effects of poison **2** sthg that relieves or counteracts ⟨*an* ~ *to the mechanization of our society*⟩ [ME *antidot,* fr L *antidotum,* fr Gk *antidotos,* fr fem of *antidotos* given as an antidote, fr *antididonai* to give as an antidote, fr *anti-* + *didonai* to give – more at ²DATE] – **antidotal** /ˌantiˈdohtl/ *adj*

ˌantiˈdromic /-ˈdromik/ *adj, esp of a nerve impulse or fibre* proceeding or conducting in a direction opposite to the usual one [*anti-* + *drom-* (fr Gk *dromos* racecourse, running) + *-ic* – more at DROMEDARY]

ˈantiˌfreeze /-ˌfreez/ *n* a substance added to a liquid (e g the water in a car radiator) to lower its freezing point

antigen /ˈantijən/ *n* a protein, carbohydrate, etc that stimulates the production of an antibody when introduced into the body [ISV *anti-* + *-gen*] – **antigenic** /-ˈjenik/ *adj,* **antigenically** *adv,* **antigenicity** /-jəˈnisəti/ *n*

ˈantiˌgravity /-ˌgravəti/ *n* a supposed effect resulting from cancellation or reduction of the force of gravity – **antigravity** *adj*

ˈanti-ˌhero, *fem* **ˈanti-ˌheroine** *n* a protagonist who lacks traditional heroic qualities (e g courage) – **anti-heroic** /ˌ-- -ˈ--/ *adj*

ˌantiˈhistamine /-ˈhistəmin/ *n* any of various compounds that oppose the actions of histamine and are used esp for treating allergies and motion sickness – **antihistaminic** /-ˈminik/ *adj or n*

ˌantiˈknock /-ˈnok/ *n* a substance added to fuel to prevent knocking in an internal-combustion engine

ˈantiˌlog /-ˌlog/ *n* an antilogarithm

ˌantiˈlogarithm /-ˈlogəˌridhəm/ *n* the number corresponding to a given logarithm

ˌantimaˈcassar /-məˈkasə/ *n* a usu protective cover put over the backs or arms of upholstered seats [*anti-* + *Macassar* (*oil*) (a hairdressing), fr *Macassar*, district of Celebes in Indonesia]

ˈantiˌmatter /-ˌmatə/ *n* matter composed of antiparticles (e g antiprotons instead of protons, positrons instead of electrons, and antineutrons instead of neutrons)

ˌantimeˈtabolite /-məˈtabəˌliet/ *n* a substance (e g a sulpha drug) that prevents a living organism from using a metabolite

antimonite /ˈantiməˌniet/ *n* stibnite; an ore of antimony [G *antimonit*, fr *antimon* antimony]

antimony /ˈantiməni; *NAm* ˈantiˌmohni/ *n* a trivalent and pentavalent brittle usu metallic metalloid element used esp as a constituent of alloys ☞ PERIODIC TABLE [ME *antimonie*, fr ML *antimonium*, perh modif of Ar *ithmid*, of Hamitic origin; akin to Egypt *sdm* antimony, Copt *stēm*] – **antimonial** /ˌantiˈmohnyəl, -ni·əl/ *adj*, **antimonious** *adj*

anting /ˈanting/ *n* the deliberate placing by some songbirds of living ants among their feathers

ˈantiˌnode /-ˌnohd/ *n* a region of maximum amplitude situated between adjacent nodes in a vibrating body [ISV] – **antinodal** /-ˈnohdl/ *adj*

ˌantiˈnomian /-ˈnohmi·ən/ *n* one who denies the universality of moral laws; *specif* an adherent of the (heretical) view that those whose salvation is preordained are freed from all moral restraints [ML *antinomus*, fr L *anti-* + Gk *nomos* law] – **antinomian** *adj*, **antinomianism** *n*

antinomy /anˈtinəmi/ *n* a contradiction or conflict between 2 apparently valid principles [G *antinomie*, fr L *antinomia* conflict of laws, fr Gk, fr *anti-* + *nomos* law – more at NIMBLE]

ˌantiˈoxidant /-ˈoksid(ə)nt/ *n or adj* (a substance) that inhibits oxidation reactions

ˌantiˈparticle /-ˈpahtikl/ *n* an elementary particle identical to another in mass but opposite to it in electric and magnetic properties that when brought together with its counterpart produces mutual annihilation

antipasto /ˈantiˌpastoh/ *n, pl* **antipastos** HORS D'OEUVRE – used esp with reference to Italian food [It, fr *anti-* (fr L *ante-*) + *pasto* food, fr L *pastus*, fr *pastus*, pp of *pascere* to feed – more at FOOD]

ˌantipaˈthetic /-pəˈthetik/ *adj* **1** feeling or causing aversion or opposition **2** opposed in nature or character *to* – **antipathetically** *adv*

antipathy /anˈtipəthi/ *n* a fixed aversion or dislike; a distaste [L *antipathia*, fr Gk *antipatheia*, fr *antipathēs* of opposite feelings, fr *anti-* + *pathos* experience – more at PATHOS]

ˌantipersonˈnel /-puhsəˈnel/ *adj, of a weapon* (designed) for use against people

ˌantiˈperspirant /-ˈpuhspirənt/ *n* a substance used to check excessive perspiration

antiphon /ˈantifən, -fon/ *n* a verse, usu from Scripture, said or sung usu before and after a canticle, psalm, or psalm verse as part of the liturgy [LL *antiphona* – more at ANTHEM] – **antiphonal** /anˈtifənl/ *adj*

antiphonary /anˈtifən(ə)ri/ *also* **antiphonal** /anˈtifənl/ *n* a book containing the choral parts of the Divine Office

antiphony /anˈtifəni/ *n* responsive alternation between 2 groups, esp of singers

antipodal /anˈtipədl/ *adj* **1** of the antipodes; *specif* situated at the opposite side of the earth or moon ⟨*an ~ meridian*⟩ ⟨*an ~ continent*⟩ **2** diametrically opposite ⟨*an ~ point on a sphere*⟩

antipodes /anˈtipəˌdeez/ *n pl the* region of the earth diametrically opposite; *specif, often cap* Australasia [ME *antipodes*, pl, people dwelling at opposite points on the globe, fr L, fr Gk, fr pl of *antipod-*, *antipous* with feet opposite, fr *anti-* + *pod-*, *pous* foot – more at FOOT] – **antipodean** /anˌtipəˈdee·ən/ *adj*

antipope /ˈantiˌpohp/ *n* one elected or claiming to be pope in opposition to the pope canonically chosen [MF *antipape*, fr ML *antipapa*, fr *anti-* + *papa* pope]

antipyretic /ˌantipie(ə)ˈretik/ *n or adj* (sthg, esp a drug) that reduces fever

[1]**antiquarian** /ˌantiˈkweəri·ən/ *n* one who collects or studies antiquities [L *antiquarius* antiquary]

[2]**antiquarian** *adj* **1** of antiquarians or antiquities **2** *of books or prints* old (and rare) – **antiquarianism** *n*

antiquary /ˈantikwəri/ *n* an antiquarian

antiquated /ˈantiˌkwaytid/ *adj* **1** outmoded or discredited by reason of age; out-of-date **2** advanced in age

[1]**antique** /anˈteek/ *adj* **1** belonging to or surviving from earlier, esp classical, times; ancient ⟨*ruins of an ~ city*⟩ **2** old-fashioned **3** made in an earlier period and therefore valuable ⟨*~ mirrors*⟩; *also* suggesting the style of an earlier period [MF, fr L *antiquus*, fr *ante* before – more at ANTE-]

[2]**antique** *n* **1** *the* ancient Greek or Roman style in art **2** a relic or object of ancient times **3** a work of art, piece of furniture, or decorative object made at an earlier period and sought by collectors

antiquity /anˈtikwəti/ *n* **1** ancient times; *esp* the period before the Middle Ages **2** the quality of being ancient **3** *pl* relics or monuments of ancient times [ME *antiquite*, fr MF *antiquité*, fr L *antiquitat-*, *antiquitas*, fr *antiquus*]

antirrhinum /ˌantiˈrienəm/ *n* any of a large genus of plants (e g the snapdragon or a related plant) of the figwort family with bright-coloured 2-lipped flowers [NL, genus name, fr L, snapdragon, fr Gk *antirrhinon*, fr *anti-* like (fr *anti* against, equivalent to) + *rhin-*, *rhis* nose – more at ANTI-]

ˌanti-ˈSemitism *n* hostility towards Jews – **anti-Semitic** *adj*, **anti-Semite** *n*

antisepsis /ˌantiˈsepsis/ *n* the inhibiting of the growth of microorganisms by antiseptic means

[1]**ˌantiˈseptic** /-ˈseptik/ *adj* **1a** opposing sepsis (in living tissue), specif by arresting the growth of microorganisms, esp bacteria **b** of, acting or protecting like, or using an antiseptic **2a** scrupulously clean; aseptic **b** extremely neat or orderly, esp to the point of being bare or uninteresting **3** impersonal, detached [*anti-* + Gk *sēptikos* putrefying, septic] – **antiseptically** *adv*

[2]**antiseptic** *n* an antiseptic substance; *also* a germicide

antiserum /'--,--, ,--'--/ *n* a serum containing antibodies [ISV]

,anti'social /-'sohsh(ə)l/ *adj* **1** hostile or harmful to organized society **2a** averse to the society of others; unsociable **b** *Br* UNSOCIAL 2

antistrophe /an'tistrəfi/ *n* the second of 2 inversely corresponding metrical parts [LL, fr Gk *antistrophē*, fr *anti-* + *strophē* strophe] – **antistrophic** /,anti'strofik/ *adj*, **antistrophically** *adv*

,antisym'metric /-si'metrik/ *adj* **1** relating to or being a relation (e g 'is a subset of') that implies equality of any 2 quantities for which it holds in both directions **2** having a form which would be symmetrical if the signs of the numbers describing 1 half were reversed

antithesis /an'tithəsis/ *n, pl* **antitheses** /-seez/ **1a** a contrast of ideas expressed by a parallel arrangement of words (e g in 'action, not words') **b** opposition, contrast **c** the direct opposite ⟨*his ideas are the ~ of mine*⟩ **2** the second stage of a reasoned argument, in contrast to the thesis [LL, fr Gk, lit., opposition, fr *antitithenai* to oppose, fr *anti-* + *tithenai* to set – more at [1]DO]

antithetical /,anti'thetikl/, **antithetic** *adj* **1** constituting or marked by antithesis **2** directly opposed – **antithetically** *adv*

,anti'toxin /-'toksin/ *n* (a serum containing) an antibody capable of neutralizing the specific toxin that stimulated its production in the body [ISV] – **antitoxic** *adj*

,anti'trades /-'traydz/ *n pl* westerly winds that move counter to the trade winds and become the prevailing westerly winds of middle latitudes

,anti'trust /-'trust/ *adj* of the US laws to protect trade from monopolies or unfair business practices [*anti-* + [1]*trust*]

,anti'tussive /-'tusiv/ *n or adj* (sthg) that controls or prevents coughing

'anti,type /-,tiep/ *n* **1** sthg or sby that is represented or foreshadowed by a type or symbol **2** an opposite type

,anti'venin /-'venin/ *n* (a serum containing) an antitoxin to a venom [ISV]

antler /'antlə/ *n* (a branch of) the solid periodically shed (much branched) horn of an animal of the deer family [ME *aunteler*, fr MF *antoillier*, fr (assumed) VL *anteoculare*, fr neut of *anteocularis* located before the eye, fr L *ante-* + *oculus* eye – more at EYE] – **antlered** *adj*

antonomasia /,antonə'mayzh(y)ə, -zyə/ *n* **1** the substitution of an epithet or title for a proper name (e g *his honour* for a judge) **2** the use of a proper name to denote a class (e g a *Solomon* for a wise ruler) [L, fr Gk, fr *antonomazein* to name instead, fr *anti-* instead, against + *onomazein* to name, fr *onoma* name – more at NAME]

antonym /'antənim/ *n* a word having the opposite meaning [*anti* + *-onym*] – **antonymous** /an'tonimәs/ *adj*, **antonymy** /-mi/ *n*

antrum /'antrəm/ *n, pl* **antra** /-trə/ the cavity of a hollow organ or sinus [LL, fr L, cave, fr Gk *antron*] – **antral** *adj*

anuran /ə'nyooərən/ *n or adj* (a) salientian [deriv of *a-* + Gk *oura* tail – more at SQUIRREL]

anus /'aynəs/ *n* the rear excretory opening of the alimentary canal ☞ DIGESTION [L; akin to OIr *āinne* anus]

anvil /'anvil/ *n* **1** a heavy, usu steel-faced, iron block on which metal is shaped **2** a towering anvil-shaped cloud **3** the incus ☞ NERVE [ME *anfilt*, fr OE; akin to OHG *anafalz* anvil; both fr a prehistoric WGmc compound whose first constituent is represented by OE *an* on, and whose second is akin to Sw dial *filta* to beat; akin to L *pellere* to beat – more at ON, FELT]

anxiety /ang'zie·əti/ *n* **1a** apprehensive uneasiness of mind, usu over an impending or anticipated ill **b** an ardent or earnest wish ⟨*~ to please*⟩ **c** a cause of anxiety **2** an abnormal overwhelming sense of apprehension and fear, often with doubt about one's capacity to cope with the threat [L *anxietas*, fr *anxius*]

anxious /'ang(k)shəs/ *adj* **1** troubled, worried **2** causing anxiety; worrying **3** ardently or earnestly wishing *to* [L *anxius*; akin to L *angere* to strangle, distress – more at ANGER] – **anxiously** *adv*, **anxiousness** *n*

[1]any /'eni/ *adj* **1** one or some indiscriminately; whichever is chosen ⟨*~ plan is better than none*⟩ **2** one, some, or all; whatever: e g **a** of whatever number or quantity; being even the smallest number or quantity of ⟨*have you ~ money?*⟩ ⟨*never get ~ letters*⟩ **b** no matter how great ⟨*at ~ cost*⟩ **c** no matter how ordinary or inadequate ⟨*wear just ~ old thing*⟩ **3** being an appreciable number, part, or amount of – not in positive statements ⟨*not for ~ length of time*⟩ [ME, fr OE *ǣnig*; akin to OHG *einag* any, OE *ān* one – more at ONE]

[2]any *pron, pl* **any** **1** any person; anybody ⟨*~ of us*⟩ **2a** any thing **b** any part, quantity, or number ⟨*hardly ~ of it*⟩

[3]any *adv* to any extent or degree; AT ALL ⟨*not feeling ~ better*⟩

anybody /'eni,bodi, -bədi/ *pron* any person ⟨*has ~ lost their glasses?*⟩

'any,how /-,how/ *adv* **1** in a haphazard manner ⟨*thrown down all ~*⟩ **2** anyway

any'more /-'maw/ *adv* at the present time; now – usu in negatives

'anyone /-wun, -wən/ *pron* anybody

'any,place /-,plays/ *adv, NAm* anywhere

'any,road /-,rohd/ *adv, Br* anyway – nonstandard

[1]'any,thing /-,thing/ *pron* any thing whatever ⟨*do ~ for a quiet life*⟩ – **anything but** not at all; far from

[2]anything *adv* in any degree; AT ALL ⟨*isn't ~ like so cold*⟩

'any,way /-,way/ *adv* **1** in any case, inevitably ⟨*going to be hanged ~*⟩ **2** – used when resuming a narrative ⟨*well, ~, I rang the bell*

[1]'any,where /-,weə/ *adv* **1** in, at, or to any place ⟨*too late to go ~*⟩ **2** to any extent; AT ALL ⟨*isn't ~ near ready*⟩ **3** – used to indicate limits of variation ⟨*~ from 40 to 60*⟩

[2]anywhere *n* any place

Anzac /'anzak/ *n* a soldier from Australia or New Zealand, esp in WW I [*A*ustralian and *N*ew *Z*ealand *A*rmy *C*orps]

aorist /'ayərist, 'eərist/ *n* a verb inflection (e g in Greek) expressing simple occurrence of a past action without reference to its completeness, duration, or repetition [LL & Gk; LL *aoristos*, fr Gk, fr *aoristos* undefined, fr *a* + *horistos* definable, fr *horizein* to define – more at HORIZON] – **aorist** *adj*, **aoristic** /-'ristik/ *adj*, **aoristically** *adv*

aorta /ay'awtə/ *n, pl* **aortas, aortae** /-ti/ the great artery that carries blood from the left side of the heart to be distributed by branch arteries throughout the body ☞ ANATOMY [NL, fr Gk *aortē*, fr *aeirein* to lift] – **aortal** *adj*, **aortic** *adj*

aortic arch /ay'awtik/ *n* any of a series of paired arterial branches in vertebrate embryos that connect the front and back arterial systems in front of the heart and persist in a complete form only in adult fishes

à outrance /,ah 'oohtronhs (*Fr* a utrɑ̃s)/ *adv* to the bitter end; unsparingly [F, lit., to excess]

¹ap- – see AD-

²ap- – see APO-

apace /ə'pays/ *adv* at a quick pace; swiftly [ME, prob fr MF *à pas* on step]

Apache /ə'pachi; *sense 3* ə'pash/ *n, pl* **Apaches,** *esp collectively* **Apache** **1** a member of a group of N American Indian peoples of the SW USA **2** any of the Athapaskan languages of the Apache people **3** *not cap* a member of a gang of (Parisian) criminals [Sp, prob fr Zuñi *Ápachu*, lit., enemy; (3) F, fr *Apache* Apache Indian]

apanage /'apənij/ *n* a grant made to a dependent member of the royal family or a principal liege man [F – more at APPANAGE]

apart /ə'paht/ *adv* **1a** at a distance (from one another in space or time) ⟨*tried to keep ~ from the family squabbles*⟩ ⟨*towns 20 miles ~*⟩ **b** at a distance in character or opinions ⟨*their ideas are worlds ~*⟩ **2** so as to separate one from another ⟨*can't tell the twins ~*⟩ **3** excluded from consideration ⟨*joking ~, what shall we do?*⟩ **4** in or into 2 or more parts ⟨*had to take the engine ~*⟩ [ME, fr MF *a part*, lit., to the side]

a'part from *prep* **1** in addition to; besides ⟨*haven't time, quite ~ the cost*⟩ **2** EXCEPT FOR ⟨*excellent ~ a few blemishes*⟩

apartheid /ə'paht·(h)ayt, -(h)iet/ *n* racial segregation; *specif* a policy of segregation and discrimination against non-Europeans in the Republic of S Africa [Afrik, lit., separateness]

apartment /a'pahtmənt/ *n* **1** a single room in a building **2** a suite of rooms used for living quarters ⟨*the Royal ~s*⟩ **3** *chiefly NAm* a flat [F *appartement*, fr It *appartamento*] – **apartmental** /-'mentl/ *adj*

a'partment ,house *n, NAm* a block of flats

apathetic /,apə'thetik/ *adj* **1** having or showing little or no feeling; spiritless **2** lacking interest or concern; indifferent [*apathy* + *-etic* (as in *pathetic*)] – **apathetically** *adv*

apathy /'apəthi/ *n* **1** lack of feeling or emotion; impassiveness **2** lack of interest or concern; indifference [Gk *apatheia*, fr *apathēs* without feeling, fr *a-* + *pathos* emotion – more at PATHOS]

apatite /'apətiet/ *n* any of a group of calcium phosphate minerals occurring in phosphate rock, bones, and teeth; *specif* calcium fluorophosphate [G *apatit*, fr Gk *apatē* deceit]

¹ape /ayp/ *n* **1** a (large semierect tailless or short-tailed Old World) monkey: **a** a chimpanzee **b** a gorilla **c** any similar primate **2a** a mimic **b** a large uncouth person [ME, fr OE *apa*; akin to OHG *affo* ape] – **apelike** *adj*

²ape *vt* to imitate closely but often clumsily and ineptly – **aper** *n*

apeak /ə'peek/ *adj or adv* vertical ⟨*with oars ~*⟩ [alter. of earlier *apike*, prob fr *a-* + *pike* mountain]

'ape,man *n* a primate intermediate in character between human beings and the great apes

aperçu /apuh'sooh (*Fr* apɛrsy)/ *n, pl* **aperçus** /~/ **1** an immediate impression; *esp* an insight **2** a brief survey or conspectus; an outline [F, fr pp of *apercevoir* to perceive]

aperient /ə'piəri·ənt/ *n or adj* (a) laxative [adj L *aperient-, aperiens*, prp of *aperire* to uncover, open; n fr adj]

aperiodic /,aypiəri'odik/ *adj* **1** of irregular occurrence ⟨*~ floods*⟩ **2** not having periodic vibrations; not oscillatory – **aperiodically** *adv*, **aperiodicity** /,ay,piəri·ə'disəti/ *n*

aperitif /ə,perə'teef, -'---/ *n* an alcoholic drink taken before a meal to stimulate the appetite [F *apéritif* aperient, aperitif, fr MF *aperitif*, adj, aperient, fr ML *aperitivus*, irreg fr L *aperire*]

aperture /'apəchə/ *n* **1** an open space; a hole, gap **2a** (the diameter of) the opening in an optical (photographic) system through which the light passes ☞ CAMERA **b** the diameter of the objective lens or mirror of a telescope [ME, fr L *apertura*, fr *apertus*, pp of *aperire* to open – more at WEIR]

apetalous /ə'petələs/ *adj* having no petals – **apetaly** *n*

apex /'aypeks/ *n, pl* **apexes, apices** /'aypə,seez/ **1a** the uppermost peak; the vertex ⟨*the ~ of a mountain*⟩ **b** the narrowed or pointed end; the tip ⟨*the ~ of the tongue*⟩ **2** the highest or culminating point ⟨*the ~ of his career*⟩ [L, summit, small rod at top of priest's cap; prob akin to L *aptus* fastened, attached – more at APT]

aphaeresis /ə'ferəsis, ə'fiə-/ *n, pl* **aphaereses** /-seez/ the loss of 1 or more sounds or letters at the beginning of a word (e g in *bus* for *omnibus*) [LL, fr Gk *aphairesis*, lit., taking off, fr *aphairein* to take away, fr *apo-* + *hairein* to take] – **aphaeretic** /,afə'retik/ *adj*

aphasia /ə'fayzh(y)ə, -zyə/ *n* (partial) loss of the power to use or understand words, usu resulting from brain damage – compare ALEXIA [NL, fr Gk, fr *a-* + *-phasia*] – **aphasiac** /-zi,ak/ *adj*, **aphasic** /-zik/ *n or adj*

aphelion /ə'feelyən/ *n, pl* **aphelia** /-lyə/ the point in the path of a planet, comet, etc that is farthest from the sun – compare PERIHELION [NL, fr *apo-* + Gk *hēlios* sun – more at ¹SOLAR]

aphid /'ayfid/ *n* a greenfly or related small sluggish insect that sucks the juices of plants

aphis /'ayfis/ *n, pl* **aphides** /'ayfi,deez/ an aphid (of a common genus) [NL *Aphid-, Aphis*, genus name, fr NGk *aphis*, perh alter. of *koris* bug]

aphorism /'afəriz(ə)m/ *n* a concise pithy formulation of a truth; an adage [MF *aphorisme*, fr LL *aphorismus*, fr Gk *aphorismos* definition, aphorism, fr *aphorizein* to define, fr *apo-* + *horizein* to bound – more at HORIZON] – **aphorize** *vi*, **aphorist** *n*, **aphoristic** /-'ristik/ *adj*, **aphoristically** *adv*

aphrodisiac /,afrə'diziak/ *n or adj* (a substance) that stimulates sexual desire [adj Gk *aphrodisiakos* sexual, fr *aphrodisia* sexual pleasures, fr neut pl of *aphrodisios* of Aphrodite, fr *Aphroditē*, goddess of love; n fr adj] – **aphrodisiacal** /,afrədi'zie·əkl/ *adj*

apian /'aypi·ən/ *adj* of bees [L *apianus*, fr *apis*]

apiarian /,aypi'eəri·ən/ *adj* of beekeeping or bees

apiarist /'aypi·ərist/ *n* a beekeeper

apiary /'aypi·əri/ *n* a place where (hives or colonies of) bees are kept, esp for their honey [L *apiarium*, fr *apis* bee]

apical /'aypikl, a-/ *adj* of, situated at, or forming an apex [prob fr NL *apicalis*, fr L *apic-, apex*] – **apically** *adv*

apices /'aypə,seez/ *pl of* APEX

apiculture /'aypi,kulchə/ *n* the keeping of bees, esp on a large scale [prob fr F, fr L *apis* bee + F *culture*] – **apicultural** /,aypi'kulchərəl, '--,---/ *adj*, **apiculturist** *n*

apiece /ə'pees/ *adv* for each one; individually [ME *a pece*, fr [3]*a* + *pece* piece]

apish /'aypish/ *adj* resembling an ape: e g **a** slavishly imitative **b** extremely silly or affected – **apishly** *adv*, **apishness** *n*

aplanatic /,ayplə'natik/ *adj, esp of a lens (system)* free from spherical aberration [*a-* + Gk *planasthai* to wander – more at PLANET]

aplasia /ay'playzh(y)ə, -zyə/ *n* incomplete or faulty development of an organ or part [NL, fr [2]*a-* + *-plasia*] – **aplastic** /ay'plastik/ *adj*

aplenty /ə'plenti/ *adj* enough and to spare; in abundance ⟨*money ~ for all his needs*⟩

aplomb /ə'plum, ə'plom/ *n* complete composure or self-assurance; poise [F, lit., perpendicularity, fr MF, fr *a plomb*, lit., according to the plummet]

apnoea, *chiefly NAm* **apnea** /'apni·ə/ *n* **1** transient cessation of respiration **2** asphyxia [NL, fr *a-* + *-pnoea*]

apo-, ap- *prefix* **1** away from; off ⟨aphelion⟩ ⟨apogee⟩ **2** detached; separate ⟨apocarpous⟩ [ME, fr MF & L; MF, fr L, fr Gk, fr *apo* – more at OF]

apocalypse /ə'pokəlips/ *n* **1a** any of a number of early Jewish and Christian works, written esp under an assumed name, and characterized by symbolic imagery, which describe the establishment of God's kingdom **b** *cap* REVELATION 2 – usu + *the* **2** sthg viewed as a prophetic revelation [ME, revelation, Revelation, fr LL *apocalypsis*, fr Gk *apokalypsis*, fr *apokalyptein* to uncover, fr *apo-* + *kalyptein* to cover – more at HELL]

apocalyptic /ə,pokə'liptik/ *also* **apocalyptical** /-kl/ *adj* **1** of or resembling an apocalypse **2** forecasting the ultimate destiny of the world; prophetic **3** foreboding imminent disaster; terrible [LGk *apokalyptikos*, fr Gk *apokalyptein*] – **apocalyptically** *adv*

apochromatic /,apəkrə'matik/ *adj, esp of a lens (system)* free from chromatic and spherical aberration ⟨*an ~ lens*⟩ [ISV]

apocrine /'apəkrin, -kreen/ *adj* (coming from a gland) producing a fluid secretion by separation of part of the cytoplasm from the secreting cells [ISV *apo-* + Gk *krinein* to separate – more at CERTAIN]

apocrypha /ə'pokrifə/ *n* **1** (a collection of) writings or statements of dubious authenticity **2** *sing or pl in constr, cap* books included in the Septuagint and Vulgate but excluded from the Jewish and Protestant canons of the Old Testament – usu + *the* [ML, fr LL, neut pl of *apocryphus* secret, not canonical, fr Gk *apokryphos* obscure, fr *apokryptein* to hide away, fr *apo-* + *kryptein* to hide – more at CRYPT]

apocryphal /ə'pokrif(ə)l/ *adj* **1** *often cap* of or resembling the Apocrypha **2** of doubtful authenticity – **apocryphally** *adv*, **apocryphalness** *n*

apodal /'apədl/, **apodous** /'apədəs/ *adj* having no (appendages analogous to) feet ⟨*eels are ~*⟩ [Gk *apod-, apous*, fr *a-* + *pod-, pous* foot – more at FOOT]

apodeictic /,apə'diektik/ *adj* apodictic

apodictic /,apə'diktik/ *adj* expressing, or of the nature of, necessary truth or absolute certainty [L *apodicticus*, fr Gk *apodeiktikos*, fr *apodeiknynai* to demonstrate, fr *apo-* + *deiknynai* to show – more at DICTION] – **apodictically** *adv*

apodosis /ə'podəsis/ *n, pl* **apodoses** /-seez/ the main clause of a conditional sentence – compare PROTASIS [NL, fr Gk, fr *apodidonai* to give back, deliver, fr *apo-* + *didonai* to give – more at [2]DATE]

apoenzyme /,apoh'enziem/ *n* a protein that forms an active enzyme by combination with a coenzyme [ISV]

apogamy /ə'pogəmi/ *n* development of a sporophyte from a gametophyte without fertilization [ISV] – **apogamous** *adj*, **apogamic** /,apə'gamik/ *adj*

apogee /'apəjee/ *n* **1** the point farthest from a planet or other celestial body reached by any object orbiting it – compare PERIGEE **2** the farthest or highest point; the culmination ⟨*Aegean civilization reached its ~ in Crete*⟩ [F *apogée*, fr NL *apogaeum*, fr Gk *apogaion*, fr neut of *apogeios, apogaios* far from the earth, fr *apo-* + *gē* earth] – **apogean** /,apə'jee·ən/ *adj*

apologetic /ə,polə'jetik/ *adj* **1a** offered in defence or vindication **b** offered by way of excuse or apology ⟨*an ~ smile*⟩ **2** regretfully acknowledging fault or failure; contrite [LL *apologeticus*, fr Gk *apologētikos*, fr *apologeisthai* to defend, fr *apo-* + *logos* speech] – **apologetically** *adv*

a,polo'getics *n pl but sing or pl in constr* **1** systematic reasoned argument in defence (e g of a doctrine) **2** a branch of theology devoted to the rational defence of Christianity

apologia /,apə'lohjyə/ *n* a reasoned defence in speech or writing, esp of a faith, cause, or institution [LL]

apologist /ə'poləjist/ *n* the author of an apologia

apolog·ize, -ise /ə'poləjiez/ *vi* to make an apology

apologue /'apəlog/ *n* an allegorical narrative, usu with a moral [F, fr L *apologus*, fr Gk *apologos*, fr *apo-* + *logos* speech, narrative]

apology /ə'poləji/ *n* **1a** an apologia **b** EXCUSE 1 **2** an admission of error or discourtesy accompanied by an expression of regret **3** a poor substitute *for* [MF or LL; MF *apologie*, fr LL *apologia*, fr Gk, fr *apo-* + *logos* speech – more at LEGEND]

apolune /'apəloohn/ *n* the point in the path of a body orbiting the moon that is farthest from the centre of the moon – compare PERILUNE [*apo-* + L *luna* moon – more at LUNAR]

apomict /'apəmikt/ *n* sthg produced by or reproducing by apomixis [prob back-formation fr ISV *apomictic*, fr *apo-* + Gk *mignynai* to mix – more at MIX] – **apomictic** /-'miktik/ *adj*, **apomictically** *adv*

apomixis /,apə'miksis/ *n, pl* **apomixes** /-'mikseez/ reproduction involving the production of seed without fertilization [NL, fr *apo-* + Gk *mixis* act of mixing, fr *mignynai*]

apophthegm /'apə,them/ *n* a short, pithy, and instructive saying [F or NL; F *apophthegme*, perh fr NL *apophthegma*, fr Gk *apophthegmat-, apophthegma*, fr *apophthengesthai* to speak out, fr *apo-* + *phthengesthai* to utter] – **apophthegmatic** /,apətheg'matik/, **apophthegmatical** *adj*, **apophthegmatically** *adv*

apoplectic /,apə'plektik/ *adj* **1** of, causing, affected with, or showing symptoms of apoplexy **2** violently excited (e g from rage) [F or LL; F *apoplectique*, fr LL *apoplecticus*, fr Gk *apoplēktikos*, fr *apoplēssein*] – **apoplectically** *adv*

apoplexy /ˈapəˌpleksi/ *n* ²STROKE 5 [ME *apoplexie*, fr MF & LL; MF, fr LL *apoplexia*, fr Gk *apoplēxia*, fr *apoplēssein* to cripple by a stroke, fr *apo-* + *plēssein* to strike – more at PLAINT]

aport /əˈpawt/ *adv* on or towards the left side of a ship ⟨*steer the helm* ~⟩

aposematic /ˌapəsiˈmatik/ *adj, esp of insect coloration* conspicuous and serving to warn [*apo-* + Gk *sēmat-*, *sēma* sign] – **aposematically** *adv*

aposiopesis /ˌapəzie·əˈpeesis/ *n, pl* **aposiopeses** /-ˌseez/ the leaving of a thought incomplete, usu by a sudden breaking off of a sentence [LL, fr Gk *aposiōpēsis*, fr *aposiōpan* to be quite silent, fr *apo-* + *siōpan* to be silent, fr *siōpē* silence] – **aposiopetic** /-ˈpetik/ *adj*

apostasy /əˈpostəsi/ *n* **1** renunciation of a religious faith **2** abandonment of a previous loyalty; defection [ME *apostasie*, fr LL *apostasia*, fr Gk, lit., revolt, fr *aphistasthai* to revolt, fr *apo-* + *histasthai* to stand – more at STAND]

apostate /əˈpostayt/ *n* one who commits apostasy – **apostate** *adj*

apostat·ize, -ise /əˈpostətiez/ *vi* to commit apostasy

a posteriori /ˌay poˌstiəriˈawri/ *adj* **1** inductive **2** relating to or derived by reasoning from observed facts – compare A PRIORI [L, lit., from the latter] – **a posteriori** *adv*

apostle /əˈpos(ə)l/ *n* **1** one sent on a mission; *esp* any of an authoritative New Testament group sent out to preach the gospel and made up esp of Jesus's original 12 disciples and Paul **2a** one who first advocates an important belief or system **b** an ardent supporter; an adherent ⟨*an* ~ *of liberal tolerance*⟩ [ME, fr OF & OE; OF *apostle* & OE *apostol*, fr LL *apostolus*, fr Gk *apostolos*, fr *apostellein* to send away, fr *apo-* + *stellein* to send – more at ¹STALL] – **apostleship** *n*

apostolic /ˌapəˈstolik/ *adj* **1** of an apostle or the New Testament apostles **2a** of the divine authority vested in the apostles held (e g by Roman Catholics, Anglicans, and Eastern Orthodox) to be handed down through the successive ordinations of bishops **b** of the pope as the successor to the apostolic authority vested in St Peter – **apostolicity** /əˌpostəˈlisəti/ *n*

¹**apostrophe** /əˈpostrəfi/ *n* the addressing, rhetorically, of a usu absent person or a usu personified thing [L, fr Gk *apostrophē*, lit., act of turning away, fr *apostrephein* to turn away, fr *apo-* + *strephein* to turn – more at STROPHE] – **apostrophize** *vb*, **apostrophic** /ˌapəˈstrofik/ *adj*

²**apostrophe** *n* a mark ' used to indicate the omission of letters or figures, the possessive case, or the plural of letters or figures [MF & LL; MF, fr LL *apostrophus*, fr Gk *apostrophos*, fr *apostrophos* turned away, fr *apostrephein*] – **apostrophic** /ˌapəˈstrofik/ *adj*

aˌpothecaries' ˈweight /əˈpothək(ə)riz/ *n* the series of units of weight used formerly by pharmacists and based on the ounce of 8 drachms and the drachm of 3 scruples or 60 grains ☞ UNIT

apothecary /əˈpothək(ə)ri/ *n, archaic or NAm* **1** a pharmacist **2** PHARMACY 2 [ME *apothecarie*, fr ML *apothecarius*, fr LL, shopkeeper, fr L *apotheca* storehouse, fr Gk *apothēkē*, fr *apotithenai* to put away, fr *apo-* + *tithenai* to put – more at ¹DO]

apothegm /ˈapəthem/ *n, NAm* an apophthegm

apotheosis /əˌpothiˈohsis/ *n, pl* **apotheoses** /-seez/ **1** deification **2** *the* perfect example ⟨*she is the* ~ *of womanhood*⟩ [LL, fr Gk *apotheōsis*, fr *apotheoun* to deify, fr *apo-* + *theos* god] – **apotheosize** /ˌapəˈthee·əˌsiez, əˈpothi·əˌsiez/ *vt*

appal, *NAm chiefly* **appall** /əˈpawl/ *vt* **-ll-** to overcome with consternation, horror, or dismay [ME *appallen*, fr MF *apalir*, fr OF, fr *a-* (fr L *ad-*) + *palir* to grow pale, fr L *pallescere*, incho of *pallēre* to be pale – more at ¹FALLOW] – **appalling** *adj*, **appallingly** *adv*

Appaloosa /ˌapəˈloohsə, -zə/ *n* (any of) a N American breed of rugged saddle horses with a mottled skin and vertically striped hooves [prob fr *Palouse*, an Indian people of Washington and Idaho, USA]

appanage /ˈapənij/ *n* **1** apanage **2** a usual accompaniment [F *apanage*, fr OF, fr *apaner* to provide for a younger offspring, fr OProv *apanar* to support, fr *a-* (fr L *ad-*) + *pan* bread, fr L *panis* – more at FOOD]

apparat /ˈapərat, ˌ--ˈ-/ *n* APPARATUS 2 [Russ]

apparatchik /ˌapəˈrachik/ *n, pl* **apparatchiks, apparatchiki** /-ˈrachiki/ a member of a Communist apparat [Russ, fr *apparat*]

apparatus /ˈapəraytəs, --ˈ--; *NAm also* -ˈratəs/ *n, pl* **apparatuses, apparatus** **1a** (a piece of) equipment designed for a particular use, esp for a scientific operation **b** a group of organs having a common function **2** the administrative bureaucracy of an organization, esp a political party [L, fr *apparatus*, pp of *apparare* to prepare, fr *ad-* + *parare* to prepare – more at PARE]

¹**apparel** /əˈparəl/ *vt* **-ll-** (*NAm* **-l-, -ll-**) **1** to put clothes on; dress – chiefly fml **2** to adorn, embellish – chiefly poetic [ME *appareillen*, fr OF *apareillier* to prepare, fr (assumed) VL *apparicularc*, irreg fr L *apparare*]

²**apparel** *n* **1** garments, clothing – chiefly fml **2** sthg that clothes or adorns ⟨*the bright* ~ *of spring*⟩ – chiefly poetic

apparent /əˈparənt/ *adj* **1** easily seen or understood; plain, evident **2** seemingly real but not necessarily so **3** having an absolute right to succeed to a title or estate ⟨*the heir* ~⟩ [ME, fr OF *aparent*, fr L *apparent-*, *apparens*, prp of *apparēre* to appear] – **apparently** *adv*

apˌparent hoˈrizon *n* HORIZON 1a

apˈparent ˌtime *n* the time of day indicated by a sundial

apparition /ˌapəˈrish(ə)n/ *n* **1a** an unusual or unexpected sight; a phenomenon **b** a ghostly figure **2** the act of becoming visible; appearance [ME *apparicioun*, fr LL *apparition-*, *apparitio* appearance, fr L *apparitus*, pp of *apparēre*] – **apparitional** *adj*

¹**appeal** /əˈpeel/ *n* **1** a legal proceeding by which a case is brought to a higher court for review ☞ LAW **2a(1)** an application (e g to a recognized authority) for corroboration, vindication, or decision **(2)** a call by members of the fielding side in cricket, esp by the bowler, for the umpire to decide whether a batsman is out **b** an earnest plea for aid or mercy; an entreaty **3** the power of arousing a sympathetic response; attraction ⟨*the theatre has lost its* ~ *for him*⟩

²**appeal** *vt* to take (a case) to a higher court ~ *vi* **1**

to take a case to a higher court **2a** to call on another for corroboration, vindication, or decision **b** to make an appeal in cricket **3** to make an earnest plea or request **4** to arouse a sympathetic response ***USE*** often + *to* [ME *appelen* to accuse, appeal, fr MF *apeler,* fr L *appellare,* fr *appellere* to drive to, fr *ad-* + *pellere* to drive – more at FELT] – **appealer** *n,* **appealable** *adj,* **appealability** /-lə'biləti/ *n*

appealing /ə'peeling/ *adj* **1** having appeal; pleasing **2** marked by earnest entreaty; imploring – **appealingly** *adv*

appear /ə'piə/ *vi* **1a** to be or become visible ⟨*the sun* ~s *on the horizon*⟩ **b** to arrive ⟨~s *promptly at 8 each day*⟩ **2** to come formally before an authoritative body **3** to give the impression of being; seem ⟨~s *happy enough*⟩ **4** to come into public view ⟨*first* ~ed *on a television variety show*⟩ [ME *apperen,* fr OF *aparoir,* fr L *apparēre,* fr *ad-* + *parēre* to show oneself; akin to Gk *peparein* to display]

appearance /ə'piərəns/ *n* **1** the coming into court of a party in an action or his/her lawyer **2** a visit or attendance that is seen or noticed by others ⟨*put in an* ~ *at the party*⟩ **3a** an outward aspect; a look ⟨*had a fierce* ~⟩ **b** an external show; a semblance ⟨*although hostile, he tried to preserve an* ~ *of neutrality*⟩ **c** *pl* an outward or superficial indication that hides the real situation ⟨*would do anything to keep up* ~s⟩ [APPEAR + -ANCE]

appease /ə'peez/ *vt* **1** to pacify, calm **2** to cause to subside; allay ⟨~ *his hunger*⟩ **3** to conciliate (esp an aggressor) by concessions [ME *appesen,* fr OF *apaisier,* fr *a-* (fr L *ad-*) + *pais* peace – more at PEACE] – **appeasable** *adj,* **appeasement** *n,* **appeaser** *n*

[1]**appellant** /ə'pelənt/ *adj* appellate

[2]**appellant** *n* one who appeals against a judicial decision

appellate /ə'pelət/ *adj* of or recognizing appeals ⟨*an* ~ *court*⟩ [L *appellatus,* pp of *appellare*]

appellation /,apə'laysh(ə)n/ *n* an identifying name or title

appellation contrôlée /,kontroh'lay (*Fr* apəlasjɔ̃ kɔ̃trole)/ *n* a government certification of a French wine guaranteeing that it originates from a specified geographical area and meets that locality's standards of production [F, lit., controlled appellation]

appellative /ə'pelətiv/ *adj* of or being a common noun – **appellatively** *adv*

append /ə'pend/ *vt* to attach or add, esp as a supplement or appendix [F *appendre,* fr LL *appendere,* fr L, to weigh, fr *ad-* + *pendere* to weigh – more at PENDANT]

appendage /ə'pendij/ *n* **1** sthg appended to sthg larger or more important **2** a limb, seta, or other subordinate or derivative body part

appendant /ə'pend(ə)nt/ *adj* **1** associated as an accompaniment or attendant circumstance **2** attached as an appendage – **appendant** *n*

appendectomy /,apən'dektəmi, ,apen-/ *n, NAm* an appendicectomy

appendicectomy /ə,pendi'sektəmi/ *n* surgical removal of the vermiform appendix [L *appendic-, appendix* + E *-ectomy*]

appendicitis /ə,pendi'sietəs/ *n* inflammation of the vermiform appendix [NL]

appendix /ə'pendiks/ *n, pl* **appendixes, appendices** /-di,seez/ **1** a supplement (e g containing explanatory or statistical material), usu attached at the end of a piece of writing **2** the vermiform appendix or similar bodily outgrowth ☞ DIGESTION [L *appendic-, appendix* appendage, fr *appendere*]

apperception /,apuh'sepsh(ə)n/ *n* **1** introspective self-consciousness **2** mental perception; *esp* the understanding of sthg perceived in terms of previous experience [F *aperception,* fr *apercevoir* to perceive] – **apperceive** /,apuh'seev/ *vt,* **apperceptive** /-'septiv/ *adj*

appertain /,apə'tayn/ *vi* to belong or be connected as a rightful or customary part, possession, or attribute; pertain – usu + *to* [ME *apperteinen,* fr MF *apartenir,* fr LL *appertinēre,* fr L *ad-* + *pertinēre* to belong – more at PERTAIN]

appetite /'apətiet/ *n* **1** a desire to satisfy an internal bodily need; *esp* an (eager) desire to eat **2** a strong desire demanding satisfaction; an inclination [ME *apetit,* fr MF, fr L *appetitus,* fr *appetitus,* pp of *appetere* to strive after, fr *ad-* + *petere* to go to – more at FEATHER] – **appetitive** /-,tietiv/ *adj*

appet·izer, -iser /'apətiezə/ *n* a food or drink that stimulates the appetite and is usu served before a meal

appet·izing, -ising /'apətiezing/ *adj* appealing to the appetite, esp in appearance or aroma – **appetizingly** *adv*

applaud /ə'plawd/ *vb* to express approval (of), esp by clapping the hands [MF or L; MF *applaudir,* fr L *applaudere,* fr *ad-* + *plaudere* to applaud] – **applaudable** *adj,* **applauder** *n*

applause /ə'plawz/ *n* **1** approval publicly expressed (e g by clapping the hands) **2** praise [ML *applausus,* fr L, clashing noise, fr *applausus,* pp of *applaudere*]

apple /'apl/ *n* **1** (the fleshy, edible, usu rounded, red, yellow, or green fruit of) a tree of the rose family **2** a fruit or other plant structure resembling an apple [ME *appel,* fr OE *æppel;* akin to OHG *apful* apple, OSlav *ablŭko*] – **apple of someone's eye** sby or sthg greatly cherished ⟨*his daughter is the* apple of his eye⟩ – **she's apples** *Austr* everything's fine – infml

apple-pie bed *n, Br* a bed made with the sheet folded back as a practical joke, so that one cannot lie out straight

apple-pie order *n* perfect order

'apple-,polish *vb, NAm* to attempt to ingratiate oneself (with) [fr the tradition of schoolchildren giving a shiny apple to their teacher] – **apple-polisher** *n*

,apples and 'pears *n pl, Br* stairs – slang [rhyming slang]

'Appleton ,layer /'aplt(ə)n/ *n* F LAYER [Sir Edward *Appleton* †1965 E physicist]

appliance /ə'plie·əns/ *n* **1** an instrument or device designed for a particular use; *esp* a domestic machine or device powered by gas or electricity (e g a food mixer, vacuum cleaner, or cooker) **2** BRACE 4e [APPLY + -ANCE]

applicable /ə'plikəbl/ *adj* appropriate – **applicability** /-kə'biləti/ *n*

applicant /'aplikənt/ *n* one who applies

application /,apli'kaysh(ə)n/ *n* **1a** an act of applying **b** a use to which sthg is put **c** close attention; diligence **2** a request, petition **3** a lotion **4** capacity for practical use; relevance [ME *applicacioun,* fr L *application-, applicatio* inclination, fr *applicatus,* pp of *applicare*] – **applicative** /ə'plikətiv/ *adj,* **applicatory** /ə'plikətri/ *adj*

applicator /ˈaplikaytə/ *n* a device for applying a substance (e g medicine or polish)

applied /əˈplied/ *adj* put to practical use; *esp* applying general principles to solve definite problems ⟨~ *sciences*⟩

[1]**appliqué** /əˈpleekay, ˌapleeˈkay/ *n* a cutout decoration fastened (e g by sewing) to a larger piece of material; *also* the decorative work formed in this manner [F, pp of *appliquer* to put on, fr L *applicare*]

[2]**appliqué** *vt* **appliquéing** /-kaying/ to apply (e g a decoration or ornament) to a larger surface

apply /əˈplie/ *vt* **1a** to bring to bear; put to use, esp for some practical purpose ⟨~ *pressure*⟩ ⟨~ *the brakes*⟩ **b** to lay or spread on ⟨~ *varnish to a table*⟩ **2** to devote (e g oneself) with close attention or diligence – usu + *to* ⟨*should* ~ *himself to his work*⟩ ~ *vi* **1** to have relevance – usu + *to* ⟨*this rule* applies *to new members only*⟩ **2** to make a request, esp in writing ⟨~ *for a job*⟩ [ME *applien*, fr MF *aplier*, fr L *applicare*, fr *ad-* + *plicare* to fold – more at [1]PLY] – **applier** /əˈplie·ə/ *n*

appoggiatura /əˌpojəˈtooərə/ *n* an embellishing note preceding an essential melodic note, used chiefly in the 18th c ☞ MUSIC [It, lit., support, fr *appoggiare* to cause to lean, fr (assumed) VL *appodiare*, fr L *ad-* + *podium* support]

appoint /əˈpoynt/ *vt* **1** to fix or name officially **2** to select for an office or position **3** to declare the disposition of (an estate) to sby [ME *appointen*, fr MF *apointier* to arrange, fr *a-* (fr L *ad-*) + *point*]

apˈpointed *adj* equipped, furnished

appointee /ˌapoynˈtee, əˌpoynˈtee/ *n* one who is appointed

appointive /əˈpoyntiv/ *adj* of or filled by appointment ⟨*an* ~ *office*⟩

apˈpointment /-mənt/ *n* **1** an act of appointing; a designation ⟨*fill a vacancy by* ~⟩ **2** an office or position held by sby who has been appointed to it rather than voted into it **3** an arrangement for a meeting **4** *pl* equipment, furnishings

apportion /əˈpawsh(ə)n/ *vt* to divide and share out in just proportion or according to a plan; allot [MF *apportionner*, fr *a-* (fr L *ad-*) + *portionner* to portion] – **apportionment** *n*

apposite /ˈapəzit/ *adj* highly pertinent or appropriate; apt [L *appositus*, fr pp of *apponere* to place near, fr *ad-* + *ponere* to put – more at POSITION] – **appositely** *adv*, **appositeness** *n*

apposition /ˌapəˈzish(ə)n/ *n* a grammatical construction in which 2 usu adjacent nouns or noun phrases have the same referent and stand in the same syntactic relation to the rest of a sentence (e g *the poet* and *Burns* in 'a biography of the poet Burns") – **appositional** *adj*, **appositionally** *adv*

appraisal /əˈprayz(ə)l/ *n* an act or instance of appraising; *specif* a valuation of property by an authorized person [APPRAISE + [2]-AL]

appraise /əˈprayz/ *vt* to evaluate the worth, significance, or status of; *esp* to give an expert judgment of the value or merit of [ME *appreisen*, fr MF *aprisier*, fr OF, fr *a-* (fr L *ad-*) + *prisier* to appraise – more at [3]PRIZE] – **appraisement** *n*, **appraiser** *n*, **appraising** *adj*, **appraisingly** *adv*

appreciable /əˈpreesh(y)əbl/ *adj* **1** capable of being perceived or measured **2** fairly large ⟨*an* ~ *distance*⟩ – **appreciably** *adv*

appreciate /əˈpreeshiayt, -siayt/ *vt* **1a** to understand the nature, worth, quality, or significance of **b** to recognize with gratitude; value or admire highly **2** to increase the value of ~ *vi* to increase in value [LL *appretiatus*, pp of *appretiare*, fr L *ad-* + *pretium* price – more at PRICE] – **appreciative** /-ətiv/ *adj*, **appreciatively** *adv*, **appreciator** /-ˌaytə/ *n*, **appreciatory** /-ət(ə)ri/ *adj*

appreciation /əˌpreeshiˈaysh(ə)n, -si-/ *n* **1a** sensitive awareness; *esp* recognition of aesthetic values **b** a judgment, evaluation; *esp* a favourable critical estimate **c** an expression of admiration, approval, or gratitude **2** an increase in value

apprehend /ˌapriˈhend/ *vt* **1** to arrest, seize ⟨~ *a thief*⟩ **2** to understand, perceive ~ *vi* to understand [ME *apprehenden*, fr L *apprehendere*, lit., to seize, fr *ad-* + *prehendere* to seize – more at PREHENSILE]

apprehensible /ˌapriˈhensəbl/ *adj* capable of being apprehended – **apprehensibly** *adv*

apprehension /ˌapriˈhensh(ə)n/ *n* **1** the act or power of comprehending ⟨*a man of dull* ~⟩ **2** arrest, seizure – used technically in Scottish law **3** anxiety or fear, esp of future evil; foreboding [ME, fr LL *apprehension-*, *apprehensio*, fr L *apprehensus*, pp of *apprehendere*]

apprehensive /ˌapriˈhensiv, -ziv/ *adj* viewing the future with anxiety, unease, or fear – often + *for* or *of* – **apprehensively** *adv*, **apprehensiveness** *n*

[1]**apprentice** /əˈprentis/ *n* **1** one who is learning an art or trade **a** from an employer to whom he/she is bound by indenture **b** by practical experience under skilled workers **2** an inexperienced person; a novice [ME *aprentis*, fr MF, fr OF, fr *aprendre* to learn, fr L *apprendere*, *apprehendere*] – **apprenticeship** *n*

[2]**apprentice** *vt* to set at work as an apprentice

appressed /əˈprest/ *adj* lying flat against sthg ⟨*leaves* ~ *to the stem*⟩ [L *appressus*, pp of *apprimere* to press to, fr *ad-* + *premere* to press – more at [2]PRESS]

apprise /əˈpriez/ *vt* to give notice to; tell – usu + *of*; fml [F *appris*, pp of *apprendre* to learn, teach, fr OF *aprendre*]

appro /ˈaproh/ *n*, *Br* – **on appro** ON APPROVAL – infml

[1]**approach** /əˈprohch/ *vt* **1a** to draw closer to **b** to come very near to in quality, character, etc **2a** to make advances to, esp in order to create a desired result ⟨*was* ~ed *by several film producers*⟩ **b** to begin to consider or deal with ⟨~ *the subject with an open mind*⟩ ~ *vi* to draw nearer [ME *approchen*, fr OF *aprochier*, fr LL *appropiare*, fr L *ad-* + *prope* near; akin to L *pro* before – more at FOR]

[2]**approach** *n* **1a** an act or instance of approaching **b** an approximation **2** a manner or method of doing sthg, esp for the first time ⟨*a highly individual* ~ *to language*⟩ **3** a means of access ⟨*the* ~es *to the city*⟩ **4a** a golf shot from the fairway towards the green **b** (the steps taken on) the part of a tenpin bowling alley from which a bowler must deliver the ball **5** the final part of an aircraft flight before landing **6** an advance made to establish personal or business relations – usu pl

approachable /əˈprohchəbl/ *adj* easy to meet or deal with [[1]APPROACH + -ABLE] – **approachability** /-ˈbiləti/ *n*

approbation /ˌaprəˈbaysh(ə)n/ *n* formal or official approval; sanction [ME, fr MF, fr L *approbation-*, *approbatio*, fr *approbatus*, pp of *approbare*] – **approbatory** /əˈprohbət(ə)ri/ *adj*

[1]**appropriate** /ə'prohpri,ayt/ *vt* **1** to take exclusive possession of **2** to set apart (specif money) for a particular purpose or use **3** to take or make use of without authority or right [ME *appropriaten,* fr LL *appropriatus,* pp of *appropriare,* fr L *ad-* + *proprius* own] – **appropriable** /-pri·əbl/ *adj,* **appropriator** /-,aytə/ *n*

[2]**appropriate** /ə'prohpri·ət/ *adj* especially suitable or compatible; fitting – **appropriately** *adv,* **appropriateness** *n*

appropriation /ə,prohpri'aysh(ə)n/ *n* sthg appropriated; *specif* money set aside by formal action for a particular use [[1]APPROPRIATE + -ION] – **appropriative** /-ətiv/ *adj*

approval /ə'proohvl/ *n* **1** a favourable opinion or judgment **2** formal or official permission [APPROVE +[2]-AL] – **on approval** *of goods supplied commercially* to be returned without payment if found unsatisfactory

approve /ə'proohv/ *vt* **1** to have or express a favourable opinion of **2a** to accept as satisfactory **b** to give formal or official sanction to; ratify ⟨*Parliament* ~d *the proposed policy*⟩ ~ *vi* to take a favourable view – often + *of* ⟨*doesn't* ~ *of fighting*⟩ [ME *approven,* fr OF *aprover,* fr L *approbare,* fr *ad-* + *probare* to prove – more at PROVE] – **approvingly** *adv*

[1]**approximate** /ə'proksimət/ *adj* nearly correct or exact ☞ SYMBOL [LL *approximatus,* pp of *approximare* to come near, fr L *ad-* + *proximare* to come near – more at PROXIMATE] – **approximately** *adv*

[2]**approximate** /ə'proksimayt/ *vt* **1** to bring near or close – often + *to* **2** to come near to; approach, esp in quality or number ~ *vi* to come close – usu + *to*

approximation /ə,proksi'maysh(ə)n/ *n* sthg that is approximate; *esp* a mathematical quantity that is close in value but not equal to a desired quantity [[2]APPROXIMATE + -ION] – **approximative** /ə'proksimətiv/ *adj,* **approximatively** *adv*

appurtenance /ə'puhtinəns/ *n* an accessory [ME, fr AF *apurtenance,* fr OF *apartenance,* fr *apartenir* to belong – more at APPERTAIN] – **appurtenant** *adj or n*

après-ski /,apray 'skee (*Fr* apre ski/ *adj or n* (of or for) social activity after a day's skiing [F *après* after + *ski* ski, skiing]

apricot /'ayprikot/ *n* **1** (the oval orange-coloured fruit of) a temperate-zone tree of the rose family closely related to the peach and plum **2** an orange pink colour [alter. of earlier *abrecock,* deriv of Ar *al-birqūq* the apricot]

April /'ayprəl/ *n* the 4th month of the Gregorian calendar [ME, fr OF & L; OF *avrill,* fr L *Aprilis*]

,April 'fool *n* the victim of a joke or trick played on April Fools' Day

,April 'Fools' ,Day *n* April 1 characteristically marked by the playing of practical jokes

a priori /ay pree'awri, ah, -rie/ *adj* **1a** relating to or derived by reasoning from self-evident propositions; deductive – compare A POSTERIORI **b** of or relating to sthg that can be known by reason alone **c** true or false by definition or convention alone ⟨~ *statements*⟩ **2** without examination or analysis; presumptive [L, from the former] – **a priori** *adv,* **apriority** /-'orəti/ *n*

apron /'aypran/ *n* **1** a garment usu tied round the waist and used to protect clothing **2** sthg that suggests or resembles an apron in shape, position, or use: e g **a** the part of a stage that projects in front of the curtain **b** the extensive paved area by an airport terminal or in front of aircraft hangars [ME, alter. (by incorrect division of *a napron*) of *napron,* fr MF *naperon,* dim. of *nape* cloth, modif of L *mappa* napkin, towel]

'apron ,strings *n pl* dominance, esp of a man by his mother or wife ⟨*still tied to his mother's* ~⟩

[1]**apropos** /,aprə'poh/ *adv* **1** at an opportune time **2** BY THE WAY [F *à propos,* lit., to the purpose]

[2]**apropos** *adj* both relevant and opportune

[3]**apropos** *prep* APROPOS OF

,apro'pos of *prep* concerning; WITH REGARD TO

apse /aps/ *n* **1** a projecting part of a building (e g a church) that is usu semicircular or polygonal and vaulted **2** APSIS 1 [ML & L; ML *apsis,* fr L]

apsidal /'apsidl/ *adj* of an apse

apsis /'apsis/ *n, pl* **apsides** /'apsideez/ **1** the point in an astronomical orbit at which the distance of the body from the centre of attraction is either greatest or least **2** APSE 1 [NL *apsid-, apsis,* fr L, arch, orbit, fr Gk *hapsid-, hapsis,* fr *haptein* to fasten]

apt /apt/ *adj* **1** ordinarily disposed; likely – usu + *to* **2** suited to a purpose; relevant **3** keenly intelligent and responsive ⟨*an* ~ *pupil*⟩ [ME, fr L *aptus,* lit., fastened, fr pp of *apere* to fasten; akin to L *apisci* to reach, *apud* near, Skt *āpta* fit] – **aptly** *adv,* **aptness** *n*

apterous /'aptərəs/ *adj* lacking wings ⟨~ *insects*⟩ [Gk *apteros,* fr *a-* + *pteron* wing – more at FEATHER]

aptitude /'aptityoohd, -choohd/ *n* **1** a natural ability; a talent, esp for learning **2** general fitness or suitability – usu + *for* – **aptitudinal** /,apti'tyoohd(ə)nl, -'chooh-/ *adj,* **aptitudinally** *adv*

Aquadag /'akwə,dag/ *trademark* – used for a colloidal suspension of fine particles of graphite in water for use as a lubricant

aqua fortis /,akwə 'fawtis/ *n* NITRIC ACID [NL, lit., strong water]

aqualung /'akwə,lung/ *n* cylinders of compressed air, oxygen, etc carried on the back and connected to a face mask for breathing underwater [L *aqua* water + E *lung*]

aquamarine /,akwəmə'reen/ *n* **1** a transparent blue to green beryl used as a gemstone **2** a pale blue to light greenish blue colour [NL *aqua marina,* fr L, sea water]

[1]**aquaplane** /'akwə,playn/ *n* a board towed behind a fast motorboat and ridden by sby standing on it

[2]**aquaplane** *vi* **1** to ride on an aquaplane **2** *of a car* to go out of control by sliding on water lying on the surface of a wet road – **aquaplaner** *n*

,aqua 'regia /'reji·ə, 'ree-/ *n* a mixture of nitric and hydrochloric acids that dissolves gold or platinum [NL, lit., royal water]

aquarelle /,akwə'rel/ *n* a painting in thin usu transparent watercolours [F, fr obs It *acquarella* (now *acquerello*), fr *acqua* water, fr L *aqua*] – **aquarellist** /-'relist/ *n*

aquarist /'akwərist/ *n* one who keeps an aquarium

aquarium /ə'kweəri·əm/ *n, pl* **aquariums, aquaria** /-ri·ə/ **1** a glass tank, artificial pond, etc in which living aquatic animals or plants are kept **2** an establishment where collections of living aquatic organisms are exhibited [fr neut of L *aquarius* of water, fr *aqua*]

Aquarius /ə'kweəri·əs/ *n* (sby born under) the 11th sign of the zodiac in astrology, which is pictured as a man pouring water ☞ SYMBOL [L, lit., water carrier] – **Aquarian** *adj or n*

[1]**aquatic** /ə'kwotik, -kwa-/ *adj* **1** growing,living in, or frequenting water **2** taking place in or on water ⟨~ *sports*⟩ – **aquatically** *adv*

[2]**aquatic** *n* **1** an aquatic animal or plant **2** *pl but sing or pl in constr* water sports

aquatint /'akwətint/ *n* (a print made by) a method of etching a printing plate that enables tones similar to watercolour washes to be reproduced [It *acqua tinta* dyed water] – **aquatint** *vt*, **aquatinter** *n*, **aquatintist** *n*

aquavit /'akwəvit/ *n* a colourless Scandinavian spirit flavoured with caraway seeds [Sw, Dan, & Norw *akvavit*, fr ML *aqua vitae*]

,**aqua 'vitae** /'veetie, 'vie-/ *n* **1** ALCOHOL 1 **2** a strong spirit (e g brandy or whisky) [ME, fr ML, lit., water of life]

aqueduct /'akwə,dukt/ *n* a conduit, esp an arched structure over a valley, for carrying water [L *aquaeductus*, fr *aquae* (gen of *aqua*) + *ductus* act of leading – more at DUCT]

aqueous /'akwi·əs, 'ay-/ *adj* of, resembling, or made from, with, or by water [ML *aqueus*, fr L *aqua*] – **aqueously** *adv*

,**aqueous 'humour** *n* a transparent liquid occupying the space between the lens and the cornea of the eye ☞ NERVE

aquifer /'akwifə/ *n* a water-bearing layer of permeable rock, sand, or gravel [NL, fr L *aqua* + *-fer*] – **aquiferous** /a'kwifərəs/ *adj*

aquilegia /,akwi'leej(y)ə/ *n* a columbine [NL]

aquiline /'akwilien/ *adj* **1** of or like an eagle **2** *of the human nose* hooked [L *aquilinus*, fr *aquila* eagle] – **aquilinity** /,akwi'linəti/ *n*

aquiver /ə'kwivə/ *adj* marked by trembling or quivering

[1]**-ar** /-ə *also* -ah/ *suffix* (*n* → *adj*) of, relating to, or being ⟨*molecul*ar⟩ ⟨*spectacul*ar⟩; resembling ⟨*oracul*ar⟩ [ME, fr L *-aris*, alter. of *-alis* -al]

[2]**-ar** *suffix* (→ *n*) [2]-ER ⟨*begg*ar⟩ ⟨*schol*ar⟩

Arab /'arəb/ *n* **1a** a member of a Semitic people orig of the Arabian peninsula and now widespread throughout the Middle East and N Africa **b** a member of an Arabic-speaking people **2** *not cap* **a** a homeless vagabond; *esp* an outcast boy or girl **b** a mischievous or annoying child **3** a typically intelligent, graceful, and swift horse of an Arabian stock [ME, fr L *Arabus, Arabs*, fr Gk *Arab-, Araps*, fr Ar *'Arab*] – **Arab** *adj*

[1]**arabesque** /,arə'besk/ *adj* (in the style) of arabesque [F, fr It *arabesco* in Arabian style, fr *Arabo* Arab, fr L *Arabus*]

[2]**arabesque** *n* **1** a decorative design or style that combines natural motifs (e g flowers or foliage) to produce an intricate pattern **2** a posture in ballet in which the dancer is supported on one leg with one arm extended forwards and the other arm and leg backwards

Arabian /ə'raybi·ən/ *n* **1** a native or inhabitant of Arabia **2** ARAB 3 [*Arabia*, peninsula in SW Asia] – **Arabian** *adj*

[1]**Arabic** /'arəbik/ *adj* **1** (characteristic) of Arabia, Arabians, or the Arabs **2** of or being Arabic

[2]**Arabic** *n* a Semitic language, now the prevailing speech of Arabia, Jordan, Lebanon, Syria, Iraq, Egypt, and parts of N Africa ☞ ALPHABET, LANGUAGE

arabic·ize, -ise /ə'rabisiez/ *vt, often cap* to adapt (a language or elements of a language) to Arabic usage

,**Arabic 'numeral** *n, often not cap A* any of the number symbols 0, 1, 2, 3, 4, 5, 6, 7, 8, 9 ☞ NUMBER

Arabist /'arəbist/ *n* a specialist in Arabic language or culture

arab·ize, -ise /'arəbiez/ *vt, often cap* **1** to cause to acquire Arabic customs, manners, speech, or outlook **2** to arabicize

arable /'arəbl/ *n or adj* (land) being or fit to be farmed for crops [adj MF or L; MF, fr L *arabilis*, fr *arare* to plough; akin to OE *erian* to plough, Gk *aroun*; n fr adj] – **arability** /,arə'biləti/ *n*

arachnid /ə'raknid/ *n* any of a class (e g spiders, mites, ticks, and scorpions) of arthropods whose bodies have 2 segments of which the front bears 4 pairs of legs [deriv of Gk *arachnē* spider] – **arachnid** *adj*

arachnoid /ə'raknoyd/ *n* a thin membrane covering the brain and spinal cord and lying between the dura mater and the pia mater [NL *arachnoides*, fr Gk *arachnoeidēs* like a cobweb, fr *arachnē* spider, spider's web]

arak /'arak, 'arək/ *n* **1** E Indian rum produced from molasses and a small quantity of dried red rice **2** arrack [Ar *'araq* sweat, juice, liquor]

Araldite /'arəldiet/ *trademark* – used for various (adhesive) epoxy resins

Aramaic /,arə'mayik/ *n* a Semitic language of the Aramaeans, a pre-Christian people of Syria and Upper Mesopotamia, that was used in SW Asia by non-Aramaean peoples including the Jews after the Babylonian exile ☞ ALPHABET [L *Aramaeus*, fr Gk *Aramaios*, fr Heb *'Ărām* Aram, ancient name for Syria]

Aran /'arən/ *n* a style of knitting that produces a fabric consisting of vertical patterned bands and that is usu in a thick cream-coloured wool [*Aran* Islands, Eire]

Araucanian /ə,raw'kaynyən, ,araw-, -ni·ən/ *also* **Araucan** /ə'rawkən/ *n* a member, or the language, of a group of American Indian peoples of Chile and adjacent parts of Argentina ☞ LANGUAGE [Sp *araucano*, fr *Arauco*]

araucaria /,araw'keəri·ə/ *n* a monkey-puzzle or related tree of the cyprus family [NL, genus name, fr *Arauco*, province in Chile]

Arawak /'arəwak, -wahk/ *n, pl* **Arawaks,** *esp collectively* **Arawak** a member, or the language, of an American Indian people living chiefly on the coast of Guyana

Arawakan /,arə'wakən, -'wahkən/ *n, pl* **Arawakans,** *esp collectively* **Arawakan** a member, or the language family, of a group of American Indian peoples of S America and the W Indies ☞ LANGUAGE

arbalest, arbalist /'ahbəlist/ *n* a large medieval military steel crossbow [ME *arblast*, fr OE, fr OF *arbaleste*, fr LL *arcuballista*, fr L *arcus* bow + *ballista* – more at ARROW] – **arbalester** *n*

arbiter /'ahbitə/ *n* a person or agency with absolute power of judging and determining [ME *arbitre*, fr MF, fr L *arbitr-, arbiter*]

arbitrament /'ahbitrəmənt/ *n* the judgment given

by an arbitrator [ME, fr MF *arbitrement*, fr *arbitrer* to give judgment, fr L *arbitrari*, fr *arbitr-*, *arbiter*]

arbitrary /ˈahbitrəri/ *adj* **1** depending on choice or discretion **2a** arising from unrestrained exercise of the will **b** selected at random and without reason **3** despotic, tyrannical – **arbitrarily** /ˈahbitrərəli, ˌahbiˈtrerəli/ *adv*, **arbitrariness** *n*

arbitrate /ˈahbitrayt/ *vi* to act as arbitrator ~ *vt* **1** to act as arbiter upon **2** to submit for decision to an arbitrator – **arbitrative** /-ˌtraytiv/ *adj*

arbitration /ˌahbiˈtraysh(ə)n/ *n* the settlement of a disputed issue by an arbitrator [ARBITRATE + -ION] – **arbitrational** *adj*

arbitrator /ˈahbiˌtraytə/ *n* **1** sby chosen to settle differences between 2 parties in dispute **2** an arbiter

arbor /ˈahbə/ *n* a spindle or axle of a wheel [L, tree, shaft]

arboreal /ˌahˈbawri·əl/ *adj* of, resembling, inhabiting, or frequenting a tree or trees [L *arboreus* of a tree, fr *arbor*] – **arboreally** *adv*

arboreous /ˌahˈbawri·əs/ *adj* **1** wooded **2** arboreal

arborescent /ˌahbəˈres(ə)nt/ *adj* resembling a tree in properties, growth, structure, or appearance – **arborescence** *n*, **arborescently** *adv*

arboretum /ˌahbəˈreetəm, ahˈboritəm/ *n, pl* **arboretums, arboreta** /-tə/ a place where trees and shrubs are cultivated for study and display [NL, fr L, place grown with trees, fr *arbor*]

arboriculture /ˈahbəriˌkulchə/ *n* the cultivation of trees and shrubs – **arboriculturist** /ˌahbəriˈkulchərist, ahˌbori-/ *n*

arbor·ize, -ise /ˈahbəriez/ *vi* to assume a treelike appearance ⟨*the nerve fibres* ~d⟩ – **arborization** /-rieˈzaysh(ə)n/ *n*

arborvitae /ˌahbawˈvietee, -ˈveetee/ *n* any of various ornamental evergreen trees of the cyprus family [NL *arbor vitae*, lit., tree of life]

arbour, *NAm chiefly* **arbor** /ˈahbə/ *n* a bower of (latticework covered with) shrubs, vines, or branches [ME *erber* plot of grass, arbour, fr OF *herbier* plot of grass, fr *herbe* herb, grass, fr L *herba*]

arbutus /ahˈbyoohtəs/ *n* any of a genus of white- or pink-flowered shrubs and trees of the heath family [NL, genus name, fr L, strawberry tree]

[1]**arc** /ahk/ *n* **1** the apparent path described by a celestial body **2** sthg arched or curved **3** a sustained luminous discharge of electricity across a gap in a circuit or between electrodes; *also* ARC LAMP **4** a continuous portion of a curve (e g of a circle or ellipse) ☞ MATHEMATICS [ME *ark*, fr MF *arc* bow, fr L *arcus* bow, arch, arc – more at ARROW]

[2]**arc** *vi* to form an electric arc

[3]**arc** *adj* INVERSE 2 – used with the trigonometric and hyperbolic functions ⟨~ *sine*⟩ ⟨*if y is the cosine of θ then θ is the* ~ *cosine of* y⟩ ☞ SYMBOL [*arc sine* arc or angle (corresponding to the) sine (of so many degrees)]

arcade /ahˈkayd/ *n* **1** a long arched gallery or building **2** a passageway or avenue (e g between shops) [F, fr It *arcata*, fr *arco* arch, fr L *arcus*] – **arcaded** *adj*

Arcadia /ahˈkaydi·ə/ *n* a usu idealized rural region or scene of simple pleasure and quiet [L *Arcadia*, fr Gk *Arkadia*, pastoral region of ancient Greece] – **Arcadian** *adj*

Arcady /ˈahkədi/ *n* Arcadia

arcane /ahˈkayn/ *adj* known or knowable only to an initiate; secret [L *arcanus*, fr *arca* chest – more at ARK]

[1]**arch** /ahch/ *n* **1** a typically curved structural member spanning an opening and resisting lateral or vertical pressure (e g of a wall) ☞ ARCHITECTURE **2** sthg (e g the vaulted bony structure of the foot) resembling an arch in form or function **3** an archway [ME *arche*, fr OF, fr (assumed) VL *arca*, fr L *arcus* – more at ARROW]

[2]**arch** *vt* **1** to span or provide with an arch **2** to form or bend into an arch ~ *vi* to form an arch

[3]**arch** *adj* **1** principal, chief ⟨*an* arch-*villain*⟩ ⟨*an* ~ *rebel*⟩ **2a** cleverly sly and alert **b** playfully saucy [*arch-*; (2) as in *archrogue*] – **archly** *adv*, **archness** *n*

[1]**arch-** /ahch-/ *prefix* **1** chief; principal ⟨arch*bishop*⟩ **2** extreme; most fully embodying the qualities of (a specified usu undesirable human type) ⟨arch*rogue*⟩ ⟨arch*enemy*⟩ [ME *arche-*, *arch-*, fr OE *arce-* & OF *arch-*, both fr LL *arch-* & L *archi-*, fr Gk *arch-*, *archi-*, fr *archein* to begin, rule; akin to Gk *archē* beginning, rule, *archos* ruler]

[2]**arch-** – see ARCHI-

-arch /-ahk/ *comb form* (→ *n*) ruler; leader ⟨*matri*arch⟩ ⟨*olig*arch⟩ [ME *-arche*, fr OF & LL & L; OF *-arche*, fr LL *-archa*, fr L *-arches*, *-archus*, fr Gk *-archēs*, *-archos*, fr *archein*]

archae- /ahki-/, **archaeo-,** *chiefly NAm* **arche-** *comb form* ancient; primitive ⟨archaeo*pteryx*⟩ ⟨archaeo*logy*⟩ [Gk *archaio-*, fr *archaios* ancient, fr *archē* beginning]

Archaean, *chiefly NAm Archean* /ahˈkee·ən/ *adj or n* (of or being) the (earlier part of the) Precambrian [Gk *archaios*]

archaeology /ˌahkiˈoləji/ *n* the scientific study of material remains (e g artefacts and dwellings) of past human life and activities [F *archéologie*, fr LL *archaeologia* antiquarian lore, fr Gk *archaiologia*, fr *archaio-* + *-logia* -logy] – **archaeological** /-əˈlojikl/ *adj*, **archaeologically** *adv*, **archaeologist** /ˌahkiˈoləjist/ *n*

archaeopteryx /ˌahkiˈoptəriks/ *n* an extinct primitive bird with some reptilian characteristics [NL, genus name, fr *archae-* + Gk *pteryx* wing; akin to Gk *pteron* wing – more at FEATHER]

Archaeozoic /ˌahki·əˈzoh·ik/ *adj or n* (of or being) the earliest era of geological history ☞ EVOLUTION

archaic /ahˈkayik/ *adj* **1** (characteristic) of an earlier or more primitive time; antiquated **2** no longer used in ordinary speech or writing [F or Gk; F *archaïque*, fr Gk *archaïkos*, fr *archaios*] – **archaically** *adv*

archaism /ahˈkayiz(ə)m/ *n* **1** the use of archaic diction or style **2** an instance of archaic usage; *esp* an archaic word or expression **3** sthg outmoded or old-fashioned [NL *archaïsmus*, fr Gk *archaïsmos*, fr *archaios*] – **archaist** *n*, **archaize** *vb*, **archaistic** /-ˈistik/ *adj*

archangel /ˌahkˈaynjəl, ˈ-ˌ--/ *n* a chief angel [ME, fr OF or LL; OF *archangele*, fr LL *archangelus*, fr Gk *archangelos*, fr *arch-* + *angelos* angel] – **archangelic** /-anˈjelik/ *adj*

archbishop /ˌahchˈbishəp/ *n* a bishop at the head of an ecclesiastical province, or one of equivalent honorary rank [ME, fr OE *arcebiscop*, fr LL *archiepiscopus*, fr LGk *archiepiskopos*, fr *archi-* + *epis-*

kopos bishop – more at BISHOP] – **archbishopric** /-rik/ *n*

,arch'deacon /-'deekən/ *n* a clergyman having the duty of assisting a diocesan bishop, esp in administrative work [ME *archedeken*, fr OE *arcediacon*, fr LL *archidiaconus*, fr LGk *archidiakonos*, fr Gk *archi-* + *diakonos* deacon] – **archdeaconate** /-nət/ *n*

,arch'diocese /-'die·əsis/ *n* the diocese of an archbishop – **archdiocesan** /-die'osisən/ *adj*

,arch'duchess /-'duchis/ *n* **1** the wife or widow of an archduke **2** a woman having in her own right the rank of archduke [F *archiduchesse*, fem of *archiduc* archduke, fr MF *archeduc*]

,arch'duke /-'dyoohk/ *n* a sovereign prince [MF *archeduc*, fr *arche-* arch- + *duc* duke] – **archducal** /'dyoohk(ə)l/ *adj*, **archduchy** /-'duchi/ *n*, **archdukedom** /-d(ə)m/ *n*

arche-, archeo- *comb form, chiefly NAm* archae-

Archean /ah'kee·ən/ *adj or n, chiefly NAm* Archaean

archegonium /,ahki'gohnyəm, -ni·əm/ *n, pl* **archegonia** /-nyə, -ni·ə/ the flask-shaped female sex organ of mosses, ferns, and some conifers [NL, fr Gk *archegonos* originator, fr *archein* to begin + *gonos* procreation; akin to Gk *gignesthai* to be born – more at ARCH-, KIN] – **archegonial** *adj*, **archegoniate** /-ayt, -ət/ *n or adj*

archer /'ahchə/ *n* one who practises archery [ME, fr OF, fr LL *arcarius*, alter. of *arcuarius*, fr *arcuarius* of a bow, fr L *arcus* bow – more at ARROW]

'archer,fish /-,fish/ *n* any of several small E Indian fishes that catch insects by stunning them with drops of water ejected from the mouth

archery /'ahchəri/ *n* the art, practice, skill, or sport of shooting arrows from a bow

archetype /'ahki,tiep/ *n* **1** an original pattern or model; a prototype **2** IDEA 1a **3** an inherited idea or mode of thought derived from the collective unconscious [L *archetypum*, fr Gk *archetypon*, fr neut of *archetypos* archetypal, fr *archein* + *typos* type] – **archetypal** /,ahki'tiepl/, **archetypical** /-'tipikl/ *adj*, **archetypally** /-'tiep(ə)l·i/, **archetypically** /-'tipikli/ *adv*

archi- /ahki-/, **arch-** *prefix* **1** chief; principal ⟨archi*trave*⟩ **2** primitive; original; primary [F or L; F, fr L, fr Gk – more at ARCH-]

archiepiscopal /,ahki·i'piskəpl/ *adj* of an archbishop [ML *archiepiscopalis*, fr LL *archiepiscopus* archbishop – more at ARCHBISHOP] – **archiepiscopally** /-pəli/ *adv*, **archiepiscopate** /-pət, -,payt/ *n*

archimandrite /,ahki'mandriet/ *n* a dignitary in the Eastern church ranking below a bishop [LL *archimandrites*, fr LGk *archimandritēs*, fr Gk *archi-* + LGk *mandra* monastery, fr Gk, fold, pen]

Archimedes' screw /,ahki'meediz/ *n* a device made of a tube bent spirally round an axis, or of a broad-threaded screw encased by a cylinder, and used to raise water [*Archimedes* †212 BC Gk mathematician & inventor]

archipelago /,ahki'peləgoh, ,ahchi-/ *n, pl* **archipelagoes, archipelagos** (an expanse of water with) a group of scattered islands [*Archipelago* Aegean Sea, fr It *Arcipelago*, lit., chief sea, fr *arci-* (fr L *archi-*) + Gk *pelagos* sea – more at [1]FLAKE] – **archipelagic** /-pə'lajik/ *adj*

architect /'ahkitekt/ *n* **1** sby who designs buildings and superintends their construction **2** sby who devises, plans, and achieves a difficult objective [MF *architecte*, fr L *architectus*, fr Gk *architektōn* master builder, fr *archi-* + *tektōn* builder, carpenter – more at TECHNICAL]

architectonic /,ahkitek'tonik/ *adj* **1** of or according with the principles of architecture **2** resembling architecture in structure or organization [L *architectonicus*, fr Gk *architektonikos*, fr *architektōn*] – **architectonically** *adv*

,architec'tonics *n pl but sing or pl in constr, also* **architectonic** **1a** the systematic arrangement of knowledge **b** the system of structure **2** the art or science of architecture

architecture /'ahki,tekchə/ *n* **1** the art, practice, or profession of designing and erecting buildings; *also* a method or style of building **2** product or work of architecture ⟨*the beautiful ~ of Prague*⟩ – **architectural** /-'tekchərəl/ *adj*, **architecturally** *adv*

architrave /'ahki,trayv/ *n* **1** the lowest part of an entablature resting immediately on the capital of the column **2** the moulded frame round a rectangular recess or opening (e g a door) *USE* ☞ ARCHITECTURE [MF, fr OIt, fr *archi-* + *trave* beam, fr L *trabs*]

archival /ah'kievl/ *adj* relating to, contained in, or constituting archives

[1]**archive** /'ahkiev/ *n* a place in which public records or historical documents are preserved; *also* the material preserved – often pl with sing. meaning [F & L; F, fr L *archivum*, fr Gk *archeion* government house (in pl, official documents), fr *archē* rule, government]

[2]**archive** *vt* to file or collect (e g records or documents) in a repository (e g an archive)

archivist /'ahkivist/ *n* sby in charge of archives

archon /'ahkon/ *n* a chief magistrate in ancient Athens [L, fr Gk *archōn*, fr prp of *archein*]

archway /'ahch,way/ *n* (an arch over) a way or passage that runs beneath arches

-archy /-ahki/ *comb form* (→ *n*) rule; government ⟨*mon*archy⟩ [ME *-archie*, fr MF, fr L *-archia*, fr Gk, fr *archein* to rule – more at ARCH-]

'arc ,lamp /ahk/ *n* a type of electric lamp that produces light by an arc made when a current passes between 2 incandescent electrodes surrounded by gas

arctic /'ahktik/ *adj* **1** *often cap* of the N Pole or the surrounding region **2a** extremely cold; frigid **b** cold in temper or mood [ME *artik*, fr L *arcticus*, fr Gk *arktikos*, fr *arktos* bear, Ursa Major, north; akin to L *ursus* bear]

,arctic 'circle *n, often cap A&C* the parallel of latitude approx 66 ½ degrees north of the equator that circumscribes the north polar region

arcuate /'ahkyoo·ət, -ayt/ *adj* curved like a bow ⟨*an ~ cloud*⟩ [L *arcuatus*, pp of *arcuare* to bend like a bow, fr *arcus* bow – more at ARROW] – **arcuately** /-ətli/ *adv*

'arc-,weld *vt* to weld (metal parts) by means of an electric arc struck between 2 electrodes or 1 electrode and the metal – **arc welding** *n*

arc weld *n* a weld made by arc welding

-ard /ahd/ *suffix* (→ *n*) one characterized by or associated with (a usu undesirable specified action, state, or quality) ⟨*dull*ard⟩ [ME, fr OF, of Gmc origin; akin to OHG *-hart* (in personal names such as *Gērhart* Gerard), OE *heard* hard]

ardent /'ahd(ə)nt/ *adj* characterized by warmth of

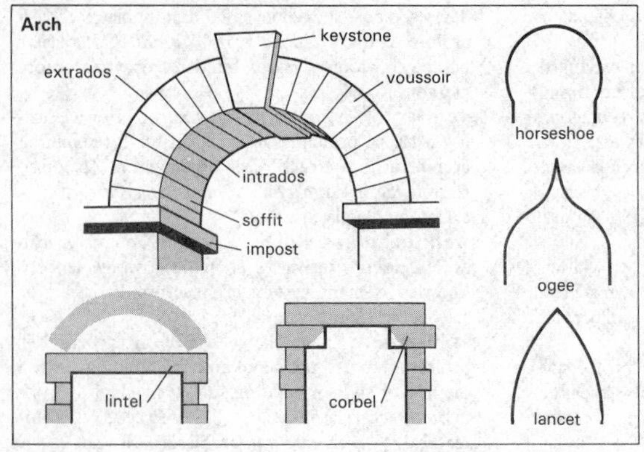
Arch
keystone
extrados
voussoir
horseshoe
intrados
soffit
impost
ogee
lintel
corbel
lancet

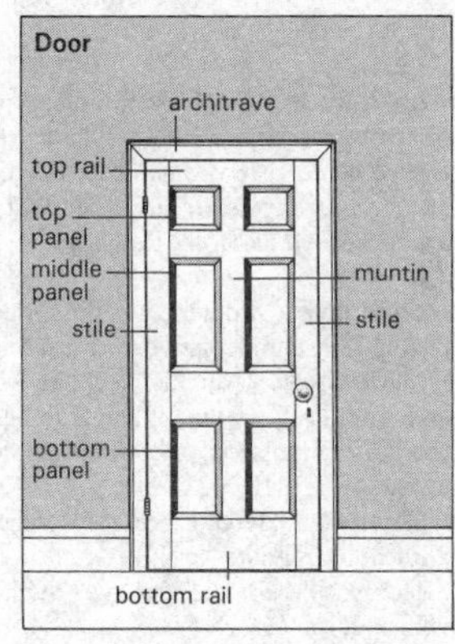
Door
architrave
top rail
top panel
middle panel
muntin
stile
stile
bottom panel
bottom rail

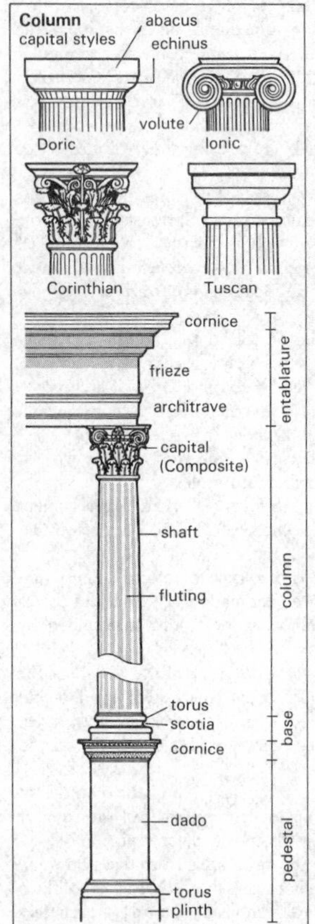
Column
capital styles
abacus
echinus
volute
Doric
Ionic
Corinthian
Tuscan
cornice
frieze
architrave
entablature
capital (Composite)
shaft
fluting
column
torus
scotia
cornice
base
dado
pedestal
torus
plinth

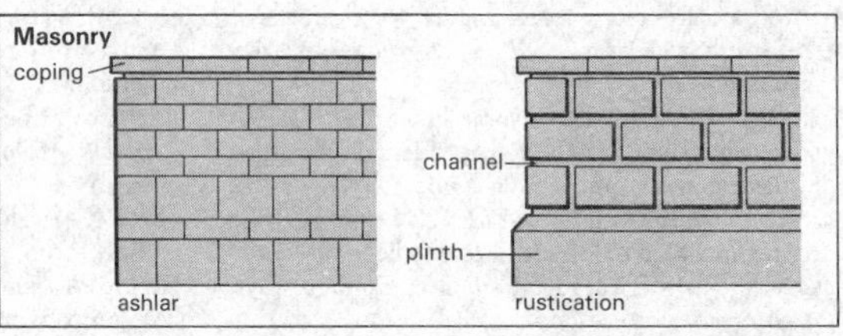
Masonry
coping
channel
plinth
ashlar
rustication

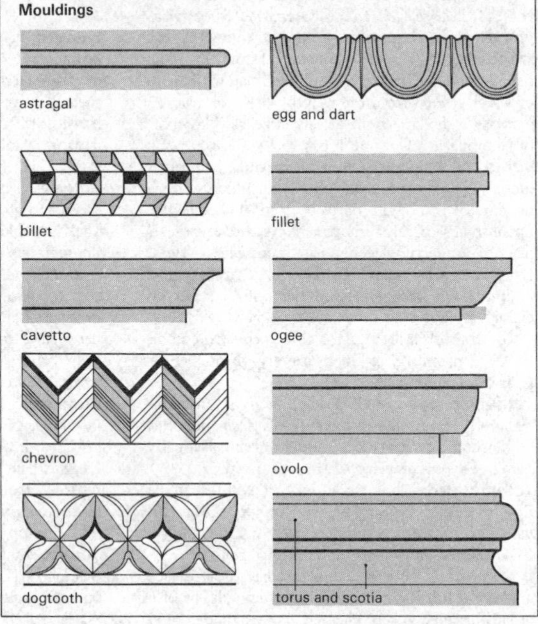
Mouldings
astragal
egg and dart
billet
fillet
cavetto
ogee
chevron
ovolo
dogtooth
torus and scotia

☞ BUILDING

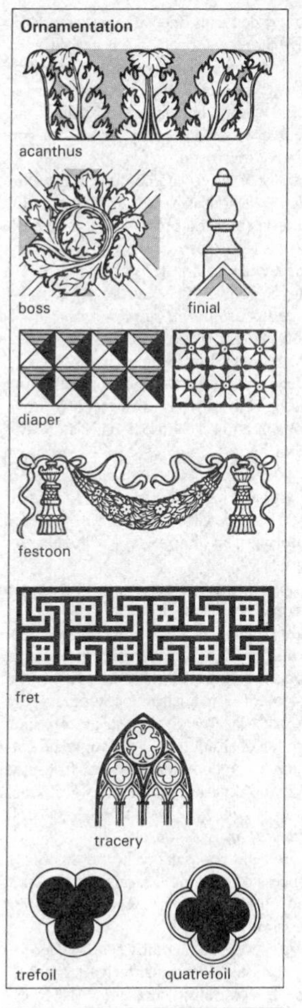
Ornamentation
acanthus
boss
finial
diaper
festoon
fret
tracery
trefoil
quatrefoil

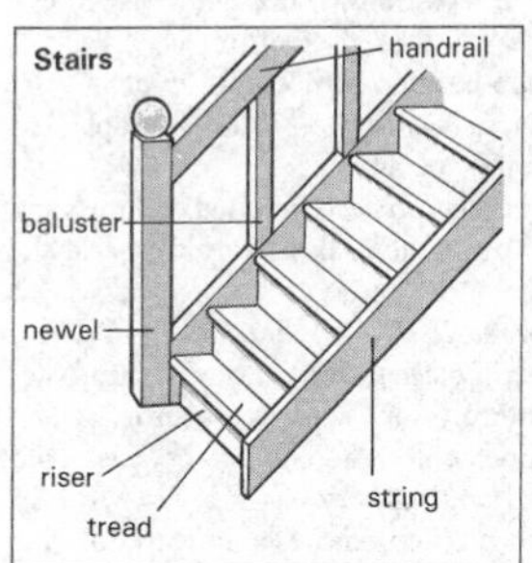
Stairs
handrail
baluster
newel
riser
tread
string

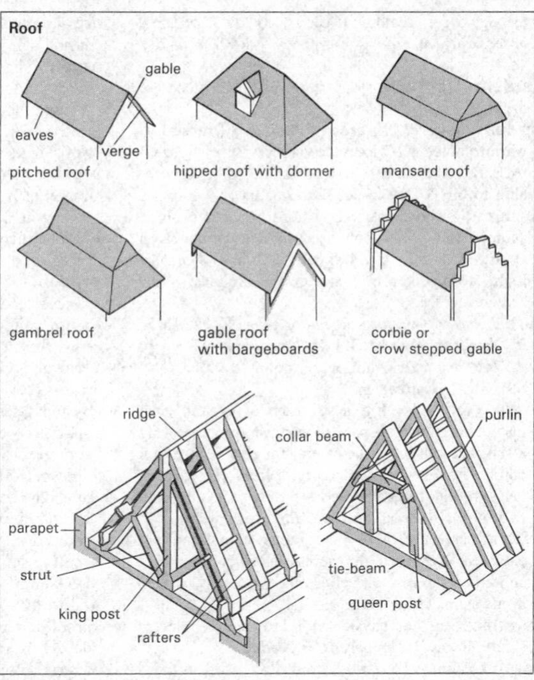
Roof
gable
eaves
verge
pitched roof
hipped roof with dormer
mansard roof
gambrel roof
gable roof
with bargeboards
corbie or
crow stepped gable
ridge
purlin
collar beam
parapet
strut
king post
rafters
tie-beam
queen post

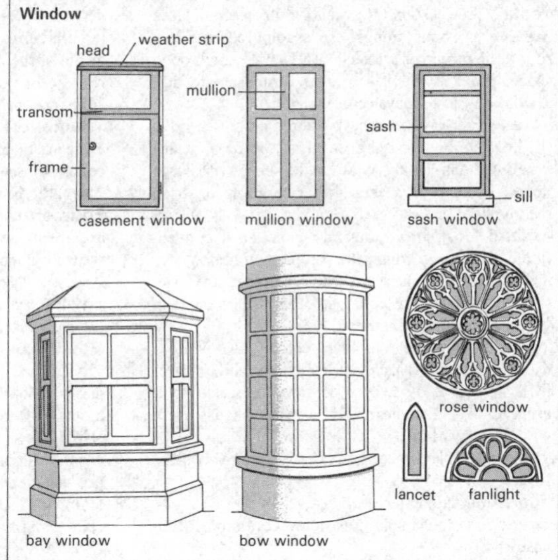
Window
weather strip
head
mullion
transom
sash
frame
sill
casement window
mullion window
sash window
rose window
lancet
fanlight
bay window
bow window

feeling; eager, zealous [ME, fr MF, fr L *ardent-, ardens*, prp of *ardēre*] – **ardency** /-si/ *n*, **ardently** *adv*

,**ardent 'spirits** *n pl* strong distilled alcoholic drinks

ardour, *NAm chiefly* **ardor** /'ahdə/ *n* **1** (transitory) warmth of feeling **2** extreme vigour or intensity; zeal [ME, fr MF & L; MF, fr L *ardor*, fr *ardēre* to burn; akin to OHG *essa* forge, L *aridus* dry]

arduous /'ahdyoo·əs/ *adj* **1** hard to accomplish or achieve; difficult, strenuous **2** hard to climb; steep [L *arduus* high, steep, difficult; akin to ON *örthigr* high, steep, Gk *orthos* straight] – **arduously** *adv*, **arduousness** *n*

[1]**are** /ə; *strong* ah/ *pres 2 sing or pres pl of* BE [ME, fr OE *earun*; akin to ON *eru, erum* are, OE *is* is]

[2]**are** /ah/ *n* a metric unit of area equal to $100m^2$ ☞ UNIT [F, fr L *area*]

area /'eəri·ə/ *n* **1** a level piece of ground **2** a particular extent of space or surface, or one serving a special function **3** the extent, range, or scope of a concept, operation, or activity; a field [L, piece of level ground, threshing floor, fr *arēre* to be dry; akin to L *ardor*] – **areal** /'eəri·əl/ *adj*, **areally** *adv*

arena /ə'reenə/ *n* **1** (a building containing) an enclosed area used for public entertainment **2** a sphere of interest or activity; a scene [L *harena, arena* sand, sandy place]

arenaceous /,ari'nayshəs/ *adj* growing or living in sandy places [L *arenaceus*, fr *arena*]

aren't /ahnt/ **1** are not **2** am not – used in questions

areola /ə'ree·ələ/ *n, pl* **areolae** /-li/ a small area between or round things; *esp* a coloured ring (e g round the nipple or a vesicle) [NL, fr L, small open space, dim. of *area*] – **areolar** *adj*, **areolate** *adj*, **areolation** /ə,ree·ə'laysh(ə)n, ,ari·ə-/ *n*

arête /ə'ret, ə'rayt/ *n* a sharp-crested mountain ridge [F, lit., fishbone, fr LL *arista*, fr L, beard of grain]

argali /'ahgəli/ *n* an Asiatic wild sheep with large horns, or any of several other large wild sheep [Mongolian]

,**Argand 'diagram** /,ahgənd, -gand/ *n* a conventional diagram in which the complex number $x + iy$ is represented by the point whose rectangular Cartesian coordinates are *x* and *y* [Jean Robert *Argand* †1822 Swiss mathematician]

argent /'ahjənt/ *n* **1** a silver colour; *also* white – used in heraldry **2** *archaic* the metal or colour silver [ME, fr MF & L; MF, fr L *argentum*; akin to L *arguere* to make clear, Gk *argyros* silver, *argos* white] – **argent** *adj*

argentic /ah'jentik/ *adj* of or containing (bivalent) silver

argentine /'ahjəntien/ *adj* silver, silvery

argentous /ah'jentəs/ *adj* of or containing (univalent) silver

argie-bargie /,ahji 'bahji/ *n* argy-bargy

argil /'ahjil/ *n* (potter's) clay [ME, fr L *argilla*, fr Gk *argillos*; akin to Gk *argos* white]

argillaceous /,ahji'layshəs/ *adj* of or containing clay or clay minerals

arginine /'ahjinien/ *n* an amino acid that is a chemical base and is found in most proteins [G *arginin*]

Argive /'ahgiev, -jiev/ *adj* of Greece; *esp* of the Achaean city of Argos [L *Argivus*, fr Gk *Argeios*, lit., of Argos, fr *Argos*, city-state of ancient Greece] – **Argive** *n*

argol /'ahgol/ *n* crude tartar deposited in wine casks during aging [ME *argoile*, prob fr AF *argoil*]

argon /'ahgon/ *n* a noble gaseous element found in the air and volcanic gases and used esp as a filler for vacuum tubes and electric light bulbs ☞ PERIODIC TABLE [Gk, neut of *argos* idle, lazy, fr *a-* + *ergon* work; fr its relative inertness]

argosy /'ahgəsi/ *n* a large merchant sailing ship [modif of It *ragusea* Ragusan vessel, fr *Ragusa*, city & port in Dalmatia (now Dubrovnik, Yugoslavia)]

argot /'ahgoh/ *n* a (more or less secret) vocabulary peculiar to a particular group [F]

arguably /'ahgyoo·əbli/ *adv* as can be argued ⟨~ *the best black cellist around at present*⟩

argue /'ahgyooh/ *vi* **1** to give reasons for or against sthg; reason **2** to contend or disagree in words ~ *vt* **1** to give evidence of; indicate **2** to consider the reasons for and against; discuss **3** to (try to) prove by giving reasons; maintain **4** to persuade by giving reasons ⟨~d *him out of going*⟩ **5** to give reasons or arguments in favour of ⟨*his letter* ~s *restraint*⟩ [ME *arguen*, fr MF *arguer* to accuse, reason & L *arguere* to make clear; MF *arguer*, fr L *argutare* to prate, fr *argutus* clear, noisy, fr pp of *arguere*] – **arguable** *adj*, **arguer** *n*

argufy /'ahgyoofie/ *vt* to dispute ~ *vi* to wrangle *USE* infml – **argufier** /-,fie·ə/ *n*

argument /'ahgyoomənt/ *n* **1** a reason given in proof or rebuttal **2a** the act or process of arguing; debate **b** a coherent series of reasons offered **c** a quarrel, disagreement **3** an abstract or summary, esp of a literary work **4a** any of the variables which determine the value of a function **b** the angle indicating the direction of a complex number from the origin of the Argand diagram ⟨*if* a + ib *is written as* re^{i} $C\theta$ or r$(cos\theta + isin\theta)$ *then* θ *is the* ~⟩ [ME, fr MF, fr L *argumentum*, fr *arguere*]

argumentation /,ahgyoomən'taysh(ə)n, -men-/ *n* **1** the act or process of forming reasons and drawing conclusions and applying them to a case in discussion **2** debate, discussion

argumentative /,ahgyoo'mentətiv/ *adj* given to argument; disputatious – **argumentatively** *adv*

Argus /'ahgəs/ *n* a watchful guardian [L, fr Gk *Argos*, a legendary 100-eyed creature]

argy-bargy, argie-bargie /,ahji 'bahji/ *n, chiefly Br* (a) lively discussion; (a) dispute – infml [redupl of Sc & E dial *argy*, alter. of *argue*]

aria /'ahri·ə/ *n, pl* **arias** an accompanied melody sung (e g in an opera) by 1 voice [It, lit., atmospheric air, modif of L *aer*]

-arian /-'eəri·ən/ *suffix* (→ *n*) **1** believer in ⟨*Unitarian*⟩; advocate of ⟨*vegetarian*⟩ **2** one who pursues (a specified interest or activity) ⟨*antiquarian*⟩ ⟨*librarian*⟩ **3** one who is (so many decades) old ⟨*octogenarian*⟩ [L *-arius* -ary]

Arianism /'eəri·ə,niz(ə)m/ *n* the (heretical) doctrine that the divinity of the Son is of an inferior nature to that of the Father [*Arius* †336 Gk theologian] – **Arian** *adj or n*

arid /'arid/ *adj* **1** excessively dry; *specif* having insufficient rainfall to support agriculture **2** lacking in interest and life [F or L; F *aride*, fr L *aridus* – more at ARDOUR] – **aridity** /ə'ridəti/ *n*, **aridness** *n*

ariel /'eəri·əl/ *n* an Asian and African gazelle [Ar *aryal*, var of *ayyil* stag]

Aries /'eəriz, -reez/ *n* (sby born under) the 1st sign of the zodiac in astrology, which is pictured as a ram

☞ SYMBOL [L, lit., ram; akin to Gk *eriphos* kid, OIr *heirp* doe] – **Arian** /ˈeəri·ən/ *adj or n*

aright /əˈriet/ *adv* rightly, correctly [ME, fr OE *ariht*, fr [1]*a-* + *riht* right]

aril /ˈaril/ *n* an exterior covering of some seeds (e g those of yew) that develops after fertilization [prob fr NL *arillus*, fr ML, raisin, grape seed] – **ariled** /ˈarild/ *adj*, **arillate** /ˈari,layt/ *adj*

arise /əˈriez/ *vi* **arose** /əˈrohz/; **arisen** /əˈriz(ə)n/ **1a** to originate from a source – often + *from* **b** to come into being or to attention **2** to get up, rise – chiefly fml [ME *arisen*, fr OE *ārīsan*, fr *ā-*, perfective prefix + *rīsan* to rise]

aristocracy /,ariˈstokrəsi/ *n* **1** (a state with) a government in which power is vested in a small privileged usu hereditary noble class **2** *sing or pl in constr* a (governing) usu hereditary nobility **3** *sing or pl in constr* the whole group of those believed to be superior (e g in wealth, rank, or intellect) [MF & LL; MF *aristocratie*, fr LL *aristocratia*, fr Gk *aristokratia*, fr *aristos* best + *-kratia* -cracy]

aristocrat /ˈaristəkrat, əˈri-/ *n* **1** a member of an aristocracy; *esp* a noble **2** one who has the bearing and viewpoint typical of the aristocracy

aristocratic /,aristəˈkratik, ə,ri-/ *adj* belonging to, having the qualities of, or favouring aristocracy [MF *aristocratique*, fr ML *aristocraticus*, fr Gk *aristokratikos*, fr *aristos* + *-kratikos* -cratic] – **aristocratically** *adv*

Aristotelian, Aristotelean /,aristəˈteeli·ən, -stoh-/ *adj* of Aristotle's doctrines or his principles of logic [*Aristotle* †322 BC Gk philosopher] – **Aristotelian** *n*, **Aristotelianism** /-li·ə,niz(ə)m/ *n*

arithmetic /əˈrithmətik/ *n* **1** a branch of mathematics that deals with real numbers and calculations with them **2** computation, calculation [ME *arsmetrik*, fr OF *arismetique*, fr L *arithmetica*, fr Gk *arithmētikē*, fr fem of *arithmētikos* arithmetical, fr *arithmein* to count, fr *arithmos* number; akin to Gk *arariskein* to fit] – **arithmetic** /,arithˈmetik/, **arithmetical** *adj*, **arithmetically** *adv*, **arithmetician** /ə,rithməˈtish(ə)n, ,arith-/ *n*

,arith,metic ˈmean /,arithˈmetik/ *n* a value found by dividing the sum of a set of terms by the number of terms ☞ STATISTICS, SYMBOL

,arith,metic proˈgression *n* a sequence (e g 3, 5, 7, 9) in which the difference between any term and its predecessor is constant

-arium /-ˈeəri·əm, -ˈahri·əm/ *suffix* (→ *n*), *pl* **-ariums, -aria** /-ri·ə/ thing or place relating to or connected with ⟨*planet*arium⟩ ⟨*aqu*arium⟩ [L, fr neut of *-arius* -ary]

ark /ahk/ *n* **1** a ship; *esp* (one like) the one built by Noah to escape the Flood **2a** the sacred chest representing to the Hebrews the presence of God among them **b** a repository for the scrolls of the Torah [ME, fr OE *arc*; akin to OHG *arahha* ark; both fr a prehistoric Gmc word borrowed fr L *arca* chest; akin to L *arcēre* to hold off, defend, Gk *arkein*]

[1]**arm** /ahm/ *n* **1** (the part between the shoulder and the wrist of) the human upper limb **2** sthg like or corresponding to an arm: e g **a** the forelimb of a vertebrate animal **b** a limb of an invertebrate animal **3** an inlet of water (e g from the sea) **4** might, authority ⟨*the long ~ of the law*⟩ **5** a support (e g on a chair) for the elbow and forearm **6** a sleeve **7** a functional division of a group or activity [ME, fr OE *earm*; akin to L *armus* shoulder, Gk *harmos* joint, L *arma* weapons, *ars* skill, Gk *arariskein* to fit] – **armed** *adj*, **armful** *n*, **armless** *adj*, **armlike** *adj* – **at arm's length** far enough away to avoid intimacy

[2]**arm** *vt* **1** to supply or equip with weapons **2** to provide with sthg that strengthens or protects **3** to fortify morally **4** to equip for action or operation ⟨*~ a bomb*⟩ *~ vi* to prepare oneself for struggle or resistance [ME *armen*, fr OF *armer*, fr L *armare*, fr *arma* weapons, tools]

[3]**arm** *n* **1a** a weapon; *esp* a firearm – usu pl **b** a combat branch (e g of an army) **2** *pl* the heraldic insignia of a group or body (e g a family or government) **3** *pl* **a** active hostilities **b** military service or profession [ME *armes* (pl) weapons, fr OF, fr L *arma*] – **up in arms** angrily rebellious and protesting strongly ⟨*the entire community are* up in arms *about the proposed motorway*⟩

armada /ahˈmahdə/ *n*, *pl* **armadas** a fleet of warships; *specif*, *cap* that sent against England by Spain in 1588 [Sp, fr ML *armata* army, fleet, fr L, fem of *armatus*, pp of *armare*]

armadillo /,ahməˈdiloh/ *n*, *pl* **armadillos** any of several burrowing chiefly nocturnal S American mammals with body and head encased in an armour of small bony plates [Sp, fr dim. of *armado* armed one, fr L *armatus*]

Armageddon /,ahməˈged(ə)n/ *n* **1** (the site or time of) a final and conclusive battle between the forces of good and evil **2** a vast decisive conflict [Gk *Armageddōn, Harmagedōn*, scene of the battle foretold in Rev 16:14–16]

Armagnac /ˈahmənyak/ *n* a dry brandy produced in the Gers district of France [F, fr *Armagnac*, region in SW France]

armament /ˈahməmənt/ *n* **1** a military or naval force **2** the military strength, esp in arms and equipment, of a ship, fort, or combat unit, nation, etc **3** the process of preparing for war [F *armement*, fr L *armamenta* (pl) utensils, military or naval equipment, fr *armare* to arm, equip]

armamentarium /,ahməmənˈteəri·əm/ *n*, *pl* **armamentaria** /-ri·ə/ the equipment and methods available, esp in medical treatment [L, armoury, fr *armamenta*]

armature /ˈahməchə/ *n* **1** an offensive or defensive structure in a plant or animal (e g teeth or thorns) **2a** the central rotating part of an electric motor or generator **b** a framework on which a modeller in clay, wax, etc builds up his/her work [L *armatura* armour, equipment, fr *armatus*]

[1]**armchair** /ˈahm,cheə/ *n* a chair with armrests

[2]**armchair** *adj* **1** remote from direct dealing with practical problems ⟨*~ strategists*⟩ **2** sharing vicariously in another's experiences ⟨*an ~ traveller*⟩

Armenian /ahˈmeenyən, -ni·ən/ *n* **1** a member of a people living chiefly in Armenia **2** the Indo-European language of the Armenians ☞ LANGUAGE [*Armenia* (fr L, fr Gk), former kingdom in W Asia, now divided between USSR, Turkey, & Iran] – **Armenian** *adj*

ˈarm,hole /-,hohl/ *n* an opening for the arm in a garment

armiger /ˈahmijə/ *n* **1** a squire **2** a person entitled to bear heraldic arms [ML, fr L, armour-bearer, fr *armiger* bearing arms, fr *arma* arms + *-ger* -gerous] – **armigeral** /ahˈmijərəl/, **armigerous** /-rəs/ *adj*

,armillary ˈsphere /ˈahmiləri, -ˈ---/ *n* an old astronomical instrument composed of rings representing the positions of important circles of the celestial sphere [F *sphère armillaire*, fr ML *armilla*, fr L, bracelet, iron ring, fr *armus* arm, shoulder; akin to OE *earm* arm]

armistice /'ahmistis/ *n* a temporary suspension of hostilities; a truce [F or NL; F, fr NL *armistitium*, fr L *arma* + *-stitium* (as in *solstitium* solstice)]

'Armistice ,Day *n* **1** *Br* REMEMBRANCE SUNDAY – used before the official adoption of *Remembrance Sunday* after WW II **2** *NAm* VETERANS DAY – used before the official adoption of *Veterans Day* in 1954 [fr the armistice terminating WW I on November 11, 1918]

armlet /'ahmlit/ *n* **1** a band (e g of cloth or metal) worn round the upper arm **2** a small arm (e g of the sea)

armorial /ah'mawri·əl/ *adj* of or bearing heraldic arms [*armory* (heraldry)] – **armorially** *adv*

armour, *Nam chiefly* **armor** /'ahmə/ *n* **1a** a defensive covering for the body; *esp* a covering (e g of metal) worn in combat **b** a usu metallic protective covering (e g for a ship, fort, aircraft, or car) **2** armoured forces and vehicles (e g tanks) [ME *armure*, fr OF, fr L *armatura* – more at ARMATURE] – **armour** *vt*, **armourless** *adj*

,armour-'clad *adj* sheathed in or protected by armour

armoured /'ahməd/ *adj* consisting of or equipped with vehicles protected with armour plate

armourer /'ahmərə/ *n* **1** sby who makes or looks after armour or arms **2** sby who repairs, assembles, and tests firearms

,armour 'plate *n* a defensive covering of hard metal plates for combat vehicles and vessels

armoury /'ahməri/ *n* (a collection of or place for storing) arms and military equipment

'arm,pit /-,pit/ *n* the hollow beneath the junction of the arm and shoulder

'arm,rest /-,rest/ *n* a support for the arm

'arm ,wrestling *n* a contest in which 2 opponents grip each other's usu right hand and set the corresponding elbow on a surface, then attempt to force each other's arm down

army /'ahmi/ *n* **1a** a large organized force for war on land **b** *often cap* the complete military organization of a nation for land warfare ☞ RANK **2** a great multitude **3** a body of people organized to advance a cause ⟨*the Salvation* Army⟩ [ME *armee*, fr MF, fr ML *armata* – more at ARMADA]

arnica /'ahnikə/ *n, pl* **arnicas** any of several related composite plants [NL, genus name]

'A-,road *n* a main road of high standard

aroma /ə'rohmə/ *n, pl* **aromas** **1a** a distinctive, pervasive, and usu pleasant or savoury smell **b** the bouquet of a wine **2** a distinctive quality or atmosphere [ME *aromat* spice, fr OF, fr L *aromat-, aroma*, fr Gk *arōmat-, arōma*]

[1]aromatic /,arə'matik/ *adj* **1** of or having an aroma: **a** fragrant **b** having a strong esp pungent or spicy smell **2** *of a chemical compound* having a molecular structure containing a ring, specif containing (a group like) a benzene ring – **aromatically** /,arə'matikli/ *adv*, **aromaticity** /,arəmə'tisəti, ə,rohmə-/ *n*, **aromaticness** /,arə'matiknis/ *n*, **aromatize** /ə'rohmə,tiez/ *vt*, **aromatization** /-tie'zaysh(ə)n/ *n*

[2]aromatic *n* sthg aromatic

arose /ə'rohz/ *past of* ARISE

[1]around /ə'rownd/ *adv, chiefly NAm* **1** round **2** ABOUT 3, 5 [ME, fr [1]*a-* + *round*, n]

[2]around *prep, chiefly NAm* **1** round **2** ABOUT 1, 2a, 5

[3]around *adj, chiefly NAm* **1** ABOUT 1 ⟨*has been up and ~ for 2 days*⟩ **2** in existence, evidence, or circulation ⟨*the most intelligent of the artists ~ today* – R M Coates⟩

arouse /ə'rowz/ *vt* **1** to awaken from sleep **2** to rouse to action; excite, esp sexually [*a-* (as in *arise*) + *rouse*] – **arousal** /-zl/ *n*

arpeggio /ah'pejioh/ *n, pl* **arpeggios** (the sounding of) a chord whose notes are played in succession, not simultaneously ☞ MUSIC [It, fr *arpeggiare* to play on the harp, fr *arpa* harp, of Gmc origin; akin to OHG *harpha* harp]

arquebus /'ahkwibəs/ *n* a heavy but portable matchlock gun usu fired from a support [MF *harquebuse, arquebuse*, deriv of MLG *hakebusse*, fr *haken* hook + *busse* gun] – **arquebusier** /,ahkwibə'siə/ *n*

arrack, arak /'arak, 'arək/ *n* an Asian alcoholic spirit that is a distillation of the fermented mash of rice and molasses and to which has been added the fermented sap of the coconut palm [Ar *'araq* sweat, juice, liquor]

arraign /ə'rayn/ *vt* **1** to charge before a court **2** to accuse of wrong, inadequacy, or imperfection [ME *arreinen*, fr MF *araisner*, fr OF, fr *a-* (fr L *ad-*) + *raisnier* to speak, fr (assumed) VL *rationare*, fr L *ration-, ratio* reason – more at REASON] – **arraignment** *n*

arrange /ə'raynj/ *vt* **1** to put in order or into sequence or relationship **2** to make preparations for; plan **3** to bring about an agreement concerning; settle ⟨*~ an exchange of prisoners of war*⟩ **4** to adapt (a musical composition) by scoring for different voices or instruments ~ *vi* to make plans ⟨*~ to go on holiday*⟩ [ME *arangen*, fr MF *arangier*, fr OF, fr *a-* + *rengier* to set in a row, fr *reng* row – more at [2]RANK] – **arranger** *n*

ar'rangement /-mənt/ *n* **1a** a preliminary measure; a preparation ⟨*travel ~s*⟩ **b** an adaptation of a musical composition for different voices or instruments **c** an informal agreement or settlement, esp on personal, social, or political matters **d** an agreement with a bank that allows one to draw money without notice from a branch other than that at which one has one's account ⟨*have you got an ~?*⟩ **2** sthg made by arranging constituents or things together ⟨*a floral ~*⟩ [ARRANGE + -MENT]

arrant /'arənt/ *adj* notoriously without moderation; extreme ⟨*an ~ fool*⟩ [alter. of *errant*] – **arrantly** *adv*

arras /'arəs/ *n, pl* **arras** a wall hanging or screen made of tapestry [ME, fr *Arras*, city in France]

[1]array /ə'ray/ *vt* **1** to set or place in order; marshal **2** to dress or decorate, esp in splendid or impressive clothes; adorn [ME *arrayen*, fr OF *arayer*, fr (assumed) VL *arredare*, fr L *ad-* + a base of Gmc origin; akin to Goth *garaiths* arranged – more at READY] – **arrayer** *n*

[2]array *n* **1** military order ⟨*forces in ~*⟩ **2a** clothing, garments **b** rich or beautiful apparel; finery **3** an imposing group; a large number **4** a number of mathematical elements arranged in rows and columns **5** an arrangement of computer memory elements (e g magnetic cores) in a single plane

arrear /ə'riə/ *n* **1** an unfinished duty **2** an unpaid and overdue debt *USE* usu pl with sing. meaning [ME *arrere* behind, backwards, fr MF, fr (assumed) VL *ad retro* backwards, fr L *ad* to + *retro* backwards, behind – more at [1]AT, RETRO-] – **arrearage** /ə'riərij/ *n* – **in arrears** behind in the discharge of obligations

[1]**arrest** /ə'rest/ *vt* **1a** to bring to a stop ⟨*sickness* ~ed *his activities*⟩ **b** to make inactive **2** to seize, capture; *specif* to take or keep in custody by authority of law **3** to catch and fix or hold ⟨~ *the attention*⟩ [ME *aresten*, fr MF *arester* to rest, arrest, fr (assumed) VL *arrestare*, fr L *ad-* + *restare* to remain, rest] – **arrester, arrestor** *n*, **arrestment** *n*

[2]**arrest** *n* **1a** the act of stopping **b** the condition of being stopped ⟨*cardiac* ~⟩ **2** the taking or detaining of sby in custody by authority of law **3** a device for arresting motion – **under arrest** in legal custody

ar,restable of'fence *n* a serious offence for which anyone can make an arrest without a warrant ☞ LAW

arresting /ə'resting/ *adj* catching the attention; striking – **arrestingly** *adv*

arrhythmia /ə'ridhmi·ə/ *n* an (abnormal) alteration in rhythm of the heartbeat [NL, fr Gk, lack of rhythm, fr *arrhythmos* unrhythmical, fr *a-* + *rhythmos* rhythm] – **arrhythmic** /-mik/, **arrhythmical** *adj*, **arrhythmically** *adv*

arrière-'pensée /,arieə 'ponsay, ,--- -'- (*Fr* arjɛ:r pɔ̃se)/ *n* a mental reservation [F, fr *arrière* behind + *pensée* thought]

arris /'aris/ *n, pl* **arris, arrises** the sharp ridge or prominent angle formed by the meeting of 2 surfaces, esp in mouldings [prob modif of MF *areste*, lit., fishbone, fr LL *arista* – more at ARÊTE]

arrival /ə'rievl/ *n* **1** the attainment of an end or state **2** sby or sthg that has arrived [ARRIVE + [2]-AL]

arrive /ə'riev/ *vi* **1** to reach a destination **2** to come ⟨*the moment has* ~d⟩ **3** to achieve success [ME *ariven*, fr OF *ariver*, fr (assumed) VL *arripare* to come to shore, fr L *ad-* + *ripa* shore – more at RIVE] – **arriver** *n* – **arrive at** to reach by effort or thought ⟨*have* arrived at *a decision*⟩

arrogance /'arəgəns/ *n* aggressive conceit [ME, fr L *arrogant-, arrogans*, prp of *arrogare*] – **arrogant** /-gənt/ *adj*, **arrogantly** *adv*

arrogate /'arəgayt/ *vt* to claim or seize without justification, on behalf of oneself or another [L *arrogatus*, pp of *arrogare*, fr *ad-* + *rogare* to ask – more at [1]RIGHT] – **arrogation** /,arə'gaysh(ə)n/ *n*

arrondissement /,arən'deesmənt (*Fr* arɔ̃dismɑ̃)/ *n* **1** a parliamentary division of a French department **2** an administrative district of some large French cities, esp Paris [F]

[1]**arrow** /'aroh/ *n* **1** a projectile shot from a bow, usu having a slender shaft, a pointed head, and feathers at the end **2** sthg shaped like an arrow; *esp* a mark to indicate direction [ME *arwe*, fr OE; akin to Goth *arhwazna* arrow, L *arcus* bow, arch, arc]

[2]**arrow** *vt* to indicate with an arrow ⟨*the location is* ~ed *on the map*⟩

'arrow,head /-,hed/ *n* **1** the pointed front part of an arrow **2** sthg shaped like an arrowhead **3** any of several related (water) plants with leaves shaped like arrowheads

'arrow,root /-,rooht/ *n* (a tropical American plant whose roots yield) a nutritive starch used esp as a thickening agent in cooking [fr its use by American Indians to heal wounds from poisoned arrows]

arse /ahs/ *n* **1** the buttocks **2** the anus *USE* vulg [ME *ars, ers*, fr OE *ærs, ears*; akin to OHG & ON *ars* buttocks, Gk *orrhos*, Arm *oṙ*, Hitt *arraš*, OIr *err* tail]

'arse,hole /,hohl/ *n* the anus – vulg

arsenal /'ahsənl, 'ahsnəl/ *n* **1** an establishment for the manufacture or storage of arms and military equipment; an armoury **2** a store, repertory [It *arsenale*, modif of Ar *dār ṣinā'ah* house of manufacture]

arsenic /'ahsnik/ *n* **1** a trivalent and pentavalent semimetallic steel-grey poisonous element ☞ PERIODIC TABLE **2** an extremely poisonous trioxide of arsenic, used esp as an insecticide [ME, fr MF & L; MF, fr L *arsenicum*, fr Gk *arsenikon, arrhenikon* yellow orpiment, fr Syr *zarnig*, of Iranian origin; akin to Av *zaranya* gold, Skt *hari* yellowish] – **arsenic** /ah'senik/ *adj*, **arsenical** *adj or n*, **arsenious** /ah'seenyəs, -ni·əs/ *adj*

arsis /'ahsis/ *n, pl* **arses** /'ahseez/ a stressed syllable in a metrical foot [LL & Gk; LL, raising of the voice, accented part of foot, fr Gk, upbeat, unaccented part of foot, lit., act of lifting, fr *aeirein, airein* to lift]

arson /'ahsən/ *n* the criminal act of setting fire to property in order to cause destruction [obs F, fr OF, fr *ars*, pp of *ardre* to burn, fr L *ardēre* – more at ARDOUR] – **arsonist** *n*

[1]**art** /aht/ *archaic pres 2 sing of* BE [ME, fr OE *eart*; akin to ON *est, ert* (thou) art, OE *is* is]

[2]**art** *n* **1** a skill acquired by experience, study, or observation **2** *pl* the humanities as contrasted with science **3a** the conscious use of skill and creative imagination, esp in the production of aesthetic objects; *also* works so produced **b** (any of the) fine arts or graphic arts **4** decorative or illustrative elements in printed matter [ME, fr OF, fr L *art-, ars* – more at [1]ARM]

[3]**art** *adj* **1** composed, designed, or created with conscious artistry ⟨*an* ~ *song*⟩ **2** designed for decorative purposes ⟨~ *pottery*⟩

-art – see -ARD

art deco /,ah(t) 'dekoh/ *n, often cap A&D* a decorative style of the 1920s and 1930s characterized esp by bold flowing lines and the use of new materials (e g plastic) [F *Art Déco*, fr *Exposition Internationale des Arts Décoratifs*, an exhibition of decorative arts held in Paris in 1925]

artefact, artifact /'ahtifakt/ *n* **1a** a usu simple object (e g a tool or ornament) produced by human workmanship **b** a product of civilization ⟨*an* ~ *of the jet age*⟩ **2** sthg (e g a structure seen in the microscope) unnaturally present through extraneous influences (e g from defects in the staining procedure) [L *arte*, abl of *art-, ars* skill + *factum*, neut of *factus*, pp of *facere* to make, do – more at [1]ARM, [1]DO] – **artefactual** /ahti'faktyooəl, -chooəl/ *adj*

artel /ah'tel/ *n* a workers' or peasants' cooperative in the USSR [Russ *artel'*, fr It *artieri*, pl of *artiere* artisan, fr *arte* art]

artemisia /,ahtə'mizi·ə, -'misi·ə, -'mizh(y)ə/ *n* wormwood or a related strong-smelling composite herb or shrub [NL, genus name, fr L, artemisia, fr Gk]

arteri- /ahtiəri-/, **arterio-** *comb form* **1** artery ⟨arter*itis*⟩ **2** arterial and ⟨arterio*venous*⟩ [MF, fr LL, fr Gk *artēri-, artērio-*, fr *artēria* artery]

arterial /ah'tiəri·əl/ *adj* **1** of or (being the bright red blood) contained in an artery **2** of or being a main road – **arterially** *adv*

arterial·ize, -ise /ah'tiəri·əliez/ *vt* to transform (venous blood) into arterial blood by oxygenation – **arterialization** /-lie'zaysh(ə)n/ *n*

arteriole /ah'tiəriohl/ *n* a very small artery connecting a larger artery with (small blood vessels like) capillaries ☞ ANATOMY [F or NL; F *artériole*, prob fr NL *arteriola*, dim. of L *arteria*] – **arteriolar** /-ri'ohlə/ *adj*

arteriosclerosis /ah,tiəriohskle'rohsis/ *n* abnormal thickening and hardening of the arterial walls [NL] – **arteriosclerotic** /-sklə'rotik/ *adj or n*

artery /'ahtəri/ *n* **1** any of the branching elastic-walled blood vessels that carry blood from the heart to the lungs and through the body – compare VEIN ☞ ANATOMY **2** an esp main channel (e g a river or road) of transport or communication [ME *arterie*, fr L *arteria*, fr Gk *artēria*; akin to Gk *aortē* aorta]

ar,tesian 'well /ah'teezh(ə)n, -zi·ən/ *n* a well by which water reaches the surface with little or no pumping [F *artésien*, lit., of Artois, fr OF, fr *Arteis* Artois, region of France]

'art ,film *n* a film produced for predominantly aesthetic rather than commercial purposes

'art ,form *n* a recognized form (e g a symphony) or medium (e g sculpture) of artistic expression

artful /'ahtf(ə)l/ *adj* adroit in attaining an end, often by deceitful or indirect means; crafty [²ART + ¹-FUL] – **artfully** *adv*, **artfulness** *n*

arthr- /ahthr-/, **arthro-** *comb form* joint ⟨arthr*itis*⟩ ⟨arthro*pod*⟩ [L, fr Gk, fr *arthron*; akin to Gk *arariskein* to fit – more at ¹ARM]

arthritic /ah'thritik/ *adj* of or affected with arthritis – **arthritic** *n*, **arthritically** *adv*

arthritis /ah'thrietəs/ *n, pl* **arthritides** /ah'thrieti,deez/ usu painful inflammation of 1 or more joints [L, fr Gk, fr *arthron*]

arthrodesis /ah'throdisis/ *n, pl* **arthrodeses** /-seez/ the surgical immobilization of a joint so that the bones grow solidly together [NL, fr *arthr-* + Gk *desis* binding, fr *dein* to bind]

arthropod /'ahthrə,pod/ *n* any of a phylum of invertebrate animals (e g insects, arachnids, and crustaceans) with a jointed body and limbs and usu an outer skin made of chitin and moulted at intervals [NL *Arthropoda*, group name, fr *arthr-* + Gk *pod-*, *pous* foot – more at FOOT]

artic /ah'tik/ *n, Br* an articulated lorry – infml

artichoke /'ahti,chohk/ *n* **1a** a tall composite plant like a thistle **b** the partly edible flower head of the artichoke, used as a vegetable **2** JERUSALEM ARTICHOKE [It dial. *articiocco*, fr Ar *al-khurshūf* the artichoke]

¹article /'ahtikl/ *n* **1a(1)** a separate clause, item, provision, or point in a document **(2)** *pl* a written agreement specifying conditions of apprenticeship **b** a piece of nonfictional prose, usu forming an independent part of a magazine, newspaper, etc **2** an item of business; a matter **3** a word or affix (e g *a*, *an*, and *the*) used with nouns to give indefiniteness or definiteness **4a** a particular or separate object or thing, esp viewed as a member of a class of things ⟨*several* ~s *of clothing*⟩ ⟨~s *of value*⟩ **b** a thing of a particular and distinctive kind ⟨*the genuine* ~⟩ [ME, fr OF, fr L *articulus* joint, division, dim. of *artus* joint; akin to Gk *arariskein* to fit – more at ¹ARM]

²article *vt* to bind by articles (e g of apprenticeship)

articular /ah'tikyoolə/ *adj* of a joint ⟨~ *cartilage*⟩ [ME *articuler*, fr L *articularis*, fr *articulus*]

¹articulate /ah'tikyoolət/ *adj* **1a** divided into syllables or words meaningfully arranged **b** having the power of speech **c** expressing oneself readily, clearly, or effectively; *also* expressed in this manner **2** jointed [NL *articulatus*, fr L *articulus*] – **articulacy** /-ləsi/ *n*, **articulately** *adv*, **articulateness** *n*

²articulate /ah'tikyoolayt/ *vt* **1a** to utter distinctly **b** to give clear and effective utterance to ⟨~ *one's grievances*⟩ **2** to unite with a joint ~ *vi* **1** to utter articulate sounds **2** to become united or connected (as if) by a joint [L *articulatus*, pp of *articulare*, fr *articulus*] – **articulative** /-lətiv/ *adj*, **articulator** /-,laytə/ *n*, **articulatory** /-lətri/ *adj*

ar'ticulated *adj, chiefly Br* having 2 parts flexibly connected and intended to operate as a unit ⟨*an* ~ *lorry*⟩

articulation /ah,tikyoo'laysh(ə)n, ,---'--/ *n* **1a** the action or manner of jointing or interrelating **b** the state of being jointed or interrelated **2** a (movable) joint (between plant or animal parts) **3a** the (verbal) expression of thoughts and feelings **b** the act or manner of articulating sounds **4** the occlusion of teeth

artifact /'ahtifakt/ *n* an artefact – **artifactual** /-'faktyooəl, -chooəl/ *adj*

artifice /'ahtifis/ *n* **1** an artful device, expedient, or stratagem; a trick **2** clever or artful skill; ingenuity [MF, fr L *artificium*, fr *artific-*, *artifex* artificer, fr L *art-*, *ars* skill + *facere* to make, do – more at ¹ARM, ¹DO]

artificer /ah'tifisə, 'ahtifisə/ *n* **1** a skilled or artistic worker or craftsman **2** a military or naval mechanic

artificial /,ahti'fish(ə)l/ *adj* **1** made by human skill and labour, often to a natural model; man-made ⟨*an* ~ *limb*⟩ ⟨~ *diamonds*⟩ **2a** lacking in natural quality; affected **b** imitation, sham [ME, fr MF or L; MF *artificiel*, fr L *artificialis*, fr *artificium*] – **artificiality** /-,fishi'aləti/ *n*, **artificially** /-'fish(ə)li/ *adv*, **artificialness** *n*

,arti,ficial insemi'nation *n* introduction of semen into the uterus or oviduct by other than natural means

,arti,ficial respi'ration *n* the rhythmic forcing of air into and out of the lungs of sby whose breathing has stopped

artillery /ah'tiləri/ *n* **1** large-calibre mounted firearms (e g guns, howitzers, missile launchers, etc) **2** *sing or pl in constr* a branch of an army armed with artillery [ME *artillerie* military equipment, missile-throwing weapons, fr MF]

artisan /'ahti,zan, ,--'-, 'ahtiz(ə)n/ *n* **1** a skilled manual worker (e g a carpenter, plumber, or tailor) **2** a member of the urban proletariat [MF, fr OIt *artigiano*, fr *arte* art, fr L *art-*, *ars*]

artist /'ahtist/ *n* **1a** one who professes and practises an imaginative art **b** a person skilled in a fine art **2** a skilled performer; *specif* an artiste **3** one who is proficient in a specified and usu dubious activity; an expert ⟨*rip-off* ~⟩ – infml **4** *Austr & NAm* a fellow or character, esp of a specified sort – infml

artiste /ah'teest/ *n* a skilled public performer; *specif* a musical or theatrical entertainer [F]

artistic /ah'tistik/ *adj* **1** concerning or characteristic of art or artists **2** showing imaginative skill in arrangement or execution – **artistically** *adv*

artistry /'ahtistri/ *n* **1** artistic quality **2** artistic ability

'artless /-lis/ *adj* **1** free from artificiality; natural ⟨~ *grace*⟩ **2** free from deceit, guile, or craftiness; sincerely simple – **artlessly** *adv*, **artlessness** *n*

art nouveau /,ah(t) nooh'voh/ *n, often cap A&N* a decorative style of late 19th-c origin, characterized esp by curved lines and plant motifs [F, lit., new art]

'art ,paper *n, Br* paper coated with china clay and used esp for halftone illustrations

artsy-craftsy /,ahtsi 'krahftsi/ *adj, NAm* arty-crafty

'art,work /-,wuhk/ *n* ART 4

arty /'ahti/ *adj* showily or pretentiously artistic ⟨~ *lighting and photography*⟩ – **artily** *adv*, **artiness** *n*

arty-crafty /,ahti 'krahfti/ *adj* arty; *esp* affectedly simple or rustic in style – infml [fr the phrase *arts and crafts*]

arum /'eərəm/ *n* a cuckoopint or related Old World plant with flowers in a fleshy spathe (partially) surrounded by a leafy bract [NL, genus name, fr L, arum, fr Gk *aron*]

arvo /'ahvoh/ *n, Austr & NZ* the afternoon – infml [alter. of *af*ternoon + *-o*]

¹-ary /-(ə)ri/ *suffix* (→ *n*) **1** thing belonging to or connected with ⟨*ov*ary⟩; *esp* place or repository of or for ⟨*libr*ary⟩ ⟨*avi*ary⟩ **2** one belonging to, connected with, or engaged in ⟨*function*ary⟩ ⟨*mission*ary⟩ [ME *-arie*, fr OF & L; OF *-aire, -arie*, fr L *-arius, -aria, -arium*, fr *-arius*, adj suffix]

²-ary *suffix* (→ *adj*) of or connected with ⟨*budget*ary⟩ ⟨*milit*ary⟩ [ME *-arie*, fr MF & L; MF *-aire*, fr L *-arius*]

¹Aryan /'eəri·ən, 'ahri·ən/ *adj* **1** *of language* Indo-European **2** of speakers of Indo-European or Indo-Iranian languages **3a** of a supposed ethnic type represented by early speakers of Indo-European languages **b** Nordic [Skt *ārya* noble, belonging to the people speaking an Indo-European dialect who migrated into N India]

²Aryan *n* **1** a member of a people speaking an Indo-European language **2** a Nordic **3** a gentile

aryl /'aril/ *n* a radical (e g phenyl) derived from an aromatic hydrocarbon by the removal of 1 hydrogen atom [ISV *ar*omatic + *-yl*]

¹as /əz; *strong* az/ *adv* **1** to the same degree or amount; equally ⟨~ *deaf as a post*⟩ **2** when considered in a specified form or relation – usu used before a preposition or participle ⟨*my opinion* ~ *distinguished from his*⟩ [ME, fr OE *eallswā* likewise, just as – more at ALSO]

²as *conj* **1a** to the same degree that ⟨*deaf* ~ *a post*⟩ – usu used as a correlative after *as* or *so* to introduce a comparison ⟨*as long ago* ~ *1930*⟩ or as a result ⟨*so clearly guilty* ~ *to leave no doubt*⟩ **b** – used after *same* or *such* to introduce an example or comparison ⟨*in the same building* ~ *my brother*⟩ ⟨*such trees* ~ *oak or pine*⟩ **c** – used after *so* to introduce the idea of purpose ⟨*he hid so* ~ *not to get caught*⟩ **2** in the way that ⟨*do* ~ *I say, not* ~ *I do*⟩ – used before *so* to introduce a parallel ⟨~ *the French like their wine, so the British like their beer*⟩ **3** in accordance with what ⟨*quite good* ~ *boys go*⟩ ⟨*late,* ~ *usual*⟩ **4** while, when ⟨*spilt the milk* ~ *she got up*⟩ **5** regardless of the fact that; though ⟨*naked* ~ *I was, I rushed out*⟩ **6** for the reason that; seeing ⟨~ *it's raining, let's make toffee*⟩ – **as is** in the present condition without modification ⟨*bought the clock at an auction* as is⟩ – infml – **as it is** IN REALITY – **as it were** SO TO SPEAK – **as often as not** at least half the time

³as *pron* **1** a fact that; and this ⟨*is ill,* ~ *you can see*⟩ ⟨*unaccustomed* ~ *I am to public speaking*⟩ **2** which also; and so ⟨*plays football,* ~ *do his brothers*⟩

⁴as *prep* **1** LIKE 1a, 2 **2** in the capacity, character, role, or state of ⟨*works* ~ *an editor*⟩ ⟨*they regard her* ~ *clever*⟩

⁵as /as/ *n, pl* **asses** /'aseez, 'asiz/ (a unit of value represented by) a bronze coin of ancient Rome [L]

as- – see AD-

asafoetida, *NAm chiefly* **asafetida** /,asə'fetidə/ *n* the fetid gum resin of various oriental plants of the carrot family used in cookery [ME *asafetida*, fr ML *asafoetida*, fr Per *azā* mastic + L *foetida*, fem of *foetidus* fetid]

asbestos /ə'spestos, -zb-, -sb-/ *n* either of 2 minerals composed of thin flexible fibres, used to make noncombustible, nonconducting, or chemically resistant materials [ME *albestron* mineral supposed to be inextinguishable when set on fire, prob fr MF, fr ML *asbeston*, alter. of L *asbestos*, fr Gk, unslaked lime, fr *asbestos* inextinguishable, fr *a-* + *sbennynai* to quench; akin to Lith *gesti* to be extinguished]

asbestosis /,aspe'stohsis, -zb-, -sb-/ *n, pl* **asbestoses** /-,seez/ a disease of the lungs due to the inhalation of asbestos particles [NL]

asc-, asco- *comb form* ascomycete ⟨asco*carp*⟩ [NL, fr *ascus*]

ascarid /'askərid/ *n* the common roundworm, parasitic in the human intestine, or a related nematode [deriv of LL *ascarid-, ascaris* intestinal worm, fr Gk *askarid-, askaris*; akin to Gk *skairein* to gambol – more at CARDINAL]

ascaris /'askəris/ *n, pl* **ascarides** /as'karideez/ an ascarid [LL]

ascend /ə'send/ *vi* **1** to move or slope gradually upwards; rise **2a** to rise from a lower level or degree ⟨~ *to power*⟩ **b** to go back in time or in order of genealogical succession ~ *vt* **1** to go or move up **2** to succeed to; begin to occupy – esp in *ascend the throne* [ME *ascenden*, fr L *ascendere*, fr *ad-* + *scandere* to climb – more at SCAN] – **ascendable, ascendible** *adj*, **ascending** *adj*

ascendance *also* **ascendence** /ə'send(ə)ns/ *n* ascendancy

ascendancy *also* **ascendency** /ə'send(ə)nsi/ *n* controlling influence; domination

¹ascendant *also* **ascendent** /ə'send(ə)nt/ *n* **1** *the* degree of the zodiac that rises above the eastern horizon at any moment (e g at one's birth) **2** a state or position of dominant power or importance – esp in *in the ascendant* **3** an ancestor [ME *ascendent*, fr ML *ascendent-, ascendens*, fr L, prp of *ascendere*]

²ascendant *also* **ascendent** *adj* **1** rising **2** superior, dominant – **ascendantly** *adv*

ascension /ə'sensh(ə)n/ *n* the act or process of ascending [ME, fr L *ascension-, ascensio*, fr *ascensus*, pp of *ascendere*]

A'scension ˌDay *n* the Thursday 40 days after Easter observed in commemoration of Christ's ascension into Heaven

ascent /ə'sent/ *n* **1a** the act of going, climbing, or travelling up **b** a way up; an upward slope or path **2** an advance in social status or reputation; progress [fr *ascend*, by analogy with *descend* : *descent*]

ascertain /ˌasə'tayn/ *vt* to find out or learn with certainty [ME *acertainen* to make certain, fr MF *acertainer*, fr *a-* (fr L *ad-*) + *certain*] – **ascertainable** *adj*

ascetic /ə'setik/ *also* **ascetical** /-kl/ *adj* **1** practising strict self-denial as a spiritual discipline **2** austere in appearance, manner, or attitude [Gk *askētikos*, lit., laborious, fr *askētēs* one that exercises, hermit, fr *askein* to work, exercise] – **ascetic** *n*, **ascetically** *adv*, **asceticism** /-ˌsiz(ə)m/ *n*

ascidian /ə'sidi·ən/ *n* any of an order of tunicates (e g the sea squirt); *broadly* a tunicate [NL *Ascidia*, genus name, fr Gk *askidion*, dim. of *askos* wineskin, bladder]

ascites /ə'sieteez/ *n, pl* **ascites** accumulation of usu blood-derived watery fluid in the abdomen [ME *aschytes*, fr LL *ascites*, fr Gk *askitēs*, fr *askos* wineskin, bladder] – **ascitic** /ə'sitik/ *adj*

asco- – see ASC-

ascomycete /ˌaskə'mieseet/ *n* any of a class of higher fungi (e g yeast) in which the spores are formed in asci [deriv of Gk *askos* + *mykēt-*, *mykēs* fungus; akin to L *mucus*] – **ascomycetous** /-mie'seetəs/ *adj*

ascorbate /ə'skawbayt/ *n* a salt of ascorbic acid

asˌcorbic 'acid /ə'skawbik/ *n* VITAMIN C [*a-* + NL *scorbutus* scurvy – more at SCORBUTIC]

ascribe /ə'skrieb/ *vt* to refer or attribute (sthg) *to* a supposed cause or source [ME *ascriven*, fr MF *ascrivre*, fr L *ascribere*, fr *ad-* + *scribere* to write – more at [1]SCRIBE] – **ascribable** *adj*

ascription /ə'skripsh(ə)n/ *n* the act of ascribing; attribution [LL *ascription-*, *ascriptio*, fr L, written addition, fr *ascriptus*, pp of *ascribere*]

ascus /'askəs/ *n, pl* **asci** /'askie/ the membranous oval or tubular spore sac of an ascomycete [NL, fr Gk *askos* wineskin, bladder]

asdic /'azdik/ *n* sonar [*A*nti-*S*ubmarine *D*etection *I*nvestigation *C*ommittee]

-ase /-ayz, -ays, -əz/ *suffix* (→ *n*) enzyme ⟨*protease*⟩ [F, fr *diastase*]

asepsis /ay'sepsis, ə-, a-/ *n* **1** the condition of being aseptic **2** the methods of making or keeping sthg aseptic [NL]

aseptic /ay'septik, ə-, a-/ *adj* **1** preventing infection ⟨~ *techniques*⟩ **2** free or freed from disease-causing microorganisms ⟨*an* ~ *operating theatre*⟩ [ISV] – **aseptically** *adv*

asexual /ay'seksyooəl, -'seksh(ə)l, ə-/ *adj* **1** lacking sex (organs) **2** produced without sexual action or differentiation **3** without expression of or reference to sexual interest – **asexually** *adv*

aˌsexual repro'duction *n* reproduction (e g cell division or spore formation) without union of individuals or germ cells

as 'far as *conj* INSOFAR AS

'as for *prep* concerning; IN REGARD TO – used esp in making a contrast ⟨~ *the others, they'll arrive later*⟩

'as from *prep* not earlier or later than ⟨*takes effect* ~ *July 1st*⟩

[1]**ash** /ash/ *n* **1** (the tough elastic wood of) any of a genus of tall pinnate-leaved trees of the olive family **2** the ligature æ used in Old English to represent a low front vowel [ME *asshe*, fr OE *æsc*; akin to OHG *ask* ash, L *ornus* wild mountain ash; (2) OE *æsc*, name of the corresponding runic letter]

[2]**ash** *n* **1a** the solid residue left when material is thoroughly burned or oxidized **b** fine particles of mineral matter from a volcano ☞ GEOGRAPHY **2** *pl* the remains of sthg destroyed by fire ⟨*a new city built on the* ~es *of the old*⟩ **3** *pl* the remains of a dead body after cremation or disintegration [ME *asshe*, fr OE *asce*; akin to OHG *asca* ash, L *aridus* dry – more at ARDOUR] – **ashless** *adj*

ashamed /ə'shaymd/ *adj* **1** feeling shame, guilt, or disgrace **2** restrained by fear of shame ⟨*was* ~ *to beg*⟩ [ME, fr OE *āscamod*, pp of *āscamian* to shame, fr *ā-*, perfective prefix + *scamian* to shame] – **ashamedly** /-midli/ *adv*

Ashanti /ə'shanti/ *n, pl* **Ashantis**, *esp collectively* **Ashanti** **1** a member of a W African people of Ghana **2** the dialect of Akan spoken by the Ashanti [Ashanti *A*[1] *san*[3] *te*[1]]

'ash ˌcan *n, NAm* a dustbin

[1]**ashen** /'ash(ə)n/ *adj* of or made from the wood of the ash tree

[2]**ashen** *adj* **1** consisting of or resembling ashes **2** deadly pale; blanched ⟨*his face was* ~ *with fear*⟩

Ashes /'ashiz/ *n pl* a trophy played for in a series of cricket test matches between England and Australia – + *the* [fr a jesting reference to the ashes of the dead body of English cricket after an Australian victory in 1882]

Ashkenazi /ˌashkə'nahzi/ *n, pl* **Ashkenazim** /-'nazim/ a member of the central European Yiddish-speaking branch of Jewry – compare SEPHARDI [Heb *Ashkĕnāzī*] – **Ashkenazic** /-'nazik/ *adj*

ashlar /'ashlə/ *n* **1** (masonry of) hewn or squared stone ☞ ARCHITECTURE **2** a thin squared and dressed stone for facing a wall of rubble or brick [ME *asheler*, fr MF *aisselier* a transverse beam, fr OF, fr *ais* board, fr L *axis*, alter. of *assis*]

ashore /ə'shaw/ *adv* on or to the shore

'ashˌpan /-ˌpan/ *n* a tray fitted under the grate in a fire and into which ashes fall

ashram /'ashrəm, -ram/ *n* the hermitage of a Hindu sage; *broadly* any Hindu religious retreat [Skt *āśrama*, fr *ā* towards + *śrama* religious exercise]

'ashˌtray /-ˌtray/ *n* a (small) receptacle for tobacco ash and cigar and cigarette ends

ˌAsh 'Wednesday *n* the first day of Lent [fr the custom of sprinkling ashes on penitents' heads]

ashy /'ashi/ *adj* **1** of ashes **2** [2]ASHEN 2

Asian /'aysh(ə)n, 'ayzh(ə)n/ *adj* (characteristic) of the continent of Asia or its people [L *Asianus*, fr Gk *asianos*, fr *Asia*] – **Asian** *n*

Asiatic /ˌayzi'atik, ˌayzhi-/ *adj* Asian – **Asiatic** *n*

[1]**aside** /ə'sied/ *adv or adj* **1** to or towards the side ⟨*stepped* ~⟩ **2** out of the way ⟨*put his work* ~⟩ **3** apart; IN RESERVE **4** APART 3 [ME, fr [1]*a-* + *side*]

[2]**aside** *n* **1** an utterance meant to be inaudible; *esp* an actor's speech supposedly not heard by other characters on stage **2** a digression

a'side from *prep, chiefly NAm* APART FROM

as 'if *conj* **1** as it would be if ⟨*it was* ~ *he had lost his best friend*⟩ **2** as one would do if ⟨*shook his head* ~ *to say no*⟩ **3** that ⟨*it's not* ~ *she's poor*⟩ **4** – used in emphatic repudiation of a notion ⟨~ *I cared!*⟩

asinine /'asinien/ *adj* stupid [L *asininus* of or like an ass, fr *asinus* ass] – **asininely** *adv*, **asininity** /-'ninəti/ *n*

ask /ahsk/ *vt* **1a** to call on for an answer ⟨*I* ~ed *him about his trip*⟩ **b** to put a question about ⟨*I* ~ed *his whereabouts*⟩ **c** to put or frame (a question) ⟨~ *a question of him*⟩ **2a** to make a request of ⟨*she* ~*ed her teacher for help*⟩ **b** to make a request for ⟨*she* ~ed *help from her teacher*⟩ **3** to behave in such a way as to provoke (an unpleasant response) ⟨*just* ~ing *to be given a good hiding*⟩ **4** to set as a price ⟨~ed *£1500 for the car*⟩ **5** to invite ⟨~ *him to dinner*⟩ ~ *vi* to seek information ⟨*he* ~ed *after the old man's health*⟩ [ME *asken*, fr OE *āscian*; akin to OHG *eiscōn* to ask, L *aeruscare* to beg] – **asker** *n*

askance /ə'skahns/ *adv* with disapproval or distrust – esp in *look askance* [perh fr It *a scancio* obliquely]

askew /ə'skyooh/ *adv or adj* awry [prob fr [1]*a-* + *skew*] – **askewness** *n*

'**asking ,price** /'ahsking/ *n* the price set by the seller

aslant /ə'slahnt/ *prep, adv, or adj* (over or across) in a slanting direction

asleep /ə'sleep/ *adj* **1** in a state of sleep **2** dead – euph **3** lacking sensation; numb

as 'long as *conj* **1** providing, while; SO LONG AS **2** *chiefly NAm* since; INASMUCH AS ⟨~ *you're going, I'll go too*⟩

aslope /ə'slohp/ *adj or adv* in a sloping or slanting position or direction

as 'much as *adv* even; SO MUCH AS

asocial /ay'sohsh(ə)l/ *adj* **1** lacking the capacity for social interaction **2** antisocial

'**as of** *prep, chiefly NAm* AS FROM

asp /asp/ *n* a small venomous snake of Egypt, variously identified as a cobra or cerastes [ME *aspis*, fr L, fr Gk]

asparagine /ə'sparəjeen, -jin/ *n* an amino acid that is an amide of aspartic acid found in most proteins [F, fr L *asparagus*]

asparagus /ə'sparəgəs/ *n* (any of a genus of Old World perennial plants of the lily family including) a tall plant widely cultivated for its edible young shoots [NL, genus name, fr L, asparagus plant, fr Gk *asparagos*; akin to Gk *spargan* to swell – more at [1]SPARK]

a,spartic 'acid /ə'spahtik/ *n* an amino acid found in most proteins [ISV, irreg fr L *asparagus*]

aspect /'aspekt/ *n* **1a** the position of planets or stars with respect to one another, held by astrologers to influence human affairs; *also* the apparent position (e g conjunction) of a body in the solar system with respect to the sun **b** a position facing a particular direction ⟨*the house has a southern* ~⟩ **c** the manner of presentation of an aerofoil, hydrofoil, etc to a gas or liquid through which it is moving **2a** appearance to the eye or mind **b** a particular feature of a situation, plan, or point of view **3** (a set of inflected verb forms that indicate) the nature of an action as to its beginning, duration, completion, or repetition (e g in *I swim* and *I am swimming*) [ME, fr L *aspectus*, fr *aspectus*, pp of *aspicere* to look at, fr *ad-* + *specere* to look – more at SPY] – **aspectual** /a'spekchooəl/ *adj*

'**aspect ,ratio** *n* a ratio of one dimension to another: e g **a** the ratio of an aerofoil's span to its mean chord **b** the ratio of the width tc the height of a screen or image (e g in television or the cinema)

aspen /'aspən/ *n* any of several poplars with leaves that flutter in the lightest wind [alter. of ME *asp*, fr OE *æspe*; akin to OHG *aspa* aspen, Latvian *apsa*]

aspergillus /,aspə'jiləs/ *n, pl* **aspergilli** /-lie/ any of a genus of fungi including many common moulds [NL, genus name, fr *aspergillum* brush for sprinkling water, fr L *aspergere*]

asperity /ə'sperəti/ *n* **1** rigour, hardship **2** roughness of surface; unevenness **3** roughness of manner or temper; harshness [ME *asprete*, fr OF *aspreté*, fr *aspre* rough, fr L *asper*]

asperse /ə'spuhs/ *vt* to sprinkle, esp with holy water [L *aspersus*, pp of *aspergere*, fr *ad-* + *spargere* to scatter – more at [1]SPARK]

aspersion /ə'spuhsh(ə)n/ *n* **1** a sprinkling with water, esp in religious ceremonies **2** a calumnious or unwarranted doubt ⟨*he cast* ~s *on her integrity*⟩

asphalt /'asfalt, -felt, ash-; *NAm* 'asfawlt/ *n* **1** a brown to black bituminous substance found in natural beds and also obtained as a residue in petroleum or coal tar refining **2** an asphaltic composition used for surfacing roads and footpaths [ME *aspalt*, fr LL *aspaltus*, fr Gk *asphaltos*] – **asphaltic** /-tik/ *adj*

'**asphaltum** /-təm/ *n* asphalt [alter. of ME *aspaltoun, aspalt*]

asphodel /'asfə,del/ *n* any of various Old World plants of the lily family with long spikes of flowers [L *asphodelus*, fr Gk *asphodelos*]

asphyxia /ə'sfiksi·ə/ *n* a lack of oxygen in the body, usu caused by interruption of breathing, and resulting in unconsciousness or death [NL, fr Gk, stopping of the pulse, fr *a-* + *sphyzein* to throb] – **asphyxiate** /-siayt/ *vb*, **asphyxiation** /-si'aysh(ə)n/ *n*, **asphyxiator** /-si,aytə/ *n*

aspic /'aspik/ *n* a clear savoury jelly (e g of fish or meat stock) used as a garnish or to make a meat, fish, etc mould [F, lit., asp]

aspidistra /,aspi'distrə/ *n* any of various Asiatic plants of the lily family with large leaves, often grown as house plants [NL, irreg fr Gk *aspid-, aspis* shield]

[1]**aspirate** /'aspirət/, **aspirated** /'aspiraytid/ *adj* pronounced with aspiration [L *aspiratus*, pp of *aspirare*]

[2]**aspirate** /'aspirayt/ *vt* **1** to pronounce (a vowel, consonant, or word) with an *h*-sound **2** to draw or remove (e g blood) by suction

[3]**aspirate** /'aspirət/ *n* **1** (a character, esp *h*, representing) an independent /h/ sound **2** an aspirated consonant (e g the *p* of *pit*) **3** material removed by aspiration

aspiration /,aspi'raysh(ə)n/ *n* **1** the pronunciation or addition of an aspirate **2** a drawing of sthg in, out, up, or through (as if) by suction: e g **a** the act of breathing (sthg in) **b** the withdrawal of fluid from the body **3a** a strong desire to achieve sthg high or great **b** an object of such desire

aspirator /'aspiraytə/ *n* an apparatus for aspirating (fluid, tissue, etc from the body)

aspire /ə'spie·ə/ *vi* to seek to attain or accomplish a particular goal – usu + *to* ⟨~d *to a career in medicine*⟩ [ME *aspiren*, fr MF or L; MF *aspirer*, fr L *aspirare*, lit., to breathe upon, fr *ad-* + *spirare* to breathe – more at SPIRIT] – **aspirant** /'aspirənt/ *n or adj*, **aspirer** /ə'spie(ə)rə/ *n*

aspirin /'asprin/ *n, pl* **aspirin, aspirins** (a tablet containing) a derivative of salicylic acid used for relief of pain and fever [ISV, fr *acetyl* + *spir*aeic acid (former name of salicylic acid), fr NL *Spiraea*, genus of shrubs – more at SPIRAEA]

as re'gards /ri'gahdz/ *prep* with respect to; IN REGARD TO

as re'spects /ri'spekts/ *prep* with respect to; IN REGARD TO

[1]**ass** /as/ *n* **1** the donkey or a similar long-eared hardy gregarious mammal related to and smaller than the horse **2** a stupid, obstinate, or perverse person or thing ⟨*saying that the law is an* ~⟩ [ME, fr OE *assa*, perh fr OIr *asan*, fr L *asinus*]

[2]**ass** *n, chiefly NAm* the arse [by alter.]

assail /ə'sayl/ *vt* **1** to attack violently with blows or words **2** to prey on ⟨~ed *by doubts*⟩ [ME *assailen*, fr OF *asaillir*, fr (assumed) VL *assalire*, alter. of L *assilire* to leap upon, fr *ad-* + *salire* to leap – more at SALLY] – **assailable** *adj*, **assailant** *n*

assassin /ə'sasin/ *n* **1** *cap* any of a secret order of Muslims who at the time of the Crusades committed secret murders **2** a murderer; *esp* one who murders a politically important person, for money or from fanatical motives [ML *assassinus*, fr Ar *ḥashshā-shīn*, pl of *ḥashshāsh* one who smokes or chews hashish]

assassinate /ə'sasinayt/ *vt* to murder suddenly or secretly, usu for political reasons – **assassination** /-'naysh(ə)n/ *n*, **assassinator** /-,naytə/ *n*

[1]**assault** /ə'sawlt/ *n* **1** a violent physical or verbal attack **2a** an attempt to do or immediate threat of doing unlawful personal violence **b** rape **3** an attempt to attack a fortification by a sudden rush [ME *assaut*, fr OF, fr (assumed) VL *assaltus*, fr *assaltus*, pp of *assalire*]

[2]**assault** *vt* **1** to make an (indecent) assault on **2** to rape – **assaulter** *n*, **assaultive** *adj*

[1]**assay** /ə'say/ *n* analysis of an ore, drug, etc to determine the presence, absence, or quantity of 1 or more components [ME, fr OF *essai, assai* test, effort – more at ESSAY]

[2]**assay** *vt* **1a** to analyse (e g an ore) for 1 or more valuable components **b** to judge the worth or quality of **2** to try, attempt – fml – **assayer** *n*

assegai, assagai /'asigie/ *n* a slender iron-tipped hardwood spear used in southern Africa [deriv of Ar *az-zaghāya* the assegai, fr *al-* the + *zaghāya* assegai]

assemblage /ə'semblij/ *n* **1** a collection of people or things; a gathering **2** a three-dimensional collage made from scraps, junk, and odds and ends (e g of cloth, wood, stone etc) [ASSEMBLE + -AGE]

assemble /ə'sembl/ *vb* **assembling** /ə'sembling/ *vt* **1** to bring together (e g in a particular place or for a particular purpose) **2** to fit together the parts of ~ *vi* to gather together; convene [ME *assemblen*, fr OF *assembler*, fr (assumed) VL *assimulare*, fr L *ad-* + *simul* together – more at SAME] – **assembler** *n*

assembly /ə'sembli/ *n* **1** a company of people gathered for deliberation and legislation, entertainment, or worship; *specif* a morning gathering of a school for prayers and/or for the giving out of notices **2** *cap* a legislative body **3a** an assemblage **b** assembling or being assembled **4** a bugle, drum, etc signal for troops to assemble or fall in **5** (a collection of parts assembled by) the fitting together of manufactured parts into a complete machine, structure, etc [ME *assemblee*, fr MF, fr OF, fr *assembler*]

as'sembly ,line *n* **1** an arrangement of machines, equipment, and usu workers in which work passes through successive operations until the product is assembled **2** a process for turning out a finished product in a mechanically efficient but often cursory manner

[1]**assent** /ə'sent/ *vi* to agree to sthg [ME *assenten*, fr OF *assenter*, fr L *assentari*, fr *assentire*, fr *ad-* + *sentire* to feel – more at SENSE] – **assentor, assenter** *n*

[2]**assent** *n* acquiescence, agreement

assert /ə'suht/ *vt* **1** to state or declare positively and often forcefully **2** to demonstrate the existence of [L *assertus*, pp of *asserere*, fr *ad-* + *serere* to join – more at SERIES] – **assertor** *n* – **assert oneself** to compel recognition of esp one's rights

assertion /ə'suhsh(ə)n/ *n* a declaration, affirmation [ASSERT + -ION]

assertive /ə'suhtiv/ *adj* characterized by bold assertion; dogmatic – **assertively** *adv*, **assertiveness** *n*

asses /'asiz/ *pl of* AS *or of* ASS

assess /ə'ses/ *vt* **1a** to determine the rate or amount of (e g a tax) **b** to impose (e g a tax) according to an established rate **2** to make an official valuation of (property) for the purposes of taxation **3** to determine the importance, size, or value of [ME *assessen*, prob fr ML *assessus*, pp of *assidēre*, fr L, to sit beside, assist in the office of a judge – more at ASSIZE] – **assessable** *adj*, **assessment** *n*

assessor /ə'sesə/ *n* **1** a specialist who advises a court **2** an official who assesses property for taxation **3** *chiefly Br* sby who investigates and values insurance claims

asset /'aset/ *n* **1a** *pl* the total property of a person, company, or institution; *esp* that part which can be used to pay debts **b** a single item of property **2** an advantage, resource **3** *pl* the items on a balance sheet showing the book value of property owned [back-formation fr *assets*, sing., sufficient property to pay debts and legacies, fr AF *asetz*, fr OF *assez* enough, fr (assumed) VL *ad satis*, fr L *ad* to + *satis* enough – more at AT, SAD]

'asset-,stripping *n* selling the assets of a profitable enterprise in order to maximize short-term profits

asseverate /ə'sevərayt/ *vt* to affirm solemnly – fml [L *asseveratus*, pp of *asseverare*, fr *ad-* + *severus* severe] – **asseveration** /-'raysh(ə)n/ *n*, **asseverative** /-rətiv/ *adj*

assiduity /,asi'dyooh·əti/ *n* **1** diligence **2** solicitous or obsequious attention to a person

assiduous /ə'sidyoo·əs/ *adj* marked by careful unremitting attention or persistent application; sedulous [L *assiduus*, fr *assidēre*] – **assiduously** *adv*, **assiduousness** *n*

[1]**assign** /ə'sien/ *vt* **1** to transfer (property) to another, esp in trust or for the benefit of creditors **2** to appoint to a post or duty **3** to fix authoritatively; specify, designate [ME *assignen*, fr OF *assigner*, fr L *assignare*, fr *ad-* + *signare* to mark, fr *signum* mark, sign] – **assignability** /-nə'biləti/ *n*, **assignable** *adj*, **assigner, assignor** *n*

[2]**assign** *n* **1** ASSIGNEE 1, 2 **2** sby to whom property or a right is legally transferred

assignation /,asig'naysh(ə)n/ *n* **1** the act of assigning; *also* the assignment made **2** a meeting, esp a secret one with a lover ⟨*returned from an* ~ *with his mistress* – W B Yeats⟩ – **assignational** *adj*

assignee /,asie'nee/ *n* **1** a person to whom an

assignment is made **2** a person appointed to act for another **3** ASSIGN 2

assignment /ə'sienmənt/ *n* **1a** a position, post, or job to which one is assigned **b** a specified task or amount of work assigned by authority **2** (a document effecting) the legal transfer of property [[1]ASSIGN + -MENT]

assimilate /ə'similayt/ *vt* **1a** to take in or absorb into the system (as nourishment) **b** to absorb; *esp* to take into the mind and fully comprehend **2a** to make similar – usu + *to* or *with* **b** to absorb into a cultural tradition **3** to compare, liken – usu + *to* or *with* ~ *vi* to become assimilated [ML *assimilatus*, pp of *assimilare*, fr L *assimulare* to make similar, fr *ad-* + *simulare* to make similar, simulate] – **assimilable** /-ləbl/ *adj*, **assimilative** /-lətiv/ *adj*, **assimilator** /-laytə/ *n*, **assimilatory** /ə'similətri/ *adj*

assimilation /ə,simi'laysh(ə)n/ *n* adaptation of a sound to an adjacent sound (e g the *p* in *cupboard*) [ASSIMILATE + -ION]

[1]**assist** /ə'sist/ *vi* **1** to give support or aid **2** to be present as a spectator ~ *vt* to give support or aid to [MF or L; MF *assister* to help, stand by, fr L *assistere*, fr *ad-* + *sistere* to cause to stand; akin to L *stare* to stand – more at STAND] – **assistance** *n*, **assistant** *n*

[2]**assist** *n* the officially recorded action of a player who by throwing a ball in baseball or by passing a ball or puck in basketball, lacrosse, or ice hockey enables a teammate to put an opponent out or score a goal

assize /ə'siez/ *n, often cap* the periodical sessions of the superior courts formerly held in every English county for trial of civil and criminal cases – usu pl with sing. meaning [ME *assise*, fr OF, session, settlement, fr *asseoir* to seat, fr (assumed) VL *assedēre*, fr L *assidēre* to sit beside, assist in the office of a judge, fr *ad-* + *sedēre* to sit – more at SIT]

associable /ə'soh·sh(y)əbl, -si·əbl/ *adj* capable of being associated, joined, or connected in thought – **associability** /-ə'biləti/ *n*

[1]**associate** /ə'sohs(h)iayt/ *vt* **1** to join as a friend, companion, or partner in business ⟨~ *ourselves with a larger firm*⟩ **2** to bring together in any of various ways (e g in memory, thought, or imagination) ~ *vi* **1** to come together as partners, friends, or companions **2** to combine or join with other parts; unite *USE* often + *with* [ME *associat* associated, fr L *associatus*, pp of *associare* to unite, fr *ad-* + *sociare* to join, fr *socius* companion – more at SOCIAL] – **associatory** /-s(h)i·ətri/ *adj*

[2]**associate** /ə'sohs(h)i·ət/ *adj* **1** closely connected (e g in function or office) with another **2** having secondary or subordinate status ⟨~ *membership in a society*⟩

[3]**associate** /ə'sohs(h)i·ət, -ayt/ *n* **1** a fellow worker; partner, colleague **2** a companion, comrade **3** sthg closely connected with or usu accompanying another **4** one admitted to a subordinate degree of membership ⟨*an* ~ *of the Royal Academy*⟩ – **associateship** /-s(h)i·ət/ *n*

association /ə,sohs(h)i'aysh(ə)n/ *n* **1** an organization of people having a common interest; a society, league **2** sthg linked in memory, thought, or imagination with a thing or person; a connotation **3** the formation of mental connections between sensations, ideas, memories, etc **4** the formation of polymers by loose chemical linkage (e g through hydrogen bonds) **5** an ecological community with usu 2 or more dominant species uniformly distributed [[1]ASSOCIATE + -ION] – **associational** /-s(h)i'aysh(ə)nl/ *adj*

as,sociation 'football *n* soccer ☞ SPORT

associationism /ə,sohs(h)i'ayshəniz(ə)m/ *n* a theory that explains mental life in terms of the association of ideas

associative /ə'sohs(h)i·ətiv/ *adj* **1** dependent on or acquired by association or learning **2** operating on elements such that when the order of the elements is preserved the result is independent of the grouping ⟨*addition is* ~ *since* $(a + b) + c = a + (b + c)$⟩ – **associatively** *adv*, **associativity** /-s(h)i·ə'tivəti/ *n*

assonance /'asənəns/ *n* **1** resemblance of sound in words or syllables **2** repetition of esp only the vowel sounds (e g in *stony* and *holy*) or only the consonant sounds, as an alternative to rhyme [F, fr L *assonare* to answer with the same sound, fr *ad-* + *sonare* to sound – more at [3]SOUND] – **assonant** *adj or n*

as 'soon as *conj* immediately at or just after the time that

assort /ə'sawt/ *vt* to distribute into groups of a like kind; classify ~ *vi* to suit or match well or ill with sthg [MF *assortir*, fr *a-* (fr L *ad-*) + *sorte* sort] – **assortative** /-tətiv/ *adj*, **assorter** *n*

as'sorted *adj* **1** consisting of various kinds **2** suited by nature, character, or design; matched ⟨*an ill*-assorted *pair*⟩

as'sortment /-mənt/ *n* a collection of assorted things or people [ASSORT + -MENT]

assuage /ə'swayj/ *vt* to lessen the intensity of (pain, suffering, desire, etc); ease [ME *aswagen*, fr OF *assouagier*, fr (assumed) VL *assuaviare*, fr L *ad-* + *suavis* sweet – more at SWEET] – **assuagement** *n*

assume /ə'syoohm/ *vt* **1a** to take to or upon oneself; undertake **b** to invest oneself formally with (an office or its symbols) **2** to seize, usurp **3** to pretend to have or be; feign **4** to take as granted or true; suppose – often + *that* [ME *assumen*, fr L *assumere*, fr *ad-* + *sumere* to take – more at CONSUME] – **assumability** /-mə'biləti/ *n*, **assumable** *adj*, **assumably** *adv*

assumption /ə'sum(p)sh(ə)n/ *n* **1a** the taking up of a person into heaven **b** *cap* August 15 observed in commemoration of the assumption of the Virgin Mary **2** the act of laying claim to or taking possession of sthg **3a** the supposition that sthg is true **b** a fact or statement (e g a proposition, axiom, or postulate) taken for granted [ME, fr LL *assumption-, assumptio*, fr L, taking up, fr *assumptus*, pp of *assumere*]

assumptive /ə'sum(p)tiv/ *adj* taken for granted

assurance /ə'shawrəns, -'shooə-/ *n* **1a** a pledge, guarantee **b** *chiefly Br* (life) insurance **2a** the quality or state of being sure or certain; freedom from doubt **b** confidence of mind or manner; *also* excessive self-confidence; brashness **3** sthg that inspires or tends to inspire confidence [ASSURE + -ANCE]

assure /ə'shaw, -'shooə/ *vt* **1** to make safe; insure (esp life or safety) **2** to give confidence to; reassure **3** to inform positively **4** to guarantee the happening or attainment of; ensure [ME *assuren*, fr MF *assurer*, fr ML *assecurare*, fr L *ad-* + *securus* secure]

[1]**as'sured** *adj* **1** characterized by self-confidence ⟨*an* ~ *dancer*⟩ **2** satisfied as to the certainty or truth of a matter; convinced – **assuredly** /-ridli/ *adv*, **assuredness** /-ridnis/ *n*

[2]**assured** *n, pl* **assured, assureds** an insured person

assurer, assuror /ə'shawrə, ə'shooərə/ *n* a person or firm that assures; an insurer

Assyrian /ə'siri·ən/ *n* **1** a member of an ancient Semitic race forming the Assyrian nation **2** the Semitic language of the Assyrians – **Assyrian** *adj*

Assyriology /ə,siri'oləji/ *n* the study of the history, language, and antiquities of ancient Assyria and Babylonia – **Assyriologist** *n*, **Assyriological** /-ri·ə'lojikl/ *adj*

-ast /-ast/ *suffix* (→ *n*) one practising or given to ⟨*iconoclast*⟩ ⟨*enthusiast*⟩ [ME, fr L *-astes*, fr Gk *-astēs*, fr verbs in *-azein*]

astarboard /ə'stahbəd, -,bawd/ *adv* on or towards the right side of a ship ⟨*steer the helm* ~⟩

astatic /ə'statik, ay-/ *adj* **1** not stable or steady **2** not tending to take a fixed or definite position or direction [[2]*a-* + *static*] – **astatically** *adv*, **astaticism** /-ti,siz(ə)m/ *n*

astatine /'astəteen, -tin/ *n* a radioactive halogen element similar to iodine and formed by radioactive decay or made artificially ☞ PERIODIC TABLE [Gk *astatos* unsteady, fr *a-* + *statos* standing, fr *histanai* to cause to stand – more at STAND]

aster /'astə/ *n* **1** any of various chiefly autumn-blooming leafy-stemmed composite plants with often showy heads **2** a system of cytoplasmic rays typically arranged radially about a centrosome at either end of the mitotic spindle [(1) NL, genus name, fr L, aster, fr Gk *aster-*, *astēr* star, aster; (2) NL, fr Gk *aster-*, *astēr* – more at STAR]

-aster /-a(h)stə, -əstə/ *suffix* (*n* → *n*) one who is an inferior, worthless, or false kind of ⟨*criticaster*⟩ ⟨*poetaster*⟩ [ME, fr L, suffix denoting partial resemblance]

[1]**asterisk** /'astərisk/ *n* a sign * used as a reference mark, esp to denote the omission of letters or words or to show that sthg is doubtful or absent ☞ SYMBOL [LL *asteriscus*, fr Gk *asteriskos*, lit., little star, dim. of *aster-*, *astēr*]

[2]**asterisk** *vt* to mark with an asterisk; star

asterism /'astəriz(ə)m/ *n* **1a** a constellation **b** a small group of stars **2** a star-shaped figure visible in some crystals under reflected or transmitted light [Gk *asterismos*, fr *asterizein* to arrange in constellations, fr *aster-*, *astēr*]

astern /ə'stuhn/ *adv or adj* **1** behind the stern; to the rear **2** at or towards the stern of a ship **3** backwards ⟨*the captain signalled full* ~⟩

[1]**asteroid** /'astəroyd/ *n* any of thousands of small planets mostly between Mars and Jupiter ☞ ASTRONOMY [Gk *asteroeidēs* starlike, fr *aster-*, *astēr*] – **asteroidal** /-'roydl/ *adj*

[2]**asteroid** *adj* **1** starlike **2** of or like a starfish

asthenia /əs'theenyə, -ni·ə/ *n* lack or loss of strength; debility [NL, fr Gk *astheneia*, fr *asthenēs* weak, fr *a-* + *sthenos* strength]

asthenic /əs'thenik/ *adj* of or exhibiting asthenia; weak

asthma /'as(th)mə/ *n* (an allergic condition marked by attacks of) laboured breathing with wheezing and usu coughing, gasping, and a sense of constriction in the chest [ME *asma*, fr ML, modif of Gk *asthma*] – **asthmatic** /as(th)'matik/ *adj or n*, **asthmatically** *adv*

as 'though *conj* AS IF

astigmatic /,astig'matik/ *adj* affected with, relating to, or correcting astigmatism [[2]*a-* + Gk *stigmat-*, *stigma* mark – more at STIGMA] – **astigmatically** *adv*

astigmatism /a'stigmətiz(ə)m, ə-/ *n* a defect of an optical system (e g a lens or the eye) in which rays from a single point fail to meet in a focal point, resulting in a blurred image

astir /ə'stuh/ *adj* **1** in a state of bustle or excitement **2** out of bed; up [Sc *asteer*, fr [1]*a-* + *steer*, var of *stir*]

Asti spumante /,asti spoo'manti, spyooh-/ *n* an Italian sparkling white wine [It, lit., sparkling Asti, fr *Asti*, town in Italy]

'**as to** *prep* **1a** with regard or reference to; about – used esp with questions and speculations **b** AS FOR **2** by; ACCORDING TO ⟨*graded* ~ *size and colour*⟩

astonish /ə'stonish/ *vt* to strike with sudden wonder or surprise [prob fr earlier *astony* (fr ME *astonen*, *astonien*, fr OF *estoner*, fr – assumed – VL *extonare*, fr L *ex-* + *tonare* to thunder) + *-ish* (as in *abolish*) – more at THUNDER] – **astonishing** *adj*, **astonishingly** *adv*, **astonishment** *n*

astound /ə'stownd/ *vt* to fill with bewilderment and wonder [prob fr *astound* (adj), fr ME *astoned*, fr pp of *astonen*] – **astounding** *adj*, **astoundingly** *adv*

astr-, astro- *comb form* star; heavens; outer space ⟨astro*physics*⟩ [ME *astro-*, fr OF, fr L *astr-*, *astro-*, fr Gk, fr *astron* – more at STAR]

astraddle /ə'stradl/ *adv or prep* astride

astragal /'astrəgl/ *n* a narrow half-round moulding ☞ ARCHITECTURE [L *astragalus*, fr Gk *astragalos* anklebone, moulding]

astragalus /a'stragələs, ə-/ *n*, *pl* **astragali** /-lie/ a bone nearest the body in the tarsus of the foot of a bird, mammal, etc [NL, fr Gk *astragalos*]

astrakhan, astrachan /,astrə'kahn, -'kan, -kən/ *n*, *often cap* **1** karakul of Russian origin **2** a woollen fabric with curled and looped pile [*Astrakhan*, city in USSR]

astral /'astrəl/ *adj* **1** (consisting) of stars **2** (consisting) of a spiritual substance held in theosophy to be the material of which sby's supposed second body is made up, that can be seen by specially gifted people [LL *astralis*, fr L *astrum* star, fr Gk *astron* – more at STAR] – **astrally** *adv*

astray /ə'stray/ *adv or adj* **1** off the right path or route **2** in error; away from a proper or desirable course or development [ME, fr MF *estraié* wandering, fr *estraier* to stray – more at STRAY]

[1]**astride** /ə'stried/ *adv* with the legs wide apart

[2]**astride** *prep* **1** on or above and with 1 leg on each side of **2** extending over or across; spanning

[1]**astringent** /ə'strinj(ə)nt/ *adj* **1** capable of making firm the soft tissues of the body; styptic **2** rigidly severe; austere [prob fr MF, fr L *astringent-*, *astringens*, prp of *astringere* to bind fast, fr *ad-* + *stringere* to bind tight – more at [2]STRAIN] – **astringency** *n*, **astringently** *adv*

[2]**astringent** *n* an astringent substance

astro- – see ASTR-

astrolabe /'astrə,layb/ *n* an instrument used, before the invention of the sextant, to observe the position of celestial bodies [ME, fr MF & ML; MF, fr ML *astrolabium*, fr LGk *astrolabion*, dim. of Gk *astrolabos*, fr *astr-* + *lambanein* to take – more at LATCH]

astrology /ə'stroləji/ *n* the art or practice of determining the supposed influences of the planets on human affairs [ME *astrologie*, fr MF, fr L astrologia, fr Gk, fr astr- + -logia -logy] – **astrologer** /ə'strolәjә/ *n*, **astrological** /ˌastrə'lojikl/ *adj*, **astrologically** *adv*

astronaut /'astrəˌnawt/ *n* sby who travels beyond the earth's atmosphere [*astr-* + *-naut* (as in *aeronaut*)]

astronautics /ˌastrə'nawtiks/ *n pl but sing or pl in constr* the science of the construction and operation of vehicles for travel in space – **astronautic, astronautical** *adj*, **astronautically** *adv*

astronomer /ə'stronəmə/ *n* sby who is skilled in or practises astronomy

astronomical /ˌastrə'nomikl/, **astronomic** /-'nomik/ *adj* enormously or inconceivably large – infml [ASTRONOMY + -ICAL] – **astronomically** *adv*

ˌastroˌnomical 'unit *n* a unit of length used in astronomy, equal to the mean distance of the earth from the sun or about 149,600,000km (about 93 million mi) ☞ PHYSICS, UNIT

astronomy /ə'stronəmi/ *n* a branch of science dealing with the celestial bodies 👁 [ME *astronomie*, fr OF, fr L *astronomia*, fr Gk, fr *astr-* + *-nomia* -nomy]

astrophysics /ˌastroh'fiziks/ *n pl but sing or pl in constr* a branch of astronomy dealing with the physical and chemical constitution of the celestial bodies [ISV] – **astrophysical** *adj*, **astrophysicist** *n*

Astroturf /'astrəˌtuhf/ *trademark* – used for an artificial grasslike surface that is used for lawns and sports fields

astute /ə'styooht, ə'schooht/ *adj* shrewdly perspicacious [L *astutus*, fr *astus* craft] – **astutely** *adv*, **astuteness** *n*

asunder /ə'sundə/ *adv or adj* **1** into parts ⟨*torn* ~⟩ **2** apart from each other in position ⟨*wide* ~⟩

as 'yet *adv* up to this or that time

asylum /ə'sieləm/ *n* **1** a place of refuge for criminals, debtors, etc; a sanctuary **2** a place of retreat and security; a shelter **3a** the protection from the law or refuge afforded by an asylum **b** protection from arrest and extradition given by a nation to political refugees **4** an institution for the care of the destitute or afflicted, esp the insane [ME, fr L, fr Gk *asylon*, neut of *asylos* inviolable, fr *a-* + *sylon* right of seizure]

asymmetric /aysi'metrik/, **asymmetrical** /-kl/ *adj* **1** not symmetrical **2** *of an atom or group* bonded to several different atoms or groups [Gk *asymmetria* lack of proportion, fr *asymmetros* ill-proportioned, fr [2]*a-* + *symmetros* symmetrical – more at SYMMETRY] – **asymmetrically** *adv*, **asymmetry** /ay'simətri/ *n*

ˌasymˌmetric 'bars *n pl but sing or pl in constr* (a women's gymnastics event using) a pair of wooden bars supported horizontally one 1.5m (about 5ft) and the other 2.3m (about 7ft 6in) above the floor, usu with a common base

asymptomatic /ˌaysimptə'matik/ *adj* presenting no symptoms of disease – **asymptomatically** *adv*

asymptote /'asimtoht/ *n* a straight line that is approached more and more closely by a curve but not met by it ☞ MATHEMATICS [prob fr (assumed) NL *asymptotus*, fr Gk *asymptōtos*, fr *asymptōtos* not meeting, fr [2]*a-* + *sympiptein* to meet – more at SYMPTOM] – **asymptotic** /-'totik/ *adj*, **asymptotically** *adv*

asynchrony /ay'singkrəni/, **asynchronism** /-ˌniz(ə)m/ *n* an absence or lack of concurrence in time [[1]*a-* + *synchrony*] – **asynchronous** /-krənəs/ *adj*, **asynchronously** *adv*

[1]**at** /ət; *strong* at/ *prep* **1** – used to indicate presence or occurrence in, on, or near a place imagined as a point ⟨~ *a hotel*⟩ ⟨*sick* ~ *heart*⟩; compare IN 1a(3) **2** – used to indicate the goal or direction of an action or motion ⟨*aim* ~ *the target*⟩; compare TO 1 **3a** – used to indicate occupation or employment ⟨~ *the controls*⟩ ⟨~ *tea*⟩ **b** when it comes to (an occupation or employment) ⟨*an expert* ~ *chess*⟩ **4** – used to indicate situation or condition ⟨~ *liberty*⟩ ⟨~ *risk*⟩ **5** in response to ⟨*laugh* ~ *his jokes*⟩ **6** – used to indicate position on a scale (e g of cost, speed, or age) ⟨~ *90 mph*⟩ **7** – used to indicate position in time ⟨~ *3 o'clock*⟩ ⟨~ *weekends*⟩ **8** from a distance of ⟨*shot him* ~ *30 paces*⟩ [ME, fr OE *æt*; akin to OHG *az* at, L *ad*] – **at a** as a result of only 1; by or during only 1 ⟨*drank it* at a *gulp*⟩ ⟨*reduce prices* at a *stroke*⟩ ⟨*2* at a *time*⟩ – **at it** doing it; *esp* busy ⟨*been hard* at it *all day*⟩ – **at that 1** at that point and no further ⟨*let it go* at that⟩ **2** which makes it more surprising; IN ADDITION ⟨*she says sack him, and maybe I will* at that⟩

[2]**at** /aht/ *n, pl* **at** ☞ *Laos* at NATIONALITY [Siamese]

at- – see AD-

at 'all *adv* to the least extent or degree; under any circumstances ⟨*not* ~ *far*⟩ ⟨*very seldom if* ~⟩ – **not at all** – used in answer to thanks or to an apology

ataractic /ˌatə'raktik/ *n* a tranquillizer [Gk *ataraktos* calm, fr *a-* + *tarassein* to disturb] – **ataractic** *adj*

ataraxic /ˌatə'raksik/ *n* an ataractic [Gk *ataraxia* calmness, fr *a-* + *tarassein*] – **ataraxic** *adj*

atavism /'atəviz(ə)m/ *n* (an individual or character showing) recurrence in (the parts of) an organism of a form typical of ancestors more remote than the parents [F *atavisme*, fr L *atavus* ancestor] – **atavist** /-vist/ *n*, **atavistic** /-'vistik/ *adj*, **atavistically** *adv*

ataxia /ə'taksi·ə/ *n* **1** lack of order; confusion **2** an inability to coordinate voluntary muscular movements that is symptomatic of some nervous disorders [Gk, fr [2]*a-* + *tassein* to put in order – more at TACTICS] – **ataxic** /ə'taksik/ *adj*

ate /et, ayt/ *past of* EAT

[1]**-ate** /-ət, -ayt/ *suffix* (→ *n*) **1** product of (a specified process) ⟨*distillate*⟩ ⟨*condensate*⟩ ⟨*initiate*⟩ **2** chemical compound or complex anion derived from (a specified compound or element) ⟨*phenolate*⟩ ⟨*ferrate*⟩; *esp* salt or ester of (a specified acid with a name ending in *-ic* and not beginning with *hydro-*) ⟨*sulphate*⟩ [ME *-at*, fr OF, fr L *-atus*, *-atum*, masc & neut of *-atus*, pp ending; (2) NL *-atum*, fr L]

[2]**-ate** *suffix* (→ *n*) **1** office, function, or rank of ⟨*consulate*⟩ ⟨*doctorate*⟩ **2** individual or group of people holding (a specified office or rank) or having (a specified function) ⟨*electorate*⟩ ⟨*candidate*⟩ [ME *-at*, fr OF, fr L *-atus*, fr *-atus*, pp ending]

[3]**-ate, -ated** *suffix* (→ *adj*) **1** being in or brought to (a specified state) ⟨*passionate*⟩ ⟨*inanimate*⟩ **2** marked by having ⟨*craniate*⟩ ⟨*loculated*⟩ **3** resembling; having the shape of ⟨*pinnate*⟩ ⟨*foliate*⟩ [ME *-at*, fr L *-atus*, fr pp ending of 1st conjugation verbs, fr *-a-*, stem vowel of 1st conjugation + *-tus*, pp suffix – more at [1]-ED]

[4]**-ate** *suffix* (→ *vb*) **1** act (in a specified way) ⟨*pontificate*⟩ ⟨*remonstrate*⟩ **2** act (in a specified

Relative sizes of the planets

Scale of space

Outside the solar system, the kilometre is too small a unit for distance measurement – even the nearest star is 40 million million km away. Astronomers instead use units based on the time it takes light to travel the distance. Earth–Moon is thus a distance of $1\frac{1}{4}$ light-seconds; Sun–Earth $8\frac{1}{3}$ light-minutes. Star and galaxy distances are measured in *light-years*: one light-year is 9.5 million million km.

* light from this galaxy was setting out when the Earth and solar system were being born

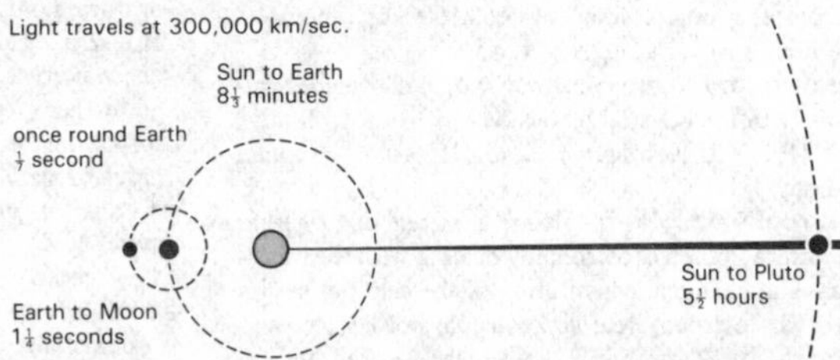

Orbits of the planets

Most planetary orbits lie within the same plane (the ecliptic); however, the orbit of Pluto lies slightly out of this plane, and until 1999 Pluto will be nearer to the Sun than Neptune.

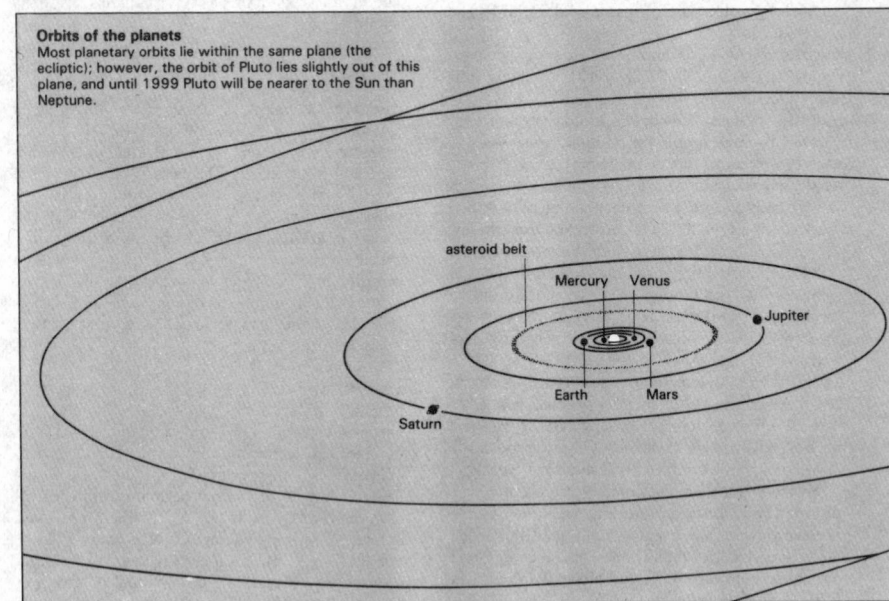

asteroid belt
Mercury
Venus
Jupiter
Earth
Mars
Saturn

Planets

The Earth is one of nine planets orbiting the Sun. The four planets nearest the Sun are relatively small and rocky, like the Earth. The outer planets are huge globes of compressed gases – chiefly hydrogen, helium, methane, and ammonia. The outermost planet, Pluto, is a small solid icy world. Saturn's rings consist of billions of small ice blocks only a metre across, independently orbiting the planet; Jupiter and Uranus have rings too faint to be seen from Earth.

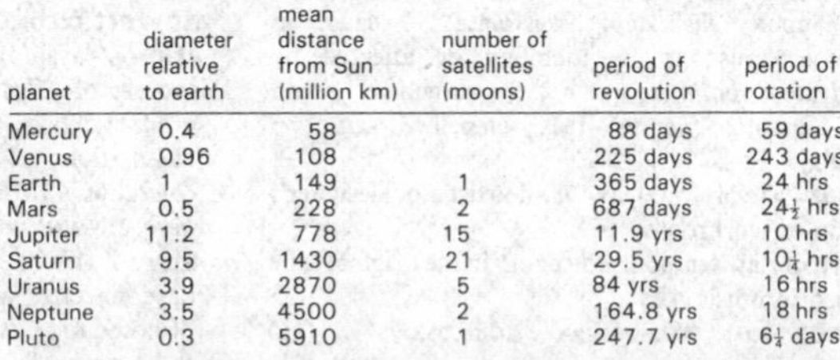

planet	diameter relative to earth	mean distance from Sun (million km)	number of satellites (moons)	period of revolution	period of rotation
Mercury	0.4	58		88 days	59 days
Venus	0.96	108		225 days	243 days
Earth	1	149	1	365 days	24 hrs
Mars	0.5	228	2	687 days	24½ hrs
Jupiter	11.2	778	15	11.9 yrs	10 hrs
Saturn	9.5	1430	21	29.5 yrs	10¼ hrs
Uranus	3.9	2870	5	84 yrs	16 hrs
Neptune	3.5	4500	2	164.8 yrs	18 hrs
Pluto	0.3	5910	1	247.7 yrs	6½ days

Comets

A comet is a block of ice and dust about 10 km in diameter, following a very elongated orbit. As it approaches the Sun, the ice evaporates and can grow into a spectacular tail.

name	period of revolution about Sun (years)	closest approach to Sun (millions of kilometres)	farthest point from Sun (millions of kilometres)
Encke	3.3	51	610
Halley	76	88	5,300
Ikeya-Seki	25,000	1	25,000
Kohoutek	75,000	21	500,000

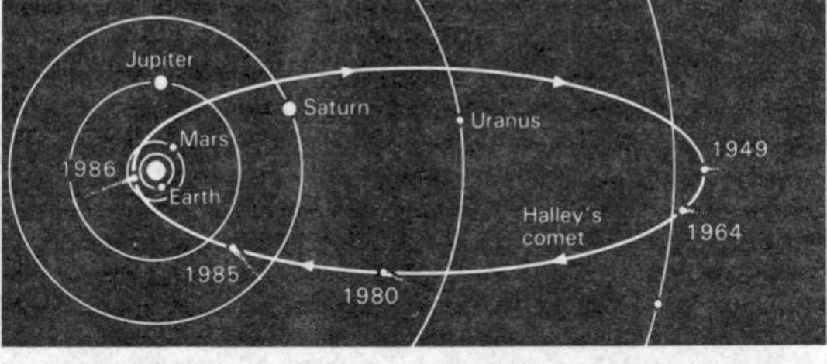

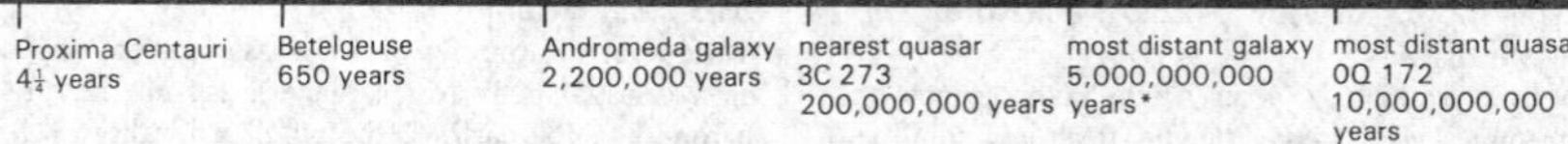

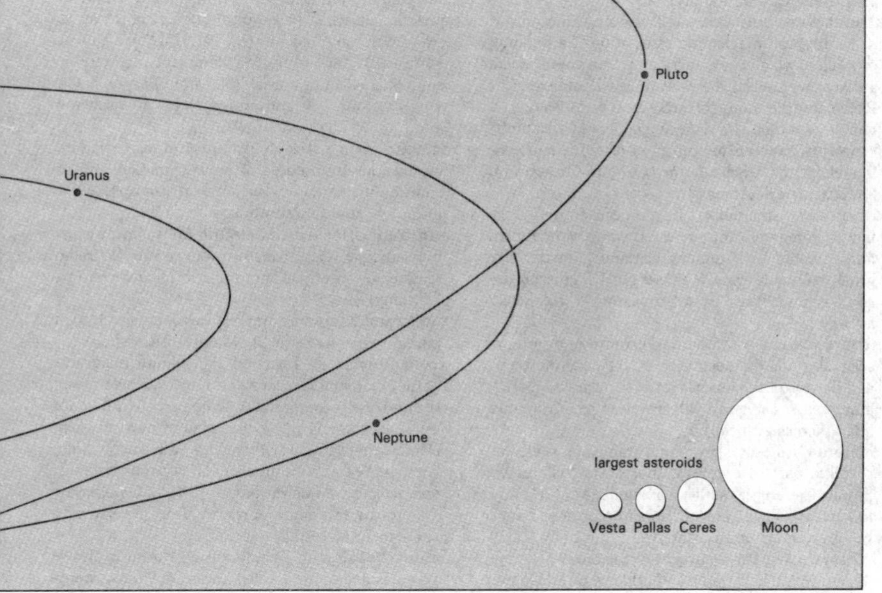

way) upon ⟨*insul*ate⟩ ⟨*assassin*ate⟩ **3** cause to become; cause to be modified or affected by ⟨*activ*ate⟩ ⟨*pollin*ate⟩ **4** provide with ⟨*substanti*ate⟩ ⟨*aer*ate⟩ [ME *-aten*, fr L *-atus*, pp ending]

atelier /ə'teliay, 'atəlyay/ *n* an artist's or designer's studio or workroom [F]

a tempo /,ah 'tempoh/ *adv or adj* in the original time – used in music [It]

Athabascan, Athabaskan /,athə'baskən/ *n* (an) Athapaskan

,Atha'nasian ,Creed /,athə'nayzh(ə)n, -sh(ə)n/ *n* a Christian creed originating in Europe about AD 400 and relating esp to the Trinity and Incarnation [St *Athanasius* †373 Gk patriarch & theologian]

Athapaskan, Athapascan /,athə'paskən/ *n* **1** a language stock of the Na-dene group of N America ☞ LANGUAGE **2** a member of a people speaking an Athapaskan language [Cree *Athap-askaw*, an Athapaskan people, lit., grass or reeds here and there]

atheism /'aythi·iz(ə)m/ *n* the belief or doctrine that there is no deity [MF *athéisme*, fr *athée* atheist, fr Gk *atheos* godless, fr *a-* + *theos* god] – **atheist** /'aythi·ist/ *n*, **atheistic** /-'istik/, **atheistical** *adj*, **atheistically** *adv*

atheling /'athəling/ *n* an Anglo-Saxon prince or nobleman [ME, fr OE *ætheling*, fr *æthelu* nobility; akin to OHG *adal* nobility]

athenaeum, atheneum /,athə'nee·əm, ə'theeni·əm/ *n* **1** a literary or scientific association **2** a building or room in which books, periodicals, and newspapers are kept for use [L *Athenaeum*, a school in ancient Rome for the study of arts, fr Gk *Athēnaion*, a temple of Athene, fr *Athēnē*, goddess of wisdom]

Athenian /ə'theenyən, -ni·ən/ *n or adj* (a native or inhabitant) of Athens [*Athens*, city in Greece, fr L *Athenae*, fr Gk *Athēnai*]

atheroma /,athə'rohmə/ *n* fatty degeneration of the inner lining of the arteries [NL *atheromat-*, *atheroma*, fr L, a tumour containing matter like gruel, fr Gk *athērōma*, fr *athēra* gruel] – **atheromatosis** /-,rohmə'tohsis/ *n*, **atheromatous** /-'rohmətəs/ *adj*

atherosclerosis /,athərohsklə'rohsis/ *n* arteriosclerosis with the deposition of fatty substances in and fibrosis of the inner layer of the arteries [NL, fr *atheroma* + *sclerosis*] – **atherosclerotic** /-sklə'rotik/ *adj*, **atherosclerotically** *n*

athlete /'athleet/ *n* sby who is trained in, skilled in, or takes part in exercises, sports, etc that require physical strength, agility, or stamina [ME, fr L *athleta*, fr Gk *athlētēs*, fr *athlein* to contend for a prize, fr *athlon* prize, contest]

,athlete's 'foot *n* ringworm of the feet

athletic /ath'letik/ *adj* **1** of athletes or athletics **2** characteristic of an athlete; *esp* vigorous, active – **athletically** *adv*, **athleticism** /-ti,siz(ə)m/ *n*

ath'letics *n pl but sing or pl in constr, Br* competitive walking, running, throwing, and jumping sports collectively

ath,letic sup'port *n* a jockstrap

at 'home *n* a reception given at one's home

-athon /-əthən, -athon/ *comb form* (→ *n*) contest of endurance ⟨*talk*athon⟩ [*marathon*]

¹athwart /ə'thwawt/ *adv* **1** across, esp in an oblique direction **2** in opposition to the right or expected course [ME, fr ¹*a-* + *thwart*]

²athwart *prep* **1** across **2** in opposition to

-ation /-'aysh(ə)n/ *suffix* (*vb* → *n*) **1** action or process of ⟨*flirt*ation⟩ ⟨*comput*ation⟩ **2** result or product of (a specified action or process) ⟨*alter*ation⟩ ⟨*plant*ation⟩ **3** state or condition of ⟨*el*ation⟩ ⟨*agit*ation⟩ [ME *-acioun*, fr OF *-ation*, fr L *-ation-*, *-atio*, fr *-atus* -ate + *-ion-*, *-io* -ion]

-ative /-ətiv/ *suffix* (*vb*, *n* → *adj*) **1** of, relating to, or connected with ⟨*authorit*ative⟩ **2** tending to; disposed to ⟨*talk*ative⟩ ⟨*lax*ative⟩ [ME, fr MF *-atif*, fr L *-ativus*, fr *-atus* + *-ivus* -ive]

Atlantic /ət'lantik/ *adj* of or found near the Atlantic ocean [L *Atlanticus*, fr Gk *Atlantikos*, fr *Atlantis* Atlantic Ocean, fr *Atlant-*, *Atlas*]

atlas /'atləs/ *n* **1** *cap* one who bears a heavy burden **2** a bound collection of maps, charts, or tables **3** the first vertebra of the neck [L *Atlant-*, *Atlas*, fr Gk, mythological giant holding up the heavens; (2) fr title of book of maps by Gerhardus Mercator †1594 Flemish cartographer]

atman /'atmən/ *n*, *often cap* **1** the innermost essence of each individual according to Hinduism **2** the supreme universal self according to Hinduism; BRAHMAN 1b [Skt *ātman*, lit., breath, soul; akin to OHG *ātum* breath]

atmosphere /'atməsfiə/ *n* **1** a mass of gas enveloping a celestial body (e g a planet); *esp* all the air surrounding the earth **2** the air of a locality **3** a surrounding influence or environment **4** a unit of pressure chosen to be a typical pressure of the air at sea level and equal to 101,325N/m^2 (about 14.7lb/in^2) ☞ UNIT **5** a dominant aesthetic or emotional effect or appeal [NL *atmosphaera*, fr Gk *atmos* vapour + L *sphaera* sphere] – **atmosphered** *adj*

atmospheric /,atmə'sferik/ *adj* **1** of, occurring in, or like the atmosphere **2** having, marked by, or contributing aesthetic or emotional atmosphere ⟨~ *music*⟩ – **atmospherically** *adv*

,atmo'spherics *n pl* (the electrical phenomena causing) audible disturbances produced in a radio receiver by electrical atmospheric phenomena (e g lightning)

atoll /'atol, ə'tol/ *n* a coral reef surrounding a lagoon [*atolu*, native name in the Maldive islands]

atom /'atəm/ *n* **1** any of the minute indivisible particles of which according to ancient materialism the universe is composed **2** a tiny particle; a bit ⟨*not an* ~ *of truth in it*⟩ **3** the smallest particle of an element that can exist either alone or in combination, consisting of various numbers of electrons, protons, and neutrons **4** nuclear power [ME, fr L *atomus*, fr Gk *atomos*, fr *atomos* indivisible, fr ²*a-* + *temnein* to cut – more at TOME]

'atom ,bomb *n* **1** a bomb whose violent explosive power is due to the sudden release of atomic energy derived from the splitting of the nuclei of plutonium, uranium, etc by neutrons in a very rapid chain reaction **2** HYDROGEN BOMB – **atom-bomb** *vt*

atomic /ə'tomik/ *adj* **1** of or concerned with atoms, atom bombs, or atomic energy **2** *of a chemical element* existing as separate atoms – **atomically** *adv*

atomic bomb *n* ATOM BOMB

atomic clock *n* a precision clock that is regulated by the natural vibration frequencies of an atomic system

atomic energy *n* energy liberated in an atom bomb,

nuclear reactor, etc by changes in the nucleus of an atom ☞ ENERGY

atomicity /,atə'misəti/ *n* the number of atoms in the molecule of a (gaseous) element [ATOMIC + -ITY]

atomic mass *n* the mass of an atom usu expressed in atomic mass units

atomic mass unit *n* a unit of mass used in atomic and nuclear physics equal to $^1/_{12}$ of the atomic mass of the most abundantly occurring isotope of carbon

atomic number *n* the number of protons in the nucleus of an atom which is characteristic of a chemical element and determines its place in the periodic table

atomic pile *n* REACTOR 2

atomic theory *n* the theory that all material substances are composed of atoms of a relatively small number of types and all the atoms of the same type are identical

atomic weight *n* the ratio of the average mass of an atom of an element to the mass of an atom of the most abundantly occurring isotope of carbon

atomism /'atəmiz(ə)m/ *n* a doctrine that the universe is composed of simple indivisible minute particles – **atomist** *n*

atomistic /atə'mistik/ *adj* **1** of atoms or atomism **2** composed of many simple elements; *also* divided into unconnected or antagonistic fragments ⟨*an* ~ *society*⟩ – **atomistically** *adv*

atom·ize, -ise /'atəmiez/ *vt* to reduce to minute particles or to a fine spray – **atomization** /-'zaysh(ə)n/ *n*

atomizer /'atəmiezə/ *n* an instrument for atomizing usu a perfume or disinfectant

atonal /a'tohnl, ay-/ *adj* organized without reference to a musical key and using the notes of the chromatic scale impartially [²a- + *tonal*] – **atonalism** *n*, **atonalist** *n*, **atonally** *adv*, **atonalistic** /a,tohnə'listik, ay-/ *adj*, **atonality** *n* /,atoh'naləti, ,ay-/

atone /ə'tohn/ *vi* to supply satisfaction *for*; make amends *for* ⟨*the* atoning *death of Christ*⟩ [ME *atonen* to become reconciled, fr *at on* in harmony, fr *at* + *on* one]

a'tonement /-mənt/ *n* **1** *often cap* the expiation of mankind's original sin through the death of Christ **2** reparation for an offence or injury; satisfaction [ATONE + -MENT]

atonic /ə'tonik, a-/ *adj* **1** characterized by atony **2** not accented – **atonicity** /,ato'nisəti, ,ay-/ *n*

atony /'atəni/ *n* lack, esp by a contractile organ, of physiological tone [LL *atonia*, fr Gk, fr *atonos* without tone, fr *a-* + *tonos* tone]

atopy /'atəpi/ *n* a prob hereditary tendency to asthma, hay fever, urticaria, and other allergies [Gk *atopia* uncommonness, fr *atopos* out of the way, uncommon, fr *a-* + *topos* place] – **atopic** /ay'topik/ *adj*

-ator /-aytə/ *suffix* (→ *n*) ¹-OR ⟨*commentator*⟩ [ME *-atour*, fr OF & L; OF, fr L *-ator*, fr *-atus* -ate + *-or*]

ATP *n* a derivative of adenine that is reversibly converted, esp to ADP, with the release of the cellular energy required for many metabolic reactions [adenosine *tri*phosphate]

atresia /ə'treezyə, -zh(y)ə/ *n* absence or closure of a natural body passage (e g the anus) [NL, fr ²a- + Gk *trēsis* perforation, fr *tetrainein* to pierce – more at THROW]

atrium /'atri·əm, 'ay-/ *n, pl* **atria** /'atri·ə, 'ay-/ *also* **atriums** **1** an inner courtyard open to the sky (e g in a Roman house) **2** an anatomical cavity or passage; *specif* a chamber of the heart that receives blood from the veins and forces it into a ventricle or ventricles ☞ ANATOMY [(1) L; (2) NL, fr L] – **atrial** *adj*

atrocious /ə'trohshəs/ *adj* **1** extremely wicked, brutal, or cruel; barbaric **2** of very poor quality ⟨~ *handwriting*⟩ [L *atroc-*, *atrox* gloomy, atrocious, fr *atr-*, *ater* black + *-oc-*, *-ox* (akin to Gk *ōps* eye) – more at EYE] – **atrociously** *adv*, **atrociousness** *n*

atrocity /ə'trosəti/ *n* **1** being atrocious **2** an atrocious act, object, or situation

¹atrophy /'atrəfi/ *n* **1** (sometimes natural) decrease in size or wasting away of a body part or tissue **2** a wasting away or progressive decline; degeneration [LL *atrophia*, fr Gk, fr *atrophos* ill fed, fr *a-* + *trephein* to nourish; akin to Gk *thrombos* clot, curd] – **atrophic** /ə'trofik/ *adj*

²atrophy *vb* to (cause to) undergo atrophy

atropine /'atrəpeen, -pin/ *n* an alkaloid found in deadly nightshade and used in medicine to inhibit the parasympathetic nervous system [G *atropin*, fr NL *Atropa*, genus name of belladonna, fr Gk *Atropos*, one of the 3 mythical Fates]

attaboy /'atə,boy/ *interj, chiefly NAm* – used to encourage, or express admiration [alter. of *that's the boy*]

attach /ə'tach/ *vt* **1** to seize by legal authority **2** to bring (oneself) into an association **3** to appoint to serve with an organization for special duties or for a temporary period **4** to fasten **5** to ascribe, attribute ~ *vi* to become attached; stick ***USE*** often + *to* [ME *attachen*, fr MF *attacher*, fr OF *estachier*, fr *estache* stake, of Gmc origin; akin to OE *staca* stake] – **attachable** *adj*

attaché /ə'tashay/ *n* a technical expert on a diplomatic staff [F, pp of *attacher*]

at'taché ,case *n* a small thin case used esp for carrying papers

at'tached *adj* feeling affection or liking

at'tachment /-mənt/ *n* **1** a seizure by legal process **2a** fidelity – often + *to* ⟨~ *to a cause*⟩ **b** an affectionate regard **3** a device attached to a machine or implement **4** the physical connection by which one thing is attached to another [ATTACH + -MENT]

¹attack /ə'tak/ *vt* **1** to set upon forcefully in order to damage, injure, or destroy **2** to take the initiative against in a game or contest **3** to assail with unfriendly or bitter words **4** to begin to affect or to act on injuriously **5** to set to work on, esp vigorously ~ *vi* to make an attack [MF *attaquer*, fr (assumed) OIt *estaccare* to attach, fr *stacca* stake, of Gmc origin; akin to OE *staca*] – **attacker** *n*

²attack *n* **1** the act of attacking; an assault **2** a belligerent or antagonistic action or verbal assault – often + *on* **3** the beginning of destructive action (e g by a chemical agent) **4** the setting to work on some undertaking **5** a fit of sickness or (recurrent) disease **6a** an attempt to score or to gain ground in a game **b** *sing or pl in constr* the attacking players in a team or the positions occupied by them; *specif* the bowlers in a cricket team ⟨*the Yorkshire* ~ *gave nothing away*⟩ **7** the act or manner of beginning a musical tone or phrase ⟨*a sharp* ~⟩

attain /ə'tayn/ *vt* to reach as an end; achieve ~ *vi* to come or arrive by motion, growth, or effort – + *to* [ME *atteynen*, fr OF *ataindre*, fr (assumed) VL *attangere*, fr L *attingere*, fr *ad-* + *tangere* to touch – more at TANGENT] – **attainable** *adj*, **attainableness, attainability** /ə,taynə'biləti/ *n*

attainder /ə'tayndə/ *n* a penalty enforced until 1870 by which sby sentenced to death or outlawry forfeited his/her property and civil rights [ME *attaynder*, fr MF *ataindre* to accuse, attain]

attainment /ə'taynmənt/ *n* sthg attained; an accomplishment [ATTAIN + -MENT]

attar /'atə/ *n* a fragrant essential oil (e g from rose petals); *also* a fragrance [Per *'atir* perfumed, fr Ar, fr *'itr* perfume]

1**attempt** /ə'tempt/ *vt* to make an effort to do, accomplish, solve, or effect, esp without success [L *attemptare*, fr *ad-* + *temptare* to touch, try – more at TEMPT] – **attemptable** *adj*

2**attempt** *n* **1** the act or an instance of attempting; *esp* an unsuccessful effort **2** an attack, assault – often + *on*

attend /ə'tend/ *vt* **1** to take charge of; LOOK AFTER **2** to go or stay with as a companion, nurse, or servant **3** to be present with; accompany, escort **4** to be present at ~ *vi* **1a** to apply oneself ⟨~ *to your work*⟩ **b** to deal with **2** to apply the mind or pay attention; heed *USE* – often + *to* [ME *attenden*, fr OF *atendre*, fr L *attendere*, lit., to stretch to, fr *ad-* + *tendere* to stretch – more at THIN] – **attender** *n*

attendance /ə'tend(ə)ns/ *n* **1** the number of people attending **2** the number of times a person attends, usu out of a possible maximum [ATTEND + -ANCE]

at'tendance ,centre *n* a centre at which a young offender is obliged to attend regularly instead of going to prison

1**attendant** /ə'tend(ə)nt/ *adj* accompanying or following as a consequence

2**attendant** *n* one who attends another to perform a service; *esp* an employee who waits on customers ⟨*a car park* ~⟩

attention /ə'tensh(ə)n/ *n* **1** attending, esp through application of the mind to an object of sense or thought **2** consideration with a view to action **3a** an act of civility or courtesy, esp in courtship – usu pl **b** sympathetic consideration of the needs and wants of others **4** a formal position of readiness assumed by a soldier – usu as a command [ME *attencioun*, fr L *attention-*, *attentio*, fr *attentus*, pp of *attendere*] – **attentional** *adj*

at'tention ,span *n* the length of time during which an individual is able to concentrate

attentive /ə'tentiv/ *adj* **1** mindful, observant **2** solicitous **3** paying attentions (as if) in the role of a suitor – **attentively** *adv*, **attentiveness** *n*

1**attenuate** /ə'tenyooayt/ *vt* **1** to make thin **2** to lessen the amount, force, or value of; weaken **3** to reduce the severity, virulence, or vitality of ~ *vi* to become thin or fine; diminish [L *attenuatus*, pp of *attenuare* to make thin, fr *ad-* + *tenuis* thin – more at THIN] – **attenuation** /ə,tenyoo'aysh(ə)n/ *n*

2**attenuate** *adj* tapering gradually ⟨*an* ~ *leaf*⟩ ☞ PLANT

attenuator /ə'tenyoo,aytə/ *n* a device for attenuating; *esp* one for reducing the amplitude of an electrical signal

attest /ə'test/ *vt* **1a** to affirm to be true **b** to authenticate esp officially **2** to be proof of; bear witness to **3** to put on oath ~ *vi* to bear witness, testify – often + *to* [MF *attester*, fr L *attestari*, fr *ad-* + *testis* witness – more at TESTAMENT] – **attester** *n*, **attestation** /,ate'staysh(ə)n/ *n*

attic /'atik/ *n* a room or space immediately below the roof of a building [F *attique* low storey or wall above an entablature, fr *attique* of Attica, fr L *Atticus*; fr the use of this feature in the Attic order of architecture]

1**Attic** *adj* (characteristic) of Attica or Athens [L *Atticus*, fr Gk *Attikos*, fr *Attikē* Attica, state of ancient Greece]

2**Attic** *n* a Greek dialect of ancient Attica which became the literary language of the Greek-speaking world

1**attire** /ə'tie·ə/ *vt* to put garments on; dress, array; *esp* to clothe in fancy or rich garments [ME *attiren*, fr OF *atirier*, fr *a-* (fr L *ad-*) + *tire* order, rank, of Gmc origin; akin to OE *tīr* glory; akin to L *deus* god – more at DEITY]

2**attire** *n* dress, clothes; *esp* splendid or decorative clothing

attitude /'atityoohd/ *n* **1** the arrangement of the parts of a body or figure; a posture **2** a feeling, emotion, or mental position with regard to a fact or state **3** a manner assumed for a specific purpose **4** a ballet position in which one leg is raised at the back and bent at the knee **5** the position of an aircraft or spacecraft relative to a particular point of reference (e g the horizon) [F, fr It *attitudine*, fr *attitudine* aptitude, fr LL *aptitudin-*, *aptitudo* fitness, fr L *aptus* fit – more at APT] – **attitudinal** /-'tyoohdinl/ *adj*

attitudin·ize, -ise /,ati'tyoohdiniez/ *vi* to assume an affected mental attitude; pose

atto- *comb form* one million million millionth (10^{-18}) part of ⟨atto*gram*⟩ ☞ PHYSICS [ISV, fr Dan or Norw *atten* eighteen, fr ON *āttjān*; akin to OE *eahtatīene* eighteen]

attorney /ə'tuhni/ *n* **1** sby with legal authority to act for another **2** *NAm* a lawyer [ME *attourney*, fr MF *atorné*, pp of *atorner* to agree to become tenant to a new owner of the same property, fr OF, fr *a-* (fr L *ad-*) + *torner* to turn] – **attorneyship** /-,ship/ *n*

at,torney 'general *n, pl* **attorneys general, attorney generals** *often cap A&G* the chief legal officer of a nation or state

attract /ə'trakt/ *vt* to cause to approach or adhere: e g **a** to pull to or towards oneself or itself ⟨*a magnet* ~*s iron*⟩ **b** to draw by appeal to interest, emotion, or aesthetic sense ⟨~ *attention*⟩ ~ *vi* to possess or exercise the power of attracting sthg or sby ⟨*opposites* ~⟩ [ME *attracten*, fr L *attractus*, pp of *attrahere*, fr *ad-* + *trahere* to draw – more at DRAW] – **attractable** *adj*, **attractor** *n*, **attractive** *adj*, **attractively** *adv*, **attractiveness** *n*

attractant /ə'trakt(ə)nt/ *n or adj* (a pheromone or other substance) that attracts sthg, esp insects

attraction /ə'traksh(ə)n/ *n* **1** a characteristic that elicits interest or admiration – usu pl **2** the action or power of drawing forth a response (e g interest or affection); an attractive quality **3** a force between unlike electric charges, unlike magnetic poles, etc, resisting separation **4** sthg that attracts or is intended to attract people by appealing to their desires and tastes [ATTRACT + -ION]

1**attribute** /'atribyooht/ *n* **1** an inherent characteristic **2** an object closely associated with a usu specified person, thing, or office **3** a subordinate word or phrase that grammatically limits the meaning of another; *esp* an adjective [ME, fr L *attributus*, pp of *attribuere* to attribute, fr *ad-* + *tribuere* to bestow – more at TRIBUTE]

[2]**attribute** /ə'tribyooht/ *vt* to reckon as originating in an indicated fashion – usu + *to* – **attributable** *adj*, **attributer** *n*, **attribution** /,atri'byoohsh(ə)n/ *n* – **attribute to 1** to explain by indicating as a cause **2** to regard as a characteristic of (a person or thing)

attributive /ə'tribyootiv/ *adj* **1** relating to or of the nature of an attribute **2** directly preceding a modified noun (e g *city* in *city streets*) – compare PREDICATIVE – **attributive** *n*, **attributively** *adv*

attrition /ə'trish(ə)n/ *n* **1** sorrow for one's sins arising from fear of punishment – compare CONTRITION **2** the act of rubbing together; friction; *also* the act of wearing or grinding down by friction **3** the act of weakening or exhausting by constant harassment or abuse ⟨*war of* ~⟩ [L *attrition-, attritio*, fr *attritus*, pp of *atterere* to rub against, fr *ad-* + *terere* to rub – more at THROW; (1) ME *atricioun*, fr (assumed) ML *attrition-, attritio*, fr L] – **attritional** *adj*

attune /ə'tyoohn/ *vt* to bring into harmony; tune – **attunement** *n*

atypical /,ay'tipikl/ *adj* not typical; irregular – **atypically** *adv*, **atypicality** /ay,tipi'kaləti/ *n*

aubade /'oh,bahd/ *n* a love song or poem associated with morning [F, fr (assumed) OProv *aubada*, fr OProv *alba, auba* dawn, fr (assumed) VL *alba*, fr L, fem of *albus* white]

aubergine /'ohbəzheen, -jeen/ **1** (the edible usu smooth dark purple ovoid fruit of) the eggplant **2** a deep reddish purple colour [F, fr Catal *albergínia*, fr Ar *al-bādhinjān* the eggplant, fr *al* the + *bādhinjān* eggplant, fr Per *bādingān*]

aubrietia /aw'breeshə/ *n* any of various trailing spring-flowering rock plants of the mustard family [NL, genus name, fr Claude *Aubriet* †1742 F painter of flowers & animals]

auburn /'awbən/ *adj or n* (of) a reddish brown colour [adj ME *auborne* blond, fr MF, fr ML *alburnus* whitish, fr L *albus*; n fr adj]

au courant /,oh kooh'ronh (*Fr* o kurɑ̃)/ *adj* **1** fully informed; up-to-date **2** fully familiar; conversant [F, lit., in the current]

[1]**auction** /'awksh(ə)n/ *n* **1** a public sale of property to the highest bidder – compare PRIVATE TREATY **2** the act or process of bidding in some card games [L *auction-, auctio*, lit., increase, fr *auctus*, pp of *augēre* to increase – more at EKE OUT]

[2]**auction** *vt* to sell at an auction – often + *off* ⟨~ed *off the silver*⟩

auction bridge *n* a form of bridge differing from contract bridge in that tricks made in excess of the contract are scored towards game

auctioneer /,awksh(ə)n'iə/ *n* an agent who sells goods at an auction – **auctioneer** *vt*

audacious /aw'dayshəs/ *adj* **1a** intrepidly daring; adventurous **b** recklessly bold; rash **2** insolent [MF *audacieux*, fr *audace* boldness, fr L *audacia*, fr *audac-, audax* bold, fr *audēre* to dare, fr *avidus* eager – more at AVID] – **audaciously** *adv*, **audaciousness** *n*, **audacity** /aw'dasəti/ *n*

audible /'awdəbl/ *adj* heard or capable of being heard [LL *audibilis*, fr L *audire* to hear; akin to Gk *aisthanesthai* to perceive, Skt *āvis* evidently] – **audibly** *adv*, **audibility** /,awdə'biləti/ *n*

audience /'awdi·əns/ *n* **1a** a formal hearing or interview ⟨*an* ~ *with the pope*⟩ **b** an opportunity of being heard ⟨*the court refused him* ~⟩ **2** *sing or pl in constr* a group of listeners or spectators [ME, fr MF, fr L *audientia*, fr *audient-, audiens*, prp of *audire*]

[1]**audio** /'awdioh/ *adj* **1** of or being acoustic, mechanical, or electrical frequencies corresponding to those of audible sound waves, approx 20 to 20,000Hz **2a** of sound or its reproduction, esp high-fidelity reproduction **b** relating to or used in the transmission or reception of sound – compare VIDEO [*audio-*]

[2]**audio** *n* the transmission, reception, or reproduction of sound

audio- *comb form* **1** hearing ⟨audio*meter*⟩ **2** sound ⟨audio*phile*⟩ **3** auditory and ⟨audio*visual*⟩ [L *audire* to hear]

audiology /,awdi'oləji/ *n* the biology of hearing – **audiologist** *n*, **audiological** /,awdi·ə'lojikl/ *adj*

audiometer /,awdi'omitə/ *n* an instrument for measuring the sharpness of hearing – **audiometry** /-tri/ *n*, **audiometric** /,awdioh'metrik/ *adj*

audiophile /'awdioh,fiel/ *n* sby with a keen interest in the reproduction of sounds, esp music from high-fidelity broadcasts or recordings

audiovisual /,awdioh'viz(h)yooəl/ *adj* of (teaching methods using) both hearing and sight

[1]**audit** /'awdit/ *n* (the final report on) a formal or official examination and verification of an account book [ME, fr L *auditus* act of hearing, fr *auditus*, pp]

[2]**audit** *vt* to perform an audit on – **auditable** *adj*

[1]**audition** /aw'dish(ə)n/ *n* **1** the power or sense of hearing **2** the act of hearing; *esp* a critical hearing **3** a trial performance to appraise an entertainer's abilities [MF or L; MF, fr L *audition-, auditio*, fr *auditus*, pp of *audire* to hear]

[2]**audition** *vt* to test (e g for a part) in an audition ~ *vi* to give a trial performance – usu + *for*

auditive /'awditiv/ *adj* auditory

auditor /'awditə/ *n* **1** one who hears or listens; *esp* a member of an audience **2** one authorized to perform an audit

auditorium /,awdi'tawri·əm/ *n, pl* **auditoria** /-ri·ə/, **auditoriums** the part of a public building where an audience sits [L, fr *auditus*, pp]

auditory /'awdit(ə)ri/ *adj* of or experienced through hearing [LL *auditorius*, fr L *auditus*, pp]

au fait /,oh 'fay/ *adj* **1** fully competent; capable **2** fully informed; familiar *with* [F, lit., to the point]

auf Wiedersehen /,owf 'veedəzayn (*Ger* auf viːdəzeːən)/ *interj* – used to express farewell [G, lit., till seeing again]

Augean stable /aw'jee·ən/ *n* a very filthy or corrupt condition or place – usu pl with sing. meaning [*Augean* fr L *Augeas*, legendary King of Elis in Greece, fr Gk *Augeias*; fr the legend that his stable was uncleaned for 30 years until Hercules cleaned it]

auger /'awgə/ *n* **1** a tool for boring holes in wood consisting of a shank with a central tapered screw and a pair of cutting lips with projecting spurs that cut the edge of the hole – compare GIMLET **2** any of various instruments or devices shaped like an auger [ME, alter. (by incorrect division of *a nauger*) of *nauger*, fr OE *nafogār*; akin to OHG *nabugēr* auger; both fr a prehistoric WGmc-NGmc compound whose constituents are represented by OE *nafu* nave & *gār* spear]

¹**aught** /awt/ *pron* 1 all ⟨*for ~ I care*⟩ 2 *archaic* anything [ME, fr OE *āwiht*, fr *ā* ever + *wiht* creature, thing – more at ¹AYE]

²**aught** *n* a zero, cipher [alter. (by incorrect division of *a naught*) of *naught*]

¹**augment** /awg'ment/ *vi* to become greater, increase ~ *vt* 1 to make greater, more numerous, larger, or more intense 2 to add an augment to [ME *augmenten*, fr MF *augmenter*, fr LL *augmentare*, fr *augmentum* increase, fr *augēre* to increase – more at EKE OUT] – **augmentable** *adj*, **augmenter, augmentor** *n*, **augmentation** /,awgmen'taysh(ə)n/ *n*

²**augment** /'awgment/ *n* a prefixed or lengthened initial vowel marking past tense, esp in Greek and Sanskrit verbs

augmentative /awg'mentətiv/ *adj* 1 able to augment 2 *of a word or affix* indicating large size and sometimes awkwardness – **augmentative** *n*

augmented *adj*, *of a musical interval* made a semitone greater than major or perfect

au gratin /,oh 'gratin (*Fr* o gratɛ̃)/ *adj* covered with breadcrumbs or grated cheese and browned under a grill [F, lit., with the burnt scrapings from the pan]

¹**augur** /'awgə/ *n* one held to foretell events by omens; a soothsayer; *specif* an official diviner of Ancient Rome [L; prob akin to L *augēre* to increase]

²**augur** *vt* 1 to foretell, esp from omens 2 to give promise of; presage ~ *vi* to predict the future, esp from omens

augury /'awgyoori/ *n* 1 predicting the future from omens or portents 2 an omen, portent

august /aw'gust/ *adj* marked by majestic dignity or grandeur [L *augustus*; akin to L *augēre* to increase] – **augustly** *adv*, **augustness** *n*

August /'awgəst/ *n* the 8th month of the Gregorian calendar [ME, fr OE, fr L *Augustus*, fr *Augustus* Caesar † AD 14 1st Roman emperor]

Augustan /aw'gust(ə)n/ *adj* (characteristic) of a the age of Augustus Caesar b the neoclassical period in English literature – **Augustan** *n*

¹**Augustinian** /,awgə'stini·ən/ *adj* of St Augustine of Hippo, his doctrines, or any of the monastic orders claiming descent from his precepts [St *Augustine* †430 Numidian church father & Bishop of Hippo] – **Augustinianism** *n*

²**Augustinian** *n* a member of an Augustinian order; *specif* a friar of the Hermits of St Augustine founded in 1256 and devoted to educational, missionary, and parish work

auk /awk/ *n* a puffin, guillemot, razorbill, or related short-necked diving seabird of the northern hemisphere [Norw or Icel *alk, alka*, fr ON *ālka*; akin to L *olor* swan]

auld /awld/ *adj, chiefly Scot* old [ME (northern), var of ME *ald*, fr OE *eald* old – more at OLD]

,**auld lang 'syne** /lang 'sien; *often* zien/ *n* the good old times [Sc, lit., old long ago]

au naturel /,oh natyoo'rel/ *adj* 1 in natural style or condition 2 uncooked or cooked plainly 3 naked – euph [F]

aunt /ahnt/ *n* 1a the sister of one's father or mother b the wife of one's uncle 2 – often used as a term of affection for a woman who is a close friend of a young child or its parents [ME, fr OF *ante*, fr L *amita*; akin to OHG *amma* mother, nurse, Gk *amma* nurse]

auntie, aunty /'ahnti/ *n* an aunt – infml

,**Aunt 'Sally** /'sali/ *n* 1 an effigy of a woman at which objects are thrown at a fair 2 *Br* an easy target of criticism or attack

¹**au pair** /,oh 'peə/ *n* a foreign girl who does domestic work for a family in return for room and board and the opportunity to learn the language of the family [F, on even terms]

²**au pair** *vi* to work as an au pair

aur- /awr-/, **auri-** *comb form* 1 ear ⟨*aural*⟩ ⟨*auriscope*⟩ 2 aural and ⟨*aurinasal*⟩ [L, fr *auris* – more at ¹EAR]

aura /'awrə/ *n* 1 a distinctive atmosphere surrounding a given source 2 a luminous radiation; a nimbus 3 a sensation experienced before an attack of a brain disorder, esp epilepsy [ME, fr L, air, breeze, fr Gk; akin to Gk *aēr* air]

aural /'awrəl/ *adj* of the ear or the sense of hearing – **aurally** *adv*

aurar /'owrah/ *pl of* EYRIR ☞ *Iceland* at NATIONALITY

aureole /'awriohl/, **aureola** /aw'ree·ələ, ə-/ *n* 1 a radiant light surrounding the head or body of a representation of a holy figure – compare NIMBUS 2 the halo surrounding the sun, moon etc when seen through thin cloud [ME *aureole* heavenly crown worn by saints, fr ML *aureola*, fr L, fem of *aureolus* golden – more at ORIOLE] – **aureole** *vt*

au revoir /,oh rə'vwah (*Fr* o rəvwa:r)/ *n* goodbye – often used interjectionally [F, lit., till seeing again]

auric /'awrik/ *adj* of or derived from (trivalent) gold [L *aurum* gold – more at ORIOLE]

auricle /'awrikl/ *n* 1a PINNA 2 b an atrium of the heart – not now in technical use 2 an ear-shaped lobe [L *auricula*, fr dim. of *auris* ear]

auricular /aw'rikyoolə/ *adj* 1 of or using the ear or the sense of hearing 2 told privately ⟨*an ~ confession*⟩ 3 understood or recognized by the sense of hearing 4 of an auricle

auriferous /aw'rifərəs/ *adj* gold-bearing [L *aurifer*, fr *aurum* + *-fer* -ferous]

Aurignacian /,awrig'naysh(ə)n/ *adj* of an Upper Palaeolithic culture characterized by finely made artefacts of stone and bone, cave paintings, and engravings [F *aurignacien*, fr *Aurignac*, village in France]

aurochs /'awroks/ *n, pl* **aurochs** an extinct European ox held to be a wild ancestor of domestic cattle [G, fr OHG *ūrohso*, fr *ūro* aurochs + *ohso* ox; akin to OE *ūr* aurochs – more at OX]

aurora /aw'rawrə/ *n, pl* **auroras, aurorae** /-ri/ dawn [L – more at EAST] – **auroral** *adj*, **aurorean** /-ri·ən/ *adj*

au,rora au'stralis /aw'strahlis/ *n* a phenomenon in the S hemisphere corresponding to the aurora borealis [NL, lit., southern dawn]

au,rora bore'alis /bawri'ahlis/ *n* a luminous electrical phenomenon in the N hemisphere, esp at high latitudes, that consists of streamers or arches of light in the sky [NL, lit., northern dawn]

aurous /'awrəs/ *adj* of or containing (univalent) gold [ISV, fr L *aurum* gold – more at ORIOLE]

auscultation /,awskəl'taysh(ə)n/ *n* the act of listening to the heart, lungs, etc as a medical diagnostic aid [L *auscultation-, auscultatio* act of listening, fr *auscultatus*, pp of *auscultare* to listen; akin to L *auris* ear – more at ¹EAR] – **auscultate** /'awskəl,tayt/ *vt*

auspice /'awspis/ *n* 1 a (favourable) prophetic sign

2 *pl* kindly patronage and guidance [L *auspicium*, fr *auspic-*, *auspex* diviner by birds, fr *avis* bird + *specere* to look, look at – more at AVIARY, SPY]

auspicious /aw'spish(ə)s/ *adj* **1** affording a favourable auspice; propitious **2** attended by good auspices; prosperous – **auspiciously** *adv*, **auspiciousness** *n*

Aussie /'ozi/ *n* an Australian – infml [*Aus*tralian + *-ie*]

austere /aw'stiə, o'stiə/ *adj* **1** stern and forbidding in appearance and manner **2** rigidly abstemious; self-denying **3** unadorned, simple [ME, fr MF, fr L *austerus*, fr Gk *austēros* harsh, severe; akin to Gk *hauos* dry] – **austerely** *adv*, **austereness** *n*

austerity /aw'sterəti, o-/ *n* **1** an austere act, manner, or attitude **2** enforced or extreme economy

Austin /'ostin/ *adj or n* Augustinian [ME *Austyn*, modif of LL *Augustinus* Augustine]

[1]**Austr-, Austro-** *comb form* south; southern ⟨Austro*asiatic*⟩ [ME *austr-*, fr L, fr *Austr-*, *Auster* south wind; akin to L *aurora* dawn – more at EAST]

[2]**Austr-, Austro-** *comb form* Austrian and ⟨Austro-*Hungarian*⟩ [prob fr NL, fr *Austria*]

austral /'awstrəl/ *adj* southern

Australasian /,ostrə'layzh(y)ən; *also* ,aw-/ *n or adj* (a native or inhabitant) of Australasia [*Australasia*, islands of the S & central Pacific, fr F *Australasie*]

Au'stralia ,Day /o'straylyə; *also* aw-/ *n* the first Monday after January 25 observed as a national holiday in Australia in commemoration of the landing of the British at Sydney Cove in 1788

[1]**Australian** /o'straylyən; *also* aw-/ *n* **1** a native or inhabitant of Australia **2** the speech of the aboriginal inhabitants of Australia ☞ LANGUAGE **3** English as spoken and written in Australia [*Australia*, continent of the southern hemisphere]

[2]**Australian** *adj* **1** (characteristic) of Australia **2** of or being a biogeographic region that comprises Australia and the islands north of it from the Celebes eastwards, Tasmania, New Zealand, and Polynesia

Australoid /'ostrəloyd/ *adj* of an ethnic group including the Australian aborigines and other peoples of southern Asia and Pacific islands [*Australia* + E *-oid*] – **Australoid** *n*

australopithecine /,ostrəloh'pithəseen/ *adj* of extinct southern African manlike creatures with near-human teeth and a relatively small brain [deriv of L *australis* southern (fr *Austr-*, *Auster*) + Gk *pithēkos* ape] – **australopithecine** *n*

Austroasiatic *also* **Austro-Asiatic** /,ostroh,ayzi'atik, -,ayzhi-/ *adj* of or constituting a family of languages once widespread over NE India and SE Asia

Austronesian /,ostrə'neezh(ə)n/ *adj* of or constituting a family of Pacific languages including Indonesian, Melanesian, Micronesian, and Polynesian [*Austronesia*, islands of the southern Pacific]

aut-, auto- *comb form* **1** self; same one; of or by oneself ⟨auto*biography*⟩ ⟨auto*didact*⟩ **2** automatic; self-acting; self-regulating ⟨auto*dyne*⟩ [Gk, fr *autos* same, -self, self]

autarchic /,aw'tahkik/, **autarchical** /-kl/ *adj* of or marked by autarchy

autarchy /'awtahki/ *n* absolute sovereignty [Gk *autarchia*, fr *aut-* + *-archia* -archy]

autarky *also* **autarchy** /'awtahki/ *n* national (economic) self-sufficiency and independence [G *autarkie*, fr Gk *autarkeia*, fr *autarkēs* self-sufficient, fr *aut-* + *arkein* to defend, suffice – more at ARK] – **autarkic** /aw'tahkik/, **autarkical** *adj*

authentic /aw'thentik/ *adj* **1** worthy of belief as conforming to fact or reality; trustworthy **2** not imaginary, false, or imitation; genuine [ME *autentik*, fr MF *autentique*, fr LL *authenticus*, fr Gk *authentikos*, fr *authentēs* perpetrator, master, fr *aut-* + *-hentēs* (akin to Gk *anyein* to accomplish, Skt *sanoti* he gains)] – **authentically** *adv*, **authenticity** /,awthen'tisəti/ *n*

authenticate /aw'thentikayt/ *vt* to (serve to) prove the authenticity of – **authenticator** *n*, **authentication** /aw,thenti'kaysh(ə)n/ *n*

author /'awthə/, *fem* **authoress** /-res, -ris/ *n* **1a** the writer of a literary work **b** (the books written by) sby whose profession is writing **2** sby or sthg that originates or gives existence; a source [ME *auctour*, fr ONF, fr L *auctor* promoter, originator, author, fr *auctus*, pp of *augēre* to increase – more at EKE OUT] – **authorial** /aw'thawri·əl/ *adj*

authoritarian /aw,thori'teəri·ən/ *adj* of or favouring submission to authority rather than personal freedom – **authoritarian** *n*, **authoritarianism** *n*

authoritative /aw'thoritətiv/ *adj* **1a** having or proceeding from authority; official **b** entitled to credit or acceptance; conclusive **2** dictatorial, peremptory – **authoritatively** *adv*, **authoritativeness** *n*

authority /aw'thorəti/ *n* **1a** a book, quotation, etc referred to for justification of one's opinions or actions **b** a conclusive statement or set of statements **c** an individual cited or appealed to as an expert **2a** power to require and receive submission; the right to expect obedience **b** power to influence or command **c** a right granted by sby in authority; authorization **3a** *pl the* people in command **b** persons in command; *specif* government **c** *often cap* a governmental administrative body **4a** grounds, warrant ⟨*had excellent* ~ *for his strange actions*⟩ **b** convincing force; weight ⟨*his strong tenor lent* ~ *to the performance*⟩ [ME *auctorite*, fr OF *auctorité*, fr L *auctoritat-*, *auctoritas* opinion, decision, power, fr *auctor*]

author·ize, -ise /'awthəriez/ *vt* **1** to invest with authority or legal power; empower – often + infin **2** to establish (as if) by authority; sanction – **authorizer** *n*, **authorization** /-'zaysh(ə)n/ *n*

Authorized Version *n* an English version of the Bible prepared under James I, published in 1611, and widely used by Protestants

'**authorship** /-ship/ *n* **1** the profession or activity of writing **2** the identity of the author of a literary work ⟨*the* ~ *of* Hamlet *is not seriously disputed*⟩

autism /'awtiz(ə)m/ *n* a disorder of childhood development marked esp by inability to form relationships with other people [NL *autismus*, fr L *aut-* + *-ismus* -ism] – **autistic** /aw'tistik/ *adj*

auto /'awtoh/ *n, pl* **autos** *chiefly NAm* MOTOR CAR [short for *automobile*]

[1]**auto-** – see AUT-

[2]**auto-** *comb form* self-propelling; automotive ⟨autocycle⟩ [*automobile*, adj (self-propelling)]

autoantibody /,awtoh'antibodi/ *n* an antibody that combines with a constituent of an individual's own tissues rather than with foreign matter (e g bacteria)

autobahn /'awtoh,bahn/ *n* a German motorway [G, fr *auto* car + *bahn* track, way]

autobiography /,awtəbie'ogrəfi/ *n* the biography of

a person written by him-/herself; *also* such writing considered as a genre – **autobiographer** *n*, **autobiographic** /,awtə,bie·ə'grafik/, **autobiographical** *adj*

autocephalous /,awtoh'sefələs/ *adj, esp of Eastern national churches* independent of external, esp patriarchal, authority [LGk *autokephalos*, fr Gk *aut-* + *kephalē* head – more at CEPHALIC]

autochthon /aw'tokthən/ *n, pl* **autochthons, autochthones** /-neez/ **1** an aborigine, native **2** an autochthonous plant, animal, etc [Gk *autochthōn*, fr *aut-* + *chthōn* earth – more at HUMBLE] – **autochthonism** *n*

autochthonous /aw'tokthənəs/ *adj* indigenous, native – compare ALLOCHTHONOUS – **autochthonously** *adv*, **autochthony** *n*

[1]**autoclave** /'awtoh,klayv/ *n* an apparatus (e g for sterilizing) using superheated steam under pressure [F, fr *aut-* + L *clavis* key – more at CLAVICLE]

[2]**autoclave** *vt* to subject to the action of an autoclave

autocracy /aw'tokrəsi/ *n* government by an autocrat

autocrat /'awtəkrat/ *n* **1** one who rules with unlimited power **2** a dictatorial person [F *autocrate*, fr Gk *autokratēs* ruling by oneself, absolute, fr *aut-* + *kratos* strength, power – more at HARD] – **autocratic** /,awtə'kratik/ *adj*, **autocratically** *adv*

autocross /'awtoh,kros/ *n* the sport of racing motor cars on usu grass tracks against the clock [*auto* + *cross (country)*]

autocue /'awtoh,kyooh/ *n* a device that enables a person (e g a newsreader) being televised to read a script without averting his/her eyes from the camera

auto-da-fé /,awtoh dah 'fay/ *n, pl* **autos-da-fé** /~/ the burning of a heretic; *esp* the ceremonial execution of sby condemned by the Spanish Inquisition [Pg *auto da fé*, lit., act of the faith]

,auto'didact /-'diedakt/ *n* a person who is self-taught [Gk *autodidaktos* self-taught, fr *aut-* + *didaktos* taught, fr *didaskein* to teach] – **autodidactic** / -'daktik/ *adj*

,autoe'roticism /-i'rotisiz(ə)m/ *n* autoerotism

,auto'erotism /-'eərətiz(ə)m/ *n* sexual gratification obtained by oneself without the participation of another person – **autoerotic** /i'rotik/ *adj*, **autoerotically** *adv*

autogamy /aw'togəmi/ *n* self-fertilization [ISV] – **autogamous** *adj*

autogenous /aw'tojənəs/, **autogenic** /,awtə'jenik/ *adj* originating or derived from sources within the same individual ⟨*an ~ graft*⟩ [Gk *autogenēs*, fr *aut-* + *-genēs* born, produced – more at -GEN] – **autogenously** /aw'tojənəsli/ *adv*

autogiro *also* **autogyro** /,awtə'jie·əroh/ *n, pl* **autogiros** *also* **autogyros** an aircraft that resembles a helicopter and has a propeller for forward motion and a freely rotating horizontal rotor for lift [fr *Autogiro*, a trademark]

autograft /'awtə,grahft, -,graft/ *n* a transplant from one part to another part of the same body – **autograft** *vt*

[1]**autograph** /'awtə,grahf, -,graf/ *n* an identifying mark, specif a person's signature, made by the individual him-/herself [LL *autographum*, fr L, neut of *autographus* written with one's own hand, fr Gk *autographos*, fr *aut-* + *-graphos* written – more at -GRAPH] – **autography** /aw'tografi/ *n*

[2]**autograph** *vt* to write one's signature in or on

Autoharp /'awtoh,hahp/ *trademark* – used for a zither with button-controlled dampers for selected strings

autoimmune /,awtohi'myoohn/ *adj* of or caused by autoantibodies; *specif, of a disease* caused by the production of large numbers of autoantibodies – **autoimmunity** *n*, **autoimmunization** /-,imyoo nie'zaysh(ə)n/ *n*

autointoxication /,awtoh·in,toksi'kaysh(ə)n/ *n* a state of being poisoned by toxic substances produced within the body [ISV]

autologous /aw'toləgəs/ *adj* derived from the same individual [*aut-* + *-ologous* (as in *homologous*)]

autolysis /aw'toləsis/ *n* breakdown of all or part of a cell or tissue by self-produced enzymes [NL] – **autolyse** /'awtə,liez/ *vb*, **autolytic** /,awtə'litik/ *adj*

automate /'awtəmayt/ *vt* **1** to operate by automation **2** to convert to largely automatic operation ~ *vi* to undergo automation [back-formation fr *automation*] – **automatable** *adj*

[1]**automatic** /,awtə'matik/ *adj* **1a** acting or done spontaneously or unconsciously **b** resembling an automaton; mechanical **2** having a self-acting or self-regulating mechanism ⟨*an ~ car with ~ transmission*⟩ **3** *of a firearm* repeatedly ejecting the empty cartridge shell, introducing a new cartridge, and firing it [Gk *automatos* self-acting, fr *aut-* + *-matos* (akin to L *ment-, mens* mind) – more at MIND] – **automatically** *adv*, **automaticity** /,awtəmə'tisəti/ *n*

[2]**automatic** *n* an automatic machine or apparatus; *esp* an automatic firearm or vehicle

,auto,matic 'pilot *n* a device for automatically steering a ship, aircraft, or spacecraft

automation /awtə'maysh(ə)n/ *n* **1** the technique of making an apparatus, process, or system operate automatically **2** automatic operation of an apparatus, process, or system by mechanical or electronic devices that take the place of human operators ['*automatic*]

automatism /aw'tomətiz(ə)m/ *n* **1** an automatic action **2** a theory that conceives of the body as a machine, with consciousness being merely an accessory [F *automatisme*, fr *automate* automaton, fr L *automaton*] – **automatist** *n*

automaton /aw'tomət(ə)n; *also* ,awtə'mayt(ə)n/ *n, pl* **automatons, automata** /-tə/ **1** a mechanism having its own power source; *also* a robot **2** a person who acts in a mechanical fashion [L, fr Gk, neut of *automatos*]

automobile /'awtəmə,beel/ *n, NAm* MOTOR CAR ☞ CAR [F, fr *aut-* + *mobile* mobile] – **automobile** *vi*, **automobilist** /,awtə'mohbəlist, -'beelist/ *n*

,auto'motive /-'mohtiv/ *adj* of or concerned with motor vehicles

,auto'nomic /-'nomik/ *adj* **1** acting or occurring involuntarily ⟨*~ reflexes*⟩ **2** relating to, affecting, or controlled by the autonomic nervous system – **autonomically** *adv*

autonomic nervous system *n* a part of the vertebrate nervous system that supplies smooth and cardiac muscle and glandular tissues with nerves and consists of the sympathetic nervous system and the parasympathetic nervous system

autonomous /aw'tonəməs/ *adj* self-governing, independent [Gk *autonomos* independent, fr *aut-* + *nomos* law – more at NIMBLE] – **autonomously** *adv*

autonomy /aw'tonəmi/ *n* **1** self-determined freedom and esp moral independence **2** self-government; *esp* the degree of political independence possessed by a minority group, territorial division, etc – **autonomist** *n*

autopilot /ˈawtoh,pielət/ *n* AUTOMATIC PILOT

autopsy /ˈawtopsi/ *n* a postmortem examination [Gk *autopsia* act of seeing with one's own eyes, fr *aut-* + *opsis* sight, fr *opsesthai* to be going to see – more at OPTIC] – **autopsy** *vt*

autoradiograph /,awtohˈraydi·ə,grahf, -,graf/, **,autoradio,gram** /-,gram/ *n* an image produced by radiation from a radioactive substance in an object in close contact with a photographic film or plate [ISV] – **autoradiographic** /-,raydi·əˈgrafik/ *adj*, **autoradiography** /-ray diˈogrəfi/ *n*

ˈauto,route /-,rooht/ *n* a French motorway [F, fr *auto*mobile + *route* road – more at ROUTE]

autos-da-fé /,awtoh dah ˈfay/ *pl of* AUTO-DA-FÉ

autosome /ˈawtə,sohm/ *n* a chromosome other than a sex chromosome – **autosomal** /,awtəˈsohml/ *adj*, **autosomally** *adv*

autosport /ˈawtoh,spawt/ *n* motorcycle and motor vehicle racing and rallying

ˈauto,strada /-,strahdə/ *n, pl* **autostradas, autostrade** /-day/ an Italian motorway [It, fr *auto*mobile + *strada* street, fr LL *strata* paved road – more at STREET]

,autosugˈgestion /-səˈjeschən/ *n* an influencing of one's attitudes, behaviour, or physical condition by mental processes other than conscious thought [ISV] – **autosuggest** *vt*

autotomy /awˈtotəmi/ *n* reflex separation of a part (e g a lizard's tail) from the body [ISV] – **autotomous** *adj*, **autotomic** /,awtəˈtomik/ *adj*

autotrophic /,awtəˈtrofik/ *adj* able to live and grow on carbon from carbon dioxide or carbonates and nitrogen from a simple inorganic compound – compare HETEROTROPHIC [prob fr G *autotroph*, fr Gk *autotrophos* supplying one's own food, fr *aut-* + *trephein* to nourish – more at ATROPHY] – **autotrophically** *adv*, **autotroph** /ˈawtətrohf/ *n*

autumn /ˈawtəm/ *n* **1** the season between summer and winter, extending, in the northern hemisphere, from the September equinox to the December solstice **2** a period of maturity or the early stages of decline [ME *autumpne*, fr L *autumnus*] – **autumnal** /awˈtumnəl/ *adj*, **autumnally** *adv*

autumn crocus *n* an autumn-blooming plant of the lily family

auxesis /awkˈseesis, -gz-/ *n* growth; *specif* increase of cell size without cell division [NL, fr Gk *auxēsis* increase, growth, fr *auxein* to increase – more at EKE OUT] – **auxetic** /awkˈsetik, -gz-/ *adj*, **auxetically** *adv*

¹auxiliary /awgˈzilyəri/ *adj* **1** subsidiary **2** being a verb (e g *be, do,* or *may*) used typically to express person, number, mood, voice, or tense, usu accompanying another verb **3** supplementary [L *auxiliaris*, fr *auxilium* help; akin to Gk *auxein* to increase]

²auxiliary *n* **1** an auxiliary person, group, or device **2** an auxiliary verb **3** a member of a foreign force serving a nation at war

auxin /ˈawksin/ *n* (an analogue of) a plant hormone that promotes growth [ISV, fr Gk *auxein*] – **auxinic** /awkˈsinik/ *adj*, **auxinically** *adv*

auxotrophic /,awksəˈtrohfik/ *adj* requiring a specific growth substance beyond the minimum required for normal metabolism and reproduction ⟨~ *mutants of bacteria*⟩ [Gk *auxein* to increase + *-o-* + E *-trophic*] – **auxotroph** /ˈawksə-/ *n*

¹avail /əˈvayl/ *vb* to be of use or advantage (to) [ME *availen*, prob fr *a-* (as in *abaten* to abate) + *vailen* to avail, fr OF *valoir* to be of worth, fr L *valēre* – more at WIELD] – **avail oneself of** to make use of; take advantage of

²avail *n* benefit, use – chiefly after *of* or *to* and in negative contexts ⟨*of little* ~⟩ ⟨*to no* ~⟩

available /əˈvayləbl/ *adj* **1** present or ready for immediate use **2** accessible, obtainable **3** qualified or willing to do sthg or to assume a responsibility ⟨~ *candidates*⟩ **4** present in such chemical or physical form as to be usable (e g by a plant) ⟨~ *nitrogen*⟩ ⟨~ *water*⟩ [ME, advantageous, beneficial, fr *availen* + *-able*] – **availableness** *n*, **availably** *adv*, **availability** /ə,vayləˈbiləti/ *n*

¹avalanche /ˈavəlahnch/ *n* **1** a large mass of snow, rock, ice, etc falling rapidly down a mountain **2** a sudden overwhelming rush or accumulation of sthg [F, fr F dial. *lavantse, avalantse*]

²avalanche *vi* to descend in an avalanche ~ *vt* to overwhelm, flood

¹avant-garde /,avong ˈgahd/ *n* *the* group of people who create or apply new ideas and techniques in any field, esp the arts; *also* such a group that is extremist, bizarre, or arty and affected [F, vanguard] – **avant-gardism** *n*, **avant-gardist** *n*

²avant-garde *adj* of the avant-garde or artistic work that is new and experimental

avarice /ˈavəris/ *n* excessive or insatiable desire for wealth or gain; cupidity [ME, fr OF, fr L *avaritia*, fr *avarus* avaricious, fr *avēre* to covet – more at AVID] – **avaricious** /,avəˈrishəs/ *adj*, **avariciously** *adv*, **avariciousness** *n*

avast /əˈvahst/ *vb imper* – a nautical command to stop or cease [perh fr D *houd vast* hold fast]

avatar /ˈavətah/ *n* **1** an earthly incarnation of a Hindu deity **2a** an incarnation in human form **b** an embodiment (e g of a concept or philosophy), usu in a person [Skt *avatāra* descent, fr *avatarati* he descends, fr *ava-* away + *tarati* he crosses over – more at UKASE, THROUGH]

ave /ˈahvay, -vi/ *n, often cap* HAIL MARY [ME, fr L, hail!]

,Ave Maˈria /məˈree·ə/ *n* HAIL MARY [ME, fr ML, hail, Mary!]

avenge /əˈvenj/ *vt* **1** to take vengeance on behalf of **2** to exact satisfaction for (a wrong) by punishing the wrongdoer [ME *avengen*, prob fr *a-* (as in *abaten* to abate) + *vengen* to avenge, fr OF *vengier* – more at VENGEANCE] – **avenger** *n*

avens /ˈavinz/ *n, pl* **avens** /~/ any of a genus of perennial plants of the rose family with white, purple, or yellow flowers [ME *avence*, fr OF]

aventurine /əˈventyoorin, -reen/ *n* **1** glass containing opaque sparkling particles of foreign material **2** a translucent quartz spangled with mica or other mineral [F, fr *aventure* chance – more at ADVENTURE]

avenue /ˈavənyooh/ *n* **1** a line of approach **2** a broad passageway bordered by trees **3** an often broad street or road **4** *chiefly Br* a tree-lined walk or driveway to a large country house situated off a main road [MF, fr fem of *avenu*, pp of *avenir* to come to, fr L *advenire* – more at ADVENTURE]

aver /əˈvuh/ *vt* **-rr- 1** to allege, assert **2** to declare positively – fml [ME *averren*, fr MF *averer*, fr ML *adverare* to confirm as authentic, fr L *ad-* + *verus* true – more at VERY] – **averment** *n*

[1]**average** /'avərij, 'avrij/ *n* **1** a partial loss or damage sustained by a ship or cargo; *also* a charge arising from this, usu distributed among all chargeable with it **2** a single value representative of a set of other values; *esp* ARITHMETIC MEAN ☞ STATISTICS **3** a level (e g of intelligence) typical of a group, class, or series **4** a ratio expressing the average performance of a sports team or sportsman as a fraction of the number of opportunities for successful performance – compare LAW OF AVERAGES [modif of MF *avarie* damage to ship or cargo, fr OIt *avaria*, fr Ar *'awārīyah* damaged merchandise]

[2]**average** *adj* **1** equalling an arithmetic mean **2a** about midway between extremes **b** not out of the ordinary; common – **averagely** *adv*, **averageness** *n*

[3]**average** *vi* to be or come to an average ⟨*the gain* ~d *out to 20 per cent*⟩ ~ *vt* **1** to do, get, or have on average or as an average sum or quantity ⟨~s *12 hours of work a day*⟩ **2** to find the arithmetic mean of **3** to bring towards the average **4** to have an average value of ⟨*a colour* averaging *a pale purple*⟩

averse /ə'vuhs/ *adj* having an active feeling of repugnance or distaste – + *to* or *from* [L *aversus*, pp of *avertere* – more at AVERT] – **aversely** *adv*, **averseness** *n*

aversion /ə'vuhsh(ə)n/ *n* **1** a feeling of settled dislike for sthg; antipathy **2** *chiefly Br* an object of aversion; a cause of repugnance [LL *aversion-*, *aversio*, fr L, the act of turning away, fr *aversus*] – **aversive** /-siv/ *adj*

a'version ,therapy *n* therapy intended to change antisocial behaviour or a habit by association with unpleasant sensations

avert /ə'vuht/ *vt* **1** to turn away or aside (e g the eyes) in avoidance **2** to see coming and ward off; avoid, prevent [ME *averten*, fr MF *avertir*, fr L *avertere*, fr *ab-* + *vertere* to turn – more at [1]WORTH]

Avesta /ə'vestə/ *n* the book of the sacred writings of Zoroastrianism [MPer *Avastāk*, lit., original text]

Avestan /ə'vest(ə)n/ *n* an ancient sacred language of old Iranian – **Avestan** *adj*

avian /'ayvi·ən/ *adj* of or derived from birds [L *avis*]

aviary /'ayvyəri/ *n* a place for keeping birds [L *aviarium*, fr *avis* bird; akin to Gk *aetos* eagle]

aviation /,ayvi'aysh(ə)n/ *n* **1** the operation of heavier-than-air aircraft **2** aircraft manufacture, development, and design [F, fr L *avis*]

aviator /'ayviaytə/, *fem* **aviatrix** /-triks/ *n* the pilot of an aircraft [F *aviateur*, fr *avi-* (fr L *avis*) + *-ateur* (as in *amateur*)]

avid /'avid/ *adj* urgently or greedily eager; keen [F or L; F *avide*, fr L *avidus*, fr *avēre* to covet; akin to Goth *awiliuth* thanks, Gk *enēēs* gentle] – **avidly** *adv*, **avidness** *n*, **avidity** /ə'vidəti/ *n*

avidin /'avidin, ə'vidin/ *n* a protein found in white of egg that combines with biotin and makes it inactive [fr its avidity for biotin]

avifauna /,ayvi'fawnə/ *n* the (kinds of) birds of a region, period, or environment [NL, fr L *avis* + NL *fauna*] – **avifaunal** *adj*, **avifaunally** *adv*, **avifaunistic** /-faw'nistik/ *adj*

avionics /,ayvi'oniks/ *n pl but sing or pl in constr* the development and production of electronic equipment for aircraft and space vehicles; *also, pl in constr* the devices and systems so developed [*avi*ation elec*tronics*] – **avionic** *adj*

avitaminosis /,ay,vitəmi'nohsis, ,a-/ *n, pl* **avitaminoses** /-seez/ disease resulting from a deficiency of 1 or more vitamins [NL] – **avitaminotic** /-'notik/ *adj*

avo /'avooh/ *n, pl* **avos** ☞ *Macao* at NATIONALITY [Pg, fr *avo* fractional part, fr *-avo* ordinal suffix (as in *oitavo* eighth, fr L *octavus*)]

avocado /,avə'kahdoh/ *n, pl* **avocados** *also* **avocadoes** (a tropical American tree of the laurel family bearing) a pulpy green or purple pear-shaped edible fruit [Sp, alter. of *aguacate*, fr Nahuatl *ahuacatl*, short for *ahuacacuahuitl*, lit., testicle tree]

avocation /,avə'kaysh(ə)n/ *n* a subordinate occupation pursued in addition to one's vocation, esp for enjoyment; a hobby [L *avocation-*, *avocatio*, fr *avocatus*, pp of *avocare* to call away, fr *ab-* + *vocare* to call, fr *voc-*, *vox* voice – more at VOICE] – **avocational** *adj*, **avocationally** *adv*

avocet /'avəset/ *n* a black and white wading bird with webbed feet and a slender upward-curving bill [F & It; F *avocette*, fr It *avocetta*]

Avogadro's constant /,avə'gadrohz/ *n* the number of molecules that occurs in 1 mole of substance; 6.023×10^{23} ☞ PHYSICS [Count Amedeo *Avogadro* †1856 It chemist & physicist]

Avogadro's number *n* AVOGADRO'S CONSTANT

avoid /ə'voyd/ *vt* **1a** to keep away from; shun **b** to prevent the occurrence or effectiveness of **c** to refrain from **2** to make legally void [ME *avoiden*, fr OF *esvuidier*, fr *es-* (fr L *ex-*) + *vuidier* to empty – more at [3]VOID] – **avoidable** *adj*, **avoidably** *adv*, **avoidance** *n*, **avoider** *n*

avoirdupois /,avwahdooh'pwah, ,avədə'poyz/, **avoirdupois weight** *n* the series of units of weight based on the pound of 16 ounces and the ounce of 16 drams ☞ UNIT [ME *avoir de pois* goods sold by weight, fr OF, lit., goods of weight]

avouch /ə'vowch/ *vt* **1** to declare as a matter of fact; affirm **2** to vouch for; corroborate **3a** to acknowledge (e g an act) as one's own **b** to confess, avow *USE* fml or archaic [ME *avouchen* to cite as authority, fr MF *avochier* to summon, fr L *advocare* – more at ADVOCATE] – **avouchment** *n*

avow /ə'vow/ *vt* **1** to declare assuredly **2** to acknowledge openly, bluntly, and without shame [ME *avowen*, fr OF *avouer*, fr L *advocare*] – **avower** *n*, **avowal** *n*, **avowedly** /-idli/ *adv*

avulsion /ə'vulsh(ə)n/ *n* a forcible separation or detachment: e g **a** a tearing away of a body part accidentally or surgically **b** a sudden cutting off of land from a property by flood, currents, etc [L *avulsion-*, *avulsio*, fr *avulsus*, pp of *avellere* to tear off, fr *ab-* + *vellere* to pluck, pull]

avuncular /ə'vungkyoolə/ *adj* **1** of an uncle **2** kindly, genial [L *avunculus* maternal uncle – more at UNCLE]

await /ə'wayt/ *vt* **1** to wait for **2** to be in store for [ME *awaiten*, fr ONF *awaitier*, fr *a-* (fr L *ad-*) + *waitier* to watch – more at [1]WAIT]

[1]**awake** /ə'wayk/ *vb* **awoke** /ə'wohk/ *also* **awaked; awoken** /ə'wohkən/ *vi* **1** to emerge from sleep or a sleeplike state **2** to become conscious or aware of sthg – usu + *to* ⟨awoke *to their danger*⟩ ~ *vt* **1** to arouse from sleep or a sleeplike state **2** to make active; stir up ⟨awoke *old memories*⟩ [ME *awaken*

(fr OE *awacan*, fr [1]*a-* + *wacan* to awake, arise, be born) & *awakien*, fr OE *awacian*, fr [1]*a-* + *wacian* to be awake, watch – more at [1]WAKE]

[2]**awake** *adj* **1** roused (as if) from sleep **2** fully conscious; aware – usu + *to*

awaken /ə'waykən/ *vb* to awake [ME *awakenen*, fr OE *awæcnian*, fr *a-* + *wæcnian* to waken] – **awakener** *n*

[1]**award** /ə'wawd/ *vt* **1** to give by judicial decree **2** to confer or bestow as being deserved or needed [ME *awarden* to decide, fr ONF *eswarder*, fr *es-* (fr L *ex-*) + *warder* to guard, of Gmc origin; akin to OHG *wartēn* to watch] – **awardable** *adj*, **awarder** *n*

[2]**award** *n* **1** a final decision; *esp* the decision of arbitrators in a case submitted to them **2** sthg that is conferred or bestowed, esp on the basis of merit or need

aware /ə'weə/ *adj* having or showing realization, perception, or knowledge; conscious – often + *of* [ME *iwar*, fr OE *gewær*, fr *ge-* (associative prefix) + *wær* wary – more at CO-, WARY] – **awareness** *n*

awash /ə'wosh/ *adj* **1** covered with water; flooded **2** marked by an abundance

[1]**away** /ə'way/ *adv* **1** on the way; along ⟨*get ~ early*⟩ **2** from here or there; hence, thence ⟨*go ~ and leave me alone!*⟩ **3a** in a secure place or manner ⟨*locked ~*⟩ ⟨*tucked ~*⟩ **b** in another direction; aside ⟨*looked ~*⟩ **4** out of existence; to an end ⟨*echoes dying ~*⟩ ⟨*laze ~ the afternoon*⟩ **5** from one's possession ⟨*gave ~ a fortune*⟩ **6a** on, uninterruptedly ⟨*clocks ticking ~*⟩ **b** without hesitation or delay ⟨*do it right ~*⟩ **7** by a long distance or interval; far ⟨*~ back in 1910*⟩ [ME *away, on way*, fr OE *aweg, on weg*, fr *a, on* + *weg* way – more at WAY]

[2]**away** *adj* **1** absent from a place; gone ⟨*~ for the weekend*⟩ **2** distant ⟨*a lake 10 miles ~*⟩ **3** played on an opponent's grounds ⟨*an ~ game*⟩

awe /aw/ *vt or n* (to inspire with) an emotion compounded of dread, veneration, and wonder [n ME, fr ON *agi*; akin to OE *ege* awe, Gk *achos* pain; vb fr n]

awed /awd/ *adj* showing awe ⟨*~ respect*⟩

aweigh /ə'way/ *adj, of an anchor* raised just clear of the bottom of a body of water [[1]*a-* + [1]*weigh* 4]

awesome /'aws(ə)m/ *adj* inspiring or expressing awe – **awesomely** *adv*, **awesomeness** *n*

'awe,struck /-,struk/ *also* **awestricken** /-,strikən/ *adj* filled with awe

[1]**awful** /'awf(ə)l/ *adj* **1** extremely disagreeable or objectionable **2** exceedingly great ⟨*an ~ lot to do*⟩ – used as an intensive; chiefly infml [AWE + [1]-FUL] – **awfully** *adv*, **awfulness** *n*

[2]**awful** *adv* very, extremely – nonstandard

awkward /'awkwəd/ *adj* **1** lacking dexterity or skill, esp in the use of hands; clumsy **2** lacking ease or grace (e g of movement or expression) **3a** lacking social grace and assurance **b** causing embarrassment ⟨*an ~ moment*⟩ **4** poorly adapted for use or handling **5** requiring caution ⟨*an ~ diplomatic situation*⟩ **6** deliberately obstructive [ME *awkeward* in the wrong direction, fr *awke* turned the wrong way, fr ON *öfugr*; akin to OHG *abuh* turned the wrong way, L *opacus* obscure] – **awkwardly** *adv*, **awkwardness** *n*

awl /awl/ *n* a pointed instrument for marking surfaces or making small holes (e g in leather) [ME *al*, fr ON *alr*; akin to OHG *āla* awl, Skt *ārā*]

awn /awn/ *n* any of the slender bristles at the end of the flower spikelet in some grasses (e g barley) [ME, fr OE *agen*, fr ON *ögn*; akin to OHG *agana* awn, OE *ecg* edge – more at EDGE] – **awned** *adj*, **awnless** *adj*

awning /'awning/ *n* **1** an often canvas rooflike cover, used to protect sthg (e g a shop window or a ship's deck) from sun or rain **2** a shelter resembling an awning [origin unknown] – **awninged** /'awningd/ *adj*

awoken /ə'wohkən/ *past part of* AWAKE

AWOL /'aywol/ *adj, often not cap* absent without leave [*a*bsent *w*ithout *l*eave]

awry /ə'rie/ *adv or adj* **1** in a turned or twisted position or direction; askew **2** out of the right or hoped-for course; amiss [ME *on wry*, fr *on* + *wry*]

[1]**axe,** *NAm chiefly* **ax** /aks/ *n* **1** a tool that has a cutting edge parallel to the handle and is used esp for felling trees and chopping and splitting wood **2** drastic reduction or removal (e g of personnel) [ME, fr OE *æx*; akin to OHG *ackus* axe, L *ascia*, Gk *axinē*] – **axe to grind** an ulterior often selfish purpose to further

[2]**axe,** *NAm chiefly* **ax** *vt* **1a** to hew, shape, dress, or trim with an axe **b** to chop, split, or sever with an axe **2** to remove abruptly (e g from employment or from a budget)

axel /'aksl/ *n* a jump in ice-skating from one skate with 1½ turns in the air and a return to the other skate [*Axel* Paulsen *fl* 1890 Norw figure skater]

'axe,man /-,man/ *n* one who wields an axe; *specif* a usu psychopathic criminal

axial /'aksi·əl/, **axal** /'aksl/ *adj* **1** of or functioning as an axis **2** situated round, in the direction of, on, or along an axis – **axially** *adv*, **axiality** /,aksi'aləti/ *n*

axil /'aksl/ *n* the angle between a branch or leaf and the axis from which it arises [NL *axilla*, fr L]

axilla /ak'silə/ *n, pl* **axillas, axillae** /-li/ the armpit [L]

axillary /ak'siləri/ *adj* **1** of or located near the armpit **2** situated in or growing from an axil

axiology /,aksi'oləji/ *n* inquiry into values, esp in ethics [Gk *axios* + ISV *-logy*] – **axiological** /-si·ə'lojikl/ *adj*

axiom /'aksi·əm/ *n* **1** a principle, rule, or maxim widely accepted on its intrinsic merit; a generally recognized truth **2a** a proposition regarded as a self-evident truth **b** a postulate [L *axioma*, fr Gk *axiōma*, lit., honour, fr *axioun* to think worthy, fr *axios* worth, worthy; akin to Gk *agein* to drive – more at AGENT]

axiomatic /,aksi·ə'matik/ *adj* of or having the nature of an axiom; *esp* self-evident [MGk *axiōmatikos*, fr Gk, honourable, fr *axiōmat-*, *axiōma*] – **axiomatically** *adv*

axis /'aksis/ *n, pl* **axes** /-seez/ **1a** a straight line about which a body or a geometric figure rotates or may be supposed to rotate **b** a straight line with respect to which a body or figure is symmetrical **c** any of the reference lines of a coordinate system **2a** the second vertebra of the neck on which the head and first vertebra pivot **b** any of various parts that are central, fundamental, or that lie on or constitute an axis **3** a plant stem **4** any of several imaginary reference lines used in describing a crystal structure **5** a partnership or alliance (e g the one between

Germany and Italy in WW II) *USE (1)* ☞ MATHEMATICS [L, axis, axle; akin to OE *eax* axis, axle, Gk *axōn*, L *axilla* armpit, *agere* to drive – more at AGENT]

'axis ,deer *n* a white-spotted deer of India and other parts of S Asia [NL *axis*, fr L, a wild animal of India]

axle /'aksl/ *n* **1** a shaft on or with which a wheel revolves **2** a rod connecting a pair of wheels of a vehicle; *also* an axletree ☞ CAR [ME *axel-* (as in *axeltre*)]

'axle,tree /-,tree/ *n* a fixed bar or beam with bearings at each end on which wheels (e g of a cart) revolve [ME *axeltre*, fr ON *öxultrē*, fr *öxull* axle + *trē* tree]

Axminster /'aks,minstə/ *n* (a carpet woven in) a weave in which pile tufts are inserted into a backing during its weaving according to a predetermined arrangement of colours and patterns – compare WILTON [*Axminster*, town in England]

axolotl /'aksəlotl, ,aksə'lotl/ *n* any of several salamanders of mountain lakes of Mexico [Nahuatl, lit., water doll]

axon /'akson/ *n* a usu long projecting part of a nerve cell that usu conducts impulses away from the cell body [NL, fr Gk *axōn*] – **axonal** *adj*, **axonic** /,ak'sonik/ *adj*

ayah /'ie·ə/ *n* a native nurse or maid in India [Hindi *āyā*, fr Pg *aia*, fr L *avia* grandmother]

ayatollah /,ie·ə'tolə/ *n* a leader of Iranian Shiite Islam [Per *āyatollāh*, fr Ar *āyatullāh* manifestation of God]

[1]aye *also* **ay** /ay/ *adv* ever, always, continually [ME *aye, ai*, fr ON *ei*; akin to OE *ā* always, L *aevum* age, lifetime, Gk *aiōn* age]

[2]aye *also* **ay** /ie/ *adv* yes – used as the correct formal response to a naval order ⟨~, ~, *sir*⟩ [perh fr ME *ye, yie* – more at YEA]

[3]aye *also* **ay** /ie/ *n* an affirmative vote or voter

aye-aye /'ie ,ie/ *n* a nocturnal lemur of Madagascar ☞ ENDANGERED [F, fr Malagasy *aiay*]

Aylesbury /'aylzb(ə)ri/ *n* any of a breed of large white domestic ducks [*Aylesbury*, town in England]

Aymara /'iemə,rah/ *n, pl* **Aymaras**, *esp collectively* **Aymara** a member, or the language, of an American Indian people of Bolivia and Peru ☞ LANGUAGE [Sp *Aymará*]

Ayrshire /'eə,shiə/ *n* any of a breed of hardy dairy cattle that are usu spotted red, brown, or white in colour [*Ayrshire* (Ayr), county of Scotland]

A-Z /,ay tə 'zed/ *n, Br* an indexed street atlas of a town

az- /əz-, az-/, **azo-** *comb form* containing nitrogen, esp as the bivalent group N=N ⟨azo*benzene*⟩ [ISV, fr *azote* nitrogen]

aza-, az- *comb form* containing nitrogen in place of carbon and usu the bivalent group NH for the group CH_2 or a single trivalent nitrogen atom for the group CH ⟨aza*guanine*⟩ [ISV *az-* + *-a-*]

azalea /ə'zaylyə/ *n* any of a group of rhododendrons with funnel-shaped flowers and usu deciduous leaves [NL, genus name, fr Gk, fem of *azaleos* dry; akin to L *aridus* dry]

azeotrope /ə'zee·ətrohp/ *n* a mixture of liquids whose boiling point does not change during distillation [ISV [2]*a-* + *zeo-* (fr Gk *zein* to boil) + *-trope*, fr Gk *tropos* turn, way – more at YEAST, TROPE] – **azeotropic** /,ayzi·ə'tropik/ *adj*

azide /'ay,zied, 'a-/ *n* a compound containing the group N_3 combined with an element or radical – **azido** /-doh/ *adj*

azimuth /'aziməth/ *n* **1** an arc of the horizon expressed as the clockwise angle measured between a fixed point (e g true N or true S) and the vertical circle passing through the centre of an object **2** horizontal direction [ME, fr (assumed) ML, fr Ar *as-sumūt* the azimuth, pl of *as-samt* the way] – **azimuthal** /,azi'moohthl/ *adj*, **azimuthally** *adv*

azimuthal projection *n* a projection of the earth's surface onto a tangential plane

azo /'ayzoh, 'a-/ *adj* relating to or containing the bivalent group N=N united at both ends to carbon [*az-*]

azo dye *n* any of numerous versatile dyes containing azo groups

azoic /ay'zoh·ik, a-/ *adj* having no life; *specif* of the geological time that antedates life ☞ EVOLUTION [[2]*a-* + Gk *zōē* life – more at QUICK]

azotobacter /ə'zohtə,baktə, ay-/ *n* any of a genus of large rod-shaped or spherical bacteria that occur in soil and sewage and fix atmospheric nitrogen [NL, genus name, fr ISV *azote* nitrogen (irreg fr *a-* + Gk *zōē* + NL *bacterium*]

Aztec /'aztek/ *n* **1** a member of the Nahuatlan people that founded the Mexican empire conquered by Cortes in 1519 **2** the language of the Aztecs [Sp *Azteca*, fr Nahuatl, pl of *aztecatl*] – **Aztecan** *adj*

azure /'azyooə, 'ay-, -zhə/ *n* **1a** sky blue **b** blue – used in heraldry **2** *archaic* LAPIS LAZULI [ME *asur*, fr OF *azur*, prob fr OSp, modif of Ar *lāzaward*, fr Per *lāzhuward*] – **azure** *adj*

azurite /'azyooriet, 'ay-, -zhə-/ *n* (a semiprecious stone derived from) a blue mineral that is a carbonate of copper [F, fr *azur* azure]

azygous, azygos /'azigəs/ *adj* not being one of a pair ⟨*an* ~ *vein*⟩ [NL *azygos*, fr Gk, unyoked, fr [2]*a-* + *zygon* yoke – more at YOKE]

B

b /bee/ *n, pl* **b's, bs** *often cap* **1a** (a graphic representation of or device for reproducing) the 2nd letter of the English alphabet **b** a speech counterpart of orthographic *b* **2** the 7th note of a C-major scale **3** one designated *b,* esp as the 2nd in order or class **4** a grade rating a student's work as good but short of excellent **5** sthg that is the supporting item of 2 things ⟨*a* ~*-movie*⟩ **6** – used euphemistically for any offensive word beginning with the letter *b*

baa, ba /bah/ *vi or n* (to make) the bleat of a sheep [imit]

baal /bahl, 'bay·əl/ *n, pl* **baals, baalim** /-lim/ *often cap* any of numerous Canaanite and Phoenician local deities [Heb *ba'al* lord] – **baalism** *n, often cap*

baas /bahs/ *n, SAfr* a master, boss [Afrik, fr MD *baes*]

'baas,skap /-,skap/ *n, SAfr* WHITE SUPREMACY [Afrik, lit., mastership, fr *baas*]

babbitt /'babit/ *n* a babbitt-metal lining for a bearing

babbitt metal *n* an alloy, esp of tin, copper, antimony, and lead, used for lining bearings [Isaac *Babbitt* †1862 US inventor]

babble /'babl/ *vb* **babbling** /'babling, 'babl·ing/ *vi* **1a** to utter meaningless or unintelligible sounds **b** to talk foolishly; chatter **2** to make a continuous murmuring sound ~ *vt* **1** to utter in an incoherently or meaninglessly repetitious manner **2** to reveal by talk that is too free [ME *babelen,* prob of imit origin] – **babble** *n,* **babblement** *n,* **babbler** /'bablə/ *n*

babe /bayb/ *n* **1** a naive inexperienced person **2a** an infant, baby – chiefly poetic **b** a girl, woman – slang; usu as a noun of address [ME, baby, prob of imit origin]

Babel /'baybl/ *n, often not cap* **1** a confusion of sounds or voices **2** a scene of noise or confusion [the Tower of *Babel* (fr Heb *Bābhel,* fr Assyr-Bab *bāb-ilu* gate of god), biblical structure (Gen 11:4–9) intended to reach heaven which incurred the wrath of God, who punished the builders by making their speech mutually unintelligible]

babirusa, babirussa, babiroussa /,babə'roohsə/ *n* a large pig of the E Indies, the male of which has large backward-curving tusks [Malay *bābīrūsa,* fr *bābī* hog + *rūsa* deer]

baboon /bə'boohn/ *n* any of several large African and Asiatic primates having doglike muzzles and usu short tails [ME *babewin,* fr MF *babouin,* fr *baboue* grimace] – **baboonish** *adj*

babu /'bah,booh/ *n* **1** a Hindu gentleman – a form of address corresponding to *Mr* **2** an Indian with some education in English – chiefly derog [Hindi *bābū,* lit., father]

babul /bah'boohl, '- -/ *n* an acacia tree widespread in N Africa and across Asia that yields gum arabic and tannins as well as fodder and timber [Per *babūl*]

¹baby /'baybi/ *n* **1a(1)** an extremely young child; *esp* an infant **(2)** an unborn child ⟨*my* ~ *started kicking before I was 4 months pregnant*⟩ **(3)** an extremely young animal **b** the youngest of a group **2** an infantile person **3** a person or thing for which one feels special responsibility or pride **4** a person; *esp* a girl, woman – slang; usu as a noun of address [ME, fr *babe*] – **babyish** *adj,* **babyhood** /-hood/ *n*

²baby *adj* very small ⟨*use* ~ *mushrooms*⟩

³baby *vt* to tend or indulge with often excessive or inappropriate care

'baby ,buggy *n* **1** a lightweight foldable pushchair **2** *NAm* a pram

,baby 'grand *n* a small grand piano

Babylonian /,babi'lohnyən, -ni·ən/ *n or adj* (a native or inhabitant or the Akkadian language) of ancient Babylonia or Babylon [*Babylon,* ancient city of *Babylonia,* ancient country of SW Asia]

'baby-,minder *n chiefly Br* a childminder for babies or preschool children – **baby-minding** *n*

'baby-,sit *vi* **-tt-; baby-sat** to care for a child, usu for a short period while the parents are out [back-formation fr *baby-sitter*] – **baby-sitter** *n*

'baby ,talk *n* the imperfect speech used by or to small children

baccalaureate /,bakə'lawri·ət/ *n* the academic degree of bachelor [ML *baccalaureatus,* fr *baccalaureus* bachelor, alter. of *baccalarius*]

baccarat /'bakərah, --'-/ *n* a card game in which 3 hands are dealt and players may bet on either or both hands against the dealer's [F *baccara*]

bacchanal /'bakənl/ *n* **1a** a devotee of Bacchus; *esp* one who celebrates the Bacchanalia **b** a reveller **2** drunken revelry or carousal; bacchanalia [L *bacchanalis* of Bacchus, fr *Bacchus,* god of wine, fr Gk *Bakchos*] – **bacchanal** *adj*

bacchanalia /,bakə'naylyə/ *n, pl* **bacchanalia** **1** *pl, cap* a Roman festival of Bacchus celebrated with dancing, song, and revelry **2** a drunken feast; an orgy [L, pl, fr neut pl of *bacchanalis*] – **bacchanalian** *adj or n*

bacchante /bə'kanti/ *n* a priestess or female follower of Bacchus; a maenad [F, fr L *bacchant-, bacchans,* prp of *bacchari* to celebrate the festival of Bacchus]

baccy /'baki/ *n, chiefly Br* tobacco – infml [by shortening & alter.]

¹bach /bakh/ *n, NZ* a simple dwelling; *esp* a shack or chalet [prob short for *bachelor*]

²bach /bahkh/ *n, Welsh* – used as a term of endearment, usu after a person's name ⟨*how are you Dai* ~*?*⟩ [W, lit., little (one)]

bachelor /'bachələ, 'bachlə/ *n* **1** a recipient of what is usu the lowest degree conferred by a college or university ⟨~ *of arts*⟩ **2a** an unmarried man **b** a man past the usual age for marrying or one who seems unlikely to marry **3** a male animal (e g a fur seal) without a mate during breeding time [ME *bacheler,* fr OF, prob fr ML *baccalarius* tenant farmer, squire, advanced student, of Celtic origin; akin to IrGael *bachlach* shepherd, peasant, fr OIr *bachall* staff, fr L *baculum*] – **bachelordom** *n,* **bachelorhood** *n*

'**bachelor ,girl** *n* an unmarried girl or woman who lives independently

bacillary /bə'siləri/ *adj* of or caused by bacilli [ML & NL *bacillus*]

bacillus /bə'siləs/ *n, pl* **bacilli** /-lie/ a usu rod-shaped bacterium; *esp* one that causes disease [NL, fr ML, small staff, rod, dim. of L *baculus* staff, alter. of *baculum*]

[1]**back** /bak/ *n* **1a** the rear part of the human body, esp from the neck to the end of the spine **b** the corresponding part of a quadruped or other lower animal **2a** the side or surface behind the front or face; the rear part; *also* the farther or reverse side **b** sthg at or on the back for support ⟨*the ~ of a chair*⟩ **3** (the position of) a primarily defensive player in some games (e g soccer) [ME, fr OE *bæc*; akin to OHG *bah* back] – **backless** *adj* – **with one's back to the wall** in a situation from which one cannot retreat and must either fight or be defeated

[2]**back** *adv* **1a(1)** to, towards, or at the rear ⟨*tie one's hair ~*⟩ **(2)** away (e g from the speaker) ⟨*stand ~ and give him air*⟩ **b** in or into the past or nearer the beginning; ago ⟨*3 years ~*⟩ **c** in or into a reclining position ⟨*lie ~*⟩ **d** in or into a delayed or retarded condition ⟨*set them ~ on the schedule*⟩ **2a** to, towards, or in a place from which sby or sthg came ⟨*put it ~ on the shelf*⟩ **b** to or towards a former state ⟨*thought ~ to his childhood*⟩ **c** in return or reply ⟨*ring me ~*⟩ – **back and forth** backwards and forwards repeatedly

[3]**back** *adj* **1a** at or in the back ⟨*~ door*⟩ **b** distant from a central or main area; remote ⟨*~ roads*⟩ **c** articulated at or towards the back of the oral passage **2** being in arrears ⟨*~ pay*⟩ **3** not current ⟨*~ number of a magazine*⟩

[4]**back** *vt* **1a** to support by material or moral assistance – often + *up* **b** to substantiate – often + *up* ⟨*~ up an argument with forceful illustrations*⟩ **c(1)** to countersign, endorse **(2)** to assume financial responsibility for ⟨*~ an enterprise*⟩ **2** to cause to go back or in reverse **3a** to provide with a back **b** to be at the back of **4** to place a bet on (e g a horse) ~ *vi* **1** to move backwards **2** *of the wind* to shift anticlockwise – compare VEER **3** to have the back in the direction of sthg ⟨*my house ~s onto the golf course*⟩

'**back,ache** /-,ayk/ *n* a (dull persistent) pain in the back

back away *vi* to move back (e g from a theoretical position); withdraw

,**back 'bench** *n* any of the benches in Parliament on which rank and file members sit – usu pl – **back-bencher** *n*

'**back,bite** /-,biet/ *vb* **backbit** /-,bit/; **backbitten** /-,bit(ə)n/ to say mean or spiteful things about (sby) – **backbiter** *n*

'**back,board** /-,bawd/ *n* a rounded or rectangular board behind the basket on a basketball court

,**back 'boiler** *n, chiefly Br* a domestic boiler fitted at the back of and heated by an esp coal or gas fire

'**back,bone** /-,bohn/ *n* **1** SPINAL COLUMN **2a** a chief mountain ridge, range, or system **b** the foundation or most substantial part of sthg **3** a firm and resolute character

'**back,breaking** /-,brayking/ *adj* physically taxing or exhausting

'**back,chat** /-,chat/ *n, chiefly Br* impudent or argumentative talk made in reply, esp by a subordinate – infml

'**back,cloth** /-,kloth/ *n, Br* **1** a painted cloth hung across the rear of a stage **2** BACKGROUND 1a, 3

'**back,comb** /-,kohm/ *vt* to comb (the hair) against the direction of growth starting with the short underlying hairs in order to produce a bouffant effect

'**back,date** /-,dayt/ *vt* to apply (e g a pay rise) retrospectively – compare POSTDATE

back down *vi* to retreat from a commitment or position

'**back,drop** /-,drop/ *n* a backcloth

backer /'bakə/ *n* **1** one who supports, esp financially **2** *Br* one who has placed a bet [[4]BACK + [2]-ER]

[1]'**back,fire** /-,fie·ə/ *n* a premature explosion in the cylinder or an explosion in the exhaust system of an internal-combustion engine

[2],**back'fire** *vi* **1** to make or undergo a backfire **2** to have the reverse of the desired or expected effect

'**back-for,mation** *n* the formation of a word by subtraction from an existing word; *also* a word so formed (e g *burgle* from *burglar*)

'**back,gammon** /-,gamən/ *n* a board game played with dice and counters in which each player tries to move his/her counters along the board and at the same time to block or capture his/her opponent's counters [perh fr [3]*back* + ME *gamen, game* game]

'**back,ground** /-,grownd/ *n* **1a** the scenery or ground behind sthg **b** the part of a painting or photograph that depicts what lies behind objects in the foreground **2** an inconspicuous position ⟨*in the ~*⟩ **3a** the conditions that form the setting within which sthg is experienced **b** information essential to the understanding of a problem or situation **c** the total of a person's experience, knowledge, and education

'**background ,noise** *n* intrusive sound that interferes with received or recorded electronic signals

[1]'**back,hand** /-,hand/ *n* **1** a stroke in tennis, squash, etc made with the back of the hand turned in the direction of movement; *also* the side of the body on which this is made **2** handwriting whose strokes slant downwards from left to right

[2]**backhand, backhanded** /,-'--/ *adv* with a backhand

[3]**backhand** *vt* to do, hit, or catch backhand

,**back'handed** /-'handid/ *adj* **1** using or made with a backhand **2** *of writing* being backhand **3** indirect, devious; *esp* sarcastic ⟨*a ~ compliment*⟩ – **backhandedly** *adv*

'**back,hander** /-,handə/ *n* **1** a backhanded blow or stroke **2** *Br* a backhanded remark **3** a bribe – infml

backing /'baking/ *n* **1** sthg forming a back **2a** support, aid **b** endorsement

'**back,lash** /-,lash/ *n* **1** a sudden violent backward movement or reaction **2** a strong adverse reaction – **backlasher** *n*

'**back,lift** /-,lift/ *n* a backswing

'**back,log** /-,log/ *n* **1** a reserve **2** an accumulation of tasks not performed, orders unfulfilled, or materials not processed [[3]*back* + *log*; orig sense, large log of wood at back of fire]

'back,most /-,mohst/ *adj* farthest back

'back ,number *n* sby or sthg that is out of date; *esp* an old issue of a periodical or newspaper

,back of be'yond *n* a remote inaccessible place ⟨*an old house in the ~*⟩

back off *vi* BACK DOWN

back out *vi* to withdraw, esp from a commitment or contest

1'back,pack /-,pak/ *n* **1** a piece of equipment designed to be carried on the back while in use ⟨*an oxygen ~ for lunar exploration*⟩ **2** *chiefly NAm* a rucksack

2backpack *vb, chiefly NAm* to hike carrying (food, equipment, etc in) a backpack – **backpacker** *n*

'back ,passage *n, chiefly Br* the rectum – euph

'back,pedal /-,pedl/ *vi* **1** to move backwards (e g in boxing) **2** to back down from or reverse a previous opinion or stand

,back'room /-'roohm, -'room/ *adj* of or being a directing group that exercises its authority in an inconspicuous and indirect way

'back,scattering /-,skatəring/ *n* the scattering of radiation backwards due to reflection from particles of the medium traversed

back seat *n* an inferior position ⟨*won't take a ~ to anyone*⟩

,back-seat 'driver *n* a passenger in a motor car who offers unwanted advice to the driver

,back'side /-'sied/ *n* the buttocks

'back,sight /-,siet/ *n* the sight nearest the eye on a firearm

'back,slap /-,slap/ *vi* **-pp-** to display excessive cordiality or good fellowship – **backslapper** *n*

'back,slide /-,slied/ *vi* **-slid** /-,slid/; **-slid, -slidden** /-,slid(ə)n/ to lapse morally or in the practice of religion – **backslider** *n*

'back,space /-,spays/ *vi* to press a key on a typewriter which causes the carriage to move back 1 space

'back,spin /-,spin/ *n* spin of a ball with the part furthest from the ground turning in a direction opposite to that of the ball's forward motion – compare TOP SPIN

1,back'stage /-'stayj/ *adv* **1** in or to a backstage area **2** in private, secretly

2'back,stage *adj* **1** of or occurring in the parts of a theatre that cannot be seen by the audience **2** of the inner working or operation (e g of an organization)

'back,stairs /-,steəz/ *adj* **1** secret, furtive ⟨*~ political deals*⟩ **2** sordid, scandalous ⟨*~ gossip*⟩

'back,stay /-,stay/ *n* a stay extending aft from a masthead to the stern or side of a ship ☞ SHIP

'back,stitch /-,stich/ *n* a method of hand sewing in which each new stitch is formed by inserting the needle a stitch length behind and bringing it out a stitch length in front of the end of the previous stitch – **backstitch** *vb*

'back,stop /-,stop/ *n* **1** sthg at the back serving as a stop **2** the catcher in baseball

'back,street /-,street/ *adj* made, done, or acting illegally or surreptitiously ⟨*~ abortion*⟩

'back,stroke /-,strohk/ *n* a swimming stroke executed on the back – **backstroker** *n*

'back,swing /-,swing/ *n* the movement of a bat, arm, etc backwards to a position from which the forward or downward swing is made

'back,sword /-,sawd/ *n* a single-edged sword

,back-to-'back *n* a 2-storey terraced house built with its back against the back of a parallel terrace

,back to 'front *adv* **1** in such a way that the back and the front are reversed in position **2** thoroughly; INSIDE OUT ⟨*learnt the Highway Code ~*⟩

'back,track /-,trak/ *vi* **1** to retrace a path or course **2** to reverse a position or stand

'back,up /-,up/ *n* **1** sby or sthg that serves as a substitute, auxiliary, or alternative **2** sby or sthg that gives support

back up *vt* to support (sby), esp in argument or in playing a team game ~ *vi* to back up a teammate

'backveld, backveldt /-velt, -felt/ *n, SAfr* a remote or culturally backward area – compare BUNDU [3*back* + Afrik *veld* field]

'backward /-wood/ *adj* **1a** directed or turned backwards **b** done or executed backwards ⟨*a ~ somersault*⟩ **2** retarded in development **3** of or occupying a fielding position in cricket behind the batsman's wicket ☞ SPORT **4** *chiefly NAm* diffident, shy – **backwardly** *adv*, **backwardness** *n*

backwardation /,bakwoo'daysh(ə)n/ *n, Br* a premium paid by a seller to a buyer of shares to postpone delivery until a future day of settlement – compare CONTANGO [*backward* + *-ation*]

'backwards, *chiefly NAm* **backward** *adv* **1** towards the back **2** with the back foremost **3** in a reverse direction; towards the beginning ⟨*say the alphabet ~*⟩ **4** perfectly; BY HEART ⟨*knows it all ~*⟩ **5** towards the past **6** towards a worse state – **bend/fall/lean over backwards** to make extreme efforts, esp in order to please or conciliate

'back,wash /-,wosh/ *n* **1a** a backward movement in air, water, etc produced by a propelling force (e g the motion of oars) **b** the backward movement of a receding wave **2** a usu unwelcome consequence or by-product of an event; an aftermath

'back,water /-,wawtə/ *n* **1** a stagnant pool or inlet kept filled by the opposing current of a river; *broadly* a body of water turned back in its course **2** a place or condition that is isolated or backward, esp intellectually

'backwoods /-woodz/ *n, pl but sing or pl in constr* a remote or culturally backward area – usu + *the* – **backwoodsman** *n*

bacon /'baykən/ *n* (the meat cut from) the cured and often smoked side of a pig ☞ MEAT [ME, fr MF, of Gmc origin; akin to OHG *bahho* side of bacon, *bah* back]

'bacon ,pig *n* a pig reared to produce a certain proportion of lean meat to fat and suitable for use as bacon, gammon, and ham

bacteraemia /,baktə'reemi·ə/ *n* the usu transient presence of microorganisms, esp bacteria, in the blood [NL, alter. of *bacteriaemia*, fr *bacteri-* + *-aemia* (fr Gk *aimia*, fr *haima* blood)]

bacteri- /baktiəri-/, **bacterio-** *comb form* bacteria ⟨bac teri*al*⟩ ⟨bacterio*lysis*⟩ [NL *bacterium*]

bacteria /bak'tiəri·ə/ *pl of* BACTERIUM

bactericide /bak'tiəri,sied/ sthg that kills bacteria – **bactericidal** /bak,tiəri'siedl/ *adj*, **bactericidally** *adv*

bacteriology /bak,tiəri'oləji/ *n* **1** a science that deals with bacteria **2** bacterial life and phenomena ⟨*the ~ of a water supply*⟩ [ISV] – **bacteriologist** *n*, **bacteriologic** /-ə'lojik/, **bacteriological** *adj*, **bacteriologically** *adv*

bac,teri'olysis /-'oləsis/ *n* destruction or dissolution of bacterial cells [NL] – **bacteriolytic** /-ə'litik/ *adj*

bac'teriophage /-ə,fayj/ *n* any of various specific viruses that attack bacteria [ISV] – **bacteriophagic** /-,tiəri·ə'fajik/ *adj*, **bacteriophagous** /-,tiəri'afəgəs/ *adj*, **bacteriophagy** /-,tiəri'ofəji/ *n*

bac,terio'stasis /-oh'staysis/ *n* inhibition of the growth of bacteria without their destruction [NL]

bacterium /bak'tiəri·əm/ *n, pl* **bacteria** /-ri·ə/ any of a group of microscopic organisms that live in soil, water, organic matter, or the bodies of plants and animals and are important to human beings because of their chemical effects and because many of them cause diseases ☞ PLANT [NL, fr Gk *baktērion* staff; akin to L *baculum* staff] – **bacterial** *adj*, **bacterially** *adv*

,Bactrian 'camel /'baktri·ən/ *n* CAMEL 1b [fr its habitat in *Bactria*, ancient country of SW Asia]

[1]**bad** /bad/ *adj* **worse** /wuhs/; **worst** /wuhst/ **1a** failing to reach an acceptable standard; poor, inadequate **b** unfavourable **c** no longer acceptable, because of decay or disrepair ⟨*~ fish*⟩ ⟨*the house was in ~ condition*⟩ **2a** morally objectionable **b** mischievous, disobedient **3** unskilful, incompetent – often + *at* ⟨*~ at crosswords*⟩ **4** disagreeable, unpleasant ⟨*~ news*⟩ **5a** injurious, harmful ⟨*smoking is ~ for your health*⟩ **b** worse than usual; severe ⟨*a ~ cold*⟩ **6** incorrect, faulty ⟨*~ grammar*⟩ **7a** suffering pain or distress; unwell ⟨*he felt ~ because of his cold*⟩ **b** unhealthy, diseased ⟨*~ teeth*⟩ **8** sorry, unhappy ⟨*felt ~ after slighting a friend*⟩ **9** invalid, worthless ⟨*a ~ cheque*⟩ ⟨*a ~ coin*⟩ **10** *of a debt* not collectible [ME, perh fr OE *bæddel* hermaphrodite] – **bad** *adv*, **badly** *adv*, **badness** *n* – **in someone's bad books** out of favour with sby

[2]**bad** *n* an evil or unhappy state

,bad 'blood *n* ill feeling; bitterness

baddie, baddy /'badi/ *n* sby or sthg bad; *esp* an opponent of the hero (e g in fiction or the cinema) – infml

bade /bed, bad/ *past of* BID

badge /baj/ *n* **1** a device or token, esp of membership in a society or group **2** a characteristic mark **3** an emblem awarded for a particular accomplishment [ME *bage, bagge*] – **badge** *vt*

[1]**badger** /'bajə/ *n* (the pelt or fur of) any of several sturdy burrowing nocturnal mammals widely distributed in the northern hemisphere [prob fr *badge*; fr the white mark on its forehead]

[2]**badger** *vt* to harass or annoy persistently [fr the sport of baiting badgers]

badinage /'badi,nahzh, -nij/ *n* playful repartee; banter [F, fr *badiner* to joke]

'bad,lands /-,landz/ *n pl, chiefly NAm* a barren region marked by extensive rock erosion and fantastic hill formations

,bad 'lot *n* a disreputable or dishonest person

,badly 'off *adj* in an unsatisfactory condition; *esp* not having enough money

badminton /'badmint(ə)n/ *n* a court game played with light long-handled rackets and a shuttle volleyed over a net [*Badminton*, estate in Gloucestershire, where it was first played]

[1]**baffle** /bafl/ *vt* **baffling** /'bafling, 'bafl·ing/ to throw into puzzled confusion; perplex [prob alter. of ME (Sc) *bawchillen* to denounce, discredit publicly] – **bafflement** *n*, **baffler** /'baflə/ *n*, **bafflingly** /'baflingli/ *adv*

[2]**baffle** *n* **1** a device (e g a plate, wall, or screen) to deflect, check, or regulate flow (e g of a fluid or light) **2** a structure that reduces the exchange of sound waves between the front and back of a loudspeaker

'baffling ,wind *n* a light wind that frequently shifts from one point to another

[1]**bag** /bag/ *n* **1a** a usu flexible container for holding, storing, or carrying sthg **b** a handbag or shoulder bag **2** sthg resembling a bag; *esp* a sagging in cloth **3a** a quantity of game (permitted to be) taken **b** spoils, loot **4** *pl chiefly Br* lots, masses – infml ⟨*has ~s of money*⟩ **5** a slovenly unattractive woman ⟨*silly old ~*⟩ – slang **6** a way of life – slang [ME *bagge*, fr ON *baggi*] – **bagful** *n* – **bag and baggage 1** with all one's belongings **2** entirely, wholesale – **in the bag** as good as achieved; already certain before the test – infml

[2]**bag** *vb* **-gg-** *vi* **1** to swell out; bulge **2** to hang loosely ~ *vt* **1** to cause to swell **2** to put into a bag **3a** to take (animals) as game **b** to get possession of, seize; *also* to steal

bagasse /bə'gas/ *n* the residue of sugarcane, grapes, etc left after a product (e g juice) has been extracted [F]

bagatelle /,bagə'tel/ *n* **1** TRIFLE 1 **2** a game in which balls must be put into or through cups or arches at one end of an oblong table [F, fr It *bagattella*]

bagel /'baygl/ *n* a hard glazed ring-shaped bread roll [Yiddish *beygel*, deriv of OHG *boug* ring; akin to OE *bēag* ring]

baggage /'bagij/ *n* **1** portable equipment, esp of a military force **2** superfluous or useless things, ideas, or practices **3** *NAm* luggage, esp for travel by sea or air **4** a good-for-nothing woman; a pert girl – infml [ME *bagage*, fr MF, fr *bague* bundle; (4) prob modif of MF *bagasse*, fr OProv *bagassa*]

baggy /'bagi/ *adj* loose, puffed out, or hanging like a bag ⟨*~ trousers*⟩ – **baggily** *adv*, **bagginess** *n*

,bag of 'waters *n* the double-walled fluid-filled sac that encloses and protects the foetus in the womb and that breaks, releasing its fluid, during the birth process

'bag,pipe /-,piep/ *n* a wind instrument consisting of a leather bag, mouth tube, chanter, and drone pipes – often pl with sing. meaning but sing. or pl in constr – **bagpiper** *n*

bags /bagz/ *n pl in constr, pl* **bags** OXFORD BAGS

baguette /ba'get/ *n* **1** a small moulding like, but smaller than, the astragal **2** (a gem having) the shape of a long narrow rectangle **3** a long thin French loaf [F, lit., rod]

bah /bah/ *interj* – used to express disdain

Baha'i /bə'hah·i/ *n, pl* **Baha'is** an adherent of a religious movement originating among Shia Muslims in Iran in the 19th c and emphasizing the spiritual unity of mankind [Per *bahā'ī*, lit., of glory, fr *bahā* glory] – **Baha'i** *adj*, **Bahaism** *n*, **Bahaist** *n*

Bahasa Indonesia /bah'hahsə/ *n* a branch of the Austronesian language family of the E Indies that is the official language of Indonesia [Indonesian *bahasa indonésia*, lit., Indonesian language]

baht /baht/ *n, pl* **bahts, baht** ☞ *Thailand* at NATIONALITY [Thai *bāt*]

[1]**bail** /bayl/ *n* **1** security deposited as a guarantee that sby temporarily freed from custody will return to stand trial **2** temporary release on bail **3** one who provides bail [ME, custody, security for appearance, fr MF, custody, fr *baillier* to have in charge, deliver,

fr ML *bajulare* to control, fr L, to carry a load, fr *bajulus* porter]

[2]**bail** *vt* **1** to deliver (property) in trust to another for a special purpose and for a limited period **2** to release on bail **3** to procure the release of (a person in custody) by giving bail – often + *out* [(1) AF *baillier,* fr F, to deliver; (2, 3) [1]*bail*] – **bailable** *adj,* **bailee** /ˌbay'lee/ *n,* **bailment** *n,* **bailor** /'baylə/ *n*

[3]**bail** *n* **1** either of the 2 crosspieces that lie on the stumps to form the wicket in cricket ☞ SPORT **2** *chiefly Br* a device for confining or separating animals [ME *baille* bailey, fr OF]

[4]**bail,** *Br also* **bale** *n* a container used to remove water from a boat [ME *baille,* fr MF, bucket, fr ML *bajula* water vessel, fr fem of L *bajulus*]

[5]**bail,** *Br also* **bale** *vt* to clear (water) from a boat by collecting in a bail, bucket etc and throwing over the side ~ *vi* to parachute from an aircraft ***USE*** (*vt & vi*) usu + *out* – **bailer** /'baylə/ *n*

bailey /'bayli/ *n* (the space enclosed by) the outer wall of a castle or any of several walls surrounding the keep – compare WARD 1 ☞ CHURCH [ME *bailli,* fr OF *baille, balie* palisade, bailey]

'**Bailey ˌbridge** *n* a prefabricated bridge built from interchangeable latticed steel panels [Sir Donald *Bailey* b1901 E engineer]

bailie /'bayli/ *n* a Scottish municipal magistrate [ME]

bailiff /'baylif/ *n* **1** an official employed by a sheriff to serve writs, make arrests, etc **2** *chiefly Br* one who manages an estate or farm [ME *baillif, bailie,* fr OF *baillif,* fr *bail* custody, jurisdiction – more at [1]BAIL] – **bailiffship** *n*

bailiwick /'bayliwik/ *n* the area of jurisdiction of a bailie or bailiff [ME *baillifwik,* fr *baillif* + *wik* dwelling place, village, fr OE *wīc;* akin to OHG *wich* dwelling place, town; both fr a prehistoric WGmc word borrowed fr L *vicus* village – more at VICINITY]

bail out, *Br also* **bale out** *vt* to help from a predicament; release from difficulty

bain-marie /banh mə'ree (*Fr* bɛ̃ mari)/ *n* a vessel of hot or boiling water into which another vessel, containing food, is placed, in order to cook or heat the food gently – compare DOUBLE SAUCEPAN [F, fr MF, lit., bath (of) Mary]

bairn /beən/ *n, chiefly Scot & N Eng* a child [ME *bern, barn,* fr OE *bearn* & ON *barn;* akin to OHG *barn* child]

[1]**bait** /bayt/ *vt* **1** to provoke, tease, or exasperate with unjust, nagging, or persistent remarks **2** to harass (e g a chained animal) with dogs, usu for sport **3** to provide with bait ⟨~ *a hook*⟩ [ME *baiten,* fr ON *beita;* akin to OE *bǣtan* to bait, *bītan* to bite] – **baiter** *n*

[2]**bait** *n* **1a** sthg used in luring, esp to a hook or trap **b** a poisonous material placed where it will be eaten by pests **2** a lure, temptation [ON *beit* pasturage & *beita* food; akin to OE *bītan* to bite]

baiza /'biezah/ *n* ☞ *Oman* at NATIONALITY [colloq Ar, fr Hindi *paisā*]

baize /bayz/ *n* a woollen cloth, resembling felt, used chiefly for covering and lining sthg (e g table tops or drawers) [MF *baies,* pl of *baie* baize, fr fem of *bai* bay-coloured]

[1]**bake** /bayk/ *vt* **1** to cook (e g food) by dry heat, esp in an oven **2** to dry or harden by subjecting to heat ~ *vi* **1** to cook food (e g bread and cakes) by baking **2** to become baked **3** to become extremely hot ⟨*I'll have to stop sunbathing, I'm* baking⟩ [ME *baken,* fr OE *bacan;* akin to OHG *bahhan* to bake, Gk *phōgein* to roast] – **baker** *n*

[2]**bake** *n, NAm* a social gathering at which (baked) food is served

'**bakeˌhouse** /-ˌhows/ *n* a place for baking food, esp bread [ME *bakhous,* fr *baken* to bake + *hous* house]

Bakelite /'baykəliet/ *trademark* – used for any of various synthetic resins and plastics

ˌ**baker's 'dozen** /'baykəz/ *n* thirteen [prob fr a former practice of selling 13 loaves for 12 to guard against accusations of giving short weight]

bakery /'bayk(ə)ri/ *n* a place for baking or selling baked goods, esp bread and cakes

'**baking ˌpowder** /'bayking/ *n* a powder that consists of a bicarbonate and an acid substance used in place of yeast as a raising agent in making scones, cakes, etc

'**baking ˌsoda** *n* SODIUM BICARBONATE

baksheesh /'bakˌsheesh, -'-/ *n, pl* **baksheesh** money given as a tip [Per *bakhshīsh,* fr *bakhshīdan* to give; akin to Gk *phagein* to eat, Skt *bhajati* he allots]

balaclava /ˌbalə'klahvə/, **balaclava helmet** *n, often cap B* a knitted pull-on hood that covers the ears, neck, and throat ☞ GARMENT [*Balaclava* (now usu Balaklava), village in the Crimea, USSR, where a battle of the Crimean War was fought on 25 Oct 1854]

balalaika /ˌbalə'liekə/ *n* a musical instrument of Russian origin, usu having 3 strings and a triangular body which is played by plucking [Russ]

[1]**balance** /'baləns/ *n* **1** an instrument for weighing: e g **a** a centrally-supported beam that has 2 scalepans of equal weight suspended from its ends **b** any device that measures weight and force **2** a counterbalancing weight, force, or influence **3** stability produced by even distribution of weight on each side of a vertical axis **4a** equilibrium between contrasting, opposing, or interacting elements **b** equality between the totals of the 2 sides of an account **5** an aesthetically pleasing integration of elements **6** the ability to retain one's physical equilibrium **7** the weight or force of one side in excess of another ⟨*the* ~ *of the evidence lay on the side of the defendant*⟩ **8a** (a statement of) the difference between credits and debits in an account **b** sthg left over; a remainder **c** an amount in excess, esp on the credit side of an account **9** mental and emotional steadiness **10** the point on the trigger side of a rifle at which the weight of the ends balance each other [ME, fr OF, fr (assumed) VL *bilancia,* fr LL *bilanc-, bilanx* having two scalepans, fr L *bi-* + *lanc-, lanx* plate; akin to OE *eln* ell] – **balanced** *adj* – **in the balance** in an uncertain critical position; with the fate or outcome about to be determined – **on balance** all things considered

[2]**balance** *vt* **1a(1)** to compute the difference between the debits and credits of (an account) **(2)** to pay the amount due on **b** to arrange so that one set of elements exactly equals another ⟨~ *a mathematical equation*⟩ **2a** to counterbalance, offset **b** to equal or equalize in weight, number, or proportion **3** to compare the relative importance, value, force, or weight of; ponder **4** to bring to a state or position of balance ~ *vi* **1** to become balanced or established in balance ⟨*sat* balancing *on the fence*⟩ **2** to be an equal

counterpoise – often + *with* **3** to waver, hesitate ⟨*a mind that* ~s *and deliberates*⟩ – **balancer** *n*

'balance ,beam *n* (a gymnastic event using) a narrow horizontal wooden beam supported 1.2m (about 4ft) above the floor and used for balancing exercises

,balance of 'payments *n* the difference over a period of time between a country's payments to and receipts from abroad

,balance of 'power *n* an equilibrium of power sufficient to prevent one nation from imposing its will upon another

,balance of 'trade *n* the difference in value between a country's imports and exports

'balance ,sheet *n* a statement of financial condition at a given date

'balance ,wheel *n* a wheel that regulates or stabilizes the motion of a mechanism (e g a watch or clock)

Balante /bə'lahnt/ *n, pl* **Balantes,** *esp collectively* **Balante** a member, or the language, of a Negro people of Senegal and Angola [F, fr Balante *Bulanda*]

balas /'baləs/ *n* a gemstone consisting of a mixture of oxides of aluminium, iron and manganese and having a pale rose-red or orange colour [ME, fr MF *balais,* fr Ar *balakhsh,* fr *Balakhshān,* ancient region of Afghanistan]

balata /bə'lahtə/ *n* the dried juice of tropical American trees of the sapodilla family that is used as an alternative to gutta-percha, esp in belting and golf balls; *also* a tree yielding this [Sp, of Cariban origin; akin to Galibi *balata*]

balboa /bal'boh·ə/ *n* ☞ *Panama* at NATIONALITY [Sp, fr Vasco Núñez de *Balboa* †1517 Sp explorer]

balcony /'balkəni/ *n* **1** a platform built out from the wall of a building and enclosed by a railing or low wall **2** a gallery inside a building (e g a theatre) [It *balcone,* fr OIt, scaffold, of Gmc origin; akin to OHG *balko* beam – more at BALK] – **balconied** *adj*

bald /bawld/ *adj* **1a** lacking a natural or usual covering (e g of hair, vegetation, or nap) **b** having little or no tread ⟨~ *tyres*⟩ **2** unadorned, undisguised ⟨*the* ~ *truth*⟩ **3** *of an animal* marked with white, esp on the head or face [ME *balled*; akin to OE *bǣl* fire, pyre, Dan *baeldet* bald, L *fulica* coot, Gk *phalios* having a white spot] – **baldish** *adj,* **baldly** *adv,* **baldness** *n*

,bald 'eagle *n* an eagle of N America that has a white head and neck when mature and eats fish and carrion

balderdash /'bawldədash/ *n* nonsense – often as a generalized expression of disagreement [origin unknown]

'bald-,faced *adj, NAm* barefaced

baldie /'bawldi/ *n* a bald person – usu as a noun of address; infml

balding /'bawlding/ *adj* becoming bald

baldric /'bawldrik/ *n* an often ornamented belt worn over one shoulder and across the body to support a sword, bugle, etc [ME *baudry, baudrik*]

[1]**bale** /bayl/ *n* a large bundle of goods; *specif* a large closely pressed package of merchandise bound and usu wrapped for storage or transportation [ME, fr OF, of Gmc origin; akin to OHG *balla* ball] – **bale** *vt*

[2]**bale** *n or vb, Br* [4/5]BAIL

baleen /bə'leen/ *n* whalebone [ME *baleine* whale, baleen, fr L *balaena* whale, fr Gk *phallaina*; akin to Gk *phallos* penis – more at [1]BLOW]

ba,leen 'whale *n* WHALEBONE WHALE

baleful /'baylf(ə)l/ *adj* **1** deadly or pernicious in influence **2** gloomily threatening [arch *bale* (evil, sorrow), fr ME, fr OE *bealu*] – **balefully** *adv,* **balefulness** *n*

bale out *vt, Br* BAIL OUT

[1]**balk,** *chiefly Br* **baulk** /bawlk, bawk/ *n* **1** a ridge of land left unploughed **2** a roughly squared beam of timber **3** the area behind the balk lines on a billiard table [ME *balke,* fr OE *balca*; akin to OHG *balko* beam, L *fulcire* to prop, Gk *phalanx* log, phalanx]

[2]**balk,** *chiefly Br* **baulk** *vt* to check or stop (as if) by an obstacle; hinder, thwart ~ *vi* **1** to stop short and refuse to proceed **2** to refuse abruptly – often + *at* ⟨~ed *at the suggestion*⟩ – **balker** *n*

balkan·ize, -ise /'bawlkəniez/ *vt, often cap* to divide (e g a region) into smaller and often mutually hostile units [*Balkan* peninsula, SE Europe; fr the way in which this territory has been divided into many small states] – **balkanization** /-'zaysh(ə)n/ *n, often cap*

'balk ,line *n* any of 4 lines parallel to the cushions of a billiard table; *specif* the line at one end behind which the cue balls are placed at the start of many games

[1]**ball** /bawl/ *n* **1** a round or roundish body or mass: **a** a solid or hollow spherical or egg-shaped body used in a game or sport **b** a spherical or conical projectile; *also* projectiles used in firearms ⟨*powder and* ~⟩ **c** the rounded slightly raised fleshy area at the base of a thumb or big toe **2** a delivery or play of the ball in cricket, baseball, etc ⟨*bowled by a good* ~⟩ **3** a game in which a ball is thrown, kicked, or struck; *specif, NAm* baseball **4a** a testis – usu pl; vulg **b** *pl* nonsense – often used interjectionally; vulg [ME *bal,* fr ON *böllr*; akin to OE *bealluc* testis, OHG *balla* ball, OE *bula* bull] – **on the ball** marked by being knowledgeable and competent; alert – infml – **start/set/keep the ball rolling** to begin/continue sthg

[2]**ball** *vb* **1** to form or gather into a ball **2** to have sexual intercourse (with) – vulg

[3]**ball** *n* **1** a large formal gathering for social dancing **2** a very pleasant experience; a good time – infml [F *bal,* fr OF, fr *baller* to dance, fr LL *ballare,* fr Gk *ballizein*; akin to Skt *balbalīti* he whirls]

ballad /'baləd/ *n* **1** a narrative composition in rhythmic verse suitable for singing **2** a (slow, romantic or sentimental) popular, esp narrative, song [ME *balade* song sung while dancing, song, fr MF, fr OProv *balada* dance, song sung while dancing, fr *balar* to dance, fr LL *ballare*] – **balladic** /,bə'ladik/ *adj*

ballade /bə'lahd, ba-/ *n* a fixed verse form of usu 3 stanzas with recurrent rhymes, a short concluding verse, and an identical refrain for each part [ME *balade,* fr MF, ballad, ballade]

,ball-and-'socket ,joint *n* a joint (e g in the hip) in which a rounded part moves within a cuplike socket so as to allow free movement in many directions ☞ ANATOMY

[1]**ballast** /'baləst/ *n* **1a** heavy material carried in a ship to improve stability **b** heavy material that is carried on a balloon or airship to steady it and can be jettisoned to control the rate of descent **2** sthg that gives stability, esp in character or conduct **3** gravel or broken stone laid in a bed for railway lines or the

lower layer of roads [prob fr LG, of Scand origin; akin to Dan & Sw *barlast* ballast; akin to OE *bær* bare & to OE *blæst* load]

²**ballast** *vt* **1** to steady or equip (as if) with ballast **2** to fill in (e g a railway bed) with ballast

,**ball 'bearing** *n* a bearing having minimal friction in which hardened steel balls roll easily in a groove between a shaft and a support; *also* any of the balls in such a bearing

'**ball ,boy,** *fem* '**ball ,girl** *n* a tennis-court attendant who retrieves balls for the players

'**ball ,cock** *n* an automatic valve (e g in a cistern) controlled by the rise and fall of a float at the end of a lever

ballerina /,balə'reenə/ *n* a female, esp principal, ballet dancer [It, fr *ballare* to dance, fr LL]

ballet /'balay; *NAm also* bə'lay/ *n* **1** (a group that performs) artistic dancing in which the graceful flowing movements are based on conventional positions and steps **2** a theatrical art form using ballet dancing, music, and scenery to convey a story, theme, or atmosphere [F, fr It *balletto*, dim. of *ballo* dance, fr *ballare*] – **balletic** /ba'letik/ *adj*

balletomane /'balitəmayn, bə'letəmayn/ *n* a devotee of ballet [*ballet* + *-o-* + *-mane* (fr *mania*)] – **balletomania** /,balitə'maynyə/ *n*

ballista /bə'listə/ *n, pl* **ballistae** an ancient military device often in the form of a crossbow for hurling large missiles [L, fr (assumed) Gk *ballistēs*, fr *ballein* to throw – more at DEVIL]

ballistic /bə'listik/ *adj* **1** of ballistics **2** actuated by a sudden impulse (e g one due to an electric discharge) [L *ballista*] – **ballistically** *adv*

bal,listic 'missile *n* a missile propelled and guided in ascent but falling freely in descent

bal'listics *n pl but sing or pl in constr* **1** the science dealing with the motion of projectiles in flight **2** (the study of) the individual characteristics of and firing processes in a firearm or cartridge

'**ball ,joint** *n* BALL-AND-SOCKET JOINT

,**ball 'lightning** *n* a rare form of lightning consisting of luminous balls that may move along solid objects or float in the air

ballock /'bolək, 'bawlək/ *n* a bollock

¹**balloon** /bə'loohn/ *n* **1** an envelope filled with hot air or a gas lighter than air so as to rise and float in the atmosphere **2** an inflatable usu brightly coloured rubber bag used as a toy **3** a line enclosing words spoken or thought by a character, esp in a cartoon [F *ballon* large football, balloon, fr It dial. *ballone* large football, aug of *balla* ball, of Gmc origin]

²**balloon** *vt* to inflate, distend ~ *vi* **1** to ascend or travel in a balloon **2** to swell or puff out; expand – often + *out* **3** to increase rapidly **4** to travel in a high curving arc

³**balloon** *adj* relating to, resembling, or suggesting a balloon ⟨*a ~ sleeve*⟩

bal'loon ,glass *n, chiefly Br* a short-stemmed drinking glass with a pear-shaped bowl, used esp for brandy

ballooning /bə'loohning/ *n* the act or sport of riding in a balloon – **balloonist** *n*

bal'loon ,tyre *n* a large tyre that is inflated to low pressure to provide cushioning over rough surfaces

¹**ballot** /'balət/ *n* **1** (a sheet of paper, or orig a small ball, used in) secret voting **2** the right to vote **3** the number of votes cast [It *ballotta*, fr It dial., dim. of *balla* ball]

²**ballot** *vi* to vote by ballot ~ *vt* to ask for a vote from ⟨*the union* ~ed *the members*⟩ – **balloter** *n*

ballottement /bə'lotmənt/ *n* a sharp upward pushing with a finger to detect a floating object, esp as a test for pregnancy or a floating kidney [F, lit., act of tossing, shaking, fr *ballotter* to toss, fr MF *baloter*, fr *balotte* little ball, fr It dial *ballotta*]

'**ball ,park** *n, NAm* a park in which ball games, esp baseball, are played – **in the ball park** approximately correct – slang

'**ball,point** /-,poynt/, ,**ballpoint 'pen** *n* a pen having as the writing point a small rotating metal ball that inks itself by contact with an inner magazine

,**ballroom 'dancing** /'bawlroohm, -room/ *n* a usu formal type of dancing done esp by couples for recreation, exhibition, or competition

'**balls-,up,** *NAm* **ball-up** *n* a state of muddled confusion caused by a mistake – slang

balls up, *NAm* **ball up** *vb* to make or become badly muddled or confused – slang

bally /'bali/ *adj or adv, Br* ¹BLOODY 4, ³BLOODY – euph [euphemism]

ballyhoo /,bali'hooh/ *n, pl* **ballyhoos** **1** a noisy demonstration or talk **2** flamboyant, exaggerated, or sensational advertising or propaganda [origin unknown] – **ballyhoo** *vt*

balm /bahm/ *n* **1** an aromatic and medicinal resin **2** an aromatic preparation (e g a healing ointment) **3** any of various aromatic plants of the mint family **4** sthg that soothes, relieves, or heals physically or emotionally [ME *basme, baume*, fr OF, fr L *balsamum* balsam, fr Gk *balsamon*]

,**balm of 'Gilead** /'giliad/ **1** (a small evergreen African and Asian tree yielding) a fragrant oleoresin used esp in perfumery **2** either of 2 poplars: **a** a hybrid northern tree with broad heart-shaped leaves **b** BALSAM POPLAR [*Gilead*, region of ancient Palestine known for its balm (Jer 8:22)]

balmy /'bahmi/ *adj* **1a** having the qualities of balm; soothing **b** mild **2** barmy [(2) by alter.] – **balmily** *adv*, **balminess** *n*

baloney /bə'lohni/ *n* nonsense – often as a generalized expression of disagreement [perh alter. of *bologna (sausage)*]

balsa /'bawlsə, 'bolsə/ *n* (the strong very light wood of) a tropical American tree [Sp]

balsam /'bals(ə)m, 'bol-/ *n* **1** (a preparation containing) an oily and resinous substance flowing from various plants **2a** any of several trees yielding balsam **b** any of a widely distributed genus of watery-juiced annual plants (e g touch-me-not) **3** BALM 4 [L *balsamum*] – **balsamic** /-'samik/ *adj*

,**balsam 'fir** *n* a coniferous American tree from which Canada balsam is prepared

,**balsam 'poplar** *n* a N American poplar that is often cultivated as a shade tree and yields balsam

Balti /'bahlti, 'bawlti/ *n* a Tibeto-Burman language of N Kashmir

Baltic /'bawltik, 'bol-/ *adj* **1** of the Baltic sea or Lithuania, Latvia, and Estonia **2** of a branch of the Indo-European languages containing Latvian, Lithuanian, and Old Prussian [ML *(mare) balticum* Baltic sea]

,**Balto-Sla'vonic** /,bawltoh, ,bol-/ *n* a subfamily of Indo-European languages consisting of the Baltic and the Slavonic branches

baluster /'baləstə/ *n* an upright rounded, square, or vase-shaped support (e g for the rail of a staircase balustrade) ☞ ARCHITECTURE [F *balustre*, fr It *balaustro*, fr *balaustra* wild pomegranate flower, fr L *balaustium*, fr Gk *balaustion*; fr its shape]

balustrade /,balə'strayd, 'balə,strayd/ *n* a row of balusters topped by a rail; *also* a usu low parapet or barrier [F, fr It *balaustrata*, fr *balaustro*]

Bambara /bam'bahrə/ *n, pl* **Bambaras,** *esp collectively* **Bambara** a member, or the Mande language, of a Negroid people of the upper Niger ☞ LANGUAGE

bambino /bam'beenoh/ *n, pl* **bambinos, bambini** /-ni/ a representation of the infant Christ [It, dim. of *bambo* child]

bamboo /bam'booh/ *n, pl* **bamboos** any of various chiefly tropical giant grasses including some with strong hollow stems used for building, furniture, or utensils [Malay *bambu*] – **bamboo** *adj*

,bamboo 'curtain *n, often cap B&C* a political, military, and ideological barrier between China and the capitalist world

bamboozle /bam'boohzl/ *vt* to deceive by trickery [origin unknown] – **bamboozlement** *n*

[1]**ban** /ban/ *vt* **-nn-** to prohibit, esp by legal means or social pressure [ME *bannen* to summon, curse, fr OE *bannan* to summon; akin to OHG *bannan* to command, L *fari* to speak, Gk *phanai* to say, *phōnē* sound, voice]

[2]**ban** *n* **1** an ecclesiastical curse, excommunication **2** a legal or social prohibition [ME (orig sense, summoning of vassals for military service), partly fr *bannen* & partly fr OF *ban*, of Gmc origin; akin to OHG *bannan* to command]

[3]**ban** *n, pl* **bani** ☞ *Romania* at NATIONALITY [Romanian]

banal /bə'nahl/ *adj* lacking originality, freshness, or novelty; trite, hackneyed [F, fr MF, of compulsory feudal service, possessed in common, commonplace, fr *ban*] – **banally** *adv*, **banality** /bə'naləti/ *n*

banana /bə'nahnə/ *n* (a tropical tree that bears) an elongated usu tapering fruit with soft pulpy flesh enclosed in a soft usu yellow rind that grows in bunches reminiscent of the fingers of a hand [Sp or Pg; Sp, fr Pg, of African origin; akin to Wolof *banäna* banana]

ba'nana re,public *n* a small tropical country that is politically unstable and usu economically underdeveloped – derog [fr the dependence of some small tropical countries on their fruit-exporting trade]

ba'nanas *adj* mad – infml ⟨*call him that and he goes* ~⟩ [prob fr *banana oil* (nonsense, insincere or mad talk)]

[1]**band** /band/ *n* **1** a strip or belt serving to join or hold things together **2** a ring of elastic **3** a more or less well-defined range of wavelengths, frequencies, or energies of light waves, radio waves, sound waves, etc **4** an elongated surface or section with parallel or roughly parallel sides **5** a narrow strip serving chiefly as decoration: e g **a** a narrow strip of material applied as trimming to an article of dress **b** *pl* 2 cloth strips sometimes worn at the front of the neck as part of clerical, legal, or academic dress **6** a strip distinguishable in some way (e g by colour, texture, or composition) **7** *Br* a group of pupils assessed as being of broadly similar ability – compare STREAM [ME *bande* strip, fr MF, fr (assumed) VL *binda*, of Gmc origin; akin to OHG *binta* fillet; akin to OE *bindan* to bind]

[2]**band** *vt* **1** to fasten a band to or tie up with a band **2** to gather together for a purpose; unite **3** *Br* to divide (pupils) into bands ~ *vi* **1** to unite for a common purpose; confederate – often + *together* ⟨*they all* ~ed *together to fight the enemy*⟩ **2** to divide pupils into bands – **bander** *n*

[3]**band** *n sing or pl in constr* a group of people, animals, or things; *esp* a group of musicians organized for ensemble playing and using chiefly woodwind, brass, and percussion instruments – compare ORCHESTRA [MF *bande* troop]

[1]**bandage** /'bandij/ *n* a strip of fabric used esp to dress and bind up wounds [MF, fr *bande* strip]

[2]**bandage** *vt* to bind, dress, or cover with a bandage – **bandager** *n*

'Band-,Aid *trademark* – used for a small adhesive plaster with a gauze pad

bandanna, bandana /ban'danə/ *n* a large colourful patterned handkerchief [Hindi *b adhnū* tie-dyeing, tie-dyed cloth, fr *b adhnā* to tie, fr Skt *badhnāti* he ties; akin to OE *bindan*]

'band,box /-,boks/ *n* a usu cylindrical box of cardboard or thin wood used esp for holding hats

bandeau /'bandoh; *NAm* -'-/ *n, pl* **bandeaux** /'bandoh(z); *NAm* ban'doh(z)/ a band of material worn round the head to keep the hair in place [F, dim. of *bande* strip]

banded /'bandid/ *adj* marked with bands

banderilla /,bandə'ree(l)yə/ *n* a decorated barbed dart thrust into the neck or shoulders of the bull in a bullfight [Sp, dim. of *bandera* banner]

banderillero /,bandəree(l)'yeəroh/ *n, pl* **banderilleros** one who thrusts in banderillas in a bullfight [Sp, fr *banderilla*]

banderole, banderol /,bandə'rohl/ *n* a long narrow forked flag or streamer [F *banderole*, fr It *banderuola*, dim. of *bandiera* banner, of Gmc origin; akin to Goth *bandwo* sign – more at BANNER]

bandicoot /'bandikooht/ *n* **1** any of several very large distinctive rats of India and Ceylon **2** any of various small insect and plant-eating marsupial mammals of Australia, Tasmania, and New Guinea [Telugu *pandikokku*]

bandit /'bandit/ *n, pl* **bandits** *also* **banditti** /ban'deeti/ **1** an outlaw; *esp* a member of a band of marauders **2** a political terrorist [It *bandito*, fr pp of *bandire* to banish, of Gmc origin; akin to OHG *bannan* to command – more at [1]BAN] – **banditry** *n*

'band,leader /-,leedə/ *n* the director of a dance band

'band,master /-,mahstə/ *n* a conductor of an esp military band

bandolier, bandoleer /,bandə'liə/ *n* a belt worn over the shoulder and across the chest with pockets or loops for cartridges [MF *bandouliere*, deriv of OSp *bando* band, of Gmc origin; akin to Goth *bandwo* sign]

'band ,saw *n* a power saw having an endless steel blade running over pulleys

'bandsman /-mən/ *n* a member of a musical band

'band,stand /-,stand/ *n* a usu roofed stand or platform for a band to perform on outdoors

'band,wagon /-,wagən/ *n* a party, faction, or cause that attracts adherents by its timeliness, momentum, etc [[3]*band* + *wagon*] – **jump/climb on the bandwagon** to attach oneself to a successful cause or enterprise in the hope of personal gain

'band,width /-,width/ *n* the range of frequencies

within which an electrical device (e g an amplifier) operates acceptably

[1]**bandy** /'bandi/ *vt* **1** to exchange (words) in an argumentative, careless, or lighthearted manner **2** to use in a glib or offhand manner – often + *about* [prob fr MF *bander* to be tight, to hit to and fro, fr *bande* strip – more at [1]BAND]

[2]**bandy** *n* a game similar to ice hockey played esp in the Baltic countries [perh fr MF *bandé*, pp of *bander*]

[3]**bandy** *adj* **1** *of legs* bowed **2** bowlegged [prob fr *bandy* (hockey stick)] – **bandy-legged** /'legid/ *adj*

bane /bayn/ *n* **1** poison – esp in combination ⟨*rats-bane*⟩ **2** a cause of death, ruin, or trouble [ME, fr OE *bana*; akin to OHG *bano* death, Av *banta* ill] – **baneful** *adj*

[1]**bang** /bang/ *vt* **1** to strike sharply; bump ⟨*fell and* ~ ed *his knee*⟩ **2** to knock, beat, or strike hard, often with a sharp noise **3** to have sexual intercourse with – vulg ~ *vi* **1** to strike with a sharp noise or thump ⟨*the falling chair* ~ ed *against the wall*⟩ **2** to produce a sharp often explosive noise or noises [prob of Scand origin; akin to Icel *banga* to hammer]

[2]**bang** *n* **1** a resounding blow; a thump **2** a sudden loud noise – often used interjectionally **3** a quick burst of energy ⟨*start off with a* ~⟩ **4** an act of sexual intercourse – vulg

[3]**bang** *adv* **1** right, directly **2** exactly ⟨*arrived* ~ *on 6 o'clock*⟩ ***USE*** infml

[4]**bang** *n* a short squarely-cut fringe of hair – usu pl with sing. meaning [prob short for *bangtail* (short tail)]

banger /'bang·ə/ *n, Br* **1** a firework that explodes with a loud bang **2** a sausage **3** an old usu dilapidated car ***USE*** *(2&3)* infml [[1]BANG + [2]-ER]

Bangladeshi /,bang·glə'deshi/ *adj* (characteristic) of Bangladesh [*Bangladesh* (formerly East Pakistan), country of S Asia]

bangle /'bang·gl/ *n* a rigid usu ornamental bracelet or anklet slipped or clasped on [Hindi *ba·ngli*]

,**bang-'on** *adj or adv, Br* just what is needed; first-rate – infml

bang up *vt, chiefly Br* to raise ⟨*to* bang up *an executive's salary*⟩ – infml [[1]*bang*]

banian /'banyən/ *n* a banyan

banish /'banish/ *vt* **1** to require by authority to leave a place, esp a country **2** to dispel [ME *banishen*, fr MF *baniss-*, stem of *banir*, of Gmc origin; akin to OHG *bannan* to command – more at [1]BAN] – **banisher** *n*, **banishment** *n*

banister *also* **bannister** /'banistə/ *n* a handrail with its upright supports guarding the edge of a staircase – often pl with sing. meaning [alter. of *baluster*]

banjo /'banjoh, -'-/ *n, pl* **banjos** *also* **banjoes** a stringed instrument with a drumlike body that is strummed with the fingers [prob of African origin; akin to Kimbundu *mbanza*, a similar instrument] – **banjoist** *n*

[1]**bank** /bangk/ *n* **1a** a mound, pile, or ridge (e g of earth or snow) **b** a piled up mass of cloud or fog **c** an undersea elevation rising esp from the continental shelf **2** the rising ground bordering a lake or river or forming the edge of a cut or hollow **3** the lateral inward tilt of a surface along a curve or of a vehicle when following a curved path [ME, prob of Scand origin; akin to ON *bakki* bank; akin to OE *benc* bench – more at BENCH]

[2]**bank** *vt* **1** to surround with a bank **2** to keep *up* to ensure slow burning **3** to build (a road or railway) with the outer edge of a curve higher than the inner ~ *vi* **1** to rise in or form a bank – often + *up* **2a** to incline an aircraft laterally when turning **b(1)** *of an aircraft* to incline laterally **(2)** to follow a curve or incline, specif in racing

[3]**bank** *n* **1** a bench for the rowers of a galley **2** a row of keys on an alphabetic keyboard (e g of a typewriter) [ME, fr OF *banc* bench, of Gmc origin; akin to OE *benc*]

[4]**bank** *n* **1** an establishment for the custody, loan, exchange, or issue of money and for the transmission of funds **2** a person conducting a gambling house or game; *specif* the banker in a game of cards **3** a supply of sthg held in reserve: e g **a** the money, chips, etc held by the bank or banker for use in a gambling game **b** the pool of pieces belonging to a game (e g dominoes) from which the players draw **4** a place where data, human organs, etc are held available for use when needed [ME, fr MF or OIt; MF *banque*, fr OIt *banca*, lit., bench, of Gmc origin; akin to OE *benc*]

[5]**bank** *vi* to deposit money or have an account in a bank ⟨*where do you* ~?⟩ ~ *vt* to deposit in a bank – **bank on** to depend or rely on; COUNT ON

bankable /'bangkəbl/ *adj* acceptable to or at a bank

'**bank,book** /-,book/ *n* the depositor's book in which a bank enters a record of his/her account

[1]**banker** /'bangkə/ *n* **1** one who engages in the business of banking **2** the player who keeps the bank in various games

[2]**banker** *n* a man or boat employed in the cod fishery on the Newfoundland banks

'**banker's ,card** *n, Br* CHEQUE CARD

,**bank 'holiday** *n* **1** *often cap B&H* a public holiday in the British Isles on which banks and most businesses are closed by law **2** *NAm* a period when banks are closed often by government fiat

banking /'bangking/ *n* the business of a bank or a banker

'**bank ,note** *n* a promissory note issued by a bank, payable to the bearer on demand without interest, and acceptable as money

[1]**bankrupt** /'bangkrupt/ *n* **1a** an insolvent person whose estate is administered under the bankruptcy laws for the benefit of his/her creditors **b** one who becomes insolvent **2** one who is destitute of a usu specified quality or thing ⟨*a moral* ~⟩ [modif of MF & OIt; MF *banqueroute* bankruptcy, fr OIt *bancarotta*, fr *banca* bank + *rotta* broken, fr L *rupta*, fem of *ruptus*, pp of *rumpere* to break – more at [4]BANK, BEREAVE]

[2]**bankrupt** *vt* **1** to reduce to bankruptcy **2** to impoverish

[3]**bankrupt** *adj* **1** reduced to a state of financial ruin; *specif* legally declared a bankrupt **2a** broken, ruined ⟨*a* ~ *professional career*⟩ **b** destitute – + *of* or *in*

bankruptcy /'bangk,rupsi/ *n* **1** being bankrupt **2** utter failure, impoverishment, or destitution

banner /'banə/ *n* **1a** a usu square flag bearing heraldic arms; *broadly* [4]FLAG 1 **b** an ensign displaying a distinctive or symbolic device or legend; *esp* one presented as an award of honour or distinction **2** a headline in large type running across a newspaper page **3** a strip of cloth on which a sign is painted **4** a name, slogan, or goal associated with a particular group or ideology – often + *under* [ME *banere*, fr

OF, of Gmc origin; akin to Goth *bandwo* sign; akin to ON *benda* to give a sign]

banneret *also* **bannerette** /ˌbanəˈret/ *n* a small banner [ME *baneret,* fr OF, fr *banere*]

bannerol /ˌbanəˈrohl/ *n* a banderole [MF, var of *banderole*]

bannister /ˈbanistə/ *n* a banister

bannock /ˈbanək/ *n* a usu unleavened flat bread or biscuit made with oatmeal or barley meal [ME *bannok,* prob fr ScGael *bannach*]

banns /banz/ *n pl* the public announcement, esp in church, of a proposed marriage – chiefly in *publish/read the banns* [pl of *bann,* fr ME *bane, ban* proclamation, ban]

[1]**banquet** /ˈbangkwit/ *n* an elaborate ceremonial meal for numerous people often in honour of a person; a feast [MF, fr OIt *banchetto,* fr dim. of *banca* bench, bank]

[2]**banquet** *vb* to provide with or partake of a banquet – **banqueter** *n*

banquette /bangˈket (*Fr* bɑ̃kɛt)/ *n* **1** a raised step along the inside of a parapet or trench for soldiers or guns **2** a built-in upholstered bench along a wall [F, fr Prov *banqueta,* dim. of *banc* bench, of Gmc origin; akin to OE *benc* bench]

banshee /ˈbanshee *also* -ˈ-/ *n* a female spirit in Gaelic folklore whose wailing warns of approaching death in a household [ScGael *bean-sìth,* fr or akin to OIr *ben side* woman of fairyland]

[1]**bantam** /ˈbant(ə)m/ *n* any of numerous small domestic fowl [*Bantam,* former residency in Java]

[2]**bantam** *adj* small, diminutive

ˈ**bantam,weight** /-ˌwayt/ *n* a boxer who weighs not more than 8st 6lb (about 53.5kg) if professional or more than 51kg (about 8st) but not more than 54kg (about 8st 7lb) if amateur

[1]**banter** /ˈbantə/ *vi* to speak or act playfully or wittily [origin unknown] – **banterer** *n,* **banteringly** *adv*

[2]**banter** *n* good-natured repartee; badinage

banting /ˈbanting/ *n, archaic* a method of reducing a person's weight based on a low carbohydrate and fat intake [William *Banting* †1878 E undertaker & writer on dieting]

Bantu /ˈbantooh; *also* -ˈ-/ *n, pl* **Bantus,** *esp collectively* **Bantu** **1** a member of a group of Negroid peoples inhabiting equatorial and southern Africa **2** a group of African languages spoken generally at and south of the Equator ☞ LANGUAGE

bantustan /ˌbantoohˈstan, -ˈstahn/ *n, often cap* an all-black partially self-governing enclave in the Republic of S Africa [*Bantu* + *-stan* land (as in *Hindustan*)]

banyan /ˈbanyan/ *n* an Indian tree of the fig family with branches that send out shoots which grow down to the soil and root to form secondary trunks [earlier *banyan* (Hindu merchant), fr Hindi *baniyā*; fr a banyan pagoda erected under a tree of the species in Iran]

banzai /banˈzie/ *n* – used as a Japanese cheer or battle cry [Jap, lit., 10,000 years]

baobab /ˈbayoh,bab, ˈbayə-, ˈbow,bab/ *n* a broad-trunked Old World tropical tree with an edible acid fruit resembling a gourd and bark used in making paper, cloth, and rope [prob native name in Africa]

bap /bap/ *n* a soft thin-crusted usu flour-dusted bread roll that may be of various shapes and sizes according to regional custom [origin unknown]

baptism /ˈbaptiz(ə)m/ *n* **1** the ritual use of water for purification, esp in the Christian sacrament of admission to the church **2** an act, experience, or ordeal by which one is purified, sanctified, initiated, or named – **baptismal** /-ˈtizməl/ *adj,* **baptismally** *adv*

baptismal name /bapˈtizməl/ *n* CHRISTIAN NAME 1

baptism of fire *n* an initial experience (e g a soldier's first battle) that is a severe ordeal [orig sense fr trans of LGk *baptisma pyros,* a spiritual baptism by gift of the Holy Spirit; now usu taken to refer to artillery fire]

baptist /ˈbaptist/ *n* **1** one who baptizes **2** *cap* a member of a Protestant denomination which reserves baptism to full believers – **Baptist** *adj*

baptistery, **baptistry** /ˈbaptistri/ *n* a part of a church or formerly a separate building used for baptism

bapt·ize, -ise /bapˈtiez, ˈ--/ *vt* **1** to administer baptism to **2a** to purify or cleanse spiritually, esp by a purging experience or ordeal **b** to initiate, launch **3** to give a name to (as if) at baptism; christen ~ *vi* to administer baptism [ME *baptizen,* fr OF *baptiser,* fr LL *baptizare,* fr Gk *baptizein* to dip, baptize, fr *baptos* dipped, fr *baptein* to dip; akin to ON *kafa* to dive] – **baptizer** *n*

[1]**bar** /bah/ *n* **1a** a straight piece (e g of wood or metal), that is longer than it is wide and has any of various uses (e g as a lever, support, barrier, or fastening) **b** a solid piece or block of material that is usu rectangular and considerably longer than it is wide **c** a usu rigid piece (e g of wood or metal) longer than it is wide that is used as a handle or support; *specif* a barre **2** sthg that obstructs or prevents passage, progress, or action: e g **a** the extinction of a claim in law **b** an intangible or nonphysical impediment **c** a submerged or partly submerged bank (e g of sand) along a shore or in a river, often obstructing navigation **3a** [6]DOCK; *also* the railing that encloses the dock **b** *often cap* **(1)** *sing or pl in constr* the whole body of barristers **(2)** the profession of barrister **c** a barrier beyond which nonmembers of Parliament may not pass **4** a straight stripe, band, or line much longer than it is wide: e g **a** any of 2 or more horizontal stripes on a heraldic shield **b** STRIPE 2 **c** a strip of metal attached to a military medal to indicate an additional award of the medal **5a(1)** a counter at which food or esp alcoholic drinks are served **(2)** a room or establishment whose main feature is a bar for the serving of alcoholic drinks **b** a place where goods, esp a specified commodity, are sold or served across a counter ⟨*a shoe* ~⟩ **6** (a group of musical notes and rests that add up to a prescribed time value, bounded on each side on the staff by) a bar line ☞ MUSIC **7** a small loop or crosspiece of oversewn threads used, esp on garments, as a fastening (e g for a hook), for joining, or for strengthening sthg [ME *barre,* fr OF]

[2]**bar** *vt* **-rr-** **1a** to fasten with a bar **b** to place bars across to prevent movement in, out, or through **2** to mark with stripes **3a** to shut in or out (as if) by bars **b** to set aside the possibility of; RULE OUT **4a** to interpose legal objection to **b** to prevent, forbid ⟨*no holds* ~red⟩

[3]**bar** *prep* except

[4]**bar** *adv, of odds in betting* being offered for all the unnamed competitors ⟨*20 to 1* ~⟩

[5]bar *n* a unit of pressure equal to 100,000N/m² (about 14.5lb/in²) ☞ UNIT [G, fr Gk *baros*]

bar-, baro- *comb form* weight; pressure ⟨barometer⟩ [Gk *baros*; akin to Gk *barys* heavy – more at GRIEVE]

[1]barb /bahb/ *n* **1a** a sharp projection extending backwards from the point of an arrow, fishhook, etc, and preventing easy extraction **b** a biting or pointedly critical remark or comment **2** any of the side branches of the shaft of a feather ☞ ANATOMY **3** a plant hair or bristle ending in a hook [ME *barbe* barb, beard, fr MF, fr L *barba* – more at BEARD]

[2]barb *vt* to provide (e g an arrow) with a barb

[3]barb *n* any of a northern African breed of horses that are noted for speed and endurance and are related to Arabs [F *barbe*, fr It *barbero*, fr *barbero* of Barbary, fr *Barberia* Barbary, coastal region in Africa]

barbarian /bah'beəri·ən/ *adj* **1** of a land, culture, or people alien and usu believed to be inferior to and more savage than one's own **2** lacking refinement, learning, or artistic or literary culture [L *barbarus*] – **barbarian** *n*, **barbarianism** *n*

barbaric /bah'barik/ *adj* **1** (characteristic) of barbarians; *esp* uncivilized **2** savage, barbarous – **barbarically** *adv*

barbarism /'bahbə,riz(ə)m/ *n* **1** (use of) a word or action unacceptable by contemporary standards; *also* the practice or display of barbarian ideas, acts, or attitudes **2** a barbarian or barbarous social or intellectual condition; backwardness

barbarity /bah'barəti/ *n* **1** barbarism **2** (an act or instance of) barbarous cruelty; inhumanity

barbar·ize, -ise /'bahbəriez/ *vb* to make or become barbarous – **barbarization** /-'zaysh(ə)n/ *n*

barbarous /'bahb(ə)rəs/ *adj* **1** uncivilized **2** lacking culture or refinement **3** mercilessly harsh or cruel [L *barbarus*, fr Gk *barbaros* foreign, ignorant] – **barbarously** *adv*, **barbarousness** *n*

,Barbary 'ape /'bahbəri/ *n* a tailless monkey of N Africa and Gibraltar [*Barbary*, region of Africa]

[1]barbecue /'bahbi,kyooh/ *n* **1** a (portable) fireplace over which meat and fish are roasted **2** meat roasted over an open fire or barbecue pit **3** a social gathering, esp in the open air, at which barbecued food is served [AmerSp *barbacoa*, prob fr Taino]

[2]barbecue *vt* to roast or grill on a rack over hot coals or on a revolving spit in front of or over a source of cooking heat, esp an open fire – **barbecuer** *n*

barbed /bahbd/ *adj* **1** having barbs **2** characterized by pointed and biting criticism – **barbedness** *n*

,barbed 'wire *n* twisted wires armed at intervals with sharp points

[1]barbel /'bahbl/ *n* a European freshwater fish with 4 barbels on its upper jaw [ME, fr MF, fr (assumed) VL *barbellus*, dim. of L *barbus* barbel, fr *barba* beard – more at BEARD]

[2]barbel *n* a slender tactile projecting organ on the lips of certain fishes (e g catfish) used in locating food [obs F, fr MF, dim. of *barbe* barb, beard]

barbell /'bah,bel/ *n* a bar with adjustable weighted discs attached to each end that is used for exercise and in weight lifting

barber /'bahbə/ *n* sby, esp a man, whose occupation is cutting and dressing men's hair and shaving [ME, fr MF *barbeor*, fr *barbe* beard, fr L *barba*] – **barber** *vb*

barberry /'bahb(ə)ri, -,beri/ *n* any of a genus of shrubs having spines, yellow flowers, and oval red berries [by folk etymology fr ME *barbere*, fr MF *barbarin*, fr Ar *barbāris*]

'barber,shop /-,shop/ *n* unaccompanied vocal harmonizing of popular songs, esp by a male quartet [fr former custom of men in barbershops forming quartets for impromptu singing]

barber's pole *n* a red and white striped pole fixed to the front of a barber's shop

barbette /bah'bet/ *n* **1** a mound of earth or a protected platform from which guns fire over a parapet **2** the armour protection of a turret on a warship [F, dim. of *barbe* headdress]

barbican /'bahbikən/ *n* an outer defensive work; *esp* a tower at a gate or bridge [ME, fr OF *barbacane*, fr ML *barbacana*]

barbital /'bahbi,tal/ *n, NAm* barbitone [*barbit*uric + *-al* (as in *Veronal*)]

barbitone /'bahbi,tohn/ *n, Br* a barbiturate that is a hypnotic formerly much used in sleeping pills [*barbit*uric + *-one*]

barbiturate /bah'bityoorət/ *n* **1** a salt or ester of barbituric acid **2** any of several derivatives of barbituric acid (e g thiopentone and phenobarbitone) that are used esp in the treatment of epilepsy and were formerly much used in sleeping pills

,barbi,turic 'acid /,bahbi'tyooərik/ *n* an acid used in the manufacture of barbiturate drugs and plastics [part trans of G *barbitursäure*, irreg fr the name *Barbara* + ISV *uric* + G *säure* acid]

barbule /'bah,byoohl/ *n* any of the small outgrowths that fringe the barbs of a feather ☞ ANATOMY [L *barbula* little beard]

barcarole, barcarolle /,bahkə'rohl/ *n* (music imitating) a Venetian boat song with a beat suggesting a rowing rhythm [F *barcarolle*, fr It *barcarola*, fr *barcarolo* gondolier, fr *barca* barque, fr LL]

[1]bard /bahd/ *n* **1** sby, specif a Celtic poet-singer, who composed, sang, or recited verses on heroes and their deeds **2** a poet; *specif* one recognized or honoured at an eisteddfod **3** *cap* – used as an epithet for Shakespeare; + *the* [ME, fr ScGael & MIr; akin to W *bardd* poet] – **bardic** *adj*

[2]bard, barde *n* a strip of pork fat, bacon, etc for covering lean meat before roasting [MF *barde* armour or ornamental covering for a horse, fr OSp *barda*, fr Ar *barda'ah*] – **bard** *vt*

bardolatry /bah'dolətri/ *n* idolatry of Shakespeare [*Bard (of Avon)*, epithet of William Shakespeare †1616 E poet & dramatist + id*olatry*] – **bardolater** *n*

[1]bare /beə/ *adj* **1** lacking a natural, usual, or appropriate covering, esp clothing **2** open to view; exposed – often in *lay bare* **3a** unfurnished, empty ⟨*the cupboard was* ~⟩ **b** destitute *of* **4a** having nothing left over or added; scant, mere ⟨*the* ~ *necessities*⟩ **b** undisguised, unadorned ⟨*the* ~ *facts*⟩ [ME, fr OE *bær*; akin to OHG *bar* naked, Lith *basas* barefoot] – **bareness** *n*

[2]bare *vt* to make or lay bare; uncover, reveal

'bare,back /-,bak/, **'bare,backed** *adv or adj* on the bare back of a horse without a saddle

bare bones *n pl* the barest essentials, facts, or elements

,bare'faced /-'fayst/ *adj* lacking scruples; shameless [[1]BARE + -FACED] – **barefacedly** /-'faystli, -'faysidli/ *adv*, **barefacedness** *n*

'bare,foot /-,foot/, **barefooted** /-'footid/ *adv or adj* without shoes, socks, stockings, etc; with the feet bare

barefoot doctor *n* a villager, esp in Asia, who has been given some medical training and who is the first person consulted by sick people in his/her community

,bare-'handed *adv or adj* **1** without gloves **2** without tools or weapons ⟨*fight an animal* ~⟩

,bare'headed /-'hedid/ *adv or adj* without a covering for the head – **bareheadedness** *n*

barely /'beəli/ *adv* **1** scarcely, hardly **2** in a meagre manner; scantily ⟨*a* ~ *furnished room*⟩

[1]bargain /'bahgən/ *n* **1** an agreement between parties concerning the terms of a transaction between them or the course of action each pursues in respect to the other **2** an advantageous purchase **3** a transaction, situation, or event regarded in the light of its good or bad results ⟨*make the best of a bad* ~⟩ – **into the bargain** also

[2]bargain *vi* **1** to negotiate over the terms of a purchase, agreement, or contract **2** to come to terms; agree [ME *bargainen*, fr MF *bargaignier*, of Gmc origin; akin to OE *borgian* to borrow] – **bargainer** *n* – **bargain for** to be at all prepared for; EXPECT 2a

'bargain ,basement *n* a section of a shop where merchandise is sold at reduced prices

[1]barge /bahj/ *n* **1a** a flat-bottomed boat used chiefly for the transport of goods on inland waterways or between ships and the shore; *also* NARROW BOAT **b** a flat-bottomed coastal sailing vessel with leeboards instead of a keel **2a** a large naval motorboat used by flag officers **b** an ornate carved vessel used on ceremonial occasions [ME, fr OF, fr LL *barca*]

[2]barge *vi* **1** to move in a headlong or clumsy fashion **2** to intrude *in* or *into* [fr the slow heavy motion of a barge]

'barge,board /-,bawd/ *n* an often ornamented board attached to the sloping edge of a gabled roof ☞ ARCHITECTURE [origin unknown]

bargee /bah'jee/ *n, Br* sby who works on a barge

barilla /bə'rilə/ *n* either of 2 European saltworts or a related Algerian plant [Sp *barrilla*]

baritone /'baritohn/ *n* **1** (a person with) a male singing voice between bass and tenor **2** a member of a family of instruments having a range next below that of the tenor [F *baryton* or It *baritono*, fr Gk *barytonos* deep sounding, fr *barys* heavy + *tonos* tone – more at GRIEVE] – **baritone** *adj*, **baritonal** /-'tohnl/ *adj*

barium /'beəri·əm/ *n* a soft bivalent metallic element of the alkaline-earth group ☞ PERIODIC TABLE [NL, fr *bar-*] – **baric** /'barik/ *adj*

barium meal *n* a solution of barium sulphate swallowed by a patient to make the stomach or intestines visible in X-ray pictures

[1]bark /bahk/ *vi* **1** to make (a sound similar to) the short loud cry characteristic of a dog **2** to speak in a curt, loud, and usu angry tone; snap ~ *vt* to utter in a curt, loud, and usu angry tone [ME *berken*, fr OE *beorcan*; akin to ON *berkja* to bark, Lith *burgėti* to growl] – **barker** *n* – **bark up the wrong tree** to proceed under a misapprehension

[2]bark *n* **1** (a sound similar to) the sound made by a barking dog **2** a short sharp peremptory utterance – **barkless** *adj*

[3]bark *n* the tough exterior covering of a woody root or stem [ME, fr ON *bark-*, *börkr*; akin to MD & MLG *borke* bark] – **barkless** *adj*

[4]bark *vt* to abrade the skin of

[5]bark *n* **1** *NAm* a barque **2** a boat – poetic [ME, fr MF *barque*, fr OProv *barca*, fr LL]

'bark ,beetle *n* any of several beetles that bore under the bark of trees both as larva and adult

'bar,keeper /-,keepə/, **barkeep** /-,keep/ *n, NAm* a barman

barley /'bahli/ *n* a widely cultivated cereal grass whose seed is used to make malt and in foods (e g breakfast cereals and soups) and stock feeds [ME *barly*, fr OE *bærlic* of barley; akin to OE *bere* barley, L *far* spelt]

,barley 'wine *n* a strong ale

'bar ,line *n* a vertical line across a musical staff before the first beat of a bar ☞ MUSIC

barm /bahm/ *n* yeast formed during the fermenting of beer [ME *berme*, fr OE *beorma*; akin to L *fermentum* yeast, *fervēre* to boil – more at [2]BURN]

'barman /-mən/, *fem* **'bar,maid** /-,mayd/ *n* one who serves drinks in a bar

bar mitzvah /,bah 'mitsvə/ *n, often cap B&M* (the initiatory ceremony of) a Jewish youth of 13 who assumes adult religious duties and responsibilities [Heb *bar miṣwāh*, lit., son of the (divine) law]

barmy /'bahmi/ *adj* **1** frothy with barm **2** slightly mad; foolish – infml

barn /bahn/ *n* **1** a usu large farm building for storage, esp of feed, cereal products, etc **2** an unusually large and usu bare building ⟨*a great* ~ *of a house*⟩ [ME *bern*, fr OE *bereærn*, fr *bere* barley + *ærn* place] – **barny** *adj*

barnacle /'bahnəkl/ *n* any of numerous marine crustaceans that are free-swimming as larvae but fixed to rocks or floating objects as adults [fr former belief that the barnacle (goose) was generated from this crustacean] – **barnacled** *adj*

'barnacle ,goose *n* a European goose that breeds in the arctic [ME *barnakille*, alter. of *bernake*, fr ML *bernaca*]

'barn ,dance *n* a type of country dance, esp a round dance or a square dance with called instructions; *also* a social gathering for such dances

,barn 'door *n* a movable flap on a (theatre) light used to control the shape of the beam

barney /'bahni/ *vi or n, Br* (to engage in) a quarrel or row – infml [perh fr the name *Barney*]

'barn ,owl *n* a widely distributed owl that nests esp in barns and other buildings

'barn,storm /-,stawm/ *vb, chiefly NAm vi* **1** to tour in theatrical performances **2** to pilot an aeroplane on sightseeing flights or in exhibition stunts, esp in rural districts ~ *vt* to travel across while barnstorming [*barn* + [2]*storm*; fr itinerant actors performing in barns] – **barnstormer** *n*

'barn,yard /-,yahd/ *n* a farmyard

baro- – see BAR-

barograph /'barə,grahf, -,graf/ *n* a recording barometer [ISV] – **barographic** /-'grafik/ *adj*

barometer /bə'romitə/ *n* **1** an instrument for determining the pressure of the atmosphere and hence for assisting in predicting the weather or measuring the height of an ascent **2** sthg that serves to register fluctuations (e g in public opinion) – **barometry** *n*, **barometric** /,barə'metrik/, **barometrical** *adj*, **barometrically** *adv*

baron /'barən/ *n* **1a** a feudal tenant holding his rights and title by military or other honourable service directly from a sovereign ruler **b** a lord of the realm **2a** a member of the lowest rank of the peerage in Britain **b** a European nobleman **3** a man of great power or influence in a specified field of activity **4** a joint of meat consisting of 2 loins or sirloins joined by the backbone ⟨*a ~ of beef*⟩ [ME, fr OF, of Gmc origin; akin to OHG *baro* freeman; (4) prob fr punning *sirloin* as 'Sir Loin'']

baronage /'barənij/ *n* NOBILITY 2

baroness /,barə'nes/ *n* **1** the wife or widow of a baron **2** a woman having in her own right the rank of a baron

baronet /,barə'net, 'barənit/ *n* the holder of a rank of honour below a baron and above a knight

baronetage /'barənətij/ *n* the whole body of baronets

baronetcy /'barənətsi/ *n* the rank of a baronet

baronial /bə'rohni·əl/ *adj* **1** of or befitting a baron or the baronage **2** stately, ample

barony /'barəni/ *n* the domain or rank of a baron

baroque /bə'rok/ *adj* (typical) of a style of artistic expression prevalent esp in the 17th c that is marked by extravagant forms and elaborate and sometimes grotesque ornamentation [F, lit., irregular, fr Pg *barroco* or Sp *barrueco* irregular pearl] – **baroquely** *adv*

barouche /bə'roohsh/ *n* a 4-wheeled horse-drawn carriage with a high driver's seat at the front and a folding top over the rear seats [G *barutsche*, fr It *biroccio*, deriv of LL *birotus* two-wheeled, fr L *bi-* + *rota* wheel – more at ROLL]

barque *NAm chiefly* **bark** /bahk/ *n* a sailing vessel with the rearmost of usu 3 masts fore-and-aft rigged and the others square-rigged [ME *bark*, fr MF *barque*, fr OProv *barca*, fr LL]

barquentine /'bahkən,teen/ *n* a 3-masted sailing vessel with the foremast square-rigged and the other masts fore-and-aft rigged [*barque* + *-entine*, alter. of *-antine* (as in *brigantine*)]

[1]**barrack** /'barək/ *n* **1** (a set or area of) buildings for lodging soldiers in garrison – often pl with sing. meaning but sing. or pl in constr **2** a large building characterized by extreme plainness or dreary uniformity with others – usu pl with sing. meaning but sing. or pl in constr [F *baraque* hut, fr Catal *barraca*]

[2]**barrack** *vt* to lodge in barracks

[3]**barrack** *vi* **1** *chiefly Br* to jeer, scoff **2** *chiefly Austr & NZ* to root, cheer – usu + *for* ~ *vt* **1** *chiefly Br* to shout at derisively; jeer **2** *chiefly Austr & NZ* to support (e g a sports team), esp by shouting encouragement [prob fr *borak* nonsense, banter (in a native language of Australia)] – **barracker** *n*

barrack square *n* an area for drill practice near a barracks

barracouta /,barə'koohtə/ *n* a large food fish of Pacific seas [modif of AmerSp *barracuda*]

barracuda /,barə'kyoohdə/ *n, pl* **barracuda,** *esp for different types* **barracudas** any of several predatory fishes of warm seas that include excellent food fishes as well as forms regarded as poisonous [AmerSp]

[1]**barrage** /'barahzh/ *n* an artificial dam placed in a watercourse or estuary [F, fr *barrer* to bar, fr *barre* bar]

[2]**barrage** *n* **1** a barrier, esp of intensive artillery fire, to hinder enemy action **2** a rapid series (e g of questions) [F (*tir de*) *barrage* barrier fire] – **barrage** *vt*

'**barrage bal,loon** *n* a large captive balloon used to support wires or nets to prevent the approach of low-flying enemy aircraft

barramunda /,barə'moondə/ *n* any of several Australian freshwater fishes used for food [native name in Australia]

barramundi /,barə'moondi/ *n* a barramunda

barrator *also* **barrater** /'barətə/ *n* one who engages in barratry

barratry /'barətri/ *n* **1** a fraudulent breach of duty by the master or crew of a ship **2** persistent litigation [ME *barratrie*, fr MF *baraterie* deception, fr *barater* to deceive, exchange]

barre /bah/ *n* a horizontal handrail used by ballet dancers while exercising [F, bar]

[1]**barrel** /'barəl/ *n* **1** an approximately cylindrical vessel with bulging sides and flat ends constructed from wooden staves bound together with hoops; *also* any similar vessel **2** a drum or cylindrical part: e g **a** the discharging tube of a gun **b** the part of a fountain pen or pencil containing the ink or lead **c** a cylindrical or tapering housing containing the lenses, iris diaphragm, etc of a camera or other piece of optical equipment **3** the trunk, esp of a quadruped [ME *barel*, fr MF *baril*] – **barrelled,** *NAm* **barreled** *adj* – **over a barrel** at a disadvantage; in an awkward situation so that one is helpless ⟨*he had me* over a barrel *so I had to give in*⟩ – infml

[2]**barrel** *vt* **-ll-** (*NAm* **-l-**, **-ll-**) to put or pack in a barrel

'**barrel,house** /-,hows/ *n* a style of jazz characterized by a heavy beat and simultaneous improvisation by players [*barrelhouse* (a cheap drinking and dancing establishment)]

'**barrel ,organ** *n* a musical instrument consisting of a revolving cylinder studded with pegs that open a series of valves to admit air from a bellows to a set of pipes

barren /'barən/ *adj* **1** not reproducing: e g **a** *of a female or mating* incapable of producing offspring **b** habitually failing to fruit **2** not productive; *esp* producing inferior or scanty vegetation **3** lacking, devoid *of* **4** lacking interest, information, or charm [ME *bareine*, fr OF *baraine*] – **barrenly** *adv*, **barrenness** *n*

[1]**barricade** /'barikayd, --'-/ *vt* **1** to block off, stop up, or defend with a barricade **2** to prevent access to by means of a barricade

[2]**barricade** *n* **1** an obstruction or rampart thrown up across a way or passage to check the advance of the enemy **2** a barrier, obstacle [F, fr MF, fr *barriquer* to barricade, fr *barrique* barrel]

barrier /'bari·ə/ *n* **1** a material object (e g a stockade, fortress, or railing) or set of objects that separates, demarcates, or serves as a barricade **2** sthg immaterial that impedes or separates ⟨~s *of reserve*⟩ **3** a factor that tends to restrict the free movement, mingling, or interbreeding of individuals or populations [ME *barrere*, fr MF *barriere*, fr *barre*]

barrier reef *n* a coral reef roughly parallel to a shore and separated from it by a lagoon

barring /'bahring/ *prep* excepting

barrio /'bahrioh, 'ba-/ *n, pl* **barrios** a Spanish-speaking neighbourhood in a city or town in the USA, esp in the Southwest [Sp, fr Ar *barrī* of the open country, fr *barr* outside, open country]

barrister /'baristə/, **,barrister-at-'law** *n* a lawyer who has the right to plead as an advocate in an

English or Welsh superior court – compare SOLICITOR ['bar + -i- + -ster]

'barroom /-,roohm, -room/ *n* BAR 5a(2)

¹barrow /'baroh/ *n* a large mound of earth or stones over the remains of the dead; a tumulus [ME *bergh*, fr OE *beorg*; akin to OHG *berg* mountain, Skt *brhant* high]

²barrow *n* a male pig castrated before sexual maturity [ME *barow*, fr OE *bearg*; akin to OHG *barug* barrow, OE *borian* to bore]

³barrow *n* a cart with a shallow box body, 2 wheels, and shafts for pushing it [ME *barew*, fr OE *bearwe*; akin to OE *beran* to carry – more at ²BEAR]

'barrow ,boy *n* a man or boy who sells goods (e g fruit or vegetables) from a barrow

,bar 'sinister *n* **1** an imaginary heraldic shape or representation indicating bastardy **2** the condition of being of illegitimate birth

'bar,tender /-,tendə/ *n, chiefly NAm* a barman

¹barter /'bahtə/ *vi* to trade by exchanging one commodity for another without the use of money ~ *vt* **1** to exchange (as if) by bartering **2** to part with unwisely or for an unworthy return – + *away* [ME *bartren*, fr MF *barater*] – **barterer** *n*

²barter *n* the carrying on of trade by bartering

bartizan /'bahtiz(ə)n, ,bahti'zan/ *n* a corner turret, parapet, etc projecting from a building [ME *bretasinge*, fr *bretasce* parapet – more at BRATTICE]

baryon /'bari·ən/ *n* any of a group of elementary particles (e g a hyperon) that are fermions and have a mass equal to or greater than that of the proton [ISV *bary-* (fr Gk *barys* heavy) + ²*-on* – more at GRIEVE] – **baryonic** /-'onik/ *adj*

barytes /bə'rieteez/ *n* naturally occurring barium sulphate [Gk *barytēs* weight, fr *barys* heavy]

basal /'bays(ə)l/ *adj* **1** of, situated at, or forming the base **2** of the foundation, base, or essence; fundamental – **basally** *adv*

basal metabolic rate *n* the rate at which heat is given off by an organism at complete rest

,basal me'tabolism *n* the rate at which energy is used in a fasting and resting organism using energy solely to maintain vital cellular activity, respiration, and circulation

basalt /'ba(y)sawlt, bə'sawlt/ *n* a dense to fine-grained dark igneous rock consisting essentially of a feldspar and usu pyroxene [L *basaltes*, MS var of *basanites* touchstone, fr Gk *basanitēs* (*lithos*), fr *basanos* touchstone, fr Egypt *bhnw*] – **basaltic** /-'sawltik/ *adj*

bascule /'baskyool, 'baskyoohl/ *n* (a bridge raised or lowered by) a counterbalancing apparatus [F, seesaw]

¹base /bays/ *n* **1a** the bottom of sthg; a foundation **b** the lower part of a wall, pier, or column considered as a separate architectural feature ☞ ARCHITECTURE **c** a side or face of a geometrical figure on which it is regarded as standing ☞ MATHEMATICS **d** that part of an organ by which it is attached to another structure nearer the centre of a living organism **2a** a main ingredient **b** a supporting or carrying ingredient **3** the fundamental part of sthg; a basis **4a** a centre from which a start is made in an activity or from which operations proceed **b** a line in a survey which serves as the origin for computations **c** the locality or installations on which a military force relies for supplies or from which it starts operations **d(1)** the number with reference to which a number system is constructed **(2)** a number with reference to which logarithms are computed **e** ROOT 6 **5a** the starting place or goal in various games **b** any of the stations at each of the 4 corners of the inner part of a baseball field to which a batter must run in turn in order to score a run **6** the middle region of a transistor that controls the current flow **7** any of various typically water-soluble and acrid or brackish tasting chemical compounds that are capable of taking up a hydrogen ion from or donating an unshared pair of electrons to an acid to form a salt **8** *also* **base component** that part of a transformational grammar that consists of rules and a lexicon and that generates the deep structures of a language [ME, fr MF, fr L *basis*, fr Gk, step, base, fr *bainein* to go – more at COME] – **based** *adj*, **baseless** *adj*

²base *vt* **1** to make, form, or serve as a base for **2** to use as a base or basis for; establish, found – usu + *on* or *upon*

³base *adj* constituting or serving as a base

⁴base *adj* **1a** *of a metal* of comparatively low value and having relatively inferior properties (e g resistance to corrosion) – compare NOBLE 3 **b** containing a larger than usual proportion of base metals **2** lacking higher values; degrading ⟨*a drab ~ way of life*⟩ **3** of relatively little value [ME *bas* short, low, bass, fr MF, fr ML *bassus* short, low] – **basely** *adv*, **baseness** *n*

'base,ball /-,bawl/ *n* (the ball used in) a game played with a bat and ball between 2 teams of 9 players each on a large field centring on 4 bases arranged in a square that mark the course a batter must run to score

'base,board /-,bawd/ *n, NAm* SKIRTING BOARD

'base,born /-,bawn/ *adj* **1** of humble or illegitimate birth **2** *archaic* mean, ignoble [⁴*base*]

'base,line /-,lien/ *n* the back line at each end of a court in tennis, badminton, etc ☞ SPORT

'basement /-mənt/ *n* the part of a building that is wholly or partly below ground level [prob fr ¹*base* + *-ment*] – **basementless** *adj*

basenji /bə'senji/ *n* any of an African breed of small compact curly-tailed dogs that seldom bark [of Bantu origin; akin to Lingala *basenji*, pl of *mosenji* native]

¹bash /bash/ *vt* **1** to strike violently; *also* to injure or damage by striking; smash – often + *in* or *up* **2** to make a violent attack on *USE* infml [prob imit] – **basher** *n*

²bash *n* **1** a forceful blow **2** *chiefly Br* a try, attempt ⟨*have a ~ at it*⟩ **3** *NAm* a festive social gathering; a party *USE* infml

bashful /'bashf(ə)l/ *adj* **1** socially shy or timid **2** characterized by, showing, or resulting from extreme sensitiveness or self-consciousness [obs *bash* (to be abashed), fr ME *basshen*, short for *abasshen*, *abaishen* – more at ABASH] – **bashfully** *adv*, **bashfulness** *n*

¹basic /'baysik, -zik/ *adj* **1** of or forming the base or essence; fundamental **2** constituting or serving as the minimum basis or starting point **3a** of, containing, or having the character of a chemical base **b** having an alkaline reaction; being an alkali **4** *of rock* containing relatively little silica **5** of, being, or made by a steelmaking process in which the furnace is lined with material containing relatively little silica – **basically** *adv*, **basicity** /bay'sisəti/ *n*

²basic *n* sthg basic; a fundamental

BASIC /'baysik/ *n* a high-level computer language for programming and interacting with a computer in a wide variety of applications [*B*eginner's *A*ll-purpose *S*ymbolic *I*nstruction *C*ode]

Basic English *n* a simplified version of English with a vocabulary of 850 words designed for teaching and international communication

basic slag *n* a slag used in the basic process of steelmaking and useful as a fertilizer

basidiomycete /bə,sidioh'mieseet, -,----'-/ *n* any of a large class of higher fungi bearing spores on a basidium and including rusts, mushrooms, and puffballs [deriv of NL *basidium* + Gk *mykēt-, mykēs* fungus – more at MYC-] – **basidiomycetous** /-mie'seetəs/ *adj*

ba'sidio,spore /-,spaw/ *n* a spore produced by a basidium [NL *basidium* + E *-o-* + *spore*] – **basidiosporous** /bə,sidioh'spawrəs, bə,sidi'ospərəs/ *adj*

basidium /bə'sidi·əm/ *n, pl* **basidia** /-di·ə/ a specialized cell on a basidiomycete bearing usu 4 basidiospores [NL, fr L *basis*] – **basidial** *adj*

basil /'baz(ə)l/ *n* any of several plants of the mint family; *esp* SWEET BASIL [MF *basile*, fr LL *basilicum*, fr Gk *basilikon*, fr neut of *basilikos*]

basilar /'basilə, 'bazilə/ *adj* of or situated at the base [irreg fr *basis*]

basilar membrane *n* a membrane in the cochlea of the inner ear that vibrates in response to sound waves

basilica /bə'zilikə, bə'si-/ *n* **1** an oblong building used in ancient Rome as a place of assembly or as a lawcourt and usu ending in an apse **2** an early Christian church similar to a Roman basilica **3** a Roman Catholic church given certain ceremonial privileges [L, fr Gk *basilikē*, fr fem of *basilikos* royal, fr *basileus* king] – **basilican** *adj*

basilisk /'basilisk, 'bazi-/ *n* **1** a mythical reptile whose breath and glance were fatal **2** any of several crested tropical American lizards related to the iguanas [ME, fr L *basiliscus*, fr Gk *basiliskos*, fr dim. of *basileus*] – **basilisk** *adj*

basin /'bays(ə)n/ *n* **1a** a round open usu metal or ceramic vessel with a greater width than depth and sides that slope or curve inwards to the base, used typically for holding water for washing **b** a bowl with a greater depth than width esp for holding, mixing, or cooking food ⟨*a pudding* ~⟩ **c** the contents of a basin **2a** a dock built in a tidal river or harbour **b** a (partly) enclosed water area, esp for ships **3a** a depression in the surface of the land or ocean floor **b** the region drained by a river and its tributaries **4** an area of the earth in which the strata dip from the sides towards the centre [ME, fr OF *bacin*, fr LL *bacchinon*] – **basinal** *adj*, **basined** *adj*

basis /'baysis/ *n, pl* **bases** /'bayseez/ **1** a foundation **2** the principal component of sthg **3** a basic principle or way of proceeding [L – more at ¹BASE]

bask /bahsk/ *vi* **1** to lie in, or expose oneself to, a pleasant warmth or atmosphere **2** to enjoy sby's favour or approval – usu + *in* [ME *basken*, fr ON *bathask*, refl of *batha* to bathe; akin to OE *bæth* bath]

basket /'bahskit/ *n* **1a** a rigid or semirigid receptacle made of interwoven material (e g osiers, cane, wood, or metal) **b** any of various lightweight usu wood containers **c** the contents of a basket **2** sthg that resembles a basket, esp in shape or use **3** a net open at the bottom and suspended from a metal ring that constitutes the goal in basketball **4** a collection, group ⟨*the* ~ *of major world currencies*⟩ **5** *Br* a person of a specified type ⟨*she's a nice old* ~⟩ – infml [ME, prob fr (assumed) ONF *baskot*; akin to OF *baschoue* wooden vessel; both fr L *bascauda* dishpan, of Celt origin; akin to MIr *basc* necklace – more at FASCIA; (5) euphemism for *bastard*] – **basketful** *n*, **basketlike** *adj*

'basket,ball /-,bawl/ *n* (the ball used in) an indoor court game between 2 teams of 5 players each who score by tossing a large ball through a raised basket

'basket ,chair *n* a wickerwork armchair

basketry /'bahskitri/ *n* (the art or craft of making) baskets or objects woven like baskets

'basket ,weave *n* a textile weave resembling the chequered pattern of a plaited basket

'basket,work /-,wuhk/ *n* basketry

basking shark /'bahsking/ *n* a large species of shark that often lies near the water surface

bas mitzvah /,bas 'mitzvə/ *n, often cap B&M* a Jewish girl who at about 13 years of age assumes religious responsibilities [Heb *bath miṣwāh*, lit., daughter of the (divine) law]

basophil /'baysə,fil, 'bayzə-/, **basophile** /-,fiel/ *n* a white blood cell with basophilic granules – compare EOSINOPHIL ☞ ANATOMY

,baso'philic /-'filik/ *adj* staining readily with dyes that are chemical bases ⟨*some blood cells contain* ~ *granules*⟩ [ISV *base* + *-o-* + *-philic*]

Basque /bask, bahsk/ *n* a member of a people inhabiting the W Pyrenees or their language ☞ LANGUAGE [F, fr L *Vasco*] – **Basque** *adj*

bas-relief /,bas ri'leef, ,bah, ,bahs, '- -,-/ *n* sculptural relief in which the design projects very slightly from the surrounding surface – compare HIGH RELIEF [F, fr *bas* low + *relief* raised work]

¹bass /bas/ *n, pl* **bass**, *esp for different types* **basses** any of numerous edible spiny-finned fishes [ME *base*, alter. of OE *bærs*; akin to OE *byrst* bristle – more at BRISTLE]

²bass /bays/ *adj* **1** deep or grave in tone **2a** of low pitch **b** of or having the range or part of a bass [ME *bas* base]

³bass /bays/ *n* **1** the lowest part in 4-part harmony **2a** (a person with) the lowest adult male singing voice **b** a member of a family of instruments having the lowest range; *esp* a double bass or bass guitar

⁴bass /bas/ *n* a coarse tough fibre from palm trees [alter. of *bast*]

bass clef /bays/ *n* a clef placing the F below middle C on the fourth line of the staff ☞ MUSIC

bass drum /bays/ *n* a large drum with 2 heads that gives a booming sound of low indefinite pitch

basset /'basit/, **'basset ,hound** *n* (any of) a breed of short-legged hunting dogs with very long ears [F *basset*, fr MF, fr *basset* short, fr *bas* low – more at ⁴BASE]

bassist /'baysist/ *n* a double bass player

basso /'basoh/ *n, pl* **bassos, bassi** /-si/ an (operatic) bass singer [It, fr ML *bassus*, fr *bassus* short, low]

bassoon /bə'soohn/ *n* a double-reed woodwind instrument with a usual range 2 octaves lower than the oboe [F *basson*, fr It *bassone*, fr *basso*] – **bassoonist** *n*

,basso pro'fundo /prə'foondoh/ *n, pl* **basso profun-**

dos (a person with) an exceptionally low bass singing voice [It, lit., deep bass]

bass viol /bays/ *n* VIOLA DA GAMBA

bast /bast/ *n* **1** phloem **2** a strong woody fibre obtained chiefly from the phloem of certain plants [ME, fr OE *bæst*; akin to OHG & ON *bast*]

[1]**bastard** /'bahstəd, 'ba-/ *n* **1** an illegitimate child **2** sthg spurious, irregular, inferior, or of questionable origin **3a** an offensive or disagreeable person – often + *you* as a generalized term of abuse **b** a fellow of a usu specified type ⟨*poor old* ~⟩ – infml [ME, fr OF *bastart, bastard*, perh fr *fils de bast*, lit., son of the barn] – **bastardly** *adj*

[2]**bastard** *adj* **1** illegitimate **2** of an inferior or less typical type, stock, or form **3** lacking genuineness or authority; false

bastard·ize, -ise /'bahstədiez, 'ba-/ *vt* **1** to declare illegitimate **2** to debase – **bastardization** /-die'zaysh(ə)n/ *n*

bastard wing *n* the projecting part of a bird's wing corresponding to a mammal's thumb and bearing a few short feathers

bastardy /'bahstədi, 'ba-/ *n* the quality or state of being a bastard; illegitimacy

[1]**baste** /bayst/ *vt* TACK 1b [ME *basten*, fr MF *bastir*, of Gmc origin; akin to OHG *besten* to patch; akin to OE *bæst* bast] – **baster** *n*

[2]**baste** *vt* to moisten (e g meat) at intervals with melted butter, dripping, etc during cooking, esp roasting [origin unknown] – **baster** *n*

[3]**baste** *vt* to beat severely or soundly; thrash [prob fr ON *beysta*; akin to OE *bēatan* to beat]

Ba'stille ,Day /ba'steel/ *n* July 14 observed in France as a national holiday in commemoration of the fall of the Bastille in 1789

bastinade /,basti'nahd/ *n* a bastinado

bastinado /,basti'naydoh/ *n, pl* **bastinadoes** **1** (a blow or beating with) a stick or cudgel **2** the punishment of beating the soles of the feet with a stick [Sp *bastonada*, fr *bastón* stick, fr LL *bastum*] – **bastinado** *vt*

basting /'baysting/ *n* a severe beating [fr gerund of [3]*baste*]

bastion /'basti·ən/ *n* **1** a projecting part of a fortification **2** a fortified area or position **3** sthg considered a stronghold; a bulwark [MF, fr *bastille* fortress, modif of OProv *bastida*, fr *bastir* to build, of Gmc origin; akin to OHG *besten* to patch] – **bastioned** *adj*

[1]**bat** /bat/ *n* **1** a stout solid stick; a club **2** a sharp blow; a stroke **3** a (wooden) implement used for hitting the ball in cricket, baseball, table tennis, etc **4a** a batsman **b** a turn at batting in cricket, baseball, etc **5** a hand-held implement shaped like a table-tennis bat for guiding aircraft when landing or taxiing [ME, fr OE *batt*, prob of Celt origin; akin to Gaulish anda*bata*, a gladiator – more at BATTLE] – **off one's own bat** through one's own efforts, esp without being prompted

[2]**bat** *vb* **-tt-** *vt* to strike or hit (as if) with a bat ~ *vi* **1** to strike a ball with a bat **2** to take one's turn at batting, esp in cricket

[3]**bat** *n* any of an order of nocturnal flying mammals with forelimbs modified to form wings [alter. of ME *bakke*, prob of Scand origin; akin to OSw natt*bakka* bat]

[4]**bat** *vt* **-tt-** to blink, esp in surprise or emotion ⟨*never* ~ted *an eyelid*⟩ [prob alter. of *bate* (to beat wings), fr ME *baten*, fr MF *batre* to beat – more at DEBATE]

batch /bach/ *n* **1** the quantity baked at 1 time **2a** the quantity of material produced at 1 operation or for use at 1 time **b** a group of jobs to be run on a computer at 1 time with the same program ⟨~ *processing*⟩ **3** a group of people or things; a lot [ME *bache*; akin to OE *bacan* to bake]

[1]**bate** /bayt/ *vt, archaic* to restrain [ME *baten*, short for *abaten* to abate] – **with bated breath** anxiously, worriedly

[2]**bate** *n* a rage, temper – slang [var of *bait*, perh back-formation fr *baited* harassed, tormented]

Batesian mimicry /'baytsi·ən/ *n* resemblance of a harmless species to another that is protected from predators by repellent qualities (e g unpleasant taste) [Henry Walter *Bates* †1892 E naturalist]

[1]**bath** /bahth/ *n, pl* **baths** /bahths; *sense 3 often* bahdhz/ **1** a washing or soaking (e g in water or steam) of all or part of the body **2a** water used for bathing ⟨*run a* ~⟩ **b** a vessel for bathing in; *esp* one that is permanently fixed in a bathroom **c** (a vat, tank, etc holding) a specified type of liquid used for a special purpose (e g to keep samples at a constant temperature) **3a** a building containing an apartment or a series of rooms designed for bathing **b** SWIMMING POOL – usu pl with sing. meaning but sing. or pl in constr **c** a spa **d** *NAm* a bathroom ***USE*** (*3a&3c*) usu pl with sing. meaning [ME, fr OE *bæth*; akin to OHG *bad* bath, OE *bacan* to bake]

[2]**bath** *vb, Br vt* to give a bath to ~ *vi* to take a bath

bath-, batho- *comb form* depth ⟨batho*meter*⟩ [ISV, fr Gk *bathos*, fr *bathys* deep – more at BATHY-]

,Bath 'bun *n* a sweet yeast-leavened bun containing dried fruit (e g raisins and sultanas) and topped with sugar crystals [*Bath*, town in England]

'bath ,chair *n, often cap B* a usu hooded wheelchair [*Bath*, town in England]

'Bath ,chap *n* [4]CHAP 1; *esp* the flesh of a jaw or lower cheek of a pig used as food [*Bath*, town in England]

[1]**bathe** /baydh/ *vt* **1** to wash or soak in a liquid (e g water) **2** to moisten **3** to apply water or a liquid medicament to **4** to suffuse, esp with light ~ *vi* **1** to take a bath **2** to swim (e g in the sea or a river) for pleasure **3** to become immersed or absorbed [ME *bathen*, fr OE *bathian*; akin to OE *bæth* bath] – **bather** *n*

[2]**bathe** *n, Br* an act of bathing, esp in the sea

bathetic /bə'thetik/ *adj* characterized by bathos [*bathos* + *-etic* (as in *pathetic*)] – **bathetically** *adv*

bathhouse /'bahth,hows/ *n* a building equipped for people to take baths

'bathing ,beauty /'baydhing/ *n* a woman in a swimming costume who is a contestant in a beauty contest

'bathing ,hut *n* a hut for bathers to undress in

'bathing ,suit *n* SWIMMING COSTUME

'bath ,mat *n* **1** a usu washable mat, often of absorbent material, placed beside a bath **2** a mat of nonslip material, esp rubber, placed in a bath to prevent the bather from slipping

batholith /'bathəlith/ *n* a deep-sited dome-shaped mass of intrusive igneous rock [ISV] – **batholithic** /-'lithik/ *adj*

bathometer /bə'thomitə/ *n* an instrument for measuring depths in water

bathos /'baythos/ *n* **1** a sudden descent from the sublime to the commonplace or absurd; an anticlimax **2** exceptional commonplaceness; triteness [Gk, lit., depth]

'bath,robe /-,rohb/ *n* a loose usu absorbent robe worn before and after having a bath

'bathroom /-,roohm, -room/ *n* **1** a room containing a bath or shower and usu a washbasin and toilet **2** a toilet – chiefly euph

'bath ,salts *n pl but sing or pl in constr* a usu coloured compound for perfuming or softening bathwater

bathy- *comb form* **1** deep; depth ⟨bathy*metry*⟩ ⟨bathy*pelagic*⟩ **2** deep-sea ⟨bathy*sphere*⟩ [ISV, fr Gk, fr *bathys* deep; akin to Skt *gāhate* he dives into]

bathyscaphe /'bathiskayf, -skaf/ *n* a navigable submersible ship for deep-sea exploration [ISV *bathy-* + Gk *skaphē* light boat]

bathysphere /'bathisfiə/ *n* a strongly built diving sphere for deep-sea observation

batik /'batik/ *n* (a fabric or design printed by) an Indonesian method of hand-printing by coating with wax the parts to be left undyed [Malay, fr Jav, painted]

batiste /bə'teest/ *n* a fine soft sheer fabric of plain weave made of various fibres [F]

batman /'batmən/ *n* a British officer's servant [*bat* (pack-saddle, luggage), fr MF *bat*, deriv of Gk *bastazein* to carry]

baton /'bat(ə)n, 'ba,ton, bə'ton (*Fr* batõ)/ *n* **1** a cudgel, truncheon **2** a staff borne as a symbol of office **3** a wand with which a conductor directs a band or orchestra **4** a stick or hollow cylinder passed by each member of a relay team to the succeeding runner [F *bâton*, fr OF *baston*, fr LL *bastum* stick]

'baton ,charge /'bat(ə)n/ *n* a charge by police or troops wielding batons

batrachian /bə'trayki·ən/ *n* a frog, toad, or other vertebrate amphibian animal [deriv of Gk *batrachos* frog] – **batrachian** *adj*

bats /bats/ *adj, chiefly Br* batty ⟨*he's gone* ~⟩ – infml [prob fr the phrase *to have bats in the belfry* to be crazy]

'batsman /-mən/ *n* sby who bats or is batting, esp in cricket ☞ SPORT – **batsmanship** *n*

battalion /bə'talyən/ *n sing or pl in constr* **1** a large body of organized troops **2** a military unit composed of a headquarters and 2 or more companies **3** a large group [MF *bataillon*, fr OIt *battaglione*, aug of *battaglia* company of soldiers, battle, fr LL *battalia* combat – more at BATTLE]

¹batten /'bat(ə)n/ *vi* [orig sense, to improve, grow fat, thrive; prob fr ON *batna* to improve] – **batten on 1** to make oneself selfishly dependent on (sby) ⟨battened on *his rich relatives*⟩ **2** to seize on (an excuse, argument, etc)

²batten *n* **1** a thin narrow strip of squared timber **2a** a thin strip of wood, plastic, etc inserted into a sail to keep it flat and taut **b** a slat used to secure the tarpaulins and hatch covers of a ship **3** a strip holding a row of floodlights [F *bâton*]

³batten *vt* to provide or fasten (e g hatches) with battens – often + *down*

¹batter /'batə/ *vt* **1** to beat persistently or hard so as to bruise, shatter, or demolish **2** to wear or damage by hard usage or blows ⟨*a* ~ed *old hat*⟩ ~ *vi* to strike heavily and repeatedly; beat [ME *bateren*, prob freq of *batten* to bat, fr *bat*]

²batter *n* a mixture that consists essentially of flour, egg, and milk or water and is thin enough to pour or drop from a spoon; *also* batter mixture (e g that used for coating fish) when cooked – compare DOUGH [ME *bater*, prob fr *bateren*]

³batter *vi* to slope upwards and backwards *vt* to cause (e g a wall) to slope upwards and backwards [origin unknown]

⁴batter *n* an upwards and backwards slope of the outer face of a structure

⁵batter *n* the player who is batting in baseball [²BAT + ²-ER]

'battering ,ram /'batəring/ *n* an ancient military siege engine consisting of a large wooden beam with a head of iron used for beating down walls

battery /'bat(ə)ri/ *n* **1a** the act of battering **b** the unlawful application of any degree of force to a person without his/her consent **2** a grouping of similar artillery guns (e g for tactical purposes) **3** *sing or pl in constr* a tactical and administrative army artillery unit equivalent to an infantry company **4** one or more cells connected together to provide an electric current: e g **a** STORAGE CELL **b** DRY CELL; *also* a connected group of dry cells **5a** a number of similar articles, items, or devices arranged, connected, or used together; a set, series **b(1)** a large number of small cages in which egg-laying hens are kept **(2)** a series of cages or compartments for raising or fattening animals, esp poultry **c** an impressive or imposing group; an array **6** the position of readiness of a gun for firing [MF *batterie*, fr OF, fr *battre* to beat, fr L *battuere* – more at BATTLE]

batting /'bating/ *n* layers or sheets of raw cotton or wool used esp for lining quilts [fr gerund of ²*bat*]

¹battle /'batl/ *n* **1** a general hostile encounter between armies, warships, aircraft, etc **2** a combat between 2 people **3** an extended contest, struggle, or controversy [ME *batel*, fr OF *bataille* battle, fortifying tower, battalion, fr LL *battalia* combat, alter. of *battualia* fencing exercises, fr L *battuere* to beat, of Celt origin; akin to Gaulish anda*bata*, a gladiator; akin to L *fatuus* foolish, Russ *bat* cudgel]

²battle *vb* **battling** /'batling, 'batl·ing/ *vi* **1** to engage in battle; fight **2** to contend with full strength, craft, or resources; struggle ~ *vt* **1** to fight against **2** to force (e g one's way) by battling – **battler** *n*

'battle-,axe *n* a quarrelsome domineering woman

'battle ,cruiser *n* a large heavily-armed warship faster than a battleship

'battle,dress /-,dres/ *n* the uniform worn by soldiers in battle

battlement /'batlmənt/ *n* a parapet with indentations that surmounts a wall and is used for defence or decoration – compare CRENELLATION ☞ CHURCH [ME *batelment*, fr MF *bataille* fortifying tower] – **battlemented** /-,mentid/ *adj*

,battle 'royal *n, pl* **battles royal, battle royals 1** a fight or contest between more than 2 opponents, esp until only the winner remains on his/her feet or in the ring **2** a violent struggle or heated dispute

'battle,ship /-,ship/ *n* the largest and most heavily armed and armoured type of warship [short for *line-of-battle ship*]

battue /ba't(y)ooh/ *n* (a hunt using) the beating of woods and bushes to flush game [F, fr *battre* to beat]

batty /'bati/ *adj* mentally unstable; crazy – infml [[3]*bat* + [1]*-y* – more at BATS] – **battiness** *n*

bauble /'bawbl/ *n* **1** a trinket or trifle **2** a jester's staff [ME *babel*, fr MF]

baud /bawd, bohd/ *n, pl* **baud** *also* **bauds** any of several units of data transmission speed; *specif* one equal to 1 bit of data per second [*baud* (telegraphic transmission speed unit), fr J M E *Baudot* †1903 F inventor]

Bauhaus /'bow,hows/ *adj* (characteristic) of a German school of design established in 1919 and noted esp for a programme that synthesized technology, craftsmanship, and design aesthetics [G *Bauhaus*, lit., architecture house, academy founded in Weimar, Germany]

baulk /baw(l)k/ *vb or n, chiefly Br* (to) balk

bauxite /'bawksiet/ *n* a mineral that is an impure mixture of earthy hydrous aluminium oxides and hydroxides and is the principal ore of aluminium [F, fr Les *Baux*, place near Arles, France] – **bauxitic** /bawk'sitik/ *adj*

Bavarian /bə'veəri·ən/ *n* a native or inhabitant of Bavaria or the High German dialect spoken there [*Bavaria*, region of Germany] – **Bavarian** *adj*

bawbee, baubee /baw'bee/ *n, Scot* **1** a trifle **2** *archaic* an English halfpenny [prob fr Alexander Orrok, laird of Sille*bawby fl* 1541 Sc master of the mint; original sense, a 16th-c Sc coin]

bawd /bawd/ *n* a woman who keeps a house of prostitution; a madam [ME *bawde*, perh fr MF *baud* bold, merry]

bawdry /'bawdri/ *n* bawdy [ME *bawderie*, fr *bawde*]

[1]**bawdy** /'bawdi/ *adj* boisterously or humorously indecent [*bawd* + *-y*] – **bawdily** *adv*, **bawdiness** *n*

[2]**bawdy** *n* suggestive, coarse, or obscene language [prob fr [1]*bawdy*]

[1]**bawl** /bawl/ *vb* **1** to yell, bellow **2** to cry, wail [ME *baulen*, prob of Scand origin; akin to Icel *baula* to low] – **bawler** *n*

[2]**bawl** *n* a loud prolonged cry

bawl out *vt, chiefly NAm* to reprimand loudly or severely – infml

[1]**bay** /bay/ *adj, esp of a horse* of the colour bay [ME, fr MF *bai*, fr L *badius*; akin to OIr *buide* yellow]

[2]**bay** *n* **1** a horse with a bay-coloured body and black mane, tail, and points **2** a reddish brown colour

[3]**bay** *n* **1** any of several shrubs or trees resembling the laurel **2** an honorary garland or crown, esp of laurel, given for victory or excellence [ME, berry, fr MF *baie*, fr L *baca*]

[4]**bay** *n* **1** a division of a part of a building (e g the walls or roof) or of the whole building **2** a main division of a structure; *esp* a compartment in the fuselage of an aircraft ⟨*the forward instrument* ~⟩ [ME, fr MF *baée* opening, fr OF, fr fem of *baé*, pp of *baer* to gape, yawn, fr ML *batare*]

[5]**bay** *vi* to bark with prolonged tones [ME *baien, abaien*, fr OF *abaiier*, of imit origin]

[6]**bay** *n* **1** the position of one unable to retreat and forced to face a foe or danger ⟨*brought his quarry to* ~⟩ **2** the position of one kept off or repelled with difficulty ⟨*police kept the rioters at* ~⟩ [ME *bay, abay*, fr OF *abai*, fr *abaiier*]

[7]**bay** *n* (a land formation resembling) an inlet of a sea, lake, etc, usu smaller than a gulf ☞ GEOGRAPHY [ME *baye*, fr MF *baie*]

'**bay ,leaf** *n* the leaf of the European laurel used dried in cooking

[1]**bayonet** /,bayə'net, '---/ *n* a blade attached to the muzzle of a firearm and used in hand-to-hand combat [F *baïonnette*, fr *Bayonne*, city in France]

[2]**bayonet** *vt* to stab or drive (as if) with a bayonet ~ *vi* to use a bayonet

,**bay 'rum** *n* a fragrant cosmetic and medicinal liquid from the (oil of the) leaves of a W Indian tree of the myrtle family

,**bay 'salt** *n* common salt obtained by evaporating sea water – compare ROCK SALT [[7]*bay*]

,**bay 'window** *n* a window or series of windows projecting outwards from the wall ☞ ARCHITECTURE [[4]*bay*]

bazaar /bə'zah/ *n* **1** an (Oriental) market consisting of rows of shops or stalls selling miscellaneous goods **2** a fair for the sale of miscellaneous articles, esp for charitable purposes [Per *bāzār*]

bazooka /bə'zoohkə/ *n* an individual infantry antitank rocket launcher [*bazooka* (a crude musical instrument made of pipes and a funnel)]

,**BC'G ,vaccine** *n* a vaccine used to protect people against tuberculosis [*b*acillus *C*almette-*G*uérin, fr Albert *Calmette* †1933 and Camille *Guérin* †1961 F bacteriologists]

bdellium /'deli·əm/ *n* a gum resin similar to myrrh obtained from various trees of the E Indies and Africa [ME, fr L, fr Gk *bdellion*]

be /bi, bee; *strong* bee/ *vb, pres 1 sing* **am** /əm, m; *strong* am/; *2 sing* **are** /ə; *strong* ah/; *3 sing* **is** /z; *strong* iz/; *pl* **are**; *pres subjunctive* **be**; *pres part* **being**; *past 1&3 sing* **was** /wəz; *strong* woz/; *2 sing* **were** /wə; *strong* **wuh/**; *pl* **were**; *past subjunctive* **were**; *past part* **been /bin, been;** *strong* been/ *vi* **1a** to equal in meaning; have the same connotation as ⟨*January* is *the first month*⟩ ⟨*let* x ~ *10*⟩ **b** to represent, symbolize ⟨*God* is *love*⟩ ⟨*Olivier* was *hamlet*⟩ ⟨*Valentino* was *romance*⟩ **c** to have identity with ⟨*it's me*⟩ ⟨*the first person I met* was *my brother*⟩ ⟨*the difficulty* is *finding them*⟩ **d** to belong to the class of ⟨*the fish* is *a trout*⟩ **e** to occupy a specified position in space ⟨*the book* is *on the table*⟩ ⟨*where* are *the Grampians?*⟩ **f** to take place at a specified time; occur ⟨*the concert* was *last night*⟩ **g** to have a specified qualification ⟨*the leaves* are *green*⟩ ⟨~ *quick*⟩, destination ⟨~ *off*⟩, origin ⟨*she* is *from India*⟩, occupation ⟨*what's he up to?*⟩, function or purpose ⟨*it's for you*⟩ ⟨*it's to cut with*⟩, cost or value ⟨*the book* is *£5*⟩, or standpoint ⟨~ *against terrorism*⟩ **2** to have reality or actuality; exist ⟨*I think, therefore I* am⟩ ⟨*once upon a time there* was *a castle*⟩ ~ *va* **1** – used with the past participle of transitive verbs as a passive-voice auxiliary ⟨*the money* was *found*⟩ ⟨*the house is* ~ing *built*⟩ **2** – used as the auxiliary of the present participle in progressive tenses expressing continuous action ⟨*he* is *reading*⟩ ⟨*I have* been *sleeping*⟩ or arrangement in advance ⟨*we* are *leaving tomorrow*⟩ **3** – used with the past participle of some intransitive verbs as an auxiliary forming archaic perfect tenses ⟨*my father* is *come* – Jane Austen⟩ **4** – used with *to* and an infinitive to express destiny ⟨*he* was *to become famous*⟩ ⟨*they* were *to have been married*⟩, arrangement in advance ⟨*I* am *to interview him today*⟩, obligation or necessity ⟨*you* are *not to smoke*⟩, or possibility ⟨*it* was *nowhere to be found*⟩ ⟨*you* were*n't to know*⟩ *USE vi* (*1*) used regularly as the linking verb of simple ***predication; used in the past subjunctive or often in the indicative to express unreal conditions*** *if I* were *you*〉〈*if I* wasn't *a Catholic – Daily Mirror*〉; often in British English ***used of groups in the plural form*** *Somerset* were *28 for 2 – The Observer*〉 [ME *been*, fr OE *bēon*; akin to OHG *bim* am, L *fui* I have been, *futurus* about to be, *fieri* to become, be done, Gk *phynai* to be born, be by nature, *phyein* to bring forth – more at AM, [1]ARE, IS, WAS, WERE]

be- /bi-/ *prefix* **1** (*vb* → *vb*) on; round; all over 〈be*daub*〉 〈be*smear*〉 **2** (*vb* → *vb*) to a great or greater degree; thoroughly 〈be*fuddle*〉 〈be*rate*〉 〈be*labour*〉 **3** (*adj* → *adj*) wearing (a specified article of dress) 〈be*wigged*〉 〈be*ribboned*〉 〈be*spectacled*〉 **4** (*vb* → *vb*) about; to; at; upon; against; across 〈be*stride*〉 〈be*speak*〉 **5** (*adj, n* → *vb*) make; cause to be; treat as 〈be*little*〉 〈be*fool*〉 〈be*friend*〉 **6** (*n* → *vb*) affect, afflict, provide, or cover with, esp excessively 〈be*calmed*〉 〈be*devil*〉 [ME, fr OE *bi-, be-*; akin to OE *bī* by, near – more at BY]

[1]**beach** /beech/ *n* a (gently sloping) seashore or lakeshore usu covered by sand or pebbles; *esp* the part of this between the high and low water marks [origin unknown]

[2]**beach** *vt* to run or drive ashore

'beach,comber /-,kohmə/ *n* one who searches along a shore for useful or salable flotsam and jetsam; *esp* a white man on the islands of the S Pacific who earns a living by doing this – **beachcomb** *vb*

'beach,head /-,hed/ *n* an area on a hostile shore occupied to secure further landing of troops and supplies

beach-la-mar /,beech lə 'mah/ *n* BÊCHE-DE-MER 2 [by folk etymology]

beacon /'beekən/ *n* **1** a signal fire commonly on a hill, tower, or pole; *also, Br* a high conspicuous hill suitable for or used in the past for such a fire **2a** a signal mark used to guide shipping **b** a radio transmitter emitting signals for the guidance of aircraft **3** a source of light or inspiration [ME *beken*, fr OE *bēacen* sign; akin to OHG *bouhhan* sign]

[1]**bead** /beed/ *n* **1** a small ball (e g of wood or glass) pierced for threading on a string or wire **2** *pl* (a series of prayers and meditations made with) a rosary **3** a small ball-shaped body: e g **a** a drop of liquid **b** a small metal knob on a firearm used as a front sight **4** a projecting rim, band, or moulding ☞ CAR [ME *bede* prayer, prayer bead, fr OE *bed, gebed* prayer; akin to OE *biddan* to entreat, pray – more at BID]

[2]**bead** *vt* **1** to adorn or cover with beads or beading **2** to string together like beads ~ *vi* to form into a bead

beading /'beeding/ *n* **1** material adorned with or consisting of beads **2a** a narrow moulding of rounded often semicircular cross section **b** a moulding that resembles a string of beads **3** a narrow openwork insertion or trimming (e g on lingerie)

beadle /'beedl/ *n* a minor parish official whose duties include ushering and preserving order at services [ME *bedel*, fr OE *bydel*; akin to OHG *butil* bailiff, OE *bēodan* to command – more at BID]

beadroll /'beed,rohl/ *n* a list of names; a catalogue [fr the reading in church of a list of names of people for whom prayers are to be said]

beady /'beedi/ *adj, esp of eyes* small, round, and shiny with interest or greed [[1]BEAD + [1]-Y]

beagle /'beegl/ *n* (any of) a breed of small short-legged smooth-coated hounds [ME *begle*]

beagling /'beegling/ *n* hunting on foot with beagles – **beagler** *n*

beak /beek/ *n* **1a** the bill of a bird; *esp* the bill of a bird of prey adapted for striking and tearing ☞ ANATOMY **b** any of various rigid projecting mouth structures (e g of a turtle); *also* the long sucking mouth of some insects **2** a pointed structure or formation: **a** a metal-tipped beam projecting from the bow of an ancient galley for ramming an enemy ship **b** the pouring spout of a vessel **c** a projection suggesting the beak of a bird **3** the human nose – infml **4** *chiefly Br* **a** a magistrate – slang **b** a schoolmaster – slang [ME *bec*, fr OF, fr L *beccus*, of Gaulish origin] – **beaked** *adj*

beaker /'beekə/ *n* **1** a large drinking cup with a wide mouth; a mug **2** a cylindrical flat-bottomed vessel usu with a pouring lip that is used esp by chemists and pharmacists [ME *biker*, fr ON *bikarr*, prob fr OS *bikeri*; akin to OHG *behhari* beaker; both fr a prehistoric WGmc word borrowed fr ML *bicarius* beaker, fr Gk *bikos* earthen jug]

'Beaker ,Folk /'beekə/ *n pl* a prehistoric people living in Europe in the early Bronze Age whose culture was characterized by finely decorated beakers buried with their dead

,be-all and 'end-all *n the* chief factor; *the* essential element – often derog

[1]**beam** /beem/ *n* **1a** a long piece of heavy often squared timber suitable for use in construction **b** the part of a plough to which the handles, standard, and coulter are attached **c** the bar of a balance from which scales hang **d** any of the principal horizontal supporting members of a building or across a ship **e** the width of a ship at its widest part **f** an oscillating lever joining an engine piston rod to a crank, esp in one type of stationary steam engine (a ~ engine) **2a** a ray or shaft of radiation, esp light **b** a collection of nearly parallel rays (e g X rays) or of particles (e g electrons) moving in nearly parallel paths **c** (the course indicated by) a radio signal transmitted continuously in one direction as an aircraft navigation aid **3** the main stem of a deer's antler **4** the width of the buttocks 〈*broad in the* ~〉 – infml [ME *beem*, fr OE *bēam* tree, beam; akin to OHG *boum* tree] – **off (the) beam** wrong, irrelevant – **on the beam** proceeding or operating correctly

[2]**beam** *vt* **1** to emit in beams or as a beam, esp of light **2** to aim (a broadcast) by directional aerials ~ *vi* to smile with joy

,beam-'ends *n pl, Br* buttocks – infml – **on her beam-ends** *of a ship* about to capsize

beamer /'beemə/ *n* a usu intimidatory delivery of the ball in cricket that passes or hits the batsman at above waist height before it bounces [[2]BEAM + [2]-ER]

beamy /'beemi/ *adj, of a ship* broad in the beam

bean /been/ *n* **1a** (the often edible seed of) any of various erect or climbing leguminous plants **b** a bean pod used when immature as a vegetable **c** (a plant producing) any of various seeds or fruits that resemble beans or bean pods **2a** a valueless item 〈*not worth a* ~〉 **b** the smallest possible amount of money 〈*gave up my job and haven't a* ~〉 ***USE*** (*2*) infml [ME *bene*, fr OE *bēan*; akin to OHG *bōna* bean]

'bean,bag /-,bag/ *n* a small fabric bag that is filled with beans and used in games or as a toy

'bean,feast /-,feest/ *n, Br* a festivity, celebration – infml

beano /'beenoh/ *n, pl* **beanos** a beanfeast – infml [by shortening & alter.]

'bean,pole /-,pohl/ *n* a very tall thin person – infml

'bean ,shoots *n pl* BEAN SPROUTS

'bean ,sprouts *n pl* the sprouts of bean seeds, esp of the mung bean, used as a vegetable

[1]**bear** /beə/ *n, pl* **bears,** (*1*) **bears** *or esp collectively* **bear 1** any of a family of large heavy mammals that have long shaggy hair and a short tail and feed largely on fruit and insects as well as on flesh **2** a surly, uncouth, or shambling person **3** one who sells securities or commodities in expectation of a fall in price – compare [1]BULL 2 [ME *bere,* fr OE *bera;* akin to OE *brūn* brown; (3) prob fr proverbial phrase *selling the bearskin before catching the bear*]

[2]**bear** *vb* **bore** /baw/; **borne** *also* **born** /bawn/ *vt* **1a** to carry, transport ⟨~ *gifts*⟩ – often in combination ⟨*air*borne *troops*⟩ **b** to carry or own as equipment ⟨~ *arms*⟩ **c** to entertain mentally ⟨~ *malice*⟩ **d** to behave, conduct **e** to have or show as a feature ⟨~ *scars*⟩ ⟨~ *no relationship*⟩ **f** to give as testimony ⟨~ *false witness*⟩ **g** to have as an identification ⟨bore *the name of John*⟩ **2a** to give birth to – compare BORN **b** to produce as yield ⟨~ *apples*⟩ **c** to contain – often in combination ⟨*oil-*bearing *shale*⟩ **3a** to support the weight of **b** to accept the presence of; tolerate ⟨~ *pain*⟩ ⟨*couldn't* ~ *his wife's family*⟩ **c** to sustain, incur ⟨~ *the cost*⟩ ⟨~ *the responsibility*⟩ **d** to admit of; allow ⟨*it won't* ~ *repeating*⟩ ~ *vi* **1a** to become directed ⟨*bring guns to* ~ *on a target*⟩ – compare BRING TO BEAR **b** to go or extend in a usu specified direction ⟨*the road* ~s *to the right*⟩ **2** to apply, have relevance ⟨*facts* ~ing *on the situation*⟩ **3** to support weight or strain **4** to produce fruit; yield [ME *beren,* fr OE *beran;* akin to OHG *beran* to carry, L *ferre,* Gk *pherein*] – **bear fruit** to come to satisfying fruition or production – **bear in mind** to think of, esp as a warning; remember – **bear with** to show patience or indulgence towards ⟨bear with *the old bore for a while longer*⟩

'bear,baiting /-,bayting/ *n* the practice of setting dogs on a captive bear that was formerly a popular entertainment

[1]**beard** /biəd/ *n* **1** the hair that grows on the lower part of a man's face, usu excluding the moustache **2** a hairy or bristly appendage or tuft (e g on a goat's chin) [ME *berd,* fr OE *beard;* akin to OHG *bart* beard, L *barba*] – **bearded** *adj,* **beardedness** *n,* **beardless** *adj*

[2]**beard** *vt* to confront and oppose with boldness, resolution, and often effrontery; defy [[1]*beard;* fr idea of facing an opponent]

bear down *vt* to overcome, overwhelm ~ *vi* **1** to exert full strength and concentrated attention **2** *of a woman in childbirth* to exert concentrated downward pressure in an effort to expel the child from the womb – **bear down on 1** to weigh heavily on **2** to come towards purposefully or threateningly

bearer /'beərə/ *n* **1** a porter **2** a plant yielding fruit **3** a pallbearer **4** one holding an order for payment, esp a bank note or cheque [[2]BEAR + [2]-ER]

'bear ,garden *n* a scene of great noise or tumult [fr the rowdiness of bearbaiting]

'bear ,hug *n* a rough tight embrace

bearing /'beəring/ *n* **1** the manner in which one bears or conducts oneself **2** the act, power, or time of bringing forth offspring or fruit **3a** an object, surface, or point that supports **b** a machine part in which another part turns or slides – often pl with sing. meaning **4** an emblem or figure on a heraldic shield **5a** the compass direction of one point (with respect to another) **b** a determination of position **c** *pl* comprehension of one's position, environment, or situation ⟨*lost his* ~s⟩ **d** a relation, connection, significance – usu + *on* ⟨*has no* ~ *on the matter*⟩

'bearing ,rein *n* a checkrein

bearish /'beərish/ *adj* marked by, tending to cause, or fearful of falling prices (e g in a stock market) [[1]BEAR + -ISH] – **bearishly** *adv,* **bearishness** *n*

béar,naise 'sauce /,bayə'nayz/ *n, often cap B* a rich sauce made with butter and egg yolks, and flavoured with wine, onion and tarragon [F *béarnaise,* fem of *béarnais* of Béarn, fr *Béarn,* region & former province of France]

bear out *vt* to confirm, substantiate ⟨*research* bore out *his theory*⟩

'bear,skin /-,skin/ *n* an article made of the skin of a bear; *esp* a tall black military hat worn by the Brigade of Guards ☞ GARMENT

bear up *vt* to support, encourage ~ *vi* to summon up courage, resolution, or strength ⟨bearing up *under the strain*⟩

beast /beest/ *n* **1a** an animal as distinguished from a plant **b** a 4-legged mammal as distinguished from human beings, lower vertebrates, and invertebrates **c** an animal under human control **2** a contemptible person [ME *beste,* fr OF, fr L *bestia*]

beastings /'beestingz/ *n pl but sing or pl in constr, NAm* beestings

[1]**beastly** /'beestli/ *adj* **1** bestial **2** abominable, disagreeable ⟨~ *weather*⟩ – **beastliness** *n*

[2]**beastly** *adv* very ⟨*a* ~ *cold day*⟩ – infml

,beast of 'burden *n* an animal employed to carry heavy material or perform other heavy work (e g pulling a plough)

[1]**beat** /beet/ *vb* **beat; beaten** /'beet(ə)n/, **beat** *vt* **1** to strike repeatedly: **a** to hit repeatedly so as to inflict pain – often + *up* **b** to strike directly against (sthg) forcefully and repeatedly ⟨*shores* ~en *by heavy waves*⟩ **c** to flap or thrash at vigorously ⟨*a trapped bird* ~ing *the air*⟩ **d** to strike at or range over (as if) in order to rouse game **e** to mix (esp food) by stirring; whip **f** to strike repeatedly in order to produce music or a signal **2a** to drive or force by blows ⟨*to* ~ *off the savage dogs*⟩ **b** to pound into a powder, paste, or pulp **c** to make by repeated treading or driving over ⟨~ *a path*⟩ **d(1)** to dislodge by repeated hitting ⟨~ *the dust from the carpet*⟩ **(2)** to lodge securely by repeated striking ⟨~ *a stake into the ground*⟩ **e** to shape by beating; *esp* to flatten thin by blows ⟨*gold* ~en *into foil*⟩ **f** to sound or express, esp by drumbeat ⟨~ *a tattoo*⟩ **3** to cause to strike or tap repeatedly ⟨~ *his foot nervously on the ground*⟩ **4a** to overcome, defeat; *also* to surpass **b** to prevail despite ⟨~ *the odds*⟩ **c** to leave dispirited, irresolute, or hopeless ⟨*a failure at 50, a* ~en *man*⟩ **d** to be or to bowl a ball that is too good for (a batsman) to hit **5** to act ahead of, usu so as to forestall – chiefly in *beat someone to it* **6** to indicate by beating **7** to bewilder, baffle – infml ~ *vi* **1a** to dash, strike ⟨*the rain was* ~ing *on the roof*⟩ **b** to glare or strike with oppressive intensity ⟨*the sun was* ~ing *down*⟩ **2a** to pulsate, throb **b** to sound on

being struck ⟨*the drums were ~ing*⟩ **3a** to strike the air; flap ⟨*the birds wings ~ frantically*⟩ **b** to strike cover or range (as if) in order to find or rouse game **4** to progress with much difficulty; *specif, of a sailing vessel* to make way at sea against the wind by a series of alternate tacks across the wind [ME *beten*, fr OE *bēatan*; akin to OHG *bōzan* to beat, L *-futare* to beat, *fustis* club] – **beat about the bush** to fail to come to the point in conversation by talking indirectly or evasively – **beat it** to hurry away; scram – infml – **beat one's brains out** to try intently to resolve sthg difficult by thinking

[2]**beat** *n* **1a** a single stroke or blow, esp in a series; *also* a pulsation, throb **b** a sound produced (as if) by beating **2** each of the pulsations of amplitude produced by the mixing of sine waves (e g sound or radio waves) having different frequencies **3a** (the rhythmic effect of) a metrical or rhythmic stress in poetry or music **b** the tempo indicated to a musical performer **4** an area or route regularly patrolled, esp by a policeman **5** TACK 3b **6** a deadbeat – infml – **beatless** *adj*

[3]**beat** *adj* **1** of or being beatniks ⟨*~ poets*⟩ **2** exhausted – infml [short for *beaten*, pp of *beat*]

[4]**beat** *n* a beatnik

beaten /'beet(ə)n/ *adj* **1** hammered into a desired shape ⟨*~ gold*⟩ **2** defeated

beater /'beetə/ *n* **1a** any of various hand-held implements for whisking or beating ⟨*a carpet ~*⟩ ⟨*an egg ~*⟩ **b** a rotary blade attached to an electric mixer **c** a stick for beating a gong **2** one who strikes bushes or other cover to rouse game [[1]BEAT + [2]-ER]

beatific /,bee·ə'tifik/ *adj* **1** of, possessing, or imparting beatitude **2** having a blissful or benign appearance; saintly, angelic ⟨*a ~ smile*⟩ [L *beatificus* making happy, fr *beatus* happy, fr pp of *beare* to bless; akin to L *bonus* good – more at BOUNTY] – **beatifically** *adv*

beatify /bee'atifie/ *vt* **1** to make supremely happy **2** to authorize the veneration of (a dead person) by Catholics by giving the title 'Blessed" [MF *beatifier*, fr LL *beatificare*, fr L *beatus*] – **beatification** /-fi'kaysh(ə)n/ *n*

beating /'beeting/ *n* **1** injury or damage inflicted by striking with repeated blows **2** a throbbing **3** a defeat

beatitude /bi'atityoohd, -choohd/ *n* **1a** a state of utmost bliss **b** – used as a title for a primate, esp of an Eastern church **2** any of a series of sayings of Jesus beginning in the Authorized version of the Bible 'Blessed are" [L *beatitudo*, fr *beatus*]

beatnik /'beetnik/ *n* a person, esp in the 1950s and 1960s, who rejected the moral attitudes of established society (e g by unconventional behaviour and dress) [[3]*beat* + *-nik*]

beau /boh/ *n, pl* **beaux, beaus** /bohz/ **1** a lover **2** *archaic* a dandy [F, fr *beau* beautiful, fr L *bellus* pretty]

'**Beaufort** ,**scale** /'bohfawt/ *n* a scale in which the force of the wind is indicated by numbers from 0 to 12 [Sir Francis *Beaufort* †1857 E admiral]

,**beau i'deal** *n, pl* **beau ideals** the perfect type or model – often + *of* [F *beau idéal* ideal beauty]

Beaujolais /'bohzhəlay/ *n* a chiefly red table wine made in southern Burgundy in France [F, fr *Beaujolais*, region of central France]

[1]**beaut** /byooht/ *n, chiefly Austr & NZ* BEAUTY 3 – infml

[2]**beaut** *adj, Austr & NZ* fine, marvellous – infml

beauteous /'byoohti·əs, -tyəs/ *adj, archaic* beautiful [ME, fr *beaute*] – **beauteously** *adv*, **beauteousness** *n*

beautician /byooh'tish(ə)n/ *n* sby who gives beauty treatments [*beauty* + *-ician*]

beautiful /'byoohtif(ə)l/ *adj* **1** having qualities of beauty; exciting aesthetic pleasure or keenly delighting the senses **2** generally pleasing; excellent – **beautifully** *adv*, **beautifulness** *n*

beautiful people *n pl, often cap B&P* members of the jet set

beautify /'byoohtifie/ *vt* to make beautiful; embellish – **beautifier** /-,fie·ə/ **beautification** /-fi'kaysh(ə)n/ *n*

beauty /'byoohti/ *n* **1** the qualities in a person or thing that give pleasure to the senses or pleasurably exalt the mind or spirit; loveliness **2** a beautiful person or thing; *esp* a beautiful woman **3** a brilliant, extreme, or conspicuous example or instance ⟨*that mistake was a ~*⟩ **4** a particularly advantageous or excellent quality ⟨*the ~ of my idea is that it costs so little*⟩ [ME *beaute*, fr OF *biauté*, fr *bel, biau* beautiful, fr L *bellus* pretty; akin to L *bonus* good – more at BOUNTY]

'**beauty** ,**sleep** *n* sleep considered as being beneficial to a person's beauty

'**beauty** ,**spot** *n* a beautiful scenic area

beaux esprits /,bohz e'spree (*Fr* boz ɛspri)/ *pl of* BEL ESPRIT

[1]**beaver** /'beevə/ *n, pl* **beavers,** (*1a*) **beavers** *or esp collectively* **beaver** **1a** a large semiaquatic rodent mammal that has webbed hind feet, a broad flat tail, and builds dams and underwater lodges **b** the fur or pelt of the beaver **2** a hat made of beaver fur or a fabric imitation **3** a heavy fabric of felted wool napped on both sides **4** an energetic hard-working person [ME *bever*, fr OE *beofor*; akin to OHG *bibar* beaver, OE *brūn* brown]

[2]**beaver** *vi* to work energetically ⟨*~ing away at the problem*⟩

[3]**beaver** *n* **1** a piece of armour protecting the lower part of the face **2** a helmet visor [ME *baviere*, fr MF]

'**beaver**,**board** /-,bawd/ *n* a fibreboard used esp for partitions and ceilings [fr *Beaver Board*, a trademark]

bebop /'bee,bop/ *n* bop [imit] – **bebopper** *n*

becalm /bi'kahm/ *vt* to keep motionless by lack of wind – usu pass [*be-* + [3]*calm*]

[1]**because** /bi'koz, bə-, -kəz/ *conj* **1** for the reason that; since ⟨*he rested ~ he was tired*⟩ **2** and the proof is that ⟨*they must be in, ~ the light's on*⟩ [ME *because that, because*, fr *by cause that*]

[2]**because** *adv* because of sthg forgotten or unmentionable – infml ⟨*I did it, well, just ~*⟩

be'cause of *prep* **1** as a result of **2** for the sake of

beccafico /,bekə'feekoh/ *n, pl* **beccaficos, beccaficoes** any of various European songbirds that are sometimes eaten [It, fr *beccare* to peck + *fico* fig, fr L *ficus*]

béchamel /'bayshəmel (*Fr* beʃamɛːl)/ *n* a white sauce made with roux and milk in which vegetables and herbs have been infused – compare VELOUTÉ [F *sauce béchamelle*, fr Louis de *Béchamel* †1703 F courtier]

bêche-de-mer /,besh də 'meə/ *n* **1** a trepang **2** *cap*

B&M a pidgin English used esp in the W Pacific [F, lit., sea grub]

[1]**beck** /bek/ *n, NEng* a brook; *esp* a pebbly mountain stream [ME *bek*, fr ON *bekkr*; akin to OE *bæc* brook, OHG *bah*, MIr *būal* flowing water]

[2]**beck** *n* [ME, nod, bow, gesture of command, fr *becken, beknen*] – **at someone's beck and call** in continual readiness to obey any command from sby

becket /'bekit/ *n* a bracket, loop of rope, hook, etc for securing tackle or spars [origin unknown]

beckon /'bekən/ *vi* **1** to summon or signal, typically with a wave or nod **2** to appear inviting ~*vt* to beckon to [ME *beknen*, fr OE *biecnan*, fr *bēacen* sign – more at BEACON] – **beckon** *n*

become /bi'kum/ *vb* **became** /bi'kaym/; **become** *vi* **1** to come into existence **2** to come to be ⟨~ *sick*⟩ ⟨became *party leader*⟩ ~*vt* to suit or be suitable to ⟨*her clothes* ~ *her*⟩ [ME *becomen* to come to, become, fr OE *becuman*, fr *be-* + *cuman* to come] – **become of** to happen to ⟨*what* became of *that girl who always came top?*⟩

becoming /bi'kuming/ *adj* suitable, fitting; *esp* attractively suitable – **becomingly** *adv*

[1]**bed** /bed/ *n* **1a** a piece of furniture on or in which one may lie and sleep and which usu includes bedstead, mattress, and bedding **b** a place of sexual relations; *also* LOVEMAKING 2 **c** a place for sleeping or resting **d** sleep; *also* a time for sleeping ⟨*took a walk before* ~⟩ **e** the use of a bed for the night **2** a flat or level surface: e g **a** (plants grown in) a plot of ground, esp in a garden, prepared for plants **b** the bottom of a body of water; *also* an area of sea or lake bottom supporting a heavy growth of a specified organism ⟨*an oyster* ~⟩ **3** a supporting surface or structure; *esp* the foundation that supports a road or railway **4** STRATUM 1a **5** a mass or heap resembling a bed ⟨*a* ~ *of ashes*⟩; *esp* a heap on which sthg else is laid ⟨*coleslaw on a* ~ *of lettuce*⟩ [ME, fr OE *bedd*; akin to OHG *betti* bed, L *fodere* to dig] – **in bed** in the act of sexual intercourse ⟨*found him* in bed *with another woman*⟩

[2]**bed** *vb* **-dd-** *vt* **1a** to provide with a bed or bedding; settle in sleeping quarters **b** to go to bed with, usu for sexual intercourse **2a** to embed **b** to plant or arrange (garden plants, vegetable plants, etc) in beds – often + *out* **c** to base, establish **3** to lay flat or in a layer ~*vi* **1a** to find or make sleeping accommodation **b** to go to bed **2** to form a layer **3** to lie flat or flush *USE* (*vt 1a; vi 1, 2*) often + *down*

,bed and 'breakfast *n, Br* a night's lodging and breakfast the following morning

'bed,bug /-,bug/ *n* a wingless bloodsucking bug that sometimes infests beds

'bed,clothes /-,klohdhz/ *n pl* the covers (e g sheets and blankets) used on a bed

bedder /'bedə/ *n* **1** a woman servant, employed esp to make beds, at a Cambridge college – compare GYP, SCOUT **2** a bedding plant

[1]**bedding** /'beding/ *n* **1** bedclothes **2** a bottom layer; a foundation **3** material to provide a bed for livestock **4** a stratified rock formation [ME, fr OE, fr *bedd*]

[2]**bedding** *adj, of a plant* appropriate or adapted for culture in open-air beds [fr gerund of [2]*bed*]

beddy-byes /'bedi ,biez/ *n pl but sing or pl in constr* bed – used by or to children [blend of *bed* and *bye-byes*]

bedeck /bi'dek/ *vt* to clothe with finery; deck out

bedevil /bi'devl/ *vt* **1** to possess (as if) with a devil; bewitch **2** to change for the worse; spoil, frustrate **3** to torment maliciously; harass – **bedevilment** *n*

'bed,fellow /-,feloh/ *n* **1** one who shares a bed **2** a close associate; an ally ⟨*political* ~s⟩

bedlam /'bedləm/ *n* a place, scene, or state of uproar and confusion [*Bedlam*, popular name for the Hospital of St Mary of Bethlehem, London, a lunatic asylum, fr ME *Bedlem* Bethlehem] – **bedlam** *adj*

'bed ,linen *n* the sheets and pillowcases used on a bed

'bed,maker /-,maykə/ *n* BEDDER 1

'bed,mate /-,mayt/ *n* one who shares one's bed; *esp* a sexual partner

,bed of 'roses *n* a place or situation of agreeable ease

bedouin, beduin /'bedwin, 'bedooh·in/ *n, pl* **bedouins,** *esp collectively* **bedouin** *often cap* a nomadic Arab of the Arabian, Syrian, or N African deserts [F *bédouin*, fr Ar *badāwi, bidwān*, pl of *badawi* desert dweller]

'bed,pan /-,pan/ *n* a shallow vessel used by a person in bed for urination or defecation

'bed,post /-,pohst/ *n* a usu turned or carved post of a bedstead

bedraggle /bi'dragl/ *vt* to wet thoroughly [*be-* + *draggle* (to make wet by dragging), freq of *drag*]

be'draggled *adj* **1** left wet and limp (as if) by rain **2** soiled and stained (as if) by trailing in mud

'bed,ridden /-,rid(ə)n/ *adj* confined (e g by illness) to bed [alter. of ME *bedrede, bedreden*, fr OE *bedreda*, fr *bedreda* one confined to bed, fr *bedd* bed + *-rida, -reda* rider, fr *rīdan* to ride]

'bed,rock /-,rok/ *n* **1** the solid rock underlying unconsolidated surface materials (e g soil) **2** the basis of sthg – **bedrock** *adj*

[1]**'bedroom** /-,roohm, -room/ *n* a room furnished with a bed and intended primarily for sleeping

[2]**bedroom** *adj* dealing with, suggestive of, or inviting sexual relations ⟨*a* ~ *farce*⟩

,bedset'tee /-se'tee/ *n, Br* an upholstered sofa that can be converted into a single or double bed usu by lowering its hinged back – compare STUDIO COUCH

'bed,side /-,sied/ *adj* **1** of or conducted at the bedside **2** suitable for a person in bed ⟨~ *reading*⟩

,bedside 'manner *n* the manner with which a medical doctor deals with his/her patients

'bed-,sit *n, Br* a bed-sitter – infml

,bed-'sitter *n, Br* a single room serving as both bedroom and sitting room [*bed*room + *sitt*ing room + *-er*]

,bed-'sitting-,room *n, Br* a bed-sitter

'bed,sore /-,saw/ *n* a sore caused by prolonged pressure on the tissue of a bedridden invalid

'bed,spread /-,spred/ *n* a usu ornamental cloth cover for a bed

'bed,spring /-,spring/ *n* a spring supporting a mattress

'bed,stead /-,sted/ *n* the framework of a bed [ME *bedstede*, fr *bed* + *stede* place – more at STEAD]

'bed,straw /-,straw/ *n* any of a genus of plants of the madder family having angled stems, opposite or whorled leaves, and small flowers [fr its use for mattresses]

'bed ,table *n* a small table placed at the bedside; *also* a table that fits over a bed and has an adjustable height

beduin /'bedwin, 'bedooh·in/ *n, pl* **beduins,** *esp collectively* **beduin** a bedouin

'bed-,wetting *n* involuntary discharge of urine occurring in bed during sleep – **bed wetter** *n*

bee /bee/ *n* **1** a social 4-winged insect often kept in hives for the honey that it produces; *broadly* any of numerous insects that differ from the related wasps, esp in the heavier hairier body and legs and in sometimes having a pollen basket ☞ ANATOMY **2** *NAm* a gathering of people for a usu specified purpose ⟨*a sewing* ~⟩ [ME, fr OE *bēo*; akin to OHG *bīa* bee, Lith *bitis*] – **beelike** *adj* – **bee in one's bonnet** an obsession about a specified subject or idea

Beeb /beeb/ *n, Br* – used for *the* BBC; humor [by shortening & alter.]

'bee,bread /-,bred/ *n* bitter yellowish brown pollen (mixed with honey by bees as food)

beech /beech/ *n, pl* **beeches, beech** (the wood of) any of a genus of hardwood deciduous trees with smooth grey bark and small edible triangular nuts [ME *beche*, fr OE *bēce*; akin to OE *bōc* beech, OHG *buohha*, L *fagus*, Gk *phēgos* oak] – **beechen** *adj*

beech mast *n* the nuts of the beech (when lying on the ground)

'bee ,eater *n* (any of) a family of brightly coloured slender-billed insect-eating chiefly tropical Old World birds

[1]**beef** /beef/ *n, pl* **beefs,** *(2a)* **beeves** /beevz/, **beef,** *NAm chiefly* **beefs** **1** the flesh of a bullock, cow, or other adult domestic bovine animal ☞ MEAT **2a** an ox, cow, or bull in a (nearly) full-grown state; *esp* a bullock or cow fattened for food ⟨*a herd of good* ~⟩ **b** a dressed carcass of a beef animal **3** muscular flesh; brawn **4** a complaint – infml [ME, fr OF *buef* ox, beef, fr L *bov-*, *bos* head of cattle – more at [1]cow]

[2]**beef** *vt* to add weight, strength, or power to – usu + *up* ~ *vi* to complain – infml

'beef,cake /-,kayk/ *n* a photographic display of muscular male physiques – infml; compare CHEESECAKE

'beef,eater /-,eetə/ *n* YEOMAN OF THE GUARD – not used technically [*beef* + *eater*; orig sense, a well-fed servant]

'beefsteak ,fungus /'beef,stayk/ *n* a bright red edible pore fungus that grows on dead trees

'beef,wood /-,wood/ *n* (a tree yielding) any of several hard heavy reddish Australian or W Indian woods

beefy /'beefi/ *adj* **1** full of beef **2** brawny, powerful

beehive /'bee,hiev/ *n* **1** HIVE 1 **2** a scene of crowded activity – **beehive** *adj*

'bee,line /-,lien/ *n* a straight direct course [fr the belief that nectar-laden bees return to their hives in a direct line]

been /bin, been; *strong* been/ *past part of* BE; *specif* paid a visit ⟨*has the postman* ~*?*⟩

'bee ,orchid *n* any of several European plants of the orchid family with velvety flowers resembling bees

[1]**beep** /beep/ *n* a sound (e g from a horn or electronic device) that serves as a signal or warning [imit]

[2]**beep** *vi* **1** to sound a horn **2** to make a beep ~ *vt* to cause (e g a horn) to sound – **beeper** *n*

beer /biə/ *n* **1** an alcoholic drink brewed from fermented malt flavoured with hops **2** a carbonated nonalcoholic or fermented slightly alcoholic drink flavoured with roots or other plant parts ⟨*ginger* ~⟩ [ME *ber*, fr OE *bēor*; akin to OHG *bior* beer]

,beer and 'skittles *n pl but sing or pl in constr* a situation of agreeable ease

beery /'biəri/ *adj* **1** affected or caused by beer ⟨~ *voices*⟩ **2** smelling or tasting of beer ⟨*a* ~ *tavern*⟩

,bee's 'knees *n pl but sing in constr* one who or that which is outstandingly good – infml; + *the*

beestings, *NAm* **beastings** /'beestingz/ *n pl but sing or pl in constr* the colostrum, esp of a cow [ME *bestynge*, fr OE *bȳsting*, fr *bēost*]

beeswax /'beez,waks/ *n* a yellowish plastic substance secreted by bees that is used by them for constructing honeycombs and is used as a wood polish

beet /beet/ *n* **1** any of various plants of the goosefoot family with a swollen root used as a vegetable, as a source of sugar, or for forage **2** *NAm* beetroot [ME *bete*, fr OE *bēte*, fr L *beta*]

[1]**beetle** /'beetl/ *n* **1** any of an order of insects that have 4 wings of which the front pair are modified into stiff coverings that protect the back pair at rest **2** a game in which the players attempt to be the first to complete a stylized drawing of a beetle in accordance with the throwing of a dice [ME *betylle*, fr OE *bitula*, fr *bītan* to bite]

[2]**beetle** *vi* **beetling** /'beetling/ *Br* to move swiftly ⟨~d *off down the road*⟩ – infml

[3]**beetle** *n* a heavy wooden tool for hammering or ramming [ME *betel*, fr OE *bīetel*; akin to OE *bēatan* to beat]

beetling /'beetling/ *adj* prominent and overhanging ⟨~ *brows*⟩ [ME *bitel-browed* with overhanging brows, prob fr *betylle, bitel* beetle]

beetroot /'beetrooht/ *n, pl* **beetroot, beetroots** *chiefly Br* a cultivated beet with a red edible root that is a common salad vegetable

befall /bi'fawl/ *vb* **befell** /bi'fel/; **befallen** /bi'fawlən/ to happen (to), esp as if by fate [ME *befallen*, fr OE *befeallan*, fr *be-* + *feallan* to fall]

befit /bi'fit/ *vt* **-tt-** to be proper or becoming to

befitting /bi'fiting/ *adj* suitable, appropriate – **befittingly** *adv*

befog /bi'fog/ *vt* **-gg-** **1** to make foggy; obscure **2** to confuse

[1]**before** /bi'faw/ *adv* **1** so as to be in advance of others; ahead **2** earlier in time; previously ⟨*haven't we met* ~*?*⟩ ⟨*had left a week* ~⟩ [ME, adv & prep, fr OE *beforan*, fr *be-* + *foran* before, fr *fore*]

[2]**before** *prep* **1a** IN FRONT OF **b** under the jurisdiction or consideration of ⟨*the case* ~ *the court*⟩ **2** preceding in time; earlier than **3** in a higher or more important position than ⟨*put quantity* ~ *quality*⟩ **4** under the onslaught of

[3]**before** *conj* **1** earlier than the time when **2** rather than

beforehand /bi'faw,hand/ *adv or adj* **1** in anticipation **2** ahead of time – **beforehandedness** *n*

befriend /bi'frend/ *vt* to become a friend of purposely; show kindness and understanding to

befuddle /bi'fudl/ *vb* **befuddling** /bi'fudling/ **1** to muddle or stupefy (as if) with drink **2** to confuse, perplex – **befuddlement** *n*

beg /beg/ *vb* **-gg-** *vt* **1** to ask for as a charity ⟨~ged *alms*⟩ **2** to ask earnestly (for); entreat ⟨~ *a favour*⟩

⟨~ged *her to stay*⟩ **3a** to evade, sidestep ⟨~ged *the real problems*⟩ **b** to assume as established or proved without justification ⟨~ *the question*⟩ ~ *vi* **1** to ask for alms or charity **2a** to ask earnestly ⟨~ged *for mercy*⟩ **b** to ask permission – usu + an infinitive ⟨*I* ~ *to differ*⟩ **3** *of a dog* to sit up and hold out the forepaws [ME *beggen*, prob alter. of OE *bedecian*]

beget /bi'get/ *vt* **-tt-; begot**/bi'got/, *archaic* **begat** /bi'gat/; **begotten** /bi'gotn/, **begot** **1** to procreate as the father; sire **2** to produce as an effect; cause [ME *begeten*, alter. of *beyeten*, fr OE *bigietan* – more at GET] – **begetter** *n*

[1]**beggar** /'begə/ *n* **1** one who lives by asking for gifts **2** a pauper **3** a person; *esp* a fellow – infml ⟨*lucky* ~⟩ [ME *beggere, beggare*, fr *beggen* to beg + *-ere, -are* -er; (3) partly euphemism for *bugger*]

[2]**beggar** *vt* **1** to reduce to beggary **2** to exceed the resources or abilities of ⟨*it* ~s *description*⟩

'**beggarly** /-li/ *adj* **1** marked by extreme poverty **2** contemptibly mean, petty, or paltry – **beggarliness** *n*

beggary /'begəri/ *n* poverty, penury [[1]BEGGAR + [2]-Y]

begin /bi'gin/ *vb* **-nn-; began** /bi'gan/; **begun** /bi'gun/ *vi* **1a** to do the first part of an action; start ⟨*if you're all ready, we'll* ~⟩ **b** to undergo initial steps ⟨*work on the project* began *in May*⟩ **2a** to come into existence; arise ⟨*the war* began *in 1939*⟩ **b** to have a starting point ⟨*the alphabet* ~s *with* A⟩ ~ *vt* **1** to set about the activity of ⟨*the children* began *laughing*⟩ **2** to call into being; found ⟨~ *a dynasty*⟩ **3** to come first in ⟨A ~s *the alphabet*⟩ **4** to do or succeed in, in the least degree ⟨*can't* ~ *to describe her beauty*⟩ [ME *beginnen*, fr OE *beginnan*; akin to OHG *biginnan* to begin, OE *onginnan*] – **beginner** *n*

beginning /bi'gining/ *n* **1** the point at which sthg begins; the start **2** the first part **3** the origin, source **4** a rudimentary stage or early period – usu pl

beg off *vi* to ask to be released from sthg

begone /bi'gon/ *vi* to go away; depart – usu in the infin or esp the imperative [ME, fr *be gone* (imper)]

begonia /bi'gohni·ə/ *n* any of a large genus of tropical plants that have asymmetrical leaves and are widely cultivated as ornamental garden and house plants [NL, genus name, fr Michel *Bégon* †1710 F governor of Santo Domingo]

begorra /bi'gorə/ *interj, Irish* – used as a mild oath [euphemism for *by God*]

begrudge /bi'gruj/ *vt* **1** to give or concede reluctantly ⟨*he* ~d *every minute taken from his work*⟩ **2** to envy the pleasure or enjoyment of ⟨*they* ~ *him his wealth*⟩ – **begrudger** *n*, **begrudgingly** *adv*

beguile /bi'giel/ *vt* **1** to deceive, hoodwink **2** to while away, esp by some agreeable occupation **3** to please or persuade by the use of wiles; charm ⟨*her ways* ~d *him*⟩ ~ *vi* to deceive by wiles – **beguilement** *n*, **beguiler** *n*, **beguilingly** *adv*

beguine /bi'geen/ *n* a vigorous popular W Indian dance [AmerF *béguine*, fr F *béguin* flirtation]

behalf /bi'hahf/ *n* [ME, benefit, support, fr *by* + *half* half, side] – **on behalf of,** *NAm* **in behalf of** in the interest of; as a representative of

behave /bi'hayv/ *vb* **1** to conduct (oneself) in a specified way ⟨*she has been* behaving *badly*⟩ **2** to conduct (oneself) properly ⟨*you must learn to* ~ *yourself in company*⟩ [ME *behaven*, fr *be-* + *haven* to have, hold – more at HAVE] – **behaver** *n*

behaviour, *NAm chiefly* **behavior** /bi'hayvyə/ *n* **1a** anything that an organism does involving action and response to stimulation **b** the response of an individual, group, or species to its environment **2** the way in which sthg (e g a machine) functions [alter. of ME *behavour*, fr *behaven*] – **behavioural** *adj*, **behaviourally** *adv*

behaviourism /bi'hayvyə,riz(ə)m/ *n* a theory holding that the proper concern of psychology is the objective study of behaviour and that information derived from introspection is not admissible psychological evidence

behaviour therapy *n* therapy intended to change an abnormal behaviour (e g a phobia) by conditioning the patient to respond normally

behead /bi'hed/ *vt* to cut off the head of; decapitate

behest /bi'hest/ *n* an urgent prompting or insistent request ⟨*returned home at the* ~ *of his friends*⟩ [ME, promise, command, fr OE *behǣs* promise, fr *behātan* to promise, fr *be-* + *hātan* to command, promise]

[1]**behind** /bi'hiend/ *adv* **1a** in the place, situation, or time that is being or has been departed from ⟨*I've left the keys* ~ – *SEU S*⟩ **b** in, to, or towards the back ⟨*look* ~⟩ **2a** in a secondary or inferior position **b** IN ARREARS ⟨~ *in his payments*⟩ **c** slow [ME *behinde*, fr OE *behindan*, fr *be-* + *hindan* from behind; akin to OE *hinder* behind – more at [2]HIND]

[2]**behind** *prep* **1a(1)** at or to the back or rear of ⟨*look* ~ *you*⟩ **(2)** remaining after (sby who has departed) ⟨*left a great name* ~ *him*⟩ **b** obscured by ⟨*malice* ~ *the mask of friendship*⟩ **2** – used to indicate backwardness ⟨~ *his classmates in performance*⟩, delay ⟨~ *schedule*⟩, or deficiency ⟨*lagged* ~ *last year's sales*⟩ **3a** in the background of ⟨*the conditions* ~ *the strike*⟩ **b** in a supporting position at the back of ⟨*solidly* ~ *their candidate*⟩ – **behind the times** old-fashioned, out-of-date

[3]**behind** *n* the buttocks – slang [[1]*behind*]

behindhand /bi'hiend,hand/ *adj* **1** behind schedule; IN ARREARS ⟨*he was* ~ *with the rent*⟩ **2** lagging behind the times; backward

be,hind-the-'scenes *adj* kept, made, or held in secret

behold /bi'hohld/ *vb* **beheld** /bi'held/ *vt* to see, observe ~ *vi archaic* – used in the imper to call attention [ME *beholden* to keep, behold, fr OE *behealdan*, fr *be-* + *healdan* to hold] – **beholder** *n*

beholden /bi'hohldn/ *adj* under obligation for a favour or gift; indebted *to* [ME, fr pp of *beholden*]

behoof /bi'hoof, bi'hoohf/ *n* advantage, profit [ME *behof*, fr OE *behōf*; akin to OE *hebban* to raise – more at HEAVE]

behoove /bi'hoohv/ *vb, NAm* to behove

behove /bi'hohv/ *vb* to be incumbent (on), or necessary, proper, or advantageous (for) ⟨*it* ~s *us to fight*⟩ [ME *behoven*, fr OE *behōfian*, fr *behōf*]

beige /bayzh, bayj/ *n* a yellowish grey colour [F] – **beige** *adj*, **beigy** *adj*

[1]**being** /'bee·ing/ *n* **1a** the quality or state of having existence **b** conscious existence; life ⟨*the mother who gave him his* ~⟩ **2** the qualities that constitute an existent thing; the essence; *esp* personality **3** a

living thing; *esp* a person [ME, fr gerund of *been, bēon* to be – more at BE]

[2]**being** *adj* [prp of *be*] – **for the time being** for the moment

bel /bel/ *n* 10 decibels [Alexander Graham *Bell* †1922 US inventor]

belabour /bi'laybə/ *vt* **1** to work on or at to absurd lengths ⟨~ *the obvious*⟩ **2a** to beat soundly **b** to assail, attack

belated /bi'laytid/ *adj* delayed beyond the usual time [pp of arch *belate* (to make late)] – **belatedly** *adv*, **belatedness** *n*

[1]**belay** /bi'lay/ *vt* **1** to secure or make fast (e g a rope) by turns round a support or bitt **2** to stop **3a** to secure (a person) at the end of a rope **b** to secure (a rope) to a person or object ~ *vi* **1** to be belayed **2** to stop; LEAVE OFF – in the imper ⟨~ *there*⟩ **3** to make a rope fast [ME *beleggen* to beset, fr OE *belecgan*, fr *be-* + *lecgan* to lay]

[2]**belay** *n* **1** a method or act of belaying a rope or person in mountain climbing **2** (sthg to which is attached) a mountain climber's belayed rope

bel canto /ˌbel 'kantoh/ *n* operatic singing stressing ease, purity, evenness of tone production, and an agile and precise vocal technique [It, lit., beautiful singing]

belch /belch/ *vi* **1** to expel gas suddenly from the stomach through the mouth **2** to erupt, explode, or detonate violently **3** to issue forth spasmodically; gush ~ *vt* **1** to eject or emit violently **2** to expel (gas) suddenly from the stomach through the mouth [ME *belchen*, fr OE *bealcian*] – **belch** *n*

beldam, beldame /'beldəm, -dam/ *n* an old woman; *esp* a hag [ME *beldam* grandmother, fr MF *bel* beautiful + ME *dam*]

beleaguer /bi'leegə/ *vt* **1** to surround with an army so as to prevent escape; besiege **2** to beset, harass [D *belegeren*, fr *be-* (akin to OE *be-*) + *leger* camp; akin to OHG *legar* bed – more at [1]LAIR]

belemnite /'beləmniet/ *n* a conical pointed fossil shell of any of an order of extinct cephalopod molluscs [F *bélemnite*, fr Gk *belemnon* dart; akin to Gk *ballein* to throw – more at DEVIL] – **belemnitic** /-'nitik/ *adj*

bel esprit /ˌbel e'spree (*Fr* bɛl ɛspri)/ *n, pl* **beaux esprits** /ˌbohz e'spree (*Fr* boz ɛspri)/ a person with a fine and gifted mind [F, lit., fine mind]

belfry /'belfri/ *n* (a room in which a bell is hung in) a bell tower, esp when associated with a church ☞ CHURCH [ME *belfrey*, alter. of *berfrey*, fr MF *berfrei*, deriv of Gk *pyrgos phoretos* movable war tower]

Belgian /'belj(ə)n/ *n or adj* (a native or inhabitant) of Belgium [*Belgium*, country in NW Europe]

ˌBelgian 'hare *n* (any of) a breed of slender dark-red domestic rabbits

Belgo- /belgoh-/ *comb form* Belgian and ⟨Belgo-*English*⟩ [*Belgian*]

Belial /'beeli·əl/ *n* worthlessness, wickedness – often personified in the Bible ⟨*children of* ~⟩ [Gk, fr Heb *bělīya'al*]

belie /bi'lie/ *vt* **belying** **1** to give a false impression of **2** to show (sthg) to be false [ME *belien*, fr OE *belēogan*, fr *be-* + *lēogan* to lie – more at [3]LIE] – **belier** *n*

belief /bi'leef/ *n* **1** trust or confidence in sby or sthg **2** sthg believed; *specif* a tenet or body of tenets held by a group **3** conviction of the truth of some statement or the reality of some being, thing, or phenomenon, esp when based on examination of evidence [ME *beleave*, prob alter. of OE *gelēafa*, fr *ge-*, associative prefix + *lēafa*; akin to OE *lȳfan*]

believe /bi'leev/ *vi* **1a** to have a firm religious faith **b** to accept sthg trustfully and on faith ⟨*people who ~ in the natural goodness of man*⟩ **2** to have a firm conviction as to the reality or goodness of sthg ⟨~ *in exercise*⟩ ~ *vt* **1** to consider to be true or honest ⟨~ *the reports*⟩ **2** to hold as an opinion; think ⟨*I ~ it will rain soon*⟩ *USE* (*vi*) often + *in* [ME *beleven*, fr OE *belēfan*, fr *be-* + *lȳfan, lēfan* to allow, believe; akin to OHG *gilouben* to believe, OE *lēof* dear – more at LOVE] – **believable** *adj*, **believer** *n*

Beˌlisha 'beacon /bə'leeshə/ *n* a flashing light in an amber globe mounted on a usu black and white striped pole that marks a zebra crossing [Leslie Hore-*Belisha* †1957 E politician]

belittle /bi'litl/ *vt* **belittling** /bi'litling, -'litl·ing/ to undermine the value of ⟨~s *her efforts*⟩ – **belittlement** *n*, **belittler** *n*

[1]**bell** /bel/ *n* **1** a hollow metallic device, usu cup-shaped with a flaring mouth if operated manually, and saucer-shaped if part of an electrical or clockwork device, that vibrates and gives forth a ringing sound when struck **2** *the* sound of a bell as a signal; *specif* one to mark the start of the last lap in a running or cycling race or the start or end of a round in boxing, wrestling, etc **3a** a bell rung to tell the hour **b** a half-hour subdivision of a watch on shipboard indicated by the strokes of a bell **4** sthg bell-shaped: e g **a** the corolla of any of many flowers **b** the flared end of a wind instrument [ME *belle*, fr OE; akin to OE *bellan* to roar – more at BELLOW]

[2]**bell** *vt* **1** to provide with a bell **2** to make bell-mouthed ~ *vi* to take the form of a bell; flare

[3]**bell** *vi, of a stag or hound* to make a resonant bellowing or baying sound [ME *bellen*, fr OE *bellan*]

belladonna /ˌbelə'donə/ *n* (an atropine-containing extract of) deadly nightshade [It, lit., beautiful lady; fr its use as a cosmetic]

belladonna lily *n* a plant of the daffodil family noted for its fragrant usu white or pink flowers

'bell-ˌbottoms *n pl* trousers with wide flaring bottoms ☞ GARMENT – **bell-bottom** *adj*

'bellˌboy /-ˌboy/ *n, chiefly NAm* [1]PAGE

'bell ˌbuoy *n* a buoy fitted with a warning bell which is rung by the action of the waves

belle /bel/ *n* a popular and attractive girl or woman ⟨*bathing* ~s⟩ ⟨*the ~ of the ball*⟩ [F, fr fem of *beau* beautiful – more at BEAU]

belles lettres /ˌbel 'letrə, 'letə (*Fr* bɛl lɛtr)/ *n pl but sing in constr* (light, entertaining, usu sophisticated) literature that has no practical or informative function [F, lit., fine letters] – **belletrist** /-'letrist/ *n*

'bellˌflower /-ˌflowə/ *n* any of a genus of plants (e g the harebell) having usu showy bell-shaped flowers

'bell ˌheather *n* a western European heather

bellhop /-ˌhop/ *n, NAm* [1]PAGE 2 [short for *bell-hopper*]

bellicose /'belikohs/ *adj* disposed to or fond of quarrels or wars [ME, fr L *bellicosus*, fr *bellicus* of war, fr *bellum* war] – **bellicosely** *adv*, **bellicoseness** *n*, **bellicosity** /-'kosəti/ *n*

-bellied /-belid/ *comb form* (*adj* → *adj*) having (such) a belly ⟨*a big*-bellied *man*⟩

belligerence /bə'lij(ə)rəns/, **belligerency** /-si/ *n* **1** an aggressive or truculent attitude, atmosphere, or disposition 2 the state of being at war or in conflict; *specif* the status of a legally recognized belligerent

bel'ligerent /-rənt/ *adj* **1** engaged in legally recognized war **2** inclined to or exhibiting assertiveness, hostility, or combativeness [modif of L *belligerant-, belligerans*, prp of *belligerare* to wage war, fr *belliger* waging war, fr *bellum* + *gerere* to wage – more at CAST] – **belligerent** *n*, **belligerently** *adv*

'bell ˌjar *n* a bell-shaped usu glass vessel that is designed to cover objects or to contain gases or a vacuum

'bell ˌmetal *n* bronze with a high tin content, used for bells

bellow /'beloh/ *vi* **1** to make the loud deep hollow sound characteristic of a bull **2** to shout in a deep voice ~ *vt* to bawl ⟨~s *the orders*⟩ [ME *belwen*, fr OE *bylgian*; akin to OE & OHG *bellan* to roar, Skt *bhāsate* he talks] – **bellow** *n*

bellows /'belohz/ *n, pl* **bellows** **1** a device that by alternate expansion and contraction supplies a current of air – often pl with sing. meaning **2** a pleated expandable part in a camera [ME *bely, below, belwes* – more at BELLY]

'bell,pull /-ˌpool/ *n* (a handle or knob attached to) a cord by which one rings a bell

'bell ˌpush *n* a button that is pushed to ring a bell

'bell,wether /-ˌwedhə/ *n* a male sheep that leads the flock; *broadly* a leader who is followed blindly [ME, fr *belle* bell + *wether*; fr the practice of belling the leader of a flock]

¹belly /'beli/ *n* **1a** ABDOMEN 1 **b(1)** the undersurface of an animal's body **(2)** a cut of pork consisting of this part of the body ☞ MEAT **c** the womb, uterus **d** the stomach and associated organs **2** an internal cavity; the interior **3** a surface or object curved or rounded like a human belly [ME *bely* bellows, belly, fr OE *belg* bag, skin; akin to OHG *balg* bag, skin, OE *blāwan* to blow]

²belly *vb* to swell, fill ⟨*the sails* bellied⟩

¹'belly,ache /-ˌayk/ *n* colic

²bellyache *vi* to complain whiningly or peevishly; find fault – infml – **bellyacher** *n*

'belly ˌbutton *n* NAVEL 1 – infml

'belly ˌdance *n* a usu solo dance emphasizing movements of the belly – **belly dance** *vi*, **belly dancer** *n*

'belly ˌflop *n* a dive into water in which the front of the body strikes flat against the surface – **belly flop** *vi*

'bellyful /-f(ə)l/ *n* an excessive amount ⟨*a* ~ *of advice*⟩ – infml

'belly-ˌland *vi* to land an aircraft on its undersurface without the use of landing gear – **belly landing** *n*

'belly ˌlaugh *n* a deep hearty laugh

belong /bi'long/ *vi* **1** to be in a proper situation (e g according to ability or social qualification), position, or place **2** to be attached or bound *to* by birth, allegiance, dependency, or membership **3** to be an attribute, part, or function of a person or thing ⟨*nuts and bolts* ~ *to a car*⟩ **4** to be properly classified ⟨*whales* ~ *among the mammals*⟩ [ME *belongen*, fr *be-* + *longen* to be suitable, fr *along (on)* because (of)] – **belong to** to be the property of

belonging /bi'long·ing/ *n* **1** a possession – usu pl **2** close or intimate relationship ⟨*a sense of* ~⟩

ˌBelo'russian /ˌbeloh-/ *n or adj* (a) Byelorussian

beloved /bi'luvid, bi'luvd/ *n or adj, pl* **beloved** (sby) dearly loved – usu in fml or religious contexts

¹below /bi'loh/ *adv* **1** in, on, or to a lower place, floor, or deck; *specif* on earth or in or to Hades or hell **2** UNDER 2 **3** under the surface of the water or earth [*be-* + *low*, adj]

²below *prep* **1** in or to a lower place than; under **2** inferior to (e g in rank) **3** not suitable to the rank of; BENEATH 2 **4** covered by; underneath **5** downstream from **6** UNDER 4 ⟨~ *the age of 18*⟩

³below *n, pl* **below** *the* thing or matter written or discussed lower on the same page or on a following page

⁴below *interj* – used by a climber to warn others below to beware of falling stones or rocks

bel paese /ˌbel pah'ayzay/ *n, often cap B&P* a mild soft creamy Italian cheese with a thin dark yellow rind [It, lit., beautiful country]

¹belt /belt/ *n* **1** a strip of material worn round the waist or hips or over the shoulder for decoration or to hold sthg (e g clothing or a weapon) **2** an endless band of tough flexible material for transmitting motion and power or conveying materials **3** an area characterized by some distinctive feature (e g of culture, geology, or life forms); *esp* one suited to a specified crop [ME, fr OE; akin to OHG *balz* belt; both fr a prehistoric WGmc-NGmc word borrowed fr L *balteus* belt] – **belted** *adj*, **beltless** *adj* – **below the belt** in an unfair way ⟨*alluding to his past misdeeds in that way was really hitting* below the belt⟩ – **under one's belt** as part of one's experience; having been attained

²belt *vt* **1a** to encircle or fasten with a belt **b** to strap on **2a** to beat (as if) with a belt; thrash **b** to strike, hit – infml **3** to sing in a forceful manner or style – usu + *out*; infml ~ *vi* to move or act in a vigorous or violent manner – infml

³belt *n* a jarring blow; a whack – infml

belting /'belting/ *n* **1** belts collectively **2** material for belts

belt up *vi, Br* SHUT UP – infml

'beltway /-ˌway/ *n, chiefly NAm* RING ROAD

beluga /bi'loohgə/ *n* **1** a white sturgeon of the Black sea, Caspian sea, and their tributaries **2** a whale that is white when adult [Russ, fr *belyĭ* white; akin to Gk *phainein* to show – more at FANCY]

belvedere /'belvidiə/ *n* a turret, cupola, etc placed esp on the roof of a house to command an extensive view [It, lit., beautiful view]

bemoan /bi'mohn/ *vt* to express regret, displeasure, or deep grief over; lament

bemuse /bi'myoohz/ *vt* to make confused; bewilder – **bemusedly** /-zidli/ *adv*, **bemusement** *n*

Bence-Jones protein /ˌbens 'johnz/ *n* a protein that occurs abnormally in the blood serum and urine in some cancers of the bone marrow, esp multiple myeloma, and occas in other bone diseases [Henry *Bence-Jones* †1873 E physician & chemist]

¹bench /bench/ *n* **1a** a long usu backless seat (e g of wood or stone) for 2 or more people **b** a thwart in a boat **2a** *often cap* **(1)** a judge's seat in court **(2)** the office of judge or magistrate ⟨*appointed to the* ~⟩ **b** *sing or pl in constr* the judges or magistrates **(1)** hearing a particular case **(2)** collectively **3a(1)** a seat for an official (e g a judge or magistrate) **(2)** the office or dignity of such an official **b** any of the long seats on which members sit in Parliament **4** a long worktable [ME, fr OE *benc*; akin to OHG *bank* bench]

[2]**bench** *vt* **1** to exhibit (a dog) at a show **2** *NAm* to remove from or keep out of a game

bencher /'benchə/ *n, Br* any of the chief or governing members of any of the Inns of Court [[1]BENCH + [2]-ER]

'**bench,mark** /-,mahk/ *n* **1** a point of reference (e g a mark on a permanent object indicating height above sea level) from which measurements may be made, esp in surveying **2** sthg that serves as a standard by which others may be measured

[1]**bend** /bend/ *n* any of various knots for fastening one rope to another or to an object – compare HITCH [ME, band, fr OE, fetter]

[2]**bend** *vb* **bent** /bent/ *vt* **1** to force into or out of a curve or angle **2** to fasten ⟨~ *a sail to its yard*⟩ **3** to make submissive; subdue **4a** to cause to turn from a course; deflect **b** to guide or turn towards sthg; direct ⟨*he* bent *his steps homewards*⟩ **5** to direct strenuously or with interest; apply ⟨bent *themselves to the task*⟩ **6** to alter or modify to make more acceptable, esp to oneself ⟨~ *the rules*⟩ ~ *vi* **1** to move or curve out of a straight line or position **2** to incline the body, esp in submission; bow **3** to yield, compromise [ME *bendan*, fr OE *bendan*; akin to OE *bend* fetter] – **bend over backwards** to make extreme efforts

[3]**bend** *n* **1** bending or being bent **2** a curved part, esp of a road or stream **3** *pl but sing or pl in constr* CAISSON DISEASE ⟨*a case of the* ~s⟩ – **round the bend** mad, crazy – infml ⟨*thought his friends must have gone* round the bend⟩

bender /'bendə/ *n* a drinking spree – infml [[2]BEND + [2]-ER]

bendy /'bendi/ *adj* **1** PLIABLE 1a **2** having many bends

[1]**beneath** /bi'neeth/ *adv* **1** in or to a lower position; below **2** directly under; underneath [ME *benethe*, fr OE *beneothan*, fr *be-* + *neothan* below; akin to OE *nithera* nether]

[2]**beneath** *prep* **1a** in or to a lower position than; below **b** directly under, esp so as to be close or touching **2** not suitable to; unworthy of ⟨~ *contempt*⟩ **3** under the control, pressure, or influence of

Benedicite /,beni'disitay, -tee/ *n* a hymn of praise to God beginning 'All the works of the Lord, bless ye the Lord'' [ME, fr LL, bless ye, imper pl of *benedicere* to bless; fr the first word of the hymn]

Benedictine /,beni'dikteen, -tin/ *n* **1** a monk or a nun of any of the congregations following the rule of St Benedict and devoted esp to scholarship **2** *often not cap* a brandy-based liqueur made orig by French Benedictine monks – **Benedictine** *adj*

benediction /,beni'diksh(ə)n/ *n* **1** the invocation of a blessing; *esp* the short blessing with which public worship is concluded **2** *often cap* a Roman Catholic or Anglo-Catholic devotion including the exposition of the Host and the blessing of the people with it [ME *benediccioun*, fr LL *benediction-*, *benedictio*, fr *benedictus*, pp of *benedicere* to bless, fr L, to speak well of, fr *bene* well + *dicere* to say – more at BOUNTY, DICTION]

Benedictus /,beni'diktəs/ *n* **1** a liturgical text from Mt 21:9 beginning 'Blessed is he that cometh in the name of the Lord'' **2** a canticle from Lk 1:68 beginning 'Blessed be the Lord God of Israel'' [LL, blessed, fr pp of *benedicere*; fr its first word]

benefaction /,beni'faksh(ə)n/ *n* **1** the act of doing good, esp by generous donation **2** a benefit conferred; *esp* a charitable donation [LL *benefaction-*, *benefactio*, fr L *bene factus*, pp of *bene facere* to do good to, fr *bene* + *facere* to do – more at DO]

benefactor /'beni,faktə/, *fem* **benefactress** /-tris/ *n* one who gives aid; *esp* one who makes a gift or bequest to a person, institution, etc

benefice /'benifis/ *n* an ecclesiastical office to which an income is attached [ME, fr MF, fr ML *beneficium*, fr L, favour, promotion, fr *beneficus* beneficent, fr *bene* + *facere*] – **benefice** *vt*

beneficent /bi'nefis(ə)nt/ *adj* doing or producing good; *esp* performing acts of kindness and charity [back-formation fr *beneficence*, fr L *beneficentia*, fr *beneficus*] – **beneficently** *adv*, **beneficence** /-s(ə)ns/ *n*

beneficial /,beni'fish(ə)l/ *adj* **1** conferring benefits; conducive to personal or social well-being **2** receiving or entitling one to receive advantage or profit, esp from property ⟨*the* ~ *owner of an estate*⟩ [L *beneficium* favour, benefit] – **beneficially** *adv*, **beneficialness** *n*

beneficiary /,beni'fish(ə)ri/ *n* **1** one who benefits from sthg **2** one who receives the income or proceeds of a trust, will, or insurance policy – **beneficiary** *adj*

beneficiate /,beni'fishi,ayt/ *vt* to treat (a raw material) so as to improve properties – **beneficiation** /-'aysh(ə)n/ *n*

[1]**benefit** /'benifit/ *n* **1a** sthg that promotes well-being; an advantage **b** good, welfare ⟨*did it for his* ~⟩ **2a** financial help in time of need (e g sickness, old age, or unemployment) **b** a payment or service provided for under an annuity, pension scheme, or insurance policy **3** an entertainment, game, or social event to raise funds for a person or cause [ME, fr AF *benfet*, fr L *bene factum*, fr neut of *bene factus*]

[2]**benefit** *vb* **-t-** (*NAm* **-t-, -tt-**) *vt* to be useful or profitable to ~ *vi* to receive benefit

,**benefit of 'clergy** *n* **1** the former clerical privilege of being tried in an ecclesiastical court **2** the ministration or sanction of the church – chiefly humor ⟨*a couple living together without* ~⟩

,**benefit of the 'doubt** *n* *the* assumption of innocence in the absence of complete proof of guilt

Benelux /'beniluks/ *n* (the customs union formed in 1947 between) Belgium, the Netherlands, and Luxembourg ⟨*the* ~ *countries*⟩ [*Be*lgium + *Ne*therlands + *Lux*embourg]

benevolent /bi'nevələnt/ *adj* **1** marked by or disposed to doing good; charitable **2** indicative of or characterized by goodwill ⟨~ *smiles*⟩ [ME, fr L *benevolent-*, *benevolens*, fr *bene* + *volent-*, *volens*, prp of *velle* to wish – more at WILL] – **benevolence** *n*, **benevolently** *adv*, **benevolentness** *n*

Bengali /ben'gawli, beng'gawli/ *n* **1** a native or inhabitant of Bengal **2** a native or inhabitant of Bangladesh **3** the modern Indic language of Bengal ☞ LANGUAGE [Hindi *Baṅgālī*, fr *Baṅgāl* Bengal] – **Bengali** *adj*

benighted /bi'nietid/ *adj* intellectually, morally, or socially unenlightened [fr pp of *benight* (to overtake by darkness or night), fr *be-* + [1]*night*] – **benightedly** *adv*, **benightedness** *n*

benign /bi'nien/ *adj* **1** gentle, gracious **2** favourable, mild ⟨*a* ~ *climate*⟩ **3** *of a tumour* not malignant [ME *benigne*, fr MF, fr L *benignus*, fr *bene* well +

gigni to be born, passive of *gignere* to beget – more at BOUNTY, KIN] – **benignly** *adv*, **benignity** /bi'nignəti/ *n*

benignant /bi'nignənt/ *adj* BENIGN 1, 2 [*benign* + *-ant* (as in *malignant*)] – **benignantly** *adv*, **benignancy** /-nənsi/ *n*

[1]**bent** /bent/ *n* **1a** a reedy grass **b** a stalk of stiff coarse grass **2** any of a genus of grasses including important pasture and lawn grasses [ME, grassy place, bent grass, fr OE *beonot-*; akin to OHG *binuz* rush]

[2]**bent** *adj* **1** changed from an original straight or even condition by bending; curved **2** set *on* ⟨*was ~ on winning*⟩ **3** *Br* homosexual – slang **4** *Br* corrupt; CROOKED 2 – slang [ME, fr pp of *benden* to bend]

[3]**bent** *n* **1** a strong inclination or interest; a bias **2** a special ability or talent ⟨*a ~ for art*⟩ [irreg fr [2]*bend*]

Benthamism /'benthə,miz(ə)m/ *n* the utilitarian philosophy of Jeremy Bentham [Jeremy *Bentham* †1832 E philosopher] – **Benthamite** /-,miet/ *n*

benthos /'benthos/ *n* organisms that live on or at the bottom of bodies of water [NL, fr Gk, depth, deep sea; akin to Gk *bathys* deep – more at BATHY-] – **benthic** /'benthik/ *adj*

bentonite /'bentəniet/ *n* an absorbent clay used esp to give bulk to paper, drugs, etc [Fort *Benton*, Montana, USA] – **bentonitic** /-'nitik/ *adj*

'bent,wood /-,wood/ *adj* made of wood that is steamed and bent into shape for use in furniture

benumb /bi'num/ *vt* to make inactive or numb; deaden [ME *benomen*, fr *benomen, benome*, pp of *benimen* to deprive, fr OE *beniman*, fr *be-* + *niman* to take – more at NIMBLE]

benz- /benz-/, **benzo-** *comb form* related to benzene or benzoic acid ⟨benzo*phenone*⟩ ⟨benz*yl*⟩ [ISV, fr *benzoin*]

benzaldehyde /ben'zaldihied/ *n* a liquid chemical compound found in essential oils (e g in peach kernels) and used in flavouring and perfumes, as a solvent, and in the synthesis of dyes [G *benzaldehyd*, fr *benz-* + *aldehyd* aldehyde]

Benzedrine /'benzədrin, -dreen/ *trademark* – used for a type of amphetamine

benzene /'benzeen/ *n* an inflammable poisonous liquid hydrocarbon used in the synthesis of organic chemical compounds and as a solvent [ISV *benz-* + *-ene*] – **benzenoid** /'benzənoyd/ *adj*

'benzene ,ring *n* the structural arrangement of 6 carbon atoms that exists in the molecules of benzene and many other organic chemical compounds

benzine /'benzeen/ *n* any of various volatile inflammable petroleum distillates used esp as solvents or motor fuels [G *benzin*, fr *benz-*]

benzodiazepine /,benzohdie'ayzipin/ *n* any of several chemically related synthetic drugs (e g diazepam, chlordiazepoxide, and nitrazepam) widely used as tranquillizers, sedatives, and hypnotics [*benz-* + *di-* + *az-* + *epoxide* + *-ine*]

ben,zoic 'acid /ben'zoh·ik/ *n* an organic acid used esp as a food preservative, in medicine, and in organic synthesis [ISV, fr *benzoin*]

benzoin /'benzoh·in, -'--, 'benzoyn/ *n* (any of various trees found in SE Asia yielding) a hard fragrant yellowish balsamic resin used esp in medicines [MF *benjoin*, fr OCatal *benjuí*, fr Ar *lubān jāwi*, lit., frankincense of Java]

benzol /'benzol/ *n* (unrefined) benzene [G, fr *benz-* + *-ol*]

bequeath /bi'kweeth, bi'kweedh/ *vt vt* **1** to give or leave (sthg, esp personal property) by will – compare DEVISE 2 **2** to transmit; HAND DOWN ⟨*ideas ~ed to us by the 19th c*⟩ [ME *bequethen*, fr OE *becwethan*, fr *be-* + *cwethan* to say – more at QUOTH] – **bequeathal** /bi'kweedhəl/ *n*

bequest /bi'kwest/ *n* **1** the act of bequeathing **2** a legacy [ME, irreg fr *bequethen*]

berate /bi'rayt/ *vt* to scold or condemn vehemently [*be-* + *rate* (to chide), fr ME *raten*]

Berber /'buhbə/ *n* **1** a member of a Caucasian people of N Africa **2** (any of various N African languages comprising) a Hamitic branch of the Afro-Asiatic language family [Ar *Barbar*]

berberine /'buhbəreen/ *n* a bitter alkaloid obtained from the roots of various plants (e g barberry) and used esp as a tonic [G *berberin*, fr NL *berberis* barberry root, fr ML *barberis*, fr Ar *barbāris*]

berceuse /beə'suhz/ *n, pl* **berceuses** /~/ (a musical composition in the style of) a lullaby [F, fr *bercer* to rock]

bereave /bi'reev/ *vt* **bereaved, bereft** /bi'reft/ to rob or deprive *of* sby or sthg held dear, esp through death [ME *bereven*, fr OE *berēafian*, fr *be-* + *rēafian* to rob; akin to OHG *roubōn* to rob, L *rumpere* to break, *ruere* to rush, dig up] – **bereavement** *n*

be'reaved *n or adj, pl* **bereaved** (*the* person) suffering the death of a loved one

bereft /bi'reft/ *adj* **1** deprived or robbed *of*; completely without sthg ⟨*~ of all hope*⟩ **2** bereaved

beret /'beray/ *n* a cap with a tight headband, a soft full flat top, and no peak [F *berret*, fr Prov – more at BIRETTA]

[1]**berg** /buhg/ *n* an iceberg

[2]**berg** *n, SAfr* a mountain – often in place-names [Afrik, fr MD *bergh, berch*; akin to OHG *berg* mountain]

bergamot /'buhgəmot/ *n* a pear-shaped orange whose rind yields an essential oil used in perfumery [prob fr *Bergamo*, town in Italy]

bergschrund /'beəg,shroont/ *n* a crevasse at the top of a mountain glacier [G, fr *berg* mountain + *schrund* crack]

beriberi /'beri,beri, ,--'--/ *n* a deficiency disease marked by degeneration of the nerves and caused by a lack of or inability to assimilate vitamin B_1 [Sinhalese *bæribæri*]

berk /buhk/ *n, Br* a burk – slang

Berkeleian, Berkeleyan /bah'klee·ən, 'bahkli·ən/ *adj* (characteristic) of Bishop Berkeley or his theory that only what is immediately perceived is real [George *Berkeley* †1753 Ir bishop & philosopher] – **Berkeleian** *n*, **Berkeleianism** *n*

berkelium /bə'keeli·əm/ *n* an artificially produced radioactive metallic element ☞ PERIODIC TABLE [NL, fr *Berkeley*, city in California, USA]

berm, berme /buhm/ *n* **1** a narrow shelf between a ditch and the base of a parapet in a fortification **2** a narrow path beside a road, canal, etc [F *berme*, fr D *berm* strip of ground along a dyke; akin to ME *brimme* brim]

Bermuda rig /bə'myoohdə/ *n* a fore-and-aft rig with a tall mainmast and triangular mainsail [*Bermuda* Islands in the W Atlantic ocean]

Ber,muda 'shorts *n pl* knee-length shorts ☞ GARMENT

[1]**berry** /'beri/ *n* **1a** a small, pulpy, and usu edible fruit (e g a strawberry or raspberry) **b** a simple fruit (e g a currant, grape, tomato, or banana) with a pulpy or fleshy pericarp – used technically in botany **2** an egg of a fish or lobster [ME *berye*, fr OE *berie*; akin to OHG *beri* berry] – **berried** *adj*, **berrylike** *adj*

[2]**berry** *vi* **1** to bear or produce berries **2** to gather or seek berries

[1]**berserk** /bə'zuhk, buh-/ *n* any of a type of ancient Scandinavian warrior who fought in a wild frenzy [ON *berserkr*, fr *björn* bear + *serkr* shirt]

[2]**berserk** *adj* frenzied, esp with anger; crazed – usu in *go berserk* – **berserk** *adv*

berserker /bə'zuhkə/ *n* a berserk

[1]**berth** /buhth/ *n* **1** safe distance for manoeuvring maintained between a ship and another object **2** an allotted place for a ship when at anchor or at a wharf **3** a place for sleeping (e g a bunk), esp on a ship or train **4a** a place, position ⟨*earned the number 2* ~⟩ **b** a job, post – infml [prob fr [2]*bear* + *-th*] – **give a wide berth to** to remain at a safe distance from; avoid

[2]**berth** *vt* **1** to bring into a berth; dock **2** to allot a berth to ~ *vi* to come into a berth

-berther /-buhthə/ *comb form* (→ *n*) sthg having berths of a specified kind or number

beryl /'beril/ *n* a mineral that is a silicate of beryllium and aluminium, occurs as green, yellow, pink, or white crystals, and is used as a gemstone – compare AQUAMARINE, EMERALD [ME, fr OF *beril*, fr L *beryllus*, fr Gk *bēryllos*, of Indic origin; akin to Skt *vaiḍūrya* cat's-eye gem]

beryllium /bə'rili·əm/ *n* a light strong bivalent metallic element ☞ PERIODIC TABLE [NL, fr Gk *bēryllion*, dim. of *bēryllos*]

beseech /bi'seech/ *vt* **besought** /-sawt/, **beseeched** **1** to beg for urgently or anxiously ⟨besought *a favour of her*⟩ **2** to request earnestly; implore ⟨*do not go, I* ~ *you*⟩ [ME *besechen*, fr *be-* + *sechen* to seek] – **beseechingly** *adv*

beset /bi'set/ *vt* **1** to trouble or assail constantly ⟨~ *by fears*⟩ **2** to surround and (prepare to) attack ⟨~ *by the enemy*⟩ [ME *besetten* to set round, encompass, fr OE *besettan*, fr *be-* + *settan* to set] – **besetment** *n*

besetting /bi'seting/ *adj* constantly causing temptation or difficulty; continuously present ⟨*a* ~ *sin*⟩

beside /bi'sied/ *prep* **1a** by the side of ⟨*walk* ~ *me*⟩ **b** in comparison with **c** on a par with **d** unconnected with; wide of ⟨~ *the point*⟩ **2** besides [ME, adv & prep, fr OE *be sīdan* at or to the side, fr *be* at (fr *bī*) + *sīdan*, dat & acc of *sīde* side – more at BY] – **beside oneself** in a state of extreme agitation or excitement

[1]**be'sides** *adv* **1** as an additional factor or circumstance ⟨*has a wife and 6 children* ~⟩ **2** moreover, furthermore

[2]**besides** *prep* **1** other than; unless we are to mention ⟨*who* ~ *John would say that?*⟩ **2** as an additional circumstance to ⟨~ *being old, she is losing her sight*⟩

besiege /bi'seej/ *vt vt* **1** to surround with armed forces **2a** to crowd round; surround closely **b** to press with questions, requests, etc; importune – **besieger** *n*

besmirch /bi'smuhch/ *vt* to sully, soil

besom /'beez(ə)m/ *n* BROOM 2; *esp* one made of twigs [ME *beseme*, fr OE *besma*; akin to OHG *besmo* broom]

besotted /bi'sotid/ *adj* **1** made dull or foolish, esp by infatuation **2** drunk, intoxicated [fr pp of *besot* (to make dull or foolish), fr *be-* + *sot* (to befool)]

bespatter /bi'spatə/ *vt* to spatter

bespeak /bi'speek/ *vt* **bespoke** /-'spohk/; **bespoken** /-'spohkən/ **1** to hire, engage, or claim beforehand **2** to indicate, signify ⟨*her performance* ~s *considerable practice*⟩ ***USE*** fml

bespectacled /bi'spektəkld/ *adj* wearing glasses

bespoke /bi'spohk/ *adj*, *Br* **1** made-to-measure; *broadly* made or arranged according to particular requirements **2** dealing in or producing articles that are made to measure ⟨*a* ~ *tailor*⟩ [pp of *bespeak*]

besprinkle /bi'springkl/ *vt* to sprinkle [ME *besprengeln*, freq of *besprengen*, fr OE *besprengan*]

,**Bessemer con'verter** /'besimə/ *n* the furnace used in the Bessemer process

'**Bessemer ,process** *n* a steelmaking process in which air is blasted through molten pig iron to remove impurities [Sir Henry *Bessemer* †1898 E engineer & inventor]

[1]**best** /best/ *adj*, *superlative of* GOOD **1** excelling all others (e g in ability, quality, integrity, or usefulness) ⟨*the* ~ *student*⟩ **2** most productive of good ⟨*what is the* ~ *thing to do*⟩ **3** most, largest ⟨*for the* ~ *part of a week*⟩ **4** reserved for special occasions ⟨*got out the* ~ *sherry glasses*⟩ [ME, fr OE *betst*; akin to OE *bōt* remedy – more at BETTER]

[2]**best** *adv*, *superlative of* WELL **1** in the best manner; to the best extent or degree ⟨*a Wednesday would suit me* ~ *– SEU S*⟩ **2** BETTER 2 ⟨*is* ~ *avoided*⟩ ⟨*we'd* ~ *go*⟩ – **as best** in the best way ⟨*climbed over* as best *he could*⟩

[3]**best** *n*, *pl* **best** **1** the best state or part ⟨*never at my* ~ *before breakfast*⟩ ⟨*the* ~ *of life is over at 20*⟩ **2** sby or sthg that is best ⟨*can ride with the* ~ *of them*⟩ **3** the greatest degree of good or excellence ⟨*always demand the* ~ *of my pupils*⟩ **4** one's maximum effort ⟨*did my* ~⟩ **5** best clothes ⟨*Sunday* ~⟩ **6** a winning majority ⟨*the* ~ *of 3 games*⟩ – **at best** even under the most favourable circumstances; seen in the best light – **make the best of** to cope with an unfavourable situation in the best and most optimistic manner possible

[4]**best** *vt* to get the better of; outdo

,**best ,end of 'neck** *n* a cut of lamb, veal, etc from between the lower end of the neck and the loin ☞ MEAT

bestial /'besti·əl/ *adj* **1** of beasts **2** marked by brutal or inhuman instincts or desires; *specif* sexually depraved [ME, fr MF, fr L *bestialis*, fr *bestia* beast] – **bestialize** *vt*, **bestially** *adv*

bestiality /,besti'aləti/ *n* bestial behaviour; *specif* sexual relations between a human being and an animal [BESTIAL + -ITY]

bestiary /'besti·əri/ *n* a medieval allegorical or moralizing work about real or imaginary animals [ML *bestiarium*, fr L, neut of *bestiarius* of beasts, fr *bestia*]

bestir /bi'stuh/ *vt* to stir up; rouse to action

,**best 'man** *n* the principal attendant of a bridegroom at a wedding

bestow /bi'stoh/ *vt* to present as a gift – usu + *on*

or *upon* [ME *bestowen*, fr *be-* + *stowe* place – more at STOW] – **bestowal** *n*

bestrew /bi'strooh/ *vt* **bestrewed; bestrewed, bestrewn** /-'stroohn/ **1** to strew **2** to lie scattered over

bestride /bi'stried/ *vt* **bestrode** /-'strohd/; **bestridden** /-'stridən/ **1** to ride, sit, or stand astride; straddle **2** to tower over; dominate

,best-'seller *n* **1** sthg, esp a book, which has sold in very large numbers, usu over a given period **2** an author or performer whose works sell in very large numbers – **best-selling** *adj*

[1]**bet** /bet/ *n* **1a** the act of risking a sum of money or other stake on the forecast outcome of a future event (e g a race or contest), esp in competition with a second party **b** a stake so risked **c** an outcome or result on which a stake is gambled **2** an opinion, belief ⟨*my ~ is it will pour with rain*⟩ **3** a plan of action; course ⟨*your best ~ is to call a plumber*⟩ – infml [origin unknown]

[2]**bet** *vb* **bet** *also* **betted; -tt-** *vt* **1** to stake as a bet – usu + *on* or *against* **2** to make a bet with (sby) **3** to be convinced that ⟨*I ~ they don't turn up*⟩ – infml ~ *vi* to lay a bet – **bet one's bottom dollar** to be virtually certain – infml – **you bet** you may be sure; certainly – slang

beta /'beetə; *NAm usu* 'baytə/ *n* **1a** the 2nd letter of the Greek alphabet **b** B 4 **2** – used to designate the second brightest star of a constellation [Gk *bēta*, of Sem origin; akin to Heb *bēth*, 2nd letter of the Heb alphabet]

,beta-,adre'nergic /,adri'nuhjik/ *adj* of or being a beta-receptor ⟨~ *blocking action*⟩

'beta-,blocker *n* a drug (e g propranolol) that inhibits the action of adrenalin and similar compounds and is used esp to treat high blood pressure

betake /bi'tayk/ *vt* **betook** /-'took/; **betaken** /-'taykən/ to cause (oneself) to go – fml

,beta-oxi'dation *n* gradual breakdown of fatty acids, esp in mitochondria

'beta ,particle *n* an electron or positron ejected from the nucleus of an atom during radioactive decay

'beta ,ray *n* a stream of beta particles

'beta-re,ceptor *n* a receptor for neurotransmitters (e g adrenalin) in the sympathetic nervous system whose stimulation is associated esp with dilation of small blood vessels and increased heart rate and output – compare ALPHA-RECEPTOR

betatron /'beetətron/ *n* an accelerator in which electrons are propelled by the inductive action of a rapidly varying magnetic field [ISV]

betel /'beetl/ *n* a climbing pepper whose leaves are chewed together with betel nut and lime, esp by SE Asians, to stimulate the flow of saliva [Pg, fr Tamil *ve r rilai*]

'betel ,nut *n* the astringent seed of the betel palm [fr its being chewed with betel leaves]

'betel ,palm *n* an Asiatic palm that has an orange-coloured fruit [*betel* nut]

bête noire /,bet 'nwah/ *n, pl* **bêtes noires** /~/ a person or thing strongly detested [F, lit., black beast]

bethel /'beth(ə)l/ *n* **1** a Nonconformist chapel **2** a place of worship for seamen [Heb *bēth' ēl* house of God]

bethink /bi'thingk/ *vt* **bethought** /-'thawt/ *archaic* to cause (oneself) to be reminded or to consider – usu + *of*

betide /bi'tied/ *vt* to happen to; befall ⟨*woe ~ them if they're late!*⟩ ~ *vi* to happen, esp as if by fate ⟨*we shall remain friends, whatever may ~*⟩ ***USE*** fml or poetic; used only in the 3rd pers sing. pres subj ***and infin*** [ME *betiden*, fr *be-* + *tiden* to happen, fr OE *tīdan*; akin to MD *tiden* to go, come, OE *tīd* time]

bêtise /be'teez/ *n, pl* **bêtises** /~/ (an act of) stupidity [F, fr *bête* foolish, fr *bête* fool, beast]

betoken /bi'tohkən/ *vt* **1** to give evidence of; show **2** to presage, portend

betony /'betəni/ *n* any of several plants of the mint family [ME *betone*, fr OF *betoine*, fr L *vettonica, betonica*, fr *Vettones*, an ancient Spanish people]

betray /bi'tray/ *vt* **1** to deceive, lead astray **2a** to deliver to an enemy by treachery **b** to be a traitor to ⟨~ed *his people*⟩ **3a** to fail or desert, esp in time of need **b** to disappoint the hopes, expectation, or confidence of **4a** to be a sign of (sthg one would like to hide) **b** to disclose, deliberately or unintentionally, in violation of confidence [ME *betrayen*, fr *be-* + *trayen* to betray, fr OF *traïr*, fr L *tradere* – more at TRAITOR] – **betrayal** *n*, **betrayer** *n*

betroth /bi'trohth, -'trohdh/ *vt* **betrothed** /-dhd/, **betrothing** /-dhing/ to promise to marry or give in marriage [ME *betrouthen*, fr *be-* + *trouthe* truth, troth – more at TRUTH]

betrothal /bi'trohdhəl/ *n* a mutual promise or contract for a future marriage [BETROTH + [2]-AL]

be'trothed *n* the person to whom one is betrothed

[1]**better** /'betə/ *adj, comparative of* GOOD *or of* WELL **1** more than half ⟨*for the ~ part of a month*⟩ **2** improved in health; recovered **3** of greater quality, ability, integrity, usefulness, etc [ME *bettre*, fr OE *betera*; akin to OE *bōt* remedy, Skt *bhadra* fortunate]

[2]**better** *adv, comparative of* WELL **1** in a better manner; to a better extent or degree **2a** to a higher or greater degree ⟨*he knows the story ~ than you do*⟩ **b** more wisely or usefully ⟨*is ~ avoided*⟩ ⟨*I'd ~ not go round at lunchtime – SEU S*⟩

[3]**better** *n, pl* **better,** (1b) **betters 1a** sthg better **b** one's superior, esp in merit or rank – usu pl **2** *the* advantage, victory ⟨*get the ~ of him*⟩ – **for better or for worse** whatever the outcome

[4]**better** *vt* **1** to make better: e g **a** to make more tolerable or acceptable ⟨*trying to ~ the lot of slum dwellers*⟩ **b** to make more complete or perfect **2** to surpass in excellence; excel ~ *vi* to become better

,better 'half *n* a spouse; *esp* a wife – humor

'betterment /-mənt/ *n* an improvement [[4]BETTER + -MENT]

'betting ,shop /'beting/ *n, Br* a bookmaker's shop

bettor, better /'betə/ *n* one who bets

[1]**between** /bi'tween/ *prep* **1a** through the common action of; jointly engaging ⟨~ *them, they managed to lay the carpet*⟩ **b** in shares to each of ⟨*divided ~ his 4 children*⟩ **2a** in or into the time, space, or interval that separates ⟨*in ~ the rafters*⟩ **b** in intermediate relation to ⟨*a colour ~ blue and grey*⟩ **3a** from one to the other of ⟨*travelling ~ London and Paris*⟩ **b** serving to connect or separate ⟨*dividing line ~ fact and fancy*⟩ **4** in point of comparison of ⟨*not much to choose ~ them*⟩ **5** taking together the total effect of; WHAT WITH ⟨*kept very busy ~ cooking, writing, and gardening*⟩ [ME *betwene*, prep & adv, fr OE *betwēonum*, fr *be-* + *-twēonum*

(dat pl) (akin to Goth *tweihnai* two each); akin to OE *twā* two] – **between you and me** in confidence

²**between** *adv* in or into an intermediate space or interval

betweentimes /-,tiemz/ *adv* at or during intervals

betweenwhiles /-,wielz/ *adv* betweentimes

betwixt /bi'twikst/ *adv or prep, archaic* between [ME, fr OE *betwux*, fr *be-* + *-twux* (akin to Goth *tweihnai*)]

be,twixt and be'tween *adv or adj* in a midway position; neither one thing nor the other

¹**bevel** /'bevl/ *n* **1** the angle or slant that one surface or line makes with another when they are not at right angles **2** an instrument consisting of 2 rules or arms jointed together and opening to any angle for drawing angles or adjusting surfaces to be given a bevel [(assumed) MF, fr OF *baïf* with open mouth, fr *baer* to yawn, fr ML *batare*]

²**bevel** *vb* **-ll-** (*NAm* **-l-, -ll-**), /'bevl·ing/ *vt* to cut or shape to a bevel ~ *vi* to incline, slant

'**bevel ,gear** *n* (a system of gears having) a pair of toothed wheels that work shafts inclined to each other

beverage /'bev(ə)rij/ *n* a liquid for drinking; *esp* one that is not water [ME, fr MF *bevrage*, fr *beivre* to drink, fr L *bibere* – more at POTABLE]

bevvy /'bevi/ *n, dial Br* any alcoholic drink; *esp* beer – slang [by shortening & alter. fr *beverage*]

bevy /'bevi/ *n* a group or collection, esp of girls [ME *bevey*]

bewail /bi'wayl/ *vt* to express deep sorrow for; lament

beware /bi'weə/ *vb* to be wary (of) ⟨~ *the Ides of March!*⟩ ⟨~ *of the dog!*⟩ – usu in imper and infin [ME *been war*, fr *been* to be + *war* careful – more at BE, WARY]

bewilder /bi'wildə/ *vt* to perplex or confuse, esp by a complexity, variety, or multitude of objects or considerations [*be-* + arch *wilder* (to lead astray, perplex), prob irreg fr *wilderness*] – **bewilderedly** *adv*, **bewilderingly** *adv*, **bewilderment** *n*

bewitch /bi'wich/ *vt* **1a** to influence or affect, esp injuriously, by witchcraft **b** to cast a spell over **2** to attract as if by the power of witchcraft; enchant ⟨~ed *by her beauty*⟩ – **bewitchingly** *adv*, **bewitchment** *n*

¹**beyond** /bee'ond/ *adv* **1** on or to the farther side; farther **2** as an additional amount; besides [ME, prep & adv, fr OE *begeondan*, fr *be-* + *geondan* beyond, fr *geond* yonder]

²**beyond** *prep* **1** on or to the farther side of; at a greater distance than **2a** out of the reach or sphere of ⟨~ *repair*⟩ **b** in a degree or amount surpassing ⟨~ *my wildest dreams*⟩ **c** out of the comprehension of **3** BESIDES 2 **4** later than; past

³**beyond** *n* **1** sthg that lies beyond **2** sthg that lies outside the scope of ordinary experience; *specif* ²HEREAFTER

bezant /'bezənt, bə'zant/ *n* SOLIDUS 1 [ME *besant*, fr MF, fr ML *Byzantius* Byzantine, fr *Byzantium*, ancient name of Istanbul, city in Turkey]

bezel /'bez(ə)l/ *n* **1** a sloping edge, esp on a cutting tool **2** the (upper) faceted portion of a gem **3** a rim or groove that holds a transparent covering of a watch, clock, headlight, etc [prob F dial., alter. of F *biseau*]

bezique /bə'zeek/ *n* (the combination of the queen of spades and jack of diamonds held in) a card game for 2 people that is played with a double pack of 64 cards [F *bésique*]

Bhagavad Gita /,bahgəvahd 'geetah/ *n* a Hindu devotional scripture consisting chiefly of discourses of Krishna in poetic form [Skt *Bhagavadgītā*, lit., song of the blessed one (Krishna)]

bhakti /'bahkti/ *n* devotion to a deity constituting a way to salvation in Hinduism [Skt, lit., portion]

bhang /bang/ *n* a mild form of cannabis used esp in India [Hindi *bh ag*]

B-horizon /bee/ *n* the subsurface layer of soil that is frequently enriched by substances from the surface layer

¹**bi-** /bie-/ *prefix* **1a** two ⟨bi*parous*⟩ ⟨bi*lingual*⟩ **b** appearing or occurring every 2 ⟨bi*monthly*⟩ ⟨bi*weekly*⟩ **c** into two parts ⟨bi*sect*⟩ **2a** twice; doubly; on both sides ⟨bi*convex*⟩ ⟨bi*serrate*⟩ **b** appearing or occurring twice in ⟨bi*weekly*⟩ – often disapproved of in this sense because of the likelihood of confusion with sense 1b; compare SEMI- **3** located between, involving, or affecting 2 (specified symmetrical parts) ⟨bi*aural*⟩ **4** DI- 2 ⟨bi*phenyl*⟩ **5** acid salt ⟨bi*carbonate*⟩ [ME, fr L; akin to OE *twi-*]

²**bi-, bio-** *comb form* life ⟨bio*graphy*⟩; living organisms or tissue ⟨bio*logy*⟩ [Gk, fr *bios* mode of life – more at QUICK]

bi'annual /-'anyooəl/ *adj* occurring twice a year – **biannually** *adv*

¹**bias** /'bie·əs/ *n* **1** a line diagonal to the grain of a fabric, often used in the cutting of garments for smoother fit – usu + *the* ⟨*cut on the* ~⟩ **2a** an inclination of temperament or outlook; *esp* a personal prejudice **b** a bent, tendency **c** a tendency of an estimate to deviate in one direction from a true value (e g because of non-random sampling) **3** (the property of shape or weight causing) the tendency of a bowl used in the game of bowls to take a curved path when rolled **4** a voltage applied to a device (e g the grid of a thermionic valve) to enable it to function normally [MF *biais*, fr OProv] – **on the bias** askew, obliquely

²**bias** *adj, esp of fabrics and their cut* diagonal, slanting – **bias** *adv*

³**bias** *vt* **-s-, -ss- 1a** to give a prejudiced outlook to **b** to influence unfairly **2** to apply an electrical bias to

biased /'bie·əst/ *adj* exhibiting or characterized by bias

biathlon /bie'athlən/ *n* an athletic contest consisting of combined cross-country skiing and rifle shooting [¹*bi-* + Gk *athlon* contest]

bib /bib/ *n* **1** a covering (e g of cloth or plastic) placed over a child's front to protect his/her clothes **2** a small rectangular section of a garment (e g an apron or dungarees) extending above the waist [prob fr arch *bib* (to drink), fr ME *bibben*, perh fr L *bibere*]

,bib and 'tucker /'tukə/ *n* an outfit of clothing – usu in *best bib and tucker*; infml

bibber /'bibə/ *n* sby given to drinking alcohol; a tippler [arch *bib* (to drink) + ²*-er* – more at BIB]

bibcock *also* **bibb cock** /'bib,kok/ *n* a tap with a bent-down nozzle [prob fr *bib* + *cock*]

bibelot /'bib(ə)loh/ *n pl* **bibelots** /-loh(z)/ a small ornament or decorative object; a trinket, curio [F]

bible /'biebl/ *n* **1a** *cap* the sacred book of Christians comprising the Old Testament and the New Testament **b** any book containing the sacred writings of a religion **2** *cap* a copy or an edition of the Bible **3** an authoritative book ⟨*the fisherman's* ~⟩ [ME, fr OF, fr ML *biblia*, fr Gk, pl of *biblion* book, dim. of *byblos* papyrus, book, fr *Byblos*, ancient Phoenician city from which papyrus was exported]

'Bible ,Belt *n* an area characterized by ardent religious fundamentalism; *esp* such an area in the southern USA

biblical /'biblikl/ *adj* **1** of or in accord with the Bible **2** suggestive of the Bible or Bible times [ML *biblicus*, fr *biblia*] – **biblically** *adv*

biblicism /'biblisiz(ə)m/ *n, often cap* narrow or exclusive use of the Bible – **biblicist** *n, often cap*

biblio- *comb form* book ⟨biblio*graphy*⟩ [MF, fr L, fr Gk, fr *biblion*]

bibliography /bibli'ogrəfi/ *n* **1** the history, identification, or description of writings and publications **2** a list of writings relating to a particular topic, written by a particular author, issued by a particular publisher, etc **3** a list of the works referred to in a text or consulted by the author in its production [prob fr NL *bibliographia*, fr Gk, the copying of books, fr *biblio-* + *-graphia* -graphy] – **bibliographer** *n*, **bibliographic** /-ə'grafik/, **bibliographical** *adj*, **bibliographically** *adv*

bibliophile /'bibli·ə,fiel/ *n* a lover or collector of books [F, fr *biblio-* + *-phile*] – **bibliophilic** /-'filik/ *adj*, **bibliophilism** /,bibli'ofiliz(ə)m/ *n*, **bibliophilist** /-'ofilist/ *n*, **bibliophily** /-'ofili/ *n*

bibliotheca /,bibli·ə'theekə/ *n, pl* **bibliothecas, bibliothecae** /-kee, -see/ a collection of books [L, fr Gk *bibliothēkē*, fr *biblio-* + *thēkē* case; akin to Gk *tithenai* to put, place – more at DO] – **bibliothecal** /-'theekəl/ *adj*

bibulous /'bibyooləs/ *adj* prone to over-indulgence in alcoholic drinks [L *bibulus*, fr *bibere* to drink – more at POTABLE] – **bibulously** *adv*, **bibulousness** *n*

bicameral /,bie'kam(ə)r(ə)l/ *adj* having 2 legislative chambers ['*bi-* + *cameral* (of or relating to a chamber), fr LL *camera* room – more at CHAMBER] – **bicameralism** *n*

bicarb /'bie,kahb/ *n* SODIUM BICARBONATE – infml

bicarbonate /bie'kahbənət/ *n* an acid carbonate; *esp* SODIUM BICARBONATE [ISV]

biccy, bicky, bikky /'biki/ *n, Br* a biscuit – infml [by shortening & alter.]

bice /bies/ *n* a dull blue or green pigment [ME *bis*, fr *bis* (adj) dark grey, fr MF]

bicentenary /,biesen'teenəri, -'te-/ *n or adj* (the celebration) of a 200th anniversary

bicentennial /,biesen'teni·əl/ *n or adj* (a) bicentenary

biceps /'bieseps/ *n* the large muscle at the front of the upper arm that bends the arm at the elbow when it contracts; *broadly* any muscle attached in 2 places at one end [NL *bicipit-*, *biceps*, fr L, two-headed, fr *bi-* + *capit-*, *caput* head – more at HEAD]

bicker /'bikə/ *vi* to engage in petulant or petty argument [ME *bikeren*] – **bicker** *n*, **bickerer** *n*

biconcave /,bie'konkayv/ *adj* concave on both sides [ISV] – **biconcavity** /-kon'kavəti, -kən-/ *n*

biconvex /,bie'konveks, ,biekən'veks/ *adj* convex on both sides [ISV] – **biconvexity** /,biekən'veksəti/ *n*

biculturalism /bie'kulchərəliz(ə)m/ *n* the existence of 2 distinct cultures in 1 nation ⟨*Canada's* ~⟩ – **bicultural** *adj*

bicuspid /bie'kuspid/ *n or adj* (a tooth) having or ending in 2 points [adj NL *bicuspid-*, *bicuspis*, fr *bi-* + L *cuspid-*, *cuspis* point; n fr adj]

bi,cuspid 'valve *n* the heart valve consisting of 2 flaps that stops blood flowing back from the left ventricle to the left atrium

bicycle /'biesikl/ *vi or n* **bicycling** /'biesikling/ (to ride) a 2 wheeled pedal-driven vehicle with handlebars and a saddle [n F, fr *bi-* + *-cycle* (as in *tricycle*); vb fr n] – **bicycler** /-klə/ *n*, **bicyclist** /-klist/ *n*

bicyclic /,bie'siklik, -'sie-/ *adj* consisting of or arranged in 2 cycles or circles [ISV]

¹bid /bid/ *vb* **bade** /bad, bed/, **bid,** (*3*) **bid; bidden** /'bidn/, **bid** *also* **bade; -dd-** *vt* **1a** to issue an order to; tell ⟨*he did as he was* ~⟩ **b** to invite to come **2** to give expression to ⟨bade *him a tearful farewell*⟩ **3a** to offer (a price) for payment or acceptance (e g at an auction) **b** to make a bid of or in (a suit at cards) ~ *vi* to make a bid [partly fr ME *bidden* to request, entreat, fr OE *biddan*; akin to OHG *bitten* to entreat, Skt *bādhate* he harasses; partly fr ME *beden* to offer, command, fr OE *bēodan*; akin to OHG *biotan* to offer, Gk *pynthanesthai* to learn by inquiry] – **bidder** *n* – **bid fair** to seem likely; show promise ⟨*she* bids fair *to become extremely attractive*⟩

²bid *n* **1a** the act of one who bids **b** a statement of what one will give or take for sthg; *esp* an offer of a price **c** sthg offered as a bid **2** an opportunity to bid **3** (an announcement of) the amount of tricks to be won, suit to be played in, etc in a card game **4** an attempt to win or achieve sthg ⟨*a* ~ *for power*⟩

biddable /'bidəbl/ *adj* **1** easily led or controlled; docile **2** capable of being reasonably bid – **biddably** /-bli/ *adv*, **biddability** /-'biləti/ *n*

bidding /'biding/ *n* order, command ⟨*came at my* ~⟩

¹biddy /'bidi/ *n, chiefly NAm* HEN 1a; *also* a young chicken – infml [perh imit]

²biddy *n* a woman ⟨*an eccentric old* ~⟩ – usu derog [dim. of the name *Bridget*]

'biddy-,bid *n* (the burr of) a grassland plant of New Zealand of the rose family [modif of Maori *piripiri*]

'biddy-,biddy *n* the biddy-bid

bide /bied/ *vi* **bode** /bohd/, **bided** /'biedid/; **bided** *archaic or dial* to remain awhile; stay [ME *biden*, fr OE *bīdan*; akin to OHG *bītan* to wait, L *fidere* to trust, Gk *peithesthai* to believe] – **bider** *n* – **bide one's time** to wait until the appropriate time comes to initiate action or to proceed

bidet /'beeday/ *n* a low fixture used esp for bathing the external genitals and the anus [F, small horse, bidet, fr MF, fr *bider* to trot]

bid up *vt* to raise the price of (e g property in an auction) by a succession of increasing offers

Biedermeier, Biedermaier /'beedə,mie·ə/ *adj* **1** of or suggesting a conventional and unimaginative style of furniture and interior decoration popular among the middle classes in Germany in the 19th c **2** conventional or philistine in attitude [Gottlieb *Biedermeier*, fictitious simple German bourgeois, ostensible author of poems by Adolf Kussmaul †1902 & others]

biennial /bie'eni·əl/ *adj* **1** occurring every 2 years **2** *of a plant* growing vegetatively during the first year and fruiting and dying during the second – **biennial** *n*, **biennially** *adv*

biennium /bie'eni·əm/ *n, pl* **bienniums, biennia**

/-ni·ə/ a period of 2 years [L, fr *bi-* + *annus* year – more at ANNUAL]

bier /biə/ *n* a stand on which a corpse or coffin is placed; *also* a coffin together with its stand [ME *bere*, fr OE *bǣr*; akin to OE *beran* to carry – more at ²BEAR]

bifacial /bie'faysh(ə)l/ *adj* **1** having opposite surfaces alike ⟨~ *leaves*⟩ **2** having 2 fronts or faces

biff /bif/ *n* a whack, blow – infml [prob imit] – **biff** *vt*

bifid /'biefid/ *adj* divided into 2 equal lobes or parts by a central cleft ⟨*a* ~ *petal*⟩ [L *bifidus*, fr *bi-* + *-fidus* -fid] – **bifidly** *adv*, **bifidity** /-'fidəti/ *n*

bifilar /,bie'fielə/ *adj* involving 2 threads or wires ⟨~ *suspension of a pendulum*⟩ [ISV *bi-* + L *filum* thread] – **bifilarly** *adv*

bifocal /bie'fohk(ə)l/ *adj* **1** having 2 focal lengths **2** having 1 part that corrects for near vision and 1 for distant vision ⟨*a* ~ *lens*⟩ [ISV]

bi'focals *n pl* glasses with bifocal lenses

biform /'bie,fawm/ *adj* combining the qualities or forms of 2 distinct kinds of individuals [L *biformis*, fr *bi-* + *forma* form]

bifurcate /'biefuh,kayt, 'bi-, -fə-/ *vi* to divide into 2 branches or parts [ML *bifurcatus*, pp of *bifurcare*, fr L *bifurcus* two-pronged, fr *bi-* + *furca* fork] – **bifurcate** /-kət, -kayt/ *adj*, **bifurcation** /-'kaysh(ə)n/ *n*

¹**big** /big/ *adj* **-gg-** **1** of great force ⟨*a* ~ *storm*⟩ **2a** large in bulk or extent; *also* large in number or amount ⟨*a* ~ *house*⟩ ⟨*a* ~ *fleet*⟩ **b** conducted on a large scale ⟨~ *business*⟩ **c** important in influence, standing, or wealth ⟨*the* ~ *4 banks*⟩ **3a** advanced in pregnancy ⟨~ *with child*⟩ **b** full to bursting; swelling ⟨~ *with rage*⟩ **4** *of the voice* loud and resonant **5a** elder ⟨*my* ~ *sister*⟩ **b** older, grown-up ⟨*when I'm a* ~ *girl, I'm going to be a nurse*⟩ **6a** chief, outstanding ⟨*the* ~ *issue of the campaign*⟩ ⟨*his* ~ *moment*⟩ **b** of great importance or significance ⟨*a* ~ *decision*⟩ **7a** pretentious, boastful ⟨~ *talk*⟩ **b** magnanimous, generous ⟨*that's very* ~ *of you*⟩ **8** popular ⟨*Frank Sinatra is very* ~ *in Las Vegas*⟩ – infml [ME, prob of Scand origin; akin to Norw dial. *bugge* important man; akin to OE *bȳl* boil, Skt *bhūri* abundant] – **biggish** *adj*, **bigness** *n*

²**big** *adv* **1a** outstandingly ⟨*made it* ~ *in New York*⟩ **b** on a grand scale ⟨*think* ~!⟩ **2** pretentiously ⟨*he talks* ~⟩ *USE* infml

bigamy /'bigəmi/ *n* the crime of going through a marriage ceremony with one person while legally married to another [ME *bigamie*, fr ML *bigamia*, fr L *bi-* + LL *-gamia* -gamy, fr Gk, fr *gamos* marriage; akin to L *gener* son-in-law] – **bigamist** *n*, **bigamous** *adj*, **bigamously** *adv*

,big 'bang ,theory *n* a theory in cosmology: the universe originated from the explosion of a single mass of material so that the components are still flying apart – compare STEADY STATE THEORY

,Big 'Brother *n* (the leader of) a ruthless all-powerful government [*Big Brother*, omnipotent head of state in the novel *1984* by George Orwell †1950 E writer]

big bud *n* any of several plant diseases caused by a gall mite

,big 'dipper /'dipə/ *n* **1** *often cap B&D, Br* ROLLER COASTER **2** *cap B&D, NAm* URSA MAJOR

,big 'end *n* the end of an engine's connecting rod nearest the crankpin

,big 'game *n* **1** large animals hunted or fished for sport **2** an important objective; *esp* one involving risk

,big 'gun *n* sby or sthg important or powerful – infml

'big,head /-,hed/ *n* a conceited person – infml

'big ,head *n* an exaggerated opinion of one's importance – infml – **bigheaded** *adj*

,big'hearted /-'hahtid/ *adj* generous and kindly – **bigheartedly** *adv*, **bigheartedness** *n*

bight /biet/ *n* **1a** the middle part of a slack rope **b** a loop in a rope **2** (a hollow formed by) a bend of a river, coast, mountain chain, etc [ME, bend, angle, fr OE *byht*; akin to OE *būgan* to bend – more at ¹BOW]

'big,mouthed /-,mowdhd, -,mowtht/ *adj* loud-mouthed

,big 'name *n* a very famous or important performer or personage – **big-name** *adj*

,big 'noise *n* BIG SHOT – infml

bigot /'bigət/ *n* one who is obstinately or intolerantly devoted to his/her own religion, opinion, etc [MF, hypocrite, bigot] – **bigoted** *adj*, **bigotedly** *adv*, **bigotry** /-tri/ *n*

'big ,shot *n* an important person – infml

,big 'stick *n* (the threat of using) force – infml

'big ,time *n* *the* highest rank, esp among entertainers – infml – **big-time** *adj*, **big-timer** *n*

,big 'top *n* the main tent of a circus

,big 'tree *n* a very large Californian evergreen tree of the pine family

,big 'wheel *n* **1** an amusement device consisting of a large upright power-driven wheel carrying seats that remain horizontal round its rim **2** BIG SHOT

'big,wig /-,wig/ *n* an important person – infml

¹**bijou** /'bee,zhooh/ *n, pl* **bijous, bijoux** /-,zhooh(z)/ a small dainty usu ornamental piece of delicate workmanship; a jewel [F, fr Bret *bizou* ring, fr *biz* finger; akin to W *bys* finger]

²**bijou** *adj, esp of a house* desirably elegant and usu small

bijouterie /bi'zhooht(ə)ri/ *n* a collection of trinkets or ornaments; jewellery [F, fr *bijou*]

bike /biek/ *vi or n* (to ride) **1** a bicycle **2** a motorcycle [by shortening & alter.]

bikini /bi'keeni/ *n* a woman's brief 2-piece garment resembling bra and pants worn for swimming or sunbathing [F, fr *Bikini*, atoll of the Marshall islands]

bikky /'biki/ *n* a biccy – infml

bilabial /bie'laybi·əl/ *n or adj* (a consonant) produced with both lips (e g /b, p, m/) [ISV]

bilateral /bie'lat(ə)rəl/ *adj* **1** having 2 sides **2** BIPARTITE 2 – **bilateralism** *n*, **bilaterally** *adv*, **bilateralness** *n*

bi,lateral 'symmetry *n* a pattern of symmetry in which the organism is divisible into essentially identical halves by 1 plane only

bilberry /'bilb(ə)ri/ *n* (the bluish edible fruit of) a dwarf bushy European shrub of the heath family that grows on moorland [*bil-* (prob of Scand origin; akin to Dan *bølle* whortleberry) + *berry*]

bilbo /'bilboh/ *n* an iron bar with sliding shackles formerly used to confine the feet of prisoners – usu pl with sing. meaning [perh fr *Bilbao, Bilboa*, town in Spain]

bile /biel/ *n* **1** a yellow or greenish fluid secreted by the liver into the intestines to aid the digestion of fats

☞ DIGESTION **2** inclination to anger [F, fr L *bilis*; akin to W *bustl* bile]

¹bilge /bilj/ *n* **1** the (space inside the) lowest usu rounded part of a ship's hull between the keel and the vertical sides ☞ SHIP **2** stale or worthless remarks or ideas – infml [prob modif of MF *boulge, bouge* leather bag, curved part – more at BUDGET]

²bilge *vt* to damage (a ship) in the bilge ~ *vi* to suffer damage in the bilge

'bilge ,keel *n* a longitudinal projection attached to a ship's hull or the bilge on either side to reduce rolling and support the weight of the vessel when grounded

'bilge ,water *n* foul water that collects in the bilge of a ship

bilharzia /bil'hahzi·ə/ *n* **1** a schistosome **2** schistosomiasis [NL, fr Theodor *Bilharz* †1862 G zoologist] – **bilharzial** *adj*

bilharziasis /,bilhah'zie·əsis/ *n, pl* **bilharziases** /-seez/ schistosomiasis [NL, fr *bilharzia* + *-iasis*]

biliary /'bilyəri/ *adj* of or conveying bile or bile-conveying structures ⟨~ *disorders*⟩ [F *biliare*, fr L *bilis*]

bilingual /bie'ling·gwəl/ *adj* **1** of, containing, or expressed in 2 languages **2** using or able to use 2 languages with the fluency of a native speaker [L *bilinguis*, fr *bi-* + *lingua* tongue – more at TONGUE] – **bilingual** *n*, **bilingualism** *n*, **bilingually** *adv*

bilious /'bili·əs/ *adj* **1** marked by or suffering from disordered liver function, esp excessive secretion of bile **2** peevish, ill-natured **3** *of colours* extremely distasteful; sickly ⟨*a ~ green*⟩ – infml [MF *bilieux*, fr L *biliosus*, fr *bilis*] – **biliously** *adv*, **biliousness** *n*

bilirubin /,bili'roohbin/ *n* a reddish yellow pigment occurring in bile, blood, urine, and gallstones [L *bilis* + *ruber* red – more at RED]

bilk /bilk/ *vt* to cheat out of what is due [perh alter. of ²*balk*] – **bilker** *n*

¹bill /bil/ *n* **1** (a mouthpart resembling) the jaws of a bird together with variously shaped and coloured horny coverings and often specialized for a particular diet **2** a projection of land like a beak [ME *bile*, fr OE; akin to OE *bill* (weapon)]

²bill *vi* to caress affectionately – chiefly in *bill and coo*

³bill *n* **1** a long staff with a hook-shaped blade used as a weapon up to the 18th c **2** a billhook [ME *bil*, fr OE *bill*; akin to OHG *bill* pickaxe, Gk *phitros* log]

⁴bill *n* **1** a draft of a law presented to a legislature ☞ LAW **2** a paper carrying a statement of particulars **3a** (an itemized account of) charges due for goods or services **b** a statement of a creditor's claim **4a** a written or printed notice advertising an event of interest to the public (e g a theatrical entertainment) **b** an item (e g a film or play) in a programme entertainment **5** *chiefly NAm* ²NOTE 3c [ME, fr ML *billa*, alter. of *bulla*, fr L, bubble, boss]

⁵bill *vt* **1** to submit a bill of charges to **2a** to advertise, esp by posters or placards **b** to arrange for the presentation of as part of a programme

billabong /'biləbong/ *n, Austr* **1a** a blind channel leading out from a river **b** a usu dry stream bed that is filled seasonally **2** a backwater forming a stagnant pool [native name in Australia]

'bill,board /-,bawd/ *n, chiefly NAm* HOARDING 2 [⁴*bill* + *board*]

-billed /-bild/ *comb form* (→ *adj*) having (such) a bill ⟨*hard*-billed⟩

¹billet /'bilit/ *n* **1a** an official order directing that a member of a military force be provided with board and lodging (e g in a private home) **b** quarters assigned (as if) by a billet **2** a position, job ⟨*a lucrative ~*⟩ [ME *bylet* short document, fr MF *billette*, dim. of *bulle* document, fr ML *bulla*]

²billet *vt* to provide (e g soldiers) with a billet

³billet *n* **1** a small thick piece of wood (e g for firewood) **2** a usu small bar of iron, steel, etc **3** a Romanesque architectural moulding or ornamentation consisting of raised short cylinders or square pieces placed at regular intervals ☞ ARCHITECTURE [ME *bylet*, fr MF *billete*, dim. of *bille* log, of Celt origin; akin to OIr *bile* sacred tree]

billet-doux /,bili 'dooh, ,beeyay/ *n, pl* **billets-doux** /~/ a love letter [F *billet doux*, lit., sweet letter]

'bill,fold /-,fohld/ *n, NAm* WALLET 1 [short for earlier *billfolder*, fr ⁴*bill* 5]

'bill,head /-,hed/ *n* (the heading of) a printed form used for bills

'bill,hook /-,hook/ *n* a cutting tool, used esp for pruning, that has a blade with a hooked point [³*bill* + *hook*]

billiards /'bilyədz/ *n pl but sing in constr* any of several games played on an oblong table by driving small balls against one another or into pockets with a cue; *specif* one with 3 balls in which scores are made by causing a cue ball to hit 2 object balls in succession – compare POOL [MF *billard* billiard cue, billiards, fr *bille*] – **billiard** *adj*

billing /'biling/ *n* **1** ADVERTISING 2 ⟨*advance ~*⟩ **2** the relative prominence given to a name (e g of an actor) in advertising programmes ⟨*top ~*⟩ [⁵*bill*]

billion /'bilyən/ *n* **1** a thousand millions (10^9) **2** an indefinitely large number – often pl with sing. meaning **3** *Br* a million millions (10^{12}) ***USE*** *(1&3)* ☞ NUMBER [F, fr *bi-* + *-illion* (as in *million*)] – **billion** *adj*, **billionth** *adj or n*

billionaire /,bilyə'neə/ *n* one whose wealth is estimated at a billion or more money units (e g pounds or dollars) [*billion* + *-aire* (as in *millionaire*)]

,bill of ex'change *n* an unconditional written order from one person to another to pay a specified sum of money to a designated person

,bill of 'fare *n* a menu

,bill of 'lading *n* a receipt signed usu by the agent or owner of a ship listing goods (to be) shipped

,bill of 'quantities *n, Br* a statement of work and materials involved in a construction job

,bill of 'rights *n, often cap B&R* a summary in law (e g the English Statute of 1689) of fundamental rights and privileges guaranteed by the state

,bill of 'sale *n* a formal document for the conveyance or transfer of title to goods and personal property

billon /'bilən/ *n* gold or silver heavily alloyed with a less valuable metal [F, fr MF, fr *bille* log – more at ³BILLET]

¹billow /'biloh/ *n* **1** a great wave, esp in the open sea **2** a rolling swirling mass (e g of flame or smoke) [prob fr ON *bylgja*; akin to OHG *balg* bag – more at BELLY] – **billowy** *adj*

²billow *vb* to (cause to) rise, roll, bulge, or swell out (as if) in billows

'bill,poster /-,pohstə/ *n* one who pastes up advertisements and public notices on hoardings – **billposting** *n*

'bill,sticker /-,stikə/ *n* a billposter – **billsticking** *n*

[1]**billy** /'bili/, **'billy ,club** *n, NAm* TRUNCHEON 2 [prob fr *Billy*, nickname for *William*]

[2]**billy,** *chiefly Austr* **'billy,can** *n* a can of metal or enamelware with an arched handle and a lid, used for outdoor cooking or carrying food or liquid [prob fr the name *Billy*]

'billy ,goat *n* a male goat – infml [fr the name *Billy*]

billy-o /'bilioh/ *n* [prob fr the name *Billy*] – **like billy-o/billy-oh** very much; vigorously ⟨*was raining* like billy-o⟩

bilobed /'bie,lohbd/ *adj* divided into 2 lobes

biltong /'biltong/ *n, chiefly SAfr* strips of lean meat dried in the sun [Afrik, fr *bil* buttock + *tong* tongue]

bimetallic /,biemi'talik/ *adj* (of or being a device with a part) composed of 2 different metals, esp ones that expand by different amounts when heated – **bimetal** *adj or n*

bimillenary /,biemi'lenəri/, **bimillenial** /-ni·əl/ *n or adj* (the celebration) of a 2000th anniversary

bimolecular /biemə'lekyoolə/ *adj* **1** of or formed from 2 molecules **2** being 2 molecules thick [ISV] – **bimolecularly** *adv*

bimonthly /,bie'munthli/ *adj or adv* (occurring) every 2 months or twice a month

[1]**bin** /bin/ *n* **1** a container used for storage (e g of flour, grain, bread, or coal) **2** a partitioned case or stand for storing and aging bottles of wine **3** *Br* a wastepaper basket, dustbin, or similar container for rubbish [ME *binn*, fr OE, manger, basket, prob of Celt origin; akin to Gaulish *benna* wicker-bodied cart, Gk *phatnē* manger]

[2]**bin** *vt* **-nn-** to put or store (esp bottled wine) in a bin

bin- *comb form* [1]BI- ⟨bin*aural*⟩ [ME, fr LL, fr L *bini* two by two; akin to OE *twīn* twine]

binary /'bienəri/ *adj* **1** consisting of or marked by 2 things or parts **2a** of, being, or belonging to a system of numbers having 2 as its base ⟨*the* ~ *digits 0 and 1*⟩ **b** involving a choice or condition of 2 alternatives (e g on or off) ⟨~ *logic*⟩ **3** having 2 musical subjects or 2 complementary sections ⟨~ *form*⟩ [LL *binarius*, fr L *bini*] – **binary** *n*

,binary 'fission *n* asexual reproduction of a cell by division into 2 parts

,binary 'star *n* a system of 2 stars that revolve round each other

binaural /,bien'awrəl/ *adj* **1** of or used with both ears **2** stereophonically (recorded and) played to the hearer via headphones [ISV] – **binaurally** *adv*

[1]**bind** /biend/ *vb* **bound** /bownd/ *vt* **1a** to make secure by tying (e g with cord) or tying together **b** to confine or restrict (as if) with bonds ⟨*he was* bound *and thrown into prison*⟩ **c** to put under a (legal) obligation ⟨*we are all* bound *to keep the law*⟩ **2** to wrap round with sthg (e g cloth) so as to enclose or cover **3** to encircle, gird **4a** to cause to stick together ⟨*add an egg to* ~ *the mixture*⟩ **b** to take up and hold (e g by chemical forces); combine with ⟨*enzymes* ~ *their substrates*⟩ **5** to constipate **6** to make binding; settle ⟨*a deposit* ~s *the sale*⟩ **7** to protect, strengthen, cover, or decorate with (a) binding **8** to cause to be attached (e g by gratitude or affection) ~*vi* **1** to form a cohesive mass **2** to become hindered from free operation; jam **3** to complain – infml [ME *binden*, fr OE *bindan*; akin to OHG *bintan* to bind, Gk *peisma* cable]

[2]**bind** *n* a nuisance, bore – infml – **in a bind** *chiefly NAm* in trouble or difficulty – infml

binder /'biendə/ *n* **1** a person who binds books **2** a usu detachable cover (e g for holding sheets of paper) **3** sthg (e g tar or cement) that produces or promotes cohesion in loosely assembled substances ☞ BUILDING [[1]BIND + [2]-ER]

[1]**binding** /'biending/ *n* a material or device used to bind: e g **a** a covering that fastens the leaves of a book **b** a narrow strip of fabric used to finish raw edges [[1]BIND + [2]-ING]

[2]**binding** *adj* imposing an obligation ⟨*a* ~ *promise*⟩

'binding ,energy *n* the energy required to break up a molecule, atom, or atomic nucleus completely into its constituent particles

bind over *vt* to impose a specific legal obligation on ⟨*he was* bound over *to keep the peace*⟩

'bind,weed /-,weed/ *n* any of various twining plants with usu large showy trumpet-shaped flowers

bine /bien/ *n* a twining stem or flexible shoot (e g of the hop) [alter. of [2]*bind* (sthg that binds)]

,Binet-Si'mon ,scale /,beenay see'mohn/ *n* an intelligence test consisting of graded tasks for children of successive ages [Alfred *Binet* †1911 & Théodore *Simon* †1961 F psychologists]

binge /binj/ *n* an unrestrained indulgence in sthg; *esp* a drunken revel – infml [E dial. *binge* (to drink heavily)]

[1]**bingo** /'bing·goh/ *interj* **1** – used to express the suddenness or unexpectedness of an event **2** – used as an exclamation to show that one has won a game of bingo [alter. of *bing* (interj suggesting a sharp ringing sound), of imit origin]

[2]**bingo** *n* a game of chance played with cards having numbered squares corresponding to numbers drawn at random and won by covering or marking off all or a predetermined number of such squares

binman /'bin,man, -mən/ *n, pl* **binmen** /-,men, -mən/ *Br* a dustman

binnacle /'binəkl/ *n* a case, stand, etc containing a ship's compass [alter. of ME *bitakle*, fr OPg or OSp; OPg *bitácola* & OSp *bitácula*, fr L *habitaculum* dwelling place, fr *habitare* to inhabit – more at HABITATION]

binocular /bi'nokyoolə/ *adj* of, using, or adapted to the use of both eyes ⟨*good* ~ *vision*⟩ – **binocularly** *adv*

bi'noculars *n pl, pl* **binoculars** a binocular optical instrument; *esp* field glasses or opera glasses

binomial /bie'nohmyəl/ *n or adj* (a mathematical expression) consisting of 2 terms connected by a plus sign or minus sign [n NL *binomium*, fr ML, neut of *binomius* having two names, alter. of L *binominis*, fr *bi-* + *nomin-, nomen* name – more at NAME; adj fr n] – **binomially** *adv*

bi'nomial ,theorem *n* a theorem by means of which a binomial may be raised to any power by a formula

binominal /bie'nominl/ *adj, of taxonomic nomenclature* consisting of or using 2 Latin names

bint /bint/ *n, Br* a girl or woman – chiefly derog [Ar, girl, daughter]

binturong /bin'tooərong/ *n* an Asiatic civet with a prehensile tail [Malay]

bio- – see [2]BI-

bioassay /ˌbie·ohˈasay, -əˈsay/ *n* the determination of the relative strength of a substance (e g a drug) by comparing its effect on a test organism with that of a standard preparation [*bio*logical *assay*] – **bioassay** /-əˈsay/ *vt*

biochemistry /ˌbie·ohˈkeməstri/ *n* chemistry that deals with the chemical compounds and processes occurring in organisms [ISV] – **biochemist** *n,* **biochemical** *adj,* **biochemically** *adv*

biodegradable /ˌbie·ohdeeˈgraydəbl/ *adj* capable of being broken down, esp into simpler harmless products, by the action of living beings (e g microorganisms) [[2]*bi-* + *degrade* + *-able*] – **biodegradability** /-dəˈbiləti/ *n,* **biodegrade** /-ˌdeeˈgrayd/ *vb,* **biodegradation** /-ˌdeegrəˈdaysh(ə)n, -de-/ *n*

ˌbioenerˈgetics /-ˌenəˈjetiks/ *n pl but sing in constr* the biology of energy transformations and exchanges within and between living things and their environments – **bioenergetic** *adj*

ˌbioengiˈneering /-ˌenjiˈniəring/ *n* the application to biological or medical science of engineering principles or equipment

ˌbioˈfeedback /-ˈfeedˌbak/ *n* the technique of making unconscious or involuntary bodily processes perceptible to the senses in order to affect them by conscious mental control

ˌbioˈgenesis /-ˈjenəsis/ *n* **1** the development of living things from preexisting living things **2** biosynthesis [NL] – **biogenetic** /-jəˈnetik/ *adj*

biogenic /ˌbie·ohˈjenik/ *adj* produced by living organisms – **biogenicity** /ˌbie·ohjəˈnisəti/ *n*

ˌbiogeoˈgraphical /-jee·əˈgrafikl/, **ˌbiogeoˈgraphic** *adj* of or being a geographical region viewed in terms of its plants and animals

biography /bieˈogrəfi/ *n* **1** a usu written account of a person's life **2** biographical writing as a literary genre [LGk *biographia,* fr Gk *bi-* + *-graphia* -graphy] – **biographer** *n,* **biographical** /ˌbie·əˈgrafikl/, **biographic** *adj,* **biographically** *adv*

ˌbioˌlogical ˈclock /ˌbie·əˈlojikl/ *n* the inherent timing mechanism responsible for various cyclic responses (e g changes in hormone levels) of living beings

biological control *n* control of pests by interference with their ecological environment

biological oxygen demand *n* the amount of oxygen required by microorganisms in water, that can be used as an indicator of pollution

bioˌlogical ˈwarfare *n* warfare involving the use of (disease-causing) living organisms, or chemicals harmful to plants

biology /bieˈoləji/ *n* **1** a science that deals with the structure, function, development, distribution, and life processes of living organisms **2a** the plant and animal life of a region or environment **b** the biology of an organism or group [G *biologie,* fr *bi-* + *-logie* -logy] – **biologist** *n,* **biological** /bie·əˈlojikl/ *adj,* **biologically** *adv*

bioluminescence /ˌbie·ohˌloohmiˈnes(ə)ns/ *n* (the emission of) light from living organisms [ISV] – **bioluminescent** *adj*

biomass /ˈbie·ohˌmas/ *n* the amount of living matter present in a region (e g in a unit area or volume of habitat)

biome /ˈbie·ohm/ *n* a major type of ecological community ⟨*the grassland* ~⟩ ☞ PLANT [[2]*bi-* + *-ome*]

biometrics /ˌbie·əˈmetriks/ *n pl but sing or pl in constr* biometry

biometry /bieˈomətri/ *n* the statistical analysis of biological observations and phenomena [ISV] – **biometric** /ˌbie·əˈmetrik/, **biometrical** *adj*

bionic /bieˈonik/ *adj* **1** involving bionics; *also* having or being a bionically designed part (e g a limb) **2** having exceptional abilities or powers – not used technically – **bionically** *adv*

biˈonics *n pl but sing or pl in constr* **1** a science concerned with the application of biological systems to engineering problems **2** the use of mechanical parts to replace or simulate damaged parts of a living thing [[2]*bi-* + *-onics* (as in *electronics*)]

bionomics /ˌbie·ohˈnomiks/ *n pl but sing in constr* ecology [*bionomic,* adj, prob fr F *bionomique,* fr *bionomie* ecology, fr *bi-* + *-nomie* -nomy] – **bionomic, bionomical** *adj,* **bionomically** *adv*

-biont /-bie·ont/ *comb form* (→ *n*) one having a (specified) mode of life ⟨*haplo*biont⟩ [prob fr G, modif of Gk *biount-, biōn,* prp of *bioun* to live, fr *bios* life]

biophysics /bie·ohˈfiziks/ *n pl but sing or pl in constr* biology concerned with the application of physics to biological problems – **biophysical** *adj,* **biophysicist** /-ˈfizisist/ *n*

biopsy /ˈbieˌopsi/ *n* the removal and examination of tissue, cells, or fluids from the living body [ISV [2]*bi-* + Gk *opsis* appearance – more at OPTIC]

biorhythm /ˈbie·ohˌridhəm/ *n* a supposed periodic fluctuation in the activity of the biological processes of a living thing that is held to affect and determine mood, behaviour, and performance – usu pl – **biorhythmic** /ˌbie·ohˈridhmik/ *adj,* **biorhythmically** *adv*

bioscope /ˈbie·əˌskohp/ *n, chiefly SAfr* CINEMA 2 – infml [[2]*bi-* + *-scope*]

-biosis /-bieˈohsis/ *comb form* (→ *n*), *pl* **-bioses** /-seez/ mode of life ⟨*sym*biosis⟩ [NL, fr Gk *biōsis,* fr *bioun* to live, fr *bios*] – **biotic** *comb form* (→ *adj*)

biosphere /ˈbie·əˌsfiə/ *n* the part of the world in which life exists

biosynthesis /ˌbie·ohˈsinthəsis/ *n, pl* **biosyntheses** /-seez/ the production of a chemical compound by a living organism [NL] – **biosynthetic** /-ˈthetik/ *adj,* **biosynthetically** *adv*

biota /bieˈohtə/ *n* the flora and fauna of a region [NL, fr Gk *biotē* life; akin to Gk *bios*]

biotic /bieˈotik/ *adj* of life; *esp* caused or produced by living organisms [Gk *biōtikos,* fr *bioun*]

biotin /ˈbie·ətin/ *n* a growth-controlling vitamin of the vitamin B complex found esp in yeast, liver, and egg yolk [ISV, fr Gk *biotos* life, sustenance; akin to Gk *bios*]

bipartisan /ˌbieˈpahtizn/ *adj* of or involving 2 parties

bipartite /ˌbieˈpahtiet/ *adj* **1** being in 2 parts **2** *of a treaty, contract, etc between 2 parties* **a** having 2 correspondent parts, one for each party **b** affecting both parties in the same way **3** cleft (almost) into 2 parts ⟨*a* ~ *leaf*⟩ [L *bipartitus,* pp of *bipartire* to divide in two, fr *bi-* + *partire* to divide, fr *part-, pars* part] – **bipartitely** *adv,* **bipartition** /ˌbie pahˈtish(ə)n/ *n*

biped /ˈbieped/ *n* a 2-footed animal [L *biped-, bipes,* fr [1]*bi-* + *ped-, pes* foot – more at FOOT] – **biped, bipedal** /-ˈpeedl/ *adj*

biplane /ˈbieˌplayn/ *n* an aeroplane with 2 pairs of

wings placed one above and usu slightly forward of the other

bipolar /ˌbieˈpohlə/ *adj* having or involving 2 (oppositely charged) poles – **bipolarity** /ˌbiepəˈlarəti/ *n*

[1]**birch** /buhch/ *n* **1** (the hard pale close-grained wood of) any of a genus of deciduous usu short-lived trees or shrubs typically having a layered outer bark that peels readily **2** a birch rod or bundle of twigs for flogging [ME, fr OE *beorc*; akin to OHG *birka* birch, L *fraxinus* ash tree, OE *beorht* bright – more at BRIGHT] – **birch, birchen** /ˈbuhchən/ *adj*

[2]**birch** *vt* to whip (as if) with a birch

bird /buhd/ *n* **1** any of a class of warm-blooded vertebrates with the body more or less completely covered with feathers and the forelimbs modified as wings ☞ ANATOMY **2a** a (peculiar) fellow – chiefly infml **b** *chiefly Br* a girl – infml **3** a hissing or jeering expressive of disapproval or derision – chiefly in *give somebody the bird/get the bird*; infml **4** *Br* TIME 5b – slang [ME, fr OE *bridd*; (4) short for rhyming slang *birdlime* time] – **birdlike** *adj* – **for the birds** trivial, worthless – infml

birdbath /-ˌbahth/ *n* a usu ornamental basin for birds to bathe in

ˈ**birdˌbrain** /-ˌbrayn/ *n* a silly or stupid person – infml – **birdbrained** *adj*

ˈ**birdˌcall** /-ˌkawl/ *n* a device for imitating the call of a bird

ˈ**bird ˌdog** *n, NAm* a gundog trained to hunt or retrieve birds

[1]**birdie** /ˈbuhdi/ *n* **1** a (little) bird – used esp by or to children **2** a golf score of 1 stroke less than par on a hole

[2]**birdie** *vt* **birdieing** /ˈbuhdi·ing/ to play (a hole in golf) in 1 stroke under par

ˈ**birdˌlime** /-ˌliem/ *n* **1** a sticky substance that is smeared on twigs to snare small birds **2** the droppings of birds

ˌ**bird of ˈparadise** *n* any of numerous brilliantly coloured plumed birds of the New Guinea area

ˌ**bird of ˈpassage** *n* **1** a migratory bird **2** a person who leads a wandering or unsettled life

ˌ**bird of ˈprey** *n* a hawk, vulture, or other bird that feeds on carrion or on meat taken by hunting

ˈ**birdˌseed** /-ˌseed/ *n* a mixture of hemp, millet, and other seeds used for feeding caged and wild birds

ˈ**bird's-ˌeye** *n* any of numerous plants with small bright-coloured flowers – often in combination

ˌ**bird's-eye ˈview** *n* **1** a view from above; an aerial view **2** a brief and general summary; an overview

ˌ**bird's-foot ˈtrefoil** *n* any of a genus of leguminous plants with claw-shaped pods and usu yellow flowers

ˈ**bird's-ˌnesting** *n* the practice of searching for birds' nests, esp in order to steal the eggs

ˌ**bird's nest ˈsoup** *n* a soup made from the gelatinous nest of any of several S Asiatic swifts

ˈ**birdˌstrike** /-ˌstriek/ *n* a collision between a bird and an aircraft

ˈ**bird-ˌwatching** *n* the observation or identification of birds in their natural environment – **bird-watcher** *n*

birefringence /ˌbieriˈfrinj(ə)ns/ *n* the refraction of light in 2 slightly different directions to form 2 rays [ISV] – **birefringent** *adj*

bireme /ˈbiereem/ *n* a galley with 2 banks of oars [L *biremis*, fr [1]*bi-* + *remus* oar – more at ROW]

biretta /biˈretə/ *n* a square cap with 3 ridges on top worn by (Roman Catholic) clergy ☞ GARMENT [It *berretta*, fr OProv *berret* cap, irreg fr LL *birrus* cloak with a hood, of Celt origin; akin to MIr *berr* short]

birk /buhk/ *n, Br* a burk – slang

Biro /ˈbieroh/ *trademark* – used for a ballpoint pen

birth /buhth/ *n* **1a** the emergence of a new individual from the body of its parent **b** the act or process of bringing forth young from within the body **2** the fact of being born, esp at a particular time or place ⟨*a Frenchman by* ~⟩ **3** (noble) lineage or extraction ⟨*marriage between equals in* ~⟩ **4** a beginning, start ⟨*the* ~ *of an idea*⟩ **5** natural or inherited tendency ⟨*an artist by* ~⟩ [ME, fr ON *byrth*; akin to OE *beran* – more at [2]BEAR]

ˈ**birth cerˌtificate** *n* an official record of sby's parentage and date and place of birth

ˈ**birth conˌtrol** *n* control of the number of children born, esp by preventing or lessening the frequency of conception; *broadly* contraception

birthday /ˈbuhthday, -di/ *n* **1a** the day of a person's birth **b** a day of origin **2** an anniversary of a birth ⟨*her 21st* ~⟩

ˈ**birthday ˌsuit** *n* nothing but bare skin; nakedness ⟨*a photograph of her at 6 months in her* ~⟩ – humor

ˈ**birthˌmark** /-ˌmahk/ *n* a usu red or brown blemish on the skin at birth

ˈ**birthˌrate** /-ˌrayt/ *n* the number of (live) births per unit of population (e g 1000 people) in a period of time (e g 1 year)

ˈ**birthˌright** /-ˌriet/ *n* sthg (e g a privilege or possession) to which a person is entitled by birth

bis- /bis-/ *comb form* twice; doubled – esp in complex chemical expressions ⟨bis*(methylphenyl) mercury*⟩ [L *bis*, fr OL *dvis*; akin to OHG *zwiro* twice, L *duo* two – more at TWO]

biscuit /ˈbiskit/ *n* **1** earthenware or porcelain after the first firing and before glazing **2** a light yellowish brown colour **3** *Br* any of several variously-shaped small usu unleavened thin dry crisp bakery products that may be sweet or savoury **4** *NAm* a soft cake or bread (e g a scone) made without yeast [ME *bisquite* dry crisp bread, fr MF *bescuit*, fr (*pain*) *bescuit* twice-cooked bread]

bise /beez/ *n* a cold dry northerly or northeasterly wind of S France, Switzerland, and Italy [ME, fr OF, of Gmc origin]

bisect /bieˈsekt/ *vt* to divide into 2 (equal) parts ~ *vi* to cross, intersect – **bisection** /bieˈseksh(ə)n/ *n*

bisector /bieˈsektə/ *n* a straight line that bisects an angle or a line [BISECT + [1]-OR]

bisexual /bieˈseksyoo(ə)l, -sh(ə)l/ *adj* **1a** possessing characteristics of both sexes **b** sexually attracted to both sexes **2** of or involving both sexes – **bisexual** *n*, **bisexually** *adv*, **bisexuality** /ˌbieseksyooˈaləti, -sek shoo-/ *n*

bishop /ˈbishəp/ *n* **1** a clergyman ranking above a priest, having authority to ordain and confirm, and typically governing a diocese **2** either of 2 chess pieces of each colour allowed to move diagonally across any number of consecutive unoccupied squares [ME *bisshop*, fr OE *bisceop*, fr LL *episcopus*, fr Gk *episkopos*, lit., overseer, fr *epi-* + *skeptesthai* to look – more at SPY] – **bishophood** *n*

bishopric /ˈbishəprik/ *n* **1** a diocese **2** the office of bishop [ME *bisshopriche*, fr OE *bisceoprīce*, fr *bisceop* + *rīce* kingdom – more at RICH]

bismuth /ˈbizməth/ *n* a heavy chiefly trivalent metallic element ☞ PERIODIC TABLE [obs G *bismut* (now *wismut*), modif of *wismut*, fr *wise* meadow + *mut* claim to a mine] – **bismuthic** /bizˈmudhik, -ˈmyoohdhik/ *adj*

bison /ˈbiesn/ *n, pl* **bison** 1 a large shaggy-maned European bovine mammal that is now nearly extinct 2 BUFFALO 2 [L *bisont-*, *bison*, of Gmc origin; akin to OHG *wisant* aurochs; akin to OPruss *wissambrs* aurochs]

[1]**bisque** /bisk/ *n* an advantage (e g an extra turn in croquet) allowed to an inferior player [F]

[2]**bisque** *n* a thick cream soup (e g of shellfish or game) [F]

[3]**bisque** *n* BISCUIT 1; *esp* a type of white unglazed ceramic ware [by shortening & alter.]

bistort /biˈstawt/ *n* a European plant with twisted roots and a spike of usu pink flowers [MF *bistorte*, fr (assumed) ML *bistorta*, fr L *bis-* + *torta*, fem of *tortus*, pp of *torquēre* to twist – more at TORTURE]

bistre /ˈbeestə, -strə/ *n* (the yellowish to dark colour of) a pigment used in art [F]

bistro /beestroh/ *n, pl* **bistros** a small bar, restaurant, or tavern [F]

[1]**bit** /bit/ *n* **1** a bar of metal or occas rubber attached to the bridle and inserted in the mouth of a horse **2** the biting or cutting edge or part of a tool; *also* a replaceable drilling, boring, etc part of a compound tool **3** sthg that curbs or restrains **4** the part of a key that enters the lock and acts on the bolt and tumblers [ME *bitt*, fr OE *bite* act of biting; akin to OE *bītan* to bite]

[2]**bit** *vt* **-tt-** to put a bit in the mouth of (a horse)

[3]**bit** *n* **1a** a small piece or quantity of anything (e g food) ⟨*a ~ of cake*⟩ ⟨*a ~ of string*⟩ ⟨*a little ~ more*⟩ **b(1)** a usu specified small coin ⟨*a fivepenny ~*⟩ **(2)** a money unit worth ⅛ of a US dollar **c** a part, section ⟨*couldn't hear the next ~*⟩ **2** sthg small or unimportant of its kind: e g **a** a brief period; a while **b(1)** an indefinite usu small degree, extent, or amount ⟨*is a ~ of a rascal*⟩ ⟨*every ~ as powerful*⟩ **(2)** an indefinite small fraction ⟨*3 inches and a ~*⟩ – infml **3** all the items, situations, or activities appropriate to a given style, role, etc ⟨*rejected the whole love and marriage ~*⟩ **4** a small but necessary piece of work ⟨*doing their ~ for Britain by refusing a pay rise*⟩ **5** a young woman – slang [ME, piece bitten off, morsel of food, fr OE *bita*; akin to OE *bītan*] – **a bit 1** somewhat, rather ⟨a bit *difficult*⟩ – infml **2** the smallest or an insignificant amount or degree ⟨*not* a bit *sorry*⟩ – infml – **a bit much** a little more than one wants to endure – **a bit of all right** *Br* sby or sthg very pleasing; *esp* a sexually attractive person – infml – **bit by bit** little by little – **bit on the side** (a person with whom one has) occasional sexual intercourse usu outside marriage – **to bits** TO PIECES

[4]**bit** *n* (the physical representation in a computer or electronic memory of) a unit of computer information equivalent to the result of a choice between 2 alternatives (e g *on* or *off*) [*bi*nary dig*it*]

[1]**bitch** /bich/ *n* **1** the female of the dog or similar flesh-eating animals **2** a malicious, spiteful, and domineering woman **3** a complaint – infml [ME *bicche*, fr OE *bicce*; akin to OE *bæc* back]

[2]**bitch** *vi* to complain – infml

bitchy /ˈbichi/ *adj* characterized by malicious, spiteful, or arrogant behaviour – **bitchily** *adv*, **bitchiness** *n*

[1]**bite** /biet/ *vb* **bit** /bit/; **bitten** /ˈbit(ə)n/ *also* **bit** *vt* **1a** to seize with teeth or jaws, so that they enter, grip, or wound **b** to sting with a fang or other specialized part of the body ⟨*the midges are* biting *me*⟩ **c** to remove or sever with the teeth **2** to cut or pierce (as if) with an edged weapon **3** to cause sharp pain or stinging discomfort to **4** to take strong hold of; grip ~ *vi* **1** to bite or have the habit of biting sthg ⟨*does that dog ~?*⟩ **2** *of a weapon or tool* to cut, pierce **3** to have a sharp penetrating effect ⟨*the sauce really* ~s⟩ **4** *of fish* to take a bait **5** to take or maintain a firm hold [ME *biten*, fr OE *bītan*; akin to OHG *bīzan* to bite, L *findere* to split] – **biter** *n* – **bite off more than one can chew** to undertake more than one can perform – **bite the dust 1** to fall dead, esp in battle **2** to be finished or defeated ⟨*another of his schemes has* bitten the dust⟩

[2]**bite** *n* **1a** the amount of food taken with 1 bite; a morsel **b** a small amount of food; a snack **2** a wound made by biting **3** the hold or grip by which friction is created or purchase is obtained **4** a sharp incisive quality or effect

biting /ˈbieting/ *adj* having the power to bite ⟨*a ~ wind*⟩; *esp* sharp, cutting ⟨*~ irony*⟩ – **bitingly** *adv*

ˌbit of ˈwork *n, pl* **bits of work** a person – derog ⟨*a nasty ~*⟩

ˈbit ˌpart *n* a small acting part, usu with spoken lines

ˈbit ˌplayer *n* a player of bit parts

ˌbits and ˈbobs /bobz/ *n pl* ODDS AND ENDS

ˌbits and ˈpieces *n pl* ODDS AND ENDS

bitt /bit/ *n* either of a pair of posts on a ship's deck for securing ropes [perh fr ON *biti* beam; akin to OE *bōt* boat]

[1]**bitter** /ˈbitə/ *adj* **1a** being or inducing an acrid, astringent, or disagreeable taste similar to that of quinine that is one of the 4 basic taste sensations – compare SALT, SOUR, SWEET **b** distressing, galling ⟨*a ~ sense of shame*⟩ **2a** intense, severe ⟨*~ enemies*⟩ **b** very cold ⟨*a ~ winter*⟩ **c** cynical, rancorous ⟨*~ contempt*⟩ **3** expressive of severe grief or regret ⟨*~ tears*⟩ [ME, fr OE *biter*; akin to OHG *bittar* bitter, OE *bītan*] – **bitterish** *adj*, **bitterly** *adv*, **bitterness** *n*

[2]**bitter** *adv, NAm* bitterly

[3]**bitter** *n* **1** *pl but sing or pl in constr* a usu alcoholic solution of bitter and often aromatic plant products used esp in preparing mixed drinks or as a mild tonic **2** *Br* a very dry beer heavily flavoured with hops

ˌbitter ˈend *n* *the* last extremity, however painful or calamitous [prob orig fr *bitter end* (the end of a ship's anchoring cable), fr *bitter* (a turn of cable round the bitts), fr *bitt*]

bitterling /ˈbitəling/ *n* a small central European freshwater fish resembling the carp [G, fr *bitter* bitter (fr OHG *bittar*) + *-ling* -ling]

bittern /ˈbitən/ *n* any of various small or medium-sized herons with a characteristic booming cry [ME *bitoure*, fr MF *butor*, deriv of L *butio*]

ˈbitter ˌprinciple *n* any of various strongly bitter-tasting substances (e g aloin) extracted from plants

[1]**ˈbitterˌsweet** /-ˌsweet/ *n* a rambling poisonous nightshade with purple-and-yellow flowers

[2]**bittersweet** *adj* bitter and sweet at the same time;

esp pleasant but with elements of suffering or regret ⟨*a ~ ballad*⟩ – **bittersweetly** *adv*, **bittersweetness** *n*

bitty /ˈbiti/ *adj* scrappy, disjointed [[3]BIT + [1]-Y] – **bittily** *adv*

bitumen /ˈbityoomin/ *n* any of various mixtures of hydrocarbons (e g tar) that occur naturally or as residues after heating petroleum, coal, etc [ME *bithumen* mineral pitch, fr L *bitumin-, bitumen*] – **bituminoid** /biˈtyoohmiˌnoyd/ *adj*, **bituminize** /biˈtyoohmiˌniez/ *vt*, **bituminization** /-ˈzaysh(ə)n/ *n*

bituminous /biˈtyoohminəs/ *adj* resembling, containing, or impregnated with bitumen

bivalent /bieˈvaylənt/ *adj* **1** having a valency of 2 **2** *of chromosomes* that become associated in pairs during meiotic cell division – **bivalent** *n*

bivalve /ˈbieˌvalv/ *n or adj* (a mollusc) having a shell composed of 2 valves

[1]**bivouac** /ˈbivoo·ak/ *n* a usu temporary encampment under little or no shelter [F, fr LG *biwake*, fr *bi* at + *wake* guard]

[2]**bivouac** *vi* **-ck-** to make a bivouac; camp

biweekly /ˌbieˈweekli/ *n, adj, or adv* (a publication) issued or occurring **a** every 2 weeks **b** twice a week

biyearly /ˌbieˈyiəli/ *adj* **1** biennial **2** biannual

bizarre /biˈzah/ *adj* **1** odd, extravagant, eccentric **2** involving sensational contrasts or incongruities [F, fr It *bizzarro*] – **bizarrely** *adv*, **bizarreness** *n*

blab /blab/ *vb* **-bb-** *vt* to reveal (a secret) ~ *vi* to talk indiscreetly or thoughtlessly [ME *blabbe* one who blabs; akin to ME *blaberen* to blabber] – **blab** *n*

blabber /ˈblabə/ *vi* to babble ~ *vt* to say indiscreetly [ME *blaberen*, prob of imit origin] – **blabber** *n*

ˈ**blabberˌmouth** /-ˌmowth/ *n* one who talks too much

[1]**black** /blak/ *adj* **1a** of the colour black **b** very dark in colour ⟨*his face was ~ with rage*⟩ **2** *often cap* **a** having dark pigmentation; *esp* of the Negro race ⟨*~ Americans*⟩ **b** of black people or culture ⟨*~ literature*⟩ **3** dressed in black ⟨*the ~ Prince*⟩ **4** dirty, soiled ⟨*hands ~ with dirt*⟩ **5a** having or reflecting little or no light ⟨*~ water*⟩ ⟨*a ~ night*⟩ **b** *of coffee* served without milk or cream **6a** thoroughly sinister or evil ⟨*a ~ deed*⟩ **b** indicative of hostility, disapproval, or discredit ⟨*met only with ~ looks*⟩ **7a** very dismal or calamitous ⟨*~ despair*⟩ **b** marked by the occurrence of disaster ⟨*~ Friday*⟩ **8** showing a profit ⟨*a ~ financial statement*⟩ – compare RED 4 **9** characterized by grim, distorted, or grotesque humour **10** bought, sold, or operating illegally and esp in contravention of official economic regulations ⟨*the ~ economy*⟩ ⟨*~ food*⟩ **11** *chiefly Br* subject to boycott by trade-union members [ME *blak*, fr OE *blæc*; akin to OHG *blah* black, L *flagrare* to burn, Gk *phlegein*, OE *bǣl* fire – more at BALD] – **blackish** *adj*, **blackly** *adv*, **blackness** *n*

[2]**black** *n* **1** a black pigment or dye **2** the colour of least lightness that belongs to objects that neither reflect nor transmit light **3** sthg black; *esp* black clothing ⟨*looks good in ~*⟩ **4** one who belongs wholly or partly to a dark-skinned race; *esp* a Negro **5** (the player playing) the dark-coloured pieces in a board game (e g chess) for 2 players **6** (nearly) total absence of light ⟨*the ~ of night*⟩ **7** the condition of being financially in credit or solvent or of making a profit – usu + *in the*; compare RED 3

[3]**black** *vt* **1** to make black **2** *chiefly Br* to declare (e g a business or industry) subject to boycott by trade-union members

blackamoor /ˈblakəˌmaw, -ˌmooə/ *n, archaic* BLACK 4 [irreg fr *black* + *Moor*]

ˌ**black-and-ˈblue** *adj* darkly discoloured from blood that has leaked under the skin by bruising

ˌ**Black and ˈTan** *n* a member of the Royal Irish Constabulary resisting the armed movement for Irish independence in 1921 [fr the colour of the uniform]

ˌ**black-and-ˈwhite** *adj* **1** reproducing visual images in tones of grey rather than in colours ⟨*~ television*⟩ **2a** sharply divided into 2 groups or sides **b** evaluating things as either all good or all bad ⟨*~ morality*⟩

ˌ**black and ˈwhite** *n* **1** writing, print **2** a drawing or print done in black and white or in monochrome **3** black-and-white reproduction of visual images, esp by photography or television

ˈ**blackˌball** /-ˌbawl/ *vt* **1** to vote against (esp a candidate for membership of a club) **2** to ostracize [fr the black ball sometimes used to register an adverse vote in a ballot] – **blackball** *n*

black ban *n, Austr* a blacking, boycott

ˌ**black ˈbear** *n* the common American bear

ˈ**black ˌbelt** *n* (one who has) a rating of expert in judo, karate, etc

ˈ**blackberry** /-b(ə)ri/ *n* (the usu black seedy edible fruit of) any of various prickly shrubs of the rose family

ˌ**black ˈbile** *n* the one of the 4 humours in medieval physiology that was believed to be secreted by the kidneys or spleen and to cause melancholy

ˈ**blackˌbird** /-ˌbuhd/ *n* **1** a common Old World thrush the male of which is black with an orange beak and eye rim **2** any of several American birds

ˈ**blackˌboard** /-ˌbawd/ *n* a hard smooth usu dark surface for writing or drawing on with chalk

ˌ**black ˈbody** *n* an ideal body or surface that completely absorbs all radiant energy falling upon it with no reflection

ˌ**black ˈbook** *n* a book containing a blacklist

ˌ**black ˈbox** *n* **1** a usu electronic device, esp one that can be plugged in or removed as a unit, whose internal mechanism is hidden from or mysterious to the user **2** FLIGHT RECORDER

ˌ**black ˈbryony** *n* a herbaceous Old World climbing plant that bears red poisonous berries

ˈ**blackˌbuck** /-ˌbuk/ *n* a common medium-sized Indian antelope

ˌ**black ˈbun** *n, Scot* a rich dark fruit cake or bread often encased in pastry

ˈ**blackˌcap** /-ˌkap/ *n* a small Old World warbler with a black crown

ˌ**black ˈcap** *n* a black head-covering formerly worn by a judge in Britain when passing the death sentence

ˈ**blackˌcock** /-ˌkok/ *n* the (male) black grouse

blackcurrant /ˈblakˌkurənt, ˌ-ˈ--/ *n* (the small black edible fruit of) a widely cultivated European currant

ˈ**blackˌdamp** /-ˌdamp/ *n* a mixture containing carbon dioxide that occurs as a mine gas and is incapable of supporting life or flame

ˌ**black ˈdeath** *n, often cap B&D* a form of plague epidemic in Europe and Asia in the 14th c [fr the black patches formed on the skin of its victims]

ˌblack 'diamond *n* **1** *pl* COAL 2 **2** carbonado

blacken /'blakən/ *vi* to become dark or black ⟨*the sky* ~s⟩ ~ *vt* **1** to make dark or black **2** to defame, sully – **blackener** *n*

ˌblack 'eye *n* a discoloration of the skin round the eye from bruising

ˌblack-eyed 'pea *n* (the edible seed of) a leguminous plant widely cultivated in warm areas for food and green manure

'blackˌfellow /-ˌfeloh/ *n* an Australian aborigine – derog

'blackˌfish /-ˌfish/ *n* **1** any of numerous dark-coloured fishes; *esp* a tautog **2** the female salmon just after spawning

'blackˌfly /-ˌflie/ *n, pl* **blackflies,** *esp collectively* **blackfly** (an infestation by) any of several small dark-coloured insects

ˌblack 'friar *n* a Dominican friar [fr the black mantle worn by Dominicans]

ˌblack 'gold *n* crude oil

ˌblack 'grouse *n* a large Eurasian grouse of which the male is black and the female mottled

blackguard /'blagəd, -ˌgahd/ *n* a coarse or unscrupulous person; a scoundrel – now often humor ['*black* + *guard*; orig sense, the kitchen servants of a large household] – **blackguardism** /'blagədiz(ə)m/ *n,* **blackguardly** /'blagədli/ *adj or adv*

'blackˌhead /-ˌhed/ *n* a small usu dark-coloured oily plug blocking the duct of a sebaceous gland, esp on the face

ˌblack 'hole *n* a celestial body, prob formed from a collapsed star, with a very high density and an intense gravitational field, from which no radiation can escape

ˌblack 'ice *n, Br* transparent slippery ice (e g on a road)

blacking /'blaking/ *n* **1** a paste, polish, etc applied to an object to make it black **2** a boycotting of business, industry, etc by trade-union members

[1]'blackˌjack /-ˌjak/ *n* **1** [2]PONTOON **2** *NAm* a cosh [(1) *black* + [1]*jack* 5; (2) *black* + [1]*jack* 2]

[2]'blackˌjack *vt, NAm* to strike with a blackjack

ˌblack 'lead /led/ *n* graphite

'blackˌleg /-ˌleg/ *n, chiefly Br* a worker hostile to trade unionism or acting in opposition to union policies

ˌblack 'letter *n* a heavier angular style of type or lettering used esp by early European printers ☞ ALPHABET

ˌblack 'light *n* invisible ultraviolet or infrared light

'blackˌlist /-ˌlist/ *n* a list of people or organizations who are disapproved of or are to be punished or boycotted – **blacklist** *vt*

ˌblack 'magic *n* magic performed with the aim of harming or killing sby or sthg

'blackˌmail /-ˌmayl/ *n* **1** (money obtained by) extortion by threats, esp of exposure of secrets that would lead to loss of reputation, prosecution, etc **2** political, industrial, or moral pressure to do sthg that is considered undesirable ['*black* + *mail* (tribute, payment), fr ME *male, maille,* fr OE *māl* agreement, pay, fr ON *māl* speech, agreement] – **blackmail** *vt*

Black Maria /ˌblak mə'rie·ə/ *n* an enclosed motor vehicle used by police to carry prisoners [prob fr the name *Maria*]

ˌblack 'market *n* illicit trade in commodities or currencies in violation of official regulations (e g rationing)

ˌblack marke'teer /ˌmahki'tiə/ *n* one who trades on a black market

ˌBlack 'Mass *n* a travesty of the Christian mass ascribed to worshippers of Satan

ˌBlack 'Muslim *n* a member of an exclusively black chiefly US Muslim sect that advocates a strictly separate black community

'blackˌout /-ˌowt/ *n* **1** a period of darkness enforced as a precaution against air raids, or caused by a failure of electrical power **2** a temporary loss or dulling of vision, consciousness, or memory **3** a holding back or suppression of sthg ⟨*a* ~ *of news about the invasion*⟩ **4** a usu temporary loss of radio signal (e g during the reentry of a spacecraft)

black out *vi* **1** to become enveloped in darkness **2** to undergo a temporary loss of vision, consciousness, or memory **3** to extinguish or screen all lights for protection, esp against air attack ~ *vt* **1** to cause to black out **2** to suppress, esp by censorship ⟨black out *the news*⟩

ˌBlack 'Panther *n* a member of a militant organization of US blacks

ˌblack 'pepper *n* a pungent condiment prepared from the dried black-husked berries of an E Indian plant used either whole or ground – compare WHITE PEPPER

ˌblack 'power *n* the mobilization of the political and economic power of US blacks, esp to further racial equality

ˌblack 'pudding *n, chiefly Br* a very dark sausage made from suet and a large proportion of pigs blood – compare WHITE PUDDING

ˌBlack 'Rod *n* the principal usher of the House of Lords [fr his staff of office]

ˌblack 'sheep *n* a disreputable member of a respectable group, family, etc

'Blackˌshirt /-ˌshuht/ *n* a member of a fascist organization having a black shirt as part of its uniform

'blackˌsmith /-ˌsmith/ *n* one who works iron, esp at a forge [fr his working with iron, known as black metal] – **blacksmithing** *n*

'black ˌspot *n, Br* a stretch of road on which accidents occur frequently

ˌblack 'tea *n* tea that is dark in colour from complete fermentation of the leaf before drying

'blackˌthorn /-ˌthawn/ *n* a European spiny shrub of the rose family with hard wood and small white flowers

ˌblack-'tie *adj* characterized by or requiring the wearing of semiformal evening dress by men including a dinner jacket and a black bow tie ⟨*a* ~ *dinner*⟩ – compare WHITE-TIE

'blackˌtop /-ˌtop/ *n, NAm* a bituminous material used esp for surfacing roads – **blacktop** *vt*

black up *vi* to put on black make-up, esp in order to play a Negro role

ˌblack 'velvet *n* a drink that is a mixture of stout and champagne or cider

ˌblackwater 'fever /'blakˌwawtə/ *n* a severe form of malaria in which the urine becomes dark-coloured

ˌblack 'widow *n* a venomous New World spider of which the female is black with an hourglass-shaped red mark on the underside of the abdomen

bladder /'bladə/ *n* **1a** a membranous sac in animals that serves as the receptacle of a liquid or contains gas; *esp* the urinary bladder ☞ DIGESTION **b** VESICLE 1a **2** a bag filled with a liquid or gas (e g the air-filled rubber one inside a football) [ME, fr OE *blǣdre*; akin to OHG *blātara* bladder, OE *blāwan* to blow]

bladder campion *n* a white-flowered plant of the pink family with a large membranous globular calyx

'bladder,wort /-,wuht/ *n* any of a genus of the butterwort family of chiefly aquatic plants with vesicular floats or insect traps

'bladder ,wrack /rak/ *n* a common brown seaweed used in making kelp and as a manure

blade /blayd/ *n* **1** (the flat expanded part, as distinguished from the stalk, of) a leaf, esp of a grass, cereal, etc **2a** the broad flattened part of an oar, paddle, bat, etc **b** an arm of a screw propeller, electric fan, steam turbine, etc **c** the broad flat or concave part of a machine (e g a bulldozer) that comes into contact with material to be moved **d** a broad flat body part; *specif* the scapula – used chiefly in naming cuts of meat ☞ MEAT **3a** the cutting part of a knife, razor, etc **b** a sword **c** the runner of an ice skate **4** *archaic* a dashing lively man – now usu humor [ME, fr OE *blæd*; akin to OHG *blat* leaf, L *folium*, Gk *phyllon*, OE *blōwan* to blossom – more at [3]BLOW]

bladed /'blaydid/ *adj* having blades – often in combination ⟨*broad*-bladed *leaves*⟩

blaeberry /'blayb(ə)ri/ *n, Scot* the bilberry [ME (northern) *blaberie*, fr *bla* dark blue (fr ON *blār*) + *berry*]

blah /blah/ *n* silly or pretentious chatter or nonsense – infml [imit]

blain /blayn/ *n* an inflammatory swelling or sore [ME, fr OE *blegen*; akin to MLG *bleine* blain, OE *blāwan* to blow]

[1]blame /blaym/ *vt* **1** to find fault with; censure **2a** to hold responsible for sthg reprehensible ⟨~ *him for everything*⟩ **b** to place responsibility for (sthg reprehensible) – + *on* ⟨~s *it on me*⟩ [ME *blamen*, fr OF *blamer*, fr LL *blasphemare* to blaspheme, fr Gk *blasphēmein*] – **blamable** *adj*, **blamably** *adv*, **blamer** *n*

[2]blame *n* **1** an expression of disapproval or reproach **2** responsibility for sthg reprehensible ⟨*they must share the* ~ *for the crime*⟩ – **blameful** *adj*, **blamefully** *adv*, **blameless** *adj*, **blamelessly** *adv*, **blamelessness** *n*

'blame,worthy /-,wuhthi/ *adj* deserving blame – **blameworthiness** *n*

blanch /blahnch/ *vt* **1** to take the colour out of: **a** to bleach (a growing plant) by excluding light **b** to scald or parboil (e g almonds or food for freezing) in water or steam in order to remove the skin from, whiten, or stop enzymatic action **2** to make ashen or pale ⟨*fear* ~es *the cheek*⟩ ~ *vi* to become white or pale ⟨~ed *when he heard the news*⟩ [ME *blaunchen*, fr MF *blanchir*, fr OF *blanche*, fem of *blanc*, adj, white] – **blancher** *n*

blancmange /blə'monj, -'monzh/ *n* a usu sweetened and flavoured dessert made from gelatinous or starchy substances (e g cornflour) and milk [ME *blancmanger*, fr MF *blanc manger*, lit., white food]

blanco /'blangkoh/ *vt* **blancoes; blancoing; blancoed** to treat with Blanco

Blanco *trademark* – used for a substance used esp in the armed forces to whiten or colour belts and webbing

bland /bland/ *adj* **1a** smooth, soothing ⟨*a* ~ *smile*⟩ **b** unperturbed ⟨*a* ~ *confession of guilt*⟩ **2a** not irritating or stimulating; mild ⟨*a* ~ *diet*⟩ **b** dull, insipid ⟨~ *stories with little plot or action*⟩ [L *blandus*] – **blandly** *adv*, **blandness** *n*

blandishment /'blandishmənt/ *n* a coaxing or flattering act or utterance – often pl [*blandish* (to coax, flatter), fr ME *blandishen*, fr MF *blandiss-*, stem of *blandir*, fr L *blandiri*, fr *blandus*] – **blandish** *vb*

[1]blank /blangk/ *adj* **1a** dazed, nonplussed ⟨*stared in* ~ *dismay*⟩ **b** expressionless ⟨*a* ~ *stare*⟩ **2a** lacking interest, variety, or change ⟨*a* ~ *prospect*⟩ **b** devoid of covering or content; *esp* free from writing ⟨~ *paper*⟩ **c** not filled in ⟨*a* ~ *cheque*⟩ **3** absolute, unqualified ⟨*a* ~ *refusal*⟩ **4** having a plain or unbroken surface where an opening is usual ⟨*a* ~ *arch*⟩ [ME, white, fr MF *blanc*, of Gmc origin; akin to OHG *blanch* white; akin to L *flagrare* to burn – more at BLACK] – **blankly** *adv*, **blankness** *n*

[2]blank *n* **1** an empty space **2a** a void ⟨*my mind was a* ~ *during the test*⟩ **b** a vacant or uneventful period ⟨*a long* ~ *in history*⟩ **3** a dash substituted for an omitted word **4a** a piece of material prepared to be made into sthg (e g a key or coin) by a further operation **b** a cartridge loaded with powder but no bullet

[3]blank *vt* **1a** to make blank – usu + *out* **b** to block – usu + *off* ⟨~ed off *the tunnel*⟩ **2** *NAm* to keep (an opposing team) from scoring

,blank 'cheque *n* **1** a signed cheque with the amount unspecified **2** complete freedom of action or control; CARTE BLANCHE

[1]blanket /'blangkit/ *n* **1** a large thick usu rectangular piece of fabric (e g woven from wool or acrylic yarn) used esp as a bed covering or a similar piece of fabric used as a body covering (e g for a horse) **2** a thick covering or layer ⟨*a* ~ *of snow*⟩ [ME, fr OF *blankete*, fr *blanc*]

[2]blanket *vt* to cover (as if) with a blanket ⟨*new grass* ~s *the slope*⟩

[3]blanket *adj* applicable in all instances or to all members of a group or class

'blanket ,bath *n* a wash given to a bedridden person

'blanket ,stitch *n* a widely spaced loop stitch used esp round the edges of thick fabrics (e g blankets) instead of hemming in order to prevent fraying – compare BUTTONHOLE STITCH – **blanket-stitch** *vt*

,blank 'verse *n* unrhymed verse, esp in iambic pentameters

blanquette /blong'ket/ *n* a stew of white meat (e g veal) in a white sauce [F]

blare /bleə/ *vi* to emit loud and harsh sound ~ *vt* **1** to sound loudly and usu harshly **2** to proclaim loudly or sensationally ⟨*headlines* ~d *his defeat*⟩ [ME *bleren*; akin to OE *blǣtan* to bleat] – **blare** *n*

blarney /'blahni/ *n* **1** smooth wheedling talk; flattery **2** nonsense [*Blarney stone*, a stone in Blarney Castle, near Cork, Eire, held to give skill in flattery to those who kiss it] – **blarney** *vb*

blasé /'blahzay, -'-/ *adj* indifferent to pleasure or excitement as a result of excessive indulgence or enjoyment; *also* sophisticated [F, fr pp of *blaser* to exhaust by indulgence]

blaspheme /blas'feem/ *vb* to speak of or address (God or sthg sacred) with impiety [ME *blasfemen*, fr LL *blasphemare* – more at BLAME] – **blasphemer** *n*

blasphemy /ˈblasfəmi/ *n* (the act of showing) contempt or lack of reverence for God or sthg (considered) sacred – **blasphemous** *adj*, **blasphemously** *adv*, **blasphemousness** *n*

[1]**blast** /blahst/ *n* **1** a violent gust of wind **2** the sound produced by air blown through a wind instrument or whistle **3a** a stream of air or gas forced through a hole **b** a violent outburst **c** the continuous draught forced through a blast furnace **4** a sudden pernicious influence or effect ⟨*the ~ of a huge epidemic*⟩ **5** (a violent wave of increased atmospheric pressure followed by a wave of decreased atmospheric pressure produced in the vicinity of) an explosion or violent detonation **6** speed, capacity ⟨*going full ~ down the road*⟩ **7** the utterance of the word *blast* as a curse [ME, fr OE *blǣst*; akin to OHG *blāst* blast, OE *blāwan* to blow]

[2]**blast** *vi* **1** to produce loud harsh sounds **2a** to use an explosive **b** to shoot **3** to shrivel, wither ~ *vt* **1** to injure (as if) by the action of wind; blight **2** to shatter, remove, or open (as if) with an explosive ⟨*~ a new course for the stream*⟩ **3** to apply a forced draught to **4** to cause to blast off ⟨*will ~ themselves from the moon's surface*⟩ **5a** to denounce vigorously ⟨*judge ~*s *police methods*⟩ **b** to curse, damn **c** to hit vigorously and effectively **6** to defeat decisively ⟨*they ~*ed *the home team*⟩ – **blaster** *n*, **blasting** *n or adj*

[3]**blast** *interj, Br* – used to express annoyance; slang

blast-, blasto- *comb form* bud; embryo; germ ⟨blasto*cyst*⟩ ⟨blast*ula*⟩ [G, fr Gk, fr *blastos*]

-blast /-blast/ *comb form* (→ *n*) formative cell; cell layer ⟨*erythro*blast⟩; *also* formative unit, esp of living matter [NL *-blastus*, fr Gk *blastos* bud, shoot; akin to OE *molda* top of the head, Skt *mūrdhan* head]

blasted /ˈblahstid/ *adj* **1a** withered **b** damaged (as if) by an explosive, lightning, or the wind **2** confounded, detestable ⟨*this ~ weather*⟩ – infml

ˈ**blast ˌfurnace** *n* a furnace, esp for converting iron ore into iron, in which combustion is forced by a current of air under pressure

-blastic /-ˈblastik/ *comb form* (→ *adj*) having (such or so many) buds, cells, or cell layers ⟨*megalo*blastic⟩ [ISV, fr *-blast*]

blastocoel, blastocoele /ˈblastəˌseel/ *n* the cavity of a blastula [ISV] – **blastocoelic** /-ˈseelik/ *adj*

blastocyst /ˈblastəsist/ *n* the modified blastula of a placental mammal

blast off *vi, esp of rocket-propelled missiles and vehicles* TAKE OFF 3 – **blast-off** /ˈ--/ *n*

blastomere /ˈblastəˌmiə/ *n* a cell produced during cleavage of an egg [ISV] – **blastomeric** /ˌblastəˈmerik/ *adj*

blastula /ˈblastyoolə/ *n, pl* **blastulas, blastulae** /-li/ the embryo of a metazoan animal at the stage in its development succeeding the morula, typically having the form of a hollow fluid-filled cavity bounded by a single layer of cells – compare GASTRULA, MORULA [NL, fr Gk *blastos*] – **blastular** *adj*, **blastulation** /-ˈlaysh(ə)n/ *n*

blatant /ˈblayt(ə)nt/ *adj* **1** noisy, esp in a vulgar or offensive manner **2** completely obvious, conspicuous, or obtrusive, esp in a crass or offensive manner [perh fr L *blatire* to chatter] – **blatantly** *adv*, **blatancy** /-si/ *n*

blather /ˈbladhə/ *n* foolish voluble talk [ON *blathr* nonsense, fr *blathra* to talk nonsense] – **blather** *vi*, **blatherer** /-rə/ *n*

[1]**blaze** /blayz/ *n* **1a** an intensely burning flame or sudden fire **b** intense direct light, often accompanied by heat ⟨*the ~ of noon*⟩ **2a** a dazzling display ⟨*a ~ of flowers*⟩ **b** a sudden outburst ⟨*a ~ of fury*⟩ **c** brilliance ⟨*the ~ of the jewels*⟩ **3** *pl* HELL 2a – usu as an interjection or as a generalized term of abuse ⟨*go to ~*s⟩ [ME *blase*, fr OE *blæse* torch; akin to OE *bǣl* fire – more at BALD]

[2]**blaze** *vi* **1a** to burn intensely ⟨*the sun ~*d *overhead*⟩ **b** to flare up ⟨*he suddenly ~*d *with anger*⟩ **2** to be conspicuously brilliant or resplendent **3** to shoot rapidly and repeatedly ⟨*~*d *away at the target*⟩ – **blazingly** *adv*

[3]**blaze** *vt* to make public or conspicuous – chiefly in *blaze abroad* [ME *blasen*, fr MD *blāsen* to blow; akin to OHG *blāst* blast]

[4]**blaze** *n* **1** a broad white mark on the face of an animal, esp a horse **2** a trail marker; *esp* a mark made on a tree by cutting off a piece of the bark [G *blas*, fr OHG *plas*; akin to OE *blæse*]

[5]**blaze** *vt* **1** to mark (e g a trail) with blazes **2** to lead or pioneer in (some direction or activity) – chiefly in *blaze the trail*

blazer /ˈblayzə/ *n* a jacket, esp with patch pockets, that is for casual wear or is part of a school uniform [[2]BLAZE + [2]-ER]

[1]**blazon** /ˈblayz(ə)n/ *n* **1** COAT OF ARMS **2** the proper formal description of heraldic arms or charges [ME *blason*, fr MF]

[2]**blazon** *vt* **1** to proclaim widely – often + *forth* **2** to describe (heraldic arms or charges) in technical terms – **blazoner** *n*, **blazoning** *n*

ˈ**blazonry** /-ri/ *n* **1** blazon **2** dazzling display

[1]**bleach** /bleech/ *vt* **1** to remove colour or stains from **2** to make whiter or lighter, esp by physical or chemical removal of colour ~ *vi* to grow white or lose colour [ME *blechen*, fr OE *blǣcean*; akin to OE *blāc* pale, *bǣl* fire – more at BALD] – **bleachable** *adj*

[2]**bleach** *n* **1** a preparation used in bleaching **2** the degree of whiteness obtained by bleaching

ˈ**bleaching ˌpowder** /ˈbleeching/ *n* a white powder consisting chiefly of calcium hydroxide, calcium chloride, and calcium hypochlorite used as a bleach, disinfectant, or deodorant

[1]**bleak** /bleek/ *adj* **1** exposed, barren, and often windswept **2** cold, raw **3a** lacking in warmth or kindness **b** not hopeful or encouraging ⟨*a ~ outlook*⟩ **c** severely simple or austere [ME *bleke* pale; prob akin to OE *blāc*] – **bleakish** *adj*, **bleakly** *adv*, **bleakness** *n*

[2]**bleak** *n* a small European river fish [ME *bleke*, prob fr ON *bleikja*]

blear /bliə/ *vt* **1** to make (the eyes) bleary **2** to blur [ME *bleren*]

bleary /ˈbliəri/ *adj* **1** *of the eyes or vision* dull or dimmed, esp from fatigue or sleep **2** poorly outlined or defined – **blearily** *adv*, **bleariness** *n*

[1]**bleat** /bleet/ *vi* **1** to make (a sound like) the cry characteristic of a sheep or goat **2a** to talk complainingly or with a whine **b** to blather ~ *vt* to utter in a bleating manner [ME *bleten*, fr OE *blǣtan*; akin to L *flēre* to weep, OE *bellan* to roar – more at BELLOW] – **bleater** *n*

²bleat *n* (a sound like) the characteristic cry of a sheep or goat

bleb /bleb/ *n* a small blister [perh alter. of *blob*]

¹bleed /bleed/ *vb* **bled** /bled/ *vi* **1a** to emit or lose blood **b** to die or be wounded, esp in battle ⟨*men who* bled *for their country*⟩ **2** to feel anguish, pain, or sympathy **3** to lose some constituent (e g sap or dye) by exuding it or by diffusion **4** to be printed so as to run off an edge of a page after trimming ~ *vt* **1** to remove or draw blood from **2** to extort money from **3** to draw sap from (a tree) **4** to extract or let out some of (a contained substance) from (a container) **5** to cause (e g a printed illustration) to bleed; *also* to trim (e g a page) so that some of the printing bleeds **6** to extract or drain the vitality or lifeblood from ⟨*high taxes* ~ing *private enterprise*⟩ [ME *bleden*, fr OE *blēdan*, fr *blōd* blood]

²bleed *n* an act or instance of bleeding, esp by a haemophiliac

bleeder /ˈbleedə/ *n* **1** a haemophiliac **2** a worthless person – slang [¹BLEED + ²-ER]

bleeding /ˈbleeding/ *adj or adv* ¹BLOODY 4, ³BLOODY – slang

ˌbleeding ˈheart *n* any of various plants of the fumitory family with usu red or pink heart-shaped flowers

¹bleep /bleep/ *n* **1** a short high-pitched sound (e g from electronic equipment) **2** a bleeper [imit]

²bleep *vt* **1** to call (sby) by means of a bleeper **2** to replace (recorded words) with a bleep or other sound – usu + *out* ⟨*all the obscenities were* ~ed out⟩ ~ *vi* to emit a bleep

bleeper /ˈbleepə/ *n* a portable radio receiver that emits a bleep as a signal that the wearer is required

blemish /ˈblemish/ *vt or n* (to spoil the perfection of by) a noticeable imperfection [vb ME *blemisshen*, fr MF *blesmiss-*, stem of *blesmir* to make pale, wound, of Gmc origin; akin to G *blass* pale; akin to OE *blæse* torch – more at ¹BLAZE; n fr vb]

blench /blench/ *vi* to draw back or flinch from lack of courage [ME *blenchen* to deceive, blench, fr OE *blencan* to deceive; akin to ON *blekkja* to impose on]

¹blend /blend/ *vb* **blended** *also* **blent** /blent/ *vt* **1** to mix; *esp* to combine or associate so that the separate constituents cannot be distinguished **2** to prepare by thoroughly intermingling different varieties or grades ~ *vi* **1a** to mix or intermingle thoroughly **b** to combine into an integrated whole **2** to produce a harmonious effect [ME *blenden*, modif of ON *blanda*; akin to OE *blandan* to mix, Lith *blandus* thick (of soup)]

²blend *n* **1** an act or product of blending ⟨*our own* ~ *of tea*⟩ **2** a word (e g *brunch*) produced by combining other words or parts of words

blende /blend/ *n* sphalerite [G, fr *blenden* to blind, fr OHG *blenten*; akin to OE *blind*]

blender /ˈblendə/ *n* an electric appliance for grinding or mixing; *specif* a liquidizer [¹BLEND + ²-ER]

blenny /ˈbleni/ *n* any of numerous usu small and elongated and often scaleless sea fishes [L *blennius*, a sea fish, fr Gk *blennos*]

blephar- /blefə-/, **blepharo-** *comb form* eyelid ⟨ble*pharitis*⟩ [NL, fr Gk, fr *blepharon*]

blesbok /ˈbles,bok/ *n* a S African antelope that has a large white spot on the face [Afrik, fr *bles* blaze + *bok* male antelope]

bless /bles/ *vt* **blessed** *also* **blest** /blest/ **1** to hallow or consecrate by religious rite, esp by making the sign of the cross **2** to invoke divine care for **3a** to praise, glorify ⟨~ *His holy name*⟩ **b** to speak gratefully of ⟨~ed *him for his kindness*⟩ **4** to confer prosperity or happiness on **5** – used in exclamations chiefly to express mild or good-humoured surprise ⟨~ *my soul, what's happened now?*⟩ **6** *archaic* to protect, preserve [ME *blessen*, fr OE *blētsian*, fr *blōd* blood; fr the use of blood in consecration]

blessed /ˈblesid/ *adj* **1a** *often cap* holy; venerated ⟨*the* Blessed *Sacrament*⟩ **b** *cap* – used as a title for a beatified person ⟨Blessed *Oliver Plunket*⟩ **2** – used as an intensive ⟨*no one gave us a* ~ *penny*⟩ – **blessedly** *adv*, **blessedness** *n*

blessing /ˈblesing/ *n* **1a** the invocation of God's favour upon a person ⟨*the congregation stood for the* ~⟩ **b** approval **2** sthg conducive to happiness or welfare **3** grace said at a meal

blether /ˈbledhə/ *vi or n* (to) blather [Sc, var of *blather*]

blew /blooh/ *past of* BLOW

blewits /ˈblooh·its/ *n* an edible mushroom that is lilac when young [prob irreg fr *blue*]

¹blight /bliet/ *n* **1** (an organism that causes) a disease or injury of plants resulting in withering, cessation of growth, and death of parts without rotting **2** sthg that impairs, frustrates, or destroys **3** a condition of disorder or decay ⟨*urban* ~⟩ [origin unknown]

²blight *vt* **1** to affect (e g a plant) with blight **2** to impair, frustrate ~ *vi* to suffer from or become affected with blight

blighter /ˈblietə/ *n, chiefly Br* a fellow; *esp* one held in low esteem – infml [²BLIGHT + ²-ER]

blighty /ˈblieti/ *n, often cap, Br* **1** (a wound forcing a return home to) Britain **2** leave *USE* slang; used esp by British soldiers [by folk etymology fr Hindi *bilāyatī, wilāyatī* foreign country, England, fr Ar *wilāyat* province, country]

blimey /ˈbliemi/ *interj, chiefly Br* – used for expressing surprise; slang [short for *gorblimey*, alter. of *God blind me*]

blimp /blimp/ *n* **1** a nonrigid airship **2** *cap* COLONEL BLIMP [prob based on ³*limp*] – **blimpish** *adj*, **blimpishly** *adv*, **blimpishness** *n*

¹blind /bliend/ *adj* **1a** unable to see; sightless **b** of or designed for sightless people **2a** unable or unwilling to discern or judge ⟨~ *to all arguments*⟩ **b** not based on reason, evidence, or knowledge ⟨~ *faith*⟩ **3** completely insensible ⟨*in a* ~ *stupor*⟩ **4** without sight or knowledge of anything that could serve for guidance beforehand **5** performed solely by the use of instruments within an aircraft ⟨*a* ~ *landing*⟩ **6** hidden from sight; concealed ⟨*a* ~ *corner*⟩ ⟨~ *stitch*⟩ **7** having only 1 opening or outlet ⟨*a* ~ *alley*⟩ **8** having no opening for light or passage ⟨*a* ~ *wall*⟩ [ME, fr OE; akin to OHG *blint* blind, OE *blandan* to mix – more at BLEND] – **blindly** *adv*, **blindness** *n*

²blind *vt* **1** to make blind **2** to rob of judgment or discernment **3** to dazzle ~ *vi Br* to swear ⟨*cursing and* ~ing⟩ – infml – **blindingly** *adv* – **blind with science** to impress or overwhelm with a display of usu technical knowledge

³blind *n* **1** sthg to hinder sight or keep out light: e g **a** a window shutter **b** *chiefly Br* an awning **c** a flexible screen (e g a strip of cloth) usu mounted on a roller for covering a window **d** a curtain **e** VENETIAN BLIND **2** a cover, subterfuge **3** *NAm* [3]HIDE

[4]**blind** *adv* **1** to the point of insensibility ⟨*~ drunk*⟩ **2** without seeing outside an aircraft ⟨*to fly ~*⟩ **3** – used as an intensive ⟨*swore ~ he wouldn't escape*⟩

,blind 'alley *n* a fruitless or mistaken course or direction

,blind 'date *n* a date between people who have not previously met

blinder /'bliendə/ *n* **1** *Br* sthg outstanding; *esp* an outstanding piece of play in cricket or football – infml **2** *NAm* BLINKER 3 [[2]BLIND + [2]-ER]

'blind,fold /-,fohld/ *vt or n* **1** (to cover the eyes of with) a piece of material (e g a bandage) for covering the eyes to prevent sight **2** (to hinder from seeing or esp understanding with) sthg that obscures vision or mental awareness [vb ME *blindfellen, blindfelden* to strike blind, blindfold, fr *blind* + *fellen* to fell; n fr vb]

blinding /'bliending/ *n* material (e g sand or gravel) used to fill crevices, esp in a new road [fr gerund of *blind* (to fill gaps in, clog), fr [2]*blind*]

blindman's buff /,bliend,manz 'buf/ *n* a group game in which a blindfolded player tries to catch and identify another player [*buff* (blow, buffet), fr ME *buffe*, fr MF, of imit origin]

'blind ,side *n* the side away from which one is looking

'blind ,spot *n* **1a** the point in the retina where the optic nerve enters that is not sensitive to light **b** a part of a visual field that cannot be seen or inspected ⟨*the car has a bad ~*⟩ **2** an area in which one lacks knowledge, understanding, or discrimination

'blind,worm /-,wuhm/ *n* a slowworm

[1]**blink** /blingk/ *vi* **1** to close and open the eyes involuntarily **2** to shine intermittently **3a** to wink *at* **b** to look with surprise or dismay *at* ~ *vt* **1** to cause (one's eyes) to blink **2** to evade, shirk [ME *blinken* to open one's eyes]

[2]**blink** *n* **1** a glimmer, sparkle **2** a usu involuntary shutting and opening of the eye **3** iceblink **– on the blink** not working properly ⟨*the light switch is* on the blink⟩ – infml

blinker /'blingkə/ *n* **1** a warning or signalling light that flashes on and off **2** *pl* an obstruction to sight or discernment **3** *chiefly Br* either of 2 flaps, one on each side of a horse's bridle, allowing only frontal vision [[1]BLINK + [2]-ER] – **blinker** *vt*, **blinkered** *adj*

blinking /'blingking/ *adj or adv*, *Br* [1]BLOODY 4, [3]BLOODY – euph

blintze /'blintsə/, **blintz** /blints/ *n* a thin folded filled pancake [Yiddish *blintse*, fr Russ *blinets*, dim. of *blin* pancake]

blip /blip/ *n* **1** a bleep **2** an image on a radar screen [imit]

bliss /blis/ *n* **1** complete happiness **2** paradise, heaven [ME *blisse*, fr OE *bliss*; akin to OE *blīthe* blithe] – **blissful** *adj*, **blissfully** *adv*, **blissfulness** *n*

[1]**blister** /'blistə/ *n* **1** a raised part of the outer skin containing watery liquid **2** an enclosed raised spot (e g in paint) resembling a blister **3** a disease of plants marked by large swollen patches on the leaves **4** any of various structures that bulge out ⟨*an aircraft's radar ~*⟩ [ME, modif of OF or MD; OF *blostre* boil, fr MD *bluyster* blister; akin to OE *blǣst* blast] – **blistery** *adj*

[2]**blister** *vi* to become affected with a blister ~ *vt* **1** to raise a blister on **2** to attack harshly

'blister ,copper *n* copper that has a black blistered surface, is almost pure, and occurs as an intermediate product in copper refining

blistering /'blistəring/ *adj* **1** extremely intense or severe **2** *of speed* extremely high – **blisteringly** *adv*

blithe /bliedh/ *adj* **1** lighthearted, merry, cheerful ⟨*hail to thee, ~ spirit* – P B Shelley⟩ **2** casual, heedless ⟨*~ unconcern*⟩ [ME, fr OE *blīthe*; akin to OHG *blīdi* joyous, OE *bǣl* fire – more at BALD] – **blithely** *adv*

blithering /'blidhəring/ *adj* talking nonsense; babbling; *broadly* utterly stupid ⟨*you ~ idiot!*⟩ – infml [fr prp of *blither*, alter. of *blather*]

blitz /blits/ *n* **1a** a blitzkrieg **b** an intensive aerial bombardment; *specif, often cap the* bombardment of British cities by the German air force in 1940 and 1941 **2** an intensive nonmilitary campaign ⟨*a ~ against the unions*⟩ – chiefly journ – **blitz** *vb*

'blitz,krieg /-,kreeg/ *n* a violent swift surprise campaign conducted by coordinated air and ground forces [G, fr *blitz* lightning + *krieg* war]

blizzard /'blizəd/ *n* **1** a long severe snowstorm **2** an intensely strong cold wind filled with fine snow **3** an overwhelming rush or deluge ⟨*the ~ of mail at Christmas*⟩ [origin unknown] – **blizzardy** *adj*

bloated /'blohtid/ *adj* **1** unpleasantly swollen **2** much larger than is warranted ⟨*a ~ estimate*⟩ [fr pp of *bloat* (to swell), fr *bloat* swollen, alter. of ME *blout*, perh fr ON *blautr* soft, soaked]

bloater /'blohtə/ *n* a large herring or mackerel lightly salted and briefly smoked [obs *bloat* (to cure)]

blob /blob/ *n* **1a** a small drop of liquid ⟨*a ~ of ink*⟩ **b** a small drop or lump of sthg viscous or thick **2** sthg ill-defined or amorphous [ME]

bloc /blok/ *n* a (temporary) combination of individuals, parties, or nations for a common purpose [F, lit., block]

[1]**block** /blok/ *n* **1** a compact usu solid piece of substantial material (e g wood or stone): e g **a** a mould or form on which articles are shaped or displayed **b** a rectangular building unit that is larger than a brick **c** a usu cubical and solid wooden or plastic building toy that is usu provided in sets **d** the metal casting that contains the cylinders of an internal-combustion engine **2** HEAD 1 – slang **3a** an obstacle **b** an obstruction of an opponent's play in sports, esp in football, hockey, etc **c** interruption of the normal physiological function (e g transmission of nerve impulses) of a tissue or organ **4** a wooden or metal case enclosing 1 or more pulleys **5** (a ballet shoe with) a solid toe on which a dancer can stand on points **6a** a quantity or number of things dealt with as a unit **b** a part of a building or set of buildings devoted to a particular use **c** *chiefly NAm* (the distance along 1 side of) a usu rectangular space (e g in a town) enclosed by streets and usu occupied by buildings **d** BLOCK SECTION **7** a piece of engraved or etched material (e g wood or metal) from which impressions are printed [ME *blok*, fr MF *bloc*, fr MD *blok*; akin to OHG *bloh* block, MIr *blog* fragment]

[2]**block** *vt* **1a** to make unsuitable for passage or progress by obstruction **b** to hinder the passage, progress, or accomplishment of (as if) by interposing an

obstruction **c** to shut off from view ⟨*trees* ~ing *the sun*⟩ **d** to obstruct or interfere usu legitimately with (e g an opponent) in various games or sports **e** to prevent normal functioning of **2** to make (2 or more lines of writing or type) flush at the left or at both margins **3** to arrange (e g a school timetable) in long continuous periods ~ *vi* to block an opponent in sports – **blockage** *n*, **blocker** *n*

[1]**blockade** /blə'kayd, blo-/ *n* **1** the surrounding or blocking of a particular enemy area to prevent passage of people or supplies **2** an obstruction

[2]**blockade** *vt* to subject to a blockade – **blockader** *n*

,**block and 'tackle** *n* an arrangement of pulley blocks with associated rope or cable for hoisting or hauling

'**block,board** /-,bawd/ *n* material made of parallel wooden strips glued edge to edge and finished on top and underneath with thin wooden sheets

'**block-,booking** *n* a booking of a number of places (e g theatre seats) at 1 time

'**block,buster** /-,bustə/ *n* **1** a huge high-explosive demolition bomb **2** sby or sthg particularly outstanding or effective *USE* infml

block diagram *n* a diagram (e g of a system or process) in which labelled figures (e g rectangles) and interconnecting lines represent the relationship of parts

'**block,head** /-,hed/ *n* an extremely dull or stupid person

'**block,house** /-,hows/ *n* **1** a building made of heavy timbers with loopholes for firing through, observation, etc, formerly used as a fort **2** an observation post built to withstand heat, blast, radiation, etc

block in *vt* to sketch the outlines of, in a design

,**block 'letter** *n* a simple capital letter ⟨*write in* block letters, *please*⟩

block mountain *n* a horst ☞ GEOGRAPHY

block out *vt* BLOCK IN

'**block ,plane** *n* a small plane made with the blade set at a low pitch and used chiefly on end grains of wood

block release *n* a short course of full-time study for which a worker is released by his/her employer – compare DAY RELEASE

block section *n* a length of railway track of defined limits, the use of which is governed by block signals

block signal *n* a signal at the entrance of a block section to control trains entering and using that block section

block system *n* a system by which a railway track is divided into short sections and trains are controlled by signals

bloke /blohk/ *n, chiefly Br* a man – infml [perh fr Shelta]

[1]**blond** /blond/ *adj* **1a** *of hair* of a flaxen, golden, light auburn, or pale yellowish brown colour **b** of a pale white or rosy white colour ⟨~ *skin*⟩ **c** being a blond ⟨*a handsome* ~ *youth*⟩ **2a** of a light colour **b** of the colour blond [F] – **blondish** *adj*

[2]**blond** *n* **1** sby with blond hair and often a light complexion and blue or grey eyes **2** a light yellowish brown to dark greyish yellow colour

blonde /blond/ *n or adj* (a) blond – used esp for or in relation to women ⟨*a smiling* ~⟩ [F, fem of *blond*]

[1]**blood** /blud/ *n* **1a** the usu red fluid that circulates in the heart, arteries, capillaries, and veins of a vertebrate animal, carrying nourishment and oxygen to, and bringing away waste products from, all parts of the body ☞ ANATOMY **b** a comparable fluid of an invertebrate animal **2a** lifeblood; *broadly* life **b** human lineage; *esp* the royal lineage **c** kinship **d** descent from parents **3a** temper, passion **b** the one of the 4 humours in medieval physiology that was believed to cause sanguinity **4** people or ideas of the specified, esp innovative, kind ⟨*need some fresh* ~ *in the organization*⟩ **5** *archaic* a dashing lively esp young man; a rake – now usu humor [ME, fr OE *blōd*; akin to OHG *bluot* blood]

[2]**blood** *vt* **1** to stain or wet with blood; *esp* to mark the face of (an inexperienced fox hunter) with the blood of the fox **2** to give an initiating experience to (sby new to a particular field of activity)

'**blood,bath** /-,bahth/ *n* a great slaughter; a massacre

,**blood 'brother** *n* either of 2 men pledged to mutual loyalty, esp by a ceremonial mingling of each other's blood – **blood brotherhood** *n*

'**blood ,count** *n* (the determination of) the number of blood cells in a definite volume of blood

'**blood,curdling** /-,kuhdling/ *adj* arousing horror ⟨~ *screams*⟩ – **bloodcurdlingly** *adv*

-blooded /-bludid/ *comb form* (→ *adj*) having (such) blood or (such) a temperament ⟨*cold*-blooded⟩ ⟨*warm*-blooded⟩

'**blood ,feud** *n* a murderous feud between clans or families

'**blood ,group** *n* any of the classes into which human beings can be separated on the basis of the presence or absence of specific antigens in their blood

'**blood,guilt** /-,gilt/ *n* guilt resulting from bloodshed

'**blood ,heat** *n* a temperature approximating to that of the human body; about 37°C or 98°F

'**blood,hound** /-,hownd/ *n* **1** a large powerful hound of European origin remarkable for its acuteness of smell and poor sight **2** a person (e g a detective) who is keen in pursuing or tracking sby or sthg down

'**bloodless** /-lis/ *adj* **1** deficient in or free from blood **2** not accompanied by the shedding of blood ⟨*a* ~ *victory*⟩ **3** lacking in spirit or vitality **4** lacking in human feeling ⟨~ *statistics*⟩ – **bloodlessly** *adv*, **bloodlessness** *n*

'**blood,letting** /-,leting/ *n* **1** phlebotomy **2** bloodshed

'**blood,line** /-,lien/ *n* a group of related individuals, esp with distinctive characteristics

'**blood ,money** *n* **1** money obtained at the cost of another's life **2** money paid to the next of kin of a slain person

'**blood ,platelet** /'playtlit/ *n* any of the minute cytoplasmic discs in the blood of vertebrates that assist in blood clotting and are non-nucleated in humans

'**blood ,poisoning** *n* septicaemia

'**blood ,pressure** *n* pressure that is exerted by the blood on the walls of the blood vessels, esp arteries, and that varies with the age and health of the individual

,**blood 'red** *adj* having the colour of blood

'**blood-re,lation** *n* a person related by consanguinity

'**blood ,serum** *n* the watery portion of the blood

excluding the blood cells; *also* blood plasma from which the fibrin has been removed

'blood,shed /-,shed/ *n* **1** the shedding of blood **2** the taking of life

'blood,shot /-,shot/ *adj, of an eye* having the white part tinged with red

'blood ,sport *n* a field sport (e g fox hunting or beagling) in which animals are killed – derog; not used technically

'blood,stain /-,stayn/ *n* a discoloration caused by blood – **bloodstained** *adj*

'blood,stock /-,stok/ *n sing or pl in constr* horses of Thoroughbred breeding, esp when used for racing

'blood,stone /-,stohn/ *n* a translucent green quartz gemstone sprinkled with red spots

'blood,stream /-,streem/ *n* the flowing blood in a circulatory system

'blood,sucker /-,sukə/ *n* **1** a leech **2** a person who extorts money from another – **bloodsucking** *adj*

'blood ,sugar *n* (the concentration of) the glucose in the blood

'blood ,test *n* a test of the blood (e g to ascertain the nature of an infection or to detect leukaemia)

'blood,thirsty /-,thuhsti/ *adj* eager for bloodshed – **bloodthirstily** *adj*, **bloodthirstiness** *n*

'blood ,type *n* BLOOD GROUP

'blood ,vessel *n* any of the vessels through which blood circulates in an animal ☞ ANATOMY

'blood,worm /-,wuhm/ *n* any of various reddish annelid worms often used as bait for fish

¹bloody /'bludi/ *adj* **1** smeared, stained with, or containing blood **2** accompanied by or involving bloodshed **3a** murderous, bloodthirsty **b** merciless, cruel **4** – used as an intensive; slang [ME, fr OE *blōdig*, fr *blōd* blood] – **bloodily** *adv*, **bloodiness** *n*

²bloody *vt* to make bloody

³bloody *adv* – used as an intensive; slang ⟨*not* ~ *likely!*⟩

,Bloody 'Mary /'meəri/ *n, pl* **Bloody Marys** a cocktail consisting chiefly of vodka and tomato juice [prob fr *Bloody Mary*, nickname of Mary I of England †1558; fr its red colour]

,bloody-'minded *adj* deliberately obstructive or unhelpful – **bloody-mindedness** *n*

¹bloom /bloohm/ *n* a thick bar of hammered or rolled iron or steel [ME *blome* lump of metal, fr OE *blōma*]

²bloom *n* **1a** a flower **b** the flowering state ⟨*the roses in* ~⟩ **c** an excessive growth of phytoplankton **2** a time of beauty, freshness, and vigour ⟨*the* ~ *of youth*⟩ **3a** a delicate powdery coating on some fruits and leaves **b** cloudiness on a film of varnish or lacquer **c** a mottled surface that appears on chocolate, often due to incorrect temperatures in manufacture or storage **4** a rosy or healthy appearance [ME *blome*, fr ON *blom*; akin to OE *blōwan* to blossom – more at ³BLOW] – **bloomy** *adj*

³bloom *vi* **1a** to produce or yield flowers **b** to support abundant plant life ⟨*make the desert* ~⟩ **2a** to flourish ⟨~ing *with health*⟩ **b** to reach maturity; blossom ⟨*their friendship* ~ed *over the weeks*⟩ **3** *of a body of water* to become densely populated with microorganisms, esp plankton

bloomer /'bloohmə/ *n* a stupid blunder – infml [³BLOOM + ²-ER]

bloomers /'bloohməz/ *n pl* a woman's undergarment with full loose legs gathered at the knee [Amelia *Bloomer* †1894 US feminist]

blooming /'blooming, 'blooh-/ *adj, chiefly Br* – used as a generalized intensive; euph ⟨*that* ~ *idiot*⟩ [prob euphemism for *bloody*]

blooper /'bloohpə/ *n, NAm* an embarrassing public blunder – infml [*bloop* (a grating or howling sound), of imit origin]

¹blossom /'blosəm/ *n* **1a** the flower of a plant; *esp* the flower that produces edible fruits **b** the mass of bloom on a single plant **2** a high point or stage of development [ME *blosme*, fr OE *blōstm*; akin to OE *blōwan*] – **blossomy** *adj*

²blossom *vi* **1** to bloom **2** to come into one's own; develop ⟨*a* ~ing *talent*⟩

¹blot /blot/ *n* **1** a soiling or disfiguring mark; a spot **2** a mark of reproach; a blemish [ME]

²blot *vb* **-tt-** *vt* **1** to spot, stain, or spatter with a discolouring substance **2** to dry or remove with an absorbing agent (e g blotting paper) ~ *vi* **1** to make a blot **2** to become marked with a blot – **blot one's copybook** to mar one's previously good record or standing

³blot *n* a backgammon counter exposed to capture [perh fr Dan *blot* naked, exposed]

blotch /bloch/ *n* **1** an imperfection, blemish **2** an irregular spot or mark (e g of colour or ink) [prob partly alter. (influenced by ¹*blot*) of *botch* (swelling), & partly fr OF *bloche* clod of earth] – **blotch** *vt*, **blotchily** *adv*; **blotchy** *adj*

blot out /blot/ *vt* **1** to obscure, eclipse **2** to destroy; WIPE OUT

blotter /'blotə/ *n* a piece of blotting paper

'blotting ,paper /'bloting/ *n* a spongy unsized paper used to absorb ink

blotto /'blotoh/ *adj, Br* extremely drunk – slang [prob irreg fr ²*blot*]

blouse /blowz/ *n* a usu loose-fitting woman's upper garment that resembles a shirt or smock and is waist-length or longer [F]

blouson /'bloohzon, 'blowzon/ *n* a short loose jacket or blouse usu closely fitted at the waist [F, fr *blouse*]

¹blow /bloh/ *vb* **blew** /blooh/; **blown** /blohn/ *vi* **1** *of air* to move with speed or force ⟨*it's* ~ing *hard tonight*⟩ **2** to send forth a current of gas, esp air ⟨blew *on his cold hands*⟩ **3** to make a sound by blowing ⟨*the whistle* blew⟩ **4** to boast **5a** to pant **b** *of a whale* to eject moisture-laden air from the lungs through the blowhole **6** *of an electric fuse* to melt when overloaded **7** *of a tyre* to lose the contained air through a spontaneous puncture – usu + *out* ~ *vt* **1a** to set (gas or vapour) in motion **b** to act on with a current of gas or vapour **2** to damn, disregard – infml ⟨~ *the expense*⟩ **3** to produce or shape by the action of blown or injected air ⟨~ing *bubbles*⟩ ⟨~ing *glass*⟩ **4** to deposit eggs or larvae on or in – used with reference to an insect **5** to shatter, burst, or destroy by explosion – compare BLOW UP **6** to cause (a fuse) to blow **7** to rupture by too much pressure ⟨blew *a gasket*⟩ **8** to squander (money or an advantage) ⟨blew *£50 on a dress*⟩ ⟨blew *his chance*⟩ – slang **9** to leave hurriedly ⟨blew *town*⟩ – slang [ME *blowen*, fr OE *blāwan*; akin to OHG *blāen* to blow, L *flare*, Gk *phallos* penis] – **blow hot and cold** to act changeably by alternately favouring and rebuffing – **blow off steam** to release pent-up emotions – **blow one's own trumpet** to praise oneself; boast – **blow one's top** to become furious; explode with anger – infml – **blow the gaff** *Br* to let out a usu discreditable secret – **blow someone's mind** **1** to cause sby to hallucinate – slang **2** to amaze sby – infml – **blow the whistle on** **1** to bring (sthg secret) into the open – slang **2** to inform against – slang

²**blow** *n* **1** a strong wind or windy storm **2** an act or instance of blowing **3** a walk or other outing in the fresh air – infml

³**blow** *vt* **blew** /blooh/; **blown** /blohn/ to cause (e g flowers or blossom) to open out, usu just before dropping ⟨*these roses are* ~n⟩ [ME *blowen*, fr OE *blōwan*; akin to OHG *bluoen* to bloom, L *florēre* to bloom, *flor-*, *flos* flower]

⁴**blow** *n* ²BLOOM 1b ⟨*lilacs in full* ~⟩ – poetic

⁵**blow** *n* **1** a hard stroke delivered with a part of the body or with an instrument **2** *pl* a hostile or aggressive state – esp in *come to blows* **3** a forcible or sudden act or effort ⟨*a* ~ *for freedom*⟩ **4** a shock or misfortune [ME (northern) *blaw*]

'**blow,back** /-,bak/ *n* a recoil-operated action of a firearm in which no locking or inertia mechanism hinders the rearward motion of the bolt or breechblock; *also* an automatic firearm using such an action

,**blow-by-'blow** *adj* minutely detailed ⟨*a* ~ *account*⟩

,**blow-'dry** *vt* to blow warm air over, through, or onto (e g the hair) until dry – **blow-dry** /'-,-/ *n*, **blow-drier** *n*

blower /'bloh·ə/ *n* **1** sby or sthg that blows or is blown **2** a device for producing a current of air or gas **3** *Br the* telephone – infml

'**blow,fly** /-,flie/ *n* any of various 2-winged flies that deposit their eggs or maggots esp on meat or in wounds; *esp* a bluebottle

'**blow,gun** /-,gun/ *n* BLOWPIPE 2

'**blow,hard** /-,hahd/ *n* a braggart

'**blow,hole** /-,hohl/ *n* **1** a nostril in the top of the head of a whale, porpoise, or dolphin **2** a hole in the ice to which aquatic mammals (e g seals) come to breathe

blow in *vi* to arrive casually or unexpectedly – infml

'**blow,lamp** /-,lamp/ *n* a small portable burner that produces an intense flame and has a pressurized fuel tank

blown /blohn/ *adj* **1** swollen **2** flyblown [ME *blowen*, fr pp of *blowen* to blow]

'**blow,out** /-,owt/ *n* **1** a large meal –infml **2** a bursting of a container (e g a tyre) by pressure of the contents on a weak spot **3** an uncontrolled eruption of an oil or gas well

blow out *vi* **1** to become extinguished by a gust **2** *of an oil or gas well* to erupt out of control ~ *vt* to extinguish by a gust

blow over *vi* to pass away without effect

'**blow,pipe** /-,piep/ *n* **1** a small tube for blowing air, oxygen, etc into a flame to direct and increase the heat **2** a tube for propelling a projectile (e g a dart) by blowing **3** a long metal tube used by a glassblower

blowsy *also* **blowzy** /'blowzi/ *adj* **1** having a coarse ruddy complexion **2** *esp of a woman* slovenly in appearance and usu fat [E dial. *blowse*, *blowze* (wench, slattern)]

'**blow,torch** /-,tawch/ *n* a blowlamp

'**blow,up** /-,up/ *n* **1** an explosion **2** an outburst of temper **3** a photographic enlargement

blow up *vt* **1** to shatter or destroy by explosion **2** to build up or exaggerate to an unreasonable extent **3** to fill up with a gas, esp air ⟨blow up *a balloon*⟩ **4** to make a photographic enlargement of ~ *vi* **1a** to explode **b** to be disrupted or destroyed (e g by explosion) **c** to become violently angry **2a** to become filled with a gas, esp air **b** to become expanded to unreasonable proportions **3** to come into being; arise

blowy /'bloh·i/ *adj* windy ⟨*a* ~ *March day*⟩

¹**blubber** /'blubə/ *n* the fat of large marine mammals, esp whales [ME *bluber* bubble, foam, prob of imit origin] – **blubbery** *adj*

²**blubber** *vi* to weep noisily ~ *vt* to utter while weeping *USE* infml [ME *blubren* to make a bubbling sound, fr *bluber*]

³**blubber** *adj* puffed out; thick ⟨~ *lips*⟩

blubbery /'blubəri/ *adj* ³BLUBBER

¹**bludgeon** /'blujən/ *n* a short club used as a weapon [perh modif of OF *bougeon*, dim. of *bouge*, *bolge* club]

²**bludgeon** *vt* **1** to hit or beat with a bludgeon **2** to overcome by aggressive argument

¹**blue** /blooh/ *adj* **1** of the colour blue **2** discoloured through cold, anger, bruising, or fear **3** bluish grey ⟨*a* ~ *cat*⟩ **4a** low in spirits **b** depressing, dismal **5** CONSERVATIVE 1 **6a** obscene, pornographic ⟨*a* ~ *film*⟩ **b** off-colour, risqué ⟨~ *jokes*⟩ [ME, fr OF *blou*, of Gmc origin; akin to OHG *blāo* blue; akin to L *flavus* yellow, OE *bǣl* fire – more at BALD] – **bluely** *adv*, **blueness** *n* – **once in a blue moon** very rarely – **until one is blue in the face** unsuccessfully for ever ⟨*you can complain* until you're blue in the face *but no one will listen*⟩

²**blue** *n* **1** a colour whose hue is that of the clear sky and lies between green and violet in the spectrum **2a** a blue pigment or dye **b** a blue preparation used to whiten clothes in laundering **3** blue clothing ⟨*dressed in* ~⟩ **4a(1)** the sky **(2)** the far distance **b** the sea **5** any of numerous small chiefly blue butterflies **6** *often cap, Br* a usu notional award given to sby who has played in a sporting contest between Oxford and Cambridge universities; *also* sby who has been given such an award **7** *Austr* a quarrel, row – infml – **out of the blue** without warning; unexpectedly ⟨*she just turned up* out of the blue *expecting a meal*⟩

³**blue** *vb* **blueing, bluing** /'blooh·ing/ to (cause to) turn blue

⁴**blue** *vt* **blueing, bluing** *Br* to spend lavishly and wastefully – infml [prob fr *blew*, pp of ¹*blow* (see sense 8)]

,**blue 'baby** *n* a baby with a bluish tint, usu from a congenital heart defect

'**blue,beard** /-,biəd/ *n* a man who marries and kills one wife after another [*Bluebeard*, a folklore character]

'**blue,bell** /-,bel/ *n* **1** any of various plants of the lily family bearing blue bell-shaped flowers; *esp* the wild hyacinth **2** *chiefly Scot* the harebell

'**blueberry** /-b(ə)ri/ *NAm* -,beri/ *n* (the edible blue or blackish berry of) any of several shrubs of the heath family

'**blue,bird** /-,buhd/ *n* any of several small N American songbirds

,**blue-'black** *adj* dark blue

,**blue 'blood** *n* high or noble birth – **blue-blooded** *adj*

blue book *n* an official parliamentary report or document [fr colour of cover]

¹blue,bottle /-,botl/ *n* **1** CORNFLOWER 2 **2** any of several blowflies of which the abdomen or the whole body is iridescent blue, that make a loud buzzing noise in flight **3** *Austr & SAfr* a small blue jellyfish with 1 tentacle

,blue 'cheese *n* cheese marked with veins of greenish blue mould

blue chip *n* a stock issue of high investment quality that usu pertains to a substantial well-established company and enjoys public confidence in its worth and stability – **blue-chip** *adj*

,blue-'collar *adj* of or being the class of manual wage-earning employees whose duties call for the wearing of work clothes or protective clothing – compare WHITE-COLLAR

,blue-eyed 'boy *n* a favourite – often derog ⟨*teacher's* ~⟩

'blue,fish /-,fish/ *n* an active voracious fish that is found in all warm seas

'blue,grass /-,grahs/ *n* **1** *NAm* MEADOW GRASS **2** a type of country music played on unamplified stringed instruments [(2) fr *Bluegrass* State, nickname of Kentucky, USA, where such music prob originated]

blue-green alga *n* any of a class of algae that have their chlorophyll masked by bluish green pigments ☞ PLANT

blue gum *n* any of several Australian eucalyptuses grown for their wood

'blue ,john /jon/ *n* a blue form of fluorite used esp for jewellery and ornaments [fr the name *John*]

,blue-'pencil *vt* to edit by correcting or deleting – **blue penciller** *n*

,blue 'peter /'peetə/ *n* a blue signal flag with a white square in the centre, used to indicate that a merchant vessel is ready to sail [fr the name *Peter*]

'blue,print /-,print/ *n* **1** a photographic print in white on a bright blue ground, used esp for copying maps and plans **2** a detailed programme of action ⟨*a* ~ *for victory*⟩ – **blueprint** *vt*

blue ribbon *n* a ribbon of blue fabric worn as an honour or award, esp by members of the Order of the Garter

blues /bloohz/ *n, pl* **blues** **1** *sing or pl in constr* low spirits; melancholy – + *the* **2** (a song in) a melancholy style of music characterized by flattened thirds or sevenths where a major interval would be expected in the melody and harmony ⟨*singing the* ~⟩ – **bluesy** /'bloohzi/ *adj*

'blue,stocking /-,stoking/ *n* a woman with intellectual or literary interests – derog [*Bluestocking* Society, 18th-c literary club]

'blue ,tit *n* a widely distributed European tit that has a bright blue crown and a mostly yellow underside

,blue 'vitriol *n* a hydrated copper sulphate

blue whale *n* a rorqual that is the largest living animal and is found esp in northern European waters ☞ ENDANGERED

bluey /'blooh·i/ *n, Austr* a bundle carried by a bushman; swag [fr the blue blanket commonly used to wrap the bundle]

¹bluff /bluf/ *adj* **1** rising steeply with a broad, flat, or rounded front **2** good-naturedly frank and outspoken [obs D *blaf* flat; akin to MLG *blaff* smooth] – **bluffly** *adv*, **bluffness** *n*

²bluff *n* a high steep bank; a cliff

³bluff *vt* **1** to deceive (an opponent) in cards by a bold bet on an inferior hand with the result that the opponent withdraws a winning hand **2** to deceive by pretence or an outward appearance of strength, confidence, etc ~ *vi* to bluff sby [prob fr D *bluffen* to boast, play a kind of card game] – **bluffer** *n*

⁴bluff *n* an act or instance of bluffing

bluish /'blooh·ish/ *adj* having a tinge of blue; rather blue – **bluishness** *n*

¹blunder /'blundə/ *vi* **1** to move unsteadily or confusedly **2** to make a blunder [ME *blundren*] – **blunderer** *n*, **blunderingly** *adv*

²blunder *n* a gross error or mistake resulting from stupidity, ignorance, or carelessness

blunderbuss /'blundə,bus/ *n* an obsolete short firearm with a large bore and usu a flaring muzzle [by folk etymology fr obs D *donderbus*, fr D *donder* thunder + obs D *bus* gun]

¹blunt /blunt/ *adj* **1** insensitive, dull **2** having an edge or point that is not sharp **3a** aggressively outspoken **b** direct, straightforward [ME] – **bluntly** *adv*, **bluntness** *n*

²blunt *vt* to make less sharp or definite

¹blur /bluh/ *n* **1** a smear or stain **2** sthg vague or indistinct [perh akin to ME *bleren* to blear] – **blurry** *adj*, **blurriness** *n*

²blur *vb* **-rr-** *vt* **1** to obscure or blemish by smearing **2** to make indistinct or confused ~ *vi* to become vague, indistinct, or confused – **blurringly** *adv*

blurb /bluhb/ *n* a short publicity notice, esp on a book cover [coined by Gelett Burgess †1951 US humorist]

blurt out /bluht/ *vt* to utter abruptly and impulsively [prob imit]

¹blush /blush/ *vi* **1** to become red in the face, esp from shame, modesty, or embarrassment **2** to feel shame or embarrassment [ME *blusshen*, fr OE *blyscan* to redden, fr *blȳsa* flame; akin to OHG *bluhhen* to burn brightly] – **blushingly** *adv*

²blush *n* **1** a reddening of the face, esp from shame, confusion, or embarrassment **2** a red or rosy tint – **blushful** *adj*

blusher /'blushə/ *n* a cream or powder for adding colour to the cheeks [¹BLUSH + ²-ER]

¹bluster /'blustə/ *vi* **1** to blow in stormy gusts **2** to talk or act in a noisily self-assertive or boastful manner [ME *blustren*, prob fr MLG *blüsteren*] – **blusterer** *n*, **blusteringly** *adv*

²bluster *n* **1** a violent blowing **2** loudly boastful or threatening talk – **blusterous** *adj*, **blustery** *adj*

bo /boh/ *n, chiefly NAm* a fellow – used chiefly in infml address [perh short for E dial. *bor* (friend, neighbour)]

BO /,bee 'oh/ *n* a disagreeable smell, esp of stale perspiration, given off by a person's body [*B*ody *O*dour]

boa /'boh·ə/ *n* **1** a large snake (e g the boa constrictor, anaconda, or python) that crushes its prey **2** a long fluffy scarf of fur, feathers, or delicate fabric [L, a water snake]

,boa con'strictor *n* a tropical American boa that reaches a length of 3m (about 10ft) or more

boar /baw/ *n* **1a** an uncastrated male pig **b** the male of any of several mammals (e g a guinea pig or badger) **2** the Old World wild pig from which most domestic pigs derive [ME *bor*, fr OE *bār*; akin to OHG & OS *bēr* boar] – **boarish** *adj*

[1]board /bawd/ *n* **1** the distance that a sailing vessel makes on 1 tack **2a** a usu long thin narrow piece of sawn timber **b** *pl* STAGE 2a(2), (3) **3a** a table spread with a meal **b** daily meals, esp when provided in return for payment **4** *sing or pl in constr* **a** a group of people having managerial, supervisory, or investigatory powers ⟨~ *of directors*⟩ ⟨~ *of examiners*⟩ **b** an official body ⟨*the gas* ~⟩ **5** a flat usu rectangular piece of material designed or marked for a special purpose (e g for playing chess, ludo, backgammon, etc or for use as a blackboard or surfboard) **6a** any of various wood pulps or composition materials formed into stiff flat rectangular sheets **b** cardboard **7** *archaic* TABLE 1 [ME *bord* piece of sawed lumber, border, ship's side, fr OE; akin to OHG *bort* ship's side, Skt *bardhaka* carpenter] – **boardlike** *adj* – **on board** aboard

[2]board *vt* **1** to come up against or alongside (a ship), usu to attack **2** to go aboard (e g a ship, train, aircraft, or bus) **3** to cover with boards – + *over* or *up* ⟨~ *up a window*⟩ **4** to provide with regular meals and usu lodging for a fixed price ~ *vi* to take one's meals, usu as a paying customer

boarder /'bawdə/ *n* **1** a lodger **2** a resident pupil at a boarding school [[2]BOARD + [2]-ER]

boardinghouse /'bawding,hows/ *n* a lodging house that supplies meals

'boarding ,school *n* a school at which meals and lodging are provided

Board of Trade *n* a British government department concerned with commerce and industry that in 1970 was absorbed into the Department of Trade and Industry

board out *vb* to (cause to) receive regular board and usu lodging away from home ⟨boarded *the cat* out *while they were on holiday*⟩

'boardroom /-,roohm, -room/ *n* a room in which board meetings are held

'board,walk /-,wawk/ *n, NAm* a walk often constructed of planking, usu beside the sea

boart /'boh·ət, bawt/ *n* bort

[1]boast /bohst/ *n* **1** an act of boasting **2** a cause for pride [ME *boost*] – **boastful** *adj*, **boastfully** *adv*, **boastfulness** *n*

[2]boast *vi* to praise oneself ~ *vt* **1** to speak of or assert with excessive pride **2** to have or display as notable or a source of pride – **boaster** *n*

[3]boast *n* a usu defensive shot in squash made from a rear corner of the court and hitting a side wall before the front wall [prob fr F *bosse* protuberance, place where the ball hits the wall]

[1]boat /boht/ *n* **1** a small open vessel or craft for travelling across water **2** a usu small ship ⟨*left England on the Calais* ~⟩ **3** a boat-shaped utensil or dish ⟨*a gravy* ~⟩ [ME *boot*, fr OE *bāt*; akin to ON *beit* boat] – **in the same boat** in the same situation or predicament

[2]boat *vi* to use a boat, esp for recreation

boatel, botel /boh'tel/ *n* a waterside hotel with berths to accommodate people travelling by boat [blend of *boat* and *hotel*]

boater /'bohtə/ *n* a stiff straw hat with a shallow flat crown and a brim [[2]BOAT + [2]-ER]

'boat,hook /-,hook/ *n* a pole with a hook at one end, used esp for fending off or holding boats alongside

'boat,house /-,hows/ *n* a shed for boats

'boatman /-mən/ *n* one who works with or hires out esp pleasure boats – **boatmanship, boatsmanship** *n*

boatswain /'bohz(ə)n, 'bohs(ə)n/ *n* a petty officer on a merchant vessel or warrant officer in the navy who supervises all work done on deck and is responsible esp for routine maintenance of the ship's structure [ME *bootswein*, fr *boot* boat + *swein* boy, servant]

,boatswain's 'chair *n* a support suspended by ropes and pulleys and used for work high on the side of a ship, tall building, etc

'boat ,train *n* an express train that takes people to or from a ship

[1]bob /bob/ *vb* **-bb-** *vt* **1** to move up and down in a short quick movement ⟨~ *one's head*⟩ **2** to perform (a respectful gesture, esp a curtsy) briefly ~ *vi* **1** to move down and up briefly or repeatedly ⟨*a cork* ~bed *in the water*⟩ **2** to curtsy briefly **3** to try to seize a suspended or floating object with the teeth ⟨~ *for apples at a Halloween party*⟩ [ME *boben* to strike, move with a jerk, prob of imit origin] – **bobber** *n*

[2]bob *n* **1** a short quick down-and-up motion **2** (a method of bell ringing using) a modification of the order in change ringing

[3]bob *n* **1a** *Scot* a nosegay **b** a knot or twist (e g of ribbons or hair) **c** a haircut for a woman or girl in which the hair hangs loose just above the shoulders **2** FLOAT 1a **3** a hanging ball or weight on a plumb line or kite's tail **4** *pl* a small insignificant item ⟨*bits and* ~s⟩ [ME *bobbe* bunch, cluster]

[4]bob *vt* **-bb-** **1** to cut shorter; crop ⟨~ *a horse's tail*⟩ **2** to cut (hair) in a bob

[5]bob *n, pl* **bob** *Br* a shilling; *also* the sum of 5 new pence – infml [perh fr *Bob*, nickname for *Robert*]

bobbin /'bobin/ *n* **1** a cylinder or spindle on which yarn or thread is wound (e g for use in spinning, sewing, or lacemaking) **2** a coil of insulated wire or the reel it is wound on [F *bobine*]

[1]bobble /'bobl/ *vi* **bobbling** /'bobling, 'bobl·ing/ to move jerkily down and up briefly or repeatedly [freq of [1]*bob*]

[2]bobble *n* **1** a bobbling movement **2** a small often fluffy ball (e g of wool) used for ornament or trimming ⟨*curtains with plush* ~s – H E Bates⟩ ⟨*a* ~ *hat*⟩

bobby /'bobi/ *n, Br* a policeman – infml [*Bobby*, nickname for *Robert*, after Sir *Robert* Peel †1850 E statesman, who organized the London police force]

'bobby ,socks, bobby sox /soks/ *n pl, chiefly NAm* socks reaching above the ankle, esp for girls [fr the name *Bobby*]

'bobby-,soxer /,soksə/ *n, NAm* an adolescent girl – chiefly derog

'bob,cat /-,kat/ *n* a common N American lynx [[3]*bob*; fr its stubby tail]

'bob,sleigh /-,slay/ *n* **1** either of a pair of short sledges joined by a coupling **2** a large usu metal sledge for 2 or 4 people used in racing [perh fr [3]*bob*]

'bob,tail /-,tayl/ *n* a horse or dog with a bobbed tail [[3]*bob*] – **bobtail, bobtailed** *adj*

bob up *vi* to emerge, arise, or appear suddenly or unexpectedly ⟨*the question* bobbed up *again*⟩

Boche /bosh/ *n, pl* **Boches,** *esp collectively* **Boche** a German (soldier) – derog [F (slang), rascal, German, prob short for *alboche*, alter. of *allemand* German]

bod /bod/ *n* a person – infml ⟨*an odd* ~⟩ [short for *body*]
bode /bohd/ *vt* to augur, presage ⟨*this* ~s *ill for the future*⟩ [ME *boden*, fr OE *bodian*; akin to OE *bēodan* to proclaim – more at BID] – **bodement** /'bohdmənt/ *n*
bodega /boh'deegə, -'daygə/ *n* **1** a storehouse for wine **2** a shop that sells wine [Sp, fr L *apotheca* storehouse – more at APOTHECARY]
bodge /boj/ *vt* to botch – infml [by alter.]
bodhisattva, boddhisattva /,bohdi'satvə/ *n* a being that according to Buddhism has attained perfect enlightenment but compassionately refrains from entering nirvana in order to save others [Skt *bodhisattva* one whose essence is enlightenment, fr *bodhi* enlightenment + *sattva* being]
bodice /'bodis/ *n* the part of a dress that is above the waist [alter. of *bodies*, pl of [1]*body* (see sense 3A)]
-bodied /-bodid/ *comb form* (*adj, n* → *adj*) having (such) a body ⟨*full*-bodied⟩ ⟨*glass*-bodied⟩
[1]**bodily** /'bodəli/ *adj* of the body ⟨~ *comfort*⟩ ⟨~ *organs*⟩
[2]**bodily** *adv* **1** IN THE FLESH, IN PERSON **2** as a whole; altogether
bodkin /'bodkin/ *n* **1a** a small sharp slender instrument for making holes in cloth **b** a long ornamental hairpin **2** a blunt thick needle with a large eye used to draw tape or ribbon through a loop or hem **3** *archaic* a dagger, stiletto [ME]
body /'bodi/ *n* **1a(1)** the organized physical substance of a living animal or plant ☞ ANATOMY **(2)** a corpse **b** a human being; a person **2a** the main part of a plant or animal body, esp as distinguished from limbs and head **b** the main, central, or principal part: e g **(1)** the nave of a church **(2)** the part of a vehicle on or in which the load is placed **3a** the part of a garment covering the body or trunk **b** the central part of printed or written matter **c** the sound box or pipe of a musical instrument **4a** a mass of matter distinct from other masses ⟨*a* ~ *of water*⟩ **b** any of the 7 planets in old astronomy **c** sthg that embodies or gives concrete reality to a thing; *specif* a material object in physical space **5** *sing or pl in constr* a group of people or things: e g **a** a fighting unit **b** a group of individuals organized for some purpose ⟨*a legislative* ~⟩ **6a** compactness or firmness of texture **b** comparative richness of flavour in wine [ME, fr OE *bodig*; akin to OHG *botah* body]
'body ,blow *n* a serious setback
,body 'corporate *n* CORPORATION 2
body forth *vt* to represent, symbolize
'body,guard /-,gahd/ *n* an escort whose duty it is to protect a person from bodily harm
,bodyline 'bowling /'bodilien/ *n* intimidatory fast bowling in cricket aimed persistently at the batsman's body and directed esp towards the leg side
'body ,louse *n* a sucking louse that feeds on the body and lives in people's clothing
,body 'politic *n* a group of people under a single government
'body ,snatcher *n* one who formerly dug up corpses illegally for dissection
'body,surf /-,suhf/ *vi* to surf without a surfboard by planing on the chest and stomach – **bodysurfer** *n*
'body,work /-,wuhk/ *n* the structure or form of a vehicle body
Boer /'baw·ə, 'boh·ə/ *n* a S African of Dutch descent [D, lit., farmer – more at BOOR]
boffin /'bofin/ *n, chiefly Br* a scientific expert; *esp* one involved in technological research – infml [origin unknown]
Bofors gun /'bohfəz/ *n* a light automatic antiaircraft gun [*Bofors*, munition works in Sweden]
bog /bog/ *n* **1** (an area of) wet spongy poorly-drained ground **2** *Br* TOILET 2 – slang [of Celt origin; akin to OIr *bocc* soft; akin to OE *būgan* to bend – more at [1]BOW; (2) short for *bog-house*] – **boggy** *adj*
,bog 'aspho,del /'asfə,del/ *n* either of 2 bog plants of the lily family
'bog,bean /-,been/ *n* a bog plant with pinkish white flowers
bog down *vb* **-gg-** *vt* to cause to sink (as if) into a bog; impede ~ *vi* to become impeded
bogey *also* **bogy, bogie** /'bohgi/ *n, pl* **bogeys** *also* **bogies** **1** a spectre, ghost **2** a source of fear, perplexity, or harassment **3** a golf score of 1 stroke over par on a hole [prob alter. of *bogle*]
'bogey,man /-,man/ *n* a bugbear; *esp* a monstrous imaginary figure used to threaten children
[1]**boggle** /'bogl/ *vi* **boggling** /'bogling/ **1** to be startled or amazed ⟨*the mind* ~s⟩ **2** to hesitate because of doubt, fear, or scruples [perh fr *bogle*] – **boggle** *n*
[2]**boggle** *n* a bogle
bogie *also* **bogey, bogy** /'bohgi/ *n, pl* **bogies** *also* **bogeys** *chiefly Br* a swivelling framework with 1 or more pairs of wheels and springs to carry and guide 1 end of a railway vehicle [origin unknown]
bogle /'bohgl/ *n, dial Br* a goblin, spectre; *also* an object of fear or loathing [E dial. (Sc & northern), terrifying apparition; akin to ME *bugge* scarecrow, spectre – more at BUG]
'bog ,myrtle /'muhtl/ *n* a densely branched shrub that grows in boggy land and has aromatic leaves
bogus /'bohgəs/ *adj* spurious, sham [*bogus* (a machine for making counterfeit money)] – **bogusness** *n*
bohea /boh'hee/ *n, often cap* a black tea [Chin (Pek) *wu*[3]*-i*[2], hills in China where it was grown]
Bohemian /boh'heemyən, -mi·ən/ *n* **1a** a native or inhabitant of Bohemia **b** the group of Czech dialects used in Bohemia **2** a person (e g a writer or artist) living an unconventional life [*Bohemia*, region (former kingdom) of Czechoslovakia] – **bohemian** *adj, often cap*
'Bohr ,theory /'boh·ə/ *n* a theory in physical chemistry: an atom consists of a positively charged nucleus about which revolves 1 or more electrons [Niels *Bohr* †1962 Dan physicist]
[1]**boil** /boyl/ *n* a localized pus-filled swelling of the skin resulting from infection in a skin gland [alter. of ME *bile*, fr OE *bȳl* – more at BIG]
[2]**boil** *vi* **1a** *of a fluid* to change into (bubbles of) a vapour when heated **b** to come to the boiling point (of the contents) ⟨*the kettle's* ~ing⟩ **2** to bubble or foam violently; churn **3** to be excited or stirred ⟨*made his blood* ~⟩ **4** to undergo the action of a boiling liquid (e g in cooking) ~ *vt* **1** to subject to the action of a boiling liquid (e g in cooking) ⟨~ *eggs*⟩ **2** to heat to the boiling point (of the contents) [ME *boilen*, fr OF *boillir*, fr L *bullire* to bubble, fr *bulla* bubble]
[3]**boil** *n* the act or state of boiling; BOILING POINT ⟨*keep it on the* ~⟩
boil down *vt* **1** to reduce in bulk by boiling **2** to

condense or summarize ~*vi* to amount *to* ⟨*her speech* boiled down *to a plea for more money*⟩

,boiled 'sweet *n* a sweet of boiled sugar

boiler /'boylə/ *n* **1** a vessel used for boiling **2** the part of a steam generator in which water is converted into steam under pressure **3** a tank in which water is heated or hot water is stored [[2]BOIL + [2]-ER]

'boiler ,suit *n, chiefly Br* a one-piece outer garment combining shirt and trousers, worn chiefly to protect clothing

[1]boiling /'boyling/ *adj* suitable for boiling ⟨*a ~ fowl*⟩

[2]boiling *adv* to an extreme degree; very ⟨*~ mad*⟩ ⟨*~ hot*⟩

'boiling ,point *n* **1** the temperature at which a liquid boils **2** the point at which a person loses his/her self-control

boil over *vi* **1** to overflow while boiling **2** to lose one's temper

boil up *vi* to rise towards a dangerous level (e g of unrest)

boisterous /'boyst(ə)rəs/ *adj* **1** noisily and cheerfully rough **2** stormy, wild [ME *boistous* rough] – **boisterously** *adv*, **boisterousness** *n*

Bokmål /'boohkmohl/ *n* a literary form of Norwegian adapted from written Danish – compare NYNORSK [Norw, lit., book language]

bola /'bohlə/ *n* a S American weapon consisting of 2 or more heavy balls attached to the ends of a cord for hurling at and entangling an animal [AmerSp *bolas*, fr pl of Sp *bola* ball]

bolas /'bohləs/ *n* a bola

[1]bold /bohld/ *adj* **1** showing or requiring a fearless adventurous spirit **2** impudent, presumptuous **3** departing from convention or tradition **4** standing out prominently; conspicuous **5** (set) in boldface [ME, fr OE *beald*; akin to OHG *bald* bold] – **boldly** *adv*, **boldness** *n*

[2]bold *n* boldface

'bold,face /-,fays/ *n* (printing in) the thickened form of a typeface used to give prominence or emphasis

bole /bohl/ *n* the trunk of a tree [ME, fr ON *bolr*]

bolection /boh'leksh(ə)n/ *n* a moulding that projects (e g from between panels on a wall) [origin unknown]

bolero /bə'leəroh; *sense 2* 'boləroh/ *n, pl* **boleros 1** (music for) a type of Spanish dance **2** a loose waist-length jacket open at the front [Sp, perh fr *bola* ball]

boletus /bə'leetəs, boh-/ *n, pl* **boletuses, boleti** /-tie/ any of a genus of fleshy fungi, some of which are edible [NL, genus name, fr L, a fungus, fr Gk *bōlitēs*]

bolide /'bohlied, -lid/ *n* a large (exploding) meteor [F, fr L *bolid-, bolis* arrow-shaped meteor, fr Gk, lit., missile, javelin, fr *ballein* to throw – more at DEVIL]

bolivar /bo'leevah/ *n, pl* **bolivars, bolivares** /,boli'vahrays/ ☞ *Venezuela* at NATIONALITY [AmerSp *bolívar*, fr Simón *Bolívar* †1830 Venezuelan soldier & statesman]

boll /bohl/ *n* the seed pod of cotton or similar plants [ME]

bollard /'bolahd, -ləd/ *n* **1** a post on a wharf round which to fasten mooring lines **2** a bitt **3** *Br* a short post (e g on a kerb or traffic island) to guide vehicles or forbid access [perh irreg fr *bole*]

bollock /'bolək/ *n, Br* **1** a testicle – usu pl **2** *pl* nonsense, rubbish – often used interjectionally *USE* vulg [ME *ballock*, fr OE *bealluc* – more at BALL]

bollocking /'boləking/ *n, Br* a severe reprimand – vulg

boll weevil /bohl/ *n* a weevil that infests the cotton plant

bologna sausage /bə'lonyə/ *n* a large smoked sausage made of beef, veal, and pork [*Bologna*, town in Italy]

bolometer /bə'lomitə, boh-/ *n* a very sensitive electrical instrument used in the detection and measurement of heat radiation [Gk *bolē* beam of light + E *-o-* + *-meter*] – **bolometric** /,bolə'metrik, ,boh-/ *adj*, **bolometrically** *adv*

boloney /bə'lohni/ *n* baloney

Bolshevik /'bolshəvik/ *n, pl* **Bolsheviks** *also* **Bolsheviki** /,bolshə'veeki/ **1** a member of the more radical wing of the Russian Social Democratic party that seized power in Russia in 1917 **2** COMMUNIST 1 – derog [Russ *bol'shevik*, fr *bol'she* larger; fr their forming the majority group of the party] – **Bolshevik** *adj*, **bolshevism** /-,viz(ə)m/ *n, often cap*, **bolshevize** /-,viez/ *vt*, **Bolshevization** /-vie'zaysh(ə)n/ *n*

Bolshevist /'bolshəvist/ *n or adj* (a) Bolshevik

[1]bolshie, bolshy /'bolshi/ *n* a Bolshevik – infml [by shortening & alter.]

[2]bolshie, bolshy *adj, Br* obstinate and argumentative; stubbornly uncooperative – infml – **bolshiness** *n*

[1]bolster /'bolstə/ *n* **1** a long pillow or cushion placed across the head of a bed, usu under other pillows **2** a structural part (e g in machinery) that eliminates friction or provides support ☞ BUILDING [ME, fr OE; akin to OE *belg* bag – more at BELLY]

[2]bolster *vt* to give support to; reinforce ⟨*~ed up his pride*⟩ – **bolsterer** *n*

[1]bolt /bolt, bohlt/ *n* **1a** a short stout usu blunt-headed arrow shot from a crossbow **b** a lightning stroke; a thunderbolt **2a** a sliding bar or rod used to fasten a door **b** the part of a lock that is shot or withdrawn by the key **3** a roll of cloth or wallpaper of a standard length **4a** a metal rod or pin for fastening objects together **b** a screw-bolt with a head suitable for turning with a spanner **5** a rod or bar that closes the breech of a breech-loading firearm [ME, fr OE; akin to OHG *bolz* crossbow bolt, Lith *beldėti* to beat]

[2]bolt *vi* **1** to move rapidly; dash ⟨*she ~ed for the door*⟩ **2a** to dart off or away; flee **b** to break away from control **3** to produce seed prematurely **4** *NAm* to break away from or oppose one's political party ~*vt* **1** to flush, start ⟨*~ rabbits*⟩ **2** to secure with a bolt **3** to attach or fasten with bolts **4** to swallow (e g food) hastily or without chewing – **bolter** *n*

[3]bolt *adv* in a rigidly erect position ⟨*sat ~ upright*⟩

[4]bolt *n* a dash, run [[2]*bolt*]

[5]bolt *vt* to sift (e g flour) [ME *bulten*, fr OF *buleter*, of Gmc origin; akin to MHG *biuteln* to sift, fr *biutel* bag, fr OHG *būtil*] – **bolter** *n*

,bolt from the 'blue *n* a completely unexpected occurrence

'bolt-,hole *n* **1** a hole into which an animal runs for safety **2** a means of rapid escape or place of refuge

boltrope /'bolt,rohp, 'bohlt-/ *n* a strong rope stitched to the edges of a sail to prevent it tearing or fraying

bolus /'bohləs/ *n* **1** a large pill **2** a soft mass of food that has been chewed but not swallowed [LL, fr Gk *bōlos* lump]

[1]**bomb** /bom/ *n* **1a** any of several explosive or incendiary devices typically detonated by impact or a timing mechanism and usu dropped from aircraft, thrown or placed by hand, or fired from a mortar **b** ATOM BOMB; *broadly* nuclear weapons – + *the* **2** a rounded mass of lava exploded from a volcano **3** *Br* a large sum of money ⟨*she's made a* ~⟩ – infml **4** *NAm* a failure, flop – infml [F *bombe*, fr It *bomba*, prob fr L *bombus* deep hollow sound, fr Gk *bombos*, of imit origin] – **a bomb** *Br* very successfully – infml ⟨*our act goes down* a bomb *in Britain* – *News of the World*⟩

[2]**bomb** *vt* to attack with bombs; bombard ~ *vi* to fail; FALL FLAT – infml

bombard /bom'bahd, '--/ *vt* **1** to attack with heavy artillery or with bombers **2** to attack vigorously or persistently (e g with questions) **3** to subject to the impact of electrons, alpha rays, or other rapidly moving particles [MF *bombarder*, fr *bombarde*, kind of cannon, prob fr L *bombus*] – **bombardment** *n*

bombardier /ˌbombə'diə/ *n* **1** a noncommissioned officer in the British artillery **2** a US bomber-crew member who aims and releases the bombs

bombast /'bombast/ *n* pretentious inflated speech or writing [MF *bombace*, fr ML *bombac-*, *bombax* cotton, alter. of L *bombyc-*, *bombyx* silkworm, silk, fr Gk *bombyk-*, *bombyx*] – **bombastic** /bom'bastik/ *adj*, **bombastically** *adv*

ˌBombay 'duck /bom'bay/ *n* a small fish found off S Asiatic coasts and eaten dried and salted with curry [*Bombay*, city in India]

bombazine /'bombəˌzeen, ˌ--'-/ *n* a silk fabric woven in twill weave and dyed black [MF *bombasin*, fr ML *bombacinum*, *bombycinum* silken texture, fr L, neut of *bombycinus* of silk, fr *bombyc-*, *bombyx*]

'bomb ˌbay *n* a bomb-carrying compartment in the underside of a combat aircraft

bomb disposal *n* the making safe of unexploded bombs

bombe /bomb/ *n* a frozen dessert made in a round or cone-shaped mould [F, lit., bomb]

bomber /'bomə/ *n* **1** an aircraft designed for bombing **2** sby who throws or places bombs

'bomber ˌjacket *n* a short jacket with elasticated waistband and cuffs

'bombˌshell /-ˌshel/ *n* **1** BOMB 1a **2** sby or sthg that has a stunning or devastating effect ⟨*the book was a political* ~⟩

'bombˌsight /-ˌsiet/ *n* a sighting device for aiming bombs

'bombˌsite /-ˌsiet/ *n* an area of ground on which buildings have been destroyed by bombing, esp from the air

bona fide /ˌbohnə 'fiedi/ *adj* genuine, sincere [L, in good faith]

ˌbona 'fides /'fiediz/ *n sing or pl in constr* honest intentions; sincerity [L, good faith]

bonanza /bə'nanzə/ *n* **1** an exceptionally large and rich mass of ore in a mine **2** sthg (unexpectedly) considered valuable, profitable, or rewarding ⟨*the oil* ~⟩ [Sp, lit., calm, fair weather, fr ML *bonacia*, alter. of L *malacia* calm at sea, fr Gk *malakia*, lit., softness, fr *malakos* soft]

Bonapartism /'bohnəˌpahˌtiz(ə)m/ *n* support of the French emperors Napoleon I or Napoleon III or their dynasty [*Bonaparte, Buonaparte*, family name of the dynasty] – **Bonapartist** /-ˌpahtist/ *n or adj*

bonbon /'bonˌbon/ *n* SWEET 2b; *specif* one with a chocolate or fondant coating and fondant centre that sometimes contains fruits and nuts [F (baby talk), redupl of *bon* good, fr L *bonus* – more at BOUNTY]

bonce /bons/ *n*, *Br* the head – infml [E dial *bonce* (large marble)]

[1]**bond** /bond/ *n* **1** sthg (e g a fetter) that binds or restrains **2** a binding agreement **3a** a mechanism by means of which atoms, ions, or groups of atoms are held together in a molecule or crystal **b** an adhesive or cementing material **4** sthg that unites or binds ⟨*the* ~s *of friendship*⟩ **5a** a legally enforceable agreement to pay **b** a certificate of intention to pay the holder a specified sum, with or without other interest, on a specified date **6** the system of overlapping bricks in a wall ☞ BUILDING **7** the state of imported goods retained by customs authorities until duties are paid **8** a strong durable paper, now used esp for writing and typing [ME *band, bond*, fr ON *band*; akin to OE *bindan* to bind – more at [1]BAND]

[2]**bond** *vt* **1** to overlap (e g bricks) for solidity of construction **2** to put (goods) in bond until duties and taxes are paid **3a** to cause to stick firmly **b** to hold together in a molecule or crystal by chemical bonds ~ *vi* to cohere (as if) by means of a bond – **bondable** *adj*, **bonder** *n*

bondage /'bondij/ *n* **1** the tenure or service of a villein, serf, or slave **2a** slavery, serfdom **b** subjugation to a controlling person or force **c** a form of sexual gratification involving the physical restraint of one partner ⟨~ *fantasies*⟩ [ME, fr *bonde* peasant, serf, fr OE *bōnda* householder, fr ON *bōndi*]

bonded /'bondid/ *adj* **1** used for or being goods in bond ⟨*a* ~ *warehouse*⟩ **2** composed of 2 or more layers of fabric held together by an adhesive ⟨~ *fabrics*⟩

'bondˌholder /-ˌhohldə/ *n* one who holds a government or company bond

'bondman /-mən/, *fem* **'bondˌwoman** *n* a slave, serf [ME *bondeman*, fr *bonde*]

bondsman /'bondzmən/ *n* a slave, serf

'bondˌstone /-ˌstohn/ *n* a stone long enough to extend through the full thickness of a wall

[1]**bone** /bohn/ *n* **1a** (any of the hard body structures composed of) the largely calcium-containing connective tissue of which the adult skeleton of most vertebrate animals is chiefly composed ☞ ANATOMY **b** (a structure made of) baleen, ivory, or another hard substance resembling bone **2** *the* essential or basic part or level; *the* core ⟨*cut expenses to the* ~⟩ **3** *pl* the core of one's being ⟨*I felt in my* ~s *that she was lying*⟩ **4** a subject or matter of dispute ⟨*a* ~ *of contention*⟩ **5a** *pl* thin bars of bone, ivory, or wood held in pairs between the fingers and used to produce musical rhythms **b** a strip of whalebone or steel used to stiffen a corset or dress **c** *pl* dice **d** a domino [ME *bon*, fr OE *bān*; akin to OHG & ON *bein* bone] – **boned** /bohnd/ *adj*, **boneless** *adj* – **bone to pick** a matter to argue or complain about

[2]**bone** *vt* **1** to remove the bones from **2** to stiffen (a garment) with bones – **boner** *n*

[3]**bone** *adv* absolutely, utterly – chiefly in *bone dry, bone idle*

'bone ˌash *n* the white porous residue, chiefly of calcium phosphate, produced from bones heated to a high temperature in air

ˌ**bone ˈchina** *n* a type of translucent and durable white hard-paste porcelain made from a mixture of bone ash and kaolin

ˈ**boneˌhead** /-ˌhed/ *n* a stupid person – infml – **boneheaded** /-ˈhedid/ *adj*

ˈ**bone ˌmeal** *n* fertilizer or feed made of crushed or ground bone

ˈ**boneˌsetter** /-ˌsetə/ *n* a person, esp one who is not a licensed physician, who sets broken or dislocated bones

ˈ**bone ˌshaker** *n* an early bicycle with solid tyres

bone up *vi* to try to master necessary information in a short time, esp for a special purpose ⟨*better* bone up *on those theories before the exam*⟩ – infml [prob fr ²*bone*]

bonfire /ˈbonfie·ə/ *n* a large fire built in the open air [ME *bonefire* a fire of bones, fr *bon* bone + *fire*]

ˈ**Bonfire ˌNight** *n* GUY FAWKES NIGHT

bong /bong/ *n* a deep resonant sound, esp of a large bell [imit] – **bong** *vi*

¹**bongo** /ˈbong·goh/ *n, pl* **bongos,** *esp collectively* **bongo** any of 3 large striped antelopes of tropical Africa [of African origin]

²**bongo** *n, pl* **bongos** *also* **bongoes** either of a pair of small tuned drums played with the hands [AmerSp *bongó*] – **bongoist** /-ist/ *n*

bonhomie /ˌbonoˈmee, boˈnomi/ *n* good-natured friendliness [F, fr *bonhomme* good-natured man, fr *bon* good + *homme* man]

bonito /bəˈneetoh/ *n, pl* **bonitos,** *esp collectively* **bonito** any of various medium-sized tunas [Sp, fr *bonito* pretty, fr L *bonus* good]

bonkers /ˈbongkəz/ *adj, chiefly Br* mad, crazy – infml [origin unknown]

bon mot /ˌbon ˈmoh (*Fr* bɔ̃ mo)/ *n, pl* **bons mots, bon mots** /ˌbon ˈmoh(z) (*Fr* ~)/ a witticism [F, lit., good word]

bonnet /ˈbonit/ *n* **1** a cloth or straw hat tied under the chin, now worn chiefly by children **2** *Br* the hinged metal covering over the engine of a motor vehicle [ME *bonet,* fr MF, fr ML *abonnis*]

bonny /ˈboni/ *adj, chiefly Br* attractive, comely [ME *bonie,* fr OF *bon* good, fr L *bonus* – more at BOUNTY] – **bonnily** *adv*

bonsai /bonˈsie/ *n, pl* **bonsai** (the art of growing) a potted plant dwarfed by special methods of culture [Jap]

bonspiel /ˈbonˌspeel, -spəl/ *n* a match or tournament between curling clubs [perh fr D *bond* league + *spel* game]

bontebok /ˈbontəˌbok/ *n* a S African antelope that is now almost extinct [Afrik, fr *bont* spotted + *bok* male antelope]

bon ton /ˌbon ˈtonh (*Fr* bɔ̃ tɔ̃)/ *n* the fashionable style or thing [F, lit., good tone]

bonus /ˈbohnəs/ *n* **1** sthg given in addition to what is usual or strictly due **2** money or an equivalent given in addition to an employee's usual remuneration [L, good – more at BOUNTY]

bon vivant /(*Fr* bɔ̃ vivɑ̃)/ *n, pl* **bons vivants, bon vivants** /~/ a person with cultivated and refined tastes, esp in regard to food and drink [F, lit., good liver]

bon viveur /(*Fr* vivœːr)/ *n, chiefly Br* BON VIVANT

bon voyage /ˌbon vwahˈyahj, -yahzh (*Fr* bɔ̃ vwajɑːʒ)/ *n* a farewell – often used interjectionally [F, lit., good journey]

bony, boney /ˈbohni/ *adj* **1** consisting of or resembling bone **2a** full of bones **b** having large or prominent bones **3** skinny, scrawny

ˈ**bony ˌfish** *n* any of a major group of fishes comprising all those with a bony rather than a cartilaginous skeleton and including the salmon, carp, herring, etc; a teleost

bonze /bonz/ *n* a Chinese or Japanese Buddhist monk [F, fr Pg *bonzo,* fr Jap *bonsō*]

¹**boo** /booh/ *interj* – used to express contempt or disapproval or to startle or frighten [ME *bo*]

²**boo** *n, pl* **boos** a shout of disapproval or contempt

³**boo** *vb* to show scorn or disapproval (of) by uttering 'boo"

¹**boob** /boohb/ *n* **1** a stupid mistake; a blunder – infml **2** BREAST 1 – slang [short for *booby*]

²**boob** *vi* to make a stupid mistake – infml

¹**booby** /ˈboohbi/ *n* **1** an awkward foolish person **2** any of several small gannets of tropical seas **3** the poorest performer in a group [modif of Sp *bobo,* fr L *balbus* stammering, prob of imit origin]

²**booby** *n* BREAST 1 – vulg [alter. of *bubby,* perh imit of the noise made by a sucking infant]

ˈ**booby ˌhatch** *n, NAm* MADHOUSE 1

ˈ**booby ˌprize** *n* an award for the poorest performance in a contest

ˈ**booby ˌtrap** *n* **1** a trap for the unwary or unsuspecting **2** a harmless-looking object concealing an explosive device that is set to explode by remote control or if touched – **booby-trap** *vt*

boodle /ˈboohdl/ *n* money, esp when stolen or used for bribery – slang [D *boedel* estate, lot, fr MD; akin to ON *būth* booth]

boogie /ˈboohgi/ *n* boogie-woogie

ˌ**boogie-ˈwoogie** /ˈwoohgi/ *n* a style of playing blues on the piano characterized by a steady rhythmic bass and a simple, often improvised, melody [origin unknown]

¹**book** /book/ *n* **1a** a set of written, printed, or blank sheets bound together into a volume **b** a long written or printed literary composition **c** a major division of a treatise or literary work **d** a record of business transactions – usu pl ⟨*their* ~s *show a profit*⟩ **2** *cap the* Bible **3** sthg regarded as a source of enlightenment or instruction **4** a packet of (paper, cardboard, etc) commodities (e g tickets, stamps, or matches) bound together **5** the bets registered by a bookmaker **6** the number of tricks that must be won at cards before any trick can have scoring value – compare ODD TRICK [ME, fr OE *bōc*; akin to OHG *buoh* book, OE *bōc* beech; prob fr the early Germanic practice of carving runes on beechwood tablets – more at BEECH] – **bookful** *n,* **booklet** *n* – **by/according to the book** by following previously laid down instructions and not using personal initiative ⟨*it's safer to go* by the book *than risk making a mistake*⟩ – **in one's book** in one's own opinion ⟨in my book *this is the way to handle it*⟩ – **one for the book** an act or occurrence worth noting

²**book** *vt* **1** to reserve or make arrangements for in advance ⟨~ *2 seats at the theatre*⟩ **2a** to take the name of with a view to prosecution **b** to enter the name of (a player) in a book for a violation of the rules usu involving foul play – used with reference to a rugby or soccer player ~ *vi* **1** to reserve sthg in advance ⟨~ *up through your travel agent*⟩ **2** *chiefly Br* to register in a hotel – **booker** *n*

[3]**book** *adj* **1** derived from books; theoretical **2** shown by books of account

bookable /ˈbookəbl/ *adj, chiefly Br* **1** that may be reserved in advance **2** that makes a player liable to be booked by a referee

ˈ**book,binding** /-ˌbiending/ *n* the craft or trade of binding books – **bookbinder** *n*, **bookbindery** /-d(ə)ri/ *n*

ˈ**book,case** /-ˌkays/ *n* a piece of furniture consisting of a set of shelves to hold books

ˈ**book,end** /-ˌend/ *n* a support placed at the end of a row of books

bookie /ˈbooki/ *n* a bookmaker [by shortening & alter.]

booking /ˈbooking/ *n* **1** an engagement or scheduled performance **2** a reservation **3** an instance of being booked by a referee [[2]BOOK + [2]-ING]

ˈ**booking ,office** *n, chiefly Br* an office where tickets are sold and bookings made, esp at a railway station

bookish /ˈbookish/ *adj* **1** relying on theoretical knowledge rather than practical experience **2** literary as opposed to colloquial [[1]BOOK + -ISH] – **bookishly** *adv*, **bookishness** *n*

ˈ**book,keeper** /-ˌkeepə/ *n* one who records the accounts or transactions of a business – **bookkeeping** *n*

ˈ**book ,lung** *n* a saclike breathing organ in many arachnids containing numerous thin folds of membrane arranged like the leaves of a book

ˈ**book,maker** /-ˌmaykə/ *n* sby who determines odds and receives and pays off bets [[1]BOOK + MAKER] – **bookmaking** *n*

ˈ**book,man** /-ˌman/ *n* **1** a litterateur **2** a bookseller

ˈ**book,mark** /-ˌmahk/, ˈ**book,marker** /-ˌmahkə/ *n* sthg used to mark a place in a book

Book of Common Prayer *n* the service book of the Anglican Church

ˈ**book,plate** /-ˌplayt/ *n* a label that is usu placed inside the cover of a book to identify the owner

ˈ**book,rest** /-ˌrest/ *n* an (adjustable) support for an open book

ˈ**book,seller** /-ˌselə/ *n* sby who sells books; *specif* the owner or manager of a bookshop

ˈ**book,shop** /-ˌshop/ *n* a shop where books are the main items offered for sale

ˈ**book,stall** /-ˌstawl/ *n* a stall where books, magazines, and newspapers are sold

ˈ**book ,token** *n* a gift token exchangeable for books

book up *vt* to reserve all the accommodation in or services of – usu pass

ˈ**book,worm** /-ˌwuhm/ *n* **1** any of various insect larvae that feed on the binding and paste of books **2** a person unusually fond of reading and study

Boolean /ˈboohli·ən/ *adj* of or being a system in logic that symbolically represents certain relationships between entities (e g sets, propositions, or states of computer logic circuits) ⟨~ *algebra*⟩ ⟨~ *expression*⟩ [George *Boole* †1864 E mathematician]

[1]**boom** /boohm/ *n* **1** a spar at the foot of the mainsail in fore-and-aft rig that is attached at its fore end to the mast ☞ SHIP **2** a long movable arm used to manipulate a microphone **3** a barrier across a river or enclosing an area of water to keep logs together; *also* the enclosed logs **4** a cable or line of spars extended across a river or the mouth of a harbour as a barrier to navigation [D, tree, beam; akin to OHG *boum* tree – more at BEAM]

[2]**boom** /boom, boohm/ *vi* **1** to make a deep hollow sound or cry **2** to experience a rapid increase in activity or importance ⟨*business was* ~ing⟩ ~ *vt* to cause to resound [imit]

[3]**boom** /boom, boohm/ *n* **1** a booming sound or cry **2a** rapid settlement and development (e g of a town) **b** a rapid growth or increase in a specified area ⟨*the baby* ~⟩ **c** a rapid widespread expansion of economic activity

boomer /ˈboohmə/ *n, Austr* a large male kangaroo [[2]BOOM + [2]-ER]

boomerang /ˈboohmə,rang/ *n* **1** a bent piece of wood shaped so that it returns to its thrower and used by Australian aborigines as a hunting weapon **2** an act or utterance that backfires on its originator [native name in Australia] – **boomerang** *vi*

boomslang /ˈboohm,slang/ *n* a large venomous tree snake of southern Africa [Afrik, fr *boom* tree + *slang* snake]

[1]**boon** /boohn/ *n* **1** a benefit or favour, esp when given in answer to a request **2** a timely benefit; a blessing [ME, fr ON *bōn* petition; akin to OE *bēn* prayer, *bannan* to summon – more at [1]BAN]

[2]**boon** *adj* close, intimate, and convivial – esp in *boon companion* [ME *bon*, fr MF, good – more at BONNY]

boor /booə, baw/ *n* a coarse, ill-mannered, or insensitive person [D *boer* peasant, farmer; akin to OE *būan* to dwell – more at [1]BOWER] – **boorish** *adj*

[1]**boost** /boohst/ *vt* **1** to push or shove up from below **2** to increase, raise ⟨*plans to* ~ *production*⟩ **3** to encourage, promote ⟨*extra pay to* ~ *morale*⟩ **4** to increase the force, pressure, or amount of; *esp* to raise the voltage of or across (an electric circuit) [origin unknown]

[2]**boost** *n* **1** a push upwards **2** an increase in amount **3** an act that promotes or encourages

booster /ˈboohstə/ *n* **1** an auxiliary engine which assists (e g at take-off) by providing a large thrust for a short time ☞ SPACE **2** a supplementary dose increasing or renewing the effectiveness of a medicament [[1]BOOST + [2]-ER]

[1]**boot** /booht/ *n* [arch *boot* (profit, avail), fr ME, fr OE *bōt* remedy; akin to OE *bet*era better] – **to boot** besides

[2]**boot** *n* **1a** an outer covering for the human foot that extends above the ankle and has a stiff or thick sole and heel **b** a stout shoe, esp for sports ⟨*football* ~s⟩ **2** an instrument of torture that crushes the leg and foot **3** a blow or kick delivered (as if) by a booted foot **4** *Br* the major luggage compartment of a motor car **5** summary discharge or dismissal – slang; chiefly in *give/get the boot* [ME, fr MF *bote*] – **booted** *adj* – **put/stick the boot in 1** *chiefly Br* to cause added distress to one who is already defeated – infml **2** to act with brutal decisiveness – infml

[3]**boot** *vt* to kick

ˈ**boot,black** /-ˌblak/ *n* sby who cleans and shines shoes

bootee, bootie /ˈbooh,tee, -ˈ-/ *n* **1** a short boot **2** an infant's sock worn in place of a shoe

booth /booth/ *n, pl* **booths** /boohths, boohdhz/ **1** a stall or stand for the sale or exhibition of goods **2** a small enclosure affording privacy (e g for telephoning, dining, etc) [ME *bothe*, of Scand origin; akin to

ON *būth* booth; akin to OE *būan* to dwell – more at [1]BOWER]

'boot,jack /-,jak/ *n* a device (e g of metal or wood) shaped like the letter V and used in pulling off boots

'boot,lace /-,lays/ *n, Br* a long stout shoelace

[1]**'boot,leg** /-,leg/ *adj or n, chiefly NAm* (being) smuggled or illegally produced alcoholic drink [fr former practice of carrying a concealed bottle of liquor in the top of a boot]

[2]**bootleg** *vb, chiefly NAm* to manufacture, sell, or transport for sale (esp alcoholic drink) contrary to law

'bootless /-lis/ *adj* useless, unprofitable – fml [[1]*boot* + *-less*] – **bootlessly** *adv,* **bootlessness** *n*

'boot,lick /-,lik/ *vi* to attempt to gain favour by a cringing or flattering manner – infml – **bootlicker** *n*

boot out *vt* to eject or discharge summarily ⟨*was* booted out *of office*⟩ – infml

boots *n, pl* **boots** *Br* a servant who polishes shoes and carries luggage, esp in a hotel [fr pl of [2]*boot*]

'boot,straps /,straps/ *n* – **haul/pull oneself up by one's own bootstraps** to improve oneself or one's situation by one's own unaided efforts

booty /'boohti/ *n* **1** plunder taken (e g in war) **2** a rich gain or prize [modif of MF *butin,* fr MLG *būte* exchange]

[1]**booze** /boohz/ *vi* to drink intoxicating liquor to excess – slang [ME *bousen,* fr MD or MFlem *būsen*; akin to MHG *būs* swelling] – **boozily** *adv,* **boozy** *adj*

[2]**booze** *n* **1** intoxicating drink; *esp* spirits **2** a drinking spree *USE* slang

boozer /'boohzə/ *n* a public house – slang [[1]BOOZE + [2]-ER]

'booze-,up *n* **1** BOOZE 2 **2** a drunken party *USE* slang

[1]**bop** /bop/ *vt or n* **-pp-** (to strike with) a blow (e g of the fist) – infml [imit]

[2]**bop** *n* jazz characterized by unusual chord structures, syncopated rhythm, and harmonic complexity and innovation [short for *bebop*] – **bopper** *n*

[3]**bop** *vi* **-pp-** to dance (e g in a disco) in a casual and unrestricted manner, esp to popular music – infml

bora /'bawrə/ *n* a violent cold northerly wind of the Adriatic [It dial., fr L *boreas* – more at BOREAL]

bo,racic 'acid /bə'rasik/ *n* BORIC ACID [ML *borac-, borax* borax]

borage /'borij, 'burij/ *n* a coarse hairy blue-flowered European herb [ME, fr MF *bourage*]

borate /'bawrayt/ *n* a salt or ester of a boric acid

borax /'bawraks/ *n* natural or synthetic hydrated sodium borate used esp as a flux, cleansing agent, and water softener [ME *boras,* fr MF, fr ML *borac-, borax,* fr Ar *būraq,* fr Per *būrah*]

borazon /'bawrə,zon/ *n* a substance that consists of a boron nitride and is as hard as diamond but more resistant to high temperature [*boron* + *az-* + *-on*]

Bordeaux /baw'doh/ *n, pl* **Bordeaux** /baw'doh(z)/ a red or white wine of the Bordeaux region of France

bordello /baw'deloh/ *n, pl* **bordellos** a brothel [It, fr OF *bordel,* fr *borde* hut, of Gmc origin; akin to OE *bord* board]

[1]**border** /'bawdə/ *n* **1** an outer part or edge **2** a boundary, frontier ⟨*crossed the* ~ *into Italy*⟩ **3** a narrow bed of planted ground (e g beside a path) **4** an ornamental design at the edge of sthg (e g printed matter, fabric, or a rug) [ME *bordure,* fr MF, fr OF, fr *border* to border, fr *bort* border, of Gmc origin; akin to OE *bord*] – **bordered** *adj*

[2]**border** *vt* **1** to put a border on **2** to adjoin at the edge or boundary – **borderer** *n* – **border on 1** BORDER 2 ⟨*the USA* borders on *Canada*⟩ **2** to resemble closely ⟨*his devotion* borders on *the ridiculous*⟩

'Border ,collie *n* (any of) a breed of rough-haired, often black-and-white, stocky dogs that are the dogs most commonly used in Britain for herding sheep [fr its origin in the borderlands between England and Scotland]

bordereau /,bawdə'roh/ *n, pl* **bordereaux** /-'roh(z)/ a detailed memorandum; *esp* one containing a list of documents [F]

'border,line /-,lien/ *adj* **1** verging on one or other place or state without being definitely assignable to either **2** not quite meeting accepted standards (e g of morality or good taste) ⟨*a* ~ *joke*⟩

'border ,line *n* a line of demarcation

'Border ,terrier *n* a small terrier of British origin with a harsh dense coat and close undercoat

[1]**bore** /baw/ *vt* **1** to pierce (as if) with a rotary tool **2** to form or construct by boring ~ *vi* **1a** to make a hole by boring **b** to drill a mine or well **2** to make one's way steadily or laboriously [ME *boren,* fr OE *borian*; akin to OHG *borōn* to bore, L *forare* to bore, *ferire* to strike]

[2]**bore** *n* **1** a hole made (as if) by boring **2a** an interior cylindrical cavity ⟨*the* ~ *of a thermometer*⟩ **b** [1]BARREL 2a **3a** the size of a hole **b** the interior diameter of a tube **c** the diameter of an engine cylinder

[3]**bore** *past of* BEAR

[4]**bore** *n* a tidal flood that moves swiftly as a steep-fronted wave in a channel, estuary, etc [(assumed) ME *bore* wave, fr ON *bāra*]

[5]**bore** *n* a tedious person or thing [perh fr [1]*bore*]

[6]**bore** *vt* to weary by being dull or monotonous – **boring** *adj,* **boringly** *adv*

boreal /'bawri·əl/ *adj, often cap* of or growing in northern and mountainous parts of the northern hemisphere ☞ PLANT [ME *boriall,* fr LL *borealis,* fr L *boreas* north wind, north, fr Gk, fr *Boreas,* god of the north wind]

boredom /'bawd(ə)m/ *n* the state of being bored

'bore,hole /-,hohl/ *n* a hole drilled in the earth to obtain water, oil, etc

borer /'bawrə/ *n* a tool used for boring [[1]BORE + [2]-ER]

boric /'bawrik/ *adj* of or containing boron

,boric 'acid *n* a white solid acid used esp as a weak antiseptic

boride /'bawried/ *n* a binary compound of boron, usu with a more electropositive element or radical

born /bawn/ *adj* **1a** brought into existence (as if) by birth **b** by birth; native ⟨*British*-born⟩ **2** having a specified character or situation from birth ⟨*a* ~ *leader*⟩ ⟨*nobly* ~⟩ [ME, fr OE *boren,* pp of *beran* to carry – more at [2]BEAR]

,born-a'gain *adj* having undergone a conversion, esp to evangelical Christianity

borne /bawn/ *past part of* BEAR

boron /'bawron/ *n* a trivalent metalloid element found in nature only in combination ☞ PERIODIC TABLE [*borax* + *-on* (as in *carbon*)] – **boronic** /baw'ronik/ *adj*

borough /'burə/ *n* **1** a British urban constituency **2a** a municipal corporation in certain states of the USA **b** any of the 5 political divisions of New York City [ME *burgh*, fr OE *burg* fortified town; akin to OHG *burg* fortified place, OE *beorg* mountain – more at [1]BARROW]

borrow /'boroh/ *vt* **1** to take or receive with the intention of returning ⟨~ *a book*⟩ **2a** to appropriate for one's own use **b** to copy or imitate **3** to take (1) from a figure of the minuend in subtraction and add it as 10 to the next lowest figure ~ *vi* to borrow sthg ⟨*English* ~s *from other languages*⟩ [ME *borwen*, fr OE *borgian*; akin to OE *beorgan* to preserve – more at BURY] – **borrower** *n*

borsch /bawsh/ *n* borscht

borscht /bawsht/ *n* a soup made primarily from beetroots and served hot or cold, often with sour cream [Russ *borshch*]

borstal /'bawstl/ *n, often cap, Br* a penal institution for young offenders [*Borstal*, village in Kent, England, site of first such institution]

bort, boart /bawt/ *n* imperfectly crystallized diamond (fragments) used as an abrasive [prob fr D *boort*]

bortsch /bawch, bawshch/ *n* borscht

borzoi /'bawzoy, -'-/ *n* any of a breed of large long-haired dogs developed in Russia, esp for pursuing wolves [Russ *borzoĭ*, fr *borzoĭ* swift; akin to L *festinare* to hasten]

boscage *also* **boskage** /'boskij/ *n* a growth of trees or shrubs [ME *boskage*, fr MF *boscage*, fr OF, fr *bois*, *bosc* forest, perh of Gmc origin; akin to ME *bush*]

bosh /bosh/ *n* nonsense – infml [Turk *boş* empty, useless]

bosky /'boski/ *adj, archaic* full of trees; wooded [E dial. *bosk* (bush), fr ME *bush, bosk*]

[1]**bosom** /'boozəm/ *n* **1** the front of the human chest; *esp* the female breasts **2a** the breast considered as the centre of secret thoughts and emotions **b** close relationship ⟨*in the* ~ *of her family*⟩ **3** the part of a garment covering the breast [ME, fr OE *bōsm*; akin to OHG *buosam* bosom, Skt *bhūri* abundant – more at BIG]

[2]**bosom** *adj* close, intimate ⟨~ *friends*⟩

-bosomed *comb form* (*adj* → *adj*) having (such) a bosom ⟨*big*-bosomed⟩

bosomy /'boozəmi/ *adj* having large breasts

boson /'bohson/ *n* a particle (e g a photon, meson, or alpha particle) that obeys relations stated by Bose and Einstein and whose spin is either zero or an integral number [Satyendranath *Bose* †1974 Indian physicist + E [2]*-on*] – **bosonic** /boh'sonik/ *adj*

[1]**boss** /bos/ *n* **1a** a protuberant part or body ⟨*a* ~ *of granite*⟩ ⟨*a* ~ *on an animal's horn*⟩ **b** a raised ornamentation **c** a carved ornament concealing the intersection of the ribs of a vault or panelled ceiling ☞ ARCHITECTURE, CHURCH **2** the enlarged part of a shaft, esp on which a wheel is mounted [ME *boce*, fr OF, fr (assumed) VL *bottia*]

[2]**boss** *n* **1** one who exercises control or authority; *specif* one who directs or supervises workers **2** a politician who controls a party organization (e g in the USA) [D *baas* master; akin to Fris *baes* master]

[3]**boss** *vt* **1** to act as director or supervisor of **2** ORDER 2a – often + *about* or *around* *USE* infml

bossa nova /ˌbosə 'nohvə/ *n* (music for) a Brazilian dance similar to the samba [Pg, lit., new trend]

ˌboss-'eyed *adj, Br* having a squint; cross-eyed – infml [perh fr [1]*boss*]

bossy /'bosi/ *adj* domineering, dictatorial – infml – **bossiness** *n*

bosun /'bohz(ə)n, 'bohs(ə)n/ *n* a boatswain

boˌtanic 'garden /bə'tanik/ *n* a place in which plant collections are grown for display and scientific study – often pl with sing. meaning

botan·ize, -ise /'botəniez/ *vi* to collect plants for botanical investigation; *also* to study plants, esp on a field trip

botany /'botəni/ *n* **1** a branch of biology dealing with plant life **2a** the plant life (of a region) **b** the properties and life phenomena exhibited by a plant, plant type, or plant group [back-formation fr *botanic*, fr F *botanique*, fr Gk *botanikos* of herbs, fr *botanē* pasture, herb, fr *boskein* to feed; akin to Lith *gauja* herd] – **botanist** *n*, **botanic** *adj* /bə'tanik/, **botanical** *adj*, **botanically** *adv*

ˌbotany 'wool *n* a fine grade of (Australian) merino wool [*Botany* Bay, region of New South Wales in Australia]

[1]**botch** /boch/ *vt* **1** to repair, patch, or assemble in a makeshift or inept way **2** to foul up hopelessly; bungle *USE* infml [ME *bocchen*] – **botcher** *n*

[2]**botch** *n* **1** sthg botched; a mess **2** a clumsy patchwork *USE* infml – **botchy** *adj*

botel /boh'tel/ *n* a boatel

botfly /'botˌflie/ *n* any of various heavy-bodied 2-winged flies with larvae parasitic in the alimentary canals of human beings and other large mammals [*bot* (larva of the botfly), perh modif of ScGael *boiteag* maggot]

[1]**both** /bohth/ *adj* being the 2; affecting or involving the one as well as the other ⟨~ *his feet*⟩ [ME *bothe*, fr ON *bāthir*; akin to OHG *beide* both]

[2]**both** *pron pl in constr* the one as well as the other ⟨~ *of the books*⟩ ⟨*we're* ~ *well*⟩

[3]**both** *conj* – used to indicate and stress the inclusion of each of 2 or more things specified by coordinated words or word groups ⟨*she* ~ *speaks and writes Swahili*⟩

[1]**bother** /'bodhə/ *vt* **1** to cause to be troubled or perplexed **2a** to annoy or inconvenience **b** – used as a mild interjection of annoyance ~ *vi* **1** to feel mild concern or anxiety **2** to take pains; take the trouble [perh fr IrGael *bodhar* deaf, bothered]

[2]**bother** *n* **1** (a cause of) mild discomfort, annoyance, or worry **2** unnecessary fussing **3** a minor disturbance ⟨*there was a spot of* ~ *here today*⟩

botheration /ˌbodhə'raysh(ə)n/ *n* **1** bothering or being bothered **2** – used as a mild interjection of annoyance

'bothersome /-s(ə)m/ *adj* causing bother; annoying

bothy /'bothi/ *n, Scot* **1** a small outbuilding on a farm which formerly provided accommodation for farmworkers **2** a small hut in the mountains which provides shelter for mountaineers and hill walkers [Sc, prob fr obs Sc *both* booth, fr ME *bothe* – more at BOOTH]

'bo ˌtree /boh/ *n* the pipal tree [Sinhalese *bō*, fr Skt *bodhi*]

[1]**bottle** /'botl/ *n* **1a** a rigid or semirigid container, esp for liquids, usu of glass or plastic, with a comparatively narrow neck or mouth **b** the contents of a

bottle **2a** intoxicating drink – slang ⟨*hit the* ~⟩ **b** bottled milk used to feed infants **3** *Br* NERVE 3b – slang [ME *botel,* fr MF *bouteille,* fr ML *butticula,* dim. of LL *buttis* cask] – **bottleful** *n*

[2]**bottle** *vt* **bottling** /ˈbotling/ **1** to put into a bottle **2** *Br* to preserve (e g fruit) by storage in glass jars – **bottler** /ˈbotlə/ *n*

ˈ**bottle-ˌfeed** *vt* **bottle-fed** /fed/ to feed (e g an infant) by means of a bottle

bottle green *adj or n* very dark green

ˈ**bottleˌneck** /-ˌnek/ *n* **1a** a narrow stretch of road **b** a point or situation where free movement or progress is held up **2** a style of guitar playing using an object (e g a metal bar or the neck of a bottle) pressed against the strings to produce the effect of one note sliding into another

ˌ**bottle-nosed ˈdolphin** *n* any of various moderately large stout-bodied toothed whales with a prominent beak and long curved dorsal fin

bottle up *vt* to confine as if in a bottle; restrain ⟨bottling up *their anger*⟩

[1]**bottom** /ˈbotəm/ *n* **1a** the underside of sthg **b** a surface on which sthg rests **c** the buttocks, rump **2** the ground below a body of water **3** the part of a ship's hull lying below the water **4a** the lowest, deepest, or farthest part or place **b** the lowest or last place in order of precedence ⟨*started work at the* ~⟩ **c** the transmission gear of a motor vehicle giving lowest speed of travel **d** the lower part of a two-piece garment – often pl with sing. meaning ⟨*pyjama* ~s⟩ **5** low-lying land along a watercourse **6** a basis, source **7** *archaic* a ship; *esp* a merchant ship [ME *botme,* fr OE *botm*; akin to OHG *bodam* bottom, L *fundus,* Gk *pythmēn*] – **bottomed** *adj* – **at bottom** really, basically

[2]**bottom** *vt* to provide with a bottom or foundation ~ *vi* to reach the bottom – usu + *out* – **bottomer** *n*

[3]**bottom** *adj* **1** of or situated at the bottom **2** frequenting the bottom ⟨~ *fishes*⟩ – **bottommost** /-mohst, -məst/

ˌ**bottom ˈdrawer** *n, Br* (a drawer for storing) a young woman's collection of clothes and esp household articles, kept in anticipation of her marriage

ˈ**bottomless** /-lis/ *adj* **1** extremely deep **2** boundless, unlimited [[1]BOTTOM + -LESS] – **bottomlessly** *adv,* **bottomlessness** *n*

bottomry /ˈbotəmri/ *n* a contract by which a ship is pledged as security for a loan to be repaid at the end of a successful voyage [modif of D *bodemerij,* fr *bodem* bottom, ship; akin to OHG *bodam*]

botulin /ˈbotyoolin, ˈbochəlin/ *n* a toxin that is the direct cause of botulism [prob fr NL *botulinus,* a spore-forming bacterium, fr L *botulus* sausage]

botulism /ˈbotyooˌliz(ə)m, -chə-/ *n* acute often fatal food poisoning caused by botulin in (preserved) food

bouclé, boucle /ˈboohklay/ *n* (a fabric made from) an uneven yarn of 3 plies, one of which forms loops at intervals [F *bouclé* curly, fr pp of *boucler* to curl, fr *boucle* buckle, curl]

boudoir /ˈboohdwah/ *n* a woman's dressing room, bedroom, or private sitting room [F, fr *bouder* to pout]

bouffant /ˈboohfong/ *adj* puffed out ⟨*a* ~ *hairstyle*⟩ ⟨~ *sleeves*⟩ [F, fr MF, fr prp of *bouffer* to puff]

bougainvillaea /ˌboohgənˈvilyə/ *n* any of a genus of ornamental tropical American woody climbing plants with brilliant purple or red floral bracts [NL, fr Louis Antoine de *Bougainville* †1811 F navigator]

bough /bow/ *n* a (main) branch of a tree [ME, shoulder, bough, fr OE *bōg*; akin to OHG *buog* shoulder, Gk *pēchys* forearm] – **boughed** /bowd/ *adj*

bought /bawt/ *past of* BUY

bougie /ˈboozhi/ *n* a tapering cylindrical instrument for introduction into a tubular passage of the body [F, lit., wax candle, fr *Bougie,* seaport in Algeria]

bouillabaisse /ˌbooh·yəˈbes (*Fr* bujabɛs)/ *n* a highly seasoned fish stew made with at least 2 kinds of fish [F]

bouillon /ˈbooh·yong (*Fr* bujɔ̃)/ *n* a thin clear soup made usu from lean beef [F, fr OF *boillon,* fr *boillir* to boil]

boulder /ˈbohldə/ *n* a large stone or mass of rock [short for *boulder stone,* fr ME *bulder ston,* part trans of a word of Scand origin; akin to Sw dial *bullersten* large stone in a stream, fr *buller* noise + *sten* stone]

ˈ**boulder ˌclay** *n* a glacial deposit of pebbles, rock, etc in clay

[1]**boule** /boohl/ *n* **1** an orig French game similar to bowls in which usu metal balls are thrown or rolled in an attempt to place them nearer to a jack than the opponent's balls **2** a synthetically-formed pear-shaped mass of sapphire, spinel, etc with the atomic structure of a single crystal [F, ball, fr MF, fr L *bulla* bubble]

[2]**boule, boulle** /boohl, byoohl/ *n* buhl

boulevard /ˈboohləˌvahd, -ˌvah/ *n* a broad avenue, usu lined by trees [F, modif of MD *bolwerc* bulwark]

[1]**bounce** /bowns/ *vt* **1** to cause to rebound ⟨~ *a ball*⟩ **2** to return (a cheque) as not good because of lack of funds in the payer's account – infml ~ *vi* **1** to rebound after striking **2** to move violently, noisily, or with a springing step ⟨~d *into the room*⟩ **3** to be returned by a bank as not good – infml [ME *bounsen* to beat, thump, prob of imit origin]

[2]**bounce** *n* **1a** a sudden leap or bound **b** a rebound **2** verve, liveliness

bounce back *vi* to recover quickly from a blow or defeat

bouncer /ˈbownsə/ *n* **1** a man employed in a public place to restrain or remove disorderly people **2** a fast intimidatory short-pitched delivery of a cricket ball that passes or hits the batsman at above chest height after bouncing [[1]BOUNCE + [2]-ER]

bouncing /ˈbownsing/ *adj* enjoying good health; robust

bouncing bet *n, often cap 2nd B* soapwort [*Bet,* nickname for *Elizabeth*]

bouncy /ˈbownsi/ *adj* **1** buoyant, exuberant **2** that bounces readily – **bouncily** *adv*

[1]**bound** /bownd/ *adj* going or intending to go ⟨~ *for home*⟩ ⟨*college-*bound⟩ [ME *boun* ready, prepared to go, fr ON *būinn,* pp of *būa* to dwell, prepare; akin to OHG *būan* to dwell – more at BOWER]

[2]**bound** *n* **1** a limiting line; a boundary **2** sthg that limits or restrains ⟨*beyond the* ~s *of decency*⟩ *USE* usu pl with sing. meaning [ME, fr OF *bodne,* fr ML *bodina*]

[3]**bound** *vt* **1** to set limits to **2** to form the boundary of *USE* usu pass

[4]**bound** *adj* **1a** confined ⟨*desk*-bound⟩ **b** certain, sure *to* ⟨*~ to rain soon*⟩ **2** placed under legal or moral obligation ⟨*I'm ~ to say*⟩ ⟨*duty*-bound⟩ **3** held in chemical or physical combination ⟨*~ water in a molecule*⟩ **4** always occurring in combination with another linguistic form (e g *un-* in *unknown* and *-er* in *speaker*) [ME *bounden*, fr pp of *binden* to bind]

[5]**bound** *n* **1** a leap, jump **2** a bounce [MF *bond*, fr *bondir* to leap, fr (assumed) VL *bombitire* to hum, fr L *bombus* deep hollow sound – more at BOMB]

[6]**bound** *vi* **1** to move by leaping **2** to rebound, bounce

boundary /'bownd(ə)ri/ *n* **1** sthg, esp a dividing line, that indicates or fixes a limit or extent **2a** the marked limits of a cricket field **b** (the score of 4 or 6 made by) a stroke in cricket that sends the ball over the boundary

bounden /'bowndən/ *adj* made obligatory; binding – esp in *bounden duty* [ME]

bounder /'bowndə/ *n* a cad – not now in vogue [[6]BOUND + [2]-ER]

'**boundless** /-lis/ *adj* limitless [[2]BOUND + -LESS] – **boundlessly** *adv*, **boundlessness** *n*

,**bound 'up** *adj* closely involved or associated *with*

bounteous /'bowntyəs, -ti·əs/ *adj* giving or given freely [ME *bountevous*, fr MF *bontif* kind, fr OF, fr *bonté*] – **bounteously** *adv*, **bounteousness** *n*

bountiful /'bowntif(ə)l/ *adj* **1** generous, liberal **2** abundant, plentiful ⟨*a ~ harvest*⟩ – **bountifully** *adv*, **bountifulness** *n*

bounty /'bownti/ *n* **1** generosity **2** sthg given generously **3a** a financial inducement or reward, esp when offered by a government for some act or service **b** a payment to encourage the killing of vermin or dangerous animals [ME *bounte* goodness, fr OF *bonté*, fr L *bonitat-*, *bonitas*, fr *bonus* good, fr OL *duenos*; akin to MHG *zwīden* to grant, L *bene* well]

bouquet /booh'kay/ *n* **1** a bunch of flowers fastened together **2** a distinctive and characteristic fragrance (e g of wine) [F, fr MF, thicket, fr ONF *bosquet*, fr OF *bosc* forest – more at BOSCAGE]

,**bouquet 'garni** /'gahni/ *n* a small bunch of herbs (e g thyme, parsley, and a bay leaf) for use in flavouring stews and soups [F, lit., garnished bouquet]

bourbon /'buhbən, 'booəbən (*Fr* burbɔ̃)/ *n* **1** *cap* a member of a royal dynasty who ruled in France, Spain, etc **2** a whisky distilled from a mash made up of not less than 51 per cent maize plus malt and rye **3** *often cap, chiefly NAm* an extreme political reactionary [*Bourbon*, seigniory in France; (2) *Bourbon* County, Kentucky, USA] – **bourbonism** /-,niz(ə)m/ *n, often cap*

[1]**bourgeois** /'booəzhwah, 'baw-/ *n, pl* **bourgeois** **1** a middle-class person **2** one whose behaviour and views are influenced by bourgeois values or interests **3** *pl* the bourgeoisie [MF, burgher, fr OF *borjois*, fr *borc* town, fr L *burgus* fortified place, of Gmc origin; akin to OHG *burg* fortified place – more at BOROUGH]

[2]**bourgeois** *adj* **1** middle-class **2** marked by a narrow-minded concern for material interests and respectability **3** capitalist

bourgeoisie /,booəzhwah'zee/ *n sing or pl in constr* MIDDLE CLASS [F, fr *bourgeois*]

[1]**bourn, bourne** /bawn/ *n* a small stream [ME *burn*, *bourne*, fr OE; akin to OHG *brunno* spring of water, L *fervēre* to boil]

[2]**bourn, bourne** *n, archaic* a boundary, limit [MF *bourne*, fr OF *bodne* – more at [2]BOUND]

bourrée /'booray/ *n* (a musical composition suitable for) a 17th-c French dance usu in duple time [F]

bourse /booəs, baws/ *n* EXCHANGE 4a; *specif* a European stock exchange [F, lit., purse, fr ML *bursa* – more at PURSE]

bout /bowt/ *n* **1** a spell of activity ⟨*a ~ of work*⟩ **2** an athletic match (e g of boxing) **3** an outbreak or attack of illness, fever, etc [E dial. (a trip going and returning in ploughing), fr ME *bought* bend]

boutique /booh'teek/ *n* a small fashionable shop selling specialized goods; *also* a small shop within a large department store [F, shop]

bouzouki *also* **bousouki** /boo'zoohki/ *n* a long-necked Greek stringed instrument that resembles a mandolin [NGk *mpouzouki*, prob fr Turk *büyük* large]

bovine /'bohvien/ *adj* **1** of oxen or cows **2** like an ox or cow (e g in being slow, stolid, or dull) [LL *bovinus*, fr L *bov-*, *bos* ox, cow – more at COW]

Bovril /'bovril/ *trademark* – used for a concentrated beef extract

bovver /'bovə/ *n, Br* rowdy or violent disturbance; aggro ⟨*~ boys*⟩ [alter. of *bother*]

[1]**bow** /bow/ *vi* **1** to submit, yield **2** to bend the head, body, or knee in respect, submission, or greeting ~ *vt* **1** to incline (e g the head), esp in respect, submission, or shame **2** to express by bowing [ME *bowen*, fr OE *būgan*; akin to OHG *biogan* to bend, Skt *bhujati* he bends] – **bow and scrape** to act in an obsequious manner

[2]**bow** /bow/ *n* a bending of the head or body in respect, submission, or greeting

[3]**bow** /boh/ *n* **1** a bend, arch **2** a strip of wood, fibreglass, or other flexible material held bent by a strong cord connecting the 2 ends and used to shoot an arrow **3** an often ornamental slipknot (e g for tying a shoelace) **4** (a stroke made with) a resilient wooden rod with horsehairs stretched from end to end, used in playing an instrument of the viol or violin family [ME *bowe*, fr OE *boga*; akin to OE *būgan*]

[4]**bow** /boh/ *vb* **1** to (cause to) bend into a curve **2** to play (a stringed instrument) with a bow

[5]**bow** /bow/ *n* **1** the forward part of a ship – often pl with sing. meaning ☞ SHIP **2** [2]BOWMAN; *specif* one who rows in the front end of a boat [prob fr Dan *bov* shoulder, bow, fr ON *bōgr*; akin to OE *bōg* bough]

bowdler·ize, -ise /'bowdləriez/ *vt* to expurgate (e g a book) by omitting or modifying parts considered vulgar [Thomas *Bowdler* †1825 E editor] – **bowdlerizer** *n*, **bowdlerization** /-rie'zayshən/ *n*

bowel /'bowəl/ *n* **1** (a specified division of) the intestine or gut – usu pl with sing. meaning **2** *pl* the innermost parts ⟨*~s of the earth*⟩ [ME, fr OF *boel*, fr MF *botellus*, fr L, dim. of *botulus* sausage] – **bowelless** *adj*

[1]**bower** /'bowə/ *n* **1** an attractive dwelling or retreat **2** a (garden) shelter made with tree boughs or vines twisted together **3** a boudoir – poetic [ME *bour* dwelling, fr OE *būr*; akin to OE & OHG *būan* to dwell, OE *bēon* to be] – **bowery** /-ri/ *adj*

[2]**bower** *n* a ship's principal anchor carried in the bows [[5]*bow* + [2]*-er*]

'bow,head /'boh,hed/ *n* an Arctic right whale

'bowie ,knife /'boh·i/ *n* a stout hunting knife with a sharpened part on the back edge curved concavely to the point [James *Bowie* †1836 US soldier]

¹bowl /bohl/ *n* **1** any of various round hollow vessels used esp for holding liquids or food or for mixing food **2** the contents of a bowl **3a** the hollow of a spoon or tobacco pipe **b** the receptacle of a toilet **4a** a bowl-shaped geographical region or formation **b** *NAm* a bowl-shaped structure; *esp* a sports stadium [ME *bolle*, fr OE *bolla*; akin to OHG *bolla* blister, OE *blāwan* to blow] – **bowled** /bohld/ *adj*, **bowlful** *n*

²bowl *n* **1** a ball used in bowls that is weighted or shaped to give it a bias **2** *pl but sing in constr* a game played typically outdoors on a green, in which bowls are rolled at a target jack in an attempt to bring them nearer to it than the opponent's bowls [ME *boule*, fr MF, fr L *bulla* bubble]

³bowl *vi* **1a** to participate in a game of bowling **b** to play or roll a ball in bowls or bowling **c** to play as a bowler in cricket **2** to travel in a vehicle smoothly and rapidly – often + *along* ~ *vt* **1a** to roll (a ball) in bowling **b** to score by bowling ⟨~s *150*⟩ **2a** to deliver (a ball) to a batsman in cricket **b** to dismiss (a batsman in cricket) by breaking the wicket – used with reference to a bowled ball or a bowler

,bow'legged /-'leg(i)d/ *adj* having legs that are bowed outwards at the knees – **bowlegs** /,boh'legz/ *n pl*

¹bowler /'bohlə/ *n* the person who bowls in a team sport; *specif* a member of the fielding side who bowls (as a specialist) the ball in cricket ☞ SPORT [³BOWL + ²-ER]

²bowler, ,bowler 'hat *n* a stiff felt hat with a rounded crown and a narrow brim [*Bowler*, 19th-c family of E hatters]

bowline /'boh,lien/ *n* **1** a rope attached to a square sail that is used to keep the windward edge of the sail taut and at a steady angle to the wind ☞ SHIP **2** a knot used to form a non-slipping loop at the end of a rope [ME *bouline*, perh fr *bowe* bow + *line*]

bowling /'bohling/ *n* any of several games in which balls are rolled at 1 or more objects

'bowling ,alley *n* (a building or room containing) a long narrow enclosure or lane with a smooth usu wooden floor for bowling or playing skittles

'bowling ,crease *n* either of the lines drawn perpendicularly across a cricket pitch in line with each wicket – compare POPPING CREASE ☞ SPORT

'bowling ,green *n* a smooth close-cut area of turf for playing bowls

bowl out *vt* to dismiss all the members of (the batting side) in cricket

bowl over *vt* **1** to strike with a swiftly moving object **2** to overwhelm with surprise

¹bowman /'bohmən/ *n* an archer [³*bow*]

²bowman *n* a boatman, oarsman, etc in the front of a boat [⁵*bow*]

Bowman's capsule /'bohmənz/ *n* the thin membranous capsule surrounding each glomerulus in the kidneys of vertebrates [Sir William *Bowman* †1892 E surgeon]

bow out /bow/ *vi* to retire, withdraw

'bow ,saw /boh/ *n* a saw having a narrow blade held under tension, esp by a light bow-shaped frame

bowsprit /'boh,sprit/ *n* a spar projecting forwards from the bow of a ship ☞ SHIP [ME *bouspret*, prob fr MLG *bōchsprēt*, fr *bōch* bow + *sprēt* pole]

,bow 'tie /boh/ *n* a short tie fastened in a bow

,bow 'window /boh/ *n* a curved bay window ☞ ARCHITECTURE

bowwow /'bow,wow/ *n* **1** the bark of a dog – often used imitatively **2** a dog – used esp by or to children [imit]

bowyer /'bohyə/ *n* sby who makes or sells bows for archery

¹box /boks/ *n, pl* **box, boxes** any of several evergreen shrubs or small trees used esp for hedges [ME, fr OE, fr L *buxus*, fr Gk *pyxos*]

²box *n* **1a** a rigid container having 4 sides, a bottom, and a cover **b** the contents of a box **2a** a small compartment (e g for a group of spectators in a theatre) **b(1)** PENALTY AREA **(2)** PENALTY BOX **3a** a boxlike protective case (e g for machinery) **b** a shield to protect the genitals, worn esp by batsmen and wicketkeepers in cricket **c** a structure that contains a telephone for use by members of a specified organization ⟨*police* ~⟩ ⟨*AA or RAC* ~⟩ **4** a small simple sheltering or enclosing structure **5** *Br* a gift given to tradesmen at Christmas **6** *Br* television; *specif* a television set – + *the*; infml [ME, fr OE, fr LL *buxis*, fr Gk *pyxis*, fr *pyxos*] – **boxful** *n*, **boxy** /'boksi/ *adj*, **boxiness** *n*

³box *vt* **1** to provide with a box **2** to enclose (as if) in a box – + *in* or *up* **3** to hem in (e g an opponent in soccer) – usu + *in* – **box the compass 1** to name the 32 points of the compass in their order **2** to make a complete reversal

⁴box *n* a punch or slap, esp on the ear [ME]

⁵box *vt* **1** to slap (e g the ears) with the hand **2** to engage in boxing with ~ *vi* to engage in boxing

Box and Cox /koks/ *adv or adj, Br* alternating; IN TURN [eponymous characters, who share a room but never meet, in play by J M Morton †1891 E dramatist]

'box,car /-,kah/ *n, NAm* ³VAN 2

¹boxer /'boksə/ *n* one who engages in the sport of boxing

²boxer *n* a compact medium-sized short-haired dog of a breed originating in Germany [G, fr E ¹*boxer*]

Boxer *n* a member of a Chinese secret society which was opposed to foreign influence in China and whose rebellion was suppressed in 1900 [approx trans of Chin (Pek) *i⁴he²ch'üan²*, lit., righteous harmonious fist]

'boxer ,shorts *n pl* men's loose-fitting underpants ☞ GARMENT

'box-,girder *n* a hollow rectangular girder

boxing /'boksing/ *n* the art of attack and defence with the fists practised as a sport

'Boxing ,Day *n* December 26, observed as a public holiday in Britain (apart from Scotland) and elsewhere in the Commonwealth, on which service workers (e g postmen) were traditionally given Christmas boxes

'boxing ,glove *n* a heavily padded leather mitten worn in boxing

'box ,junction *n* a road junction at which a pattern of crosshatched yellow lines on the road warns the road-user not to enter until his/her exit is clear

'box ,kite *n* a tailless kite consisting of 2 or more open-ended connected boxes

'box ,number *n* the number of a box or pigeon hole at a newspaper or post office where arrangements are made for replies to advertisements or other mail to be sent

'box ,office *n* **1** an office (e g in a theatre) where tickets of admission are sold **2** sthg that enhances ticket sales ⟨*the publicity is all good* ~⟩

'box ,pleat *n* a pleat made by forming 2 folded edges, one facing right and the other left – compare INVERTED PLEAT

'boxroom /-,roohm, -room/ *n, Br* a small storage room (e g for trunks) in a private house

'box ,spanner *n* a spanner that is shaped to enclose a nut, bolt head, etc

'box,wood /-,wood/ *n* the very close-grained heavy tough hard wood of the box tree

[1]boy /boy/ *n* **1a** a male child from birth to puberty **b** a son **c** an immature male; a youth **d** a boyfriend **2** a fellow, person ⟨*the* ~s *at the office*⟩ **3** a male servant – sometimes taken to be offensive [ME; akin to Fris *boi* boy] – **boyhood** /-hood/ *n*, **boyish** *adj*, **boyishly** *adv*, **boyishness** *n*

[2]boy *interj, chiefly NAm* – used to express esp excitement or surprise

boycott /'boykot/ *vt* to engage in a concerted refusal to have dealings with (e g a person, shop, or organization), usu to express disapproval or to force acceptance of certain conditions [C C *Boycott* †1897 E land agent in Ireland who was ostracized for refusing to reduce rents] – **boycott** *n*, **boycotter** *n*

'boy,friend /-,frend/ *n* **1** a frequent or regular male companion of a girl or woman **2** a male lover

boyo /'boyoh/ *n, pl* **boyos** /-ohz/ *Irish & Welsh* a boy, lad [*boy* + *-o*]

,boy 'scout *n* SCOUT 4 – no longer used technically

boysenberry /'boyzənb(ə)ri/ *n* (the fruit of) a spring shrub developed by crossing several varieties of blackberry and raspberry [Rudolph *Boysen fl*1923 US horticulturist + E *berry*]

bra /brah/ *n, pl* **bras** a woman's closely fitting undergarment with cups for supporting the breasts [short for *brassiere*, fr obs F *brassière* bodice, fr OF *braciere* arm protector, fr *braz* arm, fr L *bracchium* – more at BRACE]

[1]braai /brie/ *n, SAfr* BARBECUE 1, 3; *also* an area (e g a patio) intended for a braai [short for *braaivleis*]

[2]braai *vt, SAfr* to barbecue

braaivleis /'brie,flays/ *n, SAfr* BARBECUE 1, 3 [Afrik, lit., grilled meat, fr *braai* to grill + *vleis* meat]

[1]brace /brays/ *n, pl* **braces,** (*1*) **braces,** *after a determiner* **brace** **1** two of a kind; a pair ⟨*several* ~ *of quail*⟩ **2** sthg (e g a clasp) that connects or fastens **3** a crank-shaped instrument for turning a drilling bit **4a** a diagonal piece of structural material that serves to strengthen **b** a rope attached to a yard on a ship that swings the yard horizontally to trim the sail ☞ SHIP **c** *pl* straps worn over the shoulders to hold up trousers **d** an appliance for supporting a weak leg or other body part **e** a dental fitting worn to correct irregular teeth **5a** a mark { or } used to connect words or items to be considered together **b** (this mark connecting) 2 or more musical staves the parts of which are to be performed simultaneously [ME, pair, clasp, fr MF, two arms, fr L *bracchia*, pl of *bracchium* arm, fr Gk *brachiōn*, fr compar of *brachys* short – more at BRIEF]

[2]brace *vt* **1a** to prepare for use by making taut **b** to prepare, steel ⟨~ *yourself for the shock*⟩ **2** to turn (a sail yard) by means of a brace **3** to provide or support with a brace ⟨*heavily* ~d *because of polio*⟩

bracelet /'brayslit/ *n* **1** an ornamental band or chain worn round the wrist **2** sthg (e g handcuffs) resembling a bracelet [ME, fr MF, dim. of *bras* arm, fr L *bracchium*]

[1]bracer /'braysə/ *n* an arm or wrist protector, esp for use by an archer [ME, fr MF *braciere*, fr OF, fr *braz* arm, fr L *bracchium*]

[2]bracer *n* a drink (e g of an alcoholic beverage) taken as a stimulant [[2]BRACE + [2]-ER]

brace up *vb* to (cause to) have more courage, spirit, and cheerfulness

brachi- /bra(y)ki-/, **brachio-** *comb form* arm ⟨brachi*ate*⟩ ⟨brachio*pod*⟩ [L *bracchium, brachium* – more at BRACE]

brachial /'bra(y)ki·əl/ *adj* of or located in (a part like) an arm ⟨*a* ~ *artery*⟩

brachiate /'bra(y)ki·ət, -ayt/ *vi* to progress by swinging from one hold to another by the arms – used technically – **brachiation** /-'aysh(ə)n/ *n*

brachiopod /'bra(y)ki·ə,pod/ *n* any of a phylum of mostly extinct marine invertebrate animals with shells composed of 2 halves hinged together ☞ EVOLUTION [deriv of L *bracchium* + Gk *pod-, pous* foot – more at FOOT] – **brachiopod** *adj*

brachy- *comb form* short ⟨brachy*dactylous*⟩ [Gk, fr *brachys* – more at BRIEF]

brachycephalic /,brakisi'falik/ *adj* having a short or broad head [NL *brachycephalus*, fr Gk *brachy-* + *kephalē* head – more at CEPHALIC] – **brachycephaly** /-'sefəli/ *n*

bracing /'braysing/ *adj* refreshing, invigorating ⟨*a* ~ *breeze*⟩

bracken /'brakən/ *n* (a dense growth of) a common large coarse fern of esp moorland, that is poisonous to grazing animals [ME *braken*, prob of Scand origin; akin to OSw *brække* fern]

[1]bracket /'brakit/ *n* **1** an overhanging projecting fixture or member that is designed to support a vertical load or strengthen an angle **2a** PARENTHESIS 1b **b** either of a pair of marks [ ] used in writing and printing to enclose matter or in mathematics and logic to show that a complex expression should be treated as a single unit **c** ANGLE BRACKET **d** BRACE 5b **3** (the distance between) a pair of shots fired usu in front of and beyond a target to aid in range-finding **4** any of a graded series of income groups ⟨*the £20,000 income* ~⟩ [MF *braguette* codpiece, fr dim. of *brague* breeches, fr OProv *braga*, fr L *braca*, fr Gaulish *brāca*, of Gmc origin; akin to OHG *bruoh* breeches – more at BREECH]

[2]bracket *vt* **1** to place (as if) within brackets **2** to provide or fasten with brackets **3** to put in the same category; associate – usu + *together* **4a** to get a range by firing in front of and behind (a target) **b** to establish a margin on either side of (e g an estimation)

brackish /'brakish/ *adj* slightly salty ⟨~ *water*⟩ [D *brac* salty; akin to MLG *brac* salty] – **brackishness** *n*

bract /brakt/ *n* **1** a usu small leaf near a flower or floral axis **2** a leaf borne on a floral axis [NL *bractea*, fr L, thin metal plate] – **bracteal** *adj*, **bracteate** /-ət, -ayt/ *adj*, **bracted** *adj*

bracteole /'braktiohl/ *n* a small or secondary bract, esp on a floral axis [NL *bracteola*, fr L, dim. of *bractea*] – **bracteolate** /brak'tee·ələt, -layt, 'brakti·ə-layt/ *adj*

brad /brad/ *n* a thin wedged-shaped nail having a slight projection at the top of one side instead of a head [ME, fr ON *broddr* spike; akin to OE *byrst* bristle – more at BRISTLE]

bradawl /'brad,awl/ *n* an awl; *esp* one used by a woodworker

bradycardia /,bradi'kahdi·ə/ *n* relatively slow heart action, whether physiological or pathological – compare TACHYCARDIA [NL, fr Gk *bradys* slow + NL *-cardia*]

bradykinin /,bradi'kienin/ *n* a local polypeptide hormone that is a kinin, is formed in injured tissue, and prob plays a part in inflammatory processes [Gk *bradys* slow]

brae /bray/ *n, chiefly Scot* a hillside, esp along a river [ME *bra*, fr ON *brā* eyelash; akin to OE *bregdan* to move quickly – more at BRAID]

¹**brag** /brag/ *n* a card game resembling poker [*brag* (boast); fr the boast or challenge made by one player to another]

²**brag** *vb* **-gg-** to talk or assert boastfully – **bragger** *n*

braggadocio /,bragə'dochioh -'dokioh/ *n* empty boasting [*Braggadocchio*, personification of boasting in the poem *The Faerie Queene* by Edmund Spenser †1599 E poet]

braggart /'bragət/ *n* a loud arrogant boaster – **braggart** *adj*

Brahma /'brahmə/ *n* **1** BRAHMAN 1b **2** the creator deity of the Hindu sacred triad – compare SIVA, VISHNU [Skt *brahman*]

Brahman /'brahmən/ *n* **1a** a Hindu of the highest caste traditionally assigned to the priesthood **b** the impersonal ground of all being in Hinduism **2** any of an Indian breed of humped cattle; *also* a large vigorous heat-resistant and tick-resistant animal developed in the USA by interbreeding Indian cattle [Skt *brāhmana*, lit., having to do with prayer, fr *brahman*, neut, prayer] – **Brahmanic** /-'manik/ *adj*

Brahmanism /'brahmə,niz(ə)m/ *n* orthodox Hinduism adhering to the pantheism of the Vedas and to the ancient sacrifices and family ceremonies

Brahmin /'brahmin/ *n* **1** (a) Brahman **2** *NAm* an intellectually and socially cultivated but aloof person – **Brahminism** *n*, **Brahminical** /-'minikl/ *adj*

¹**braid** /brayd/ *vt* **1** *chiefly NAm* PLAIT 2 **2** to ornament, esp with ribbon or braid [ME *breyden*, lit., to move suddenly, fr OE *bregdan*; akin to OHG *brettan* to draw (a sword), Gk *phorkon* something white or wrinkled] – **braider** *n*

²**braid** *n* **1** a narrow piece of fabric, esp plaited cord or ribbon, used for trimming **2** *chiefly NAm* a length of plaited hair

¹**brail** /brayl/ *n* a rope fastened to the edge or end of a sail and used for hauling the sail up or in [ME *brayle*, fr AF *braiel*, fr OF, strap]

²**brail** *vt* to take in (e g a sail) by the brails

braille /brayl/ *n, often cap* a system of writing or printing for the blind that uses characters made up of raised dots [Louis *Braille* †1852 F teacher of the blind]

¹**brain** /brayn/ *n* **1a** the portion of the vertebrate central nervous system that constitutes the organ of thought and neural coordination, is made up of neurons and supporting and nutritive structures, is enclosed within the skull, and is continuous with the spinal cord ☞ NERVE **b** a nervous centre in invertebrates comparable in position and function to the vertebrate brain **2a(1)** an intellect, mind ⟨*has a good* ~⟩ **(2)** intellectual endowment; intelligence – often pl with sing. meaning ⟨*plenty of* ~s *in that family*⟩ **b(1)** a very intelligent or intellectual person **(2)** the chief planner of an organization or enterprise – usu pl with sing. meaning but sing. in constr **3** an automatic device (e g a computer) that performs 1 or more of the functions of the human brain for control or computation [ME, fr OE *brægen*; akin to MLG *bregen* brain, Gk *brechmos* front part of the head] – **on the brain** as an obsession; continually in mind ⟨*I've got that tune* on the brain *again*⟩

²**brain** *vt* **1** to kill by smashing the skull **2** to hit hard on the head – infml

'**brain,child** /-,chield/ *n* a product of one's creative imagination

'**brain ,death** *n* the death of a human being determined by the assessment that his/her brain has irreversibly ceased to function

'**brain ,drain** *n* *the* loss of highly qualified workers and professionals through emigration

-brained *comb form* (*adj, n* → *adj*) having (such) a brain ⟨*feather*brained⟩

'**brainless** /-lis/ *adj* stupid, foolish – **brainlessly** *adv*, **brainlessness** *n*

'**brain,power** /-,powə/ *n* intellectual ability; intelligence

'**brain ,stem** *n* the part of the brain connecting the spinal cord with the forebrain and cerebrum

'**brain,storm** /-,stawm/ *n* **1** a fit of insanity **2** *chiefly NAm* BRAIN WAVE 2

'**brain,storming** /-,stawming/ *n, NAm* a problem-solving technique that involves the spontaneous contribution of ideas from all members of a group

'**brains ,trust** *n sing or pl in constr, chiefly Br* a group of expert advisers, esp assembled to answer questions of immediate or current interest

'**brain,teaser** /-,teezə/ *n* a logical or mathematical puzzle

'**brain,washing** /-,woshing/ *n* a systematic attempt to instil beliefs into sby, often in place of beliefs already held [trans of Chin (Pek) *hsi*[3] *nao*[3]] – **brainwash** *vt*, **brainwash** *n*, **brainwasher** *n*

'**brain ,wave** *n* **1** a rhythmic fluctuation of voltage between parts of the brain **2** a sudden bright idea

brainy /'brayni/ *adj* intelligent, clever – infml – **braininess** *n*

braise /brayz/ *vt* to cook (e g meat) slowly by first sautéeing in hot fat and then simmering gently in very little liquid in a closed container [F *braiser*, fr *braise* live coals, fr OF *brese*]

¹**brake** /brayk/ *n* **1** a device for arresting usu rotary motion, esp by friction **2** sthg that slows down or stops movement or activity [ME, bridle, curb] – **brakeless** *adj*

²**brake** *vt* to slow or stop by a brake ~ *vi* **1** to operate, manage, or apply a brake, esp on a vehicle **2** to become slowed by a brake

³**brake** *n* an area of overgrown rough or marshy land [ME *-brake*] – **braky** /'brayki/ *adj*

⁴**brake** *n* ESTATE CAR [*break* (carriage frame used for breaking horses), fr ¹*break*]

brake horsepower *n* the useful power of an engine as calculated from the resistance to a brake or dynamometer applied to the shaft or flywheel

'**brake ,van** *n, Br* GUARD'S VAN

bramble /'brambl/ *n* a rough prickly shrub, esp a blackberry [ME *brembel*, fr OE *brēmel*; akin to OE *brōm* broom] – **brambly** *adj*

brambling /'brambling/ *n* a brightly coloured Old World finch [prob fr *bramble* + *-ing*]

Bramley /'bramli/ *n* a large green variety of cooking apple [Matthew *Bramley* *fl*1850 E butcher & reputed first grower of the fruit]

bran /bran/ *n* the broken husk of cereal grain separated from the flour or meal by sifting [ME, fr OF]

[1]**branch** /brahnch/ *n* **1** a secondary shoot or stem (e g a bough) arising from a main axis (e g of a tree) **2a** TRIBUTARY 2 **b** a side road or way **c** a slender projection (e g the tine of an antler) **3** a distinct part of a complex whole: e g **a** a division of a family descending from a particular ancestor **b** a distinct area of knowledge ⟨*pathology is a ~ of medicine*⟩ **c** a division or separate part of an organization [ME, fr OF *branche*, fr LL *branca* paw] – **branched** *adj*, **branchless** *adj*, **branchlet** /'brahnchlit/ *n*, **branchy** /-chi/ *adj*

[2]**branch** *vi* **1** to put forth branches **2** to spring out (e g from a main stem)

branchia /'brangki·ə/ *n, pl* **branchiae** /-ki,ee/ [2]GILL 1 [L, sing., fr Gk, pl of *branchion* gill; akin to Gk *bronchos* windpipe – more at CRAW] – **branchial** /-ki·əl/, **branchiate** /-ki·ət, -ki·ayt/ *adj*

branchiopod /'brangki·ə,pod/ *n* any of a group of aquatic crustaceans (e g a brine shrimp) typically having a long body, a carapace, and many pairs of leaflike appendages [deriv of Gk *branchia* gills + *pod-*, *pous* foot – more at FOOT] – **branchiopod, branchiopodan** /,brangki'opədən; *also* ,brangki·ə'pohdən/ *adj*, **branchiopodous** /,brangki'opədəs; *also* ,brangki·ə'pohdəs/ *adj*

branch out *vi* to extend activities ⟨*the business is* branching out *all over the state*⟩

[1]**brand** /brand/ *n* **1** a charred piece of wood **2a** a mark made by burning with a hot iron, or with a stamp or stencil, to identify manufacture or quality or to designate ownership (e g of cattle) **b(1)** a mark formerly put on criminals with a hot iron **(2)** a mark of disgrace ⟨*the ~ of poverty*⟩ **3a** a class of goods identified by name as the product of a single firm or manufacturer **b** a characteristic or distinctive kind ⟨*a lively ~ of humour*⟩ **4** a tool used to produce a brand **5** a sword – poetic [ME, torch, sword, fr OE; akin to OE *bærnan* to burn]

[2]**brand** *vt* **1** to mark with a brand **2** to stigmatize **3** to impress indelibly – **brander** *n*

brandish /'brandish/ *vt* to shake or wave (e g a weapon) menacingly or ostentatiously [ME *braundisshen*, fr MF *brandiss-*, stem of *brandir*, fr OF, fr *brand* sword, of Gmc origin; akin to OE *brand*]

,brand-'new *adj* conspicuously new and unused

brandy /'brandi/ *n* a spirit distilled from wine or fermented fruit juice ⟨*plum ~*⟩ [short for *brandywine*, fr D *brandewijn*, fr MD *brantwijn*, fr *brant* burnt, distilled + *wijn* wine]

'brandy ,snap *n* a very thin cylindrical ginger biscuit sometimes flavoured with brandy

brant /brant/ *n, pl* **brants,** *esp collectively* **brant** *chiefly NAm* BRENT GOOSE

[1]**brash** /brash/ *n* a mass of fragments (e g of ice) [obs *brash* (to breach a wall), prob fr MF *breche* breach]

[2]**brash** *adj* **1** impetuous, rash **2** uninhibitedly energetic or demonstrative **3** aggressively self-assertive; impudent [origin unknown] – **brashly** *adv*, **brashness** *n*

brass /brahs/ *n* **1** an alloy of copper and zinc **2a** *sing or pl in constr* the brass instruments of an orchestra or band **b** a usu brass memorial tablet **c** bright metal fittings or utensils **3** brazen self-assurance **4** *sing or pl in constr* BRASS HATS **5** *chiefly N Eng* money ***USE*** (*3, 4, & 5*) infml [ME *bras*, fr OE *bræs*; akin to MLG *bras* metal] – **brass** *adj*

,brass 'band *n* a band consisting (chiefly) of brass and percussion instruments

brasserie /'bras(ə)ri/ *n* a restaurant that serves beer [F, fr MF *brasser* to brew, fr OF *bracier*, fr L *braces*, a kind of wheat]

,brass 'farthing *n* a trivial amount

,brass 'hat *n* a high-ranking military officer – infml

brassica /'brasikə/ *n* any of a large genus of Old World temperate-zone plants of the mustard family that includes many important vegetables and crop plants (e g cabbage, turnip, mustard, and rape) [NL, genus name, fr L, cabbage]

brassiere /'brazi·ə/ *n* a bra – fml

brass instrument *n* any of a group of wind instruments with a long usu curved cylindrical or conical metal tube, a mouthpiece against which the player's lips vibrate, and usu valves or a slide for producing all the notes within the instrument's range

,brass 'tacks *n pl* details of immediate practical importance – esp in *get down to brass tacks*

brassy /'brahsi/ *adj* **1** shamelessly bold; brazen **2** resembling brass, esp in colour – **brassily** *adv*, **brassiness** *n*

brat /brat/ *n* an (ill-mannered) child [perh fr E dial. *brat* (ragamuffin)]

brattice /'bratis/ *n* an esp temporary wooden or cloth partition for directing air in a mine [ME *bretais, bretasce* parapet, fr OF *bretesche*, fr ML *breteschia*] – **brattice** *vt*

bravado /brə'vahdoh/ *n, pl* **bravadoes, bravados** (a display of) blustering swaggering conduct [MF *bravade* & OSp *bravata*, fr OIt *bravata*, fr *bravare* to challenge, show off, fr *bravo*]

[1]**brave** /brayv/ *adj* **1** courageous, fearless **2** excellent, splendid ⟨*a ~ new world*⟩ [MF, fr OIt & OSp *bravo* courageous, wild, fr L *barbarus* barbarous] – **bravely** *adv*

[2]**brave** *vt vt* to face or endure with courage

[3]**brave** *n* a N American Indian warrior

bravery /'brayv(ə)ri/ *n* courage, valour

[1]**bravo** /'brahvoh/ *n, pl* **bravos, bravoes** a villain, desperado; *esp* a hired assassin [It, fr *bravo*, adj, brave]

[2]**bravo** /brah'voh/ *n, pl* **bravos** a shout of approval – often used interjectionally in applauding a performance

Bravo /'brah,voh/ *n* – a communications code word for the letter *b*

bravura /brə'v(y)ooərə/ *n* **1** a flamboyant brilliant style **2** a musical passage requiring exceptional agility and technical skill in execution **3** a show of daring or brilliance [It, lit., bravery, fr *bravare*]

braw /braw/ *adj, chiefly Scot* good or fine, esp in appearance or dress [modif of MF *brave*]

[1]**brawl** /brawl/ *vi* **1** to quarrel or fight noisily **2** *of*

water to make a loud confused bubbling sound [ME *brawlen*] – **brawler** *n*

2**brawl** *n* **1** a noisy quarrel or fight **2** a brawling noise

brawn /brawn/ *n* **1a** strong muscles **b** muscular strength **2** pork trimmings, esp the meat from a pig's head, boiled, chopped, and pressed into a mould [ME, fr MF *braon* muscle, of Gmc origin; akin to OE *brǣd* flesh]

brawny /'brawni/ *adj* muscular, strong – **brawnily** *adv*, **brawniness** *n*

1**bray** /bray/ *vi* to utter the loud harsh cry characteristic of a donkey ~ *vt* to utter or play loudly, harshly, or discordantly [ME *brayen*, fr OF *braire* to cry, fr (assumed) VL *bragere*, of Celt origin; akin to MIr *braigid* he breaks wind; akin to L *frangere* to break – more at BREAK] – **bray** *n*

2**bray** *vt* to crush or grind finely [ME *brayen*, fr MF *broiier*, of Gmc origin; akin to OHG *brehhan* to break – more at BREAK]

braze /brayz/ *vt* to solder with an alloy (e g of brass and silver) that melts on contact with the heated metals being joined [prob fr F *braser*, fr OF, to burn, fr *brese* live coals] – **brazer** *n*

1**brazen** /'brayz(ə)n/ *adj* **1** resembling or made of brass **2** sounding harsh and loud like struck brass **3** contemptuously bold [ME *brasen*, fr OE *bræsen*, fr *bræs* brass] – **brazenly** *adv*, **brazenness** *n*

2**brazen** *vt* to face with defiance or impudence – esp in *brazen it out*

,**brazen-'faced** *adj* BRAZEN 3

1**brazier** /'brayzi·ə, 'brayzhə/ *n* one who works in brass [ME *brasier*, fr *bras* brass]

2**brazier** *n* a receptacle or stand for holding burning coals [F *brasier*, fr OF, fire of hot coals, fr *brese*]

Bra'zil ,nut /brə'zil/ *n* (a tall S American tree that bears) a roughly triangular oily edible nut [*Brazil*, country in S America]

bra'zil,wood /-,wood/ *n* (the red or purple dye obtained from) the heavy wood of any of various tropical leguminous trees [Sp *brasil*, fr *brasa* live coals; fr its colour]

1**breach** /breech/ *n* **1** infraction or violation (e g of a law, obligation, or standard) ⟨~ *of contract*⟩ **2** a gap (e g in a wall) made by battering **3** a break in customarily friendly relations **4** a leap, esp of a whale out of water [ME *breche*, fr OE *bryce*; akin to OE *brecan* to break]

2**breach** *vt* **1** to make a breach in ⟨~ *the city walls*⟩ **2** to break, violate ⟨~ *an agreement*⟩

,**breach of 'promise** *n* violation of a promise, esp to marry

,**breach of the 'peace** *n* an instance of disorderly conduct

1**bread** /bred/ *n* **1** a food consisting essentially of flour or meal which is baked and usu leavened, esp with yeast **2** food, sustenance ⟨*our daily* ~⟩ **3a** livelihood ⟨*earns his daily* ~ *as a labourer*⟩ **b** money – slang [ME *breed*, fr OE *brēad*; akin to OHG *brōt* bread, OE *brēowan* to brew] – **bread upon the waters** resources chanced or charitable deeds performed without expectation of return

2**bread** *vt* to cover with breadcrumbs ⟨*a* ~ed *pork chop*⟩

,**bread-and-'butter** *adj* **1a** basic, fundamental ⟨*wages, housing, and other* ~ *issues*⟩ **b** dependable, routine ⟨*the* ~ *repertoire of an orchestra*⟩ **2** sent or given as thanks for hospitality ⟨*a* ~ *letter*⟩

,**bread and 'butter** *n* a means of sustenance or livelihood

,**bread and 'circuses** *n pl* entertainment provided at public expense; *also* a palliative offered to avert potential discontent [trans of L *panis et circenses*]

'**bread,basket** /-,bahskit/ *n* the stomach – slang

1'**bread,crumb** /-,krum/ *n* a small fragment of bread

2**breadcrumb** *vt* 2BREAD

'**bread,fruit** /-,frooht/ *n* the large starchy fruit of a tropical tree that has white flesh with a breadlike texture

'**bread,line** /-,lien/ *n* **1** *Br* the level of income required for subsistence **2** *chiefly NAm* a queue of people waiting to receive food given in charity

breadth /bret·th, bredth/ *n* **1** distance from side to side **2a** sthg of full width ⟨*a* ~ *of cloth*⟩ **b** a wide expanse ⟨~s *of grass*⟩ **3a** catholicity, scope **b** liberality of views or taste [obs *brede* breadth (fr ME, fr OE *brǣdu*, fr *brād* broad) + *-th* (as in *length*)]

'**breadthways** /-,wayz, -wiz/, '**breadth,wise** /-,wiez/ *adv or adj* in the direction of the breadth ⟨*a course of bricks laid* ~⟩

'**bread,winner** /-,winə/ *n* one whose wages are a family's livelihood – **breadwinning** *n*

1**break** /brayk/ *vb* **broke** /brohk/; **broken** /'brohkən/ *vt* **1a** to separate into parts with suddenness or violence **b** to fracture ⟨~ *an arm*⟩ **c** to rupture ⟨~ *the skin*⟩ **2** to violate, transgress ⟨~ *the law*⟩ **3a** to force a way through or into ⟨*the silence was* broken *by a dog barking*⟩ **b** to escape by force from ⟨*he* broke *jail*⟩ **4** to make or effect by cutting or forcing through ⟨~ *a trail through the woods*⟩ **5** to disrupt the order or compactness of ⟨~ *ranks*⟩ **6a** to defeat utterly; destroy **b** to crush the spirit of **c(1)** to train (an animal, esp a horse) for the service of human beings **(2)** to inure, accustom ⟨*a horse* broken *to the saddle*⟩ **d** to exhaust in health, strength, or capacity **7a** to ruin financially **b** to reduce in rank **8a** to reduce the force or intensity of ⟨*the bushes will* ~ *his fall*⟩ **b** to cause failure and discontinuance of (a strike) by measures outside bargaining processes **9** to exceed, surpass ⟨~ *a record*⟩ ⟨~ *the speed limit*⟩ **10** to ruin the prospects of ⟨*could make or* ~ *her career*⟩ **11a** to stop or interrupt **b** to open and bring about suspension of operation ⟨~ *an electric circuit*⟩ **c** to destroy the unity or completeness of ⟨*they must be kept together; I don't want to* ~ *the collection*⟩ **d** to destroy the uniformity of ⟨*the straight line of the horizon was* broken *by a rocky outcrop*⟩ **12** to cause to discontinue a habit ⟨*tried to* ~ *him of smoking*⟩ **13** to make known; tell ⟨~ *the bad news gently*⟩ **14a** to solve (a code or cipher system); CRACK 3a **b** to demonstrate the falsity of (an alibi) **15** to split into smaller units, parts, or processes; divide ⟨~ *a £10 note*⟩ – often + *up* or *down* **16** to open the operating mechanism of (a gun) ~ *vi* **1** to escape with sudden forceful effort – often + *out* or *away* ⟨~ *out of jail*⟩ ⟨broke *away from the main bunch*⟩ **2a** to come into being, esp suddenly ⟨*day was* ~ing⟩ ⟨*the storm* broke⟩ **b** to come to pass; occur ⟨*report news stories as they* ~⟩ **3** to effect a penetration ⟨~ *through enemy lines*⟩ **4** to take a different course; depart ⟨~ *from tradition*⟩ **5** to make a sudden dash ⟨~ *for cover*⟩ **6** to separate after a clinch in boxing **7** to come apart or split into pieces; burst, shatter **8** *of a wave* to curl over and disintegrate in surf or foam **9** *of weather* to change suddenly, esp after a fine spell

10 to give way in disorderly retreat **11a** to fail in health, strength, or control ⟨*may* ~ *under questioning*⟩ **b** to become inoperative because of damage, wear, or strain **12** to end a relationship, agreement, etc *with* **13** *esp of a ball bowled in cricket* to change direction of forward travel on bouncing **14** *of a voice* to alter sharply in tone, pitch, or intensity; *esp* to shift abruptly from one register to another ⟨*her voice* ~ing *with emotion*⟩ ⟨*boys' voices* ~ *at puberty*⟩ **15** *of a horse* to fail to keep a prescribed gait **16** to interrupt one's activity for a brief period ⟨~ *for lunch*⟩ **17** to make the opening shot of a game of snooker, billiards, or pool **18a** to fold, lift, or come apart at a seam, groove, or joint **b** *of cream* to separate during churning into liquid and fat **19** *chiefly NAm* to happen, develop ⟨*for the team to succeed, everything has to* ~ *right*⟩ [ME *breken*, fr OE *brecan*; akin to OHG *brehhan* to break, L *frangere*] – **breakable** *adj or n* – **break a leg** to be successful in a performance – used in the theatre to wish another luck – **break cover** to emerge abruptly from a hiding place ⟨*the hunted fox* broke cover⟩ – **break even** to achieve a balance between expenditure and income; *esp* to recover precisely what one spends ⟨*the church fete only* broke even *this year*⟩ – **break into** **1a** to begin abruptly ⟨*the horse* breaks into *a gallop*⟩ **b** to give voice or expression to abruptly ⟨*she* broke into *song*⟩ ⟨broke into *a laugh*⟩ **2** to enter by force ⟨*thieves* broke into *the house*⟩ **3** to make entry or entrance into ⟨*trying to* break into *show business*⟩ **4** to interrupt ⟨*kept* breaking into *the conversation*⟩ – **break new ground** to make or show new discoveries; pioneer ⟨breaking new ground *in genetic engineering*⟩ – **break service/break someone's service** to win a game against the server (e g in tennis) – **break someone's heart** to cause sby heartbreak – **break the back** to do or overcome the largest or hardest part – **break the ice** to overcome initial reserve – **break wind** to expel gas from the intestine through the anus

[2]**break** *n* **1** an act or action of breaking **2a** a condition produced (as if) by breaking; a gap ⟨*a* ~ *in the clouds*⟩ **b** a rupture in previously good relations **c** a gap in an otherwise continuous electric circuit **3** the action or act of breaking in, out, or forth ⟨*a jail* ~⟩ **4** a dash, rush ⟨*make a* ~ *for it*⟩ **5** the act of separating after a clinch in boxing **6a** a change or interruption in a continuous process or trend ⟨*it makes a* ~⟩ **b** a change from the status quo ⟨*a sharp* ~ *with tradition*⟩ **c** a respite from work or duty; *specif* a daily pause for play and refreshment at school **d** a planned interruption in a radio or television programme ⟨*a* ~ *for the commercial*⟩ **7a** the opening shot in a game of snooker, billiards, or pool **b** change in direction of forward travel, esp of a cricket ball on bouncing because of spin imparted by the bowler **c** a slow ball bowled in cricket that deviates in a specified direction on bouncing ⟨*an off* ~⟩ **d** the act or an instance of breaking an opponent's service in tennis **e** failure of a horse to maintain a prescribed gait **f** (a score made by) a sequence of successful shots or strokes (e g in snooker) **8** a notable variation in pitch, intensity, or tone in the voice **9** a place, situation, or time at which a break occurs: e g **a** the point where one musical register changes to another **b** a short ornamental passage inserted between phrases in jazz **10a** a stroke of esp good luck **b** an opportunity, chance ⟨*give me a* ~⟩

breakage /ˈbraykij/ *n* **1** sthg broken – usu pl **2** allowance for things broken (e g in transit) [[1]BREAK + -AGE]

[1]**breakaway** /ˈbraykə,way/ *n* **1** sby or sthg that breaks away **2** a breaking away (e g from a group or tradition); a withdrawing

[2]**breakaway** *adj* **1** favouring independence from an affiliation; withdrawing ⟨*a* ~ *faction formed a new party*⟩ **2** *chiefly NAm* made to break or bend easily ⟨~ *road signs for highway safety*⟩

ˈ**break,down** /-,down/ *n* **1** a failure to function **2** a physical, mental, or nervous collapse **3** failure to progress or have effect ⟨*a* ~ *of negotiations*⟩ **4** the process of decomposing ⟨~ *of food during digestion*⟩ **5** a division into categories; a classification **6** a whole analysed into parts; *specif* an account in which the transactions are recorded under various categories

break down *vt* **1a** to cause to fall or collapse by breaking or shattering **b** to make ineffective ⟨break down *legal barriers*⟩ **c** to put an end to; suppress ⟨*he tried to* break down *their opposition*⟩ **2a** to divide into parts or categories **b** to separate into simpler substances **c** to take apart, esp for storage or shipment ~ *vi* **1a** to become inoperative through breakage or wear **b** to become inapplicable or ineffective; deteriorate ⟨*relations began to* break down⟩ **2a** to be susceptible to analysis or subdivision ⟨*the outline* breaks down *into 3 parts*⟩ **b** to undergo decomposition **3** to lose one's composure completely ⟨*he* broke down *and wept*⟩

ˈ**break,down ,lorry** *n* a lorry fitted with equipment suitable for repairing or towing disabled or immobilized motor vehicles

[1]**breaker** /ˈbraykə/ *n* **1** a wave breaking into foam **2** a user of Citizens' Band radio – slang [[1]BREAK + [2]-ER]

[2]**breaker** *n* a small water cask [by folk etymology fr Sp *barrica*]

,**break-ˈeven** *adj or n* (of or being) the point at which profit equals loss

breakfast /ˈbrekfəst/ *n* (food prepared for) the first meal of the day, esp when taken in the morning [ME *brekfast*, fr *breken* to break + [4]*fast*] – **breakfast** *vb*, **breakfaster** *n*

break in *vi* **1** to enter a house or building by force **2a** to interrupt a conversation **b** to intrude ~ *vt* **1** to accustom to a certain activity ⟨break in *a new reporter*⟩ **2** to use or wear until comfortable or working properly

ˈ**breaking ,point** /ˈbrayking/ *n* the point at which a person gives way under stress

ˈ**break,neck** /-,nek/ *adj* extremely dangerous ⟨~ *speed*⟩

break off *vi* **1** to become detached; separate **2** to stop abruptly ⟨break off *in the middle of a sentence*⟩ ~ *vt* to discontinue ⟨break off *diplomatic relations*⟩

ˈ**break,out** /-,owt/ *n* a violent or forceful breaching of a restraint (e g imprisonment or siege)

break out *vi* **1** to become affected with a skin eruption ⟨broke out *in a rash*⟩ **2** to develop or emerge with suddenness and force ⟨*a riot* broke out⟩ **3** to escape ~ *vt* **1** to take from shipboard stowage ready for use **2** to unfurl (a flag) at the mast

ˈ**break,through** /-,throoh/ *n* **1** an act or point of

breaking through an obstruction **2** an attack that penetrates enemy lines **3** a sudden advance, esp in knowledge or technique ⟨*a medical* ~⟩

'break,up /-,up/ *n* **1** a dissolution, disruption ⟨*the ~ of a marriage*⟩ **2** a division into smaller units **3** *chiefly Can* the spring thaw

break up *vt* **1** to disrupt the continuity of ⟨*too many footnotes can* break up *a text*⟩ **2** to decompose ⟨break up *a chemical*⟩ **3** to bring to an end ⟨*it* broke up *their marriage*⟩ **4a** to break into pieces (e g for salvage); scrap **b** to crumble **5a** to distress ⟨*his wife's death really* broke *him* up⟩ – infml **b** *chiefly NAm* to cause to laugh heartily – infml ~ *vi* **1a** to come to an end ⟨*their partnership* broke up⟩ **b** to separate, split up ⟨*Simon and Mary have* broken up⟩ **2** to lose morale or composure ⟨*he is likely to* break up *under attack*⟩; *also* to give way to laughter **3** *Br, of a school* to disband for the holidays

'break,water /-,wawtə/ *n* an offshore structure (e g a wall) used to protect a harbour or beach from the force of waves

¹bream /breem/ *n, pl* **bream,** *esp for different types* **breams 1** any of various European freshwater fishes related to the carps and minnows **2** any of various freshwater sunfishes [ME *breme,* fr MF, of Gmc origin; akin to OHG *brahsima* bream, *brettan* to draw (a sword) – more at BRAID]

²bream *vt* ³GRAVE [prob fr D *brem* furze]

¹breast /brest/ *n* **1** either of 2 protuberant milk-producing glandular organs situated on the front of the chest in the human female and some other mammals; *broadly* a discrete mammary gland **2** the fore part of the body between the neck and the abdomen ☞ MEAT **3** sthg (e g a swelling or curve) resembling a breast **4** the seat of emotion and thought; the bosom – fml [ME *brest,* fr OE *brēost*; akin to OHG *brust* breast, Russ *bryukho* belly]

²breast *vt* **1** to contend with resolutely; confront ⟨~ *the rush-hour traffic*⟩ **2a** to meet or lean against with the breast or front ⟨*the swimmer* ~ed *the waves*⟩ **b** to thrust the chest against ⟨*the sprinter* ~ed *the tape*⟩ **3** *chiefly Br* to climb, ascend

'breast,bone /-,bohn/ *n* the sternum ☞ ANATOMY

'breast-,feed *vt* to feed (a baby) with the milk from the breast rather than a bottle

'breast,plate /-,playt/ *n* **1** a metal plate worn as defensive armour for the chest **2** PLASTRON 2

'breast,stroke /-,strohk/ *n* a swimming stroke executed on the front by thrusting the arms forwards while kicking outwards and backwards with the legs, then sweeping the arms backwards – **breast-stroker** *n*

breastsummer /'bres(t)səmə/ *n* a bressumer [¹*breast* + ⁴*summer*]

'breast,work /-,wuhk/ *n* a temporary fortification, usu consisting of a low parapet

breath /breth/ *n* **1a** a slight fragrance or smell **b** a slight indication; a suggestion ⟨*the faintest ~ of scandal*⟩ **2a** the faculty of breathing **b** an act of breathing **c** opportunity or time to breathe; respite **3** a slight movement of air **4** air inhaled and exhaled in breathing **5** spirit, animation [ME *breth,* fr OE *brǣth*; akin to OHG *brādam* breath, OE *beorma* yeast – more at BARM] – **out of breath** breathing very rapidly (e g from strenuous exercise) – **under one's breath** in a whisper

breathalyse *also* **breathalyze** /'brethə,liez/ *vt* to test (e g a driver) for the level of alcohol in exhaled breath [back-formation fr *breathalyser*]

'breatha,lyser *also* **breathalyzer** /-,liezə/ *n* a device used to test the alcohol content in the blood of a motorist, usu consisting of a plastic bag into which the subject blows through crystals which turn green if the alcohol level is too high [*breath* + an*alyse* + ²*-er*]

breathe /breedh/ *vi* **1** to draw air into and expel it from the lungs **2** to live **3** to pause and rest before continuing **4** *of wind* to blow softly **5** *of wine* to be exposed to the beneficial effects of air after being kept in an airtight container (e g a bottle) ~ *vt* **1a** to send *out* by exhaling ⟨~d *garlic over him*⟩ **b** to instil (as if) by breathing ⟨~ *new life into the movement*⟩ **2a** to utter, express ⟨*don't ~ a word of it to anyone*⟩ **b** to make manifest; display ⟨*the novel* ~s *despair*⟩ **3** to allow (e g a horse) to rest after exertion **4** to inhale [ME *brethen,* fr *breth*] – **breathe down someone's neck** to keep sby under constant or too close surveillance ⟨*parents always* breathing down his neck⟩ – **breathe easily/freely** to enjoy relief (e g from pressure or danger)

breather /'breedhə/ *n* **1** a small vent in an otherwise airtight enclosure (e g a crankcase) **2** a break in activity for rest or relief – infml [BREATHE + ²-ER]

breathing /'breedhing/ *n* either of the marks ʻ and ʼ used in writing Greek to indicate aspiration or its absence

'breathing ,space *n* a pause in a period of activity, esp for rest and recuperation

breathless /'brethlis/ *adj* **1** not breathing; *esp* holding one's breath due to excitement or suspense **2a** gasping; OUT OF BREATH **b** gripping, intense ⟨~ *tension*⟩ **3** without any breeze; stuffy ⟨*a ~ summer's afternoon*⟩ – **breathlessly** *adv,* **breathlessness** *n*

'breath,taking /-,tayking/ *adj* **1** making one breathless **2** exciting, thrilling ⟨*a ~ stock car race*⟩ – **breathtakingly** *adv*

'breath ,test *n, Br* a test made with a breathalyser

breathy /'brethi/ *adj* characterized or accompanied by the audible passage of breath – **breathily** *adv,* **breathiness** *n*

breccia /'breki·ə, 'brechi·ə/ *n* a rock consisting of angular fragments embedded in sand, clay, etc [It]

Brechtian /'brekhti·ən/ *adj* combining left-wing political orientation with irony and avant-garde dramatic technique [Bertolt *Brecht* †1956 G dramatist]

breech /breech/ *n* **1** the buttocks **2** the part of a firearm at the rear of the barrel [ME, breeches, fr OE *brēc,* pl of *brōc* leg covering; akin to OHG *bruoh* breeches, OE *brecan* to break]

breech birth *n* a birth in which the rear end of the baby appears first

'breech,block /-,blok/ *n* the block that closes the rear of the barrel against the force of the charge in breech-loading firearms

breech delivery *n* BREECH BIRTH

breeches /'brichiz, 'breechiz/ *n pl* **1** knee-length trousers, usu closely fastened at the lower edges **2** jodhpurs that are baggy at the thigh and close fitting and fastened with buttons from the knee to the ankle [ME – more at BREECH]

breeches buoy *n* a seat in the form of a pair of canvas breeches hung from a life buoy running on a rope leading to a place of safety for use in rescue at sea

ˈbreech,loader /-ˌlohdə/ *n* a firearm that is loaded at the breech – **breech-loading** *adj*

¹breed /breed/ *vb* **bred** /bred/ *vt* **1a** to produce (offspring) by hatching or gestation **b** to rear; BRING UP 1 ⟨*born and* bred *in Somerset*⟩ **2** to produce, engender ⟨*despair often* ~s *violence*⟩ **3** to propagate (plants or animals) sexually and usu under controlled conditions **4** to inculcate by training ⟨~ *good behaviour*⟩ **5** to produce (a fissile element) in a nuclear chain reaction ~ *vi* **1** to produce offspring by sexual union **2** to propagate animals or plants [ME *breden*, fr OE *brēdan*; akin to OE *brōd* brood] – **breeder** *n*

²breed *n* **1** a group of animals or plants, often specially selected, visibly similar in most characteristics **2** race, lineage **3** class, kind ⟨*a new* ~ *of radicals*⟩

breeder reactor /ˈbreedə/ *n* a nuclear reactor in which more radioactive fuel is produced than is consumed ☞ ENERGY

breeding /ˈbreeding/ *n* **1** ancestry **2** behaviour; *esp* that showing good manners **3** the sexual propagation of plants or animals

ˈbreeding ˌground *n* a place or set of circumstances favourable to the propagation of certain ideas, movements, etc

breeks /breeks/ *n pl, chiefly Scot* breeches [ME (northern) *breke*, fr OE *brēc*]

¹breeze /breez/ *n* **1** a light gentle wind; *also* a wind of between 4 and 31 mph **2** a slight disturbance or quarrel – infml **3** *chiefly NAm* sthg easily done; a cinch – infml [MF *brise* NE wind, perh alter. of *bise* cold N wind] – **breezeless** *adj*

²breeze *vi* **1** to come *in* or *into*, or move *along*, swiftly and airily ⟨*she* ~d *in as if nothing had happened*⟩ **2** to make progress quickly and easily ⟨~ *through the books*⟩ – infml

³breeze *n* ashy residue from the making of coke or charcoal [prob modif of F *braise* cinders]

ˈbreeze-ˌblock *n* a rectangular building block made of breeze mixed with sand and cement

breezy /ˈbreezi/ *adj* **1** windy, fresh **2** brisk, lively **3** insouciant, airy – **breezily** *adv*, **breeziness** *n*

bremsstrahlung /ˈbrem,s(h)trahləng/ *n* the electromagnetic radiation produced by the sudden slowing down of a charged particle in an intense electric field [G, lit., decelerated radiation]

ˈBren ˌgun /bren/ *n* a gas-operated magazine-fed light machine gun [*Br*no, city in Czechoslovakia + *En*field, town in England]

ˌbrent ˈgoose /brent/ *also* **brant** /brant/ *n* any of several small dark geese that breed in the Arctic and migrate southwards [origin unknown]

bressumer /ˈbresəmə/ *n* a large supporting beam set across an opening (e g a fireplace) [alter. of *breastsummer*]

brethren /ˈbredhrin/ *pl of* BROTHER – chiefly in fml address or in referring to the members of a profession, society, or sect

Breton /ˈbret(ə)n/ *n* **1** a native or inhabitant of Brittany **2** the Celtic language of the Bretons ☞ LANGUAGE [F, fr ML *Briton-*, *Brito*, fr L, Briton] – **Breton** *adj*

breve /breev/ *n* **1** a curved mark ˘ used to indicate a short vowel or a short or unstressed syllable ☞ SYMBOL **2** a note equal in time value to 2 semibreves or 4 minims ☞ MUSIC [L, neut of *brevis* brief – more at ¹BRIEF]

¹brevet /ˈbrevit/ *n* a commission giving a military officer higher nominal rank than that for which he receives pay [ME, an official message, fr MF, fr OF, dim. of *bref*, *brief* letter – more at ²BRIEF]

²brevet *vt* **-tt-, -t-** to confer a usu specified rank on by brevet

breviary /ˈbrevi·əri, ˈbree-, -yəri/ *n*, *often cap* **1** a book containing the prayers, hymns, psalms, and readings for the canonical hours **2** DIVINE OFFICE [L *breviarium*, fr *brevis* – more at ¹BRIEF]

brevity /ˈbrevəti/ *n* **1** shortness of duration; the quality of being brief **2** expression in few words; conciseness [L *brevitas*, fr *brevis*]

¹brew /brooh/ *vt* **1** to prepare (e g beer or ale) by steeping, boiling, and fermentation or by infusion and fermentation **2** to contrive, plot – often + *up* ⟨~ *up a plan*⟩ **3** to prepare (e g tea) by infusion in hot water ~ *vi* **1** to brew beer or ale **2** to be in the process of formation ⟨*a storm is* ~ing *in the east*⟩ – often + *up* **3** *chiefly Br* to undergo infusion ⟨*left the tea to* ~⟩ [ME *brewen*, fr OE *brēowan*; akin to L *fervēre* to boil – more at ²BURN] – **brewer** *n*

²brew *n* **1a** a brewed beverage **b(1)** an amount brewed at once **(2)** the quality of what is brewed ⟨*likes a nice strong* ~⟩ **c** a product of brewing **2** the process of brewing

ˌbrewer's ˈdroop /ˈbrooh·əz/ *n, Br* an inability to achieve penile erection after drinking too much alcohol – slang

brewer's yeast *n* a yeast used in brewing and as a source of vitamins of the B complex

brewery /ˈbrooh·əri/ *n* an establishment in which beer or ale is brewed

ˈBrewster ˌsessions /ˈbroohstə/ *n pl* the annual sittings of magistrates at which licences to sell alcoholic drink are issued or renewed [arch *brewster* (brewer)]

brew up *vi, Br* to make tea

¹briar /ˈbrie·ə/ *n* ¹BRIER

²briar *n* **1** ²BRIER **2** a tobacco pipe made from the root of a brier

¹bribe /brieb/ *vt* to induce or influence (as if) by bribery ~ *vi* to practise bribery – **bribable** *adj*, **briber** *n*

²bribe *n* sthg, esp money, given or promised to influence the judgment or conduct of a person [ME, something stolen, fr MF, bread given to a beggar]

bribery /ˈbrieb(ə)ri/ *n* the act or practice of giving or taking a bribe

bric-a-brac /ˈbrik ə ˌbrak/ *n* miscellaneous small articles, usu of ornamental or sentimental value; curios [F *bric-à-brac*]

¹brick /brik/ *n* **1** a usu rectangular unit for building or paving purposes, typically not exceeding 215mm x 102mm x 65mm (about 8in × 3¾in × 2¼in) and made of moist clay hardened by heat ☞ BUILDING **2** a rectangular compressed mass (e g of ice cream) **3** a reliable stout hearted person; a stalwart ⟨*Angela, you're a real* ~⟩ – infml [ME *bryke*, fr MF *brique*, fr MD *bricke*; akin to OE *brecan* to break]

²brick *vt* to close, face, or pave with bricks – usu + *up* ⟨~ed *up a disused entrance*⟩

ˈbrick,bat /-ˌbat/ *n* **1** a fragment of a hard material (e g a brick); *esp* one used as a missile **2** a critical remark

'brick,field /-,feeld/ *n, Br* a place where bricks are made

brickie /'briki/ *n* a bricklayer – infml

'brick,layer /-,layə/ *n* a person who is employed to lay bricks – **bricklaying** *n*

,brick 'red *adj or n* reddish brown

'brick,work /-,wuhk/ *n* (the part of) a structure made from bricks and mortar ☞ BUILDING

'brick,yard /-,yahd/ *n* a brickfield

bridal /'briedl/ *adj* of or for a bride or wedding; nuptial

bride /bried/ *n* a woman at the time of her wedding [ME, fr OE *brȳd*; akin to OHG *brūt* bride]

'bride,groom /-,groohm, -,groom/ *n* a man at the time of his wedding [ME *bridegome*, fr OE *brȳdguma*; akin to OHG *brūtigomo* bridegroom; both fr a prehistoric NGmc-WGmc compound whose constituents are represented by OE *brȳd* & by OE *guma* man – more at HOMAGE]

'brides,maid /-,mayd/ *n* an unmarried girl or woman who attends a bride

[1]**bridge** /brij/ *n* **1a** a structure spanning a depression or obstacle and supporting a roadway, railway, canal, or path **b** a time, place, or means of connection or transition **2a** the upper bony part of the nose **b** an arch serving to raise the strings of a musical instrument **c** a raised platform on a ship from which it is directed **d** the support for a billiards or snooker cue formed esp by the hand **3a** sthg (e g a partial denture permanently attached to adjacent natural teeth) that fills a gap **b** a connection (e g an atom or bond) that joins 2 different parts of a molecule (e g opposite sides of a ring) [ME *brigge*, fr OE *brycg*; akin to OHG *brucka* bridge, OSlav *brŭvŭno* beam]

[2]**bridge** *vt* to make a bridge over or across; *also* to cross (e g a river) by a bridge – **bridgeable** *adj*

[3]**bridge** *n* any of various card games for usu 4 players in 2 partnerships in which players bid for the right to name a trump suit, and in which the hand of the declarer's partner is exposed and played by the declarer; *specif* CONTRACT BRIDGE [alter. of earlier *biritch*, of unknown origin]

'bridge,head /-,hed/ *n* **1a** a fortification protecting the end of a bridge nearest an enemy **b** the area round the end of a bridge **2** an advanced position, usu beyond a bridge, (to be) seized in hostile territory as a foothold for further advance

,bridge 'roll *n* a small finger-shaped soft roll [prob fr [1]*bridge*]

'bridge,work /-,wuhk/ *n* a dental bridge

'bridging ,loan /'brijing/ *n* a short-term loan made to sby awaiting finalization of a long-term loan or mortgage

[1]**bridle** /'briedl/ *n* **1** a framework of leather straps buckled together round the head of a draught or riding animal, including the bit and reins, used to direct and control it **2** a length of secured cable, esp on a boat, to which a second cable can be attached (e g for mooring) **3** a curb, restraint ⟨*set a ~ on his power*⟩ [ME *bridel*, fr OE *brīdel*; akin to OE *bregdan* to move quickly – more at BRAID]

[2]**bridle** *vb* **bridling** /'briedling/ *vt* **1** to put a bridle on **2** to restrain or control (as if) with a bridle ⟨*you must learn to ~ your tongue*⟩ ~ *vi* to show hostility or resentment (e g because of an affront), esp by drawing back the head and chin

'bridle ,path *n* a track or right of way suitable for horseback riding

'bridle,way /-,way/ BRIDLE PATH

bridoon /bri'doohn/ *n* a light snaffle bit used esp with a curb in a double bridle [F *bridon*, fr *bride* bridle]

Brie /bree/ *n* a large round cream-coloured soft cheese ripened through bacterial action [F, fr *Brie*, district in France]

[1]**brief** /breef/ *adj* **1** short in duration or extent **2** in few words; concise [ME *bref, breve*, fr MF *brief*, fr L *brevis*; akin to OHG *murg* short, Gk *brachys*] – **briefly** *adv*, **briefness** *n*

[2]**brief** *n* **1** a papal directive, less binding than a bull **2a** a synopsis, summary **b(1)** a statement of a client's case drawn up for the instruction of counsel **(2)** a case, or piece of employment, given to a barrister **c** a set of instructions outlining what is required, and usu setting limits to one's powers (e g in negotiating) ⟨*her ~ was to reduce British payments*⟩ **3** *pl* short close-fitting pants ☞ GARMENT [ME *bref*, fr MF, fr ML *brevis*, fr LL, summary, fr L *brevis*, adj] – **in brief** in a few words; briefly

[3]**brief** *vt* **1** to provide with final instructions or necessary information ⟨~ *journalists about the situation*⟩ **2** *Br* to retain (a barrister) as legal counsel

'brief,case /-,kays/ *n* a flat rectangular case for carrying papers or books

briefing /'breefing/ *n* (a meeting to give out) final instructions or necessary information

[1]**brier, briar** /'brie·ə/ *n* a plant with a woody, thorny, or prickly stem [ME *brere*, fr OE *brēr*] – **briery** *adj*

[2]**brier, briar** *n* a heath of S Europe with a root used for making pipes [F *bruyère* heath, fr (assumed) VL *brucaria*, fr LL *brucus* heather, of Celt origin; akin to OIr *froech* heather; akin to Gk *ereikē* heather]

[1]**brig** /brig/ *n* a 2-masted square-rigged sailing vessel [short for *brigantine*]

[2]**brig** *n* a prison in the US Navy [prob fr [1]*brig*]

[1]**brigade** /bri'gayd/ *n* **1** a large section of an army usu composed of a headquarters, several fighting units (e g infantry battalions or armoured regiments), and supporting units **2** an organized or uniformed group of people (e g firemen) [F, fr It *brigata*, fr *brigare*]

[2]**brigade** *vt* to form or unite into a brigade

brigadier /,brigə'diə/ *n* ☞ RANK [F, fr *brigade*]

,brigadier 'general *n* ☞ RANK

brigalow /'brigəloh/ *n, Austr* any of several species of acacia forming thick scrub [native name in Australia]

brigand /'brigənd/ *n* one who lives by plunder, usu as a member of a group; a bandit [ME *brigaunt*, fr MF *brigand*, fr OIt *brigante*, fr *brigare* to fight, fr *briga* strife, of Celt origin; akin to OIr *brig* strength] – **brigandage** *n*, **brigandism** *n*

brigandine /'brigan,deen, -din/ *n* medieval body armour of mail or plate [ME, fr MF, fr *brigand*]

brigantine /'brigən,teen/ *n* a 2-masted square-rigged sailing vessel differing from a brig in not carrying a square mainsail [MF *brigantin*, fr OIt *brigantino*, fr *brigante*]

bright /briet/ *adj* **1a** radiating or reflecting light; shining **b** radiant with happiness ⟨~ *faces*⟩ **2** *of a colour* of high saturation or brilliance **3a** intelligent, clever **b** lively, charming ⟨*be ~ and jovial among your guests* – Shak⟩ **c** promising, talented [ME, fr

OE *beorht*; akin to OHG *beraht* bright, Skt *bhrājate* it shines] – **bright** *adv*, **brightly** *adv*, **brightness** *n*

,bright and 'early *adv* very early in the morning – infml

brighten /'brietn/ *vb* to make or become bright or brighter – often + *up* – **brightener** *n*

bright lights *n pl* (*the* false gaiety and allure of) an urban area offering a variety of entertainments

'Bright's di,sease /'briets/ *n* any of several kidney diseases marked by albumin in the urine [Richard *Bright* †1858 E physician]

'bright,work /-,wuhk/ *n* polished or plated metalwork

brill /bril/ *n, pl* **brill** (a European flatfish related to) the turbot [perh fr Corn *brȳthel* mackerel]

[1]**brilliant** /'brilyənt, -li·ənt/ *adj* **1** very bright; glittering **2a** striking, distinctive ⟨*a ~ example*⟩ **b** having great intellectual ability **3** of high quality; good – infml [F *brillant*, prp of *briller* to shine, fr It *brillare*, prob fr *brillo* beryl, fr L *beryllus*] – **brilliance** *n*, **brilliancy** *n*, **brilliantly** *adv*

[2]**brilliant** *n* a gem, esp a diamond, cut with numerous facets for maximum brilliance

brilliantine /'brilyən,teen/ *n* a preparation for making hair glossy and smooth

[1]**brim** /brim/ *n* **1** the edge or rim of a hollow vessel, a natural depression, or a cavity **2** the projecting rim of a hat [ME *brimme*; akin to MHG *brem* edge] – **brimless** *adj*

[2]**brim** *vi* **-mm-** to be full to the brim

brimful /,brim'fool/ *adj* full to the brim; ready to overflow

-brimmed /-brimd/ *comb form* (→ *adj*) having (such) a brim ⟨*a wide*-brimmed *hat*⟩

brim over *vi* to overflow a brim

brimstone /'brim,stohn/ *n* SULPHUR 1 [ME *brinston*, prob fr *birnen* to burn + *ston* stone]

brindle /'brindl/ *n* a brindled colour [*brindled, brindle*, adj]

brindled /'brind(ə)ld/ *adj* having obscure dark streaks or flecks on a grey or tawny ground [alter. of arch *brinded*, fr ME *brende, brended*; prob akin to OE *brand* brand, fire – more at BRAND]

[1]**brine** /brien/ *n* water (almost) saturated with common salt [ME, fr OE *brȳne*; akin to MD *brīne* brine, L *fricare* to rub – more at FRICTION] – **briny** *adj*, **brininess** *n*

[2]**brine** *vt* to treat with brine (e g by soaking)

Bri'nell ,number /bri'nel/ *n* a number expressing the hardness of a metal or alloy [Johann *Brinell* †1925 Sw engineer]

bring /bring/ *vt* **brought** /brawt/ **1a** to convey (sthg) to a place or person; come with or cause to come **b(1)** to attract ⟨*his screams* brought *the neighbours*⟩ **(2)** to force, compel ⟨*cannot ~ myself to do it*⟩ **(3)** to cause to achieve a particular condition ⟨*~ water to the boil*⟩ **2a** to cause to occur, lead to ⟨*winter will ~ snow and ice*⟩ **b** to initiate ⟨*~ legal action*⟩ **c** to offer, present ⟨*~ an argument*⟩ **3** PREFER 3 ⟨*~ a charge*⟩ **4** to sell for (a price) ⟨*the car should ~ £800*⟩ [ME *bringen*, fr OE *bringan*; akin to OHG *bringan* to bring, W *hebrwng* to accompany] – **bringer** *n* – **bring home** to make unmistakably clear to – **bring to bear 1** to put to use ⟨bring *knowledge* to bear *on the problem*⟩ **2** to apply, exert ⟨bring *pressure* to bear *on the management*⟩ – **bring to book 1** to put in a position in which one must answer for one's acts **2** to cause to be reproved – **bring to light** to disclose, reveal – **bring to mind** to cause to be recalled – **bring up the rear** to come last

bring about *vt* to cause to take place; effect

bring down *vt* **1** to cause to fall or come down **2** to kill by shooting ⟨brought *the bear* down *with one shot*⟩ **3** to reduce **4** to cause to be depressed – usu pass – **bring the house down** to win the enthusiastic approval of the audience

bring forth *vt* **1** to bear ⟨brought forth *fruit*⟩ **2** to give birth to; produce **3** to offer, present ⟨brought forth *arguments to justify her conduct*⟩

bring forward *vt* **1** to produce to view; introduce **2** to carry (a total) forward (e g to the top of the next page)

bring in *vt* **1** to produce as profit or return ⟨*this will* bring in *the money*⟩ **2** to introduce **3** to pronounce (a verdict) in court **4** to earn ⟨*she* brings in *a good salary*⟩

bring off *vt* to carry to a successful conclusion; achieve, accomplish

bring on *vt* **1** to cause to appear or occur **2** to improve, help

bring out *vt* **1** to make clear **2a** to present to the public; *specif* to publish **b** to introduce (a young woman) formally to society **3** to utter **4** to cause (sby) to be afflicted with a rash, spots, etc – usu + *in* **5** to encourage to be less reticent – esp in *bring somebody out of him-/herself* **6** *chiefly Br* to instruct or cause (workers) to go on strike

bring round *vt* **1** to cause to adopt a particular opinion or course of action; persuade **2** to restore to consciousness; revive

bring to *vt* **1** to cause (a boat) to lie to or come to a standstill **2** BRING ROUND 2

bring up *vt* **1** to educate, rear **2** to cause to stop suddenly **3** to bring to attention; introduce **4** to vomit

brinjal /'brinjəl/ *n* an aubergine [Pg *bringella, beringela*, fr Ar *bādhinjān*, fr Per *bādingān*]

brink /bringk/ *n* **1** an edge; *esp* the edge at the top of a steep place **2** *the* verge, onset ⟨*on the ~ of war*⟩ [ME, prob of Scand origin; akin to ON *brekka* slope; akin to L *front-, frons* forehead]

brinkmanship /'bringkmən,ship/ *n* the art of going to the very brink of conflict, danger, etc before drawing back [*brink* + *-manship* (as in *horsemanship*)]

briny /'brieni/ *n* (the water of) *the* sea [*briny*, adj, fr *brine* + *-y*]

brio /'bree·oh/ *n* enthusiastic vigour; vivacity, verve [It]

brioche /bree'osh/ *n* a light slightly sweet bread roll made with a rich yeast dough [F, fr MF dial., fr *brier* to knead, of Gmc origin; akin to OHG *brehhan* to break – more at BREAK]

briquette, briquet /bri'ket/ *n* a compacted block, usu of coal-dust [F *briquette*, dim. of *brique* brick]

brisk /brisk/ *adj* **1** keenly alert; lively **2** fresh, invigorating ⟨*~ weather*⟩ **3** energetic, quick ⟨*a ~ pace*⟩ **4** sharp in tone or manner – chiefly euph [prob modif of MF *brusque* – more at BRUSQUE] – **briskly** *adv*, **briskness** *n*

brisket /'briskit/ *n* a joint of beef cut from the breast; *broadly* the breast or lower chest of a 4-legged animal ☞ MEAT [ME *brusket*; akin to OE *brēost* breast]

brisling, bristling /'brizling, 'bris-/ *n* a small herring that resembles a sardine [Norw *brisling*, fr LG *bretling*, fr *bret* broad; akin to OE *brād* broad]

[1]**bristle** /'brisl/ *n* a short stiff coarse hair or filament [ME *bristil*, fr *brust* bristle, fr OE *byrst*; akin to OHG *burst* bristle, L *fastigium* top]

[2]**bristle** *vb* **bristling** /'brisling, 'brisl·ing/ *vi* **1a** to rise and stand stiffly erect ⟨*quills* bristling *in all directions*⟩ **b** to raise the bristles (e g in anger) **2** to take on an aggressive attitude or appearance (e g in response to a slight) **3** to be filled or thickly covered (*with* sthg suggestive of bristles) ~ *vt* **1** to provide with bristles **2** to make bristly; ruffle

'bristle,tail /-,tayl/ *n* any of various wingless insects with 2 or 3 slender bristles at the hind end of the body

bristly /'brisli/ *adj* **1a** consisting of or resembling bristles **b** thickly covered with bristles **2** tending to bristle easily; belligerent

'Bristol ,fashion /'bristl/ *adj* in good order; spick-and-span – usu in *all shipshape and Bristol fashion* [*Bristol*, England, important seaport]

'bristols *n pl, Br* breasts – vulg [rhyming slang *Bristol (City)* titty, breast]

Brit /brit/ *n* a British person – infml

Bri'tannia ,metal /bri'tanyə/ *n* a silver-white alloy of tin, antimony, and copper [*Britannia*, poetic name for Great Britain, fr L]

Britannia silver *n* silver of at least 95.84 per cent purity

Britannic /bri'tanik/ *adj* British – fml ⟨*Her ~ Majesty*⟩

britches /'brichiz/ *n pl* breeches

[1]**British** /'british/ *n* **1** the Celtic language of the ancient Britons **2** *pl in constr* the people of Britain **3** *chiefly NAm* English as typically spoken and written in Britain [ME *Bruttische* of Britain, fr OE *Brettisc*, of Celt origin; akin to W *Brython* Briton]

[2]**British** *adj* of Britain, its people, or their language ☞ HISTORY – **Britishness** *n*

Britisher /'britishə/ *n, chiefly NAm* BRITON 2

,British 'Summer ,Time *n* time 1 hour ahead of Greenwich Mean Time that is used in Britain during the summer and is the same as Central European Time – compare DAYLIGHT SAVING TIME

,British 'thermal ,unit *n* the quantity of heat required to raise the temperature of 1lb of water by 1°F under standard conditions ☞ UNIT

Briton /'brit(ə)n/ *n* **1** a member of any of the peoples inhabiting Britain before the Anglo-Saxon invasions **2** a native, inhabitant, or subject of Britain [ME *Breton*, fr MF & L; MF, fr L *Briton-*, *Brito*, of Celt origin; akin to W *Brython*]

brittle /'britl/ *adj* **1a** easily broken or cracked **b** insecure, frail ⟨*a ~ friendship*⟩ **2** easily hurt or offended; sensitive ⟨*a ~ personality*⟩ **3** sharp, tense ⟨*a ~ sound*⟩ **4** lacking warmth or depth of feeling ⟨*~ gaiety*⟩ [ME *britil*; akin to OE *brēotan* to break, Skt *bhrūna* embryo] – **brittlely** /'britl·i/ *adv*, **brittleness** *n*

brittle star *n* any of a subclass or class of starfish that have slender flexible arms

[1]**broach** /brohch/ *n* **1** any of various pointed or tapered tools: e g **a** a bit for boring holes **b** a tool for tapping casks **2** a spit for roasting meat [ME *broche*, fr MF, fr (assumed) VL *brocca*, fr L, fem of *broccus* projecting]

[2]**broach** *vt* **1a** to pierce (a container, esp a cask or bottle) prior to using the contents; tap **b** to open up or break into (e g a store or stock of sthg) and start to use **2** to open up (a subject) for discussion

[3]**broach** *vi*, *of a boat* to change direction dangerously, esp so as to lie broadside to the waves – usu + *to* ~ *vt* to cause (a boat) to broach [perh fr [2]*broach*]

[1]**broad** /brawd/ *adj* **1a** having ample extent from side to side or between limits ⟨*~ shoulders*⟩ **b** in width; across ⟨*made the path 10 feet ~*⟩ **2** extending far and wide; spacious ⟨*the ~ plains*⟩ **3a** open, full – esp in *broad daylight* **b** plain, obvious ⟨*a ~ hint*⟩ **4** marked by lack of restraint or delicacy; coarse **5a** liberal, tolerant **b** widely applicable or applied; general **6** relating to the main points ⟨*~ outlines*⟩ **7** dialectal, esp in pronunciation **8** *of a vowel* open – used specif of *a* pronounced as /ah/ [ME *brood*, fr OE *brād*; akin to OHG *breit* broad] – **broadly** *adv*

[2]**broad** *adv* in a broad manner; fully

[3]**broad** *n* **1** the broad part ⟨*~ of his back*⟩ **2** *often cap, Br* a large area of fresh water formed by the broadening of a river – usu pl; used chiefly with reference to such formations found in E Anglia **3** a prostitute – slang **4** *chiefly NAm* a woman – slang

,broad 'arrow *n* **1** an arrow with a flat barbed head **2** *Br* a mark like a broad arrow that identifies government property, including clothing formerly worn by convicts

,broad 'bean *n* (the large flat edible seed of) a widely cultivated Old World leguminous plant

[1]**broadcast** /'brawd,kahst/ *adj* cast or scattered in all directions [[2]*broad* + *cast*, fr pp of [1]*cast*]

[2]**broadcast** *n* **1** the act of transmitting by radio or television **2** a single radio or television programme *USE* ☞ TELEVISION

[3]**broadcast** *vb* **broadcast** *also* **broadcasted** *vt* **1** to scatter or sow (seed) broadcast **2** to make widely known **3** to transmit as a broadcast, esp for widespread reception ☞ TELEVISION ~ *vi* **1** to transmit a broadcast **2** to speak or perform on a broadcast programme – **broadcaster** *n*

[4]**broadcast** *adv* to or over a broad area

,Broad 'Church *adj* of 19th-c liberal Anglicanism

'broad,cloth /-,kloth/ *n* a twilled napped woollen or worsted fabric with a smooth lustrous finish and dense texture

broaden /'brawdn/ *vb vb* to make or become broad

'broad ,jump *n, NAm* LONG JUMP

'broad,leaf /-,leef/ *adj* broad-leaved

,broad-'leaved *adj* having broad leaves; *specif, of a tree* not coniferous

'broad,loom /-,loohm/ *n or adj* (a carpet) woven on a wide loom

,broad-'minded *adj* tolerant of varied views, unconventional behaviour, etc; liberal – **broad-mindedly** *adv*, **broad-mindedness** *n*

'broad,sheet /-,sheet/ *n* **1** a large sheet of paper printed on 1 side only; *also* sthg (e g an advertisement) printed on a broadsheet **2** a newspaper whose page depth is the full size of a rotary press plate – compare TABLOID

[1]**'broad,side** /-,sied/ *n* **1** the side of a ship above the waterline **2** a broadsheet **3a** (the simultaneous firing of) all the guns on 1 side of a ship **b** a forceful verbal or written attack

[2]**broadside** *adv* with the broadside or broader side towards a given object or point

A TABLE OF MAJOR EVENTS IN BRITISH HISTORY

Period	Date	Event
PRE-ROMAN TIMES	**10,000 BC**	Ice cap recedes. Land bridge between Britain and Continent covered with water.
		Old Stone Age (Palaeolithic) culture – reindeer hunting.
	9000–8000	*Middle Stone Age (Mesolithic) culture – deer hunting, shaped flints, oxen.*
	4500 (ca)	*Malemose (Mesolithic) culture.*
	2700	*Windmill Hill culture (Neolithic). Slash & burn farming.* Indo-Europeans enter S.E. Britain.
		Megaliths – Stonehenge. Ancestors of Picts in Scotland. *Dead buried in barrows.*
	1800	*Bronze Age men arrive. Round burial mounds. 'Iberian' type.*
		'Beaker People' distinctive pottery.
	1000	
	800	*Some immigration in S.E. England by early Celtic tribes.*
		Cremation of dead. Aryan languages.
		Ploughs.
	500	*Hallstatt Celts (early Iron Age) enter S.E. England.*
		Two language types. 'Goidels' (ancestors of Irish, Scottish Highlanders, Manx), 'Brythons' (ancestors of Welsh and Cornish).
	375	*Hallstatt Celts occupy all southern England. Trade in tin with Continent.*
	323	*Hallstatt Celts in all England. 'Iberians' still dominate Scotland, Ireland.*
	301	*Hallstatt Celts move into Scotland.*
	250	*Hallstatt Celts move further into Scotland.*
	220	*Hallstatt Celts reach Highlands. La Tène Celts (same as Gauls) enter S.E. England.*
	190	*La Tène Celts dominate south of England. Hallstatt Celts dominate all but east Highlands & Ireland.*
	150	*Hallstatt Celts squeezed by Ligurian resurgence from Highlands, La Tène occupation of Lowlands.*
	75	*La Tène Celts in England. 'Iberians' in Scotland and Ireland.*
	55	Julius Caesar crosses to Britain from Gaul to reconnoitre for future invasion.
	54	Caesar's second visit.
	44	*Belgae (a strong confederation of Gauls) occupy S.E. England – heavy plough.*
		Much trade with province of Gaul. Ford at site of London develops into a trading post after Claudian conquest.
AD1		
ROMAN OCCUPATION BEGINS	**43**	Emperor Claudius conquers east and south. Defeats Caractacus and captures Camulodunum (Colchester).
	47	Governor of Britain establishes frontier from Severn to Trent.
	51	Caractacus defeated in Wales.
	61	Boudicca (Boadicea) leads Iceni tribe in rebellion.
	62	Boudicca defeated.
	68	Tribe of Brigantes defects.
	74	Brigantes defeated.
	78	Wales finally subjugated.
	81–84	Agricola builds fortresses between Forth and Clyde to contain Picts.
	99–110	Isca (Exeter), Deva (Chester), and Eboracum (York) – fortresses rebuilt in stone.
100		
		Romans established five self-governing cities (St. Albans, Colchester, Lincoln, Gloucester, and York) and divided the rest of the country into tribal districts ruled by loyal Celtic chiefs, where possible.
	117	Revolt in northern Britain.
	120	Hadrian visits Britain, starts Hadrian's Wall from Solway to Tyne.
	139–42	Romans advance north, build Antonine Wall from Forth to Clyde.
	155–58	Revolt in Scotland put down.
	180	Revolt in Scotland. Antonine Wall broken.
	197	Maeatae overrun Hadrian's Wall. Destroy Eboracum. Romans regain control, rebuild forts.
200		
	205–08	Hadrian's Wall rebuilt. Emperor Severus leads campaign against Caledonians.
	211	Severus dies at Eboracum.
	212	Caracalla divides Britain into two provinces, grants Roman citizenship to all free provincials.
	259–74	Britain forms part of Gallic Empire under Postumus and his successors.
		Religion of Mithras popular with soldiers and merchants.
	287	Carausius, commander of the British fleet, usurps Britain and northern Gaul.
	293	Carausius killed and replaced by Allectus.
	296	Constantius Caesar recaptures Britain, builds up Deva and Eboracum – reorganizes Britain into four provinces.
300		
	306	Emperor Constantius dies at Eboracum.
	313–14	After Edict of Toleration recognized Christian Church, three British bishops attended Council of Arles.
	343–60	Attempts to pacify Picts and Scots.
	364	Raids by Picts, Scots, Attacotti, Saxons.
	367	Invasion by Picts, Scots, Attacotti, Saxon pirates. Count of Saxon Shore killed, Duke of Britain defeated.
	369	Count Theodosius restores Roman control.
	383–88	Revolt by Magnus Maximus. Defeated by Theodosius. Hadrian's Wall overrun and never rebuilt.

☞ HISTORY

400	**406–10**	All Roman legions removed from Britain. British cities must defend themselves.
	432–61?	*St Patrick brings Christianity to Ireland.*
	446	British make final appeal to Rome for protection.
	449	Vortigern invites Hengest and Horsa and other Saxons to help defend Britain against the Picts. Instead, they establish a Jutish kingdom in Kent and many more Saxons enter Britain.
	460–80	Ambrosius Aurelianus, Romano-British leader, keeps Saxons in S.E. England.
	490 (ca)	Arthur, Romano-British leader, defeats Saxons at Mount Badon and delays their westward expansion.
500	**511**	Arthur killed at Battle of Camlann.
	550–90	West Saxons defeat Welsh at Deorham, Gloucestershire but are then checked.
		Christianity survives in Wales throughout this period.
	563	*St Columba brings Irish Christianity to Scotland. Founds monastery at Iona.*
	591	Augustine, a Roman monk, brings Roman Christianity to Kent under King Ethelbert.
	600	First Archbishop of Canterbury.
600	**616**	Northumbrian Saxons separate Britons in Wales from those in the North by winning battle at Chester.
	627	Edwin King of Northumbria is converted to Roman Christianity by Ethelberga and Paulinus from Kent.
		Founding of Edinburgh. Saxons occupy lowlands.
	633	Penda of Mercia, champion of paganism, kills Edwin, but *Irish Christianity takes root in Northumbria under the leadership of Aidan from Iona. He founded Lindisfarne monastery.*
	655	Oswy reunites Northumbria, kills Penda. Mercia accepts Christianity.
	664	Synod of Whitby. Oswy decides that the North will accept the authority of Roman Christianity.
		Cultural flowering of Anglo-Saxon literature – Caedmon the poet. Learning fostered by Theodore of Tarsus, next Archbishop of Canterbury. Latin and Greek scholarship. Schools.
	690	Laws of Ine of Wessex written down.
700	**673–735**	*Venerable Bede writes 'History of the English Church and People' at Jarrow.*
		Heptarchy of the seven Saxon kingdoms takes shape. Northumbria, Mercia, Wessex, Kent, Sussex, East Anglia, Essex. First three are dominant.
	757–96	Offa II rules Mercia. Dyke built as defence from Welsh, Mercia strongest kingdom.
	787	First appearance of Danes at Weymouth.
		Alcuin of York takes English learning to court of Charlemagne.
800	**800**	Century of Viking raids.
	825	Egbert breaks Mercia's power. Wessex now strongest kingdom.
		Saxons have moots to decide on actions. Annual Witanmoots.
	851	Danes attempt major invasion by sea.
	866–71	Danes settle on land and raid on horseback.
	871–900	Alfred the Great.
	877	Danes fail at second invasion attempt at Swanage. Alfred drives them from Exeter.
	878	Alfred defeats Danes, under Guthrum, at Ethandune. Guthrum accepts Christianity and agrees to live in Danelaw by peace of Wedmore. There are further Danish raids by sea, however. *Alfred revives schooling, learning. 'Anglo-Saxon Chronicle' started.*
900	**900–40**	Edward the Elder and Athelstan conquer Danelaw and become first kings of all England, though York not finally defeated until 954.
	937	Athelstan defeats league of Scots, British, and Danes at Brunanburgh.
	959–75	Edgar next strong king. Supports Dunstan's reforms of monasteries, inspired by Clunic reforms in France. Dunstan becomes Archbishop of Canterbury. Unites crown and church interests.
	975–79	Edward the Martyr's short reign ends in murder.
	979–1016	Ethelred the Redeless (Unready) fails to resist new Danish invasions.
1000	**1001**	Danish land tax – Danegeld, is paid.
	1002	Ethelred massacres Danes.
	1003–13	Sweyn Fork-beard raids England in revenge.
	1016	Edmund Ironside elected king after Ethelred dies, but he is defeated by Danes and murdered.
	1016	Canute, King of Denmark, Norway, and Hebrides, becomes King of England – reconciles English and Danes, church and state.
	1031	Malcolm II of Scotland swears allegiance to Canute.
	1036	Canute dies. Succeeded by short reigns of Harthacanute and Harald.
	1042–66	Edward the Confessor. Norman influence increases in England.
		Robert of Jumièges becomes Archbishop of Canterbury and leads Norman party against Godwin, Earl of Wessex.
	1053	Godwin dies. Harold becomes Earl of Wessex.
	1066	Edward dies. Harold elected king by Witan.
		Harold defeats Tostig and Harald Hardrada at Stamford Bridge.
		William, Duke of Normandy, defeats English at Battle of Hastings.

BRITISH ISLES

WILLIAM I

1066

1068 William completes conquest of southern England.

1069 Edgar and Edwin of Northumbria and Morcar of Mercia rebel. William defeats them and lays waste the North.

1070–71 Hereward the Wake stands at Ely, but is defeated.

1070 The Norman Lanfranc becomes Archbishop of Canterbury.

1075 William suppresses Norman barons and consolidates his rule by building castles, granting land to barons who owe duty directly to him.

1086 Salisbury Decree regulates feudal system in England.

1086 Domesday Survey made for taxation.

1087

WILLIAM II 'RUFUS'

1089–93 No Archbishop of Canterbury until Anselm.

1100 William mysteriously killed.

1100

HENRY I

1106 Henry and Anselm compromise on powers of church and state.

Curia Regis and Exchequer become separate.

1120 Henry's legitimate male heir dies at sea.

1128 Council swears allegiance to Matilda, Henry's daughter, wife of Geoffrey Plantagenet.

STEPHEN

1135–54 War of Succession between Stephen and Matilda.

Cistercian monasteries founded, especially in North, on wasteland. Develop sheep farming, later to become basis of England's wool trade.

1153 Peace of Wallingford settles inheritance on Matilda's son.

HENRY II

1154 First Plantagenet king of England.

1154 Thomas à Becket becomes Chancellor. Nicholas Breakspear becomes Adrian IV, only English Pope.

1162 Chancellor Thomas à Becket becomes Archbishop of Canterbury. Becket and Henry quarrel about church authority.

1170 Thomas à Becket murdered.

RICHARD I

1189

1190–93 Richard joins Third Crusade.

1194–98 Hubert Walter rules while Richard is in Normandy.

1199–1200 'Justices of the Peace' begin.

1200

JOHN

1206–13 John struggles with Pope Innocent III about election of Stephen Langdon as Archbishop of Canterbury. After papal interdict of 5 years, John agrees.

HENRY III

1216 Magna Carta establishes basic rights of free man.

Founding of colleges at Oxford and Cambridge during this reign.

1244 Barons demand power to supervise Treasury.

1263 Simon de Montfort reforms Parliament; invites two knights from each shire, two burghers from each town.

1265 Simon de Montfort killed; rebellion crushed.

1272 Wars against French, Scots, Welsh.

EDWARD I

1290 Edward I expels Jews.

1295 'Model Parliament', with representatives from towns and shires, grants money for wars against Scots and French.

1300

EDWARD II

1307 Edward I dies marching against Robert Bruce.

1312 Edward II's favourite, Piers Gaveston, killed by barons who take power.

1322 Edward recovers powers of crown from barons.

1326–27 Queen Isabella and Roger Mortimer, with barons, depose Edward, who is killed.

EDWARD III

1327

1330 Edward III takes full power from Isabella and Mortimer.

Black Death ravages Europe, kills a third of the English.

1351–65 Series of statutes makes England more independent of continental and papal laws. Statute of Labourers fixes wages and prices.

1377 John of Gaunt dominant in Parliament.

RICHARD II

John Wycliffe preaches Lollardry, translates Bible into English.

1381 Peasants' Revolt against taxes, restrictions. Peasants defeated.

1388 *Geoffrey Chaucer writes 'Canterbury Tales'.*

1398–99 Henry Bolingbroke and Richard II struggle for Crown. Richard II captured. Dies in 1400.

HENRY IV

1399 First Lancastrian king of England.

WALES

By 1100 Normans establish Marcher Lords on border.

1194–1240 Llewelyn the Great reconquers Powys.

1263–65 Llewelyn ap Griffith supports Simon de Montfort.

1277–84 Conquest of Wales by Edward I. Castles built to keep power.

1300–1425 *Traditional tales, now called 'Mabinogion' and 'Book of Taliessen', written down.*

SCOTLAND

1100 Scottish kingship was Anglo-Norman.

1124–53 David I invades England during Stephen's wars.

1138 Scots clansmen lose Battle of the Standard.

1290 Succession crisis. Edward I chooses John Balliol.

1297 William Wallace defeats English at Stirling.

1298 English defeat Wallace at Falkirk.

1314 Robert Bruce defeats English at Bannockburn. Becomes king till 1327.

1346 Scots invade England, but lose battle at Neville's Cross. Scots retain independence, and ally with French henceforth.

IRELAND

1014 Brian Boru fails to unite Celts, but stops Normans at Clontarf.

1169–71 Richard de Clare leads adventurers in conquering Ireland, with support of Pope Adrian IV.

1394 Richard II visits Ireland, reforms administration.

1399 Richard II returns to Ireland to crush rebellion.

EUROPE

1087 William killed in Normandy.

1096 Robert, Duke of Normandy, joins First Crusade.

1106 Henry defeats Robert in Normandy and imprisons him.

1113–21 Wars in France.

Henry rules England, Normandy, Brittany, Anjou, Maine, Touraine, Aquitaine (from his wife Eleanor), and Toulouse.

1189 Henry II dies after sons' rebellion.

1199 Richard killed in France.

1202–04 John loses all French possessions except Aquitaine to Philip II of France.

1226 Great Council refuses payment to Pope. Early example of English independence.

Edward makes many attempts to regain French lands.

France supports barons against Edward II.

1337–1453 Hundred Years War between France and England, caused by French support for Scotland, French attacks in Gascony, and interference with English wool trade. Key events to 1399–

1) English victory at Crécy 1346.

2) English capture French King at Poitiers, 1356.

3) Treaty of Brétigny, 1360. England gains S.W. France.

4) War renewed, 1369. Black Prince sacks Limoges 1370. French win back some territories.

1350–72 Sea battles with Spain.

BRITISH ISLES

1400

1400–15 Welsh rebel under Owen Glendower. Gradually worn down.

1406 Parliament gains control of all public grants of money.

1408 Last of three revolts of Percys put down.

HENRY V

1413 Henry has support of Parliament.

Lollards persecuted during this reign.

HENRY VI

1422 Henry V dies, leaving infant son.

Duke of Gloucester becomes Regent.

1445 Henry VI marries Margaret of Anjou as move towards peace with France – she later supports him during Wars of the Roses.

1450 Rivalry between House of Lancaster and York begins.

1453 First attack of mental illness in Henry VI. Duke of York becomes Protector.

1455–85 Wars of the Roses.

1455 First battle in St. Albans.

EDWARD IV

1461

1461 Edward IV defeats Henry at Towton.

1469 *Sir Thomas Malory writes 'Morte d'Arthur'.*

1470 Earl of Warwick restores Henry VI.

1471 Edward defeats Henry at Tewkesbury. Henry killed in the Tower.

1477 *Caxton sets up first printing press in England at Westminster.*

1480 War with Scotland.

EDWARD V

1483

1483 Edward V and his brother Richard, Princes in the Tower, put to death.

RICHARD III

1485 Richard III killed at Bosworth.

HENRY VII

1485 First Tudor king of England.

1486 Henry marries Elizabeth of York.

1487 Henry defeats pretender Lambert Simnel, Star Chamber begins. Henry consolidates power, strengthens courts, raises revenue.

1492–99 Perkin Warbeck tries to gain Crown, supported by Scotland.

1499 *Erasmus visits England.*

1500

1503 James IV of Scotland marries Henry's daughter, Margaret. Attempt at alliance, not successful.

HENRY VIII

1509

1509 Henry marries Catherine of Aragon, to ally with Spain.

1516 *Sir Thomas More writes 'Utopia'.*

1521–33 Henry attempts to divorce Catherine.

1521 Henry starts divorce proceedings against Catherine – protracted negotiations lead to separation from Rome.

1533 Henry marries Anne Boleyn. Thomas Cranmer becomes Archbishop of Canterbury.

1534 Act of Supremacy. Henry becomes head of English Church.

1535 Sir Thomas More and Cardinal Fisher executed.

1536 Dissolution of monasteries begins. Tyndale dies.

1538 *Great Bible issued, in English.*

Henry has four other wives, only one of whom, Jane Seymour, gives him a male heir.

EDWARD VI

1547

1549 *Cranmer publishes 'Book of Common Prayer' – its use is enforced by law.*

1553 Lady Jane Grey, Queen for nine days.

MARY

1553

1554 Wyatt's rebellion in favour of Protestantism suppressed. Mary marries Philip of Spain.

1555 Persecution of Protestants. Cranmer executed.

ELIZABETH I

1558

1559 English Church restored to its former position under Henry VIII.

1568 Mary Queens of Scots imprisoned.

1577–80 *Drake's voyage around the world.*

1581 Jesuit missions to England.

1587 Mary Queen of Scots executed.

1588 English prevent invasion by Spanish Armada.

1590 *Edmund Spenser's 'Faerie Queen' published.*

Cultural flowering at Elizabeth's court.

1599 Earl of Essex fails to put down Irish Rebellion under Earl of Tyrone.

1600 Essex executed.

IRELAND

1487 Yorkist intrigues against Henry VII.

1494 Poyning's Law placed Irish Parliament under English rule.

SCOTLAND

1513 James IV and many nobles killed at Flodden.

1542–67 Reign of Mary Stuart.

1542–59 Regency of Mary of Guise.

1559 Rise of John Knox, Calvinist reformer.

1561–68 Mary Stuart in Scotland. Scots disapprove of her religion and marriages to Darnley and Bothwell.

1567 Mary's son James becomes James VI of Scotland.

1568 Mary flees to England, leaving James in Scotland.

1603 James VI of Scotland becomes James I of England.

EUROPE

1415–53 Second half of Hundred Years War.
Key events –
1) English victories at Harfleur and Agincourt, 1415.
2) Treaty of Troyes gives Henry the French throne 1420.
3) Joan of Arc revives French spirit 1429.
4) French conquer all English-held lands except Calais 1453.

1475 Louis XI grants pension to Edward to obtain peace, but supports Scots in their war.

1493 Pope Alexander VI divides New World between Spain and Portugal with Line of Demarcation.

1512–13 Henry and Wolsey wage war against France.

1517 Luther begins his protest against Rome.

1521 Field of the Cloth of Gold. Henry negotiates with Francis I of France and – separately – with Emperor Charles.

1525 Charles defeats Francis at Pavia. Wolsey's continental adventures unpopular at home.

1547 Peace with France.

1558 Loss of Calais, last French possession.

1572 St Bartholomew's Day Massacre of Protestants in France forces Elizabeth to head the Protestant cause.

1585 Elizabeth briefly assists Dutch rebellion against Hapsburgs. Leicester's expedition defeated.
East India Company founded.

BRITISH ISLES

1600

JAMES I

1601 Poor Law.

1603 First Stuart king of England and Ireland

1605 Gunpowder Plot foiled.

1611 *Authorized version of the Bible.*

1614–21 Parliament suspended. Beginnings of struggle with King.

1616 *William Shakespeare dies.*

Arts: Donne, Suckling, Jonson, Marvell, Herbert, Campion, Inigo Jones.

CHARLES I

1625

1628 Petition of Right limits King's power. Buckingham assassinated.

1629–41 Charles governs without Parliament, by advice of Archbishop Laud and Sir Thomas Wentworth. Charles observes no limits to his power.

1640–41 Charles recalls Parliament, which refuses money to fight Scots.

1642–46 First Civil War.

1645 Cromwell's new model army wins at Naseby.

1648–49 Second Civil War, Parliament against army.

CROMWELL COMMON WEALTH

1649 Charles I executed.

1651 *Hobbes 'Leviathan'.*

1653 Cromwell becomes Lord Protector.

Society of Friends (Quakers) develop during this period.

CHARLES II

1660 Restoration of monarchy.

1661–65 Clarendon Code enforces religious conformity.

1662 *Royal Society chartered.*

1663 *Milton's 'Paradise Lost'.*

1665 Great Plague in London.

1666 Great Fire in London.

Christopher Wren designs new buildings, churches.

Arts: Pepys, Evelyn, Dryden, Purcell.

1678 *Bunyan's 'Pilgrim's Progress'.*

JAMES II

1685

1687 James II suspends many laws.

Newton's 'Principia' published.

1688–89 'Glorious revolution'. Rulers limited by law and Parliament Bill of Rights.

WILLIAM III and MARY

1689

1694 Mary dies.

1693–94 National Debt and Bank of England begin.

1700

1701 Acts of Settlement, concerning the Succession.

Arts: Pope, Defoe, Swift. Vanbrugh designs Blenheim.

ANNE

1702

GEORGE I

1714 First Hanoverian king of Great Britain.

1720 Speculative scheme, South Sea Bubble, collapses.

1721–42 Robert Walpole, first Prime Minister. Cabinet-style government begins. Whigs dominant.

1722 Workhouses for poor begin.

GEORGE II

1727

1729 John and Charles Wesley start Methodist movement.

1756 William Pitt the Elder came to power.

1756–63 Seven Years War (against France).

Results: England gains decisive power in Canada (Wolfe captures Quebec) and India (Clive captures Plassey). Attempts to raise taxes and quarter soldiers antagonize the American colonies.

GEORGE III

1760

1760–90's *Beginnings of 'Agricultural Revolution' (crop rotation, animal breeding, fertilization) and 'Industrial Revolution' (advances in spinning, weaving, iron manufacture) lead to growth of large cities eg Birmingham and Manchester and change in working pattern of most people. Population expands.*

1776–81 American War of Independence; colonists supported by French.

1776 *Publication of Adam Smith's 'Wealth of Nations'.*

Arts: Reynolds, Gainsborough, Fielding, Burns, Scott, Johnson, Gibbon, Hogarth, Heppelwhite, Chippendale.

1787 Society for Abolition of Slave Trade founded.

1796 *Jenner inoculates against smallpox.*

IRELAND

1641 Catholic Rising in Ireland.

1649 Cromwell begins subjugation of Ireland. Harsh rule.

1690 William III defeats Irish and James II at the Boyne.

SCOTLAND

1638 Scots reject Anglican Liturgy – their invasion of England sparks civil war.

1650–51 Cromwell defeats Scots.

1689 Jacobite Scots defeat English at Killiecrankie but lose at Dunkeld.

1692 Glencoe Massacre of Jacobite Highlanders.

1707 Union of Scotland and England.

1745 'The Forty-Five' rebellion led by Bonnie Prince Charlie fails.

1746 Final defeat of Jacobite Highlanders at Culloden.

EUROPE

1618–48 Thirty Years War in Germany.

1623–30 Alternate periods of peace and war with Spain and France.

Charles I marries Henrietta Maria of France.

Wars led to conflict between King and Parliament.

1651 Navigation Act passed against Dutch shipping.

1652–54 First Dutch War.

1665–67 Second Dutch War.

1672–74 Third Dutch War.

1702–14 England enters war of Spanish succession against Louis XIV. Churchill, Duke of Marlborough, wins at Blenheim and Ramillies.

1714 Treaty of Utrecht.

English gain Gibraltar.

French support Jacobites in this period.

English try to hold balance of power in Europe during this century.

1739 War of Jenkins' Ear against Spain.

1744–48 War of the Austrian succession. England supports Prussia and Austria. Against France.

1759 English support Frederick the Great of Prussia.

1789 *French Revolution influences English thought.*

1793 Louis XVI executed.

1799 England joins Russia and Austria against France.

WIDER WORLD

1607 First successful settlement in Virginia.

1620 Pilgrims settle in Plymouth, Massachusetts.

1630's Massachusetts, Connecticut, Rhode Island, Maryland settled.

1639 Fort St George established in Madras, India.

1660's Carolina, New Jersey settled.

England kept New York after Second Dutch War.

1665 Quakers in New Jersey.

1668 Bombay granted to East India Company.

1682 Settlement of Pennsylvania and Delaware.

1732 Georgia founded.

1740's and **1750's** French and Spanish forces fight English in America and India. French try to wear down East India Company's power in Madras, Bombay, and Fort William.

1768 *Captain Cook's first voyage to Australia and New Zealand.*

1784 Cabinet gains control of East India Company.

1786 First Australian penal colony.

1791 Upper and Lower Canada granted representative governments.

1793 French and English fight in West Indies.

1795 England takes Cape of Good Hope, Ceylon, Java, and Malaccas from Dutch.

BRITISH ISLES

1800

1800 Pitt's Combination Acts suppress trade unions – repealed in 1824.

Arts: Austen, Keats, Wordsworth, Blake, Turner, Constable, Coleridge.

1815 Corn Laws passed to protect agriculture.

1819 Peterloo Massacre followed by Six Acts.

GEORGE IV

1820

1825 *Stockton and Darlington Railway.*

1826–29 Peel reforms penal code, establishes police force.

WILLIAM IV

1830

1832 Reform Bill corrects Parliamentary representation.

1833 First Factory Act provides for inspection.

1834 Grand National Consolidated Trades Union formed.

Poor Law Amendment Act increases workhouses.

VICTORIA

1837

1838–48 Chartist movement for greater democracy.

1846 Repeal of Corn Laws by Peel to help Ireland.

1847 Ten Hour Factory Act. *Marx publishes 'Communist Manifesto'.*

1848 Public Health Act.

Arts: Dickens, Thackeray, Tennyson, Hopkins, George Eliot, Wilde.

1859 *Darwin's 'Origin of Species' – basis of evolutionary theory.*

1867 Second Reform Bill extended vote to working classes.

1870 Liberal reforms under Gladstone begin: elementary education by schools boards, secrecy in voting. Local government boards, civil service reformed.

1874 Third Reform Bill extends vote to rural workers.

1888–89 Unskilled workers form unions after Dock Strike.

1898 *Wireless communication by Marconi.*

1900

1900 Foundation of Labour Party.

EDWARD VII

1901

1902 Balfour's Education Act improves system.

1905 The Pankhursts' Women's Suffrage agitation.

1906–11 Lloyd-George's liberal reforms; provision of school meals, medical care, old age pensions. Probation system, Labour Exchange, Council housing, Unemployment and Health Insurance. Restriction of House of Lords' power, regulations of industries.

GEORGE V

1910

1914 Home Rule for Ireland passed, but deferred.

1914–18 First World War.

1918 Votes granted to women over 30.

1919 *Atom split by Rutherford.*

1924 First Labour Government – Ramsay MacDonald.

1926 General Strike. *Baird demonstrates television.*

1928 Conditions of women's vote same as men's.

1929 *Fleming discovers penicillin.*

World-wide economic depression.

1931 Ramsay MacDonald's national government adopts severe economy measures. Statute of Westminster.

1936 Abdication crisis. *Keynes 'Theory of Employment'.*

EDWARD VIII

GEORGE VI

1936

1939–45 Second World War.

1940 Churchill becomes Prime Minister.

1944 Butler's Education Act.

1945 Labour Government establishes Welfare State, under Attlee. Based on ideas put forward during the war: National Health Service, nationalization of railways and mines, town and country planning. Post-war housing crisis.

ELIZABETH II

1952

1956 *First nuclear power station in the world at Calder Hall.*

First CND (Campaign for Nuclear Disarmament) march from Aldermaston.

1971 Decimal currency.

1970's Deepening economic difficulties, made worse by increases in oil prices. Some relief from North Sea oil. Efforts to control prices and incomes.

1979 Prime Minister Thatcher introduces 'monetarism' in attempt to stabilize economy.

Arts: Hardy, Joyce, Shaw, D.H. Lawrence, Masefield, Huxley, Dylan Thomas, Yeats, Wells, Woolf, Britten, Walton.

IRELAND

1801 Union with Great Britain.

1823 O'Connell founds Catholic Association.

1845–46 Great potato famine – many people emigrated.

1916 Easter Rising starts active rebellion.

1922 Partition into Ulster and Irish Free State (a Dominion).

1937 Republic of Eire formed.

1939–45 Eire neutral in war.

1969–present. Troubles in Ulster.

EUROPE

1800–15 (1800 English take Malta).

Napoleonic wars.

1805 Nelson wins at Trafalgar.

1808 and **1815** Wellington's victories in Spain and at Waterloo.

1815 Treaty of Vienna settled Europe according to Metternich's plan.

1829 Independence of Greece supported by Britain.

1848 European revolutions influence thought in England. Greatest Chartist demonstration.

1854–56 Crimean War in Russia. *Florence Nightingale begins reform of nursing techniques.* Palmerston Prime Minister.

1867 *'Das Kapital' published. Deeply affects political thought.*

1878 Treaty of Berlin settles Anglo-Russian conflict over Turkey.

1907 Anglo-Russian Treaty.

1911 Agadir crisis.

1912–13 Balkan Wars.

1917 Russian Revolution.

1919 Attempt at fair adjustment of boundaries. Treaty of Versailles.

1922 Mussolini takes power in Italy.

1928 Kellogg-Briand Pact.

1933 Hitler takes power in Germany.

1938 Hitler takes Austria, Czechoslovakia.

1948 Russian control of Eastern Europe.

1948–49 Berlin airlift.

1949 North Atlantic Treaty Organization (NATO).

1960 'Cold War' intensifies, 'U-2' spy plane caught over Russia.

1970's 'Detente' with Russia.

1973 Britain enters Common Market under Heath.

1980's Revival of disarmament movements.

WIDER WORLD

1807 Slave trade abolished.

1812 United States enters war against English.

West Indies

Britain controls Jamaica, Bahamas, British Honduras, Barbados.

1833 Slavery abolished throughout Empire.

India and China

1818 British control all India.

1839–41 British try to conquer Afghanistan.

1840–42 Opium War with China. England gets Hong Kong.

1857 Indian Mutiny.

1858 Secretary of State supersedes East India Company.

1885 British take upper Burma.

Africa

1819 English settlers in Cape Town.

1836 Boers' Great Trek.

1879 Zulu War. *Livingstone explores.*

1889 Rhodesia founded.

1899–1902 Boer War.

1906 South Africa becomes self-governing.

Near East

Britain ready to take power when Ottoman Empire falters.

1885 General Gordon shot at Khartoum.

1898 Kitchener conquers Sudan.

League of Nations.

1931 Japanese invade Manchuria.

1935 Mussolini invades Abyssinia.

1945 First atomic bombs end war.

United Nations founded.

1947 India independent.

1948 Palestine and Burma independent.

1950–3 Korean War.

1956 Egypt seizes control of Suez Canal. Anthony Eden tries to take it by force.

1948–58 Rebellions in Malaya.

1956 Pakistan independent.

1960 Ghana, Cyprus independent.

1962 Uganda, Tanganyika independent – also Jamaica, Trinidad and Tobago, Nigeria.

1963 Greeks and Turks fight in Cyprus. Kenya self-governing.

1969 Malawi, Gambia, Malta independent.

1965 Rhodesia declares independence (UDI).

1967 Britain withdraws from Aden

1980 Rhodesia gains independence as Zimbabwe.

1981 Barbados independent.

,broad-'spectrum *adj* effective against various insects or microorganisms ⟨*a ~ antibiotic*⟩

'broad,sword /-,sawd/ *n* a sword with a broad blade for cutting rather than thrusting

Broadway /'brawdway/ *n* the New York commercial theatre and amusement world [*Broadway,* street in New York on or near which were once located most of the city's legitimate theatres] – **Broadway** *adj*

Brobdingnagian /,brobding'nagi·ən/ *adj* gigantic, towering [*Brobdingnag,* imaginary country inhabited by giants in *Gulliver's Travels* by Jonathan Swift †1745 Ir satirist]

brocade /brə'kayd/ *n* a rich (silk) fabric woven with raised patterns [Sp *brocado,* fr Catal *brocat,* fr It *broccato,* fr *broccare* to spur, brocade, fr *brocco* small nail, fr L *broccus* projecting] – **brocade** *vt,* **brocaded** *adj*

brocatelle /,brokə'tel/ *n* a stiff fabric with patterns in high relief [F, fr It *broccatello,* dim. of *broccato*]

broccoli /'brokəli/ *n* **1** a large hardy cauliflower **2 broccoli, sprouting broccoli** a branching form of cauliflower whose young shoots are used for food [It, pl of *broccolo* flowering top of a cabbage, dim. of *brocco* small nail, sprout]

broch /brokh, brawkh/ *n* any of several ancient fortified circular towers found in the N and W of Scotland and adjacent islands [Sc *broch, bruch,* lit., borough, fr ME (Sc) *brugh,* alter. of ME *burgh* – more at BOROUGH]

brochette /bro'shet, broh-/ *n* (food grilled on) a skewer [F, fr OF *brochete,* fr *broche* pointed tool – more at BROACH]

brochure /'brohshə, broh'shooə/ *n* a small pamphlet [F, fr *brocher* to sew, fr MF, to prick, fr OF *brochier,* fr *broche*]

brock /brok/ *n, archaic* a badger – now used chiefly in stories as a name for the badger [ME, fr OE *broc,* of Celt origin; akin to W *broch* badger]

brocket /'brokit/ *n* **1** a male red deer 2 years old – compare PRICKET **2** any of several small S American deer with unbranched horns [ME *broket,* prob modif of ONF *brocard, brockart* fallow deer 1 year old]

broderie anglaise /,brohdəri 'ong·glez, ,--- -'-/ **1** openwork embroidery, usu in white thread, on white fine cloth **2** cloth embroidered with broderie anglaise [F, lit., English embroidery]

¹brogue /brohg/ *n* a stout walking shoe characterized by decorative perforations on the uppers ☞ GARMENT [IrGael & ScGael *brōg,* fr MIr *brōc,* fr ON *brōk* leg covering; akin to OE *brōc* leg covering – more at BREECH]

²brogue *n* a dialect or regional pronunciation; *esp* an Irish accent [perh fr IrGael *barrōg* wrestling hold, bond (as in *barrōg teangan* lisp, lit., hold of the tongue)]

broil /broyl/ *vt* to cook by direct exposure to radiant heat (e g over a fire); *specif, NAm* to grill *~ vi* to become extremely hot [ME *broilen,* fr MF *bruler* to burn, modif of L *ustulare* to singe, fr *ustus,* pp of *urere* to burn]

broiler /'broylə/ *n* a bird suitable for grilling; *esp* a young chicken [BROIL + ²-ER]

¹broke /brohk/ *past of* BREAK

²broke *adj* penniless – infml; compare STONY-BROKE [ME, alter. of *broken*]

broken /'brohkən/ *adj* **1** violently separated into parts; shattered **2a** having undergone or been subjected to fracture ⟨*a ~ leg*⟩ **b** *of a land surface* irregular, interrupted, or full of obstacles ⟨*~ ground*⟩ **c** not fulfilled; violated ⟨*a ~ promise*⟩ **d** discontinuous, interrupted **3a** made weak or infirm **b** subdued completely; crushed ⟨*a ~ spirit*⟩ **c** not working; defective **4a** cut off; disconnected **b** adversely affected or disrupted by marital separation or divorce ⟨*~ marriage*⟩ ⟨*a ~ home*⟩ **c** imperfect ⟨*~ English*⟩ [ME, fr OE *brocen,* fr pp of *brecan* to break] – **brokenly** *adv,* **brokenness** *n*

,broken-'down *adj* **1** in a state of disrepair; wrecked, dilapidated **2** spiritually or physically ill or exhausted

,broken'hearted /-'hahtid/ *adj* overcome by grief or despair

,broken 'wind /wind/ *n* a chronic respiratory disease of horses marked by a persistent cough and heaving of the flanks – **broken-winded** *adj*

broker /'brohkə/ *n* **1** one who acts as an intermediary (e g in a business deal) **2** an agent who negotiates contracts of purchase and sale (e g of commodities or securities) [ME, negotiator, fr (assumed) AF *brocour,* akin to OF *broche* pointed tool, tap of a cask – more at BROACH]

brokerage /'brohk(ə)rij/ *n* **1** the business of a broker **2** the fee or commission for transacting business as a broker

broking /'brohking/ *n* BROKERAGE 1 [fr prp of obs *broke* (to negotiate), prob back-formation fr *broker*]

brolga /'brolgə/ *n* an Australian bird that is a large crane with grey plumage [native name in Australia]

brolly /'broli/ *n, chiefly Br* an umbrella – infml [by shortening & alter.]

brom- /brohm-/, **bromo-** *comb form* bromine ⟨bromo*benzene*⟩ [prob fr F *brome,* fr Gk *brōmos* bad smell]

bromate /'brohmayt/ *n* a salt of bromic acid

bromeliad /broh'meeliad/ *n* any of a family of chiefly tropical American plants including the pineapple and various ornamental plants [NL *Bromelia,* genus of tropical American plants, fr Olaf *Bromelius* †1705 Sw botanist]

bromic /'brohmik/ *adj* of or containing (pentavalent) bromine

,bromic 'acid *n* an unstable strongly oxidizing acid

bromide /'brohmied/ *n* **1** a compound of bromine with another element or radical; *esp* any of various bromides formerly used as sedatives **2** a commonplace or hackneyed statement or notion

bromine /'brohmeen, -min/ *n* a nonmetallic element, usu occurring as a deep red corrosive toxic liquid ☞ PERIODIC TABLE [F *brome* bromine + E *-ine*]

bronch- /brongk-/, **broncho-** *comb form* bronchial tube; bronchial ⟨bronch*itis*⟩ [prob fr F, throat, fr LL, fr Gk, fr *bronchos* – more at CRAW]

bronchi- /brongki-/, **bronchio-** *comb form* bronchial tubes ⟨bronchi*ectasis*⟩ [NL, fr *bronchia,* pl, branches of the bronchi, fr Gk, dim. of *bronchos* bronchus]

bronchial /'brongki·əl/ *adj* of the bronchi or their ramifications in the lungs – **bronchially** *adv*

bronchiectasis /,brongki'ektəsis/ *n* abnormal dilation of the bronchial tubes, often as a result of infection [NL]

bronchiole /'brongkiohl/ *n* a minute thin-walled branch of a bronchus ☞ DIGESTION [NL *bronchiolum*, dim. of *bronchia*] – **bronchiolar** /,brongki'ohlə/ *adj*

bronchitis /brong'kietəs/ *n* (a disease marked by) acute or chronic inflammation of the bronchial tubes accompanied by a cough and catarrh [NL] – **bronchitic** /brong'kitik/ *adj*

bronchopneumonia /,brongkohnyoo'mohnyə, -ni·ə/ *n* pneumonia involving many widely scattered but small patches of lung tissue [NL]

bronchus /'brongkəs/ *n, pl* **bronchi** /'brongki, -kie/ either of the 2 main branches of the windpipe ☞ DIGESTION [NL, fr Gk *bronchos*]

bronco /'brongkoh/ *n, pl* **broncos** an unbroken or imperfectly broken horse of western N America [MexSp, fr Sp, rough, wild]

brontosaurus /,brontə'sawrəs/ *n* any of various large 4-legged and prob plant-eating dinosaurs [deriv of Gk *brontē* thunder (akin to Gk *bremein* to roar) + *sauros* lizard – more at SAURIAN]

[1]**bronze** /bronz/ *vt* **1** to give the appearance of bronze to **2** to make brown or tanned

[2]**bronze** *n* **1** any of various copper-base alloys; *esp* one containing tin **2** a sculpture or artefact made of bronze **3** a yellowish-brown colour **4** BRONZE MEDAL ⟨*won a ~ in the 100 metres*⟩ [F, fr It *bronzo*, perh fr Per *birinj, pirinj* copper] – **bronze** *adj*, **bronzy** *adj*

'**Bronze ,Age** *n* the period of human culture characterized by the use of bronze or copper tools and weapons

,**bronze 'medal** *n* a medal of bronze awarded to sby who comes third in a competition – **bronze medallist** *n*

brooch /brohch/ *n* an ornament worn on clothing and fastened by means of a pin [ME *broche* pointed tool, brooch – more at BROACH]

[1]**brood** /broohd/ *n* **1a** young birds, insects, etc hatched or cared for at one time **b** the children in one family – humor **2** a group having a common nature or origin [ME, fr OE *brōd*; akin to OE *beorma* yeast – more at BARM]

[2]**brood** *vi* **1** *of a bird* to sit on eggs in order to hatch them **2a** to dwell gloomily *on*; worry *over* or *about* **b** to be in a state of depression – **broodingly** *adv*

[3]**brood** *adj* kept for breeding ⟨*a ~ mare*⟩

brooder /'broohdə/ *n* a heated structure used for raising young fowl [[2]BROOD + [2]-ER]

broody /'broohdi/ *adj* **1** *of fowl* being in a state of readiness to brood eggs **2** given or conducive to introspection; contemplative, moody **3** *of a woman* feeling a strong desire or urge to be a mother – infml – **broodiness** *n*

[1]**brook** /brook/ *vt* to tolerate; STAND FOR ⟨*she would ~ no interference with her plans*⟩ [ME *brouken* to use, enjoy, fr OE *brūcan*; akin to OHG *brūhhan* to use, L *frui* to enjoy]

[2]**brook** *n* a usu small freshwater stream [ME, fr OE *brōc*; akin to OHG *bruoh* marshy ground]

broom /broohm, broom/ *n* **1** any of various leguminous shrubs with long slender branches, small leaves, and usu showy yellow flowers **2** a brush for sweeping composed of a bundle of firm stiff twigs, bristles, or fibres (e g of nylon) bound to or set on a long handle [ME, fr OE *brōm*; akin to OHG *brāmo* bramble, MF *brimme* brim]

'**broom,rape** /-,rayp/ *n* any of various leafless plants that grow as parasites on the roots of other plants [trans of ML *rapum genistae*; fr the parasitic growth of one species on the roots of broom]

'**broom,stick** /-,stik/ *n* the long thin handle of a broom

brose /brohz/ *n, chiefly Scot* a porridge made with boiling milk, water, or other liquid and oatmeal [perh alter. of Sc *bruis* broth, fr ME *brewes*, fr OF *broez*, nom sing. & acc pl of *broet*, dim. of *breu*, of Gmc origin]

broth /broth/ *n* **1a** the stock in which meat, fish, cereal grains, or vegetables have been cooked **b** a thin soup made from stock **2** a liquid medium for culturing esp bacteria [ME, fr OE; akin to OHG *brod* broth, L *fervēre* to boil – more at [2]BURN]

brothel /'broth(ə)l, 'brodh(ə)l/ *n* a premises (e g a house) in which the services of prostitutes can be bought [ME, worthless fellow, prostitute, fr *brothen*, pp of *brethen* to waste away, go to ruin, fr OE *brēothan* to waste away; akin to OE *brēotan* to break – more at BRITTLE]

brother /'brudhə/ *n, pl* **brothers,** (*3, 4, & 5*) **brothers** *also* **brethren** /'bredhrin/ **1** a male having the same parents as another person; *also* a half brother or stepbrother **2a** a kinsman **b** one, esp a male, who shares with another a common national or racial origin **3** a fellow member – used as a title in some evangelical denominations **4** one, esp a male, who is related to another by a common tie or interest **5** a member of a men's religious order who is not in holy orders ⟨*a lay ~*⟩ [ME, fr OE *brōthor*; akin to OHG *bruodor* brother, L *frater*, Gk *phratēr* member of the same clan]

'**brotherhood** /-hood/ *n* **1** the quality or state of being brothers **2a** an association (e g a religious body) for a particular purpose **b** (an idea of) fellowship between all human beings ⟨*universal ~*⟩ [ME *brotherhede, brotherhod*, alter. of *brotherrede*, fr OE *brōthorrǣden*, fr *brōthor* + *rǣden* condition – more at KINDRED]

'**brother-in-,law** *n, pl* **brothers-in-law** **1** the brother of one's spouse **2** the husband of one's sister

'**brotherly** /-li/ *adj* **1** of, resembling, or appropriate to brothers, esp in feeling or showing platonic affection **2** filled with fellow feeling, sympathy, or compassion ⟨*she was overwhelmed with ~ love for the homeless*⟩ – **brotherliness** *n*, **brotherly** *adv*

brougham /'brooh(ə)m/ *n* a light closed 4-wheeled horse-drawn carriage [Henry Peter *Brougham*, Baron Brougham and Vaux †1868 Sc jurist]

brought /brawt/ *past of* BRING

brouhaha /'brooh·hah,hah/ *n* a hubbub, uproar [F]

brow /brow/ *n* **1a** an eyebrow **b** the forehead **2** the top or edge of a hill, cliff, etc [ME, fr OE *brū*; akin to ON *brūn* eyebrow, Gk *ophrys*]

'**brow,band** /-,band/ *n* the part of a bridle crossing the horse's forehead and preventing the headpiece from slipping back

'**brow,beat** /-,beet/ *vt* **browbeat; browbeaten** to intimidate, coerce, or bully by a persistently threatening or dominating manner ⟨*union members ~en into accepting a cut in salary*⟩

-browed /-browd/ *comb form* (→ *adj*) having (such) a brow or brows ⟨*beetle-browed*⟩

[1]**brown** /brown/ *adj* **1** of the colour brown; *esp* of dark or tanned complexion **2** (made with ingredients that are) partially or wholly unrefined or unpolished ⟨~ *sugar*⟩ [ME *broun*, fr OE *brūn*; akin to OHG *brūn* brown, Gk *phrynē* toad]

[2]**brown** *n* any of a range of dark colours between red and yellow in hue – **brownish** *adj*, **browny** *adj*

[3]**brown** *vb* to make or become brown (e g by sautéing)

brown ale *n* a sweet, dark, heavily malted beer

brown alga *n* any of many algae, with a predominantly brown colour, that are mostly seaweeds

brown bear *n* any of several bears predominantly brown in colour; *esp* a European bear

brown coal *n* lignite

ˌbrowned-ˈoff *adj, chiefly Br* annoyed; FED UP – infml [*browned* fr pp of [3]*brown*]

brown fat *n* a heat-producing tissue that is present in significant amounts in hibernating mammals, human infants, and adults acclimatized to cold

brownie /ˈbrowni/ *n* **1** a good-natured goblin believed to perform household chores at night **2** **brownie guide, brownie** a member of the most junior section of the (British) Guide movement for girls aged from 7 to 10 **3** *chiefly NAm* a small square or rectangle of rich chocolate cake containing nuts [[1]*brown*]

browning /ˈbrowning/ *n* a substance (e g caramelized sugar) used to give a brown colour (e g to gravy)

ˌbrown ˈsauce *n* a sauce usu made from a roux combined with meat stock – compare WHITE SAUCE

ˈbrownˌshirt /-ˌshuht/ *n, often cap* a Nazi; *esp* STORM TROOPER 1 [trans of G *braunhemd*; fr the uniform worn by Nazis]

ˌbrown ˈstudy *n* a state of serious absorption or abstraction; a reverie

ˌbrown ˈtrout *n* a speckled European trout used for food

[1]**browse** /browz/ *n* **1** tender shoots, twigs, and leaves of trees and shrubs that provide food for animals (e g deer) **2** a period of time spent browsing ⟨*had a good ~ in the library*⟩ [prob modif of MF *brouts*, pl of *brout* sprout, fr OF *brost*, of Gmc origin; akin to OS *brustian* to sprout; akin to OE *brēost* breast]

[2]**browse** *vt* to feed on (browse) ~ *vi* **1** *of animals* to nibble at leaves, grass, or other vegetation **2** to read or search idly *through* a book or a mass of things (e g in a shop), in the hope of finding sthg interesting – **browser** *n*

brucellosis /ˌbroohsəˈlohsis, -siz/ *n* a serious long-lasting disease, esp of human beings and cattle, caused by a bacterium [NL *brucella*, a genus of bacteria, fr Sir David *Bruce* †1931 Br bacteriologist]

bruin /ˈbrooh·in/ *n* – used chiefly in stories as a name for the bear [D, name of the bear in the medieval poem *Reynard the Fox*]

[1]**bruise** /broohz/ *vt* **1** to inflict a bruise on **2** to crush (e g leaves or berries) by pounding **3** to wound, injure; *esp* to inflict psychological hurt on ~ *vi* to be damaged by a bruise ⟨*tomatoes ~ easily*⟩ [ME *brusen, brisen*, fr MF & OE; MF *bruisier* to break (of Celt origin; akin to OIr *brūu* I shatter) & OE *brȳsan* to bruise (akin to OIr *brūu*, L *frustum* piece)]

[2]**bruise** *n* **1a** an injury involving rupture of small blood vessels and discoloration without a break in the skin **b** an injury to plant tissue involving underlying damage and discoloration without a break in the skin **2** an injury, esp to the feelings

bruiser /ˈbroohzə/ *n* a large burly man; *specif* a prizefighter

bruit /ˈbrooh·ee/ *n* any of several usu abnormal sounds (e g a heart murmur) that can be detected in a medical examination [ME, fr MF, fr OF, noise]

Brumaire /ˈbroohmeə (*Fr* brymɛːr)/ *n* the 2nd month of the French revolutionary calendar corresponding to 23 October–21 November [F, fr *brume* fog, winter, fr L *bruma* winter solstice, winter, fr *brevis* brief]

brumby /ˈbrumbi/ *n, Austr & NZ* a wild or unbroken horse [prob native name in Queensland, Australia]

brummagem /ˈbrumәjim/ *n or adj* (sthg) cheap, inferior, or showy [*Brummagem*, alter. of *Birmingham*, city in England, formerly famed for cheap manufactured goods]

Brummy /ˈbrumi/ *n or adj* (a native or inhabitant or the dialect) of Birmingham – infml [by shortening & alter. fr *Brummagem*]

brunch /brunch/ *n* a meal, usu taken in the middle of the morning, that combines a late breakfast and an early lunch [*b*reakfast + l*unch*]

brunette, *NAm also* **brunet** /broohˈnet/ *n or adj* (sby, esp a young adult woman,) having dark hair and usu a relatively dark complexion [F *brunet* (masc) & *brunette* (fem), fr OF, fr *brun* brown, fr ML *brunus*, of Gmc origin; akin to OHG *brūn* brown – more at BROWN]

brunt /brunt/ *n* the principal force or stress (e g of an attack) – esp in *bear the brunt of* [ME]

[1]**brush** /brush/ *n* **1** (land covered with) scrub vegetation **2** *chiefly NAm & Austr* brushwood [ME *brusch*, fr MF *broce*, fr OF]

[2]**brush** *n* **1** an implement composed of filaments (e g of hair, bristle, nylon, or wire) set into a firm piece of material and used esp for grooming hair, painting, sweeping, or scrubbing **2** a bushy tail, esp of a fox **3** a conductor (e g a piece of carbon or braided copper wire) that makes electrical contact between a stationary and a moving part **4** an act of brushing **5** a quick light touch or momentary contact in passing ⟨*felt the ~ of her coat*⟩ [ME *brusshe*, fr MF *broisse*, fr OF *broce*]

[3]**brush** *vt* **1a** to apply a brush to **b** to apply with a brush **2** to remove with sweeping strokes (e g of a brush) – usu + *away* or *off* ⟨~ed *the dirt off her coat*⟩ **3** to pass lightly over or across; touch gently against in passing

[4]**brush** *vi* to move lightly, heedlessly, or rudely – usu + *by* or *past* [ME *bruschen* to rush, fr MF *brosser* to dash through underbrush, fr *broce*]

[5]**brush** *n* a brief antagonistic encounter or skirmish ⟨*had a ~ with authority*⟩ [ME *brusche* rush, hostile collision, fr *bruschen*]

brushed *adj, of a fabric* finished with a nap ⟨~ *cotton*⟩

ˈbrushˌfire /-ˌfie·ə/ *adj* involving military mobilization only on a small and local scale ⟨~ *border wars*⟩ [*brush fire* (a fire involving brush but not full-sized trees)]

ˈbrush-ˌoff *n* a quietly curt or disdainful dismissal; a rebuff – infml

brush off *vt* to dispose of in an offhand way; dismiss

brush up *vi* to tidy one's clothes, hair, etc ⟨*wanted* *to wash and* brush up *when they arrived*⟩ ~ *vt* to renew one's skill in; refresh one's memory of ⟨*she'll have to* brush up *her French*⟩ – **brushup** /'- ,-/ *n* – **brush up on** BRUSH UP *vt*

[1]**'brush,wood** /-,wood/ *n* **1** twigs or small branches, esp when cut or broken **2** a thicket of shrubs and small trees

[1]**'brush,work** /-,wuhk/ *n* (a particular artist's) technique of applying paint with a brush

brusque /brusk, broosk, broohsk/ *adj* blunt or abrupt in manner or speech, often to the point of rudeness [F *brusque*, fr It *brusco*, fr ML *bruscus* butcher's-broom] – **brusquely** *adv*, **brusqueness** *n*

brusquerie /,bruskə'ree, ,broo-, ,brooh-, '---/ *n* abruptness of manner [F, fr *brusque*]

,Brussels 'carpet /'bruslz/ *n* a carpet with a looped woollen pile fixed onto a strong linen base [*Brussels*, city in Belgium]

,Brussels 'lace *n* any of various fine laces, esp with (appliqué) floral designs

,brussels 'sprout *n, often cap B* (any of the many edible small green buds that grow on the stem of) a plant of the mustard family

brut /brooht (*Fr* bryt)/ *adj, of champagne* very dry; *specif* containing less than 1.5 per cent sugar by volume [F, lit., rough]

brutal /'broohtl/ *adj* **1** grossly ruthless or unfeeling ⟨*a ~ slander*⟩ **2** cruel, cold-blooded ⟨*a ~ attack*⟩ **3** harsh, severe ⟨*~ weather*⟩ **4** unpleasantly accurate and incisive ⟨*~ truth*⟩ [[1]BRUTE + [1]-AL] – **brutally** *adv*, **brutality** /brooh'taləti/ *n*

brutal·ize, -ise /'brooht(ə)l,iez/ *vt* **1** to make brutal, unfeeling, or inhuman ⟨*people ~d by poverty and disease*⟩ **2** to beat brutally – **brutalization** /-ie'zaysh(ə)n/ *n*

[1]**brute** /brooht/ *adj* **1** characteristic of an animal in quality, action, or instinct: e g **a** cruel, savage **b** not working by reason; mindless ⟨*~ instinct*⟩ **2** purely physical ⟨*~ strength*⟩ [ME, fr MF *brut* rough, fr L *brutus* stupid, lit., heavy; akin to L *gravis* heavy – more at [1]GRIEVE]

[2]**brute** *n* **1** a beast **2** a brutal person – **brutish** *adj*, **brutishly** *adv*

bruxism /'bruksiz(ə)m/ *n* the habit of unconsciously gritting or grinding the teeth, esp in situations of stress or during sleep [irreg fr Gk *brychein* to gnash the teeth + E *-ism*]

bryology /brie'oləji/ *n* a branch of botany that deals with mosses and liverworts [Gk *bryon* moss + ISV *-logy*]

bryony /'brie·əni/ *n* any of a genus of climbing plants of the cucumber family [L *bryonia*, fr Gk *bryōnia*; akin to Gk *bryon*]

bryophyte /'brie·ə,fiet/ *n* any of a division of nonflowering plants comprising the mosses and liverworts ☞ PLANT [deriv of Gk *bryon* + *phyton* plant; akin to Gk *phyein* to bring forth – more at BE] – **bryophytic** /-'fitik/ *adj*

bryozoan /,brie·ə'zoh·ən/ *n* (any of) a phylum or class of aquatic animals that reproduce by budding and usu form colonies [NL *Bryozoa*, class name, fr Gk *bryon* + NL *-zoa*] – **bryozoan** *adj*

Brython /'brith(ə)n/ *n* **1** a member of the British branch of Celts **2** a speaker of a Brythonic language [W] – **Brythonic** /bri'thonik/ *adj*

Brythonic /bri'thonik/ *n* the group of the Celtic languages comprising Welsh, Cornish, and Breton – **Brythonic** *adj*

,B 'Special *n* a member of a former part-time volunteer police force in N Ireland

bub /bub/ *n* BREAST 1 – usu pl; slang [perh imit of noise made by a sucking infant]

bubal /'byoohbl/ *n* a large hartebeest of northern Africa that is now almost extinct [NL *bubalis*, fr Gk *boubalis*, an African antelope]

[1]**bubble** /'bubl/ *vi* **bubbling** /'bubling, 'bubl·ing/ **1** to form or produce bubbles **2** to make a sound like the bubbles rising in liquid ⟨*a brook* bubbling *over rocks*⟩ **3** to be highly excited or overflowing (with a feeling) ⟨bubbling *over with happiness*⟩ [ME *bublen*, prob of imit origin]

[2]**bubble** *n* **1a** a usu small body of gas within a liquid or solid **b** a thin spherical usu transparent film of liquid inflated with air or vapour **c** a transparent dome **2** sthg that lacks firmness or reality; *specif* an unreliable or speculative scheme **3** a sound like that of bubbling

,bubble and 'squeak *n, chiefly Br* a dish consisting of usu leftover potato, cabbage, and sometimes meat, fried together [fr the noise of frying]

'bubble ,bath *n* (a bath to which has been added) a perfumed, usu liquid or granular, preparation that produces foam when added to water

'bubble ,chamber *n* a chamber in which the path of an ionizing particle is made visible by a string of bubbles, usu in liquid hydrogen

'bubble ,gum *n* a chewing gum that can be blown into large bubbles

'bubble ,memory *n* a large capacity computer memory that stores information, usu magnetically ☞ COMPUTER

[1]**bubbly** /'bubli/ *adj* **1** full of bubbles **2** overflowing with good spirits or liveliness; vivacious ⟨*a ~ personality*⟩

[2]**bubbly** *n* champagne; *broadly* any sparkling wine – infml

Bube /'booh,bay/ *n, pl* **Bubes,** *esp collectively* **Bube** a member, or the Bantu language, of the people of Fernando Po

bubo /'byoohboh/ *n, pl* **buboes** an inflamed swelling of a lymph gland, esp in the groin or armpit [ML *bubon-*, *bubo*, fr Gk *boubōn* groin, gland, bubo] – **bubonic** *adj*

bu,bonic 'plague /byoo'bonik, byooh-/ *n* plague characterized by the formation of buboes

buccal /'bukl/ *adj* of or involving the cheeks or the cavity of the mouth [L *bucca* cheek – more at POCK]

buccaneer /,bukə'niə/ *n* **1** a freebooter preying on Spanish ships and settlements, esp in the W Indies in the 17th c; *broadly* a pirate **2** an unscrupulous adventurer, esp in politics or business [F *boucanier*, fr *boucaner* to smoke meat on a grid over a fire] – **buccaneer** *vi*

[1]**buck** /buk/ *n, pl* **bucks,** (*1*) **bucks,** *esp collectively* **buck** **1a** a male animal, esp a male deer, antelope, rabbit, rat, etc **b** an antelope **2** a dashing fellow; a dandy **3** VAULTING HORSE **4** *NAm* DOLLAR 2 – slang [ME, fr OE *bucca* stag, he-goat; akin to OHG *boc* he-goat, MIr *bocc*; (4) perh short for *buckskin*, regarded as a unit of exchange in early NAm commerce]

[2]**buck** *vi* **1** *of a horse or mule* to spring into the air with the back curved and come down with the forelegs stiff and the head lowered **2** to refuse assent; balk **3** *chiefly NAm* to move or react jerkily ~ *vt* **1**

to throw (e g a rider) by bucking **2** to fail to comply with; run counter to ⟨~ *the system*⟩

[3]**buck** *n* **1** an object formerly used in poker to mark the next player to deal; *broadly* sthg used as a reminder **2** *the* responsibility – esp in *pass the buck* [short for earlier *buckhorn knife*]

'**buck,bean** /-,been/ *n* the bogbean

'**buck,board** /-,bawd/ *n, NAm* a 4-wheeled horse-drawn vehicle with a sprung platform [obs *buck* (body of a wagon) + E *board*]

bucked /bukt/ *adj* pleased, encouraged ⟨*felt very ~ to hear the news*⟩

[1]**bucket** /'bukit/ *n* **1** a large open container, usu round, with tapering sides and a semicircular handle on top, used esp for holding or carrying liquids **2** sthg resembling a bucket, esp in shape or function: e g **a** the scoop of an excavating machine **b** any of the receptacles on the rim of a waterwheel **c** any of the vanes of a turbine rotor **3** *pl* large quantities ⟨~s *of blood*⟩ – infml [ME, fr AF *buket*, fr OE *būc* pitcher, belly; akin to OHG *būh* belly, Skt *bhūri* abundant – more at BIG]

[2]**bucket** *vt* to draw or lift in buckets ~ *vi* **1** to move about jerkily or recklessly **2** *chiefly Br* BUCKET DOWN

bucket down *vi, chiefly Br* **1** *of rain* to fall heavily **2** to rain very hard ⟨*it's been* bucketing down *all day*⟩

'**bucketful** /-f(ə)l/ *n, pl* **bucketfuls, bucketsful** as much as a bucket will hold

'**bucket ,seat** *n* a round-backed separate seat for 1 person in a motor car, aircraft, etc

[1]**buckle** /'bukl/ *n* a fastening consisting of a rigid rim, usu with a hinged pin, used to join together 2 loose ends (e g of a belt or strap) or for ornament [ME *bocle*, fr MF, boss of a shield, buckle, fr L *buccula*, dim. of *bucca* cheek – more at POCK]

[2]**buckle** *vb* **buckling** /'bukling, 'bukl·ing/ *vt* **1** to fasten with a buckle **2** to cause to bend, give way, or crumple ~ *vi* **1** to bend, warp ⟨*the pavement* ~d *in the heat*⟩ **2** to yield; GIVE WAY ⟨*one who does not ~ under pressure*⟩

[3]**buckle** *n* a distorted formation due to buckling

buckle down *vi* to apply oneself vigorously ⟨*about time she* buckled down *to her work*⟩

buckler /'buklə/ *n* a small round shield held by a handle at arm's length [ME *bocler*, fr OF, shield with a boss, fr *bocle*]

,**buckle 'to** *vi* to brace oneself or gather up one's strength to put effort into work ⟨*we must* buckle to *and start writing the dictionary*⟩

buckling /'bukling/ *n* a herring smoked until lightly cooked – compare KIPPER [G *bückling*]

bucko /'bukoh/ *n, pl* **buckoes** **1** one who is domineering and bullying; a swaggerer **2** *chiefly Irish* a young fellow; a lad [[1]*buck* + *-o*]

buckram /'bukrəm/ *n* a fabric of cotton or linen, with a stiff finish, used for interlinings in garments, for stiffening in hats, and in bookbinding [ME *bukeram*, fr OF *boquerant*, fr OProv *bocaran*, fr *Bokhara*, city in central Asia]

buckshee /'bukshee, -'-/ *adj or adv, Br* without charge; free – slang [Hindi *bakhśiś* gratuity, gift, fr Per *bakhshish* – more at BAKSHEESH]

buckshot /'buk,shot/ *n* a coarse lead shot used esp for shooting large animals

'**buck,skin** /-,skin/ *n* a soft pliable usu suede-finished leather – **buckskin** *adj*

'**buck,thorn** /-,thawn/ *n* any of a genus of often thorny trees or shrubs

,**buck'tooth** /-'toohth/ *n* a large projecting front tooth – **buck-toothed** *adj*

buck up *vi* **1** to become encouraged **2** to hurry up ~ *vt* **1** to improve, smarten **2** to raise the morale or spirits of ⟨*the news* bucked *her* up *no end*⟩ [[2]*buck*]

'**buck,wheat** /-,weet/ *n* **1** any of a genus of plants of the dock family that have pinkish white flowers and triangular seeds **2** the seed of a buckwheat, used as a cereal grain [D *boekweit*, fr MD *boecweit*, fr *boec-* (akin to OHG *buohha* beech tree) + *weit* wheat – more at BEECH]

bucolic /byooh'kolik/ *adj* **1** of shepherds or herdsmen; pastoral **2** (typical) of rural life [L *bucolicus*, fr Gk *boukolikos*, fr *boukolos* cowherd, fr *bous* head of cattle + *-kolos* (akin to L *colere* to cultivate) – more at [1]COW, WHEEL] – **bucolically** *adv*

[1]**bud** /bud/ *n* **1** a small protuberance on the stem of a plant that may develop into a flower, leaf, or shoot **2** sthg not yet mature or fully developed: e g **a** an incompletely opened flower **b** an outgrowth of an organism that becomes a new individual [ME *budde*; akin to OE *budda* beetle, Skt *bhūri* abundant – more at BIG]

[2]**bud** *vb* **-dd-** *vi* **1** *of a plant* to put forth buds **2** to develop by way of outgrowth **3** to reproduce asexually by forming and developing buds ~ *vt* **1** to produce or develop from buds **2** to graft a bud into (a plant of another kind), usu in order to propagate a desired variety

Buddha /'boodə/ *n* **1** sby who has attained the perfect enlightenment sought in Buddhism **2** a representation of Gautama Buddha [Skt, enlightened]

Buddhism /'boodiz(ə)m/ *n* an eastern religion growing out of the teaching of Gautama Buddha that one can be liberated from the suffering inherent in life by mental and moral self-purification – **Buddhist** *n or adj*

budding /'buding/ *adj* being in an early and usu promising stage of development ⟨~ *novelists*⟩

buddleia /'budli·ə/ *n* any of a genus of shrubs or trees with showy clusters of usu yellow or violet flowers [NL, genus name, fr Adam *Buddle* †1715 E botanist]

buddy /'budi/ *n, chiefly NAm* **1** a companion, partner **2** [3]MATE 1c ***USE*** infml [prob baby talk alter. of *brother*]

budge /buj/ *vb* **1** to (cause to) move or shift ⟨*the mule wouldn't ~*⟩ **2** to (force or cause to) change an opinion or yield ⟨*couldn't ~ her on the issue*⟩ [MF *bouger*, fr (assumed) VL *bullicare*, fr L *bullire* to bubble, boil – more at [2]BOIL]

budgerigar /'buj(ə)ri,gah/ *n* a small Australian bird that belongs to the same family as the parrots and is often kept in captivity [native name in Australia]

[1]**budget** /'bujit/ *n* **1** a statement of a financial position for a definite period of time (e g for the following year), that is based on estimates of expenditures and proposals for financing them **2** a plan of how money will be spent or allocated ⟨*a weekly ~*⟩ **3** the amount of money available for, required for, or assigned to a particular purpose [ME *bowgette* pouch, wallet, fr MF *bougette*, dim. of *bouge* leather bag, fr L *bulga*, of Gaulish origin; akin to MIr *bolg* bag; akin to OE *belg, bælg* bag – more at BELLY] – **budgetary** /-t(ə)ri/ *adj*

²budget *vt* to plan or provide for the use of (e g money, time, or manpower) in detail ~ *vi* to arrange or plan a budget

budgie /'buji/ *n* a budgerigar – infml [by shortening & alter.]

¹buff /buf/ *n* **1** a strong supple oil-tanned leather produced chiefly from cattle hides **2** *the* bare skin – chiefly in *in the buff* **3** (a) pale yellowish brown **4** a device (e g a stick or pad) with a soft absorbent surface used for polishing sthg **5** one who has a keen interest in and wide knowledge of a specified subject; an enthusiast ⟨*a film* ~⟩ [MF *buffle* wild ox, fr OIt *bufalo*; (5) earlier *buff* (an enthusiast about going to fires), fr the buff overcoats worn by volunteer firemen in New York City *ab* 1820] – **buff** *adj*

²buff *vt* **1** to polish, shine **2** to give a velvety surface like that of buff to (leather) – **buffer** *n*

buffalo /'bufəloh/ *n, pl* **buffaloes** *also* **buffalos,** *esp collectively* **buffalo 1** WATER BUFFALO **2** a large N American wild ox with short horns, heavy forequarters, and a large muscular hump; *also* any similar wild ox [It *bufalo* & Sp *búfalo*, fr LL *bufalus*, alter. of L *bubalus*, fr Gk *boubalos* African gazelle, irreg fr *bous* head of cattle – more at ¹COW]

¹buffer /'bufə/ *n* an (ineffectual) fellow – chiefly in *old buffer*; infml [origin unknown]

²buffer *n* **1** any of various devices for reducing the effect of an impact; *esp, Br* a spring-loaded metal disc on a railway vehicle or at the end of a railway track **2** a device that serves to protect sthg, or to cushion against shock **3** a person who shields another, esp from annoying routine matters **4** (a solution containing) a substance capable in solution of neutralizing both acids and bases and thereby maintaining the original acidity or basicity of the solution **5** a temporary storage unit (e g in a computer); *esp* one that accepts information at one rate and delivers it at another [*buff* (to react like a soft body when struck)]

³buffer *vt* **1** to lessen the shock of; cushion **2** to add a buffer to (e g a solution); *also* to buffer a solution of (a substance)

buffer state *n* a small neutral state lying between 2 larger potentially rival powers

¹buffet /'bufit/ *n* **1** a blow, esp with the hand **2** sthg that strikes with telling force [ME, fr MF, fr OF, dim. of *buffe*]

²buffet /'bufit/ *vt* **1** to strike sharply, esp with the hand; cuff **2** to strike repeatedly; batter ⟨*the waves* ~ed *the shore*⟩ **3** to use roughly; treat unpleasantly ⟨~ed *by life*⟩

³buffet /'boofay/ *n* **1** a sideboard or cupboard often used for the display of tableware **2** a counter for refreshments **3** a meal set out on tables or a sideboard for diners to help themselves **4** *chiefly Br* a self-service restaurant or snack bar [F]

bufflehead /'bufl,hed/ *n* a small N American diving duck [arch *buffle* (buffalo) + *head*]

buffo /'bufoh/ *n, pl* **buffi** /'bufi/, **buffos** a clown, buffoon; *specif* a male singer of comic roles in opera [It, fr *buffone*]

buffoon /bə'foohn/ *n* **1** a ludicrous figure; a clown **2** a rough and noisy fool [MF *bouffon*, fr OIt *buffone*, fr ML *bufon-*, *bufo*, fr L, toad] – **buffoonery** *n*

¹bug /bug/ *n* **1** any of several insects commonly considered obnoxious; *esp* a bedbug **2** an unexpected defect or imperfection ⟨*we'll need to iron the* ~s *out*⟩ **3** a disease-producing germ; *also* a disease caused by it – not used technically **4** a concealed listening device **5** a temporary enthusiasm; a craze – infml [ME *bugge* spectre, goblin; akin to Norw dial. *bugge* important man – more at BIG]

²bug *vt* **-gg- 1a** to plant a concealed listening device in **b** to eavesdrop on by means of a mechanical bug **2** to bother, annoy – infml ⟨*don't* ~ *me with petty details*⟩

bugaboo /'bugə,booh/ *n, pl* **bugaboos** *chiefly NAm* a bugbear [prob of Celt origin; akin to W *bwcibo* the Devil (fr *bwci* hobgoblin + *bo* scarecrow), Corn *buccaboo*]

bugbear /'bug,beə/ *n* an object or (persistent) source of fear, concern, or difficulty ⟨*this national* ~ *of inflation*⟩ [prob fr ¹*bug* + ¹*bear*]

¹bugger /'bugə/ *n* **1** a sodomite **2a** a worthless or contemptible person, esp male **b** a creature; *esp* a man ⟨*poor* ~⟩ **3** *chiefly Br* a cause of annoyance or difficulty *USE* (*except 1*) vulg [MF *bougre* heretic, sodomite, fr ML *Bulgarus*, lit., Bulgarian]

²bugger *vt* **1** to practise sodomy on **2a** – used interjectionally to express contempt or annoyance ⟨~ *Tom! We'll go without him*⟩ **b** to damage or ruin, usu because of incompetence – often + *up* **3** to exhaust; WEAR OUT **4** *Br* to be evasive with or misleading to – + *around* or *about* ⟨*don't* ~ *me about*⟩ ~ *vi Br* to fool *around* or *about*, esp by dithering or being indecisive *USE* (*except 1*) vulg

,bugger 'all *n, Br* nothing ⟨*there's* ~ *else to do*⟩ – vulg

,bugger 'off *vi, Br* to go away – vulg

buggery /'bugəri/ *n* sodomy

¹buggy /'bugi/ *adj* infested with bugs

²buggy *n* a light one-horse carriage [origin unknown]

¹bugle /'byoohgl/ *n* a European annual plant of the mint family that has spikes of blue flowers [ME, fr OF, fr LL *bugula*]

²bugle *n* a valveless brass instrument that is used esp for military calls [ME, buffalo, instrument made of buffalo horn, bugle, fr OF, fr L *buculus*, dim. of *bos* head of cattle – more at ¹COW]

³bugle *vi* to sound a bugle – **bugler** /'byoohglə/ *n*

bugloss /'byooh,glos/ *n* any of several coarse hairy plants of the borage family [MF *buglosse*, fr L *buglossa*, irreg fr Gk *bouglōssos*, fr *bous* head of cattle + *glōssa* tongue – more at ¹COW, ²GLOSS]

buhl, boulle /boohl/ *n* inlaid decoration of tortoiseshell or ornamental metalwork (e g brass) used in cabinetwork [André Charles *Boulle* †1732 F cabinet-maker]

buhr, burr /buh/ *n* buhrstone

'buhr,stone /-,stohn/ *n* (a millstone cut from) a silica rock used for millstones [prob fr ¹*burr* + *stone*]

¹build /bild/ *vb* **built** /bilt/ *vt* **1** to construct by putting together materials gradually into a composite whole **2** to cause to be constructed **3** to develop according to a systematic plan, by a definite process, or on a particular base **4** to increase or enlarge ~ *vi* **1** to engage in building **2a** to increase in intensity ⟨~ *to a climax*⟩ **b** to develop in extent ⟨*outside the arena a queue was already* ~ing⟩ [ME *bilden*, fr OE *byldan*; akin to OE *būan* to dwell – more at ¹BOWER]

²build *n* the physical proportions of a person or

animal; *esp* a person's figure of a usu specified type ⟨*an athletic* ~⟩

builder /'bildə/ *n* sby who contracts to build and supervises building operations [[1]BUILD + [2]-ER]

build in *vt* to construct or develop as an integral part

building /'bilding/ *n* **1** a permanent structure (e g a school or house) usu having walls and a roof 👁 **2** the art, business, or act of assembling materials into a structure

'building ,line *n* a line fixed with respect to the frontage of a plot of land beyond which the owner may not build

'building so,ciety *n* any of various British organizations in which the public can invest money, and which advance money for house purchase

'build,up /-,up/ *n* **1** sthg produced by building up ⟨*deal with the* ~ *of traffic*⟩ **2** praise or publicity, esp given in advance ⟨*sales were slow in spite of the* ~ *the product received*⟩

build up *vt* **1** to develop gradually by increments ⟨built up *a library*⟩ **2** to promote the esteem of; praise ~ *vi* to accumulate or develop appreciably ⟨*clouds* building up *on the horizon*⟩

built /bilt/ *adj* proportioned or formed in a specified way ⟨*a slightly* ~ *girl*⟩

,built-'in *adj* **1** forming an integral part of a structure ⟨~ *cupboards*⟩ **2** inherent

,built-'up *adj* **1** made of several sections or layers fastened together **2** well-filled or fully covered with buildings ⟨*a* ~ *area*⟩

bulb /bulb/ *n* **1a** a short stem base of a plant (e g the lily, onion, or hyacinth), with 1 or more buds enclosed in overlapping membranous or fleshy leaves, that is formed underground as a resting stage in the plant's development – compare CORM, TUBER **b** a tuber, corm, or other fleshy structure resembling a bulb in appearance **c** a plant having or developing from a bulb **2** INCANDESCENT LAMP **3** a rounded or swollen anatomical structure [L *bulbus*, fr Gk *bolbos* bulbous plant; akin to Arm *bolk* radish]

bulbous /'bulbəs/ *adj* **1** growing from or bearing bulbs **2** resembling a bulb, esp in roundness ⟨*a* ~ *nose*⟩ – **bulbously** *adv*

bulbul /'bool,bool/ *n* any of various songbirds of Asia and Africa that live in groups [Per, fr Ar]

Bulgarian /bul'geəri·ən, bool-/ *n* **1 Bulgarian** *also* **Bulgar** a native or inhabitant of Bulgaria **2** the Slavonic language of the Bulgarians ☞ LANGUAGE [*Bulgaria*, country in SE Europe] – **Bulgarian** *adj*

[1]**bulge** /bulj/ *n* **1** BILGE 1 **2** a swelling or convex curve on a surface, usu caused by pressure from within or below **3** a sudden and usu temporary expansion (e g in population) [MF *boulge, bouge* leather bag, curved part – more at BUDGET] – **bulgy** *adj*

[2]**bulge** *vi vi* to jut out; swell ⟨*eaten so much I'm* bulging⟩

bulimia /byooh'limi·ə/ *n* an abnormal and constant craving for food [NL, fr Gk *boulimia* great hunger, fr *bous* head of cattle + *limos* hunger – more at [1]COW, LESS]

[1]**bulk** /bulk/ *n* **1a** spatial dimension; *esp* volume **b** roughage **2a** voluminous or ponderous mass – often used with reference to the shape or size of a corpulent person **b** a structure, esp when viewed as a mass of material ⟨*the shrouded* ~s *of snow-covered cars*⟩ **3** the main or greater part *of* [ME, heap, bulk, fr ON *bulki* cargo] – **in bulk** in large amounts or quantities; *esp, of goods bought and sold* in amounts or quantities much larger than as usu packaged or purchased

[2]**bulk** *vt* **1** to cause to swell or to be thicker or fuller; pad – often + *out* ⟨*had to* ~ *the text out to 20,000 words*⟩ **2** to gather into a mass ~ *vi* to appear as a factor; loom ⟨*a consideration that* ~s *large in everyone's thinking*⟩

[3]**bulk** *adj* (of materials) in bulk ⟨~ *cement*⟩

'bulk,head /-,hed/ *n* a partition or wall separating compartments (e g in an aircraft or ship) [*bulk* (structure projecting from a building) + *head*]

bulky /'bulki/ *adj* **1** having too much bulk; *esp* unwieldy **2** corpulent – chiefly euph – **bulkily** *adv*, **bulkiness** *n*

[1]**bull** /bool/ *n* **1a** an adult male bovine animal **b** an adult male elephant, whale, or other large animal **2** one who buys securities or commodities in expectation of a price rise or who acts to effect such a rise – compare BEAR **3** BULL'S-EYE 3a [ME *bule*, fr OE *bula*; akin to OE *blāwan* to blow; (2) prob developed as a companion to *bear*]

[2]**bull** *adj* BULLISH 1

[3]**bull** *vt* to try to increase the price of (e g stocks) or in (a market)

[4]**bull** *n* **1** a papal edict on a subject of major importance **2** an edict, decree [ME *bulle*, fr ML *bulla* seal, sealed document, fr L, bubble, amulet]

[5]**bull** *n* **1** empty boastful talk; nonsense **2** *Br* unnecessary or irksome fatigues or discipline, esp in the armed forces ***USE*** slang [short for *bullshit*]

bulla /'boolə, 'bulə/ *n, pl* **bullae** /-li/ **1** a hollow thin-walled rounded bony prominence **2** a large blister or vesicle [NL, fr L] – **bullous** *adj*

bullace /'boolis/ *n* a European plum tree that bears small oval fruit in clusters [ME *bolace*, fr MF *beloce*, fr ML *bolluca*]

'bull ,ant *n* BULLDOG ANT

'bull,dog /-,dog/ *n* **1** a thickset muscular short-haired dog of an English breed that has widely separated forelegs and a short neck **2** a proctor's attendant at Oxford or Cambridge

'bulldog ,ant *n, chiefly Austr* a large ant with a painful sting

'bulldog ,clip *n* a large clip made from 2 flat metal bars and a spring, used to clamp sheets of paper together

bulldoze /'bool,dohz/ *vt* **1** to bully **2** to move, clear, gouge out, or level off with a bulldozer **3** to force insensitively or ruthlessly [perh fr [1]*bull* + alter. of *dose*]

'bull,dozer /-,dohzə/ *n* a tractor-driven machine with a broad blunt horizontal blade that is used for clearing land, building roads, etc [BULLDOZE + [2]-ER]

bullet /'boolit/ *n* **1** a small round or elongated missile designed to be fired from a firearm; *broadly* CARTRIDGE 1a **2** sthg resembling a bullet [MF *boulette* small ball & *boulet* missile, dims. of *boule* ball – more at [2]BOWL] – **bulletproof** *adj*

,bullet'headed /-'hedid/ *adj* **1** having a rounded solid-looking head **2** bullheaded

bulletin /'boolətin/ *n* **1** a brief public notice; *specif* a brief news item intended for immediate publication **2** a short programme of news items on radio or television [F, fr It *bullettino*, dim. of *bulla* papal edict, fr ML – more at [4]BULL] '**bulletin ,board** *n, NAm* a notice-board

'**bull,fight** /-,fiet/ *n* a spectacle (in an arena) in which bulls are ceremonially excited, fought with, and in Hispanic tradition killed, for public entertainment – **bullfighter** *n*

'**bull,finch** /-,finch/ *n* a European finch, the male of which has a rosy red breast and throat

'**bull,frog** /-,frog/ *n* a heavy-bodied deep-voiced frog

'**bull,head** /-,hed/ *n* any of various small river fishes with a big head; *esp* a miller's thumb

,**bull'headed** /-'hedid/ *adj* stupidly stubborn; headstrong – **bullheadedly** *adv*, **bullheadedness** *n*

'**bull,horn** /-,hawn/ *n* a megaphone

bullion /'boolyən/ *n* gold or silver (in bars) that has not been minted [ME, fr AF, mint]

bullish /'boolish/ *adj* **1** suggestive of a bull (e g in brawniness) **2** marked by, tending to cause, or hopeful of rising prices (e g in a stock market)

,**bull 'neck** *n* a thick short powerful neck – **bull-necked** *adj*

bullock /'boolək/ *n* **1** a young bull **2** a castrated bull [ME *bullok*, fr OE *bulluc*, dim. of *bull*]

'**bull,ring** /-,ring/ *n* an arena for bullfights

'**bull-,roarer** *n* a wooden slat tied to the end of a thong and whirled to make a roaring sound, used esp by Australian aborigines in religious rites

'**bull ,session** *n, NAm* an informal group discussion [[5]*bull*]

'**bull's-,eye** *n* **1** a small thick disc of glass inserted (e g in a ship's deck) to let in light **2** a very hard round usu peppermint sweet **3a** (a shot that hits) the centre of a target **b** sthg that precisely attains a desired end **4** (a lantern having) a simple lens of short focal distance

'**bull,shit** /-,shit/ *n* nonsense – vulg [[1]*bull* + *shit*]

'**bulls,wool** /-,wool/ *n, Austr & NZ* nonsense – infml [[1]*bull* + *wool*]

,**bull 'terrier** *n* a short-haired terrier of a breed originated in England by crossing the bulldog with a breed of terrier

[1]**bully** /'booli/ *n* **1** a browbeating person; *esp* one habitually cruel to others weaker than him-/herself **2** a hired ruffian [orig senses, sweetheart, fine fellow, bravo; prob modif of D *boel* lover, fr MHG *buole*]

[2]**bully** *adj* [*bully* (fine, first-rate), prob fr [1]*bully*] – **bully for** – used to congratulate a specified person, sometimes ironically ⟨*well* bully for *you!*⟩

[3]**bully** *vt* to treat abusively; intimidate

[4]**bully, 'bully-,off** *n* a procedure for starting play in a hockey match in which 2 opposing players face each other and alternately strike the ground and the opponent's stick 3 times before attempting to gain possession of the ball [origin unknown]

[5]**bully** *vt* to put (a hockey ball) in play with a bully ~ *vi* to start or restart a hockey match with a bully – usu + *off*

bully beef, bully *n* beef that has been preserved with salt and tinned [prob modif of F (*bœuf*) *bouilli* boiled beef]

'**bully,boy** /-,boy/ *n* a rough man, esp a hired thug

bulrush /'bool,rush/ *n* **1** any of a genus of annual or perennial sedges **2** the papyrus – used in the Bible **3** *Br* either of 2 reedmaces [ME *bulrysche*]

bulwark /'boolək/ *n* **1a** a solid wall-like structure raised for defence; a rampart **b** a breakwater, seawall **2a** a strong support or protection ⟨*education as a ~ of democracy*⟩ **b** a defence ⟨*a pay rise of 30 per cent would be a ~ against inflation*⟩ **3** the side of a ship above the upper deck – usu pl with sing. meaning [ME *bulwerke*, fr MD *bolwerc*, fr MHG, fr *bole* plank + *werc* work]

[1]**bum** /bum/ *n, chiefly Br* the buttocks – slang [ME *bom*]

[2]**bum** *vt* **-mm-** *Br* to have anal intercourse with – vulg

[3]**bum** *vb* **-mm-** *vi* to spend time idly and often travelling casually ⟨~*med around for 3 years before she got a job*⟩ – usu + *around*; slang ~ *vt* to obtain by begging; cadge ⟨*can I ~ a fag off you?*⟩ – slang [prob back-formation fr [1]*bummer*]

[4]**bum** *n* **1** *NAm* an idler, loafer; *specif* a vagrant, tramp **2** *chiefly NAm* an incompetent worthless person **3** *NAm* one who devotes his/her time to a specified recreational activity ⟨*a ski ~*⟩ ⟨*a beach ~*⟩ *USE* slang [prob short for *bummer*]

[5]**bum** *adj, chiefly NAm* **1** inferior, worthless ⟨~ *advice*⟩ **2** disabled ⟨*a ~ knee*⟩ *USE* slang

[1]**bumble** /'bumbl/ *vi* **bumbling** /'bumbling, 'bumbl·ing/ DRONE 1 [ME *bomblen* to boom, of imit origin]

[2]**bumble** *vi* **bumbling** /'bumbling/ **1** to speak in a faltering manner **2** to proceed unsteadily; stumble – often + *along* [prob alter. of *bungle*] – **bumbler** /'bumblə/ *n*, **bumblingly** /'bumblingli/ *adv*

'**bumble,bee** /-,bee/ *n* any of numerous large robust hairy bees

'**bum,boat** /-,boht/ *n* a boat that brings commodities for sale to larger ships [prob fr LG *bumboot*, fr *bum* tree + *boot* boat]

bumf, bumph /bumf/ *n, Br* (undesirable or superfluous) paperwork – infml [*bumf* (toilet paper), short for *bumfodder*, fr [1]*bum* + *fodder*]

[1]**bummer** /'bumə/ *n, chiefly NAm* [4]BUM 1 [prob modif of G *bummler* loafer, fr *bummeln* to dangle, loaf]

[2]**bummer** *n* an unpleasant experience (e g a bad reaction to a hallucinogenic drug) – infml [[5]*bum* + *-er*]

[1]**bump** /bump/ *vt* **1** to strike or knock with force **2** to collide with **3** to dislodge with a jolt ~ *vi* **1** to knock against sthg with a forceful jolt – often + *into* **2** to proceed in a series of bumps [imit] – **bump into** to encounter, esp by chance

[2]**bump** *n* **1** a sudden forceful blow or jolt **2** a rounded projection from a surface: e g **a** a swelling of tissue **b** a natural protuberance of the skull **3** a thrusting of the hips forwards in an erotic manner – compare [2]GRIND 3a **4** *pl the* act of holding a child by his/her arms and legs and swinging him/her into the air and back to the ground ⟨*gave her the* ~s *on her birthday*⟩

[1]**bumper** /'bumpə/ *n* **1** a brimming cup or glass **2** sthg unusually large [prob fr *bump* (to bulge)]

[2]**bumper** *adj* unusually large ⟨*a ~ crop*⟩

[3]**bumper** *n* **1** a metal or rubber bar, usu at either end of a motor vehicle, for absorbing shock or minimizing damage in collision **2** a bouncer [[1]BUMP + [2]-ER]

bumpkin /'bum(p)kin/ *n* an awkward and unsophisticated rustic ⟨*a country ~*⟩ [perh fr Flem *bommekijn* small cask, fr MD, fr *bomme* cask]

bump off *vt* to murder – slang

bumptious /'bum(p)shəs/ *adj* self-assertive in a presumptuous, obtuse, and often noisy manner; obtrus-

Cavity wall
This consists of two parallel 'skins' of brickwork with a gap of 50–75mm in between. The gap prevents damp penetrating to the inside of the house and acts as insulation. The brickwork is joined by metal ties.

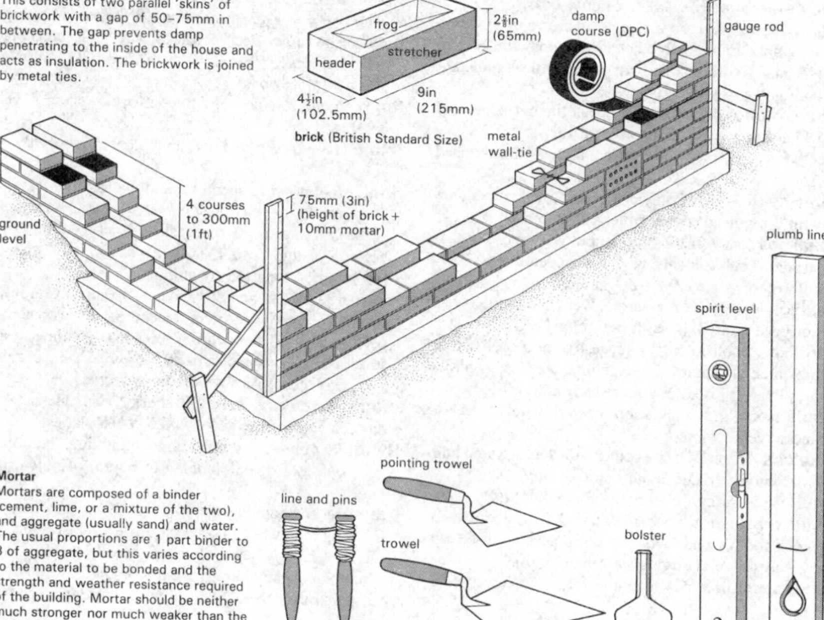

Mortar
Mortars are composed of a binder (cement, lime, or a mixture of the two), and aggregate (usually sand) and water. The usual proportions are 1 part binder to 3 of aggregate, but this varies according to the material to be bonded and the strength and weather resistance required of the building. Mortar should be neither much stronger nor much weaker than the materials with which it is used.

Bonds

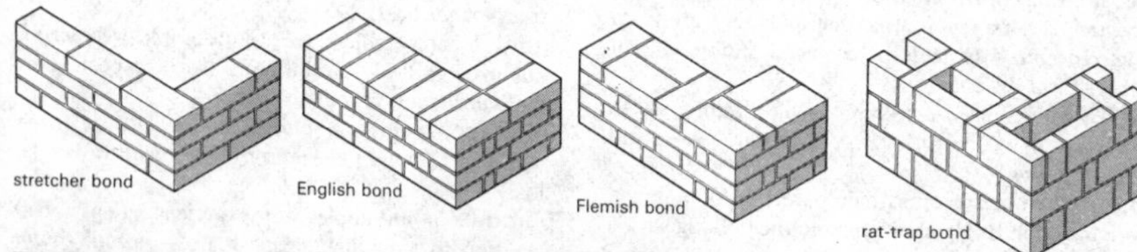

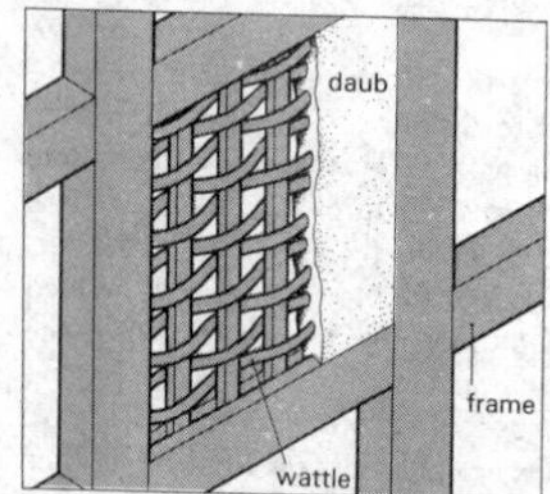

Wattle and daub was used to fill in the basic timber frame of a house. Poles were slotted into the framework, and twigs or reeds were then woven around them into a hurdle pattern. A layer of clay (daub) was then applied and sometimes coated with plaster.

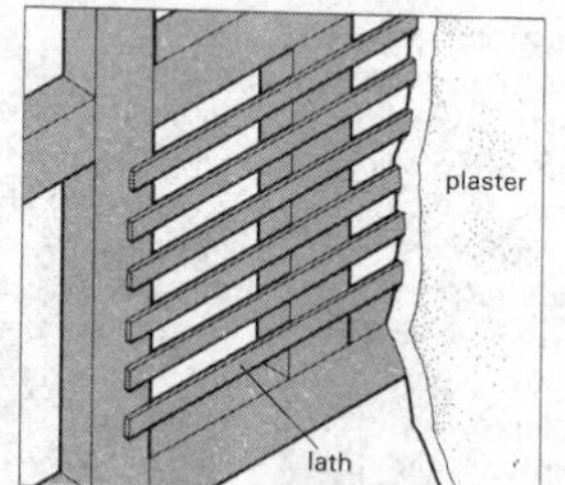

Lath and plaster consisted of laths nailed to a timber frame and covered with plaster.

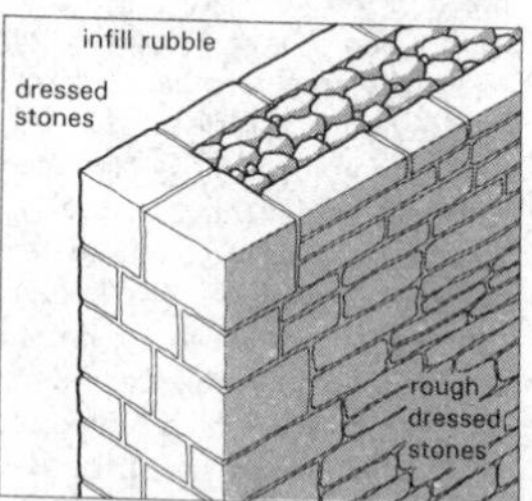

Stone walling is divided into two types – rubble and ashlar. Ashlar is a term used only of finely squared and jointed masonry.

 ARCHITECTURE

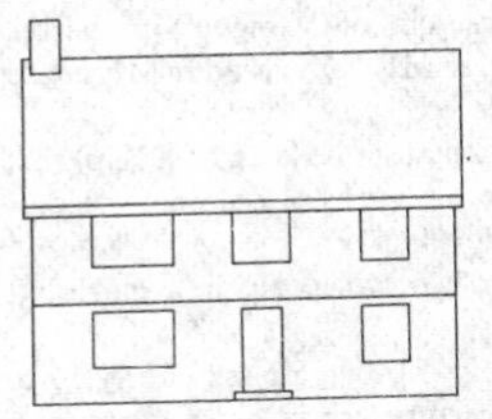

elevation

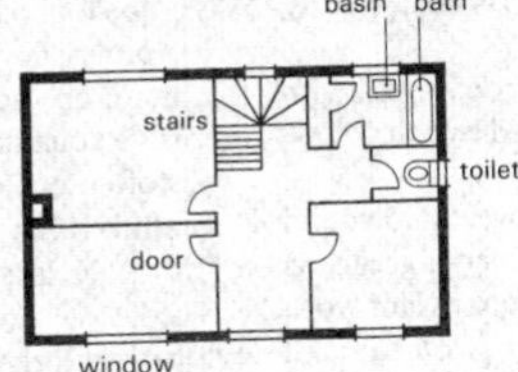

first floor plan

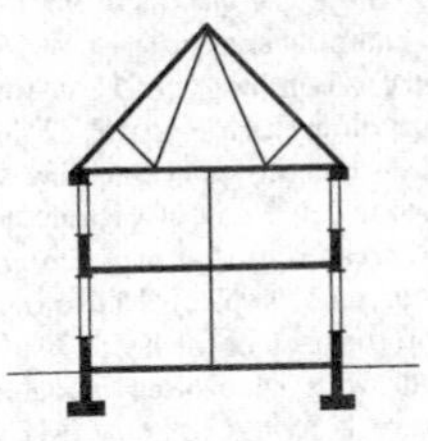

section

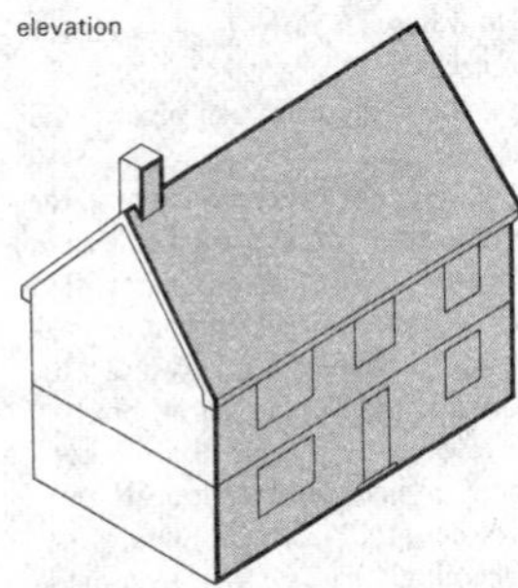

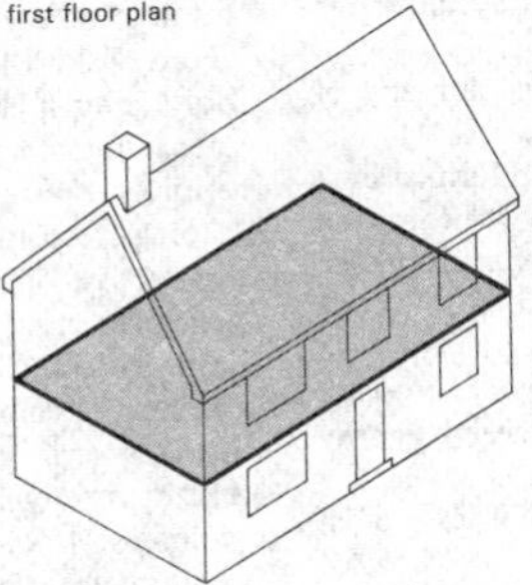

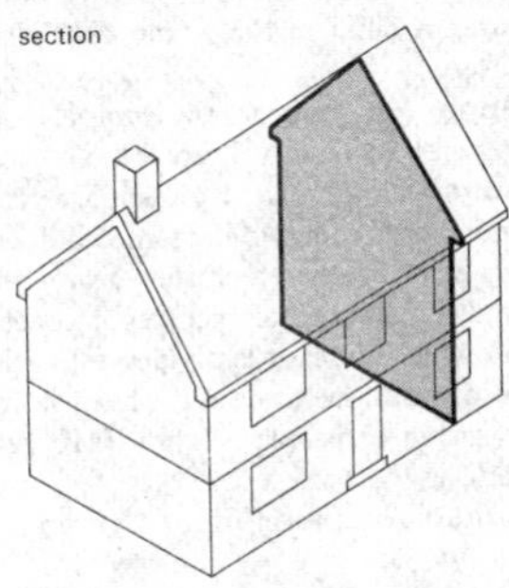

Traditional building styles

Timber frame house. The wattle and daub infilling of boxframed timber houses was, from the 17th century, often replaced with brickwork, sometimes using a herringbone pattern.

Cob and thatch. Cob is clay or pressed earth reinforced with straw or hair. It is durable if protected from damp at top and bottom.

Flint walling is found in S and E England. The corners, doors, and windows are reinforced with brick or stone.

Pantiles are S-shaped tiles made of clay, which is fired and sometimes glazed. They are now used by architects to give a 'Mediterranean' look to a house.

Pargetting or raised and cut plasterwork on timber frame houses, fashionable in E Anglia in the 16th and 17th centuries.

Weatherboarding was used for houses from the 18th century, when imports of soft wood reached areas where timber-built houses were common.

ive [[1]bump + -tious (as in *fractious*)] – **bumptiously** *adv*, **bumptiousness** *n*

bumpy /'bumpi/ *adj* **1** having or covered with bumps; uneven ⟨*a* ~ *road*⟩ **2** marked by jolts ⟨*a* ~ *ride*⟩ – **bumpily** *adv*, **bumpiness** *n*

bun /bun/ *n* **1** any of various usu sweet and round small bread rolls that may contain added ingredients (e g currants or spice) **2** a usu tight knot of hair worn esp on the back of the head **3a** *chiefly N Eng* a small round sweet cake often made from a sponge-cake mixture **b** *Scot* BLACK BUN [ME *bunne*] – **bun in the oven** a child in the womb ⟨*she's got a* bun in the oven⟩

Buna /'b(y)oohnə/ *trademark* – used for any of several artificial rubbers

[1]**bunch** /bunch/ *n* **1** a compact group formed by a number of things of the same kind, esp when growing or held together; a cluster **2** *sing or pl in constr* the main group (e g of cyclists) in a race **3** *pl, Br* a style in which the hair is divided into 2 lengths and tied, usu one on each side of the head **4** *sing or pl in constr* a group of people – infml [ME *bunche*] – **bunchy** *adj*

[2]**bunch** *vb* to form (into) a group or cluster – often + *up*

bund /bund/ *n* an embankment or causeway used to control or retain water or oil [Hindi *band*, fr Per; akin to OE *binden* to bind]

[1]**bundle** /'bundl/ *n* **1a** a collection of things held loosely together **b** a package **c** a collection, conglomerate **2** a small band of mostly parallel nerve or other fibres **3** a great deal; mass ⟨*that will be a* ~ *of fun*⟩ ⟨*he's a* ~ *of nerves*⟩ **4** a sizable sum of money – slang [ME *bundel*, fr MD; akin to OE *byndel* bundle, *bindan* to bind]

[2]**bundle** *vt* **bundling** /'bundling, 'bundl·ing/ **1** to make into a bundle or package **2** to hustle or hurry unceremoniously ⟨~d *the children off to school*⟩ **3** to hastily deposit or stuff *into* a suitcase, box, drawer, etc

bundle up *vb* to dress warmly

bundling /'bundling, 'bundl·ing/ *n* a former custom whereby a courting couple occupied the same bed without undressing [fr gerund of [2]*bundle*]

bundu /'boondooh/ *n*, *SAfr* the bush, veld [Bantu]

'bun-,fight *n*, *Br* **1** an informal gathering of a group; tea-party ⟨*are you going to the post-graduates'* ~*?*⟩ **2** a confused disturbance in which people are jostling and shoving, esp in a confined space *USE* infml

[1]**bung** /bung/ *n* the stopper in the bunghole of a cask; *broadly* sthg used to plug an opening [ME, fr MD *bonne, bonghe*, prob fr LL *puncta* puncture, fr L, fem of *punctus*, pp of *pungere* to prick – more at PUNGENT]

[2]**bung** *vt* **1** to plug, block, or close (as if) with a bung – often + *up* **2** *chiefly Br* to throw, toss **3** *Br* to put ⟨~ *that record on*⟩ *USE (except 1)* infml

bungalow /'bung·gəloh/ *n* a usu detached or semidetached 1-storied house [Hindi *baṅglā*, lit., (house) in the Bengal style]

'bung,hole /-,hohl/ *n* a hole for emptying or filling a cask

bungle /'bung·gl/ *vt* **bungling** /'bung·gling, 'bung·gl·ing/ to perform clumsily; mishandle, botch [perh of Scand origin; akin to Icel *banga* to hammer] – **bungler** /'bung·glə/ *n*, **bungling** /'bung·gling/ *adj*

bunion /'bunyən/ *n* an inflamed swelling at the side of the foot on the first joint of the big toe [prob irreg fr *bunny* (swelling), fr ME *bony*, prob fr MF *bugne* bump on the head]

[1]**bunk** /bungk/ *n* **1** a built-in bed (e g on a ship) that is often one of a tier of berths **2** a sleeping place – infml [prob short for *bunker*]

[2]**bunk** *vi* to sleep or bed *down*, esp in a makeshift bed

[3]**bunk** *n* [origin unknown] – **do a bunk** *chiefly Br* to make a hurried departure, esp in order to escape – slang

[4]**bunk** *n* nonsense, humbug ⟨*history is* ~ – Henry Ford⟩ [short for *bunkum*]

bunk bed *n* either of 2 single beds usu placed one above the other

[1]**bunker** /'bungkə/ *n* **1** a bin or compartment for storage; *esp* one on a ship for storing fuel **2a** a protective embankment or dugout; *esp* a fortified chamber mostly below ground **b** a golf course hazard that is an area of sand-covered bare ground with 1 or more embankments [Sc *bonker* chest, box]

[2]**bunker** *vt* to place or store (esp fuel) in a bunker

bunkum /'bungkəm/ *n* insincere or foolish talk; nonsense [*Buncombe* county, North Carolina, USA; fr the defence of a seemingly irrelevant speech made by its congressional representative, that he was speaking to·Buncombe]

bunny /'buni/ *n* RABBIT 1 – usu used by or to children [E dial. *bun* (rabbit)]

,Bunsen 'burner /'buns(ə)n/ *n* a gas burner in which air is mixed with the gas to produce an intensely hot blue flame [Robert *Bunsen* †1899 G chemist]

[1]**bunt** /bunt/ *n* **1a** the middle part of a square sail ☞ SHIP **b** the bunched part of a furled sail **2** the baggy part of a fishing net [perh fr LG, bundle, fr MLG; akin to OE *byndel* bundle]

[2]**bunt** *n* a disease of wheat caused by either of 2 parasitic fungi [origin unknown]

[3]**bunt** *vt* to strike or push (as if) with the head; butt [alter. of *butt*] – **bunter** *n*

[1]**bunting** /'bunting/ *n* any of various birds that have short strong beaks and are related to the finches [ME]

[2]**bunting** *n* (flags or decorations made of) a lightweight loosely woven fabric [perh fr E dial. *bunt* (to sift)]

buntline /'buntlin, -,lien/ *n* any of the ropes attached to a square sail for hauling it up to the yard for furling ☞ SHIP

[1]**buoy** /boy/ *n* a distinctively shaped and marked float moored to the bottom **a** as a navigational aid to mark a channel or hazard **b** for mooring a ship [ME *boye*, fr (assumed) MF *boie*, of Gmc origin; akin to OE *bēacen* sign – more at BEACON]

[2]**buoy** *vt* **1** to mark (as if) by a buoy **2a** to keep afloat **b** to support, sustain **3** to raise the spirits of ⟨*hope* ~s *him up*⟩ *USE* (*2 & 3*) usu + *up* [(1) [1]*buoy*; (2, 3) prob fr Sp *boyar* to float, fr *boya* buoy, fr (assumed) MF *boie*]

buoyancy /'boyənsi/ *n* **1a** the tendency of a body to float or to rise when submerged in a fluid **b** the power of a fluid to exert an upward force on a body placed in it **2** resilience, vivacity

buoyant /'boyənt/ *adj* **1** capable of floating **2** cheerful, resilient – **buoyantly** *adv*

bur /buh/ *n* [1]BURR

buran /ˈbooh,rahn/ *n* a violent winter storm of the steppes of the USSR [Russ]

burble /ˈbuhbl/ *vi* **burbling** /ˈbuhbling, ˈbuhbl·ing/ **1** to make a bubbling sound; gurgle **2** to babble, prattle **3** *of airflow* to become turbulent [ME *burblen*, prob of imit origin] – **burble** *n*

burbot /ˈbuhbət/ *n, pl* **burbot** *also* **burbots** a freshwater fish of the cod family that has barbels on the mouth [ME *borbot*, fr MF *bourbotte*, fr *bourbeter* to burrow in the mud, fr OF, fr *bourbe* mud]

[1]**burden** /ˈbuhd(ə)n/ *n* **1a** sthg that is carried; a load **b** a duty, responsibility **2** sthg oppressive or wearisome; an encumbrance **3** capacity for carrying cargo ⟨*a ship of a hundred tons* ~⟩ [ME, fr OE *byrthen*; akin to OE *beran* to carry – more at [2]BEAR]

[2]**burden** *vt* to load, oppress

[3]**burden** *n* **1** a chorus, refrain **2** a central topic; a theme [alter. of *bourdon* drone bass (e g in a bagpipe), fr ME *burdoun*, fr MF *bourdon* bass pipe, of imit origin]

,burden of ˈproof *n* the duty of proving an assertion

ˈburdensome /-səm/ *adj* imposing or constituting a burden; oppressive

burdock /ˈbuhdok/ *n* any of a genus of coarse composite plants bearing prickly spherical flower heads [[1]*burr, bur* + [1]*dock*]

bureau /ˈbyooəroh/ *n, pl* **bureaus** *also* **bureaux** /-rohz/ **1a** a specialized administrative unit; *esp* a government department **b** an establishment for exchanging information, making contacts, or coordinating activities **2** *Br* a writing desk; *esp* one with drawers and a sloping top [F, desk, cloth covering for desks, fr OF *burel* woollen cloth, fr (assumed) OF *bure*, fr LL *burra* shaggy cloth]

bureaucracy /byooəˈrokrəsi/ *n* **1** government characterized by specialization of functions, adherence to fixed rules, and a hierarchy of authority; *also* the body of appointed government officials **2** a system of public administration marked by excessive officialism [F *bureaucratie*, fr *bureau* + *-cratie* -cracy] – **bureaucratize** /-,tiez/ *vt*, **bureaucratization** *n*, **bureaucratic** /,byooərəˈkratik/ *adj*, **bureaucratically** *adv*

bureaucrat /ˈbyooərə,krat/ *n* a member of a bureaucracy; *esp* a government official who follows a rigid routine

burette, *NAm also* **buret** /byooˈret/ *n* a graduated glass tube with a small aperture and stopcock for measuring usu small quantities of liquid [F *burette*, fr MF, cruet, fr *buire* pitcher, alter. of OF *buie*, of Gmc origin; akin to OE *būc* pitcher – more at BUCKET]

burgage /ˈbuhgij/ *n* a tenure by which land in an English or Scottish town was held for a yearly rent [ME, property held by burgage tenure, fr MF *bourgage*, lit., burgage, fr OF, fr *bourg, borc* town, fr L *burgus* fortified place, of Gmc origin; akin to OHG *burg* fortified place – more at BOROUGH]

burgee /ˈbuhjee/ *n* a swallow-tailed or triangular flag flown, esp by racing yachts, for identification [perh fr F dial *bourgeais* shipowner]

burgeon /ˈbuhj(ə)n/ *vi* **1** to send forth new growth (e g buds or branches) **2** to grow and expand rapidly [ME *burjonen*, fr *burjon* bud, fr OF, fr (assumed) VL *burrion-, burrio*, fr LL *burra* shaggy cloth]

burger /ˈbuhgə/ **1** a savoury flat cake, usu of minced meat, that is eaten grilled or fried; *esp* a hamburger **2** a sandwich made with a burger, usu in a bread roll (topped with a usu specified food such as cheese) *USE* usu in combination ⟨*beef*burger⟩ ⟨*cheese*burger⟩ [ham*burger*]

burgess /ˈbuhjis/ *n, archaic* a citizen of a British borough [ME *burgeis*, fr OF *borjois*, fr *borc*]

burgh /ˈburə/ *n* a borough; *specif* a town in Scotland that has a charter [ME – more at BOROUGH]

burgher /ˈbuhgə/ *n* an inhabitant of an esp medieval borough or a town

burglar /ˈbuhglə/ *n* sby who commits burglary [AF *burgler*, fr ML *burglator*, prob alter. of *burgator*, fr *burgatus*, pp of *burgare* to commit burglary, fr L *burgus* fortified place] – **burglarize** *vt, chiefly NAm*

burglary /ˈbuhgləri/ *n* the offence of unlawfully entering a building with criminal intent, esp to steal

burgle /ˈbuhgl/ *vt* **burgling** /ˈbuhgling, ˈbuhgl·ing/ to commit an act of burglary against [back-formation fr *burglar*]

burgomaster /ˈbuhgə,mahstə/ *n* the mayor of a town in certain European countries [part modif, part trans of D *burgemeester*, fr *burg* town + *meester* master]

burgoo /ˈbuh,gooh, ,-ˈ-/ *n* porridge, esp as formerly served to sailors [perh fr Ar *burghul*]

Burgundy /ˈbuhgəndi/ *n* a red or white table wine from the Burgundy region of France

burial /ˈberi·əl/ *n* the act, process, or ceremony of burying esp a dead body [ME *beriel, berial*, back-formation fr *beriels* (taken as a plural), fr OE *byrgels*; akin to OS *burgisli* tomb, OE *byrgan* to bury – more at BURY]

burin /ˈbyooərin/ *n* **1** an engraver's steel cutting tool **2** a prehistoric flint tool with a bevelled point [F]

burk, berk *also* **birk** /buhk/ *n, Br* a stupid person; a fool [short for rhyming slang *Berkshire* (or perh *Berkeley*) *Hunt* cunt]

burke /buhk/ *vt* **1** to suffocate or strangle in order to obtain a body to be sold for dissection **2a** to suppress quietly or indirectly ⟨~ *an inquiry*⟩ **b** to bypass, avoid – derog ⟨~ *an issue*⟩ [William *Burke* †1829 Ir criminal executed for this crime]

[1]**burl** /buhl/ *vt* to finish (cloth), esp by repairing loose threads and knots [ME, fr *burle* knot or lump in thread or cloth, deriv of LL *burra* shaggy cloth] – **burler** *n*

[2]**burl** *n, Austr* a try, attempt – esp in *give it a burl* [prob alter. of *whirl* (as in *give it a whirl*)]

burlap /ˈbuhlap/ *n* a coarse heavy plain-woven fabric, usu of jute or hemp, used for sacking and in furniture and linoleum manufacture [alter. of earlier *borelapp*]

[1]**burlesque** /buhˈlesk/ *n* **1** a literary or dramatic work that uses exaggeration or imitation to ridicule **2** mockery, usu by caricature **3** a US stage show usu consisting of short turns, comic sketches, and striptease acts [*burlesque*, adj (comic, droll), fr F, fr It *burlesco*, fr *burla* joke, fr Sp] – **burlesque** *adj*

[2]**burlesque** *vt* to imitate in a humorous or derisive manner; mock

burly /ˈbuhli/ *adj* strongly and heavily built [ME, comely, noble, well-built; prob akin to OE *borlīce* extremely, excellently, OHG *burlīh* lofty, excellent] – **burliness** *n*

Burmese /buhˈmeez/ *n, pl* **Burmese** (the Tibeto-Burman language of) a native or inhabitant of

Burma ☞ LANGUAGE [*Burma*, country in SE Asia] – **Burmese** *adj*

[1]**burn** /buhn/ *n, chiefly Scot* a small stream [ME – more at [1]BOURN]

[2]**burn** *vb* **burnt** /buhnt/, **burned** /buhnd, buhnt/ *vi* **1a** to consume fuel and give off heat, light, and gases **b** to undergo combustion **c** to undergo nuclear fission or nuclear fusion **d** to give off light ⟨*a light* ~ing *in the window*⟩ **2a** *of the ears or face* to become very red and feel uncomfortably hot **b** to produce or undergo a painfully stinging or smarting sensation ⟨*fingers* ~ing *from the cold*⟩ **c** to receive sunburn ⟨*kind of skin that* ~s *easily*⟩ **d(1)** to long passionately; [1]DIE 3 ⟨~ing *to tell the story*⟩ **(2)** to be filled *with*; experience sthg strongly ⟨~ing *with fury*⟩ **3** to become charred, scorched, or destroyed by fire or the action of heat ⟨*the potatoes are* ~ing⟩ ~ *vt* **1a** to cause to undergo combustion; *esp* to destroy by fire ⟨~ed *the rubbish*⟩ **b** to use as fuel **2a** to transform by exposure to heat or fire ⟨~ *clay to bricks*⟩ **b** to produce by burning ⟨~ *a hole in the sleeve*⟩ **3a** to injure or damage by exposure to fire, heat, radiation, caustic chemicals, or electricity **b** to execute by burning ⟨~ *heretics at the stake*⟩ **c** to char or scorch by exposing to fire or heat **4** to harm, exploit – often pass [ME *birnan*, fr OE *byrnan*, vi, *bærnan*, vt; akin to OHG *brinnan* to burn, L *fervēre* to boil] – **burnable** *adj* – **burn one's bridges/boats** to cut off all means of retreat – **burn the candle at both ends** to use one's resources or energies to excess; *esp* to be active at night as well as by day – **burn the midnight oil** to work or study far into the night

[3]**burn** *n* **1a** injury or damage resulting (as if) from burning **b** a burned area ⟨*a* ~ *on the table top*⟩ **c** a burning sensation ⟨*the* ~ *of iodine on a cut*⟩ **2** a firing of a spacecraft rocket engine in flight

burner /'buhnə/ *n* the part of a fuel-burning device (e g a stove or furnace) where the flame is produced [[2]BURN + [2]-ER]

burnet /'buhnit/ *n* any of a genus of plants of the rose family with flowers arranged in spikes [ME, fr OF *burnete*, fr *brun* brown – more at BRUNETTE]

'burnet ,moth *n* any of various day-flying moths with bright metallic wings

burning /'buhning/ *adj* **1a** on fire **b** ardent, intense ⟨~ *enthusiasm*⟩ **2a** affecting (as if) with heat ⟨*a* ~ *fever*⟩ **b** resembling that produced by a burn ⟨*a* ~ *sensation on the tongue*⟩ **3** of fundamental importance; urgent ⟨*one of the* ~ *issues of our time*⟩ – **burningly** *adv*

,burning 'bush *n* any of several plants with red fruit or foliage

burnish /'buhnish/ *vt* to make shiny or lustrous, esp by rubbing; polish [ME *burnischen*, fr MF *bruniss-*, stem of *brunir*, lit., to make brown, fr *brun*] – **burnishing** *adj or n*

burnous /,buh'noohs/ *n* a hooded cloak traditionally worn by Arabs and Moors [F, fr Ar *burnus*, fr Gk *birros*]

burn out *vt* **1** to cause to be no longer active, having completed a course of development ⟨*the disease had* burnt *itself* out⟩ **2** to exhaust by excessive physical or mental activity ⟨*she was a* burnt-out *case at 30*⟩ **3** to cause to burn out ~ *vi* to cease to conduct electricity when the enclosed filament or conducting wire has melted

,burnt 'umber *n* (the dark reddish brown colour of) umber calcined to give it a reddish hue – compare RAW UMBER

burn up *vt vt* to drive along extremely fast ⟨burn up *the motorway*⟩ – infml – **burn-up** *n*

[1]**burp** /buhp/ *n* a belch – infml [imit]

[2]**burp** *vb* to (cause to) belch – infml

[1]**burr, bur** /buh/ *n* **1** a rough or prickly covering of a fruit or seed **2** sthg that sticks or clings **3** a thin rough edge left after cutting or shaping metal, plastic, etc **4** the pronunciation of /r/ in a W country or Northumberland accent **5** a small drill; *also* a bit used in a dentist's or surgeon's burr **6** a rough whirring sound [ME *burre*; akin to OE *byrst* bristle – more at BRISTLE] – **burred** *adj*, **burry** *adj*

[2]**burr** *vi* to make a whirring sound ~ *vt* to pronounce with a burr

[3]**burr** *n* buhr

burro /'booroh/ *n, pl* **burros** *chiefly NAm* a small donkey (used as a pack animal) [Sp, irreg fr *borrico*, fr LL *burricus* small horse]

[1]**burrow** /'buroh/ *n* a hole or excavation in the ground made by a rabbit, fox, etc for shelter and habitation [ME *borow*]

[2]**burrow** *vt* **1** to construct or excavate by tunnelling ⟨~ed *its way beneath the hill*⟩ **2** to make a motion suggestive of burrowing with; nestle ⟨*she* ~ed *her grubby hand into mine*⟩ ~ *vi* **1** to conceal oneself (as if) in a burrow **2a** to make a burrow **b** to progress (as if) by digging **3** to make a motion suggestive of burrowing; snuggle, nestle ⟨~ed *against her back for warmth*⟩ **4** to make a search as if by digging ⟨~ed *into her pocket for a 10p piece*⟩ – **burrower** *n*

bursa /'buhsə/ *n, pl* **bursas, bursae** /'buhsi/ a small sac or pouch (between a tendon and a bone) [NL, fr ML, bag, purse – more at PURSE] – **bursal** *adj*

bursar /'buhsə/ *n* **1** an officer (e g of a monastery or college) in charge of funds **2** *chiefly Scot* the holder of a bursary [ML *bursarius*, fr *bursa*]

bursary /'buhs(ə)ri/ *n* **1** a bursar's office **2** a grant of money to a needy student [ML *bursaria*, fr *bursa*]

bursitis /,buh'sietəs/ *n* inflammation of a bursa of the knee, shoulder, elbow, or other joint [NL, fr *bursa*]

[1]**burst** /buhst/ *vb* **burst** *vi* **1** to break open, apart, or into pieces, usu from impact or because of pressure from within **2a** to give way from an excess of emotion ⟨*his heart will* ~ *with grief*⟩ **b** to give vent suddenly to a repressed emotion ⟨~ *into tears*⟩ **3a** to emerge or spring suddenly ⟨~ *out of a house*⟩ **b** to launch, plunge ⟨~ *into song*⟩ **4** to be filled to breaking point or to the point of overflowing ~ *vt* **1** to cause to break open or into pieces, usu by means of pressure from within **2** to produce (as if) by bursting [ME *bersten*, fr OE *berstan*; akin to OHG *brestan* to burst, MIr *brosc* noise] – **burst at the seams** to be large or full to the point of discomfort

[2]**burst** *n* **1** a sudden usu temporary outbreak **2** an explosion, eruption **3** a sharp temporary increase (of speed, energy, etc) **4** a volley of shots

burst out *vi* to begin suddenly ⟨*he* burst out *laughing*⟩ ~ *vt* to exclaim suddenly

bury /'beri/ *vt vt* **1** to dispose of by depositing (as if) in the earth; *esp* to inter **2** to conceal, hide ⟨*the report was* buried *under miscellaneous papers*⟩ **3** to put completely out of mind; HAVE DONE WITH ⟨~ing *their differences*⟩ **4** to submerge, engross – usu + *in*

⟨buried *herself in her books*⟩ [ME *burien*, fr OE *byrgan*; akin to OE *beorgan* to preserve, OHG *bergan* to shelter, Russ *berech'* to save] – **bury the hatchet** to settle a disagreement; become reconciled

¹bus /bus/ *n, pl* **-s-**, *chiefly NAm* **-ss-** **1** a large motor-driven passenger vehicle operating usu according to a timetable along a fixed route **2** a busbar [short for *omnibus*]

²bus *vb* **-s-, -ss-** *vi* to travel by bus ~ *vt* to transport by bus; *specif, chiefly NAm* to transport (children) by bus to a school in another district where the pupils are of a different race, in order to create integrated classes

busbar /'bus,bah/ *n* a conductor or an assembly of conductors connected to several similar circuits in an electrical or electronic system [²omni*bus* + *bar*]

busby /'buzbi/ *n* **1** a military full-dress fur hat worn esp by hussars **2** the bearskin worn by the Brigade of Guards – not used technically ***USE*** ☞ GARMENT [prob fr the name *Busby*]

¹bush /boosh/ *n* **1a** a (low densely branched) shrub **b** a close thicket of shrubs **2** a large uncleared or sparsely settled area (e g in Africa or Australia), usu scrub-covered or forested **3a** a bushy tuft or mass ⟨*a ~ of black hair*⟩ **b** ²BRUSH 2 [ME; akin to OHG *busc* forest]

²bush *vt* to support, protect, etc with bushes ~ *vi* to extend like or resemble a bush

³bush, bushing *n* a usu removable cylindrical lining for an opening used to limit the size of the opening, resist abrasion, or serve as a guide [D *bus* bushing, box, fr MD *busse* box, fr LL *buxis* – more at ²BOX]

⁴bush *vt* to provide (a bearing, shaft, etc) with a bush

'bush ,baby *n* a member of either of 2 genera of small active nocturnal tree-dwelling African primates

'bush,buck /-,buk/ *n, pl* **bushbucks,** *esp collectively* **bushbuck** a small tropical African striped forest antelope [trans of Afrik *bosbok*]

'bush,craft /-,krahft/ *n* skill and experience in living in the bush

bushed *adj* **1** perplexed, confused **2** *chiefly Austr* lost, esp in the bush **3** tired, exhausted – infml [¹BUSH + ¹-ED]

bushel /'booshl/ *n* **1** any of various units of dry capacity ☞ UNIT **2** a container holding a bushel [ME *busshel*, fr OF *boissel*, fr (assumed) OF *boisse* one sixth of a bushel, of Celt origin; akin to MIr *boss* palm of the hand]

'bushland /-lənd, -,land/ *n* ¹BUSH 2

'bushman /-mən/ *n* **1** *cap* a member, or the language, of a race of nomadic hunters of southern Africa **2** *chiefly Austr* sby who lives in the bush and is experienced in bushcraft [(1) modif of obs Afrik *boschjesman*, fr *boschje* (dim. of *bosch* forest) + Afrik *man*]

'bush,master /-,mahstə/ *n* a tropical American pit viper that is the largest New World venomous snake

'bush,ranger /-,raynjə/ *n* **1** a frontiersman, woodsman **2** *Austr* an outlaw living in the bush

bush telegraph *n* the rapid unofficial communication of news, rumours, etc by word of mouth

bushwhack /'boosh,wak/ *vi* **1** to clear a path through thick woods **2** to live or hide out in the woods **3** to fight in or attack from the bush ~ *vt* to ambush [back-formation fr *bushwhacker*] – **bushwhacker** *n*, **bushwhacking** *n*

bushy /'booshi/ *adj* **1** full of or overgrown with bushes **2** growing thickly or densely – **bushily** *adv*, **bushiness** *n*

business /'biznis/ *n* **1a** a role, function **b** an immediate task or objective; a mission **c** a particular field of endeavour ⟨*the best in the ~*⟩ **2a** a usu commercial or mercantile activity engaged in as a means of livelihood **b** one's regular employment, profession, or trade **c** a commercial or industrial enterprise ⟨*sold her ~ and retired*⟩; *also* such enterprises ⟨*~ seldom acts as a unit*⟩ **d** economic transactions or dealings ⟨*ready to take his ~ elsewhere unless service improved*⟩ **3** an affair, matter ⟨*a strange ~*⟩ **4** movement or action performed by an actor **5a** personal concern ⟨*none of your ~*⟩ **b** proper motive; justifying right ⟨*you have no ~ asking me that*⟩ **6** serious activity ⟨*immediately got down to ~*⟩ [ME *bisinesse*, fr *bisy* busy + *-nesse* -ness] – **like nobody's business** extraordinarily well

'business,like /-,liek/ *adj* **1** (briskly) efficient **2** serious, purposeful

'businessman /-mən, -,man/, *fem* **'business,woman** *n* **1** sby professionally engaged in commercial transactions; *esp* a business executive **2** sby with financial flair ⟨*I'm not much of a ~*⟩

busk /busk/ *vi, chiefly Br* to sing or play an instrument in the street (e g outside a theatre) in order to earn money [origin unknown] – **busker** *n*

buskin /'buskin/ *n* a laced boot reaching halfway up the calf or to the knee [perh modif of Sp *borcegui*]

'bus ,lane *n, Br* a traffic lane for buses only

busman /'busmən/ *n, chiefly Br* sby who works on a bus

,busman's 'holiday *n* a holiday spent doing one's usual work

'bus-,shelter *n* a structure giving protection against bad weather at a bus-stop

'bus-,stop *n* a place, usu marked by a standardized sign, where people may board and alight from buses

¹bust /bust/ *n* **1** a sculpture of the upper part of the human figure including the head, neck, and usu shoulders **2** the upper part of the human torso between neck and waist; *esp* the (size of the) breasts of a woman [F *buste*, fr It *busto*, fr L *bustum* tomb]

²bust *vb* **busted** *also* **bust** *vt* **1a** to break, smash; *also* to make inoperative ⟨*~ my watch this morning*⟩ **b** to bring to an end; BREAK UP 3 – often + *up* **2a** to arrest **b** to raid ⟨*police ~ed the flat below looking for heroin*⟩ ~ *vi* **1a** to burst ⟨*laughing fit to ~*⟩ **b** BREAK DOWN 1a **2** to lose a game or turn by exceeding a limit (e g the count of 21 in pontoon) ***USE*** (*vt; vi 1*) infml [alter. of *burst*] – **bust a gut** to exert oneself; make a great effort – infml

³bust *n* a police raid or arrest – infml

⁴bust *adj* **1** broken – chiefly infml **2** bankrupt – chiefly in *go bust*; infml

bustard /'bustəd/ *n* any of a family of usu large Old World and Australian game birds [ME, modif of MF *bistarde*, fr OIt *bistarda*, fr L *avis tarda*, lit., slow bird]

buster /'bustə/ *n* **1** sby or sthg that breaks or breaks up ⟨*crime ~s*⟩ **2** *chiefly NAm* PAL 2a – usu as a form of address ⟨*thanks a million, ~*⟩

[1]**bustle** /ˈbusl/ *vi* **bustling** /ˈbusling, ˈbusl·ing/ to move briskly and often ostentatiously [prob alter. of obs *buskle* (to prepare), freq of *busk*] – **bustling** /ˈbusling/ *adj*, **bustlingly** *adv*

[2]**bustle** *n* noisy and energetic activity ⟨*the hustle and ~ of the big city*⟩

[3]**bustle** *n* a pad or framework worn to expand and support fullness at the back of a woman's skirt [origin unknown]

ˈ**bust-ˌup** *n* **1** a breaking up or apart ⟨*the ~ of their marriage*⟩ **2** a quarrel *USE* infml

busty /ˈbusti/ *adj* having large breasts

[1]**busy** /ˈbizi/ *adj* **1** engaged in action; occupied **2** full of activity; bustling ⟨*a ~ seaport*⟩ **3** foolishly or intrusively active; meddlesome **4** full of detail ⟨*a ~ design*⟩ **5** *NAm, esp of a telephone* in use [ME *bisy*, fr OE *bisig*; akin to MD & MLG *besich* busy] – **busily** /ˈbizəli/ *adv*, **busyness** /ˈbizinis/ *n*

[2]**busy** *vt* to make (esp oneself) busy; occupy ⟨*he* busied *himself with the ironing*⟩

ˈ**busyˌbody** /-ˌbodi/ *n* an officious or inquisitive person

ˌ**busy** ˈ**lizzie** /ˈlizi/ *n* a common house plant that bears usu pink, scarlet, or crimson flowers almost continuously [[1]*busy* + *Lizzie*, nickname for *Elizabeth*]

[1]**but** /bət; *strong* but/ *conj* **1a** were it not ⟨*would collapse ~ for your help*⟩ **b** without the necessary accompaniment that – used after a negative ⟨*it never rains ~ it pours*⟩ **c** otherwise than; that not ⟨*I don't know ~ what I'll go*⟩ **2a** on the contrary; on the other hand – used to join coordinate sentence elements of the same class or function expressing contrast ⟨*I meant to tell you ~ you weren't here*⟩ **b** and nevertheless; and yet ⟨*poor ~ proud*⟩ **c** – introducing an expression of protest or enthusiasm ⟨*~ that's ridiculous*⟩ or embarking on a new topic ⟨*~ to continue B*⟩ [ME, fr OE *būtan*, prep & conj, outside, without, except, except that; akin to OHG *būzan* without, except; both fr a prehistoric WGmc compound whose constituents are represented by OE *be* by & OE *ūtan* outside; akin to OE *ūt* out – more at BY, OUT]

[2]**but** *prep* **1a** with the exception of; barring ⟨*we're all here ~ Mary*⟩ **b** other than ⟨*this letter is nothing ~ an insult*⟩ **c** not counting ⟨*the next house ~ 2*⟩ **2** *Scot* without, lacking

[3]**but** *adv* **1** only, merely ⟨*he is ~ a child*⟩ **2** to the contrary ⟨*who knows ~ that he may succeed*⟩ **3** – used for emphasis ⟨*get there ~ fast*⟩ **4** *NE Eng & Austr* however, though ⟨*it's pouring with rain, warm ~*⟩

[4]**but** /but/ *n* a doubt, objection ⟨*there are no ~s about it*⟩

butadiene /ˌbyoohtəˈdie·een, ˌ---ˈ-/ *n* an inflammable gaseous hydrocarbon used in making synthetic rubbers [ISV *butane* + *di-* + *-ene*]

butane /ˈbyoohtayn/ *n* an inflammable gaseous hydrocarbon of the alkane series used esp as a fuel (e g in cigarette lighters) [ISV *butyric* + *-ane*]

[1]**butch** /booch/ *n, chiefly Br* a male or female homosexual who plays the masculine role in a relationship [*Butch*, a nickname for boys, prob short for *butcher*]

[2]**butch** *adj, chiefly Br* aggressively masculine in appearance – used, often disparagingly, of both women and (esp homosexual) men

[1]**butcher** /ˈboochə/ *n* **1a** sby who slaughters animals or dresses their flesh **b** sby who deals in meat **2** sby who kills ruthlessly or brutally [ME *bocher*, fr OF *bouchier*, fr *bouc* he-goat, prob of Celt origin; akin to MIr *bocc* he-goat – more at [1]BUCK]

[2]**butcher** *vt* **1** to slaughter and prepare for market **2** to kill in a barbarous manner **3** to spoil, ruin – **butcherer** *n*

ˈ**butcher-ˌbird** *n* any of various shrikes

ˈ**butchers** *n, pl* **butchers** *Br* LOOK 1 – slang [rhyming slang *butcher's (hook)*]

ˌ**butcher's-ˈbroom** *n* a European plant with stiff-pointed leaflike twigs used for brooms

butchery /ˈbooch(ə)ri/ *n* **1** the preparation of meat for sale **2** cruel and ruthless slaughter of human beings **3** the action of spoiling or ruining **4** *chiefly Br* a slaughterhouse

butler /ˈbutlə/ *n* **1** a manservant in charge of the wines and spirits **2** the chief male servant of a household [ME *buteler*, fr OF *bouteillier* bottle bearer, fr *bouteille* bottle – more at BOTTLE]

[1]**butt** /but/ *vb* to strike or shove (sthg) with the head or horns [ME *butten*, fr OF *boter*, of Gmc origin; akin to OHG *bōzan* to beat – more at [1]BEAT]

[2]**butt** *n* a blow or thrust, usu with the head or horns

[3]**butt** *n* **1a** a backstop for catching missiles shot at a target **b** a target **c** *pl* a range, specif for archery or rifle practice **d** a low mound, wall, etc from behind which sportsmen shoot at game birds **2** an object of abuse or ridicule; a victim [ME; partly fr MF *but* target, end, of Gmc origin; akin to ON *būtr* log, LG *butt* blunt; partly fr MF *bute* backstop, fr *but* target]

[4]**butt** *vi* to abut – usu + *against* or *onto* ~ *vt* **1** to place end to end or side to side without overlapping **2** to join by means of a butt joint [partly fr [3]*butt*, partly fr [5]*butt*]

[5]**butt** *n* **1** the end of a plant or tree nearest the roots **2** the thicker or handle end of a tool or weapon **3** an unused remainder; *esp* the unsmoked remnant of a cigar or cigarette [ME; prob akin to ME *buttok* buttock, LG *butt* blunt, OHG *bōzan* to beat]

[6]**butt** *n* a large cask, esp for wine, beer, or water [ME, fr MF *botte*, fr OProv *bota*, fr LL *buttis*]

butte /byooht/ *n, chiefly NAm* an isolated hill with steep sides [F, knoll, fr MF *bute* mound of earth serving as a backstop]

[1]**butter** /ˈbutə/ *n* **1** a pale yellow solid emulsion of fat globules, air, and water made by churning milk or cream and used as food **2a** any of various vegetable oils remaining solid or semisolid at ordinary temperatures ⟨*cocoa ~*⟩ **b** any of various food spreads made with or having the consistency of butter ⟨*peanut ~*⟩ [ME, fr OE *butere*; akin to OHG *butera* butter; both fr a prehistoric WGmc word borrowed fr L *butyrum* butter, fr Gk *boutyron*, fr *bous* cow + *tyros* cheese] – **butterless** *adj*

[2]**butter** *vt* to spread or cook with butter

ˈ**butterˌball** /-ˌbawl/ *n* a chubby person – infml

ˈ**butter ˌbean** *n* **1** a (large dried) lima bean **2** SIEVA BEAN

ˈ**butterˌbur** /-ˌbuh/ *n* a large Eurasian plant with very large leaves and reddish-purple flowers

ˈ**butterˌcup** /-ˌkup/ *n* any of many plants with usu bright yellow flowers that commonly grow in fields and as weeds

ˈ**butterˌfat** /-ˌfat/ *n* the natural fat of milk and chief constituent of butter

ˈbutter,fingered /-,fing·gəd/ *adj* apt to let things fall or slip through the fingers; careless – infml

ˈbutter,fingers /-,fing·gəz/ *n, pl* **butterfingers** a butterfingered person – infml

ˈbutter,fish /-,fish/ *n* any of numerous fishes with a slippery coating of mucus

ˈbutter,fly /-,flie/ *n* **1** any of numerous slender-bodied day-flying insects with large broad often brightly coloured wings ☞ ANATOMY **2** a person chiefly occupied with the pursuit of pleasure **3** a swimming stroke executed on the front by moving both arms together forwards out of the water and then sweeping them back through the water **4** *pl* queasiness caused esp by nervous tension – infml [ME *butterflie,* fr OE *buterflēoge,* fr *butere* butter + *flēoge* fly; perh fr former belief that butterflies steal milk and butter]

ˈbutterfly ,fish *n* a fish having either variegated colours, broad expanded fins, or both; *esp* a European blenny

ˈbutterfly ,nut *n* WING NUT

ˈbutterfly ,valve *n* a damper or valve consisting of a disc turning round an axis on the diameter of the disc

ˈbutter,milk /-,milk/ *n* **1** the liquid left after butter has been churned from milk or cream **2** cultured milk made by the addition of suitable bacteria to milk

ˈbutter,nut /-,nut/ *n* (the edible oily nut of) an American tree of the walnut family

ˈbutter,scotch /-,skoch/ *n* (the flavour of) a brittle toffee made from brown sugar, syrup, butter, and water

butter up *vt* to charm with lavish flattery; cajole – infml

ˈbutter,wort /-,wuht/ *n* any of a genus of insect-eating plants of damp places

¹buttery /ˈbut(ə)ri/ *n* a room (e g in a college) in which food and drink are served or sold [ME *boterie,* fr MF, fr *botte* cask, butt – more at ⁶BUTT]

²buttery *adj* similar to or containing butter

butt in *vi vi* **1** to meddle, intrude **2** to interrupt

ˈbutt ,joint *n* a joint made by placing the ends or sides of the parts together without overlap and often with reinforcement

buttock /ˈbutək/ *n* the back of a hip that forms one of the 2 fleshy parts on which a person sits [ME *buttok* – more at ⁵BUTT]

¹button /ˈbut(ə)n/ *n* **1** a small knob or disc secured to an article (e g of clothing) and used as a fastener by passing it through a buttonhole or loop **2** an immature whole mushroom **3** a guard on the tip of a fencing foil **4** PUSH BUTTON **5** sthg of little value ⟨*not worth a* ~⟩ [ME *boton,* fr MF, fr OF, fr *boter* to thrust – more at ¹BUTT] – **buttonless** *adj*

²button *vt* to close or fasten (as if) with buttons – often + *up* ⟨~ *up your overcoat*⟩ ~ *vi* to have buttons for fastening ⟨*this dress* ~s *at the back*⟩

ˈbutton-,down *adj, of a collar* having the ends fastened to the garment with buttons

¹ˈbutton,hole /-,hohl/ *n* **1** a slit or loop through which a button is passed **2** *chiefly Br* a flower worn in a buttonhole or pinned to the lapel

²buttonhole *vt* **1** to provide with buttonholes **2** to sew with buttonhole stitch – **buttonholer** *n*

³buttonhole *vt* to detain in conversation [alter. of *buttonhold* (to detain sby by holding the buttons on his clothes)]

ˈbuttonhole ,stitch *n* a closely worked loop stitch used to make a firm or neat edge (e g on a buttonhole) – compare BLANKET STITCH

ˈbutton,hook /-,hook/ *n* a hook for drawing small buttons through buttonholes

ˈbuttons *n, pl* **buttons** *Br* a bellboy – infml [fr rows of buttons on his jacket]

ˈbutton-,through *adj, of a garment* fastened from the top to the bottom with buttons ⟨*a* ~ *skirt*⟩

buttress /ˈbutris/ *n* **1** a structure built against a wall or building to provide support or reinforcement **2** a projecting part of a mountain **3** sthg that supports or strengthens ⟨*a* ~ *of the cause of peace*⟩ [ME *butres,* fr MF *bouterez,* fr OF *boterez,* fr *boter*] – **buttress** *vt,* **buttressed** *adj*

ˈbutt ,weld *n* a butt joint made by welding – **butt-weld** *vt,* **butt welding** *n*

butty /ˈbuti/ *n, dial Br* a sandwich – infml [ˈ*butt*er + ⁴*-y*]

butut /booh'tooht/ *n* ☞ *The Gambia* at NATIONALITY [native name in the Gambia]

butyl /ˈbyoohtil, -tiel/ *n* a univalent radical C_4H_9 derived from butane [ISV *butyric* + *-yl*]

butyr- /byooti-/, **butyro-** *comb form* **1** butyric ⟨butyr*al*⟩ **2** butyric acid ⟨butyr*ate*⟩ [ISV, fr *butyric*]

butyraceous /,byoohtiˈrayshəs/ *adj* buttery – used technically [L *butyrum* butter – more at BUTTER]

butyric /byoohˈtirik/ *adj* relating to or producing butyric acid [F *butyrique,* fr L *butyrum*]

bu,tyric ˈacid *n* an unpleasant-smelling fatty acid found esp in rancid butter

buxom /ˈbuks(ə)m/ *adj* attractively or healthily plump; *specif* full-bosomed [ME *buxsum* compliant, gracious, fr (assumed) OE *būhsum,* fr OE *būgan* to bend – more at ¹BOW] – **buxomness** *n*

¹buy /bie/ *vb* **bought** /bawt/ *vt* **1** to acquire possession or rights to the use of by payment, esp of money; purchase **2** to obtain, often by some sacrifice ⟨bought *peace with their lives*⟩ **3** to bribe, hire **4** to be the purchasing equivalent of ⟨*the pound* ~s *less today than it used to*⟩ **5** to believe, accept ⟨*OK, I'll* ~ *that*⟩ – slang ~ *vi* to make a purchase [ME *byen,* fr OE *bycgan*; akin to Goth *bugjan* to buy] – **buy time** to delay an imminent action or decision; stall

²buy *n* an act of buying; a purchase

buyer /ˈbie·ə/ *n* one who selects and buys stock to be sold in an esp large shop [¹BUY + ²-ER]

ˈbuyer's ,market *n* a market in which supply exceeds demand, buyers have a wide range of choice, and prices tend to be low – compare SELLER'S MARKET

buy in *vt* to obtain (a stock or supply of sthg) by purchase, esp in anticipation of need; *also* to complete an outstanding securities transaction by purchase against the account of (a delaying or defaulting speculator or dealer) – **buy-in** /ˈ- ,-/ *n*

buy off *vt* to make a payment to in order to avoid some undesired course of action (e g prosecution)

buy out *vt* **1** to purchase the share or interest of ⟨bought out *his partner*⟩ **2** to free (e g from military service) by payment – usu + *of* ⟨bought *himself* out *of the army*⟩

buy up *vt* **1** to purchase a controlling interest in (e g a company), esp by acquiring shares **2** to buy the entire available supply of

¹buzz /buz/ *vi* **1** to make a low continuous vibratory sound like that of a bee **2** to be filled with a confused murmur ⟨*the room* ~ed *with excitement*⟩ **3** to make a signal with a buzzer ~ *vt* **1** to cause to buzz **2** to fly over or close to in order to threaten or warn ⟨*the airliner was* ~ed *by fighters during its approach*⟩ **3** to summon or signal with a buzzer [ME *bussen*, of imit origin]

²**buzz** *n* **1** a persistent vibratory sound **2a** a confused murmur or flurry of activity **b** rumour, gossip **3** a signal conveyed by a buzzer or bell; *specif* a telephone call – infml **4** *chiefly NAm* a pleasant stimulation; a kick – infml

buzzard /'buzəd/ *n* **1** a contemptible, greedy, or grasping person **2** *chiefly Br* a common large European hawk with soaring flight, or a similar related bird **3** *chiefly NAm* a (large) bird of prey (e g the turkey buzzard) [ME *busard*, fr OF, alter. of *buison*, fr L *buteon-, buteo*]

buzzer /'buzə/ *n* an electric signalling device that makes a buzzing sound [¹BUZZ + ²-ER]

buzz off *vi* to go away quickly – slang

'**buzz ,saw** *n, chiefly NAm* CIRCULAR SAW

'**buzz,word** /-,wuhd/ *n* a usu technical word or phrase unintelligible to laymen

bwana /'bwahnə/ *n, chiefly E Africa* a master, boss – often as a term of address [Swahili, fr Ar *abūna* our father]

¹**by** /bie/ *prep* **1a** in proximity to; near ⟨*standing* ~ *the window*⟩ **b** on the person or in the possession of ⟨*keep a spare set* ~ *me*⟩ **2a** through (the medium of); via ⟨*enter* ~ *the door*⟩ ⟨*delivered* ~ *hand*⟩ **b** 11°15' in the direction of (another compass point up to 90° away) ⟨*north* ~ *east*⟩ **c** up to and then beyond; past ⟨*went right* ~ *him*⟩ **3a** in the circumstances of; during ⟨*studied* ~ *night*⟩ **b** not later than ⟨*in bed* ~ *2 am*⟩ **4a(1)** through the instrumentality or use of ⟨~ *bus*⟩ ⟨*what did he mean* ~ *that?*⟩ **(2)** through the action or creation of ⟨*a trio* ~ *Mozart*⟩ **b(1)** sired by – compare OUT OF 2c **(2)** with the participation of (the other parent) ⟨*his daughter* ~ *his first wife*⟩ **5** with the witness or sanction of ⟨*swear* ~ *Heaven*⟩ **6a** in conformity with ⟨*acted* ~ *the rules*⟩ ⟨*opened it* ~ *mistake*⟩ **b** in terms of ⟨*paid* ~ *the hour*⟩ ⟨*called her* ~ *name*⟩ **c** from the evidence of ⟨*judge* ~ *appearances*⟩ **d** with the action of ⟨*began* ~ *scolding her*⟩ ⟨*alarmed him* ~ *driving too fast*⟩ **7** with respect to ⟨*French* ~ *birth*⟩ **8** to the amount or extent of ⟨*better* ~ *far*⟩ **9** in successive units or increments of ⟨~ *inches*⟩ ⟨*day* ~ *day*⟩ ⟨*succeeded little* ~ *little*⟩ **10** – used in division as the inverse of *into* ⟨*divide 70* ~ *35*⟩, in multiplication ⟨*multiply 10* ~ *4*⟩, and in measurements ⟨*a room 15ft* ~ *20ft*⟩ **11** *chiefly Scot* in comparison with; beside [ME, prep & adv, fr OE, prep, *be, bī*; akin to OHG *bī* by, near, L *ambi-* on both sides, around, Gk *amphi*] – **by oneself 1** alone, unaccompanied ⟨*standing* by himself *watching the others playing*⟩ **2** unaided ⟨*did her shoes up all* by herself⟩

²**by** *adv* **1a** close at hand; near ⟨*when nobody was* ~⟩ **b** at or to another's home ⟨*stop* ~ *for a chat*⟩ **2** past ⟨*saw him go* ~⟩ **3** aside, away; *esp* in or into reserve ⟨*keep a few bottles* ~⟩

,**by and 'by** *adv* soon

,**by and 'large** *adv* ON THE WHOLE, IN GENERAL

'**by-,blow** *n* an indirect blow

¹**bye, by** /bie/ *n* **1** sthg of secondary importance **2** the passage to the next round of a tournament allowed to a competitor without an opponent **3** a run scored in cricket off a ball that passes the batsman without striking the bat or body – compare LEG BYE, EXTRA [alter. of ²*by*] – **by the bye** BY THE WAY

²**bye, by** *interj* – used to express farewell [short for *goodbye*]

¹**bye-bye, by-by** /'- ,-, ,- '-/ *interj* – used to express farewell [baby-talk redupl of *goodbye*]

²'**bye-,bye,** '**by-,by** *n* bed, sleep – usu pl with sing. meaning ⟨*go to* ~s⟩; usu used by or to children

'**by-e,lection** *also* '**bye-e,lection** *n* a special election to fill a vacancy

'**bye-,line** *n* GOAL LINE – infml

Byelorussian, Belorussian /,b(y)eloh'rushən/ *n* **1** a native or inhabitant of Byelorussia in the USSR **2** the Slavonic language of the Byelorussians ☞ LANGUAGE – **Byelorussian** *adj*

¹**bygone** /'bie,gon/ *adj* earlier, past; *esp* outmoded

²**bygone** *n* an esp domestic artefact of an early and disused type – **let bygones be bygones** to forgive and forget past quarrels

bylaw, byelaw /'bie,law/ *n* a local or secondary law or regulation ☞ LAW [ME *bilawe*, prob fr (assumed) ON *bȳlög*, fr ON *bȳr* town + *lög* law]

'**by-,line** *n* **1** a secondary line; a sideline **2** the author's name printed with a newspaper or magazine article

¹'**by,pass** /-,pahs/ *n* **1** a passage to one side; *esp* a road built so that through traffic can avoid a town centre **2** a channel carrying a fluid round a part and back to the main stream

²**bypass** *vt* **1** to avoid by means of a bypass **2** to neglect or ignore, usu intentionally; circumvent

'**by,path** /-,pahth/ *n* a byway

'**by,play** /-,play/ *n* action engaged in on the side while the main action proceeds (e g during a dramatic production)

'**by-,product** *n* sthg produced (e g in manufacturing) in addition to a principal product

byre /'bie-ə/ *n, chiefly Br* a cow shed [ME, fr OE *bȳre*; akin to OE *būr* dwelling – more at ¹BOWER]

Byronic /bie'ronik/ *adj* displaying a self-conscious romanticism [fr the characteristics of the life and writings of George Gordon, Lord *Byron* †1824 E poet] – **Byronically** *adv*

byssinosis /,bisi'nohsis/ *n, pl* **byssinoses** /-seez/ a chronic lung disorder associated with the prolonged inhalation of cotton dust [NL, fr L *byssinus* of fine linen, fr Gk *byssinos*, fr *byssos* byssus]

byssus /'bisəs/ *n, pl* **byssuses, byssi** /-sie/ a tuft of filaments by which some bivalve molluscs (e g mussels) attach themselves to a surface [NL, fr L, linen cloth, fr Gk *byssos* flax, of Sem origin; akin to Heb *būṣ* linen cloth]

bystander /'bie,standə/ *n* one present but not involved in a situation or event

byte /biet/ *n* a string of adjacent binary digits that is often shorter than a word and is processed by a computer as a unit; *esp* one that is 8 bits long [perh alter. of ²*bite*]

'**by,way** /-,way/ *n* **1** a little-used road **2** a secondary or little known aspect ⟨*the author takes us down the* ~s *of medieval literature*⟩

'**by,word** /-,wuhd/ *n* **1** a proverb **2** (the name of) sby or sthg taken as representing some usu bad quality ⟨*a* ~ *for cruelty*⟩

,**by-your-'leave** *n* a request for permission – esp in *without so much as a by-your-leave*

Byzantine /bi'zantien, bie-, -teen/ *adj* **1** (characteristic) of the ancient city of Byzantium or its empire **2** of or in a style of architecture developed in the Byzantine Empire in the 5th and 6th c, featuring a central dome carried over a square space and much use of mosaics **3** intricately tortuous; labyrinthine [LL *Byzantinus*, fr *Byzantium*, ancient name of Istanbul, city in Turkey] – **Byzantine** *n*

C

c /see/ *n, pl* **c's, cs** **1** (a graphic representation of or device for reproducing) the 3rd letter of the English alphabet **2** a speech counterpart of orthographic *c* **3** the keynote of a C-major scale **4** one designated *c*, esp as the 3rd in order or class **5** a grade rating a student's work as fair or mediocre in quality **6a** one hundred ☞ NUMBER **b** *chiefly NAm* a sum of $100 – slang

ca' /kah, kaw/ *vb or n, Scot* (to) call

cab /kab/ *n* **1** a taxi **2** the part of a locomotive, lorry, crane, etc that houses the driver and operating controls [short for *cabriolet*]

cabal /kə'bal/ *vi or n* **-ll-** (to unite in or form) a clandestine or unofficial faction, esp in political intrigue [F *cabale* cabala, intrigue, cabal, fr ML *cabbala* cabala, fr LHeb *qabbālāh*, lit., received (lore)] – **cabalist** /'kabl·ist, kə'balist/ *n*

cabala, cabbala, cabbalah *also* **kabala, kabbala, kabbalah** /kə'bahlə, 'kabələ/ *n, often cap* **1** a system of esoteric Jewish mysticism **2a** a traditional, esoteric, occult, or secret matter **b** esoteric doctrine or mysterious art [ML *cabbala*] – **cabalism** /'kabə,liz(ə)m/ *n*, **cabalist** *n*, **cabalistic** /,kabə'listik/ *adj*

caballero /,kabə'lyeəroh, kabə'yeəroh/ *n, pl* **caballeros** a Spanish gentleman or knight [Sp, fr LL *caballarius* horseman – more at CAVALIER]

cabaret /'kabəray/ *n* a stage show or series of acts provided at a nightclub, restaurant, etc [F, lit., tavern, fr ONF, prob irreg fr LL *camera* chamber]

cabbage /'kabij/ *n* **1** a cultivated plant that has a short stem and a dense globular head of usu green leaves used as a vegetable **2a** one who has lost control of his/her esp mental and physical faculties as the result of illness or accident **b** an inactive and apathetic person *USE* (*2*) infml [ME *caboche*, fr ONF, head]

'cabbage ,palm *n* a palm with edible cabbage-like buds at the end of the stem

,cabbage 'white *n* any of several related largely white butterflies whose caterpillars feed on cabbage

cabby, cabbie /'kabi/ *n* a taxi driver – infml [*cab* + *-y*]

caber /'kaybə/ *n* a roughly trimmed tree trunk that is tossed for distance in a Scottish sport [ScGael *cabar*]

[1]**cabin** /'kabin/ *n* **1a** a room or compartment on a ship or boat for passengers or crew **b** a compartment in an aircraft for cargo, crew, or passengers **2** a small usu single-storied dwelling of simple construction **3** *chiefly Br* CAB 2 [ME *cabane*, fr MF, fr OProv *cabana* hut, fr ML *capanna*]

[2]**cabin** *vt* to confine – chiefly poetic

'cabin ,boy *n* a boy employed as a servant on board a ship

'cabin ,class *n* a class of accommodation on a passenger ship superior to tourist class and inferior to first class

'cabin ,cruiser *n* a private motorboat with living accommodation

[1]**cabinet** /'kab(i)nit/ *n* **1a** a case for storing or displaying articles **b** an upright case housing a radio or television set **2** *sing or pl in constr, often cap* a body of advisers of a head of state, who formulate government policy [MF, small room, dim. of ONF *cabine* gambling house]

[2]**cabinet** *adj* of a governmental cabinet

'cabinet,maker /-,maykə/ *n* a craftsman who makes fine furniture in wood – **cabinetmaking** *n*

'cabinet,work /-,wuhk/ *n* high quality woodwork produced by a cabinetmaker

[1]**cable** /'kaybl/ *n* **1a** a strong thick rope **b** a wire rope or metal chain of great tensile strength **2** an assembly of electrical conductors insulated from each other and surrounded by a sheath ☞ TELEVISION **3** a cablegram **4 cable, cable length** a nautical unit of length equal to about **a** *Br* 185m (202yd) **b** *NAm* 219m (240yd) [ME, fr ONF, fr ML *capulum* lasso, fr L *capere* to take – more at HEAVE]

[2]**cable** *vb* **cabling** /'kaybl·ing, 'kaybling/ *vt* **1** to fasten or provide with a cable or cables **2a** to transmit (a message) by submarine cable **b** to communicate with or inform (a person) by cablegram **3** to make into (a form resembling) a cable ~ *vi* to communicate by means of a cablegram

'cable ,car *n* a carriage made to be moved on a cable railway or along an overhead cable

'cablegram /-,gram, -grəm/ *n* a message sent by a submarine cable

'cable-,laid *adj, of a rope* composed of 3 ropes twisted together each containing 3 strands

cable railway *n* a railway along which the carriages are pulled by an endless cable operated by a stationary motor; [2]FUNICULAR

'cable ,stitch *n* a knitting stitch that produces a twisted rope-like pattern

cable television *n* cablevision

'cable,vision /-,vizh(ə)n/ *n* a system in which television signals reach the television by cable rather than by a separate aerial ☞ TELEVISION

'cable,way /-,way/ *n* a suspended cable along which carriers (e g cable cars) can be pulled

cabman /'kabmən/ *n* a taxi driver

cabochon /'kabə,shon/ *n* (the form of) a convex highly polished gem, cut without facets [MF, aug of ONF *caboche* head] – **cabochon** *adv*

caboodle /kə'boohdl/ *n* a collection, lot ⟨*sell the whole* ~⟩ – infml [prob fr *ca-* (intensive prefix, prob of imit origin) + *boodle* (lot, large amount)]

caboose /kə'boohs/ *n* **1** a ship's galley **2** *NAm* a wagon attached to a goods train, usu at the rear, mainly for the use of the train crew [prob fr D *kabuis*, fr MLG *kabūse*]

cabotage /ˈkabəˌtahzh/ *n* trade or transport in coastal waters or between 2 points within a country [F, fr *caboter* to sail along the coast]
cabriole /ˈkabriˌohl/ *n* a curved furniture leg, often ending in an ornamental foot [F, caper]
cabriolet /ˌkabriohˈlay/ *n* a light 2-wheeled 1-horse carriage with upward-curving shafts [F, fr dim. of *cabriole* caper, alter. of MF *capriole*]
cac- /kak-/, **caco-** *comb form* bad; unpleasant ⟨cacogenics⟩ ⟨cacophony⟩ [NL, fr Gk *kak-*, *kako-*, fr *kakos* bad]
ca' canny /ˌkah ˈkani, ˌkaw/ *n, dial Br* a go-slow [E dial. & Sc *ca'canny* to proceed cautiously, fr *ca'* to call, drive + *canny* cautious(ly)] – **ca' canny** *vi, dial Br*
cacao /kəˈkah·oh, -ˈkayoh/ *n, pl* **cacaos** (a S American tree bearing) the fatty seeds which are used, partly fermented and dried, in making cocoa, chocolate, and cocoa butter [Sp, fr Nahuatl *cacahuatl* cacao beans]
cachalot /ˈkashəlot/ *n* SPERM WHALE [F]
cache /kash/ *n* **1** a hiding place, esp for provisions or weapons **2** sthg hidden or stored in a cache [F, fr *cacher* to press, hide, fr (assumed) VL *coacticare* to press together, fr L *coactare* to compel, fr *coactus*, pp of *cogere* to compel – more at COGENT] – **cache** *vt*
cachet /ˈkashay, kəˈshay/ *n* **1** [3]SEAL 1; *esp* one used as a mark of official approval **2** (a characteristic feature or quality conferring) prestige **3** sthg other than the postmark that is stamped by hand on a postal item [MF, fr *cacher* to press, hide]
cachexia /kəˈkeksi·ə/ *also* **cachexy** /kəˈkeksi, ˈkakeksi/ *n* general physical wasting, usu associated with chronic disease [LL *cachexia*, fr Gk *kachexia* bad condition, fr *kak-* cac- + *hexis* condition, fr *echein* to have, be disposed – more at SCHEME] – **cachetic** /kəˈketik/ *adj*
cachinnate /ˈkakinayt/ *vi* to laugh loudly or immoderately – fml [L *cachinnatus*, pp of *cachinnare*, of imit origin] – **cachinnation** /-ˈnaysh(ə)n/ *n*
cachou /ˈkashooh, kəˈshooh/ *n* **1** catechu **2** a pill or lozenge used to sweeten the breath [F, fr Pg *cachu*, fr Malayalam *kāccu*]
cachucha /kəˈchoohchə/ *n* a lively Andalusian solo dance in triple time done with castanets [Sp, small boat, cachucha]
ˌcack-ˈhanded /kak/ *adj, Br* **1** awkward, clumsy –infml **2** left-handed – derog [origin unknown]
cackle /ˈkakl/ *vi* **cackling** /ˈkakl·ing, ˈkakling/ **1** to make the sharp broken noise or cry characteristic of a hen, esp after laying **2** to laugh in a way suggestive of a hen's cackle **3** [1]CHATTER 2 [ME *cakelen*, of imit origin] – **cackle** *n*, **cackler** /ˈkaklə, ˈkakl·ə/ *n*
caco- *comb form* – see CAC-
cacodemon /ˌkakəˈdeemən/ *n* an evil spirit; a demon [Gk *kakodaimōn*, fr *kak-* cac- + *daimōn* spirit] – **cacodemonic** /-diˈmonik/ *adj*
cacography /kəˈkogrəfi, ka-/ *n* bad handwriting or spelling – compare CALLIGRAPHY – **cacographical** /ˌkakəˈgrafikl/ *adj*
cacomistle /ˈkakəˌmisl/ *n* a flesh-eating mammal related to and resembling the raccoon [MexSp, fr Nahuatl *tlacomiztli*, fr *tlaco* half + *miztli* mountain lion]
cacophony /kəˈkofəni/ *n* harsh or discordant sound; dissonance [F *cacaphonie*, fr NL *cacaphonia*, fr Gk *kakophōnia*, fr *kak-* cac- + *phōnē* sound] – **cacophonous** *adj*
cactus /ˈkaktəs/ *n, pl* **cacti** /-tie/, **cactuses** any of a family of plants that have fleshy stems and scaly or spiny branches instead of leaves and are found esp in dry areas (e g deserts) [NL, genus name, fr L, a thistle-like plant, fr Gk *kaktos*]
cad /kad/ *n* an unscrupulous or dishonourable man – derog; not now in vogue [E dial., unskilled assistant, short for Sc *caddie*] – **caddish** *adj*
cadaver /kəˈdavə, -ˈdahvə, -ˈdayvə/ *n* a corpse, usu intended for dissection [L, fr *cadere* to fall]
cadaverous /kəˈdav(ə)rəs/ *adj* **1** (suggestive) of a corpse **2a** unhealthily pale; pallid, livid **b** gaunt, emaciated – **cadaverously** *adv*
caddie, caddy /ˈkadi/ *n* one who assists a golfer, esp by carrying clubs [F *cadet* military cadet] – **caddie, caddy** *vi*
ˈcaddis ˌfly /ˈkadis/ *n* any of an order of 4-winged insects with aquatic larvae
ˈcaddis ˌworm *n* the larva of a caddis fly [prob alter. of obs *codworm*, fr *cod* (bag) + *worm*; fr the case or tube in which it lives]
caddy /ˈkadi/ *n* a small box or tin used esp for holding tea [Malay *kati*, a unit of weight]
-cade /-kayd/ *comb form* (*n* → *n*) procession ⟨*motor*cade⟩ [*cavalcade*]
cadence /ˈkayd(ə)ns/, **ˈcadency** /-si/ *n* **1a** the rhythm and intonations in language **b** a falling inflection of the voice **2** a concluding strain; *specif* a musical chord sequence moving to a harmonic close or point of rest and giving the sense of harmonic completion **3** the modulated and rhythmic recurrence of a sound [ME, fr OIt *cadenza*, fr *cadere* to fall, fr L – more at CHANCE] – **cadenced** *adj*, **cadential** /kayˈdensh(ə)l/ *adj*
cadent /ˈkayd(ə)nt/ *adj* having a rhythmic fall in pitch or tone [L *cadent-*, *cadens*, prp of *cadere*]
cadenza /kəˈdenzə/ *n* a technically showy sometimes improvised solo passage in a concerto [It, cadence, cadenza]
cadet /kəˈdet/ *n* **1a** a younger brother or son **b** (a member of) a younger branch of a family **2** sby training to be an officer in the armed forces or a policeman **3** a young person receiving basic military training, esp at school [F, fr F dial. *capdet* chief, fr LL *capitellum*, dim. of L *capit-*, *caput* head – more at HEAD] – **cadetship** *n*
cadge /kaj/ *vb* to get (sthg) by asking and usu imposing on sby's hospitality or good nature – infml [back-formation fr Sc *cadger* carrier, huckster, fr ME *cadgear*, fr *caggen* to tie] – **cadger** *n*
cadi /ˈkahdi, ˈkay-/ *n* a qadi
cadmium /ˈkadmi·əm/ *n* a bluish-white soft toxic bivalent metallic element used esp in platings and bearing metals ☞ PERIODIC TABLE [NL, fr L *cadmia* calamine – more at CALAMINE; fr the occurrence of its ores together with calamine]
cadre /ˈkahdə/ *n* **1** a permanent nucleus of an esp military organization, capable of rapid expansion if necessary **2** (a member of) a group of activists working for the Communist party cause [F, fr It *quadro*, fr L *quadrum* square – more at [1]QUARREL]
caduceus /kəˈdyoohsi·əs/ *n, pl* **caducei** /-siˌie/ the symbolic staff of an ancient Greek or Roman herald [L, modif of Gk *karykeion*, fr *karyx*, *kēryx* herald; akin to OE *hrēth* glory] – **caducean** /-si·ən, -shən/ *adj*

caducity /kə'dyoohsəti/ *n* **1** the quality of being transitory or perishable **2** senility *USE* fml [F *caducité*, fr *caduc* transitory, fr L *caducus*]

caducous /kə'dyoohkəs/ *adj, esp of floral organs of plants* falling off early [L *caducus* tending to fall, transitory, fr *cadere* to fall – more at CHANCE]

caecum, *NAm chiefly* **cecum** /'seekəm/ *n* a cavity open at 1 end; *esp* the pouch in which the large intestine begins and into which the ileum opens ☞ DIGESTION [NL, fr L *intestinum caecum*, lit., blind intestine] – **caecal** *adj*, **caecally** *adv*

caen- /seen-/, **caeno-** cain-

Caerphilly /keə'fili, kah-, kə-/ *n* a mild white moist cheese [*Caerphilly*, urban district in Wales]

Caesar /'seezə/ *n* **1** any of the Roman emperors who succeeded Augustus Caesar – used as a title **2** *often not cap* a powerful ruler [Gaius Julius *Caesar* †44 BC Roman statesman] – **Caesarean, Caesarian** /si'zeəri·ən/ *adj*

caesarean, cae,sarean 'section, caesarian, *NAm* **cesarean** /si'zeəri·ən/ *n* a surgical incision of the abdominal and uterine walls for the delivery of offspring [fr the belief that Julius Caesar was so born]

caesious /'seezi·əs/ *adj* bluish or greyish green [L *caesius* bluish grey]

caesium, *NAm chiefly* **cesium** /'seezi·əm/ *n* a silver-white soft element of the alkali metal group ☞ PERIODIC TABLE [NL, fr L *caesius*]

caesura /si'zyooərə, -'zhooərə/ *n, pl* **caesuras, caesurae** /-ri/ a break or pause in usu the middle of a line of verse [LL, fr L, act of cutting, fr *caedere* to cut – more at CONCISE] – **caesural** *adj*

café /'kafay/ *n* **1** *chiefly Br* a small restaurant or coffeehouse serving light meals and nonalcoholic drinks **2** *NAm* BAR 5a(2) [F, coffee, café, fr Turk *kahve* – more at COFFEE]

,café au 'lait /oh 'lay (*Fr* kafɛ o lɛ)/ *n* **1** coffee with usu hot milk in about equal parts **2** the colour of coffee with milk [F, coffee with milk]

cafeteria /,kafə'tiəri·ə/ *n* a restaurant in which the customers serve themselves or are served at a counter and take the food to tables to eat [AmerSp *cafetería* retail coffee store, fr Sp *café* coffee]

caff /kaf/ *n, Br* CAFÉ 1; *esp* a cheap plain one – infml [by shortening & alter.]

caffeine /'kafeen/ *n* an alkaloid found esp in tea and coffee that acts as a stimulant and diuretic [G *kaffein*, fr *kaffee* coffee, fr F *café*] – **caffeinic** /ka'feenik, ,kafee'inik/ *adj*

caftan, kaftan /'kaftan/ *n* a loose ankle-length garment with long sleeves, traditionally worn by Arabs ☞ GARMENT [Russ *kaftan*, fr Turk, fr Per *qaftān*]

¹cage /kayj/ *n* **1** a box or enclosure of open construction for animals **2** a barred cell or fenced area for prisoners **3** a framework serving as a support ⟨*the steel ~ of a skyscraper*⟩ **4** an enclosure resembling a cage in form or purpose [ME, fr OF, fr L *cavea* cavity, cage, fr *cavus* hollow – more at ¹CAVE]

²cage *vt* to put or keep (as if) in a cage

'cage ,bird *n* a bird (suitable for keeping) in a cage

cagey *also* **cagy** /'kayji/ *adj* **1** hesitant about committing oneself **2** wary of being trapped or deceived; shrewd *USE* infml [origin unknown] – **cagily** *adv*, **caginess** *also* **cageyness** *n*

cagoule /'kagoohl/ *n* a long waterproof anorak [F, hood, cowl, fr LL *cuculla* monk's cowl]

cahoot /kə'hooht/ *n* a partnership, league – usu pl with sing. meaning; infml; usu in *in cahoots* [perh fr F *cahute* cabin, hut]

caiman /'kaymən/ *n, pl* **caimans,** *esp collectively* **caiman** a cayman

cain-, caino-, caen-, caeno-, *chiefly NAm* **cen-, ceno-** *comb form* new; recent ⟨Caino*zoic*⟩ [Gk *kain-*, *kaino-*, fr *kainos* – more at RECENT]

-caine /-kayn/ *comb form* (→ *n*) synthetic anaesthetic resembling cocaine ⟨*ligno*caine⟩ [G *-kain*, fr *kokain* cocaine]

Cainozoic /,kaynə'zoh·ik/ *adj or n* (of or being) an era of geological history that extends from the beginning of the Tertiary period to the present ☞ EVOLUTION

cairn /keən/ *n* a pile of stones built as a memorial or landmark [ME *carne*, fr ScGael *carn*; akin to OIr & W *carn* cairn] – **cairned** *adj*

cairngorm /'keən,gawm/ *n* a yellow or smoky-brown quartz [*Cairngorm*, mountain in Scotland]

,cairn 'terrier *n* a small compactly built terrier of Scottish origin [fr its use in hunting among cairns]

caisson /'kays(ə)n, kə'soohn/ *n* **1** a chest or wagon for artillery ammunition **2a** a watertight chamber used for construction work under water or as a foundation **b** a float for raising a sunken vessel **c** a hollow floating box or a boat used as a floodgate for a dock or basin **3** COFFER 4 [F, aug of *caisse* box, fr OProv *caisa*, fr L *capsa* chest, case – more at ²CASE]

caisson disease *n* pain, paralysis, and often collapse caused by the release of gas bubbles in tissue on too rapid reduction of pressure (e g in deep-sea diving)

cajole /kə'johl/ *vt* to persuade or deceive with deliberate flattery, esp in the face of reluctance [F *cajoler* to chatter like a jay in a cage, cajole, alter. of MF *gaioler*, fr ONF *gaiole* birdcage, fr LL *caveola*, dim. of L *cavea* cage – more at CAGE] – **cajolement** *n*, **cajoler** *n*, **cajolery** /kə'johl(ə)ri/ *n*

¹cake /kayk/ *n* **1a** a usu fried or baked often unleavened breadlike food – usu in combination ⟨*oat*cake⟩ **b** (a shaped mass of) any of various sweet baked foods made from a basic mixture of flour and sugar, usu with fat, eggs, and a raising agent **c** a flattened usu round mass of (baked or fried) food ⟨*a fish ~*⟩ **2** a block of compressed or congealed matter ⟨*a ~ of ice*⟩ [ME, fr ON *kaka*; akin to OHG *kuocho* cake]

²cake *vt* to encrust ~*vi* to form or harden into a mass

'cake,walk /-,wawk/ *n* **1** (the music for) a stage dance characterized by strutting movements **2** an easy task – infml [fr former practice of giving a cake as a prize to the most accomplished dancer] – **cakewalk** *vi*, **cakewalker** *n*

'Calabar ,bean /'kalə,bah/ *n* the dark brown poisonous seed of a tropical African climbing plant [*Calabar*, city in Nigeria]

calabash /'kalə,bash/ *n* (a container or utensil made from the hard shell of) a gourd [F & Sp; F *calebasse* gourd, fr Sp *calabaza*, prob fr Ar *qar'ah yābisah* dry gourd]

calaboose /ˈkalə,boohs, ,- -ˈ-/ *n, dial NAm* a (local) jail [Sp *calabozo* dungeon]
calabrese /,kaləˈbrayzi, -ˈbree-/ *n* a type of sprouting broccoli [It, Calabrian, fr *Calabria*, region of Italy]
calamander /,kaləˈmandə/ *n* the black-striped wood of an E Indian tree, used for furniture [prob fr D *kalamanderhout* calamander wood]
calamine /ˈkaləmien/ *n* a pink powder of zinc oxide or carbonate with a small amount of ferric oxide, used in soothing or cooling lotions [F, ore of zinc, fr ML *calamina*, alter. of L *cadmia*, fr Gk *kadmeia*, lit., Theban (earth), fr fem of *kadmeios* Theban, fr *Kadmos* Cadmus, legendary founder of Thebes, ancient city of Greece]
calamint /ˈkaləmint/ *n* any of a genus of plants of the mint family [ME *calament*, fr OF, fr ML *calamentum*, fr Gk *kalaminthē*]
calamity /kəˈlaməti/ *n* **1** a state of deep distress caused by misfortune or loss **2** an extremely grave event; a disaster [MF *calamité*, fr L *calamitat-, calamitas*; akin to L *clades* destruction – more at [1]HALT] – **calamitous** *adj*, **calamitously** *adv*, **calamitousness** *n*
calandria /kəˈlandri·ə/ *n* a vessel through which a set of pipes pass, used as a heat-exchanger [Sp, lit., lark]
calc-, calci- *comb form* calcium; calcium salt ⟨*calcify*⟩ ⟨*calcareous*⟩ [L *calc-, calx* lime – more at CHALK]
calcaneum /kalˈkayni·əm/ *n, pl* **calcanea** /-ni·ə/ the calcaneus [L, fr *calc-, calx* heel; akin to Gk *kōlon* limb, *skelos* leg]
calcaneus /kalˈkayni·əs/ *n, pl* **calcanei** /-ni,ie/ a tarsal bone that in human beings is the great bone of the heel [LL, heel, alter. of L *calcaneum*]
calcareous /kalˈkeəri·əs/ *adj* **1** resembling, containing, or consisting of calcium compounds, esp calcium carbonate **2** growing on limestone or in soil impregnated with lime [L *calcarius* of lime, fr *calc-, calx* lime] – **calcareously** *adv*, **calcareousness** *n*
calceolaria /,kalsi·əˈleəri·ə/ *n* any of a genus of tropical American plants of the figwort family with showy pouch-shaped flowers [NL, genus name, fr L *calceolus* small shoe, dim. of *calceus* shoe, fr *calc-, calx* heel]
calces /ˈkal,seez/ *pl of* CALX
calciferol /kalˈsifə,rol/ *n* VITAMIN D_2 [blend of *calciferous* and *ergosterol*]
calciferous /kalˈsif(ə)rəs/ *adj* producing or containing calcium carbonate
calcify /ˈkalsifie/ *vb* **1** to make or become hardened by deposition of calcium salts, esp calcium carbonate **2** to make or become inflexible or unchangeable – **calcific** /kalˈsifik/ *adj*, **calcification** /,kalsifiˈkaysh(ə)n/ *n*
calcine /ˈkalsin, -sien/ *vt* to heat (e g inorganic materials) without melting usu in order to drive off volatile matter or to bring about oxidation or powdering of the material ~ *vi* to be calcined [ME *calcenen*, fr MF *calciner*, fr L *calc-, calx* lime – more at CHALK] – **calcination** /,kalsiˈnaysh(ə)n/ *n*
calcite /ˈkalsiet/ *n* calcium carbonate in the form of limestone, chalk, marble, etc – **calcitic** /-ˈsitik/ *adj*
calcitonin /,kalsiˈtohnin/ *n* a polypeptide hormone produced by the thyroid gland, that tends to lower the level of calcium in the blood plasma [*calci-* + [1]*tonic* + *-in*]
calcium /ˈkalsi·əm/ *n* a silver-white bivalent metallic element of the alkaline-earth group occurring only in combination ☞ PERIODIC TABLE [NL, fr L *calc-, calx* lime]
,calcium ˈcarbide *n* a usu dark grey compound that produces acetylene when mixed with water
,calcium ˈcarbonate *n* a compound found in nature as calcite, limestone, etc, and in bones and shells
,calcium ˈphosphate *n* any of several phosphates that occur naturally in phosphate rock, teeth, and bones and are used in fertilizers and animal feeds
calculable /ˈkalkyooləbl/ *adj* subject to or ascertainable by calculation – **calculably** *adv*, **calculability** /-ləˈbiləti/ *n*
calculate /ˈkalkyoolayt/ *vt* **1** to determine by mathematical processes **2** to reckon by exercise of practical judgment; estimate ~ *vi* **1** to make a calculation **2** to forecast consequences **3** to count, rely – + *on* or *upon* [L *calculatus*, pp of *calculare*, fr *calculus* pebble (used in reckoning), dim. of *calc-, calx* stone used in gambling, lime – more at CHALK]
calculated /ˈkalkyoolaytid/ *adj* **1a** worked out by mathematical calculation **b** engaged in, undertaken, or displayed after reckoning or estimating the probability of success ⟨*a ~ risk*⟩ **2** shrewdly planned to accomplish a purpose **3** apt, likely *to* – **calculatedly** *adv*, **calculatedness** *n*
calculating /ˈkalkyoolayting/ *adj* **1** used for making calculations ⟨*a ~ machine*⟩ **2** marked by shrewd consideration of self-interest; scheming – **calculatingly** *adv*
calculation /,kalkyooˈlaysh(ə)n/ *n* **1** (the result of) the process or an act of calculating **2** studied care in planning, esp to promote self-interest – **calculative** /ˈkalkyoolətiv/ *adj*
calculator /ˈkalkyoolaytə/ *n* **1** an electronic or mechanical machine for performing mathematical operations **2** a set or book of tables used in calculating [CALCULATE + [1]-OR]
calculous /ˈkalkyooləs/ *adj* caused or characterized by a pathological calculus or calculi
calculus /ˈkalkyooləs/ *n, pl* **calculi** /-lie/ *also* **calculuses** **1a** an abnormal hard stony mass (e g of cholesterol) in the kidney, gall bladder, or other hollow organ **b** [1]TARTAR 2 **2a** a method of computation or calculation in a special symbolic notation **b** the mathematical methods comprising differential and integral calculus [L, pebble, stone in the bladder or kidney, stone used in reckoning]
caldera /kalˈdeərə/ *n* a wide volcanic crater formed by violent explosion or subsidence of the volcano [Sp, lit., cauldron, fr LL *caldaria*]
caldron /ˈkawldrən/ *n* a cauldron
Caledonian /,kaləˈdohnyən, -ni·ən/ *adj* of (ancient) Scotland, esp the Highlands [NL *Caledonia* Scotland, fr L, part of N Britain] – **Caledonian** *n*
calefactory /,kaliˈfakt(ə)ri/ *n* a heated monastery room used as a sitting room [ML *calefactorium*, fr L *calefactus*, pp of *calefacere* to warm – more at CHAFE]
[1]**calendar** /ˈkaləndə/ *n* **1** a system for fixing the beginning, length, and divisions of the civil year and arranging days and longer divisions of time (e g weeks and months) in a definite order **2** a tabular display of the days of 1 year **3** a chronological list of events or activities [ME *calender*, fr AF or ML;

AF *calender*, fr ML *kalendarium*, fr L, moneylender's account book, fr *kalendae* calends]

[2]**calendar** *vt* to enter in a calendar

calender /'kalǝndǝ/ *n* a machine for pressing cloth, rubber, paper, etc between rollers or plates (e g for smoothing and glazing) [MF *calandre*, modif of Gk *kylindros* cylinder – more at CYLINDER] – **calender** *vt*

calends, kalends /'kalindz/ *n pl but sing or pl in constr* the first day of the ancient Roman month [ME *kalendes*, fr L *kalendae, calendae*]

[1]**calf** /kahf/ *n, pl* **calves** /kahvz/ *also* **calfs,** *(2)* **calfs** **1a** the young of the domestic cow or a closely related mammal (e g a bison) **b** the young of some large animals (e g the elephant and whale) **2** calfskin ⟨*the book was bound in fine* ~⟩ **3** a small mass of ice broken off from a coastal glacier, iceberg, etc [ME, fr OE *cealf*; akin to OHG *kalb* calf, ON *kālfi* calf of the leg, L *galla* gallnut] – **calflike** *adj* – **in calf** *of a cow* pregnant

[2]**calf** *n, pl* **calves** the fleshy back part of the leg below the knee [ME, fr ON *kālfi*]

'calf ,love *n* PUPPY LOVE

,calf's-foot 'jelly *n* jelly made from gelatin obtained by boiling calves' feet

'calf,skin /-,skin/ *n* a high-quality leather made from the skin of a calf

Calgon /'kalgon/ *trademark* –used for a water softener that is a complex phosphate of sodium

calibrate /'kali,brayt/ *vt* **1** to determine the calibre of (e g a thermometer tube) **2** to determine, adjust, or mark the graduations of (e g a thermometer) **3** to determine the correct reading of (an arbitrary or inaccurate scale or instrument) by comparison with a standard – **calibrator** *n*

calibration /,kali'braysh(ǝ)n/ *n* a set of graduations that indicate values or positions –usu pl with sing. meaning [CALIBRATE + -ION]

calibre, *NAm chiefly* **caliber** /'kalibǝ/ *n* **1** the internal or external diameter of a round body (e g a bullet or other projectile) or a hollow cylinder (e g a gun barrel) **2a** degree of mental capacity or moral quality **b** degree of excellence or importance [MF, fr OIt *calibro*, fr Ar *qālib* shoemaker's last]

caliche /kǝ'leechi/ *n* the nitrate-bearing gravel or rock of the sodium nitrate deposits of Chile and Peru [AmerSp, fr Sp, flake of lime, fr *cal* lime, fr L *calx* – more at CHALK]

calico /'kalikoh/ *n, pl* **calicoes, calicos** **1** white unprinted cotton cloth of medium weight, orig imported from India **2** *NAm* brightly printed cotton fabric [*Calicut*, city in India] – **calico** *adj*

'calico ,printing *n* a process of making coloured designs on cotton fabrics (e g calico)

californium /,kali'fawnyǝm, -ni·ǝm/ *n* a radioactive element made by bombarding curium 242 with alpha particles ☞ PERIODIC TABLE [NL, fr *California*, state of USA]

Calinago /,kali'nahgoh/ *n* an Arawakan language of the Lesser Antilles and Central America

calipash /'kali,pash/ *n* a fatty gelatinous dull greenish edible substance next to the upper shell of a turtle [perh native name in W Indies]

calipee /'kali,pee/ *n* a fatty gelatinous light yellow edible substance next to the lower shell of a turtle [perh native name in W Indies]

caliper /'kalipǝ/ *vt or n, chiefly NAm* (to) calliper

caliph, calif /'kalif, 'kay-/ *n* a secular and spiritual head of Islam claiming descent from Muhammad [ME *caliphe*, fr MF *calife*, fr Ar *khalīfah* successor] – **caliphal** *adj*, **caliphate** /-ǝt, -ayt/ *n*

calisthenics /,kalis'theniks/ *n pl but sing or pl in constr, chiefly NAm* callisthenics – **calisthenic** *adj*

calix /'kaliks, 'kay-/ *n, pl* **calices** /-li,seez/ CALYX 2 [L *calic-, calix* – more at CHALICE]

calk /kawk/ *vt* to caulk – **calker** *n*

[1]**call** /kawl/ *vi* **1a** to speak loudly or distinctly so as to be heard at a distance; shout **b** to make a request or demand ⟨~ *for an investigation*⟩ **c** *of an animal* to utter a characteristic note or cry **2** to make a demand in card games (e g for a particular card or for a show of hands) **3** *of a batsman* to indicate vocally to one's batting partner whether one intends to take a run or not **4** to make a brief visit – often + *in* or *by* ⟨~ed *in at the pub*⟩ **5** *chiefly NAm* to (try to) get into communication by telephone – often + *up* ~ *vt* **1a** to utter or announce in a loud distinct voice – often + *out* **b** to read aloud (e g a list of names) ⟨*the teacher* ~ed *the register every morning*⟩ **2a** to command or request to come or be present ⟨~ed *to testify*⟩ **b** to cause to come; bring ⟨~s *to mind an old saying*⟩ **c** to summon to a particular activity, employment, or office ⟨*was* ~ed *to active duty*⟩ **d** to invite or command to meet; convoke ⟨~ *a meeting*⟩ **3** to rouse from sleep **4** to give the order for; bring into action ⟨~ *a strike against the company*⟩ **5a** to make a demand in bridge for (a card or suit) **b** to require (a player) to show the hand in poker by making an equal bet **6** to attract (e g game) by imitating a characteristic cry **7a** to rule on the status of (e g a tennis serve) ⟨*the serve was* ~ed *out by the umpire*⟩ **b** *of a cricket umpire* to pronounce the bowling delivery to be illegal ⟨*Griffin was* ~ed *for throwing*⟩ **8** to give the calls for (a square dance) **9** to suspend ⟨*time was* ~ed⟩ **10** to speak of or address by a specified name; give a name to ⟨~ *her Kitty*⟩ **11a** to regard or characterize as a certain kind; consider ⟨*can hardly be* ~ed *generous*⟩ **b** to consider for purposes of an estimate or for convenience ⟨~ *it an even quid*⟩ **12** to predict, guess ⟨~ *the toss of a coin*⟩ **13** *chiefly NAm* to (try to) get into communication with by telephone –often + *up* [ME *callen*, prob fr ON *kalla*; akin to OE hilde*calla* battle herald, OHG *kallōn* to talk loudly, OSlav *glasŭ* voice] – **callable** *adj*, **caller** *n* – **call a spade a spade** to speak frankly and usu bluntly – **called to the bar** admitted as a barrister – **call for** **1** to call to get; collect **2** to require as necessary or appropriate ⟨*it* called for *all her strength*⟩ **3** to demand, order ⟨*legislation* calling for *the establishment of new schools*⟩ – **call in/into question** to cast doubt upon ⟨called in question *the validity of his statement*⟩ – **call it a day** to stop whatever one has been doing at least for the present – **call it quits** **1** CALL IT A DAY **2** to acknowledge that the advantage is now even – **call on/upon** **1** to require, oblige ⟨*may be* called on *to do several jobs*⟩ **2** to appeal to; invoke ⟨*universities are* called upon *to meet the needs of a technological world*⟩ – **call someone's bluff** to challenge and expose an empty pretence or threat – **call the shots/the tune** to be in charge or control; determine the policy or procedure – **call to account** to hold responsible; reprimand ⟨called to account *for violation of the rules*⟩ – **call**

to order to order (a meeting) to observe the customary rules

[2]**call** *n* **1a** an act of calling with the voice **b** the cry of an animal (e g a bird) **c** (an instrument used to produce) an imitation of an animal's cry made to attract the animal **2a** a request or command to come or assemble **b** a summons or signal on a drum, bugle, or pipe **c** a summoning of actors to the stage (e g for rehearsal) **3a** admission to the bar as a barrister **b** a divine vocation **c** a strong inner prompting to a course of action **d** the attraction or appeal of a particular activity or place ⟨*the* ~ *of the wild*⟩ **4a** a demand, request **b** need, justification ⟨*there was no* ~ *for such rudeness*⟩ **5** a short usu formal visit ⟨*a courtesy* ~⟩ **6** the name (e g of a suit in a card game) or thing called **7** the act of calling in a card game **8** the act of telephoning ☞ TELECOMMUNICATION **9** a direction or a succession of directions for a square dance rhythmically called to the dancers **10** a usu vocal ruling made by an official of a sports contest – **on call 1** available for use ⟨*the company car is always* on call *for you*⟩ **2** ready to respond to a summons or command ⟨*a doctor* on call⟩ – **within call** within hearing or reach of a call or summons

calla /'kalə/,**'calla ,lily** *n* any of several plants of the arum family; *esp* a European plant that grows in wet places [NL, genus name, modif of Gk *kallaia* cock's wattles]

'call ,box *n, Br* a public telephone box

'call,boy /-,boy/ *n* **1** a person who tells actors when it is time to go on stage **2** *chiefly NAm* a hotel page

call down *vt* to invoke, request ⟨call down *a blessing on the crops*⟩

'call ,girl *n* a prostitute who accepts appointments by telephone

calligraphy /kə'ligrəfi/ *n* (beautiful or elegant) handwriting – compare CACOGRAPHY ☞ ALPHABET [F or Gk; F *calligraphie*, fr Gk *kalligraphia*, fr *kalli-* beautiful (fr *kallos* beauty) + *-graphia* -graphy; akin to Gk *kalos* beautiful, Skt *kalya* healthy] – **calligrapher, calligraphist** *n*, **calligraphic** /,kali'grafik/ *adj*, **calligraphically** *adv*

call in *vt* **1a** to withdraw from an advanced position ⟨call in *the outposts*⟩ **b** to withdraw from circulation ⟨call in *bank notes and issue new ones*⟩ **2** to summon to one's aid or for consultation ⟨call in *an arbitrator to settle the dispute*⟩

calling /'kawling/ *n* **1** a strong inner impulse towards a particular course of action, esp when accompanied by conviction of divine influence **2** a vocation, profession

'calling ,card *n, NAm* VISITING CARD

[1]**calliper,** *chiefly NAm* **caliper** /'kalipə/ *n* **1** a measuring instrument with 2 arms that can be adjusted to determine thickness, diameter, or distance between surfaces – usu pl with sing. meaning ⟨*a pair of* ~s⟩ **2** a support for the human leg extending from the knee or thigh to the foot [alter. of *calibre*]

[2]**calliper,** *chiefly NAm* **caliper** *vt* to measure (as if) with callipers

callisthenics, *chiefly NAm* **calisthenics** /,kalis'theniks/ *n pl but sing or pl in constr* (the art or practice of) systematic rhythmic bodily exercises performed usu without apparatus [Gk *kallos* beauty + *sthenos* strength – more at CALLIGRAPHY] – **callisthenic** *adj*

call off *vt* **1** to draw away; divert ⟨call *the dogs* off!⟩ **2** to cancel ⟨call *the trip* off⟩

,call of 'nature *n* the urge to urinate or defecate – euph

callose /'kalohs/ *n* a carbohydrate component of plant cell walls [L *callosus* callous]

callosity /kə'losəti/ *n* (an area of) marked or abnormal hardness and thickness

callous /'kaləs/ *adj* **1** hardened and thickened **2** unfeeling; *esp* unsympathetic [MF *calleux*, fr L *callosus*, fr *callum, callus* callous skin; akin to Skt *kiṇa* callosity] – **callously** *adv*, **callousness** *n*

call out *vt* **1** to summon into action ⟨call out *the guard*⟩ **2** to challenge to a duel **3** to order a strike of ⟨call out *the steelworkers*⟩

callow /'kaloh/ *adj* **1** *of a bird* not yet fully fledged **2** lacking adult attitudes; immature ⟨~ *youth*⟩ [ME *calu* bald, fr OE; akin to OHG *kalo* bald] – **callowness** *n*

'call ,sign *n* the combination of letters or letters and numbers assigned to an operator, activity, or station for identification of a radio broadcast

'call-,up *n* an order to report for military service

call up *vt* **1** to bring to mind; evoke **2** to summon before an authority **3** to summon together or collect (e g for a united effort) ⟨call up *all his forces for the attack*⟩ **4** to summon for active military duty

callus /'kaləs/ *n* **1** a hard thickened area on skin or bark **2** a mass of connective tissue formed round a break in a bone and changed into bone during healing **3** soft tissue that forms over a cut plant surface **4** a tumour of plant tissue [L]

[1]**calm** /kahm; *NAm* kah(l)m/ *n* **1a** the absence of winds or rough water; stillness **b** a state in which the wind has a speed of less than 1km/h (about ⅝mph) **2** a state of repose free from agitation [ME *calme*, fr MF, fr OIt *calma*, fr LL *cauma* heat, fr Gk *kauma*, fr *kaiein* to burn – more at CAUSTIC]

[2]**calm** *adj* **1** marked by calm; still ⟨*a* ~ *sea*⟩ **2** free from agitation or excitement ⟨*a* ~ *manner*⟩ – **calmly** *adv*, **calmness** *n*

[3]**calm** *vb* to make or become calm

calmative /'kahmətiv; *NAm* 'kah(l)mətiv/ *n or adj* (a) sedative [[3]*calm* + *-ative* (as in *sedative*)]

calomel /'kalə,mel, -məl/ *n* MERCUROUS CHLORIDE [prob fr (assumed) NL *calomelas*, fr Gk *kalos* beautiful + *melas* black – more at CALLIGRAPHY, MULLET]

Calor gas /'kalə/ *trademark* – used for butane gas in liquid form that is contained in portable cylinders and used as a fuel (e g for domestic heating)

[1]**caloric** /kə'lorik/ *n* a hypothetical weightless fluid formerly held to be responsible for the phenomena of heat and combustion [F *calorique*, fr L *calor*]

[2]**caloric** *adj* of heat or calories – **calorically** *adv*

calorie *also* **calory** /'kaləri/ *n* **1a** the quantity of heat required to raise the temperature of 1g of water by 1°C under standard conditions ☞ UNIT **b** a kilocalorie; *also* an equivalent unit expressing the energy-producing value of food when oxidized **2** an amount of food having an energy-producing value of 1 kilocalorie [F *calorie*, fr L *calor* heat, fr *calēre* to be warm – more at LEE]

calorific /,kalə'rifik/ *adj* of heat production [F or L; F *calorifique*, fr L *calorificus*, fr *calor*]

calorimeter /,kalə'rimitə/ *n* any of several devices for measuring heat taken up or given out [ISV, fr L *calor*] – **calorimetry** *n*, **calorimetric** /ˌkalərəˈmetrik/ *adj*, **calorimetrically** *adv*

calque /kalk/ *n* LOAN TRANSLATION [F, lit., copy, fr *calquer* to trace, fr It *calcare* to trample, trace, fr L, to trample, fr *calc-, calx* heel]

calthrop /ˈkalthrəp/ *n* a caltrop

caltrop *also* **caltrap** /ˈkaltrəp/ *n* **1** WATER CHESTNUT 1 **2** a device with 4 metal points arranged so that 1 always projects upwards, used to hinder enemy horses, vehicles, etc [ME *calketrappe* star thistle, fr OE *calcatrippe*, fr ML *calcatrippa*]

calumet /ˈkalyooˌmet/ *n* a long highly ornamented pipe of the N American Indians smoked esp on ceremonial occasions in token of peace [AmerF, fr F dial, straw, fr LL *calamellus*, dim. of L *calamus* reed, fr Gk *kalamos*]

calumniate /kəˈlumniayt/ *vt* to slander – fml – **calumniator** *n*, **calumniation** /-niˈaysh(ə)n/ *n*

calumny /ˈkaləmni/ *n* (the act of uttering) a false charge or misrepresentation maliciously calculated to damage another's reputation [MF & L; MF *calomnie*, fr L *calumnia*, fr *calvi* to deceive; akin to OE *hōl* calumny, Gk *kēlein* to beguile] – **calumnious** /kəˈlumni·əs/ *adj*, **calumniously** *adv*

calvados /ˈkalvədos/ *n, often cap* apple brandy [F, fr *Calvados*, department of Normandy, France]

calvary /ˈkalvəri/ *n* **1** an open-air representation of the crucifixion of Christ **2** an experience of intense mental suffering [*Calvary*, the hill near Jerusalem where Jesus was crucified]

calve /kahv/ *vb* **1** to give birth to (a calf) **2** *of an ice mass* to release (a calf) [ME *calven*, fr OE *cealfian*, fr *cealf* calf]

calves *pl of* CALF

Calvinism /ˈkalviniz(ə)m/ *n* the theological system of Calvin and his followers, marked by emphasis on the sovereignty of God and esp by the doctrine of predestination [John *Calvin* †1564 F theologian] – **Calvinist** *n or adj*, **Calvinistic** /-ˈnistik/ *adj*, **Calvinistically** *adv*

calx /kalks/ *n, pl* **calxes, calces** /-ˌseez/ the crumbly residue left when a metal or mineral has been subjected to intense heat [ME *cals*, fr L *calx* lime – more at CHALK]

calypso /kəˈlipsoh/ *n, pl* **calypsos** *also* **calypsoes** an improvised ballad, usu satirizing current events, in a style originating in the W Indies [perh fr *Calypso*, island nymph in Homer's *Odyssey*] – **calypsonian** /kəˌlipˈsohnyən, ˌkalip-/ *n or adj*

calyx /ˈkaliks, ˈkay-/ *n, pl* **calyxes, calyces** /-liˌseez/ **1** the outer usu green or leafy part of a flower or floret, consisting of sepals **2 calyx, calix** a cuplike animal structure [L *calyc-, calyx*, fr Gk *kalyx* – more at CHALICE] – **calyceal** /ˌkaliˈsee·əl, ˌkay-/ *adj*

cam /kam/ *n* a mechanical device (e g a wheel attached to an axis at a point other than its centre) that transforms circular motion into intermittent or back-and-forth motion [perh fr F *came*, fr G *kamm*, lit., comb, fr OHG *kamb*]

camaraderie /ˌkaməˈrahdəri, -ˈradəri/ *n* friendly good humour amongst comrades [F, fr *camarade* comrade]

¹camber /ˈkambə/ *vb* to (cause to) curve upwards in the middle [F *cambrer*, fr MF *cambre* curved, fr L *camur* – more at CHAMBER]

²camber *n* **1** a slight convexity or arching (e g of a beam or road) **2** an arrangement of the wheels of a motor vehicle so as to be closer together at the bottom than at the top

ˌcamberwell ˈbeauty /ˈcambəˌwel/ *n, often cap C&B, Br* a dark brown butterfly with yellow-bordered wings [*Camberwell*, district of London]

cambium /ˈkambi·əm/ *n, pl* **cambiums, cambia** /-bi·ə/ a thin layer of cells between the xylem and phloem of most plants that divides to form more xylem and phloem [NL, fr ML, exchange, fr L *cambiare* to exchange – more at CHANGE] – **cambial** *adj*

Cambodian /ˌkamˈbohdi·ən/ *n* **1** a Kampuchean **2** KHMER 2 [*Cambodia*, former name of Kampuchea, country in SE Asia] – **Cambodian** *adj*

Cambrian /ˈkambri·ən/ *adj* **1** Welsh **2** of or being the earliest geological period of the Palaeozoic era ☞ EVOLUTION [ML *Cambria* Wales, fr W *Cymry* Welshmen] – **Cambrian** *n*

cambric /ˈkambrik/ *n* a fine thin white linen or cotton fabric [obs Flem *Kameryk* Cambrai, city in France]

¹came /kaym/ *past of* COME

²came /kaym/ *n* a slender grooved lead rod used to hold together panes of glass, esp in a lattice or stained-glass window [origin unknown]

camel /ˈkaməl/ *n* **1** either of 2 large ruminant mammals used as draught and saddle animals in (African and Asian) desert regions: **a** the 1-humped Arabian camel **b** the 2-humped Bactrian camel **2** a float used to lift submerged ships **3** a light yellowish brown colour [ME, fr OE & ONF, fr L *camelus*, fr Gk *kamēlos*, of Sem origin; akin to Heb & Phoenician *gāmāl* camel]

ˈcamelˌback /-ˌbak/ *n* an uncured rubber compound used for retreading pneumatic tyres

ˈcamel ˌhair *n* cloth, usu of a light tan colour with a soft silky texture, made from the hair of a camel or a mixture of this and wool

camellia *also* **camelia** /kəˈmeelyə/ *n* an ornamental greenhouse shrub with glossy evergreen leaves and roselike flowers, or a related shrub or tree of the tea family [NL *Camellia*, genus name, fr *Camellus* (Georg Josef Kamel) †1706 Moravian Jesuit missionary]

camelopard /kəˈmeləˌpahd/ *n, archaic* a giraffe [LL *camelopardus*, alter. of L *camelopardalis*, fr Gk *kamēlopardalis*, fr *kamēlos* + *pardalis* leopard]

Camembert /ˈkaməmbeə (*Fr* kamɑ̃bɛːr)/ *n* a round thin-rinded soft rich cheese [F, fr *Camembert*, town in Normandy, France]

cameo /ˈkamioh/ *n, pl* **cameos** **1a** a gem carved in relief; *esp* a small piece of sculpture cut in relief in one layer with another contrasting layer serving as background **b** a small medallion with a profiled head in relief **2** a usu brief part in literature or film that reveals or highlights character, plot, or scene **3** a small dramatic role often played by a well-known actor [It] – **cameo** *adj or vt*

camera /ˈkamrə/ *n* **1** *often cap* the treasury department of the papal curia **2** a lightproof box having an aperture, and esp a lens, for recording the image of an object on a light-sensitive material: e g **a** one containing photographic film for producing a permanent record 👁 **b** one containing a device which converts the image into an electrical signal (e g for television transmission) ***USE*** *(2)* ☞ TELEVISION, VIDEO [LL, room – more at CHAMBER]

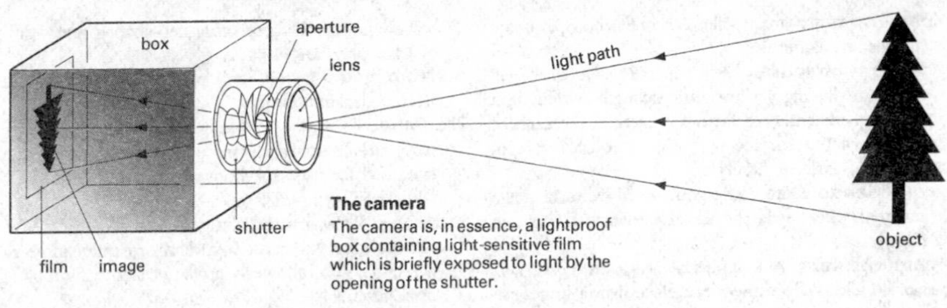

The camera
The camera is, in essence, a lightproof box containing light-sensitive film which is briefly exposed to light by the opening of the shutter.

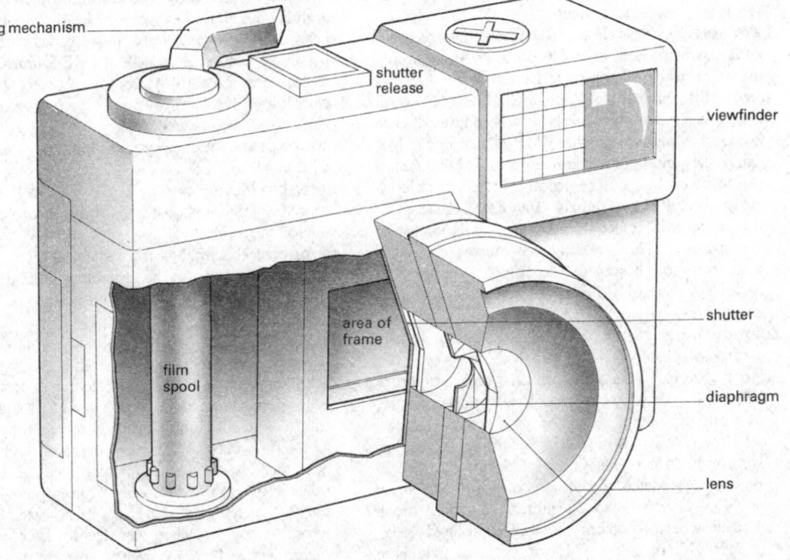

Lens
The image is brought into focus on the film by adjusting the distance (focal length) between a compound lens and the film. This lens consists of a combination of converging and diverging elements which work together to produce an image that is free from aberration. The simplest compound lens, shown below, comprises a converging element with a weaker diverging element made in a different type of glass to correct the errors caused by using a converging element on its own.

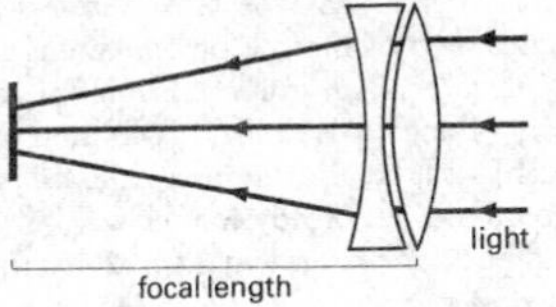

Aperture/diaphragm
This consists of a ring of thin metal blades, between the elements of the lens, which can be opened or closed to increase or decrease the diameter of the aperture at the centre, thus controlling the amount of light entering the camera. The aperture is calibrated in 'F'-stops, each successive stop either halving or doubling the amount of light admitted.

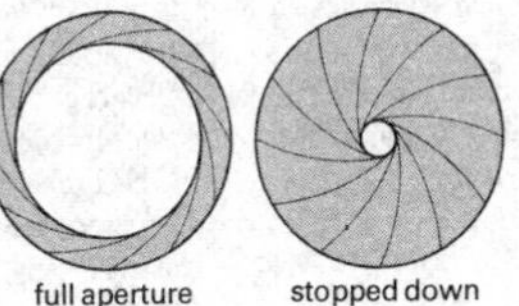

Shutter
This controls the length of time for which light is allowed to enter the camera. The shutter shown here consists of a set of thin metal blades, located behind the compound lens, which are normally completely closed and which open briefly for the required exposure when the shutter is released.

Film
Film can be obtained in either cartridge or spool form, and in a range of speeds. The winding mechanism moves the film through the camera, frame by frame, by means of sprockets which fit into the holes at the sides of the film. The film speed refers to its sensitivity to light. Fast film is used for dark conditions and short exposures, eg action photography. Slow film is used for portraits and high definition photographs.

ˈcameraman /-ˌman, -mən/ *n* one who operates a (television) camera

ˌcamera obˈscura /əbˈskyooərə/ *n* a darkened enclosure having an aperture through which light from outside enters to form an image of the exterior view on a flat surface (e g a ground glass screen) [NL, lit., dark chamber]

camerlengo /ˌkaməˈleng·goh/ *n, pl* **camerlengos** a cardinal who heads the papal treasury [It *camarlingo*]

camiknickers /ˈkamiˌnikəz/ *n pl in constr, pl* **camiknickers** *Br* a one-piece close-fitting undergarment worn by women, that combines a camisole and knickers – **camiknicker** *adj*

camisole /ˈkamiˌsohl/ *n* a short bodice worn as an undergarment by women [F, prob fr OProv *camisolla*, dim. of *camisa* shirt, fr LL *camisia*]

camomile, chamomile /ˈkaməmiel/ *n* any of several strong-scented composite plants whose flower heads are used in herbal remedies [ME *camemille*, fr ML *camomilla*, modif of L *chamaemelon*, fr Gk *chamaimēlon*, fr *chamai* on the ground + *mēlon* apple]

[1]**camouflage** /ˈkaməˌflahzh, -ˌflahj/ *n* **1** the disguising of esp military equipment or installations with nets, paint, etc **2a** concealment by means of disguise ☞ DEFENCE **b** sthg (e g a disguise) designed to deceive or conceal [F, fr *camoufler* to disguise, fr It *camuffare*]

[2]**camouflage** *vt* to conceal or disguise by camouflage – **camouflageable** /-ˌflahzhəbl, -jəbl/ *adj*

[1]**camp** /kamp/ *n* **1a** a ground on which temporary shelters (e g tents) are erected **b** a temporary shelter or group of shelters erected on such ground **c** a new settlement (e g in a lumbering or mining region) **2** *sing or pl in constr* a group of people engaged in promoting or defending a theory or position ⟨*Liberal and Conservative* ~s⟩ **3a** military service or life **b** a place where troops are housed or trained [MF, prob fr ONF or OProv, fr L *campus* plain, field; akin to OHG *hamf* crippled, Gk *kampē* bend]

[2]**camp** *vi* **1** to pitch or occupy a camp **2** to live temporarily in a camp or outdoors

[3]**camp** *adj* **1** homosexual **2** exaggeratedly effeminate **3** deliberately and outrageously artificial, affected, or inappropriate, esp to the point of tastelessness *USE* infml [origin unknown] – **campily** *adv*, **campness** *n*, **campy** *adj*

[4]**camp** *vi or n* (to engage in) a camp style, manner, etc – infml –**camp it up** to act or behave in an affected or esp exaggeratedly effeminate manner – infml

[1]**campaign** /ˌkamˈpayn/ *n* **1** a connected series of military operations forming a distinct phase of a war **2** active military life; [1]CAMP 3a **3** a connected series of operations designed to bring about a particular result [F *campagne*, prob fr It *campagna* level country, campaign, fr LL *campania* level country, fr L, the level country round Naples]

[2]**campaign** *vi* to go on, engage in, or conduct a campaign – **campaigner** *n*

campanile /ˌkampəˈneeli/ *n, pl* **campaniles, campanili** /~/ a usu freestanding bell tower [It, fr *campana* bell, fr LL]

campanology /ˌkampəˈnoləji/ *n* the art of bell ringing [NL *campanologia*, fr LL *campana* + NL *-o-* + *-logia* -logy] – **campanologist** *n*

campanula /kəmˈpanyoolə/ *n* a bellflower [NL, dim. of LL *campana*]

campanulate /kəmˈpanyoolət, -layt/ *adj* bell-shaped [NL *campanula* bell-shaped part, dim. of LL *campana*]

ˌcamp ˈbed *n* a small collapsible bed, usu of fabric stretched over a frame

camper /ˈkampə/ *n* **1** a person who temporarily stays in a tent, caravan, etc **2** a motor vehicle equipped for use as temporary accommodation (e g while holidaying) [[2]CAMP + [2]-ER]

camp follower *n* **1** a civilian, esp a prostitute, who follows a military unit to attend or exploit military personnel **2** a follower who is not of the main body of adherents

camphor /ˈkamfə/ *n* a tough gummy volatile fragrant compound obtained esp from the wood and bark of an evergreen tree and used as a liniment, plasticizer, and insect repellent [ME *caumfre*, fr AF, fr ML *camphora*, fr Ar *kāfūr*, fr Malay *kāpūr*] – **camphoraceous** /-ˈrayshəs/ *adj*, **camphoric** /kamˈforik/ *adj*

camphorate /ˈkamfərayt/ *vt* to impregnate or treat with camphor

campion /ˈkampi·ən/ *n* **1** RED CAMPION **2** WHITE CAMPION **3** BLADDER CAMPION [prob fr obs *campion* (champion)]

campong /ˈkampong/ *n* a kampong

campus /ˈkampəs/ *n* the grounds and buildings of a geographically self-contained university [L, plain – more at [1]CAMP]

camshaft /ˈkamˌshahft/ *n* a shaft to which a cam is fastened

[1]**can** /kən; *strong* kan/ *verbal auxiliary, pres sing & pl* **can;** *past* **could** /kəd; *strong* kood/ **1a** know how to ⟨*he* ~ *read*⟩ **b** be physically or mentally able to ⟨*I* ~*'t think why*⟩ **c** may perhaps – chiefly in questions ⟨*what* ~ *they want?*⟩ **d** be logically inferred or supposed to – chiefly in negatives ⟨*he* ~ *hardly have meant that*⟩; compare [1]MUST 4 **e** be permitted by conscience or feeling to ⟨~ *hardly blame him*⟩ **f** be inherently able or designed to ⟨*everything that money* ~ *buy*⟩ **g** be logically able to ⟨*2 + 2* ~ *also be written 3 + 1*⟩ **h** be enabled by law, agreement, or custom to **2** have permission to – used interchangeably with *may* **3** will – used in questions with the force of a request ⟨~ *you hold on a minute, please?*⟩ **4** will have to ⟨*if you don't like it you* ~ *lump it*⟩ [ME (1 & 3 sing. pres indic), fr OE; akin to OHG *kan* (1 & 3 sing. pres indic) know, am able, OE *cnāwan* to know – more at KNOW] – **can keep it** – used in rejection of sthg distasteful ⟨*if that's their famous temple they* can keep it⟩

[2]**can** /kan/ *n* **1** a usu cylindrical receptacle: **a** a vessel for holding liquids **b** TIN 2a; *esp* a tin containing a beverage (e g beer) **2** *NAm* TOILET 2 – infml **3** *chiefly NAm* jail – slang [ME *canne*, fr OE; akin to OHG *channa* can] – **canful** *adj* – **in the can** *of a film or videotape* completed and ready for release

[3]**can** *vt* **-nn- 1** to pack or preserve in a tin **2** *chiefly NAm* to put a stop or end to – slang – **canner** *n*

Canada balsam /ˈkanədə/ *n* a sticky yellow to green resin from the balsam fir that is used as a transparent cement, esp in microscopy [*Canada*, country in N America]

ˌCanada ˈgoose *n* a chiefly grey wild goose characterized by a black head and neck and a white patch under the throat

Canadian /kəˈnaydi·ən/ *n or adj* (a native or inhabitant) of Canada

Caˌnadian ˈpondˌweed *n* a submerged plant of

slow-moving water put in garden ponds to increase the oxygen content of the water

canaille /kə'nayəl, kə'nie/ *n sing or pl in constr* rabble, riffraff [F, fr It *canaglia*, fr *cane* dog, fr L *canis* – more at HOUND]

canal /kə'nal/ *n* **1** a channel, watercourse **2** a tubular anatomical channel **3** an artificial waterway for navigation, drainage, or irrigation [ME, fr L *canalis* pipe, channel, fr *canna* reed – more at CANE]

canal·ize, -ise /'kanəliez/ *vt* **1** to provide with or make into a canal or channel **2** to direct into preferred channels – **canalization** /-'zaysh(ə)n/ *n*

canapé /'kanəpay, -pi/ *n* an appetizer consisting of a piece of bread, biscuit, etc, topped with a savoury spread [F, lit., sofa, fr ML *canopeum, canapeum* mosquito net – more at CANOPY]

canard /kə'nahd, 'kanahd/ *n* **1** a false or unfounded report or story; a hoax **2** (an aeroplane with) a small surface providing stability or control mounted in front of the main supporting surface on an aeroplane or hydrofoil [F, lit., duck; (1) fr MF *vendre des canards à moitié* to cheat, lit., to half-sell ducks]

canary /kə'neəri/ *n* a small usu green to yellow finch of the Canary islands, widely kept as a cage bird [MF *canarie*, fr OSp *canario*, fr *Islas Canarias* Canary Islands]

ca,nary 'yellow *adj or n* vivid yellow

canasta /kə'nastə/ *n* **1** a form of rummy usu for 4 players using 2 full packs plus jokers **2** a combination of 7 cards of the same rank in canasta [Sp, lit., basket]

cancan /'kan,kan/ *n* a dance performed by women, characterized by high kicking usu while holding up the front of a full ruffled skirt [F]

[1]cancel /'kansl/ *vb* **-ll-** (*NAm* **-l-, -ll-**), /'kansl·ing/ *vt* **1a** to mark or strike out for deletion **b** to omit, delete **2a** to make void; countermand, annul ⟨~ *a magazine subscription*⟩ **b** to bring to nothingness; destroy **c** to match in force or effect; offset – often + *out* ⟨*his irritability* ~led *out his natural kindness* – Osbert Sitwell⟩ **3** to call off, usu without intending to reschedule to a later time **4a** to remove (a common divisor) from a numerator and denominator **b** to remove (equivalents) on opposite sides of an equation or account **5** to deface (a stamp), usu with a set of parallel lines, so as to invalidate reuse ~ *vi* to neutralize each other's strength or effect; counterbalance – usu + *out* [ME *cancellen*, fr MF *canceller*, fr LL *cancellare*, fr L, to make like a lattice, fr *cancelli* (pl), dim. of *cancer* lattice, alter. of *carcer* prison] – **cancellable** *adj*, **canceller** /'kansl·ə/ *n*

[2]cancel *n* a cancellation

cancellation, *NAm also* **cancelation** /,kansə'laysh(ə)n/ *n* **1** sthg cancelled, esp a seat in an aircraft, theatre performance, etc **2** a mark made to cancel sthg (e g a postage stamp) [[1]CANCEL + -ATION]

cancellous /'kansələs, kan'seləs/ *adj, of bone* porous [NL *cancelli* intersecting bony plates and bars in cancellous bone, fr L, lattice]

cancer /'kansə/ *n* **1** *cap* (sby born under) the 4th zodiacal constellation, pictured as a crab ☞ SYMBOL **2** (a condition marked by) a malignant tumour of potentially unlimited growth **3** a source of evil or anguish ⟨*the* ~ *of hidden resentment – Irish Digest*⟩ [ME, fr L, lit., crab; akin to Gk *karkinos* crab, cancer] – **cancerous** *adj*, **cancerously** *adv*

Cancerian /kan'siəri·ən, -'seə-/ *n* sby born under the 4th sign of the zodiac – **Cancerian** *adj*

cancroid /'kang,kroyd/ *adj* **1** crablike **2** cancer-like [L *cancr-, cancer* crab, cancer]

candela /kan'daylə, -'deelə/ *n* the SI unit of luminous intensity ☞ PHYSICS [L, candle]

candelabra /,kandl'ahbrə/ *n* a candelabrum

candelabrum /,kandl'ahbrəm/ *n, pl* **candelabra** /-brə/ *also* **candelabrums** a branched candlestick or lamp with several lights [L, fr *candela*]

candescent /kan'des(ə)nt/ *adj* glowing or dazzling, esp from great heat – fml [L *candescent-, candescens*, prp of *candescere*, incho of *candēre*] – **candescence** /-s(ə)ns/ *n*

candid /'kandid/ *adj* **1** indicating or suggesting complete sincerity **2** disposed to criticize severely; blunt [F & L; F *candide*, fr L *candidus* bright, white, fr *candēre* to shine, glow; akin to LGk *kandaros* ember] – **candidly** *adv*, **candidness** *n*

candida /'kandidə/ *n* any of a genus of parasitic yeastlike fungi that includes the causative agent of thrush [NL, genus name, fr L, fem of *candidus* white]

candidate /'kandidayt, -dət/ *n* **1** one who is nominated or qualified for, or aspires to an office, membership, or award **2** one who is taking an examination **3** sthg suitable for a specified action or process [L *candidatus*, fr *candidatus* clothed in white, fr *candidus* white; fr the white toga worn by candidates for office in ancient Rome] – **candidacy** /-dəsi/ *n*

candidature /'kandidəchə/ *n, chiefly Br* being a candidate; *esp* standing for election

candidiasis /,kandi'die·əsis/ *n* a disease (e g of the vagina) resulting from an infection by a candida [NL]

[1]candle /'kandl/ *n* **1** a usu long slender cylindrical mass of tallow or wax enclosing a wick that is burnt to give light **2** sthg resembling a candle in shape or use ⟨*a sulphur* ~ *for fumigation*⟩ **3** a candela [ME *candel*, fr OE, fr L *candela*, fr *candēre*] – **not worth the candle** *chiefly Br* not worth the effort; not justified by the result

[2]candle *vt* to examine (eggs) for staleness, blood clots, or fertility by holding between the eye and a light – **candler** /'kandlə/ *n*

'Candlemas /-məs/ *n* February 2 observed as a church festival in commemoration of the presentation of Christ in the temple and the purification of the Virgin Mary [ME *candelmasse*, fr OE *candelmæsse*, fr *candel* + *mæsse* mass, feast; fr the candles blessed and carried in celebration of the feast]

'candle,power /-,powə/ *n* luminous intensity expressed in candelas

'candle,stick /-,stik/ *n* a holder with a socket for a candle

'candle,wick /-,wik/ *n* a very thick soft cotton yarn; *also* fabric made with this yarn usu with a raised tufted pattern, used esp for bedspreads

'candle,wood /-,wood/ *n* slivers of resinous wood burned for light

candour, *NAm chiefly* **candor** /'kandə/ *n* unreserved and candid expression; forthrightness [F & L; F *candeur*, fr L *candor*, fr *candēre* – more at CANDID]

[1]candy /'kandi/ *n* **1** crystallized sugar formed by boiling down sugar syrup **2** *chiefly NAm* SWEET 2b [ME *sugre candy*, part trans of MF *sucre candi*, part trans of OIt *zucchero candi,* fr *zucchero* sugar + Ar *qandī* candied, fr *qand* cane sugar] – **candy** *adj*

[2]**candy** *vt* to encrust or glaze (e g fruit or fruit peel) with sugar

'**candy ,floss** /flos/ *n* a light fluffy mass of spun sugar, usu wound round a stick as a sweet

'**candy,tuft** /-,tuft/ *n* any of a genus of plants of the mustard family cultivated for their white, pink, or purple flowers [*Candy* (now *Candia*) Crete, Greek island + E *tuft*]

[1]**cane** /kayn/ *n* **1a** a hollow or pithy usu flexible jointed stem (e g of bamboo) **b** an elongated flowering or fruiting stem (e g of a raspberry) **c** any of various tall woody grasses or reeds; *esp* sugarcane **2a** a walking stick; *specif* one made of cane **b** (*the* use of) a cane or rod for flogging **c** a length of split rattan for use in basketry [ME, fr MF, fr OProv *cana,* fr L *canna,* fr Gk *kanna,* of Sem origin; akin to Ar *qanāh* hollow stick, reed]

[2]**cane** *vt* **1** to beat with a cane; *broadly* to punish **2** to weave or furnish with cane ⟨~ *the seat of a chair*⟩

'**cane ,sugar** *n* sugar obtained from sugarcane

[1]**canine** /'kaynien/ *adj* of or resembling a dog or (members of) the family of flesh-eating mammals that includes the dogs, wolves, jackals, and foxes [L *caninus,* fr *canis* dog – more at HOUND]

[2]**canine** *n* **1** any of the 4 conical pointed teeth each of which lies between an incisor and the first premolar on each side of both the top and bottom jaws ☞ DIGESTION **2** DOG 1

canister *also* **cannister** /'kanistə/ *n* **1** a small usu metal box or tin for holding a dry product (e g tea or shot) **2** encased shot for close-range antipersonnel artillery fire [L *canistrum* basket, fr Gk *kanastron,* fr *kanna* reed]

[1]**canker** /'kangkə/ *n* **1a(1)** an erosive or spreading sore **(2)** an area of local tissue death in a plant **b** any of various inflammatory animal diseases **2** a source of corruption or debasement [ME, fr ONF *cancre,* fr L *cancer* crab, cancer] – **cankerous** *adj*

[2]**canker** *vt* to corrupt with a malignancy of mind or spirit ~ *vi* **1** to become infested with canker **2** to undergo corruption

cannabin /'kanəbin/ *n* a dark cannabis-containing resin [L *cannabis*]

cannabis /'kanəbis/ *n* the dried flowering spikes of the female hemp plant, sometimes smoked in cigarettes for their intoxicating effect – compare HASHISH, MARIJUANA [L, hemp, fr Gk *kannabis,* fr the source of OE *hænep* hemp]

canned /kand/ *adj* **1** recorded for mechanical or electronic reproduction; *esp* prerecorded for addition to a sound track or a videotape ⟨~ *laughter*⟩ ⟨~ *music*⟩ **2** drunk – slang [[3]CAN + [1]-ED]

'**cannel ,coal** /'kanl/ *n* a bituminous coal that burns brightly [prob fr E dial *cannel* (candle), fr ME *candel*]

cannelloni /,kanə'lohni/ *n* large tubular rolls of pasta (filled with meat, cheese, etc) [It, pl of *cannellone* tubular noodle, aug of *cannello* segment of a stalk of cane, small tube, fr *canna* cane, reed, fr L – more at CANE]

cannery /'kanəri/ *n* a factory for canning foods

cannibal /'kanibl/ *n* **1** a human being who eats human flesh **2** an animal that eats its own kind [NL *Canibalis* Carib, fr Sp *Caníbal,* fr Arawakan *Caniba, Carib,* of Cariban origin; akin to Carib *Galibi* Caribs, lit., strong men] – **cannibal** *adj,* **cannibalism** *n,* **cannibalistic** /-'istik/ *adj*

cannibal·ize, -ise /'kanibl,iez/ *vt* to dismantle (e g a machine) in order to provide spare parts for others – **cannibalization** /-ie'zaysh(ə)n/ *n*

cannister /'kanistə/ *n* a canister

[1]**cannon** /'kanən/ *n, pl* **cannons, cannon 1** a usu large gun mounted on a carriage **2** an automatic shell-firing gun mounted esp in an aircraft [MF *canon,* fr It *cannone,* lit., large tube, aug of *canna* reed, tube, fr L, cane, reed – more at CANE]

[2]**cannon** *n, Br* a shot in billiards in which the cue ball strikes each of 2 object balls [alter. of *carom*]

[3]**cannon** *vi* **1a** to collide – usu + *into* **b** to collide with and be deflected *off* sthg **2** *Br* to make a cannon in billiards

cannonade /,kanə'nayd/ *vb or n* (to attack with) heavy continuous artillery fire

'**cannon,ball** /-,bawl/ *n* a round solid missile made for firing from an old type of cannon

'**cannon ,bone** *n* the leg bone between the hock joint and the fetlock in hoofed mammals ☞ ANATOMY [F *canon,* lit., cannon]

'**cannon ,fodder** *n* people regarded merely as material to be used in armed conflict

'**cannonry** /-ri/ *n* **1** a cannonade **2** artillery

cannot /'kanot, -nət, kə'not/ can not – **cannot but/cannot help but** to be bound to; must ⟨could not but *smile at the answer*⟩

cannula /'kanyoolə/ *n, pl* **cannulas, cannulae** /-li/ a small tube for insertion into a body cavity or duct [NL, fr L, dim. of *canna* reed – more at CANE]

cannulation /,kanyoo'laysh(ə)n/ *n* the insertion of a cannula – **cannulate** /-layt/ *vt*

canny /'kani/ *adj* **1** cautious and shrewd; *specif* thrifty **2** *Scot & NE Eng* careful, steady **3** *NE Eng* agreeable, comely [[1]*can* + [1]*-y*] – **cannily** *adv,* **canniness** *n*

[1]**canoe** /kə'nooh/ *n* **1** a long light narrow boat with sharp ends and curved sides usu propelled by paddling **2** *chiefly Br* a kayak [F, fr NL *canoa,* fr Sp, fr Arawakan, of Cariban origin; akin to Galibi *canaoua*]

[2]**canoe** *vi* to travel in or paddle a canoe, esp as a recreation or sport ~ *vt* to transport in a canoe – **canoeist** *n*

[1]**canon** /'kanən/ *n* **1a** a regulation or dogma decreed by a church council **b** a provision of canon law **2** the series of prayers forming the unvarying part of the Mass **3a** an authoritative list of books accepted as Holy Scripture **b** the authentic works of a writer **4a** an accepted principle, rule, or criterion **b** a body of principles, rules, or standards **5** a musical composition for 2 or more voice parts in which the melody is repeated by the successively entering voices [ME, fr OE, fr LL, fr L, ruler, rule, model, standard, fr Gk *kanōn* (akin to Gk *kanna* reed – more at CANE); (2) ME, prob fr OF, fr LL, fr L; (3) ME, fr LL, fr L; (5) LGk *kanōn,* fr Gk]

[2]**canon** *n* **1** a clergyman belonging to the chapter of a cathedral or collegiate church **2** CANON REGULAR [ME *canoun,* fr AF *canunie,* fr LL *canonicus* one living under a rule, fr L, according to rule, fr Gk *kanonikos,* fr *kanōn*]

cañon /'kanyən/ *n* a canyon

canoness /'kanənəs, -,nes/ *n* a woman living in a community under a religious rule but not under a perpetual vow

canonical /kə'nonikl/, **canonic** /kə'nonik/ *adj* **1** of an esp ecclesiastical or musical canon **2** conforming to a general rule; orthodox **3** accepted as forming the canon of scripture **4** reduced to the simplest or clearest equivalent form ⟨*a ~ matrix*⟩ – **canonically** *adv*, **canonicity** /,kanə'nisəti/ *n*

canonical hour *n* any of the daily offices of devotion that compose the Divine Office – compare MATINS, LAUD, PRIME, TERCE, SEXT, NONE, VESPERS, COMPLINE

ca'nonicals *n pl* the vestments prescribed by canon for an officiating clergyman

canonist /'kanənist/ *n* a specialist in canon law

canon·ize, -ise /'kanəniez/ *vt* **1** to recognize officially as a saint **2** to attribute authoritative sanction or approval to [ME *canonizen*, fr ML *canonizare*, fr LL *canon* catalogue of saints, fr L, standard] – **canonization** /-'zaysh(ə)n/ *n*

,canon 'law *n* the usu codified law governing a church

,canon 'regular *n, pl* **canons regular** a member of any of several Roman Catholic open religious communities

canoodle /kə'noohdl/ *vi* **canoodling** /kə'noohdling/ to caress or cuddle (with sby) – infml [perh fr E dial. *canoodle* (donkey, fool, silly lover)]

canopic jar /kə'nohpik/ *n, often cap C* a jar in which the ancient Egyptians preserved the viscera of an embalmed body [*Canopus*, city of ancient Egypt]

[1]**canopy** /'kanəpi/ *n* **1a** a cloth covering suspended over a bed **b** a cover (e g of cloth) fixed or carried above a person of high rank or a sacred object **c** an awning, marquee **d** anything which seems like a cover ⟨*the ~ of the heavens*⟩ ⟨*a ~ of branches*⟩ **2** an ornamental rooflike structure **3a** the transparent enclosure over an aircraft cockpit **b** the lifting or supporting surface of a parachute [ME *canope*, fr ML *canopeum* mosquito net, fr L *conopeum*, fr Gk *kōnōpion*, fr *kōnōps* mosquito]

[2]**canopy** *vt* to cover (as if) with a canopy

canst /kənst; *strong* kanst/ *archaic pres 2 sing of* [1]CAN

[1]**cant** /kant/ *n* **1a** a sudden thrust that produces some displacement **b** the displacement so caused **2** an oblique or slanting surface; a slope [ME, prob fr MD or ONF; MD, edge, corner, fr ONF, fr L *canthus*, *cantus* iron tyre, perh of Celt origin; akin to W *cant* rim; akin to Gk *kanthos* corner of the eye]

[2]**cant** *vt* **1** to give a cant or oblique edge to; bevel **2** to set at an angle; tip or tilt up or over ~ *vi* **1** to pitch to one side; lean **2** to slope

[3]**cant** *vi* to speak in cant or jargon [prob fr ONF *canter* to tell, lit., to sing, fr L *cantare* – more at CHANT]

[4]**cant** *n* **1** jargon; *specif* the argot of the underworld **2** a set or stock phrase **3** the insincere expression of platitudes or sentiments, esp those suggesting piety

can't /kahnt/ can not

cantabile /kan'tahbili, -lay/ *adv* in a singing manner – used in music [It, fr LL *cantabilis* worthy to be sung, fr L *cantare*]

Cantabrigian /,kantə'briji·ən/ *n* a student or graduate of Cambridge University [ML *Cantabrigia* Cambridge]

cantaloupe, cantaloup /'kantə,loohp/ *n* a muskmelon with a hard ridged rind and reddish orange flesh [*Cantalupo*, former papal villa near Rome, Italy]

cantankerous /,kan'tangkərəs/ *adj* ill-natured, quarrelsome [perh irreg fr obs *contack* (contention)] – **cantankerously** *adv*, **cantankerousness** *n*

cantata /kan'tahtə/ *n* a usu religious choral composition comprising choruses, solos, recitatives, and interludes [It, fr L, sung mass, ecclesiastical chant, fr fem of *cantatus*, pp of *cantare*]

'cant ,dog *n* CANT HOOK [[1]*cant*]

canteen /kan'teen/ *n* **1** a shop providing supplies in a camp **2** a dining hall **3** a partitioned chest or box for holding cutlery **4** a usu cloth-covered flask carried by a soldier, traveller, etc and containing a liquid, esp drinking water [F *cantine* bottle case, sutler's shop, fr It *cantina* wine cellar, fr *canto* corner, fr L *canthus* iron tyre – more at [1]CANT]

[1]**canter** /'kantə/ *vi* to progress or ride at a canter ~ *vt* to cause to canter [short for obs *canterbury*, fr *canterbury*, n (canter), fr *Canterbury*, England; fr the supposed gait of pilgrims to Canterbury]

[2]**canter** *n* **1** a 3-beat gait of a quadruped, specif a horse, resembling but smoother and slower than the gallop **2** a ride at a canter

,Canterbury 'bell /'kantəb(ə)ri/ *n* any of several tall plants cultivated for their large showy bell-shaped flowers [*Canterbury*, city in England]

cantharis /'kanthəris/ *n, pl* **cantharides** /kan'tharideez/ SPANISH FLY [ME & L; ME *cantharide*, fr L *cantharid-*, *cantharis*, fr Gk *kantharid-*, *kantharis*]

'cant ,hook *n* a stout wooden lever with a metal-clad end used esp in handling logs [[1]*cant*]

canticle /'kantikl/ *n* a song; *specif* any of several liturgical songs (e g the Magnificat) taken from the Bible [ME, fr L *canticulum*, dim. of *canticum* song, fr *cantus*, pp of *canere* to sing]

Canticles /'kantikleez/ *n pl but sing in constr* SONG OF SOLOMON

cantilever /'kanti,leevə/ *n* a projecting beam or member supported at only 1 end: e g **a** a bracket-shaped member supporting a balcony or a cornice **b** either of the 2 beams or trusses that when joined directly or by a suspended connecting member form a span of a cantilever bridge [perh fr [1]*cant* + *-i-* + *lever*]

cantle /'kantl/ *n* the upward-curving rear part of a saddle [ME *cantel*, fr ONF, dim. of *cant* edge, corner – more at [1]CANT]

canto /'kantoh/ *n, pl* **cantos** a major division of a long poem [It, fr L *cantus* song, fr *cantus*, pp of *canere* to sing – more at CHANT]

[1]**canton** /'kanton, -'-/ *n* **1** a small territorial division of a country (e g Switzerland or France) **2** a rectangle in the right chief corner of a heraldic shield [MF, fr It *cantone*, fr *canto* corner, fr L *canthus* iron tyre; (2) MF, fr OProv, fr *cant* edge, corner, fr L *canthus*] – **cantonal** /'kant(ə)nl, kan'tonl/ *adj*

[2]**canton** /kan'ton; *sense 2* kən'toohn/ *vt* **1** to divide into cantons **2** [2]BILLET

Cantonese /,kantə'neez/ *n, pl* **Cantonese** **1** a native or inhabitant of Canton **2** the dialect of Chinese spoken in and near Canton [*Canton*, city in China] – **Cantonese** *adj*

cantonment /kən'toohnmənt/ *n* (a group of usu temporary structures for) the housing of troops [F *cantonnement*, fr *cantonner* to billet troops]

cantor /'kantaw/ *n* a singer who leads liturgical

music (e g in a synagogue) [L, singer, fr *cantus*, pp of *canere* to sing]

Canuck /kə'nuk/ *n* **1** the language of the French Canadians – derog **2** *chiefly Can* FRENCH CANADIAN – slang [prob alter. of *Canadian*]

canvas *also* **canvass** /'kanvəs/ *n* **1** a firm closely woven cloth usu of linen, hemp, or cotton used for clothing, sails, tents etc **2** a set of sails; sail **3** a cloth surface suitable for painting on in oils; *also* the painting on such a surface **4** a coarse cloth so woven as to form regular meshes as a basis for embroidery or tapestry **5** the floor of a boxing or wrestling ring [ME *canevas*, fr ONF, fr (assumed) VL *cannabaceus* hempen, fr L *cannabis* hemp – more at CANNABIS] – **canvaslike** *adj* – **under canvas** living in a tent

'canvas,back /-,bak/ *n* a N American wild duck closely related to the European pochard [fr its colour]

canvass *also* **canvas** /'kanvəs/ *vt* **1** to examine in detail; *specif, NAm* to examine (votes) officially for authenticity **2** to discuss, debate **3** to visit (e g a voter) in order to solicit political support or to ascertain opinions ~ *vi* to seek orders or votes; solicit [obs *canvas* (to toss in a canvas sheet, trounce, castigate)] – **canvass** *n*, **canvasser** *also* **canvaser** *n*

canyon, cañon /'kanyən/ *n* a deep valley or gorge [AmerSp *cañón*, prob alter. of obs Sp *callón*, aug of *calle* street, fr L *callis* footpath]

caoutchouc /'kow,choohk/ *n* [1]RUBBER 2 [F, fr obs Sp *cauchuc* (now *caucho*), fr Quechua]

[1]**cap** /kap/ *n* **1a** a soft usu flat head covering with a peak and no brim **b** (one who has gained) a head covering awarded to a player selected for a special, specif national, sports team or who is a regular member of esp a cricket team **2** a natural cover or top: e g **a** a usu unyielding overlying rock or soil layer **b** the pileus **c** (a patch of distinctively coloured feathers on) the top of a bird's head **3** sthg that serves as a cover or protection, esp for the end or top of an object **4** a mortarboard ⟨*students dressed in ~ and gown*⟩ ☞ GARMENT **5** the uppermost part; the top **6** a small container holding an explosive charge (e g for a toy pistol or for priming the charge in a firearm) **7** the symbol ∩ indicating the intersection of 2 sets – compare CUP 8 **8** *Br* DUTCH CAP [ME *cappe*, fr OE *cæppe*, fr LL *cappa* head-covering, cloak] – **capful** *n*

[2]**cap** *vt* **-pp-** **1a** to provide or protect with a cap **b** to give a cap to as a symbol of honour or rank **2** to form a cap over; crown ⟨*the mountains were ~ped with mist* – John Buchan⟩ **3** to follow with sthg more noticeable or significant; outdo

capability /,kaypə'biləti/ *n* **1** being capable **2** a feature or faculty capable of development; potential **3** the capacity for an indicated use or development

capable /'kaypəbl/ *adj* **1** susceptible ⟨*a remark ~ of being misunderstood*⟩ **2** having the attributes or traits required to perform a specified deed or action ⟨*he is ~ of murder*⟩ **3** able ⟨*her ~ fingers*⟩ *USE* (*except 3*) + *of* [MF or LL; MF *capable*, fr LL *capabilis*, irreg fr L *capere* to take – more at HEAVE] – **capableness** *n*, **capably** /'kaypəbli/ *adv*

capacious /kə'payshəs/ *adj* able to hold a great deal [L *capac-, capax*, fr *capere*] – **capaciously** *adv*, **capaciousness** *n*

capacitance /kə'pasit(ə)ns/ *n* **1** the ability of a conductor or system of conductors and insulators to store electric charge ☞ PHYSICS **2** the measure of capacitance equal to the ratio of the charge induced to the potential difference *USE* ☞ VIDEO [*capacity*] – **capacitive** /kə 'pasətiv/ *adj*, **capacitively** *adv*

capacitor /kə'pasətə/ *n* a component in an electrical circuit that provides capacitance and usu consists of an insulator sandwiched between 2 oppositely charged conductors

capacity /kə'pasəti/ *n* **1a** the ability to receive, accommodate, or deal with sthg **b** an ability to contain ⟨*a jug with a ~ of 2pt*⟩ ☞ UNIT **c** the maximum amount that can be contained or produced ⟨*working at ~*⟩ ⟨*a ~ crowd*⟩ **2** legal competence or power **3a** ability, calibre **b** POTENTIAL 1 **4** a position or role assigned or assumed ⟨*in his ~ as judge*⟩ [ME *capacite*, fr MF *capacité*, fr L *capacitat-, capacitas*, fr *capac-, capax*]

,cap and 'bells *n, pl* **caps and bells** the traditional dress of a court jester

,cap and 'gown *n sing or pl in constr* academicals

caparison /kə'paris(ə)n/ *n* **1** an ornamental covering for a horse, esp a warhorse in former times **2** rich clothing; adornment [MF *caparaçon*, fr OSp *caparazón*] – **caparison** *vt*

[1]**cape** /kayp/ *n* a peninsula or similar land projection jutting out into water [ME *cap*, fr MF, fr OProv, fr L *caput* head – more at HEAD]

[2]**cape** *n* a sleeveless outer (part of a) garment that fits closely at the neck and hangs loosely from the shoulders – compare [1]CLOAK 1 [prob fr Sp *capa* cloak, fr LL *cappa* head covering, cloak]

,Cape 'Coloured *n* a person of mixed black and white ancestry in S Africa [*Cape* of Good Hope, province of S Africa] – **Cape Coloured** *adj*

,Cape 'Dutch *n, archaic* Afrikaans [*Cape* of Good Hope]

,Cape 'hunting ,dog *n* any of a species of wild African predatory dogs that live in grasslands south and east of the Sahara and hunt in packs ☞ FOOD [*Cape* of Good Hope]

capelin /'kap(ə)lin/ *n* a small fish of northern seas related to the smelts [CanF *capelan*, fr F, codfish, fr OProv, chaplain, codfish, fr ML *cappellanus* chaplain – more at CHAPLAIN]

[1]**caper** /'kaypə/ *n* **1** any of a genus of low prickly shrubs of the Mediterranean region **2** a greenish flower bud or young berry of the caper, pickled and used as a seasoning, garnish, etc [back-formation fr earlier *capers* (taken as a plural), fr ME *caperis*, fr L *capparis*, fr Gk *kapparis*]

[2]**caper** *vi* to leap about in a carefree way; prance [prob by shortening & alter. fr *capriole*]

[3]**caper** *n* **1** a joyful leap **2** a high-spirited escapade; a prank **3** *chiefly NAm* an illegal enterprise; a crime – infml

capercaillie /,kapə'kayli/, **capercailzie** /-'kaylzi/ *n* the largest Old World grouse [ScGael *capalcoille*, lit., horse of the woods]

capillarity /,kapi'larəti/ *n* the elevation or depression of the surface of a liquid in contact with a solid (e g in a fine-bore tube) that depends on the relative attraction of the molecules of the liquid for each other and for those of the solid [[1]CAPILLARY + -ITY]

[1]**capillary** /kə'piləri/ *adj* **1a** resembling a hair, esp in slender elongated form **b** *of a tube, passage, etc* having a very fine bore **2** involving, held by, or

resulting from surface tension **3** of capillaries or capillarity [F or L; F *capillaire*, fr L *capillaris*, fr *capillus* hair]

[2]**capillary** *n* a capillary tube; *esp* any of the smallest blood vessels connecting arteries with veins and forming networks throughout the body ☞ ANATOMY

,cap in 'hand *adv* in a deferential manner

[1]**capital** /'kapitl/ *adj* **1a** punishable by death ⟨*a* ~ *crime*⟩ **b** involving execution ⟨~ *punishment*⟩ **2** *of a letter* of or conforming to the series (e g A, B, C rather than a, b, c) used to begin sentences or proper names **3a** of the greatest importance or influence ⟨*the* ~ *importance of criticism in the work of creation itself* – T S Eliot⟩ **b** being the seat of government **4** excellent ⟨*a* ~ *book*⟩ – not now in vogue [ME, fr L *capitalis*, fr *capit-*, *caput* head – more at HEAD]

[2]**capital** *n* **1a** (the value of) a stock of accumulated goods, esp at a particular time and in contrast to income received during a particular period **b** accumulated possessions calculated to bring in income **c** *sing or pl in constr* people holding capital **d** a sum of money saved **2** an esp initial capital letter ☞ ALPHABET **3** a city serving as a seat of government ☞ MAP [F or It; F, fr It *capitale*, fr *capitale*, adj, chief, principal, fr L *capitalis*; (2,3) fr [1]*capital*] – **make capital of/out of** to turn (a situation) to one's advantage

[3]**capital** *n* the top part or piece of an architectural column ☞ ARCHITECTURE [ME *capitale*, modif of ONF *capitel*, fr LL *capitellum* small head, top of column, dim. of L *capit-*, *caput*]

,capital 'assets *n pl* tangible or intangible long-term assets

,capital 'gain *n* the profit from the sale of a capital asset (e g a house) – usu pl with sing. meaning ⟨capital-gains *tax*⟩

capital goods *n pl* goods used in producing other commodities rather than for sale to consumers

,capital-in'tensive *adj* using or requiring a capital investment that is large in relation to other inputs or needs – compare LABOUR- INTENSIVE 1

capitalism /'kapitl,iz(ə)m/ *n* an economic system characterized by private ownership and control of the means of production, distribution, and exchange and by the profit motive [[2]*capital* + *-ism*]

[1]**capitalist** /'kapitl·ist/ *n* **1** a person with (invested) capital; *broadly* a very wealthy person **2** one who favours capitalism

[2]**capitalist, capitalistic** /-'istik/ *adj* **1** owning capital ⟨*the* ~ *class*⟩ **2** practising, advocating, or marked by capitalism ⟨~ *nations*⟩ – **capitalistically** *adv*

capital·ize, -ise /'kapitl,iez/ *vt* **1** to write or print in capitals or with an initial capital **2** to convert into capital ⟨~ *the company's reserve fund*⟩ **3** to convert (a periodic payment) into an equivalent capital sum ⟨~d *annuities*⟩ **4** to supply capital for ~ *vi* to gain by turning sthg to advantage – usu + *on* – **capitalization** /-ie'zaysh(ə)n/ *n*

capital ship *n* a warship (e g a battleship) of the first rank in size and importance

capitation /,kapi'taysh(ə)n/ *n* a uniform payment or charge made per person [LL *capitation-*, *capitatio* poll tax, fr L *capit-*, *caput*]

capitol /'kapitl/ *n* **1** a building in which a US legislative body meets **2** *cap* the building in which Congress meets at Washington [L *Capitolium*, temple of Jupiter on the Capitoline hill in Rome]

capitular /kə'pityoolə, -choolə/ *adj* of an ecclesiastical chapter [ML *capitularis*, fr *capitulum* chapter]

capitulate /kə'pityoolayt, -choo-/ *vi* **1** to surrender, often after negotiation of terms **2** to cease resisting; acquiesce [ML *capitulatus*, pp of *capitulare* to distinguish by heads or chapters, fr LL *capitulum*]

capitulation /kə,pityoo'laysh(ə)n, -choo-/ *n* **1** an agreement between governments **2** the act or agreement of sby who surrenders **3** a surrender, acquiescence

capitulum /kə'pityooləm, -chooləm/ *n, pl* **capitula** /-lə/ a rounded or flattened cluster of stalkless flowers, often simulating 1 larger flower ☞ PLANT [NL, fr L, small head – more at CHAPTER]

capo /'kapoh, 'kay-/ *n, pl* **capos** a movable bar attached to the fingerboard esp of a guitar to raise the pitch of the strings [short for *capotasto*, fr It, lit., head of fingerboard]

capon /'kaypən, -pon/ *n* a castrated male chicken [ME, fr OE *capūn*, prob fr ONF *capon*, fr L *capon-*, *capo*; akin to Gk *koptein* to cut] – **caponize** *vt*

cappuccino /,kapoo'cheenoh/ *n* coffee made with espresso and hot milk [It, lit., Capuchin; fr the likeness of its colour to that of a Capuchin's habit]

caprice /kə'prees/ *n* **1a** a sudden and seemingly unmotivated change of mind **b** a sudden and unpredictable change or series of changes ⟨*the* ~s *of the weather*⟩ **2** a disposition to change one's mind impulsively [F, fr It *capriccio*, lit., head with hair standing on end, shudder, fr *capo* head (fr L *caput*) + *riccio* hedgehog, fr L *ericius* – more at HEAD, URCHIN]

capricious /kə'prishəs/ *adj* governed or characterized by caprice; apt to change suddenly or unpredictably – **capriciously** *adv*, **capriciousness** *n*

Capricorn /'kaprikawn/ *n* (sby born under) the 10th zodiacal constellation, pictured as a creature resembling a goat with the tail of a fish ☞ SYMBOL [ME *Capricorne*, fr L *Capricornus*, fr *caper* goat + *cornu* horn – more at HORN] – **Capricornian** /-'kawni·ən/ *adj or n*

capriole /'kapriohl/ *n* a vertical leap made by a trained horse with a backward kick of the hind legs at the height of the leap [MF or OIt; MF *capriole*, fr OIt *capriola*, fr *capriolo* roebuck, fr L *capreolus* goat, roebuck, fr *capr-*, *caper* he-goat; akin to OE *hæfer* goat, Gk *kapros* wild boar] – **capriole** *vi*

ca,proic 'acid /kə'proh·ik/ *n* a liquid fatty acid used in flavourings and medicine [ISV, fr L *capr-*, *caper*]

Capsian /'kapsi·ən/ *adj* of a Palaeolithic culture of N Africa and S Europe [F *capsien*, fr L *Capsa* Gafsa, oasis in Tunisia]

capsicum /'kapsikəm/ *n* (the many-seeded usu fleshy-walled fruit of) any of a genus of tropical herbaceous plants and shrubs of the nightshade family – compare HOT PEPPER, SWEET PEPPER [NL, genus name, perh fr L *capsa* case]

capsid /'kapsid/ *n* the outer protein shell of a virus particle [L *capsa* case + E [2]*-id* – more at [2]CASE] – **capsidal** *adj*

capsize /kap'siez/ *vb* to (cause to) overturn ⟨~ *a canoe*⟩ [origin unknown]

capstan /'kapstən/ *n* **1** a mechanical device consisting of an upright drum round which a rope, hawser, etc is fastened, used for moving or raising heavy weights **2** a rotating shaft that drives tape at a constant speed in a tape recorder [ME]

capstone /'kap,stohn/ *n* a copingstone ['*cap*]

capsulate /'kapsyoolət, -layt/, **capsulated** /-,laytid/ *adj* enclosed in a capsule

capsule /'kapsyoohl, -yool/ *n* **1** a membrane or sac **a** enclosing a body part **b** surrounding a microorganism **2** a closed plant receptacle containing spores or seeds **3** a usu gelatin shell enclosing a drug for swallowing **4** a compact usu rounded container **5** a detachable pressurized compartment, esp in a spacecraft or aircraft, containing crew and controls; *also* a spacecraft ☞ SPACE **6** a usu metal, wax, or plastic covering that encloses the top of a bottle, esp of wine, and protects the cork [F, fr L *capsula*, dim. of *capsa* box – more at ²CASE] – **capsular** /'kapsyoolə/ *adj*

capsul·ize, -ise /'kapsyoo,liez/ *vt* to formulate or state in a brief or compact way

¹**captain** /'kaptin/ *n* **1a** ☞ RANK **b** an officer in charge of a ship **c** a pilot of a civil aircraft **2** a distinguished military leader **3** a leader of a team, esp a sports team **4** a dominant figure ⟨~s *of industry*⟩ **5** *Br* the head boy or girl at a school **6** *NAm* a fire or police officer [ME *capitane*, fr MF *capitain*, fr LL *capitaneus*, adj & n, chief, fr L *capit-*, *caput* head – more at HEAD] – **captaincy** /-si/ *n*, **captainship** *n*

²**captain** *vt* to be captain of

caption /'kapshən/ *n* **1** a heading or title, esp of an article or document **2** a comment or description accompanying a pictorial illustration **3** a film subtitle [ME *capcioun*, fr L *caption-*, *captio* act of taking, fr *captus*, pp of *capere* to take – more at HEAVE] – **caption** *vt*, **captionless** *adj*

captious /'kapshəs/ *adj* marked by an often ill-natured inclination to stress faults and raise objections [ME *capcious*, fr MF or L; MF *captieux*, fr L *captiosus*, fr *captio* act of taking, deception] – **captiously** *adv*, **captiousness** *n*

captivate /'kaptivayt/ *vt* to fascinate or charm irresistibly – **captivatingly** *adv*, **captivation** /-'vaysh(ə)n/ *n*

captive /'kaptiv/ *adj* **1a** taken and held as prisoner, esp by an enemy in war **b** kept within bounds; confined **c** held under control **2** in a situation that makes departure or inattention difficult ⟨*a ~ audience*⟩ [ME, fr L *captivus*, fr *captus*, pp of *capere*] – **captive** *n*, **captivity** /kap'tivəti/ *n*

captor /'kaptə/ *n* one who or that which holds another captive [LL, fr L *captus*]

¹**capture** /'kapchə/ *n* **1** the act of gaining control or possession **2** one who or that which has been captured **3** the acquisition by an atom, molecule, ion, or nucleus of an additional elementary particle, often with associated emission of radiation [MF, fr L *captura*, fr *captus*]

²**capture** *vt* **1** to take captive; win, gain ⟨~ *a city*⟩ **2** to preserve in a relatively permanent form ⟨*how well the scene was* ~d *on film*⟩ **3** to remove (e g a chess piece) from the playing board according to the rules of a game **4** to bring about the capture of (an elementary particle)

capuchin /kə'pyoohchin, -shin/ *n* **1** *cap* a member of an austere branch of the Franciscan Order founded in 1528 **2** a hooded cloak worn by women in former times **3** a S American monkey with hair on its crown shaped like a monk's cowl [MF, fr OIt *cappuccino*, fr *cappuccio* hood, fr *cappa* cloak, fr LL; fr his cowl]

capybara /,kapi'bahrə/ *n* a large tailless mainly aquatic S American rodent [Pg *capibara*, fr Tupi]

car /kah/ *n* **1** a vehicle moving on wheels: **a** a chariot of war or of triumph – chiefly poetic **b** a railway carriage; *esp* one used for a specific purpose ⟨*buffet* ~⟩ ⟨*sleeping* ~⟩ **c** MOTOR CAR 👁 **2** the passenger compartment of an airship or balloon **3** *NAm* the cage of a lift [ME *carre*, fr AF, fr L *carra*, pl of *carrum*, alter. of *carrus*, of Celt origin; akin to OIr & MW *carr* vehicle; akin to L *currere* to run]

carabineer, carbinier /,karəbi'niə/ *n* a soldier armed with a carbine [F *carabinier*, fr *carabine* carbine]

carabiner *also* **karabiner** /,karə'beenə/ *n* an oblong ring with an openable side that is used in mountaineering to hold freely running rope [G *karabiner*]

carabinieri /,karəbi'nyeəri/ *n pl* the Italian national police force [It, pl of *carabiniere*, fr F *carabinier* carabineer]

caracal /'karəkal, ,--'-/ *n* a long-legged medium-sized cat of Africa and Asia [F, fr Sp, fr Turk *karakulak*, lit., black-ear, fr *kara* black + *kulak* ear]

caracul /'karəkl/ *n* (a) karakul

carafe /kə'rahf, -'raf, 'karəf/ *n* a (glass) bottle used to hold water or wine, esp at table [F, fr It *caraffa*, fr Ar *gharrāfah*]

caramel /'karəməl, -mel/ *n* **1** a brittle brown somewhat bitter substance obtained by heating sugar and used as a colouring and flavouring agent **2** a chewy usu quite soft caramel-flavoured toffee [F, fr Sp *caramelo*, fr Pg, icicle, caramel, fr LL *calamellus* small reed – more at SHAWM] – **caramelize** *vb*

carapace /'karə,pays/ *n* a hard case (e g of chitin) covering (part of) the back of a turtle, crab, etc [F, fr Sp *carapacho*]

carat /'karət/ *n* **1** a unit of weight for precious stones equal to 200mg **2** *NAm chiefly* **karat** a unit of fineness for gold equal to $\frac{1}{24}$ part of pure gold in an alloy [MF, prob fr ML *carratus*, fr Ar *qīrāt* bean pod, a small weight, fr Gk *keration* carob bean, a small weight, fr dim. of *kerat-*, *keras* horn – more at HORN]

¹**caravan** /'karə,van/ *n* **1a** *sing or pl in constr* a company of travellers on a journey through desert or hostile regions; *also* a train of pack animals **b** a group of vehicles travelling together **2** *Br* a covered vehicle designed to be towed by a motor car or horse and to serve as a dwelling when parked [It *caravana*, fr Per *kārwān*]

²**caravan** *vi* **-nn-** (*NAm* **-n-, -nn-**) to have a holiday in a caravan

caravanner /'karə,vanə/ *n*, *Br* one who goes camping with a caravan

caravanserai /,karə'vansərie/, *NAm chiefly* **caravansary** /-səri/ *n*, *pl* **caravanserais, caravanserai** a usu large inn in Eastern countries that is built round a courtyard and used as a resting place for caravans [Per *kārwānsarāī*, fr *kārwān* caravan + *sarāī* palace, inn]

caravel /'karə,vel/ *n* a small 15th- and 16th-c ship with broad bows, high narrow poop, and triangular sails [MF *caravelle*, fr OPg *caravela*]

caraway /'karəway/ *n* a usu white-flowered aromatic plant with pungent seeds used as a flavouring

[ME, prob fr ML *carvi*, fr Ar *karawyā*, fr Gk *karon*]

carb-, carbo- *comb form* carbon; carbonic; carbonyl; carboxyl ⟨carb *ide*⟩ ⟨carbo*hydrate*⟩ [F, fr *carbone*]

carbamate /'kahbə,mayt/ *n* a salt or ester of carbamic acid

car,bamic 'acid /kah'bamik/ *n* an acid known in the form of salts and esters in the blood and urine of mammals [ISV *carb-* + *am*ide + *-ic*]

carbamide /'kahbəmied/ *n* urea [ISV *carb-* + *amide*]

carbanion /kah'ban,ie·ən/ *n* an organic ion carrying a negative charge on a carbon atom – compare CARBONIUM

carbide /'kahbied/ *n* a compound of carbon with a more electropositive element; *esp* CALCIUM CARBIDE [ISV]

carbine /'kahbien/ *n* **1** a short light rifle or musket orig carried by cavalry **2** a short light gas-operated magazine-fed automatic rifle [F *carabine*, fr MF *carabin* carabineer]

carbinol /'kahbinol/ *n* (an alcohol derived from) methanol – not now used technically [ISV, fr obs G *karbin* methyl, fr G *karb-* carb-]

carbohydrate /,kahbə'hiedrayt, -boh-/ *n* any of various compounds of carbon, hydrogen, and oxygen (e g sugars, starches, and celluloses) formed by green plants and constituting a major class of energy-providing animal foods

car,bolic 'acid /kah'bolik/ *n* phenol [ISV *carb-* + L *oleum* oil – more at OIL]

carbon /'kahb(ə)n/ *n* **1** a nonmetallic chiefly tetravalent element occurring as diamond, graphite, charcoal, coke, etc and as a constituent of coal, petroleum, carbonates (e g limestone), and organic compounds ☞ PERIODIC TABLE **2a** a sheet of carbon paper **b** CARBON COPY 1 **3** a piece of carbon used as an element in a voltaic cell [F *carbone*, fr L *carbon-*, *carbo* ember, charcoal] – **carbonless** *adj*

carbon 14 *n* a heavy radioactive carbon isotope (of mass number 14) used in carbon dating

carbonaceous /,kahbə'nayshəs/ *adj* relating to, resembling, containing, or composed of carbon

carbonado /,kahbə'naydoh/ *n, pl* **carbonados** opaque dark-coloured diamond used as an abrasive [Pg, lit., carbonated, fr *carbone* carbon, fr F]

[1]**carbonate** /'kahbənət, -nayt/ *n* a salt or ester of carbonic acid

[2]**carbonate** /'kahbənayt/ *vt* **1** to convert into a carbonate **2** to impregnate with carbon dioxide; aerate ⟨*a* ~d *beverage*⟩ – **carbonation** /-'naysh(ə)n/ *n*

,carbon 'black *n* carbon as a colloidal black substance (e g soot)

,carbon 'copy *n* **1** a copy made with carbon paper **2** a duplicate or exact replica

'carbon ,cycle *n* **1** the fusion reaction thought to be the energy source of most stars, in which 4 hydrogen atoms fuse to form a helium atom **2** the cycle of carbon in living things in which carbon dioxide from the air is caused to react by photosynthesis to form organic nutrients and is ultimately restored to the inorganic state by respiration and rotting

,carbon 'dating *n* the dating of ancient material (e g an archaeological specimen) by recording the amount of carbon 14 remaining

,carbon di'oxide *n* a heavy colourless gas that does not support combustion, is formed esp by the combustion and decomposition of organic substances, and is absorbed from the air by plants in photosynthesis

,carbon di'sulphide *n* a colourless inflammable poisonous liquid used esp as a solvent for rubber

car,bonic 'acid /kah'bonik/ *n* a weak acid that is a solution of carbon dioxide in water and whose salts are carbonates

carbonic acid gas *n* CARBON DIOXIDE

carboniferous /,kahbə'nif(ə)rəs/ *adj* **1** producing or containing carbon or coal **2** *cap* of or being the period of the Palaeozoic era between the Devonian and the Permian in which coal deposits formed ☞ EVOLUTION – **Carboniferous** *n*

carbonium /kah'bohni·əm/ *n* an organic ion carrying a positive charge on a carbon atom – compare CARBANION [*carb-* + *-onium*]

carbon·ize, -ise /'kahb(ə)n,iez/ *vt* to convert into carbon or a carbon-containing residue ~ *vi* to become carbonized; char – **carbonization** /-ie'zaysh(ə)n/ *n*

,carbon mo'noxide *n* a colourless odourless very toxic gas formed as a product of the incomplete combustion of carbon

carbonnade /,kahbə'nayd/ *n* a rich beef stew made with beer [F]

'carbon ,paper *n* (a sheet of) thin paper coated on 1 side with dark pigment, used to make copies by placing between 2 sheets of paper, so that the pigment is transferred to the lower sheet by the pressure of writing or typing on the upper

,carbon ,tetra'chloride /,tetrə'klawried/ *n* a colourless noninflammable toxic liquid used as an industrial solvent and a starting material in organic synthesis

carbonyl /'kahbənil/ *n* **1** a bivalent radical CO occurring in aldehydes, ketones, carboxylic acids, esters, acid halides, and amides **2** a compound of the carbonyl radical with a metal – **carbonylic** /-'nilik/ *adj*

Carborundum /,kahbə'roondəm/ *trademark* – used for various abrasives

carboxy-, carbox- *comb form* carboxyl

carboxyl /kah'boksil/ *n* a univalent radical COOH contained in organic acids [ISV] – **carboxylic** /-'silik/ *adj*

carboxylase /kah'boksilayz, -lays/ *n* an enzyme that catalyses a chemical reaction in which a carboxyl group is added or removed [ISV]

[1]**carboxylate** /kah'boksilayt/ *n* a salt or ester of a carboxylic acid

[2]**carboxylate** *vt* to introduce 1 or more carboxyl groups into (a compound) – **carboxylation** /-'laysh(ə)n/ *n*

,carbox,ylic 'acid /,kahbək'silik/ *n* an organic acid (e g acetic acid) containing 1 or more carboxyl groups

carboy /'kah,boy/ *n* a large usu roughly spherical glass or plastic container for liquids [Per *qarāba*, fr Ar *qarrābah* demijohn]

carbuncle /'kah,bungkl/ *n* **1** a red gemstone, usu a garnet, cut in a domed shape without facets **2** a painful local inflammation of the skin and deeper tissues with multiple openings for the discharge of pus [ME, fr MF, fr L *carbunculus* small coal, carbuncle, dim. of *carbon-*, *carbo* charcoal, ember] – **carbuncled** *adj*, **carbuncular** /kah'bungkyoolə/ *adj*

A transverse front-wheel drive engine

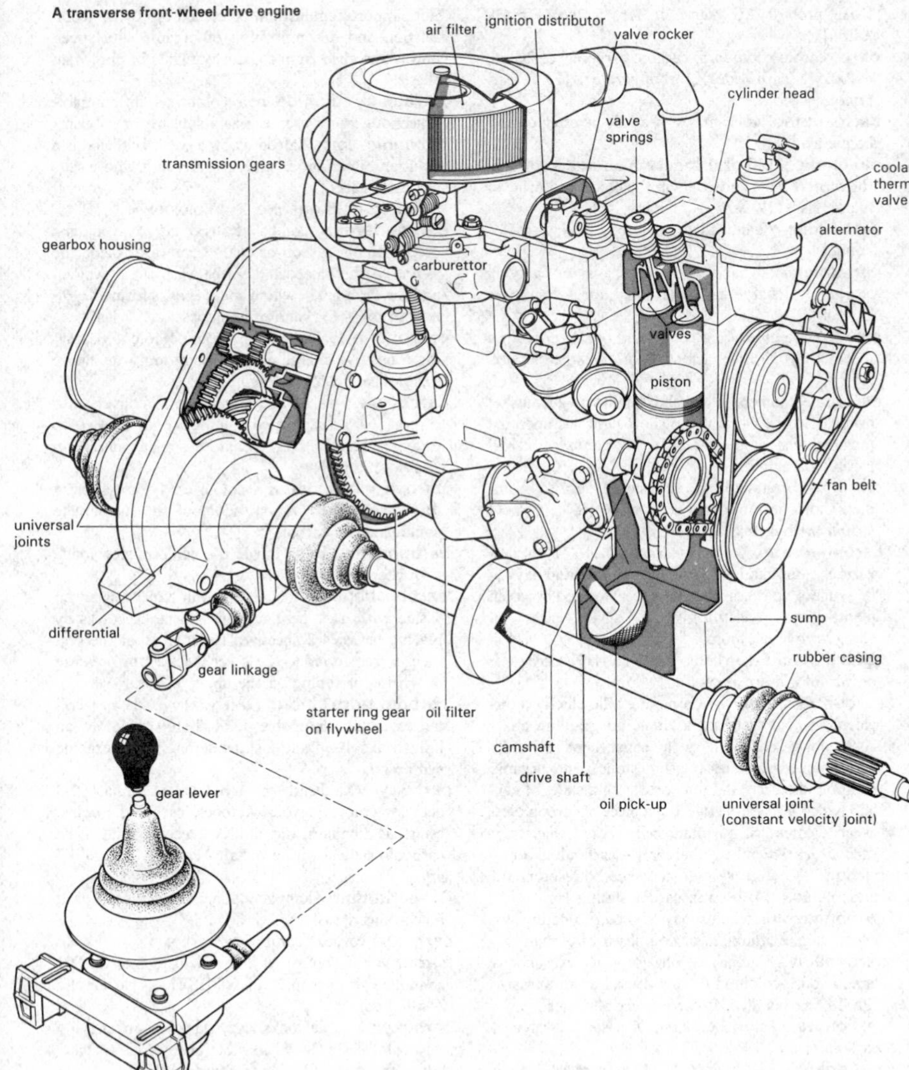

The gearbox is the means by which torque is multiplied and transmitted from the engine to the drive shafts. The different gears allow the engine to operate near its optimum rpm, whatever the speed at which the car is moving.

The camshaft opens the inlet valves and the exhaust valves in the right sequence and at the right time. If (as here) it is not mounted above them, it reaches them through pushrods and rockers.

The universal joints transmit torque from the differential to each front wheel hub through a drive-shaft, which they allow to move as the wheel rises or falls over bumps. Because the wheels have also to be steered, yet must be driven smoothly, a special kind of universal joint is used, known as a constant-velocity joint.

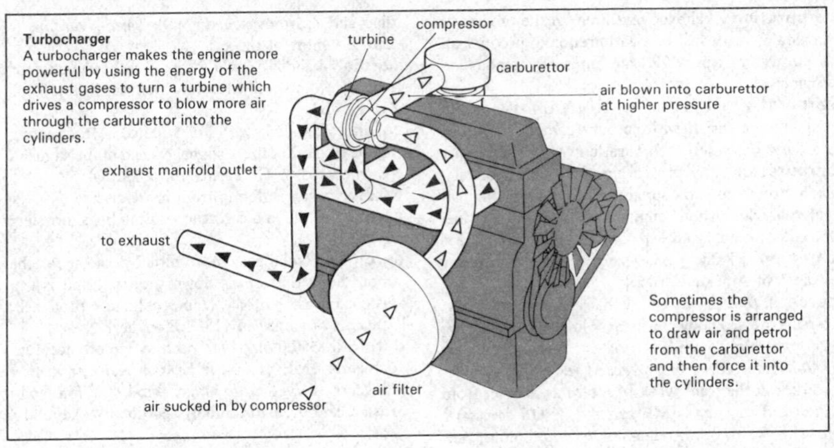

Turbocharger
A turbocharger makes the engine more powerful by using the energy of the exhaust gases to turn a turbine which drives a compressor to blow more air through the carburettor into the cylinders.

compressor
turbine
carburettor
air blown into carburettor at higher pressure
exhaust manifold outlet
to exhaust
air filter
air sucked in by compressor

Sometimes the compressor is arranged to draw air and petrol from the carburettor and then force it into the cylinders.

A radial tyre

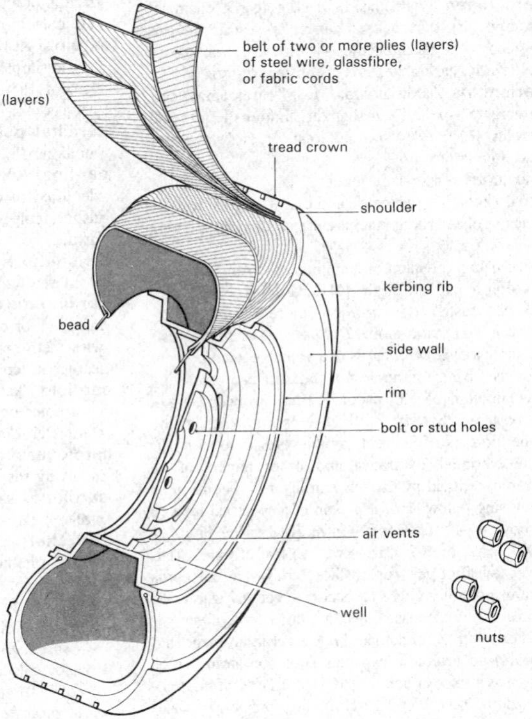

belt of two or more plies (layers) of steel wire, glassfibre, or fabric cords
carcass of one or more plies (layers) of fabric cords laid radially (directly from bead to bead)
tread crown
shoulder
kerbing rib
bead
side wall
rim
bolt or stud holes
air vents
well
nuts

Disc brake

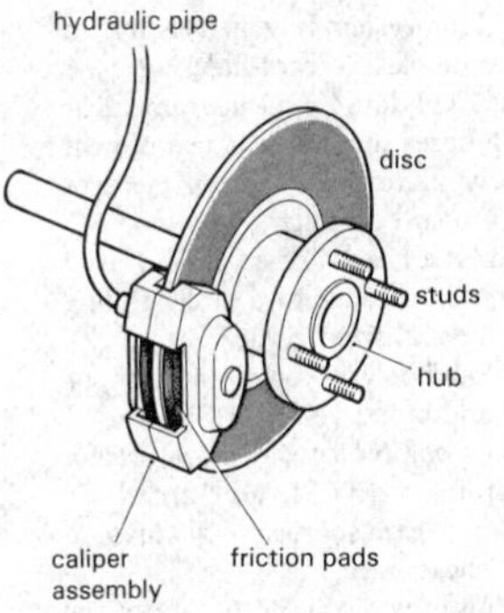

hydraulic pipe
disc
studs
hub
caliper assembly
friction pads

Disc brakes. When the brake pedal is pressed, resulting pressure in the hydraulic system makes the caliper assembly push the two friction pads together so that they grip the brake disc and slow the wheel.

carburation /ˌkahbyooˈraysh(ə)n/ *n* the process of mixing air with fuel in a carburettor to produce an explosive mixture for an internal combustion engine

carburet /ˈkahbyooret/ *vt* **-tt-** (*NAm* **-t-, -tt-**) to combine or enrich with carbon (compounds) [obs *carburet* (carbide)] – **carburetion** /-ˈray shən/ *n*

carburettor, *NAm* **carburetor** /ˌkahbyooˈretə, ˌkahbəˈretə/ *n* an apparatus for supplying an internal-combustion engine with vaporized fuel mixed with air in an explosive mixture ☞ CAR

carcajou /ˈkahkəjooh, -ˌzhooh/ *n* a wolverine [CanF, of AmerInd origin]

carcass, *Br also* **carcase** /ˈkahkəs/ *n* **1** a dead body; *esp* the dressed body of a meat animal **2** the decaying or worthless remains of a structure ⟨*the half-submerged* ~ *of a wrecked vessel*⟩ **3** a framework; *esp* the framework of a tyre as distinct from the tread ☞ CAR [MF *carcasse*, fr OF *carcois*]

carcin- /kahsin-/, **carcino-** *comb form* tumour; cancer ⟨carcino*genic*⟩ [Gk *karkin-*, *karkino-*, fr *karkinos* – more at CANCER]

carcinogen /ˈkahsinəjən/ *n* sthg (e g a chemical compound) that causes cancer – **carcinogenesis** /-ˈjenəsis/ *n*, **carcinogenic** /-ˈjenik/ *adj*, **carcinogenically** *adv*, **carcinogenicity** /ˌkahsinəjəˈnisəti/ *n*

carcinoma /ˌkahsiˈnohmə/ *n, pl* **carcinomas, carcinomata** /-mətə/ a malignant tumour of epithelial origin [L, fr Gk *karkinōma* cancer, fr *karkinos*] – **carcinomatous** *adj*

ˈcar ˌcoat *n* a ¾-length coat

¹card /kahd/ *vt* to cleanse and disentangle (fibres) by the use of a carding machine preparatory to spinning – **carder** *n*

²card *n* an implement or machine for carding fibres or raising a nap on cloth [ME *carde*, fr MF, fr LL *cardus* thistle, fr L *carduus* – more at CHARD]

³card *n* **1** PLAYING CARD **2** *pl but sing or pl in constr* a game played with cards **3** a valuable asset or right for use in negotiations **4** a flat stiff usu small and rectangular piece of paper or thin cardboard: e g **a** a postcard **b** VISITING CARD **c** PROGRAMME 1a; *esp* one for a sporting event **d** GREETINGS CARD **5** *pl, Br* the National Insurance and other papers of an employee, held by his/her employer **6** a comical or amusing fellow **7** *Br* a person of a specified type ⟨*a knowing* ~⟩ *USE* (*6&7*) infml [ME *carde*, modif of MF *carte*, prob fr OIt *carta*, lit., leaf of paper, fr L *charta* leaf of papyrus, fr Gk *chartēs*] – **on the cards** quite possible; likely to occur – **get/ask for one's cards** to be dismissed/resign from employment

cardamom /ˈkahdəməm/ *n* (an E Indian plant that bears) an aromatic capsular fruit containing seeds used as a spice or condiment [L *cardamomum*, fr Gk *kardamōmon*, blend of *kardamon* peppergrass and *amōmon*, an Indian spice plant]

¹ˈcardˌboard /-ˌbawd/ *n* material of similar composition to paper but thicker and stiffer [³*card* + *board*]

²cardboard *adj* **1** made (as if) of cardboard **2** unreal, insubstantial ⟨*the story has too many* ~ *characters*⟩

ˈcard-ˌcarrying *adj* being a fully paid-up member, esp of the Communist party [fr the assumption that such a person carries a membership card]

cardi- /kahdi-/, **cardio-** *comb form* heart; cardiac ⟨cardio *gram*⟩ ⟨cardio*graph*⟩ ⟨cardio*logy*⟩; cardiac and ⟨cardio*vascular*⟩ [Gk *kardi-*, *kardio-*, fr *kardia* – more at HEART]

-cardia /-kahdi·ə/ *comb form* (→ *n*) heart action or location (of a specified type) ⟨*tachy*cardia⟩ [NL, fr Gk *kardia*]

¹cardiac /ˈkahdiak/ *adj* **1** of, situated near, or acting on the heart **2** of the oesophageal end of the stomach [L *cardiacus*, fr Gk *kardiakos*, fr *kardia*]

²cardiac *n* sby suffering from heart disease

cardie /ˈkahdi/ *n* a cardigan – infml [by shortening & alter.]

cardigan /ˈkahdigən/ *n* a knitted garment for the upper body that opens down the front and is usu fastened with buttons [James Thomas Brudenell, 7th Earl of *Cardigan* †1868 E soldier]

¹cardinal /ˈkahdinl/ *adj* of primary importance; fundamental [ME, fr OF, fr LL *cardinalis*, fr L, of a hinge, fr *cardin-*, *cardo* hinge; akin to OE *hratian* to rush, Gk *skairein* to gambol] – **cardinally** /ˈkahdinli/ *adv*

²cardinal *n* a member of a body of high officials of the Roman Catholic church whose powers include the election of a new pope – **cardinalate** /-lət, -ˌlayt/ *n*, **cardinalship** *n*

cardinal number *n* a number (e g 1, 2, 3) that is used in simple counting and that indicates how many elements there are in a collection – compare ORDINAL NUMBER ☞ NUMBER

ˌcardinal ˈpoint *n* any of the 4 principal compass points north, south, east, and west

ˌcardinal ˈvirtue *n* any of the 4 natural virtues identified in classical literature, namely prudence, justice, temperance, and fortitude; *broadly* any major virtue

card index *n, Br* a filing system in which each item is entered on a separate card – **card-index** *vt*

ˈcarding maˌchine /ˈkahding/ *n* an instrument or machine for carding fibres that consists usu of bent wire teeth set closely in rows in a thick piece of leather fastened to a board or roller

cardioid /ˈkahdioyd/ *n* a heart-shaped curve traced by a point on the circumference of a circle rolling completely round an equal-sized circle

cardiovascular /ˌkahdiohˈvaskyoolə/ *adj* of or involving the heart and blood vessels [ISV]

-cardium /-kahdi·əm/ *comb form* (→ *n*), *pl* **-cardia** /-di·ə/ heart ⟨*epi*cardium⟩ [NL, fr Gk *kardia*]

ˈcardˌsharp /-ˌshahp/, **ˈcardˌsharper** /-ˌshahpə/ *n* one who habitually cheats at cards

¹care /keə/ *n* **1** a cause for anxiety ⟨*the* ~*s of the world*⟩ **2** close attention; effort ⟨*took* ~ *over the drawing*⟩ **3** change, supervision ⟨*under the doctor's* ~⟩; *specif, Br* guardianship and supervision of children by a local authority **4** sby or sthg that is an object of attention, anxiety, or solicitude ⟨*the flower garden was her special* ~⟩ [ME, fr OE *caru*; akin to OHG *kara* lament, L *garrire* to chatter]

²care *vi* **1a** to feel trouble or anxiety **b** to feel interest or concern – often + *about* **2** to give care ⟨~ *for the sick*⟩ **3** to have a liking or taste *for* ~ *vt* **1** to be concerned about ⟨*nobody* ~s *what I do*⟩ **2** to wish ⟨*if you* ~ *to go*⟩

careen /kəˈreen/ *vt* **1** to cause (a boat) to lean over on one side **2** to clean, caulk, or repair (a boat) in this position ~ *vi* **1a** to careen a boat **b** to undergo this process **2** to heel over **3** *chiefly NAm* to career [MF *carène* keel, fr OIt *carena*, fr L *carina*, lit., nutshell; akin to Gk *karyon* nut]

[1]career /kə'riə/ *n* **1** the course of (a particular sphere of) a person's life ⟨*Churchill's* ~ *as a politician*⟩ **2** a field of employment in which one expects to remain; *esp* such a field which requires special qualifications and training [MF *carrière*, fr OProv *carriera* street, fr ML *carraria* road for vehicles, fr L *carrus* car]

[2]career *vi* to move swiftly in an uncontrolled fashion ⟨*the car* ~ed *off the road*⟩

[3]career *adj* of or engaged in an occupation which offers a long-term series of opportunities for advancement, usu within some specified organization or business ⟨*a* ~ *diplomat*⟩

ca'reer ,girl *adj* a woman who puts advancement in her career or profession before marriage or motherhood

careerist /kə'riərist/ *n* one who is intent on advancing his/her career, often at the expense of personal integrity – **careerism** *n*

carefree /'keə,free/ *adj* free from anxiety or responsibility ⟨~ *holidays*⟩

'careful /-f(ə)l/ *adj* **1** exercising or taking care **2a** marked by attentive concern **b** cautious, prudent ⟨*be* ~ *of the horses*⟩ – often + *to* and an infinitive ⟨*be* ~ *to switch off the machine*⟩ – **carefully** *adv*, **carefulness** *n*

'careless /-lis/ *adj* **1** not taking care **2a** negligent, slovenly ⟨*writing that is* ~ *and full of errors*⟩ **b** unstudied, spontaneous ⟨~ *grace*⟩ **3a** free from care; untroubled ⟨~ *days*⟩ **b** indifferent, unconcerned ⟨~ *of the consequences*⟩ – **carelessly** *adv*, **carelessness** *n*

[1]caress /kə'res/ *n* **1** a kiss **2** a caressing touch or stroke [F *caresse*, fr It *carezza*, fr *caro* dear, fr L *carus* – more at CHARITY]

[2]caress *vt* **1** to touch or stroke lightly and lovingly **2** to touch or affect gently or soothingly ⟨*music that* ~es *the ear*⟩ – **caresser** *n*, **caressingly** *adv*

caret /'karət/ *n* a mark ‸ or ᴧ or ⟩ used on written or printed matter to indicate an insertion to be made [L, it is lacking, fr *carēre* to lack, be without – more at CASTE]

'care,taker /-,taykə/ *n* **1** one who takes care of the house or land of an owner, esp during his/her absence **2** one who keeps clean a large and/or public building (e g a school or office), looks after the heating system, and carries out minor repairs **3** sby or sthg temporarily installed in office ⟨*a* ~ *government*⟩

'care,worn /-,wawn/ *adj* showing the effects of grief or anxiety ⟨*a* ~ *face*⟩

carful /'kahfool/ *n* as much or as many as a car will hold

cargo /'kahgoh/ *n, pl* **cargoes, cargos** the goods conveyed in a ship, aircraft, or vehicle; freight [Sp, load, charge, fr *cargar* to load, fr LL *carricare* – more at CHARGE]

'cargo ,cult *n* a millenarian movement of the SW Pacific characterized by a belief in the imminent return of the gods or tribal ancestors in ships or aircraft bearing an abundance of (western) goods with them

Carib /'karib/ *n* **1** a member of an American Indian people of northern S America and the Lesser Antilles **2** the language of the Caribs [NL *Caribes* (pl), fr Sp *Caribe*, fr Arawakan *Carib* – more at CANNIBAL]

Cariban /'karəbən, kə'reebən/ *n* a member, or the language family, of a group of American Indian peoples of northern S America, the lesser Antilles, and nearby coasts ☞ LANGUAGE

Caribbean /,kari'bee.ən/ *adj* of the Caribs, the eastern and southern W Indies, or the Caribbean sea [NL *Caribbaeus*, fr *Caribes*]

caribou /'kari,booh/ *n, pl* **caribous,** *esp collectively* **caribou** any of several large N American antlered deer [CanF, of Algonquian origin]

[1]caricature /'karikəchə, -chooə, -tyooə/ *n* **1** exaggeration of features or characteristics, often to a ludicrous or grotesque degree **2** a comic or satirical representation, esp in literature or art, that has the qualities of caricature **3** a distortion so gross or inferior as to seem like a caricature [It *caricatura*, lit., act of loading, fr *caricare* to load, fr LL *carricare*] – **caricatural** /,karikə'chooərəl, -'tyooərəl/ *adj*, **caricaturist** /'karikə ,chooərist, -,tyooərist/ *n*

[2]caricature /'karikə,chooə, -,tyooə/ *vt* to make or draw a caricature of; represent in caricature

caries /'keəreez, -riz/ *n, pl* **caries** progressive decay of a tooth or sometimes a bone, caused by microorganisms [L, decay; akin to Gk *kēr* death]

carillon /kə'rilyən/ *n* a set of bells sounded by hammers controlled from a keyboard [F, alter. of OF *quarregnon*, fr LL *quaternion-*, *quaternio* set of four – more at QUATERNION]

carina /kə'reenə, -'rienə/ *n, pl* **carinas, carinae** /-ni/ a keel-shaped anatomical part [NL, fr L, keel – more at CAREEN]

carinate /'karinayt/ *also* **'cari,nated** *adj* keeled, ridged ⟨*a* ~ *sepal*⟩

carioca /,kari'ohkə/ *n* **1** *cap* a native or inhabitant of Rio de Janeiro **2** (the music for) a dance resembling the samba [Pg, fr Tupi]

carious /'keəri·əs/ *adj* affected with caries [L *cariosus*, fr *caries*]

cark /kahk/ *vb, archaic* to (cause to) be anxious [ME *carken*, lit., to load, burden, fr ONF *carquier*, fr LL *carricare*]

carl, carle /kahl/ *n, archaic* a man of the common people [ME, fr OE *-carl*, fr ON *karl* man, carl; akin to OE *ceorl* churl – more at CHURL]

carline, carlin /'kahlin/ *n, chiefly Scot* an old woman or witch [ME *kerling*, fr ON, fr *karl* man]

'car,load /,-lohd/ *n* a load that fills a car

Carmelite /'kahmə,liet/ *n* a member of the Roman Catholic mendicant Order of Our Lady of Mount Carmel founded in the 12th c [ME, fr ML *carmelita*, fr *Carmel* Mount Carmel, Palestine, where the order was founded] – **Carmelite** *adj*

carminative /kah'minətiv/ *adj* causing expulsion of gas from the alimentary canal to relieve colic or gripes [F *carminatif*, fr L *carminatus*, pp of *carminare* to card, fr *carmin-*, *carmen* card, fr *carrere* to card – more at CHARD] – **carminative** *n*

carmine /'kahmin/ *n* **1** a rich crimson or scarlet pigment **2** a vivid red [F *carmin*, fr ML *carminium*, irreg fr Ar *qirmiz* kermes + L *minium* – more at MINIUM]

carnage /'kahnij/ *n* great slaughter (e g in battle) [MF, flesh of slain animals or men, fr ML *carnaticum* tribute consisting of animals or meat, fr L *carn-*, *caro*]

carnal /'kahnl/ *adj* **1** given to or marked by physical and esp sexual pleasures and appetites **2** temporal, worldly [ME, fr ONF or LL; ONF, fr LL *carnalis*, fr L *carn-*, *caro* flesh; akin to Gk *keirein* to cut –

more at SHEAR] – **carnality** /kah'naləti/ *n*, **carnally** /'kahnl·i/ *adv*

carnassial /kah'nassi·əl/ *adj* of or being the large long cutting teeth of a carnivore [F *carnassier* carnivorous, deriv of L *carn-, caro*] – **carnassial** *n*

carnation /kah'naysh(ə)n/ *n* **1** light red or pink **2** any of numerous cultivated usu double-flowered pinks [MF, fr OIt *carnagione*, fr *carne* flesh, fr L *carn-, caro*]

carnauba /kah'nowbə/ *n* a fan-leaved Brazilian palm with an edible root, whose leaves yield a wax used in polishes [Pg]

carnelian /kah'neelyən/ *n* (a) cornelian [by alter.]

carnet /'kahnay, -'- (*Fr* karnɛ)/ *n* a customs document permitting free movement of a vehicle across a frontier or temporary duty free import (e g of goods en route to another country) [F, lit., notebook, fr MF *quernet*, fr L *quaterni* set of four – more at QUATERNION]

carnival /'kahnivl/ *n* **1** a period of merrymaking before Lent, esp in Roman Catholic countries **2** an instance of merrymaking or feasting **3a** an exhibition or organized programme of entertainment; a festival **b** *chiefly NAm* a travelling circus or funfair [It *carnevale*, alter. of earlier *carnelevare*, lit., removal of meat, fr *carne* flesh (fr L *carn-, caro*) + *levare* to remove, fr L, to raise]

carnivore /'kahni,vaw/ *n* a flesh-eating animal; *esp* any of an order of flesh-eating mammals ☞ FOOD [deriv of L *carnivorus*]

carnivorous /kah'niv(ə)rəs/ *adj* **1** of or being a carnivore; *specif* flesh-eating **2** *of a plant* feeding on nutrients obtained from animal tissue, esp insects [L *carnivorus*, fr *carn-, caro* flesh + *-vorus* -vorous] – **carnivorously** *adv*, **carnivorousness** *n*

carob /'karəb/ *n* (the edible pod of) a Mediterranean evergreen leguminous tree with red flowers [MF *carobe*, fr ML *carrubium*, fr Ar *kharrūbah*]

[1]**carol** /'karəl/ *n* a popular seasonal usu religious song or ballad; *esp* a Christmas song or hymn [ME *carole*, fr OF, modif of LL *choraula* choral song, fr L, choral accompanist, fr Gk *choraulēs*, fr *choros* chorus + *aulein* to play a reed instrument, fr *aulos*, a reed instrument]

[2]**carol** *vb* **-ll-** (*NAm* **-l-**, **-ll-**) to sing (joyfully)

Caroline /'karəlien/, **Carolean** /,karə'lee·ən/ *adj* of or relating to Charles – used esp with reference to Charles I and Charles II of England [NL *carolinus*, fr ML *Carolus* Charles]

Carolingian /,karə'linji·ən/ *n or adj* (a member) of a medieval Frankish dynasty who ruled in France, Germany, and Italy [adj F *carolingien*, fr ML *karolingi* French people, prob fr (assumed) OHG *karling* Frenchman, fr *Karl* Charles; n fr adj]

carom /'karəm/ *n or vi*, *NAm* [2]/[3]CANNON [n by shortening & alter. fr obs *carambole*, fr Sp *carambola*; vb fr n]

carotene /'karəteen/ *n* any of several orange or red hydrocarbon plant pigments convertible to vitamin A [ISV, fr LL *carota* carrot]

carotenoid *also* **carotinoid** /kə'rotənoyd/ *n* a carotene or similar animal or plant pigment – **carotenoid** *adj*

carotid /kə'rotid/ *adj or n* (of or being) the chief artery or pair of arteries that supply the head with blood [adj F or Gk; F *carotide*, fr Gk *karōtides* carotid arteries, fr *karoun* to stupefy; akin to Gk *kara* head – more at CEREBRAL; n fr adj]

carotid body *n* a small body of tissue at the point in the neck where the carotid artery forks that is sensitive to change in the oxygen content of blood

carousal /kə'rowzl/ *n* a carouse

[1]**carouse** /kə'rowz/ *n* a drunken revel [MF *carrousse*, fr *carous*, adv, completely, all out (in *boire carous* to empty the cup), fr G *garaus*]

[2]**carouse** *vi* **1** to drink alcoholic beverages heavily or freely **2** to take part in a drinking bout

carousel, *NAm also* **carrousel** /,karə'sel, -'zel/ *n* **1** a rotating stand or delivery system ⟨*a luggage ~ at the airport*⟩ **2** *chiefly NAm* a merry-go-round [F *carrousel* tournament for horsemen, fr It *carosello*]

[1]**carp** /kahp/ *vi* to find fault or complain querulously and often unnecessarily – infml; usu + *at* [ME *carpen*, of Scand origin; akin to Icel *karpa* to dispute]

[2]**carp** *n, pl* **carps**, *esp collectively* **carp** (a fish resembling or related to) a large Old World soft-finned freshwater fish often farmed for food [ME *carpe*, fr MF, fr LL *carpa*, prob of Gmc origin; akin to OHG *karpfo* carp]

carp- /kahp-/, **carpo-** *comb form* fruit ⟨carp*ology*⟩ [F & NL, fr Gk *karp-, karpo-*, fr *karpos* – more at HARVEST]

-carp /-kahp/ *comb form* (→ *n*) part of a fruit ⟨*meso*carp⟩; fruit ⟨*schizo*carp⟩ [NL *-carpium*, fr Gk *-karpion*, fr *karpos*]

'car ,park *n, chiefly Br* an area or building set aside for parking motor vehicles

carpel /'kahpl/ *n* any of the structures of a flowering plant that constitute the female (innermost) part of a flower and usu consist of an ovary, style, and stigma ☞ PLANT [NL *carpellum*, fr Gk *karpos* fruit] – **carpellary** /'kahpl·əri/ *adj*, **carpellate** /-ət, -ayt/ *adj*

[1]**carpenter** /'kahpintə/ *n* a woodworker; *esp* one who builds or repairs large-scale structural woodwork [ME, fr ONF *carpentier*, fr L *carpentarius* carriage-maker, fr *carpentum* carriage, of Celt origin; akin to OIr *carr* vehicle – more at CAR]

[2]**carpenter** *vi* to follow the trade of a carpenter ⟨*~ed when he was young*⟩ ~ *vt* to put together, often in a mechanical manner

carpentry /'kahpintri/ *n* **1** the art or trade of a carpenter; *specif* the art of shaping and assembling structural woodwork **2** timberwork constructed by a carpenter

[1]**carpet** /'kahpit/ *n* **1** a heavy woven or felted material used as a floor covering; *also* a floor covering made of this fabric **2** a surface resembling or suggesting a carpet ⟨*a ~ of leaves*⟩ [ME, fr MF *carpite*, fr OIt *carpita*, fr *carpire* to pluck, modif of L *carpere* to pluck – more at HARVEST] – **on the carpet** before an authority for censure or reprimand

[2]**carpet** *vt* **1** to cover (as if) with a carpet ⟨*snowdrops ~ the lawn*⟩ **2** to reprimand – infml

'carpet,bag /-,bag/ *n* a bag made of carpet fabric, common in the 19th c

'carpet,bagger /-,bagə/ *n* **1** a Northerner who went to the American South after the Civil War in search of personal gain **2** a nonresident who meddles in the politics of a locality [fr their carrying all their belongings in carpetbags]

carpeting /'kahpiting/ *n* (material for) carpets

-carpic /-kahpik/ *comb form* (→ *adj*) -carpous ⟨*poly*carpic⟩ [prob fr NL *-carpicus*, fr Gk *karpos* fruit]

carpo- – see CARP-

'car,port /-,pawt/ *n* a usu open-sided shelter for cars

carpospore /'kahpə,spaw/ *n* a diploid spore of a red alga – **carposporic** /-'sporik/ *adj*

-carpous /-kahpəs/ *comb form* (→ *adj*) having (such) fruit or (so many) fruits ⟨*poly*carpous⟩ [NL *-carpus*, fr Gk *-karpos*, fr *karpos* fruit – more at HARVEST] – **-carpy** /-kahpi/ *comb form* (→ *n*)

carpus /'kahpəs/ *n, pl* **carpi** /-pie/ (the bones of) the wrist ☞ ANATOMY [NL, fr Gk *karpos* – more at WHARF] – **carpal** *adj*

carrack /'karak/ *n* a large square-rigged trading vessel of the 14th to 17th c that was sometimes equipped for warfare [ME *carrake*, fr MF *caraque*, fr OSp *carraca*, fr Ar *qarāqir*, pl of *qurqūr* merchant ship]

carrageen *also* **carragheen** /'karəgeen/ *n* a dark purple branching edible seaweed [*Carragheen*, town near Waterford, Eire]

carrageenan /,karə'geenən/, **carragheenan** /~/, **carrageenin** /-nin/ *n* a colloid extracted esp from carrageen and used esp as a suspending, thickening, and clarifying agent (e g in foods) [*carrageen* + [3]*-an* or *-in*]

carrefour /,karə'fooə, -'faw/ *n* a place where 4 ways meet; a crossroads [MF, fr LL *quadrifurcum*, neut of *quadrifurcus* having 4 forks, fr L *quadri-* + *furca* fork]

carrel /'karəl/ *n* a partitioned area or cubicle used for individual study, esp in a library [alter. of ME *carole* round dance, ring – more at CAROL]

carriage /'karij/ *n* **1** the act of carrying **2** the manner of bearing the body; posture **3** the price or cost of carrying ⟨~ *paid*⟩ **4** a wheeled vehicle; *esp* a horse-drawn passenger-carrying vehicle designed for private use **5** a movable part of a machine that supports some other part ⟨*a typewriter* ~⟩ **6** *Br* a railway passenger vehicle; a coach [ME *cariage*, fr ONF, fr *carier* to transport in a vehicle – more at CARRY]

'carriage ,trade *n* trade from rich people

'carriage,way /-,way/ *n, Br* the part of a road used by vehicular traffic; *specif* LANE 2b

carrick bend /'karik/ *n* a knot used to join the ends of 2 large ropes [prob fr obs *carrick* (carrack), fr ME *carrake, carryk*]

carrier /'kari·ə/ *n* **1** a bearer, messenger **2** an individual or organization that contracts to transport goods, messages, etc **3a** a container for carrying **b** a device, platform, machine, etc that carries ⟨*a luggage* ~ *on a bicycle*⟩ **4** a bearer and transmitter of a causative agent of disease; *esp* one who is immune to the disease **5a** a usu inactive accessory substance; VEHICLE 1 **b** a substance (e g a catalyst) by whose agency some element or group is transferred from one compound to another **6** a radio or electrical wave of relatively high frequency that can be modulated by a signal (e g representing sound or vision information), esp in order to transmit that signal **7** a mobile hole or electron capable of carrying an electric charge in a semiconductor **8** AIRCRAFT CARRIER [CARRY + [2]-ER]

carrier bag /'--- ,-, ,--- '-/ *n, Br* a bag of plastic or thick paper used for carrying goods, esp shopping

'carrier ,pigeon *n* a homing pigeon (used to carry messages)

carrion /'kari·ən/ *n* **1** dead and putrefying flesh **2** sthg corrupt or rotten [ME *caroine*, fr AF, fr (assumed) VL *caronia*, irreg fr L *carn-, caro* flesh – more at CARNAL]

carrion crow *n* the common European black crow

carronade /,karə'nayd/ *n* a short-barrelled muzzle-loaded large-calibre gun formerly used esp on ships [*Carron*, town in Scotland, where it was first made]

carrot /'karət/ *n* **1** (a biennial plant with) a usu orange spindle-shaped root eaten as a vegetable **2** a promised and often illusory reward or advantage ⟨*offered them the* ~ *of promotion*⟩ [MF *carotte*, fr LL *carota*, fr Gk *karōton*]

carroty /'karəti/ *adj* bright orange-red in colour

carrousel /,karə'sel, -'zel/ *n, NAm* a carousel

[1]carry /'kari/ *vt* **1** to support and move (a load); transport **2a** to convey, conduct **b** to support ⟨*this beam* carries *the weight of the upper storeys*⟩ **3** to lead or influence by appeal to the emotions **4** to transfer from one place to another; *esp* to transfer (a digit corresponding to a multiple of 10) to the next higher power of 10 in addition **5a** to wear or have on one's person ⟨*I never* ~ *money on me*⟩ **b** to bear on or within oneself ⟨*is* ~ing *an unborn child*⟩ **c** to have as a mark, attribute, or property ⟨~ *a scar*⟩ **6** to have as a consequence, esp in law; involve ⟨*the crime* carried *a heavy penalty*⟩ **7** to hold (e g one's person) in a specified manner ⟨carries *himself well*⟩ **8** to sing with reasonable correctness of pitch ⟨~ *a tune*⟩ **9a** to keep in stock for sale **b** to provide sustenance for; support ⟨*land* ~ing *100 head of cattle*⟩ **10** to maintain through financial support or personal effort ⟨*he* carried *the magazine single-handedly*⟩ **11** to extend or prolong in space, time, or degree ⟨~ *a principle too far*⟩ **12** to gain victory for **13a** to broadcast **b** to publish ⟨*newspapers* ~ *weather reports*⟩ **14** to perform with sufficient ability to make up for the poor performance of (e g a partner or teammate) **15** to hoist and maintain (a sail) in use ~ *vi* **1** to act as a bearer **2a** to reach or penetrate to a distance ⟨*voices* ~ *well*⟩ **b** to convey itself to a reader or audience **3** to undergo or allow carriage in a specified way [ME *carien*, fr ONF *carier* to transport in a vehicle, fr *car* vehicle, fr L *carrus* – more at CAR] – **carry a torch** to be in love, esp without reciprocation; cherish a longing or devotion ⟨*she still* carries a torch *for him even though their engagement is broken*⟩ – **carry the can** to bear the responsibility; accept the blame – infml – **carry the day** to win, prevail

[2]carry *n* **1** the range of a gun or projectile or of a struck or thrown ball **2** portage

carry away *vt* to arouse to a high and often excessive degree of emotion or enthusiasm – usu passive

'carry,cot /-,kot/ *n, chiefly Br* a small lightweight boxlike bed, usu with 2 handles, in which a baby can be carried

carry forward *vt* to transfer (e g a total) to the succeeding column, page, or book relating to the same account

,carrying-'on *n, pl* **carryings-on** rowdy, excited, or improper behaviour – infml

carry off *vt* **1** to cause the death of ⟨*the plague* carried off *thousands*⟩ **2** to perform easily or successfully ⟨*the leading lady* carried off *her part brilliantly*⟩ **3** to gain possession or control of; capture ⟨carried off *the prize*⟩

'carry,on /-,on/ *n, NAm* a piece of luggage suitable for a passenger to carry on board an aircraft

'carry-,on *n* an instance of rowdy, excited, or improper behaviour; a to-do – infml

carry on *vt* to conduct, manage ⟨carry on *a business*⟩ *vi* **1** to behave in a rowdy, excited, or improper manner ⟨*embarrassed by the way he* carries on⟩ **2** to continue one's course or activity, esp in spite of obstacles or discouragement **3** *Br* to flirt; *also* to have a love affair – usu + *with*

'carry,out /-,owt/ *n* **1** *chiefly Scot* food or esp alcoholic drink bought to be consumed off the premises **2** *chiefly NAm & Scot* a takeaway

carry out *vt* **1** to put into execution ⟨carry out *a plan*⟩ **2** to bring to a successful conclusion; complete, accomplish

carry over *vt* CARRY FORWARD ~ *vi* to persist from one stage or sphere of activity to another

carry through *vt* CARRY OUT ~ *vi* to survive, persist ⟨*feelings that* carry through *to the present*⟩

carse /kahs/ *n, Scot* low fertile land beside a river [ME *cars, kerss*]

carsick /'kah,sik/ *adj* suffering from the motion sickness associated with travelling by car – **carsickness** *n*

[1]**cart** /kaht/ *n* **1** a heavy 2-wheeled or 4-wheeled vehicle used for transporting bulky or heavy loads (e g goods or animal feed) **2** a lightweight 2-wheeled vehicle drawn by a horse, pony, or dog **3** a small wheeled vehicle [ME, prob fr ON *kartr*; akin to OE *cræt* cart, OE *cradol* cradle]

[2]**cart** *vt* **1** to carry or convey (as if) in a cart **2** to take or drag away without ceremony or by force – infml; usu + *off* ⟨*they* ~ed *him off to jail*⟩ **3** to carry by hand – infml – **carter** *n*

cartage /'kahtij/ *n* the act of carting; *also* the charge for this

carte blanche /,kaht 'blonh·sh (*Fr* kart blɑ̃ʃ)/ *n* full discretionary power ⟨*was given* ~ *to furnish the house*⟩ [F, lit., blank document]

,carte du 'jour /dooh 'zhooə/ *n, pl* **cartes du jour** /~/ a menu; *esp* that of a particular day [F, lit., card of the day]

cartel /kah'tel/ *n* a combination of independent commercial enterprises designed to limit competition [MF, letter of defiance, fr OIt *cartello*, lit., placard, fr *carta* leaf of paper – more at [3]CARD]

Cartesian /kah'teezh(y)ən, -zyən/ *adj* of or used in the philosophy of René Descartes [NL *cartesianus*, fr Renatus *Cartesius* (René Descartes) †1650 F philosopher] – **Cartesian** *n*, **Cartesianism** *n*

Cartesian coordinate *n* a coordinate measured from 1 of 2 or 3 straight-line axes perpendicular to one another

'cart ,horse *n* any large powerful draught horse (e g a Clydesdale)

Carthusian /kah'thyoohzh(y)ən, -zyən/ *n or adj* (a member) of an austere contemplative religious order founded by St Bruno in 1084 [n ML *cartusiensis*, irreg fr OF *Chartrouse*, mother house of the Carthusian order, near Grenoble, town in France; adj fr n]

cartilage /'kahtilij/ *n* (a structure composed of) a translucent elastic tissue that makes up most of the skeleton of very young vertebrates and becomes mostly converted into bone in adult higher vertebrates ☞ ANATOMY [L *cartilagin-, cartilago*; akin to L *cratis* wickerwork – more at HURDLE] – **cartilaginous** /,kahti'lajinəs/ *adj*

cartilaginous fish /,kahti'lajinəs/ *n* **1** any of a major group of fishes comprising all those with a cartilaginous rather than a bony skeleton and including the sharks, dogfishes, and rays; an elasmobranch **2** a cyclostome

'cart,load /-,lohd/ *n* as much as a cart will hold

cartogram /'kahtə,gram/ *n* a map showing statistical information presented in diagrammatic form [F *cartogramme*, fr *carte* + *-gramme* -gram]

cartography /kah'togrəfi/ *n* map making [F *cartographie*, fr *carte* card, map + *-graphie* -graphy – more at [3]CARD] – **cartographer** *n*, **cartographic** /,kahtə'grafik/, **cartographical** *adj*

cartomancy /'kahtə,mansi/ *n* the telling of fortunes by means of playing cards [F *cartomancie*, fr *carte* card + *-o-* + *mancie* -mancy]

carton /'kaht(ə)n/ *n* a box or container made of plastic, cardboard, etc [F, fr It *cartone* pasteboard]

cartoon /kah'toohn/ *n* **1** a preparatory design, drawing, or painting (e g for a fresco) **2a** a satirical drawing commenting on public and usu political matters **b** STRIP CARTOON **3** ANIMATED CARTOON [It *cartone* pasteboard, cartoon, aug of *carta* leaf of paper – more at [3]CARD] – **cartoon** *vb*, **cartoonist** *n*

cartouche *also* **cartouch** /kah'toohsh/ *n* **1** an ornate or ornamental frame **2** an oval or oblong figure (e g on ancient Egyptian monuments) enclosing a ruler's name [F *cartouche* cartridge with paper case, fr It *cartoccio*, fr *carta*]

cartridge /'kahtrij/ *n* **1a** a tube of metal, paper, etc containing a complete charge, a primer, and often the bullet or shot for a firearm **b** a case containing an explosive charge for blasting **2** the part of the arm of a record player holding the stylus and the mechanism that converts movements of the stylus into electrical signals **3** a case containing a reel of magnetic tape designed for insertion into a tape recorder [alter. of earlier *cartage*, modif of MF *cartouche*]

'cartridge ,belt *n* a belt with a series of loops for holding cartridges

'cartridge ,paper *n* a stiff rough-surfaced close-grained paper (e g for drawing)

cartulary /'kahtyooləri/ *n* a collection of records or charters [ML *chartularium*, fr *chartula* charter – more at CHARTER]

[1]**'cart,wheel** /-,weel/ *n* a sideways handspring with arms and legs extended

[2]**cartwheel** *vi* to perform cartwheels

'cart,wright /-,riet/ *n* sby who makes and repairs carts

caruncle /'karəngkl/ *n* a naked fleshy outgrowth (e g a domestic fowl's wattle) [obs F *caruncule*, fr L *caruncula* little piece of flesh, dim. of *caro* flesh – more at CARNAL] – **caruncular** /kə'rungkyoolə/ *adj*, **carunculate** /-lət/, **carunculated** /-,laytid/ *adj*

carve /kahv/ *vt* **1a** to cut so as to shape **b** to produce by cutting ⟨~d *his initials in the soft sandstone*⟩ **2** to make or acquire (a career, reputation, etc) through one's own efforts – often + *out* ⟨~d *out a place for himself in the firm*⟩ **3** to cut (food, esp meat) into pieces or slices ~ *vi* **1** to cut up and serve meat **2** to work as a sculptor or engraver [ME *kerven*, fr OE *ceorfan*; akin to MHG *kerben* to notch, Gk *graphein* to scratch, write]

carvel /'kahvl/ *n* a caravel [ME *carvile*, fr MF *caravelle, carvelle*]

'carvel-,built *adj, of a boat* built with the planks meeting flush at the seams [prob fr D *karveel-*, fr *karveel* caravel, fr MF *carvelle*]

carven /'kahvən/ *adj* wrought or ornamented by carving; carved – poetic

carver /'kahvə/ **1** a long sharp knife used for carving meat **2** *pl* a knife and fork used for carving and serving meat [CARVE + [2]-ER]

'carve-,up *n* **1** a competitive event in which the result has been irregularly decided beforehand – infml **2** a division into parts; *esp* the sharing out of loot – slang

carve up *vt* **1** to divide into parts or shares ⟨carved up *the inheritance between them*⟩ **2** to wound with a knife – slang

carving /'kahving/ *n* **1** the act or art of one who carves **2** a carved object or design

'car ,wash *n* (an area containing) an automatic machine for washing cars, usu consisting of 1 large horizontal and 2 large upright revolving brushes through which water and soap are sprayed

caryatid /'kari·ə,tid, ,kari'atid, kə'rie·ətid/ *n, pl* **caryatids, caryatides** /,kari'atideez, kə,rie·ə'teediz/ a draped female figure used as a column to support an entablature [L *caryatides*, pl, fr Gk *karyatides* priestesses of Artemis at Caryae, caryatids, fr *Karyai* Caryae, town in Greece]

caryopsis /,kari'opsis/ *n, pl* **caryopses** /-seez/, **caryopsides** /-si,deez/ a small 1-seeded dry fruit (e g of grasses) in which the fruit and seed are fused together in a single grain [NL, fr Gk *karyon* nut + *opsis* appearance]

Casanova /kasə'nohvə/ *n* a (promiscuous and unscrupulous) male lover [Giacomo Girolamo *Casanova* †1798 It adventurer]

casbah *also* **kasbah** /'kaz,bah/ *n* (a market in) the older Arab section of a N African city [F, fr Ar dial. *qaṣbah*]

[1]cascade /kas'kayd/ *n* **1** a steep usu small fall of water; *esp* one of a series of such falls **2a** sthg arranged in a series or in a succession of stages so that each stage derives from or acts on the product of the preceding stage ⟨*a* ~ *amplifier*⟩ **b** an arrangement of fabric (e g lace) that falls in a wavy line **3** sthg falling or rushing forth in profusion ⟨*a* ~ *of flowers*⟩ [F, fr It *cascata*, fr *cascare* to fall, fr (assumed) VL *casicare*, fr L *casus*, pp of *cadere* to fall]

[2]cascade *vi* to fall (as if) in a cascade ~ *vt* to connect in a cascade arrangement

cascara /ka'skahrə/ *n* **1 cascara, cascara buckthorn** a buckthorn of the Pacific coast of the USA **2 cascara, cascara sagrada** the dried bark of cascara buckthorn, used as a mild laxative [Sp *cáscara* bark, fr *cascar* to crack, break, fr (assumed) VL *quassicare* to shake, break, fr L *quassare* – more at QUASH; (2) *cascara sagrada* AmerSp, lit., sacred bark]

[1]case /kays/ *n* **1a** a set of circumstances or conditions; a situation **b** a situation or object requiring investigation or action **2** an (inflectional) form of a noun, pronoun, or adjective indicating its grammatical relation to other words **3a** a suit or action that reaches a court of law **b(1)** the evidence supporting a conclusion ⟨*the* ~ *for bringing back hanging*⟩ **(2)** an argument; *esp* one that is convincing **4a** an instance of disease or injury; *also* a patient suffering from a specific illness **b** an instance that directs attention to a situation or exhibits it in action; an example **5** a peculiar person; a character – infml [ME *cas*, fr OF, fr L *casus* fall, chance, fr *casus*, pp of *cadere* to fall – more at CHANCE] – **in any case** without regard to or in spite of other considerations; whatever else is done or is the case ⟨*war is inevitable* in any case⟩ – **in case 1** as a precaution; as a precaution against the event that ⟨*take a towel anyway just* in case *you want to swim*⟩ **2** *chiefly NAm* if – **in case of 1** in the event of ⟨in case of *trouble, yell*⟩ **2** for fear of; as a precaution against ⟨*posted sentries* in case of *attack*⟩

[2]case *n* **1** a box or receptacle for holding sthg: e g **a** a glass-panelled box for the display of specimens (e g in a museum) **b** *chiefly Br* a suitcase **c** a box together with its contents **2** a pair – chiefly with reference to pistols **3a** an outer covering ⟨*a pastry* ~⟩ **b** a stiff book cover that is made apart from the book and glued onto it **4** a shallow divided tray for holding printing type [ME *cas*, fr ONF *casse*, fr L *capsa* chest, case, fr *capere* to take – more at HEAVE]

[3]case *vt* **1** to enclose in or cover with a case; encase **2** to inspect or study (e g a house), esp with intent to rob – slang

'case,book /-,book/ *n* a book containing records of illustrative cases for reference (e g in law or medicine)

cased /kayst/ *adj, of a book* being a hardback

'case ,harden *vt* **1** to harden the surface of (iron or steel) **2** to make callous – **case-hardened** *adj*

case history *n* a record of history, environment, and relevant details (e g of individual behaviour or condition), esp for use in analysis, illustration, or diagnosis

casein /'kaysi·in, -seen/ *n* a protein in milk that is precipitated by (lactic) acid or rennet, is the chief constituent of cheese, and is used in making plastics [prob fr F *caséine*, fr L *caseus* cheese]

,case in 'point *n* a relevant example

'case ,law *n* law established by previous judicial decisions ☞ LAW

'case ,load *n* the number of cases handled in a particular period (e g by a court or clinic)

casemate /'kays,mayt/ *n* a fortified position or chamber or an armoured enclosure on a warship from which guns are fired [MF, fr OIt *casamatta*]

casement /'kaysmənt/ *n* (a window with) a sash that opens on hinges at the side ☞ ARCHITECTURE [ME, hollow moulding, prob fr ONF *encassement* frame, fr *encasser* to enshrine, frame, fr *en-* + *casse*]

caseous /'kaysi·əs/ *adj* of or like cheese [L *caseus* cheese]

'case ,shot *n* an artillery projectile consisting of a number of balls or metal fragments enclosed in a case

case study *n* an analysis of a person, institution, or community based on details concerning development, environment, etc

casette /kə'set/ *n* a cassette

'case,work /-,wuhk/ *n* social work involving direct consideration of the problems of individual people or families – **caseworker** *n*

[1]cash /kash/ *n* **1** ready money **2** money or its equivalent paid promptly at the time of purchase

[MF or OIt; MF *casse* money box, fr OIt *cassa*, fr L *capsa* chest – more at ²CASE]

²**cash** *vt* **1** to pay or obtain cash for ⟨~ *a cheque*⟩ **2** to lead and win a bridge trick with (the highest remaining card of a suit)

³**cash** *n, pl* **cash** (a money unit equivalent to) a small Chinese or Indian coin [Pg *caixa*, fr Tamil *kācu*, a small copper coin, fr Skt *karsa*, a weight of gold or silver; akin to OPer *karsha-*, a weight]

ˌcash-and-ˈcarry *adj* sold for cash and collected by the purchaser

ˈcash ˌcard *n* a card that is issued by a bank and allows the holder to operate a cash-dispensing machine

ˈcash ˌcrop *n* a crop (e g cotton or sugar beet) produced for sale rather than for use by the grower

ˈcash ˌdesk *n* a desk (e g in a shop) where payment for purchases is taken

cashew /ˈkashooh, kəˈshooh, kaˈshooh/ *n* (the edible kidney-shaped nut of) a tropical American tree of the sumach family [Pg *acajú, cajú*, fr Tupi *acajú*]

¹**cashier** /kaˈshiə/ *vt* to dismiss, usu dishonourably, esp from service in the armed forces [D *casseren*, fr MF *casser* to discharge, annul – more at QUASH]

²**cashier** *n* **1** one employed to receive cash from customers, esp in a shop **2** one who collects and records payments (e g in a bank) [D or MF; D *kassier*, fr MF *cassier*, fr *casse* money box]

cash in *vt* to convert into cash ⟨cashed in *all his bonds*⟩ ~ *vi* to exploit a financial or other advantage – usu + *on* ⟨cashing in *on the success of recent peace initiatives*⟩

cashmere /ˈkashmiə, -ˈ-/ *n* (yarn or fabric made from) fine wool from the undercoat of the Kashmir goat [*Cashmere*, var of *Kashmir*, region of the Indian subcontinent]

ˈcash ˌregister *n* a machine that has a drawer for cash and is used to record and display the amount of each purchase and the money received

casing /ˈkaysing/ *n* sthg that encases; material for encasing

casino /kəˈseenoh/ *n, pl* **casinos** a building or room used for social amusements, specif gambling [It, fr *casa* house, fr L, cabin]

cask /kahsk/ *n* **1** a barrel-shaped container, usu for holding liquids **2** a cask and its contents; *also* the quantity contained in a cask [MF *casque* helmet, fr Sp *casco* potsherd, skull, helmet, fr *cascar* to break – more at CASCARA]

casket /ˈkahskit/ *n* **1** a small usu ornamental chest or box (e g for jewels) **2** *NAm* a coffin [ME, modif of MF *cassette*]

casque /kask/ *n* a helmet [MF – more at CASK]

Cassandra /kəˈsahndrə, -ˈsan-/ *n* one who predicts misfortune or disaster [L, fr Gk *Kassandra*, daughter of King Priam of Troy in Gk legend]

cassava /kəˈsahvə/ *n* (the fleshy edible starch-yielding rootstock of) any of several tropical plants of the spurge family [Sp *cazabe* cassava bread, fr Taino *caçábi*]

¹**casserole** /ˈkasərohl/ *n* **1** a heatproof dish with a cover in which food may be baked and served **2** the savoury food cooked and served in a casserole [F, saucepan, fr MF, irreg fr *casse* ladle, dripping pan, deriv of Gk *kyathos* ladle]

²**casserole** *vt* to cook (food) slowly in a casserole

cassette, casette /kəˈset/ *n* **1** a lightproof container for holding film or plates that can be inserted into a camera **2** a small case containing magnetic tape that can be inserted into a tape recorder [F *cassette* casket, fr MF, dim. of ONF *casse* case]

cassia /ˈkasi·ə/ *n* **1** a coarse cinnamon bark **2** senna [ME, fr OE, fr L, fr Gk *kassia*, of Sem origin; akin to Heb *qĕṣīʿāh* cassia]

cassis /ˈkasees/ *n* a liqueur made from blackcurrants and used esp as a flavouring (e g in white wine) [F, blackcurrant, fr L *cassia*]

cassiterite /kəˈsitəriet/ *n* tin dioxide occurring as a brown or black mineral [F *cassitérite*, fr Gk *kassiteros* tin]

cassock /ˈkasək/ *n* an ankle-length garment worn by the Roman Catholic and Anglican clergy or by laymen assisting in services [MF *casaque*, fr Per *kazhāghand* padded jacket, fr *kazh* raw silk + *āghand* stuffed]

cassoulet /ˈkasəˌlay/ *n* a stew of haricot beans and mixed meats [F, fr F dial., lit., stone dish, dim. of *cassolo* bowl, dim. of *casso* ladle, deriv of Gk *kyathos* ladle]

cassowary /ˈkasəˌweəri/ *n* any of several large flightless Australasian birds closely related to the emu [Malay *kĕsuari*]

¹**cast** /kahst/ *vb* **cast** *vt* **1a** to cause to move by throwing ⟨~ *a fishing line*⟩ **b** to direct ⟨~ *a shadow*⟩ ⟨~ *doubt on the enterprise*⟩ **c(1)** to send forth; emit ⟨*the fire* ~s *a warm glow*⟩ **(2)** to place as if by throwing ⟨~ *a spell*⟩ ⟨*was* ~ *into prison*⟩ **d** to deposit (a vote) formally **e(1)** to throw off or away ⟨*the horse* ~ *a shoe*⟩ **(2)** to shed, moult **(3)** *of an animal* to give birth to (prematurely) **2** to calculate (a horoscope) by means of astrology **3a** to arrange into a suitable form or order **b** to assign a part for (e g a play) or to (e g an actor) **4a** to shape (e g metal or plastic) by pouring into a mould when molten **b** to form by casting ~ *vi* **1** to throw out a line and lure with a fishing rod **2** to look round; seek – + *about* or *around* ⟨*she* ~ *around uncertainly for somewhere to sit*⟩ **3** to veer **4** to take form in a mould [ME *casten*, fr ON *kasta*; akin to ON *kös* heap, & perh to L *gerere* to carry, wage] – **cast anchor** to lower the anchor; to anchor – **cast lots** DRAW LOTS

²**cast** *n* **1a** an act of casting **b** a throw of a (fishing) line or net **2** *sing or pl in constr* the set of performers in a dramatic production **3** the distance to which sthg can be thrown **4a** a turning of the eye in a particular direction **b** a slight squint in the eye **5a** a reproduction (e g of a statue) formed by casting **b** an impression taken from an object with a molten or plastic substance **c** ¹PLASTER 3 **6a** a modification of a colour by a trace of some added colour ⟨*grey with a greenish* ~⟩ **b** a tinge, suggestion **7** a shape, appearance ⟨*the delicate* ~ *of her features*⟩ **8** the excrement of an earthworm

castanet /ˌkastəˈnet/ *n* either of a pair of small usu wooden or plastic shells clicked together in the hand and used esp by dancers – usu pl [Sp *castañeta*, fr *castaña* chestnut, fr L *castanea* – more at CHESTNUT]

castaway /ˈkahstəˌway/ *n* a person who is cast adrift or ashore as a result of a shipwreck or as a punishment – **castaway** *adj*

cast away *vt* to cause (a person or vessel) to be shipwrecked – usu passive

caste /kahst/ *n* **1** any of the hereditary social groups in Hinduism that restrict the occupations of their members and their association with members of other castes **2a** a social class **b** the prestige conferred by caste **3** the system of social division by castes **4** a specialized form of a social insect (e g a soldier or worker ant) adapted to carry out a particular function in the colony [Pg *casta*, lit., race, lineage, fr fem of *casto* pure, chaste, fr L *castus*; akin to L *carēre* to be without, Gk *keazein* to split, Skt *śasati* he cuts to pieces]

castellan /ˈkastilən/ *n* a governor or warden of a castle or fort [ME *castelleyn*, fr ONF *castelain*, fr L *castellanus* occupant of a castle, fr *castellanus* of a castle, fr *castellum* castle]

castellated /ˈkastiˌlaytid/ *adj* having battlements like a castle [ML *castellatus*, pp of *castellare* to fortify, fr L *castellum*]

caster /ˈkahstə/ *n* **1** a machine that casts type **2** [2]CASTOR 1, 2 [[1]CAST + [2]-ER]

caster sugar *n* finely granulated white sugar

castigate /ˈkastigayt/ *vt* to punish or reprimand severely – fml [L *castigatus*, pp of *castigare* – more at CHASTEN] – **castigator** /-ˈgaytə/ *n*, **castigation** /-ˈgaysh(ə)n/ *n*

castile soap /kaˈsteel/ *n*, *often cap C* a fine hard bland soap made from olive oil and sodium hydroxide [*Castile*, region of Spain]

Castilian /kaˈstilyən/ *n* **1** a native or inhabitant of Castile **2** (the official and literary language of Spain based on) the dialect of Castile – **Castilian** *adj*

casting /ˈkahsting/ *n* **1** sthg cast in a mould **2** sthg cast out or off

casting vote *n* a deciding vote cast in the event of a tie

ˌcast-ˈiron *adj* **1** capable of withstanding great strain; strong, unyielding ⟨*a ~ stomach*⟩ **2** impossible to disprove or falsify ⟨*a ~ alibi*⟩

ˌcast ˈiron *n* a hard brittle alloy of iron, carbon, and silicon cast in a mould

[1]**castle** /ˈkahsl/ *n* **1** a large fortified building or set of buildings ☞ CHURCH **2** a stronghold **3** [3]ROOK [ME *castel*, fr OE, fr ONF, fr L *castellum* fortress, castle, dim. of *castrum* fortified place]

[2]**castle** *vb* **castling** /ˈkahsl·ing/ to move (a chess king) 2 squares towards a rook and then place the rook on the square on the other side of the king

ˌcastle in the ˈair *n* an impractical scheme; a daydream

ˈcastˌoff /-ˌof/ *n* **1** a cast-off article (e g of clothing) – usu pl **2** an estimate of the space that will be required for a given amount of text when printed

ˌcast-ˈoff *adj* thrown away or discarded, esp because outgrown or no longer wanted ⟨*~ clothes*⟩ ⟨*a ~ lover*⟩

cast off *vt* **1** to unfasten or untie (a boat or line) **2** to remove (a stitch or stitches) from a knitting needle in such a way as to prevent unravelling **3** to get rid of; discard ⟨cast off *all restraint*⟩ **4** to measure (an amount of text) to determine the space it will take up when printed ~ *vi* **1** to unfasten or untie a boat or a line **2** to finish a knitted article by casting off all the stitches

cast on *vb* to place (a stitch or stitches) on a knitting needle for beginning or enlarging a knitted article

[1]**castor** /ˈkahstə/ *n* a strong-smelling substance consisting of dried glands taken from near the anus of the beaver, used esp in making perfume [ME, bever, fr L, fr Gk *kastōr*, fr *Kastōr* Castor, hero or demigod of Greek mythology]

[2]**castor, caster** /ˈkahstə/ *n* **1** a small wheel set in a swivel mounting on the base of a piece of furniture, machinery, etc **2** a container with a perforated top for sprinkling powdered or granulated foods, esp sugar – compare SHAKER [[1]CAST + [1]-OR, [2]-ER]

ˌcastor ˈoil *n* a pale viscous oil from the beans of a tropical Old World plant, used esp as a purgative [prob fr its former use as a substitute for castor in medicine]

cast out *vt* to drive out; expel

castrate /kaˈstrayt/ *vt* **1** to deprive of sexual organs: **a** to remove the testes of; geld **b** to remove the ovaries of; spay **2** to deprive of vitality or vigour; emasculate [L *castratus*, pp of *castrare*; akin to Skt *śasati* he cuts to pieces – more at CASTE] – **castrate** /ˈ--/ *n*, **castration** /kaˈstraysh(ə)n/ *n*

castrato /kaˈstrahtoh/ *n*, *pl* **castrati** /-ti/ a singer castrated in boyhood to preserve the high range of his voice [It, fr pp of *castrare* to castrate, fr L]

Castroism /ˈkastrohˌiz(ə)m/ *n* the political principles and policies of Fidel Castro [Fidel *Castro* *b*1927 Cuban premier] – **Castroite** /-ˌiet/ *n*

[1]**casual** /ˈkazh(y)ooəl, kazyooəl/ *adj* **1** subject to, resulting from, or occurring by chance **2a** occurring without regularity; occasional **b** employed for irregular periods ⟨*a ~ labourer*⟩ **3a** feeling or showing little concern; nonchalant **b** informal, natural; *also* designed for informal wear [ME, fr MF & LL; MF *casuel*, fr LL *casualis*, fr L *casus* fall, chance – more at [1]CASE] – **casually** *adv*, **casualness** *n*

[2]**casual** *n* a casual or migratory worker

casualty /ˈkazh(y)ooəlti, -zyooəl-/ *n* **1** a member of a military force killed or wounded in action **2** a person or thing injured, lost, or destroyed ⟨*small firms will be the first* casualties *of these policies*⟩ [ME *casuelte* chance, mischance, loss, fr ML *casualitas*, fr LL *casualis*]

casuistry /ˈkazh(y)ooˌistri, ˈkazyooistri/ *n* **1** a method or doctrine dealing with particular ethical problems **2** the false application of general principles to particular instances, esp with regard to morals or law [*casuist* (one who studies cases of conscience), prob fr Sp *casuista*, fr L *casus* fall, chance, case – more at [1]CASE] – **casuist** *n*, **casuistic** /-ˈistik/, **casuistical** *adj*

casus belli /ˌkahsoos ˈbeli/ *n*, *pl* **casus belli** /ˈbelie/ an event or action that brings about a war [NL, occasion of war]

[1]**cat** /kat/ *n* **1a** a small domesticated flesh-eating mammal kept as a pet or for catching rats and mice **b** any of a family of carnivores that includes the domestic cat, lion, tiger, leopard, jaguar, cougar, lynx, and cheetah **2** a malicious woman **3** a cat-o'-nine-tails **4** a player or devotee of jazz – slang **5** a (male) person – slang [ME, fr OE *catt*; akin to OHG *kazza* cat; both fr a prehistoric NGmc-WGmc word prob borrowed fr LL *cattus*, *catta* cat]

[2]**cat** *n* CATAMARAN 2 – infml

cata-, cat-, cath- *prefix* down ⟨cata*pult*⟩ ⟨cata*rrh*⟩ [Gk *kata-*, *kat-*, *kath-*, fr *kata* down, in accordance with, by; akin to L *com-* with – more at co-]

catabolism /kəˈtabəliz(ə)m/ *n* destructive metabolism involving the release of energy and resulting in the breakdown of complex materials (e g glucose) – compare ANABOLISM [Gk *katabolē* throwing down, fr *kataballein* to throw down, fr *kata-* + *ballein* to throw – more at DEVIL] – **catabolize** *vb*, **catabolic** /ˌkatəˈbolik/ *adj*

catabolite /kəˈtabəliet/ *n* a (waste) product of catabolism

catachresis /ˌkatəˈkreesis/ *n, pl* **catachreses** /-seez/ use of the wrong word for the context [L, fr Gk *katachrēsis* misuse, fr *katachrēsthai* to use up, misuse, fr *kata-* + *chrēsthai* to use] – **catachrestic** /-ˈkrestik/, **catachrestical** *adj*

cataclysm /ˈkatəˌkliz(ə)m/ *n* **1** a flood, deluge **2** a violent geological change of the earth's surface **3** a momentous event marked by violent upheaval and destruction [F *cataclysme*, fr L *cataclysmos*, fr Gk *kataklysmos*, fr *kataklyzein* to flood, fr *kata-* + *klyzein* to wash] – **cataclysmal** /ˌkatəˈklizməl/, **cataclysmic** /-ˈklizmik/ *adj*

catacomb /ˈkatəˌkoohm/ *n* **1** a galleried subterranean cemetery with recesses for tombs **2** an underground passageway or group of passageways; a labyrinth *USE* often pl with sing. meaning [MF *catacombe*, prob fr OIt *catacomba*, fr LL *catacumbae*, pl]

catadromous /kəˈtadrəməs/ *adj* living in fresh water and going to the sea to spawn ⟨~ *eels*⟩ [prob fr NL *catadromus*, fr *cata-* + *-dromus* -dromous]

catafalque /ˈkatəˌfalk/ *n* an ornamental structure supporting or bearing a coffin (e g during a lying in state) [It *catafalco*, fr (assumed) VL *catafalicum* scaffold, fr *cata-* + L *fala* siege tower]

Catalan /ˈkatəˌlan, -lən/ *n* **1** a native or inhabitant of Catalonia **2** the Romance language of Catalonia, Valencia, and the Balearic islands ☞ LANGUAGE [Sp *Catalán*] – **Catalan** *adj*

catalectic /ˌkatəˈlektik/ *adj* lacking a syllable at the end of a line of verse [LL *catalecticus*, fr Gk *katalēktikos*, fr *katalēgein* to leave off, fr *kata-* + *lēgein* to stop – more at SLACK]

catalepsy /ˈkatəˌlepsi/ *n* a trancelike state associated with schizophrenia in which the body remains rigid and immobile for prolonged periods [ME *catalempsi*, fr ML *catalepsia*, fr LL *catalepsis*, fr Gk *katalēpsis*, lit., act of seizing, fr *katalambanein* to seize, fr *kata-* + *lambanein* to take – more at LATCH] – **cataleptic** /-ˈleptik/ *adj or n*

catalo /ˈkatəloh/ *n, pl* **cataloes, catalos** a cattalo

[1]**catalogue,** *NAm chiefly* **catalog** /ˈkatəlog/ **1** (a pamphlet or book containing) a complete list of items arranged systematically with descriptive details **2** a list, series ⟨*a* ~ *of disasters*⟩ [ME *cateloge*, fr MF *catalogue*, fr LL *catalogus*, fr Gk *katalogos*, fr *katalegein* to list, enumerate, fr *kata-* + *legein* to gather, speak – more at LEGEND]

[2]**catalogue,** *NAm chiefly* **catalog** *vt* **1** to enter in a catalogue; *esp* to classify (books or information) descriptively **2** to make a catalogue of

catalyse, *NAm* **catalyze** /ˈkatəliez/ *vt* to bring about the catalysis of (a chemical reaction)

catalysis /kəˈtaləsis/ *n, pl* **catalyses** /-seez/ a change, esp an increase, in the rate of a chemical reaction induced by a catalyst [Gk *katalysis* dissolution, fr *katalyein* to dissolve, fr *kata-* cata- + *lyein* to dissolve, release – more at LOSE]

catalyst /ˈkatəlist/ *n* **1** a chemical agent that causes catalysis **2** a substance (e g an enzyme) that changes, esp increases, the rate of a chemical reaction but itself remains chemically unchanged **3** sby or sthg whose action inspires further and usu more important events [fr *catalysis*, by analogy to *analysis* : *analyst*]

catalytic /ˌkatəˈlitik/ *adj* causing or involving catalysis

catamaran /ˈkatəməˌran, -rahn, ˌ---ˈ-/ *n* **1** a raft made of logs or pieces of wood lashed together **2** a boat with twin hulls side by side [Tamil *kaṭṭumaram*, fr *kaṭṭu* to tie + *maram* tree]

catamite /ˈkatəˌmiet/ *n* a boy kept by a pederast [L *catamitus*, fr *Catamitus* Ganymede, cupbearer of the gods, fr Etruscan *Catmite*, fr Gk *Ganymēdēs*]

catamount /ˈkatəˌmownt/ *n* a cat-a-mountain

ˌ**cat-a-ˈmountain** *n* a leopard, puma, or similar wild cat [ME *cat of the mountaine*]

ˌ**cat-and'mouse** *adj* consisting of continuous chasing and near captures and escapes

cataplexy /ˈkatəˌpleksi/ *n* sudden temporary paralysis following a strong emotional stimulus (e g shock) [G *kataplexie*, fr Gk *kataplēxis*, fr *kataplēssein* to strike down, terrify, fr *kata-* + *plēssein* to strike – more at PLAINT]

[1]**catapult** /ˈkatəpoolt, -pult/ *n* **1** an ancient military device for hurling missiles **2** a device for launching an aeroplane at flying speed (e g from an aircraft carrier) **3** *Br* a Y-shaped stick with a piece of elastic material fixed between the 2 prongs, used for shooting small objects (e g stones) [MF or L; MF *catapulte*, fr L *catapulta*, fr Gk *katapaltēs*, fr *kata-* + *pallein* to hurl, brandish – more at POLEMIC]

[2]**catapult** *vb* **1** to throw or launch (a missile) by means of a catapult **2** to (cause to) move suddenly or abruptly ⟨*was* ~ed *from rags to riches overnight*⟩

cataract /ˈkatərakt/ *n* **1** clouding of (the enclosing membrane of) the lens of the eye; *also* the clouded area **2a** a (large steeply-descending) waterfall **b** steep rapids in a river **c** a downpour, deluge [L *cataracta* waterfall, portcullis, fr Gk *kataraktēs*, fr *katarassein* to dash down, fr *kata-* cata- + *arassein* to strike, dash; (1) MF or ML; MF *cataracte*, fr ML *cataracta*, fr L, portcullis]

catarrh /kəˈtah/ *n* (the mucus resulting from) inflammation of a mucous membrane, esp in the human nose and air passages [MF or LL; MF *catarrhe*, fr LL *catarrhus*, fr Gk *katarrhous*, fr *katarrhein* to flow down, fr *kata-* + *rhein* to flow – more at STREAM] – **catarrhal** /-rəl/ *adj*

catastrophe /kəˈtastrəfi/ *n* **1** a momentous, tragic, and unexpected event of extreme gravity **2** CATACLYSM 2 [Gk *katastrophē*, fr *katastrephein* to overturn, fr *kata-* + *strephein* to turn – more at STROPHE] – **catastrophic** /ˌkatəˈstrofik/ *adj*, **catastrophically** *adv*

catatonia /ˌkatəˈtohnyə, -ni·ə/ *n* (a psychological disorder, esp schizophrenia, marked by) catalepsy [NL, fr G *katatonie*, fr *kata-* cata- + NL *tonus*] – **catatonic** /-ˈtonik/ *adj or n*

ˈ**catˌboat** /-ˌboht/ *n* a sailing boat with a mast positioned close to the bows and a single sail [perh fr *cat*, a former type of cargo ship]

ˈ**cat ˌburglar** *n, Br* a burglar who enters buildings by climbing up walls, drainpipes, etc

ˈ**catˌcall** /-ˌkawl/ *n* a loud or raucous cry expressing disapproval – **catcall** *vb*

[1]**catch** /kach/ *vb* **caught** /kawt/ *vt* **1a** to capture or seize, esp after pursuit **b** to take or entangle (as if) in a snare ⟨caught *in a web of deceit*⟩ **c** to discover unexpectedly; surprise ⟨caught *in the act*⟩ **d** to

check suddenly or momentarily **e** to cause to become entangled, fastened, or stuck ⟨~ *a sleeve on a nail*⟩ **2a** to seize; *esp* to intercept and keep hold of (a moving object), esp in the hands ⟨~ *the ball*⟩ **b** to dismiss (a batsman in cricket) by catching the ball after it has been hit and before it has touched the ground **3a** to contract; become infected with ⟨~ *a cold*⟩ **b** to hit, strike ⟨~ *the mood of the occasion*⟩ **c** to receive the force or impact of **4** to attract, arrest ⟨*tried to* ~ *his attention*⟩ **5** to take or get momentarily or quickly ⟨~ *a glimpse of her friend*⟩ **6** to be in time for ⟨~ *the bus*⟩ ⟨~ *the last post*⟩ **7** to grasp with the senses or the mind ~ *vi* **1** to become caught **2** *of a fire* to start to burn **3** BURN 3 ⟨*the sugar* caught *on the bottom of the pan*⟩ [ME *cacchen*, fr ONF *cachier* to hunt, fr (assumed) VL *captiare*, alter. of L *captare* to chase, fr *captus*, pp of *capere* to take – more at HEAVE] – **catchable** *adj* – **catch a crab** to make a faulty stroke in rowing – **catch it** to incur blame, reprimand, or punishment – infml – **catch one's breath 1** to rest long enough to restore normal breathing **2** to stop breathing briefly, usu under the influence of strong emotion – **catch someone on the hop** to find sby unprepared – infml

[2]**catch** *n* **1** sthg caught; *esp* the total quantity caught at one time ⟨*a large* ~ *of fish*⟩ **2** a game in which a ball is thrown and caught **3** sthg that retains or fastens ⟨*the safety* ~ *of her brooch was broken*⟩ **4** an often humorous or coarse round for 3 or more voices **5** a concealed difficulty; a snag ⟨*there must be a* ~ *in it somewhere*⟩ **6** an eligible marriage partner – infml

catch 22 *n, often cap C* a predicament from which a victim is unable to extricate him-/herself because the means of escape is precluded by prior conditions [*Catch-22*, novel by Joseph Heller *b*1923 US writer]

'catch,all /-,awl/ *n* sthg intended to include or cover miscellaneous cases, items, circumstances, etc ⟨*a* ~ *category*⟩

,catch-as-,catch-'can *n* a style of wrestling in which all holds are allowed and in which a fall is gained by pinning an opponent's shoulders to the ground

'catch ,crop *n* a crop planted between the rows of the main crop or grown between the harvesting of a main crop and the planting of another

'catch,cry /-,krie/ *n, Austr* a slogan; TAG 4a, 4b ⟨*resort to 1950s* catchcries *about red perils – The Australian*⟩

catcher /'kachə/ *n* a baseball player who stands behind the batter to catch balls that the batter fails to hit [[1]CATCH + [2]-ER]

'catch,fly /-,flie/ *n* any of various plants with sticky stems on which small insects are caught

catching /'kaching/ *adj* **1** infectious, contagious **2** alluring, attractive

catchment /'kachmənt/ *n* the action of collecting a substance or material (e g water); *also* the amount collected

'catchment ,area *n* **1** the area from which a lake, reservoir, etc gets its rainwater **2** a geographical area from which people are drawn to attend a particular school, hospital, etc

catch on *vi* **1** to become popular ⟨*the new fashion quickly* caught on *in Britain*⟩ **2** to understand, learn – often + *to*; infml

catch out *vt* to expose or detect in wrongdoing or error – usu passive

catchpenny /'kach,peni; *adj also* 'kachpəni/ *n or adj* (sthg) worthless but designed to appear attractive, esp by being showy – derog

'catch,phrase /-,frayz/ *n* an arresting phrase that enjoys short-lived popularity

catchup /'kachəp/ *n, chiefly NAm* ketchup

catch up *vt* **1a** to pick up, often abruptly ⟨caught *the child* up *in her arms*⟩ **b** to ensnare, entangle – usu + *up*; usu passive **c** to engross, absorb – usu + *in*; usu passive **2** to act or move fast enough to draw level with ⟨*we'll* catch *you* up *later*⟩ ~ *vi* **1** to act or move fast enough to draw level ⟨*we'll* catch up *with you later*⟩ **2** to acquaint oneself or deal with sthg belatedly – + *on* or *with* ⟨*I must* catch up *on the bookkeeping*⟩

'catch,word /-,wuhd/ *n* **1** a word placed so as to assist a reader when turning a page **2** a word or expression associated with some school of thought or political movement; a slogan

catchy /'kachi/ *adj* **1** tending to attract the interest or attention ⟨*a* ~ *title*⟩ **2** easy to remember and reproduce ⟨*a* ~ *tune*⟩

cate /kayt/ *n, archaic* a dainty or choice morsel – usu pl [ME, article of purchased food, short for *acate*, fr ONF *acat* purchase, fr *acater* to buy, fr (assumed) VL *accaptare*, fr L *acceptare* to accept]

catechism /'katə,kiz(ə)m/ *n* **1** instruction by question and answer **2** a manual for catechizing; *specif* a summary of religious doctrine, often in the form of questions and answers **3** a set of formal questions put as a test – **catechismal** /-'kizməl/ *adj*

catech·ize, -ise /'katə,kiez/ *vt* **1** to teach systematically, esp by using question and answer; *specif* to teach the articles of faith of a religion in such a manner **2** to question systematically or searchingly [LL *catechizare*, fr Gk *katēchein* to teach, lit., to din into, fr *kata-* cata- + *ēchein* to resound, fr *ēchē* sound – more at ECHO] – **catechist** *n*, **catechizer** /-,kiezə/ *n*, **catechization** /-kie'zaysh(ə)n/ *n*

catechol /'katə,kohl, -,chohl/ *n* pyrocatechol

catecholamine /,katə'kohləmeen, -'choh-/ *n* any of various amines (e g adrenalin and dopamine) that function as hormones, neurotransmitters, or both, and are related to pyrocatechol

catechu /'katə,chooh/ *n* any of several dry astringent substances obtained from tropical Asiatic plants [prob fr Malay *kachu*, of Dravidian origin; akin to Tamil & Kannada *kācu* catechu]

catechumen /,katə'kyoohmin/ *n* a person receiving instruction in Christian doctrine and discipline before admission to membership of a church [ME *cathecumyn*, fr MF *cathecumine*, fr LL *catechumenus*, fr Gk *katēchoumenos*, prp passive of *katēchein* to teach]

categorical /,katə'gorikl/ *also* **,cate'goric** /-'gorik/ *adj* absolute, unqualified ⟨*a* ~ *denial*⟩ [LL *categoricus*, fr Gk *katēgorikos*, fr *katēgoria* affirmation, category] – **categorically** *adv*

categorical imperative *n* a moral obligation that is unconditionally and universally binding

categor·ize, -ise /'katəgə,riez/ *vt* to put into a category; classify – **categorization** /-rie'zaysh(ə)n/ *n*

category /'katəg(ə)ri/ *n* **1** a general or fundamental form or class of terms, things, or ideas (e g in philosophy) **2** a division within a system of classification [LL *categoria*, fr Gk *katēgoria* predication, category, fr *katēgorein* to accuse, affirm, predicate, fr *kata-* cata- + *agora* public assembly – more at GREGARIOUS]

catena /kə'teenə/ *n, pl* **catenae** /-ni/, **catenas** a connected series of related things, esp of comments on the Scriptures by early Christian theologians [ML, fr L, chain – more at CHAIN]

catenary /'katən(ə)ri/ *n* the curve formed by a perfectly flexible cord of uniform density and cross section hanging freely from 2 fixed points [NL *catenaria*, fr L, fem of *catenarius* of a chain, fr *catena*] – **catenary** *adj*

catenate /'katənayt/ *vt* to connect in a series; link – fml [L *catenatus*, pp of *catenare*, fr *catena*] – **catenation** /-'naysh(ə)n/ *n*

cater /'kaytə/ *vi* **1** to provide and serve a supply of usu prepared food **2** to supply what is required or desired – usu + *for* or *to* ⟨~ed *to her whims all day long*⟩ [obs *cater* (buyer of provisions), fr ME *catour*, short for *acatour*, fr AF, fr ONF *acater* to buy – more at CATE] – **caterer** *n*

catercorner /,kaytə'kawnə/, **,cater-'cornered** *adv or adj, NAm* (situated) in a diagonal or oblique position ⟨*the house stood* ~ *across the square*⟩ [obs *cater* (a four on cards or dice; deriv of L *quattuor* four) + E *corner*]

caterpillar /'katə,pilə/ *n* a wormlike larva, specif of a butterfly or moth ☞ ANATOMY [ME *catyrpel*, fr ONF *catepelose*, lit., hairy cat]

Caterpillar *trademark* – used for a tractor designed to travel over rough or soft ground and propelled by 2 endless metal belts

caterwaul /'katə,wawl/ *vi* to cry noisily [ME *caterwawen*] – **caterwaul** *n*

'cat,fish /-,fish/ *n* any of numerous large-headed fishes with long barbels

'cat ,flu *n* an often fatal viral disease of the respiratory system of domestic cats

'cat,gut /-,gut/ *n* a tough cord usu made from sheep intestines and used esp for the strings of musical instruments and tennis rackets and for surgical sutures

cath- – see CATA-

Cathar /'ka,thah/ *n, pl* **Cathari** /'kathə,rie/, **Cathars** a member of any of several medieval self-denying Manichaean Christian sects [LL *cathari* (pl), fr LGk *katharoi*, fr Gk, pl of *katharos*, adj] – **Catharism** /'kathə,riz(ə)m/ *n*

catharsis /kə'thahsis/ *n, pl* **catharses** /-seez/ **1** purgation **2** purification or purgation of the emotions through drama **3** the process of bringing repressed ideas and feelings to consciousness and expressing them, esp during psychoanalysis [NL, fr Gk *katharsis*, fr *kathairein* to cleanse, purge, fr *katharos* pure] – **cathartic** *adj*

Cathay /ka'thay, kə-/ *n, archaic* China [ML *Cataya, Kitai*, of Turkic origin]

'cat,head /-,hed/ *n* a projecting part near the bow of a ship to which the anchor is hoisted and secured

cathedra /kə'theedrə/ *n* a bishop's throne [L, chair – more at CHAIR]

cathedral /kə'theedrəl/ *n* a church that is the official seat of a diocesan bishop [LL *cathedralis*, prob short for (assumed) *ecclesia cathedralis* church containing a cathedra]

cathepsin /kə'thepsin/ *n* any of several intracellular enzymes that occur esp in lysosomes and break down proteins [Gk *kathepsein* to digest (fr *kata-* cata- + *hepsein* to boil) + E *-in*]

'catherine ,wheel /'kath(ə)rin/ *n, often cap C* a firework in the form of a wheel that spins as it burns [St *Catherine* of Alexandria †*ab*307 Christian martyr tortured on a spiked wheel]

catheter /'kathətə/ *n* a tubular device for insertion into a hollow body part (e g a blood vessel), usu to inject or draw off fluids or to keep a passage open [LL, fr Gk *kathetēr*, fr *kathienai* to send down, fr *kata-* cata- + *hienai* to send – more at [2]JET] – **catheterize** /-,riez/ *vt*

cathexis /kə'theksis/ *n, pl* **cathexes** /-seez/ investment of mental or emotional energy in a person, object, or idea [NL (intended as trans of G *besetzung*), fr Gk *kathexis* holding, fr *katechein* to hold fast, occupy, fr *kata-* cata- + *echein* to have, hold – more at SCHEME] – **cathect** /kə'thekt/ *vt*, **cathectic** *adj*

cathode /'ka,thohd/ *n* the electrode by which electrons leave an external circuit and enter a device; *specif* the positive terminal of a primary cell or of a storage battery that is delivering current – compare ANODE [Gk *kathodos* way down, fr *kata-* + *hodos* way] – **cathodal** /kə'thohdl/ *adj*, **cathodic** /kə'thodik/ *adj*

cathode ray *n* a beam of high-speed electrons projected from the heated cathode of a vacuum tube

cathode-ray tube *n* a vacuum tube in which a beam of electrons is projected onto a fluorescent screen to provide a visual display (e g a television picture) ☞ TELEVISION

catholic /'kath(ə)lik/ *adj* **1** comprehensive, universal; *esp* broad in sympathies or tastes **2** *cap* **a** of or forming the entire body of worshippers that constitutes the Christian church **b** of or forming the ancient undivided Christian church or a church claiming historical continuity from it; *specif* ROMAN CATHOLIC [MF & LL; MF *catholique*, fr LL *catholicus*, fr Gk *katholikos* universal, general, fr *katholou* in general, fr *kata* by + *holos* whole – more at CATA-, SAFE] – **catholicism** /kə'tholə,siz(ə)m/ *n*, **catholicize** *vb*

Catholic *n* a member of a Catholic church; *specif* ROMAN CATHOLIC

catholicity /,kathə'lisəti/ *n* **1** liberality of sentiments or views **2** universality

catholicon /kə'tholi,kon, -kən/ *n* a cure-all, panacea [F or ML; F, fr ML, fr Gk *katholikon*, neut of *katholikos*]

cation /'kat,ie·ən/ *n* a positively charged ion (that moves towards the cathode in an electrolysed solution) – compare ANION [Gk *kation*, neut of *katiōn*, prp of *katienai* to go down, fr *kata-* cata- + *ienai* to go – more at ISSUE] – **cationic** /-ie'onik/ *adj*

catkin /'kat,kin/ *n* a hanging spike-shaped densely crowded group of flowers without petals (e g in a willow) [obs D *katteken*, lit., kitten; fr its resemblance to a cat's tail]

'cat,mint /-,mint/ *n* a blue-flowered plant of the mint family whose strong scent is attractive to cats

'cat,nap /-,nap/ *n* a brief period of sleep, esp during the day – **catnap** *vi*

'cat,nip /-,nip/ *n* catmint [[1]*cat* + obs *nep* (catnip), fr ME, fr OE *nepte*, fr L *nepeta*]

,cat-o'-'nine-,tails *n, pl* **cat-o'-nine-tails** a whip made of usu 9 knotted cords fastened to a handle [fr the resemblance of its scars to the scratches of a cat]

catoptric /kə'toptrik/ *adj* of a mirror or reflected light; *also* produced by reflection [Gk *katoptrikos*, fr *katoptron* mirror, fr *katopsesthai* to be going to observe, fr *kata-* cata- + *opsesthai* to be going to see – more at OPTIC]

cat's cradle *n* a game in which a string looped in a pattern on the fingers of one person's hands is transferred to the hands of another so as to form a different figure

'cats,ear /-,iə/ *n* any of various yellow European composite plants

'cat's-,eye *n, pl* **cat's-eyes** **1** any of various gems (e g a chrysoberyl or a chalcedony) that reflect a narrow band of light from within **2** a small reflector set in a road, usu in a line with others, to reflect vehicle headlights

'cat's-,paw *n, pl* **cat's-paws** **1** a light breeze that ruffles the surface of water in irregular patches **2** sby used by another as a tool or dupe **3** a hitch in a rope onto which a tackle may be hooked [(2) fr the fable of a monkey that used a cat's paw to draw chestnuts from a fire]

'cat's-,tail *n* **1** timothy **2** reedmace

'cat,suit /-,s(y)ooht/ *n* a tightly fitting 1-piece garment combining top and trousers

catsup /'katsəp/ *n, chiefly NAm* ketchup

cattalo, catalo /'katəloh/ *n, pl* **cattaloes, cattalos** a cross between the American buffalo and domestic cattle [*cat*tle + buff*alo*]

cattery /'katəri/ *n* a place for the breeding or care of cats

cattle /'katl/ *n, pl* bovine animals kept on a farm, ranch, etc [ME *catel*, fr ONF, personal property, fr ML *capitale*, fr L, neut of *capitalis* of the head – more at [1]CAPITAL]

'cattle ,grid *n, Br* a shallow ditch in a road covered by parallel bars spaced far enough apart to prevent livestock from crossing

'cattleman /-mən, -,man/ *n* one who tends or raises cattle

'cattle,stop /-,stop/ *n, NZ* CATTLE GRID

catty /'kati/ *adj* slyly spiteful; malicious [CAT + [1]-Y] – **cattily** *adv*, **cattiness** *n*

'cat,walk /-,wawk/ *n* **1** a narrow walkway (e g round a machine) **2** a narrow stage in the centre of a room on which fashion shows are held

Caucasian /kaw'kayzh(y)ən/ *adj* **1** of Caucasus or its inhabitants **2** of the white race of mankind as classified according to physical features [*Caucasus, Caucasia*, region of USSR] – **Caucasian** *n*, **Caucasoid** /'kawkə,soyd/ *adj or n*

caucus /'kawkəs/ *n* a closed political meeting to decide on policy, select candidates, etc [prob of Algonquian origin]

caudal /'kawdl/ *adj* **1** of or being a tail **2** situated at or directed towards the hind part of the body [NL *caudalis*, fr L *cauda* tail]

caudate /'kawdayt/ *also* **caudated** /-,daytid/ *adj* having a tail or tail-like appendage

caudillo /kaw'deelyoh, kow-, -'dheelyoh/ *n, pl* **caudillos** a Spanish or Latin American military dictator [Sp, fr LL *capitellum* small head – more at CADET]

caught /kawt/ *past of* CATCH

caul /kawl/ *n* **1** the large fatty fold of membrane covering the intestines **2** the inner foetal membrane of higher vertebrates, esp when covering the head at birth [ME *calle*, fr MF *cale*]

cauldron, caldron /'kawldrən/ *n* **1** a large open metal pot used for cooking over an open fire **2** sthg that resembles a boiling cauldron ⟨*a* ~ *of intense emotions*⟩ [ME, alter. of *cauderon*, fr ONF, dim. of *caudiere*, fr LL *caldaria*, fr L, warm bath, fr fem of *caldarius* suitable for warming, fr *calidus* warm, fr *calēre* to be warm]

caulescent /kaw'les(ə)nt/ *adj, of a plant* having a stem that shows above the ground [ISV, fr L *caulis*]

cauliflower /'koli,flowə/ *n* (a plant closely related to the cabbage with) a compact head of usu white undeveloped flowers eaten as a vegetable [It *cavolfiore*, fr *cavolo* cabbage (fr LL *caulus*, fr L *caulis* stem, cabbage) + *fiore* flower, fr L *flor-, flos* – more at HOLE]

,cauliflower 'ear *n* an ear thickened and deformed through injury (e g from repeated blows in boxing)

cauline /'kawleen, -lien/ *adj* of or growing on (the upper part of) a stem – compare [1]RADICAL 1a [prob fr NL *caulinus*, fr L *caulis*]

caulk, calk /kawk/ *vt* to stop up and make watertight (e g the seams of a boat, cracks in wood, etc) by filling with a waterproof material [ME *caulken*, fr ONF *cauquer* to trample, fr L *calcare*, fr *calc-, calx* heel] – **caulker** *n*

cauri /'kawri/ *n, pl* **cauris** ☞ *Guinea* at NATIONALITY [prob native name in Guinea]

causal /'kawzl/ *adj* **1** expressing or indicating cause; causative ⟨*a* ~ *clause introduced by* since *or* because⟩ **2** of or being a cause ⟨*the* ~ *agent of a disease*⟩ – **causally** *adv*

causality /kaw'zaləti/ *n* **1** a causal quality or agency **2** the relation between a cause and its effect

causation /kaw'zaysh(ə)n/ *n* **1** the act or process of causing **2** the act or agency by which an effect is produced

causative /'kawzətiv/ *adj* **1** effective or operating as a cause or agent **2** expressing causation – **causative** *n*, **causatively** *adv*

[1]cause /kawz/ *n* **1a** sby or sthg that brings about an effect **b** an agent that brings sthg about **c** a reason for an action or condition; a motive **2** a ground for legal action **3** a principle or movement worth defending or supporting [ME, fr OF, fr L *causa*] – **causeless** *adj*

[2]cause *vt* to serve as the cause or occasion of – **causer** *n*

'cause /kəz; *strong* koz/ *conj* because – nonstandard

cause célèbre /,kohz say'leb(rə) (*Fr* koːz selɛbr)/ *n, pl* **causes célèbres** /~ ~/ **1** a legal case that excites widespread interest **2** a notorious incident or episode [F, lit., celebrated case]

causerie /'kohz(ə)ri/ *n* **1** an informal conversation; a chat **2** a short informal written composition, esp on a literary subject [F, fr *causer* to chat, fr L *causari* to plead, discuss, fr *causa*]

causeway /'kawz,way/ *n* a raised road or path, esp across wet ground or water [ME *cauciwey*, fr *cauci* raised path + *wey* way]

[1]caustic /'kostik, 'kaw-/ *adj* **1** capable of destroying or eating away by chemical action; corrosive **2** incisive, biting ⟨~ *wit*⟩ **3** of or being the envelope of rays reflected or refracted by a curved surface [L *causticus*, fr Gk *kaustikos*, fr *kaiein* to burn; akin to Lith *kulé* smut of plants] – **caustically** *adv*, **causticity** /-'stisəti/ *n*

²**caustic** *n* a curve or surface formed by (the intersection of) the envelope of rays reflected or refracted by a curved surface

caustic lime *n* ¹LIME 2a

caustic soda *n* SODIUM HYDROXIDE

cauter·ize, -ise /'kawtə,riez/ *vt* to sear or destroy (e g a wound or body tissue) with a cautery, esp in order to rid of infection – **cauterization** /-rie'zaysh(ə)n/ *n*

cautery /'kawtəri/ *n* **1** cauterization **2** an instrument (e g a hot iron) or caustic chemical used to cauterize tissue [L *cauterium*, fr Gk *kautērion* branding iron, fr *kaiein*]

¹**caution** /'kawsh(ə)n/ *n* **1** a warning, admonishment; *specif* an official warning given to sby who has committed a minor offence **2** prudent forethought intended to minimize risk; care **3** sby or sthg that causes astonishment or amusement – infml ⟨*she's a proper* ~⟩ [L *caution-, cautio* precaution, fr *cautus*, pp of *cavēre* to be on guard – more at HEAR] – **cautionary** *adj*

²**caution** *vt* **1a** to advise caution to; warn; *specif* to warn (sby under arrest) that his/her words will be recorded and may be used in evidence **b** to admonish, reprove; *specif* to give an official warning to ⟨~ed *for disorderly conduct*⟩ **2** *of a soccer referee* ²BOOK 2b ~ *vi* to urge, warn ⟨~ed *against an excess of alcohol*⟩

cautious /'kawshəs/ *adj* careful, prudent – **cautiously** *adv*, **cautiousness** *n*

cavalcade /'kavl,kayd, ,--'-/ *n* **1** PROCESSION 1; *esp* one of riders or carriages **2** a dramatic sequence or procession; a series [MF, ride on horseback, fr OIt *cavalcata*, fr *cavalcare* to go on horseback, fr LL *caballicare*, fr L *caballus* horse; akin to Gk dial *kaballeion* horse-drawn vehicle]

¹**cavalier** /,kavə'liə/ *n* **1** a gentleman of former times trained in arms and horsemanship; *specif* a mounted soldier **2** a gallant gentleman of former times; *esp* one in attendance on a lady **3** *cap* an adherent of Charles I of England, esp during the Civil War [MF, fr OIt *cavaliere*, fr OProv *cavalier*, fr LL *caballarius* horseman, fr L *caballus*]

²**cavalier** *adj* **1** debonair **2** given to or characterized by offhand dismissal of important matters **3** *cap* of the party of Charles I of England – **cavalierly** *adv*

cavalletto /,kavə'letoh/ *n pl* **cavalletti** /-ti/ a low training rail for horses to jump [It, lit., little horse, dim. of *cavallo* horse, fr L *caballus*]

cavalry /'kavəlri/ *n, sing or pl in constr* **1** a branch of an army consisting of mounted troops **2** a branch of a modern army consisting of armoured vehicles [It *cavalleria* cavalry, chivalry, fr *cavaliere*]

cavalry twill *n* a strong fabric woven in a double twill and used orig for riding breeches

cavatina /,kavə'teenə/ *n* **1** a short simple operatic solo **2** an instrumental composition in a similar style, usu having a slow tempo [It, fr *cavata* production of sound from an instrument, fr *cavare* to dig out, fr L, to make hollow, fr *cavus*]

¹**cave** /kayv/ *n* **1** a natural chamber (e g underground or in the side of a hill or cliff) having a usu horizontal opening on the surface **2** *Br* a formal withdrawing or group of people withdrawing from a political party [ME, fr OF, fr L *cava*, fr *cavus* hollow; akin to ON *hūnn* cub, Gk *kyein* to be pregnant, *koilos* hollow, Skt *śvayati* he swells; (2) fr *cave of Adullam*, where David was joined by malcontents (I Sam 22:1, 2)]

²**cave** *vt* to form a cave in or under; hollow out ~ *vi* to explore cave or pothole systems – **caver** *n*

³**cave** /kay'vee/ *interj, Br* – used as a warning call among schoolchildren, esp at public school; compare KEEP CAVE [L, beware, fr *cavēre* to beware, be on guard]

caveat /'kavi·at, 'kay-/ *n* **1** a cautionary remark or statement; a warning – fml **2** an official notice to a court to suspend a proceeding until the opposition has been heard [L, let him beware, fr *cavēre*]

,caveat 'emptor /'emptaw/ *n* the principle in commerce which states that without a guarantee the buyer takes the risk of quality upon him-/herself [NL, let the buyer beware]

'cave ,dweller *n* one who dwells in a cave

cave in *vt* to cause to fall in or collapse ~ *vi* **1** to fall in or collapse **2** to cease to resist; submit – infml

'cave,man /-,man/ *n* **1** a cave dweller, esp of the Stone Age **2** a man who acts in a rough primitive manner, esp towards women

cavendish /'kavəndish/ *n, often cap* tobacco that is softened by moisture, usu sweetened, and pressed into flat cakes [prob fr the name *Cavendish*]

cavern /'kavən/ *n* a large usu underground chamber or cave [ME *caverne*, fr MF, fr L *caverna*, fr *cavus*] – **cavernous** *adj*, **cavernously** *adv*

cavesson /'kavəsən/ *n* a stiff padded noseband used for breaking in horses [modif of It *cavezzone* halter with noseband, aug of *cavezza* halter, irreg fr L *capitium* opening in tunic for head, fr *capit-, caput* head]

cavetto /kə'vetoh/ *n, pl* **cavetti** /-ti/ a concave moulding having a curve that in cross section approximates to a quarter circle ☞ ARCHITECTURE [It, fr *cavo* hollow, fr L *cavus*]

caviar, caviare /'kaviah/ *n* **1** the salted roe of large fish (e g sturgeon) eaten as a delicacy **2** sthg considered too delicate or lofty for mass appreciation ⟨*will be* ~ *to the multitude*⟩ [earlier *cavery, caviarie*, fr obs It *caviari*, pl of *caviaro*, fr Turk *havyar*]

cavil /'kavil, -vl/ *vi* **-ll-** (*NAm* **-l-, -ll-**), /'kavl·ing/ to raise trivial and frivolous objections [L *cavillari* to jest, cavil, fr *cavilla* raillery] – **cavil** *n*, **caviller** *n*

cavitate /'kavitayt/ *vb* to form cavities or bubbles (in)

cavitation /,kavi'taysh(ə)n/ *n* (the pitting and wearing away of a solid surface due to) the formation of partial vacuums in a liquid by the swift movement of a solid body (e g a propeller) or by high-frequency sound waves [*cavity* + *-ation*]

cavity /'kavəti/ *n* an empty or hollowed-out space within a mass; *specif* a decaying hollow in a tooth [MF *cavité*, fr LL *cavitas*, fr L *cavus* hollow]

cavity wall *n* a wall built in 2 thicknesses, the air space between providing insulation ☞ BUILDING

cavort /kə'vawt/ *vi* **1** to prance **2** to engage in extravagant behaviour [perh alter. of *curvet* (a leap made by a horse), modif of It *corvetta*, deriv of L *curvare* to bend, curve]

cavy /'kayvi/ *n* a guinea pig or related short-tailed S American rodent [NL *Cavia*, genus name, fr obs Pg *çavía* (now *savía*), fr Tupi *sawiya* rat]

caw /kaw/ *vi* to utter (a sound like) the harsh raucous cry of the crow [imit] – **caw** *n*

cay /kee, kay/ *n* a low island or reef of sand or coral [Sp *cayo* – more at [4]KEY]

,cayenne 'pepper /kay'en/ *n* **1** a pungent red condiment consisting of the ground dried pods and seeds of hot peppers – compare CHILLI, PAPRIKA **2** a hot pepper, esp a cultivated capsicum [alter. (influenced by *Cayenne*, town in French Guiana) of earlier *cayan*, modif of Tupi *kyinha*]

cayman, caiman /'kaymən, 'kie-/ *n, pl* **caymans,** *esp collectively* **cayman** any of several Central and S American crocodilians related to the alligators [Sp *caimán*, prob fr Carib *caymán*]

cayuse /'kie,yoohs, ,-'-/ *n, dial W US* a N American Indian pony [*Cayuse*, native name for a N American Indian people]

'C ,clef *n* a movable clef indicating middle C by its placement on 1 of the lines of the staff ☞ MUSIC

[1]cease /sees/ *vt* to bring to an end; terminate ⟨~ *this noise!*⟩ ~ *vi* **1** to come to an end ⟨*when will this quarrelling* ~*?*⟩ **2** to bring an activity or action to an end; discontinue ⟨*cried for hours without* ceasing⟩ [ME *cesen*, fr OF *cesser*, fr L *cessare* to delay, fr *cessus*, pp of *cedere*]

[2]cease *n* stopping, cessation ⟨*without* ~⟩

,cease-'fire *n* (a military order for) a cessation of firing or of active hostilities

'ceaseless /-lis/ *adj* continuing endlessly; constant – **ceaselessly** *adv*, **ceaselessness** *n*

cecum /'seekəm/ *n, pl* **ceca** /-kə/ *NAm* the caecum – **cecal** *adj*

cedar /'seedə/ *n* (the fragrant wood of) any of a genus of usu tall evergreen coniferous trees of the pine family [ME *cedre*, fr OF, fr L *cedrus*, fr Gk *kedros*; akin to Lith *kadagys* juniper]

cede /seed/ *vt* to yield or surrender (e g territory), usu by treaty [F or L; F *céder*, fr L *cedere* to go, withdraw, yield; prob akin to L *cis* on this side and to Gk *hodos* road, way, L *sedēre* to sit] – **ceder** *n*

cedi /'saydi/ *n, pl* **cedi** /~/ ☞ *Ghana* at NATIONALITY [Fante *sedi* small shell]

cedilla /sə'dilə/ *n* a mark ¸ × placed under a letter (e g ç in French) to indicate an alteration or modification of its usual phonetic value (e g in the French *façade*) ☞ SYMBOL [Sp, the obs letter *ç* (actually a medieval form of the letter *z*), cedilla, fr dim. of *ceda, zeda* the letter *z*, fr LL *zeta*, fr Gk *zēta*]

Ceefax /'see,faks/ *trademark* – used for a service provided by the BBC which transmits information (e g the weather or sports results) on usu special channels ☞ TELEVISION

ceilidh /'kayli/ *n* an informal party for esp Scottish or Irish dancing and music [IrGael *cēilidhe* & ScGael *cēilidh*, fr MIr *cēlide*, fr OIr *cēle, cēile* companion, husband; akin to L *civis* citizen]

ceiling /'seeling/ *n* **1** the overhead inside surface of a room **2** the height above the ground of the base of the lowest layer of clouds **3** a prescribed or actual maximum height at which an aircraft can fly **4** an upper usu prescribed limit ⟨*a* ~ *on rents and wages*⟩ [ME *celing*, fr *celen* to furnish with a ceiling, prob fr (assumed) MF *celer*, fr L *caelare* to carve, fr *caelum* chisel, fr *caedere* to cut]

celadon /'selədon, -dn/ *n* **1** a greyish green colour **2** (a type of pottery having) a greyish green ceramic glaze [F *céladon*, fr *Céladon*, languid lover in the romance *L'Astrée* by Honoré d'Urfé †1625 F writer]

celandine /'selən,dien/ *n* **1** *also* **greater celandine** a yellow-flowered biennial plant of the poppy family **2** *also* **lesser celandine** a common yellow-flowered European perennial plant of the buttercup family [ME *celidoine*, fr MF, fr L *chelidonia*, fr fem of *chelidonius* of the swallow, fr Gk *chelidonios*, fr *chelidon-, chelidōn* swallow]

-cele /-seel/ *comb form* (→ *n*) hernia ⟨*meningo*cele⟩ [MF, fr L, fr Gk *kēlē*; akin to OE *hēala* hernia, OSlav *kyla*]

celebrant /'selibrənt/ *n* the priest officiating at the Eucharist [CELEBRATE + [1]-ANT]

celebrate /'selibrayt/ *vt* **1** to perform (a sacrament or solemn ceremony) publicly and with appropriate rites ⟨~ *the mass*⟩ **2a** to mark (a holy day or feast day) ceremonially **b** to mark (a special occasion) with festivities or suspension of routine activities **3** to hold up for public acclaim; extol ⟨*his poetry* ~s *the glory of nature*⟩ ~ *vi* **1** to officiate at a religious ceremony **2** to observe a special occasion, usu with festivities [L *celebratus*, pp of *celebrare* to frequent, celebrate, fr *celebr-, celeber* much frequented, famous; akin to L *celer*] – **celebration** /-'braysh(ə)n/ *n*, **celebrator** /-,braytə/ *n*, **celebratory** /'selibrət(ə)ri/ *adj*

'cele,brated *adj* widely known and often referred to – **celebratedness** *n*

celebrity /sə'lebrəti/ *n* **1** the state of being famous **2** a well-known and widely acclaimed person

celeriac /sə'le(ə)riak/ *n* a type of celery grown for its thickened edible root [irreg fr *celery*]

celerity /sə'lerəti/ *n* rapidity of motion or action – fml [ME *celerite*, fr MF *célérité*, fr L *celeritat-, celeritas*, fr *celer* swift]

celery /'seləri/ *n* a European plant of the carrot family with leafstalks eaten cold or hot as a vegetable [prob fr It dial. *seleri*, pl of *selero*, modif of LL *selinon*, fr Gk]

celesta /sə'lestə/ *n* a keyboard instrument with hammers that strike steel plates producing a tone like that of a glockenspiel [F *célesta*, alter. of *céleste*, lit., heavenly, fr L *caelestis*]

celeste /sə'lest/ *n* a celesta

celestial /sə'lesti·əl/ *adj* **1** of or suggesting heaven or divinity; divine **2** of or in the sky or visible heavens ⟨*a* ~ *body*⟩ [ME, fr MF, fr L *caelestis*, fr *caelum* sky; akin to Skt *citra* bright] – **celestially** *adv*

celestial sphere *n* an imaginary sphere of infinite radius against which the celestial bodies appear to be projected

celiac /'seeliak/ *adj, NAm* coeliac

celibate /'selibət/ *n* one who is unmarried and does not have sexual intercourse, esp because of a religious vow [L *caelibatus*, fr *caelib-, caelebs* unmarried; akin to Skt *kevala* alone & to OE *libban* to live] – **celibacy** /-bəsi/ *n*, **celibate** /-bət/ *adj*

cell /sel/ *n* **1** a 1-room dwelling occupied esp by a hermit or recluse **2a** a barely furnished room for 1 person (e g in a convent or monastery) **b** a small room in a prison for 1 or more inmates **3** a small compartment (e g in a honeycomb), receptacle, cavity (e g one containing seeds in a plant ovary), or bounded space **4** the smallest structural unit of living matter consisting of nuclear and cytoplasmic material bounded by a semipermeable membrane and capable of functioning either alone or with others in all fundamental life processes **5a** a vessel (e g a cup or jar) containing electrodes and an electrolyte either for generating electricity by chemical action or for use in electrolysis **b** a single unit in a device for producing an electrical effect as a result of exposure to radiant energy **6** the primary unit of a political, esp Communist, organization **7** a basic subdivision of a computer memory that is addressable and can hold 1 unit (e g a word) of a computer's basic operating data [ME, fr OE, religious house, & OF *celle* hermit's cell, fr L *cella* small room; akin to L *celare* to conceal – more at HELL]

[1]**cellar** /'selə/ *n* **1** an underground room; *esp* one used for storage **2** an individual's stock of wine [ME *celer*, fr AF, fr L *cellarium* storeroom, fr *cella*]

[2]**cellar** *vt* to store or place (e g wine) in a cellar

cellarage /'selərij/ *n* **1** cellar space, esp for storage **2** the charge made for storage in a cellar

cellarer /'selərə/ *n* an official (e g in a monastery) in charge of provisions [ME *celerer*, fr OF, fr LL *cellariarius*, fr L *cellarium*]

cell division *n* the process by which 2 daughter cells are formed from a parent cell – compare MEIOSIS, MITOSIS

-celled /-seld/ *comb form* (*adj* → *adj*) having (such or so many) cells ⟨*single*-celled *organisms*⟩

cello /'cheloh/ *n, pl* **cellos** a large stringed instrument of the violin family tuned an octave below the viola [short for *violoncello*] – **cellist** /'chelist/ *n*

cellobiose /ˌselə'bie·ohs, -ohz/ *n* a faintly sweet disaccharide obtained from cellulose [ISV *cell*ulose + *-o-* + *biose* (disaccharide), fr [1]*bi-* + *-ose*]

cellophane /'seləˌfayn/ *n* regenerated cellulose in the form of thin transparent sheets, used esp for wrapping goods [F, fr *cell*ulose + *-phane* (as in *diaphane* diaphanous, fr ML *diaphanus*)]

'cell ˌsap *n* cytoplasm

cellular /'selyoolə/ *adj* **1** of, relating to, or consisting of cells **2** containing cavities; porous **3** having a very open weave ⟨*a* ~ *blanket*⟩ [NL *cellularis*, fr *cellula* living cell, fr L, dim. of *cella* small room] – **cellularly** *adv*, **cellularity** /ˌselyoo'larəti/ *n*

cellule /'selyoohl/ *n* a small cell [L *cellula*]

cellulite /'selyooˌliet/ *n* a type of body fat held to be caused by water retention, and producing a dimpled effect on the skin (e g of the thigh)

cellulitis /ˌselyoo'lietəs/ *n* diffuse, esp subcutaneous, inflammation of body tissue [NL, fr *cellula*]

celluloid /'selyooˌloyd/ *n* film for the cinema; *also* FILM 3 [fr *Celluloid*, a trademark] – **celluloid** *adj*

Celluloid *trademark* – used for a tough inflammable thermoplastic composed essentially of cellulose nitrate and camphor

cellulose /'selyooˌlohs/ *n* **1** a polysaccharide of glucose units that constitutes the chief part of plant cell walls, occurs naturally in cotton, kapok, etc, and is the raw material of many manufactured goods (e g paper, rayon, and cellophane) **2** paint or lacquer of which the main constituent is cellulose nitrate or acetate [F, fr *cellule* living cell, fr NL *cellula*]

ˌcellulose 'acetate *n* any of several compounds formed esp by the action of acetic acid on cellulose and used for making textile fibres, packaging sheets, photographic films, and varnishes

ˌcellulose 'nitrate *n* any of several compounds formed by the action of nitric acid on cellulose and used for making explosives, plastics, rayon, and varnishes

ˌcell 'wall *n* the firm nonliving wall, formed usu from cellulose, that encloses and supports most plant cells

Celsius /'selsi·əs/ *adj* relating to, conforming to, or being a scale of temperature on which water freezes at 0° and boils at 100° under standard conditions ☞ PHYSICS, UNIT [Anders *Celsius* †1744 Sw astronomer]

celt /selt/ *n* a prehistoric stone or metal implement shaped like a chisel or axe head [LL *celtis* chisel]

Celt, Kelt /kelt/ *n* **1** a member of a division of the early Indo-European peoples extending at various times from the British Isles and Spain to Asia Minor **2** a modern Gael, Highland Scot, Irishman, Welshman, Cornishman, Manxman, or Breton [F *Celte*, sing. of *Celtes*, fr L *Celtae*]

[1]**Celtic, Keltic** /'keltik/ *adj* (characteristic) of the Celts or their languages

[2]**Celtic, Keltic** *n* a branch of Indo-European languages comprising Welsh, Cornish, Breton, Irish, Scots Gaelic, and Manx, which is now confined to Brittany and parts of the British Isles ☞ LANGUAGE – **Celticist** /'keltisist/ *n*

ˌCeltic 'cross *n* a Latin cross with a ring centred on the intersection of the 2 shafts ☞ SYMBOL

ˌCeltic 'fringe *n, often cap F* Cornwall, Wales, Ireland, and Highland Scotland considered as a cultural and political grouping

cembalo /'chembəˌloh/ *n, pl* **cembali** /-li/, **cembalos** a harpsichord [It]

[1]**cement** /si'ment/ *n* **1** a powder consisting of alumina, silica, lime, iron oxide, and magnesia pulverized together and burnt in a kiln, that is used as the binding agent in mortar and concrete ☞ BUILDING **2** a substance (e g a glue or adhesive) used for sticking objects together **3** sthg serving to unite firmly ⟨*a common tradition is the* ~ *which holds the community together*⟩ **4** cementum **5** an adhesive preparation used for filling teeth, attaching dental crowns, etc **6** concrete – not used technically [ME *sement*, fr OF *ciment*, fr L *caementum* stone chips used in making mortar, fr *caedere* to cut – more at CONCISE] – **cementitious** /ˌsemen'tishəs, ˌsee-/ *adj*

[2]**cement** *vt* **1** to unite or make firm (as if) by the application of cement **2** to overlay with concrete

cementation /ˌsemen'taysh(ə)n, ˌsee-/ *n* the process of heating a solid surrounded by a powder so that the solid is changed by chemical combination with the powder; *esp* the heating of iron surrounded by charcoal to make steel [[2]CEMENT + -ATION]

cementite /si'mentiet/ *n* the compound of iron and carbon in steel, cast iron, and iron-carbon alloys [[1]*cement*]

cementum /si'mentəm/ *n* the thin bony layer enclosing the base of a tooth [NL, fr L *caementum*]

cemetery /'semətri/ *n* a burial ground; *esp* one not in a churchyard [ME *cimitery*, fr MF *cimitere*, fr LL *coemeterium*, fr Gk *koimētērion* sleeping chamber, burial place, fr *koiman* to put to sleep; akin to L *cunae* cradle]

cen-, ceno- *comb form, chiefly NAm* cain-, caino-

-cene /-seen/ *comb form* (→ *adj*) recent – in names of geological periods ⟨*Eocene*⟩ [Gk *kainos*]

cenobite /'seenohˌbiet/ *n, chiefly NAm* a coenobite – **cenobitic** /ˌseenə'bitik/, **cenobitical** *adj*

cenospecies /'seenoh,spees(h)iz/ *n* a species which, owing to its closely related genotype, is capable of interbreeding with another [*coen-* + *species*]

cenotaph /'senə,tahf/ *n* a tomb or monument erected in honour of a person or group of people whose remains are elsewhere; *specif, cap* that standing in Whitehall in London in memory of the dead of WWs I and II [F *cénotaphe*, fr L *cenotaphium*, fr Gk *kenotaphion*, fr *kenos* empty + *taphos* tomb; akin to Arm *sin* empty – more at EPITAPH]

cense /sens/ *vt* to perfume, or burn incense at [ME *censen*, prob short for *encensen* to incense, fr MF *encenser*, fr LL *incensare*, fr *incensum* incense]

censer /'sensə/ *n* a covered incense burner swung on chains during certain religious rituals

[1]**censor** /'sensə/ *n* **1** either of 2 magistrates of early Rome who acted as census takers, inspectors of morals, etc **2** an official who examines publications, films, letters, etc and has the power to suppress objectionable (e g obscene or libellous) matter **3** a supposed mental agency that represses certain unacceptable ideas and desires before they reach consciousness [L, fr *censēre* to assess, tax; akin to Skt *śaṁsati* he recites] – **censorial** /sen'sawri·əl/ *adj*

[2]**censor** *vt* to subject to censorship

censorious /sen'sawri·əs/ *adj* severely critical; given to censure [L *censorius* of a censor, fr *censor*] – **censoriously** *adv*, **censoriousness** *n*

censorship /'sensə,ship/ *n* **1** the act, practice, or duties of a censor; *esp* censorial control **2** the office, power, or term of a Roman censor **3** the repression in the mind of unacceptable ideas and desires

[1]**censure** /'senshə/ *n* **1** a judgment involving condemnation **2** the act of blaming or condemning sternly **3** an official reprimand [L *censura*, fr *censēre*]

[2]**censure** *vt* to find fault with and criticize as blameworthy – **censurable** *adj*, **censurer** *n*

census /'sensəs/ *n* **1** a periodic counting of the population and gathering of related statistics (e g age, sex, or social class) carried out by government **2** a usu official count or tally [L, fr *censēre*]

cent /sent/ *n* (a coin or note representing) a unit worth $^{1}/_{100}$ of the basic money unit of certain countries (e g the American dollar) ☞ NATIONALITY [MF, hundred, fr L *centum* – more at HUNDRED]

centaur /'sen,taw/ *n* any of a race of mythological creatures having the head, arms, and upper body of a man, and the lower body and back legs of a horse [ME, fr L *Centaurus*, fr Gk *Kentauros*]

centaury /'sen,tawri/ *n* any of a genus of low-growing plants of the gentian family [ME *centaure*, fr MF *centaurée*, fr ML *centaurea*, fr L *centaureum*, fr Gk *kentaureion*, fr *Kentauros*]

centavo /sen'tahvoh/ *n, pl* **centavos** (a coin or note representing) a unit worth $^{1}/_{100}$ of the basic money unit of certain Spanish or Portuguese-speaking countries (e g Chile, Cuba, Mexico, Portugal) ☞ NATIONALITY [Sp, lit., hundredth, fr L *centum* hundred]

centenarian /,sentə'neəri·ən/ *n* sby who is (more than) 100 years old – **centenarian** *adj*

centenary /sen'teenəri, -'tenəri/ *n* (the celebration of) a 100th anniversary [LL *centenarium*, fr L *centenarius* of a hundred, fr *centeni* one hundred each, fr *centum* hundred – more at HUNDRED] – **centenary** *adj*

centennial /sen'teni·əl/ *n, chiefly NAm* a centenary [L *centum* + E *-ennial* (as in *biennial*)] – **centennial** *adj*, **centennially** *adv*

center /'sentə/ *vb or n, NAm* (to) centre

centesimal /sen'tesiməl/ *adj* marked by or relating to division into hundredths [L *centesimus* hundredth, fr *centum*]

centesimo /sen'tesimoh/ *n, pl* **centesimos** ☞ *Uruguay* at NATIONALITY [Sp *centésimo*]

centi- /senti-/ *comb form* **1** hundred ⟨centi*pede*⟩ **2** one hundredth (10^{-2}) part of (a specified unit) ⟨centi*metre*⟩ ☞ PHYSICS, UNIT [F & L; F, hundredth, fr L, hundred, fr *centum*]

centigrade /'senti,grayd/ *adj* Celsius ☞ UNIT [F, fr L *centi-* hundred + F *grade*]

centigram /'senti,gram/ *n* one hundredth of a gram ☞ UNIT [F *centigramme*, fr *centi-* + *gramme* gram]

centilitre /'senti,leetə/ *n* one hundredth of a litre (about 0.35 fl oz) ☞ UNIT

centime /'sonteem/ *n* (a note or coin representing) a unit worth $^{1}/_{100}$ of the basic money unit of certain French-speaking countries (e g Algeria, Belgium, France) ☞ NATIONALITY [F, fr *cent* hundred, fr L *centum*]

centimetre /'sentimeetə/ *n* one hundredth of a metre (about 0.4in) ☞ UNIT

centimetre-gram-second *adj* of or being a system of units based on the centimetre, the gram, and the second

centimo /'sentimoh/ *n, pl* **centimos** (a coin or note representing) a unit worth $^{1}/_{100}$ of the basic money unit of Spain and certain South American countries ☞ NATIONALITY [Sp *céntimo*]

centipede /'senti,peed/ *n* any of a class of many-segmented arthropods with each segment bearing 1 pair of legs [L *centipeda*, fr *centi-* + *ped-*, *pes* foot – more at FOOT]

cento /'sentoh/ *n, pl* **centones** /sen'tohneez/, **centos** a literary work made up of quotations from other works [LL, fr L, patchwork garment; akin to OHG *hadara* rag, Skt *kanthā* patched garment]

centr-, centri-, centro- *comb form* centre ⟨centri*fugal*⟩ ⟨centr*oid*⟩ [Gk *kentr-*, *kentro-*, fr *kentron* centre – more at CENTRE]

central /'sentrəl/ *adj* **1** containing or constituting a centre **2** of primary importance; principal ⟨*the ~ character of the novel*⟩ **3a** at, in, or near the centre ⟨*the plains of ~ N America*⟩ **b** easily accessible; convenient ⟨*our house is very ~ for the shops*⟩ **4** having overall power or control ⟨*decided by the ~ committee*⟩ **5** of, originating in, or comprising the central nervous system [L *centralis*, fr *centrum* centre – more at CENTRE] – **centrally** *adv*, **centrality** /sen'traləti/ *n*

,central 'bank *n* the main banking institution of a country, usu dealing with government or inter-bank transactions rather than those of private individuals

Central European Time *n* the standard time, 1 hour ahead of Greenwich Mean Time, which is used by most countries of Western and Central Europe in the first time zone east of Greenwich

,central 'heating *n* a system of heating whereby heat is produced at a central source (e g a boiler) and carried by pipes to radiators or air vents throughout a building (e g a house or office block)

centralism /'sentrə,liz(ə)m/ *n* the practice or principle of concentrating power and control in a central authority – **centralist** *n or adj*, **centralistic** /ˌsentrə'listik/ *adj*

central·ize, -ise /'sentrə,liez/ *vi* to come to or gather round a centre; *specif* to gather under central control (e g of government) ~ *vt* to bring to a centre; consolidate; *specif* to bring (power, authority, etc) under central control – **centralizer** *n*, **centralization** /-lie'zaysh(ə)n/ *n*

ˌcentral 'nervous ˌsystem *n* the part of the nervous system which in vertebrates consists of the brain and spinal cord and which coordinates the activity of the entire nervous system

central processing unit *n* PROCESSOR 1b

[1]centre, *NAm chiefly* **center** /'sentə/ *n* **1** the point round which a circle or sphere is described; *broadly* the centre of symmetry **2a** a place, esp a collection of buildings, round which a usu specified activity is concentrated ⟨*a shopping* ~⟩ **b** sby or sthg round which interest is concentrated ⟨*the* ~ *of the controversy*⟩ **c** a source from which sthg originates ⟨*a propaganda* ~⟩ **d** a region of concentrated population ⟨*an urban* ~⟩ **3** a group of nerve cells having a common function ⟨*respiratory* ~⟩ **4** the middle part (e g of a stage) **5** *often cap* a group, party, etc holding moderate political views ⟨*the possible formation of a new* ~ *party*⟩ **6a** a player occupying a middle position in the forward line of a team (e g in football or hockey) **b** an instance of passing the ball from a wing to the centre of a pitch or court (e g in football) **7** (a recess containing) a rod with a conical end which supports a workpiece in a lathe or grinding machine and about or with which the workpiece revolves **8** a temporary wooden framework on which an arch is supported during construction [ME *centre*, fr MF, fr L *centrum*, fr Gk *kentron* sharp point, centre of a circle, fr *kentein* to prick; akin to OHG *hantag* pointed, Latvian *sīts* hunting spear]

[2]centre, *NAm chiefly* **center** *vi* **1** to have a centre; focus – usu + *round* or *on* **2** to come to or towards a centre or central area **3** to centre a ball, puck, etc ~ *vt* **1** to place or fix in or at a centre or central area ⟨~ *the picture on the wall*⟩ **2** to gather to a centre; concentrate ⟨~s *her hopes on her son*⟩ **3** to adjust (e g lenses) so that the axes coincide **4** to pass (e g a ball or puck) from either side towards the middle of the playing area

'centreˌboard /-ˌbawd/ *n* a retractable keel used esp in small yachts

centre circle *n* a circle of 9.15m (10yd) radius in the middle of a soccer pitch ☞ SPORT

centred /'sentəd/ *adj* having a centre – often in combination ⟨*a dark*-centred *flower*⟩

'centreˌfold /-ˌfohld/ *n* (a pictorial display covering) the 2 facing pages in the centre of a newspaper or magazine ⟨~ *pinup*⟩

ˌcentre-'forward *n* (the position of) a player in hockey, soccer, etc positioned in the middle of the forward line ☞ SPORT

ˌcentre-'half *n* (the position of) a player in hockey, soccer, etc positioned in the middle of the halfback line ☞ SPORT

ˌcentre of 'gravity *n* **1** CENTRE OF MASS **2** the point at which the entire weight of a body may be considered as concentrated so that if supported at this point the body would remain in equilibrium in any position

ˌcentre of 'mass *n* the point at which the entire mass of a body or system of bodies may be considered as concentrated

'centreˌpiece /-ˌpees/ *n* **1** an ornament (e g of flowers) placed in the centre of a table **2** the most important or outstanding item

centre spread *n* a centrefold

ˌcentre-three-'quarter *n* (the position of) either of the 2 players in rugby positioned in the middle of the three-quarter-back line

centri- /sentri-/ – see CENTR-

centric /'sentrik/ *adj* central [Gk *kentrikos* of the centre, fr *kentron*] – **centrically** *adv*, **centricity** /sen'trisəti/ *n*

-centric /-sentrik/ *comb form* (→ *adj*) having (such) a centre ⟨*con*centric⟩ or (such or so many) centres ⟨*poly*centric⟩; having (sthg specified) as a centre ⟨*helio*centric⟩ [ML *-centricus*, fr L *centrum* centre]

centrifugal /ˌsentri'fyoohg(ə)l, sen'trifyoog(ə)l/ *adj* **1** proceeding or acting in a direction away from a centre or axis **2** using or acting by centrifugal force ⟨*a* ~ *pump*⟩ **3** tending away from centralization; separatist ⟨~ *tendencies in modern society*⟩ [NL *centrifugus*, fr *centr-* + L *fugere* to flee – more at FUGITIVE]

centrifugal force *n* the force that appears to act outwardly from the centre of rotation of an object moving along a circular path

centrifuge /'sentri,fyoohj, -ˌfyoohzh/ *vt or n* (to subject to centrifugal action, esp in) a machine using centrifugal force, esp for separating substances of different densities [n F, fr *centrifuge* centrifugal, fr NL *centrifugus*; vb fr n] – **centrifugation** /-fyooh'gaysh(ə)n/ *n*

centriole /'sentri,ohl/ *n* either of a pair of organelles consisting of 9 microtubules arranged cylindrically, which are found in many animal cells and function in the formation of the mitotic apparatus [G *zentriol*, fr *zentrum* centre]

centripetal /'sentri,petl, sen'tripitl/ *adj* **1** proceeding or acting in a direction towards a centre or axis **2** tending towards centralization; unifying [NL *centripetus*, fr *centr-* + L *petere* to go to, seek – more at FEATHER] – **centripetally** /sen'tripit(ə)li/ *adv*

centrist /'sentrist/ *n*, *often cap* a member of a moderate party; *broadly* one holding moderate political views – **centrism** *n*

centro- – see CENTR-

centroid /'sentroyd/ *n* CENTRE OF MASS – **centroidal** /sen'troydl/ *adj*

centromere /'sentrə,miə/ *n* the point on a chromosome by which it appears to attach to the spindle in mitosis [ISV] – **centromeric** /-'merik, -'miərik/ *adj*

centrosome /'sentrə,sohm/ *n* (the region of clear cytoplasm that contains) a centriole [G *zentrosom*, fr *zentr-* centr- + *-som* -some] – **centrosomic** /-'sohmik/ *adj*

centrosphere /'sentrə,sfiə/ *n* the central part of the earth composed of very dense material [ISV]

centrum /'sentrəm/ *n*, *pl* **centrums, centra** /-trə/ the body of a vertebra [L – more at CENTRE]

centurion /sen'tyooəri·ən/ *n* an officer commanding a Roman century [ME, fr MF & L; MF, fr L *centurion-*, *centurio*, fr *centuria*]

century /'senchəri/ *n* **1** a subdivision of the ancient Roman legion orig consisting of 100 men **2** a group, sequence, or series of 100 like things; *specif* 100 runs made by a cricketer in 1 innings **3** a period of 100 years; *esp* any of the 100-year periods reckoned forwards or backwards from the conventional date of the birth of Christ [L *centuria*, irreg fr *centum* hundred]

century plant *n* a Mexican agave that matures and flowers once after many years of growth and then dies

cep /sep/ *n* any of several edible fungi having a sponge-like underside; *esp* one with a shiny brown cap and white underside considered a delicacy esp in France and Germany [F *cèpe*, fr F dial. *cep* tree trunk, mushroom, fr L *cippus* stake, post]

cephal-, cephalo- *comb form* head ⟨cephal*ic*⟩; head and ⟨cephalo*thorax*⟩ [L, fr Gk *kephal-, kephalo-*, fr *kephalē*]

cephalic /si'falik/ *adj* **1** of or relating to the head **2** directed towards or situated on, in, or near the head [MF *céphalique*, fr L *cephalicus*, fr Gk *kephalikos*, fr *kephalē* head; akin to OHG *gebal* skull, ON *gafl* gable] – **cephalically** *adv*

-cephalic, -cephalous *comb form* (→ *adj*) having (such) a head or (so many) heads ⟨*brachy*-cephalic⟩

cephalic index *n* the ratio of the maximum breadth of the head to its maximum length multiplied by 100 – compare CRANIAL INDEX

cephalochordate /,sefəloh'kawdayt/ *n* a lancelet

cephalopod /'sef(ə)lə,pod/ *n* any of a class of tentacled molluscs that includes the squids, cuttlefishes, and octopuses [deriv of *cephal-* + Gk *pod-, pous* foot – more at FOOT] – **cephalopod** *adj*, **cephalopodan** /,sefə'lopədən; *also* ,sef(ə)lə'pohdən/ *adj or n*

cephalosporin /,sef(ə)lə'spawrin/ *n* any of several antibiotics with actions similar to those of penicillin [NL *Cephalosporium*, genus of fungi + *-in*]

cephalothorax /,sef(ə)lə'thawraks/ *n* the united head and thorax of an arachnid or higher crustacean [ISV]

Cepheid /'sefi·id/ *n* any of a class of pulsating stars with regularly varying light intensities [L *Cepheus*, a northern constellation, fr *Cepheus*, mythical king of Ethiopia and father of Andromeda, fr Gk *Kēpheus*]

[1]**ceramic** /sə'ramik/ *adj* of or being (the manufacture of) a product (e g porcelain or brick) made from a nonmetallic mineral (e g clay) by firing at high temperatures [Gk *keramikos*, fr *keramos* potter's clay, pottery]

[2]**ceramic** *n* **1** *pl but sing in constr* the art or process of making ceramic articles **2** a product of ceramic manufacture – **ceramist** /sə'ramist, 'serəmist/, **ceramicist** /sə'raməsist/ *n*

cerastes /si'rasteez/ *n* a venomous viper of the Near East that has a horny projection over each eye [ME, fr L, fr Gk *kerastēs*, lit., horned, fr *keras*]

cerat-, cerato-, kerat-, kerato- *comb form* **1** horn; horny ⟨cerat*odus*⟩ ⟨kerat*in*⟩ **2** – see KERAT- 1 [NL, fr Gk *kerat-, kerato-*, fr *keras* horn – more at HORN]

cercaria /suh'keəri·ə/ *n, pl* **cercariae** /-ri,ee/ a usu tadpole-shaped larval trematode worm produced in a mollusc host by a redia [NL, fr Gk *kerkos* tail] – **cercarial** *adj*

cere /siə/ *n* a usu waxy swelling at the base of a bird's beak [ME *sere*, fr MF *cere*, fr ML *cera*, fr L, wax]

[1]**cereal** /'siəri·əl/ *adj* of or relating to (the plants that produce) grain [F or L; F *céréale*, fr L *cerealis* of Ceres, of grain, fr *Ceres*, goddess of agriculture]

[2]**cereal** *n* **1** (a grass or other plant yielding) grain suitable for food **2** a food made from grain and usu eaten with milk and sugar at breakfast

cerebellum /,serə'beləm/ *n, pl* **cerebellums, cerebella** /-lə/ a large part of the back of the brain which projects outwards and is concerned esp with coordinating muscles and maintaining equilibrium ☞ NERVE [ML, fr L, dim. of *cerebrum*] – **cerebellar** *adj*

cerebr-, cerebro- *comb form* **1** brain; cerebrum ⟨cerebr*ation*⟩ **2** cerebral and ⟨cerebro*spinal*⟩ [*cerebrum*]

cerebral /'serəbrəl/ *adj* **1a** of the brain or the intellect **b** of or being the cerebrum **2a** appealing to the intellect ⟨~ *drama*⟩ **b** primarily intellectual in nature ⟨*a ~ society*⟩ [F *cérébral*, fr L *cerebrum* brain; akin to Gk *kara* head, *keras* horn – more at HORN] – **cerebrally** *adv*

,cerebral 'cortex *n* the outer layer of grey matter in the brain whose chief function is the coordination of higher nervous activity

,cerebral 'hemisphere *n* either of the 2 hollow convoluted lateral halves of the cerebrum of the brain

,cerebral 'palsy *n* a disability resulting from damage to the brain before or during birth and characterized by speech disturbance and lack of muscular coordination – compare SPASTIC PARALYSIS

cerebrate /'serəbrayt/ *vi* to use the mind; think – fml [back-formation fr *cerebration*, fr *cerebrum*] – **cerebration** /-'braysh(ə)n/ *n*

cerebrospinal /,serəbroh'spienl/ *adj* of the brain and spinal cord

cerebrospinal fluid *n* a liquid like blood serum that is secreted from the blood into the ventricles of the brain

,cerebro'vascular /-'vaskyoolə/ *adj* of or involving the brain and the blood vessels supplying it

cerebrum /'seribrəm/ *n, pl* **cerebrums, cerebra** /-brə/ **1** BRAIN 1a **2** the expanded front portion of the brain that in higher mammals overlies the rest of the brain and consists of the 2 cerebral hemispheres ☞ NERVE [L]

cerecloth /-,kloth/ *n* waxed cloth formerly used esp for wrapping a dead body [alter. of earlier *cered cloth* (waxed cloth)]

cerement /'siəmənt/ *n, archaic* a shroud for the dead – usu pl with sing. meaning [*cere* (to wax, wrap in a cerecloth; fr ME *ceren*, fr MF *cirer*, fr L *cerare*, fr *cera* wax) + *-ment*]

[1]**ceremonial** /,serə'mohnyəl, -ni·əl/ *adj* marked by, involved in, or belonging to ceremony – **ceremonialism** *n*, **ceremonialist** *n*, **ceremonially** *adv*

[2]**ceremonial** *n* **1a** a ceremonial act or action **b** a usu prescribed system of formalities or rituals **2** (a book containing) the order of service in the Roman Catholic church

ceremonious /,serə'mohnyəs, -ni·əs/ *adj* **1** ceremonial **2** devoted to form and ceremony; punctilious – **ceremoniously** *adv*, **ceremoniousness** *n*

ceremony /'serəməni/ *n* **1** a formal act or series of acts prescribed by ritual, protocol, or convention ⟨*the marriage ~*⟩ **2** (observance of) established procedures of civility or politeness [ME *ceremonie*, fr MF *cérémonie*, fr L *caerimonia*]

Cerenkov radiation /chir'(y)engkəf, -kof/ *n* light

produced by charged particles (e g electrons) passing through a transparent medium at a speed greater than that of light in the same medium [P A *Cherenkov* b1904 Russ physicist]

cerise /sə'rees, -'reez/ *n or adj* (a) light purplish red [F, lit., cherry, fr LL *ceresia* – more at CHERRY]

cerium /'siəri·əm/ *n* a malleable ductile metallic element that is the most abundant of the rare-earth group ☞ PERIODIC TABLE [NL, fr *Ceres*, goddess of agriculture] – **ceric** /'siərik, 'serik/ *adj*

cermet /'suhmit/ *n* an alloy of a heat-resistant ceramic material and a metal, used esp for turbine blades [*cer*amic + *met*al]

ceroplastic /,si(ə)roh'plastik; *also* -'plah-/ *adj* **1** of or relating to modelling in wax **2** modelled in wax [Gk *kēroplastikos*, fr *kēros* wax + *plastikos* plastic]

cert /suht/ *n, Br* CERTAINTY 1; *esp* a horse that is sure to win a race – infml ⟨*a dead ~ for the 4.30*⟩

[1]**certain** /'suhtn/ *adj* **1** fixed, settled ⟨*guaranteed a ~ percentage of the profit*⟩ **2a** of a particular but unspecified character, quantity, or degree ⟨*the house has a ~ charm*⟩ **b** named but not known ⟨*a ~ Bill Clarke*⟩ **3a** established beyond doubt or question; definite ⟨*it is ~ that we exist*⟩ **b** unerring, dependable ⟨*her discernment was ~*⟩ **4a** inevitable ⟨*the ~ advance of age and decay*⟩ **b** incapable of failing; sure – + infinitive ⟨*she is ~ to do well*⟩ **5a** assured in mind; convinced ⟨*I'm ~ she saw me*⟩ **b** assured in action; sure ⟨*be ~ you catch your train*⟩ [ME, fr OF, fr (assumed) VL *certanus*, fr L *certus*, fr pp of *cernere* to sift, discern, decide; akin to Gk *krinein* to separate, decide, judge, *keirein* to cut – more at SHEAR] – **certainly** *adv* – **for certain** as a certainty; assuredly

[2]**certain** *pron, pl in constr* certain ones ⟨*~ of the questions raised were thought to be irrelevant*⟩

certainty /-ti/ *n* **1** sthg certain **2** the quality or state of being certain

[1]**certificate** /sə'tifikət/ *n* a document containing a certified statement; *esp* one declaring the status or qualifications of the holder ⟨*a birth ~*⟩ [ME *certificat*, fr MF, fr ML *certificatum*, fr LL, neut of *certificatus*, pp of *certificare* to certify]

[2]**certificate** /sə'tifikayt/ *vt* to testify to, authorize by, or award with a certificate – **certification** /,suhtifi'kaysh(ə)n/ *n*, **certificatory** /,suh'tifikət(ə)ri, ,suhtifi'kayt(ə)ri/ *adj*

Certificate of Secondary Education *n* a British examination in any of many subjects, which is less academic than the O level, and is taken usu at the age of about 16

certify /'suhtifie/ *vt* **1a** to confirm, esp officially in writing **b** to declare officially as being true or as meeting a standard **c** to declare officially the insanity of **2** to certificate, license ⟨*a* certified *teacher*⟩ **3** *chiefly NAm* to guarantee the payment or value of (a cheque) by endorsing on the front [ME *certifien*, fr MF *certifier*, fr LL *certificare*, fr L *certus* certain – more at CERTAIN] – **certifiable** /-,fie·əbl/ *adj*, **certifiably** *adv*, **certifier** /-,fie·ə/ *n*

certiorari /,suhtiaw'reəri, -shiaw-/ *n* a writ of a superior court calling for the records of proceedings in an inferior court [ME, fr L, to be informed; fr the use of this word in the writ]

certitude /'suhti,tyoohd/ *n* the state of being or feeling certain [ME, fr LL *certitudo*, fr L *certus*]

cerulean /si'roohli·ən/ *adj* deep sky blue in colour [L *caeruleus* dark blue]

cerumen /si'roohmən/ *n* the yellow waxy secretion from the outer ear [NL, irreg fr L *cera* wax, prob fr Gk *kēros*; akin to Lith *korys* honeycomb] – **ceruminous** /si'roohminəs/ *adj*

ceruse /'siə,roohs, si'roohs/ *n* white lead as a pigment [ME, fr MF *céruse*, fr L *cerussa*]

cervic-, cervici-, cervico- *comb form* neck; cervix ⟨cervic*itis*⟩; cervical and ⟨cervico*thoracic*⟩ [L *cervic-, cervex* neck]

cervical /'suhvikl/ *adj* of a neck or cervix

cervine /'suh,vien/ *adj* of or resembling deer [L *cervinus* of a deer, fr *cervus* stag, deer – more at HART]

cervix /'suhviks/ *n, pl* **cervices** /-viseez/, **cervixes 1** (the back part of) the neck **2** a constricted portion of an organ or body part; *esp* the narrow outer end of the uterus ☞ REPRODUCTION [L *cervic-, cervix*]

cesarean *also* **cesarian** /si'zeəri·ən/ *n, NAm* a caesarean – **cesarean** *also* **cesarian** *adj*

cesium /'seezi·əm/ *n, NAm* caesium

cessation /si'saysh(ə)n/ *n* a temporary or final stop; an ending [ME *cessacioun*, fr MF *cessation*, fr L *cessation-, cessatio* delay, idleness, fr *cessatus*, pp of *cessare* to delay, be idle – more at CEASE]

cesser /'sesə/ *n* an ending or cessation in law (e g of interest or liability) [MF, fr *cesser* to cease]

cession /'sesh(ə)n/ *n* the act or an instance of yielding rights, property, or esp territory [ME, fr MF, fr L *cession-, cessio*, fr *cessus*, pp of *cedere* to withdraw – more at CEDE]

cesspit /'ses,pit/ *n* **1** a pit for the disposal of refuse (e g sewage) **2** a corrupt or squalid place [*cess*pool + *pit*]

cesspool /'ses,poohl/ *n* an underground basin for liquid waste (e g household sewage) [by folk etymology fr ME *suspiral* vent, cesspool, fr MF *souspirail* ventilator, fr *soupirer* to sigh, fr L *suspirare*, lit., to draw a long breath, fr *sub-* up + *spirare* to breathe – more at SPIRIT]

cestode /'ses,tohd/ *n* any of a subclass of parasitic flatworms including the tapeworms, usu living in the intestines [deriv of Gk *kestos* girdle] – **cestode** *adj*

cesura /si'zhooərə/ *n* a caesura

cetacean /si'taysh(ə)n/ *n* any of an order of aquatic, mostly marine, mammals that includes the whales, dolphins, and porpoises [deriv of L *cetus* whale, fr Gk *kētos*] – **cetacean** *adj*, **cetaceous** /-shəs/ *adj*

cetane /'see,tayn/ *n* a colourless oily hydrocarbon found in petroleum [ISV *cet-* (deriv of L *cetus*) + *-ane*] – **cetyl** /'seetl/ *adj*

cetane number *n* a measure of the ignition properties of a diesel fuel – compare OCTANE NUMBER

cetane rating *n* CETANE NUMBER

ceteris paribus /,ketəris 'paribəs, 'pah-/ *adv* all other things being equal – fml [NL]

cha /chah/ *n* [1]CHAR

Chablis /'shabli/ *n, pl* **Chablis** /~/ a very dry white table wine produced in northern Burgundy [F, fr *Chablis*, town in France]

cha-cha /'chah ,chah/, **,cha-cha-'cha** *n* (a piece of music for performing) a fast rhythmic ballroom dance of Latin American origin [AmerSp *cha-cha-cha*] – **cha-cha** *vi*

chaconne /shə'kon/ *n* **1** an old Spanish dance tune resembling the passacaglia **2** a musical composition in 3_4 time typically consisting of variations on a repeated succession of chords [F & Sp; F *chaconne,* fr Sp *chacona*]

chad /chad/ *n* small pieces of paper or cardboard produced in punching paper tape or data cards; *also* a piece of chad [perh fr Sc, gravel]

Chad *n* a branch of the Afro-Asiatic language family comprising numerous languages of N Nigeria and the Cameroons [Lake *Chad,* central Africa]

chador, chadar, chuddar, chudder /ˈchudə/ *n* a large cloth serving as a veil and head covering worn by women in India and Iran; *esp* one, usu black, worn by Islamic women in Iran as a sign of religious orthodoxy [Hindi *caddar,* fr Per *chaddar*]

chaeta /ˈkeetə/ *n, pl* **chaetae** /-ˌtee/ a bristle, seta [NL, fr Gk *chaitē* long flowing hair] – **chaetal** *adj*

chaetognath /ˈkeetəgˌnath/ *n* any of a phylum of small free-swimming marine worms with movable curved bristles on either side of the mouth [deriv of Gk *chaitē* + *gnathos* jaw – more at GNATH-] – **chaetognath** *adj,* **chaetognathan** /keeˈtognəthən/ *adj or n*

[1]**chafe** /chayf/ *vt* **1** to irritate, vex **2** to warm (part of the body) by rubbing **3a** to rub so as to wear away **b** to make sore (as if) by rubbing ~ *vi* **1** to feel irritation or discontent; fret ⟨~s *at his restrictive desk job*⟩ **2** to become sore or uncomfortable as a result of rubbing [ME *chaufen* to warm, fr MF *chaufer,* fr (assumed) VL *calfare,* alter. of L *calefacere,* fr *calēre* to be warm + *facere* to make – more at [1]DO]

[2]**chafe** *n* (injury or wear caused by) friction

chafer /ˈchayfə/ *n* a cockchafer or related large beetle [ME *cheaffer,* fr OE *ceafor;* akin to OE *ceafl* jowl – more at JOWL]

[1]**chaff** /chaf, chahf/ *n* **1** the seed coverings and other debris separated from the seed in threshing grain **2** worthless matter – esp in *separate the wheat from the chaff* **3** chopped straw, hay, etc used for animal feed **4** material (e g strips of foil) ejected into the air to reflect enemy radar waves and so prevent detection [ME *chaf,* fr OE *ceaf;* akin to OHG *cheva* husk] – **chaffy** *adj*

[2]**chaff** *n* light jesting talk; banter [prob fr [1]*chafe*]

[3]**chaff** *vt* to tease good-naturedly ~ *vi* to jest, banter

chaffinch /ˈchafinch/ *n* a European finch with a reddish breast, a bluish head, and white wing bars [ME, fr OE *ceaffinc,* fr *ceaf* + *finc* finch]

ˈchafing ˌdish /ˈchayfing/ *n* a dish for cooking or keeping food warm, esp over a spirit burner at the table [ME *chafing,* prp of *chaufen, chafen* to warm]

ˈChagas' diˌsease /ˈshahgəs(iz)/ *n* an often fatal tropical American disease caused by a trypanosome and characterized esp by high fever [Carlos *Chagas* †1934 Brazilian physician]

chagrin /ˈshagrin/ *vt or n* (to subject to) mental distress caused by humiliation, disappointment, or failure [n F, fr *chagrin* sad; vb fr n]

chai /chie/ *n, pl* **chais** a building for the fermentation and storage of wine [F, alter. of *quai* quay, platform]

Chaima /ˈchiemə/ *n* a member, or the language, of a Cariban people of Venezuela

[1]**chain** /chayn/ *n* **1a** a series of usu metal links or rings connected to or fitted into one another and used for various purposes (e g support or restraint) **b** an ornament or badge of office consisting of such a series of links **c(1)** a measuring instrument of 100 links used in surveying **(2)** a unit of length equal to 66ft (about 20.12m) ☞ UNIT **2** sthg that confines, restrains, or secures – usu pl ⟨*the* ~s *of ignorance*⟩ **3a** a series of linked or connected things ⟨*a* ~ *of events*⟩ ⟨*a mountain* ~⟩ **b** a group of associated establishments (e g shops or hotels) under the same ownership ⟨*a* ~ *of supermarkets*⟩ **c** a number of atoms or chemical groups united like links in a chain [ME *cheyne,* fr OF *chaeine,* fr L *catena;* akin to L *cassis* net]

[2]**chain** *vt* to fasten, restrict, or confine (as if) with a chain – often + *up* or *down*

ˈchain ˌgang *n, sing or pl in constr* a gang of convicts chained together, usu while doing hard labour outside prison

ˈchain ˌletter *n* a letter containing a request that copies of it, sometimes together with money or goods, be sent to a specified number of other people who should then repeat the process

ˈchain ˌmail *n* flexible armour of interlinked metal rings

ˈchain ˌprinter *n* a line printer in which the type is carried on a continuous band past a line of hammers

chain reaction *n* **1** a series of events so related to each other that each one initiates the next **2** a self-sustaining chemical or nuclear reaction yielding energy or products that cause further reactions of the same kind

ˈchain ˌsaw *n* a portable power saw that has teeth linked together to form a continuous revolving chain

ˈchain-ˌsmoke *vb* to smoke (esp cigarettes) continually, usu by lighting one cigarette from the previous one smoked

ˈchain ˌstitch *n* an ornamental embroidery or crochet stitch that resembles a linked chain

ˈchain ˌstore *n* any of several usu retail shops under the same ownership and selling the same lines of goods

ˈchainˌwheel /-ˌweel/ *n* a sprocket wheel (e g on a bicycle) that transmits power

[1]**chair** /cheə/ *n* **1** a seat for 1 person, usu having 4 legs and a back and sometimes arms **2a** an office or position of authority or dignity; *specif* a professorship ⟨*holds a university* ~⟩ **b** a chairman **3** SEDAN CHAIR **4** a deep-grooved metal block fastened to a sleeper to hold a rail in place [ME *chaiere,* fr OF, fr L *cathedra,* fr Gk *kathedra,* fr *kata-* cata- + *hedra* seat – more at SIT]

[2]**chair** *vt* **1** to install in office **2** to preside as chairman of **3** *chiefly Br* to carry shoulder-high in acclaim ⟨*the time you won your town the race we* ~ed *you through the market place* –A E Housman⟩

ˈchair ˌlift *n* a ski lift with seats for passengers

ˈchairman /-mən/, *fem* **ˈchairˌlady, ˈchairˌwoman** *n* **1** one who presides over or heads a meeting, committee, organization, or board of directors **2** a radio or television presenter; *esp* one who coordinates unscripted or diverse material **3** a carrier of a sedan chair – **chairmanship** *n*

ˈchairˌperson /-ˌpuhs(ə)n/ *n, pl* **chairpersons** a chairman or chairwoman

chaise /shez, shayz/ *n* a light carriage, usu having 2 wheels and a folding top [F, chair, chaise, alter. of OF *chaiere*]

ˌchaise ˈlongue /long·g/ *n, pl* **chaise longues** *also* **chaises longues** /~ long·g(z)/ a low sofa with only 1 armrest, on which one may recline [F, lit., long chair]

chalaza /kəˈlahzə, -ˈla-/ *n, pl* **chalazae** /-zi/, **chalazas** either of a pair of spiral bands in the white of a bird's egg that extend from the yolk and are attached to opposite ends of the lining membrane [NL, fr Gk, hailstone; akin to Per *zhāla* hail] – **chalazal** *adj*

chalcedony /kalˈsidəni, -ˈsedəni/ *n* a translucent quartz that is often pale blue or grey and is used as a gemstone [ME *calcedonie*, a precious stone, fr LL *chalcedonius*, fr Gk *Chalkēdōn* Chalcedon, former city in Turkey] – **chalcedonic** /ˌkalsiˈdonik/ *adj*

chalcid /ˈkalsid/ *n* any of various related and typically minute insects parasitic in the larval state on the larvae or pupae of other insects [deriv of Gk *chalkos* copper] – **chalcid** *adj*

chalcopyrite /ˌkalkəˈpieriet/ *n* a brassy-yellow mineral consisting of copper-iron sulphide [NL *chalcopyrites*, fr Gk *chalkos* + L *pyrites*]

Chaldean /kalˈdee·ən/ *n* **1** a member of an ancient Semitic people once dominant in Babylonia **2** the Semitic language of the Chaldeans [L *Chaldaeus* Chaldean, astrologer, fr Gk *Chaldaios*, fr *Chaldaia* Chaldea, region of ancient Babylonia] – **Chaldean** *adj*

Chaldee /ˈkalˌdee, ˌ-ˈ-/ *n* **1** the Aramaic vernacular that was the original language of some parts of the Old Testament **2** (a) Chaldean [ME *Caldey*, prob fr MF *chaldée*, fr L *Chaldaeus*]

chalet /ˈshalay/ *n* **1** a hut used by herdsmen in the Alps **2a** a usu wooden house with a steeply sloping roof and widely overhanging eaves, common esp in Switzerland **b** a small house or hut used esp for temporary accommodation (e g at a holiday camp) [F]

chalice /ˈchalis/ *n* **1** a drinking cup; a goblet **2** an esp gold or silver cup used to hold the wine at communion [ME, fr AF, fr L *calic-, calix*; akin to Gk *kalyx* calyx]

[1]**chalk** /chawk/ *n* **1** a soft white, grey, or buff limestone composed chiefly of the shells of small marine organisms **2** a short stick of chalk or chalky material used esp for writing and drawing [ME, fr OE *cealc*; akin to OHG & MLG *kalk* lime; all fr a prehistoric WGmc word borrowed fr L *calc-, calx* lime, fr Gk *chalix* pebble; akin to Gk *skallein* to hoe – more at SHELL] – **chalky** *adj*

[2]**chalk** *vt* **1** to rub or mark with chalk **2** to write or draw with chalk **3** to set down or add up (as if) with chalk – usu + *up* ⟨~ *up the score*⟩ ~ *vi*, *Br* to act as scorer for a darts match

chalk out *vt* to delineate roughly; sketch ⟨chalk out *a plan of action*⟩

chalk up *vt* **1** to ascribe, credit; *specif* to charge to sby's account ⟨chalk *it* up *to me*⟩ **2** to attain, achieve ⟨chalked up *a record score for the season*⟩

[1]**challenge** /ˈchalinj/ *vt* **1** to order to halt and prove identity ⟨*the sentry* ~d *the stranger at the gates*⟩ **2** to dispute, esp as being unjust, invalid, or outmoded; impugn ⟨*uncovered new data that* ~s *old assumptions*⟩ **3** to question formally the legality or legal qualifications of (e g a juror) **4a** to defy boldly; dare **b** to call out to duel, combat, or competition **5** to stimulate by testing the skill of (sby or sthg) ⟨*maths* ~s *him*⟩ **6** to administer infective (antigenic) material to (an organism) in order to ascertain whether experimental immunization has been effective [ME *chalengen* to accuse, fr OF *chalengier*, fr L *calumniari* to accuse falsely, fr *calumnia* calumny] – **challenger** *n*, **challenging** *adj*, **challengingly** *adv*

[2]**challenge** *n* **1a** a calling to account or into question; a protest **b** a command given by a sentry, watchman, etc to halt and prove identity **c** a questioning of right or validity **2a** a summons that is threatening or provocative; *specif* a call to a duel **b** an invitation to compete **3** (sthg having) the quality of being demanding or stimulating ⟨*the job presented a real* ~⟩ **4** a test of immunity by reexposure to infective (antigenic) material after specific immunization with it

chalone /ˈkaˌlohn/ *n* a local hormone that controls, esp by inhibition, the growth and differentiation of tissue cells [Gk *chalōn*, prp of *chalan* to slacken]

[1]**chamber** /ˈchaymbə/ *n* **1** a natural or artificial enclosed space or cavity **2a(1)** a room where a judge hears private cases – usu pl with sing. meaning **(2)** *pl* a set of rooms used by a group of barristers **b** a reception room in an official or state building **3** (a hall used by) a legislative or judicial body; *esp* either of 2 houses of a legislature **4** the part of a gun that holds the charge or cartridge **5** *archaic* a room; *esp* a bedroom [ME *chambre*, fr OF, fr LL *camera*, fr L, arched roof, fr Gk *kamara* vault; akin to L *camur* curved]

[2]**chamber** *vt* to accommodate (e g a charge) in the chamber of a firearm

chamberlain /ˈchaymbəlin/ *n* **1** a chief officer of a royal or noble household **2** a treasurer (e g of a corporation) [ME, fr OF *chamberlayn*, of Gmc origin; akin to OHG *chamarling* chamberlain, fr *chamara* chamber, fr LL *camera*]

ˈchamberˌmaid /-ˌmayd/ *n* a maid who cleans bedrooms and makes beds (e g in a hotel)

ˈchamber ˌmusic *n* music written for a small group of instruments

ˌChamber of ˈCommerce *n* an association of businessmen to promote commercial and industrial interests in the community

ˌchamber of ˈhorrors *n* a hall in which objects of macabre interest (e g instruments of torture) are exhibited; *broadly* any horrifying or frightening place, situation, etc

ˈchamber ˌorchestra *n* a small orchestra, usu with 1 player for each instrumental part

ˈchamber ˌpot *n* a bowl-shaped receptacle for urine and faeces, used chiefly in the bedroom

[1]**chambré** /ˈshombray (*Fr* ʃɑ̃ːbre)/ *adj*, *of wine* at room temperature [F, fr pp of *chambrer* to put in a room, fr *chambre* room]

[2]**chambré** *vt* **ˈchamˌbréing** /-ˌbraying/ to bring (wine) to room temperature

chameleon /shəˈmeelyən, kə-/ *n* **1** any of a group of Old World lizards with a long tongue, a prehensile tail, and the ability to change the colour of the skin **2** sby or sthg changeable; *specif* a fickle person [ME *camelion*, fr MF, fr L *chamaeleon*, fr Gk *chamaileōn*, fr *chamai* on the ground + *leōn* lion – more at HUMBLE] – **chameleonic** /-liˈonik/ *adj*

[1]**chamfer** /ˈchamfə/ *n* a bevelled edge [MF *chanfreint*, fr pp of *chanfraindre* to bevel, fr *chant* edge (fr L *canthus* iron tyre) + *fraindre* to break, fr L *frangere* – more at [1]CANT, BREAK]

[2]**chamfer** *vt* to cut a chamfer on

chammy, shammy /'shami/ *n* CHAMOIS 2 [by shortening & alter.]

chamois /'shamwah/ *n, pl* **chamois** *also* **chamoix** /'shamwah(z)/ **1** a small goatlike antelope of Europe and the Caucasus **2** a soft pliant leather prepared from the skin of the chamois or sheep, used esp as a cloth for polishing [MF, fr LL *camox*]

chamomile /'kamə,miel/ *n* camomile

[1]**champ** /champ/ *vt* **1** to munch (food) noisily **2** to gnaw, bite ~ *vi* **1** to make biting or gnashing movements **2** to eat noisily **3** to show impatience or eagerness – usu in *champ at the bit* ⟨*the children were* ~ing *at the bit to get on board*⟩ [perh imit]

[2]**champ** *n* a champion – infml

champagne /sham'payn/ *n* a white sparkling wine made in the old province of Champagne in France [F, fr *Champagne*, region of France]

champaign /sham'payn/ *n* an expanse of level open country; a plain [ME *champaine*, fr MF *champagne*, fr LL *campania* – more at CAMPAIGN] – **champaign** *adj*

champers /'shampəz/ *n, Br* champagne – infml [by shortening & alter.]

champerty /'champəti/ *n* an illegal action whereby an outsider aids sby involved in a law suit (e g by paying for his/her defence) in the hope of receiving a share of the property, money, etc at stake [ME *champartie*, fr MF *champart* field rent, fr *champ* field (fr L *campus*) + *part* portion – more at [1]CAMP, [1]PART] – **champertous** *adj*

champignon /'shompin,yonh (*Fr* ʃɑ̃piɲɔ̃)/ *n* any of various edible mushrooms, esp the common meadow mushroom [MF, fr *champagne*]

[1]**champion** /'champi·ən/ *n* **1** a militant supporter of, or fighter for, a cause or person ⟨*an outspoken* ~ *of civil rights*⟩ **2** one who shows marked superiority; *specif* the winner of a competitive event [ME, fr OF, fr ML *campion-, campio*, of WGmc origin]

[2]**champion** *vt* to protect or fight for as a champion

[3]**champion** *adj, chiefly N Eng* superb, splendid – infml

'champion,ship /-,ship/ *n* **1** the act of championing; defence ⟨*his* ~ *of freedom of speech*⟩ **2** a contest held to determine a champion

champlevé /'shomlə,vay, ,--'- (*Fr* ʃɑ̃ləve)/ *adj or n* (in) a style of enamel decoration in which the enamel colours are fired in shallow depressions pressed or cut into a metal surface – compare CLOISONNÉ [F]

[1]**chance** /chahns/ *n* **1a** an event without discernible human intention or observable cause ⟨*this is a strange* ~ *that throws you and me together* – Charles Dickens⟩ **b** the incalculable (assumed) element in existence; that which determines unaccountable happenings ⟨*we met by* ~⟩ **2** a situation favouring some purpose; an opportunity **3** an opportunity of dismissing a batsman in cricket **4a** the possibility of a specified or favourable outcome in an uncertain situation ⟨*we have almost no* ~ *of winning*⟩ **b** *pl* the more likely indications ⟨~s *are he's already heard the news*⟩ **5** a risk ⟨*took a* ~ *on it*⟩ [ME, fr OF, fr (assumed) VL *cadentia* fall, fr L *cadent-, cadens*, prp of *cadere* to fall; akin to Skt *śad* to fall] – **chance** *adj*, **chanceless** *adj*

[2]**chance** *vi* **1** to take place or come about by chance; happen ⟨*it* ~d *that the street was empty*⟩ **2** to come or light *on* or *upon* by chance ⟨~d *on the idea*⟩ ~ *vt* to accept the hazard of; risk

chancel /'chahnsl/ *n* the part of a church containing the altar and seats for the clergy and choir ☞ CHURCH [ME, fr MF, fr LL *cancellus* lattice, fr L *cancelli*; fr the latticework enclosing it]

chancellery, chancellory /'chahns(ə)ləri/ *n* **1** the position or department of a chancellor **2** the office or staff of an embassy or consulate

chancellor /'chahns(ə)lə/ *n* **1a** the secretary of a nobleman, prince, or king **b** LORD CHANCELLOR **c** a Roman Catholic priest heading a diocesan chancery **2** the titular head of a British university **3** a usu lay legal officer of an Anglican diocese **4** the chief minister of state in some European countries [ME *chanceler*, fr OF *chancelier*, fr LL *cancellarius* doorkeeper, secretary, fr *cancellus*] – **chancellorship** *n*

Chancellor of the Duchy of Lancaster *n* a British government minister who has no direct responsibility for a government department but is usu a member of the cabinet

,chancellor of the ex'chequer *n, often cap C&E* a member of the British cabinet in charge of public finances

chancery /'chahnsəri/ *n* **1a Chancery Division, Chancery** a division of the High Court having jurisdiction over causes in equity ☞ LAW **b** a US court of equity **2** a record office for public archives or those of ecclesiastical, legal, or diplomatic proceedings **3a** a chancellor's court or office **b** the office in which the business of a Roman Catholic diocese is transacted and recorded **c** CHANCELLERY 2 [ME *chancerie*, alter. of *chancellerie* chancellery, fr OF, fr *chancelier*]

chancre /'shangkə/ *n* the initial lesion of some diseases, specif syphilis [F, fr L *cancer*] – **chancrous** /-krəs/ *adj*

chancroid /'shang,kroyd/ *n* a bacterial venereal disease – **chancroidal** /shang'kroydl, '-,--/ *adj*

chancy /'chahnsi/ *adj* uncertain in outcome or prospect; risky [[1]CHANCE + [1]-Y] – **chancily** *adj*, **chanciness** *n*

chandelier /,shandə'liə/ *n* a branched often ornate lighting fixture suspended from a ceiling [F, lit., candlestick, modif of L *candelabrum*]

chandler /'chahndlə/ *n* a retail dealer in supplies and equipment of a specified kind ⟨*a ship's* ~⟩ ⟨*a corn* ~⟩ [ME *chandeler* maker or seller of candles, fr MF *chandelier*, fr OF, fr *chandelle* candle, fr L *candela*]

chandlery /'chahndləri/ *n* **1** a place where candles are kept **2** the business or merchandise of a chandler

[1]**change** /chaynj/ *vt* **1a** to make different **b** to give a different position, direction, status, or aspect to ⟨*we* ~d *our thinking on the matter*⟩ ⟨*stop* changing *your mind*⟩ **c** to exchange, reverse – often + *over* or *round* ⟨*just* ~ *the speaker leads over*⟩ **2a** to replace with another ⟨*let's* ~ *the subject*⟩ **b** to move from one to another ⟨~ *sides*⟩ **c** to exchange for an equivalent sum or comparable item **d** to undergo a loss or modification of ⟨*foliage* changing *colour*⟩ **e** to put fresh clothes or covering on ⟨~ *a bed*⟩ ~ *vi* **1** to become different ⟨*her mood* ~s *every hour*⟩ **2** *of the moon* to pass from one phase to another **3** to go from one vehicle of a public transport system to another **4** *of the (male) voice* to shift to a lower register; BREAK 9a **5** to undergo transformation, transition, or conversion ⟨*winter* ~d *to spring*⟩ ⟨*most industries have* ~d *to the metric system*⟩ **6** to put

on different clothes **7** to engage in giving sthg and receiving sthg in return – usu + *with* [ME *changen*, fr OF *changier*, fr L *cambiare* to exchange, of Celt origin; akin to OIr *camm* crooked; akin to Gk *skambos* crooked] – **changer** *n* – **change hands** to pass from the possession of one person to that of another

[2]**change** *n* **1a** a (marked) alteration ⟨*has undergone a ~ since he was married*⟩ **b** a substitution ⟨*a ~ of players*⟩ **c** the passage of the moon from one phase to another; *specif* the coming of the new moon **2** an alternative set, esp of clothes **3a** money of lower denominations received in exchange for an equivalent sum of higher denominations ⟨*have you got ~ for a pound?*⟩ **b** money returned when a payment exceeds the amount due **c** coins of low denominations ⟨*a pocketful of ~*⟩ **4** an order in which a set of bells is struck in change ringing – **changeful** *adj*, **changefully** *adv*, **changefulness** n, **changeless** *adj*, **changelessly** *adv*, **changelessness** *n*

changeable /'chaynjəbl/ *adj* **1** able or apt to vary **2** capable of being altered or exchanged **3** fickle – **changeableness** *n*, **changeably** *adv*, **changeability** /-'biləti/ *n*

change down *vi* to engage a lower gear in a motor vehicle

changeling /'chaynjling/ *n* a child secretly exchanged for another in infancy; *specif* a half-witted or ugly elf-child left in place of a human child by fairies

,change of 'heart *n* a complete reversal in attitude

,change of 'life *n the* menopause

'change-,over *n* a conversion to a different system or function

'change ,ringing *n* the art or practice of ringing a set of tuned (church) bells in continually varying order

change up *vi* to engage a higher gear in a motor vehicle

'changing ,room /'chaynjing/ *n* a room in which one changes one's clothes (e g for sport)

[1]**channel** /'chanl/ *n* **1a** the bed where a stream of water runs **b** the deeper part of a river, harbour, or strait **c** a narrow region of sea between 2 land masses **d** a path along which information passes or can be stored (e g on a recording tape) ⟨*there is no sound coming from the left ~ of the stereo*⟩ **e** a course or direction of thought, action, or communication – often pl with sing. meaning ⟨*used official ~s to air his grievance*⟩ **f(1)** a band of frequencies of sufficient width for a transmission (e g from a radio or television station) **(2)** a television station ⟨*switch over to another ~*⟩ ☞ TELEVISION **2** a usu tubular passage, esp for liquids **3** a long gutter, groove, or furrow ☞ ARCHITECTURE [ME *chanel*, fr OF, fr L *canalis* pipe, channel – more at CANAL]

[2]**channel** *vt* **-ll-** (*NAm* **-l-**, **-ll-**), **channelling** /'chanl·ing/ **1** to form or wear a channel in **2** to convey into or through a channel; direct ⟨*~ his energy into constructive activities*⟩

channel·ize, -ise /'chanl,iez/ *vt* to channel – **channelization** /-ie'zaysh(ə)n/ *n*

chanson /'shans(ə)n (*Fr* ʃɑ̃sɔ̃)/ *n, pl* **chansons** /'shans(ə)nz (*Fr* ~)/ a (French cabaret) song [F, fr L *cantion-*, *cantio*, fr *cantus*, pp]

[1]**chant** /chahnt/ *vi* **1** to sing a chant **2** to recite in a monotonous tone ~ *vt* to utter as in chanting [ME *chaunten*, fr MF *chanter*, fr L *cantare*, fr *cantus*, pp of *canere*; akin to OE *hana* cock, Gk *kanachē* ringing sound]

[2]**chant** *n* **1** (the music or performance of) a repetitive melody used for liturgical singing in which as many syllables are assigned to each note as required **2** a rhythmic monotonous utterance or song

chanter /'chahntə/ *n* the reed pipe of a bagpipe with finger holes on which the melody is played [[1]CHANT + [2]-ER]

chanterelle /,shantə'rel, ,shon-/ *n* a rich-yellow edible mushroom [F, fr NL *cantharella*, dim. of L *cantharus* drinking-vessel]

chanteuse /,shan'tuhz, ,shon-/ *n, pl* **chanteuses** /~/ a female (nightclub or cabaret) singer [F, fem of *chanteur* singer, fr *chanter*]

chanticleer /,chanti'kliə/ *n* – used as a poetic name of the domestic cock [ME *Chantecleer*, cock in verse narratives, fr OF *Chantecler*, cock in the poem *Roman de Renart*]

Chantilly, Chantilly lace /shon'tili, shan-/ *n* a delicate lace with a 6-sided mesh ground and a floral or scrolled design [*Chantilly*, town in France]

chantry /'chahntri/ *n* (a chapel or altar founded under) an endowment for the chanting of masses for the founder's soul ☞ CHURCH [ME *chanterie*, fr MF, singing, fr *chanter*]

Chanukah /'hahnoo,kah/ *n* Hanukkah

chaos /'kayos/ *n* **1** *often cap* the confused unorganized state of primordial matter before the creation of distinct forms – compare COSMOS 1 **2a** a state of utter confusion **b** a confused mass [L, fr Gk – more at [1]GUM] – **chaotic** /kay'otik/ *adj*, **chaotically** *adv*

[1]**chap** /chap/ *n* a man, fellow – infml [short for *chapman* (merchant, pedlar), fr ME, fr OE *cēapman*, fr *cēap* trade + *man*]

[2]**chap** *vb* **-pp-** to (cause to) open in slits or cracks ⟨*~ped lips*⟩ [ME *chappen*; akin to MD *cappen* to cut down]

[3]**chap** *n* a crack in the skin caused by exposure to wind or cold

[4]**chap** *n* **1** (the fleshy covering of) a jaw **2** the lower front part of the face *USE* usu pl with sing. meaning [prob fr [2]*chap*]

chaparral /,shapə'ral/ *n* a dense (N American) area of shrubs or dwarf trees, esp evergreen oaks ☞ PLANT [Sp, fr *chaparro* dwarf evergreen oak, fr Basque *txapar*]

chapati, chapatti /chə'pati, -'pahti/ *n, pl* **chapati, chapaties, chapatis, chapatti, chapatties, chapattis** a thin unleavened usu round bread [Hindi *capati*, fr Skt *carpaṭi* thin cake, fr *carpaṭa* flat]

chape /chayp/ *n* the metal mounting or trimming of (the point of) a scabbard [ME, scabbard, fr MF, cape, fr LL *cappa*]

[1]**chapel** /'chapl/ *n* **1a** a place of worship serving a residence or institution **b** a room or bay in a church for prayer or minor religious services **2** a choir of singers belonging to a chapel **3** a chapel service or assembly **4** *sing or pl in constr* the members of a trade union, esp in a printing office **5** a place of worship used by a Christian group other than an established church ⟨*a nonconformist ~*⟩ [ME, fr OF *chapele*, fr ML *cappella*, fr dim. of LL *cappa* cloak; fr the cloak of St Martin of Tours preserved in a chapel built for that purpose]

[2]**chapel** *adj, chiefly Br* belonging to a Nonconformist church

ˌ**chapel of** ˈ**ease** *n* a dependent church built to accommodate parishioners living in remote areas

[1]**chaperon, chaperone** /ˈshapəˌrohn/ *n* one delegated to ensure propriety; *esp* a married or older woman who accompanies a younger woman on social occasions [F *chaperon,* lit., hood, fr MF, head covering, fr *chape*]

[2]**chaperon, chaperone** *vt* to act as chaperon to; escort – **chaperonage** *n*

chapfallen /ˈchapˌfawlən/ *adj* depressed, dejected [[4]*chap* + *fallen*]

chaplain /ˈchaplin/ *n* **1** a clergyman in charge of a chapel **2** a clergyman officially attached to a branch of the armed forces, an institution, or a family or court [ME *chapelain,* fr OF, fr ML *cappellanus,* fr *cappella*] – **chaplaincy** /-si/ *n,* **chaplainship** *n*

chaplet /ˈchaplit/ *n* **1** a wreath to be worn on the head **2a** a string of beads **b** a part of a rosary comprising 5 decades [ME *chapelet,* fr MF, fr OF, dim. of *chapel* hat, garland, fr ML *cappellus* head covering, fr LL *cappa*] – **chapleted** /ˈchaplitid/ *adj*

chaps /chaps/ *n pl* leather leggings worn over the trousers, esp by N American ranch hands [modif of MexSp *chaparreras*]

chapter /ˈchaptə/ *n* **1a** a major division of a book **b** sthg resembling a chapter in being a significant specified unit ⟨*breaking his leg was the final event in a* ~ *of accidents*⟩ **2** (a regular meeting of) the canons of a cathedral or collegiate church, or the members of a religious house **3** a local branch of a society or fraternity [ME *chapitre* division of a book, meeting of canons, fr OF, fr LL *capitulum* division of a book & ML, meeting place of canons, fr L, dim. of *capit-, caput* head – more at HEAD]

ˌ**chapter and** ˈ**verse** *n* (a full specification of the source of) a piece of information [fr custom of citing passages in the Bible by chapter and verse number]

ˈ**chapter** ˌ**house** *n* the building or rooms where a chapter meets

[1]**char, charr** /chah/ *n, pl* **chars,** *esp collectively* **char** any of a genus of small-scaled trouts [origin unknown]

[2]**char** *vb* **-rr-** *vt* **1** to convert to charcoal or carbon, usu by heat; burn **2** to burn slightly; scorch ~ *vi* to become charred [back-formation fr *charcoal*]

[3]**char** *vi* **-rr-** to work as a cleaning woman [back-formation fr *charwoman*]

[4]**char** *n, Br* a charwoman – infml

[5]**char, cha** *n, Br* TEA 2 – infml [Hindi *cā,* fr Chin (Pek) *ch'a*[2]]

charabanc /ˈsharəˌbang/ *n, Br* an (old-fashioned) motor coach used for sightseeing [F *char à bancs,* lit., wagon with benches]

character /ˈkarəktə/ *n* **1a** a distinctive mark, usu in the form of a stylized graphic device **b** a graphic symbol (e g a hieroglyph or alphabet letter) used in writing or printing **c(1)** style of writing or printing **(2)** CIPHER 2 **2a** (any of) the mental or ethical qualities that make up and distinguish the individual **b(1)** (a group or kind distinguished by) a feature used to categorize things (e g organisms) **(2)** an inherited characteristic **(3)** the sum of the distinctive qualities characteristic of a breed, type, etc; the (distinctive) main or essential nature of sthg ⟨*a wine of great* ~⟩ ⟨*the unique* ~ *of the town*⟩ **3a** a person, esp one marked by notable or conspicuous traits ⟨*one of the real* ~s *in Westminster today*⟩ **b** any of the people portrayed in a novel, film, play, etc ⟨*he plays the main* ~ *in the film*⟩ **4** (good) reputation ⟨~ *assassination*⟩ **5** moral strength; integrity ⟨*a man of* ~⟩ [ME *caracter,* fr MF *caractère,* fr L *character* mark, distinctive quality, fr Gk *charaktēr,* fr *charassein* to scratch, engrave; akin to Lith *žerti* to scratch] – **characterless** *adj* – **in/out of character** in/not in accord with a person's usual qualities, traits, or behaviour

character actor *n* an actor capable of portraying personalities often markedly different from his/her own

[1]**characteristic** /ˌkarəktəˈristik/ *adj* serving to reveal and distinguish the individual character; typical – **characteristically** *adv*

[2]**characteristic** *n* **1** a distinguishing trait, quality, or property **2** the integral part of a common logarithm

character·ize, -ise /ˈkarəktəˌriez/ *vt* **1** to describe the character or quality of; delineate ⟨~d *him as soft-spoken yet ambitious*⟩ **2** to be a characteristic of; distinguish ⟨*a cool light fragrance* ~s *the cologne*⟩ – **characterization** /-ˈzaysh(ə)n/ *n*

charade /shəˈrahd; *NAm* -ˈrayd/ *n* **1** *pl but sing or pl in constr* a game in which one team acts out each syllable of a word or phrase while the other tries to guess what is being represented **2** a ridiculous pretence [F, fr Prov *charrado* conversation]

charcoal /ˈchahˌkohl/ *n* **1** a dark or black porous carbon prepared by partly burning vegetable or animal substances (e g wood or bone) **2** fine charcoal used in pencil form for drawing [ME *charcole*]

chard /chahd/ *n* a beet with large edible dark green leaves and succulent stalks [F *carde,* fr OProv *cardo* thistle-like vegetable, fr L *carduus* thistle, artichoke; akin to MLG *harst* rake, L *carrere* to card]

Charentais /ˌsharonˈtay (*Fr* ʃarɑ̃tɛ)/ *n* a small round melon with a yellowish green rind and faintly scented orange flesh [F *charentais* of Charente, fr *Charente,* department of France]

[1]**charge** /chahj/ *vt* **1a(1)** to place a usu powder charge in (a firearm) **(2)** to load or fill to capacity ⟨~ *the blast furnace with ore*⟩ **b(1)** to restore the active materials in (a storage battery) by the passage of a direct current in the opposite direction to that of discharge **(2)** to give an electric charge to **c** to place a heraldic charge on **d** to fill with (passionate) emotion, feeling, etc ⟨*the music is* ~d *with excitement*⟩ ⟨*a highly* ~d *issue*⟩ **2** to command or exhort with right or authority ⟨*I* ~ *you not to leave*⟩ **3a** to blame ⟨~s *him as the instigator*⟩ **b** to make an assertion against; accuse ⟨~s *him with armed robbery*⟩ **c** to place the blame for ⟨~ *her failure to negligence*⟩ **d** to assert as an accusation ⟨~s *that he distorted the data*⟩ **4** to rush violently at; attack; *also* to rush into (an opponent), usu illegally, in soccer, basketball, etc **5a(1)** to impose a financial obligation on ⟨~ *his estate with debts incurred*⟩ **(2)** to impose as financial obligation ⟨~ *debts to an estate*⟩ **b(1)** to fix or ask as fee or payment **(2)** to ask payment of (a person) ⟨~ *a client for expenses*⟩ **c** to record (an item) as an expense, debt, obligation, or liability ⟨~ *it to my account*⟩ ~ *vi* **1** to rush forwards (as if) in assault **2** to ask or set a price [ME *chargen,* fr OF *chargier,* fr LL *carricare,* fr L *carrus* wheeled vehicle – more at CAR] – **chargeable** *adj* – **charge with** to impose (a task or responsibility) on

[2]**charge** *n* **1** a shape, representation, or design

depicted on a heraldic achievement – compare DEVICE 3 **2a** the quantity that an apparatus is intended to receive and fitted to hold; *esp* the quantity of explosive for a gun or cannon **b** power, force ⟨*the emotional ~ of the drama*⟩ **c(1)** a basic property of matter that occurs in discrete natural units and is considered as negative (e g when belonging to an electron) or positive (e g when belonging to a proton) **(2)** a definite quantity of electricity; *esp* the charge that a storage battery is capable of yielding **3a** an obligation, requirement **b** control, supervision ⟨*has ~ of the home office*⟩ ⟨*I leave you in ~*⟩ **c** sby or sthg committed to the care of another **4a** an instruction, command **b** instructions given by a judge to a jury **5** the price demanded or paid for sthg ⟨*no admission ~*⟩ **6** an accusation, indictment, or statement of complaint **7** a violent rush forwards (e g in attack)

chargé d'affaires /ˌshahzhay daˈfeə/ *n, pl* **chargés d'affaires** /~ daˈfeə(z)/ **1** a diplomat who substitutes for an ambassador **2** a diplomatic representative inferior in rank to an ambassador [F, lit., one charged with affairs]

chargehand /ˈchahjˌhand/ *n, Br* a workman in charge of a group of workers or a job

ˈcharge ˌnurse *n* a usu male nurse in charge of a hospital ward – compare SISTER 4

[1]**charger** /ˈchahjə/ *n* a large flat meat dish [ME *chargeour*, akin to ME *chargen* to charge]

[2]**charger** *n* a horse for battle or parade [[1]CHARGE + [2]-ER]

ˈcharge ˌsheet *n* a police record of charges made and people to be tried in a magistrate's court

chariot /ˈchari·ət/ *n* **1** a light 4-wheeled pleasure or state carriage **2** a 2-wheeled horse-drawn vehicle of ancient times used in warfare and racing [ME, fr MF, fr OF, fr *char* wheeled vehicle, fr L *carrus*]

charioteer /ˌchari·əˈtiə/ *n* the driver of a chariot

charisma /kəˈrizmə/ *n* the special magnetic appeal, charm, or power of an individual (e g a political leader) that inspires popular loyalty and enthusiasm [Gk, favour, gift, fr *charizesthai* to favour, fr *charis* grace; akin to Gk *chairein* to rejoice – more at YEARN] – **charismatic** /ˌkarizˈmatik/ *adj*

charitable /ˈcharitəbl/ *adj* **1a** liberal in giving to the poor; generous **b** of or giving charity ⟨*~ institutions*⟩ **2** merciful or kind in judging others; lenient – **charitableness** *n*, **charitably** *adv*

charity /ˈcharəti/ *n* **1** benevolent goodwill towards or love of humanity **2a** kindly generosity and helpfulness, esp towards the needy or suffering; *also* aid given to those in need **b** an institution engaged in relief of the poor, sick, etc **c** public provision for the relief of the needy **3a** a gift for public benevolent purposes **b** an institution (e g a hospital) funded by such a gift **4** lenient judgment of others [ME *charite*, fr OF *charité*, fr LL *caritat-, caritas* Christian love, fr L, dearness, fr *carus* dear; akin to Skt *kāma* love]

charivari /ˌshahriˈvahri/ *n* a noisy and raucous medley of sounds; a din [F, fr LL *caribaria* headache, fr Gk *karēbaria*, fr *kara, karē* head + *barys* heavy – more at CEREBRAL, [1]GRIEVE]

charlady /ˈchahˌlaydi/ *n, Br* a charwoman

charlatan /ˈshahlət(ə)n/ *n* **1** QUACK 1 **2** one who pretends, usu ostentatiously, to have special knowledge or ability; a fraud [It *ciarlatano*, alter. of *cerretano*, lit., inhabitant of Cerreto, fr *Cerreto*, village in Italy] – **charlatanism, charlatanry** *n*

Charles's Wain /ˌchahlziz ˈwayn/ *n* URSA MAJOR [ME *Charlewayn*, fr OE *Charles Wægn* the waggon of Charles (Charlemagne, 'Charles the Great" †814 Frankish king)]

Charleston /ˈchahlstən/ *vi or n* (to dance) a lively ballroom dance in which the heels are swung sharply outwards on each step [*Charleston*, city in South Carolina, USA]

charlie /ˈchahli/ *n, Br* one who is or appears to be absurd or silly; a fool [rhyming slang *Charlie (Hunt)* cunt]

Charlie – a communications code word for the letter *c* [fr the name *Charlie*, dim. of *Charles*]

charlock /ˈchahˌlok/ *n* a wild mustard that is a weed of cultivated ground [ME *cherlok*, fr OE *cerlic*]

[1]**charm** /chahm/ *n* **1** an incantation **2** sthg worn to ward off evil or to ensure good fortune **3a** a quality that fascinates, allures, or delights **b** *pl* physical graces or attractions, esp of a woman **4** a small ornament worn on a bracelet or chain **5** a quantum property postulated to account for unexpectedly long lifetimes of particles that have quantum numbers identical to other elementary particles [ME *charme*, fr OF, fr L *carmen* song, fr *canere* to sing – more at CHANT] – **charmless** *adj*

[2]**charm** *vt* **1a** to affect (as if) by magic; bewitch **b** to soothe or delight by compelling attraction ⟨*~s the women with his suave manner*⟩ **2** to control (an animal) by the use of rituals (e g the playing of music) held to have magical powers ⟨*~ a snake*⟩ ~ *vi* to have the effect of a charm; fascinate

charmer /ˈchahmə/ *n* an attractive or captivating person – chiefly infml [[2]CHARM + [2]-ER]

charming /ˈchahming/ *adj* extremely pleasing or delightful; entrancing – **charmingly** *adv*

ˈcharnel ˌhouse /ˈchahn(ə)l/ *n* a building or chamber in which bodies or bones are deposited [ME *charnel*, fr MF, fr ML *carnale*, fr LL, neut of *carnalis* of the flesh – more at CARNAL]

Charolais /ˈsharəˌlay/ *n* any of a French breed of large white cattle used primarily for beef and crossbreeding [*Charolais*, district in E France]

charpoy /ˈchahˌpoy/ *n* a lightweight Indian bedstead [Hindi *cārpāī*]

charr /chah/ *n, pl* **charrs**, *esp collectively* **charr** [1]CHAR

[1]**chart** /chaht/ *n* **1a** an outline map showing the geographical distribution of sthg (e g climatic or magnetic variations) **b** a navigator's map **2a** a sheet giving information in tabular form; *esp, pl* *the* list of best-selling popular gramophone records (produced weekly) **b** [1]GRAPH **c** a schematic, usu large, diagram **d** a sheet of paper ruled and graduated for use in a recording instrument (e g on an electrocardiograph) [MF *charte*, fr L *charta* piece of papyrus, document – more at [3]CARD]

[2]**chart** *vt* **1** to make a chart of **2** to lay out a plan for **3** to display or mark (as if) on a chart

[1]**charter** /ˈchahtə/ *n* **1** a formal written instrument or contract **2a** a document that creates and defines the rights of a city, educational institution, or company **b** CONSTITUTION 4 **3** a special privilege, immunity, or exemption **4** a total or partial lease of a ship, aeroplane, etc for a particular use or group of people ⟨*low-cost travel on ~ flights to Greece and*

Spain⟩ [ME *chartre*, fr OF, fr ML *chartula*, fr L, dim. of *charta*]

[2]**charter** *vt* **1a** to establish or grant by charter **b** to certify as qualified ⟨*a* ~ed *accountant*⟩ ⟨*a* ~ed *surveyor*⟩ **2** to hire or lease for usu exclusive and temporary use ⟨~ed *a boat*⟩ – **charterer** *n*

,**chartered ac'countant** /'chahtəd/ *n, Br* a professionally qualified accountant

'**charter,house** /-,hows/ *n* a Carthusian monastery [by folk etymology fr MF *chartrouse*, irreg fr *Chartosse* (now *Chartreuse*), site in France of the first Carthusian monastery]

'**charter ,member** *n* an original member of a society or corporation

'**charter,party** /-,pahti/ *n* a contract for the hire of (part of) a ship for the conveyance of cargo or passengers [F *charte partie*, fr ML *charta partita*, lit., divided charter]

Chartism /'chah,tiz(ə)m/ *n* the principles and practices of a body of 19th-c English political reformers [ML *charta* charter, fr L, document] – **Chartist** *n*

Chartreuse /,shah'truhz/ *trademark* – used for an aromatic usu green or yellow liqueur

charwoman /'chah,woomən/ *n* a cleaning woman; *esp, Br* one employed in a private house [*chare* (chore) + *woman*]

chary /'cheəri/ *adj* **1** cautious; *esp* wary of taking risks **2** slow to grant or accept ⟨*a man very* ~ *of compliments*⟩ [ME, sorrowful, dear, fr OE *cearig* sorrowful, fr *caru* sorrow – more at CARE] – **charily** *adv*, **chariness** *n*

[1]**chase** /chays/ *vt* **1a** to follow rapidly or persistently; pursue ⟨*he's too old to* ~ *women*⟩ **b** to hunt **2** to cause to depart or flee; drive ⟨~ *the dog out of the pantry*⟩ **3** *chiefly Br* to investigate (a matter) or contact (a person, company, etc) in order to obtain information or (hasten) results – usu + *up* ~ *vi* **1** to chase an animal, person, or thing – usu + *after* **2** to rush, hasten ⟨~d *all over town looking for a place to stay*⟩ [ME *chasen*, fr MF *chasser*, fr (assumed) VL *captiare* – more at CATCH]

[2]**chase** *n* **1a** the act of chasing; pursuit **b** *the* hunting of wild animals **2** sthg pursued; a quarry **3** a tract of unenclosed land set aside for the breeding of animals for hunting and fishing **4** a steeplechase

[3]**chase** *vt* **1** to ornament (metal) by indenting with a hammer and tools that have no cutting edge **2** to make by such ornamentation ⟨~ *a monogram*⟩ [ME *chassen*, modif of MF *enchasser* to set (a jewel)]

[4]**chase** *n* **1** a groove cut in a surface for a pipe, wire, etc **2** the part of a cannon enclosing the barrel between the trunnions and the mouth of the muzzle [F *chas* eye of a needle, fr LL *capsus* enclosed space, fr L, cage, alter. of *capsa* box – more at [2]CASE]

[5]**chase** *n* a rectangular steel or iron frame into which printing type or blocks are locked for printing or platemaking [prob fr F *châsse* frame, fr L *capsa*]

chaser /'chaysə/ *n* **1** a glass or swallow of a mild drink (e g beer) taken after spirits; *also* a drink of spirits taken after a mild drink (e g beer) **2** a horse that is a steeplechaser [[1]CHASE + [2]-ER]

chasm /'kaz(ə)m/ *n* **1** a deep cleft in the earth **2** an apparently unbridgeable gap ⟨*a political* ~ *between the 2 countries*⟩ [L *chasma*, fr Gk; akin to L *hiare* to yawn – more at YAWN]

chassé /'shasay/ *vi or n* **chasséing** /'sha,saying/ (to make) a sliding dance step resembling a glissade [n F, fr pp of *chasser* to chase; vb fr n]

chassepot /'shas,poh, 'shasə,poh/ *n* a breech-loading rifle closed with a sliding bolt and firing paper cartridges [F, fr Antoine *Chassepot* †1905 F inventor]

chassis /'shasi/ *n, pl* **chassis** /'shasiz/ **1** a supporting framework for the body of a vehicle (e g a car) **2** the frame on which the electrical parts of a radio, television, etc are mounted [F *châssis*, fr (assumed) VL *capsicum*, fr L *capsa* box – more at [2]CASE]

chaste /chayst/ *adj* **1** abstinent from (unlawful or immoral) sexual intercourse; celibate **2** pure in thought and act; modest **3** severely simple in design or execution; austere ⟨*he wrote in a pure* ~ *style*⟩ [ME, fr OF, fr L *castus* pure – more at CASTE] – **chastely** *adv*, **chasteness** *n*, **chastity** /'chastəti/ *n*

chasten /'chays(ə)n/ *vt* **1** to correct by punishment or suffering; discipline **2** to subdue, restrain [alter. of obs *chaste* (to chasten), fr ME *chasten*, fr OF *chastier*, fr L *castigare*, fr *castus* + *-igare* (fr *agere* to drive) – more at AGENT] – **chastener** *n*

chastise /chas'tiez/ *vt* **1** to inflict punishment on, esp by whipping **2** to subject to severe reproof or criticism [ME *chastisen*, alter. of *chasten*] – **chastisement** *n*, **chastiser** *n*

'**chastity ,belt** /'chastəti/ *n* a device consisting of a belt with an attachment passing between the legs, designed to prevent sexual intercourse on the part of the woman wearing it

chasuble /'chazyoobl/ *n* a sleeveless outer vestment worn by the officiating priest at mass ☞ GARMENT [F, fr LL *casubla* hooded garment]

[1]**chat** /chat/ *vi* **-tt-** to talk in an informal or familiar manner [ME *chatten*, short for *chatteren*]

[2]**chat** *n* **1** (an instance of) light familiar talk; *esp* (a) conversation **2** a stonechat, whinchat, or related bird [(2) prob imit]

château /'shatoh/ *n, pl* **châteaus, châteaux** /'shatohz/ **1** a feudal castle or large country house in France **2** a French vineyard estate [F, fr OF *chastel*, fr L *castellum* castle]

chatelain /'shatə,layn/ *n* a castellan [MF *châtelain*, fr L *castellanus* occupant of a castle]

chatelaine /'shatə,layn/ *n* **1** the mistress of a castle or large house **2** a clasp with a short chain formerly used to attach small articles (e g keys) to a woman's belt [F *châtelaine*, fem of *châtelain*]

chatoyant /shə'toyənt/ *n or adj* (a gem) having a changeable lustre or colour [adj F, fr prp of *chatoyer* to shine like a cat's eyes; n fr adj] – **chatoyancy** *n*

'**chat ,show** /chat/ *n* a radio or television programme in which people, esp celebrities, engage in discussion or are interviewed

chattel /'chatl/ *n* an item of personal property – usu in *goods and chattels* [ME *chatel* property, fr OF, fr ML *capitale* – more at CATTLE]

[1]**chatter** /'chatə/ *vi* **1** to produce rapid successive inarticulate sounds suggestive of language ⟨*squirrels* ~ed *angrily*⟩ **2** to talk idly, incessantly, or fast; jabber **3a** *esp of teeth* to click repeatedly or uncontrollably (e g from cold) **b** *of a cutting tool (e g a drill)* to vibrate rapidly whilst cutting [ME *chatteren*, of imit origin] – **chatterer** *n*

[2]**chatter** *n* **1** the sound or (vibrating) action of chattering **2** idle talk; prattle

'**chatter,box** /-,boks/ *n* one who engages in much idle talk – infml

chatty /'chati/ *adj* **1** fond of chatting; talkative **2** having the style and manner of light familiar conversation ⟨*a* ~ *letter*⟩ *USE* infml – **chattily** *adv*, **chattiness** *n*

chat up *vt, Br* to engage (sby) in friendly conversation for an ulterior motive, esp with amorous intent – infml

chaudfroid /ˌshoh'fwah (*Fr* ʃofrwa)/ *n* (a dish of cold meat, fish, etc cooked with) a creamy sauce containing aspic that sets to a jelly [F, lit., hot-cold, fr *chaud* hot (fr L *calidus*) + *froid* cold (fr L *frigidus*)]

[1]**chauffeur** /ˌshoh'fuh, 'shohfə/ *n* a person employed to drive a private passenger-carrying motor vehicle, esp a car [F, lit., stoker, fr *chauffer* to heat, fr MF *chaufer* – more at CHAFE]

[2]**chauffeur** *vi* to work as a chauffeur ~ *vt* to transport (a person) or drive (e g a car) as (if) a chauffeur

chaulmoogra /ˌchawl'moohgrə/ *n* any of several E Indian trees that yield an acrid oil formerly used in treating leprosy and skin diseases [Beng *cāulmugrā*]

chauvinism /'shohvəˌniz(ə)m/ *n* **1** excessive or blind patriotism **2** undue attachment to one's group, cause, or place ⟨*male* ~⟩ [F *chauvinisme*, fr Nicolas *Chauvin fl* 1815 F soldier of excessive patriotism and devotion to Napoleon] – **chauvinist** *n*, **chauvinistic** /-'nistik/ *adj*, **chauvinistically** *adv*

chaw /chaw/ *vt or n, dial* (to) chew (esp a quid of tobacco) [by alter.]

[1]**cheap** /cheep/ *n* [ME *chep* bargain, fr OE *cēap* trade; akin to OHG *kouf* trade; both fr a prehistoric Gmc stem borrowed fr L *caupo* tradesman] – **on the cheap** at minimum expense; cheaply ⟨*schools that are run* on the cheap⟩

[2]**cheap** *adj* **1a** (relatively) low in price; *esp* purchasable below the market price or the real value **b** charging a low price ⟨*a* ~ *supermarket*⟩ **c** depreciated in value (e g by currency inflation) ⟨~ *dollars*⟩ **2** gained with little effort ⟨*a* ~ *victory*⟩; *esp* gained by contemptible means ⟨~ *laughs*⟩ ⟨~ *thrill*⟩ **3a** of inferior quality or worth; tawdry, sleazy **b** contemptible because of lack of any fine or redeeming qualities ⟨~ *election gimmickry*⟩ **4** *of money* obtainable at a low rate of interest **5** *NAm* stingy – **cheap, cheaply** *adv*, **cheapish** *adj*, **cheapness** *n*

cheapen /'cheep(ə)n/ *vb* to make or become **a** cheap in price or value **b** lower in esteem **c** tawdry, vulgar, or inferior

[1]**'cheap-ˌjack** /jak/ *n* sby, esp a pedlar, who sells cheap wares [*cheap* + the name *Jack*]

[2]**cheap-jack** *adj* **1** inferior, cheap, or worthless ⟨~ *film companies*⟩ **2** characterized by unscrupulous opportunism ⟨~ *speculators*⟩

cheapskate /'cheepˌskayt/ *n, chiefly NAm* a miserly or stingy person [*cheap* + *skate* (fellow, miser)]

[1]**cheat** /cheet/ *n* **1** a fraudulent deception; a fraud **2** one who cheats; a pretender, deceiver [earlier *cheat* forfeited property, fr ME *chet* escheat, short for *eschete* – more at ESCHEAT]

[2]**cheat** *vt* **1** to deprive of sthg valuable by deceit or fraud **2** to influence or lead by deceit or fraud **3** to defeat the purpose or blunt the effects of ⟨~ *winter of its dreariness* – Washington Irving⟩ ~ *vi* **1a** to practise fraud or deception **b** to violate rules dishonestly (e g at cards or in an exam) **2** to be sexually unfaithful – usu + *on* – **cheater** *n*

[1]**check** /chek/ *n* **1** exposure of a chess king to an attack from which it must be protected or moved to safety – often used interjectionally **2** a sudden stoppage of a forward course or progress; an arrest **3** a sudden pause or break in a progression **4** one who or that which arrests, limits, or restrains; a restraint **5a** a standard for testing and evaluation; a criterion **b** an inspection, examination, test, or verification **6a** (a square in) a pattern of squares (of alternating colours) **b** a fabric woven or printed with such a design **7** a crack or break, esp in a piece of timber **8** *NAm* a cheque **9a** *chiefly NAm* a ticket or token showing ownership or identity or indicating payment made ⟨*a luggage* ~⟩ **b** *NAm* a counter in various games **c** *NAm* a bill, esp for food and drink in a restaurant **10** *NAm* [2]TICK 2 [ME *chek*, fr OF *eschec*, fr Ar *shāh*, fr Per, lit., king; (6) ME *chek*, short for *cheker* chequer] – **in check** under restraint or control ⟨*held the enemy* in check⟩

[2]**check** *vt* **1** to put (a chess opponent's king) in check **2a** to slow or bring to a stop; brake **b** to block the progress of (e g an ice-hockey player) **3a** to restrain or diminish the action or force of; control **b** to ease off and then secure again (e g a rope) **4a** to compare with a source, original, or authority; verify **b** to inspect for satisfactory condition, accuracy, safety, or performance – sometimes + *out* or *over* **5** to mark into squares; chequer – usu in past part **6** *chiefly NAm* to note or mark with a tick – often + *off* **7a** *NAm* CHECK IN 2 **b** *chiefly NAm* to leave or accept for safekeeping in a cloakroom or left-luggage office – often + *in* **8** *chiefly dial* to rebuke, reprimand ~ *vi* **1a** *of a dog* to stop in a chase, esp when scent is lost **b** to halt through caution, uncertainty, or fear **2a** to investigate and make sure ⟨~ed *on the passengers' safety*⟩ **b** *chiefly NAm* to correspond point for point; tally ⟨*the description* ~s *with the photograph*⟩ – often + *out* ⟨*his story* ~ed *out*⟩ – **checkable** *adj*, **checker** *n* – **check into** to check in at ⟨check into *a hotel*⟩ – **check up on 1** to examine for accuracy or truth, esp in order to corroborate information ⟨check up on *the facts*⟩ **2** to make thorough inquiries about ⟨*police* checked up on *her*⟩

[1]**checker** /'chekə/ *n* **1** *chiefly NAm* a chequer **2** *NAm* a draughtsman [(2) back-formation fr *checkers*]

[2]**checker** *vt, chiefly NAm* to chequer

checkers /'chekəz/ *n pl but sing in constr, NAm* the game of draughts [pl of *checker* (chessboard), fr ME *cheker*, fr OF *eschequier*, fr *eschec*]

check in *vi* to report one's presence or arrival; *esp* to arrive and register at a hotel or airport ~ *vt* **1** to return or accept the return of ⟨check in *the equipment after use*⟩ **2** to deposit (luggage) for transport, esp by air

checklist /'chekˌlist/ *n* an inventory, catalogue; *esp* a complete list of checks to be made

[1]**checkmate** /ˌchek'mayt/ *vt* **1** to thwart or counter completely **2** to check (a chess opponent's king) so that escape is impossible [ME *chekmaten*, fr *chekmate*, interj used to announce checkmate, fr MF *eschec mat*, fr Ar *shāh māt*, fr Per, lit., the king is left helpless]

[2]**ˌcheck'mate** *n* **1a** the act of checkmating **b** the situation of a checkmated king **2** complete defeat *USE* (*1*) often used interjectionally

checkout /'chek,owt/ *n* a cash desk equipped with a cash register in a self-service shop

check out *vi* to complete the formalities for leaving, esp at a hotel ~*vt* to have the removal of (sthg) recorded ⟨check out *a library book*⟩

checkpoint /'chek,poynt/ *n* a location where inspection (e g of travellers) may take place

checkrein /'chek,rayn/ *n* a short rein attached from the bit to the saddle to prevent a horse from lowering its head

checkroom /'chek,roohm, -room/ *n, NAm* a room in which luggage, parcels, or coats may be left for safekeeping

checkup /'chek,up/ *n* a (general physical) examination

checkweighman /'chek,waymən, -man/ *n* a colliery worker employed on behalf of the miners to check the weighing of coal against company estimates

Cheddar /'chedə/ *n* a hard smooth-textured cheese with a flavour that ranges from mild to strong as the cheese matures [*Cheddar,* village in Somerset, England]

[1]**cheek** /cheek/ *n* **1** the fleshy side of the face below the eye and above and to the side of the mouth **2** either of 2 paired facing parts (e g the jaws of a vice) **3** insolent boldness; impudence **4** a buttock – infml [ME *cheke,* fr OE *cēace;* akin to MLG *kāke* jawbone]

[2]**cheek** *vt* to speak rudely or impudently to – infml

'cheek,bone /-,bohn/ *n* (the bone forming) the prominence below the eye

,cheek by 'jowl *adv* very close together

-cheeked *comb form* (→ *adj*) having (such) cheeks ⟨*rosy*-cheeked⟩

'cheek ,pouch *n* a pouch in the cheek of a monkey, hamster, etc for holding food

cheeky /'cheeki/ *adj* impudent, insolent [[1]CHEEK + [1]-Y] – **cheekily** *adv,* **cheekiness** *n*

cheep /cheep/ *vi or n* (to utter) a faint shrill sound characteristic of a young bird [imit]

[1]**cheer** /chiə/ *n* **1** state of mind or heart; spirit ⟨*be of good ~* – Matthew 9:2(AV)⟩ **2** happiness, gaiety **3** sthg that gladdens **4** a shout of applause or encouragement [ME *chere* face, cheer, fr OF, face] – **cheerless** *adj,* **cheerlessly** *adv,* **cheerlessness** *n*

[2]**cheer** *vt* **1a** to instil with hope or courage; comfort **b** to make glad or happy **2** to urge *on* or encourage, esp by shouts ⟨~ed *the team on*⟩ **3** to applaud with shouts ~*vi* **1** to grow or be cheerful; rejoice **2** to utter a shout of applause or triumph ***USE*** (*vt 1; vi 1*) usu + *up* – **cheerer** *n*

'cheerful /-f(ə)l/ *adj* **1a** full of good spirits; merry **b** ungrudging ⟨~ *obedience*⟩ **2** conducive to good cheer; likely to dispel gloom ⟨*a ~ sunny room*⟩ – **cheerfully** *adv,* **cheerfulness** *n*

cheerio /,chiəri'oh/ *interj, chiefly Br* – used to express farewell [*cheery* + *-o*]

'cheer,leader /-,leedə/ *n* one, esp a female, who leads organized cheering (e g at a N American football game)

cheers /chiəz/ *interj* – used as a toast and sometimes as an informal farewell or expression of thanks

cheery /'chiəri/ *adj* marked by or causing good spirits; cheerful – **cheerily** *adv,* **cheeriness** *n*

[1]**cheese** /cheez/ *n* **1** (an often cylindrical cake of) a food consisting of coagulated, compressed, and usu ripened milk curds **2** sthg resembling cheese in consistency or a cylindrical cake of cheese **3** a fruit preserve with the consistency of cream cheese [ME *chese,* fr OE *cēse;* akin to OHG *kāsi* cheese; both fr a prehistoric WGmc word borrowed fr L *caseus* cheese; akin to OE *hwatherian* to foam, Skt *kvathati* he boils] – **cheesy** *adj,* **cheesiness** *n*

[2]**cheese** *n* an important person; a boss – slang; chiefly in *big cheese* [prob fr Hindi *chīz* thing, fr Per]

'cheese,cake /-,kayk/ *n* **1** a baked or refrigerated dessert consisting of a soft filling, usu containing cheese, in a biscuit or pastry case **2** a photographic display of shapely and scantily clothed female figures – infml; compare BEEFCAKE

'cheese,cloth /-,kloth/ *n* a very fine unsized cotton gauze [fr its use in cheesemaking]

,cheesed 'off *adj, chiefly Br* browned-off – slang [prob fr *cheese* (to stop, run away)]

cheesehead /'cheez,hed/ *adj, of a screw or bolt* having a squat cylindrical head

cheeseparing /'cheez,peəring/ *n* miserly or petty economizing; stinginess – **cheeseparing** *adj*

cheetah /'cheetə/ *n* a long-legged spotted swift-moving African and formerly Asiatic cat with nonretractile claws [Hindi *cītā,* fr Skt *citrakāya* tiger, fr *citra* bright + *kāya* body]

chef /shef/ *n* a skilled cook; *esp* the chief cook in a restaurant or hotel [F, short for *chef de cuisine* head of the kitchen]

chef d'oeuvre /,shay 'duhvə (*Fr* ʃɛ dœːvr)/ *n, pl* **chefs d'oeuvre** /~/ an (artistic or literary) masterpiece [F *chef-d'oeuvre,* lit., leading work]

Chehalis /chə'haylis/ *n, pl* **Chehalises,** *esp collectively* **Chehalis** a member, or the language, of an American Indian people of Washington in the NW USA [*Chehalis,* village in the state of Washington, USA]

cheka /'chekə/ *n, often cap* the Soviet secret police between 1917 and 1922 [Russ, fr *che* + *ka,* names of initial letters of *Chrezvychainaya Kommissiya* extraordinary commission]

chela /'keelə/ *n, pl* **chelae** /-li/ a pincerlike claw of a crustacean (e g a crab) or arachnid (e g a scorpion) [NL, fr Gk *chēlē* claw]

[1]**chelate** /'kee,layt/ *adj* **1** resembling or having chelae **2** of or having a molecular structure in which a metal ion is held by 1 or more coordinate bonds – **chelate** /-layt, -lət/ *n*

[2]**chelate** *vb* to react (with) so as to form a chelate structure – **chelation** /ki'laysh(ə)n/ *n*

,Chelsea 'bun /'chelsi/ *n* a sweet yeast-leavened bun containing currants, raisins, etc and shaped in a flat coil [*Chelsea,* district of London]

,Chelsea 'pensioner *n* a veteran or disabled soldier living at the Chelsea Royal Hospital

chem- /kem-/, **chemo-** *also* **chemi-** *comb form* **1** chemical; chemistry ⟨chemo*therapy*⟩ ⟨chemo*taxis*⟩ **2** chemically ⟨chemi*sorb*⟩ [NL, fr LGk *chēmeia* alchemy, prob fr *chyma* fluid, fr *chein* to pour]

[1]**chemical** /'kemikl/ *adj* **1** of, used in, or produced by chemistry **2** acting, operated, or produced by chemicals – **chemically** /'kemikli/ *adv*

[2]**chemical** *n* a substance (e g an element or chemical compound) obtained by a chemical process or used for producing a chemical effect

,chemical engi'neering *n* engineering dealing with the industrial application of chemistry

,chemical 'warfare *n* warfare using poisonous or harmful chemicals

chemico- *comb form* CHEM- 1 ⟨chemico*physical*⟩

chemiluminescence /ˌkemiˌloohmiˈnes(ə)ns/ *n* light (e g bioluminescence) produced by chemical reaction [ISV] – **chemiluminescent** *adj*

chemin de fer /shəˌmanh də ˈfeə (*Fr* ʃəmɛ̃ də fɛr)/ *n, pl* **chemins de fer** /~/ a card game resembling baccarat in which only 2 hands are dealt and any number of players may bet against the dealer [F, lit., railway]

chemise /shəˈmeez/ *n* **1** a woman's one-piece undergarment **2** a usu loose straight-hanging dress [ME, fr OF, shirt, fr LL *camisia*]

chemisorb /ˌkemiˈsawb/, **chemosorb** /ˈkemə-/ *vt* to take up and hold, usu irreversibly, by chemical forces [*chem-* + *-sorb* (as in *adsorb*)] – **chemisorption** /-ˈsawpsh(ə)n, -ˈzaw-/ *n*

chemist /ˈkemist/ *n* **1** one who is trained in chemistry **2** *Br* (a pharmacist, esp in) a retail shop where medicines and miscellaneous articles (e g cosmetics and films) are sold [NL *chimista*, short for ML *alchimista* alchemist]

chemistry /ˈkemistri/ *n* **1** a science that deals with the composition, structure, and properties of substances and of the transformations they undergo **2a** the composition and chemical properties of a substance **b** chemical processes and phenomena (e g of an organism) ⟨*blood* ~⟩

chemmy /ˈshemi/ *n* CHEMIN DE FER [by shortening & alter.]

chemo- – see CHEM-

chemoreceptor /ˈkeemohriˌseptə, ke-/ *n* a sense organ (e g a taste bud) that responds to chemical stimuli [ISV] – **chemoreception** /-riˌsepsh(ə)n/ *n*

chemosphere /ˈkeməˌsfiə/ *n* the mesosphere

chemotaxis /ˌkeemohˈtaksis, ke-/ *n* orientation or movement of an organism in relation to chemical agents [NL] – **chemotactic** /-ˈtaktik/ *adj*

chemotherapy /ˌkeemohˈtherəpi, ˌke-/ *n* the use of chemical agents in the treatment or control of disease [ISV] – **chemotherapeutic** /-ˌtherəˈpyoohtik/ *adj*, **chemotherapist** /-ˈtherəpist/ *n*

chemotropism /kiˈmotrəˌpiz(ə)m, ˌkeeməˈtrohpiz(ə)m/ *n* orientation of cells or organisms (e g bacteria) in relation to chemical stimuli [ISV] – **chemotropic** /ˌkeemohˈtropik, ˌke-/ *adj*

chenille /shəˈneel/ *n* a (wool, cotton, silk, or rayon) yarn with protruding pile; *also* a fabric with a pile face and a chenille yarn weft [F, lit., caterpillar, fr L *canicula*, dim. of *canis* dog; fr its hairy appearance – more at HOUND]

cheongsam /ˈchongˌsam/ *n* a dress with a slit skirt and a mandarin collar worn esp by oriental women [Chin (Cant) *ch'eūng shaam*, lit., long gown]

cheque /chek/ *n, chiefly Br* a written order for a bank to pay money as instructed; *also* a printed form on which such an order is usually written [alter. of [1]*check*]

ˈchequeˌbook /-ˌbook/ *n* a book containing unwritten cheques

ˈcheque ˌcard *n* a card issued to guarantee that the holder's cheques up to a specific amount will be honoured by the issuing bank

[1]**chequer**, *chiefly NAm* **checker** /ˈchekə/ *n* [1]CHECK 6a [ME *cheker*, fr OF *eschequier*, fr *eschec* check]

[2]**chequer**, *chiefly NAm* **checker** *vt* **1** to variegate with different colours or shades; *esp* to mark with squares of (2) alternating colours **2** to vary with contrasting elements or situations ⟨*a* ~ed *career*⟩ *USE* usu in past part

cherish /ˈcherish/ *vt* **1a** to hold dear; feel or show affection for **b** to keep or cultivate with care and affection; nurture **2** to keep in the mind deeply and with affection ⟨*still* ~es *that memory*⟩ [ME *cherisshen*, fr MF *cheriss-*, stem of *cherir* to cherish, fr OF, fr *chier* dear, fr L *carus* – more at CHARITY] – **cherishable** *adj*

chernozem /ˌchuhnəˈzem, -ˈzhom/ *n* a dark-coloured humus-rich soil found in temperate to cool climates [Russ, lit., black earth]

Cherokee /ˌcherəˈkee/ *n, pl* **Cherokees,** *esp collectively* **Cherokee** (a member or the Iroquoian language of) a N American Indian people orig of Tennessee and N Carolina ☞ LANGUAGE [prob fr Creek *tciloki* people of a different speech]

cheroot /shəˈrooht/ *n* a cigar cut square at both ends [Tamil *curuṭṭu*, lit., roll]

cherry /ˈcheri/ *n* **1** (the wood or small pale yellow to deep red or blackish fruit of) any of numerous trees and shrubs of the rose family, often cultivated for their fruit or ornamental flowers **2** light red [ME *chery*, fr ONF *cherise* (taken as a plural), fr LL *ceresia*, fr L *cerasus* cherry tree, fr Gk *kerasos* – more at CORNEL] – **cherry** *adj*, **cherrylike** *adj*

chersonese /ˈkuhsəˌneez, -ˌnees/ *n* a peninsula – chiefly poetic [L *chersonesus*, fr Gk *chersonēsos*, fr *chersos* dry land + *nēsos* island]

chert /chuht/ *n* a flintlike silica [origin unknown] – **cherty** *adj*

cherub /ˈcherəb/ *n, pl* **cherubs,** (*1*) **cherubim** /ˈcherəbim/ **1** a biblical attendant of God or of a holy place, often represented as a being with large wings, a human head, and an animal body **2a** a beautiful usu winged child in painting and sculpture **b** an innocent-looking usu chubby and pretty person [L, fr Gk *cheroub*, fr Heb *kĕrūbh*] – **cherubic** *adj*

chervil /ˈchuhvil/ *n* an aromatic plant of the carrot family whose leaves are used as a herb [ME *cherville*, fr OE *cerfille*; akin to OHG *kervila* chervil]

chess /ches/ *n* a game for 2 players each of whom moves his/her 16 chessmen according to fixed rules across a chessboard and tries to checkmate his/her opponent's king [ME *ches*, fr OF *esches*, acc pl of *eschec* check at chess – more at CHECK]

ˈchessˌboard /-ˌbawd/ *n* a board used in chess, draughts, etc that is divided into usu 64 equal squares of 2 alternating colours

chessman /-ˌman/ *n, pl* **chessmen** /-mən, -ˌmen/ any of the pieces (1 king, 1 queen, 2 rooks, 2 bishops, 2 knights, and 8 pawns) used by each side in playing chess

chest /chest/ *n* **1a** a box with a lid used esp for the safekeeping of belongings **b** a usu small cupboard used esp for storing medicines or first-aid supplies **c** a case in which a commodity (e g tea) is shipped **2** the part of the body enclosed by the ribs and breastbone [ME, fr OE *cest*; akin to OHG & ON *kista* chest] – **chestful** *n*

-chested /-chestid/ *comb form* (→ *adj*) having (such) a chest ⟨*flat*-chested⟩ ⟨*deep*-chested⟩

chesterfield /ˈchestəˌfeeld/ *n* a heavily padded usu leather sofa [prob fr a 19th-c Earl of *Chesterfield*]

[1]**chestnut** /ˈches(t)ˌnut/ *n* **1** (the nut or wood of) a tree or shrub of the beech family; *esp* SPANISH CHESTNUT **2** reddish brown **3** HORSE CHESTNUT **4** a chestnut-coloured animal, specif a horse **5** the small

callus on the inner side of a horse's leg ☞ ANATOMY **6** an often repeated joke or story; *broadly* anything repeated excessively [ME *chasteine, chesten* chestnut tree, fr MF *chastaigne*, fr L *castanea*, fr Gk *kastanea*]

[2]**chestnut** *adj* of the colour chestnut

,chest of 'drawers /drawz/ *n* a piece of furniture containing a set of drawers (e g for holding clothes)

chesty /'chesti/ *adj* **1** of, inclined to, symptomatic of, or suffering from disease of the chest ⟨*a ~ cough*⟩ – not used technically **2** having prominent breasts – slang

che'val ,glass /shə'val/ *n* a full-length mirror in a frame by which it may be tilted [F *cheval* horse, support]

chevalier /,shevə'liə/ *n* a member of certain orders of merit (e g the French Legion of Honour) [F, knight, horseman, fr MF, fr LL *caballarius* – more at CAVALIER]

cheviot /'cheevi·ət, 'che-/ *n* **1** *often cap* any of a breed of hardy hornless sheep **2** a fabric made from the wool of cheviot sheep [*Cheviot* hills, England and Scotland]

chevron /'shevrən/ *n* a figure, pattern, or object having the shape of an (inverted) V; *esp* a sleeve badge that usu consists of 1 or more chevron-shaped stripes and indicates the wearer's rank ☞ ARCHITECTURE [ME, fr MF, rafter, chevron, fr (assumed) VL *caprion-, caprio* rafter; akin to L *caper* goat]

chevrotain /'shevrətayn, -tin/ *n* any of several very small hornless ruminant mammals of tropical Asia and W Africa [F, dim. of *chevrot* kid, fawn, fr MF, dim. of *chèvre* goat, fr L *capra* she-goat, fem of *capr-, caper* he-goat]

[1]**chew** /chooh/ *vb* to crush, grind, or gnaw (esp food) (as if) with the teeth [ME *chewen*, fr OE *cēowan*; akin to OHG *kiuwan* to chew, OSlav *žīvati*] – **chewable** *adj*, **chewer** *n*, **chewy** *adj*

[2]**chew** *n* **1** the act of chewing **2** sthg for chewing ⟨*a ~ of tobacco*⟩

'chewing ,gum /'chooh·ing/ *n* a flavoured usu sweetened insoluble material (e g chicle) for chewing

chew over *vt* to meditate on; think about reflectively – infml

Cheyenne /,shie'an, -'en/ *n, pl* **Cheyennes,** /~/ *esp collectively* **Cheyenne** (a member or the language of) a N American Indian people of the W plains of the USA [CanF, fr Dakota *Shaiyena*, fr *shaia* to speak strangely]

chez /shay/ *prep* at or to the home of [F]

chi /kie/ *n* the 22nd letter of the Greek alphabet [Gk *chei*]

chiack /'chie·ək/ *vb, chiefly Austr* to make derisive remarks (about) [alter. of *chi-hike, chi-ike* (a shout of greeting or derision)] – **chiack** *n*

Chianti /ki'anti/ *n* a dry (red) Italian table wine [It, fr *Chianti*, district of Tuscany, Italy]

chiao /chow/ *n, pl* **chiao** /~/ a jiao [Chin (Pek) *chiao*[3]]

chiaroscuro /ki,ahrə'skooəroh/ *n, pl* **chiaroscuros** **1** pictorial representation in terms of light and shade **2** the arrangement or treatment of light and shade in a painting [It, fr *chiaro* clear, light + *oscuro* obscure, dark]

chiasma /ki'azmə/ *n, pl* **chiasmata** /-mətə/ an anatomical cross-shaped configuration; *esp* that between paired chromatids considered to be the point where genetic material is exchanged [NL, X-shaped form, fr Gk, crosspiece, fr *chiazein* to mark with a chi, fr *chi* (x)] – **chiasmic, chiasmatic** /,kee·əz'matik/ *adj*

chibouk, chibouque /chi'boohk/ *n* a long-stemmed Turkish tobacco pipe [F *chibouque*, fr Turk *çibuk*]

chic /sheek, shik/ *adj or n* (having or showing) elegance and sophistication, esp of dress or manner [F] – **chicly** *adv*, **chicness** *n*

chicane /shi'kayn/ *n* **1** a series of tight turns in opposite directions in an otherwise straight stretch of a road-racing course **2** a hand of cards containing no trumps [F, deception, obstacle, fr MF, fr *chicaner* to quibble, obstruct justice]

chicanery /shi'kayn(ə)ri/ *n* **1** deception by the use of fallacious or irrelevant arguments **2** a piece of sharp practice or legal trickery – **chicane** *vb*

chichi /'shee,shee/ *adj or n* **1** showy, frilly, or elaborate (ornamentation) **2** unnecessarily elaborate or affected (behaviour, style, etc) [F]

chick /chik/ *n* **1** a young bird; *esp* a (newly hatched) chicken ☞ LIFE CYCLE **2** a young woman – slang [short for *chicken*]

[1]**chicken** /'chikin/ *n* **1** the common domestic fowl, esp when young; *also* its flesh used as food **2** a young person – chiefly in *he/she is no chicken* **3a** a contest in which the participants put themselves in danger to see who is most brave **b** a coward – slang *USE* (*2&3a*) infml [ME *chiken*, fr OE *cicen* young chicken; akin to OE *cocc* cock]

[2]**chicken** *adj* scared – infml

'chicken ,feed *n* a small and insignificant amount, esp of money – infml

,chicken'hearted /-'hahtid/ *adj* timid, cowardly

,chicken-'livered *adj* timid, cowardly

chicken out *vi* to lose one's nerve – infml

'chicken ,pox /poks/ *n* an infectious virus disease, esp of children, that is marked by mild fever and a rash of small blisters

'chicken ,wire *n* a light galvanized wire netting with a hexagonal mesh [fr its use for making enclosures for chickens]

chick-pea /'chik ,pee/ *n* (the hard edible seed of) an Asiatic leguminous plant [by folk etymology fr ME *chiche*, fr MF, fr L *cicer*]

chickweed /'chik,weed/ *n* any of various low-growing small-leaved plants of the pink family that occur commonly as weeds

chicle /'chikl/ *n* a gum from the latex of the sapodilla used as the chief ingredient of chewing gum [Sp, fr Nahuatl *chictli*]

chicory /'chik(ə)ri/ *n* a usu blue-flowered European perennial composite plant widely grown for its edible thick roots and as a salad plant; *also* the ground roasted root used as a coffee additive [ME *cicoree*, fr MF *cichorée, chicorée*, fr L *cichoreum*, fr Gk *kichoreia*]

chide /chied/ *vb* **chid** /chid/, **chided; chid, chidden** /'chid(ə)n/, **chided** to rebuke (sby) angrily; scold [ME *chiden*, fr OE *cīdan* to quarrel, chide, fr *cīd* strife] – **chidingly** *adv*

[1]**chief** /cheef/ *n* **1** (a broad band across) the upper part of a heraldic field **2** the head of a body of people or an organization; a leader ⟨*~ of police*⟩ [ME, fr OF, head, chief, fr L *caput* head – more at HEAD] – **chiefdom** /-d(ə)m/, **chiefship** *n*

[2]**chief** *adj* **1** accorded highest rank or office ⟨~ *librarian*⟩ **2** of greatest importance or influence ⟨*the ~ reasons*⟩

ˌchief ˈjustice *n* the presiding judge of a supreme court of justice (e g the US Supreme Court)

chiefly /ˈcheefli/ *adv* **1** most importantly; principally, especially **2** for the most part; mostly, mainly

chief master sergeant *n* ☞ RANK

ˌchief of ˈstaff *n* the senior officer of an armed forces staff that serves a commander

ˌchief ˌpetty ˈofficer *n* ☞ RANK

chieftain /ˈcheeftən/, *fem* **chieftainess** /-ˈnes/ *n* a chief, esp of a band, tribe, or clan [ME *chieftaine*, fr MF *chevetain*, fr LL *capitaneus* chief – more at CAPTAIN] – **chieftainship** *n*

chieftaincy /ˈcheeftənsi/ *n* **1** the rank, dignity, office, or rule of a chieftain **2** a region or a people ruled by a chief

ˌchief techˈnician *n* ☞ RANK

ˌchief ˈwarrant ˌofficer *n* ☞ RANK

chiffchaff /ˈchifˌchaf/ *n* a small greyish European warbler [imit]

chiffon /ˈshifon, -ˈ-/ *n* a sheer (silk) fabric [F, lit., rag, fr *chiffe* old rag, alter. of MF *chipe*, fr ME *chip* chip]

chiffonier /ˌshifəˈniə/ *n* a high narrow chest of drawers [F *chiffonnier*, fr *chiffon*]

chigger /ˈchigə/ *n* a chigoe [by alter.]

chignon /shiˈnyon, ˈshee-/ *n* a usu large smooth knot of hair worn esp at the nape of the neck [F, fr MF *chaignon* chain, collar, nape]

chigoe /ˈsheegoh/ *n* **1** a tropical flea, the female of which burrows under the skin **2** HARVEST MITE [of Cariban origin; akin to Galibi *chico* chigoe]

Chihuahua /chiˈwah·wə/ *n* a very small round-headed large-eared dog of Mexican origin [MexSp, fr *Chihuahua*, state & city in Mexico]

chilblain /ˈchilˌblayn/ *n* an inflammatory sore, esp on the feet or hands, caused by exposure to cold [[3]*chill* + *blain*]

child /chield/ *n, pl* **children** /ˈchildrən/ **1** an unborn or recently born person **2a** a young person, esp between infancy and youth **b** a childlike or childish person **c(1)** a person not yet of (a legally specified) age **(2)** sby under the age of 14 – used in English law; compare YOUNG PERSON **3a** a son or daughter ⟨*left the estate to her* ~ren⟩ **b** a descendant ⟨*the* Children *of David*⟩ **4** one strongly influenced by another or by a place or state of affairs ⟨*a ~ of the depression*⟩ **5** a product, result ⟨*dreams; which are the* ~ren *of an idle brain* – Shak⟩ [ME, fr OE *cild*; akin to Goth *kilthei* womb, Skt *jaṭhara* belly] – **childless** *adj*, **childlessness** *n* – **with child** *of a woman* PREGNANT 3

child benefit *n* a (weekly) allowance paid through the post office for each child in a family

ˈchildˌbirth /-ˌbuhth/ *n* parturition

childe /chield/ *n, often cap, archaic* a young man of noble birth [var of *child*]

childhood /ˈchieldˌhood/ *n* **1** the state or period of being a child **2** an early period in the development of sthg ⟨*there was a ~ of religion as there was a ~ of science – TLS*⟩

childish /ˈchieldish/ *adj* **1** of or befitting a child or childhood **2** marked by or suggestive of immaturity ⟨*a ~ spiteful remark*⟩ – **childishly** *adv*, **childishness** *n*

childlike /ˈchieldˌliek/ *adj* marked by innocence and trust [CHILD + -LIKE]

childly /ˈchieldli/ *adj* childlike – poetic

childminder /ˈchieldˌmiendə/ *n, chiefly Br* one who looks after other people's children, esp when both parents are at work – **childminding** *n*

childproof /ˈchieldˌproohf/ *n* not liable to damage or misuse by children; *specif* designed to be impossible for children to open ⟨*a ~ lock*⟩

ˌChildren of ˈIsrael *n pl* *the* Jewish people

ˈchild's ˌplay *n* an extremely simple task or act

ˌChile ˈpine /ˈchili/ *n* a monkey puzzle [*Chile*, country in S America]

ˌChile ˌsaltˈpetre /ˌsawltˈpeetə/ *n* (naturally occurring) sodium nitrate

chiliad /ˈkiliˌad/ *n* **1** a group of 1000 **2** a period of 1000 years [LL *chiliad-*, *chilias*, fr Gk, fr *chilioi* thousand – more at MILE]

chiliasm /ˈkiliˌaz(ə)m/ *n* MILLENARIANISM 1 [NL *chiliasmus*, fr LL *chiliastes* one who believes in chiliasm, fr *chilias*] – **chiliast** /-ˌast/ *n*, **chiliastic** /-ˈastik/ *adj*

[1]**chill** /chil/ *vi* **1** to become cold **2** to catch a chill **3** *of a metal* to become surface-hardened by sudden cooling ~ *vt* **1a** to make cold or chilly **b** to make (esp food or drink) cool, esp without freezing **2** to affect as if with cold; dispirit **3** to harden the surface of (metal) by sudden cooling [ME *chillen*, fr *chile* cold, frost, fr OE *cele*; akin to OE *ceald* cold] – **chillingly** *adv*

[2]**chill** *adj* CHILLY 1, 2 – **chillness** *n*

[3]**chill** *n* **1a** a (disagreeable) sensation of coldness **b** COMMON COLD **2** a moderate but disagreeable degree of cold **3** coldness of manner ⟨*felt the ~ of his opponent's stare*⟩

chilli, chili /ˈchili/ *n, pl* **chillies, chilies** the pod of a hot pepper used either whole or ground as a pungent condiment – compare CAYENNE PEPPER [Sp *chile*, fr Nahuatl *chilli*]

chilly /ˈchili/ *adj* **1** noticeably (unpleasantly) cold **2** lacking warmth of feeling; distant, unfriendly **3** tending to arouse fear or apprehension ⟨~ *details*⟩ – **chilliness** *n*

ˌChiltern ˈHundreds /ˈchiltən/ *n pl* a nominal office for which an MP applies in order to resign his/her seat [*Chiltern Hundreds*, district of Buckinghamshire, England, whose stewardship is a nominal office]

chimaera /kiˈmiərə, kie-/ *n* **1** any of a family of marine cartilaginous fishes with a tapering tail **2** a chimera [(1) NL, genus name, fr L, chimera]

[1]**chime** /chiem/ *n* **1a** a musically tuned set of bells **b** a set of objects (e g hanging metal bars or tubes) that sound like bells when struck **2a** the sound of a set of bells – usu pl with sing. meaning **b** a musical sound like that of bells [ME, cymbal, fr OF *chimbe*, fr L *cymbalum*]

[2]**chime** *vi* **1** to make the sounds of a chime **2** to be or act in accord ⟨*the music and the mood* ~d *well together*⟩ ~ *vt* **1** to cause to chime **2** to signal or indicate by chiming ⟨*the clock* ~d *midnight*⟩ – **chimer** *n*

[3]**chime** /chiem/, **chimb** /chim/ *n* the projecting rim of a barrel [ME *chimbe*, fr OE *cimb-*; akin to OE *camb* comb]

chime in *vi* **1** to break into a conversation or discussion, esp in order to express an opinion **2** to combine harmoniously – often + *with*

chimera /ki'miərə, kie-/ *n* **1a** *cap* a fire-breathing female mythological monster that had a lion's head, a goat's body, and a serpent's tail **b** an imaginary monster made up of incongruous parts **2a** an illusion or fabrication of the mind; *esp* an unrealizable dream **b** a terror that exists only in the mind **3** an individual, organ, or part consisting of tissues of diverse genetic constitution and occurring esp in plants and most frequently at a graft union [L *chimaera*, fr Gk *chimaira* she-goat, chimera; akin to Gk *cheimōn* winter – more at HIBERNATE] – **chimeric,** /ki'merik, kie-/ **chimerical** *adj*, **chimerically** *adv*

chimney /'chimni/ *n* **1** a vertical structure incorporated into a building and enclosing a flue or flues for carrying off smoke; *esp* the part of such a structure extending above a roof **2** a structure through which smoke and gases (e g from a furnace or steam engine) are discharged **3** a tube, usu of glass, placed round a flame (e g of an oil lamp) to serve as a shield **4** a narrow cleft, vent, etc (e g in rock) ☞ GEOGRAPHY [ME, fr MF *cheminée*, fr LL *caminata*, fr L *caminus* furnace, fireplace, fr Gk *kaminos*; akin to Gk *kamara* vault]

'chimney ,breast *n* the wall that encloses a chimney and projects into a room

'chimney ,corner *n* a seat by or within a large open fireplace

'chimney,piece /-,pees/ *n* a mantelpiece

'chimney ,pot *n* a usu earthenware pipe at the top of a chimney

'chimney ,stack *n* **1** a masonry, brickwork, etc chimney rising above a roof and usu containing several flues **2** a tall chimney, typically of circular section, serving a factory, power station, etc

'chimney ,sweep *n* one whose occupation is cleaning soot from chimney flues

chimp /chimp/ *n* a chimpanzee – infml

chimpanzee /,chimpan'zee/ *n* a tree-dwelling anthropoid ape of equatorial Africa that is smaller and less fierce than the gorilla [Kongo dial. *chimpenzi*]

chin /chin/ *n* the lower portion of the face lying below the lower lip and including the prominence of the lower jaw [ME, fr OE *cinn*; akin to OHG *kinni* chin, L *gena* cheek, Gk *genys* jaw, cheek]

china /'chienə/ *n* **1** porcelain; *also* vitreous porcelain ware (e g dishes and vases) for domestic use **2** chinaware; *broadly* crockery ⟨*set the table with the good* ~⟩ **3** *chiefly Br* BONE CHINA [Per *chīnī* Chinese porcelain]

'china ,clay *n* kaolin

chinagraph /'chienə,grahf, -,graf/ *n* a pencil that will write on china or glass

chinaman /'chienəmən/ *n* **1** a ball bowled by a slow left-hander in cricket that breaks from the off to the leg side on bouncing as viewed by a right-handed batsman **2** *cap* a native of China – derog [(1) perh from bowling of this type by Ellis Achong *b*1904 Chinese-born West Indian cricketer]

'China,town /-,town/ *n* the Chinese quarter of a city

'china,ware /-,weə/ *n* tableware made of china

chinchilla /,chin'chilə/ *n* **1** (the soft pearly-grey fur of) a S American rodent the size of a large squirrel ☞ ENDANGERED **2** (any of) a breed of domestic rabbit with long white or greyish fur; *also* (any of) a breed of cat with similar fur [Sp]

chin-chin /,chin 'chin/ *interj, Br* – used as an informal greeting, farewell, or toast [Chin (Pek) *ch'ing* [3], *ch'ing* [3]-*ch'ing* [3], phrase of salutation]

Chindit /'chindit/ *n* a member of an Allied force fighting behind Japanese lines in Burma during WW II [Burmese *chinthé* fabulous lionlike animal]

[1]chine /chien/ *n, Br* a steep-sided ravine, esp in Dorset or the Isle of Wight [ME, crack, chasm, fr OE *cine, cinu*; akin to OE *cīnan* to gape, crack]

[2]chine *n* **1** (a cut of meat including the whole or part of) the backbone **2** a (mountain) ridge **3** the intersection of the bottom and sides of a boat [ME, fr MF *eschine*, of Gmc origin; akin to OHG *scina* shinbone, needle – more at SHIN]

[3]chine *vt* to separate the backbone from the ribs of (a joint of meat); *also* to cut through the backbone of (a carcass)

Chinese /,chie'neez/ *n, pl* **Chinese** **1** a native or inhabitant of China **2** a group of related Sino-Tibetan tone languages used by the people of China; *specif* Mandarin ☞ ALPHABET, LANGUAGE [*China*, country in Asia] – **Chinese** *adj*

Chinese copy *n* an exact imitation or duplicate that includes defects as well as desired qualities

Chinese leaf *n* either of 2 Asiatic types of cabbage widely used in oriental cookery

Chinese puzzle *n* an intricate or ingenious puzzle

,Chinese 'wall *n* an apparently insurmountable barrier; *esp* a serious obstacle to understanding [*Chinese Wall*, a defensive wall built in the 3rd c BC between China and Mongolia]

chinese water deer *n* a small deer with no antlers that has become established in parts of Britain and France

Chinese white *n* a white zinc oxide pigment

[1]chink /chingk/ *n* **1** a small slit or fissure ⟨*a* ~ *in the curtain*⟩ **2** a means of evasion or escape; a loophole ⟨*a* ~ *in the law*⟩ [prob alter. of ME *chin, chine* crack, fissure – more at [1]CHINE]

[2]chink *n* a short sharp sound [imit] – **chink** *vb*

Chink *n* a native of China – derog [alter. of *Chinese*]

chinless /'chinlis/ *adj, Br* lacking firmness of purpose; ineffectual – infml [CHIN + -LESS]

Chino- *comb form* Chinese and ⟨Chino-*Japanese*⟩ – compare SINO-

chinoiserie /shee'nwahzəri, ,---'-/ *n* (an object or decoration in) a style in art and interior design that copies Chinese features or motifs [F, fr *chinois* Chinese, fr *Chine* China]

chinook /shə'nook; *also* chi'noohk, -'nook/ *n* **1** a warm moist southwesterly wind of the NW coast of the USA **2** a warm dry westerly wind of the E slopes of the Rocky mountains [Chehalis *Tsinúk* a member of an American Indian people of Oregon]

Chinook Jargon *n* a mixture of American Indian languages, French, and English, formerly used as a lingua franca in the NW USA and in W Canada and Alaska

chintz /chints/ *n* a (glazed) printed plain-weave fabric, usu of cotton [earlier *chints*, pl of *chint*, fr Hindi *ch 60 t*]

chintzy /'chintsi/ *adj* **1** made or decorated (as if) with chintz **2** gaudy, cheap

'chin-,wag *n* a conversation, chat – infml

[1]chip /chip/ *n* **1a** a small usu thin and flat piece (e g of wood or stone) cut, struck, or flaked off **b** a small thin slice or piece of fruit, chocolate, etc **2** a counter used as a token for money in gambling games **3** a flaw left after a chip is removed **4** (the small piece of semiconductor, esp silicon, on which is constructed) an integrated circuit ☞ COMPUTER **5** CHIP SHOT **6a** *chiefly Br* a strip of potato fried in deep fat **b** *NAm & Austr* [3]CRISP [ME] **– chip off the old block** a child that resembles either of his/her parents **– chip on one's shoulder** a challenging, belligerent, or embittered attitude **– when the chips are down** when the crucial or critical point has been reached ⟨when the chips are down *you have only yourself to depend on*⟩

[2]**chip** *vb* **-pp-** *vt* **1a** to cut or hew with an edged tool **b(1)** to cut or break (a small piece) from sthg **(2)** to cut or break a fragment from **2** to kick or hit (a ball, pass, etc) in a short high arc ~ *vi* **1** to break off in small pieces **2** to play a chip shot

'**chip,board** /-,bawd/ *n* an artificial board made from compressed wood chips and glue

chip in *vi* **1** to contribute ⟨*everyone* chipped in *for the gift*⟩ **2** to interrupt or add a comment to a conversation between other people ~ *vt* to contribute ⟨chipped in *£1 for the gift*⟩ ***USE*** infml

chipmunk /'chip,mungk/ *n* any of numerous small striped American squirrels [alter. of earlier *chitmunk*, of Algonquian origin; akin to Ojibwa *atchitamõ* squirrel]

chipolata /,chipə'lahtə/ *n* a small thin sausage [F, fr It *cipollata*, fr fem of *cipollato* with onions, fr *cipolla* onion, fr LL *cepula*, dim. of L *cepa* onion]

Chippendale /'chipən,dayl/ *adj or n* (of or being) an 18th-c English furniture style characterized by graceful outline and fine ornamentation [Thomas *Chippendale* †1779 E cabinet-maker & designer]

chipper /'chipə/ *adj* cheerful, bright [prob fr E dial. *kipper* (lively)]

chippy /'chipi/ *n* **1** a carpenter **2** *Br* a shop selling fish and chips ***USE*** infml [[1]*chip* + [1]*-y*]

'**chip ,shot** *n* a short shot in golf that lofts the ball to the green and allows it to roll

chir- /kir-/, **chiro-** *comb form* hand ⟨chiro*practic*⟩ [L, fr Gk *cheir-*, *cheiro-*, fr *cheir*; akin to Hitt *kesar* hand]

chiral /'kierəl/ *adj, esp of a crystal or molecule* not able to be superimposed on its mirror image [*chir-* + *-al*; lit., handed, i e asymmetric] – **chirality** /-'raləti/ *n*

Chi-Rho /,kie 'roh/ *n, pl* **Chi-Rhos** a Christian monogram and symbol formed from the first 2 letters (X and P) of the Greek word for *Christ* [*chi* + *rho*]

chirography /kie'rogrəfi/ *n* handwriting, penmanship – **chirographer** *n*, **chirographic** /,kierə'grafik/, **chirographical** *adj*

chiromancy /'kirə,mansi/ *n* palmistry [prob fr MF *chiromancie*, fr ML *chiromantia*, fr Gk *cheir-* chir- + *-manteia* -mancy – more at -MANCY] – **chiromancer** *n*

chironomid /ki'ronəmid/ *n* any of a family of nonbiting midges [deriv of Gk *cheironomos* one who gestures with his hands]

chiropody /ki'ropədi, shi-/ *n* the care and treatment of the human foot in health and disease [*chir-* + *pod-*; fr its original concern with both hands and feet] – **chiropodist** *n*

chiropractic /'kirə,praktik/ *n* a system of healing disease that employs manipulation and adjustment of body structures (e g the spinal column) [*chir-* + Gk *praktikos* practical, operative – more at PRACTICAL] – **chiropractor** *n*

chiropter /ki'roptə/, **chiropteran** /-rən/ *n* [3]BAT [deriv of Gk *cheir* hand + *pteron* wing – more at FEATHER] – **chiropteran** *adj*

chirp /chuhp/ *vi or n* (to make or speak in a tone resembling) the characteristic short shrill sound of a small bird or insect [imit]

chirpy /'chuhpi/ *adj* lively, cheerful – infml [CHIRP + [1]-Y] – **chirpily** *adv*, **chirpiness** *n*

chirr /chuh/ *vi or n* (to make) the trilled sound characteristic of certain insects (e g a grasshopper) [imit]

chirrup /'chirəp/ *vi or n* (to) chirp [imit]

chirurgeon /ki'ruhj(ə)n/ *n, archaic* a surgeon [ME *cirurgian*, fr OF *cirurgien*, fr *cirurgie* surgery]

[1]**chisel** /'chizl/ *n* a metal tool with a cutting edge at the end of a blade used in dressing, shaping, or working wood, stone, metal, etc [ME, fr ONF, prob alter. of *chisoir* goldsmith's chisel, fr (assumed) VL *caesorium* cutting instrument, fr L *caesus*, pp of *caedere* to cut – more at CONCISE]

[2]**chisel** *vb* **-ll-** (*NAm* **-l-**, **-ll-**), /'chizl·ing/ **1** to cut or work (as if) with a chisel **2** to trick, cheat, or obtain (sthg) by cheating ⟨*he's* ~led *me out of my prize*⟩ – slang – **chiseller** *n*

'**chiselled**, *NAm chiefly* **chiseled** sharply defined; clear-cut ⟨~ *features*⟩

'**chi-,square** /kie/, **chi-squared** *n* a statistic that indicates the agreement between a set of observed values and a set of values derived from a theoretical model ☞ SYMBOL

[1]**chit** /chit/ *n* an immature often disrespectful young woman, usu of slight build ⟨*a mere* ~ *of a girl*⟩ [ME *chitte* kitten, cub]

[2]**chit** *n* a small slip of paper with writing on it; *esp* an order for goods [Hindi *ciṭṭhī*]

chital /'cheetl/ *n* AXIS DEER [Hindi *cītal*, fr Skt *citrala* variegated, fr *citra* spotted, bright]

chitarrone /,keetə'rohni/ *n* a bass or contrabass of the lute family [It, aug of *chitarra* guitar, fr Gk *kithara* lyre]

chitchat /'chit,chat/ *vi or n* **-tt-** (to make) small talk; gossip – infml [redupl of *chat*]

chitin /'kietin/ *n* a horny polysaccharide that forms part of the hard outer covering of esp insects and crustaceans [F *chitine*, fr Gk *chitōn* chiton, tunic] – **chitinous** *adj*

chiton /'kieton, -tn/ *n* any of an order of marine molluscs with a shell of many plates [NL, genus name, fr Gk *chitōn* tunic, of Sem origin; akin to Heb *kuttōneth* tunic]

chitterling /'chitə,ling/ *n* a section of the smaller intestines of pigs, esp when prepared as food – usu pl [ME *chiterling*]

chivalrous /'shiv(ə)lrəs/ *adj* **1** having the characteristics (e g valour or gallantry) of a knight **2** (characteristic) of knight-errantry **3a** honourable, generous **b** graciously courteous and considerate, esp to women [ME, fr MF *chevalereus*, fr *chevalier* horseman] – **chivalrously** *adv*, **chivalrousness** *n*

chivalry /'shiv(ə)lri/ *n* **1** the system, spirit, or customs of medieval knighthood **2** the qualities (e g courage, integrity, and consideration) of an ideal knight; chivalrous conduct **3** *archaic, sing or pl in constr* mounted men-at-arms [ME *chivalrie*, fr OF *chevalerie*, fr *chevalier*] – **chivalric** /-rik/ *adj*

chive /chiev/ *n* a perennial plant related to the onion and used esp to flavour and garnish food – usu pl with sing. meaning [ME, fr ONF, fr L *cepa* onion]

chivvy, chivy /ˈchivi/ *vt* **1** to tease or annoy with persistent petty attacks; harass **2** to rouse to activity – often + *up* or *along* ***USE*** infml [prob fr E dial. *Chevy Chase* (chase, confusion), fr title of a ballad celebrating a battle in the Cheviot hills in 1388]

chlamydomonas /ˌklamidəˈmohnəs/ *n* any of a genus of single-celled green algae that have 2 flagella and are common in fresh water [NL, genus name, fr L *chlamyd-, chlamys* mantle + NL *monas* monad]

chlor-, chloro- *comb form* **1** green ⟨chloro*phyll*⟩ ⟨chloro*sis*⟩ **2** (containing) chlorine ⟨chlor*ic*⟩ ⟨chloro*promazine*⟩ [NL, fr Gk, fr *chlōros* greenish yellow – more at YELLOW]

ˌchloral ˈhydrate, chloral /ˈklawrəl/ *n* a synthetic drug used as a sedative and hypnotic

chloramphenicol /ˌklawramˈfenikol/ *n* a broad-spectrum antibiotic used esp to treat typhoid fever [*chlor-* + *am*id- + *phe*n- + *ni*tr- + glyc*ol*]

chlorate /ˈklawrayt/ *n* a salt containing the radical ClO_3

chlordane /ˈklawˌdayn/ *n* a chlorinated insecticide [*chlor-* + in*dane* (an oily cyclic hydrocarbon)]

chlordiazepoxide /ˌklawdieˌaziˈpoksied/ *n* a synthetic drug similar to diazepam and used esp as a tranquillizer and to treat the withdrawal symptoms of alcoholism – compare LIBRIUM [*chlor-* + *di-* + *az-* + *epoxide*]

chlorella /kləˈrelə/ *n* any of a genus of single-celled green algae [NL, genus name, fr Gk *chlōros*]

chloride /ˈklawried/ *n* a compound of chlorine with another element or radical; *esp* a salt or ester of hydrochloric acid [G *chlorid*, fr *chlor-* + *-id* -ide]

chlorinate /ˈklawriˌnayt/ *vt* to treat or cause to combine with (a compound of) chlorine – **chlorinator** *n*, **chlorination** n /-ˈnaysh(ə)n/

chlorine /ˈklawreen/ *n* a halogen element that is isolated as a pungent heavy greenish yellow gas ☞ PERIODIC TABLE

chlorite /ˈklawriet/ *n* a salt containing the radical ClO_2 [prob fr F, fr *chlor-*]

chloro- – see CHLOR-

chloroform /ˈkloraˌfawm/ *vt or n* (to anaesthetize with) a colourless volatile liquid used esp as a solvent and formerly as a general anaesthetic [n F *chloroforme*, fr *chlor-* + *formyle* formyl; fr its having been regarded as a trichloride of this radical; vb fr n]

chlorohydrin /ˌklawrohˈhiedrin/ *n* a chlorinated glycol or polyhydroxy alcohol [ISV, fr *chlor-* + *hydr-*]

Chloromycetin /ˌklawrohmieˈseetin/ *trademark* – used for chloramphenicol

chlorophyll /ˈklorəfil/ *n* **1** the green photosynthetic colouring matter of plants found in the chloroplasts **2** a waxy green chlorophyll-containing substance extracted from green plants and used as a colouring agent or deodorant [F *chlorophylle*, fr *chlor-* + Gk *phyllon* leaf – more at BLADE]

chloroplast /ˈklawrohˌplast/ *n* a chlorophyll-containing organelle that is the site of photosynthesis and starch formation in plant cells [ISV]

chloroquine /ˈklawrohˌkween/ *n* an antimalarial drug [*chlor-* + *qu*inol *ine*]

chlorosis /klawˈrohsis/ *n* **1** an iron-deficiency anaemia of young girls characterized by a greenish colour of the skin **2** a diseased condition in green plants marked by yellowing or blanching [NL] – **chlorotic** /klawˈrotik/ *adj*

chlorothiazide /ˌklawrohˈthie·əzied/ *n* a thiazide diuretic drug used esp in the treatment of high blood pressure and oedema

chlorous /ˈklawrəs/ *adj* of or obtained from (trivalent) chlorine

chlorpromazine /ˌklawˈprohməˌzeen/ *n* a derivative of phenothiazine used widely as a tranquillizer, esp to suppress disturbed behaviour (e g in the treatment of schizophrenia) – compare LARGACTIL [*chlor-* + *pro*pyl + *m*ethyl + phenothi*azine*]

chlorpropamide /ˌklawˈpropəmied/ *n* a sulphonylurea drug taken orally to reduce blood sugar in the treatment of mild diabetes mellitus [*chlor-* + *prop*ane + *amide*]

choc-ice /ˈchok ˌies/ *n, Br* a bar of ice cream covered in chocolate [short for *chocolate ice*]

[1]**chock** /chok/ *n* a wedge or block placed under a door, barrel, wheel, etc to prevent movement [origin unknown]

[2]**chock** *vt* **1** to provide, stop, or make fast (as if) with chocks **2** to raise or support on blocks

[3]**chock** *adv* as closely or as completely as possible [[1]*chock*]

chock-a-block /ˌchok ə ˈblok/ *adj or adv* tightly packed; in a very crowded condition [*chock* + [1]*a-* on + *block*, orig the position of a tackle when both blocks are together]

chocolate /ˈchoklət/ *n* **1** a paste, powder, or solid block of food prepared from (sweetened or flavoured) ground roasted cacao seeds **2** a beverage made by mixing chocolate with usu hot water or milk **3** a sweet made or coated with chocolate **4** dark brown [Sp, fr Nahuatl *xocoatl*] – **chocolate** *adj*

ˈchocolate-ˌbox *adj* superficially pretty or sentimental ⟨*a ~ painting of a farmhouse*⟩ [fr the pictures commonly seen on boxes of chocolates]

choctaw /ˈchokˌtaw/ *n* a half turn in ice-skating from an edge of one foot to the opposite edge of the other foot – compare MOHAWK 2 [*Choctaw*, a N American Indian people]

[1]**choice** /choys/ *n* **1** the act of choosing; selection **2** the power of choosing; an option **3a** sby or sthg chosen **b** the best part; the elite **4** a sufficient number and variety to choose among [ME *chois*, fr OF, fr *choisir* to choose, of Gmc origin; akin to OHG *kiosan* to choose – more at CHOOSE]

[2]**choice** *adj* **1** worthy of being chosen **2** selected with care; well chosen **3** of high quality – **choicely** *adv*, **choiceness** *n*

choir /kwie·ə/ *n* **1** *sing or pl in constr* an organized company of singers **2** the part of a church occupied by the singers or the clergy; *specif* the part of the chancel between the sanctuary and the nave ☞ CHURCH [ME *quer*, fr OF *cuer*, fr ML *chorus*, fr L, chorus]

ˈchoirˌboy /-ˌboy/ *n* a boy singer in a (church) choir

ˈchoir ˌorgan *n* a division of an organ having mostly soft stops

ˈchoir ˌschool *n* a school primarily intended for the boys of a cathedral or college choir

[1]**choke** /chohk/ *vt* **1** to check the normal breathing of by compressing or obstructing the windpipe, or by poisoning available air **2** to stop or suppress expression of or by; silence ⟨*a ban designed to ~*

discussion⟩ – often + *back* or *down* **3a** to restrain the growth or activity of ⟨*the flowers were* ~d *by the weeds*⟩ **b** to obstruct by filling up or clogging ⟨*leaves* ~d *the drain*⟩ **c** to fill completely; jam ~ *vi* **1** to become choked in breathing **2a** to become obstructed or checked **b** to become speechless or incapacitated, esp from strong emotion – usu + *up* **3** to lose one's composure and fail to perform effectively in a critical situation [ME *choken*, alter. of *achoken*, fr OE *acēocian*]

²**choke** *n* sthg that obstructs passage or flow: e g **a** a valve in the carburettor of a petrol engine for controlling the amount of air in a fuel air mixture **b** an inductor **c** a narrowing towards the muzzle in the bore of a gun **d** a device allowing variation of the choke of a shotgun

³**choke** *n* the fibrous (inedible) central part of a globe artichoke [back-formation fr *artichoke*, prob by confusion with ²*choke*]

chokeberry /'chohkb(ə)ri/ *n* (the small astringent berry of) a shrub of the rose family that has brilliant autumn foliage

choked /chohkt/ *adj, Br* **1** angry, resentful **2** emotionally moved; touched *USE* infml

chokedamp /'chohk,damp/ *n* blackdamp

choker /'chohkə/ *n* **1** a high stiff (clerical) collar **2** a short necklace or decorative band that fits closely round the throat [¹CHOKE + ²-ER]

chokey, choky /'chohki/ *n, Br* PRISON 2 – slang [Hindi *chaukī* shed, lock-up]

choko /'chohkoh/ *n, pl* **chokos** *Austr & NZ* a succulent cucumber-like vegetable [AmerSp *chocho*, fr Nahuatl *chayotli*]

chol-, chole-, cholo- *comb form* bile; gall ⟨chol*ate*⟩ ⟨chol*esterol*⟩ [Gk *chol-, cholē-, cholo-*, fr *cholē, cholos* – more at ¹GALL]

cholangiography /kə,lanji'ogrəfi/ *n* X-ray photography of the bile ducts [*chol-* + *angi-* + *-graphy*] – **cholangiographic** /kə,lanji·ə'grafik/ *adj*

cholate /'koh,layt/ *n* a salt or ester of cholic acid

cholecystectomy /,kohləsi'stektəmi/ *n* surgical removal of the gall bladder [NL *cholecystis* gallbladder (fr *chol-* + Gk *kystis* bladder) + ISV *-ectomy*]

cholecystitis /,kohləsi'stietəs/ *n* inflammation of the gall bladder [NL, fr *cholecystis*]

cholecystokinin /,kohlə,sistə'kienin/ *n* a hormone secreted by the lining of the duodenum that regulates the emptying of the gall bladder and secretion of enzymes by the pancreas [NL *cholecystis* + E *-o-* + *kinin*]

choler /'kolə, 'kohlə/ *n* **1** anger, irascibility – fml **2a** *archaic* YELLOW BILE **b** *obs* BILE 1a **3** *obs* the state of being bilious [ME *coler*, fr MF *colere*, fr L *cholera* bilious disease, fr Gk, fr *cholē*]

cholera /'kolərə/ *n* (any of several diseases of human beings and domestic animals similar to) an often fatal infectious epidemic disease caused by a bacterium and marked by severe gastrointestinal disorders [ME *colera* bile, fr L *cholera*] – **choleraic** /-'rayik/ *adj*

choleric /'kolərik/ *adj* **1** easily moved to (excessive) anger; irascible **2** angry, irate *USE* fml

cholesterol /kə'lestərol/ *n* a hydroxy steroid that is present in animal and plant cells and is a possible factor in hardening of the arteries [F *cholésterine*, fr *chol-* + Gk *stereos* solid]

choli /'chohli/ *n* a (short-sleeved) close-fitting bodice worn under a sari ☞ GARMENT [Hindi *colī*, fr Skt *cola, coḍa*]

,**cholic 'acid** /'kohlik/ *n* a bile acid important in fat digestion [Gk *cholikos* bilious, fr *cholē*]

choline /'kohleen/ *n* a naturally occurring substance that is a vitamin of the vitamin B complex essential to liver function [ISV]

cholinergic /,kohli'nuhjik/ *adj* **1** *of autonomic nerve fibres* releasing or activated by the neurotransmitter acetylcholine **2** resembling acetylcholine, esp in physiological action [ISV acetyl*choline* + Gk *ergon* work – more at ¹WORK]

chomp /chomp/ *vb* to champ [by alter.]

chondr-, chondri-, chondro- *comb form* cartilage ⟨chondro*blast*⟩ [NL, fr Gk *chondr-, chondro-*, fr *chondros* grain, cartilage]

chondrite /'kondriet/ *n* a granular meteorite [ISV, fr Gk *chondros* grain] – **chondritic** /kon'dritik/ *adj*

chondrule /'kondroohl/ *n* any of the rounded stony granules often found embedded in meteorites [Gk *chondros* grain]

choose /choohz/ *vb* **chose** /chohz/; **chosen** /'chohz(ə)n/ *vt* **1a** to select freely and after consideration **b** to decide on; *esp* to elect ⟨chose *her as leader*⟩ **2a** to decide ⟨chose *to go by train*⟩ **b** to wish ⟨*I* ~ *not to do it*⟩ ~ *vi* to make a selection [ME *chosen*, fr OE *cēosan*; akin to OHG *kiosan* to choose, L *gustare* to taste] – **chooser** *n*

choosy, choosey /'choohzi/ *adj* fastidiously selective; particular

¹**chop** /chop/ *vb* **-pp-** *vt* **1a** to cut into or sever, usu by a blow or repeated blows of a sharp instrument ⟨~ *down a tree*⟩ **b** to cut into pieces – often + *up* **2** to strike (a ball) so as to impart backspin **3** to subject to the action of a chopper ⟨~ *a beam of light*⟩ ~ *vi* to make a quick stroke or repeated strokes (as if) with a sharp instrument [ME *chappen, choppen* – more at ²CHAP]

²**chop** *n* **1** a forceful usu slanting blow or stroke (as if) with an axe or cleaver **2** a small cut of meat often including part of a rib ☞ MEAT **3** an uneven motion of the sea, esp when wind and tide are opposed **4** abrupt removal; *esp* ¹SACK 4 – + *the*; infml

³**chop** *vi* **-pp-** *esp of the wind* to change direction [ME *chappen, choppen* to barter, fr OE *cēapian*] – **chop and change** to keep changing one's mind, plans, etc – **chop logic** to argue with minute oversubtle distinctions

⁴**chop** *n* (a licence validated by) a seal or official stamp such as was formerly used in China or India [Hindi *chāp* stamp]

,**chop-'chop** *adv or interj* without delay; quickly – infml [Pidgin E, redupl of *chop* fast – more at CHOPSTICK]

'**chop,house** /-,hows/ *n* a restaurant specializing in meat dishes, esp chops or steaks

chopper /'chopə/ *n* **1** a short-handled axe or cleaver **2** a device that interrupts an electric current or a beam of radiation (e g light) at short regular intervals **3** a helicopter – infml [¹CHOP + ²-ER]

choppy /'chopi/ *adj, of the sea or other expanse of water* rough with small waves [³*chop*]

chops /chops/ *n pl* (the fleshy covering of) the jaw ⟨*the hungry dog licked his* ~⟩ [alter. of ⁴*chap*]

'**chop,stick** /-,stik/ *n* either of 2 slender sticks held between thumb and fingers, used chiefly in oriental countries to lift food to the mouth [Pidgin E, fr *chop* fast (of Chinese origin; akin to Cant *kap*) + E *stick*]

chopsuey /,chop'sooh·i/ *n* a Chinese dish of shredded meat or chicken with bean sprouts and other vegetables, usu served with rice and soy sauce [Chin (Cant) *shap sui* odds and ends, fr *shap* various + *sui* bits]

choral /'kawrəl/ *adj* accompanied with or designed for singing (by a choir) [F or ML; F *choral*, fr ML *choralis*, fr L *chorus*] – **chorally** *adv*

chorale *also* **choral** /ko'rahl/ *n* **1** (music composed for) a usu German traditional hymn or psalm for singing in church **2** *sing or pl in constr* a chorus, choir [G *choral*, short for *choralgesang* choral song]

[1]**chord** /kawd/ *n* a combination of notes sounded together [alter. of ME *cord*, short for *accord*]

[2]**chord** *n* **1** CORD 3a **2** a straight line joining 2 points on a curve ☞ MATHEMATICS **3** an individual emotion or disposition ⟨*touch the right* ~⟩ **4** the straight line joining the leading and trailing edges of an aerofoil [alter. of [1]*cord*]

chordal /'kawdl/ *adj* **1** of or suggesting a chord **2** relating to music characterized more by harmony than counterpoint

chordate /'kaw,dayt, -dət/ *n or adj* (any) of a phylum or subkingdom of animals including the vertebrates that have at some stage of development a notochord, a central nervous system along the back, and gill clefts [deriv of L *chorda* cord]

'chord ,organ *n* an electronic or reed organ with buttons to produce simple chords

chore /chaw/ *n* **1** a routine task or job **2** a difficult or disagreeable task [alter. of *chare*, fr ME *char* turn, piece of work, fr OE *cierr*]

chorea /ko'ree·ə/ *n* a nervous disorder marked by spasmodic movements of limbs and facial muscles and by lack of coordination [NL, fr L, dance, fr Gk *choreia*, fr *choros* chorus] – **choreic** /ko'ree·ik/ *adj or n*

choreography /,kori'ogrəfi/ *n* **1** the art of representing dance steps and sequences in symbols **2** stage dancing as distinguished from social or ballroom dancing **3** the composition and arrangement of a ballet or other dance for the stage [F *chorégraphie*, fr Gk *choreia* + F *-graphie* -graphy] – **choreographer** *n*, **choreograph** /'kori·ə,grahf, -,graf/ *vb*, **choreographic** /-'grafik/ *adj*, **choreographically** *adv*

choric /'korik/ *adj* of or being in the style of a (Greek) chorus

chorion /'kawri·ən/ *n* the outer embryonic membrane of higher vertebrates that is associated with the allantois in the formation of the placenta [NL, fr Gk] – **chorionic** /-'onik/ *adj*

chorister /'koristə/ *n* a singer in a choir; *specif* a choirboy [ME *querister*, fr AF *cueristre*, fr ML *chorista*, fr L *chorus*]

'C-ho,rizon *n* the layer of soil lying beneath the B-horizon and consisting of weathered rock

choroid /'kaw,royd/, **choroid coat** *n* a membrane containing large pigment cells that lies between the retina and the sclera of the vertebrate eye ☞ NERVE [NL *choroides* resembling the chorion, fr Gk *chorioeidēs*, fr *chorion*] – **choroid** *adj*

chortle /'chawtl/ *vi* **chortling** /'chawtl·ing, 'chawtling/ to laugh or chuckle, esp in satisfaction or exultation [blend of *chuckle* and *snort*] – **chortle** *n*, **chortler** /'chawtlə/ *n*

[1]**chorus** /'kawrəs/ *n* **1** (the part of a drama sung or spoken by) a character (e g in Elizabethan drama) or group of singers and dancers (e g in Greek drama) who comment on the action **2** *sing or pl in constr* **a** an organized company of singers who sing in concert; *specif* a body of singers who sing the choral parts of a work (e g in opera) **b** a group of dancers and singers supporting the featured players in a musical or revue ⟨*a* ~ *girl*⟩ **3a** a part of a song or hymn recurring at intervals **b** a composition sung by a chorus **4** sthg performed, sung, or uttered simultaneously by a number of people or animals [L, ring dance, chorus, fr Gk *choros*] – **in chorus** in unison

[2]**chorus** *vb* to sing or utter in chorus

chose /chohz/ *past of* CHOOSE

[1]**chosen** /'chohz(ə)n/ *adj* selected or marked for favour or special privilege ⟨*granted to a* ~ *few*⟩ [ME, fr pp of *chosen* to choose]

[2]**chosen** *n pl in constr* *the* people who are the object of divine favour

chough /chuf/ *n* an Old World bird of the crow family that has red legs, a red beak, and glossy black plumage [ME]

,choux 'pastry /shooh/ *n* a light pastry made with an egg-enriched dough and used for profiteroles, eclairs, etc [F *choux*, pl of *chou*, lit., cabbage, fr L *caulis* stalk – more at HOLE]

[1]**chow** /chow/ *n* food – infml [perh fr Chin (Pek) *chiao* C3 meat dumpling]

[2]**chow** *also* **'chow ,chow** *n* a heavy-coated broad-headed dog with a blue-black tongue [fr a Chin dial. word akin to Cant *kaú* dog]

'chow-,chow *n* a Chinese preserve of ginger, fruits, and peel in heavy syrup [Pidgin E, mixture]

chowder /'chowdə/ *n* a thick (clam or other seafood) soup or stew [F *chaudière* kettle, contents of a kettle, fr LL *caldaria* – more at CAULDRON]

chow mein /,chow 'mayn/ *n* a Chinese dish of fried noodles usu mixed with shredded meat or poultry and vegetables [Chin (Pek) *ch'ao*[3] *mien*[4], fr *ch'ao*[3] to fry + *mien*[4] dough]

chrism /'kriz(ə)m/ *n* consecrated oil used in Greek and Roman Catholic churches, esp in baptism, confirmation, and ordination [ME *crisme*, fr OE *crisma*, fr LL *chrisma*, fr Gk, ointment, fr *chriein* to anoint; akin to OE *grēot* grit, sand]

chrisom *also* **chrysom** /'kriz(ə)m/ *n* a white cloth or robe put on a child at baptism as a symbol of innocence and formerly also used as a shroud for infants [ME *crisom*, short for *crisom cloth*, fr *crisom* chrism + *cloth*]

'chrisom ,child *n* a child that dies in its first month

Christ /kriest/ *n* **1** the Messiah **2** Jesus [ME *Crist*, fr OE, fr L *Christus*, fr Gk *Christos*, lit., anointed, fr *chriein*] – **Christlike** *adj*

christen /'kris(ə)n/ *vt* **1a** BAPTIZE 1, 3 **b** to name at baptism **2** to name or dedicate (e g a ship or bell) by a ceremony suggestive of baptism **3** to name **4** to use for the first time – infml [ME *cristnen*, fr OE *cristnian*, fr *cristen* Christian, fr L *christianus*]

Christendom /'kris(ə)ndəm, 'krist-/ *n* the community of people or nations professing Christianity [ME *cristendom*, fr OE *cristendōm*, fr *cristen*]

christening /'kris(ə)ning/ *n* the ceremony of baptizing and naming a child

[1]Christian /ˈkristi·ən/ *n* **1a** an adherent of Christianity **b** a member of a Christian denomination, esp by baptism **2** a good or kind person regardless of religion [L *christianus*, adj & n, fr Gk *christianos*, fr *Christos*]

[2]Christian *adj* **1** of or consistent with Christianity or Christians **2** commendably decent or generous ⟨*has a very ~ concern for others*⟩ – **Christianize** /-ˌniez/ *vt*, **Christianization** /-nieˈzaysh(ə)n/ *n*, **Christianly** *adv*

ˈChristian ˌera *n* the period dating from the birth of Christ

christiania /ˌkristiˈahnyə, -ni·ə/ *n* STEM CHRISTIE [*Christiania*, former name of Oslo, city in Norway]

Christianity /ˌkristiˈanəti/ *n* **1** the religion based on the life and teachings of Jesus Christ and the Bible **2** conformity to (a branch of) the Christian religion

ˈChristian ˌname *n* **1** a name given at christening (or confirmation) **2** a forename

ˌChristian ˈScience *n* a religion founded by Mary Baker Eddy in 1866 that includes a practice of spiritual healing – **Christian Scientist** *n*

Christmas /ˈkrisməs/ *n* **1** a festival of the western Christian churches on December 25 that commemorates the birth of Christ and is usu observed as a public holiday **2 Christmas, Christmastide** /-ˌtied/ the festival season from Christmas Eve till the Epiphany (January 6) [ME *Christemasse*, fr OE *Cristes mæsse*, lit., Christ's mass] – **Christmassy** /ˈkrisməsi/ *adj*

Christmas cactus *n* a branching winter-flowering S American cactus with showy red flowers

ˌChristmas ˈEve *n* the (evening of the) day before Christmas day

ˌChristmas ˈrose *n* a European winter-flowering plant of the buttercup family that has white or purplish flowers

ˈChristmas ˌtree *n* an evergreen or artificial tree decorated with lights, tinsel, etc at Christmas

Christo- *comb form* Christ ⟨Christo*centric*⟩ ⟨Christo*logy*⟩

Christogram /ˈkriestəˌgram, ˈkris-/ *n* a graphic symbol of Christ; *esp* the Chi-Rho [Gk *Christos* Christ + E *-gram*]

chrom- /krohm-/, **chromo-** *comb form* **1** chromium ⟨chrom*ize*⟩ **2a** colour; coloured ⟨chromo*plast*⟩ **b** pigment ⟨chromo*phore*⟩ [F, fr Gk *chrōma* colour]

chroma /ˈkrohmə/ *n* a quality of colour combining hue and saturation [Gk *chrōma*]

chromat-, chromato- *comb form* colour ⟨chromat*icity*⟩ [Gk *chrōmat-, chrōma*]

chromate /ˈkrohˌmayt/ *n* a salt or ester of chromic acid [F, fr Gk *chrōma*]

chromatic /krohˈmatik/ *adj* **1a** of colour sensation or (intensity of) colour **b** highly coloured **2a** of or giving all the notes of the chromatic scale **b** characterized by frequent use of intervals or notes outside the diatonic scale [Gk *chrōmatikos*, fr *chrōmat-, chrōma* skin, colour, modified tone; akin to OE *grēot* sand – more at GRIT] – **chromatically** *adv*, **chromaticism** /-tiˌsiz(ə)m/ *n*

chroˌmatic aberˈration /ˌabəˈraysh(ə)n/ *n* optical aberration caused by the differences in refraction of the different colours of the spectrum and characterized by coloured outlines round an image

chromaticity /ˌkrohməˈtisəti/ *n* a quality of a colour in terms of its purity and dominant or complementary wavelength [CHROMATIC + -ITY]

chromatic scale *n* a musical scale consisting entirely of semitones

chromatid /ˈkrohmətid/ *n* either of the paired strands of a chromosome

chromatin /ˈkrohmətin/ *n* a complex of DNA with proteins that forms the chromosomes in the cell nucleus and is readily stained – **chromatinic** /-ˈtinik/ *adj*

chromatogram /krohˈmatəgram/ *n* the visual record (e g the pattern remaining in the absorbent medium) of the components separated by chromatography

chromatography /ˌkrohməˈtogrəfi/ *n* the separation of chemicals from a mixture by passing the mixture as a solution or vapour over or through a substance (e g paper) which adsorbs the chemicals to differing extents – **chromatograph** /krohˈmatəgrahf, -graf/ *vt*, **chromatographic** /ˌkrohmətəˈgrafik/ *adj*, **chromatographically** *adv*

chromatophore /krohˈmatəfaw/ *n* a pigment-bearing cell or organelle; *esp* any of the cells found in the surface layer of an animal capable of causing skin-colour changes by expanding or contracting [ISV]

chrome /krohm/ *n* **1** (a pigment formed from) chromium **2** (sthg with) a plating of chromium [F, fr Gk *chrōma*]

-chrome /-krohm/ *comb form* (→ *n, adj*) **1** coloured thing ⟨*helio*chrome⟩; coloured ⟨*poly*chrome⟩ **2** colouring matter ⟨*uro*chrome⟩ [ML *-chromat-, -chroma* coloured thing, fr Gk *chrōmat-, chrōma*]

ˌchrome ˈyellow *n* a yellow pigment consisting essentially of lead chromate

chromic /ˈkrohmik/ *adj* of or derived from (trivalent) chromium

ˌchromic ˈacid *n* a corrosive acid whose salts are chromates

chrominance /ˈkrohminəns/ *n* the colour information in a colour television signal [*chrom-* + lum*inance*]

chromite /ˈkrohˌmiet/ *n* a mineral that consists of a magnetic oxide of iron and chromium [G *chromit*, fr *chrom-*]

chromium /ˈkrohmyəm, -mi·əm/ *n* a blue-white metallic element found naturally only in combination and used esp in alloys and in electroplating ☞ PERIODIC TABLE [NL, fr F *chrome*]

chromo- – see CHROM-

chromolithograph /ˌkrohmohˈlithəˌgrahf, -ˌgraf/ *n* a picture printed in colours from a series of stones prepared by the lithographic process – **chromolithographic** /-ˌlithəˈgrafik/ *adj*, **chromolithography** /-liˈthogrəfi/ *n*

chromomere /ˈkrohməˌmiə/ *n* any of the small bead-shaped concentrations of chromatin that are arranged in a line along the chromosome [ISV] – **chromomeric** /-ˈmerik/ *adj*

chromophore /ˈkrohməˌfaw/ *n* a chemical group that gives rise to colour in a compound [ISV] – **chromophoric** /-ˈforik/ *adj*

chromoplast /ˈkrohməˌplast/ *n* a coloured body in a plant cell that contains no chlorophyll but usu contains red or yellow pigment (e g carotene) [ISV]

chromoprotein /ˌkrohmohˈprohteen/ *n* a compound (e g haemoglobin) of a protein with a metal-containing pigment (e g haem)

chromosome /'krohmə,sohm, -,zohm/ *n* any of the gene-carrying bodies that contain DNA and protein and are found in the cell nucleus [ISV] – **chromosomal** /-'sohml, -'zohml/ *adj*, **chromosomally** *adv*

'**chromosome ,number** *n* the usu constant number of chromosomes characteristic of a particular species of animal or plant

chromosphere /'krohmə,sfiə/ *n* the lower layer of the sun's atmosphere that is immediately above the photosphere and consists chiefly of hydrogen; *also* a similar part of the atmosphere of any star – **chromospheric** /-'sferik/ *adj*

chromous /'krohməs/ *adj* of or derived from (bivalent) chromium

chron-, chrono- *comb form* time ⟨chrono*logy*⟩ [Gk, fr *chronos*]

chronic /'kronik/ *adj* **1a** *esp of an illness* marked by long duration or frequent recurrence – usu contrasted with ACUTE 4 **b** suffering from a chronic disease **2a** always present or encountered; *esp* constantly troubling ⟨*~ financial difficulties*⟩ **b** habitual, persistent ⟨*a ~ grumbler*⟩ **3** *Br* bad, terrible – infml [F *chronique*, fr Gk *chronikos* of time, fr *chronos*] – **chronically** *adv*, **chronicity** /kro'nisəti/ *n*

[1]**chronicle** /'kronikl/ *n* **1** a usu continuous and detailed historical account of events arranged chronologically without analysis or interpretation **2** a narrative [ME *cronicle*, fr AF, alter. of OF *chronique*, fr L *chronica*, fr Gk *chronika*, fr neut pl of *chronikos*]

[2]**chronicle** *vt* **chronicling** /'kronikl·ing/ **1** to record (as if) in a chronicle **2** to list, describe – **chronicler** /-klə/ *n*

'**chronicle ,play** *n* a play with a historical theme consisting usu of rather loosely connected episodes chronologically arranged

Chronicles /'kroniklz/ *n pl but sing in constr* either of 2 historical books of canonical Jewish and Christian Scripture

chronogram /'krohnə,gram/ *n* a phrase in which some letters are Roman numerals that make a date when added together – **chronogrammatic** /-grə'matik/, **chronogrammatical** *adj*

chronograph /'krohnə,grahf, -,graf/ *n* an instrument for accurately measuring and recording time intervals – **chronographic** /-'grafik/ *adj*, **chronography** /krə'nogrəfi/ *n*

chronological /,kronə'lojikl, ,kroh-/ *also* **chronologic** /-'lojik/ *adj* of or arranged in or according to the order of time ⟨*~ tables of British history*⟩ – **chronologically** *adv*

chronology /krə'noləji/ *n* **1** (the scientific study or use of) a method for setting past events in order of occurrence **2** an arrangement in order of occurrence; *specif* such an arrangement presented in tabular or list form [NL *chronologia*, fr *chron-* + *-logia* -logy] – **chronologer, chronologist** *n*, **chronologize** *vt*

chronometer /krə'nomitə/ *n* an instrument for measuring time; *esp* one designed to keep time with great accuracy

chronometry /krə'nomətri/ *n* (the science of) accurate time measurement – **chronometric** /,kronə'metrik, ,kroh-/, **chronometrical** *adj*, **chronometrically** *adv*

chrys- /kris-/, **chryso-** *comb form* gold; yellow ⟨chryso*lite*⟩ [Gk, fr *chrysos*]

chrysalid /'krisəlid/ *n* a chrysalis

chrysalis /'krisəlis/ *n, pl* **chrysalides** /kri'salə,deez/, **chrysalises** **1** (the case enclosing) a pupa, esp of a butterfly or moth **2** a sheltered state or stage of being or growth ⟨*ready to emerge from the ~ of adolescence*⟩ [L *chrysallid-, chrysallis* gold-coloured pupa of butterflies, fr Gk, fr *chrysos* gold, of Sem origin]

chrysanthemum /kri'zanthiməm/ *n* any of various (cultivated) composite plants with brightly coloured often double flower heads [L, fr Gk *chrysanthemon*, fr *chrys-* + *anthemon* flower; akin to Gk *anthos* flower]

chrysoberyl /'krisə,berəl/ *n* a usu yellow or pale green mineral consisting of beryllium aluminium oxide and used as a gem [L *chrysoberyllus*, fr Gk *chrysobēryllos*, fr *chrys-* + *bēryllos* beryl]

chrysolite /'krisə,liet/ *n* olivine [ME *crisolite*, fr OF, fr L *chrysolithos*, fr Gk, fr *chrys-* + *-lithos* -lite]

chrysom /'kriz(ə)m/ *n* a chrisom

chrysotile /'krisə,tiel/ *n* a type of fibrous silky asbestos [G *chrysotil*, fr *chrys-* + *-til* fibre, fr Gk *tillein* to pluck]

chthonic /'thonik/, **chthonian** /'thohnyən, -ni·ən/ *adj* of the underworld; infernal ⟨*~ deities*⟩ [Gk *chthon-, chthōn* earth – more at HUMBLE]

chub /chub/ *n, pl* **chub**, *esp for different types* **chubs** (a marine or freshwater fish similar to) a European freshwater fish of the carp family [ME *chubbe*]

Chubb /chub/ *trademark* – used for a type of lock with a device for jamming the bolt if an attempt is made to pick it

chubby /'chubi/ *adj* of large proportions; plump ⟨*a ~ boy*⟩ [*chub* + *-y*] – **chubbiness** *n*

[1]**chuck** /chuk/ *n* – used as a term of endearment [ME *chuk*, fr *chukken* to make a clucking noise, of imit origin]

[2]**chuck** *vt* **1** to pat, tap ⟨*~ed her under the chin*⟩ **2a** to toss, throw **b** to discard – often + *out* or *away* **3** to leave; GIVE UP 2 ⟨*~ed his job*⟩ – often + *in* or *up* *USE (except 1)* infml [perh fr MF *chuquer, choquer* to knock]

[3]**chuck** *n* **1** a pat or nudge under the chin **2** a throw – infml

[4]**chuck** *n* **1** a cut of beef that includes most of the neck and the area about the shoulder blade ☞ MEAT **2** a device for holding a workpiece (e g for turning on a lathe) or tool (e g in a drill) [E dial. *chuck* (lump, log), prob var of *chock*]

chuckle /chukl/ *vi* **chuckling** /'chukling/ to laugh inwardly or quietly [prob freq of *chuck* (to make a clucking noise)] – **chuckle** *n*, **chucklesome** /-s(ə)m/ *adj*, **chucklingly** /'chuklingli/ *adv*

chucklehead /'chukl,hed/ *n* a blockhead – infml [*chuckle* (lumpish) + *head*] – **chuckleheaded** /-'hedid/ *adj*

chuck out *vt* to eject (a person) from a place or an office; dismiss – infml – **chucker-out** *n*

'**chuck ,wagon** *n, NAm* a wagon carrying a stove and provisions for cooking (e g on a ranch) [E dial (NAm) *chuck* (food)]

chuff /chuf/ *vi or n* (to produce or move with) a sound made (as if) by a steam engine releasing steam regularly [imit]

chuffed /chuft/ *adj, Br* pleased – infml [E dial *chuff* (fat, proud, happy)]

chug /chug/ *vi or n* **-gg-** (to move or go with) a usu repetitive dull explosive sound made (as if) by a labouring engine [imit]

chukar /chu'kah/ *n, pl* **chukar, chukars** a largely grey and black Indian partridge [Hindi *cakor*]

chukka /'chukə/ *n* **1** a chukker **2 chukka, chukka boot** a usu ankle-length leather boot (worn for playing polo)

chukker /'chukə/ *n* any of the periods of play in a polo game [Hindi *cakkar* circular course, fr Skt *cakra* wheel, circle – more at WHEEL]

[1]**chum** /chum/ *n* a close friend; a mate – infml; no longer in vogue [perh by shortening & alter. fr *chamber fellow* (roommate)]

[2]**chum** *vi* **-mm-** to form a friendship, esp a close one – usu + *(up) with*; no longer in vogue

chummy /'chumi/ *adj* friendly, intimate – infml – **chummily** *adv*, **chumminess** *n*

chump /chump/ *n* **1** a cut of meat taken from between the loin and hindleg, esp of a lamb, mutton, or pork carcass ☞ MEAT **2** a fool, duffer – infml [perh blend of *chunk* and *lump*] – **off one's chump** OFF ONE'S HEAD

chunder /'chundə/ *vb, chiefly Austr*, to vomit – slang [origin unknown]

chunk /chungk/ *n* **1** LUMP 1; *esp* one of a firm or hard material (e g wood) **2** a (large) quantity ⟨*put a sizable ~ of money on the race*⟩ – infml [perh alter. of E dial. *chuck* (lump, log)]

chunky /'chungki/ *adj* **1** stocky **2** filled with chunks ⟨*~ marmalade*⟩ **3** *of materials, clothes, etc* thick and heavy – **chunkily** *adv*, **chunkiness** *n*

chunnel /'chunl/ *n, often cap* a proposed tunnel under the English channel [blend of *channel* and *tunnel*]

chunter /'chuntə/ *vi, Br* to talk or mutter incessantly and usu irrelevantly – often + *on*; infml [prob imit]

[1]**church** /chuhch/ *n* **1** a building for public (Christian) worship; *esp* a place of worship used by an established church – compare CHAPEL 5 👁 **2** *often cap* institutionalized religion; *esp* the established Christian religion of a country **3** *cap* a body or organization of religious believers: e g **a** the whole body of Christians **b** DENOMINATION 2 **c** CONGREGATION 2 **4** an occasion for public worship ⟨*goes to ~ every Sunday*⟩ **5** the clerical profession ⟨*considered the ~ as a possible career*⟩ [ME *chirche*, fr OE *cirice*; akin to OHG *kirihha* church; both fr a prehistoric WGmc word derived fr LGk *kyriakon*, fr Gk, neut of *kyriakos* of the lord, fr *kyrios* lord, master, fr *kyros* power] – **churchly** *adj*, **churchman,** /-mən/ *fem* **churchwoman** *n*

[2]**church** *adj* **1** of a church **2** *chiefly Br* being a member of the established state church – compare [2]CHAPEL

ˌ**Church 'Army** *n* an Anglican organization for social work founded on the model of the Salvation Army

churching /'chuhching/ *n* a ceremony in which a woman after childbirth is received and blessed in church – **church** *vt*

church mode *n* any of several modes prevalent in medieval music

ˌ**Church of 'England** *n* the established episcopal church of England

ˌ**Church of 'Scotland** *n* the established presbyterian church of Scotland

church school *n* a (primary) school controlled in part by a church

ˌ**church'warden** /'-wawd(ə)n/ *n* **1** either of 2 lay parish officers in Anglican churches with responsibility esp for parish property and alms **2** a long-stemmed (clay) tobacco pipe

churchy /'chuhchi/ *adj* marked by strict conformity or zealous adherence to the forms or beliefs of a church

'**churchˌyard** /-ˌyahd/ *n* an enclosed piece of ground surrounding a church; *esp* one used as a burial ground

churl /chuhl/ *n* **1a** a rude ill-bred person **b** a mean morose person **2** *archaic* a rustic, countryman [ME, fr OE *ceorl* man, ceorl; akin to Gk *gēras* old age – more at [1]CORN]

churlish /'chuhlish/ *adj* **1** lacking refinement or sensitivity **2** rudely uncooperative; surly – **churlishly** *adv*, **churlishness** *n*

[1]**churn** /chuhn/ *n* **1** a vessel used in making butter in which milk or cream is agitated to separate the oily globules from the watery medium **2** *Br* a large metal container for transporting milk [ME *chyrne*, fr OE *cyrin*; akin to OE *corn* grain; fr the granular appearance of cream as it is churned – more at [1]CORN]

[2]**churn** *vt* **1** to agitate (milk or cream) in a churn in order to make butter **2** to stir or agitate violently *~ vi* **1** to work a churn **2** to produce or be in violent motion

churn out *vt* to produce prolifically and mechanically, usu without great concern for quality – chiefly infml

churr /chuh/ *vi or n* (to make) a vibrant or whirring noise characteristic of certain insects and birds (e g the partridge) [imit]

chute /shooht/ *n* **1** a waterfall, rapid, etc **2** an inclined plane, channel, or passage down which things may pass **3** a parachute – infml [F, fr OF, fr *cheoir* to fall, fr L *cadere* – more at CHANCE]

chutney /'chutni/ *n* a thick condiment or relish of Indian origin that contains fruits, sugar, vinegar, and spices [Hindi *caṭnī*]

chutzpah *also* **chutzpa** /'khootspah, 'hootspah/ *n* brazen audacity – infml [Yiddish, fr LHeb *ḥuṣpāh*]

chyle /kiel/ *n* lymph that is milky from emulsified fats and is produced during intestinal absorption of fats [LL *chylus*, fr Gk *chylos* juice, chyle, fr *chein* to pour – more at [4]FOUND] – **chylous** /'kieləs/ *adj*

chylomicron /ˌkieloh'miekron/ *n* a microscopic drop of fat occurring in the blood during fat digestion and assimilation [Gk *chylos* + *mikron*, neut of *mikros* small]

chyme /kiem/ *n* the semifluid mass of partly digested food expelled by the stomach into the duodenum [NL *chymus*, fr LL, chyle, fr Gk *chymos* juice, fr *chein*] – **chymous** *adj*

chymotrypsin /ˌkiemoh'tripsin/ *n* an enzyme that breaks down proteins and is released into the intestines from the pancreas during digestion [*chyme* + *-o-* + *trypsin*]

ciao /chow/ *interj* – used to express greeting or farewell [It, fr It dial., alter. of *schiavo* (I am your) slave, fr ML *sclavus*]

ciborium /si'bawri·əm/ *n, pl* **ciboria** /-ri·ə/ **1** a goblet-shaped vessel for holding the consecrated bread used at Communion **2** a freestanding vaulted canopy supported by 4 columns over a high altar [ML, fr L, cup, fr Gk *kibōrion*]

cicada /si'kahdə, -'kaydə/ *n* any of a family of insects that have large transparent wings and whose males produce a shrill singing noise [NL, genus name, fr L, cicada]

cicala /si'kahlə/ *n* a cicada [It, fr ML, alter. of L *cicada*]

cicatrice /'sikətrees/ *n* a cicatrix

cicatrix /'sikə,triks/ *n, pl* **cicatrices** /,sikə'trieseez, si'kaytri,seez/ **1** a scar resulting after a flesh wound has healed **2** a mark resembling a scar: e g **a** a mark left on a stem after the fall of a leaf or bract **b** HILUM 1a [L *cicatric-, cicatrix*] – **cicatricial** /,sikə'trish(ə)l/ *adj*

cicatr·ize, -ise /'sikə,triez/ *vt* [1]SCAR ~ *vi* to heal by forming a scar – **cicatrization** /-'zaysh(ə)n/ *n*

cicerone /,sisə'rohni, ,chichə-/ *n, pl* **ciceroni** /~/ one who acts as a guide to antiquities; *broadly* a guide, mentor [It, fr *Cicerone* Cicero †43 BC Roman orator & statesman]

cichlid /'siklid/ *n* any of a family of mostly tropical spiny-finned freshwater fishes [deriv of Gk *kichlē* thrush, a kind of wrasse; akin to Gk *chelidōn* swallow – more at CELANDINE]

cicisbeo /,chichiz'bayoh/ *n, pl* **cicisbei** /-'bay,ee/ a lover or gallant [It]

-cide /-sied/ *comb form* (→ *n*) **1** killer ⟨*insecticide*⟩ **2** killing ⟨*suicide*⟩ [MF, fr L *-cida* (1) & *-cidium* (2), fr *caedere* to cut, kill – more at CONCISE] – **-cidal** *comb form* (→ *adj*)

cider, *Br also* **cyder** /'siedə/ *n* fermented often sparkling apple juice [ME *sidre*, fr OF, fr LL *sicera* strong drink, fr Gk *sikera*, fr Heb *shēkhār*]

cig /sig/ *n* a cigarette – infml

cigar /si'gah/ *n* a small roll of tobacco leaf for smoking [Sp *cigarro*]

cigarette, *NAm also* **cigaret** /,sigə'ret/ *n* a narrow cylinder of cut tobacco enclosed in paper for smoking; *also* a similar roll of a herbal or narcotic substance [F *cigarette*, dim. of *cigare* cigar, fr Sp *cigarro*]

cigarillo /,sigə'riloh, -'reelyoh/ *n, pl* **cigarillos** a very small cigar [Sp *cigarrillo*, dim. of *cigarro*]

ciliary /'silyəri/ *adj* **1** of cilia **2** of or being the ciliary body

ciliary body *n* the ringlike muscular body supporting the lens of the eye ☞ NERVE

cilium /'sili·əm/ *n, pl* **cilia** /-li·ə/ **1** an eyelash **2** a minute hairlike part; *esp* one capable of a lashing movement that produces locomotion in a single-celled organism [NL, fr L, eyelid] – **ciliate** /-ət, -ayt/, **ciliated** /-aytid/ *adj*, **ciliation** /-'aysh(ə)n/ *n*

[1]**cinch** /sinch/ *n* **1** *NAm* GIRTH 1 **2a** a task performed with ease **b** sthg certain to happen ***USE*** (*2*) infml [Sp *cincha*, fr L *cingula* girdle, girth, fr *cingere*]

[2]**cinch** *vt* **1** *NAm* to fasten or tighten a girth round (a horse) – often + *up* **2** to make certain of; assure – infml

cinchona /sing'kohnə/ *n* (the dried quinine-containing bark of) any of a genus of S American trees and shrubs of the madder family [NL, genus name, fr Countess of *Chinchón* †1641 vicereine of Peru]

cinchonine /'singkəneen/ *n* an alkaloid found esp in cinchona bark and used like quinine

cincture /'singkchə/ *n* a girdle, belt; *esp* a cloth cord or sash worn round an ecclesiastical vestment or the habit of a religious order [L *cinctura* girdle, fr *cinctus*, pp of *cingere* to gird; akin to Skt *kāñcī* girdle]

cinder /'sində/ *n* **1** (a fragment of) slag (e g from a blast furnace or volcano) **2** a fragment of ash **3** a piece of partly burned material (e g coal) that will burn further but will not flame [ME *sinder*, fr OE; akin to OHG *sintar* dross, slag, OSlav *sędra* stalactite] – **cindery** *adj*

Cinderella /,sində'relə/ *n* **1** sby or sthg that suffers undeserved neglect **2** sby or sthg that is suddenly raised from obscurity to honour or importance [*Cinderella*, heroine of a fairy-tale]

cine- /sini-/ *comb form* relating to the cinema ⟨cine*camera*⟩ ⟨cine*film*⟩ [*cinema*]

cineaste /'siniast/ *n* a devotee of films [F *cinéaste*]

cinecamera /'sini,kamrə/ *n* a simple hand-held camera for making usu amateur films

cinema /'sinimə/ *n* **1a** films considered esp as an art form, entertainment, or industry – usu + *the* **b** the art or technique of making films; *also* the effects appropriate to film **2** *chiefly Br* a theatre where films are shown [short for *cinematograph*]

cinemagoer /'sinimə,goh·ə/ *n* one who frequently attends films – **cinemagoing** *n or adj*

Cinemascope /'sinimə,skohp/ *trademark* – used for a method of film projection employing a cylindrical lens, an extra-wide screen, and usu stereophonic sound

cinematic /,sini'matik/ *adj* **1** made and presented as a film ⟨~ *fantasies*⟩ **2** of or suitable for (the making of) films – **cinematically** *adv*

cinematograph /,sini'matə,grahf, -,graf/ *n, chiefly Br* a film camera or projector [F *cinématographe*, fr Gk *kinēmat-, kinēma* movement (fr *kinein* to move) + *-o-* + *-graphe* -graph]

cinematography /,sinimə'tografi/ *n* the art or science of cinema photography – **cinematographer** *n*, **cinematographic** /sini,matə'grafik/ *adj*, **cinematographically** *adv*

,cinema 'verité /'veritay/ *n* the art or technique of film-making so as to convey documentary-style realism [F *cinéma-vérité*, lit., truth cinema]

cineole /'siniohl/ *n* a liquid with a camphor smell contained in many essential oils, esp that of eucalyptus [ISV, by transposition fr NL *oleum cinae* wormseed oil]

Cinerama /,sinə'rahmə/ *trademark* – used for a method of film projection employing 3 projectors, an extra-wide concave screen, and stereophonic sound

cineraria /,sinə'reəri·ə/ *n* any of several composite pot plants with heart-shaped leaves and clusters of bright flower heads [NL, fr L, fem of *cinerarius* of ashes, fr *ciner-, cinis* ashes]

cinerarium /,sinə'reəri·əm/ *n, pl* **cineraria** /-ri·ə/ a place where the ashes of the cremated dead are kept [L, fr *ciner-, cinis*] – **cinerary** /'sinərəri/ *adj*

Cingalese /,sing·gə'leez/ *n, pl* **Cingalese** (a) Sinhalese

cinnabar /'sinəbah/ *n* **1** naturally occurring red mercuric sulphide **2** a European moth with greyish black fore wings marked with red and clear reddish pink hind wings [ME *cynabare*, fr MF & L; MF *cenobre*, fr L *cinnabaris*, fr Gk *kinnabari*, of non-IE origin; akin to Ar *zinjafr* cinnabar]

The parish church

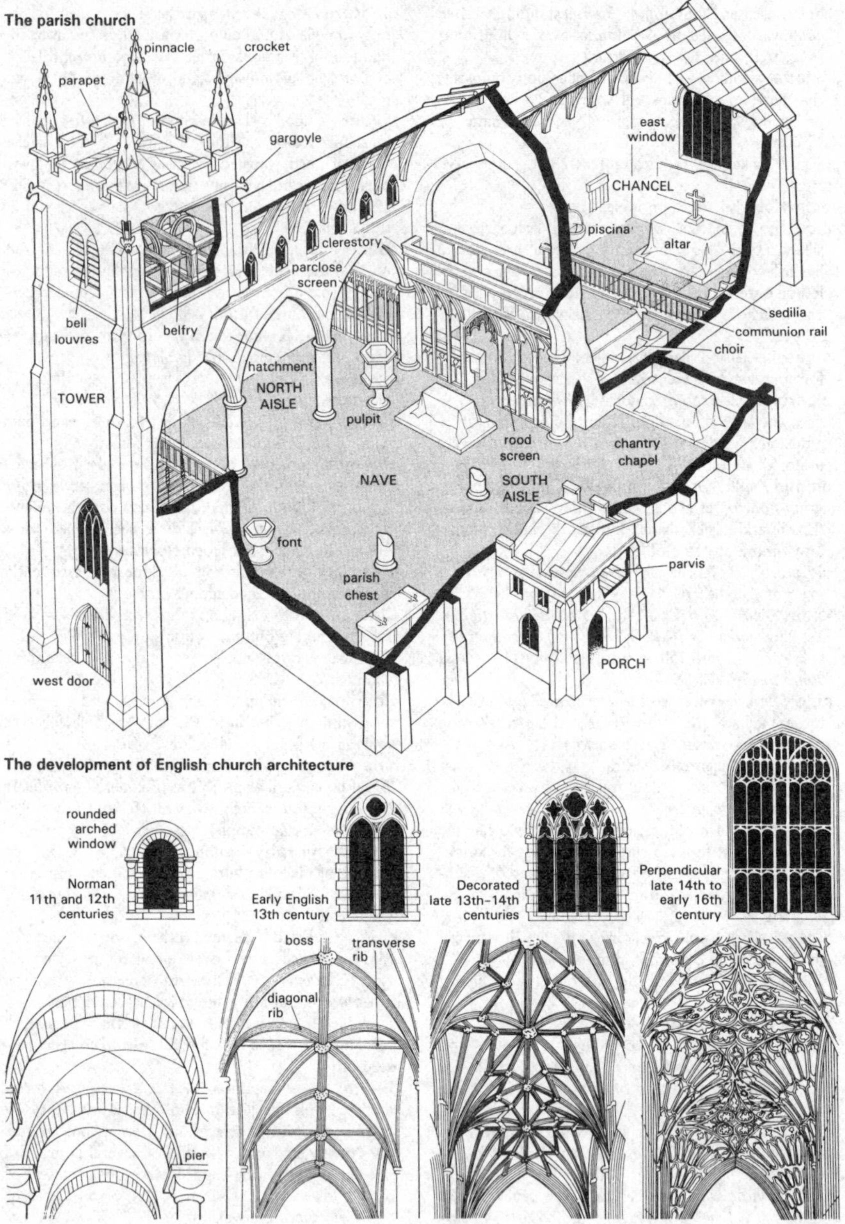
pinnacle
crocket
parapet
gargoyle
east window
CHANCEL
piscina
altar
clerestory
parclose screen
bell
louvres
belfry
sedilia
communion rail
choir
hatchment
NORTH AISLE
TOWER
pulpit
rood screen
chantry chapel
NAVE
SOUTH AISLE
font
parish chest
parvis
PORCH
west door
The development of English church architecture
rounded arched window
Norman 11th and 12th centuries
Early English 13th century
Decorated late 13th–14th centuries
Perpendicular late 14th to early 16th century
boss
transverse rib
diagonal rib
pier
groined vault
ribbed vault
lierne vault
fan vault

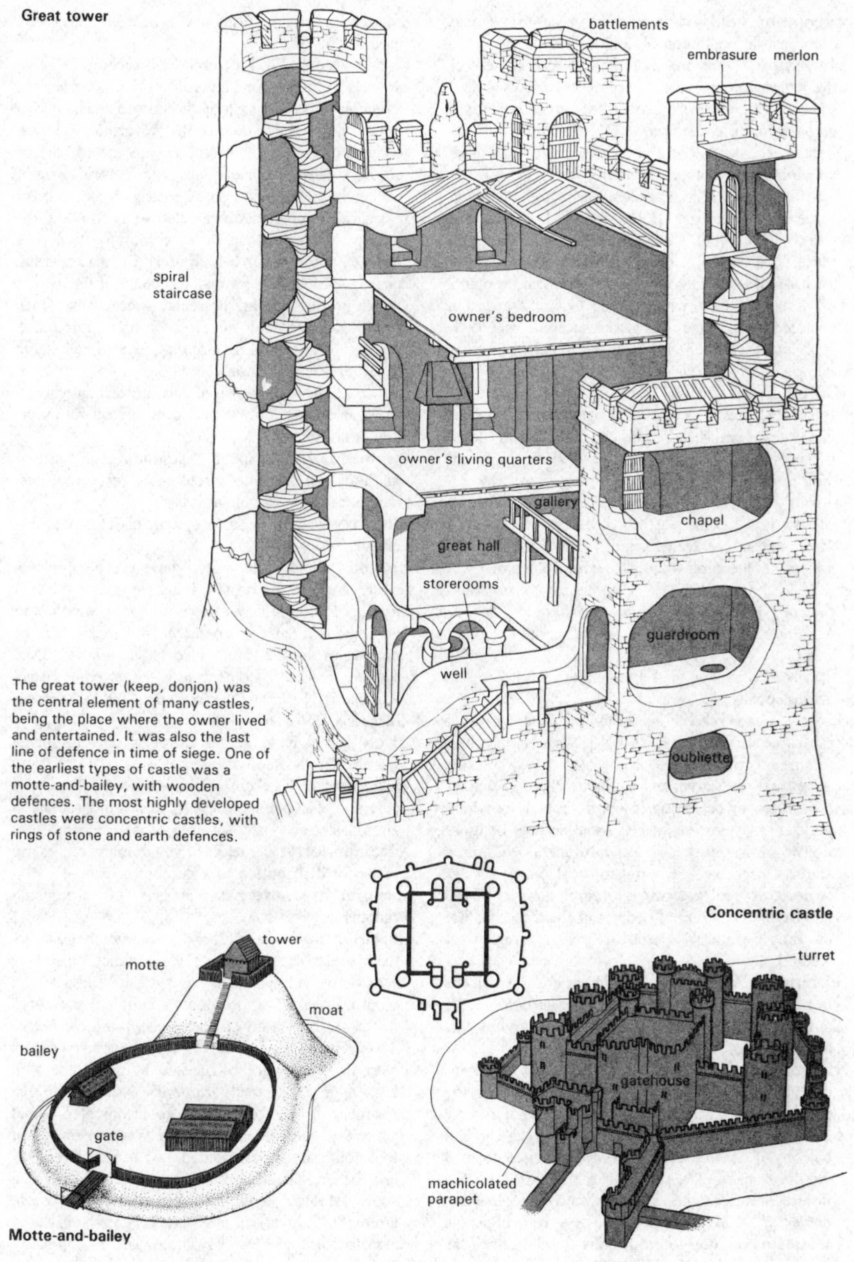

The great tower (keep, donjon) was the central element of many castles, being the place where the owner lived and entertained. It was also the last line of defence in time of siege. One of the earliest types of castle was a motte-and-bailey, with wooden defences. The most highly developed castles were concentric castles, with rings of stone and earth defences.

cin,namic 'acid /sə'namik/ *n* an odourless acid found esp in cinnamon oil and storax

cinnamon /'sinəmən/ *n* **1** (any of several trees of the laurel family with) an aromatic bark used as a spice **2** light yellowish brown [ME *cynamone*, fr L *cinnamomum, cinnamon*, fr Gk *kinnamōmon, kinnamon*, of non-IE origin; akin to Heb *qinnāmōn* cinnamon] – **cinnamic** /sə'namik/ *adj*

cinquecento /,chingkwi'chentoh/ *n* the 16th century, esp in Italian art [It, lit., five hundred, fr *cinque* five (fr L *quinque*) + *cento* hundred, fr L *centum* – more at HUNDRED] – **cinquecentist** *n*

cinquefoil /'singk,foyl/ *n* **1** any of a genus of plants of the rose family with 5-lobed leaves **2** a design enclosed by 5 joined arcs arranged in a circle [ME *sink foil*, fr MF *cincfoille*, fr L *quinquefolium*, fr *quinque* five + *folium* leaf – more at BLADE]

'Cinque ,Port /singk/ *n* any of orig 5 and now 7 towns on the SE coast of England with ancient privileges because of their importance in naval defence [back-formation fr *Cinque Ports*, pl, fr OF *cinq ports* five ports, fr L *quinque portus*]

[1]**cipher** *also* **cypher** /'siefə/ *n* **1a** ZERO 1 **b** sby who or sthg that has no worth or influence; a nonentity **2a** a method of transforming a text in order to conceal its meaning – compare CODE 3b **b** a message in code **3** any of the Arabic numerals **4** a combination of symbolic letters; *esp* a monogram [ME, fr MF *cifre*, fr ML *cifra*, fr Ar *ṣifr* empty, cipher, zero]

[2]**cipher** *also* **cypher** *vt* **1** to encipher **2** to compute arithmetically

circa /'suhkə/ *prep* at, in, or of approximately – used esp with dates ⟨*born* ~ *1600*⟩ [L, fr *circum* round – more at CIRCUM-]

circadian /suh'kaydi·ən/ *adj* being, having, characterized by, or occurring in approximately day-long periods or cycles (e g of biological activity or function) ⟨~ *rhythms*⟩ ⟨~ *leaf movements*⟩ [L *circa* about + *dies* day + E *-an* – more at DEITY]

Circassian /suh'kasi·ən/ *n or adj* (a member or the language) of a group of peoples of the Caucasus not of Indo-European speech [*Circassia*, region of Russia]

circinate /'suhsi,nayt/ *adj* rolled or coiled (with the top as a centre) ⟨~ *fern fronds unfolding*⟩ [L *circinatus*, pp of *circinare* to round, fr *circinus* pair of compasses, fr *circus*] – **circinately** *adv*

[1]**circle** /'suhkl/ *n* **1a** a closed plane curve every point of which is equidistant from a fixed point within the curve **b** the plane surface bounded by such a curve **2** sthg in the form of (an arc of) a circle: e g **a** a balcony or tier of seats in a theatre **b** a circle formed on the surface of a sphere (e g the earth) by the intersection of a plane **3** cycle, round ⟨*the wheel has come full* ~⟩ **4** *sing or pl in constr* a group of people sharing a common interest, activity, or leader ⟨*the gossip of court* ~s⟩ *USE* (*1*) ☞ MATHEMATICS [ME *cercle*, fr OF, fr L *circulus*, dim. of *circus* ring, circus, fr or akin to Gk *krikos, kirkos* ring]

[2]**circle** *vb* **circling** /'suhkling, 'suhkl·ing/ *vt* **1** to enclose (as if) in a circle **2** to move or revolve round ~ *vi* to move (as if) in a circle – **circler** /'suhklə, 'suhkl·ə/ *n*

circlet /'suhklit/ *n* a little circle; *esp* a circular ornament

circlip /'suh,klip/ *trademark* – used for a clip that encircles a tubular fitting and is held in place by its natural tension

circuit /'suhkit/ *n* **1** a closed loop encompassing an area **2a** a course round a periphery **b** a racetrack **3a** a regular tour (e g by a judge) round an assigned area or territory **b** the route travelled **c** a group of church congregations with 1 pastor (e g in the Methodist church) **4a** the complete path of an electric current, usu including the source of energy **b** an array of electrical components connected so as to allow the passage of current **c** a 2-way communication path between points (e g in a computer) **5a** an association or league of similar groups **b** a chain of theatres at which productions are presented successively [ME, fr MF *circuite*, fr L *circuitus*, fr pp of *circumire, circuire* to go round, fr *circum-* + *ire* to go – more at ISSUE] – **circuital** *adj*

'circuit ,breaker *n* a switch that automatically interrupts an electric circuit under an infrequent abnormal condition

circuitous /suh'kyooh·itəs/ *adj* indirect in route or method; roundabout – **circuitously** *adv*, **circuitousness, circuity** /-'kyooh·əti/ *n*

circuitry /'suhkitri/ *n* (a system of) electrical circuits

[1]**circular** /'suhkyoolə/ *adj* **1** having the form of a circle **2** moving in or describing a circle or spiral **3** marked by the fallacy of assuming sthg which is to be demonstrated ⟨~ *arguments*⟩ **4** marked by or moving in a cycle **5** intended for circulation [ME *circuler*, fr MF, fr LL *circularis*, fr L *circulus* circle] – **circularity** /-'larəti/ *n*, **circularly** /-ləli/ *adv*, **circularness** /-lə,nis/ *n*

[2]**circular** *n* a paper (e g a leaflet or advertisement) intended for wide distribution

circular·ize, -ise /'suhkyoolə,riez/ *vt* **1** to send circulars to **2** to publicize, esp by means of circulars – **circularization** /-rie 'zaysh(ə)n/ *n*

,circular 'letter *n* a letter of which many copies are made for distribution to a number of people

circular measure *n* the measure of an angle in radians

,circular 'saw *n* a power-driven saw that has its teeth set on the edge of a revolving metal disc

circulate /'suhkyoo,layt/ *vi* **1** to move in a circle, circuit, or orbit; *esp* to follow a course that returns to the starting point ⟨*blood* ~s *through the body*⟩ **2** to pass from person to person or place to place: e g **a** to flow without obstruction **b** to become well known or widespread ⟨*rumours* ~d *through the town*⟩ **c** to go from group to group at a social gathering **d** to come into the hands of readers; *specif* to become sold or distributed ~ *vt* to cause to circulate [L *circulatus*, pp of *circulare*, fr *circulus* circle] – **circulatable** /-,laytəbl/ *adj*, **circulative** /-lətiv/ *adj*, **circulator** /-,laytə/ *n*, **circulatory** /-lətri/ *adj*

circulation /,suhkyoo'laysh(ə)n/ *n* **1** a flow **2** orderly movement through a circuit; *esp* the movement of blood through the vessels of the body induced by the pumping action of the heart **3a** passage or transmission from person to person or place to place; *esp* the interchange of currency ⟨*coins in* ~⟩ **b** the extent of dissemination; *esp* the average number of copies of a publication sold over a given period

'circulatory ,system /'suhkyoolətri, ,suhkyoo'-layt(ə)ri/ *n* the system of blood, blood and lymphatic vessels, and heart concerned with the circulation of the blood and lymph ☞ ANATOMY

circum- /suhkəm-/ *prefix* round; about ⟨*circumnavigate*⟩ [OF or L; OF, fr L, fr *circum*, fr *circus* circle – more at CIRCLE]

,circum'ambulate /-'ambyoolayt/ *vt* to walk round, esp in a ritual fashion – fml [LL *circumambulatus*, pp of *circumambulare*, fr L *circum-* + *ambulare* to walk]

circumcise /'suhkəm,siez/ *vt* to cut off the foreskin of (a male) or the clitoris of (a female) [ME *circumcisen*, fr L *circumcisus*, pp of *circumcidere*, fr *circum-* + *caedere* to cut – more at CONCISE] – **circumciser** *n*

,circum'cision /-'sizh(ə)n/ *n* **1** a Jewish rite of circumcising performed on male infants as a sign of inclusion in the Jewish religious community **2** *cap* January 1 observed as a church festival in commemoration of the circumcision of Jesus [CIRCUMCISE + -ION]

circumference /suh'kumfərəns/ *n* **1** the perimeter of a circle ☞ MATHEMATICS **2** the external boundary or surface of a figure or object [ME, fr MF, fr L *circumferentia*, fr *circumferre* to carry round, fr *circum-* + *ferre* to carry – more at [2]BEAR] – **circumferential** /-,kumfə'rensh(ə)l/ *adj*

[1]**circumflex** /'suhkəm,fleks/ *adj* marked with or having the sound indicated by a circumflex [L *circumflexus*, pp of *circumflectere* to bend round, mark with a circumflex, fr *circum-* + *flectere* to bend]

[2]**circumflex** *n* an accent mark ˆ ×, ˆ , or ˜ used in various languages to mark length, contraction, or a particular vowel quality ☞ SYMBOL

,circumlo'cution /-lə'kyoohsh(ə)n/ *n* **1** the use of an unnecessarily large number of words to express an idea **2** evasive speech [L *circumlocution-*, *circumlocutio*, fr *circum-* + *locutio* speech, fr *locutus*, pp of *loqui* to speak] – **circumlocutious** /-'kyoohshəs/ *adj*, **circumlocutory** /-'lokyoot(ə)ri/ *adj*

,circum'lunar /-'loohnə/ *adj* revolving round or surrounding the moon

,circum'navigate /-'navigayt/ *vt* to go round; *esp* to travel completely round (the earth), esp by sea [L *circumnavigatus*, pp of *circumnavigare* to sail round, fr *circum-* + *navigare* to navigate] – **circumnavigator** *n*, **circumnavigation** /-'gaysh(ə)n/ *n*

,circum'polar /-'pohlə/ *adj* **1** *of a celestial body* continually visible above the horizon **2** surrounding or found near a pole of the earth

'circum,scribe /-,skrieb/ *vt* **1** to surround by a physical or imaginary line **2** to restrict the range or activity of definitely and clearly **3** to draw round (a geometrical figure) so as to touch at as many points as possible [L *circumscribere*, fr *circum-* + *scribere* to write, draw – more at [1]SCRIBE]

,circum'scription /-'skripsh(ə)n/ *n* (a) circumscribing or being circumscribed; *esp* (the act of imposing) a restriction [L *circumscription-*, *circumscriptio*, fr *circumscriptus*, pp of *circumscribere*]

'circum,spect /-,spekt/ *adj* careful to consider all circumstances and possible consequences; prudent [ME, fr MF or L; MF *circonspect*, fr L *circumspectus*, fr pp of *circumspicere* to look around, be cautious, fr *circum-* + *specere* to look – more at SPY] – **circumspection** /-'speksh(ə)n/ *n*, **circumspectly** /-,spektli/ *adv*

circumstance /'suhkəm,stahns, -stans, -stəns/ *n* **1** a condition or event that accompanies, causes, or determines another; *also* the sum of such conditions or events ⟨*economic* ~⟩ **2a** a state of affairs; an occurrence ⟨*open rebellion was a rare* ~⟩ – often pl with sing. meaning ⟨*a victim of* ~s⟩ **b** *pl* situation with regard to material or financial welfare ⟨*he was in easy* ~s⟩ **3** attendant formalities and ceremony ⟨*pomp and* ~⟩ **4** an incident viewed as part of a narrative or course of events; a fact [ME, fr MF, fr L *circumstantia*, fr *circumstant-*, *circumstans*, prp of *circumstare* to stand round, fr *circum-* + *stare* to stand – more at STAND] – **in/under the circumstances** because of the conditions; considering the situation

'circumstanced *adj* placed in specified circumstances, esp in regard to property or income

circumstantial /,suhkəm'stansh(ə)l, -'stahnsh(ə)l/ *adj* **1** belonging to, consisting in, or dependent on circumstances **2** pertinent but not essential; incidental – **circumstantiality** /-shi'aləti/ *n*, **circumstantially** /-sh(ə)l·i/ *adv*

,circum,stantial 'evidence *n* evidence that tends to prove a fact indirectly by proving other events or circumstances which afford a basis for drawing conclusions

circumstantiate /,suhkəm'stanshi,ayt/ *vt* to supply with circumstantial evidence or support

,circum'vallate /-'valayt/ *adj* surrounded (as if) by a rampart [L *circumvallatus*, pp of *circumvallare* to surround with a wall, fr *circum-* + *vallare* to fortify with a wall, fr *vallum* rampart – more at WALL] – **circumvallation** /-va'laysh(ə)n/ *n*

,circum'vent /-'vent/ *vt* to check or evade, esp by ingenuity or stratagem [L *circumventus*, pp of *circumvenire*, fr *circum-* + *venire* to come – more at COME] – **circumvention** /-'vensh(ə)n/ *n*

circus /'suhkəs/ *n* **1a** a large circular or oval stadium used esp for sports contests or spectacles **b** a public spectacle **2a** (the usu covered arena housing) an entertainment in which a variety of performers (e g acrobats and clowns) and performing animals are involved in a series of unrelated acts **b** an activity suggestive of a circus (e g in being a busy scene of noisy or frivolous action) **3** *Br* a road junction in a town partly surrounded by a circle of buildings – usu in proper names ⟨*Piccadilly* Circus⟩ [L, ring, circus – more at CIRCLE] – **circusy** *adj*

ciré /'siray (*Fr* sire)/ *n* (a fabric with) a highly glazed finish, usu achieved by waxing and heating [F, fr pp of *cirer* to wax, fr *cire* wax, fr L *cera* – more at CERUMEN]

cire perdue /,siə peə'dooh (*Fr* siːr pɛrdy)/ *n* a process used in metal casting in which a clay impression of an object (e g a statue) is formed from a wax model which is then melted away leaving a mould into which molten metal can be poured [F *(moulage à) cire perdue*, lit., lost wax casting]

'cirl ,bunting /suhl/ *n* a small yellow olive and black European bunting [NL *cirlus*, specific epithet, fr It *cirlo*, of imit origin]

cirque /suhk/ *n* **1** a deep steep-walled basin on a mountain ☞ GEOGRAPHY **2** *archaic* CIRCUS 1a [F, fr L *circus*]

cirr-, cirri-, cirro- *comb form* cirrus ⟨cirri*ped*⟩ ⟨cirr*ose*⟩ ⟨cirro*stratus*⟩ [NL *cirrus*]

cirrhosis /si'rohsis/ *n*, *pl* **cirrhoses** /-,seez/ hardening (of the liver) caused by excessive formation of connective tissue [NL, fr Gk *kirrhos* orange-coloured] – **cirrhotic** /-'rotik/ *adj or n*

cirriped /ˈsiri,ped/, **cirripede** /-,peed/ *n* a barnacle or related marine crustacean permanently attached (e g to a rock) as an adult [deriv of NL *cirr-* + L *ped-, pes* foot – more at FOOT] – **cirriped** *adj*

cirrocumulus /,sirohˈkyoohmyooləs/ *n* a cloud formation consisting of small white rounded masses at a high altitude, usu in regular groupings forming a mackerel sky [NL]

cirrostratus /,sirohˈstrahtəs/ *n* a uniform layer of high stratus clouds that are darker than cirrus ☞ WEATHER [NL]

cirrus /ˈsirəs/ *n, pl* **cirri** /-rie/ **1** TENDRIL 1 **2** a slender usu flexible (invertebrate) animal appendage **3** a wispy white cloud formation usu of minute ice crystals formed at high altitudes ☞ WEATHER [NL, fr L, curl]

cis /sis/ *adj* characterized by having identical atoms or groups on the same side of the molecule – usu ital; often in combination ⟨cis- *dichloroethylene*⟩; compare TRANS [L, on this side]

cis- /sis-/ *prefix* on this side of ⟨cis*pontine*⟩ ⟨cis*atlantic*⟩ [L, fr *cis* – more at HE]

cisalpine /sisˈalpien/ *adj* south of the Alps

cislunar /sisˈloohnə/ *adj* between the earth and the moon ⟨~ *space*⟩

cissy, sissy /ˈsisi/ *n, Br* **1** an effeminate boy or man **2** a cowardly person *USE* infml [*cissy*, alter. of *sissy*, fr *sis* (short for *sister*) + [1]*-y*] – **cissy** *adj*

cist /sist/ *n* a neolithic or Bronze Age stone burial chamber [W, chest, fr L *cista*]

Cistercian /siˈstuhsh(ə)n/ *n* a member of an austere Benedictine order founded by St Robert of Molesme in 1098 at Cîteaux in France [ML *Cistercium* Cîteaux] – **Cistercian** *adj*

cistern /ˈsist(ə)n/ *n* an artificial reservoir for storing liquids, esp water: e g **a** a tank at the top of a house or building **b** a water reservoir for a toilet **c** *chiefly NAm* a usu underground tank for storing rainwater [ME, fr OF *cisterne*, fr L *cisterna*, fr *cista* box, chest]

cistron /ˈsistron/ *n* a gene consisting of a segment of DNA which codes for a particular enzyme, RNA molecule, etc [*cis-* + *trans-* + [2]*-on*] – **cistronic** /-ˈstronik/ *adj*

citadel /ˈsitədl, -,del/ *n* **1** a fortress; *esp* one that commands a city **2** a stronghold [MF *citadelle*, fr OIt *cittadella*, dim. of *cittade* city, fr ML *civitat-, civitas* – more at CITY]

citation /sieˈtaysh(ə)n/ *n* **1a** an act of citing or quoting **b** a quotation **2** a mention; *specif* specific reference in a military dispatch to meritorious conduct – **citational** *adj*

cite /siet/ *vt* **1** to call upon to appear before a court **2** to quote by way of example, authority, precedent, or proof ⟨~ *Biblical passages*⟩ **3** to refer to or name; *esp* to mention formally in commendation or praise [MF *citer* to cite, summon, fr L *citare* to put in motion, rouse, summon, fr *citus*, pp of *ciēre* to stir, move] – **citable** *adj*

cithara /ˈsithərə, ˈki-/ *n* an ancient Greek stringed instrument of the lyre family with a wooden sounding board [L, fr Gk *kithara*]

cithern /ˈsidhuhn/ *n* a cittern

citizen /ˈsitiz(ə)n/ *n* **1** an inhabitant of a city or town; *esp* a freeman **2** a (native or naturalized) member of a state [ME *citizein*, fr AF *citezein*, alter. of OF *citeien*, fr *cité* city] – **citizenly** *adj*, **citizenship** *n*

ˈ**citizenry** /-ri/ *n sing or pl in constr* the whole body of citizens

,**Citizens' ˈBand** *n* a system of radio communication by which private individuals, esp drivers, can transmit messages to one another

citr-, citri-, citro- *comb form* **1** citrus ⟨citri*culture*⟩ **2** citric acid ⟨citr*ate*⟩ [NL, fr *Citrus*, genus name]

citrate /ˈsitrayt, ˈsie-/ *n* a salt or ester of citric acid [ISV]

,**citric ˈacid** /ˈsitrik/ *n* an acid occurring in lemons, limes, etc, formed as an intermediate in cell metabolism, and used as a flavouring [ISV]

,**citric ˈacid ,cycle** *n* KREBS CYCLE

[1]**citrine** /ˈsitrin/ *adj* resembling a lemon, esp in colour [ME, fr MF *citrin*, fr ML *citrinus*, fr L *citrus* citron tree]

[2]**citrine** *n* semiprecious yellow quartz

citron /ˈsitrən/ *n* **1** a (tree that bears) fruit like the lemon but larger and with a thicker rind **2** the preserved rind of the citron, used esp in cakes and puddings [ME, fr MF, fr OProv, modif of L *citrus* citron tree]

citronella /,sitrəˈnelə/ *n* a fragrant S Asian grass that yields an oil used in perfumery and as an insect repellent [NL, fr F *citronnelle* lemon balm, fr *citron*]

citrous /ˈsitrəs/ *adj* of or being citrus trees or their fruit

citrus /ˈsitrəs/ *n, pl* **citrus, citruses** any of several often thorny trees and shrubs of the rue family grown in warm regions for their edible thick-rinded juicy fruit (e g the orange or lemon) [NL, genus name, fr L, citron tree] – **citrus** *adj*

cittern /ˈsitən/ *n* a plucked stringed instrument popular esp in Renaissance England [blend of *cither* and *gittern*]

city /ˈsiti/ *n* **1a** a large town **b** an incorporated British town that has a cathedral or has had civic status conferred on it ☞ COUNTY **c** a usu large chartered municipality in the USA **2** a city-state **3a** *the* financial and commercial area of London **b** *cap, sing or pl in constr the* influential financial interests of the British economy [ME *citie* large or small town, fr OF *cité* capital city, fr ML *civitat-, civitas*, fr L, citizenship, state, city of Rome, fr *civis* citizen – more at HOME]

,**city ˈfather** *n* an important official or prominent citizen of a city

,**city ˈhall** *n* the chief administrative building of a city

,**city ˈslicker** *n, NAm* a slicker – infml

,**city-ˈstate** *n* an autonomous state consisting of a city and surrounding territory

civet /ˈsivit/ *n* a thick yellowish musky-smelling substance extracted from a pouch near the sexual organs of the civet cat and used in perfumery [MF *civette*, fr OIt *zibetto*, fr Ar *zabād* civet perfume]

ˈ**civet ,cat** *n* a long-bodied short-legged flesh-eating African mammal from which civet is obtained

civic /ˈsivik/ *adj* of a citizen, a city, or citizenship [L *civicus*, fr *civis* citizen] – **civically** /-kli/ *adv*

ˈ**civic ,centre** *n, Br* an area where a planned group of the chief public buildings of a town are situated

ˈ**civics** *n pl but sing or pl in constr* a social science dealing with the rights and duties of citizens

civies /ˈsiviz/ *n pl* civvies

civil /ˈsivl/ *adj* **1** of citizens ⟨~ *liberties*⟩ **2** adequately courteous and polite; not rude **3** relating to private rights as distinct from criminal proceedings ☞ LAW **4** *of time* based on the sun and legally recognized for use in ordinary affairs **5** of or involving the general public as distinguished from special (e g military or religious) affairs [ME, fr MF, fr L *civilis*, fr *civis*] – **civilly** /'siv(ə)l·i/ *adv*

,civil de'fence *n, often cap C&D* protective measures organized by and for civilians against hostile attack, esp from the air, or natural disaster

,civil ,diso'bedience *n* refusal to obey governmental demands (e g payment of tax) as a means of forcing concessions

,civil engi'neer *n* an engineer whose training or occupation is in the designing and construction of large-scale public works (e g roads or bridges) – **civil engineering** *n*

civilian /si'vilyən/ *n* one who is not in the army, navy, air force, or other uniformed public body – **civilian** *adj*, **civilianize** /-,niez/ *vt*, **civilianization** /-nie'zaysh(ə)n/ *n*

civility /si'viləti/ *n* **1** courtesy, politeness **2** a polite act or expression – usu pl

civil·ization, -isation /,sivilie'zaysh(ə)n, -li-/ *n* **1a** a relatively high level of cultural and technological development **b** the culture characteristic of a particular time or place **2** the process of becoming civilized **3** life in a place that offers the comforts of the modern world; *specif* life in a city – often humor

civil·ize, -ise /'siv(ə)l,iez/ *vt* **1** to cause to develop out of a primitive state; *specif* to bring to a technically advanced and rationally ordered stage of cultural development **2** to educate, refine – **civilizable** *adj*, **civilizer** *n*

'civil·ized, -ised *adj* of or being peoples or nations in a state of civilization

,civil 'law *n, often cap C&L* **1** ROMAN LAW **2** the body of private law developed from Roman law as distinct from common law **3** the law established by a nation or state for its own jurisdiction (e g as distinct from international law) **4** the law of private rights ☞ LAW

,civil 'liberty *n* a right or freedom of the individual citizen in relation to the state (e g freedom of speech); *also* such rights or freedoms considered collectively – **civil libertarian** *n*

'civil ,list *n* an annual allowance by Parliament for the expenses of the monarch and royal family

,civil 'marriage *n* a marriage involving a civil contract but no religious rite

,civil 'rights *n pl* CIVIL LIBERTIES; *esp* those of status equality between races or groups – **civil righter, civil rightist** *n*

,civil 'servant *n* a member of a civil service

,civil 'service *n sing or pl in constr* the administrative service of a government or international agency, exclusive of the armed forces

,civil 'war *n* a war between opposing groups of citizens of the same country

civvies, civies /'siviz/ *n pl* civilian as distinguished from military clothes – slang [by shortening & alter.]

'civvy ,street /'sivi/ *n, often cap C&S, Br* civilian life as opposed to life in the services – slang

clachan /'klak(h)ən, 'klah-/ *n, Scot & Irish* a small village; a hamlet [ME, fr ScGael]

¹clack /klak/ *vi* **1** CHATTER 2 – infml **2** to make an abrupt striking sound or sounds ~*vt* to cause to make a clatter [ME *clacken*, of imit origin] – **clacker** *n*

²clack *n* **1** rapid continuous talk; chatter – infml **2** a sound of clacking

¹clad /klad/ *adj* being covered or clothed ⟨*ivy*-clad *buildings*⟩ ⟨~ *in tweeds*⟩ [pp of *clothe*]

²clad *vt* **-dd-; clad** to cover with cladding

³clad *n* cladding

cladding /'klading/ *n* a thin covering or overlay (e g of stone on a building or metal on a metal core)

cladistics /klə'distiks/ *n pl but sing in constr* a theory that describes the relationship between types of organism on the assumption that their sharing of a unique characteristic (e g the hair of mammals) possessed by no other organism indicates their descent from a single common ancestor [*clade* (group of organisms evolved from a common ancestor; fr Gk *klados* branch) + *-istics* (as in *statistics*)]

cladode /'kladohd/ *n* a branch that closely resembles a leaf and often bears leaves or flowers [NL *cladodium*, fr Gk *klados* branch] – **cladodial** /-'dohdi·əl/ *adj*

¹claim /klaym/ *vt* **1a** to ask for, esp as a right ⟨~ed *Supplementary Benefit*⟩ **b** to require, demand **c** to take; ACCOUNT FOR 3 ⟨*plague* ~ed *thousands of lives*⟩ **2** to take as the rightful owner **3** to assert in the face of possible contradiction; maintain ⟨~ed *that he'd been cheated*⟩ [ME *claimen*, fr OF *clamer*, fr L *clamare* to cry out, shout; akin to L *calare* to call – more at ¹LOW] – **claimable** *adj*, **claimer** *n*

²claim *n* **1** a demand for sthg (believed to be) due ⟨*insurance* ~⟩ **2a** a right or title to sthg **b** an assertion open to challenge ⟨*a* ~ *to fame*⟩ **3** sthg claimed; *esp* a tract of land staked out

claimant /'klaymənt/ *n* one who asserts a right or entitlement

clairvoyance /kleə'voyəns/ *n* **1** the power or faculty of discerning objects not apparent to the physical senses **2** the ability to perceive matters beyond the range of ordinary perception [F, fr *clairvoyant* clear-sighted, fr *clair* clear (fr L *clarus*) + *voyant*, prp of *voir* to see, fr L *vidēre*] – **clairvoyant** *adj or n*

clam /klam/ *n* **1** any of numerous edible marine molluscs (e g a scallop) living in sand or mud **2** a freshwater mussel [*clam*, n (clamp), fr OE *clamm* bond, fetter; fr the clamping action of the shells]

'clam,bake /-,bayk/ *n, NAm* **1** an outdoor party; *esp* a seashore outing where food is cooked on heated rocks covered by seaweed **2** a gathering characterized by noisy sociability; *esp* a political rally [*clam* + *bake*]

clamber /'klambə/ *vi* to climb awkwardly or with difficulty [ME *clambren*; akin to OE *climban* to climb] – **clamberer** *n*

clammy /'klami/ *adj* being damp, clinging, and usu cool [ME, prob fr *clammen* to smear, stick, fr OE *clǣman*; akin to OE *clǣg* clay] – **clammily** *adv*, **clamminess** *n*

clamour, *NAm chiefly* **clamor** /'klamə/ *vi or n* **1** (to engage in) noisy shouting **2** (to make) a loud continuous noise **3** (to make) insistent public expression (e g of support or protest) ⟨*the* ~ *for representation*⟩ [n ME *clamor*, fr MF *clamour*, fr L *clamor*, fr *clamare* to cry out; vb fr n] – **clamorous** *adj*, **clamorously** *adv*, **clamourousness** *n*

¹clamp /klamp/ *n* **1** a device that holds or compresses 2 or more parts firmly together **2** a heap of wooden sticks or bricks for burning, firing, etc [ME, prob fr (assumed) MD *klampe*; akin to OE *clamm* bond, fetter]

[2]**clamp** *vt* **1** to fasten (as if) with a clamp ⟨~ *an artery*⟩ **2** to hold tightly

[3]**clamp** *n, Br* a heap of potatoes, turnips, etc covered over with straw or earth [prob fr D *klamp* heap]

clamp down *vi* to impose restrictions; *also* to make restrictions more stringent – **clamp-down** *n*

clam up *vi* to become silent – infml

clan /klan/ *n* **1a** a (Highland Scots) Celtic group of households descended from a common ancestor **b** a group of people related by family ⟨*the Kennedy* ~⟩ **2** a usu close-knit group united by a common interest or common characteristics [ME, fr ScGael *clann* offspring, clan, fr OIr *cland* plant, offspring, fr L *planta* plant] – **clansman** /'klanzmən/ *n*

clandestine /klan'destin, 'klandəstin/ *adj* held in or conducted with secrecy; surreptitious [MF or L; MF *clandestin*, fr L *clandestinus*, irreg fr *clam* secretly; akin to L *celare* to hide – more at HELL] – **clandestinely** *adv*

clang /klang/ *vi* **1** to make a loud metallic ringing sound ⟨*anvils* ~ed⟩ **2** *esp of a crane or goose* to utter a harsh cry ~ *vt* to cause to clang ⟨~ *a bell*⟩ [L *clangere*; akin to Gk *klazein* to scream, bark, OE *hlōwan* to low] – **clang** *n*

clanger /'klang·ə/ *n, Br* a blunder – infml [*clang* + [2]-*er*]

clangour, *NAm chiefly* **clangor** /'klang(g)ə/ *vi or n* (to make) a resounding clang or medley of clangs ⟨*the* ~ *of hammers*⟩ [n L *clangor*, fr *clangere*; vb fr n] – **clangorous** *adj*, **clangorously** *adv*

[1]**clank** /klangk/ *vb* to (cause to) make a clank or series of clanks [prob imit] – **clankingly** *adv*

[2]**clank** *n* a sharp brief metallic sound

clannish /'klanish/ *adj* tending to associate only with a select group of similar background, status, or interests [CLAN + -ISH] – **clannishly** *adv*, **clannishness** *n*

[1]**clap** /klap/ *vb* **-pp-** *vt* **1** to strike (e g 2 flat hard surfaces) together so as to produce a loud sharp percussive noise **2a** to strike (the hands) together repeatedly, usu in applause **b** to applaud **3** to strike with the flat of the hand in a friendly way **4** to place, put, or set, esp energetically – infml ⟨~ *him in irons*⟩ ⟨*finest vessel I ever* ~ped *eyes on*⟩ ~ *vi* **1** to produce a sharp percussive noise **2** to applaud [ME *clappen*, fr OE *clæppan*; akin to OHG *klaphōn* to beat, L *gleba* clod – more at [1]CLIP]

[2]**clap** *n* **1** a loud sharp percussive noise, specif of thunder **2** a friendly slap ⟨*a* ~ *on the shoulder*⟩ **3** the sound of clapping hands; *esp* applause

[3]**clap** *n* VENEREAL DISEASE; *esp* gonorrhoea – slang [MF *clapoir* bubo]

clapboard /'klabəd, 'klap,bawd/ *n, NAm* weatherboard [part trans of D *klaphout* stave wood] – **clapboard** *vt*

,**clapped 'out** *adj, chiefly Br, esp of machinery* (old and) worn-out; liable to break down irreparably – infml

clapper /'klapə/ *n* the tongue of a bell [[1]CLAP + [2]-ER] – **like the clappers** *Br* as fast as possible – infml; + *run* or *go*

'**clapper-,board** *n* a hinged board containing identifying details of the scene to be filmed that is held before the camera and banged together to mark the beginning and end of each take

claptrap /'klap,trap/ *n* pretentious nonsense; rubbish – infml [[2]*clap* + [1]*trap*; fr its attempt to win applause]

claque /klak/ *n sing or pl in constr* **1** a group hired to applaud at a performance **2** a group of self-interested obsequious flatterers [F, fr *claquer* to clap, of imit origin]

clarence /'klarəns/ *n* a closed 4-wheeled 4-passenger carriage [Duke of *Clarence*, later William IV of England †1837]

claret /'klarit/ *n* **1** a dry red Bordeaux **2** a dark purplish red colour [ME, fr MF (*vin*) *claret* clear wine, fr *claret* clear, fr *cler* clear] – **claret** *adj*

clarify /'klari,fie/ *vt* **1** to make (e g a liquid) clear or pure, usu by freeing from suspended matter **2** to make free from confusion **3** to make understandable ~ *vi* to become clear [ME *clarifien*, fr MF *clarifier*, fr LL *clarificare*, fr L *clarus* clear – more at CLEAR] – **clarification** /,klarifi'kaysh(ə)n/ *n*, **clarifier** /'klari,fie·ə/ *n*

clarinet /,klari'net/ *n* a single-reed woodwind instrument with a usual range from D below middle C upwards for 3½ octaves [F *clarinette*, prob deriv of ML *clarion-*, *clario*] – **clarinettist**, *NAm chiefly* **clarinetist** /-'netist/ *n*

[1]**clarion** /'klari·ən/ *n* (the sound of) a medieval trumpet [ME, fr MF & ML; MF *clairon*, fr ML *clarion-*, *clario*, fr L *clarus* clear]

[2]**clarion** *adj* brilliantly clear ⟨*a* ~ *call to action*⟩

clarity /'klarəti/ *n* the quality or state of being clear [ME *clarite*, fr L *claritat-*, *claritas*, fr *clarus*]

clarkia /'klahki·ə/ *n* a showy annual N American garden plant of the evening-primrose family [NL, fr William *Clark* †1838 US explorer]

clary /'kleəri/ *n* any of several plants of the mint family, closely related to sage [ME *clarie*, fr MF *sclaree*, fr ML *sclareia*]

[1]**clash** /klash/ *vi* **1** to make a clash ⟨*cymbals* ~ed⟩ **2a** to come into conflict **b** to form a displeasing combination; not match ⟨*these colours* ~⟩ ~ *vt* to cause to clash [imit] – **clasher** *n*

[2]**clash** *n* **1** a noisy usu metallic sound of collision **2a** a hostile encounter **b** a sharp conflict ⟨*a* ~ *of opinions*⟩

[1]**clasp** /klahsp/ *n* **1** a device for holding objects or parts of sthg together ⟨*the* ~ *of a necklace*⟩ **2** a holding or enveloping (as if) with the hands or arms [ME *claspe*]

[2]**clasp** *vt* **1** to fasten (as if) with a clasp **2** to enclose and hold with the arms; *specif* to embrace **3** to seize (as if) with the hand; grasp

clasper /'klahspə/ *n* a male copulatory structure of some insects and fishes [[2]CLASP + [2]-ER]

'**clasp ,knife** *n* a large single-bladed folding knife having a catch to hold the blade open

[1]**class** /klahs/ *n* **1a** *sing or pl in constr* a group sharing the same economic or social status in a society consisting of several groups with differing statuses – often pl with sing. meaning ⟨*the labouring* ~es⟩ **b(1)** social rank **(2)** the system of differentiating society by classes **c** high quality; elegance **2** *sing or pl in constr* a body of students meeting regularly to study the same subject **3** a group, set, or kind sharing common attributes: e g **a** a category in biological classification ranking above the order and below the phylum or division **b** a grammatical cat-

egory **4a** a division or rating based on grade or quality **b** *Br* a level of university honours degree awarded to a student according to merit ⟨*what* ~ *did she get?*⟩ [F *classe*, fr L *classis* group called to arms, class of citizens; akin to L *calare* to call – more at [1]LOW]

[2]**class** *vt* to classify

'class-,conscious *adj* **1** actively aware of one's common status with others in a particular class **2** taking part in class war – **class-consciousness** *n*

[1]**classic** /'klasik/ *adj* **1a** of recognized value or merit; serving as a standard of excellence **b** both traditional and enduring ⟨*a* ~ *heritage*⟩ **c** characterized by simple tailored and elegant lines that remain in fashion year after year ⟨*a* ~ *suit*⟩ **2** CLASSICAL 2 **3a** authoritative, definitive **b** being an example that shows clearly the characteristics of some group of things or occurrences; archetypal [F or L; F *classique*, fr L *classicus* of the highest class of Roman citizens, of the first rank, fr *classis*]

[2]**classic** *n* **1a** a literary work of ancient Greece or Rome **b** *pl* Greek and Latin literature, history, and philosophy considered as an academic subject **2a** (the author of) a work of lasting excellence **b** an authoritative source **3** a classic example; archetype **4** an important long-established sporting event; *specif, Br* any of 5 flat races for horses (e g the Epsom Derby)

classical /'klasikl/ *adj* **1** standard, classic **2** of the (literature, art, architecture, or ideals of the) ancient Greek and Roman world **3a** of or being (a composer of) music of the late 18th c and early 19th c characterized by an emphasis on simplicity, objectivity, and proportion **b** of or being music in the educated European tradition that includes such forms as chamber music, opera, and symphony as distinguished from folk, popular music, or jazz **4a** both authoritative and traditional **b(1)** of or being systems or methods that constitute an accepted although not necessarily modern approach to a subject ⟨~ *Mendelian genetics*⟩ **(2)** not involving relativity, wave mechanics, or quantum theory ⟨~ *physics*⟩ **5** concerned with instruction in the classics [L *classicus*]

classicality /,klasi'kaləti/ *n* the quality or state of being classic or classical

classically /'klasikli/ *adv* in a classic or classical manner

classicism /'klasi,siz(ə)m/, **classicalism** /'klasikl,iz(ə)m/ *n* **1a** the principles or style embodied in classical literature, art, or architecture **b** a classical idiom or expression **2** adherence to traditional standards (e g of simplicity, restraint, and proportion) that are considered to have universal and lasting worth – **classicalist** /-k(ə)l,ist/, **classicist** /-,sist/ *n*, **classicistic** /-'sistik/ *adj*

classic·ize, -ise /'klasisiez/ *vt* to make classic or classical

classification /,klasifi'kaysh(ə)n/ *n* **1** classifying **2a** systematic arrangement in groups according to established criteria; *specif* taxonomy **b** a class, category – **classificatorily** /-'kayt(ə)rəli/ *adv*, **classificatory** /,klasifi'kayt(ə)ri, klə'sifikət(ə)ri/ *adj*

classified /'klasi,fied/ *adj* withheld from general circulation for reasons of national security ⟨~ *information*⟩

classify /'klasi,fie/ *vt* **1** to arrange in classes **2** to assign to a category – **classifiable** /-,fie·əbl/ *adj*, **classifier** /-,fie·ə/ *n*

classless /'klahslis/ *adj* **1** free from class distinction ⟨*a* ~ *society*⟩ **2** belonging to no particular social class – **classlessness** *n*

'class,mate /-,mayt/ *n* a member of the same class in a school or college

'classroom /-room, -,roohm/ *n* a room where classes meet

'class ,war *n* the struggle for power between workers and property owners assumed by Marxist theory to develop in a capitalist society

classy /'klahsi/ *adj* elegant, stylish – infml – **classiness** *n*

clastic /'klastik/ *adj* made up of fragments of preexisting rocks [ISV, fr Gk *klastos* broken, fr *klan* to break – more at [1]HALT] – **clastic** *n*

clathrate /'klath,rayt/ *adj* of or being a compound formed by the inclusion of molecules of one kind in the crystal lattice of another [L *clathratus*, fr *clathri* (pl) lattice, fr Gk *klēithron* bar, fr *kleiein* to close – more at [4]CLOSE] – **clathrate** *n*

[1]**clatter** /'klatə/ *vi* **1** to make a clatter ⟨*the dishes* ~ed *on the shelf*⟩ **2** to move or go with a clatter ⟨~ed *down the stairs*⟩ **3** to prattle ~ *vt* to cause to clatter [ME *clatren*, fr (assumed) OE *clatrian*, of imit origin] – **clatterer** *n*, **clatteringly** *adv*

[2]**clatter** *n* **1** a rattling sound (e g of hard bodies striking together) ⟨*the* ~ *of pots and pans*⟩ **2** a commotion ⟨*the midday* ~ *of the business district*⟩ – **clattery** *adj*

claudication /,klawdi'kaysh(ə)n/ *n* lameness, limping [L *claudication-*, *claudicatio*, fr *claudicatus*, pp of *claudicare* to limp, fr *claudus* lame; akin to L *claudere* to close – more at [4]CLOSE]

clause /klawz/ *n* **1** a distinct article or condition in a formal document **2** a phrase containing a subject and predicate and functioning either in isolation or as a member of a complex or compound sentence [ME, fr OF, clause, fr ML *clausa* close of a rhetorical period, fr L, fem of *clausus*, pp of *claudere* to close] – **clausal** *adj*

claustral /'klawstrəl/ *adj* cloistral [ME, fr ML *claustralis*, fr *claustrum* cloister – more at CLOISTER]

claustrophobia /,klostrə'fohbi·ə, ,klaw-/ *n* abnormal dread of being in closed or confined spaces [NL, fr L *claustrum* bar, bolt + NL *phobia* – more at CLOISTER] – **claustrophobic** /-'fohbik/ *adj*

clavate /'klay,vayt, -vət/ *adj* club-shaped [NL *clavatus*, fr L *clava* club, fr *clavus* nail, knot in wood] – **clavately** *adv*, **clavation** /-'vaysh(ə)n/ *n*

clavichord /'klavi,kawd/ *n* an early usu rectangular keyboard instrument [ML *clavichordium*, fr L *clavis* key + *chorda* string – more at CORD] – **clavichordist** *n*

clavicle /'klavikl/ *n* a bone of the vertebrate shoulder typically linking the shoulder blade and breastbone; the collarbone ☞ ANATOMY [F *clavicule*, fr NL *clavicula*, fr L, dim. of L *clavis* key; akin to Gk *kleid-*, *kleis* key, L *claudere* to close – more at [4]CLOSE] – **clavicular** /klə'vikyoolə/ *adj*

clavier /'klavi·ə/ *n* a usu unspecified keyboard instrument [G *klavier*, fr F *clavier*, fr OF, key-bearer, fr L *clavis* key] – **clavierist** /'klavyərist/ *n*

claviform /'klavi,fawm/ *adj* club-shaped [L *clava* club]

[1]**claw** /klaw/ *n* **1** (a part resembling or limb having) a sharp usu slender curved nail on an animal's toe **2** any of the pincerlike organs on the end of some limbs of a lobster, scorpion, or similar arthropod **3** sthg (e g the forked end of a claw hammer) resembling a claw [ME *clawe*, fr OE *clawu* hoof, claw; akin to ON *klō* claw, OE *cliewen* ball – more at CLEW] – **clawed** *adj*

[2]**claw** *vt* to rake, seize, dig, or make (as if) with claws ~ *vi* to scrape, scratch, dig, or pull (as if) with claws

claw back *vt* to take back, esp by taxation – **claw-back** /'- ,-/ *n*

'**claw ,hammer** *n* a hammer with one end of the head forked for pulling out nails

clay /klay/ *n* **1a** (soil composed chiefly of) an earthy material that is soft when moist but hard when fired, is composed mainly of fine particles of aluminium silicates, and is used for making brick, tile, and pottery **b** thick and clinging earth or mud **2a** a substance that resembles clay and is used for modelling **b** the human body as distinguished from the spirit [ME, fr OE *clǣg*; akin to OHG *klīwa* bran, LL *glut-*, *glus* glue, MGk *glia*] – **clayey** /'klay·i/ *adj*, **clayish** *adj*

claymore /'klay,maw/ *n* a large single-edged broadsword formerly used by Scottish Highlanders [ScGael *claidheamh mōr*, lit., great sword]

,**clay 'pigeon** *n* a saucer-shaped object usu made of baked clay and hurled into the air as a target for shooting at with a shotgun

[1]**clean** /kleen/ *adj* **1a** (relatively) free from dirt or pollution ⟨*changed into ~ clothes*⟩ **b** free from contamination or disease **c** relatively free from radioactive fallout ⟨*a ~ atomic explosion*⟩ **2** unadulterated, pure **3a** free from illegal, immoral, or disreputable activities ⟨*a ~ record*⟩ **b** free from the use of obscenity ⟨*I just don't know any ~ jokes!*⟩ **c** observing the rules; fair ⟨*a ~ fight*⟩ **4** thorough, complete ⟨*a ~ break with the past*⟩ **5** relatively free from error or blemish; clear; *specif* legible ⟨*~ copy*⟩ **6a** characterized by clarity, precision, or deftness ⟨*architecture with ~ almost austere lines*⟩ **b** not jagged; smooth ⟨*a ~ edge*⟩ **c** *of a ship or aircraft* well streamlined [ME *clene*, fr OE *clǣne*; akin to OHG *kleini* delicate, dainty, Gk *glainoi* ornaments] – **cleanly** *adv*, **cleanness** *n*

[2]**clean** *adv* **1a** so as to leave clean ⟨*a new broom sweeps ~*⟩ **b** in a clean manner ⟨*fight ~*⟩ **2** all the way; completely ⟨*the bullet went ~ through his arm*⟩

[3]**clean** *vt* **1** to make clean – often + *up* **2a** to strip, empty **b** to deprive of money or possessions – often + *out* ⟨*they ~ed him out completely*⟩; infml ~ *vi* to undergo cleaning – **cleanable** *adj*

[4]**clean** *n* an act of cleaning away dirt

,**clean-'cut** *adj* **1** cut so that the surface or edge is smooth and even **2** sharply defined **3** of wholesome appearance

cleaner /'kleenə/ *n* **1** sby whose occupation is cleaning rooms or clothes **2** a substance, implement, or machine for cleaning – **to the cleaners** to or through the experience of being deprived of all one's money – infml

cleanliness /'klenlinis/ *n* fastidiousness in keeping things or one's person clean – **cleanly** /'kleenli/ *adj*

cleanse /klenz/ *vb* to clean [ME *clensen*, fr OE *clǣnsian* to purify, fr *clǣne* clean]

cleanser /'klenzə/ *n* a preparation (e g a scouring powder or skin cream) used for cleaning [CLEANSE + [2]-ER]

,**clean-'shaven** *adj* with the hair, specif of the beard and moustache, shaved off

,**clean 'sweep** *n* **1** a capture of all the prizes at stake in a contest or competition **2** a wholesale removal (e g of staff or out-of-date material)

clean up *vi* to make a large esp sweeping gain (e g in business or gambling) ~ *vt* to remove by cleaning – **cleanup** /'-,-/ *n*

[1]**clear** /kliə/ *adj* **1a** bright, luminous **b** free from cloud, mist, haze, or dust ⟨*a ~ day*⟩ **c** untroubled, serene ⟨*a ~ gaze*⟩ **2** clean, pure: e g **a** free from blemishes **b** easily seen through; transparent **3a** easily heard **b** easily visible; plain **c** free from obscurity or ambiguity; easily understood **4a** capable of sharp discernment; keen ⟨*this problem needs a ~ mind*⟩ **b** free from doubt; sure ⟨*we are not ~ what to do*⟩ **5** free from guilt ⟨*a ~ conscience*⟩ **6a** net ⟨*a ~ profit*⟩ **b** unqualified, absolute ⟨*a ~ victory*⟩ **c** free from obstruction or entanglement **d** full ⟨*6 ~ days*⟩ [ME *clere*, fr OF *cler*, fr L *clarus* clear, bright; akin to L *calare* to call – more at [1]LOW] – **clearly** *adv*, **clearness** *n*

[2]**clear** *adv* **1** clearly ⟨*to cry loud and ~*⟩ **2** *chiefly NAm* all the way ⟨*can see ~ to the mountains today*⟩

[3]**clear** *vt* **1a** to make transparent or translucent **b** to free from unwanted material – often + *out* ⟨*~ out that cupboard*⟩ **2a** to free from accusation or blame; vindicate **b** to certify as trustworthy ⟨*~ a man for top secret military work*⟩ **3a** to rid (the throat) of phlegm; *also* to make a rasping noise in (the throat) **b** to erase accumulated totals or stored data from (e g a calculator or computer memory) **4** to authorize or cause to be authorized **5a** to free from financial obligation **b(1)** to settle, discharge ⟨*~ an account*⟩ **(2)** to deal with until finished or settled ⟨*~ the backlog of work*⟩ **c** to gain without deduction ⟨*~ a profit*⟩ **d** to put through a clearinghouse **6a** to get rid of; remove ⟨*~ the plates from the table*⟩ – often + *off*, *up*, or *away* ⟨*~ away the rubbish*⟩ **b** to kick or pass (the ball) away from the goal as a defensive measure in soccer **7** to go over without touching ⟨*the horse ~ed the jump*⟩ ~ *vi* **1a** to become clear – often + *up* ⟨*it ~ed up quickly after the rain*⟩ **b** to go away; vanish ⟨*the symptoms ~ed gradually*⟩ – sometimes + *off*, *out* ⟨*told him to ~ out*⟩, or *away* ⟨*after the mist ~ed away*⟩ **c** to sell **2** to pass through a clearinghouse – **clearable** *adj*, **clearer** *n* – **clear the air** to remove elements of hostility, tension, confusion, or uncertainty from the mood or temper of the time – **clear the decks** to get things ready for action

[4]**clear** *n* a high long arcing shot in badminton – **in the clear** **1** free from guilt or suspicion **2** in plaintext; not in code or cipher

clearance /'kliərəns/ *n* **1a** an authorization **b** a sale to clear out stock **c** the removal of buildings, people, etc from the space they previously occupied ⟨*the Highland ~s*⟩ ⟨*slum ~*⟩ **d** a clearing of the ball in soccer **2** the distance by which one object clears another, or the clear space between them [[3]CLEAR + -ANCE]

'**clear,cole** /-,kohl/ *n* a priming of size mixed with

ground chalk or white lead and used esp in house painting [part trans of F *claire colle*, fr *claire* clear + *colle* glue]

,clear-'cut *adj* **1** sharply outlined; distinct **2** free from ambiguity or uncertainty

,clear'headed /-'hedid/ *adj* **1** not confused; sensible, rational **2** having no illusions about a state of affairs; realistic – **clearheadedly** *adv*, **clearheadedness** *n*

clearing /'kliəring/ *n* an area of land cleared of wood and brush [[3]CLEAR + [2]-ING]

'clearing ,bank *n* a bank that is a member of a clearinghouse

'clearing,house /-,hows/ *n* an establishment maintained by banks for settling mutual claims and accounts

,clear-'sighted *adj* CLEARHEADED 2; *esp* having perceptive insight – **clear-sightedly** *adv*, **clear-sightedness** *n*

clear up *vt* **1** to tidy up **2** to explain ⟨clear up *the mystery*⟩

'clear,way /-,way/ *n*, *Br* a road on which vehicles may stop only in an emergency

cleat /kleet/ *n* **1a** a wedge-shaped piece fastened to sthg and serving as a support or check **b** a wooden or metal fitting, usu with 2 projecting horns, round which a rope may be made fast **2a** a projecting piece (e g on the bottom of a shoe) that provides a grip **b** *pl* shoes equipped with cleats [ME *clete* wedge, fr (assumed) OE *clēat*; akin to MHG *klōz* lump – more at CLOUT]

cleavage /'kleevij/ *n* **1** the property of a crystal or rock (e g slate) of splitting along definite planes **2** (a) division **3** CELL DIVISION **4** the splitting of a molecule into simpler molecules **5** (the space between) a woman's breasts, esp when exposed by a low-cut garment [[2]CLEAVE + -AGE]

[1]cleave /kleev/ *vi* **cleaved, clove** /klohv/ to stick firmly and closely or loyally and steadfastly – usu + *to* [ME *clevien*, fr OE *clifian*; akin to ON *klīfa* to cling to, OE *clǣg* clay]

[2]cleave *vb* **cleaved** *also* **cleft** /kleft/, **clove** /klohv/; **cleaved** *also* **cleft, cloven** /'klohv(ə)n/ *vt* to divide or pass through (as if) by a cutting blow; split ~ *vi* to split, esp along the grain [ME *cleven*, fr OE *clēofan*; akin to ON *kljūfa* to split, L *glubere* to peel, Gk *glyphein* to carve] – **cleavable** *adj*

cleaver /'kleevə/ *n* a butcher's implement for cutting animal carcasses into joints or pieces [[2]CLEAVE + [2]-ER]

cleavers /'kleevəz/ *n pl but sing or pl in constr* an annual plant of the madder family that bears small white flowers and stiff prickles that make it stick to surfaces [ME *clivre*, alter. of OE *clife* burdock, cleavers; akin to OE *clifian* to adhere]

clef /klef/ *n* a sign placed on a musical staff to indicate the pitch represented by the notes following it ☞ MUSIC [F, lit., key, fr L *clavis* – more at CLAVICLE]

cleft /kleft/ *n* **1** a space or opening made by splitting; a fissure **2** a usu V-shaped indented formation; a hollow between ridges or protuberances [ME *clift*, fr OE *geclyft*; akin to OE *clēofan* to cleave]

,cleft 'lip *n* a harelip

,cleft 'palate *n* a congenital fissure of the roof of the mouth

,cleft 'stick *n*, *chiefly Br* DILEMMA 2

cleg /kleg/ *n*, *Br* a dull-grey biting fly; a horsefly [ME, fr ON *kleggi*]

clematis /klə'maytəs, 'klemətis/ *n* a usu climbing or scrambling plant of the buttercup family with 3 leaflets on each leaf and usu white, pink, or purple flowers [NL, genus name, fr L, fr Gk *klēmatis* brushwood, clematis, fr *klēmat-*, *klēma* twig, fr *klan* to break – more at [1]HALT]

clemency /'klemənsi/ *n* disposition to be merciful, esp to moderate the severity of punishment due

clement /'klemənt/ *adj* **1** inclined to be merciful; lenient ⟨*a* ~ *judge*⟩ **2** *of weather* pleasantly mild [ME, fr L *clement-*, *clemens*] – **clemently** *adv*

clementine /'klemənteen/ *n* a small practically seedless citrus fruit that is a cross between an orange and a tangerine and has slightly acid pink-tinged flesh [F *clémentine*]

clench /klench/ *vt* **1** CLINCH 1, 2 **2** to hold fast; clutch **3** to set or close tightly ⟨~ed *his teeth*⟩ ⟨~ed *his fists*⟩ [ME *clenchen*, fr OE *-clencan*; akin to OE *clingan* to cling]

clepsydra /'klepsidrə/ *n*, *pl* **clepsydras, clepsydrae** /-dri/ WATER CLOCK [L, fr Gk *klepsydra*, fr *kleptein* to steal + *hydōr* water – more at KLEPHT, WATER]

clerestory, clearstory /'kliə,stawri/ *n* **1** the part of an outside wall of a room or building that rises above an adjoining roof ⟨~ *windows*⟩ ☞ CHURCH **2** *chiefly NAm* a raised ventilating section of a railway carriage roof [ME, fr *clere* clear + *story* storey]

clergy /'kluhji/ *n sing or pl in constr* a group ordained to perform pastoral or sacerdotal functions in an organized religion, esp a Christian church [ME *clergie*, fr OF, knowledge, learning, fr *clerc* clergyman]

'clergyman /-mən/ *n* an ordained minister

cleric /'klerik/ *n* a member of the clergy; *specif* one in orders below the grade of priest [LL *clericus*]

[1]clerical /'klerikl/ *adj* **1** (characteristic) of the clergy, a clergyman, or a cleric **2** of a clerk or office worker – **clerically** *adv*

[2]clerical *n* **1** a clergyman **2** an adherent of clericalism **3** *pl* clerical clothes

,clerical 'collar *n* a narrow stiff upright white collar fastening at the back and worn by clergymen

'clerical,ism /-,iz(ə)m/ *n* a policy promoting ecclesiastical influence in secular matters – **clericalist** *n*

clerihew /'kleri,hyooh/ *n* a witty pseudo-biographical 4-line verse [Edmund *Clerihew* Bentley †1956 E writer]

clerisy /'klerəsi/ *n sing or pl in constr* members of the learned professions considered as a group [G *klerisei* clergy, fr ML *clericia*, fr LL *clericus* cleric]

[1]clerk /klahk; *NAm* kluhk/ *n* **1** a cleric **2a** sby whose occupation is keeping records or accounts or doing general office work ⟨*a filing* ~⟩ **b** *NAm* SHOP ASSISTANT [ME, fr OF *clerc* & OE *cleric*, *clerc*, both fr LL *clericus*, fr LGk *klērikos*, fr Gk *klēros* lot, inheritance (in allusion to Deut 18:2); akin to Gk *klan* to break – more at [1]HALT] – **clerkly** *adj*, **clerkship** *n*

[2]clerk *vi* to act or work as a clerk

,clerk of the 'course *n* an official who has direct charge of the running of a horse-race or motor-race meeting

,clerk of the 'works *n* the person in charge of building works in a particular place

,clerk 'regular *n, pl* **clerks regular** a member of an open Roman Catholic order with pastoral duties

,Cleveland 'bay /'kleevlənd/ *n* (any of) a breed of powerful bay riding horses [*Cleveland*, district (and now county) of England]

clever /'klevə/ *adj* **1a** skilful or adroit *with* the hands or body; nimble **b** mentally quick and resourceful; intelligent **2** marked by wit or ingenuity; *also* thus marked but lacking depth or soundness [ME *cliver*, prob of Scand origin; akin to ON *kljūfa* to split – more at [2]CLEAVE] – **cleverish** *adj*, **cleverly** *adv*, **cleverness** *n*

,clever-'dick /dik/ *n, Br* SMART ALEC – infml

clevis /'klevis/ *n* a usu U-shaped metal shackle with the ends drilled to receive a pin or bolt used for attaching or suspending parts [earlier *clevi*, prob of Scand origin; akin to ON *kljūfa* to split]

[1]**clew** /klooh/ *n* **1** CLUE 1 **2** *also* **clue** (a metal loop attached to) the lower or after corner of a sail SHIP [ME *clewe* ball of thread, fr OE *cliewen*; akin to OHG *kliuwa* ball, Skt *glau* lump]

[2]**clew** *vt* **1** CLUE 2 **2** *also* **clue** to haul (a sail) by ropes through the clews

cliché /'klee,shay/ *n* **1** a hackneyed phrase or expression; *also* the idea expressed by it **2** a hackneyed theme or situation [F, lit., stereotype, fr pp of *clicher* to stereotype, of imit origin] – **cliché** *adj*, **clichéd** *adj*

[1]**click** /klik/ *n* **1** a slight sharp sound **2** a sharp speech sound in some languages made by the sudden inrush of air at the release of an occlusion in the mouth [prob imit]

[2]**click** *vt* to strike, move, or produce with a click ⟨~ed *his heels together*⟩ ~ *vi* **1** to operate with or make a click **2a** to strike up an immediately warm friendship, esp with sby of the opposite sex **b** to succeed ⟨*a film that* ~s⟩ **c** *Br* to cause sudden insight or recognition ⟨*the name* ~ed⟩ – sometimes in *click into place* *USE* (*2*) infml

'click ,beetle *n* any of a family of beetles able to right themselves with a click when turned over

'click ,stop *n* a setting of a control device (e g for the length of exposure given by the shutter of a camera) that is distinguished by positive engagement and usu by a click

client /'klie·ənt/ *n* **1** a vassal, state, etc under the protection of another ⟨~ *states*⟩ **2a** sby who engages or receives the advice or services of a professional person or organization **b** a customer [ME, fr MF & L; MF *client*, fr L *client-*, *cliens*; akin to L *clinare* to lean – more at [1]LEAN] – **clientage** /-tij/ *n*, **cliental** /klie'entl, 'klie·əntl/ *adj*

clientele /,klee·on'tel/ *n sing or pl in constr* a body of clients ⟨*a shop that caters to an exclusive* ~⟩ [F *clientèle*, fr L *clientela*, fr *client-*, *cliens*]

cliff /klif/ *n* a very steep high face of rock, earth, ice, etc [ME *clif*, fr OE; akin to OE *clifian* to adhere to] – **cliffy** *adj*

'cliff-,hanger *n* **1** an adventure serial or melodrama, usu presented in instalments each ending in suspense **2** a contest or situation whose outcome is in doubt to the very end

[1]**climacteric** /,klie'maktərik, ,kliemək'terik/ *adj* of or being a critical period (e g of life) [L *climactericus*, fr Gk *klimaktērikos*, fr *klimaktēr* critical point, lit., rung of a ladder, fr *klimak-*, *klimax* ladder]

[2]**climacteric** *n* **1** a major turning point or critical stage; *specif* one supposed to occur at intervals of 7 years **2** the menopause; *also* a corresponding period in the male during which sexual activity and competence are reduced

climactic /klie'maktik/ *adj* of or being a climax – **climactically** *adv*

climate /'kliemət/ *n* **1** (a region of the earth having a specified) average course or condition of the weather over a period of years as shown by temperature, wind, rain, etc **2** the prevailing state of affairs or feelings of a group or period; a milieu ⟨*a* ~ *of fear*⟩ [ME *climat*, fr MF, fr LL *climat-*, *clima*, fr Gk *klimat-*, *klima* inclination, latitude, climate, fr *klinein* to lean – more at [1]LEAN] – **climatic** /-'matik/ *adj*, **climatically** *adv*

climatology /,kliemə'toləji/ *n* a branch of meteorology dealing with climates – **climatological** /-tə'lojikl/ *adj*, **climatologically** *adv*, **climatologist** /-'toləjist/ *n*

[1]**climax** /'klie,maks/ *n* **1a** the highest point; a culmination **b** the point of highest dramatic tension or a major turning point in some action (e g of a play) **c** an orgasm **2** a relatively stable final stage reached by a (plant) community in its ecological development [L, fr Gk *klimax* ladder, fr *klinein* to lean]

[2]**climax** *vi* to come to a climax

climb /kliem/ *vi* **1a** to go gradually upwards; rise ⟨*watching the smoke* ~⟩ **b** to slope upwards ⟨*the road* ~s *steadily*⟩ **2a** to go *up*, *down*, etc on a more or less vertical surface using the hands to grasp or give support **b** *of a plant* to ascend in growth (e g by twining) **3** to get *into* or *out of* clothing, usu with some haste or effort ~ *vt* **1** to go upwards on or along, to the top of, or over ⟨~ *a hill*⟩ **2** to draw or pull oneself up, over, or to the top of, by using hands and feet ⟨~ *a tree*⟩ **3** to grow up or over [ME *climben*, fr OE *climban*; akin to OE *clamm* bond, fetter] – **climb** *n*, **climbable** /'klieməbl/ *adj*, **climber** /'kliemə/ *n*

climb down *vi* BACK DOWN – **climb-down** *n*

'climbing-,frame /'klieming/ *n, Br* a framework for children to climb on

'climbing ,iron *n* a crampon

clime /kliem/ *n* CLIMATE 1 – usu pl with sing. meaning; chiefly poetic [LL *clima*]

clin-, **clino-** *comb form* incline; slant ⟨clino*meter*⟩ [NL, fr Gk *klinein* to lean – more at [1]LEAN]

[1]**clinch** /klinch/ *vt* **1** to turn over or flatten the protruding pointed end of (e g a driven nail) **2** to fasten in this way ~ *vi* to hold an opponent (e g in boxing) at close quarters [prob alter. of *clench*] – **clinchingly** *adv*

[2]**clinch** *n* **1** a fastening by means of a clinched nail, rivet, or bolt **2** an act or instance of clinching in boxing

clincher /'klinchə/ *n* a decisive fact, argument, act, or remark [[1]CLINCH + [2]-ER]

cline /klien/ *n* a graded series of differences in shape or physiology shown by a group of related organisms, usu along a line of environmental or geographical transition; *broadly* a continuum [Gk *klinein* to lean] – **clinal** /'klienl/ *adj*, **clinally** *adv*

-cline /-klien/ *comb form* (→ *n*) slope ⟨*mono*cline⟩ [back-formation fr *-clinal* (sloping), fr Gk *klinein*] – **-clinal** *comb form* (→ *adj*), **-clinic** *comb form* (→ *adj*)

cling /kling/ *vi* **clung** /klung/ **1a** to stick as if glued firmly **b** to hold (on) tightly or tenaciously **2a** to have a strong emotional attachment or dependence **b**

esp of a smell to linger [ME *clingen*, fr OE *clingan*; akin to OHG *klunga* tangled ball of thread, MIr *glacc* hand] – **clingy** *adj*

'cling,stone /-,stohn/ *n* a fruit (e g a peach) whose flesh sticks strongly to the stone

clinic /'klinik/ *n* **1** a class of medical instruction in which patients are examined and discussed **2** a meeting held by an expert or person in authority, to which people bring problems for discussion and resolution ⟨*an MP's weekly ~ for her constituents*⟩ **3a** a facility (e g of a hospital) for the diagnosis and treatment of outpatients **b** a usu private hospital [F *clinique*, fr Gk *klinikē* medical practice at the sick-bed, fr fem of *klinikos* of a bed, fr *klinē* bed, fr *klinein* to lean, recline – more at [1]LEAN]

clinical /'klinikl/ *adj* **1** involving, based on, or noticeable from direct observation of the patient ⟨~ *psychology*⟩ **2** analytic, detached [CLINIC + [1]-AL] – **clinically** *adv*

clinician /kli'nish(ə)n/ *n* sby qualified in clinical medicine, psychiatry, etc as distinguished from one specializing in laboratory or research techniques

[1]clink /klingk/ *vb* to (cause to) give out a slight sharp short metallic sound [ME *clinken*, of imit origin] – **clink** *n*

[2]clink *n* PRISON 2 – slang [*Clink*, a former prison in Southwark, London]

clinker /'klingkə/ *n* stony matter fused by fire; slag [alter. of earlier *klincard* (a hard yellowish Dutch brick), fr obs D *klinkaard*]

'clinker-,built *adj* having the lower edge of each external plank or plate overlapping the upper edge of the one below it ⟨*a ~ boat*⟩ [*clinker*, n (clinch)]

clino- – see CLIN-

clinometer /kli'nomitə, 'klie-/ *n* any of various instruments for measuring angles of slope – **clinometric** /,klinə'metrik, ,klie-/ *adj*, **clinometry** /-'nomətri/ *n*

clint /klint/ *n* a limestone block in a horizontal limestone surface broken up by clefts [ME, perh fr MLG *klint* cliff, crag]

[1]clip /klip/ *vt* **-pp-** to clasp or fasten with a clip [ME *clippen* to embrace, encompass, clutch, fr OE *clyppan*; akin to OHG *klāftra* fathom, L *gleba* clod, *globus* globe]

[2]clip *n* **1** any of various devices that grip, clasp, or hold **2** (a device to hold cartridges for charging) a magazine from which ammunition is fed into the chamber of a firearm **3** a piece of jewellery held in position by a spring clip

[3]clip *vb* **-pp-** *vt* **1a** to cut (off) (as if) with shears **b** to cut off the end or outer part of **c** [3]EXCISE **2** to abbreviate in speech or writing **3** to hit with a glancing blow; *also* to hit smartly ⟨~ped *him round the ear*⟩ – infml ~ *vi* to clip sthg [ME *clippen*, fr ON *klippa*]

[4]clip *n* **1a** the product of (a single) shearing (e g of sheep) **b** a section of filmed material **2a** an act of clipping **b** the manner in which sthg is clipped **3** a sharp blow **4** a rapid rate of motion *USE* (*3&4*) infml

'clip,board /-,bawd/ *n* a small writing board with a spring clip for holding papers

'clip-,clop /klop/ *vi or n* (to make) a rhythmic repeated sound characteristically produced by horses' hooves – infml [imit]

'clip ,joint *n* **1** a place of public entertainment (e g a nightclub) that defrauds, overcharges, etc **2** a business establishment that makes a practice of over-charging *USE* slang [[3]*clip* (to overcharge, swindle) + [1]*joint*]

'clip-,on *adj* of or being sthg that clips on ⟨~ *ear-rings*⟩

clip on *vi* to be capable of being fastened by an attached clip

'clip-,ons *n pl* sunglasses that clip onto spectacles

clipper /'klipə/ *n* **1** an implement for cutting or trimming hair or nails – usu pl with sing. meaning **2** a fast sailing ship, esp with long slender lines, a sharply raked bow, and a large sail area [[3]CLIP + [2]-ER]

clippie /'klipi/ *n, Br* a female bus conductor – infml [[3]*clip* (to punch a hole, i e in a bus ticket)]

clipping /'kliping/ *n, chiefly NAm* CUTTING 2

clique /kleek/ *n sing or pl in constr* a highly exclusive and often aloof group of people held together by common interests, views, etc [F] – **cliquey, cliquy** *adj*, **cliquish** *adj*, **cliquishly** *adv*, **cliquishness** *n*

clitoris /'klitəris, 'klie-/ *n* a small erectile organ at the front or top part of the vulva that is a centre of sexual sensation in females ☞ REPRODUCTION [NL, fr Gk *kleitoris*] – **clitoral** /-t(ə)rəl/, **clitoric** /-'torik/ *adj*

cloaca /kloh'aykə/ *n, pl* **cloacae** /-kee, -see/ **1** a conduit for sewage **2** the chamber into which the intestinal, urinary, and generative canals discharge, esp in birds, reptiles, amphibians, and many fishes [L; akin to Gk *klyzein* to wash] – **cloacal** *adj*

[1]cloak /klohk/ *n* **1** a sleeveless outer garment that usu fastens at the neck and hangs loosely from the shoulders – compare [2]CAPE **2** sthg that conceals; a pretence, disguise [ME *cloke*, fr ONF *cloque* bell, cloak, fr ML *clocca* bell; fr its shape]

[2]cloak *vt* to cover or hide (as if) with a cloak

,cloak-and-'dagger *adj* dealing in or suggestive of melodramatic intrigue and action usu involving espionage

'cloakroom /-room, -,roohm/ *n* **1** a room in which outdoor clothing or luggage may be left during one's stay **2** *chiefly Br* a room with a toilet – euph

[1]clobber /'klobə/ *n, Br* gear, paraphernalia; *esp* clothes worn for a usu specified purpose or function – infml [prob alter. of *clothes*]

[2]clobber *vt* **1** to hit with force **2** to defeat overwhelmingly *USE* infml [origin unknown]

cloche /klosh/ *n* **1** a translucent cover used for protecting outdoor plants **2** a woman's usu soft close-fitting hat with a deeply rounded crown and narrow brim ☞ GARMENT [F, lit., bell, fr ML *clocca*]

[1]clock /klok/ *n* **1** a device other than a watch for indicating or measuring time **2** a recording or metering device with a dial and indicator attached to a mechanism: e g **a** a speedometer **b** *Br* a milometer **3** *Br* a face – slang [ME *clok*, fr MD *clocke* bell, clock, fr ONF or ML; ONF *cloque* bell, fr ML *clocca*, of Celt origin; akin to MIr *clocc* bell] – **clocklike** *adj* – **round the clock 1** continuously for 24 hours; day and night without cessation **2** without relaxation and heedless of time

[2]clock *vt* **1** to time with a stopwatch or electric timing device – used chiefly in sports **2a** to register on a mechanical recording device **b** *Br* to attain a time, speed, etc, of – often + *up*; infml **3** to hit ⟨~ed *him on the jaw*⟩ – infml – **clocker** *n*

[3]clock *n* an ornamental pattern on the outside ankle

or side of a stocking or sock [prob fr *clock* (bell); fr its original bell-like shape]

clock in *vi* to record the time of one's arrival or commencement of work by punching a card in a time clock

clock off *vi* CLOCK OUT

clock on *vi* CLOCK IN

clock out *vi* to record the time of one's departure or stopping of work by punching a card in a time clock

'clock-,watcher /,wochə/ *n* a person (e g a worker) who keeps close watch on the passage of time in order not to work a single moment longer than he/she has to – **clock-watching** *n*

'clock,wise /-,wiez/ *adv* in the direction in which the hands of a clock rotate as viewed from in front – **clockwise** *adj*

'clock,work /-,wuhk/ *n* machinery that operates in a manner similar to that of a mechanical clock; *specif* machinery powered by a coiled spring ⟨*a ~ toy*⟩ – **like clockwork** smoothly and with no hitches

clod /klod/ *n* **1** a lump or mass, esp of earth or clay **2** an oaf, dolt **3** a gristly cut of beef taken from the neck ☞ MEAT [ME, alter. of *clot*] – **cloddish** *adj*, **cloddishness** *n*, **cloddy** *adj*

clodhopper /'klod,hopə/ *n* **1** a clodhopping person – infml **2** a large heavy shoe – chiefly humor

'clod,hopping /-,hoping/ *adj* **1** boorish **2** *Br* awkward, clumsy *USE* infml

[1]clog /klog/ *n* **1** a weight attached, esp to an animal, to hinder motion **2** a shoe, sandal, or overshoe with a thick typically wooden sole [ME *clogge* short thick piece of wood]

[2]clog *vb* **-gg-** *vt* **1** to halt or retard the progress, operation, or growth of **2a** to obstruct so as to hinder motion in or through **b** to block ⟨*the drain is* ~ged *up*⟩ ~ *vi* to become blocked *up*

cloisonné /,klwahzo'nay, '--,-/ *adj or n* (in) a style of enamel decoration in which the enamel is fired in raised sections separated by fine wire or thin metal strips – compare CHAMPLEVÉ [F, fr pp of *cloisonner* to partition]

cloister /'kloystə/ *n* **1a** a monastic establishment **b** *the* monastic life **2** a covered passage on the side of an open court, usu having one side walled and the other an open arcade or colonnade [ME *cloistre*, fr OF, fr ML *claustrum*, fr L, bar, bolt, fr *clausus*, pp of *claudere* to close – more at [4]CLOSE]

cloistered /'kloystəd/ *adj* **1** suggestive of the seclusion of a monastic cloister ⟨~ *calm*⟩ **2** surrounded with a cloister ⟨~ *gardens*⟩

cloistral /'kloystrəl/ *adj* (suggestive) of a cloister

[1]clone /klohn/ *n* **1** an individual that is asexually produced and is therefore identical to its parent **2** all such progeny of a single parent – used technically [Gk *klōn* twig, slip; akin to Gk *klan* to break] – **clonal** /'klohnl/ *adj*, **clonally** *adv*

[2]clone *vt* to cause to grow (as if) as a clone

clonk /klongk/ *vb* to make a thumping sound (on), as if from the impact of a hard object on a hard but hollow surface [imit] – **clonk** *n*

clonus /'klohnəs/ *n* a rapid succession of alternating contractions and partial relaxations of a muscle that occurs in some nervous diseases [NL, fr Gk *klonos* turmoil; akin to L *celer* swift] – **clonic** /-nik/ *adj*, **clonicity** /-'nisəti/ *n*

clop /klop/ *n* a sound made (as if) by a hoof or shoe against a hard surface [imit] – **clop** *vi*

[1]close /klohz/ *vt* **1a** to move so as to bar passage ⟨~ *the gate*⟩ **b** to deny access to ⟨~ *the park*⟩ **c** to suspend or stop the operations of; *also* to discontinue or dispose of (a business) permanently – often + *down* **2a** to bring to an end ⟨~ *an account*⟩ **b** to conclude discussion or negotiation about ⟨*the question is* ~d⟩; *also* to bring to agreement or settlement ⟨~ *a deal*⟩ **3** to bring or bind together the parts or edges of ⟨*a* ~d *fist*⟩ ~ *vi* **1a** to contract, swing, or slide so as to leave no opening ⟨*the door* ~d *quietly*⟩ **b** to cease operation ⟨*the factory* ~d *down*⟩ ⟨*the shops* ~ *at 9 pm*⟩; *specif, Br* to stop broadcasting – usu + *down* **2** to draw near, esp in order to fight – usu + *with* **3** to come to an end [ME *closen*, fr OF *clos-*, stem of *clore*, fr L *claudere*] – **closable, closeable** /'klohzəbl/ *adj*, **closer** /'klohzə/ *n* – **close one's doors** **1** to refuse admission ⟨*the nation* closed its doors *to immigrants*⟩ **2** to go out of business ⟨*after nearly 40 years he had to* close his doors *for lack of trade*⟩ – **close one's eyes to** to ignore deliberately – **close ranks** to unite in a concerted stand, esp to meet a challenge – **close the door** to be uncompromisingly obstructive ⟨*his attitude* closed the door *to further negotiation*⟩

[2]close /klohz/ *n* a conclusion or end in time or existence ⟨*the decade drew to a* ~⟩

[3]close /klohs; *sense 2 also* klohz/ *n* **1** a road closed at one end **2** *Br* the precinct of a cathedral [ME *clos*, lit., enclosure, fr OF *clos*, fr L *clausum*, fr neut of *clausus*, pp]

[4]close /klohs/ *adj* **1** having no openings; closed **2a** confined, cramped ⟨~ *quarters*⟩ **b** articulated with some part of the tongue close to the palate ⟨*a* ~ *vowel*⟩ **3** restricted, closed ⟨*the* ~ *season*⟩ **4** secretive, reticent ⟨*she was very* ~ *about her past*⟩ **5** strict, rigorous ⟨*keep* ~ *watch*⟩ ⟨*under* ~ *arrest*⟩ **6** hot and stuffy **7** having little space between items or units; compact, dense ⟨~ *texture*⟩ **8** very short or near to the surface ⟨*the barber gave him a* ~ *shave*⟩ **9** near; *esp* adjacent ⟨*he and I are* ~ *relations*⟩ **10** intimate, familiar ⟨~ *collaboration*⟩ **11a** searching, minute ⟨*a* ~ *study*⟩ **b** faithful to an original ⟨*a* ~ *copy*⟩ **12** evenly contested or having a (nearly) even score ⟨*a* ~ *game*⟩ [ME *clos*, fr MF, fr L *clausus*, pp of *claudere* to shut, close; akin to Gk *kleiein* to close, OHG *sliozan*] – **closely** *adv*, **closeness** *n* – **close to home** within one's personal interests so that one is strongly affected ⟨*the audience felt that the speaker's remarks hit pretty* close to home⟩

[5]close /klohs/ *adv* in or into a close position or manner; near ⟨*come* ~ *to ruining us*⟩ – **close on** almost ⟨close on *500 people*⟩

,close 'call /klohs/ *n* a narrow escape

,close-'cropped /klohs/ *adj* clipped short ⟨~ *hair*⟩

closed /klohzd/ *adj* **1a** not open **b** enclosed ⟨*a* ~ *porch*⟩ **2a** forming a self-contained unit allowing no additions ⟨~ *system*⟩ **b(1)** traced by a moving point that returns to its starting point without retracing its path ⟨*a* ~ *curve*⟩; *also* so formed that every plane section is a closed curve ⟨*a* ~ *surface*⟩ **(2)** characterized by mathematical elements that when subjected to an operation produce only elements of the same set ⟨*the set of whole numbers is* ~ *under addition and multiplication*⟩ **(3)** containing all the limit points of every subset ⟨*a* ~ *set*⟩ **3a** confined to a few ⟨~ *membership*⟩ **b** rigidly excluding outside influence ⟨*a* ~ *mind*⟩

ˌclosed ˈcircuit *n* **1** a television installation in which the signal is transmitted by wire to a limited number of receivers, usu in 1 location **2** a connected array of electrical components that will allow the passage of current – **closed-circuit** *adj*

closedown /ˈklohzˌdown/ *n* the act or result of closing down; *esp* the end of a period of broadcasting

ˌclosed ˈshop *n* an establishment which employs only union members – compare OPEN SHOP

closefisted /ˌklohsˈfistid/ *adj* tightfisted

ˌclose-ˈhauled /klohs/ *adj or adv* with the sails set for sailing as near directly into the wind as possible

close in /klohz/ *vi* **1** to gather in close all round with an oppressing effect ⟨*despair* closed in *on her*⟩ **2** to approach from various directions to close quarters, esp for an attack or arrest ⟨*at dawn the police* closed in⟩ **3** to grow dark ⟨*the short November day was already* closing in – Ellen Glasgow⟩

ˌclose-ˈknit /klohs/ *adj* bound together by close ties

close out /klohz/ *vb, NAm* to (attempt to) dispose of (goods), esp by selling at reduced prices

ˌclose ˈquarters /klohs/ *n pl* immediate contact or close range ⟨*fought at* ~⟩

ˈclose ˌseason /klohs/ *n, Br* a period during which it is illegal to kill or catch certain game or fish

ˌclose ˈshave /klohs/ *n* a narrow escape – infml

[1]closet /ˈklozit/ *n* **1** a small or private room **2** WATER CLOSET **3** *chiefly NAm* a cupboard [ME, fr MF, dim. of *clos* enclosure]

[2]closet *vt* **1** to shut (oneself) up (as if) in a closet **2** to take into a closet for a secret interview

ˈclose-ˌup /klohs/ *n* **1** a photograph or film shot taken at close range **2** a view or examination of sthg from a small distance away

clostridium /kloˈstridi·əm/ *n, pl* **clostridia** /-di·ə/ any of various spore-forming soil or intestinal bacteria that cause gas gangrene, tetanus, and other diseases [NL, genus name, fr Gk *klōstēr* spindle, fr *klōthein* to spin] – **clostridial** *adj*

[1]closure /ˈklohzhə/ *n* **1** closing or being closed **2** the ending of a side's innings in cricket by declaration **3** the closing of debate in a legislative body, esp by calling for a vote – compare GUILLOTINE [ME, fr MF, fr L *clausura*, fr *clausus*, pp of *claudere* to close – more at [4]CLOSE; (3) trans of F *clôture*, alter. of MF *closure*]

[2]closure *vt* to close (a debate) by closure

[1]clot /klot/ *n* **1a** a roundish viscous lump formed by coagulation of a portion of liquid (e g cream) **b** a coagulated mass produced by clotting of blood **2** *Br* a stupid person – infml [ME, fr OE *clott*; akin to MHG *klōz* lump, ball – more at CLOUT]

[2]clot *vb* **-tt-** *vi* **1** to become a clot; form clots **2** *of blood* to undergo a sequence of complex chemical and physical reactions that results in conversion from liquid form into a coagulated mass ~ *vt* to cause to clot

cloth /kloth/ *n, pl* **cloths** /klodhz, kloths/ **1** a pliable material made usu by weaving, felting, or knitting natural or synthetic fibres and filaments **2** a piece of cloth adapted for a particular purpose: e g **a** a tablecloth **b** a dishcloth **c** a duster **3** (the distinctive dress of) a profession or calling distinguished by its dress; *specif the* clergy [ME, fr OE *clāth*; akin to OE *clīthan* to adhere to, LL *glut-*, *glus* glue]

ˌcloth-ˈcap *adj, Br* working-class – infml [fr the cloth caps commonly worn, esp formerly, by working-class men]

clothe /klohdh/ *vt* **clothed, clad** /klad/ **1a** to cover (as if) with clothing; dress **b** to provide with clothes **2** to express or enhance by suitably significant language [ME *clothen*, fr OE *clāthian*, fr *clāth* cloth, garment]

ˌcloth-ˈeared /iəd/ *adj, Br* (irritatingly) deficient in hearing – infml; chiefly humor

clothes /klohdhz/ *n pl* **1** articles of material (e g cloth) worn to cover the body, for warmth, protection, or decoration ☞ GARMENT **2** bedclothes [ME, fr OE *clāthas*, pl of *clāth* cloth, garment]

ˈclothes ˌbasket *n* a basket used for storing clothes that are to be washed

ˈclothes ˌbrush *n* a small stiff brush for removing dirt from clothes

ˈclothesˌhorse /-ˌhaws/ *n* **1** a frame on which to hang clothes, esp for drying or airing indoors **2** *chiefly NAm* a conspicuously dressy person – derog

ˈclothesˌline /-ˌlien/ *n* a line (e g of cord or nylon) on which clothes may be hung to dry, esp outdoors

ˈclothes ˌmoth *n* any of several small yellowish moths whose larvae eat wool, fur, hair, etc

ˈclothes ˌpeg *n* a wooden or plastic clip or forked device used for holding clothes or washing on a line

ˈclothesˌpin /-ˌpin/ *n, NAm* CLOTHES PEG

clothier /ˈklohdhiə/ *n* sby who makes or sells cloth or clothing [ME, alter. of *clother*, fr *cloth*]

clothing /ˈklohdhing/ *n* clothes

cloture /ˈklohchə/ *n, NAm* CLOSURE 3 – **cloture** *vt*

[1]cloud /klowd/ *n* **1a** a visible mass of particles of water or ice at a usu great height in the air ☞ WEATHER **b** a light filmy, puffy, or billowy mass seeming to float in the air **2** any of many masses of opaque matter in interstellar space **3** a great crowd or multitude; a swarm, esp of insects ⟨~s *of mosquitoes*⟩ **4** sthg that obscures or blemishes ⟨*their reputation is under a* ~⟩ [ME, rock, cloud, fr OE *clūd*; akin to Gk *gloutos* buttock] – **cloudless** *adj*, **cloudlet** *n*

[2]cloud *vi* **1** to grow cloudy – usu + *over* or *up* **2a** *of facial features* to become troubled, apprehensive, etc **b** to become blurred, dubious, or ominous ~ *vt* **1a** to envelop or obscure (as if) with a cloud **b** to make opaque or murky by condensation, smoke, etc **2** to make unclear or confused **3** to taint, sully ⟨*a* ~ed *reputation*⟩ **4** to cast gloom over

ˈcloudberry /-b(ə)ri, -ˌberi/ *n* (the pale amber edible fruit of) a creeping plant closely related to the raspberry [[1]*cloud* + *berry*; perh fr its shape]

ˈcloudˌburst /-ˌbuhst/ *n* a sudden very heavy fall of rain

ˈcloud ˌchamber *n* a vessel containing saturated water vapour whose sudden expansion reveals the passage of an ionizing particle (e g an alpha particle) by a trail of visible droplets

ˌcloud ˈnine *n* a feeling of extreme well-being or elation – usu + *on*; infml [*nine* prob an arbitrary number, *seven* being sometimes used instead]

cloudy /ˈklowdi/ *adj* **1** (having a sky) overcast with clouds **2** not clear or transparent ⟨~ *beer*⟩ ⟨*a ~ mirror*⟩ – **cloudily** *adv*, **cloudiness** *n*

[1]clout /klowt/ *n* **1** *dial chiefly N Eng & Scot* CLOTH 2; *specif* a piece of cloth or rag used for household tasks (e g polishing or cleaning) – often in combination ⟨*dish*clout⟩ **2** a blow or lusty hit with the hand, cricket bat, etc **3** influence; *esp* effective political power *USE* (*2&3*) infml [ME, fr OE *clūt*; akin to MHG *klōz* lump, Russ *gluda*]

[2]clout *vt* to hit forcefully – infml

'clout ,nail *n* a nail with a large flat head [*clout* (iron plate used to keep wood from wearing)]

[1]clove /klohv/ *n* any of the small bulbs (e g in garlic) developed as parts of a larger bulb [ME, fr OE *clufu*; akin to OE *clēofan* to cleave]

[2]clove *past of* CLEAVE

[3]clove *n* (a tree of the myrtle family that bears) a flower bud that is used dried as a spice [alter. of ME *clowe*, fr OF *clou* (*de girofle*), lit., nail of clove, fr L *clavus* nail]

'clove ,hitch *n* a knot used to secure a rope temporarily to a spar or another rope [ME *cloven, clove* divided, fr pp of *clevien* to cleave]

cloven /'klohv(ə)n/ *past part of* [2]CLEAVE

,cloven 'foot *n* a foot (e g of a sheep) divided into 2 parts at the end farthest from the body – **cloven-footed** *adj*

,cloven 'hoof *n* CLOVEN FOOT – **cloven-hoofed** *adj*

clover /'klohvə/ *n* any of a genus of leguminous plants having leaves with 3 leaflets and flowers in dense heads [ME, fr OE *clāfre*; akin to OHG *klēo* clover] – **in clover** in prosperity or in pleasant circumstances

'clover,leaf /-,leef/ *n, pl* **cloverleafs, cloverleaves** /-,leevz/ a road junction whose plan resembles the arrangement of leaves in a 4-leaved clover and that connects 2 major roads at different levels

clown /klown/ *n* **1** a jester in an entertainment (e g a play); *specif* a grotesquely dressed comedy performer in a circus **2** one who habitually plays the buffoon; a joker [perh fr MF *coulon* settler, fr L *colonus* colonist, farmer – more at COLONY] – **clown** *vi*, **clownery** /'klownəri/ *n*, **clownish** *adj*, **clownishly** *adv*, **clownishness** *n*

cloy /kloy/ *vt* to surfeit with an excess, usu of sthg orig pleasing ~ *vi* to cause surfeit [ME *acloien* to lame, fr MF *encloer* to drive in a nail, fr ML *inclavare*, fr L *in* + *clavus* nail] – **cloyingly** /'kloyingli/ *adv*

[1]club /klub/ *n* **1a** a heavy stick thicker at one end than the other and used as a hand weapon **b** a stick or bat used to hit a ball in golf and other games **c** a light spar **2a** a playing card marked with 1 or more black figures in the shape of a cloverleaf **b** *pl but sing or pl in constr* the suit comprising cards identified by this figure **3a** *sing or pl in constr* **(1)** an association of people for a specified object, usu jointly supported and meeting periodically ⟨*judo ~*⟩ **(2)** an often exclusive association of people that has premises available as a congenial place of retreat or temporary residence or for dining at **b** the meeting place or premises of a club **c** a group of people who agree to make regular payments or purchases in order to secure some advantage ⟨*book ~*⟩ **d** a nightclub [ME *clubbe*, fr ON *klubba*; akin to OHG *kolbo* club, OE *clamm* bond] – **in the club** *of a woman* pregnant – infml

[2]club *vb* **-bb-** *vt* to beat or strike (as if) with a club ~ *vi* to combine to share a common expense or object – usu + *together*

clubbable, clubable /'klubəbl/ *adj* sociable

clubbed *adj* club-shaped

'club ,chair *n* a deep low thickly upholstered armchair, often with a rather low back and heavy sides and arms

,club'foot /-'foot/ *n* a misshapen foot twisted out of position from birth – **clubfooted** /,-'--/ *adj*

'club ,moss *n* any of an order of primitive vascular plants ☞ PLANT [trans of NL *muscus clavatus*; fr the club-shaped spore-producing vessels in some species]

'club,root /-,rooht/ *n* a disease of cabbages and related plants characterized by swellings or distortions of the root

,club 'sandwich *n* a sandwich of 3 slices of bread with 2 layers of filling

[1]cluck /kluk/ *vi* **1** to make a cluck **2** to express fussy interest or concern – usu + *over*; infml ~ *vt* to call with a cluck [imit]

[2]cluck *n* the characteristic guttural sound made by a hen

[1]clue /klooh/ *n* **1** *also* **clew** sthg that guides via intricate procedure to the solution of a problem **2** CLEW 2 [ME *clewe* ball of thread – more at CLEW]

[2]clue *vt* **clueing, cluing 1** CLEW 2 **2** *also* **clew** to inform – usu + *in* or *up*; infml ⟨~ *me in on how it happened*⟩

'clueless /-lis/ *adj, Br* hopelessly ignorant or lacking in sense – infml [[1]CLUE + -LESS]

[1]clump /klump/ *n* **1** a compact group of things of the same kind, esp trees or bushes; a cluster **2** a compact mass **3** a heavy tramping sound [prob fr LG *klump*; akin to OE *clamm* bond] – **clumpy** *adj*

[2]clump *vi* **1** to tread clumsily and noisily **2** to form clumps ~ *vt* to arrange in or cause to form clumps

clumsy /'klumzi/ *adj* **1a** awkward and ungraceful in movement or action **b** lacking tact or subtlety ⟨*a ~ joke*⟩ **2** awkwardly or poorly made; unwieldy [prob fr obs *clumse* (benumbed with cold), of Scand origin] – **clumsily** *adv*, **clumsiness** *n*

clung /klung/ *past of* CLING

[1]cluster /'klustə/ *n* a compact group formed by a number of similar things or people; a bunch: e g **a** a group of faint stars or galaxies that appear close together and have common properties (e g distance and motion) **b** the group of 4 cups that connect the teats of a cow to a milking machine [ME, fr OE *clyster*; akin to OE *clott* clot] – **clustery** *adj*

[2]cluster *vt* to collect into a cluster ~ *vi* to grow or assemble in a cluster

'cluster ,bomb *n* a bomb that explodes to release many smaller usu incendiary or fragmentation missiles

[1]clutch /kluch/ *vt* to grasp or hold (as if) with the hand or claws, esp tightly or suddenly ~ *vi* **1** to seek to grasp and hold – often + *at* **2** to operate the clutch on a motor vehicle [ME *clucchen*, fr OE *clyccan*; akin to MIr *glacc* hand – more at CLING]

[2]clutch *n* **1** (the claws or a hand in) the act of grasping or seizing firmly **2** (a lever or pedal operating) a coupling used to connect and disconnect a driving and a driven part of a mechanism

[3]clutch *n* a nest of eggs or a brood of chicks; *broadly* a group, bunch [alter. of E dial. *cletch* (hatching, brood)]

'clutch ,bag *n* a small handbag with no handle

[1]clutter /'klutə/ *vt* to fill or cover with scattered or disordered things – often + *up* [ME *clotteren* to clot, fr *clot*]

[2]clutter *n* **1a** a crowded or confused mass or collection **b** scattered or disordered material **2** interfering echoes visible on a radar screen caused by reflection from objects other than the target

Clydesdale /'kliedz,dayl/ *n* a heavy draught horse with heavily feathered legs [*Clydesdale*, region of Scotland, where it originated]

clypeus /'klipi·əs/ *n, pl* **clypei** /-pi,ie/ a plate on the front of an insect's head [NL, fr L, round shield]

co- /koh-/ *prefix* **1** with; together; joint ⟨co*exist*⟩ ⟨co*heir*⟩ ⟨co*education*⟩ **2** in or to the same degree ⟨co*extensive*⟩ **3a** associate; fellow ⟨co*author*⟩ ⟨co-*star*⟩ **b** deputy; assistant ⟨co*pilot*⟩ [ME, fr L, fr *com-*; akin to OE *ge-*, perfective and collective prefix, Gk *koinos* common]

coacervate /koh'asəvayt/ *n* a mass of colloidal droplets held together by electrostatic attractive forces [L *coacervatus*, pp of *coacervare* to heap up, fr *co-* + *acervus* heap] – **coacervate** /,koh·ə'suhvət/ *adj*, **coacervation** /,koh,asə'vaysh(ə)n/ *n*

[1]coach /kohch/ *n* **1a** a large usu closed four-wheeled carriage – compare STAGE 4c **b** a railway carriage **c** a usu single-deck bus used esp for long-distance or charter work **2a** a private tutor **b** sby who instructs or trains a performer, sportsman, etc [ME *coche*, fr MF, fr G *kutsche*, prob fr Hung *kocsi (szekér)* wagon from Kocs, fr *Kocs*, village in Hungary]

[2]coach *vt* **1** to train intensively by instruction, demonstration, and practice **2** to act as coach to ~ *vi* **1** to go in a coach **2** to instruct, direct, or prompt as a coach – **coacher** *n*

'coach,built /-,bilt/ *adj*, *of a vehicle body* built to individual requirements by craftsmen – **coachbuilder** *n*

'coachman /-mən/ *n* a man who drives or whose business is to drive a coach or carriage

'coach,work /-,wuhk/ *n* the bodywork of a road or rail vehicle

coadjutor /,koh'ajətə/ *n* an assistant; *specif* a bishop assisting a diocesan bishop and often having the right of succession [ME *coadjutour*, fr MF *coadjuteur*, fr L *coadjutor*, fr *co-* + *adjutor* aid, fr *adjutus*, pp of *adjuvare* to help – more at AID] – **coadjutor** *adj*

coagulant /koh'agyoolənt/ *n* sthg that produces coagulation

coagulate /koh'agyoolayt/ *vb* to (cause to) become viscous or thickened into a coherent mass; curdle, clot [L *coagulatus*, pp of *coagulare* to curdle, fr *coagulum* curdling agent, fr *cogere* to drive together – more at COGENT] – **coagulable** /-ləbl/ *adj*, **coagulability** /-lə'biləti/ *n*, **coagulation** /-'laysh(ə)n/ *n*

coagulum /koh'agyooləm/ *n, pl* **coagula** /-lə/, **coagulums** a coagulated mass [L, coagulant]

coal /kohl/ *n* **1** a piece of glowing, burning, or burnt carbonized material (e g partly burnt wood) **2** a (small piece or broken up quantity of) black or blackish solid combustible mineral consisting chiefly of carbonized vegetable matter and widely used as a natural fuel ☞ ENERGY [ME *col*, fr OE; akin to OHG & ON *kol* burning ember, IrGael *gual* coal]

,coal 'black *adj* absolutely black; very black

coalesce /,koh·ə'les/ *vi* to unite into a whole; fuse [L *coalescere*, fr *co-* + *alescere* to grow – more at OLD] – **coalescence** *n*, **coalescent** *adj*

'coal,field /-,feeld/ *n* a region in which deposits of coal occur

'coal,fish /-,fish/ *n* any of several blackish or dark-backed fishes; *esp* a coley

'coal ,gas *n* gas made from burning coal; *esp* gas made by carbonizing bituminous coal and used for heating and lighting

'coal,hole /-,hohl/ *n* **1** a hole or chute for receiving coal **2** *Br* a compartment for storing coal

coalition /,koh·ə'lish(ə)n/ *n* **1a** an act of coalescing; a union **b** a body formed by the union of orig distinct elements **2** *sing or pl in constr* a temporary alliance (e g of political parties) for joint action (e g to form a government) [MF, fr L *coalitus*, pp of *coalescere*] – **coalitionist** *n*

'coal ,measures *n pl* beds of coal with the associated rocks

,coal 'tar *n* tar obtained by the distilling of bituminous coal and used esp in making dyes and drugs

'coal ,tit *n* a small black-crowned European tit with a white patch on the neck

coaming /'kohming/ *n* a raised frame (e g round a hatchway in the deck of a ship) to keep out water [perh irreg fr *comb*]

coarctate /koh'ahktayt/ *adj* constricted – used technically [L *coarctatus*, pp of *coartare* to press together, fr *co-* + *artus* narrow, confined; akin to L *artus* joint – more at ARTICLE] – **coarctation** /-'taysh(ə)n/ *n*

coarse /kaws/ *adj* **1** of ordinary or inferior quality or value; common **2a(1)** composed of relatively large particles ⟨*~ sand*⟩ **(2)** rough in texture or tone ⟨*~ cloth*⟩ ⟨*a ~ bell*⟩ **b** adjusted or designed for heavy, fast, or less delicate work ⟨*a ~ saw with large teeth*⟩ **c** not precise or detailed with respect to adjustment or discrimination **3** crude or unrefined in taste, manners, or language [ME *cors*, prob fr *course*, n (the common run of things)] – **coarsely** *adv*, **coarseness** *n*

'coarse ,fish *n, chiefly Br* any freshwater fish not belonging to the salmon family – **coarse fishing** *n*

coarsen /'kaws(ə)n/ *vb* to make or become coarse

[1]coast /kohst/ *n* the land near a shore; the seashore [ME *cost*, fr MF *coste*, fr L *costa* rib, side; akin to OSlav *kostĭ* bone] – **coastal** *adj*, **coastally** *adv*, **coastwards** /-woodz/ *adv*

[2]coast *vt* to sail along the shore of ~ *vi* **1** to sail along the shore **2a** to slide, glide, etc downhill by the force of gravity **b** to move along (as if) without further application of propulsive power **c** to proceed easily without special application of effort or concern

coaster /'kohstə/ *n* **1** a small vessel trading from port to port along a coast **2a** a tray or stand, esp of silver, for a decanter **b** a small mat used, esp under a drinks glass, to protect a surface [[2]COAST + [2]-ER]

'coast,guard /-,gahd/ *n* (a member of) a force responsible for maintaining lookout posts round the coast of the UK for mounting rescues at sea, preventing smuggling, etc

'coast,line /-,lien/ *n* the outline or shape of a coast ☞ GEOGRAPHY

[1]coat /koht/ *n* **1** an outer garment that has sleeves and usu opens the full length of the centre front **2** the external covering of an animal **3** a protective layer; a coating [ME *cote*, fr OF, of Gmc origin; akin to OHG *kozza* coarse mantle] – **coated** *adj*

[2]coat *vt* to cover or spread with a protective or enclosing layer – **coater** *n*

¹**coat ,hanger** *n* ²HANGER

coati /koh'ahti/ *n* a tropical American mammal related to the raccoon but with a longer body and tail and a long flexible snout [Pg *coatí*, fr Tupi]

co,ati'mundi /-'moondi/ *n* a coati [Tupi]

coating /'kohting/ *n* a layer of one substance covering another

,coat of 'arms *n, pl* **coats of arms** (a tabard or surcoat embroidered with) a set of distinctive heraldic shapes or representations, usu depicted on a shield, that is the central part of a heraldic achievement [trans of F *cotte d'armes*]

'**coat ,tails** *n pl* two long tapering skirts at the back of a man's coat

coax /kohks/ *vt* **1** to influence or gently urge by caresses or flattery; wheedle **2** to draw or gain by means of gentle urging or flattery ⟨~ed *an answer out of her*⟩ **3** to manipulate with great perseverance and skill towards a desired condition [earlier *cokes*, fr *cokes*, n (simpleton)]

coaxial /koh'aksi·əl/ *adj* mounted on concentric shafts – **coaxially** *adv*

coaxial cable *n* a conductor for high-frequency electrical signals (e g telephone or television signals) consisting of a tube of electrically conducting material containing, and separated by a layer of insulation from, a central conducting wire

¹**cob** /kob/ *n* **1** a male swan **2** CORNCOB 1 **3** (any of) a breed of short-legged stocky horses **4** *Br* a small rounded usu crusty loaf [ME *cobbe* leader; akin to OE *cot* cottage – more at ¹COT] – **cobby** *adj*

²**cob** *n* a building material used chiefly in SW England and consisting of natural clay or chalk mixed with straw or hair as a binder; *also* a house built of cob ☞ BUILDING [perh fr ¹*cob* (rounded mass, lump)]

cobalt /'koh,bawlt/ *n* a tough divalent or trivalent silver-white magnetic metallic element ☞ PERIODIC TABLE [G *kobalt*, alter. of *kobold*, lit., goblin, fr MHG *kobolt*; fr its occurrence in silver ore, believed to be due to goblins] – **cobaltic** /koh'bawltik/ *adj*, **cobaltous** /koh'bawltəs/ *adj*

,cobalt 'blue *n* a greenish blue pigment consisting essentially of cobalt oxide and alumina

cobber /'kobə/ *n, Austr* a man's male friend; a mate – infml [prob fr Yiddish *chaber* comrade, fr Heb]

¹**cobble** /'kobl/ *vt* **cobbling** /'kobling, 'kobl·ing/ **1** to repair (esp shoes); *also* to make (esp shoes) **2** to make or assemble roughly or hastily – usu + *together* [ME *coblen*, perh back-formation fr *cobelere* cobbler]

²**cobble** *n* a naturally rounded stone of a size suitable for paving a street [back-formation fr *cobblestone*]

³**cobble** *vt* to pave with cobblestones

cobbler /'koblə/ *n* **1** a mender or maker of leather goods, esp shoes **2** *pl, Br* nonsense, rubbish – often used interjectionally; infml [ME *cobelere*; (2) rhyming slang *cobbler's (awls)* balls, testicles]

'**cobble,stone** /-,stohn/ *n* a cobble [ME, fr *cobble*- (prob fr *cob* lump, round object) + *stone*] – **cobblestoned** *adj*

coble /'kohbl, 'kobl/ *n* a flat-bottomed fishing boat with a lugsail [ME]

cobnut /'kob,nut/ *n* (the nut of) a European hazel [*cob* (lump, round object)]

Cobol, COBOL /'kohbol/ *n* a high-level computer language designed for business applications [*com*mon *b*usiness *o*riented *l*anguage]

cobra /'kobrə, 'kohbrə/ *n* any of several venomous Asiatic and African snakes that have grooved fangs and when excited expand the skin of the neck into a hood [Pg *cobra (de capello)*, lit., hooded snake, fr L *colubra* snake]

cobweb /'kob,web/ *n* **1** (a) spider's web **2** a single thread spun by a spider [ME *coppeweb*, fr *coppe* spider (fr OE ātor*coppe*) + *web*; akin to MD *coppe* spider] – **cobwebbed** *adj*, **cobwebby** *adj*

coca /'kohkə/ *n* (the dried cocaine-containing leaves of) a S American shrub [Sp, fr Quechua *kúka*]

cocaine /,koh'kayn, kə-/ *n* an alkaloid that is obtained from coca leaves, has been used as a local anaesthetic, and is a common drug of abuse that can result in psychological dependence – **cocainism** /-,niz(ə)m/ *n*

coccidiosis /kok,sidi'ohsis/ *n, pl* **coccidioses** /-seez/ a disease of birds (e g poultry) and mammals (e g sheep) caused by coccidia [NL]

coccidium /kok'sidi·əm/ *n, pl* **coccidia** /-di·ə/ any of an order of protozoans usu parasitic in the lining of the digestive tract of vertebrates [NL, dim. of *coccus*]

coccus /'kokəs/ *n, pl* **cocci** /'kok(s)ie/ a spherical bacterium [NL, fr Gk *kokkos*] – **coccal** /-kəl/ *adj*, **coccoid** /-koyd/ *adj*

coccyx /'koksiks/ *n, pl* **coccyges** /-si,jeez/ *also* **coccyxes** the end of the spinal column below the sacrum in human beings and the tailless apes [NL, fr Gk *kokkyx* cuckoo, coccyx; fr its resemblance to a cuckoo's beak] – **coccygeal** /kok'siji·əl/ *adj*

Cochin China /,kohchin 'chienə, ,kochin/ *n* any of an Asian breed of large domestic fowl with thick plumage and densely feathered legs and feet [*Cochin China*, region of Vietnam]

cochineal /,kochi'neel/ *n* a red dyestuff consisting of the dried bodies of female cochineal insects, used esp as a colouring agent for food [MF & Sp; MF *cochenille*, fr OSp *cochinilla* wood louse, cochineal]

,cochi'neal ,insect *n* a small bright red insect that feeds on cactus

cochlea /'kokli·ə/ *n, pl* **cochleas, cochleae** /-li,ee/ a coiled part of the inner ear of higher vertebrates that is filled with liquid through which sound waves are transmitted to the auditory nerve ☞ NERVE [NL, fr L, snail, snail shell, fr Gk *kochlias*, fr *kochlos* land snail; akin to Gk *konchē* mussel] – **cochlear** *adj*

¹**cock** /kok/ *n* **1a** the (adult) male of various birds, specif the domestic fowl **b** the male of fish, crabs, lobsters, and other aquatic animals **2** a device (e g a tap or valve) for regulating the flow of a liquid **3** the hammer of a firearm or its position when cocked ready for firing **4** *Br* – used as a term of infml address to a man **5** the penis – vulg **6** *Br* nonsense, rubbish – slang [ME *cok*, fr OE *cocc*, of imit origin]

²**cock** *vi* to set the hammer of a firearm ready for firing ~ *vt* **1a** to draw back and set the hammer of (a firearm) for firing **b** to draw or bend back in preparation for throwing or hitting **2a** to set erect ⟨*the dog* ~ed *its ears*⟩ **b** to turn, tip, or tilt, usu to one side ⟨~ed *his head inquiringly*⟩ **3** to turn up (e g the brim of a hat) [*cock* (to swagger, stick up), fr ME *cocken* to quarrel, fight, fr *cok* cock] – **cock a snook** to react with disdain or defiance ⟨cock a snook *at authority*⟩

³**cock** *n* a small pile (e g of hay) [ME *cok*, of Scand origin]

[4]**cock** *vt* to put (e g hay) into cocks

cockade /ko'kayd/ *n* an ornament (e g a rosette or knot of ribbon) worn on the hat as a badge [modif of F *cocarde*, fr fem of *cocard* vain, fr *coq* cock, fr OF *coc*, of imit origin] – **cockaded** *adj*

cock-a-hoop /,kok ə 'hoohp/ *adj* triumphantly boastful; exulting – infml [fr the phrase *to set cock a hoop* to be festive]

,cock-a-'leekie /ə 'leeki/ *n* a chicken and leek soup [alter. of *cockie* (dim. of [1]*cock*) + *leekie*, dim. of *leek*]

,cock-and-'bull *adj* of or being an incredible and apparently concocted story – infml

cockatiel /,kokə'teel/ *n* a small grey Australian parrot with a crested yellow head [D *kaketielje*, deriv of Malay *kakatua*]

cockatoo /,kokə'tooh/ *n, pl* **cockatoos** any of numerous large noisy usu showy and crested chiefly Australasian parrots [D *kaketoe*, fr Malay *kakatua*, fr *kakak* elder sibling + *tua* old]

cockatrice /'kokətris, -tries/ *n* a mythical serpent that was hatched from a cock's egg and had a deadly glance [ME *cocatrice*, fr MF *cocatris* mongoose, cockatrice, fr ML *cocatric-*, *cocatrix* mongoose]

cockchafer /'kok,chayfə/ *n* a large European beetle destructive to vegetation [[1]*cock* + *chafer*]

'cock,crow /-,kroh/ *n* dawn

,cocked 'hat *n* a hat with brim turned up at 3 places to give a 3-cornered shape ☞ GARMENT

cockerel /'kok(ə)rəl/ *n* a young male domestic fowl [ME *cokerelle*, fr OF dial. *kokerel*, dim. of OF *coc*]

,cocker 'spaniel /'kokə/ *n* a small spaniel with long ears and silky coat [*cocking* (woodcock hunting)]

,cock'eyed /-'ied/ *adj* **1** having a squint **2a** askew, awry **b** somewhat foolish or mad ⟨*a ~ scheme*⟩ *USE* infml – **cockeyedly** /-'ie(i)dli/ *adv*, **cockeyedness** /-'ie(i)dnis/ *n*

'cock,fighting /-,fieting/ *n* the setting of specially bred cocks, usu fitted with metal spurs, to fight each other for public entertainment – **cockfight** *n*

[1]**cockle** /'kokl/ *n* CORN COCKLE [ME, fr OE *coccel*]

[2]**cockle** *n* (the ribbed shell of) a (common edible) bivalve mollusc [ME *cokille*, fr MF *coquille* shell, modif of L *conchylia*, pl of *conchylium*, fr Gk *konchylion*, fr *konchē* conch]

[3]**cockle** *n* a pucker or wrinkle [MF *coquille*] – **cockle** *vb*

'cockle,shell /-,shel/ *n* **1** the shell of a cockle, scallop, or similar mollusc **2** a light flimsy boat

cockney /'kokni/ *n* **1** a native of London and now esp of the E End of London **2** the dialect of (the E End of) London [ME *cokeney* pampered child, (effeminate) townsman, lit., cocks' egg, fr *coken* (gen pl of *cok* cock) + *ey* egg, fr OE *ǣg*] – **cockney** *adj*, **cockneyfy** /-ni,fie/ *vt*, **cockneyish** *adj*, **cockneyism** /-ni,iz(ə)m/ *n*

,cock of the 'walk *n* one who dominates or is self-assertive, esp overbearingly

'cock,pit /-,pit/ *n* **1a** a pit or enclosure for cockfights **b** a place noted for bloody, violent, or prolonged conflict **2a** the rear part of the lowest deck of a sailing warship used as officers' quarters and for treating the wounded **b** a recess below deck level from which a small vessel (e g a yacht) is steered **c** a space in the fuselage of an aeroplane for the pilot (and crew) ☞ FLIGHT **d** the driver's compartment in a racing or sports car

'cock,roach /-,rohch/ *n* any of numerous omnivorous usu dark brown chiefly nocturnal insects that include some that are domestic pests [by folk etymology fr Sp *cucaracha*, irreg fr *cuca* caterpillar]

,cock'sure /-'shooə, -'shaw/ *adj* cocky – infml [prob fr [1]*cock* + *sure*] – **cocksurely** *adv*, **cocksureness** *n*

[1]**cocktail** /'kok,tayl/ *n* **1a** a drink of mixed spirits or of spirits mixed with flavourings **b** sthg resembling or suggesting such a drink; *esp* a mixture of diverse elements **2a** an appetizer of tomato juice, shellfish, etc **b** a dish of finely chopped mixed fruits [prob fr [1]*cock* + *tail*]

[2]**cocktail** *adj* of, appropriate to accompany, or set aside for cocktails or a cocktail party ⟨*the ~ hour*⟩ ⟨*a ~ dress*⟩

cock up *vt, chiefly Br* to spoil or render a failure by bungling or incompetence – slang – **cock-up** /'-,-/ *n*

[1]**cocky** /'koki/ *adj* marked by overconfidence or presumptuousness – infml [[1]*cock* + *-y*] – **cockily** *adv*, **cockiness** *n*

[2]**cocky** *n, Austr & NZ* one who owns a small farm [by shortening & alter. fr *cockatoo*; fr orig contemptuous comparison of such farmers to voracious transient birds]

coco /'koh,koh/ *n, pl* **cocos** COCONUT PALM [Sp & Pg; Sp, fr Pg *côco*, lit., bogeyman]

cocoa /'koh,koh/ *n* **1** the cacao tree **2a** powdered ground roasted cacao seeds from which some fat has been removed – compare CHOCOLATE 1 **b** a beverage made by mixing cocoa with usu hot milk [modif of Sp *cacao*]

,cocoa 'butter *n* a pale vegetable fat with a low melting point obtained from cacao seeds

coconut *also* **cocoanut** /'kohkə,nut/ *n* the large oval fruit of the coconut palm whose outer fibrous husk yields coir and whose nut contains thick edible meat and a thick sweet milk; *also* COCONUT PALM

'coconut ,palm *n* a tall (American) tropical palm

'coconut ,shy *n* a stall at a funfair where one throws balls at coconuts on stands

[1]**cocoon** /kə'koohn/ *n* **1** (an animal's protective covering similar to) a (silk) envelope which an insect larva forms about itself and in which it passes the pupa stage **2** a (protective) covering like a cocoon (e g for an aeroplane in storage) **3** a sheltered or insulated state of existence [F *cocon*, fr Prov *coucoun*, fr *coco* shell, fr L *coccum* outgrowth on a tree, fr Gk *kokkos* grain, seed, kermes berry]

[2]**cocoon** *vt* to wrap or envelop, esp tightly, (as if) in a cocoon

cocotte /ko'kot, kə-/ *n* a courtesan [F]

[1]**cod** /kod/, **'cod,fish** *n, pl* **cod** (the flesh of) a soft-finned N Atlantic food fish or related Pacific fish [ME]

[2]**cod** *n, Br* nonsense – slang [short for *codswallop*]

coda /'kohdə/ *n* **1** a concluding musical section that is formally distinct from the main structure ☞ MUSIC **2** sthg that serves to round out or conclude sthg, esp a literary or dramatic work, and that has an interest of its own [It, lit., tail, fr L *cauda*]

coddle /'kodl/ *vt* **coddling** /'kodling, 'kodl·ing/ **1** to cook (esp eggs) slowly in a liquid just below the boiling point **2** to treat with extreme care; pamper [perh fr *caudle*] – **coddler** /'kodlə, 'kodl·ə/ *n*

[1]**code** /kohd/ *n* **1** a systematic body of laws, esp with statutory force **2** a system of principles or maxims

⟨*moral* ~⟩ **3a** a system of signals for communication **b** a system of symbols used to represent assigned and often secret meanings – compare CIPHER 2a **4** GENETIC CODE [ME, fr MF, fr L *caudex, codex* trunk of a tree, tablet of wood covered with wax for writing on, book; akin to L *cudere* to beat – more at HEW] – **codeless** *adj*

[2]**code** *vt* **1** to put into the form or symbols of a code **2** to specify (an amino acid, protein, etc) in terms of the genetic code ~ *vi* to be or contain the genetic code *for* an amino acid, protein, etc – **codable** /'kohdəbl/ *adj*, **coder** /'kohdə/ *n*

codeine /'koh,deen/ *n* a derivative of morphine that is weaker in action than morphine and is given orally to relieve pain and coughing [F *codéine*, fr Gk *kōdeia* poppyhead, fr *kōos* cavity; akin to Gk *koilos* hollow]

'code ,name *n* a name that for secrecy or convenience is used in place of an ordinary name

codex /'koh,deks/ *n, pl* **codices** /-di,seez/ a manuscript book, esp of biblical or classical texts [L]

'cod,fish /-,fish/ *n* a cod

codger /'kojə/ *n* an old and mildly eccentric man – esp in *old codger*; infml [prob alter. of *cadger*]

codicil /'kohdisil/ *n* **1** a modifying clause added to a will **2** an appendix, supplement [MF *codicille*, fr L *codicillus*, dim. of *codic-, codex* book] – **codicillary** /,kohdi'siləri/ *adj*

codify /'kohdi,fie/ *vt* **1** to reduce to a code **2** to express in a systematic form – **codifiable** /-,fie·əbl/ *adj*, **codifiability** /-,fie·ə'biləti/ *n*, **codification** /-fi'kaysh(ə)n/ *n*

codlin /'kodlin/ *n* [2]CODLING

[1]**codling** /'kodling/ *n* a young cod [ME, fr [1]*cod* + *-ling*]

[2]**codling** *n* any of several elongated greenish cooking apples [alter. of ME *querdlyng*]

'codling ,moth *n* a small moth whose larva lives in apples, pears, etc

'codlin ,moth *n* CODLING MOTH

,cod-liver 'oil *n* an oil obtained from the liver of the cod and closely related fishes and used as a source of vitamins A and D

codon /'kohdon/ *n* a group of 3 adjacent nucleotides in RNA or DNA that codes for a particular amino acid or starts or stops protein synthesis [[1]*code* + [2]*-on*]

'cod,piece /-,pees/ *n* a flap or bag concealing an opening in the front of men's breeches, esp in the 15th and 16th c ☞ GARMENT [ME *codpese*, fr *cod* bag, scrotum (fr OE *codd*) + *pese* piece]

cods /kodz/ *n, Br* nonsense – slang [short for *codswallop*]

codswallop /'kodz,woləp/ *n, chiefly Br* nonsense – slang [origin unknown]

coed /,koh'ed/ **1** a coeducational school **2** *NAm* a female student in a coeducational institution *USE* infml [short for *coeducational*] – **coed** *adj*

coeducation /,koh·edyoo'kaysh(ə)n, -ejoo-/ *n* the education of students of both sexes at the same institution – **coeducational** *adj*, **coeducationally** *adv*

coefficient /,koh·i'fish(ə)nt/ *n* **1** any of the factors, esp variable quantities, that are multiplied together in a mathematical product considered in relation to a usu specified factor ⟨*in the expression* 5xy *the* ~ *of* xy *is* 5⟩ **2** a number that serves as a measure of some property or characteristic (e g of a device or process) ⟨~ *of expansion of a metal*⟩ [NL *coefficient-, coefficiens*, fr L *co-* + *efficient-, efficiens* efficient]

coelacanth /'seelə,kanth/ *n* any of a family of mostly extinct fishes [deriv of Gk *koilos* hollow + *akantha* thorn, spine – more at [1]CAVE] – **coelacanthine** /-'kanthien/, **coelacanthous** /-'kanthəs/ *adj*

-coele, -coel /-,seel/ *comb form* (→ *n*) cavity; chamber ⟨*blas* ocoele⟩ ⟨*entero*coele⟩ [prob fr NL *-coela*, fr neut pl of *-coelus* hollow, concave, fr Gk *-koilos*, fr *koilos*]

coelenterate /see'lentərayt, -rət/ *n* any of a phylum of invertebrate animals including the corals, sea anemones, and jellyfishes [deriv of Gk *koilos* + *enteron* intestine – more at INTER-] – **coelenterate** *adj*

coeliac, *NAm chiefly* **celiac** /'seeli,ak/ *adj* of the abdominal cavity [L *coeliacus*, fr Gk *koiliakos*, fr *koilia* cavity, fr *koilos*]

'coeliac di,sease *n* defective digestion of fats in the intestines, esp in young children

coelom /'seeləm/ *n, pl* **coeloms, coelomata** /,see'lohmətə/ the usu epithelium-lined space between the body wall and the digestive tract in animals more advanced than the lower worms [G, fr Gk *koilōma* cavity, fr *koilos*] – **coelomic** /see'lohmik/ *adj*

'coelo,mate /-,mayt/ *n or adj* (an animal) having a coelom

coen- /seen-/, **coeno-** *comb form* common; general ⟨*coe* nocyte⟩ ⟨*coeno*bite⟩ [NL, fr Gk *koin-, koino-*, fr *koinos* – more at CO-]

coenobite, *NAm chiefly* **cenobite** /'seenə,biet/ *n* a member of a monastic community [LL *coenobita*, fr *coenobium* monastery, fr LGk *koinobion*, deriv of Gk *koin-* coen- + *bios* life] – **coenobitic** /-'bitik/ *adj*

coenocyte /'seenə,siet/ *n* a syncytium [ISV] – **coenocytic** /-'sitik/ *adj*

coenzyme /,koh'enziem/ *n* a nonprotein compound that combines with a protein to form an active enzyme and whose activity cannot be destroyed by heat – **coenzymatic** /koh,enzie'matik, -zi-/ *adj*, **coenzymatically** *adv*

,co,enzyme 'A *n* a coenzyme that occurs in all living cells and is essential to the metabolism of carbohydrates, fats, and some amino acids

coerce /koh'uhs/ *vt* **1** to restrain or dominate by authority or force **2** to compel to an act or choice – often + *into* **3** to enforce or bring about by force or threat [L *coercēre*, fr *co-* + *arcēre* to shut up, hold off – more at ARK] – **coercible** *adj*, **coercive** /-siv/ *adj*, **coercion** /koh'uhsh(ə)n/ *n*

coeval /koh'eevl/ *adj* of the same or equal age, antiquity, or duration [L *coaevus*, fr *co-* + *aevum* age, lifetime – more at AGE] – **coeval** *n*, **coevality** /,koh·i'valəti/ *n*

coexist /,koh·ig'zist/ *vi* **1** to exist together or at the same time **2** to live in peace with each other – **coexistence** *n*, **coexistent** *adj*

coextensive /,koh·ik'stensiv/ *adj* having the same scope or boundaries in space or time – **coextensively** *adv*

cofactor /,koh'faktə, '-,--/ *n* a substance that acts with another substance to bring about certain effects; *esp* a coenzyme

coffee /'kofi/ *n* **1a** a beverage made by percolation, infusion, or decoction from the roasted seeds of a coffee tree; *also* these seeds either green or roasted **b** COFFEE TREE **2** a cup of coffee **3** a time when coffee is drunk [It & Turk; It *caffè*, fr Turk *kahve*, fr Ar *qaḥwa*]

'coffee,house /-,hows/ *n* an establishment that sells refreshments and commonly serves as an informal club

'coffee-,table *adj, of a publication* being outsize and lavishly produced (e g with extensive use of full-colour illustrations) as if for display on a coffee table ⟨*a pompous ~ tome – TLS*⟩

coffee table *n* a low table usu placed in a living room

'coffee ,tree *n* a large African evergreen shrub or small tree of the madder family, widely cultivated in warm regions for its seeds

coffer /'kofə/ *n* **1** a chest, box; *esp* a strongbox **2** a treasury, exchequer; *broadly* a store of wealth – usu pl with sing. meaning **3a** a caisson **b** a cofferdam **4** a recessed decorative panel in a vault, ceiling, etc [ME *coffre*, fr OF, fr L *cophinus* basket, fr Gk *kophinos*]

cofferdam /'kofə,dam/ *n* a watertight enclosure from which water is pumped to allow construction or repair (e g of a pier or ship's hull)

coffin /'kofin/ *n* **1** a box or chest for the burial of a corpse **2** the horny body forming the hoof of a horse's foot [ME, basket, receptacle, fr MF *cofin*, fr L *cophinus*] – **coffin** *vt*

'coffin ,bone *n* the bone enclosed within the hoof of the horse

¹cog /kog/ *n* **1** a tooth on the rim of a wheel or gear **2** a subordinate person or part [ME *cogge*, of Scand origin; akin to Norw *kug* cog; akin to OE *cycgel* cudgel] – **cogged** *adj*

²cog *vt* **-gg-** to direct the fall of (dice) fraudulently [*cog* (a trick)]

cogent /'kohj(ə)nt/ *adj* appealing forcibly to the mind or reason; convincing ⟨*~ evidence*⟩ [L *cogent-, cogens*, prp of *cogere* to drive together, collect, fr *co-* + *agere* to drive – more at AGENT] – **cogency** /-j(ə)nsi/ *n*, **cogently** *adv*

cogitate /'kojitayt/ *vi* to ponder, usu intently and objectively; meditate ~ *vt* to cogitate on ***USE*** fml [L *cogitatus*, pp of *cogitare* to think, think about, fr *co-* + *agitare* to drive, agitate – more at AGITATE] – **cogitation** /-'taysh(ə)n/ *n*, **cogitative** /-tətiv/ *adj*

cogito /'kojitoh/ *n* the principle that one's existence can be conclusively established by the fact that one thinks [NL *cogito, ergo sum* I think, therefore I am (theorem stated by René Descartes †1650 F philosopher)]

cognac /'konyak/ *n* a French brandy, specif one from the departments of Charente and Charente-Maritime distilled from white wine [F, fr *Cognac*, town in France]

¹cognate /'kog,nayt/ *adj* **1** related by blood, esp on the mother's side **2a** related by derivation or borrowing or by descent from the same ancestral language ⟨*German* vater *is ~ with* father⟩ **b** *of a noun* related in form and meaning to the verb of which it is the object **3** of the same or similar nature [L *cognatus*, fr *co-* + *gnatus, natus*, pp of *nasci* to be born; akin to L *gignere* to beget – more at KIN] – **cognately** *adv*, **cognateness, cognation** /kog'naysh(ə)n/ *n*

²cognate *n* sthg (e g a word) cognate with another

cognition /kog'nish(ə)n/ *n* (a product of) the act or process of knowing that involves the processing of sensory information and includes perception, awareness, and judgment [ME *cognicioun*, fr L *cognition-, cognitio*, fr *cognitus*, pp of *cognoscere* to become acquainted with, know, fr *co-* + *gnoscere* to come to know – more at KNOW] – **cognitional** /-'nish(ə)nl/ *adj*, **cognitive** /'kognətiv/ *adj*

cogn·izable, -isable /'kognizəbl, kog'niezəbl/ *adj* capable of being judicially heard and determined – fml or technical – **cognizably** *adv*

cogn·izance, -isance /'kogniz(ə)ns/ *n* **1** jurisdiction, control **2** the ability to perceive or understand **3** notice, heed ⟨*take ~ of a fault*⟩ ***USE*** fml or technical [ME *conisaunce*, fr OF *conoissance*, fr *conoistre* to know, fr L *cognoscere*]

cogn·izant, -isant /'kogniz(ə)nt/ *adj* having special or certain knowledge, often from firsthand sources – fml or technical [back-formation fr *cognizance*]

cognomen /kog'nohmin/ *n, pl* **cognomens, cognomina** /-'nominə, -'noh-/ **1** a surname; *esp* the family (and usu 3rd) name of sby named in the ancient Roman fashion **2** a name; *esp* a descriptive nickname – fml or humor [L, irreg fr *co-* + *nomen* name – more at NAME] – **cognominal** /-'nominl/ *adj*

cognoscente /,konyoh'shenti, ,kognə-/ *n, pl* **cognoscenti** /~/ a person having or claiming expert knowledge; a connoisseur [obs It (now *conoscente*), fr *cognoscente*, adj, wise, fr L *cognoscent-, cognoscens*, prp of *cognoscere*]

'cog,wheel /-,weel/ *n* a wheel with cogs or teeth

cohabit /koh'habit/ *vi* to live or exist together, specif as husband and wife [LL *cohabitare*, fr L *co-* + *habitare* to inhabit, fr *habitus*, pp of *habēre* to have] – **cohabitant** *n*, **cohabitation** *n*

cohere /koh'hiə/ *vi* **1** to hold together firmly as parts of the same mass; *broadly* to stick, adhere **2a** to become united in ideas or interests **b** to be logically or aesthetically consistent [L *cohaerēre*, fr *co-* + *haerēre* to stick – more at HESITATE]

coherent /koh'hiərənt/ *adj* **1** having the quality of cohering **2a** logically consistent ⟨*a ~ argument*⟩ **b** showing a unity of thought or purpose **3** relating to, composed of, or producing (electromagnetic) waves in phase with each other ⟨*~ light*⟩ [MF or L; MF *cohérent*, fr L *cohaerent-, cohaerens*, prp of *cohaerēre*] – **coherence** /-rəns/, **coherency** *n*, **coherently** *adv*

cohesion /koh'heezh(ə)n/ *n* the act or process of cohering [L *cohaesus*, pp of *cohaerēre*] – **cohesionless** *adj*, **cohesive** /-'heesiv, -ziv/ *adj*, **cohesively** *adv*, **cohesiveness** *n*

cohort /'koh,hawt/ *n* **1a** a group of soldiers; *esp, sing or pl in constr* a division of a Roman legion **b** a band, group **c** a group of individuals having age, class membership, or other statistical factors in common in a study of the population **2** *chiefly NAm* a companion, accomplice [MF & L; MF *cohorte*, fr L *cohort-, cohors* – more at COURT]

¹coif /koyf/ *n* a close-fitting cap: e g **a** a hoodlike bonnet worn by nuns under a veil **b** a protective usu metal skullcap formerly worn under a hood of mail [ME *coife*, fr MF, fr LL *cofea*]

²coif *vt* **-ff-** **1** to cover or dress (as if) with a coif **2** to arrange (hair) by brushing, combing, or curling

coiffe /kwahf/ *n* a hairstyle [ME *coife, coyffe* coif]

coiffeur /kwah'fuh (*Fr* kwafœːr)/ *n* a hairdresser [F, fr *coiffer*]

coiffeuse /kwah'fuhz (*Fr* kwaføːz)/ *n* a female hairdresser [F, fem of *coiffeur*]

coiffure /kwah'f(y)ooə (*Fr* kwafyːr)/ *n* a hairstyle [F, fr *coiffer* to cover with a coif, arrange (hair), fr *coife*] – **coiffured** *adj*

[1]**coil** /koyl/ *vt* to wind into rings or spirals ~ *vi* **1** to move in a circular, spiral, or winding course **2** to form or lie in a coil [MF *coillir, cuillir* to gather – more at CULL] – **coilability** /-lə'biləti/ *n*

[2]**coil** *n* **1a** (a length of rope, cable, etc gathered into) a series of loops; a spiral **b** a single loop of a coil **2** a number of turns of wire, esp in spiral form, usu for electromagnetic effect or for providing electrical resistance **3** a series of connected pipes in rows, layers, or windings **4** (a stamp from) a roll of postage stamps

[1]**coin** /koyn/ *n* **1** a usu thin round piece of metal issued as money **2** metal money [ME, fr MF, wedge, corner, fr L *cuneus* wedge]

[2]**coin** *vt* **1a** to make (a coin), esp by stamping; mint **b** to convert (metal) into coins **2** to create, invent ⟨~ *a phrase*⟩ **3** to make or earn (money) rapidly and in large quantity – often in *coin it*

coinage /'koynij/ *n* **1** coining or (a large number of) coins **2** sthg (e g a word) made up or invented

'coin-,box *n* a telephone whose operation is paid for by the insertion of coins; *also* the box attached to such a telephone that receives the coins

coincide /,koh·in'sied/ *vi* **1** to occupy the same place in space or time **2** to correspond in nature, character, function, or position **3** to be in accord or agreement; concur [ML *coincidere*, fr L *co-* + *incidere* to fall on, fr *in-* + *cadere* to fall – more at CHANCE]

coincidence /koh'insid(ə)ns; *sense* also ,koh·in'sied(ə)ns/ *n* **1** the act or condition of coinciding; a correspondence **2** (an example of) the chance occurrence at the same time or place of 2 or more events that appear to be related or similar – **coincidental** /,koh·insi'dentl/ *adj*, **coincidentally** *adv*

coincident /koh'insid(ə)nt/ *adj* **1** occupying the same space or time ⟨~ *points*⟩ **2** of similar nature; harmonious [F, fr ML *coincident-, coincidens*, prp of *coincidere*] – **coincidently** *adv*

coiner /'koynə/ *n, chiefly Br* sby who makes counterfeit coins [[2]COIN + [2]-ER]

'coin-,op /op/ *n* a self-service laundry where the machines are operated by coins

coir /'koyə/ *n* a stiff coarse fibre from the husk of a coconut [Tamil *kayiṛu* rope]

coition /koh'ish(ə)n/ *n* coitus [LL, fr L *coition-, coitio* a coming together, fr *coitus*, pp of *coire* to come together, fr *co-* + *ire* to go – more at ISSUE] – **coitional** *adj*

coitus /'koytəs, 'koh·itəs/ *n* the natural conveying of semen to the female reproductive tract; *broadly* SEXUAL INTERCOURSE [L, fr *coitus*, pp] – **coital** *adj*, **coitally** *adv*

,coitus inter'ruptus /intə'ruptəs/ *n* coitus which is purposely interrupted in order to prevent ejaculation of sperm into the vagina [NL, interrupted coitus]

,coitus reser'vatus /rezuh'vahtəs/ *n* COITUS INTERRUPTUS [NL, coitus held back]

[1]**coke** /kohk/ *n* a solid porous fuel that remains after gases have been driven from coal by heating [ME; akin to Sw *kälk* pith, Gk *gelgis* bulb of garlic]

[2]**coke** *vt* to convert (coal) into coke

[3]**coke** *n* cocaine – slang [by shortening & alter.]

col /kol/ *n* a depression or pass in a mountain ridge or range [F, fr MF, neck, fr L *collum*]

[1]**col-** – see COM-

[2]**col-, coli-, colo-** *comb form* **1** colon ⟨co*litis*⟩ ⟨colo*stomy*⟩ **2** colon bacillus ⟨coli*form*⟩ ⟨coli*phage*⟩ [NL, fr L *colon*]

[1]**cola** /'kohlə/ *pl of* [1] [2]COLON

[2]**cola** *also* **kola** /'kohlə/ *n* a carbonated soft drink flavoured with extract from coca leaves, kola nut, sugar, caramel, and acid and aromatic substances [fr *Coca-Cola*, a trademark]

colander /'koləndə; *also* 'ku-/, **cullender** /'kuləndə/ *n* a perforated bowl-shaped utensil for washing or draining food [ME *colyndore*, prob modif of OProv *colador*, fr ML *colatorium*, fr L *colatus*, pp of *colare* to sieve, fr *colum* sieve]

cola nut *n* KOLA NUT

col arco /kol 'ahkoh/ *adv* with the bow – used in music; compare PIZZICATO [It]

colatitude /,koh'latityoohd/ *n* the difference between a degree of latitude and 90°

colchicine /'kolchiseen, 'kolki-/ *n* an alkaloid extracted from the corms or seeds of the meadow saffron and used esp to inhibit division of the cell nucleus in mitosis and in the treatment of gout

colchicum /'kolchikəm, 'kolki-/ *n* (the colchicine-containing dried corm or seed of) the meadow saffron or a related plant [NL, genus name, fr L, a kind of plant with a poisonous root, fr Gk *kolchikon*, lit., product of Colchis, fr *Colchis*, ancient country in Asia]

[1]**cold** /kohld/ *adj* **1** having a low temperature, often below some normal temperature or below that compatible with human comfort **2a** marked by lack of warm feeling; unemotional; *also* unfriendly ⟨*a ~ stare*⟩ **b** marked by deliberation or calculation ⟨*a ~ act of aggression*⟩ **3a** previously cooked but served cold ⟨~ *meats*⟩ **b** not (sufficiently) hot or heated **c** made cold ⟨~ *drinks*⟩ **d** *of a process* performed on an unheated material ⟨~ *conditioning of steel prior to rolling*⟩ **4a** depressing, cheerless **b** producing a sensation of cold; chilling ⟨~ *blank walls*⟩ **c** COOL 5 **5a** dead **b** unconscious ⟨*knocked out* ~⟩ **6a** retaining only faint scents, traces, or clues ⟨*a ~ trail*⟩ **b** far from a goal, object, or solution sought **c** stale, uninteresting ⟨~ *news*⟩ **7** presented or regarded in a straightforward way; impersonal ⟨*the ~ facts*⟩ **8** unprepared **9** intense yet without the usual outward effects ⟨*a ~ fury*⟩ [ME, fr OE *ceald, cald*; akin to OHG *kalt* cold, L *gelu* frost, *gelare* to freeze] – **coldish** *adj*, **coldly** *adv*, **coldness** *n* – **in cold blood** with premeditation; deliberately

[2]**cold** *n* **1a** a condition of low temperature **b** cold weather **2** bodily sensation produced by relative lack of heat; chill **3** a bodily disorder popularly associated with chilling; *specif* COMMON COLD **4** a state of neglect or deprivation – esp in *come/bring in out of the cold*

[3]**cold** *adv* with utter finality; absolutely ⟨*was turned down* ~⟩

,cold-'blooded *adj* **1a** done or acting without consideration or compunction; ruthless ⟨~ *murder*⟩ **b** concerned only with the facts; emotionless **2** having a body temperature not internally regulated but approximating to that of the environment – compare WARM-BLOODED – **cold-bloodedly** *adv*, **cold-bloodedness** *n*

cold chisel *n* a chisel made of steel of a strength and temper suitable for chipping or cutting cold metal

,cold 'comfort *n* scant consolation

,cold 'cream *n* a thick oily often perfumed cream for cleansing and soothing the skin of the neck, face, etc

,cold 'feet *n pl* apprehension or doubt strong enough to prevent a planned course of action

'cold ,frame *n* a usu glass-covered frame without artificial heat used to protect plants and seedlings

,cold 'front *n* an advancing edge of a cold air mass

,cold 'shoulder *n* intentionally cold or unsympathetic treatment – usu + *the* – **cold-shoulder** *vt*

'cold ,sore *n* (herpes simplex when occurring as) 1 or more blisters appearing round or inside the mouth

,cold 'storage *n* a condition of being held or continued without being acted on; abeyance

,cold 'sweat *n* concurrent perspiration and chill, usu associated with fear, pain, or shock

,cold 'turkey *n* **1** *NAm* blunt language or procedure **2** (the shivering, nausea, feelings of fear, etc resulting from) the abrupt complete cessation of the use of an addictive narcotic drug by an addict – infml

'cold ,type *n* composition or typesetting done without the casting of metal, esp produced directly by a typewriter mechanism

'cold ,war *n* **1** a conflict carried on by methods short of military action **2** a hostile but nonviolent relationship – **cold warrior** *n*

'cold ,wave *n* a period of unusually cold weather

cole /kohl/ *n* cabbage, broccoli, kohlrabi, or a related (edible) plant of the cabbage family [ME, fr OE *cāl*, fr L *caulis* stem, cabbage – more at HOLE]

coleoptera /,koli'optərə/ *n pl* the insects that are beetles [NL, deriv of Gk *koleon* sheath + *pteron* wing – more at FEATHER] – **coleopterist** *n*, **coleopterous** *adj*

coleopteran /,koli'optərən/ *n* [1]BEETLE 1 – **coleopteran** *adj*

coleoptile /,koli'optiel/ *n* the first leaf produced by a germinating seed of grasses and some related plants, that forms a protective sheath round the bud that develops into the shoot [NL *coleoptilum*, fr Gk *koleon* + *ptilon* down; akin to Gk *pteron*]

coleslaw /'kohl,slaw/ *n* a salad of raw sliced or chopped white cabbage – compare SAUERKRAUT [D *koolsla*, fr *kool* cabbage + *sla* salad]

coleus /'kohli·əs/ *n, pl* **coleuses** any of a large genus of plants of the mint family including many grown for their showy foliage [NL, genus name, fr Gk *koleos, koleon* sheath]

coley /'kohli/ *n, pl* **coley,** *esp for different types* **coleys** *Br* an important N Atlantic food fish closely related to the cod [prob by shortening & alter. fr *coalfish*]

coli- – see [2]COL-

colic /'kolik/ *n* a paroxysm of abdominal pain localized in the intestines or other hollow organ and caused by spasm, obstruction, or twisting [ME, fr MF *colique*, fr L *colicus* colicky, fr Gk *kōlikos*, fr *kōlon*, alter. of *kolon* colon] – **colicky** *adj*

coliseum /,kolə'see·əm/ *n* **1** *cap* COLOSSEUM 1 **2** **coliseum, colosseum** a large building (e g a stadium or theatre) used for public entertainments [ML *Colisseum, Colosseum*]

colitis /kə'lietəs, koh-/ *n* inflammation of the colon [NL]

coll-, collo- *comb form* **1** glue ⟨coll*agen*⟩ ⟨coll*odion*⟩ **2** colloid ⟨collo*type*⟩ [NL, fr Gk *koll-, kollo-*, fr *kolla* – more at PROTOCOL]

collaborate /kə'labərayt/ *vi* **1** to work together or with another (e g in an intellectual endeavour) **2** to cooperate with an enemy of one's country [LL *collaboratus*, pp of *collaborare* to labour together, fr L *com-* + *laborare* to labour] – **collaborator** *n*, **collaborative** /-rətiv/ *adj*, **collaboration** /-'raysh(ə)n/ *n*

collaborationism /kə,labə'rayshəniz(ə)m/ *n* collaboration with an enemy – **collaborationist** *adj or n*

collage /'kolahzh/ *n* **1** an (abstract) composition made of pieces of paper, wood, cloth, etc fixed to a surface **2** an assembly of diverse fragments ⟨*a* ~ *of ideas*⟩ [F, gluing, fr *coller* to glue, fr *colle* glue, fr (assumed) VL *colla*, fr Gk *kolla*] – **collagist** *n*

collagen /'koləjən/ *n* an insoluble protein that occurs as fibres in connective tissue (e g tendons) and in bones and yields gelatin and glue on prolonged heating with water [Gk *kolla* + ISV *-gen*] – **collagenic** /,kolə'jenik/ *adj*, **collagenous** /kə'lajinəs/ *adj*

[1]**collapse** /kə'laps/ *vi* **1** to break down completely; disintegrate **2** to fall in or give way abruptly and completely (e g through compression) **3** to lose force, value, or effect suddenly **4** to break down in energy, stamina, or self-control through exhaustion or disease; *esp* to fall helpless or unconscious **5** to fold down into a more compact shape ⟨*a telescope that* ~s⟩ ~ *vt* to cause to collapse [L *collapsus*, pp of *collabi*, fr *com-* + *labi* to fall, slide – more at SLEEP] – **collapsible** *adj*, **collapsibility** /-sə'biləti/ *n*

[2]**collapse** *n* **1a** an (extreme) breakdown in energy, strength, or self-control **b** an airless state of (part of) a lung **2** the act or an instance of collapsing

[1]**collar** /'kolə/ *n* **1** a band, strip, or chain worn round the neck: e g **a** a band that serves to finish or decorate the neckline of a garment; *esp* one that is turned over **b** a band fitted about the neck of an animal **c** a part of the harness of draught animals that fits over the shoulders and takes the strain when a load is drawn **d** a protective or supportive device worn round the neck **2** sthg resembling a collar (e g a ring or round flange to restrain motion or hold sthg in place) **3** any of various animal structures or markings similar to a collar in appearance or form **4** a cut of bacon from the neck of a pig ☞ MEAT [ME *coler*, fr OF, fr L *collare*, fr *collum* neck; akin to ON & OHG *hals* neck, OE *hwēol* wheel – more at WHEEL] – **collared** *adj*, **collarless** *adj*

[2]**collar** *vt* **1a** to seize by the collar or neck; *broadly* to apprehend **b** to get control of **2** to buttonhole *USE* infml

'collar ,beam *n* a horizontal beam in a roof, that connects 2 opposite rafters at a place higher than their base – compare TIE-BEAM ☞ ARCHITECTURE

'collar,bone /-,bohn/ *n* the clavicle ☞ ANATOMY

collate /kə'layt/ *vt* **1** to collect and compare carefully in order to verify and often to integrate or arrange in order **2** to appoint (a priest) to a Church of England benefice of which the bishop is the patron **3** to assemble in proper order ⟨~ *printed sheets*⟩ [back-formation fr *collation*] – **collator** *n*

[1]**collateral** /kə'lat(ə)rəl/ *adj* **1** accompanying as secondary or subordinate **2** belonging to the same ancestral stock but not in a direct line of descent –

usu contrasted with *lineal* **3** parallel or corresponding in position, time, or significance **4** of or being collateral [ME, prob fr MF, fr ML *collateralis*, fr L *com-* + *lateralis* lateral] – **collaterally** *adv*, **collaterality** /-'raləti/ *n*

[2]**collateral** *n* **1** a collateral relative **2** property pledged by a borrower to protect the interests of the lender

collation /kə'laysh(ə)n/ *n* **1** a light meal; *esp* one allowed on fast days in place of lunch or supper **2** the act, process, or result of collating [(1) ME, fr ML *collation-*, *collatio*, fr LL, conference, fr L, bringing together, comparison, fr *collatus* (pp of *conferre* to bring together, bestow upon), fr *com-* + *latus*, pp of *ferre* to carry; (2) ME, fr L *collation-*, *collatio*]

colleague /'koleeg/ *n* a fellow worker, esp in a profession [MF *collegue*, fr L *collega*, fr *com-* + *legare* to appoint, depute – more at LEGATE]

[1]**collect** /'kolikt/ *n* a short prayer comprising an invocation, petition, and conclusion; *specif, often cap* one preceding the Epistle read at Communion [ME *collecte*, fr OF, fr ML *collecta*, short for *oratio ad collectam* prayer upon assembly]

[2]**collect** /kə'lekt/ *vt* **1a** to bring together into 1 body or place; *specif* to assemble a collection of **b** to gather or exact from a number of sources ⟨~ *taxes*⟩ **2** to accumulate, gather ⟨*books* ~ *dust*⟩ **3** to gain or regain control of ⟨~ *his thoughts*⟩ **4** to claim as due and receive possession or payment of ⟨~ *social security*⟩ **5** to provide transport or escort for ⟨~ *the children from school*⟩ **6** *chiefly Br* to gain, obtain ~ *vi* **1** to come together in a band, group, or mass; gather ⟨*the troops* ~ed⟩ **2a** to assemble a collection **b** to receive payment ⟨~ing *on his insurance*⟩ [L *collectus*, pp of *colligere* to collect, fr *com-* + *legere* to gather] – **collectible, collectable** *adj*

[3]**collect** /kə'lekt/ *adv or adj, NAm* to be paid for by the receiver ⟨*send the package* ~⟩ ⟨*a* ~ *telephone call*⟩

collected /kə'lektid/ *adj* **1** exhibiting calmness and composure **2** *of a gait or horse* (performed) in a state of collection – compare EXTENDED – **collectedly** *adv*, **collectedness** *n*

collection /kə'leksh(ə)n/ *n* **1** sthg collected; *esp* an accumulation of objects gathered for study, comparison, or exhibition **2** a standard pose of a well-schooled and responsive riding horse with its head arched and its hocks well under the body [[2]COLLECT + -ION]

[1]**collective** /kə'lektiv/ *adj* **1** denoting a number of individuals considered as 1 group ⟨flock *is a* ~ *word*⟩ **2** *of a fruit* MULTIPLE 4 **3** of, made, or held in common by a group of individuals ⟨~ *responsibility*⟩ **4** collectivized ⟨*a* ~ *farm*⟩ – **collectively** *adv*

[2]**collective** *n* **1** *sing or pl in constr* a collective body; a group **2** a cooperative organization; *specif* a collective farm

col,lective 'bargaining *n* negotiation between an employer and union representatives usu on wages, hours, and working conditions

col,lective se'curity *n* the maintenance by common action of the security of all members of an association of nations

col,lective un'conscious *n* that part of a person's unconscious which is inherited and shared with all other people

collectivism /kə'lekti,viz(ə)m/ *n* a political or economic theory advocating collective control, esp over production and distribution – **collectivist** *adj or n*, **collectivistic** /-'vistik/ *adj*, **collectivistically** *adv*

collectiv·ize, -ise /kə'lektiviez/ *vt* to organize under collective control – **collectivization** /-'zaysh(ə)n/ *n*

collector /kə'lektə/ *n* **1a** an official who collects funds, esp money **b** one who makes a collection ⟨*a stamp* ~⟩ **2** a conductor maintaining contact between moving and stationary parts of an electric circuit **3** a region in a transistor that collects charge carriers – **collectorship** *n*

colleen /ko'leen/ *n* **1** an Irish girl **2** *Irish* a girl [IrGael *cailīn*]

college /'kolij/ *n* **1** a building used for an educational or religious purpose **2a** a self-governing endowed constituent body of a university offering instruction and often living quarters but not granting degrees **b** an institution offering vocational or technical instruction ⟨*business* ~⟩ ⟨*art* ~⟩ **3** an organized body of people engaged in a common pursuit **4** *chiefly Br* a public school or private secondary school; *also* a state school for older pupils ⟨*a Sixth-form* ~⟩ *USE* (except 1) sing. or pl in constr [ME, fr MF, fr L *collegium* society, fr *collega* colleague – more at COLLEAGUE] – **college** *adj*

collegial /kə'leeji·əl/ *adj* **1** COLLEGIATE 1, 2 **2** characterized by equal sharing of authority, esp by Roman Catholic bishops – **collegially** *adv*, **collegiality** /-'aləti/ *n*

collegian /kə'leejən/ *n* a member of a college

collegiate /kə'leeji·ət/ *adj* **1** of a collegiate church **2** of or comprising a college **3** COLLEGIAL 2 [ML *collegiatus*, fr L *collegium*] – **collegiately** *adv*

col,legiate 'church *n* a church other than a cathedral that has a chapter of canons

collenchyma /kə'lengkimə/ *n* a plant tissue of growing stems, leaf midribs, etc that consists of living (elongated) cells with irregularly thickened walls – compare PARENCHYMA, SCLERENCHYMA [NL] – **collenchymatous** /,kolən'kiemətəs, -'ki-/ *adj*

collet /'kolit/ *n* a metal band, collar, ferrule, or flange; *esp* a circle or flange in which a gem is set [MF, dim. of *col* collar, fr L *collum* neck – more at COLLAR]

collide /kə'lied/ *vi* **1** to come together forcibly **2** to come into conflict [L *collidere*, fr *com-* + *laedere* to injure by striking]

collie /'koli/ *n* a large dog of any of several varieties of a breed developed in Scotland, esp for use in herding sheep and cattle [prob fr E dial. *colly* (black)]

collier /'kolyə/ *n* **1** a coal miner **2** a ship for transporting coal [ME *colier* charcoal-burner, fr *col* coal]

colliery /'kolyəri/ *n* a coal mine and its associated buildings

colligative /kə'ligətiv/ *adj* depending on the number rather than the nature of particles (e g molecules) ⟨*pressure is a* ~ *property*⟩ [L *colligatus*, pp of *colligare* to bind together, fr *com-* + *ligare* to tie]

collimate /'kolimayt/ *vt* **1** to make (e g rays of light) parallel **2** to adjust the line of sight of (a telescope, theodolite, etc) [L *collimatus*, pp of *collimare*, MS var of *collineare* to make straight, fr *com-* + *linea* line] – **collimation** /-'maysh(ə)n/ *n*

collimator /'koli,maytə/ *n* a device (e g in a telescope or spectroscope) for producing a beam of parallel rays of radiation (e g light)

collinear /ˌkoh'lini·ə/ *adj* lying on or passing through the same straight line [ISV] – **collinearity** /-ˌlini'arəti/ *n*

collision /kə'lizh(ə)n/ *n* **1** an act or instance of colliding; a clash **2** an encounter between particles (e g atoms or molecules) resulting in exchange or transformation of energy [ME, fr L *collision-, collisio*, fr *collisus*, pp of *collidere*] – **collisional** *adj*

col'lision ˌcourse *n* a course or approach that would result in collision or conflict if continued unaltered

collo- – see COLL-

collocate /'koləkayt/ *vt* to set or arrange in a place or position; *esp* to set side by side – fml ~ *vi*, *of a linguistic element* to form part of a collocation [L *collocatus*, pp of *collocare*, fr *com-* + *locare* to place, fr *locus* place – more at [1]STALL]

collocation /ˌkolə'kaysh(ə)n/ *n* the act or result of placing or arranging together; *specif* a noticeable arrangement or joining together of linguistic elements (e g words) – **collocational** *adj*

collodion /kə'lohdi·ən/ *n* a viscous solution of pyroxylin, used esp as a coating for wounds or for photographic films [modif of NL *collodium*, fr Gk *kollōdēs* glutinous, fr *kolla* glue]

colloid /'koloyd/ *n* **1a** a substance composed of particles that are too small to be seen with a light microscope but too large to form a true solution and that will typically diffract a beam of light – compare CRYSTALLOID **b** a system consisting of a colloid together with the gaseous, liquid, or solid medium in which it is dispersed **2** a gelatinous substance found in tissues, esp in disease [ISV *coll-* + *-oid*] – **colloidal** /ko'loydl/ *adj*, **colloidally** *adv*

collop /'koləp/ *n* a small (meat) slice; an escalope [ME]

colloquial /kə'lohkwi·əl/ *adj* used in, characteristic of, or using the style of familiar and informal conversation; conversational – **colloquial** *n*, **colloquially** *adv*, **colloquiality** /-'aləti/ *n*

colloquialism /kə'lohkwi·əˌliz(ə)m/ *n* **1** a colloquial expression **2** colloquial style

colloquium /kə'lohkwi·əm/ *n, pl* **colloquiums, colloquia** /-kwi·ə/ a conference, seminar – compare SYMPOSIUM 2a [L, colloquy]

colloquy /'koləkwi/ *n* a formal conversation or dialogue [L *colloquium*, fr *colloqui* to converse, fr *com-* + *loqui* to speak]

collude /kə'loohd/ *vi* to conspire, plot [L *colludere*, fr *com-* + *ludere* to play, fr *ludus* game – more at LUDICROUS]

collusion /kə'loohzh(ə)n/ *n* secret agreement or cooperation for an illegal or deceitful purpose [ME, fr MF, fr L *collusion-, collusio*, fr *collusus*, pp of *colludere*] – **collusive** /-siv, -ziv/ *adj*, **collusively** *adv*

collyrium /kə'liəri·əm/ *n, pl* **collyriums, collyria** /-ri·ə/ an eye lotion [L, fr Gk *kollyrion* pessary, eye salve, fr dim. of *kollyra* roll of bread]

collywobbles /'koliˌwoblz/ *n pl* **1** stomachache **2** qualms, butterflies *USE* + *the*; infml [prob alter. of *colic* + *wobbles*]

colo- – see [2]COL-

'colobus ˌmonkey /'koləbəs/ *n* any of various long-tailed African monkeys· [NL *colobus*, genus name, fr Gk *kolobos* docked, mutilated; fr the rudimentary thumb]

cologne /kə'lohn/ *n* TOILET WATER [*Cologne*, city in Germany] – **cologned** *adj*

[1]**colon** /'kohˌlon/ *n, pl* **colons, cola** /-lə/ the part of the large intestine that extends from the caecum to the rectum ☞ DIGESTION [L, fr Gk *kolon*] – **colonic** /kə'lonik/ *adj*

[2]**colon** *n, pl* **colons, cola** /-lə/ **1** a punctuation mark : used chiefly to direct attention to matter that follows, to introduce the words of a speaker (e g in a play), in various references (e g in John 4:10), and, esp in NAm, between the parts of an expression of time in hours and minutes **2** the sign : used in a ratio where it is usu read as 'to" (e g in 4:1), or in phonetic transcription (e g in i:) where it signals a change in length and in vowel quality [L, part of a poem, fr Gk *kōlon* limb, part of a strophe]

[3]**colon** */koh'lon/ n, pl* **colones** /-nays/ ☞ *Costa Rica, El Salvador* at NATIONALITY [Sp *colón*]

'colon baˌcillus /'kohˌlon/ *n* any of various bacilli that normally live in intestines of vertebrate animals

colonel /'kuhnl/ *n* ☞ RANK [alter. of *coronel*, fr MF, modif of OIt *colonnello* column of soldiers, colonel, dim. of *colonna* column, fr L *columna*] – **colonelcy** *n*

ˌColonel 'Blimp /blimp/ *n* a pompous person with out-of-date or ultraconservative views; *broadly* a reactionary [*Colonel Blimp*, cartoon character created by David Low †1963 Br cartoonist] – **Colonel Blimpism** *n*

[1]**colonial** /kə'lohnyəl, -ni·əl/ *adj* **1** (characteristic) of a colony **2** *often cap* made or prevailing in America before 1776 ⟨~ *architecture*⟩ **3** possessing or composed of colonies ⟨*Britain's* ~ *empire*⟩ – **colonialize** *vt*, **colonially** *adv*, **colonialness** *n*

[2]**colonial** *n* a member or inhabitant of a (British Crown) colony

colonialism /kə'lohni·əˌliz(ə)m/ *n* (a policy based on) control by a state over a dependent area or people – **colonialist** *n or adj*, **colonialistic** /-'listik/ *adj*

colonist /'kolənist/ *n* **1** a member or inhabitant of a colony **2** one who colonizes or settles in a new country

colon·ize, -ise /'koləniez/ *vt* to establish a colony in, on, or of ~ *vi* to make or establish a colony; settle – **colonizer** *n*, **colonization** /-'zaysh(ə)n/ *n*

colonnade /ˌkolə'nayd/ *n* a row of columns, usu supporting an entablature [F, fr It *colonnato*, fr *colonna* column] – **colonnaded** *adj*

colony /'koləni/ *n* **1** a body of settlers living in a new territory but subject to control by the parent state; *also* their territory **2** a distinguishable localized population within a species ⟨*a* ~ *of termites*⟩ **3a** a mass of microorganisms, usu growing in or on a solid medium **b** all the units of a compound animal (e g a coral) **4** (the area occupied by) a group of individuals with common interests living close together ⟨*an artists'* ~⟩ **5** a group of people segregated from the general public ⟨*a leper* ~⟩ ⟨*a penal* ~⟩ [ME *colonie*, fr MF & L; MF, fr L *colonia*, fr *colonus* farmer, colonist, fr *colere* to cultivate – more at WHEEL]

colophon /'kohləˌfon/ *n* **1** a statement at the end of a book or manuscript, giving facts about its production **2** an identifying device used by a printer or publisher [L, fr Gk *kolophōn* summit, finishing touch]

colophony /koˈlofəni/ *n* rosin [ME *colophonie,* deriv of Gk *Kolophōn* Colophon, an Ionian city]

color /ˈkulə/ *vb or n, chiefly NAm* (to) colour

ˌColoˌrado ˈbeetle /ˌkoləˈrahdoh/ *n* a black-and-yellow striped beetle that feeds on the leaves of the potato [*Colorado,* state of USA]

coloration, *Br also* **colouration** /ˌkuləˈraysh(ə)n/ *n* **1** COLOURING 1c(1), COMPLEXION 1 ⟨*the dark ~ of his skin*⟩ **2** use or choice of colours (e g by an artist) **3** an arrangement or range of colours ⟨*the brilliant ~ of a butterfly's wing*⟩

coloratura /ˌkolərəˈtyooərə/ *n* (a singer who uses) elaborate embellishment in vocal music [obs It, lit., colouring, fr LL, fr L *coloratus,* pp of *colorare* to colour, fr *color*]

colorimeter /ˌkuloˈrimitə/ *n* an instrument used for chemical analysis by comparison of a liquid's colour with standard colours [ISV] – **colorimetry** /-tri/ *n,* **colorimetric** /-ˈmetrik/ *adj*

colossal /kəˈlos(ə)l/ *adj* of or like a colossus; *esp* of very great size or degree ⟨*a ~ building*⟩ ⟨*a ~ blunder*⟩ – **colossally** *adv*

colosseum /ˌkoləˈsee·əm/ *n* **1 Colosseum, Coliseum** an amphitheatre built in Rome in the first c AD **2** COLISEUM 2 [ML, fr L, neut of *colosseus* colossal, fr *colossus*]

Colossians /kəˈlosh(ə)nz/ *n pl but sing in constr* a book of the New Testament attributed to St Paul and addressed to the Christians of Colossae

colossus /kəˈlosəs/ *n, pl* **colossuses, colossi** /-sie/ **1** a statue of gigantic size **2** sby or sthg remarkably preeminent [L, fr Gk *kolossos*]

colostomy /kəˈlostəmi/ *n* surgical formation of an artificial anus [ISV [2]*col-* + *-stomy*]

colostrum /kəˈlostrəm/ *n* the milk that is secreted for a few days after giving birth and is characterized by high protein and antibody content [L] – **colostral** *adj*

[1]**colour,** *NAm chiefly* **color** /ˈkulə/ *n* **1a** the visual sensation (e g red or grey) caused by the wavelength of perceived light that enables one to differentiate otherwise identical objects **b** the aspect of objects and light sources that may be described in terms of hue, lightness, and saturation for objects and hue, brightness, and saturation for light sources **c** a hue, esp as opposed to black, white, or grey **2** an outward often deceptive show; an appearance (of authenticity) ⟨*his wounds gave ~ to his story*⟩ **3** the tint characteristic of good health **4a** an identifying badge, pennant, or flag (e g of a ship or regiment) **b** coloured clothing distinguishing one as a member of a usu specified group or as a representative of a usu specified person or thing **c** any of the 5 principal heraldic tinctures azure, vert, sable, gules, and purpure **5** character, nature ⟨*showed himself in his true ~s*⟩ **6** the use or combination of colours (e g by painters) **7** vitality, interest ⟨*the play had a good deal of ~ to it*⟩ **8** a pigment **9** tonal quality in music **10** skin pigmentation other than white, characteristic of race **11** *Br* the award made to a regular member of a team ⟨*got my cricket ~s*⟩ *USE (4a, 4b, 5, & 11)* usu pl with sing. meaning [ME *colour,* fr OF, fr L *color;* akin to L *celare* to conceal – more at HELL]

[2]**colour,** *NAm chiefly* **color** *vt* **1a** to give colour to **b** to change the colour of **2** to change as if by dyeing or painting: e g **a** to misrepresent, distort **b** to influence, affect ⟨*~ his judgment*⟩ *~ vi* to take on or impart colour; *specif* to blush – **colourant** *n*

colourable /ˈkul(ə)rəbl/ *adj* seemingly valid or genuine; plausible – **colourably** *adv*

colouration /ˌkuləˈraysh(ə)n/ *n, Br* coloration

ˈcolour ˌbar *n* a social or legal barrier that prevents coloured people from participating with whites in various activities or restricts their opportunities

ˈcolour-ˌblind *adj* (partially) unable to distinguish 1 or more colours – **colour blindness** *n*

[1]**ˈcoloured** *adj* **1** having colour **2** marked by exaggeration or bias **3a** of a race other than the white; *esp* BLACK 2 **b** *often cap* of mixed race – esp of S Africans of mixed descent

[2]**coloured** *n, pl* **coloureds, coloured** *often cap* a coloured person

colourfast /ˈkuləˌfahst/ *adj* having colour that will not fade or run – **colourfastness** *n*

ˈcolour ˌfilter *n* FILTER 3b

ˈcolourful /-f(ə)l/ *adj* **1** having striking colours **2** full of variety or interest – **colourfully** *adv,* **colourfulness** *n*

colouring /ˈkuləring/ **1a** (the effect produced by combining or) applying colours **b** sthg that produces colour **c(1)** natural colour **(2)** COMPLEXION 1 ⟨*her dark ~*⟩ **2** an influence, bias **3** a timbre, quality

colourist /ˈkulərist/ *n* one, esp a painter, who colours or deals with colour

colourless /ˈkuləlis/ *adj* lacking colour: e g **a** pallid **b** dull, uninteresting – **colourlessly** *adv,* **colourlessness** *n*

ˈcolour ˌscheme *n* a systematic combination of colours ⟨*the ~ of a room*⟩

ˈcolour ˌsergeant *n* ☞ RANK

ˌcolour ˈsupplement *n, Br* an illustrated colour magazine published as a supplement to a usu Sunday newspaper

colourway /ˈkuləˌway/ *n* COLOUR SCHEME

-colous /-kələs/ *comb form* (→ *adj*) living or growing in or on ⟨*areni*colous⟩ [L *-cola* inhabitant; akin to L *colere* to inhabit – more at WHEEL]

colporteur /ˈkolˌpawtə/ *n* a seller of religious books [F, alter. of MF *comporteur,* fr *comporter* to bear, peddle]

colt /kohlt, kolt/ *n* **1** a young male horse that is either sexually immature or has not attained an arbitrarily designated age **2** a novice; *esp* a cricketer or rugby player in a junior team [ME, fr OE; akin to OE *cild* child]

coltish /ˈkohltish, ˈkol-/ *adj* **1** frisky, playful **2** of or resembling a colt – **coltishly** *adv,* **coltishness** *n*

coltsfoot /ˈkohltsˌfoot, ˈkolts-/ *n, pl* **coltsfoots** a composite plant whose yellow flower heads appear early in spring before the leaves [fr the shape of the leaves]

colubrine /ˈkoləˌbrin, -ˌbrien/ *adj* of or resembling a snake [L *colubrinus,* fr *coluber, colubra* snake]

columbarium /ˌkoləmˈbeəri·əm/ *n, pl* **columbaria** /-ri·ə/ a structure (e g in a crematorium) lined with recesses for urns containing ashes of those who have been cremated [L, lit., dovecote, fr *columba* dove]

columbine /ˈkoləmbien/ *n* any of a genus of plants of the buttercup family with showy spurred flowers [ME, fr ML *columbina,* fr L, fem of *columbinus* dovelike, fr *columba* dove; akin to OHG *holuntar* elder tree, Gk *kolymbos* a bird, *kelainos* black]

columbium /kəˈlumbi·əm/ *n, NAm* niobium [NL, fr *Columbia* the USA, fr Christopher *Columbus* †1506 It navigator]

column /ˈkoləm/ *n* **1a** a vertical arrangement of

items or a vertical section of printing on a page ⟨*a ~ of figures*⟩ **b** a special and usu regular feature in a newspaper or periodical **2** a pillar that usu consists of a round shaft, a capital, and a base ☞ ARCHITECTURE **3** sthg resembling a column in form, position, or function ⟨*a ~ of water*⟩ **4** a long narrow formation of soldiers, vehicles, etc in rows [ME *columne*, fr MF *colomne*, fr L *columna*, fr *columen* top; akin to L *collis* hill – more at HILL] – **columned** /'koləmd/ *adj*

columnar /'koləmnə/ *adj* **1** of or characterized by columns **2** of, being, or composed of tall narrow (somewhat) cylindrical epithelial cells

columnist /'koləmnist/ *n* one who writes a newspaper or magazine column

colza /'kolzə/ *n* **1** rape or another cole whose seed is used as a source of oil **2** rapeseed [F, fr D *koolzaad*, fr MD *coolsaet*, fr *coole* cabbage + *saet* seed]

com-, col-, con- *prefix* with; together; jointly – usu *com-* before *b, p,* or *m* ⟨com*mingle*⟩, *col-* before *l* ⟨col*linear*⟩, and *con-* before other sounds ⟨con*centrate*⟩ [ME, fr OF, fr L, with, together, thoroughly – more at CO-]

[1]coma /'kohmə/ *n* a state of deep unconsciousness caused by disease, injury, etc [NL, fr Gk *kōma* deep sleep]

[2]coma *n, pl* **comae** /'kohmi/ **1** the head of a comet, usu containing a nucleus **2** an optical aberration in which the image of a point source becomes a comet-shaped blur [L, hair, fr Gk *komē*] – **comatic** /koh'matik/ *adj*

Comanche /kə'manchi/ *n, pl* **Comanches,** *esp collectively* **Comanche** a member of a N American Indian people ranging from Wyoming and Nebraska into New Mexico and NW Texas ☞ LANGUAGE [Sp, of Shoshonean origin; perh akin to Hopi *kománči* scalp lock]

comatose /'kohmə,tohs, -,tohz/ *adj* **1** of or suffering from coma **2** characterized by lethargy and sluggishness; torpid ⟨*a ~ economy*⟩ [F *comateux*, fr Gk *kōmat-, kōma*]

[1]comb /kohm/ *n* **1a** a toothed instrument used esp for adjusting, cleaning, or confining hair **b** a structure resembling such a comb; *esp* any of several toothed devices used in handling or ordering textile fibres **c** a currycomb **2** a fleshy crest on the head of a domestic fowl or a related bird **3** a honeycomb [ME, fr OE *camb*; akin to OHG *kamb* comb, Gk *gomphos* tooth] – **combed** /kohmd/ *adj*, **comblike** *adj*

[2]comb *vt* **1** to draw a comb through for the purpose of arranging or cleaning **2** to pass across with a scraping or raking action **3a** to eliminate (e g with a comb) by a thorough going over – usu + *out* **b** to search or examine systematically **4** to use with a combing action ~ *vi* , *of a wave* to roll over or break into foam

[1]combat /'kombat, kəm'bat/ *vb* **-tt-** (*NAm* **-t-, -tt-**) *vi* to engage in combat; fight ~ *vt* **1** to fight with; battle **2** to struggle against; *esp* to strive to reduce or eliminate ⟨*~ inflation*⟩ [MF *combattre*, fr (assumed) VL *combattere*, fr L *com-* + *battuere* to beat – more at BATTLE]

[2]combat /'kombat/ *n* **1** a fight or contest between individuals or groups **2** a conflict, controversy **3** active fighting in a war – **combat** *adj*

combatant /'kombətənt, kəm'bat(ə)nt/ *n* a person, nation, etc that is (ready to be) an active participant in combat – **combatant** *adj*

'combat fa,tigue *n* SHELL SHOCK

combative /'kombətiv/ *adj* marked by eagerness to fight or contend – **combatively** *adv*, **combativeness** *n*

combe /koohm/ *n, Br* a coomb

comber /'kohmə/ *n* ROLLER 2 [[2]COMB + [2]-ER]

combination /,kombi'naysh(ə)n/ *n* **1a** a result or product of combining **b** a group of people working as a team **2** any of the different sets of a usu specified number of individuals that can be chosen from a group and are considered without regard to order within the set **3** *pl* any of various 1-piece undergarments for the upper and lower parts of the body and legs **4** a (process of) combining, esp to form a chemical compound – **combinational** *adj*

,combi'nation ,lock *n* a lock with a mechanism operated by the selection of a specific combination of letters or numbers

combinative /'kombinətiv, -,naytiv/ *adj* **1** tending or able to combine **2** resulting from combination

combinatorial /,kombinə'tawri·əl/ *adj* **1** of or involving combinations **2** of or relating to the manipulation of mathematical elements within finite sets ⟨*~ mathematics*⟩

[1]combine /kəm'bien/ *vt* **1a** to bring into such close relationship as to obscure individual characters; merge **b** to cause to unite into a chemical compound **2** to cause to mix together **3** to possess in combination ~ *vi* **1a** to become one **b** to unite to form a chemical compound **2** to act together [ME *combinen*, fr MF *combiner*, fr LL *combinare*, fr L *com-* + *bini* two by two – more at BIN-] – **combiner** *n*, **combinable** *adj*, **combinability** /-nə'biləti/ *n*

[2]combine /'kombien/ *n* **1** a combination of people or organizations, esp in industry or commerce, to further their interests **2 combine, combine harvester** a harvesting machine that cuts, threshes, and cleans grain while moving over a field

'combing ,wool /'kohming/ *n* long-staple strong-fibred wool suitable for combing, used esp in the manufacture of worsteds

com'bining ,form /kəm'biening/ *n* a linguistic form (e g *Franco-*) that cannot stand alone but forms compounds with other free or bound forms

combo /'komboh/ *n, pl* **combos** a usu small jazz or dance band [*comb*ination + *-o*]

combust /kəm'bust/ *vb* to burn [L *combustus*, pp of *comburere* to burn up, irreg fr *com-* + *urere* to burn]

combustible /kəm'bustəbl/ *adj* **1** capable of (easily) being set on fire **2** easily excited – **combustible** *n*, **combustibly** *adv*, **combustibility** /-stə'biləti/ *n*

combustion /kəm'buschən/ *n* **1** a chemical reaction, esp an oxidation, in which light and heat are evolved ☞ FLIGHT **2** a slower chemical oxidation – **combustive** *adj*

[1]come /kum/ *vb* **came** /kaym/; **come** *vi* **1a** to move towards sthg nearer, esp towards the speaker; approach ⟨*~ here*⟩ ⟨came *running to her mother*⟩ **b** to move or journey nearer, esp towards or with the speaker, with a specified purpose ⟨*he* came *to see us*⟩ ⟨*~ and see what's going on*⟩ **c(1)** to reach a specified position in a progression ⟨*now we ~ to the section on health*⟩ ⟨came *short of his goal*⟩ **(2)** to arrive, appear,occur ⟨*the time has ~*⟩ ⟨*they* came *by train*⟩ – used in the subjunctive mood before an expression of future time ⟨*a year ago* ~ *March*⟩ **d(1)** to approach, reach, or fulfil a specified condition ⟨*this* ~s *near perfection*⟩ – often + *to* ⟨came *to his senses*⟩ ⟨~ *to the throne*⟩ ⟨*what are things* coming *to?*⟩ **(2)** – used with a following infinitive to express arrival at a condition ⟨came *to regard him as a friend*⟩ or chance occurrence ⟨*how did you* ~ *to be invited?*⟩ **2a** to happen, esp by chance ⟨*no harm will* ~ *to you*⟩ ⟨~ *what may*⟩ ⟨*how* ~s *it that you're at home?*⟩ **b(1)** to extend, reach ⟨*her dress* came *to her ankles*⟩ **(2)** to amount ⟨*that* ~s *to 75p exactly*⟩ **c** to originate, arise, or be the result *of* ⟨*wine* ~s *from grapes*⟩ ⟨~s *of sturdy stock*⟩ ⟨*this* ~s *of not changing your socks*⟩ **d** to fall within the specified limits, scope, or jurisdiction ⟨*rabbits* ~ *under rodents*⟩ ⟨*this* ~s *within the terms of the treaty*⟩ **e** to issue *from* ⟨*a sob* came *from her throat*⟩ **f** to be available or turn out, usu as specified ⟨*this model* ~s *in several sizes*⟩ ⟨*good clothes* ~ *expensive*⟩ **g** to be or belong in a specified place or relation ⟨*the address* ~s *above the date*⟩; *also* TAKE PLACE ⟨*Monday* ~s *after Sunday*⟩ **h** to take form ⟨*the story won't* ~⟩ **3** to become ⟨*it* came *untied*⟩ ⟨*the handle* came *off*⟩; *esp* to reach a culminating state ⟨*it all* came *right in the end*⟩ – compare GO 13c **4** to experience orgasm – infml ~ *vt* **1a** to move nearer by traversing ⟨*has* ~ *several miles*⟩ **b** to reach some state after traversing ⟨*has* ~ *a long way from humble beginnings*⟩ **2** to take on the aspect of; play the role of – infml ⟨*don't* ~ *the old soldier with me*⟩ [ME *comen*, fr OE *cuman*; akin to OHG *queman* to come, L *venire*, Gk *bainein* to walk, go] – **as it comes** without stipulated additions; *specif* NEAT 1a – **come a cropper 1** *chiefly Br* to have a fall or an accident – infml **2** to fail completely – slang – **come across** to meet with or find by chance ⟨came across *an interesting problem*⟩ – **come by** to get possession of; acquire ⟨*good jobs are hard to* come by⟩ – **come clean** to tell the whole story; confess – infml – **come home to roost** to rebound upon the perpetrator – **come into** to acquire as a possession or inheritance ⟨came into *a fortune*⟩ – **come it** *chiefly Br* to act with bold disrespect ⟨*don't* come it *over me*⟩ – slang – **come off it** to cease foolish or pretentious talk or behaviour – usu used imperatively; infml – **come one's way** to fall to one's lot – **come over** to seize suddenly and strangely ⟨*what's* come over *you?*⟩ – **come through** to survive (e g an illness) – **come to** to be a question of ⟨*hopeless when it* comes to *arithmetic*⟩ – **come to a head** to arrive at a culminating point or crisis – **come to grief** to end badly; fail – **come to oneself 1** COME TO **2** to regain self-control – **come to pass** HAPPEN 2 – fml – **come unstuck** COME TO GRIEF ⟨*the government* came unstuck *over food prices*⟩ – infml – **come upon** to meet with or find by chance – **to come** in the future; coming ⟨*in years* to come⟩ – **whether one is coming or going** – used to suggest frenetic disorder and bewilderment ⟨*don't know* whether I'm coming or going⟩

[2]**come** *interj* – used to express encouragement or to urge reconsideration ⟨~, ~, *it's not as bad as that*⟩

come about *vi* **1** to occur; TAKE PLACE **2** to change direction ⟨*the wind has* come about *into the north*⟩ **3** *of a ship* to turn onto a new tack

come across *vi* **1** to provide sthg demanded or expected, esp sex or money **2** to produce an impression ⟨*he* comes across *as a persuasive speaker*⟩

,come a'gain *interj* – used as a request for a remark to be repeated; infml

come along *vi* **1** to appear ⟨*wouldn't just marry the first man that* came along⟩ **2** to hurry – usu imperative

'come,back /-,bak/ *n* **1a** a means of redress **b** a retrospective criticism of a decision **2** a return to a former state or condition **3** a sharp or witty reply; a retort – infml

come back *vi* **1** to return to memory ⟨*it's all* coming back *to me now*⟩ **2** to reply, retort **3** to regain a former condition or position

Comecon /'komi,kon/ *n* an economic organization formed in 1949 by the countries of the Soviet bloc to coordinate their economies, and promote mutual aid [*Co*uncil for *M*utual *Econ*omic Assistance]

comedian /kə'meedi·ən/, *fem* **comedienne** /kə,meedi'en/ *n* **1** an actor who plays comic roles **2** one, esp a professional entertainer, who aims to be amusing [*comedienne* fr F *comédienne*, fem of *comédien* comedian]

comedic /kə'meedik/ *adj* of comedy

comedo /'komidoh/ *n*, *pl* **comedones** /,komi'dohneez/ a blackhead [NL, fr L, glutton, fr *comedere* to eat – more at COMESTIBLE]

'come,down /-,down/ *n* a striking descent in rank or dignity – infml

come down *vi* **1** to formulate and express one's opinion or decision ⟨came down *in favour of abortion on demand*⟩ **2** *of an aircraft, missile, etc* to land; *esp* to crash **3** to become ill ⟨*they* came down *with measles*⟩ **4** *Br* to return from a university

comedy /'komədi/ *n* **1a** a drama of light and amusing character, typically with a happy ending **b** (a work in) the genre of (dramatic) literature dealing with comic or serious subjects in a light or satirical manner – compare TRAGEDY 1 **2** a ludicrous or farcical event or series of events **3** the comic aspect of sthg [ME, fr MF *comedie*, fr L *comoedia*, fr Gk *kōmōidia*, fr *kōmos* revel + *aeidein* to sing – more at ODE]

,come-'hither *adj* sexually inviting ⟨*that* ~ *look in his eyes*⟩

come in *vi* **1** to arrive ⟨*I was there when the train* came in⟩ **2** to finish as specified, esp in a competition ⟨came in *third*⟩ **3a** to function in a specified manner; be of use ⟨*to* come in *handy*⟩ **b** to make reply to a signal ⟨came in *loud and clear*⟩ **4** to assume a role or function ⟨*that's where you* come in⟩ – **come in for** to become subject to ⟨coming in for *increasing criticism*⟩

comely /'kumli/ *adj* of pleasing appearance; not plain [ME *comly*, alter. of OE *cȳmlic* glorious, fr *cȳme* lovely, fine; akin to OHG *kūmig* weak, Gk *goan* to lament] – **comeliness** *n*

come off *vi* **1** to finish or emerge from sthg in a specified condition ⟨came off *well in the contest*⟩ **2** to succeed ⟨*that didn't quite* come off⟩ **3** to happen, occur **4** to become detached

'come-,on *n* **1** *chiefly NAm* an attraction or enticement (e g in sales promotion) to induce an action **2** an instance of sexually provocative enticement – infml

come on *vi* **1** to advance or begin by degrees ⟨*as darkness* came on, *it got harder to see*⟩ **2** – used in cajoling, pleading, defiance, or encouraging ⟨come on, *you can do it*⟩ 3 COME ALONG 2 4 to appear on the radio, television, or stage 5 *chiefly NAm* to project a specified appearance ⟨comes on *as a Liberal in his speeches*⟩

come out *vi* **1a** to come to public notice; be published **b** to become evident ⟨*this will* come out *in the full analysis*⟩ **2a** to declare oneself, esp in public utterance ⟨came out *in favour of the popular candidate*⟩ **b** to present oneself openly as homosexual **3** to end up; TURN OUT ⟨*everything will* come out *right*⟩ **4** to make a debut; *specif* to make one's first appearance in society as a debutante – **come out in the wash 1** to become known in the course of time **2** to reach a satisfactory conclusion – **come out with** to utter or say, usu unexpectedly

come over *vi* **1a** to change from one side (e g of a controversy) to the other **b** to drop in casually ⟨come over *any time; we're always in*⟩ **2** COME ACROSS 2 ⟨*she* comes over *as a very sincere person*⟩ **3** *Br* to become ⟨*she* came over *all queer*⟩

comer /'kumə/ *n* **1** sby who comes or arrives ⟨*all* ~s⟩ **2** *chiefly NAm* sby making rapid progress or showing promise

come round *vi* **1** COME TO **2** to accede to a particular opinion or course of action **3** COME ABOUT 2

comestible /kə'mestəbl/ *n* food – usu pl with sing. meaning; fml [MF, edible, fr ML *comestibilis*, fr L *comestus*, pp of *comedere* to eat, fr *com-* + *edere* to eat]

comet /'komit/ *n* a celestial body that follows a usu highly elliptical orbit round the sun and consists of an indistinct head usu surrounding a bright nucleus, often with a long tail which points away from the sun ☞ ASTRONOMY, SYMBOL [ME *comete*, fr OE *cometa*, fr L, fr Gk *komētēs*, lit., long-haired, fr *koman* to wear long hair, fr *komē* hair] – **cometary** /-t(ə)ri/ *adj*

come through *vi* **1** to do what is needed or expected **2** to become communicated

,come 'to *vi* to recover consciousness

come up *vi* **1** to rise in rank or status ⟨*an officer who* came up *from the ranks*⟩ **2** to arise inevitably or by chance ⟨*any problems that* come up⟩ **3** to appear before a magistrate ⟨*he* came up *for speeding*⟩ **4** to become, esp after cleaning ⟨*the table* came up *like new*⟩ – **come up with** to provide, esp in dealing with a problem or challenge ⟨came up with *a better solution*⟩

,come-'uppance /'up(ə)ns/ *n* a deserved rebuke or penalty [*come up* + *-ance*]

comfit /'kumfit/ *n* a sweetmeat consisting of a nut, seed, piece of fruit, etc coated and preserved with sugar [ME *confit*, fr MF, fr pp of *confire* to prepare, fr L *conficere*, fr *com-* + *facere* to make – more at [1]DO]

[1]**comfort** /'kumfət/ *n* **1** (sby or sthg that provides) consolation or encouragement in time of trouble or worry **2** contented well-being – **comfortless** *adj*

[2]**comfort** *vt* **1** to cheer up **2** to ease the grief or trouble of; console [ME *comforten*, fr OF *conforter*, fr LL *confortare* to strengthen greatly, fr L *com-* + *fortis* strong] – **comfortingly** *adv*

comfortable /'kumftəbl/ *adj* **1a** providing or enjoying contentment and security ⟨*a* ~ *income*⟩ **b** providing or enjoying physical comfort ⟨*a* ~ *armchair*⟩ **2a** causing no worry or doubt ⟨~ *assumptions that require no thought*⟩ **b** free from stress or tension ⟨*a* ~ *routine*⟩ – **comfortably** /-bli/ *adv*

comforter /'kumfətə/ *n* **1** *cap* HOLY SPIRIT **2a** a knitted scarf **b** *chiefly NAm* a quilt, eiderdown [[2]COMFORT + [2]-ER]

'comfort ,station *n, NAm* a public toilet (e g at a petrol station) – euph

comfrey /'kumfri/ *n* any of a genus of (tall) plants of the borage family whose coarse hairy leaves are much used in herbal medicine [ME *cumfirie*, fr OF, fr L *conferva*, a water plant, fr *confervēre* to boil together, heal, fr *com-* + *fervēre* to boil]

comfy /'kumfi/ *adj* comfortable – infml [by shortening & alter.]

[1]**comic** /'komik/ *adj* **1** of or marked by comedy **2** causing laughter or amusement; funny [L *comicus*, fr Gk *kōmikos*, fr *kōmos* revel]

[2]**comic** *n* **1** a comedian **2** a magazine consisting mainly of strip-cartoon stories **3** *pl, NAm* the part of a newspaper devoted to strip cartoons

comical /'komikl/ *adj* being of a kind to excite laughter, esp because of a startlingly or unexpectedly humorous impact ⟨*he thought her hat was* ~⟩ – **comically** *adv*

,comic 'opera *n* opera with humorous episodes and usu some spoken dialogue and a sentimental plot

'comic ,strip *n* STRIP CARTOON

Cominform /'komin,fawm/ *n* an organization operating from 1947 to 1956 to coordinate the activities of 9 European Communist parties [*Com*munist *Inform*ation Bureau]

[1]**coming** /'kuming/ *n* an act or instance of arriving ⟨~s *and goings*⟩

[2]**coming** *adj* **1** immediately due in sequence or development; next ⟨*the* ~ *year*⟩ **2** gaining in importance; up-and-coming

Comintern /'komin,tuhn/ *n* an international of Socialist organizations operating from 1919 to 1943 [Russ *Komintern*, fr *Kom*munisticheskiĭ *Intern*ational Communist International]

comity /'komiti/ *n* harmony, fellowship; *specif* the recognition by courts of one jurisdiction of the laws and decisions of another [L *comitat-*, *comitas* courtesy, fr *comis* courteous, fr OL *cosmis*, fr *com-* + *-smis* (akin to Skt *smayate* he smiles) – more at SMILE]

,comity of 'nations *n* the courtesy and friendship of nations, marked esp by recognition of each other's laws

comma /'komə/ *n* **1** a punctuation mark , used esp as a mark of separation within the sentence **2** a butterfly with a silvery comma-shaped mark on the underside of the hind wing [LL, fr L, part of a sentence, fr Gk *komma* segment, clause, fr *koptein* to cut – more at CAPON]

'comma ba,cillus *n* a bacterium that causes cholera

[1]**command** /kə'mahnd/ *vt* **1** to direct authoritatively; order **2a** to have at one's immediate disposal **b** to be able to ask for and receive ⟨~s *a high fee*⟩ **c** to overlook or dominate (as if) from a strategic position **d** to have military command of as senior officer ~ *vi* to be commander; be supreme [ME *comanden*, fr OF *comander*, fr (assumed) VL *commandare*, alter. of L *commendare* to commit to one's charge – more at COMMEND] – **commandable** *adj*

[2]**command** *n* **1** an order given **2** (the activation of a device by) an electrical signal **3a** the ability or power to control; the mastery **b** the authority or right to command ⟨*the officer in* ~⟩ **c** facility in use

⟨*a good ~ of French*⟩ **4** *sing or pl in constr* the unit, personnel, etc under a commander

[3]**command** *adj* done on command or request ⟨*a ~ performance*⟩

commandant /,komən'dant, -'dahnt/ *n* a commanding officer

commandeer /,komən'diə/ *vt* **1** to seize for military purposes **2** to take arbitrary or forcible possession of [Afrik *kommandeer*, fr F *commander* to command, fr OF *comander*]

commander /kə'mahndə/ *n* ☞ RANK [[1]COMMAND + [2]-ER] – **commandership** *n*

com,mander-in-'chief *n* one who is in supreme command of an armed force

commanding /kə'mahnding/ *adj* **1** having command; being in charge ⟨*a ~ officer*⟩ **2** dominating or having priority ⟨*a ~ position of a castle*⟩ ⟨*a ~ lead*⟩ **3** deserving or expecting respect and obedience ⟨*a ~ voice*⟩ – **commandingly** *adv*

com'mandment /-mənt/ *n* sthg commanded; *specif* any of the biblical Ten Commandments

commando /kə'mahndoh/ *n, pl* **commandos, commandoes** (a member of) a usu small military unit for surprise raids [Afrik *kommando*, fr D *commando* command, fr Sp *comando*, fr *comandar* to command, fr F *commander*]

com'mand ,paper *n* a government report laid before Parliament at the command of the crown

com'mand ,post *n* the headquarters of a military unit in the field

commedia dell'arte /kə,maydi·ə del 'ahti/ *n* Italian comedy of the 16th–18th c, improvised from standardized situations and stock characters [It, lit., comedy of art]

comme il faut /,kom eel 'foh/ *adj* conforming to accepted standards; proper [F, lit., as it should be]

commemorate /kə'meməravt/ *vt* **1** to call to formal remembrance **2** to mark by some ceremony or observation; observe **3** to serve as a memorial of [L *commemoratus*, pp of *commemorare*, fr *com-* + *memorare* to remind of, fr *memor* mindful – more at MEMORY] – **commemorative** /-rətiv/ *adj*, **commemoration** /-'raysh(ə)n/ *n*

commence /kə'mens/ *vb* to start, begin – fml [ME *comencen*, fr MF *comencer*, fr (assumed) VL *cominitiare*, fr L *com-* + LL *initiare* to begin, fr L, to initiate] – **commencement** *n*

commend /kə'mend/ *vt* **1** to entrust for care or preservation **2** to recommend as worthy of confidence or notice [ME *commenden*, fr L *commendare*, fr *com-* + *mandare* to entrust – more at MANDATE] – **commendable** *adj*, **commendably** *adv*

commendation /,komən'daysh(ə)n/ *n* sthg (e g a formal citation) that commends – **commendatory** /kə'mendət(ə)ri/ *adj*

commensal /kə'mens(ə)l/ *adj* living in a state of commensalism [ME, fr ML *commensalis*, fr L *com-* + LL *mensalis* of the table, fr L *mensa* table] – **commensal** *n*, **commensally** *adv*

com'mensalism /-,iz(ə)m/ *n* the association of 2 species whereby one or both species obtain benefits (e g food or protection) without either species being harmed ☞ DEFENCE

commensurable /kə'mensh(ə)rəbl/ *adj* having a common measure; *esp* divisible by a common unit an integral number of times – **commensurably** *adv*, **commensurability** /-rə'biləti/ *n*

commensurate /kə'menshərət/ *adj* **1** (approximately) equal in measure or extent; coextensive **2** corresponding in size, extent, amount, or degree; proportionate ⟨*was given a job ~ with his abilities*⟩ [LL *commensuratus*, fr L *com-* + LL *mensuratus*, pp of *mensurare* to measure, fr L *mensura* measure – more at MEASURE] – **commensurately** *adv*, **commensuration** /-'raysh(ə)n/ *n*

[1]**comment** /'koment/ *n* **1** a note explaining or criticizing the meaning of a piece of writing ⟨*~s printed in the margin*⟩ **2a** an observation or remark expressing an opinion or attitude **b** a judgment expressed indirectly ⟨*this film is a ~ on current moral standards*⟩ [ME, fr LL *commentum*, fr L, invention, fr neut of *commentus*, pp of *comminisci* to invent, fr *com-* + *-minisci* (akin to *ment-*, *mens* mind) – more at MIND]

[2]**comment** *vi* to explain or interpret sthg by comment; *broadly* to make a comment ⟨*~ed on the match*⟩

commentary /'komənt(ə)ri/ *n* **1** a systematic series of explanations or interpretations (e g of a piece of writing) **2** a series of spoken remarks and comments used as a broadcast description of some event ⟨*a running ~ on the match*⟩

commentate /'koməntayt/ *vi* to act as a commentator; *esp* to give a broadcast commentary [back-formation fr *commentator*]

commentator /'komən,taytə/ *n* a person who provides a commentary; *specif* one who reports and discusses news or sports events on radio or television

commerce /'komuhs/ *n* the exchange or buying and selling of commodities, esp on a large scale [MF, fr L *commercium*, fr *com-* + *merc-*, *merx* merchandise]

[1]**commercial** /kə'muhsh(ə)l/ *adj* **1a(1)** engaged in work designed for the market **(2)** (characteristic) of commerce **(3)** having or being a good financial prospect ⟨*found oil in ~ quantities*⟩ **b(1)** *esp of a chemical* average or inferior in quality **(2)** producing work to a standard determined only by market criteria **2a** viewed with regard to profit ⟨*a ~ success*⟩ **b** designed for a large market **3** supported by advertisers ⟨*~ TV*⟩ – **commercially** *adv*

[2]**commercial** *n* an advertisement broadcast on radio or television

com,mercial 'art *n* graphic art put to commercial use, esp in advertising – **commercial artist** *n*

com'mercial,ism /-,iz(ə)m/ *n* **1** commercial spirit, institutions, or methods **2** excessive emphasis on profit – **commercialist** *n*, **commercialistic** /-'istik/ *adj*

com'mercial·,ize, -ise /-,iez/ *vt* **1a** to manage on a business basis for profit **b** to make commercial **2** to exploit for profit – **commercialization** /-'zaysh(ə)n/ *n*

com,mercial 'traveller *n, Br* SALES REPRESENTATIVE

commie /'komi/ *n* a communist – chiefly derog [by shortening & alter.]

commingle /ko'ming·gl/ *vb* to combine into a common fund or stock

comminute /'kominyooht/ *vt* to reduce to minute particles; pulverize [L *comminutus*, pp of *comminuere*, fr *com-* + *minuere* to lessen] – **comminution** /,komi'nyoohsh(ə)n/ *n*

commis /kə'mee/ *n, pl* **commis** /~/ a junior or

assistant in a hotel, catering establishment, etc ⟨*a ~ chef*⟩ [F, fr *commis*, pp of *commettre* to commit, entrust, fr L *committere* to connect, entrust]

commiserate /kə'mizərayt/ *vi* to feel or express sympathy *with* sby; condole ⟨*~ over their hard luck*⟩ [L *commiseratus*, pp of *commiserari*, fr *com-* + *miserari* to pity, fr *miser* wretched] – **commiserative** /-rətiv/ *adj*, **commiseration** /-'raysh(ə)n/ *n*

commissar /,komi'sahr/ *n* **1** a Communist party official assigned to a military unit to teach party principles and ideals **2** the head of a government department in the USSR until 1946 [Russ *komissar*, fr G *kommissar*, fr ML *commissarius*]

commissariat /,komi'seəri·ət/ *n* **1** the department of an army that organizes food supplies **2** a government department in the USSR until 1946 [NL *commissariatus*, fr ML *commissarius*; (2) Russ *komissariat*, fr G *kommissariat*, fr NL *commissariatus*]

commissary /'komis(ə)ri/ *n* **1** an officer in charge of military supplies **2** *NAm* (a store for) equipment, food supplies, etc, esp of a military force [ME *commissarie*, fr ML *commissarius*, fr L *commissus*, pp]

[1]**commission** /kə'mish(ə)n/ *n* **1a** a formal warrant granting various powers **b** (a certificate conferring) military rank above a certain level **2** an authorization or command to act in a prescribed manner or to perform prescribed acts; a charge **3** authority to act as agent for another; *also* sthg to be done by an agent **4a** *sing or pl in constr* a group of people directed to perform some duty **b** *often cap* a government agency **5** an act of committing sthg **6** a fee, esp a percentage, paid to an agent or employee for transacting a piece of business or performing a service [ME, fr MF, fr L *commission-*, *commissio* act of bringing together, fr *commissus*, pp of *committere*] – **in/into commission 1** *of a ship* ready for active service **2** in use or in condition for use – **on commission** with commission serving as partial or full pay for work done – **out of commission 1** out of active service or use **2** out of working order

[2]**commission** *vt* **1a** to confer a formal commission on **b** to order, appoint, or assign to perform a task or function ⟨*the writer who was ~ed to do the biography*⟩ **2** to put (a ship) in commission

commissionaire /kə,mishə'neə/ *n, chiefly Br* a uniformed attendant at a cinema, theatre, office, etc [F *commissionnaire*, fr *commission*]

commissioner /kə'mishənə/ *n* **1** a member or the head of a commission **2** the government representative in a district, province, etc – **commissionership** *n*

Com,missioner for 'Oaths *n, Br* sby authorized to administer oaths or affirmations or to take affidavits

commissure /'komisyooə, -syə/ *n* **1** the place where 2 parts are joined; a closure **2** a connecting band of nerve tissue in the brain or spinal cord [ME, fr MF or L; MF, fr L *commissura* a joining, fr *commissus*, pp] – **commissural** /kə'misyooərəl, ,komi'syooərəl/ *adj*

commit /kə'mit/ *vt* **-tt- 1a** to entrust **b** to place in a prison or mental institution **c** to transfer, consign ⟨*~ something to paper*⟩ **2** to carry out (a crime, sin, etc) **3a** to obligate, bind **b** to assign to some particular course or use ⟨*all available troops were ~ted to the attack*⟩ [ME *committen*, fr L *committere* to connect, entrust, fr *com-* + *mittere* to send] – **committable** *adj*

com'mitment /-mənt/ *n* **1** an act of committing to a charge or trust; *esp* a consignment to an institution **2a** an agreement or pledge to do sthg in the future **b** sthg pledged **c** loyalty to a system of thought or action

committal /kə'mitl/ *n* commitment or consignment (e g to prison or the grave)

committee /kə'miti/ *n sing or pl in constr* a body of people delegated **a** to report on, investigate, etc some matter ⟨*a parliamentary ~*⟩ **b** to organize or administrate a society, event, etc ⟨*the fête ~*⟩ [ME, one to whom a charge is committed, fr *committen*] – **committeeman** /-mən, -,man/ *n*, **committeewoman** *n*

committee of the whole house *n, often cap C, W, & H* the whole membership of a legislative house operating as a committee under informal rules

com'mittee ,stage *n* the stage in parliamentary procedure between the second reading and the third reading when a bill is discussed in detail in committee ☞ LAW

commode /kə'mohd/ *n* **1** a low chest of drawers **2** a boxlike structure or chair with a removable seat covering a chamber pot [F, fr *commode*, adj, suitable, convenient, fr L *commodus*, fr *com-* + *modus* measure – more at METE]

commodious /kə'mohdi·əs/ *adj* comfortably or conveniently spacious; roomy – fml [ME, useful, fr MF *commodieux*, fr ML *commodiosus*, irreg fr L *commodum* convenience, fr neut of *commodus*] – **commodiously** *adv*, **commodiousness** *n*

commodity /kə'modəti/ *n* **1** sthg useful or valuable **2a** a product possessing utility; sthg that can be bought and sold **b** an article of trade or commerce, esp when delivered for shipment [ME *commoditee*, fr MF *commodité*, fr L *commoditat-*, *commoditas*, fr *commodus*]

commodore /'komədaw/ *n* **1** ☞ RANK **2** the senior captain of a merchant shipping line **3** the chief officer of a yacht club [prob modif of D *commandeur* commander, fr F, fr OF *comandeor*, fr *comander* to command]

[1]**common** /'komən/ *adj* **1** of the community at large; public ⟨*work for the ~ good*⟩ **2a** belonging to or shared by 2 or more individuals or by all members of a group **b** belonging equally to 2 or more quantities ⟨*a ~ denominator*⟩ ⟨*a ~ factor*⟩ **3a** occurring or appearing frequently; familiar ⟨*a ~ sight*⟩ **b** of the familiar kind **4a** widespread, general ⟨*being ~ knowledge*⟩ **b** characterized by a lack of privilege or special status ⟨*the ~ people*⟩ **c** simply satisfying accustomed criteria (and no more); elementary ⟨*~ decency*⟩ **5a** falling below ordinary standards; second-rate **b** lacking refinement **6** either masculine or feminine in gender [ME *commun*, fr OF, fr L *communis* – more at [1]MEAN] – **commonly** *adv*, **commonness** *n*

[2]**common** *n* **1** *pl* the common people – used chiefly in a historical context **2** *pl* food or provisions (shared jointly by all members of an institution) – esp in *short commons* **3** *pl but sing or pl in constr, often cap* **a** the political group or estate made up of commoners **b** HOUSE OF COMMONS ☞ LAW **4** a right which sby may have on another's land **5** a piece of land open to use by all: e g **a** undivided land used esp for pasture **b** a more or less treeless expanse of undevel-

oped land available for recreation **6a** a religious service suitable for any of various festivals **b** the ordinary of the Mass **7** *Br* COMMON SENSE – slang – **in common** shared together – used esp of shared interests, attitudes, or experience ⟨*we had a lot* in common⟩

commonality /ˌkomə'naləti/ *n* **1** possession of common features or attributes or of some degree of standardization; commonness **2** a common feature or attribute [ME *communalitie,* alter. of *communalte*]

commonalty /'komənəlti/ *n* (the political estate formed by) the common people [ME *communalte,* fr OF *comunalté,* fr *comunal* communal]

'common ˌchord *n* TRIAD 2

ˌcommon 'cold *n* inflammation of the mucous membranes of the nose, throat, mouth, etc caused by a virus and lasting for a short time

ˌcommon 'core *n* the compulsory subjects in a British school curriculum

Common Entrance examination *n, often cap 2nd E* an examination taken, esp by boys between the ages of 12 and 14, for admission to a British public school

commoner /'komənə/ *n* **1** a member of the common people; sby not of noble rank **2** a student (e g at Oxford) who is not supported by the college endowments

ˌcommon 'fraction *n* a fraction in which both the numerator and denominator are expressed as numbers and are separated by a horizontal or slanted line – compare DECIMAL

ˌcommon-'law *adj* **1** of the common law **2** recognized in law without solemnization of marriage ⟨*his ~ wife*⟩

ˌcommon 'law *n* the body of uncodified English law that forms the basis of the English legal system – compare EQUITY 2 ☞ LAW

ˌcommon 'logarithm *n* a logarithm whose base is 10

ˌcommon 'market *n* an economic unit formed to remove trade barriers among its members; *specif, often cap C&M the* European economic community

ˌcommon 'multiple *n* a multiple of each of 2 or more numbers or expressions

ˌcommon 'noun *n* a noun that may occur with limiting modifiers (e g *a* or *an, some, every,* and *my*) and that designates any one of a class of beings or things

ˌcommon or 'garden *adj* ordinary, everyday – infml

¹'commonˌplace /-ˌplays/ *n* **1** an obvious or trite observation **2** sthg taken for granted [trans of L *locus communis* widely applicable argument, trans of Gk *koinos topos*]

²commonplace *adj* routinely found; ordinary, unremarkable – **commonplaceness** *n*

'common ˌroom *n* a room or set of rooms in a school, college, etc for the recreational use of the staff or students

ˌcommon 'salt *n* SALT 1a

ˌcommon 'sense *n* sound and prudent (but often unsophisticated) judgment – **commonsense** *adj,* **commonsensical** /-'sensikl/ *adj*

'common ˌtime *n* the musical metre marked by 4 crotchets per bar

'commonˌwealth /-ˌwelth/ *n* **1** a political unit: e g **a** one founded on law and united by agreement of the people for the common good **b** one in which supreme authority is vested in the people **2** *cap* the English state from 1649 to 1660 **3** a state of the USA **4** *cap* a federal union of states – used officially of Australia **5** *often cap* a loose association of autonomous states under a common allegiance; *specif* an association consisting of Britain and states that were formerly British colonies [ME *commen wealthe,* fr *commen, commun* common + *wealthe, welthe* welfare, wealth]

'common ˌyear *n* a calendar year containing no additional day to make it coincide with the solar year

commotion /kə'mohsh(ə)n/ *n* **1** a state of civil unrest or insurrection **2** a disturbance, tumult **3** noisy confusion and bustle [ME, fr MF, fr L *commotion-, commotio,* fr *commotus,* pp of *commovēre* to agitate, fr *com-* + *movēre* to move]

communal /'komyoonl/ *adj* **1** of a commune or communes **2** of a community **3** shared ⟨*~ activity*⟩ [F, fr LL *communalis,* fr L *communis*] – **communalize** *vt,* **communally** *adv,* **communality** /-'naləti/ *n*

'communalˌism /-ˌiz(ə)m/ *n* social organization on a communal basis – **communalist** *n or adj*

communard /'komyooˌnahd/ *n* **1** *cap* one who participated in the Commune of Paris in 1871 **2** one who lives in a commune [F]

¹commune /kə'myoohn/ *vi* **1** to receive Communion **2** to communicate intimately [ME *communen* to converse, administer Communion, fr MF *comunier* to converse, administer or receive Communion, fr LL *communicare,* fr L]

²commune /'koˌmyoohn/ *n* **1** the smallest administrative district of many (European) countries **2** *sing or pl in constr* an often rural community of unrelated individuals or families organized on a communal basis [F, alter. of MF *comugne,* fr ML *communia,* fr L, neut pl of *communis*]

communicable /kə'myoohnikəbl/ *adj, esp of a disease* transmittable – **communicableness** *n,* **communicably** *adv,* **communicability** /-kə 'biləti/ *n*

communicant /kə'myoohnikənt/ *n* **1** a church member who receives or is entitled to receive Communion **2** an informant [COMMUNICATE + ¹-ANT] – **communicant** *adj*

communicate /kə'myoohniˌkayt/ *vt* **1** to convey knowledge of or information about; make known **2** to cause to pass from one to another *~ vi* **1** to receive Communion **2** to transmit information, thought, or feeling so that it is satisfactorily received or understood **3** to give access to each other; connect ⟨*the rooms ~*⟩ [L *communicatus,* pp of *communicare* to impart, participate, fr *communis* common – more at ¹MEAN] – **communicator** *n,* **communicatory** /-kət(ə)ri/ *adj*

communication /kəˌmyoohni'kaysh(ə)n/ *n* **1** a verbal or written message **2** (the use of a common system of symbols, signs, behaviour, etc for the) exchange of information **3** *pl* **a** a system (e g of telephones) for communicating **b** a system of routes for moving troops, supplies, etc **4** *pl but sing or pl in constr* techniques for the effective transmission of information, ideas, etc [COMMUNICATE + -ION] – **communicational** *adj*

comˌmuni'cation ˌcord *n, Br* a device (e g a chain or handle) in a railway carriage that may be pulled in an emergency to sound an alarm

communicative /kə'myoohnikətiv/ *adj* **1** tending to communicate; talkative **2** of communication – **communicatively** *adv*, **communicativeness** *n*

communion /kə'myoohnyən, -ni·ən/ *n* **1a** *often cap* the religious service celebrating the Eucharist in Protestant churches **b** the act of receiving the Eucharist **2** intimate fellowship or rapport **3** a body of Christians having a common faith and discipline [ME, fr L *communion-, communio* mutual participation, fr *communis*]

communiqué /kə'myoohni,kay/ *n* BULLETIN 1 [F, fr pp of *communiquer* to communicate, fr L *communicare*]

communism /'komyooniz(ə)m/ *n* **1a** a theory advocating elimination of private property **b** a system in which goods are held in common and are available to all as needed **2** *cap* **a** a doctrine based on revolutionary Marxian socialism and Marxism-Leninism that is the official ideology of the USSR **b** a totalitarian system of government in which a single party controls state-owned means of production [F *communisme*, fr *commun* common]

communist /'komyoonist/ *n, often cap* **1** an adherent or advocate of Communism **2** a left-wing revolutionary – **communist** *adj, often cap*, **communistic** /-'nistik/ *adj, often cap*

communitarian /kə,myoohni'teəri·ən/ *adj* of or based on social organization in small communes – **communitarian** *n*, **communitarianism** *n*

community /kə'myoohnəti/ *n* **1** *sing or pl in constr* **a** a group of people living in a particular area **b** all the interacting populations of various living organisms in a particular area **c** a group of individuals with some common characteristic (e g profession, religion, or status) **d** a body of people or nations having a common history or common interests ⟨*the international* ~⟩ **2** society in general **3a** joint ownership or participation **b** common character; likeness ⟨*bound by* ~ *of interests*⟩ **c** social ties; fellowship **d** the state or condition of living in a society [ME *comunete*, fr MF *comuneté*, fr L *communitat-, communitas*, fr *communis*]

com'munity ,centre *n* a building or group of buildings for the educational and recreational activities of a community

com'munity ,chest *n, NAm* a general fund accumulated from subscriptions to pay for social-welfare requirements in a community

com'munity ,home *n, Br* a local-authority centre for housing juvenile offenders and deprived children

com,munity 'service ,order *n* a judicial order requiring a convicted person to do unpaid work on behalf of the community

commun·ize, -ise /'komyooniez/ *vt* to make communal or Communist [back-formation fr *communization*] – **communization** /-'zaysh(ə)n/ *n*

commutation /,komyoo'taysh(ə)n/ *n* **1** a replacement; *specif* a substitution of one form of payment or charge for another **2** an act or process of commuting **3** the process of converting an alternating current to a direct current [ME, fr MF, fr L *commutation-, commutatio*, fr *commutatus*, pp of *commutare*]

,commu'tation ,ticket *n, NAm* a ticket sold, usu at a reduced rate, for a fixed number of trips over the same route during a limited period – compare SEASON TICKET

commutative /kə'myoohtətiv/ *adj* **1** of or showing commutation **2** combining elements to produce a result that is independent of the order in which the elements are taken ⟨*a* ~ *group*⟩ ⟨*addition of the positive integers is* ~⟩

commutator /'komyoo,taytə/ *n* a device for reversing the direction of an electric current; *esp* a device on a motor or generator that converts alternating current to direct current

commute /kə'myooht/ *vt* **1** to convert (e g a payment) into another form **2** to exchange (a penalty) for another less severe ~ *vi* **1** to travet back and forth regularly (e g between home and work) **2** *of 2 mathematical operators* to give a commutative result [L *commutare* to change, exchange, fr *com-* + *mutare* to change] – **commutable** *adj*, **commuter** *n*

[1]**compact** /kəm'pakt/ *adj* **1** having parts or units closely packed or joined **2** succinct, terse ⟨*a* ~ *statement*⟩ **3** occupying a small volume because of efficient use of space ⟨*a* ~ *camera*⟩ [ME, firmly put together, fr L *compactus*, fr pp of *compingere* to put together, fr *com-* + *pangere* to fasten – more at PACT] – **compactly** *adv*, **compactness** *n*

[2]**compact** *vt* **1a** to knit or draw together; combine, consolidate **b** to press together; compress **2** to make up by connecting or combining; compose – **compactible** *adj*, **compaction** /kəm'paksh(ə)n/ *n*, **compactor** *n*

[3]**compact** /'kom,pakt/ *n* sthg compact or compacted: e g **a** a small slim case for face powder **b** a medium-sized US motor car

[4]**compact** /'kom,pakt/ *n* an agreement, contract [L *compactum*, fr neut of *compactus*, pp of *compacisci* to make an agreement, fr *com-* + *pacisci* to contract]

[1]**companion** /kəm'panyən/ *n* one who accompanies another; a comrade [ME *compainoun*, fr OF *compagnon*, fr LL *companion-, companio*, fr L *com-* + *panis* bread, food] – **companionate** /-nət/ *adj*, **companionship** *n*

[2]**companion** *n* (a covering at the top of) a companionway [by folk etymology fr D *kampanje* poop deck]

companionable /kəm'panyənəbl/ *adj* marked by, conducive to, or suggestive of companionship; sociable – **companionableness** *n*, **companionably** *adv*

com'panion,way /-,way/ *n* a ship's stairway from one deck to another [[2]*companion*]

company /'kump(ə)ni/ *n* **1a** friendly association with another; fellowship ⟨*I enjoy her* ~⟩ **b** companions, associates ⟨*know a person by the* ~ *he keeps*⟩ **c** *sing or pl in constr* visitors, guests ⟨*having* ~ *for dinner*⟩ **2** *sing or pl in constr* **a** a group of people or things ⟨*a* ~ *of horsemen*⟩ **b** a unit of soldiers composed usu of a headquarters and 2 or more platoons **c** an organization of musical or dramatic performers **d** the officers and men of a ship **3a** *sing or pl in constr* an association of people for carrying on a commercial or industrial enterprise **b** those members of a partnership firm whose names do not appear in the firm name ⟨*John Smith and* Company⟩ [ME *companie*, fr OF *compagnie*, fr *compain* companion, fr LL *companio*]

,company 'officer *n* an army officer of the rank of second lieutenant, lieutenant, or captain

,company 'secretary *n* a senior officer of a company who typically supervises its financial and legal aspects

comparable /'komp(ə)rəbl/ *adj* **1** capable of or suitable for comparison **2** approximately equivalent; similar ⟨*fabrics of ~ quality*⟩ – **comparableness** *n*, **comparably** *adv*, **comparability** /-rə'biləti/ *n*

[1]**comparative** /kəm'parətiv/ *adj* **1** of or constituting the degree of grammatical comparison expressing increase in quality, quantity, or relation **2** considered as if in comparison to sthg else as a standard; relative ⟨*a ~ stranger*⟩ **3** characterized by the systematic comparison of phenomena ⟨*~ anatomy*⟩ – **comparatively** *adv*, **comparativeness** *n*

[2]**comparative** *n* the comparative degree or form in a language

comparator /kəm'parətə/ *n* a device for comparing sthg with a similar thing or with a standard measure

[1]**compare** /kəm'peə/ *vt* **1** to represent as similar; liken **2** to examine the character or qualities of, esp in order to discover resemblances or differences **3** to inflect or modify (an adjective or adverb) according to the degrees of comparison ~ *vi* **1** to bear being compared ⟨*it just doesn't ~*⟩ **2** to be equal or alike – + *with* [ME *comparen*, fr MF *comparer*, fr L *comparare* to couple, compare, fr *compar* like, fr *com-* + *par* equal]

[2]**compare** *n* COMPARISON 1b ⟨*beauty beyond ~*⟩

comparison /kəm'paris(ə)n/ *n* **1a** the representing of one thing or person as similar to or like another **b** an examination of 2 or more items to establish similarities and dissimilarities **2** identity or similarity of features ⟨*several points of ~ between the 2 authors*⟩ **3** the modification of an adjective or adverb to denote different levels of quality, quantity, or relation [ME, fr MF *comparaison*, fr L *comparation-*, *comparatio*, fr *comparatus*, pp of *comparare*]

compartment /kəm'pahtmənt/ *n* **1** any of the parts into which an enclosed space is divided **2** a separate division or section [MF *compartiment*, fr It *compartimento*, fr *compartire* to mark out into parts, fr LL *compartiri* to share out, fr L *com-* + *partiri* to share, fr *part-*, *pars* part, share] – **compartment** *vt*, **compartmental** /,kompaht'mentl/ *adj*

compartmental·ize, -ise /,kompaht'ment(ə)l,iez/ *vt* to separate into isolated compartments; *also* to keep in isolated categories ⟨*~d knowledge*⟩ – **compartmentalization** /-'zaysh(ə)n/ *n*

[1]**compass** /'kumpəs/ *vt* **1** to devise or contrive often with craft or skill; plot **2a** to encompass **b** to travel entirely round ⟨*~ the earth*⟩ **3** to achieve; BRING ABOUT **4** to comprehend ***USE*** fml [ME *compassen*, fr OF *compasser* to measure, fr (assumed) VL *compassare* to pace off, fr L *com-* + *passus* pace] – **compassable** *adj*

[2]**compass** *n* **1a** a boundary, circumference ⟨*within the ~ of the city walls*⟩ **b** range, scope ⟨*the ~ of a voice*⟩ **2a** an instrument that indicates directions, typically by means of a freely-turning needle pointing to magnetic north **b** an instrument for drawing circles or transferring measurements that consists of 2 legs joined at 1 end by a pivot – usu pl with sing. meaning

'**compass ,card** *n* the circular card attached to the needles of a mariner's compass showing the 32 points of the compass

compassion /kəm'pash(ə)n/ *n* sympathetic consciousness of others' distress together with a desire to alleviate it [ME, fr MF or LL; MF, fr LL *compassion-*, *compassio*, fr *compassus*, pp of *compati* to sympathize, fr L *com-* + *pati* to bear, suffer – more at PATIENT] – **compassionless** *adj*

compassionate /kəm'pash(ə)nət/ *adj* **1** having or showing compassion; sympathetic **2** granted because of unusual, distressing circumstances affecting an individual – used of special privileges (e g extra leave of absence) – **compassionately** *adv*, **compassionateness** *n*

compatible /kəm'patəbl/ *adj* **1** capable of existing together in harmony **2a** being or relating to a television system in which colour transmissions may be received on unmodified black-and-white sets **b** being or relating to an audio system allowing stereo signals to be treated as mono by unmodified mono equipment [MF, fr ML *compatibilis*, lit., sympathetic, fr LL *compati*] – **compatibleness** *n*, **compatibly** *adv*, **compatibility** /-tə'biləti/ *n*

compatriot /kəm'patri·ət/ *n* a fellow countryman [F *compatriote*, fr LL *compatriota*, fr L *com-* + LL *patriota* fellow countryman – more at PATRIOT] – **compatriotic** /-tri'otik/ *adj*

compeer /'kom,piə/ *n* an equal, peer [modif of L *compar*, fr *compar*, adj, like – more at COMPARE]

compel /kəm'pel/ *vt* **-ll-** **1** to drive or force irresistibly *to* do sthg ⟨*poverty ~led him to work*⟩ **2** to cause to occur by overwhelming pressure ⟨*exhaustion of ammunition ~led their surrender*⟩ [ME *compellen*, fr MF *compellir*, fr L *compellere*, fr *com-* + *pellere* to drive – more at FELT] – **compellable** *adj*

compelling /kəm'peling/ *adj* having an irresistible power of attraction – **compellingly** *adv*

compendious /kəm'pendi·əs/ *adj* comprehensive but relatively brief – **compendiously** *adv*, **compendiousness** *n*

compendium /kəm'pendi·əm/ *n, pl* **compendiums, compendia** /-di·ə/ **1** a brief summary of a larger work or of a field of knowledge; an abstract **2** a collection of indoor games and puzzles [ML, fr L, saving, shortcut, fr *compendere* to weigh together, fr *com-* + *pendere* to weigh – more at PENDANT]

compensate /'kompənsayt/ *vt* **1** to have an equal and opposite effect to; counterbalance **2** to make amends to, esp by appropriate payment ⟨*~ a neighbour for damage to his property*⟩ ~ *vi* to supply an equivalent *for* [L *compensatus*, pp of *compensare*, fr *compensus*, pp of *compendere*] – **compensative** /-,saytiv/ *adj*, **compensator** *n*, **compensatory** /'kom pen,sayt(ə)ri, kəm'pensət(ə)ri/ *adj*

compensation /,kompen'saysh(ə)n, -pən-/ *n* **1a** increased functioning or development of one organ to compensate for a defect in another **b** the alleviation of feelings of inferiority, frustration, failure, etc in one field by increased endeavour in another **2** a recompense; *specif* payment for damage or loss – **compensational** *adj*

[1]**compere** /'kompeə/ *n, Br* the presenter of a radio or television programme, esp a light entertainment programme [F *compère*, lit., godfather, fr ML *compater*, fr L *com-* + *pater* father]

[2]**compere** *vb, Br* to act as compere (for)

compete /kəm'peet/ *vi* to strive consciously or unconsciously for an objective; *also* to be in a state of rivalry [LL *competere* to seek together, fr L, to come together, agree, be suitable, fr *com-* + *petere* to go to, seek – more at FEATHER]

competence /'kompit(ə)ns/ *also* **competency** /-si/

n **1** the quality or state of being competent **2** the innate human capacity to acquire, use, and understand language – compare PERFORMANCE 6, LANGUE **3** a sufficiency of means for the necessities and conveniences of life – fml

competent /'kompit(ə)nt/ *adj* **1a** having requisite or adequate ability ⟨*a ~ workman*⟩ **b** showing clear signs of production by a competent agent (e g a workman or writer) ⟨*a ~ novel*⟩ **2** legally qualified [ME, suitable, fr MF & L; MF, fr L *competent-, competens*, fr prp of *competere* to be suitable] – **competently** *adv*

competition /,kompə'tish(ə)n/ *n* **1** the act or process of competing; rivalry **2** a usu organized test of comparative skill, performance, etc; *also, sing or pl in constr* the others competing with one ⟨*keep ahead of the ~*⟩ **3** the competing of 2 or more parties to do business with a third party **4** competing demand by 2 or more (kinds of) organisms for some environmental resource in short supply [LL *competition-, competitio*, fr L *competitus*, pp of *competere*]

competitive /kəm'petətiv/ *adj* **1** relating to, characterized by, or based on competition; *specif, of wages and prices* at least as good as those offered by competitors **2** inclined or desiring to compete – **competitively** *adv*, **competitiveness** *n*

competitor /kəm'petitə/ *n* sby who or sthg that competes; a rival

compilation /,kompi'laysh(ə)n/ *n* sthg compiled [COMPILE + -ATION]

compile /kəm'piel/ *vt* **1** to collect into 1 work **2** to compose out of materials from other documents [ME *compilen*, fr MF *compiler*, fr L *compilare* to plunder]

compiler /kəm'pielə/ *n* a computer program that translates instructions written in a high-level symbolic language (e g Cobol) into machine code [COMPILE + [2]-ER]

complacency /kəm'plays(ə)nsi/ *also* **complacence** *n* self-satisfaction accompanied by unawareness of actual dangers or deficiencies

complacent /kəm'plays(ə)nt/ *adj* self-satisfied ⟨*a ~ smile*⟩ [L *complacent-, complacens*, prp of *complacēre* to please greatly, fr *com-* + *placēre* to please – more at PLEASE] – **complacently** *adv*

complain /kəm'playn/ *vi* **1** to express feelings of discontent ⟨~ed *about the heat*⟩ ⟨~ed *it was too hot*⟩ **2** to make a formal accusation or charge [ME *compleynen*, fr MF *complaindre*, fr (assumed) VL *complangere*, fr L *com-* + *plangere* to lament – more at PLAINT] – **complainer** *n*, **complainingly** *adv*

complainant /kəm'playnənt/ *n* one who makes a complaint; *specif* the party in a legal action or proceeding who makes a complaint

complaint /kəm'playnt/ *n* **1** an expression of discontent **2a** sthg that is the cause or subject of protest or outcry **b** a bodily ailment or disease [ME *compleynte*, fr MF *complainte*, fr OF, fr *complaindre*]

complaisant /kəm'plays(ə)nt/ *adj* **1** marked by an inclination to please or comply **2** tending to consent to others' wishes [F, fr MF, fr prp of *complaire* to gratify, acquiesce, fr L *complacēre* to please greatly] – **complaisance** *n*, **complaisantly** *adv*

[1]complement /'komplimənt/ *n* **1a** sthg that fills up or completes **b** the quantity required to make sthg complete; *specif* COMPANY 2d **c** either of 2 mutually completing parts; a counterpart **2a** an angle or arc that when added to a given angle or arc equals 90° **b** a number that when added to another number of the same sign yields zero if the significant digit farthest to the left is discarded **3** an added word or expression by which a predication is made complete (e g *president* in 'they elected him president'') **4** the protein in blood serum that in combination with antibodies causes the destruction of antigens (e g bacteria) [ME, fr L *complementum*, fr *complēre*] – **complemental** /-'mentl/ *adj*

[2]complement *vt* to be complementary to

complementary /,kompli'ment(ə)ri/ *adj* **1** serving to fill out or complete **2** mutually supplying each other's lack **3** of or constituting either of a pair of contrasting colours that produce a neutral colour when combined **4** of the precise pairing of bases between 2 strands of DNA or RNA such that the sequence of bases on one strand determines that on the other **5** *of a pair of angles* having the sum of 90° – **complementary** *n*, **complementariness** *n*, **complementarily** /-'mentrəli/ *adv*, **complementarity** /-'tarəti/ *n*

[1]complete /kəm'pleet/ *adj* **1** having all necessary parts, elements, or steps **2** whole or concluded ⟨*after 2 ~ revolutions about the sun*⟩ **3** thoroughly competent; highly proficient **4a** fully carried out; thorough ⟨*a ~ renovation*⟩ **b** total, absolute ⟨*~ silence*⟩ [ME *complet*, fr MF, fr L *completus*, fr pp of *complēre* to fill up, complete, fr *com-* + *plēre* to fill – more at [1]FULL] – **completely** *adv*, **completeness** *n*, **completive** *adj*

[2]complete *vt* **1** to bring to an end; *esp* to bring to a perfected state ⟨*~ a painting*⟩ **2a** to make whole or perfect ⟨*the church* ~s *the charm of this village*⟩ **b** to mark the end of ⟨*a rousing chorus* ~s *the show*⟩ **c** to execute, fulfil ⟨*~ a contract*⟩ – **completion** /kəm'pleesh(ə)n/ *n*

[1]complex /'kompleks/ *adj* **1a** composed of 2 or (many) more parts **b(1)** *of a word* having a bound form as 1 or both of its immediate constituents (e g *unmanly*) **(2)** *of a sentence* consisting of a main clause and 1 or more subordinate clauses **2** hard to separate, analyse, or solve **3** of or being a complex number [L *complexus*, pp of *complecti* to embrace, comprise (a multitude of objects), fr *com-* + *plectere* to braid – more at [1]PLY] – **complexly** *adv*, **complexity** /kəm'pleksəti/ *n*

[2]complex *n* **1** a whole made up of complicated or interrelated parts ⟨*a shopping ~*⟩ **2a** a group of repressed related desires and memories that usu adversely affects personality and behaviour **b** an exaggerated reaction to sthg ⟨*has a ~ about flying*⟩ – compare THING 10a

complex fraction *n* a fraction having fractions for the numerator, or the denominator, or both – compare SIMPLE FRACTION

complexion /kəm'pleksh(ə)n/ *n* **1** the appearance of the skin, esp of the face **2** overall aspect or character ⟨*that puts a different ~ on things*⟩ [ME, fr MF, fr ML *complexion-, complexio*, fr L, combination, fr *complexus*, pp] – **complexional** *adj*, **complexioned** *adj*

complex number *n* a number containing both real and imaginary parts ☞ NUMBER

compliance /kəm'plie·əns/ *n* **1** the act or process of complying (readily) with the wishes of others **2** a disposition to yield to others **3** (a measure of) the ease of overcoming a restoring force (e g a spring) – **compliant** *adj*, **compliantly** *adv*

complicate /'komplikayt/ *vt* **1** to combine, esp in an involved or inextricable manner **2** to make complex or difficult [L *complicatus*, pp of *complicare* to fold together, fr *com-* + *plicare* to fold – more at [1]PLY]

complicated /'kompli,kaytid/ *adj* **1** consisting of parts intricately combined **2** difficult to analyse, understand, or explain – **complicatedly** *adv*, **complicatedness** *n*

complication /,kompli'kaysh(ə)n/ *n* **1a** intricacy, complexity **b** an instance of making difficult, involved, or intricate **c** a complex or intricate feature or element **d** a factor or issue that occurs unexpectedly and changes existing plans, methods, or attitudes – often pl **2** a secondary disease or condition developing in the course of a primary disease

complicity /kəm'plisəti/ *n* (an instance of) association or participation (as if) in a wrongful act [F *complicité*, fr *complice* accomplice, fr LL *complic-*, *complex* partner]

[1]**compliment** /'kompliment/ *n* **1** an expression of esteem, affection, or admiration; *esp* a flattering remark **2** *pl* best wishes; regards [F, fr It *complimento*, fr Sp *cumplimiento*, fr *cumplir* to be courteous]

[2]**compliment** /'kompli,ment/ *vt* **1** to pay a compliment to **2** to present with a token of esteem

complimentary /,kompli'ment(ə)ri/ *adj* **1** expressing or containing a compliment **2** given free as a courtesy or favour ⟨~ *tickets*⟩ – **complimentarily** *adv*

compline /'komplin/ *n, often cap* the last of the canonical hours, said before retiring at night [ME *complie, compline*, fr OF *complie*, modif of LL *completa*, fr L, fem of *completus* complete]

comply /kəm'plie/ *vi* to conform or adapt one's actions to another's wishes or to a rule [It *complire*, fr Sp *cumplir* to complete, perform what is due, be courteous, fr L *complēre* to complete] – **complier** *n*

[1]**component** /kəm'pohnənt/ *n* **1** a constituent part; an ingredient **2** any of the vector terms added to form a vector sum or resultant [L *component-*, *componens*, prp of *componere* to put together – more at COMPOUND] – **componential** /,kompə'nensh(ə)l/ *adj*

[2]**component** *adj* serving or helping to constitute; constituent

comport /kəm'pawt/ *vi* to be fitting; accord ⟨*acts that ~ with ideals*⟩ ~ *vt* to behave (oneself) in a manner conformable to what is right, proper, or expected *USE* fml [MF *comporter* to bear, conduct, fr L *comportare* to bring together, fr *com-* + *portare* to carry – more at [1]FARE]

compose /kəm'pohz/ *vt* **1a** to form by putting together ⟨~ *a collage with those pictures*⟩ **b** to form the substance of; MAKE UP – chiefly passive ⟨~d *of many ingredients*⟩ **c** SET 11c **2a** to create by mental or artistic labour; produce ⟨~ *a sonnet*⟩ **b** to formulate and write (a piece of music) **3** to settle (a point of disagreement) **4** to free from agitation; calm, settle ⟨~ *oneself*⟩ ~ *vi* to practise composition [MF *composer*, fr L *componere* (perf indic *composui*) – more at COMPOUND]

composed /kəm'pohzd/ *adj* free from agitation; COLLECTED 1 – **composedly** /-zidli/ *adv*, **composedness** /-zidnis/ *n*

composer /kəm'pohzə/ *n* a person who writes music [COMPOSE + [2]-ER]

com'posing ,stick /kəm'pohzing/ *n* a tray with an adjustable slide into which type is set

[1]**composite** /'kompəzit/ *adj* **1** made up of distinct parts: e g **a** *cap* of a Roman order of architecture that combines Ionic with Corinthian ☞ ARCHITECTURE **b** of or belonging to a very large family of plants, including the dandelion, daisy, and sunflower, typically having florets arranged in dense heads that resemble single flowers **2** combining the typical or essential characteristics of individuals making up a group ⟨*a ~ portrait of mystics known to the painter*⟩ [L *compositus*, pp of *componere*] – **compositely** *adv*

[2]**composite** *n* sthg composite; a compound

composition /,kompə'zish(ə)n/ *n* **1a** the act or process of composing; *specif* arrangement into proper proportion or relation and esp into artistic form **b** (the production of) an arrangement of type for printing **2** the factors or parts which go to make sthg; *also* the way in which the factors or parts make up the whole **3** an agreement by which a creditor accepts partial payment **4** a product of mixing or combining various elements or ingredients **5** an intellectual creation: e g **a** a piece of writing; *esp* a school essay **b** a written piece of music, esp of considerable size and complexity [ME *composicioun*, fr MF *composition*, fr L *composition-*, *compositio*, fr *compositus*] – **compositional** *adj*, **compositionally** *adv*

compositor /kəm'pozitə/ *n* sby who sets type

compos mentis /,kompəs 'mentis/ *adj* of sound mind, memory, and understanding [L, lit., having mastery of one's mind]

[1]**compost** /'kompost/ *n* a mixture of decayed organic matter used for fertilizing and conditioning land [MF, fr ML *compostum*, fr L, neut of *compositus*, *compostus*, pp of *componere* to put together]

[2]**compost** *vt* to convert (e g plant debris) to compost – **composter** *n*

composure /kəm'pohzhə/ *n* calmness or repose, esp of mind, bearing, or appearance

compote /'kompot/ *n* a dessert of fruit cooked in syrup and usu served cold [F, fr OF *composte*, fr L *composta*, fem of *compostus*, pp]

[1]**compound** /kəm'pownd/ *vt* **1** to put together (parts) so as to form a whole; combine ⟨~ *ingredients*⟩ **2** to form by combining parts ⟨~ *a medicine*⟩ **3a** to pay (interest) on both the accumulated interest and the principal **b** to add to; augment ⟨*to ~ an error*⟩ **4** to agree for a consideration not to prosecute (an offence) ⟨~ *a felony*⟩ ~ *vi* to become joined in a compound [ME *compounen*, fr MF *compondre*, fr L *componere*, fr *com-* + *ponere* to put – more at POSITION] – **compoundable** *adj*, **compounder** *n*

[2]**compound** /'kompownd/ *adj* **1** composed of or resulting from union of (many similar) separate elements, ingredients, or parts **2** involving or used in a combination **3** *of a sentence* having 2 or more main clauses [ME *compouned*, pp of *compounen*]

[3]**compound** /'kompownd/ *n* **1** a word consisting of components that are words, combining forms, or affixes (e g *houseboat, anthropology*) **2** sthg formed by a union of elements or parts; *specif* a distinct substance formed by combination of chemical elements in fixed proportion by weight

[4]**compound** /'kompownd/ *n* a fenced or walled-in

area containing a group of buildings, esp residences [by folk etymology fr Malay *kampong* group of buildings, village]

compound eye *n* an arthropod eye consisting of a number of separate visual units ☞ ANATOMY

,compound 'fracture *n* a bone fracture produced in such a way as to form an open wound

,compound 'interest *n* interest computed on the original principal plus accumulated interest

compound lens *n* LENS 1b ☞ CAMERA

comprehend /,kompri'hend/ *vt* **1** to grasp the nature, significance, or meaning of; understand **2** to include ⟨*the park* ~s *all of the land beyond the river*⟩ – fml [ME *comprehenden*, fr L *comprehendere*, fr *com-* + *prehendere* to grasp – more at PREHENSILE] – **comprehendible** *adj*

comprehensible /,kompri'hensəbl/ *adj* capable of being comprehended; intelligible – **comprehensibleness** *n*, **comprehensibly** *adv*, **comprehensibility** /-sə'biləti/ *n*

comprehension /,kompri'hensh(ə)n/ *n* **1a** grasping with the intellect; understanding **b** knowledge gained by comprehending **c** the capacity for understanding fully **2** a school exercise testing understanding of a passage [MF & L; MF, fr L *comprehension-, comprehensio*, fr *comprehensus*, pp of *comprehendere* to understand, comprise]

[1]**comprehensive** /,kompri'hensiv/ *adj* **1** covering completely or broadly; inclusive ⟨~ *insurance*⟩ **2** having or exhibiting wide mental grasp ⟨~ *knowledge*⟩ **3** *chiefly Br* of or being the principle of educating in 1 unified school nearly all children above the age of 11 from a given area regardless of ability ⟨~ *education*⟩ – **comprehensively** *adv*, **comprehensiveness** *n*

[2]**comprehensive** *n, Br* a comprehensive school

[1]**compress** /kəm'pres/ *vt* **1** to press or squeeze together **2** to reduce in size or volume as if by squeezing ~ *vi* to be compressed [ME *compressen*, fr LL *compressare* to press hard, fr L *compressus*, pp of *comprimere* to compress, fr *com-* + *premere* to press] – **compressible** *adj*, **compressibility** /-sə'biləti/ *n*

[2]**compress** /'kompres/ *n* a pad pressed on a body part (e g to ease the pain and swelling of a bruise) [MF *compresse*, fr *compresser* to compress, fr LL *compressare*]

compressed /kəm'prest/ *adj* **1** pressed together; reduced in size or volume (e g by pressure) **2** flattened as though subjected to compressing – **compressedly** /-'presidli, -'prestli/ *adv*

compression /kəm'presh(ə)n/ *n* **1** a compressing or being compressed **2** (the quality of) the process of compressing the fuel mixture in a cylinder of an internal-combustion engine – **compressional** *adj*

compressor /kəm'presə/ *n* sthg that compresses; *esp* a machine for compressing gases ☞ FLIGHT

comprise /kəm'priez/ *vt* **1** to include, contain **2** to be made up of **3** to make up, constitute [ME *comprisen*, fr MF *compris*, pp of *comprendre*, fr L *comprehendere*]

[1]**compromise** /'komprəmiez/ *n* **1a** the settling of differences through arbitration or through consent reached by mutual concessions **b** a settlement reached by compromise **c** sthg blending qualities of 2 different things ⟨*a* ~ *solution*⟩ **2** a concession to sthg disreputable or prejudicial ⟨*a* ~ *of principles*⟩ [ME, mutual promise to abide by an arbiter's decision, fr MF *compromis*, fr L *compromissum*, fr neut of *compromissus*, pp of *compromittere* to promise mutually, fr *com-* + *promittere* to promise – more at PROMISE]

[2]**compromise** *vt* **1** to adjust or settle by mutual concessions **2** to expose to discredit or scandal ~ *vi* to come to agreement by mutual concession – **compromiser** *n*

Comptometer /komp'tomitə/ *trademark* – used for a calculating machine

comptroller /kən'trohlə; *also* ,kom(p)'trohlə/ *n* CONTROLLER 1 [ME, alter. of *conterroller* controller] – **comptrollership** *n*

compulsion /kəm'pulsh(ə)n/ *n* **1a** compelling or being compelled **b** a force or agency that compels **2** a strong impulse to perform an irrational act [ME, fr MF or LL; MF, fr LL *compulsion-, compulsio*, fr L *compulsus*, pp of *compellere* to compel]

compulsive /kəm'pulsiv/ *adj* of, caused by, like, or suffering from a psychological compulsion or obsession – **compulsively** *adv*, **compulsiveness** *n*

compulsory /kəm'puls(ə)ri/ *adj* **1** mandatory, enforced ⟨~ *arbitration*⟩ **2** involving compulsion or obligation; coercive ⟨~ *legislation*⟩ – **compulsorily** /-s(ə)rəli/ *adv*

compunction /kəm'pungksh(ə)n/ *n* **1** anxiety arising from awareness of guilt; remorse **2** a twinge of misgiving; a scruple ⟨*cheated without* ~⟩ [ME *compunccioun*, fr MF *componction*, fr LL *compunction-, compunctio*, fr L *compunctus*, pp of *compungere* to prick hard, sting, fr *com-* + *pungere* to prick – more at PUNGENT] – **compunctious** /-'pungkshəs/ *adj*

compurgation /,kompuh'gaysh(ə)n/ *n* a method of trial abolished in 1833 by which a person could be acquitted if witnesses swore to his/her innocence and veracity [LL *compurgation-, compurgatio*, fr L *compurgatus*, pp of *compurgare* to clear completely, fr *com-* + *purgare* to purge]

compurgator /'kompuh,gaytə/ *n* one who testifies to the innocence or veracity of another

computation /,kompyoo'taysh(ə)n/ *n* **1** the use or operation of a computer **2** (a system of) calculating; *also* the amount calculated [COMPUTE + -ATION] – **computational** *adj*

compute /kəm'pyooht/ *vt* to determine, esp by mathematical means; *also* to determine or calculate by means of a computer ~ *vi* **1** to make calculation; reckon **2** to use a computer [L *computare* – more at [1]COUNT] – **computable** *adj*, **computability** /-tə'biləti/ *n*

computer /kəm'pyoohtə/ *n* a programmable electronic device that can store, retrieve, and process data 👁 [COMPUTE + [2]-ER]

computer·ize, -ise /kəm'pyoohtə,riez/ *vt* **1** to carry out, control, or conduct by means of a computer **2** to equip with computers – **computerization** /-'zaysh(ə)n/ *n*

comrade /'komrid, -rayd/ *n* **1a** an intimate friend or associate; a companion **b** a fellow soldier **2** a communist [MF *comarade* group sleeping in one room, roommate, companion, fr OSp *comarada*, fr *cámara* room, fr LL *camera, camara*; (2) fr its use as a form of address by communists] – **comradely** *adj*, **comradeliness** *n*, **comradeship** *n*

comsat /'kom,sat/ *n* an artificial satellite used for relaying radio waves (e g for intercontinental communication) [*com*munications *sat*ellite]

The diagram on the right shows the flow of information (data) within a computer system. Information or instructions can be displayed on the screen of the VDU and put into the computer (input) by typing on the keyboard. The processor takes information from the VDU and either stores it on disk or processes it as directed by a set of instructions in the computer called the program. The processor can also retrieve stored information and show it on the VDU screen, or print it on paper through the line printer (printout), or copy it to magnetic tape for library storage or despatch to another computer.
The illustration below shows what the elements of a business computer might look like.

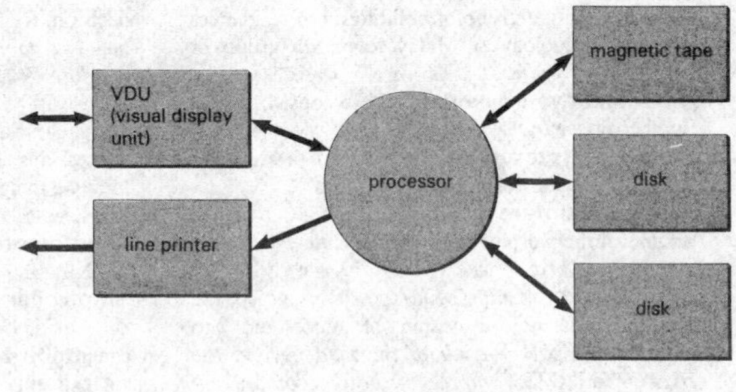

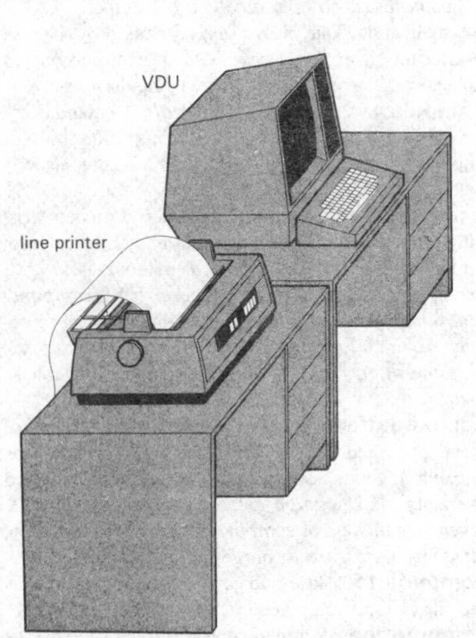

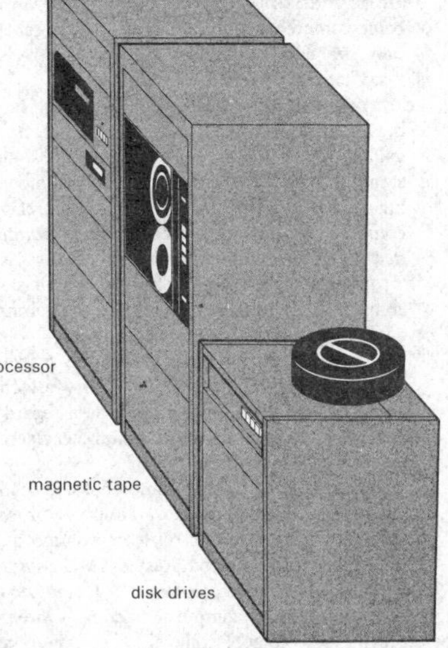

There are several ways of storing data in a form which is accessible to a computer. Magnetic tape, in the form of reel-to-reel, cassette, or cartridge, can store a comparatively large amount of information but the computer may take a long time to find the data it requires. Disks, whether rigid or floppy, have a shorter access time, and solid-state devices are quickest of all, though at present they have a limited storage capacity.

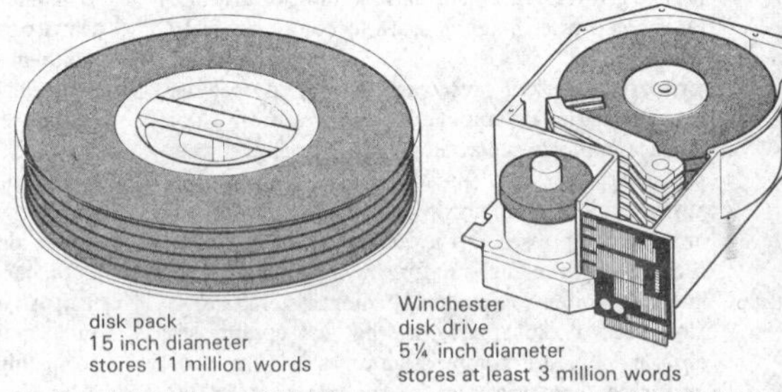

disk pack
15 inch diameter
stores 11 million words

Winchester
disk drive
5¼ inch diameter
stores at least 3 million words

TELEVISION

The microcomputer shown on the right is of the kind that might be used by a small business or home enthusiast. Floppy disks are used to store the data, and a small printer provides hard copy. The most elementary of home computers consist of a microprocessor, a TV set to act as a screen, and a cassette recorder for storage.

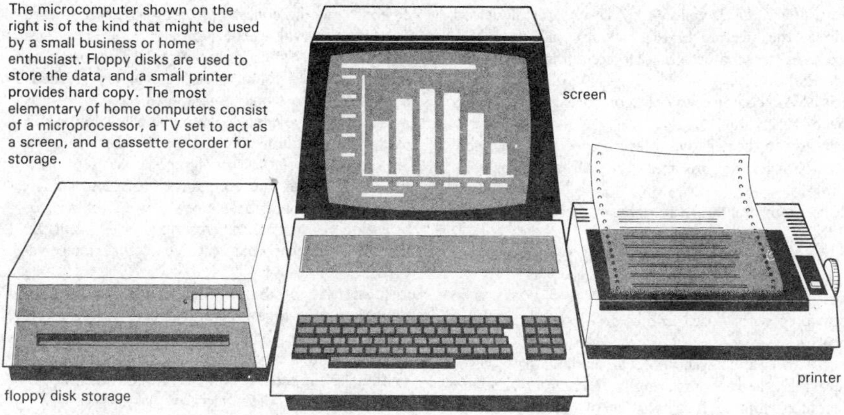

screen

printer

floppy disk storage

microprocessor

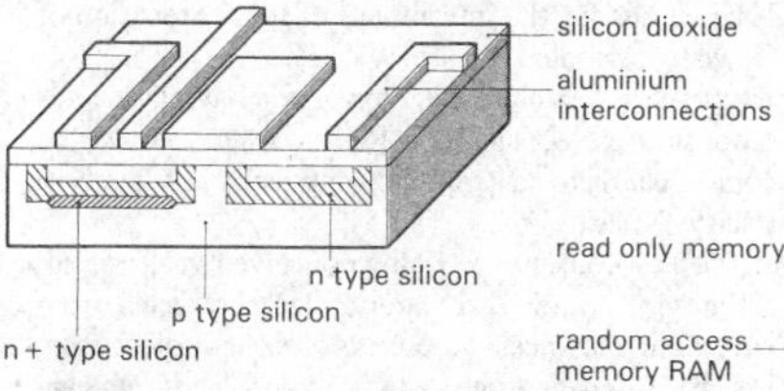

silicon dioxide

aluminium interconnections

n type silicon

p type silicon

n + type silicon

Silicon chips are made from wafers of pure silicon crystal, treated so that complete electrical circuits are formed within the solid material (solid-state). The wafer is first etched, then 'doped' with phosphorus and boron to produce n and p type silicon. Finally aluminium interconnections are laid down with more silicon dioxide. Chips may be made into data storage units (memories), processors (microprocessors), or a combination of both (the microcomputer shown here is the kind of chip used in a programmable pocket computer).

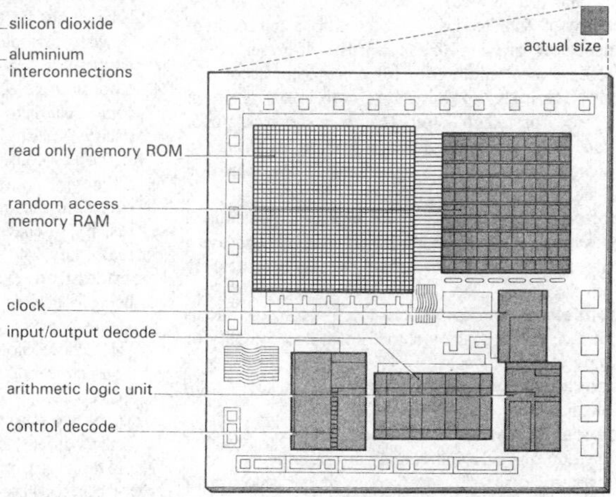

actual size

read only memory ROM

random access memory RAM

clock

input/output decode

arithmetic logic unit

control decode

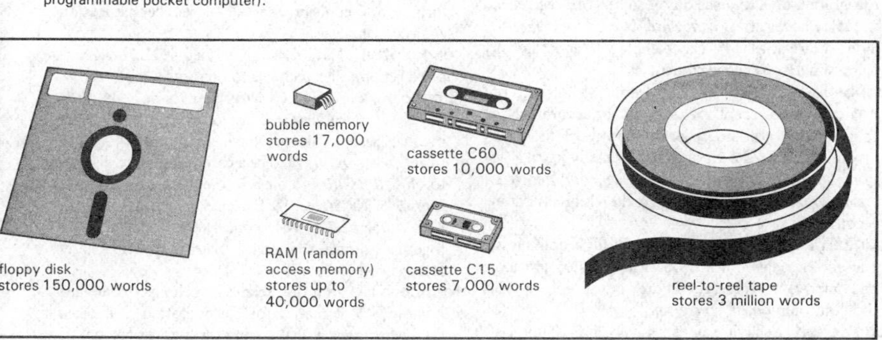

[1]**con,** *NAm chiefly* **conn** /kon/ *vt* **-nn-** to conduct or direct the steering of (e g a ship) [alter. of ME *condien* to conduct, fr MF *conduire,* fr L *conducere*]

[2]**con,** *NAm chiefly* **conn** *n* the control exercised by one who cons a ship

[3]**con** *adv* on the negative side; in opposition ⟨*so much has been written pro and* ~⟩ [ME, short for *contra*]

[4]**con** *n* (sby holding) the opposing or negative position

[5]**con** *vt* **-nn-** 1 to swindle, trick 2 to persuade, cajole *USE* slang [*confidence (trick)*] – **con** *n*

[6]**con** *n* a convict – slang

[7]**con** *prep* with – used in music ⟨~ sordini⟩ [It]

con- – see COM-

conation /koh'naysh(ə)n/ *n* an instinct, drive, wish, craving, etc to act purposefully [L *conation-, conatio* act of attempting, fr *conatus*, pp of *conari* to attempt – more at DEACON] – **conational** *adj,* **conative** /'konətiv, 'koh-/ *adj*

conatus /koh'naytəs/ *n, pl* **conatus** a natural tendency or striving (e g towards self-preservation) [NL, fr L, attempt, effort, fr *conatus*, pp]

concatenate /kon'katənayt/ *vt* to link together in a series or chain – fml [LL *concatenatus*, pp of *concatenare* to link together, fr L *com-* + *catenare* to chain, fr *catena* chain] – **concatenation** /-'naysh(ə)n/ *n*

concave /,kon'kayv, '--/ *adj* hollowed or rounded inwards like the inside of a bowl [MF, fr L *concavus,* fr *com-* + *cavus* hollow – more at [1]CAVE] – **concavely** *adv*

concavity /kon'kavəti, kən-/ *n* **1** a concave line or surface or the space included in it **2** the quality or state of being concave

concavo-concave /kon,kayvoh kon'kayv/ *adj* biconcave

concavo-convex /kon,kayvoh kon'veks/ *adj* concave on one side and convex on the other

conceal /kən'seel/ *vt* **1** to prevent disclosure or recognition of **2** to place out of sight [ME *concelen,* fr MF *conceler,* fr L *concelare,* fr *com-* + *celare* to hide – more at HELL] – **concealable** *adj,* **concealer** *n,* **concealingly** *adv,* **concealment** *n*

concede /kən'seed/ *vt* **1** to grant as a right or privilege **2a** to accept as true, valid, or accurate **b** to acknowledge grudgingly or hesitantly **3** to allow involuntarily ⟨~d *2 more goals*⟩ – chiefly journ ~ *vi* to make concession; yield [F or L; F *concéder,* fr L *concedere,* fr *com-* + *cedere* to yield – more at CEDE] – **conceder** *n*

conceit /kən'seet/ *n* **1** excessively high opinion of oneself **2a** a fanciful idea **b** an elaborate, unusual, and cleverly expressed figure of speech [ME, thought, opinion, fr *conceiven*]

con'ceited *adj* having an excessively high opinion of oneself – **conceitedly** *adv,* **conceitedness** *n*

conceivable /kən'seevəbl/ *adj* capable of being conceived; imaginable – **conceivableness** *n,* **conceivably** *adv,* **conceivability** /-və'biləti/ *n*

conceive /kən'seev/ *vt* **1** to become pregnant with (young) **2a** to cause to originate in one's mind ⟨~ *a prejudice against him*⟩ **b** to form a conception of; evolve mentally; visualize **3** to be of the opinion – fml ~ *vi* **1** to become pregnant **2** to have a conception *of* [ME *conceiven,* fr OF *conceivre,* fr L *concipere* to take in, conceive, fr *com-* + *capere* to take – more at HEAVE] – **conceiver** *n*

[1]**concentrate** /'kons(ə)ntrayt/ *vt* **1a** to bring or direct towards a common centre or objective; focus **b** to gather into 1 body, mass, or force ⟨*power was* ~d *in a few able hands*⟩ **2a** to make less dilute **b** to express or exhibit in condensed form ⟨*the author* ~s *his message in the last paragraph*⟩ ~ *vi* **1** to draw towards or meet in a common centre **2** to gather, collect **3** to concentrate one's powers, efforts, or attention ⟨~ *on a problem*⟩ [*com-* + L *centrum* centre] – **concentrative** /-,traytiv/ *adj,* **concentrator** *n*

[2]**concentrate** *n* sthg concentrated; *esp* a feed for animals rich in digestible nutrients

concentration /,konsən'traysh(ə)n/ *n* **1** direction of attention to a single object **2** a concentrated mass or thing **3** the relative content of a (chemical) component; strength [[1]CONCENTRATE + -ION]

concentration camp *n* a camp where political prisoners, refugees, etc are confined; *esp* any of the Nazi camps for the internment or mass execution of (Jewish) prisoners during WW II

concentric /kən'sentrik, kon-/ *adj* having a common centre ⟨~ *circles*⟩ [ML *concentricus,* fr L *com-* + *centrum* centre] – **concentrically** *adv,* **concentricity** /-'trisəti/ *n*

concept /'konsept/ *n* **1** sthg conceived in the mind; a thought, notion **2** a generic idea abstracted from particular instances [L *conceptum,* neut of *conceptus,* pp] – **conceptual** /kən'septyooəl/ *adj,* **conceptually** *adv*

conception /kən'sepsh(ə)n/ *n* **1a** conceiving or being conceived **b** an embryo, foetus **2** a general idea; a concept **3** the originating of sthg in the mind [ME *concepcioun,* fr OF *conception,* fr L *conception-, conceptio,* fr *conceptus,* pp of *concipere* to take in, conceive] – **conceptional** *adj,* **conceptive** *adj*

conceptual art /kən'septyooəl/ *n* art in which the artist's intent is to convey a concept rather than create an art object

conceptual·ize, -ise /kən'septyooəliez, -choo-/ *vt* to form a concept of – **conceptualization** /-'zaysh(ə)n/ *n*

conceptus /kən'septəs/ *n* a foetus [L, one conceived, fr pp of *concipere* to conceive]

[1]**concern** /kən'suhn/ *vt* **1** to relate to; be about ⟨*the novel* ~s *3 soldiers*⟩ **2** to have an influence on; involve; *also* to be the business or affair of ⟨*the problem* ~s *us all*⟩ **3** to be a care, trouble, or distress to ⟨*his ill health* ~s *me*⟩ **4** to engage, occupy ⟨~s *himself with trivia*⟩ [ME *concernen,* fr MF & ML; MF *concerner,* fr ML *concernere,* fr LL, to sift together, mingle, fr L *com-* + *cernere* to sift – more at CERTAIN]

[2]**concern** *n* **1** sthg that relates or belongs to one ⟨*it's not my* ~⟩ **2** matter for consideration **3** marked interest or regard, usu arising through a personal tie or relationship **4** a business or manufacturing organization or establishment

con'cerned *adj* **1** anxious ⟨~ *for his safety*⟩ ⟨~ *to discover the truth*⟩ **2a** interestedly engaged ⟨~ *with books and music*⟩ **b** (culpably) involved ⟨*arrested all* ~⟩

concerning /kən'suhning/ *prep* relating to; with reference to

concert /'konsuht, -sət; *sense 2 usu* 'konsət/ *n* **1** an instance of working together; an agreement – esp in *in concert (with)* **2** a public performance of music or dancing; *esp* a performance, usu by a group of musicians, that is made up of several individual compositions [F, fr It *concerto*, fr *concertare* to negotiate, fr LL, fr L, to contend, fr *com-* + *certare* to strive, fr *certus* decided – more at CERTAIN]

concerted /kən'suhtid/ *adj* **1a** planned or done together; combined ⟨*a* ~ *effort*⟩ **b** performed in unison ⟨~ *artillery fire*⟩ **2** arranged in parts for several voices or instruments – **concertedly** *adv*, **concertedness** *n*

,concert 'grand /'konsət/ *n* a grand piano of the largest size for concerts

[1]concertina /,konsə'teenə/ *n* a small hexagonal musical instrument of the accordion family [*concert* + *-ina*]

[2]concertina *vi* **concertinaed** /-nəd/; **concertinaing** /-nə·ing/ *Br* to become compressed in the manner of a concertina being closed, esp as a result of a crash

concertino /,konchə'teenoh/ *n, pl* **concertinos** a short concerto [It, dim. of *concerto*]

concertmaster /'konsət,mahstə/ *n, chiefly NAm* LEADER 5a [G *konzertmeister*, fr *konzert* concert + *meister* master]

concerto /kən'cheətoh, -'chuh-/ *n, pl* **concerti** /-ti/, **concertos** a piece for 1 or more soloists and orchestra, usu with 3 contrasting movements [It, fr *concerto* concert]

con,certo 'grosso /'grosoh/ *n, pl* **concerti grossi** /'grosi/ a piece for a small group of solo instruments and full orchestra [It, lit., big concerto]

'concert ,pitch /'konsət/ *n* **1** a tuning standard of usu 440 Hz for A above middle C **2** a high state of fitness, tension, or readiness

concession /kən'sesh(ə)n/ *n* **1** the act or an instance of conceding **2** a grant of land, property, or a right made, esp by a government, in return for services or for a particular use **3** a reduction of demands or standards made esp to accommodate shortcomings [F or L; F, fr L *concession-, concessio*, fr *concessus*, pp of *concedere* to concede] – **concessional** *adj*, **concessionally** *adv*, **concessionary** *adj*

concessionaire /kən,seshə'neə/ *n* the owner or beneficiary of a concession [F *concessionnaire*, fr *concession*]

concessive /kən'sesiv/ *adj* denoting the yielding or admitting of a point ⟨*a* ~ *clause beginning with 'although'*⟩ – **concessively** *adv*

conch /konch, kongk/ *n, pl* **conches** /'konchiz/, **conchs** **1** (the spiral shell of) any of various large marine gastropod molluscs **2** (the plain semidome of) an apse [L *concha* mussel, mussel shell, fr Gk *konchē*; (2) It *conca* semidome, apse, fr LL *concha*, fr L]

conch-, concho- *comb form* shell ⟨*conchology*⟩ [Gk *konch-, koncho-*, fr *konchē*]

concha /'kongkə/ *n, pl* **conchae** /-ki/ sthg shell-shaped; *esp* the largest and deepest concavity of the external ear [L, shell] – **conchal** *adj*

conchoidal /kong'koydl/ *adj, esp of a crystal fracture* shaped like the smooth curved inner surface of a mussel or oyster shell [Gk *konchoeidēs* like a mussel, fr *konchē*] – **conchoidally** *adv*

conchology /kong'koləji/ *n* the branch of zoology that deals with shells – **conchologist** *n*

conchy, conchie /'konchi/ *n, chiefly Br* CONSCIENTIOUS OBJECTOR – derog [by shortening & alter.]

concierge /,konsi'eəzh/ *n* sby who is employed as doorkeeper, caretaker, etc, esp in France [F, modif of L *conservus* fellow slave, fr *com-* + *servus* slave]

conciliar /kən'sili·ə/ *adj* of or issued by a council [L *concilium* council] – **conciliarly** *adv*

conciliate /kən'sili·ayt/ *vt* **1** to reconcile **2** to appease [L *conciliatus*, pp of *conciliare* to assemble, unite, win over, fr *concilium* assembly, council – more at COUNCIL] – **conciliator** *n*, **conciliative** /-ətiv/ *adj*, **conciliatory** /-ət(ə)ri/ *adj*, **conciliation** /-'aysh(ə)n/ *n*

concinnity /kən'sinəti/ *n* neatness and elegance, esp of literary style – fml [L *concinnitas*, fr *concinnus* skilfully put together]

concise /kən'sies/ *adj* marked by brevity of expression or statement; free from all elaboration and superfluous detail [L *concisus*, fr pp of *concidere* to cut up, fr *com-* + *caedere* to cut, strike; akin to MHG *heie* mallet, Arm *xait'* to prick] – **concisely** *adv*, **conciseness** *n*

concision /kən'sizh(ə)n/ *n* conciseness [ME, fr L *concision-, concisio*, fr *concisus*, pp]

conclave /'kongklayv, 'kon-/ *n* a private meeting or secret assembly; *esp* the assembly of Roman Catholic cardinals secluded continuously while electing a pope [ME, fr MF or ML; MF, fr ML, fr L, room that can be locked up, fr *com-* + *clavis* key – more at CLAVICLE]

conclude /kən'kloohd/ *vt* **1** to bring to an end, esp in a particular way or with a particular action ⟨~ *a meeting with a prayer*⟩ **2a** to arrive at as a logically necessary inference ⟨~d *that her argument was sound*⟩ **b** to decide ⟨~d *he would wait a little longer*⟩ **c** to come to an agreement on; effect ⟨~ *a sale*⟩ ~ *vi* END 1 [ME *concluden*, fr L *concludere* to shut up, end, infer, fr *com-* + *claudere* to shut – more at [4]CLOSE]

conclusion /kən'kloohzh(ə)n/ *n* **1** a reasoned judgment; an inference; *specif* the inferred proposition of a syllogism **2a** a result, outcome **b** a final summing up (e g of an essay) **3** an act or instance of concluding [ME, fr MF, fr L *conclusion-, conclusio*, fr *conclusus*, pp of *concludere*]

conclusive /kən'kloohsiv, -ziv/ *adj* putting an end to debate or question, esp by reason of irrefutability – **conclusively** *adv*, **conclusiveness** *n*

concoct /kən'kokt/ *vt* to prepare (e g a meal, story, etc) by combining diverse ingredients [L *concoctus*, pp of *concoquere* to cook together, fr *com-* + *coquere* to cook] – **concocter** *n*, **concoctive** *adj*, **concoction** /-'koksh(ə)n/ *n*

[1]concomitant /kon'komit(ə)nt, kən-/ *adj* accompanying, esp in a subordinate or incidental way [L *concomitant-, concomitans*, prp of *concomitari* to accompany, fr *com-* + *comitari* to accompany, fr *comit-, comes* companion – more at [3]COUNT] – **concomitance** *n*, **concomitantly** *adv*

[2]concomitant *n* sthg that accompanies or is collaterally connected with sthg else; an accompaniment

concord /'kongkawd, 'kon-/ *n* **1a** a state of agreement; harmony **b** a harmonious combination of simultaneously heard notes **2** a treaty, covenant **3** grammatical agreement [ME, fr OF *concorde*, fr L *concordia*, fr *concord-, concors* agreeing, fr *com-* + *cord-, cor* heart – more at HEART]

concordance /kəng'kawd(ə)ns, kən-/ *n* **1** an alphabetical index of the principal words in a book or an author's works, with their immediate contexts **2** agreement [ME, fr MF, fr ML *concordantia*, fr L *concordant-, concordans*]

concordant /kəng'kawd(ə)nt, kən-/ *adj* consonant, harmonious [ME, fr MF, fr L *concordant-, concordans*, prp of *concordare* to agree, fr *concord-, concors*] – **concordantly** *adv*

concordat /kon'kawdat, kən-/ *n* a compact, covenant; *specif* one between a pope and a sovereign or government [F, fr ML *concordatum*, fr L, neut of *concordatus*, pp of *concordare*]

concourse /'kongkaws, 'kon-/ *n* **1** a coming, gathering, or happening together ⟨*a large* ~ *of people*⟩ **2a** an open space where roads or paths meet **b** an open space or main hall (e g in a station) [ME, fr MF & L; MF *concours*, fr L *concursus*, fr *concursus*, pp of *concurrere* to run together – more at CONCUR]

concrescence /kəng'kres(ə)ns, kən-/ *n* a growing together; a coalescence [L *concrescentia*, fr *concrescent-, concrescens*, prp of *concrescere*] – **concrescent** *adj*

[1]**concrete** /'kongkreet, 'kon-/ *adj* **1** *of a noun* naming a thing rather than a quality, state, or action **2a** characterized by or belonging to immediate experience of actual things or events **b** specific, particular ⟨~ *proposals*⟩ **c** real, tangible ⟨~ *evidence*⟩ **3** relating to or made of concrete [ME, coalesced, fr L *concretus*, fr pp of *concrescere* to grow together, fr *com-* + *crescere* to grow – more at CRESCENT] – **concretely** *adv*, **concreteness** *n*

[2]**concrete** *n* a hard strong building material made by mixing a cementing material (e g portland cement) and a mineral aggregate (e g sand and gravel) with sufficient water to cause the cement to set and bind the entire mass

[3]**concrete** /kəng'kreet, kən-; *sense 2 usu* 'kongkreet, 'kon-/ *vt* **1** to form into a solid mass; solidify **2** to cover with, form of, or set in concrete ~ *vi* to become concreted

'concrete ,music /'kongkreet, 'kon-/ *n* MUSIQUE CONCRÈTE

'concrete ,poetry *n* poetry whose effect depends partly on its typographical arrangement

concretion /kəng'kreesh(ə)n, kən-/ *n* **1** a hard usu inorganic mass formed (abnormally) in a living body **2** a mass of deposited mineral matter in rock [[3]CONCRETE + -ION] – **concretionary** *adj*

concret·ize, -ise /'kongkree,tiez, 'kon-/ *vt* to make concrete, specific, or definite ⟨*tried to* ~ *his ideas*⟩

concubinage /'kongkyoobinij, kən'kyooh-/ *n* being or having a concubine

concubine /'kongkyoobien, 'kon-/ *n* a woman who lives with a man as his wife; MISTRESS 5; *esp* a woman who lives with a man in addition to his lawful wife or wives [ME, fr OF, fr L *concubina*, fr *com-* + *cubare* to lie – more at [2]HIP]

concupiscence /kəng'kyoohpis(ə)ns, kən-/ *n* strong desire; *esp* lust [ME, fr MF, fr LL *concupiscentia*, fr L *concupiscent-, concupiscens*, prp of *concupiscere* to desire ardently, fr *com-* + *cupere* to desire] – **concupiscent** *adj*

concur /kən'kuh/ *vi* **-rr-** **1** to happen together; coincide **2** to act together to a common end or single effect **3** to express agreement ⟨~ *with an opinion*⟩ [ME *concurren*, fr L *concurrere*, fr *com-* + *currere* to run]

concurrence /kən'kurəns/ *n* **1a** agreement or union in action **b(1)** agreement in opinion or design **(2)** consent **2** a coming together; a conjunction

concurrent /kən'kurənt/ *adj* **1a** meeting or intersecting in a point **b** running parallel **2** operating or occurring at the same time [ME, fr MF & L; MF, fr L *concurrent-, concurrens*, prp of *concurrere*] – **concurrent** *n*, **concurrently** *adv*

concuss /kən'kus/ *vt* to affect with concussion [L *concussus*, pp]

concussion /kən'kush(ə)n/ *n* **1** a hard blow or collision **2** (a jarring injury to the brain often resulting in unconsciousness caused by) a stunning or shattering effect from a hard blow [MF or L; MF, fr L *concussion-, concussio*, fr *concussus*, pp of *concutere* to shake violently, fr *com-* + *quatere* to shake] – **concussive** /-siv/ *adj*, **concussively** *adv*

condemn /kən'dem/ *vt* **1** to declare to be utterly reprehensible, wrong, or evil, usu after considering evidence **2a** to prescribe punishment for; *specif* to sentence to death **b** to sentence, doom **3** to declare unfit for use or consumption **4** to declare (e g contraband) convertible to public use [ME *condemnen*, fr OF *condemner*, fr L *condemnare*, fr *com-* + *damnare* to condemn – more at DAMN] – **condemnable** /kən'deməbl, -'demnəbl/ *adj*, **condemnatory** *adj*

condemnation /,kondəm'naysh(ə)n, -dem-/ *n* **1** censure, blame **2** the act of judicially convicting **3** the state of being condemned

con'demned ,cell *n* a prison cell for people condemned to death

condensate /kən'densayt/ *n* a (liquid) product of condensation

condensation /,kondən'saysh(ə)n, -den-/ *n* **1a** chemical combination between molecules with elimination of a simple molecule (e g water) to form a new, more complex compound **b** a change to a denser form (e g from vapour to liquid) **2** a product of condensing; *specif* an abridgment of a literary work [CONDENSE + -ATION] – **condensational** *adj*

condense /kən'dens/ *vt* to make denser or more compact; *esp* to subject to condensation ~ *vi* to undergo condensation [ME *condensen*, fr MF *condenser*, fr L *condensare*, fr *com-* + *densare* to make dense, fr *densus* dense] – **condensable** *adj*

condenser /kən'densə/ *n* **1a** a lens or mirror used to concentrate light on an object **b** an apparatus for condensing gas or vapour **2** a capacitor – now used chiefly in the motor trade [CONDENSE + [2]-ER]

condescend /,kondi'send/ *vi* to waive the privileges of rank ⟨~ed *to eat with subordinates*⟩; *broadly* to descend to less formal or dignified action or speech [ME *condescenden*, fr MF *condescendre*, fr LL *condescendere*, fr L *com-* + *descendere* to descend]

condescending /,kondi'sending/ *adj* showing or characterized by condescension; patronizing – **condescendingly** *adv*

condescension /,kondi'sensh(ə)n/ *n* **1** voluntary descent from one's rank or dignity in relations with an inferior **2** a patronizing attitude [LL *condescension-, condescensio*, fr *condescensus*, pp of *condescendere*]

condign /kən'dien/ *adj* deserved, appropriate ⟨~ *punishment*⟩ – fml [ME *condigne*, fr MF, fr L *condignus* very worthy, fr *com-* + *dignus* worthy – more at DECENT] – **condignly** *adv*

condiment /'kondimənt/ *n* sthg used to enhance the flavour of food; *esp* seasoning [ME, fr MF, fr L *condimentum*, fr *condire* to pickle, fr *condere* to build, store up, fr *com-* + *-dere* to put – more at [1]DO]

[1]**condition** /kən'dish(ə)n/ *n* **1** sthg essential to the appearance or occurrence of sthg else; a prerequisite ⟨*one of the necessary* ~s *for producing a pure chemical acid is clean apparatus*⟩ **2** a protasis **3** a favourable or unfavourable state of sthg ⟨*delayed by the* ~ *of the road*⟩ **4a** a state of being **b** social status; rank **c** a usu defective state of health or appearance ⟨*a heart* ~⟩ **d** a state of physical fitness or readiness for use ⟨*the car was in good* ~⟩ ⟨*exercising to get into* ~⟩ **e** *pl* attendant circumstances ⟨*under present* ~s⟩ [ME *condicion*, fr MF, fr L *condicion-*, *condicio* terms of agreement, condition, fr *condicere* to agree, fr *com-* + *dicere* to say, determine – more at DICTION]

[2]**condition** *vt* **1** to put into a proper or desired state for work or use **2** to give a certain condition to **3a** to adapt to a surrounding culture **b** to modify so that an act or response previously associated with one stimulus becomes associated with another – **conditionable** *adj*, **conditioner** *n*

conditional /kən'dish(ə)nl/ *adj* **1** subject to, implying, or dependent on a condition ⟨*a* ~ *promise*⟩ **2** expressing, containing, or implying a supposition ⟨*the* ~ *clause* if he speaks⟩ **3** CONDITIONED 3 – **conditional** *n*, **conditionally** *adv*, **conditionality** /-'aləti/ *n*

conditional discharge *n* a penalty involving merely compliance with some condition, imposed by a court for a minor or technical offence – compare ABSOLUTE DISCHARGE

conditioned /kən'dish(ə)nd/ *adj* **1** CONDITIONAL 1 **2** brought or put into a specified state **3** *esp of a reflex* determined or established by conditioning

condole /kən'dohl/ *vi* to express sympathetic sorrow ⟨*we* ~ *with you in your misfortune*⟩ [LL *condolēre*, fr L *com-* + *dolēre* to feel pain; akin to Gk *daidalos* ingeniously formed] – **condolatory** *adj*

condolence /kən'dohləns/ *n* (an expression of) sympathy with another in sorrow

condom /'kondəm/ *n* a sheath, usu of rubber, worn over the penis (e g to prevent conception or venereal infection during sexual intercourse) [perh fr name of its inventor, but his identity is unknown]

condominium /,kondə'minyəm, -ni·əm/ *n* **1** (a territory under) joint sovereignty by 2 or more nations **2** *NAm* (individual ownership of) a unit in a multi-unit structure (e g a block of flats) [NL, fr L *com-* + *dominium* domain]

condone /kən'dohn/ *vt* to pardon or overlook voluntarily; tacitly accept; *esp* to treat as if harmless or of no importance ⟨~ *corruption in politics*⟩ [L *condonare* to forgive, fr *com-* + *donare* to give – more at DONATION] – **condoner** *n*, **condonable** *adj*, **condonation** /,kondə'naysh(ə)n, -doh-/ *n*

condor /'kondaw/ *n* a very large vulture of the high Andes with bare head and neck [Sp *cóndor*, fr Quechua *kúntur*]

condottiere /,kondo'tyeəri/ *n*, *pl* **condottieri** /~/ a (leading) member of a band of mercenaries in Europe between the 14th and 16th c [It]

conduce /kən'dyoohs/ *vi* to lead or tend *to* a particular and usu desirable result; contribute [ME *conducen* to conduct, fr L *conducere* to conduct, conduce, fr *com-* + *ducere* to lead – more at [1]TOW] – **conducive** *adj*

[1]**conduct** /'kondukt/ *n* **1** the act, manner, or process of carrying on; management **2** a mode or standard of personal behaviour, esp as based on moral principles [alter. of ME *conduit*, fr OF, act of leading, escort, fr ML *conductus*, fr L *conductus*, pp of *conducere*]

[2]**conduct** /kən'dukt/ *vt* **1** to bring (as if) by leading; guide ⟨~ *tourists through a museum*⟩ **2** to carry on or out, usu from a position of command or control ⟨~ *a siege*⟩ ⟨~ *an experiment*⟩ **3a** to convey in a channel, pipe, etc **b** to act as a medium for transmitting (e g heat or light) **4** to behave in a specified manner ⟨~ed *himself appallingly*⟩ **5** to direct the performance or execution of (e g a musical work or group of musicians) ~ *vi* **1** to act as leader or director, esp of an orchestra **2** to have the property of transmitting heat, sound, electricity, etc – **conductible** *adj*, **conductive** *adj*, **conductibility** /-tə'biləti/ *n*

conductance /kən'dukt(ə)ns/ *n* **1** conducting power **2** the readiness with which a conductor transmits an electric current

conduction /kən'duksh(ə)n/ *n* **1** the act of conducting or conveying **2** transmission through or by means of a conductor **3** the transmission of an electrical impulse through (nerve) tissue

conductivity /,konduk'tivəti/ *n* the quality or power of conducting or transmitting

conductor /kən'duktə/ *n* **1** a collector of fares on a public conveyance, esp a bus **2** one who directs the performance of musicians **3** a substance or body capable of transmitting electricity, heat, sound, etc **4** *chiefly NAm* GUARD 6 [[2]CONDUCT + [1]-OR] – **conductorial** /,konduk'tawri·əl/ *adj*

con'ductor ,rail *n* a rail for conducting current to an electric locomotive or train

conductress /kən'duktris/ *n* a female bus conductor

conduit /'kondit, 'kondwit, 'kondyoo·it/ *n* **1** a channel through which sthg (e g a fluid) is conveyed **2** a pipe, tube, or tile for protecting electric wires or cables [ME, fr MF, lit., act of leading]

condyle /'kondil/ *n* a prominence of a bone forming part of a joint [F & L; F, fr L *condylus* knuckle, fr Gk *kondylos*] – **condylar** /-lə/ *adj*, **condyloid** /-loyd/ *adj*

condyloma /,kondi'lohmə/ *n* a warty growth on the skin or mucous membrane, usu near the anus and genitals [NL, fr Gk *kondylōma*, fr *kondylos*] – **condylomatous** /-'lomətəs, -'loh-/ *adj*

[1]**cone** /kohn/ *n* **1** a mass of overlapping woody scales that, esp in trees of the pine family, are arranged on an axis and bear seeds between them; *broadly* any of several similar flower or fruit clusters **2a** a solid generated by rotating a right-angled triangle about a side other than its hypotenuse **b** a solid figure tapering evenly to a point from a circular base **3a** any of the relatively short light receptors in the retina of vertebrates that are sensitive to bright light and function in colour vision – compare ROD 3 **b** any of many somewhat conical tropical gastropod molluscs **c** the apex of a volcano ☞ GEOGRAPHY **d** a crisp cone-shaped wafer for holding a portion of ice cream [MF or L; MF, fr L *conus*, fr Gk *kōnos* – more at HONE]

[2]**cone** *vt* **1** to bevel like the slanting surface of a cone **2** to mark off (e g a road) with cones

coney /'kohni/ *n* **1** a cony **2** rabbit fur [ME *conies*, pl – more at CONY]

confab /'konfab/ *vi or n* **-bb-** (to have) a chat or discussion – infml [short for *confabulate, confabulation*]

confabulate /kən'fabyoolayt/ *vi* **1** to chat **2** to hold a discussion *USE* humor [L *confabulatus*, pp of *confabulari*, fr *com-* + *fabulari* to talk, fr *fabula* story – more at FABLE] – **confabulatory** /-lət(ə)ri/ *adj*, **confabulation** /-'laysh(ə)n/ *n*

confection /kən'feksh(ə)n/ *n* a fancy or rich dish (e g a cream cake or preserve) or sweetmeat [ME *confeccioun*, fr MF *confection*, fr LL *confection-, confectio*, fr L, preparation, fr *confectus*, pp of *conficere* to prepare – more at COMFIT] – **confectionary** *adj*

confectioner /kən'fekshənə/ *n* a manufacturer of or dealer in confectionery

confectionery /kən'fekshənri/ *n* **1** confections, sweets **2** the confectioner's art or business **3** a confectioner's shop

confederacy /kən'fed(ə)rəsi/ *n* **1** a league or compact for mutual support or common action; an alliance **2** an unlawful association; a conspiracy **3** a league or alliance for common action; *esp, cap* the 11 states withdrawing from the USA in 1860 and 1861 – **confederal** *adj*, **confederalist** *n*

[1]**confederate** /kən'fed(ə)rət/ *adj* **1** united in a league; allied **2** *cap* of or relating to the Confederacy [ME *confederat*, fr LL *confoederatus*, pp of *confoederare* to unite by a league, fr L *com-* + *foeder-, foedus* compact – more at FEDERAL]

[2]**confederate** *n* **1** an ally, accomplice **2** *cap* an adherent of the Confederacy

[3]**confederate** /kən'fedə,rayt/ *vt* to unite in a confederacy ~ *vi* to band together – **confederative** /-rətiv/ *adj*

confederation /kən,fedə'raysh(ə)n/ *n* a league [[3]CONFEDERATE + -ION]

confer /kən'fuh/ *vb* **-rr-** *vt* to bestow (as if) from a position of superiority ~ *vi* to come together to compare views or take counsel; consult [L *conferre* to bring together, fr *com-* + *ferre* to carry – more at [2]BEAR] – **conferrable** *adj*, **conferral** *n*, **conferrer** *n*, **conferee** /,konfə'ree/ *n*

conference /'konf(ə)rəns/ *n* **1a** a usu formal interchange of views; a consultation **b** a meeting of 2 or more people for the discussion of matters of common concern **2** a representative assembly or administrative organization of a denomination, organization, association, etc – **conferential** /,konfə'rensh(ə)l/ *adj*

confess /kən'fes/ *vt* **1** to make known (e g sthg wrong or damaging to oneself); admit **2a** to acknowledge (sin) to God or a priest **b** to receive the confession of (a penitent) **3** to declare faith in or adherence to ~ *vi* **1a** to acknowledge one's sins or the state of one's conscience to God or a priest **b** to hear a confession **2** to admit [ME *confessen*, fr MF *confesser*, fr OF, fr *confes* having confessed, fr L *confessus*, pp of *confitēri* to confess, fr *com-* + *fatēri* to confess; akin to L *fari* to speak – more at [1]BAN] – **confessable** *adj*, **confessor** *n*

confessedly /kən'fesidli/ *adv* by confession; admittedly

confession /kən'fesh(ə)n/ *n* **1** a disclosure of one's sins **2** a statement of what is confessed: e g **a** a written acknowledgment of guilt by a party accused of an offence **b** a formal statement of religious beliefs **3** an organized religious body having a common creed – **confessional** *adj*, **confessionalism** *n*, **confessionalist** *n*, **confessionally** *adv*

confessional /kən'fesh(ə)nl/ *n* **1** a place where a priest hears confessions **2** *the* practice of confessing to a priest

confetti /kən'feti/ *n* small bits of brightly coloured paper meant to be thrown (e g at weddings) [It, pl of *confetto* sweetmeat, fr ML *confectum*, fr L, neut of *confectus*, pp of *conficere* to prepare]

confidant, *fem* **confidante** /'konfi,dant, ,- -'-/ *n* one to whom secrets are entrusted; *esp* an intimate [F *confident* (fem *confidente*), fr It *confidente*, fr *confidente* confident, trustworthy, fr L *confident-, confidens*]

confide /kən'fied/ *vi* to show confidence *in* by imparting secrets ~ *vt* to tell confidentially [ME *confiden*, fr MF or L; MF *confider*, fr L *confidere*, fr *com-* + *fidere* to trust – more at BIDE]

confidence /'konfid(ə)ns/ *n* **1** faith, trust ⟨*their* ~ *in God's mercy*⟩ **2** a feeling or consciousness of one's powers being sufficient, or of reliance on one's circumstances **3** the quality or state of being certain ⟨*they had every* ~ *of success*⟩ **4a** a relationship of trust or intimacy ⟨*took his friend into his* ~⟩ **b** reliance on another's discretion ⟨*their story was told in strictest* ~⟩ **c** legislative support ⟨*vote of* ~⟩ **5** sthg said in confidence; a secret

'**confidence ,man** *n* a conman

'**confidence ,trick** *n* a swindle performed by a person who pretends to be sthg that he/she is not

confident /'konfid(ə)nt/ *adj* **1** characterized by assurance; *esp* self-reliant **2** full of conviction; certain [L *confident-, confidens*, fr prp of *confidere*] – **confidently** *adv*

confidential /,konfi'densh(ə)l/ *adj* **1** private, secret **2** marked by intimacy or willingness to confide ⟨*a* ~ *tone*⟩ – **confidentially** *adv*, **confidentialness** *n*, **confidentiality** /-shi'aləti/ *n*

configuration /kən,figoo'raysh(ə)n, -,figyoo-/ *n* **1a** (relative) arrangement of parts **b** sthg (e g a figure, contour, pattern, or apparatus) produced by such arrangement **c** the relative positions in space of the atoms in a chemical compound **2** a gestalt ⟨*personality* ~⟩ [LL *configuration-, configuratio* similar formation, fr L *configuratus*, pp of *configurare* to form from or after, fr *com-* + *figurare* to form, fr *figura* figure] – **configurational** *adj*, **configurationally** *adv*, **configurative** /-'fig(y)oorətiv/ *adj*

[1]**confine** /kən'fien/ *vt* **1** to keep within limits; restrict **2a** to shut up; imprison **b** to keep indoors or in bed, esp just before childbirth ⟨*she was* ~d *2 days before the baby was due*⟩ – usu passive – **confiner** *n*

[2]**confine** /'konfien/ *n* **1** bounds, borders **2** outlying parts; limits *USE* usu pl with sing. meaning [MF or L; MF *confines*, pl, fr L *confine* border, fr neut of *confinis* adjacent, fr *com-* + *finis* end]

confined /kən'fiend/ *adj* **1** kept within confines **2** restricted to quarters; *esp* undergoing childbirth

con'finement /-mənt/ *n* confining or being confined, esp in childbirth

confirm /kən'fuhm/ *vt* **1** to make firm or firmer; strengthen **2** to give approval to; ratify ⟨~ *a treaty*⟩ **3** to administer the rite of confirmation to **4** to make certain of; remove doubt about by authoritative act or indisputable fact ⟨*I* ~ *our offer of the job*⟩ ⟨*served to* ~ *me in my suspicions*⟩ [ME *confirmen*, fr OF *confirmer*, fr L *confirmare*, fr *com-* + *firmare* to make firm, fr *firmus* firm] – **confirmable** *adj*, **confirmability** /-mə'biləti/ *n*

confirmation /,konfə'maysh(ə)n/ *n* **1** a rite admitting a person to full membership of a church **2** confirming proof; corroboration [CONFIRM + -ATION] – **confirmational** **confirmatory** /kən'fuhmət(ə)ri/ *adj*

confirmed /kən'fuhmd/ *adj* **1a** made firm; strengthened **b** being so fixed in habit as to be unlikely to change ⟨*a* ~ *bachelor*⟩ **2** having received the rite of confirmation – **confirmedly** /-midli/ *adv*, **confirmedness** /-m(i)dnis/ *n*

confiscable /kən'fiskəbl, kon-/ *adj* liable to confiscation

confiscate /'konfiskayt/ *vt* to seize (as if) by authority [L *confiscatus*, pp of *confiscare* to confiscate, fr *com-* + *fiscus* treasury – more at FISCAL] – **confiscator** *n*, **confiscation** /,konfi'skaysh(ə)n/ *n*, **confiscatory** /kon'fiskət(ə)ri, kən-/ *adj*

confiteor /kon'fiti·aw/ *n* a liturgical form of confession of sins used esp in the Roman Catholic church [ME, fr L, I confess, fr *confitēri* to confess – more at CONFESS]

conflagration /,konflə'graysh(ə)n/ *n* a (large disastrous) fire [L *conflagration-*, *conflagratio*, fr *conflagratus*, pp of *conflagrare* to burn, fr *com-* + *flagrare* to burn – more at BLACK]

conflate /kən'flayt/ *vt* to bring together; fuse ⟨~ *2 texts into 1*⟩ [L *conflatus*, pp of *conflare* to blow together, fuse, fr *com-* + *flare* to blow – more at [1]BLOW] – **conflation** /kən'flaysh(ə)n/ *n*

[1]**conflict** /'konflikt/ *n* **1** a sharp disagreement or clash (e g between divergent ideas, interests, or people) **2** (distress caused by) mental struggle resulting from incompatible impulses **3** a hostile encounter (e g a fight, battle, or war) [ME, fr L *conflictus* act of striking together, fr *conflictus*, pp of *confligere* to strike together, fr *com-* + *fligere* to strike – more at PROFLIGATE]

[2]**conflict** /kən'flikt/ *vi* to be in opposition (to another or each other); disagree – **confliction** *n*

conflicting /kən'flikting/ *adj* being in conflict or opposition; incompatible ⟨~ *reports*⟩ – **conflictingly** *adv*

confluence /'konfloo·əns/, **confluency** /-si/ *n* **1** a coming or flowing together; a meeting or gathering at 1 point **2** the (place of) union of 2 or more streams

[1]**confluent** /'konfloo·ənt/ *adj* flowing or coming together; *also* run together [L *confluent-*, *confluens*, prp of *confluere* to flow together, fr *com-* + *fluere* to flow – more at FLUID]

[2]**confluent** *n* a confluent stream

confocal /,kon'fohkl/ *adj* having the same foci ⟨~ *ellipses*⟩ ⟨~ *lenses*⟩ – **confocally** *adv*

conform /kən'fawm/ *vt* to give the same shape, outline, or contour to; bring into harmony or accord ~ *vi* **1** to be similar or identical **2** to be obedient or compliant; *esp* to adapt oneself to prevailing standards or customs [ME *conformen*, fr MF *conformer*, fr L *conformare*, fr *com-* + *formare* to form, fr *forma* form] – **conformer** *n*, **conformism** *n*, **conformist** *n*

conformable /kən'fawməbl/ *adj* **1** corresponding in form or character; similar – usu + *to* **2** *of geological strata* following in unbroken sequence – **conformably** *adv*

conformal /kən'fawml, kon-/ *adj* leaving the size of the angle between corresponding curves unchanged; *esp, of a map* representing small areas in their true shape [LL *conformalis* having the same shape, fr L *com-* + *formalis* formal, fr *forma*]

conformation /,konfə'maysh(ə)n/ *n* **1** adaptation **2a** CONFORMITY 1 **b** the way in which sthg is formed; shape, structure [CONFORM + -ATION] – **conformational** *adj*

conformity /kən'fawməti/ *n* **1** correspondence in form, manner, or character; agreement ⟨*behaved in* ~ *with his beliefs*⟩ **2** an act or instance of conforming **3** action in accordance with a specified standard or authority; obedience ⟨~ *to social custom*⟩

confound /kən'fownd/ *vt* **1** to put to shame; discomfit ⟨*a performance that* ~ed *his critics*⟩ **2** to refute ⟨*sought to* ~ *his arguments*⟩ **3** to damn – used as a mild interjection of annoyance ⟨~ *him!*⟩ **4** to throw into confusion or perplexity **5** to increase the confusion of ⟨*confusion worse* ~ed – John Milton⟩ [ME *confounden*, fr OF *confondre*, fr L *confundere* to pour together, confuse, fr *com-* + *fundere* to pour – more at [4]FOUND] – **confounder** *n*

con'founded *adj* damned ⟨*that* ~ *cat!*⟩ – **confoundedly** *adv*

confraternity /,konfrə'tuhnəti/ *n* a society devoted to a religious or charitable cause [ME *confraternite*, fr MF *confraternité*, fr ML *confraternitat-*, *confraternitas*, fr *confrater* fellow, brother, fr L *com-* + *frater* brother – more at BROTHER]

confront /kən'frunt/ *vt* **1** to face, esp in challenge; oppose **2a** to cause to meet; bring face to face *with* ⟨~ *a reader with statistics*⟩ **b** to be faced with ⟨*the problems that one* ~s *are enormous*⟩ [MF *confronter* to border on, confront, fr ML *confrontare* to bound, fr L *com-* + *front-*, *frons* forehead, front – more at BRINK] – **confronter** *n*

confrontation /,konfrən'taysh(ə)n/ *n* **1** a face-to-face meeting **2** (an instance of) the clashing of forces or ideas; a conflict ⟨*sit-ins*, ~s *and riot* – *Power & Authority in British Universities*⟩ [CONFRONT + -ATION] – **confrontational** *adj*, **confrontationism** *n*, **confrontationist** *n*

Confucian /kən'fyoohsh(ə)n/ *adj* of the Chinese philosopher Confucius †479 BC or his teachings or followers – **Confucian** *n*, **Confucianism** *n*

confuse /kən'fyoohz/ *vt* **1a** to make embarrassed; abash **b** to disturb or muddle in mind or purpose ⟨*his question* ~d *me*⟩ **2a** to make indistinct; blur ⟨*stop* confusing *the issue*⟩ **b** to mix indiscriminately; jumble **c** to fail to differentiate from another often similar or related thing ⟨~ *Socialism with Communism*⟩ **3** *archaic* to bring to ruin [back-formation fr ME *confused* perplexed, fr MF *confus*, fr L *confusus*, pp of *confundere*] – **confused** *adj*, **confusedly** /-zidli/ *adv*, **confusing** *adj*, **confusingly** *adv*

confusion /kən'fyoohzh(ə)n/ *n* **1** an instance of confusing or being confused **2** (a) disorder, muddle

confute /kən'fyooht/ *vt* to overwhelm in argument; refute conclusively [L *confutare*, fr *com-* + *-futare* to beat – more at [1]BEAT] – **confutation** /,konfyooh'taysh(ə)n/ *n*

conga /'kong·gə/ *n* **1** a dance involving 3 steps followed by a kick and performed by a group, usu in single file **2** a tall narrow bass drum beaten with the hands [AmerSp, fr Sp, fem of *congo* of the Congo, fr *Congo*, region in Africa]

congeal /kən'jeel/ *vt* **1** to bring from a fluid to a solid state (as if) by cold; to coagulate **2** to make rigid, inflexible, or immobile ~ *vi* to become congealed [ME *congelen*, fr MF *congeler*, fr L *congelare*, fr *com-* + *gelare* to freeze – more at COLD] – **congealable** *adj*, **congealment** *n*

congelation /ˌkonji'laysh(ə)n/ *n* the process or result of congealing

congener /kən'jeenə/ *n* **1** a member of the same taxonomic genus as another plant or animal **2** sby or sthg resembling another in nature or action **3** a secondary product (e g an aldehyde or ester) retained in an alcoholic beverage and important in determining its flavour and in causing hangovers [L, of the same kind, fr *com-* + *gener-*, *genus* kind – more at KIN] – **congeneric** /ˌkonjə'nerik/ *adj*, **congenerous** /kən'jenərəs/ *adj*

congenial /kən'jeenyəl, -ni·əl/ *adj* **1** existing or associated together harmoniously – often + *with* **2** pleasant; *esp* agreeably suited to one's nature, tastes, or outlook [*com-* + *genius*] – **congenially** *adv*, **congeniality** /-ni'aləti/ *n*

congenital /kən'jenitl/ *adj* **1a** existing at or dating from birth ⟨~ *idiocy*⟩ **b** constituting an essential characteristic; inherent ⟨~ *fear of snakes*⟩ **2** being such by nature ⟨*a* ~ *liar*⟩ [L *congenitus*, fr *com-* + *genitus*, pp of *gignere* to beget – more at KIN] – **congenitally** *adv*

conger /'kong·gə/, ˌ**conger** '**eel** *n* any of various related (large) edible sea eels [ME *congre*, fr OF, fr L *congr-*, *conger*, fr Gk *gongros*; akin to ON *kökkr* ball, L *gingiva* gum]

congest /kən'jest/ *vt* **1** to cause an excessive fullness of the blood vessels of (e g an organ) **2** to clog ⟨*traffic* ~*ed the highways*⟩ [L *congestus*, pp of *congerere* to bring together, fr *com-* + *gerere* to bear – more at CAST] – **congestion** *n*, **congestive** *adj*

[1]**conglomerate** /kən'glomərət/ *adj* made up of parts from various sources or of various kinds [L *conglomeratus*, pp of *conglomerare* to roll together, fr *com-* + *glomerare* to wind into a ball, fr *glomer-*, *glomus* ball]

[2]**conglomerate** /kən'glomərayt/ *vt* to accumulate ~ *vi* to gather into a mass or coherent whole ⟨*numbers of dull people* ~d *round her* – Virginia Woolf⟩ – **conglomerator** *n*, **conglomerative** /-rətiv/ *adj*

[3]**conglomerate** /kən'glomərət/ *n* **1** a composite mixture; *specif* (a) rock composed of variously-sized rounded fragments in a cement **2** a widely diversified business company – **conglomeratic** /-'ratik/ *adj*

conglomeration /kənˌglomə'raysh(ə)n/ *n* a mixed coherent mass [[2]CONGLOMERATE + -ION]

congrats /kən'grats/ *n pl* congratulations – infml

congratulate /kən'gratyoolayt, -choo-/ *vt* to express pleasure to (a person) on account of success or good fortune [L *congratulatus*, pp of *congratulari* to wish joy, fr *com-* + *gratulari* to wish joy, fr *gratus* pleasing – more at GRACE] – **congratulator** *n*, **congratulatory** /-lət(ə)ri/ *adj*

congratulation /kənˌgratyoo'laysh(ə)n, -choo-/ *n* a congratulatory expression – usu pl with sing. meaning [CONGRATULATE + -ION]

congregate /'kong·griˌgayt/ *vb* to (cause to) gather together [ME *congregaten*, fr L *congregatus*, pp of *congregare*, fr *com-* + *greg-*, *grex* flock – more at GREGARIOUS]

congregation /ˌkong·gri'gaysh(ə)n/ *n* **1** an assembly of people; *esp* such an assembly for religious worship **2** a religious community; *esp* an organized body of believers in a particular locality [CONGREGATE + -ION]

congregational /ˌkong·gri'gaysh(ə)nl/ *adj* **1** of a congregation **2** *often cap* of (a body of) Protestant churches governed by the assembly of the local congregation – **congregationalism** *n, often cap*, **congregationalist** *n or adj, often cap*

congress /'kong·gres, -gris/ *n* **1** a formal meeting of delegates for discussion and usu action on some question **2** the supreme legislative body of a nation; *esp, cap* that of the USA **3** an association, usu made up of delegates from constituent organizations **4** the act or action of coming together and meeting – fml [L *congressus*, fr *congressus*, pp of *congredi* to come together, fr *com-* + *gradi* to go – more at GRADE] – **congressional** /kən'gresh(ə)nl/ *adj*, **congressionally** *adv*

congressman /'kong·gresmən, -gris-/, *fem* '**congress,woman** *n* a member of a congress

congruence /'kong·grooəns/, **congruency** /-si/ *n* the quality or state of agreeing or coinciding

congruent /'kong·grooənt/ *adj* **1** congruous **2** being exactly the same in size and shape ⟨~ *triangles*⟩ – compare SIMILAR 3 ☞ SYMBOL [L *congruent-*, *congruens*, prp of *congruere*] – **congruently** *adv*

congruity /kən'grooh·əti/ *n* being congruent or congruous

congruous /'kong·grooəs/ *adj* **1** in agreement, harmony, or correspondence **2** conforming to the circumstances or requirements of a situation; appropriate – fml ⟨*a* ~ *room to work in* – G B Shaw⟩ [L *congruus*, fr *congruere* to come together, agree, fr *com-* + *-gruere* (akin to Gk *zachreēs* attacking violently)] – **congruously** *adv*, **congruousness** *n*

conic /'konik, 'kohnik/, ˌ**conic** '**section** *n* **1** a plane curve, line, or point that is the intersection of a plane and a cone **2** a curve generated by a point which moves so that the ratio of its distance from a fixed point to its distance from a fixed line is constant *USE* ☞ MATHEMATICS

conical /'konikl/, **conic** /'konik, 'kohnik/ *adj* **1** resembling a cone in shape **2** of a cone – **conically** *adv*, **conicity** /koh'nisəti/ *n*

conidiophore /koh'nidi·əfaw/ *n* a structure (on a fungal hypha) that bears conidia [NL *conidium* + ISV *-phore*] – **conidiophorous** /-ˌnidi'of(ə)rəs/ *adj*

conidium /koh'nidi·əm/ *n, pl* **conidia** /-di·ə/ an asexual spore (e g of a fungus or bacterium) [NL, fr Gk *konis* dust – more at INCINERATE] – **conidial** *adj*

conifer /'konifə, 'koh-/ *n* any of an order of mostly evergreen trees and shrubs including pines, cypresses, and yews, that bear ovules naked on the surface of scales rather than enclosed in an ovary ☞ PLANT [deriv of L *conifer* cone-bearing, fr *conus* cone + *-fer*] – **coniferous** /-'nif(ə)rəs/ *adj*

coniine /'kohni·een, -in, 'kohˌneen/ *n* an alkaloid that is the principal poison in hemlock [G *koniin*, fr LL *conium*]

conjectural /kən'jekch(ə)rəl/ *adj* of the nature of or involving or based on conjecture – **conjecturally** *adv*

[1]**conjecture** /kən'jekchə/ *n* **1** the drawing of conclusions from inadequate evidence **2** a conclusion

reached by surmise or guesswork [ME, fr MF or L; MF, fr L *conjectura*, fr *conjectus*, pp of *conicere*, lit., to throw together, fr *com-* + *jacere* to throw – more at [2]JET]

[2]**conjecture** *vt* **1** to arrive at by conjecture **2** to make conjectures as to ~ *vi* to form conjectures – **conjecturer** *n*

conjoin /kən'joyn/ *vi* to join together, esp for a common purpose [ME *conjoinen*, fr MF *conjoindre*, fr L *conjungere*, fr *com-* + *jungere* to join – more at YOKE]

conjoint /kən'joynt/ *adj* related to, made up of, or carried on by 2 or more in combination; joint, united [ME, fr MF, pp of *conjoindre*] – **conjointly** *adv*

conjugal /'konjoogl/ *adj* of the married state or married people and their relationship [MF or L; MF, fr L *conjugalis*, fr *conjug-*, *conjux* husband, wife, fr *conjungere* to join, unite in marriage] – **conjugally** *adv*, **conjugality** /-'galəti/ *n*

,conjugal 'rights *n pl* the right of sexual intercourse between husband and wife

conjugant /'konjoogənt/ *n* either of a pair of conjugating gametes or organisms

[1]**conjugate** /'konjoogət, -gayt/ *adj* **1** having features in common but opposite or inverse in some particular **2** derived from the same root ⟨~ *words*⟩ [ME *conjugat*, fr L *conjugatus*, pp of *conjugare* to unite, fr *com-* + *jugare* to join, fr *jugum* yoke – more at YOKE] – **conjugately** /-gətli/ *adv*, **conjugateness** /-gətnis/ *n*

[2]**conjugate** /'konjoogayt/ *vt* to give in prescribed order the various inflectional forms of (a verb) ~ *vi* **1** to become joined together **2** to pair and fuse in genetic conjugation

[3]**conjugate** /'konjoogət, -gayt/ *n* sthg conjugate; a product of conjugating

conjugated /'konjoo,gaytid/ *adj* formed by the combination of 2 compounds or combined with another compound ⟨*a* ~ *protein*⟩

conjugation /,konjoo'gaysh(ə)n/ *n* **1a** (a diagrammatic arrangement of) the inflectional forms of a verb **b** a class of verbs having the same type of inflectional forms **2a** fusion of (similar) gametes with union of their nuclei that in algae, fungi, etc replaces the typical fertilization of higher forms **b** the one-way transfer of DNA between bacteria in cellular contact [[2]CONJUGATE + -ION] – **conjugational** *adj*, **conjugationally** *adv*, **conjugative** /'konjoo,gaytiv/ *adj*

conjunct /kən'jungkt/ *adj* joint, united [ME, fr L *conjunctus*, pp of *conjungere*]

conjunction /kən'jungksh(ə)n/ *n* **1** joining together; being joined together **2** occurrence together in time or space; concurrence **3** the apparent meeting or passing of 2 or more celestial bodies – compare OPPOSITION 1 ☞ SYMBOL **4** a word (e g *and* or *when*) that joins together sentences, clauses, phrases, or words – **conjunctional** *adj*, **conjunctionally** *adv*

conjunctiva /kən'jungktivə/ *n*, *pl* **conjunctivas, conjunctivae** /-vi/ the mucous membrane that lines the inner surface of the eyelids and is continued over part of the eyeball [NL, fr LL, fem of *conjunctivus* conjoining, fr L *conjunctus*] – **conjunctival** /,konjungk'tievl, kən'jungktivl/ *adj*, **conjunctivitis** /-ti'vietəs/ *n*

conjunctive /kən'jung(k)tiv/ *adj* **1** connective **2** being or functioning like a conjunction – **conjunctive** *n*, **conjunctively** *adv*

conjuncture /kən'jung(k)chə/ *n* a combination of circumstances or events usu producing a crisis; a juncture

conjuration /,konjoo'raysh(ə)n/ *n* **1** the act or process of conjuring **2** a magic spell **3** a solemn appeal

conjure /'konjə, 'kun-; *vt sense 2* kən'jooə/ *vt* **1a** to summon by invocation or by uttering a spell, charm, etc **b(1)** to affect or effect (as if) by magical powers **(2)** to imagine, contrive – often + *up* ⟨*to* ~ *up imaginary dangers*⟩ **2** *archaic* to charge or entreat earnestly or solemnly ~ *vi* **1** to make use of magical powers **2** to use a conjurer's tricks [ME *conjuren*, fr OF *conjurer*, fr L *conjurare* to swear together, fr *com-* + *jurare* to swear – more at [1]JURY]

conjurer, conjuror /'konjoorə, 'kun-/ *n* one who performs tricks by sleight of hand or illusion

[1]**conk** /kongk/ *n* (a punch on) the nose – infml [prob alter. of *conch*]

[2]**conk** *vt* to hit (someone) on the head, esp the nose – infml

[3]**conk** *vi* **1** to break down; *esp* to stall ⟨*the motor suddenly* ~ed *out*⟩ **2** to faint ***USE*** usu + *out*; infml [prob imit]

conker /'kongkə/ *n* **1** *pl but sing in constr* a British game in which each player in turn swings a conker on a string to try to break one held on its string by his/her opponent **2** the large seed of the horse chestnut, esp as used in playing conkers [*conch* + [2]*-er*; fr the original use of a snail shell on a string in the game]

conman /'kon,man/ *n* one who engages in confidence tricks; a swindler

conn /kon/ *vt or n*, *NAm* [1] [2]CON

connate /'konayt/ *adj*, *of plant or animal parts* congenitally or firmly united [LL *connatus*, pp of *connasci* to be born together, fr L *com-* + *nasci* to be born – more at NATION] – **connately** *adv*

connect /kə'nekt/ *vt* **1** to join or fasten together, usu by some intervening thing **2** to place or establish in relationship ~ *vi* **1** to be or become joined ⟨*the 2 rooms* ~ *through a hallway*⟩ **2** to make a successful hit or shot [L *conectere, connectere*, fr *com-* + *nectere* to bind] – **connectable** *also* **connectible** *adj*, **connector** *also* **connecter** *n*

connected /kə'nektid/ *adj* **1** joined or linked together **2** having a social, professional, or commercial relationship – **connectedly** *adv*, **connectedness** *n*

con'necting rod /kə'nekting/ *n* a rod that transmits power from a part of a machine in reciprocating motion (e g a piston) to another that is rotating (e g a crankshaft)

connection, *chiefly Br* **connexion** /kə'neksh(ə)n/ *n* **1a** causal or logical relationship ⟨*the* ~ *between 2 ideas*⟩ **b** contextual relations or associations ⟨*in this* ~ *the word has a different meaning*⟩ **2a** sthg that connects; a link ⟨*a loose* ~ *in the wiring*⟩ **b** an arrangement that assists communication or transport; *specif* a train, aeroplane, etc that one should transfer to at a particular station, airport, etc ⟨missed their ~ at Crewe⟩ **3** a person connected with others, esp by marriage, kinship, or common interest ⟨*has powerful* ~s *in high places*⟩ **4** a social, professional, or commercial relationship: e g **a** an arrangement to execute orders or advance interests of another ⟨*a* *firm's foreign* ~s⟩ **b** a source of contraband (e g illegal drugs) **5** a religious denomination [L *connexion-, connexio,* fr *conexus,* pp of *conectere*] – **connectional** *adj* – **in connection with** with reference to; concerning

[1]**connective** /kəˈnektiv/ *adj* tending to connect – **connectively** *adv,* **connectivity** /ˌkonekˈtivəti/ *n*

[2]**connective** *n* sthg that connects; *esp* a conjunction

connective tissue *n* any of various tissues (e g bone or cartilage) that pervade, support, and bind together other tissues and organs

ˈconning ˌtower /ˈkoning/ *n* a raised observation tower and usu entrance on the deck of a submarine

conniption /kəˈnipsh(ə)n/ *n, NAm* a fit of rage, hysteria, or alarm [origin unknown]

connivance /kəˈniev(ə)ns/ *n* knowledge of and active or passive consent to wrongdoing [CONNIVE + -ANCE]

connive /kəˈniev/ *vi* **1** to pretend ignorance of or fail to take action against sthg one ought to oppose **2a** to be indulgent or in secret sympathy **b** to cooperate secretly or have a secret understanding; conspire ***USE*** often + *at* [F or L; F *conniver,* fr L *conivēre, connivēre* to close the eyes, connive, fr *com-* + *-nivēre* (akin to *nictare* to wink); akin to OE & OHG *hnīgan* to bow, L *nicere* to beckon] – **conniver** *n*

connoisseur /ˌkonəˈsuh, -ˈsooə/ *n* **1** an expert judge in matters of taste or appreciation (e g of art) **2** one who enjoys with discrimination and appreciation of subtleties ⟨*a* ~ *of fine wines*⟩ [obs F (now *connaisseur*), fr OF *connoisseor,* fr *connoistre* to know, fr L *cognoscere* – more at COGNITION] – **connoisseurship** *n*

connote /kəˈnoht/ *vt* **1** to convey in addition to exact explicit meaning ⟨*all the misery that poverty* ~s⟩ **2** to be associated with or inseparable from as a consequence or accompaniment ⟨*the remorse so often* ~d *by guilt*⟩ **3** to imply or indicate as a logically essential attribute of sthg denoted [ML *connotare,* fr L *com-* + *notare* to note] – **connotation** /ˌkonəˈtaysh(ə)n/ *n,* **connotational, connotative** /ˈkonəˌtaytiv, kəˈnohtətiv/ *adj*

connubial /kəˈnyoohbi·əl/ *adj* conjugal [L *conubialis,* fr *conubium, connubium* marriage, fr *com-* + *nubere* to marry – more at NUPTIAL] – **connubially** *adv,* **connubiality** /-biˈaləti/ *n*

conoid /ˈkohˌnoyd/, **conoidal** /kohˈnoydl/ *adj* shaped (nearly) like a cone – **conoid** *n*

conquer /ˈkongkə/ *vt* **1** to gain or acquire by force of arms; subjugate ⟨~ed *England*⟩ **2** to overcome by force of arms; vanquish ⟨~ed *Harold*⟩ **3** to gain mastery over ⟨~ed *the mountain*⟩ ⟨~ed *his fear*⟩ ~ *vi* to be victorious ⟨*we will* ~ *or die*⟩ [ME *conqueren* to acquire, conquer, fr OF *conquerre,* fr (assumed) VL *conquaerere,* fr L *conquirere* to search for, collect, fr *com-* + *quaerere* to ask, search] – **conqueror** *n*

conquest /ˈkon(g)kwest/ *n* **1** conquering **2a** sthg conquered; *esp* territory appropriated in war – often pl **b** a person who has been won over, esp by love or sexual attraction [ME, fr OF, fr (assumed) VL *conquaesitus,* alter. of L *conquisitus,* pp of *conquirere*]

conquistador /konˈk(w)istədaw/ *n, pl* **conquistadores** /-ˈdawrays, -reez/, **conquistadors** one who conquers; *specif* any of the Spanish conquerors of America [Sp, deriv of L *conquirere*]

consanguineous /ˌkonsangˈgwini·əs/ *adj* of the same blood or origin; *specif* descended from the same ancestor [L *consanguineus,* fr *com-* + *sanguin-, sanguis* blood – more at SANGUINE] – **consanguineously** *adv,* **consanguinity** /-ˈgwinəti/ *n*

conscience /ˈkonsh(ə)ns/ *n* **1** the consciousness of the moral quality of one's own conduct or intentions, together with a feeling of obligation to refrain from doing wrong **2** conformity to the dictates of conscience; conscientiousness ⟨~ *argues against it*⟩ [ME, fr OF, fr L *conscientia,* fr *conscient-, consciens,* prp of *conscire* to be conscious, be conscious of guilt, fr *com-* + *scire* to know – more at SCIENCE] – **conscienceless** *adj* – **in all conscience** by any standard of fairness

conscience clause *n* a clause in a law exempting those who object on moral or religious grounds

ˈconscience ˌmoney *n* money paid usu anonymously to relieve the conscience

conscientious /ˌkonshiˈenshəs/ *adj* **1** governed by or conforming to the dictates of conscience; scrupulous **2** meticulous or careful, esp in one's work; *also* hard-working [F *conscientieux,* fr ML *conscientiosus,* fr L *conscientia* conscience] – **conscientiously** *adv,* **conscientiousness** *n*

consciˌentious obˈjector *n* one who refuses to serve in the armed forces or bear arms, esp on moral or religious grounds – **conscientious objection** *n*

[1]**conscious** /ˈkonshəs/ *adj* **1** perceiving with a degree of controlled thought or observation **2** personally felt **3** capable of or marked by thought, will, intention, or perception **4** having mental faculties undulled by sleep, faintness, or stupor; awake **5** done or acting with critical awareness ⟨*made a* ~ *effort to avoid the same mistakes*⟩ **6** marked by awareness of or concern for sthg specified ⟨*a fashion-*conscious *shopper*⟩ [L *conscius,* fr *com-* + *scire* to know] – **consciously** *adv*

[2]**conscious** *n* CONSCIOUSNESS 3 – used in Freudian psychology

consciousness /ˈkonshəsnis/ *n* **1** concern, awareness ⟨*class* ~⟩ **2** the totality of conscious states of an individual **3** the upper level of mental life of which sby is aware, as contrasted with unconscious processes

[1]**conscript** /ˈkonskript/ *n or adj* (sby) conscripted [adj MF, fr L *conscriptus,* pp of *conscribere* to enrol, fr *com-* + *scribere* to write – more at [1]SCRIBE; n fr adj]

[2]**conscript** /kənˈskript/ *vt* to enlist compulsorily, esp for military service – **conscription** /kənˈskripsh(ə)n/ *n*

consecrate /ˈkonsikrayt/ *vt* **1** to ordain to a religious office, esp that of bishop **2a** to make or declare sacred by a solemn ceremony **b** to prepare (bread and wine used at communion) to be received as Christ's body and blood **c** to devote to a purpose with deep solemnity or dedication **3** to make inviolable or venerable ⟨*principles* ~d *by the weight of history*⟩ [ME *consecraten,* fr L *consecratus,* pp of *consecrare,* fr *com-* + *sacrare* to consecrate – more at SACRED] – **consecrator** *n,* **consecration** /-ˈkraysh(ə)n/ *n,* **consecratory** /-ˈkraytəri/ *adj*

consecutive /kənˈsekyootiv/ *adj* following one after the other in order without gaps [F *consécutif,* fr L *consecutus,* pp of *consequi* to follow – more at

CONSEQUENT] – **consecutively** *adv*, **consecutiveness** *n*

consensual /kən'sensyoo·əl/ *adj* involving or made by mutual consent [L *consensus* + E *-al*] – **consensually** *adv*

consensus /kən'sensəs/ *n* **1** general agreement; unanimity **2** the judgment arrived at by most of those concerned [L, fr *consensus*, pp of *consentire*]

[1]consent /kən'sent/ *vi* to give assent or approval; agree *to* [ME *consenten*, fr L *consentire*, fr *com-* + *sentire* to feel – more at SENSE] – **consenter** *n*, **consentingly** *adv*

[2]consent *n* compliance in or approval of what is done or proposed by another; acquiescence

consenting adult /kən'senting/ *n* an adult who consents to sexual, esp homosexual, acts

consequence /'konsikwəns/ *n* **1** sthg produced by a cause or necessarily following from a set of conditions **2** a conclusion arrived at by reasoning **3a** importance in terms of power to produce an effect; moment **b** social importance – **in consequence** as a result; consequently

consequent /'konsikwənt/ *adj* following as a result or effect [MF, fr L *consequent-*, *consequens*, prp of *consequi* to follow along, fr *com-* + *sequi* to follow – more at SUE]

consequential /,konsi'kwensh(ə)l/ *adj* **1** consequent **2** of the nature of a secondary result; indirect **3** having significant consequences; important ⟨*a grave and ~ event*⟩ – **consequentially** *adv*, **consequentialness, consequentiality** /-shi'aləti/ *n*

consequently /'konsikwəntli/ *adv* as a result; in view of the foregoing

conservancy /kən'suhv(ə)nsi/ *n* **1a** conservation **b** (an area protected by) an organization designated to conserve and protect the environment **2** *Br* a board regulating a river or port [alter. of obs *conservacy* (conservation), fr AF *conservacie*, fr ML *conservatia*, fr L *conservatus*, pp]

conservation /,konsə'vaysh(ə)n/ *n* careful preservation and protection, esp of a natural resource, the quality of the environment, or plant or animal species, to prevent exploitation, destruction, etc ☞ ENERGY [ME, fr MF, fr L *conservation-*, *conservatio*, fr *conservatus*, pp of *conservare*] – **conservational** *adj*, **conservationist** *n*

conservatism /kən'suhvətiz(ə)m/ *n* **1** (a political philosophy based on) the disposition to preserve what is established **2** *cap* the principles and policies of a Conservative party **3** the tendency to prefer an existing situation to change

[1]conservative /kən'suhvətiv/ *adj* **1a** of or being a philosophy of conservatism; traditional **b** *cap* advocating conservatism; *specif* of or constituting a British political party associated with support of established institutions and opposed to radical change **2a** moderate, cautious ⟨*a ~ estimate*⟩ **b** marked by or relating to traditional norms of taste, elegance, style, or manners ⟨*a ~ suit*⟩ – **conservatively** *adv*, **conservativeness** *n*

[2]conservative *n* **1** *cap* a supporter of a Conservative party **2** one who keeps to traditional methods or views

conservatoire /kən'suhvətwah/ *n* a school specializing in any one of the fine arts ⟨*a ~ of music*⟩ [F, fr It *conservatorio* home for foundlings, music school, fr L *conservatus*, pp]

conservator /kən'suhvətə, 'konsə,vaytə/ *n* **1** a museum official responsible for the care, restoration, etc of exhibits **2** an official charged with the protection of sthg affecting public welfare and interests – **conservatorial** /kən,suhvə'tawri·əl/ *adj*

conservatory /kən'suhvət(ə)ri/ *n* **1** a greenhouse, usu forming a room of a house, for growing or displaying ornamental plants **2** *chiefly NAm* a conservatoire

[1]conserve /kən'suhv/ *vt* **1a** to keep in a state of safety or wholeness ⟨*~ wild life*⟩ **b** to avoid wasteful or destructive use of ⟨*~ natural resources*⟩ **2** to preserve, esp with sugar **3** to maintain (mass, energy, momentum, etc) constant during a process of chemical or physical change [ME *conserven*, fr MF *conserver*, fr L *conservare*, fr *com-* + *servare* to keep, guard, observe; akin to OE *searu* armour, Av *haurvaiti* he guards] – **conserver** *n*

[2]conserve /kən'suhv, 'konsuhv/ *n* a preserve of fruit boiled with sugar that is used like jam

consider /kən'sidə/ *vt* **1** to think about with care or caution **2** to gaze on steadily or reflectively **3** to think of as specified; regard as being ⟨*~ thrift essential*⟩ ⟨*their works are well ~ed abroad*⟩ **4** to have as an opinion ⟨*~ed that he was wrong*⟩ ~ *vi* to reflect, deliberate ⟨*paused a moment to ~*⟩ [ME *consideren*, fr MF *considerer*, fr L *considerare*, lit., to observe the stars, fr *com-* + *sider-*, *sidus* star – more at SIDEREAL]

considerable /kən'sid(ə)rəbl/ *adj* **1** worth consideration; significant **2** large in extent or degree ⟨*a ~ number*⟩ – **considerably** *adv*

considerate /kən'sid(ə)rət/ *adj* marked by or given to consideration of the rights and feelings of others – **considerately** *adv*, **considerateness** *n*

consideration /kən,sidə'raysh(ə)n/ *n* **1** continuous and careful thought ⟨*after long ~*⟩ **2a** sthg considered as a basis for thought or action; a reason **b** a taking into account **3** thoughtful and sympathetic or solicitous regard **4a** a recompense, payment ⟨*for a small ~*⟩ **b** an element of inducement that distinguishes a legally binding contract from a mere promise – **in consideration of 1** in recompense or payment for **2** ON ACCOUNT OF, BECAUSE OF

con'sidered *adj* matured by extended thought ⟨*his ~ opinion*⟩

[1]considering /kən'sid(ə)ring/ *prep* taking into account ⟨*he did well ~ his limitations*⟩

[2]considering *conj* in view of the fact that ⟨*~ he was new at the job, he did quite well*⟩

consign /kən'sien/ *vt* **1** to give over to another's care **2** to give, transfer, or deliver into the hands or control of another; *also* to assign *to* sthg as a destination or end [MF *consigner*, fr L *consignare*, fr *com-* + *signum* sign, mark, seal] – **consignable** *adj*, **consignor** *n*

consignee /,konsie'nee/ *n* one to whom sthg is consigned

consignment /kən'sienmənt/ *n* sthg consigned, esp in a single shipment [CONSIGN + -MENT]

consist /kən'sist/ *vi* **1** to lie, reside *in* ⟨*liberty ~s in the absence of obstructions* – A E Housman⟩ **2** to be made up or composed *of* ⟨*breakfast ~ed of cereal, milk, and fruit*⟩ [MF & L; MF *consister*, fr L *consistere*, lit., to stand together, fr *com-* + *sistere* to take a stand; akin to L *stare* to stand – more at STAND]

consistency /kən'sist(ə)nsi/ *also* **consistence** *n* **1**

internal constancy of constitution or character; persistency **2** degree of resistance of **a** a liquid to movement ⟨*the ~ of thick syrup*⟩ **b** a soft solid to deformation ⟨*the ~ of clay*⟩ **3a** agreement or harmony of parts or features to one another or a whole; *specif* ability to be asserted together without contradiction **b** harmony of conduct or practice with past performance or stated intent ⟨*followed his own advice with ~*⟩

consistent /kən'sist(ə)nt/ *adj* **1** marked by harmonious regularity or steady continuity; free from irregularity, variation, or contradiction ⟨*a ~ style in painting*⟩ **2** converging to the true value of a statistical parameter estimated as the sample becomes large ⟨*a ~ estimator*⟩ [L *consistent-, consistens,* prp of *consistere*] – **consistently** *adv*

consistory /kən'sist(ə)ri/ *n* a church tribunal or governing body; *esp* one made up of the Pope and cardinals [ME *consistorie,* fr MF, fr ML & LL; ML *consistorium* church tribunal, fr LL, imperial council, fr L *consistere*] – **consistorial** /,konsi'stawri·əl, kən,si-/*adj*

consistory court *n* a diocesan court in the Church of England

consociation /kən,sohshi'aysh(ə)n, -si'aysh(ə)n/ *n* an ecological community with a single dominant organism [L *consociation-, consociatio* alliance, fr *consociatus,* pp of *consociare* to associate, fr *com-* + *socius* companion – more at SOCIAL] – **consociational** *adj*

consol /kən'sol, 'kon,sol/ *n* an interest-bearing government bond having no maturity date but redeemable on call – usu pl [short for *Consolidated Annuities,* British government securities]

,conso'lation ,prize /,konsə'laysh(ə)n/ *n* a prize given to one who just fails to gain a major prize in a contest

[1]console /kən'sohl/ *vt* to alleviate the grief or sense of loss of [F *consoler,* fr L *consolari,* fr *com-* + *solari* to console – more at SILLY] – **consolingly** *adv,* **consolable** *adj,* **consolation** /,konsə'laysh(ə)n/ *n,* **consolatory** /kən'solət(ə)ri/ *adj*

[2]console /'konsohl, 'konsl/ *n* **1** a carved bracket projecting from a wall to support a shelf or cornice **2** the desk containing the keyboards, stops, etc of an organ **3a** a control panel; *also* a cabinet in which a control panel is mounted **b** the part of a computer used for communication between the operator and the computer **4** a cabinet (e g for a radio or television set) designed to rest directly on the floor [F, fr MF, short for *consolateur* bracket in human shape, lit., consoler, fr L *consolator,* fr *consolatus,* pp of *consolari*]

'console ,table /'konsohl, 'konsl/ *n* a table fixed to a wall and supported by brackets

consolidate /kən'solidayt/ *vt* **1** to join together into 1 whole; unite ⟨*~ several small school districts*⟩ **2** to make firm or secure; strengthen ⟨*~ their hold on first place*⟩ **3** to form into a compact mass *~ vi* to become consolidated; *specif* to merge ⟨*the 2 companies ~*d⟩ [L *consolidatus,* pp of *consolidare* to make solid, fr *com-* + *solidus* solid] – **consolidator** *n*

consolidation /kən,soli'daysh(ə)n/ *n* uniting or being united; *esp* the unification of 2 or more companies by dissolution of existing ones and creation of a single new company – compare MERGER 2 [CONSOLIDATE + -ION]

consommé /kən'somay, ,konsə'may/ *n* a thin clear meat soup made from meat broth [F, fr pp of *consommer* to complete, boil down, fr L *consummare* to complete, fr *com-* + *summa* sum]

consonance /'kons(ə)nəns/ *n* **1a** correspondence or recurrence of sounds, esp in words; assonance **b** an agreeable combination of musical notes in harmony **2** harmony or agreement among components – fml [ME, fr MF, fr L *consonantia,* fr *consonant-, consonans*]

[1]consonant /'kons(ə)nənt/ *n* (a letter or other symbol representing) any of a class of speech sounds (e g /p/, /g/, /n/, /l/, /s/, /r/) characterized by constriction or closure at 1 or more points in the breath channel ☞ ALPHABET [ME, fr L *consonant-, consonans,* fr prp of *consonare*] – **consonantal** /,konsə'nantl/ *adj*

[2]consonant *adj* **1** marked by musical consonances **2** having similar sounds ⟨*~ words*⟩ **3** in agreement or harmony; free from elements making for discord – fml [MF, fr L *consonant-, consonans,* prp of *consonare* to sound together, agree, fr *com-* + *sonare* to sound] – **consonantly** *adv*

[1]consort /'konsawt/ *n* **1** an associate **2** a spouse – compare PRINCE CONSORT [ME, fr MF, fr L *consort-, consors,* lit., one who shares a common lot, fr *com-* + *sort-, sors* lot, share]

[2]consort *n* **1** a conjunction, association ⟨*he ruled in ~ with his father*⟩ **2a** a group of musicians performing esp early music **b** a set of musical instruments (e g viols or recorders) of the same family played together [MF *consorte,* fr *consort*]

[3]consort /kən'sawt/ *vi* **1** to keep company *with* ⟨*~*ing *with criminals*⟩ **2** to accord, harmonize *with* ⟨*the illustrations ~ admirably with the text – TLS*⟩ *USE* fml

consortium /kən'sawti.əm/ *n, pl* **consortia** /-ti·ə/ *also* **consortiums** a business or banking agreement or combination [L, fellowship, fr *consort-, consors*]

conspectus /kən'spektəs/ *n, pl* **conspectuses** a survey, summary; *esp* a brief one providing an overall view [L, fr *conspectus,* pp of *conspicere*]

conspicuous /kən'spikyoo·əs/ *adj* **1** obvious to the eye or mind **2** attracting attention; striking [L *conspicuus,* fr *conspicere* to get sight of, fr *com-* + *specere* to look – more at SPY] – **conspicuously** *adv,* **conspicuousness** *n*

conspiracy /kən'spirəsi/ *n* **1** (the offence of) conspiring together ⟨*~ to murder*⟩ **2a** an agreement among conspirators **b** *sing or pl in constr* a group of conspirators [ME *conspiracie,* fr L *conspiratus,* pp of *conspirare*]

con,spiracy of 'silence *n* an agreement to keep silent, esp in order to promote or protect selfish interests

conspirator /kən'spirətə/ *n* one who conspires; a plotter

conspiratorial /kən,spirə'tawri.əl, ,kon-/ *adj* (suggestive) of a conspiracy or conspirator – **conspiratorially** *adv*

conspire /kən'spie.ə/ *vi* **1a** to join in a plot **b** to scheme **2** to act together ⟨*circumstances ~*d *to defeat his efforts*⟩ [ME *conspiren,* fr MF *conspirer,* fr L *conspirare* to breathe together, agree, conspire, fr *com-* + *spirare* to breathe – more at SPIRIT]

constable /'konstəbl, 'kun-/ *n* **1** a high officer of a medieval royal or noble household **2** the warden or governor of a royal castle or a fortified town **3** *Br* a policeman; *specif* one ranking below sergeant [ME *conestable,* fr OF, fr LL *comes stabuli,* lit., officer of the stable]

[1]**constabulary** /kən'stabyooləri/ *n sing or pl in constr* **1** the police force of a district or country **2** an armed police force organized on military lines ⟨*the Royal Ulster* Constabulary⟩

[2]**constabulary** *adj* of a constable or constabulary

constancy /'konstənsi/ *n* **1** fidelity, loyalty **2** freedom from change

[1]**constant** /'konstənt/ *adj* **1** marked by steadfast resolution or faithfulness; exhibiting constancy of mind or attachment ⟨*his ~ friend for years*⟩ **2** invariable, uniform **3** continually occurring or recurring; regular [ME, fr MF, fr L *constant-, constans,* fr prp of *constare* to stand firm, be consistent, fr *com-* + *stare* to stand – more at STAND] – **constantly** *adv*

[2]**constant** *n* sthg invariable or unchanging: e g **a** a number that has a fixed value in a given situation or universally or that is characteristic of some substance or instrument ☞ PHYSICS **b** a number that is assumed not to change value in a given mathematical discussion **c** a term in logic with a fixed designation

constantan /'konstəntan/ *n* an alloy of copper and nickel used for electrical resistors and in thermocouples [fr the constancy of its resistance under change of temperature]

constellation /,konstə'laysh(ə)n/ *n* **1** any of many arbitrary configurations of stars supposed to fill the outlines of usu mythical figures **2** a cluster, group, or configuration; *esp* a large or impressive one [ME *constellacioun,* fr MF *constellation,* fr LL *constellation-, constellatio,* fr *constellatus* studded with stars, fr L *com-* + *stella* star – more at STAR] – **constellatory** /kən'stelət(ə)ri/ *adj*

consternation /,konstə'naysh(ə)n/ *n* amazed dismay that hinders or throws into confusion [F or L; F, fr L *consternation-, consternatio,* fr *consternatus,* pp of *consternare* to bewilder, alarm, fr *com-* + *-sternare* (akin to OE *starian* to stare)]

constipate /'konstipayt/ *vt* to cause constipation in [ML *constipatus,* pp of *constipare,* fr L, to crowd together, fr *com-* + *stipare* to press together – more at STIFF]

constipation /,konsti'paysh(ə)n/ *n* **1** abnormally delayed or infrequent passage of faeces **2** impairment or blockage of proper functioning

constituency /kən'stityoo·ənsi, -'stichoo-/ *n* (the residents in) an electoral district

[1]**constituent** /kən'stityoo·ənt, -choo-/ *n* **1** an essential part; a component **2** a resident in a constituency [F *constituant,* fr MF, fr prp of *constituer* to constitute, fr L *constituere*]

[2]**constituent** *adj* **1** serving to form, compose, or make up a unit or whole; component **2** having the power to frame or amend a constitution ⟨*a ~ assembly*⟩ [L *constituent-, constituens,* prp of *constituere*] – **constituently** *adv*

constitute /'konstityooht, -chooht/ *vt* **1** to appoint to an often specified office, function, or dignity ⟨~d *authorities*⟩ ⟨~d *himself their representative*⟩ **2** to establish; SET UP: e g **a** to establish formally **b** to give legal form to **3** to form, make, be ⟨*12 months ~ a year*⟩ ⟨*unemployment* ~s *a major problem*⟩ [L *constitutus,* pp of *constituere* to set up, constitute, fr *com-* + *statuere* to set – more at STATUTE]

constitution /,konsti'tyoohsh(ə)n/ *n* **1** the act of establishing, making, or setting up **2a** the physical and mental structure of an individual **b** the factors or parts which go to make sthg; composition; *also* the way in which these parts or factors make up the whole **3** the way in which a state or society is organized **4** (a document embodying) the fundamental principles and laws of a nation, state, or social group

[1]**constitutional** /,konsti'tyoohsh(ə)nl/ *adj* **1** relating to, inherent in, or affecting the constitution of body or mind **2** being in accordance with or authorized by the constitution of a state or society ⟨*a ~ government*⟩ **3** regulated according to a constitution ⟨*a ~ monarchy*⟩ **4** of a constitution – **constitutionalize** *vt,* **constitutionality** /-sh(ə)n'aləti/ *n*

[2]**constitutional** *n* a walk taken for one's health

,consti'tutionalism /-iz(ə)m/ *n* adherence to constitutional principles; *also* a constitutional system of government – **constitutionalist** *n*

constitutional law *n* law dealing with the powers, organization, and responsibilities of government ☞ LAW

constitutionally /,konsti'tyoohsh(ə)nl·i/ *adv* **1a** in accordance with one's mental or bodily constitution ⟨~ *unable to grasp subtleties*⟩ **b** in structure, composition, or physical constitution **2** in accordance with a constitution ⟨*was not ~ eligible to fill the office*⟩

constitutive /kən'stityootiv/ *adj* having the power to enact or establish – **constitutively** *adv*

constrain /kən'strayn/ *vt* **1** to force by imposed stricture or limitation ⟨*necessity* ~s *me to work*⟩ ⟨*the evidence* ~s *belief*⟩ **2** to force or produce in an unnatural or strained manner ⟨*a* ~ed *smile*⟩ **3** to hold within narrow confines; *also* to clasp tightly [ME *constrainen,* fr MF *constraindre,* fr L *constringere* to constrict, constrain, fr *com-* + *stringere* to draw tight – more at [2]STRAIN] – **constrainedly** /-nidli/ *adv*

constraint /kən'straynt/ *n* **1a** constraining or being constrained **b** a constraining agency or force; a check ⟨*put legal* ~s *on the board's activities*⟩ **2a** repression of one's own feelings, behaviour, or actions **b** a sense of being constrained; embarrassment [ME, fr MF *constrainte,* fr *constraindre*]

constrict /kən'strikt/ *vt* **1a** to make narrow **b** to compress, squeeze ⟨~ *a nerve*⟩ **2** to set or keep within limits [L *constrictus,* pp of *constringere*] – **constrictive** *adj,* **constriction** /kən'striksh(ə)n/ *n*

constrictor /kən'striktə/ *n* **1** a muscle that contracts a cavity or orifice or compresses an organ **2** a snake (e g a boa constrictor) that kills prey by compressing it in its coils [CONSTRICT + [1]-OR]

[1]**construct** /kən'strukt/ *vt* **1** to make or form by combining parts; build **2** to set in logical order **3** to draw (a geometrical figure) with suitable instruments and under given conditions [L *constructus,* pp of *construere,* fr *com-* + *struere* to build – more at STRUCTURE] – **constructible** *adj,* **constructor** *n*

[2]**construct** /'konstrukt/ *n* sthg constructed, esp mentally

construction /kən'struksh(ə)n/ *n* **1** the arrangement and connection of morphemes, words, or groups of words into some higher unit (e g a phrase or clause) **2** the process, art, or manner of constructing; *also* sthg constructed ☞ BUILDING **3** the act or result of construing, interpreting, or explaining – **constructional** *adj,* **constructionally** *adv*

constructive /kən'struktiv/ *adj* **1** (judicially) implied rather than explicit ⟨~ *permission*⟩ **2** of or involved in construction **3** suggesting improvement or development ⟨~ *criticism*⟩ – **constructively** *adv*, **constructiveness** *n*

constructivism /kən'strukti,viz(ə)m/ *n* a nonfigurative art movement originating in Russia about 1914 and concerned with the aesthetic effects of the juxtaposition of (geometric) forms and various kinds of surface quality (e g colour, tone, texture, etc) and the use of modern industrial materials (e g glass and plastic) – **constructivist** *adj or n*

construe /kən'strooh/ *vt* **1** to analyse the syntax of (e g a sentence or sentence part) **2** to understand or explain the sense or intention of ⟨~d *my actions as hostile*⟩ **3** to translate closely ~ *vi* to construe a sentence or sentence part, esp in connection with translating [ME *construen*, fr LL *construere*, fr L, to construct] – **construable** *adj*

consubstantial /,konsəb'stansh(ə)l/ *adj, esp of the 3 persons of the Trinity* of the same substance [LL *consubstantialis*, fr L *com-* + *substantia* substance]

consubstantiation /,konsəb,stanshi'aysh(ə)n, -si'aysh(ə)n/ *n* (the Anglican doctrine of) the actual presence and combination of the body and blood of Christ with the bread and wine used at Communion – compare TRANSUBSTANTIATION

consul /'kons(ə)l/ *n* **1a** either of 2 elected chief magistrates of the Roman republic **b** any of 3 chief magistrates of France from 1799 to 1804 **2** an official appointed by a government to reside in a foreign country to look after the (commercial) interests of citizens of the appointing country [ME, fr L, fr *consulere* to consult] – **consulship** *n*, **consular** /'konsyoolə/ *adj*

consulate /'konsyoolət/ *n* **1** a government by consuls **2** the residence, office, or jurisdiction of a consul

,consul 'general *n, pl* **consuls general** a senior diplomatic consul stationed in an important place or having jurisdiction in several places or over several consuls

consult /kən'sult/ *vt* **1** to ask the advice or opinion of ⟨~ *a doctor*⟩ **2** to refer to ⟨~ *a dictionary*⟩ ~ *vi* **1** to deliberate together; confer **2** to serve as a consultant [MF or L; MF *consulter*, fr L *consultare*, fr *consultus*, pp of *consulere* to deliberate, consult] – **consulter** *n*

consultancy /kən'sult(ə)nsi/ *n* **1** an agency that provides consulting services **2** consultation

consultant /kən'sult(ə)nt/ *n* **1** one who consults sby or sthg **2** an expert who gives professional advice or services **3** the most senior grade of British hospital doctor, usu having direct clinical responsibility for hospital patients – **consultantship** *n*

consultation /,kons(ə)l'taysh(ə)n/ *n* **1** a council, conference **2** the act of consulting or conferring

consultative /kən'sultətiv/ *adj* of or intended for consultation; advisory ⟨*a* ~ *committee*⟩

consulting /kən'sulting/ *adj* **1** providing professional or expert advice ⟨*a* ~ *architect*⟩ **2** of a (medical) consultation or consultant

consumables /kən'syoohməblz/ *n pl* food, provisions

consume /kən'syoohm/ *vt* **1** to do away with completely; destroy ⟨*fire* ~d *several buildings*⟩ **2a** to spend wastefully; squander **b** to use or use up ⟨*work* ~s *time*⟩ ⟨*furnaces* ~ *fuel*⟩ **3** to eat or drink, esp in great quantity or eagerly **4** to engage fully; engross ⟨*she was* ~d *with curiosity*⟩ ~ *vi* to waste or burn away; perish [ME *consumen*, fr MF or L; MF *consumer*, fr L *consumere*, fr *com-* + *sumere* to take up, take, fr *sub-* up + *emere* to take – more at SUB-, REDEEM] – **consumable** *adj*, **consumingly** *adv*

consumer /kən'syoohmə/ *n* **1** a customer for goods or services **2** an organism requiring complex organic compounds for food, which it obtains by preying on other organisms or by eating particles of organic matter ☞ FOOD [CONSUME + [2]-ER] – **consumership** *n*

con'sumer ,goods *n pl* goods (e g food, clothing, and domestic appliances) that are not used in further manufacturing processes

consumerism /kən'syoohmə,riz(ə)m/ *n* **1** the promotion and protection of the consumer's interests **2** the theory that an increasing consumption of goods is economically desirable – **consumerist** *n*

[1]**consummate** /kən'sumət, 'konsyoomət, -sə-, -su-/ *adj* **1** extremely skilled and accomplished ⟨*a* ~ *liar*⟩ **2** of the highest degree ⟨~ *skill*⟩ ⟨~ *cruelty*⟩ [ME, fr L *consummatus*, pp of *consummare* to sum up, finish, fr *com-* + *summa* sum] – **consummately** *adv*

[2]**consummate** /'konsyoomayt, -sə-, -su-/ *vt* to make (a marriage) complete by sexual intercourse – **consummative** /-,maytiv/ *adj*, **consummator** *n*

consummation /,konsə'maysh(ə)n, -su-, -syoo-/ *n* **1** the consummating of a marriage **2** the ultimate end; a goal [[2]CONSUMMATE + -ION]

consumption /kən'sumsh(ə)n, -'sumpsh(ə)n/ *n* **1** the act or process of consuming **2** the utilization of economic goods in the satisfaction of wants or in the process of production, resulting chiefly in their destruction, deterioration, or transformation **3** (a progressive wasting of the body, esp from) lung tuberculosis [ME *consumpcioun*, fr L *consumption-consumptio*, fr *consumptus*, pp of *consumere*]

consumptive /kən'sum(p)tiv/ *adj* of or affected with consumption (of the lungs) – **consumptive** *n*, **consumptively** *adv*

[1]**contact** /'kontakt/ *n* **1a** (an instance of) touching **b** (a part made to form) the junction of 2 electrical conductors through which a current passes **2a** association, relationship ⟨*she needs human* ~⟩ **b** connection, communication ⟨*keep in* ~!⟩ **c** the act of establishing communication with sby or observing or receiving a significant signal from a person or object ⟨*radar* ~ *with Mars*⟩ **3** one serving as a carrier or source ⟨*our* ~ *in Berlin*⟩ [F or L; F, fr L *contactus*, fr *contactus*, pp of *contingere* to have contact with – more at CONTINGENT]

[2]**contact** /'kontakt, kon'takt, kən-/ *vt* **1** to bring into contact **2a** to enter or be in contact with; join **b** to get in communication with ⟨~ *your local agent*⟩ ~ *vi* to make contact

[3]**contact** /'kontakt/ *adj* maintaining, involving, or activated or caused by contact ⟨~ *explosives*⟩

,contact ,inhi'bition *n* the cessation of movement and growth of one cell when in contact with another, observed esp in tissue cultures

'contact ,lens *n* a thin lens designed to fit over the cornea of the eye, esp for the correction of a visual defect

contact print *n* a photographic print made with a negative in contact with a photographic paper, plate, or film

contagion /kən'tayj(ə)n, -jyən/ *n* **1a** the transmission of a disease by (indirect) contact **b** (a virus, bacterium, etc that causes) a contagious disease **2** corrupting influence or contact [ME, fr MF & L; MF, fr L *contagion-, contagio,* fr *contingere* to have contact with, pollute]

contagious /kən'tayjəs, -jyəs/ *adj* **1** communicable by contact; catching **2** bearing contagion **3** exciting similar emotions or conduct in others ⟨~ *enthusiasm*⟩ – **contagiously** *adv,* **contagiousness** *n*

con,tagious a'bortion *n* brucellosis or other disease of domestic animals causing abortion

contain /kən'tayn/ *vt* **1** to keep within limits; hold back or hold down: e g **a** to restrain, control ⟨~ *yourself!*⟩ **b** to check, halt ⟨~ *the enemy's attack*⟩ **c** to follow successfully a policy of containment towards **d** to prevent (an enemy, opponent, etc) from advancing or attacking **2a** to have within; hold **b** to comprise, include ⟨*the bill* ~s *several new clauses*⟩ **3** to be divisible by, usu without a remainder [ME *conteinen,* fr OF *contenir,* fr L *continēre* to hold together, hold in, contain, fr *com-* + *tenēre* to hold – more at THIN] – **containable** *adj*

container /kən'taynə/ *n* a receptacle for the shipment of goods; *specif* a metal packing case, standardized for mechanical handling, usu forming a single lorry or rail-wagon load [CONTAIN + [2]-ER]

container·ization, -isation /kən,taynərie'zaysh(ə)n/ *n* a shipping method in which a large amount of material is packaged together in 1 large container

container·ize, -ise /kən'taynəriez/ *vt* **1** to ship by containerization **2** to convert to the use of containers ⟨*plans to* ~ *the ports*⟩

con'tainer ,ship *n* a ship for carrying cargo in containers

containment /kən'taynmənt/ *n* preventing the expansion of a hostile power or ideology [CONTAIN + -MENT]

contaminant /kən'taminənt/ *n* sthg that contaminates

contaminate /kən'taminayt/ *vt* **1a** to soil, stain, or infect by contact or association **b** to make inferior or impure by adding sthg ⟨*iron* ~d *with phosphorus*⟩ **2** to make unfit for use by the introduction of unwholesome or undesirable elements [L *contaminatus,* pp of *contaminare;* akin to L *contagio* contagion] – **contaminator** *n,* **contamination** /-'naysh(ə)n/ *n,* **contaminative** /kən'taminətiv/ *adj*

contango /kən'tang·goh/ *n, pl* **contangos** *Br* a premium paid by a buyer to a seller of shares to postpone delivery until a future day of settlement – compare BACKWARDATION [perh alter. of *continue*]

conte /konht, kawnt (*Fr* kɔ̃t)/ *n* a tale or short story, esp of adventure [F]

contemn /kən'tem/ *vt* to view or treat with contempt; scorn – fml [ME *contempnen,* fr MF *contempner,* fr L *contemnere,* fr *com-* + *temnere* to despise – more at STAMP] – **contemner** *also* **contemnor** /-nə/ *n*

contemplate /'kontəmplayt/ *vt* **1** to view or consider with continued attention; meditate on **2** to have in view as contingent or probable or as an end or intention ⟨*what do you* ~ *doing?*⟩ ~ *vi* to ponder, meditate [L *contemplatus,* pp of *contemplari,* fr *com-* + *templum* space marked out for observation of auguries – more at [1]TEMPLE] – **contemplator** *n*

contemplation /,kontəm'playsh(ə)n, -tem-/ *n* **1** meditation on spiritual things as a private devotion **2** an act of considering with attention; a study **3** the act of regarding steadily

contemplative /'kontəm,playtiv, -tem-, kən'templətiv/ *adj* **1** of or involving contemplation **2** of a religious order devoted to prayer and penance – **contemplative** *n,* **contemplatively** /-,playtivli/ *adv,* **contemplativeness** *n*

contemporaneous /kən,tempə'raynyəs, kon-, -ni·əs/ *adj* CONTEMPORARY 1 [L *contemporaneus,* fr *com-* + *tempor-, tempus* time – more at TEMPORAL] – **contemporaneously** *adv,* **contemporaneousness, contemporaneity** /kən,temp(ə)rə'nayəti, -'nee·əti/ *n*

[1]**contemporary** /kən'temp(ə)rəri, -pri/ *adj* **1** happening, existing, living, or coming into being during the same period of time **2** marked by characteristics of the present period; modern [*com-* + L *tempor-, tempus*] – **contemporarily** *adv*

[2]**contemporary** *n* sby or sthg contemporary with another; *specif* one of about the same age as another

contempt /kən'tem(p)t/ *n* **1a** the act of despising; the state of mind of one who despises **b** lack of respect or reverence for sthg **2** the state of being despised ⟨*he is held in* ~⟩ **3** obstruction of the administration of justice in court; *esp* wilful disobedience to or open disrespect of a court [ME, fr L *contemptus,* fr *contemptus,* pp of *contemnere*]

contemptible /kən'tem(p)təbl/ *adj* worthy of contempt – **contemptibleness** *n,* **contemptibly** *adv*

contemptuous /kən'tem(p)choo·əs, -tyoo·əs/ *adj* manifesting, feeling, or expressing contempt [L *contemptus* contempt] – **contemptuously** *adv,* **contemptuousness** *n*

contend /kən'tend/ *vi* **1** to strive or vie in contest or rivalry or against difficulties **2** to strive in debate; argue ~ *vt* to maintain, assert ⟨~ed *that he was right*⟩ [MF or L; MF *contendre,* fr L *contendere,* fr *com-* + *tendere* to stretch – more at THIN] – **contender** *n*

[1]**content** /kən'tent/ *adj* happy, satisfied ⟨~ *to wait quietly*⟩ [ME, fr MF, fr L *contentus,* fr pp of *continēre* to hold in, contain] – **contentment** *n*

[2]**content** /kən'tent/ *vt* **1** to appease the desires of; satisfy **2** to limit (oneself) in requirements, desires, or actions – usu + *with*

[3]**content** /kən'tent/ *n* freedom from care or discomfort; satisfaction

[4]**content** /'kontent/ *n* **1a** that which is contained – usu pl with sing. meaning ⟨*the jar's* ~s⟩ ⟨*the drawer's* ~s⟩ **b** *pl* the topics or matter treated in a written work ⟨*table of* ~s⟩ **2a** the substance, gist ⟨~ *as opposed to form*⟩ **b** the events, physical detail, and information in a work of art – compare FORM 9b **3** the matter dealt with in a field of study **4** the amount of specified material contained; proportion ⟨*the lead* ~ *of paint*⟩ [ME, fr L *contentus,* pp of *continēre* to contain]

contented /kən'tentid/ *adj* marked by satisfaction with one's possessions, status, or situation; happy – **contentedly** *adv,* **contentedness** *n*

contention /kən'tensh(ə)n/ *n* **1** (an act or instance of) contending **2** a point advanced or maintained in a debate or argument [ME *contencioun,* fr MF, fr L *contention-, contentio,* fr *contentus,* pp of *contendere* to contend]

contentious /kən'tenshəs/ *adj* **1** exhibiting an often perverse and wearisome tendency to quarrels and disputes 2 likely to cause contention ⟨*a ~ argument*⟩ – **contentiously** *adv*, **contentiousness** *n*

[1]**contest** /kən'test/ *vt* to make the subject of dispute, contention, or litigation *~vi* to strive, vie [MF *contester*, fr L *contestari* (*litem*) to bring an action at law, fr *contestari* to call to witness, fr *com-* + *testis* witness – more at TESTAMENT] – **contestable** *adj*, **contester** *n*

[2]**contest** /'kontest/ *n* **1** a struggle for superiority or victory **2** a competitive event; COMPETITION 2; *esp* one adjudicated by a panel of specially chosen judges

contestant /kən'test(ə)nt/ *n* **1** one who participates in a contest **2** one who contests an award or decision

context /'kontekst/ *n* **1** the parts surrounding a written or spoken word or passage that can throw light on its meaning **2** the interrelated conditions in which sthg exists or occurs [ME, weaving together of words, fr L *contextus* connection of words, coherence, fr *contextus*, pp of *contexere* to weave together, fr *com-* + *texere* to weave – more at TECHNICAL] – **contextual** /kən'tekschoo·əl, -tyoo·əl/ *adj*, **contextually** *adv*

contiguous /kən'tigyoo.əs/ *adj* **1** in actual contact; touching along a boundary or at a point **2** next or near in time or sequence [L *contiguus*, fr *contingere* to have contact with – more at CONTINGENT] – **contiguously** *adv*, **contiguousness** *n*, **contiguity** /,konti'gyooh·əti/ *n*

continence /'kontinəns/ *n* **1** self-restraint from yielding to impulse or desire **2** ability to refrain from a bodily activity; the state of being continent [ME, fr MF, fr L *continentia*, fr *continent-*, *continens*]

[1]**continent** /'kontinənt/ *adj* **1** exercising continence **2** not suffering from incontinence of the urine or faeces [ME, fr MF, fr L *continent-*, *continens*, fr prp of *continēre* to hold in – more at CONTAIN] – **continently** *adv*

[2]**continent** *n* **1** any of the (7) great divisions of land on the globe **2** *cap the* continent of Europe as distinguished from the British Isles [L *continent-*, *continens* continuous mass of land, mainland, fr *continent-*, *continens*, prp of *continēre*]

[1]**continental** /,konti'nentl/ *adj* (characteristic) of a continent, esp Europe – **continentally** *adv*

[2]**continental** *n* an inhabitant of a continent, esp Europe

continental breakfast *n* a light breakfast, typically of bread rolls with preserves and coffee

,conti,nental 'drift *n* the (supposed) drifting apart of the continents from being a solid land mass ☞ GEOGRAPHY

,conti,nental 'quilt *n* a duvet

,conti,nental 'shelf *n* the gently sloping part of the ocean floor that borders a continent and ends in a steeper slope to the ocean depths

Continental System *n* *the* attempt to blockade Britain begun by Napoleon in 1806

contingency /kən'tinj(ə)nsi/ *n* **1** an event that may occur; *esp* an undesirable one **2** an event that is liable to accompany another event [MF or ML; MF *contingence*, fr ML *contingentia*, fr LL, possibility, fr L *contingent-*, *contingens*, prp of *contingere* to touch on all sides, to happen]

con'tingency ,table *n* a table that shows the correlation between 2 variables

[1]**contingent** /kən'tinj(ə)nt/ *adj* **1** happening by chance or unforeseen causes **2** dependent *on* or conditioned by sthg else **3** not logically necessary; *esp* empirical [ME, fr MF, fr L *contingent-*, *contingens*, prp of *contingere* to have contact with, befall, fr *com-* + *tangere* to touch – more at [1]TANGENT] – **contingently** *adv*

[2]**contingent** *n* a quota or share, esp of people supplied from or representative of an area, group, or military force

continual /kən'tinyoo·əl, -yool/ *adj* **1** continuing indefinitely without interruption ⟨*~ fear*⟩ **2** recurring in steady rapid succession [ME, fr MF, fr L *continuus* continuous] – **continually** *adv*

continuance /kən'tinyoo·əns/ *n* **1** the act or process of continuing in a state, condition, or course of action **2** *NAm* adjournment of court proceedings

continuant /kən'tinyoo·ənt/ *n* a consonant (e g /l/ or /f/) that may be prolonged – compare STOP 7 [CONTINUE + [1]-ANT] – **continuant** *adj*

continuation /kən,tinyoo'aysh(ə)n/ *n* **1** the act or process of continuing in a state or activity **2** resumption after an interruption **3** sthg that continues, increases, or adds

continue /kən'tinyooh/ *vi* **1** to maintain a condition, course, or action without interruption **2** to remain in existence; endure **3** to remain in a place or condition; stay **4** to resume an activity after interruption *~vt* **1a** to maintain (a condition, course, or action) without interruption; CARRY ON ⟨*~s walking*⟩ **b** to prolong; *specif* to resume after interruption **2** to cause to continue **3** to say further ⟨*'We must fight for freedom", ~*d *the speaker*⟩ **4** *NAm* to postpone (a legal proceeding) [ME *continuen*, fr MF *continuer*, fr L *continuare*, fr *continuus*] – **continuer** *n*

continuity /,konti'nyooh·əti/ *n* **1a** uninterrupted connection, succession, or union **b** persistence without essential change **c** uninterrupted duration in time **2** sthg that has, displays, or provides continuity: e g **a** a script or scenario in the performing arts; *esp* one giving the details of the sequence of individual shots **b** speech or music used to link parts of an entertainment, esp a radio or television programme **3** an example of the property characteristic of a continuous mathematical function

,conti'nuity ,girl *n* sby responsible for ensuring consistency between individual shots after a break in filming

continuo /kən'tinyoo,oh/ *n*, *pl* **continuos** a bass part for a keyboard or stringed instrument written as a succession of bass notes with figures that indicate the required chords; *also* (the instruments playing) a continuo accompaniment [It, fr *continuo* continuous, fr L *continuus*]

continuous /kən'tinyoo·əs/ *adj* **1** marked by uninterrupted extension in space, time, or sequence **2** *of a function* having an arbitrarily small numerical difference between the value at any one point and the value at any other point sufficiently near the first point [L *continuus*, fr *continēre* to hold together – more at CONTAIN] – **continuously** *adv*, **continuousness** *n*

con,tinuous as'sessment *n* appraisal of the value of a student's work throughout a course as a means of awarding his/her final mark or degree

continuum /kən'tinyoo·əm/ *n*, *pl* **continua** /-nyoo·ə/, **continuums** **1** sthg (e g duration or extension) absolutely continuous and homogeneous that can be described only by reference to sthg else (e g numbers) **2a** sthg in which a fundamental common character is discernible amid a series of imperceptible or indefinite variations ⟨*the* ~ *of experience*⟩ **b** an uninterrupted ordered sequence [L, neut of *continuus*]

contort /kən'tawt/ *vb* to twist in a violent manner; deform ⟨*his features* ~ed *with fury*⟩ ⟨~ *spelling and grammar*⟩ [L *contortus*, pp of *contorquēre*, fr *com-* + *torquēre* to twist – more at TORTURE] – **contortive** *adj*, **contortion** /kən'tawsh(ə)n/ *n*

contortionist /kən'tawsh(ə)nist/ *n* **1** an acrobat who specializes in unnatural body postures **2** one who extricates him-/herself from a dilemma by complicated but doubtful arguments – **contortionistic** /-'istik/ *adj*

¹contour /'kon,tooə/ *n* **1** (a line representing) an outline, esp of a curving or irregular figure **2 contour, contour line** a line (e g on a map) connecting points of equal elevation or height [F, fr It *contorno*, fr *contornare* to round off, sketch in outline, fr L *com-* + *tornare* to turn in a lathe, fr *tornus* lathe]

²contour *vt* **1a** to shape the contour of **b** to shape so as to fit contours **2** to construct (e g a road) in conformity to a contour

contra- /kontrə-/ *prefix* **1** against; contrary; contrasting ⟨contra*distinction*⟩ ⟨contra*ception*⟩ **2** pitched below normal ⟨contra*bass*⟩ [ME, fr L, fr *contra* against, opposite – more at ⁴COUNTER]

contraband /'kontrə,band/ *n* goods or merchandise whose import, export, or possession is forbidden; *also* smuggled goods [It *contrabbando*, fr ML *contrabannum*, fr *contra-* + *bannus, bannum* decree, of Gmc origin; akin to OHG *ban* command] – **contraband** *adj*

,contra'bass /-'bays/ *n* DOUBLE BASS

,contrabas'soon /-bə'soohn/ *n* a double-reed woodwind instrument having a range an octave lower than that of the bassoon

contracept /,kontrə'sept/ *vi* to prevent conception or impregnation [back-formation fr *contraception*]

contraception /,kontrə'sepsh(ə)n/ *n* prevention of conception or impregnation [*contra-* + *conception*] – **contraceptive** /-'septiv/ *adj*

contraceptive /,kontrə'septiv/ *n* a method or device used in preventing conception; *esp* a condom

¹contract /'kontrakt/ *n* **1a** (a document containing) a legally binding agreement between 2 or more people or parties **b** a betrothal **2** an undertaking to win a specified number of tricks in bridge [ME, fr L *contractus*, fr *contractus*, pp of *contrahere* to draw together, make a contract, reduce in size, fr *com-* + *trahere* to draw – more at DRAW]

²contract /kən'trakt; *vt sense* ' *and vi sense* ' *usu* 'kontrakt/ *vt* **1** to undertake by contract **2a** to catch (an illness) **b** to incur as an obligation ⟨~ *a debt*⟩ **3** to knit, wrinkle ⟨*a frown* ~ed *his brow*⟩ **4** to reduce to a smaller size (as if) by squeezing or forcing together **5** to shorten (e g a word) ~ *vi* **1** to make a contract **2** to draw together so as to become smaller or shorter ⟨*metal* ~s *on cooling*⟩ ⟨*muscles* ~ *involuntarily in tetanus*⟩ [partly fr MF *contracter* to agree upon, fr L *contractus*, n; partly fr L *contractus*, pp of *contrahere* to draw together] – **contractible** /kən'traktəbl/ *adj*, **contractibility** /-tə'biləti/ *n*

,contract 'bridge /'kontrakt/ *n* a form of bridge in which overtricks do not count towards game bonuses – compare AUCTION BRIDGE

contractile /kən'traktiel/ *adj* having the power or property of contracting ⟨*a* ~ *protein*⟩ – **contractility** /,kontrak'tiləti/ *n*

con,tractile 'vacuole *n* a vacuole in a protozoan organism that contracts to discharge fluid from the body

contract in *vb* to agree to inclusion (of) in a particular scheme

contraction /kən'traksh(ə)n/ *n* **1** the shortening and thickening of a muscle (fibre) **2** (a form produced by) a shortening of a word, syllable, or word group [²CONTRACT + -ION] – **contractional** *adj*, **contractive** *adj*

contractor /kən'traktə, 'kontraktə/ *n* one who contracts to perform work, esp building work, or to provide supplies, usu on a large scale

contract out *vb* to agree to exclusion (of) from a particular scheme

contractual / kən'traktyoo·əl, -choo·əl/ *adj* of or constituting a contract [L *contractus* contract] – **contractually** *adv*

contracture /kən'trakchə/ *n* a permanent shortening of muscle, tendon, scar tissue, etc producing deformity [²CONTRACT + -URE]

contradict /,kontrə'dikt/ *vt* **1** to state the contrary of (a statement or speaker) **2** to deny the truthfulness of (a statement or speaker) [L *contradictus*, pp of *contradicere*, fr *contra-* + *dicere* to say, speak – more at DICTION] – **contradictable** *adj*, **contradictor** *n*

contradiction /,kontrə'diksh(ə)n/ *n* **1** a logical inconsistency ⟨*a* ~ *in terms*⟩ **2** an opposition or conflict inherent in a system or situation [CONTRADICT + -ION]

¹contradictory /,kontrə'dikt(ə)ri/ *n* a proposition so related to another that if one is true the other must be false and if one is false the other must be true [CONTRADICT + ¹-ORY]

²contradictory *adj* **1** given to or marked by contradiction **2** serving to contradict – **contradictorily** *adv*, **contradictoriness** *n*

,contradi'stinction /-di'stingksh(ə)n/ *n* distinction by contrast – **contradistinctive** *adj*, **contradistinctively** *adv*

,contradi'stinguish /-di'sting·gwish/ *vt* to distinguish by contrast of qualities

contrail /'kontrayl/ *n* a streak of condensed water vapour created in the air by the passage of an aircraft or rocket at high altitudes [*con*densation *trail*]

,contra'indicate /-'indikayt/ *vt* to make (a treatment or procedure) inadvisable ⟨*a drug that is* ~d *in pregnancy*⟩ – **contraindication** /-indi'kaysh(ə)n/ *n*, **contraindicative** /-in'dikətiv/ *adj*

,contra'lateral /-'lat(ə)rəl/ *adj* situated or appearing on or affecting the opposite side of the body – compare IPSILATERAL [ISV]

contralto /kən'traltoh, kən'trahltoh/ *n, pl* **contraltos** **1** (a person with) the lowest female singing voice **2** the part sung by a contralto [It, fr *contra-* + *alto*]

contraption /kən'trapsh(ə)n/ *n* a newfangled or complicated device; a gadget [perh blend of *contrivance, trap*, and *invention*]

contrapuntal /,kontrə'puntl/ *adj* of counterpoint [It *contrappunto* counterpoint, fr ML *contrapunctus*] – **contrapuntally** *adv*

contrariety /,kontrə'rie.əti/ *n* opposition, disagreement – fml [ME *contrariete*, fr MF *contrarieté*, fr LL *contrarietat-*, *contrarietas*, fr L *contrarius* contrary]

contrariwise /'kontrəri,wiez, kən'treə-/ *adv* conversely; VICE VERSA [[2]CONTRARY + -WISE]

[1]**contrary** /'kontrəri/ *n* **1** a fact or condition incompatible with another **2** either of a pair of opposites **3** either of 2 terms (e g true and false) that cannot both simultaneously be said to be true of the same subject **– on the contrary** just the opposite; no **– to the contrary 1** to the opposite effect ⟨*if I hear nothing* to the contrary *I'll accept that explanation*⟩ **2** notwithstanding

[2]**contrary** /'kontrəri; *sense 4 often* kən'treəri/ *adj* **1** completely different or opposed **2** opposite in position, direction, or nature **3** *of wind or weather* unfavourable **4** obstinately self-willed; inclined to oppose the wishes of others [ME *contrarie*, fr MF *contraire*, fr L *contrarius*, fr *contra* opposite] – **contrarily** /'kontrərəli/ *adv*, **contrariness** /'kontrərinis; *sense 4 often* kən'treərinis/ *n*

'**contrary to** /'kontrəri/ *prep* in opposition to

[1]**contrast** /'kontrahst/ *n* **1a** juxtaposition of dissimilar elements (e g colour, tone, or emotion) in a work of art **b** degree of difference between the lightest and darkest parts of a painting, photograph, television picture, etc **2** comparison of similar objects to set off their dissimilar qualities **3** a person or thing against which another may be contrasted – **contrastive** /kən'trahstiv/ *adj*, **contrastively** *adv*

[2]**contrast** /kən'trahst/ *vi* to exhibit contrast ~ *vt* **1** to put in contrast **2** to compare in respect to differences [F *contraster*, fr MF, to oppose, resist, alter. of *contrester*, fr (assumed) VL *contrastare*, fr L *contra-* + *stare* to stand – more at STAND] – **contrastable** *adj*

contravene /,kontrə'veen/ *vt* to go or act contrary to ⟨~ *a law*⟩ [MF or LL; MF *contrevenir*, fr LL *contravenire*, fr L *contra-* + *venire* to come – more at COME] – **contravener** *n*

contravention /,kontrə'vensh(ə)n/ *n* a violation or infringement [MF, fr LL *contraventus*, pp of *contravenire*]

contretemps /'kon(h)trə,tonh, 'kawntrə-, -tong (*Fr* kõtrətɑ̃)/ *n*, *pl* **contretemps** /-(z) (*Fr* ~)/ a minor setback, disagreement, or confrontation [F, fr *contre-* counter- + *temps* time, fr L *tempus* – more at TEMPORAL]

contribute /kən'tribyooht, 'kontri-/ *vt* **1** to give in common with others **2** to supply (e g an article) for a publication ~ *vi* **1** to help bring about an end or result **2** to supply articles to a publication [L *contributus*, pp of *contribuere*, fr *com-* + *tribuere* to grant – more at TRIBUTE] – **contributive** /kən'tribyootiv/ *adj*, **contributively** *adv*, **contributor** /kən'tribyootə/ *n*

contribution /,kontri'byoohsh(ə)n/ *n* the act of contributing; *also* sthg contributed

[1]**contributory** /kən'tribyoot(ə)ri/ *adj* **1** contributing to a common fund or enterprise **2** of or forming a contribution **3** financed by contributions; *specif*, *of an insurance or pension plan* contributed to by both employers and employees

[2]**contributory** *n* sby liable in British law to contribute towards meeting the debts of a bankrupt company

contrite /kən'triet/ *adj* **1** grieving and penitent for sin or shortcoming **2** showing contrition [ME *contrit*, fr MF, fr ML *contritus*, fr L, bruised, fr pp of *conterere* to grind, bruise, fr *com-* + *terere* to rub – more at THROW] – **contritely** *adv*, **contriteness** *n*

contrition /kən'trish(ə)n/ *n* sorrow for one's sins, arising esp from the love of God rather than fear of punishment – compare ATTRITION [CONTRITE + -ION]

contrivance /kən'triev(ə)ns/ *n* **1** contriving or being contrived **2** sthg contrived; *esp* a mechanical device

contrive /kən'triev/ *vt* **1a** to devise, plan **b** to create in an inventive or resourceful manner **2** to bring about; manage [ME *controven*, *contreven*, fr MF *controver*, fr LL *contropare* to compare] – **contriver** *n*

con'trived *adj* unnatural and forced

[1]**control** /kən'trohl/ *vt* **-ll- 1** to check, test, or verify **2a** to exercise restraining or directing influence over **b** to have power over; rule [ME *controllen*, fr MF *contreroller*, fr *contrerolle* copy of an account, audit, fr *contre-* counter- + *rolle* roll, account] – **controllable** *adj*, **controllability** /-lə'biləti/ *n*

[2]**control** *n* **1** power to control, direct, or command **2a** (an organism, culture, etc used in) an experiment in which the procedure or agent under test in a parallel experiment is omitted and which is used as a standard of comparison in judging experimental effects **b** a mechanism used to regulate or guide the operation of a machine, apparatus, or system – often pl **c** an organization that directs a space flight ⟨*mission* ~⟩ **d** a personality or spirit believed to be responsible for the actions of a spiritualistic medium at a séance

controller /kən'trohlə/ *n* **1a** a public-finance official **b** a chief financial officer, esp of a business enterprise **2** one who controls or has power to control [ME *conterroller*, fr MF *contrerolleur*, fr *contrerolle*] – **controllership** *n*

controlling interest /kən'trohling/ *n* sufficient share ownership in a company to have control over policy

con'trol ,panel *n* a panel on which are mounted devices (e g dials and switches) used in the remote control and monitoring of electrified or mechanical apparatus ☞ FLIGHT

con'trol ,surface *n* a movable aerofoil or fin of an aircraft or ship that allows the position of the vehicle relative to the ground or water to be changed

con'trol ,unit *n* (a prison installation providing) a special punitive regime of total isolation for especially violent prisoners

controversial /,kontrə'vuhsh(ə)l/ *adj* of, given to, or arousing controversy – **controversialism** *n*, **controversialist** *n*, **controversially** *adv*

controversy /'kontrə,vuhsi; *also* kən'trovəsi/ *n* (a) debate or dispute, esp in public or in the media [ME *controversie*, fr L *controversia*, fr *controversus* disputable, lit., turned opposite, fr *contro-* (akin to *contra-*) + *versus*, pp of *vertere* to turn]

controvert /'kontrə,vuht, ,--'-/ *vt* to deny or dispute – fml [back-formation fr *controversy*] – **controverter** /'kontrə,vuhtə/ *n*, **controvertible** /-'vuhtəbl/ *adj*

contumacious /,kontyoo'mayshəs/ *adj* stubbornly disobedient; rebellious – fml [ME *contumacie* insubordinacy, fr L *contumacia*, fr *contumac-*, *contumax* insubordinate, fr *com-* + *tumēre* to swell, be proud – more at THUMB] – **contumaciously** *adv*, **contumacy** /'kontyoomәsi/ *n*

contumely /kon'tyoohmili, 'kontyoomili/ *n* abusive and contemptuous language or treatment – fml [ME *contumelie,* fr MF, fr L *contumelia*; perh akin to L *contumacia*] – **contumelious** /ˌkontyoo'meelyəs/ *adj,* **contumeliously** *adv*

contuse /kən'tyoohz/ *vt* to bruise (tissue) [MF *contuser,* fr L *contusus,* pp of *contundere* to crush, bruise, fr *com-* + *tundere* to beat – more at [1]STINT] – **contusion** /-zh(ə)n/ *n*

conundrum /kə'nundrəm/ *n* **1** a riddle; *esp* one whose answer is or involves a pun **2** an intricate and difficult problem [origin unknown]

conurbation /ˌkonuh'baysh(ə)n/ *n* a grouping of several previously separate towns to form 1 large community [*com-* + L *urb-, urbs* city]

convalesce /ˌkonvə'les/ *vi* to recover gradually after sickness or weakness [L *convalescere,* fr *com-* + *valescere* to grow strong, fr *valēre* to be strong, be well – more at WIELD] – **convalescence** *n,* **convalescent** *adj or n*

convection /kən'veksh(ə)n/ *n* (the transfer of heat by) the circulatory motion that occurs in a gas or liquid at a nonuniform temperature owing to the variation of density with temperature [LL *convection-, convectio,* fr L *convectus,* pp of *convehere* to bring together, fr *com-* + *vehere* to carry – more at WAY] – **convect** *vb,* **convectional** *adj,* **convective** *adj*

convector /kən'vektə/ *n* a heating unit from which heated air circulates by convection [CONVECT + [1]-OR]

convene /kən'veen/ *vi* to come together in a body ~ *vt* **1** to summon before a tribunal **2** to cause to assemble [ME *convenen,* fr MF *convenir* to come together]

convenience /kən'veenyəns, -ni·əns/ *n* **1** fitness or suitability **2** an appliance, device, or service conducive to comfort **3** a suitable time; an opportunity ⟨*at your earliest* ~⟩ **4** personal comfort or advantage **5** *Br* PUBLIC CONVENIENCE [ME, fr MF, fr L *convenientia,* fr *convenient-, conveniens*]

con'venience ˌfood *n* commercially prepared food (e g cake mixes or tinned meat) requiring little or no further preparation before eating

convenient /kən'veenyənt, -ni·ənt/ *adj* **1** suited to personal comfort or to easy use **2** suited to a particular situation **3** near at hand; easily accessible [ME, fr L *convenient-, conveniens,* fr prp of *convenire* to come together, be suitable] – **conveniently** *adv*

convenor, convener /kən'veenə/ *n, chiefly Br* **1** a member of a group or esp committee responsible for calling meetings; *broadly* a chairperson **2** an elected union official responsible for coordinating the work of shop stewards in an establishment [CONVENE + [1]-OR]

convent /'konv(ə)nt, -vent/ *n* a local community or house of a religious order or congregation; *esp* an establishment of nuns [ME *covent,* fr OF, fr ML *conventus,* fr L, assembly, fr *conventus,* pp of *convenire*]

conventicle /kən'ventikl/ *n* **1** an (irregular or unlawful) assembly or meeting **2** a (clandestine) assembly for religious worship **3** a meetinghouse [ME, fr L *conventiculum,* dim. of *conventus* assembly] – **conventicler** *n*

convention /kən'vensh(ə)n/ *n* **1a** an agreement or contract, esp between states or parties **b** an agreement between enemies (e g concerning the exchange of prisoners) **2** a generally agreed principle or practice **3** an assembly **4a** (an) accepted social custom or practice **b** an established artistic technique or practice ⟨*the* ~s *of the stream-of-consciousness novel*⟩ **c** an agreed system of bidding or playing that conveys information between partners in bridge or another card game [ME, fr MF or L; MF, fr L *convention-, conventio,* fr *conventus,* pp of *convenire* to come together, be suitable, fr *com-* + *venire* to come – more at COME]

conventional /kən'vensh(ə)nl/ *adj* **1a** conforming to or sanctioned by convention **b** lacking originality or individuality **2** *of warfare* not using atom or hydrogen bombs – **conventionalism** *n,* **conventionalist** *n,* **conventionalize** *vt,* **conventionally** *adv,* **conventionality** /-'aləti/ *n*

conventual /kən'ventyoo(ə)l, -choo(ə)l/ *adj* of or befitting a convent or monastic life [ME, fr MF or ML; MF, fr ML *conventualis,* fr *conventus* convent] – **conventually** *adv*

converge /kən'vuhj/ *vi* **1** to move together towards a common point; meet **2** to come together in a common interest or focus **3** *of (the value of a term in) a mathematical series* to approach a limit as the number of terms increases without limit ~ *vt* to cause to converge [ML *convergere,* fr L *com-* + *vergere* to bend, incline – more at WRENCH]

convergence /kən'vuhj(ə)ns/, **convergency** /-si/ *n* **1** a converging, esp towards union or uniformity; *esp* coordinated movement of the eyes resulting in reception of an image on corresponding retinal areas **2** independent development in unrelated organisms of similar characters, often associated with similar environments or behaviour

convergent /kən'vuhj(ə)nt/ *adj* **1** tending to move towards 1 point or to approach each other **2** exhibiting convergence **3** mathematically converging to a limit ⟨*a* ~ *series*⟩

conversant /kən'vuhs(ə)nt/ *adj* having knowledge or experience; familiar *with* [ME *conversaunt,* fr MF *conversant,* fr L *conversant-, conversans,* prp of *conversari* to associate with] – **conversantly** *adv*

conversation /ˌkonvə'saysh(ə)n/ *n* **1** (an instance of) informal verbal exchange of feelings, opinions, or ideas **2** an exchange similar to conversation; *esp* real-time interaction with a computer, esp through a keyboard [ME *conversacioun,* fr MF *conversation,* fr L *conversation-, conversatio,* fr *conversatus,* pp of *conversari* to live, keep company with] – **conversational** *adj,* **conversationally** *adv*

conversationalist /ˌkonvə'saysh(ə)nl·ist/ *n* one who converses a great deal or who excels in conversation

conversazione /ˌkonvəsatsi'ohni/ *n, pl* **conversaziones** /-neez/, **conversazioni** /-ni/ a meeting for informal discussion of intellectual or cultural matters [It, lit., conversation, fr L *conversation-, conversatio*]

[1]converse /kən'vuhs/ *vi* **1** to exchange thoughts and opinions in speech; talk **2** to carry on an exchange similar to a conversation; *esp* to interact with a computer [ME *conversen,* fr MF *converser,* fr L *conversari* to live, keep company with, fr *conversus,* pp of *convertere* to turn round]

[2]converse /'konˌvuhs/ *n* conversation – fml

[3]converse /'konˌvuhs/ *adj* reversed in order, relation, or action; opposite [L *conversus,* pp of *convertere*] – **conversely** *adv*

[4]**converse** /'kon,vuhs/ *n* sthg converse to another; *esp* a proposition in logic in which the subject and predicate terms have been interchanged ⟨*'no* P *is* S" *is the* ~ *of 'no* S *is* P"⟩

conversion /kən'vuhsh(ə)n/ *n* **1** converting or being converted **2** (an experience associated with) a definite and decisive adoption of a religious faith **3** sthg converted from one use to another **4** the unlawful exercising of rights to personal property belonging to another **5** the alteration of a building to a different purpose; *also* a building so altered **6** (the score resulting from) an opportunity to kick a goal awarded to the scoring team after a try in rugby **7 conversion, conversion hysteria** bodily symptoms (e g paralysis) appearing as a result of mental conflict without a physical cause [ME, fr MF, fr L *conversion-, conversio,* fr *conversus,* pp of *convertere*] – **conversional** *adj*

[1]**convert** /kən'vuht/ *vt* **1a** to win over from one persuasion or party to another **b** to bring about a religious conversion in **2a** to alter the physical or chemical nature or properties of, esp in manufacturing **b** to change from one form or function to another; *esp* to make (structural) alterations to (a building or part of a building) **c** to exchange for an equivalent **3** to complete (a try) in rugby by successfully kicking a conversion ~ *vi* to undergo conversion [ME *converten,* fr OF *convertir,* fr L *convertere,* to turn round, transform, convert, fr *com-* + *vertere* to turn] – **converter** *n*

[2]**convert** /'konvuht/ *n* a person who has experienced an esp religious conversion

[1]**convertible** /kən'vuhtəbl/ *adj* **1** capable of being converted **2** *of a motor vehicle* having a top that may be lowered or removed ⟨*a* ~ *sports car*⟩ **3** capable of being exchanged for a specified equivalent (e g another currency) – **convertibleness** *n,* **convertibly** *adv*

[2]**convertible** *n* a convertible motor car

convex /,kon'veks; *not attrib* kən'veks/ *adj* curved or rounded outwards like the outside of a bowl [MF or L; MF *convexe,* fr L *convexus* vaulted, concave, convex, fr *com-* + *-vexus*; akin to OE *wōh* crooked, bent – more at PREVARICATE] – **convexly** *adv*

convexity /kən'veksəti/ *n* a convex line, surface, or part [CONVEX + -ITY]

convexo-concave /kən,veksoh kon'kayv/ *adj* concavo-convex

convey /kən'vay/ *vt* **1** to take or carry from one place to another **2** to impart or communicate (e g feelings or ideas) **3** to transmit, transfer; *specif* to transfer (property or the rights to property) to another [ME *conveyen,* fr OF *conveier* to accompany, escort, fr (assumed) VL *conviare,* fr L *com-* + *via* way – more at VIA]

conveyance /kən'vayəns/ *n* **1** a document by which rights to property are transferred **2** a means of transport; a vehicle [CONVEY + -ANCE]

conveyancing /kən'vayənsing/ *n* the act or business of transferring rights to property – **conveyancer** *n*

conveyer, conveyor /kən'vayə/ *n* a mechanical apparatus for carrying articles or bulk material (e g by an endless moving belt) [CONVEY + [2]-ER]

[1]**convict** /kən'vikt/ *vt* **1** to find or prove to be guilty **2** to convince of error or sinfulness [ME *convicten,* fr L *convictus,* pp of *convincere* to refute, convict]

[2]**convict** /'konvikt/ *n* a person serving a (long-term) prison sentence

conviction /kən'viksh(ə)n/ *n* **1** convicting or being convicted, esp in judicial proceedings **2a** a strong persuasion or belief **b** the state of being convinced

convince /kən'vins/ *vt* to cause to believe; persuade [L *convincere* to refute, convict, prove, fr *com-* + *vincere* to conquer – more at VICTOR]

convincing /kən'vinsing/ *adj* having the power to overcome doubt or disbelief; plausible – **convincingly** *adv,* **convincingness** *n*

convivial /kən'vivi·əl/ *adj* relating to or fond of eating, drinking, and good company [LL *convivialis,* fr L *convivium* banquet, fr *com-* + *vivere* to live – more at [1]QUICK] – **convivially** *adv,* **conviviality** /-'aləti/ *n*

convocation /,konvə'kaysh(ə)n, -voh-/ *n* **1** an assembly of people called together: e g **a** either of the 2 provincial assemblies of bishops and representative clergy of the Church of England ⟨*the* ~ *of York*⟩ **b** a ceremonial assembly of graduates of a college or university **2** the act of calling together [ME, fr MF, fr L *convocation-, convocatio,* fr *convocatus,* pp of *convocare*] – **convocational** *adj*

convoke /kən'vohk/ *vt* to call together to a formal meeting [MF *convoquer,* fr L *convocare,* fr *com-* + *vocare* to call – more at VOICE]

convolute /'konvəlooht, ,--'-/ *vb* to twist or coil [L *convolutus,* pp of *convolvere,* fr *com-* + *volvere* to roll – more at VOLUBLE]

,**convo'luted** *adj* **1** having convolutions **2** involved, intricate ⟨*a* ~ *argument*⟩

convolution /,konvə'loohsh(ə)n/ *n* **1** any of the irregular ridges on the surface of the brain, esp of the cerebrum of higher mammals **2** sthg intricate or complicated [CONVOLUTE + -ION] – **convolutional** *adj*

convolvulus /kən'volvyooləs/ *n, pl* **convolvuluses, convolvuli** /-lie/ any of a genus of usu twining plants (e g bindweed) [NL, fr L *convolvere* to roll together]

[1]**convoy** /'konvoy/ *vt* to accompany or escort, esp for protection [ME *convoyen,* fr MF *conveier, convoier* – more at CONVEY]

[2]**convoy** *n* **1** convoying or being convoyed **2** *sing or pl in constr* a group of ships, military vehicles, etc moving together, esp with a protective escort; *also* such an escort

convulsant /kən'vuls(ə)nt/ *adj* causing convulsions – **convulsant** *n*

convulse /kən'vuls/ *vt* **1** to shake or agitate violently, esp (as if) with irregular spasms **2** to cause to laugh helplessly [L *convulsus,* pp of *convellere* to pluck up, convulse, fr *com-* + *vellere* to pluck – more at VULNERABLE]

convulsion /kən'vulsh(ə)n/ *n* **1** an abnormal violent and involuntary contraction or series of contractions of the muscles **2a** a violent disturbance **b** an uncontrolled fit; a paroxysm – **convulsionary** *adj*

convulsive /kən'vulsiv/ *adj* constituting, producing, or affected with a convulsion – **convulsively** *adv,* **convulsiveness** *n*

cony, coney /'kohni/ *n* **1** a rabbit **2** a pika **3** a hyrax [ME *conies,* pl, fr OF *conis,* pl of *conil,* fr L *cuniculus*]

[1]**coo** /kooh/ *vi* **cooed, coo'd 1** to make (a sound similar to) the low soft cry characteristic of a dove

or pigeon **2** to talk lovingly or appreciatively [imit] – **coo** *n*

[2]**coo** *interj, Br* – used to express surprise; infml [origin unknown]

cooee /'kooh·ee/ *interj, Br* – used to make one's presence known or to attract sby's attention at a distance [origin unknown] – **cooee** *vi*

[1]**cook** /kook/ *n* sby who prepares food for eating [ME, fr OE *cōc*; akin to OHG *koch*; both fr a prehistoric WGmc word borrowed fr L *coquus*, fr *coquere* to cook; akin to OE *āfigen* fried, Gk *pessein* to cook]

[2]**cook** *vi* **1** to prepare food for eating, esp by subjection to heat **2** to undergo the process of being cooked ⟨*the rice is* ~ing *now*⟩ **3** to occur, happen – infml ⟨*what's* ~ing?⟩ ~ *vt* **1** to prepare (e g food) for eating by a heating process **2** to subject to the action of heat or fire – **cook someone's goose** to ruin sby irretrievably – **cook the books** to falsify financial accounts in order to deceive

'**cook,book** /-,book/ *n* COOKERY BOOK; *broadly* a book of detailed instructions (e g as used in statistics)

cooker /'kookə/ *n* **1** an apparatus, appliance, etc for cooking; *esp* one typically consisting of an oven, hot plates or rings, and a grill fixed in position **2** a variety, esp of fruit, not usu eaten raw [[2]COOK + [2]-ER]

cookery /'kook(ə)ri/ *n* the art or practice of cooking

'**cookery ,book** *n* a book of recipes and instructions for preparing and cooking food

'**cook,house** /-,hows/ *n* a kitchen set up outdoors, at a campsite, or on board ship

cookie, cooky /'kooki/ *n* **1a** *Scot* a plain bun **b** *NAm* a sweet flat or slightly leavened biscuit **2** *chiefly NAm* a person, esp of a specified type – infml ⟨*a tough* ~⟩ [D *koekje*, dim. of *koek* cake]

cooking /'kooking/ *adj* suitable for or used in cooking ⟨~ *apples*⟩ ⟨~ *utensils*⟩

'**cook,out** /-,owt/ *n, chiefly NAm* (the meal eaten at) an outing at which food is cooked and served in the open

cook up *vt* to concoct, improvise – infml

[1]**cool** /koohl/ *adj* **1** moderately cold; lacking in warmth **2a** dispassionately calm and self-controlled **b** lacking friendliness or enthusiasm **c** of or being an understated, restrained, and melodic style of jazz – compare HOT 2d **3** disrespectful, impudent ⟨*a* ~ *reply*⟩ **4** bringing or suggesting relief from heat ⟨*a* ~ *dress*⟩ **5** *of a colour* producing an impression of being cool; *specif* in the range blue to green **6** showing sophistication by a restrained or detached manner **7** – used as an intensive; infml ⟨*paid a* ~ *million for it*⟩ **8** very good; excellent – slang [ME *col*, fr OE *cōl*; akin to OHG *kuoli* cool, OE *ceald* cold] – **coolish** *adj*, **coolly** *also* **cooly** *adv*, **coolness** *n*

[2]**cool** *vi* **1** to become cool; lose heat or warmth **2** to lose enthusiasm or passion ~ *vt* **1** to make cool; impart a feeling of coolness to – often + *off* or *down* **2** to moderate the excitement, force, or activity of – **cool it** to become calm or quiet; relax – infml ⟨*just* cool it, *will you, so I can think*⟩ – **cool one's heels** to wait or be kept waiting for a long time, esp (as if) from disdain or discourtesy

[3]**cool** *n* **1** a cool atmosphere or place **2** poise, composure – infml ⟨*don't lose your* ~⟩

[4]**cool** *adv* in a casual and nonchalant manner – infml ⟨*play it* ~⟩

coolabah, coolibah /'koohlə,bah/ *n, Austr* any of several eucalyptuses or gum trees [native name in Australia]

coolant /'koohlənt/ *n* a liquid or gas used in cooling, esp in an engine ☞ ENERGY

cool down *vi* to allow a violent emotion (e g rage) to pass

cooler /'koohlə/ *n* **1a** a container for cooling liquids **b** *NAm* a refrigerator **2** a prison cell – slang [[2]COOL + [2]-ER]

,**cool'headed** /-'hedid/ *adj* not easily excited

coolie /'koohli/ *n* an unskilled labourer or porter, usu in or from the Far East, hired for low or subsistence wages [Hindi *kulī*]

'**coolie ,hat** *n* a shallow conical hat, usu of straw, worn esp to protect the head from the heat of the sun

,**cooling-'off** *adj* designed to allow passions to cool or to permit negotiation between parties ⟨*a* ~ *period*⟩

coomb, coombe, combe /koohm/ *n, Br* a valley or basin, esp on a hillside or running up from the coast [of Celt origin; akin to W *cwm* valley]

coon /koohn/ *n* **1** *chiefly NAm* a raccoon **2** a Negro – derog [short for *raccoon*]

'**coon,skin** /-,skin/ *n* the skin or pelt of the raccoon

[1]**coop** /koohp/ *n* **1** a cage or small enclosure or building, esp for housing poultry **2** a confined space [ME *cupe*; akin to OE *cȳpe* basket, *cot* cot]

[2]**coop** *vt* **1** to confine in a restricted space – usu + *up* **2** to place or keep in a coop – often + *up*

co-op /'koh ,op/ *n* a cooperative

cooper /'koohpə/ *n* a maker or repairer of barrels, casks, etc [ME *couper, cowper*, fr MD *cūper* (fr *cūpe* cask) or MLG *kūper*, fr *kūpe* cask; MD *cūpe* & MLG *kūpe*, fr L *cupa*; akin to Gk *kypellon* cup – more at HIVE] – **cooper** *vb*, **cooperage** *n*

cooperate /koh'opərayt/ *vi* to act or work with another or others for a common purpose [LL *cooperatus*, pp of *cooperari*, fr L *co-* + *operari* to work – more at OPERATE] – **cooperator** *n*

cooperation /koh,opə'raysh(ə)n/ *n* **1** a common effort **2** association for common benefit [COOPERATE + -ION]

[1]**cooperative** /koh'op(ə)rətiv/ *adj* **1** showing cooperation or a willingness to work with others **2** of, or organized as, a cooperative – **cooperatively** *adv*, **cooperativeness** *n*

[2]**cooperative** *n* an enterprise (e g a shop) or organization (e g a society) owned by and operated for the benefit of those using its services ⟨*a housing* ~⟩

co-opt /,koh 'opt/ *vt* **1** to choose or elect as a member; *specif, of a committee* to draft onto itself as an additional member **2** to gain the participation or services of; assimilate [L *cooptare*, fr *co-* + *optare* to choose] – **co-optation** /,koh ,op'taysh(ə)n/ *n*, **co-optative** /'optətiv/ *adj*, **co-option** /'opsh(ə)n/ *n*, **co-optive** *adj*

[1]**coordinate** /koh'awd(ə)nət, -di-/ *adj* **1** equal in rank, quality, or significance **2** relating to or marked by coordination [L *co-* + *ordinatus*, pp of *ordinare* to arrange, fr *ordin-, ordo* order] – **coordinately** *adv*, **coordinateness** *n*

[2]**coordinate** *n* **1** any of a set of numbers used in specifying the location of a point on a line, on a

surface, or in space **2** *pl* outer garments, usu separates, in harmonizing colours, materials, and pattern

[3]**coordinate** /koh'awd(ə)nayt, -di-/ *vt* to combine in a common action; harmonize ~ *vi* to be or become coordinate, esp so as to act together harmoniously [LL or L; LL *coordinatus*, pp of *coordinare*, fr L *co-* + *ordinare*] – **coordination** /-'aysh(ə)n/ *n*, **coordinative** *adj*, **coordinator** /-,aytə/ *n*

co,ordinate 'bond /koh'awd(ə)nət, -di-/ *n* a covalent chemical bond for which the electrons are supplied by only 1 of the 2 atoms it joins

coordinated /koh'awd(ə)n,aytid, -di-/ *adj* able to move one's body efficiently and usu gracefully in sports, gymnastics, etc

co,ordinate ge'ometry /koh'awd(ə)nət, -di-/ *n* ANALYTICAL GEOMETRY

coot /kooht/ *n* **1** any of various slaty-black water birds of the rail family that somewhat resemble ducks **2** a foolish person – infml [ME *coote*; akin to D *koet* coot]

cootie /'koohti/ *n*, *NAm* BODY LOUSE – infml [perh modif of Malay *kutu*]

[1]**cop** /kop/ *vt* **-pp-** to get hold of; catch; *specif*, *Br* to arrest – slang [perh fr D *kapen* to steal, fr Fris *kāpia* to take away; akin to OHG *kouf* trade – more at CHEAP] – **cop it** *Br* to be in serious trouble – slang

[2]**cop** *n*, *Br* a capture, arrest – esp in *a fair cop*; slang – **not much cop** *chiefly Br* fairly bad; worthless – slang

[3]**cop** *n* a policeman – infml [short for [2]*copper*]

copaiba /koh'piebə, -'pay-, ,kohpə'eebə/ *n* (a S American tree yielding) an oleoresin used esp in varnishes [Sp & Pg; Sp, fr Pg *copaíba*, of Tupian origin; akin to Guarani *cupaiba* copaiba]

copal /'kohp(ə)l/ *n* a resin from various tropical trees used esp in varnishes [Sp, fr Nahuatl *copalli* resin]

coparcener /koh'pahs(ə)nə/ *n* joint heir [*co-* + *parcener* (partner, joint heir), fr AF, fr OF *parçonier*, fr *parçon* portion, fr L *partition-*, *partitio* partition]

copartner /koh'pahtnə/ *n* a partner – **copartnership** *n*

[1]**cope** /kohp/ *n* a long ecclesiastical vestment resembling a cape, worn on special occasions (e g processions) [ME, fr OE *-cāp*, fr LL *cappa* head covering]

[2]**cope** *vt* to supply or cover with a cope or coping

[3]**cope** *vi* to deal with a problem or task effectively – usu + *with* [ME *copen*, fr MF *couper* to strike, cut, fr OF, fr *coup* blow, fr LL *colpus*, alter. of L *colaphus*, fr Gk *kolaphos* buffet]

copeck /'kohpek/ *n* a kopeck

copepod /'kohpə,pod/ *n* any of a large subclass of usu minute freshwater and marine crustaceans [deriv of Gk *kōpē* oar + *pod-*, *pous* foot] – **copepod** *adj*

Copernican /koh'puhnikən, kə'puh-/ *adj* of Copernicus or the belief that the earth rotates daily on its axis and the planets revolve in orbits round the sun [Nicolaus *Copernicus* †1543 Pol astronomer] – **Copernican** *n*, **Copernicanism** *n*

'cope,stone /-,stohn/ *n* a copingstone

copier /'kopi·ə/ *n* a machine for making copies, esp by photocopying or xeroxing [[2]COPY + [2]-ER]

'co-,pilot /koh/ *n* a qualified aircraft pilot who assists or relieves the pilot but is not in command

coping /'kohping/ *n* the final, usu sloping, course of brick, stone, etc on the top of a wall ☞ ARCHITECTURE

'coping ,saw *n* a narrow-bladed saw used in cutting curved outlines in thin wood [fr prp of *cope* (to cut, notch)]

'coping,stone /-,stohn/ *n*, *chiefly Br* a stone forming (part of) a coping

copious /'kohpi.əs, 'kohpyəs/ *adj* **1** plentiful, lavish ⟨*a* ~ *harvest*⟩ **2** profuse in words or expression [ME, fr L *copiosus*, fr *copia* abundance, fr *co-* + *ops* wealth – more at OPULENT] – **copiously** *adv*, **copiousness** *n*

copita /koh'peetə/ *n* a tulip-shaped glass used esp for sherry [Sp, dim. of *copa* cup]

coplanar /koh'playnə/ *adj* lying or acting in the same plane – **coplanarity** /,kohplay'narəti/ *n*

copolymer·ize, -ise /koh'polimәriez/ *vb* to polymerize (e g 2 different monomers) together – **copolymer** *n*, **copolymerization** /-'zaysh(ə)n/ *n*

'cop-,out *n* an act of copping out – infml

cop out *vi* to avoid an unwanted responsibility or commitment – infml

[1]**copper** /'kopə/ *n* **1** a common reddish metallic element that is ductile and malleable and one of the best conductors of heat and electricity ☞ PERIODIC TABLE **2** a coin or token made of copper or bronze and usu of low value **3** any of various small butterflies with usu copper-coloured wings **4** *chiefly Br* a large metal vessel used, esp formerly, for boiling clothes [ME *coper*, fr OE; akin to OHG *kupfar* copper; both fr a prehistoric WGmc-NGmc word borrowed fr LL *cuprum* copper, fr L (*aes*) *Cyprium*, lit., Cyprian metal] – **coppery** *adj*

[2]**copper** *n* a policeman – infml [[1]*cop*]

copperas /'kopərəs/ *n* a green hydrated (ferrous) iron sulphate [alter. of ME *coperose*, fr MF, fr (assumed) VL *cuprirosa*, fr LL *cuprum* + L *rosa* rose]

,copper 'beech *n* a variety of beech with copper-coloured leaves

,copper-'bottomed *adj*, *chiefly Br* completely safe; reliable ⟨*a* ~ *currency*⟩ ⟨*a* ~ *promise*⟩ – infml

'copper,plate /-,playt/ *n* handwriting modelled on engravings in copper and marked by lines of sharply contrasting thickness; *broadly* formal and ornate handwriting

,copper py'rites *n* chalcopyrite

'copper,smith /-,smith/ *n* sby who works in, or produces articles of, copper

coppice /'kopis/ *n* a thicket, grove, etc of small trees (originating mainly from shoots or root suckers rather than seed) [MF *copeiz*, fr *couper* to cut – more at [3]COPE] – **coppice** *vb*

copr-, copro- *comb form* dung; faeces ⟨copr*olite*⟩ [NL, fr Gk *kopr-*, *kopro-*, fr *kopros*; akin to Skt *śakṛt* dung]

copra /'koprə/ *n* dried coconut meat yielding coconut oil [Pg, fr Malayalam *koppara*]

coprolite /'koprəliet/ *n* fossil excrement – **coprolitic** /-'litik/ *adj*

coprophagous /ko'profəgəs/ *adj* feeding on dung ⟨*a* ~ *beetle*⟩ [Gk *koprophagos*, fr *kopr-* + *-phagos* -phagous] – **coprophagy** /-ji/ *n*

coprophilia /,koprə'fili.ə/ *n* a marked, esp sexual, interest in excrement [NL] – **coprophiliac** /-li,ak/ *n*

copse /kops/ *n* a coppice [by alter.]

Copt /kopt/ *n* a member of a people descended from the ancient Egyptians [Ar *qubt* Copts, fr Coptic *gyptios* Egyptian, fr Gk *aigyptios*]

Coptic /ˈkoptik/ *adj* of the Copts, their Afro-Asiatic liturgical language, or their church – **Coptic** *n*

copula /ˈkopyoolə/ *n* a verb (e g a form of *be* or *seem*) that links a subject and a complement [L, bond]

copulate /ˈkopyoolayt/ *vi* to engage in sexual intercourse [L *copulatus*, pp of *copulare* to join, fr *copula*] – **copulation** /-ˈlaysh(ə)n/ *n*, **copulatory** /-lətri/ *adj*

¹**copulative** /ˈkopyoolətiv/ *adj* **1a** joining together coordinate words or word groups and expressing addition of their meanings **b** functioning as a copula **2** of copulation – **copulatively** *adv*

²**copulative** *n* a copulative word

¹**copy** /ˈkopi/ *n* **1** an imitation, transcript, or reproduction of an original work **2** any of a series of esp mechanical reproductions of an original impression **3** (newsworthy) material ready to be printed or photoengraved [ME *copie*, fr MF, fr ML *copia*, fr L, abundance – more at COPIOUS]

²**copy** *vt* **1** to make a copy of **2** to model oneself on ~ *vi* **1** to make a copy **2** to undergo copying ⟨*the document did not* ~ *well*⟩

ˈ**copy,book** /-ˌbook/ *n* a book formerly used in teaching penmanship and containing models for imitation

ˈ**copy-,book** *adj, Br* completely correct; proper

ˈ**copy,cat** /-ˌkat/ *n* one who slavishly imitates the behaviour or practices of another – used chiefly by children

ˈ**copy-,edit** *vb* to prepare (manuscript copy) for printing, esp by correcting errors and specifying style – **copy editor** *n*

ˈ**copy,hold** /-ˌhohld/ *n* (land held by) a former type of land tenure in England established by a transcript of the manorial records – **copyholder** *n*

copyist /ˈkopi.ist/ *n* one who makes copies

ˈ**copy,reader** /-ˌreedə/ *n* COPY EDITOR; *also* one who edits newspaper copy and adds in headlines

¹ˈ**copy,right** /-ˌriet/ *n* the exclusive legal right to reproduce, publish, and sell a literary, musical, or artistic work ☞ SYMBOL – **copyright** *adj*

²**copyright** *vt* to secure a copyright on

ˈ**copy,taster** /-ˌtaystə/ *n, Br* a journalist who selects potential copy

ˈ**copy,writer** /-ˌrietə/ *n* a writer of advertising or publicity copy

coquetry /ˈkokətri, ˈkoh-/ *n* flirtatious behaviour or attitude

coquette /koˈket, kə-, koh-/ *n* a woman who tries to gain the attention and admiration of men without sincere affection [F, fem of *coquet* wanton, fr dim. of *coq* cock] – **coquettish** *adj*

coquina /koˈkeenə/ *n* a soft whitish limestone formed of broken shells and corals [Sp, prob irreg dim. of *concha* shell]

cor /kaw/ *interj, Br* – used to express surprise or incredulity; slang [euphemism for *God*]

coracle /ˈkorəkl/ *n* a small (nearly) circular boat of a traditional Welsh or Irish design made by covering a wicker frame with waterproof material [W *corwgl*]

coracoid /ˈkorəkoyd/ *adj* of or being a (cartilage) bone that extends from the shoulder blade to or towards the breast bone of many vertebrates [NL *coracoides*, fr Gk *korakoeidēs*, lit., like a raven, fr *korak-*, *korax* raven – more at ¹RAVEN] – **coracoid** *n*

coral /ˈkorəl/ *n* **1** (the hard esp red deposit produced as a skeleton chiefly by) a colony of anthozoan polyps **2** a piece of (red) coral **3a** a bright reddish mass of ovaries (e g of a lobster or scallop) **b** deep orange-pink [ME, fr MF, fr L *corallium*, fr Gk *korallion*] – **coral** *adj*, **coralloid** /-loyd/, **coralloidal** /-ˈloydl/ *adj*

¹**coralline** /ˈkorəlien/ *adj* of or like coral or a coralline [F *corallin*, fr LL *corallinus*, fr L *corallium*]

²**coralline** *n* **1** any of a family of hardened calcium-containing red seaweeds **2** any of various aquatic invertebrate animals, specif a bryozoan or hydroid, that live in colonies and resemble coral

ˈ**coral ,snake** *n* (a harmless snake resembling) any of several brilliantly coloured venomous chiefly tropical New World snakes

cor anglais /ˌkawr ˈong·glay ,- -ˈ- (*Fr* kɔr ɑ̃glɛ/ *n* a double-reed woodwind instrument similar to, and with a range a fifth lower than, the oboe [F, English horn]

¹**corbel** /ˈkawbl/ *n* a projection from a wall which supports a weight; *esp* one stepped upwards and outwards from a vertical surface ☞ ARCHITECTURE [ME, fr MF, fr dim. of *corp* raven, fr L *corvus* – more at ¹RAVEN]

²**corbel** *vt* **-ll-** (*NAm* **-l-**, **-ll-**) to supply with or make into a corbel

corbie /ˈkawbi/ *n, chiefly Scot* CARRION CROW; *also* a raven [ME, modif of OF *corbin*, fr L *corvinus* of a raven, fr *corvus* raven]

corbie gable *n* a gable with stepped sides ☞ ARCHITECTURE

corbie step *n* any of the series of steps on the sloping sides of a corbie gable ☞ ARCHITECTURE – **corbie stepped** *adj*

¹**cord** /kawd/ *n* **1** (a length of) long thin flexible material consisting of several strands (e g of thread or yarn) woven or twisted together **2** a moral, spiritual, or emotional bond **3a** an anatomical structure (e g a nerve) resembling a cord **b** an electric flex **4** a unit of cut wood usu equal to $128ft^3$ (about $3.63m^3$); *also* a stack containing this amount of wood **5a** a rib like a cord on a textile **b(1)** a fabric made with such ribs **(2)** *pl* trousers made of corduroy [ME, fr OF *corde*, fr L *chorda* string, fr Gk *chordē* – more at YARN]

²**cord** *vt* **1** to provide, bind, or connect with a cord **2** to pile up (wood) in cords – **corder** *n*

cordage /ˈkawdij/ *n* ropes, esp in a ship's rigging [¹CORD + -AGE]

cordate /ˈkawdayt/ *adj* heart-shaped ☞ PLANT [NL *cordatus*, fr L *cord-*, *cor*] – **cordately** *adv*

corded /ˈkawdid/ *adj* **1** bound or fastened with cords **2** striped or ribbed (as if) with cord; twilled

¹**cordial** /ˈkawdi.əl/ *adj* **1** warmly and genially affable ⟨*a most* ~ *welcome*⟩ **2** sincerely or deeply felt [ME, fr ML *cordialis*, fr L *cord-*, *cor* heart – more at HEART] – **cordially** *adv*, **cordialness, cordiality** /-ˈaləti/ *n*

²**cordial** *n* **1** a stimulating medicine **2** a nonalcoholic sweetened fruit drink; a fruit syrup

cordillera /ˌkawdiˈlyeərə/ *n* (any of the ranges in) a parallel series of mountain ranges [Sp, fr *cordilla*, dim. of *cuerda* cord, chain, fr L *chorda*] – **cordilleran** *adj*

cordite /'kawdiet/ *n* a smokeless explosive for propelling bullets, shells, etc made from nitroglycerine, guncotton, and petroleum jelly [[1]*cord* + [1]*-ite*]

cordless /'kawdlis/ *adj, of an electrical device* containing the source of electrical power within itself; *esp* battery powered [[1]CORD + -LESS]

cordoba /'kawdəbə/ *n* ☞ *Nicaragua* at NATIONALITY [Sp *córdoba*, fr Francisco Fernández de *Córdoba* †1526 Sp explorer]

[1]**cordon** /'kawd(ə)n/ *n* **1a** *sing or pl in constr* a line of troops, police, etc enclosing an area **b** a line or ring of people or objects **2** a plant, esp a fruit-tree, trained to a single stem by pruning off all side shoots [F, lit., ornamental cord, ribbon, dim. of *corde* cord]

[2]**cordon** *vt* to form a protective or restrictive cordon round – often + *off*

cordon bleu /,kawdonh 'bluh (*Fr* kɔrdɔ̃ blø)/ *adj or n* (typical of or being) sby with great skill or distinction in (classical French) cookery ⟨~ *cooking*⟩ [F, lit., blue cordon]

,cordon ,sani'taire /sani'teə (*Fr* ~ sanitɛːr/ *n* **1** a barrier round an infected region, policed to prevent the spread of infection **2** a buffer zone [F, lit., sanitary cordon]

cordovan /'kawdəv(ə)n/ *n* a soft fine-grained leather, often of horsehide, orig made in Cordoba [OSp *cordován*, fr *Córdova* (now *Córdoba*), city in Spain]

corduroy /'kawd(ə)roy/ *n* **1** a durable usu cotton pile fabric with lengthways ribs or wales **2** *chiefly NAm* a road built of logs laid side by side [perh fr [1]*cord* + obs *duroy* (coarse woollen fabric)]

cordwainer /'kawd,waynə/ *n, archaic* a shoemaker [arch *cordwain* (cordovan), fr ME *cordwane*, fr MF *cordoan*, fr OSp *cordován*] – **cordwainery** *n*

'cord,wood /-,wood/ *n* wood piled or sold in cords; *also* standing timber suitable for use as fuel

[1]**core** /kaw/ *n* **1** a central or interior part, usu distinct from an enveloping part: e g **a** the usu inedible central part of an apple, pineapple, etc **b** the portion of a foundry mould that shapes the interior of a hollow casting **c** a cylindrical portion removed from a mass for inspection; *specif* such a portion of rock got by boring **d(1)** a piece of ferromagnetic material (e g iron) serving to concentrate and intensify the magnetic field resulting from a current in a surrounding coil **(2)** a tiny ring-shaped piece of magnetic material (e g ferrite) used in computer memories **(3) core, core memory, core storage** a computer memory consisting of an array of cores strung on fine wires **e** the central part of a planet, esp the earth **f** a piece of stone (e g flint) from which flakes have been struck for making primitive weapons or tools **g** a conducting wire with its insulation in an electric cable **h** a subject which is central in a course of studies **2** the essential, basic, or central part (e g of an individual, class, or entity) [ME]

[2]**core** *vt* to remove a core from – **corer** *n*

corepressor /,kohri'presə/ *n* a substance that activates a particular genetic repressor (e g by combining with it)

co-respondent /,koh ri'spond(ə)nt/ *n* a person claimed to have committed adultery with the respondent in a divorce case

corgi /'kawgi/ *n, pl* **corgis** (any of) either of 2 varieties of short-legged long-backed dogs with fox-like heads, orig developed in Wales [W, fr *cor* dwarf + *ci* dog; akin to OIr *cū* dog, OE *hund* – more at HOUND]

coriander /,kori'andə/ *n* (the aromatic ripened dried fruits used for flavouring of) an Old World plant of the carrot family [ME *coriandre*, fr OF, fr L *coriandrum*, fr Gk *koriandron*]

Corinthian /kə'rinthi·ən/ *adj* **1** (characteristic) of (inhabitants of) Corinth **2** of the lightest and most ornate of the 3 Greek orders of architecture characterized esp by a bell-shaped capital decorated with acanthus leaves ☞ ARCHITECTURE [L *Corinthiensis*, fr *Corinthus* Corinth, city in ancient Greece, fr Gk *Korinthos*] – **Corinthian** *n*

Co'rinthians *n pl but sing in constr* either of 2 books of the New Testament attributed to St Paul and addressed to the Christians of Corinth

Coriolis force /,kori'ohlis/ *n* a force arising as a result of the earth's rotation that deflects moving objects to the right in the northern hemisphere and to the left in the southern hemisphere [Gaspard G *Coriolis* †1843 F civil engineer]

[1]**cork** /kawk/ *n* **1a** the elastic tough outer tissue of the cork oak used esp for stoppers and insulation **b** the phellem of a plant **2** a usu cork stopper, esp for a bottle **3** an angling float [ME, cork, bark, prob fr Ar *qurq*, fr L *cortic-, cortex*] – **corky** *adj*

[2]**cork** *vt* to fit or close with a cork

corkage /'kawkij/ *n* a charge made for serving alcoholic drink, esp wine, in a restaurant; *esp* one made for serving drink bought elsewhere [[1]CORK + -AGE]

corked /'kawkt/ *adj, of wine* having an unpleasant smell and taste as a result of being kept in a bottle sealed with a leaky cork

corker /'kawkə/ *n* sthg or sby astonishing or superlative – infml; no longer in vogue [[2]CORK + [2]-ER] – **corking** *adj or adv*

'cork ,oak *n* a S European and N African oak from whose bark cork is obtained

[1]**'cork,screw** /-,skrooh/ *n* an implement for removing corks from bottles, typically consisting of a pointed spiral piece of metal attached to a handle

[2]**corkscrew** *vt* to twist into a spiral ~ *vi* to move in a winding course

[3]**corkscrew** *adj* spiral ⟨*a* ~ *staircase*⟩

'cork,wood /-,wood/ *n* the balsa or other tree with light or corky wood

corm /kawm/ *n* a rounded thick underground plant stem base with buds and scaly leaves – compare BULB, TUBER [NL *cormus*, fr Gk *kormos* tree trunk, fr *keirein* to cut – more at SHEAR]

cormorant /'kawmərənt/ *n* a common dark-coloured web-footed European seabird with a long neck, hooked bill, and white throat and cheeks; *also* any of several related seabirds [ME *cormeraunt*, fr MF *cormorant*, fr OF *cormareng*, fr *corp* raven + *marenc* of the sea, fr L *marinus*]

[1]**corn** /kawn/ *n* **1** a small hard seed **2** (the seeds of) the important cereal crop of a particular region (e g wheat and barley in Britain) **3** SWEET CORN **4** sthg corny – infml [ME, fr OE; akin to OHG & ON *korn* grain, L *granum*, Gk *gēras* old age]

[2]**corn** *vt* to preserve or season with salt or brine ⟨~ed *beef*⟩

[3]**corn** *n* a local hardening and thickening of skin (e g on the top of a toe) [ME *corne*, fr MF, horn, corner, fr L *cornu* horn, point]

'corn,cob /-,kob/ *n* **1** the axis on which the edible kernels of sweet corn are arranged **2** an ear of sweet corn

'corn ,cockle *n* a poisonous annual purple-flowered plant of the pink family that is a now rare weed of cornfields

'corn,crake /-,krayk/ *n* a common Eurasian short-billed rail

'corn ,dolly *n* an article of woven straw that orig had ritual significance but is now used for decoration

cornea /kaw'nee·ə, 'kawni·ə/ *n* the hard transparent part of the coat of the eyeball that covers the iris and pupil ☞ NERVE [ML, fr L, fem of *corneus* horny, fr *cornu*] – **corneal** *adj*

cornel /'kawnl/ *n* dogwood or a related plant [deriv of L *cornus* cornel cherry tree; akin to Gk *kerasos* cherry tree]

cornelian /kaw'neelyən/ *n* a hard reddish chalcedony used in jewellery [ME *corneline*, fr MF, perh fr *cornelle* cornel]

corneous /'kawni·əs/ *adj* HORNY 1 [L *corneus*]

[1]corner /'kawnə/ *n* **1a** the point where converging lines, edges, or sides meet; an angle **b** the place of intersection of 2 streets or roads **c** a piece designed to form, mark, or protect a corner (e g of a book) **2** the angular space between meeting lines, edges, or borders: e g **a** the area of a playing field or court near the intersection of the sideline and the goal line or baseline **b** any of the 4 angles of a boxing ring; *esp* that in which a boxer rests between rounds **3** *sing or pl in constr* a contestant's group of supporters, adherents, etc **4** CORNER KICK; *also* CORNER HIT **5a** a private, secret, or remote place ⟨*a quiet* ~ *of a small Welsh town*⟩ ⟨*a hole and* ~ *business*⟩ **b** a difficult or embarrassing situation; a position from which escape or retreat is difficult ⟨*talked himself into a tight* ~⟩ **6** control or ownership of enough of the available supply of a commodity or security to permit manipulation of esp the price **7** a point at which significant change occurs – often in *turn a corner* [ME, fr OF *cornere*, fr *corne* horn, corner] – **cornered** *adj* – **round the corner** imminent; AT HAND ⟨*promised that good times were just* round the corner⟩

[2]corner *vt* **1a** to drive into a corner **b** to catch and hold the attention of, esp so as to force into conversation **2** to get a corner on ⟨~ *the wheat market*⟩ ~ *vi* to turn a corner ⟨*this car* ~s *well*⟩

-cornered /-kawnəd/ *comb form* (→ *adj*) **1** having such or so many corners **2** having so many participants or contestants

'corner ,hit *n* a free hit, esp in hockey or shinty, awarded to the attacking side when a member of the defending side has sent the ball over his/her own goal line

'corner ,kick *n* a free kick in soccer that is taken from the corner of the field and is awarded to the attacking team when a member of the defending team has sent the ball behind his/her own goal line

'corner,stone /-,stohn/ *n* **1** a block of stone forming a part of a corner or angle in a wall; *specif* FOUNDATION STONE **2** the most basic element; a foundation

'corner,wise /-,wiez/ *also* **'corner,ways** /-,wayz/ *adv* diagonally

[1]cornet /'kawnit/ *n* **1** a valved brass instrument resembling a trumpet but with a shorter tube and less brilliant tone **2** sthg shaped like a cone: e g **a** a piece of paper twisted for use as a container **b** an ice cream cone [ME, fr MF, fr dim. of *corn* horn, fr L *cornu*] – **cornetist, cornettist** /'kawnitist, kaw'netist/ *n*

[2]cornet *n* the former fifth commissioned officer of a British cavalry troop who carried the standard [MF *cornette* type of headdress, standard, standard-bearer, fr *corne* horn, fr L *cornu*]

'corn,flakes /-,flayks/ *n pl* toasted flakes of maize eaten as a breakfast cereal

'corn,flour /-,flowə/ *n* a finely ground flour made from maize, rice, etc and used esp as a thickening agent in cooking

'corn,flower /-,flowə/ *n* **1** CORN COCKLE **2** a usu bright-blue-flowered European composite (garden) plant

cornice /'kawnis/ *n* **1a** the ornamental projecting piece that forms the top edge of a building, pillar, etc; *esp* the top projecting part of an entablature ☞ ARCHITECTURE **b** an ornamental plaster moulding between wall and ceiling **2** a decorative band of metal or wood used to conceal curtain fixtures **3** an overhanging mass of snow, ice, etc on a mountain [MF, fr It] – **corniced** *adj*

corniche /kaw'neesh/ *n* a road built along a coast, esp along the face of a cliff [F *cornice, corniche*, lit., cornice]

[1]Cornish /'kawnish/ *adj* (characteristic) of Cornwall [*Corn*wall, county of England + E *-ish*]

[2]Cornish *n* the ancient Celtic language of Cornwall ☞ LANGUAGE

'Corn ,Laws *n pl* a series of laws in force in Britain before 1846 restricting the import of foreign grain

'corn ,mari,gold *n* a European composite golden-yellow-flowered plant that is a weed of cornfields

'corn ,pone /pohn/ *n, S & Mid US* a bread made with maize and baked or fried [[1]*corn* + *pone* bread, of Algonquian origin; akin to Delaware *äpân* baked]

'corn ,silk *n* the silky styles on an ear of maize

'corn,starch /-,stahch/ *n* cornflour

cornucopia /,kawnyoo'kohpi·ə/ *n* **1** a goat's horn overflowing with fruit and corn used to symbolize abundance **2** an inexhaustible store; an abundance **3** a vessel shaped like a horn or cone [LL, fr L *cornu copiae* horn of plenty] – **cornucopian** *adj*

corny /'kawni/ *adj* **1** tiresomely simple and sentimental; trite **2** hackneyed – infml [[1]CORN + [1]-Y] – **cornily** *adv*, **corniness** *n*

corolla /kə'rolə/ *n* the petals of a flower constituting the inner floral envelope [NL, fr L, dim. of *corona*] – **corollate** /kə'rolət, 'korəlayt/ *adj*

corollary /kə'roləri/ *n* **1** a direct conclusion from a proved proposition **2** sthg that naturally follows or accompanies [ME *corolarie*, fr LL *corollarium*, fr L, money paid for a garland, gratuity, fr *corolla*] – **corollary** *adj*

corona /kə'rohnə/ *n* **1** the concave moulding on the upper part of a classical cornice **2a** a usu coloured circle of usu diffracted light seen round and close to a luminous celestial body (e g the sun or moon) **b** the tenuous outermost part of the atmosphere of the sun and other stars appearing as a halo round the moon's black disc during a total eclipse of the sun **c** the upper portion of a bodily part (e g a tooth or the skull) **d** a circular appendage on the inner side of the corolla in the daffodil, jonquil, etc **3** a long straight-sided cigar with a roundly blunt sealed mouth end [L, garland, crown, cornice – more at [1]CROWN; (3) fr *La Corona*, a trademark]

coronach /'korənəkh, -nək/ *n* a Scottish or Irish funeral dirge [ScGael *corranach* & IrGael *coránach*, fr MIr *com-* together + (assumed) MIr *rānach* outcry, weeping]

coronal /'korənl/ *adj* **1** of a corona or crown **2** lying in the direction of the coronal suture – **coronally** *adv*

,coronal 'suture *n* the join between the parietal and frontal bones extending across the top of the skull

[1]**coronary** /'korən(ə)ri/ *adj* (of or being the arteries or veins) of the heart [CORONA + [2]-ARY]

[2]**coronary** *n* CORONARY THROMBOSIS

,coronary throm'bosis /throm'bohsis/ *n* the blocking of a coronary artery of the heart by a blood clot, usu causing death of heart muscle tissue

coronation /,korə'naysh(ə)n/ *n* the act or ceremony of investing a sovereign or his/her consort with the royal crown [ME *coronacion*, fr MF *coronation*, fr *coroner* to crown]

coroner /'korənə/ *n* a public officer whose principal duty is to inquire into the cause of any death which there is reason to suppose might not be due to natural causes [ME, an officer of the crown, fr AF, fr OF *corone* crown, fr L *corona*]

coronet /'korənit/ *n* **1** a small crown **2** an ornamental wreath or band for the head **3** the lower part of a horse's pastern where the horn ends in skin ☞ ANATOMY [MF *coronette*, fr OF *coronete*, fr *corone*]

corpora /'kawpərə/ *pl of* CORPUS

[1]**corporal** /'kawp(ə)rəl/ *adj* of or affecting the body ⟨~ *punishment*⟩ [ME, fr MF, fr L *corporalis*, fr *corpor-*, *corpus* body] – **corporality** /-'aləti/ *n*, **corporally** *adv*

[2]**corporal** *n* ☞ RANK [MF, lowest noncommissioned officer, alter. of *caporal*, fr OIt *caporale*, fr *capo* head, fr L *caput* – more at HEAD]

corporate /'kawp(ə)rət/ *adj* **1a** INCORPORATED 2 **b** of a company **2** of or formed into a unified body of individuals **3** **corporate, corporative** (formed according to the principles) of corporatism ⟨*a ~ state*⟩ [L *corporatus*, pp of *corporare* to make into a body, fr *corpor-*, *corpus*] – **corporately** *adv*

corporation /,kawpə'raysh(ə)n/ *n* **1** *sing or pl in constr* the municipal authorities of a town or city **2** a body made up of more than 1 person which is formed and authorized by law to act as a single person with its own legal identity, rights, and duties **3** an association of employers and employees or of members of a profession in a corporate state **4** a potbelly – humor

,corpo'ration ,tax *n* tax levied on the profits of limited companies

corporatism /'kawp(ə)rə,tiz(ə)m/ *n* the organization of a society into corporations serving as organs of political representation (e g in Fascist Italy) – **corporatist** *adj*

corporeal /kaw'pawri·əl/ *adj* having, consisting of, or relating to a physical material body: e g **a** not spiritual **b** not immaterial or intangible; substantial [L *corporeus* of the body, fr *corpor-*, *corpus*] – **corporealness** *n*, **corporeally** *adv*, **corporeality** /-ri'aləti/ *n*

corposant /'kawpəz(ə)nt/ *n* SAINT ELMO'S FIRE [Pg *corpo-santo*, lit., holy body]

corps /kaw/ *n, pl* **corps** /kawz/ **1** *sing or pl in constr* an army unit usu consisting of 2 or more divisions (organized for a particular purpose) **2** any of various associations of German university students [F, fr L *corpus* body]

corps de ballet /,kaw də 'balay, *NAm* ba'lay/ *n, pl* **corps de ballet** /~/ the ensemble of a ballet company [F]

corpse /kawps/ *n* a dead (human) body [ME *corps*, fr MF, fr L *corpus*]

corpulence /'kawpyooləns/, **corpulency** /-si/ *n* the state of being excessively fat; obesity [MF *corpulence*, fr L *corpulentia*, fr *corpulentus* large-bodied, fr *corpus*] – **corpulent** *adj*

corpus /'kawpəs/ *n, pl* **corpora** /'kawpərə/ **1** the body or corpse of a human or animal **2** the main body or corporeal substance of a thing; *esp* the main part of a bodily structure or organ ⟨*the ~ of the uterus*⟩ **3a** a collection or body of writings or works (e g of 1 author or artist), esp of a particular kind or on a particular subject **b** a body of spoken and/or written language for linguistic study [ME, fr L]

,corpus al'latum /ə'laytəm/ *n, pl* **corpora allata** /,kawpərə ə'laytə/ either of a pair of organs that lie behind the brain of many insects and secrete esp juvenile hormones [NL, lit., applied body]

corpus callosum /kə'lohs(ə)m/ *n, pl* **corpora callosa** /,kawpərə ko'lohsə/ a wide band of nerve fibres joining the cerebral hemispheres in the brains of humans and other higher mammals [NL, lit., callous body]

,Corpus 'Christi /'kristi/ *n* the Thursday after Trinity Sunday observed, esp by Roman Catholics, in honour of the Eucharist [ME, fr ML, lit., body of Christ]

corpuscle /'kawpəsl, -pu-, kaw'pusl/ *n* **1** a minute particle **2a** a living (blood) cell ☞ ANATOMY **b** any of various very small multicellular parts of an organism [L *corpusculum*, dim. of *corpus*] – **corpuscular** /kaw'puskyoolə/ *adj*

,corpus de'licti /di'likti/ *n, pl* **corpora delicti** /,kawpərə ~/ the body of facts showing that a breach of the law has taken place; *esp* the body of the victim in a case of murder [NL, lit., body of the crime]

,corpus 'luteum /'loohti·əm/ *n, pl* **corpora lutea** /,kawpərə 'loohti·ə/ a reddish-yellow mass of hormone-secreting tissue that forms in the mammalian ovary after ovulation and quickly returns to its original state if the ovum is not fertilized [NL, lit., yellowish body]

corrade /kə'rayd/ *vb vb* to erode by abrasion ⟨~d *rocks*⟩ [L *corradere* to scrape together, fr *com-* + *radere* to scrape – more at RAT] – **corrasion** /kə'rayzh(ə)n/ *n*, **corrasive** /kə'raysiv, -ziv/ *adj*

[1]**corral** /kə'rahl, ko-, kaw-, -ral/ *n* **1** a pen or enclosure for confining livestock **2** an enclosure made with wagons for defence of an encampment [Sp, fr (assumed) VL *currale* enclosure for vehicles, fr L *currus* cart, fr *currere* to run – more at CAR]

[2]**corral** *vt* **-ll- 1** to enclose in a corral **2** to arrange (wagons) so as to form a corral

[1]**correct** /kə'rekt/ *vt* **1** to alter or adjust so as to counteract some imperfection or failing **2a** to punish (e g a child) with a view to reforming or improving **b** to point out the faults of ⟨~*ing essays*⟩ [ME *correcten*, fr L *correctus*, pp of *corrigere*, fr *com-* + *regere* to lead straight – more at [1]RIGHT] – **correctable**

adj, **corrective** *adj or n*, **correctively** *adv*, **corrector** *n*

[2]**correct** *adj* **1** conforming to an approved or conventional standard **2** true, right [ME, corrected, fr L *correctus*, fr pp of *corrigere*] – **correctly** *adv*, **correctness** *n*

correction /kə'reksh(ə)n/ *n* **1a** an amendment **b** a rebuke, punishment **2a** sthg substituted, esp written, in place of what is wrong **b** a quantity applied by way of correcting (e g in adjusting an instrument) [[1]CORRECT + -ION] – **correctional** *adj*

[1]**correlate** /'korilayt, -lət/ *n* either of 2 things so related that one directly implies the other (e g husband and wife) [back-formation fr *correlation*] – **correlate** *adj*

[2]**correlate** /'korilayt/ *vi* to have reciprocal or mutual relationship ~ *vt* **1** to establish a mutual or reciprocal relation of **2** to relate so that to each member of one set or series a corresponding member of another is assigned – **correlatable** *adj*

correlation /,kori'laysh(ə)n/ *n* **1** a relation of phenomena as invariable accompaniments of each other **2** an interdependence between mathematical variables, esp in statistics ☞ STATISTICS [ML *correlation-*, *correlatio*, fr L *com-* + *relation-*, *relatio* relation] – **correlational** *adj*

correlative /kə'relətiv, ko-/ *adj* naturally related; corresponding – **correlative** *n*, **correlatively** *adv*

correspond /,kori'spond/ *vi* **1a** to be in conformity or agreement; suit, match – usu + *to* or *with* **b** to be equivalent or parallel **2** to communicate *with* a person by exchange of letters [MF or ML; MF *correspondre*, fr ML *correspondēre*, fr L *com-* + *respondēre* to respond]

correspondence /,kori'spond(ə)ns/ *n* **1a** the agreement of things with one another **b** a particular similarity **c** an association of 1 or more members of one set with each member of another set **2a** (communication by) letters **b** the news, information, or opinion contributed by a correspondent to a newspaper or periodical

,corre'spondence ,college *n* a college that teaches nonresident students by post

[1]**correspondent** /,kori'spond(ə)nt/ *adj* **1** corresponding **2** fitting, conforming ***USE*** + *with* or *to* [ME, fr MF or ML; MF, fr ML *correspondent-*, *correspondens*, prp of *correspondēre*]

[2]**correspondent** *n* **1** one who communicates with another by letter **2** one who has regular commercial relations with another **3** one who contributes news or comment to a publication or radio or television network ⟨*a war* ~⟩

corresponding /,kori'sponding/ *adj* **1a** agreeing in some respect (e g kind, degree, position, or function) **b** related, accompanying **2** participating at a distance and by post ⟨*a* ~ *member of the society*⟩ – **correspondingly** *adv*

corrida /ko'reedhə, -də/ *n* a bullfight [Sp, lit., act of running]

corridor /'koridaw, -də/ *n*, **1** a passage (e g in a hotel or railway carriage) onto which compartments or rooms open **2** a usu narrow passageway or route: e g **a** a narrow strip of land through foreign-held territory **b** a restricted path for air traffic **3** a strip of land that by geographical characteristics is distinct from its surroundings [MF, fr OIt *corridore*, fr *correre* to run, fr L *currere* – more at CAR]

corrie /kori/ *n*, *chiefly Scot* a steep-sided bowl-like valley in the side of a mountain; a cwm, cirque [ScGael *coire*, lit., kettle]

corrigendum /,kori'jendəm/ *n*, *pl* **corrigenda** /-də/ an error in a printed work, shown with its correction on a separate sheet [L, neut of *corrigendus*, gerundive of *corrigere* to correct]

corroborant /kə'robərənt/ *adj*, *archaic*, *of a medicine* having an invigorating effect [L *corroborant-*, *corroborans*, prp of *corroborare*]

corroborate /kə'robərayt/ *vt* to support with evidence or authority; make more certain [L *corroboratus*, pp of *corroborare*, fr *com-* + *robor-*, *robur* strength] – **corroborative** /-b(ə)rətiv/, **corroboratory** /-b(ə)rətri/ *adj*, **corroborator** /-bə,raytə/ *n*, **corroboration** /-'raysh(ə)n/ *n*

corroboree /kə'robəri/ *n* **1** a nocturnal Australian aboriginal festivity with songs and symbolic dances to celebrate important events **2** *Austr* **a** a noisy festivity **b** a tumult [native name in New South Wales, Australia]

corrode /kə'rohd/ *vt* **1** to eat or wear (esp metal) away gradually, esp by chemical action **2** to weaken or destroy (as if) by corrosion ~ *vi* to undergo corroding [ME *corroden*, fr L *corrodere* to gnaw to pieces, fr *com-* + *rodere* to gnaw – more at RAT] – **corrodible** *adj*

corrosion /kə'rohzh(ə)n/ *n* the action or process of corroding; *also* the product of such a process [ME, fr LL *corrosion-*, *corrosio* act of gnawing, fr L *corrosus*, pp of *corrodere*]

corrosive /kə'rohsiv, -ziv/ *adj* **1** corroding ⟨~ *acids*⟩ ⟨~ *action*⟩ ☞ SYMBOL **2** bitingly sarcastic – **corrosive** *n*, **corrosively** *adv*, **corrosiveness** *n*

co,rrosive 'sublimate *n* mercuric chloride

corrugate /'korəgayt, -roo-/ *vb* to shape or become shaped into alternating ridges and grooves; furrow ⟨~d *cardboard*⟩ ⟨~d *iron*⟩ [L *corrugatus*, pp of *corrugare*, fr *com-* + *ruga* wrinkle – more at ROUGH] – **corrugation** /-'gaysh(ə)n/ *n*

[1]**corrupt** /kə'rupt/ *vt* **1a** to change from good to bad in morals, manners, or actions; *also* to influence by bribery **b** to degrade with unsound principles or moral values **2** to alter from the original or correct form or version ~ *vi* to become corrupt [ME *corrupten*, fr L *corruptus*, pp of *corrumpere*, fr *com-* + *rumpere* to break – more at BEREAVE] – **corrupter**, **corruptor** *n*, **corruptible** *adj*, **corruptibly** *adv*, **corruptibility** /-tə'biləti/ *n*, **corruptive** *adj*

[2]**corrupt** *adj* **1a** morally degenerate and perverted **b** characterized by bribery **2** having been vitiated by mistakes or changes ⟨*a* ~ *text*⟩ [ME, fr MF or L; MF, fr L *corruptus*, fr pp of *corrumpere*] – **corruptly** *adv*, **corruptness** *n*

corruption /kə'rupsh(ə)n/ *n* **1** impairment of integrity, virtue, or moral principle **2** decay, decomposition **3** inducement by bribery to do wrong **4** a departure from what is pure or correct [[1]CORRUPT + -ION]

corsage /kaw'sahzh/ *n* an arrangement of flowers to be worn by a woman, esp on the bodice [F, bust, bodice, fr OF, bust, fr *cors* body, fr L *corpus*]

corsair /'kawseə/ *n* a pirate; *esp* a privateer of the Barbary coast [MF & OIt; MF *corsaire* pirate, fr OProv *corsari*, fr OIt *corsaro*, fr ML *cursarius*, fr L *cursus* course – more at COURSE]

corselette /,kawsə'let/, **corselet** /'kawslit/ *n*, a one-piece undergarment combining girdle and bra [fr *Corselette*, a trademark]

[1]**corset** /'kawsit/ *n* a boned supporting undergarment for women, extending from beneath the bust to below the hips, and designed to give shape to the figure; *also* a similar garment worn by men and women, esp in cases of injury [ME, fr OF, dim. of *cors*]

[2]**corset** *vt* to restrict closely

corsetiere /,kawseti'eə, kaw,se-/ *n* sby who makes, fits, or sells corsets, girdles, or bras [F *corsetière*, fem of *corsetier*, fr *corset*]

corsetry /'kawsitri/ *n* (women's) undergarments that give support or shape

corslet, corselet /'kawslit/ *n* a piece of armour for the trunk but usu not the arms or legs [MF *corselet*, dim. of *cors* body, bodice]

cortege /kaw'tayzh, -'teəzh/ *also* **cortège** /kaw'tezh/ *n* **1** a train of attendants; a retinue **2** a procession; *esp* a funeral procession [F *cortège*, fr It *corteggio*, fr *corteggiare* to court, fr *corte* court, fr L *cohort-, cohors* throng – more at COURT]

cortex /'kawteks/ *n, pl* **cortices** /'kawtiseez/, **cortexes** **1** a plant bark (e g cinchona) used medicinally **2** the outer part of the kidney, adrenal gland, a hair, etc; *esp* the outer layer of grey matter of the brain ☞ NERVE **3** the layer of (parenchymatous) tissue between the inner vascular tissue and the outer epidermal tissue of a green plant [L *cortic-, cortex* bark – more at CUIRASS]

cortical /'kawtikl/ *adj* **1** (consisting) of a cortex **2** involving or resulting from the action or condition of the cerebral cortex – **cortically** *adv*

corticate /'kawtikət, -kayt/ *adj* having a cortex

cortico- /kawtikoh-/ *comb form* **1** cortex ⟨cortico*steroid*⟩ **2** cortical and ⟨cortico*spinal*⟩

corticoid /'kawtikoyd/ *n* a corticosteroid

corticosteroid /,kawtikoh'stiəroyd/ *n* (a synthetic drug with actions similar to those of) any of several steroids (e g cortisone) produced by the cortex of the adrenal gland [ISV]

corticotrophin /,kawtikoh'trohfin/ *n* ADRENOCORTICOTROPHIC HORMONE [*cortico-* + *troph*ic + *-in*]

corticotropin /,kawtikoh'trohpin/ *n* corticotrophin [*cortico-* + [3]*trop*ic + *-in*]

cortisol /'kawtisol, -zol, -sohl, -zohl/ *n* hydrocortisone [*corti*sone + *-ol*]

cortisone /'kawtisohn, -zohn/ *n* a glucocorticoid steroid hormone that is produced by the cortex of the adrenal gland [alter. of *corticosterone* (steroid hormone of the adrenal cortex)]

corundum /kə'rundəm/ *n* a very hard natural or synthetic mineral that consists of aluminium oxide, exists in various colours, and is used as an abrasive and a gemstone – compare RUBY, SAPPHIRE [Tamil *kuruntam*, fr Skt *kuruvinda* ruby]

coruscate /'korəskayt/ *vi* to sparkle, flash ⟨*her* coruscating *wit*⟩ [L *coruscatus*, pp of *coruscare*] – **coruscation** *n*

corvée /'kaw,vay, ,-'-/ *n* labour exacted in lieu of taxes by public authorities [ME *corvee*, fr MF, fr ML *corrogata*, fr L, fem of *corrogatus*, pp of *corrogare* to collect, requisition, fr *com-* + *rogare* to ask – more at [1]RIGHT]

corvette /kaw'vet/ *n* **1** a small sailing warship with a flush deck **2** a small highly manoeuvrable armed escort ship [F]

corvine /'kawvien/ *adj* of or related to the crows; resembling a crow [L *corvinus*, fr *corvus* raven – more at [1]RAVEN]

corymb /'korim(b)/ *n* a flat-topped inflorescence; *specif* one in which the flower stalks are attached at different levels on the main axis ☞ PLANT [F *corymbe*, fr L *corymbus* cluster of fruit or flowers, fr Gk *korymbos*] – **corymbed** *adj*, **corymbose** /-,bohs/ *adj*, **corymbosely** *adv*

coryphaeus /,kori'fee·əs/ *n, pl* **coryphaei** /-'fee·ie/ the leader of a Greek chorus [L, leader, fr Gk *koryphaios*, fr *koryphē* summit; akin to L *cornu*]

coryphée /,kawri'fay/ *n* a ballet dancer who dances in a small group instead of in the corps de ballet or as a soloist [F, fr L *coryphaeus*]

coryza /kə'riezə/ *n* short-lasting infectious inflammation of the upper respiratory tract; *esp* COMMON COLD [LL, fr Gk *koryza* nasal mucus; akin to OHG *hroz* nasal mucus, Skt *kardama* mud] – **coryzal** *adj*

[1]**cos** /kəz; *strong* koz/ *conj* because – used in writing to represent a casual or childish pronunciation [by shortening & alter.]

[2]**cos** /koz/, **'cos ,lettuce** *n* a long-leaved variety of lettuce [*Kos, Cos*, Gk island]

cosecant /koh'seekənt, -'se-/ *n* the trigonometric function that is the reciprocal of the sine [NL *cosecant-, cosecans*, fr *co-* + *secant-, secans* secant]

coseismal /,koh'siezməl/ *n or adj* (a line joining points) simultaneously affected by the same phase of seismic shock [*co-* + *seism-* + *-al*]

cosh /kosh/ *vt or n, chiefly Br* (to strike with) a short heavy rod often enclosed in a softer material and used as a hand weapon [perh fr Romany *kosh* stick]

cosine /'koh,sien/ *n* the trigonometric function that for an acute angle in a right-angled triangle is the ratio between the side adjacent to the angle and the hypotenuse ☞ MATHEMATICS [NL *cosinus*, fr *co-* + ML *sinus* sine]

[1]**cosmetic** /koz'metik/ *n* a cosmetic preparation for external use

[2]**cosmetic** *adj* of or intended to improve beauty (e g of the hair or complexion) ⟨~ *surgery*⟩; *broadly* intended to improve the outward appearance [Gk *kosmētikos* skilled in adornment, fr *kosmein* to arrange, adorn, fr *kosmos* order] – **cosmetically** *adv*, **cosmetology** /,kozmi'toləji/ *n*, **cosmetologist** *n*

cosmetician /,kozmi'tish(ə)n/ *n* sby who is professionally trained in the use of cosmetics

cosmic /'kozmik/ *also* **cosmical** /-kl/ *adj* **1** of the universe in contrast to the earth alone **2** great in extent, intensity, or comprehensiveness [Gk *kosmikos*, fr *kosmos* order, universe] – **cosmically** *adv*

,cosmic 'dust *n* very fine particles of solid matter in any part of the universe

,cosmic 'ray *n* a stream of highly energetic radiation reaching the earth's atmosphere from space – usu pl with sing. meaning

cosmodrome /'kozmə,drohm/ *n* an establishment for launching esp Soviet space vehicles [Russ *kosmodrom*, fr *kosmo*navt cosmonaut + *-drom* -drome]

cosmogony /koz'mogəni/ *n* (a theory of) the creation or origin of the universe [NL *cosmogonia*, fr Gk *kosmogonia*, fr *kosmos* + *gonos* offspring] – **cosmogonist** *n*, **cosmogonic** /-'gonik/, **cosmogonical** *adj*

cosmography /koz'mogrəfi/ *n* **1** a general description of the world or the universe **2** a branch of science dealing with the constitution of the universe

[ME *cosmographie*, fr LL *cosmographia*, fr Gk *kosmographia*, fr *kosmos* + *-graphia* -graphy] – **cosmographer** *n*, **cosmographic** /ˌkozmə'grafik/, **cosmographical** *adj*, **cosmographically** *adv*

cosmology /koz'moləji/ *n* **1** a theoretical account of the nature of the universe **2** astronomy dealing with the origin, structure, and space-time relationships of the universe [NL *cosmologia*, fr Gk *kosmos* + NL *-logia* -logy] – **cosmologic** /ˌkozmə'lojik/, **cosmological** *adj*, **cosmologically** *adv*, **cosmologist** /koz'moləjist/ *n*

cosmonaut /'kozməˌnawt/ *n* a usu Soviet astronaut ☞ SPACE [part trans of Russ *kosmonavt*, fr Gk *kosmos* + Russ *-navt* (as in *aeronavt* aeronaut)]

[1]**cosmopolitan** /ˌkozmə'polit(ə)n/ *adj* **1** having worldwide rather than provincial scope or bearing **2** marked by a sophistication that comes from wide and often international experience **3** composed of people, constituents, or elements from many parts of the world **4** *of a plant, animal, etc* found in most parts of the world and under varied ecological conditions – **cosmopolitanism** *n*

[2]**cosmopolitan** *n* a cosmopolite

cosmopolite /koz'mopəliet/ *n* a cosmopolitan person or organism [NL *cosmopolites*, fr Gk *kosmopolitēs*, fr *kosmos* + *politēs* citizen] – **cosmopolitism** /koz'mopəˌlieˌtiz(ə)m, -ləˌtiz(ə)m, ˌkozmə'poliˌtiz(ə)m/ *n*

cosmos /'kozmos/ *n* **1** an orderly universe – compare CHAOS **2** a complex and orderly system that is complete in itself **3** any of a genus of tropical American composite plants grown for their yellow or red flower heads [G *kosmos*, fr Gk]

cossack /'kosak/ *n* a member of a people of the SE USSR famous for their skill as horsemen [Russ *kazak* & Ukrainian *kozak*, fr Turk *kazak* free person]

cosset /'kosit/ *vt* to treat as a pet; pamper [*cosset* (pet lamb), perh deriv of OE *cotsæta* cottager]

[1]**cost** /kost/ *n* **1a** the price paid or charged for sthg **b** the expenditure (e g of effort or sacrifice) made to achieve an object **2** the loss or penalty incurred in gaining sthg **3** *pl* expenses incurred in litigation – **costless** *adj* – **at all costs** regardless of the price or difficulties – **to one's cost** to one's disadvantage or loss

[2]**cost** *vb* **cost,** (*vt* 2) **costed** *vi* **1** to require a specified expenditure ⟨*the best goods ~ more*⟩ **2** to require the specified effort, suffering, or loss ~ *vt* **1** to cause to pay, suffer, or lose ⟨*frequent absences ~ him his job*⟩ ⟨*your suggestion would ~ us too much time*⟩ **2** to estimate or set the cost of [ME *costen*, fr MF *coster*, fr L *constare* to stand firm, to cost – more at CONSTANT]

costa /'kostə/ *n, pl* **costae** /'kosti/ (the front vein of an insect wing or other part that resembles) a rib [L – more at COAST] – **costal** *adj*, **costate** /'kostayt/ *adj*

'**cost acˌcounting** *n* the systematic recording and analysis of the costs of material, labour, and overheads that are incurred during production – **cost accountant** *n*

'**co-ˌstar** /koh/ *n* a star who has equal billing with another leading performer in a film or play – **co-star** *vb*

ˌ**cost-ef'fective** *adj* economically worthwhile – **cost-effectiveness** *n*

costermonger /'kostəˌmung·gə/ *n, Br* a seller of articles, esp fruit or vegetables, from a street barrow or stall [alter. of obs *costardmonger*, fr *costard* (large apple) + *monger*]

costive /'kostiv/ *adj* affected with or causing constipation [ME, fr MF *costivé*, pp of *costiver* to constipate, fr L *constipare*] – **costively** *adv*, **costiveness** *n*

costly /'kostli/ *adj* **1** valuable, expensive **2** made at great expense or with considerable sacrifice – **costliness** *n*

costmary /'kostˌmeəri/ *n* a composite plant that resembles tansy and is used as a herb and in flavouring [ME *costmarie*, fr *coste* costmary (fr OE *cost*, fr L *costum*, fr Gk *kostos*, a fragrant root) + *Marie* the Virgin Mary]

ˌ**cost of 'living** *n* the cost of purchasing those goods and services which are included in an accepted standard level of consumption

ˌ**cost-of-'living ˌindex** *n* RETAIL PRICE INDEX

'**cost-ˌplus** *adj* calculated on the basis of a fixed fee or a percentage added to actual cost ⟨*~ pricing*⟩

'**cost-ˌpush** *n* an increase or upward trend in production costs, sometimes considered to result in increased consumer prices irrespective of the level of demand – compare DEMAND-PULL – **cost-push** *adj*

[1]**costume** /'kostyoohm, 'kostyoom/ *n* **1** a distinctive fashion in coiffure, jewellery, and apparel of a period, country, class, or group **2** a set of garments suitable for a specified occasion, activity, or season **3** a set of garments belonging to a specific time, place or, character, worn in order to assume a particular role (e g in a play or at a fancy-dress party) *USE* ☞ GARMENT [F, fr It, custom, dress, fr L *consuetudin-*, *consuetudo* custom – more at CUSTOM] – **costumey** *adj*

[2]**costume** *vt* **1** to provide with a costume **2** to design costumes for ⟨*~ a play*⟩

[3]**costume** *adj* characterized by the use of costumes ⟨*a ~ ball*⟩ ⟨*a ~ drama*⟩

ˌ**costume 'jewellery** *n* inexpensive jewellery typically worn attached to clothing rather than on the body

costumier /ko'styoohmi·ə/, **costumer** /'kostyoohmə, -yoo-, ko'styoohmə/ *n* sby who deals in or makes costumes (e g for theatrical productions) [F]

[1]**cosy,** *NAm chiefly* **cozy** /'kohzi/ *adj* **1** enjoying or affording warmth and ease; snug **2a** marked by the intimacy of the family or a close group **b** self-satisfied, complacent [prob of Scand origin; akin to Norw *koselig* snug, cosy] – **cosily** *adv*

[2]**cosy,** *NAm chiefly* **cozy** *n* a covering, esp for a teapot, designed to keep the contents hot

[1]**cot** /kot/ *n* a small house; a cottage – poetic [ME, fr OE; akin to ON *kot* small hut, L *guttur* throat]

[2]**cot** *n* **1** a lightweight bedstead **2** a small bed with high enclosing sides, esp for a child **3** *chiefly NAm* CAMP BED [Hindi *khāṭ* bedstead, fr Skt *khaṭvā*, of Dravidian origin; akin to Tamil *kaṭṭil* bedstead]

cotangent /koh'tanj(ə)nt, '-,--/ *n* the trigonometric function that is the reciprocal of the tangent [NL *cotangent-*, *cotangens*, fr *co-* + *tangent-*, *tangens* tangent]

'**cot-ˌdeath** *n* the death of a young baby from no apparent disease

cote /koht/ *n* a shed or coop for small domestic animals, esp pigeons [ME, fr OE]

coterie /'kohtəri/ *n* a close group of people with a

unifying common interest or purpose [F, fr MF, tenants, fr (assumed) MF *cotier* peasant occupying a cottage, fr ML *cotarius*]

coterminous /koh'tuhminəs/ *adj* **1** having the same boundaries ⟨~ *states*⟩ **2** coextensive in scope or duration ⟨~ *interests*⟩ [alter. of *conterminous*, fr L *conterminus*, fr *com-* + *terminus* boundary – more at TERM] – **coterminously** *adv*

cotidal /,koh'tiedl/ *adj* indicating equality in the tides or a coincidence in the time of high or low tide

cotillion *also* **cotillon** /kə'tilyən/ *n* **1** an elaborate French dance with frequent changing of partners **2** *NAm* a formal ball [F *cotillon*, lit., petticoat, fr OF, fr *cote* coat]

cotoneaster /kə,tohni'astə/ *n* any of a genus of Old World flowering shrubs of the rose family [NL, genus name, fr L *cydonia, cotoneum* quince + NL *-aster*]

Cotswold /'kots,wohld, -wəld/ *n* a sheep of a large long-woolled English breed [*Cotswold* hills, England]

cotta /'kotə/ *n* a waist-length surplice [ML, of Gmc origin; akin to OHG *kozza* coarse mantle – more at COAT]

cottage /'kotij/ *n* a small house, esp in the country [ME *cotage*, fr (assumed) AF, fr ME *cot*] – **cottager** *n*, **cottagey** *adj*

,cottage 'cheese *n* a soft white bland cheese made from the curds of skimmed milk

,cottage 'hospital *n*, *Br* a small hospital without resident doctors

cottage industry *n* an industry whose work force consists of family units working at home with their own equipment

,cottage 'pie *n* a shepherd's pie esp made with minced beef

cotter /'kotə/ *n* a wedge-shaped or tapered piece used to fasten parts of a structure together [origin unknown]

'cotter ,pin *n* (a pin for securing) a cotter; *also* SPLIT PIN

[1]**cotton** /'kot(ə)n/ *n* **1** (a plant producing or grown for) a soft usu white fibrous substance composed of the hairs surrounding the seeds of various tropical plants of the mallow family **2a** fabric made of cotton **b** yarn spun from cotton [ME *coton*, fr MF, fr Ar *qutn*]

[2]**cotton** *vi* to come to understand; CATCH ON 2 – usu + *on* or *onto*; infml

'cotton ,gin *n* a machine for separating the seeds, seed cases, and foreign material from cotton

'cotton ,grass *n* any of a genus of sedges with tufted spikes

'cotton,seed ,cake /'kot(ə)n,seed/ *n* a compressed mass of cotton seeds used for feeding cattle

'cotton,wood /-,wood/ *n* a poplar of the USA with a tuft of cottony hairs on the seed

,cotton 'wool *n* **1** raw cotton; *esp* cotton pressed into sheets used esp for lining, cleaning, or as a surgical dressing **2** an overprotected comfortable environment

cottony /'kot(ə)ni/ *adj* covered with (soft long) hairs [[1]COTTON + [1]-Y]

cotyl- /kotil-/, **cotyli-**, **cotylo-** *comb form* (organ or part like a) cup ⟨cotyl*oid*⟩ [Gk *kotyl-, kotylo-*, fr *kotylē*]

-cotyl /-'kotil/ *comb form* (→ *n*) cotyledon ⟨*di*cotyl⟩ [*cotyledon*]

cotyledon /,koti'leed(ə)n/ *n* **1** a lobule of the placenta of a mammal **2** the first leaf or either of the first pair or whorl of leaves developed by the embryo of a seed plant [NL, fr Gk *kotylēdōn* cup-shaped hollow, fr kotylē cup] – **cotyledonal** *adj*, **cotyledonary, cotyledonous** *adj*

[1]**couch** /kowch/ *vt* **1** to lower to and hold in an attacking position ⟨~ed *his lance*⟩ **2** to treat (a cataract) by displacing the lens of the eye **3** to phrase in a specified manner ⟨~ed *in hostile terms*⟩ – fml ~ *vi*, *of an animal* to lie down to sleep; *also* to lie in ambush [ME *couchen*, fr MF *coucher*, fr L *collocare* to set in place – more at COLLOCATE]

[2]**couch** *n* **1** a piece of furniture for sitting or lying on **a** with a back and usu armrests **b** with a low back and raised head-end **2** a long upholstered seat with a headrest for patients to lie on during medical examination or psychoanalysis **3** the den of an animal (e g an otter)

couchette /kooh'shet/ *n* a seat in a railway-carriage compartment that converts into a bunk [F, dim. of *couche* couch]

'couch ,grass /'kowch, 'koohch/ *n* any of several grasses that spread rapidly by long creeping underground stems and are difficult to eradicate [alter. of *quitch grass*]

coudé /'koohday, -'-/ *adj* (of or relating to a telescope) constructed so that light is reflected to a focus at a fixed place where the holder for a photographic plate, spectrograph, etc may be mounted [F *coudé* bent like an elbow, fr *coude* elbow, fr L *cubitum* – more at [2]HIP]

cougar /'koohgə/ *n*, *pl* **cougars**, *esp collectively* **cougar** *chiefly NAm* a puma [F *couguar*, fr NL *cuguacuarana*, modif of Tupi *suasuarana*, lit., false deer, fr *suasú* deer + *rana* false]

[1]**cough** /kof/ *vi* **1** to expel air from the lungs suddenly with an explosive noise **2** to make a noise like that of coughing ~ *vt* to expel by coughing ⟨~ *up mucus*⟩ [ME *coughen*, fr (assumed) OE *cohhian*; akin to MHG *kūchen* to breathe heavily]

[2]**cough** *n* **1** a condition marked by repeated or frequent coughing **2** an act or sound of coughing

'cough ,drop *n* a medicated sweet for relieving coughing and soothing a sore throat

cough up *vb* to produce or hand over (esp money or information) unwillingly – infml

could /kəd; *strong* kood/ *verbal auxiliary* **1** *past of* CAN – used in the past ⟨*he found he* ~ *go*⟩, in the past conditional ⟨*he said he would go if he* ~⟩, as an alternative to *can* suggesting less force or certainty ⟨*you* ~ *be right*⟩, as a polite form in the present ⟨~ *you do this for me*⟩, as an alternative to *might* expressing purpose in the past ⟨*wrote it down so that I* ~ *remember it*⟩, and as an alternative to *ought* or *should* ⟨*you* ~ *at least apologize*⟩ **2** feel impelled to ⟨*I* ~ *wring her neck*⟩ [ME *couthe, coude*, fr OE *cūthe*; akin to OHG *konda* could]

couldn't /'koodnt/ could not

coulee /'koohli/ *also* **coulée** /'koohlay/ *n* **1** a thick stream of lava **2** *NAm* a (deep) ravine [CanF *coulée*, fr F, flowing, flow of lava, fr *couler* to flow, fr L *colare* to strain, fr *colum* sieve]

couloir /'koohlwah/ *n* a gorge in a mountainside [F, lit., strainer, fr LL *colatorium*, fr L *colatus*, pp of *colare*]

coulomb /'kooh,lom, -lohm, -'-/ *n* the SI unit of electric charge ☞ PHYSICS [Charles A de *Coulomb* †1806 F physicist]

coulter /'kohltə/ *n* a blade or sharp disc attached to the beam of a plough that makes a vertical cut in the ground in front of the ploughshare [ME *colter,* fr OE *culter* & OF *coltre,* both fr L *culter* ploughshare]

coumarin /'koohmərin/ *n* a compound with the smell of new-mown hay obtained from plants or made synthetically and used esp in perfumery [F *coumarine,* fr *coumarou* tonka bean tree, fr Sp or Pg; Sp *coumarú,* fr Pg, fr Tupi]

coumarone /'koohmə,rohn/ *n* a compound obtained from coal tar and used to make resins that are used in varnishes, printing inks, etc [ISV *coumarin* + *-one*]

[1]**council** /'kownsl, -sil/ *n* **1** an assembly, meeting **2a** *sing or pl in constr* an elected or appointed body with administrative, legislative, or advisory powers **b** a locally-elected body having power over a parish, district, county, etc [ME *counceil,* fr OF *concile,* fr L *concilium,* fr *com-* + *calare* to call – more at [1]LOW]

[2]**council** *adj* **1** used by a council ⟨*a* ~ *chamber*⟩ **2** *Br* provided, maintained, or operated by local government ⟨~ *flats*⟩

councillor /'kowns(ə)lə, -silə/, *NAm also* **councilor** *n* a member of a council

,**council of 'ministers** *n sing or pl in constr, often cap C&M* CABINET 2

[1]**counsel** /'kownsl/ *n, pl* **counsels,** (*4*) **counsel 1** advice **2** deliberation, consultation **3** thoughts or intentions – chiefly in *keep one's own counsel* **4a** a barrister engaged in the trial of a case in court **b** a lawyer appointed to advise a client [ME *conseil,* fr OF, fr L *consilium,* fr *consulere* to consult]

[2]**counsel** *vt* **-ll-** (*NAm* **-l, -ll-**), /'kownsl·ing/ to advise

counselling /'kownsl·ing/, *NAm chiefly* **counseling** *n* professional guidance in personal and social matters

counsellor, *NAm chiefly* **counselor** /'kownsl·ə/ *n* **1** an adviser **2** *NAm* a lawyer; *specif* a counsel

,**counsel of per'fection** *n* a piece of excellent but impracticable advice

[1]**count** /kownt/ *vt* **1a** to reckon or name by units or groups so as to find the total number of units involved – often + *up* **b** to name the numbers in order up to and including **c** to include in a tallying and reckoning ⟨*about 100 copies if you* ~ *the damaged ones*⟩ **2** to consider ⟨~ *yourself lucky*⟩ **3** to include or exclude (as if) by counting ⟨~ *me in*⟩ ~ *vi* **1a** to name the numbers in order by units or groups ⟨~ *in tens*⟩ **b** to count the units in a group **2** to rely *on* or *upon* sby or sthg **3** to have value or significance ⟨*these are the men who really* ~⟩ [ME *counten,* fr MF *compter,* fr L *computare,* fr *com-* + *putare* to consider – more at PAVE] – **countable** *adj* – **count on** to look forward to as certain; anticipate ⟨counted on *winning*⟩

[2]**count** *n* **1a** the action or process of counting **b** a total obtained by counting **2a** an allegation in an indictment ⟨*guilty on all* ~s⟩ **b** a specific point under consideration; an issue ⟨*disagreed on several* ~s⟩ **3** the total number of individual things in a given unit or sample ⟨*blood* ~⟩ **4** the calling out of the seconds from 1 to 10 when a boxer has been knocked down during which he must rise or be defeated **5** any of various measures of the fineness of a textile yarn – compare TEX, DENIER, [4]PICK 2 **6** *chiefly NAm the* score

[3]**count** *n* a European nobleman corresponding in rank to a British earl [MF *comte,* fr LL *comit-, comes,* fr L, companion, one of the imperial court, fr *com-* + *ire* to go – more at ISSUE]

'**count,down** /-,down/ *n* a continuous counting backwards to zero of the time remaining before an event, esp the launching of a space vehicle – **count down** *vi*

[1]**countenance** /'kownt(ə)nəns/ *n* **1** composure ⟨*keep one's* ~⟩ **2** a face; *esp* the face as an indication of mood, emotion, or character **3** moral support; sanction ***USE*** fml [ME *contenance,* fr MF, fr ML *continentia,* fr L, restraint, fr *continent-, continens,* prp of *continēre* to hold together – more at CONTAIN]

[2]**countenance** *vt* to extend approval or support to – fml

[1]**counter** /'kowntə/ *n* **1** a small disc of metal, plastic, etc used in counting or in games **2** sthg of value in bargaining; an asset **3** a level surface (e g a table) over which transactions are conducted or food is served or on which goods are displayed [ME *countour,* fr MF *comptouer,* fr ML *computatorium* computing place, fr L *computatus,* pp of *computare*] – **over the counter** without a prescription ⟨*cough mixture available* over the counter⟩ – **under the counter** by surreptitious means; in an illicit and private manner

[2]**counter** *n* a device for indicating a number or amount [ME, fr MF *conteor,* fr *compter* to count]

[3]**counter** *vt* **1** to act in opposition to; oppose **2** to nullify the effects of; offset ⟨*tried to* ~ *the trend towards bureaucratization*⟩ ~ *vi* to meet attacks or arguments with defensive or retaliatory steps [ME *countren,* fr MF *contre*]

[4]**counter** *adv* in an opposite, contrary, or wrong direction [ME *contre,* fr MF, fr L *contra* against, opposite; akin to L *com-* with, together – more at CO-]

[5]**counter** *n* **1** the contrary, opposite **2** an overhanging stern of a vessel **3a** the (blow resulting from the) making of an attack while parrying (e g in boxing or fencing) **b** an agency or force that offsets; a check

[6]**counter** *adj* **1** marked by or tending towards an opposite direction or effect **2** showing opposition, hostility, or antipathy

counter- *prefix* **1a** contrary; in the opposite direction ⟨counter*march*⟩ **b** opposing; retaliatory ⟨counter*offensive*⟩ **2** complementary; corresponding ⟨counter*part*⟩ **3** duplicate; substitute ⟨counter*foil*⟩ [ME *contre-,* fr MF, fr *contre*]

counteract /,kowntə'rakt/ *vt* to lessen or neutralize the usu ill effects of by an opposing action – **counteraction** /-'raksh(ə)n/ *n,* **counteractive** *adj*

,**counterat'tack** /-ə'tak/ *vb* to make an attack (against) in reply to an enemy's attack – **counterattack** /'---,-/ *n*

'**counterat,traction** /-ə,traksh(ə)n/ *n* an attraction that competes with another

[1]'**counter,balance** /-,baləns/ *n* **1** a weight that balances another **2** a force or influence that offsets or checks an opposing force

[2],**counter'balance** *vt* to oppose or balance with an equal weight or force

'**counter,blast** /-,blahst/ *n* an energetic and often vociferous reaction or response

'**counter,change** /-,chaynj/ *vt* **1** to interchange, transpose **2** CHEQUER 1a ~ *vi* to change places or parts

'**counter,charge** /-,chahj/ *n* a charge made to counter another charge or to oppose an accuser

'**counter,claim** /-,klaym/ *n* an opposing claim, esp in law – **counterclaim** /,--'-/ *vi*

,**counter'clockwise** /-'klokwiez/ *adj or adv, chiefly NAm* anticlockwise

'**counter,culture** /-,kulchə/ *n* a culture with values that run counter to established social norms

'**counter,current** /-,kurənt/ *adj* (involving interaction between materials) flowing in opposite directions

,**counter'espionage** /-'espi·ənahzh/ *n* espionage directed towards detecting and thwarting enemy espionage

'**counterex,ample** /-ig,zahmpl/ *n* an example that disproves a theorem, proposition, etc

[1]**counterfeit** /'kowntəfit, -feet/ *vb* to imitate or copy (sthg) closely, esp with intent to deceive or defraud – **counterfeiter** *n*

[2]**counterfeit** *adj* **1** made in imitation of sthg else with intent to deceive or defraud **2** insincere, feigned ⟨~ *sympathy*⟩ [ME *countrefet*, fr MF *contrefait*, fr pp of *contrefaire* to imitate, fr *contre-* + *faire* to make, fr L *facere* – more at [1]DO]

[3]**counterfeit** *n* **1** a forgery **2** sthg likely to be mistaken for sthg of higher value

'**counter,foil** /-,foyl/ *n* a detachable part of a cheque, ticket, etc usu kept as a record or receipt

,**counterin'telligence** /-in'telij(ə)ns/ *n* organized activity of an intelligence service designed to block an enemy's sources of information

,**counter'irritant** /-'irit(ə)nt/ *n* sthg applied locally to produce surface inflammation with the object of reducing inflammation in tissue underneath – **counterirritant** *adj*

[1]**countermand** /,kowntə'mahnd, '--,-/ *vt* **1** to revoke (a command) by a contrary order **2** to order back (e g troops) by a superseding contrary order [ME *countermaunden*, fr MF *contremander*, fr *contre-* counter- + *mander* to command, fr L *mandare*]

[2]**countermand** *n* (the giving of) a contrary order revoking an earlier one

'**counter,march** /-,mahch/ *n* a movement in marching by which a unit of troops reverses direction while keeping the same order – **countermarch** /,--'-/ *vi*

'**counter,measure** /-,mezhə/ *n* a measure designed to counter another action or state of affairs

[1]'**counter,mine** /-,mien/ *n* a tunnel for intercepting an enemy mine

[2]**countermine** *vt* to intercept with a countermine ~ *vi* to lay down countermines

'**counter,move** /-,moohv/ *n* a move designed to counter another move

,**counterof'fensive** /-ə'fensiv/ *n* a military offensive undertaken from a previously defensive position

'**counter,pane** /-,payn/ *n* a bedspread [alter. of ME *countrepointe*, modif of MF *coute pointe*, lit., embroidered quilt]

'**counter,part** /-,paht/ *n* **1** a duplicate **2** sthg that completes; a complement **3** one having the same function or characteristics as another; an equivalent

[1]'**counter,point** /-,poynt/ *n* **1a** one or more independent melodies added above or below a given melody **b** the combination of 2 or more independent melodies into a single harmonic texture **2a** a complementing or contrasting item **b** use of contrast or interplay of elements in a work of art [MF *contrepoint*, fr ML *contrapunctus*, fr L *contra-* counter- + ML *punctus* musical note, melody, fr L, act of pricking, fr *punctus*, pp of *pungere* to prick – more at PUNGENT]

[2]**counterpoint** *vt* **1** to compose or arrange in counterpoint **2** to set off or emphasize by contrast or juxtaposition

'**counter,poise** /-,poyz/ *n* **1** a counterbalance **2** a state of balance; equilibrium [ME *countrepeis*, fr MF *contrepeis, contrepois*, fr *contre-* + *peis, pois* weight – more at [2]POISE] – **counterpoise** *vt*

,**counterpro'ductive** /-prə'duktiv/ *adj* tending to hinder the attainment of a desired end

,**counter,revo'lution** /-,revə'loohsh(ə)n/ *n* a revolution directed towards overthrowing the system established by a previous revolution – **counterrevolutionary** *adj or n*, **counterrevolutionist** *n*

'**counter,scarp** /-,skahp/ *n* the outer wall of a ditch in a fortification [MF *countrescarpe*, fr *contre-* counter- + *escarpe* scarp]

'**counter,shaft** /-,shahft/ *n* a shaft that is driven by a main shaft and transmits motion to a working part

[1]'**counter,sign** /-,sien/ *n* a password or secret signal given by one wishing to pass a guard

[2]**countersign** *vt* to add one's signature to (a document) as a witness of another signature – **countersignature** /-,signəchə/ *n*

'**counter,sink** /-,singk/ *vt* **countersunk** /-,sungk/ **1** to enlarge (a hole), esp by bevelling, so that the head of a bolt, screw, etc will fit below or level with the surface **2** to set the head of (e g a screw) below or level with the surface

'**counter,tenor** /-,tenə/ *n* (a person with) an adult male singing voice higher than tenor [ME *countretenour*, fr MF *contreteneur*, fr *contre-* + *teneur* tenor]

,**counter'vail** /-'vayl/ *vt* to counterbalance, offset [ME *countrevailen*, fr MF *contrevaloir*, fr *contre-* counter- + *valoir* to be worth, fr L *valēre* – more at WIELD]

'**counter,weight** /-,wayt/ *n* a counterbalance – **counterweight** *vt*

countess /'kowntis, -tes/ *n* **1** the wife or widow of an earl or count **2** a woman having in her own right the rank of an earl or count

countinghouse /'kownting,hows/ *n* a building, room, or office used for keeping account books and transacting business

'**countless** /-lis/ *adj* too numerous to be counted; innumerable

,**count 'palatine** *n* **1** a high judicial official in the Holy Roman Empire **2** a count of the Holy Roman Empire having imperial powers in his own domain

countrified *also* **countryfied** /'kuntrified/ *adj* **1** rural, rustic **2** unsophisticated [*country* + *-fied* (as in *glorified*)]

country /'kuntri/ *n* **1** an indefinite usu extended expanse of land; a region **2a** the land of a person's birth, residence, or citizenship **b** a political state or nation or its territory ☞ MAP **3** *sing or pl in constr* a *the* populace **b** *the* electorate ⟨*the government was forced to go to the* ~⟩ **4** rural as opposed to urban areas **5** COUNTRY MUSIC [ME *contree*, fr OF *contrée*, fr ML *contrata*, fr L *contra* against, on the opposite side]

,country and 'western *n* COUNTRY MUSIC

'country ,club *n* a sporting or social club set in a rural area

,country 'cousin *n* one who is unaccustomed to or confused by the bustle and sophistication of city life

,country 'dance *n* any of various native or folk dances for several pairs of dancers typically arranged in square or circular figures or in 2 long rows facing a partner

,country 'house *n* a house, mansion, or estate in the country

'countryman /-mən/, *fem* **'country,woman** *n* **1** an inhabitant or native of a specified country **2** a compatriot **3** one living in the country or having country ways

'country ,music *n* music derived from or imitating the folk style of the southern USA or the Western cowboy

,country 'seat *n* a mansion or estate in the country that is the hereditary property of 1 family

'country,side /-,sied/ *n* a rural area

¹county /'kownti/ *n* **1a** any of the territorial divisions of Britain and Ireland constituting the chief units for administrative, judicial, and political purposes **b** *sing or pl in constr* the people of a county **2** the largest local government unit in various countries (e g the USA) [ME *counte*, fr OF *conté*, fr ML *comitatus*, fr LL, office of a count, fr *comit-*, *comes* count – more at ³COUNT]

²county *adj* **1** of a county **2** *Br* characteristic of or belonging to the English landed gentry ⟨*a* ~ *accent*⟩

,county 'borough *n* a borough which until 1974 had the local-government powers of a county

,county 'court *n, often cap 1st C* a local civil court in England which is presided over by a judge and deals with relatively minor claims ☞ LAW

,county 'palatine *n* the territory of a count palatine or earl palatine

,county 'seat *n, NAm* COUNTY TOWN

,county 'town *n, chiefly Br* a town that is the seat of the government of a county ☞ COUNTY

¹coup /kohp/ *vb, chiefly Scot* to overturn, upset [ME *coupen* to strike, fr MF *couper* – more at ³COPE]

²coup /kooh/ *n, pl* **coups** /koohz/ **1** a brilliant, sudden, and usu highly successful stroke or act **2** COUP D'ETAT [F, blow, stroke – more at ³COPE]

coup de grâce /,kooh də 'grahs, 'gras (*Fr* ku də gras)/ *n, pl* **coups de grâce** /~ ~ ~/ **1** a fatal blow or shot administered to end the suffering of a mortally wounded person or animal **2** a decisive finishing stroke [F, lit., stroke of mercy]

,coup de 'main /də 'manh (*Fr* də mɛ̃)/ *n, pl* **coups de main** /~ ~ ~/ a sudden forceful attack [F, lit., stroke of the hand]

,coup d'é 'tat /day'tah (*Fr* deta)/ *n, pl* **coups d'état** /~ ~/ the violent overthrow of an existing government by a small group [F, lit., stroke of state]

,coup de théâtre /də tay'ahtr(ə)/ *n, pl* **coups de théâtre** /~ ~ ~/ a sudden sensational turn of events, esp in a play; *also* a spectacular piece of staging or stagecraft [F *coup de théâtre*, lit., stroke of theatre]

,coup 'd'oeil /duh·i (*Fr* dœːj)/ *n, pl* **coups d'oeil** /~ ~/ a brief survey; a glance [F, lit., stroke of the eye]

coupe /koohp/ *n* (a cold dessert of fruit and ice cream served in) a small goblet-shaped dish [F, cup, fr LL *cuppa* – more at CUP]

coupé /'koohpay; *sense 2 also* koohp/, **coupe** /koohp/ *n* **1** a 4-wheeled horse-drawn carriage for 2 passengers with an outside seat for the driver **2** a closed 2-door motor car for usu 2 people [F *coupé*, fr pp of *couper* to cut]

¹couple /'kupl/ *vb* **coupling** /'kupling/ *vt* **1** to unite or link ⟨~d *his praise with a request*⟩ **2a** to fasten together; connect **b** to bring (2 electric circuits) into such close proximity as to permit mutual influence **3** to join in marriage ~ *vi* **1** to copulate **2** to join

²couple *n, pl* **couples, couple** **1** *sing or pl in constr* 2 people paired together; *esp* a married or engaged couple **2a** 2 things considered together; a pair **b** an indefinite small number; a few ⟨*a* ~ *of days ago*⟩ – infml **3** 2 equal and opposite forces that act along parallel lines and cause rotation [ME, pair, bond, fr OF *cople*, fr L *copula* bond, fr *co-* + *apere* to fasten – more at APT]

³couple *adj* two – + a ⟨*a* ~ *more drinks*⟩

coupler /'kuplə/ *n* a device on a keyboard instrument by which keyboards or keys are connected to play together [¹COUPLE + ²-ER]

couplet /'kuplit/ *n* a unit of 2 successive, usu rhyming, lines of verse [MF, dim. of *cople*]

coupling /'kupling/ *n* a device that serves to connect the ends of adjacent parts or objects [¹COUPLE + ²-ING]

coupon /'koohpon/ *n* a form handed over in order to obtain an article, service, or accommodation: e g **a** a detachable ticket or certificate that entitles the holder to sthg **b** a voucher given with a purchase that can be exchanged for goods **c** a part of a printed advertisement to be cut off for use as an order form or enquiry form **d** a printed entry form for a competition, esp the football pools [F, fr OF, piece, fr *couper* to cut – more at ³COPE]

courage /'kurij/ *n* mental or moral strength to confront and withstand danger, fear, or difficulty; bravery [ME *corage*, fr OF, fr *cuer* heart, fr L *cor* – more at HEART] – **courageous** /kə'rayjəs/ *adj*, **courageously** *adv*

courante /kooh'rahn(h)t (*Fr* kurɑ̃ːt)/ *n* a musical composition or movement (e g in a suite) in quick triple time [MF, fr *courir* to run, fr L *currere*]

courgette /kaw'zhet, kooə-/ *n* (the plant that bears) a variety of small vegetable marrow cooked and eaten as a vegetable [F dial., dim. of *courge* gourd, fr L *cucurbita*]

courier /'koori·ə/ *n* **1a** a member of a diplomatic service who carries state or embassy papers **b** one who carries secret information, contraband, etc **2** a tourist guide employed by a travel agency [MF *courrier*, fr OIt *corriere*, fr *correre* to run, fr L *currere*]

¹course /kaws/ *n* **1** the act or action of moving in a path from point to point **2** the path over which sthg moves: e g **a** a racecourse **b** the direction of travel, usu measured as a clockwise angle from north **c** WATERCOURSE **d** GOLF COURSE **3a** usual procedure or normal action ⟨*the law must take its* ~⟩ **b** a chosen

The British Isles – political

☞ MAP

manner of conducting oneself; a plan of action ⟨*our wisest ~ is to retreat*⟩ **c** progression through a series of acts or events or a development or period ⟨*in the ~ of the year*⟩ **4a** a series of educational activities relating to a subject, esp when constituting a curriculum ⟨*a management ~*⟩ **b** a particular medical treatment administered over a designated period **5a** a part of a meal served at one time **b** a row; *esp* a continuous horizontal layer of brick or masonry throughout a wall ☞ BUILDING [ME, fr OF, fr L *cursus*, fr *cursus*, pp of *currere* to run – more at CAR] – **of course 1** as might be expected; naturally **2** admittedly; TO BE SURE

[2]**course** *vt* **1** to hunt or pursue (e g hares) with dogs that follow by sight **2** to follow close upon; pursue ~ *vi of a liquid* to run or pass rapidly (as if) along an indicated path ⟨*blood* coursing *through his veins*⟩

[3]**course** *adv* OF COURSE – infml

courser /'kawsə/ *n* any of various African and Asian birds noted for their swift running [[2]COURSE + [2]-ER]

[1]**court** /kawt/ *n* **1a** the residence or establishment of a dignitary, esp a sovereign **b** *sing or pl in constr* **(1)** the sovereign and his officers and advisers who are the governing power **(2)** the family and retinue of a sovereign **c** a reception held by a sovereign **2a** a manor house or large building (e g a block of flats) surrounded by usu enclosed grounds – archaic except in proper names ⟨*Hampton* Court⟩ ⟨*Withdean* Court⟩ **b** a space enclosed wholly or partly by a building **c** (a division of) a rectangular space walled or marked off for playing lawn tennis, squash, basketball, etc **d** a yard surrounded by houses, with only 1 opening onto a street **3a** (a session of) an official assembly for the transaction of judicial business **b** *sing or pl in constr* judicial officers in session **4** *sing or pl in constr* an assembly with legislative or administrative powers **5** conduct or attention intended to win favour ⟨*pay ~ to the king*⟩ [ME, fr OF, fr L *cohort-, cohors* enclosure, throng, cohort, fr *co-* + *-hort-, -hors* (akin to *hortus* garden)]

[2]**court** *vt* **1** to act so as to invite or provoke ⟨~s *disaster*⟩ **2a** to seek the affections of; woo **b** *of an animal* to perform actions to attract (a mate) **3** to seek to win the favour of ~ *vi of a man and woman* to be involved in a relationship that may lead to marriage

court bouillon /,kaw booh'yonh/ *n* a stock made with vegetables, herbs, and often wine in which fish is or has been cooked [F *court-bouillon*, fr *court* short + *bouillon* bouillon]

'**court ,card** *n* a king, queen, or jack in a pack of cards [alter. of *coat card*; fr the coats worn by the figures depicted]

Courtelle /,kaw'tel/ *trademark* – used for an acrylic fibre

courteous /'kuhtyəs, -ti·əs, *also* 'kaw-/ *adj* showing respect and consideration for others [ME *corteis*, fr OF, fr *court* court] – **courteously** *adv*, **courteousness** *n*

courtesan /,kawti'zan, '--,-/ *n* a prostitute with a courtly, wealthy, or upper-class clientele [MF *courtisane*, fr OIt *cortigiana* woman courtier, fem of *cortigiano* courtier, fr *corte* court, fr L *cohort-, cohors*]

[1]**courtesy** /'kuhtəsi/ *n* **1** courteous behaviour **2** a courteous act or expression [ME *corteisie*, fr OF, fr *corteis*] – **by courtesy of** through the kindness, generosity, or permission granted by (a person or organization)

[2]**courtesy** *adj* granted, provided, or performed by way of courtesy ⟨*made a ~ call on the ambassador*⟩

'**courtesy of** *prep* BY COURTESY OF

'**courtesy ,title** *n* a title commonly accepted though without legal validity

courthouse /'kawt,hows/ *n, chiefly NAm* a building in which courts of law are regularly held

courtier /'kawtyə/ *n* one in attendance at a royal court

courtly /'kawtli/ *adj* of a quality befitting the court; elegant, refined – **courtliness** *n*

,**courtly 'love** *n* a medieval conventionalized code prescribing the conduct and emotions of ladies and their lovers

[1],**court-'martial** *n, pl* **courts-martial** *also* **court-martials** (a trial by) a court of commissioned officers that tries members of the armed forces

[2]**court-martial** *vt* **-ll-** (*NAm* **-l-**, **-ll-**) to try by court-martial

,**court of a'ppeal** *n, often cap C&A* a court hearing appeals from the decisions of lower courts ☞ LAW

,**Court of ,Criminal Ap'peal** *n* the supreme court of appeal in Scotland for criminal cases ☞ LAW

,**court of in'quiry** *n* a board of people appointed to ascertain the causes of an accident, disaster, etc

,**court of 'record** *n* a court whose recorded proceedings are valid as evidence of fact

,**Court of 'Session** *n* the highest civil court in Scotland ☞ LAW

,**Court of St 'James's** *n* the court of the British sovereign [*St James's* Palace, London, former seat of the British court]

'**court ,plaster** *n* an adhesive plaster, esp of silk coated with isinglass and glycerin [fr its use for beauty spots by ladies at royal courts]

'**court,ship** /-,ship/ *n* the act, process, or period of courting

,**court 'shoe** *n* a plain high-heeled women's shoe with no fastenings ☞ GARMENT [fr its use as part of dress at court]

'**court,yard** /-,yahd/ *n* an open court or enclosure adjacent to a building

couscous /'koohs,koohs/ *n* a N African dish of crushed or coarsely ground wheat steamed and served with meat, vegetables, and spices [F, fr Ar *kuskus*, fr *kuskasa* to pound, pulverize]

cousin /'kuzn/ *n* **1a** a child of one's uncle or aunt **b** a relative descended from one's grandparent or more remote ancestor in a different line **2** – formerly used as a title by a sovereign in addressing a nobleman [ME *cosin*, fr OF, fr L *consobrinus*, fr *com-* + *sobrinus* cousin on the mother's side, fr *soror* sister – more at SISTER] – **cousinhood** /-hood/ *n*, **cousinship** *n*

couture /,kooh'tyooə/ *n* **1** the business of designing and making fashionable custom-made women's clothing; *also* the designers and establishments engaged in this business **2** HAUTE COUTURE [F, fr OF *cousture* sewing, fr (assumed) VL *consutura*, fr L *consutus*, pp of *consuere* to sew together, fr *com-* + *suere* to sew – more at SEW]

couturier /kooh'tyooəri·ə, -ri·ay/, *fem* **couturière** /kooh,tyooəri'eə/ *n* (the proprietor of or designer for) an establishment engaged in couture [F, dressmaker, fr OF *cousturier* tailor's assistant, fr *cousture*]

couvade /kooh'vahd/ *n* a custom among some peoples by which a father retires to bed at the birth of his child as if bearing it himself [F, fr MF, cowardly inactivity, fr *cover* to sit on, brood over – more at COVEY]

covalency /koh'vaylənsi/ *n* valency characterized by the sharing of (pairs of) electrons between combining atoms; *also* the number of such pairs an atom can share when forming covalent bonds – **covalent** *adj*, **covalently** *adv*

co,valent 'bond /koh'vaylənt/ *n* a nonionic chemical bond formed by shared (pairs of) electrons between combining atoms

covariance /,koh'veəri·əns/ *n* the expected value of the product of the deviations of 2 random variables from their respective means

[1]cove /kohv/ *n* **1** a small sheltered area; *esp* an inlet or bay **2** a (deep) recess in (the side of) a mountain **3** a concave moulding, esp at the point where a wall meets a ceiling or floor [ME, den, fr OE *cofa*; akin to OE *cot*]

[2]cove *vt* to make in a hollow concave form

[3]cove *n, Br* a man, fellow – slang; no longer in vogue [prob fr Romany *kova* thing, person]

coven /'kuvn, 'kovn/ *n sing or pl in constr* an assembly or band of witches [ME *covin* band, fr MF, fr ML *convenium* agreement, fr L *convenire* to agree – more at CONVENTION]

[1]covenant /'kuv(ə)nənt, 'kov-/ *n* **1** a solemn agreement **2** a written promise [ME, fr OF, fr prp of *covenir* to agree, fr L *convenire*]

[2]covenant *vb* to promise by or enter into a covenant

covenanter, covenantor /'kuv(ə)nəntə, 'ko-/ *n* **1** sby who makes a covenant **2** *cap* an adherent of the Scottish National Covenant of 1638

Coventry /'kov(ə)ntri; *also* 'ku-/ *n* a state of ostracism or exclusion – chiefly in *send to Coventry* [*Coventry*, city in England]

[1]cover /'kuvə/ *vt* **1a** to guard from attack **b(1)** to have within the range of one's guns **(2)** to hold within range of an aimed firearm **c(1)** to insure **(2)** to afford protection against or compensation for **d** to mark (an opponent) in order to obstruct play **e** to make sufficient provision for (a demand or charge) by means of a reserve or deposit ⟨*his balance was insufficient to ~ his cheque*⟩ **2a** to hide from sight or knowledge; conceal – usu + *up* ⟨*~ up a scandal*⟩ **b** to lie or spread over; envelop ⟨*snow ~ed the ground*⟩ **3** to lay or spread sthg over **4** to extend thickly or conspicuously over the surface of ⟨*~ed in spots*⟩ **5** to place or set a cover or covering over **6a** *of a male animal* to copulate with (a female animal) **b** to sit on and incubate (eggs) **7** to invest with a large or excessive amount of sthg ⟨*~s himself with glory*⟩ **8** to play a higher-ranking card on (a previously played card) **9** to include, consider, or take in ⟨*this book ~s the whole Renaissance*⟩ **10a** to have as one's territory or field of activity ⟨*one salesman ~s the whole county*⟩ **b** to report news about **11** to pass over; traverse ⟨*~ed 5 miles at great speed*⟩ ~ *vi* **1** to conceal sthg illicit, blameworthy, or embarrassing from notice – usu + *up* **2** to act as a substitute or replacement during an absence – chiefly in *cover for someone* [ME *coveren*, fr OF *covrir*, fr L *cooperire*, fr *co-* + *operire* to close, cover] – **cover one's tracks** to conceal evidence of one's past actions in order to elude pursuit or investigation – **cover the ground** **1** to cover a distance with adequate speed **2** to deal with an assignment or examine a subject thoroughly

[2]cover *n* **1** sthg that protects, shelters, or guards: e g **a** natural shelter for an animal **b(1)** a position affording shelter from attack **(2)** (the protection offered by) a force supporting a military operation **(3)** COVERAGE 3a **2** sthg that is placed over or about another thing: **a** a lid, top **b** (the front or back part of) a binding or jacket of a book **c** an overlay or outer layer (e g for protection) ⟨*a chair ~*⟩ **d** a roof **e** a cloth (e g a blanket) used on a bed ⟨*threw back the ~s*⟩ **f** sthg (e g vegetation or snow) that covers the ground **g** the extent to which clouds obscure the sky **3a** sthg that conceals or obscures ⟨*under ~ of darkness*⟩ **b** a masking device; a pretext **4** an envelope or wrapper for postal use ⟨*under separate ~*⟩ **5a** cover-point, extra cover, or a cricket fielding position between them ☞ SPORT **b** *pl the* fielding positions in cricket that lie between point and mid-off ☞ SPORT

coverage /'kuv(ə)rij/ *n* **1** the act or fact of covering **2** inclusion within the scope of discussion or reporting ⟨*news ~*⟩ **3a** the total range of risks covered by the terms of an insurance contract **b** the number or percentage of people reached by a communications medium

'cover-,all *adj* comprehensive

'cover ,charge *n* a charge (e g for service) made by a restaurant or nightclub in addition to the charge for food and drink

'cover ,girl *n* an attractive girl whose picture appears on a magazine cover

'cover ,glass *n* a piece of very thin glass used to cover material on a glass microscope slide

[1]covering /'kuv(ə)ring/ *n* sthg that covers or conceals

[2]covering *adj* containing an explanation of an accompanying item ⟨*a ~ letter*⟩

'coverlet /-lit/ *n* a bedspread [ME, alter. of *coverlite*, fr AF *coverelyth*, fr OF *covrir* to cover + *lit* bed, fr L *lectus* – more at [1]LIE]

'cover ,note *n, Br* a provisional insurance document providing cover between acceptance of a risk and issue of a full policy

'cover-,point *n* a fielding position in cricket further from the batsman than point and situated between mid-off and point ☞ SPORT

[1]covert /'kuvət, -vuht, 'ko-/ *adj* not openly shown; secret [ME, fr OF, pp of *covrir* to cover] – **covertly** *adv*, **covertness** *n*

[2]covert *n* **1a** a hiding place; a shelter **b** a thicket affording cover for game **2** a feather covering the bases of the wing or tail feathers of a bird ☞ ANATOMY

'cover-,up *n* a device or course of action that conceals sthg (e g sthg illegal)

covet /'kovit, 'ku-/ *vt* to desire (what belongs to another) inordinately or culpably [ME *coveiten*, fr OF *coveitier*, fr *coveitié* desire, modif of L *cupiditat-*, *cupiditas*, fr *cupidus* desirous, fr *cupere* to desire]

covetous /'kovitəs, 'ku-/ *adj* showing an inordinate desire for esp another's wealth or possessions – **covetously** *adv*, **covetousness** *n*

covey /'kuvi/ *n* **1** a mature bird or pair of birds with a brood of young; *also* a small flock **2** a company, group [ME, fr MF *covee*, fr OF, fr *cover* to sit on, brood over, fr L *cubare* to lie – more at [2]HIP]

[1]**cow** /kow/ *n* **1** the mature female of cattle or of any animal the male of which is called *bull* **2** a domestic bovine animal regardless of sex or age **3** a woman; *esp* one who is unpleasant **4** *chiefly Austr* a cause of annoyance or difficulty ***USE*** *(3&4)* vulg [ME *cou*, fr OE *cū*; akin to OHG *kuo* cow, L *bos* head of cattle, Gk *bous*, Skt *go*] – **till the cows come home** FOREVER 1

[2]**cow** *vt* to intimidate with threats or a show of strength [prob of Scand origin; akin to Dan *kue* to subdue]

cowage, cowhage /'kowij/ *n* a tropical leguminous climbing plant whose pods are covered with barbed hairs that cause severe itching [Hindi *kav ac*]

coward /'kowəd/ *n* one who lacks courage or resolve [ME, fr OF *coart*, fr *coe* tail, fr L *cauda*]

cowardice /'kowədis/ *n* lack of courage or resolve [ME *cowardise*, fr OF *coardise*, fr *coart*]

[1]**'cowardly** /-li/ *adv* in a cowardly manner

[2]**cowardly** *adj* resembling or befitting a coward ⟨*a ~ retreat*⟩ – **cowardliness** *n*

'cow,bane /-,bayn/ *n* a tall perennial Eurasian plant or similar poisonous plant of the carrot family

'cow,bell /-,bel/ *n* a bell hung round the neck of a cow to make a sound by which it can be located

'cow,boy /-,boy/, *fem* **'cow,girl** *n* **1** one who tends or drives cattle; *esp* a usu mounted cattle ranch hand in N America **2a** one who employs irregular or unscrupulous methods, esp in business **b** a person who uses underhand or dubious means to get his own way ***USE*** *(2)* infml

'cowboy ,boot *n* a boot with a high arch and heel and usu fancy stitching ☞ GARMENT

'cowboy ,hat *n* a wide-brimmed hat with a large soft crown

'cow,catcher /-,kachə/ *n, chiefly NAm* an apparatus on the front of a locomotive or tram for removing obstacles from the track

cower /'kowə/ *vi* to crouch down or shrink away (e g in fear) from sthg menacing [ME *couren*, of Scand origin; akin to Norw *kura* to cower; akin to Gk *gyros* circle, OE *cot*]

'cow,fish /-,fish/ *n* **1** a sirenian **2** any of various small brightly coloured fishes with projections resembling horns over the eyes

cowhage /'kowij/ *n* cowage

'cow,hand /-,hand/ *n* a cowherd or cowboy

'cow,herd /-,huhd/ *n* one who tends cows

'cow,hide /-,hied/ *n* **1** leather made from the hide of a cow **2** *NAm* a coarse leather whip

cowl /kowl/ *n* **1a** a hood or long hooded cloak, esp of a monk **b** a draped neckline on a garment resembling a folded-down hood **2a** a chimney covering designed to improve ventilation **b** a cowling [ME *cowle*, fr OE *cugele*, fr LL *cuculla* monk's hood, fr L *cucullus* hood] – **cowled** *adj*

'cow,lick /-,lik/ *n* a tuft of hair that sticks up, esp over the forehead [fr its appearance of having been licked by a cow]

cowling /'kowling/ *n* a removable metal covering over an engine, esp in an aircraft

'cowman /-mən/ *n* a cowherd or cowboy

,co-'worker /,koh/ *n* a fellow worker

'cow,pat /-,pat/ *n* a small heap of cow dung

'cow,pea /-,pee/ *n* BLACK-EYED PEA

'cow,pox /-,poks/ *n* a mild disease of the cow that when communicated to humans gives protection against smallpox

cowrie, cowry /'kowri/ *n* any of numerous marine gastropod molluscs with glossy and often brightly coloured shells, formerly used as money in parts of Africa and Asia [Hindi *kauṛī*]

'cow,slip /-,slip/ *n* a common European plant of the primrose family with fragrant yellow or purplish flowers [ME *cowslyppe*, fr OE *cūslyppe*, lit., cow dung, fr *cūcow* + *slypa, slyppe* paste – more at [5]SLIP]

cox /koks/ *vb or n* (to) coxswain – **coxless** *adj*

coxa /'koksə/ *n, pl* **coxae** /-si/ the basal segment of a limb of an insect, spider, etc ☞ ANATOMY [L, hip; akin to OHG *hāhsina* hock, Skt *kakṣa* armpit] – **coxal** *adj*

coxcomb /'koks,kohm/ *n* a conceited foolish person; a fop [ME *cokkes comb*, lit., cock's comb]

[1]**coxswain** /'koksn, -,swayn/ *n* **1** a sailor who commands and usu steers a ship's boat **2** the steersman of a racing rowing boat who usu directs the crew [ME *cokswayne*, fr *cok* small boat + *swain* servant] – **coxswainless** *adj*

[2]**coxswain** *vb* to command or steer as coxswain

coy /koy/ *adj* **1a** (affectedly) shy **b** provocatively playful or coquettish **2** showing reluctance to make a definite commitment or face unpalatable facts [ME, quiet, shy, fr MF *coi* calm, fr L *quietus* quiet] – **coyly** *adv*, **coyness** *n*

coyote /'koyoht, -'-, -'ohti, kie'ohti/ *n, pl* **coyotes,** *esp collectively* **coyote** a small N American wolf [MexSp, fr Nahuatl *coyotl*]

coypu /'koyp(y)ooh/ *n, pl* **coypus,** *esp collectively* **coypu** a S American aquatic rodent with webbed feet now commonly found in E Anglia [AmerSp *coipú*, fr Araucan *coypu*]

[1]**cozy** /'kohzi/ *adj, NAm* cosy

[2]**cozy** *n, chiefly NAm* a cosy

[1]**crab** /krab/ *n* **1** any of numerous chiefly marine crustaceans usu with the front pair of limbs modified as grasping pincers and a short broad flattened carapace; *also* the flesh of this cooked and eaten as food **2** *pl* infestation with crab lice [ME *crabbe*, fr OE *crabba*; akin to OHG *krebiz* crab, OE *ceorfan* to carve]

[2]**crab** *vb* **-bb-** *vt* **1** to cause to move sideways or in an indirect or diagonal manner **2** to head (an aircraft) by means of the rudder into a crosswind to counteract drift ~ *vi* to move sideways indirectly or diagonally

[3]**crab** *n* CRAB APPLE [ME *crabbe*, perh fr *crabbe* [1]crab]

[4]**crab** *vb* **-bb-** *vt* to make sullen; sour ⟨*old age has ~bed his nature*⟩ ~ *vi* to carp, grouse ⟨*always ~s about the weather*⟩ – infml [ME *crabben*, prob back-formation fr *crabbed*]

[5]**crab** *n* an ill-tempered person – infml

'crab ,apple *n* (a tree that bears) a small usu wild sour apple [[3]*crab*]

crabbed /'krabid/ *adj* **1** morose, peevish **2** difficult to read or understand ⟨*~ handwriting*⟩ [ME, partly fr *crabbe* [1]crab, partly fr *crabbe* [3]crab] – **crabbedly** *adv*, **crabbedness** *n*

crabby /'krabi/ *adj* cross, ill-tempered – infml [[5]*crab*]

'crab,grass /-,grahs/ *n* a grass with freely rooting creeping stems that grows as a weed in lawns

ˈcrab ˌlouse *n* a sucking louse that infests the pubic region of the human body

ˈcrabˌwise /-ˌwiez/ *adv* **1** sideways **2** in a sidling or cautiously indirect manner

¹crack /krak/ *vi* **1** to make a sudden sharp explosive noise ⟨*the whip* ~s⟩ **2a** to break or split apart **b** to develop fissures **3a** to lose control or effectiveness under pressure – often + *up* **b** to fail in tone, volume, etc ⟨*his voice* ~ed⟩ **4** *esp of hydrocarbons* to break up into simpler chemical compounds when heated, usu with a catalyst ~ *vt* **1a** to break so that fissures appear on the surface ⟨~ *a mirror*⟩ **b** to break with a crack ⟨~ *nuts*⟩ **2** to tell (a joke) **3a** to puzzle out and expose, solve, or reveal the mystery of ⟨~ *a code*⟩ **b** to break into ⟨~ *a safe*⟩ **c** to break through (e g a barrier) so as to gain acceptance or recognition **4** to cause to make a sudden sharp noise ⟨~ *one's knuckles*⟩ **5a** to subject (esp heavy hydrocarbons) to cracking, esp to produce petrol **b** to produce (e g petrol) by cracking **6** to open (e g a can or bottle) for drinking – infml [ME *crakken*, fr OE *cracian*; akin to Skt *jarate* it crackles – more at CRANE]

²crack *n* **1** a sudden sharp loud noise ⟨*the* ~ *of rifle fire*⟩ **2a** a line or narrow opening that marks a break; a fissure ⟨*a* ~ *in the ice*⟩ **b** a narrow opening; a chink ⟨*leave the door open a* ~⟩ **3** a broken tone of the voice **4** a sharp resounding blow ⟨*gave him a* ~ *on the head*⟩ **5** a witty remark; a quip – infml **6** an attempt, try *at* – infml

³crack *adj* of superior quality or ability ⟨*a* ~ *shot*⟩ – infml

ˈcrackˌdown /-ˌdown/ *n* an act or instance of cracking down

crack down *vi* to take regulatory or disciplinary action – usu + *on*

cracked *adj* **1** marked by harshness, dissonance, or failure to sustain a tone ⟨*a* ~ *voice*⟩ **2** mentally disordered; crazy – infml

cracker /ˈkrakə/ *n* **1a** a (folded) usu paper cylinder containing an explosive that is discharged to make a noise **b** a brightly coloured paper and cardboard tube that makes a cracking noise when pulled sharply apart and usu contains a toy, paper hat, or other party item **2** *pl* a nutcracker **3** a thin often savoury biscuit **4** the equipment in which cracking, esp of petroleum, is carried out **5** *Br* sthg or sby exceptional; *esp* an outstandingly attractive girl or woman – infml [¹CRACK + ²-ER]

crackerjack *also* **crackajack** /ˈkrakəjak/ *n, chiefly NAm* sby or sthg of marked excellence – infml [¹*crack* + ²*-er* + *jack*] – **crackerjack** *adj*

ˈcrackers *adj, chiefly Br* mad, crazy – infml [prob alter. of *cracked*]

cracking /ˈkraking/ *adv* very, extremely ⟨*a* ~ *good book*⟩ – infml; no longer in vogue

¹crackle /ˈkrakl/ *vb* **crackling** /ˈkrakling, ˈkrakl·ing/ *vi* **1** to make a crackle ⟨*the fire* ~s *on the hearth*⟩ **2** CRAZE ~ *vt* **1** to crush or crack with a snapping sound **2** CRAZE 1 [freq of ¹*crack*]

²crackle *n* **1** the noise of repeated small cracks or reports **2** a network of fine cracks on an otherwise smooth surface – **crackly** /ˈkrakli/ *adj*

crackling /ˈkrakling/ *n* **1** the crisp skin of roast meat, esp pork **2** the crisp residue left after the rendering of animal fat, esp lard – usu pl with sing. meaning

cracknel /ˈkrakn(ə)l/ *n* a hard brittle biscuit [ME *krakenelle*, prob modif of MF *craquelin*, fr MD *crākeline*, fr *crāken* to crack]

ˌcrack of ˈdawn *n* the first light of dawn

ˌcrack of ˈdoom *n* the thunderclap heralding the Day of Judgment

ˈcrackˌpot /-ˌpot/ *n* sby with eccentric ideas; a crank – infml [¹*crack* + *pot* (head)] – **crackpot** *adj*

ˈcracksman /-mən/ *n* a burglar – infml

ˈcrack-ˌup *n* **1** a mental collapse; NERVOUS BREAKDOWN **2** a collapse, breakdown

crack up *vt* to present in (excessively) favourable terms ⟨*wasn't all that it was* cracked up *to be*⟩ – infml ~ *vi* to undergo a physical or mental collapse

-cracy /-krəsi/ *comb form* (→ *n*) **1** rule; government ⟨*demo*cracy⟩ **2** powerful or dominant social or political class ⟨*aristo*cracy⟩ **3** state having a (specified) government or ruling class ⟨*merito*cracy⟩ [MF & LL; MF *-cratie*, fr LL *-cratia*, fr Gk *-kratia*, fr *kratos* strength, power – more at HARD]

¹cradle /ˈkraydl/ *n* **1a** a baby's bed or cot, usu on rockers **b** a framework of wood or metal used as a support, scaffold, etc **2a** the earliest period of life; infancy ⟨*from the* ~ *to the grave*⟩ **b** a place of origin ⟨~ *of civilization*⟩ [ME *cradel*, fr OE *cradol*; akin to OHG *kratto* basket, Skt *grantha* knot]

²cradle *vt* **cradling** /ˈkraydling/ **1** to place or keep (as if) in a cradle **2** to shelter or hold protectively

¹craft /krahft/ *n, pl* **crafts,** (*5*) **craft** *also* **crafts** **1** skill in planning, making, or executing; dexterity – often in combination ⟨*stage*craft⟩ **2** an activity or trade requiring manual dexterity or artistic skill; *broadly* a trade, profession **3** skill in deceiving to gain an end **4** *sing or pl in constr* the members of a trade or trade association **5a** a (small) boat **b** an aircraft **c** a spacecraft [ME, strength, skill, fr OE *cræft*; akin to OHG *kraft* strength]

²craft *vt* to make (as if) using skill and dexterity ⟨*a beautifully* ~ed *novel*⟩

ˈcraftsman /-mən/, *fem* **ˈcraftsˌwoman** *n* **1** a workman who practises a skilled trade or handicraft **2** one who displays a high degree of manual dexterity or artistic skill – **craftsmanlike** *adj*, **craftsmanship** *n*

crafty /ˈkrahfti/ *adj* showing subtlety and guile – **craftily** *adv*, **craftiness** *n*

crag /krag/ *n* a steep rugged rock or cliff [ME, of Celt origin; akin to OIr *crec* crag]

craggy /ˈkragi/ *adj* rough, rugged ⟨*a* ~ *face*⟩ – **cragginess** *n*

ˈcragsman /-mən/ *n* sby skilled in climbing crags

crake /krayk/ *n* a (short-billed) rail (e g the corncrake) [ME, prob fr ON *krāka* crow or *krākr* raven; akin to OE *crāwan* to crow]

cram /kram/ *vb* **-mm-** *vt* **1** to pack tight; jam ⟨~ *a suitcase with clothes*⟩ **2** to thrust forcefully **3** to prepare hastily for an examination **4** to eat voraciously; bolt – infml ~ *vi* **1** to study hastily and intensively for an examination **2** to eat greedily or until uncomfortably full – infml [ME *crammen*, fr OE *crammian*; akin to Gk *ageirein* to collect]

crambo /ˈkramboh/ *n, pl* **cramboes** a game in which a player gives a word or line of verse to be matched in rhyme by other players [alter. of earlier *crambe*, fr L, cabbage, fr Gk *krambē*]

ˌcram-ˈfull /kram/ *adj* as full as can be

crammer /ˈkramə/ *n, Br* a school or teacher that prepares students intensively for an examination – infml [CRAM + ²-ER]

[1]**cramp** /kramp/ *n* **1** a painful involuntary spasmodic contraction of a muscle **2** *pl* severe abdominal pain [ME *crampe*, fr MF, of Gmc origin; akin to LG *krampe* hook]

[2]**cramp** *n* **1** a usu metal device bent at the ends and used to hold timbers or blocks of stone together **2** a clamp [LG or obs D *krampe* hook; akin to OE *cradol* cradle]

[3]**cramp** *vt* **1** to affect with cramp **2a** to confine, restrain **b** to restrain from free expression – esp in *cramp someone's style* **3** to fasten or hold with a clamp

crampon /'krampon/ *n* **1** a hooked mechanical device for lifting heavy objects – usu pl with sing. meaning **2** a metal frame with downward- and forward-pointing spikes that is fixed to the sole of a boot for climbing slopes of ice or hard snow [MF *crampon*, of Gmc origin; akin to LG *krampe*]

cranberry /'kranb(ə)ri/ *n* any of various plants of the heath family; *also* the red acid berry of such plants used in making sauces and jellies [part trans of LG *kraanbere*, fr *kraan* crane + *bere* berry]

[1]**crane** /krayn/ *n* **1** any of a family of tall wading birds ☞ ENDANGERED **2** a machine for moving heavy weights by means of a projecting swinging arm or a hoisting apparatus supported on an overhead track [ME *cran*, fr OE; akin to OHG *krano* crane, Gk *geranos*, L *grus*, Skt *jarate* it crackles]

[2]**crane** *vt* **1** to raise or lift (as if) by a crane **2** to stretch (e g the neck), esp in order to see better ~ *vi* to stretch one's neck, esp in order to see better ⟨*I* ~d *out of the window*⟩

'**crane ,fly** *n* any of numerous long-legged slender two-winged flies that resemble large mosquitoes but do not bite

cranesbill /'kraynz,bil/ *n* GERANIUM 1

crani-, **cranio-** /krayni-/ *comb form* **1** cranium ⟨crani*ate*⟩ **2** cranial and ⟨cranio*sacral*⟩ [ML *cranium*]

,**cranial 'index** /'kraynyəl, -ni·əl/ *n* the ratio of the maximum breadth of the skull to its maximum height multiplied by 100 – compare CEPHALIC INDEX

,**cranial 'nerve** *n* any of the (12 pairs of) nerves that leave the lower surface of the brain to connect with the body, esp the head and face

craniate /'krayni·ət, -,ayt/ *n or adj* (one) having a skull

craniology /,krayni'oləji/ *n* a science dealing with variations in size, shape, and proportions of the skull among the different races of human beings [prob fr G *kraniologie*, fr *kranio-* crani- + *-logie* -logy]

cranium /'kraynyəm, -ni·əm/ *n, pl* **craniums, crania** /-nyə, -ni·ə/ the skull; *specif* the part that encloses the brain ☞ ANATOMY [ML, fr Gk *kranion*; akin to Gk *kara* head – more at CEREBRAL] – **cranial** *adj*

[1]**crank** /krangk/ *n* **1** a part of an axle or shaft bent at right angles by which reciprocating motion is changed into circular motion or vice versa **2** an eccentric person; *also* one who is excessively enthusiastic or fastidious about sthg [ME *cranke*, fr OE *cranc-* (as in *crancstaef*, a weaving instrument); akin to OE *cradol* cradle]

[2]**crank** *vi* to turn a crank (e g in starting an engine) ~ *vt* **1** to bend into the shape of a crank **2** to provide or fasten with a crank **3a** to move or operate (as if) by a crank **b** to start by use of a crank – often + *up*

[3]**crank** *adj, of a boat* easily capsized [short for *crank-sided* (easily tipped)]

'**crank,case** /-,kays/ *n* the housing of a crankshaft

'**crank,pin** /-,pin/ *n* the pin which forms the handle of a crank or to which the connecting rod is attached

'**crank,shaft** /-,shahft/ *n* a shaft driven by or driving a crank ☞ CAR

cranky /'krangki/ *adj* **1** *of machinery* working erratically; unpredictable **2** ECCENTRIC 2 **3** *NAm* bad-tempered [[1]*crank* & [3]*crank*] – **crankily** *adv*, **crankiness** *n*

cranny /'krani/ *n* a small crack or slit; a chink [ME *crany*, fr MF *cren, cran* notch] – **crannied** /'kranid/ *adj*

[1]**crap** /krap/ *n* **1a** excrement **b** an act of defecation **2** nonsense, rubbish – slang; sometimes used as an interjection *USE* (*1*) vulg [ME *crappe* chaff, residue from rendered fat, fr MD, piece torn off, fr *crappen* to break off]

[2]**crap** *vi* **-pp-** to defecate – vulg

crappy /'krapi/ *adj* of very poor quality – slang [[1]*crap*]

craps /kraps/ *n pl but sing or pl in constr* a gambling game played with 2 dice [LaF, fr F *crabs, craps*, fr E *crabs* lowest throw at hazard, fr pl of [1]*crab*] – **crap** *adj*

crapulent /'krapyoolənt/ *adj* crapulous [LL *crapulentus*, fr L *crapula* drunkenness, fr Gk *kraipalē*]

crapulous /'krapyooləs/ *adj* **1** marked by excessive indulgence, esp in alcohol **2** suffering the effects of excessive drinking of alcohol *USE* fml [LL *crapulosus*, fr L *crapula*]

craquelure /'krakəl(y)ooə/ *n* fine cracks on the surface of old paintings caused by decay of pigment and varnish [F, fr *craqueler* to crack, crackle, fr *craquer*, of imit origin]

[1]**crash** /krash/ *vt* **1a** to break violently and noisily; smash **b** to damage (an aircraft) in landing **c** to damage (a vehicle) by collision **2a** to cause to make a crashing sound ⟨~ *the cymbals together*⟩ **b** to force (e g one's way) with loud crashing noises **3** to enter without invitation or payment ⟨~ *the party*⟩ – infml **4** to cause (e g a computer system or program) to crash ~ *vi* **1a** to break or go to pieces (as if) with violence and noise **b** to crash an aircraft or vehicle **c** to be involved in a crash **2** to make a crashing noise **3** to move or go (as if) with a crash **4** to spend the night in a (makeshift) place; go to sleep ⟨*can I* ~ *on your floor tonight?*⟩ – sometimes + *out*; slang **5** *esp of a computer system or program* to become (suddenly) completely inoperative [ME *crasschen*]

[2]**crash** *n* **1** a loud noise (e g of things smashing) ⟨*a* ~ *of thunder*⟩ **2** a breaking to pieces (as if) by collision; *also* an instance of crashing ⟨*a plane* ~⟩ **3** a sudden decline or failure (e g of a business) ⟨*the Wall Street* ~⟩

[3]**crash** *adj* designed to achieve an intended result in the shortest possible time ⟨*a* ~ *diet*⟩

[4]**crash** *n* a coarse fabric made orig of linen, used for draperies, clothing, etc [prob fr Russ *krashenina* coloured linen]

'**crash ,barrier** *n* a barrier to prevent vehicles accidentally colliding or leaving the road

'crash-,dive *vb* (to cause) to descend or dive steeply and quickly – used esp with reference to an aircraft or submarine – **crashdive** *n*

'crash ,helmet *n* a helmet that is worn (e g by motorcyclists) to protect the head in the event of an accident

crashing /'krashing/ *adj* utter, absolute ⟨*a ~ bore*⟩

,crash-'land *vb* to land (an aircraft) under emergency conditions, usu with some damage to the craft – **crash landing** *n*

'crash ,pad *n* a place where free temporary accommodation is available – infml

crass /kras/ *adj* **1** insensitive, coarse ⟨*~ behaviour*⟩ **2** deplorably great; complete ⟨*~ stupidity*⟩ [L *crassus* thick, gross] – **crassitude** /'krasityoohd/ *n*, **crassly** *adv*, **crassness** *n*

-crat /-krat/ *comb form* (→ *n*) **1** advocate or partisan of (a specified form of government) ⟨*demo*crat⟩ **2** member of (a specified ruling class) ⟨*pluto*crat⟩ ⟨*techno*crat⟩ [F *-crate*, back-formation fr *-cratie* -cracy] – **-cratic** /-'kratik/ *comb form* (→ *adj*)

¹crate /krayt/ *n* **1** a usu wooden framework or box for holding goods (e g fruit, bottles, etc), esp during transit **2** the contents of a crate [L *cratis* wickerwork – more at HURDLE]

²crate *vt* to pack in a crate

¹crater /'kraytə/ *n* **1** a (bowl-shaped) depression: e g **a** round the mouth of a volcano **b** formed by the impact of a meteorite **2** a hole in the ground made by an explosion **3** a jar or vase with a wide mouth used in classical antiquity for mixing wine and water [L, mixing bowl, crater, fr Gk *kratēr*, fr *kerannynai* to mix; akin to Skt *āśīrta* mixed]

²crater *vt* to form craters in

cravat /krə'vat/ *n* a decorative band or scarf worn round the neck, esp by men ☞ GARMENT [F *cravate*, fr *Cravate* Croatian]

crave /krayv/ *vt* **1** to have a strong or urgent desire for **2** to ask for earnestly; beg ⟨*I ~ the court's indulgence*⟩ – fml ~ *vi* to have a strong desire; yearn ⟨*~s after affection*⟩ [ME *craven*, fr OE *crafian*; akin to OHG *krāpfo* hook, OE *cradol* cradle]

craven /'krayv(ə)n/ *adj* completely lacking in courage; cowardly [ME *cravant*, perh fr OF *crevant*, prp of *crever* to burst, break, fr L *crepare*] – **craven** *n*, **cravenly** *adv*, **cravenness** *n*

craving /'krayving/ *n* a great desire or longing ⟨*a ~ for tobacco*⟩

craw /kraw/ *n* **1** the crop of a bird or insect **2** the stomach, esp of an animal [ME *crawe*, fr (assumed) OE *crawa*; akin to Gk *bronchos* windpipe, throat, L *vorare* to devour – more at VORACIOUS]

crawfish /'kraw,fish/ *n, chiefly NAm* a crayfish

¹crawl /krawl/ *vi* **1** to move slowly in a prone position (as if) without the use of limbs **2** to move or progress slowly or laboriously **3** CREEP 3b **4a** to be alive or swarming (as if) with creeping things **b** to have the sensation of insects creeping over one ⟨*the story made her flesh ~*⟩ **5** to behave in a servile manner – infml ~ *vt* to move upon (as if) in a creeping manner ⟨*the meanest man who ever ~ed the earth*⟩ [ME *crawlen*, fr ON *krafla*; akin to OE *crabba* crab]

²crawl *n* **1a** crawling **b** slow or laborious motion ⟨*traffic moving at a ~*⟩ **2** the fastest swimming stroke, executed lying on the front and consisting of alternating overarm strokes combined with kicks with the legs

crawler /'krawlə/ *n* **1** a vehicle (e g a crane) that travels on endless metal belts **2** a servile person – infml [¹CRAWL + ²-ER]

crawly /'krawli/ *adj* creepy

crayfish /'kray,fish/ *n* **1** any of numerous freshwater crustaceans resembling the lobster but usu much smaller **2** SPINY LOBSTER [by folk etymology fr ME *crevis*, fr MF *crevice*, of Gmc origin; akin to OHG *krebiz* crab – more at CRAB]

crayon /'krayon, -ən/ *vt or n* (to draw or colour with) a stick of coloured chalk or wax used for writing or drawing [F, crayon, pencil, fr dim. of *craie* chalk, fr L *creta*]

¹craze /krayz/ *vt* **1** to produce minute cracks on the surface or glaze of **2** to make (as if) insane ⟨*~d by pain and fear*⟩ ~ *vi* to develop a mesh of fine cracks [ME *crasen* to crush, craze, of Scand origin; akin to OSw *krasa* to crush]

²craze *n* **1** an exaggerated and often short-lived enthusiasm; a fad **2** fine cracks in a surface or coating of glaze, enamel, etc

crazy /'krayzi/ *adj* **1** mad, insane **2a** impractical ⟨*a ~ idea*⟩ **b** unusual, eccentric **3** extremely enthusiastic *about*; very fond – **crazily** *adv*, **craziness** *n* – **like crazy** to an extreme degree ⟨*everyone dancing* like crazy⟩ – infml

,crazy 'paving *n, Br* a paved surface made up of irregularly shaped paving stones

¹creak /kreek/ *vi* to make a prolonged grating or squeaking noise [ME *creken* to croak, of imit origin]

²creak *n* a prolonged rasping, grating, or squeaking noise (e g of an unoiled hinge) – **creaky** *adj*, **creakily** *adv*

¹cream /kreem/ *n* **1** the yellowish part of milk containing butterfat, that forms a surface layer when milk is allowed to stand **2a** a food (e g a sauce or cake filling) prepared with or resembling cream in consistency, richness, etc **b** a biscuit, chocolate, etc filled with (a soft preparation resembling) whipped cream **c** sthg with the consistency of thick cream; *esp* a usu emulsified medicinal or cosmetic preparation ⟨*skin ~*⟩ **3** the choicest part **4** a pale yellowish white colour [ME *creime, creme*, fr MF *craime, cresme*, fr LL *cramum*, of Celt origin; akin to W *cramen* scab] – **creamily** *adv*, **creaminess** *n*, **creamy** *adj*

²cream *vi* **1** to form cream or a surface layer like the cream on milk **2** to break into a creamy froth ~ *vt* **1a** SKIM 1c **b** to take away (the choicest part) – usu + *off* ⟨*~ off the brightest students*⟩ **2** to provide, prepare, or treat with cream or a cream sauce **3** to work or blend to the consistency of cream ⟨*~ butter and sugar*⟩ **4** to cause to form a surface layer of or like cream **5** *NAm* to defeat completely – infml

,cream 'cheese *n* a mild white soft unripened cheese made from whole milk enriched with cream

creamer /'kreemə/ *n* **1** a device for separating cream from milk **2** a small vessel (e g a jug) for serving cream

creamery /'kreeməri/ *n* an establishment where butter and cheese are made or where milk and milk products are prepared or sold – compare DAIRY 3

,cream of 'tartar /'tahtə/ *n* potassium hydrogen tartrate occurring as a white powder and used esp in baking powder

[1]**crease** /krees/ *n* **1** a line or mark made (as if) by folding a pliable substance **2a** an area surrounding the goal in lacrosse, hockey, etc into which an attacking player may not precede the ball or puck **b** the bowling crease, popping crease, or return crease of a cricket pitch [prob alter. of earlier *creaste*, fr ME *creste* crest] – **creaseless** *adj*

[2]**crease** *vt* **1** to make a crease in or on; wrinkle **2** *chiefly Br* **a** to cause much amusement to – often + *up* **b** to tire out ~ *vi* to become creased *USE* (*2*) infml

create /kri'ayt/ *vt* **1** to bring into existence ⟨*God* ~d *the heaven and the earth* – Gen 1:1 (AV)⟩ **2a** to invest with a new form, office, or rank ⟨*was* ~d *a peer of the realm*⟩ **b** to produce, cause ⟨~d *a disturbance*⟩ **3** to design, invent ~ *vi Br* to make a loud fuss about sthg – infml [ME *createn*, fr L *creatus*, pp of *creare*]

creatine /'kree·ə,teen/ *n* a substance that occurs esp in the muscles of vertebrates either free or as creatine phosphate [ISV, fr Gk *kreat-*, *kreas* flesh – more at RAW]

,**creatine 'phosphate** *n* a derivative of creatine that is an energy source for the contraction of the muscles of vertebrates

creatinine /kree'atineen/ *n* a compound formed from the breakdown of creatine and found in muscle, blood, urine, etc [G *kreatinin*, fr *kreatin* creatine]

creation /kri'aysh(ə)n/ *n* **1** *often cap* the act of bringing the world into ordered existence **2** sthg created: e g **a** the world **b** creatures singly or collectively **c** an original work of art **d** a product of some minor art or craft (e g dressmaking or cookery) showing unusual flair or immagination – often derog ⟨*a hideous* ~ *in mauve and magneta tulle*⟩ [CREATE + -ION]

creationist /kri'ayshənist/ *n or adj* (an adherent) of a theory that all forms of life were created simultaneously by God, and did not evolve from earlier forms

creative /kri'aytiv/ *adj* **1** marked by or requiring the ability or power to create; given to creating **2** having the quality of sthg imaginatively created ⟨*the* ~ *arts*⟩ – **creatively** *adv*, **creativeness** *n*

creator /kri'aytə/ *n* a person who creates, usu by bringing sthg new or original into being; *esp, cap* GOD 1

creature /'kreechə/ *n* **1a** sthg created ⟨~s *of fantasy*⟩ **b** a lower animal ⟨*the* ~s *of the woods*⟩ **2a** an animate being; *esp* a non-human one **b** a human being; a person **3** one who is the servile dependant or tool of another [ME, fr OF, fr LL *creatura*, fr L *creatus*] – **creatural** *adj*, **creatureliness** *n*, **creaturely** *adj*

creature comforts *n pl* material things that give bodily comfort

crèche /kresh/ *n* **1** a representation of the Nativity scene **2** *chiefly Br* a centre where children under school age are looked after while their parents are at work [F, fr OF *creche* manger, crib, of Gmc origin; akin to OHG *krippa* manger – more at CRIB]

credence /'kreedəns/ *n* acceptance of sthg as true or real ⟨*give* ~ *to gossip*⟩ [ME, fr MF or ML; MF, fr ML *credentia*, fr L *credent-*, *credens*, prp of *credere* to believe, trust – more at CREED]

'**credence ,table** *n* a Renaissance side table or sideboard used chiefly for valuable plate [MF, fr OIt *credenza*]

credential /kri'densh(ə)l/ *n* sthg, esp a letter, that gives proof of identity, status, or authority – usu pl with sing. meaning

credenza /kri'denzə/ *n* CREDENCE TABLE [It, lit., belief, confidence, fr ML *credentia*]

,**credi'bility ,gap** /,kredə'biləti/ *n* (a lack of credibility arising from) a discrepancy between what is claimed and what is perceived to be true

credible /'kredəbl/ *adj* offering reasonable grounds for belief [ME, fr L *credibilis*, fr *credere*] – **credibly** *adv*, **credibility** /,kredə'biləti/ *n*

[1]**credit** /'kredit/ *n* **1a** the balance in a person's favour in an account **b** an amount or sum placed at a person's disposal by a bank and usu to be repaid with interest **c** time given for payment for goods or services provided but not immediately paid for ⟨*long-term* ~⟩ **d** an entry on the right-hand side of an account constituting an addition to a revenue, net worth, or liability account **2** credence **3** influence derived from enjoying the confidence of others; standing **4** a source of honour or repute ⟨*a* ~ *to her parents*⟩ **5** acknowledgment, approval ⟨~ *where* ~ *is due*⟩ **6a** a line, note, or name that acknowledges the source of an item **b** an acknowledgment of a contributor by name that appears at the beginning or end of a film or television programme **7a** recognition that a student has fulfilled a course requirement **b** the passing of an examination at a level well above the minimum though not with distinction [MF, fr OIt *credito*, fr L *creditum* something entrusted to another, loan, fr neut of *creditus*, pp of *credere*] – **on credit** with the cost charged to one's account and paid later ⟨*bought his new tape recorder* on credit⟩

[2]**credit** *vt* **1** to believe **2a** to enter on the credit side of an account **b** to place to the credit of ⟨~ *an account*⟩ – compare DEBIT **3a** to ascribe some usu favourable characteristic to – + *with* ⟨~ *me with some intelligence*⟩ **b** to attribute *to* some person ⟨*they* ~ *the invention to him*⟩ [partly fr [1]*credit*; partly fr L *creditus*, pp]

creditable /'kreditəbl/ *adj* **1** worthy of esteem or praise **2** *NAm* capable of being attributed *to* – **creditably** *adv*

'**credit ,card** *n* a card provided by a bank, agency, or business allowing the holder to obtain goods and services on credit

creditor /'kreditə/ *n* one to whom a debt is owed

'**credit-,worthy** *adj* qualifying for commercial credit – **credit-worthiness** *n*

credo /'kreedoh, 'kray-/ *n, pl* **credos** **1** a creed **2** *cap* a musical setting of the creed in a sung mass [ME, fr L, I believe]

credulity /kri'dyoohləti/ *n* undue willingness to believe; gullibility

credulous /'kredyooləs/ *adj* ready to believe, esp on slight evidence [L *credulus*, fr *credere*] – **credulously** *adv*, **credulousness** *n*

Cree /kree/ *n, pl* **Crees**, *esp collectively* **Cree** a member, or the Algonquian language, of an American Indian people of Manitoba and Saskatchewan [short for earlier *Christens*, fr CanF *Christino*, prob modif of Ojibwa *Kenistenoag*]

creed /kreed/ *n* **1** a brief conventionalized statement of religious belief; *esp* such a statement said or sung as part of Christian worship **2** a set of fundamental beliefs [ME *crede*, fr OE *crēda*, fr L *credo* (first word of the Apostles' and Nicene Creeds), fr *credere* to believe, trust, entrust; akin to OIr *cretim* I believe, Skt *śrad-dadhāti* he believes] – **creedal** *adj*, **credal** *adj*

creek /kreek/ *n* **1** *chiefly Br* a small narrow inlet of a lake, sea, etc **2** *chiefly NAm & Austr* a brook [ME *crike, creke*, fr ON *-kriki* bend; akin to ON *krōkr* hook – more at [1]CROOK] – **up the creek 1** in trouble – infml **2** wrong, mistaken – infml

Creek *n* a member, or the Muskogean language, of a confederacy of American Indian peoples of Alabama, Georgia, and Florida

creel /kreel/ *n* a wickerwork container (e g for newly caught fish) [ME *creille, crele*, prob fr (assumed) MF *creille* grill, fr L *craticula*, dim. of *cratis* wickerwork – more at HURDLE]

[1]**creep** /kreep/ *vi* **crept** /krept/ **1** to move along with the body prone and close to the ground **2a** to go very slowly ⟨*the hours* crept *by*⟩ **b** to go timidly or cautiously so as to escape notice **c** to enter, advance, or develop gradually or slowly ⟨*a note of irritation* crept *into her voice*⟩ **3a** CRAWL 4b **b** *of a plant* to spread or grow over a surface by clinging with tendrils, roots, etc or rooting at intervals **4** to change shape permanently due to prolonged stress or exposure to high temperatures [ME *crepen*, fr OE *crēopan*; akin to Gk *grypos* curved, bent]

[2]**creep** *n* **1** a movement of or like creeping **2** the slow change of dimensions of an object due to prolonged exposure to high temperature or stress **3** a distressing sensation, esp of apprehension or disgust, like that caused by insects creeping over one's flesh – usu pl with sing. meaning ⟨*gives me the* ~s⟩; infml **4** *Br* an obnoxious or ingratiatingly servile person – infml

creeper /'kreepə/ *n* **1a** a creeping plant **b** a bird (e g a tree creeper) that creeps about on trees or bushes **c** a creeping insect or reptile **2** a grapnel [[1]CREEP + [2]-ER]

creeping jenny /,kreeping 'jeni/ *n* a yellow-flowered trailing perennial plant of the primrose family [*Jenny*, nickname for *Jane*]

creepy /'kreepi/ *adj* producing a sensation of shivery apprehension ⟨*a* ~ *horror story*⟩

,creepy-'crawly /'krawli/ *n, Br* a small creeping or scuttling creature (e g a spider) – infml

cremate /kri'mayt/ *vt* to reduce (a dead body) to ashes by burning [L *crematus*, pp of *cremare* to burn up, cremate] – **cremation** /-'maysh(ə)n/ *n*

crematorium /,kremə'tawri·əm/ *n, pl* **crematoriums, crematoria** /-ri·ə/ a place where cremation is carried out

crème /krem (*Fr* krɛm)/ *n, pl* **crèmes** /krem(z) (*Fr* ~)/ CREAM 2a, b [F, fr OF *cresme* – more at CREAM]

crème de la crème /,krem də lah 'krem/ *n* the very best [F, lit., cream of the cream]

,crème de 'menthe /də 'mont (*Fr* də mɑ̃:t)/ *n* a sweet green or white mint-flavoured liqueur [F, lit., cream of mint]

crenate /'kreenayt/, **crenated** *adj* having the margin cut into rounded scallops ⟨*a* ~ *leaf*⟩ ☞ PLANT [NL *crenatus*, fr ML *crena* notch] – **crenation** /-'naysh(ə)n/ *n*

crenel /'krenl/, **crenelle** /krə'nel/ *n* a crenellation [MF *crenel*, fr OF, dim. of *cren* notch, fr *crener* to notch; akin to ML *crena* notch]

crenellated /'krenə,laytid/ *adj* having battlements

crenellation /,krenə'laysh(ə)n/ *n* an indentation in a battlement ☞ CHURCH

creole /'kree,ohl/ *adj, often cap* of Creoles or their language

Creole *n* **1** a person of European descent in the W Indies or Spanish America **2** a white descendant of early French or Spanish settlers of the Gulf States of the USA **3** a person of mixed French or Spanish and Negro descent **4** *not cap* a language based on 2 or more languages that serves as the native language of its speakers [F *créole*, fr Sp *criollo*, fr Pg *crioulo* white person born in the colonies]

[1]**creosote** /'kree·ə,soht/ *n* **1** a clear or yellowish oily liquid obtained from wood tar and used as an antiseptic **2** a brownish oily liquid obtained from coal tar and used esp as a wood preservative [G *kreosot*, fr Gk *kreas* flesh + *sōtēr* preserver, fr *sōzein* to preserve, fr *sōs* safe – more at RAW, THUMB; fr its antiseptic properties]

[2]**creosote** *vt* to treat with creosote

crepe, crêpe /krayp/ *n* **1** a light crinkled fabric woven from any of various fibres **2** a small very thin pancake [F *crêpe*, fr MF *crespe*, fr *crespe* curled, fr L *crispus*] – **crepey, crepy** *adj*

,crepe de 'chine /də 'sheen/ *n, often cap 2nd C* a soft fine crepe, orig of silk [F *crêpe de Chine*, lit., crepe from China]

,crepe 'paper *n* thin paper with a crinkled or puckered texture

,crepe 'rubber *n* crude or synthetic rubber in the form of crinkled sheets, used esp for shoe soles

,crepe 'sole *n* (a shoe with) a crepe rubber sole

crepitate /'krepitayt/ *vi* to crackle [L *crepitatus*, pp of *crepitare* to crackle, fr *crepitus*, pp of *crepare* to rattle, crack – more at [1]RAVEN]

crepitation /,krepi'taysh(ə)n/ *n* **1** a crackling sound heard from the lungs that is characteristic of pneumonia **2** a grating sound produced by the fractured ends of a bone moving against each other [CREPITATE + -ION]

crepitus /'krepitəs/ *n* crepitation [L, fr pp of *crepare*]

crept /krept/ *past of* CREEP

crepuscular /kri'puskyoolə/ *adj* **1** active in the twilight ⟨~ *insects*⟩ **2** of or resembling twilight; dim – fml [L *crepusculum* twilight, fr *creper* dusky]

[1]**crescendo** /krə'shendoh/ *n, pl* **crescendos, crescendoes 1** a gradual increase; *esp* a gradual increase in volume in a musical passage **2** a crescendo musical passage ***USE*** ☞ MUSIC [It, lit., growing, fr L *crescendum*, gerund of *crescere* to grow] – **crescendo** *vi*

[2]**crescendo** *adv or adj* with an increase in volume – used in music ☞ MUSIC

crescent /'krezənt/ *n* **1** the figure of the moon at any stage between new moon and first quarter or last quarter and the succeeding new moon **2** sthg shaped like a crescent and consisting of a concave and a convex curve [ME *cressant*, fr MF *creissant*, fr prp of *creistre* to grow, increase, fr L *crescere*; akin to OHG *hirsi* millet, L *creare* to create, Gk *koros* boy]

cresol /'kreesol, -sohl/ *n* a phenol used esp as a disinfectant [ISV, irreg fr *creosote*]

cress /kres/ *n* any of numerous plants of the mustard family that have mildly pungent leaves and are used in salads and as a garnish [ME *cresse*, fr OE *cærse, cressa*; akin to OHG *kressa* cress]

¹crest /krest/ *n* **1a** a showy tuft or projection on the head of an animal, esp a bird **b** the plume, emblem, etc worn on a knight's helmet **c(1)** a symbol of a family, office, etc that appears as a figure on top of the helmet in a heraldic achievement **(2)** COAT OF ARMS – not used technically in heraldry **d** the upper muscular ridge of a horse's neck from which the mane grows **2** the ridge or top, esp of a wave, roof, or mountain **3** *the* climax, culmination ⟨*at the ~ of his fame*⟩ [ME *creste*, fr MF, fr L *crista*; akin to OE *hrisian* to shake, L *curvus* curved – more at ¹CROWN] – **crestless** *adj*

²crest *vt* **1** to provide with a crest; crown **2** to reach the crest of ~ *vi*, *of waves* to rise to a crest

crested /ˈkrestid/ *adj* **1** having a crest **2** marked or decorated with a crest ⟨~ *crockery*⟩

crestfallen /ˈkrest,fawlən/ *adj* disheartened, dejected

cretaceous /kriˈtayshəs/ *adj* **1** resembling or containing chalk **2** *cap* of or being the last period of the Mesozoic era ☞ EVOLUTION [L *cretaceus*, fr *creta* chalk] – **cretaceous** *n*, **cretaceously** *adv*

cretin /ˈkretin/ *n* sby afflicted with cretinism; *broadly* an imbecile, idiot [F *crétin*, fr F dial. *cretin* Christian, human being, kind of idiot found in the Alps, fr L *christianus* Christian] – **cretinous** *adj*

cretinism /ˈkreti,niz(ə)m/ *n* (congenital) physical stunting and mental retardation caused by severe deficiency of the thyroid gland in infancy

cretonne /ˈkree,ton, kriˈton/ *n* a strong unglazed cotton or linen cloth used esp for curtains and upholstery [F, fr *Creton*, town in Normandy, France]

crevasse /krəˈvas/ *n* a deep fissure, esp in a glacier ☞ GEOGRAPHY [F, fr OF *crevace*]

crevice /ˈkrevis/ *n* a narrow opening resulting from a split or crack [ME, fr MF *crevace*, fr OF, fr *crever* to break, fr L *crepare* to crack – more at ¹RAVEN]

¹crew /krooh/ *chiefly Br past of* CROW

²crew *n sing or pl in constr* **1** a company of men working on 1 job or under 1 foreman **2a** the personnel of a ship or boat (excluding the captain and officers) **b** members of a crew ⟨*the captain and 50* ~⟩ **c** the people who man an aircraft in flight **3** a number of people temporarily associated – infml [ME *crue*, lit., reinforcement, fr MF *creue* increase, fr *creistre* to grow – more at CRESCENT] – **crewless** *adj*, **crewman** /-mən/ *n*

³crew *vb* to serve as a member of a crew (on)

ˈcrew ,cut *n* a very short bristly haircut, esp for a man

crewel /ˈkrooh·əl/ *n* loosely twisted worsted yarn used in embroidery and tapestry [ME *crule*]

ˈcrewel,work /-,wuhk/ *n* embroidery design worked with crewel

¹crib /krib/ *n* **1** a manger for feeding animals **2** an enclosure, esp with barred or slatted sides: e g **a** a stall for a stabled animal **b** CRADLE 1a **c** a bin for storage **3a** a set of cards contributed to equally by each player in cribbage for the dealer to use in scoring **b** cribbage **4** a literal translation; *esp* one used surreptitiously by students **5** *Br* a building considered with a view to unlawful entry **6** *chiefly NAm* COT 2 [ME, fr OE *cribb*; akin to OHG *krippa* manger, Gk *griphos* reed basket, OE *cradol* cradle]

²crib *vb* **-bb-** *vt* **1** to confine, cramp **2** to provide with or put into a crib **3** to pilfer, steal; *esp* to plagiarize ~ *vi* **1** to steal, plagiarize **2** to use a crib; cheat – **cribber** *n*

cribbage /ˈkribij/ *n* a card game for 2 to 4 players each attempting to form various counting combinations of cards [¹*crib*]

ˈcrib ,biting *n* a bad habit of horses in which they gnaw (e g at the manger) while slobbering, salivating, and sucking in air

cribriform /ˈkribri,fawm/ *adj* pierced with small holes [L *cribrum* sieve; akin to L *cernere* to sift – more at CERTAIN]

¹crick /krik/ *n* a painful spasmodic condition of the muscles of the neck, back, etc [ME *cryk*]

²crick *vt* to cause a crick in (the neck, back, etc)

¹cricket /ˈkrikit/ *n* a leaping insect noted for the chirping sounds produced by the male [ME *criket*, fr MF *criquet*, of imit origin]

²cricket *n* a game played with a bat and ball on a large field with 2 wickets near its centre by 2 sides of 11 players each ☞ SPORT [MF *criquet* stake used as goal in a bowling game] – **cricketer** *n* – **not cricket** against the dictates of fair play; not honourable

cricoid /ˈkriekoyd/ *adj* of or being a ring-shaped cartilage of the larynx [NL *cricoides*, fr Gk *krikoeidēs* ring-shaped, fr *krikos* ring – more at CIRCLE]

crier /ˈkrie·ə/ *n* an officer who makes announcements in a court [¹CRY + ²-ER]

crikey /ˈkrieki/ *interj, chiefly Br* – used to express surprise; no longer in vogue [euphemism for *Christ*]

crime /kriem/ *n* **1** (a) violation of law **2** a grave offence, esp against morality **3** criminal activity **4** sthg deplorable, foolish, or disgraceful ⟨*it's a ~ to waste good food*⟩ – infml [ME, fr L *crimen* accusation, fault, crime]

¹criminal /ˈkriminl/ *adj* **1** involving or being a crime **2** relating to crime or its punishment ⟨~ *law*⟩ ⟨*a ~ court*⟩ ☞ LAW **3** guilty of crime **4** disgraceful, deplorable – infml [ME, fr MF or LL; MF *criminel*, fr LL *criminalis*, fr L *crimin-*, *crimen* crime, accusation] – **criminally** *adv*, **criminality** /,krimiˈnaləti/ *n*

²criminal *n* one who has committed or been convicted of a crime

criminate /ˈkriminayt/ *vt* **1** to accuse of a crime **2** to incriminate [L *criminatus*, pp of *criminari*, fr *crimin-*, *crimen*] – **crimination** /-ˈnaysh(ə)n/ *n*

criminology /,krimiˈnoləji/ *n* the study of crime, criminals, and penal treatment [It *criminologia*, fr L *crimin-*, *crimen* + It *-o-* + *-logia* -logy] – **criminologist** *n*, **criminological** /,kriminəˈlojikl/ *adj*

¹crimp /krimp/ *vt* **1** to make wavy, or curly ⟨~ *her hair*⟩ **2** to roll or curl the edge of (e g a steel panel) **3** to pinch or press together in order to seal or join [D or LG *krimpen* to shrivel; akin to LG *krampe* hook – more at CRAMP] – **crimp** *n*, **crimper** *n*

²crimp *n or vt* (one employed) to entrap or force (men) into joining the army or navy [perh fr ¹*crimp*]

Crimplene /ˈkrimpleen/ *trademark* – used for a textured continuous-filament polyester yarn

¹crimson /ˈkrimz(ə)n/ *adj or n* (a) deep purplish red [n ME *crimisin*, fr OSp *cremesín*, fr Ar *qirmizī*, fr *qirmiz* kermes; adj fr n]

²crimson *vb* to make or become crimson

cringe /krinj/ *vi* **1** to shrink or wince, esp in fear or servility **2** to behave with fawning self-abasement [ME *crengen*; akin to OE *cringan* to yield, *cradol* cradle]

cringle /'kring·gl/ *n* an eyelet or loop worked into the edge of a sail for attaching a rope [LG *kringel*, dim. of *kring* ring; akin to OE *cradol* cradle]

[1]**crinkle** /'kringkl/ *vb* **crinkling** /'kringkling/ *vi* **1** to wrinkle **2** to rustle ~*vt* to cause to crinkle [ME *crynkelen*; akin to OE *cringan* to yield]

[2]**crinkle** *n* a wrinkle – **crinkly** /'kringkli/ *adj*

crinoid /'krienoyd/ *n* any of a large class of echinoderms having a cup-shaped body with 5 or more feathery arms [deriv of Gk *krinon* lily] – **crinoid** *adj*

crinoline /'krinəlin/ *n* (a padded or hooped petticoat supporting) a full skirt as worn by women in the 19th c ☞ GARMENT [F, fr It *crinolino*, fr *crino* horsehair (fr L *crinis* hair; akin to L *crista* crest) + *lino* flax, linen, fr L *linum*]

criollo /kri'oh(l)yoh/ *n, pl* **criollos** a person born and usu raised in Latin America; *esp* one of Spanish descent [Sp – more at CREOLE]

cripes /krieps/ *interj, Br* – used to express surprise; no longer in vogue [euphemism for *Christ*]

[1]**cripple** /'kripl/ *n* a lame or partly disabled person or animal [ME *cripel*, fr OE *crypel*; akin to OE *crēopan* to creep – more at CREEP]

[2]**cripple** *vt* **crippling** /'kripling/ **1** to make a cripple; lame **2** to deprive of strength, efficiency, wholeness, or capability for service

crisis /'kriesis/ *n, pl* **crises** /-seez/ **1a** the turning point for better or worse in an acute disease (e g pneumonia) **b** a sudden attack of pain, distress, etc **2** an unstable or crucial time or situation; *esp* TURNING POINT [L, fr Gk *krisis*, lit., decision, fr *krinein* to decide – more at CERTAIN]

[1]**crisp** /krisp/ *adj* **1a** easily crumbled; brittle **b** desirably firm and fresh ⟨*a ~ apple*⟩ **c** newly made or prepared ⟨*a ~ pound note*⟩ **2** sharp, clean-cut, and clear ⟨*a ~ illustration*⟩ **3** decisive, sharp ⟨*a ~ manner*⟩ **4** *of weather* briskly cold; fresh; *esp* frosty [ME, curled, fr OE, fr L *crispus*; akin to L *curvus* curved – more at [1]CROWN] – **crisply** *adv*, **crispness** *n*

[2]**crisp** *vt* **1** to curl, crimp **2** to make or keep crisp ⟨*~ the bread in the oven*⟩ ~*vi* to become crisp – **crisper** *n*

[3]**crisp** *n, chiefly Br* a thin slice of (flavoured or salted) fried potato, usu eaten cold

'**crisp,bread** /-,bred/ *n* a plain dry unsweetened biscuit made from crushed grain (e g rye)

crispen /'krispən/ *vb* to make or become crisp

crispy /'krispi/ *adj* crisp – **crispiness** *n*

[1]**crisscross** /'kris,kros/ *adj or n* (marked or characterized by) crisscrossing or a crisscrossed pattern [obs *christcross, crisscross* (mark of a cross)]

[2]**crisscross** *vt* **1** to mark with intersecting lines **2** to pass back and forth through or over ~*vi* to go or pass back and forth

crista /'kristə/ *n, pl* **cristae** /-ti/ any of the inwardly projecting folds of the inner membrane of a mitochondrion [NL, fr L, crest]

criterion /krie'tiəri·ən/ *n, pl* **criteria** /-ri·ə/ *also* **criterions** a standard on which a judgment or decision may be based [Gk *kritērion*, fr *kritēs* judge, fr *krinein* to judge, decide – more at CERTAIN] – **criterial** *adj*

critic /'kritik/ *n* one who criticizes: e g **a** one who evaluates works of art, literature, or music, esp as a profession **b** one who tends to judge harshly or to be over-critical of minor faults [L *criticus*, fr Gk *kritikos*, fr *kritikos* able to discern or judge, fr *krinein* to judge]

critical /'kritikl/ *adj* **1a** inclined to criticize severely and unfavourably **b** consisting of or involving criticism ⟨*~ writings*⟩ **c** exercising or involving careful judgment or judicious evaluation **2a** relating to or being a measurement, point, etc at which some quality, property, or phenomenon undergoes a marked change ⟨*~ temperature*⟩ **b** crucial, decisive ⟨*~ test*⟩ **c** being in or approaching a state of crisis **3** *of a nuclear reactor* sustaining an energy-producing chain reaction – **critically** *adv*, **criticality** /-'kaləti/ *n*

,**critical 'angle** *n* **1** the smallest angle of incident light reflected onto an interior surface at which total internal reflection takes place **2** the angle of attack at which the flow about an aerofoil changes abruptly, with corresponding abrupt changes in the lift and drag ☞ FLIGHT

,**critical 'mass** *n* the minimum mass of fissile material that can sustain a nuclear chain reaction

criticism /'kriti,siz(ə)m/ *n* **1a** the act of criticizing, usu unfavourably **b** a critical observation or remark **c** a critique **2** the art or act of analysing and evaluating esp the fine arts, literature, or literary documents

critic·ize, -ise /'kriti,siez/ *vt* **1** to consider the merits and demerits of and judge accordingly; evaluate **2** to stress the faults of ~*vi* to criticize sthg or sby

critique /kri'teek/ *n* an act of criticizing; *esp* a critical estimate or discussion (e g an article or essay) [alter. of arch *critic* (criticism), fr Gk *kritikē*]

critter /'kritə/ *n, dial* a creature [by alter.]

[1]**croak** /krohk/ *vi* **1a** to make a croak **b** to speak in a hoarse throaty voice **2** to die – slang ~*vt* **1** to utter (gloomily) in a hoarse raucous voice ⟨*the raven that ~s the fatal entrance of Duncan* – Shak⟩ **2** to kill – slang [ME *croken*, of imit origin]

[2]**croak** *n* a deep hoarse cry characteristic of a frog or toad; *also* a similar sound – **croaky** *adj*

Croatian /kroh'aysh(ə)n/, **Croat** /'kroh,at/ *n* **1** a native or inhabitant of Croatia **2** a south Slavonic language spoken by the Croatians and written in the Latin alphabet – compare SERB ☞ LANGUAGE [*Croatia*, region of SE Europe now part of Yugoslavia] – **Croatian** *adj*

[1]**crochet** /'krohshay/ *n* crocheted work [F, hook, crochet, fr MF, dim. of *croche* hook, of Scand origin; akin to ON *krōkr* hook – more at [1]CROOK]

[2]**crochet** *vt* to form (e g a garment or design) by drawing a single continuous yarn or thread into a pattern of interlocked loops using a hooked needle ~*vi* to do or make crochet work – **crocheter** /-,shayə/ *n*

crocidolite /kroh'sidəliet/ *n* a blue or green asbestos mineral that is a fibrous silicate of sodium and iron [G *krokydolith*, fr Gk *krokyd-, krokys* nap on cloth + G *-lith* -lite]

[1]**crock** /krok/ *n* **1** a thick earthenware pot or jar **2** a piece of broken earthenware used esp to cover the bottom of a flowerpot [ME, fr OE *crocc*; akin to MHG *krūche* crock]

[2]**crock** *n* **1** an old (broken-down) vehicle **2** an (elderly) disabled person *USE* infml [ME *crok* old disabled animal, prob of Scand origin; akin to Norw dial. *krokje* broken-down horse or person]

[3]**crock** *vt* to cause to become disabled ~*vi* BREAK DOWN 1a *USE* (*vt & vi*) sometimes + *up*; infml

crockery /ˈkrokəri/ *n* earthenware or china tableware, esp for everyday domestic use

crocket /ˈkrokit/ *n* an architectural ornament in the form of curved and bent foliage placed at regular intervals on the edge of a gable, spire, or canopy ☞ CHURCH [ME *croket*, fr ONF *croquet* hook, dim. of *croc* hook, of Scand origin; akin to ON *krōkr* hook]

ˈ**crock ˌpot** *n* a deep round vessel with a removable inner bowl and a heating element that is used to cook food slowly at a low temperature

crocodile /ˈkrokədiel/ *n* **1** any of several tropical or subtropical large voracious thick-skinned long-bodied aquatic reptiles; *broadly* a crocodilian ☞ LIFE CYCLE **2** the skin of a crocodile; *also* leather prepared from this **3** *Br* a line of people (e g schoolchildren) walking in pairs [ME & L; ME *cocodrille*, fr OF, fr ML *cocodrillus*, alter. of L *crocodilus*, fr Gk *krokodilos* lizard, crocodile, fr *krokē* pebble + *drilos* worm]

ˈ**crocodile ˌtears** *n pl* false or affected tears; hypocritical sorrow [fr ancient belief that crocodiles shed tears over their prey]

crocodilian /ˌkrokəˈdili·ən/ *n* a crocodile, alligator, or related (extinct) reptile – **crocodilian** *adj*

crocus /ˈkrohkəs/ *n, pl* **crocuses** any of a large genus of usu early-flowering plants of the iris family bearing a single usu brightly-coloured long-tubed flower [NL, genus name, fr L, saffron, fr Gk *krokos*, of Sem origin]

croft /kroft/ *n, chiefly Br* **1** a small enclosed field usu adjoining a house **2** a small farm on often poor land, esp in Scotland, worked by a tenant [ME, fr OE; akin to OE *crēopan* to creep – more at CREEP] – **crofter** *n*

crofting /ˈkrofting/ *n, chiefly Br* the system of working the land as crofts

croissant /ˈkwahsong (*Fr* krwasɔ̃)/ *n* a usu flaky rich crescent-shaped roll of bread or yeast- leavened pastry [F, lit., crescent, fr MF *creissant*]

Cro-Magnon /ˌkroh ˈmanyən, ˈmagnən/ *n* a tall erect race of human beings known from skeletal remains found chiefly in S France and classified as the same species as recent human beings [*Cro-Magnon*, a cave near Les Eyzies, France]

cromlech /ˈkromlək/ *n* a dolmen [W, lit., bent stone]

crone /ˈkrohn/ *n* a withered old woman [ME, fr ONF *carogne*, lit., carrion, fr (assumed) VL *caronia* – more at CARRION]

crony /ˈkrohni/ *n* a close friend, esp of long standing; a chum – infml; often derog ⟨*old* cronies *down at the pub*⟩ [alter. of obs *chrony*, prob fr Gk *chronios* long-lasting, fr *chronos* time]

¹**crook** /krook/ *n* **1** an implement or part of sthg having a bent or hooked shape **2** a shepherd's staff **3** a bend, curve ⟨*she carried the parcel in the* ~ *of her arm*⟩ **4** a person given to criminal practices; a thief, swindler – infml [ME *crok*, fr ON *krōkr* hook; akin to OE *cradol* cradle]

²**crook** *vt* BEND 1 ⟨*I* ~ed *my neck so I could see*⟩ ~ *vi* to curve, wind

³**crook** *adj, Austr & NZ* **1** ill, sick **2** not in correct working order **3** bad, unpleasant *USE* infml [perh alter. of *cronk* (ill), fr Yiddish or G *krank*, fr MHG *kranc* weak]

crooked /ˈkrookid/ *adj* **1** having a crook or curve; bent **2** not morally straightforward; dishonest **3** *Austr* bad-tempered; angry – **crookedly** *adv*, **crookedness** *n*

croon /kroohn/ *vi* to sing usu sentimental popular songs in a low or soft voice ~ *vt* to sing in a crooning manner [ME *croynen* to bellow, fr MD *cronen*; akin to OE *cran* crane] – **croon** *n*, **crooner** *n*

¹**crop** /krop/ *n* **1** (the stock or handle of) a riding whip, esp with a short stock and a loop on the end **2** a pouched enlargement of the gullet of many birds in which food is stored and prepared for digestion **3** a short haircut **4a** (the total production of) a plant or animal product that can be grown and harvested extensively ⟨*a large apple* ~⟩ **b** a group or quantity appearing at any one time ⟨*a new* ~ *of students*⟩ [ME, craw, head of a plant, yield of a field, fr OE *cropp*; akin to OHG *kropf* goitre, craw, OE *crēopan* to creep – more at CREEP]

²**crop** *vb* **-pp-** *vt* **1a** to remove the upper or outer parts of ⟨~ *a hedge*⟩ **b** to harvest ⟨~ *trout*⟩ **c** to cut short; trim **2** to grow as or to cause (land) to bear a crop ⟨~ *more wheat next year*⟩ ~ *vi* **1** to feed by cropping sthg **2** to yield or bear a crop

¹**cropper** /ˈkropə/ *n* a plant that yields a crop of a usu specified quality or amount [²CROP + ²-ER]

²**cropper** *n* **1** a severe fall **2** a sudden or complete disaster *USE* chiefly in *come a cropper*; infml [prob fr E dial. *crop* (neck), fr ¹*crop*]

crop up *vi* to happen or appear unexpectedly or casually – infml

croquet /ˈkrohkay/ *n* **1** a game in which wooden balls are driven by mallets through a series of hoops set out on a lawn **2** the driving away of an opponent's croquet ball by striking one's own ball placed against it [F dial., hockey stick, fr ONF, crook, dim. of *croc* hook, of Scand origin] – **croquet** *vt*

croquette /krohˈket/ *n* a small (rounded) piece of minced meat, vegetable, etc coated with egg and breadcrumbs and fried in deep fat [F, fr *croquer* to crunch, of imit origin]

crore /kraw/ *n, pl* **crores** /krawz/ *also* **crore** a money unit worth 10 million rupees or 100 lakhs [Hindi *karor*]

crosier, crozier /ˈkrohzhə/ *n* a staff resembling a shepherd's crook carried by bishops as a symbol of office [ME *croser* crosier bearer, fr MF *crossier*, fr *crosse* crosier, of Gmc origin; akin to OE *crycc* crutch – more at CRUTCH]

¹**cross** /kros/ *n* **1a** an upright stake with a transverse beam used, esp by the ancient Romans, for execution **b** *often cap* the cross on which Jesus was crucified **2a** the Crucifixion **b** an affliction, trial **3** a figure or design consisting of an upright bar intersected by a horizontal one; *specif* one used as a Christian emblem **4** a monument shaped like or surmounted by a cross ⟨*the market* ~⟩ **5** a mark formed by 2 intersecting lines crossing at their midpoints that is used as a signature, to mark a position, to indicate that sthg is incorrect, or to indicate a kiss in a letter – compare ²TICK 2 **6** a badge, emblem, or decoration shaped like a cross **7a** the crossing of dissimilar individuals; *also* the resulting hybrid **b** sby who or sthg that combines characteristics of 2 different types or individuals **8** a hook delivered over the opponent's lead in boxing **9** the act of crossing the ball in soccer [ME, fr OE, fr ON or OIr; ON *kross*, fr (assumed) OIr *cross*, fr L *cruc-*, *crux* – more at RIDGE] – **on the cross** on the bias; diagonally

²**cross** *vt* **1a** to lie or be situated across **b** to intersect

2 to make the sign of the cross on or over 3 to cancel by marking a cross on or drawing a line through 4 to place or fold crosswise ⟨~ *the arms*⟩ 5 to run counter to; oppose 6 to go across 7a to draw a line across ⟨~ *one's* t's⟩ b to draw 2 parallel lines across (a cheque) so that it can only be paid directly into a bank account 8 to cause (an animal or plant) to interbreed with one of a different kind; hybridize 9 to kick or pass (the ball) across the field in soccer, specif from the wing into the goal area ~*vi* 1 to move, pass, or extend across sthg – usu + *over* 2 *of letters, travellers, etc* to meet and pass 3 to interbreed, hybridize 4 to cross the ball in soccer – **cross the floor** *of a member of parliament* to transfer allegiance to the opposing party – **cross swords** to come into conflict – **cross one's mind** to occur to one

[3]**cross** *adj* 1 lying or moving across 2 mutually opposed ⟨~ *purposes*⟩ 3 involving mutual interchange; reciprocal 4a irritable, grumpy b angry, annoyed 5 crossbred, hybrid – **crossly** *adv*, **crossness** *n*

[4]**cross** *adv* not parallel; crosswise

'cross,bar /-,bah/ *n* a transverse bar (e g between goalposts)

'cross ,bench *n* any of the benches in the House of Lords for members who belong to neither government nor opposition parties – usu pl [[3]*cross*] – **crossbencher** *n*

crossbill /'kros,bil/ *n* any of a genus of finches with strongly curved crossed mandibles that feed esp on the seeds of conifers

crossbones /'kros,bohnz/ *n pl* 2 leg or arm bones placed or depicted crosswise – compare SKULL AND CROSSBONES

crossbow /'kros,boh/ *n* a short bow mounted crosswise near the end of a wooden stock and used to fire bolts and stones – **crossbowman** /-mən/ *n*

'cross,bred /-,bred/ *adj* hybrid; *specif* produced by interbreeding 2 pure but different breeds, strains, or varieties – **crossbred** *n*

[1]**'cross,breed** *vb* **'cross,bred** *vt* to hybridize or cross (esp 2 varieties or breeds of the same species) ~*vi* to undergo crossbreeding

[2]**crossbreed** *n* a hybrid

,cross-'buttock *n* a throw in which a wrestler pulls his opponent forwards over his hip

,cross-'check *vb* to check (information) for validity or accuracy by reference to more than 1 source – **cross-check** *n*

[1]**,cross-'country** *adj* 1 proceeding over countryside and not by roads 2 racing or travelling over the countryside instead of over a track or run – **cross-country** *adv*

[2]**,cross-'country** *n* cross-country running, horse riding, etc

'cross,court /-,kawt/ *adv or adj* towards the diagonally opposite side of a tennis, basketball, etc court

,cross-'cultural *adj* dealing with or drawing a comparison between different cultures

'cross,current /-,kurənt/ *n* a conflicting tendency – usu pl ⟨*political* ~s⟩

'cross,cut /-,kut/ *vt* to intersperse with contrasting images – **crosscut** *n*

'cross,cut ,saw *n* a saw designed to cut across the grain of wood – compare RIPSAW

'cross-,dresser *n* a transvestite

crosse /kros/ *n* the long-handled netted stick used in lacrosse [F, lit., crosier – more at CROSIER]

crossed /krost/ *adj, of a telephone line* connected in error to 2 or more telephones

,cross-ex'amine *vt* to question closely (esp a witness in a law court) in order to check answers or elicit new information – **cross-examination** *n*, **cross-examiner** *n*

,cross-'eye *n* 1 a squint in which the eye turns towards the nose 2 *pl* eyes affected with cross-eye – **cross-eyed** *adj*

,cross-,fertil·i'zation, -isation *n* 1a fertilization by the joining of ova with pollen or sperm from a different individual – compare SELF-FERTILIZATION b cross-pollination 2 interaction, esp of a broadening or productive nature – **cross-fertilize** /,- '---/ *vb*

'cross,fire /-,fie·ə/ *n* 1 firing from 2 or more points in crossing directions 2 rapid or heated interchange

,cross-'grained *adj* 1 having the grain or fibres running diagonally, transversely, or irregularly 2 difficult to deal with; intractable

'cross ,hair *n* a fine wire or thread seen through the eyepiece of an optical instrument and used as a reference mark

,cross'hatch /-'hach/ *vt* to shade with a series of intersecting parallel lines – **cross-hatching** *n*

'cross,head /-,hed/ *n* 1 a sliding metal block between a piston rod and a connecting rod, esp in a steam engine 2 a centred headline, esp between paragraphs in a newspaper column

crossing /'krosing/ *n* 1 a traversing or travelling across 2a a place or structure (e g on a street or over a river) where pedestrians or vehicles may cross b LEVEL CROSSING c a place where railway lines, roads, etc cross each other

,crossing-'over *n* the interchange of (segments of) genes between homologous chromosomes during meiotic cell division

,cross-'legged /'legid; *also* legd/ *adv or adj* 1 with legs crossed and knees spread wide apart ⟨*sat* ~ *on the floor*⟩ 2 with one leg placed over and across the other

'cross-,link *n* an atom, group, etc connecting parallel chains in a polymer or other complex chemical molecule – **cross-link** *vb*, **cross-linkable** *adj*, **cross-linkage** *n*

,cross 'multiply *vi* to find the 2 products obtained by multiplying the numerator of each of 2 fractions by the denominator of the other – **cross multiplication** /,- ---'--/

,cross of Lor'raine /lə'rayn, lə'ren (*Fr* lɔrɛn)/ *n* a cross having 2 horizontal crossbars intersecting the upright, one above and one below the middle of the upright, the upper crossbar being shorter than the lower ☞ SYMBOL [*Lorraine*, region in NE France]

crosspatch /'kros,pach/ *n* a bad-tempered person – infml [[3]*cross* + *patch* (fool)]

'cross,piece /-,pees/ *n* a horizontal member (e g of a structure)

crossply /'kros,plie/ *n or adj* (a tyre) with the cords arranged crosswise to strengthen the tread

,cross-,polli'nation *n* the transfer of pollen from one flower to the stigma of another – compare SELF-POLLINATION – **cross-pollinate** *vt*

,cross 'product *n* VECTOR PRODUCT

,cross-'purposes *n pl* – **at cross purposes** having a mutual misunderstanding or deliberately conflicting approach

,cross-re'fer *vb* **-rr-** *vt* **1** to direct (a reader) from one page or entry (e g in a book) to another **2** to refer from (a secondary entry) to a main entry ~ *vi* to make a cross-reference

[1]**,cross-'reference** *n* an indication at one place (e g in a book or filing system) of the existence of relevant information at another place

[2]**,cross-'reference** *vb* to cross-refer

,cross-re'sistance *n* tolerance (e g of bacteria) to a normally poisonous substance (e g an antibiotic) acquired by exposure to a chemically related substance

'cross,road /-,rohd/ *n* **1** the place where 2 or more roads intersect **2a** a central meeting place ⟨*the* ~s *of the world*⟩ **b** a crucial point, esp where a decision must be made ⟨*at a* ~s *in her career*⟩ *USE* usu pl with sing. meaning but sing. or pl in constr

'cross-,section *n* **1** (a drawing of) a surface made by cutting across sthg, esp at right angles to its length **2** the probability of an encounter between particles (resulting in a specified effect) ⟨*the ionization* ~⟩ **3** a representative sample ⟨*a* ~ *of society*⟩ – **cross-sectional** /,- '---/ *adj*

'cross-,stitch *n* (needlework using) a stitch in the shape of an X formed by crossing one stitch over another – **cross-stitch** *vb*

'cross-,talk *n* **1** unwanted signals in a communication channel that come from another channel **2** *Br* rapid exchange of repartee (e g between comedians)

'cross,trees /-treez/ *n pl* a pair of horizontal crosspieces on a mast to which supporting ropes are attached ☞ SHIP

'cross,ways /-,wayz/ *adv* crosswise, diagonally

'cross,wind /-,wind/ *n* a wind blowing in a direction not parallel to the course of a vehicle, aircraft, etc

cross wire *n* CROSS HAIR

'cross,wise /-,wiez/ *adv* so as to cross sthg; across ⟨*logs laid* ~⟩

'cross,word ,puzzle /'kros,wuhd/ *n* a puzzle in which words are entered in a pattern of numbered squares in answer to correspondingly numbered clues in such a way that the words read across and down ☞ WORD

crotch /kroch/ *n* **1** an angle formed where 2 branches separate off from a tree trunk **2** the angle between the inner thighs where they meet the human body [prob alter. of *crutch*] – **crotched** *adj*

crotchet /'krochit/ *n* a musical note with the time value of half a minim or 2 quavers ☞ MUSIC [ME *crochet*, lit., hook, fr MF – more at CROCHET]

crotchety /'krochiti/ *adj* bad-tempered ⟨*a* ~ *old man*⟩ – infml [*crotchet* (idiosyncrasy)] – **crotchetiness** *n*

croton /'kroht(ə)n/ *n* an E Indian plant yielding an oil formerly used as a drastic purgative; *also* a related plant of the spurge family [NL, genus name, fr Gk *krotōn* castor-oil plant]

crouch /krowch/ *vi* to lower the body by bending the legs [ME *crouchen*, perh fr MF *crochir* to become hook-shaped, fr *croche* hook] – **crouch** *n*

[1]**croup** /kroohp/ *n* the rump of a quadruped ☞ ANATOMY [ME *croupe*, fr OF, of Gmc origin; akin to OHG *kropf* craw – more at CROP]

[2]**croup** *n* a spasmodic laryngitis, esp of infants, marked by periods of difficult breathing and a hoarse cough [E dial. *croup* (to cry hoarsely, cough), prob of imit origin] – **croupous** *adj*, **croupy** *adj*

croupier /'kroohpi·ə, -ay/ *n* an employee of a gambling casino who collects and pays out bets at the gaming tables [F, lit., rider on the croup of a horse, fr *croupe* croup]

crouton /'kroohton/ *n* a small cube of crisp toasted or fried bread served with soup or used as a garnish [F *croûton*, dim. of *croûte* crust, fr MF *crouste*]

[1]**crow** /kroh/ *n* **1** the carrion or hooded crow or a related large usu entirely glossy black bird **2** a crowbar [ME *crowe*, fr OE *crāwe*; akin to OHG *krāwa* crow, OE *crāwan* to crow] – **as the crow flies** in a straight line

[2]**crow** *vi* **crowed,** (*I*) **crowed** *also* **crew** /krooh/ **1** to make the loud shrill cry characteristic of a cock **2** *esp of an infant* to utter sounds of happiness or pleasure **3a** to exult gloatingly, esp over another's misfortune **b** to brag exultantly or blatantly [ME *crowen*, fr OE *crāwan*]

[3]**crow** *n* **1** the characteristic cry of the cock **2** a triumphant cry

crowbar /'kroh,bah/ *n* an iron or steel bar for use as a lever that is wedge-shaped at the working end [[1]*crow* + *bar*; prob fr the forked end, like a crow's foot, it sometimes has]

crowberry /'krohb(ə)ri/ *n* (the tasteless black berry of) any of several low shrubby evergreen plants, esp of arctic or mountainous regions

[1]**crowd** /krowd/ *vi* **1** to press close ⟨*people* ~ing *through the narrow gates*⟩ **2** to collect in numbers; throng ~ *vt* **1a** to fill by pressing or thronging together ⟨*people* ~ed *the hall*⟩ **b** to force or thrust into a small space ⟨~ed *books onto the shelves*⟩ **2** to push, force ⟨~ed *us off the pavement*⟩ **3** to hoist more (sail) than usual for greater speed – usu + *on* **4** to press close to; jostle **5** to put pressure on – infml [ME *crouden*, fr OE *crūdan*; akin to MHG *kroten* to crowd, OE *crod* multitude, MIr *gruth* curds]

[2]**crowd** *n sing or pl in constr* **1** a large number of people gathered together without order; a throng **2** people in general – + *the* **3** a large number of things close together and in disorder **4** a specified social group ⟨*the in* ~⟩

crowded /'krowdid/ **1** filled with numerous people, things, or events **2** pressed or forced into a small space ⟨~ *spectators*⟩

crowd out *vt* **1** to exclude by depriving of space or time **2** to fill to capacity by coming or collecting together

'crowd,puller /-,poolə/ *n, chiefly Br* sby or sthg that attracts large crowds – infml

crowfoot /'kroh,foot/ *n, pl* **crowfoots** any of numerous plants, esp of the buttercup family, with lobed leaves shaped like a crow's foot

[1]**crown** /krown/ *n* **1** a reward of victory or mark of honour; *esp* the title representing the championship in a sport **2** a (gold and jewel-encrusted) headdress worn as a symbol of sovereignty **3a** the topmost part of the skull or head **b** the summit of a slope, mountain, etc **c** the upper part of the foliage of a tree or shrub **d** the part of a hat or cap that covers the crown of the head **e** (an artificial substitute for) the part of a tooth visible outside the gum ☞ DIGESTION **4** a wreath, band, or circular ornament for the head, esp worn as a symbol of victory **5** *often cap* **a** the sovereign as head of state; *also* sovereignty **b** the government under a constitutional monarchy **6** the

high point or culmination **7a** a British coin worth 25 pence (formerly 5 shillings) **b** a size of paper usu 20 x 15in (508 × 381mm) **8a** a koruna **b** a krona **c** a krone **9** the part of a flowering plant at which stem and root merge [ME *coroune, crowne*, fr OF *corone*, fr L *corona* wreath, crown, fr Gk *korōnē*; akin to Gk *korōnos* curved, L *curvus*, MIr *cruind* round] – **crowned** *adj*

[2]**crown** *vt* **1a** to place a crown on the head of, esp as a symbol of investiture ⟨~ed *her queen*⟩ **b** to recognize, usu officially, as (the leader in a particular field) **2** to bestow sthg on as a mark of honour or reward **3** to surmount, top; *esp* to put a draughtsman on top of (another draughtsman) to make a king **4** to bring to a successful conclusion **5** to put an artificial crown on (a tooth) **6** to hit on the head – infml [ME *corounen*, fr OF *coroner*, fr L *coronare*, fr *corona*]

,crown 'canopy *n* the cover formed by the topmost branches of trees in a forest

,crown 'colony *n, often cap C&C* a colony of the Commonwealth over which the British government retains some control

,Crown 'Court *n* a local criminal court in England and Wales having jurisdiction over serious offences ☞ LAW

,crown 'glass *n* a glass of relatively low refractive index and dispersion, used esp in lenses

,crown 'green *n* a bowling green which slopes downwards slightly from its centre to its outer edge

,crown 'jewels *n pl* the jewels (e g crown and sceptre) belonging to a sovereign's regalia

,crown of 'thorns *n* a starfish of the Pacific region that is covered with long spines and feeds on the coral of coral reefs

,crown 'prince *n* an heir apparent to a crown or throne

,crown prin'cess *n* **1** the wife of a crown prince **2** a female heir apparent or heir presumptive to a crown or throne

'crown ,saw *n* a saw with teeth at the edge of a hollow cylinder that is used to cut circular holes

'crow's-,foot *n, pl* **'crow's-,feet** **1** any of the wrinkles round the outer corners of the eyes – usu pl **2** crowfoot

'crow's ,nest *n* a partly enclosed high lookout platform (e g on a ship's mast)

'crow ,step *n* CORBIE STEP ☞ ARCHITECTURE – **crow stepped** *adj*

crozier /'krohzhə/ *n* a crosier

cruces /'kroohseez/ *pl of* CRUX

crucial /'kroohshəl/ *adj* **1** important or essential to the resolving of a crisis; decisive **2** of the greatest importance or significance [F, fr L *cruc-, crux* cross – more at RIDGE] – **crucially** *adv*

crucian /'kroohsh(ə)n/, **,crucian 'carp** *n* a European carp [modif of LG *karuse*, fr MHG *karusse*, fr Lith *karusis*]

crucible /'kroohsibl/ *n* **1** a vessel for melting and calcining a substance at a very high temperature **2** a severe test [ME *corusible*, fr ML *crucibulum*, modif of OF *croiseul*]

crucifer /'kroohsifə/ *n* **1** a person who carries a cross, esp at the head of an ecclesiastical procession **2** any plant of the mustard family, including the cabbage, stock, cress, etc [deriv of L *cruc-, crux* + *-fer*] – **cruciferous** /krooh'sif(ə)rəs/ *adj*

crucifix /'kroohsifiks/ *n* a representation of Christ on the cross [ME, fr LL *crucifixus* the crucified Christ, fr *crucifixus*, pp of *crucifigere* to crucify, fr L *cruc-, crux* + *figere* to fasten]

crucifixion /,kroohsi'fiksh(ə)n/ *n* **1** the act of crucifying **2** *cap* the crucifying of Christ

cruciform /'kroohsi,fawm/ *adj* forming or arranged in a cross [L *cruc-, crux* + E *-form*] – **cruciformly** *adv*

crucify /'kroohsi,fie/ *vt* **1** to execute by nailing or binding the hands and feet to a cross and leaving to die **2** to treat cruelly; torture, persecute [ME *crucifien*, fr OF *crucifier*, fr LL *crucifigere*]

cruck /kruk/ *n, Br* either of a pair of curved timbers forming a main roof support and extending to the ground [ME *crokke*, prob var of *crok* crook]

crud /krud/ *n* **1** a deposit or incrustation of filth, grease, etc – infml **2** a disagreeable or contemptible substance or person – slang [ME *curd, crudd*] – **cruddy** *adj*

[1]**crude** /kroohd/ *adj* **1** existing in a natural state and unaltered by processing **2** vulgar, gross **3** rough or inexpert in plan or execution **4** tabulated without being broken down into classes ⟨~ *death rate*⟩ [ME, fr L *crudus* raw – more at RAW] – **crudely** *adv*, **crudeness** *n*

[2]**crude** *n* a substance, esp petroleum, in its natural unprocessed state

crudity /'kroohdəti/ *n* **1** being crude **2** sthg crude

cruel /'krooh·əl/ *adj* **-ll-** (*NAm* **-l-**, **-ll-**) **1** liking to inflict pain or suffering; pitiless **2** causing suffering; painful [ME, fr OF, fr L *crudelis*, irreg fr *crudus*] – **cruelly** *adv*, **cruelness** *n*

'cruelty /-ti/ *n* **1** being cruel **2** (an instance of) cruel behaviour [ME *cruelte*, fr OF *cruelté*, fr L *crudelitat-, crudelitas*, fr *crudelis*]

cruet /'krooh·it/ *n* **1** a vessel to hold wine or water for the Eucharist **2** a small usu glass bottle or jug that holds oil or vinegar for use at table **3** a small container (e g a pot or shaker) for holding a condiment, esp salt, pepper, or mustard, at table **4** a set of cruets, usu on a stand [ME, fr AF, dim. of OF *crue*, of Gmc origin; akin to OE *crocc* crock]

[1]**cruise** /kroohz/ *vi* **1** to travel by sea for pleasure **2** to go about or patrol the streets without any definite destination ⟨*a* cruising *taxi*⟩ **3a** *of an aircraft* to fly at the most efficient operating speed **b** *of a vehicle* to travel at an economical speed that can be maintained for a long distance **4** to make progress easily **5** to search (e g in public places) for an esp homosexual partner – slang [D *kruisen* to make a cross, cruise, fr MD *crucen*, fr *crūce* cross, fr L *cruc-, crux* – more at RIDGE]

[2]**cruise** *n* an act or instance of cruising; *esp* a sea voyage for pleasure

'cruise ,missile *n* a long-distance low-flying missile that is supported in flight by aerofoils, is guided by an inbuilt computerized navigation system, and typically carries a nuclear warhead

cruiser /'kroohzə/ *n* **1** CABIN CRUISER **2** a large fast lightly armoured warship [[1]CRUISE + [2]-ER]

'cruiser,weight /-,wayt/ *n* a professional boxer who weighs between 12st 7lb (about 79.4kg) and 13st 8lb (almost 86.2kg)

[1]**crumb** /krum/ *n* **1** a small fragment, esp of bread **2** a small amount ⟨*a* ~ *of comfort*⟩ **3a** (loose crumbly soil or other material resembling) the soft part of

bread inside the crust **b** a small lump consisting of soil particles **4** a worthless person – slang [ME *crumme,* fr OE *cruma;* akin to MHG *krume* crumb]

²crumb *vt* **1** to break up into crumbs **2** to cover or thicken with crumbs

¹crumble /'krumbl/ *vb* **crumbling** /'krumbling/ to break or fall into small pieces; disintegrate – often + *away* [alter. of ME *kremelen,* freq of OE *gecrymian* to crumble, fr *cruma*] – **crumbly** /'krumbli/ *adj*

²crumble *n* a dessert of stewed fruit topped with a crumbly mixture of fat, flour, and sugar

crumbs /krumz/ *interj, chiefly Br* – used to express surprise or consternation; infml [euphemism for *Christ*]

crumhorn, krummhorn /'krum,hawn/ *n* a Renaissance woodwind instrument with a double reed and a hooked tube [G *krummhorn,* fr *krumm* crooked + *horn* horn]

crummy, crumby /'krumi/ *adj* **1** miserable, filthy **2** of poor quality; worthless *USE* slang [ME *crumme* crumb]

¹crump /krump/ *vi* **1** to crunch **2** to explode heavily [imit]

²crump *n* **1** a crunching sound **2** a shell, bomb – infml

crumpet /'krumpit/ *n* **1** a small round cake made from an unsweetened leavened batter that is cooked on a griddle and usu toasted before serving **2** *Br* women collectively as sexual objects – slang ⟨*a piece of* ~⟩ [perh fr ME *crompid* (*cake*) wafer, lit., curled-up cake, fr *crumped,* pp of *crumpen* to curl up, fr *crump, crumb* crooked]

¹crumple /'krumpl/ *vb* **crumpling** /'krumpling/ *vt* to press, bend, or crush out of shape; rumple ~ *vi* **1** to become crumpled **2** to collapse ⟨*her face* ~d *at the news*⟩ – often + *up* [(assumed) ME *crumplen,* freq of ME *crumpen*]

²crumple *n* a wrinkle or crease made by crumpling

¹crunch /krunch/ *vb* **1** to chew or bite (sthg) with a noisy crushing sound **2** to (cause to) make a crushing sound **3** to make (one's way) with a crushing sound [alter. of *craunch,* prob of imit origin]

²crunch *n* **1** an act or sound of crunching **2** *the* critical or decisive situation or moment – infml

crunchy /'krunchi/ *adj* crisp, brittle – **crunchiness** *n*

crupper /'krupə/ *n* a leather loop passing under a horse's tail and buckled to the saddle to prevent the saddle from slipping forwards [ME *cruper,* fr OF *crupiere,* fr *croupe* hindquarters]

crural /'krooərəl/ *adj* of the thigh or leg; *specif* femoral [L *crur-, crus* leg]

crusade /krooh'sayd/ *n* **1** *cap* any of the medieval Christian military expeditions to win the Holy Land from the Muslims **2** a reforming enterprise undertaken with zeal and enthusiasm [blend of MF *croisade* and Sp *cruzada;* both derivs of L *cruc-, crux* cross] – **crusade** *vi*

cruse /kroohz, kroohs/ *n* a small earthenware jar or pot for holding oil, water, etc [ME; akin to OE *crūse* pitcher]

¹crush /krush/ *vt* **1** to alter or destroy the structure of by pressure or compression **2** to reduce to particles by pounding or grinding **3** to subdue, overwhelm ⟨~ed *the revolt*⟩ ⟨*a* ~ing *remark*⟩ **4** to crowd, push ~ *vi* to become crushed ⟨*eggshells* ~ *easily*⟩ [ME *crusshen,* fr MF *cruisir,* of Gmc origin; akin to MLG *krossen* to crush] – **crushable** *adj,* **crusher** *n*

²crush *n* **1** a crowding together, esp of many people **2** (the object of) an intense usu brief infatuation – infml

'crush ,barrier *n* a barrier erected to control crowds

crust /krust/ *n* **1a** the hardened exterior of bread **b** a piece of this or of bread grown dry or hard **2** the pastry cover of a pie **3a** a hard or brittle surface layer (e g of soil or snow) **b** the outer rocky layer of the earth **c** a deposit built up on the inside of a wine bottle during long aging **d** a hard deposit (on the skin); *esp* a scab **4** a superficial hardness of behaviour ⟨*break through her* ~ *of reserve*⟩ [ME, fr L *crusta;* akin to OE *hrūse* earth, Gk *kryos* icy cold] – **crust** *vb,* **crustal** *adj*

crustacean /kru'staysh(ə)n/ *n, pl* **crustaceans, crustacea** /-shə/ any of a large class of mostly aquatic arthropods with a carapace, a pair of appendages on each segment, and 2 pairs of antennae, including the lobsters, crabs, woodlice, etc [NL *Crustacea,* group name, fr neut pl of *crustaceus*] – **crustacean** *adj*

crustaceous /kru'stayshəs/ *adj* of, having, or forming a crust or shell; of or being a crustacean [NL *crustaceus,* fr L *crusta* crust, shell]

crusted /'krustid/ *adj* covered with or having formed a crust

crusty /'krusti/ *adj* **1** having a hard well-baked crust **2** surly, uncivil – **crustily** *adv,* **crustiness** *n*

crutch /kruch/ *n* **1a** a staff of wood or metal typically fitting under the armpit to support a disabled person in walking **b** a prop, stay **2** the crotch of an animal or human **3** the part of a garment that covers the human crotch [ME *crucche,* fr OE *crycc;* akin to OHG *krucka* crutch, OE *cradol* cradle]

crux /kruks, krooks/ *n, pl* **cruxes** *also* **cruces** /'krooh,seez/ **1** a puzzling or difficult problem **2** an essential or decisive point ⟨*the* ~ *of the matter*⟩ [L *cruc-, crux* cross, torture – more at RIDGE]

,crux an'sata /an'saytə/ *n, pl* **cruces ansatae** /-ti/ an ankh [NL, lit., cross with a handle]

cruzeiro /krooh'zeəroh/ *n, pl* **cruzeiros** ☞ *Brazil* at NATIONALITY [Pg]

¹cry /krie/ *vi* **1** to call loudly; shout (e g in fear or pain) **2** to weep, sob **3** *of a bird or animal* to utter a characteristic sound or call **4** to require or suggest strongly a remedy – usu + *out for;* infml ~ *vt* **1** to utter loudly; shout **2** to proclaim publicly; advertise ⟨~ *their wares*⟩ [ME *crien,* fr OF *crier,* fr L *quiritare* to cry out for help (from a citizen), to scream, fr *Quirit-, Quiris* Roman citizen] – **cry over spilt milk** to express vain regrets for what cannot be recovered or undone – **cry wolf** to raise a false alarm and risk the possibility that a future real need will not be taken seriously – **for crying out loud** used to express exasperation and annoyance; infml

²cry *n* **1** an inarticulate utterance of distress, rage, pain, etc **2** a loud shout **3** a watchword, slogan ⟨*'death to the invader" was the* ~⟩ **4** a general public demand or complaint **5** a spell of weeping ⟨*have a good* ~⟩ **6** the characteristic sound or call of an animal or bird **7** pursuit – in *in full cry*

cry- /krie-/, **cryo-** *comb form* cold; low temperature; freezing ⟨cryogen⟩ [G *kryo-,* fr Gk, fr *kryos* – more at CRUST]

'cry,baby /-,baybi/ *n* one who cries or complains too easily or frequently – infml

cry down *vt* to disparage, depreciate

crying /'krie·ing/ *adj* calling for notice ⟨*a ~ shame*⟩

cry off *vt* to call off (e g an agreement) ~ *vi* , *chiefly Br* to withdraw; BACK OUT

cryogen /'krie·əjən/ *n* a substance used in producing low temperatures; a refrigerant

cryogenic /,krie·ə'jenik/ *adj* of, involving, or being (the production of) very low temperatures – **cryogenically** *adv*

,cryo'genics *n pl but sing or pl in constr* the physics of the production and effects of very low temperatures

cryolite /'krie·ə,liet/ *n* a mineral consisting of sodium-aluminium fluoride, found in Greenland and used in making soda and aluminium [ISV]

cryostat /'krie·ə,stat/ *n* an apparatus for maintaining a constant low temperature [ISV]

cryosurgery /,krie·oh'suhj(ə)ri/ *n* surgery in which extreme chilling is used to destroy or cut tissue – **cryosurgical** *adj,* **cryosurgeon** /'--,--, ,--'--/ *n*

crypt /kript/ *n* a chamber (e g a vault) wholly or partly underground; *esp* a vault under the main floor of a church [L *crypta*, fr Gk *kryptē*, fr fem of *kryptos* hidden, fr *kryptein* to hide; akin to ON *hreysar* heap of stones, Lith *krauti* to pile up] – **cryptal** *adj*

crypt- /kript-/, **crypto-** *comb form* **1** hidden; obscure ⟨crypto*genic*⟩ **2** secret; unavowed ⟨crypto*fascist*⟩ [NL, fr Gk *kryptos*]

cryptic /'kriptik/ *adj* **1** secret, occult **2** intended to be obscure or mysterious **3** serving to conceal ⟨~ *coloration in animals*⟩ **4** making use of cipher or code [LL *crypticus*, fr Gk *kryptikos*, fr *kryptos*] – **cryptically** *adv*

crypto /'kriptoh/ *n, pl* **cryptos** one who supports or belongs secretly to a party, sect, or other group [*crypt-*]

cryptocrystalline /,kriptə'kristl,ien/ *adj* having minute crystals distinguishable only under the microscope [ISV]

cryptogam /'kriptə,gam/ *n* a plant (e g a fern, moss, or fungus) reproducing by means of spores and not producing flowers or seed [deriv of Gk *kryptos* + *-gamia* -gamy] – **cryptogamic** /,kriptə'gamik/ *adj,* **cryptogamous** /krip'togəməs/ *adj*

cryptogenic /,kriptə'jenik/ *adj* of obscure or unknown origin ⟨*a ~ disease*⟩

cryptogram /'kriptə,gram/ *n* a communication in cipher or code [F *cryptogramme*, fr *crypt-* + *-gramme* -gram] – **cryptogrammic** /-'gramik/ *adj*

cryptography /krip'tografi/ *n* **1** secret writing; cryptic symbolization **2** the preparation of cryptograms, ciphers, or codes [NL *cryptographia*, fr *crypt-* + *-graphia* -graphy] – **cryptographer** *n,* **cryptographic** /,kriptə'grafik/ *adj*

[1]crystal /'kristl/ *n* **1** (almost) transparent and colourless quartz **2** sthg resembling crystal in transparency and colourlessness **3** a chemical substance in a form that has a regularly repeating internal arrangement of atoms and often regularly arranged external plane faces **4** (an object made of) a clear colourless glass of superior quality **5** the transparent cover over a watch or clock dial **6** an electronic component containing crystalline material used as a frequency-determining element [ME *cristal*, fr OF, fr L *crystallum*, fr Gk *krystallos* ice, crystal]

[2]crystal *adj* **1** consisting of or resembling crystal; clear, lucid **2** relating to or using a crystal ⟨*a ~ microphone*⟩

,crystal 'ball *n* **1** a usu crystal sphere traditionally used by fortune-tellers **2** a means or method of predicting future events

,crystal 'clear *adj* perfectly clear

'crystal ,gazing *n* **1** the art or practice of concentrating on a crystal ball to aid divination **2** the attempt to predict future events or make difficult judgments, esp without adequate data – **crystal gazer** *n*

crystall-, crystallo- *comb form* crystal ⟨crystall*iferous*⟩ [Gk *krystallos*]

crystalline /'kristl,ien/ *adj* composed of crystal or crystals [ME *cristallin*, fr MF & L; MF, fr L *crystallinus*, fr Gk *krystallinos*, fr *krystallos*] – **crystallinity** /-'inəti/ *n*

crystalline lens *n* the lens of the eye in vertebrates

crystallite /'kristl,iet/ *n* a minute unspecific mineral form, esp in glassy volcanic rocks, that marks the first step in crystallization [G *kristallit*, fr Gk *krystallos*] – **crystallitic** /-'itik/ *adj*

crystall·ize, -ise *also* **crystal·ize, -ise** /'kristl,iez/ *vt* **1** to cause to form crystals or assume crystalline form **2** to cause to take a definite form ⟨*tried to ~ his thoughts*⟩ **3** to coat (e g fruit) with (sugar) crystals ~ *vi* to become crystallized – **crystallizable** *adj,* **crystallized** *adj,* **crystallizer** *n,* **crystallization** /-ie'zaysh(ə)n/ *n*

crystallography /,kristl'ogrəfi/ *n* the science dealing with the forms and structures of crystals – **crystallographer** *n,* **crystallographic** /-ə'grafik/, **crystallographical** *adj,* **crystallographically** *adv*

crystalloid /'kristl,oyd/ *n* a substance that forms a true solution and is capable of being crystallized – compare COLLOID 1a – **crystalloid, crystalloidal** /-'oydl/ *adj*

cry up *vt* to praise highly; extol

ctenoid /'te(e)noyd/ *adj* (having or consisting of scales) with a toothed margin ⟨*a ~ fish*⟩ [ISV, fr Gk *ktenoeidēs*, fr *kten-*, *kteis* comb – more at PECTINATE]

ctenophore /'tenəfaw/ *n* any of a phylum of sea animals superficially resembling jellyfishes but swimming by means of 8 bands of thin flat cilia-bearing plates [deriv of Gk *kten-*, *kteis* + *pherein* to carry – more at [2]BEAR] – **ctenophoran** /ti'nofərən/ *adj*

cuadrilla /kwah'dree(l)yə/ *n sing or pl in constr* the team helping the matador in a bullfight [Sp, dim. of *cuadra* square, fr L *quadra*]

cub /kub/ *n* **1** the young of a flesh-eating mammal (e g a bear or lion) **2** an inexperienced newspaper reporter **3** CUB SCOUT [origin unknown]

,cuban 'heel /'kyoohbən/ *n* a broad medium-high heel on a shoe or boot [*Cuba*, island in the W Indies]

cubbing /'kubing/ *n, Br* the hunting of young foxes [*cub* + *-ing*]

cubby /'kubi/, **'cubby,hole** /-,hohl/ *n* a snug or cramped space [obs *cub* (cattle-pen), fr D *kub* thatched roof; akin to OE *cofa* den – more at [1]COVE]

[1]cube /kyoohb/ *n* **1a** the regular solid of 6 equal square sides **b** a block of anything so shaped ⟨*a bouillon ~*⟩ **2** the product got by multiplying together 3 equal numbers [ME, fr L *cubus*, fr Gk *kybos* cube, vertebra – more at [2]HIP]

[2]**cube** *vt* **1** to raise to the third power **2** to cut into cubes – **cuber** *n*

cubeb /'kyooh,beb/ *n* the dried unripe berry of a tropical shrub of the pepper family formerly used in medicine, esp as a urinary antiseptic [MF *cubebe*, fr OF, fr ML *cubeba*, fr Ar *kubābah*]

,**cube 'root** *n* a number whose cube is a given number

cubic /'kyoohbik/ *adj* **1** cube-shaped **2** of or being a crystal system characterized by 3 equal axes at right angles **3a** three-dimensional **b** being the volume of a cube whose edge is a specified unit ⟨~ *metre*⟩ **4** of or involving (terms of) the third power or order – **cubicly** *adv*, **cubic** *n*, **cubically** *adv*

cubical /'kyoohbikl/ *adj* cubic; *esp* shaped like a cube – **cubically** *adv*

cubicle /'kyoohbikl/ *n* **1** a sleeping compartment partitioned off from a large room **2** a small partitioned space or compartment [L *cubiculum*, fr *cubare* to lie, recline – more at [2]HIP]

cubiform /'kyoohbi,fawm/ *adj* cube-shaped [L *cubus* + E *-form*]

cubism /'kyooh,biz(ə)m/ *n* a 20th-c art movement that stresses abstract form, esp by displaying several aspects of the same object simultaneously [F *cubisme*, fr *cube* + *-isme* -ism] – **cubist** *n*, **cubist, cubistic** /kyooh'bistik/ *adj*

cubit /'kyoohbit/ *n* any of various ancient units of length based on the length of the forearm from the elbow to the tip of the middle finger ☞ UNIT [ME, fr L *cubitum* elbow, cubit – more at [2]HIP]

cuboid /'kyoohboyd/ *adj* (being one of the tarsal bones of many higher animals that is) approx cube-shaped – **cuboid** *n*, **cuboidal** /kyooh'boydl, '---/

'**cub ,scout** *n* a member of the most junior section of the (British) Scout movement

'**cucking ,stool** /'kuking/ *n* a seat to which culprits were formerly tied to be pelted, jeered at, or plunged into water [ME *cucking stol*, lit., defecating chair]

[1]**cuckold** /'kukohld, 'kookohld/ *n* a man whose wife is adulterous [ME *cokewold*, prob deriv of OF *cucuault*, fr *cucu* cuckoo]

[2]**cuckold** *vt* to make a cuckold of (a husband) – **cuckolder** *n*, **cuckoldry** *n*

[1]**cuckoo** /'kookooh/ *n, pl* **cuckoos** **1** (any of a large family of birds including) a greyish brown European bird that lays its eggs in the nests of other birds which hatch them and rear the offspring **2** the characteristic call of the cuckoo [ME *cuccu*, of imit origin]

[2]**cuckoo** *adj* deficient in sense or intelligence; silly – infml

'**cuckoo ,clock** *n* a clock that announces the hours by sounds resembling a cuckoo's call

'**cuckoo,flower** /-,flowə/ *n* a European and American usu lilac-flowered plant of the mustard family, that grows in wet places

'**cuckoo,pint** /-,pient/ *n* a European arum that has a large pale green leaflike bract surrounding a spike of dense tiny purple flowers, and bears a cluster of red berries as fruit [ME *cuccupintel*, fr *cuccu* + *pintel* pintle]

'**cuckoo ,spit** *n* (a frothy secretion exuded on plants by the larva of) a froghopper

cucumber /'kyoohkumbə/ *n* (a climbing plant with) a long green edible fruit cultivated as a garden vegetable and eaten esp in salads [ME, fr MF *cocombre*, fr L *cucumer-*, *cucumis*]

'**cucumber ,tree** *n* any of several American magnolias whose fruit resembles a small cucumber

cucurbit /kyooh'kuhbit/ *n* a plant of the cucumber family [ME *cucurbite*, fr MF, fr L *cucurbita* gourd]

cud /kud/ *n* food brought up into the mouth by a ruminating animal from its first stomach to be chewed again [ME *cudde*, fr OE *cwudu*; akin to OHG *kuti* glue, Skt *jatu* gum]

cudbear /'kud,beə/ *n* a reddish dye obtained from lichens [irreg fr *Cuthbert* Gordon, 18th-c Sc chemist]

[1]**cuddle** /'kudl/ *vb* **cuddling** /'kudling, 'kudl·ing/ *vt* to hold close for warmth or comfort or in affection ~ *vi* to lie close; nestle, snuggle [origin unknown]

[2]**cuddle** *n* an act of cuddling

'**cuddlesome** /-s(ə)m/ *adj* cuddly

cuddly /'kudli, 'kudl·i/ *adj* suitable for cuddling; lovable

[1]**cuddy** /'kudi/ *n* a small cabin or shelter under a boat's foredeck [origin unknown]

[2]**cuddy, cuddie** *n, dial Br* **1** a donkey **2** a blockhead [perh fr *Cuddy*, nickname for *Cuthbert*]

[1]**cudgel** /'kuj(ə)l/ *n* a short heavy club [ME *kuggel*, fr OE *cycgel*; akin to MHG *kugele* ball, OE *cot* hut – more at [1]COT]

[2]**cudgel** *vt* **-ll-** (*NAm* **-l-**, **-ll-**), /'kujl·ing/ to beat (as if) with a cudgel

cudweed /'kud,weed/ *n* any of several composite plants with silky or woolly foliage

[1]**cue** /kyooh/ *n* **1a** a signal to a performer to begin a specific speech or action **b** sthg serving a comparable purpose; a hint **2** a feature of sthg that determines the way in which it is perceived [prob fr *qu*, abbr (used as a direction in actors' copies of plays) of L *quando* when]

[2]**cue** *vt* **cuing, cueing** to give a cue to; prompt

[3]**cue** *n* a leather-tipped tapering rod for striking the ball in billiards, snooker, etc [F *queue*, lit., tail, fr L *cauda*]

[4]**cue** *vb* **cuing, cueing** *vt* to strike with a cue ~ *vi* to use a cue

'**cue ,ball** *n* the ball in billiards, snooker, etc that is struck by a cue

cuesta /'kwestə/ *n* a hill or ridge with a steep face on one side and a gentle slope on the other [Sp, fr L *costa* side, rib – more at COAST]

[1]**cuff** /kuf/ *n* **1** a fold or band at the end of a sleeve which encircles the wrist **2** a turned-up hem of a trouser leg **3** a handcuff – usu pl; infml [ME, glove, mitten] – **cuffless** *adj* – **off the cuff** without preparation

[2]**cuff** *vt* to strike, esp (as if) with the palm of the hand [perh fr obs *cuff* (glove), fr ME]

[3]**cuff** *n* a blow with the hand, esp when open; a slap

'**cuff ,link** *n* a usu ornamental device consisting of 2 linked parts used to fasten a shirt cuff

cuffuffle /kə'fufl/ *n, Br* a fuss, rumpus – infml [E dial. (Sc) *curfuffle* disorder, agitation]

cui bono /,kwee 'bonoh/ *n* a principle that probable responsibility for an act or event lies with sby having sthg to gain [L, to whose advantage?]

cuirass /kwi'ras/ *n* a piece of armour consisting of a (joined backplate and) breastplate [ME *curas*, fr MF *curasse*, fr LL *coreacea*, fem of *coreaceus* leathern, fr L *corium* skin, leather; akin to OE *heortha* deerskin, L *cortex* bark, Gk *keirein* to cut – more at SHEAR]

cuirassier /ˌkwirəˈsiə/ *n* a cavalry soldier wearing a cuirass

cuish /kwish/ *n* a cuisse

cuisine /kwiˈzeen/ *n* a manner of preparing or cooking food; *also* the food prepared [F, lit., kitchen, fr LL *coquina* – more at KITCHEN]

cuisse /kwis, kwees/ *n* a piece of armour for the front of the thigh [ME *cusseis*, pl, fr MF *cuissaux*, pl of *cuissel*, fr *cuisse* thigh, fr L *coxa* hip – more at COXA]

cul-de-sac /ˈkul di ˌsak/ *n, pl* **culs-de-sac** /~/ *also* **cul-de-sacs** /saks/ **1** an (anatomical) pouch or tube with only 1 opening **2** a street, usu residential, closed at 1 end [F, lit., bottom of the bag]

culinary /ˈkulin(ə)ri/ *adj* of the kitchen or cookery [L *culinarius*, fr *culina* kitchen – more at KILN]

¹cull /kul/ *vt* **1** to select from a group; choose **2** to identify and remove the rejects from (a flock, herd, etc) **3** to control the size of a population of (animals) by killing a limited number [ME *cullen*, fr MF *cuillir*, fr L *colligere* to bind together – more at ²COLLECT] – **culler** *n*

²cull *n* **1** culling **2** a culled animal

cullender /ˈkuləndə/ *n* a colander

¹culm /kulm/ *n* ⁴SLACK [ME]

²culm *n* the stem of a grass or other monocotyledonous plant [L *culmus* stalk – more at HAULM]

culminant /ˈkulminənt/ *adj*, *of a celestial body* on the meridian

culminate /ˈkulminayt/ *vi* **1** *of a celestial body* to be at the meridian; be directly overhead **2** to reach the highest or a climactic or decisive point – often + *in* [ML *culminatus*, pp of *culminare*, fr LL, to crown, fr L *culmin-*, *culmen* top – more at HILL] – **culmination** /-ˈnaysh(ə)n/ *n*

culottes /kooˈlots/ *n pl* short trousers having the appearance of a skirt and worn by women ☞ GARMENT [F *culotte* breeches, fr dim. of *cul* backside, fr L *culus*] – **culotte** *adj*

culpable /ˈkulpəbl/ *adj* meriting condemnation or blame 〈~ *negligence*〉 [ME *coupable*, fr MF, fr L *culpabilis*, fr *culpare* to blame, fr *culpa* guilt] – **culpableness** *n*, **culpably** *adv*, **culpability** /-ˈbiləti/ *n*

culprit /ˈkulprit/ *n* one guilty of a crime or a fault [AF *cul* (abbr of *culpable* guilty) + *prest, prit* ready (i e to prove it), fr L *praestus* – more at PRESTO]

cult /kult/ *n* **1** (the body of adherents of) **a** a system of religious beliefs and ritual 〈*the ~ of the Virgin Mary*〉 **b** a religion regarded as unorthodox or spurious **2** (a group marked by) great devotion, often regarded as a fad, to a person, idea, or thing [F & L; F *culte*, fr L *cultus* care, adoration, fr *cultus*, pp of *colere* to cultivate – more at WHEEL] – **cultic** *adj*, **cultism** *n*, **cultist** *n*

cultivar /ˈkultiˌvah, -ˌveə/ *n* an organism of a kind originating and kept under cultivation [*culti*vated + *var*iety]

cultivate /ˈkultivayt/ *vt* **1** to prepare or use (land, soil, etc) for the growing of crops; *also* to break up the soil about (growing plants) **2a** to foster the growth of (a plant or crop) **b** CULTURE 2a **c** to improve by labour, care, or study; refine 〈~ *the mind*〉 **3** to further, encourage 〈~ *a friendship*〉 [ML *cultivatus*, pp of *cultivare*, fr *cultivus* cultivable, fr L *cultus*, pp] – **cultivatable** *adj*, **cultivation** /-ˈvaysh(ə)n/ *n*

ˈcultivated *adj* refined, educated

cultivator /ˈkultivaytə/ *n* an implement to break up the soil (while crops are growing) [CULTIVATE + ¹-OR]

¹culture /ˈkulchə/ *n* **1** cultivation, tillage **2** the development of the mind, esp by education **3a** enlightenment and excellence of taste acquired by intellectual and aesthetic training **b** intellectual and artistic enlightenment as distinguished from vocational and technical skills **4a** the socially transmitted pattern of human behaviour that includes thought, speech, action, institutions, and artefacts **b** the customary beliefs, social forms, etc of a racial, religious, or social group **5** (a product of) the cultivation of living cells, tissue, viruses, etc in prepared nutrient media [ME, fr MF, fr L *cultura*, fr *cultus*, pp] – **cultural** *adj*, **culturally** *adv*

²culture *vt* **1** to cultivate **2a** to grow (bacteria, viruses, etc) in a culture **b** to start a culture from 〈~ *a specimen of urine*〉

cultured /ˈkulchəd/ *adj* cultivated

cultured pearl *n* a natural pearl grown under controlled conditions and usu induced by inserting a foreign body into the mouth of the oyster

ˈculture ˌshock *n* psychological and social disorientation caused by confrontation with a new or alien culture

ˈculture-ˌvulture *n* one who has an avid though uncritical interest in culture – humor

cultus /ˈkultəs/ *n* a cult [L, adoration]

culverin /ˈkulvərin/ *n* **1** an early musket **2** a long cannon of relatively light construction used in the 16th and 17th c [ME, fr MF *couleuvrine*, fr *couleuvre* snake, fr L *colubra*]

culvert /ˈkulvət/ *n* a construction that allows water to pass over or under an obstacle (e g a road or canal) [origin unknown]

cum /kum/ *prep* with; combined with; along with 〈*lounge ~ dining room*〉 [L; akin to L *com-* – more at CO-]

cumber /ˈkumbə/ *vt* **1** to clutter up; hamper **2** to burden ***USE*** fml [ME *cumbren*]

ˈcumbersome /-s(ə)m/ *adj* unwieldy because of heaviness and bulk – **cumbersomely** *adv*, **cumbersomeness** *n*

cumbrous /ˈkumbrəs/ *adj* cumbersome – **cumbrously** *adv*, **cumbrousness** *n*

cumin /ˈkumin, ˈkyoohmin/ *n* a plant of the carrot family cultivated for its aromatic seeds used as a flavouring [ME, fr OE *cymen*; akin to OHG *kumin* cumin; both fr a prehistoric WGmc word borrowed fr L *cuminum*, fr Gk *kyminon*, of Sem origin]

cummerbund /ˈkuməˌbund/ *n* a broad waistsash worn esp with men's formal evening wear [Hindi *kamarband*, fr Per, fr *kamar* waist + *band*]

cumquat /ˈkumˌkwot/ *n* a kumquat

cumul- /kyoohmyool-/, **cumuli-**, **cumulo-** *comb form* cumulus and 〈cumulo*cirrus*〉 [NL, fr L *cumulus*]

cumulate /ˈkyoohmyoolayt/ *vt vt* to accumulate [L *cumulatus*, pp of *cumulare*, fr *cumulus* mass] – **cumulate** *adj*, **cumulation** /-ˈlaysh(ə)n/ *n*

cumulative /ˈkyoohmyoolətiv/ *adj* **1a** made up of accumulated parts **b** increasing by successive additions **2** formed by adding new material of the same kind 〈*a ~ book index*〉 – **cumulatively** *adv*, **cumulativeness** *n*

cumulonimbus /ˌkyoohmyooloh'nimbəs/ *n* a cumulus cloud formation often in the shape of an anvil, extending to great heights and characteristic of thunderstorm conditions ☞ WEATHER [NL]

ˌ**cumulo'stratus** /-'strahtəs/ *n* a cumulus cloud formation with a horizontal base [NL]

cumulus /'kyoohmyooləs/ *n, pl* **cumuli** /-lie, -li/ a massive cloud formation with a flat base and rounded outlines often piled up like a mountain ☞ WEATHER [NL, fr L]

cuneate /'kyoohni·ət, -ayt/ *adj* having a narrow triangular shape with the smallest angle towards the base ⟨*a* ~ *leaf*⟩ ☞ PLANT [L *cuneatus*, fr *cuneus* wedge; akin to Skt *śūla* spear] – **cuneately** *adv*

[1]**cuneiform** /'kyoohni,fawm/ *adj* **1** wedge-shaped **2** composed of or written in the wedge-shaped characters used in ancient Assyrian, Babylonian, and Persian inscriptions ⟨~ *alphabet*⟩ [prob fr F *cunéiforme*, fr MF, fr L *cuneus* + MF *-iforme* -iform]

[2]**cuneiform** *n* **1** cuneiform writing **2** a cuneiform part

cunnilinctus /ˌkuni'lingktəs/ *n* cunnilingus [NL, fr L *cunnus* vulva + *linctus* act of licking, fr pp of *lingere* to lick – more at LICK]

ˌ**cunni'lingus** /-'ling·gəs/ *n* oral stimulation of the vulva or clitoris [NL, fr L, one who licks the vulva, fr *cunnus* + *lingere*]

[1]**cunning** /'kuning/ *adj* **1** dexterous, ingenious **2** devious, crafty **3** *NAm* prettily appealing; cute [ME, fr prp of *can* know] – **cunningly** *adv*, **cunningness** *n*

[2]**cunning** *n* craft, slyness

cunt /kunt/ *n* **1** the female genitals **2** sexual intercourse – used by men **3** *Br* an unpleasant person ***USE*** vulg [ME *cunte*; akin to MLG *kunte* female pudenda, MHG *kotze* prostitute]

[1]**cup** /kup/ *n* **1** a small open drinking vessel that is usu bowl-shaped and has a handle on 1 side **2** the consecrated wine of the Communion **3** that which comes to one in life (as if) by fate ⟨~ *of happiness*⟩ **4** (a competition or championship with) an ornamental usu metal cup offered as a prize **5a** sthg resembling a cup **b** either of 2 parts of a garment, esp a bra, that are shaped to fit over the breasts **6** any of various usu alcoholic and cold drinks made from mixed ingredients ⟨*cider* ~⟩ – compare [4]PUNCH **7** the capacity of a cup; *specif, chiefly NAm* CUPFUL 2 **8** the symbol ∪ indicating the union of 2 sets – compare CAP 7 [ME *cuppe*, fr OE; akin to OHG *kopf* cup; both fr a prehistoric WGmc word borrowed fr LL *cuppa* cup, alter. of L *cupa* tub; akin to OE *hȳf* hive] – **cuplike** *adj* – **in one's cups** [2]DRUNK 1

[2]**cup** *vt* **-pp-** **1** to treat or draw blood from by cupping **2** to form into the shape of a cup ⟨~ped *his hands*⟩

cupboard /'kubəd/ *n* a shelved recess or freestanding piece of furniture with doors, for storage of utensils, food, clothes, etc [ME *cupbord*, fr *cuppe* cup + *bord* board, table]

'**cupboard** ˌ**love** *n* insincere love professed for the sake of gain

cupel /'kyoohpl, kyoo'pel/ *vt or n* **-ll-** (*NAm* **-ll-**, **-l-**), /'kyoohpl·ing, kyoo'peling/ (to refine or test for purity in) a small shallow porous usu bone-ash cup used to separate precious metals from lead [F *coupelle*, dim. of *coupe* cup, fr LL *cuppa*] – **cupeller** *n*, **cupellation** /ˌkyoohpə'laysh(ə)n/ *n*

cupful /'kupf(ə)l/ *n, pl* **cupfuls** *also* **cupsful** **1** as much as a cup will hold **2** *chiefly NAm* a unit of measure equal to 8fl oz (about 0.23l) ☞ UNIT

Cupid /'kyoohpid/ *n* **1** the Roman god of erotic love **2** *not cap* a representation of Cupid as a winged naked boy often holding a bow and arrow [L *Cupido*, fr *cupido* desire, fr *cupere* to desire]

cupidity /kyooh'pidəti/ *n* inordinate desire for wealth; avarice, greed [ME *cupidite*, fr MF *cupidité*, fr L *cupiditat-, cupiditas* – more at COVET]

Cupid's bow *n* (the shape, used esp to describe the upper lip, of) a bow formed from 2 convexly curved pieces of metal, wood, etc

ˌ**cup of 'tea** *n* sthg one likes or is suited to – infml

cupola /'kyoohpələ/ *n* **1** a small domed structure built on top of a roof **2** a vertical cylindrical furnace for melting pig iron [It, fr L *cupula*, dim. of *cupa* tub]

cuppa /'kupə/ *n, chiefly Br* a cup of tea – infml [short for *cuppa tea*, pronunciation spelling of *cup of tea*]

cupping /'kuping/ *n* the application to the skin of a previously heated glass vessel, in which a partial vacuum develops, in order to draw blood to the surface (e g for bleeding)

cupr-, cupri-, cupro- *comb form* copper ⟨cupri*ferous*⟩; copper and ⟨cupro*nickel*⟩ [LL *cuprum* – more at [1]COPPER]

cuprammonium rayon /ˌkyoohprə'mohnyəm, -ni·əm/ *n* a rayon made from cellulose dissolved in an ammonia-containing copper solution

cupreous /'kyoohpri·əs/ *adj* containing or resembling copper; coppery [LL *cupreus*, fr *cuprum*]

cupric /'kyoohprik/ *adj* of or containing (bivalent) copper

cuprite /'kyoohpriet/ *n* red copper oxide occurring as a mineral [G *kuprit*, fr LL *cuprum*]

ˌ**cupro-'nickel** /'kyoohproh/ *n* an alloy of usu 7 parts of copper and 3 parts of nickel used esp in British silver coins

cuprous /'kyoohprəs/ *adj* of or containing (univalent) copper

'**cup-ˌtie** *n* a match in a knockout competition for a cup

cupule /'kyoohpyoohl/ *n* a cup-shaped anatomical structure [NL *cupula*, fr LL, dim. of L *cupa* tub – more at CUP]

cur /kuh/ *n* **1** a mongrel or inferior dog **2** a surly or cowardly fellow [ME, short for *curdogge*, fr (assumed) ME *curren* to growl + ME *dogge* dog; akin to OE *cran* crane]

curaçao *also* **curaçoa** /kyooərə'sow, -'soh, '---/ *n* a liqueur flavoured with the peel of bitter oranges [D *curaçao*, fr *Curaçao*, island in the Netherlands Antilles]

curacy /'kyooərəsi/ *n* the (term of) office of a curate

curare, curari /kyoo'rahri/ *n* a dried extract of a climbing plant that contains the drug tubocurarine, used in arrow poisons by S American Indians and in medicine to produce muscular relaxation [Pg & Sp *curare*, fr Carib *kurari*]

curarine /kyoo'rahrin, -reen/ *n* any of several alkaloids found in curare

curar·ize, -ise /kyoo'rahriez/ *vt* to treat (as if) with curare, esp so as to produce muscular relaxation (e g in surgery) – **curarization** /kyooˌrahri'zaysh(ə)n/ *n*

curate /'kyooərət/ *n* a clergyman serving as assistant (e g to a rector) in a parish [ME, clergyman, fr ML *curatus*, fr *cura* cure of souls, fr L, care]

curate's egg *n, Br* sthg with both good and bad parts [fr the story of a curate who, given a stale egg by his bishop, declared that parts of it were excellent]

curative /'kyooərətiv/ *adj* relating to or used in the cure of diseases – **curative** *n*, **curatively** *adv*

curator /kyoo'raytə/ *n* sby in charge of a place of exhibition (e g a museum or zoo) [L, fr *curatus*, pp of *curare* to care, fr *cura* care] – **curatorship** *n*, **curatorial** /,kyooərə'tawri·əl/ *adj*

[1]**curb** /kuhb/ *n* **1a** a chain or strap that is used to restrain a horse and is attached to the sides of the bit and passes below the lower jaw **b** a bit used esp with a curb chain or strap, usu in a double bridle **2** a sprain in a ligament just below a horse's hock **3** a check, restraint **4** an edge or margin that strengthens or confines **5** *chiefly NAm* a kerb [MF *courbe* curve, curved piece of wood or iron, fr *courbe* curved, fr L *curvus*]

[2]**curb** *vt* **1** to put a curb on **2** to check, control

curd /kuhd/ *n* **1** the thick casein-rich part of coagulated milk used as a food or made into cheese **2** a rich thick fruit preserve made with eggs, sugar, and butter **3** the edible head of a cauliflower or a similar related plant [ME] – **curdy** *adj*

curdle /'kuhdl/ *vb* **curdling** /'kuhdling/ **1** to form curds (in); *specif* to separate into solid curds and liquid ⟨*overheating* ~d *the milk*⟩ **2** to spoil, sour [freq of *curd* (to thicken, congeal)]

[1]**cure** /kyooə/ *n* **1** spiritual or pastoral charge **2** (a drug, treatment, etc that gives) relief or esp recovery from a disease **3** sthg that corrects a harmful or troublesome situation; a remedy **4** a process or method of curing [ME, fr OF, fr ML & L; ML *cura* cure of souls, fr L, care] – **cureless** *adj*

[2]**cure** *vt* **1a** to restore to health, soundness, or normality **b** to bring about recovery from **2a** to rectify **b** to free (sby) from sthg objectionable or harmful **3** to prepare by chemical or physical processing; *esp* to preserve (meat, fish, etc) by salting, drying, smoking, etc ~ *vi* **1** to undergo a curing process **2** to effect a cure – **curable** *adj*, **curableness** *n*, **curably** *adv*, **curer** *n*, **curability** /,kyooərə'biləti/ *n*

curé /'kyooəray/ *n* a French parish priest [OF, fr ML *curatus* – more at CURATE]

'**cure-,all** *n* a remedy for all ills; a panacea

curettage /kyoo'retij/ *n* a surgical scraping or cleaning (e g of the womb) by means of a curette

curette, curet /kyoo'ret/ *n* a scoop, loop, or ring used in curettage [F *curette*, fr *curer* to cure, fr L *curare*, fr *cura*] – **curette** *vt*

curfew /'kuhfyooh/ *n* **1** a regulation imposed on all or particular people, esp during times of civil disturbance, requiring their withdrawal from the streets by a stated time **2** a signal (e g the sounding of a bell) announcing the beginning of a time of curfew **3a** the hour at which a curfew becomes effective **b** the period during which a curfew is in effect [ME, fr MF *covrefeu*, signal given to bank the hearth fire, curfew, fr *covrir* to cover + *feu* fire, fr L *focus* hearth]

curia /'kyooəri·ə/ *n, pl* **curiae** /-ri,ee/ **1** a division of an ancient Roman tribe **2** *often cap* the administration and governmental apparatus of the Roman Catholic church [L, fr *co-* + *vir* man – more at VIRILE] – **curial** *adj*

curie /'kyooəri/ *n* a unit of radioactivity equal to 3.7 $\times 10^{10}$ disintegrations per second [Marie *Curie* †1934 Pol-F chemist]

curio /'kyooərioh/ *n, pl* **curios** sthg considered novel, rare, or bizarre [short for *curiosity*]

curiosa /,kyooəri'ohzə, -sə/ *n pl* unusual or pornographic books [NL, fr L, neut pl of *curiosus*]

curiosity /,kyooəri'osəti/ *n* **1** desire to know **2** inquisitiveness, nosiness **3** a strange, interesting, or rare object, custom, etc

curious /'kyooəri·əs/ *adj* **1** eager to investigate and learn **2** inquisitive, nosy **3** strange, novel, or odd [ME, fr MF *curios*, fr L *curiosus* careful, inquisitive, fr *cura* cure] – **curiously** *adv*, **curiousness** *n*

curium /'kyooəri·əm/ *n* an artificially produced radioactive trivalent metallic element ☞ PERIODIC TABLE [NL, fr Marie *Curie* & Pierre *Curie* †1906 F chemists]

[1]**curl** /kuhl/ *vt* **1** to form into waves or coils **2** to form into a curved shape; twist **3** to provide with curls ~ *vi* **1a** to grow in coils or spirals **b** to form curls or twists **2** to move or progress in curves or spirals **3** to play the game of curling [ME *curlen*, fr *crul* curly, prob fr MD; akin to OHG *krol* curly, OE *cradol* cradle]

[2]**curl** *n* **1** a curled lock of hair **2** sthg with a spiral or winding form; a coil **3** curling or being curled ⟨*a ~ of the lip*⟩ **4** a (plant disease marked by the) rolling or curling of leaves

curler /'kuhlə/ *n* a small cylinder on which hair is wound for curling [[1]CURL + [2]-ER]

curlew /'kuhlyooh/ *n, pl* **curlews**, *esp collectively* **curlew** any of various largely brownish (migratory) wading birds with long legs and a long slender down-curved bill [ME, fr MF *corlieu*, of imit origin]

curlicue *also* **curlycue** /'kuhli,kyooh/ *n* a decorative curve or flourish (e g in handwriting) [*curly* + *cue* (a braid of hair)]

curling /'kuhling/ *n* a game in which 2 teams, of 4 players each, slide heavy round flat-bottomed stones over ice towards a target circle marked on the ice [prob fr gerund of [1]*curl*] – **curler** *n*

'**curl,paper** /-,paypə/ *n* a piece of paper round which a lock of hair to be curled is wound

curly /'kuhli/ *adj* tending to curl; having curls – **curliness** *n*

,**curly 'kale** /kayl/ *n* KALE 1

curmudgeon /kə'mujən/ *n* a crusty ill-tempered (old) man [origin unknown] – **curmudgeonly** *adj*

curragh, currach /'kurə, 'kurəkh/ *n, Irish* **1** marshy wasteland **2** a coracle [ScGael *curach* & IrGael *currach*; akin to MIr *curach* coracle]

currant /'kurənt/ *n* **1** a small seedless type of dried grape used in cookery **2** (a shrub of the gooseberry family bearing) a redcurrant, blackcurrant, or similar acid edible fruit [ME *raison of Coraunte*, lit., raisin of Corinth, fr *Corinth*, region & city of Greece]

currency /'kurənsi/ *n* **1a** circulation as a medium of exchange ⟨*sixpences are no longer in* ~⟩ **b** (the state of being in) general use, acceptance, or prevalence **2** sthg (e g coins and bank notes) that is in circulation as a medium of exchange ☞ NATIONALITY

[1]**current** /'kurənt/ *adj* **1a** elapsing now ⟨*during the ~ week*⟩ **b** occurring in or belonging to the present time **2** used as a medium of exchange **3** generally accepted, used, or practised at the moment [ME

curraunt, fr OF *curant*, prp of *courre* to run, fr L *currere* – more at CAR] – **currently** *adv*, **currentness** *n*

[2]**current** *n* **1a** the part of a body of gas or liquid that moves continuously in a certain direction **b** the swiftest part of a stream **c** a (tidal) movement of lake, sea, or ocean water **2** a tendency to follow a certain or specified course **3** a flow of electric charge; *also* the rate of such flow ☞ PHYSICS

current account *n, chiefly Br* a bank account against which cheques may be drawn and on which interest is usu not payable – compare DEPOSIT ACCOUNT

curriculum /kəˈrikyooləm/ *n, pl* **curricula** /-lə/ *also* **curriculums** the courses offered by an educational institution or followed by an individual or group [NL, fr L, running, fr *currere*] – **curricular** *adj*

curˌriculum ˈvitae /ˈveetie/ *n, pl* **curricula vitae** /-lə/ a summary of sby's career and qualifications, esp as relevant to a job application [L, course of (one's) life]

currish /ˈkuhrish/ *adj* ignoble [CUR + -ISH] – **currishly** *adv*

[1]**curry** /ˈkuri/ *vt* **1** to dress the coat of (e g a horse) with a currycomb **2** to dress (tanned leather) [ME *currayen*, fr OF *correer* to prepare, curry, fr (assumed) VL *conredare*, fr L *com-* + a base of Gmc origin; akin to Goth *garaiths* arrayed – more at READY] – **currier** *n* – **curry favour** to seek to gain favour by flattery or attention [*favour* by folk-etymology fr ME *favel* chestnut horse (symbolizing hypocrisy), fr OF *fauvel*]

[2]**curry** *also* **currie** /ˈkuri/ *n* a food or dish seasoned with a mixture of spices or curry powder [Tamil-Malayalam *ka ri*]

[3]**curry** *vt* to flavour or cook with curry powder or sauce

currycomb /ˈkuriˌkohm/ *n* a metal comb with rows of teeth or serrated ridges, used esp to clean grooming brushes or to curry horses – **currycomb** *vt*

ˈcurry ˌpowder *n* a condiment consisting of several pungent ground spices (e g cayenne pepper, fenugreek, and turmeric)

[1]**curse** /kuhs/ *n* **1** an utterance (of a deity) or a request (to a deity) that invokes harm or injury; an imprecation **2** an evil or misfortune that comes (as if) in response to imprecation or as retribution **3** a cause of misfortune **4** menstruation – + *the*; infml [ME *curs*, fr OE]

[2]**curse** *vt* **1** to call upon divine or supernatural power to cause harm or injury to; *also* to doom, damn **2** to use profanely insolent language against **3** to bring great evil upon; afflict ~ *vi* to utter curses; swear

cursed /kuhsid, kuhst/ *also* **curst** /kuhst/ *adj* under or deserving a curse – **cursedly** /ˈkuhsidli/ *adv*, **cursedness** /ˈkuhsidnis/ *n*

[1]**cursive** /ˈkuhsiv/ *adj* running, coursing; *esp* written in flowing, usu slanted, strokes with the characters joined in each word ☞ ALPHABET [F or ML; F *cursif*, fr ML *cursivus*, lit., running, fr L *cursus*, pp of *currere* to run] – **cursively** *adv*, **cursiveness** *n*

[2]**cursive** *n* cursive writing

cursor /ˈkuhsə/ *n* a transparent slide with a reference hairline for precisely locating marks on a scientific instrument (e g a slide rule) [obs *cursor* (runner), fr ME, fr L, fr *cursus*, pp]

cursorial /kuhˈsawri·əl/ *adj, of (a part of) an animal* adapted to running

cursory /ˈkuhsəri/ *adj* rapid and often superficial; hasty [LL *cursorius* of running, fr L *cursus* running, fr *cursus*, pp] – **cursorily** /kuhs(ə)rəli/ *adv*, **cursoriness** *n*

curt /kuht/ *adj* marked by rude or peremptory shortness; brusque [L *curtus* shortened – more at SHEAR] – **curtly** *adv*, **curtness** *n*

curtail /kuhˈtayl/ *vt* to cut short, limit [alter. of obs *curtal* (to dock an animal's tail), fr *curtal* (animal with a docked tail), fr MF *courtault*, fr *court* short, fr L *curtus*] – **curtailer** *n*, **curtailment** *n*

[1]**curtain** /ˈkuht(ə)n/ *n* **1** a hanging fabric screen that can usu be drawn back or up; *esp* one used at a window **2** a device or agency that conceals or acts as a barrier – compare IRON CURTAIN **3a** a castle wall between 2 neighbouring bastions **b** an exterior wall that carries no load **4a** the movable screen separating the stage from the auditorium of a theatre **b** the ascent or opening (e g at the beginning of a play) of a stage curtain; *also* its descent or closing **c** CURTAIN CALL **d** *pl* the end; *esp* death – infml [ME *curtine*, fr OF, fr LL *cortina*, fr L *cohort-*, *cohors* enclosure, court – more at COURT]

[2]**curtain** *vt* **1** to furnish (as if) with curtains **2** to veil or shut off (as if) with a curtain

ˈcurtain ˌcall *n* an appearance by a performer after the final curtain of a play in response to the applause of the audience

ˈcurtain ˌraiser *n* **1** a short play presented before the main full-length drama **2** a usu short preliminary to a main event

curtana /kuhˈtahnə, -ˈtaynə/ *n* a sword without a point, carried at the coronation of English monarchs as a symbol of mercy [ME, deriv of AF *curtain*, fr OF *cortain*, name of the broken sword of the legendary hero Roland, fr *cort* short]

curtilage /ˈkuhtəlij/ *n* a piece of ground within the fence surrounding a house [ME, fr OF *cortillage*, fr *cortil* courtyard, fr *cort* court]

[1]**curtsy, curtsey** /ˈkuhtsi/ *n* an act of respect on the part of a woman, made by bending the knees and lowering the head and shoulders [alter. of *courtesy*]

[2]**curtsy, curtsey** *vi* to make a curtsy

curule /ˈkyooəroohl/ *adj* of a folding seat that is like a stool, reserved in ancient Rome for the use of the highest dignitaries [L *curulis*, alter. of *currulis* of a chariot, fr *currus* chariot, fr *currere* to run]

curvaceous *also* **curvacious** /kuhˈvayshəs/ *adj, of a woman* having a pleasingly well-developed figure with attractive curves – infml

curvature /ˈkuhvəchə/ *n* **1** (a measure or amount of) curving or being curved **2a** an abnormal curving (e g of the spine) **b** a curved surface of an organ (e g the stomach) [L *curvatura*, fr *curvatus*, pp of *curvare*]

[1]**curve** /kuhv/ *vi* to have or make a turn, change, or deviation from a straight line without sharp breaks or angularity ~ *vt* to cause to curve [L *curvare*, fr *curvus* curved]

[2]**curve** *n* **1** a curving line or surface **2** sthg curved (e g a curving line of the human body) **3** a representation on a graph of a varying quantity (e g speed, force, or weight) **4** a distribution indicating the relative performance of individuals measured against one another – **curvy** *adj*

curvilinear /ˌkuhviˈlinyə, -ni·ə/ *adj* consisting of or bounded by curved lines [L *curvus* + *linea* line] – **curvilinearly** *adv*, **curvilinearity** /-ˌlini'arəti/ *n*

cuscus /'kuskəs/ *n* any of several tree-dwelling (New Guinea) phalangers [NL, fr a native name in New Guinea]

cushat /'kushət/ *n, chiefly Scot* a woodpigeon [ME *cowschote*, fr OE *cūscote*]

'Cushing's diˌsease /'kooshingz/ *n* CUSHING'S SYNDROME

'Cushing's ˌsyndrome *n* obesity, esp of the face, and muscular weakness caused by an excess of glucocorticoid hormones (e g cortisone) often resulting from prolonged therapeutic administration [Harvey *Cushing* †1939 US surgeon]

[1]**cushion** /'kooshən/ *n* **1** a soft pillow or padded bag; *esp* one used for sitting, reclining, or kneeling on **2** a bodily part resembling a pad **3** a pad of springy rubber along the inside of the rim of a billiard table off which balls bounce **4** sthg serving to mitigate the effects of disturbances or disorders [ME *cusshin*, fr MF *coissin*, fr (assumed) VL *coxinus*, fr L *coxa* hip – more at COXA] – **cushionless** *adj*, **cushiony** *adj*

[2]**cushion** *vt* **1** to furnish with a cushion **2a** to mitigate the effects of **b** to protect against force or shock **3** to slow gradually so as to minimize the shock or damage to moving parts

Cushitic /koo'shitik/ *n* a branch of the Afro-Asiatic language family comprising various languages of E Africa [*Cush* (Kush), ancient country of NE Africa] – **Cushitic** *adj*

cushy /'kooshi/ *adj* entailing little hardship or effort; easy ⟨*a* ~ *job*⟩ – infml [Hindi *khush* pleasant, fr Per *khush*] – **cushily** *adv*, **cushiness** *n*

cusp /kusp/ *n* a point, apex: e g **a** either horn of a crescent moon **b** a pointed projection formed by or arising from the intersection of 2 arcs or foils **c(1)** a point on the grinding surface of a tooth **(2)** a fold or flap of a heart valve [L *cuspis* point] – **cuspate** /'kuspit, 'kuspayt/ *adj*

cuspidor /'kuspidaw/ *n* a spittoon [Pg *cuspidouro* place for spitting, fr *cuspir* to spit, fr L *conspuere*, fr *com-* + *spuere* to spit – more at SPEW]

[1]**cuss** /kus/ *n* **1** a curse **2** a fellow ⟨*a harmless old* ~⟩ *USE* infml [alter. of *curse*]

[2]**cuss** *vb* to curse – infml – **cusser** *n*

cussed /'kusid/ *adj* **1** cursed **2** obstinate, cantankerous *USE* infml – **cussedly** *adv*, **cussedness** *n*

custard /'kustəd/ *n* **1** a semisolid usu sweetened and often baked mixture made with milk and eggs **2** a sweet sauce made with milk and eggs or a commercial preparation of coloured cornflour [ME *custarde, crustade*, a kind of pie, prob deriv of OF *crouste* crust]

'custard ˌapple *n* (any of a genus of chiefly tropical American trees or shrubs bearing) a soft-fleshed edible fruit

custodial /ku'stohdi·əl/ *adj* **1** of guardianship or custody **2** of or involving legal detention ⟨*a* ~ *sentence*⟩

custodian /ku'stohdi·ən/ *n* one who guards and protects or maintains; *esp* the curator of a public building – **custodianship** *n*

custody /'kustədi/ *n* **1a** the state of being cared for or guarded **b** imprisonment, detention **2** the act or right of caring for a minor, esp when granted by a court of law; guardianship [ME *custodie*, fr L *custodia* guarding, fr *custod-, custos* guardian]

[1]**custom** /'kustəm/ *n* **1a** an established socially accepted practice **b** long-established practice having the force of law **c** the usual practice of an individual **d** the usages that regulate social life **2a** *pl* duties or tolls imposed on imports or exports **b** *pl but sing or pl in constr* the agency, establishment, or procedure for collecting such customs **3** *chiefly Br* business patronage [ME *custume*, fr OF, fr L *consuetudin-, consuetudo*, fr *consuetus*, pp of *consuescere* to accustom, fr *com-* + *suescere* to accustom; akin to *suus* one's own – more at SUICIDE]

[2]**custom** *adj, Nam* made or performed according to personal order ⟨~ *clothes*⟩

customary /'kustəm(ə)ri/ *adj* established by or according to custom; usual – **customarily** /'kustəmrəli, ˌkustə'merəli/ *adv*, **customariness** /'kustəm(ə)rinis/ *n*

ˌcustom-'built *adj* built to individual specifications

customer /'kustəmə/ *n* **1** one who purchases a commodity or service **2** an individual, usu having some specified distinctive trait ⟨*a tough* ~⟩ [ME *custumer*, fr *custume*]

custom·ize, -ise /'kustəmiez/ *vt* to build, fit, or alter according to individual specifications

ˌcustom-'made *adj* made to individual specifications ⟨*a* ~ *suit*⟩

'customsˌhouse /-ˌhows/ *n* a building where customs are collected and where vessels are entered and cleared

[1]**cut** /kut/ *vb* **-tt-; cut** *vt* **1a(1)** to penetrate (as if) with an edged instrument **(2)** to castrate (a usu male animal) **b** to hurt the feelings of ⟨*his cruel remark* ~ *me deeply*⟩ **c** [1]CHOP 2 **d** to experience the emergence of (a tooth) through the gum **2a** to trim, pare **b** to shorten by omissions **c** to dilute, adulterate ⟨~ *the whisky with water*⟩ **d** to reduce in amount ⟨~ *costs*⟩ **e** EDIT 1b **3a** to mow or reap ⟨~ *hay*⟩ **b(1)** to divide into parts with an edged instrument ⟨~ *bread*⟩ **(2)** to fell, hew ⟨~ *timber*⟩ **c** to play a cut in cricket at (a ball) or at the bowling of (a bowler) **4a** to divide into segments **b** to intersect, cross **c** to break, interrupt ⟨~ *our supply lines*⟩ **d(1)** to divide (a pack of cards) into 2 portions **(2)** to draw (a card) from the pack **5a** to refuse to recognize (an acquaintance) **b** to stop (a motor) by opening a switch **c** to terminate the filming of (a scene in a film) **6a** to make or give shape to (as if) with an edged tool ⟨~ *stone*⟩ ⟨~ *a diamond*⟩ **b** to record sounds on (a gramophone record) **7a** to perform, make ⟨~ *a caper*⟩ ⟨~ *a dash*⟩ **b** to give the appearance or impression of ⟨~ *a fine figure*⟩ **8a** to stop, cease ⟨~ *the nonsense*⟩ – infml **b** to absent oneself from (e g a class) – infml ~ *vi* **1a** to function (as if) as an edged tool **b** to be able to be separated, divided, or marked with a sharp instrument ⟨*cheese* ~s *easily*⟩ **c** to perform the operation of dividing, severing, incising, or intersecting **d(1)** to make a stroke with a whip, sword, etc **(2)** to play a cut in cricket **e** to wound feelings or sensibilities **f** to cause constriction or chafing **g** to be of effect, influence, or significance ⟨*an analysis that* ~s *deep*⟩ **2a** to cut a pack of cards, esp in order to decide who deals **b** to draw a card from the pack **3a** to move swiftly ⟨*a yacht* ~*ting through the water*⟩ **b** to describe an oblique or diagonal line **c** to change sharply in direction; swerve **d** to make an abrupt transition from one sound or image to another in film, radio, or television **4** to stop filming or recording [ME *cutten*] – **cut**

corners to perform some action in the quickest, easiest, or cheapest way – **cut no ice** to fail to impress; have no importance or influence – infml – **cut short** 1 to abbreviate 2 INTERRUPT 1

[2]**cut** *n* **1** sthg cut (off): e g **a** a length of cloth varying from 40 to 100yd (44 to 109m) in length **b** the yield of products cut, esp during 1 harvest **c** a (slice cut from a) piece from a meat carcass or a fish ☞ MEAT **d** a share ⟨*took his* ~ *of the profits*⟩ **2a** a canal, channel, or inlet made by excavation or worn by natural action **b(1)** an opening made with an edged instrument **(2)** a gash, wound **c** a surface or outline left by cutting **d** a passage cut as a roadway **3a** a gesture or expression that hurts the feelings **b** a stroke or blow with the edge of sthg sharp **c** a lash (as if) with a whip **d** the act of reducing or removing a part ⟨*a* ~ *in pay*⟩ **e** (the result of) a cutting of playing cards **4a** a sharp downward blow or stroke; *also* backspin **b** an attacking stroke in cricket played with the bat held horizontally and sending the ball on the off side **5** an abrupt transition from one sound or image to another in film, radio, or television **6a** the shape and style in which a thing is cut, formed, or made ⟨*clothes of a good* ~⟩ **b** a pattern, type **c** a haircut – **a cut above** superior (to); of higher quality or rank (than)

cut along *vi vi* to leave, go away – infml

,cut-and-'dried *adj* completely decided; not open to further discussion

cutaneous /kyooh'taynyəs, -ni·əs/ *adj* of or affecting the skin [NL *cutaneus*, fr L *cutis* skin – more at [4]HIDE] – **cutaneously** *adv*

cutaway /'kutəway/ *adj* having or showing parts cut away or absent

'cut,back /-,bak/ *n* **1** sthg cut back **2** a reduction

cut back *vt* **1** to shorten by cutting; prune ⟨cut back *a rose tree*⟩ **2** to reduce, decrease ⟨cut back *expenditure*⟩ ~ *vi* **1** to interrupt the sequence of a plot (e g of a film) by returning to events occurring previously **2** CUT DOWN; *esp* to economize

cut down *vt* **1** to strike down and kill or incapacitate **2** to reduce, curtail ⟨cut down *expenses*⟩ ~ *vi* to reduce or curtail volume or activity ⟨cut down *on his smoking*⟩ – **cut down to size** to reduce from an exaggerated importance to true or suitable stature

cute /kyooht/ *adj* attractive or pretty, esp in a dainty or delicate way – infml [short for *acute*] – **cutely** *adv*, **cuteness** *n*

,cut 'glass *n* glass ornamented with patterns cut into its surface by an abrasive wheel and then polished

cuticle /'kyoohtikl/ *n* a skin or outer covering: e g **a** the (dead or horny) epidermis of an animal **b** a thin fatty film on the external surface of many higher plants [L *cuticula*, dim. of *cutis* skin] – **cuticular** /kyooh'tikyoolə/ *adj*

cutie, cutey /'kyoohti/ *n* an attractive person; *esp* a pretty girl – infml [*cute* + *-ie*]

'cutie-,pie *adj* odiously sweet – infml

cut in *vi* **1** to thrust oneself into a position between others or belonging to another **2** to join in sthg suddenly ⟨cut in *on the conversation*⟩ **3** to take 1 of a dancing couple as one's partner **4** to become automatically connected or started in operation ~ *vt* **1** to introduce into a number, group, or sequence **2** to include, esp among those benefiting or favoured ⟨cut *them* in *on the profits*⟩

cutis /'kyoohtis/ *n, pl* **cutes** /-,teez/, **cutises** the dermis [L – more at [4]HIDE]

cutlass *also* **cutlas** /'kutləs/ *n* a short curved sword, esp as used formerly by sailors [MF *coutelas*, aug of *coutel* knife, fr L *cultellus*, dim. of *culter* knife, ploughshare]

cutler /'kutlə/ *n* one who deals in, makes, or repairs cutlery [ME, fr MF *coutelier*, fr LL *cultellarius*, fr L *cultellus*]

cutlery /'kutləri/ *n* **1** edged or cutting tools; *esp* implements (e g knives, forks, and spoons) for cutting and eating food **2** the business of a cutler

cutlet /'kutlit/ *n* **1** (a flat mass of minced food in the shape of) a small slice of meat from the neck of lamb, mutton, or veal ☞ MEAT **2** a cross-sectional slice from between the head and centre of a large fish – compare STEAK [F *côtelette*, fr OF *costelette*, dim. of *coste* rib, side, fr L *costa* – more at COAST]

cutline /'kut,lien/ *n* **1** a caption, legend **2** a horizontal line about 1.8m (6ft) high on the front wall of a squash court, above which the ball must be hit when serving ☞ SPORT

'cut,off /-,of/ *n* **1** (a device for) cutting off **2** the point, date, or period for a cutoff – **cutoff** *adj*

cut off *vt* **1** to strike off; sever **2** to bring to an untimely end **3** to stop the passage of ⟨cut off *supplies*⟩ **4** to shut off, bar ⟨*the fence* cut off *his view*⟩ **5** to separate, isolate ⟨cut *himself* off *from his family*⟩ **6** to disinherit **7a** to stop the operation of; turn off **b** to stop or interrupt while in communication ⟨*the operator* cut *me* off⟩

'cut,out /-,owt/ *n* **1** sthg cut out or off from sthg else **2** a device that cuts out; *esp* one that is operated automatically by an excessive electric current – **cutout** *adj*

[1]**cut out** *vt* **1** to form or shape by cutting, erosion, etc **2** to take the place of; supplant **3** to put an end to; desist from ⟨cut out *smoking*⟩ **4a** to remove or exclude (as if) by cutting **b** to make inoperative ~ *vi* to cease operating

[2]**,cut 'out** *adj* naturally fitted or suited ⟨*not* ~ *to be an actor*⟩

,cut-'price *adj* selling or sold at a discount

cutter /'kutə/ *n* **1a** one whose work is cutting or involves cutting (e g of cloth or film) **b** an instrument, machine, machine part, or tool that cuts **2a** a ship's boat for carrying stores or passengers **b** a fore-and-aft rigged sailing boat with a single mast and 2 foresails **c** a small armed boat in the US coastguard [[1]CUT + [2]-ER]

[1]**'cut,throat** /-,throht/ *n* a murderous thug

[2]**cutthroat** *adj* **1** murderous, cruel **2** ruthless, unprincipled ⟨~ *competition*⟩

cutthroat razor *n* a razor with a rigid steel cutting blade hinged to a case that forms a handle when the razor is open for use

[1]**cutting** /'kuting/ *n* **1** sthg cut (off or out): e g **a** a part of a plant stem, leaf, root, etc capable of developing into a new plant **b** a harvest **c** *chiefly Br* an excavation or cut, esp through high ground, for a canal, road, etc **d** *chiefly Br* an item cut out of a publication **2** sthg made by cutting

[2]**cutting** *adj* **1** designed for cutting; sharp, edged **2** *of wind* marked by sharp piercing cold **3** likely to wound the feelings of another; *esp* sarcastic – **cuttingly** *adv*

cuttlebone /'kutl,bohn/ *n* the internal shell of the cuttlefish used in the form of a powder for polishing or as a mineral supplement to the diet of cage birds [ME *cotul* cuttlefish (fr OE *cudele*) + E *bone*]

cuttlefish /'kutl,fish/ *n* a 10-armed marine cephalopod mollusc differing from the related squids in having a hard internal shell [ME *cotul* + E *fish*]
cutty /'kuti/ *adj, chiefly Scot* (cut) short [²*cut* + *-y*]
¹**cut up** *vt* **1** to cut into parts or pieces **2** to subject to hostile criticism; censure ~ *vi NAm* to behave in a comic, boisterous, or unruly manner – **cut up rough** to express often obstreperous resentment
²,**cut 'up** *adj* deeply distressed; grieved – infml
'**cut,water** /-,wawtə/ *n* the foremost part of a ship's bow
'**cut,worm** /-,wuhm/ *n* any of various chiefly nocturnal caterpillars (that feed on plant stems near ground level)
cuvette /kyooh'vet/ *n* a small often transparent laboratory vessel, specif for holding samples in a spectrophotometer [F, dim. of *cuve* tub, fr L *cupa* – more at CUP]
cwm /koohm/ *n* CIRQUE 1 [W, valley]
-cy /-si/ *suffix* (*n, adj* → *n*) **1** action or practice of ⟨*mendican*cy⟩ ⟨*pira*cy⟩ **2** rank or office of ⟨*baronet*cy⟩ ⟨*papa*cy⟩ **3** body or class of ⟨*magistra*cy⟩ **4** quality or state of ⟨*accura*cy⟩ ⟨*bankrupt*cy⟩ ***USE*** often replacing a ***final*** *-t* or *-te* of the base word [ME *-cie*, fr OF, fr L *-tia*; partly fr *-t-* (final stem consonant) + *-ia* -y; partly fr Gk *-tia, -teia*, fr *-t-* (final stem consonant) + *-ia, -eia* -y]
cyan /'sie,an, -ən/ *n* a greenish blue colour [Gk *kyanos*]
cyan-, cyano- *comb form* **1** dark blue; blue ⟨cyano*sis*⟩ **2** cyanide ⟨cyano*genetic*⟩; *also* containing a cyanide group ⟨cyano*benzene*⟩ [G, fr Gk *kyan-, kyano-*, fr *kyanos* dark blue enamel]
cyanamide /sie'anəmied/ *n* (a caustic organic acid whose calcium salt is) calcium cyanamide [ISV]
cyanic /sie'anik/ *adj* **1** relating to or containing cyanogen **2** of a blue or bluish colour [ISV]
cyanide /'sie·ənied/ *n* (a usu extremely poisonous salt of hydrocyanic acid or a nitrile, containing) the univalent chemical radical -CN [ISV]
cyanoacrylate /,sie·ənoh'akrilayt, sie,anoh-/ *n* any of several liquid acrylate monomers that are used as very rapidly setting strong adhesives in industry and medicine
cyanocobalamin /,sie·ənohkoh'baləmin, sie,anoh-/ *also* **cyanocobalamine** /-,meen/ *n* VITAMIN B_{12} [*cyan-* + *cobalt* + vit*amin*] – **cyanocobalamic** /-bə'lamik/ *n*
cyanogen /sie'anəjin/ *n* a colourless inflammable extremely poisonous gas [F *cyanogène*, fr *cyan-* + *gène* -gen]
cyanophyte /sie'anəfiet/ *n* BLUE-GREEN ALGA
cyanosed /'sieə,nohzd, -nohst/ *adj* affected with cyanosis
cyanosis /,sie·ən'nohsis/ *n* bluish or purplish discoloration (of the skin) due to deficient oxygenation of the blood [NL, fr Gk *kyanōsis* dark blue colour, fr *kyan-* cyan-] – **cyanotic** /-'notik/ *adj*
cybernated /'siebə,naytid/ *adj* involving cybernation ⟨*a* ~ *bakery*⟩
cybernation /,siebə'naysh(ə)n/ *n* the automatic control of a process or operation (e g in manufacturing) by means of computers [*cyber*netics + *-ation*]
cybernetics /,siebə'netiks/ *n pl but sing or pl in constr* the comparative study of the automatic control systems formed by the nervous system and brain and by mechanical-electrical communication systems [Gk *kybernētēs* pilot, governor (fr *kybernan* to steer, govern) + E *-ics*] – **cybernetic** *adj*
cycad /'siekad/ *n* any of an order of tropical gymnospermous trees resembling palms ☞ EVOLUTION, PLANT [NL *Cycad-, Cycas*]
cycl-, cyclo- *comb form* **1** circle ⟨cyclo*meter*⟩ **2** having a cyclic molecular structure ⟨cyclo*hexane*⟩ [NL, fr Gk *kykl-, kyklo-*, fr *kyklos*]
cyclamate /'sieklǝmayt, -mət, 'siklə-/ *n* a synthetic compound used, esp formerly, as an artificial sweetener [*cyclo*hexyl (fr *cyclohe*xane + *-yl*) + sulpha*mate* (fr *sulpham*ic + *-ate*)]
cyclamen /'sikləmən/ *n* any of a genus of plants of the primrose family with showy drooping flowers [NL, genus name, fr Gk *kyklaminos*]
¹**cycle** /'siekl/ *n* **1a** (the time needed to complete) a series of related events happening in a regularly repeated order **b** one complete performance of a periodic process (e g a vibration or electrical oscillation) **2** a group of poems, plays, novels, or songs on a central theme **3** a bicycle, motorcycle, tricycle, etc [F or LL; F, fr LL *cyclus*, fr Gk *kyklos* circle, wheel, cycle – more at WHEEL]
²**cycle** *vi* **cycling** /'siekling/ **1a** to pass through a cycle **b** to recur in cycles **2** to ride a cycle; *specif* to bicycle – **cycler** *n*
'**cycle ,track** *n* a path reserved for esp pedal cycles
'**cycle,way** /-,way/ *n* CYCLE TRACK
cyclic /'siklik, 'sieklik/, '**cyclical** /-kl/ *adj* **1** of or belonging to a cycle **2** of or containing a ring of atoms ⟨*benzene is a* ~ *compound*⟩ – **cyclically, cyclicly** *adv*
cyclic AMP *n* a nucleotide in each molecule of which a phosphate group is joined at 2 places to an adenosine group, and which functions as a regulator of processes occurring inside cells (e g those caused by hormones)
cyclist /'sieklist/ *n* one who rides a cycle
cycl·ize, -ise /'siek(ə)l,iez, 'si-/ *vt vt* to make (a chemical compound) form 1 or more rings in the molecular structure – **cyclization** /-ie'zaysh(ə)n/ *n*
cyclo- – see CYCL-
'**cyclo-,cross** /'siekloh/ *n* the sport of racing bicycles on cross-country courses that usu require the contestant to carry his/her bicycle at some stage
cyclohexane /,siekloh'heksayn/ *n* a cyclic hydrocarbon found in petroleum and used esp as a solvent and in organic synthesis [ISV]
¹**cycloid** /'siekloyd, 'si-/ *n* a curve traced by a point on the circumference of a circle that rolls along a straight line [F *cycloïde*, fr Gk *kykloeidēs* circular, fr *kyklos*] – **cycloidal** /sie'kloydl, si-, '---/ *adj*
²**cycloid** *adj* circular; *esp* arranged or progressing in circles
cyclometer /sie'klomitə/ *n* a device designed to record the revolutions of a wheel and often the distance traversed by a wheeled vehicle, esp a bicycle
cyclone /'sieklohn/ *n* **1a** a storm or system of winds that rotates about a centre of low atmospheric pressure, advances at high speeds, and often brings abundant rain ☞ WEATHER **b** a tornado **c** ³LOW 1b **2** any of various centrifugal devices for separating materials (e g solid particles from gases or liquids) [modif of Gk *kyklōma* wheel, coil, fr *kykloun* to go round, fr *kyklos* circle] – **cyclonic** /sie'klonik/ *adj*, **cyclonically** *adv*

cyclopedia, cyclopaedia /ˌsiekləˈpeedi·ə/ *n* an encyclopedia – **cyclopedic** /-ˈpeedik/ *adj*

cyclosis /sieˈklohsis/ *n* the slow, usu circular, movement of cytoplasm within a living cell [NL, fr Gk *kyklōsis* encirclement, fr *kykloun* to go round]

cyclostome /ˈsiekləˌstohm, ˈsi-/ *n or adj* (any) of a class of primitive fishlike vertebrates comprising the hagfishes and lampreys [deriv of Gk *kykl-* + *stoma* mouth – more at STOMACH]

[1]**cyclostyle** /ˈsiekləˌstiel/ *n* a machine for making multiple copies that uses a stencil cut by a pen whose tip is a small rowel [fr *Cyclostyle*, a trademark]

[2]**cyclostyle** *vt* to make multiple copies of by using a cyclostyle

cyclothymia /ˌsieklohˈthiemi·ə, ˌsi-/ *n* a condition marked by abnormal swings between elated and depressed moods [NL, fr G *zyklothymie*, fr *zykl-* cycl- + *-thymie* -thymia] – **cyclothymic** /-ˈthiemik/ *adj*

cyclotron /ˈsiekləˌtron/ *n* a particle accelerator in which protons, ions, etc are propelled by an alternating electric field in a constant magnetic field [*cycl-* + *-tron*; fr the circular movement of the particles]

cyder /ˈsiedə/ *n, Br* cider

cygnet /ˈsignit/ *n* a young swan [ME *sygnett*, fr MF *cygne* swan, fr L *cycnus, cygnus*, fr Gk *kyknos*]

cylinder /ˈsilində/ *n* **1a** a surface traced by a straight line moving in a circle or other closed curve round and parallel to a fixed straight line **b** the space bounded by a cylinder and 2 parallel planes that cross it **c** a hollow or solid object with the shape of a cylinder and a circular cross-section **2a** the piston chamber in an engine ☞ CAR **b** any of various rotating parts (e g in printing presses) **c** a cylindrical clay object inscribed with cuneiform characters [MF or L; MF *cylindre*, fr L *cylindrus*, fr Gk *kylindros*, fr *kylindein* to roll; akin to OE *sceol* squinting, L *scelus* crime, Gk *skelos* leg, *skolios* crooked] – **cylindered** *adj*

cylindrical /siˈlindrikl/, **cylindric** /-drik/ *adj* (having the form) of a cylinder – **cylindrically** *adv*

cymbal /ˈsimbl/ *n* a concave brass plate that produces a clashing tone when struck with a drumstick or against another cymbal [ME, fr OE *cymbal* & MF *cymbale*, fr L *cymbalum*, fr Gk *kymbalon*, fr *kymbē* bowl – more at HUMP] – **cymbalist** *n*

cymbidium /simˈbidi·əm/ *n* any of a genus of tropical Old World orchids with showy boat-shaped flowers [NL, genus name, fr L *cymba* boat, fr Gk *kymbē* bowl, boat]

cyme /siem/ *n* an inflorescence in which all floral axes end in a single flower (and the main axis bears the central and first-opening flower with subsequent flowers developing from side shoots) ☞ PLANT [NL *cyma*, fr L, cabbage sprout, fr Gk *kyma* swell, wave, cabbage sprout, fr *kyein* to be pregnant] – **cymose** /-mohs, -mohz/ *adj*, **cymosely** *adv*

Cymric /ˈkumrik, ˈkimrik/ *adj* (characteristic) of the Brythonic Celts or their language; *specif* Welsh [W *Cymry* Brythonic Celts, Welshmen, pl of *Cymro* Welshman]

cynic /ˈsinik/ *n* **1** *cap* an adherent of an ancient Greek school of philosophers who held that virtue is the highest good and that its essence lies in mastery over one's desires and wants **2a** one who is habitually pessimistic or sardonic **b** one who sarcastically doubts the existence of human sincerity or of any motive other than self-interest [MF or L; MF *cynique*, fr L *cynicus*, fr Gk *kynikos*, lit., like a dog, fr *kyn-, kyōn* dog – more at HOUND] – **cynic, cynical** *adj*, **cynically** *adv*, **cynicism** /ˈsiniˌsiz(ə)m/ *n*

cynosure /ˈsinəˌzyooə, ˈsie-, -ˌshooə/ *n* a centre of attraction or attention [MF & L; MF, Ursa Minor, guide, fr L *cynosura* Ursa Minor, fr Gk *kynosoura*, fr *kynos oura* dog's tail]

Cynthia /ˈsinthi·ə/ *n* the moon personified – poetic [L, goddess of the moon, fr fem of *Cynthius* of Cynthus, fr *Cynthus*, mountain on Delos, Greek island, where she was born]

cypher /ˈsiefə/ *vb or n, chiefly Br* (to) cipher

cypress /ˈsieprəs/ *n* (the wood of) any of a genus of evergreen gymnospermous trees with aromatic overlapping leaves resembling scales [ME, fr OF *ciprès*, fr L *cyparissus*, fr Gk *kyparissos*]

Cypriot, Cypriote /ˈsipri·ət/ *n or adj* (a native or inhabitant) of Cyprus [F *cypriote*, fr *Cyprus*, island in the Mediterranean]

cypripedium /ˌsipriˈpeedi·əm/ *n* the lady's slipper or a related orchid usu with large showy drooping flowers [NL, genus name, fr LL *Cypris*, a name for Venus, goddess of love & beauty + Gk *pedilon* sandal]

cyproterone /sieˈprotərohn/ *n* CYPROTERONE ACETATE [prob fr *cycl-* + *progesterone*]

cyˌproterone ˈacetate *n* a synthetic steroid that inhibits the secretion of androgenic steroids (e g testosterone) and is used esp to treat some male sexual disorders

Cyrillic /siˈrilik/ *adj* of or constituting an alphabet used for writing various Slavic languages (e g Old Church Slavonic and Russian) ☞ ALPHABET [St *Cyril* †869 apostle of the Slavs, reputed inventor of the Cyrillic alphabet]

cyst /sist/ *n* **1** a closed sac (e g of watery liquid or gas) with a distinct membrane, developing (abnormally) in a plant or animal **2** a body resembling a cyst: e g **a** (a capsule formed about) a microorganism in a resting or spore stage **b** a resistant cover about a parasite when inside the host [NL *cystis*, fr Gk *kystis* bladder, pouch] – **cystoid** *adj or n*

cyst- /sist-/, **cysti-, cysto-** *comb form* bladder ⟨cysti*tis*⟩; sac ⟨cysto*carp*⟩ [F, fr Gk *kyst-, kysto-*, fr *kystis*]

-cyst /-sist/ *comb form* (→ *n*) bladder; sac ⟨*blasto*cyst⟩ [NL *-cystis*, fr Gk *kystis*]

cysteine /ˈsistiˌeen, ˈsistayn/ *n* a sulphur-containing amino acid found in many proteins and readily convertible to cystine [ISV, fr *cystine* + *-ein*]

cystic /ˈsistik/ *adj* **1** (composed) of or containing a cyst or cysts **2** of the urinary or gall bladder

ˌcystic fiˈbrosis /fieˈbrohsis/ *n* a common often fatal hereditary disease appearing in early childhood and marked esp by faulty digestion and difficulty in breathing

cystine /ˈsisteen, -in/ *n* a sulphur-containing amino acid found in many proteins [fr its discovery in bladder stones]

cystitis /siˈstietəs/ *n* inflammation of the urinary bladder [NL]

cyt- /siet-/, **cyto-** *comb form* **1** cell ⟨cyto*logy*⟩ **2** cytoplasm ⟨cyto*kinesis*⟩ [G *zyt-, zyto-*, fr Gk *kytos* hollow vessel – more at [4]HIDE]

-cyte /-siet/ *comb form* (→ *n*) cell ⟨*leuco*cyte⟩ [NL *-cyta*, fr Gk *kytos* hollow vessel]

cytidine /'sietədeen, 'si-/ *n* a nucleoside containing cytosine [*cyt*osine + *-idine*]

cytochrome /'sietə,krohm/ *n* any of several enzymes that function in intracellular energy generation as transporters of electrons, esp to oxygen, by undergoing successive oxidation and reduction

cytokinesis /,sietohkie'neesis, -ki-/ *n* the cleavage of the cytoplasm of a cell into daughter cells following division of the nucleus [NL, fr *cyt-* + Gk *kinēsis* motion] – **cytokinetic** /-kie'netik, -ki-/ *adj*

cytology /sie'toləji/ *n* the biology of (the structure, function, multiplication, pathology, etc of) cells [ISV] – **cytologist** *n*, **cytological** /,sietə'lojikl/, **cytologic** *adj*, **cytologically** *adv*

cytoplasm /'sietə,plaz(ə)m/ *n* the substance of a plant or animal cell outside the organelles (e g the nucleus and mitochondria) [ISV] – **cytoplasmic** /-'plazmik/ *adj*, **cytoplasmically** *adv*

cytosine /'sietə,seen/ *n* a pyrimidine base that is one of the 4 bases whose order in a DNA or RNA chain codes genetic information – compare ADENINE, GUANINE, THYMINE, URACIL [ISV *cyt-* + *-ose* + *-ine*]

cytosol /'sietoh,sol/ *n* the cytoplasm

cytotoxin /,sietə'toksin/ *n* a substance with a toxic effect on cells – **cytotoxic** *adj*, **cytotoxicity** /-tok'sisəti/ *n*

czar /zah/ *n* a tsar

czardas /'chahdash/ *n, pl* **czardas** /~/ a Hungarian dance in which the dancers start slowly and finish rapidly [Hung *csárdás*]

Czech /chek/ *n* **1** a native or inhabitant of Czechoslovakia; *specif* a Slav of W Czechoslovakia **2** the Slavonic language of the Czechs ☞ LANGUAGE [Czech *Čech*] – **Czech** *adj*

D

d /dee/ *n, pl* **d's, ds** *often cap* **1** (a graphic representation of or device for reproducing) the 4th letter of the English alphabet **2** five hundred ☞ NUMBER **3** the 2nd note of a C-major scale **4** one designated *d,* esp as the 4th in order or class, or as a mark of lesser quality than *a, b,* or *c* **5** sthg shaped like the letter D: e g **a** a semicircle on a billiard table used chiefly when returning a potted cue ball to the table **b** the metal loop on the cheek piece of the bit of a bridle

d- *prefix* dextrorotatory ⟨d-*tartaric acid*⟩ [ISV, fr *dextr-*]

[1]**-d** *suffix* **1** – used to form the past participle of regular weak verbs that end in *e* ⟨*love*d⟩ ⟨*fade*d⟩; compare [1]-ED 1 **2** – used to form adjectives of identical meaning from Latin-derived adjectives ending in *-ate* ⟨*crenulate*d⟩ **3** [1]-ED 2 – used to form adjectives from nouns ending in *e* ⟨*brogue*d⟩ ⟨*bow-tie*d⟩

[2]**-d** *suffix* (→ *vb*) – used to form the past tense of regular weak verbs that end in *e*; compare [2]-ED

[3]**-d** *suffix* (→ *adj*), *NAm* – used after the figure 2 or 3 to indicate the ordinal number second or third ⟨*2*d⟩ ⟨*53*d⟩

d' *vb* do ⟨d'*you know*⟩

'd *vb* **1** had **2** would **3** did ⟨*when'd she go?*⟩ – used in questions; infml

da /dah/ *n, dial Br* a father, daddy [baby talk]

[1]**dab** /dab/ *n* **1** a sudden feeble blow or thrust; a poke **2** a gentle touch or stroke (e g with a sponge); a pat [ME *dabbe,* prob of imit origin]

[2]**dab** *vb* **-bb-** *vt* **1** to touch lightly, and usu repeatedly; pat **2** to apply lightly or irregularly; daub ~ *vi* to make a dab

[3]**dab** *n* **1** a daub, patch **2** *pl, Br* fingerprints – infml [alter. of *daub*]

[4]**dab** *n* a flatfish; *esp* any of several flounders [AF *dabbe*]

[5]**dab** *n* DAB HAND – infml

dabble /'dabl/ *vb* **dabbling** /'dabling/ *vt* to wet slightly or intermittently by dipping in a liquid ⟨*she* ~d *her fingers in the river*⟩ ~ *vi* **1** to paddle, splash, or play (as if) in water **2** to work or concern oneself superficially ⟨~s *in art*⟩ [perh freq of [2]*dab*]

dabbler /'dablə/ *n* sby not deeply engaged in or concerned with sthg [DABBLE + [2]-ER]

dabbling /'dabling/ *n* a superficial or intermittent interest or study

dabchick /'dab,chik/ *n* any of several small grebes [prob irreg fr obs *dop* (to dive) + *chick*]

,dab 'hand /dab/ *n, chiefly Br* sby skilful *at*; an expert – infml [*dab* perh alter. of *adept*]

dace /days/ *n, pl* **dace** a small freshwater European fish [ME, fr MF *dars,* fr ML *darsus*]

dacha /'dahchə/ *n* a Russian country cottage used esp in the summer [Russ, lit., gift; fr its frequently being the gift of a ruler]

dachshund /'daksənd/ *n* (any of) a breed of dogs of German origin with a long body, short legs, and long drooping ears [G, fr *dachs* badger + *hund* dog]

Dacron /'dakron/ *trademark* – used for a synthetic polyester textile fibre

dactyl /'daktil/ *n* a metrical foot consisting of 1 long and 2 short, or 1 stressed and 2 unstressed, syllables (e g in *tenderly*) [ME *dactile,* fr L *dactylus,* fr Gk *daktylos,* lit., finger; fr the three syllables having the first one longest, like the joints of the finger] – **dactylic** /dak'tilik/ *adj or n*

dactylology /,dakti'loləji/ *n* the art of communicating ideas by sign language [Gk *daktyl-* of a finger + E *-logy*]

-dactylous /-daktiləs/ *comb form* (→ *adj*) having (such or so many) fingers or toes ⟨*di*dactylous⟩ [Gk *-daktylos,* fr *daktylos*]

dad /dad/ *n* a father – infml [prob baby talk]

dada /'dahdah/ *n, often cap* a movement in art and literature based on deliberate irrationality and negation of traditional artistic values [F, fr (baby talk) *dada* hobby-horse] – **dadaism** *n, often cap,* **dadaist** *n, often cap,* **dadaistic** /-'istik/ *adj, often cap*

daddy /'dadi/ *n* a father – infml [*dad* + [4]*-y*]

,daddy 'longlegs /'long,legz/ *n, pl* **daddy longlegs 1** CRANE FLY **2** *NAm* a harvestman

dado /'daydoh/ *n, pl* **dadoes 1** the part of a pedestal or plinth between the base and the cornice ☞ ARCHITECTURE **2** the lower part of an interior wall when specially decorated or faced; *also* the decoration adorning this part of a wall [It, die, plinth]

daemon /'deemən/ *n* **1** an attendant power or spirit; a genius **2** a supernatural being of Greek mythology **3** DEMON 1 [LL, evil spirit – more at DEMON]

daffodil /'dafədil/ *n* any of various plants with flowers that have a large typically yellow corona elongated into a trumpet shape; *also* a related bulb-forming plant [prob fr D *de affodil* the asphodel, fr *de* the (fr MD) + *affodil* asphodel, fr MF *afrodille,* fr L *asphodelus,* fr Gk *asphodelos*]

daft /dahft/ *adj* **1** silly, foolish **2** *chiefly Br* fanatically enthusiastic ⟨~ *about football*⟩ ***USE*** infml [ME *dafte* gentle, stupid; akin to OE *gedæfte* mild, gentle, ME *defte* gentle, deft, L *faber* smith] – **daft** *adv,* **daftly** *adv,* **daftness** *n*

[1]**dag** /dag/ *n* a piece of matted or manure-coated wool – usu pl [ME *dagge*]

[2]**dag** *vt* **-gg-** to remove dags from (sheep)

dagga /'dahgə, 'dah·khə/ *n, SAfr* cannabis [Afrik, fr Hottentot *daga-b*]

dagger /'dagə/ *n* **1** a short sharp pointed weapon for stabbing **2** a sign † used as a reference mark or to indicate a death date ☞ SYMBOL [ME] – **at daggers drawn** in bitter conflict

dago /'daygoh/ *n, pl* **dagos, dagoes** sby of Italian, Spanish, or Portuguese birth or descent – derog [alter. of earlier *diego,* fr *Diego,* a common Sp forename]

daguerreotype /dəˈger(i)ə,tiep/ *n* an early photograph produced on a silver or a silver-covered copper plate [F *daguerréotype*, fr L J M *Daguerre* †1851 F painter & inventor + F *-o-* + *type*] – **daguerreotype** *vt*

dah /dah/ *n* ²DASH 6 – used when articulating Morse code [imit]

dahlia /ˈdayli·ə, ˈdah-/ *n* any of an American genus of composite (garden) plants with showy flower heads and roots that form tubers [NL, genus name, fr Anders *Dahl* †1789 Sw botanist]

Dáil /doyl, diel/, **Dáil Éireann** /~ ˈeərən/ *n* the lower house of parliament in Eire [IrGael, assembly]

¹**daily** /ˈdayli/ *adj* **1a** occurring, made, or acted on every day **b** *of a newspaper* issued every weekday **c** of or providing for every day **2** covering the period of or based on a day ⟨~ *statistics*⟩ [ME *dayly*, fr OE *dæglic*, fr *dæg* day + *-līc* -ly – more at DAY] – **dailiness** *n*

²**daily** *adv* every day; every weekday

³**daily** *n* **1** a newspaper published daily from Monday to Saturday **2** *Br* a charwoman who works on a daily basis

,daily ˈdozen *n* a series of physical exercises to be performed daily

daimon /ˈdiemohn/ *n, pl* **daimones** /ˈdiemənееz/, **daimons** DAEMON 1, 2 [Gk *daimōn*] – **daimonic** /-ˈmonik/ *adj*

¹**dainty** /ˈdaynti/ *n* sthg particularly nice to eat; a delicacy [ME *deinte*, fr OF *deintié*, fr L *dignitat-*, *dignitas* dignity, worth]

²**dainty** *adj* **1** attractively prepared and served **2** delicately beautiful **3a** fastidious **b** showing avoidance of anything rough – **daintily** *adv*, **daintiness** *n*

daiquiri /dieˈkiəri, də-, ˈdakiri/ *n* a cocktail made of rum, lime juice, and sugar [*Daiquirí*, town in Cuba]

¹**dairy** /ˈdeəri/ *n* **1** a room, building, etc where milk is processed and butter or cheese is made **2** farming concerned with the production of milk, butter, and cheese **3** an establishment for the sale or distribution of milk and milk products – compare CREAMERY [ME *deyerie*, fr *deye* dairymaid, fr OE *dǣge* kneader of bread; akin to OE *dāg* dough – more at DOUGH]

²**dairy** *adj* of or concerned with (the production of) milk (products)

ˈdairying /-ing/ *n* the business of operating a dairy or producing milk products

dairyman /-mən/, *fem* **ˈdairy,maid** /-,mayd/ *n* one who operates or works for a dairy (farm)

dais /ˈday·is/ *n* a raised platform; *esp* one at the end of a hall [ME *deis*, fr OF, fr L *discus* dish, quoit – more at DISH]

daisy /ˈdayzi/ *n* a composite plant with well-developed ray flowers in its flower head: e g **a** a common short European plant with a yellow disc and white or pink ray flowers **b** OXEYE DAISY [ME *dayeseye*, fr OE *dægesēage*, fr *dæg* day + *ēage* eye]

ˈdaisy ,chain *n* a string of linked daisies threaded through each other's stalks

Dakota /dəˈkohtə/ *n, pl* **Dakotas**, *esp collectively* **Dakota** a member, or the language, of an American Indian people of the N Mississippi valley

,Dalai ˈLama /ˈdalie/ *n* the spiritual head of Tibetan Buddhism [Mongolian *dalai* ocean]

dalasi /dahˈlahsi/ *n* ☞ *The Gambia* at NATIONALITY [native name in the Gambia]

dale /dayl/ *n* a vale, valley [ME, fr OE *dæl*; akin to OHG *tal* valley, Gk *tholos* rotunda]

Dalek /ˈdahlik/ *n* any of a race of ruthlessly aggressive fictional creatures protected by distinctive metallic shells containing their life-support systems [name of creatures in television science-fiction series 'Dr Who']

dalliance /ˈdali·əns/ *n* a dallying: e g **a** amorous or erotically stimulating activity **b** a frivolous action

dally /ˈdali/ *vi* **1a** to act playfully; *esp* to flirt **b** to deal lightly; toy **2** to waste time; dawdle [ME *dalyen*, fr AF *dalier*] – **dallier** *n*

dalmatian /dalˈmaysh(ə)n/ *n, often cap* (any of) a breed of medium-sized dogs with a white short-haired coat with black or brown spots [fr the supposed origin of the breed in *Dalmatia*, region of Yugoslavia]

dalmatic /dalˈmatik/ *n* a wide-sleeved outer garment with slit sides worn by a deacon or prelate; *also* a similar robe worn by sovereigns or emperors at coronations or other ceremonies ☞ GARMENT [LL *dalmatica*, fr L, fem of *dalmaticus* Dalmatian, fr *Dalmatia*]

ˈDalton ,plan /ˈdawltən/ *n* a method of progressive education whereby pupils assume responsibility for their own pace of work [*Dalton*, town in Massachusetts, USA, site of first school to use the plan]

¹**dam** /dam/ *n* a female parent – used esp with reference to domestic animals [ME *dam, dame* lady, dam – more at DAME]

²**dam** *n* **1** a barrier preventing the flow of a fluid; *esp* a barrier across a watercourse **2** a body of water confined by a dam [ME]

³**dam** *vt* **-mm- 1** to provide or restrain with a dam **2** to stop up; block

¹**damage** /ˈdamij/ *n* **1** loss or harm resulting from injury to person, property, or reputation **2** *pl* compensation in money imposed by law for loss or injury **3** expense, cost – infml ⟨*what's the* ~?⟩ [ME, fr OF, fr *dam* damage, fr L *damnum*]

²**damage** *vt* to cause damage to ~ *vi* to become damaged – **damager** *n*

damar /ˈdamə/ *n* dammar

¹**damascene** /ˈdaməseen/ *n* the characteristic markings of Damascus steel [L *Damascenus* of Damascus, fr *Damascus*, city in Syria]

²**damascene** *vt* to ornament (e g iron or steel) with wavy patterns like those of watered silk or with inlaid work of precious metals [MF *damasquiner*, fr *damasquin* of Damascus]

Damascus steel /dəˈmaskəs/ *n* damascened steel used esp for sword blades

¹**damask** /ˈdamәsk/ *n* **1** a reversible lustrous fabric (e g of linen, cotton, or silk) having a plain background woven with patterns **2** greyish red [ME *damaske*, fr ML *damascus*, fr *Damascus*]

²**damask** *adj* **1** made of or resembling damask **2** of the colour damask

,damask ˈrose *n* a large fragrant pink rose cultivated esp as a source of attar of roses [obs *Damask* (of Damascus), fr obs *Damask* (Damascus)]

dame /daym/ *n* **1** a woman of rank, station, or authority: e g **a** the wife or daughter of a lord **b** a female member of an order of knighthood – used as a title preceding the Christian name **2a** an elderly woman; *specif* a comic one in pantomime played usu by a male actor **b** *chiefly NAm* a woman – infml [ME, fr OF, fr L *domina*, fem of *dominus* master; akin to L *domus* house – more at TIMBER]

'dame ,school *n* a school in which reading and writing were taught by a woman in her home

dame's violet *n* a Eurasian plant of the mustard family widely cultivated for its spikes of fragrant white or purple flowers

damfool /,dam'foohl/ *adj* extremely foolish or stupid – infml [alter. of [3]*damn* + *fool*]

dammar, damar *also* **dammer** /'damə/ *n* any of various resins derived from trees and used esp in inks and varnishes [Malay *damar*]

dammit /'damit/ *interj* – used to express annoyance; slang [by alter. of [1]*damn* + *it*] – **as near as dammit** almost exactly

[1]damn /dam/ *vt* **1** to condemn to a punishment or fate; *esp* to condemn to hell **2** to condemn as a failure by public criticism **3** to bring ruin on **4** to curse – often used as an interjection to express annoyance ⟨~ *it all!*⟩ ~ *vi* to curse, swear [ME *dampnen*, fr OF *dampner*, fr L *damnare*, fr *damnum* damage, loss, fine] – **I'll be damned** – used to express astonishment – **I'll be damned if** I emphatically do not or will not ⟨I'll be damned if *I'll go*⟩

[2]damn *n* **1** the utterance of the word *damn* as a curse **2** the slightest bit ⟨*I couldn't care a* ~⟩ – chiefly in negative phrases

[3]damn *adj or adv* – used as an intensive – **damn well** beyond doubt or question; certainly ⟨*better* damn well *marry that boy – Spare Rib*⟩

damnable /'damnəbl/ *adj* **1** liable to or deserving condemnation **2** very bad; detestable ⟨~ *weather*⟩ – **damnableness** *n*, **damnably** *adv*

,damn 'all *n*, *Br & Can* nothing at all – slang

damnation /dam'naysh(ə)n/ *n* damning or being damned

damnatory /'damnət(ə)ri/ *adj* expressing, imposing, or causing condemnation

damned /damd/ *adj or adv* **damneder** /-də/; **damnedest, damndest** /-dist/ [3]DAMN

damnedest, damndest /'damdist/ *n* utmost, best – chiefly in *do one's damnedest* ⟨*doing her* ~ *to succeed*⟩; infml

damnify /'damnifie/ *vt* to cause loss or damage to [MF *damnifier*, fr OF, fr LL *damnificare*, fr L *damnificus* injurious, fr *damnum* damage]

damning /'daming/ *adj* causing or leading to condemnation or ruin ⟨*presented some* ~ *testimony*⟩ – **damningly** *adv*

damosel, damozel /'daməzel/ *n* a damsel

[1]damp /damp/ *n* **1** a noxious gas, esp in a coal mine **2** moisture, humidity **3** DAMPER 2 ⟨*the bad news cast a* ~ *on his spirits*⟩ **4** *archaic* fog, mist [MD or MLG, vapour; akin to OHG *damph* vapour, OE *dim* dim] – **damp-proof** /'- ,-/ *adj*

[2]damp *vt* **1a** to diminish the activity or intensity of ⟨~ *the fire in the furnace*⟩ – often + *down* **b** to reduce progressively the vibration or oscillation of (e g sound waves) **2** to dampen ~ *vi* to diminish progressively in vibration or oscillation

[3]damp *adj* slightly or moderately wet – **damply** *adv*, **dampness** *n*, **dampish** *adj*

'damp ,course, damp-proof course *n* a horizontal damp-resistant layer near the ground in a masonry wall ☞ BUILDING

dampen /'dampən/ *vt vt* **1** to check or diminish the activity or vigour of (esp feelings) ⟨*nothing could* ~ *his spirits*⟩ **2** to make damp **3** DAMP 1b – **dampener** *n*

damper /'dampə/ *n* **1** a device that damps: e g **a** a valve or plate (e g in the flue of a furnace) for regulating the draught **b** a small felted block which prevents or stops the vibration of a piano string **c** a device (e g a shock absorber) designed to bring a mechanism to rest with minimum oscillation **2** a dulling or deadening influence ⟨*put a* ~ *on the celebration*⟩ **3** *Austr & NZ* unleavened bread made with flour and water and baked in the ashes of a fire

,damp 'squib *n*, *Br* sthg that ends feebly, esp after a promising start – infml

damsel /'damzəl/ *n*, *archaic* a young woman; a girl [ME *damesel*, fr OF *dameisele*, fr (assumed) VL *domnicella* young noblewoman, dim. of L *domina* lady]

'damsel,fly /-,flie/ *n* any of numerous insects distinguished from the related dragonflies esp by projecting stalked wings that are folded above the body when the insect is at rest

damson /'damzən/ *n* (the small acid purple fruit of) an Asiatic plum that is a cultivated bullace [ME, fr L *prunum damascenum*, lit., plum of Damascus]

dan /dan/ *n* a level of expertise in an Oriental martial art (e g judo) [Jap]

[1]dance /dahns/ *vi* **1** to engage in or perform a dance **2** to move quickly up and down or about ~ *vt* **1** to perform or take part in as a dancer **2** to bring or accompany into a specified condition by dancing ⟨~d *her way to fame*⟩ [ME *dauncen*, fr OF *dancier*] – **danceable** /-səbl/ *adj*, **dancer** *n*

[2]dance *n* **1** (an act or instance or the art of) a series of rhythmic and patterned bodily movements usu performed to music **2** a social gathering for dancing **3** a piece of music for dancing to

,dance of 'death *n* DANSE MACABRE

dandelion /'dandi,lie·ən/ *n* any of a genus of yellow-flowered composite plants including one that occurs virtually worldwide as a weed ☞ PLANT [MF *dent de lion*, lit., lion's tooth]

dander /'dandə/ *n* anger, temper – chiefly in *have/get one's dander up*; infml [perh fr *dander*, *dunder* (ferment)]

Dandie Dinmont terrier /,dandi 'dinmont/ *n* (a dog of) a breed of terriers with short legs, a long body, and a rough coat [*Dandie Dinmont*, character owning 2 such dogs in the novel *Guy Mannering* by Sir Walter Scott †1832 Sc writer]

dandify /'dandifie/ *vt* to cause to resemble a dandy – **dandification** /-fi'kaysh(ə)n/ *n*

dandle /'dandl/ *vt* **dandling** /'dandling, 'dandl·ing/ to move (e g a baby) up and down in one's arms or on one's knee in affectionate play [origin unknown]

dandruff /'dandruf, -drəf/ *n* a scurf that comes off the scalp in small white or greyish scales [prob fr *dand-* (origin unknown) + *-ruff*, of Scand origin; akin to ON *hrūfa* scab; akin to OHG *hruf* scurf, Lith *kraupus* rough] – **dandruffy** *adj*

[1]dandy /'dandi/ *n* a man who gives exaggerated attention to dress and demeanour [perh fr *Dandy*, nickname for *Andrew*] – **dandyish** *adj*, **dandyishly** *adv*, **dandyism** *n*

[2]dandy *adj*, *NAm* very good; first-rate – infml; not now in vogue

'**dandy ,brush** *n* a coarse brush used in grooming horses

Dane /dayn/ *n* a native or inhabitant of Denmark [ME *Dan*, fr ON *Danr*]

danegeld /'dayn,geld/ *n, often cap* an annual tax levied in the 10th, 11th, and 12th cs, prob imposed orig to buy off Danish invaders in England or to maintain forces to oppose them [ME, fr *Dane* (gen pl of *Dan* Dane) + *geld* tribute, payment, fr OE *gield*; akin to OE *gieldan* to pay (for), reward – more at YIELD]

Danelaw /'dayn,law/ *n* (the law in force in) the part of England held by the Danes before the Norman Conquest in 1066

danger /'daynjə/ *n* **1** exposure to the possibility of injury, pain, or loss **2** a case or cause of danger ⟨*the* ~s *of mining*⟩ [ME *daunger*, fr OF *dangier*, alter. of *dongier*, fr (assumed) VL *dominiarium*, fr L *dominium* ownership]

'**danger ,list** *n* a list of those (e g hospital patients) in danger (e g of dying)

'**danger ,money** *n* extra pay for dangerous work

dangerous /'daynj(ə)rəs/ *adj* **1** exposing to or involving danger **2** able or likely to inflict injury – **dangerously** *adv*, **dangerousness** *n*

dangle /'dang·gl/ *vb* **dangling** /'dang·gling/ *vi* to hang or swing loosely ~ *vt* **1** to cause to dangle; swing **2** to display enticingly ⟨~d *the possibility before them*⟩ [prob of Scand origin; akin to Dan *dangle* to dangle] – **dangler** *n*, **danglingly** *adv*

Daniel /'danyəl/ *n* (an Old Testament book of narratives, visions and prophecies which tells of) a Jewish hero, who, as an exile in Babylon, interpreted dreams, gave accounts of apocalyptic visions, and was divinely delivered from a den of lions

[1]**Danish** /'daynish/ *adj* (characteristic) of Denmark

[2]**Danish** *n* the Germanic language of the Danes ☞ LANGUAGE

,Danish 'blue *n* a soft strongly flavoured Danish cheese with blue veins

,Danish 'pastry *n* (a piece of) confectionery made from a rich yeast dough with a sweet filling

dank /dangk/ *adj* unpleasantly moist or wet [ME *danke*, prob of Scand origin] – **dankly** *adv*, **dankness** *n*

danse macabre /,donhs mə'kahbrə, mə'kahb (*Fr* dɑ̃:s maka:br)/ *n* (a dance symbolizing) a medieval artistic theme in which death leads people to the grave [F, lit., macabre dance]

danseur /donh'suh (*Fr* dɑ̃sœ:r)/ *n* a male ballet dancer [F, fr *danser* to dance]

danseuse /donh'suhz (*Fr* dɑ̃sø:z)/ *n* a female ballet dancer [F, fem of *danseur*]

dap /dap/ *vi* **-pp-** to fish by allowing the bait to touch the surface of the water lightly [perh alter. of [2]*dab*]

daphne /'dafni/ *n* any of a genus of Eurasian shrubs [NL, genus name, fr L, laurel, fr Gk *daphnē*]

daphnia /'dafni·ə/ *n* any of a genus of minute freshwater crustaceans used as food for aquarium fish [NL, genus name]

dapper /'dapə/ *adj, esp of a small man* neat and spruce as regards clothing and demeanour [ME *dapyr*, fr MD *dapper* quick, strong; akin to OHG *tapfar* heavy, OSlav *debelŭ* thick] – **dapperly** *adv*, **dapperness** *n*

dapple /'dapl/ *vb* **dappling** /'dapling, 'dapl·ing/ to mark or become marked with rounded patches of varying shade [ME *dappel-grey*, adj, grey variegated with spots of different colour] – **dapple** *n*

dapsone /'dapsohn/ *n* a synthetic antibacterial drug used esp as the major treatment for leprosy [*di*aminodi*p*henyl-*s*ulph*one*]

Darby and Joan /,dahbi ənd 'john/ *n* a happily married elderly couple [prob fr *Darby & Joan*, couple in an 18th-c song]

[1]**dare** /deə/ *vb* **dared,** *archaic* **durst** /duhst/ *vi* to have sufficient courage or impudence (to) ⟨*no one* ~d *say a word*⟩ ⟨*try it if you* ~⟩ ~ *vt* **1a** to challenge to perform an action, esp as a proof of courage ⟨~d *him to jump*⟩ **b** to confront boldly; defy ⟨~d *the anger of her family*⟩ **2** to have the courage to contend against, venture, or try [ME *dar* (1 & 3 sing. pres indic), fr OE *dear*; akin to OHG gi*tar* (1 & 3 sing. pres indic) dare, L in*festus* hostile] – **darer** *n*

[2]**dare** *n* a challenge to a bold act ⟨*foolishly took a* ~⟩

daredevil /'deə,devl/ *n or adj* (sby) recklessly bold – **daredevilry** /-ri/ *n*

daren't /deənt/ dare not

daresay /,deə'say/ *vb pres 1 sing* venture to say (so); think (it) probable; suppose (so) [ME *(I) dar sayen* I venture to say]

[1]**daring** /'deəring/ *adj* adventurously bold in action or thought ⟨~ *acrobats*⟩ ⟨~ *crimes*⟩ – **daringly** *adv*, **daringness** *n*

[2]**daring** *n* venturesome boldness

dariole /'dariohl/ *n* (a dish cooked or set in) a small cup-shaped mould for cakes, jellies, creams, etc [F, fr MF, pastry filled with cream]

Darjeeling /dah'jeeling/ *n* a high-quality tea grown esp in the mountainous districts of N India [*Darjeeling*, city in India]

[1]**dark** /dahk/ *adj* **1** (partially) devoid of light **2a** (partially) black **b** *of a colour* of (very) low lightness **3a** arising from or showing evil traits or desires; evil **b** dismal, sad ⟨*took a* ~ *view of the future*⟩ **c** lacking knowledge or culture **4** not fair; swarthy ⟨*her* ~ *good looks*⟩ **5** secret ⟨*kept his plans* ~⟩ **6** *of a theatre* temporarily not presenting any production [ME *derk*, fr OE *deorc*; akin to OHG *tarchannen* to hide, Gk *thrassein* to trouble] – **darkish** *adj*, **darkly** *adv*, **darkness** *n*

[2]**dark** *n* **1a** the absence of light; darkness **b** a place or time of little or no light; night, nightfall ⟨*after* ~⟩ **2** a dark or deep colour – **in the dark** in ignorance ⟨*kept the public* in the dark *about the agreement*⟩

'**Dark ,Ages** *n pl* the period from about AD 476 to about 1000

darken /'dahkən/ *vb* to make or become dark or darker – **darkener** *n*

,dark 'horse *n* sby or sthg (e g a contestant) little known, but with a potential much greater than the evidence would suggest

'**dark ,lantern** *n* a lantern that can be closed to conceal the light

darkling /'dahkling/ *adj* **1** dark **2** done or taking place in the dark *USE* chiefly poetic [ME *derkelyng*, fr *derk* dark + *-lyng* -ling]

'**darkroom** /-,roohm, -room/ *n* a room with no light or with a safelight for handling and processing light-sensitive photographic materials

'**darksome** /-səm/ *adj* dark – poetic

darky, darkey /'dahki/ *n* a Negro – derog ['*dark* + [1]*-y*]

¹darling /ˈdahling/ *n* **1a** a dearly loved person **b** DEAR 1b **2** a favourite ⟨*the critics'* ~⟩ [ME *derling*, fr OE *dēorling*, fr *dēore* dear]

²darling *adj* **1** dearly loved; favourite **2** charming ⟨*a* ~ *little house*⟩ – used esp by women

¹darn /dahn/ *vt* to mend (sthg) with interlacing stitches woven across a hole or worn part ⟨~ *a sock*⟩ [prob fr F dial. *darner*] – **darner** *n*

²darn *n* a place that has been darned ⟨*a sweater full of* ~s⟩

³darn *vb* to damn [euphemism] – **darned** *adj or adv*

⁴darn *adj or adv* damned

darnel /ˈdahnl/ *n* any of several grasses that are common weeds [ME]

¹dart /daht/ *n* **1a** a small projectile with a pointed shaft at one end and flights of feather, plastic, etc at the other **b** *pl but sing in constr* a game in which darts are thrown at a dartboard **2** sthg with a slender pointed shaft or outline; *specif* a stitched tapering fold put in a garment to shape it to the figure **3** a quick movement; a dash [ME, fr MF, of Gmc origin; akin to OHG *tart* dart]

²dart *vt* **1** to throw with a sudden movement **2** to thrust or move with sudden speed **3** to put a dart or darts in (a garment or part of a garment) ~ *vi* to move suddenly or rapidly ⟨~ed *across the road*⟩

ˈdart,board /-,bawd/ *n* a circular target used in darts that is divided, usu by wire, into different scoring areas

darter /ˈdahtə/ *n* any of several fish-eating birds related to the cormorants but having a long slender neck [²DART + ²-ER]

Dartmoor pony /ˈdahtmaw, -mooə/ *n* (any of) an old breed of small shaggy English ponies [*Dartmoor*, region of SW England]

Darwinian /dahˈwinyən, -ni·ən/ *adj* of (the theories or followers of) Charles Darwin, or Darwinism [Charles *Darwin* †1882 E naturalist] – **Darwinian** *n*

Darwinism /ˈdahwi,niz(ə)m/ *n* a theory of evolution asserting that all the groups of plants and animals have arisen by natural selection – **Darwinist** *n*, **darwinist, darwinistic** /-ˈnistik/ *adj, often cap*

¹dash /dash/ *vt* **1** to strike or knock violently **2** to break by striking or knocking **3** to destroy, ruin ⟨*the news* ~ed *her hopes*⟩ **4** *Br* DAMN 4 – euph ⟨~ *it all*⟩ ~ *vi* **1** to move with sudden speed ⟨~ed *through the rain*⟩ **2** to smash [ME *dasshen*, prob of imit origin; (4) euphemism]

²dash *n* **1** (the sound produced by) a sudden burst or splash **2a** a stroke of a pen **b** a punctuation mark – used esp to indicate a break in the thought or structure of a sentence **3** a small but significant addition ⟨*a* ~ *of salt*⟩ **4** liveliness of style and action; panache **5** a sudden onset, rush, or attempt **6** a signal (e g a flash or audible tone) of relatively long duration that is one of the 2 fundamental units of Morse code – compare ¹DOT 4 **7** *Br* PRIME 5

dashboard /ˈdash,bawd/ *n* a panel extending across a motor car, aeroplane, or motorboat below the windscreen and usu containing dials and controls

dashiki /dəˈsheeki/ *n* a usu brightly coloured loose-fitting pull-on shirt traditionally worn in W Africa [alter. of Yoruba *danshiki*]

dashing /ˈdashing/ *adj* **1** marked by vigorous action; spirited **2** marked by smartness, esp in dress and manners – **dashingly** *adv*

dash off *vt* to complete or execute (e g writing or drawing) hastily ⟨dash off *a letter*⟩

dashpot /ˈdash,pot/ *n* a device for cushioning or damping a movement (e g of a mechanical part) to avoid shock

dassie /ˈdahsi/ *n* a hyrax of southern Africa [Afrik]

dastard /ˈdastəd/ *n, archaic* a coward; *esp* one who commits malicious acts [ME, perh fr ON *dæstr* exhausted]

ˈdastardly /-li/ *adj, archaic* despicably malicious or cowardly – **dastardliness** *n*

data /ˈdahtə, ˈdaytə/ *n pl but sing or pl in constr* factual information (e g measurements or statistics) used as a basis for reasoning, discussion, or calculation ⟨*all the essential* ~ *are here – TLS*⟩ ⟨*any* ~ *he could glean was valuable – TLS*⟩ [pl of *datum*]

ˈdata ,bank *n* a collection of data organized esp for rapid search and retrieval (e g by computer) ☞ COMPUTER

ˈdata ,base *n* the data that is accessible to a data-processing system (e g a computer) ☞ COMPUTER

,data ˈprocessing *n* the conversion (e g by computer) of crude information into usable or storable form ☞ COMPUTER – **data processor** *n*

¹date /dayt/ *n* (the oblong edible fruit of) a tall palm [ME, fr OF, deriv of L *dactylus*, fr Gk *daktylos*, lit., finger]

²date *n* **1a** the time reckoned in days or larger units at which an event occurs ⟨*the* ~ *of her birth*⟩ **b** a statement of such a time ⟨*the* ~ *on the letter*⟩ **2** the period of time to which sthg belongs **3a** an appointment for a specified time; *esp* a social engagement between 2 people of opposite sex – infml **b** *NAm* a person of the opposite sex with whom one has a date – infml [ME, fr MF, fr LL *data*, fr *data* (as in *data Romae* given at Rome), fem of L *datus*, pp of *dare* to give; akin to Gk *didonai* to give] – **to date** up to the present moment

³date *vt* **1** to determine the date of ⟨~ *an antique*⟩ **2** to record the date of **3a** to mark with characteristics typical of a particular period **b** to show up plainly the age of ⟨*his knickerbockers* ~ *him*⟩ **4** *chiefly NAm* to make or have a date with (a person of the opposite sex) – infml ~ *vi* **1** to have been in existence – usu + *from* **2** to become old-fashioned ⟨*clothes that never* ~⟩ – **datable, dateable** /ˈdaytəbl/ *adj*, **dater** *n*

ˈdated *adj* **1** provided with a date ⟨*a* ~ *document*⟩ **2** out-of-date, old-fashioned – **datedly** *adv*, **datedness** *n*

dateless /ˈdaytlis/ *adj* **1** having no date **2** timeless

ˈdate,line /-,lien/ *n* **1** a line in a written document or publication giving the date and place of composition or issue **2** INTERNATIONAL DATE LINE – **dateline** *vt*

ˈdate,stamp /-,stamp/ *n* (the mark made by) a device for stamping a date

dative /ˈdaytiv/ *n* (a form in) a grammatical case expressing typically the indirect object of a verb, the object of some prepositions, or a possessor [ME *datif*, fr L *dativus*, lit., relating to giving, fr *datus*] – **dative** *adj*

dative bond *n* COORDINATE BOND [fr the donation of electrons by one of the atoms]

datum /ˈdahtəm; *NAm* ˈdaytəm/ *n, pl* (*1*) **data** /-tə/,

(*2*) **datums** **1** sthg given or admitted, esp as a basis for reasoning or drawing conclusions **2** sthg used as a basis for measuring or calculating [L, fr neut of *datus*]

datura /də'tyooərə/ *n* the thorn apple or a related, usu very poisonous, plant of the nightshade family [NL, genus name, fr Hindi *dhatūrā* jimsonweed]

[1]**daub** /dawb/ *vt* **1** to cover or coat with soft adhesive matter; plaster **2** to coat with a dirty substance **3** to apply (e g colouring material) crudely (to) ~ *vi* to paint without much skill [ME *dauben*, fr OF *dauber*, deriv of L *dealbare* to whiten, whitewash, plaster, fr *de-* + *albus* white] – **dauber** *n*

[2]**daub** *n* **1** material used to daub walls ⟨*wattle and* ~⟩ **2** a daubing **3** sthg daubed on; a smear **4** a crude picture

daube /dohb/ *n* a stew of meat, esp beef, braised in red wine [F]

[1]**daughter** /'dawtə/ *n* **1a** a human female having the relation of child to parent **b** a female descendant – often pl **2a** a human female having a specified origin or affiliation ⟨*a* ~ *of the Church*⟩ **b** sthg considered as a daughter ⟨*French is a* ~ *(language) of Latin*⟩ **3** an isotope formed as the immediate product of the radioactive decay of an element [ME *doughter*, fr OE *dohtor*; akin to OHG *tohter* daughter, Gk *thygatēr*] – **daughterless** *adj*, **daughterly** *adj*

[2]**daughter** *adj* **1** having the characteristics or relationship of a daughter **2** of the first generation of offspring, molecules, etc produced by reproduction, division, or replication ⟨*the* ~ *cells*⟩

'**daughter-in-,law** *n, pl* **daughters-in-law** the wife of one's son

daunt /dawnt/ *vt* to lessen the courage of; inspire awe in [ME *daunten*, fr OF *danter*, alter. of *donter*, fr L *domitare* to tame, fr *domitus*, pp of *domare* – more at TAME]

daunting /'dawnting/ *adj* discouraging, disheartening ⟨*a* ~ *task*⟩ – **dauntingly** *adv*

'**dauntless** /-lis/ *adj* fearless ⟨*a* ~ *hero*⟩ – **dauntlessly** *adv*, **dauntlessness** *n*

dauphin /'dohfanh (*Fr* dofɛ̃)/ *n, often cap* the eldest son of a king of France [MF *dalfin*, fr OF, title of lords of the Dauphiné, fr *Dalfin*, a surname]

dauphine /'dohfeen (*Fr* dofin)/ *n, often cap* the wife of the dauphin [F]

davenport /'davən,pawt/ *n* **1** a small compact writing desk **2** *chiefly NAm* a large upholstered sofa; *esp* one that converts into a bed [prob fr the name *Davenport*]

davit /'davit/ *n* any of 2 or more projecting arms on a vessel which are used as cranes, esp for lowering boats [prob fr the name *David*]

Davy Jones's locker /,dayvi 'johnziz/ *n* the bottom of the sea [*Davy Jones*, legendary spirit of the sea]

'**Davy ,lamp** /'dayvi/ *n* an early safety lamp used in mines [Sir Humphry *Davy* †1829 E chemist & inventor]

daw /daw/ *n* a jackdaw [ME *dawe*; akin to OHG *taha* jackdaw]

dawdle /'dawdl/ *vi* **dawdling** /'dawdling/ *vi* **1** to spend time idly ⟨~ *over one's coffee*⟩ **2** to move lackadaisically [origin unknown] – **dawdle** *n*, **dawdler** /'dawdlə/ *n*

[1]**dawn** /dawn/ *vi* **1** to begin to grow light as the sun rises **2** to begin to appear or develop **3** to begin to be perceived or understood ⟨*the truth finally* ~ed *on him*⟩ [ME *dawnen*, prob back-formation fr *dawning* daybreak, alter. of *dawing*, fr OE *dagung*, fr *dagian* to dawn]

[2]**dawn** *n* **1** the first appearance of light in the morning **2** a first appearance; a beginning ⟨*the* ~ *of the space age*⟩

day /day/ *n* **1** the time of light when the sun is above the horizon between one night and the next **2** the time required by a celestial body, specif the earth, to turn once on its axis **3** the solar day of 24 hours beginning at midnight **4** a specified day or date ⟨*wash* ~⟩ **5** a specified time or period ⟨*in grandfather's* ~⟩ **6** the conflict or contention of the day ⟨*played hard and won the* ~⟩ **7** the time established by usage or law for work, school, or business ⟨*an 8-hour* ~⟩ **8** an era [ME, fr OE *dæg*; akin to OHG *tag* day] – **day in, day out** DAY AFTER DAY – **from day to day** [2]DAILY

,**day after 'day** *adv* for an indefinite or seemingly endless number of successive days

Dayak /'die,ak/ *n* (a) Dyak

daybed /'day,bed/ *n* a narrow bed or couch for rest or sleep during the day

'**day,break** /-,brayk/ *n* DAWN 1

'**day,dream** /-,dreem/ *n* a visionary, usu wish-fulfilling, creation of the waking imagination – **daydream** *vi*

Dayglo /'day,glow/ *trademark* – used for a type of paint which glows in natural daylight

'**day,light** /-,liet/ *n* **1** DAWN 1 **2** knowledge or understanding of sthg that has been obscure ⟨*began to see* ~ *on the problem*⟩ **3** *pl* mental soundness or stability; wits ⟨*scared the* ~s *out of her*⟩ – infml

,**daylight 'robbery** *n, Br* an instance of exorbitant pricing or charging – infml

daylight saving time *n, chiefly NAm* time usu 1 hour ahead of standard time and used esp during the summer – compare BRITISH SUMMER TIME

'**day ,lily** *n* any of various Eurasian plants of the lily family cultivated for their short-lived flowers

day nursery *n* a public centre for the care of young children

,**Day of A'tonement** *n* YOM KIPPUR

,**day of 'reckoning** *n* a time when the results of mistakes or misdeeds are felt, or when offences are punished

day release *n* a system in Britain whereby workers are allowed days off work to attend educational courses

,**day-re'turn** *n, Br* a ticket sold for a return journey on the same day and usu at a reduced rate if used outside rush hours

days /dayz/ *adv, chiefly NAm* by day repeatedly; on any day

'**day,spring** /-,spring/ *n* DAWN 1 – poetic

'**day,star** /-,stah/ *n* **1** MORNING STAR **2** SUN 1a

,**day-to-'day** *adj* **1** taking place, made, or done in the course of successive days ⟨~ *problems*⟩ **2** providing for a day at a time with little thought for the future ⟨*lived an aimless* ~ *existence*⟩

daze /dayz/ *vt* to stupefy, esp by a blow; stun [ME *dasen*, fr ON *dasa* (in *dasask* to become exhausted)] – **daze** *n*, **dazedly** /'dayzidli/ *adv*, **dazedness** /'dayz(i)dnis/ *n*

dazzle /'dazl/ *vb* **dazzling** /'dazling/ *vi* **1** to lose clear vision, esp from looking at bright light **2a** to shine brilliantly **b** to arouse admiration by an impressive display ~ *vt* **1** to overpower or temporarily blind (the sight) with light **2** to impress deeply, overpower, or confound with brilliance ⟨~d *the crowd with her oratory*⟩ [freq of *daze*] – **dazzle** *n*, **dazzler** *n*, **dazzlingly** *adv*

'D ,day /dee/ *n* a day set for launching an operation; *specif* June 6, 1944, on which the Allies began the invasion of France in WW II [*D*, abbr for *day*]

DDT *n* a synthetic chlorinated water-insoluble insecticide that tends to accumulate in food chains and is poisonous to many vertebrates [*d*ichloro-*d*iphenyl-*t*richloro-ethane]

de- /dee-/ *prefix* **1a** do the opposite of (a specified action) ⟨de*populate*⟩ ⟨de*compose*⟩ **b** reverse of ⟨de-*empha sis*⟩ ⟨de*industrialization*⟩ **2a** remove (sthg specified) from ⟨de*louse*⟩ ⟨de*capitate*⟩ **b** remove from (sthg specified) ⟨de*throne*⟩ **3** reduce ⟨de*value*⟩ **4** alight from (a specified thing) ⟨de*train*⟩ [ME, fr OF *de-*, *des-*, partly fr L *de-* from, down, away (fr *de*) and partly fr L *dis-*; L *de* akin to OIr *di* from, OE *tō* to – more at TO, DIS-]

deacon /'deekən/ *n* a subordinate officer in a Christian church: e g **a** a clergyman ranking below a priest and, in the Anglican and Roman Catholic churches, usu a candidate for ordination as priest **b** an assistant minister in a Lutheran parish **c** any of a group of laymen with administrative and sometimes spiritual duties in various Protestant churches [ME *dekene*, fr OE *dēacon*, fr LL *diaconus*, fr Gk *diakonos*, lit., servant, fr *dia-* + *-konos* (akin to en*konein* to be active); akin to L *conari* to attempt]

deaconess /,deekə'nes, '---/ *n* a woman assisting in the ministry of a Protestant church

deactivate /dee'aktivayt/ *vt* to make inactive or ineffective – **deactivator** *n*, **deactivation** /-'vaysh(ə)n/ *n*

[1]dead /ded/ *adj* **1** deprived of life; having died **2a(1)** having the appearance of death; deathly ⟨*in a ~ faint*⟩ **(2)** lacking power to move, feel, or respond; numb **b** very tired **c** grown cold; extinguished ⟨~ *coals*⟩ **3a** inanimate, inert ⟨~ *matter*⟩ **b** barren, infertile ⟨~ *soil*⟩ **4a(1)** no longer having power or effect ⟨*a ~ law*⟩ ⟨*a ~ battery*⟩ **(2)** no longer having interest, relevance, or significance ⟨*a ~ issue*⟩ **b** no longer used; obsolete ⟨*a ~ language*⟩ **c** no longer existing ⟨*charity is ~*⟩ **d** lacking in activity **e** lacking elasticity or springiness **f** out of action or use; *specif* free from any connection to a source of voltage and free from electric charges **g** temporarily out of play ⟨*a ~ ball*⟩ **5** not imparting motion or power although otherwise functioning ⟨*a ~ rear axle*⟩ **6** lacking warmth, odour, vigour, or taste **7a** absolutely uniform ⟨~ *level*⟩ **b** exact ⟨~ *centre of the target*⟩ **c** abrupt ⟨*brought to a ~ stop*⟩ **d** complete, absolute ⟨*a ~ silence*⟩ ⟨*a ~ loss*⟩ ⟨*a ~ giveaway*⟩ **8** lacking in gaiety or animation – chiefly infml [ME *deed*, fr OE *dēad*; akin to ON *dauthr* dead, *deyja* to die – more at [1]DIE] – **deadness** *n*

[2]dead *n* **1** *pl in constr* dead people or animals **2** the state of being dead ⟨*raised him from the ~* – Col 2:12(RSV)⟩ **3** the time of greatest quiet or inactivity ⟨*the ~ of night*⟩

[3]dead *adv* **1** absolutely, utterly ⟨~ *certain* ⟩ **2** suddenly and completely ⟨*stopped ~*⟩ **3** directly, exactly ⟨~ *ahead*⟩ ⟨~ *on time*⟩ **4** *Br* very, extremely ⟨~ *lucky*⟩ – infml

dead-'ball ,line *n* **1** a line at each end of a rugby pitch, not more than 23m (about 25yd) behind the goal line, beyond which the ball is out of play ☞ SPORT **2** a soccer goal line

dead bat *n* a cricket bat held loosely so that a ball striking it will not travel far through the air

deadbeat /'ded,beet/ *n*, *chiefly NAm* a loafer

,dead 'duck *n* sby or sthg (e g a scheme) unlikely to succeed; a nonstarter – infml

deaden /'dedən/ *vt vt* **1** to deprive of liveliness, brilliance, sensation, or force **2** to make (e g a wall) impervious to sound [DEAD + [2]-EN] – **deadener** *n*, **deadeningly** *adv*

,dead-'end *adj* **1a** lacking opportunities for advancement ⟨*a ~ job*⟩ **b** lacking an exit ⟨*a ~ street*⟩ **2** made aggressively antisocial by a dead-end existence ⟨~ *kids*⟩

,dead 'end *n* **1** an end (e g of a street) without an exit **2** a position, situation, or course of action that leads no further

deadening /'dedəning/ *n* material used to soundproof walls or floors

'dead ,hand *n* **1** mortmain **2** the oppressive influence of the past

,dead'head /-'hed/ *vt*, *Br* to remove dead flower heads from (a plant)

,dead 'heat *n* an inconclusive finish to a race or other contest, in which the fastest time, highest total, etc is achieved by more than one competitor – **dead-heat** *vi*

,dead 'letter *n* **1** a law that has lost its force without being formally abolished **2** an undeliverable and unreturnable letter

'dead,light /-,liet/ *n* a metal cover or shutter fitted inside a porthole to keep out light and water

deadline /'dedlien/ *n* **1** a boundary beyond which it is not possible or permitted to pass **2** a date or time before which sthg (e g the presentation of copy for publication) must be done

deadlock /'dedlok/ *n* **1** a lock that can be opened and shut only by a key **2** inaction or neutralization resulting from the opposition of equally powerful and uncompromising people or factions; a standstill **3** a tied score – **deadlock** *vt*

[1]deadly /'dedli/ *adj* **1** likely to cause or capable of producing death ⟨*a ~ disease*⟩ ⟨*a ~ instrument*⟩ **2a** aiming to kill or destroy; implacable ⟨*a ~ enemy*⟩ **b** unerring ⟨~ *accuracy*⟩ **c** marked by determination or extreme seriousness ⟨*she was in ~ earnest*⟩ **3** lacking animation; dull ⟨~ *bores*⟩ ⟨*a ~ conversation*⟩ **4** intense, extreme ⟨~ *fear*⟩ – **deadliness** *n*

[2]deadly *adv* **1** suggesting death ⟨~ *pale*⟩ **2** extremely ⟨~ *serious*⟩

,deadly 'night,shade /'niet,shayd/ *n* a European poisonous nightshade that has dull purple flowers and black berries

,deadly 'sin *n* any of the 7 sins of pride, covetousness, lust, anger, gluttony, envy, and sloth held to lead to damnation

,dead ,man's 'handle *n*, *Br* a handle that requires constant pressure to allow operation (e g of a train or tram)

,dead ,men's 'fingers *n* a fleshy soft coral of European coastal waters

[1]deadpan /ded'pan/ *adj* impassive, expressionless [*dead* + *pan*, n (face)]

[2]deadpan *adv* in a deadpan manner

,dead 'reckoning *n* the calculation without celestial observations of the position of a ship or aircraft, from the record of the courses followed, the distance travelled, etc – **dead reckon** *vb*, **dead reckoner** *n*

'dead,weight /-,wayt/ *n* **1** the unrelieved weight of an inert mass **2** a ship's total weight including cargo, fuel, stores, crew, and passengers

'dead,wood /-,wood/ *n* useless personnel or material

deaf /def/ *adj* **1** (partially) lacking the sense of hearing **2** unwilling to hear or listen *to*; not to be persuaded ⟨~ *to reason*⟩ [ME *deef*, fr OE *dēaf*; akin to Gk *typhlos* blind, *typhein* to smoke, L *fumus* smoke – more at FUME] – **deafish** *adj*, **deafly** *adv*, **deafness** *n*

'deaf-,aid *n, Br* HEARING AID

deafen /'defən/ *vt* to make deaf ~ *vi* to cause deafness or stun sby with noise – **deafeningly** *adv*

,deaf-'mute *n or adj* (one who is) deaf and dumb

[1]**deal** /deel/ *n* **1** a usu large or indefinite quantity or degree; a lot ⟨*a great* ~ *of support*⟩ ⟨*a good* ~ *faster*⟩ **2a** the act or right of distributing cards to players in a card game **b** HAND 9b [ME *deel*, fr OE *dǣl*; akin to OE *dāl* division, portion, OHG *teil* part]

[2]**deal** *vb* **dealt** /delt/ *vt* **1a** to give as sby's portion; apportion **b** to distribute (playing cards) to players in a game **2** to administer, bestow ⟨~t *him a blow*⟩ ~ *vi* **1** to distribute the cards in a card game **2** to concern oneself or itself ⟨*the book* ~s *with education*⟩ **3a** to trade **b** to sell or distribute sthg as a business ⟨~ *in insurance*⟩ **4** to take action with regard to sby or sthg ⟨~ *with an offender*⟩

[3]**deal** *n* **1** a transaction **2** treatment received ⟨*a raw* ~⟩ **3** an arrangement for mutual advantage

[4]**deal** *n* (a sawn piece of) fir or pine timber [MD or MLG *dele* plank; akin to OHG *dili* plank] – **deal** *adj*

dealer /'deelə/ *n* **1** sby who deals in goods or services **2** sby or sthg that deals playing cards [[2]DEAL + [2]-ER]

dealing /'deeling/ *n* **1** *pl* friendly or business interactions **2** a method of business; a manner of conduct [ME *deling*, fr gerund of *delen* to deal]

[1]**dean, dene** /deen/ *n, Br* a narrow wooded valley containing a stream [ME *dene*, fr OE *denu*]

[2]**dean** *n* **1a** the head of the chapter of a collegiate or cathedral church – often used as a title **b** RURAL DEAN **2** the head of a university division, faculty, or school **3** a doyen [ME *deen*, fr MF *deien*, fr LL *decanus*, lit., chief of ten, fr L *decem* ten – more at TEN] – **deanship** *n*

deanery /'deenəri/ *n* the office, jurisdiction, or official residence of a clerical dean

[1]**dear** /diə/ *adj* **1** highly valued; much loved – often used in address ⟨~ *Sir*⟩ **2** expensive **3** heartfelt ⟨*her* ~est *wish*⟩ [ME *dere*, fr OE *dēore*] – **dear** *adv*, **dearly** *adv*, **dearness** *n*

[2]**dear** *n* **1a** a loved one; a sweetheart **b** – used as a familiar or affectionate form of address **2** a lovable person

[3]**dear** *interj* – used typically to express annoyance or dismay ⟨*oh* ~⟩ [prob short for *dear God* or *dear Lord*]

dearth /duhth/ *n* an inadequate supply; a scarcity [ME *derthe*, fr *dere* dear, costly]

deary /'diəri/ *n* a dear person – used chiefly in address

death /deth/ *n* **1** a permanent cessation of all vital functions; the end of life **2** the cause or occasion of loss of life ⟨*drinking was the* ~ *of him*⟩ **3** *cap* death personified, usu represented as a skeleton with a scythe **4** the state of being dead **5** extinction, disappearance [ME *deeth*, fr OE *dēath*; akin to ON *dauthi* death, *deyja* to die – more at [1]DIE] – **at death's door** seriously ill – **to death** beyond all acceptable limits; excessively ⟨*bored* to death⟩

'death,bed /-,bed/ *n* – **on one's deathbed** near the point of death

'death,blow /-,bloh/ *n* a destructive or killing stroke or event

'death ,cap *n* a very poisonous toadstool

'death ,cell *n* CONDEMNED CELL

'death ,duty *n, chiefly Br* tax levied on the estate of a dead person – often pl with sing. meaning

'deathless /-lis/ *adj* immortal, imperishable ⟨~ *fame*⟩ – **deathlessly** *adv*, **deathlessness** *n*

'deathly /-li/ *adj* (suggestive) of death ⟨*a* ~ *pallor*⟩ – **deathly** *adv*

'death ,mask *n* a cast taken from the face of a dead person

'death ,rate *n* the number of deaths per 1000 people in a population over a given period

'death ,rattle *n* a gurgling sound produced by air passing through mucus in the lungs and throat of a dying person

'death's-,head *n* a human skull symbolic of death

death's-head moth *n* a very large European hawkmoth with skull-shaped markings on its back

'death ,trap *n* a potentially lethal structure or place

'death ,warrant *n* a warrant for the execution of a death sentence

'death,watch /-,woch/ *n* a vigil kept with the dead or dying [*death* + *watch* (vigil)]

deathwatch beetle *n* any of various small wood-boring beetles common in old buildings

'death-,wish *n* a usu unconscious desire for the death of another or oneself

deb /deb/ *n* a debutante – infml – **debby** *adj*

debacle /di'bahkəl/ *n* **1** a tumultuous breakup of ice in a river **2** a violent disruption (e g of an army); a rout **3** a complete failure; a fiasco [F *débâcle*, fr *débâcler* to unbar, fr MF *desbacler*, fr *des-* de- + *bacler* to bar, fr OProv *baclar*, fr (assumed) VL *bacculare*, fr L *baculum* staff – more at BACTERIUM]

debag /,dee'bag/ *vt* **-gg-** *Br* to remove the trousers of as a joke or punishment – infml [*de-* + *bags* (trousers)]

debar /,dee'bah/ *vt* **-rr-** to bar *from* having, doing, or undergoing sthg; preclude [ME *debarren*, fr MF *desbarrer* to unbar, fr *des-* de- + *barrer* to bar] – **debarment** *n*

debark /,dee'bahk/ *vt* to remove the bark from (a tree)

debase /di'bays/ *vt* **1** to lower in status, esteem, quality, or character **2a** to reduce the intrinsic value of (a coin) by increasing the content of low-value metal **b** to reduce the exchange value of (a monetary unit) [*de-* + [4]*base*] – **debasement** *n*, **debaser** *n*

debatable /di'baytəbl/ *adj* **1** claimed by more than 1 country ⟨~ *territory*⟩ **2** open to debate; questionable

[1]**debate** /di'bayt/ *n* a contention by words or arguments; *esp* the formal discussion of a motion **a** in parliament **b** between 2 opposing sides

[2]**debate** *vi* **1a** to contend in words **b** to discuss a

question by considering opposed arguments **2** to participate in a debate ~ *vt* **1** to argue about **2** to consider [ME *debaten*, fr MF *debatre*, fr OF, fr *de-* + *batre* to beat, fr L *battuere* – more at BATTLE] – **debater** *n*

[1]**debauch** /di'bawch/ *vt* **1** to lead away from virtue or excellence **2** to make excessively intemperate or sensual [MF *debaucher*, fr OF *desbauchier* to scatter, rough-hew (timber), fr *des-* de- + *bauch* beam, of Gmc origin; akin to OHG *balko* beam] – **debaucher** *n*

[2]**debauch** *n* **1** an act or occasion of debauchery **2** an orgy

debauchee /di,baw'chee/ *n* one given to debauchery [F *débauché*, fr pp of *débaucher*]

debauchery /di'bawchəri/ *n* excessive indulgence in the pleasures of the flesh

debenture /di'benchə/ *n, Br* a loan secured on the assets of a company in respect of which the company must pay a fixed interest before any dividends are paid to its own shareholders [ME *debentur*, fr L, they are due, fr *debēre* to owe]

debilitate /di'bilitayt/ *vt* to impair the strength of; enfeeble [L *debilitatus*, pp of *debilitare* to weaken, fr *debilis*] – **debilitation** /-'taysh(ə)n/ *n*

debility /di'biləti/ *n* a weakness or infirmity [MF *debilité*, fr L *debilitat-*, *debilitas*, fr *debilis* weak]

[1]**debit** /'debit/ *n* **1a** (an entry in an account that is) a record of money owed **b** the sum of the items so entered **2** a charge against a bank account [L *debitum* debt]

[2]**debit** *vt* **1** to enter as a debit **2** to charge to the debit of ⟨~ *an account*⟩ – compare CREDIT 2b

debonair /,debə'neə/ *adj* **1** suave, urbane **2** light-hearted, nonchalant [ME *debonere*, fr OF *debonaire*, fr *de bonne aire* of good family or nature] – **debonairly** *adv*, **debonairness** *n*

debouch /di'bowch/ *vi vi* to emerge or issue, esp from a narrow place into a wider place [F *déboucher*, fr *dé-* de- + *bouche* mouth, fr L *bucca* cheek – more at POCK]

de'bouchment /-mənt/ *n* a mouth or outlet, esp of a river [DEBOUCH + -MENT]

debridement /di'breedmənt/ *n* the surgical removal, esp from a wound, of dead, lacerated, or contaminated tissue [F *débridement*, fr *débrider* to remove unhealthy tissue, lit., to unbridle, fr MF *desbrider*, fr *des-* de- + *bride* bridle, fr MHG *bridel*]

debrief /,dee'breef/ *vt* to interrogate (a person) on return from a mission in order to obtain useful information

debris /'debri/ *n* **1** the remains of sthg broken down or destroyed **2a** an accumulation of fragments of rock **b** accumulated rubbish or waste [F *débris*, fr MF, fr *debriser* to break to pieces, fr OF *debrisier*, fr *de-* + *brisier* to break, of Celt origin]

debt /det/ *n* **1** a state of owing ⟨*heavily in* ~⟩ **2** sthg owed; an obligation ⟨*couldn't pay her* ~s⟩ [ME *dette, debte*, fr OF *dette* something owed, fr (assumed) VL *debita*, fr L, pl of *debitum* debt, fr neut of *debitus*, pp of *debēre* to owe, fr *de-* + *habēre* to have – more at HABIT] – **debtless** *adj* – **in someone's debt** owing sby gratitude; indebted to sby

debtor /'detə/ *n* one who owes a debt

debug /,dee'bug/ *vt* **-gg-** **1** to eliminate errors in or malfunctions of ⟨~ *a computer program*⟩ **2** to remove a concealed microphone or wiretapping device from

debunk /,dee'bungk/ *vt* to expose the falseness of [*de-* + [4]*bunk*] – **debunker** *n*

debus /,dee'bus/ *vb* **-ss-** *vt* to unload (e g military stores) from a vehicle ~ *vi* to get out of a motor vehicle [*de-* + *bus*]

debut /'dayb(y)ooh/ *n* **1** a first public appearance **2** a formal entrance into society [F *début*, fr *débuter* to begin, fr MF *desbuter* to play first, fr *des-* de- + *but* starting point, goal – more at [3]BUTT] – **debut** *vi*

debutant /'debyoo,tont/ *n* sby making a debut [F *débutant*, fr prp of *débuter*]

debutante /'debyoo,tont/ *n* a woman making a debut; *esp* a young woman making her formal entrance into society [F *débutante*, fem of *débutant*]

deca- /dekə-/, **dec-, deka-, dek-** *comb form* ten (10^1) ⟨de camerous⟩ ⟨decathlon⟩ ☞ PHYSICS [ME, fr L, fr Gk *deka-*, *dek-*, fr *deka* – more at TEN]

decade /'dekayd; *also* di'kayd/ *n* **1** a group, set, or sequence of 10 **2** a period of 10 years **3** a division of the rosary containing 10 Hail Marys [ME, fr MF *décade*, fr LL *decad-*, *decas*, fr Gk *dekad-*, *dekas*, fr *deka*]

decadence /'dekədəns/ *n* **1** being decadent **2** a period of decline [MF, fr ML *decadentia*, fr LL *decadent-*, *decadens*, prp of *decadere* to fall, sink – more at DECAY]

decadent /'dekədənt/ *adj* **1** marked by decay or decline, esp in moral or cultural standards **2** tending to gratify one's desires, appetites, or whims in an excessive or unrestrained manner [back-formation fr *decadence*] – **decadently** *adv*

decaffeinated /,dee'kafinaytid/ *adj, of coffee* having had most of the caffeine removed

decagon /'dekəgon/ *n* a polygon of 10 angles and 10 sides ☞ MATHEMATICS [NL *decagonum*, fr Gk *dekagōnon*, fr *deka-* deca- + *-gōnon* -gon]

decal /'dee,kal, di'kal, 'dekəl/ *n, chiefly NAm* a design or picture, esp on specially prepared paper, for transfer to another surface; a transfer [short for *decalcomania*, fr F *décalcomanie*, fr *décalquer* to copy by tracing + *manie* mania]

decalcify /,dee'kalsifie/ *vt* to remove calcium or calcium compounds from (bones, teeth, soil, etc) [ISV] – **decalcification** /-fi'kaysh(ə)n/ *n*

decalitre /'dekə,leetə/ *n* ten litres (about 2.2gall) [F *décalitre*, fr *déca-* deca + *litre* litre]

Decalogue /'dekəlog/ *n* TEN COMMANDMENTS [ME *decaloge*, fr LL *decalogus*, fr Gk *dekalogos*, fr *deka-* + *logos* word – more at LEGEND]

decamp /,dee'kamp/ *vi* **1** to break up a camp **2** to depart suddenly; abscond [F *décamper*, fr MF *descamper*, fr *des-* de- + *camper* to camp] – **decampment** *n*

decant /di'kant/ *vt* **1** to pour from one vessel into another, esp a decanter **2** to draw off without disturbing the sediment [NL *decantare*, fr L *de-* + ML *cantus* side, fr L, iron tyre – more at [1]CANT] – **decantation** /,deekan'taysh(ə)n/ *n*

decanter /di'kantə/ *n* an ornamental glass bottle used for serving an alcoholic drink, esp wine [DECANT + [2]-ER]

decapitate /di'kapitayt/ *vt* to cut off the head of [LL *decapitatus*, pp of *decapitare*, fr L *de-* + *capit-*, *caput* head – more at HEAD] – **decapitator** /-,taytə/ *n*, **decapitation** /-'taysh(ə)n/ *n*

decapod /'dekə,pod/ *n* any of an order of crustaceans including the shrimps, lobsters, and crabs that have stalked eyes, 5 pairs of appendages, and the head and thorax fused and covered by a carapace [NL *Decapoda*, order name] – **decapod** *adj*, **decapodal** /di'kapədl/ *adj*, **decapodan** /di'kapəd(ə)n; *also* ,dekə'pohd(ə)n/ *adj or n*, **decapodous** /-dəs/ *adj*

decarbon·ize, -ise /,dee'kahbəniez/ *vt* to remove carbon from [ISV] – **decarbonizer** *n*

decasyllabic /,dekəsi'labik/ *adj* consisting of 10 syllables [prob fr F *décasyllabique*, fr Gk *dekasyllabos*, fr *deka-* deca- + *syllabē* syllable] – **decasyllabic** *n*, **decasyllable** /'dekə,siləbl/ *n*

decathlete /di'kathleet/ *n* sby who competes in the decathlon

decathlon /di'kathlon/ *n* a men's athletic contest in which each competitor competes in 10 running, jumping, and throwing events [F *décathlon*, fr *déca-* deca- + Gk *athlon* contest]

[1]**decay** /di'kay/ *vi* **1** to decline from a sound or prosperous condition **2** to decrease gradually in quantity, activity, or force; *specif* to undergo radioactive decay **3** to fall into ruin **4** to decline in health, strength, or vigour **5** to undergo decomposition ~ *vt* to destroy by decomposition [ME *decayen*, fr ONF *decaïr*, fr LL *decadere* to fall, sink, fr L *de-* + *cadere* to fall – more at CHANCE] – **decayer** *n*

[2]**decay** *n* **1** a gradual decline in strength, soundness, prosperity, or quality **2** a wasting or wearing away; ruin **3** (a product of) rot; *specif* decomposition of organic matter (e g proteins), chiefly by bacteria in the presence of oxygen **4** a decline in health or vigour **5** decrease in quantity, activity, or force; *esp* spontaneous disintegration of an atom or particle (e g a meson) usu with the emission of radiation

Decca /'dekə/ *trademark* – used for a navigational aid that makes use of chains of long-wave radio transmitters to define position in terms of the phase relationships of the radio waves

decease /di'sees/ *n* death – fml [ME *deces*, fr MF, fr L *decessus* departure, death, fr *decessus*, pp of *decedere* to depart, die, fr *de-* + *cedere* to go – more at CEDE] – **decease** *vi*

de'ceased *n or adj, pl* **deceased** (sby) no longer living; *esp* (sby) recently dead

decedent /di'seed(ə)nt/ *n, NAm* a deceased person – used chiefly in law [L *decedent-, decedens*, prp of *decedere*]

deceit /di'seet/ *n* **1** the act or practice of deceiving; deception **2** the quality of being deceitful [ME *deceite*, fr OF, fr L *decepta*, fem of *deceptus*, pp of *decipere*]

de'ceitful /-f(ə)l/ *adj* having a tendency or disposition to deceive: **a** not honest **b** deceptive, misleading – **deceitfully** *adv*, **deceitfulness** *n*

deceive /di'seev/ *vt vt* to cause to accept as true or valid what is false or invalid; delude ~ *vi* to practise deceit [ME *deceiven*, fr OF *deceivre*, fr L *decipere*, fr *de-* + *capere* to take – more at HEAVE] – **deceivable** *adj*, **deceiver** *n*, **deceivingly** *adv*

decelerate /,dee'selərayt/ *vb* to (cause to) move at decreasing speed [*de-* + *accelerate*] – **decelerator** *n*, **deceleration** /-'raysh(ə)n/ *n*

December /di'sembə/ *n* the 12th month of the Gregorian calendar [ME *Decembre*, fr OF, fr L *December* (tenth month), fr *decem* ten – more at TEN]

Decembrist /di'sembrist/ *n* a participant in the unsuccessful uprising against the Tzar Nicholas I in December 1825

decemvir /di'semvə/ *n* any of a ruling body of 10, specif of 10 magistrates in ancient Rome [L, back-formation fr *decemviri*, pl, fr *decem* + *viri*, pl of *vir* man – more at VIRILE] – **decemviral** /-vərəl/ *adj*, **decemvirate** /-vərət/ *n*

decency /'deesənsi/ *n* **1** propriety, decorum **2** a standard of propriety – usu pl [DECENT + -CY]

decennial /di'senyəl, -ni·əl/ *adj* consisting of, lasting for, or occurring every 10 years – **decennial** *n*, **decennially** *adv*

decennium /di'senyəm, -ni·əm/ *n, pl* **decenniums, decennia** /-nyə, -ni·ə/ a period of 10 years [L, fr *decem* + *annus* year – more at ANNUAL]

decent /'dees(ə)nt/ *adj* **1** conforming to standards of propriety, good taste, or morality; *specif* clothed according to standards of propriety **2** free from obscenity **3** adequate, tolerable ⟨~ *wages*⟩ ⟨~ *housing*⟩ ⟨*grow a* ~ *beard*⟩ **4** *chiefly Br* obliging, considerate ⟨*jolly* ~ *of you*⟩ – infml [MF or L; MF, fr L *decent-, decens*, prp of *decēre* to be fitting; akin to L *decus* honour, *dignus* worthy, Gk *dokein* to seem, seem good] – **decently** *adv*

decentral·ization, -isation /dee,sentrəlie'zaysh(ə)n/ *n* **1** the distribution of functions and powers from a central authority to regional authorities, departments, etc **2** the redistribution of population and industry from urban centres to outlying areas – **decentralizationist** *n*

decentral·ize, -ise /,dee'sentrəliez/ *vt* to bring about the decentralization of ~ *vi* to undergo decentralization

deception /di'sepsh(ə)n/ *n* **1a** the act of deceiving **b** the fact or condition of being deceived **2** sthg that deceives; a trick [ME *decepcioun*, fr MF *deception*, fr LL *deception-, deceptio*, fr L *deceptus*, pp of *decipere* to deceive] – **deceptional** *adj*

deceptive /di'septiv/ *adj* tending or having power to deceive; misleading – **deceptively** *adv*, **deceptiveness** *n*

decerebrate /,dee'serəbrayt/ *vt* to remove or inactivate the brain of – **decerebrate** *adj*, **decerebration** /-'braysh(ə)n/ *n*

deci- /desi-, desə/ *comb form* one tenth part of (a specified unit) ⟨deci*litre*⟩ ☞ PHYSICS [F *déci-*, fr L *decimus* tenth, fr *decem* ten – more at TEN]

decibel /'desibel/ *n* **1** a unit for expressing the ratio of 2 amounts of electric or acoustic signal power equal to 10 times the common logarithm of this ratio **2** a unit for expressing the intensity of sounds on a scale from zero for the average least perceptible sound to about 130 for the average pain level [ISV *deci-* + *bel*]

decide /di'sied/ *vt* **1** to arrive at a solution that ends uncertainty or dispute about ⟨~ *the borderline issues*⟩ **2** to bring to a definitive end **3** to induce to come to a choice ~ *vi* to make a choice or judgment [ME *deciden*, fr MF *decider*, fr L *decidere*, lit., to cut off, fr *de-* + *caedere* to cut – more at CONCISE] – **decider** *n*, **decidable** *adj*, **decidability** /-də'biləti/ *n*

de'cided *adj* **1** unquestionable ⟨*a* ~ *advantage*⟩ **2** free from doubt or hesitation ⟨*a woman of* ~ *opinions*⟩ – **decidedly** *adv*, **decidedness** *n*

deciding /di'sieding/ *adj* DECISIVE 1

decidua /di'sidyoo·ə/ *n, pl* **deciduae** /-i/ a part of the lining of the womb that in women and other higher mammals undergoes special changes in preparation for pregnancy and is cast off during menstruation or while giving birth [NL, fr L, fem of *deciduus*] – **decidual** *adj*

deciduous /di'sidyoo·əs/ *adj* **1** (having parts) that fall off or are shed seasonally or at a particular stage in development ⟨~ *teeth*⟩ ⟨*a* ~ *tree*⟩ **2** ephemeral, transitory – fml [L *deciduus*, fr *decidere* to fall off, fr *de-* + *cadere* to fall – more at CHANCE] – **deciduously** *adv*, **deciduousness** *n*

decigram /'desi,gram/ *n* one tenth of a gram (.0035oz) ☞ UNIT [F *décigramme*, fr *déci-* + *gramme* gram]

decilitre /'desi,leetə/ *n* one tenth of a litre (about 0.18pt) ☞ UNIT

[1]**decimal** /'desiməl/ *adj* **1** numbered or proceeding by tens: **a** based on the number 10 **b** subdivided into units which are tenths, hundredths, etc of another unit **c** expressed in a decimal fraction **2** using a decimal system (e g of coinage) ⟨*when Britain went* ~⟩ [(assumed) NL *decimalis*, fr ML, of a tithe, fr L *decima* tithe – more at DIME] – **decimally** *adv*

[2]**decimal, ,decimal 'fraction** *n* a fraction that is expressed as a sum of integral multiples of powers of $^1/_{10}$ by writing a dot followed by 1 digit for the number of tenths, 1 digit for the number of hundredths, and so on (e g 0.25 = $^{25}/_{100}$) – compare COMMON FRACTION

decimal·ize, -ise /'desimə,liez/ *vt* to convert to a decimal system ⟨~ *currency*⟩ – **decimalization** /-lie'zaysh(ə)n/ *n*

,decimal 'point *n* the dot at the left of a decimal fraction

decimate /'desimayt/ *vt* **1** to kill every tenth man of (e g mutinous soldiers) **2** to destroy a large part of [L *decimatus*, pp of *decimare*, fr *decimus* tenth, fr *decem* ten] – **decimation** /-'mayshən/ *n*

decimetre /'desi,meetə/ *n* one tenth of a metre (about 3.9in)

decipher /di'siefə/ *vt* **1a** to convert into intelligible form **b** to decode **2** to make out the meaning of despite obscurity [*de-* + *cipher*] – **decipherable** *adj*, **decipherer** *n*, **decipherment** *n*

decision /di'sizh(ə)n/ *n* **1a** deciding **b** a conclusion arrived at after consideration **2** a report of a conclusion ⟨*the* ~ *appeared in all the newspapers*⟩ **3** promptness and firmness in deciding ⟨*a man of courage and* ~⟩ [MF, fr L *decision-, decisio*, fr *decisus*, pp of *decidere* to decide] – **decisional** *adj*

decisive /di'siesiv/ *adj* **1** having the power or quality of deciding; conclusive **2** marked by or indicative of determination or firmness; resolute **3** unmistakable, unquestionable ⟨*a* ~ *victory*⟩ – **decisively** *adv*, **decisiveness** *n*

[1]**deck** /dek/ *n* **1** a platform in a ship serving usu as a structural element and forming the floor for its compartments **2** sthg resembling the deck of a ship: e g **a** a level or floor of a bus with more than 1 floor **b** the roadway of a bridge **c** TAPE DECK **d** RECORD DECK **3** *NAm* a pack of playing cards **4** *the* ground – infml; chiefly in *hit the deck* [prob modif of (assumed) LG *verdeck* (whence G *verdeck*), fr (assumed) MLG *vordeck*, fr MLG *vordecken* to cover, fr *vor-* (akin to OHG *fur-* for-) + *decken* to cover] – **decked** *adj*

[2]**deck** *vt* to array, decorate – often + *out* [D *dekken* to cover; akin to OHG *decken* to cover]

'deck ,chair *n* an adjustable folding chair made of canvas stretched over a wooden frame

decker /'dekə/ *n* sthg with a deck or a specified number of levels, floors, or layers – often in combination ⟨*double*-decker *bus*⟩

'deck,hand /-,hand/ *n* a seaman who performs manual duties

'deck,house /-,hows/ *n* a cabin built on a ship's upper deck

decking /'deking/ *n* a deck; *also* material for a deck

deckle /'dekl/ *n* a part of a paper-making machine that determines the width of the web [G *deckel*, lit., cover, fr *decken* to cover, fr OHG]

deckle edge *n* a rough untrimmed edge of paper – **deckle-edged** /,dekl 'ejd/ *adj*

'deck ,tennis *n* a game in which players toss a quoit back and forth over a net stretched across a small court [fr its being played chiefly on the decks of ocean liners]

declaim /di'klaym/ *vi* **1** to speak rhetorically **2** to speak pompously or bombastically ~ *vt* to deliver rhetorically; *specif* to recite in elocution [ME *declamen*, fr L *declamare*, fr *de-* + *clamare* to cry out; akin to L *calare* to call – more at [1]LOW] – **declaimer** *n*, **declamation** /,deklə'maysh(ə)n/ *n*

declamatory /di'klamət(ə)ri/ *adj* of or marked by declamation [L *declamatorius*, fr *declamatus*, pp of *declamare*]

declarant /di'kleərənt/ *n* sby who makes a legal declaration [DECLARE + -ANT]

declaration /,deklə'raysh(ə)n/ *n* **1** sthg declared **2** a document containing such a declaration [DECLARE + -ATION]

declarative /di'klarətiv/ *adj* **1** constituting a statement rather than a command or a question ⟨~ *sentence*⟩ **2** declaratory – **declaratively** *adv*

declaratory /di'klarət(ə)ri/ *adj* serving to declare, set forth, or explain

declare /di'kleə/ *vt* **1** to make known formally or explicitly **2** to make evident; show **3** to state emphatically; affirm ⟨~s *his innocence*⟩ **4** to make a full statement of (one's taxable or dutiable income or property) **5a** to announce (e g a trump suit) in a card game **b** to meld (a combination of playing cards) in canasta, rummy, etc ~ *vi* **1** to make a declaration **2** to avow one's support **3** *of a captain or team* to announce one's decision to end one's side's innings in cricket before all the batsmen are out [ME *declaren*, fr MF *declarer*, fr L *declarare*, fr *de-* + *clarare* to make clear, fr *clarus* clear – more at CLEAR] – **declarable** *adj* – **declare war** to commence hostilities; *specif* to make a formal declaration of intention to go to war

declarer /di'kleərə/ *n* the player in bridge who was the first on his/her side to bid the trump suit and plays both his/her own hand and that of the dummy [DECLARE + [2]-ER]

déclassé /,day'klasay/ *adj* fallen or lowered in class, rank, etc [F, fr pp of *déclasser* to remove from a class]

declassify /,dee'klasifie/ *vt* to declare (e g information) no longer secret

declension /di'klensh(ə)n/ *n* **1** a schematic arrangement of noun, adjective, or pronoun inflections **2** a class of nouns or adjectives having the same type of inflectional forms [prob alter. of earlier *declenson*, modif of MF *declinaison*, fr LL *declination-, declinatio*, fr L, grammatical inflection, turning aside, fr *declinatus*, pp of *declinare* to inflect, turn aside] – **declensional** *adj*

declination /ˌdekli'naysh(ə)n/ *n* **1** angular distance (e g of a star) N or S from the celestial equator **2** a formal refusal **3** the angle between a compass needle and the geographical meridian, equal to the difference between magnetic and true north [ME *declinacioun*, fr MF *declination*, fr L *declination-, declinatio* turning aside, altitude of the pole] – **declinational** *adj*

[1]**decline** /di'klien/ *vi* **1a** to slope downwards; descend **b** to bend down; droop **2a** *of a celestial body* to sink towards setting **b** to draw towards a close; wane **3** to refuse ~ *vt* **1** to give in prescribed order the grammatical forms of (a noun, pronoun, or adjective) **2a** to refuse to undertake, engage in, or comply with ⟨~ *battle*⟩ **b** to refuse courteously ⟨~ *an invitation*⟩ [ME *declinen*, fr MF *decliner*, fr L *declinare* to turn aside, inflect, fr *de-* + *clinare* to incline – more at [1]LEAN] – **declinable** *adj*

[2]**decline** *n* **1** the process of declining: **a** a gradual physical or mental decay **b** a change to a lower state or level **2** the period during which sthg is approaching its end **3** a downward slope

declinometer /ˌdekli'nomitə/ *n* an instrument for measuring astronomical or magnetic declination [ISV *declino-* (fr *declination*) + *-meter*]

declivity /di'klivəti/ *n* **1** downward inclination **2** a descending slope *USE* fml [L *declivitat-, declivitas*, fr *declivis* sloping down, fr *de-* + *clivus* slope, hill; akin to L *clinare*] – **declivitous** *adj*

decoct /di'kokt/ *vt* **1** to extract the essence of by boiling **2** to boil down; concentrate [L *decoctus*, pp of *decoquere*, fr *de-* + *coquere* to cook – more at COOK] – **decoction** /di'koksh(ə)n/ *n*

decode /ˌdee'kohd/ *vt* to convert (a coded message) into intelligible language – **decoder** *n*

decoke /ˌdee'kohk/ *vt, Br* to remove carbon deposits from (e g an internal-combustion engine) – **decoke** *n*

décolletage /ˌdaykol'tahzh (*Fr* dekɔltaːʒ)/ *n* the low-cut neckline of a dress [F, action of cutting or wearing a low neckline, fr *décolleter*]

décolleté /ˌdaykol'tay, -'-- (*Fr* dekɔlte)/ *adj* **1** wearing a strapless or low-necked dress **2** low-necked [F, fr pp of *décolleter* to give a low neckline to, fr *dé-* de- + *collet* collar, fr OF *colet*, fr *col* collar, neck, fr L *collum* neck]

decolon·ize, -ise /ˌdee'koləniez/ *vt* to free from colonial status – **decolonization** *n*

decolor·ize, -ise, *chiefly Br* **decolour·ize, -ise** /ˌdee'kuləriez/ *vt* to remove colour from – **decolorizer** *n*, **decolorization** /-rie'zaysh(ə)n/ *n*

decommission /ˌdeekə'mish(ə)n/ *vt* to remove (a ship) from service

decompose /ˌdeekəm'pohz/ *vt vt* **1** to separate into constituent parts, elements, atoms, etc **2** to rot ~ *vi* to undergo chemical breakdown; decay, rot ☞ FOOD [F *décomposer*, fr *dé-* de + *composer* to compose] – **decomposer** *n*, **decomposable** *adj*, **decomposability** /-zə'biləti/ *n*, **decomposition** /ˌdeekompə'zish(ə)n/ *n*, **decompositional** *adj*

decompress /ˌdeekəm'pres/ *vt* to release from pressure or compression – **decompression** /-'presh(ə)n/ *n*

ˌ**decom'pression** ˌ**sickness** *n* CAISSON DISEASE

decongestant /ˌdeekən'jest(ə)nt/ *n* sthg (e g a drug) that relieves congestion

decontaminate /ˌdeekən'taminayt/ *vt* to rid of contamination (e g radioactivity) – **decontamination** /-'naysh(ə)n/ *n*

decor, décor /'dekaw/ *n* **1** the style and layout of interior decoration and furnishings **2** a stage setting [F *décor*, fr *décorer* to decorate, fr L *decorare*]

decorate /'dekərayt/ *vt* **1a** to add sthg ornamental to **b** to apply new coverings of paint, wallpaper, etc to the interior or exterior surfaces of **2** to award a mark of honour to [L *decoratus*, pp of *decorare*, fr *decor-, decus* ornament, honour – more at DECENT]

'**Decorated** *adj* of a Gothic style of architecture prevalent in Britain from the late 13th to the mid 14th c characterized by ogee arches and elaborate ornamentation ☞ CHURCH

decoration /ˌdekə'raysh(ə)n/ *n* **1** an ornament ⟨*Christmas* ~s⟩ **2** a badge of honour (e g a medal) [DECORATE + -ION]

decorative /'dek(ə)rətiv/ *adj* serving to decorate; *esp* purely ornamental rather than functional – **decoratively** *adv*, **decorativeness** *n*

decorator /'dekəˌraytə/ *n* one who designs or executes interior decoration and furnishings [DECORATE + [1]-OR]

decorous /'dekərəs/ *adj* marked by propriety and good taste; correct [L *decorus*, fr *decor* beauty, grace; akin to L *decēre* to be fitting – more at DECENT] – **decorously** *adv*, **decorousness** *n*

decorticate /ˌdee'kawtikayt/ *vt* **1** to peel the husk, bark or other outer covering from **2** to remove (part of) the cortex from (e g the brain) [L *decorticatus*, pp of *decorticare* to remove the bark from, fr *de-* + *cortic-, cortex* bark – more at CUIRASS] – **decorticator** *n*, **decortication** /-'kaysh(ə)n/ *n*

decorum /di'kawrəm/ *n* propriety and good taste in conduct or appearance [L, fr neut of *decorus*]

decoupage, découpage /ˌdaykooh'pahzh (*Fr* dekupaːʒ)/ *n* the art of applying decorative cutouts (e g of paper) which are then coated with varnish, lacquer, etc [F *découpage*, lit., act of cutting out, fr MF, fr *decouper* to cut out, fr *de-* + *couper* to cut – more at [3]COPE]

decouple /ˌdee'kupl/ *vt, chiefly Br* to isolate (e g systems, esp oscillating electrical systems) one from another so that they behave independently

[1]**decoy** /'deekoy, di'koy/ *n* **1** a pond into which wild fowl are lured for capture **2** sthg used to lure or lead another into a trap **3** sby or sthg used to distract or divert the attention (e g of an enemy) [prob fr D *de kooi*, lit., the cage, fr *de* the + *kooi* cage, fr L *cavea* – more at CAGE]

[2]**decoy** *vt* to lure or entice (as if) by a decoy

[1]**decrease** /di'krees/ *vb* to (cause to) grow progressively less (e g in size, amount, number, or intensity) [ME *decreessen*, fr (assumed) AF *decreistre*, fr L *decrescere*, fr *de-* + *crescere* to grow – more at CRESCENT] – **decreasingly** *adv*

[2]**decrease** /'deeˌkrees, di'krees/ *n* **1** the process of decreasing **2** the amount by which sthg decreases

[1]**decree** /di'kree/ *n* **1** an order usu having legal force **2a** a religious rule made by a council or titular head **b** a foreordaining will **3** a judicial decision, esp in an equity, probate, or divorce court [ME, fr MF *decré*, fr L *decretum*, fr neut of *decretus*, pp of *decernere* to

decide, fr *de-* + *cernere* to sift, decide – more at CERTAIN]

[2]**decree** *vt* to command or impose by decree ⟨~ *an amnesty*⟩ – **decreer** /di'kree·ə/ *n*

decree nisi /di,kree 'neezi, -zie, 'niesie/ *n* a provisional decree of divorce that is made absolute after a fixed period unless cause to the contrary is shown [L *nisi* unless, fr *ne-* not + *si* if]

decrepit /di'krepit/ *adj* **1** wasted and weakened (as if) by the infirmities of old age **2a** worn-out **b** fallen into ruin or disrepair [ME, fr MF, fr L *decrepitus*, fr *de-* + *crepitus*, pp of *crepare* to crack, creak] – **decrepitly** *adv*, **decrepitude** /-tyoohd/ *n*

decrepitate /di'krepitayt/ *vt* to roast or calcine (e g a salt) so as to cause crackling or until crackling stops ~ *vi* to become decrepitated [prob fr (assumed) NL *decrepitatus*, pp of *decrepitare*, fr L *de-* + *crepitare* to crackle – more at CREPITATE] – **decrepitation** /-'taysh(ə)n/ *n*

decrescendo /,deekrə'shendoh/ *n, adv, or adj, pl* **decrescendos** (a) diminuendo [It, lit., decreasing, fr L *decrescendum*, gerund of *decrescere*]

decrescent /di'kres(ə)nt/ *adj* decreasing, waning [alter. of earlier *decressant*, prob fr AF, prp of (assumed) AF *decreistre* to decrease]

decretal /di'kreetl/ *n* an authoritative papal decision on a point of canon law [ME *decretale*, fr MF, fr LL *decretalis* of a decree, fr L *decretum* decree]

decretory /di'kreet(ə)ri/ *adj* relating to or fixed by a decree or decision [L *decretorius*, fr *decretus*]

decry /di'krie/ *vt* **1** to depreciate (e g a coin) officially or publicly **2** to express strong disapproval of [F *décrier*, fr OF *descrier*, fr *des-* de- + *crier* to cry] – **decrier** *n*

decumbent /di'kumb(ə)nt/ *adj, of a plant* lying on the ground except for a raised apex or extremity [L *decumbent-*, *decumbens*, prp of *decumbere* to lie down, fr *de-* + *-cumbere* to lie down – more at SUCCUMB]

decuple /'dekyoopl/ *adj* **1** tenfold **2** taken in groups of 10 [F *décuple*, fr MF, fr LL *decuplus*, fr L *decem* ten + *-plus* multiplied by – more at TEN, DOUBLE]

decussate /di'kusayt, -sət/ *adj, of leaves* arranged in pairs each at right angles to the next pair above or below ☞ PLANT [L *decussatus*, pp of *decussare* to intersect, fr *decussis* Roman numeral X, intersection, irreg fr *decem* ten + *ass-*, *as* unit, copper coin – more at ACE] – **decussately** *adv*

decussation /,deekə'saysh(ə)n/ *n* a crossed tract of nerve fibres passing between parts of the body on opposite sides of the brain or spinal cord; a commissure [DECUSSATE + -ION]

dedicate /'dedikayt/ *vt* **1** CONSECRATE 2A **2a** to set apart to a definite use **b** to assign permanently to a goal or way of life **3** to inscribe or address (a book, song, etc) to somebody or something as a mark of esteem or affection ⟨~ *a book to a friend*⟩ [ME, fr L *dedicatus*, pp of *dedicare* to affirm, dedicate, fr *de-* + *dicare* to proclaim, dedicate] – **dedicator** *n*, **dedicatee** /,dedikə'tee/ *n*

'**dedicated** *adj* **1** devoted to a cause, ideal, or purpose; zealous ⟨*a* ~ *scholar*⟩ **2** given over to a particular purpose ⟨*a* ~ *process control computer*⟩ – **dedicatedly** *adv*

dedication /,dedi'kaysh(ə)n/ *n* **1** a devoting or setting aside for a particular, specif religious, purpose **2** a phrase or sentence that dedicates **3** self-sacrificing devotion [DEDICATE + -ION] – **dedicative** /'dedikətiv/ *adj*, **dedicatory** /'dedikət(ə)ri/ *adj*

deduce /di'dyoohs/ *vt* to establish by deduction; *specif* to infer from a general principle – compare INDUCE 3 [L *deducere*, lit., to lead away, fr *de-* + *ducere* to lead – more at TOW] – **deducible** /-səbl/ *adj*

deduct /di'dukt/ *vt* to subtract (an amount) from a total [L *deductus*, pp of *deducere*] – **deductible** *adj*, **deductibility** /-tə'biləti/ *n*

deduction /di'duksh(ə)n/ *n* **1a** an act of taking away **b** sthg that is or may be subtracted **2** (the deriving of) a necessary conclusion reached by reasoning; *specif* an inference in which a particular conclusion is drawn from general premises

deductive /di'duktiv/ *adj* **1** of or employing mathematical or logical deduction **2** capable of being deduced from premises; inferential – **deductively** *adv*

[1]**deed** /deed/ *n* **1** sthg that is done ⟨*evil* ~s⟩ **2** an illustrious act or action; a feat, exploit **3** the act of performing ⟨*never mistake the word for the* ~⟩ **4** a signed (and sealed) written document containing some legal transfer, bargain, or contract [ME *dede*, fr OE *dǣd*; akin to OE *dōn* to do] – **deedless** *adj*

[2]**deed** *vt, NAm* to convey or transfer by deed

'**deed ,poll** *n, pl* **deeds poll** a deed made and executed by 1 party only ['*deed* + *poll*, adj (having the edges cut even rather than indented), fr [2]*poll*]

deejay /'dee,jay/ *n* DISC JOCKEY [*d*isc *j*ockey]

deem /deem/ *vt* to judge, consider – fml ⟨*would* ~ *it an honour*⟩ [ME *demen*, fr OE *dēman*; akin to OHG *tuomen* to judge, OE *dōm* judgment]

[1]**deep** /deep/ *adj* **1** extending far from some surface or area: e g **a** extending far downwards ⟨*a* ~ *well*⟩ **b** (extending) far from the surface of the body **c** extending well back from a front surface ⟨*a* ~ *cupboard*⟩ **d(1)** near the outer limits of the playing area or far from an attacking movement **(2)** of or occupying a fielding position in cricket far from the batsman ☞ SPORT **2** having a specified extension in an implied direction ⟨*shelf 20 inches* ~⟩ ⟨*cars parked 3-*deep⟩ **3a** difficult to understand ⟨*may be true, but it's too* ~ *for me*⟩ **b** capable of profound thought ⟨*a* ~ *thinker*⟩ **c** engrossed, involved ⟨*a man* ~ *in debt*⟩ **d** intense, extreme ⟨~ *sleep*⟩ ⟨~ *sin*⟩ **4a** *of a colour* high in saturation and low in lightness **b** having a low musical pitch or pitch range **5** remote in time or space [ME, fr OE *dēop*; akin to OHG *tiof* deep, OE *dyppan* to dip – more at DIP] – **deeply** *adv*, **deepness** *n* – **in deep water** in difficulty or distress; unable to manage

[2]**deep** *adv* **1a(1)** to a great depth ⟨*still waters run* ~⟩ **(2)** deep to a specified degree – usu in combination ⟨*ankle-*deep *in mud*⟩ **b** well within the boundaries ⟨*a house* ~ *in the woods*⟩ **2** far on; late ⟨*danced* ~ *into the night*⟩ **3** in a deep position ⟨*the wingers were playing* ~⟩ **4** far back in space or time ⟨*had its roots* ~ *in the Dark Ages*⟩

[3]**deep** *n* **1** a vast or immeasurable extent; an abyss **2a** *the* sea **b** any of the very deep portions of a body of water, esp the sea

deepen /'deep(ə)n/ *vb* to make or become deeper or more profound

,**deep-'freeze** *vt* **-froze** /frohz/; **-frozen** /'frohz(ə)n/ to freeze or store (e g food) in a freezer

deep freeze *n* a freezer

,deep-'fry *vt* to fry (food) by complete immersion in hot fat or oil – **deep-fryer** *n*

,deep 'kiss *n* FRENCH KISS

,deep-'rooted *adj* firmly established ⟨*a* ~ *loyalty*⟩

,deep-'seated *adj* **1** situated far below the surface ⟨*a* ~ *inflammation*⟩ **2** firmly established ⟨*a* ~ *tradition*⟩

'deep ,structure *n* a formal representation of the underlying meaning of a sentence

deer /diə/ *n, pl* **deer** *also* **deers** **1** any of several ruminant mammals of which most of the males and some of the females bear antlers **2** *archaic* an animal; *esp* a small mammal [ME, deer, animal, fr OE *dēor* beast; akin to OHG *tior* wild animal, Skt *dhvaṁsati* he perishes]

'deer,hound /-,hownd/ *n* (any of) a breed of tall dogs like but larger than the greyhound

'deer,stalker /-,stawkə/ *n* a close-fitting hat with peaks at the front and the back and flaps that may be folded down as coverings for ears ☞ GARMENT [fr its suitability to be worn by a person stalking deer]

deface /di'fays/ *vt* to mar the external appearance of [ME *defacen*, fr MF *desfacier*, fr OF, fr *des-* de- + *face*] – **defacement** *n*, **defacer** *n*

[1]**de facto** /di 'faktoh, day/ *adv* in reality; actually [NL]

[2]**de facto** *adj* existing in fact; effective ⟨*a* ~ *state of war*⟩ – compare DE JURE

defaecate /'defəkayt/ *vb, chiefly Br* to defecate – **defaecation** /-'kaysh(ə)n/ *n*

defalcate /'deefal,kayt/ *vi* to embezzle – fml [ML *defalcatus*, pp of *defalcare*, fr L *de-* + *falc-, falx* sickle] – **defalcator** *n*, **defalcation** /-fal'kaysh(ə)n/ *n*

defame /di'faym/ *vt* to injure the reputation of by libel or slander [ME *diffamen, defamen*, fr MF & L; ME *diffamen*, fr MF *diffamer*, fr L *diffamare*, fr *dis-* + *fama* fame; ME *defamen*, fr MF *defamer*, fr ML *defamare*, fr L *de-* + *fama*] – **defamation** /,defə'maysh(ə)n/ *n*, **defamatory** /di'famətri/ *adj*, **defamer** *n*

defat /,dee'fat/ *vt* to remove fat from

[1]**default** /di'fawlt/ *n* failure to act, pay, appear, or compete [ME *defaute, defaulte*, fr OF *defaute*, fr (assumed) VL *defallita*, fr fem of *defallitus*, pp of *defallere* to be lacking, fail, fr L *de-* + *fallere* to deceive] – **in default of** in the absence of

[2]**default** *vi* to fail to meet an esp financial obligation ~ *vt* **1** to fail to perform, pay, or make good **2** to declare to be in default – **defaulter** *n*

defeasance /di'feez(ə)ns/ *n* a rendering null or void [ME *defesance*, fr AF, fr OF *deffesant*, prp of *deffaire*]

defeasible /di'feezəbl/ *adj* capable of being annulled – **defeasibility** /-zə'biləti/ *n*

[1]**defeat** /di'feet/ *vt* **1a** to nullify ⟨~ *an estate*⟩ **b** to frustrate ⟨~ *a hope*⟩ **2** to win victory over ⟨~ *the opposing team*⟩ [ME *deffeten*, fr MF *deffait*, pp of *deffaire* to destroy, fr ML *disfacere*, fr L *dis-* + *facere* to do – more at [1]DO]

[2]**defeat** *n* **1** an overthrow, esp of an army in battle **2** the loss of a contest

defeatism /di'feetiz(ə)m/ *n* acceptance of or resignation to defeat – **defeatist** *n or adj*

defecate, *Br also* **defaecate** /'defəkayt/ *vb* to discharge (esp faeces) from the bowels [L *defaecatus*, pp of *defaecare*, fr *de-* + *faec-, faex* dregs] – **defecation** /-'kaysh(ə)n/ *n*

[1]**defect** /'deefekt/ *n* **1** an imperfection that impairs worth or usefulness ⟨*a hearing* ~⟩ **2** an irregularity (e g a foreign atom) in the lattice of a crystal [ME *defaicte*, fr MF *defect*, fr L *defectus* lack, fr *defectus*, pp of *deficere* to desert, fail, fr *de-* + *facere*]

[2]**defect** /di'fekt/ *vi* to desert a cause or party, often in order to espouse another [L *defectus*, pp] – **defector** *n*, **defection** /di'feksh(ə)n/ *n*

[1]**defective** /di'fektiv/ *adj* **1** lacking sthg essential; faulty ⟨*a* ~ *pane of glass*⟩ ⟨~ *eyesight*⟩ **2** lacking 1 or more of the usual grammatical inflections – **defectively** *adv*, **defectiveness** *n*

[2]**defective** *n* one who is subnormal physically or mentally

defence, *NAm chiefly* **defense** /di'fens/ *n* **1** the act or action of defending **2a** a means or method of defending; *also, pl* a defensive structure **b** an argument in support or justification **c** a defendant's denial, answer, or strategy **3** *sing or pl in constr* **a** a defending party or group (e g in a court of law) **b** defensive players, acts, or moves in a game or sport **4** the military resources of a country ⟨~ *budget*⟩ [ME, fr OF, fr (assumed) VL *defensa*, fr L, fem of *defensus*, pp of *defendere*] – **defenceless** *adj*, **defencelessly** *adv*, **defencelessness** *n*

de'fence ,mechanism *n* an (unconscious) mental process (e g projection or repression) that prevents the entry of unacceptable or painful thoughts into consciousness

defend /di'fend/ *vt* **1a** to protect from attack **b** to maintain by argument in the face of opposition or criticism **c** to attempt to prevent an opponent from scoring in (e g a goal) **2** to act as legal representative in court for ~ *vi* **1** to take action against attack or challenge **2** to play or be in defence [ME *defenden*, fr OF *defendre*, fr L *defendere*, fr *de-* + *-fendere* to strike; akin to OE *gūth* battle, war, Gk *theinein* to strike] – **defendable** *adj*

defendant /di'fend(ə)nt/ *n* a person, company, etc against whom a criminal charge or civil claim is made – compare PLAINTIFF [DEFEND + -ANT]

defender /di'fendə/ *n* sby who plays in a defensive position in a sport ☞ SPORT [DEFEND + [2]-ER]

defensible /di'fensəbl/ *adj* capable of being defended [ME, fr LL *defensibilis*, fr *defensus*] – **defensibly** *adv*, **defensibility** /-sə'biləti/ *n*

[1]**defensive** /di'fensiv/ *adj* **1** serving to defend **2a** devoted to resisting or preventing aggression or attack; *also* disposed (as if) to ward off expected criticism or critical inquiry **b** of or relating to the attempt to keep an opponent from scoring – **defensively** *adv*, **defensiveness** *n*

[2]**defensive** *n* – **on the defensive** being prepared for expected aggression, attack, or criticism

[1]**defer** /di'fuh/ *vt* **-rr-** to delay; PUT OFF 2a [ME *deferren, differren*, fr MF *differer*, fr L *differre* to postpone, be different – more at DIFFER] – **deferment** *n*, **deferrable** *adj*, **deferral** *n*, **deferrer** *n*

[2]**defer** *vi* **-rr-** *vi* to submit *to* another's opinion, usu through deference or respect [ME *deferren, differren*, fr MF *deferer, defferer*, fr LL *deferre*, fr L, to bring down, bring, fr *de-* + *ferre* to carry – more at [2]BEAR]

deference /'def(ə)rəns/ *n* respect and esteem due a superior or an elder [[2]DEFER + -ENCE] – **in deference to** because of respect for

deferential /ˌdefəˈrensh(ə)l/ *adj* showing or expressing deference ⟨~ *attention*⟩ [L *deferent-, deferens,* prp of *deferre*] – **deferentially** *adv*

deferred /diˈfuhd/ *adj* withheld for or until a stated time ⟨*a* ~ *payment*⟩

deferred share *n, chiefly Br* a fixed-dividend share that ranks after an ordinary share in the claim on dividends – compare PREFERENCE SHARE, ORDINARY SHARE

defiance /diˈfie·əns/ *n* a disposition to resist; contempt of opposition [DEFY + -ANCE] – **defiant** *adj,* **defiantly** *adv* – **in defiance of** despite; CONTRARY TO

defibrillate /ˌdeeˈfibrilayt/ *vt* to restore the normal regular beating and rhythm of (a heart) – **defibrillator** /-ˌlaytə/ *n,* **defibrillatory** /-lətri/ *adj,* **defibrillative** /-lətiv/ *adj,* **defibrillation** /-ˈlaysh(ə)n/ *n*

deficiency /diˈfish(ə)nsi/ *n* **1** being deficient **2** a shortage of substances necessary to health

deficiency disease *n* a disease (e g scurvy) caused by a lack of essential vitamins, minerals, etc in the diet

deficiency payment *n* a payment made to farmers by the British government until Britain joined the EEC in 1973 to make up the difference between the market price for agricultural products and the guaranteed minimum price

deficient /diˈfish(ə)nt/ *adj* **1** lacking in some necessary quality or element **2** not up to a normal standard or complement [L *deficient-, deficiens,* prp of *deficere* to be wanting – more at [1]DEFECT] – **deficiently** *adv*

deficit /ˈdefəsit/ *n* **1** a deficiency in amount or quality **2** an excess of expenditure over revenue [F *déficit,* fr L *deficit* it is wanting, fr *deficere*]

de fide /di ˈfiedi/ *adj or adv* (held) as an obligatory article of faith [NL, from faith]

[1]**defilade** /ˌdefiˈlayd/ *vt* to arrange (fortifications) so as to protect from enemy fire [prob fr *de-* + *-filade* (as in *enfilade*)]

[2]**defilade** *n* the act or process of defilading

[1]**defile** /diˈfiel/ *vt* **1** to make unclean or impure **2** to deprive of virginity [ME *defilen,* alter. of *defoulen* to trample, defile, fr OF *defouler* to trample, fr *de-* + *fouler* to trample, lit., to full – more at [5]FULL] – **defilement** *n,* **defiler** *n*

[2]**defile** *vi* to march off in a file [F *défiler,* fr *dé-* de- + *filer* to move in a column – more at [5]FILE]

[3]**defile** *n* a narrow passage or gorge [F *défilé,* fr pp of *défiler*]

define /diˈfien/ *vt* **1a** to fix or mark the limits of; demarcate **b** to make clear or precise in outline ⟨*the issues aren't too well* ~d⟩ **2a** to be the essential quality or qualities of; identify ⟨*whatever* ~s *us as human*⟩ **b** to set forth the meaning of ⟨~ *a word*⟩ ~ *vi* to make a definition [ME *definen,* fr MF & L; MF *definer,* fr L *definire,* fr *de-* + *finire* to limit, end, fr *finis* boundary, end] – **definable** *adj,* **definer** *n*

defining /diˈfiening/ *adj* RESTRICTIVE 2

definite /ˈdefinət/ *adj* **1** having distinct or certain limits **2a** free of all ambiguity, uncertainty, or obscurity **b** unquestionable, decided ⟨*a* ~ *advantage*⟩ **3** designating an identified or immediately identifiable person or thing ⟨*the* ~ *article* the⟩ [L *definitus,* pp of *definire*] – **definitely** *adv,* **definiteness** *n*

definite integral *n* a number that is the difference between the values of the indefinite integral of a given function at the limits of a given interval ☞ SYMBOL

definition /ˌdefiˈnish(ə)n/ *n* **1a** a word or phrase expressing the essential nature of a person, word, or thing; a meaning **b** the action or process of stating such a meaning **2a** the action or power of making definite and clear **b(1)** distinctness of outline or detail (e g in a photograph) **(2)** clarity, esp of musical sound in reproduction [DEFINITE + -ION] – **definitional** *adj*

definitive /diˈfinətiv/ *adj* **1** serving to provide a final solution ⟨*a* ~ *victory*⟩ **2** authoritative and apparently exhaustive ⟨*a* ~ *biography*⟩ **3** *of a postage stamp* issued as one of the normal stamps of the country or territory of use – **definitively** *adv,* **definitiveness** *n*

deflagrate /ˈdefləgrayt/ *vb* to (cause to) burn rapidly with sparks and intense heat – compare DETONATE [L *deflagratus,* pp of *deflagrare* to burn down, fr *de-* + *flagrare* to burn – more at BLACK] – **deflagration** /-ˈgraysh(ə)n/ *n*

deflate /diˈflayt, ˌdee-/ *vt* **1** to release air or gas from **2a** to reduce in size or importance **b** to reduce in self-confidence or self-importance, esp suddenly **3** to reduce (a price level) or cause (the availability of credit or the economy) to contract ~ *vi* to lose firmness (as if) through the escape of contained gas [*de-* + *-flate* (as in *inflate*)] – **deflator** *n*

deflation /diˈflaysh(ə)n, ˌdee-/ *n* **1a** a contraction in the volume of available money and credit, and thus in the economy, esp as a result of government policy **b** a decline in the general level of prices **2** the erosion of soil by the wind [DEFLATE + -ION] – **deflationary** *adj*

deflect /diˈflekt/ *vb* to turn from a straight course or fixed direction [L *deflectere* to bend down, turn aside, fr *de-* + *flectere* to bend] – **deflective** *adj,* **deflector** *n*

deflection, *Br also* **deflexion** /diˈfleksh(ə)n/ *n* (the amount or degree of) deflecting

defloration /ˌdeflawˈraysh(ə)n, ˌdee-/ *n* deflowering or being deflowered [ME *defloracioun,* fr LL *defloration-, defloratio,* fr *defloratus,* pp of *deflorare*]

deflower /ˌdeeˈflowə/ *vt* to deprive of virginity; ravish [ME *deflouren,* fr MF or LL; MF *deflorer,* fr LL *deflorare,* fr L *de-* + *flor-, flos* flower] – **deflowerer** *n*

defocus /ˌdeeˈfohkəs/ *vb* **-ss-, -s-** *vb* to put or go out of focus

defog /ˌdeeˈfog/ *vt* **-gg-** *NAm* to demist – **defogger** *n*

defoliant /ˌdeeˈfohli·ənt/ *n* a chemical applied to plants to cause the leaves to drop off prematurely [*defoliate* (fr LL *defoliatus,* pp of *defoliare* to strip of leaves, fr *de-* + *folium* leaf) + *-ant*] – **defoliate** *vt or adj,* **defoliation** *n,* **defoliator** *n*

deforest /diˈforist/ *vt* to clear of forests – **deforestation** /-ˈstay sh(ə)n/ *n*

deform /diˈfawm/ *vt* **1** to spoil the form or appearance of **2** to make hideous or monstrous **3** to alter the shape of by stress ~ *vi* to become misshapen or changed in shape [ME *deformen,* fr MF or L; MF *deformer,* fr L *deformare,* fr *de-* + *formare* to form, fr *forma* form] – **deformation** /ˌdefəˈmaysh(ə)n/ *n,* **deformational** *adj*

deformed /diˈfawmd/ *adj* distorted or unshapely in form

deformity /diˈfawməti/ *n* **1** the state of being

Defence against predators

Animals are equipped with a variety of protective adaptations designed to prevent them from being eaten by other animals. Camouflage, disguise, noxiousness, and mimicry are primary defence mechanisms that operate regardless of whether a predator is present. Bluffs, threats, and group cooperation are secondary defence mechanisms, being brought into effect when a predator is encountered. However, the most common secondary defence mechanism is flight; most animals will choose to flee rather than stand and fight.

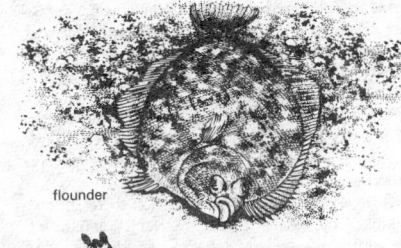

flounder

Camouflage

The most elaborate camouflage is disruptive coloration: the stripes running across the zebra's body break up its outline, thus enabling it to merge into its surroundings. Many species change their coloration to conform to the character of their environment. Moulting enables the rock ptarmigan to change its white winter plumage for patchy brown plumage that blends with the partially exposed ground when the snow melts in the spring. The flounder has sensitive colour vision with which it registers the subtlest colour gradations, and is thus able to reproduce the colour and texture of the sea bottom.

zebra

rock ptarmigan in spring and winter plumage

Disguise

Lying disguised as an inanimate, inedible object is an effective means of escaping capture by a predator. The stick insect can resemble a twig growing from a branch, by lying head downwards and extending its body outwards, at an angle, from the branch.

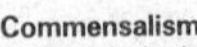

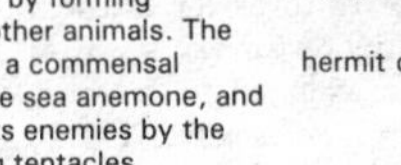

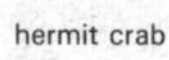

Commensalism

Some relatively defenceless species protect themselves by forming associations with other animals. The hermit crab lives in a commensal association with the sea anemone, and is protected from its enemies by the anemone's stinging tentacles.

Noxiousness
Many animals are vividly coloured with red, yellow, orange, black, or white to warn predators that they are poisonous or have a disagreeable means of retaliation. The European salamander's black and yellow coloration advertises the poisons secreted from skin glands on the surface of its body. The orange and black Monarch butterfly contains poisons from milkweed plants on which the caterpillar feeds. The skunk's black and white stripes warn attackers of the putrid-smelling spray that it ejects from its anal glands when threatened.

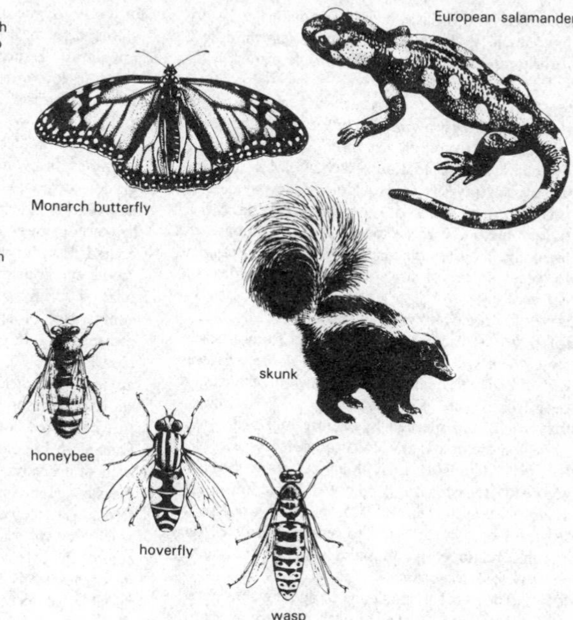

Mimicry
Numerous non-noxious species mimic the appearance of unpalatable vividly coloured animals to escape the attention of predators. The harmless, yellow and black striped hoverfly resembles the honeybee and the wasp, and even buzzes in a threatening manner when disturbed, thus protecting itself from attack.

Bluffs and threats
Animals under attack often try to frighten the predator away by bluffs or threats. Birds ruffle their feathers in order to appear larger and more formidable. The eyed hawkmoth reveals huge false eyes on its underwings to scare attackers. Many predators will not eat carrion, so the grass snake, when threatened, feigns death by rolling on its back with mouth open and tongue lolling.

Group cooperation
Some herds of animals, instead of scattering when danger threatens, work together to fend off attackers. Musk-oxen bulls form a defensive ring, with their horns pointing outwards, round the cows and calves of the herd, presenting a united front against preying wolf packs.

deformed **2** a physical blemish or distortion; a disfigurement [ME *deformite*, fr MF *deformité*, fr L *deformitat-, deformitas*, fr *deformis* deformed, fr *de-* + *forma*]

defraud /di'frawd/ *vt* to cheat of sthg [ME *defrauden*, fr MF *defrauder*, fr L *defraudare*, fr *de-* + *fraudare* to cheat, fr *fraud-, fraus* fraud] – **defrauder** *n*, **defraudation** /-'daysh(ə)n/ *n*

defray /di'fray/ *vt* to provide for the payment of [MF *deffrayer*, fr *des-* de- + *frayer* to expend, fr OF, fr (assumed) OF *frai* expenditure, lit., damage by breaking, fr L *fractum*, neut of *fractus*, pp of *frangere* to break – more at BREAK] – **defrayable** *adj*, **defrayal** *n*

defrock /,dee'frok/ *vt* to unfrock

defrost /,dee'frost/ *vt* **1** to thaw out from a frozen state ⟨~ *meat*⟩ **2** to free from ice ⟨~ *the refrigerator*⟩ **3** *NAm* to demist ~ *vi* to thaw out, esp from a deep-frozen state – **defroster** *n*

deft /deft/ *adj* marked by facility and skill [ME *defte* – more at DAFT] – **deftly** *n*, **deftness** *n*

defunct /di'fungkt/ *adj* no longer existing or in use; *esp* dead [L *defunctus*, fr pp of *defungi* to finish, die, fr *de-* + *fungi* to perform – more at FUNCTION]

defuse /,dee'fyoohz/ *vt* **1** to remove the fuse from (a mine, bomb, etc) **2** to make less harmful, potent, or tense ⟨~ *the crisis*⟩

defy /di'fie/ *vt* **1** to challenge to do sthg considered impossible; dare **2** to face with assured power of resistance; show no fear of nor respect for ⟨~ *public opinion*⟩ **3** to resist attempts at ⟨*the paintings* ~ *classification*⟩ [ME *defyen* to renounce faith in, challenge, fr OF *defier*, fr *de-* + *fier* to entrust, fr (assumed) VL *fidare*, alter. of L *fidere* to trust – more at BIDE] – **defier** *n*

dégagé /,dayga'zhay/ *adj* FREE AND EASY 1 ⟨*clothes with a* ~ *look*⟩ [F, fr pp of *dégager* to redeem a pledge, free, fr OF *desgagier*, fr *des-* de- + *gage* pledge – more at GAGE]

degas /,dee'gas/ *vt* **-ss-** to remove gas from

degauss /,dee'gows, -'gaws/ *vt* to demagnetize; *esp* to demagnetize (a steel ship), esp as a protection against magnetic mines – **degausser** *n*

1**degenerate** /di'jen(ə)rət/ *adj* **1a** having declined in nature, character, structure, function, etc from an ancestral or former state **b** having sunk to a condition below that which is normal to a type; *esp* having sunk to a lower and usu peculiarly corrupt state **2** characterized by or made of atoms stripped of their electrons and packed very densely ⟨*a* ~ *star*⟩ [ME *degenerat*, fr L *degeneratus*, pp of *degenerare* to degenerate, fr *de-* + *gener-, genus* race, kind – more at KIN] – **degenerately** *adv*, **degenerateness** *n*, **degeneracy** /-rəsi/ *n*

2**degenerate** *n* sthg or esp sby degenerate; *esp* one showing signs of reversion to an earlier cultural or evolutionary stage

3**degenerate** /di'jenərayt/ *vi* **1** to pass from a higher to a lower type or condition; deteriorate **2** to sink into a low intellectual or moral state **3** to decline from a former thriving or healthy condition **4** to evolve or develop into a less autonomous or complex form ⟨~d *into parasites*⟩ – **degenerative** /-rətiv/ *adj*, **degeneration** /-'raysh(ə)n/ *n*

deglutition /,deeglooh'tish(ə)n/ *n* the act or process of swallowing [F *déglutition*, fr L *deglutitus*, pp of *deglutire* to swallow down, fr *de-* + *glutire, gluttire* to swallow – more at GLUTTON]

degrade /di'grayd/ *vt* **1a** to lower in grade, rank, or status; demote **b** to reduce the quality of; *specif* to impair with respect to some physical property **2** to bring to low esteem or into disrepute ⟨degrading *vices*⟩ **3** ERODE 1c **4** to decompose (a chemical compound) ~ *vi* **1** to degenerate **2** *of a chemical compound* to decompose [ME *degraden*, fr MF *degrader*, fr LL *degradare*, fr L *de-* + *gradus* step, grade] – **degradable** *adj*, **degrader** *n*, **degradingly** *adv*, **degradation** /,degrə'daysh(ə)n/ *n*

degree /di'gree/ *n* **1** a step or stage in a process, course, or order of classification ⟨*advanced by* ~s⟩ **2a** the extent or measure of an action, condition, or relation **b** any of the (sets of) forms used in the comparison of an adjective or adverb **c** a legal measure of guilt or negligence ⟨*guilty of murder in the first* ~⟩ **d** a positive and esp considerable amount ⟨*eccentric to a* ~⟩ **3** the civil condition or status of a person ⟨*people of high* ~⟩ **4** an academic title conferred **a** on students in recognition of proficiency **b** honorarily **5** a division or interval of a scale of measurement; *specif* any of various units for measuring temperature **6** a 360th part of the circumference of a circle ☞ SYMBOL **7a** the rank of algebraic expression that for a monomial term is the sum of the exponents of the variable factors and for a polynomial is the sum of the exponents of the variable factors of the highest degree ⟨x^2y^3z *and* $x^6 + y^2 + 2z$ *are both of the 6th degree*⟩ **b** the greatest power of the derivative of highest order in a differential equation [ME, fr OF *degré*, fr (assumed) VL *degradus*, fr L *de-* + *gradus*] – **degreed** *adj* – **to a degree** **1** to a remarkable extent **2** in a small way

de'gree-,day *n* a unit that represents 1 degree of declination from a given point (e g 65°) in the mean daily outdoor temperature and that is used to measure heat requirements

de,gree of 'freedom *n* any of a limited characteristic number of ways in which a body or system may move

de haut en bas /də ,oh on(h) 'bah (*Fr* də o ɑ̃ bɑ)/ *adj or adv* having a superior or condescending manner [F, lit., from top to bottom]

dehisce /di'his/ *vi* to split (open); *also* to discharge contents by so splitting ⟨*anthers* dehiscing *at maturity*⟩ [L *dehiscere* to split open, fr *de-* + *hiscere* to gape; akin to L *hiare* to yawn – more at YAWN] – **dehiscence** *n*, **dehiscent** *adj*

dehuman·ize, -ise /,dee'hyoohməniez/ *vt* to divest of human qualities or personality – **dehumanization** /-'zaysh(ə)n/ *n*

dehumidify /,deehyooh'midifie/ *vt* to remove moisture from (e g air) – **dehumidification** /-fi'kaysh(ə)n/ *n*, **dehumidifier** *n*

dehydr- /deehiedr-/, **dehydro-** *comb form* with hydrogen removed ⟨dehydro*cortisone*⟩

dehydrate /,deehie'drayt/ *vt* **1** to remove (bound) water from (a chemical compound, foods, etc) **2** to make dry and uninteresting in style or character ~ *vi* to lose water or body fluids (abnormally) – **dehydrator** *n*, **dehydration** /-'draysh(ə)n/ *n*

dehydrogenase /,dee'hiedrəjə,nayz, ,deehie'drojənayz, -nays/ *n* an enzyme that accelerates the oxidation of or removal of hydrogen from a compound [ISV]

deictic /'diektik/ *adj* DEMONSTRATIVE 2 ⟨this, that,

and those *have a ~ function*⟩ [Gk *deiktikos*, fr *deiktos*, verbal of *deiknynai* to show]

deify /'dee·ifie, 'day-/ *vt* **1a** to make a god of **b** to take as an object of worship **2** to glorify as of supreme worth ⟨~ *money*⟩ [ME *deifyen*, fr MF *deifier*, fr LL *deificare*, fr L *deus* god] – **deification** /-ifi'kaysh(ə)n/ *n*

deign /dayn/ *vi* to condescend ⟨*she barely* ~ed *to acknowledge their greeting*⟩ ~ *vt* to condescend to give or offer [ME *deignen*, fr OF *deignier*, fr L *dignare, dignari*, fr *dignus* worthy – more at DECENT]

deion·ize, -ise /,dee'ie·əniez/ *vt* to remove ions from (esp water) – **deionization** /-'zaysh(ə)n/ *n*

deism /'dee·iz(ə)m, 'day-/ *n, often cap* a movement or system of thought advocating natural religion based on human reason rather than revelation; *specif* a chiefly 18th-c doctrine asserting that although God created the universe he does not intervene in its functioning [F *déisme*, fr L *deus* god + F *-isme* -ism] – **deist** *n, often cap,* **deistic** /-'istik/ *adj,* **deistically** *adv*

deity /'dee·əti, 'day-/ *n* **1a** the rank or essential nature of a god **b** *cap the* Supreme Being; GOD 1 **2** a god or goddess ⟨*the* deities *of ancient Greece*⟩ **3** one exalted or revered as supremely good or powerful [ME *deitee*, fr MF *deité*, fr LL *deitat-, deitas*, fr L *deus* god; akin to OE *Tīw*, god of war, L *divus* god, *dies* day, Gk *dios* heavenly]

déjà vu /,dayzhah 'vooh (*Fr* deʒa vy)/ *n* **1** the illusion of remembering scenes and events when they are experienced for the first time **2** sthg excessively or unpleasantly familiar [F, adj, already seen]

dejected /di'jektid/ *adj* cast down in spirits; depressed [*deject* (to depress), fr ME *dejecten* to throw down, fr L *dejectus*, pp of *deicere*, fr *de-* + *jacere* to throw] – **dejectedly** *adv,* **dejectedness** *n*

dejection /di'jeksh(ə)n/ *n* lowness of spirits

de jure /,di 'jooəri/ *adv or adj* by (full legal) right ⟨*recognition extended ~ to the new government*⟩ – compare DE FACTO [NL]

deka- /dekə-/, **dek-** – see DECA-

dekko /'dekoh/ *n, Br* a look, glance – slang [Hindi *dekho* look!, imper pl of *dekhnā* to see, fr Skt *dṛś* to see; akin to Skt *dṛṣṭi* seeing, sight, eye]

delaine /də'layn/ *n* a lightweight, often print, woollen dress fabric [F *(mousseline) de laine* (muslin) of wool]

Delaware /'deləweə/ *n, pl* **Delawares,** *esp collectively* **Delaware** a member, or the Algonquian language, of an American Indian people orig of the Delaware valley

[1]**delay** /di'lay/ *n* **1** delaying or (an instance of) being delayed **2** the time during which sthg is delayed

[2]**delay** *vt* **1** to postpone **2** to stop, detain, or hinder for a time ~ *vi* **1** to move or act slowly **2** to pause momentarily [ME *delayen*, fr OF *delaier*, fr *de-* + *laier* to leave, alter. of *laissier*, fr L *laxare* to slacken – more at RELAX] – **delayer** *n,* **delaying** *adj*

del credere /,del 'kredəri/ *n* a guarantee of a buyer's solvency given by a commission agent, usu in return for an additional commission [It, of belief, of trust] – **del credere** *adj or adv*

delectable /di'lektəbl/ *adj* **1** highly pleasing; delightful **2** delicious [ME, fr MF, fr L *delectabilis*, fr *delectare* to delight – more at DELIGHT] – **delectableness** *n,* **delectably** *adv,* **delectability** /-tə'biləti/ *n*

delectation /,delek'taysh(ə)n, ,dee-/ *n* **1** DELIGHT 1 **2** enjoyment [ME *delectacioun*, fr MF or L; MF *delectation*, fr L *delectation-, delectatio*, fr *delectatus*]

delegable /'deligəbl/ *adj* capable of being delegated

delegacy /'deligəsi/ *n* **1a** the act of delegating **b** an appointment as delegate **2** *sing or pl in constr* a body of delegates; a board

[1]**delegate** /'deligət/ *n* a person delegated to act for another; *esp* a representative to a conference [ME *delegat*, fr ML *delegatus*, fr L, pp of *delegare* to delegate, fr *de-* + *legare* to send – more at LEGATE]

[2]**delegate** /'deligayt/ *vt* **1** to entrust (e g a duty or responsibility) to another **2** to appoint as one's representative ~ *vi* to assign responsibility or authority

delegation /,deli'gaysh(ə)n/ *n* **1** the act of empowering to act for another **2** *sing or pl in constr* a group of people chosen to represent others [[2]DELEGATE + -ION]

delete /di'leet/ *vt* to eliminate, esp by blotting out, cutting out, or erasing [L *deletus*, pp of *delēre* to wipe out, destroy, fr *de-* + *-lēre* (akin to L *linere* to smear) – more at LIME]

deleterious /,deli'tiəri·əs/ *adj* harmful, detrimental – fml [Gk *dēlētērios*, fr *dēleisthai* to hurt] – **deleteriously** *adv,* **deleteriousness** *n*

deletion /di'leesh(ə)n/ *n* sthg deleted [L *deletion-, deletio* destruction, fr *deletus*]

delft /delft/ *n* tin-glazed Dutch earthenware with blue and white or polychrome decoration [*Delft*, town in the Netherlands]

deli /'deli/ *n, pl* **delis** DELICATESSEN 2

[1]**deliberate** /di'lib(ə)rət/ *adj* **1** characterized by or resulting from careful and thorough consideration **2** characterized by awareness of the consequences; wilful **3** slow, unhurried ⟨*walked with a ~ step*⟩ [L *deliberatus*, pp of *deliberare* to weigh in mind, ponder, irreg fr *de-* + *libra* scale, pound] – **deliberately** *adv,* **deliberateness** *n*

[2]**deliberate** /di'libərayt/ *vt* to think about deliberately and often with formal discussion before reaching a decision ~ *vi* to ponder issues and decisions carefully

deliberation /di,libə'raysh(ə)n/ *n* **1** deliberating or being deliberate **2** a discussion and consideration of pros and cons – **deliberative** /di'lib(ə)rətiv/ *adj,* **deliberatively** *adv,* **deliberativeness** *n*

delicacy /'delikəsi/ *n* **1** sthg pleasing to eat that is considered rare or luxurious **2** the quality or state of being dainty ⟨*lace of great* ~⟩ **3** frailty, fragility **4** precise and refined perception or discrimination **5a** refined sensibility in feeling or conduct **b** avoidance of anything offensive or disturbing

delicate /'delikət/ *adj* **1a** pleasing to the senses in a mild or subtle way **b** marked by daintiness or charm of colour, line, or proportion **2a** marked by keen sensitivity or subtle discrimination ⟨~ *perception*⟩ **b** fastidious, squeamish **3a** marked by extreme precision **b** having or showing extreme sensitivity ⟨*a ~ instrument*⟩ **4** calling for or involving meticulously careful treatment ⟨*the ~ balance of power*⟩ **5a** very finely made **b(1)** fragile **(2)** weak, sickly **c** marked by or requiring tact ⟨*touches on a ~ subject*⟩ [ME *delicat*, fr L *delicatus* delicate, addicted to pleasure;

akin to L *delicere* to allure] – **delicately** *adv*, **delicateness** *n*

delicatessen /ˌdelikə'tes(ə)n/ *n* **1** *pl in constr* (delicacies and foreign) foods ready for eating (e g cooked meats) **2** a shop where delicatessen are sold [obs G (now *delikatessen*), pl of *delicatesse* delicacy, fr F *délicatesse*, prob fr OIt *delicatezza*, fr *delicato* delicate, fr L *delicatus*]

delicious /di'lishəs/ *adj* **1** affording great pleasure; delightful **2** highly pleasing to one of the bodily senses, esp of taste or smell [ME, fr OF, fr LL *deliciosus*, fr L *deliciae* delight, fr *delicere* to allure] – **deliciously** *adv*, **deliciousness** *n*

[1]**delight** /di'liet/ *n* **1** great pleasure or satisfaction; joy **2** sthg that gives great pleasure ⟨*a* ~ *to behold*⟩

[2]**delight** *vi* to take great pleasure *in* doing sthg ~ *vt* to give enjoyment or satisfaction to ⟨~ed *the audience with his performance*⟩ [ME *deliten*, fr OF *delitier*, fr L *delectare*, fr *delectus*, pp of *delicere* to allure, fr *de-* + *lacere* to allure; akin to OE *læl* switch, L *laqueus* snare] – **delighter** *n*

de'lighted *adj* highly pleased – **delightedly** *adv*, **delightedness** *n*

de'lightful /-f(ə)l/ *adj* highly pleasing – **delightfully** *adv*, **delightfulness** *n*

delimit /di'limit/ *vt* to fix the limits of ⟨~ *a boundary*⟩ [F *délimiter*, fr L *delimitare*, fr *de-* + *limitare* to limit, fr *limit-*, *limes* boundary, limit – more at [1]LIMB]

delimitate /di'limitayt/ *vt* to delimit – **delimitative** /di'limitətiv/ *adj*, **delimitation** /-'taysh(ə)n/ *n*

delineate /di'liniayt/ *vt* **1** to show by drawing lines in the shape of **2** to describe in usu sharp or vivid detail [L *delineatus*, pp of *delineare*, fr *de-* + *linea* line] – **delineator** *n*, **delineative** /-ətiv/ *adj*, **delineation** /-'aysh(ə)n/ *n*

delinquency /di'lingkwənsi/ *n* (the practice of engaging in) antisocial or illegal conduct – used esp when emphasis is placed on maladjustment rather than criminal intent [[2]DELINQUENT + -CY]

[1]**delinquent** /di'lingkwənt/ *n* a delinquent person

[2]**delinquent** *adj* **1** guilty of wrongdoing or of neglect of duty **2** marked by delinquency ⟨~ *behaviour*⟩ [L *delinquent-*, *delinquens*, prp of *delinquere* to fail, offend, fr *de-* + *linquere* to leave – more at LOAN] – **delinquently** *adv*

deliquesce /ˌdeli'kwes/ *vi* to melt away; *specif, of a compound* to dissolve gradually in water attracted and absorbed from the air [L *deliquescere*, fr *de-* + *liquescere*, incho of *liquēre* to be fluid – more at LIQUID] – **deliquescence** *n*, **deliquescent** *adj*

delirious /di'liəri·əs/ *adj* (characteristic) of or affected by delirium – **deliriously** *adv*, **deliriousness** *n*

delirium /di'liəri·əm/ *n* **1** confusion, frenzy, disordered speech, hallucinations, etc occurring as a (temporary) mental disturbance **2** frenzied excitement [L, fr *delirare* to deviate, be crazy, fr *de-* + *lira* furrow – more at LEARN]

deˌlirium 'tremens /'tremenz/ *n* a violent delirium with tremors induced by chronic alcoholism [NL, lit., trembling delirium]

deliver /di'livə/ *vt* **1** to set free **2** to hand over; convey ⟨~ *the milk*⟩ **3a** to assist in giving birth ⟨*she was* ~ed *of a fine boy*⟩ **b** to aid in the birth of **c** to give birth to **4** to utter ⟨~ed *her speech effectively*⟩ **5** to aim or guide (e g a blow) to an intended target or destination ~ *vi* to produce the promised, desired, or expected results – infml [ME *deliveren*, fr OF *delivrer*, fr LL *deliberare*, fr L *de-* + *liberare* to liberate] – **deliverable** *adj*, **deliverer** *n*

deliverance /di'liv(ə)rəns/ *n* **1** liberation, rescue **2** an opinion or verdict expressed publicly [DELIVER + -ANCE]

delivery /di'liv(ə)ri/ *n* **1** DELIVERANCE 1 **2a** the act of handing over **b** a physical or legal transfer **c** sthg delivered at 1 time or in 1 unit ⟨*milk* deliveries⟩ **3** the act of giving birth **4** the uttering of a speech; *also* the manner or style of uttering in speech or song **5** the act or manner or an instance of sending forth, throwing, or bowling [ME *deliverie*, fr *deliveren*]

de'liveryman /-mən, -ˌman/ *n, pl* **deliverymen** /-mən, -ˌmen/ a van driver who delivers wholesale or retail goods to customers, usu over a regular local route

dell /del/ *n* a small secluded hollow or valley, esp in a forest [ME *delle*; akin to MHG *telle* ravine, OE *dæl* valley – more at DALE]

delouse /ˌdee'lows/ *vt* to remove lice from

Delphic /'delfik/, **Delphian** /'delfi·ən/ *adj* **1** of ancient Delphi or its oracle **2a** ambiguous **b** obscure, enigmatic [*Delphi*, town in ancient Greece] – **delphically** *adv*

delphinium /del'fini·əm/ *n* any of a genus of plants of the buttercup family with deeply cut leaves and flowers in showy spikes [NL, genus name, fr Gk *delphinion* larkspur, dim. of *delphin-*, *delphis* dolphin – more at DOLPHIN]

delta /'deltə/ *n* **1a** the 4th letter of the Greek alphabet **b** [1]D 4 **2** a triangular alluvial deposit at the mouth of a river ☞ GEOGRAPHY **3** an increment of a variable [ME *deltha*, fr Gk *delta*, of Sem origin; akin to Heb *dāleth*, 4th letter of the Heb alphabet] – **deltaic** /del'tayik/ *adj*

Delta – a communications code word for the letter *d*

'delta ˌwing *n* an approximately triangular aircraft wing with a (nearly) straight rearmost edge – **delta-winged** *adj*

deltoid /'deltoyd/ *n* a large triangular muscle covering the shoulder joint and acting to raise the arm to the side [NL *deltoides*, fr Gk *deltoeidēs* shaped like a delta, fr *delta*]

delude /di'loohd/ *vt* to mislead the mind or judgment of; deceive, trick [ME *deluden*, fr L *deludere*, fr *de-* + *ludere* to play – more at LUDICROUS] – **deluder** *n*, **deludingly** *adv*

[1]**deluge** /'delyoohj, -yoohzh/ *n* **1a** a great flood; *specif, cap the* Flood recorded in the Old Testament (Gen 6:8) **b** a drenching fall of rain **2** an overwhelming amount or number ⟨*a* ~ *of criticism*⟩ ⟨*a* ~ *of letters*⟩ [ME, fr MF, fr L *diluvium*, fr *diluere* to wash away, fr *dis-* + *lavere* to wash]

[2]**deluge** *vt* **1** to overflow with water; inundate **2** to overwhelm, swamp

delusion /di'loohzh(ə)n/ *n* **1** deluding or being deluded **2a** sthg delusively believed **b** (a mental state characterized by) a false belief (about the self or others) that persists despite the facts and occurs esp in psychotic states [ME, fr L *delusion-*, *delusio*, fr *delusus*, pp of *deludere*] – **delusional** *adj*, **delusionary** /-n(ə)ri/ *adj*

delusive /di'loohsiv, -ziv/ *adj* **1** likely to delude **2** constituting a delusion – **delusively** *adv*, **delusiveness** *n*

delusory /di'loohz(ə)ri, -s(ə)ri/ *adj* deceptive, delusive

delustre /ˌdee'lustə/ *vt* to reduce the sheen of (e g yarn or fabric)

de luxe /di 'luks/ *adj* notably luxurious or elegant [F, lit., of luxury]

delve /delv/ *vi vi* **1** to dig or work (as if) with a spade **2** to make a careful or detailed search for information ⟨~d *into the past*⟩ [ME *delven*, fr OE *delfan*; akin to OHG *telban* to dig] – **delver** *n*

demagnet·ize, -ise /ˌdee'magnitiez/ *vt* to cause not to have magnetic properties or a magnetic field – **demagnetizer** *n*, **demagnetization** /-'zaysh(ə)n/ *n*

demagogue, *NAm also* **demagog** /'deməgog/ *n* **1** a leader of the common people in ancient times **2** an agitator who makes use of popular prejudices in order to gain power [Gk *dēmagōgos*, fr *dēmos* people (akin to Gk *daiesthai* to divide) + *agōgos* leading, fr *agein* to lead – more at TIDE, AGENT] – **demagoguery** /-ˌgog(ə)ri/ *n*, **demagogy** /-ˌgogi/ *n*, **demagogic** /-'gogik, -'gojik/, **demagogical** *adj*, **demagogically** *adv*

[1]**demand** /di'mahnd/ *n* **1** an act of demanding or asking, esp with authority; a claim **2a** an expressed desire for ownership or use **b** willingness and ability to purchase a commodity or service **c** the quantity of a commodity or service wanted at a specified price and time **3** a desire or need *for*; the state of being sought after ⟨*gold is in great* ~⟩ ⟨*a great* ~ *for teachers*⟩ – **on demand** whenever the demand is made ⟨*feed the baby* on demand⟩

[2]**demand** *vi* to make a demand; ask ~ *vt* **1** to ask or call for with authority; claim as due or just ⟨~ *payment of a debt*⟩ **2** to call for urgently, peremptorily, or insistently **3** to ask authoritatively or earnestly to be informed of ⟨~ *the reason for her visit*⟩ **4** to require [ME *demaunden*, fr MF *demander*, fr ML *demandare*, fr L *de-* + *mandare* to enjoin – more at MANDATE] – **demandable** *adj*, **demander** *n*

demandant /di'mahndənt/ *n* one who makes a demand or claim

demanding /di'mahnding/ *adj* exacting – **demandingly** *adv*

de'mand-ˌpull *n* an increase or upward trend in spendable money, sometimes considered to result in increased competition for available goods and services and a corresponding increase in consumer prices – compare COST-PUSH – **demand-pull** *adj*

demantoid /di'mantoyd/ *n* a green garnet [G, fr obs G *demant* diamond, fr MHG *diemant*, fr OF *diamant*]

demarcate /'deemahˌkayt/ *vt* **1** to mark the limits of **2** to set apart; separate [back-formation fr *demarcation*]

demarcation *also* **demarkation** /ˌdeemah'kaysh(ə)n/ *n* the marking of limits or boundaries, esp between areas of work to be carried out by members of particular trade unions ⟨*a* ~ *dispute*⟩ [Sp *demarcación* & Pg *demarcação*, fr *demarcar* to delimit, fr *de-* + *marcar* to mark, fr It *marcare*, of Gmc origin; akin to OHG *marha* boundary – more at [1]MARCH]

demarche /'dayˌmahsh/ *n* **1** a course of action; a manoeuvre **2** a diplomatic manoeuvre [F *démarche*, lit., gait, fr MF, fr *demarcher* to march, fr OF *demarchier*, fr *de-* + *marchier* to march]

dematerial·ize, -ise /ˌdeemə'tiəri·əliez/ *vb* to deprive of or lose material form or qualities

deme /deem/ *n* a unit of local government in ancient Attica or modern Greece [Gk *dēmos*, lit., people]

demean /di'meen/ *vt* to degrade, debase [*de-* + *mean*]

demeanour, *NAm chiefly* **demeanor** /di'meenə/ *n* behaviour towards others; outward manner [earlier *demeanure*, fr *demean* (to behave) + *-ure*; *demean* fr ME *demenen*, fr OF *demener* to conduct, guide, fr *de-* + *mener* to lead, drive, fr L *minare*, fr *minari* to threaten]

demented /di'mented/ *adj* insane; *also* crazy [arch *dement* (to drive mad), fr LL *dementare*, fr L *dement-*, *demens*] – **dementedly** *adv*, **dementedness** *n*

dementia /di'mensh(y)ə/ *n* **1** deteriorated mentality due to damage to or (natural) deterioration of the brain ⟨*senile* ~⟩ **2** madness, insanity [L, fr *dement-*, *demens* mad, fr *de-* + *ment-*, *mens* mind – more at MIND] – **demential** *adj*

deˌmentia 'praecox /'preekoks/ *n* schizophrenia [NL, lit., premature dementia]

demerara sugar /ˌdemə'reərə/ *n* brown crystallized unrefined cane sugar from the W Indies [*Demerara*, region of Guyana]

demerit /ˌdee'merit, '-ˌ--/ *n* **1** a quality that deserves blame or lacks merit; a fault, defect **2** *NAm* a bad mark given to an offender [ME, fr MF *demerite*, fr *de-* + *merite* merit]

demersal /di'muhsl/ *adj* of or living near the bottom of the sea – compare PELAGIC [L *demersus*, pp of *demergere* to sink, fr *de-* + *mergere* to dip, sink, plunge]

demesne /di'mayn, -'meen/ *n* **1** legal possession of land as one's own **2** land actually occupied by the owner and not held by tenants **3a** the land attached to a mansion **b** landed property; an estate **c** a region, realm [ME, alter. of *demeyne*, fr OF *demaine* – more at DOMAIN]

demi- /demi-/ *prefix* **1** half ⟨demi*semiquaver*⟩ **2** partly belonging to (a specified type or class) ⟨demi*god*⟩ [ME, fr *demi*, fr MF, fr L *dimidius*, prob back-formation fr *dimidiare* to halve, fr *dis-* + *medius* mid – more at MID]

demigod /'demiˌgod/, *fem* **'demiˌgoddess** *n* **1a** a mythological superhuman being with less power than a god **b** an offspring of a union between a mortal and a god **2** a person so outstanding that he/she seems to approach the divine

demijohn /'demiˌjon/ *n* a narrow-necked large bottle of glass or stoneware [by folk etymology fr F *dame-jeanne*, lit., Lady Jane]

demilitar·ize, -ise /ˌdee'militəriez/ *vt* to strip of military forces, weapons, etc – **demilitarization** /-'zaysh(ə)n/ *n*

demimondaine /ˌdemimon'dayn/ *n* a woman of the demimonde [F *demi-mondaine*, fr fem of *demi-mondain*, fr *demi-monde*]

ˌdemi'monde /-'mond/ *n* **1** *sing or pl in constr* a class of women on the fringes of respectable society who were supported by wealthy lovers **2** a demimondaine **3** *sing or pl in constr* a group engaged in activity of doubtful legality or propriety [F *demi-monde*, fr *demi-* + *monde* world, fr L *mundus*]

demineral·ize, -ise /ˌdee'min(ə)rəˌliez/ *vt* to remove

the mineral matter from (e g water) – **demineralizer** *n*, **demineralization** /-'zaysh(ə)n/ *n*

[1]**demise** /di'miez/ *vt* **1** to convey (e g an estate) by will or lease **2** to transmit by succession or inheritance ~ *vi* to pass by descent or bequest ⟨*the property* ~d *to the king*⟩

[2]**demise** *n* **1** the conveyance of an estate or transfer of sovereignty by demising **2a** death – technical, euph, or humor **b** a cessation of existence or activity – fml or humor [MF, fem of *demis*, pp of *demettre* to dismiss, fr L *demittere* to send down, fr *de-* + *mittere* to send – more at SMITE]

demisemiquaver /,demisemi'kwayvə/ *n* a musical note with the time value of ½ of a semiquaver ☞ MUSIC

demission /di'mish(ə)n/ *n* a resignation, abdication – fml [MF, fr L *demission-*, *demissio* lowering, fr *demissus*, pp of *demittere*]

demist /,dee'mist/ *vt*, *Br* to remove mist from (e g a car windscreen) – **demister** *n*

demit /di'mit/ *vb* **-tt-** to resign – fml [MF *demettre*]

demitasse /'demi,tas/ *n* a small cup of, or for, black coffee [F *demi-tasse*, fr *demi-* + *tasse* cup, fr MF, fr Ar *ṭass*, fr Per *tast*]

'**demi,urge** /-,uhj/ *n* **1** a Gnostic subordinate deity who is the creator of the material world **2** sthg that is an autonomous creative force or decisive power [LL *demiurgus*, fr Gk *dēmiourgos*, lit., one who works for the people, fr *dēmios* of the people (fr *dēmos* people) + *-ourgos* worker (fr *ergon* work) – more at DEMAGOGUE, WORK] – **demiurgeous** /-'uhjəs/ *adj*, **demiurgic** /-'uhjik/, **demiurgical** *adj*, **demiurgically** *adv*

,**demi-vi'erge** /vi'eəzh, 'vyeəzh/ *n* a woman who engages in sexual activity while retaining her physiological virginity [F, lit., half virgin, fr *demi-* + *vierge* virgin, fr L *virgin-*, *virgo*]

demo /'demoh/ *n*, *pl* **demos** **1** DEMONSTRATION 4 **2** *cap NAm* DEMOCRAT 2

[1]**demob** /,dee'mob/ *vt*, *chiefly Br* to demobilize

[2]**demob** *n*, *chiefly Br* a demobilization

demobil·ize, -ise /,dee'mohbiliez/ *vt* **1** to disband **2** to discharge from military service – **demobilization** /-'zaysh(ə)n/ *n*

democracy /di'mokrəsi/ *n* **1a** government by the people **b** (a political unit with) a government in which the supreme power is exercised by the people directly or indirectly through a system of representation usu involving free elections **2** the absence of class distinctions or privileges [MF *democratie*, fr LL *democratia*, fr Gk *dēmokratia*, fr *dēmos* + *-kratia* -cracy]

democrat /'deməkrat/ *n* **1a** an adherent of democracy **b** one who practises social equality **2** *cap* a member of the Democratic party of the USA

democratic /,demə'kratik/ *adj* **1** of or favouring democracy or social equality **2** *often cap* of or constituting a political party of the USA associated with policies of social reform and internationalism – **democratically** *adv*, **democratize** /di'mokrətiez/ *vt*, **democratization** /-tie'zaysh(ə)n/ *n*, **democratizer** /di'mokrətiezə/*n*

démodé /,daymoh'day/ *adj* no longer fashionable; out-of-date [F, fr *dé-* de- + *mode* fashion]

demodulate /,dee'modyoolayt/ *vt* to extract the information (e g a video signal) from (a modulated carrier wave) – **demodulator** *n*, **demodulation** /-'laysh(ə)n/ *n*

demography /di'mogrəfi/ *n* the statistical study of human populations, esp with reference to size and density, distribution, and vital statistics [F *démographie*, fr Gk *dēmos* people + F *-graphie* -graphy] – **demographer** *n*, **demographic** /,demə'grafik/ *adj*, **demographically** *adv*

demoiselle /dəmwah'zel/ *n* a damselfly [F, fr OF *dameisele* – more at DAMSEL]

demolish /di'molish/ *vt* **1** to destroy, smash, or tear down **2** to eat up – infml [MF *demoliss-*, stem of *demolir*, fr L *demoliri*, fr *de-* + *moliri* to construct, fr *moles* mass – more at [3]MOLE] – **demolisher** *n*

demolition /,demə'lish(ə)n/ *n* the act or an instance of demolishing [MF & L; MF, fr L *demolition-*, *demolitio*, fr *demolitus*, pp of *demoliri*] – **demolitionist** *n*

demon /'deemən/ *n* **1a** an evil spirit **b** an evil or undesirable emotion, trait, or state **2** DAEMON 1, 2 **3** one who has unusual drive or effectiveness ⟨*a* ~ *for work*⟩ [ME, fr LL & L; LL *daemon* evil spirit, fr L, divinity, spirit, fr Gk *daimōn*] – **demonism** *n*, **demonize** *vt*, **demonization** /,deemənie'zaysh(ə)n/ *n*, **demonology** /,deemə'noləji/ *n*

demonet·ize, -ise /,dee'munitiez/ *vt* to stop using (a metal) as a money standard [F *démonétiser*, fr *dé-* de- + L *moneta* coin – more at [1]MINT] – **demonetization** /di,munitie'zaysh(ə)n/

[1]**demoniac** /di'mohniak/ *also* **demoniacal** /,deemoh'nie·əkl/ *adj* **1** possessed or influenced by a demon **2** demonic [ME *demoniak*, fr LL *daemoniacus*, fr Gk *daimoniakos*, fr *daimon-*, *daimōn*] – **demoniacally** *adv*

[2]**demoniac** *n* one regarded as possessed by a demon

demonic /di'monik/ *also* **demonical** /-kl/ *adj* (suggestive) of a demon; fiendish ⟨~ *cruelty*⟩ – **demonically** *adv*

demonstrable /di'monstrəbl/ *adj* **1** capable of being demonstrated **2** apparent, evident – **demonstrableness** *n*, **demonstrably** *adv*, **demonstrability** /di,monstrə'biləti/ *n*

demonstrate /'demənstrayt/ *vt* **1** to show clearly **2a** to prove or make clear by reasoning or evidence **b** to illustrate and explain, esp with many examples **3** to show or prove the application, value, or efficiency of to a prospective buyer ~ *vi* **1** to make or give a demonstration **2** to take part in a demonstration ⟨demonstrating *against the abortion bill*⟩ [L *demonstratus*, pp of *demonstrare*, fr *de-* + *monstrare* to show – more at MUSTER]

demonstration /,demən'straysh(ə)n/ *n* **1** an outward expression or display **2a(1)** conclusive evidence; proof **(2)** a proof in which the conclusion is the immediate sequence of reasoning from premises **b** a showing and explanation of the merits of a product to a prospective buyer **c** a display of an action or process ⟨*cooking* ~⟩ **3** a show of armed force **4** a mass meeting, procession, etc to display group feelings (e g about grievances or political issues) [DEMONSTRATE + -ION] – **demonstrational** *adj*

[1]**demonstrative** /di'monstrətiv/ *adj* **1** demonstrating sthg to be real or true **2** pointing out the one referred to and distinguishing it from others of the same class ⟨~ *pronouns*⟩ **3** given to or marked by

display of feeling – **demonstratively** *adv*, **demonstrativeness** *n*

²**demonstrative** *n* a demonstrative word or morpheme

demonstrator /'demən,straytə/ *n* one who demonstrates: e g **a** a junior staff member who demonstrates experiments in a university science department **b** sby who participates in a demonstration ⟨*the* ~s *were given a police escort*⟩

demoral·ize, -ise /di'morə,liez/ *vt* to weaken the morale or self-respect of; discourage, dispirit – **demoralizingly** *adv*, **demoralization** /di,morəlie'zaysh(ə)n/ *n*

demos /'deemos/ *n*, *often cap* the populace personified [Gk *dēmos* – more at DEMAGOGUE]

demote /di'moht/ *vt* to reduce to a lower grade or rank [*de-* + *-mote* (as in *promote*)] – **demotion** /di'mohsh(ə)n/ *n*

demotic /di'motik/ *adj* **1** of the people **2** of or written in a simplified form of the ancient Egyptian hieratic writing **3** of the Modern Greek vernacular [Gk *dēmotikos*, fr *dēmotēs* commoner, fr *dēmos*] – **demotic** *n*

demount /,dee'mownt/ *vt* **1** to remove from a mounted position **2** to disassemble, dismantle – **demountable** *adj*

demulcent /di'muls(ə)nt/ *adj*, *of a medicine* soothing [L *demulcent-*, *demulcens*, prp of *demulcēre* to soothe, fr *de-* + *mulcēre* to soothe] – **demulcent** *n*

¹**demur** /di'muh/ *vi* **-rr-** **1** to put in a demurrer **2** to take exception; (mildly) object [ME *demeoren* to linger, fr OF *demorer*, fr L *demorari*, fr *de-* + *morari* to linger, fr *mora* delay – more at MEMORY] – **demurral** *n*, **demurrable** *adj*

²**demur** *n* **1** a hesitation ⟨*men who follow fashion without* ~⟩ **2** objection, protest

demure /di'myooə/ *adj* **1** reserved, modest **2** affectedly modest, reserved, or serious; coy [ME, perh fr MF *demorer*, *demourer* to linger] – **demurely** *adv*, **demureness** *n*

demurrer /di'muhrə/ *n* **1** a legal objection that assumes the truth of the matter alleged by the opponent, but asserts that it is insufficient in law to sustain his/her claim, and that he/she should not be allowed to proceed – no longer used in English law **2** an objection [MF *demorer*, vb]

demy /di'mie/ *n* a size of paper usu 22½ × 17½in (572 × 444mm) [ME *demi* half – more at DEMI-]

demyelinate /dee'mie·ili,nayt/ *vt* to remove or destroy the myelin of (a nerve fibre) – **demyelination** /-'naysh(ə)n/ *n*

demystify /dee'mistifie/ *vt* to eliminate the mystery from; clarify ⟨~ *the law*⟩ – **demystification** /di,mistifi'kaysh(ə)n/ *n*

demytholog·ize, -ise /,deemi'tholəjiez/ *vt* to eliminate the mythical elements or associations of – **demythologization** /,deemi ,tholəjie'zaysh(ə)n/ *n*

den /den/ *n* **1** the lair of a wild, usu predatory, animal **2** a centre of secret, esp unlawful, activity ⟨*an opium* ~⟩ **3** a comfortable usu secluded room [ME, fr OE *denn*; akin to OE *denu* valley, OHG *tenni* threshing floor, Gk *thenar* palm of the hand]

denarius /di'neəri·əs/ *n*, *pl* **denarii** /di'neəri,ie/ a small silver coin of ancient Rome [ME, fr L – more at DENIER]

denational·ize, -ise /dee'nashən(ə)l,iez/ *vt* **1** to divest of national status, character, or rights **2** to remove from ownership or control by the state – **denationalization** /,dee,nashən(ə)lie'zaysh(ə)n/ *n*

denature /dee'naychə/ *vt* **1** to make (alcohol) unfit for drinking **2** to modify (e g a protein) by heat, acid, etc so that some of the original structure of the molecule is lost and its properties are changed – **denaturant** /dee'naychərənt, -'nachə-/ *n*, **denaturation** /dee ,naychə'raysh(ə)n, -,nachə-/ *n*

denazify /,dee'nayzifie, ,dee'nahtsi,fie/ *vt* to rid of Nazism and its influence – **denazification** /,deenayzifi'kaysh(ə)n, dee,nahtsifi'kaysh(ə)n/ *n*

dendr-, dendro- *comb form* tree ⟨dendr*oid*⟩; branching like a tree ⟨dendr*ite*⟩ [Gk, fr *dendron*; akin to Gk *drys* tree – more at TREE]

dendrite /'dendriet/ *n* **1** (a mineral marked with) a branching crystal form **2** any of the (branching) extensions from a nerve cell that conduct impulses towards the body of the cell – **dendritic** /den'dritik/ *also* **dendritical** *adj*, **dendritically** *adv*

dendrochronology /,dendrohkrə'noləji/ *n* the dating of events and variations in climate by comparative study of the annual growth rings in wood

dene /deen/ *n* ¹DEAN

dengue /'deng·gi/ *n* an infectious short-lasting virus disease characterized esp by pain in the joints [Sp]

deniable /di'nie·əbl/ *adj* capable of being denied

denial /di'nie·əl/ *n* **1** a refusal to satisfy a request or desire **2a** a refusal to admit the truth or reality (e g of a statement or charge) **b** an assertion that an allegation is false **3** a refusal to acknowledge sby or sthg; a disavowal

denier /'deeni·ə, 'deenyə/ *n* a unit of fineness for silk, rayon, or nylon yarn equal to the fineness of a yarn weighing 1g for each 9000m – compare TEX [ME *denere*, fr MF *denier*, fr L *denarius*, coin worth ten asses, fr *denarius* containing ten, fr *deni* ten each, fr *decem* ten – more at TEN]

denigrate /'denigrayt/ *vt* **1** to cast aspersions on; defame **2** to belittle [L *denigratus*, pp of *denigrare*, fr *de-* + *nigrare* to blacken, fr *nigr-*, *niger* black] – **denigrator** *n*, **denigratory** /-t(ə)ri/ *adj*, **denigration** /,deni'graysh(ə)n/ *n*

denim /'denəm/ *n* **1** a firm durable twilled usu blue cotton fabric used esp for jeans **2** *pl* denim trousers; *esp* blue jeans [F (*serge*) *de Nîmes* serge of Nîmes, town in France]

denitrify /,dee'nietri,fie/ *vt* to remove (a compound of) nitrogen from; to convert the nitrogen in (a nitrate or nitrite) to gaseous nitrogen released into the atmosphere – **denitrification** /dee,nietrifi'kaysh(ə)n/ *n*

denizen /'deniz(ə)n/ *n* **1** an inhabitant **2** a naturalized plant or animal [ME *denysen*, fr MF *denzein*, fr OF, inner, fr *denz* within, fr LL *deintus*, fr L *de-* + *intus* within – more at ENT-]

denominate /di'nominayt/ *vt* to give a name to – fml [L *denominatus*, pp of *denominare*, fr *de-* + *nominare* to name – more at NOMINATE]

denomination /di,nomi'naysh(ə)n/ *n* **1** a name, designation; *esp* a general name for a category **2** a religious organization or sect **3** a grade or degree in a series of values or sizes (e g of money) [DENOMINATE + -ION]

denominational /di,nomi'naysh(ə)nl/ *adj* of a particular religious denomination ⟨*a* ~ *school*⟩ – **denominationally** *adv*

de,nomi'national,ism /-,iz(ə)m/ *n* the narrowly

exclusive emphasizing of denominational differences – **denominationalist** *n*

denominative /di'nominativ/ *adj* conferring or constituting a name [L *de* from + *nomin-, nomen* name] – **denominative** *n*

denominator /di'nomi,naytə/ *n* the part of a vulgar fraction that is below the line and that in fractions with 1 as the numerator indicates into how many parts the unit is divided; a divisor

denotation /,deenoh'taysh(ə)n/ *n* **1** a direct specific meaning as distinct from a connotation **2** a denoting term; a name **3** the totality of subjects of which a term may be predicated, esp in logic [DENOTE + -ATION]

denote /di'noht/ *vt* **1** to indicate ⟨*the swollen bellies that ~ starvation*⟩ **2** to be a sign or mark for ⟨*red ~s danger*⟩ **3** to have the meaning of; mean [MF *denoter*, fr L *denotare*, fr *de-* + *notare* to note] – **denotative** /-tətiv/ *adj*

denouement /day'noohmonh/ *n* **1** the resolution of the main complication in a literary work **2** the outcome of a complex sequence of events [F *dénouement*, lit., untying, fr MF *desnouement*, fr *desnouer* to untie, fr OF *desnoer*, fr *des-* de- + *noer* to tie, fr L *nodare*, fr *nodus* knot]

denounce /di'nowns/ *vt* **1** to condemn, esp publicly, as deserving censure or punishment **2** to inform against; accuse **3** to announce formally the termination of (e g a treaty) [ME *denouncen*, fr OF *denoncier* to proclaim, fr L *denuntiare*, fr *de-* + *nuntiare* to report – more at ANNOUNCE] – **denouncement** *n*, **denouncer** *n*

de novo /di 'nohvoh/ *adv* over again; anew [L]

dense /dens/ *adj* **1** marked by high density, compactness, or crowding together of parts ⟨*~ undergrowth*⟩ ⟨*a ~ fog*⟩ **2** sluggish of mind; stupid **3** demanding concentration to follow or comprehend ⟨*~ prose*⟩ [L *densus*; akin to Gk *dasys* thick with hair or leaves] – **densely** *adv*, **denseness** *n*

density /'densəti/ *n* **1** the quantity per unit volume, unit area, or unit length: e g **a** the mass of a substance or distribution of a quantity per unit of volume or space **b** the average number of individuals or units per unit of space ⟨*a population ~*⟩ **2** the degree of opaqueness of sthg translucent [DENSE + -ITY]

[1]**dent** /dent/ *n* **1** a depression or hollow made by a blow or by pressure **2** an adverse effect ⟨*made a ~ in the weekly budget*⟩ [ME, blow, alter. of *dint*]

[2]**dent** *vt* to make a dent in or on

dent- /dent-/, **denti-**, **dento-** *comb form* tooth; teeth ⟨den*tiform*⟩ ⟨denti*frice*⟩ [ME *denti-*, fr L, fr *dent-, dens* tooth – more at TOOTH]

[1]**dental** /'dentl/ *adj* **1** of the teeth or dentistry **2** articulated with the tip or blade of the tongue against or near the upper front teeth [L *dentalis*, fr *dent-, dens*] – **dentalize** *vt*, **dentally** *adv*

[2]**dental** *n* a dental consonant

,dental 'floss *n* a waxed thread used to clean between the teeth

dentalium /den'tayli·əm/ *n, pl* **dentalia** /-li·ə/ a tooth shell or related shellfish [NL, genus name, fr L *dentalis*]

dentate /'dentayt/, **'dentated** *adj* having teeth or pointed conical projections ⟨*a ~ leaf*⟩ ☞ PLANT [L *dentatus*, fr *dent-, dens*] – **dentately** *adv*, **dentation** /den'taysh(ə)n/ *n*

dentifrice /'denti,fris/ *n* a powder, paste, or liquid for cleaning the teeth [MF, fr L *dentifricium*, fr *denti-* + *fricare* to rub – more at FRICTION]

dentin /'dentin/ *n, NAm* dentine

dentine /'denteen/ *n* a calcium-containing material, similar to but harder and denser than bone, of which the principal mass of a tooth is composed ☞ DIGESTION – **dentinal** *adj*

dentist /'dentist/ *n* one who treats diseases, malformations, and injuries to the teeth, mouth, etc and who makes and inserts false teeth [F *dentiste*, fr *dent*] – **dentistry** *n*

dentition /den'tish(ə)n/ *n* **1** the emergence of teeth from the gums **2** the number, kind, and arrangement of a human being's or other animal's teeth [L *dentition-, dentitio*, fr *dentitus*, pp of *dentire* to cut teeth, fr *dent-, dens*]

dento- /dentoh-/ – see DENT-

denture /'denchə, -chooə/ *n* an artificial replacement for 1 or more teeth; *esp, pl* a set of false teeth [F, fr MF, fr *dent*]

denuclear·ize, -ise /,dee'nyoohkli·ə,riez/ *vt* to remove nuclear arms from – **denuclearization** /dee,nyoohkli·ərie'zaysh(ə)n/ *n*

denude /di'nyoohd/ *vt* **1a** to strip of all covering **b** to lay bare by erosion **2** to remove an important possession or quality from; strip ⟨*~d of his dignity*⟩ [L *denudare*, fr *de-* + *nudus* bare – more at NAKED] – **denudation** /,deenyooh'daysh(ə)n/ *n*

denumerable /di'nyoohm(ə)rəbl/ *adj, of a mathematical set* having elements that can be numbered successively; countable – **denumerably** *adv*, **denumerability** /-rə'biləti/ *n*

denunciation /di,nunsi'aysh(ə)n/ *n* a (public) condemnation [L *denuntiation-, denuntiatio*, fr *denuntiatus*, pp of *denuntiare* to denounce]

deny /di'nie/ *vt* **1** to declare to be untrue or invalid; refuse to accept **2** to disown, repudiate **3a** to give a negative answer to **b** to refuse to grant ⟨*~ a request*⟩ **c** to restrain (oneself) from self-indulgence [ME *denyen*, fr OF *denier*, fr L *denegare*, fr *de-* + *negare* to deny – more at NEGATE]

deodar /'dee·ohdah, 'dee·ə-/ *n* an East Indian cedar [Hindi *deodār*, fr Skt *devadāru*, lit., timber of the gods, fr *deva* god + *dāru* wood]

,deo'dara /-'dah·rə/ *n* a deodar

deodorant /dee'ohdərənt/ *n* a preparation that destroys or masks unpleasant smells – **deodorant** *adj*

deodor·ize, -ise /dee'ohdəriez/ *vt* to destroy or prevent the unpleasant smell of – **deodorizer** *n*, **deodorization** /dee,ohdərie'zaysh(ə)n/

deontology /,dee·on'toləji/ *n* a theory or examination of the nature of moral obligation [Gk *deont-, deon* that which is obligatory, fr neut of prp of *dein* to lack, be needful] – **deontologist** *n*, **deontological** /dee,ontə'lojikl/ *adj*

Deo volente /,day·oh vo'lenti/ *adv* God being willing [L]

deoxy- /dee·oksi-/ *comb form* containing fewer hydroxide groups in the molecule ⟨deoxy*ribonucleic acid*⟩ [ISV]

deoxygenate /,dee'oksijinayt/ *vt* to remove oxygen from – **deoxygenation** /dee,oksiji'naysh(ə)n/ *n*

deoxyribonucleic acid /di,oksi,riebohnyooh'klayik/ *n* DNA [*deoxyribose* + *nucleic acid*]

deoxyribonucleotide /di,oksi,rieboh'nyoohkli·ə,tied/ *n* any of several nucleotides that contain deoxyribose and some of which are constituents of DNA

deoxyribose /dee,oksi'riebohz/ *n* a pentose sugar occurring esp in deoxyribonucleotides [ISV *deoxy-* + *ribose*]

depart /di'paht/ *vi* **1** to go away; leave **2** to turn aside; deviate *from* ~ *vt* to go away from; leave [ME *departen* to divide, go away, fr OF *departir,* fr *de-* + *partir* to divide, fr L *partire,* fr *part-, pars* part]

de'parted *adj* **1** bygone **2** having died, esp recently – euph

department /di'pahtmənt/ *n* **1a** a major division of a government **b** a division of an institution or business that provides a specified service or deals with a specified subject ⟨*sales* ~⟩ **c** a major administrative subdivision (e g in France) **d** a section of a department store **2** a distinct sphere (e g of activity or thought) – infml ⟨*that's not my* ~⟩ [F *département,* fr MF, fr *departir*] – **departmental** /,deepaht'mentl/ *adj,* **departmentally** *adv,* **departmentalize** /,deepaht'mentl·iez/ *vt,* **departmentalization** /-'zaysh(ə)n/ *n*

de'partment ,store *n* a large shop, selling a wide variety of goods, arranged in several departments

departure /di'pahchə/ *n* **1a** the act of going away **b** a setting out (e g on a new course of action) **2** the distance due east or west travelled by a ship in its course **3** deviation, divergence

depend /di'pend/ *vi* **1** to be determined by or based on some condition or action **2a** to place reliance or trust **b** to be dependent, esp for financial support **3** to hang down ***USE*** (*1&2*) + *on* or *upon* [ME *dependen,* fr MF *dependre,* modif of L *dependēre,* fr *de-* + *pendēre* to hang – more at PENDANT]

dependable /di'pendəbl/ *adj* reliable [DEPEND + -ABLE] – **dependableness** *n,* **dependably** *adv,* **dependability** /di,pendə'biləti/ *n*

dependant, *NAm chiefly* **dependent** /di'pendənt/ *n* a person who relies on another for esp financial support

dependence *also* **dependance** /di'pendəns/ *n* **1** being influenced by or subject to another **2** reliance, trust **3** a need for or reliance on a drug: **a** compulsive physiological need for a habit-forming drug (e g heroin); addiction **b** psychological need for a drug after a period of use; habituation [DEPEND + -ENCE]

dependency /di'pend(ə)nsi/ *n* sthg that is dependent on sthg else; *specif* a territorial unit under the jurisdiction of a nation but not formally annexed to it

dependent /di'pend(ə)nt/ *adj* **1** determined or conditioned by another; contingent **2** relying on another for support **3** subject to another's jurisdiction **4** SUBORDINATE 3 ***USE*** (*1&2*) + *on* or *upon* [ME *dependant,* fr MF, prp of *dependre*] – **dependently** *adv*

depersonal·ize, -ise /,dee'puhsənl·iez/ *vt* **1** to deprive of the sense of personal identity **2** to make impersonal – **depersonalization** /-'zaysh(ə)n/ *n*

depict /di'pikt/ *vt* **1** to represent by a picture **2** to describe [L *depictus,* pp of *depingere,* fr *de-* + *pingere* to paint – more at PAINT] – **depicter** *n,* **depiction** /di'piksh(ə)n/ *n*

depilate /'depilayt/ *vt* to remove hair from [L *depilatus,* pp of *depilare,* fr *de-* + *pilus* hair – more at [5]PILE] – **depilation** /,depi'laysh(ə)n/ *n,* **depilatory** /di'pilət(ə)ri/ *adj or n*

deplete /di'pleet/ *vt* to reduce in amount by using up; exhaust, esp of strength or resources [L *depletus,* pp of *deplēre,* fr *de-* + *plēre* to fill – more at [1]FULL] – **depletion** /di'pleesh(ə)n/ *n*

deplorable /di'plawrəbl/ *adj* **1** lamentable ⟨*a* ~ *accident*⟩ **2** extremely bad – **deplorableness** *n,* **deplorably** *adv*

deplore /di'plaw/ *vt* **1** to feel or express grief for **2** to regret or disapprove of strongly [MF or L; MF *deplorer,* fr L *deplorare,* fr *de-* + *plorare* to wail] – **deploringly** *adv*

deploy /di'ploy/ *vt* **1** to spread out (e g troops or ships), esp in battle formation **2** to utilize or arrange as if deploying troops ~ *vi* to move in being deployed [F *déployer,* fr L *displicare* to scatter – more at DISPLAY] – **deployable** *adj,* **deployment** *n*

deplume /,dee'ploohm/ *vt* to pluck the feathers of [ME *deplumen,* fr MF *deplumer,* fr ML *deplumare,* fr L *de-* + *pluma* feather – more at [1]FLEECE]

depolar·ize, -ise /,dee'pohləriez/ *vt* to prevent or remove polarization of (e g a dry battery or a cell membrane) – **depolarizer** *n,* **depolarization** /di,pohlərie'zaysh(ə)n/ *n*

depolitic·ize, -ise /,deepə'litisiez/ *vt* to make nonpolitical ⟨~ *foreign aid*⟩

[1]**deponent** /di'pohnənt/ *adj, of a verb* occurring with passive or middle voice forms but with active voice meaning [LL *deponent-, deponens,* fr L, prp of *deponere*]

[2]**deponent** *n* **1** a deponent verb **2** one who gives (written) evidence

depopulate /,dee'popyoolayt/ *vt* to reduce greatly the population of ~ *vi* to decrease in population [L *depopulatus,* pp of *depopulari,* fr *de-* + *populari* to ravage] – **depopulator** *n,* **depopulation** /-'laysh(ə)n/ *n*

deport /di'pawt/ *vt* **1a** to expel (e g an alien) legally from a country **b** to transport (e g a convicted criminal) to a penal colony or place of exile **2** to behave or conduct (oneself) in a specified manner – fml [L *deportare* to carry away, fr *de-* + *portare* to carry; (2) MF *deporter,* fr L *deportare*] – **deportation** /,deepaw'taysh(ə)n/ *n,* **deportee** /,deepaw'tee/ *n*

de'portment /-mənt/ *n* **1** *Br* the manner in which one stands, sits, or walks; posture **2** *NAm* behaviour, conduct

depose /di'pohz/ *vt* **1** to remove from a position of authority (e g a throne) **2** to testify under oath or by affidavit ~ *vi* to bear witness [ME *deposen,* fr OF *deposer,* fr LL *deponere* (perf indic *deposui*), fr L, to put down; (2) ME *deposen,* fr ML *deponere,* fr LL]

[1]**deposit** /di'pozit/ *vt* **1** to place, esp for safekeeping or as a pledge; *esp* to put in a bank **2a** to lay down; place **b** to let fall (e g sediment) [L *depositus,* pp of *deponere*] – **depositor** *n*

[2]**deposit** *n* **1** depositing or being deposited **2a** money deposited in a bank **b** money given as a pledge or down payment **3** a depository **4** sthg laid down; *esp* (an accumulation of) matter deposited by a natural process ☞ GEOGRAPHY

de'posit ac,count *n, chiefly Br* an account (e g in a bank) on which interest is usu payable and from which withdrawals can be made usu only by prior arrangement – compare CURRENT ACCOUNT

depositary /di'pozit(ə)ri/ *n* a person to whom sthg is entrusted

deposition /,depə'zish(ə)n, ,dee-/ *n* **1** removal from a position of authority **2** a (written and sworn) statement presented as evidence **3** an act or process of depositing – **depositional** *adj*

depository /di'pozit(ə)ri/ *n* **1** a depositary **2** a place where sthg is deposited, esp for safekeeping

[1]**depot** /'depoh/ *n* **1a** a place for the storage of military supplies **b** a place for the reception and training of military recruits; a regimental headquarters **2a** a place for storing goods **b** a store, depository **3a** *Br* an area (e g a garage) in which buses or trains are stored, esp for maintenance **b** *NAm* a railway station [F *dépôt*, fr ML *depositum*, fr L, neut of *depositus*]

[2]**depot** *adj, of a (dose of a) drug* designed to act over a long period

deprave /di'prayv/ *vt* to corrupt morally; pervert [ME *depraven*, fr MF *depraver*, fr L *depravare* to pervert, fr *de-* + *pravus* crooked, bad] – **depravedly** /-vidli/ *adv*, **depraver** *n*, **depravation** /,deprə'vaysh(ə)n/ *n*

depravity /di'pravəti/ *n* (an instance of) moral corruption [DEPRAVE + -ITY]

deprecate /'deprikayt/ *vt* to express disapproval of, esp mildly or regretfully [L *deprecatus*, pp of *deprecari* to avert by prayer, fr *de-* + *precari* to pray – more at PRAY] – **deprecatingly** *adv*, **deprecation** /,depri'kaysh(ə)n/ *n*

deprecatory /'deprikayt(ə)ri/ *adj* **1** apologetic **2** disapproving – **deprecatorily** *adv*

depreciate /di'prees(h)iayt/ *vt* **1** to lower the price or estimated value of **2** to belittle, disparage ~ *vi* to lessen in value; fall [LL *depretiatus*, pp of *depretiare*, fr L *de-* + *pretium* price – more at PRICE] – **depreciable** /di'preesh(i)əbl/ *adj*, **depreciator** *n*, **depreciative** /-sh(i)ətiv/, **depreciatory** /-si·ət(ə)ri, -shi-/ *adj*, **depreciation** /de,preesi'aysh(ə)n, -shi-/ *n*

depredate /'depridayt/ *vb* to plunder, ravage [LL *depraedatus*, pp of *depraedari*, fr L *de-* + *praedari* to plunder – more at PREY] – **depredator** *n*, **depredatory** /-t(ə)ri/ *adj*, **depredation** /,depri'daysh(ə)n/ *n*

depress /di'pres/ *vt* **1** to push or press down ⟨~ *a typewriter key*⟩ **2** to lessen the activity or strength of **3** to sadden, dispirit **4** to decrease the market value or marketability of [ME *depressen*, fr MF *depresser*, fr L *depressus*, pp of *deprimere* to press down, fr *de-* + *premere* to press – more at [2]PRESS] – **depressingly** *adv*

depressant /di'pres(ə)nt/ *n* sthg (e g a drug) that depresses function or activity ⟨*alcohol acts as a* ~ *of the brain*⟩ – **depressant** *adj*

de'pressed *adj* **1** low in spirits; sad **2** lowered or sunken, esp in the centre **3** suffering from economic depression ⟨*a* ~ *area*⟩

depressing /di'presing/ *adj* causing emotional depression ⟨*a* ~ *story*⟩ – **depressingly** *adv*

depression /di'presh(ə)n/ *n* **1** the angular distance of a celestial body below the horizon **2a** a pressing down; a lowering **b** (a mental disorder marked by inactivity, difficulty in thinking and concentration, and esp by) sadness or dejection **c** a lowering of activity, vitality, amount, force, etc **3** a depressed place or part; a hollow **4** [3]LOW 1b ☞ WEATHER **5** a period of low general economic activity marked esp by rising levels of unemployment [DEPRESS + -ION]

[1]**depressive** /di'presiv/ *adj* **1** tending to depress **2** of, characterized by, or liable to psychological depression – **depressively** *adv*

[2]**depressive** *n* one who suffers from periods of psychological depression

depressor /di'presə/ *n* **1** a muscle that draws down a part – compare LEVATOR **2** a device for pressing a part down or aside [LL, fr L *depressus*]

deprivation /,depri'vaysh(ə)n/ *n* **1** an act of depriving; a loss **2** being deprived; privation

deprive /di'priev/ *vt* **1** to take sthg away from **2** to remove (e g a clergyman) from office **3** to withhold sthg from ⟨*he threatened to* ~ *them of their rights*⟩ *USE* (*1&3*) + *of* [ME *depriven*, fr ML *deprivare*, fr L *de-* + *privare* to deprive – more at PRIVATE]

de'prived *adj* lacking the necessities of life or a good environment ⟨*culturally* ~ *children*⟩

depth /depth/ *n* **1a(1)** a deep place in a body of water ⟨*found in the* ~s *of the ocean*⟩ **(2)** a part that is far from the outside or surface ⟨*the* ~s *of the woods*⟩ **b(1)** a profound or intense state (e g of thought or feeling) ⟨*the* ~s *of despair*⟩ **(2)** the worst, most intensive, or severest part ⟨*the* ~s *of winter*⟩ **2a** the perpendicular measurement downwards from a surface **b** the distance from front to back **3** the quality of being deep **4** the degree of intensity ⟨~ *of a colour*⟩ *USE* (*1*) often pl with sing. meaning [ME, prob fr *dep* deep] – **in depth** with great thoroughness ⟨*haven't studied it* in depth⟩ – **out of one's depth 1** in water that is deeper than one's height **2** beyond one's ability to understand

'**depth ,bomb** *n* DEPTH CHARGE

'**depth ,charge** *n* an explosive projectile for use underwater, esp against submarines

'**depth psy,chology** *n* the investigation of the unconscious; psychoanalysis

deputation /,depyoo'taysh(ə)n/ *n sing or pl in constr* a group of people appointed to represent others [DEPUTE + -ATION]

[1]**depute** /di'pyooht/ *vt* to delegate [ME *deputen* to appoint, fr MF *deputer*, fr LL *deputare* to assign, fr L, to consider (as), fr *de-* + *putare* to consider – more at PAVE]

[2]**depute** *n, Scot* a deputy [ME, fr MF *deputé, depute*, pp of *deputer*]

deput·ize, -ise /'depyoo,tiez/ *vi* to act as a deputy *for*

deputy /'depyooti/ *n* **1** a person (e g a second-in-command) appointed as a substitute with power to act for another **2** a member of the lower house of some legislative assemblies [ME, fr MF *deputé*, pp of *deputer*]

derail /,dee'rayl/ *vt* to cause (e g a train) to leave the rails ~ *vi* to be derailed [F *dérailler*, fr *dé-* de- + *rail*, fr E] – **derailment** *n*

derange /di'raynj/ *vt* to disturb the operation or functions of [F *déranger*, fr OF *desrengier*, fr *de-* + *reng* place – more at [2]RANK] – **derangement** *n*

de'ranged *adj* mad, insane

derby /'dahbi/ *n* **1** *cap* a flat race for 3-year-old horses over 1½mi (about 2.9km) held annually at Epsom in England **2** a usu informal race or contest for a specified category of contestant ⟨*a donkey* ~⟩ **3** a sporting match against a major local rival **4** *chiefly NAm* [2]BOWLER [Edward Stanley, 12th Earl of *Derby* †1834]

[1]**derelict** /'derəlikt/ *adj* **1** left to decay **2** *chiefly NAm* lacking a sense of duty; negligent [L *derelictus*, pp of *derelinquere* to abandon, fr *de-* + *relinquere* to leave – more at RELINQUISH]

[2]**derelict** *n* **1** sthg voluntarily abandoned; *specif* a

ship abandoned on the high seas **2** a down-and-out

dereliction /,derə'liksh(ə)n/ *n* **1** (intentional) abandonment or being abandoned **2** a recession of water leaving permanently dry land **3a** conscious neglect ⟨~ *of duty*⟩ **b** a fault, shortcoming

derepress /,deeri'pres/ *vt* to activate (a gene) by releasing from a blocked state – **derepression** /,deeri'presh(ə)n/ *n*

derestrict /,deeri'strikt/ *vt* to cancel or remove a restriction, esp a speed limit, from – **deristriction** /,deeri'striksh(ə)n/ *n*

deride /di'ried/ *vt* to mock, scorn [L *deridēre*, fr *de-* + *ridēre* to laugh – more at RIDICULOUS]

de rigueur /də ri'guh (*Fr* də rigœːr)/ *adj* required by fashion, etiquette, or custom [F, compulsory, lit., of strictness]

derision /di'rizh(ə)n/ *n* deriding or being derided [ME, fr MF, fr LL *derision-, derisio*, fr L *derisus*, pp of *deridēre*]

derisive /di'riesiv, -ziv/ *adj* showing derision; mocking, scornful – **derisively** *adv*

derisory /di'riez(ə)ri/ *adj* **1** derisive **2** worthy of derision; ridiculous; *specif* contemptibly small ⟨*a* ~ *pay offer*⟩

derivation /,deri'vaysh(ə)n/ *n* **1a** the formation of a word from another word or root, esp with an affix **b** an act of tracing or stating the derivation of a word **c** ETYMOLOGY 1 **2a** the source, origin **b** descent ⟨*a family of Scottish* ~⟩ **3** DERIVATIVE 2 **4** an act of deriving – **derivational** *adj*

[1]**derivative** /di'rivətiv/ *adj* **1** formed by derivation **2** made up of derived elements; not original – **derivatively** *adv*

[2]**derivative** *n* **1** a word formed by derivation **2** sthg derived **3** the limit of the ratio of the change in a function to the corresponding change in its independent variable as the latter change approaches zero **4** a chemical related structurally to and (theoretically) derivable from another

derive /di'riev/ *vt* **1a** to obtain or receive, esp from a specified source **b** to obtain (a chemical) from a parent substance **2** to infer, deduce **3a** to trace the derivation of **b** to form by derivation ~ *vi* to come as a derivative *from* [ME *deriven*, fr MF *deriver*, fr L *derivare*, fr *de-* + *rivus* stream – more at RISE] – **derivable** *adj*

derm /duhm/ *n* **1** the dermis **2** SKIN 2a [NL *derma* & *dermis*]

derm-, derma-, dermo- *comb form* dermat- ⟨derma*l*⟩ [NL, fr Gk *derm-, dermo-*, fr *derma*, fr *derein* to skin – more at [2]TEAR]

-derm /-duhm/ *comb form* (→ *n*) skin; layer ⟨*ecto*derm⟩ ⟨*pachy*derm⟩ [prob fr F *-derme*, fr Gk *derma*]

derma /'duhmə/ *n* the dermis [NL, fr Gk]

-derma /-duhmə/ *comb form* (→ *n*), *pl* **-dermas, -dermata** /-duhmahtə/ skin; skin ailment ⟨*sclero*derma⟩ [NL, fr Gk *dermat-, derma* skin] – **-dermatous** *comb form* (→ *adj*)

dermat- /duhmət-/, **dermato-** *comb form* skin ⟨der mat*itis*⟩ ⟨dermato*logy*⟩ [Gk, fr *dermat-, derma*]

dermatitis /,duhmə'tietəs/ *n* a disease or inflammation of the skin [NL]

dermatology /,duhmə'toləji/ *n* a branch of medicine dealing with (diseases of) the skin – **dermatologist** /-'toləjist/ *n*, **dermatologic** /-tə'lojik/, **dermatological** *adj*

dermis /'duhmis/ *n* (the sensitive vascular inner layer of) the skin ☞ NERVE [NL, fr LL *-dermis*] – **dermal** *adj*

-dermis /-duhmis/ *comb form* (→ *n*) layer of skin or tissue ⟨*epi*dermis⟩ [LL, fr Gk, fr *derma*]

dernier cri /,deənyay 'kree (*Fr* dɛrnje kri)/ *n* the newest fashion [F, lit., last cry]

derogate /'derəgayt/ *vb* [LL *derogatus*, pp of *derogare*, fr L, to annul (a law), detract, fr *de-* + *rogare* to ask, propose (a law) – more at [1]RIGHT] – **derogation** /,derə'gaysh(ə)n/ *n*, **derogative** /di'rogətiv/ *adj* – **derogate from** to impair by taking away a part; detract from – fml

derogatory /di'rogət(ə)ri/ *adj* expressing a low opinion; disparaging – **derogatorily** /di'rogət(ə)rəli/ *adv*

derrick /'derik/ *n* **1** a hoisting apparatus employing a tackle rigged at the end of a beam **2** a framework over an oil well or similar hole, for supporting drilling tackle ☞ ENERGY [obs *derrick* (hangman, gallows), fr *Derick*, surname of 17th-c E hangman]

derriere, derrière /'deri·eə/ *n* the buttocks – euph or humor [F *derrière*, fr *derrière*, adj, hinder, fr OF *deriere*, adv, behind, fr L *de retro*, fr *de* from + *retro* back – more at DE-, RETRO-]

derring-do /,dering 'dooh/ *n* daring action ⟨*deeds of* ~⟩ [alter. of ME *dorring don* daring to do, fr *dorring* (gerund of *dorren* to dare) + *don* to do]

derringer /'derinjə/ *n* a short-barrelled pistol of large calibre [Henry *Deringer* †1868 US inventor]

derris /'deris/ *n* (an insecticidal extract of) any of a genus of tropical leguminous shrubs and climbing plants [NL, genus name, fr Gk, skin, fr *derein* to skin – more at [2]TEAR]

derv /duhv/ *n* fuel oil for diesel engines [*d*iesel-*e*ngined *r*oad *v*ehicle]

dervish /'duhvish/ *n* a member of a Muslim religious order noted for devotional exercises (e g bodily movements leading to a trance) [Turk *derviş*, lit., beggar, fr Per *darvēsh*]

desalinate /,dee'salinayt/ *vt* to remove salt from (esp sea water) – **desalinator** *n*, **desalination** /,deesali'naysh(ə)n/ *n*

desalt /,dee'sawlt/ *vt* to desalinate – **desalter** *n*

[1]**descant** /'des,kant/ *n* a counterpoint superimposed on a simple melody and usu sung by some or all of the sopranos [ME *dyscant*, fr ONF & ML; ONF *descant*, fr ML *discantus*, fr L *dis-* + *cantus* song – more at CHANT]

[2]**descant** /des'kant, dis-/ *vi* **1** to sing or play a descant **2** to talk or write at considerable length *on* or *upon*

descant recorder *n, chiefly Br* the member of the recorder family with the highest range

descend /di'send/ *vi* **1** to pass from a higher to a lower level **2** to pass from the general to the particular **3** to pass by inheritance **4** to incline, lead, or extend downwards ⟨*the road* ~s *to the river*⟩ **5a** to come down or make a sudden attack – usu + *on* or *upon* **b** to make a sudden disconcerting visit or appearance – usu + *on* or *upon*; chiefly humor **6** to proceed from higher to lower in a sequence or gradation **7** to sink in status or dignity; stoop ~ *vt* to pass, move, or extend down or down along ⟨*he* ~ed *the steps*⟩ [ME *descenden*, fr OF *descendre*, fr

L *descendere*, fr *de-* + *scandere* to climb – more at SCAN]

descendant, *NAm also* **descendent** /di'send(ə)nt/ *n* sby or sthg descended or deriving from another [MF & L; MF *descendant*, fr L *descendent-*, *descendens*, prp of *descendere*]

de'scended *adj* having as an ancestor; sprung *from*

descendeur /,deson'duh/ *n* any of several devices allowing a controlled descent of a rope in abseiling [F, fr *descendre*]

descent /di'sent/ *n* **1** the act or process of descending **2** a downward step (e g in status or value) **3a** derivation from an ancestor; birth, lineage **b** transmission of an estate by inheritance **c** a transmission from a usu earlier source; a derivation **4a** a downward inclination; a slope **b** a descending way (e g a staircase) **5** a sudden hostile raid or attack [ME, fr MF *descente*, fr *descendre*]

describe /di'skrieb/ *vt* **1** to give an account of in words **2** to trace the outline of [L *describere*, fr *de-* + *scribere* to write – more at [1]SCRIBE] – **describable** *adj*

description /di'skripsh(ə)n/ *n* **1** an account intended to convey a mental image of sthg experienced **2** kind, sort ⟨*people of every* ~⟩ [ME *descripcioun*, fr MF & L; MF *description*, fr L *description-*, *descriptio*, fr *descriptus*, pp of *describere*]

descriptive /di'skriptiv/ *adj* **1** serving to describe, esp vividly **2** *of a modifier* expressing the quality, kind, or condition of what is denoted by the modified term; not limiting or demonstrative (e g *hot* in 'hot water") – **descriptively** *adv*

descry /di'skrie/ *vt* to notice or see, esp at a distance – fml [ME *descrien*, fr OF *descrier* to proclaim, decry]

desecrate /'desikrayt/ *vt* to violate the sanctity of; profane [*de-* + *-secrate* (as in *consecrate*)] – **desecrator** *n*, **descration** /,desi 'kraysh(ə)n/ *n*

desegregate /,dee'segrigayt/ *vt* to eliminate (racial) segregation in – **desegregation** /-'gaysh(ə)n/ *n*

desensit·ize, -ise /,dee'sensətiez/ *vt* **1** to make (sby previously sensitive) insensitive or nonreactive to a sensitizing agent **2** to make (a photographic material) less sensitive or completely insensitive to radiation – **desensitizer** *n*, **desensitization** /-'zaysh(ə)n/ *n*

[1]**desert** /'dezət/ *n* **1** (a desolate region like) a dry barren region incapable of supporting much life ☞ PLANT **2** an area or place that is deprived of or devoid of sthg important ⟨*a cultural* ~⟩ [ME, fr OF, fr LL *desertum*, fr L, neut of *desertus*, pp of *deserere* to desert, fr *de-* + *serere* to join together – more at SERIES] – **desertic** /-tik/ *adj*

[2]**desert** /di'zuht/ *n* deserved reward or punishment – usu pl with sing. meaning ⟨*got her just* ~s⟩ [ME *deserte*, fr OF, fr fem of *desert*, pp of *deservir* to deserve]

[3]**desert** /di'zuht/ *vt* **1** to leave, usu without intending to return **2a** to abandon or forsake, esp in time of need **b** to abandon (military service) without leave ~ *vi* to quit one's post, (military) service, etc without leave or justification [F *déserter*, fr LL *desertare*, fr *desertus*] – **deserter** *n*

Desert /'dezət/ *trademark* – used for an ankle-high laced suede boot with a rubber sole

desertion /di'zuhsh(ə)n/ *n* the abandonment of a post or relationship and the moral and legal obligations attached to it ⟨*sued for divorce on grounds of* ~⟩ [[3]DESERT + -ION]

deserve /di'zuhv/ *vb* to be worthy of or suitable for (some recompense or treatment) [ME *deserven*, fr OF *deservir*, fr L *deservire* to serve zealously, fr *de-* + *servire* to serve] – **deservedly** /-vidli/ *adv*

deserving /di'zuhving/ *adj* meriting (financial) aid

desex /,dee'seks/ *vt* **1** to castrate, spay **2** to desexualize

desexual·ize, -ise /,dee'seksyoo(ə)liez, -shəliez/ *vt* to deprive of sexuality, sexual power, or the qualities appropriate to one or other sex – **desexualization** /-'zaysh(ə)n/ *n*

deshabille /,dayza'beel, dis-/, **déshabillé** /,dayza'bee,ay/ *n* the state of being only partially or carelessly dressed [F *déshabillé*, fr pp of *déshabiller* to undress, fr *dés* dis- + *habiller* to dress, fr *bille* log – more at [3]BILLET]

desiccate /'desikayt/ *vt* **1** to dry up **2** to preserve (a food) by drying to dehydrate [L *desiccatus*, pp of *desiccare* to dry up, fr *de-* + *siccare* to dry, fr *siccus* dry] – **desiccant** *n*, **desiccator** *n*, **desiccative** /-,kaytiv/ *adj*, **desiccation** /,desi'kaysh(ə)n/ *n*

desideratum /di,zidə'raytəm, -'rah-/ *n*, *pl* **desiderata** /-tə/ sthg desired as necessary – fml [L, neut of *desideratus*, pp of *desiderare* to desire]

[1]**design** /di'zien/ *vt* **1a** to conceive and plan out in the mind **b** to devise for a specific function or end **2a** to draw the plans for **b** to create or execute according to a plan; devise ~ *vi* **1** to conceive or execute a plan **2** to draw, lay out, or prepare a design [MF *designer*, fr L *designare*, fr *de-* + *signare* to mark, mark out – more at [2]SIGN] – **designer** *n*, **designedly** /-nidli/ *adv*

[2]**design** *n* **1** a mental plan or scheme **2a** a particular purpose held in view **b** deliberate purposeful planning ⟨*more by accident than by* ~⟩ **3** *pl* dishonest, hostile, or acquisitive intent – + *on* **4** (the act of producing) a drawing, plan, or pattern showing the details of how sthg is to be constructed **5** the arrangement of the elements of a work of art or artefact **6** a decorative pattern

[1]**designate** /'dezignət, -nayt/ *adj* chosen for an office but not yet installed ⟨*ambassador* ~⟩ [L *designatus*, pp of *designare*]

[2]**designate** /'dezignayt/ *vt* **1** to indicate; POINT OUT **2** to call by a distinctive name or title **3** to nominate for a specified purpose, office, or duty – **designator** *n*, **designatory** /,dezig'nayt(ə)ri/ *adj*

designation /,dezig'naysh(ə)n/ *n* **1** the act of indicating or identifying **2** a distinguishing name or title **3** appointment to an office, post, or service

designing /di'ziening/ *adj* crafty, scheming

desirable /di'zie·ərəbl/ *adj* **1** causing (sexual) desire; attractive **2** worth seeking or doing as advantageous, beneficial, or wise – **desirableness** *n*, **desirably** *adv*, **desirability** /di,zie·ərə'biləti/ *n*

[1]**desire** /di'zie·ə/ *vt* **1** to long or hope for **2** to express a wish for; request **3** to wish to have sexual relations with [ME *desiren*, fr OF *desirer*, fr L *desiderare*, fr *de-* + *sider-*, *sidus* star]

[2]**desire** *n* **1** a conscious impulse towards an object or experience promising enjoyment or satisfaction **2** a (sexual) longing or craving **3** a formal request or petition **4** sthg desired

desirous /di'zie·ərəs/ *adj* eagerly wanting; desiring – fml

desist /di'zist/ *vi* to cease to proceed or act – fml [MF *desister*, fr L *desistere*, fr *de-* + *sistere* to stand, stop; akin to L *stare* to stand] – **desistance** *n*

desk /desk/ *n* **1a** a table with a sloping or horizontal surface and often drawers and compartments, that is designed esp for writing and reading **b** a church lectern **c** a table, counter, or booth at which cashiers, clerks, etc work **d** a music stand **2** a division of an organization specializing in a usu specified phase of activity [ME *deske*, fr ML *desca*, modif of OIt *desco* table, fr L *discus* dish, disc – more at DISH]

desk research *n* research conducted by examining existing data (e g published statistics)

desm- /desm-/, **desmo-** *comb form* bond; ligament [NL, fr Gk, fr *desmos*, fr *dein* to bind – more at DIADEM]

desman /'desmən/ *n, pl* **desmans** any of several aquatic insect-eating mammals resembling moles ☞ ENDANGERED [short for Sw *desmansråtta*, fr *desman* musk + *råtta* rat]

[1]**desolate** /'dezələt/ *adj* **1** deserted, uninhabited **2** forsaken, forlorn **3** barren, lifeless ⟨*a ~ landscape*⟩ [ME *desolat*, fr L *desolatus*, pp of *desolare* to abandon, fr *de-* + *solus* alone] – **desolately** *adv*, **desolateness** *n*

[2]**desolate** /'dezəlayt/ *vt* **1** to deprive of inhabitants **2** to lay waste – **desolator** /-,laytə/ *n*

desolation /,dezə'laysh(ə)n/ *n* **1** devastation, ruin **2** a barren wasteland **3** misery, wretchedness [DESOLATE + -ION]

desorb /,dee'sawb/ *vt* to free from an absorbed or adsorbed state – **desorption** /-'sawpsh(ə)n/

desoxy- /desoksi-/ *comb form* deoxy-

[1]**despair** /di'speə/ *vi* to lose all hope or confidence ⟨*~ of winning*⟩ [ME *despeiren*, fr MF *desperer*, fr L *desperare*, fr *de-* + *sperare* to hope; akin to L *spes* hope – more at SPEED] – **despairingly** *adv*

[2]**despair** *n* **1** utter loss of hope **2** a cause of hopelessness ⟨*that child is the ~ of his parents*⟩

despatch /di'spach/ *vb or n* (to) dispatch

desperado /,despə'rahdoh/ *n, pl* **desperadoes, desperados** a bold, reckless, or violent person, esp a criminal [prob alter. of obs *desperate* (desperado), fr *desperate*, adj]

desperate /'desp(ə)rət/ *adj* **1** being (almost) beyond hope **2a** reckless because of despair **b** undertaken as a last resort ⟨*a ~ remedy*⟩ **3** suffering extreme need or anxiety ⟨*~ for money*⟩ **4** fraught with extreme danger or impending disaster [L *desperatus*, pp of *desperare*] – **desperately** *adv*, **desperateness** *n*

desperation /,despə'raysh(ə)n/ *n* **1** loss of hope and surrender to despair **2** extreme recklessness caused by hopelessness

despicable /di'spikəbl/ *adj* morally contemptible [LL *despicabilis*, fr L *despicari* to despise] – **despicableness** *n*, **despicably** *adv*

despise /di'spiez/ *vt* **1** to regard with contempt or distaste **2** to regard as negligible or worthless [ME *despisen*, fr OF *despis-*, stem of *despire*, fr L *despicere*, fr *de-* + *specere* to look – more at SPY] – **despiser** *n*

despite /di'spiet/ *prep* notwithstanding; IN SPITE OF ⟨*ran ~ her injury*⟩ [short for *in despite of; despite*, n (contempt, defiance), fr ME, fr OF *despit*, fr L *despectus*, fr *despectus*, pp of *despicere*]

despoil /di'spoyl/ *vt* to plunder, pillage [ME *despoylen*, fr OF *despoillier*, fr L *despoliare*, fr *de-* + *spoliare* to strip, rob – more at [2]SPOIL] – **despoiler** *n*, **despoilment** *n*

despoliation /di,spohli'aysh(ə)n/ *n* plundering or being plundered [LL *despoliation-*, *despoliatio*, fr *despoliatus*, pp of *despoliare*]

despond /di'spond/ *n* despondency [*despond* (to become discouraged), fr L *despondēre*, fr *de-* + *spondēre* to promise solemnly – more at SPOUSE]

despondency /di'spondənsi/ *n* dejection, depression [DESPONDENT + -CY]

despondent /di'spond(ə)nt/ *adj* feeling extreme discouragement or dejection [L *despondent-*, *despondens*, prp of *despondēre*] – **despondently** *adv*

despot /'despot/ *n* **1** a ruler with absolute power **2** a person exercising power abusively or tyrannically [MF *despote*, fr Gk *despotēs*; akin to Skt *dampati* lord of the house; both fr a prehistoric IE compound whose constituents are akin to L *domus* house and to L *potis* able – more at TIMBER, POTENT] – **despotic** /di'spotik/ *adj*, **despotically** *adv*

despotism /'despə,tiz(ə)m/ *n* **1** rule by a despot; absolutism **2** despotic exercise of power

desquamate /'deskwə,mayt/ *vi* to peel off in scales [L *desquamatus*, pp of *desquamare*, fr *de-* + *squama* scale] – **desquamation** /,deskwə'maysh(ə)n/ *n*

dessert /di'zuht/ *n* a usu sweet course or dish served at the end of a meal [MF, fr *desservir* to clear the table, fr *des-* de- + *servir* to serve, fr L *servire*]

des'sert,spoon /-,spoohn/ *n* **1** a spoon intermediate in size between a teaspoon and a tablespoon and used for eating dessert **2** a dessertspoonful

des'sert,spoonful /-f(ə)l/ *n* **1** as much as a dessertspoon can hold **2** a unit of measure equal to about 8.9cm³ (about 2½ fluid drachms) ☞ UNIT

dessert wine *n* a usu sweet wine often served with dessert

destalin·ize, -ise /,dee'stahliniez, -stal-/ *vi* to dismantle the system associated with Stalin and his rule [Joseph *Stalin* †1953 Russ political leader] – **destalinization** /-'zaysh(ə)n/ *n*

destination /,desti'naysh(ə)n/ *n* a place which is set for the end of a journey or to which sthg is sent [DESTINE + -ATION]

destine /'destin/ *vt* **1** to designate or dedicate in advance **2** to direct or set apart for a specified purpose or goal ⟨*freight ~d for English ports*⟩ *USE* usu pass [ME *destinen*, fr OF *destiner*, fr L *destinare*, fr *de-* + *-stinare* (akin to L *stare* to stand) – more at STAND]

destiny /'destini/ *n* **1** the power or agency held to determine the course of events **2** sthg to which a person or thing is destined; fortune **3** a predetermined course of events [ME *destinee*, fr MF, fr fem of *destiné*, pp of *destiner*]

destitute /'destityooht/ *adj* **1** lacking sthg necessary or desirable – + *of* ⟨*a heart ~ of feeling*⟩ **2** lacking the basic necessities of life; extremely poor [ME, fr L *destitutus*, pp of *destituere* to abandon, deprive, fr *de-* + *statuere* to set up – more at STATUTE] – **destitution** /-'tyoohsh(ə)n/ *n*

destrier /'destri·ə/ *n, archaic* a war-horse, charger [ME, fr OF, fr *destre* right hand, fr L *dextra*, fr fem of *dexter*]

destroy /di'stroy/ *vt* **1** to demolish, ruin **2a** to put an end to; kill **b** to make ineffective; neutralize [ME *destroyen*, fr OF *destruire*, fr (assumed) VL *destrugere*, alter. of L *destruere*, fr *de-* + *struere* to build – more at STRUCTURE]

destroyer /di'stroyə/ *n* a fast multi-purpose warship smaller than a cruiser [DESTROY + [2]-ER]

[1]**destruct** /di'strukt/ *vt, NAm* to destroy [back-formation fr *destruction*] – **destructible** *adj*, **destructibility** /-tə'biləti/ *n*

[2]**destruct** *n* the deliberate destruction of a device (e g a rocket)

destruction /di'struksh(ə)n/ *n* **1** destroying or being destroyed **2** a cause of ruin or downfall [ME *destruccioun*, fr MF *destruction*, fr L *destruction-, destructio*, fr *destructus*, pp of *destruere*]

destructive /di'struktiv/ *adj* **1** causing destruction **2** designed or tending to destroy; negative ⟨~ *criticism*⟩ – **destructively** *adv*, **destructiveness** *n*, **destructivity** /,deestruk'tivəti/ *n*

destructor /di'struktə/ *n* an incinerator for refuse [DESTRUCT + [1]-OR]

desuetude /'deswityoohd, di'syooh·i,tyoohd/ *n* discontinuance from use; disuse – fml [F or L; F *désuétude*, fr L *desuetudo*, fr *desuetus*, pp of *desuescere* to become unaccustomed, fr *de-* + *suescere* to become accustomed; akin to L *sui* of oneself – more at SUICIDE]

desultory /'desəlt(ə)ri, 'dez-/ *adj* passing aimlessly from one subject or activity to another [L *desultorius*, fr *desultus*, pp of *desilire* to leap down, fr *de-* + *salire* to leap – more at [2]SALLY] – **desultorily** *adv*, **desultoriness** *n*

detach /di'tach/ *vt* **1** to separate, esp from a larger mass and usu without causing damage **2** to separate from a parent organization for a special purpose ⟨~ *a ship from the fleet*⟩ [F *détacher*, fr OF *destachier*, fr *des-* de- + *-tachier* (as in *atachier* to attach)] – **detachable** *adj*, **detachably** *adv*, **detachability** /di,tachə'biləti/ *n*

de'tached *adj* **1** standing by itself; *specif* not sharing any wall with another building **2** free from prejudice or emotional involvement; aloof – **detachedly** *adv*

de'tachment /-mənt/ *n* **1** a detaching, separation **2** *sing or pl in constr* a body of troops, ships, etc separated from the main body for a special mission **3** freedom from bias

[1]**detail** /'dee,tayl/ *n* **1** extended treatment of or attention to particular items **2a** a small and subordinate part; *specif* part of a work of art considered or reproduced in isolation **b** a part considered separately from the whole **c** an individual relevant part or fact – usu pl ⟨*can you let me have the* ~s *by tonight*⟩ **3a** *sing or pl in constr* a small military detachment selected for a particular task **b** the task to be performed by a military detail [F *détail*, fr OF *detail* slice, piece, fr *detaillier* to cut in pieces, fr *de-* + *taillier* to cut – more at TAILOR] – **in detail** item by item; thoroughly

[2]**detail** *vt* **1** to report in detail **2** to assign to a particular task or place

'de,tailed *adj* marked by abundant detail or thorough treatment

detain /di'tayn/ *vt* **1** to hold or retain (as if) in custody ⟨~ed *in hospital overnight*⟩ **2** to delay; HOLD BACK 1 [ME *deteynen*, fr MF *detenir*, fr L *detinēre*, fr *de-* + *tenēre* to hold – more at THIN]

detainee /,deetay'nee/ *n* a person held in custody, esp for political reasons

detainer /di'taynə/ *n* **1** the withholding from the rightful owner of sthg which has lawfully come into the possession of the holder **2** (a writ authorizing) detention in custody [AF *detener*, fr *detener* to detain, fr L *detinēre*]

detect /di'tekt/ *vt* to discover the existence or presence of [ME *detecten*, fr L *detectus*, pp of *detegere* to uncover, detect, fr *de-* + *tegere* to cover – more at THATCH] – **detectable** *adj*, **detection** /di'teksh(ə)n/ *n*, **detectability** /di,tektə'biləti/ *n*

[1]**detective** /di'tektiv/ *adj* **1** used in detecting sthg **2** of detectives or their work ⟨*a* ~ *novel*⟩

[2]**detective** *n* a policeman or other person engaged in investigating crimes, detecting lawbreakers, or getting information that is not readily accessible

detector /di'tektə/ *n* an electrical circuit for separating an (audio) signal from a (radio) carrier [DETECT + [1]-OR]

detent /di'tent/ *n* a device that locks or unlocks one mechanical part in relation to another, esp in a clock [F *détente*, fr MF *destente*, fr *destendre* to slacken, fr OF, fr *des-* de- + *tendre* to stretch, fr L *tendere* – more at THIN]

détente, detente /day'tonht/ *n* a relaxation of strained relations (e g between ideologically opposed nations) [F]

detention /di'tensh(ə)n/ *n* **1** detaining or being detained, esp in custody **2** *chiefly Br* the keeping in of a pupil after school hours as a punishment [MF or LL; MF, fr LL *detention-, detentio*, fr L *detentus*, pp of *detinēre* to detain]

de'tention ,centre *n, Br* an institution for the detention of young offenders for short periods

deter /di'tuh/ *vt* **-rr-** to discourage or prevent from acting [L *deterrēre*, fr *de-* + *terrēre* to frighten – more at TERROR] – **determent** *n*, **deterable** *adj*

detergent /di'tuhj(ə)nt/ *n* a cleansing agent; *specif* any of various synthetic (water-soluble) compounds that are chemically different from soaps and are able to keep oils, dirt, etc in suspension and act as wetting agents [F or L; F *détergent*, fr L *detergent-, detergens*, prp of *detergēre* to wipe off, cleanse, fr *de* from, away + *tergēre* to wipe off – more at TERSE]

deteriorate /di'tiəri·ə,rayt/ *vb* to grow or make or worse [LL *deterioratus*, pp of *deteriorare*, fr L *deterior* worse, fr *de-* + *-ter* (suffix as in L *uter* which of two) + *-ior* (compar suffix) – more at WHETHER, [1]-ER] – **deteriorative** /-ri·ərətiv/ *adj*, **deterioration** /di,tiəri·ə'raysh(ə)n/ *n*

determinable /di'tuhminəbl/ *adj* **1** capable of being determined, definitely ascertained, or decided upon **2** liable to be terminated – **determinably** *adv*

determinant /di'tuhminənt/ *n* **1** sthg that determines, fixes, or conditions **2** an array of symbols or numbers written in the form of a square matrix bordered on either side by a vertical line; *also* a value assigned to a determinant obtained by manipulating its elements according to a certain rule **3** a gene

determinate /di'tuhminət/ *adj* **1** fixed, established **2** conclusively determined; definitive [ME, fr L *determinatus*, pp of *determinare*] – **determinately** *adv*, **determinateness** *n*, **determinacy** /-nəsi/ *n*

determination /di,tuhmi'naysh(ə)n/ *n* **1** a judicial decision settling a controversy **2a** firm intention **b** the ability to make and act on firm decisions; resoluteness

determinative /di'tuhminətiv/ *n or adj* (sthg) serving to determine – **determinatively** *adv*

determine /di'tuhmin/ *vt* **1a** to fix conclusively or authoritatively **b** to settle, decide ⟨~ *the rights and wrongs of a case*⟩ **2a** to fix beforehand **b** to regulate ⟨*demand* ~s *the price*⟩ **3a** to ascertain the intent, nature, or scope of **b** to set an end to ⟨~ *an estate*⟩ ~ *vi* **1** to come to a decision **2** to come to an end or become void [ME *determinen*, fr MF *determiner*, fr L *determinare*, fr *de-* + *terminare* to limit, fr *terminus* boundary, limit – more at TERM]

de'termined *adj* **1** decided, resolved ⟨*was* ~ *to learn to drive*⟩ **2** firm, resolute ⟨*a very* ~ *woman*⟩ – **determinedly** *adv*, **determinedness** *n*

determiner /di'tuhminə/ *n* a word that limits the meaning of a noun and comes before a descriptive adjective modifying the same noun (e g *his* in 'his new car") [DETERMINE + [2]-ER]

determinism /di'tuhmi,niz(ə)m/ *n* **1** a doctrine that all phenomena are determined by preceding occurrences; *esp* the doctrine that all human acts, choices, etc are causally determined and that free will is illusory **2** a belief in predestination – **determinist** *n or adj*, **deterministic** /di,tuhmi'nistik/ *adj*, **deterministically** *adv*

[1]**deterrent** /di'terənt/ *adj* serving to deter [L *deterrent-, deterrens*, prp of *deterrēre* to deter] – **deterrence** *n*, **deterrently** *adv*

[2]**deterrent** *n* sthg that deters; *esp* a (nuclear) weapon that is held in readiness by one nation or alliance in order to deter another from attacking

detest /di'test/ *vt* to feel intense dislike for; loathe [ME *detesten*, fr L *detestari*, lit., to curse while calling a deity to witness, fr *de-* + *testari* to call to witness – more at TESTAMENT] – **detestable** *adj*, **detestably** *adv*

detestation /,deete'staysh(ə)n/ *n* extreme dislike; abhorrence

dethrone /,dee'throhn/ *vt* DEPOSE 1 – **dethronement** *n*

detinue /'detinyooh/ *n* (a common-law action against) the unlawful detention of a piece of personal property [ME *detenewe*, fr MF *detenue* detention, fr fem of *detenu*, pp of *detenir* to detain]

detonate /'detənayt/ *vb* to (cause to) explode with sudden violence ⟨~ *an atom bomb*⟩ – compare DEFLAGRATE [L *detonatus*, pp of *detonare* to thunder down, fr *de-* + *tonare* to thunder – more at THUNDER] – **detonatable** *adj*, **detonative** /-,naytiv, -nətiv/ *adj*

detonation /,detə'naysh(ə)n/ *n* **1** the action or process of detonating **2** premature combustion in an internal-combustion engine that results in knocking

detonator /'detənaytə/ *n* **1** a device used for detonating a high explosive **2** a device, clipped on to a railway line, that detonates as a train passes to warn of esp fog or emergency

[1]**detour** /'dee,tooə/ *n* a deviation from a course or procedure; *specif* a way that is an alternative to a shorter or planned route [F *détour*, fr OF *destor*, fr *destorner* to divert, fr *des-* de- + *torner* to turn – more at [1]TURN]

[2]**detour** *vi* to make a detour ~ *vt* to send by a roundabout route

detoxicate /,dee'toksikayt/ *vt* to detoxify [*de-* + L *toxicum* poison – more at TOXIC] – **detoxicant** *n*, **detoxication** /di,toksi'kaysh(ə)n/ *n*

detoxify /,dee'toksifie/ *vt* to remove a poison or toxin from – **detoxification** /di,toksifi 'kaysh(ə)n/ *n*

detract /di'trakt/ *vi* to take away sthg desirable – usu + *from* [ME *detracten*, fr L *detractus*, pp of *detrahere* to withdraw, disparage, fr *de-* + *trahere* to draw – more at DRAW]

detraction /di'traksh(ə)n/ *n* belittling, disparagement – **detractive** *adj*

detractor /di'traktə/ *n* one who denigrates sby or his/her ideas or beliefs ⟨*her* ~s *were more vociferous than her followers*⟩

detrain /,dee'trayn/ *vb* to alight or remove from a railway train – **detrainment** *n*

detriment /'detrimənt/ *n* (a cause of) injury or damage [ME, fr MF or L; MF, fr L *detrimentum*, fr *deterere* to wear away, impair, fr *de-* + *terere* to rub – more at THROW]

detrimental /,detri'mentl/ *adj* harmful, damaging – **detrimentally** *adv*

detrition /di'trish(ə)n/ *n* a wearing away, esp by rubbing [ML *detrition-, detritio*, fr L *detritus*]

detritus /di'trietəs/ *n, pl* **detritus** /~/ **1** loose material (e g rock fragments or organic particles) produced by disintegration **2** debris caused by disintegration [F *détritus*, fr L *detritus*, pp of *deterere*] – **detrital** /di'trietl/ *adj*

de trop /də'troh (*Fr* də tro)/ *adj* not wanted or needed; superfluous [F]

Dettol /'detl/ *trademark* – used for a disinfectant containing chlorinated phenols

detumescence /,deetyooh'mes(ə)ns/ *n* subsidence or diminution of swelling – **detumescent** *adj*

deuce /dyoohs/ *n* **1** a playing card or the face of a dice representing the number 2 **2** a tie in a game (e g tennis) after which a side must score 2 consecutive clear points to win **3a** the devil, the dickens – formerly used as an interjection or intensive **b** sthg very bad or remarkable of its kind ⟨*a* ~ *of a mess*⟩ [MF *deus* two, fr L *duos*, acc masc of *duo* two; (3) prob fr LG *duus* deuce (the worst throw at dice; hence, exclamation of dismay) – more at TWO]

deuced /dyoohst, 'dyoohsid/ *adj* damned, confounded – **deuced, deucedly** /dyoohst, 'dyoohsidli/ *adv*

deus ex machina /'dayəs eks 'makinə/ *n* sby or sthg (e g in fiction or drama) that appears or is introduced suddenly and unexpectedly and provides a contrived solution to an apparently insoluble difficulty [NL, a god from a machine, trans of Gk *theos ek mēchanēs*]

deuter- /dyootə-/, **deutero-** *comb form* deuterium; containing deuterium ⟨deuter*ated*⟩ ⟨deutero *alkanes*⟩ [ISV]

deuterate /'dyoohtə,rayt/ *vt* to introduce deuterium into (a compound) – **deuteration** /-'raysh(ə)n/ *n*

deuterium /dyooh'tiəri·əm/ *n* the hydrogen isotope that is twice the mass of ordinary hydrogen [NL, fr Gk *deuteros* second]

Deuteronomy /,dyoohtə'ronəmi/ *n* the fifth book of the Old Testament containing Mosaic laws and narrative [ME *Deutronomie*, fr LL *Deuteronomium*, fr Gk *Deuteronomion*, fr *deuteros* + *nomos* law – more at NIMBLE]

deutoplasm /'dyoohtoh,plaz(ə)m/ *n* the nonliving nutritive material in the substance of a cell; *esp* the yolk or food reserves of an egg [ISV, fr *deuto-* secondary (deriv of Gk *deuteros*) + *plasm*] – **deutoplasmic** /,dyoohtoh'plazmik/ *adj*

Deutsche Mark /'doych ,mahk (ər dɔɪtʃə mark)/

n ☞ *Germany (Federal Republic)* at NATIONALITY [G, German mark]

deutzia /'dyoohtsi·ə, 'doytsi·ə/ *n* any of a genus of the saxifrage family of ornamental shrubs with white or pink flowers [NL, fr Jean *Deutz* †1784? D patron of botanical research]

devaluation /,dee,valyoo'aysh(ə)n/ *n* **1** a reduction in the exchange value of a currency **2** a lessening, esp of status or stature

devalue /,dee'valyooh/, **devaluate** /dee'valyoo,ayt/ *vt* **1** to reduce the exchange value of (money) **2** to lessen the value or reputation of ~ *vi* to institute devaluation

Devanagari /,dayvə'nahgəri/ *n* an alphabet used for writing Sanskrit and various modern languages of India ☞ ALPHABET [Skt *devanāgarī*, fr *deva* divine + *nāgarī* script of the city; akin to L *divus* divine – more at DEITY]

devastate /'devəstayt/ *vt* **1** to reduce to ruin; lay waste **2** to have a shattering effect on; overwhelm ⟨*a* devastating *attack on his work*⟩ [L *devastatus*, pp of *devastare*, fr *de-* + *vastare* to lay waste – more at WASTE] – **devastatingly** *adv*, **devastator** *n*, **devastation** /-'staysh(ə)n/ *n*

develop /di'veləp/ *vt* **1a** to unfold gradually or in detail; expound **b** to show signs of ⟨~ *an illness*⟩ **c** to subject (exposed photograph material) esp to chemicals, in order to produce a visible image; *also* to make visible by such a method **d** to elaborate by the unfolding of a musical idea and by the working out of rhythmic and harmonic changes in the theme **2** to bring out the possibilities of **3a** to promote the growth of ⟨~ed *her muscles*⟩ **b** to make more available or usable ⟨~ *its resources*⟩ **c** to build on or change the use of (a tract of land) **d** to move (a chess piece) to a position providing more opportunity for effective use **4** to cause to grow, mature, or increase **5** to acquire gradually ⟨~ *a taste for good wine*⟩ ~ *vi* **1a** to go through a process of natural growth, differentiation, or evolution by successive changes **b** to evolve; *broadly* to grow **2** to become gradually visible or apparent **3** to develop one's pieces in chess [F *développer*, fr OF *desvoloper*, fr *des-* de- + *voloper* to wrap] – **developable** *adj*

de'veloped *adj* having achieved a high economic level of industrial production and a high standard of living ⟨~ *nation*⟩

developer /di'veləpə/ *n* **1** a chemical used to develop exposed photographic materials **2** a person who develops real estate; *esp* sby who improves and subdivides land and builds and sells houses on it [DEVELOP + [2]-ER]

developing /di'veləping/ *adj* UNDERDEVELOPED 2

de'velopment /-mənt/ *n* **1** the act, process, or result of developing **2** being developed – **developmental** /di,veləp'mentl/ *adj*, **developmentally** *adv*

de'velopment ,area *n*, *Br* an area of high unemployment where government encouragement is given to new industries

[1]deviant /'deevi·ənt/ *adj* **1** deviating, esp from a norm **2** characterized by deviation – **deviance, deviancy** *n*

[2]deviant *n* a person whose behaviour differs markedly from the norm

[1]deviate /'deevi,ayt/ *vi* to stray, esp from a topic, principle, or accepted norm or from a straight course [LL *deviatus*, pp of *deviare*, fr L *de-* + *via* way – more at VIA] – **deviator** *n*, **deviatory** /'deevi·ət(ə)ri/ *adj*

[2]deviate /'deevi·ət, -ayt/ *n*, *chiefly NAm* a deviant

deviation /,deevi'aysh(ə)n/ *n* **1** deflection of a compass needle caused by local magnetic influences **2** the difference between a value in a frequency distribution and a fixed number ☞ STATISTICS **3** departure from an established party line **4** departure from accepted norms of behaviour ⟨*sexual* ~⟩ [[1]DEVIATE + -ION] – **deviationism** *n*, **deviationist** *n*

device /di'vies/ *n* **1a** a scheme to trick or deceive **b** sthg elaborate or intricate in design **c** sthg (e g a figure of speech or a dramatic convention) designed to achieve a particular artistic effect **d** a piece of equipment or a mechanism designed for a special purpose or function **2** *pl* desire, will ⟨*left to her own* ~s⟩ **3a** an emblematic design used in a heraldic achievement – compare CHARGE 1 **b** a motto [ME *devis, devise*, fr OF, division, intention, fr *deviser* to divide, regulate, tell – more at DEVISE]

[1]devil /'devl/ *n* **1** *often cap* the supreme spirit of evil in Jewish and Christian belief, the tempter of mankind, the leader of all apostate angels, and the ruler of hell **2** a malignant spirit; a demon **3** an extremely cruel or wicked person; a fiend **4** a high-spirited, reckless, or energetic person **5** a junior legal counsel working without payment to gain experience **6a** a person of the specified type ⟨*poor* ~⟩ ⟨*lucky* ~⟩ **b** sthg provoking, difficult, or trying ⟨*this type of bottle is the very* ~ *to open*⟩ **c** – used as an interjection or intensive ⟨*what the* ~ *is that?*⟩ *USE* (*6*) infml [ME *devel*, fr OE *dēofol*, fr LL *diabolus*, fr Gk *diabolos*, lit., slanderer, fr *diaballein* to throw across, slander, fr *dia-* + *ballein* to throw; akin to OHG *quellan* to well, gush]

[2]devil *vb* **-ll-** (*NAm* **-l-, -ll-**), /'devl·ing/ *vt* to season (food) highly, esp with peppery condiments ⟨~led *kidneys*⟩ ~ *vi* to serve or function as a legal devil

'devil,fish /-,fish/ *n*, *Br* ANGLER FISH

devilish /'devl·ish/ *adj* (characteristic) of a devil ⟨~ *tricks*⟩ – **devilishly** *adv*

,devil-may-'care *adj* heedless of authority or convention

devilment /'devlmənt/ *n* wild mischief

devilry /'devlri/ *n* **1** action performed with the help of the devil; witchcraft **2** (an act of) mischief

,devil's 'advocate *n* **1** the Roman Catholic official who presents the possible objections to claims to canonization or to the title 'Blessed'' **2** a person who champions the less accepted or approved cause, esp for the sake of argument [trans of NL *advocatus diaboli*]

,devil's 'coach ,horse *n* a large flesh-eating rove beetle

deviltry /'devltri/ *n* devilry

devious /'deevi·əs, -vyəs/ *adj* **1** deviating from a fixed or straight course **2** deviating from a right, accepted, or common course **3** not straightforward or wholly sincere [L *devius*, fr *de* from + *via* way – more at DE-, VIA] – **deviously** *adv*, **deviousness** *n*

[1]devise /di'viez/ *vt* **1a** to formulate in the mind; invent **b** to plan, plot **2** to give or leave (real property) by will – compare BEQUEATH 1 [ME *devisen*, fr OF *deviser* to divide, regulate, tell, modif of (assumed) VL *divisare*, fr L *divisus*, pp of *dividere* to divide] – **devisable** *adj*, **devisal** *n*, **diviser** *n*

[2]devise *n* **1** a devising act or clause **2** property devised by will

devisee /di,vie'zee, ,devi'zee/ *n* sby to whom a devise of property is made

devisor /di'viezə/ *n* sby who devises property in a will

devital·ize, -ise /,dee'vietl,iez/ *vt* to deprive of life, vigour, or effectiveness

devoice /,dee'voys/ *vt* to pronounce (a sometimes or formerly voiced sound) without vibration of the vocal cords

devoid /di'voyd/ *adj* not having or using; lacking – + *of* [ME, prob short for *devoided*, pp of *devoiden* to vacate, fr MF *desvuidier* to empty, fr OF, fr *des-* dis- + *vuidier* to empty – more at [3]VOID]

devolution /,deevə'loohsh(ə)n/ *n* **1** the passage of rights, property, etc to a successor **2** delegation or conferral to a subordinate **3** the surrender of functions and powers to regional or local authorities by a central government; *specif* such a surrender of powers to Scottish and Welsh authorities by the UK government [ML *devolution-, devolutio*, fr L *devolutus*, pp of *devolvere*] – **devolutionary** /-n(ə)ri/ *adj*, **devolutionist** *n*

devolve /di'volv/ *vt* **1** to transfer from one person to another; HAND DOWN 1, 2 **2** to surrender by devolution ~ *vi* **1** to pass by transmission or succession **2** to fall or be passed, usu as an obligation or responsibility ***USE*** (*vi*) usu + *on* or *upon* [ME *devolven*, fr L *devolvere*, fr *de-* + *volvere* to roll – more at VOLUBLE]

Devonian /de'vohnyən, -ni·ən/ *adj* **1** of Devon **2** of or being the period of the Palaeozoic era between the Silurian and the Carboniferous ☞ EVOLUTION [*Devon*, county in England] – **Devonian** *n*

devote /di'voht/ *vt* **1** to set apart for a special purpose; dedicate *to* **2** to give (oneself) over wholly *to* [L *devotus*, pp of *devovēre*, fr *de-* + *vovēre* to vow]

de'voted *adj* loyally attached ⟨*a* ~ *friend*⟩ – **devotedly** *adv*

devotee /,devə'tee/ *n* **1** a deeply religious person **2** a keen follower or supporter; an enthusiast ⟨*a* ~ *of opera*⟩

devotion /di'vohsh(ə)n/ *n* **1a** piety **b** a special act of prayer or supplication – usu pl **2a** devoting or being devoted **b** ardent love, affection, or dedication – **devotional** *adj*, **devotionally** *adv*

devour /di'vowə/ *vt* **1** to eat up greedily or ravenously **2** to swallow up; consume ⟨~ed *by fire*⟩ **3** to preoccupy, absorb ⟨~ed *by guilt*⟩ **4** to take in eagerly through the mind or senses ⟨~s *books*⟩ [ME *devouren*, fr MF *devourer*, fr L *devorare*, fr *de-* + *vorare* to devour – more at VORACIOUS] – **devourer** *n*

devout /di'vowt/ *adj* **1** devoted to religion; pious **2** sincere, genuine ⟨*a* ~ *hope*⟩ [ME *devot*, fr OF, fr LL *devotus*, fr L, pp of *devovēre*] – **devoutly** *adv*, **devoutness** *n*

dew /dyooh/ *n* moisture that condenses on the surfaces of cool bodies, esp at night [ME, fr OE *dēaw*; akin to OHG *tou* dew, Gk *thein* to run]

Dewar flask /'dyooh·ə/ *n* a glass or metal vacuum flask that is used esp in laboratories for storing liquefied gases [Sir James *Dewar* †1923 Sc chemist & physicist]

dewberry /'dyoohb(ə)ri/ *n* (the berry of) any of several shrubs resembling the blackberry

'dew,claw /-,klaw/ *n* (a claw or hoof at the end of) a vestigial digit not reaching to the ground on the foot of a mammal – **dewclawed** *adj*

Dewey decimal classification /'dyooh·i/ *n* a book classification whereby main classes are shown by a 3-digit number and subdivisions by numbers after a decimal point [Melvil *Dewey* †1931 US librarian]

'dew,fall /-,fawl/ *n* (the time of) deposition of dew

dewlap /'dyoohlap/ *n* a hanging fold of skin under the neck of an animal (e g a cow) – **dewlapped** *adj*

'dew ,point *n* the temperature of the air at which dew begins to be deposited

'dew ,pond *n* a shallow usu artificial pond thought to be filled by the condensation of dew

dewy /'dyooh·i/ *adj* moist (as if) with dew – **dewily** *adv*, **dewiness** *n*

,dewy-'eyed *adj* naively credulous or trusting

dexamethasone /,deksə'methəzohn, -sohn/ *n* a synthetic steroid that is a widely used glucocorticoid [perh fr *Dexa*myl, a trademark + *meth*yl + *-sone* (as in *cortisone*)]

Dexedrine /'deksədrin/ *trademark* – used for a preparation of dextroamphetamine sulphate

dexie /'deksi/ *n* a Dexedrine tablet [*Dex*edrine + *-ie*]

dexter /'dekstə/ *adj* of or being the side of a heraldic shield at the right of a person wearing it [L, of or on the right; akin to Gk *dexios* situated on the right, L *decēre* to be fitting – more at DECENT] – **dexter** *adv*

dexterity /dek'sterəti/ *n* **1** skill and ease in using the hands **2** mental quickness [MF or L; MF *dexterité*, fr L *dexteritat-, dexteritas*, fr *dexter*]

dexterous, dextrous /'dekstrəs/ *adj* **1** skilful with the hands **2** mentally adroit [L *dextr-, dexter* dextral, skilful] – **dexterously** /'dekst(ə)rəsli/ *adv*

dextr- *comb form* **1 dextr-, dextro-** on or towards the right; right ⟨dextr*al*⟩ **2** DEXTRO- 2 [LL, fr L *dextr-, dexter*]

dextral /'dekstrəl/ *adj* of or inclined to the right: e g **a** right-handed **b** *of the shell of a gastropod mollusc* having whorls that turn in an anticlockwise direction from the top to the bottom as viewed with the top towards the observer – compare SINISTRAL – **dextrally** *adv*, **dextrality** /dek'stralәti/ *n*

dextran /'dekstrən/ *n* **1** any of numerous polysaccharides that yield only glucose on hydrolysis **2** a compound obtained from dextran and used as a plasma substitute [*dextr*ose + *-an*]

dextrin /'dekstrin/ *n* any of various soluble gummy polysaccharides used as adhesives and as sizes for paper and textiles [F *dextrine*, fr *dextr-*]

dextro- /dekstroh-/ *comb form* **1** DEXTR- 1 ⟨dextro*cardia*⟩ **2 dextro-, dextr-** dextrorotatory ⟨dextro*tartaric acid*⟩

,dextroam,phetamine 'sulphate /,dekstroh·am 'fetəmin/ *n* an amphetamine now used esp to treat abnormal sudden lapses into deep sleep – compare DEXEDRINE

dextrorotary /,dekstroh'roht(ə)ri/ *adj* dextrorotatory

dextrorotatory /,dekstroh'rohtətri, -roh'taytəri/ *adj* turning clockwise or towards the right; *esp* rotating the plane of polarization of light towards the right ⟨~ *crystals*⟩ – compare LAEVOROTATORY – **dextrorotation** /-roh'taysh(ə)n/ *n*

dextrorse /'dekstraws, -'-/ *adj* **1** *of a plant* twining spirally upwards round an axis from left to right – compare SINISTRORSE **2** DEXTRAL b [NL *dextrorsus*, fr L, towards the right, fr *dextr-* + *versus,* pp of *vertere* to turn – more at WORTH] – **dextrorsely** *adv*

dextrose /ˈdekstrohz, ˈdekstrohs/ *n* dextrorotatory glucose

dextrous /ˈdekstrəs/ *adj* dexterous

dhal /dahl/ *n* a pulse having split cotyledons that is cultivated in India [Hindi *dāl*]

dharma /ˈdahmə/ *n* the fundamental concept of law, both natural and moral, in Hinduism and Buddhism, based on the principle of everything in the universe acting according to its essential nature or proper station [Skt, fr *dhārayati* he holds; akin to L *firmus* firm] – **dharmic** /-mik/ *adj*

dhobi /ˈdohbi/ *n* an Indian washerman or washerwoman [Hindi *dhobī*]

dhoti /ˈdohti/ *n, pl* **dhotis** a loincloth worn by Hindu men [Hindi *dhotī*]

dhow /dow/ *n* an Arab lateen-rigged boat, usu having a long overhanging bow and a high poop [Ar *dāwa*]

di- /die-/ *comb form* **1** twice; twofold; double ⟨di*chromatic*⟩ **2** containing 2 atoms, groups, or chemical equivalents in the molecular structure ⟨di*chloride*⟩ [ME, fr MF, fr L, fr Gk; akin to OE *twi-*]

dia- /die·ə-/ *also* **di-** *prefix* through ⟨dia*positive*⟩; across ⟨dia*meter*⟩ [ME, fr OF, fr L, fr Gk, through, apart, fr *dia*; akin to L *dis-*]

diabetes /ˌdie·əˈbeetis, -teez/ *n* any of various abnormal conditions characterized by the secretion and excretion of excessive amounts of urine; *specif* DIABETES MELLITUS [L, fr Gk *diabētēs*, fr *diabainein* to cross over, fr *dia-* + *bainein* to go – more at COME]

ˌdiaˌbetes inˈsipidus /inˈsipidəs/ *n* a disorder of the pituitary gland characterized by intense thirst and by the excretion of large amounts of urine [NL, lit., insipid diabetes]

ˌdiaˌbetes ˈmellitus /ˈmelitəs/ *n* a disorder of the process by which the body uses sugars and other carbohydrates in which not enough insulin is produced or the cells become resistant to its action and which is characterized typically by abnormally great amounts of sugar in the blood and urine [NL, lit., honey-sweet diabetes]

[1]**diabetic** /ˌdie·əˈbetik/ *adj* **1** of diabetes or diabetics **2** affected with diabetes

[2]**diabetic** *n* a person affected with diabetes

diablerie /deeˈahbləri/ *n* sorcery; BLACK MAGIC [F, fr OF, fr *diable* devil, fr LL *diabolus* – more at DEVIL]

diabol-, diabolo- *comb form* devil ⟨diabol*ism*⟩ [ME *deabol-*, fr MF *diabol-*, fr LL, fr Gk, fr *diabolos* – more at DEVIL]

diabolic /ˌdie·əˈbolik/ *adj* **1** (characteristic) of the devil; fiendish **2** DIABOLICAL 2 [ME *deabolik*, fr MF *diabolique*, fr LL *diabolicus*, fr *diabolus*] – **diabolically** *adv,* **diabolicalness** *n*

diabolical /ˌdie·əˈbolikl/ *adj* **1** DIABOLIC 1 **2** *chiefly Br* dreadful, appalling ⟨*it's ~ the way he treats his wife*⟩ ⟨*that meal was ~*⟩ – infml

diabolism /dieˈabəliz(ə)m/ *n* dealings with, possession by, or worship of the devil – **diabolist** *n*

diabol·ize, -ise /dieˈabəliez/ *vt* to represent as or make diabolic

diachronic /ˌdie·əˈkronik/ *adj* of or dealing with the historical development of phenomena, esp language – compare SYNCHRONIC – **diachronically** *adv*

diaconal /dieˈakənəl/ *adj* of a deacon or deaconess [LL *diaconalis*, fr *diaconus* deacon – more at DEACON]

diaconate /dieˈakənit, -nayt/ *n* the (period of) office of a deacon or deaconess

diacritic /ˌdie·əˈkritik/ *n* a mark near or through an orthographic or phonetic character or combination of characters indicating a changed phonetic value – compare ACCENT 3a

diacritical /ˌdie·əˈkritikl/ *also* **diacritic** *adj* **1** serving as a diacritic **2** serving to distinguish; distinctive [Gk *diakritikos* separative, fr *diakrinein* to distinguish, fr *dia-* + *krinein* to separate – more at CERTAIN]

diadelphous /ˌdie·əˈdelfəs/ *adj* united so as to form 2 sets ⟨*the stamens of leguminous plants are ~*⟩ [*di-* + *-adelphous* – more at MONADELPHOUS]

diadem /ˈdie·əˌdem/ *n* **1** a crown; *specif* a headband worn as a badge of royalty **2** regal power or dignity [ME *diademe*, fr OF, fr L *diadema*, fr Gk *diadēma*, fr *diadein* to bind round, fr *dia-* + *dein* to bind; akin to Alb *duai* sheaf, Skt *dāman* rope]

diaeresis, *chiefly NAm* **dieresis** /dieˈiərisis/ *n, pl* **diaereses** /-ˌseez/ **1** a mark ¨ placed over a vowel to indicate pronunciation as a separate syllable (e g in *naïve*) ☞ SYMBOL **2** the break in a verse caused by the coincidence of the end of a foot with the end of a word [LL *diaeresis*, fr Gk *diairesis*, fr *diairein* to divide, fr *dia-* + *hairein* to take] – **diaeretic** /ˌdie·əˈretik/ *adj*

diagnose /ˈdie·əgnohz/ *vt* to recognize (e g a disease) by signs and symptoms [back-formation fr *diagnosis*] – **diagnosable, diagnoseable** /ˌdie·əgˈnohzəbl/ *adj*

diagnosis /ˌdie·əgˈnohsis/ *n, pl* **diagnoses** /-seez/ **1** the art or act of identifying a disease from its signs and symptoms **2** (a statement resulting from) the investigation of the cause or nature of a problem or phenomenon [NL, fr Gk *diagnōsis*, fr *diagignōskein* to distinguish, fr *dia-* + *gignōskein* to know – more at KNOW]

[1]**diagnostic** /ˌdie·əgˈnostik/ *also* **diagnostical** /-kl/ *adj* of or involving diagnosis – **diagnostically** *adv*

[2]**diagnostic** *n* the art or practice of diagnosis – often pl with sing. meaning – **diagnostician** /-noˈstish(ə)n/ *n*

[1]**diagonal** /dieˈag(ə)nl/ *adj* **1** joining 2 nonadjacent angles of a polygon or polyhedron **2** running in an oblique direction from a reference line (e g the vertical) [L *diagonalis*, fr Gk *diagōnios* from angle to angle, fr *dia-* + *gōnia* angle; akin to Gk *gony* knee – more at KNEE] – **diagonalize** *vt,* **diagonally** *adv*

[2]**diagonal** *n* **1** a diagonal straight line or plane ☞ MATHEMATICS **2** a diagonal direction **3** SOLIDUS 2

[1]**diagram** /ˈdie·əˌgram/ *n* **1** a line drawing made for mathematical or scientific purposes **2** a drawing or design that shows the arrangement and relations (e g of parts) [Gk *diagramma*, fr *diagraphein* to mark out by lines, fr *dia-* + *graphein* to write – more at CARVE] – **diagrammatic** /ˌdie·əgrəˈmatik/ *also* **diagrammatical** *adj,* **diagrammatically** *adv*

[2]**diagram** *vt* **-mm-** (*NAm* **-m-, -mm-**) to represent in the form of a diagram

diagrammat·ize, -ise /ˌdie·əˈgramətiez/ *vt* to diagram

[1]**dial** /ˈdie·əl/ *n* **1** a sundial **2** the graduated face of a

timepiece **3a** a face on which some measurement is registered, usu by means of numbers and a pointer **b** a disc-shaped control on an electrical or mechanical device ⟨*a telephone* ~⟩ **4** *Br* a person's face – slang [ME, fr L *dies* day – more at DEITY]

²dial *vb* **-ll-** (*NAm* **-l-**, **-ll-**) *vt* to operate a dial so as to select ⟨~ led *the number*⟩ ~ *vi* **1** to manipulate a dial **2** to make a call on a dial telephone

dialect /ˈdie·əlekt/ *n* a regional, social, or subordinate variety of a language, usu differing distinctively from the standard or original language [MF *dialecte*, fr L *dialectus*, fr Gk *dialektos* conversation, dialect, fr *dialegesthai* to converse – more at DIALOGUE] – **dialectal** /-ˈlektl/ *adj*, **dialectally** *adv*

dialectic /ˌdie·əˈlektik/ *n* **1a** development through the stages of thesis, antithesis, and synthesis in accordance with (systems derived from) Hegel's logic **b** the theoretical application of dialectical materialism, esp in Marxist investigation of economics and the social sciences **2** a systematic reasoning, exposition, or argument that juxtaposes opposed or contradictory ideas and usu seeks to resolve their conflict **3** the dialectical tension or opposition between 2 interacting forces or elements *USE* (*1a&2*) usu pl with sing. meaning but sing. or pl in constr [ME *dialetik* intellectual investigation by means of dialogue, fr MF *dialetique*, fr L *dialectica*, fr Gk *dialektikē*, fr fem of *dialektikos* of conversation, fr *dialektos*]

dialectical /ˌdie·əˈlektikl/ *also* **dialectic** *adj* **1** of or in accordance with dialectic **2** (characteristic) of a dialect – **dialectically** *adv*

diaˌlectical maˈterialism *n* the Marxist theory that the material basis of a reality constantly changes in a dialectical process that is independent of thought

dialectician /ˌdie·əlekˈtish(ə)n/ *n* **1** one who is skilled in or practises dialectic **2** a student of dialects

dialectology /ˌdie·əlekˈtoləji/ *n* the study of dialect [ISV] – **dialectologist** *n*, **dialectological** /-ˌlektəˈlojikl/ *adj*, **dialectologically** *adv*

dialogic /ˌdie·əˈlojik/ *also* **dialogical** /-kl/ *adj* of or characterized by dialogue ⟨~ *writing*⟩ – **dialogically** *adv*

dialogist /dieˈaləjist/ *n* **1** one who participates in a dialogue **2** a writer of dialogues – **dialogistic** /ˌdie·aləˈjistik/ *adj*

dialogue, *NAm also* **dialog** /ˈdie·əlog/ *n* **1** a literary work in conversational form **2a** a conversation between 2 or more people or between a person and sthg else (e g a computer) **b** an exchange of ideas and opinions **3** the conversational element of literary or dramatic composition **4** discussion or negotiation between 2 nations, factions, groups, etc with conflicting interests ⟨*the continuing governmental policy of* ~ *between East and West*⟩ [MF, fr OF, fr L *dialogus*, fr Gk *dialogos*, fr *dialegesthai* to converse, fr *dia-* + *legein* to speak]

dialysate /dieˈalisayt/, **dialyzate** /-zayt/ *n* the material that passes through the membrane in dialysis; *also* the liquid into which this material passes [*dialysis* or *dialyze* + *-ate*]

dialyse, *NAm* **dialyze** /ˈdie·əˌliez/ *vt* to subject to dialysis ~ *vi* to undergo dialysis – **dialysable** *adj*, **dialyser** *n*

dialysis /dieˈaləsis/ *n, pl* **dialyses** /-ˌseez/ the separation of substances in solution by means of their unequal diffusion through semipermeable membranes; *esp* the purification of blood by such means [NL, fr Gk, separation, fr *dialyein* to dissolve, fr *dia-* + *lyein* to loosen – more at LOSE] – **dialytic** /ˌdie·əˈlitik/ *adj*

diamagnet /ˈdie·əˌmagnit/, **diamagnetic** /-magˈnetik/ *n* a diamagnetic substance [*diamagnet* back-formation fr *diamagnetic*, adj]

diamagnetic /ˌdie·əmagˈnetik/ *adj* of or being a substance that in a magnetic field is (slightly) attracted towards points of lower field intensity – **diamagnetism** /-ˈmagniˌtiz(ə)m/ *n*

diamanté /ˌdee·əˈmanti, diə-/ *n* (cloth or other material decorated with) sparkling particles, esp powdered crystal [F, fr pp of *diamanter* to set with diamonds, fr *diamant* diamond]

diamantiferous /ˌdee·əmanˈtifərəs/ *adj* yielding diamonds

diameter /dieˈamitə/ *n* **1** a line passing through the centre of a geometrical figure or body **2** the length of a straight line through the centre of an object (e g a circle) *USE* ☞ MATHEMATICS [ME *diametre*, fr MF, fr L *diametros*, fr Gk, fr *dia-* + *metron* measure – more at MEASURE] – **diametral** /dieˈamitrəl/ *adj*

diametric /ˌdie·əˈmetrik/, **diametrical** /-kl/ *adj* **1** of or constituting a diameter **2** completely opposed or opposite – **diametrically** *adv*

¹diamond /ˈdie·əmənd/ *n* **1** a (piece of) very hard crystalline carbon that is highly valued as a precious stone, esp when flawless and transparent, and is used industrially as an abrasive and in rock drills **2** a square or rhombus orientated so that the diagonals are horizontal and vertical **3a** a playing card marked with 1 or more red diamond-shaped figures **b** *pl but sing or pl in constr* the suit comprising cards identified by this figure **4** the entire playing field or the area enclosed by the bases in baseball [ME *diamaunde*, fr MF *diamant*, fr LL *diamant-*, *diamas*, alter. of L *adamant-*, *adamas*, hardest metal, diamond, fr Gk] – **diamondiferous** /ˌdie·əmənˈdif(ə)rəs/ *adj*

²diamond *adj* of, marking, or being a 60th or 75th anniversary ⟨~ *wedding*⟩

ˈdiamondˌback /-ˌbak/ *n* a large and deadly rattlesnake of the southern USA [fr the diamond-shaped markings on its back]

diandrous /dieˈandrəs/ *adj* having 2 stamens

dianthus /dieˈanthəs/ *n* ³PINK [NL, genus name, fr Gk *dios* heavenly + *anthos* flower – more at DEITY, ANTHOLOGY]

diapason /ˌdie·əˈpayz(ə)n, -s(ə)n/ *n* **1a** a full deep burst of harmonious sound **b** a principal organ stop extending through the range of the instrument **2** the entire range of musical tones **3** the range, scope [ME, fr L, fr Gk (*hē*) *dia pasōn* (*chordōn symphōnia*) the concord through all the notes, fr *dia* through + *pasōn*, gen fem pl of *pas* all – more at DIA-, PAN-]

diapause /ˈdie·əˌpawz/ *n* a period (e g in an insect) of arrested development between periods of activity [Gk *diapausis* pause, fr *diapauein* to pause, fr *dia-* + *pauein* to stop – more at PAUSE]

¹diaper /ˈdiepə, ˈdie·əpə/ *n* **1** a soft usu white linen or cotton fabric used for tablecloths or towels **2** an ornamental pattern consisting of one or more small repeated units of design (e g geometric figures) ☞ ARCHITECTURE **3** *chiefly NAm* a nappy [ME *diapre*, fr MF, fr ML *diasprum*]

²diaper *vt* to ornament with diaper designs

diaphanous /die'afənəs/ *adj* so fine as to be almost transparent [ML *diaphanus*, fr Gk *diaphanēs*, fr *diaphainein* to show through, fr *dia-* + *phainein* to show – more at FANCY] – **diaphanously** *adv*, **diaphanousness** *n*

diaphoretic /,die·əfə'retik/ *adj*, *esp of a drug* causing sweating [LL *diaphoreticus*, fr Gk *diaphorētikos*, fr *diaphorētos*, verbal of *diaphorein* to perspire, fr *dia-* + *pherein* to carry – more at [2]BEAR]

diaphragm /'die·ə,fram/ *n* **1** the partition separating the chest and abdominal cavities in mammals ☞ DIGESTION **2** a dividing membrane or thin partition, esp in a tube **3** a partition in a plant or the body or shell of an invertebrate animal **4** a device that limits the aperture of a lens or optical system ☞ CAMERA **5** a thin flexible disc that is free to vibrate (e g in an earphone) **6** DUTCH CAP [ME *diafragma*, fr LL *diaphragma*, fr Gk, fr *diaphrassein* to barricade, fr *dia-* + *phrassein* to enclose] – **diaphragmatic** /,die·əfrag'matik/ *adj*, **diaphragmatically** *adv*

diapositive /,die·ə'pozətiv/ *n* a transparent photographic positive; *specif* [2]SLIDE 5b

diarchy /'die,ahki/ *n* dyarchy

diarist /'die·ərist/ *n* one who keeps a diary

diarrhoea, *NAm chiefly* **diarrhea** /,die·ə'riə/ *n* abnormally frequent intestinal evacuations with more or less fluid faeces [ME *diaria*, fr LL *diarrhoea*, fr Gk *diarrhoia*, fr *diarrhein* to flow through, fr *dia-* + *rhein* to flow – more at STREAM] – **diarrhoeal, diarrhoeic** /-'riə·ik, -'ree·ik/ *also* **diarrhoetic** /-'riətik, -'reetik/ *adj*

diary /'die·əri/ *n* **1** (a book containing) a daily record of personal experiences or observations **2** *chiefly Br* a book with dates marked in which memoranda can be noted [L *diarium*, fr *dies* day – more at DEITY]

Diaspora /die'aspərə/ *n* **1** the settling, or area of settlement, of Jews outside Palestine after the Babylonian exile **2** *sing or pl in constr* the Jews living outside Palestine or modern Israel [Gk, dispersion, fr *diaspeirein* to scatter, fr *dia-* + *speirein* to sow – more at SPROUT]

diastase /'die·ə,stayz, -,stays/ *n* amylase; *esp* a mixture of amylases from malt [F, fr Gk *diastasis* separation, interval, fr *diistanai* to separate, fr *dia-* + *histanai* to cause to stand – more at STAND] – **diastatic** /,die·ə'statik/ *adj*

diastole /die'astəli/ *n* a rhythmically recurrent expansion; *esp* the dilation of the cavities of the heart during which they fill with blood – compare SYSTOLE [Gk *diastolē* dilatation, fr *diastellein* to expand, fr *dia-* + *stellein* to send – more at [1]STALL] – **diastolic** /,die·ə'stolik/ *adj*

diastrophism /die'astrəfiz(ə)m/ *n* major deformation of the earth's crust that produces continents, ocean basins, mountains, etc [Gk *diastrophē* twisting, fr *diastrephein* to distort, fr *dia-* + *strephein* to twist – more at STROPHE] – **diastrophic** /,die·ə'strofik/ *adj*, **diastrophically** *adv*

diathermanous /,die·ə'thuhmənəs/ *adj* DIATHERMIC 1 [Gk *diatherman-*, stem of *diathermainein* to heat through]

diathermic /,die·ə'thuhmik/ *adj* **1** transmitting infrared radiation **2** of or using diathermy ⟨~ *treatment*⟩

diathermy /'die·ə,thuhmi/ *n* the generation of heat in tissue by electric currents for medical or surgical purposes [ISV]

diathesis /die'athəsis/ *n, pl* **diatheses** /-,seez/ a constitutional predisposition towards an abnormality or disease [NL, fr Gk, lit., arrangement, fr *diatithenai* to arrange, fr *dia-* + *tithenai* to set – more at DO] – **diathetic** /,die·ə'thetik/ *adj*

diatom /'die·ətəm, -,tom/ *n* any of a class of minute single-celled algae with hard shell-like skeletons that are composed of silica and form kieselguhr [deriv of Gk *diatomos* cut in half, fr *diatemnein* to cut through, fr *dia-* + *temnein* to cut – more at TOME] – **diatomaceous** /,die·ətə'mayshəs/ *adj*

diatomic /,die·ə'tomik/ *adj* **1** consisting of 2 atoms **2** having 2 replaceable atoms or radicals [ISV]

diatomite /,die'atəmiet/ *n* kieselguhr

diatonic /,die·ə'tonik/ *adj* relating to a major or minor musical scale of 8 notes to the octave without chromatic deviation [LL *diatonicus*, fr Gk *diatonikos*, fr *diatonos* stretching, fr *diateinein* to stretch out, fr *dia-* + *teinein* to stretch – more at THIN] – **diatonically** *adv*

diatribe /'die·ə,trieb/ *n* a (lengthy) piece of bitter and abusive criticism [L *diatriba*, fr Gk *diatribē* pastime, discourse, fr *diatribein* to spend (time), wear away, fr *dia-* + *tribein* to rub]

diazepam /die'azəpam/ *n* a synthetic tranquillizer that is also used as a sedative and muscle relaxant, esp before surgical operations – compare VALIUM [*di-* + *az-* + *epoxide* + *-am* (compound related to ammonia)]

diazo /die'azoh/ *adj* **1** of or containing a radical composed of 2 nitrogen atoms united to a single carbon atom **2** of or containing a diazonium ion [ISV *diaz-*, *diazo-*, fr *di-* + *az-*]

diazonium /,die·ə'zohni·əm/ *n* an ion that is composed of 2 nitrogen atoms united to 1 carbon atom and usu exists in salts that are used in the manufacture of azo dyes [ISV *di-* + *az-* + *-onium*]

dibasic /die'baysik/ *adj* **1** *of an acid* having 2 replaceable hydrogen atoms **2** containing 2 atoms of a univalent metal **3** *of a base or a basic salt* having 2 hydroxyl groups

dibber /'dibə/ *n* a dibble [by alter.]

[1]**dibble** /'dibl/ *n* a small pointed hand implement used to make holes in the ground for plants, seeds, or bulbs [ME *debylle*]

[2]**dibble** *vt* **1** to plant with a dibble **2** to make holes in (soil) (as if) with a dibble

dibs /dibz/ *n pl* money, esp in small amounts – slang [prob short for *dibstones* (jacks), fr obs *dib* (to dab)]

[1]**dice** /dies/ *n, pl* **dice** /~/ **1a** a small cube that is marked on each face with from 1 to 6 spots so that spots on opposite faces total 7 and that is used to determine arbitrary values in various games **b** a gambling game played with dice **2** a small cubical piece (e g of food) [ME *dyce*, fr *dees*, *dyce*, pl of *dee* die, fr MF *dé*] – **no dice** of no avail; no use – infml

[2]**dice** *vt* **1a** to cut (e g food) into small cubes **b** to ornament with square markings **2** to gamble using dice ⟨~ *his money away*⟩ ~ *vi* **1** to play games with dice **2** to take a chance ⟨~ *with death*⟩ [ME *dycen*, fr *dyce*] – **dicer** /'diesə/ *n*

dicey /'diesi/ *adj* risky, unpredictable – infml [[1]*dice* + *-y*]

dich- /diek-/, **dicho-** *comb form* in two; apart

⟨di chogamous⟩ ⟨dichotomy⟩ [LL, fr Gk, fr *dicha*; akin to Gk *di-*]

dichlor- /dieklaw-/, **dichloro-** *comb form* containing 2 atoms of chlorine in the molecular structure ⟨dichloro*ethylene*⟩

dichloride /ˌdie'klawried/ *n* a compound containing 2 atoms of chlorine combined with an element or radical

dichlorvos /ˌdie'klawvos, -vəs/ *n* an insecticide used esp against insects in houses, shops, etc [*dichlor-* + *vi*nyl + phos*phate*]

dichotomous /die'kotəməs/ *adj* **1** dividing into 2 parts **2** of, involving, or arising from dichotomy [LL *dichotomos*, fr Gk, fr *dich-* + *temnein* to cut – more at TOME] – **dichotomously** *adv*, **dichotomousness** *n*

dichotomy /die'kotəmi/ *n* **1** a division into 2 esp mutually exclusive or contradictory groups **2** a (repeated) branching (into 2 branches) [Gk *dichotomia*, fr *dichotomos*]

dichroism /'diekroh,iz(ə)m/ *n* **1** the property of certain crystals of differing in colour when viewed in the direction of 2 different axes **2** the property of a surface of reflecting light of one colour and transmitting light of other colours – **dichroic** /die'krohik/ *adj*

dichromate /ˌdie'krohmayt, -mət/ *n* a usu orange to red chromium salt containing 2 atoms of chromium in the molecule [ISV]

dichromatic /ˌdiekroh'matik/ *adj* **1** having or using 2 colours **2** having 2 colour varieties or colour phases independent of age or sex ⟨*a* ~ *bird*⟩ [*di-* + *chromatic*] – **dichromatism** /die'krohmə,tiz(ə)m/ *n*

dick /dik/ *n* **1** *chiefly Br* a person ⟨*clever* ~⟩ **2** a detective **3** the penis – vulg *USE* (*1&2*) infml [*Dick*, nickname for *Richard*; (2) prob by shortening & alter.]

dickens /'dikinz/ *n* devil, deuce – used as an interjection or intensive [euphemism]

Dickensian /di'kenzi·ən/ *adj* (suggestive) of aspects of Victorian England, esp urban squalor or conviviality [Charles *Dickens* †1870 E novelist]

dicker /'dikə/ *vi* **1** to bargain, haggle **2** to hesitate, dither [origin unknown]

dickey, dicky *also* **dickie** /'diki/ *n* **1** a false front of a shirt **2** *chiefly Br* **a** the driver's seat in a carriage **b** a folding seat at the back of a carriage or motor car [*Dicky*, nickname for *Richard*]

'dickey,bird /-ˌbuhd/ *n* **1** a small bird – used by or to children **2** so much as a single word ⟨*never said a* ~⟩ – infml [*Dicky*, nickname for *Richard*; (2) rhyming slang *dickeybird* word]

dicky /'diki/ *adj, Br* in a weak or unsound condition – infml ⟨*a* ~ *heart*⟩ [origin unknown]

dicot /'die,kot/ *n* a dicotyledon

dicotyledon /die,koti'leedn, ,---'--/ *n* a plant with 2 seed leaves ☞ PLANT [deriv of NL *di-* + *cotyledon*] – **dicotyledonous** /ˌdiekot-/

dicoumarol /ˌdie'koohmərol/ *n* a drug that is taken by mouth to delay the clotting of blood, esp in the treatment of thrombosis [fr *Dicumarol*, a trademark]

dicrotic /ˌdie'krotik/ *adj, of the pulse* having a double beat (e g in certain feverish states) [Gk *dikrotos* having a double beat] – **dicrotism** /'diekrə,tiz(ə)m/ *n*

Dictaphone /'diktə,fohn/ *trademark* – used for a dictating machine

[1]**dictate** /dik'tayt/ *vi* **1** to give dictation **2** to speak or act with authority; prescribe ~ *vt* **1** to speak or read for a person to transcribe or for a machine to record **2** to impose, pronounce, or specify with authority [L *dictatus*, pp of *dictare* to assert, dictate, fr *dictus*, pp of *dicere* to say – more at DICTION]

[2]**dictate** /'diktayt/ *n* **1** an authoritative rule, prescription, or command **2** a ruling principle – usu pl ⟨*according to the* ~s *of his conscience*⟩

dic'tating ma,chine /dik'tayting/ *n* a machine designed for the recording of dictated matter

dictation /dik'taysh(ə)n/ *n* **1** PRESCRIPTION 2 **2a** the act or manner of uttering words to be transcribed **b** material that is dictated or transcribed

dictator /dik'taytə/ *n* **1** a person granted absolute emergency power, esp in ancient Rome **2** an absolute ruler; *esp* one who has seized power unconstitutionally and uses it oppressively [L, fr *dictatus*]

dictatorial /ˌdiktə'tawri·əl/ *adj* **1** of a dictator **2** arrogantly domineering – **dictatorially** *adv*, **dictatorialness** *n*

dic'tator,ship /-ˌship/ *n* **1** the office of dictator **2** total or absolute control; leadership, rule **3** a state or form of government where absolute power is concentrated in one person or a small clique

diction /'diksh(ə)n/ *n* **1** choice of words, esp with regard to correctness or clearness **2** pronunciation and enunciation of words in speaking or singing [L *diction-*, *dictio* speaking, style, fr *dictus*, pp of *dicere* to say; akin to OE *tēon* to accuse, L *dicare* to proclaim, dedicate, Gk *deiknynai* to show, *dikē* judgment, right] – **dictional** *adj*, **dictionally** *adv*

dictionary /'dikshən(ə)ri/ *n* **1** a reference book containing words, terms, or names, usu alphabetically arranged, together with information about them, esp their forms, pronunciations, functions, etymologies, meanings, syntactic and idiomatic uses, and applications **2** a reference book giving for words of one language equivalents in another **3** a list (e g of synonyms or hyphenation instructions) stored in machine-readable form (e g on a computer disk) for reference by an automatic system (e g for computerized typesetting) [ML *dictionarium*, fr LL *diction-*, *dictio* word, fr L, speaking]

dictum /'diktəm/ *n, pl* **dicta** /-tə/ *also* **dictums** **1** an authoritative statement on some topic; a pronouncement **2** OBITER DICTUM 1 [L, fr neut of *dictus*]

dicty- /dikti-/, **dictyo-** *comb form* net; network ⟨dic tyo*stele*⟩ ⟨dictyo*some*⟩ [NL, fr Gk *dikty-*, *diktyo-*, fr *diktyon*, fr *dikein* to throw]

dictyosome /'dikti·ə,sohm/ *n* GOLGI BODY

did /did/ *past of* DO

didactic /die'daktik/ *adj* **1** intended to teach sthg, esp a moral lesson **2** having a tendency to teach in an authoritarian manner [Gk *didaktikos*, fr *didaskein* to teach] – **didactically** *adv*, **didacticism** /-ti,siz(ə)m/ *n*

diddle /'didl/ *vt* **diddling** /'didl·ing, 'didling/ to cheat, swindle – infml [prob fr Jeremy *Diddler*, character in the play *Raising the Wind* by James Kenny †1849 E dramatist] – **diddler** *n*

diddums /'didəmz/ *interj* – used to express commiseration to a child [baby-talk alter. of *did you/he/she*]

didgeridoo /ˌdijəri'dooh/ *n* an Australian wind instrument with a long wooden tube [imit]

didicoi, didicoy /'didi,koy/ *n, pl* **didicois, didicoys** *Br* an itinerant tinker, traveller, etc (who is not a true Romany) [Romany]

didn't /'didnt/ did not

didst /didst/ *archaic past 2 sing of* DO

didymium /,die'dimi·əm, di-/ *n* a mixture of rare-earth elements made up chiefly of neodymium and praseodymium [NL, fr Gk *didymos* double, twin, testicle, fr *dyo* two – more at TWO]

[1]**die** /die/ *vi* **dying** **1** to stop living; suffer the end of physical life ☞ SYMBOL **2** to pass out of existence, cease ⟨*his anger* ~d *at these words*⟩ **3** to long keenly or desperately ⟨dying *to go*⟩ **4** to stop ⟨*the motor* ~d⟩ [ME *dien*, fr or akin to ON *deyja* to die; akin to OHG *touwen* to die, OIr *duine* human being]

[2]**die** *n, pl (1)* **dice** /dies/, *(2&3)* **dies** /diez/ **1** a dice **2** DADO 1 **3** any of various tools or devices for giving a desired shape, form, or finish to a material or for impressing an object or material [ME *dee*, fr MF *dé*] – **the dice are loaded** all the elements of a situation are combined to work – usu + *against* or *in favour of* ⟨*I will never get the job,* the dice are loaded *in favour of him*⟩ – **the die is cast** the irrevocable decision or step has been taken

'die-,cast *vt* **die-cast** to make by forcing molten plastic, metal, etc into a die – **die-cast** *adj*

diecious /die'eeshəs/ *adj, NAm* dioecious

die down *vi* **1** *of a plant* to undergo death of the parts lying above ground **2** to diminish, subside

'die-,hard *n or adj* (one) strongly resisting change – **die-hardism** *n*

dieldrin /'dee·əl,drin/ *n* a persistent chlorine-containing insecticide [*Diels-Alder* reaction, fr Otto *Diels* †1954 & Kurt *Alder* †1958 G chemists]

dielectric /,die·i'lektrik/ *n* a substance that can transmit an electrical effect by electrostatic induction but not by conduction; an insulator [*dia-* + *electric*] – **dielectric** *adj*

diene /'die,een/ *n* a compound containing 2 double bonds [*di-* + *-ene*]

die out *vi* to become extinct

dieresis /,die·ə'reesis/ *n, chiefly NAm* a diaeresis

diesel /'deezl/ *n* **1** (a vehicle driven by) a diesel engine **2 diesel, diesel oil** a heavy mineral oil used as fuel in diesel engines [Rudolph *Diesel* †1913 G mechanical engineer]

,diesel-e'lectric *adj* of or using the combination of a diesel engine driving an electric generator ⟨*a* ~ *locomotive*⟩ – **diesel-electric** *n*

'diesel ,engine *n* an internal-combustion engine in which fuel is ignited by air compressed to a sufficiently high temperature

Dies Irae /,dee·ayz 'iərie/ *n* a medieval Latin hymn sung in requiem masses [ML, day of wrath; fr the first words of the hymn]

[1]**diet** /'die·ət/ *n* **1** the food and drink habitually taken by a group, animal, or individual **2** the kind and amount of food prescribed for a person or animal for a special purpose (e g losing weight) [ME *diete*, fr OF, fr L *diaeta* prescribed diet, fr Gk *diaita*, lit., manner of living, fr *dia-* + *-aita* (akin to Gk *aisa* share)]

[2]**diet** *vb* to (cause to) eat and drink sparingly or according to prescribed rules – **dieter** *n*

[3]**diet** *n* any of various national or provincial legislatures [ML *dieta* day's journey, assembly, fr L *dies* day – more at DEITY]

[1]**dietary** /'die·ət(ə)ri/ *n* the kinds and amounts of food available to or eaten by an individual, group, or population

[2]**dietary** *adj* of (the rules of) a diet – **dietarily** /'die·ət(ə)rəli/ *adv*

dietetic /,die·ə'tetik/ *adj* **1** of diet **2** adapted for use in special diets – **dietetically** *adv*

,die'tetics *n pl but sing or pl in constr* the application of the principles of nutrition to feeding

di,ethyl 'ether /die'ethl, -'eethl, -thiel/ *n* ETHER 3a

diethylstilboestrol /die,ethlstil'bestrol, die,eethl-, -thiel-/ *n* stilboestrol [ISV]

dietitian, dietician /,die·ə'tish(ə)n/ *n* a specialist in dietetics [*dietitian* irreg fr [1]*diet*]

differ /'difə/ *vi* **1a** to be unlike; be distinct *from* **b** to change from time to time; vary **2** to disagree ⟨*people who* ~ *on religious matters*⟩ [ME *differen*, fr MF or L; MF *differer* to postpone, be different, fr L *differre*, fr *dis-* + *ferre* to carry – more at [2]BEAR]

difference /'difrəns/ *n* **1a** unlikeness between 2 or more people or things **b** the degree or amount by which things differ **2** a disagreement, dispute; dissension ⟨*unable to settle their* ~s⟩ **3** the degree or amount by which things differ in quantity or measure; *specif* REMAINDER 2b(1) **4** a significant change in or effect on a situation

different /'difrənt/ *adj* **1** partly or totally unlike; dissimilar – + *from*, chiefly Br *to*, or chiefly NAm *than* **2a** distinct **b** various **c** another **3** unusual, special [MF, fr L *different-, differens*, prp of *differre*] – **differently** *adv*, **differentness** *n*

differentia /,difə'renshyə/ *n, pl* **differentiae** /-shi,ee/ the mark or feature that distinguishes one member of a general class from another; *esp* a trait distinguishing species from other species of the same genus [L, difference, fr *different-, differens*]

[1]**differential** /,difə'renshəl/ *adj* **1a** of or constituting a difference **b** based on or resulting from a differential ⟨~ *freight charges*⟩ **c** functioning or proceeding differently or at a different rate **2** of or involving a differential or differentiation **3** of quantitative differences – **differentially** *adv*

[2]**differential** *n* **1** the product of the derivative of a function of one variable with the increment of the independent variable ⟨*for a function* f(x) *the* ~ *is* f(x)dx⟩ **2** the amount of a difference between comparable individuals or classes; *specif* the amount by which the remuneration of distinct types of worker differs **3** (a case covering) a differential gear

diffe,rential 'calculus *n* a branch of mathematics dealing chiefly with the rate of change of functions with respect to their variables

diffe,rential e'quation *n* an equation containing differentials or derivatives of functions

differential gear *n* an arrangement of gears in a vehicle that allows one of the wheels imparting motion to turn (e g in going round a corner) faster than the other

differentiate /,difə'renshiayt/ *vt* **1** to obtain the mathematical derivative of **2** to mark or show a difference in **3** to cause differentiation of in the course of development **4** to express the specific difference of ~ *vi* **1** to recognize a difference *between* **2** to become distinct or different in character **3** to undergo differentiation – **differentiability** /-shi·ə'biləti/ *n*, **differentiable** /-shi·əbl/ *adj*

differentiation /,difə,renshi'aysh(ə)n/ *n* **1** development into more complex, numerous, or varied forms **2a** modification of body parts for performance of particular functions **b** all the processes whereby apparently similar cells, tissues, and structures attain their adult forms and functions [DIFFERENTIATE + -ION]

difficult /'difik(ə)lt/ *adj* **1** hard to do, make, carry out, or understand ⟨*a ~ climb*⟩ ⟨*a ~ text*⟩ **2a** hard to deal with, manage, or please ⟨*a ~ child*⟩ **b** puzzling [back-formation fr *difficulty*] – **difficultly** *adv*

difficulty /'difik(ə)lti/ *n* **1** being difficult **2** an obstacle or impediment **3** a cause of (financial) trouble or embarrassment – usu pl with sing. meaning [ME *difficulte*, fr L *difficultas*, irreg fr *difficilis*, fr *dis-* + *facilis* easy – more at FACILE]

diffident /'difid(ə)nt/ *adj* **1** lacking in self-confidence **2** reserved, unassertive [L *diffident-, diffidens*, prp of *diffidere* to distrust, fr *dis-* + *fidere* to trust – more at BIDE] – **diffidently** *adv*, **diffidence** /-d(ə)ns/ *n*

diffract /di'frakt/ *vt* to cause (a beam of light) to become a set of light and dark or coloured bands in passing by the edge of an opaque body, through narrow slits, etc [back-formation fr *diffraction*, fr NL *diffraction-, diffractio*, fr L *diffractus*, pp of *diffringere* to break apart, fr *dis-* + *frangere* to break – more at BREAK] – **diffraction** /di'fraksh(ə)n/ *n*

diffraction grating *n* GRATING 3

[1]**diffuse** /di'fyoohs/ *adj* **1** not concentrated or localized; scattered **2** lacking conciseness; verbose [L *diffusus*, pp of *diffundere* to spread out, fr *dis-* + *fundere* to pour – more at [4]FOUND] – **diffusely** *adv*, **diffuseness** *n*

[2]**diffuse** /di'fyoohz/ *vt* **1** to spread out freely in all directions **2** to break up and distribute (incident light) by reflection ~ *vi* **1** to spread out or become transmitted **2** to undergo diffusion [MF or L; MF *diffuser*, fr L *diffusus*, pp] – **diffuser** *n*, **diffusible** *adj*, **diffusive** /-siv/ *adj*

diffusion /di'fyoohzh(ə)n/ *n* **1** diffusing or being diffused **2** being long-winded **3a** the process whereby particles of liquids, gases, or solids intermingle as the result of their spontaneous movement **b** reflection of light by a rough reflecting surface – **diffusional** *adj*

[1]**dig** /dig/ *vb* **-gg-; dug** /dug/ *vi* **1** to turn up, loosen, or remove earth **2** to understand ~ *vt* **1** to break up, turn, or loosen (earth) with an implement **2** to bring to the surface (as if) by digging; unearth **3** to hollow out by removing earth; excavate ⟨*~ a hole*⟩ **4** to drive down into; thrust **5** to poke, prod ⟨*~ him in the ribs*⟩ **6a** to pay attention to; notice **b** to understand, appreciate *USE* (*vi 2; vt 6*) slang [ME *diggen*]

[2]**dig** *n* **1a** a thrust, poke **b** a cutting or snide remark **2** an archaeological excavation (site) **3** *pl, chiefly Br* LODGING 2b [(3) short for *diggings*]

digamy /'digəmi/ *n* a second marriage after the termination of the first [LL *digamia*, fr LGk, fr Gk *digamos* married to two people, fr *di-* + *-gamos* -gamous]

digastric /,die'gastrik/ *adj, of a muscle* having 2 enlarged parts separated by a tendon [NL *digastricus*, fr *di-* + *gastricus* gastric]

digenesis /,die'jenəsis/ *n* successive reproduction by sexual and asexual methods [NL] – **digenetic** /,dieji'netik/ *adj*

[1]**digest** /'diejest/ *n* **1** a systematic compilation of laws **2** a literary abridgment [ME *Digest* compilation of Roman laws ordered by Justinian, fr LL *Digesta*, pl, fr L, collection of writings arranged under headings, fr neut pl of *digestus*, pp of *digerere* to arrange, distribute, digest, fr *dis-* + *gerere* to carry – more at CAST]

[2]**digest** /di'jest, die-/ *vt* **1** to distribute or arrange systematically **2** to convert (food) into a form the body can use **3** to assimilate mentally **4** to soften or decompose or extract soluble ingredients from by heat and moisture or chemicals **5** to compress into a short summary ~ *vi* to become digested [ME *digesten*, fr L *digestus*] – **digester** *n*, **digestible** /di'jestəbl/ *adj*, **digestibility** /-jestə'biləti/ *n*

digestion /di'jeschən/ *n* the process or power of digesting sthg, esp food

[1]**digestive** /di'jestiv/ *n* sthg that aids digestion

[2]**digestive** *adj* of, causing, or promoting digestion – **digestively** *adv*, **digestiveness** *n*

digger /'digə/ *n* **1** a tool or machine for digging **2** a private soldier from Australia or New Zealand, esp in WW I – infml [[1]DIG + [2]-ER]

'**digger** ,**wasp** *n* a burrowing wasp

diggings /'digingz/ *n pl* **1** material dug out **2** a place of excavating, esp for ore, metals, or precious stones

dig in *vt* to incorporate by burying in the soil ~ *vi* **1** to dig defensive positions **2** to hold stubbornly to a position; defend doggedly (e g when batting in cricket) **3** to begin eating – infml – **dig one's heels in** to refuse to move or change one's mind; be stubborn

digit /'dijit/ *n* **1a** any of the Arabic numerals from 1 to 9, usu also including 0 **b** any of the elements that combine to form numbers in a system other than the decimal system **2** a finger or toe **3** a unit of measurement equal to ¾in (about 1.9cm) UNIT [ME, fr L *digitus* finger, toe – more at TOE]

digital /'dijitl/ *adj* **1** of or with the fingers or toes **2** of calculation by numerical methods which use discrete units **3** of data in the form of numerical digits TELECOMMUNICATION, VIDEO **4** *of an automatic device* presenting information in the form of numerical digits – **digitally** *adv*

,**digital com'puter** *n* a computer that operates with numbers expressed as discrete pulses representing digits – compare ANALOGUE COMPUTER

digitalis /,diji'tahlis/ *n* (the dried leaf of) the common foxglove (containing several compounds which are important as drugs used esp as powerful heart stimulants) [NL, genus name, fr L, of a finger, fr *digitus*; fr its finger-shaped corolla]

digital·ize, -ise /'dijitl,iez/ *vt* to digitize

digitate /'dijitayt/ *adj* **1** having fingers or toes **2** having divisions arranged like the fingers of a hand ⟨*a ~ leaf*⟩ PLANT – **digitately** *adv*, **digitation** /,diji'taysh(ə)n/ *n*

digiti- /dijiti-/ *comb form* digit; finger; toe ⟨digiti*form*⟩ [F, fr L *digitus*]

digitigrade /'dijiti,grayd/ *adj* (designed for) walking on the toes with the back of the foot more or less raised – compare PLANTIGRADE [F, fr *digiti-* + *grade*]

digit·ize, -ise /'dijitiez/ *vt* to put (e g data) into digital notation – **digitizer** *n*, **digitization** /-'zaysh(ə)n/ *n*

digitoxin /,diji'toksin/ *n* a compound that is the most active constituent of digitalis [ISV, blend of NL *Digitalis* and ISV *toxin*]

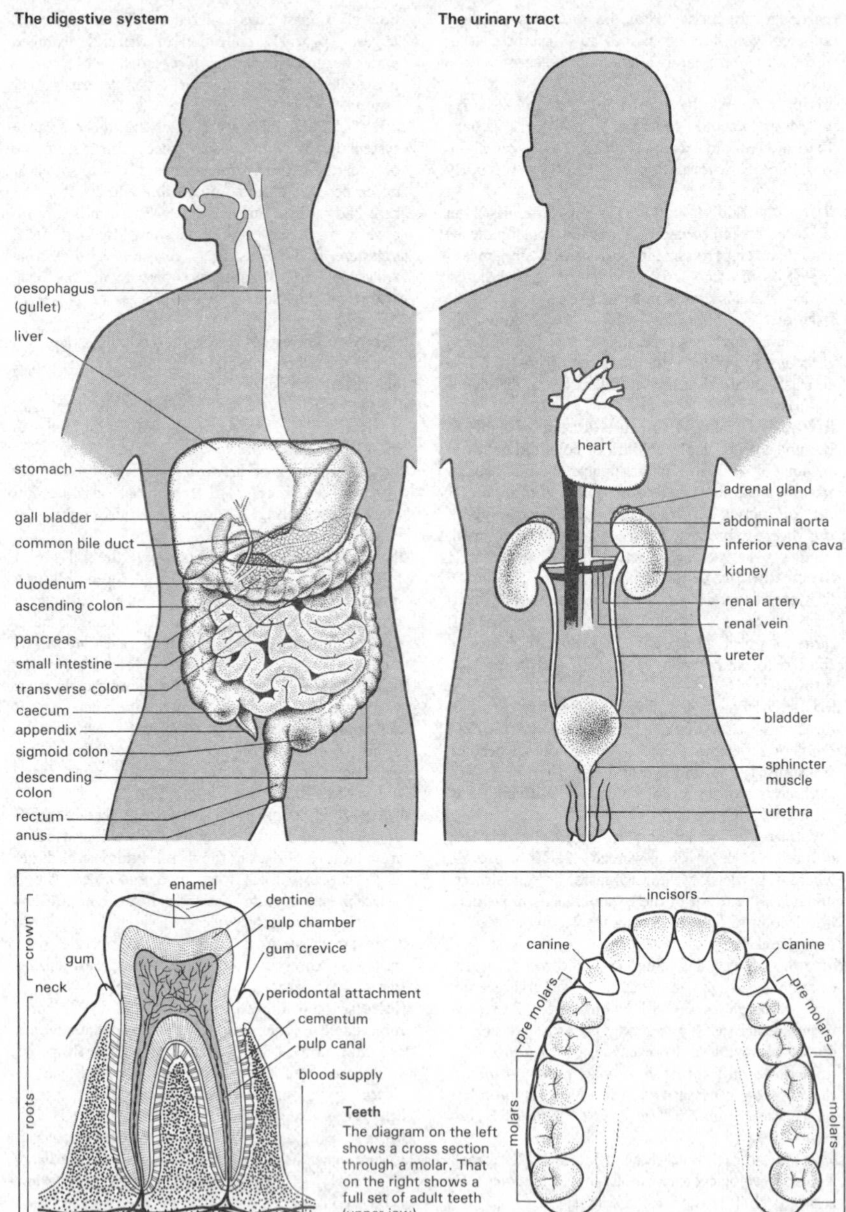

Teeth
The diagram on the left shows a cross section through a molar. That on the right shows a full set of adult teeth (upper jaw).

☞ ANATOMY, NERVE, REPRODUCTION

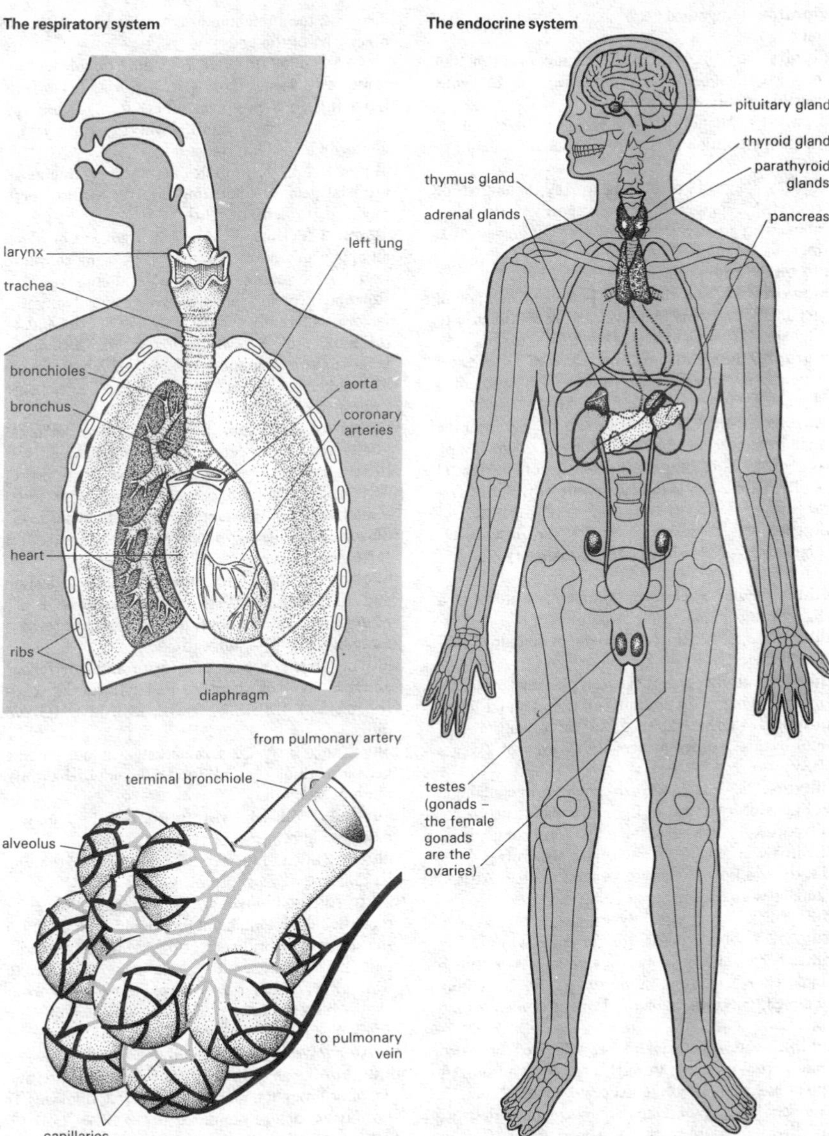

The exchange of gases in the lungs takes place in the terminal bronchioles, where blood in the capillaries passes close to the lining membrane allowing oxygen to be absorbed and carbon dioxide to be given up.

The endocrine glands produce hormones which are the chemical messengers that keep the body healthy, controlling such functions as growth and sexual development. The pituitary gland, in conjunction with the hypothalamus, controls the activity and secretions of the other endocrine glands.

dignified /ˈdignified/ *adj* showing or having dignity

dignify /ˈdignifie/ *vt* to confer dignity or distinction on [MF *dignifier*, fr LL *dignificare*, fr L *dignus* worthy – more at DECENT]

dignitary /ˈdignit(ə)ri/ *n* a person of high rank or holding a position of dignity or honour – **dignitary** *adj*

dignity /ˈdignəti/ *n* **1** being worthy, honoured, or esteemed **2** high rank, office, or position **3** stillness of manner; gravity [ME *dignete*, fr OF *digneté*, fr L *dignitat-*, *dignitas*, fr *dignus*]

dig out *vt* to find, unearth

digoxin /diˈjoksin, dig-/ *n* a poisonous compound obtained from some foxgloves and used similarly to digitalis [ISV *dig-* (fr NL *Digitalis*) + *toxin*]

digraph /ˈdie,grahf, -,graf/ *n* a group of 2 successive letters, esp whose phonetic value is a single sound – **digraphic** /dieˈgrafik/ *adj*, **digraphically** *adv*

digress /diˈgres, die-/ *vi* to turn aside, esp from the main subject in writing or speaking [L *digressus*, pp of *digredi*, fr *dis-* + *gradi* to step – more at GRADE] – **digressive** /-siv/ *adj*, **digressively** *adv*, **digressiveness** *n*

digression /diˈgresh(ə)n, die-/ *n* (an instance of) digressing – **digressional** *adj*, **digressionary** /-n(ə)ri/ *adj*

dihal-, **dihalo-** *comb form* containing 2 atoms of a halogen in the molecular structure

[1]**dihedral** /,dieˈheedrəl/ *adj* having or contained by 2 flat surfaces

[2]**dihedral** *n* the angle between an esp upwardly inclined wing of an aircraft and a horizontal line

dihybrid /,dieˈhiebrid/ *n or adj* (an organism, cell, etc) having 2 different versions of each of 2 genes [ISV]

dihydr- /diehiedr-/, **dihydro-** *comb form* containing 2 atoms of hydrogen in the molecular structure

dihydroxy- /diehiedroksi-/ *comb form* containing 2 hydroxyl groups in the molecular structure

dik-dik /ˈdik ,dik/ *n* any of several small E African antelopes [native name in E Africa]

[1]**dike** /diek/ *vb or n* (to) dyke

[2]**dike** *n* a lesbian – derog [origin unknown]

diktat /dikˈtat/ *n* a harsh settlement or ruling imposed by a victor or authority [G, lit., something dictated, fr NL *dictatum*, fr L, neut of *dictatus*, pp of *dictare* to dictate]

dilapidated /diˈlapidaytid/ *adj* decayed or fallen into partial ruin, esp through neglect or misuse [fr pp of *dilapidate* (to bring to decay or partial ruin), fr L *dilapidatus*, pp of *dilapidare* to squander, destroy, fr *dis-* + *lapidare* to throw stones, fr *lapid-*, *lapis* stone] – **dilapidation** /di,lapiˈdaysh(ə)n/ *n*

dilatation /,diləˈtaysh(ə)n/ *n* **1a** the condition of being stretched beyond normal dimensions ⟨~ *of the stomach*⟩ **b** DILATION 2 **2** expanding or being expanded **3** a dilated part or formation – **dilatational** *adj*

dilate /diˈlayt, die-/ *vt* to distend ~ *vi* **1** to comment at length *on* or *upon* **2** to become wide [ME *dilaten*, fr MF *dilater*, fr L *dilatare*, lit., to spread wide, fr *dis-* + *latus* wide – more at LATITUDE] – **dilatable** *adj*, **dilator** /dieˈlaytə/ *n*, **dilative** *adj*, **dilatability** /die,laytəˈbiləti/ *n*

diˈlated *adj* expanded, widened – **dilatedly** *adv*, **dilatedness** *n*

dilation /diˈlaysh(ə)n, die-/ *n* **1** dilating or being dilated **2** the stretching or enlarging of an organ or other part of the body

dilatory /ˈdilət(ə)ri/ *adj* **1** tending or intended to cause delay **2** slow, tardy [LL *dilatorius*, fr L *dilatus* (pp of *differre* to postpone, differ), fr *dis-* + *latus*, pp of *ferre* to carry – more at DIFFER, TOLERATE] – **dilatorily** *adv*, **dilatoriness** *n*

dildo /ˈdildoh/ *n*, *pl* **dildos** an object serving as an artificial penis for inserting into the vagina [perh modif of It *diletto* delight]

dilemma /diˈlemə, die-/ *n* **1** an argument in which an opponent's position is refuted by being shown to lead to 2 or more unacceptable alternatives **2** a situation involving choice between 2 equally unsatisfactory alternatives [LL, fr LGk *dilēmmat-*, *dilēmma*, prob back-formation fr Gk *dilēmmatos* involving two assumptions, fr *di-* + *lēmmat-*, *lēmma* assumption – more at LEMMA] – **dilemmatic** /,diləˈmatik, ,die-/ *adj*

dilettante /,diliˈtanti/ *n*, *pl* **dilettanti** /,diliˈtanti/ **dilettantes** /-tiz/ a person with a superficial interest in an art or a branch of knowledge [It, fr prp of *dilettare* to delight, fr L *delectare* – more at [2]DELIGHT] – **dilettante** *adj*, **dilettantish** *adj*, **dilettantism** *n*

diligence /ˈdilij(ə)ns/ *n* steady application and effort [MF, fr L *diligentia*, fr *diligent-*, *diligens*]

diligent /ˈdilij(ə)nt/ *adj* showing steady application and effort [ME, fr MF, fr L *diligent-*, *diligens*, fr prp of *diligere* to esteem, love, fr *di-* + *legere* to select – more at LEGEND] – **diligently** *adv*

dill /dil/ *n* a European plant with aromatic foliage and seeds, both of which are used in flavouring foods (e g pickles) [ME *dile*, fr OE; akin to OHG *tilli* dill]

dilly /ˈdili/ *n*, *NAm* a remarkable or outstanding person or thing – infml [obs *dilly*, adj (delightful), alter. of *delightful*]

dillydally /ˈdili,dali/ *vi* to waste time by loitering; dawdle – infml [redupl of *dally*]

diluent /ˈdilyoo·ənt/ *n or adj* (an agent for) diluting [L *diluent-*, *diluens*, prp of *diluere*]

[1]**dilute** /dieˈlooht, -ˈlyooht/ *vt* **1** to make thinner or more liquid by adding another liquid **2** to diminish the strength or brilliance of by adding more liquid, light, etc **3** to attenuate [L *dilutus*, pp of *diluere* to wash away, dilute, fr *di-* + *lavere* to wash – more at LYE] – **diluter**, **dilutor** *n*, **dilutive** /-tiv/ *adj*, **dilution** /dieˈloohsh(ə)n, -ˈlyooh-/ *n*

[2]**dilute** *adj* weak, diluted – **diluteness** *n*

diluvial /diˈloohvyəl, -vi·əl/, **diluvian** /-vyən, -vi·ən/ *adj* of or brought about by a flood [LL *diluvialis*, fr L *diluvium* deluge – more at DELUGE]

[1]**dim** /dim/ *adj* **-mm-** **1** giving out a weak or insufficient light **2a** seen indistinctly ⟨*a ~ shape loomed out of the fog*⟩ **b** characterized by an unfavourable or pessimistic attitude – esp in *take a dim view of* **3** not seeing clearly ⟨*the old man's eyes were ~*⟩ **4** lacking intelligence; stupid – infml [ME, fr OE; akin to OHG *timber* dark, Skt *dhamati* he blows] – **dimly** *adv*, **dimness** *n*

[2]**dim** *vb* **-mm-** *vt* **1** to make dim **2** *NAm* DIP 4 ~ *vi* to become dim

dime /diem/ *n* a coin worth $^1/_{10}$ of a US dollar [ME, tenth part, tithe, fr MF, fr L *decima*, fr fem of *decimus* tenth, fr *decem* ten – more at TEN]

[1]**dimension** /diˈmensh(ə)n, die-/ *n* **1a(1)** extension in 1 direction **(2)** any of a group of parameters necessary and sufficient to determine uniquely eacl

element of a system of usu mathematical entities ⟨*the surface of a sphere has 2* ~s⟩ **b** the size of extension in 1 or all directions **c** the range over which sthg extends; the scope – usu pl with sing. meaning **d** an aspect ⟨*gave a whole new* ~ *to the problem*⟩ **2** any of the fundamental quantities, specif mass, length, and time, which combine to make a derived unit – usu pl ⟨*velocity has the* ~s *of length divided by time*⟩ [ME, fr MF, fr L *dimension-*, *dimensio*, fr *dimensus*, pp of *dimetiri* to measure out, fr *dis-* + *metiri* to measure – more at MEASURE] – **dimensional** *adj*, **dimensionally** *adv*, **dimensionless** *adj*, **dimensionality** /-,mensh(ə)'naləti/ *n*

[2]**dimension** *vt* to indicate the dimensions on (a drawing)

dimer /'diemə/ *n* a compound formed by the union of 2 radicals or 2 molecules of a simpler compound [ISV *di-* + *-mer* (as in *polymer*)] – **dimerize** *vt*, **dimeric** /die'merik/ *adj*, **dimerization** /,die mərie'zaysh(ə)n/ *n*

dimerous /'dimərəs/ *adj*, *of an insect or plant part* consisting of 2 parts [NL *dimerus*, fr L *di-* + NL *-merus* -merous] – **dimerism** *n*

dimethyl- /diemethil-, -mee-, -thiel/ *comb form* containing 2 methyl groups in the molecular structure

dimethyltryptamine /,diemethil'triptəmeen,-mee-, -thiel-/ an easily synthesized hallucinogenic drug [*dimethyl-* + *tryptophan* + *amine*]

diminish /di'minish/ *vt* **1** to make or cause to appear less **2** to lessen the reputation of; belittle ~ *vi* to become gradually less; dwindle [ME *deminishen*, alter. of *diminuen*, fr MF *diminuer*, fr LL *diminuere*, alter. of L *deminuere*, fr *de* + *minuere* to lessen – more at MINOR] – **diminishable** *adj*, **diminishment** *n*

di'minished *adj*, *of a musical interval* made a semitone less than perfect or minor ⟨*a* ~ *fifth*⟩

di,minished re,sponsi'bility *n* limitation of a person's criminal responsibility due to mental abnormality or instability

di,minishing re'turns /di'minishing/ *n pl* a rate of yield that beyond a certain point fails to increase in proportion to additional investments of labour or capital

diminuendo /di,minyoo'endoh/ *n, adv, or adj, pl* **diminuendos** (a musical passage played) with a decrease in volume ☞ MUSIC [It, lit., diminishing, fr LL *diminuendum*, gerund of *diminuere*]

diminution /,dimi'nyoohsh(ə)n/ *n* a diminishing or decrease [ME *diminucioun*, fr MF *diminution*, fr ML *diminution-*, *diminutio*, alter. of L *deminution-*, *deminutio*, fr *deminutus*, pp of *deminuere*] – **diminutional** *adj*

[1]**diminutive** /di'minyootiv/ *n* a diminutive word, affix, or name [ME *diminutif*, fr ML *diminutivum*, alter. of LL *deminutivum*, fr neut of *deminutivus*]

[2]**diminutive** *adj* **1** indicating small size and sometimes lovableness or triviality – used in connection with affixes and words formed with them (e g *duckling*), with clipped forms (e g *Jim*), and with altered forms (e g *Peggy*) **2** exceptionally small; tiny – **diminutively** *adv*, **diminutiveness** *n*

dimissory /di'misəri/ *adj* **1** giving permission to be ordained in another bishop's diocese ⟨*a* ~ *letter*⟩ **2** granting leave to depart – fml [ML *dimissorius*, fr LL, submitting a matter to a higher court, fr L *dimissus*, pp of *dimittere* to dismiss]

dimity /'dimiti/ *n* a corded cotton fabric woven with checks or stripes [alter. of ME *demyt*, prob fr MGk *dimitos* of double thread, fr Gk *di-* + *mitos* warp thread]

dimmer /'dimə/ *n* a device for regulating the brightness of electric lighting [[2]DIM + [2]-ER]

dimorphism /,die'mawfiz(ə)m/ *n* the occurrence, combination, or existence of 2 distinct forms: e g **a** the existence of 2 different forms of a species, distinguished by size, colour, etc **b** the existence of an organ (e g the leaves of a plant) in 2 different forms **c** crystallization of a chemical compound in 2 different forms [ISV] – **dimorphic** /-fik/, **dimorphous** *adj*

[1]**dimple** /'dimpl/ *n* **1** a slight natural indentation in the cheek or another part of the human body **2** a depression or indentation on a surface [ME *dympull*; akin to OHG *tumphilo* whirlpool, OE *dyppan* to dip – more at DIP] – **dimply** /'dimpli/ *adj*

[2]**dimple** *vb* to mark with or form dimples

dimwit /'dim,wit/ *n* a stupid or mentally slow person – infml – **dim-witted** /,- '--/ *adj*, **dim-wittedly** /'witidli/ *adv*, **dim-wittedness** *n*

[1]**din** /din/ *n* a loud continued discordant noise [ME, fr OE *dyne*; akin to ON *dynr* din, Skt *dhvanati* it roars]

[2]**din** *vi* **-nn-** to make a din ⟨*the music* ~ned *in their ears*⟩ – **din into** to instil into by perpetual repetition

dinar /'dee,nah/ *n* (a coin or note representing) a money unit of certain Arab countries and Yugoslavia ☞ NATIONALITY [Ar *dīnār*, fr Gk *dēnarion* denarius, fr L *denarius*]

dine /dien/ *vi* to eat dinner ~ *vt* to entertain to dinner ⟨*wined and* ~d *us splendidly*⟩ [ME *dinen*, fr OF *diner*, fr (assumed) VL *disjejunare* to break one's fast, fr L *dis-* + LL *jejunare* to fast, fr L *jejunus* fasting] – **dine off/on/upon** to eat (sthg) as one's meal, esp one's dinner

diner /'dienə/ *n* **1** sby who is dining **2a** *NAm* a small restaurant, often beside the road **b** *chiefly NAm* DINING CAR

dinette /,die'net/ *n* a small (part of a) room set aside for eating meals in [*dine* + *-ette*]

dingbats /'ding,bats/ *n pl but sing or pl in constr, Austr & NZ* an attack of nervous anxiety – + *the*; slang [origin unknown]

[1]**dingdong** /'ding,dong/ *n* **1** the ringing sound produced by repeated strokes, esp on a bell **2** a rapid heated exchange of words or blows – infml [imit]

[2]**dingdong** *adj* **1** of or resembling the sound of a bell **2** with the advantage (e g in an argument or race) passing continually back and forth from one participant, side, etc to the other – infml

dinghy /'ding·gi/ *n* **1** a small boat often carried on a ship and used esp as a lifeboat or to transport passengers to and from shore **2** a small open sailing boat **3** a rubber life raft [Bengali *diṅgi* & Hindi *ḍiṅgī*]

dingle /'ding·gl/ *n* a small narrow wooded valley [ME, abyss]

dingo /'ding·goh/ *n, pl* **dingoes** a wild dog of Australia [native name in Australia]

dingy /'dinji/ *adj* **1** dirty, discoloured **2** shabby, squalid [origin unknown] – **dingily** *adv*, **dinginess** *n*

'dining ,car /'diening/ *n* a railway carriage where meals are served

dining room /'-- -, '-- ,-/ *n* a room set aside for eating meals in

dinitro- /,die'nietroh-/ *comb form* containing 2 nitro groups in the molecular structure

dinkum /'dingkəm/ *adj, Austr* real, genuine – infml [prob fr E dial. *dinkum*, n (work)]

dinky /'dingki/ *adj* **1** *chiefly Br* neat and dainty **2** *chiefly NAm* small, insignificant ***USE*** infml [Sc *dink* neat]

dinner /'dinə/ *n* **1** (the food eaten for) the principal meal of the day taken either in the evening or at midday **2** a formal evening meal or banquet [ME *diner*, fr OF, fr *diner* to dine]

'dinner ,jacket *n* a usu black jacket for men's semiformal evening wear

'dinner ,lady *n, Br* a woman who supervises children during mealtimes at school

dinosaur /'dienə,saw/ *n* **1** any of a group of extinct, typically very large flesh- or plant-eating reptiles, most of which lived on the land; *broadly* any large extinct reptile **2** an organization or institution that is unwieldy and outdated ⟨*Britain's industrial* ~s⟩ [deriv of Gk *deinos* terrible + *sauros* lizard – more at DIRE, SAURIAN] – **dinosaurian** /-'sawri·ən/ *adj or n*, **dinosauric** /-'sawrik/ *adj*

dinothere /'dienə,thiə/ *n* any of a genus of extinct mammals similar to elephants but with a pair of downward-directed tusks [NL *Deinotherium*, genus name, fr Gk *deinos* + NL *-therium* beast, animal, fr Gk *thērion*, dim. of *thēr*]

dint /dint/ *n* [ME, stroke, blow, fr OE *dynt*] – **by dint of** by means or application of

dinucleotide /die'nyoohkli·ətied/ *n* a nucleotide consisting of 2 units each composed of ribose or deoxyribose combined with a phosphate group and a nitrogen-containing base

diocesan /,die'osisən/ *n* a bishop having jurisdiction over a diocese

diocese /'die·əsis/ *n* the area under the jurisdiction of a bishop [ME *diocise*, fr MF, fr LL *diocesis*, alter. of *dioecesis*, fr L, administrative division, fr Gk *dioikēsis* administration, administrative division, fr *dioikein* to keep house, govern, fr *dia-* + *oikein* to dwell, manage, fr *oikos* house – more at VICINITY] – **diocesan** /die'osisən/ *adj*

diode /'die,ohd/ *n* **1** a thermionic valve having only an anode and a cathode **2** a semiconductor device having only 2 terminals [ISV]

dioecious, *NAm also* **diecious** /,die'eeshəs/ *adj* having male and female reproductive organs in different individuals or plants – compare MONOECIOUS [deriv of Gk *di-* + *oikos* house] – **dioeciously** *adv*, **dioecism** /-,siz(ə)m/ *n*

Dionysiac /,die·ə'niz(h)iak, -'nis(h)-/ *adj* Dionysian [L *dionysiacus*, fr Gk *dionysiakos*, fr *Dionysos* Dionysus] – **Dionysiac** *n*

Dionysian /,die·ə'niz(h)yən, -'nis(h)-/ *adj* of or relating to (the worship of) Dionysus, the Greek god of wine

dioptre, *NAm chiefly* **diopter** /,die'optə/ *n* a unit of measurement of the refractive power of lenses equal to the reciprocal of the focal length in metres [*diopter* (an optical instrument), fr MF *dioptre*, fr L *dioptra*, fr Gk, fr *dia-* + *opsesthai* to be going to see]

dioptric /die'optrik/ *adj* **1** refractive **2** produced by means of refraction [Gk *dioptrikos* of a diopter (instrument), fr *dioptra*]

diorama /,die·ə'rahmə/ *n* **1** a scenic representation in which an artificially lit translucent painting is viewed through an opening **2a** a three-dimensional representation in which miniature modelled figures, buildings, etc are displayed against a painted background **b** a life-size museum exhibit of an animal or bird in realistic natural surroundings against a painted background **3** a small-scale set used in films and television [F, fr *dia-* + *-orama* (as in *panorama*, fr E)] – **dioramic** /-'ramik/ *adj*

diorite /'die·əriet/ *n* a granular igneous rock commonly of acid feldspar and hornblende [F, irreg fr Gk *diorizein* to distinguish, fr *dia-* + *horizein* to define – more at HORIZON] – **dioritic** /-'ritik/ *adj*

dioxide /,die'oksied/ *n* an oxide containing 2 atoms of oxygen [ISV]

[1]dip /dip/ *vb* **-pp-** *vt* **1a** to plunge or immerse in a liquid (e g in order to moisten or dye) **b** to immerse (e g a sheep) in an antiseptic or parasite-killing solution **2** to lift up (water, grain etc) by scooping or ladling **3** to lower and then raise again ⟨~ *a flag in salute*⟩ **4** to lower (the beam of a vehicle's headlights) so as to reduce glare ~ *vi* **1a** to plunge into a liquid and quickly emerge **b** to immerse sthg in a processing liquid or finishing material **2** to drop down or decrease suddenly **3** to reach inside or below sthg, esp so as to take out part of the contents – usu + *in* or *into* **4** to incline downwards from the plane of the horizon [ME *dippen*, fr OE *dyppan*; akin to OHG *tupfen* to wash, Lith *dubus* deep] – **dip into 1** to make inroads into for funds ⟨dipped into *the family's savings*⟩ **2** to read superficially or in a random manner ⟨dipped into *a book while he was waiting*⟩

[2]dip *n* **1** a brief bathe for sport or exercise **2a** a sharp downward course; a drop **b** the angle that a stratum or similar geological feature makes with a horizontal plane **3** the angle formed with the horizon by a magnetic needle rotating in the vertical plane **4** a hollow, depression **5a** a sauce or soft mixture into which food is dipped before being eaten **b** a liquid preparation into which an object or animal may be dipped (e g for cleaning or disinfecting) **6** a pickpocket – slang

dipeptide /,die'peptied/ *n* a peptide having 2 molecules of amino acid in its molecular structure

diphase /'die,fayz/, **diphasic** /-'fayzik/ *adj* having 2 phases

di,phenox,ylate ,hydro'chloride /,diefe'noksilayt, -feen-/ *n* a drug used to treat the symptoms of diarrhoea – compare LOMOTIL [*diphenoxylate* fr *di-* + *phen-* + *ox-* + *-yl* + *-ate*]

diphosgene /die'fosjeen/ *n* a liquid compound used as a poison gas in WW 1 [ISV]

diphtheria /dif'thiəri·ə, dip-/ *n* an acute infectious disease caused by a bacterium and marked by fever and the formation of a false membrane, esp in the throat, causing difficulty in breathing [NL, fr F *diphthérie*, fr Gk *diphthera* leather; fr the toughness of the false membrane] – **diphtherial, diphtherian** *adj*, **diphtheritic** /-thə'ritik/ *adj*, **diphtheroid** *adj*

diphthong /'difthong, 'dip-/ *n* **1** a gliding monosyllabic vowel sound (e g /oy/ in *toy*) that starts at or near the articulatory position for one vowel and moves to or towards the position of another **2** a digraph **3** either of the ligatures æ or œ [ME *diptonge*, fr MF *diptongue*, fr LL *dipthongus*, fr Gk *diphthongos*, fr *di-* + *phthongos* voice, sound] – **diphthongal** /-'thong(g)l/ *adj*

diphthong·ize, -ise /'difthong(g)iez, 'dip-/ *vb* to change into or pronounce as a diphthong – **diphthongization** /-'zaysh(ə)n/ *n*

diphy- /difi-/, **diphyo-** *comb form* double; bipartite ⟨diphy*odont*⟩ [NL, fr Gk *diphy-*, fr *diphyēs*, fr *di-* + *phyein* to bring forth – more at BE]

dipl-, diplo- *comb form* double; twofold ⟨diplo*pia*⟩ [Gk, fr *diploos* – more at DOUBLE]

diplococcus /,diploh'kokəs/ *n, pl* **diplococci** /-kok(s)ie/ any of a genus of bacteria that includes some serious pathogens [NL, genus name] – **diplococcal, diplococcic** /-sik/ *adj*

diplodocus /di'plodəkəs/ *n* any of a genus of very large plant-eating dinosaurs [NL, genus name, fr *dipl-* + Gk *dokos* beam, fr *dekesthai, dechesthai* to receive; akin to L *decēre* to be fitting – more at DECENT]

diploid /'diployd/ *n or adj* (a cell or organism) having double the basic number of chromosomes arranged in homologous pairs – compare HAPLOID, POLYPLOID

diploma /di'plohmə/ *n* **1** an official or state document **2** a document conferring some honour or privilege **3** (a certificate of) a qualification, usu in a more specialized subject or at a lower level than a degree [L, passport, diploma, fr Gk *diplōma* folded paper, passport, fr *diploun* to double, fr *diploos*]

diplomacy /di'plohməsi/ *n* **1** the art and practice of conducting international relations **2** skill and tact in handling affairs

diplomat /'dipləmat/ *n* **1** one (e g an ambassador) employed in diplomacy **2** one skilled in dealing with people tactfully and adroitly [F *diplomate*, back-formation fr *diplomatique*]

diplomate /'diplə,mayt/ *n* one who holds a diploma [*diploma* + [1]*-ate*]

diplomatic /,diplə'matik/ *adj* **1** exactly reproducing the original ⟨*a* ~ *edition*⟩ **2** of diplomats or international relations **3** employing tact and conciliation [(1) NL *diplomaticus*, fr L *diplomat-, diploma*; (2, 3) F *diplomatique* connected with documents regulating international relations, fr NL *diplomaticus*] – **diplomatically** *adv*

,diplo,matic im'munity *n* the exemption from local laws and taxes accorded to diplomatic staff abroad

diplomatist /di'plohmətist/ *n* a person skilled or employed in diplomacy

diplopia /di'plohpi·ə, -pyə/ *n* a disorder of vision in which 2 images of a single object are seen because of unequal action of the eye muscles [NL] – **diplopic** /-pik/ *adj*

diplopod /'diplə,pod/ *n* a millipede [deriv of Gk *dipl-* + *pod-, pous* foot – more at FOOT] – **diplopodous** /dip'lopədəs/ *adj*

diplotene /'diploh,teen/ *n* a stage of meiotic cell division during which the paired chromosomes begin to separate [ISV] – **diplotene** *adj*

dipole /'die,pohl/ *n* **1a** a pair of equal and opposite electric charges, or magnetic poles of opposite sign, separated by a small distance **b** a molecule having such charges **2** a radio aerial consisting of 2 horizontal rods in line, with their ends slightly separated [ISV] – **dipole, dipolar** /-'pohlə/ *adj*

dipper /'dipə/ *n* **1** sthg (e g a long-handled cup) used for dipping **2** any of several diving birds **3** *cap, chiefly NAm* **a Dipper, Big Dipper** URSA MAJOR **b** URSA MINOR [[1]DIP + [2]-ER]

dippy /'dipi/ crazy, eccentric – slang [perh alter. of *dipso*, short for *dipsomaniac*]

dipsomania /,dipsoh'maynyə, -ni·ə, ,dipsə-/ *n* an uncontrollable craving for alcoholic drinks [NL, fr Gk *dipsa* thirst + LL *mania*] – **dipsomaniac** *n*, **dipsomaniacal** /-mə'nie·əkl/ *adj*

dipstick /'dip,stik/ *n* a graduated rod for measuring the depth of a liquid (e g the oil in a car's engine)

dipteran /'diptərən/ *n* TWO-WINGED FLY [deriv of Gk *dipteros*] – **dipteran** *adj*

dipterous /'diptərəs/ *adj* **1** having 2 wings or winglike appendages **2** of the two-winged flies [NL *dipterus*, fr Gk *dipteros*, fr *di-* + *pteron* wing – more at FEATHER]

diptych /'diptik/ *n* **1** a 2-leaved hinged writing tablet **2** a painting or carving done on 2 hinged panels and used esp as an altarpiece [LL *diptycha*, pl, fr Gk, fr neut pl of *diptychos* folded in two, fr *di-* + *ptychē* fold]

dire /die·ə/ *adj* **1** dreadful, awful **2** warning of disaster; ominous ⟨*a* ~ *forecast*⟩ **3** desperately urgent ⟨~ *need*⟩ [L *dirus*; akin to Gk *deinos* terrible, Skt *dvesti* he hates] – **direly** *adv*, **direness** *n*

[1]**direct** /di'rekt, die-/ *vt* **1a** to mark (e g a letter or parcel) with a name and address **b** to address or aim (e g a remark) **2** to cause to turn, move, point, or follow a straight course ⟨~ed *her eyes heavenward*⟩ **3** to show or point out the way for **4a** to control and regulate the activities or course of **b** to control the organization and performance of; supervise ⟨~ed *the latest science fiction film*⟩ **c** to order or instruct with authority ⟨*police* ~ed *the crowd to move back*⟩ **d** to train and usu lead performances of; *specif, chiefly NAm* to conduct ⟨~ed *the orchestra in a new work*⟩ ~ *vi* to act as director [ME *directen*, fr L *directus*, pp of *dirigere* to set straight, direct – more at DRESS]

[2]**direct** *adj* **1a** going from one point to another in time or space without deviation or interruption; straight **b** going by the shortest way ⟨*the* ~ *route*⟩ **2a** stemming immediately from a source, cause, or reason ⟨~ *result*⟩ **b** passing in a straight line of descent from parent to offspring ⟨~ *ancestor*⟩ **3** frank, straightforward **4a** operating without an intervening agency **b** effected by the action of the people or the electorate and not by representatives **5** consisting of or reproducing the exact words of a speaker or writer ⟨~ *speech*⟩ – compare INDIRECT 4 **6** diametric, exact ⟨*was a* ~ *contradiction of all he'd said before*⟩ **7** *of a celestial body* moving in the general planetary direction from W to E; not retrograde [ME, fr L *directus*, fr pp of *dirigere*] – **directness** *n*

[3]**direct** *adv* **1** from point to point without deviation; by the shortest way ⟨*write to him* ~⟩ **2** without an intervening agency or stage

direct action *n* action that seeks to achieve an end by the most immediately effective means (e g boycott or strike)

direct current *n* an electric current flowing in 1 direction only; *esp* such a current that is substantially constant in value

direct grant *n, often cap D&G* a grant of money given direct by the Department of Education and Science to certain British schools, which are obliged to admit a number of non-fee-paying pupils ⟨*a ~ school*⟩

direction /di'reksh(ə)n, die-/ *n* **1** guidance or supervision of action **2a** the act, art, or technique of directing an orchestra, film, or theatrical production **b** a word, phrase, or sign indicating the appropriate tempo, mood, or intensity of a passage or movement in music **3** *pl* explicit instructions on how to do sthg or get to a place ⟨*read the* ~s *on the packet*⟩ ⟨*asked for* ~s *to King's Cross*⟩ **4a** the line or course along which sby or sthg moves or is aimed ⟨*drove off in the ~ of London*⟩ **b** the point towards which sby or sthg faces ⟨*which ~ does this house face?*⟩ **5a** a tendency, trend **b** a guiding or motivating purpose ⟨*had a new sense of* ~⟩

directional /di'reksh(ə)nl, die-/ *adj* **1** of or indicating direction in space: e g **a** suitable for detecting the direction from which radio signals come, or for sending out signals in 1 direction only ⟨*a ~ aerial*⟩ **b** of or being a device that operates more efficiently in one direction than in others **2** relating to direction or guidance, esp of thought or effort – **directionality** /-'aləti/ *n*

di'rection ,finder *n* an aerial used to determine the direction of incoming radio waves

[1]**directive** /di'rektiv, die-/ *adj* **1** serving to direct, guide, or influence **2** serving to provide a direction

[2]**directive** *n* an authoritative instruction issued by a high-level body or official

[1]**di'rectly** /-li/ *adv* **1** in a direct manner **2a** without delay; immediately **b** soon, shortly

[2]**directly** *conj, chiefly Br* immediately after; as soon as – infml

di'rect ,method *n* a method of foreign-language teaching, placing the emphasis on oral work and minimal use of the student's own language

direct object *n* a grammatical object representing the primary goal or the result of the action of its verb (e g *me* in 'he hit me' and *house* in 'we built a house')

director /di'rektə, die-/ *n* **1** the head of an organized group or administrative unit **2** a member of a governing board entrusted with the overall direction of a company **3** sby who has responsibility for supervising the artistic and technical aspects of a film or play – compare PRODUCER 3a [[1]DIRECT + [1]-OR] – **directorship** *n*, **directorial** /di,rek'tawri·əl, ,direk-/ *adj*

directorate /di'rektərət, die-/ *n* **1** the office of director **2** a board of directors (e g of a company)

directory /di'rekt(ə)ri, die-/ *n* **1** a book or collection of directions or rules, esp concerning forms of worship **2** an alphabetical or classified list (e g of names, addresses, telephone numbers, etc) [ML *directorium*, fr neut of LL *directorius* directorial, fr L *directus*, pp]

direct proportion *n* a proportion of 2 variables whose ratio is constant

directrix /di'rektriks, die-/ *n, pl* **directrixes** /-triksiz/ *also* **directrices** /-tri,seez/ a fixed curve by relation to which a conic section is described ☞ MATHEMATICS [ML, fem of LL *director*, fr L *directus*, pp]

direct tax *n* a tax (e g income tax) exacted directly from the person, organization, etc on whom it is levied – compare INDIRECT TAX

dirge /duhj/ *n* **1** a song or hymn of grief or lamentation, esp intended to accompany funeral or memorial rites **2** a slow mournful piece of music [ME *dirige*, the Office of the Dead, fr the first word of a LL antiphon, fr L, imper of *dirigere*]

dirham /diə'ham, də'ram/ *n* ☞ *Libya, Morocco, Qatar, United Arab Emirates* at NATIONALITY [Ar, fr L *drachma* drachma]

[1]**dirigible** /'dirijəbl, -'---/ *adj* capable of being steered [L *dirigere*]

[2]**dirigible** *n* an airship [*dirigible* (*balloon*)]

dirigisme /,deeree'zheezm(ə) (*Fr* diriʒism)/ *n* state control of the economy and social institutions – chiefly derog [F, fr *diriger* to direct, fr L *dirigere*] – **dirigiste** /-'zheest, (*Fr* -ʒist)/ *adj*

dirk /duhk/ *n* a long straight-bladed dagger, used esp by Scottish Highlanders [Sc *durk*]

dirndl /'duhndl/ *n* a full skirt with a tight waistband ☞ GARMENT [short for G *dirndlkleid*, fr G dial. *dirndl* girl + G *kleid* dress]

dirt /duht/ *n* **1a** excrement **b** a filthy or soiling substance (e g mud or grime) **c** sby or sthg worthless or contemptible **2** [3]SOIL 2a **3a** obscene or pornographic speech or writing **b** scandalous or malicious gossip [ME *drit*, fr ON; akin to OE *drītan* to defecate, L *foria* diarrhoea]

,dirt 'cheap *adj or adv* (sold) at a very low price – infml

[1]**dirty** /'duhti/ *adj* **1a** not clean or pure; marked or contaminated with dirt **b** causing sby or sthg to become soiled or covered with dirt ⟨~ *jobs*⟩ **2a** base, sordid ⟨*war is a ~ business*⟩ **b** unsportsmanlike, unfair ⟨~ *players*⟩ **c** low, despicable ⟨~ *tricks*⟩ **3a** indecent, obscene ⟨~ *language*⟩ **b** sexually illicit ⟨*a ~ weekend*⟩ **4** *of weather* rough, stormy **5** *of colour* not clear and bright; dull ⟨*drab* dirty*-pink walls*⟩ **6** conveying resentment or disgust ⟨*gave him a ~ look*⟩ **7** producing considerable fallout ⟨~ *bombs*⟩ – **dirtily** *adv*, **dirtiness** *n*

[2]**dirty** *vb* to make or become dirty

dis- /dis-/ *prefix* **1a** do the opposite of (a specified action) ⟨dis*establish*⟩ ⟨dis*appear*⟩ **b** deprive of, remove (sthg specified) from ⟨dis*arm*⟩ ⟨dis*member*⟩ **c** exclude or expel from ⟨dis*bar*⟩ **2** opposite or absence of ⟨dis*array*⟩ ⟨dis*belief*⟩ **3** not ⟨dis*agreeable*⟩ ⟨dis*honest*⟩ **4** completely ⟨dis*annul*⟩ ⟨dis*gruntled*⟩ **5** dys- ⟨dis*function*⟩ [ME *dis-, des-*, fr OF & L; OF *des-, dis-*, fr L *dis-*, lit., apart; akin to OE *te-* apart, L *duo* two – more at TWO; (5) by folk etymology]

disability /,disə'biləti/ *n* **1a** the condition of being disabled; *specif* inability to do sthg (e g pursue an occupation) because of physical or mental impairment **b** sthg that disables; a handicap **2** a legal disqualification

disable /dis'aybl/ *vt* **1** to deprive of legal right, qualification, or capacity **2** to make incapable or ineffective; *esp* to deprive of physical soundness; cripple – **disablement** *n*

disabuse /,disə'byoohz/ *vt* to free from a mistaken impression or judgment [F *désabuser*, fr *dés-* dis- + *abuser* to abuse]

disaccharide /,die'sakəried/ *n* any of a class of sugars (e g sucrose) that, on hydrolysis, yield 2 monosaccharide molecules

[1]**disadvantage** /,disəd'vahntij/ *n* **1** loss or damage, esp to reputation or finances **2a** an unfavourable, inferior, or prejudicial situation ⟨*we were at a* ~⟩ **b** sby or sthg which causes one to be in an unfavourable condition or position; a handicap ⟨*her poor health is*

a great ~ *to her*⟩ [ME *disavauntage*, fr MF *desavantage*, fr OF, fr *des-* + *avantage* advantage]

[2]**disadvantage** *vt* to place at a disadvantage

ˌ**disadˈvantaged** *adj* underprivileged, esp socially

disadvantageous /ˌdisadvənˈtayjəs/ *adj* 1 prejudicial, unfavourable 2 derogatory, disparaging – **disadvantageously** *adv*, **disadvantageousness** *n*

disaffect /ˌdisəˈfekt/ *vt* to alienate the affection or loyalty of – **disaffection** /-əˈfeksh(ə)n/ *n*

ˌ**disafˈfected** *adj* discontented and resentful, esp towards authority

disaffiliate /ˌdisəˈfiliayt/ *vb* to end, or separate from, an affiliation or connection – **disaffiliation** /-ˈaysh(ə)n/ *n*

disaffirm /ˌdisəˈfuhm/ *vt* to annul or repudiate (e g a legal settlement) – **disaffirmance** *n*, **disaffirmation** /ˌdisafəˈmaysh(ə)n, -ˌ--ˈ--/ *n*

disagree /ˌdisəˈgree/ *vi* 1 to be unlike or at variance 2 to differ in opinion – usu + *with* 3 to have a bad effect – usu + *with* ⟨*fried foods* ~ *with me*⟩ [ME *disagreen*, fr MF *desagreer*, fr *des-* + *agreer* to agree]

disagreeable /disəˈgree·əbl/ *adj* 1 unpleasant, objectionable 2 peevish, ill-tempered – **disagreeableness** *n*, **disagreeably** *adv*, **disagreeability** /-ˈbiləti/ *n*

ˌ**disaˈgreement** /-mənt/ *n* 1 a lack of correspondence; a disparity 2 a difference of opinion; an argument [DISAGREE + -MENT]

disallow /ˌdisəˈlow/ *vt* to refuse to admit or recognize – **disallowance** *n*

disambiguate /ˌdisamˈbigyooˌayt/ *vt* to remove (possible) ambiguity from (e g a phrase or sentence) – **disambiguation** /-ˈaysh(ə)n/ *n*

disannul /ˌdisəˈnul/ *vt* to annul, cancel

disappear /ˌdisəˈpiə/ *vi* 1 to pass from view suddenly or gradually 2 to cease to be or to be known 3 to leave or depart, esp secretly – infml – **disappearance** *n*

disappoint /ˌdisəˈpoynt/ *vt* to fail to meet the expectation or hope of; *also* to sadden by so doing [MF *desapointier*, fr *des-* dis- + *apointier* to arrange – more at APPOINT] – **disappointing** *adj*, **disappointingly** *adv*

ˌ**disapˈpointed** *adj* defeated in expectation or hope; thwarted – **disappointedly** *adv*

ˌ**disapˈpointment** /-mənt/ *n* 1 disappointing or being disappointed 2 sby or sthg that disappoints

disapprobation /ˌdisˌaprəˈbaysh(ə)n/ *n* disapproval – fml

disapproval /ˌdisəˈproohv(ə)l/ *n* unfavourable opinion; censure

disapprove /ˌdisəˈproohv/ *vt* to refuse approval to; reject ~ *vi* to have or express an unfavourable opinion *of* – **disapprover** *n*, **disapprovingly** *adv*

disarm /disˈahm/ *vt* 1a to deprive of a weapon or weapons b to deprive of a means of attack or defence c to make (e g a bomb) harmless, esp by removing a fuse or warhead 2 to dispel the hostility or suspicion of ~ *vi* 1 to lay aside arms 2 to reduce or abolish weapons and armed forces [ME *desarmen*, fr MF *desarmer*, fr OF, fr *des-* + *armer* to arm] – **disarmament** /-məmənt/ *n*

disarming /disˈahming/ *adj* allaying criticism or hostility – **disarmingly** *adv*

disarrange /ˌdisəˈraynj/ *vt* to disturb the arrangement or order of – **disarrangement** *n*

[1]**disarray** /ˌdisəˈray/ *n* a lack of order or sequence; disorder

[2]**disarray** *vt* to throw or place into disorder [ME *disarayen*, fr MF *desarroyer*, fr OF *desareer*, fr *des-* + *areer* to array]

disarticulate /ˌdisahˈtikyoolayt/ *vb* to (cause to) become disjointed – **disarticulation** /-ˈlaysh(ə)n/ *n*

disassemble /ˌdisəˈsembl/ *vt* to take (e g a machine) apart – **disassembly** *n*

disassociate /ˌdisəˈsohs(h)iayt/ *vt* to dissociate – **disassociation** /-ˈaysh(ə)n/ *n*

disaster /diˈzahstə/ *n* 1 a sudden event bringing great damage, loss, or destruction; *broadly* an unfortunate occurrence 2 a failure ⟨*was a complete* ~ *as a teacher*⟩ – infml [MF & OIt; MF *desastre*, fr OIt *disastro*, lit., unfavourable aspect of a star, fr *dis-* (fr L) + *astro* star, fr L *astrum* – more at ASTRAL] – **disastrous** /-trəs/ *adj*, **disastrously** *adv*

diˈsaster ˌarea *n* an area officially declared to be the scene of a disaster and therefore qualified to receive emergency loans and supplies

disavow /ˌdisəˈvow/ *vt* to deny knowledge of or responsibility for; repudiate – fml [ME *desavowen*, fr MF *desavouer*, fr OF, fr *des-* dis- + *avouer* to avow] – **disavowal** *n*

disband /disˈband/ *vb* to (cause to) break up and separate; disperse [MF *desbander*, fr *des-* + *bande* band] – **disbandment** *n*

disbar /disˈbah/ *vt* to deprive (a barrister) of the right to practise; expel from the bar – **disbarment** *n*

disbelief /ˌdisbiˈleef/ *n* mental rejection of sthg as untrue

disbelieve /ˌdisbiˈleev/ *vb* to reject or withhold belief (in) – **disbeliever** *n*

disbud /ˌdisˈbud/ *vt* **-dd-** to remove (superfluous) buds from (e g a plant), esp in order to improve the quality of bloom

disburden /disˈbuhd(ə)n/ *vt* to unburden – **disburdenment** *n*

disburse /disˈbuhs/ *vt* 1 to pay out, esp from a fund 2 to make a payment in settlement of; defray – fml [MF *desbourser*, fr OF *desborser*, fr *des-* + *borser* to get money, fr *borse* purse, fr ML *bursa* – more at PURSE] – **disbursement** *n*, **disburser** *n*

disc, *NAm chiefly* **disk** /disk/ *n* 1a a thin flat circular object b an apparently flat figure or surface (e g of a planet) ⟨*the solar* ~⟩ 2 any of various round flat anatomical structures; *esp* any of the cartilaginous discs between the spinal vertebrae ⟨*suffering from a slipped* ~⟩ ☞ ANATOMY 3 a gramophone record 4 DISK 1a 5 any of the sharp-edged concave circular cutting blades of a harrow [L *discus* – more at DISH]

discalced /disˈkalst/ *adj, of a friar or nun* barefoot or wearing only sandals [part trans of L *discalceatus*, fr *dis-* + *calceatus*, pp of *calceare* to put on shoes, fr *calceus* shoe, fr *calc-*, *calx* heel]

[1]**discard** /disˈkahd/ *vt* 1a to throw out (a playing card) from one's hand b to play (any card from a suit different from the one led except a trump) when unable to follow suit 2 to get rid of as useless or superfluous ~ *vi* to discard a playing card

[2]**discard** *n* 1 the act of discarding in a card game 2 sby or sthg discarded; *esp* a discarded card

ˈ**disc ˌbrake** *n* a brake that operates by the friction of a calliper pressing against the sides of a rotating disc ☞ CAR

discern /di'suhn/ *vt* **1** to detect with one of the senses, esp vision **2** to perceive or recognize mentally [ME *discernen*, fr MF *discerner*, fr L *discernere* to separate, distinguish between, fr *dis-* apart + *cernere* to sift – more at DIS-, CERTAIN] – **discerner** *n*, **discernible** *also* **discernable** *adj*, **discernibly** *adv*

discerning /di'suhning/ *adj* showing insight and understanding; discriminating – **discerningly** *adv*

di'scernment /-mənt/ *n* skill in discerning; keen insight [DISCERN + -MENT]

[1]**discharge** /dis'chahj/ *vt* **1a** to unload **b** to release from an obligation **2a** to shoot ⟨~ *a gun*⟩ **b** to release from custody or care **c** to send or pour out; emit **3a** to dismiss from employment or service **b** to fulfil (e g a debt or obligation) by performing an appropriate action **c** to annul legally **4** to remove an electric charge from or reduce the electric charge of ~ *vi* **1** to throw off or deliver a load, charge, or burden **2a** *of a gun* to be fired **b** to pour out (fluid) contents **3** to lose or reduce an electric charge [ME *dischargen*, fr MF *descharger*, fr LL *discarricare*, fr L *dis-* + LL *carricare* to load – more at CHARGE] – **dischargeable** *adj*, **dischargee** /-'jee/ *n*, **discharger** *n*

[2]**discharge** /'dischahj, -'-/ *n* **1a** the relieving of an obligation, accusation, or penalty **b** a certificate of release or payment **2** the act of discharging or unloading **3a** legal release from confinement **b** an acquittal **4** the act or an instance of firing a missile or missiles ⟨*an artillery* ~⟩ **5a** a flowing or pouring out **b** sthg that is discharged or emitted ⟨*a purulent* ~⟩ **6** release or dismissal, esp from an office or employment **7a** a usu brief flow of an electric charge through a gas, usu with associated light emission **b** the conversion of the chemical energy of a battery into electrical energy

'discharge ,lamp *n* a lamp which contains gas or vapour at very low pressure and through which conduction causing luminosity takes place when a high potential difference is applied

disciple /di'siepl/ *n* **1** one who accepts and assists in spreading another's doctrines; a follower **2** any of the followers of Christ during his life on earth; *esp* any of Christ's 12 appointed followers [ME, fr OE *discipul* & OF *desciple*, fr LL and L; LL *discipulus* follower of Jesus Christ in his lifetime, fr L, pupil] – **discipleship** *n*, **discipular** /di'sipyoolə/ *adj*

disciplinarian /,disipli'neəri·ən/ *n* one who enforces or advocates (strict) discipline or order – **disciplinarian** *adj*

disciplinary /,disi'plinəri/ *adj* **1** of or involving discipline; corrective ⟨~ *action*⟩ **2** of a particular field of study

[1]**discipline** /'disiplin/ *n* **1** a field of study **2** training of the mind and character designed to produce obedience and self-control **3** punishment, chastisement **4a** order obtained by enforcing obedience (e g in a school or army) **b** self-control **5** a system of rules governing conduct [ME, fr MF & L; MF, fr L *disciplina* teaching, learning, fr *discipulus* pupil] – **disciplinal** /-,plinl/ *adj*

[2]**discipline** *vt* **1** to punish or penalize for the sake of discipline **2** to train by instruction and exercise, esp in obedience and self-control **3** to bring (a group) under control ⟨~ *troops*⟩ – **disciplinable** *adj*, **discipliner** *n*

'disc ,jockey *n* one who introduces records of popular usu contemporary music (e g on a radio programme or at a discotheque)

disclaim /dis'klaym/ *vi* to make a disclaimer ~ *vt* **1** to renounce a legal claim to **2** to deny, disavow [AF *disclaimer*, fr *dis-* + *claimer* to claim, fr OF *clamer*]

disclaimer /dis'klaymə/ *n* **1** a denial of legal responsibility **2** a denial, repudiation [AF, fr *disclaimer*, vb]

disclose /dis'klohz/ *vt* **1** to expose to view **2** to make known; reveal to public knowledge [ME *disclosen*, fr MF *desclos-*, stem of *desclore* to disclose, fr ML *disclaudere* to open, fr L *dis-* + *claudere* to close – more at [4]CLOSE] – **discloser** *n*

disclosure /dis'klohzhə/ *n* **1** (an instance of) disclosing; an exposure **2** sthg disclosed; a revelation

disco /'diskoh/ *n, pl* **discos** **1** a collection of popular records together with the equipment for playing them **2** a discotheque – infml [short for *discotheque*]

discography /di'skogrəfi/ *n* **1** a descriptive list of gramophone records **2** the study of recorded music [F *discographie*, fr *disc-* + *-graphie* -graphy] – **discographer** *n*, **discographical** /,diskə'grafikl/ *also* **discographic** *adj*, **discographically** *adv*

discoid /'diskoyd/ *adj* resembling a disc or discus [LL *discoides* quoit-shaped, fr Gk *diskoeidēs*, fr *diskos* disc]

discolour /dis'kulə/ *vb* to (cause to) change colour for the worse; stain [ME *discolouren*, fr MF *descolourer*, fr LL *discolorari*, fr L *discolor* of another colour, fr *dis-* + *color* colour] – **discoloration** *n*

discombobulate /,diskəm'bobyoo,layt/ *vt, NAm* to upset, confuse [prob alter. of *discompose*]

discomfit /dis'kumfit/ *vt* **1** to frustrate the plans of; thwart **2** to cause perplexity and embarrassment to; disconcert [ME *discomfiten*, fr OF *desconfit*, pp of *desconfire*, fr *des-* + *confire* to prepare – more at COMFIT] – **discomfiture** /-fichə/ *n*

[1]**discomfort** /dis'kumfət/ *vt* to make uncomfortable or uneasy [ME *discomforten*, fr MF *desconforter*, fr OF, fr *des-* + *conforter* to comfort]

[2]**discomfort** *n* (sthg causing) mental or physical unease

discompose /,diskəm'pohz/ *vt* to destroy the composure of – fml – **discomposure** /-'pohzhə/ *n*

disconcert /,diskən'suht/ *vt* to disturb the composure of; fluster [obs F *disconcerter*, alter. of MF *desconcerter*, fr *des-* + *concerter* to concert] – **disconcerting** *adj*, **disconcertingly** *adv*

disconnect /,diskə'nekt/ *vt* to sever the connection of or between; *specif* CUT OFF 7B – **disconnection** /-'neksh(ə)n/ *n*

,discon'nected *adj* disjointed, incoherent – **disconnectedly** *adv*, **disconnectedness** *n*

disconsolate /dis'konsələt/ *adj* dejected, downcast [ME, fr ML *disconsolatus*, fr L *dis-* + *consolatus*, pp of *consolari* to console] – **disconsolately** *adv*, **disconsolateness** *n*, **disconsolation** /,dis,konsə'laysh(ə)n/ *n*

[1]**discontent** /,diskən'tent/ *n* **1** lack of contentment; dissatisfaction **2** one who is discontented; a malcontent

[2]**discontent** *vt* to make discontented

,discon'tented *also* **discontent** *adj* restlessly unhappy; dissatisfied

,discon'tentment /-mənt/ *n* DISCONTENT 1

discontinue /,diskən'tinyooh/ *vt* to cease, stop;

specif to cease production of ⟨*this line has been* ~d⟩ ~ *vi* to come to an end [ME *discontinuen*, fr MF *discontinuer*, fr ML *discontinuare*, fr L *dis-* + *continuare* to continue] – **discontinuance** *n*

discontinuous /,diskən'tinyoo·əs/ *adj* lacking sequence, coherence, or continuity – **discontinuously** *adv*, **discontinuity** /,diskonti'nyooh·əti/ *n*

discord /'diskawd/ *n* **1** lack of agreement or harmony; conflict **2a** dissonance **b** a harsh unpleasant combination of sounds [ME *discorde*, deriv of L *discord-*, *discors* discordant, fr *dis-* + *cord-*, *cor* heart – more at HEART]

discordant /dis'kawd(ə)nt/ *adj* **1** disagreeing; AT VARIANCE **2** relating to a discord; dissonant ⟨~ *tones*⟩ – **discordance, discordancy** *n*, **discordantly** *adv*

discotheque /'diskə,tek/ *n* a nightclub for dancing to usu recorded music [F *discothèque*, fr *disque* disc, record + *-o-* + *-thèque* (as in *bibliothèque* library)]

[1]**discount** /'diskownt/ *n* a reduction made from the gross amount or value of sthg: e g **a** a reduction in the price of goods, accorded esp to special or trade customers **b** a reduction in the amount due on a bill of exchange, debt, etc when paid promptly or before the specified date – **at a discount** below the usual price

[2]**discount** /'diskownt; *sense 2* dis'kownt/ *vt* **1a** to make a deduction from, usu for cash or prompt payment **b** to sell or offer for sale at a discount **c** to buy or sell (a bill of exchange) before maturity at below the stated price **2a** to leave out of account as unimportant, unreliable, or irrelevant; disregard **b** to underestimate the importance of; minimize **3** to take (e g a future event) into account in present arrangements or calculations [modif of F *décompter*, fr OF *desconter*, fr ML *discomputare*, fr L *dis-* + *computare* to count – more at [1]COUNT] – **discountable** /-'---/ *adj*

discountenance /dis'kownt(ə)nəns/ *vt* **1** to abash, disconcert **2** to discourage by showing disapproval – fml

discourage /dis'kurij/ *vt* **1** to deprive of confidence; dishearten **2a** to hinder, deter *from* **b** to attempt to prevent, esp by showing disapproval [MF *descorager*, fr OF *descoragier*, fr *des-* dis- + *corage* courage] – **discouragement** *n*

[1]**discourse** /'diskaws/ *n* **1** a talk, conversation **2** (orderly expression of ideas in) a formal speech or piece of writing [ME *discours*, fr ML & LL *discursus*; ML, argument, fr LL, conversation, fr L, act of running about, fr *discursus*, pp of *discurrere* to run about, fr *dis-* + *currere* to run – more at CAR]

[2]**discourse** /'--, -'-/ *vi* **1** to express one's ideas in speech or writing **2** to talk, converse ***USE*** usu + *on* or *upon* – **discourser** *n*

discourteous /dis'kuhtyəs, -'kaw-, -ti·əs/ *adj* rude, impolite – **discourteously** *adv*, **discourteousness** *n*

discourtesy /dis'kuhtəsi, -'kaw-/ *n* (an instance of) rudeness; (an) incivility

discover /di'skuvə/ *vt* **1** to obtain sight or knowledge of for the first time **2** to make known or visible – fml [ME *discoveren*, fr OF *descovrir*, fr LL *discooperire*, fr L *dis-* + *cooperire* to cover – more at COVER] – **discoverable** *adj*, **discoverer** *n*

discovery /di'skuv(ə)ri/ *n* **1a** the act or an instance of discovering or revealing **b** an obligatory disclosure of documents or facts by a party to a legal action **2** sby or sthg discovered

[1]**discredit** /dis'kredit/ *vt* **1** to refuse to accept as true or accurate **2** to cast doubt on the accuracy, authority, or reputation of

[2]**discredit** *n* **1** (sby or sthg causing) loss of credit or reputation **2** loss of belief or confidence; doubt

discreditable /dis'kreditəbl/ *adj* bringing discredit or disgrace – **discreditably** *adv*

discreet /di'skreet/ *adj* **1** judicious in speech or conduct; *esp* capable of maintaining a prudent silence **2** unpretentious, modest ⟨*the house was furnished with* ~ *elegance*⟩ [ME, fr MF *discret*, fr ML *discretus*, fr L, pp of *discernere* to separate, distinguish between – more at DISCERN] – **discreetly** *adv*, **discreetness** *n*

discrepant /di'skrep(ə)nt/ *adj* disagreeing; AT VARIANCE [L *discrepant-*, *discrepans*, prp of *discrepare* to sound discordantly, fr *dis-* + *crepare* to rattle, creak – more at [1]RAVEN] – **discrepancy** *n*, **discrepantly** *adv*

discrete /di'skreet/ *adj* **1** individually distinct **2** consisting of distinct or unconnected elements [ME, fr L *discretus*] – **discretely** *adv*, **discreteness** *n*

discretion /di'skresh(ə)n/ *n* **1** the quality of being discreet **2** the ability to make responsible decisions **3a** individual choice or judgment ⟨*left the decision to his* ~⟩ **b** power of free decision within legal bounds ⟨*reached the age of* ~⟩

discretionary /di'skresh(ə)nri/ *adj* **1** left to or exercised at one's own discretion ⟨~ *powers*⟩ **2** subject to the discretion of another

discriminant /di'skriminənt/ *n* a mathematical expression providing a criterion for the behaviour of another more complicated expression, relation, or set of relations

discriminate /di'skrimi,nayt/ *vt* to distinguish (e g objects or ideas) by noting differences ⟨~ *good from bad*⟩ ~ *vi* **1a** to make a distinction ⟨~ *between fact and fancy*⟩ **b** to show good judgment or discernment **2** to treat sby differently and esp unfavourably on the grounds of race, sex, religion, etc [L *discriminatus*, pp of *discriminare*, fr *discrimin-*, *discrimen* distinction, fr *discernere* to distinguish between – more at DISCERN] – **discriminator** *n*

discriminating /di'skrimi,nayting/ *adj* **1** discerning, judicious **2** discriminatory – **discriminatingly** *adv*

discrimination /di,skrimi'naysh(ə)n/ *n* **1** the act or process of responding to different sensory stimuli in different ways **2** discernment and good judgment, esp in matters of taste **3** prejudicial treatment (e g on the grounds of race or sex) [DISCRIMINATE + -ION] – **discriminational** *adj*

discriminative /di'skriminətiv/ *adj* discriminatory

discriminatory /di'skriminət(ə)ri/ *adj* showing esp unfavourable discrimination ⟨*a* ~ *law*⟩ – **discriminatorily** *adv*

discursive /di'skuhsiv, -ziv/ *adj* **1** passing usu unmethodically from one topic to another; digressive **2** proceeding by logical argument or reason [ML *discursivus*, fr L *discursus*, pp of *discurrere* to run about – more at DISCOURSE] – **discursively** *adv*, **discursiveness** *n*

discus /'diskəs/ *n, pl* **discuses** (the athletic field event involving the throwing of) a solid disc, between 180mm and 219mm (about 7 to 9in) in diameter, that is thicker in the centre than at the edge [L – more at DISH]

discuss /di'skus/ *vt* to consider or examine (a topic) in speech or writing [ME *discussen*, fr L *discussus*, pp of *discutere*, fr *dis-* apart + *quatere* to shake] – **discussable, discussible** *adj*

discussion /di'skush(ə)n/ *n* (an instance of) consideration of a question in open debate or conversation

[1]**disdain** /dis'dayn/ *n* contempt for sthg regarded as worthless or insignificant; scorn [ME *desdeyne*, fr OF *desdeign*, fr *desdeignier*]

[2]**disdain** *vt* **1** to regard with disdain **2** to refuse or abstain from because of disdain ⟨*she* ~ed *to answer him*⟩ [ME *desdeynen*, fr MF *desdeignier*, fr (assumed) VL *disdignare*, fr L *dis-* + *dignare* to deign – more at DEIGN]

dis'dainful /-f(ə)l/ *adj* feeling or showing disdain – **disdainfully** *adv*, **disdainfulness** *n*

disease /di'zeez/ *n* **1** a condition of (a part of) a living animal or plant body that impairs the performance of a vital function; (a) sickness, malady **2** a harmful or corrupt development, situation, condition, etc ⟨*the* ~ *of prejudice*⟩ [ME *disese* uneasiness, sickness, fr MF *desaise*, fr *des-* dis- + *aise* ease] – **diseased** *adj*

diseconomy /,disi'konəmi/ *n* **1** a lack of economy **2** (a factor responsible for) an increase in costs

disembark /,disim'bahk/ *vb* to (cause to) alight from a ship, plane, etc [MF *desembarquer*, fr *des-* + *embarquer* to embark] – **disembarkation** /,disimbah'kaysh(ə)n, -em-/ *n*

disembody /,disim'bodi/ *vt* to divest of a body or material existence

disembogue /,disim'bohg/ *vb, of a stream, river, etc* to pour (itself) forth (as if) from a channel – fml [modif of Sp *desembocar*, fr *des-* dis- (fr L *dis-*) + *embocar* to put into the mouth, fr *en* in (fr L *in*) + *boca* mouth, fr L *bucca* – more at POCK]

disembowel /,disim'bowəl/ *vt* to remove the bowels or entrails of; eviscerate – **disembowelment** *n*

disembroil /,disim'broyl/ *vt* to free from a confused or entangled state or situation

disenchant /,disin'chahnt/ *vt* to rid of an illusion [MF *desenchanter*, fr *des-* + *enchanter* to enchant] – **disenchanter** *n*, **disenchanting** *adj*, **disenchantingly** *adv*, **disenchantment** *n*

disencumber /,disin'kumbə/ *vt* to free from an encumbrance [MF *desencombrer*, fr *des-* + *encombrer* to encumber]

disendow /,disin'dow/ *vt* to strip of an endowment – **disendowment** *n*

disenfranchise /,disin'frahnchiez, -'fran-/ *vt* to deprive of a franchise or right; *esp* to deprive (sby) of the right to vote or (a place) of the right to send representatives to an elected body – **disenfranchisement** /-'frahnchizmənt, -'fran-, -,chiezmənt/ *n*

disengage /,dising'gayj/ *vt* **1** to release or detach from sthg that engages or entangles **2** to remove (e g troops) from combat areas ~ *vi* **1** to detach or release oneself; *specif, esp of troops* to withdraw **2** to move one's fencing sword to the other side of an opponent's sword in order to attack [F *désengager*, fr MF, fr *des-* + *engager* to engage] – **disengagement** *n*

disentail /,disin'tayl/ *vt* to free (an estate) from entail

disentangle /,disin'tang·gl/ *vb* to (cause to) become free from entanglements: unravel – **disentanglement** *n*

disequilibrium /,diseekwi'libri·əm, -ekwi-/ *n* loss or lack of equilibrium

disestablish /,disi'stablish/ *vt* to deprive (esp a national church) of established status – **disestablishment** *n*

[1]**disfavour** /dis'fayvə/ *n* **1** disapproval, dislike **2** the state of being disapproved of ⟨*fell into* ~⟩ [prob fr MF *desfaveur*, fr *des-* dis- + *faveur* favour, fr OF *favor*]

[2]**disfavour** *vt* to regard or treat with disfavour

disfigure /dis'figə/ *vt* to spoil the appearance or quality of; mar [ME *disfiguren*, fr MF *desfigurer*, fr *des-* + *figure*] – **disfigurement** *n*

disfranchise /dis'frahnchiez, -'fran-/ *vt* to disenfranchise – **disfranchisement** /dis'frahnchizmənt, -'fran-, -,chiezmənt/

disfrock /dis'frok/ *vt* to unfrock

dis'function /dis'fungksh(ə)n/ *n* dysfunction

disgorge /dis'gawj/ *vt* **1a** to discharge with force; *specif* to vomit **b** to give up on request or under pressure **2** to discharge the contents of (e g one's stomach) ~ *vi* to discharge contents ⟨*where the river* ~s *into the sea*⟩ [MF *desgorger*, fr *des-* + *gorge* throat]

[1]**disgrace** /dis'grays/ *vt* **1** to bring reproach or shame to **2** to cause to lose favour or standing

[2]**disgrace** *n* **1a** loss of favour, honour, or respect; shame **b** the state of being out of favour ⟨*she's in* ~⟩ **2** sby or sthg shameful ⟨*his manners are a* ~⟩ [MF, fr OIt *disgrazia*, fr *dis-* (fr L) + *grazia* grace, fr L *gratia* – more at GRACE]

dis'graceful /-f(ə)l/ *adj* shameful, shocking – **disgracefully** *adv*, **disgracefulness** *n*

disgruntled /dis'gruntld/ *adj* aggrieved and dissatisfied [fr pp of *disgruntle* (to aggrieve), fr *dis-* + *gruntle* (to grumble), fr ME *gruntlen*, freq of *grunt*]

[1]**disguise** /dis'giez/ *vt* **1** to change the appearance or nature of in order to conceal identity ⟨~d *himself as a tramp*⟩ **2** to hide the true state or character of [ME *disgisen*, fr MF *desguiser*, fr OF, fr *des-* + *guise*] – **disguisedly** /-zidli/ *adv*, **disguisement** *n*

[2]**disguise** *n* **1** (the use of) sthg (e g clothing) to conceal one's identity **2** an outward appearance that misrepresents the true nature of sthg ⟨*a blessing in* ~⟩

[1]**disgust** /dis'gust/ *n* strong aversion aroused by sby or sthg physically or morally distasteful

[2]**disgust** *vt* to arouse repugnance or aversion in [MF *desgouster*, fr *des-* dis- + *goust* taste, fr L *gustus*; akin to L *gustare* to taste – more at CHOOSE] – **disgusted** *adj*, **disgustedly** *adv*

[1]**dish** /dish/ *n* **1a** a shallow open often circular or oval vessel used esp for holding or serving food; *broadly* any vessel from which food is eaten or served **b** a dishful **c** *pl the* utensils and tableware used in preparing, serving, and eating a meal ⟨*wash the* ~es⟩ **2** a type of food prepared in a particular way ⟨*a delicious meat* ~⟩ **3** sthg resembling a dish in shape: e g **a** a directional aerial, esp for receiving radio or television transmissions or microwaves, having a concave usu parabolic reflector ☞ TELEVISION **b** a hollow or depression **4** an attractive person – infml [ME, fr OE *disc* plate; akin to OHG *tisc* plate, table; both fr a prehistoric WGmc word

borrowed fr L *discus* quoit, disc, dish, fr Gk *diskos*, fr *dikein* to throw]

[2]**dish** *vt* **1** to make concave like a dish **2** *chiefly Br* to ruin or spoil (e g a person or his/her hopes) – infml

dishabille /ˌdisəˈbeel/ *n* deshabille

disharmony /disˈhahməni/ *n* lack of harmony; discord – **disharmonious** /ˌdishahˈmohnyəs, -ni·əs/ *adj*

dishcloth /-ˌkloth/ *n* a cloth for washing or drying dishes

dishearten /disˈhaht(ə)n/ *vt* to cause to lose enthusiasm or morale; discourage – **disheartening** *adj*, **dishearteningly** *adv*, **disheartenment** *n*

dished /disht/ *adj* **1** concave **2** *of a pair of vehicle wheels* fixed so as to be nearer together at the bottom than the top

dishevel /diˈshevl/ *vt* **-ll-** (*NAm* **-l-**, **-ll-**), /diˈshevl·ing/ to make untidy or disordered [back-formation fr *dishevelled*]

diˈshevelled, *NAm chiefly* **disheveled** *adj*, *esp of a person's hair or appearance* unkempt, untidy [ME *discheveled*, part trans of MF *deschevelé*, fr pp of *descheveler* to disarrange the hair, fr *des-* + *chevel* hair, fr L *capillus*]

ˈ**dishful** /-f(ə)l/ *n* the amount a dish contains or will hold

dishonest /disˈonist/ *adj* not honest, truthful, or sincere [ME, fr MF *deshoneste*, fr *des-* + *honeste* honest] – **dishonestly** *adv*

dishonesty /disˈonisti/ *n* (an instance of) lack of honesty or integrity

[1]**dishonour** /disˈonə/ *n* **1** (sby or sthg causing) loss of honour or reputation **2** a state of shame or disgrace [ME, fr OF *deshonor*, fr *des-* + *honor* honour]

[2]**dishonour** *vt* **1** to treat in a degrading or disrespectful manner **2** to bring shame on **3** to refuse to accept or pay (e g a cheque)

dishonourable /disˈon(ə)rəbl/ *adj* base, shameful – **dishonourably** *adv*

dish out *vt* to give or distribute freely ⟨*always* dishing out *advice*⟩ – infml

dish up *vt* **1** to put (a meal, food, etc) onto dishes; serve **2** to produce or present (e g facts) ⟨*has been* dishing up *the same lessons for years*⟩ – infml ~ *vi* to put food onto dishes ready to be eaten ⟨*I'm* dishing up *now*⟩

ˈ**dishˌwasher** /-ˌwoshə/ *n* a person or electrical machine that washes dishes

ˈ**dishˌwater** /-ˌwawtə/ *n* water in which dishes have been washed

dishy /ˈdishi/ *adj*, *chiefly Br*, *of a person* attractive – infml [[1]*dish* 4 + *-y*]

[1]**disillusion** /ˌdisiˈloohzh(ə)n, -ˈlyooh-/ *n* the state of being disillusioned

[2]**disillusion** *vt* to reveal the usu unpleasant truth (e g about sby or sthg admired) to; disenchant – **disillusionment** *n*

ˌ**disilˈlusioned** *adj* bitter or depressed as a result of having been disillusioned ⟨*feeling very* ~ *with government policies*⟩

disincentive /ˌdisinˈsentiv/ *n* sthg that discourages action or effort; a deterrent

disinclination /ˌdisingkliˈnaysh(ə)n/ *n* (an) unwillingness to do sthg; mild dislike

disinclined /ˌdisinˈkliend/ *adj* unwilling

disinfect /ˌdisinˈfekt/ *vt* to cleanse of infection, esp by destroying harmful microorganisms [MF *desinfecter*, fr *des-* + *infecter* to infect] – **disinfection** /-ˈfeksh(ə)n/ *n*

disinfectant /ˌdisinˈfekt(ə)nt/ *n* a chemical that destroys harmful microorganisms

disinfest /ˌdisinˈfest/ *vt* to rid of insects, rodents, or other pests – **disinfestation** /ˌdisinfeˈstaysh(ə)n/ *n*

disinflation /ˌdisinˈflaysh(ə)n/ *n* a reduction of inflation without the general reduction in economic activity associated with deflation – **disinflationary** *adj*

disingenuous /ˌdisinˈjenyoo·əs/ *adj* insincere; *also* falsely frank or naive in manner – **disingenuously** *adv*, **disingenuousness** *n*

disinherit /ˌdisinˈherit/ *vt* to deprive (an heir) of the right to inherit; *broadly* to deprive of a special right or privilege – **disinheritance** *n*

disintegrate /disˈintigrayt/ *vt* **1** to break up into fragments or constituent elements **2** to destroy the unity or cohesion of ~ *vi* **1** to break into fragments or constituent elements **2** to lose unity or cohesion **3** *esp of a nucleus* to undergo a change in composition (e g by emitting radioactive particles or dividing into smaller units) – **disintegrator** *n*, **disintegrative** /-ˌgraytiv/ *adj*, **disintegration** /-ˈgraysh(ə)n/ *n*

disinter /ˌdisinˈtuh/ *vt* **1** to remove from a grave or tomb **2** to bring to light; unearth – **disinterment** *n*

disinterest /disˈintrest, -trəst/ *n* **1** lack of interest; apathy – disapproved of by some speakers **2** lack of self-interest; disinterestedness

disˈinterested *adj* **1** uninterested – disapproved of by some speakers **2** free from selfish motive or interest; impartial – **disinterestedly** *adv*, **disinterestedness** *n*

disinvestment /ˌdisinˈvestmənt/ *n* reduction or termination of investment, esp by realizing assets or not replacing capital equipment

disjoin /disˈjoyn/ *vb* to (cause to) become detached [MF *desjoindre*, fr L *disjungere*, fr *dis-* + *jungere* to join – more at YOKE]

disjoint /disˈjoynt/ *vt* **1** to disturb the orderly arrangement of **2** to take apart at the joints

disˈjointed *adj* lacking orderly sequence; incoherent – **disjointedly** *adv*, **disjointedness** *n*

disjunct /ˈdisjungkt/ *n* an adverbial linguistic form (e g *frankly* in 'frankly, I'm annoyed") that expresses an evaluation of what is said [*disjunct*, adj (separate, discontinuous), fr L *disjunctus*, pp of *disjungere*]

disjunction /disˈjungksh(ə)n/ *n* **1** (a) cleavage, separation **2a** INCLUSIVE DISJUNCTION **b** EXCLUSIVE DISJUNCTION

[1]**disjunctive** /disˈjungktiv/ *n* a disjunctive conjunction – see [2]DISJUNCTIVE 1b

[2]**disjunctive** *adj* **1a** being, belonging to, or characterizing a logical disjunction **b** expressing an alternative or opposition between the meanings of the words connected (e g in the question 'Is he old or young? ', *or* is a disjunctive conjunction) **2** marked by breaks or separation – fml – **disjunctively** *adv*

disk /disk/ *n* **1a** *Br also* **disc** a round flat plate coated with a magnetic substance on which data for a computer is stored ☞ COMPUTER **b disk, disk pack** a computer storage device consisting of a stack of disks rotating at high speed, each disk having its own head to read and write data ☞ COMPUTER **2** *chiefly NAm* a disc

[1]**dislike** /disˈliek/ *vt* to regard with dislike

[2]**dislike** *n* (an object of) a feeling of aversion or disapproval

dislocate /ˈdislə,kayt/ *vt* **1** to put out of place; *esp* to displace (e g a bone or joint) from normal connection **2** to put (plans, machinery, etc) out of order; disrupt [ML *dislocatus*, pp of *dislocare*, fr L *dis-* + *locare* to locate]

dislocation /,disləˈkaysh(ə)n/ *n* **1** displacement of 1 or more bones at a joint **2** a discontinuity in the lattice structure of a crystal **3** disruption of an established order or course [DISLOCATE + -ION]

dislodge /disˈloj/ *vt* to force out of or remove from a fixed or entrenched position [ME *disloggen*, fr MF *desloger*, fr *des-* + *loger* to lodge, fr *loge* lodge]

disloyal /disˈloyəl/ *adj* untrue to obligations or ties; unfaithful [MF *desloial*, fr OF, fr *des-* + *loial* loyal] – **disloyally** *adv*, **disloyalty** *n*

dismal /ˈdizm(ə)l/ *adj* causing or expressing gloom or sadness [ME, fr *dismal*, n, days marked as unlucky in medieval calendars, fr AF, fr ML *dies mali*, lit., evil days] – **dismally** *adv*, **dismalness** *n*

dismantle /disˈmantl/ *vt* **1** to strip of furniture, equipment, etc **2** to take to pieces [MF *desmanteler*, fr *des-* + *mantel* mantle] – **dismantlement** *n*

dismast /disˈmahst/ *vt* to remove or break off the mast of (a ship)

[1]**dismay** /diˈsmay, diz-/ *vt* to fill with dismay [ME *dismayen*, fr (assumed) OF *desmaiier*, fr OF *des-* + *-maiier* (as in *esmaiier* to dismay), fr (assumed) VL *-magare*, of Gmc origin] – **dismayingly** *adv*

[2]**dismay** *n* sudden consternation or apprehension

disˈmember *vt* **1** to cut or tear off the limbs or members of **2** to divide up (e g a territory) into parts [ME *dismembren*, fr OF *desmembrer*, fr *des-* + *membre* member] – **dismemberment** *n*

dismiss /disˈmis/ *vt* **1** to allow to leave; send away **2** to remove or send away from employment or service **3a** to put out of one's mind; reject as unworthy of serious consideration **b** to put out of judicial consideration; refuse a further hearing to (e g a court case) **4** to bowl out (a batsman or side) in cricket [modif of L *dimissus*, pp of *dimittere*, fr *dis-* apart + *mittere* to send – more at DIS-, SMITE] – **dismissal** *n*, **dismissible** *adj*

dismissive /disˈmisiv/ *adj* disdainful

dismount /disˈmownt/ *vi* to alight from a horse, bicycle, etc ~ *vt* **1** to throw down or remove from horseback **2** to remove from a mounting [prob modif of MF *desmonter*, fr *des-* + *monter* to mount]

disobedient /,disəˈbeedi·ənt/ *adj* refusing or failing to obey [ME, fr MF *desobedient*, fr *des-* + *obedient*] – **disobedience** *n*, **disobediently** *adv*

disobey /,disəˈbay/ *vb* to fail to obey [ME *disobeyen*, fr MF *desobeir*, fr *des-* + *obeir* to obey]

disoblige /,disəˈbliej/ *vt* **1** to go counter to the wishes of **2** to inconvenience [F *désobliger*, fr MF, fr *des-* + *obliger* to oblige]

[1]**disorder** /disˈawdə/ *vt* **1** to throw into confusion or disorder **2** to disturb the good health of; upset

[2]**disorder** *n* **1** lack of order; confusion **2** breach of the peace or public order ⟨*troubled times marked by social* ~s⟩ **3** an abnormal physical or mental condition; an ailment

disˈorderly /-li/ *adj* **1a** untidy, disarranged **b** unruly, violent **2** offensive to public order ⟨*charged with being drunk and* ~⟩ – **disorderliness** *n*

disorderly house *n* a brothel

disorgan·ize, -ise /disˈawgəniez/ *vt* to throw into disorder or confusion [F *désorganiser*, fr *dés-* dis- + *organiser* to organize] – **disorganization** /-ˈzaysh(ə)n/ *n*

disˈorgan·ized, -ised *adj* lacking coherence or system

disorient /disˈawrient, -ənt/ *vt, chiefly NAm* to disorientate [F *désorienter*, fr *dés-* dis- + *orienter* to orient, fr MF, fr *orient*, n]

disorientate /disˈawri·ən,tayt/ *vt* **1** to deprive of the normal sense of position, relationship, or identity **2** to confuse – **disorientation** /-ˈtaysh(ə)n/ *n*

disown /disˈohn/ *vt* **1** to refuse to acknowledge as one's own **2** to repudiate any connection with

disparage /diˈsparij/ *vt* to speak slightingly of; belittle [ME *disparagen* to degrade by marriage below one's class, discredit, fr MF *desparagier* to marry below one's class, fr OF, fr *des-* dis- + *parage* extraction, lineage, fr *per* peer] – **disparagement** *n*, **disparaging** *adj*, **disparagingly** *adv*

disparate /ˈdispərət/ *adj* markedly distinct in quality or character [L *disparatus*, pp of *disparare* to separate, fr *dis-* + *parare* to prepare – more at PARE] – **disparately** *adv*, **disparateness** *n*

disparity /diˈsparəti/ *n* (a) difference or inequality [MF *desparité*, fr LL *disparitat-*, *disparitas*, fr L *dis-* + LL *paritat-*, *paritas* parity]

dispassionate /disˈpash(ə)nət/ *adj* not influenced by strong feeling; *esp* calm, impartial – **dispassionately** *adv*, **dispassionateness** *n*

[1]**dispatch** /diˈspach/ *vt* **1** to send off or away promptly, esp to a particular place or to carry out a particular, usu official, task **2a** to carry out or complete (e g a task) rapidly or efficiently **b** to get through; consume quickly – infml ⟨*soon* ~ed *that chocolate cake*⟩ **3** to kill, esp with quick efficiency – euph [Sp *despachar* or It *dispacciare*, fr Prov *despachar* to get rid of, fr MF *despeechier* to set free, fr OF, fr *des-* + *-peechier* (as in *empeechier* to hinder) – more at IMPEACH] – **dispatcher** *n*

[2]**dispatch** *n* **1** a sending off (e g of a communication or messenger) **2a** a message; *esp* an important official diplomatic or military message **b** a news item sent in by a correspondent to a newspaper **3** promptness and efficiency **4** an act of killing; *specif* a murder – euph

dispel /diˈspel/ *vt* **-ll-** to drive away; disperse [L *dispellere*, fr *dis-* + *pellere* to drive, beat – more at FELT]

dispensable /diˈspensəbl/ *adj* that can be dispensed with; inessential – **dispensability** /-ˈbiləti/ *n*

dispensary /diˈspens(ə)ri/ *n* a part of a hospital or chemist's shop where drugs, medical supplies, etc are dispensed

dispensation /,dispenˈsaysh(ə)n/ *n* **1a** an esp divine ordering of human affairs **b** a particular arrangement or provision made by God, providence, or nature **c** a usu specified religious system, esp considered as controlling human affairs during a particular period **2a** an exemption from a law, vow, etc; *specif* permission to disregard or break a rule of Roman Catholic church law **b** a formal authorization [DISPENSE + -ATION] – **dispensational** *adj*

dispense /diˈspens/ *vt* **1a** to deal out, distribute **b** to administer (e g law or justice) **2** to give a dispensation to; exempt *from* **3** to prepare and give out (drugs, medicine, etc on prescription) [ME *dispensen*, fr ML & L; ML *dispensare* to grant dispensation, fr L, to distribute, fr *dispensus*, pp of *dispendere* to weigh out, fr *dis-* + *pendere* to weigh – more at SPAN] – **dispense with 1** DISCARD 2 **2** to do without

dispenser /di'spensə/ *n* **1** a container or machine that dispenses items (e g of food) or usu fixed quantities (e g of drink) **2** a person who dispenses medicines [DISPENSE + 2-ER]

dispersant /di'spuhs(ə)nt/ *n* a dispersing agent; *esp* a substance used to disperse and stabilize fine particles of one substance in another – **dispersant** *adj*

disperse /di'spuhs/ *vt* **1a** to cause to break up or scatter ⟨*they* ~d *the meeting*⟩ **b** to spread over a wide area **c** to cause to evaporate or vanish **2a** to subject (e g light) to dispersion **b** to distribute (e g fine particles) more or less evenly throughout a liquid ~ *vi* **1** to break up in random fashion; scatter **2** to become dispersed; dissipate [ME *dysparsen*, fr MF *disperser*, fr L *dispersus*, pp of *dispergere* to scatter, fr *dis-* + *spargere* to scatter – more at 1SPARK] – **dispersal** *n*, **dispersedly** /-sidli/ *adv*, **disperser** *n*, **dispersible** *adj*, **dispersive** *adj*, **dispersively** *adv*, **dispersiveness** *n*

dispersion /di'spuhsh(ə)n/ *n* **1** *cap the* Diaspora **2** the extent to which the values of a frequency distribution are scattered around an average **3** the separation of light into colours by refraction or diffraction with formation of a spectrum; *also* the separation of nonhomogeneous radiation into components in accordance with some characteristic (e g energy, wavelength, or mass) **4a** a dispersed substance **b** a system consisting of a dispersed substance and the medium in which it is dispersed; COLLOID 1b [DISPERSE + -ION]

dispirit /di'spirit/ *vt* to dishearten, discourage [*dis-* + *spirit*] – **dispirited** *adj*, **dispiritedly** *adv*, **dispiritedness** *n*

displace /dis'plays/ *vt* **1a** to remove from or force out of the usual or proper place **b** to remove from office **2** to take the place of; replace; *specif* to take the place of (e g an atom) in a chemical reaction [prob fr MF *desplacer*, fr *des-* dis- + *place*] – **displaceable** *adj*

dis,placed 'person *n* sby who has been forced to leave his/her country because of war, revolution, etc; a refugee

dis'placement /-mənt/ *n* **1a** the volume or weight of a fluid (e g water) displaced by a body (e g a ship) of equal weight floating in it **b** the difference between the initial position of a body and any later position **2** the transfer of emotions from the object that orig evoked them to a substitute (e g in dreams) [DISPLACE + -MENT]

1display /di'splay/ *vt* **1** to expose to view; show **2** to exhibit, esp ostentatiously ~ *vi* to make a breeding display [ME *displayen*, fr AF *despleier*, fr L *displicare* to scatter, fr *dis-* + *plicare* to fold – more at 1PLY]

2display *n* **1a(1)** a presentation or exhibition of sthg in open view ⟨*a fireworks* ~⟩ **(2)** an esp ostentatious show or demonstration **b** an arrangement of type or printing designed to catch the eye (e g in headlines and title pages) **c** an eye-catching arrangement exhibiting sthg (e g goods for sale) **d** a device (e g a cathode-ray tube screen) that presents information in visual form ⟨*a visual* ~ *unit*⟩ **2** a pattern of behaviour exhibited esp by male birds in the breeding season

displease /dis'pleez/ *vb* to cause annoyance or displeasure (to) [ME *displesen*, fr MF *desplaisir*, fr (assumed) VL *displacēre*, fr L *dis-* + *placēre* to please]

displeasure /dis'plezhə/ *n* disapproval, annoyance

disport /di'spawt/ *vt* to divert or amuse (oneself) actively ~ *vi* to frolic, gambol [ME *disporten*, fr MF *desporter*, fr *des-* + *porter* to carry]

1disposable /di'spohzəbl/ *adj* **1** available for use; *specif* remaining after deduction of taxes ⟨~ *income*⟩ **2** designed to be used once and then thrown away [DISPOSE + -ABLE] – **disposability** /-'biləti/ *n*

2disposable *n* a disposable article

disposal /di'spohzl/ *n* **1a** orderly arrangement or distribution **b** management, administration **c** bestowal **d** the act or action of getting rid of sthg; *specif* the destruction or conversion of waste matter **2** the power or right to use freely ⟨*the car was at my* ~⟩ [DISPOSE + 2-AL]

dispose /di'spohz/ *vt* **1** to incline *to* – ⟨~d *to ill-health*⟩ **2** to put in place; arrange **3** to cause to have a specified attitude *towards* ⟨*unfavourably* ~d *towards her in-laws*⟩ ~ *vi* to settle a matter finally [ME *disposen*, fr MF *disposer*, fr L *disponere* to arrange (perf indic *disposui*), fr *dis-* + *ponere* to put – more at POSITION] – **dispose of 1** to get rid of (e g by finishing, selling, eating, or killing) **2** to deal with conclusively ⟨disposed of *the matter efficiently*⟩

disposition /,dispə'zish(ə)n/ *n* **1a** final arrangement; settlement **b** transfer of property, esp by will or deed **c** orderly arrangement **2a** natural temperament **b** a tendency, inclination [ME, fr MF, fr L *disposition-*, *dispositio*, fr *dispositus*, pp of *disponere*]

dispossess /,dispə'zes/ *vt* to deprive of possession or occupancy [MF *despossesser*, fr *des-* dis- + *possesser* to possess] – **dispossessor** *n*, **dispossession** /-'zesh(ə)n/ *n*

dispraise /dis'prayz/ *vt or n* (to comment on with) disapproval or censure [vb ME *dispraisen*, fr OF *despreisier*, fr *des-* dis- + *preisier* to praise; n fr vb] – **dispraisingly** *adv*

disproof /dis'proohf/ *n* **1** the act or action of disproving **2** evidence that disproves

disproportion /,disprə'pawsh(ə)n/ *n* (a) lack of proportion, symmetry, or proper relation – **disproportional** *adj*

disproportionate /,disprə'pawsh(ə)nət/ *adj* out of proportion – **disproportionately** *adv*

disprove /dis'proohv/ *vt* to prove to be false; refute [ME *disproven*, fr MF *desprover*, fr *des-* + *prover* to prove] – **disprovable** *adj*

disputant /di'spyooht(ə)nt, 'dispyoot(ə)nt/ *n* one engaged in a dispute

disputation /,dispyooh'taysh(ə)n/ *n* **1** a debate, argument **2** the oral defence of a thesis by formal logic [1DISPUTE + -ATION]

disputatious /,dispyoo'tayshəs/ *adj* inclined to dispute; argumentative – **disputatiously** *adv*, **disputatiousness** *n*

1dispute /di'spyooht/ *vi* to argue, esp angrily and persistently – often + *about* ~ *vt* **1a** to make the subject of disputation; discuss angrily **b** to call into question **2a** to struggle against; resist **b** to struggle over; contest [ME *disputen*, fr OF *desputer*, fr L *disputare* to discuss, fr *dis-* + *putare* to think] –

disputable /di'spyoohtəbl, 'dispyoo-/ *adj*, **disputably** *adv*, **disputer** *n*

[2]**dispute** *n* **1** controversy, debate ⟨*his honesty is beyond* ~⟩ **2** a quarrel, disagreement

disqualification /dis,kwolifi'kaysh(ə)n, ,---'--/ *n* **1** disqualifying or being disqualified **2** sthg that disqualifies

disqualify /dis'kwolifie/ *vt* **1** to make or declare unfit or unsuitable to do sthg **2** to declare ineligible (e g for a prize) because of violation of the rules

disquiet /dis'kwie·ət/ *vt or n* (to cause) anxiety or worry – **disquieting** *adj*, **disquietingly** *adv*

disquietude /dis'kwie·ətyoohd, -choohd/ *n* disquiet – fml

disquisition /,diskwi'zish(ə)n/ *n* a long or elaborate discussion or essay on a subject [L *disquisition-, disquisitio*, fr *disquisitus*, pp of *disquirere* to inquire diligently, fr *dis-* + *quaerere* to seek]

disrate /dis'rayt/ *vt* to reduce (e g a sailor) in rank

[1]**disregard** /,disri'gahd/ *vt* **1** to pay no attention to **2** to treat as not worthy of regard or notice

[2]**disregard** *n* lack of attention or regard; neglect – **disregardful** *adj*

disremember /,disri'membə/ *vt, chiefly NAm* to forget

disrepair /,disri'peə/ *n* the state of being in need of repair

disreputable /dis'repyootəbl/ *adj* **1** having a bad reputation; not respectable **2** dirty or untidy in appearance – **disreputableness** *n*, **disreputably** *adv*, **disreputability** /-'biləti/ *n*

disrepute /,disri'pyooht/ *n* lack of good reputation or respectability

disrespect /,disri'spekt/ *n* lack of respect or politeness – **disrespectful** *adj*, **disrespectfully** *adv*, **disrespectfulness** *n*

disrobe /dis'rohb/ *vi* to take off (esp ceremonial outer) clothing – fml or humor [MF *desrober*, fr *des-* dis- + *robe* garment – more at ROBE]

disrupt /dis'rupt/ *vt* **1** to break apart forcibly; rupture **2a** to throw into disorder **b** to interrupt the continuity of [L *disruptus*, pp of *disrumpere*, fr *dis-* + *rumpere* to break – more at BEREAVE] – **disruption** /-sh(ə)n/ *n*, **disruptive** /-tiv/ *adj*, **disruptively** *adv*, **disruptiveness** *n*

dissatisfaction /di,satis'faksh(ə)n, ,---'--/ *n* lack of satisfaction; discontent – **dissatisfactory** /-'fakt(ə)ri/ *adj*

dissatisfy /di'satisfie, dis'sa-/ *vt* to make displeased, discontented, or disappointed

dissect /di'sekt, die-/ *vt* **1** to cut (e g an animal or plant) into pieces, esp for scientific examination **2** to analyse and interpret in detail [L *dissectus*, pp of *dissecare* to cut apart, fr *dis-* + *secare* to cut – more at [2]SAW] – **dissection** /-sh(ə)n/ *n*, **dissector** *n*

disseise, disseize /dis'seez/ *vt* to deprive, esp wrongfully, of (a freehold estate in) land [ME *disseisen*, fr ML *disseisiare* & AF *disseisir*, fr OF *dessaisir*, fr *des-* + *saisir* to put in possession of – more at SEIZE]

disseisin, disseizin /dis'seezin/ *n* disseising or being disseised [ME *dysseysyne*, fr AF *disseisine*, fr OF *dessaisine*, fr *des-* dis- + *saisine* seisin]

dissemble /di'sembl/ *vt* to disguise, conceal ~ *vi* to conceal facts, intentions, or feelings under some pretence [alter. of obs *dissimule*, fr ME *dissimulen*, fr MF *dissimuler*, fr L *dissimulare* – more at DISSIMULATE] – **dissembler** *n*

disseminate /di'seminayt/ *vt* to spread about freely or widely ⟨~ *ideas*⟩ [L *disseminatus*, pp of *disseminare*, fr *dis-* + *seminare* to sow, fr *semin-, semen* seed – more at SEMEN] – **disseminator, dissemination** /-'naysh(ə)n/ n

dissension /di'sensh(ə)n/ *n* disagreement in opinion; discord [ME, fr MF, fr L *dissension-, dissensio*, fr *dissensus*, pp of *dissentire*]

[1]**dissent** /di'sent/ *vi* **1** to withhold assent **2** to differ in opinion; *specif* to reject the doctrines of an established church [ME *dissenten*, fr L *dissentire*, fr *dis-* + *sentire* to feel – more at SENSE] – **dissenter** *n*

[2]**dissent** *n* difference of opinion; *esp* religious or political nonconformity

Dissenter /di'sentə/ *n* an English Nonconformist [[1]DISSENT + [2]-ER]

dissentient /di'sensh(y)ənt/ *n or adj* (sby) disagreeing or dissenting, esp from a majority view [L *dissentient-, dissentiens*, prp of *dissentire*]

dissenting /di'senting/ *adj, often cap* Nonconformist

dissertation /,disə'taysh(ə)n/ *n* a long, detailed, usu written treatment of a subject; *specif* one submitted for a (higher) degree [L *dissertation-, dissertatio*, fr *dissertatus*, pp of *dissertare* to discourse, freq of *disserere*, fr *dis-* + *serere* to join, arrange – more at SERIES]

disservice /di'suhvis, dis'suh-/ *n* an action or deed which works to sby's disadvantage

dissever /di'sevə, dis'sevə/ *vb* to (cause to) separate or come apart – fml [ME *disseveren*, fr OF *dessevrer*, fr LL *disseparare*, fr L *dis-* + *separare* to separate] – **disseverance** *n*, **disseverment** *n*

dissident /'disid(ə)nt/ *n or adj* (sby) disagreeing strongly or rebelliously with an established opinion, group, government, etc ⟨*political* ~s⟩ [adj L *dissident-, dissidens*, prp of *dissidēre* to sit apart, disagree, fr *dis-* + *sedēre* to sit; n fr adj] – **dissidence** *n*

dissimilar /di'similə, dis'si-/ *adj* not similar; unlike – **dissimilarly** *adv*, **dissimilarity** /-'larəti/ *n*

dissimilitude /,disi'milityoohd, ,dis·si-, -choohd/ *n* lack of resemblance; dissimilarity – fml [L *dissimilitudo*, fr *dissimilis* unlike, fr *dis-* + *similis* like]

dissimulate /di'simyoolayt, dis'si-/ *vb* to dissemble [L *dissimulatus*, pp of *dissimulare*, fr *dis-* + *simulare* to simulate] – **dissimulator** *n*, **dissimulation** /-'laysh(ə)n/ *n*

dissipate /'disipayt/ *vt* **1a** to cause to disappear or scatter; dispel **b** to lose (e g heat or electricity) irrecoverably **2** to spend or use up (money, energy, etc) aimlessly or foolishly ~ *vi* to separate and scatter or vanish [L *dissipatus*, pp of *dissipare*, fr *dis-* + *supare* to throw; akin to ON *svāf* spear, Skt *svapu* broom] – **dissipater** *n*, **dissipative** /-pətiv/ *adj*

'**dissipated** *adj* given to dissipation; dissolute – **dissipatedly** *adv*, **dissipatedness** *n*

dissipation /,disi'paysh(ə)n/ *n* **1** dispersion, diffusion **2** wasteful expenditure **3** dissolute living; debauchery; *specif* excessive indulgence in alcohol [DISSIPATE + -ION]

dissociate /di'sohs(h)i,ayt/ *vt* **1** to separate from association or union with sby or sthg else; disconnect **2** to subject to chemical dissociation ~ *vi* to undergo dissociation [L *dissociatus*, pp of *dissociare*, fr *dis-*

+ *sociare* to join, fr *socius* companion – more at SOCIAL]

dissociation /di,sohsi'aysh(ə)n, -shi-/ *n* **1** the process by which a chemical combination breaks up into simpler constituents, esp as a result of the action of heat or a solvent **2** the separation of a more or less autonomous group of ideas or activities from the mainstream of consciousness, esp in cases of mental disorder [DISSOCIATE + -ION] – **dissociative** /-'sohs(h)i·ətiv/ *adj*

dissoluble /di'solyoobl, dis'so-/ *adj* capable of being dissolved or disintegrated [L *dissolubilis*, fr *dissolvere* to dissolve] – **dissolubility** /-'biləti/ *n*

dissolute /'disəlooht, -lyooht/ *adj* loose in morals; debauched [L *dissolutus*, fr pp of *dissolvere* to loosen, dissolve] – **dissolutely** *adv*, **dissoluteness** *n*

dissolution /,disə'loohsh(ə)n, -'lyooh, ,dis·sə-/ *n* **1** separation into component parts **2** disintegration, decay **3** the termination of an association, union, etc **4** the breaking up or dispersal of a group, assembly, etc [DISSOLVE + -ION]

¹dissolve /di'zolv/ *vt* **1a** to terminate officially ⟨*the marriage was* ~d⟩ **b** to cause to break up; dismiss ⟨*Parliament was* ~d *before the election*⟩ **2a** to cause to pass into solution ⟨~ *sugar in water*⟩ **b** to melt, liquefy **3** to fade out (one film or television scene) whilst fading in another ~ *vi* **1a** to pass into solution **b** to become fluid; melt **2** to fade away; disperse ⟨*the vision* ~d *before his eyes*⟩ **3** to be emotionally overcome [ME *dissolven*, fr L *dissolvere*, fr *dis-* + *solvere* to loosen – more at SOLVE] – **dissolvable** *adj*, **dissolver** *n*

²dissolve *n* an effect used in films and television in which one scene is dissolved into the next

dissonance /'disənəns/ *n* **1** a combination of discordant sounds **2** lack of agreement **3** (the sound produced by playing) an unresolved musical note or chord; *specif* an interval not included in a major or minor triad or its inversions

dissonant /'disənənt/ *adj* **1** marked by dissonance **2** incongruous [MF or L; MF, fr L *dissonant-*, *dissonans*, prp of *dissonare* to be discordant, fr *dis-* + *sonare* to sound – more at ³SOUND] – **dissonantly** *adv*

dissuade /di'swayd/ *vt* to deter or discourage *from* a course of action by persuasion [MF or L; MF *dissuader*, fr L *dissuadēre*, fr *dis-* + *suadēre* to urge]

dissuasion /di'swayzh(ə)n/ *n* the act of dissuading [MF or L; MF, fr L *dissuasion-*, *dissuasio*, fr *dissuasus*, pp of *dissuadēre*] – **dissuasive** /-siv, -ziv/ *adj*, **dissuasively** *adv*, **dissuasiveness** *n*

dissymmetry /dis'simətri/ *n* lack of symmetry – **dissymmetric** /,dis·si'metrik/ *adj*

distaff /'distahf/ *n* **1** a staff for holding the flax, tow, wool, etc in spinning **2** woman's work or domain [ME *distaf*, fr OE *distæf*, fr *dis-* (akin to MLG *dise* bunch of flax) + *stæf* staff]

'distaff ,side *n* *the* female side of a family

distal /'distl/ *adj*, *esp of an anatomical part* far from the centre or point of attachment or origin; terminal – compare PROXIMAL [*dist*ant + *-al*] – **distally** *adv*

¹distance /'dist(ə)ns/ *n* **1a** (the amount of) separation in space or time between 2 points or things **b** an extent of space or an advance along a route measured linearly; *specif* a usu particular length covered in a race ⟨*a world class runner over all* ~s⟩ **c** a distant point or place **2a** remoteness in space **b** reserve, coldness **c** difference, disparity

²distance *vt* **1** to place or keep physically or mentally at a distance **2** to outstrip

distant /'dist(ə)nt/ *adj* **1a** separated in space or time by a specified distance ⟨*a few miles* ~⟩ **b** far-off or remote in space or time ⟨*the* ~ *hills*⟩ **2** not closely related ⟨*a* ~ *cousin*⟩ **3** different in kind **4** reserved, aloof **5** coming from or going to a remote place ⟨~ *voyages*⟩ [ME, fr MF, fr L *distant-*, *distans*, prp of *distare* to stand apart, be distant, fr *dis-* + *stare* to stand – more at STAND] – **distantly** *adv*, **distantness** *n*

distaste /dis'tayst/ *n* (a) dislike, aversion

dis'tasteful /-f(ə)l/ *adj* showing or causing distaste; offensive – **distastefully** *adv*, **distastefulness** *n*

¹distemper /di'stempə/ *n* any of various animal diseases; *esp* a highly infectious virus disease occurring esp in dogs and marked by fever and disorder of the respiratory and sometimes the nervous systems [*distemper*, vb (to upset the physical condition of, derange), fr ME *distempren*, fr LL *distemperare* to temper badly, fr L *dis-* + *temperare* to temper, mingle]

²distemper *vt* to paint in or with distemper [ME *distemperen* to mix with liquid, soak, fr MF *destemprer*, fr L *dis-* + *temperare*]

³distemper *n* **1** a method of painting in which pigments are mixed with white or yolk of egg or size, esp for mural decoration **2** the paint used in the distemper process; *broadly* any of numerous water-based paints for general, esp household, use

distend /di'stend/ *vb* to (cause to) swell from internal pressure [ME *distenden*, fr L *distendere*, fr *dis-* + *tendere* to stretch – more at THIN] – **distensible** /-səbl/ *adj*, **distensibility** /-sə'biləti/ *n*, **distension** /-sh(ə)n/ *n*

distich /'di,stik/ *n* a couplet [L *distichon*, fr Gk, fr neut of *distichos* having 2 rows, fr *di-* + *stichos* row, verse; akin to Gk *steichein* to go – more at STAIR]

distichous /'distikəs/ *adj* **1** arranged in 2 vertical rows ⟨~ *leaves*⟩ ☞ PLANT **2** divided into 2 segments ⟨~ *antennae*⟩ [LL *distichus*, fr Gk *distichos*] – **distichously** *adv*

distil, *NAm chiefly* **distill** /di'stil/ *vb* **-ll-** *vt* **1** to cause to fall or exude in drops or a fine mist **2a** to subject to or transform by distillation **b** to obtain or separate *out* or *off* (as if) by distillation **c** to extract the essence of (e g an idea or subject) ~ *vi* **1** to undergo distillation **2** to condense or drop from a still after distillation **3** to appear slowly or in small quantities at a time [ME *distillen*, fr MF *distiller*, fr LL *distillare*, alter. of L *destillare*, fr *de-* + *stillare* to drip, fr *stilla* drop; akin to OE *stān* stone – more at STONE]

distillate /'distilət, -,layt/ *n* **1** a product of distillation **2** a concentrated form

distillation /,disti'laysh(ə)n/ *n* a process that consists of condensing the gas or vapour obtained from heated liquids or solids and that is used esp for purification, fractionation, or the formation of new substances

distiller /di'stilə/ *n* a person or company that makes alcohol, esp spirits, by distilling [DISTIL + ²-ER] – **distillery** *n*

distinct /di'stingkt/ *adj* **1** different, separate *from* **2** readily perceptible to the senses or mind; clear **3** definite, decided ⟨*a* ~ *possibility of rain*⟩ [ME, fr

MF, fr L *distinctus*, fr pp of *distinguere*] – **distinctly** *adv*, **distinctness** *n*

distinction /di'stingksh(ə)n/ *n* **1a** discrimination, differentiation **b** a difference made or marked; a contrast **2** a distinguishing quality or mark **3a** outstanding merit, quality, or worth ⟨*a writer of some* ~⟩ **b** special honour or recognition ⟨*passed her exam with* ~⟩

distinctive /di'stingktiv/ *adj* clearly marking sby or sthg as different from others; characteristic – **distinctively** *adv*, **distinctiveness** *n*

distingué /di'stang·gay (*Fr* distẽge/ *adj* distinguished in appearance or manner [F, fr pp of *distinguer*]

distinguish /di'sting·gwish/ *vt* **1a** to mark or recognize as separate or different – often + *from* **b** to separate into kinds, classes, or categories **c** to make (oneself) outstanding or noteworthy **d** to mark as different; characterize **2** to discern; MAKE OUT 3, 5 ~ *vi* to recognize the difference *between* [MF *distinguer*, fr L *distinguere*, lit., to separate by pricking, fr *dis-* + *-stinguere* (akin to L *instigare* to urge on) – more at [3]STICK] – **distinguishable** *adj*, **distinguishably** *adv*, **distinguishability** /-shə 'biləti/ *n*

di'stinguished *adj* **1** marked by eminence, distinction, or excellence **2** dignified in manner, bearing, or appearance

distort /di'stawt/ *vt* **1** to alter the true meaning of; misrepresent **2** to cause to take on an unnatural or abnormal shape **3** to reproduce or broadcast (radio sound, a television picture, etc) poorly or inaccurately owing to a change in the wave form of the original signal [L *distortus*, pp of *distorquēre*, fr *dis-* + *torquēre* to twist – more at TORTURE] – **distortion** /-sh(ə)n/ *n*, **distortional** *adj*

distract /di'strakt/ *vt* **1** to turn aside; divert **2** to draw (e g one's attention) to a different object [ME *distracten*, fr L *distractus*, pp of *distrahere*, lit., to draw apart, fr *dis-* + *trahere* to draw – more at DRAW] – **distractingly** *adv*, **distractible** *adj*, **distractibility** /-tə'biləti/ *n*

di'stracted *adj* **1** confused, perplexed **2** agitated – **distractedly** *adv*

distraction /di'straksh(ə)n/ *n* **1** extreme agitation or mental confusion ⟨*drove him to* ~ *with her taunts*⟩ **2** sthg that distracts; *esp* an amusement [DISTRACT + -ION] – **distractive** /-tiv/ *adj*

distrain /di'strayn/ *vb* to impose a distress (upon); *also* to seize (goods, property, etc) by way of distress [ME *distreynen*, fr OF *destreindre*, fr ML *distringere*, fr L, to draw apart, detain, fr *dis-* + *stringere* to bind tight – more at [2]STRAIN] – **distrainable** *adj*, **distrainer** *n*, **distrainment** *n*, **distrainee** /,distray'nee/ *n*

distraint /di'straynt/ *n* distraining; DISTRESS 1a [*distrain* + *-t* (as in *constraint*)]

distrait /di'stray (*Fr* distrɛ)/ *adj* absentminded [F, fr L *distractus*]

distraught /di'strawt/ *adj* mentally agitated; frantic [ME, fr L *distractus*] – **distraughtly** *adv*

[1]**distress** /di'stres/ *n* **1a** (a) seizure of goods, property, etc as a pledge or to obtain satisfaction of a claim **b** sthg distrained **2a** mental or physical anguish **b** hardship or suffering caused esp by lack of money or the necessities of life **3** a state of danger or desperate need ⟨*a ship in* ~⟩ [ME *destresse*, fr OF, fr (assumed) VL *districtia*, fr L *districtus*, pp of *distringere*] – **distressful** *adj*

[2]**distress** *vt* to cause distress to – **distressingly** *adv*

di'stressed *adj* suffering distress; *specif* impoverished ⟨~ *gentlefolk*⟩

distributary /di'stribyoot(ə)ri/ *n* a river branch flowing from and never returning to the main stream

distribute /di'stribyooht/ *vt* **1** to divide among several or many **2a** to disperse or scatter over an area **b** to give out, deliver **3** to return (e g used type) to the proper storage places [ME *distributen*, fr L *distributus*, pp of *distribuere*, fr *dis-* + *tribuere* to allot – more at TRIBUTE]

distribution /,distri'byoohsh(ə)n/ *n* **1a** distributing, apportioning **b** sthg distributed **2a** the position, arrangement, or frequency of occurrence (e g of the members of a group) over a usu specified area or length of time **b** the natural geographical range of an organism **3** an arrangement of statistical data that shows the frequency of occurrence of the values of a variable ☞ STATISTICS **4** the transport and marketing of goods between manufacturer or wholesaler and retailer – **distributional** *adj*

[1]**distributive** /di'stribyootiv/ *adj* **1** of distribution **2** denoting a word (e g *each*, *either*, or *none*) referring singly to all the members of a group – **distributively** *adv*, **distributiveness** *n*

[2]**distributive** *n* a distributive word

distributor /di'stribyootə/ *n* **1** sby employed to manage the distribution of goods **2** an apparatus for directing current to the various sparking plugs of an internal-combustion engine [DISTRIBUTE + [1]-OR]

district /'distrikt/ *n* **1** a territorial division made esp for administrative purposes **2** an area or region with a specified character or feature ⟨*a residential* ~⟩ [F, fr ML *districtus* jurisdiction, district, fr *districtus*, pp of *distringere* to distrain – more at DISTRAIN]

,district 'nurse *n*, *Br* a qualified nurse, employed by a local authority, who visits and treats patients in their own homes

distrust /dis'trust/ *vt or n* (to view with) suspicion or lack of trust – **distrustful** *adj*, **distrustfully** *adv*, **distrustfulness** *n*

disturb /di'stuhb/ *vt* **1a** to break in upon; interrupt **b** to alter the position or arrangement of **2a** to destroy the peace of mind or composure of **b** to throw into disorder **c** to put to inconvenience [ME *disturben*, *destourben*, fr OF & L; OF *destourber*, fr L *disturbare*, fr *dis-* + *turbare* to throw into disorder – more at TURBID] – **disturbingly** *adv*

disturbance /di'stuhb(ə)ns/ *n* **1** disturbing or being disturbed **2** sthg that disturbs

di'sturbed *adj* having or showing symptoms of emotional or mental instability

disubstituted /,die'substityoohtid, -chooh-/ *adj* having 2 substituted atoms or groups in a molecule

disulfiram /,diesul'fiərəm/ *n* a compound used in the treatment of alcoholism which acts by causing severe nausea when alcohol is drunk [*disulfide* (*NAm* for *disulphide*) + *thiourea* + *amyl*]

disulphide /die'sulfied/ *n* a compound containing 2 atoms of sulphur combined with an element or radical

disunion /dis'yoohnyən, -ni·ən/ *n* **1** the termination of union; separation **2** disunity

disunite /,disyoo'niet/ *vt* to divide, separate

disunity /dis'yoohnəti/ *n* lack of unity; *esp* dissension

disuse /dis'yoohs/ *n* the state of no longer being used ⟨*that word has fallen into* ~⟩

disused /dis'yoohzd/ *adj* no longer used; abandoned

dit /dit/ *n* ¹DOT 4 – used when articulating Morse code [imit]

¹**ditch** /dich/ *n* a long narrow excavation dug in the earth for defence, drainage, irrigation, etc [ME *dich,* fr OE *dīc* dyke, ditch]

²**ditch** *vt* **1a** to enclose with a ditch **b** to dig a ditch in **2** to make a forced landing of (an aircraft) on water **3** to get rid of; abandon *USE* (2&3) infml – **ditch** *n*

¹**dither** /'didhə/ *vi* to act nervously or indecisively; vacillate [ME *didderen*] – **ditherer** *n*

²**dither** *n* a state of indecision or nervous excitement ⟨*all of a* ~⟩ – **dithery** *adj*

dithi-, dithio- *comb form* containing 2 atoms of sulphur, usu in place of 2 oxygen atoms, in the molecular structure [ISV *di-* + *thi-*]

dithyramb /'dithə,ram(b)/ *n* **1** a rapturous Greek hymn in honour of Bacchus **2** a short poem or other piece of writing in a rapturous or exalted style [Gk *dithyrambos*] – **dithyrambic** /-'rambik/ *adj,* **dithyrambically** *adv*

dittany /'ditəni/ *n* a pink-flowered plant that is native to Crete [ME *ditoyne,* fr MF *ditayne,* fr L *dictamnum,* fr Gk *diktamnon*]

¹**ditto** /'ditoh/ *n* **1** a thing mentioned previously or above; the same – used to avoid repeating a word **2** *also* **ditto mark** a mark „ or " used as a sign indicating repetition usu of a word directly above in a previous line [It dial., pp of It *dire* to say, fr L *dicere* – more at DICTION]

²**ditto** *vt* to repeat the action or statement of

dittography /di'togrəfi/ *n* the unintentional repetition of letters or words in copying or printing [Gk *dittographia, dissographia,* fr *dittos, dissos* two-fold + *-graphia* -graphy] – **dittographic** /,ditə'grafik/ *adj*

ditty /'diti/ *n* a short simple song [ME *ditee,* fr OF *ditié* poem, fr pp of *ditier* to compose, fr L *dictare* to dictate, compose]

diuresis /,die·yoo'reesis/ *n* an increased excretion of urine [NL]

diuretic /,dieyoo'retik/ *n or adj* (a drug) acting to increase the flow of urine [adj ME, fr MF or LL; MF *diuretique,* fr LL *diureticus,* fr Gk *diourētikos,* fr *diourein* to urinate, fr *dia-* + *ourein* to urinate – more at URINE; n fr adj] – **diuretically** *adv*

diurnal /die'uhnl/ *adj* **1** having a daily cycle **2a** occurring during the day or daily **b** opening during the day and closing at night ⟨~ *flowers*⟩ **c** active during the day [ME, fr L *diurnalis* – more at JOURNAL] – **diurnally** *adv*

diva /'deevə/ *n, pl* **divas, dive** /-vi/ PRIMA DONNA 1 [It, lit., goddess, fr L, fem of *divus* divine, god – more at DEITY]

divagate /'dievə,gayt/ *vi* to wander from one place or subject to another; stray – fml [LL *divagatus,* pp of *divagari,* fr L *dis-* + *vagari* to wander – more at VAGARY] – **divagation** /-'gaysh(ə)n/ *n*

divalent /,die'vaylənt/ *adj* bivalent

divan /di'van, 'dievan; *sense 3* di'van/ *n* **1** the privy council of the Ottoman Empire **2** a council chamber in some Muslim countries, esp Turkey **3a** a long low couch, usu without arms or back, placed against a wall **b** a bed of a similar style without a head or foot board [Turk, fr Per *dīwān* account book]

divaricate /die'vari,kayt/ *vi* to branch off; diverge [L *divaricatus,* pp of *divaricare,* fr *dis-* + *varicare* to straddle – more at PREVARICATE] – **divaricate** /-kət, -,kayt/ *adj,* **divarication** /-'kaysh(ə)n/ *n*

¹**dive** /diev/ *vb* **dived,** *NAm also* **dove** /dohv/ *vi* **1a** to plunge into water headfirst **b** to engage in the sport of prescribed dives into water **c** to submerge ⟨*the submarine* ~d⟩ **2a** to descend or fall steeply **b** to plunge one's hand quickly *into* **c** *of an aircraft* to descend in a dive **3** to lunge or dash headlong ⟨~d *for cover*⟩ ~ *vt* **1** to cause to descend ⟨~d *his plane through the sound barrier*⟩ **2** to dip or plunge (one's hand) *into* [ME *diven, duven,* fr OE *dyfan* to dip & *dūfan* to dive; akin to OE *dyppan* to dip – more at DIP]

²**dive** *n* **1a(1)** a headlong plunge into water; *esp* one executed in a prescribed manner **(2)** an act or instance of submerging (e g by a submarine) **(3)** a steep descent of an aeroplane at greater than the maximum horizontal speed **b** a sharp decline **2** a disreputable bar, club, etc **3** a faked knockout – chiefly in *take a dive* **4** a ploy in soccer in which a player makes it appear that he has been fouled by falling over deliberately after a tackle *USE* (*except 1a*) infml

'**dive-,bomb** *vt* to bomb from an aeroplane while making a steep dive towards the target – **dive-bomber** *n*

dive in *vi* to begin or become involved in an action or activity with haste

diver /'dievə/ *n* **1** sby who dives; *esp* a person who works or explores underwater for long periods, either carrying a supply of air or having it sent from the surface **2** any of various diving birds; *specif* a loon

diverge /die'vuhj/ *vi* **1a** to move in different directions from a common point **b** to differ in character, form, or opinion – often + *from* **2** to turn aside from a path or course – often + *from* **3** to be mathematically divergent [ML *divergere,* fr L *dis-* + *vergere* to incline – more at WRENCH]

divergence /die'vuhj(ə)ns, di-/ *also* **divergency** /-si/ *n* **1a** (an instance of) diverging or being divergent **b** the amount by which sthg diverges; DIFFERENCE 3 **2** the acquisition of dissimilar characteristics by related organisms living in different environments

divergent /die'vuhj(ə)nt, di-/ *adj* **1** diverging or differing from each other **2** *of a mathematical series* having a sum that continues to increase or decrease as the number of terms increases without limit **3** causing divergence of rays ⟨*a* ~ *lens*⟩ [L *divergent-, divergens,* prp of *divergere*] – **divergently** *adv*

divers /'dievəz/ *adj, archaic* various [ME *divers, diverse*]

diverse /'die,vuhs, -'-/ *adj* **1** different, unlike **2** varied, assorted [ME *divers, diverse,* fr OF & L; OF *divers,* fr L *diversus,* fr pp of *divertere*] – **diversely** *adv,* **diverseness** *n*

diversify /,die'vuhsi,fie/ *vt* **1** to make diverse; vary **2** to divide (e g investment of funds) among different securities to reduce risk ~ *vi* to engage in varied business operations in order to reduce risk – **diversifier** *n,* **diversification** /-fi'kaysh(ə)n/ *n*

diversion /di'vuhsh(ə)n, die-/ *n* **1** a turning aside from a course, activity, or use; *specif* a detour used by traffic when the usual route is closed **2** an amusement, pastime **3** sthg that draws the attention away from the main scene of activity or operations [DIVERT + -ION] – **diversionary** /-n(ə)ri/ *adj*

diversity /di'vuhsəti, die-/ *n* **1** the condition of being different or having differences **2** a variety, assortment

divert /die'vuht/ *vt* **1a** to turn aside from one course or use to another **b** to distract **2** to entertain, amuse [ME *diverten*, fr MF & L; MF *divertir*, fr L *divertere* to turn in opposite directions, fr *dis-* + *vertere* to turn – more at [1]WORTH]

diverticulum /ˌdievə'tikyooləm/ *n, pl* **diverticula** /-lə/ a pocket or closed branch opening off a main passage, esp an abnormal pouch opening off the intestine [NL, fr L, bypath, prob alter. of *deverticulum*, fr *devertere* to turn aside, fr *de-* + *vertere*] – **diverticulitis** /-'lietəs/ *n*

divertimento /diˌvuhti'mentoh/ *n, pl* **divertimenti** /-ti/, **divertimentos** an instrumental chamber work in several movements and usu light in character [It, lit., diversion, fr *divertire* to divert, amuse, fr F *divertir*]

divertissement /di'vuhtismənt (*Fr* divɛrtismɑ̃)/ *n, pl* **divertissements** /-mənt(s) (*Fr* ~)/ **1** a ballet suite serving as an interlude **2** a divertimento **3** a diversion, entertainment [F, lit., diversion, fr *divertiss-* (stem of *divertir*)]

divest /die'vest/ *vt* **1a** to deprive or dispossess *of* property, authority, title, etc **b** to rid or free (oneself) *of* **c** to strip *of* clothing, equipment, etc **2** to take away (e g property or vested rights) ***USE*** (1c&2) fml [alter. of earlier *devest*, fr MF *desvestir*, fr ML *disvestire*, fr L *dis-* + *vestire* to clothe – more at [1]VEST] – **divestiture** /-tichə/ *n*, **divestment** *n*

[1]**divide** /di'vied/ *vt* **1** to separate into 2 or more parts, categories, divisions, etc **2a** to give out in shares; distribute **b** to set aside for different purposes ⟨~d *his time between work and play*⟩ **3a** to cause to be separate; serve as a boundary between **b** to separate into opposing sides or parties **c** to cause (a parliamentary body) to vote by division **4a** to mark divisions on ⟨~ *a sextant*⟩ **b** to determine how many times (a number or quantity) contains another number or quantity by means of a mathematical operation ⟨~ *42 by 14*⟩ ☞ SYMBOL ~ *vi* **1** to perform mathematical division ☞ SYMBOL **2a(1)** to become separated into parts **(2)** to diverge **b** to vote by division [ME *dividen*, fr L *dividere*, fr *dis-* + *-videre* to separate – more at WIDOW] – **dividable** *adj* – **divide into** to use as a divisor of ⟨divide *14* into *42*⟩

[2]**divide** *n* **1** WATERSHED 1 **2** a point or line of division

dividend /'dividend, -dənd/ *n* **1** (a pro rata share in) the part of a company's profits payable to shareholders **2** a reward, benefit ⟨*her action will pay great* ~s⟩ **3a** a number to be divided by another **b** a sum or fund to be divided and distributed [ME *divident*, fr L *dividendus*, gerundive of *dividere*]

divider /di'viedə/ *n* **1** *pl* a compasslike instrument with 2 pointed ends used for measuring or marking off lines, angles, etc **2** a partition or screen used to separate parts of a room, hall, etc [[1]DIVIDE + [2]-ER]

divination /ˌdivi'naysh(ə)n/ *n* **1** the art or practice that seeks to foresee the future or discover hidden knowledge (e g by using supernatural powers) **2** (an instance of) unusual insight or perception [ME *divinacioun*, fr L *divination-*, *divinatio*, fr *divinatus*, pp of *divinare*] – **divinatory** /di'vinət(ə)ri/ *adj*

[1]**divine** /di'vien/ *adj* **1a** of, being, or proceeding directly from God or a god **b** devoted to the worship of God or a god; sacred **2** delightful, superb – infml [ME *divin*, fr MF, fr L *divinus*, fr *divus* god – more at DEITY] – **divinely** *adv*, **divineness** *n*

[2]**divine** *n* a clergyman; *esp* one skilled in theology [ME, fr ML *divinus*, fr L, soothsayer, fr *divinus*, adj]

[3]**divine** *vt* **1** to discover, perceive, or foresee intuitively or by supernatural means **2** to discover or locate (e g water or minerals) by means of a divining rod ~ *vi* to practise divination [ME *divinen*, fr MF & L; MF *diviner*, fr L *divinare*, fr *divinus*, n] – **divinable** *adj*, **diviner** *n*

Di,vine 'Liturgy *n* the form of service used in the Eastern Orthodox celebration of Communion

Di,vine 'Office *n* the prescribed forms of prayer and ritual for daily worship used by Roman Catholic priests

di,vine 'right *n* the right of a sovereign to rule, held to derive directly from God ⟨~ *of kings*⟩; *broadly* a right which cannot be transferred

di,vine 'service *n* an esp nonsacramental service of Christian worship

'diving ,bell /'dieving/ *n* a bell-shaped metal container open only at the bottom and supplied with compressed air through a tube, in which a person can be let down under water

'diving ,suit *n* a waterproof diver's suit with a helmet that is supplied with air pumped through a tube

di'vining ,rod /di'viening/ *n* a forked rod (e g a twig) believed to dip downwards when held over ground concealing water or minerals

divinity /di'vinəti/ *n* **1** the quality or state of being divine **2a** *often cap* GOD 1 **b** a male or female deity **3** theology

divisible /di'vizəbl/ *adj* capable of being divided, esp without a remainder – **divisibility** /-'biləti/ *n*

division /di'vizh(ə)n/ *n* **1a** dividing or being divided **b** (a) distribution **2** any of the parts or sections into which a whole is divided **3** *sing or pl in constr* **a** a major army formation having the necessary tactical and administrative services to act independently **b** a naval unit of men under a single command **4a** an administrative territorial unit **b** an administrative or operating unit of an organization **5** a group of organisms forming part of a larger group; *specif* a primary category of the plant kingdom equivalent to a phylum of the animal kingdom **6** a competitive class or category (e g of a soccer league) **7** sthg that divides, separates, or marks off **8** disagreement, disunity **9** the physical separation into different lobbies of the members of a parliamentary body voting for and against a question **10** the mathematical operation of dividing one number by another [ME, fr MF, fr L *division-*, *divisio*, fr *divisus*, pp of *dividere* to divide] – **divisional** *adj*

di,vision of 'labour *n* the distribution of various parts of the process of production among different people, groups, or machines, each specializing in a particular job, to increase efficiency

divisive /di'viesiv, -ziv/ *adj* tending to cause disunity or dissension – **divisively** *adv*, **divisiveness** *n*

divisor /di'viezə/ *n* the number by which another number or quantity is divided

[1]**divorce** /di'vaws/ *n* **1** (a decree declaring) a legal

dissolution of a marriage **2** a separation, severance [ME *divorse,* fr MF, fr L *divortium,* fr *divertere, divortere* to divert, to leave one's husband]

[2]**divorce** *vt* **1a** to end marriage with (one's spouse) by divorce **b** to dissolve the marriage between **2** to end the relationship or union of; separate – usu + *from* ~ *vi* to obtain a divorce

divorcé /di'vaw'say, -'see/, *fem* **divorcée** /-'see/ *n* a divorced person [F, fr pp of *divorcer* to divorce, fr MF *divorse*]

divot /'divət/ *n* **1** a piece of turf dug out in making a golf shot **2** *Scot* a piece of turf [origin unknown]

divulge /die'vulj, di-/ *vt* to make known (e g a confidence or secret); reveal [ME *divulgen,* fr L *divulgare,* fr *dis-* + *vulgare* to make known] – **divulgence** *n*

divvy /'divi/ *n, Br* DIVIDEND 1; *esp* one paid by a Cooperative Wholesale Society – infml [by shortening & alter.]

dixie /'diksi/ *n, Br* a large metal pot in which food and drink is made or carried, esp by soldiers [Hindi *degcī,* dim. of *degcā* kettle, pot]

Dixie *n* the Southern states of the USA [name for the Southern states in the song *Dixie* (1859) by Daniel D Emmett †1904 US musician]

'dixie,land /-,land/ *n* jazz music in duple time characterized by collective improvisation [*Dixie* + *land;* fr its origin in the Southern states of the USA]

DIY *n* (the materials and equipment needed for) amateur repair, maintenance, and building work, esp around the home [*do it yourself*]

dizygotic /,diezie'gotik/ *also* **dizygous** /die'ziegəs/ *adj, of twins* fraternal [*di-* + *zygotic, -zygous*]

[1]**dizzy** /'dizi/ *adj* **1a** experiencing a whirling sensation in the head with a tendency to lose balance **b** mentally confused **2** causing or feeling giddiness or mental confusion ⟨*a* ~ *height*⟩ **3** foolish, silly – infml [ME *disy,* fr OE *dysig* stupid; akin to OHG *tusig* stupid, L *furere* to rage – more at DUST] – **dizzily** *adv,* **dizziness** *n*

[2]**dizzy** *vt* to make dizzy; bewilder – **dizzyingly** *adv*

DJ /'dee,jay/ *n* **1** DISC JOCKEY **2** DINNER JACKET

djellaba *also* **djellabah, jellaba** /jə'lahbə, 'jeləbə/ *n* a long loose outer garment with full sleeves and a hood, traditionally worn by Arabs [F *djellaba,* fr Ar *jallabah*]

djin, djinn /jin/ *n, pl* **djin, djinn** a jinn

dl- *also* **d, l-** *prefix* consisting of equal amounts of the d and l forms ⟨dl-*tartaric acid*⟩

DNA *n* any of various nucleic acids that are found esp in cell nuclei, are constructed of a double helix held together by hydrogen bonds between purine and pyrimidine bases which project inwards from 2 chains containing alternate links of deoxyribose and phosphate, and are responsible for transmitting genetic information [*d*eoxyribo*n*ucleic *a*cid]

'D-,notice *n* an official request (e g to a newspaper) that certain information be withheld from publication for security reasons [*D*efence-notice]

[1]**do** /dooh/ *vb* **does** /dəz; *strong* duz/; **did** /did/; **done** /dun/ *vt* **1** to carry out the task of; effect, perform ⟨~ *some washing*⟩ ⟨~ *overtime*⟩ **2** to put into a specified condition ⟨~ *him to death*⟩ **3** to have as a function ⟨*what's that book* ~ing *on the floor?*⟩ **4** to cause, impart ⟨*sleep will* ~ *you good*⟩ **5** to bring to an esp unwanted conclusion; finish – used esp in the past participle ⟨*that's* done *it*⟩; compare DONE 2 **6** to expend, exert ⟨did *their damnedest to hog the game*⟩ **7a** to provide ⟨*they* ~ *a mail-order service*⟩ **b** to have available for purchase; sell ⟨*they* ~ *teas here*⟩ **8** to bring into existence; produce ⟨~ *a biography of the general*⟩ **9a** to put on; perform ⟨*are* ~ing *'The Merchant of Venice" tomorrow night*⟩ **b** to play the part of; act ⟨*can* ~ *Harold Wilson very well*⟩ **c** to behave like ⟨did *a Houdini and escaped from his chains*⟩ **10a** to put in order; arrange ⟨~ *the garden*⟩ ⟨*had his hair* done⟩ **b** to clean, wash ⟨~ *the dishes*⟩ **c** to cook ⟨*likes her steak well* done⟩ **d** to decorate, furnish ⟨did *the living room in blue*⟩ **11a** to execute an artistic representation of ⟨did *her in oils*⟩ **b** to perform the appropriate professional service or services for ⟨*the barber will* ~ *you now*⟩ ⟨~ *you very well at that hotel*⟩ **12a** to work at, esp as a course of study or occupation ⟨~ *classics*⟩ ⟨*what are you* ~ing *nowadays?*⟩ **b** to solve; WORK OUT ⟨~ *a sum*⟩ **13a** to pass over; cover ⟨~ *30 miles to the gallon*⟩ **b** to travel at a (maximum) speed of ⟨~ *70 on the motorway*⟩ ⟨*this car* ~es *80*⟩ **14** to see the sights of; tour ⟨~ *12 countries in 12 days*⟩ **15** to serve out, esp as a prison sentence ⟨did *3 years*⟩ **16** to suffice, suit ⟨*worms will* ~ *us for bait*⟩ **17** – used as a substitute verb to avoid repetition ⟨*if you must make such a racket,* ~ *it somewhere else*⟩ **18a** *chiefly Br* to arrest, convict – slang ⟨*get* done *for theft*⟩ **b** *chiefly Br* to attack, hurt – slang **c** to treat unfairly; *esp* to cheat, deprive ⟨did *him out of his inheritance*⟩ – infml **d** to rob – slang ⟨~ *a shop*⟩ **19** to have sexual intercourse with (a woman or passive partner) – slang ~ *vi* **1** to act, behave ⟨~ *as I say*⟩ **2a** to fare; GET ALONG ⟨~ *well at school*⟩ ⟨*how do you* ~*?*⟩ **b** to carry on business or affairs; manage ⟨*we can* ~ *without your help*⟩ **3** to be in progress; happen ⟨*there's nothing* ~ing⟩ **4** to come to or make an end; finish – used in the past participle ⟨*have you* done *with the newspaper?*⟩; compare DONE 2 **5** to be active or busy ⟨*let us then be up and* ~ing – H W Longfellow⟩ **6** to suffice, serve ⟨*half of that will* ~⟩ **7** to be fitting; conform to custom or propriety ⟨*won't* ~ *to be late*⟩ **8a** – used as a substitute verb to avoid repetition ⟨*you sing,* ~ *you?*⟩ and, esp in British English, after a modal auxiliary ⟨*haven't heard of her yet but you will* ~⟩ **b** – used as a substitute for verb and object ⟨*he likes it and so* ~ *I*⟩ **9** – used in the imperative after another imperative to add emphasis ⟨*be quiet,* ~⟩ ~ *va* – used with the infinitive without *to* **a** to form present and past tenses in legal and parliamentary language ⟨~ *hereby bequeath*⟩ and in poetry ⟨*give what she* did *crave* – Shak⟩ **b** to form present and past tenses in declarative sentences with inverted word order ⟨*fervently* ~ *we pray* – Abraham Lincoln⟩ or in questions or negative sentences ⟨did *you hear that?*⟩ ⟨*we* don't *know*⟩ ⟨don't *go*⟩ **c** to form present and past tenses expressing emphasis ⟨*it* ~es *hurt*⟩ ⟨~ *be careful*⟩ [ME *don,* fr OE *dōn;* akin to OHG *tuon* to do, L *-dere* to put, *facere*] to make, do, Gk *tithenai* to place, set] – **doable** *adj* – **do away with 1** to put an end to; abolish **2** to put to death; kill – **do by** to deal with; treat ⟨*afraid you've been rather hard* done by⟩ – **do duty for** to act as a substitute for; serve as – **do for 1** *chiefly Br* to keep house for **2a** to wear out, exhaust **b** to bring about the death or ruin of – **do justice (to) 1a** to treat fairly or adequately **b** to show due appreciation for **2** to show in the best light ⟨*I hope he* did *himself* justice

in the examinations⟩ – **do one's bit** *Br* to make one's personal contribution, esp to a cause – **do one's block** *Austr* DO ONE'S NUT – infml – **do one's nut** to become frantic or angry – infml – **do proud** to treat or entertain splendidly – **do the dirty on** to play a sly trick on – **do something for** to improve the appearance of ⟨*that dress really* does something for *you*⟩ – **do the trick** to achieve the desired result – infml ⟨*castor oil should* do the trick⟩ – **to do with** concerned with; of concern to ⟨*a job* to do with *plastics*⟩ ⟨*nothing* to do with *you*⟩

[2]**do** *n, pl* **dos, do's** /doohz/ **1** sthg one ought to do – usu pl ⟨*gave her a list of* ~s *and don'ts*⟩ **2** *chiefly Br* a festive party or occasion – infml

[3]**do, doh** /doh/ *n* the 1st note of the diatonic scale in solmization [It]

dobbin /'dobin/ *n* – used chiefly as a familiar name for a farm horse [*Dobbin*, nickname for *Robert*]

Doberman pinscher /,dohbəmən 'pinshə/ *n* a short-haired medium-sized dog of German origin, frequently used as a guard dog [G *Dobermann pinscher*, fr Ludwig *Dobermann*, 19th-c G dog breeder + G *pinscher*, a breed of hunting dog]

dobra /'dohbrə/ *n* ☞ *São Tomé* at NATIONALITY [Pg, fr fem of obs *dobro* double, fr L *duplus*]

doc /dok/ *n* a doctor – often used as an informal term of address

docent /doh'sent/ *n* a lecturer in some US colleges and universities [obs G (now *dozent*), fr L *docent-, docens*, prp of *docēre*]

Docetism /'dohsi,tiz(ə)m, doh'setiz(ə)m/ *n* an early Christian heretical belief that Christ only seemed to have a human body and to suffer and die on the cross [Gk *Dokētai* Docetists, fr *dokein* to seem – more at DECENT] – **Docetic** /-'setik/ *adj*, **Docetist** /'dohsitist/ *n*

doch an dorris /,d(y)okh ən 'dohrəs/ *n, Scot & Irish* a parting drink [ScGael & IrGael *deoch an doruis*, lit., drink of the door]

docile /'doh,siel/ *adj* easily led or managed; tractable [L *docilis*, fr *docēre* to teach; akin to L *decēre* to be fitting – more at DECENT] – **docilely** *adv*, **docility** /-'siləti/ *n*

[1]**dock** /dok/ *n* any of a genus of coarse weeds whose leaves are used to alleviate nettle stings [ME, fr OE *docce*; akin to MD *docke* dock, ScGael *dogha* burdock]

[2]**dock** *n* the solid bony part of an animal's tail as distinguished from the hair ☞ ANATOMY [ME *dok*, fr OE *-docca* (as in *fingirdocca* finger muscle); akin to OHG *tocka* doll, ON *dokka* bundle]

[3]**dock** *vt* **1a** to remove part of the tail of **b** to cut (e g a tail) short **2** to make a deduction from (e g wages) **3** to take away (a specified amount) *from*

[4]**dock** *n* **1a** a usu artificially enclosed body of water in a port or harbour, where a ship can moor (e g for repair work to be carried out) **b** *pl the* total number of such enclosures in a harbour, together with wharves, sheds, etc **2** *chiefly NAm* a wharf [prob fr MD *docke* dock, ditch, fr L *duction-, ductio* act of leading – more at DOUCHE] – **in dock** in a garage or repair shop ⟨*my car's* in dock *at the moment*⟩

[5]**dock** *vt* **1** to haul or guide into a dock **2** to join (e g 2 spacecraft) together while in space ~ *vi* **1** to come or go into dock **2** *of spacecraft* to join together while in space

[6]**dock** *n* the prisoner's enclosure in a criminal court [Flem *docke* cage] – **in the dock** on trial ⟨*always found himself* in the dock *for his opinions*⟩

docker /'dokə/ *n* sby employed in loading and unloading ships, barges, etc [[4]*dock*]

[1]**docket** /'dokit/ *n* **1** a brief written summary of a document **2a** a document recording the contents of a shipment or the payment of customs duties **b** a label attached to goods bearing identification or instructions **c** (a copy of) a receipt **3a** *NAm* **(1)** a formal record of legal proceedings **(2)** a list of legal causes to be tried **b** *chiefly NAm* a list of business matters to be acted on [ME *doggette*]

[2]**docket** *vt* **1** to put an identifying statement or label on **2** to make an abstract of (e g legal proceedings) **3** *NAm* to place on the docket for legal action

'**dockland** /-lənd, -,land/ *n, Br* the district around the docks in a large port

'**dock,yard** /-,yahd/ *n* a place or enclosure in which ships are built or repaired

[1]**doctor** /'doktə/ *n* **1a** *also* **Doctor of the Church,** *often cap* a theologian whose doctrines the Roman Catholic church holds to be authoritative **b** a holder of the highest level of academic degree conferred by a university **2a** one qualified to practise medicine; a physician or surgeon **b** *NAm* a licensed dentist or veterinary surgeon **3** sby skilled in repairing or treating a usu specified type of machine, vehicle, etc **4** *archaic* a learned or authoritative teacher [ME *doctour* teacher, doctor, fr MF & ML; MF, fr ML *doctor*, fr L, teacher, fr *doctus*, pp of *docēre* to teach – more at DOCILE] – **doctoral** *adj*, **doctorate** /-rət/ *n*, **doctorship** *n*

[2]**doctor** *vt* **1a** to give medical treatment to **b** to repair, mend **2a** to adapt or modify for a desired end ⟨~ed *the play to suit the audience*⟩ **b** to alter in a dishonest way **3** to castrate or spay – euph ~ *vi* to practise medicine – infml

doctrinaire /,doktri'neə/ *n or adj* (one) concerned with abstract theory to the exclusion of practical considerations – chiefly derog [adj F, fr *doctrine*; n fr adj] – **doctrinairism** *n*

doctrinal /dok'trienl/ *adj* of or concerned with doctrine – **doctrinally** *adv*

doctrine /'doktrin/ *n* **1** sthg that is taught **2** a principle or the body of principles in a branch of knowledge or system of belief [ME, fr MF & L; MF, fr L *doctrina*, fr *doctor*]

[1]**document** /'dokyoomənt/ *n* an original or official paper that gives information about or proof of sthg [ME, fr MF, fr LL & L; LL *documentum* official paper, fr L, lesson, proof, fr *docēre* to teach – more at DOCILE]

[2]**document** /'dokyoo,ment/ *vt* **1** to provide documentary evidence of **2a** to support with factual evidence, references, etc **b** to be or provide a documentary account of **3** to provide (a ship) with papers required by law recording ownership, cargo, etc

[1]**documentary** /,dokyoo'ment(ə)ri/ *adj* **1** being or consisting of documents; contained or certified in writing ⟨~ *evidence*⟩ **2** presenting or based on factual material – **documentarily** /-men'terəli/ *adv*

[2]**documentary** *n* a broadcast or film that presents a factual account of a person or topic using a variety of techniques (e g narrative and interview) – compare FEATURE 3a, c – **documentarist** /-'ment(ə)rist/ *n*

documentation /,dokyoomen'taysh(ə)n/ *n* (the provision or use of) documents or documentary evidence – **documentational** *adj*

[1]dodder /'dodə/ *n* any of a genus of leafless plants of the bindweed family that are wholly parasitic on other plants [ME *doder*; akin to OE *dydring* yolk, Norw *dudra* to tremble, L *fumus* smoke – more at FUME]

[2]dodder *vi* **1** to tremble or shake from weakness or age **2** to walk feebly and unsteadily [ME *dadiren*] – **dodderer** *n*

doddered /'dodəd/ *adj* deprived of branches through age or decay ⟨*a* ~ *oak*⟩ [prob alter. of *dodded*, fr pp of E dial. *dod* (to lop), fr ME *dodden*]

doddering /'dodəring/, **doddery** /'dod(ə)ri/ *adj* weak, shaky, and slow, esp because of old age

doddle /'dodl/ *n, chiefly Br* a very easy task – infml [prob fr [2]*dodder*]

dodeca- /dohdekə-/, **dodec-** *comb form* twelve ⟨dodeca*phonic*⟩ [L, fr Gk *dōdeka-, dōdek-*, fr *dōdeka, dyōdeka*, fr *dyō, dyo* two + *deka* ten]

dodecagon /,doh'dekəgən/ *n* a polygon of 12 angles and 12 sides [Gk *dōdekagōnon*, fr *dōdeka-* + *-gōnon* -gon] – **dodecagonal** /,doh,de'kagənl/ *adj*

dodecahedron /,doh,dekə'heedrən/ *n, pl* **dodecahedrons, dodecahedra** /-drə/ a polyhedron of 12 faces [Gk *dōdekaedron*, fr *dōdeka-* + *-edron* -hedron] – **dodecahedral** /-'heedrəl/ *adj*

,dodeca'phonic /-'fonik/ *adj* twelve-tone [*dodeca-* + *phon-* + *-ic*] – **dodecaphonically** *adv*, **dodecaphonist** /doh'dekəfənist, -foh-, ,dohde'kafənist/ *n*, **dodecaphony** /-ni/ *n*

[1]dodge /doj/ *vi* to shift position suddenly and usu repeatedly (e g to avoid a blow or a pursuer) ~ *vt* **1** to evade (e g a duty) usu by trickery **2a** to avoid by a sudden or repeated shift of position **b** to avoid an encounter with [origin unknown]

[2]dodge *n* **1** a sudden movement to avoid sthg **2** a clever device to evade or trick ⟨*a tax* ~⟩

dodgem /'dojəm/, **'dodgem ,car** *n, Br* any of a number of small electric cars designed to be steered about and bumped into one another as a fun-fair amusement [[1]*dodge* + *'em*]

dodger /'dojə/ *n* one who uses clever and often dishonest methods, esp to avoid payment (e g of taxes) or responsibility [[1]DODGE + [2]-ER]

dodgy /'doji/ *adj, chiefly Br* **1** shady, dishonest ⟨*a* ~ *person*⟩ **2** risky, dangerous ⟨*a* ~ *plan*⟩ **3** liable to collapse, fail, or break down ⟨*that chair's a bit* ~⟩ *USE* infml

dodo /'doh,doh/ *n, pl* **dodoes, dodos** an extinct heavy flightless bird that formerly lived on the island of Mauritius [Pg *doudo*, fr *doudo* silly, stupid]

do down *vt, chiefly Br* **1** to cheat **2** to speak badly of; belittle

doe /doh/ *n, pl* **does,** *esp collectively* **doe** the adult female fallow deer; *broadly* the adult female of any of various mammals (e g the rabbit) or birds (e g the guinea fowl) of which the male is called a buck [ME *do*, fr OE *dā*; akin to G dial. *tē* doe]

doer /'dooh·ə/ *n* one who takes action or participates actively in sthg, rather than theorizing

does /dəz; *strong* duz/ *pres 3rd sing of* DO

doeskin /'doh,skin/ *n* **1** (leather made from) the skin of a doe **2** a smooth closely woven woollen fabric

doesn't /'duz(ə)nt/ does not

doest /'dooh·ist/ *archaic pres 2nd sing of* DO

doeth /'dooh·ith/ *archaic pres 3rd sing of* DO

doff /dof/ *vt* to take off (one's hat) in greeting or as a sign of respect [ME *doffen*, fr *don* to do + *of* off]

[1]dog /dog/ *n* **1a** a 4-legged flesh-eating domesticated mammal occurring in a great variety of breeds and prob descended from the common wolf **b** any of a family of carnivores to which the dog belongs **c** a male dog **2a** any of various usu simple mechanical devices for holding, fastening, etc that consist of a spike, rod, or bar **b** an andiron **3a** SUN DOG **b** a fogbow **4** *chiefly NAm* sthg inferior of its kind **5** an esp worthless man or fellow ⟨*a lazy* ~⟩ **6** *pl* feet **7** *pl* ruin ⟨*go to the* ~s⟩ *USE* (5, 6, &7) infml [ME, fr OE *docga*] – **doglike** *adj*

[2]dog *vt* **-gg-** to pursue closely like a dog; hound

[3]dog *adj* male ⟨*a* ~ *fox*⟩

'dog ,biscuit *n* a hard dry biscuit for dogs

'dog ,clutch *n* a clutch in which recesses in one plate are engaged by projections in the other

'dog ,collar *n* CLERICAL COLLAR – infml

'dog ,days *n pl* the hottest days in the year [fr their being reckoned from the heliacal rising of the Dog Star (Sirius)]

doge /dohj/ *n* the chief magistrate of the former republics of Venice and Genoa [It dial., fr L *duc-, dux* leader – more at DUKE]

'dog-,ear *n* the turned-down corner of a page – **dog-ear** *vt*

'dog-,eared *adj* having dog-ears; *broadly* worn, shabby

,dog-eat-'dog *adj* marked by ruthless self-interest; cutthroat

'dog-,end *n* a cigarette end – slang

'dog ,fennel *n* STINKING MAYWEED

'dog,fight /-,fiet/ *n* **1** a viciously fought contest **2** a fight between aircraft, usu at close quarters – **dogfight** *vi*

'dog,fish /-,fish/ *n* any of various small sharks

dogged /'dogid/ *adj* stubbornly determined [ME, doglike, cruel, spiteful, fr *dog, dogge* dog + *-ed*] – **doggedly** *adv*, **doggedness** *n*

doggerel /'dog(ə)rəl/ *n* (an example of) verse that is loosely styled and irregular in measure, esp for comic effect [ME *dogerel*]

doggo /'dogoh/ *adv, Br* in hiding and without moving – infml; chiefly in *lie doggo* [prob fr [1]*dog*]

doggoned /'dogond/, **doggone** /'do,gon/ *adj or adv, chiefly NAm* damned – euph [euphemism for *God-damned*]

[1]doggy /'dogi/ *adj* **1** resembling or suggestive of a dog ⟨*a* ~ *odour*⟩ **2** concerned with or fond of dogs ⟨*a* ~ *person*⟩ *USE* infml

[2]doggy, doggie /'dogi/ *n* a dog – used esp by or to children

'doggy ,bag, 'doggie ,bag *n* a bag for carrying home leftover food from a meal eaten in a restaurant [[2]*doggy*; fr the giving of such food to a pet dog]

'dog,house /-,hows/ *n, chiefly NAm* a dog kennel – **in the doghouse** in a state of disfavour – infml

,dog in the 'manger *n* a person who selfishly deprives others of sthg of no use to him-/herself [fr the fable of the dog who prevented an ox from eating hay which he himself did not want]

'dog ,Latin *n* spurious or incorrect Latin

[1]'dog,leg /-,leg/ *n* **1** a sharp bend (e g in a road) **2** an angled fairway on a golf course

[2]dogleg *adj* bent like a dog's hind leg

dogma /'dogmə/ *n* **1** an authoritative tenet or principle **2** a doctrine or body of doctrines formally and authoritatively stated by a church **3** a point of view or tenet put forth as authoritative without adequate grounds – chiefly derog [L *dogmat-, dogma*, fr Gk, fr *dokein* to seem – more at DECENT]

dogmatic /dog'matik/ *also* **dogmatical** /-kl/ *adj* **1** of dogma or dogmatics **2** characterized by or given to the use of dogmatism – chiefly derog – **dogmatically** *adv*, **dogmaticalness** *n*

dog'matics *n pl but sing or pl in constr* a branch of theology that seeks to interpret the dogmas of a religious faith

dogmatism /'dogmə,tiz(ə)m/ *n* (unwarranted or arrogant) assertion of opinion – **dogmatist** *n*

dogmat·ize, -ise /'dogmə,tiez/ *vi* to speak or write dogmatically ~ *vt* to state as a dogma or in a dogmatic manner [F *dogmatiser*, fr LL *dogmatizare*, fr Gk *dogmatizein*, fr *dogmat-, dogma*] – **dogmatization** /-'zaysh(ə)n/ *n*, **dogmatizer** *n*

do-gooder /,dooh 'goodə/ *n* an earnest often naive and ineffectual humanitarian or reformer

'dog ,paddle *n* an elementary form of swimming (e g for learners) in which the arms paddle and the legs kick – **dog-paddle** *vi*

'dog ,rose *n* a common European wild rose [trans of NL *rosa canina*]

'dogs,body /-,bodi/ *n, chiefly Br* a person who carries out routine or menial work – infml [Br naval slang *dogsbody* (pudding made of peas, junior officer)]

'dog's ,chance *n* any chance at all ⟨*didn't have a* ~⟩ – infml

'dog's ,life *n* a miserable drab existence – infml

,dog's 'mercury *n* a perennial woodland plant of the spurge family

,dogstooth 'check /'dogz,toohth/ *n* HOUNDSTOOTH CHECK

'dog-,tag *n, NAm* an identification disc for military personnel – infml

,dog-'tired *n* extremely tired – infml

'dog,tooth /-,toohth/ *n* an Early English moulding or architectural ornamentation consisting of a series of 4 leaves radiating from a raised centre ☞ ARCHITECTURE

dog violet *n* either of 2 European wild violets [trans of NL *viola canina*]

'dog,watch /-,woch/ *n* either of 2 watches (4 to 6 and 6 to 8 pm) on a ship

'dog,wood /-,wood/ *n* any of several trees and shrubs with heads of small flowers

doh /doh/ *n* ³DO

doily, doyley, doyly /'doyli/ *n* a small decorative mat, esp of paper, cloth, or plastic openwork, often placed under food, esp cakes, on a plate or stand [*Doily* or *Doyley fl* 1712 London draper]

do in *vt* **1** to kill ⟨*tried to* do *him* in *with a club*⟩ **2** to wear out, exhaust ⟨*walking all day nearly* did *us* in⟩ *USE* infml

doing /'dooh·ing/ *n* **1** the act or result of performing; action ⟨*this must be your* ~⟩ **2** effort, exertion ⟨*that will take a great deal of* ~⟩ **3** *pl* things that are done or that occur; activities [ME, fr gerund of *don* to do]

doings /'dooh·ings/ *n, pl* **doings** *also* **doingses** /-ziz/, *chiefly Br* a small object, esp one whose name is forgotten or not known ⟨*screw up that little* ~ *on the top*⟩ – infml

,do-it-your'self *adj* of or designed for use by an amateur, esp an amateur handyman – **do-it-yourselfer** *n*

dojo /'doh,joh/ *n, pl* **dojos** a school for training in various martial arts [Jap *dōjō*, fr *dō* way, art + *-jō* ground]

dolce far niente /,dolchi fah 'nyenti/ *n* carefree idleness [It, lit., sweet doing nothing]

,dolce 'vita /'veetah/ *n* a life of indolence and self-indulgence [It, lit., sweet life]

doldrums /'doldrəmz/ *n pl* **1** a depressed state of mind; *the* blues **2** an equatorial ocean region where calms, squalls, and light shifting winds prevail **3** a state of stagnation or slump [prob akin to OE *dol* foolish]

dole /dohl/ *n* **1** a distribution of food, money, or clothing to the needy **2** *the* government unemployment benefit [ME, fr OE *dāl* portion; akin to OE *dæl* part, lot]

doleful /'dohlf(ə)l/ *adj* sad, mournful [ME *dolful, doelful*, fr *dol, doel* grief, sorrow (fr OF, fr LL *dolus* pain, grief, alter. of L *dolor*) + *-ful*] – **dolefully** *adv*, **dolefulness** *n*

dole out *vt* to give, distribute, or deliver, esp in small portions

dolerite /'doləriet/ *n* any of various dark igneous rocks, esp coarse basalts [F *dolérite*, fr Gk *doleros* deceitful, fr *dolos* deceit – more at TALE; fr its being easily mistaken for diorite] – **doleritic** /-'ritik/ *adj*

dolich- /dolik-/, **dolicho-** *comb form* long ⟨dolicho*cranic*⟩ [Gk, fr *dolichos* – more at ¹LONG]

dolichocephalic /,dolikohsi'falik/ *adj* having a relatively long head [NL *dolichocephalus* dolichocephalic person, fr *dolich-* + *-cephalus* (fr Gk *kephalē* head) – more at CEPHALIC] – **dolichocephalism** /-'sefə,liz(ə)m/ *n*, **dolichocephaly** /-'sefəli/ *n*

doll /dol/ *n* **1** a small-scale figure of a human being used esp as a child's toy **2a** a (pretty but often silly) young woman – infml **b** an attractive person – slang [prob fr *Doll*, nickname for *Dorothy*] – **dollish** *adj*, **dollishly** *adv*

dollar /'dolə/ *n* **1** a taler **2** (a coin or note representing) the basic money unit of the USA, Canada, Australia, etc ☞ NATIONALITY **3** *Br* 5 shillings (25p) – slang; no longer in vogue [D or LG *daler*, fr G *taler*, short for *joachimstaler*, fr Sankt *Joachimsthal*, town in Bohemia where talers were first minted]

dollar diplomacy *n* diplomacy used by a country to promote its financial or commercial interests abroad and hence to strengthen its power

¹dollop /'doləp/ *n* a soft shapeless blob; *esp* a serving of mushy or semiliquid food ⟨*a* ~ *of mashed potato*⟩ [perh of Scand origin; akin to Norw dial. *dolp* lump]

²dollop *vt* to serve *out* carelessly or clumsily

'doll's ,house *n* a child's small-scale toy house

doll up *vt* to dress prettily or showily – infml

¹dolly /'doli/ *n* **1** DOLL 1 – used chiefly by or to children **2** a wooden-pronged instrument for beating and stirring clothes while washing them in a tub **3a** a platform on a roller or on wheels or castors for moving heavy objects **b** a wheeled platform for a film or television camera

²dolly *vi* to move a film or television camera on a dolly towards or away from a subject – usu + *in* or *out*

'dolly ,bird *n, chiefly Br* a pretty young woman, esp one who is a slavish follower of fashion and not regarded as intelligent

dolma /ˈdohlmə, -mah/ *n, pl* **dolmas, dolmades** /dohlˈmahdiz/ a vine leaf or cabbage leaf stuffed with a savoury filling [*dolma* fr Turk, lit., something stuffed, fr *dolma* stuffed; *dolmades* fr NGk, pl of *dolmas*, fr Turk *dolma*]

dolman sleeve /ˈdolmən/ *n* a sleeve very wide at the armhole and usu tight at the wrist often cut in one piece with the bodice [*dolman* (woman's coat with wide sleeves), fr F *doliman*, fr Turk *dolama* long robe with sleeves]

dolmen /ˈdolmən/ *n* a prehistoric monument consisting of 2 or more upright stones supporting a horizontal slab [F, fr Bret *tolmen*, fr *tol* table (fr L *tabula* board, plank) + *men* stone]

dolomite /ˈdoləmiet/ *n* calcium magnesium carbonate occurring as a mineral and a limestone rock [F, fr Déodat de *Dolomieu* †1801 F geologist] – **dolomitic** /-ˈmitik/ *adj*

dolorous /ˈdolərəs/ *adj* causing or expressing misery or grief – **dolorously** *adv*, **dolorousness** *n*

dolour, *NAm chiefly* **dolor** /ˈdohlə/ *n* mental suffering or anguish [ME *dolour*, fr MF, fr L *dolor* pain, grief, fr *dolēre* to feel pain, grieve – more at CONDOLE]

dolphin /ˈdolfin/ *n* **1** any of various small toothed whales with the snout elongated into a beak to varying extents **2** a spar or buoy for mooring boats [ME, fr MF *dophin, daufin*, fr OF *dalfin*, fr OProv, fr ML *dalfinus*, alter. of L *delphinus*, fr Gk *delphin-, delphis*; akin to Gk *delphys* womb, Skt *garbha*]

dolt /dohlt/ *n* an extremely dull or stupid person [prob akin to OE *dol* foolish] – **doltish** *adj*, **doltishly** *adv*, **doltishness** *n*

Dom /dom/ *n* **1** – used as a title for Benedictine, Carthusian, and Cistercian monks and some canons regular **2** – used formerly as a title preceding the Christian name of a Portuguese or Brazilian man of rank [L *dominus* master]

-dom /-d(ə)m/ *suffix* (→ *n*) **1a** rank or office of ⟨*duke*dom⟩ **b** realm or jurisdiction of ⟨*king*dom⟩ ⟨*Christen*dom⟩ **2** state or fact of being ⟨*free*dom⟩ ⟨*bore*dom⟩ **3** group or class of people having (a specified office, occupation, interest, or character) ⟨*official*dom⟩ ⟨*film*dom⟩ [ME, fr OE *-dōm*; akin to OHG *-tuom* -dom, OE *dōm* judgment – more at DOOM]

domain /dəˈmayn/ *n* **1** a territory over which control is exercised **2** a sphere of influence or activity **3** the set of values to which a variable is limited; *esp* the set of values that the independent variable of a function may take on **4** any of the small randomly oriented regions of uniform magnetization in a ferromagnetic substance [MF *domaine, demaine*, fr L *dominium*, fr *dominus* master, owner]

[1]**dome** /dohm/ *n* **1** a (nearly) hemispherical roof or vault **2** a dome-shaped (geological) structure **3** *archaic* a stately building; a mansion [F, It, & L; F *dôme* dome, cathedral, fr It *duomo* cathedral, fr ML *domus* church, fr L, house – more at TIMBER] – **domal** /ˈdohm(ə)l/ *adj*

[2]**dome** *vt* to cover with or form into a dome

ˈ**Domesday** ˌ**Book** /ˈdoohmzˌday, -di/ *n* a record of a survey of English lands made by order of William I about 1086 [ME, fr *domesday* doomsday]

[1]**domestic** /dəˈmestik/ *adj* **1** of or devoted to the home or the family **2** of one's own or some particular country; not foreign ⟨~ *politics*⟩ **3a** living near or about the habitations of human beings **b** tame; *also* bred by human beings for some specific purpose (e g food, hunting, etc) [MF *domestique*, fr L *domesticus*, fr *domus*] – **domestically** *adv*

[2]**domestic** *n* a household servant

domesticate /dəˈmestikayt/ *vt* **1** to bring (an animal or species) under human control for some specific purpose (e g for carrying loads, hunting, food, etc) **2** to cause to be fond of or adapted to household duties or pleasures – **domestication** /-ˈkaysh(ə)n/

domestic fowl *n* a chicken, turkey, or other bird developed from the jungle fowl, esp for meat or egg production

domesticity /ˌdomeˈstisəti/ *n* (devotion to) home or family life

doˌmestic ˈscience *n* instruction in the household arts

[1]**domicile** /ˈdomisiel/ *also* **domicil** /-s(i)l/ *n* a home; *esp* a person's permanent and principal home for legal purposes [MF, fr L *domicilium*, fr *domus*]

[2]**domicile** *vt* to establish in or provide with a domicile

domiciliary /ˌdomiˈsilyəri/ *adj* **1** of or being a domicile **2** taking place or attending in the home ⟨~ *visit*⟩

[1]**dominant** /ˈdominənt/ *adj* **1** commanding, controlling, or prevailing over all others **2** overlooking and commanding from a superior height **3** being the one of a pair of bodily structures that is the more effective or predominant in action ⟨*the* ~ *eye*⟩ **4** being the one of a pair of (genes determining) contrasting inherited characteristics that predominates – compare RECESSIVE 2 [MF or L; MF, fr L *dominant-, dominans*, prp of *dominari* to rule, govern] – **dominance** /-nəns/ *n*, **dominantly** *adv*

[2]**dominant** *n* **1** a socially dominant individual **2** the fifth note of a diatonic scale

dominate /ˈdominayt/ *vt* **1** to exert controlling influence or power over **2** to overlook from a superior height **3** to occupy a commanding or preeminent position in ~ *vi* **1** to have or exert mastery or control **2** to occupy a higher or superior position [L *dominatus*, pp of *dominari*, fr *dominus* master – more at DAME] **dominator** *n*, **dominative** /ˈdominətiv/ *adj*, **domination** /-ˈnaysh(ə)n/ *n*

domineer /ˌdomiˈniə/ *vi vi* to exercise arbitrary or overbearing control ⟨*a* ~ing *husband*⟩ [D *domineren*, fr F *dominer*, fr L *dominari*] – **domineeringly** *adv*

dominical /dəˈminikl/ *adj* **1** of Jesus Christ **2** of the Lord's day [LL *dominicalis*, fr *dominicus* (*dies*) the Lord's day, fr L *dominicus* of a lord, fr *dominus* lord, master]

Dominican /dəˈminikən/ *n or adj* (a member) of a preaching order of mendicant friars founded by St Dominic in 1215 [St *Dominic* (Domingo de Guzman) †1221 Sp priest]

dominie /ˈdomini/ *n, chiefly Scot* a teacher, schoolmaster [L *domine*, voc of *dominus*]

dominion /dəˈminyən, -ni·ən/ *n* **1** the power or right to rule; sovereignty **2** absolute ownership **3** *often cap* a self-governing nation of the Commonwealth other than the United Kingdom [ME *dominioun*, fr MF *dominion*, modif of L *dominium*, fr *dominus*]

Doˈminion ˌ**Day** *n* July 1 observed as a public holiday in Canada marking the grant of dominion status in 1867

domino /ˈdominoh/ *n, pl* **dominoes, dominos 1a(1)**

a long loose hooded cloak worn with a mask as a masquerade costume **(2)** a half mask worn with a masquerade costume **b** sby wearing a domino **2a** a flat rectangular block whose face is divided into 2 equal parts that are blank or bear from 1 to usu 6 dots arranged as on dice faces **b** *pl but usu sing in constr* any of several games played with a set of usu 28 dominoes [F, prob fr L *domino* (in the ritual formula *benedicamus Domino* let us bless the Lord), dat of *dominus*]

'domino ˌtheory *n* a theory that if one nation in an area, specif SE Asia, becomes Communist-controlled the same thing will happen to the neighbouring nations [fr the fact that if several dominoes are stood on end one behind the other with slight spaces between, a push on the first will make all the others topple]

dompass /'domˌpahs/ *n* an identity document that must be carried by nonwhites in S Africa – compare PASS LAW [Afrik *dompas*, fr *dom* stupid + *pas* pass]

[1]**don** /don/ *n* **1** a Spanish nobleman or gentleman – used as a title preceding the Christian name **2** a head, tutor, or fellow in a college of Oxford or Cambridge university; *broadly* a university teacher [Sp, fr L *dominus* master – more at DAME]

[2]**don** *vt* **-nn-** PUT ON 1a, b [contr of *do* + *on*]

dona /'donə/ *n* a Portuguese or Brazilian woman of rank – formerly used as a title preceding the Christian name [Pg, fr L *domina*]

doña /'donyə/ *n* a Spanish woman, esp of rank – used as a title preceding the Christian name [Sp, fr L *domina* lady]

donate /doh'nayt/ *vb* **1** to make a gift or donation (of), esp to a public or charitable cause **2** to give off or transfer (e g electrons) [back-formation fr *donation*] – **donator** *n*

donation /doh'naysh(ə)n/ *n* **1** the act of donating **2** sthg donated [ME *donatyowne*, fr L *donation-*, *donatio*, fr *donatus*, pp of *donare* to present, fr *donum* gift; akin to L *dare* to give – more at [2]DATE]

[1]**donative** /'dohnətiv/ *n* a special gift or donation

[2]**donative** *adj* subject to donation ⟨*a ~ trust*⟩ [L *donativus*, fr *donatus*]

[1]**done** /dun/ **1** *past part of* DO **2** *chiefly dial & NAm past of* DO

[2]**done** *adj* **1** conformable to social convention ⟨*it's not ~ to eat peas off your knife*⟩ **2** arrived at or brought to an end; completed **3** physically exhausted; spent **4** no longer involved; through ⟨*I'm ~ with the Army*⟩ **5** doomed to failure, defeat, or death **6** cooked sufficiently **7** arrested, imprisoned – slang ⟨*robbed a bank and got ~ for 10 years*⟩

[3]**done** *interj* – used in acceptance of a bet or transaction

'done ˌfor *adj* **1** dead or close to death **2** ruined, finished *USE* infml

Donegal /ˌdoni'gawl/, **Donegal tweed** *n* a heavy woollen fabric characterized by colourful flecks in the weft yarn [*Donegal* county, Eire]

ˌdone 'in *adj* physically exhausted – infml

[1]**dong** /dong/ *n* a penis – slang [*dong* (to sound like a bell, strike), of imit origin]

[2]**dong** /dong/ *n* ☞ *Vietnam* at NATIONALITY [Annamese]

donga /'dong·gə/ *n, SAfr* a narrow steep-sided ravine [Afrik, fr Zulu]

donjon /'dunj(ə)n, 'don-/ *n* a massive inner tower in a medieval castle ☞ CHURCH [ME – more at DUNGEON]

Don Juan /don 'jooh·ən, (*Sp* don Xwan)/ *n* a promiscuous man; *broadly* a lady-killer [*Don Juan*, legendary Spanish nobleman featured in many works of literature]

donkey /'dongki/ *n* **1** the domestic ass **2** a stupid or obstinate person [perh fr [1]*dun* + *-key* (as in *monkey*)]

'donkey ˌengine *n* a small, usu portable, auxiliary engine

'donkey ˌjacket *n* a thick hip-length hard-wearing jacket, usu blue and with a strip of (imitation) leather across the shoulders ☞ GARMENT

'donkey's ˌyears *n pl, chiefly Br* a very long time – infml

'donkeyˌwork /-ˌwuhk/ *n* hard, monotonous, and routine work – infml

donna /'donə/ *n, pl* **donne** /'donay/ an Italian woman, esp of rank – used as a title preceding the Christian name [It, fr L *domina*]

donnée /'donay/ *n, pl* **données** /-nayz/ a basic fact or assumption on which a work of fiction or drama proceeds [F, fr fem of *donné*, pp of *donner* to give, fr L *donare* to donate]

donnish /'donish/ *adj* pedantic [[1]DON + -ISH] – **donnishly** *adv*, **donnishness** *n*

donor /'dohnə/ *n* **1** a person who gives, donates, or presents **2** sby used as a source of biological material ⟨*a blood ~*⟩ **3a** a compound capable of giving up a part (e g an atom, radical, or elementary particle) for combination with an acceptor **b** an impurity that is added to a semiconductor to increase the number of mobile electrons [MF *doneur*, fr L *donator*, fr *donatus*, pp of *donare*]

[1]**don't** /dohnt/ **1** do not **2** does not – nonstandard, though sometimes used by educated speakers ⟨*there are simply certain things he ~ know* – Ezra Pound⟩

[2]**don't** *n* a prohibition – usu pl ⟨*a list of dos and ~s*⟩

doodad /'doohˌdad/ *n, chiefly NAm* a small, trivial, or decorative article – infml [origin unknown]

doodah /'doohˌdah/ *n, Br* a small article whose name is unknown or forgotten – infml [origin unknown]

doodle /'doohdl/ *vi or n* **doodling** /'doohdling, 'doohdl·ing/ (to make) an aimless scribble or sketch [perh fr *doodle* (simpleton), fr LG *dudeltopf*] – **doodler** /'doohdlə/ *n*

'doodleˌbug /-ˌbug/ *n* FLYING BOMB – infml [prob fr *doodle* (fool) + *bug*]

doolan /'doohlən/ *n, often cap, NZ* ROMAN CATHOLIC [prob fr *Doolan*, a common Irish surname]

[1]**doom** /doohm/ *n* **1** a law in Anglo-Saxon England **2a** JUDGMENT 2a; *also, archaic* a judicial condemnation **b** JUDGMENT DAY **3a** an (unhappy) destiny **b** unavoidable death or destruction; *also* environmental catastrophe – often in combination ⟨*The road forward does not lie through the despair of* doom-*watching* *B – New Scientist*⟩ [ME, fr OE *dōm*; akin to OHG *tuom* condition, state, OE *dōn* to do]

[2]**doom** *vt* **1** to destine, esp to failure or destruction **2** *archaic* to give judgment against; condemn

doomsday /'doohmzˌday, -di/ *n, often cap* JUDGMENT DAY; *broadly* some remote point in the future

⟨*if you expect people to work harder for less money, you'll have to wait from now till* ~⟩

door /daw/ *n* **1** a usu swinging or sliding barrier by which an entry is closed and opened; *also* a similar part of a piece of furniture ☞ ARCHITECTURE **2** a doorway **3** a means of access [ME *dure, dor,* fr OE *duru* door & *dor* gate; akin to OHG *turi* door, L *fores,* Gk *thyra*] – **doorless** *adj* – **at someone's door** as a charge against sby as being responsible ⟨*laid the blame* at our door⟩

ˈ**door,frame** /-,fraym/ *n* **1** a frame round the opening in which a door is fitted **2** the framework in which the panels of a door are fitted

ˈ**door,keeper** /-,keepə/ *n* a person who guards the main door to a building and lets people in and out

ˈ**door,knob** /-,nob/ *n* a knob that when turned releases a door latch

ˈ**doorman** /-mən/ *n* a (uniformed) person who tends the entrance to a hotel, theatre, etc and assists people (e g in calling taxis)

ˈ**door,mat** /-,mat/ *n* **1** a mat (e g of bristles) placed before or inside a door for wiping dirt from the shoes **2** a person who submits to bullying and indignities – infml

ˈ**door,nail** /-,nayl/ *n* a large-headed nail formerly used for the strengthening or decoration of doors – chiefly in *dead as a doornail*

ˈ**door,post** /-,pohst/ *n* an upright piece forming the side of a door opening

ˈ**door,step** /-,step/ *n* **1** a step in front of an outer door **2** *Br* a very thick slice of bread – infml

ˈ**door,stop** /-,stop/ *n* a device for holding a door open or preventing it opening too far

[1],**door-to-ˈdoor** *adj* **1** making a usu unsolicited call (e g for selling, canvassing, etc) at every residence in an area **2** providing delivery to a specified address

[2]**door-to-door** *adv* from the precise point of departure to the final point of arrival ⟨*a journey of 2 hours* ~⟩

ˈ**door,way** /-,way/ *n* an entrance into a building or room that is closed by means of a door

do over *vt, Br* to attack and injure – slang

dopa /ˈdopə/ *n* a derivative of phenylalanine; *esp* l-dopa [*d*ihydroxy*p*henyl*a*lanine]

dopamine /ˈdopə,meen/ *n* a derivative of dopa that occurs esp as a neurotransmitter in the brain [*dopa* + *amine*]

dopant /ˈdohp(ə)nt/ *n* an impurity added, usu in minute amounts, to a pure substance to alter its properties [[2]*dope*]

[1]**dope** /dohp/ *n* **1a** a thick liquid or pasty preparation **b** a preparation for giving a desired quality to a substance or surface **c** a coating (e g a cellulose varnish) applied to a surface or fabric (e g of an aeroplane or balloon) to improve strength, impermeability, or tautness **2** absorbent or adsorbent material used in various manufacturing processes (e g the making of dynamite) **3a** marijuana, opium, or another drug **b** a preparation given illegally to a racing horse, greyhound, etc to make it run faster or slower **4** a stupid person – infml **5** information, esp from a reliable source – infml [D *doop* sauce, fr *dopen* to dip; akin to OE *dyppan* to dip – more at DIP]

[2]**dope** *vt* **1** to treat or affect with dope; *esp* to give a narcotic to **2** to add an impurity to (a semiconductor) so as to give the required electrical properties ~ *vi* to take dope – **doper** *n*

dopey, dopy /ˈdohpi/ *adj* **1a** dulled by alcohol or a narcotic **b** stupefied (e g by a drug or sleep) **2** dull, stupid – infml – **dopiness** *n*

doppelgänger /ˈdopl,gengə/, **doppelganger** /-,gangə/ *n* a ghostly counterpart of a living person [G *doppelgänger,* fr *doppel-* double + *-gänger* goer]

Doppler /ˈdoplə/ *adj* of or using a shift in frequency in accordance with the Doppler effect

ˈ**Doppler ef,fect** *n* a change in the apparent frequency of sound, light, or other waves when there is relative motion between the source and the observer [Christian *Doppler* †1853 Austrian scientist & mathematician]

Dorian /ˈdawri·ən/ *n or adj* (a member) of an ancient Hellenic race settled chiefly in the Peloponnesus and Crete [L *dorius* of Doris, fr Gk *dōrios,* fr *Dōris,* region of ancient Greece]

[1]**Doric** /ˈdorik/ *adj* **1** (characteristic) of the Dorians or their language **2** of the oldest and simplest of the 3 Greek orders of architecture ☞ ARCHITECTURE

[2]**Doric** *n* **1** a dialect of ancient Greek **2** a broad rustic dialect of English, esp a Scots one

dorm /dawm/ *n* DORMITORY 1 – infml

dormant /ˈdawmənt/ *adj* **1** marked by a suspension of activity: e g **a** temporarily devoid of external activity ⟨*a* ~ *volcano*⟩ **b** temporarily in abeyance ⟨*the report lay* ~ *for several years until its suggestions were taken up by a new administration*⟩ **2** (appearing to be) asleep or inactive, esp throughout winter [ME *dormaunt* fixed, stationary, fr MF *dormant,* fr prp of *dormir* to sleep, fr L *dormire*; akin to Skt *drāti* he sleeps] – **dormancy** /-mənsi/ *n*

dormer /ˈdawmə/ *n* a window set vertically in a structure projecting through a sloping roof ☞ ARCHITECTURE [MF *dormeor* dormitory, fr L *dormitorium*]

dormie, dormy /ˈdawmi/ *adj* being ahead by as many holes in golf as remain to be played [origin unknown]

dormitory /ˈdawmət(ə)ri/ *n* **1** a large room containing a number of beds **2** a residential community from which the inhabitants commute to their places of employment ⟨*a* ~ *town*⟩ [L *dormitorium,* fr *dormitus,* pp of *dormire* to sleep]

Dormobile /ˈdawmə,beel/ *trademark* – used for a small motorized caravan

dormouse /ˈdaw,mows/ *n* any of numerous small Old World rodents having a long bushy tail [ME *dormowse,* perh fr MF *dormir* + ME *mous* mouse]

dorp /dawp/ *n, SAfr* a village [D, fr MD; akin to OHG *dorf* village]

dors- /daws-/, **dorsi-, dorso-** *comb form* **1** back ⟨dors*ad*⟩ **2** dorsal and ⟨dorso*lateral*⟩ [LL *dors-,* fr L *dorsum*]

dorsal /ˈdawsl/ *adj* relating to or situated near or on the back or top surface esp of an animal or aircraft or of any of its parts – compare VENTRAL 1b [LL *dorsalis,* fr L *dorsum* back] – **dorsally** *adv*

dorsal fin *n* a medium longitudinal vertical fin on the back of a fish or other aquatic vertebrate

[1]**dory** /ˈdawri/ *n* a flat-bottomed boat with high flaring sides [Miskito *dóri* dugout]

[2]**dory** *n* JOHN DORY

dos-à-dos /,doh za ˈdoh/ *n* a seat (e g in a carriage) designed for sitting back to back – compare TÊTE-À-TÊTE 2 [F, fr *dos-à-dos* back to back]

dosage /'dohsij/ *n* **1a** the amount of a dose of medicine **b** the giving of such a dose **2** the presence and relative representation or strength of a factor or agent

dose /dohs/ *n* **1a** the measured quantity of medicine to be taken at one time **b** the quantity of radiation administered or absorbed **2** a part of an experience to which one is exposed ⟨*a ~ of hard work*⟩ **3** an infection with a venereal disease – slang – **dose** *vt* [F, fr LL *dosis*, fr Gk, lit., act of giving, fr *didonai* to give – more at DATE]

[2]**dose** *vt* to give a dose, esp of medicine, to

dosimeter /doh'simitə/ *n* a device for measuring doses of X rays or of radioactivity [LL *dosis* + ISV *-meter*] – **dosimetric** /,dohsə'metrik/ *adj*, **dosimetry** /-'simətri/ *n*

doss /dos/ *n, chiefly Br* **1** a crude or makeshift bed, esp one in a dosshouse **2** a short sleep *USE* slang [perh fr obs *dorse, doss* (back), fr L *dorsum*]

doss down *vi, chiefly Br* to sleep or bed down in a makeshift bed – infml

dosser /'dosə/ *n, chiefly Br* a down-and-out, esp one who is forced to sleep in dosshouses

'doss,house /-,hows/ *n, chiefly Br* a hostel for derelicts

dossier /'dosi·ə, 'dosiay/ *n* a file of papers containing a detailed report or information [F, bundle of documents labelled on the back, dossier, fr *dos* back, fr L *dorsum*]

dost /dust/ *archaic pres 2 sing of* DO

[1]**dot** /dot/ *n* **1** a small spot; a speck **2a(1)** a small point made with a pointed instrument **(2)** a small round mark used in spelling or punctuation **b(1)** a point after a note or rest in music indicating augmentation of the time value by one half **(2)** a point over or under a note indicating that it is to be played staccato **3** a precise point, esp in time ⟨*arrived at 6 on the ~*⟩ **4** a signal (e g a flash or audible tone) of relatively short duration that is one of the 2 fundamental units of Morse code – compare [2]DASH 6 *USE (2b)* ☞ MUSIC [(assumed) ME, fr OE *dott* head of a boil; akin to OHG *tutta* nipple, D *dot* knot, tuft]

[2]**dot** *vb* **-tt-** *vt* **1** to mark with a dot **2** to intersperse with dots or objects scattered at random ⟨*boats ~ting the lake*⟩ ~ *vi* to make a dot

dotage /'dohtij/ *n* a state or period of senile mental decay resulting in feeblemindedness [ME, fr *doten* to dote]

dotard /'dohtəd/ *n* a person in his/her dotage

dote /doht/ *vi* **1** to exhibit mental decline of or like that of old age **2** to show excessive or foolish fondness – usu + *on* [ME *doten*; akin to MLG *dotten* to be foolish, MD *dutten* to be enraged, Icel *dotta* to nod from fatigue] – **doter** *n*, **dotingly** *adv*

doth /duth/ *archaic pres 3 sing of* DO

'dot ,product *n* SCALAR PRODUCT [[1]*dot*; fr its being commonly written $A \cdot B$]

dotterel /'dotrəl/ *n* a Eurasian plover formerly common in Britain [ME *dotrelle*, irreg fr *doten* to dote]

dottle /'dotl/ *n* (partially) unburnt tobacco left in the bowl of a pipe [ME *dottel* plug, fr (assumed) ME *dot*]

dotty /'doti/ *adj* **1** crazy, mad **2** amiably eccentric or absurd *USE* infml [alter. of Sc *dottle* fool, fr ME *dotel*, fr *doten*] – **dottily** *adv*, **dottiness** *n*

'Douay ,Version /'dooh,ay/ *n* an English 17th-c translation of the Vulgate used by Roman Catholics [*Douay, Douai*, city in France]

[1]**double** /'dubl/ *adj* **1** twofold, dual **2** consisting of 2, usu combined, similar members or parts ⟨*an egg with a ~ yolk*⟩ **3** being twice as great or as many ⟨*~ the number of expected applicants*⟩ **4** marked by duplicity; deceitful **5** folded in 2 **6** of twofold or extra size, strength, or value ⟨*a ~ Scotch*⟩ ⟨*a ~ room*⟩ **7** *of a plant or flower* having more than the normal number of petals or ray flowers – compare SINGLE [ME, fr OF, fr L *duplus*, fr *duo* two + *-plus* multiplied by; akin to Gk *diploos* double, OE *fealdan* to fold – more at TWO, [3]FOLD] – **doubleness** *n*

[2]**double** *n* **1** a double amount; *esp* a double measure of spirits **2a** a living person who closely resembles another living person **b** a wraith; a doppelgänger **c(1)** an understudy **(2)** one who resembles an actor and takes his/her place in scenes calling for special skills **3** a sharp turn or twist **4a** a bet in which the winnings and stake from a first race are bet on a second race **b** two wins in or on horse races, esp in a single day's racing **5** an act of doubling in a card game **6** the outermost narrow ring on a dartboard counting double the stated score; *also* a throw in darts that lands there – **at the double** at a fast rate between running and walking; *specif, of a military order to move* in double time

[3]**double** *adv* **1** to twice the extent or amount **2** two together

[4]**double** *vb* **doubled; doubling** /'dubling, 'dubl·ing/ *vt* **1a** to increase by adding an equal amount **b** to amount to twice the number of **c** to make a call in bridge that increases the value of tricks won or lost on (an opponent's bid) **2a** to make into 2 thicknesses; fold **b** to clench ⟨*~d his fist*⟩ **c** to cause to stoop or bend over – usu + *up* or *over* **3** to cause (troops) to move in double time **4** to cause (a billiard ball) to rebound ~ *vi* **1a** to become twice as much or as many **b** to double a bid (e g in bridge) **2** to turn back on one's course – usu + *back* **3** to become bent or folded, usu in the middle – usu + *up* or *over* **4** to serve an additional purpose – usu + *as* **5** to hurry along; *esp, of troops* to move in double time **6** *of a billiard ball* to rebound

,double-'acting *adj* acting or effective in 2 directions or ways; *esp, of an engine* being a reciprocating engine in which the working fluid (e g steam) acts on both sides of the piston

double agent *n* a spy pretending to serve one government while actually serving another

double bar *n* two adjacent vertical lines or a heavy single line marking the end of a principal section of a musical composition ☞ MUSIC

,double-'barrelled *adj* **1** *of a firearm* having 2 barrels **2** having a double purpose ⟨*asked a ~ question*⟩ **3** *of a surname* having 2 parts

,double 'bass *n* the largest instrument in the violin family tuned a fifth below the cello – **double bassist** *n*

,double 'bed *n* a bed for 2 people

,double 'bind *n* (a psychological dilemma provoked by) a situation in which a person receives conflicting cues as to his/her desired behaviour towards another, usu a parent or other family member, so that anything he/she does will be condemned; *broadly* a situation where any choice a person makes will have unpleasant consequences

,double-'blind *adj* of or being an experimental procedure which is designed to eliminate false results, in which neither the subjects nor the experimenters know the make-up of the test groups and control groups during the actual course of the experiments – compare SINGLE-BLIND

ˌdouble ˈboiler *n, chiefly NAm* DOUBLE SAUCEPAN

double bond *n* a chemical bond consisting of 2 covalent bonds between 2 atoms in a molecule

ˌdouble-ˈbreasted *adj* having a front fastening with one half of the front overlapping the other and usu a double row of buttons and a single row of buttonholes ⟨*a ~ coat*⟩ – compare SINGLE-BREASTED ☞ GARMENT

double bridle *n* a bridle consisting of 2 bits that work independently and used esp for show horses

double check *vb or n* (to make or subject to) a careful check, esp for a second time

ˌdouble ˈchin *n* a chin with a fleshy fold under it

ˌdouble ˈcream *n* thick heavy cream that contains 48 per cent butterfat and is suitable for whipping – compare SINGLE CREAM

ˌdouble-ˈcross *vt or n* (to deceive by) an act of betraying or cheating – **double-crosser** *n*

ˌdouble ˈdagger *n* a sign ≠ used as the third in the series of reference marks ☞ SYMBOL

ˌdouble-ˈdealing *adj or n* underhand or deceitful (action) – **doub le-dealer** *n*

ˌdouble-ˈdecker /ˈdekə/ *n* sthg that has 2 decks, levels, or layers; *esp* a bus with seats on 2 floors

ˌdouble deˈclutch /deeˈkluch/ *vi, Br* to change gear in a motor vehicle by disengaging the gear twice, first to pass to neutral, then to pass to the desired gear

double decomposition *n* a chemical reaction in which different kinds of molecules exchange parts to form other kinds of molecules

ˌdouble ˈdutch *n, often cap 2nd D* unintelligible or nonsensical speech or writing; gibberish – infml

ˌdouble-ˈedged *adj* having 2 purposes or possible interpretations; *specif, of a remark* seeming innocent, but capable of a malicious interpretation

ˌdouble-ˈended *adj* similar at both ends ⟨*a ~ bolt*⟩

double entendre /ˌdoohbl onˈton(h)dr (*Fr* dubl ɑ̃tɑ̃ːdr)/ *n, pl* **double entendres** /~/ an ambiguous word or expression one of whose meanings is usu risqué [obs F, lit., double meaning]

ˌdouble-ˈfaced *adj* two-faced, hypocritical

double fault *n* two consecutive service faults in tennis, squash, etc, resulting in the loss of a point or of the service – **double-fault** *vi*

ˌdouble ˈfirst *n, Br* first-class honours gained in 2 university examinations or subjects

double flat *n* a character on the musical staff indicating a drop in pitch of 2 semitones ☞ MUSIC

ˌdouble ˈglazing *n* a system of glazing in which 2 panes of glass are separated by an air space providing heat and sound insulation; *also* the 2 panes of glass so used ☞ ENERGY – **double-glaze** *vt*

ˌdoubleˈheader /-ˈhedə/ *n, NAm* two games, contests, or events held consecutively on the same programme

ˌdouble ˈhelix *n* two parallel helices arranged round the same axis; *specif* this arrangement of 2 complementary DNA strands with the bases of each strand pointing inwards and hydrogen-bonding with those of the other, that is regarded as the basic structure of the DNA of most living things

ˌdouble-ˈjointed *adj* having or being a joint that permits an exceptional degree of flexibility of the parts joined

double knit *n* a knitted fabric (e g wool) made with a double set of needles to produce a double thickness of fabric with each thickness joined by interlocking stitches

ˌdouble ˈnegative *n* a syntactic construction containing 2 negatives and having a negative meaning ⟨*"I didn't hear nothing" is a ~*⟩

ˌdouble-ˈpark *vi* to park beside a row of vehicles already parked parallel to the kerb

ˌdouble-ˈquick *adj* very quick – **double-quick** *adv*

double reed *n* two cane reeds bound and vibrating against each other and used as the mouthpiece of woodwind instruments of the oboe family

double refraction *n* birefringence

doubles /ˈdublz/ *n, pl* **doubles** a game between 2 pairs of players

double salt *n* a salt regarded as a molecular combination of 2 simple salts

double saucepan *n, Br* two interlocking saucepans, the contents of the upper being cooked or heated by boiling water in the lower

double sharp *n* a character on the musical staff indicating a rise in pitch of 2 semitones ☞ MUSIC

ˈdoubleˌspeak /-ˌspeek/ *n* double-talk

double standard *n* a principle or code that applies more rigorously to one group than to another

double star *n* (2 stars that appear to be) a binary star

double stopping *n* the simultaneous playing of 2 strings of a bowed instrument (e g a violin)

doublet /ˈdublit/ *n* **1** a man's close-fitting jacket, with or without sleeves, worn in Europe, esp in the 15th to 17th c ☞ GARMENT **2** two thrown dice showing the same number on the upper face **3** either of a pair; *specif* either of 2 words (e g *guard* and *ward*) in a language having the same derivation but a different meaning [ME, fr MF, fr *double*]

ˈdouble ˌtake *n* a delayed reaction to a surprising or significant situation – esp in *do a double take*

ˈdouble-ˌtalk *n* involved and often deliberately ambiguous language – **double-talk** *vi*, **double-talker** *n*

ˈdoubleˌthink /-ˌthingk/ *n* a simultaneous belief in 2 contradictory ideas

ˌdouble ˈtime *n* **1** a rate of marching of twice the number of steps per minute as the normal slow rate **2** payment of a worker at twice his/her regular wage rate

ˌdouble-ˈtongue *vi* to use tongue movements to produce a fast succession of detached notes on a wind instrument

double twill *n* a twill weave with intersecting diagonal lines going in opposite directions

double up *vi* to share accommodation designed for one

ˌdouble ˈvision *n* diplopia

doubloon /dubˈloohn/ *n* a former gold coin of Spain and Spanish America [Sp *doblón*, aug of *dobla*, an old Spanish coin, fr L *dupla*, fem of *duplus* double – more at DOUBLE]

doubly /ˈdubli/ *adv* **1** to twice the degree ⟨*~ pleased*⟩ **2** in 2 ways

¹doubt /dowt/ *vt* **1** to be in doubt about ⟨*he ~s everyone's word*⟩ **2a** to lack confidence in; distrust

b to consider unlikely ~ *vi* to be uncertain [ME *douten* to fear, be uncertain, fr OF *douter* to doubt, fr L *dubitare*; akin to L *dubius* dubious – more at DUBIOUS] – **doubtable** *adj*, **doubter** *n*, **doubtingly** *adv*

[2]**doubt** *n* **1** (a state of) uncertainty of belief or opinion **2** a lack of confidence; distrust **3** an inclination not to believe or accept; a reservation – **in doubt** uncertain – **no doubt** doubtless

'**doubtful** /-f(ə)l/ *adj* **1** causing doubt; open to question **2a** lacking a definite opinion; hesitant **b** uncertain in outcome; not settled **3** of questionable worth, honesty, or validity – **doubtfully** *adv*, **doubtfulness** *n*

,**doubting 'Thomas** /'toməs/ *n* a habitually doubtful person [*Thomas*, apostle of Jesus who doubted Jesus' resurrection until he had proof of it (Jn 20:24-29)]

'**doubtless** /-lis/ *adv* **1** without doubt **2** probably

douce /doohs/ *adj, chiefly Scot* sober, sedate [ME, sweet, pleasant, fr MF, fr fem of *douz*, fr L *dulcis*] – **doucely** *adv*

douche /doohsh/ *n* (a device for giving) a jet or current of fluid, directed against a part or into a cavity of the body, esp the vagina [F, fr It *doccia*, fr *docciare* to douche, fr *doccia* water pipe, prob back-formation fr *doccione* conduit, fr L *duction-, ductio* action of leading, fr *ductus*, pp of *ducere* to lead – more at [1]TOW] – **douche** *vb*

dough /doh/ *n* **1** a mixture that consists essentially of flour or meal and milk, water, or another liquid and is stiff enough to knead or roll – compare BATTER **2** money – slang [ME *dogh*, fr OE *dāg*; akin to OHG *teic* dough, L *fingere* to shape, Gk *teichos* wall] – **doughlike** *adj*

doughboy /'doh,boy/ *n* a US infantryman, esp in WW I [*doughboy* (a dumpling or piece of fried bread dough); prob fr the large round buttons on the US infantry uniform in the Civil War]

doughnut /'doh,nut/ *n* **1** a small round or ring-shaped cake that is often made with a yeast dough, filled with jam, and deep-fried **2** sthg ring-shaped; *specif* TORUS 3

doughty /'dowti/ *adj* valiant, bold – poetic [ME, fr OE *dohtig*; akin to OHG *toug* is useful, Gk *teuchein* to make] – **doughtily** /'dowtili/ *adv*, **doughtiness** *n*

doughy /'doh·i/ *adj* unhealthily pale; pasty [DOUGH + [1]-Y]

,**Douglas 'fir** /'dugləs/ *n* a tall evergreen tree of the western USA that is extensively grown for its wood [David *Douglas* †1834 Sc botanist]

,**Douglas 'spruce** *n* DOUGLAS FIR

do up *vt* **1** to repair, restore ⟨do up *old furniture*⟩ **2** to wrap up ⟨do up *a parcel*⟩ **3** to fasten (clothing or its fastenings) together ⟨*she* did *her blouse* up⟩ **4** to make more beautiful or attractive ⟨*she's* done *herself* up *for the party*⟩ – infml

dour /dowə/ *adj* **1** stern, harsh **2** gloomy, sullen [ME, prob fr Gael *dur* dull, obstinate, perh fr L *durus* hard] – **dourly** *adv*, **dourness** *n*

douroucouli /,doohrooh'koohli/ *n* any of several nocturnal S American monkeys [native name in S America]

[1]**douse, dowse** /dows/ *vt* to take (a sail) in or down [*douse* (blow, stroke), of unknown origin]

[2]**douse, dowse** *vt* **1** to plunge into or drench with water **2** to extinguish ⟨~ *the lights*⟩ [prob fr obs *douse* (to smite), fr [1]*douse*; akin to LG *dossen* to strike] – **douser** *n*

[1]**dove** /duv/ *n* **1** any of various (smaller and slenderer) types of pigeon **2** an advocate of negotiation and compromise; *esp* an opponent of war – usu contrasted with *hawk* [ME, fr (assumed) OE *dūfe*; akin to OHG *tūba* dove, & prob to OE *dēaf* deaf] – **dovish** *adj*, **dovishness** *n*

[2]**dove** /dohv/ *NAm past of* DIVE

'**dove-,colour** /duv/ *n* slightly pink warm grey – **dove-coloured** *adj*

dovecot, dovecote /'duv,kot/ *n* a small compartmented raised house or box for domestic pigeons

dovekie /'duvki/ *n* a small auk that breeds on arctic coasts [dim. of *dove*]

,**Dover 'sole** /'dohvə/ *n* a European flatfish highly valued for food [prob fr *Dover*, town in England]

'**Dover's ,powder** *n* a powder of ipecacuanha and opium used, esp formerly, as medicine [Thomas *Dover* †1742 E physician]

[1]**dovetail** /'duv,tayl/ *n* a tenon like a dove's tail and the mortise into which it fits to form a joint

[2]**dovetail** *vb* **1** to join (as if) by means of dovetails **2** to fit skilfully together to form a whole

dowager /'dowəjə/ *n* **1** a widow holding property or a title received from her deceased husband **2** a dignified elderly woman [MF *douagiere*, fr *douage* dower, fr *douer* to endow, fr L *dotare*, fr *dot-, dos* gift, dower – more at DOWRY]

dowdy /'dowdi/ *adj* **1** not neat or smart in appearance **2** old-fashioned, frumpy [*dowd* (ugly woman), fr ME *doude*] – **dowdily** *adv*, **dowdiness** *n*, **dowdyish** *adj*

[1]**dowel** /'dowəl/ *n* a usu metal or wooden pin fitting into holes in adjacent pieces to preserve their relative positions; *also* rods of wood or metal for sawing into such pins [ME *dowle*; akin to OHG *tubili* plug, LGk *typhos* wedge]

[2]**dowel** *vt* **-ll-** (*NAm* **-l-, -ll-**) to fasten by dowels

dower /'dowə/ *n* a widow's legal share during her life of her deceased husband's property – no longer used technically [ME *dowere*, fr MF *douaire*, modif of ML *dotarium* – more at DOWRY]

Dow-Jones index /,dow 'johnz/ *n* an index of the prices of securities in the USA based on the daily average price of selected lists of shares [Charles H *Dow* †1902 & Edward D *Jones* †1920 US financial statisticians]

dowlas /'dowləs/ *n* **1** a rough linen fabric used for clothing in former times **2** a strong cotton fabric of coarse yarn used esp for household cloths and towels [*Daoulas*, town in Brittany, France]

[1]**down** /down/ *n* (a region of) undulating treeless usu chalk uplands, esp in S England – usu pl with sing. meaning [ME *doun* hill, fr OE *dūn*; akin to ON *dūnn* down of feathers]

[2]**down** *adv* **1a** at or towards a relatively low level ⟨~ *into the cellar*⟩ ⟨*the river is* ~⟩ **b** downwards from the surface of the earth or water **c** below the horizon **d** downstream **e** in or into a lying or sitting position ⟨*lie* ~⟩ **f** to or on the ground, surface, or bottom ⟨*house burnt* ~⟩ ⟨*telephone wires are* ~⟩ **g** so as to conceal a particular surface ⟨*turned it face* ~⟩ **h** downstairs **2** ON THE SPOT 2; *esp* as an initial payment ⟨*paid £10* ~⟩ **3a(1)** in or into a relatively low condition or status ⟨*family has come* ~ *in the world*⟩ – sometimes used interjectionally to express opposition ⟨~ *with the oppressors!*⟩ **(2)** to prison –

often + *go* or *send* **b(1)** in or into a state of relatively low intensity or activity ⟨*calm* ~⟩ ⟨*turn the radio* ~⟩ **(2)** into silence ⟨*shouted him* ~⟩ **(3)** into a slower pace or lower gear ⟨*changed* ~ *into second*⟩ **c** lower in amount, price, figure, or rank ⟨*prices are coming* ~⟩ **d** behind an opponent ⟨*we're 3 points* ~⟩ **4a** so as to be known, recognized, or recorded, esp on paper ⟨*scribbled it* ~⟩ ⟨*you're* ~ *to speak next*⟩ – compare SET DOWN, PUT DOWN **b** so as to be firmly held in position ⟨*stick* ~ *the flap of the envelope*⟩ ⟨*don't like to feel tied* ~⟩ **c** to the moment of catching or discovering ⟨*track the criminal* ~⟩ **5** in a direction conventionally the opposite of up: e g **a** to leeward **b** in or towards the south **c** *chiefly Br* away from the capital of a country or from a university city ⟨~ *in Wiltshire*⟩ **d** to or at the front of a theatrical stage **6** DOWNWARDS 3, 4 ⟨*jewels handed* ~ *in the family*⟩ **7a** to a concentrated state ⟨*got his report* ~ *to 3 pages*⟩ – compare BOIL DOWN **b** so as to be flattened, reduced, eroded, or diluted ⟨*water* ~ *the gin*⟩ ⟨*heels worn* ~⟩ **c** completely from top to bottom ⟨*hose the car* ~⟩ [ME *doun*, fr OE *dūne*, short for *adūne, of dūne*, fr *a-* (fr *of*), *of* off, from + *dūne*, dat of *dūn* hill]

[3]**down** *adj* **1** directed or going downwards ⟨*the* ~ *escalator*⟩ **2a** depressed, dejected **b** ill ⟨~ *with flu*⟩ **3** having been finished or dealt with ⟨*eight* ~ *and two to go*⟩ **4** with the rudder to windward – used with reference to a ship's helm **5** *chiefly Br* bound in a direction regarded as down; *esp* travelling away from a large town, esp London – compare UP 9

[4]**down** *prep* **1a** down along, round, through, towards, in, into, or on **b** at the bottom of ⟨*the bathroom is* ~ *those stairs*⟩ **2** *Br* down to; to ⟨*going* ~ *the shops*⟩ – nonstandard

[5]**down** *n* a grudge, prejudice – often in *have a down on*

[6]**down** *vt* **1** to cause to go or come down **2** to drink down; swallow quickly – infml **3** to defeat – infml – **down tools** *chiefly Br* to stop working; esp [1]STRIKE 7

[7]**down** *n* a covering of soft fluffy feathers [ME *doun*, fr ON *dūnn*; akin to ON *daunn* odour, *dȳja* to shake]

,down-and-'out *n or adj* (sby) destitute or impoverished

[1]**'down,beat** /-,beet/ *n* the principally accented (e g the first) note of a bar of music

[2]**downbeat** *adj* **1** pessimistic, gloomy **2** relaxed, informal

'down-,bow /boh/ *n* a stroke in playing a bowed instrument (e g a violin) in which the bow is drawn across the strings from the heel to the tip

'down,cast /-,kahst/ *adj* **1** dejected, depressed **2** directed downwards ⟨*with* ~ *eyes*⟩

'down,draught /-,drahft/ *n* a downward movement of gas, esp air (e g in a chimney)

downer /'downə/ *n* a depressing experience or situation – infml [[6]DOWN + [2]-ER]

'down,fall /-,fawl/ *n* **1** (a cause of) a sudden fall (e g from high rank or power) **2** an often heavy fall of rain or esp snow – **downfallen** *adj*

,down'field /-'feeld/ *adv or adj* in or into the part of the field towards which the attacking team is playing

'down for *prep* being on the list to enter (e g a race or school)

,down'grade /-'grayd/ *vt* **1** to lower in rank, value, or importance **2** to alter the status of (a job) so as to lower the rate of pay

,down'hearted /-'hahtid/ *adj* downcast, dejected – **downheartedly** *adv*, **downheartedness** *n*

[1]**'down,hill** /-,hil/ *n* a skiing race downhill against time – compare SLALOM

[2]**,down'hill** *adv* **1** towards the bottom of a hill **2** towards a lower or inferior state or level – in *go downhill*

[3]**,down'hill** *adj* sloping downhill

'Downing ,Street /'downing/ *n* the British government; *also* (a spokesman for) the British prime minister ⟨*talks between Dublin and* ~⟩ ⟨~ *is expected to announce cabinet changes soon*⟩ [*Downing Street*, London, location of the British Foreign & Commonwealth Office and of the prime minister's official residence]

'down,land /-,land, -lənd/ *n* (countryside resembling) the downs

,down-'market *n* being, producing, using, or characteristic of goods designed to appeal to the lower social end of a market – **down-market** *adv*

'down on *prep* having a low opinion of or grudge against ⟨*always* ~ *him*⟩

'down ,payment *n* a deposit paid at the time of purchase or delivery

'down,pipe /-,piep/ *n* a pipe for carrying rainwater from the roof to the ground or drain

'down,pour /-,paw/ *n* a heavy fall of rain

'down,range /-,raynj/ *adv* away from a launching site and along the course of a test range ⟨*a missile landing 8000 km* ~⟩ – **downrange** *adj*

[1]**'down,right** /-,riet/ *adv* thoroughly, outright ⟨~ *mean*⟩

[2]**downright** *adj* **1** absolute, thorough ⟨*a* ~ *lie*⟩ **2** plain, blunt ⟨*a* ~ *man*⟩ – **downrightly** *adv*, **downrightness** *n*

'Down's ,syndrome /downz/ *n* a form of congenital mental deficiency in which a child is born with slanting eyes, a broad short skull, and broad hands with short fingers; mongolism [J L H *Down* †1896 E physician]

,down'stage /-'stayj/ *adv or adj* at the front of a theatrical stage; *also* towards the audience or camera

[1]**,down'stairs** /-'steəz/ *adv* down the stairs; on or to a lower floor

[2]**downstairs** *adj* situated on the main, lower, or ground floor of a building

[3]**downstairs** *n, pl* **downstairs** the lower floor of a building

,down'stream /-'streem/ *adv or adj* in the direction of the flow of a stream

'down,stroke /-,strohk/ *n* a stroke made in a downward direction

'down,time /-,tiem/ *n, chiefly NAm* time during which a machine, factory, or department is inoperative during normal working hours

'down to *prep* **1** – used to indicate a downward limit or boundary ⟨*from the manager* ~ *the office boy*⟩ **2a** to be attributed to ⟨*the murders are* ~ *the Kray gang*⟩ **b** being the responsibility of; UP TO 5

,down-to-'earth *adj* practical, realistic

'down,town /-,town/ *adv, adj, or n, chiefly NAm* (to, towards, or in) the lower part or main business district of a town or city

'down,trodden /-,trod(ə)n/ *adj* oppressed by those in power

ˈdown,turn /-ˌtuhn/ *n* a downward turn, esp towards diminished business activity

ˌdown ˈunder *adv* in or into Australia or New Zealand

downward /ˈdownwood/ *adj* **1** moving or extending downwards ⟨*the ~ path*⟩ **2** descending to a lower pitch **3** descending from a head, origin, or source – **downwardly** *adv*, **downwardness** *n*

ˈdownwards /-woodz/ *adv* **1a** from a higher to a lower place or level; in the opposite direction from up ⟨*sun sank ~*⟩ **b** downstream **c** so as to conceal a particular surface ⟨*turned it face ~*⟩ **2a** from a higher to a lower condition **b** going down in amount, price, figure, or rank ⟨*from the fourth form ~*⟩ **3** from an earlier time **4** from an ancestor or predecessor

ˌdownˈwind /-ˈwind/ *adv or adj* in the direction that the wind is blowing

downy /ˈdowni/ *adj* **1** resembling or covered in down **2** made of down

dowry /ˈdowri/ *n* the money, goods, or estate that a woman brings to her husband in marriage [ME *dowarie*, fr AF, irreg fr ML *dotarium*, fr L *dot-, dos* gift, marriage portion; akin to L *dare* to give – more at [2]DATE]

[1]**dowse** /dows/ *vt* to douse

[2]**dowse** /dowz/ *vi* to search for hidden water or minerals with a divining rod [origin unknown]

dowser /ˈdowzə/ *n* (a person using) a divining rod

ˈdowsing ˌrod /ˈdowzing/ *n* a divining rod

doxology /dokˈsoləji/ *n* a liturgical expression of praise to God [ML *doxologia*, fr LGk, fr Gk *doxa* opinion, glory (fr *dokein* to seem, seem good) + *-logia* -logy – more at DECENT]

doxy /ˈdoksi/ *n, archaic* **1** a prostitute **2** MISTRESS 4 [perh modif of obs D *docke* doll, fr MD]

doyen /ˈdoyən (*Fr* dwajɛ̃)/, *fem* **doyenne** /doyˈen (*Fr* dwajɛn)/ *n* the senior or most experienced member of a body or group ⟨*Dan Maskell, ~ of tennis commentators*⟩ [F, fr LL *decanus* dean – more at [2]DEAN]

doyley, doyly /ˈdoyli/ *n* a doily

doze /dohz/ *vi* **1** to sleep lightly **2** to fall into a light sleep – usu + *off* [prob of Scand origin; akin to ON *dūsa* to doze; akin to MHG *dosen* to be quiet, doze] – **doze** *n*, **dozer** *n*

doze away *vt* to pass (time) drowsily

dozen /ˈduzən/ *n, pl* **dozens, dozen** **1** a group of 12 **2** an indefinitely large number – usu pl with sing. meaning ⟨*I've ~s of things to do*⟩ [ME *dozeine*, fr OF *dozaine*, fr *doze* twelve, fr L *duodecim*, fr *duo* two + *decem* ten – more at TWO, TEN] – **dozen** *adj*, **dozenth** /ˈduzənth/ *adj*

dozy /ˈdohzi/ *adj* **1** drowsy, sleepy **2** *chiefly Br* stupid and slow-witted – infml – **doziness** *n*

DPN /ˌdee pee ˈen/ *n* – used, esp formerly, for NAD [*d*iphosphopyridine *n*ucleotide]

[1]**drab** /drab/ *adj* **-bb-** **1** of a dull brown colour **2** dull, cheerless [*drab* (kind of cloth), alter. of earlier *drap* (cloth), fr MF, fr LL *drappus*] – **drably** *adv*, **drabness** *n*

[2]**drab** *n* – see DRIBS AND DRABS [prob alter. of *drib*]

drabble /ˈdrabl/ *vb* **drabbling** /ˈdrabling/ to make or become wet and muddy [ME *drabelen*]

drachm /dram/ *n* **1** a drachma **2** a unit of weight equal to ⅛oz apothecary (about 3.89g) ☞ UNIT [alter. of ME *dragme* – more at DRAM]

drachma /ˈdrakmə/ *n, pl* **drachmas, drachmae** /-mi/, **drachmai** /-mie/ **1** any of various ancient Greek units of weight **2a** an ancient Greek silver coin equivalent to 6 obols **b** ☞ *Greece* at NATIONALITY [L, fr Gk *drachmē* – more at DRAM]

draconian /drayˈkohnyən, -ni·ən, drə-/, **draconic** /drayˈkonik, drə-/ *adj, often cap, esp of a law* extremely severe; drastic [L *Dracon-, Draco*, fr Gk *Drakōn* fl 621BC Athenian lawgiver]

[1]**draft** /drahft/ *n* **1** the act, result, or plan of drawing out or sketching: e g **a** a construction plan **b** a preliminary sketch, outline, or version ⟨*a rough ~ of a book*⟩ **2a** a group of individuals selected for a particular job **b** (the group of individuals resulting from) the selecting of certain animals from a herd or flock **3a** an order for the payment of money drawn by one person or bank on another **b** (an instance of) drawing from or making demands on sthg **4** *chiefly NAm* conscription – usu + *the* **5** *NAm* a draught [var of *draught*]

[2]**draft** *adj* **1** *esp of livestock* chosen from a group **2** *NAm* draught

[3]**draft** *vt* **1** to draw the preliminary sketch, version, or plan of **2** *NAm* to conscript for military service – **draftable** *adj*, **draftee** /drahfˈtee/ *n*, **drafter** *n*

draftsman /ˈdrahftsmən/ *n* sby who draws up legal documents or other writings

[1]**drag** /drag/ *n* **1** a device for dragging under water to search for objects **2a** sthg that retards motion, action, or progress **b** the retarding force acting on a body (e g an aircraft) moving through a fluid (e g air), parallel and opposite to the direction of motion **c** a burden, encumbrance **3** an object drawn over the ground to leave a scented trail (e g for dogs to follow) **4a** a drawing along or over a surface with effort or pressure **b** motion effected with slowness or difficulty **c** a drawing into the mouth of pipe, cigarette, or cigar smoke – infml **5a** woman's clothing worn by a man – slang; often in *in drag* **b** clothing – slang **6** a dull or boring person or experience – slang

[2]**drag** *vb* **-gg-** *vt* **1a** to draw slowly or heavily; haul **b** to cause to move with painful or undue slowness or difficulty **2a** to search (a body of water) with a drag **b** to catch with a dragnet or trawl **3** to bring by force or compulsion – infml ⟨*had to ~ her husband to the opera*⟩ ~ *vi* **1** to hang or lag behind **2** to trail along on the ground **3** to move or proceed laboriously or tediously – infml ⟨*the book ~s*⟩ **4** to draw tobacco smoke into the mouth – usu + *on* ⟨*~ on a cigarette*⟩; infml [ME *draggen*, fr ON *draga* or OE *dragan* – more at DRAW] – **draggingly** *adv* – **drag one's feet/heels** to act in a deliberately slow, dilatory, or ineffective manner

[3]**drag** *adj* of drag racing

ˈdrag ˌanchor *n* SEA ANCHOR

dragée /ˈdrazhay (*Fr* draʒe)/ *n* **1** a sugar-coated nut or fruit **2** a small silver-coloured sugar ball for decorating cakes [F, fr MF *dragie* – more at [3]DREDGE]

draggle /ˈdragl/ *vb* **draggling** /ˈdragling, ˈdragl·ing/ *vt* to make wet and dirty ~ *vi* **1** to trail on the ground **2** to straggle [freq of *drag*]

draggy /ˈdragi/ *adj* dull or boring ⟨*spent a really ~ evening with relations*⟩

ˈdrag,line /-ˌlien/ *n* an excavating machine in which the bucket is drawn in by cables

ˈdrag,net /-ˌnet/ *n* **1** a net drawn along the bottom of a body of water or the ground to catch fish or small game 2 a network of measures for apprehension (e g of criminals)

dragoman /ˈdragohmən/ *n, pl* **dragomans, dragomen** /-mən/ an interpreter, chiefly of Arabic, Turkish, or Persian, employed esp in the Near East [ME *drogman*, fr MF, fr OIt *dragomanno*, fr MGk *dragomanos*, fr Ar *tarjumān*, fr Aram *tūrgĕmānā*]

dragon /ˈdragən/ *n* **1** a mythical winged and clawed monster, often breathing fire **2** a fierce, combative, or very strict person [ME, fr OF, fr L *dracon-, draco* serpent, dragon, fr Gk *drakōn* serpent; akin to OE *torht* bright, Gk *derkesthai* to see, look at, Skt *darśayati* he causes to see] – **dragonish** *adj*

dragonet /ˈdragənit/ *n* any of various small often brightly coloured scaleless marine fishes constituting a family [*dragon* + *-et*]

ˈdragon,fly /-,flie/ *n* any of a suborder of long slender-bodied often brightly coloured insects that have a fine network of veins in their wings and often live near water – compare DAMSELFLY

dragonnade /,dragəˈnayd/ *n* persecution using troops; *specif* any of a series of persecutions of French Protestants under Louis XIV by soldiers who were quartered on them [F, fr *dragon* dragoon]

ˈdragon's ,blood *n* a darkened resin from the fruit of a palm used for colouring varnish and in photoengraving

¹dragoon /drəˈgoohn/ *n* a member of a European military unit formerly composed of mounted infantrymen armed with carbines [F *dragon* dragon, musket, dragoon, fr MF]

²dragoon *vt* **1** to reduce to subjection by harsh use of troops **2** to (attempt to) force into submission by persecution

ˈdrag ,race *n* an acceleration contest between cars, motorcycles, etc usu over ¼ mile (about 402m) – **drag racing** *n*

dragster /ˈdragstə/ *n* (the driver of) a vehicle, esp a motor car, built or modified for use in a drag race

ˈdrag ,strip *n* a track for drag racing

drail /drayl/ *n* a heavy fishhook used in trolling [obs *drail* (to drag, trail), perh alter. of *trail*]

¹drain /drayn/ *vt* **1a** to draw off (liquid) gradually or completely **b** to exhaust physically or emotionally **2a** to make gradually dry ⟨~ *a swamp*⟩ **b** to carry away the surface water of **c** to deplete or empty (as if) by drawing off gradually ⟨*war that* ~s *a nation of youth and wealth*⟩ **d** to empty by drinking the contents of ⟨~ed *his glass*⟩ ~ *vi* **1** to flow off gradually **2** to become gradually dry [ME *draynen*, fr OE *drēahnian*] – **drainer** *n*

²drain *n* **1** a means (e g a pipe) by which usu liquid matter is drained away **2** a gradual outflow or withdrawal **3** sthg that causes depletion; a burden – **down the drain** being used wastefully or brought to nothing ⟨*years of work went* down the drain *in the fire at his studio*⟩

drainage /ˈdraynij/ *n* **1a** draining **b** sthg drained off **2** a system of drains

ˈdraining ,board /ˈdrayning/ *n, Br* a usu grooved and often slightly sloping surface at the side of a sink unit on which washed dishes are placed to drain

ˈdrain,pipe /-,piep/ *n* a pipe that carries waste, liquid sewage, excess water, etc away from a building

,drainpipe ˈtrousers, ˈdrain,pipes *n pl* tight trousers with narrow legs ☞ GARMENT

¹drake /drayk/ *n* a mayfly; *esp* an artificial one used as bait in angling [ME, dragon, fr OE *draca*; akin to ON *dreki* dragon; both fr a prehistoric WGmc-NGmc word borrowed fr L *draco* dragon – more at DRAGON]

²drake *n* a male duck [ME; akin to OHG an*trahho* drake]

Dralon /ˈdraylon/ *trademark* – used for an acrylic fibre used chiefly in upholstery

dram /dram/ *n* **1** a unit of mass equal to $^1/_{16}$oz avoirdupois (about 1.77g) ☞ UNIT **2** *chiefly Scot* a tot of spirits, usu whisky [ME *dragme*, fr MF & LL; MF, dram, drachma, fr LL *dragma*, fr L *drachma*, fr Gk *drachmē*, lit., handful, fr *drassesthai* to grasp]

drama /ˈdrahmə/ *n* **1** a composition in verse or prose intended to portray life or character or to tell a story through action and dialogue; *specif* a play **2** dramatic art, literature, or affairs **3** a situation or set of events having the qualities of a drama [LL *dramat-, drama*, fr Gk, deed, drama, fr *dran* to do, act; prob akin to Lith *daryti* to do]

dramatic /drəˈmatik/ *adj* **1** of drama **2a** suitable to or characteristic of drama; vivid **b** striking in appearance or effect [MF & LL; MF *dramatique*, fr LL *dramaticus*, fr Gk *dramatikos*, fr *dramat-, drama*] – **dramatically** *adv*

dra,matic ˈirony *n* incongruity between a situation developed in a play and the accompanying words or actions that is understood by the audience but not by the characters

draˈmatics *n pl* **1** *sing or pl in constr* the study or practice of theatrical arts (e g acting and stagecraft) **2** dramatic behaviour; *esp* an exaggerated display of emotion

dramatis personae /,drahmətis puhˈsohnie/ *n pl* (a list of) the characters or actors in a play [NL]

dramatist /ˈdrahmətist, ˈdra-/ *n* a playwright

dramat·ize, -ise /ˈdrahmətiez, dra-/ *vt* **1** to adapt (e g a novel) for theatrical presentation **2** to present in a dramatic manner ~ *vi* **1** to be suitable for dramatization **2** to behave dramatically – **dramatizable** /-,tiezəbl/ *adj*, **dramatization** /-ˈzaysh(ə)n/ *n*

dramaturgy /ˈdramə,tuhji/ *n* the art or technique of dramatic composition and theatrical representation [G *dramaturgie*, fr Gk *dramatourgia* dramatic composition, fr *dramatourgos* dramatist, fr *dramat-, drama* + *-ourgos* worker, fr *ergon* work – more at WORK] – **dramaturgic** /,draməˈtuhjik/, **dramaturgical** *adj*, **dramaturgically** *adv*

drank /drangk/ *past of* DRINK

¹drape /drayp/ *vt* **1** to cover or decorate (as if) with folds of cloth **2** to hang or stretch loosely or carelessly ⟨~d *his legs over the chair*⟩ **3** to arrange in flowing lines or folds [ME *drapen* to weave, fr MF *draper*, fr *drap* cloth – more at DRAB] – **drapable** *also* **drapeable** *adj*, **drapability** *also* **drapeability** /,draypəˈbiləti/ *n*

²drape *n* a piece of drapery; *esp, chiefly NAm* a curtain

draper /ˈdraypə/ *n, chiefly Br* a dealer in cloth and sometimes also in clothing, haberdashery, and soft furnishings [ME, maker of cloth, fr MF *drapier*, fr OF, fr *drap*]

drapery /ˈdrayp(ə)ri/ *n* **1a** (a piece of) cloth or clothing arranged or hung gracefully, esp in loose folds **b** cloth or textile fabrics used esp for clothing or soft furnishings; *also, NAm* hangings of heavy fabric used as a curtain **2** the draping or arranging of materials **3a** *Br* the trade of a draper **b** the goods sold by a draper

drastic /'drastik/ *adj* **1** acting rapidly or violently ⟨*a ~ purgative*⟩ **2** radical in effect or action; severe [Gk *drastikos*, fr *dran* to do] – **drastically** *adv*

drat /drat/ *vt* **-tt-** to damn – euph; used as a mild oath [prob euphemism for *God rot*]

¹draught, *NAm chiefly* **draft** /drahft/ *n* **1** (the quantity of fish taken by) the act of drawing a net **2** a team of animals together with what they draw **3** the act or an instance of drinking; *also* the portion drunk in such an act **4** the act of drawing (e g from a cask); *also* a quantity of liquid so drawn **5** the depth of water a ship requires to float in, esp when loaded **6** a current of air in a closed-in space [ME *draght*; akin to OE *dragan* to draw – more at DRAW] – **on draught** *of beer or cider* ready to be served from the cask or barrel with or without the use of added gas in serving

²draught, *NAm chiefly* **draft** *adj* **1** used for drawing loads ⟨*~ oxen*⟩ **2** served from the barrel or cask ⟨*~ beer*⟩

'draught,board /-,bawd/ *n* a chessboard

draughts /drahfts/ *n pl but sing or pl in constr, Br* a game for 2 players each of whom moves his/her usu 12 draughtsmen according to fixed rules across a chessboard usu using only the black squares [ME *draghtes*, fr pl of *draght* draught, move in chess]

draughtsman /'drahftsmən/ *n* **1a** an artist skilled in drawing **b** *fem* **'draughts,woman** sby who draws plans and sketches (e g of machinery or structures) **2** *Br* a disc-shaped piece used in draughts

draughty /'drahfti/ *adj* having a cold draught blowing through

Dravidian /drə'vidi·ən, -dyən/ *n* **1** a member of any of the peoples of S India and Sri Lanka who speak Dravidian **2** any of several languages of India, Sri Lanka, and Pakistan (e g Tamil and Malayalam) [Skt *Drāvida*] – **Dravidian** *adj*

¹draw /draw/ *vb* **drew** /drooh/; **drawn** /drawn/ *vt* **1** to pull, haul **2** to cause to go in a certain direction ⟨drew *him aside*⟩ **3a** to attract ⟨*honey ~s flies*⟩ **b** to bring in, gather, or derive from a specified source ⟨*a college that ~s its students from many towns*⟩ ⟨drew *inspiration from his teacher*⟩ **c** to bring on oneself; provoke ⟨drew *enemy fire*⟩ **d** to bring out by way of response; elicit ⟨drew *cheers from the audience*⟩ **4** to inhale ⟨drew *a deep breath*⟩ **5a** to bring or pull out, esp with effort ⟨*~ a tooth*⟩ ⟨*~ a sword*⟩ **b** to extract the essence from ⟨*~ tea*⟩ **c** to disembowel ⟨*pluck and ~ a goose*⟩ **d** to cause (blood) to flow **6** to require (a specified depth) to float in **7a** to accumulate, gain ⟨*~ing interest*⟩ **b** to take (money) from a place of deposit – often + *out* **c** to use in making a cash demand ⟨*~ing a cheque on his account*⟩ **d** to receive regularly, esp from a particular source ⟨*~ a salary*⟩ **8a** to take (cards) from a dealer or pack **b** to receive or take at random ⟨drew *a winning number*⟩ **9** to bend (a bow) by pulling back the string **10** to strike (a ball) so as to impart a curved motion or backspin **11** to leave undecided or have equal scores in (a contest) **12** to produce a likeness of (e g by making lines on a surface); portray, delineate **13** to formulate or arrive at by reasoning ⟨*~ a conclusion*⟩ ⟨*~ comparisons*⟩ **14** to pull together and close (e g curtains) **15** to stretch or shape (esp metal) by pulling through dies; *also* to produce (e g a wire) thus **16** to drive game out of ~ *vi* **1** to come or go steadily or gradually ⟨*night ~s near*⟩ **2** to advance as far as a specified position ⟨drew *level*⟩ ⟨drew *up to the front door*⟩ **3a** to pull back a bowstring **b** to bring out a weapon **4a** to produce or allow a draught ⟨*the chimney ~s well*⟩ **b** *of a sail* to swell out in a wind **5** to steep, infuse ⟨*give the tea time to ~*⟩ **6** to sketch **7** to finish a competition or contest without either side winning **8a** to make a written demand for payment of money on deposit **b** to obtain resources (e g of information) ⟨*~ing from a common fund of knowledge*⟩ **9** *chiefly NAm* to suck in sthg, esp tobacco smoke – usu + *on* [ME *drawen, dragen*, fr OE *dragan*; akin to ON *draga* to draw, drag, & perh to L *trahere* to pull, draw] – **draw a blank** to fail to gain the desired object (e g information sought) – **draw lots** to decide an issue by lottery in which objects of unequal length or with different markings are used – **draw on/upon** to use as source of supply ⟨drawing on *the whole community for support*⟩ – **draw rein** to bring a horse to a stop while riding – **draw stumps** to end play in a cricket match – **draw the/a line** **1** to fix an arbitrary boundary between things that tend to merge ⟨*the difficulty of* drawing a line *between art and pornography*⟩ **2** to fix a boundary excluding what one will not tolerate or engage in – usu + *at*

²draw *n* **1a** a sucking pull on sthg held between the lips ⟨*took a ~ on his pipe*⟩ **b** *the* removing of a handgun from its holster in order to shoot **2** a drawing of lots; a raffle **3** a contest left undecided; a tie **4** sthg that draws public attention or patronage **5** the usu random assignment of starting positions in a competition, esp a competitive sport **6** *NAm* the movable part of a drawbridge

draw away *vi* to move ahead (e g of an opponent in a race) gradually

'draw,back /-,bak/ *n* an objectionable feature; a disadvantage

draw back *vi* to avoid an issue or commitment; retreat

'draw,bar /-,bah/ *n* **1** a railway vehicle coupling **2** a beam across the rear of a tractor to which implements are hitched

'draw,bridge /-,brij/ *n* a bridge made to be raised up, let down, or drawn aside so as to permit or hinder passage ☞ CHURCH

drawee /draw'ee/ *n* the person on whom an order or bill of exchange is drawn

drawer /*sense* ¹ 'draw·ə; *senses 2, 3* draw/ *n* **1** one who draws a bill of exchange or order for payment or makes a promissory note **2** an open-topped box in a piece of furniture which to open and close slides back and forth in its frame **3** *pl* an undergarment for the lower body – now usu humor [¹DRAW + ²-ER]

draw in *vt* **1** to cause or entice to enter or participate **2** to sketch roughly ⟨drawing in *the first outlines*⟩ ~ *vi* **1** *of a train* to come into a station **2** *of successive days* to grow shorter (e g in winter)

drawing /'draw·ing/ *n* **1** the art or technique of representing an object, figure, or plan by means of lines **2** sthg drawn or subject to drawing: e g **a** an amount drawn from a fund **b** a representation formed by drawing

'drawing ,board *n* **1** a board to which paper is attached for drawing on **2** a planning stage ⟨*a project still on the ~*⟩ ⟨*back to the ~*⟩

ˈdrawing ˌpin *n, Br* a pin with a broad flat head for fastening esp sheets of paper to boards

ˈdrawing ˌroom *n* **1** a formal reception room **2** LIVING ROOM – fml [short for *withdrawing room*]

¹drawl /drawl/ *vb* to speak or utter slowly and often affectedly, with vowels greatly prolonged [prob freq of *draw*] – **drawler** *n*, **drawlingly** *adv*

²drawl *n* a drawling manner of speaking – **drawly** *adj*

drawnwork /ˈdrawn,wuhk/ *n* decoration on cloth made by drawing out threads according to a pattern

draw off *vt* to remove (liquid) ~ *vi of troops* to move apart (and form new groups)

draw on *vi* to approach ⟨*night* draws on⟩ ~ *vt* **1** to cause; BRING ON 1 **2** to put on ⟨*she* drew on *her gloves*⟩

draw out *vt* **1** to remove, extract **2** to extend beyond a minimum in time; prolong **3** to cause to speak freely

ˈdraw,plate /-ˌplayt/ *n* a die with holes through which wires are drawn

ˈdraw,string /-ˌstring/ *n* a string or tape threaded through fabric, which when pulled closes an opening (e g of a bag) or gathers material (e g of curtains or clothes)

draw up *vt* **1** to bring (e g troops) into array **2** DRAFT 1 **3** to straighten (oneself) to an erect posture, esp as an assertion of dignity or resentment **4** to bring to a halt ~ *vi* to come to a halt

¹dray /dray/ *n* a strong low cart or wagon without sides, used esp by brewers [ME *draye*, a wheelless vehicle, fr OE *dræge* dragnet; akin to OE *dragan* to pull – more at DRAW]

²dray a drey

ˈdray,horse /-ˌhaws/ *n* a large and powerful horse used esp to pull drays

ˈdrayman /-mən/ *n* sby who drives a vehicle (e g a dray or lorry) for a brewery

¹dread /dred/ *vt* **1** to fear greatly **2** to be extremely apprehensive about [ME *dreden*, fr OE *drǣdan*; akin to OS an*trādan* to fear, dread, OHG in*trātan*]

²dread *n* (the object of) great fear, uneasiness, or apprehension

³dread *adj* causing or inspiring dread [ME *dred*, fr pp of *dreden*]

ˈdreadful /-f(ə)l/ *adj* **1** inspiring dread; causing great and oppressive fear **2a** extremely unpleasant or shocking **b** very disagreeable (e g through dullness or poor quality) **3** extreme ⟨~ *disorder*⟩ – **dreadfully** *adv*, **dreadfulness** *n*

dreadlocks /ˈdred,loks/ *n pl* the long matted often hennaed locks of hair worn by male Rastafarians

dreadnought /ˈdred,nawt/ *n* a battleship whose main armament consists of big guns of the same calibre [*Dreadnought*, Br battleship, the first of this type, launched in 1906]

¹dream /dreem/ *n* **1** a series of thoughts, images, or emotions occurring during sleep **2** a daydream, reverie ⟨*walked round in a* ~ *all day*⟩ **3** sthg notable for its beauty, excellence, or enjoyable quality ⟨*the new car goes like a* ~⟩ **4** a strongly desired goal; an ambition ⟨*his* ~ *of becoming president*⟩; *also* a realization of an ambition – often used attributively ⟨*a* ~ *house*⟩ [ME *dreem*, fr OE *drēam* noise, joy; akin to OHG *troum* dream, ON *draumr*, Gk *thrylos* noise, din] – **dreamful** *adj*, **dreamfully** *adv*, **dreamfulness** *n*, **dreamless** *adj*, **dreamlessly** *adv*, **dreamlessness** *n*, **dreamlike** *adj*

²dream *vb* **dreamed** /dreemd, dremt/, **dreamt** /dremt/ *vi* **1** to have a dream **2** to indulge in daydreams or fantasies ⟨~ing *of a better future*⟩ ~ *vt* **1** to have a dream of **2** to consider as a possibility; imagine **3** to pass (time) in reverie or inaction – usu + *away* – **dreamer** *n* – **dream of** to consider even the possibility of – in neg constructions ⟨*wouldn't* dream *of disturbing you*⟩

ˈdream,boat /-ˌboht/ *n* a highly attractive person of the opposite sex – infml; no longer in vogue

ˈdream,land /-ˌland/ *n* an unreal delightful region existing only in imagination or in fantasy; NEVER-NEVER LAND

ˈdream,time /-ˌtiem/ *n* a Golden Age following the Creation in the mythology of some Australian Aborigines

dream up *vt* to devise, invent – infml

dreamy /ˈdreemi/ *adj* **1** pleasantly abstracted from immediate reality **2** given to dreaming or fantasy ⟨*a* ~ *child*⟩ **3a** suggestive of a dream in vague or visionary quality **b** delightful, pleasing; *esp, of a man* sexually attractive – infml – **dreamily** *adv*, **dreaminess** *n*

drear /driə/ *adj* dreary – poetic [short for *dreary*]

dreary /ˈdriəri/ *adj* causing feelings of cheerlessness or gloom; dull [ME *drery*, fr OE *drēorig* sad, bloody, fr *drēor* gore; akin to OHG *trūrēn* to be sad, Goth *driusan* to fall, Gk *thrauein* to shatter] – **drearily** *adv*, **dreariness** *n*

¹dredge /drej/ *n* **1** an oblong frame with an attached net for gathering fish, shellfish, etc from the bottom of the sea, a river, etc **2** a machine for removing earth, mud, etc usu by buckets on an endless chain or a suction tube [prob fr Sc *dreg-* (in *dregbot* dredge boat)]

²dredge *vt* **1a** to dig, gather, or pull out with a dredge – often + *up* or *out* **b** to deepen (e g a waterway) with a dredging machine **2** to bring to light by thorough searching – usu + *up* ⟨dredging *up memories*⟩; infml ~ *vi* to use a dredge

³dredge *vt* to coat (e g food) by sprinkling (e g with flour) [obs *dredge*, n (sweetmeat), fr ME *drage, drege*, fr MF *dragie*, modif of L *tragemata* sweetmeats, fr Gk *tragēmata*, pl of *tragēma* sweetmeat, fr *trōgein* to gnaw – more at TERSE] – **dredger** *n*

dredger /ˈdrejə/ *n* a barge with an apparatus for dredging harbours, waterways, etc [²DREDGE + ²-ER]

dreg /dreg/ *n* **1** sediment; lees **2** the most undesirable part ⟨*the* ~s *of society*⟩ ***USE*** usu pl with sing. meaning [ME, fr ON *dregg*; akin to L *fraces* dregs of oil, Gk *thrassein* to trouble]

ˈD ˌregion *n* the lowest part of the ionosphere occurring between about 40 and 65km (25 and 40mi) above the surface of the earth

dreich /dreekh/ *adj, Scot* bleak, dismal ⟨*a* ~ *view over barren moors*⟩ ⟨*a* ~ *January morning*⟩ [ME *dregh, dreich*, of Scand origin; akin to ON *drjūgr* substantial, lasting]

¹drench /drench/ *n* a poisonous or medicinal drink, esp put down the throat of an animal

²drench *vt* **1** to administer a drench to (an animal) **2** to make thoroughly wet (e g with falling water or by immersion); saturate [ME *drenchen*, fr OE *drencan*; akin to OE *drincan* to drink, OHG *trenken* to cause to drink, ON *drekkja* to drown]

Dresden /'drezd(ə)n/ *n* a type of ornate and delicately coloured porcelain made at Meissen near Dresden; Meissen [*Dresden*, city in Saxony, Germany] – **Dresden** *adj*

[1]**dress** /dres/ *vt* **1** to arrange (e g troops) in the proper alignment **2a** to put clothes on **b** to provide with clothing **3** to add decorative details or accessories to; embellish ⟨~ *a Christmas tree*⟩ **4** to prepare for use or service; *esp* to prepare (e g a chicken) for cooking or eating **5a** to apply dressings or medicaments to (e g a wound) **b(1)** to arrange (the hair) **(2)** to groom and curry (an animal) **c** to kill and prepare for market **d** to cultivate, esp by applying manure or fertilizer **e** to finish the surface of (e g timber, stone, or textiles) ☞ BUILDING **f** to arrange goods on a display in (e g a shop window) ~ *vi* **1a** to put on clothing **b** to put on or wear formal, elaborate, or fancy clothes ⟨*guests were expected to ~ for dinner*⟩ **2** to align oneself properly in a line **3** *of a man* to have one's genitals lying on a specified side of the trouser crutch ⟨*do you ~ to the right or left, sir?*⟩ [ME *dressen*, fr MF *dresser*, fr OF *drecier*, fr (assumed) VL *directiare*, fr L *directus* direct, pp of *dirigere* to direct, fr *dis-* + *regere* to lead straight – more at RIGHT]

[2]**dress** *n* **1** utilitarian or ornamental covering for the human body; *esp* clothing suitable for a particular purpose or occasion **2** a 1-piece outer garment including both top and skirt usu for a woman or girl **3** covering, adornment, or appearance appropriate or peculiar to a specified time ⟨*18th-century ~*⟩ *USE* ☞ GARMENT

[3]**dress** *adj* of, being, or suitable for an occasion requiring or permitting formal dress ⟨*a ~ affair*⟩

dressage /'dresahzh, -'-/ *n* the execution by a trained horse of precise movements in response to its rider [F, preparation, straightening, training, fr *dresser* to prepare, make straight, train]

'dress ,circle *n* the first or lowest curved tier of seats in a theatre

dress down *vt* to reprove severely – **dressing down** *n*

[1]**dresser** /'dresə/ *n* **1** a piece of kitchen furniture resembling a sideboard with a high back and having compartments and shelves for holding dishes and cooking utensils **2** *chiefly NAm* a chest of drawers or bureau with a mirror [ME *dressore, dresser*, fr MF *dresseur*, fr OF *dreçor*, fr *drecier* to arrange]

[2]**dresser** *n* a person who looks after stage costumes and helps actors to dress [[1]DRESS + [2]-ER]

dressing /'dresing/ *n* **1** a seasoning, sauce, or stuffing **2** material applied to cover a wound, sore, etc **3** manure or compost to improve the growth of plants [[1]DRESS + [2]-ING]

'dressing ,gown *n* a loose robe worn esp over nightclothes or when not fully dressed

'dressing ,room *n* a room used chiefly for dressing; *esp* a room in a theatre for changing costumes and make-up

'dressing ,station *n* a station for giving first aid to the wounded

'dressing ,table *n* a table usu fitted with drawers and a mirror for use while dressing and grooming oneself

'dress,maker /-,maykə/ *n* sby who makes dresses – **dressmaking** *n*

'dress re,hearsal *n* **1** a full rehearsal of a play in costume and with stage props shortly before the first performance **2** a full-scale practice; DRY RUN 2

'dress ,shield *n* SHIELD 3

dress up *vt* **1a(1)** to clothe in best or formal clothes **(2)** to make suitable for a formal occasion (e g by adding accessories) ⟨dressing up *a smock with a gilt belt and scarves*⟩ **b** to dress in clothes suited to a particular assumed role **2** to present or cause to appear in a certain light (e g by distortion or exaggeration) ~ *vi* to get dressed up

dressy /'dresi/ *adj* **1** *of a person* showy in dress **2** *of clothes* stylish, smart **3** overly elaborate in appearance – **dressiness** *n*

drew /drooh/ *past of* DRAW

drey, dray /dray/ *n* a squirrel's nest [origin unknown]

drib /drib/ *n* – see DRIBS AND DRABS [prob back-formation fr *dribble & driblet* (drop of liquid, trifle)]

[1]**dribble** /'dribl/ *vb* **dribbled; dribbling** /'dribling/ *vi* **1** to fall or flow in drops or in a thin intermittent stream; trickle **2** to let saliva trickle from the mouth; drool **3** to come or issue in piecemeal or disconnected fashion **4a** to dribble a ball or puck **b** to proceed by dribbling **c** *of a ball* to move with short bounces ~ *vt* to propel (a ball or puck) by successive slight taps or bounces with hand, foot, or stick [freq of *drib* (to dribble), prob alter. of *drip*] – **dribbler** *n*

[2]**dribble** *n* **1** a small trickling stream or flow **2** a tiny or insignificant bit or quantity **3** an act or instance of dribbling

dribs and drabs /,dribz ən 'drabz/ *n pl* small usu scattered amounts – infml

,dried-'up *adj* wizened, shrivelled

drier *also* **dryer** /'drie·ə/ *n* **1** a substance that accelerates drying (e g of oils and printing inks) **2** any of various machines for drying sthg (e g the hair or clothes)

[1]**drift** /drift/ *n* sthg driven, propelled, or urged along or drawn (as if) by a natural agency: e g **1a** a mass of sand, snow, etc deposited (as if) by wind or water **b** rock debris deposited by natural wind, water, etc; *specif* a deposit of clay, sand, gravel, and boulders transported by (running water from) a glacier **2** a general underlying tendency or meaning, esp of what is spoken or written **3** a tool for ramming down or driving sthg, usu into or out of a hole **4** the motion or action of drifting: e g **a** a ship's deviation from its course caused by currents **b** a slow-moving ocean current **c** the lateral motion of an aircraft due to air currents **d** an easy, moderate, more or less steady flow along a spatial course **e** a gradual shift in attitude, opinion, or emotion **f** an aimless course, with no attempt at direction or control **g** a deviation from a true reproduction, representation, or reading **5** a nearly horizontal mine passage on or parallel to a vein or rock stratum **6** a gradual change in a supposedly constant characteristic of a device, esp an electrical one [ME; akin to OE *drifan* to drive – more at DRIVE] – **drifty** *adj*

[2]**drift** *vi* **1a** to become driven or carried along by a current of water or air **b** to move or float smoothly and effortlessly **2a** to move in a random or casual way **b** to become carried along aimlessly ⟨*the conversation* ~ed *from one topic to another*⟩ **3** to pile up under the force of wind or water **4** to deviate from a set adjustment ~ *vt* to pile up in a drift

drifter /'driftə/ *n* **1** sby or sthg that travels or moves about aimlessly **2** a coastal fishing boat equipped with drift nets [²DRIFT + ²-ER]

'drift ,net *n* a large fishing net that hangs vertically and is arranged to drift with the tide, currents, etc

'drift,wood /-,wood/ *n* wood cast up on a shore or beach

¹drill /dril/ *vb vt* **1a** to bore or drive a hole in (as if) by the piercing action of a drill **b** to make (e g a hole) by piercing action **2a** to instruct and exercise by repeating **b** to train or exercise in military drill ~ *vi* **1** to make a hole with a drill **2** to engage in esp military drill [D *drillen*; akin to OHG *drāen* to turn – more at THROW] – **drillable** *adj*

²drill *n* **1** (a device or machine for rotating) a tool with an edged or pointed end for making a hole in a solid substance by revolving or by a succession of blows **2** training in marching and the manual of arms **3** a physical or mental exercise aimed at improving facility and skill by regular practice **4** a marine snail that bores through oyster shells and eats the flesh **5** *chiefly Br* the approved or correct procedure for accomplishing sthg efficiently – infml

³drill *n* **1a** a shallow furrow into which seed is sown **b** a row of seed sown in such a furrow **2** a planting implement that makes holes or furrows, drops in the seed and sometimes fertilizer, and covers them with earth [perh fr arch. *drill* (rill)]

⁴drill *vt* **1** to sow (seeds) by dropping along a shallow furrow **2** to sow with seed or set with seedlings inserted in drills

⁵drill *n* a durable cotton fabric in twill weave [short for *drilling*, modif of G *drillich*, fr MHG *drilich* fabric woven with a threefold thread, fr OHG *drilīh* made up of three threads, fr L *trilic-*, *trilix*, fr *tri-* + *licium* thread]

drily /'drieli/ *adv* dryly

¹drink /dringk/ *vb* **drank** /drangk/; **drunk** /drungk/, **drank** *vt* **1a** to swallow (a liquid); *also* to swallow the liquid contents of (e g a cup) **b** to take in or suck up; absorb ⟨~ing *air into his lungs*⟩ **c** to take in or receive avidly – usu + *in* ⟨drank *in every word of the lecture*⟩ **2** to join in (a toast) **3** to bring to a specified state by taking drink ⟨drank *himself into oblivion*⟩ ~ *vi* **1** to take liquid into the mouth for swallowing **2** to drink alcoholic beverages, esp habitually or to excess [ME *drinken*, fr OE *drincan*; akin to OHG *trinkan* to drink] – **drink like a fish** to habitually drink alcohol to excess – **drink to** to drink a toast to

²drink *n* **1a** liquid suitable for swallowing **b** alcoholic drink ⟨*a* ~s *cupboard*⟩ **2** a draught or portion of liquid for drinking **3** excessive consumption of alcoholic beverages ⟨*drove him to* ~⟩ **4** OCEAN 1; *broadly* any sizable body of water – + *the*; infml

drinkable /'dringkəbl/ *adj* suitable or safe for drinking

drinker /'dringkə/ *n* one who drinks alcoholic beverages to excess [¹DRINK + ²-ER]

¹drip /drip/ *vb* **-pp-** *vt* to let fall in drops ~ *vi* **1a** to let fall drops of moisture or liquid **b** to overflow (as if) with moisture ⟨*a novel that* ~s *with sentimentality*⟩ **2** to fall (as if) in drops [ME *drippen*, fr OE *dryppan*; akin to OE *dropa* drop] – **dripper** *n*

²drip *n* **1a** the action or sound of falling in drops **b** liquid that falls, overflows, or is forced out in drops **2** a projection for throwing off rainwater **3a** a device for the administration of a liquid at a slow rate, esp into a vein **b** a substance administered by means of a drip ⟨*a saline* ~⟩ **4** a dull or inconsequential person – infml – **dripless** *adj*, **drippy** *adj*

¹,drip-'dry *vb* to dry with few or no wrinkles when hung dripping wet

²,drip-'dry *adj* made of a washable fabric that drip-dries ☞ SYMBOL

'drip-,feed *n* DRIP 3A

dripping /'driping/ *n* the fat that runs out from meat during roasting

'drip,stone /-,stohn/ *n* **1** a drip made of stone (e g over a window) **2** calcium carbonate in the form of stalactites or stalagmites

'drip ,tray *n* a tray for catching drips (e g of water from the freezing compartment of a refrigerator during defrosting)

¹drive /driev/ *vb* **drove** /drohv/; **driven** /'driv(ə)n/ *vt* **1a** to set in motion by physical force **b** to force into position by blows ⟨~ *a nail into the wall*⟩ **c** to repulse or cause to go by force, authority, or influence ⟨~ *the enemy back*⟩ ⟨drove *the thought from my mind*⟩ **d** to set or keep in motion or operation ⟨~ *machinery by electricity*⟩ **2a** to control and direct the course of (a vehicle or draught animal) **b** to convey or transport in a vehicle **3** to carry on or through energetically ⟨driving *a hard bargain*⟩ **4a** to exert inescapable or persuasive pressure on; force **b** to compel to undergo or suffer a change (e g in situation, awareness, or emotional state) ⟨drove *him crazy*⟩ **c** to urge relentlessly to continuous exertion **5** to cause (e g game or cattle) to move in a desired direction **6** to bore (e g a tunnel or passage) **7a** to propel (an object of play) swiftly **b** to play a drive in cricket at (a ball) or at the bowling of (a bowler) ~ *vi* **1** to rush or dash rapidly or with force against an obstruction ⟨*rain* driving *against the windscreen*⟩ **2** to operate a vehicle **3** to drive an object of play (e g a golf ball) [ME *driven*, fr OE *drīfan*; akin to OHG *trīban* to drive] – **drive at** to imply as an ultimate meaning or conclusion ⟨*couldn't work out what she was* driving at⟩ – **drive up the wall** to infuriate or madden (sby)

²drive *n* **1** an act of driving: e g **a** a trip in a carriage or motor vehicle **b** a shoot in which the game is driven within the range of the guns **2** a private road giving access from a public way to a building on private land **3** a (military) offensive, aggressive, or expansionist move **4** a strong systematic group effort; a campaign **5a** a motivating instinctual need or acquired desire ⟨*a sexual* ~⟩ ⟨*a* ~ *for perfection*⟩ **b** great zeal in pursuing one's ends **6a** the means for giving motion to a machine (part) ⟨*a chain* ~⟩ **b** the means by or position from which the movement of a motor vehicle is controlled or directed **7** a device including a transport and heads for reading information from or writing information onto a tape, esp magnetic tape, or disc **8** the act or an instance of driving an object of play; *esp* an attacking cricket stroke played conventionally with a straight bat and designed to send the ball in front of the batsman's wicket

'drive-,in *adj or n* (being) a place (e g a bank, cinema, or restaurant) that people can use while remaining in their cars

¹drivel /'drivl/ *vi* **-ll-** (*NAm* **-l-**, **-ll-**), /'drivl·ing/ **1** to let saliva dribble from the mouth or mucus run from the nose **2** to talk stupidly and childishly or carelessly [ME *drivelen*, fr OE *dreflian*; akin to ON *draf* malt dregs, OE *deorc* dark] – **driveller** *n*

[2]**drivel** *n* foolish or childish nonsense

driver /'drievə/ *n* **1** a coachman **2** the operator of a motor vehicle **3** an implement (e g a hammer) for driving **4** a mechanical piece for imparting motion to another piece **5** a golf club with a wooden head used in hitting the ball long distances, esp off the tee [[1]DRIVE + [2]-ER] – **driverless** *adj*

'driver ˌant *n* any of various African and Asian ants that move in vast armies

'drive ˌshaft *n* PROPELLER SHAFT ☞ CAR

'driveˌway /-ˌway/ *n* DRIVE 2

driving /'drieving/ *adj* **1** that communicates force ⟨*a ~ wheel*⟩ **2a** having great force ⟨*~ rain*⟩ **b** acting with vigour; energetic

'driving ˌseat *n* the position of top authority or control

[1]**drizzle** /'driz(ə)l/ *vb* **drizzling** /'drizl·ing/ *vi* to rain in very small drops or very lightly ~ *vt* to shed or let fall in minute drops [perh alter. of ME *drysnen* to fall, fr OE *-drysnian* to disappear; akin to Goth *driusan* to fall]

[2]**drizzle** *n* a fine misty rain ☞ WEATHER – **drizzly** /'drizli/ *adj*

drogue /drohg/ *n* **1** SEA ANCHOR **2** a small parachute for stabilizing or decelerating sthg or for pulling a larger parachute out of stowage [prob alter. of [1]*drag*]

droit /droyt (*Fr* drwa)/ *n* a legal right or due ⟨~s *of admiralty*⟩ [MF, fr ML *directum*, fr LL, neut of *directus* just, fr L, direct]

droll /drohl/ *adj* humorous, whimsical, or odd [F *drôle*, fr *drôle* scamp, fr MF *drolle*, fr MD, imp] – **drollness** *n*, **drolly** /'drohl(l)i/ *adv*

drollery /'drohləri/ *n* **1** the act or an instance of jesting or droll behaviour **2** droll humour

-drome /-ˌdrohm/ *comb form* (→ *n*) **1** sthg that runs in (such) a direction ⟨*palin*drome⟩ ⟨*loxo*drome⟩ **2** racecourse ⟨*motor*-drome⟩ ⟨*hippo*drome⟩ **3** large place specially prepared for ⟨*aero*drome⟩ [Gk *-dromos*, fr *dromos* course, racecourse, act of running; akin to Gk *dramein* to run; (2, 3) MF, fr L *-dromos*, fr Gk *dromos*] – **-dromous** /-drəməs/ *comb form* (→ *adj*)

dromedary /'droməd(ə)ri, 'drum-/ *n* a (1-humped) camel bred esp for riding [ME *dromedarie*, fr MF *dromedaire*, fr LL *dromedarius*, fr L *dromad-*, *dromas*, fr Gk, running; akin to Gk *dramein* to run, *dromos* racecourse, OE *treppan* to tread]

[1]**drone** /'drohn/ *n* **1** the male of a bee (e g the honeybee) that has no sting and gathers no honey **2** sby who lives off others **3** a remotely-controlled pilotless aircraft, missile, or ship [ME, fr OE *drān*; akin to OHG *treno* drone]

[2]**drone** *vi* **1** to make a sustained deep murmuring or buzzing sound **2** to talk in a persistently monotonous tone – **droner** *n*, **droningly** *adv*

[3]**drone** *n* **1** any of the usu 3 pipes on a bagpipe that sound fixed continuous notes **2** a droning sound **3** an unvarying sustained bass note

drongo /'drong·goh/ *n, pl* **drongos, drongoes** *chiefly Austr* a worthless person; a fool – infml [perh fr *Drongo*, name of an unsuccessful Austr racehorse]

drool /droohl/ *vi* **1a** to secrete saliva in anticipation of food **b** DRIVEL 1 **2** to make a foolishly effusive show of pleasure ~ *vt* to express sentimentally or effusively [perh alter. of *drivel*]

[1]**droop** /droohp/ *vi* **1** to hang or incline downwards **2** to become depressed or weakened; languish ~ *vt* to let droop [ME *drupen*, fr ON *drūpa*; akin to OE *dropa* drop – more at DROP] – **droopingly** *adv*

[2]**droop** *n* the condition or appearance of drooping – **droopy** *adj*

[1]**drop** /drop/ *n* **1a(1)** the quantity of fluid that falls in 1 spherical mass **(2)** *pl* a dose of medicine measured by drops **b** a minute quantity ⟨*not a ~ of pity in him*⟩ **2** sthg that resembles a liquid drop: e g **a** an ornament that hangs from a piece of jewellery (e g an earring) **b** a small globular often medicated sweet or lozenge ⟨*pear ~*⟩ ⟨*cough ~*⟩ **3a** the act or an instance of dropping; a fall **b** a decline in quantity or quality **c** (the men or equipment dropped by) a parachute descent **4a** the distance from a higher to a lower level or through which sthg drops **b** a decrease of electric potential **5** sthg that drops, hangs, or falls: e g **a** an unframed piece of cloth stage scenery **b** a hinged platform on a gallows **6** *NAm* a central point or depository to which sthg (e g mail) is brought for distribution **7** a small quantity of drink, esp alcohol; *broadly* an alcoholic drink – infml **8** (a secret place used for the deposit and collection of) letters or stolen or illegal goods – slang [ME, fr OE *dropa*; akin to Goth *driusan* to fall – more at DREARY] – **droplet** /-lit/ *n* – **at the drop of a hat** without hesitation; promptly – **have/get the drop on** *NAm* to have or get at a disadvantage – slang

[2]**drop** *vb* **-pp-** *vi* **1** to fall in drops **2a(1)** to fall, esp unexpectedly or suddenly **(2)** to descend from one level to another ⟨*his voice* ~ped⟩ **b** to fall in a state of collapse or death ⟨*he'll work until he* ~s⟩ **c** *of a card* to become played by reason of the obligation to follow suit **3a** to cease to be of concern; lapse ⟨*let the matter ~*⟩ **b** to become less ⟨*production* ~ped⟩ ~ *vt* **1a** to let fall; cause to fall **b** to drop a catch offered by (a batsman) **2a** to lower from one level or position to another **b** to cause to lessen or decrease; reduce ⟨~ped *his speed*⟩ **3** to set down from a ship or vehicle; unload; *also* to airdrop **4a** to bring down with a shot or blow **b** to cause (a high card) to drop **c** to score (a goal) with a dropkick **5a** to give up (e g an idea) **b** to leave incomplete; cease ⟨~ped *what he was doing*⟩ **c** to break off an association or connection with ⟨~ped *his old friends*⟩; *also* to leave out of a team or group **6** to leave (a letter representing a speech sound) unsounded ⟨~ *the* h *in* have⟩ **7a** to utter or mention in a casual way ⟨~ *a hint*⟩ **b** to send through the post ⟨~ *us a line soon*⟩ **8** to lose ⟨~ped *£500 on the stock market*⟩ – infml – **drop a brick/clanger** to make an embarrassing error or mistaken remark – infml

drop behind *vb* to fail to keep up (with)

drop by *vi* DROP IN

'drop-ˌforge *vt* to forge between 2 dies using a drop hammer or punch press – **drop forger** *n*

'drop ˌgoal *n* a score in rugby made with a dropkick that passes over the goal's crossbar

'drop ˌhammer *n* a power hammer raised and then released to drop on metal resting on an anvil or die

ˌdrop 'handlebars *n pl* lowered curving handlebars, esp on a racing bicycle

drop in *vi* to pay a usu brief, casual, or unexpected visit

'dropˌkick /-ˌkik/ *n* a kick made (e g in rugby) by dropping a football to the ground and kicking it at the moment it starts to rebound – **drop-kick** *vb*, **drop kicker** *n*

'drop ,leaf *n* a hinged leaf on the side or end of a table that can be folded down – compare [1]LEAF 2b(1) – **drop-leaf** *adj*

'drop-,off *n* a marked dwindling or decline ⟨*a* ~ *in attendance*⟩

drop off *vi* **1** to fall asleep **2** to decline, slump

'drop,out /-,owt/ *n* **1** one who rejects or withdraws from participation in conventional society **2** a student who fails to complete or withdraws from a course, usu of higher education **3** a spot on a magnetic tape from which data has disappeared **4** a dropkick awarded to the defending team in rugby (e g after an unconverted try)

drop out *vi* **1** to withdraw from participation **2** to make a dropout in rugby

dropper /'dropə/ *n* a short usu glass tube fitted with a rubber bulb and used to measure or administer liquids by drops [[2]DROP + [2]-ER] – **dropperful** *n*

droppings /'dropingz/ *n pl* animal dung

'drop ,shot *n* a delicate shot in tennis, badminton, squash, etc that drops quickly after crossing the net or dies after hitting a wall

dropsy /'dropsi/ *n* oedema [ME *dropesie*, short for *ydropesie*, fr OF, fr L *hydropisis*, modif of Gk *hydrōps*, fr *hydōr* water – more at WATER] – **dropsical** *adj*

droshky /'droshki/ *also* **drosky** /'droski/ *n* any of various esp Russian 2-wheeled or 4-wheeled open carriages [Russ *drozhki*, fr *droga* pole of a waggon; akin to OE *dragan* to draw]

drosophila /dro'sofilə/ *n* any of a genus of small 2-winged fruit flies extensively used in genetic research [NL, genus name, fr Gk *drosos* dew + NL *-phila*, fem of *-philus* -phil]

dross /dros/ *n* **1** the scum on the surface of molten metal **2** waste, rubbish, or foreign matter; impurities [ME *dros*, fr OE *drōs* dregs] – **drossy** *adj*

drought /drowt/ *n* **1** a prolonged period of dryness **2** a prolonged shortage of sthg [ME, fr OE *drūgath*, fr *drūgian* to dry up; akin to OE *drȳge* dry – more at DRY] – **droughty** *adj*

drouth /drowt(h)/ *n, Scot, Irish, or NAm* a drought – used poetically in other varieties of English

[1]drove /drohv/ *n* **1** a group of animals driven or moving in a body **2** a crowd of people moving or acting together [ME, fr OE *drāf*, fr *drīfan* to drive – more at DRIVE]

[2]drove *past of* DRIVE

drover /'drohvə/ *n* one who drives cattle or sheep

drown /drown/ *vi* to become drowned ~ *vt* **1a** to suffocate by submergence, esp in water **b** to submerge, esp by a rise in the water level **c** to wet thoroughly; drench ⟨~ed *the chips with ketchup*⟩ **2** to engage (oneself) deeply and strenuously ⟨~ed *himself in work*⟩ **3** to blot out (a sound) by making a loud noise ⟨*his speech was* ~ed *out by boos – New Yorker*⟩ **4** to destroy (e g a sensation or an idea) as if by drowning ⟨~ed *his sorrows in drink*⟩ [ME *drounen*]

[1]drowse /drowz/ *vi* to doze ~ *vt* to pass (time) drowsily or in dozing – usu + *away* [prob akin to Goth *driusan* to fall – more at DREARY]

[2]drowse *n* the act or an instance of dozing

drowsy /'drowzy/ *adj* **1a** sleepy **b** tending to induce sleepiness ⟨*a* ~ *summer afternoon*⟩ **c** indolent, lethargic **2** giving the appearance of peaceful inactivity – **drowsily** *adv*, **drowsiness** *n*

drub /drub/ *vt* **-bb- 1** to beat severely **2** to defeat decisively [perh fr Ar *ḍaraba*]

[1]drudge /druj/ *vi* to do hard, menial, routine, or monotonous work [ME *druggen*; prob akin to OE *drēogan* to work, endure, L *firmus* firm] – **drudger** *n*, **drudgery** /'drujəri/ *n*

[2]drudge *n* one who drudges

[1]drug /drug/ *n* **1** a substance used as (or in the preparation of) a medication **2** a substance that causes addiction or habituation [ME *drogges, drouges*, fr OF *drogue*]

[2]drug *vt* **-gg- 1** to affect or adulterate with a drug **2** to administer a drug to **3** to lull or stupefy (as if) with a drug

drugget /'drugit/ *n* a coarse durable cloth used chiefly as a floor covering [MF *droguet*, dim. of *drogue* trash, drug]

druggist /'drugist/ *n* **1** one who deals in or dispenses drugs and medicines; a pharmacist **2** *NAm* the owner or manager of a drugstore

'drug,store /-,staw/ *n, chiefly NAm* a chemist's shop; *esp* one that also sells sweets, magazines, and refreshments

druid /'drooh·id/, *fem* **druidess** /-dis/ *n, often cap* **1** a member of a pre-Christian Celtic order of priests associated with a mistletoe cult **2** an officer of the Welsh Gorsedd **3** MANDARIN 1b [L *druides, druidae*, pl, fr Gaulish *druides*; akin to OIr *druī* wizard, W *derwen* oak tree, OE *trēow* tree] – **druidic** /drooh'idik/, **druidical** *adj, often cap*

[1]drum /drum/ *n* **1** a percussion instrument usu consisting of a hollow cylinder with a drumhead stretched over each end, that is beaten with a stick or a pair of sticks in playing **2** the tympanic membrane of the ear **3** the sound made by striking a drum; *also* any similar sound **4** sthg resembling a drum in shape: e g **a** a cylindrical machine or mechanical device or part; *esp* a metal cylinder coated with magnetic material on which data (e g for a computer) may be recorded **b** a cylindrical container; *specif* a large usu metal container for liquids **5** a dwelling; PAD 6 – slang [prob fr D *trom*; akin to MHG *trumme* drum] – **drumlike** *adj*

[2]drum *vb* **-mm-** *vi* **1** to beat a drum **2** to make a succession of strokes, taps, or vibrations that produce drumlike sounds **3** to throb or sound rhythmically ⟨*blood* ~med *in his ears*⟩ ~ *vt* **1** to summon or enlist (as if) by beating a drum ⟨~med *them into service*⟩ **2** to instil (an idea or lesson) by constant repetition – usu + *into* or *out of* ⟨~med *the idea into them*⟩ **3a** to strike or tap repeatedly **b** to produce (rhythmic sounds) by such action

[3]drum *n* **1** a drumlin **2** *chiefly Scot* a long narrow hill or ridge [ScGael *druim* back, ridge, fr OIr *druimm*]

'drum,beat /-,beet/ *n* a stroke on a drum or its sound

'drum ,brake *n* a brake that operates by the friction of pads pressing against a rotating drum

'drum,fire /-,fie·ə/ *n* artillery fire so continuous as to sound like a roll on a drum

'drum,head /-,hed/ *n* the material stretched over the end of a drum

drumhead court-martial *n* a summary court-martial [fr the use of a drumhead as a table]

drumlin /'drumlin/ *n* an elongated or oval hill formed from glacial debris ☞ GEOGRAPHY [IrGael *druim* back, ridge (fr OIr *druimm*) + E *-lin* (alter. of *-ling*)]

ˌdrum 'major *n* the marching leader of a band

drummer /'drumə/ *n* **1** one who plays a drum **2** *chiefly NAm* SALES REPRESENTATIVE

drum out *vt* to dismiss ignominiously; expel ⟨drummed *him* out *of the army*⟩

'drumˌstick /-ˌstik/ *n* **1** a stick for beating a drum **2** the part of a fowl's leg between the thigh and tarsus when cooked as food

drum up *vt* **1** to bring about by persistent effort ⟨drum up *some business*⟩ **2** to invent, originate ⟨drum up *a new time-saving method*⟩

[1]drunk /drungk/ *past part of* DRINK

[2]drunk *adj* **1** under the influence of alcohol **2** dominated by an intense feeling ⟨~ *with power*⟩ **3** DRUNKEN 2b [ME *drunke*, alter. of *drunken*]

[3]drunk *n* a person who is (habitually) drunk

drunkard /'drungkəd/ *n* a person who is habitually drunk

drunken /'drungkən/ *adj* **1** DRUNK 1 **2a** given to habitual excessive use of alcohol **b** of, characterized by, or resulting from alcoholic intoxication ⟨*a* ~ *brawl*⟩ **3** unsteady or lurching as if from alcoholic intoxication [ME, fr OE *druncen*, fr pp of *drincan* to drink] – **drunkenly** *adv*, **drunkenness** *n* – **drunk in charge** driving while intoxicated

drupe /droohp/ *n* a fruit (e g a cherry or almond) that has a stone enclosed by a fleshy layer and is covered by a flexible or stiff outermost layer [NL *drupa*, fr L, overripe olive, fr Gk *dryppa* olive] – **drupaceous** /drooh'payshəs/ *adj*

drupelet /'droohplit/ *n* a small drupe; *specif* any of the individual parts of an aggregate fruit (e g the raspberry)

Druze, Druse /droohz/ *n* a member of a religious sect originating among Muslims and centred in the mountains of Lebanon and Syria [Ar *Durūz*, pl, fr Muhammed ibn-Ism'aīlal- *Darazīy* †1019 Muslim religious leader]

[1]dry /drie/ *adj* **1a** (relatively) free from a liquid, esp water **b** not in or under water ⟨~ *land*⟩ **c** lacking precipitation or humidity ⟨*a* ~ *climate*⟩ **2a** characterized by exhaustion of a supply of water or liquid ⟨*a* ~ *well*⟩ ⟨*the barrel ran* ~⟩ **b** devoid of natural moisture ⟨~ *mouth*⟩; *also* thirsty **c** no longer sticky or damp ⟨*the paint is* ~⟩ **d** *of a mammal* not giving milk ⟨*a* ~ *cow*⟩ **e** lacking freshness; stale **f** anhydrous **3a** marked by the absence or scantiness of secretions ⟨*a* ~ *cough*⟩ **b** not shedding or accompanied by tears ⟨*no* ~ *eyes*⟩ **4** prohibiting the manufacture or distribution of alcoholic beverages ⟨*a* ~ *county*⟩ – compare WET 7 **5** lacking sweetness; sec **6** solid as opposed to liquid ⟨~ *groceries*⟩ **7** functioning without lubrication ⟨*a* ~ *clutch*⟩ **8** built or constructed without a process which requires water: **a** using no mortar ⟨~ *masonry*⟩ **b** using prefabricated materials (e g plasterboard) rather than a construction involving plaster or mortar ⟨~ *wall construction*⟩ **9a** not showing or communicating warmth, enthusiasm, or feeling; impassive **b** uninteresting ⟨~ *passages of description*⟩ **c** lacking embellishment, bias, or emotional concern; plain ⟨*the* ~ *facts*⟩ **10** not yielding what is expected or desired; unproductive ⟨*a* ~ *oil field*⟩ **11** marked by a matter-of-fact, ironic, or terse manner of expression ⟨~ *wit*⟩ [ME, fr OE *drȳge*; akin to OHG *truckan* dry, MLG *drœge, drēge*, MD *drōge*] – **dryish** *adj*, **dryishly** *adv*, **dryly** *adv*, **dryness** *n*

[2]dry *vb* to make or become dry – often + *out* – **dryable** *adj*

[3]dry *n, pl* **drys** sthg dry: e g **a** a dry place **b** *chiefly Austr* the dry season

dryad /'drie·ad, -əd/ *n* a nymph of the woods in Greek mythology [L *dryad-, dryas*, fr Gk, fr *drys* tree – more at TREE]

dryasdust /ˌdrie·əz'dust/ *adj* boring, pedantic [Dr Jonas *Dryasdust*, fictitious person to whom Sir Walter Scott †1832 Sc author dedicated some of his novels] – **dryasdust** /'--ˌ-/ *n*

dry cell *n* a primary cell whose electrolyte is not a liquid

ˌdry-'clean *vb* to subject to or undergo dry cleaning ☞ SYMBOL – **dry-cleanable** *adj*, **dry cleaner** *n*

ˌdry 'cleaning *n* **1** the cleaning of fabrics or garments with organic solvents, esp chlorinated hydrocarbons, and without water **2** that which is dry-cleaned *USE* ☞ SYMBOL

dry dock *n* a dock from which the water can be pumped to allow ships to be repaired

dryer /'drie·ə/ *n* a drier

dry fly *n* an artificial angling fly designed to float on the surface of the water

dry goods *n pl, NAm* drapery as distinguished esp from hardware and groceries

ˌdry 'ice *n* solidified carbon dioxide

'dry ˌnurse *n* a nurse who takes care of but does not breast-feed another woman's baby

dry out *vi* to undergo treatment for alcoholism or drug addiction

'dryˌpoint /-ˌpoynt/ *n* an engraving made with a pointed tool (e g a needle) directly into the metal plate without the use of acid

ˌdry 'rot *n* **1** (a fungus causing) a decay of seasoned timber in which the cellulose of wood is consumed leaving a soft skeleton which is readily reduced to powder **2** decay from within, caused esp by resistance to new forces ⟨*art infected by the* ~ *of formalism* – D G Mandelbaum⟩

dry run *n* **1** a firing practice without ammunition **2** a practice exercise; a rehearsal, trial

ˌdry-'shod *adj* having or keeping dry shoes or feet

'dryˌstone /-ˌstohn/ *adj* constructed of stone without the use of mortar

dry up *vi* **1** to disappear or cease to yield (as if) by evaporation, draining, or the cutting off of a source of supply **2** to wither or die through gradual loss of vitality **3** to wipe dry dishes, cutlery, etc by hand after they have been washed **4** to stop talking; SHUT UP – infml ~ *vt* to cause to dry up

dt's /ˌdee 'teez/ *n pl, often cap D&T* DELIRIUM TREMENS

dual /'dyooh·əl/ *adj* **1** *of grammatical number* denoting reference to 2 **2a** consisting of 2 (like) parts or elements **b** having a double character or nature [L *dualis*, fr *duo* two – more at TWO] – **dual** *n*, **duality** /dyooh'aləti/ *n*, **dualize** /'dyooh·əˌliez/ *vt*, **dually** *adv*

ˌdual 'carriageˌway *n, chiefly Br* a road that has traffic travelling in opposite directions separated by a central reservation

dualism /'dyooh·əˌliz(ə)m/ *n* **1** a theory that considers reality to consist of 2 independent and irreducible substances or elements **2** the quality or state of being dual **3** a doctrine that the universe is ruled by the 2 opposing principles of good and evil – **dualist** *n*, **dualistic** /,dyooh·ə'listik/ *adj*, **dualistically** /-'listikli/ *adj*

,dual-'purpose *adj* intended for or serving 2 purposes

[1]dub /dub/ *vt* **-bb- 1a** to confer knighthood on **b** to call by a descriptive name or epithet; nickname **2** *Br* to dress (a fishing fly) [ME *dubben*, fr OE *dubbian*; akin to ON *dubba* to dub, OHG *tubili* plug] – **dubber** *n*

[2]dub *vt* **-bb- 1** to make alterations to the original sound track of (a film): e g **a** to provide with a sound track in which the voices are not those of the actors on the screen **b** to provide with a sound track in a new language ⟨*in Europe, American films are usually* ~bed *into the local language*⟩ **2** to transpose (a previous recording) to a new record **3** *chiefly Br* MIX 1b(2) [by shortening & alter. fr *double*] – **dubber** *n*

dubbin /'dubin/ *also* **dubbing** /'dubing/ *n* a dressing of oil and tallow for leather [*dubbing*, gerund of *dub* (to dress leather)] – **dubbin** *vt*

dubiety /dyooh'bie·əti/ *n* **1** the state of being doubtful **2** a doubtful matter ***USE*** fml [LL *dubietas*, fr L *dubius*]

dubious /'dyoohbi·əs/ *adj* **1** giving rise to doubt; uncertain ⟨*they considered our scheme a little* ~⟩ **2** unsettled in opinion; undecided ⟨*they were a little* ~ *about our plan*⟩ **3** of uncertain outcome ⟨*a rather* ~ *experiment*⟩ **4** of questionable value, quality, or origin ⟨*won by* ~ *means*⟩ [L *dubius*, fr *dubare* to vacillate; akin to L *duo* two – more at TWO] – **dubiously** *adv*, **dubiousness** *n*

ducal /'dyoohkl/ *adj* of or relating to a duke or duchy [MF, fr LL *ducalis* of a leader, fr L *duc-, dux* leader – more at DUKE] – **ducally** *adv*

ducat /'dukət/ *n* a usu gold coin formerly used in many European countries [ME, fr MF, fr OIt *ducato* coin with the doge's portrait on it, fr *duca* doge, fr LGk *douk-, doux* leader, fr L *duc-, dux*]

duce /'doohchi/ *n* LEADER 2c(3) [It (*Il*) *Duce*, lit., the leader, title of Benito Mussolini †1945 It dictator, fr L *duc-, dux*]

duchess /'duchis/ *n* **1** the wife or widow of a duke **2** a woman having in her own right the rank of a duke [ME *duchesse*, fr MF, fr *duc* duke]

duchy /'duchi/ *n* a dukedom [ME *duche*, fr MF *duché*, fr *duc*]

[1]duck /duk/ *n, pl* **ducks**, (*1a*) **ducks**, *esp collectively* **duck 1a** any of various swimming birds in which the neck and legs are short, the bill is often broad and flat, and the sexes are almost always different from each other in plumage **b** the flesh of any of these birds used as food **2** a female duck – compare [2]DRAKE **3** *chiefly Br* DEAR 1b – often pl with sing. meaning but sing. in constr; infml [ME *doke*, fr OE *dūce*]

[2]duck *vt* **1** to thrust momentarily under water **2** to lower (e g the head), esp quickly as a bow or to avoid being hit **3** to avoid, evade ⟨~ *the issue*⟩ ~ *vi* **1** to plunge at least one's head under the surface of water **2a** to move the head or body suddenly; dodge **b** to bow, bob **3** to evade a duty, question, or responsibility [ME *douken*; akin to OHG *tūhhan* to dive, OE *dūce* duck] – **duck** *n*

[3]duck *n* a durable closely woven usu cotton fabric [D *doek* cloth; akin to OHG *tuoh* cloth, & perh to Skt *dhvaja* flag]

[4]duck *n* a score of nought, esp in cricket [short for *duck's egg*; fr the egg-shaped number 0]

'duck,bill /-,bil/ *n* the platypus

,duck,billed 'platypus *n* the platypus

'duck,board /-,bawd/ *n* a usu wooden board or slat used to make a path over wet or muddy ground – usu pl

'ducking ,stool /'duking/ *n* a seat attached to a plank and formerly used to plunge culprits into water

duckling /'dukling/ *n* a young duck

,ducks and 'drakes *n pl but sing in constr* the pastime of skimming flat stones or shells along the surface of calm water

duck's arse *n* a (style of) haircut in which the hair at the back is cut in the shape of a duck's tail – infml

'duck,weed /-,weed/ *n* any of several small free-floating stemless plants that often cover large areas of the surface of still water

[1]ducky /'duki/ *adj* darling, sweet – infml

[2]ducky, duckie *n* DEAR 1b – infml

[1]duct /dukt/ *n* **1** a bodily tube or vessel, esp when carrying the secretion of a gland **2a** a pipe, tube, or channel that conveys a substance **b** a pipe or tubular runway for carrying an electric power line, telephone cables, or other conductors **3** a continuous tube in plant tissue [NL *ductus*, fr ML, aqueduct, fr L, act of leading, fr *ductus*, pp of *ducere* to lead – more at TOW] – **ducting** *n*

[2]duct *vt* to convey (e g a gas) through a duct

ducted /'duktid/ *adj* situated or operating in a duct

ductile /'duktiel/ *adj* **1** capable of being easily fashioned into a new form **2** *of metals* capable of being drawn out or hammered thin **3** easily led or influenced; tractable ⟨*the* ~ *masses*⟩ – infml [MF & L; MF, fr L *ductilis*, fr *ductus*, pp] – **ductility** /duk'tiləti/ *n*

,ductless 'gland /-lis/ *n* ENDOCRINE 2

ductus arteriosus /,duktəs ahtiəri'ohsəs/ *n* a short broad blood vessel that bypasses the lungs and is found normally only in the foetus [NL, lit., arterial duct]

[1]dud /dud/ *n* **1** a bomb, missile, etc that fails to explode **2** *pl* personal belongings; *esp* clothes **3** a failure **4** a counterfeit, fake ***USE*** (*2, 3, & 4*) infml [(2) ME *dudde* coarse cloak; (1, 3, 4) E dial. *dud* (weak or spiritless person), perh fr *duds* clothes, rags]

[2]dud *adj* valueless ⟨~ *cheques*⟩ – infml

dude /d(y)oohd/ *n, chiefly NAm* **1** a dandy **2** a city-dweller; *esp* a man from the eastern USA holidaying (on a ranch) in the western USA ***USE*** infml [perh fr G dial., fool] – **dudish** *adj*, **dudishly** *adv*

'dude ,ranch *n* an American cattle ranch converted into a holiday centre, offering typical ranch activities such as camping and riding

dudgeon /'dujən/ *n* indignation, resentment – esp in *in high dudgeon* [origin unknown]

[1]due /dyooh/ *adj* **1** owed or owing as a debt **2a** owed or owing as a natural or moral right ⟨*got his* ~ *reward*⟩ **b** appropriate ⟨*after* ~ *consideration*⟩ **3a** (capable of) satisfying a need, obligation, or duty – compare IN DUE COURSE **b** regular, lawful ⟨~ *proof of loss*⟩ **4** ascribable – + *to* ⟨*this advance is partly* ~ *to a few men of genius* –A N Whitehead⟩ **5** payable **6** required or expected in the prearranged or normal course of events ⟨~ *to arrive at any time*⟩ [ME, fr MF *deu*, pp of *devoir* to owe, fr L *debēre* – more at DEBT] – **in due course** after a normal passage of time; in the expected or allocated time

[2]**due** *n* sthg due or owed: e g **a** sthg esp nonmaterial that rightfully belongs to one ⟨*I don't like him, but to give him his ~ he's a good singer*⟩ **b** *pl* fees, charges

[3]**due** *adv* directly, exactly – used before points of the compass ⟨~ *north*⟩

[1]**duel** /'dyooh·əl/ *n* **1** a formal combat with weapons fought between 2 people in the presence of witnesses in order to settle a quarrel **2** a conflict between usu evenly matched antagonistic people, ideas, or forces [ML *duellum*, fr OL, war]

[2]**duel** *vi* **-ll-** (*NAm* **-l-, -ll-**) to fight a duel – **dueller** *n*, **duellist** *n*

duenna /dyooh'enə/ *n* **1** an older woman serving as governess and companion to the younger ladies in a Spanish or Portuguese family **2** a chaperon [Sp *dueña*, fr L *domina* mistress] – **duennaship** *n*

duet /dyooh'et/ *n* a (musical) composition for 2 performers [It *duetto*, dim. of *duo*]

'**due to** *prep* BECAUSE OF 1 – though disapproved by many, now used by numerous educated speakers and writers; compare [1]DUE 4

[1]**duff** /duf/ *n* a boiled or steamed pudding, often containing dried fruit [E dial., alter. of *dough*]

[2]**duff** *adj, Br* not working; worthless, useless – slang [perh back-formation fr *duffer*]

duffel, duffle /'duf(ə)l/ *n* a coarse heavy woollen material with a thick nap [D *duffel*, fr *Duffel*, town in Belgium]

'**duffel ,bag** *n* a cylindrical fabric bag, closed by a drawstring, used for carrying personal belongings [*duffer, duffle* (kit, equipment), fr *duffel*]

'**duffel ,coat** *n* a coat made of duffel that is usu thigh- or knee-length, hooded, and fastened with toggles

duffer /'dufə/ *n* an incompetent, ineffectual, or clumsy person [perh fr Sc *doofart* stupid person]

duff up *vt, Br* BEAT 1a – slang [*duff* (to fake, cheat, bungle), perh back-formation fr *duffer*]

[1]**dug** /dug/ *past of* DIG

[2]**dug** /dug/ *n* an udder; *also* a teat – usu used with reference to animals but derog when used of a woman [perh of Scand origin; akin to OSw *dæggia* to suckle; akin to OE *delu* nipple]

dugong /'dooh,gong/ *n* an aquatic plant-eating mammal related to the manatee [NL, genus name, fr Malay & Tag *duyong* sea cow]

dugout /'dug,owt/ *n* **1** a boat made by hollowing out a large log **2** a shelter dug in the ground or in a hillside, esp for troops

duiker /'diekə/ *n* any of several small African antelopes [Afrik, lit., diver, fr *duik* to dive, fr MD *dūken*; akin to OHG *tūhhan* to dive – more at [2]DUCK]

duke /dyoohk/ *n* **1** a sovereign ruler of a European duchy **2** a nobleman of the highest hereditary rank; *esp* a member of the highest rank of the British peerage **3** a fist – usu pl; slang [ME, fr OF *duc*, fr L *duc-, dux*, fr *ducere* to lead – more at TOW; (3) rhyming slang *Duke (of Yorks)* forks, fingers, hands] – **dukedom** *n*

dulcet /'dulsit/ *adj, esp of sounds* sweetly pleasant or soothing ⟨~ *tones*⟩ [ME *doucet*, fr MF, fr *douz* sweet, fr L *dulcis*] – **dulcetly** *adv*

dulcimer /'dulsimə/ *n* a stringed instrument having strings of graduated length stretched over a sounding board and played with light hammers [ME *dowcemere*, fr MF *doulcemer*, fr OIt *dolcimelo*, fr *dolce* sweet, fr L *dulcis*]

[1]**dull** /dul/ *adj* **1** mentally slow; stupid **2a** slow in perception or sensibility; insensible **b** lacking zest or vivacity; listless **3** lacking sharpness of cutting edge or point; blunt **4** not resonant or ringing ⟨*a ~ booming sound*⟩ **5** *of a colour* low in saturation and lightness **6** cloudy, overcast **7** boring, uninteresting [ME *dul*; akin to OE *dol* foolish, & prob to L *fumus* smoke – more at FUME] – **dullness, dulness** *n*, **dully** *adv*

[2]**dull** *vb* to make or become dull ⟨*eyes and ears* ~ed *by age*⟩

dullard /'duləd/ *n* a stupid or insensitive person

dulse /duls/ *n* any of several coarse edible red seaweeds [ScGael & IrGael *duileasg*; akin to W *delysg* dulse]

duly /'dyoohli/ *adv* in a due manner, time, or degree; properly ⟨*your suggestion has been ~ noted*⟩

duma /'dooh,mah/ *n* a representative council in tsarist Russia [Russ, of Gmc origin; akin to OE *dōm* judgment – more at DOOM]

dumb /dum/ *adj* **1** devoid of the power of speech **2** naturally incapable of speech ⟨~ *animals*⟩ **3** not expressed in uttered words ⟨~ *insolence*⟩ **4a** not willing to speak **b** temporarily unable to speak (e g from astonishment) ⟨*struck* ~⟩ **5** lacking some usual attribute or accompaniment **6** stupid [ME, fr OE; akin to OHG *tumb* mute, ON *tumbr*, OE *dēaf* deaf – more at DEAF] – **dumbly** /'dumli/ *adv*, **dumbness** *n*

dumbbell /'dum,bel/ *n* **1** a short bar with adjustable weights at each end used usu in pairs for weight training **2** *NAm* DUMMY 6

dumbfound, dumfound /dum'fownd/ *vt* to strike dumb with astonishment; amaze [*dumb* + *-found* (as in *confound*)]

'**dumb ,show** *n* (a play or part of a play presented by) movement, signs, and gestures without words

'**dumb,struck** /-,struk/ *adj* dumbfounded

,**dumb 'waiter** *n* **1** a movable table or stand often with revolving shelves for holding food or dishes **2** a small lift for conveying food and dishes (e g from the kitchen to the dining area of a restaurant)

dumdum /'dum,dum/ *n* a bullet that expands on impact and inflicts a severe wound [*Dum-Dum*, arsenal near Calcutta, India]

[1]**dummy** /'dumi/ *n* **1** the exposed hand in bridge played by the declarer in addition to his/her own hand; *also* the player whose hand is a dummy **2** an imitation or copy of sthg used to reproduce some of the attributes of the original; e g **a** *chiefly Br* a rubber teat given to babies to suck in order to soothe them **b** a large puppet in usu human form, used by a ventriloquist **c** a model of the human body, esp the torso, used for fitting or displaying clothes **3** a person or corporation that seems to act independently but is in reality acting for or at the direction of another **4** a pattern for a printing job showing the position of typographic elements (e g text and illustrations) **5** an instance of dummying an opponent in sports **6** a dull or stupid person – infml [[1]*dumb* + *-y*; orig sense, dumb person]

[2]**dummy** *adj* resembling or being a dummy: e g **a**

sham, artificial **b** existing in name only; fictitious ⟨*bank accounts held in ~ names*⟩

[3]**dummy** *vi* **1** to deceive an opponent (e g in rugby or soccer) by pretending to pass or release the ball while still retaining possession of it **2** *NAm* to refuse to talk – usu + *up*; slang ~ *vt* to deceive (an opponent) by dummying

'**dummy ,run** *n* a rehearsal; TRIAL RUN

[1]**dump** /dump/ *vt* **1a** to unload or let fall in a heap or mass **b** to get rid of unceremoniously or irresponsibly; abandon **2** to sell in quantity at a very low price; *specif* to sell abroad at less than the market price at home **3** to copy (data in a computer's internal storage) onto an external storage medium [perh fr D *dompen* to immerse, topple; akin to OE *dyppan* to dip – more at DIP] – **dumper** *n*

[2]**dump** *n* **1a** an accumulation of discarded materials (e g refuse) **b** a place where such materials are dumped **2** a quantity of esp military reserve materials accumulated in 1 place ⟨*arms* ~⟩ **3** an instance of dumping data stored in a computer **4** a disorderly, slovenly, or dilapidated place – infml

'**dumper ,truck** /'dumpə/, '**dump ,truck** *n* a lorry whose body may be tilted to empty the contents

dumpling /'dumpling/ *n* **1** a small usu rounded mass of leavened dough cooked by boiling or steaming often in stew **2** a short round person – humor [perh alter. of *lump*]

dumps /dumps/ *n pl* a gloomy state of mind; despondency – esp in *in the dumps*; infml [prob fr D *domp* haze, fr MD *damp*]

dumpy /'dumpi/ *adj* short and thick in build; squat [E dial. *dump* (lump)] – **dumpily** *adv*, **dumpiness** *n*

[1]**dun** /dun/ *adj* **1** of the colour dun **2** *of a horse* having a greyish or light brownish colour [ME, fr OE *dunn* – more at DUSK]

[2]**dun** *n* **1** a dun horse **2** a slightly brownish dark grey **3** (an artificial fly tied to imitate) a mayfly that has not acquired all the typical adult characteristics

[3]**dun** *vt* **-nn-** to make persistent demands upon for payment [perh short for obs *dunkirk* (privateer), fr *Dunkirk, Dunkerque* port in France]

[4]**dun** *n* **1** one who duns **2** an urgent request; *esp* a demand for payment

[5]**dun** *n* an Irish or Scottish stronghold protected by usu 2 encircling mounds or a mound and a palisade [ScGael & IrGael *dūn*]

dunce /duns/ *n* a dull or stupid person [John *Duns* Scotus †1308 Sc theologian whose once accepted writings were ridiculed in the 16th c]

dunce's cap *n* a conical cap formerly used to humiliate slow learners at school

Dun'dee ,cake /dun'dee/ *n* a fruit cake, usu decorated on top with skinned almonds [*Dundee*, city in Scotland]

dunderhead /'dundə,hed/ *n* a dunce, blockhead [perh fr D *donder* thunder + E *head*; akin to OHG *thonar* thunder – more at THUNDER] – **dunderheaded** /,dundə'hedid/ *adj*

dundrearies /dun'driəriz/ *n pl, often cap* long flowing side-whiskers worn without a beard [Lord *Dundreary*, character in the play *Our American Cousin* by Tom Taylor †1880 E dramatist]

dune /dyoohn/ *n* a hill or ridge of sand piled up by the wind ☞ GEOGRAPHY [F, fr OF, fr MD; akin to OE *dūn* down – more at DOWN]

[1]**dung** /dung/ *n* the excrement of an animal [ME, fr OE; akin to ON *dyngja* manure pile, Lith *dengti* to cover] – **dungy** /'dung·i/ *adj*

[2]**dung** *vt* to fertilize or dress with manure ~ *vi*, *of an animal* to defecate

dungaree /,dung·gə'ree/ *n* a heavy coarse durable cotton twill woven from coloured yarns; *specif* blue denim [Hindi *dūgrī*]

,dunga'rees /-reez/ *n pl* a 1-piece outer garment consisting of trousers and a bib with shoulder straps fastened at the back – **dungaree** *adj*

'**dung ,beetle** *n* a beetle that rolls balls of dung in which to lay its eggs

dungeon /'dunjən/ *n* a dark usu underground prison or vault, esp in a castle ☞ CHURCH [ME *donjon* inner tower in a castle, strong prison, fr MF, fr (assumed) ML *dominion-, dominio*, fr L *dominus* lord – more at DAME]

'**dung,hill** /-,hil/ *n* a heap of dung (e g in a farmyard)

dunk /dungk/ *vt* to dip (e g a piece of bread) into liquid (e g soup) before eating [PaG *dunke*, fr MHG *dunken*, fr OHG *dunkōn*]

dunlin /'dunlin/ *n, pl* **dunlins**, *esp collectively* **dunlin** a small widely distributed brown-backed sandpiper [[1]*dun* + *-lin* (alter. of *-ling*)]

Dunlop /'dunlop/ *n* a moist Scottish cheese similar to Cheddar [*Dunlop*, town in Ayr, Scotland]

dunnage /'dunij/ *n* **1** loose materials or padding used to prevent damage **2** (personal) baggage [origin unknown]

dunno /də'noh/ don't know – used in writing to represent nonstandard speech [by alter.]

dunnock /'dunək/ *n* a small dull-coloured European bird common in gardens and scrub [ME *dunoke*, fr [1]*dun* + *-oc, -oke* -ock]

dunny /'duni/ *n, chiefly Austr & NZ* a toilet – infml [by shortening & alter. fr *dunnaken, dannaken* (toilet), fr *danna* (human excrement)]

duo /'dyooh,oh/ *n, pl* **duos** a pair (of performers); *also* a piece (e g of music) written for 2 players [It, fr L, two – more at TWO]

duo- *comb form* two [L *duo*]

duodecimal /,dyooh·oh'desim(ə)l/ *adj* proceeding by or based on the number of 12 [L *duodecim* – more at DOZEN] – **duodecimal** *n*

,duo'decimo /-'desimoh/ *n, pl* **duodecimos** a book format in which a folded sheet forms 12 leaves; *also* a book in this format [L, abl of *duodecimus* twelfth, fr *duodecim*]

duoden-, duodeno- *comb form* duodenum ⟨duoden*itis*⟩ ⟨duodeno*gram*⟩ [NL, fr ML *duodenum*]

duodenum /,dyooh·ə'deenəm/ *n, pl* **duodena** /-nə/, **duodenums** the first part of the small intestine extending from the stomach to the jejunum ☞ DIGESTION [ME, fr ML, fr L *duodeni* twelve each, fr *duodecim* twelve; fr its length, about 12 fingers' breadth] – **duodenal** *adj*

duologue /'dyooh·ə,log/ *n* a (theatrical) dialogue between 2 people

duomo /dooh'ohmoh/ *n, pl* **duomos** a cathedral [It – more at DOME]

duotone /'dyooh·oh,tohn, 'dyooh·ə-/ *adj* of or in 2 colours

[1]**dupe** /dyoohp/ *n* one who is easily deceived or cheated [F, fr MF *duppe*, prob alter. of *huppe* hoopoe]

[2]dupe *vt* to make a dupe of; deceive – **duper** *n*, **dupery** /'dyoohpəri/ *n*

dupion /'doohpion(h)/ *n* a rough silk fabric [F *doupion*, fr It *doppione* double cocoon made by two silkworms, aug of *doppio* double, fr L *duplos*]

duple /'dyoohpl/ *adj* **1** having 2 elements; twofold **2** marked by 2 or a multiple of 2 beats per bar of music [L *duplus* double – more at DOUBLE]

[1]duplex /'dyooh,pleks/ *adj* **1** double, twofold **2** allowing telecommunication in opposite directions simultaneously [L, fr *duo* two + *-plex* -fold – more at TWO, SIMPLE]

[2]duplex *n* sthg duplex: e g **a** *NAm* a 2-family house **b** *NAm* a flat on 2 floors

[1]duplicate /'d(y)oohplikət/ *adj* **1a** consisting of or existing in 2 corresponding or identical parts or examples ⟨~ *invoices*⟩ **b** being the same as another ⟨*a* ~ *key*⟩ **2** being a card game, specif bridge, in which different players play identical hands in order to compare scores [ME, fr L *duplicatus*, pp of *duplicare* to double, fr *duplic-*, *duplex*]

[2]duplicate *n* **1** either of 2 things that exactly resemble each other; *specif* an equally valid copy of a legal document **2** a copy – **in duplicate** with an original and 1 copy ⟨*typed* ~⟩; *also* with 2 identical copies

[3]duplicate /'d(y)oohpli,kayt/ *vt* **1** to make double or twofold **2** to make an exact copy of ⟨~ *the document*⟩ ~ *vi* to replicate ⟨*DNA in chromosomes* ~s⟩ – **duplication** /-'kaysh(ə)n/ *n*, **duplicative** /-kətiv/ *adj*

duplicator /'d(y)oohpli,kaytə/ *n* a machine for making copies, esp by means other than photocopying or xeroxing [[3]DUPLICATE + [1]-OR]

duplicity /dyooh'plisəti/ *n* malicious deception in thought, speech, or action – **duplicitous** /-sitəs/ *adj*, **duplicitously** *adv*

duppy /'dupi/ *n* a usu malevolent ghost or spirit in W Indian folklore [Bube *dupe* ghost]

durable /'dyooərəbl; *also* j-/ *adj* able to exist or be used for a long time without significant deterioration [ME, fr MF, fr L *durabilis*, fr *durare* to last, endure – more at DURING] – **durableness** *n*, **durably** *adv*, **durability** /-'biləti/ *n*

'durables *n pl* consumer goods (e g vehicles and household appliances) expected to have a long lifetime

Duralumin /dyoo'ralyoomin; *also* joo-/ *trademark* – used for an alloy of aluminium, copper, manganese, and magnesium comparable in strength and hardness to soft steel

dura mater /,dyooərə 'mahtə, 'may-/ *n* the tough fibrous membrane that envelops the brain and spinal cord [ME, fr ML, lit., hard mother]

duramen /dyoo(ə)'rahmin, -'ray-; *also* j-/ *n* heartwood [NL, fr L, hardness, fr *durare* to harden, last – more at DURING]

durance /'dyooərəns; *also* j-/ *n, archaic* imprisonment – often in *durance vile* ⟨*a convict suffered* '~ *vile*" – *Irish Digest*⟩ [MF, fr *durer* to endure]

duration /dyoo(ə)'raysh(ə)n/ *n* **1** continuance in time **2** the time during which sthg exists or lasts

durative /'dyooərətiv/ *adj* of or being a verbal aspect expressing continuing action – **durative** *n*

durbar /'duh,bah/ *n* a reception held in former times by an Indian prince or a British governor or viceroy in India [Hindi *darbār*, fr Per, fr *dar* door + *bār* admission, audience]

duress /dyoo(ə)'res; *also* j-/ *n* **1** forcible restraint or restriction **2** compulsion by threat, violence, or imprisonment [ME *duresse*, fr MF *duresce* hardness, severity, fr L *duritia*, fr *durus*]

Durex /'dyooəreks/ *trademark* – used for a condom

durian /'dyooəri·ən/ *n* (an E Indian tree bearing) a large oval pleasant-tasting but foul-smelling tropical fruit with a prickly rind [Malay]

during /'dyooəring; *also* j-/ *prep* **1** throughout the whole duration of ⟨*swims every day* ~ *the summer*⟩ **2** at some point in the course of ⟨*takes his holiday* ~ *July*⟩ [ME, fr prp of *duren* to last, fr OF *durer*, fr L *durare* to harden, endure, fr *durus* hard; perh akin to Skt *dāru* wood – more at TREE]

durmast /'duh,mahst/ *n* a European oak valued esp for its dark heavy tough elastic wood [perh alter. of *dun mast*, fr [1]*dun* + *mast*]

durum /'dyooərəm; *also* j-/ *n* a hard wheat that yields a glutenous flour used esp to make pasta [NL, fr L, neut of *durus* hard]

dusk /dusk/ *n* (the darker part of) twilight ⟨*lights go on at* ~⟩ [ME *dosk, duske* dusky, alter. of OE *dox*; akin to L *fuscus* dark brown, OE *dunn* dun, *dūst* dust]

dusky /'duski/ *adj* **1** somewhat dark in colour; *esp* dark-skinned **2** shadowy, gloomy – **duskily** *adv*, **duskiness** *n*

[1]dust /dust/ *n* **1** fine dry particles of any solid matter, esp earth; *specif* the fine particles of waste that settle esp on household surfaces **2** the particles into which sthg, esp the human body, disintegrates or decays **3** sthg worthless ⟨*worldly success was* ~ *to him*⟩ **4** the surface of the ground – compare BITE THE DUST **5a** a cloud of dust ⟨*the cars raised quite a* ~⟩ **b** confusion, disturbance – esp in *kick up/raise a dust* [ME, fr OE *dūst*; akin to L *furere* to rage, Gk *thyein*] – **dustless** *adj*, **dustlike** *adj*

[2]dust *vt* **1** to make free of dust (e g by wiping or beating) **2** to prepare to use again – usu + *down* or *off* **3a** to sprinkle with fine particles ⟨~ *a cake with icing sugar*⟩ **b** to sprinkle in the form of dust ⟨~ *sugar over a cake*⟩ ~ *vi* **1** *of a bird* to work dust into the feathers **2** to remove dust (e g from household articles), esp by wiping or brushing

'dust,bin /-,bin/ *n*, *Br* a container for holding household refuse until collection

'dust ,bowl *n* a region that suffers from prolonged droughts and dust storms

'dust,cart /-,kaht/ *n*, *Br* a vehicle for collecting household waste

'dust,coat /-,koht/ *n*, *chiefly Br* a loose lightweight coat worn to protect clothing

'dust,cover /-,kuvə/ *n* **1** a dustsheet **2** DUST JACKET

'dust ,devil *n* a small whirlwind containing sand or dust

duster /'dustə/ *n* sthg that removes dust; *specif* a cloth for removing dust from household articles

'dust ,jacket *n* a removable outer paper cover for a book

'dustman /-mən/ *n*, *Br* one employed to remove household refuse

'dust,pan /-,pan/ *n* a shovel-like utensil with a handle into which household dust and litter is swept

'dust,sheet /-,sheet/ *n* a large sheet (e g of cloth)

used as a cover to protect sthg, esp furniture, from dust

'dust ,shot *n* the smallest size of shot

'dust ,storm *n* a dust-laden wind or whirlwind; *esp* a whirlwind moving across a dry region

'dust-,up *n* a quarrel, row – infml

'dust ,wrapper *n* DUST JACKET

dusty /'dusti/ *adj* **1** covered with or full of dust **2** consisting of dust; powdery **3** resembling dust, esp in consistency or colour **4** lacking vitality; dry ⟨~ *scholarship*⟩ – **dustily** *adv*, **dustiness** *n* – **not so dusty** fairly good

,dusty 'miller *n* any of several plants having leaves covered in dense white hairs

¹dutch /duch/ *adv, often cap* with each person paying for him-/herself ⟨*we always go* ~⟩ [*Dutch*]

²dutch *n, Br* one's wife – slang [by shortening & alter. fr *duchess*]

Dutch *n* **1** the Germanic language of the Netherlands ☞ LANGUAGE **2** *pl in constr* the people of the Netherlands [ME *Duche* German, fr *Duch, Duche*, adj, fr MD *duutsch*; akin to OHG *diutisc* German, Goth *thiudisko* as a gentile, *thiuda* people, Oscan *touto* city] – **Dutch** *adj*, **Dutchman** *n*

,Dutch 'auction *n* an auction in which the auctioneer gradually reduces the bidding price until a bid is received

,Dutch 'barn *n* a large barn with open sides used esp for storage of hay

,Dutch 'cap *n* a moulded cap, usu of thin rubber, that fits over the uterine cervix to act as a mechanical contraceptive barrier

,Dutch 'courage *n* courage produced by intoxication rather than inherent resolution

,Dutch 'elm di,sease *n* a fatal disease of elms caused by a fungus, spread from tree to tree by a beetle, and characterized by yellowing of the foliage and defoliation

,Dutch 'hoe *n* a garden hoe that has both edges sharpened

,Dutch 'oven *n* **1** a 3-walled metal shield used for roasting before an open fire **2** a brick oven in which food is cooked by heat radiating from the prewarmed walls

,Dutch Re'formed ,Church *n* a branch of the Calvinist Church to which the majority of Afrikaans-speaking South Africans belong

,Dutch 'treat *n* a meal or entertainment for which each person pays for him-/herself

,Dutch 'uncle *n* one who admonishes sternly and bluntly

duteous /'dyoohti·əs, -tyəs/ *adj* dutiful, obedient – fml [irreg fr *duty*]

dutiable /'dyoohti·əbl, -tyəbl/ *adj* subject to a duty ⟨~ *imports*⟩

dutiful /'dyoohtif(ə)l/ *adj* **1** filled with or motivated by a sense of duty ⟨*a* ~ *son*⟩ **2** proceeding from or expressive of a sense of duty ⟨~ *affection*⟩ – **dutifully** *adv*, **dutifulness** *n*

duty /'dyoohti/ *n* **1** conduct due to parents and superiors; respect **2a** tasks, conduct, service, or functions that arise from one's position, job, or moral obligations **b** assigned (military) service or business **3a** a moral or legal obligation **b** the force of moral obligation **4** a tax, esp on imports **5** a measure of efficiency expressed in terms of the amount of work done in relation to the energy consumed [ME *duete*, fr AF *dueté*, fr OF *deu* due]

,duty-'free *adj* exempted from duty

duumvir /dyooh'umvə, 'dyooh·əmvə/ *n* either of 2 officers or magistrates of ancient Rome constituting a board or court [L, fr *duum* (gen of *duo* two) + *vir* man]

duvet /'doohvay/ *n* a large quilt filled with insulating material (e g down, feathers, or acrylic fibre), usu placed inside a removable fabric cover and used in place of bedclothes [F, lit., down]

¹dwarf /dwawf/ *n, pl* **dwarfs, dwarves** /dwawvz/ **1** a person of unusually small stature; *esp* one whose bodily proportions are abnormal **2** an animal or plant much below normal size **3** a small manlike creature in esp Norse and Germanic mythology who was skilled as a craftsman [ME *dwerg, dwerf*, fr OE *dweorg, dweorh*; akin to OHG *twerg* dwarf] – **dwarfish** *adj*, **dwarfishness** *n*, **dwarflike** *adj*, **dwarfness** *n*

²dwarf *vt* **1** to stunt the growth of **2** to cause to appear smaller ⟨*the other buildings are* ~ed *by the skyscraper*⟩

dwarfism /'dwaw,fiz(ə)m/ *n* the condition of stunted growth

,dwarf 'star *n* a relatively small star (e g the sun) of ordinary luminosity

dwell /dwel/ *vi* **dwelt** /dwelt/, **dwelled** /dweld, dwelt/ **1** to remain for a time **2** to keep the attention directed, esp in speech or writing; linger – + *on* or *upon* ⟨dwelt *on the weaknesses in his opponent's arguments*⟩ **3** to live as a resident; reside – fml [ME *dwellen*, fr OE *dwellan* to go astray, hinder; akin to OHG *twellen* to tarry] – **dweller** *n*

dwelling /'dweling/ *n* a place (e g a house or flat) in which people live – fml or humor

dwindle /'dwindl/ *vi* **dwindling** /'dwindling/ to become steadily less in quantity; shrink, diminish [prob freq of E dial. *dwine* (to waste away), fr ME *dwinen*, fr OE *dwīnan*]

DX, Dx *n* long-range radio transmissions ⟨*when some of the best* ~ *may be heard – Radio & Electronics World*⟩ ⟨~ *listeners*⟩

DXer, Dxer *n* someone whose hobby is listening to DX

DXing, Dxing *n* the hobby of listening to DX

dy- /die-/, **dyo-** *comb form* two ⟨dy*archy*⟩ [LL, fr Gk, fr *dyo* – more at TWO]

dyad /'die,ad/ *n* a pair; *specif* COUPLE 1 – fml [LL *dyad-, dyas*, fr Gk, fr *dyo*] – **dyadic** /die'adik/ *adj*, **dyadically** *adv*

Dyak, Dayak /'die,ak/ *n* **1** (a member of) any of several Indonesian peoples of the interior of Borneo **2** the language of the Dyaks ☞ LANGUAGE [Malay *dayak* up-country]

dyarchy, diarchy /'die,ahki/ *n* a government in which power is vested in 2 rulers

dybbuk /'dibək/ *n, pl* **dybbukim** /-kim/ *also* **dybbuks** an evil spirit that inhabits the body of a living person in Jewish folklore [LHeb *dibbūq*]

¹dye /die/ *n* **1** a colour or tint produced by dyeing **2** a soluble or insoluble colouring matter [ME *dehe*, fr OE *dēah, dēag*; akin to L *fumus* smoke – more at FUME]

²dye *vt* **dyeing** to impart a new and often permanent colour to, esp by impregnation with a dye – **dyer** *n*, **dyeable** /'die·əbl/ *adj*, **dyeability** /,die·ə'biləti/ *n*

,dyed-in-the-'wool *adj* thoroughgoing, uncompromising ⟨*a* ~ *conservative*⟩

'dye,stuff /-,stuf/ *n* DYE 2

[1]**'dye,wood** /-,wood/ *n* a wood (e g fustic) yielding a dye

dying /'die·ing/ *pres part of* DIE

[1]**dyke, dike** /diek/ *n* **1** an artificial watercourse; a ditch **2** a bank, usu of earth, constructed to control or confine water **3** a barrier preventing passage, esp of sthg undesirable **4** a raised causeway **5** a body of intrusive igneous rock running across the strata ☞ GEOGRAPHY **6** *chiefly Br* a natural watercourse **7** *dial Br* a wall or fence of turf or stone [ME, fr OE *dīc* ditch, dyke; akin to MHG *tīch* pond, dyke, L *figere* to fasten, pierce]

[2]**dyke, dike** *vt* to surround or protect with a dyke

[1]**dynamic** /die'namik, di-/ *adj* **1a** of physical force or energy in motion **b** of dynamics **2a** marked by continuous activity or change ⟨*a ~ population*⟩ **b** energetic, forceful ⟨*a ~ personality*⟩ [F *dynamique*, fr Gk *dynamikos* powerful, fr *dynamis* power, fr *dynasthai* to be able] – **dynamical** *adj*, **dynamically** *adv*

[2]**dynamic** *n* a dynamic force

dy'namics *n pl but sing or pl in constr* **1** a branch of mechanics that deals with forces and their relation to the motion of bodies **2** a pattern of change or growth ⟨*population ~*⟩ **3** variation and contrast in force or intensity (e g in music)

dynamism /'dienə,miz(ə)m/ *n* **1a** a philosophical system that describes the universe in terms of the interplay of forces **b** DYNAMICS 2 **2** dynamic quality – **dynamist** *n*, **dynamistic** /-'mistik/ *adj*

[1]**dynamite** /'dienə,miet/ *n* **1** a blasting explosive that is made of nitroglycerine absorbed in a porous material **2** sby or sthg that has explosive force or effect – infml

[2]**dynamite** *vt* to destroy with dynamite – **dynamiter** *n*

dynamo /'dienəmoh/ *n, pl* **dynamos** **1** a machine by which mechanical energy is converted into electrical energy; *specif* such a device that produces direct current (e g in a motor car) ☞ ENERGY **2** a forceful energetic person [short for *dynamoelectric machine*]

dynamometer /,dienə'momitə/ *n* an instrument for measuring power exerted (e g by an engine) [F *dynamomètre*, fr Gk *dynamis* power + F *-mètre* -meter] – **dynamometric** /-moh'metrik/ *adj*, **dynamometry** /-'momitri/ *n*

dynast /'dinəst, -nast/ *n* a usu hereditary ruler [L *dynastes*, fr Gk *dynastēs*, fr *dynasthai* to be able, have power]

dynasty /'dinəsti/ *n* a succession of hereditary rulers; *also* the time during which such a dynasty rules – **dynastic** /di'nastik/ *adj*, **dynastically** *adv*

dynatron /'dienə,tron/ *n* a thermionic valve having 4 electrodes and used esp to generate oscillations [Gk *dynamis* power]

dyne /dien/ *n* the cgs unit of force; 10^{-5}N ☞ UNIT [F, fr Gk *dynamis*]

dyo- – see DY-

dys- /dis-/ *prefix* **1** abnormal; impaired ⟨dys*function*⟩ ⟨dys*plasia*⟩ **2** difficult; painful ⟨dys*uria*⟩ ⟨dys*menorrhoea*⟩ – compare EU- 1 [ME *dis-* bad, difficult, fr MF & L; MF *dis-*, fr L *dys-*, fr Gk; akin to OE *tō-*, *te-* apart, Skt *dus-* bad, difficult]

dyscrasia /dis'krayzi·ə, -zh(y)ə/ *n* an abnormal condition of the body or of one of its parts ⟨*a blood ~*⟩ [NL, fr ML, bad mixture of humours, fr Gk *dyskrasia*, fr *dys-* + *krasis* mixture, fr *kerannynai* to mix]

dysentery /'dis(ə)ntri/ *n* any of several infectious diseases characterized by severe diarrhoea, usu with passing of mucus and blood [ME *dissenterie*, fr L *dysenteria*, fr Gk, fr *dys-* + *enteron* intestine – more at INTER-] – **dysenteric** /-'terik/ *adj*

dysfunction, disfunction /dis'fungksh(ə)n/ *n* impaired or abnormal functioning – **dysfunctional** *adj*

dys'genic /-'jenik/ *adj* detrimental to the hereditary qualities of a stock

dys'genics /-'jeniks/ *n pl but sing in constr* the study of racial degeneration

dys'lexia /-'leksi·ə/ *n* a maldevelopment of reading ability in otherwise normal children due to a neurological disorder [NL, fr *dys-* + Gk *lexis* word, speech] – **dyslexic** /-sik/ *adj*

,dysmenor'rhoea /-menə'riə/ *n* painful menstruation [NL]

dys'pepsia /-'pepsi·ə/ *n* indigestion [L, fr Gk, fr *dys-* + *pepsis* digestion, fr *peptein, pessein* to cook, digest – more at COOK]

dys'peptic /-'peptik/ *adj* **1** relating to or having dyspepsia **2** showing a sour disposition; ill-tempered – **dyspeptic** *n*, **dyspeptically** *adv*

dys'phasia /-'fayzyə, -zh(y)ə/ *n* loss of or deficiency in the power to use or understand language as a result of injury to or disease of the brain [NL] – **dysphasic** /-zik/ *n or adj*

dys'phoria /-'fawri·ə/ *n* a state of feeling unwell or unhappy – compare EUPHORIA [NL, fr Gk, fr *dysphoros* hard to bear, fr *dys-* + *pherein* to bear – more at [2]BEAR] – **dysphoric** /-'forik/ *adj*

dys'plasia /-'playzi·ə, -zh(y)ə/ *n* abnormal growth or development of organs, cells, etc [NL] – **dysplastic** /-'plastik/ *adj*

dyspnoea, *chiefly NAm* **dyspnea** /disp'nee·ə/ *n* difficult or laboured breathing [L *dyspnoea*, fr Gk *dyspnoia*, fr *dyspnoos* short of breath, fr *dys-* + *pnein* to breathe – more at SNEEZE] – **dyspnoeic** /-'nee·ik/ *adj*

dys'prosium /-'prohzi·əm, -si-/ *n* an element of the rare-earth group that forms highly magnetic compounds ☞ PERIODIC TABLE [NL, fr Gk *dysprositos* hard to get at, fr *dys-* + *prositos* approachable, fr *prosienai* to approach, fr *pros-* + *ienai* to go – more at ISSUE]

dys'topia /-'tohpi·ə/ *n* an imaginary place which is depressingly wretched – compare UTOPIA [NL, fr *dys-* + *-topia* (as in *utopia*)] – **dystopian** *adj*

dys'uria /-'yooəri·ə/ *n* difficult or painful urination [NL, fr Gk *dysouria*, fr *dys-* + *-ouria* -uria]

E

e /ee/ *n, pl* **e's, es** *often cap* **1a** (a graphic representation of or device for reproducing) the 5th letter of the English alphabet **b** a speech counterpart of orthographic *e* **2** the 3rd note of a C-major scale **3** one designated *e*: e g **a** the 5th in order or class **b** the base of the system of natural logarithms having the approximate numerical value 2.71828 **4** a mark rating a student's work as poor or failing

e- *prefix* **1a** deprive of; remove (a specified quality or thing) ⟨*emasculate*⟩ ⟨*eviscerate*⟩ **b** lacking; without ⟨*edentate*⟩ ⟨*ecaudate*⟩ **2** out; on the outside ⟨*evert*⟩ **3** forth ⟨*emanate*⟩ ⟨*ejaculate*⟩ [ME, fr OF & L; OF, out, forth, away, fr L, fr *ex-*]

[1]**each** /eech/ *adj* being one of 2 or more distinct individuals considered separately and often forming a group ⟨~ *foot in turn*⟩ ⟨*they* ~ *want something different*⟩ [ME *ech*, fr OE *ǣlc*; akin to OHG *iogilīh* each; both fr a prehistoric WGmc compound whose first and second constituents respectively are represented by OE *ā* always & *gelīc* alike]

[2]**each** *pron* each one ⟨~ *of us*⟩ ⟨~ *is equally attractive*⟩

[3]**each** *adv* to or for each; apiece ⟨*tickets at £1* ~⟩

,each 'other *pron* each of 2 or more in reciprocal action or relation – not used as subject of a clause ⟨*wore* each other's *shirts*⟩ ⟨*looked at* ~ *in surprise*⟩

,each 'way *adj or adv, Br, of a bet* backing a horse, dog, etc to finish in the first two, three, or four in a race as well as to win

eager /'eegə/ *adj* marked by keen, enthusiastic, or impatient desire or interest ⟨*always* ~ *to help*⟩ [ME *egre* sharp, fierce, fr OF *aigre*, fr L *acer* – more at EDGE] – **eagerly** *adv*, **eagerness** *n*

,eager 'beaver *n* one who is unduly zealous in performing his/her assigned duties and in volunteering for more – infml

eagle /'eegl/ *n* **1** any of various large birds of prey noted for their strength, size, gracefulness, keenness of vision, and powers of flight **2** any of various emblematic or symbolic representations of an eagle: e g **a** the standard of the ancient Romans **b** the seal or standard of a nation (e g the USA) having an eagle as emblem **3** a 10-dollar gold coin of the USA **4** a golf score for 1 hole of 2 strokes less than par [ME *egle*, fr OF *aigle*, fr L *aquila*]

,eagle 'eye *n* close vigilance; careful attention ⟨*the teacher kept an* ~ *on the unruly pupil*⟩

,eagle-'eyed *adj* **1** having very good eyesight **2** looking very keenly at sthg ⟨*watched* ~ *while the cashier counted out the money*⟩ **3** good at noticing details; observant ⟨*an* ~ *employer who spots the smallest mistake*⟩

'eagle ,owl *n* an owl with prominent ear tufts that is the largest European owl

eaglet /'eeglit/ *n* a young eagle

eagre /'aygə/ *n* [4]BORE [origin unknown]

ealdorman /'awldəmən/ *n* the chief officer in a district in Anglo-Saxon England [OE – more at ALDERMAN]

-ean – see [1] [2]-AN

[1]**ear** /iə/ *n* **1a** (the external part of) the characteristic vertebrate organ of hearing and equilibrium ☞ NERVE **b** any of various organs capable of detecting vibratory motion **2** the sense or act of hearing **3** sensitivity to musical tone and pitch **4** sthg resembling an ear in shape or position; *esp* a projecting part (e g a lug or handle) **5a** sympathetic attention ⟨*gained the* ~ *of the managing director*⟩ **b** *pl* notice, awareness ⟨*it has come to my* ~s *that you are discontented*⟩ [ME *ere*, fr OE *ēare*; akin to OHG *ōra* ear, L *auris*, Gk *ous*] – **by ear** from memory of the sound without having seen the written music – **in one ear and out the other** through one's mind without making an impression ⟨*everything you say to him goes* in one ear and out the other⟩ – **up to one's ears** deeply involved; heavily implicated

[2]**ear** *n* the fruiting spike of a cereal, including both the seeds and protective structures [ME *er*, fr OE *ēar*; akin to OHG *ahir* ear, OE *ecg* edge – more at EDGE]

earache /'iə,rayk/ *n* an ache or pain in the ear

'ear,drum /-,drum/ *n* TYMPANIC MEMBRANE ☞ NERVE

eared /iəd/ *adj* having ears, esp of a specified kind or number ⟨*long*-eared *owl*⟩

'earful /-f(ə)l/ *n* **1** an outpouring of news or gossip **2** a sharp verbal reprimand ***USE*** infml

earl /uhl/ *n* a member of the British peerage ranking below a marquess and above a viscount [ME *erl*, fr OE *eorl* warrior, nobleman; akin to ON *jarl* warrior, nobleman] – **earldom** /-d(ə)m/ *n*

,earl 'marshal *n* an officer of state in England serving chiefly as a royal attendant on ceremonial occasions, as marshal of state processions, and as head of the College of Arms

'ear,lobe /-,lohb/ *n* the pendent part of the ear of humans or of some fowls

,earl 'palatine *n* an English earl having in former times royal powers within his county

[1]**early** /'uhli/ *adv* **1** at or near the beginning of a period of time, a development, or a series ⟨earlier *on in the experiment*⟩ **2** before the usual or proper time ⟨*got up* ~⟩ [ME *erly*, fr OE *ǣrlīce*, fr *ǣr* early, soon – more at ERE]

[2]**early** *adj* **1a** of or occurring near the beginning of a period of time, a development, or a series **b(1)** distant in past time **(2)** primitive **2a** occurring before the usual time **b** occurring in the near future **c** maturing or producing sooner than related forms ⟨*an* ~ *peach*⟩ – **earliness** *n*

'early ,bird *n* one who rises or arrives early

,early 'closing *n* **1** the closing of shops in a British town or district on 1 afternoon a week **2** the day on which shops close early

ˌEarly ˈEnglish *adj* of an early Gothic style of architecture, prevalent in Britain from the late 12th to the late 13th c, characterized by lancet windows and pointed arches ☞ CHURCH

[1]**earmark** /ˈiə,mahk/ *n* **1** a mark of identification on the ear of an animal **2** a distinguishing or identifying characteristic

[2]**ˈear,mark** *vt* **1** to mark (livestock) with an earmark **2** to designate (e g funds) for a specific use or owner

ˈear,muffs /-,mufs/ *n pl* a pair of ear coverings connected by a flexible band and worn as protection against cold or noise

earn /uhn/ *vt* **1** to receive (e g money) as return for effort, esp for work done or services rendered **2** to bring in as income ⟨*my shares* ~ed *nothing last year*⟩ **3a** to gain or deserve because of one's behaviour or qualities ⟨*Alexander* ~ed *the title 'The Great" by his victories in war*⟩ **b** to make worthy of or obtain for ⟨*Alexander's victories in war* ~ed *him the title 'The Great'*⟩ [ME *ernen,* fr OE *earnian*]

earner /ˈuhnə/ *n, Br* sthg profitable – slang [EARN + [2]-ER]

[1]**earnest** /ˈuhnist/ *n* a serious and intent mental state – esp in *in earnest* [ME *ernest,* fr OE *eornost;* akin to OHG *ernust* earnest]

[2]**earnest** *adj* determined and serious – **earnestly** *adv,* **earnestness** *n*

[3]**earnest** *n* **1** sthg of value, esp money, given by a buyer to a seller to seal a bargain **2** a token of what is to come; a pledge [ME *ernes, ernest,* fr OF *erres,* pl of *erre* earnest, fr L *arra,* short for *arrabo,* fr Gk *arrhabōn,* fr Heb *'ērābhōn*]

earnings /ˈuhningz/ *n pl* money earned; *esp* gross revenue

earphone /ˈiə,fohn/ *n* a device that converts electrical energy into sound waves and is worn over or inserted into the ear

ˈear,piece /-,pees/ *n* a part of an instrument (e g a telephone) to which the ear is applied for listening; *esp* an earphone

ˈear,piercing /-,piəsing/ *adj* earsplitting

ˈear,plug /-,plug/ *n* a device inserted into the outer opening of the ear for protection against water, loud noise, etc

ˈear,ring /-,ring/ *n* an ornament for the ear that is attached to the earlobe

ˈear,shot /-,shot/ *n* the range within which sthg, esp the unaided voice, may be heard

ˈear,splitting /-,spliting/ *adj* distressingly loud or shrill

[1]**earth** /uhth/ *n* **1** [1]SOIL 2a **2** the sphere of mortal or worldly existence as distinguished from spheres of spiritual life – compare HEAVEN, HELL **3a** areas of land as distinguished from sea and air **b** the solid ground **4** *often cap* the planet on which we live that is third in order from the sun ☞ ASTRONOMY, SYMBOL **5** the people of the planet earth **6** the lair of a fox, badger, etc **7** a metallic oxide formerly classed as an element **8** *chiefly Br* **a** an electrical connection to earth **b** a large conducting body (e g the earth) used as the arbitrary zero of potential **9** a huge amount of money ⟨*his suit must have cost the* ~*!*⟩ – infml [ME *erthe,* fr OE *eorthe;* akin to OHG *erda* earth, Gk *eraze* to the ground] – **earthlike** *adj,* **earthward** /-wood/ *adj or adv,* **earthwards** *adv* – **on earth** – used to intensify an interrogative pronoun ⟨*where* on earth *is it?*⟩

[2]**earth** *vt* **1** to drive (e g a fox) to hiding in its earth **2** to draw soil about (plants) – usu + *up* **3** *chiefly Br* to connect electrically with earth ~ *vi of a hunted animal* to hide in its lair

ˈearth,bound /-,bownd/ *adj* **1a** restricted to the earth **b** heading or directed towards the planet earth ⟨*an* ~ *spaceship*⟩ **2a** bound by worldly interests; lacking spiritual quality **b** pedestrian, unimaginative

ˈearth ˌcloset *n* a toilet in which earth is used to cover excreta

earthen /ˈuhdh(ə)n, -th(ə)n/ *adj* made of earth or baked clay

ˈearthen,ware /-,weə/ *n* ceramic ware made of slightly porous opaque clay fired at a low temperature – compare STONEWARE

ˈearth,light /-,liet/ *n* earthshine

ˈearth,ling /-,ling/ *n* an inhabitant of the earth, esp as contrasted with inhabitants of other planets

[1]**ˈearthly** /-li/ *adj* **1a** characteristic of or belonging to this earth **b** relating to human beings' actual life on this earth; worldly **2** possible – usu + neg or interrog ⟨*there is no* ~ *reason for such behaviour*⟩ – **earthliness** *n*

[2]**earthly** *n* a chance of success – usu + neg; infml

ˈearth ˌmother *n* **1** *often cap E&M* the female principle of fertility **2** a woman who embodies the earth mother, esp in being generously proportioned and maternal

ˈearth,nut /-,nut/ *n* the pignut

ˈearth,quake /-,kwayk/ *n* a (repeated) usu violent earth tremor caused by volcanic action or processes within the earth's crust ☞ GEOGRAPHY

ˌearth ˈscience *n* any of the sciences (e g geology) that deal with (1 or more parts of) the earth

ˈearth,shaking /-,shayking/ *adj* having tremendous importance or a widespread often violent effect – chiefly infml

ˈearth,shine /-,shien/ *n* sunlight reflected by the earth and illuminating the dark part of the moon

ˈearth,work /-,wuhk/ *n* (the construction of) an embankment, field fortification, etc made of earth

ˈearth,worm /-,wuhm/ *n* any of numerous widely distributed hermaphroditic worms that live in the soil

earthy /ˈuhthi/ *adj* **1** consisting of, resembling, or suggesting earth ⟨*an* ~ *flavour*⟩ **2** crude, coarse ⟨~ *humour*⟩ – **earthily** *adv,* **earthiness** *n*

earwig /ˈiə,wig/ *n* any of numerous insects that have slender many-jointed antennae and a pair of appendages resembling forceps [ME *erwigge,* fr OE *ēarwicga,* fr *ēare* ear + *wicga* insect – more at VETCH]

[1]**ease** /eez/ *n* **1** being comfortable: e g **a** freedom from pain, discomfort, or anxiety **b** freedom from labour or difficulty **c** freedom from embarrassment or constraint; naturalness **2** facility, effortlessness **3** easing or being eased [ME *ese,* fr OF *aise* convenience, comfort, fr L *adjacent-, adjacens* neighbourhood, fr neut of prp of *adjacēre* to lie near – more at ADJACENT] – **easeful** *adj,* **easefully** *adv* – **at ease 1** free from pain or discomfort **2** free from restraint or formality ⟨*he's quite* at *his* ease *in any kind of company*⟩ **3** standing with the feet apart and usu 1 or both hands behind the body – used esp as a military command

[2]**ease** *vt* **1** to free from sthg that pains, disquiets, or

burdens – + *of* **2** to alleviate **3** to lessen the pressure or tension of, esp by slackening, lifting, or shifting **4** to make less difficult **5** to manoeuvre gently or carefully in a specified way ⟨~d *the heavy block into position*⟩ **6** to put the helm of (a ship) towards the lee ~ *vi* **1** to decrease in activity, intensity, or severity – often + *off* or *up* ⟨*the rain is* easing *off*⟩ **2** to manoeuvre oneself gently or carefully ⟨~d *through a hole in the fence*⟩

easel /ˈeezl/ *n* a frame for supporting sthg (e g an artist's canvas) [D *ezel* ass; akin to OE *esol* ass; both fr a prehistoric EGmc-WGmc word borrowed fr L *asinus* ass]

ˈeasement /-mənt/ *n* **1** an act or means of easing or relieving **2** a right to the limited use (e g for access) of another person's ground or property

easily /ˈeezəli/ *adv* **1** without difficulty ⟨*my car will do a hundred* ~⟩ **2** without doubt; by far ⟨~ *the best*⟩

¹east /eest/ *adj or adv* towards, at, belonging to, or coming from the east ⟨*a biting* ~ *wind*⟩ ⟨*we headed* ~⟩ [ME *est*, fr OE *ēast*; akin to OHG *ōstar* to the east, L *aurora* dawn, Gk *ēōs, heōs*]

²east *n* **1** (the compass point corresponding to) the direction 90° to the right of north that is the general direction of sunrise **2a** *often cap* regions or countries lying to the east of a specified or implied point of orientation **b** *cap* regions lying to the east of Europe **3** the altar end of a church **4** sby (e g a bridge player) occupying a position designated east – **eastward** /-wood/ *adj or n*, **eastwards** *adv*

East Carribean Dollar *n* (a note or coin representing) the basic money unit of certain countries in the W Indies ☞ NATIONALITY

Easter /ˈeestə/ *n* a feast that commemorates Christ's resurrection and is observed on the first Sunday after the first full moon following March 21 [ME *estre*, fr OE *ēastre*; akin to OHG *ōstarun* (pl) Easter; both fr the prehistoric WGmc name of a pagan spring festival, akin to OE *ēast* east]

ˈEaster ˌegg *n* a (chocolate or painted and hard-boiled) egg given as a present and eaten at Easter

¹ˈeasterly /-li/ *adj or adv* east ⟨*in an* ~ *direction*⟩ ⟨*an* ~ *wind*⟩ [obs *easter* (eastern)]

²easterly *n* a wind from the east

ˌEaster ˈMonday *n* the Monday after Easter observed as a public holiday

eastern /ˈeest(ə)n/ *adj* **1** *often cap* (characteristic) of a region conventionally designated east **2** east **3 Eastern, Eastern Orthodox** ORTHODOX 2a [ME *estern*, fr OE *ēasterne*; akin to OHG *ōstrōni* eastern, OE *ēast* east] – **easternmost** /-ˌmohst/ *adj*

Easterner /ˈeest(ə)nə/ *n, chiefly NAm* a native or inhabitant of the East, esp the E USA

ˌeastern ˈhemisphere *n* the half of the earth to the east of the Atlantic ocean including Europe, Asia, and Africa

easting /ˈeesting/ *n* **1** distance due east in longitude from the preceding point of measurement **2** easterly progress

ˌeast-ˌnorthˈeast *n* a compass point midway between east and northeast

ˌeast-ˌsouthˈeast *n* a compass point midway between east and southeast

¹easy /ˈeezi/ *adj* **1** causing or involving little difficulty or discomfort ⟨*an* ~ *problem*⟩ **2a** not severe; lenient **b** readily prevailed on; compliant: e g **(1)** not difficult to deceive or take advantage of ⟨~ *prey*⟩ **(2)** readily persuaded to have sexual relations – infml **3a** plentiful in supply at low or declining interest rates ⟨~ *money*⟩ **b** less in demand and usu lower in price ⟨*gilts were* easier⟩ **4a** marked by peace and comfort ⟨*the* ~ *course of his life*⟩ **b** not hurried or strenuous ⟨*an* ~ *pace*⟩ **c** free from pain, annoyance, or anxiety **5** marked by social ease ⟨~ *manners*⟩ **6** not burdensome or straitened ⟨*bought on* ~ *terms*⟩ **7** marked by ready facility and freedom from constraint ⟨*an* ~ *flowing style*⟩ **8** *chiefly Br* not having marked preferences on a particular issue – infml [ME *esy*, fr OF *aaisié*, pp of *aaisier* to ease, fr *a-* ad- (fr L *ad-*) + *aise* ease] – **easiness** *n* – **easy on 1** lenient with ⟨*be* easy on *the boy*⟩ **2** attractive to ⟨easy on *the eyes*⟩

²easy *adv* **1** easily ⟨*promises come* ~⟩ **2** without undue speed or excitement; slowly, cautiously ⟨*take it* ~⟩ – **easy on 1** leniently with ⟨*go* easy on *the boy*⟩ **2** not too lavishly with ⟨*go* easy on *the ice, bartender*⟩

ˈeasy ˌchair *n* a large usu upholstered armchair designed for comfort and relaxation

ˌeasyˈgoing /-ˈgoh·ing/ *adj* taking life easily: e g **a** placid and tolerant **b** indolent and careless – **easygoingness** *n*

ˈeasy ˌstreet *n* a position of affluence – often + *on*; infml

eat /eet/ *vb* **ate** /et, ayt/; **eaten** /ˈeet(ə)n/ *vt* **1** to take in through the mouth and swallow as food **2** to consume gradually; corrode ⟨*the acid has* ~en *away the battery terminals*⟩ **3** to vex, bother – infml ⟨*what's* ~ing *you?*⟩ ~ *vi* to take food or a meal [ME *eten*, fr OE *etan*; akin to OHG *ezzan* to eat, L *edere*, Gk *edmenai*] – **eatable** *adj*, **eater** *n* – **eat humble pie** to apologize or retract under pressure [*humble pie* alter. of *umble pie*, fr *umbles*] – **eat one's heart out** to grieve bitterly, esp for sthg desired but unobtainable – **eat one's words** to retract what one has said – **eat out of someone's hand** to accept sby's domination

eatables /ˈeetəblz/ *n pl* food

eat out *vi* to eat away from home, esp in a restaurant

eats /eets/ *n pl* food – infml [ME *et*, fr OE *ǣt*; akin to OE *etan* to eat]

eat up *vt* **1a** to consume completely or very rapidly ⟨eat up *your greens like a good boy*⟩ **b** to absorb, preoccupy – often pass ⟨eaten up *by vanity*⟩ **2** to show avid interest in or enjoyment of ⟨*the press* ate up *the explorers' story*⟩ – infml

eau de cologne /ˌoh də kəˈlohn/ *n, pl* **eaux de cologne** /~/ TOILET WATER [F, lit., Cologne water, fr *Cologne*, city in Germany]

ˌeau-de-ˈnil /ˈneel/ *n or adj* (a) pale slightly bluish green [F, lit., Nile water, fr the *Nile*, river in Africa]

ˌeau-de-ˈvie /ˈvee/ *n, pl* **eaux-de-vie** /~/ brandy [F, lit., water of life, trans of ML *aqua vitae*]

eaves /eevz/ *n pl* the lower border of a roof that overhangs the wall ☞ ARCHITECTURE [ME *eves* (sing.), fr OE *efes*; akin to OHG *obasa* portico, OE *ūp* up – more at UP]

eavesdrop /ˈeevzˌdrop/ *vi* to listen secretly to what is said in private [prob back-formation fr *eavesdropper*, lit., one standing under the drip from the eaves] – **eavesdropper** *n*

¹ebb /eb/, **ˈebb ˌtide** *n* **1** the flowing out of the tide towards the sea **2** a point or condition of decline ⟨*relations were at a low ~*⟩ [ME *ebbe*, fr OE *ebba*; akin to MD *ebbe* ebb, OE *of* from – more at OF]

[2]**ebb** *vi* **1** *of tidal water* to recede from the flood state **2** to decline from a higher to a lower level or from a better to a worse state

ebonite /'ebəniet/ *n* a hard black vulcanized rubber [arch *ebon* (ebony) + *-ite*]

[1]**ebony** /'ebəni/ *n* (any of various tropical trees that yield) a hard heavy black wood [prob fr LL *hebeninus* of ebony, fr Gk *ebeninos*, fr *ebenos* ebony, fr Egypt *hbnj*]

[2]**ebony** *adj* **1** made of or resembling ebony **2** black, dark – usu apprec

ebullience /i'buli·əns, -yəns/, **ebulliency** /-si/ *n* the quality of being full of liveliness and enthusiasm; exuberance

ebullient /i'buli·ənt, -yənt/ *adj* **1** boiling, agitated **2** characterized by ebullience [L *ebullient-*, *ebulliens*, prp of *ebullire* to bubble out, fr *e-* + *bullire* to bubble, boil – more at [2]BOIL] – **ebulliently** *adv*

ebullition /,ebə'lish(ə)n/ *n* **1** the act, process, or state of boiling or bubbling up **2** a sudden violent outburst or display – fml

ec-, **eco-** *comb form* **1** habitat; environment ⟨eco*species*⟩ ⟨eco*physiology*⟩ **2** ecological ⟨eco*system*⟩ [LL *oeco-* household, fr Gk *oik-*, *oiko-*, fr *oikos* house – more at VICINITY]

[1]**eccentric** /ik'sentrik/ *adj* **1** not having the same centre ⟨*~ spheres*⟩ **2** deviating from established convention; odd ⟨*~ behaviour*⟩ **3a** deviating from a circular path ⟨*an ~ orbit*⟩ **b** located elsewhere than at the geometrical centre; *also* having the axis or support so located ⟨*an ~ wheel*⟩ [ML *eccentricus*, fr Gk *ekkentros*, fr *ex* out of + *kentron* centre] – **eccentrically** *adv*

[2]**eccentric** *n* **1** a mechanical device using eccentrically mounted parts to transform circular into reciprocating motion **2** an eccentric person

eccentricity /,eksen'trisəti/ *n* **1** being eccentric **2** a number that for a given conic section is the ratio of the distances from any point on the curve to the focus and the directrix

ecclesi- /ikleezi-/, **ecclesio-** *comb form* church ⟨ecclesio*graphy*⟩ [ME *ecclesi-*, fr LL *ecclesia*, fr Gk *ekklēsia* assembly of citizens, church, fr *ekkalein* to call forth, summon, fr *ex-* + *kalein* to call]

Ecclesiastes /i,kleezi'asteez/ *n* an Old Testament book ascribed to Solomon [Gk *Ekklēsiastēs*, lit., preacher (trans of Heb *Qōheleth*), fr *ekklēsiastēs* member of an assembly]

ecclesiastic /i,kleezi'astik/ *n* a clergyman

ecclesiastical /i,kleeziə'astikl/ *adj* **1** of a church, esp as a formal and established institution ⟨*~ law*⟩ **2** suitable for use in a church ⟨*~ vestments*⟩ [ME, fr LL *ecclesiasticus*, fr LGk *ekklēsiastikos*, fr Gk, of an assembly of citizens, fr *ekklēsiastēs* member of an assembly, fr *ekklēsia*] – **ecclesiastically** *adv*

ecclesiasticism /i,kleezi'astisiz(ə)m/ *n* excessive attachment to ecclesiastical forms and practices

Ecclesiasticus /i,kleezi'astikus/ *n* a didactic book of the Protestant Apocrypha included in the Roman Catholic Old Testament [LL, fr *ecclesiasticus* ecclesiastic]

ecclesiology /i,kleezi'oləji/ *n* **1** the study of church architecture and ornament **2** theological doctrine relating to the church – **ecclesiological** /-zi·ə'lojikl/ *adj*

ecdysis /'ekdisis/ *n, pl* **ecdyses** /-,seez/ the moulting or shedding of an outer layer (e g in insects and crustaceans) [NL, fr Gk *ekdysis* act of getting out]

[1]**echelon** /'eshəlon, 'ay-/ *n* **1** an arrangement of units (e g of troops or ships) resembling a series of steps **2** a particular division of a headquarters or supply organization in warfare **3** any of a series of levels or grades (e g of authority or responsibility) in some organized field of activity [F *échelon*, lit., rung of a ladder, dim. of *échelle* ladder]

[2]**echelon** *vt* to form or arrange in an echelon

echidna /i'kidnə/ *n, pl* **echidnas, echidnae** /-ni/ an egg-laying spiny-coated toothless burrowing nocturnal mammal of Australia, Tasmania, and New Guinea that feeds chiefly on ants [NL, fr L, viper, fr Gk]

echin- /ikien-/, **echino-** *comb form* **1** prickle ⟨echino*derm*⟩ **2** sea urchin ⟨echin*ite*⟩ [L, fr Gk, fr *echinos* sea urchin]

echinoderm /i'kienoh,duhm/ *n* any of a phylum of radially symmetrical marine animals consisting of the starfishes, sea urchins, and related forms [NL *Echinodermata*, phylum name, fr *echin-* + *-dermata* (fr Gk *derma* skin)] – **echinodermatous** /-'duhmətəs/ *adj*

echinoid /i'kienoyd, e'kinoyd/ *n* SEA URCHIN

echinus /i'kienəs/ *n, pl* **echini** /-nie/ **1** SEA URCHIN **2** a convex moulding beneath the abacus of a classical capital ☞ ARCHITECTURE [ME, fr L, fr Gk *echinos* hedgehog, sea urchin, architectural echinus]

[1]**echo** /'ekoh/ *n, pl* **echoes** **1a** the repetition of a sound caused by the reflection of sound waves **b** the repeated sound due to such reflection **2** sby or sthg that repeats or imitates another ⟨*his opinions were just an ~ of his superiors'*⟩ **3** a repercussion, result **4** a soft repetition of a musical phrase **5a** the reflection by an object of transmitted radar signals **b** a blip [ME *ecco*, fr MF & L; MF *echo*, fr L, fr Gk *ēchō*; akin to L *vagire* to wail, Gk *ēchē* sound] – **echoey** *adj*

[2]**echo** *vi* **1** to resound with echoes **2** to produce an echo ~ *vt* **1** to repeat, imitate **2** to send back or repeat (a sound) as an echo

Echo – a communications code word for the letter *e*

'**echo ,chamber** *n* a room with sound-reflecting walls used for making acoustic measurements and for producing echoing sound effects, esp in radio broadcasting

echoic /e'koh·ik/ *adj* **1** of an echo **2** onomatopoeic – **echoism** /'ekoh,iz(ə)m/ *n*

echolalia /,ekoh'layli·ə, -lyə/ *n* the pathological echoing of what is said by other people that is usu a symptom of mental disorder [NL] – **echolalic** /-'laylik, -'lalik/ *adj*

echolocation /'ekohlohkaysh(ə)n/ *n* the location of distant or invisible objects by means of sound waves reflected back to the sender (e g a bat or submarine) by the objects

'**echo ,sounder** *n* an instrument that uses acoustic echolocation to determine the depth of a body of water

'**echo,virus** /-,vie·ərəs/ *n* any of a group of viruses found in the gastrointestinal tract and sometimes associated with respiratory ailments and meningitis [*e*nteric *c*ytopathogenic *h*uman *o*rphan + *virus*]

éclair /i'kleə, ay-/ *n* a small light oblong cake of

choux pastry that is split and filled with cream and usu topped with (chocolate) icing [F, lit., lightning]

eclampsia /i'klampsi·ə/ *n* an attack of convulsions during pregnancy or childbirth [NL, fr Gk *eklampsis* sudden flashing, fr *eklampein* to shine forth, fr *ex* out + *lampein* to shine] – **eclamptic** /-tik/ *adj*

éclat /ay'klah (*Fr* ekla)/ *n* **1** ostentatious display **2** brilliant or conspicuous success **3** acclaim, applause [F, splinter, burst, ostentation]

1**eclectic** /e'klektik, i-/ *adj* **1** selecting or using elements from various doctrines, methods, or styles **2** composed of elements drawn from various sources [Gk *eklektikos*, fr *eklegein* to select, fr *ex* out + *legein* to gather – more at EX-, LEGEND] – **eclectically** *adv*, **eclecticism** /-ti,siz(ə)m/ *n*

2**eclectic** *n* one who uses an eclectic method or approach

1**eclipse** /i'klips/ *n* **1a** the total or partial obscuring of one celestial body by another **b** passage into the shadow of a celestial body – compare OCCULTATION, TRANSIT **2** a falling into obscurity or decay; a decline **3** the state of being in eclipse plumage ⟨*a mallard in* ~⟩ [ME, fr OF, fr L *eclipsis*, fr Gk *ekleipsis*, fr *ekleipein* to omit, fail, suffer eclipse, fr *ex* + *leipein* to leave – more at LOAN]

2**eclipse** *vt* to cause an eclipse of: e g **a** to obscure, darken **b** to surpass

e'clipse ,plumage *n* comparatively dull plumage that occurs seasonally in ducks or other birds which adopt a distinct nuptial plumage – compare NUPTIAL PLUMAGE

1**ecliptic** /i'kliptik/ *n* **1** the plane of the earth's orbit extended to meet the celestial sphere **2** a great circle drawn on a terrestrial globe making an angle of about 23° 27′ with the equator and used for illustrating and solving astronomical problems [ME *ecliptik*, fr LL *ecliptica linea*, lit., line of eclipses]

2**ecliptic** *adj* of the ecliptic or an eclipse

eclogue /'ek,log/ *n* a short poem; *esp* a pastoral dialogue [ME *eclog*, fr L *Eclogae*, title of pastoral poems by Vergil †19 BC Roman poet, lit., selections, pl of *ecloga*, fr Gk *eklogē*, fr *eklegein* to select]

eclosion /e'klozh(ə)n/ *n* the emergence of an insect from the pupal case or of a larva from the egg [F *éclosion*, fr *éclore* to hatch]

eco- – see EC-

ecology /i'koləji, ee-/ *n* (a science concerned with) the interrelationship of living organisms and their environments [G *ökologie*, fr *ök-* ec- + *-logie* -logy] – **ecological** /,eekə'lojikl, ek-/ *adj*, **ecologically** *adv*, **ecologist** /i'ko-, ee-/ *n*

econometrics /i,konə'metriks/ *n pl but sing in constr* the application of statistical methods to the study of economic data and problems [blend of *economics* and *metric*] – **econometric** *adj*, **econometrically** *adv*, **econometrician** /-mə'trish(ə)n/ *n*, **econometrist** /-'metrist/ *n*

economic /,ekə'nomik, ,ee-/ *adj* **1** of economics **2** of or based on the production, distribution, and consumption of goods and services **3** of an economy **4** having practical or industrial significance or uses; affecting material resources ⟨~ *pests*⟩ **5** profitable – **economically** *adv*

economical /,ekə'nomikl, ,ee-/ *adj* thrifty – **economically** *adv*

,eco'nomics *n pl but sing or pl in constr* **1** a social science concerned chiefly with the production, distribution, and consumption of goods and services **2** economic aspect or significance – **economist** /i'konəmist/ *n*

econom·ize, -ise /i'konə,miez/ *vi* to practise economy; be frugal – often + *on* ⟨~ *on oil*⟩ ~ *vt* to use more economically; save ⟨~ *oil*⟩ – **economizer** *n*

economy /i'konəmi/ *n* **1** thrifty and efficient use of material resources; frugality in expenditure; *also* an instance or means of economizing ⟨*the government implemented drastic* economies⟩ ⟨*bought an* economy-*size packet of soap powder*⟩ ⟨*booked an* ~ *flight to Greece*⟩ **2** efficient and sparing use of nonmaterial resources (e g effort, language, or motion) **3** the structure of economic life in a country, area, or period; *specif* an economic system [MF *yconomie*, fr ML *oeconomia*, fr Gk *oikonomia*, fr *oikonomos* household manager, fr *oikos* house + *nemein* to manage – more at VICINITY, NIMBLE]

ecospecies /'eekoh,speeshiz, 'ekoh-/ *n, pl* **ecospecies** a taxonomic species regarded as an ecological unit – **ecospecific** /-spə'sifik/ *adj*

'eco,sphere /-,sfiə/ *n* the parts of the universe habitable by living organisms; *esp* BIOSPHERE

ecossaise /,ayko'sez, eko-/ *n* (the music for) a lively folk dance in duple time [F *écossaise*, fr fem of *écossais* Scottish, fr *Écosse* Scotland]

'eco,system /-,sistəm/ *n* a complex consisting of a community and its environment functioning as a reasonably self-sustaining ecological unit in nature ☞ FOOD

ecotype /'eekə,tiep, 'ekə-/ *n* a group equivalent to a taxonomic subspecies and maintained as a distinct population by ecological and geographical factors – **ecotypic** /-'tipik/ *adj*, **ecotypically** *adv*

ecru /'aykrooh, 'ek-, -'-/ *adj or n* (of) a pale fawn colour [F *écru* unbleached, fr OF *escru*, fr *es-* completely (fr L *ex-*) + *cru* raw, fr L *crudus* – more at RAW]

ecstasy /'ekstəsi/ *n* **1** a state of very strong feeling, esp of joy or happiness **2** a (mystic or prophetic) trance [ME *extasie*, fr MF, fr LL *ecstasis*, fr Gk *ekstasis*, fr *existanai* to derange, fr *ex* out + *histanai* to cause to stand – more at EX-, STAND]

ecstatic /ik'statik, ek-/ *adj* subject to, causing, or in a state of ecstasy [ML *ecstaticus*, fr Gk *ekstatikos*, fr *existanai*] – **ecstatic** *n*, **ecstatically** *adv*

ect- /ekt-/, **ecto-** *comb form* outside; external ⟨ect*opic*⟩ ⟨ecto*derm*⟩ – compare END- 1, EXO- 1 [NL, fr Gk *ekto-*, fr *ektos*, fr *ex* out – more at EX-]

ectoblast /'ektoh,blast/ *n* the epiblast [ISV] – **ectoblastic** /-'blastik/ *adj*

'ecto,derm /-,duhm/ *n* **1** the outer cellular membrane of an animal having only 2 germ layers in the embryo (e g a jellyfish) **2** (a tissue derived from) the outermost of the 3 primary germ layers of an embryo [ISV *ect-* + Gk *derma* skin – more at DERM-] – **ectodermal** /-'duhml/, **ectodermic** /-mik/ *adj*

ectogenous /ek'tojinəs/, **ectogenic** /,ektə'jenik/ *adj, esp of pathogenic bacteria* capable of development apart from the host

ectomorph /'ektə,mawf/ *n* an ectomorphic person [*ecto*derm + *-morph*]

,ecto'morphic /-'mawfik/ *adj* having a light slender body build [*ecto*derm + *-morphic*; fr the predominance in such types of structures developed from the ectoderm]

-ectomy /-'ektəmi/ *comb form* (→ *n*) surgical removal of ⟨*gastr*ectomy⟩ [NL *-ectomia*, fr Gk *ektemnein* to cut out, fr *ex* out + *temnein* to cut – more at EX-, TOME]

ectoparasite /,ektoh'parəsiet/ *n* a parasite that lives on the exterior of its host – compare ENDOPARASITE [ISV] – **ectoparasitic** /-'sitik/ *adj*

ectopic /ek'topik/ *adj* occurring in an abnormal position or in an unusual manner or form ⟨~ *heartbeat*⟩ ⟨~ *pregnancy*⟩ [Gk *ektopos* out of place, fr *ex-* out + *topos* place – more at EX-, TOPIC] – **ectopically** *adv*

ectoplasm /'ektə,plaz(ə)m, 'ektoh-/ *n* **1** the outer relatively rigid granule-free layer of the cytoplasm of a cell – compare ENDOPLASM **2** a substance supposed to emanate from a spiritualist medium in a state of trance – **ectoplasmic** /,ektə'plazmik, ,ektoh-/ *adj*

ecumenical *also* **oecumenical** /,ekyoo'menikl, ,eek-/ *adj* **1** of or representing the whole of a body of churches ⟨*an* ~ *council*⟩ **2** promoting or tending towards worldwide Christian unity or cooperation ⟨~ *discussions*⟩ [LL *oecumenicus* worldwide, fr LGk *oikoumenikos*, fr Gk *oikoumenē* the inhabited world, fr fem of *oikoumenos*, prp passive of *oikein* to inhabit, fr *oikos* house – more at VICINITY] – **ecumenicalism** *n*, **ecumenically** *adv*, **ecumenism** /e'kyoohmə,niz(ə)m/ *n*, **ecumenist** *n*

eczema /'eks(i)mə/ *n* an inflammatory condition of the skin characterized by itching and oozing blisters [NL, fr Gk *ekzema*, fr *ekzein* to erupt, fr *ex* out + *zein* to boil – more at EX-, YEAST] – **eczematous** /ek'semətəs/ *adj*

[1]**-ed** /-d *after vowels and m,n,ng,v,z,zh,j,dh,r,l,b,g;* -id *after d,t;* -t after all others. Exceptions are given at their own entry/ *suffix* **1** – used to form the past participle of regular weak verbs that end in a consonant ⟨*end*ed⟩ ⟨*dropp*ed⟩, a vowel other than *e* ⟨*halo*ed⟩, or a final *y* that changes to *i* ⟨*cri*ed⟩; compare [1]-D 1 **2a** having; characterized by; provided with ⟨*polo-neck*ed⟩ ⟨*2-legg*ed⟩ **b** wearing; dressed in ⟨*bowler-hatt*ed⟩ ⟨*jodhpur*ed⟩ **c** having the characteristics of ⟨*bigot*ed⟩ ***USE*** (*2*) used to ***form adjectives from nouns that end in a consonant, a vowel other than*** *e*, or a final *y* that changes to *i*; compare [1]-D 2 [ME, fr OE *-ed, -od, -ad*; akin to OHG *-t*, pp ending, L *-tus*, Gk *-tos*, suffix forming verbals]

[2]**-ed** *suffix* – used to form the past tense of regular weak verbs that end in a consonant, a vowel other than *e*, or a final *y* that changes to *i*; compare [2]-D [ME *-ede, -de*, fr OE *-de, -ede, -ode, -ade*; akin to OHG *-ta*, past ending (1 sing.), & prob to OHG *-t*, pp ending]

edacious /i'dayshəs/ *adj* voracious – fml [L *edac-, edax*, fr *edere* to eat – more at EAT] – **edacity** /i'dasəti/ *n*

Edam /'eedam/ *n* a yellow mild cheese of Dutch origin usu made in flattened balls coated with red wax [*Edam*, town in the Netherlands]

edaphic /i'dafik/ *adj* of or influenced by the soil [Gk *edaphos* bottom, ground] – **edaphically** *adv*

e,daphic 'climax *n* an ecological climax resulting from soil conditions

Edda /'edə/ *n* a 13th-c collection of Old Norse mythological and heroic poems [ON, prob fr *Edda*, name of a great-grandmother in a poem] – **Eddic** *adj*

[1]**eddy** /'edi/ *n* **1** a current of water or air running contrary to the main current; *esp* a small whirlpool **2** sthg (e g smoke or fog) moving in the manner of an eddy or whirlpool [ME (Sc) *ydy*, prob fr ON *itha*; akin to OHG *ith-* again, L *et* and]

[2]**eddy** *vb* to (cause to) move in or like an eddy ⟨*the crowd* eddied *about in the marketplace*⟩

'eddy ,current *n* an electric current induced by an alternating magnetic field

edelweiss /'aydl,vies/ *n* a small perennial plant that is covered in dense fine white hairs and grows high in the Alps [G, fr *edel* noble + *weiss* white]

edema /i'deemə/ *n, NAm* oedema – **edematous** /i'demətəs/ *adj*

Eden /'eedn/ *n* **1** the garden where, according to the account in Genesis, Adam and Eve lived before the Fall **2** PARADISE 2 [LL, fr Heb *'Ēdhen*] – **Edenic** /i'denik/ *adj*

edentate /ee'dentayt/ *n or adj* (a sloth, armadillo, or other mammal in the same order) having few or no teeth [L *edentatus*, pp of *edentare* to make toothless, fr *e-* + *dent-, dens* tooth – more at TOOTH]

edentulous /ee'dentyooləs/ *adj* toothless

[1]**edge** /ej/ *n* **1a** the cutting side of a blade **b** the (degree of) sharpness of a blade **c** penetrating power; keenness ⟨*an* ~ *of sarcasm in his voice*⟩ ⟨*took the* ~ *off the criticism*⟩ **2a** the line where an object or area begins or ends; a border ⟨*the town stands on the* ~ *of a plain*⟩ **b** the narrow part adjacent to a border; the brink, verge **c** a point that marks a beginning or transition; a threshold – esp in *on the edge of* ⟨*felt herself to be on the* ~ *of insanity*⟩ **d** a favourable margin; an advantage ⟨*had the* ~ *on the competition*⟩ **3** a line where 2 planes or 2 plane faces of a solid body meet or cross **4** the edging of a cricket ball [ME *egge*, fr OE *ecg*; akin to L *acer* sharp, Gk *akmē* point] – **on edge** anxious, nervous

[2]**edge** *vt* **1** to give or supply an edge to **2** to move or force gradually in a specified way ⟨~d *him off the road*⟩ ⟨~d *her out of the leadership*⟩ **3** to incline (a ski) sideways so that 1 edge cuts into the snow **4** to hit (a ball) or the bowling of (a bowler) in cricket with the edge of the bat ~ *vi* to advance cautiously (e g by short sideways steps) ⟨*the climbers* ~d *along the cliff*⟩ ⟨*the car* ~d *round the corner*⟩ – **edger** *n*

edged /ejd/ *adj* having a specified kind of edge, boundary, or border or a specified number of edges – usu in combination ⟨*rough*-edged⟩ ⟨*two*-edged⟩

'edge ,tool *n* a tool with a sharp cutting edge

'edgeways /-,wayz, -wiz/, **edgewise** /-,wiez/ *adv* with the edge foremost; sideways

edging /'ejing/ *n* sthg that forms an edge or border

edgy /'eji/ *adj* tense, irritable; ON EDGE – **edgily** *adv*, **edginess** *n*

edh /edh/ *n* an eth

edible /'edəbl/ *adj* fit to be eaten as food [LL *edibilis*, fr L *edere* to eat – more at EAT] – **edible** *n*, **edibleness** *n*, **edibility** /-'biləti/ *n*

edict /'eedikt/ *n* **1** an official public decree **2** the order or command of an authority [L *edictum*, fr neut of *edictus*, pp of *edicere* to decree, fr *e-* + *dicere* to say – more at DICTION] – **edictal** /i'diktl/ *adj*

edification /,edifi'kaysh(ə)n/ *n* the improvement of character or the mind – fml [EDIFY + -FICATION] – **edificatory** /-'kayt(ə)ri/ *adj*

edifice /'edifis/ *n* **1** a building; *esp* a large or massive structure **2** a large abstract structure or organization

⟨*the keystone which holds together the social* ~ – R H Tawney⟩ [ME, fr MF, fr L *aedificium*, fr *aedificare*]

edify /ˈedi,fie/ *vt* to instruct and improve, esp in moral and spiritual knowledge [ME *edifien*, fr MF *edifier*, fr LL & L; LL *aedificare* to instruct or improve spiritually, fr L, to erect a house, fr *aedes* temple, house; akin to OE *ād* funeral pyre, L *aestas* summer]

edit /ˈedit/ *vt* **1a** to prepare an edition of ⟨~ed *Pope's works*⟩ **b** to assemble (e g a film or tape recording) by deleting, inserting, and rearranging material **c** to alter or adapt (e g written or spoken words), esp to make consistent with a particular standard or purpose **2** to direct the publication of ⟨~s *the local newspaper*⟩ **3** to delete – usu + *out* – **editable** *adj*

edition /iˈdish(ə)n/ *n* **1a** the form in which a text is published ⟨*paperback* ~⟩ **b** the whole number of copies published at one time ⟨*an* ~ *of 50,000*⟩ **c** the issue of a newspaper or periodical for a specified time or place ⟨*the late* ~⟩ ⟨*the Manchester* ~⟩ **2** the whole number of articles of one style put out at one time ⟨*a limited* ~ *of collectors' pieces*⟩ **3** a copy, version ⟨*she's a friendlier* ~ *of her mother*⟩ [MF, fr L *edition-*, *editio* publication, edition, fr *editus*, pp of *edere* to bring forth, publish, fr *e-* + *-dere* to put or *-dere* (fr *dare* to give) – more at DO, ²DATE]

editio princeps /i,dishio ˈprinseps, ay,ditioh ˈprinkeps/ *n, pl* **editiones principes** /-,neez -,peez/ the first printed edition, esp of an ancient or medieval text [NL, lit., first edition]

editor /ˈeditə/ *n* **1** one who edits written material, films, etc, esp as an occupation **2** a person responsible for the editorial policy and content of a (section of a) newspaper or periodical ⟨*sports* ~⟩ – **editorship** *n*

¹**editorial** /,ediˈtawri·əl/ *adj* of or written by an editor ⟨~ *policy*⟩ ⟨*an* ~ *statement*⟩ – **editorially** *adv*

²**editorial** *n* a newspaper or magazine article that gives the opinions of the editors or publishers

,**ediˈtorial·,ize, -ise** /-,iez/ *vi* **1** to express an opinion in the form of an editorial **2** to introduce personal opinion into an apparently objective report (e g by direct comment or hidden bias) – **editorializer** *n*, **editorialization** /-ˈzaysh(ə)n/ *n*

EDTA *n* an acid that forms a tight chemical compound with magnesium and potassium ions and is used esp to remove them from solutions [ethylenediaminetetraacetic acid]

educate /ˈedyoo,kayt, ˈejoo-/ *vt* **1** to provide schooling for **2** to develop mentally or morally, esp by instruction **3** to train or improve (faculties, judgment, skills, etc) [ME *educaten* to rear, fr L *educatus*, pp of *educare* to rear, educate] – **educable** *adj*, **educative** /-kətiv, -,kaytiv/ *adj*, **educator** *n*

ˈ**edu,cated** *adj* **1** having an education, esp one beyond the average **2a** trained, skilled ⟨*an* ~ *palate*⟩ **b** befitting sby educated ⟨~ *conversation*⟩ **c** based on some knowledge of fact ⟨*an* ~ *guess*⟩ – **educatedly** *adv*, **educatedness** *n*

education /,edyooˈkaysh(ə)n, -joo-/ *n* **1** educating or being educated **2** the field of study that deals with methods of teaching and learning – **educational** *adj*, **educationally** *adv*

educationalist /,edyooˈkaysh(ə)nl·ist, -joo-/, **educationist** /-ist/ *n* an educational theorist or administrator

,**edu,cational psyˈchology** *n* psychology concerned with human maturation, school learning, and evaluation of aptitude and progress by tests – **educational psychologist** *n*

educe /iˈdyoohs; *also* ij-/ *vt* **1** to elicit, develop **2** to arrive at through a consideration of the facts or evidence; infer ***USE*** fml [L *educere* to draw out, fr *e-* + *ducere* to lead – more at TOW] – **educible** *adj*, **eduction** /iˈduksh(ə)n/ *n*

Edwardian /edˈwawdi·ən, edˈwahdi·ən/ *adj* (characteristic) of Edward VII or his age (e g in complacent security and opulence)

ee /ee/ *n, pl* **een** /een/ *Scot* an eye [ME (northern), fr OE *ēage*]

¹**-ee** /-ee/ *suffix* **1** (*vt* → *n*) one to whom (a specified action) is done ⟨*appointee*⟩ ⟨*trainee*⟩ **2** (*n, adj, vb* → *n*) one who acts (in a specified way) ⟨*escapee*⟩ ⟨*absentee*⟩ [ME *-e*, fr MF *-é*, fr *-é*, pp ending, fr L *-atus*]

²**-ee** *suffix* (*n* → *n*) a particular, esp small, kind of ⟨*bootee*⟩ [prob alter. of *-y*]

eel /eel/ *n* any of numerous long snakelike fishes with a smooth slimy skin and no pelvic fins [ME *ele*, fr OE *ǣl*; akin to OHG *āl* eel] – **eellike** *adj*, **eely** *adj*

ˈ**eel,grass** /-,grahs/ *n* a plant that has very long narrow leaves and grows underwater

ˈ**eel,pout** /-,powt/ *n* any of various marine fishes resembling blennies

ˈ**eel,worm** /-,wuhm/ *n* a nematode worm; *esp* one living free in the soil or as a parasite in plants

-een /-een/ *suffix* (*n* → *n*) inferior fabric resembling (a specified fabric); imitation ⟨*velveteen*⟩ [prob fr *ratteen* (coarse woollen fabric), fr F *ratine*]

e'en /een/ *adv* even – chiefly poetic

-eer /-iə/ *suffix* (*n* → *n*) person engaged in (a specified occupation or activity) ⟨*auctioneer*⟩ ⟨*buccaneer*⟩ – often derog ⟨*profiteer*⟩ ⟨*racketeer*⟩ [MF *-ier*, fr L *-arius* – more at ¹-ARY]

e'er /eə/ *adv* ever – chiefly poetic

eerie *also* **eery** /ˈiəri/ *adj* frighteningly strange or gloomy; weird [ME *eri*, fr OE *earg* cowardly, wretched; akin to OHG *arg* cowardly, ON *argr* evil] – **eerily** *adv*, **eeriness** *n*

eff /ef/ *vi, Br* to say 'fuck" ⟨~ing *and swearing*⟩ – slang [euphemism for *fuck*] – **eff and blind** SWEAR 2 – euph

efface /iˈfays/ *vt* **1** to eliminate or make indistinct (as if) by wearing away a surface; obliterate ⟨*coins with dates* ~d *by wear*⟩ **2** to make (oneself) modestly or shyly inconspicuous [MF *effacer*, fr *ex-* + *face*] – **effaceable** *adj*, **effacement** *n*, **effacer** *n*

¹**effect** /iˈfekt/ *n* **1a** the result of a cause or agent **b** the result of purpose or intention ⟨*employed her knowledge to good* ~⟩ **2** the basic meaning; intent – esp in *to that effect* **3** power to bring about a result; efficacy **4** *pl* personal movable property; goods **5a** a distinctive impression on the human senses ⟨*the use of colour produces a very striking* ~⟩ **b** the creation of an often false desired impression ⟨*her tears were purely for* ~⟩ **c** sthg designed to produce a distinctive or desired impression – often pl ⟨*special lighting* ~s⟩ **6** the quality or state of being operative; operation ⟨*the law comes into* ~ *next week*⟩ **7** an experimental scientific phenomenon named usu after its discoverer [ME, fr MF & L; MF, fr L *effectus*, fr *effectus*, pp of *efficere* to bring about, fr *ex-* + *facere* to make, do – more at DO] – **in effect** for all

practical purposes; actually although not appearing so – **to the effect** with the meaning ⟨*issued a statement* to the effect *that he would resign*⟩

[2]**effect** *vt* **1** to bring about, often by surmounting obstacles; accomplish ⟨~ *a settlement of a dispute*⟩ **2** to put into effect; CARRY OUT ⟨*the duty of the legislature to* ~ *the will of the citizens*⟩

[1]**effective** /i'fektiv/ *adj* **1a** producing a decided, decisive, or desired effect **b** impressive, striking **2** ready for service or action ⟨~ *manpower*⟩ **3** actual, real ⟨*the* ~ *strength of the army*⟩ **4** being in effect; operative ⟨*the tax becomes* ~ *next year*⟩ – **effectiveness** *n*

[2]**effective** *n* a soldier equipped and fit for duty

ef'fectively /-li/ *adv* for all practical purposes; IN EFFECT [[1]EFFECTIVE + -LY]

effector /i'fektə/ *n* a gland, muscle, or other bodily organ that becomes active in response to stimulation

effectual /i'fektyooəl, -chooəl/ *adj* producing or able to produce a desired effect; adequate, effective – **effectualness** *n*, **effectuality** /-'aləti/ *n*

ef'fectually /-li/ *adv* for all practical purposes; IN EFFECT [EFFECTUAL + -LY]

effectuate /i'fektyoo,ayt, -choo-/ *vt* EFFECT 2 – **effectuation** /-'aysh(ə)n/ *n*

effeminate /i'feminət/ *adj* **1** *of a man* having qualities usu thought of as feminine; not manly in appearance or manner **2** marked by an unbecoming delicacy or lack of vigour ⟨~ *art*⟩ [ME, fr L *effeminatus*, fr pp of *effeminare* to make effeminate, fr *ex-* + *femina* woman – more at FEMININE] – **effeminate** *n*, **effeminacy** /-nəsi/ *n*

effendi /e'fendi/ *n, pl* **effendis** a man of property, authority, or education in an eastern Mediterranean country [Turk *efendi* master, fr NGk *aphentēs*, alter. of Gk *authentēs* – more at AUTHENTIC]

efferent /'efərənt/ *adj* conducting outwards from a part or organ; *specif* conveying nervous impulses to an effector – compare AFFERENT [F *efférent*, fr L *efferent-, efferens*, prp of *efferre* to carry outwards, fr *ex-* + *ferre* to carry – more at [2]BEAR] – **efferent** *n*, **efferently** *adv*

effervesce /,efə'ves/ *vi* **1** *of a liquid* to bubble, hiss, and foam as gas escapes **2** to show liveliness or exhilaration [L *effervescere*, fr *ex-* + *fervescere* to begin to boil, fr *fervēre* to boil – more at BURN] – **effervescence** *n*, **effervescent** *adj*, **effervescently** *adv*

effete /i'feet/ *adj* **1** worn out; exhausted **2** marked by weakness or decadent overrefinement ⟨*an* ~ *civilization*⟩ [L *effetus*, fr *ex-* + *fetus* fruitful – more at FEMININE] – **effetely** *adv*, **effeteness** *n*

efficacious /,efi'kayshəs/ *adj* having the power to produce a desired effect [L *efficac-, efficax*, fr *efficere*] – **efficacity** /,efi'kasəti/ *n*, **efficacy** /'efikəsi/ *n*, **efficaciously** *adv*, **efficaciousness** *n*

efficiency /i'fish(ə)nsi/ *n* **1** the quality or degree of being efficient **2a** efficient operation **b** the ratio of the useful energy delivered by a dynamic system to the energy supplied to it

ef'ficiency a,partment *n, NAm* a small usu furnished flat with minimal kitchen and bath facilities; a bed-sitter

efficient /i'fish(ə)nt/ *adj* **1** *of a person* able and practical; briskly competent **2** productive of desired effects, esp with minimum waste ⟨*an* ~ *method of generating electricity*⟩ [ME, fr MF or L; MF, fr L *efficient-, efficiens*, fr prp of *efficere* to bring about] – **efficiently** *adv*

effigy /'efəji/ *n* an image or representation, esp of a person; *specif* a crude figure representing a hated person [L *effigies*, fr *effingere* to form, fr *ex-* + *fingere* to shape – more at DOUGH]

effloresce /,eflaw'res/ *vi* **1** to burst into flower **2a** to change from crystals to a powder on exposure to air **b** to form or become covered with a powdery covering ⟨*bricks may* ~ *owing to the deposition of soluble salts*⟩ [L *efflorescere*, fr *ex-* + *florescere* to begin to blossom – more at FLORESCENCE]

efflorescence /,eflaw'res(ə)ns/ *n* **1** the period or state of flowering **2** the action, process, period, or result of developing and unfolding as if coming into flower; blossoming ⟨*periods of intellectual and artistic* ~ – Julian Huxley⟩ **3** the process or product of efflorescing chemically **4** a redness of the skin; an eruption – **efflorescent** *adj*

effluence /'efloo·əns/ *n* **1** sthg that flows out **2** an action or process of flowing out

[1]**effluent** /'efloo·ənt/ *adj* flowing out; emanating ⟨*an* ~ *river*⟩ [L *effluent-, effluens*, prp of *effluere* to flow out, fr *ex-* + *fluere* to flow – more at FLUID]

[2]**effluent** *n* sthg that flows out: e g **a** an outflowing branch of a main stream or lake **b** smoke, liquid industrial refuse, sewage, etc discharged into the environment, esp when causing pollution

effluvium /e'floohvi·əm, -vyəm/ *n, pl* **effluvia** /-vi·ə/ *often sing in constr*, **effluviums 1** an offensive exhalation or smell (e g from rotting vegetation) **2** a by-product, esp in the form of waste [L, act of flowing out, fr *effluere*]

efflux /'efluks/ *n* an effluence, esp of liquid or gas [L *effluxus*, pp of *effluere*] – **effluxion** /i'fluksh(ə)n/ *n*

effort /'efət/ *n* **1** conscious exertion of physical or mental power **2** a serious attempt; a try **3** sthg produced by exertion or trying ⟨*the novel was his most ambitious* ~⟩ **4** the force applied (e g to a simple machine) as distinguished from the force exerted against the load [MF, fr OF *esfort*, fr *esforcier* to force, fr *ex-* + *forcier* to force] – **effortful** *adj*, **effortless** *adj*, **effortlessly** *adv*, **effortlessness** *n*

effrontery /i'frunt(ə)ri/ *n* the quality of being shamelessly bold; insolence ⟨*the* ~ *to propound three such heresies – TLS*⟩ [F *effronterie*, deriv of LL *effront-, effrons* shameless, fr L *ex-* + *front-, frons* forehead – more at BRINK]

effulgence /i'fulj(ə)ns/ *n* radiant splendour; brilliance – fml [LL *effulgentia*, fr L *effulgent-, effulgens*, prp of *effulgēre* to shine forth, fr *ex-* + *fulgēre* to shine – more at FULGENT] – **effulgent** *adj*

[1]**effuse** /i'fyoohz/ *vt* **1** to pour out (e g a liquid) **2** to radiate, emit ~ *vi* to flow out, emanate *USE* (*vt & vi*) fml [L *effusus*, pp of *effundere*, fr *ex-* + *fundere* to pour – more at [4]FOUND]

[2]**effuse** /i'fyoohs/ *adj* spread out flat without definite form ⟨~ *lichens*⟩

effusion /i'fyoohzh(ə)n/ *n* **1** an act of effusing **2** unrestrained expression of words or feelings **3** the escape of a fluid from a containing vessel; *also* the fluid that escapes

effusive /i'fyoohsiv/ *adj* **1** unduly emotionally demonstrative; gushing **2** *of rock* characterized or formed by a nonexplosive outpouring of lava – **effusively** *adv*, **effusiveness** *n*

eft /eft/ *n* a newt [ME *evete, ewte*, fr OE *efete*]

egad /,ee'gad, i-/ *interj, archaic* – used as a mild oath [prob euphemism for *oh God*]

egalitarian /i,gali'teəri·ən/ *adj* marked by or advocating egalitarianism [F *égalitaire*, fr *égalité* equality, fr L *aequalitat-, aequalitas*, fr *aequalis* equal] – **egalitarian** *n*

e,gali'tarian,ism /-,iz(ə)m/ *n* a belief in or a philosophy advocating social, political, and economic equality among human beings

egest /,ee'jest/ *vt* to rid the body of (waste material) [L *egestus*, pp of *egerere* to carry outside, discharge, fr *e-* + *gerere* to carry – more at CAST] – **egestion** /,ee'jesch(ə)n/ *n*, **egestive** /-stiv/ *adj*

[1]**egg** /eg/ *vt* to incite to action – usu + *on* ⟨~ed *the mob on to riot*⟩ [ME *eggen*, fr ON *eggja*; akin to OE *ecg* edge – more at EDGE]

[2]**egg** *n* **1a** the hard-shelled reproductive body produced by a bird; *esp* that produced by domestic poultry and used as a food **b** an animal reproductive body consisting of an ovum together with its nutritive and protective envelopes that is capable of developing into a new individual ☞ LIFE CYCLE **c** an ovum **2** sthg resembling an egg in shape **3** a person – infml; not now in vogue ⟨*he's a good* ~*!*⟩ [ME *egge*, fr ON *egg*; akin to OE *ǣg* egg, L *ovum*, Gk *ōion*]

,egg and 'dart *n* an architectural moulding or ornamentation consisting of alternate egg-shaped figures and arrowheads ☞ ARCHITECTURE

eggar, egger /'egə, 'ay-/ *n* any of various large moths with brown bodies and wings [*eggar* alter. of *egger*, fr [2]*egg* + [2]*-er*; fr the shape of its cocoon]

'egg,cup /-,kup/ *n* a small cup without a handle used for holding a boiled egg

'egg,head /-,hed/ *n* an intellectual, highbrow – derog or humor – **eggheaded** /,eg'hedid, '-,--/ *adj*

'egg,nog /-,nog/ *n* a drink consisting of eggs beaten up with sugar, milk or cream, and often spirits (e g rum or brandy) [*egg* + *nog* (strong ale, usu alcoholic drink containing egg and milk), of unknown origin]

'egg,plant /-,plahnt/ *n* a widely cultivated plant of the nightshade family; *also, chiefly NAm* its fruit, the aubergine [fr the shape of the fruit]

[1]**'egg,shell** /-,shel/ *n* the hard exterior covering of an egg

[2]**'egg,shell** *adj* **1** *esp of china* thin and fragile **2** *esp of paint* having a slight sheen

'egg ,timer *n* an instrument like a small hourglass that runs for about 3 minutes and is used for timing the boiling of eggs

'egg ,tooth *n* a prominence on the beak or nose of an unhatched bird or reptile that is used to break through the eggshell

egis /'eejis/ *n* an aegis

eglantine /'egləntien, -teen/ *n* sweetbrier [ME *eglentyn*, fr MF *aiglent*, fr (assumed) VL *aculentum*, fr L *acus* needle; akin to L *acer* sharp – more at EDGE]

ego /'eegoh, 'egoh/ *n, pl* **egos** **1** the self, esp as contrasted with another self or the world **2** SELF-ESTEEM 1 **3** the one of the 3 divisions of the mind in psychoanalytic theory that serves as the organized conscious mediator between the person and reality, esp in the perception of and adaptation to reality – compare ID, SUPEREGO [NL, fr L, I – more at I]

,ego'centric /-'sentrik/ *adj* limited in outlook or concern to one's own activities or needs; self-centred, selfish – **egocentric** *n*, **egocentrically** *adv*, **egocentricity** /-sen'trisəti/ *n*, **egocentrism** /-'sentriz(ə)m/ *n*

,ego i'deal *n* the positive standards, ideals, and ambitions that form a person's conscious goals

'ego,ism /-,iz(ə)m/ *n* **1** (conduct based on) a doctrine that individual self-interest is or should be the foundation of morality **2** egotism

'egoist /-ist/ *n* **1** a believer in egoism **2** an egocentric or egotistic person – **egoistic** /-'istik/ *also* **egoistical** *adj*, **egoistically** *adv*

,ego'mania /-'maynyə, -ni·ə/ *n* the quality or state of being extremely egocentric – **egomaniac** *n*

egotism /'eegə,tiz(ə)m, 'egə-/ *n* **1** the practice of talking about oneself too much **2** an extreme sense of self-importance [L *ego* + E *-tism* (as in *idiotism*)] – **egotist** *n*, **egotistic** /-'tistic/, **egotistical** *adj*, **egotistically** *adv*

'ego ,trip *n* an act or series of acts that selfishly enhances and satisfies one's ego – infml – **ego-trip** *vi*, **ego-tripper** *n*

egregious /i'greej(y)əs/ *adj* conspicuously or shockingly bad; flagrant ⟨*an* ~ *mistake*⟩ – fml [L *egregius* extraordinary, distinguished, fr *e-* + *greg-, grex* herd – more at GREGARIOUS] – **egregiously** *adv*, **egregiousness** *n*

egress /'eegres/ *n* **1** going or coming out; *specif* the emergence of a celestial object from eclipse, transit, or occultation **2** a place or means of going out; an exit – fml [L *egressus*, fr *egressus*, pp of *egredi* to go out, fr *e-* + *gradi* to go – more at GRADE] – **egress** *vi*, **egression** /ee'gresh(ə)n/ *n*

egret /'eegrit, -gret/ *n* any of various herons that bear long plumes during the breeding season [ME, fr MF *aigrette*, fr OProv *aigreta*, of Gmc origin; akin to OHG *heigaro* heron]

[1]**Egyptian** /ee'jipsh(ə)n/ *adj* (characteristic) of Egypt

[2]**Egyptian** *n* **1** a native or inhabitant of Egypt **2** the Afro-Asiatic language of the ancient Egyptians to about the 3rd c AD ☞ ALPHABET

Egypto- *comb form* Egypt ⟨Egypto*logy*⟩ [prob fr F *Égypto-*, fr Gk *Aigypto-*, fr *Aigyptos* Egypt, country of NE Africa]

Egyptology /,eejip'toləji/ *n* the study of Egyptian antiquities – **Egyptologist** *n*

eh /ay/ *interj* – used to ask for confirmation or to express inquiry [ME *ey*]

eider /'iedə/ *n* **1** EIDER DUCK **2** EIDERDOWN 1

'eider,down /-,down/ *n* **1** the down of the eider duck **2** a thick warm quilt filled with eiderdown or other insulating material [prob fr G *eiderdaune*, fr Icel *æthardūnn*, fr *æthur* + *dūnn* down]

'eider ,duck *n* any of several large northern sea ducks having fine soft down [*eider* fr D, G, or Sw, fr Icel *æthur*, fr ON *æthr*]

eidetic /ie'detik/ *adj* marked by or involving extraordinarily accurate and vivid recall of visual images ⟨*an* ~ *memory*⟩ [Gk *eidētikos* of a form, fr *eidos* form] – **eidetically** *adv*

eidolon /ie'dohlon/ *n, pl* **eidolons, eidola** /-lə/ **1** a phantom, image **2** an ideal or idealized figure [Gk *eidōlon* – more at IDOL]

eigenvalue /'ieg(ə)n,valyooh/ *n* the scalar value by which an eigenvector is multiplied under its linear transformation [part trans of G *eigenwert*, fr *eigen* own, peculiar, characteristic (fr OHG *eigan*) + *wert* value – more at OWN]

'eigen,vector /-,vektə/ *n* a nonzero vector that under a given linear transformation becomes a scalar multiple of itself [ISV *eigen-* (fr G *eigen*) + *vector*]

eight /ayt/ *n* **1** ☞ NUMBER **2** the eighth in a set or series **3** sthg having 8 parts or members or a denomination of 8; *esp* (the crew of) an 8-person racing boat [ME *eighte*, fr *eighte*, adj, fr OE *eahta*; akin to OHG *ahto* eight, L *octo*, Gk *oktō*] – **eight** *adj or pron*, **eightfold** *adj or adv*

eighteen /,ay'teen/ *n* ☞ NUMBER [ME *eightetene*, adj, fr OE *eahtatīene*; akin to OE *tīen* ten] – **eighteen** *adj or pron*, **eighteenth** *adj or n*

,eigh'teenmo /-moh/ *n, pl* **eighteenmos** the size of a piece of paper cut 18 from a sheet; *also* a book, a page, or paper of this size

eighth /ayt·th/ *n* ☞ NUMBER – **eighth** *adj or adv*

eighth note *n, NAm* a quaver

'eightsome reel /-s(ə)m/ *n* a Scottish reel for 8 dancers

'Eights ,Week *n* the period in June during which boat races are held between the colleges of Oxford university and college balls take place – compare MAY WEEK [*eight* 3]

eighty /'ayti/ *n* **1** ☞ NUMBER **2** *pl* the numbers 80 to 89; *specif* a range of temperatures, ages, or dates within a century characterized by those numbers [ME *eighty*, adj, fr OE *eahtatig*, short for *hundeahtatig*, n, group of eighty, fr *hund* hundred + *eahta* eight + *-tig* group of ten; akin to OE *tīen* ten] – **eightieth** /-ti·ith/ *adj or n*, **eighty** *adj or pron*, **eightyfold** /-,fohld/ *adj or adv*

einkorn /'ien,kawn/ *n* a 1-grained type of wheat [G, fr OHG, fr *ein* one + *korn* grain – more at ONE, CORN]

Einsteinian /,ien'stieni·ən/ *adj* of Albert Einstein or his theories

einsteinium /,ien'stieni·əm/ *n* a radioactive element produced artificially ☞ PERIODIC TABLE [NL, fr Albert *Einstein* †1955 US (German-born) physicist & mathematician]

eisteddfod /ie'stedhvod/ *n, pl* **eisteddfods, eisteddfodau** /-,die/ a Welsh-language competitive festival of the arts, esp music and poetry [W, lit., session, fr *eistedd* to sit + *bod* being] – **eisteddfodic** /,eistedh'vodik/ *adj*

[1]either /'iedhə, 'ee-/ *adj* **1** being the one and the other of 2 ⟨*flowers blooming on ~ side of the path*⟩ **2** being the one or the other of 2 ⟨*take ~ road*⟩ [ME, fr OE *ǣghwæther* both, each, fr *ā* always + *ge-*, collective prefix + *hwæther* which of two, whether – more at [1]AYE, CO-]

[2]either *pron* the one or the other ⟨*could be happy with ~ of them*⟩ ⟨*don't want ~*⟩

[3]either *conj* – used before 2 or more sentence elements of the same class or function joined usu by *or* to indicate that what immediately follows is the first of 2 or more alternatives ⟨*~ sink or swim*⟩ ⟨*~ coffee, tea, or whisky*⟩

[4]either *adv* for that matter, likewise – used for emphasis after a negative or implied negation ⟨*not wise or handsome ~*⟩ ⟨*I can't swim, ~*⟩

,either-'or *adj or n* (involving) an unavoidable choice between only 2 possibilities

[1]ejaculate /i'jakyoo,layt/ *vt* **1** to eject from a living body; *specif* to eject (semen) in orgasm **2** to utter suddenly and vehemently – fml [L *ejaculatus*, pp of *ejaculari* to throw out, fr *e-* + *jaculari* to throw, fr *jaculum* dart, fr *jacere* to throw – more at [2]JET] – **ejaculation** /-'laysh(ə)n/ *n*, **ejaculatory** /i'jakyoolətri, i,jakyoo'laytəri/ *adj*

[2]ejaculate /i'jakyoolət/ *n* the semen released by a single ejaculation

eject /i'jekt/ *vt* **1** to drive out, esp by physical force ⟨*the hecklers were ~ed*⟩ **2** to evict from property ~ *vi* to escape from an aircraft by using the ejector seat [ME *ejecten*, fr L *ejectus*, pp of *eicere*, fr *e-* + *jacere*] – **ejectable** *adj*, **ejection** /-sh(ə)n/ *n*, **ejective** /-tiv/ *adj*, **ejector** *n*

ejecta /i'jektə/ *n pl but sing or pl in constr* material thrown out (e g from a volcano) [NL, fr L, neut pl of *ejectus*]

e'jector ,seat *n* an emergency escape seat that propels an occupant out and away from an aircraft by means of an explosive charge

eka- /ekə-, aykə-/ *comb form* standing or assumed to stand next in order beyond (a specified element) in the same family of the periodic table – in names of chemical elements when not yet discovered or synthesized ⟨eka*silicon (now called germanium)*⟩ ⟨eka*tantalum*⟩ [Skt *eka* one – more at ONE]

,eke 'out /eek/ *vt* **1a** to make up for the deficiencies of; supplement ⟨eked out *his income by getting a second job*⟩ **b** to make (a supply) last by economy **2** to make (e g a living) by laborious or precarious means [*eke* (to increase), fr ME *eken*, fr OE *īecan*, *ēcan*; akin to OHG *ouhhōn* to add, L *augēre* to increase, Gk *auxein*]

ekistics /i'kistiks/ *n pl but sing in constr* a science dealing with human settlements and their evolution [NGk *oikistikē*, fr fem of *oikistikos* relating to settlement, fr Gk, fr *oikizein* to settle, colonize, fr *oikos* house – more at VICINITY] – **ekistic** *adj*

ekuele /e'kwelay/ *n* ☞ *Equatorial Guinea* at NATIONALITY [native name in Equatorial Guinea]

el /el/ *n, NAm* an elevated railway

[1]elaborate /i'lab(ə)rət/ *adj* **1** planned or carried out with great care and attention to detail ⟨*~ preparations*⟩ **2** marked by complexity, wealth of detail, or ornateness; intricate ⟨*a highly ~ coiffure*⟩ [L *elaboratus*, fr pp of *elaborare* to work out, acquire by labour, fr *e-* + *laborare* to work – more at LABORATORY] – **elaborately** *adv*, **elaborateness** *n*

[2]elaborate /i'labə,rayt/ *vt* **1** to build up (complex organic compounds) from simple ingredients **2** to work out in detail; develop ~ *vi* to go into detail; add further information ⟨*need I ~?*⟩ – often + *on* ⟨*urged him to ~ on his scheme*⟩ – **elaboration** /-'raysh(ə)n/ *n*, **elaborative** /i'lab (ə)rətiv/ *adj*

élan /ay'lonh, -'lan (*Fr* elɑ̃)/ *n* vigorous spirit or enthusiasm; verve [F, fr MF *eslan* rush, fr *(s')eslancer* to rush, fr *ex-* + *lancer* to hurl – more at [2]LANCE]

eland /'eelənd/ *n* either of 2 large African antelopes [Afrik, elk, fr D, fr obs G *elend*, fr Lith *elnis*; akin to OHG *elaho* elk – more at ELK]

,élan vi'tal /vee'tal (*Fr* vital)/ *n* a vital force or creative urge, esp in the philosophy of Bergson [F]

elapse /i'laps/ *vi, of a period of time* to pass by ⟨*4 years ~d before he returned*⟩ [L *elapsus*, pp of *elabi*, fr *e-* + *labi* to slip, slide – more at SLEEP]

elasmobranch /i'lasmə,brangk, i'laz-/ *n* CARTILAGI-

NOUS FISH 1 [deriv of Gk *elasmos* metal plate (fr *elaunein*) + L *branchia* gill]

[1]**elastic** /i'lastik, i'lah-/ *adj* **1a** *of a solid* capable of recovering size and shape after deformation **b** *of a gas* capable of indefinite expansion **2** buoyant, resilient **3** capable of being easily stretched or expanded and resuming its former shape **4** capable of ready change; flexible, adaptable ⟨*an* ~ *conscience*⟩ ⟨~ *rules*⟩ ⟨~ *demand for goods*⟩ [NL *elasticus*, fr LGk *elastos* ductile, beaten, fr Gk *elaunein* to drive, beat out; akin to OIr *luid* he went] – **elastically** *adv*, **elasticity** /i,la'stisəti, ,ela'stisəti/ *n*, **elasticize** /i'lasti,siez/ *vt*

[2]**elastic** *n* **1** an elastic fabric usu made of yarns containing rubber **2** easily stretched rubber, usu prepared in cords, strings, or bands

elasticated /i'lasti,kaytid/ *adj* **1** *of fabric* made stretchy by the insertion or interweaving of elastic **2** elasticized

e,lastic 'band *n*, *Br* RUBBER BAND

elastin /i'lastin/ *n* a protein similar to collagen that is the chief component of elastic fibres of connective tissue [ISV, fr NL *elasticus*]

elastomer /i'lastəmə/ *n* any of various elastic substances resembling rubber ⟨*polyvinyl* ~s⟩ [*elastic* + *-o-* + Gk *meros* part – more at MERIT] – **elastomeric** /-'merik/ *adj*

Elastoplast /i'lastə,plahst/ *trademark* – used for an elastic adhesive plaster

elate /i'layt/ *vt* to fill with joy or pride; put in high spirits [L *elatus* (pp of *efferre* to carry out, elevate), fr *e-* + *latus*, pp of *ferre* to carry – more at TOLERATE, [2]BEAR] – **elated** *adj*, **elatedly** *adv*, **elation** /-sh(ə)n/ *n*

elater /'elətə/ *n* CLICK BEETLE [NL, genus of beetles, fr Gk *elatēr* driver, fr *elaunein*]

'E ,layer *n* a layer of the ionosphere occurring at about 95km (about 60mi) above the earth's surface that is capable of reflecting radio waves

[1]**elbow** /'elboh/ *n* **1a** the joint between the human forearm and upper arm **b** a corresponding joint in the forelimb of a vertebrate animal **2** an elbow-like pipe fitting **3** the part of a garment that covers the elbow [ME *elbowe*, fr OE *elboga*; akin to OHG *elinbogo* elbow; both fr a prehistoric NGmc-WGmc compound whose constituents are akin to OE *eln* ell & OE *boga* bow – more at ELL, [3]BOW] – **out at elbows** **1** shabbily dressed **2** POOR 1 – **up to the elbows in/with** busily engaged in

[2]**elbow** *vt* **1** to push or shove aside (as if) with the elbow; jostle ⟨~ed *him out of the way*⟩ **2** to force (e g one's way) rudely or roughly (as if) by pushing with the elbow ⟨~ed *his way into the best circles*⟩ ~ *vi* to advance by elbowing one's way

'elbow ,grease *n* hard physical effort – infml

'elbowroom /-,roohm, -room/ *n* adequate space or scope for movement, work, or operation

[1]**elder** /'eldə/ *n* any of several shrubs or small trees of the honeysuckle family [ME *eldre*, fr OE *ellærn*; prob akin to OE *alor* alder – more at ALDER]

[2]**elder** *adj* of earlier birth or greater age, esp than another related person or thing ⟨*his* ~ *brother*⟩ [ME, fr OE *ieldra*, compar of *eald* old]

[3]**elder** *n* **1** one who is older; a senior ⟨*the child trying to please his* ~s⟩ **2** one having authority by virtue of age and experience ⟨*the village* ~s⟩ **3** an official of the early church or of a Presbyterian congregation – **eldership** *n*

'elderberry /-b(ə)ri, -,beri/ *n* (the edible black or red berry of) an elder

'elderly /-li/ *adj* rather old – **elderliness** *n*

,elder 'statesman *n* an eminent senior or retired member of a group whose advice is often sought unofficially

eldest /'eldist/ *adj* of the greatest age or seniority; oldest

'eldest ,hand *n* the card player who first receives cards in the deal

El Dorado /,el də'rahdoh, do'rah-/ *n* a place of fabulous wealth, abundance, or opportunity [Sp, lit., the gilded one]

Eleatic /,eli'atik/ *n or adj* (a member) of a school of Greek philosophers founded by Parmenides and continued by Zeno that stressed unity of being and denied the existence of change [adj L *Eleaticus*, fr Gk *Eleatikos*, fr *Elea* (Velia), ancient town in S Italy; n fr adj] – **Eleaticism** /-ti,siz(ə)m/ *n*

elecampane /,elikam'payn/ *n* a large coarse European composite plant with yellow flowers [ME *elena campana*, fr ML *enula campana*, lit., field elecampane, fr *inula*, *enula* elecampane + *campana* of the field]

[1]**elect** /i'lekt/ *adj* **1** SELECT 1, 2 **2** chosen for salvation through divine mercy **3** chosen for office or position but not yet installed ⟨*the president*-elect⟩ [ME, fr L *electus* choice, fr pp of *eligere* to select, fr *e-* + *legere* to choose – more at LEGEND]

[2]**elect** *vt* **1** to select by vote for an office, position, or membership ⟨~ed *him president*⟩ **2** *of God* to choose or predestine (sby) to receive salvation **3** *chiefly NAm* to make a selection of ~ *vi* to choose, decide – fml – **election** /-sh(ə)n/ *n*

electioneer /i,leksh(ə)n'iə/ *vi* to work for a candidate or party in an election [*election* + *-eer* (as in *auctioneer*, vb)] – **electioneer** *n*

elective /ilektiv/ *adj* **1a** chosen or filled by popular election ⟨*an* ~ *office*⟩ **b** of election **2** permitting a choice; optional – **electively** *adv*, **electiveness** *n*

elector /i'lektə/ *n* **1** sby qualified to vote in an election **2** sby entitled to participate in an election: e g **a** *often cap* any of the German princes entitled to elect the Holy Roman Emperor **b** a member of the electoral college in the USA

electoral /i'lekt(ə)rəl/ *adj* of (an) election or electors

e,lectoral 'college *n sing or pl in constr* a body of electors chosen in each state to elect the president and vice-president of the USA

electorate /i'lekt(ə)rət/ *n* **1** *often cap* the territory, jurisdiction, etc of a German elector **2** *sing or pl in constr* a body of electors

electr- /ilektr-/, **electro-** *comb form* **1a** (caused by) electricity ⟨electro*magnetism*⟩ ⟨electro*chemistry*⟩ **b** electric ⟨electr*ode*⟩; electric and ⟨electro*chemical*⟩ ⟨electro*mechanical*⟩; electrically ⟨electro*positive*⟩ **2** electrolytic ⟨electro*analysis*⟩ ⟨electro*deposition*⟩ **3** electron ⟨electro*phile*⟩ [NL *electricus*]

E'lectra ,complex /i'lektrə/ *n* the Oedipus complex when it occurs in a female [*Electra*, character in Gk mythology who incites her brother to avenge their father's death by killing their mother]

electret /i'lektrət, -tret/ *n* a dielectric body in which a permanent state of electric polarization has been set up [*electr*icity + magn*et*]

[1]**electric** /i'lektrik/ *adj* **1a** of, being, supplying, producing, or produced by electricity ⟨~ *current*⟩ ⟨*an*

~ *plug*⟩ **b** operated by or using electricity ⟨*an ~ motor*⟩ **2** producing an intensely stimulating effect; thrilling ⟨*an ~ performance*⟩ **3** *of a musical instrument* electronically producing or amplifying sound ⟨*an ~ organ*⟩ [NL *electricus* produced from amber by friction, electric, fr ML, of amber, fr L *electrum* amber, alloy of gold and silver, fr Gk *ēlektron*; akin to Gk *ēlektōr* beaming sun, Skt *ulkā* meteor]

[2]**electric** *n* **1** *pl* electrical parts; electric circuitry **2** electricity – sometimes pl with sing. meaning; infml

electrical /i'lektrikl/ *adj* **1** of or connected with electricity ⟨*~ output*⟩ ⟨*~ engineering*⟩ **2** ELECTRIC 1 ⟨*~ appliances*⟩ – **electrically** *adv*

e,lectric 'blanket *n* a blanket containing an electric heating element that is used to warm a bed

e,lectric 'blue *adj or n* harshly bright slightly greenish blue

e,lectric 'chair *n* **1** a chair used in legal electrocution **2** *the* penalty of death by electrocution

e,lectric 'eel *n* a large eel-shaped fish of the Orinoco and Amazon rivers that is capable of giving a severe electric shock

e,lectric 'eye *n* PHOTOELECTRIC CELL

electrician /,elək'trish(ə)n, i,lek-/ *n* one who installs, maintains, operates, or repairs electrical equipment

electricity /i,lek'trisəti, ,ee-/ *n* **1** (the study of) the phenomena due to (the flow or accumulation of) positively and negatively charged particles (e g protons and electrons) **2** electric current; *also* electric charge ***USE*** ☞ ENERGY, PHYSICS

e,lectric 'organ *n* a specialized tract of tissue (e g in the electric eel) in which electricity is generated

e,lectric 'ray *n* any of various rays found in warm seas that can give electric shocks

e,lectric 'shock *n* [2]SHOCK 4

e,lectric 'storm *n* a violent atmospheric disturbance usu accompanied by thunder and lightning

electrify /i'lekrifie/ *vt* **1a** to charge (a body) with electricity **b** to equip for use of or supply with electric power **2** to excite, thrill – **electrification** /-fi'kaysh(ə)n/ *n*

electro- /ilektroh-/ – see ELECTR-

electrocardiogram /i,lektroh'kahdi·ə,gram/ *n* the tracing made by an electrocardiograph

,electro'cardio,graph /-,grahf, -,graf/ *n* an instrument for recording the changes of electrical potential difference occurring during the heartbeat – **electrocardiographic** /-'grafik/ *adj*, **electrocardiographically** *adv*, **electrocardiography** /-'ogrəfi/ *n*

electroconvulsive therapy /i,lektrohkən'vulsiv/ *n* a treatment for serious mental disorder, esp severe depression, in which a fit is induced by passing an electric current through the brain

electrocute /i'lektrə,kyooht/ *vt* to execute or kill by electricity [*electr-* + *-cute* (as in *execute*)] – **electrocution** /-'kyoohsh(ə)n/ *n*

electrode /i'lektrohd/ *n* a conductor used to establish electrical contact with a nonmetallic part of a circuit (e g the acid in a car battery)

electrodynamics /i,lektrohdie'namiks, -di-/ *n pl but sing in constr* physics dealing with the effects arising from the interaction of electric currents with magnets, with other electric currents, or with themselves – **electrodynamic** *adj*

e,lectroen'cephalo,gram /-in'sef(ə)lə,gram/ *n* the tracing made by an electroencephalograph [ISV]

e,lectroen'cephalo,graph /-in'sef(ə)lə,grahf, -,graf/ *n* an instrument for detecting and recording brain waves [ISV] – **electroencephalographic** /-'grafik/ *adj*, **electroencephalography** /-'logrəfi/ *n*

electroform /i'lektrə,fawm/ *vt* to form (shaped articles) by depositing material, esp a metal, on a a mould by electrolysis

electrokinetics /i,lektrohki'netiks/ *n pl but sing in constr* physics dealing with the movement of particles or liquids resulting from or producing a difference of electrical potential – **electrokinetic** *adj*

electrolysis /,elek'troləsis, i,lek-/ *n* **1** the passage of an electric current through an electrolyte to generate a gas, deposit a metal on (an object serving as) an electrode, etc **2** the destruction of hair roots, warts, moles, etc by means of an electric current [NL] – **electrolyse** /i'lektrə,liez/ *vt*

electrolyte /i'lektrə,liet/ *n* **1** a nonmetallic electric conductor (e g a salt solution) in which current is carried by the movement of ions **2** a substance that becomes an ionic conductor when dissolved in a suitable solvent or melted

electrolytic /i,lektrə'litik/ *adj* of or being electrolysis or an electrolyte – **electrolytically** *adv*

electromagnet /i,lektroh'magnit/ *n* a core of magnetizable material surrounded by a coil of wire through which an electric current is passed to make the core into a magnet

electromagnetic interaction /i,lektrohmag'netik/ *n* a fundamental interaction experienced by most elementary particles that is responsible for the emission and absorption of photons and for electric and magnetic forces

electromagnetic radiation *n* radiation consisting of a series of electromagnetic waves ☞ PHYSICS

electromagnetic spectrum *n* the entire range of wavelengths or frequencies of electromagnetic radiation extending from gamma rays to the longest radio waves and including visible light

electromagnetic unit *n* any of a series of electrical units in the cgs system based primarily on the magnetic properties of electrical currents

e,lectromag,netic 'wave *n* any of the waves that travel by inducing simultaneous periodic variations in the intensities of electric and magnetic fields and that include radio waves, infrared, visible light, ultraviolet, X rays, and gamma rays

electromagnetism /i,lektroh'magnətiz(ə)m/ *n* **1** magnetism developed (e g in an electromagnet) by a current of electricity **2** physics dealing with the physical relations between electricity and magnetism – **electromagnetic** /-mag'netik/ *adj*, **electromagnetically** *adv*

electrometer /,elek'tromitə, i,lek-/ *n* any of various instruments for detecting or measuring electrical potential differences or ionizing radiations (e g alpha rays) using the forces of attraction and repulsion existing between charged bodies

electromotive force /i,lektrə'mohtiv/ *n* the amount of energy derived from an electrical source per unit current of electricity passing through the source (e g a cell or generator)

electron /i'lektron/ *n* a negatively charged elementary particle that occurs in atoms outside the nucleus and the mass movement of which constitutes an electric current in a metal ☞ PHYSICS [*electr-* + *-on*]

electronegative /i,lektroh'negətiv/ *adj* **1** charged

with negative electric particles **2** having a tendency to attract electrons – **electronegativity** /-,negə'tivəti/ *n*

e'lectron ,gun *n* the cathode and its surrounding assembly that emits a stream of electrons (e g in a cathode-ray tube) ☞ TELEVISION

electronic /i,lek'tronik, ,eelek-/ *adj* **1** of electrons **2** of, being, or using devices constructed or working by the methods or principles of electronics – **electronically** *adv*

,elec'tronics *n pl but sing in constr* physics or technology dealing with the emission, behaviour, and effects of electrons in thermionic valves, transistors, or other electronic devices

e'lectron ,lens *n* a device (e g in an electron microscope) for focussing a beam of electrons by means of an electric or magnetic field

e,lectron 'micro,scope *n* an instrument in which a beam of electrons is used to produce an enormously enlarged image of a minute object – **electron microscopist** *n*, **electron microscopy** *n*

electron optics *n pl but sing in constr* electronics dealing with those properties of beams of electrons that are analogous to the properties of rays of light

e'lectron ,tube *n* an electronic device (e g a thermionic valve) consisting of a sealed container containing a vacuum or gas through which the flow of electrons is controlled

e'lectron ,volt *n* a unit of energy equal to the energy gained by an electron in being accelerated through a potential difference of 1 V ☞ PHYSICS, UNIT

electrophile /i'lektroh,fiel/ *n* a substance (e g a chlorine molecule) with an affinity for electrons – **electrophilic** /-'filik/ *adj*

electrophoresis /i,lektrohfə'reesis/ *n* the movement of particles through a gel or other medium in which particles are suspended under the action of an applied electric field [NL] – **electrophoretic** /-fə'retik/ *adj*, **electrophoretically** *adv*

electroplate /i'lektroh,playt/ *vt* to plate with a continuous metallic coating by electrolysis

e,lectro'positive /-'pozətiv/ *adj* **1** charged with positive electric particles **2** having a tendency to release electrons

electroscope /i'lektrə,skohp/ *n* any of various instruments for detecting the presence and positive or negative quality of an electric charge, esp as a measure of intensity of ionization of radiation [prob fr F *électroscope*] – **electroscopic** /-'skopik/ *adj*, **electroscopically** *adv*

electroshock therapy /i,lektrə'shok/ *n* ELECTROCONVULSIVE THERAPY

e,lectro'static /-'statik/ *adj* of or producing static electricity or electrostatics ⟨*an* ~ *generator*⟩ [ISV] – **electrostatically** *adv*

e,lectro'statics *n pl but sing in constr* physics dealing with phenomena due to (attractions or repulsions of) stationary electric charges

e,lectro,static 'unit *n* any of a series of electrical units in the cgs system based primarily on forces of interaction between electric charges

electrotherapy /i,lektrə'therəpi, -troh-/ *n* treatment of disease by the use of electricity

¹e'lectro,type /-,tiep/ *n* (a copy taken from) a printing plate made from a mould that is coated with metal by electrolysis then backed with lead

²electrotype *vt* to make an electrotype from (a printing surface) – **electrotyper** *n*

,electro'valent /-'vaylənt/ *adj*, *of a chemical bond* formed between positively and negatively charged ions

eleemosynary /,eli·i'mosin(ə)ri/ *adj* of, supported by, or giving charity [ML *eleemosynarius*, fr LL *eleemosyna* alms – more at ALMS]

elegant /'elig(ə)nt/ *adj* **1** gracefully refined or dignified (e g in manners, taste, or style) **2** tastefully rich or luxurious, esp in design or ornamentation ⟨~ *furnishings*⟩ **3** *of ideas* neat and simple ⟨*an* ~ *piece of reasoning*⟩ ⟨*an* ~ *mathematical proof*⟩ [MF or L; MF, fr L *elegant-, elegans*; akin to L *eligere* to select, fr *e-* + *legere* to chose – more at LEGEND] – **elegance** *n*, **elegantly** *adv*

,ele,giac 'couplet /,eli'jie·ək/ *n* a classical verse form in which dactylic hexameters alternate with pentameters

,ele,giac 'stanza *n* a quatrain in iambic pentameter with a rhyme scheme of *abab*

elegy /'eləji/ *n* **1a** a song, poem, or other work expressing sorrow or lamentation, esp for one who is dead **b** a pensive or reflective poem that is usu nostalgic or melancholy **2** a poem in elegiac couplets [L *elegia* poem in elegiac couplets, fr Gk *elegeia*, *elegeion*, fr *elegos* song of mourning] – **elegize** *vb*, **elegiac** /-'jie·ək/ *adj*, **elegiacal** *adj*, **elegiacally** *adv*

element /'eləmənt/ *n* **1a** any of the 4 substances air, water, fire, and earth formerly believed to constitute the physical universe **b** *pl* forces of nature; *esp* violent or severe weather **c** the state or sphere natural or suited to sby or sthg ⟨*at school she was in her* ~⟩ **2** a constituent part: e g **a** *pl* the simplest principles of a subject of study; the rudiments **b** any of the numbers or symbols in an array (e g a matrix) **c** a constituent of a mathematical set **d** a specified group within a human community ⟨*the rowdy* ~ *in the classroom*⟩ ⟨*the smart* ~⟩ – often pl with sing. meaning **e** any of the factors determining an outcome **f** a distinct part of a composite device; *esp* a resistor in an electric heater, kettle, etc **3** any of more than 100 fundamental substances that consist of atoms of only one kind ☞ PERIODIC TABLE **4** *pl* the bread and wine used at Communion [ME, fr OF & L; OF, fr L *elementum*]

elemental /,eli'mentl/ *adj* **1** existing as an uncombined chemical element **2** of or resembling a great force of nature ⟨~ *passions*⟩ – **elemental** *n*, **elementally** *adv*

elementary /,eli'ment(ə)ri/ *adj* **1** of or dealing with the basic elements or principles of sthg; simple ⟨*can't handle the most* ~ *decision-making*⟩ **2** ELEMENTAL 1 – **elementarily** *adv*, **elementariness** *n*

,ele,mentary 'particle *n* any of the constituents of matter and energy (e g the electron, proton, or photon) whose nature has not yet been proved to be due to the combination of other more fundamental entities

,ele'mentary ,school *n* a state school that formerly took children from the age of 5 to 13 or 14

elenchus /i'lengkəs/ *n*, *pl* **elenchi** /-kie/ a logical refutation, esp in syllogistic form [L, fr Gk *elenchos*, fr *elenchein* to shame, cross-examine, refute]

elephant /'elifənt/ *n* a very large nearly hairless mammal having the snout prolonged into a muscular trunk and 2 upper incisors developed into long tusks which provide ivory [ME, fr OF & L; OF *olifant*, fr L *elephantus*, fr Gk *elephant-*, *elephas*]

elephantiasis /,elifən'tie·əsis/ *n, pl* **elephantiases** /-,seez/ enormous enlargement of a limb or the scrotum caused by lymphatic obstruction, esp by filarial worms [NL, fr L, a kind of leprosy, fr Gk, fr *elephant-*, *elephas*]

elephantine /,eli'fantien/ *adj* **1a** huge, massive **b** clumsy, ponderous **2** of an elephant

'elephant ,seal *n* a nearly extinct large seal that has a long trunklike snout

,Eleu,sinian 'mysteries /,elyoo'sini·ən/ *n pl* the religious mysteries celebrated at ancient Eleusis in worship of Demeter and Persephone [*Eleusis*, city of ancient Greece]

elevate /'eli,vayt/ *vt* **1** to lift up; raise **2** to raise in rank or status; exalt **3** to improve morally, intellectually, or culturally **4** to raise the spirits of; elate [ME *elevaten*, fr L *elevatus*, pp of *elevare*, fr *e-* + *levare* to raise – more at LEVER]

'elevated *adj* **1** raised, esp above a surface (e g the ground) ⟨*an ~ road*⟩ **2** morally or intellectually on a high plane; lofty ⟨*~ thoughts*⟩ **3** exhilarated in mood or feeling **4** slightly tipsy – not now in vogue

elevation /,eli'vaysh(ə)n/ *n* **1** the height to which sthg is elevated: e g **a** the angle to which a gun is aimed above the horizon **b** the height above sea level **2** (the ability to achieve) a ballet dancer's or a skater's leap and seeming suspension in the air **3** an elevated place **4** being elevated **5** a geometrical projection (e g of a building) on a vertical plane ☞ BUILDING [ELEVATE + -ION] – **elevational** *adj*

elevator /'eli,vaytə/ *n* **1** sby or sthg that raises or lifts sthg up: e g **a** an endless belt or chain conveyer for raising grain, liquids, etc **b** *chiefly NAm* LIFT 9 **c** *NAm* a building for elevating, storing, discharging, and sometimes processing grain **2** a movable horizontal control surface, usu attached to the tailplane of an aircraft for controlling climb and descent ☞ FLIGHT

eleven /i'lev(ə)n/ *n* **1** ☞ NUMBER **2** the eleventh in a set or series **3** *sing or pl in constr* sthg having 11 parts or members or a denomination of 11; *esp* a cricket, soccer, or hockey team [ME *enleven*, fr *enleven*, adj, fr OE *endleofan*; akin to OHG *einlif* eleven; both fr a prehistoric Gmc compound whose first element is akin to OE *ān* one, and whose second is prob akin to OE *lēon* to lend] – **eleven** *adj or pron*, **elevenfold** *adj or adv*, **eleventh** *adj or n*

e,leven-'plus, 11-plus *n* an examination taken, esp formerly, at the age of 10-11 to determine which type of British state secondary education a child should receive

e'levenses *n pl but sometimes sing in constr, Br* light refreshment taken in the middle of the morning [irreg pl of *eleven* (o'clock)]

e,leventh 'hour *n* *the* latest possible time ⟨*won his reprieve at the ~*⟩ – **eleventh-hour** *adj*

elevon /'elivon/ *n* a control surface (of a delta-winged aircraft) combining the functions of an aileron and an elevator [*elev*ator + aileron]

elf /elf/ *n, pl* **elves** /elvz/ a (mischievous) fairy [ME, fr OE *ælf*; akin to ON *alfr* elf] – **elfish** *adj*, **elfishly** *adv*

elfin /'elfin/ *adj* of or resembling an elf, esp in being small, sprightly, or impish [irreg fr *elf*]

'elf-,lock *n* a matted lock of hair – usu pl [fr folklore belief that an elf caused it]

elicit /i'lisit/ *vt* **1** to draw forth or bring out (sthg latent or potential) **2** to call forth or draw out (a response or reaction); evoke [L *elicitus*, pp of *elicere*, fr *e-* + *lacere* to allure – more at DELIGHT] – **elicitor** *n*, **elicitation** /-'taysh(ə)n/ *n*

elide /i'lied/ *vt* to suppress or alter (e g a vowel or syllable) by elision [L *elidere* to strike out, fr *e-* + *laedere* to injure by striking]

eligible /'elijəbl/ *adj* **1** qualified to be chosen; *also* entitled ⟨*~ for promotion*⟩ ⟨*~ to retire*⟩ **2** worthy or desirable, esp as a marriage partner ⟨*an ~ young bachelor*⟩ [ME, fr MF & LL; MF, fr LL *eligibilis*, fr L *eligere* to select, fr *e-* + *legere* to chose – more at LEGEND] – **eligible** *n*, **eligibly** *adv*, **eligibility** /-'biləti/ *n*

eliminate /i'limi,nayt/ *vt* **1a** to cast out or get rid of completely; eradicate ⟨*the need to ~ poverty*⟩ **b** to set aside as unimportant; ignore **2** to expel (e g waste) from the living body **3a** to kill (a person), esp so as to remove as an obstacle **b** to remove (a competitor, team, etc) from a competition, usu by defeat [L *eliminatus*, pp of *eliminare*, fr *e-* + *limin-*, *limen* threshold] – **elimination** /-'naysh(ə)n/ *n*, **eliminative** /i'liminətiv/ *adj*, **eliminator** /-,naytə/ *n*

Elinvar /'elin,vah/ *trademark* – used for an iron alloy containing nickel and chromium and having a very low coefficient of expansion

elision /i'lizh(ə)n/ *n* **1** omission of a vowel or syllable in pronunciation (e g *I'm* for *I am*) **2** the act or an instance of eliding; omission [LL *elision-*, *elisio*, fr L *elisus*, pp of *elidere*]

élite, elite /i'leet, ay-/ *n* **1** *sing or pl in constr* a small superior group; *esp* one that has a power out of proportion to its size **2** a typewriter type producing 12 characters to the inch [F *élite*, fr OF *eslite*, fr fem of *eslit*, pp of *eslire* to choose, fr L *eligere*] – **élite** *adj*

é'li,tism, elitism /-,tiz(ə)m/ *n* (advocacy of) leadership by an élite – **élitist** *n or adj*

elixir /i'liksə, -siə/ *n* **1** an alchemist's substance supposedly capable of changing base metals into gold **2a elixir, elixir of life** a substance held to be capable of prolonging life indefinitely **b** a cure-all **3** a sweetened liquid (e g a syrup) containing a drug or medicine [ME, fr ML, fr Ar *al-iksīr* the elixir, fr *al* the + *iksīr* elixir, prob fr Gk *xērion* drying powder, fr *xēros* dry]

Elizabethan /i,lizə'beeth(ə)n/ *adj* (characteristic) of (the age of) Elizabeth I – **Elizabethan** *n*

elk /elk/ *n, pl* **elks,** *esp collectively* **elk** **1** the largest existing deer of Europe and Asia **2** *NAm* the wapiti [ME, prob fr OE *eolh*; akin to OHG *elaho* elk, Gk *elaphos* deer]

'elk,hound /-,hownd/ *n* any of a large Norwegian breed of hunting dogs with a very heavy coat

ell /el/ *n* a former English unit of length equal to 45in (about 1.14m) ☞ UNIT [ME *eln*, fr OE]

ellipse /i'lips/ *n* **1** a closed plane curve generated by a point moving in such a way that the sums of its distances from 2 fixed points is a constant; a closed plane curve obtained by plane section of a right circular cone – compare HYPERBOLA, PARABOLA ☞ MATHEMATICS **2** ellipsis [Gk *elleipsis*]

ellipsis /i'lipsis/ *n, pl* **ellipses** /-,seez/ **1** the omission of 1 or more words needed to make a construction grammatically complete **2** marks or a mark (e g ...

or *** or –) indicating the omission of letters or words [L, fr Gk *elleipsis* ellipsis, ellipse, fr *elleipein* to leave out, fall short, fr *en* in + *leipein* to leave – more at IN, LOAN]

ellipsoid /i'lipsoyd/ *n* a surface of which all the plane sections are ellipses or circles – compare HYPERBOLOID, PARABOLOID – **ellipsoid, ellipsoidal** /-'soydl/ *adj*

elliptical /i'liptikl/, **elliptic** /-tik/ *adj* **1a** of or shaped like an ellipse ☞ PLANT **b** of or marked by ellipsis or an ellipsis **2** *of speech or writing* extremely or excessively concise [Gk *elleiptikos* defective, marked by ellipsis, fr *elleipein*] – **elliptically** *adv*, **ellipticity** /-'tisəti/ *n*

elm /elm/ *n* (the wood of) any of a genus of large graceful trees [ME, fr OE; akin to OHG *elme* elm, L *ulmus*]

'elm ,bark ,beetle *n* either of 2 European beetles that transmit the fungus causing Dutch elm disease to elm trees

elocution /,elə'kyoohsh(ə)n/ *n* the art of effective public speaking, esp of good diction [ME *elocucioun*, fr L *elocution-*, *elocutio*, fr *elocutus*, pp of *eloqui*] – **elocutionary** /-shən(ə)ri/ *adj*, **elocutionist** *n*

[1]**elongate** /'elong,gayt, 'ee-/ *vt* to extend the length of ~ *vi* to grow in length [LL *elongatus*, pp of *elongare* to withdraw, fr L *e-* + *longus* long]

[2]**elongate, elongated** *adj* long in proportion to width – used esp in botany and zoology

elongation /,elong'gaysh(ə)n, ,ee-/ *n* the angular distance of one celestial body from another round which it revolves or from a particular point in the sky as viewed from earth [LL *elongare* to withdraw]

elope /i'lohp/ *vi* to run away secretly with the intention of getting married or cohabiting, usu without parental consent [AF *aloper*] – **elopement** *n*, **eloper** *n*

eloquent /'eləkwənt/ *adj* **1** characterized by fluent, forceful, and persuasive use of language **2** vividly or movingly expressive or revealing ⟨*put his arm around her in an* ~ *gesture of reassurance*⟩ [ME, fr MF, fr L *eloquent-*, *eloquens*, fr prp of *eloqui* to speak out, fr *e-* + *loqui* to speak] – **eloquence** *n*, **eloquently** *adv*

Elsan /'el,san/ *trademark* – used for a type of esp portable toilet in which chemicals are used to kill bacteria and mask the smell

else /els/ *adv* **1** apart from the person, place, manner, or time mentioned or understood ⟨*how* ~ *could he have acted*⟩ ⟨*everybody* ~ *but me*⟩ **2** also, besides ⟨*who* ~ *did you see*⟩ ⟨*there's nothing* ~ *to eat*⟩ **3** if not, otherwise ⟨*do what you are told or* ~ *you'll be sorry*⟩ ⟨*they must be coming; they'd have phoned* ~⟩ – used absolutely to express a threat ⟨*do what I tell you or* ~⟩ [ME *elles*, fr OE; akin to L *alius* other, *alter* other of two, Gk *allos* other]

,else'where /-'weə/ *adv* in or to another place ⟨*took his business* ~⟩

eluant, eluent /'elyoo·ənt/ *n* a solvent used in eluting [L *eluent-*, *eluens*, prp of *eluere*]

eluate /'elyoo·ət, -,ayt/ *n* the washings obtained by eluting [L *eluere* + E *-ate*]

elucidate /i'loohsi,dayt/ *vb* to make (sthg) lucid, esp by explanation [LL *elucidatus*, pp of *elucidare*, fr L *e-* + *lucidus* lucid] – **elucidative** *adj*, **elucidator** *n*, **elucidation** /-'daysh(ə)n/ *n*

elude /i'loohd/ *vt* **1** to avoid cunningly or adroitly **2** to escape the memory, understanding, or notice of [L *eludere*, fr *e-* + *ludere* to play – more at LUDICROUS]

elusive /i'loohsiv/ *adj* tending to elude [L *elusus*, pp of *eludere*] – **elusively** *adv*, **elusiveness** *n*, **elusion** /-zh(ə)n/ *n*

elute /ee'l(y)ooht/ *vt* to remove (adsorbed material) from an adsorbent by means of a solvent [L *elutus*, pp of *eluere* to wash out, fr *e-* + *lavere* to wash – more at LYE] – **elution** /-sh(ə)n/ *n*

elutriate /ee'l(y)oohtri,ayt/ *vt* to purify, separate, or remove by washing [L *elutriatus*, pp of *elutriare*, irreg fr *elutus*] – **elutriator** *n*

eluvium /ee'l(y)oohvi·əm, i-, -vyəm/ *n* rock debris produced by the weathering and disintegration of rock in situ [NL, fr L *eluere*] – **eluvial** *adj*

elver /'elvə/ *n* a young eel [alter. of *eelfare* (migration of eels)]

elves /elvz/ *pl of* ELF

elvish /'elvish/ *adj* elfish

Elysium /i'lizi·əm/ *n, pl* **Elysiums, Elysia** /-zi·ə/ **1** the home of the blessed after death in Greek mythology **2** PARADISE 2 [L, fr Gk *Ēlysion*] – **Elysian** *adj*

elytron /'elitron/ *n, pl* **elytra** /-trə/ either of the modified front pair of wings in beetles, cockroaches, and some other insects that serve to protect the hind pair of functional wings [NL, fr Gk *elytron* sheath, wing cover, fr *eilyein* to roll, wrap – more at VOLUBLE]

em, m /em/ *n* **1** the width of the body of a piece of type bearing the letter M used as a unit of measure of printed matter **2** [1]PICA 2

em- /im-, em-/ – see EN-

'em /(ə)m/ *pron* them – used in writing to suggest casual speech

emaciate /i'maysi,ayt/ *vb vt* to make or become excessively thin or feeble [L *emaciatus*, pp of *emaciare*, fr *e-* + *macies* leanness, fr *macer* lean – more at MEAGRE] – **emaciation** /-'aysh(ə)n/ *n*

emanate /'emə,nayt/ *vi* to come out from a source ⟨*a foul smell* ~d *from the sewer*⟩ ⟨*rumours* emanating *from high places*⟩ ~ *vt* EMIT 1 [L *emanatus*, pp of *emanare*, fr *e-* + *manare* to flow]

emanation /,emə'naysh(ə)n/ *n* **1** sthg that emanates or is produced by emanating **2** a heavy gaseous element produced by radioactive disintegration ⟨*radium* ~⟩ [EMANATE + -ION] – **emanational** *adj*, **emanative** /'emənətiv/ *adj*

emancipate /i'mansi,payt/ *vt* to free from restraint, control, or esp slavery [L *emancipatus*, pp of *emancipare*, fr *e-* + *mancipare* to transfer ownership of, fr *mancip-*, *manceps* purchaser, fr *manus* hand + *capere* to take – more at MANUAL, HEAVE] – **emancipator** *n*, **emancipation** /-'paysh(ə)n/ *n*, **emancipationist** *n*

emasculate /i'maskyoo,layt/ *vt* **1** to castrate **2** to deprive of strength, vigour, or spirit; weaken [L *emasculatus*, pp of *emasculare*, fr *e-* + *masculus* male – more at MALE] – **emasculate** *adj*, **emasculation** /-'laysh(ə)n/ *n*, **emasculator** *n*

embalm /im'bahm/ *vt* **1** to treat (a dead body) so as to give protection against decay **2** to preserve from oblivion [ME *embaumen*, fr MF *embaumer*, fr OF *embasmer*, fr *en-* + *basme* balm – more at BALM] – **embalmer** *n*, **embalmment** *n*

embankment /im'bangkmənt/ *n* a raised structure

to hold back water or to carry a roadway or railway – **embank** *vt*

embargo /im'bahgoh/ *n, pl* **embargoes** **1** an order of a government prohibiting the departure or entry of commercial ships **2** a legal prohibition on commerce ⟨*an* ~ *on arms shipments*⟩ **3** a stoppage, impediment; *esp* a prohibition [Sp, fr *embargar* to bar, fr (assumed) VL *imbarricare*, fr L *in-* + (assumed) VL *barra* bar] – **embargo** *vt*

embark /im'bahk/ *vi* **1** to go on board a boat or aircraft **2** to make a start; commence – usu + *on* or *upon* ⟨~ed *on a new career*⟩ ~ *vt* to cause to go on board a boat or aircraft [MF *embarquer*, fr OProv *embarcar*, fr *em-* (fr L *im-*) + *barca* bark] – **embarkment** *n*, **embarkation** /,embah'kaysh(ə)n/ *n*

embarrass /im'barəs/ *vt* **1** to involve in financial difficulties, esp debt **2** to cause to experience a state of self-conscious distress; disconcert ⟨*smutty stories* ~ed *her*⟩ [F *embarrasser*, fr Sp *embarazar*, fr Pg *embaraçar*] – **embarrassedly** *adv*, **embarrassingly** *adv*, **embarrassment** *n*

embassy /'embəsi/ *n* **1a** the position of an ambassador **b** an ambassador's official mission abroad **2** (the residence of) a diplomatic body headed by an ambassador [MF *ambassee*, of Gmc origin; akin to OHG *ambaht* service]

embattle /im'batl/ *vt* **1** to prepare (an army) for battle **2** to fortify (a town, position, etc) against attack **3** to provide (a building) with battlements ⟨*an* ~d *facade*⟩ [ME *embatailen*, fr MF *embatailler*, fr *en-* + *batailler* to battle]

em'battled *adj* involved in battle or conflict

embay /im'bay/ *vt* to enclose or shelter (as if) in a bay ⟨*an* ~ed *fleet*⟩

em'bayment /-mənt/ *n* **1** the formation of a bay **2** (a geographical conformation resembling) a bay

embed /im'bed/ *vt* **-dd-** to place or fix firmly (as if) in surrounding matter ⟨*a splinter was* ~ded *in his finger*⟩

embellish /im'belish/ *vt* **1** to make beautiful by adding ornaments; decorate **2** to make (speech or writing) more interesting by adding fictitious or exaggerated detail [ME *embelisshen*, fr MF *embeliss-*, stem of *embelir*, fr *en-* + *bel* beautiful – more at BEAUTY] – **embellisher** *n*, **embellishment** *n*

ember /'embə/ *n* **1** a glowing fragment (e g of coal or wood) in a (dying) fire **2** *pl* the smouldering remains of a fire **3** *pl* slowly fading emotions, memories, ideas, or responses [ME *eymere*, fr ON *eimyrja*; akin to OE *ǣmerge* ashes]

'ember ,day *n* a day set aside for fasting and prayer in Anglican and Roman Catholic churches that falls on the Wednesday, Friday, or Saturday following the first Sunday in Lent, Whitsunday, September 14, or December 13 [ME, fr OE *ymbrendæg*, fr *ymbrene* circuit, anniversary + *dæg* day]

embezzle /im'bezl/ *vt* **embezzling** /im'bezling, im'bezl·ing/ to appropriate (e g property entrusted to one's care) fraudulently to one's own use [ME *embesilen*, fr AF *embeseiller*, fr MF *en-* + *besillier* to destroy] – **embezzlement** *n*, **embezzler** *n*

embitter /im'bitə/ *vt* **1** to make bitter **2** to excite bitter feelings in – **embitterment** *n*

emblazon /im'blayz(ə)n/ *vt* **1** to display conspicuously **2a(1)** to deck in bright colours **(2)** to inscribe, adorn, or embellish (as if) with heraldic bearings or devices **b** to celebrate, extol – **emblazonment** *n*, **emblazonry** *n*

emblem /'embləm/ *n* **1** an object or a typical representation of an object symbolizing another object or idea **2** a device, symbol, or figure adopted and used as an identifying mark [ME, fr L *emblema* inlaid work, fr Gk *emblēmat-*, *emblēma*, fr *emballein* to insert, fr *en-* + *ballein* to throw – more at DEVIL]

emblematic /,emblə'matik/ *also* **emblematical** /-tikl/ *adj* of or constituting an emblem; symbolic – **emblematically** *adv*

emblemat·ize, -ise /em'blemə,tiez/ *vt* to represent (as if) by an emblem; symbolize

emblements /'embləmənts, 'emblmənts/ *n pl* crops from annual cultivation legally belonging to the tenant [ME *emblayment*, fr MF *emblaement*, fr *emblaer* to sow with grain, fr *en-* + *blee* grain]

embody /im'bodi/ *vt* **1** to give a body to (a spirit); incarnate **2** to make (e g ideas or concepts) concrete and perceptible ⟨*a chapter which* embodies *his new theory*⟩ **3** to make (e g connected ideas or principles) a part of a body or system; incorporate, include – usu + *in* ⟨*their way of life is* embodied *in their laws*⟩ **4** to represent in human or animal form; personify ⟨*men who* embodied *the idealism of the revolution*⟩ – **embodier** *n*, **embodiment** *n*

embol-, emboli-, embolo- *comb form* embolus ⟨embol*ectomy*⟩ [NL, fr *embolus*]

embolden /im'bohld(ə)n/ *vt* to make bold or courageous

embolectomy /,embə'lektəmi/ *n* surgical removal of an embolus

embolic /em'bolik/ *adj* of an embolus or an embolism

embolism /'embəliz(ə)m/ *n* (the sudden obstruction of a blood vessel by) an embolus [ME *embolisme*, fr ML *embolismus*, fr Gk *embol-* (fr *emballein* to insert, intercalate) – more at EMBLEM] – **embolismic** /-'lizmik/ *adj*

embolus /'embələs/ *n, pl* **emboli** /-,lie/ a clot, air bubble, or other particle likely to cause an embolism – compare THROMBUS [NL, fr Gk *embolos* wedge-shaped object, stopper, fr *emballein*]

emboss /im'bos/ *vt* **1** to ornament with raised work **2** to raise in relief from a surface [ME *embosen*, fr MF *embocer*, fr *en-* + *boce* boss] – **embosser** *n*, **embossment** *n*

embouchure /,ombooh'shooə/ *n* the position and use of the lips in playing a musical wind instrument [F, fr *(s')emboucher* to flow into, fr *en-* + *bouche* mouth – more at DEBOUCH]

[1]**embrace** /im'brays/ *vt* **1** to take and hold closely in the arms as a sign of affection; hug **2** to encircle, enclose **3a** to take up, esp readily or eagerly; adopt ⟨~ *a cause*⟩ **b** to avail oneself of; welcome ⟨~d *the opportunity to study further*⟩ **4** to include as a part or element of a more inclusive whole ~ *vi* to join in an embrace; hug one another [ME *embracen*, fr MF *embracer*, fr OF *embracier*, fr *en-* + *brace* two arms – more at BRACE] – **embracer** *n*, **embracingly** *adv*, **embracive** /-siv/ *adj*

[2]**embrace** *n* an act of embracing or gripping ⟨*a loving* ~⟩ ⟨*helpless in the* ~ *of terror*⟩

embranchment /im'brahnchmənt/ *n* a branching off or out (e g of a valley) [F *embranchement*, fr *(s')embrancher* to branch out, fr *en-* + *branche* branch]

embrasure /im'brayzhə/ *n* **1** a door or window aperture, esp with splayed sides that increase the width of the opening on the inside **2** an opening with sides flaring outwards in a wall or parapet, usu for a gun [F, fr obs *embraser* to widen an opening]

embrocation /,embrə'kaysh(ə)n/ *n* a liniment [LL *embrocatus*, pp of *embrocare* to rub with lotion, fr Gk *embrochē* lotion, fr *embrechein* to bathe with lotion, fr *en-* + *brechein* to wet]

embroider /im'broydə/ *vt* **1a** to ornament (e g cloth or a garment) with decorative stitches made by hand or machine **b** to form (e g a design or pattern) in ornamental needlework **2** to elaborate on (a narrative); embellish with exaggerated or fictitious details ~ *vi* **1** to do or make embroidery **2** to provide embellishments; elaborate – + *on* or *upon* [ME *embroderen*, fr MF *embroder*, fr *en-* + *broder* to embroider, of Gmc origin; akin to OE *brord* point, *byrst* bristle] – **embroiderer** *n*, **embroidery** /-d(ə)ri/ *n*

embroil /im'broyl/ *vt* **1** to throw (e g a person or affairs) into disorder or confusion **2** to involve in conflict or difficulties [F *embrouiller*, fr MF, fr *en-* + *brouiller* to broil] – **embroilment** *n*

embry- /embri-/, **embryo-** *comb form* embryo ⟨embry*ologist*⟩ [LL, fr Gk, fr *embryon*]

embryo /'embrioh/ *n, pl* **embryos** **1a** an animal in the early stages of growth before birth or hatching ☞ LIFE CYCLE **b** the developing human individual during the first 8 weeks after conception ☞ REPRODUCTION **2** a rudimentary plant within a seed **3a** sthg as yet undeveloped **b** a beginning or undeveloped state of sthg – esp in *in embryo* ⟨*plans still in* ~⟩ [ML *embryon-*, *embryo*, fr Gk *embryon*, fr *en-* + *bryein* to swell; akin to Gk *bryon* moss]

,embryo'genesis /-'jenəsis/ *n* the formation and development of the embryo – **embryogenetic** /-jə'netik/ *adj*

embryology /,embri'oləji/ *n* the biology of (the development of) embryos [F *embryologie*] – **embryologic** /,embri·ə'lojik/, **embryological** *adj*, **embryologically** *adv*, **embryologist** /-'oləjist/ *n*

embryon-, **embryoni-** *comb form* embry- [ML *embryon-*, *embryo*]

embryonic /,embri'onik/ *also* **embryonal** /em'brie·ənl/ *adj* **1** of an embryo **2** in an early stage of development – **embryonically** /,embri'onikli/ *adv*

embryophyte /'embri·ə,fiet/ *n* a plant (e g a fern or a flowering plant) that produces an embryo and develops vascular tissues

'embryo ,sac *n* the female part of a female plant consisting of a thin-walled sac containing the egg, nucleus, and other nuclei which give rise to endosperm

¹emcee /,em'see/ *n* a compere; MASTER OF CEREMONIES – infml [*m*aster of *c*eremonies]

²emcee *vb* **emceed; emceeing** to act as emcee (of) – infml

-eme /-eem/ *suffix* (→ *n*) unit of language structure ⟨*phon*eme⟩ [F *-ème* (fr *phonème* speech sound, phoneme)]

emend /i'mend/ *vt* to correct, usu by textual alterations [ME *emenden*, fr L *emendare* – more at AMEND] – **emendable** *adj*, **emender** *n*

emendate /'eemen,dayt/ *vt* to emend – **emendator** *n*, **emendatory** /i'mendət(ə)ri/ *adj*

emendation /,eemen'daysh(ə)n/ *n* (an alteration made by) the act of emending

emerald /'em(ə)rəld/ *adj or n* (of the bright green colour of) a beryl used as a gemstone [n ME *emerallde*, fr MF *esmeralde*, fr (assumed) VL *smaralda*, fr L *smaragdus*, fr Gk *smaragdos*; adj fr n]

emerge /i'muhj/ *vi* **1** to rise (as if) from an enveloping fluid; come out into view **2** to become manifest or known **3** to rise from an obscure or inferior condition [L *emergere*, fr *e-* + *mergere* to plunge – more at MERGE]

emergence /i'muhj(ə)ns/ *n* a superficial outgrowth of plant tissue (e g the thorn of a rose) [EMERGE + -ENCE]

emergency /i'muhj(ə)nsi/ *n* an unforeseen occurrence or combination of circumstances that calls for immediate action

emergent /i'muhj(ə)nt/ *adj* emerging; *esp* in the early stages of formation or development ⟨*the* ~ *countries of the world*⟩ [ME, fr L *emergent-*, *emergens*, prp of *emergere*]

emeritus /i'meritəs/, *fem* **emerita** /-tə/ *adj* holding an honorary title after retirement [L, pp of *emereri* to serve out one's term, fr *e-* + *mereri*, *merēre* to earn, deserve, serve – more at MERIT]

emery /'em(ə)ri/ *n* a dark granular mineral consisting mainly of corundum which is used for grinding and polishing [ME, fr MF *emeri*, fr OIt *smiriglio*, fr ML *smiriglum*, fr Gk *smyrid-*, *smyris*]

'emery ,board *n* a nail file of cardboard or wood covered with powdered emery

'emery ,paper *n* paper coated with emery powder for use as an abrasive

emetic /i'metik/ *n or adj* (sthg) that induces vomiting [n L *emetica*, fr Gk *emetikē*, fr fem of *emetikos* causing vomiting, fr *emein* to vomit – more at VOMIT; adj fr n] – **emetically** *adv*

émeute /ay'muht (*Fr* emøt)/ *n* a popular uprising [F]

-emia /-'eemyə, -'eemi·ə/ *comb form* (→ *n*), *NAm* -aemia

emigrant /'emigrənt/ *n* one who emigrates – **emigrant** *adj*

emigrate /'emi,grayt/ *vi* to leave one's home or country for life or residence elsewhere [L *emigratus*, pp of *emigrare*, fr *e-* + *migrare* to migrate] – **emigration** /-'graysh(ə)n/ *n*

émigré, emigré /'emigray (*Fr* emigre)/ *n* a (political) emigrant [F *émigré*, fr pp of *émigrer* to emigrate, fr L *emigrare*]

eminence /'eminəns/ *n* **1** a position of prominence or superiority – used as a title for a cardinal **2** sby or sthg high, prominent, or lofty: e g **a** a person of high rank or attainments **b** a natural geographical elevation; a height

éminence grise /aymi,nonhs 'greez (*Fr* eminɑ̃s griz)/ *n, pl* **éminences grises** /~/ one who exercises power through his/her often unsuspected influence on another person or group of people who have titular authority [F, lit., grey eminence, nickname of Père Joseph (François du Tremblay) †1638 F monk & diplomat, confidant of Cardinal Richelieu †1642 F statesman who was known as *Éminence Rouge* red eminence; fr the colours of their respective habits]

eminent /'eminənt/ *adj* **1** standing out so as to be readily seen or noted; conspicuous, notable **2** exhibiting eminence, esp in position, fame, or achievement [ME, fr MF or L; MF, fr L *eminent-*, *eminens*, prp of *eminēre* to stand out, fr *e-* + *-minēre* (akin to L *mont-*, *mons* mountain)] – **eminently** *adv*

emir /'emiə, -'-/ *n* **1** a ruler of any of various Muslim states **2** a high-ranking Turkish official of former times **3** a male descendant of Muhammad [Ar *amīr* commander]

emirate /'emirət/ *n* the position, state, power, etc of an emir

emissary /'emis(ə)ri/ *n* one sent on an often secret mission as the agent of another [L *emissarius*, fr *emissus*, pp of *emittere*]

emission /i'mish(ə)n/ *n* **1** an act or instance of emitting **2a** sthg (e g electromagnetic waves, smoke, electrons, noise, etc) sent forth by emitting **b** an effluvium – **emissive** /i'misiv/ *adj*

emissivity /,emi'sivəti, imi-/ *n* the relative power of a surface to emit heat by radiation

emit /i'mit/ *vt* **-tt- 1a** to throw or give off or out (e g light) **b** to send out; eject **2** to give utterance or voice to ⟨~ted *a groan*⟩ [L *emittere* to send out, fr *e-* + *mittere* to send – more at SMITE]

emitter /i'mitə/ *n* a region in a transistor that produces charge carriers [EMIT + [2]-ER]

Emmenthal, Emmental /'emən,tahl/ *n* a pale yellow Swiss cheese with many holes that form during ripening [*Emmenthal*, valley in Switzerland]

emmer /'emə/ *n* a hard variety of wheat [G, fr OHG *amari*]

emmet /'emit/ *n, chiefly dial* an ant [ME *emete*]

Emmy /'emi/ *n, pl* **Emmys** a statuette awarded annually by a US professional organization for notable achievement in television [alter. of *Immy*, nickname for *image orthicon* (a camera tube used in television)]

emollient /i'mohli·ənt, i'mo-, -yənt/ *n or adj* (a substance) that makes soft or gives relief [L *emollient-, emolliens*, prp of *emollire* to soften, fr *e-* + *mollis* soft – more at [1]MELT]

emolument /i'molyoomənt/ *n* the returns arising from office or employment; a salary [ME, fr L *emolumentum*, lit., miller's fee, fr *emolere* to grind up, fr *e-* + *molere* to grind – more at [2]MEAL]

emote /i'moht/ *vi* to give expression to emotion, esp theatrically [back-formation fr *emotion*]

emotion /i'mohsh(ə)n/ *n* **1** excitement **2** a mental and physical reaction (e g anger, fear, or joy) marked by strong feeling and often physiological changes that prepare the body for immediate vigorous action [MF, fr *emouvoir* to stir up, fr L *exmovēre* to move away, disturb, fr *ex-* + *movēre* to move] – **emotionless** *adj*

emotional /i'mohsh(ə)nl/ *adj* **1** of the emotions ⟨*an ~ disorder*⟩ **2** inclined to show (excessive) emotion **3** EMOTIVE 2 – **emotionalism** *n*, **emotionalist** *n*, **emotionalize** *vt*, **emotionally** *adv*, **emotionality** /-'aləti/ *n*

emotive /i'mohtiv/ *adj* **1** EMOTIONAL 1 **2** appealing to, expressing, or arousing emotion rather than reason ⟨*executions were an ~ issue*⟩ – **emotively** *adv*, **emotivity** /-'tivəti/ *n*

empanel /im'panl/ *vt* **-ll-** (*NAm* **-l-, -ll-**), /im'panl·ing/ to enrol in or on a panel ⟨~ *a jury*⟩

empathetic /,empə'thetik/ *adj* marked by empathy – **empathetically** *adv*

empathy /'empəthi/ *n* **1** the imaginative projection of a subjective state into an object, esp a work of art, so allowing it to be better understood and appreciated **2** the capacity for participation in another's feelings or ideas – **empathize** *vi*, **empathic** /em'pathik/ *adj*

emperor /'emp(ə)rə/ *n* the supreme ruler of an empire [ME, fr OF *empereor*, fr L *imperator*, lit., commander, fr *imperatus*, pp of *imperare* to command, fr *in-* + *parare* to prepare, order – more at PARE] – **emperorship** *n*

emperor penguin *n* the largest known penguin

emphasis /'emfəsis/ *n, pl* **emphases** /-,seez/ **1a** force or intensity of expression that gives special impressiveness or importance to sthg ⟨*writing with ~ on the need for reform*⟩ **b** a particular prominence given in speaking or writing to 1 or more words or syllables **2** special consideration of or stress on sthg ⟨*the school's ~ on examinations*⟩ [L, fr Gk, exposition, emphasis, fr *emphainein* to indicate, fr *en-* + *phainein* to show – more at FANCY]

emphas·ize, -ise /'emfə,siez/ *vt* to give emphasis to; place emphasis or stress on ⟨~d *the need for reform*⟩

emphatic /im'fatik/ *adj* **1** spoken with or marked by emphasis **2** tending to express oneself in forceful speech or to take decisive action [Gk *emphatikos*, fr *emphainein*] – **emphatically** *adv*

emphysema /,emfi'seemə/ *n* a disorder characterized by air-filled expansions of body tissues, esp in the lungs [NL, fr Gk *emphysēma* bodily inflation]

empire /'empie·ə/ *n* **1a** (the territory of) a large group of countries or peoples under 1 authority **b** sthg resembling a political empire; *esp* an extensive territory or enterprise under single domination or control **2** imperial sovereignty [ME, fr OF *empire, empirie*, fr L *imperium* absolute authority, empire, fr *imperare* to command]

Empire *adj* (characteristic) of a style (e g of furniture or interior decoration) popular during the first French Empire (1804-14); *specif* of a style of women's dress having a high waistline ☞ GARMENT [F, fr (*le premier*) *Empire* the first Empire of France]

empirical /em'pirikl/ *also* **empiric** *adj* originating in, based, or relying on observation or experiment rather than theory ⟨~ *data*⟩ ⟨~ *laws*⟩ [L *empiricus* doctor relying solely on experience, fr Gk *empeirikos*, fr *empeiria* experience, fr *en-* + *peiran* to attempt – more at FEAR] – **empirically** *adv*

empirical formula *n* a chemical formula showing the simplest ratio of elements in a compound rather than the total number of atoms in the molecule

empiricism /em'pirisiz(ə)m/ *n* **1** quackery **2** the practice of discovery by observation and experiment **3** a theory that all knowledge is dependent on experience of the external world – **empiricist** *n*

emplacement /im'playsmənt/ *n* **1** the situation or location of sthg **2** a prepared position for weapons or military equipment ⟨*radar* ~s⟩ [F, fr MF *emplacer* to emplace, fr *en-* + *place*] – **emplace** *vt*

emplane /im'playn/ *vb* to (cause to) board an aircraft

[1]**employ** /im'ploy/ *vt* **1a** to use in a specified way or for a specific purpose **b** to spend (time) **c** to use **2a** to engage the services of **b** to provide with a job that pays wages or a salary *USE* (1b,c) fml [ME *emploien*, fr MF *emploier*, fr L *implicare* to enfold, involve, implicate, fr *in-* + *plicare* to fold – more at PLY] – **employable** *adj*, **employer** *n*, **employability** /-ə'biləti/ *n*

[2]**employ** *n* the state of being employed, esp for wages or a salary ⟨*in the government's* ~⟩ – fml

employee, *NAm also* **employe** /,employ'ee, im,-

ploy'ee/ *n* one employed by another, esp for wages or a salary and in a position below executive level [F *employé*, fr pp of *employer* to employ]

employment /im'ploymənt/ *n* (an) activity in which one engages or is employed [[1]EMPLOY + -MENT]

em'ployment ,agency *n* an agency whose business is to find jobs for people seeking them or to find people to fill vacant jobs

em'ployment ex,change *n* LABOUR EXCHANGE

empoison /im'poyz(ə)n/ *vt* to embitter ⟨*a look of* ~ed *acceptance* – Saul Bellow⟩ [ME *empoysonen*, fr MF *empoisoner*, fr *en-* + *poison*] – **empoisonment** *n*

emporium /im'pawri·əm/ *n, pl* **emporiums, emporia** /-ri·ə/ a place of trade; *esp* a commercial centre or large shop [L, fr Gk *emporion*, fr *emporos* traveller, trader, fr *en* in + *poros* passage, journey – more at IN, FARE]

empower /im'powə/ *vt* to give official authority or legal power to – **empowerment** *n*

empress /'empris/ *n* **1** the wife or widow of an emperor **2** a woman having in her own right the rank of emperor [ME *emperesse*, fr OF, fem of *empereor* emperor]

[1]**empty** /'empti/ *adj* **1a** containing nothing; *esp* lacking typical or expected contents **b** not occupied, inhabited, or frequented ⟨~ *house*⟩ ⟨~ *streets*⟩ **2a** lacking reality or substance; hollow ⟨*an* ~ *pleasure*⟩ **b** lacking effect, value, or sincerity ⟨~ *threats*⟩ ⟨*an* ~ *gesture*⟩ **c** lacking sense; foolish ⟨*his* ~ *ideas*⟩ **3** hungry – infml [ME, fr OE *ǣmettig* unoccupied, fr *ǣmetta* leisure, fr *ǣ-* without + *-metta* (fr *mōtan* to have to) – more at [1]MUST] – **emptily** *adv*, **emptiness** *n* – **on an empty stomach** not having eaten anything

[2]**empty** *vt* **1a** to make empty; remove the contents of **b** to deprive, divest ⟨*acting* emptied *of all emotion*⟩ **c** to discharge (itself) of contents **2** to remove from what holds, encloses, or contains **3** to transfer by emptying ⟨emptied *the biscuits onto the plate*⟩ ~ *vi* **1** to become empty **2** to discharge contents ⟨*the river* empties *into the ocean*⟩ – **emptier** *n*

[3]**empty** *n* a bottle, container, vehicle, etc that has been emptied

,empty-'handed *adj* having or bringing nothing, esp because nothing has been gained or obtained ⟨*returned* ~⟩

,empty-'headed *adj* foolish, silly

empyema /,empie'eemə/ *n, pl* **empyemata** /-mətə/, **empyemas** the presence of pus in a bodily cavity [LL, fr Gk *empyēma*] – **empyemic** /-mik/ *adj*

empyreal /,empie'ree·əl/ *adj* celestial [LL *empyrius, empyreus*, fr LGk *empyrios*, fr Gk *en* in + *pyr* fire]

empyrean /,empie'ree·ən/ *adj or n* (of) the highest heavenly sphere in ancient and medieval cosmology

emu /'eemyooh/ *n* a swift-running Australian flightless bird [modif of Pg *ema* rhea]

emulate /'emyoo,layt/ *vt* **1** RIVAL 2 **2** to imitate closely; approach equality with; *specif* to imitate by means of an emulator [L *aemulatus*, pp of *aemulari*, fr *aemulus* rivalling] – **emulation** /-'laysh(ə)n/ *n*, **emulative** /'emyoolətiv/ *adj*

emulator /'emyoo,laytə/ *n* a piece of hardware or software that permits programs written for one computer to be run on another, usu newer, computer [EMULATE + [1]-OR]

emulous /'emyooləs/ *adj* ambitious or eager to emulate – **emulously** *adv*

emulsify /i'mulsifie/ *vt* to convert (e g an oil) into an emulsion – **emulsifiable** *adj*, **emulsifier** *n*, **emulsification** /-fi'kaysh(ə)n/ *n*

[1]**emulsion** /i'mulsh(ə)n/ *n* **1** (the state of) a substance (e g fat in milk) consisting of one liquid dispersed in droplets throughout another liquid ⟨~ *paint*⟩ **2** SUSPENSION 2b; *esp* a suspension of a silver compound in a gelatin solution or other solid medium for coating photographic plates, film, etc ☞ CAMERA [NL *emulsion-, emulsio*, fr L *emulsus*, pp of *emulgēre* to milk out, fr *e-* + *mulgēre* to milk; akin to OE *melcan* to milk, Gk *amelgein*] – **emulsive** /-siv/ *adj*

[2]**emulsion** *vt* to paint (e g a wall) with emulsion paint

en, n /en/ *n* the width of the body of a piece of type bearing the letter *n* used as a unit of measure of printed matter; one half of an em

[1]**en-** *also* **em-** *prefix* (→ *vb*) **1** put into or onto ⟨em*bed*⟩ ⟨en*throne*⟩; go into or onto ⟨em*bus*⟩ ⟨en*tram*⟩ **2** cause to be ⟨en*slave*⟩ ⟨en*rich*⟩ **3** provide with ⟨em*power*⟩ ⟨en*franchise*⟩ **4** so as to cover ⟨en*gulf*⟩; thoroughly ⟨en*tangle*⟩ ***USE*** usu *em* before *b, m*, or *p* [ME, fr OF, fr L *in-, im-*, fr *in*]

[2]**en-** *also* **em-** *prefix* in; within ⟨en*ergy*⟩ – usu *em-* before *b, m*, or *p* ⟨em*pathy*⟩ [ME, fr L, fr Gk, fr *en* in – more at IN]

[1]**-en** *also* **-n** /-(ə)n/ *suffix* (*n* → *adj*) made of; consisting of ⟨*earth*en⟩ ⟨*wood*en⟩ [ME, fr OE; akin to OHG *-īn* made of, L *-īnus* of or belonging to, Gk *-inos* made of, of or belonging to]

[2]**-en** *suffix* (*n, adj* → *vb*) **1a** cause to be ⟨*sharp*en⟩ ⟨*embold*en⟩ **b** cause to have ⟨*height*en⟩ **2a** become ⟨*steep*en⟩ **b** come to have ⟨*length*en⟩ [ME *-nen*, fr OE *-nian*; akin to OHG *-inōn* -en]

enable /in'aybl/ *vt* **1** to provide with the means or opportunity **2** to make possible, practical, or easy

enact /in'akt/ *vt* **1** to make into law **2** to act out, play – **enaction** /-sh(ə)n/ *n*, **enactment** *n*

[1]**enamel** /i'naml/ *vt* **-ll-** (*NAm* **-l-, -ll-**), /i'naml·ing/ to cover, inlay, or decorate with enamel [ME *enamelen*, fr MF *enamailler*, fr *en-* + *esmail* enamel, of Gmc origin; akin to OHG *smelzan* to melt – more at [2]SMELT] – **enameler** *n*, **enamelist** *n*

[2]**enamel** *n* **1** a usu opaque glassy coating applied to the surface of metal, glass, or pottery **2** sthg enamelled; *esp* enamelware **3** a substance composed of calcium phosphate that forms a thin hard layer capping the teeth ☞ DIGESTION **4** a paint that dries with a glossy appearance **5** *chiefly NAm* an often coloured coating applied to the nails to give them a smooth or glossy appearance; nail varnish

e'namel,ware /-,weə/ *n* metal household or kitchen utensils coated with enamel

enamour, *NAm chiefly* **enamor** /i'namə/ *vt* to inspire with love or liking – usu pass + *of* [ME *enamouren*, fr OF *enamourer*, fr *en-* + *amour* love – more at AMOUR]

enantiomer /i'nanti·əmə/ *n* an enantiomorph [Gk *enantios* + E *-mer*] – **enantiomeric** /-'merik/ *adj*

enantiomorph /i'nanti·ə,mawf/ *n* either of a pair of chemical compounds or crystals whose molecular structures have a mirror-image relationship to each other [Gk *enantios* opposite (fr *enanti* facing, fr *en* in + *anti* against) + ISV *-morph*] – **enantiomorphic** /-'mawfik/ *adj*, **enantiomorphism** *n*, **enantiomorphous** *adj*

enarthrosis /,enah'throhsis/ *n*, *pl* **enarthroses** /-seez/ BALL-AND-SOCKET JOINT [NL, fr Gk *enarthrōsis*]

en bloc /,om 'blok (*Fr* ɑ̃ blɔk)/ *adv or adj* as a whole; in a mass [F]

Encaenia /en'seeni·ə, -nyə/ *n pl but sing or pl in constr* an annual university ceremony (e g at Oxford) of commemoration [NL, fr L, dedication festival, fr Gk *enkainia*, fr *en* in + *kainos* new – more at IN, RECENT]

encamp /in'kamp/ *vt* to place or establish in a camp ~ *vi* to set up or occupy a camp

en'campment /-mənt/ *n* the place where a group (e g a body of troops) is encamped; a camp [ENCAMP + -MENT]

encapsulate /in'kapsyoo,layt/ *vt* **1** to enclose (as if) in a capsule **2** to epitomize, condense ~ *vi* to become encapsulated – **encapsulation** /-'laysh(ə)n/ *n*

encase /in'kays/ *vt* to enclose (as if) in a case – **encasement** *n*

encash /in'kash/ *vt*, *Br* CASH 1 – fml – **encashment** *n*

encaustic /en'kawstik, -'kos-/ *n* (a decorative technique using) a paint made from pigment mixed with melted beeswax and resin and fixed by heat after application [*encaustic*, adj, fr L *encausticus*, fr Gk *enkaustikos*, fr *enkaiein* to burn in, fr *en-* + *kaiein* to burn – more at CAUSTIC] – **encaustic** *adj*

-ence /-(ə)ns/ *suffix* (*vb* → *n*) **1** action or process of ⟨*emergence*⟩; *also* instance of (a specified action or process) ⟨*reference*⟩ ⟨*reminiscence*⟩ **2** quality or state of ⟨*dependence*⟩ ⟨*somnolence*⟩ [ME, fr OF, fr L *-entia*, fr *-ent-*, *-ens*, prp ending + *-ia* -y] – **-ent** *suffix* (*vb* → *adj* or *n*)

[1]**enceinte** /on'sant (*Fr* ɑ̃sɛ̃t)/ *adj* PREGNANT 3 [MF, fr (assumed) VL *incienta*, alter. of L *incient-*, *inciens* being with young, fr *in* + *-cient*, *-ciens* (akin to Gk *kyein* to be pregnant) – more at CAVE]

[2]**enceinte** *n* (an area enclosed by) a line of fortification [F, fr OF, enclosing wall, fr *enceindre* to surround, fr L *incingere*, fr *in-* + *cingere* to gird – more at CINCTURE]

encephal-, **encephalo-** *comb form* brain ⟨encephalitis⟩ [F *encéphal-*, fr Gk *enkephal-*, fr *enkephalos*]

encephalic /,ensi'falik/ *adj* of the brain

encephalitis /,in,sefə'lietəs/ *n*, *pl* **encephalitides** /-'litə,deez/ inflammation of the brain, usu caused by infection [NL] – **encephalitic** /-'litik/ *adj*

encephalogram /en'sef(ə)ləgram/ *n* an X-ray picture of the brain made by encephalography [ISV]

encephalograph /in'sef(ə)lə,grahf, -,graf/ *n* **1** an encephalogram **2** an electroencephalograph

encephalography /in,sef(ə)l'ogrəfi/ *n* X-ray photography of the brain after the cerebrospinal fluid has been replaced by a gas (e g air) [ISV]

en,cephalo,mye'litis /-,mie·ə'lietəs/ *n* inflammation of both the brain and spinal cord [NL]

encephalon /en'sef(ə)lon/ *n*, *pl* **encephala** /-lə/ the vertebrate brain [NL, fr Gk *enkephalos*, fr *en* in + *kephalē* head – more at IN, CEPHALIC]

enchant /in'chahnt/ *vt* **1** to bewitch **2** to attract and move deeply; delight [ME *enchanten*, fr MF *enchanter*, fr L *incantare*, fr *in-* + *cantare* to sing – more at CHANT] – **enchantment** *n*

enchanter /in'chahntə/ *n* a sorcerer [ENCHANT + [2]-ER]

en,chanter's 'night,shade *n* any of several slender European plants that bear small whitish-pink flowers

enchanting /in'chahnting/ *adj* charming – **enchantingly** *adv*

enchantress /in'chahntris/ *n* a sorceress

enchase /in'chays/ *vt* to ornament with raised or incised work (e g by engraving or inlaying) [ME *enchasen* to emboss, fr MF *enchasser* to enshrine, set, fr *en-* + *chasse* reliquary, fr L *capsa* case – more at [2]CASE]

enchilada /,enchi'lahdə/ *n* a tortilla spread with a meat filling, rolled up, and covered with a chilli sauce [AmerSp]

enchiridion /,enkie'ridi·ən/ *n*, *pl* **enchiridia** /-di·ə/ a handbook, manual [LL, fr Gk *encheiridion*, fr *en* in + *cheir* hand – more at IN, CHIR-]

encipher /in'siefə/ *vt* to convert (a message) into a cipher

encircle /in'suhkl/ *vt* **1** to form a circle round; surround **2** to move or pass completely round – **encirclement** *n*

enclave /'enklayv/ *n* a territorial or culturally distinct unit enclosed within foreign territory [F, fr MF, fr *enclaver* to enclose, fr (assumed) VL *inclavare* to lock up, fr L *in-* + *clavis* key – more at CLAVICLE]

enclitic /in'klitik/ *adj*, *of a word or particle* being without independent accent and forming part of the preceding word (e g *not* in *cannot*) [LL *encliticus*, fr Gk *enklitikos*, fr *enklinesthai* to lean on, fr *en-* + *klinein* to lean – more at LEAN] – **enclitic** *n*, **enclitically** *adv*

enclose *also* **inclose** /in'klohz/ *vt* **1a(1)** to close in completely; surround ⟨~d *the field with a high fence*⟩ **(2)** to fence off (common land) for individual use **b** to hold in; confine **2** to include in a package or envelope, esp along with sthg else ⟨*a cheque is* ~d *herewith*⟩ [ME *enclosen*, prob fr *enclos* enclosed, fr MF, pp of *enclore* to enclose, fr (assumed) VL *inclaudere*, alter. of L *includere* – more at INCLUDE]

enclosure /in'klohzhə/ *n* **1** enclosing or being enclosed **2** sthg that encloses **3** sthg enclosed: e g **a** sthg included in the same envelope or package as a letter **b** an area of enclosed ground; *esp* one reserved for a certain class of spectator in a sports ground

encode /in'kohd/ *vt* to convert (e g a body of information) from one system of communication into another; *esp* to convert (a message) into code – **encoder** *n*

encomiast /en'kohmi,ast/ *n* one who praises in encomiums [Gk *enkōmiastēs*, fr *enkōmiazein* to praise, fr *enkōmion*] – **encomiastic** /-'astik/ *adj*

encomium /en'kohmi·əm, -myəm/ *n*, *pl* **encomiums, encomia** /-mi·ə, -myə/ a usu formal expression of warm or high praise; a eulogy [L, fr Gk *enkōmion*, fr *en* in + *kōmos* revel, celebration]

encompass /in'kumpəs/ *vt* **1** to form a circle about; enclose **2** to include ⟨*a plan that* ~es *a number of aims*⟩ – **encompassment** *n*

[1]**encore** /'ong,kaw/ *n* (an audience's appreciative demand for) a performer's reappearance to give an additional or repeated performance [F, still, again]

[2]**encore** *vt* to call for an encore of or by

[1]**encounter** /in'kowntə/ *vt* **1a** to meet as an adversary or enemy **b** to engage in conflict with **2** to meet or come across, esp unexpectedly [ME *encountren*, fr OF *encontrer*, fr ML *incontrare*, fr LL *incontra* towards, fr L *in-* + *contra* against – more at [4]COUNTER]

[2]**encounter** *n* **1** a meeting or clash between hostile factions or people **2** a chance meeting

en'counter ,group *n* a group of people who meet to try and develop greater sensitivity to their own and one another's feelings

encourage /in'kurij/ *vt* **1** to inspire with courage, spirit, or hope **2** to spur on ⟨*they were* ~d *to paint by their parents*⟩ **3** to give help or patronage to (e g a process or action); promote ⟨*many companies* ~ *union membership*⟩ [ME *encoragen*, fr MF *encoragier*, fr OF, fr *en-* + *corage* courage] – **encouragement** *n*, **encouragingly** *adv*

encroach /in'krohch/ *vi* **1** to enter gradually or by stealth into the possessions or rights of another; intrude, trespass **2** to advance beyond the usual or proper limits ***USE*** usu + *on* or *upon* [ME *encrochen* to get, seize, fr MF *encrochier*, fr OF, fr *en-* + *croc, croche* hook – more at CROCHET] – **encroachment** *n*

encrust *also* **incrust** /in'krust/ *vt* to cover, line, or overlay with a crust, esp of jewels or precious metal ~ *vi* to form a crust [prob fr L *incrustare*, fr *in-* + *crusta* crust]

encrustation /,enkru'staysh(ə)n/ *n* an incrustation

encumber /in'kumbə/ *vt* **1** to weigh down, burden **2** to impede or hamper the function or activity of **3** to burden with a legal claim ⟨~ *an estate*⟩ [ME *encombren*, fr MF *encombrer*, fr OF, fr *en-* + (assumed) OF *combre* defensive barrier of felled trees]

encumbrance /in'kumbrəns/ *n* **1** sthg that encumbers; an impediment **2** a claim (e g a mortgage) against property

-ency /-(ə)nsi/ *suffix* (→ *n*) quality or state of ⟨*despondency*⟩ [ME *-encie*, fr L *-entia* – more at -ENCE]

encyclical /en'siklikl/ *n* a papal letter to the bishops of the church as a whole or to those in 1 country [*encyclical* (adj) sent to many persons or places, fr LL *encyclicus*, modif of Gk *enkyklios* circular, general, fr *en* in + *kyklos* circle, wheel]

encyclopedia, encyclopaedia /in,sieklə'peedi·ə, -dyə/ *n* a work containing general information on all branches of knowledge or comprehensive information on 1 branch, usu in articles arranged alphabetically by subject [ML *encyclopaedia* course of general education, fr Gk *enkyklios paideia* general education] – **encyclopedist** /-'peedist/ *n*

encyclopedic, encyclopaedic /in,sieklə'peedik/ *adj* (suggestive) of an encyclopedia or its methods of treating a subject; comprehensive ⟨*an* ~ *memory*⟩ – **encyclopedically** *adv*

en,cyclo'pe,dism, encyclopaedism /-'pee,diz(ə)m/ *n* encyclopedic knowledge

encyst /en'sist/ *vb* to enclose or become enclosed (as if) in a cyst – **encystment** *n*, **encystation** /,ensi'staysh(ə)n/ *n*

[1]**end** /end/ *n* **1a** the part of an area that lies at the boundary ⟨*the north* ~ *of the village*⟩; *also* the farthest point from where one is ⟨*it's at the other* ~ *of the garden*⟩ **b(1)** the point that marks the extent of sthg in space or time; the limit ⟨*at the* ~ *of the day*⟩ **(2)** the point where sthg ceases to exist ⟨*world without* ~⟩ **c** either of the extreme or last parts lengthways of an object that is appreciably longer than it is broad ⟨*a pencil with a point at either* ~⟩ **2a** (the events, sections, etc immediately preceding) the cessation of action, activity, or existence ⟨*the* ~ *of the play was its weakest part*⟩ ⟨*at the* ~ *of the war*⟩ **b** the final condition; *esp* death ⟨*the* ~ *being oblivion*⟩ **3** sthg left over; remnant **4** an aim or purpose **5** sthg or sby extreme of a kind; *the* ultimate **6a** either half of a games pitch, court, etc ⟨*change* ~s *at halftime*⟩ **b** a period of action or turn to play in bowls, curling, etc **7** a particular part of an undertaking or organization ⟨*the advertising* ~ *of a business*⟩ ***USE*** (*5 & 7*) infml [ME *ende*, fr OE; akin to OHG *enti* end, L *ante* before, Gk *anti* against] – **ended** *adj* – **in the end** ultimately – **no end 1** exceedingly **2** an endless amount; a huge quantity – **on end 1** [2]UPRIGHT ⟨*turned the table* on end *to get it through the door*⟩ **2** without a stop or letup ⟨*it rained for days* on end⟩

[2]**end** *vt* **1** to bring to an end **2** to destroy ~ *vi* **1** to come to an end **2** to reach a specified ultimate situation, condition, or rank – often + *up* ⟨~ed *up as a colonel*⟩

[3]**end** *adj* final, ultimate ⟨~ *results*⟩ ⟨~ *markets*⟩

end-, endo- /end-/ *comb form* **1** within; inside ⟨endo*skeleton*⟩ – compare ECT-, EXO- 1 **2** taking in; absorbing ⟨endo*thermal*⟩ [F, fr Gk, fr *endon* within, fr *en* in + *-don* (akin to L *domus* house) – more at IN, TIMBER]

endanger /in'daynjə/ *vt* to bring into or expose to danger or peril – **endangerment** *n*

en'dangered *adj* threatened with extinction ⟨~ *species*⟩

endarterectomy /,end,ahtə'rektəmi/ *n* surgical removal of the inner layer of an artery when it is thickened and fatty [NL *endarterium* intima of an artery (fr *end-* + *arteria* artery) + E *-ectomy*]

'end,brain /-,brayn/ *n* the front subdivision of the forebrain

endear /in'diə/ *vt* to cause to become beloved or admired – often + *to* – **endearingly** *adv*

en'dearment /-mənt/ *n* a word or act (e g a caress) expressing affection [ENDEAR + -MENT]

[1]**endeavour,** *NAm chiefly* **endeavor** /in'devə/ *vt* to attempt by exertion or effort; TRY 4 – usu + infin; fml ⟨~ing *to control her disgust*⟩ [ME *endeveren* to exert oneself, fr *en-* + *dever* duty, fr OF *deveir*, fr *devoir, deveir* to owe, be obliged, fr L *debēre* – more at DEBT]

[2]**endeavour,** *NAm chiefly* **endeavor** *n* serious determined effort ⟨*fields of* ~⟩; *also* an instance of this – fml

[1]**endemic** /en'demik/ *adj* **1** belonging or native to a particular people or region; not introduced or naturalized ⟨~ *diseases*⟩ ⟨*an* ~ *species of plant*⟩ **2** regularly occurring in or associated with a particular topic or sphere of activity [F *endémique*, fr *endémie* endemic disease, fr Gk *endēmia* action of dwelling, fr *endēmos* endemic, fr *en* in + *dēmos* people, populace – more at DEMAGOGUE] – **endemically** *adv*, **endemicity** /,ende'misəti/ *n*, **endemism** /'endə,miz(ə)m/ *n*

[2]**endemic** *n* an endemic disease or species

endergonic /,enduh'gonik/ *adj* requiring expendi-

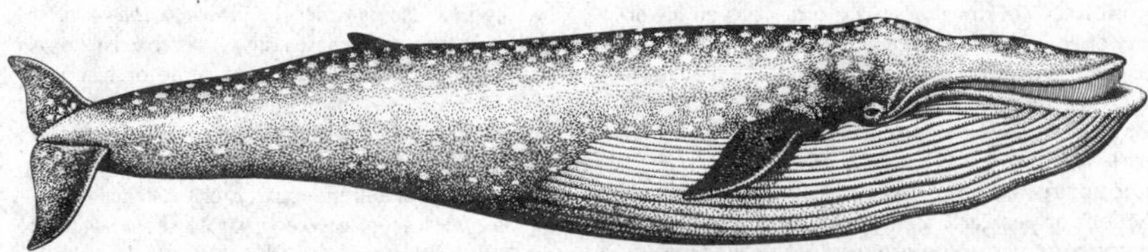

1 **The blue whale** is found throughout the world's oceans and has declined in numbers due to uncontrolled hunting for its meat and blubber. Whale hunting is now regulated by an International Convention. However, the blue whale is further threatened by commercial fishing for krill on which it feeds.

7 **The aye-aye** inhabits the coastal rainforests of northern Madagascar and is one of the world's rarest mammals. It was feared by Malagasy villagers and was killed on sight. Gradual destruction of the rainforests for agriculture has further reduced stocks.

2 **The sea otter** lives along the sheltered coasts of Alaska and California. It suffered near-extinction in the early 1920s as a result of extensive hunting for its highly valued fur.

6 **The green turtle** is widespread in warm Atlantic, Pacific, and Indian seas but is seriously threatened by over-exploitation for its meat, eggs, and hide.

3 **The giant anteater** lives in the tropical grasslands of Central and South America and, with other creatures, is threatened by the development of large areas of grassland for farming and the building of roads, railways, and towns.

4 **The chinchilla** inhabits arid regions of the Andes in South America and was hunted almost to extinction for its fur. It is now protected in Chile and widely bred in captivity.

5 **The gorilla** lives in the lowland and mountainous regions of western Africa. Its survival in the wild is threatened by agricultural development and by the demand for apes by zoos and research scientists.

Endangered species

Extinction is a natural process but it has been accelerated in recent centuries by human intervention. The greatest threat to wildlife is from the destruction of their natural habitats for urban, industrial, and agricultural development. However, excessive exploitation by hunting for skins and meat, pollution of water, and upsetting the natural equilibrium by introducing species to new regions, are factors that have endangered countless species of plant and animal life.

8 **The Pyrenean desman** lives by watercourses in the Pyrenees and mountains of northern Spain and Portugal. It is threatened with extinction as a result of pollution of the rivers and marshes, which poisons its food supply and prevents adequate oxygenation of the water.

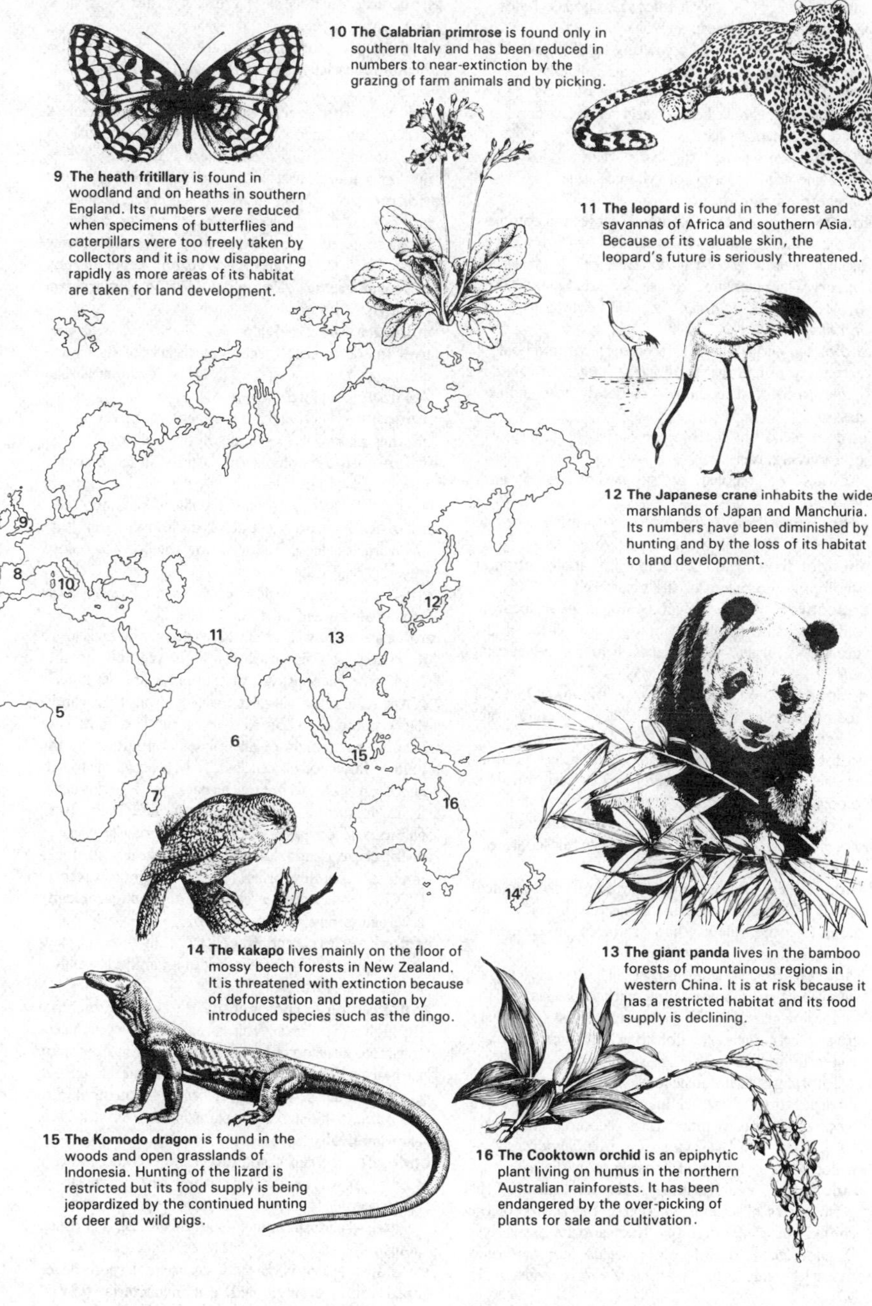

9 The heath fritillary is found in woodland and on heaths in southern England. Its numbers were reduced when specimens of butterflies and caterpillars were too freely taken by collectors and it is now disappearing rapidly as more areas of its habitat are taken for land development.

10 The Calabrian primrose is found only in southern Italy and has been reduced in numbers to near-extinction by the grazing of farm animals and by picking.

11 The leopard is found in the forest and savannas of Africa and southern Asia. Because of its valuable skin, the leopard's future is seriously threatened.

12 The Japanese crane inhabits the wide marshlands of Japan and Manchuria. Its numbers have been diminished by hunting and by the loss of its habitat to land development.

13 The giant panda lives in the bamboo forests of mountainous regions in western China. It is at risk because it has a restricted habitat and its food supply is declining.

14 The kakapo lives mainly on the floor of mossy beech forests in New Zealand. It is threatened with extinction because of deforestation and predation by introduced species such as the dingo.

15 The Komodo dragon is found in the woods and open grasslands of Indonesia. Hunting of the lizard is restricted but its food supply is being jeopardized by the continued hunting of deer and wild pigs.

16 The Cooktown orchid is an epiphytic plant living on humus in the northern Australian rainforests. It has been endangered by the over-picking of plants for sale and cultivation.

ture of energy <~ *biochemical reactions*> [*end-* + Gk *ergon* work – more at WORK]

endermic /en'duhmik/ *adj* acting by direct application to or through the skin – **endermically** *adv*

'end ,game *n* the final stage of a (specif chess) game, esp when forces have been greatly reduced – compare OPENING, MIDDLE GAME

ending /'ending/ *n* **1** the last part of a book, film, etc **2** one or more letters or syllables added to a word base, esp as an inflection

endive /'en,diev/ *n* **1** an annual or biennial composite plant that resembles a lettuce and has bitter leaves used in salads **2** *NAm* the developing crown of chicory when blanched for use as a salad plant [ME, fr MF, fr LL *endivia*, fr LGk *entubion*, fr L *intubus*]

endless /'endlis/ *adj* **1** (seeming) without end **2** extremely numerous **3** *of a belt, chain, etc* that is joined to itself at its ends – **endlessly** *adv*, **endlessness** *n*

'end ,line *n* a line marking an end or boundary, esp of a playing area

endmost /'end,mohst/ *adj* situated at the very end; farthest

endo- *comb form* **1** – see END- **2** forming a bridge between 2 atoms in a cyclic system

endocarditis /,endohkah'dietəs/ *n* inflammation of the lining and valves of the heart [NL]

endocardium /,endoh'kahdi·əm/ *n, pl* **endocardia** /-di·ə/ a thin membrane lining the cavities of the heart [NL, fr *end-* + Gk *kardia* heart] – **endocardial** *adj*

endocarp /'endə,kahp, -doh-/ *n* the inner layer of the pericarp of a fruit [F *endocarpe*] – **endocarpal** /-'kahpl/ *adj*

¹endocrine /'endohkrin, -krien, -də-/ *adj* **1** producing secretions that are discharged directly into the bloodstream <~ *system*> – compare EXOCRINE 1 **2** of or being an endocrine gland or its secretions <~ *hormone*> [ISV *end-* + Gk *krinein* to separate – more at CERTAIN]

²endocrine *n* **1** a hormone – no longer in technical use **2 endocrine, endocrine gland** the thyroid, pituitary, or other gland that produces an endocrine secretion ☞ DIGESTION

endocrinology /,endohkri'noləji, -krie-/ *n* physiology and medicine dealing with (diseases of) the endocrine glands [ISV] – **endocrinologist** /-'noləjist/ *n*, **endocrinologic** /,endohkrinə'lojik, -krie-, -də-/, **endocrinological** *adj*

endocytosis /,endohsie'tohsis/ *n* the uptake and incorporation of extracellular substances into a cell by phagocytosis or pinocytosis – compare EXOCYTOSIS [NL, fr *end-* + *-cytosis* (as in *phagocytosis*)] – **endocytotic** /-'totik/ *adj*, **endocytotically** *adv*

endoderm /'endoh,duhm/ *n* the innermost of the germ layers of an embryo that is the source of the epithelium of the digestive tract and its derivatives [F *endoderme*, fr *end-* + Gk *derma* skin – more at DERM-] – **endodermal** /-'duhml/ *adj*, **endodermally** *adv*

endoergic /,endoh'uhjik/ *adj* endothermic <~ *nuclear reactions*> [*end-* + *erg-* + *-ic*]

endogamy /en'dogəmi/ *n* marriage within one's tribe – compare EXOGAMY – **endogamous** *adj*

endogenous /en'dojinəs/ *also* **endogenic** /,endoh'jenik/ *adj* **1** growing from or on the inside **2** originating within the body – **endogenously** *adv*

endogeny /en'dojəni/ *n* growth within or from a deep-seated layer

endolymph /'endoh,limf/ *n* the watery fluid in the membranous labyrinth of the ear [ISV] – **endolymphatic** /-lim'fatik/ *adj*

endometrium /,endoh'meetri·əm/ *n, pl* **endometria** /-tri·ə/ the mucous membrane lining the uterus [NL, fr *end-* + Gk *mētra* uterus, fr *mētr-*, *mētēr* mother – more at MOTHER] – **endometrial** *adj*

endomorph /'endoh,mawf/ *n* **1** a crystal enclosed in a crystal of a different type **2** a person having a heavy rounded build, often with a marked tendency to fat [ISV; (2) *endo*derm + *-morph*] – **endomorphy** *n*, **endomorphic** /-'mawfik/ *adj*, **endomorphism** /-'mawfiz(ə)m/ *n*

endoparasite /,endoh'parəsiet/ *n* a parasite that lives in the internal organs or tissues of its host – compare ECTOPARASITE [ISV] – **endoparasitism** /-si,tiz(ə)m, -,sietiz(ə)m/ *n*

endophyte /'endoh,fiet/ *n* a plant that lives within another plant [ISV] – **endophytic** /-'fitik/ *adj*

endoplasm /'endoh,plaz(ə)m/ *n* the inner relatively fluid part of the cytoplasm of a cell – compare ECTOPLASM 1 [ISV] – **endoplasmic** /-'plazmik/ *adj*

endoradiosonde /,endoh'raydioh,sond/ *n* a tiny electronic device introduced into the body to record physiological data

'end ,organ *n* a structure (e g a muscle or sense organ) at the end of a nerve path

endorse /in'daws/ *vt* **1a** to write on the back of **b** to write (one's signature) on a cheque, bill, or note **2** to express approval of; support; *specif, chiefly NAm* to express support for (e g a political candidate) publicly **3** *Br* to record on (e g a driving licence) particulars of an offence committed by the holder [alter. of obs *endoss*, fr ME *endosen*, fr MF *endosser*, fr OF, to put on the back, fr *en-* + *dos* back, fr L *dorsum*] – **endorsable** *adj*, **endorsement** *n*, **endorser** *n*, **endorsee** /in,daw'see, ,endaw'see/ *n*

endoscope /'endə,skohp/ *n* an instrument for looking inside a hollow organ (e g the rectum or urethra) [ISV] – **endoscopic** /-'skopik/ *adj*, **endoscopically** *adv*, **endoscopy** /en'doskəpi/ *n*

endoskeleton /,endoh'skelitn/ *n* an internal skeleton or supporting framework in an animal – **endoskeletal** /-'skelitl/ *adj*

endosmosis /,endoz'mohsis/ *n* passage of material through a membrane from a region of lower concentration to a region of higher concentration – compare EXOSMOSIS [alter. of obs *endosmose*, fr F, fr *end-* + Gk *ōsmos* act of pushing, fr *ōthein* to push; akin to Skt *vadhati* he strikes] – **endosmotic** /-'motik/ *adj*, **endosmotically** *adv*

endosperm /'endoh,spuhm/ *n* a nourishing tissue in seed plants that is formed within the embryo sac [F *endosperme*, fr *end-* + Gk *sperma* seed – more at SPERM] – **endospermic** /-'spuhmik/ *adj*, **endospermous** *adj*

endospore /'endə,spaw/ *n* an asexual spore developed within a single cell, esp in bacteria [ISV] – **endosporic** /-'sporik/ *adj*, **endosporous** /en'dospərəs, ,endoh'spawrəs/ *adj*

endothelium /,endoh'theeli·əm/ *n, pl* **endothelia** /-li·ə/ an inner layer (e g of epithelium or a seed coat) [NL, fr *end-* + epi*thelium*] – **endothelial** *adj*, **endotheloid** /-'theeloyd/ *adj*

endothermic /,endoh'thuhmik/, **endothermal**

/-'thuhml/ *adj* characterized by or formed with absorption of heat [ISV]

endow /in'dow/ *vt* **1** to provide with a continuing source of income ⟨~ *a hospital*⟩ **2a** to provide *with* an ability or attribute ⟨~ed *with a natural grace*⟩ **b** CREDIT 3a – usu + *with* [ME *endowen,* fr AF *endouer,* fr MF *en-* + *douer* to endow, fr L *dotare,* fr *dot-, dos* gift, dowry – more at DOWRY]

[1]**en'dowment** /-mənt/ *n* **1** sthg endowed; *specif* the part of an institution's income derived from donations **2** a natural quality with which a person is endowed [ENDOW + -MENT]

[2]**endowment** *adj* of, being, or involving life insurance under which a certain sum is paid to the insured at the end of an agreed period or to a specified beneficiary if the insured dies within that period ⟨*an ~ policy*⟩ ⟨*an ~ mortgage*⟩

'end,paper /-,paypə/ *n* a folded sheet of paper forming the front or back inside cover and flyleaf of a book

'end ,point *n* a point marking the completion of (a stage of) a process

'end-,stopped *adj* marked by a pause at the end ⟨*an ~ line of verse*⟩

endue /in'dyooh/ *vt* to provide, endow; *also* to imbue – usu pass + *with*; fml [ME *enduen,* fr MF *enduire* to bring in, introduce, fr L *inducere* – more at INDUCE]

endurance /in'dyooərəns/ *n* the ability to withstand hardship, adversity, or stress

endure /in'dyooə/ *vi* to continue in the same state; last ~ *vt* **1** to undergo (e g a hardship), esp without giving in **2** to tolerate, permit [ME *enduren,* fr MF *endurer,* fr (assumed) VL *indurare,* fr L, to harden, fr *in-* + *durare* to harden, endure – more at DURING] – **endurable** *adj,* **endurably** *adv*

'end,ways /-,ways/, **'end,wise** /-,wiez/ *adv or adj* **1** with the end forwards (e g towards the observer) **2** in or towards the direction of the ends; lengthways **3** upright; ON END ⟨*boxes set* ~⟩ **4** end to end ⟨*put the tables together* ~⟩

-ene /-een/ *suffix* (→ *n*) unsaturated carbon compound ⟨*benz*ene⟩; *esp* aliphatic carbon compound with 1 double bond ⟨*ethyl*ene⟩ [ISV, fr Gk *-ēnē,* fem of *-ēnos,* adj suffix]

enema /'enimə/ *n, pl* **enemas** *also* **enemata** /,eni'mahtə/ **1** injection of liquid into the intestine by way of the anus (e g to ease constipation) **2** material for injection as an enema [LL, fr Gk, fr *enienai* to inject, fr *en-* + *hienai* to send – more at [2]JET]

enemy /'enəmi/ *n* **1** one who is antagonistic to another; *esp* one seeking to injure, overthrow, or confound an opponent **2** sthg harmful or deadly **3a** *sing or pl in constr* a military adversary ⟨*the ~ undertook guerrilla warfare*⟩ **b** a hostile military unit or force [ME *enemi,* fr OF, fr L *inimicus,* fr *in-* [1]in- + *amicus* friend – more at AMIABLE]

energetic /,enə'jetik/ *adj* **1** marked by energy, activity, or vigour **2** operating with power or effect; forceful **3** of energy ⟨~ *equation*⟩ [Gk *energētikos,* fr *energein* to be active, fr *energos*] – **energetically** *adv*

,ener'getics *n pl but sing in constr* a branch of mechanics that deals primarily with energy and its transformations

energ·ize, -ise /'enəjiez/ *vt* **1** to give energy to; make energetic or vigorous **2** to apply energy to so as to facilitate normal operation – **energizer** *n*

energy /'enəji/ *n* **1** the capacity of acting or being active ⟨*great intellectual* ~⟩ **2** natural power vigorously exerted ⟨*devoted all his* energies *to it*⟩ **3** the capacity for doing work ⟨*solar* ~⟩ [LL *energia,* fr Gk *energeia* activity, fr *energos* active, fr *en* in + *ergon* work – more at [1]WORK]

'energy ,level *n* **1** any of the stable states of constant energy that may be assumed by a physical system – used esp with reference to the quantum states of electrons in atoms and of nuclei **2** any of the divisions of a food chain defined by the method of obtaining food – compare TROPHIC ☞ FOOD

enervate /'enə,vayt/ *vt* to lessen the mental or physical strength or vitality of; weaken [L *enervatus,* pp of *enervare,* fr *e-* + *nervus* sinew – more at NERVE] – **enervate, enervated** *adj,* **enervation** /-'vaysh(ə)n/ *n*

en famille /on fa'mee (*Fr* ɑ̃ famiːj)/ *adv* all together as a family [F]

enfant terrible /,onfonh te'reeblə (*Fr* ɑ̃fɑ̃ tɛribl)/ *n, pl* **enfants terribles** /~/ a person whose remarks or unconventional actions cause embarrassment [F, lit., terrifying child]

enfeeble /in'feebl/ *vt* to make feeble [ME *enfeblen,* fr MF *enfeblir,* fr OF, fr *en-* + *feble* feeble] – **enfeeblement** *n*

enfeoff /in'feef/ *vt* to invest with a fief, fee, etc [ME *enfeoffen,* fr AF *enfeoffer,* fr OF *en-* + *fief*] – **enfeoffment** *n*

enfetter /en'fetə/ *vt* to bind in fetters; chain

enfilade /,enfi'layd/ *vt or n* (to subject to) gunfire directed along the length of an enemy battle line [F, fr *enfiler* to thread, enfilade, fr OF, to thread, fr *en-* + *fil* thread, fr L *filum*; vb fr n]

enfold /in'fohld/ *vt* **1** to wrap up; envelop **2** to clasp in the arms; embrace

enforce /in'faws/ *vt* **1** to give greater force to (e g an argument); reinforce **2** to impose, compel ⟨~ *obedience from them*⟩ **3** to cause (a rule or law) to be carried out effectively [ME *enforcen,* fr MF *enforcier,* fr OF, fr *en-* + *force*] – **enforceable** *adj,* **enforcement** *n,* **enforcer** *n,* **enforceability** /-sə'biləti/ *n*

enfranchise /in'franchiez/ *vt* **1** to set free (e g from slavery) **2a** to admit to the right of voting **b** to admit (a municipality) to political privileges, esp the right of Parliamentary representation [ME *enfranchisen,* fr MF *enfranchiss-,* stem of *enfranchir,* fr OF, fr *en-* + *franc* free – more at FRANK] – **enfranchisement** *n*

engage /in'gayj/ *vt* **1a** to attract and hold (sby's thoughts, attention, etc) **b** to interlock with; cause to mesh **2a** to arrange to employ (sby) **b** to arrange to obtain the services of **c** to order (a room, seat, etc) to be kept for one; reserve **3a** to hold the attention of; engross ⟨*her work* ~s *her completely*⟩ **b** to induce to participate, esp in conversation **4a** to enter into contest with ⟨~ *the enemy fleet*⟩ **b** to bring together or interlock (e g weapons) ~ *vi* **1** to pledge oneself; promise **2** to occupy one's time; participate ⟨*at university he* ~d *in gymnastics*⟩ **3** to enter into conflict ⟨*the fleets* ~d *in the Atlantic*⟩ **4** to be or become interlocked or meshed [ME *engagen,* fr MF *engagier,* fr OF, fr *en-* + *gage*]

engagé /,ong·ga'zhay (*Fr* ɑ̃gaʒe)/ *adj* actively

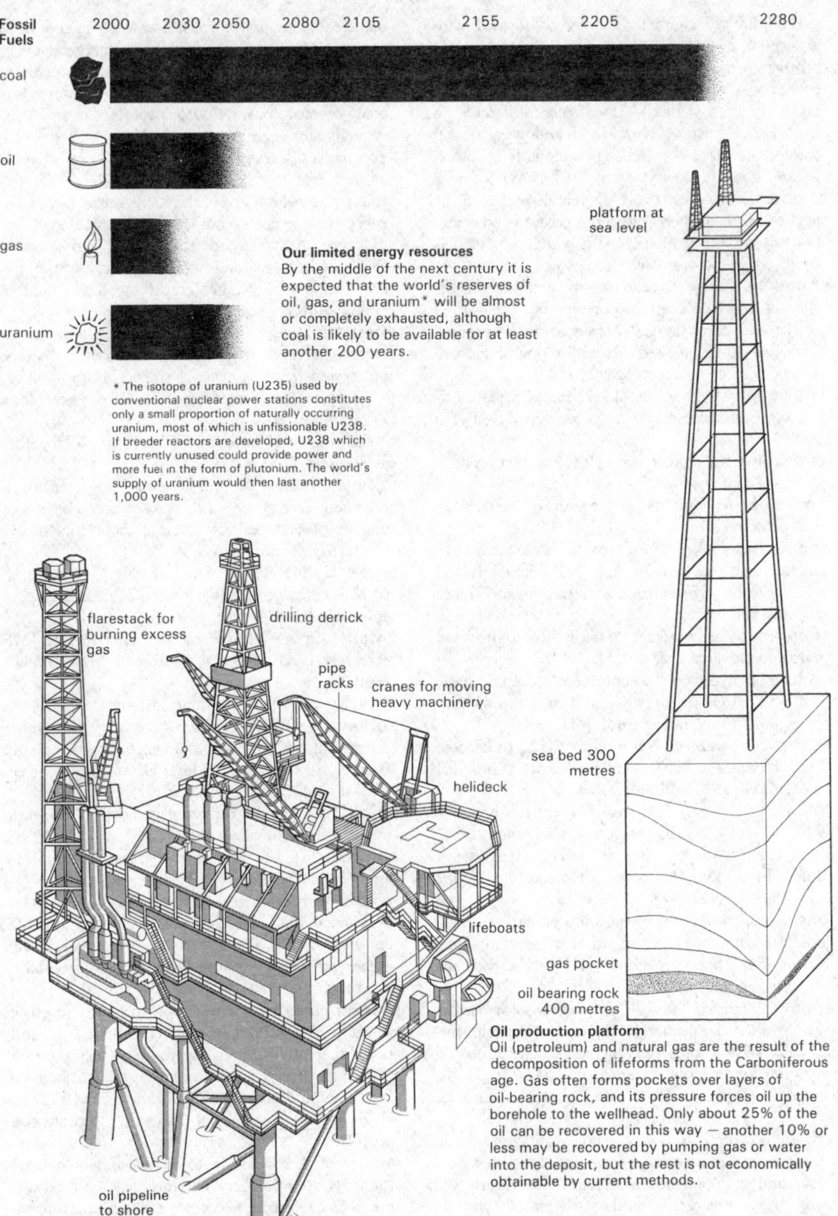

Our limited energy resources
By the middle of the next century it is expected that the world's reserves of oil, gas, and uranium* will be almost or completely exhausted, although coal is likely to be available for at least another 200 years.

* The isotope of uranium (U235) used by conventional nuclear power stations constitutes only a small proportion of naturally occurring uranium, most of which is unfissionable U238. If breeder reactors are developed, U238 which is currently unused could provide power and more fuel in the form of plutonium. The world's supply of uranium would then last another 1,000 years.

Oil production platform
Oil (petroleum) and natural gas are the result of the decomposition of lifeforms from the Carboniferous age. Gas often forms pockets over layers of oil-bearing rock, and its pressure forces oil up the borehole to the wellhead. Only about 25% of the oil can be recovered in this way – another 10% or less may be recovered by pumping gas or water into the deposit, but the rest is not economically obtainable by current methods.

Nuclear power

Nuclear power stations are similar in principle to conventional stations in that water is heated to steam to drive turbines which, in turn, produce electricity. However, the heating process, instead of burning oil or gas, is the fission of uranium 235 nuclei in a central core (the reactor). The substance surrounding the core and transferring heat to the steam generator may be water or gas, and is usually called the coolant.

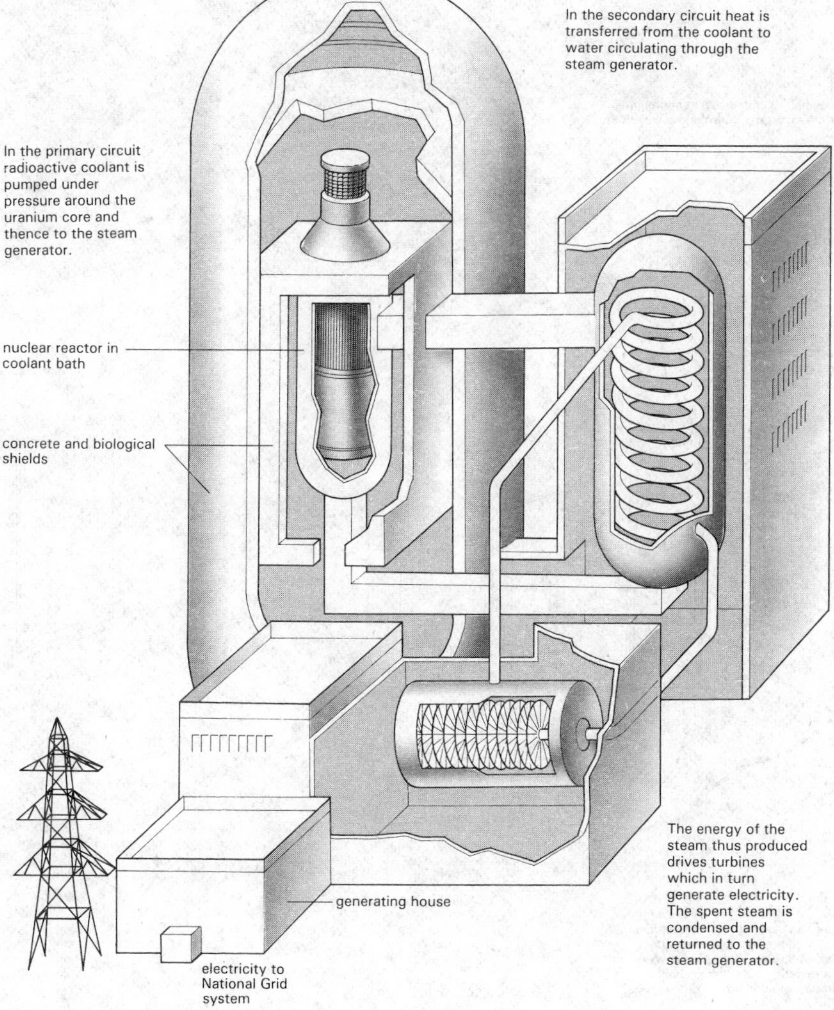

In the secondary circuit heat is transferred from the coolant to water circulating through the steam generator.

In the primary circuit radioactive coolant is pumped under pressure around the uranium core and thence to the steam generator.

nuclear reactor in coolant bath

concrete and biological shields

The energy of the steam thus produced drives turbines which in turn generate electricity. The spent steam is condensed and returned to the steam generator.

generating house

electricity to National Grid system

Energy-saving house

There are many measures that can be taken on a domestic scale to conserve and even create energy, some of which are shown on this page. The design and siting of a house also have a part to play in that small windows facing north and large windows facing south cut heat loss and make maximum use of available sunlight as a heating agent (passive solar heating).

Solar panel – a solar panel of photovoltaic solar cells converts sunlight into electricity.

Greenhouse heating

Vents in the walls and windows encourage convection airflows to heat in winter and cool in summer.

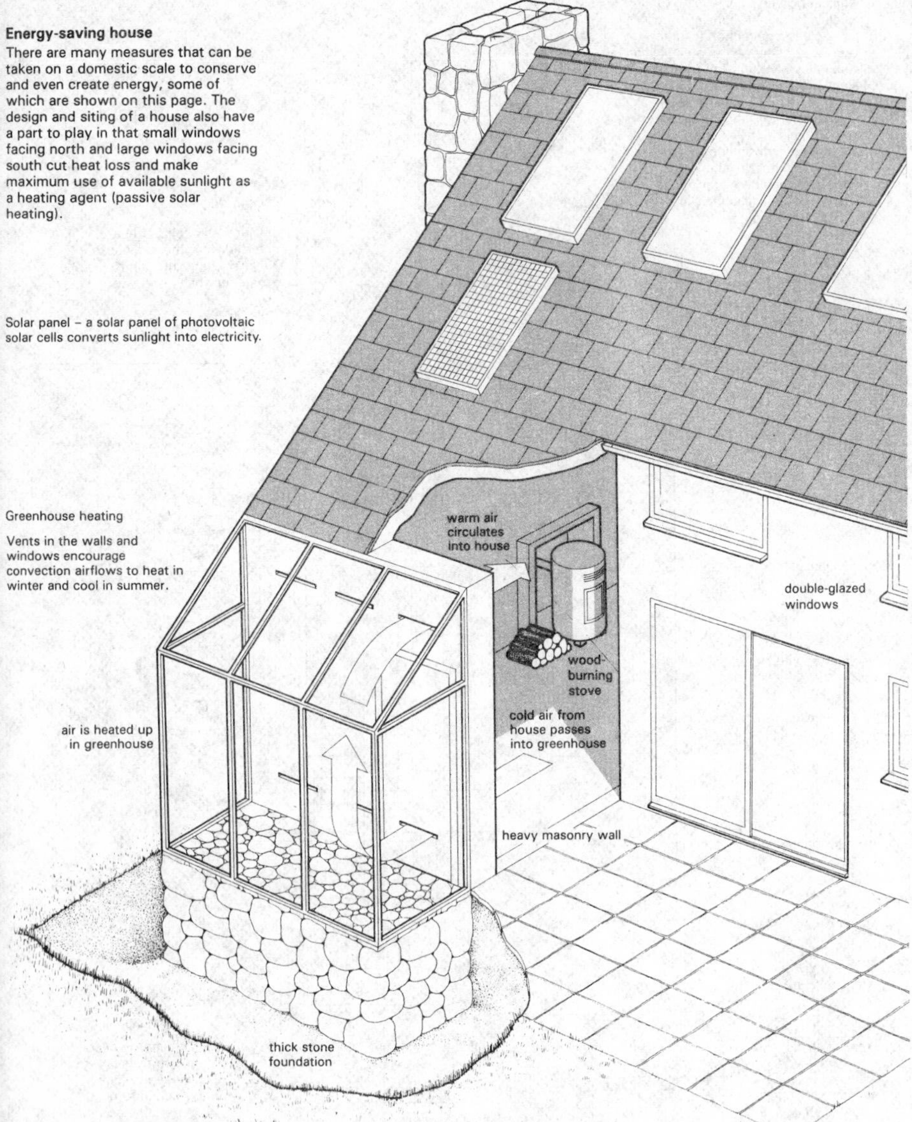

Rocks and masonry absorb heat during the day and radiate it at night. The greenhouse glass admits short wave solar radiation but traps the heat of infra red radiation.

Solar heat collectors consist of single or double glass panes backed by a dark, heat-absorbing material. When the sun shines on the panels, water circulating in fine copper pipes behind the heat absorber is warmed and transfers the heat to a heat store (an insulated water tank or in more sophisticated systems a chemical tank). Solar heat collectors are usually connected to the hot water taps via the heat store but may sometimes be linked to central heating radiators.

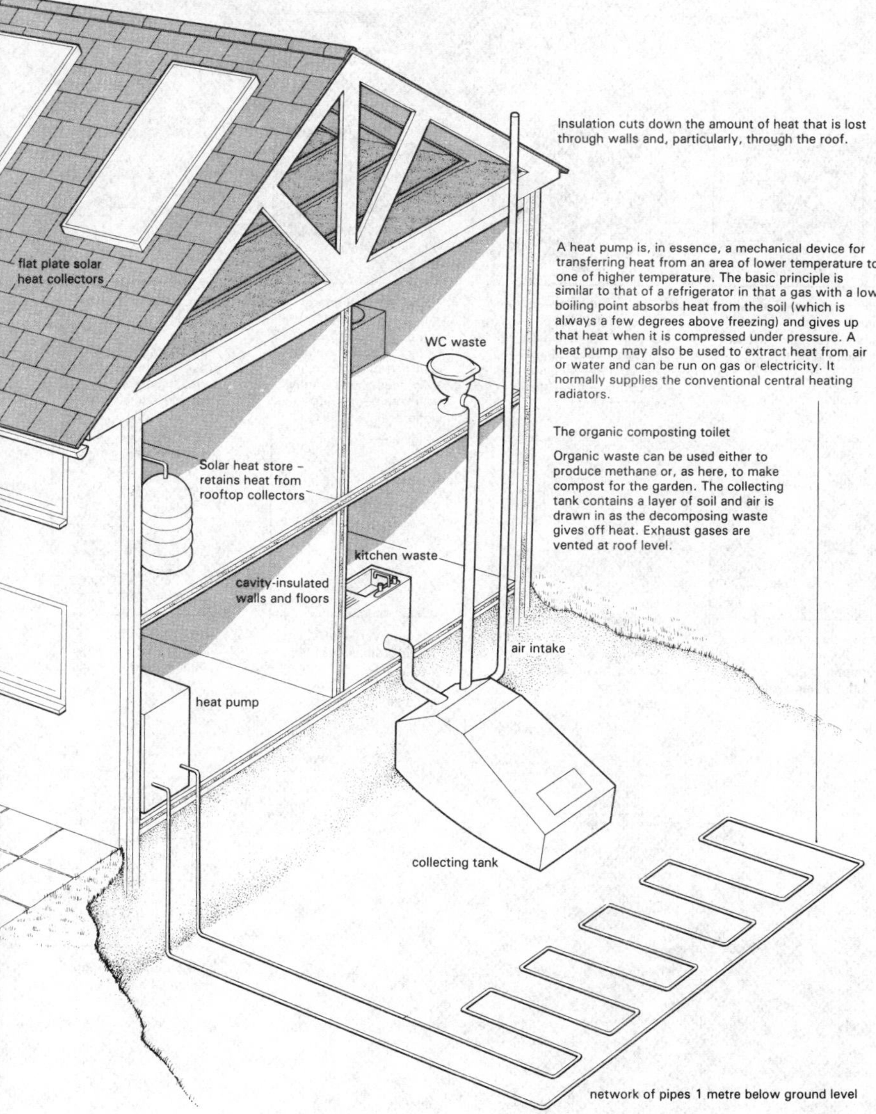

Insulation cuts down the amount of heat that is lost through walls and, particularly, through the roof.

A heat pump is, in essence, a mechanical device for transferring heat from an area of lower temperature to one of higher temperature. The basic principle is similar to that of a refrigerator in that a gas with a low boiling point absorbs heat from the soil (which is always a few degrees above freezing) and gives up that heat when it is compressed under pressure. A heat pump may also be used to extract heat from air or water and can be run on gas or electricity. It normally supplies the conventional central heating radiators.

The organic composting toilet

Organic waste can be used either to produce methane or, as here, to make compost for the garden. The collecting tank contains a layer of soil and air is drawn in as the decomposing waste gives off heat. Exhaust gases are vented at roof level.

Our alternative energy resources

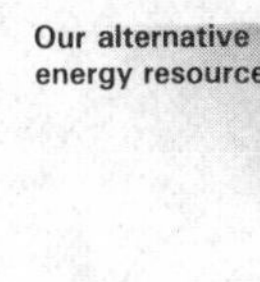

sun's energy

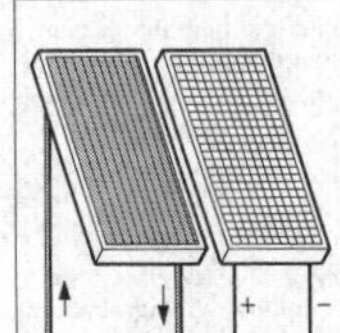

solar collectors and **solar panels** convert the sun's power into usable heat or electricity

photosynthesis — plants convert the sun's energy into organic matter which can be fermented into alcohol, decomposed for gas, or simply burnt

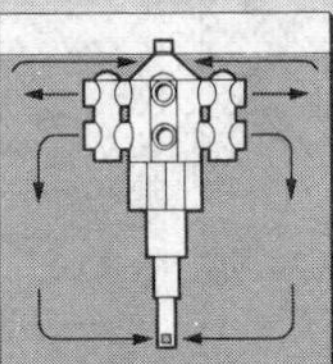

ocean thermal energy conversion — the temperature difference between surface water warmed by the sun and cold deeper water may in future be used to generate electricity

hydroelectricity — the sun's energy constantly raises water by the process of evaporation, providing the head of water necessary for hydroelectric schemes

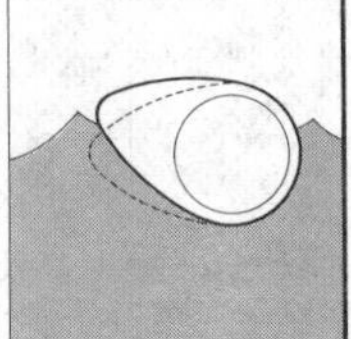

wave power — the bobbing motion of waves can be used to produce electricity

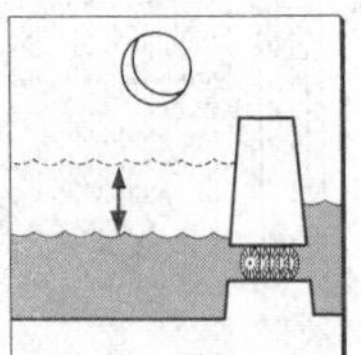

tidal power — where the tidal range is sufficiently great, power can be generated by harnessing the flow

wind power — efficient wind turbines are now being developed and offshore 'wind farms' have been proposed

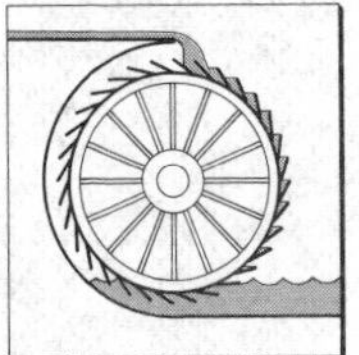

water turbine/mill — rivers provide energy on a relatively domestic scale

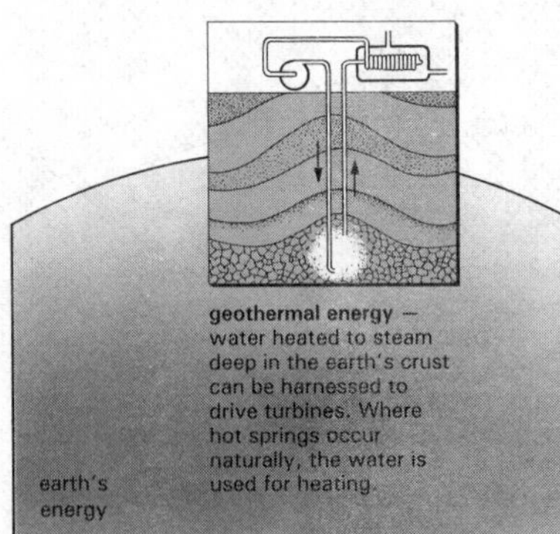

geothermal energy — water heated to steam deep in the earth's crust can be harnessed to drive turbines. Where hot springs occur naturally, the water is used for heating.

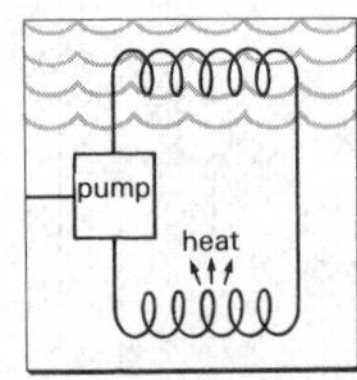

heat pump — extracts available heat from air, water, or earth

involved or committed (politically) [F, pp of *engager* to engage, fr MF *engagier*]

engaged /in'gayjd/ *adj* **1** involved in activity; occupied **2** pledged to be married **3** *chiefly Br* **a** in use ⟨*the telephone is* ~⟩ **b** reserved, booked ⟨*this table is* ~⟩

en'gagement /-mənt/ *n* **1** an agreement to marry; a betrothal **2** a pledge **3a** a promise to be present at a certain time and place **b** employment, esp for a stated time **4** a hostile encounter between military forces [ENGAGE + -MENT]

engaging /in'gayjing/ *adj* attractive, pleasing – **engagingly** *adv*

engender /in'jendə/ *vt* to cause to exist or develop; produce ⟨*angry words* ~ *strife*⟩ [ME *engendren*, fr MF *engendrer*, fr L *ingenerare*, fr *in-* + *generare* to generate]

engine /'enjin/ *n* **1** a mechanical tool ⟨*a terrible* ~ *of war*⟩ **2** a machine for converting any of various forms of energy into mechanical force and motion ☞ CAR **3** a railway locomotive [ME *engin*, fr OF, fr L *ingenium* natural disposition, talent, fr *in-* + *gignere* to beget – more at KIN] – **engineless** *adj*

-engined /-enjind/ *comb form* (→ *adj*) having (such or so many) engines ⟨*front*-engined *cars*⟩ ⟨*four*-engined *planes*⟩

¹engineer /,enji'niə/ *n* **1** a soldier who carries out engineering work **2a** a designer or builder of engines **b** a person who is trained in or follows as a profession a branch of engineering **c** a person who starts or carries through an enterprise, esp by skilful or artful contrivance ⟨*the* ~ *of the agreement*⟩ **3** a person who runs or supervises an engine or apparatus

²engineer *vt* **1** to lay out, construct, or manage as an engineer **2** to contrive, plan, or guide, usu with subtle skill and craft

engineering /,enji'niəring/ *n* **1** the art of managing engines **2** the application of science and mathematics by which the properties of matter and the sources of energy in nature are made useful to human beings

enginery /'enjinri/ *n* machines and tools; machinery

¹English /'ing·glish/ *adj* (characteristic) of England [ME, fr OE *englisc*, fr *Engle* (pl) Angles] – **Englishman** *n*, **Englishness** *n*

²English *n* **1a** the Germanic language of the people of Britain, the USA, and most Commonwealth countries ☞ LANGUAGE **b** English language, literature, or composition as an academic subject **2** *pl in constr* the people of England

English bond *n* a masonry bond in which alternate courses consist of all headers or all stretchers ☞ BUILDING

English cross bond *n* a modification of the English bond in which the joints between the bricks in the stretcher courses are not directly above each other

,English 'horn *n*, *chiefly NAm* COR ANGLAIS [trans of It *corno inglese*]

,English 'setter *n* any of a breed of gundogs characterized by a moderately long silky coat

engorge /in'gawj/ *vt* to fill (with blood) to the point of congestion ~ *vi*, *esp of an insect* to suck blood to the limit of body capacity [MF *engorgier*, fr OF, to devour, fr *en-* + *gorge* throat – more at GORGE] – **engorgement** *n*

engrailed /in'grayld/ *adj* made of or bordered by a circle of raised dots ⟨*an* ~ *coin*⟩ [ME *engreled*, fr MF *engreslé*, fr *en-* + *gresle* slender, fr L *gracilis*]

engrain /in'grayn/ *vt* to ingrain

engram *also* **engramme** /'engram/ *n* a supposed change in neural tissue postulated to account for memory [ISV] – **engrammic** /en'gramik/ *adj*

engrave /in'grayv/ *vt* **1a** to cut (a design or lettering) on a hard surface (e g metal or stone) with a sharp tool **b** to impress deeply, as if by engraving ⟨*the incident was* ~d *in his memory*⟩ **2a** to cut a design or lettering on (a hard surface) for printing; *also* to print from an engraved plate **b** to photoengrave [MF *engraver*, fr *en-* + *graver* to grave, of Gmc origin; akin to OE *grafan* to grave] – **engraver** *n*

engraving /in'grayving/ *n* (a print made from) an engraved printing surface

engross /in'grohs/ *vt* **1a** to copy or write in a large hand **b** to prepare the final text of (an official document) **2** to occupy fully the time and attention of; absorb ⟨*a scholar* ~ed *in research*⟩ ⟨*an* ~ing *problem*⟩ [ME *engrossen*, fr AF *engrosser*, prob fr ML *ingrossare*, fr L *in* + ML *grossa* large handwriting, fr L, fem of *grossus* thick] – **engrosser** *n*, **engrossment** *n*

engulf /in'gulf/ *vt* **1** to flow over and enclose; overwhelm ⟨*the mounting seas threatened to* ~ *the island*⟩ **2** *of an amoeba, phagocytic cell, etc* to take in (food) by flowing over and enclosing – **engulfment** *n*

enhance /in'hahns/ *vt* to improve (e g in value, desirability, or attractiveness); heighten [ME *enhauncen*, fr AF *enhauncer*, alter. of OF *enhaucier*, fr (assumed) VL *inaltiare*, fr L *in* + *altus* high – more at OLD] – **enhancement** *n*

enharmonic /,enhah'monik/ *adj* of or being notes that are written differently (e g A flat and G sharp) but sound the same in the tempered scale [F *enharmonique*, fr MF, of a scale employing quarter tones, fr Gk *enarmonios*, fr *en* in + *harmonia* harmony, scale] – **enharmonically** *adv*

enigma /i'nigmə/ *n* **1** intentionally obscure speech or writing; a riddle **2** sby or sthg hard to understand or explain; a puzzle [L *aenigma*, fr Gk *ainigmat-*, *ainigma*, fr *ainissesthai* to speak in riddles, fr *ainos* fable] – **enigmatic** /,enig'matik/ *adj*, **enigmatically** *adv*

enjambment, **enjambement** /in'jam·mənt (*Fr* ɑ̃ʒɑ̃bmɑ̃)/ *n* the running over of a sentence from one verse or couplet into another – compare RUN-ON [F *enjambement*, fr MF, encroachment, fr *enjamber* to straddle, encroach on, fr *en-* + *jambe* leg – more at JAMB]

enjoin /in'joyn/ *vt* **1** to order (sby) to do sthg; command **2** to impose (a condition or course of action) on sby **3** to forbid by law; prohibit *USE* fml [ME *enjoinen*, fr OF *enjoindre*, fr L *injungere*, fr *in-* + *jungere* to join – more at YOKE]

enjoy /in'joy/ *vt* **1** to take pleasure or satisfaction in **2a** to have the use or benefit of **b** to experience ⟨*he* ~ed *good health*⟩ [MF *enjoir*, fr OF, fr *en-* + *joir* to enjoy, fr L *gaudēre* to rejoice – more at JOY] – **enjoyable** *adj*, **enjoyableness** *n*, **enjoyably** *adv*, **enjoyment** *n*

enlace /in'lays/ *vt* **1** to encircle, enfold **2** to entwine, interlace [ME *enlacen*, fr MF *enlacier*, fr OF, fr *en-* + *lacier* to lace] – **enlacement** *n*

enlarge /in'lahj/ *vt* **1** to make larger **2** to reproduce in a larger form; *specif* to make a photographic enlargement of ~ *vi* **1** to grow larger **2** to speak or write at length; elaborate – often + *on* or *upon* [ME *enlargen*, fr MF *enlargier*, fr OF, fr *en-* + *large*] – **enlarger** *n*

en'largement /-mənt/ *n* a photographic print that is larger than the negative [ENLARGE + -MENT]

enlighten /in'liet(ə)n/ *vt* to cause to understand; free from false beliefs

en'lightenment /-mənt/ *n* **1** *cap* an 18th-c movement marked by a belief in universal human progress and the importance of reason and the sciences – + *the* **2** NIRVANA 1 [ENLIGHTEN + -MENT]

enlist /in'list/ *vt* **1** to engage (a person) for duty in the armed forces **2a** to secure the support and aid of ⟨~ *you in a good cause*⟩ ~ *vi* to enrol oneself in the armed forces – **enlistment** *n*

enlisted man *n* a person in the US armed forces ranking below a commissioned or warrant officer

enliven /in'liev(ə)n/ *vt* to give life, action, spirit, or interest to; animate – **enlivenment** *n*

en masse /,om 'mas (*Fr* ã mas)/ *adv* in a body; as a whole [F]

enmesh /in'mesh/ *vt* to catch or entangle (as if) in a net or mesh – **enmeshment** *n*

enmity /'enmiti/ *n* (a state of) hatred or ill will [ME *enmite*, fr MF *enemité*, fr OF *enemisté*, irreg fr *enemi* enemy]

ennead /'eniad/ *n* a group of 9 [Gk *ennead-*, *enneas*, fr *ennea* nine – more at NINE]

ennoble /in'nohbl/ *vt* **1** to make noble; elevate ⟨*believes that hard work* ~s *the human spirit*⟩ **2** to raise to the rank of the nobility [ME *ennobelen*, fr MF *ennoblir*, fr OF, fr *en-* + *noble*] – **ennoblement** *n*

ennui /on'wi (*Fr* ãn i)/ *n* weariness and dissatisfaction resulting from lack of interest or boredom [F, fr OF *enui* annoyance, fr *enuier* to annoy]

enology /,ee'noləji/ *n* oenology – **enologist** *n*

enophile /'eenoh,fiel/ *n* an oenophile

enormity /i'nawməti/ *n* **1** great wickedness ⟨*the sheer* ~ *of the crime*⟩ **2** a terribly wicked or evil act **3** the quality or state of being enormous

enormous /i'nawməs/ *adj* marked by extraordinarily great size, number, or degree [L *enormis*, fr *e*, *ex* out of + *norma* rule] – **enormously** *adv*, **enormousness** *n*

enosis /'enohsis/ *n* the (proposed) union of Cyprus and Greece [NGk *henōsis*, fr Gk, union, fr *henoun* to unite, fr *hen-*, *heis* one]

[1]**enough** /i'nuf/ *adj* fully adequate in quantity, number, or degree ⟨*not* ~ *beer*⟩ ⟨*was fool* ~ *to believe him*⟩ [ME *ynough*, fr OE *genōg;* akin to OHG *ginuog* enough; both fr a prehistoric Gmc compound whose first constituent is represented by OE *ge-* (perfective prefix) and whose second is akin to L *nancisci* to get, Gk *enenkein* to carry]

[2]**enough** *adv* **1** to a fully adequate degree; sufficiently ⟨*not cooked long* ~⟩ **2** to a tolerable degree ⟨*he understands well* ~⟩

[3]**enough** *pron, pl* **enough** a sufficient quantity or number ⟨~ *were present to constitute a quorum*⟩ ⟨*had* ~ *of their foolishness*⟩

en passant /,on pa'sonh (*Fr* ã pasã)/ *adv* in passing – used in chess of the capture of a pawn as it makes a first move of 2 squares by an enemy pawn in a position to threaten the first of these squares [F]

enplane /en'playn/ *vi, chiefly NAm* to emplane

en prise /,om 'preez (*Fr* ã priz)/ *adj, of a chess piece* exposed to capture [F]

enquire /in'kwie·ə/ *vb* to inquire

enquiry /in'kwie·əri/ *n* an inquiry

enrage /in'rayj/ *vt* to fill with rage; anger [MF *enrager* to become mad, fr OF *enragier*, fr *en-* + *rage*]

en rapport /,onh ra'paw (*Fr* ã rapɔːr)/ *adv* in harmony or agreement [F]

enrapture /in'rapchə/ *vt* to fill with delight

enrich /in'rich/ *vt* **1** to make rich or richer, esp in some desirable quality ⟨*the experience greatly* ~ed *his life*⟩ **2** to adorn, ornament ⟨~ing *the ceiling with frescoes*⟩ **3a** to make (soil) more fertile **b** to improve (a food) in nutritive value by adding nutrients (lost in processing) **c** to increase the proportion of a valuable or desirable ingredient in ⟨~ *uranium with uranium 235*⟩; *also* to add a desirable substance to ⟨~ *natural gas*⟩ [ME *enrichen*, fr MF *enrichir*, fr OF, fr *en-* + *riche* rich] – **enricher** *n*, **enrichment** *n*

enrol, *NAm also* **enroll** /in'rohl/ *vb* **-ll-** *vt* **1** to enter on a list, roll, etc **2** to prepare a final perfect copy of (a bill passed by a legislature) in written or printed form ~ *vi* to enrol oneself ⟨~ *in the history course*⟩ [ME *enrollen*, fr MF *enroller*, fr *en-* + *rolle* roll, register] – **enrolment** *n*

en route /,on 'rooht (*Fr* ã rut)/ *adv or adj* on or along the way ⟨*soon they were* ~ *to the border*⟩ [F]

ensconce /in'skons/ *vt* to settle (e g oneself) comfortably or snugly ⟨*the cat* ~d *itself in the basket*⟩ [[1]*en-* + [2]*sconce*]

ensemble /on'sombl (*Fr* ãsãːbl)/ *n* **1** a group constituting an organic whole or together producing a single effect: e g **a** concerted music of 2 or more parts **b** a complete outfit of matching garments **c** *sing or pl in constr* **(1)** the musicians engaged in the performance of a musical ensemble **(2)** a group of supporting players, singers, or dancers **2** the quality of togetherness in performance ⟨*the quartet's* ~ *was poor*⟩ [F, fr *ensemble* together, fr L *insimul* at the same time, fr *in-* + *simul* at the same time – more at SAME]

enshrine /in'shrien/ *vt* **1** to enclose (as if) in a shrine **2** to preserve or cherish, esp as sacred ⟨*they* ~d *their leader's memory in their hearts*⟩ – **enshrinement** *n*

enshroud /in'shrowd/ *vt* to shroud

ensign /'ensien; *sense* ' *naval* 'ensən/ *n* **1** a flag that is flown (e g by a ship) as the symbol of nationality **2a** a standard-bearer **b** ☞ RANK [ME *ensigne*, fr MF *enseigne*, fr L *insignia* insignia, flags]

ensilage /'ensilij/ *n* (the process of preserving) fodder (by ensiling)

ensile /en'siel, '--/ *vt* to prepare and store (fodder) for silage in a silo or pit [F *ensiler*, fr *en-* + *silo*, fr Sp]

enslave /in'slayv/ *vt* to reduce (as if) to slavery; subjugate – **enslavement** *n*, **enslaver** *n*

ensnare /in'sneə/ *vt* to take (as if) in a snare

ensue /in'syooh/ *vi* to take place afterwards or as a result [ME *ensuen*, fr MF *ensuivre*, fr OF, fr *en-* + *suivre* to follow – more at SUE]

en suite /,on 'sweet (*Fr* ã s it)/ *adv or adj* in a set or series, esp so as to form a unit ⟨*a bedroom with an* ~ *bathroom*⟩ [F]

ensure /in'shooə, -'shaw/ *vt* to make sure, certain, or safe; guarantee [ME *ensuren*, fr AF *enseurer*, prob alter. of OF *aseürer*, fr ML *assecurare* – more at ASSURE]

ent-, ento- /ent-/ *comb form* inner; within ⟨ento*blast*⟩ ⟨ento*zoa*⟩ [NL, fr Gk *entos* within; akin to L *intus* within, Gk *en* in – more at IN]

entablature /en'tablәchә/ *n* the upper section of a wall or storey, usu supported on columns or pilasters, and in classical orders consisting of architrave, frieze, and cornice ☞ ARCHITECTURE [obs F, modif of It *intavolatura*, fr *intavolare* to put on a board or table, fr *in-* (fr L) + *tavola* board, table, fr L *tabula*]

entablement /in'tayblmәnt/ *n* a platform that supports a statue and is placed above the dado [F, fr OF, fr *en-* + *table*]

[1]**entail** /in'tayl/ *vt* **1** to settle (property) so that sale or bequeathal is not permitted and inheritance is limited to (a specified class of) the owner's lineal descendants **2** to involve or imply as a necessary accompaniment or result ⟨*the project will ~ considerable expense*⟩ [ME *entailen, entaillen*, fr [1]*en-* + *taile, taille* limitation, fr MF *taille*, fr OF, fr *taillier* to cut, limit – more at TAILOR] – **entailer** *n*, **entailment** *n*

[2]**entail** *n* **1** (the rule fixing) an entailing **2** sthg entailed

entangle /in'tang·gl/ *vt* **entangling** /in'tang·gling; *also* -gl·ing/ **1** to make tangled, complicated, or confused **2** to involve in a tangle ⟨*become* ~d *in a ruinous lawsuit*⟩ – **entangler** *n*

en'tanglement /-mәnt/ *n* **1** sthg that entangles, confuses, or ensnares **2** the condition of being deeply involved

entasis /'entәsis/ *n, pl* **entases** /-,seez/ a slight convexity in the outline of a vertical architectural member (e g the shaft of a column) [Gk, lit., distension, stretching, fr *enteinein* to stretch tight, fr *en-* [2]en- + *teinein* to stretch – more at THIN]

entente /on'tont (*Fr* ɑ̃tɑ̃:t)/ *n* **1** a friendly relationship between 2 or more countries **2** *sing or pl in constr* the countries having an entente [F, fr OF, intent, understanding – more at [1]INTENT]

,entente cordi'ale /kawdi'al, -'dyal (*Fr* kɔrdjal)/ *n* ENTENTE 1; *specif* that between Britain and France in 1904 or between Britain, France, and Russia in 1908 [F, lit., cordial entente]

enter /'entә/ *vi* **1** to go or come in **2** to register as candidate in a competition ⟨*decided to ~ for the race*⟩ **3** to make a beginning ⟨~ing *upon a career*⟩ ~ *vt* **1** to go or come into ⟨~ *a room*⟩ ⟨~ing *her early thirties*⟩ **2** to inscribe, register ⟨~ *the names of qualified voters in the rolls*⟩ **3** to cause to be received, admitted, or considered – often + *for* ⟨~ *a child for a public school*⟩ **4** to put in; insert **5** to become a member of or an active participant in ⟨~ *university*⟩ ⟨~ *a race*⟩ ⟨~ *politics*⟩ **6** to put on record ⟨~ *a complaint against his partner*⟩ [ME *entren*, fr OF *entrer*, fr L *intrare*, fr *intra* within; akin to L *inter* between – more at INTER-] – **enterable** *adj* – **enter into 1** to make oneself a party to or in ⟨enter into *an important agreement*⟩ **2** to participate or share in ⟨*cheerfully* entering into *the household tasks*⟩

enter- /entә-/, **entero-** *comb form* intestine ⟨enter*itis*⟩ [Gk, fr *enteron*]

enteric /en'terik/ *adj* of the intestines

enteritis /,entә'rietәs/ *n* inflammation of the intestines, esp the human ileum, usu marked by diarrhoea [NL]

enterocoele, enterocoel /'entәroh,seel/ *n* a coelom that forms during the development of an embryo as an outgrowth from the cavity inside the gastrula – **enterocoelic** /-'seelik/ *adj*, **enterocoelous** /-'seelәs/ *adj*

enterokinase /,ent(ә)roh'kienayz, -nays/ *n* an enzyme that converts an inactive substance secreted into the intestines by the pancreas into trypsin [ISV]

enteron /'entәron/ *n* the alimentary canal or system, esp of the embryo [NL, fr Gk, intestine – more at INTER-]

enterprise /'entә,priez/ *n* **1** a (difficult or complicated) project or undertaking **2** a unit of economic organization or activity; *esp* a business organization **3** readiness to engage in enterprises [ME *enterprise*, fr MF *entreprise*, fr *entreprendre* to undertake, fr *entre-* inter- + *prendre* to take – more at [4]PRIZE] – **enterpriser** *n*

enterprising /'entә,priezing/ *adj* marked by initiative and readiness to engage in enterprises

entertain /,entә'tayn/ *vt* **1** to show hospitality to **2** to be ready and willing to think about (an idea, doubt, suggestion, etc) **3** to hold the attention of, usu pleasantly or enjoyably; divert **4** to play against (an opposing team) on one's home ground ~ *vi* to invite guests to esp one's home [ME *entertinen*, fr MF *entretenir*, fr *entre-* inter- + *tenir* to hold – more at TENABLE] – **entertainer** *n*

,enter'tainment /-mәnt/ *n* **1** sthg entertaining, diverting, or engaging **2** a public performance [ENTERTAIN + -MENT]

enthalpy /'enthәlpi, en'thalpi/ *n* a thermodynamic property of a system that is the total internal energy of the system [*en-* + Gk *thalpein* to heat]

enthral, *NAm also* **enthrall** /in'thrawl/ *vt* **-ll-** to hold the complete interest and attention of; captivate [ME *enthrallen*, fr *en-* + *thral* thrall] – **enthralment** *n*

enthrone /in'throhn/ *vt* to seat, esp ceremonially, (as if) on a throne – **enthronement** *n*

enthuse /in'thyoohz/ *vt* to make enthusiastic ⟨*proposals which shocked the orthodox and* ~d *the rebellious – TLS*⟩ ~ *vi* to show enthusiasm [back-formation fr *enthusiasm*]

enthusiasm /in'thyoohzi,az(ә)m/ *n* **1** keen and eager interest and admiration – usu + *for* or *about* **2** an object of enthusiasm [Gk *enthousiasmos*, fr *enthousiazein* to be inspired, fr *entheos* inspired, fr *en-* + *theos* god]

enthusiast /in'thyoohzi,ast/ *n* sby filled with enthusiasm; *esp* sby ardently attached to a usu specified cause, object, or pursuit ⟨*a cycling* ~⟩ – **enthusiastic** /-'astik/ *adj*, **enthusiastically** *adv*

entice /in'ties/ *vt* to tempt or persuade by arousing hope or desire [ME *enticen*, fr OF *enticier*, fr (assumed) VL *intitiare*, fr L *in-* + *titio* firebrand] – **enticement** *n*

entire /in'tie·ә/ *adj* **1** having no element or part left out ⟨*was alone the* ~ *day*⟩ **2** complete in degree; total ⟨*his* ~ *devotion to his family*⟩ **3a** consisting of 1 piece; homogeneous ⟨*the book is* ~ *in style*⟩ **b** intact ⟨*strove to keep the collection* ~⟩ **4** not castrated [ME, fr MF *entir*, fr L *integer*, lit., untouched, fr *in-* + *tangere* to touch – more at TANGENT] – **entire** *adv*, **entireness** *n*

en'tirely /-li/ *adv* **1** wholly, completely ⟨*agreed with me* ~⟩ **2** in an exclusive manner; solely ⟨*it is his fault* ~⟩

entirety /in'tie·ərəti/ *n* **1** the state of being entire or complete **2** the whole or total

entitle /in'tietl/ *vt* **1** to title **2** to give (sby) the right *to* (do or have) sthg ⟨*this ticket* ~s *the bearer to free admission*⟩ [ME *entitlen,* fr MF *entituler,* fr LL *intitulare,* fr L *in-* + *titulus* title] – **entitlement** *n*

entity /'entəti/ *n* **1a** being, existence; *esp* independent, separate, or self-contained existence **b** the existence of a thing as contrasted with its attributes **2** sthg that has separate and distinct existence [ML *entitas,* fr L *ent-, ens* existing thing, fr coined prp of *esse* to be – more at IS]

ento- /entoh-/ – see ENT-

entom- /entəm-/, **entomo-** *comb form* insect ⟨entomo*phagous*⟩ [F, fr Gk *entomon*]

entomb /in'toohm/ *vt* **1** to deposit (as if) in a tomb; bury **2** to serve as a tomb for [ME *entoumben,* fr MF *entomber,* fr *en-* + *tombe* tomb] – **entombment** *n*

entomology /,entə'moləji/ *n* zoology that deals with insects [F *entomologie,* fr Gk *entomon* insect (fr neut of *entomos* cut up, fr *en-* + *temnein* to cut) + F *-logie* -logy – more at TOME] – **entomologist** *n,* **entomological** /-mə'lojikl/ *adj,* **entomologically** *adv*

entomophagous /,entə'mofəgəs/ *adj* feeding on insects

entomophilous /,entə'mofiləs/ *adj* being normally pollinated by insects – compare ZOOPHILOUS a – **entomophily** *n*

entomostracan /,entə'mostrəkən/ *n* any of numerous simple typically small crustaceans (e g barnacles) [deriv of *entom-* + Gk *ostrakon* shell – more at OYSTER] – **entomostracan, entomostracous** *adj*

entourage /'ontoo,rahzh (*Fr* ãtura:ʒ)/ *n sing or pl in constr* a group of attendants or associates, esp of sby of high rank [F, fr MF, fr *entourer* to surround, fr *entour* around, fr *en* in (fr L *in*) + *tour* circuit – more at [2]TURN]

entr'acte /'ontrakt, -'- (*Fr* ãtrakt)/ *n* (a performance or interlude in) the interval between 2 acts of a play [F, fr *entre-* inter- + *acte* act]

entrails /'entraylz/ *n pl* internal parts; *esp* the intestines [ME *entrailles,* fr MF, fr ML *intralia,* alter. of L *interanea,* pl of *interaneum* intestine, fr neut of *interaneus* interior]

[1]**entrain** /in'trayn/ *vt, of a fluid* to draw in and transport (e g solid particles or gas) [MF *entrainer,* fr *en-* + *trainer* to draw, drag – more at [2]TRAIN] – **entrainment** *n*

[2]**entrain** *vb* to put or go aboard a train

[1]**entrance** /'entrəns/ *n* **1** the act of entering **2** the means or place of entry **3** power or permission to enter; admission **4** an arrival of a performer onto the stage or before the cameras

[2]**entrance** /in'trahns/ *vt* **1** to put into a trance **2** to fill with delight, wonder, or rapture – **entrancement** *n*

entrant /'entrənt/ *n* sby or sthg that enters or is entered; *esp* one who enters a contest

entrap /in'trap/ *vt* **-pp- 1** to catch (as if) in a trap **2** to lure into a compromising statement or act [MF *entraper,* fr *en-* + *trape* trap] – **entrapment** *n*

entreat /in'treet/ *vt* to ask urgently or plead with (sby) *for* (sthg); beg ⟨~ed *the judge for another chance*⟩ ⟨~ *his help*⟩ ~ *vi* to make an earnest request; plead [ME *entreten,* fr MF *entraitier,* fr *en-* + *traitier* to treat – more at TREAT] – **entreatingly** *adv,* **entreatment** *n*

entreaty /in'treeti/ *n* an act of entreating; a plea

entrechat /'ontrəshah (*Fr* ãtrəʃa)/ *n* a leap in which a ballet dancer repeatedly crosses his/her legs [F]

entrecote /'ontrəkot (*Fr* ãtrəko:t)/ *n* a steak cut from a boned sirloin ☞ MEAT [F *entrecôte,* fr *entre-* inter- + *côte* rib, fr L *costa* – more at COAST]

entrée, entree /'ontray (*Fr* ãtre)/ *n* **1** freedom of entry or access ⟨*had an* ~ *into the highest circles*⟩ **2a** *chiefly Br* a dish served between the usual (fish and meat) courses of a dinner **b** *chiefly NAm* the principal dish of a meal [F *entrée,* fr OF]

entremets /'ontrə,may (*Fr* ãtrəmɛ)/ *n pl but sing or pl in constr* SIDE DISH [F, fr OF *entremes,* fr L *intermissus,* pp of *intermittere* to intermit]

entrench /in'trench/ *vt* **1a** to surround with a (defensive) trench **b** to place (oneself) in a strong defensive position **2** to establish solidly, esp so as to make change difficult ~ *vi* to dig or occupy a (defensive) trench – **entrenchment** *n*

entre nous /,ontrə 'nooh (*Fr* ãtr nu)/ *adv* between ourselves, confidentially [F]

entrepôt /'ontrə,poh/ *n* a seaport, warehouse, or other intermediary centre of trade and transshipment [F]

entrepreneur /,ontrəprə'nuh (*Fr* ãtrəprənœ:r)/ *n* one who organizes, manages, and assumes the risks of a business or enterprise [F, fr OF, fr *entreprendre* to undertake] – **entrepreneurial** /-ri·əl/ *adj,* **entrepreneurship** *n*

entresol /'ontrə,sol (*Fr* ãtrəsɔl)/ *n* a mezzanine [F]

entrism /'entriz(ə)m/ *n* entryism

entropy /'entrəpi/ *n* **1** a measure of the unavailable energy in a closed thermodynamic system **2** a measure of the amount of information in a message that is based on the logarithm of the number of possible equivalent messages **3** the degradation of the matter and energy in the universe to an ultimate state of inert uniformity [G *entropie,* fr Gk *en-* + *trepein* to turn, change – more at TROPE] – **entropic** /en'tropik/ *adj*

entrust /in'trust/ *vt* **1** to confer a trust on; *esp* to deliver sthg in trust to – + *with* ⟨~ed *the bank with his savings*⟩ **2** to commit to another with confidence – + *to* ⟨~ed *his savings to the bank*⟩ – **entrustment** *n*

entry /'entri/ *n* **1** the act of entering; entrance **2** the right or privilege of entering **3** a door, gate, hall, vestibule, or other place of entrance **4a** the act of registering a record **b** a record made in a diary, account book, index, etc **c** a dictionary headword, often with its definition **5** a person, thing, or group entered in a contest; an entrant **6** the total of those entered or admitted ⟨*double the annual* ~ *to our medical schools*⟩ [ME *entre,* fr OF *entree,* fr fem of *entré,* pp of *entrer* to enter]

entryism /'entri,iz(ə)m/ *n* the practice of infiltrating a political party in order to influence that party's policy from within

entwine /in'twien/ *vb* to twine together or round

enucleate /i'nyoohkliayt/ *vt* to remove without cutting into ⟨~ *a tumour*⟩ [L *enucleatus,* pp of *enucleare,* lit., to remove the kernel from, fr *e-* +

nucleus kernel – more at NUCLEUS] – **enucleation** /-ˈay sh(ə)n/ *n*

enumerable /iˈnyoohm(ə)rəbl/ *adj* denumerable – **enumerability** /-rəˈbiləti/ *n*

enumerate /iˈnyoohmərayt/ *vt* **1** to count **2** to specify one after another; list [L *enumeratus*, pp of *enumerare*, fr *e-* + *numerare* to count, fr *numerus* number – more at NIMBLE] – **enumerator** *n*, **enumerative** /-rətiv/ *adj*, **enumeration** /-ˈraysh(ə)n/ *n*

enunciate /iˈnunsi,ayt/ *vt* **1a** to make a definite or systematic statement of; formulate **b** to announce, proclaim 〈~d *the principles to be followed by the new administration*〉 **2** to articulate, pronounce ~ *vi* to utter articulate sounds [L *enuntiatus*, pp of *enuntiare* to report, declare, fr *e-* + *nuntiare* to report – more at ANNOUNCE] – **enunciator** *n*, **enunciable** /-si·əbl/ *adj*, **enunciation** /-ˈaysh(ə)n/ *n*

enure /iˈnyooə/ *vb* to inure

enuresis /,enyooˈreesis/ *n* an involuntary discharge of urine [NL, fr Gk *enourein* to urinate in, wet the bed, fr *en-* + *ourein* to urinate] – **enuretic** /-ˈretik/ *adj or n*

envelop /inˈveləp/ *vt* **1** to enclose or enfold completely (as if) with a covering **2** to surround so as to cut off communication or retreat 〈~ *the enemy*〉 [ME *envolupen*, fr MF *envoluper, enveloper*, fr OF *envoloper*, fr *en-* + *voloper* to wrap] – **envelopment** *n*

envelope /ˈenvəlohp, ˈon-/ *n* **1** sthg that envelops; a wrapper, covering **2** a flat container, usu of folded and gummed paper (e g for a letter) **3** a membrane or other natural covering that encloses **4** a curve tangent to each of a family of curves **5** the performance limits of a machine, aircraft, etc 〈*the flight ~ of the prototype fighter was explored*〉 [F *enveloppe*, fr MF *envelope*, fr *enveloper*]

envenom /inˈvenəm/ *vt* **1** to put poison into or onto 〈~ *a weapon*〉 **2** to embitter 〈*jealousy* ~ing *his mind*〉 [ME *envenimen*, fr OF *envenimer*, fr *en-* + *venim* venom]

enviable /ˈenvi·əbl/ *adj* highly desirable – **enviableness** *n*, **enviably** *adv*

envious /ˈenvi·əs/ *adj* feeling or showing envy 〈~ *looks*〉 〈~ *of a neighbour's wealth*〉 – **enviously** *adv*, **enviousness** *n*

environ /inˈvie(ə)rən/ *vt* to encircle, surround – fml [ME *envirounen*, fr MF *environner*, fr *environ* around, fr *en* in (fr L *in*) + *viron* circle, fr *virer* to turn, fr (assumed) VL *virare*]

enˈvironment /-mənt/ *n* **1** the circumstances, objects, or conditions by which one is surrounded **2** the complex of climatic, soil, and biological factors that acts upon an organism or an ecological community – **environmental** /-ˈmentl/ *adj*, **environmentally** *adv*

en,vironˈmental,ism /-,iz(ə)m/ *n* a theory that views environment rather than heredity as the important factor in human development

en,vironˈmentalist /-ist/ *n* **1** an advocate of environmentalism **2** sby concerned about the quality of the human environment

environs /inˈvie(ə)rənz/ *n pl* the neighbourhood surrounding sthg, esp a town [F, pl of *environ*, fr MF, fr *environ*, adv & prep, round, about]

envisage /inˈvizij/ *vt* to have a mental picture of; visualize, esp in advance of an expected or hoped-for realization 〈~s *an entirely new system of education*〉 [F *envisager*, fr *en-* + *visage*]

envision /inˈvizh(ə)n/ *vt, chiefly NAm* to envisage

[1]**envoy, envoi** /ˈenvoy/ *n* the concluding remarks to a poem, essay, or book; *specif* a short fixed final stanza of a ballade [F *envoi*, lit., message, fr OF *envei*, fr *envoier* to send on one's way, fr (assumed) VL *inviare*, fr L *in-* + *via* way – more at VIA]

[2]**envoy** *n* **1** a diplomatic agent, esp one who ranks immediately below an ambassador **2** a messenger, representative [F *envoyé*, fr pp of *envoyer* to send, fr OF *envoier*]

[1]**envy** /ˈenvi/ *n* painful, resentful, or admiring awareness of an advantage enjoyed by another, accompanied by a desire to possess the same advantage; *also* an object of such a feeling [ME *envie*, fr OF, fr L *invidia*, fr *invidus* envious, fr *invidēre* to look askance at, envy, fr *in-* + *vidēre* to see – more at WIT]

[2]**envy** *vt* to feel envy towards or on account of – **envier** *n*, **envyingly** *adv*

enzootic /,enzohˈotik/ *adj, of animal diseases* peculiar to or constantly present in a particular locality [*en-* + *zo-*] – **enzootic** *n*

enzygotic /,enzieˈgotik, -zi-/ *adj, of twins* identical [*en-* + *zyg-*]

enzyme /ˈenziem/ *n* any of numerous complex proteins that are produced by living cells and catalyse specific biochemical reactions at body temperatures [G *enzym*, fr MGk *enzymos* leavened, fr Gk *en-* + *zymē* leaven] – **enzymatic** /-ˈmatik, -zi-/ *adj*, **enzymatically** *adv*, **enzymic** /enˈziemik, -ˈzi-/ *adj*, **enzymically** *adv*

enzymology /,enzieˈmoləji/ *n* science that deals with enzymes, their nature, activity, and significance [ISV] – **enzymologist** *n*

eo- /eeoh-/ *comb form* earliest; oldest 〈eo*lithic*〉 [Gk *ēō-* dawn, fr *ēōs*]

Eocene /ˈeeoh,seen/ *adj or n* (of or being) an epoch of the Tertiary between the Palaeocene and the Oligocene ☞ EVOLUTION

eohippus /,eeohˈhipəs/ *n* any of a genus of extinct small primitive 4-toed ancestors of the horse [NL, genus name, fr *eo-* + Gk *hippos* horse – more at EQUINE]

eolian /eeˈohli·ən, -lyən/ *adj, NAm* aeolian

eolith /ˈeeoh,lith, ˈee·ə,lith/ *n* a very crudely chipped flint that is the earliest form of stone tool

Eolithic /,ee·əˈlithik/ *adj* of the early period of the Stone Age characterized by the use of eoliths

eon /ˈeeon, ˈee·ən/ *n* an aeon

eosin /ˈeeoh,sin, ˈee·ə-/, **eosine** /-sin, -seen/ *n* a red fluorescent dye used esp as a biological stain [ISV, fr Gk *ēōs* dawn]

eosinophil /,ee·əˈsinəfil/, **eosinophile** /-,fiel/ *n* a white blood cell with cytoplasmic granules readily stained by eosin – compare BASOPHIL – **eosinophilic** /-ˈfilik/ *adj*

EP *n* a gramophone record with a playing time greater than a normal 45 [*e*xtended *p*lay]

ep- /ep-/ – see EPI-

epact /ˈeepakt/ *n* a period added to harmonize the lunar with the solar calendar [MF *epacte*, fr LL *epacta*, fr Gk *epaktē*, fr *epagein* to bring in, intercalate, fr *epi-* + *agein* to drive – more at AGENT]

epaulette, *NAm chiefly* **epaulet** /,epəˈlet/ *n* an ornamental (fringed) strip or pad attached to the shoulder of a garment, esp a military uniform [F *épaulette*, dim. of *épaule* shoulder, fr LL *spatula* shoulder blade, spoon, dim. of L *spatha* spoon, sword – more at [3]SPADE]

épée /'epay (*Fr* epe)/ *n* (the sport of fencing with) a sword having a bowl-shaped guard and a rigid tapering blade of triangular cross-section with no cutting edge – compare FOIL, SABRE [F, fr L *spatha*] – **épéeist** *n*

epeirogeny /,epie'rojəni/, **epeirogenesis** /e,pie(ə)roh'jenəsis/ *n* deformation of the earth's crust that produces the broader features of a continent [Gk *ēpeiros* mainland, continent + E *-geny*] – **epeirogenic** /-roh'jenik/ *adj*, **epeirogenically** *adv*

epergne /i'puhn/ *n* a (tiered or branched) centrepiece for a dinner table holding fruit, flowers, etc [prob fr F *épargne* saving]

ephedra /i'fedrə, 'efədrə/ *n* any of a large genus of nearly leafless desert shrubs [NL, genus name]

ephedrine /i'fedrin; *chem* 'efidrin, -dreen/ *n* an alkaloid orig obtained from Chinese ephedras that is used esp to relieve hay fever, asthma, and nasal congestion [NL *Ephedra*, genus of shrubs, fr L, horsetail plant, fr Gk, fr *ephedros* sitting upon, fr *epi-* + *hedra* seat – more at SIT]

ephemera /i'femərə/ *n pl* things (e g writings) of short-lived duration or interest [NL, pl of *ephemeron*]

ephemeral /i'femərəl/ *adj* **1** lasting 1 day only ⟨*an ~ fever*⟩ **2** lasting a very short time ⟨*~ pleasures*⟩ [Gk *ephēmeros* lasting a day, daily, fr *epi-* + *hēmera* day] – **ephemerally** *adv*, **ephemerality** /-'raləti/ *n*

ephemeris /i'femәris/ *n, pl* **ephemerides** /,efi'meri,deez/ a table showing the predicted position of a celestial body; *also* an astronomical almanac [L, diary, ephemeris, fr Gk *ephēmeris*, fr *ephēmeros*]

e'phemeris ,time *n* a uniform measure of time defined by the orbital motions of the planets

ephemeron /i'femə,ron/ *n, pl* **ephemera** /-rə/ *also* **ephemerons** sthg ephemeral [NL, fr Gk *ephēmeron* mayfly, fr neut of *ephēmeros*]

Ephesians /i'feezh(y)ənz/ *n pl but sing in constr* a book of the New Testament addressed to the Christians in Ephesus

ephod /'eefod/ *n* a garment worn by the Jewish high priest [Heb *ēphōdh*]

epi- /epi-/, **ep-** /ep-/ *prefix* **1** outer; external ⟨epi*dermis*⟩ **2** besides; IN ADDITION ⟨epi*logue*⟩ ⟨epi*phenomenon*⟩ **3** over; above ⟨epi*graph*⟩ [ME, fr MF & L; MF, fr L, fr Gk, fr *epi* on, at, besides, after; akin to OE *eo*fot crime]

epiblast /'epi,blast/ *n* the outer layer of an embryo at a very early stage in its development – **epiblastic** /-'blastik/ *adj*

[1]**epic** /'epik/ *adj* **1** (having the characteristics) of an epic **2a** extending beyond the usual or ordinary, esp in size or scope ⟨*his genius was ~ – TLS*⟩ **b** heroic [L *epicus*, fr Gk *epikos*, fr *epos* word, speech, poem – more at VOICE] – **epical** *adj*, **epically** *adv*

[2]**epic** *n* **1** a long narrative poem recounting the deeds of a legendary or historical hero **2** a series of events or body of legend or tradition fit to form the subject of an epic ⟨*that great environmental ~, the wreck of the Torrey Canyon – The Guardian*⟩

epicardium /,epi'kahdi·əm/ *n, pl* **epicardia** /-di·ə/ the visceral part of the pericardium that closely covers the heart [NL, fr *epi-* + Gk *kardia* heart] – **epicardial** *adj*

epicene /'epi,seen/ *adj* **1** *of a noun* having only 1 form to indicate either sex **2a** having characteristics typical of both sexes; hermaphrodite **b** effeminate **3** lacking characteristics typical of either sex; sexless [ME, fr L *epicoenus*, fr Gk *epikoinos*, fr *epi-* + *koinos* common – more at CO-] – **epicene** *n*

epicentre /'epi,sentə/ *n* **1** the part of the earth's surface directly above the place of origin of an earthquake ☞ GEOGRAPHY **2** CENTRE 2 [NL *epicentrum*, fr *epi-* + L *centrum* centre] – **epicentral** /-'sentrəl/ *adj*

,epi,conti'nental /-,konti'nentl/ *adj* lying on a continent or continental shelf

epicotyl /,epi'kotil/ *n* the portion of the axis of a plant embryo or seedling above the cotyledon [*epi-* + *cotyl*edon]

epicritic /,epi'kritik/ *adj* of or being cutaneous sensory reception marked by accurate discrimination between small degrees of sensation [Gk *epikritikos* determinative, fr *epikrinein* to decide, fr *epi-* + *krinein* to judge – more at CERTAIN]

epicure /'epikyooə/ *n* sby with sensitive and discriminating tastes, esp in food or wine [*Epicurus* †270 BC Gk philosopher] – **epicurism** *n*

Epicurean /,epikyoo'ree·ən, -'kyooəri·ən/ *n or adj* **1** (a follower) of the doctrine of the Greek philosopher Epicurus who advocated the superiority of emotional calm and intellectual pleasures **2** *often not cap* (of or suited to) an epicure – **Epicureanism** *n*

epicycle /'epi,siekl/ *n* a circle (believed in Ptolemaic astronomy to be that in which a planet moves) that itself moves round the circumference of a larger circle [ME *epicicle*, fr LL *epicyclus*, fr Gk *epikyklos*, fr *epi-* + *kyklos* circle – more at WHEEL] – **epicyclic** /-'sieklik/ *adj*

epicycloid /,epi'siekloyd/ *n* a curve traced by a point on a circle that rolls on the outside of a fixed circle

epidemic /,epi'demik/ *n or adj* (an outbreak of a disease) affecting many individuals within a population, community, or region at the same time ⟨*typhoid was ~*⟩ [adj F *épidémique*, fr MF, fr *epidemie*, n, epidemic, fr LL *epidemia*, fr Gk *epidēmia* visit, epidemic, fr *epidēmos* visiting, epidemic, fr *epi-* + *dēmos* people; n fr adj] – **epidemical** *adj*, **epidemically** *adv*, **epidemicity** /-də'misəti/ *n*

epidemiology /,epi,deemi'oləji/ *n* **1** medicine that deals with the incidence, distribution, and control of disease in a population **2** the factors controlling the presence or absence of (a cause of) disease [LL *epidemia* + ISV *-logy*] – **epidemiologic** /-ə'lojik/, **epidemiological** *adj*, **epidemiologically** *adv*, **epidemiologist** /-'oləjist/ *n*

epiderm- /epiduhm-/, **epidermo-** *comb form* epidermis ⟨epiderma*l*⟩ [*epidermis*]

epidermis /,epi'duhmis/ *n* **1a** the thin outer epithelial layer of the animal body that is derived from ectoderm and forms in vertebrates an insensitive layer over the dermis ☞ NERVE **b** any of various covering layers resembling the epidermis **2** a thin surface layer of tissue in higher plants [LL, fr Gk, fr *epi-* + *derma* skin] – **epidermal** *adj*, **epidermic** *adj*, **epidermoid** *adj*

epidiascope /,epi'die·ə,skohp/ *n* a projector for images of opaque objects or for transparencies [ISV]

epididymis /,epi'didimis/ *n, pl* **epididymides** /-,deez/ a mass of convoluted tubes at the back of the testis in which sperm is stored ☞ REPRODUCTION

[NL, fr Gk, fr *epi-* + *didymos* testicle – more at DIDYMIUM] – **epididymal** *adj*

epidural /,epi'dyooərəl/ *adj* situated on or administered outside the dura mater ⟨~ *anaesthesia*⟩ ⟨~ *structures*⟩

epifauna /,epi'fawnə/ *n* aquatic fauna living on a hard substrate (e g on a boulder in a river) [NL] – **epifaunal** *adj*

epigastric /,epi'gastrik/ *adj* lying on or over the stomach

epigeal /,epi'jee·əl/, **epigeous** /-əs/ *adj* growing, remaining, or occurring above the surface of the ground ⟨~ *germination of plants*⟩ – compare HYPOGEAL [Gk *epigaios* upon the earth, fr *epi-* + *gē* earth]

epigene /'epi,jeen/ *adj, of rock* formed or occurring on the earth's surface – compare HYPOGENE [F *épigène*, fr Gk *epigenēs* growing after, fr *epigignesthai*]

epigenesis /,epi'jenəsis/ *n* **1** development of an organism involving differentiation of an initially undifferentiated germ cell (e g a fertilized egg) **2** change in the mineral character of a rock owing to outside influences [NL] – **epigenetic** /-jə'netik/ *adj*

epiglottis /,epi'glotis/ *n* a thin plate of flexible cartilage in front of the glottis that folds back over and protects the glottis during swallowing ☞ NERVE [NL, fr Gk *epiglōttis*, fr *epi-* + *glōttis* glottis] – **epiglottal** *also* **epiglottic** *adj*

epigone /'epi,gohn/ *n* an esp inferior follower or imitator [G, fr L *epigonus* successor, fr Gk *epigonos*, fr *epigignesthai* to be born after, fr *epi-* + *gignesthai* to be born – more at KIN] – **epigonic** /-'gonik/, **epigonous** /i'pigənəs/ *adj*, **epigonism** /i'pigəniz(ə)m/ *n*

epigram /'epi,gram/ *n* **1** a short often satirical poem **2** a neat, witty, and often paradoxical remark or saying [ME *epigrame*, fr L *epigrammat-*, *epigramma*, fr Gk, fr *epigraphein* to write on, inscribe, fr *epi-* + *graphein* to write – more at CARVE] – **epigrammatic** /-grə'matik/, **epigrammatical** *adj*, **epigrammatically** *adv*, **epigrammatism** /-'gramətiz(ə)m/ *n*, **epigrammatist** *n*, **epigrammatize** *vb*

epigraph /'epi,grahf, -,graf/ *n* **1** an engraved inscription **2** a quotation at the beginning of a book, chapter, etc suggesting its theme [Gk *epigraphē*, fr *epigraphein*]

epigraphic /,epi'grafik/ *also* **epigraphical** /-kl/ *adj* of epigraphs or epigraphy – **epigraphically** *adv*

epigraphy /i'pigrəfi/ *n* **1** epigraphs collectively **2** the study of esp ancient inscriptions – **epigrapher** *n*, **epigraphist** *n*

epigynous /i'pijinəs/ *adj* **1** (having floral organs) attached to the surface of the ovary and appearing to grow from the top of it – compare HYPOGYNOUS, PERIGYNOUS **2** having epigynous floral organs – **epigyny** *n*

epilation /,epi'laysh(ə)n/ *n* the loss or removal of hair [F *épilation*, fr *épiler* to remove hair, fr *é-* e- + L *pilus* hair – more at [1]PILE]

epilepsy /'epi,lepsi/ *n* any of various disorders marked by disturbed electrical rhythms of the brain and spinal chord and typically manifested by convulsive attacks often with clouding of consciousness [MF *epilepsie*, fr LL *epilepsia*, fr Gk *epilēpsia*, fr *epilambanein* to seize, fr *epi-* + *lambanein* to take, seize – more at LATCH]

epilept-, **epilepti-**, **epilepto-** /epilept-/ *comb form* epilepsy ⟨epileptogenic⟩ [Gk *epilēpt-*, fr *epilēptos* seized by epilepsy, fr *epilambanein*]

epileptic /,epi'leptik/ *adj* of, affected with, or having the characteristics of epilepsy – **epileptic** *n*, **epileptically** *adv*

epilimnion /,epi'limnion, -ni·ən/ *n* the water above the thermocline of a lake – compare HYPOLIMNION [NL, fr *epi-* + Gk *limnion*, dim. of *limnē* marshy lake]

epilogue /'epi,log/ *n* **1** a concluding section of a literary or dramatic work that comments on or summarizes the main action or plot **2** a speech or poem addressed to the audience by an actor at the end of a play [ME *epiloge*, fr MF *epilogue*, fr L *epilogus*, fr Gk *epilogos*, fr *epilegein* to say in addition, fr *epi-* + *legein* to say – more at LEGEND]

epimer /'epimə/ *n* either of the isomers of a sugar (derivative) that differ in arrangement only in the last carbon atom of a chain that is attached to 4 different groups [*epi-* + isomer] – **epimeric** /-'merik/ *adj*

epinephrine /,epi'nefrin, i'pinəfrin, -freen/ *also* **epinephrin** /-frin/ *n, chiefly NAm* adrenalin [ISV *epi-* + Gk *nephros* kidney – more at NEPHRITIS]

epiphany /i'pifəni/ *n* **1** *cap* (January 6 observed as a church festival in commemoration of) the coming of the Magi **2** a usu sudden manifestation or perception of the essential nature or meaning of sthg [ME *epiphanie*, fr MF, fr LL *epiphania*, fr LGk, pl, prob alter. of Gk *epiphaneia* appearance, manifestation, fr *epiphainein* to manifest, fr *phainein* to show – more at FANCY] – **epiphanic** /,epi'fanik/ *adj*

epiphenomenalism /,epifə'nominl,iz(ə)m/ *n* the theory that mental processes are epiphenomena of brain processes

epiphenomenon /,epifə'nominən/ *n, pl* **epiphenomena** /-nə/ a secondary phenomenon accompanying another and caused by it – **epiphenomenal** *adj*, **epiphenomenally** *adv*

epiphysis /i'pifisis/ *n, pl* **epiphyses** /-,seez/ **1** an end of a long bone **2** PINEAL GLAND [NL, fr Gk, growth, fr *epiphyesthai* to grow on, fr *epi-* + *phyesthai* to grow, passive of *phyein* to bring forth – more at BE] – **epiphyseal** /,epi'fizi·əl/ *adj*

epiphyte /'epi,fiet/ *n* a plant that derives its moisture and nutrients from the air and rain and grows on another plant ☞ PLANT – **epiphytic** /-'fitik/ *adj*, **epiphytically** *adv*

episcopacy /i'piskəpəsi/ *n* **1** government of the church by bishops or by a hierarchy **2** an episcopate

episcopal /i'piskəpl/ *adj* **1** of a bishop **2** of, having, or constituting government by bishops **3** *cap* Anglican; *esp* of an Anglican church that is not established (e g in the USA or Scotland) [ME, fr LL *episcopalis*, fr *episcopus* bishop – more at BISHOP] – **episcopally** *adv*, **Episcopalian** /-'payli·ən, -lyən/ *n or adj*, **Episcopalianism** *n*

episcopate /i'piskəpət, -,payt/ *n* **1** the rank, office, or term of a bishop **2** a (national) body of bishops

episcope /'epi,skohp/ *n* a projector for images of opaque objects (e g photographs) [ISV *epi-* + *-scope*]

episode /'episohd/ *n* **1a** the part of an ancient Greek tragedy between 2 choric songs **b** a developed situation or incident that is integral to but separable from a continuous narrative (e g a play or novel) **c** the part of a serial presented at 1 performance **2** an event that is distinctive and separate although part of a larger series (e g in history or in sby's life) [Gk *epeisodion*, fr neut of *epeisodios* coming in besides, fr *epi-* + *eisodios* coming in, fr *eis* into (akin to Gk *en* in) + *hodos* road, journey – more at IN, CEDE]

episodic /,epi'sodik/ *also* **episodical** /-kl/ *adj* **1** made up of separate, esp loosely connected, episodes ⟨*an ~ narrative*⟩ **2** of or limited in duration or significance to a particular episode **3** occasional, sporadic – **episodically** *adv*

epistasis /i'pistəsis/ *n, pl* **epistases** /-,seez/ suppression of the effect of a gene by another gene that is not an allele of the first gene [NL, fr Gk, act of stopping, fr *ephistanai* to stop, fr *epi-* + *histanai* to cause to stand – more at STAND] – **epistatic** /,epi'statik/ *adj*

epistaxis /,epi'staksis/ *n, pl* **epistaxes** /-,seez/ a nosebleed [NL, fr Gk, fr *epistazein* to drip on, to bleed at the nose again, fr *epi-* + *stazein* to drip – more at STAGNATE]

epistemic /,epi'steemik/ *adj* of knowledge; cognitive – **epistemically** *adv*

epistemology /i,pistə'moləji/ *n* inquiry into the nature and grounds of experience, belief, and knowledge [Gk *epistēmē* knowledge, fr *epistanai* to understand, know, fr *epi-* + *histanai* to cause to stand – more at STAND] – **epistemological** /-mə'lojikl/ *adj*, **epistemologically** *adv*, **epistemologist** /-'moləjist/ *n*

epistle /i'pisl/ *n* **1** *cap* (a liturgical reading from) any of the letters (e g of St Paul) adopted as books of the New Testament **2** an esp formal letter [ME, letter, Epistle, fr OF, fr L *epistula, epistola* letter, fr Gk *epistolē* message, letter, fr *epistellein* to send to, fr *epi-* + *stellein* to send – more at [1]STALL]

e'pistle ,side *n, often cap E* the right side of an altar or chancel as one faces it [fr the custom of reading the Epistle from this side]

epistolary /i'pistəl(ə)ri/ *adj* **1** of or suitable to a letter **2** carried on by or in the form of letters ⟨*an endless sequence of ~ love affairs – TLS*⟩ **3** written in the form of a series of letters ⟨*~ novel*⟩

epistrophe /i'pistrəfi/ *n* repetition of the same word or expression at the end of a series of phrases, sentences, etc for rhetorical effect – compare ANAPHORA [Gk *epistrophē*, lit., turning about, fr *epi-* + *strophē* turning – more at STROPHE]

epitaph /'epi,tahf, -taf/ *n* **1** a commemorative inscription on a tombstone or monument **2** a brief statement commemorating a deceased person or past event [ME *epitaphe*, fr MF, fr ML *epitaphium*, fr L, funeral oration, fr Gk *epitaphion*, fr *epi-* + *taphos* tomb, funeral; akin to Gk *thaptein* to bury, Arm *damban* grave]

epitaxy /'epi,taksi/ *n* the oriented growth of one crystalline substance on another [*epi-* + *-taxy* (fr Gk *-taxia* -taxis)] – **epitaxial** /-'taksi·əl/ *adj*, **epitaxially** *adv*

epithalamium /,epithə'laymi·əm, -myəm/ *n, pl* **epithalamiums, epithalamia** /-mi·ə, -myə/ a song or poem in celebration of a bride and bridegroom [L & Gk; L *epithalamium*, fr Gk *epithalamion*, fr *epi-* + *thalamos* room, bridal chamber]

epitheli-, epithelio- /epitheeli-/ *comb form* epithelium [NL *epithelium*]

epithelium /,epi'theeli·əm, -lyəm/ *n, pl* **epithelia** /-li·ə, -lyə/ **1** a membranous cellular tissue that covers a free surface or lines a tube or cavity of an animal body and serves esp to enclose and protect the other parts of the body, to produce secretions and excretions, and to function in assimilation **2** a usu thin layer of cells that lines a cavity or tube of a plant [NL, fr *epi-* + Gk *thēlē* nipple – more at FEMININE] – **epithelial** *adj*, **epithelioid** /-li,oyd/ *adj*

epithet /'epithet/ *n* **1** a descriptive word or phrase accompanying or occurring in place of the name of a person or thing **2** a disparaging or abusive word or phrase [L *epitheton*, fr Gk, fr neut of *epithetos* added, fr *epitithenai* to put on, add, fr *epi-* + *tithenai* to put – more at DO] – **epithetic** /-'thetik/, **epithetical** *adj*

epitome /i'pitəmi/ *n* **1** a condensed account or summary, esp of a literary work **2** a typical or ideal example; an embodiment ⟨*the British monarchy itself is the ~ of tradition*⟩ [L, fr Gk *epitomē*, fr *epitemnein* to cut short, fr *epi-* + *temnein* to cut – more at TOME]

epitom·ize, -ise /i'pitəmiez/ *vt* to make or serve as an epitome of

epizootic /,epizoh'otik/ *n or adj* (a disease temporarily) affecting many animals of 1 kind at the same time – **epizootically** *adv*

epoch /'eepok/ *n* **1** a date or time selected as a point of reference (e g in astronomy) **2** a memorable event or date; *esp* TURNING POINT **3a** an extended period of time, usu characterized by a distinctive development or by a memorable series of events **b** a division of geological time less than a period and greater than an age [ML *epocha*, fr Gk *epochē* cessation, fixed point, fr *epechein* to pause, hold back, fr *epi-* + *echein* to hold – more at SCHEME] – **epochal** /'epokl/ *adj*, **epochally** *adv*

'epoch-,making *adj* uniquely or highly significant ⟨*the steam engine was an ~ invention*⟩

epode /'epohd/ *n* **1** a lyric poem in which a long line is followed by a shorter one **2** the last part of a Greek ode following the strophe and the antistrophe [L *epodos*, fr Gk *epōidos*, fr *epōidos* sung or said after, fr *epi-* + *aidein* to sing – more at ODE]

eponym /'epoh,nim, 'epə-/ *n* the person after whom sthg is (believed to be) named [Gk *epōnymos*, fr *epōnymos* eponymous, fr *epi-* + *onyma* name – more at NAME] – **eponymic** /-'nimik/ *adj*, **eponymous** /i'ponimәs/ *adj*

epos /'epos/ *n* **1** a body of poems on an epic theme that are not formally united **2** an epic poem [Gk, word, epic poem]

epoxide /i'poksied/ *n* an epoxy compound

epoxid·ize, -ise /i'poksi,diez/ *vt* to convert into an epoxy compound ⟨*~d oils*⟩

[1]**epoxy** /i'poksi/ *adj* **1** containing a 3-membered ring consisting of 1 oxygen and 2 carbon atoms **2** of an epoxy compound

[2]**epoxy** *vt* **epoxied, epoxyed** to glue with epoxy resin

epoxy resin *n* a flexible resin used esp in coatings and adhesives

epsilon /'epsilon/ *n* the 5th letter of the Greek alphabet [Gk *e psilon*, lit., simple e]

Epsom salts /'eps(ə)m/ *n pl but sing or pl in constr* hydrated magnesium sulphate used as a purgative [*Epsom*, town in Surrey, England]

equable /'ekwəbl/ *adj* uniform, even; *esp* free from extremes or sudden changes ⟨*an ~ temperament*⟩ ⟨*an ~ climate*⟩ [L *aequabilis*, fr *aequare* to make level or equal, fr *aequus*] – **equably** *adv*, **equability** /-'biləti/ *n*

1equal /'eekwəl/ *adj* **1a** of the same quantity, amount, or number as another ☞ SYMBOL **b** identical in value; equivalent **2a** like in quality, nature, or status **b** like for each member of a group, class, or society ⟨*provide ~ employment opportunities*⟩ ⟨*~ rights*⟩ **3** evenly balanced or matched ⟨*the 2 opponents were ~*⟩ **4** capable of meeting the requirements of sthg (e g a situation or task) – + *to* ⟨*he is quite ~ to the job*⟩ [ME, fr L *aequalis*, fr *aequus* level, equal]

2equal *n* sby or sthg equal ⟨*she is anyone's ~*⟩

3equal *vt* **-ll-** (*NAm* **-l-**, **-ll-**) **1** to be equal to; *esp* to be identical in value to **2** to make or produce sthg equal to

equalitarian /i,kwoli'teəri·ən/ *n or adj* (an) egalitarian – **equalitarianism** *n*

equality /i'kwoləti/ *n* the quality or state of being equal

equal·ize, -ise /'eekwə,liez/ *vt* **1** to make equal **2** to make uniform; *esp* to distribute evenly or uniformly *~ vi chiefly Br* to make sthg equal; *esp* to bring the scores level (e g in a football match) – **equalizer** *n*, **equalization** /-'zaysh(ə)n/ *n*

equally /'eekwəli/ *adv* **1** in an equal or uniform manner; evenly **2** to an equal degree; alike ⟨*respected ~ by young and old*⟩

'equals ,sign *also* **'equal ,sign** *n* a sign = indicating mathematical or logical equivalence ☞ SYMBOL

equal temperament *n* the division of the musical octave into 12 equal semitones

equanimity /,eekwə'niməti, ,ekwə-/ *n* evenness of mind or temper, esp under stress [L *aequanimitas*, fr *aequo animo* with even mind]

equate /i'kwayt/ *vt* **1** to make or set equal **2** to treat, represent, or regard as equal, equivalent, or comparable ⟨~s *dissension with disloyalty*⟩ [ME *equaten*, fr L *aequatus*, pp of *aequare*]

equation /i'kwayzh(ə)n; *sense* ' i'kwaysh(ə)n/ *n* **1** equating or being equated **2** a statement of the equality of 2 mathematical expressions – **equational** *adj*, **equationally** *adv*

equator /i'kwaytə/ *n* **1** the great circle of the celestial sphere whose plane is perpendicular to the rotational axis of the earth **2** GREAT CIRCLE; *specif* the one that is equidistant from the 2 poles of the earth and divides the earth's surface into the northern and southern hemispheres **3** a circle or circular band dividing the surface of a body into 2 usu equal and symmetrical parts ⟨*the ~ of a dividing cell*⟩ [ME, fr ML *aequator*, lit., equalizer, fr L *aequatus*; fr its containing the equinoxes] – **equatorward** /-wood/ *adj or adv*, **equatorwards** /-woodz/ *adv*

equatorial /,ekwə'tawri·əl/ *adj* **1a** of, at, or in the plane of the (earth's) equator **b** *of the climate* characterized by consistently high temperatures and rainfall throughout the year **2** being or having a support (e g for a telescope) that includes 2 axles at right angles to each other and allows a celestial body to be kept in view as the earth rotates

equerry /i'kweri, 'ekwəri/ *n* **1** an officer of a prince or noble charged with the care of horses **2** an officer of the British royal household in personal attendance on a member of the royal family [obs *escuirie*, *equerry* (stable), fr MF *escuirie* office of a squire, stable, fr *escuier*, *esquier* squire – more at ESQUIRE]

1equestrian /i'kwestri·ən/ *adj* **1a** of or featuring horses, horsemen, or horsemanship **b** representing a person on horseback **2** (composed) of knights [L *equestr-*, *equester* of a horseman, fr *eques* horseman, fr *equus* horse – more at EQUINE] – **equestrianism** *n*

2equestrian *n* sby who rides or performs on horseback

equi- *comb form* equal ⟨equi*poise*⟩; equally ⟨equi*probable*⟩ [ME, fr MF, fr L *aequi-*, fr *aequus* equal]

equiangular /,eekwi'ang·gyoolə, ,ekwi-/ *adj* having all or corresponding angles equal ⟨*an ~ triangle*⟩ ⟨*~ polygons*⟩

equidistant /,eekwi'dist(ə)nt, ,ekwi-/ *adj* equally distant [MF or LL; MF, fr LL *aequidistant-*, *aequidistans*, fr L *aequi-* + *distant-*, *distans*, prp of *distare* to stand apart] – **equidistantly** *adv*, **equidistance** *n*

equilateral /,eekwi'lat(ə)rəl, ,ekwi-/ *adj* having all sides equal ⟨*~ triangle*⟩ ☞ MATHEMATICS [LL *aequilateralis*, fr L *aequi-* + *later-*, *latus* side]

equilibrate /,eekwi'liebrayt, ,ekwi-, -'lib-, i'kwili,brayt/ *vt* to bring into or keep in equilibrium; balance *~ vi* to bring about, come to, or be in equilibrium – **equilibration** /-'braysh(ə)n/ *n*, **equilibrator** /i'kwili-/ *n*, **equilibratory** /-t(ə)ri/ *adj*

equilibrium /,eekwi'libri·əm, ,ekwi-/ *n, pl* **equilibriums, equilibria** /-bri·ə/ **1** a state of balance between opposing forces, actions, or processes (e g in a reversible chemical reaction) **2a** a state of adjustment between opposing or divergent influences or elements **b** a state of intellectual or emotional balance **3** the normal state of the animal body in respect to its environment that involves adjustment to changing conditions [L *aequilibrium*, fr *aequilibris* being in equilibrium, fr *aequi-* + *libra* weight, balance]

equine /'ekwien/ *adj* of or resembling the horse (family) [L *equinus*, fr *equus* horse; akin to OE *eoh* horse, Gk *hippos*] – **equine** *n*, **equinely** *adv*

1equinoctial /,eekwi'noksh(ə)l, ,ekwi-/ *adj* **1** relating to (the time when the sun passes) an equinox **2** relating to the regions or climate of the equinoctial line or equator

2equinoctial, equinoctial circle *n* EQUATOR 1

equinox /'ekwi,noks/ *n* **1** either of the 2 times each year that occur about March 21st and September 23rd when the sun crosses the equator and day and night are of equal length everywhere on earth **2** either of the 2 points on the celestial sphere where the celestial equator intersects the ecliptic [ME, fr MF or ML; MF *equinoxe*, fr ML *equinoxium*, alter. of L *aequinoctium*, fr *aequi-* equi- + *noct-*, *nox* night – more at NIGHT]

equip /i'kwip/ *vt* **-pp-** **1** to make ready for service, action, or use; provide with appropriate supplies **2** to dress, array [MF *equiper*, of Gmc origin; akin to OE *scip* ship]

equipage /'ekwipij/ *n* **1** material or articles used in equipment **2a** an etui **b** trappings **3** a horse-drawn carriage (with its servants)

equipment /i'kwipmənt/ *n* **1** the set of articles, apparatus, or physical resources serving to equip a person, thing, enterprise, expedition, etc **2** mental or emotional resources [EQUIP + -MENT]

equipoise /'ekwi,poyz, 'eekwi-/ *n* **1** a state of equilibrium **2** a counterbalance

equipollent /,eekwi'polənt, ,ekwi-/ *n or adj* (sthg

that is) equal in force, power, validity, or effect – fml [ME, fr MF, fr L *aequipollent-, aequipollens,* fr *aequi-* equi- + *pollent-, pollens,* prp of *pollēre* to be able] – **equipollence** *n,* **equipollency** *n*

equipotential /,eekwipə'tensh(ə)l, ,ekwi-/ *adj* of uniform potential (throughout) ⟨~ *points*⟩ ⟨*an* ~ *surface*⟩ – **equipotential** *n*

equiprobable /,eekwi'probəbl, ,ekwi-/ *adj* having the same degree of logical or mathematical probability ⟨~ *alternatives*⟩

equitable /'ekwitəbl/ *adj* **1** fair and just **2** valid in equity as distinguished from law [EQUITY + -ABLE] – **equitableness** *n,* **equitably** *adv,* **equitability** /-'biləti/ *n*

equitation /,ekwi'taysh(ə)n/ *n* the act or art of riding on horseback [MF, fr L *equitation-, equitatio,* fr *equitatus,* pp of *equitare* to ride on horseback, fr *equit-, eques* horseman, fr *equus* horse – more at EQUINE]

equity /'ekwiti/ *n* **1** justice according to natural law or right; fairness **2** a system of justice originally developed in the Chancery courts on the basis of conscience and fairness to supplement or override the more rigid common law **3a** a right, claim, or interest existing or valid in equity **b** the money value of a property or of an interest in a property in excess of claims against it **4** a share that does not bear fixed interest – usu pl [ME *equite,* fr MF *equité,* fr L *aequitat-, aequitas,* fr *aequus* equal, fair]

equivalent /i'kwivəl(ə)nt/ *adj* **1** equal in force, amount, or value **2** corresponding or virtually identical, esp in effect, function, or meaning **3** having the same chemical combining capacity ⟨~ *quantities of 2 elements*⟩ [ME, fr MF or LL; MF, fr LL *aequivalent-, aequivalens,* prp of *aequivalēre* to have equal power, fr L *aequi-* + *valēre* to be strong – more at WIELD] – **equivalence** *also* **equivalency** *n,* **equivalent** *n,* **equivalently** *adv*

equivalent weight *n* the atomic or molecular weight of a substance divided by its valency

equivocal /i'kwivəkl/ *adj* **1** subject to 2 or more interpretations; ambiguous ⟨~ *evidence*⟩ **2** questionable, suspicious [LL *aequivocus,* fr *aequi-* equi- + *voc-, vox* voice – more at VOICE] – **equivocally** *adv,* **equivocalness** *n,* **equivocality** /-'kaləti/ *n*

equivocate /i'kwivə,kayt/ *vi* to use equivocal language, esp with intent to deceive or avoid committing oneself – **equivocation** /-'kaysh(ə)n/ *n,* **equivocator** *n*

equivoque *also* **equivoke** /'ekwi,vohk, 'eekwi-/ *n* an equivocal word or phrase; *specif* a pun [F *équivoque,* fr *équivoque* equivocal, fr LL *aequivocus*]

er, ur /uh/ *interj* – used to express hesitation or doubt

¹-er /-ə/ *suffix* (→ *adj or adv*) – used to form the comparative degree of adjectives and adverbs of 1 syllable, and of some adjectives and adverbs of 2 or more syllables, that end in a consonant ⟨*hott*er⟩, a vowel other than *e,* or a final *y* that changes to *i* ⟨*dri*er⟩; compare ¹-R [ME *-er, -ere, -re,* fr OE *-ra* (in adjectives), *-or* (in adverbs); akin to OHG *-iro,* adj compar suffix, L *-ior,* Gk *-iōn*]

²-er, -ar, -ier, -r, -yer *suffix* **1** (*n* → *n*) **a** one engaged in the occupation of ⟨*furr*ier⟩ ⟨*law*yer⟩ ⟨*geograph*er⟩ **b** one belonging to or associated with ⟨*sixth-form*er⟩ **c** native of; resident of ⟨*cottag*er⟩ ⟨*London*er⟩ **d** sthg that has ⟨*three-wheel*er⟩ ⟨*four-post*er⟩ **2** (*vb* → *n*) **a** one who or that which does or performs (a specified action) ⟨*report*er⟩ ⟨*eye-open*er⟩ – sometimes added to both elements of a compound ⟨*build*er-*upp*er⟩ **b** sthg that is a suitable object of (a specified action) ⟨*broil*er⟩ ⟨*cook*er⟩ **3** (*adj* → *n*) sby or sthg that is ⟨*foreign*er⟩ ***USE*** *-yer* in a few words after *w, -ier* in a few words after other letters, *-r* in words after *e,* ***otherwise*** *-er* [ME *-er, -ere, -are, -ier, -iere;* partly fr OE *-ere* (akin to OHG *-āri;* both fr a prehistoric Gmc suffix borrowed fr L *-arius*); partly fr OF *-ier, -iere,* fr L *-arius, -aria, -arium* -ary; partly fr MF *-ere,* fr L *-ator* -or – more at ¹-ARY, ¹-OR]

era /'iərə/ *n* **1** a system of chronological notation computed from a given date as a basis ⟨*Christian* ~⟩ **2** EPOCH 2 **3a** a usu historical period set off or typified by some distinctive figure or characteristic feature ⟨*the* ~ *of space flight*⟩ **b** any of the 5 major divisions of geological time ⟨*Palaeozoic* ~⟩ ☞ EVOLUTION [LL *aera,* fr L, counters, pl of *aer-, aes* copper, money – more at ORE]

eradicate /i'radi,kayt/ *vt* **1** to pull up by the roots **2** to eliminate; DO AWAY WITH ⟨~ *ignorance by better teaching*⟩ [L *eradicatus,* pp of *eradicare,* fr *e-* + *radic-, radix* root – more at ¹ROOT] – **eradicator** *n,* **eradicable** *adj,* **eradication** /-'kaysh(ə)n/ *n,* **eradicative** /-,kaytiv/ *adj,*

erase /i'rayz/ *vt* **1a** to obliterate or rub out (e g written, painted, or engraved letters) **b** to remove (recorded matter) from a magnetic tape or wire **c** to delete from a computer storage device **2** to remove from existence or memory as if by erasing ~ *vi* to yield to being erased ⟨*pencil* ~s *easily*⟩ [L *erasus,* pp of *eradere,* fr *e-* + *radere* to scratch, scrape – more at RAT] – **erasability** /-zə'biləti/ *n,* **erasable** *adj,* **erasure** /i'rayzhə/ *n*

eraser /i'rayzə/ *n* ¹RUBBER 1b [ERASE + ²-ER]

Erastian /i'rasti·ən, -tyən/ *adj* of, characterized by, or advocating the doctrine of ecclesiastical subordination to the secular powers [Thomas *Erastus* †1583 G-Swiss physician & Zwinglian theologian] – **Erastian** *n,* **Erastianism** *n*

erbium /'uhbi·əm/ *n* a metallic element of the rare-earth group ☞ PERIODIC TABLE [NL, fr *Ytterby,* town in Sweden]

¹ere /eə/ *prep* ²BEFORE 2 – poetic [ME *er,* fr OE *ǣr,* fr *ǣr,* adv, early, soon; akin to OHG *ēr* earlier, Gk *ēri* early]

²ere *conj* before – poetic

¹erect /i'rekt/ *adj* **1a** vertical in position; upright **b** standing up or out from the body ⟨~ *hairs*⟩ **c** characterized by firm or rigid straightness (e g in bodily posture) ⟨*an* ~ *bearing*⟩ **2** in a state of physiological erection [ME, fr L *erectus,* pp of *erigere* to erect, fr *e-* + *regere* to lead straight, guide – more at ¹RIGHT] – **erectly** *adv,* **erectness** *n*

²erect *vt* **1a** to put up by the fitting together of materials or parts; build **b** to fix in an upright position **2** to elevate in status ⟨~s *a few odd notions into a philosophy*⟩ **3** to establish; SET UP 6a **4** to construct (e g a perpendicular) on a given base – **erectable** *adj,* **erector** *n*

erectile /i'rektiel/ *adj* **1** capable of being raised to an erect position; *esp, of animal tissue* capable of becoming swollen with blood to bring about the erection of a body part **2** of or involving the erection of the penis – **erectility** /-'tiləti/ *n*

erection /i'reksh(ə)n/ *n* **1** (an occurrence in the penis or clitoris of) the dilation with blood and resulting firmness of a previously flaccid body part **2** sthg erected [[2]ERECT + -ION]

'E ,region *n* the part of the ionosphere occurring between about 65 and 145km (about 40 and 90mi) above the earth's surface and containing the E layer

eremite /'erəmiet/ *n* a usu Christian hermit or recluse [ME – more at HERMIT] – **eremitic** /,erə'mitik/, **eremitical** *adj*

erepsin /i'repsin/ *n* a mixture of protein-digesting enzymes present in the intestinal juice [ISV *er-* (prob fr L *eripere* to sweep away, fr *e-* + *rapere* to sweep away) + *pepsin* – more at RAPID]

erethism /'erithiz(ə)m/ *n* abnormal responsiveness, esp of human organs and physiological systems, to stimulation [F *éréthisme*, fr Gk *erethismos* irritation, fr *erethizein* to irritate; akin to Gk *ornynai* to rouse – more at RISE] – **erethismic** /-'thizmik/ *adj*

erg /uhg/ *n* the cgs unit of work or energy; 10 Q7J [Gk *ergon* work – more at WORK]

erg- /uhg-/, **ergo-** *comb form* work ⟨ergo*nomics*⟩ [Gk, fr *ergon*]

ergo /'uhgoh/ *adv* therefore, hence [L, fr OL, because of, fr (assumed) OL *e rogo* from the direction (of)]

ergo- *comb form* ergot ⟨ergo*sterol*⟩ [F, fr *ergot*]

ergometer /uh'gomitə/ *n* an apparatus for measuring the work performed by a group of muscles – **ergometric** /,uhgə'metrik/ *adj*

ergonomics /,uhgə'nomiks/ *n pl but sing or pl in constr* a science concerned with the relationship between human beings, the machines they use, and the working environment [*erg-* + *economics*] – **ergonomic** *adj*, **ergonomist** /uh'gonəmist/ *n*

ergosterol /uh'gostərol/ *n* a steroid found esp in yeast, moulds, and ergot that is converted into vitamin D_2 by ultraviolet light [ISV]

ergot /'uhgət, -got/ *n* **1** (a fungus bearing) a black or dark purple club-shaped sclerotium that develops in place of the seed of a grass (e g rye) **2** a disease of rye and other cereals caused by an ergot fungus **3** the dried sclerotia of an ergot fungus containing ergotamine and other alkaloids used medicinally (e g to treat migraine) [F, lit., cock's spur] – **ergotic** /uh'gotik/ *adj*

ergotamine /uh'gotəmeen/ *n* an alkaloid obtained from ergot that has the pharmacological actions of ergot and is used esp in treating migraine [ISV]

ergotism /'uhgə,tiz(ə)m/ *n* an abnormal condition produced by eating grain (products) or grasses infected with ergot fungus and characterized by hallucinations and gangrene of the fingers and toes

erica /'erikə/ *n* any of a large genus of low many-branched evergreen shrubs of the heath family [NL, genus name, fr L *erice* heather, fr Gk *ereikē*] – **ericaceous** /-'kayshəs/ *adj*

Erie /'iəree/ *n* (a member or the Iroquian language of) a N American Indian people of the Lake Erie region

Erin /'erin/ *n* Ireland – chiefly poetic [OIr *Ērinn*, dat of *Ēriu* Ireland]

[1]**eristic** /e'ristik/ *also* **eristical** /-kl/ *adj* employing subtle and usu specious argument – fml [Gk *eristikos* fond of wrangling, fr *erizein* to wrangle, fr *eris* strife] – **eristically** *adv*

[2]**eristic** *n* (sby who practises) the art of disputation and polemics – fml

erk /uhk/ *n, Br* a person holding the lowest rank in the air force or navy – slang [alter. of *airc*, short for *aircraftman*]

Erlenmeyer flask /'eələn,mie·ə/ *n* a flat-bottomed conical laboratory flask [Emil *Erlenmeyer* †1909 G chemist]

ermine /'uhmin/ *n, pl* **ermines**, *esp collectively* **ermine** (the winter fur of) a stoat or related weasel that has a white winter coat usu with black on the tail [ME, fr OF, of Gmc origin; akin to OHG *harmo* weasel; akin to Lith *šarmuo* weasel]

Ernie /'uhni/ *n* an electronic device used to draw the prizewinning numbers of Premium Bonds [*E*lectronic *r*andom *n*umber *i*ndicator *e*quipment]

erode /i'rohd/ *vt* **1a** to diminish or destroy by degrees **b** to eat into or away by slow destruction of substance; corrode **c** to wear away by the action of water, wind, glacial ice, etc ☞ GEOGRAPHY **2** to produce or form by eroding ~ *vi* to undergo erosion [L *erodere* to eat away, fr *e-* + *rodere* to gnaw – more at RAT] – **erodible** *adj*

erogenous /i'rojənəs/ *also* **erogenic** /,erə'jenik/ *adj* of or producing sexual excitement (when stimulated) ⟨~ *zones*⟩ [Gk *erōs* + E *-genous, -genic*]

Eros /'iəros, 'eros/ *n* **1** all the pleasure-directed life instincts; the libido – compare THANATOS **2** sexual love [Gk *Erōs*, god of love, fr *erōs* love; akin to Gk *erasthai* to love, desire]

erosion /i'rohzh(ə)n/ *n* (an instance or product of) eroding or being eroded [MF, fr L *erosion-, erosio*, fr *erosus*, pp of *erodere*] – **erosional** *adj*, **erosionally** *adv*, **erosive** /-siv/ *adj*

erotic /i'rotik/ *adj* **1** of, concerned with, or tending to arouse sexual desire ⟨~ *art*⟩ **2** strongly affected by sexual desire [Gk *erōtikos*, fr *erōt-, erōs*] – **erotic** *n*, **erotical** *adj*, **erotically** *adv*, **eroticize** /-siez/ *vt*

erotica /i'rotikə/ *n pl but sing or pl in constr* literature or art with an erotic theme or quality [NL, fr Gk *erōtika*, neut pl of *erōtikos*]

eroticism /i'rotə,siz(ə)m/ *n* **1** an erotic theme, quality, or character **2** EROTISM 1 **3** (insistent) sexual impulse or desire – **eroticist** *n*

erotism /'erə,tiz(ə)m/ *n* **1** sexual excitement or arousal **2** EROTICISM 1, 3 [Gk *erōt-, erōs* + E *-ism*]

erotogenic /i,rotə'jenik, i,roh-/ *adj* erogenous

erotomania /i,rotə'maynyə, -roh-/ *n* (abnormally) excessive sexual desire – **erotomaniac** *n*

err /uh/ *vi* **1a** to make a mistake **b** to do wrong; sin **2** to be inaccurate or incorrect [ME *erren*, fr OF *errer*, fr L *errare*; akin to OE *ierre* wandering, angry, ON *rās* race – more at RACE]

errand /'erənd/ *n* (the object or purpose of) a short trip taken to attend to some business, often for another [ME *erend* message, business, fr OE *ǣrend*; akin to OHG *ārunti* message]

errant /'erənt/ *adj* **1** (given to) travelling, esp in search of adventure **2** going astray ⟨*an* ~ *calf*⟩; *esp* doing wrong; erring ⟨*an* ~ *child*⟩ [ME *erraunt*, fr MF *errant*, prp of *errer* to err & *errer* to travel, fr ML *iterare*, fr L *iter* road, journey – more at ITINERANT] – **errant** *n*, **errantly** *adv*

errantry /'erəntri/ *n* knight-errantry

errata /i'rahtə/ *n* (a page showing) a list of corrections [L, pl of *erratum*]

erratic /i'ratik/ *adj* **1** having no fixed course ⟨*an* ~ *comet*⟩ **2** *esp of a boulder* transported from an original resting place, esp by a glacier ☞ GEOGRA-

PHY **3** characterized by lack of consistency, regularity, or uniformity, esp in behaviour [ME, fr MF or L; MF *erratique*, fr L *erraticus*, fr *erratus*, pp of *errare*] – **erratic** *n*, **erratically** *adv*, **erraticism** /-,siz(ə)m/ *n*

erratum /i'rahtəm/ *n, pl* **errata** /-tə/ a corrigendum [L, fr neut of *erratus*]

erroneous /i'rohnyəs, -ni·əs/ *adj* containing or characterized by error; incorrect ⟨~ *assumptions*⟩ [ME, fr L *erroneus*, fr *erron-, erro* wanderer, fr *errare*] – **erroneously** *adv*, **erroneousness** *n*

error /'erə/ *n* **1a** a mistake or inaccuracy in speech, opinion, or action ⟨*a typing* ~⟩ **b** the state of being wrong in behaviour or beliefs ⟨*he realized the* ~ *of his ways*⟩ **c** an act that fails to achieve what was intended **2** the difference between an observed or calculated value and a true value [ME *errour*, fr OF, fr L *error*, fr *errare*] – **errorless** *adj* – **in error** by mistake

ersatz /'eəzatz, 'uh-/ *adj* being a usu artificial and inferior substitute; an imitation [G *ersatz-*, fr *ersatz*, n, substitute] – **ersatz** *n*

Erse /uhs/ *n* Scottish Gaelic – no longer used technically ☞ LANGUAGE [ME (Sc) *Erisch*, adj, Irish, alter. of *Irish*] – **Erse** *adj*

erstwhile /'uhst,wiel/ *adj* former, previous ⟨*his* ~ *students*⟩ [arch *erst* (formerly; fr ME *erest* earliest, first, fr OE *ǣrest*, superl of *ǣr* early) + *while*] – **erstwhile** *adv*

e,rucic 'acid /i'roohsik/ *n* a fatty acid found in the form of glycerides, esp in rapeseed oil [NL *Eruca*, genus of herbs, fr L, caterpillar, rocket plant]

eructation /i,ruk'taysh(ə)n, ,eeruk-/ *n* belching [L *eructation-, eructatio*, fr *eructatus*, pp of *eructare* to belch, fr *e-* + *ructare* to belch]

erudite /'eroodiet/ *adj* possessing or displaying extensive or profound knowledge; learned ⟨*an* ~ *scholar*⟩ [ME *erudit*, fr L *eruditus*, fr pp of *erudire* to instruct, fr *e-* + *rudis* rude, ignorant] – **eruditely** *adv*, **erudition** /-'dish(ə)n/ *n*

erupt /i'rupt/ *vi* **1a** *esp of a volcano* to release lava, steam, etc suddenly and usu violently **b(1)** to burst violently from limits or restraint **(2)** *of a tooth* to emerge through the gum **c** to become suddenly active or violent; explode ⟨*will terrorism* ~ *again?*⟩ **2** to break out (e g in a rash) ~ *vt* to force out or release suddenly or violently [L *eruptus*, pp of *erumpere* to burst forth, fr *e-* + *rumpere* to break – more at BEREAVE] – **eruptible** *adj*, **eruptive** /-tiv/ *adj*, **eruptively** *adv*

eruption /i'rupsh(ə)n/ *n* (a product of) erupting

-ery /-(ə)ri/, **-ry** *suffix* (→ *n*) **1** quality or state of having (a specified trait or mode of behaviour) ⟨*snobb*ery⟩ ⟨*treach*ery⟩ **2** art or practice of ⟨*cook*ery⟩ ⟨*skullduggery*⟩ **3** place of doing, keeping, producing, or selling (a specified thing) ⟨*fish*ery⟩ ⟨*bak*ery⟩ **4a** collection or body of ⟨*fin*ery⟩ ⟨*green*ery⟩ **b** class of (specified) goods ⟨*iron mongery*⟩ ⟨*confection*ery⟩ **5** state or condition of ⟨*slav*ery⟩ **6** all that is concerned with or characteristic of – chiefly derog ⟨*pop*ery⟩ ⟨*tomfool*ery⟩ ***USE*** *-ry* often after *d, t, l,* or *n*, otherwise *-ery* [ME *-erie*, fr OF, fr *-ier* -er + *-ie* -y]

erysipelas /,eri'sipələs/ *n* a feverish disease with intense deep red local inflammation of the skin, caused by infection by a streptococcal bacterium [ME *erisipila*, fr L *erysipelas*, fr Gk, fr *erysi-* (akin to Gk *erythros* red) + *-pelas* (akin to L *pellis* skin) – more at RED]

erythema /,eri'theemə/ *n* abnormal redness of the skin [NL, fr Gk *erythēma*, fr *erythainein* to redden, fr *erythros*] – **erythematous** /,eri'theemətəs; *also* ,erithee'mahtəs/ *adj*

erythr-, erythro- *comb form* **1** red ⟨erythro*cyte*⟩ **2** erythrocyte ⟨erythr*oid*⟩ [Gk, fr *erythros* – more at RED]

erythroblast /i'rithroh,blast/ *n* a nucleated bone-marrow cell that gives rise to red blood cells [ISV] – **erythroblastic** /-'blastik/ *adj*

erythrocyte /i'rithrə,siet/ *n* RED BLOOD CELL [ISV] – **erythrocytic** /-'sitik/ *adj*

erythromycin /i,rithrə'miesin/ *n* an antibiotic effective against many types of bacteria and some protozoans

erythropoiesis /i,rithrohpoy'eesis/ *n* the formation of red blood cells [NL, fr *erythr-* + Gk *poiēsis* creation] – **erythropoietic** /-poy'etik/ *adj*

erythropoietin /i,rithroh'poyitin, -poy'eetin/ *n* a hormone formed, esp in the kidney, in response to reduced oxygen concentration, that stimulates red blood cell formation [*erythropoietic* + *-in*]

[1]**-es** /-əz, -iz *after* s,z,sh,ch; -z *after* v *or a vowel*/ *suffix* (→ *n pl*) **1** – used to form the plural of most nouns that end in *s* ⟨*glass*es⟩, *z* ⟨*fuzz*es⟩, *sh* ⟨*bush*es⟩, *ch* ⟨*peach*es⟩, or a final *y* that changes to *i* ⟨*ladi*es⟩ and some nouns ending in *f* that changes to *v* ⟨*loav*es⟩; compare [1]-s 1 **2** [1]-s 2 [ME *-es, -s* – more at [1]-s]

[2]**-es** *suffix* (→ *vb*) – used to form the third person singular present of most verbs that end in *s* ⟨*bless*es⟩, *z* ⟨*fizz*es⟩, *sh* ⟨*hush*es⟩, *ch* ⟨*catch*es⟩, or a final *y* that changes to *i* ⟨*defi*es⟩; compare [2]-s [ME – more at [2]-s]

escadrille /'eskə,dril/ *n* an air force unit of any of several European countries (e g France) [F, flotilla, escadrille, fr Sp *escuadrilla*, dim. of *escuadra* squadron, squad – more at SQUAD]

escalade /,eskə'layd/ *n* an act of scaling (the walls of a fortification) [F, fr It *scalata*, fr *scalare* to scale, fr *scala* ladder, fr LL – more at [5]SCALE] – **escalade** *vt*, **escalader** *n*

escalate /'eskəlayt/ *vi* **1** EXPAND 1a ⟨*the matter has* ~d *into something like a major scandal – Sunday Times Magazine*⟩ **2** RISE 10b ⟨escalating *prices*⟩ ~ *vt* EXPAND 1 [back-formation fr *escalator*] – **escalation** /,eskə'laysh(ə)n/ *n*, **escalatory** /,eskə'layt(ə)ri/ *adj*

escalator /'eskəlaytə/ *n* a power-driven set of stairs arranged like an endless belt that ascend or descend continuously [fr *Escalator*, a trademark]

escallop /e'skoləp, e'skal-/ *n* a scallop

escalope /'eskə,lop/ *n* a thin boneless slice of meat; *esp* a slice of veal from the leg ☞ MEAT [F, fr MF, shell – more at SCALLOP]

escapade /'eskəpayd/ *n* a wild, reckless, and often mischievous adventure, esp one that flouts rules or convention [F, fr MF, fr OIt *scappata*, fr *scappare* to escape, fr (assumed) VL *excappare*]

[1]**escape** /i'skayp/ *vi* **1a** to get away, esp from confinement or restraint ⟨~d *from the burning building*⟩ ⟨*fantasy allows us to* ~ *from reality*⟩ **b** *of gases, liquids, etc* to leak out gradually; seep **c** *of a plant* to run wild from cultivation **2** to avoid a threatening evil ~ *vt* **1** to get or stay out of the way of; avoid ⟨~ *death*⟩ **2** to fail to be noticed or recallable by ⟨*his name* ~s *me*⟩ **3** to be produced or made by (esp a person), usu involuntarily ⟨*a yawn*

~d *him*⟩ [ME *escapen*, fr ONF *escaper*, fr (assumed) VL *excappare*, fr L *ex-* + LL *cappa* head covering, cloak] – **escapable** *adj*, **escaper** *n*, **escapee** /i,skay'pee/ *n*

[2]**escape** *n* **1** an act or instance of escaping **2** a means of escape **3** a cultivated plant run wild

[3]**escape** *adj* **1** providing a means of escape ⟨*an ~ hatch*⟩ ⟨*~ literature*⟩ **2** providing a means of evading a regulation, claim, or commitment ⟨*an ~ clause in a contract*⟩

escapement /i'skaypmənt/ *n* a device in a timepiece through which the energy of the power source is delivered to the regulatory mechanism that controls the motion of the cogwheels [[1]ESCAPE + -MENT]

escape velocity *n* the minimum velocity that a moving body (e g a rocket) must have to escape from the gravitational field of the earth or of a celestial body

escapism /i'skay,piz(ə)m/ *n* habitual diversion of the mind to purely imaginative activity or entertainment as an escape from reality or routine – **escapist** *adj or n*

escapology /,eskə'poləji/ *n* the art or practice of escaping, esp as a theatrical performance – **escapologist** *n*

escargot /e'skahgoh (*Fr* ɛskargo)/ *n, pl* **escargots** /e'skahgohz (*Fr* ~)/ a snail prepared for use as food [F, fr MF, fr OProv *escaragol*]

escarp /i'skahp/ *vt or n* (to) scarp [F *escarpe*, n, fr It *scarpa*]

escarpment /i'skahpmənt/ *n* a long cliff or steep slope separating 2 more gently sloping surfaces

-escence /-'es(ə)ns/ *suffix* (→ *n*) process of becoming ⟨*obsol*escence⟩; state or condition of being ⟨*alkal*escence⟩ ⟨*efferv*escence⟩ [MF, fr L *-escentia*, fr *-escent-*, *-escens* + *-ia* -y]

-escent /-'es(ə)nt/ *suffix* (→ *adj*) **1** being or beginning to be; slightly ⟨*conval*escent⟩ ⟨*incand*escent⟩ **2** reflecting or emitting light (in a specified way) ⟨*fluor*escent⟩ ⟨*opal*escent⟩ **3** having the properties of; resembling ⟨*arbor*escent⟩ [MF, fr L *-escent-*, *-escens*, prp suffix of incho verbs ending in *-escere*]

eschar /'eskah/ *n* a scab formed esp after a burn [ME *escare* – more at [2]SCAR]

eschatology /,eskə'toləji/ *n* **1** a branch of theology or religious belief concerned with the ultimate destiny of the universe or of mankind **2** the Christian doctrine concerning death, judgment, heaven, and hell – compare LAST THINGS [Gk *eschatos* last, farthest] – **eschatological** /,eskətə'lojikl/ *adj*, **eschatologically** *adv*

[1]**escheat** /is'cheet/ *n* the reversion of property to a government or feudal lord on the owner's dying without having made a will and without heirs; *also* property that has so reverted [ME *eschete*, fr OF, reversion of property, fr *escheoir* to fall, devolve, fr (assumed) VL *excadēre*, fr L *ex-* + (assumed) VL *cadēre* to fall, fr L *cadere* – more at CHANCE]

[2]**escheat** *vb* to (cause to) revert by escheat – **escheatable** *adj*

eschew /is'chooh/ *vt* to avoid habitually, esp on moral or practical grounds; shun – fml [ME *eschewen*, fr MF *eschiuver*, of Gmc origin; akin to OHG *sciuhen* to frighten off – more at SHY]

eschscholtzia /is'kolshə, e'shohltzi·ə/ *n* any of a genus of yellow- or red-flowered (garden) plants of the poppy family [NL, genus name, fr J F *Eschscholtz* †1831 G naturalist]

[1]**escort** /'eskawt/ *n* **1** a person, group of people, ship, aircraft, etc accompanying sby or sthg to give protection or show courtesy **2** one who accompanies another socially [F *escorte*, fr It *scorta*, fr *scorgere* to guide, fr (assumed) VL *excorrigere*, fr L *ex-* + *corrigere* to make straight, correct – more at CORRECT]

[2]**escort** /i'skawt/ *vt* to accompany as an escort

'**escort ,agency** *n* an organization that provides usu female social escorts

escritoire /,eskri'twah/ *n* a writing table or desk [obs F, writing desk, scriptorium, fr ML *scriptorium*]

escrow /'eskroh, -'-/ *n* a deed, money, piece of property, etc deposited with a third person to be delivered by him/her to a designated person only upon the fulfilment of some condition [MF *escroue* scroll] – **in escrow** in trust as an escrow

escudo /es'koohdoh/ *n, pl* **escudos** ☞ *Portugal, Cape Verde, Guinea-Bissau* at NATIONALITY [Sp & Pg, lit., shield, fr L *scutum*]

esculent /'eskyoolənt/ *n or adj* (sthg that is) edible – fml [L *esculentus*, fr *esca* food, fr *edere* to eat – more at EAT]

escutcheon /i'skuchən/ *n* **1** a shield on which a coat of arms is displayed **2** a protective or ornamental shield or plate (e g round a keyhole) [ME *escochon*, fr MF *escuchon*, fr (assumed) VL *scution-*, *scutio*, fr L *scutum* shield – more at ESQUIRE]

[1]**-ese** /-eez/ *suffix* (*n* → *adj*) of or originating in (a specified place or country) ⟨*Japan*ese⟩ ⟨*Vienn*ese⟩ [Pg *-ês* & It *-ese*, fr L *-ensis*]

[2]**-ese** *suffix* (*n* → *n*), *pl* **-ese** **1** inhabitant of ⟨*Chin*ese⟩ **2a** language of ⟨*Portugu*ese⟩ ⟨*Canton*ese⟩ **b** speech, literary style, or diction peculiar to (a specified place, person, or group) – chiefly derog ⟨*jour nal*ese⟩ ⟨*official*ese⟩

esker *also* **eskar** /'eskə/ *n* a long narrow ridge of sand and gravel deposited by a stream flowing from a retreating glacier ☞ GEOGRAPHY [IrGael *eiscir* ridge]

Eskimo *also* **Esquimau** /'eskimoh/ *n, pl* **Eskimos**, *esp collectively* **Eskimo** (a member or the language of) any of a group of peoples of N Canada, Greenland, Alaska, and E Siberia ☞ LANGUAGE [Dan *Eskimo* & F *Esquimau*, of Algonquian origin; akin to Cree *askimowew* he eats it raw] – **Eskimoan** /,eski'moh·ən/ *adj*

Eskimo dog *n* (any of) a breed of broad-chested powerful sledge dogs native to Greenland and Labrador

esophag-, **esophago-** *comb form, NAm* oesophag-, oesophago-

esoteric /,eesə'terik, ,esoh-/ *adj* **1** designed for, understood by, or restricted to a small group, esp of the specially initiated ⟨*~ knowledge*⟩ ⟨*~ pursuits*⟩ – compare EXOTERIC **2** private, confidential ⟨*an ~ purpose*⟩ [LL *esotericus*, fr Gk *esōterikos*, fr *esōterō*, compar of *eisō*, *esō* within, fr *eis* into, fr *en* in – more at IN] – **esoterically** *adv*, **esotericism** /-ri,siz(ə)m/ *n*

ESP *n* extrasensory perception [*extrasensory perception*]

espadrille /,espə'dril/ *n* a flat sandal that usu has a canvas upper and a rope sole and is tied round the ankle or leg with laces ☞ GARMENT [F]

espalier /iˈspalyə/ *n* (a fruit tree or shrub trained to grow flat against) a railing, trellis, etc [F, deriv of It *spalla* shoulder, fr LL *spatula* shoulder blade – more at EPAULETTE]

esparto /iˈspahtoh/ *n, pl* **espartos** either of 2 Spanish and Algerian grasses used esp to make rope, shoes, and paper [Sp, fr L *spartum*, fr Gk *sparton* – more at [3]SPIRE]

especial /iˈspesh(ə)l/ *adj* (distinctively or particularly) special [ME, fr MF – more at SPECIAL] – **especially** *adv*

Esperanto /ˌespəˈrantoh/ *n* an artificial international language largely based on words common to the chief European languages [Dr *Esperanto* (deriv of L *sperare* to hope), pseudonym of L L Zamenhof †1917 Pol oculist, its inventor] – **Esperantist** *n or adj*

espial /iˈspie·əl/ *n* (an act of) espying or observing

espionage /ˈespi·ənahzh, ˌ---ˈ-, -nij, iˈspie-/ *n* spying or the use of spies to obtain information ⟨*industrial* ~⟩ [F *espionnage*, fr MF, fr *espionner* to spy, fr *espion* spy, fr OIt *spione*, fr *spia*, of Gmc origin; akin to OHG *spehōn* to spy – more at SPY]

esplanade /ˌespləˈnahd, -nayd/ *n* a level open stretch of paved or grassy ground, esp along a shore [F, fr It *spianata*, fr *spianare* to level, fr L *explanare* – more at EXPLAIN]

espousal /iˈspowzl/ *n* **1** a betrothal; *also* a marriage – often pl with sing. meaning; fml **2** the adoption or support of a cause or belief

espouse /iˈspowz/ *vt* **1** to marry – fml **2** to take up and support as a cause; become attached to ⟨~ *the problems of minority groups*⟩ [ME *espousen*, fr MF *espouser*, fr LL *sponsare* to betroth, fr L *sponsus*, pp of *spondēre* to promise, betroth – more at SPOUSE] – **espouser** *n*

espresso /iˈspresoh/ *n, pl* **espressos** (an apparatus for making) coffee brewed by forcing steam through finely ground coffee beans [It (*caffè*) *espresso*, lit., pressed out coffee]

esprit /eˈspree/ *n* vivacious cleverness or wit [F, fr L *spiritus* spirit]

eˌsprit de ˈcorps /də ˈkaw/ *n* the common spirit and loyalty existing among the members of a group [F]

espy /iˈspie/ *vt* to catch sight of [ME *espien*, fr OF *espier* – more at SPY]

-esque /-ˈesk/ *suffix* (*n* → *adj*) in the manner or style of; like ⟨*statue*esque⟩ ⟨*Kafka*esque⟩ ⟨*roman*esque⟩ [F, fr It *-esco*, of Gmc origin; akin to OHG *-isc* -ish – more at -ISH]

Esquimau /ˈeskimoh/ *n, pl* **Esquimaux,** *esp collectively* **Esquimau** (an) Eskimo

esquire /iˈskwie·ə/ *n* **1** a member of the English gentry ranking below a knight **2** – used instead of Mr as a man's courtesy title and usu placed in its abbreviated form after the surname ⟨*J R Smith*, Esq⟩ **3** *archaic* a landed proprietor [ME, fr MF *esquier* squire, fr LL *scutarius*, fr L *scutum* shield; akin to OHG *sceida* sheath]

-ess /-is, -əs, -es/ *suffix* (*n* → *n*) female ⟨*act*ress⟩ ⟨*lion*ess⟩ – often derog ⟨*Negr*ess⟩ ⟨*poet*ess⟩ [ME *-esse*, fr OF, fr LL *-issa*, fr Gk]

[1]**essay** /eˈsay/ *vt* to attempt – fml – **essayer** *n*

[2]**essay** /ˈesay/ *n* **1** a usu short piece of prose writing on a specific topic **2** an (initial tentative) effort or attempt – fml [MF *essai*, fr LL *exagium* act of weighing, fr *ex-* + *agere* to drive – more at AGENT] – **essayist** *n*, **essayistic** /-ˈistik/ *adj*

essence /ˈes(ə)ns/ *n* **1a** the real or ultimate nature of an individual being or thing, esp as opposed to its existence or its accidental qualities **b** the properties or attributes by means of which sthg can be categorized or identified **2** sthg that exists, esp in an abstract form; an entity **3a** (an alcoholic solution or other preparation of) an extract, essential oil, etc possessing the special qualities of a plant, drug, etc in concentrated form **b** an odour, perfume **c** one who or that which resembles an extract in possessing a quality in concentrated form [ME, fr MF & L; MF, fr L *essentia*, fr *esse* to be – more at IS] – **in essence** in or by its very nature; essentially – **of the essence** of the utmost importance; essential ⟨*time was* of the essence⟩

[1]**essential** /iˈsensh(ə)l/ *adj* **1** of or being (an) essence; inherent **2** of the utmost importance; basic, necessary ⟨~ *foods*⟩ ⟨*an* ~ *requirement for admission to university*⟩ **3** idiopathic – **essentially** *adv*, **essentialness, essentiality** /-shiˈaləti/ *n*

[2]**essential** *n* sthg basic, indispensable, or fundamental ⟨*the* ~s *of astronomy*⟩

essential amino acid *n* an amino acid (e g lysine) that is required in the diet for normal health and growth

esˈsentialˌism /-ˌiz(ə)m/ *n* a philosophical theory that regards the essence of sthg as more important than its existence – compare EXISTENTIALISM – **essentialist** *adj or n*

esˌsential ˈoil *n* any of various volatile oils that give the characteristic smells to plants and are used esp in perfumes and flavourings – compare FIXED OIL

[1]**-est** /-ist/ *suffix* (*adj or adv* → *adj or adv*) – used to form the superlative degree of adjectives and adverbs of 1 and sometimes 2 or more syllables that end in a consonant ⟨*fatt*est⟩ ⟨*dear*est⟩, a vowel other than *e*, or a final *y* that changes to *i* ⟨*dreari*est⟩; compare [1]-ST [ME, fr OE *-st, -est, -ost*; akin to OHG *-isto* (adj superl suffix), Gk *-istos*]

[2]**-est, -st** /-ist/ *suffix* (→ *vb*) – used to form the archaic second person singular of verbs (with *thou*) [ME, fr OE *-est, -ast, -st*; akin to OHG *-ist, -ōst, -ēst*, 2 sing. ending]

establish /iˈstablish/ *vt* **1** to make firm or stable **2** to enact permanently ⟨~ *a law*⟩ **3** to bring into existence; found ⟨~ed *a republic*⟩ **4a** to set on a firm basis; place (e g oneself) in a permanent or firm usu favourable position ⟨~ed *himself as the leader*⟩ **b** to gain full recognition or acceptance of ⟨*she* ~ed *her fame as an actress*⟩ **5** to make (a church or religion) a national institution supported by civil authority **6** to put beyond doubt; prove ⟨~ed *his innocence*⟩ **7** to cause (a plant) to grow and multiply in a place where previously absent [ME *establissen*, fr MF *establiss-*, stem of *establir*, fr L *stabilire*, fr *stabilis* stable] – **establishable** *adj*, **establisher** *n*

eˈstablishment /-mənt/ *n* **1** sthg established: e g **a** a usu large organization or institution **b** a place of business or residence with its furnishings and staff **2** an established order of society: e g **a** *sing or pl in constr, often cap the* entrenched social, economic, and political leaders of a nation **b** *often cap* a controlling group ⟨*the literary* ~⟩ [ESTABLISH + -MENT]

establishmentarian /iˌstablishmənˈteəri·ən/ *adj* of or favouring the social or political establishment or esp the established religion – **establishmentarian** *n*, **establishmentarianism** *n*

estaminet /e'staminay (*Fr* ɛstaminɛ)/ *n*, *pl* **estaminets** /~/ a small café [F]

estate /i'stayt/ *n* **1** a social or political class (e g the nobility, clergy, or commons) **2a(1)** the whole of sby's real or personal property **(2)** the assets and liabilities left by sby at death **b** a large landed property, esp in the country, usu with a large house on it **3** *Br* a part of an urban area devoted to a particular type of development ⟨*a housing ~ next to an industrial ~*⟩; *specif* one devoted to housing ⟨*a council ~*⟩ **4** a state, condition – fml ⟨*men of low ~*⟩ [ME *estat*, fr MF – more at STATE]

e'state ,agent *n*, *Br* **1** an agent who is involved in the buying and selling of land and property (e g houses) **2** one who manages an estate; a steward

e'state ,car *n*, *Br* a relatively large motor car with a nearly vertical rear door and 1 compartment in which both passengers and bulky luggage can be carried

e'state ,duty *n* DEATH DUTY

[1]esteem /i'steem/ *n* favourable regard ⟨*held in high ~ by his colleagues*⟩

[2]esteem *vt* **1** to consider, deem ⟨*would ~ it a privilege*⟩ **2** to set a high value on; regard highly and prize accordingly [ME *estemen* to estimate, fr MF *estimer*, fr L *aestimare*]

ester /'estə/ *n* a (fragrant) compound formed by the reaction between an acid and an alcohol usu with elimination of water [G, fr *essigäther* ethyl acetate, fr *essig* vinegar + *äther* ether]

esterify /e'sterifie/ *vt* to convert into an ester – **esterification** /e,sterifi'kaysh(ə)n/ *n*

Esther /'estə/ *n* (a book of the Old Testament concerning) a Jewish heroine and queen of Persia [L, fr Heb *Estēr*]

esthesia /,es'theezhyə, -zyə; *also* ,ees-/ *n*, *NAm* aesthesia – **esthesis** /-sis/ *n*

esthesio- *comb form*, *NAm* aesthesio-

esthete /'eestheet/ *n*, *NAm* an aesthete – **esthetic** /is'thetik, es-/ *adj*, **esthetics** *n*

estimable /'estiməbl/ *adj* worthy of esteem – **estimableness** *n*

[1]estimate /'estimayt/ *vt* **1a** to judge approximately the value, worth, or significance of **b** to determine roughly the size, extent, or nature of **c** to produce a statement of the approximate cost of **2** to judge, conclude [L *aestimatus*, pp of *aestimare* to value, estimate] – **estimative** /-mətiv/ *adj*, **estimator** *n*

[2]estimate /'estimət/ *n* **1** the act of appraising or valuing; a calculation **2** an opinion or judgment of the nature, character, or quality of sby or sthg **3** (the numerical value of) a rough or approximate calculation **4** a statement of the expected cost of a job

estimation /,esti'maysh(ə)n/ *n* **1** ESTIMATE 2 **2a** estimating **b** the value, amount, or size arrived at in an estimate **3** esteem

Estonian /e'stohnyən, -ni·ən/ *n* a native or the Finno-Ugric language of Estonia ☞ LANGUAGE [*Estonia*, country in N Europe, now republic of USSR] – **Estonian** *adj*

estop /i'stop/ *vt* **-pp-** to impede, esp by estoppel [ME *estoppen*, fr MF *estouper*]

estoppel /i'stop(ə)l/ *n* a legal bar to alleging or denying a fact because of one's previous actions or words [prob fr MF *estoupail* bung, fr *estouper*]

estr-, **estro-** *comb form*, *NAm* oestr-

estrange /i'straynj/ *vt* to arouse enmity or indifference in (sby) in place of affection; alienate – usu + *from* ⟨~d *from her husband*⟩ [MF *estranger*, fr ML *extraneare*, fr L *extraneus* strange – more at STRANGE] – **estrangement** *n*, **estranger** *n*

estuarine /'estyooə,rin, -,rien/, **estuarial** /,estyoo'eəri·əl/ *adj* of, living in, or formed in an estuary ⟨~ *currents*⟩ ⟨~ *animals*⟩

estuary /'estyooəri/ *n* a water passage where the tide meets a river; *esp* a sea inlet at the mouth of a river [L *aestuarium*, fr *aestus* boiling, tide; akin to L *aestas* summer – more at EDIFY]

esurient /i'syooəri·ənt/ *adj* hungry, greedy – fml [L *esurient-*, *esuriens*, prp of *esurire* to be hungry, fr *edere* to eat] – **esurience**, **esuriency** *n*, **esuriently** *adv*

-et /-it, -et/ *suffix* (→ *n*) **1** small or lesser kind of ⟨*baron*et⟩ ⟨*isl*et⟩ **2** group of (a specified number) ⟨*oct*et⟩ [ME, fr OF *-et*, masc, & *-ete*, fem, fr LL *-itus* & *-ita*]

eta /'eetə/ *n* the 7th letter of the Greek alphabet [LL, fr Gk *ēta*, of Sem origin; akin to Heb *ḥēth*, 8th letter of the Heb alphabet]

et al /,et 'al/ *adv* and others [L *et alii* (masc), *et aliae* (fem), *et alia* (neut)]

etatism /ay'tatiz(ə)m/ *n* STATE SOCIALISM [F *étatisme*, fr *état* state, fr OF *estat*] – **etatist** *adj*

etc /it 'setrə/ *adv* ET CETERA

et cetera /it 'setrə/ *adv* and other things, esp of the same kind; *broadly* and so forth [L]

et'ceteras *n pl* unspecified additional items; ODDS AND ENDS

[1]etch /ech/ *vt* **1a** to produce (e g a picture or letters), esp on a plate of metal or glass, by the corrosive action of an acid **b** to subject (metal, glass, etc) to such etching **2** to delineate or impress clearly ⟨*scenes that are indelibly* ~ed *in our minds*⟩ ~ *vi* to practise etching [D *etsen*, fr G *ätzen*, lit., to feed, fr OHG *azzen*; akin to OHG *ezzan* to eat – more at EAT] – **etcher** *n*

[2]etch *n* (the action or effect of) an etching acid (on a surface)

etching /'eching/ *n* **1** the art of producing pictures or designs by printing from an etched metal plate **2** an impression from an etched plate

[1]eternal /i'tuhnl/ *adj* **1** having infinite duration; everlasting ⟨~ *life*⟩ **2** incessant, interminable **3** timeless ⟨*the ~ truths*⟩ [ME, fr MF, fr LL *aeternalis*, fr L *aeternus* eternal; akin to L *aevum* age, eternity – more at [1]AYE] – **eternalize** *vt*, **eternally** *adv*, **eternalness** *n*, **eternize** /i'tuhniez/ *vt*

[2]eternal *n* **1** *cap* GOD 1 – + *the* **2** sthg eternal

eternal triangle *n* a conflict that results from the sexual attraction between 2 people of one sex and 1 person of the other

eternity /i'tuhnəti/ *n* **1** the quality or state of being eternal **2** infinite time **3** the eternal life after death **4** a (seemingly) endless or immeasurable time ⟨*we waited an ~ for the train*⟩ [ME *eternite*, fr MF *eternité*, fr L *aeternitat-*, *aeternitas*, fr *aeternus*]

etesian winds /i'teezhyən, -zhən/ *n pl*, *often cap E* annually recurring summer winds that blow over the Mediterranean [L *etesius*, fr Gk *etēsios*, fr *etos* year – more at WETHER]

eth /eth/ *n* a letter ð used in Old English and Icelandic – compare THORN 4 [Icel]

eth-, **etho-** *comb form* ethyl ⟨eth*aldehyde*⟩ ⟨etho*chloride*⟩ [ISV]

[1]**-eth** /-ith/, **-th** /-th/ *suffix* (*vb* → *vb*) – used to form the archaic third person singular present of verbs ⟨*go*eth⟩ ⟨*do*th⟩ [ME, fr OE *-eth, -ath, -th*; akin to OHG *-it, -ōt, -ēt*, 3 sing. ending, L *-t, -it*]

[2]**-eth** /-ith/ – see [1] [2]-TH

ethane /'eethayn/ *n* an odourless gaseous hydrocarbon of the alkane group found in natural gas and used esp as a fuel [ISV, fr *ethyl*]

ethanol /'ethə,nol, 'eeth-/ *n* ALCOHOL 1

ethene /'etheen/ *n* ethylene

ether /'eethə/ *n* **1 ether, aether** (the rarefied element formerly believed to fill) the upper regions of space; the heavens **2 ether, aether** a medium formerly held to permeate all space and transmit electromagnetic waves (e g light and radio waves) **3a** a volatile inflammable liquid used esp as a solvent and formerly as a general anaesthetic **b** any of various organic compounds characterized by an oxygen atom attached to 2 carbon atoms [ME, fr L *aether*, fr Gk *aithēr*, fr *aithein* to ignite, blaze] – **etherish** *adj*, **etheric** /ee'therik, i-/ *adj*

ethereal /i'thiəri·əl; *sense 3* ,ethə'ree·əl/ *adj* **1** of the regions beyond the earth **2a** lacking material substance; intangible **b** marked by unusual delicacy, lightness, and refinement **3** of, containing, or resembling a chemical ether **4** celestial, heavenly – poetic [L *aethereus*, fr Gk *aitherios*, fr *aithēr*] – **ethereally** *adv*, **ethereality** /,ithiəri'aləti/, **etherealness** *n*, **etherealize** *vt*, **etherealization** /-ie'zaysh(ə)n/ *n*

ether·ize, -ise /'eethə,riez/ *vt* to treat or anaesthetize (as if) with ether – **etherizer** *n*, **etherization** /,eethərie'zaysh(ə)n/ *n*

ethic /'ethik/ *n* **1** *pl but sing or pl in constr* inquiry into the nature and basis of moral principles and judgments **2** a set of moral principles or values ⟨*the current materialistic* ~⟩ **3** *pl but sing or pl in constr* the principles of conduct governing an individual or a group ⟨*professional* ~s⟩ [ME *ethik*, fr MF *ethique*, fr L *ethice*, fr Gk *ēthikē*, fr *ēthikos*]

ethical /'ethikl/ *also* **ethic** *adj* **1** conforming to accepted, esp professional, standards of conduct or morality **2** *of a drug* available to the general public only on a doctor's or dentist's prescription [ME *etik*, fr L *ethicus*, fr Gk *ēthikos*, fr *ēthos* character] – **ethically** *adv*, **ethicality** /,ethi'kaləti/, **ethicalness** *n*

ethinyl /'ethənil, i'thienil, -niel/ *n* ethynyl

Ethiopian /,eethi'ohpi·ən, -pyən/ *n or adj* (a native or inhabitant) of Ethiopia [*Ethiopia*, country in NE Africa]

Ethiopic /,eethi'opik, -'ohpik/ *adj or n* (of) a Semitic language used as the Christian liturgical language in Ethiopia

ethmoid /'ethmoyd/, **ethmoidal** /eth'moydl/ *adj* of, adjoining, or being 1 or more bones of the walls and septum of the nasal cavity [F *ethmoïde*, fr Gk *ēthmoeidēs*, lit., like a strainer, fr *ēthmos* strainer] – **ethmoid** *n*

ethnarch /'ethnahk/ *n* the governor of a province or people [Gk *ethnarchēs*, fr *ethnos* nation, people + *archos* ruler]

[1]**ethnic** /'ethnik/ *adj* **1** of or being human races or large groups classed according to common traits ⟨~ *minorities*⟩ ⟨~ *groups*⟩ **2** of an exotic, esp peasant, culture ⟨~ *restaurants*⟩ [ME, fr LL *ethnicus*, fr Gk *ethnikos* national, gentile, fr *ethnos*] – **ethnicity** /,eth'nisiti, -səti/ *n*

[2]**ethnic** *n, chiefly NAm* a member of an ethnic (minority) group

ethnical /'ethnikl/ *adj* **1** ethnic **2** ethnological – **ethnically** *adv*

ethno- *comb form* race; people; cultural group ⟨*ethnocentric*⟩ [F, fr Gk *ethno-, ethn-*, fr *ethnos*]

ethnocentric /,ethnoh'sentrik/ *adj* **1** having race as a central interest **2** regarding one's own group as superior – **ethnocentrically** *adv*, **ethnocentricity** /-sen'trisəti/ *n*, **ethnocentrism** *n*

ethnography /eth'nografi/ *n* ethnology; *specif* descriptive anthropology [F *ethnographie*, fr *ethno-* + *-graphie* -graphy] – **ethnographer** *n*, **ethnographic** /,ethnoh'grafik/, **ethnographical** *adj*, **ethnographically** *adv*

ethnology /eth'noləji/ *n* a science that deals with the various forms of social relationships (e g kinship, law, religion, etc) found in esp preliterate human societies – **ethnologist** *n*, **ethnologic** /,ethnə'lojik/, **ethnological** *adj*, **ethnologically** *adv*

ethnomusicology /,ethnoh,myoohzi'koləji/ *n* the study of the music of non-European cultures – **ethnomusicologist** *n*, **ethnomusicological** /-kə'lojikl/ *adj*

ethology /i'tholəji/ *n* **1** the study of the formation and evolution of human characters and beliefs **2** the scientific study of animal behaviour [L *ethologia* art of depicting character, fr Gk *ēthologia*, fr *ēthos*] – **ethologist** *n*, **ethological** /,ithə'lojikl/ *adj*

ethos /'eethos/ *n* the distinguishing character or guiding beliefs of a person, institution, etc [NL, fr Gk *ēthos* custom, character]

ethyl /'ethil, 'eethil, -thiel/ *n* a univalent hydrocarbon radical C_2H_5 derived from ethane [ISV *eth*er + *-yl*]

,ethyl 'acetate *n* a fragrant volatile inflammable liquid ester used esp as a solvent and in flavourings

ethyl alcohol *n* ALCOHOL 1

ethylene /'ethi,leen/ *n* **1** an inflammable gaseous unsaturated hydrocarbon of the alkene group, found in coal gas and used esp in organic chemical synthesis **2** a bivalent hydrocarbon radical C_2H_4 derived from ethane – **ethylenic** /-'lenik/ *adj*

,ethylene 'glycol *n* a thick liquid alcohol used esp as an antifreeze

,ethyl 'ether *n* ETHER 3a

ethynyl, ethinyl /'ethənil, e'thienil, -niel/ *n* a radical HC≡C derived from acetylene by removal of 1 hydrogen atom [*ethyne, ethine* (acetylene) (fr *ethyl* + *-ine*) + *-yl*]

-etic /-'etik/ *suffix* (→ *adj*) [1]-IC ⟨*asc*etic⟩ – often in adjectives corresponding to nouns ending in *esis* ⟨*gen*etic⟩ ⟨*synth*etic⟩ [L & Gk; L *-eticus*, fr Gk *-etikos, -ētikos*, fr *-etos, -ētos*, ending of certain verbals]

etiolate /'eeti·ə,layt, -tioh-/ *vt* **1** to bleach and alter the natural development of (a green plant) by excluding sunlight **2** to make weak, pale, or sickly [F *étioler*, fr ONF *étieuler* to turn to stubble, fr *éteule* stubble, deriv of L *stipula* straw] – **etiolation** /,eeti·ə'laysh(ə)n, -tioh-/ *n*

etiology /,eeti'oləji/ *n, NAm* aetiology – **etiologic** /,eetiə'lojik/, **etiological** *adj*, **etiologically** *adv*

etiquette /'eti,ket/ *n* the conventionally accepted standards of proper social or professional behaviour ⟨*medical* ~⟩ [F *étiquette*, lit., ticket – more at TICKET]

Eton collar /'eetn/ *n* a large stiff turnover collar [*Eton* College, public school in England]

Etonian /ee'tonhnyən, -ni·ən/ *n or adj* (a pupil) of Eton College

etrier /'aytriay (*Fr* etrje)/ *n* a short rope ladder used in mountaineering, potholing, etc [F *étrier*, lit., stirrup]

Etruscan /i'truskən/ *n or adj* (a native or inhabitant or the language) of ancient Etruria ☞ ALPHABET [L *Etruscus* of Etruria, ancient country of Italy]

-ette /-'et/ *suffix* (*n* → *n*) **1** small or lesser kind of ⟨*kitchen*ette⟩ ⟨*cigar*ette⟩ **2** female ⟨*suffrag*ette⟩ ⟨*usher*ette⟩ **3** imitation; substitute ⟨*leather*ette⟩ ⟨*flannel*ette⟩ [ME, fr MF, fem dim. suffix, fr OF *-ete* – more at -ET]

étude /ay'tyoohd (*Fr* etyːd)/ *n* a piece of music written primarily for the practice of a technique [F, lit., study, fr MF *estude, estudie*]

etui /e'twee/ *n, pl* **etuis** /e'twee(z)/ a small ornamental case, esp for needles [F *étui*]

etymolog·ize, -ise /ˌeti'moləjiez/ *vt* to discover or give an etymology for ~ *vi* to study or formulate etymologies

etymology /ˌeti'moləji/ *n* **1** the history of the origin and development of a word or other linguistic form **2** a branch of linguistics dealing with etymologies [ME *ethimologie*, fr L *etymologia*, fr Gk, fr *etymon* + *-logia* -logy] – **etymologist** *n*, **etymological** /-mə'lojikl/ *adj*, **etymologically** *adv*

etymon /'etiˌmon/ *n, pl* **etyma** /-mə/ *also* **etymons** an earlier linguistic form from which derivatives are formed [L, fr Gk, literal meaning of a word according to its origin, fr *etymos* true; akin to Gk *eteos* true]

eu- *comb form* **1a** well; easily ⟨eu*plastic*⟩ ⟨eu*phonious*⟩ **b** good ⟨eu*pepsia*⟩ **2** true ⟨eu*chromatin*⟩ ***USE*** (1) compare DYS- 2 [ME, fr L, fr Gk, fr *ey, eu*, fr neut of *eys* good; akin to Hitt *asus* good, & perh to L *esse* to be]

eucalypt /'yoohkəˌlipt/ *n* a eucalyptus

eucalyptol /ˌyoohkə'liptol/ *n* cineole

eucalyptus /ˌyoohkə'liptəs/ *n, pl* **eucalyptuses, eucalypti** /-'liptie/ any of a genus of mostly Australian evergreen trees of the myrtle family that are widely cultivated for their gums, resins, oils, and wood [NL, genus name, fr *eu-* + Gk *kalyptos* covered, fr *kalyptein* to conceal; fr the conical covering of the buds]

eucaryote /yooh'karioht, -ət/ *n* a eukaryote – **eucaryotic** /ˌyoohˌkari'otik/ *adj*

Eucharist /'yoohkərist/ *n* (the bread and wine consecrated in) the Christian sacrament in which bread and wine, being or representing the body and blood of Christ, are ritually consumed in accordance with Christ's injunctions at the Last Supper [ME *eukarist*, fr MF *euchariste*, fr LL *eucharistia*, fr Gk, Eucharist, gratitude, fr *eucharistos* grateful, fr *eu-* + *charizesthai* to show favour, fr *charis* favour, grace, gratitude] – **eucharistic** /ˌyoohkə'ristik/ *adj, often cap*

[1]**euchre** /'yoohkə/ *n* a US card game in which a player must take at least 3 out of 5 tricks to win [origin unknown]

[2]**euchre** *vt* to prevent from winning 3 tricks in euchre

euchromatin /yooh'krohmətin/ *n* the genetically active part of chromatin that is largely composed of genes [G, fr *eu-* + *chromatin*] – **euchromatic** /-'matik/ *adj*

euclidean /yooh'klidi·ən/ *adj, often cap* of or being the geometry of Euclid that describes euclidean space [*Euclid fl ab* 300 BC Gk mathematician]

euclidean space *n, often cap E* the normal three-dimensional space in which euclidean geometry applies

eudemonism, eudaemonism /yooh'deeməˌniz(ə)m/ *n* the doctrine that personal well-being through a life governed by reason is the sole or chief good [Gk *eudaimonia* happiness, fr *eudaimōn* happy, fr *eu-* + *daimōn* spirit] – **eudemonist** *n*, **eudemonistic** /yoohˌdeemə'nistik/ *adj*

eugenic /yooh'jenik/ *adj* **1** relating to or fit for the production of good offspring **2** of eugenics [Gk *eugenēs* wellborn, fr *eu-* + *-genēs* born – more at -GEN] – **eugenically** *adv*

eu'genics *n pl but sing in constr* a science dealing with the improvement (e g by control of human mating) of the hereditary qualities of a race or breed – **eugenicist** /-nisist/ *n*

euglena /yooh'gleenə/ *n* any of a genus of green freshwater single-celled organisms that move by means of a long flagellum [NL, genus name, fr *eu-* + Gk *glēnē* eyeball, socket of a joint] – **euglenoid** /-ˌnoyd/ *adj or n*

euhemerism /yooh'heməˌriz(ə)m/ *n* interpretation of myths in terms of historical people and events [*Euhemerus*, 4th-c BC Gk mythographer] – **euhemerist** *n*, **euhemerize** *vt*, **euhemeristic** /-'ristik/ *adj*, **euhemeristically** *adv*

eukaryote, eucaryote /yooh'karioht, -ət/ *n* an organism composed of 1 or more cells typically with visibly evident nuclei – compare PROKARYOTE [*eu-* + *kary-* + *-ote* (as in *zygote*)] – **eukaryotic** /-'otik, -'ohtik/ *adj*

eulog·ize, -ise /'yoohləˌjiez/ *vt* to extol – **eulogizer** *n*

eulogy /'yoohləji/ *n* **1** a (formal) speech or piece of writing in praise of a person or thing **2** high praise [ME *euloge*, fr ML *eulogium*, fr Gk *eulogia* praise, fr *eu-* + *-logia* -logy] – **eulogist** *n*, **eulogistic** /-'jistik/ *adj*, **eulogistically** *adv*

Eumenides /yooh'meniˌdeez/ *n pl* the Furies [L, fr Gk, lit., the well-disposed ones]

eunuch /'yoohnək/ *n* **1** a castrated man employed, esp formerly, in a harem or as a chamberlain in a palace **2** a man or boy deprived of the testes or external genitals [ME *eunuk*, fr L *eunuchus*, fr Gk *eunouchos*, fr *eunē* bed + *echein* to have, have charge of – more at SCHEME] – **eunuchism** *n*, **eunuchoid** /-ˌkoyd/ *adj or n*

euonymus /yooh'oniməs/ *n* SPINDLE TREE [NL, genus name, fr L *euonymos* spindle tree, fr Gk *euōnymos*, fr *euōnymos* having an auspicious name, fr *eu-* + *onyma* name – more at NAME]

eupepsia /yooh'pepsi·ə/ *n* **1** good digestion **2** happiness, optimism ***USE*** fml [NL, fr *eu-* + *-pepsia* (as in *dyspepsia*)] – **eupeptic** /-tik/ *adj*

euphemism /'yoohfəˌmiz(ə)m/ *n* the substitution of a mild, indirect, or vague expression for an offensive or unpleasant one; *also* the expression so substituted ⟨fall asleep *is a* ~ *for* die⟩ [Gk *euphēmismos*, fr *euphēmos* auspicious, sounding good, fr *eu-* + *phēmē* speech, fr *phanai* to say, speak – more at [1]BAN] – **euphemistic** /-'mistik/ *adj*, **euphemistically** *adv*

euphem·ize, -ise /'yoohfəˌmiez/ *vb* to employ or express by a euphemism – **euphemizer** *n*

euphonious /yooh'fohnyəs, -ni·əs/ *adj* pleasing to

the ear – **euphoniously** *adv*, **euphonize** /'yoohfə,niez/ *vt*

euphonium /yooh'fohnyəm, -ni·əm/ *n* a brass instrument smaller than but resembling a tuba and having a range from B flat below the bass staff upwards for 3 octaves [Gk *euphōnos* + E *-ium* (as in *harmonium*)]

euphony /'yoohfəni/ *n* a pleasing or sweet sound, esp in speech [F *euphonie*, fr LL *euphonia*, fr Gk *euphōnia*, fr *euphōnos* sweet-voiced, musical, fr *eu-* + *phōnē* voice – more at [1]BAN] – **euphonic** /-'fonik/ *adj*, **euphonically** *adv*

euphoria /yooh'fawri·ə/ *n* an (inappropriate) feeling of well-being or elation – compare DYSPHORIA [NL, fr Gk, fr *euphoros* healthy, fr *eu-* + *pherein* to bear – more at [2]BEAR] – **euphoric** /-'forik/ *adj*, **euphorically** *adv*

euphuism /'yoohfyooh,iz(ə)m/ *n* an artificial and ornate style of writing or speaking [*Euphues*, character in prose romances by John Lyly †1606 E writer] – **euphuist** *n*, **euphuistic** /-'istik/ *adj*, **euphuistically** *adv*

Eur-, Euro- *comb form* **1** European ⟨Euro*communism*⟩; European and ⟨Eur*asian*⟩ **2** European Economic Community ⟨Euro*crat*⟩ [*Europe*]

Eurasian /yooə'rayzh(ə)n, yoo'ray-/ *adj* **1** of, growing in, or living in Europe and Asia **2** of mixed European and Asian origin – **Eurasian** *n*

eureka /yoo(ə)'reekə/ *interj* – used to express triumph at a discovery [Gk *heurēka* I have found, fr *heuriskein* to find; fr the exclamation attributed to Archimedes †212 BC Gk mathematician & inventor on finding a method for determining the purity of gold]

eurhythmic, eurythmic /yoo(ə)'ridhmik/ *adj* **1** harmonious **2** of eurhythmics

eu'rhythmics, eurythmics *n pl but sing or pl in constr* the art of harmonious bodily movement, esp through expressive timed movements in response to music [G *eurhythmie*, fr L *eurhythmia* rhythmical movement, fr Gk, fr *eurhythmos* rhythmical, fr *eu-* + *rhythmos* rhythm]

euro /'yooəroh/ *n, pl* **euros** *Austr* a large reddish grey kangaroo [native name in Australia]

Eurocommunism /,yooəroh'komyooniz(ə)m/ *n* Communism as it manifests itself in W Europe (e g in Italy and France) – **Eurocommunist** *adj or n*

'Euro,crat /-,krat/ *n* a staff member of the administrative commission of the European Economic Community – infml [*Euro*pean + *-crat* (as in *bureaucrat*)]

'Euro,dollar /-,dolə/ *n* a US dollar held (e g by a bank) outside the USA, esp in Europe [*Euro*pe + *dollar*]

[1]European /,yooərə'pee·ən/ *adj* **1** native to Europe **2** of European descent or origin **3** concerned with or affecting the whole of Europe **4** advocating European unity or alliance [L *Europaeus*, fr Gk *Europaios*, fr *Europē* Europe] – **Europeanism** *n*, **Europeanize** *vt*, **Europeanization** /,yooərə ,pee·ə·nie'zaysh(ə)n/ *n*

[2]European *n* a native or inhabitant of (the mainland of) Europe

europium /yooə'rohpi·əm, -pyəm/ *n* a bivalent and trivalent metallic element of the rare-earth group ☞ PERIODIC TABLE [NL, fr *Europa* Europe]

Eurovision /'yooərə,vizh(ə)n/ *trademark* – used for a television service enabling several chiefly W European broadcasting organizations to exchange programmes

eurythmic /yoo(ə)'ridhmik/ *adj* eurhythmic

eu'rythmics *n pl but sing or pl in constr* eurhythmics

eu,stachian 'tube /yooh'stayshyən, -shən/ *n, often cap E* a tube connecting the middle ear with the pharynx that equalizes air pressure on both sides of the eardrum ☞ NERVE [Bartolommeo *Eustachio* †1574 It anatomist]

eustatic /yooh'statik/ *adj* of or characterized by worldwide change of sea level [ISV]

eutectic /yooh'tektik/ *adj* of or being (the melting or freezing point of) an alloy or other mixture in which the constituents are in such proportions that the melting point is the lowest possible for a mixture of these substances [Gk *eutēktos* easily melted, fr *eu-* + *tēktos* melted, fr *tēkein* to melt – more at THAW] – **eutectic** *n*, **eutectoid** /-toyd/ *adj or n*

euthanasia /,yoohthə'nayzyə, -zhə, -zi·ə/ *n* the act or practice of killing (hopelessly sick or injured) individuals for reasons of mercy [Gk, easy death, fr *eu-* + *thanatos* death] – **euthanasic** /-zik/ *adj*

eutherian /yooh'thiəri·ən/ *adj or n* (of or being) a mammal of a major division comprising those mammals that have placentas [deriv of NL *eu-* + Gk *thērion* wild beast – more at TREACLE]

euthyroid /yooh'thie(ə),royd/ *adj* characterized by normal thyroid function

eutrophic /yooh'trohfik/ *adj, of a body of water* rich in dissolved nutrients (e g phosphates) but often shallow and seasonally deficient in oxygen [prob fr G *eutroph*, fr Gk *eutrophos* well nourished, nourishing, fr *eu-* + *trephein* to nourish – more at ATROPHY] – **eutrophication** /-,trohfi'kaysh(ə)n/ *n*, **eutrophy** /'yoohtrəfi; *also* yooh'trohfi/ *n*

evacuate /i'vakyoo,ayt/ *vt* **1** EMPTY 1a **2** to discharge from the body as waste **3** to remove gas, water, etc from, esp by pumping; *esp* to produce a vacuum in **4a** to remove, esp from a dangerous area **b** to withdraw from military occupation of **c** to vacate ⟨*rapidly* ~d *the burning building*⟩ ~ *vi* **1** to withdraw from a place in an organized way, esp for protection **2** to pass urine or faeces from the body [L *evacuatus*, pp of *evacuare*, fr *e-* + *vacuus* empty – more at VACUUM] – **evacuation** /i,vakyooh'aysh(ə)n/ *n*, **evacuative** /i'vakyooh·ətiv/ *adj*

evacuee /i,vakyoo'ee/ *n* a person evacuated from a dangerous place

evade /i'vayd/ *vi* to take refuge by evading sthg ~ *vt* **1** to get away from or avoid, esp by deception **2a** to avoid facing up to ⟨~d *the issue*⟩ **b** to fail to pay ⟨~ *taxes*⟩ **3** to baffle, foil ⟨*the problem* ~s *all efforts at solution*⟩ [MF & L; MF *evader*, fr L *evadere*, fr *e-* + *vadere* to go, walk – more at WADE] – **evadable** *adj*, **evader** *n*

evagination /i,vaji'naysh(ə)n/ *n* **1** everting **2** a product of eversion; an outgrowth [LL *evagination-*, *evaginatio* act of unsheathing, fr L *evaginatus*, pp of *evaginare* to unsheathe, fr *e-* + *vagina* sheath]

evaluate /i'valyoo,ayt/ *vt* to determine the amount, value, or significance of, esp by careful appraisal and study [back-formation fr *evaluation*] – **evaluation** /i,valyoo'aysh(ə)n/ *n*, **evaluative** /i'valyooətiv/ *adj*, **evaluator** /-,aytə/ *n*

evanescent /,evə'nes(ə)nt/ *adj* tending to dissipate or vanish like vapour [L *evanescent-*, *evanescens*, prp of *evanescere* – more at VANISH] – **evanescence** /-'nes(ə)ns/ *n,* **evanesce** *vi*

evangel /i'vanj(ə)l/ *n* an evangelist

evangelical /,eevan'jelikl/ *also* **evangelic** /-'jelik/ *adj* **1** of or in agreement with the Christian message as presented in the 4 Gospels **2** *often cap* Protestant; *specif* of the German Protestant church **3** *often cap* (of or being a usu Protestant denomination) emphasizing salvation by faith in the atoning death of Jesus Christ, personal conversion, and the authority of Scripture **4a** of, adhering to, or marked by fundamentalism **b** LOW CHURCH **5** evangelistic, zealous ⟨~ *ardour*⟩ [*evangel* (gospel), fr ME *evangile,* fr MF, fr LL *evangelium,* fr Gk *euangelion* good news, gospel, fr *euangelos* bringing good news, fr *eu-* + *angelos* messenger] – **Evangelical** *n,* **Evangelicalism** *n,* **evangelically** *adv*

evangelism /i'vanjə,liz(ə)m/ *n* **1** the winning or revival of personal commitments to Christ **2** militant or crusading zeal – **evangelistic** /i,vanjə'listik/ *adj,* **evangelistically** *adv*

evangelist /i'vanjəlist/ *n* **1** *often cap* a writer of any of the 4 Gospels **2** one who evangelizes; *specif* a Protestant minister or layman who preaches at special services

evangel·ize, -ise /i'vanjə,liez/ *vb* to preach the Christian gospel (to), esp with the intention of converting to Christianity – **evangelization** /i,vanjəlie'zaysh(ə)n/ *n*

evaporate /i'vapərayt/ *vi* **1a** to pass off in vapour **b** to pass off or away; disappear, fade ⟨*his fears* ~d⟩ **2** to give out vapour ~ *vt* **1** to convert into vapour **2a** to expel moisture, esp water, from ⟨~d *milk*⟩ **b** to cause to disappear or fade [ME *evaporaten,* fr L *evaporatus,* pp of *evaporare,* fr *e-* + *vapor* steam, vapour] – **evaporatable** *adj,* **evaporation** /i,vapə'raysh(ə)n/ *n,* **evaporative** /-rətiv/ *adj,* **evaporator** /-,raytə/ *n*

evasion /i'vayzh(ə)n/ *n* an act, instance, or means of evading ⟨*suspected of tax* ~⟩ [ME, fr MF or LL; MF, fr LL *evasion-, evasio,* fr L *evasus,* pp of *evadere* to evade]

evasive /i'vaysiv, -ziv/ *adj* tending or intended to evade; equivocal ⟨~ *answers*⟩ – **evasively** *adv,* **evasiveness** *n*

eve /eev/ *n* **1** the evening or the day before a special day, esp a religious holiday ⟨*Christmas* ~⟩ **2** the period immediately preceding an event ⟨*the* ~ *of the election*⟩ **3** the evening – chiefly poetic [ME *eve, even*]

evection /i'veksh(ə)n/ *n* perturbation of the moon's orbit due to the sun's attraction [L *evection-, evectio* rising, fr *evectus,* pp of *evehere* to carry out, raise up, fr *e-* + *vehere* to carry – more at WAY]

[1]**even** /'eev(ə)n/ *n, archaic* the evening – poetic [ME *even, eve,* fr OE *ǣfen*]

[2]**even** *adj* **1a** having a horizontal surface; flat, level ⟨~ *ground*⟩ **b** without break or irregularity; smooth **c** in the same plane or line – + *with* ⟨~ *with the ground*⟩ **2a** without variation; uniform ⟨*an* ~ *disposition*⟩ ⟨*an* ~ *grey sky*⟩ **b** LEVEL 3 **3a** equal ⟨*we were* ~ *after the 4th game, having won 2 each*⟩; *also* fair ⟨*an* ~ *exchange*⟩ **b** being in equilibrium **4** exactly divisible by 2 ⟨*an* ~ *number*⟩ – compare ODD 2 **5** exact, precise ⟨*an* ~ *pound*⟩ **6** fifty-fifty ⟨*she stands an* ~ *chance of winning*⟩ [ME, fr OE *efen;* akin to OHG *eban* even] – **evenly** *adv,* **evenness** *n*

[3]**even** *adv* **1** at the very time – + *as* **2a** – used as an intensive to emphasize the contrast with a less strong possibility ⟨*he looks content,* ~ *happy*⟩ ⟨*can't* ~ *walk, let alone run*⟩ **b** – used as an intensive to emphasize the comparative degree ⟨~ *better than last time*⟩ [ME, fr OE *efne,* fr *efen,* adj] – **even if** in spite of the possibility or fact that – **even now 1** at this very moment **2** in spite of what has happened – **even so** in spite of that

[4]**even** *vb* to make or become even – often + *up* or *out* – **evener** *n*

,even'handed /-'handid/ *adj* fair, impartial – **evenhandedly** *adv,* **evenhandedness** *n*

evening /'eevning/ *n* **1** the latter part of the day and the early part of the night; the time between sunset and bedtime **2** a late period (e g of time or life); the end **3** (the period of) an evening's entertainment [ME, fr OE *ǣfnung,* fr *ǣfnian* to grow towards evening, fr *ǣfen* evening; akin to OHG *āband* evening]

'evening ,dress *n* **1** clothes for formal or semiformal evening occasions **2** a dress, esp with a floor-length skirt, for wear on formal or semiformal occasions

,evening 'prayer *n, often cap E&P* the daily evening office of the Anglican church

,evening 'primrose *n* (a plant related to) a coarse plant with large yellow flowers that open in the evening

'evenings *adv, chiefly NAm* in the evening repeatedly; on any evening

,evening 'star *n* a bright planet, specif Venus, seen in the western sky at sunset

'even,song /-,song/ *n, often cap* **1** VESPERS 1 **2** EVENING PRAYER [ME, fr OE *ǣfensang,* fr *ǣfen* evening + *sang* song]

event /i'vent/ *n* **1a** a qualitative or quantitative change or complex of changes located in a restricted portion of time and space **b** a (noteworthy or important) happening or occurrence **c** a social occasion or activity **2** a contingency, case – esp in *in the event of* ⟨*in the* ~ *of my death*⟩ and (*chiefly NAm*) *in the event that* ⟨*in the* ~ *that I die*⟩ **3** any of the contests in a sporting programme or tournament [MF or L; MF, fr L *eventus,* fr *eventus,* pp of *evenire* to happen, fr *e-* + *venire* to come – more at COME] – **eventful** *adj,* **eventfully** *adv,* **eventfulness** *n,* **eventless** *adj* – **in any event, at all events** ANYWAY 1 – **in the event** *Br* when it actually happens or happened

event horizon *n* the boundary of a black hole

eventide /'eev(ə)n,tied/ *n* the evening – chiefly poetic [ME, fr OE *āefentīd,* fr *āefen* evening + *tīd* time]

eventide home *n* a home for old people

eventing /i'venting/ *n* the participation of a horse or rider in a three-day event – **eventer** *n*

eventual /i'ventyooəl, -chəl, -chooəl/ *adj* taking place at an unspecified later time; ultimately resulting ⟨*they counted on his* ~ *success*⟩ – **eventually** *adv*

eventuality /i,ventyoo'aləti, -choo-/ *n* a possible, esp unwelcome, event or outcome

eventuate /i'ventyooayt, -choo-/ *vi* to result – fml

ever /'evə/ *adv* **1** always – now chiefly in certain phrases and in combination ⟨~ *yours, John*⟩ ⟨*an ever-growing need*⟩ **2** at any time ⟨*faster than* ~⟩ – chiefly in negatives and questions ⟨*have you* ~ *met?*⟩ ⟨*he won't* ~ *do it*⟩ **3** – used as an intensive

⟨*looks ~ so angry*⟩ ⟨*as quick as ~ I can*⟩ ⟨*~ since Monday*⟩ ⟨*why ~ not?*⟩ [ME, fr OE *ǣfre*] – **ever so/such** *chiefly Br* very much – infml ⟨ever such *a nice girl*⟩ ⟨*thanks* ever so⟩

,ever and a'gain *adv* sometimes – poetic

,ever and a'non *adv* sometimes – poetic

1'ever,green /-,green/ *adj* **1** having leaves that remain green and functional through more than 1 growing season – compare DECIDUOUS 1 **2** always retaining freshness, interest, or popularity ⟨*the ~ items of the American popular repertoire* – Benny Green⟩

2evergreen *n* an evergreen plant; *also* a conifer

1everlasting /-'lahsting/ *adj* **1** lasting or enduring through all time **2a(1)** continuing long or indefinitely; perpetual **(2)** *of a plant* retaining its form or colour for a long time when dried **b** tediously persistent; ETERNAL 2 **3** lasting or wearing for a long time; durable – **everlastingly** *adv*, **everlastingness** *n*

2everlasting *n* **1** *cap* GOD 1 – + *the* **2** eternity

,ever'more /-'maw/ *adv* **1** always, forever **2** in the future

evert /i'vuht/ *vt* to turn outwards or inside out [L *evertere*, fr *e-* + *vertere* to turn – more at WORTH] – **eversible** /i'vuhsəbl/ *adj*, **eversion** /-sh(ə)n/ *n*

every /'evri/ *adj* **1** being each member without exception, of a group larger than 2 ⟨*~ word counts*⟩ ⟨*enjoyed ~ minute*⟩ ⟨*his ~ word*⟩ **2** being each or all possible ⟨*was given ~ chance*⟩ ⟨*have ~ confidence in him*⟩ **3** being once in each ⟨*go ~ third day*⟩ ⟨*change the oil ~ 5000 miles*⟩ – compare OTHER 1c [ME *everich, every*, fr OE *ǣfre ǣlc*, fr *ǣfre* ever + *ǣlc* each] – **every now and then/again, every so often** at intervals; occasionally

'every,body /-,bodi/ *pron* every person ⟨*~ decides they're a bit hungry – SEU S*⟩

'every,day /-,day/ *adj* encountered or used routinely or typically; ordinary ⟨*clothes for ~ wear*⟩ – **everydayness** *n*

'every,man /-,man/ *n* the typical or ordinary human being; MAN IN THE STREET [*Everyman*, allegorical character in *The Summoning of Everyman*, 15th-c E morality play]

'every,one /-,wun/ *pron* everybody

'every,thing /-,thing/ *pron* **1a** all that exists **b** all that is necessary or that relates to the subject ⟨*my new car has ~*⟩ **2** sthg of the greatest importance; all that counts ⟨*he meant ~ to her*⟩

'every,where /-,weə/ *adv or n* (in, at, or to) every place or the whole place

,every 'which ,way *adv, NAm* in every direction; all over the place [prob by folk etymology fr ME *everich way* every way]

evict /i'vikt/ *vt* **1a** to recover (property) from a person by a legal process **b** to remove (a tenant) from rented accommodation or land by a legal process **2** to force out [ME *evicten*, fr LL *evictus*, pp of *evincere*, fr L, to vanquish, win a point – more at EVINCE] – **evictor** *n*, **eviction** /i'viksh(ə)n/ *n*

1evidence /'evid(ə)ns/ *n* **1** an outward sign; an indication **2** sthg, esp a fact, that gives proof or reasons for believing or agreeing with sthg; *specif* information used (by a tribunal) to arrive at the truth [ME, fr MF, fr LL *evidentia*, fr L *evident-, evidens*] – **evidential** /,evi'densh(ə)l/ *adj*, **evidentially** *adv*, **evidentiary** /-'densh(y)əri/ *adj* – **in evidence** to be seen; conspicuous

2evidence *vt* to offer evidence of; show

evident /'evid(ə)nt/ *adj* clear to the vision or understanding [ME, fr MF, fr L *evident-, evidens*, fr *e-* + *vident-, videns*, prp of *vidēre* to see – more at WIT]

'evidently /-li/ *adv* **1** clearly, obviously **2** on the basis of available evidence; as seems evident

1evil /'eevl/ *adj* **-ll-** (*NAm* **-l-, -ll-**) **1a** not good morally; sinful, wicked ⟨*a thoroughly ~ doctrine*⟩ **b** arising from bad character or conduct ⟨*a man of ~ reputation*⟩ **2a** causing discomfort or repulsion; offensive ⟨*an ~ smell*⟩ **b** disagreeable ⟨*an ~ temper*⟩ **3a** pernicious, harmful **b** marked by misfortune ⟨*an ~ day*⟩ [ME, fr OE *yfel*; akin to OHG *ubil* evil] – **evil** *adv, archaic*, **evilly** *adv*, **evilness** *n*

2evil *n* **1** sthg evil; sthg that brings sorrow, distress, or calamity **2a** the fact of suffering, misfortune, or wrongdoing **b** wickedness, sin

,evil 'eye *n* (a spell put on sby with) a look believed to be capable of inflicting harm

evince /i'vins/ *vt* to show clearly; reveal – fml [L *evincere* to vanquish, win a point, fr *e-* + *vincere* to conquer – more at VICTOR] – **evincible** *adj*

eviscerate /i'visərayt/ *vt* **1** to disembowel **2** to remove an organ from (a patient); *also* to remove the contents of (an organ) **3** to deprive of vital content or force – fml [L *evisceratus*, pp of *eviscerare*, fr *e-* + *viscera* entrails] – **evisceration** /i,visə'raysh(ə)n/ *n*

evoke /i'vohk/ *vt* to call forth or up: e g **a** CONJURE 1a **b** to cite, esp with approval or for support; invoke **c** to bring to mind or recollection, esp imaginatively or poignantly ⟨*this place ~s memories of happier years*⟩ [F *évoquer*, fr L *evocare*, fr *e-* + *vocare* to call – more at VOCATION] – **evocation** /,evə'kaysh(ə)n/ *n*, **evocative** /i'vokətiv/ *adj*, **evocatively** *adv*, **evocator** /'evə,kaytə/ *n*

evolute /,eevə'looht/ *n* the curve that passes through the centres of all the circles that touch a given curve on its concave side at each point [L *evolutus*, pp of *evolvere*]

evolution /,eevə'loohsh(ə)n/ *n* **1a** a process of change and development, esp from a lower or simpler state to a higher or more complex state **b** the action or an instance of forming and giving sthg off; emission **c** a process of gradual and relatively peaceful social, political, economic, etc advance **d** sthg evolved **2** the process of working out or developing **3a** the historical development of a biological group (e g a race or species) **b** a theory that the various types of animals and plants derived from preexisting types and that the distinguishable differences are due to natural selection [L *evolution-, evolutio* unrolling, fr *evolutus*, pp of *evolvere*] – **evolutionism** *n*, **evolutionist** *n or adj*, **evolutionary** /-(ə)ri/ *adj*, **evolutionarily** /,eevə'loohsh(ə)nrəli/ *adv*

evolve /i'volv/ *vt* **1** EMIT 1a **2a** to work out, develop **b** to produce by natural evolutionary processes ~ *vi* to undergo evolutionary change [L *evolvere* to unroll, fr *e-* + *volvere* to roll – more at VOLUBLE] – **evolvable** *adj*, **evolvement** *n*

evulsion /i'vulsh(ə)n/ *n* EXTRACTION 1 [L *evulsion-, evulsio*, fr *evulsus*, pp of *evellere* to pluck out, fr *e-* + *vellere* to pluck – more at VULNERABLE]

evzone /'ev,zohn/ *n* a member of an elite (modern) Greek infantry unit [NGk *euzōnos*, fr Gk, active, lit., well-girt, fr *eu-* + *zōnē* girdle – more at ZONE]

ewe /yooh/ *n* the female of the (mature) sheep or a

related animal [ME, fr OE *ēowu*; akin to OHG *ou, ouwi* ewe, L *ovis* sheep, Gk *ois*]

Ewe *n* a Kwa language of Ghana and Togo

'ewe-,neck /yooh/ *n* a thin faultily or concavely arched neck in a dog or horse – **ewe-necked** *adj*

ewer /'yooh·ə/ *n* a wide-mouthed pitcher or jug; *esp* one used to hold water for washing or shaving [ME, fr AF, fr OF *evier*, fr (assumed) VL *aquarium*, fr L, neut of *aquarius* of water, fr *aqua* water – more at ISLAND]

[1]ex /eks, egz/ *adj* former ⟨~ *president Nixon*⟩ – often in combination ⟨*the* ex-*president*⟩ [ME, fr LL, fr L]

[2]ex *prep* **1** from a specified place or source **2a** *esp of securities* without an indicated value or right **b** free of charges until the time of removal from (a place) ⟨~ *dock*⟩ [L]

[3]ex *n* a former spouse, boyfriend, or girl friend – infml

[1]ex- /eks-, egz-/ *prefix* **1** out of; outside ⟨*exclude*⟩ ⟨*exodus*⟩ **2** cause to be ⟨*exacerbate*⟩ ⟨*exalt*⟩ **3** not ⟨*exanimate*⟩ **4** deprive of ⟨*ex propriate*⟩ ⟨*excommunicate*⟩ [ME, fr OF & L; OF, fr L, fr *ex* out of, from; akin to Gk *ex, ex-* out of, from, OSlav *iz*]

[2]ex- – see EXO-

exa- *comb form* million billion (10^{18}) ☞ PHYSICS [ISV, perh alter. of *exo-*]

exacerbate /ek'sasəbayt, ig'za-/ *vt* to make (sthg bad) worse; aggravate [L *exacerbatus*, pp of *exacerbare*, fr *ex-* + *acerbus* harsh, bitter, fr *acer* sharp – more at EDGE] – **exacerbation** /-'baysh(ə)n/ *n*

[1]exact /ig'zakt/ *vt* to demand and obtain by force, threats, etc; require ⟨*from them has been* ~ed *the ultimate sacrifice* – D D Eisenhower⟩ [ME *exacten*, fr L *exactus*, pp of *exigere* to drive out, demand, measure, fr *ex-* + *agere* to drive – more at AGENT] – **exactable** *adj*, **exactor** *also* **exacter** *n*

[2]exact *adj* **1** exhibiting or marked by complete accordance with fact **2** marked by thorough consideration or minute measurement of small factual details [L *exactus*, fr pp of *exigere*] – **exactness** *n*

exacting /ig'zakting/ *adj* making rigorous demands; *esp* requiring careful attention and precise accuracy – **exactingly** *adv*, **exactingness** *n*

exaction /ig'zaksh(ə)n/ *n* **1a** exacting **b** extortion **2** sthg exacted; *esp* a fee, reward, or contribution demanded or levied with severity or injustice

exactitude /ig'zaktityoohd/ *n* (the quality of) being exact

exactly /ig'zaktli/ *adv* **1** altogether, entirely ⟨*not* ~ *what I had in mind*⟩ **2** quite so – used to express agreement [[2]EXACT + [2]-LY]

exaggerate /ig'zajərayt/ *vt* **1** to say or believe more than the truth about **2** to make greater or more pronounced than normal; overemphasize ⟨*he* ~d *his line to gain sympathy*⟩ ~ *vi* to make an exaggeration [L *exaggeratus*, pp of *exaggerare*, lit., to heap up, fr *ex-* + *agger* heap, fr *aggerere* to carry towards, fr *ad-* + *gerere* to carry – more at CAST] – **exaggeratedly** *adv*, **exaggeratedness** *n*, **exaggerative** /-rətiv/, **exaggeratory** /-jərət(ə)ri/ *adj*, **exaggerator** /-,raytə/ *n*, **exaggeration** /-'raysh(ə)n/ *n*

exalt /ig'zawlt/ *vt* **1** to raise high, esp in rank, power, or character **2** to praise highly; glorify [ME *exalten*, fr MF & L; MF *exalter*, fr L *exaltare*, fr *ex-* + *altus* high – more at OLD] – **exaltedly** *adv*, **exalter** *n*

exaltation /,egzawl'taysh(ə)n/ *n* an excessively intensified sense of well-being, power, or importance [EXALT + -ATION]

exam /ig'zam, ik'sam/ *n* an examination

examination /ig,zami'naysh(ə)n/ *n* **1** (an) examining ⟨*a medical* ~⟩ **2** (the taking by a candidate for a university degree, Advanced level, Ordinary level, etc of) a set of questions designed to test knowledge **3** a formal interrogation (in a law court) – **examinational** *adj*, **examinatorial** /-nə'tawri·əl/ *adj*

examine /ig'zamin/ *vt* **1** to inspect closely; investigate **2a** to interrogate closely ⟨~ *a prisoner*⟩ **b** to test (e g a candidate for a university degree) by an examination in order to determine knowledge [ME *examinen*, fr MF *examiner*, fr L *examinare*, fr *examen* tongue of a balance, examination, fr *exigere* – more at EXACT] – **examinable** *adj*, **examinee** /ig,zami'nee/ *n*, **examiner** *n*

example /ig'zahmpl/ *n* **1** sthg representative of all of the group or type to which it belongs **2** sby or sthg that may be copied by other people ⟨*a good or bad* ~⟩ ⟨*set an* ~⟩ **3** (the recipient of) a punishment inflicted as a warning to others ⟨*make an* ~ *of them*⟩ **4** a problem to be solved to illustrate a rule (e g in arithmetic) [ME, fr MF, fr L *exemplum*, fr *eximere* to take out, fr *ex-* + *emere* to take – more at REDEEM] – **for example** as an example ⟨*there are many sources of air pollution; exhaust fumes,* for example⟩

exanimate /ig'zanimət, -mayt/ *adj* LIFELESS 1, 3 [L *exanimatus*, pp of *exanimare* to deprive of life or spirit, fr *ex-* + *anima* breath, soul – more at ANIMATE]

exanthema /,egzan'theemə, ,eks-/ *n* (a disease that is accompanied by) a skin rash [LL, fr Gk *exanthēma*, fr *exanthein* to bloom, erupt, fr *ex-* + *anthos* flower]

exarch /'ek,sahk/ *n* a viceroy in the Byzantine empire [LL *exarchus*, fr LGk *exarchos*, fr Gk, leader, fr *exarchein* to begin, take the lead, fr *ex-* + *archein* to rule, begin – more at ARCH-] – **exarchal** *adj*, **exarchate** /'eksah,kayt/ *n*, **exarchy** *n*

exasperate /ig'zahspə,rayt/ *vt* to anger or irritate (sby) [L *exasperatus*, pp of *exasperare*, fr *ex-* + *asper* rough] – **exasperatedly** *adv*, **exasperatingly** *adv*, **exasperation** /-'raysh(ə)n/ *n*

ex cathedra /,eks kə'theedrə/ *adv or adj* with authority ⟨~ *pronouncements*⟩ [NL, lit., from the chair]

excavate /'ekskəvayt/ *vt* **1** to form a cavity or hole in **2** to form by hollowing **3** to dig out and remove **4** to expose to view by digging away a covering ~ *vi* to make excavations [L *excavatus*, pp of *excavare*, fr *ex-* + *cavare* to make hollow – more at CAVATINA] – **excavator** *n*, **excavation** /-'vaysh(ə)n/ *n*

exceed /ik'seed/ *vt* **1** to extend beyond **2** to be greater than or superior to **3** to act or go beyond the limits of ⟨~ *the speed limit*⟩ [ME *exceden*, fr MF *exceder*, fr L *excedere*, fr *ex-* + *cedere* to go – more at CEDE]

exceedingly /ik'seedingli/, **exceeding** *adv* very, extremely

excel /ik'sel/ *vb* **-ll-** to be superior (to); surpass (others) in accomplishment or achievement – often + *at* or *in* [ME *excellen*, fr L *excellere*, fr *ex-* + *-cellere* to rise, project; akin to L *collis* hill – more at HILL]

excellence /'eks(ə)ləns/ *n* **1** *also* **excellency** being excellent **2** *also* **excellency** an excellent or valuable

Fossils
Only a few of the millions of animals that must have lived on earth are preserved as fossils. Some of the best examples of these are of marine animals with shells or exoskeletons like those shown.

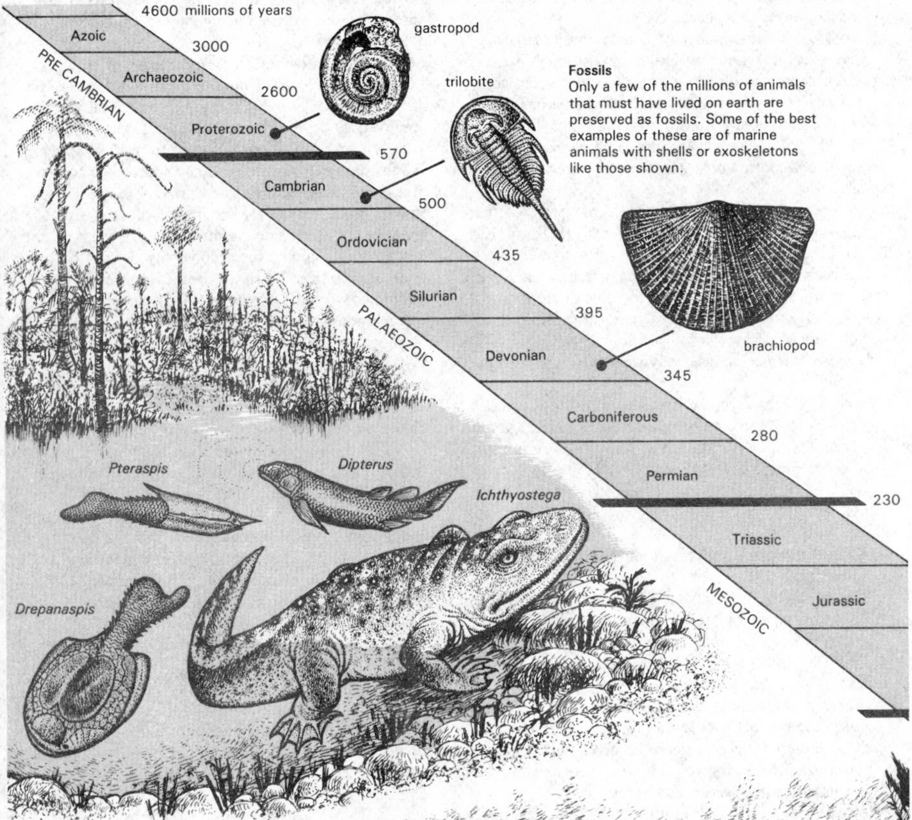

The age of fish
Fossils of many different kinds of fish have been found in rocks of the Devonian period. The fish, shown above, are pictured in a lake setting, but many fish of this era lived in both lakes and the sea. *Dipterus* probably had functional lungs and was therefore amphibious. *Ichthyostega* represents a form that is close in evolutionary development to the more advanced amphibians.

The age of mammals
The Cainozoic era began 65 million years ago and continues today. *Hyracotherium* – the earliest horse discovered – was probably hunted by *Oxyaena*. *Coryphodon* was a large plant-eater. Fossils of our own species and our closest relatives have been found only in rocks formed during the last 3.6 million years.

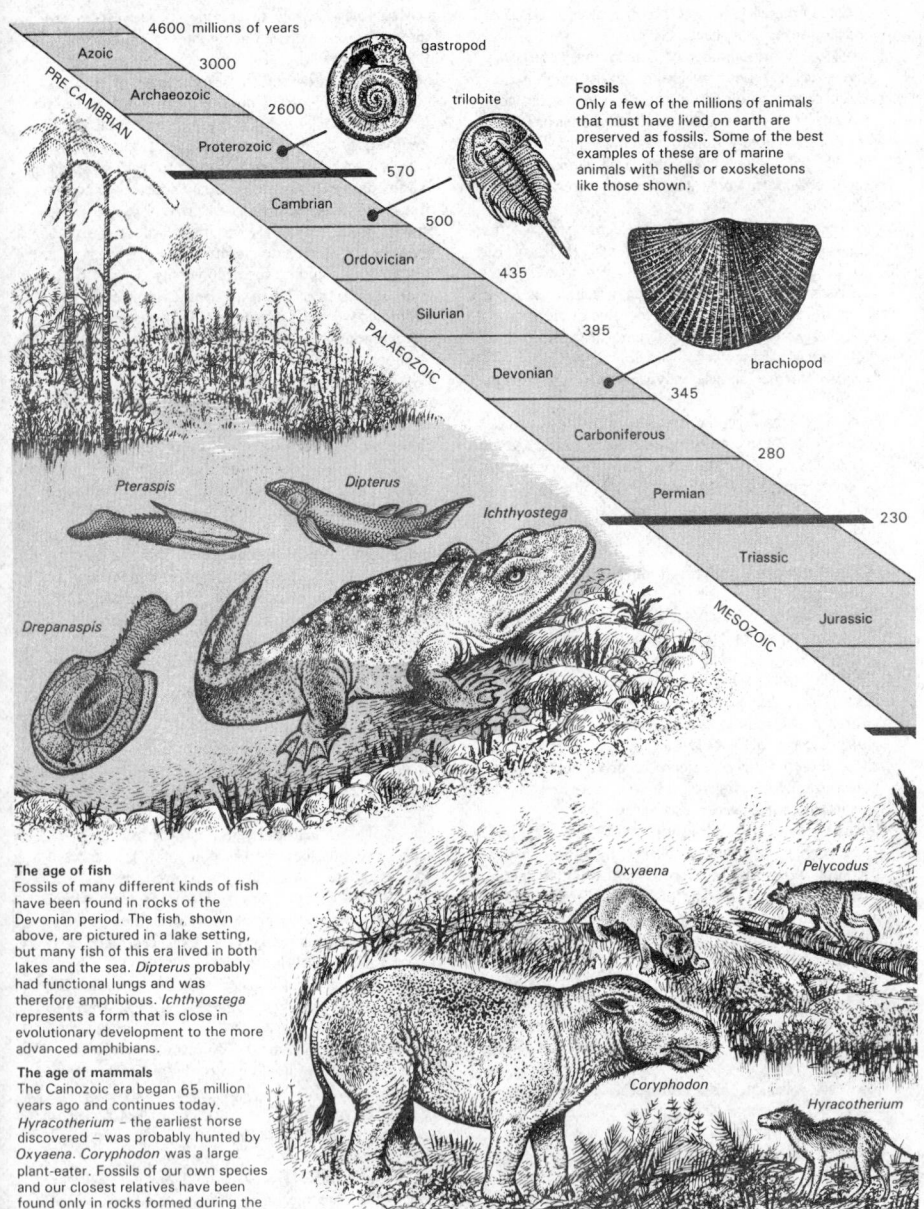

Evolution

The progressive appearance of living things supports the idea of their evolution from simple single celled organisms and can be traced in reasonable detail from fossils, though the sequence is less easy to determine for plants as their remains are rarer.

The age of reptiles
During the Mesozoic era reptiles were not only dominant on land and important in the sea but were also highly successful in the air – *Pteranodon* is the largest flying creature known. The dinosaurs became extinct about 65 million years ago and the mammals then became dominant on land.

quality; a virtue **3 Excellency, Excellence** – used as a title for certain high dignitaries (e g ambassadors) of state and church

excellent /'eksəl(ə)nt/ *adj* outstandingly good [ME, fr MF, fr L *excellent-, excellens*, fr prp of *excellere*] – **excellently** *adv*

[1]**except** /ik'sept/ *vt* to take or leave out from a number or a whole; exclude [ME *excepten*, fr MF *excepter*, fr L *exceptare*, fr *exceptus*, pp of *excipere* to take out, fr *ex-* + *capere* to take – more at HEAVE]

[2]**except** *also* **excepting** *prep* with the exclusion or exception of ⟨*daily* ~ *Sundays*⟩ ⟨*can do everything* ~ *cook*⟩

[3]**except** *also* **excepting** *conj* **1** only, but ⟨*would go* ~ *it's too far*⟩ ⟨*would have protested* ~ *that he was afraid*⟩ **2** unless ⟨~ *you repent*⟩ – fml

ex'cept for *prep* **1** but for; were it not for ⟨*couldn't have done it* ~ *your help*⟩ **2** with the exception of ⟨*all here* ~ *Mary*⟩

exception /ik'sepsh(ə)n/ *n* **1** excepting or excluding **2** sby or sthg excepted; *esp* a case to which a rule does not apply **3** question, objection ⟨*witnesses whose authority is beyond* ~ – T B Macaulay⟩

ex'ceptionable /-əbl/ *adj* likely to cause objection; objectionable – **exceptionably** *adv*, **exceptionability** /-ə'biləti/ *n*

exceptional /ik'sepsh(ə)nl/ *adj* **1** forming an exception; unusual ⟨*an* ~ *number of rainy days*⟩ **2** not average; *esp* superior – **exceptionally** *adv*, **exceptionality** /-'aləti/ *n*

[1]**excerpt** /ek'suhpt/ *vt* **1** to select (a passage) for quoting, copying, or performing **2** to take excerpts from (e g a book) [L *excerptus*, pp of *excerpere*, fr *ex-* + *carpere* to gather, pluck – more at HARVEST] – **excerpter** *also* **excerptor** *n*, **excerption** /ek'suhpsh(ə)n/ *n*

[2]**excerpt** /'ek,suhpt/ *n* a passage taken from a book, musical composition, etc

[1]**excess** /ik'ses/ *n* **1a** the exceeding of usual, proper, or specified limits **b** the amount or degree by which one thing or quantity exceeds another **2** (an instance of) undue or immoderate indulgence; intemperance **3** an amount an insured person agrees to pay him-/herself out of each claim made on an insurance policy in return for a lower premium [ME, fr MF or LL; MF *exces*, fr LL *excessus*, fr L, departure, projection, fr *excessus*, pp of *excedere* to exceed] – **excessive** *adj*, **excessively** *adv*, **excessiveness** *n* – **in excess of** more than

[2]**excess** /'ekses, ik'ses/ *adj* more than the usual, proper, or specified amount; extra ⟨*charges for* ~ *baggage*⟩

[1]**exchange** /iks'chaynj/ *n* **1a** the act of exchanging one thing for another; a trade ⟨*an* ~ *of prisoners*⟩ **b** a usu brief interchange of words or blows ⟨*had an acrimonious* ~ *with the manager*⟩ **2** sthg offered, given, or received in an exchange **3a** (the system of settling, usu by bills of exchange rather than money) debts payable currently, esp in a foreign country **b(1)** change or conversion of one currency into another **(2) exchange, exchange rate** the value of one currency in terms of another **4** a place where things or services are exchanged: e g **a** an organized market for trading in securities or commodities **b** a centre or device controlling the connection of telephone calls between many different lines ☞ TELECOMMUNICATION [ME *exchaunge*, fr MF *eschange*, fr *eschangier* to exchange, fr (assumed) VL *excambiare*, fr L *ex-* + *cambiare* to exchange – more at CHANGE]

[2]**exchange** *vt* **1a** to part with, give, or transfer in return for sthg received as an equivalent ⟨*where can I* ~ *my dollars for pounds?*⟩ ⟨*John* ~d *books with Peter*⟩ ⟨exchanging *freedom for security*⟩ **b** *of 2 parties* to give and receive (things of the same type) ⟨*the 2 armies* ~d *prisoners*⟩ ⟨*they* ~d *blows*⟩ **2** to replace by other goods ⟨*will they* ~ *clothes that don't fit?*⟩ ~ *vi* **1** to pass or become received in exchange **2** to engage in an exchange – **exchangeable** *adj*, **exchanger** *n*, **exchangeability** /-jə'biləti/ *n*

ex'change ,student *n* a student from one country allowed to study at an institution in another country in exchange for one sent to the home country of the first

exchequer /iks'chekə/ *n* **1** *cap* a former civil court having jurisdiction primarily over revenue and now merged with the Queen's Bench Division **2** *often cap* the department of state in charge of the national revenue **3** the (national or royal) treasury [ME *escheker*, fr AF, fr OF *eschequier* chessboard, counting table, fr *eschec* check – more at CHECK]

[1]**excise** /'ek,siez, ,-'-/ *n* **1** an internal tax levied on the manufacture, sale, or consumption of a commodity within a country **2** any of various taxes on privileges, often levied in the form of a licence that must be bought [obs D *excijs* (now *accijus*), fr MD, prob modif of OF *assise* session, assessment – more at ASSIZE]

[2]**excise** /ek'siez/ *vt* to impose an excise on – **excisable** *adj*

[3]**excise** *vt* to remove (as if) by cutting out [L *excisus*, pp of *excidere*, fr *ex-* + *caedere* to cut – more at CONCISE] – **excision** /ek'sizh(ə)n/ *n*

exciseman /'eksiez,man, -'-,-/ *n* an officer who inspects and rates articles liable to excise

excitable /ik'sietəbl/ *adj* capable of being readily activated or roused into a state of excitement or irritability; *specif* capable of being activated by and reacting to stimuli – **excitableness, excitability** /ik,sietə'biləti/ *n*

excite /ik'siet/ *vt* **1a** to provoke or stir up (action) ⟨~ *a rebellion*⟩ **b** to rouse to strong, esp pleasurable, feeling **c** to arouse (e g an emotional response) ⟨*the plight of the refugees* ~d *their pity*⟩ ⟨*her late arrival* ~d *much curiosity*⟩ **2** to induce a magnetic field or electric current in; *also* to induce (e g a magnetic field or an electric current) **3** to raise (e g an atom or a molecule) to a higher energy level [ME *exciten*, fr MF *exciter*, fr L *excitare*, fr *ex-* + *citare* to rouse – more at CITE] – **excitant** *n or adj*, **excitative** /-tətiv/, **excitatory** /-tət(ə)ri/ *adj*, **excitedly** *adv*, **excitement** *n*, **exciter** *n*, **exciting** *adj*, **excitingly** *adv*, **excitation** /,eksie'taysh(ə)n/ *n*

exciton /'eksi,ton/ *n* a mobile combination of a high-energy electron bound to a hole caused by the absence of an electron in a crystal (e g of silicon or another semiconductor) [ISV *excit*ation (fr *excite* + *-ation*) + *-on*] – **excitonic** /,eksə'tonik/ *adj*

exclaim /ik'sklaym/ *vi* to cry out or speak in strong or sudden emotion ⟨~ed *in delight*⟩ ~ *vt* to utter sharply, passionately, or vehemently [MF *exclamer*, fr L *exclamare*, fr *ex-* + *clamare* to cry out – more at CLAIM] – **exclaimer** *n*

exclamation /,eksklə'maysh(ə)n/ *n* exclaiming or

the words exclaimed – **exclamatory** /ik'sklamət(ə)ri/ *adj*

,excla'mation ,mark *n* a punctuation mark ! used esp after an interjection or exclamation

,excla'mation ,point *n, chiefly NAm* EXCLAMATION MARK

exclave /'eks,klayv/ *n* a portion of a country separated from the main part and surrounded by foreign territory [*ex-* + *-clave* (as in *enclave*)]

exclude /ik'skloohd/ *vt* **1a** to shut out **b** to bar from participation, consideration, or inclusion **2** to expel, esp from a place or position previously occupied [ME *excluden,* fr L *excludere,* fr *ex-* + *claudere* to close – more at [4]CLOSE] – **excludable** *adj,* **excluder** *n,* **exclusion**/-zh(ə)n/ *n,* **exclusionary** *adj*

ex'clusion ,principle /iks'kloohzh(ə)n/ *n* a principle in physics stating that no 2 electrons in an atom or molecule will be exactly equivalent

[1]**exclusive** /ik'skloohsiv, -ziv/ *adj* **1a** excluding or having power to exclude **b** limiting or limited to possession, control, use, etc by a single individual, group, etc ⟨*an ~ contract*⟩ ⟨*an ~ interview*⟩ **2a** excluding others (considered to be inferior) from participation, membership, or entry ⟨*an ~ club*⟩ **b** snobbishly aloof **3** stylish and expensive **4a** SOLE 1, 2 ⟨*~ jurisdiction*⟩ **b** whole, undivided ⟨*his ~ attention*⟩ **5** not inclusive ⟨*Monday to Friday ~*⟩ [MF *exclusif,* fr ML *exclusivus,* fr L *exclusus,* pp of *excludere*] – **exclusively** *adv,* **exclusiveness, exclusivity** /,ekslooh'sivəti/ *n*

[2]**exclusive** *n* **1** a newspaper story printed by only 1 newspaper **2** an exclusive right (e g to sell a particular product in a certain area)

ex,clusive dis'junction *n* a complex sentence in logic that is true when 1 and only 1 of its constituent sentences is true

excogitate /eks'kojitayt/ *vt* to think out; devise – fml [L *excogitatus,* pp of *excogitare,* fr *ex-* + *cogitare* to cogitate] – **excogitative** /-tətiv/ *adj,* **excogitation** /,ekskoji'taysh(ə)n/ *n*

[1]**excommunicate** /,ekskə'myoohni,kayt/ *vt* **1** to deprive officially of the rights of church membership **2** to exclude from fellowship of a group or community [ME *excommunicaten,* fr LL *excommunicatus,* pp of *excommunicare,* fr L *ex-* + LL *communicare* to communicate] – **excommunicative** /-kətiv/, **excommunicatory** /-kət(ə)ri/ *adj,* **excommunication** /-'kaysh(ə)n/ *n*

[2]**excommunicate** /,ekskə'myoohnikət, -,kayt/ *n or adj* (one who is) excommunicated

excoriate /ik'skawriayt/ *vt* **1** to wear away the skin of; abrade **2** to censure scathingly – fml [ME *excoriaten,* fr LL *excoriatus,* pp of *excoriare,* fr L *ex-* + *corium* skin, hide – more at CUIRASS] – **excoriation** /eks,kawri'aysh(ə)n/ *n*

excrement /'ekskrəmənt/ *n* faeces or other waste matter discharged from the body [L *excrementum,* fr *excernere*] – **excremental** /,ekskrə'mentl/ *adj,* **excrementitious** /,ekskrəmen'tishəs/ *adj*

excrescence /ik'skres(ə)ns/, **excrescency** /-si/ *n* an excessive or abnormal outgrowth or enlargement [ME, fr MF *excressance,* fr L *excrescentia,* fr *excrescent-, excrescens,* prp of *excrescere* to grow out, fr *ex-* + *crescere* to grow] – **excrescent** *adj*

excreta /ik'skreetə/ *n pl* excrement [NL, fr L, neut pl of *excretus*] – **excretal** *adj*

excrete /ik'skreet/ *vt* to separate and eliminate or discharge (waste) from blood or living tissue [L *excretus,* pp of *excernere* to sift out, discharge, fr *ex-* + *cernere* to sift – more at CERTAIN] – **excreter** *n,* **excretory** /-t(ə)ri/ *adj,* **excretion** /ik'skreesh(ə)n/ *n*

excruciating /ik'skroohshi,ayting/ *adj* **1** causing great pain or anguish; agonizing, tormenting ⟨*an ~ migraine*⟩ **2** very intense; extreme ⟨*~ pain*⟩ [*excruciate* fr L *excruciatus,* pp of *excruciare,* fr *ex-* + *cruciare* to crucify, fr *cruc-, crux* cross] – **excruciate** /-shi,ayt/ *vt,* **excruciatingly** *adv,* **excrutiation** /-shi'aysh(ə)n/ *n*

exculpate /'ekskul,payt, ik'skul,payt/ *vt* to clear from alleged fault, blame, or guilt [(assumed) ML *exculpatus,* pp of *exculpare,* fr L *ex-* + *culpa* blame] – **exculpation** /,ekskul'paysh(ə)n/ *n,* **exculpatory** /ik'skulpət(ə)ri/ *adj*

excursion /ik'skuhsh(ə)n/ *n* **1** a (brief) pleasure trip, usu at reduced rates **2** a deviation from a direct, definite, or proper course; *esp* a digression ⟨*needless ~s into abstruse theory*⟩ **3** (the distance travelled in) a movement outwards and back or from a mean position or axis [L *excursion-, excursio,* fr *excursus,* pp of *excurrere* to run out, extend, fr *ex-* + *currere* to run] – **excursionist** *n*

excursive /ik'skuhsiv/ *adj* digressive – **excursively** *adv,* **excursiveness** *n*

excursus /ek'skuhsəs/ *n, pl* **excursuses** *also* **excursus** an appendix or digression that contains further discussion of some point or topic [L, digression, fr *excursus,* pp]

[1]**excuse** /ik'skyoohz/ *vt* **1a** to make apology for ⟨*quietly ~d his clumsiness*⟩ **b** to try to remove blame from ⟨*~d himself for being so careless*⟩ **2** to forgive entirely or overlook as unimportant ⟨*she graciously ~d his thoughtlessness*⟩ **3** to allow to leave; dismiss ⟨*the class was ~d*⟩ **4** to be an acceptable reason for; justify – usu neg ⟨*nothing can ~ his cruelty*⟩ **5** *Br* to free from (a duty) – usu pass ⟨*the class was ~d homework*⟩ [ME *excusen,* fr OF *excuser,* fr L *excusare,* fr *ex-* + *causa* cause, explanation] – **excusal** *n,* **excusable** *adj,* **excusably** *adv,* **excusatory** /-zətri/ *adj,* **excuser** *n*

[2]**excuse** /ik'skyoohs/ *n* **1** sthg offered as grounds for being excused ⟨*he had a good ~ for being late*⟩ **2** *pl* an expression of regret for failure to do sthg or esp for one's absence ⟨*make my ~s at the party tomorrow*⟩

,ex-di'rectory *adj, Br* intentionally not listed in a telephone directory [[1]*ex-*]

exeat /'eksi,at/ *n* a formal leave of absence granted esp to a student [L, let him go out, fr *exire* to go out]

execrable /'eksikrəbl/ *adj* detestable, appalling ⟨*~ behaviour*⟩ ⟨*~ taste*⟩ – chiefly fml [EXECRATE + -ABLE] – **execrably** *adv*

execrate /'eksi,krayt/ *vt* **1** to declare to be evil or detestable; denounce **2** to detest utterly; abhor *USE* chiefly fml [L *exsecratus,* pp of *exsecrari* to put under a curse, fr *ex* + *sacr-, sacer* sacred] – **execrator** *n,* **execration** /,eksi'kraysh(ə)n/ *n,* **execrative** /-krətiv/ *adj*

executant /ig'zekyoot(ə)nt/ *n* one who executes or performs; *esp* one skilled in the technique of an art

execute /'eksi,kyooht/ *vt* **1** to carry out fully; put completely into effect **2** to put to death (legally) as a punishment **3** to make or produce (e g a work of art), esp by carrying out a design **4** to (do what is required to) make valid ⟨~ *a deed*⟩ **5** to play, perform ⟨~ *a piece of music*⟩ [ME *executen*, fr MF *executer*, back-formation fr *execution*] – **executable** *adj*

execution /ˌeksiˈkyoohsh(ə)n/ *n* **1** a putting to death as a punishment **2** a judicial writ directing the enforcement of a judgment **3** the act, mode, or result of performance ⟨*the* ~ *was perfect but the piece lacked expression*⟩ [ME, fr MF, fr L *exsecution-, exsecutio*, fr *exsecutus*, pp of *exsequi* to execute, fr *ex-* + *sequi* to follow – more at SUE]

executioner /ˌeksiˈkyoohsh(ə)nə/ *n* one who puts to death; *specif* one legally appointed to perform capital punishment

¹**executive** /igˈzekyootiv/ *adj* **1** concerned with making and carrying out laws, decisions, etc; *specif, Br* of or concerned with the detailed application of policy or law rather than its formulation **2** of, for, or being an executive ⟨*the* ~ *offices are on the top floor*⟩ [EXECUTE + -IVE]

²**executive** *n* **1** the executive branch of a government **2** an individual or group that controls or directs an organization **3** one who holds a position of administrative or managerial responsibility

executor /ˈeksiˌkyoohtə, igˈzekyootə/, *fem* **executrix** /igˈzekyooˌtriks/ *n, pl* **executors,** *fem* **executrices** /-ˌtrieseez/ one appointed to carry out the provisions of a will [ME, fr OF, fr L *exsecutor*, fr *exsecutus*] – **executory** /-(ə)ri/, **executorial** /igˌzekyooˈtawri·əl/ *adj*

exegesis /ˌeksiˈjeesis/ *n, pl* **exegeses** /-seez/ an explanation or critical interpretation of an esp biblical text; *broadly* an exposition [NL, fr Gk *exēgēsis*, fr *exēgeisthai* to explain, interpret, fr *ex-* + *hēgeisthai* to lead – more at SEEK] – **exegetic** /ˌeksiˈjetik/, **exegetical** *adj*

exegete /ˈeksiˌjeet/ *n* one who practises exegesis [Gk *exēgētēs*, fr *exēgeisthai*]

exemplar /igˈzemplə, -ˌplah/ *n* sthg that serves as a model or example; *also* a copy of a book or text [ME, fr L, fr *exemplum* example]

exemplary /igˈzempləri/ *adj* **1** deserving imitation; commendable ⟨*his conduct was* ~⟩ **2** serving as a warning ⟨~ *punishments*⟩ **3** serving as an example, instance, or illustration – **exemplarily** *adv*, **exemplariness, exemplarity** /ˌegzemˈplarəti/ *n*

exemplify /igˈzemplifie/ *vt* **1** to show or illustrate by example **2** to be an instance of or serve as an example of; typify, embody [ME *exemplifien*, fr MF *exemplifier*, fr ML *exemplificare*, fr L *exemplum*] – **exemplification** /igˌzemplifiˈkaysh(ə)n/ *n*

exemplum /igˈzempləm/ *n, pl* **exempla** /-plə/ **1** an anecdote or short story that illustrates a moral point or supports an argument **2** an example, model – chiefly fml [LL, fr L, example]

¹**exempt** /igˈzempt/ *adj* freed from some liability or requirement to which others are subject ⟨~ *from jury service*⟩ [ME, fr L *exemptus*, pp of *eximere* to take out – more at EXAMPLE]

²**exempt** *vt* to make exempt; excuse ⟨~ed *from jury service*⟩ – **exemption** /igˈzempsh(ə)n/ *n*

exequy /ˈeksikwi/ *n* a funeral ceremony – usu pl with sing. meaning; fml [ME *exequies, exequise*, sing. & pl, fr MF & L; MF *exequies*, pl, fr L *exequiae, exsequiae*, pl, fr *exequi, exsequi* to follow, perform, execute]

¹**exercise** /ˈeksəˌsiez/ *n* **1** the use of a specified power or right ⟨*the* ~ *of his authority*⟩ **2a** regular or repeated use of a faculty or body part **b** bodily exertion for the sake of developing and maintaining physical fitness **3** sthg performed or practised in order to develop, improve, or display a specific power or skill **4** a manoeuvre or drill carried out for training and discipline [ME, fr MF *exercice*, fr L *exercitium*, fr *exercitus*, pp of *exercēre* to drive on, keep busy, fr *ex-* + *arcēre* to enclose, hold off – more at ARK]

²**exercise** *vt* **1** to make effective in action; use, exert ⟨*didn't* ~ *good judgment*⟩ **2a** to use repeatedly in order to strengthen or develop **b** to train (e g troops) by drills and manoeuvres **c** to give exercise to ⟨~ *the horses*⟩ **3a** to engage the attention and effort of ⟨*the problem greatly* ~d *his mind*⟩ **b** to cause anxiety, alarm, or indignation in ⟨*citizens* ~d *about pollution*⟩ ~ *vi* to take exercise; *esp* to train – **exercisable** *adj*, **exerciser** *n*

exergue /ekˈsuhg/ *n* a space on a coin, medal, etc usu on the reverse below the central part of the design [F, fr NL *exergum*, fr Gk *ex* out of + *ergon* work]

exert /igˈzuht/ *vt* **1** to bring (e g strength or authority) to bear, esp with sustained effort; employ, wield **2** to take upon (oneself) the effort of doing sthg ⟨*he never* ~s *himself to help anyone*⟩ [L *exsertus*, pp of *exserere* to thrust out, fr *ex-* + *serere* to join – more at SERIES] – **exertion** /igˈzuhsh(ə)n/ *n*

exeunt /ˈeksiˌoont/ – used as a stage direction to specify that all or certain named characters leave the stage [L, they go out, fr *exire* to go out – more at ¹EXIT]

exfoliate /eksˈfohliayt/ *vt* to cast (e g skin or bark) off in scales, layers, etc ~ *vi* **1** to split into or shed scales, layers, surface body cells, etc **2** to come off in a thin piece **3** to grow (as if) by producing or unfolding leaves [LL *exfoliatus*, pp of *exfoliare* to strip of leaves, fr L *ex-* + *folium* leaf – more at BLADE] – **exfoliative** /-ətiv/ *adj*, **exfoliation** /-ˈaysh(ə)n/ *n*

ex gratia /ˌeks ˈgraysh(i)ə/ *adj or adv* as a favour; not compelled by legal right ⟨~ *payments*⟩ [NL]

exhalation /ˌeksəˈlaysh(ə)n, ˌeks·hə-/ *n* **1** exhaling **2** sthg exhaled or given off; an emanation

exhale /eksˈhayl, igˈzayl/ *vt* **1** to breathe out **2** to give forth (gas or vapour); emit ~ *vi* **1** to rise or be given off as vapour **2** to emit breath or vapour [ME *exalen*, fr L *exhalare*, fr *ex-* + *halare* to breathe; akin to L *anima* breath – more at ANIMATE]

¹**exhaust** /igˈzawst/ *vt* **1a** to draw off or let out completely **b** to empty by drawing off the contents; *specif* to create a vacuum in **2a** to consume entirely; USE UP ⟨~ed *our funds in a week*⟩ **b** to tire out ⟨~ed *by their efforts*⟩ **3a** to develop or deal with (a subject) to the fullest possible extent **b** to try out the whole number of ⟨~ed *all the possibilities*⟩ [L *exhaustus*, pp of *exhaurire*, fr *ex-* + *haurire* to draw; akin to MHG *œsen* to empty, Gk *auein* to take] – **exhauster** *n*, **exhaustible** *adj*, **exhaustibility** /-təˈbiləti/ *n*

²**exhaust** *n* **1** (the escape of) used gas or vapour from an engine **2** the conduit or pipe through which used gases escape ☞ CAR

exhaustion /igˈzawschən/ *n* extreme tiredness [¹EXHAUST + -ION]

exhaustive /igˈzawstiv/ *adj* comprehensive, thorough ⟨*conducted an* ~ *investigation*⟩ [¹EXHAUST + -IVE] – **exhaustively** *adv*, **exhaustiveness** *n*, **exhaustivity** /-ˈtivəti/ *n*

[1]**exhibit** /ig'zibit/ *vt* to present to view: e g **a** to show or display outwardly, esp by visible signs or actions; reveal, manifest ⟨~ed *no fear*⟩ **b** to show publicly, esp for purposes of competition or demonstration ~ *vi* to display sthg for public inspection [ME *exhibiten*, fr L *exhibitus*, pp of *exhibēre*, fr *ex-* + *habēre* to have, hold – more at GIVE] – **exhibitive** /-tiv/ *adj*, **exhibitor** *n*, **exhibitory** /-t(ə)ri/ *adj*

[2]**exhibit** *n* **1** sthg exhibited **2** sthg produced as evidence in a lawcourt **3** *chiefly NAm* EXHIBITION 1

exhibition /,eksi'bish(ə)n/ *n* **1** an act or instance of exhibiting ⟨*an ~ of ill-temper*⟩ **2** a public showing (e g of works of art or objects of manufacture) **3** *Br* a grant drawn from the funds of a school or university to help to maintain a student

exhibitioner /,eksi'bish(ə)nə/ *n*, *Br* a student who holds an exhibition

,exhi'bitionism /-iz(ə)m/ *n* **1** a perversion marked by a tendency to indecent exposure **2** the act or practice of behaving so as to attract attention to oneself – **exhibitionist** *n or adj*, **exhibitionistic** /-'istik/ *adj*

exhilarate /ig'ziləravt/ *vt* **1** to make cheerful **2** to enliven, invigorate [L *exhilaratus*, pp of *exhilarare*, fr *ex-* + *hilarare* to gladden, fr *hilarus* cheerful – more at HILARIOUS] – **exhilarative** /-rətiv/ *adj*, **exhilaration** /-'raysh(ə)n/ *n*

exhort /ig'zawt/ *vt* to urge or advise strongly ⟨~ed *them to behave well*⟩ ~ *vi* to give warnings or advice; make urgent appeals [ME *exhorten*, fr MF *exhorter*, fr L *exhortari*, fr *ex-* + *hortari* to urge, incite – more at YEARN] – **exhortative** /-tətiv/ *adj*, **exhorter** *n*

exhortation /,egzaw'taysh(ə)n/ *n* language intended to incite and encourage; *esp* an inspiring or encouraging speech or passage of writing [EXHORT + -ATION]

exhortatory /ig'zawtətri/ *adj* using exhortation; serving to exhort

exhume /eks'hyoohm, ek'syoohm, ik-/ *vt* **1** to disinter **2** to bring back from neglect or obscurity [F or ML; F *exhumer*, fr ML *exhumare*, fr L *ex* out of + *humus* earth – more at EX-, HUMBLE] – **exhumer** *n*, **exhumation** /-'maysh(ə)n/ *n*

ex hypothesi /,eks hie'pothə,sie/ *adj or adv* according to the hypothesis [NL]

exigency /'eksij(ə)nsi, ig'zij(ə)nsi/, **exigence** /'eksij(ə)ns, 'egz-/ *n* **1** an exigent state of affairs; an emergency ⟨*the cabinet must be free to act in any ~*⟩ **2** such need or necessity as belongs to the occasion; a requirement – usu pl with sing. meaning ***USE*** fml [EXIGENT + -CY]

exigent /'eksij(ə)nt, 'egz-/ *adj* **1** requiring immediate aid or action **2** exacting, demanding ***USE*** fml [L *exigent-*, *exigens*, prp of *exigere* to demand – more at EXACT] – **exigently** *adv*

exiguous /ig'zigyoo·əs/ *adj* excessively scanty; inadequate, meagre – fml [L *exiguus*, fr *exigere*] – **exiguously** *adv*, **exiguousness** *n*, **exiguity** /,eksi'gyooh·əti/ *n*

[1]**exile** /'eksiel, 'egziel/ *n* **1** enforced or voluntary absence from one's country or home **2** one who is exiled voluntarily or by authority [ME *exil*, fr MF, fr L *exilium*, fr *exul* banished person]

[2]**exile** *vt* to send into exile

exist /ig'zist/ *vi* **1a** to have being in the real world; be ⟨*do unicorns ~?*⟩ **b** to have being in specified conditions ⟨*some chemical compounds ~ only in solution*⟩ **2** to continue to be ⟨*Nazism still ~*s⟩ **3a** to have life or the functions of vitality ⟨*man cannot ~ without water*⟩ **b** to live at an inferior level or under adverse circumstances ⟨*starving people ~*ing *from one day to the next*⟩ [L *exsistere* to come into being, exist, fr *ex-* + *sistere* to stand; akin to L *stare* to stand – more at STAND]

existence /ig'zist(ə)ns/ *n* **1a** the totality of existent things **b** the state or fact of existing; life ⟨*death is an elementary fact of ~*⟩ **2** manner of living or being ⟨*pursued a solitary ~*⟩

existent /ig'zist(ə)nt/ *adj* **1** having being; existing **2** extant [L *exsistent-*, *exsistens*, prp of *exsistere*] – **existent** *n*

existential /,egzi'stensh(ə)l/ *adj* **1** of or grounded in existence ⟨~ *propositions*⟩ **2** existentialist [(2) trans of Dan *eksistentiel* & G *existential*] – **existentially** *adv*

,exi'stential,ism /-,iz(ə)m/ *n* a philosophical movement characterized by inquiry into human beings' experience of themselves in relation to the world, esp with reference to their freedom, responsibility, and isolation and the experiences (e g of anxiety and despair) in which these are revealed

,exi'stential,ist /-,ist/ *n or adj* (a follower) of existentialism – **existentialistic** /-'istik/ *adj*

existential quantifier *n* a quantifier that asserts that there exists at least 1 value of a variable

[1]**exit** /'eksit, 'egzit/ – used as a stage direction to specify who goes off stage [L, he goes out, fr *exire* to go out, fr *ex-* + *ire* to go – more at ISSUE]

[2]**exit** *n* **1** a departure of a performer from a scene **2** the act of going out or away **3** a way out of an enclosed place or space **4** death – euph [L *exitus*, fr *exitus*, pp of *exire*; (1) [1]*exit*] – **exit** *vi*

ex libris /,eks 'leebris/ *n*, *pl* **ex libris** a bookplate [NL, from the books; used before the owner's name on bookplates]

Exmoor /'eks,mooə, -,maw/ *n* (a member of) a breed of hardy ponies with thick manes native to the Exmoor district [*Exmoor*, district of SW England]

,ex 'nihilo /'neehiloh/ *adv or adj* from or out of nothing ⟨*creation ~*⟩ [L]

exo- /eksoh-/, **ex-** *comb form* **1** outside ⟨exogamy⟩; outer ⟨exo*skeleton*⟩ – compare ECT-, END- 1 **2** giving off; releasing ⟨exo*crine*⟩ [Gk *exō* out, outside, fr *ex* out of – more at EX-]

,exobi'ology /eksoh-/ *n* extraterrestrial biology – **exobiological** /-bie·ə'lojikl/ *adj*, **exobiologist** /-bie'oləjist/ *n*

exocrine /'eksə,kreen, -krin, -,krien/ *adj* **1** producing secretions that are discharged through a duct – compare ENDOCRINE 1 **2** of or being an exocrine gland or its secretions [ISV *exo-* + Gk *krinein* to separate – more at CERTAIN]

'exocrine ,gland *n* a gland (e g a sweat gland or a kidney) that releases a secretion external to an organ by means of a duct

exocytosis /,eksohsie'tohsis/ *n* the release of substances from a cell by fusion of a vesicle inside the cell with the cell membrane and release of the vesicle contents to the outside – compare ENDOCYTOSIS [NL, fr *exo-* + *-cytosis* (as in *phagocytosis*)] – **exocytic** /-'sietik/ *adj*, **exocytose** /-sie'tohz/ *vb*, **exocytotic** /-sie'totik/ *adj*

exodermis /,eksoh'duhmis/ *n* a layer of the outer living cortical cells that functions as the epidermis in roots lacking secondary thickening [NL]

exodus /'eksədəs/ *n* **1** *cap* the second book of the Old Testament, relating the flight of the Israelites from Egypt **2** a mass departure; an emigration [L, fr Gk *Exodos*, lit., road out, fr *ex-* + *hodos* road – more at CEDE]

ex officio /,eks ə'fis(h)ioh/ *adv or adj* by virtue or because of an office ⟨*the president is an ~ member of the committee*⟩ [LL]

exogamy /ek'sogəmi/ *n* marriage outside one's tribe – compare ENDOGAMY – **exogamous, exogamic** /,eksoh'gamik/ *adj*

exogenous /ek'sojinəs/ *adj* originating from the outside; due to external causes [F *exogène*, fr *exo-* + *-gène* (fr Gk *-genēs* born) – more at -GEN] – **exogenously** *adv*

exonerate /ig'zonərayt/ *vt* **1** to relieve of a responsibility, obligation, or hardship **2** to free from blame; exculpate **USE** usu + *from* ⟨~d *him from a charge of corruption*⟩ [ME *exoneraten*, fr L *exoneratus*, pp of *exonerare* to unburden, fr *ex-* + *oner-*, *onus* load] – **exonerative** /-rətiv/ *adj*, **exoneration** /-'raysh(ə)n/ *n*

exophthalmos /,eksof'thalmos, -məs/ *also* **exophthalmus** /-məs/ *n* abnormal protrusion of the eyeball [NL, fr Gk *exophthalmos* having prominent eyes, fr *ex* out + *ophthalmos* eye] – **exophthalmic** /-mik/ *adj*

exorbitant /ig'zawbit(ə)nt/ *adj, of prices, demands, etc* much greater than is reasonable; excessive [ME, abnormal, irregular, fr MF, fr LL *exorbitant-, exorbitans*, prp of *exorbitare* to deviate, fr L *ex-* + *orbita* track, rut – more at ORB] – **exorbitance** *n*, **exorbitantly** *adv*

exorc·ise, -ize /'eksaw,siez/ *vt* **1a** to expel (an evil spirit) by solemn command (e g in a religious ceremony) **b** to get rid of (e g an unpleasant thought or emotion) as if by exorcism **2** to free (e g a person or place) of an evil spirit [ME *exorcisen*, fr MF *exorciser*, fr LL *exorcizare*, fr Gk *exorkizein*, fr *ex-* + *horkizein* to bind by oath, adjure, fr *horkos* oath; akin to Gk *herkos* fence, L *sarcire* to mend] – **exorciser** *n*

exorcism /'eksaw,siz(ə)m/ *n* (a spell used in) the act of exorcising – **exorcist** /'eksəsist, -saw-/ *n*

exordium /ek'sawdi·əm, -dyəm/ *n, pl* **exordiums, exordia** /-di·ə, -dyə/ a beginning or introduction, esp to a formal speech or literary work [L, fr *exordiri* to begin, fr *ex-* + *ordiri* to begin – more at ORDER] – **exordial** *adj*

exoskeleton /,eksoh'skelitn/ *n* an external supportive (hard or bony) covering of an animal – **exoskeletal** /-'skelitl, -ski'leetl/ *adj*

exosmosis /,eksoz'mohsis/ *n* passage of material through a membrane from a region of higher concentration to a region of lower concentration – compare ENDOSMOSIS [alter. of obs *exosmose*, fr F, fr *ex-* + Gk *ōsmos* act of pushing – more at ENDOSMOSIS] – **exosmotic** /-'motik/ *adj*

exosphere /'eksoh,sfiə/ *n* the outer region of a planet's atmosphere [ISV] – **exospheric** /-'sferik/ *adj*

exostosis /,ekso'stohsis/ *n, pl* **exostoses** /-seez/ a spur or bony outgrowth from a bone [NL, fr Gk *exostōsis*, fr *ex* out of + *osteon* bone – more at EX-, OSSEOUS]

exoteric /,eksoh'terik/ *adj* **1** designed for, understood by, or suitable to be imparted to the public – compare ESOTERIC **2** not admitted or belonging to the inner or initiated circle [L & Gk; L *exotericus*, fr Gk *exōterikos*, lit., external, fr *exōterō*, compar of *exō* outside – more at EXO-] – **exoterically** *adv*

exothermic /,eksoh'thuhmik/, **exothermal** /-'thuhml/ *adj* characterized by or formed with evolution of heat [ISV] – **exothermically** *adv*

exotic /ig'zotik/ *adj* **1** introduced from another country; not native to the place where found ⟨*an ~ plant*⟩ **2** strikingly or excitingly different or unusual ⟨*an ~ dish*⟩ [L *exoticus*, fr Gk *exōtikos*, fr *exō*] – **exotic** *n*, **exotically** *adv*, **exoticness** *n*, **exoticism** /ig'zoti,siz(ə)m/ *n*

exotica /ig'zotikə/ *n pl* exotic things; *esp* literary or artistic items with an exotic theme or quality [NL, fr L, neut pl of *exoticus*]

expand /ik'spand/ *vt* **1a** to increase the size, extent, number, volume, or scope of ⟨*the company has* ~ed *its interests overseas*⟩ **b** to introduce gas into (a plastic or resin) ⟨~ed *vinyl*⟩ **2** to express in detail or in full ⟨*~ an argument*⟩ ~ *vi* **1** to become expanded ⟨ *iron* ~s *when heated*⟩ **2** ENLARGE 2 **3** to grow genial; become more sociable ⟨*only* ~s *among friends*⟩ [ME *expaunden*, fr L *expandere*, fr *ex-* + *pandere* to spread – more at FATHOM] – **expandable** *adj*

ex,panded 'metal *n* sheet metal cut and expanded into a lattice

ex'pander /-də/ *n* any of several substances (e g dextran) used as a blood or plasma substitute for increasing the blood volume [EXPAND + [2]-ER]

expanse /ik'spans/ *n* **1** sthg spread out, esp over a wide area **2** the extent to which sthg is spread out [NL *expansum*, fr L, neut of *expansus*, pp of *expandere*]

ex'pansible /-səbl/ *adj* expandable – **expansibility** /-'biləti/ *n*

expansile /ik'spansiel/ *adj* (capable) of expansion

expansion /ik'spansh(ə)n/ *n* **1** expanding or being expanded ⟨*territorial* ~⟩ **2** the increase in volume of working fluid (e g steam) in an engine cylinder **3** sthg expanded: e g **a** an expanded part **b** a fuller treatment of an earlier theme or work **4** the expanding of a mathematical expression or function in a series – **expansional** *adj*, **expansionary** /-(ə)ri/ *adj*

ex'pansion,ism /-,iz(ə)m/ *n* a policy of (territorial) expansion – **expansionist** *n*, **expansionist, expansionistic** /-'istik/ *adj*

expansive /ik'spansiv/ *adj* **1** having a capacity or tendency to expand or cause expansion **2** freely communicative; genial, effusive ⟨*she grew ~ after dinner*⟩ **3** having wide expanse or extent **4** characterized by largeness or magnificence of scale ⟨~ *living*⟩ – **expansively** *adv*, **expansiveness** *n*, **expansivity** /-'sivəti/ *n*

ex parte /,eks 'pahti, -tay/ *adv or adj* from or in the interests of 1 side only – used of legal proceedings [ML]

expatiate /ik'spayshi,ayt, ek-/ *vi* to speak or write at length or in detail, usu on a single subject – usu + *on* or *upon* [L *exspatiatus*, pp of *exspatiari* to wander, digress, fr *ex-* + *spatium* space, course – more at SPEED] – **expatiation** /-shi'aysh(ə)n/ *n*

[1]**expatriate** /eks'patriayt/ *vt* **1** to exile, banish **2** to withdraw (oneself) from residence in or allegiance to one's native country [ML *expatriatus*, pp of *expatriare* to leave one's own country, fr L *ex-* + *patria* native country, fr fem of *patrius* of a father, fr

patr-, pater father – more at FATHER] – **expatriation** /-tri'aysh(ə)n/ *n*

[2]**expatriate** /,eks'patri·ət/ *n* one who lives in a foreign country – **expatriate** *adj*

expect /ik'spekt/ *vi* **1** to look forward with anticipation **2** to be pregnant ~ *vt* **1** to anticipate or look forward to ⟨~ ed *a telephone call*⟩ **2a** to consider (an event) probable or certain ⟨~ *to be forgiven*⟩ **b** to consider reasonable, due, or necessary ⟨*he* ~ed *respect from his children*⟩ **c** to consider bound in duty or obligated ⟨*they* ~ed *him to pay his dues*⟩ **3** to suppose, think ⟨*I* ~ *that's true*⟩ – infml [L *exspectare* to look forward to, fr *ex-* + *spectare* to look at, fr *spectus*, pp of *specere* to look – more at SPY] – **expectable** *adj*, **expectably** *adv*, **expectance, expectancy** *n*, **expectedly** *adv*, **expectedness** *n*

[1]**expectant** /ik'spekt(ə)nt/ *adj* **1** characterized by expectation **2** *of a pregnant woman* expecting the birth of a child – **expectantly** *adv*

[2]**expectant** *n* one (e g a candidate for a position) who is expectant

expectation /,ekspek'taysh(ə)n/ *n* **1** expecting or sthg expected **2** prospects of inheritance – usu pl with sing. meaning **3** an expected amount or number (e g of years of life) based on statistical probability

expectorant /ik'spektərənt/ *n or adj* (sthg) that promotes expectoration

expectorate /ik'spektərayt/ *vb* **1** to eject (matter) from the throat or lungs by coughing or spitting **2** to spit (e g saliva) [prob fr (assumed) NL *expectoratus*, pp of *expectorare*, fr L, to cast out of the mind, fr *ex-* + *pector-, pectus* breast, soul] – **expectoration** /-'raysh(ə)n/ *n*

expediency /ik'speedi·ənsi, -dyənsi/ *n* **1 expediency, expedience** suitability, fitness **2** cultivation of or adherence to expedient means and methods **3** an expedient

[1]**ex'pedient** /-ənt/ *adj* **1** suitable for achieving a particular end **2** characterized by concern with what is opportune and esp by self-interest, rather than by concern with what is moral [ME, fr MF or L; MF, fr L *expedient-, expediens*, prp of *expedire* to extricate, arrange, be advantageous, fr *ex-* + *ped-, pes* foot – more at FOOT] – **expediently** *adv*

[2]**expedient** *n* a means to an end; *esp* one devised or used in case of urgent need

expedite /'ekspi,diet/ *vt* **1** to execute promptly **2** to hasten the process or progress of; facilitate *USE* fml [L *expeditus*, pp of *expedire*] – **expediter** *n*

expedition /,ekspi'dish(ə)n/ *n* **1** a journey or excursion undertaken for a specific purpose (e g for war or exploration) **2** efficient promptness; speed – fml [ME *expedicioun*, fr MF & L; MF *expedition*, fr L *expedition-, expeditio*, fr *expeditus*]

,expe'ditionary /-ri/ *adj* of or constituting an expedition; *also* sent on military service abroad ⟨*an* ~ *force*⟩

,expe'ditious /-shəs/ *adj* speedy – fml – **expeditiously** *adv*, **expeditiousness** *n*

expel /ik'spel/ *vt* **-ll- 1** to drive or force out ⟨~led *air from the lungs*⟩ **2** to drive away; *esp* to deport **3** to cut off from membership ⟨~led *from school*⟩ [ME *expellen*, fr L *expellere*, fr *ex-* + *pellere* to drive – more at FELT] – **expellable** *adj*, **expeller** *n*, **expellee** /,ekspe'lee, ik,spe'lee/ *n*

expend /ik'spend/ *vt* **1** to pay out ⟨*the new roads on which so much public money is* ~ed⟩ **2** to consume (e g time, care, or attention) by use; USE UP ⟨*projects on which he* ~ed *great energy*⟩ [ME *expenden*, fr L *expendere* to weigh out, expend, fr *ex-* + *pendere* to weigh – more at SPAN] – **expender** *n*

ex'pendable /-dəbl/ *adj* **1** normally used up in service; not intended to be kept or reused ⟨~ *supplies like pencils and paper*⟩ **2** regarded as available for sacrifice or destruction in order to accomplish an objective ⟨~ *troops*⟩ [EXPEND + -ABLE] – **expendability** /-'biləti/ *n*

expenditure /ik'spendichə/ *n* **1** the act or process of expending **2** the amount expended [irreg fr *expend*]

expense /ik'spens/ *n* **1a** sthg expended to secure a benefit or bring about a result **b** financial burden or outlay **c** *pl* the charges incurred by an employee in performing his/her duties **d** an item of business outlay chargeable against revenue in a specific period **2** a cause or occasion of usu high expenditure ⟨*a car is a great* ~⟩ [ME, fr AF or LL; AF, fr LL *expensa*, fr L, fem of *expensus*, pp of *expendere*] – **at somebody's expense** in a manner that causes sby to be ridiculed ⟨*made a joke* at my expense⟩ – **at the expense of** to the detriment of ⟨*develop a boy's physique* at the expense of *his intelligence* – Bertrand Russell⟩

ex'pense ac,count *n* an account of expenses reimbursable to an employee – **expense-account** *adj*

expensive /ik'spensiv/ *adj* **1** involving great expense ⟨*an* ~ *hobby*⟩ **2** commanding a high price; dear – **expensively** *adv*, **expensiveness** *n*

[1]**experience** /ik'spiəri·əns/ *n* **1** (the facts or events perceived by) the usu conscious perception or apprehension of reality or of an external, bodily, or mental event **2** (the knowledge, skill, or practice derived from) direct participation or observation **3** the sum total of conscious events that make up an individual life or the collective past of a community, nation, or humankind generally **4** sthg personally encountered or undergone ⟨*a terrifying* ~⟩ [ME, fr MF, fr L *experientia* act of trying, fr *experient-, experiens*, prp of *experiri* to try, fr *ex-* + *-periri* (akin to *periculum* attempt) – more at FEAR]

[2]**experience** *vt* to have experience of ⟨~d *severe hardships as a child*⟩

ex'perienced *adj* skilful or wise as a result of experience of a particular activity or of life as a whole ⟨*an* ~ *driver*⟩

experiential /ik,spiəri'ensh(ə)l/ *adj* based on or relating to experience; empirical – **experientially** *adv*

experiment /ik'sperimənt/ *n* **1** a tentative procedure or policy that is on trial **2** an operation carried out under controlled conditions in order to test or establish a hypothesis or to illustrate a known law ⟨*a scientific* ~⟩ **3** the process of making experiments [ME, fr MF, fr L *experimentum*, fr *experiri*] – **experiment** /-ment/ *vi*, **experimentation** /-men 'taysh(ə)n, -mən-/ *n*, **experimenter** *n*

experimental /ik,speri'mentl/ *adj* **1** experiential **2** based on or derived from experiment – **experimentalism** *adj*, **experimentally** *adv*

expert /'ekspuht/ *n or adj* (sby or sthg) having or showing special skill or knowledge derived from training or experience [adj ME, fr MF & L; MF, fr L *expertus*, fr pp of *experiri*; n fr adj] – **expertly** *adv*, **expertness** *n*

expertise /,ekspuh'teez/ *n* skill in or knowledge of

a particular field; know-how ⟨*technical* ~⟩ [F, fr MF, expertness, fr *expert*]

expiable /'ekspi·əbl/ *adj* capable of being expiated

expiate /'ekspi,ayt/ *vt* **1a** to eradicate the guilt incurred by (e g a sin) **b** to pay the penalty for (e g a crime) **2** to make amends for [L *expiatus*, pp of *expiare* to atone for, fr *ex-* + *piare* to atone for, appease – more at PIOUS] – **expiation** /-'aysh(ə)n/ *n*, **expiator** /-,aytə/ *n*, **expiatory** /-'ayt(ə)ri/ *adj*

expiration /,ekspie·ə'raysh(ə)n, -spi-/ *n* **1** the release of air from the lungs through the nose or mouth **2** expiry, termination [EXPIRE + -ATION]

expiratory /ik'spie·ərət(ə)ri/ *adj* of or employed in the expiration of air from the lungs

expire /ik'spie·ə/ *vi* **1** to come to an end ⟨*his term of office* ~s *this year*⟩ **2** to emit the breath **3** to die – fml ~ *vt* to breathe out (as if) from the lungs [ME *expiren*, fr MF or L; MF *expirer*, fr L *exspirare*, fr *ex-* + *spirare* to breathe – more at SPIRIT]

ex'piry /-ri/ *n* a termination, esp of a time or period fixed by law, contract, or agreement

explain /ik'splayn/ *vt* **1** to make plain or understandable **2** to give the reason for or cause of ⟨*unwilling to* ~ *his conduct*⟩ ~ *vi* to make sthg plain or understandable [ME *explanen*, fr L *explanare*, lit., to make level, fr *ex-* + *planus* level, flat – more at FLOOR] – **explainable** *adj*, **explainer** *n* – **explain oneself** to clarify one's statements or the reasons for one's conduct

explain away *vt* to avoid blame for or cause to appear insignificant by making excuses ⟨*tried to* explain away *the corruption in his department*⟩

explanation /,eksplə'naysh(ə)n/ *n* the act or process of explaining; sthg, esp a statement, that explains

explanative /ik'splanətiv/ *adj* explanatory – **explanatively** *adv*

explanatory /ik'splanət(ə)ri/ *adj* serving to explain ⟨~ *notes*⟩ – **explanatorily** *adv*

[1]**explant** /ek'splahnt/ *vt* to remove (living tissue), esp to a medium for tissue culture [*ex-* + *-plant* (as in *implant*)] – **explantation** /-'tay sh(ə)n/ *n*

[2]**explant** *n* a piece of living tissue removed from an organism and placed in a medium for tissue culture

[1]**expletive** /ek'spleetiv/ *adj* serving to fill up ⟨~ *phrases*⟩ [LL *expletivus*, fr L *expletus*, pp of *explēre* to fill out, fr *ex-* + *plēre* to fill – more at [1]FULL]

[2]**expletive** *n* **1** a word, phrase, etc inserted to fill a space without adding to the sense **2** a usu meaningless exclamatory word or phrase; *specif* one that is obscene or profane

explicable /'eksplikəbl, ek'splikəbl/ *adj* capable of being explained – **explicably** *adv*

explicate /'eksplikayt/ *vt* **1** to give a detailed explanation of **2** to develop the implications of; analyse logically [L *explicatus*, pp of *explicare*, lit., to unfold, fr *ex-* + *plicare* to fold – more at [1]PLY] – **explicator** *n*, **explicative** /'eksplikətiv, ek'spli-/ *adj*, **explicatory** /'ekspli,kayt(ə)ri, ek'splikət(ə)ri/ *adj*, **explication** /,ekspli'kaysh(ə)n/ *n*

explicit /ik'splisit/ *adj* **1** clear, unambiguous ⟨~ *instructions*⟩; *also* graphically frank ⟨~ *sex scenes*⟩ **2** fully developed or formulated [F or ML; F *explicite*, fr ML *explicitus*, fr L, pp of *explicare*] – **explicitly** *adv*, **explicitness** *n*

explode /ik'splohd/ *vt* **1** to bring (e g a belief or theory) into discredit by demonstrating falsity ⟨~ *a rumour*⟩ **2** to cause to explode or burst noisily ~ *vi* **1** to give expression to sudden, violent, and usu noisy emotion ⟨~ *with anger*⟩ **2a** to undergo a rapid chemical or nuclear reaction with the production of noise, heat, and violent expansion of gases **b** to burst or expand violently as a result of pressure ⟨*the boiler* ~d⟩ ⟨*the* exploding *population*⟩ [L *explodere* to drive off the stage by clapping, fr *ex-* + *plaudere* to clap] – **exploder** *n*

ex'ploded *adj* showing the parts separated but in correct relationship to each other ⟨*an* ~ *view of a carburettor*⟩

[1]**exploit** /'eksployt/ *n* a deed, act; *esp* a notable or heroic one [ME, outcome, success, fr OF, fr L *explicitum*, neut of *explicitus*, pp]

[2]**exploit** /ik'sployt/ *vt* **1** to turn to economic account ⟨~ *a mine*⟩; *also* to utilize **2** to take unfair advantage of for financial or other gain ⟨~s *the workers by paying low wages*⟩ – **exploitable** *adj*, **exploiter** *n*, **exploitive** *adj*, **exploitively** *adj*, **exploitability** /-tə'biləti/ *n*

exploitation /,eksploy'taysh(ə)n/ *n* **1** exploiting or being exploited **2** cashing in on a topical theme ⟨~ *movie*⟩ – **exploitative** /ik'sploytətiv/ *adj*, **exploitatively** *adv*

explore /ik'splaw/ *vt* **1** to examine or inquire into thoroughly ⟨~ *the possibilities of reaching an agreement*⟩ **2** to examine minutely, esp for diagnostic purposes **3** to travel into or through for purposes of geographical discovery ~ *vi* to make or conduct a search [L *explorare*, fr *ex-* + *plorare* to cry out; prob fr the outcry of hunters on sighting game] – **explorer** *n*, **exploration** /,eksplə'raysh(ə)n/ *n*, **explorative** /ik'splorətiv/ *adj*, **exploratively** *adv*, **exploratory** /-tri/ *adj*

explosion /ik'splohzh(ə)n/ *n* **1** exploding: e g **a** a rapid large-scale expansion, increase, or upheaval ⟨*the population* ~⟩ **b** a sudden violent outburst of emotion **2** plosion [L *explosion-*, *explosio* act of driving off by clapping, fr *explosus*, pp of *explodere*]

[1]**explosive** /ik'splohsiv, -ziv/ *adj* **1** tending or threatening to burst forth with sudden violence or noise ⟨*an* ~ *substance*⟩ ⟨*an* ~ *situation*⟩ ☞ SYMBOL **2** tending to arouse strong reactions; controversial ⟨*the play's* ~ *topicality*⟩ – **explosively** *adv*, **explosiveness** *n*

[2]**explosive** *n* **1** an explosive substance **2** a plosive, stop

expo /'ekspoh/ *n*, *pl* **expos** EXPOSITION 3

exponent /ik'spohnənt/ *n* **1** a symbol written above and to the right of a mathematical expression to indicate the operation of raising to a power ⟨*in the expression* a^3, *the* ~ 3 *indicates that* a *is cubed*⟩ **2a** sby or sthg that expounds or interprets **b** sby who advocates or exemplifies *USE* (*2*) usu + *of* [L *exponent-*, *exponens*, prp of *exponere*]

exponential /,ekspə'nensh(ə)l/ *adj* **1** involving a variable in an exponent ⟨10^x *is an* ~ *expression*⟩ **2** expressible or approximately expressible in terms of exponential functions ⟨*an* ~ *growth rate*⟩

exponential function *n* a mathematical function in which an independent variable appears in an exponent

[1]**export** /ik'spawt/ *vt* to carry or send (e g a commodity) to some other place (e g another country) for purposes of trade ~ *vi* to export sthg abroad [L *exportare*, fr *ex-* + *portare* to carry – more at [1]FARE]

– **exportable** *adj,* **exportability** /-tə'biləti/ *n,* **exporter** *n*

²**export** /'ekspawt/ *n* **1** sthg exported **2** an act of exporting

ˌ**expor'tation** /-'taysh(ə)n/ *n* an act of exporting; *also, chiefly NAm* a commodity exported

expose /ik'spohz/ *vt* **1a** to deprive of shelter or protection; lay open to attack or distressing influence ⟨~s *himself to ridicule*⟩ **b** to submit or subject to an action or influence; *specif* to subject (a photographic film, plate, or paper) to the action of radiant energy **c** to abandon (an infant) in an unsheltered place **2** to lay open to view; display: e g **a** to exhibit for public veneration **b** to reveal the face of (a playing card) **c** to engage in indecent exposure of (oneself) **3** to bring (sthg shameful) to light ⟨~d *their trickery*⟩ [ME *exposen,* fr MF *exposer,* fr L *exponere* to set forth, explain (perf indic *exposui*), fr *ex-* + *ponere* to put, place – more at POSITION] – **exposer** *n*

exposé, expose /ek'spohzay (*Fr* ɛkspoze)/ *n* **1** a formal recital or exposition of facts; a statement **2** an exposure of sthg discreditable ⟨*a newspaper* ~ *of organized crime*⟩ [F *exposé,* fr pp of *exposer*]

exposed *adj* open to view or to the elements

exposition /ˌekspə'zish(ə)n/ *n* **1** the art or practice of expounding or explaining the meaning or purpose of sthg (e g a text) **2a** a detailed explanation or elucidation, esp of sthg difficult to understand ⟨*a brilliant* ~ *of existentialism*⟩ **b** the first part of a musical composition in which the theme is presented **3** a usu international public exhibition or show (e g of industrial products) – **expositional** *adj,* **expositor** /ik'spozitə/ *n,* **expository** /ik'spozit(ə)ri/ *adj*

expositive /ik'spozətiv/ *adj* descriptive, explanatory

ex post facto /ˌeks ˌpohst 'faktoh/ *adj or adv* **1** after the fact ⟨~ *approval*⟩ **2** applied retrospectively ⟨~ *laws*⟩ [LL, from a thing done afterwards]

expostulate /ik'spostyoolayt, -chəlayt/ *vi* to reason earnestly *with* sby in order to dissuade or remonstrate – fml [L *expostulatus,* pp of *expostulare* to demand, dispute, fr *ex-* + *postulare* to ask for – more at POSTULATE] – **expostulation** /-'laysh(ə)n/ *n*

exposure /ik'spohzh(ə)/ *n* **1a** a disclosure, esp of a weakness or sthg shameful or criminal; an exposé, unmasking ⟨*continued his* ~ *of electoral frauds*⟩ **b** presentation or exposition, esp to the public by means of the mass media **c(1)** the act of exposing a sensitized photographic film, plate, or paper; *also* the duration of such an exposure **(2)** a section of a film with 1 picture on it **2a** being exposed, specif to the elements **b** the specified direction in which a building, room, etc faces ⟨*a house with a western* ~⟩ ***USE*** (*1c(1), (2)*) ☞ CAMERA [EXPOSE + -URE]

expound /ik'spownd/ *vt* to set forth, esp in careful or elaborate detail; state, explain [ME *expounden,* fr MF *expondre,* fr L *exponere* to explain – more at EXPOSE] – **expounder** *n*

¹**express** /ik'spres/ *adj* **1** firmly and explicitly stated ⟨*he disobeyed my* ~ *orders*⟩ **2** of a particular sort; specific ⟨*he came for that* ~ *purpose*⟩ **3a** (adapted or suitable for) travelling at high speed ⟨*an* ~ *highway*⟩ **b** *Br* designated to be delivered without delay by special messenger ⟨~ *mail*⟩ [ME, fr MF *expres,* fr L *expressus,* pp of *exprimere* to press out, express, fr *ex-* + *premere* to press – more at ²PRESS]

²**express** *adv* by express

³**express** *n* **1** an express vehicle **2** *Br* express mail

⁴**express** *vt* **1a** to show or represent, esp in words; state **b** to make known the opinions, feelings, etc of (oneself) ⟨~es *himself through his work*⟩ **c** to represent by a sign or symbol **2** to force out (e g the juice of a fruit) by pressure [ME *expressen,* fr MF & L; MF *expresser,* fr OF, fr *expres,* adj, fr L *expressus,* pp] – **expresser** *n,* **expressible** *adj*

expression /ik'spresh(ə)n/ *n* **1a** expressing, esp in words ⟨*freedom of* ~⟩ **b(1)** an outward manifestation or symbol ⟨*this gift is an* ~ *of my admiration for you*⟩ **(2)** a significant word or phrase **(3)** a mathematical or logical symbol or combination of symbols serving to express sthg **2a** a means or manner of expressing sthg; *esp* sensitivity and feeling in communicating or performing ⟨*read the poem with* ~⟩ **b(1)** the quality or fact of being expressive **(2)** facial aspect or vocal intonation indicative of feeling **3** (a product of) pressing out – **expressional** *adj,* **expressionless** *adj,* **expressionlessly** *adv,* **expressionlessness** *n*

ex'pressionˌism /-ˌiz(ə)m/ *n* a mode of artistic expression that attempts to depict the artist's subjective emotions and responses to objects and events – **expressionist** *n or adj,* **expressionistic** /-'istik/ *adj,* **expressionistically** *adv*

expressive /ik'spresiv/ *adj* **1** of expression ⟨*the* ~ *function of language*⟩ **2** serving to express or represent ⟨*he used foul and novel terms* ~ *of rage* – H G Wells⟩ **3** full of expression; significant ⟨*an* ~ *silence*⟩ – **expressively** *adv,* **expressiveness** *n,* **expressivity** /ˌekspre'sivəti/ *n*

expressly /ik'spresli/ *adv* **1** explicitly ⟨*I* ~ *told you not to do that*⟩ **2** for the express purpose; specially ⟨*needed a clinic* ~ *for the treatment of addicts*⟩

ex'pressˌway *n, chiefly NAm* a motorway

expropriate /ek'sprohpriˌayt/ *vt* **1** to dispossess **2** to transfer to one's own possession ⟨~d *all the land within a 10-mile radius*⟩ [ML *expropriatus,* pp of *expropriare,* fr L *ex-* + *proprius* own] – **expropriator** *n,* **expropriation** /-'aysh(ə)n/ *n*

expulsion /ik'spulsh(ə)n/ *n* expelling or being expelled [ME, fr L *expulsion-, expulsio,* fr *expulsus,* pp of *expellere* to expel] – **expulsive** /-siv/ *adj*

expunge /ik'spunj/ *vt* **1** to strike out; obliterate, erase **2** to efface completely; destroy ⟨*nothing can* ~ *his shame*⟩ ***USE*** fml [L *expungere* to mark for deletion by dots, fr *ex-* + *pungere* to prick – more at PUNGENT] – **expunction** /ik'spungksh(ə)n/ *n,* **expunger** *n*

expurgate /'ekspuhˌgayt/ *vt* to rid of sthg morally offensive; *esp* to remove objectionable parts from, before publication or presentation [L *expurgatus,* pp of *expurgare,* fr *ex-* + *purgare* to purge] – **expurgator** /-gaytə/ *n,* **expurgation** /-'gaysh(ə)n/ *n,* **expurgatorial** /ikˌspuhgə'tawri·əl/ *adj,* **expurgatory** /ik'spuhgət(ə)ri/ *adj*

exquisite /ik'skwizit, 'ekskwizit/ *adj* **1a** marked by flawless, beautiful, and usu delicate craftsmanship **b** keenly sensitive, esp in feeling; discriminating ⟨~ *taste*⟩ **2a** extremely beautiful; delightful ⟨*an* ~ *white blossom*⟩ **b** acute, intense ⟨~ *pain*⟩ [ME *exquisit* choice, ingenious, fr L *exquisitus,* fr pp of *exquirere* to search out, fr *ex-* + *quaerere* to seek] – **exquisitely** /ik'skwizitli/ *adv,* **exquisiteness** *n*

exsanguinate /ik'sang·gwiˌnayt/ *vt* to drain of blood [L *exsanguinatus* bloodless, fr *ex-* + *sanguin-, sanguis* blood] – **exsanguination** /-'nay sh(ə)n/ *n*

exserted /ek'suhtid/ *adj* projecting beyond an enclosing organ or part ⟨~ *anthers*⟩ [fr pp of *exsert* (to thrust out), fr L *exsertus, exertus,* pp of *exserere, exerere* – more at EXERT]

exstipulate /ek'stipyoolət, -,layt/ *adj, of a plant or leaf* having no stipules

extant /ek'stant/ *adj* still or currently existing ⟨~ *manuscripts*⟩ [L *exstant-, exstans,* prp of *exstare* to stand out, be in existence, fr *ex-* + *stare* to stand – more at STAND]

extemporaneous /ik,stempə'raynyəs, -ni·əs/ *adj* **1** done, spoken, performed, etc on the spur of the moment; impromptu ⟨*gave a witty* ~ *speech*⟩ **2** provided, made, or put to use as an expedient; makeshift [LL *extemporaneus,* fr L *ex tempore*] – **extemporaneously** *adv,* **extemporaneousness** *n,* **extemporaneity** /-pərə'nayəti/ *n*

extemporary /ik'stemp(ə)rəri/ *adj* extemporaneous – **extemporarily** *adv*

extempore /ik'stempəri/ *adj or adv* (spoken or done) in an extemporaneous manner ⟨*speaking* ~⟩ [L *ex tempore,* fr *ex* + *tempore,* abl of *tempus* time]

ex'tempor·ize, -ise /ik'stempə,riez/ *vi* to speak, or perform sthg, extemporaneously; improvise ~ *vt* to compose, perform, or utter extemporaneously – **extemporizer** *n,* **extemporization** /-'zaysh(ə)n/ *n*

extend /ik'stend/ *vt* **1** to spread or stretch forth; unfold ⟨~ed *both her arms*⟩ **2a** to stretch out to fullest length ⟨~ed *the sail*⟩ **b** to exert (e g a horse or oneself) to full capacity ⟨*won the race without* ~ing *himself*⟩ **3** to give or offer, usu in response to need; proffer ⟨~ing *aid to the needy*⟩ **4a** to cause to reach (e g in distance or scope) ⟨*national authority was* ~ed *over new territories*⟩ ⟨~ed *the road to the coast*⟩ **b** to prolong in time **c** to advance, further ⟨~ing *human knowledge*⟩ **5a** to enlarge **b** to increase the scope, meaning, or application of; broaden ~ *vi* **1** to stretch out in distance, space, or time ⟨*his jurisdiction* ~ed *over the whole area*⟩ **2** to reach in scope or application [ME *extenden,* fr MF or L; MF *estendre,* fr L *extendere,* fr *ex-* + *tendere* to stretch – more at THIN] – **extendable, extendible** *adj*

ex'tended *adj, of a gait or horse* performed or performing with lengthened stride and extended neck – compare COLLECTED – **extendedly** *adv,* **extendedness** *n*

ex,tended 'family *n* a family unit that includes 3 or more generations of near relatives in addition to a nuclear family in 1 household – compare NUCLEAR FAMILY

ex'tender /-də/ *n* a substance added to a product to increase its bulk or improve its physical properties [EXTEND + [2]-ER]

extensible /ik'stensəbl/, **extensile** /-siel/ *adj* capable of being extended – **extensibility** /sə'biləti/ *n*

extension /ik'stensh(ə)n/ *n* **1a** extending or being extended **b** sthg extended **2** extent, scope **3** a straightening of (a joint between the bones of) a limb **4** an increase in length of time **5** a programme of instruction for nonresident students of a university **6a** a part added (e g to a building) **b** an extra telephone connected to the principal line [ME, fr MF or LL; MF, fr LL *extension-, extensio,* fr L *extensus,* pp of *extendere*]

extensive /ik'stensiv, -ziv/ *adj* **1** having wide or considerable extent ⟨~ *reading*⟩ **2** of or being farming in which large areas of land are used with minimum outlay and labour – **extensively** *adv,* **extensiveness** *n*

extensometer /,eksten'somitə/ *n* an instrument for measuring deformations of test specimens caused by tension, compression, etc [*extension* + *-o-* + *-meter*]

extensor /ik'stensə, -saw/ *n* a muscle that produces extension

extent /ik'stent/ *n* **1** the range or distance over which sthg extends ⟨*the* ~ *of the forest*⟩ ⟨*the* ~ *of his knowledge*⟩ **2** the point or limit to which sthg extends ⟨*the* ~ *of our patience*⟩ [ME, land valuation, seizure of land, fr AF & MF; AF *extente* land valuation, fr MF, area, surveying of land, fr *extendre* to extend]

extenuate /ik'stenyoo,ayt/ *vt* to (try to) lessen the seriousness or extent of (e g a crime) by giving excuses [L *extenuatus,* pp of *extenuare,* fr *ex-* + *tenuis* thin – more at THIN] – **extenuator** *n,* **extenuatory** /-yooət(ə)ri/ *adj,* **extenuation** /-'aysh(ə)n/ *n*

[1]**exterior** /ik'stiəri·ə/ *adj* **1** on the outside or an outside surface; external **2** suitable for use on outside surfaces [L, compar of *exter, exterus* on the outside, foreign, fr *ex*] – **exteriorize** *vt,* **exteriorly** *adv,* **exteriorization** /-'zaysh(ə)n/ *n,* **exteriority** /-ri'orəti/ *n*

[2]**exterior** *n* **1a** an exterior part or surface; outside **b** an outward manner or appearance ⟨*a deceptively friendly* ~⟩ **2** a representation of an outdoor scene

exterior angle *n* **1** the angle between a side of a polygon and an extended adjacent side **2** an angle between a line crossing 2 parallel lines and either of the latter and lying outside the parallel lines ☞ MATHEMATICS

exterminate /ik'stuhmi,nayt/ *vt* to destroy completely; *esp* to kill all of ⟨~d *the mice*⟩ [L *exterminatus,* pp of *exterminare* to banish, expel, fr *ex-* + *terminus* boundary – more at TERM] – **exterminator** *n,* **extermination** /-'naysh(ə)n/ *n,* **exterminatory** /ik'stuhminət(ə)ri/ *adj*

[1]**external** /ik'stuhnl/ *adj* **1a** capable of being perceived outwardly ⟨~ *signs of a disease*⟩ **b(1)** superficial **(2)** not intrinsic or essential ⟨~ *circumstances*⟩ **2** of, connected with, or intended for the outside or an outer part **3a(1)** situated outside, apart, or beyond **(2)** arising or acting from outside ⟨*an* ~ *force*⟩ **b** of dealings with foreign countries **c** having existence independent of the mind ⟨~ *reality*⟩ [ME, fr L *externus* external, fr *exter*] – **externally** *adv,* **externality** /,ekstuh'naləti/ *n*

[2]**external** *n* an external feature or aspect – usu pl

external-combustion engine *n* a heat engine (e g a steam engine) that derives its heat energy from fuel consumed outside the engine cylinder

external degree *n* a degree taken without actually attending the university that awards it

ex,ternal ex'aminer *n* a visiting examiner who ensures impartiality and equality of standards in an examination

external·ize, -ise /ik'stuhnl,iez/ *vt* **1** to make external or externally visible **2** to attribute to causes outside the self; rationalize ⟨~s *his failure*⟩ – **externalization** /-'zaysh(ə)n/ *n*

exteroceptive /,ekstəroh'septiv/ *adj* activated by, relating to, or being stimuli received by an organism from outside [L *exter* + E *-o-* + *-ceptive* (as in *receptive*)] – **exteroceptor** *n*

exterritorial /,eks,teri'tawri·əl/ *adj* extraterritorial – **exterritoriality** /-ri'aləti/ *n*

extinct /ik'stingkt/ *adj* **1a** no longer burning **b** no longer active ⟨*an ~ volcano*⟩ **2** no longer existing ⟨*an ~ animal*⟩ **3** having no qualified claimant ⟨*an ~ title*⟩ [ME, fr L *exstinctus*, pp of *exstinguere*]

extinction /ik'stingksh(ə)n/ *n* **1** making or being extinct or (causing to be) extinguished **2** elimination or reduction of a conditioned response by not reinforcing it – **extinctive** /ik'stingktiv/ *adj*

extinguish /ik'sting·gwish/ *vt* **1a** to cause to cease burning; quench **b** to bring to an end ⟨*hope for their safety was slowly* ~ed⟩ **c** to cause extinction of (a conditioned response) **2a** to make void ⟨*~ a claim*⟩ **b** to abolish (a debt) by payment [L *exstinguere* (fr *ex-* + *stinguere* to extinguish) + E *-ish* (as in *abolish*); akin to L in*stigare* to incite – more at [3]STICK] – **extinguishable** *adj*, **extinguisher** *n*, **extinguishment** *n*

extirpate /'ekstuh,payt/ *vt* **1** to destroy completely (as if) by uprooting; annihilate **2** to cut out by surgery [L *exstirpatus*, pp of *exstirpare*, fr *ex-* + *stirp-*, *stirps* trunk, root – more at TORPID] – **extirpator** *n*, **extirpation** /-'paysh(ə)n/ *n*, **extirpative** /'ekstuh,paytiv, ik'stuhpətiv/ *adj*

extol, *NAm also* **extoll** /ik'stohl, -'stol/ *vt* **-ll-** to praise highly; glorify [ME *extollen*, fr L *extollere*, fr *ex-* + *tollere* to lift up – more at TOLERATE] – **extoller** *n*, **extolment** *n*

extort /ik'stawt/ *vt* to obtain from sby by force or threats ⟨*~ money*⟩ ⟨*~ a confession*⟩ [L *extortus*, pp of *extorquēre* to wrench out, extort, fr *ex-* + *torquēre* to twist – more at TORTURE] – **extorter** *n*, **extortive** *adj*

extortion /ik'stawsh(ə)n/ *n* extorting; *specif* the unlawful extorting of money – **extortioner** *n*, **extortionist** *n*

extortionate /ik'stawsh(ə)nət/ *adj* excessive, exorbitant – **extortionately** *adv*

[1]**extra** /'ekstrə/ *adj* **1** more than is due, usual, or necessary; additional ⟨*~ work*⟩ **2** subject to an additional charge ⟨*room service is ~*⟩ [prob short for *extraordinary*]

[2]**extra** *n* sthg or sby extra or additional: e g **a** an added charge **b** a specified edition of a newspaper ⟨*late night ~*⟩ **c** a run in cricket (e g a bye, leg bye, no-ball, or wide) that is not scored by a stroke of the bat and is not credited to a batsman's individual score **d** an additional worker; *specif* one hired to act in a group scene in a film or stage production

[3]**extra** *adv* beyond or above the usual size, extent, or amount ⟨*to work ~ hard*⟩ ⟨*they charge ~ for single rooms*⟩

extra- /ekstrə-/ *prefix* outside; beyond ⟨extra*judicial*⟩ ⟨extra*mural*⟩ [ME, fr L, fr *extra*, adv & prep, outside, except, beyond, fr *exter* on the outside – more at EXTERIOR]

extracellular /,ekstrə'selyoolə/ *adj* situated or occurring outside a cell or the cells of the body ⟨*~ digestion*⟩ ⟨*~ enzymes*⟩ – **extracellularly** *adv*

,extra 'cover *n* a fielding position in cricket between mid-off and cover and about a third of the way to the boundary ☞ SPORT

[1]**extract** /ik'strakt/ *vt* **1** to draw forth or pull out, esp against resistance or with effort ⟨*~ed a wisdom tooth*⟩ ⟨*~ed a confession*⟩ **2** to withdraw (e g a juice or fraction) by physical or chemical process; *also* to treat with a solvent so as to remove a soluble substance **3** to separate (a metal) from an ore **4** to find (a mathematical root) by calculation **5** to excerpt [ME *extracten*, fr L *extractus*, pp of *extrahere*, fr *ex-* + *trahere* to draw – more at DRAW] – **extractable, extractible** *adj*, **extractor** *n*, **extractability** /-tə'biləti/ *n*

[2]**extract** /'ekstrakt/ *n* **1** an excerpt **2 extract, extractive** /ik'straktiv/ (a solution of) the essential constituents of a complex material (e g an aromatic plant) prepared by extraction

extraction /ik'straksh(ə)n/ *n* **1** extracting **2** ancestry, origin **3** sthg extracted

extractive /ik'straktiv/ *adj* **1** tending towards or resulting in the depletion of natural resources by extraction with no provision for replenishment ⟨*~ agriculture*⟩ **2** capable of being extracted – **extractively** *adv*

ex'tractor ,fan *n* a type of ventilator, usu electrically driven, designed to expel fumes, stale air, etc

extracurricular /,ekstrəkə'rikyoolə/ *adj* **1** not falling within the scope of a regular curriculum **2** lying outside one's normal activities

extraditable /'ekstrə,dietəbl/ *adj* liable to or warranting extradition ⟨*an ~ offence*⟩

extradite /'ekstrə,diet/ *vt* **1** to hand over for extradition **2** to obtain by extradition [back-formation fr *extradition*]

extradition /,ekstrə'dish(ə)n/ *n* the surrender of an alleged criminal by one state to another having jurisdiction to try the charge [F, fr *ex-* + L *tradition-*, *traditio* act of handing over – more at TREASON]

extrados /ek'straydos/ *n, pl* **extrados** /~/, **extradoses** the convex upper surface of an arch – compare INTRADOS ☞ ARCHITECTURE [F, fr L *extra* + F *dos* back – more at DOSSIER]

extrajudicial /,ekstrəjooh'dish(ə)l/ *adj* **1** not forming part of regular legal proceedings ⟨*an ~ investigation*⟩ **2** in contravention of law ⟨*an ~ execution*⟩ – **extrajudicially** *adv*

extramarital /,ekstrə'maritl/ *adj, esp of sexual relations* involving sby other than one's spouse

extramundane /,ekstrə'mundayn, ,---'-/ *adj* situated in or relating to a region beyond the material world [LL *extramundanus*, fr L *extra* + *mundus* the world]

extramural /,ekstrə'myooərəl/ *adj* **1** outside (the walls or boundaries of) a place or organization **2** *chiefly Br* of extension courses or facilities ⟨*university ~ department*⟩ – **extramurally** *adv*

extraneous /ik'straynyəs, -ni·əs/ *adj* **1** on or coming from the outside **2** not forming an essential or vital part; irrelevant ⟨*an ~ scene that added nothing to the play*⟩ [L *extraneus* – more at STRANGE] – **extraneously** *adv*, **extraneousness** *n*

extraordinary /ik'strawdin(ə)ri/ *adj* **1a** going beyond what is usual, regular, or customary ⟨*an Act that gave him ~ powers*⟩ **b** highly exceptional; remarkable ⟨*~ beauty*⟩ **2** on or for a special function or service ⟨*an ambassador ~*⟩ ⟨*an ~ general meeting*⟩ [ME *extraordinarie*, fr L *extraordinarius*, fr *extra ordinem* out of course, fr *extra* + *ordinem*, acc of *ordin-*, *ordo* order] – **extraordinarily** *adv*, **extraordinariness** *n*

extrapolate /ek'strapə,layt/ *vt* **1** to infer (values of a variable in an unobserved interval) from values within an already observed interval **2a** to use or extend (known data or experience) in order to surmise or work out sthg unknown **b** to predict by extrapolating known data or experience [L *extra* outside + E *-polate* (as in *interpolate*) – more at EXTRA-] – **extrapolator** *n*, **extrapolative** /-lətiv/ *adj*, **extrapolation** /-'laysh(ə)n/ *n*

extrasensory /,ekstrə'sens(ə)ri/ *adj* residing beyond or outside the ordinary physical senses ⟨*instances of ~ perception*⟩

extraterrestrial /,ekstrətə'restri·əl/ *adj* originating, existing, or occurring outside the earth or its atmosphere

extraterritorial /,ekstrə,teri'tawri·əl/ *adj* outside the territorial limits of a jurisdiction

,extra,terri,tori'ality /-,teri,tawri'aləti/ *n* exemption from the jurisdiction of local law

extravagance /ik'stravəgəns/, **extravagancy** /-si/ *n* **1** an extravagant act; *specif* an excessive outlay of money **2** sthg extravagant

ex'travagant /-gənt/ *adj* **1a** lacking in moderation, balance, and restraint; excessive ⟨~ *praise*⟩ **b** excessively elaborate or showy **2a** wasteful, esp of money **b** profuse **3** exorbitant [MF, wandering, irregular, fr ML *extravagant-*, *extravagans*, fr L *extra-* + *vagant-*, *vagans*, prp of *vagari* to wander about – more at VAGARY] – **extravagantly** *adv*

extravaganza /ik,stravə'ganzə/ *n* **1** a literary or musical work marked by extreme freedom of style and structure **2** a lavish or spectacular show or event [It *estravaganza*, lit., extravagance, fr *estravagante* extravagant, fr ML *extravagant-*, *extravagans*]

extravasate /ik'stravə,sayt/ *vt* to force out or cause (e g blood) to escape from a proper vessel or channel ~ *vi* **1** to pass by infiltration from a proper vessel or channel (e g a blood vessel) into surrounding tissue **2** *esp of lava* to pour out [L *extra* + *vas* vessel – more at VASE] – **extravasate** *n*, **extravasation** /-'saysh(ə)n/ *n*

extravehicular /,ekstrəvee'ikyoolə/ *adj* taking place outside a spacecraft in flight ⟨~ *activity*⟩

extravert /'ekstrə,vuht/ *n or adj* (an) extrovert

[1]extreme /ik'streem/ *adj* **1a** existing in a very high degree ⟨~ *poverty*⟩ **b** going to great or exaggerated lengths; not moderate ⟨*an ~ right-winger*⟩ **c** exceeding the usual or expected; severe ⟨*took ~ measures*⟩ **2** situated at the farthest possible point from a centre or the nearest to an end ⟨*the country's ~ north*⟩ **3a** most advanced or thoroughgoing ⟨*the ~ avant-garde*⟩ **b** maximum ⟨*the ~ penalty*⟩ [ME, fr MF, fr L *extremus*, superl of *exter*, *exterus* on the outside – more at EXTERIOR] – **extremely** *adv*, **extremeness** *n*

[2]extreme *n* **1a** sthg situated at or marking one or other extreme point of a range ⟨~s *of heat and cold*⟩ **b** the first term or the last term of a mathematical proportion **2** a very pronounced or extreme degree ⟨*his enthusiasm was carried to an* ~⟩ **3** an extreme measure or expedient ⟨*going to* ~s⟩ – **in the extreme** to the greatest possible extent ⟨*boring* in the extreme⟩

ex,treme 'unction *n* the (Roman Catholic) sacrament of anointing and praying over sby who is dying

extremism /ik'stree,miz(ə)m/ *n* advocacy of extreme political measures; radicalism – **extremist** *n or adj*

extremity /ik'streməti/ *n* **1a** the most extreme part, point, or degree **b** a (human) hand, foot, or other limb **2** (a moment marked by) extreme misfortune and esp danger of destruction or death – compare IN EXTREMIS **3** a drastic or desperate act or measure

extricate /'ekstri,kayt/ *vt* to disentangle, esp with considerable effort ⟨*managed to ~ himself from a tricky situation*⟩ [L *extricatus*, pp of *extricare*, fr *ex-* + *tricae* trifles, perplexities] – **extricable** /-kəbl/ *adj*, **extrication** /-'kaysh(ə)n/ *n*

extrinsic /ek'strinsik, -zik/ *adj* **1** not forming part of or belonging to a thing; extraneous **2** originating from or on the outside [F & LL; F *extrinsèque*, fr LL *extrinsecus*, fr L, adv, from without; akin to L *exter* outward & *sequi* to follow – more at EXTERIOR, SUE] – **extrinsically** *adv*

extrinsic factor *n* VITAMIN B_{12} – compare INTRINSIC FACTOR

extro- *prefix* outwards ⟨extro*vert*⟩ – compare INTRO- [alter. of L *extra-*]

extrovert *also* **extravert** /'ekstrə,vuht/ *n* one whose attention and interests are directed wholly or predominantly towards what is outside the self – compare INTROVERT [deriv of L *extra-* + *vertere* to turn] – **extrovert** *adj*, **extroverted** *adj*, **extroversion** /-'vuhsh(ə)n/ *n*

extrude /ik'stroohd/ *vt* **1** to force or push out **2** to shape (e g metal or plastic) by forcing through a die ~ *vi* to become extruded [L *extrudere*, fr *ex-* + *trudere* to thrust] – **extruder** *n*, **extrudable** *adj*, **extrudability** /-də'biləti/ *n*, **extrusion** /ik'stroohzh(ə)n/ *n*

extrusive /ik'stroohsiv, -ziv/ *adj*, *of a rock* formed by crystallization of lava poured out at the earth's surface [L *extrusus*, pp of *extrudere*]

exuberant /ig'zyoohb(ə)rənt/ *adj* **1a** joyously unrestrained and enthusiastic ⟨~ *high spirits*⟩ **b** lavish and flamboyant ⟨~ *metaphors*⟩ **2** great or extreme in degree, size, or extent **3** abundant, luxuriant ⟨~ *vegetation*⟩ [ME, fr MF, fr L *exuberant-*, *exuberans*, prp of *exuberare* to be abundant, fr *ex-* + *uber* fruitful, fr *uber* udder – more at UDDER] – **exuberance** *n*, **exuberantly** *adv*

exudate /'eksyoo,dayt/ *n* exuded matter

exude /ig'zyoohd/ *vi* to ooze out ⟨*moisture* ~d *from the damp wall*⟩ ~ *vt* **1** to allow or cause to ooze or spread out in all directions ⟨~ *sweat*⟩ **2** to radiate an air of ⟨~s *charm*⟩ [L *exsudare*, fr *ex-* + *sudare* to sweat – more at SWEAT] – **exudation** /,eksyoo'daysh(ə)n/ *n*

exult /ig'zult/ *vi* to be extremely joyful; rejoice openly – usu + *at*, *in*, or *over* [MF *exulter*, fr L *exsultare*, lit., to leap up, fr *ex-* + *saltare* to leap – more at SALTIRE] – **exultance** *n*, **exultancy** /-si/ *n*, **exultant** *adj*, **exultingly** *adv*, **exultation** /,eksəl'taysh(ə)n/ *n*, **exultantly** *adv*

exurb /'eksuhb, 'egzuhb/ *n* a prosperous region outside a city and usu beyond its suburbs [*ex-* + *-urb* (as in *suburb*)] – **exurban** /ek'suhbən, egz-/ *adj*, **exurbanite** /-bə,niet/ *n*

exurbia /ek'suhbi·ə, egz-/ *n* exurbs collectively

exuviae /ig'zyoohvi,ee/ *n pl* the natural coverings of animals (e g the skins of snakes) after they have been sloughed off [L, fr *exuere* to take off, fr *ex-* + *-uere* to put on; akin to ORuss *izuti* to take off footwear] – **exuvial** /-vi·əl/ *adj*

exuviate /ig'zyoohvi,ayt/ *vb* to moult or shed (e g skin) – **exuviation** /-'aysh(ə)n/ *n*

-ey /-i/ – see [1]-Y

eyas /'ee·əs/ *n* a hawk that is a nestling [ME, alter.

(by incorrect division of *a neias*) of *neias*, fr MF *niais* fresh from the nest, fr (assumed) VL *nidax* nestling, fr L *nidus* nest – more at NEST]

[1]**eye** /ie/ *n* **1a** any of various usu paired organs of sight; *esp* a nearly spherical liquid-filled organ that is lined with a light-sensitive retina and housed in a bony socket in the skull ☞ NERVE **b** the visible parts of the eye with its surrounding structures (e g eyelashes and eyebrows) **c(1)** the faculty of seeing with eyes ⟨*a keen ~ for detail*⟩ **(2)** the faculty of intellectual or aesthetic perception or appreciation ⟨*an ~ for beauty*⟩ **d** a gaze, glance ⟨*caught his ~*⟩ **e** view, attention ⟨*in the public ~*⟩ **2a** the hole through the head of a needle **b** a (nearly) circular mark (e g on a peacock's tail) **c** a loop; *esp* one of metal or thread into which a hook is inserted – compare HOOK AND EYE **d** an undeveloped bud (e g on a potato) **e** a calm area in the centre of a tropical cyclone **f** the (differently coloured or marked) centre of a flower **3** the centre, nub ⟨*the ~ of the problem* – Norman Mailer⟩ **4** the direction from which the wind is blowing [ME, fr OE *ēage*; akin to OHG *ouga* eye, L *oculus*, Gk *ōps* eye, face] – **eyeless** *adj*, **eyelike** *adj* – **in the eye/eyes of** in the judgment or opinion of ⟨*beauty is* in the eye of *the beholder*⟩ – **my eye** – used to express mild disagreement or sometimes surprise ⟨*a diamond*, my eye! *That's glass*⟩; infml – **set/clap eyes on** to catch sight of – **with an eye to** having as an aim or purpose

[2]**eye** *vt* **eyeing, eying** to watch closely – **eyer** *n*

'**eye,ball** *n* the capsule of the eye of a vertebrate formed by the sclera and cornea that cover it, together with the structures they contain

,**eyeball-to-'eyeball** *adj* in each other's hostile presence – infml

'**eye,bath** *n* a small oval cup specially shaped for applying liquid remedies to the eye

'**eye,bolt** *n* a bolt with a looped head

'**eye,bright** *n* any of several small plants of the figwort family [fr its former use as a remedy for eye ailments]

'**eye,brow** *n* (hair growing on) the ridge over the eye

'**eye-,catching** *adj* strikingly visually attractive – **eye-catcher** *n*

eyed /ied/ *adj* having an eye or eyes, esp of a specified kind or number – often in combination ⟨*an almond-*eyed *girl*⟩

'**eyeful** /-f(ə)l/ *n* a pleasing sight; *specif* an attractive woman – infml

'**eye,glass** *n* **1** an eyepiece **2** a lens worn to aid vision; *specif* a monocle **3** *pl* glasses, spectacles

'**eye,hole** *n* a peephole

'**eye,lash** *n* (a single hair of) the fringe of hair edging the eyelid

'**eyelet** /-lit/ *n* **1** a small usu reinforced hole designed so that a cord, lace, etc may be passed through it, or used in embroidery **2** a small typically metal ring to reinforce an eyelet; a grommet [ME *oilet*, fr MF *oillet*, dim. of *oil* eye, fr L *oculus*]

'**eye,lid** *n* a movable lid of skin and muscle that can be closed over the eyeball ☞ NERVE

'**eye,liner** *n* a cosmetic for emphasizing the contours of the eyes

'**eye-,opener** *n* **1** *chiefly NAm* a drink intended to stop one feeling sleepy on waking up **2** sthg surprising and esp revelatory – infml ⟨*his behaviour was a real ~ to me*⟩ – **eye-opening** *adj*

'**eye,piece** *n* the lens or combination of lenses at the eye end of an optical instrument

'**eye ,rhyme** *n* a rhyme in which 2 words (e g *move* and *love*) appear from text spelling to rhyme but are pronounced differently

'**eye,shade** *n* a projecting front on a cap for shading the eyes

'**eye ,shadow** *n* a coloured cream or powder applied to the eyelids to accentuate the eyes

'**eye,sight** *n* SIGHT 5

'**eye,sore** *n* sthg offensive to the sight

'**eye,spot** *n* **1** a simple visual organ of pigment or pigmented cells **2** a spot of colour

'**eye,stalk** *n* either of the movable stalks bearing an eye at the tip in a crab or related crustacean

Eyetie /'ietie, -ti/ *n or adj, chiefly Br* (an) Italian – derog [by shortening & alter.]

,**eye'tooth** *n* a canine tooth of the upper jaw

eye up *vt* to look at (sby) in order to assess sexual attractiveness – infml ⟨*he was* eyeing up *the talent*⟩

'**eye,wash** *n* deceptive statements or actions; rubbish, claptrap – infml

'**eye,witness** *n* one who sees an occurrence and can bear witness to it (e g in court)

eyot /ayt, 'ay·ət/ *n* an ait

eyre /eə/ *n* (a court held on) a circuit made by itinerant medieval justices [ME *eire*, fr AF, fr OF *erre* trip, fr *errer* to travel – more at ERRANT]

eyrie /'iəri, 'eəri, 'ie·əri/ *n* **1** the nest of a bird (of prey) on a cliff or a mountain top **2** a room or dwelling situated high up ⟨*sat in his seventh floor ~ in Mayfair*⟩ [ML *aerea, eyria*, fr OF *aire*, fr L *area* area, feeding place for animals]

eyrir /'ayriə/ *n, pl* **aurar** /'aw,rah/ ☞ *Iceland* at NATIONALITY

Ezekiel /i'zeeki·əl, -kyəl/ *n* (a book of the Old Testament containing the prophesies of) a Hebrew priest of the 6th c BC [LL *Ezechiel*, fr Heb *Yĕḥezqēl*]

Ezra /'ezrə/ *n* (a book of the Old Testament attributed to) a Hebrew priest, scribe, and reformer of Judaism of the 5th c BC in Babylon and Jerusalem [LL, fr Heb *'Ezrā*]

F

f /ef/ *n, pl* **f's, fs** *often cap* **1** (a graphic representation of or device for reproducing) the 6th letter of the English alphabet **2** the 4th note of a C-major scale **3** a grade rating a student's work as failing

fa, fah /fah/ *n* the 4th note of the diatonic scale in solmization [ME, fr ML – more at GAMUT]

FA /ˌeˈfay/ *n, Br* fuck-all – euph; often in *sweet FA*

fab /fab/ *adj, Br* fabulous, great – slang; no longer in vogue

Fabian /ˈfaybi·ən, -byən/ *adj* of or being a society founded in England in 1884 to work for the gradual establishment of socialism [L *Fabianus* of or like Quintus *Fabius* Maximus †203 BC Roman general who wore down his enemies while avoiding open battles] – **Fabian** *n*, **Fabianism** *n*

fable /ˈfaybl/ *n* **1a** a legendary story of supernatural happenings **b** myths or legendary tales collectively **2** a fictitious account; a lie **3** a story intended to convey a moral; *esp* one in which animals speak and act like human beings [ME, fr MF, fr L *fabula* conversation, story, play, fr *fari* to speak – more at [1]BAN]

ˈfabled *adj* **1** fictitious **2** told or celebrated in fables; legendary

fabliau /ˈfablioh/ *n, pl* **fabliaux** /ˈfablioh(z)/ a short usu coarsely satirical verse story popular in 12th- and 13th-c France [F, fr OF, dim. of *fable*]

fabric /ˈfabrik/ *n* **1a** the basic structure of a building ⟨*the* ~ *of the theatre*⟩ **b** an underlying structure; a framework ⟨*the* ~ *of society*⟩ **2** an act of constructing; an erection **3** texture, quality – used chiefly with reference to textiles **4a** CLOTH 1 **b** a material that resembles cloth [MF *fabrique*, fr L *fabrica* workshop, structure, fr *fabr-*, *faber* smith]

ˈfabricate /-kayt/ *vt* **1** to construct or manufacture from many parts **2** to invent or create, esp in order to deceive [ME *fabricaten*, fr L *fabricatus*, pp of *fabricari*, fr *fabrica*] – **fabricator** *n*, **fabrication** /-ˈkaysh(ə)n/ *n*

fabulist /ˈfabyoolist/ *n* one who composes fables

fabulous /ˈfabyooləs/ *adj* **1** resembling things told of in fables, esp in incredible or exaggerated quality; extraordinary ⟨~ *wealth*⟩ **2** told in or based on fable **3** marvellous, great – infml ⟨*a* ~ *party*⟩ [L *fabulosus*, fr *fabula*] – **fabulously** *adv*, **fabulousness** *n*

facade *also* **façade** /fəˈsahd/ *n* **1** a face, esp the front or principal face, of a building given special architectural treatment **2** a false or superficial appearance [F *façade*, fr It *facciata*, fr *faccia* face, fr (assumed) VL *facia*]

[1]face /fays/ *n* **1** the front part of the (human) head including the chin, mouth, nose, eyes, etc and usu the forehead **2a** a facial expression; *specif* a grimace ⟨*he pulled a* ~⟩ **b** MAKE-UP 2a, b ⟨*she put her* ~ *on*⟩ **3a** an outward appearance ⟨*put a good* ~ *on it*⟩ **b** effrontery, impudence ⟨*had the* ~ *to ask for his money back*⟩ **c** dignity, reputation ⟨*afraid to lose* ~⟩ ⟨*we must save* ~ *at all costs*⟩ **4a(1)** a front, upper, or outer surface **(2)** the front of sthg with 2 or 4 sides **(3)** an exposed surface of rock **(4)** any of the plane surfaces of a geometric solid **b** a surface specially prepared: e g **(1)** the right side (e g of cloth or leather) **(2)** an inscribed, printed, or marked surface **c** the surface (e g of type) that receives the ink and transfers it to the paper **5** the exposed working surface of a mine, drift, or excavation [ME, fr OF, fr (assumed) VL *facia*, fr L *facies* make, form, face, fr *facere* to make, do – more at DO] – **in the face of/in face of** in opposition to; despite ⟨*succeed* in the face of *great difficulties*⟩ – **to someone's face** candidly in sby's presence and to his/her knowledge

[2]face *vt* **1** to meet or deal with firmly and without evasion ⟨~ *the situation calmly*⟩ **2a** to apply a facing to **b** to cover the front or surface of ⟨~d *the building with marble*⟩ **3** to have the face towards ⟨~ *the wall*⟩; *also* to front on ⟨*a house* facing *the park*⟩ **4** to turn (e g a playing card) face-up **5** to make the surface of (e g a stone) flat or smooth **6** to cause (troops) to face in a particular direction on command ~ *vi* **1** to have the face or front turned in a specified direction ⟨*the house* ~s *towards the east*⟩ **2** to turn the face in a specified direction – **face the music** to confront and endure the unpleasant consequences of one's actions – **face up to** to confront without shrinking – **face with** to confront with ⟨faced *him* with *the evidence*⟩

ˈfaceˌcloth *n* FLANNEL 3

-faced /-fayst/ *comb form* (*adj, n* → *adj*) having (such) a face or (so many) faces ⟨*two*-faced⟩

ˈface ˌflannel *n, Br* FLANNEL 3

face-harden *vt* to harden the surface of (e g steel)

ˈfaceless /-lis/ *adj* lacking identity; anonymous ⟨~ *bureaucrats*⟩ [[1]FACE + -LESS] – **facelessness** *n*

ˈface-ˌlift *n* **1** plastic surgery to remove facial defects (e g wrinkles) typical of aging **2** an alteration intended to improve appearance or utility – **face-lift** *vt*

ˈface-ˌoff *n* a method of putting a ball or puck in play in lacrosse or ice hockey in which 2 opposing players stand facing each other and on a signal attempt to gain control of the ball or puck

face out *vt* to confront defiantly or impudently ⟨faced out *the opposition*⟩

ˈface-ˌpack *n* a cream, paste, etc applied to the face to improve the complexion and remove impurities

ˈfaceˌplate /-ˌplayt/ *n* a protective cover for the human face (e g of a diver)

facer /ˈfaysə/ *n* an unexpected difficulty for which no solution is immediately clear – infml [[2]FACE + [2]-ER]

ˈface-ˌsaving *adj* serving to preserve one's dignity or reputation – **face-saver** *n*

facet /ˈfasit/ *n* **1** a small plane surface (e g of a cut gem) **2** any of the aspects from which sthg specified may be considered ⟨*another ~ of his genius*⟩ **3** the external surface of any of the usu many optical elements of the compound eye of an insect or other arthropod [F *facette*, dim. of *face*] – **faceted, facetted** *adj*

facetiae /fəˈseeshi,ee/ *n pl* **1** humorous witticisms **2** pornographic items in booksellers' catalogues [L, fr pl of *facetia* jest, fr *facetus* witty]

facetious /fəˈseeshəs/ *adj* **1** inappropriately lacking seriousness in manner; flippant ⟨*a ~ question*⟩ **2** intended to be amusing [MF *facetieux*, fr *facetie* jest, fr L *facetia*] – **facetiously** *adv*, **facetiousness** *n*

,face-to-ˈface *adj* in each other's usu hostile presence ⟨*a ~ encounter*⟩

,face to ˈface *adv* **1** in or into the usu hostile presence of (one) another **2** in or into confrontation with sthg which calls for immediate action ⟨*came ~ with the problem*⟩

ˈface ,value *n* **1** the value indicated on the face (e g of a postage stamp or a share certificate) **2** the apparent value or significance ⟨*if their results may be taken at ~*⟩

facia /ˈfashi·ə/ *n* a fascia

¹facial /ˈfaysh(ə)l/ *adj* of the face – **facially** *adv*

²facial *n* a facial beauty treatment

-facient /-faysh(ə)nt/ *comb form* (→ *adj*) making; causing ⟨*somni*facient⟩ [L *facient-, faciens*, prp of *facere* to make, do – more at DO]

facies /ˈfayshi·eez/ *n, pl* **facies** /~/ **1** the facial appearance characteristic of a particular (abnormal) condition **2** the general appearance of a particular plant, rock, etc [NL, fr L, face]

facile /ˈfasiel/ *adj* **1a** easily or readily accomplished or performed ⟨*a ~ victory*⟩ **b** specious, superficial ⟨*I am not concerned with offering any ~ solution for so complex a problem* – T S Eliot⟩ **2** used, done, or understood with ease [MF, fr L *facilis*, fr *facere*] – **facilely** *adv*, **facileness** *n*

facilitate /fəˈsilitayt/ *vt* to make easier – fml – **facilitative** /-tətiv/ *adj*, **facilitator** *n*

facilitation /fə,siliˈtaysh(ə)n/ *n* the increase in the ease with which an impulse is conducted along a particular nerve, esp resulting from repetition of the impulse [FACILITATE + -ION]

facility /fəˈsiləti/ *n* **1** the quality of being easily performed **2** the ability to perform sthg easily; aptitude **3** sthg (e g equipment) that promotes the ease of an action or operation – usu pl ⟨*provide books and other* facilities *for independent study*⟩

facing /ˈfaysing/ *n* **1a** a lining at the edge of sthg, esp a garment, for stiffening or ornament **b** *pl* the collar, cuffs, and trimmings of a uniform coat **2** an ornamental or protective layer **3** material used for facing

facsimile /fakˈsiməli/ *n* **1** an exact copy, esp of printed material **2** the transmission and reproduction of graphic material (e g typescript or pictures) by wire or radio ☞ TELECOMMUNICATION [L *fac simile* make similar] – **facsimile** *vt*

fact /fakt/ *n* **1** a thing done; *esp* a criminal act **2** the quality of having actual existence in the real world; *also* sthg having such existence **3** an event, esp as distinguished from its legal effect **4** a piece of information presented as having objective reality ⟨*that's a ~*⟩ [L *factum*, fr neut of *factus*, pp of *facere*] – **factless** *adj*, **facticity** /fakˈtisəti/ *n* – **in fact** **1** really; AS A MATTER OF FACT **2** briefly; IN SHORT

¹faction /ˈfaksh(ə)n/ *n* **1** a party or minority group within a party **2** dissension with a party or group [MF & L; MF, fr L *faction-, factio* act of making, faction – more at FASHION] – **factional** *adj*, **factionalism** *n*, **factionally** *adv*

²faction *n* the dramatized reconstruction of some real historical situation or event ⟨*~ has actually been around for quite some time Shakespeare was the first great ~ writer in his history plays* – The Guardian⟩ [blend of *fact* and *fiction*]

-faction /-ˈfaksh(ə)n/ *comb form* (→ *n*) **1** making; -fication ⟨*lique*faction⟩ **2** state ⟨*satis*faction⟩ [ME *-faccioun*, fr MF & L; MF *-faction*, fr L *-faction-, -factio* (as in *satisfaction-, satisfactio* satisfaction)] – **-factive** *comb form* (→ *adj*)

factious /ˈfakshəs/ *adj* **1** caused by or inclined to faction **2** seditious [MF or L; MF *factieux*, fr L *factiosus*, fr *factio*] – **factiously** *adv*, **factiousness** *n*

factitious /fakˈtishəs/ *adj* **1** produced by human beings rather than by natural forces **2** produced artificially; sham, unreal ⟨*created a ~ demand by spreading rumours of shortage*⟩ [L *facticius*, fr *factus*] – **factitiously** *adv*, **factitiousness** *n*

factitive /ˈfaktətiv/ *adj* of transitive verbs (e g *paint* in '*paint* the town red") that can take an objective complement as well as an object [NL *factitivus*, irreg fr L *factus*] – **factitively** *adv*

,fact of ˈlife *n, pl* **facts of life** **1** *pl* the processes and behaviour involved in (human) sex and reproduction **2** sthg that exists and must be taken into consideration

¹factor /ˈfaktə/ *n* **1** one who acts for another; an agent **2** a condition, force, or fact that actively contributes to a result **3** a gene **4** any of the numbers or symbols that when multiplied together form a product [ME, fr MF *facteur*, fr L *factor* doer, fr *factus*] – **factorship** *n*

²factor *vt* to express as the product of factors – **factorable** /-t(ə)rəbl/ *adj*

factorage /ˈfakt(ə)rij/ *n* the charges made by a factor for his services

¹factorial /fakˈtawri·əl/ *n* the product of all the positive integers from 1 to a given number ☞ SYMBOL

²factorial *adj* of a factor or a factorial

factor·ize, -ise /ˈfaktəriez/ *vt* to factor – **factorization** /-ˈzay sh(ə)n/ *n*

factory /ˈfakt(ə)ri/ *n* a building or set of buildings with facilities for manufacturing [MF *factorie* building where factors trade, fr *facteur*]

ˈfactory ,farming *n* farming using intensive methods

ˈfactory ,ship *n* the major ship of a whaling fleet

factotum /fakˈtohtəm/ *n* a servant employed to carry out many types of work [NL, lit., do everything, fr L *fac* do + *totum* everything]

factual /ˈfaktyooəl, -chooəl/ *adj* **1** of facts **2** restricted to or based on fact – **factually** *adv*, **factualness** *n*, **factuality** /-tyooˈaləti, -choo-/ *n*

facture /ˈfakchə/ *n* the manner of execution of sthg (e g an artistic work) [ME, fr MF, fr L *factura* action of making, fr *factus*]

facula /ˈfakyoolə/ *n, pl* **faculae** /-li/ a bright region of the sun's photosphere [NL, fr L, dim. of *fac-, fax* torch]

facultative /ˈfakəltətiv/ *adj* **1** permitting ⟨*~ legislation*⟩ **2** having a particular type of life or taking place under some environmental conditions but not under others ⟨*a* ~ *parasite*⟩ – compare OBLIGATE 2 – **facultatively** *adv*

faculty /ˈfakəlti/ *n* **1a** an inherent capability, power, or function of the body ⟨*the* ~ *of hearing*⟩ **b** a natural aptitude; a talent ⟨*has a* ~ *for saying the right things*⟩ **2** a group of related subject departments in a university **3** *sing or pl in constr* the members of a profession **4** (conferred) power or prerogative [ME *faculte*, fr MF *faculté*, fr ML & L; ML *facultat-, facultas* branch of learning or teaching, fr L, ability, abundance, fr *facilis* facile]

fad /fad/ *n* **1** a usu short-lived but enthusiastically pursued practice or interest; a craze **2** an idiosyncratic taste or habit ⟨*cats that have* ~s *about food*⟩ [origin unknown] – **faddish** *adj*, **faddishness** *n*, **faddism** *n*, **faddist** *n*, **faddy** *adj*

[1]**fade** /fayd/ *vi* **1** to lose freshness or vigour; wither **2** *of a brake* to lose braking power gradually, esp owing to prolonged use **3** to lose freshness or brilliance of colour **4** to disappear gradually; vanish – often + *away* ⟨*the smile* ~d *from his face*⟩ **5** to change gradually in loudness, strength, or visibility – often used of electronic signals or sounds; usu + *in* or *out* ~ *vt* to cause to fade [ME *faden*, fr MF *fader*, fr *fade* feeble, insipid, fr (assumed) VL *fatidus*, alter. of L *fatuus* fatuous, insipid]

[2]**fade** *n* an effect consisting of a fade-out or a fade-in or a combination of both

ˈ**fade-ˌin** *n* the gradual appearance of a sound or picture, usu in broadcasting or on film

ˈ**fade-ˌout** *n* the gradual disappearance of esp a sound or picture, usu in broadcasting or on film

faeces, *NAm chiefly* **feces** /ˈfeeseez/ *n pl* bodily waste discharged through the anus [ME *feces*, fr L *faec-, faex* (sing.) dregs] – **faecal** /ˈfeekl/ *adj*

faerie *also* **faery** /ˈfayəri, ˈfeəri/ *n* **1** fairyland **2** a fairy *USE* poetic [MF *faerie* – more at FAIRY] – **faery** *adj*

Faeroese, Faroese /ˌfeərohˈeez/ *n, pl* **Faeroese, Faroese** /~/ **1** an inhabitant of the Faeroes **2** the Germanic language of the Faeroese ☞ LANGUAGE [*Faeroes, Faroes*, islands in the N Atlantic] – **Faeroese** *adj*

faff /faf/ *vi, Br* to waste time over trifles; fuss – usu + *about* or *around*; infml [imit]

[1]**fag** /fag/ *vi* **-gg- 1** to act as a fag, esp in a British public school **2** to work hard; toil – infml [obs *fag* (to droop), perh fr *fag* (fag end)]

[2]**fag** *n* **1** a British public-school pupil who acts as servant to an older schoolmate **2** *chiefly Br* a tiring or boring task ⟨*it's a real* ~⟩ – infml

[3]**fag** *n* a cigarette – infml [*fag end*]

[4]**fag** *n, chiefly NAm* FAGGOT 2

ˈ**fag ˌend** *n* **1** a poor or worn-out end; a remnant **2** the extreme end ⟨*the* ~ *of one quarrel* – William Golding⟩ **USE** infml [earlier *fag* (end of a piece of cloth or a rope), fr ME *fagge* flap]

ˌ**fagged** ˈ**out** *adj* tired, exhausted – infml

[1]**faggot** /ˈfagət/ *n* **1** *NAm chiefly* **fagot a** a bundle: e g (1) a bundle of sticks (2) a bundle of pieces of wrought iron to be shaped by hammering or rolling at high temperature (3) a bunch of herbs tied together; BOUQUET GARNI **b** a round mass of minced meat (e g pig's liver) mixed with herbs and usu breadcrumbs **2** *chiefly NAm* a usu male homosexual – derog [ME *fagot*, fr MF]

[2]**faggot,** *NAm chiefly* **fagot** *vt* **1** to make a faggot of; bind together into a bundle ⟨~ed *sticks*⟩ **2** to ornament with faggoting

faggoting, *NAm chiefly* **fagoting** /ˈfagəting/ *n* **1** embroidery in which some of the horizontal threads are tied in the middle to form hourglass shapes **2** a joining, esp of cloth, lace, etc, in a similar way to faggoting

fagin /ˈfaygin/ *n* a trainer of thieves [*Fagin*, character in the novel *Oliver Twist* by Charles Dickens †1870 E novelist]

fah /fah/ *n* fa

Fahrenheit /ˈfarənˌhiet/ *adj* relating to, conforming to, or being a scale of temperature on which water freezes at 32° and boils at 212° under standard conditions ☞ UNIT [Gabriel *Fahrenheit* †1736 G physicist]

faience, faïence /fieˈahns, -ˈonhs (*Fr* fajɑ̃ːs)/ *n* tin-glazed decorated earthenware [F, fr *Faenza*, town in Italy]

[1]**fail** /fayl/ *vi* **1a** to lose strength; weaken ⟨*her health was* ~ing⟩ **b** to fade or die away ⟨*until the light* ~s⟩ **c** to stop functioning **2a** to fall short ⟨~ed *in his duty*⟩ **b** to be or become absent or inadequate ⟨*the water supply* ~ed⟩ **c** to be unsuccessful (e g in passing a test) **d** to become bankrupt or insolvent ~ *vt* **1a** to disappoint the expectations or trust of ⟨*his friends* ~ed *him*⟩ **b** to prove inadequate for or incapable of carrying out an expected service or function for ⟨*for once his wit* ~ed *him*⟩ **2** to be deficient in; lack **3** to leave undone; neglect **4a** to be unsuccessful in passing (e g a test) **b** to grade (e g a student) as not passing [ME *failen*, fr OF *faillir*, fr (assumed) VL *fallire*, alter. of L *fallere* to deceive, disappoint; prob akin to Gk *phēlos* deceitful] – **failingly** *adv*

[2]**fail** *n* **1** failure – chiefly in *without fail* **2** an examination failure

[1]**failing** /ˈfayling/ *n* a usu slight or insignificant defect in character; *broadly* a fault, imperfection

[2]**failing** *prep* in absence or default of ⟨~ *specific instructions, use your own judgment*⟩

faille /fayl/ *n* a shiny closely woven silk, rayon, or cotton fabric with transverse ribs [F]

ˈ**failˌsafe** /-ˌsayf/ *adj* designed so as to counteract automatically the effect of an anticipated possible source of failure

failure /ˈfaylyə/ *n* **1a** nonoccurrence or nonperformance; *specif* a failing to perform a duty or expected action **b** inability to perform a normal function ⟨*heart* ~⟩ **2** lack of success **3a** a falling short; a deficiency ⟨*a* ~ *in the supply of raw materials*⟩ **b** deterioration, decay **4** sby or sthg unsuccessful [alter. of earlier *failer*, fr AF, fr OF *faillir* to fail]

fain /fayn/ *adv, archaic* **1** with pleasure **2** rather [ME *fagen, fayn*, fr *fagen, fayn* happy, pleased, fr OE *fægen*; akin to ON *fegiun* happy, OE *fæger* fair]

fainéant, faineant /ˈfayni·ənt/ *adj* idle and ineffectual; indolent [F *fainéant*, n, fr MF *fait-nient*, lit., does nothing, by folk etymology fr *faignant*, fr prp of *faindre, feindre*] – **fainéant** *n*

[1]**faint** /faynt/ *adj* **1** cowardly, timid – chiefly in *faint heart* **2** weak, dizzy, and likely to faint ⟨*felt* ~⟩ **3** performed, offered, or accomplished weakly or languidly; feeble ⟨*made a* ~ *attempt at a smile*⟩ **4** lacking distinctness; *esp* dim ⟨*a* ~ *light*⟩ [ME *faint, feint*, fr OF, fr pp of *faindre, feindre* to feign, shirk – more at FEIGN] – **faintly** *adv*, **faintness** *n*

[2]faint *vi* to lose consciousness because of a temporary decrease in the blood supply to the brain (e g through exhaustion or shock)

[3]faint *n* (a condition of) fainting

,faint'hearted /-'hahtid/ *adj* lacking courage or resolution; timid – **faintheartedly** *adv*, **faintheartedness** *n*

[1]fair /feə/ *adj* **1** attractive, beautiful **2** superficially pleasing; specious ⟨*she trusted his ~ promises*⟩ **3** clean, clear ⟨*a ~ copy*⟩ **4** not stormy or foul; fine ⟨*~ weather*⟩ **5a** free from self-interest or prejudice; honest **b** conforming with the established rules; allowed ⟨*a ~ tackle*⟩ **6** favourable to a ship's course ⟨*a ~ wind*⟩ **7** light in colour; blond **8** moderately good or large; adequate ⟨*a ~ understanding of the work*⟩ **9** real, perfect – infml ⟨*a ~ treat to watch him – New Republic*⟩; compare FAIR AND SQUARE [ME *fager, fair,* fr OE *fæger*; akin to OHG *fagar* beautiful, & perh to Lith *puošti* to decorate] – **fairness** *n* – **in a fair way to** likely to

[2]fair *adv* fairly

[3]fair *vi*, *of the weather* to clear ~ *vt* to join so that the external surfaces blend smoothly

[4]fair *n* **1** a periodic gathering of buyers and sellers at a particular place and time for trade or a competitive exhibition, usu accompanied by entertainment and amusements **2a** *Br* FUN FAIR **b** an exhibition usu designed to acquaint prospective buyers or the general public with a product **3** a sale of a collection of articles usu for a charitable purpose [ME *feire,* fr OF, fr ML *feria* weekday, fair, fr LL, festal day, fr L *feriae* (pl) holidays – more at FEAST]

,fair and 'square *adv* **1** in an honest manner ⟨*won the match ~*⟩ **2** exactly, directly ⟨*hit him ~ on the nose*⟩ – **fair and square** *adj*

,fair 'dos /'dooz/ *n pl, chiefly Br* fair shares – infml [*dos* (treatment, shares), fr pl of [2]*do*]

'fair,faced /-,fayst/ *adj, of brickwork* not plastered

,fair 'game *n* sby or sthg open to legitimate pursuit, attack, or ridicule ⟨*he was ~ for our criticism*⟩

'fair,ground /-,grownd/ *n* an area where outdoor fairs, circuses, or exhibitions are held

fairing /'feəring/ *n* a smooth structure intended to reduce drag or air resistance [fr gerund of [3]*fair*]

fairish /'feərish/ *adj* fairly good ⟨*a ~ wage for those days*⟩ – infml – **fairishly** *adv*

'Fair ,Isle, Fairisle *n* (a garment or fabric in) a style of knitting having horizontal characteristically patterned bands worked in 2 or more colours against a plain background [*Fair Isle,* one of the Shetland islands, where it originated]

'fair,lead /-,leed/ *n* a block or ring that serves as a guide for a rope or chain and keeps it from chafing

'fairly /-li/ *adv* **1** completely, quite ⟨*~ bursting with pride*⟩ **2a** in a proper or legal manner ⟨*~ priced stocks*⟩ **b** impartially, honestly ⟨*a story told ~ and objectively*⟩ **3** to a full degree or extent; plainly, distinctly ⟨*had ~ caught sight of him*⟩ **4** for the most part; quite ⟨*a ~ easy job*⟩

,fair 'play *n* equitable or impartial treatment; justice

,fair-'spoken *adj* pleasant and courteous in speech ⟨*a ~ youth*⟩

'fair,way /-,way/ *n* **1** a navigable channel in a river, bay, or harbour **2** the mowed part of a golf course between a tee and a green

'fair-,weather *adj* present or loyal only in untroubled times – chiefly in *fair-weather friend*

fairy /'feəri/ *n* **1** a small mythical being having magic powers and usu human form **2** an effeminate male (homosexual) – derog [ME *fairie* fairyland, fairy people, fr OF *faerie,* fr *feie, fee* fairy, fr L *Fata,* goddess of fate, fr *fatum* fate] – **fairy** *adj,* **fairylike** *adj*

'fairy,land /-,land/ *n* **1** the land of fairies **2** a place of magical charm

'fairy ,lights *n pl, chiefly Br* small coloured electric lights for decoration, esp outdoors or on a Christmas tree

'fairy ,ring *n* (a ring of darker vegetation associated with) a ring of fungi at the edge of a body of mycelium which has grown in a circle outwards from an initial point [fr the folk belief that such rings were dancing places of the fairies]

'fairy ,story *n* FAIRY TALE

'fairy-,tale *adj* marked by **a** unusual grace or beauty **b** apparently magical success or good fortune ⟨*a ~ start to his career*⟩

'fairy ,tale *n* **1** a story which features supernatural or imaginary forces and beings **2** a made-up story, usu designed to mislead; a fabrication

fait accompli /,fayt ə'kompli, ,fet əkom'pli (*Fr* fɛt akɔ̃pli)/ *n, pl* **faits accomplis** /~/ sthg already accomplished and considered irreversible [F, accomplished fact]

faith /fayth/ *n* **1a** allegiance to duty or a person; loyalty – chiefly in *good/ bad faith* **b** fidelity to one's promises – chiefly in *keep/ break faith* **2a** belief and trust in and loyalty to God or the doctrines of a religion **b(1)** firm belief in sthg for which there is no objective proof **(2)** complete confidence **3** sthg believed with strong conviction; *esp* a system of religious beliefs [ME *feith,* fr OF *feid, foi,* fr L *fides*; akin to L *fidere* to trust – more at BIDE]

[1]'faithful /-f(ə)l/ *adj* **1** showing faith; loyal, steadfast; *specif* loyal to one's spouse in having no sexual relations outside marriage **2** firm in adherence to promises or in observance of duty; conscientious **3** true to the facts or to an original; accurate ⟨*the portrait is a ~ likeness*⟩ – **faithfully** *adv,* **faithfulness** *n*

[2]faithful *n pl* **1** *the* full church members **2** *the* body of adherents of a religion (e g Islam) **3 faithful, faithfuls** loyal followers or members ⟨*party ~s*⟩

'faith ,healing *n* a practice of attempting the cure of illnesses by prayer rather than medical techniques – **faith healer** *n*

'faithless /-lis/ *adj* **1a** lacking faith, esp religious faith **b** heedless of duty or allegiance; disloyal **2** that may not be relied on; untrustworthy ⟨*a ~ friend*⟩ – **faithlessly** *adv,* **faithlessness** *n*

[1]fake /fayk/ *vt* to coil in fakes [ME *faken*]

[2]fake *n* any of the loops of a coiled rope or cable

[3]fake *vt* **1** to alter or treat so as to impart a false character or appearance; falsify ⟨*~d all the results to suit his theories*⟩ **2a** to counterfeit, simulate **b** to feign ⟨*~d a nervous breakdown* – Michael Billington⟩ ~ *vi* **1** to engage in faking sthg; pretend **2** *NAm* to dummy [prob fr G *fegen* to sweep, thrash] – **faker** *n,* **fakery** /'fayk(ə)ri/ *n*

[4]fake *n* **1** a worthless imitation passed off as genuine **2** an impostor, charlatan

[5]fake *adj* counterfeit, phoney

fakir /'faykiə, fə'kiə, 'fahkiə, -kə/ *n* **1** a Muslim mendicant **2** an itinerant Hindu ascetic holy man [Ar *faqir*, lit., poor man]

Falangist /fə'lanjist/ *n* **1** a member of the Spanish fascist political party **2** a member of a right-wing Christian faction in the Lebanon [Sp *Falangista*, fr *Falange española* Spanish Phalanx, a fascist organization]

falcate /'falkayt/ *also* **falcated** /fal'kaytid/ *adj* hooked or curved like a sickle ☞ PLANT [L *falcatus*, fr *falc-, falx* sickle, scythe]

falchion /'fawlchən, -sh(ə)n/ *n* a broad-bladed slightly curved medieval sword [ME *fauchoun*, fr OF *fauchon*, fr *fauchier* to mow, fr (assumed) VL *falcare*, fr L *falc-, falx*]

falciform /'falsi,fawm/ *adj* falcate [L *falc-, falx* + E *-iform*]

falcon /faw(l)kən/ *n* **1** any of various hawks distinguished by long wings **2** [1]HAWK 1 [ME, fr OF, fr LL *falcon-, falco*, prob of Gmc origin; akin to OHG *falcho* falcon]

'falconer /-nə/ *n* one who hunts with hawks or who breeds or trains hawks for hunting

falconet /,falkə'net/ *n* a very small cannon used in the 16th and 17th c [*falcon* (small cannon) + *-et*]

,falcon-'gentle *n* the female peregrine falcon [ME *faucon gentil* peregrine falcon, fr MF, lit., noble falcon]

'falconry /-ri/ *n* the art of training or the sport of using falcons to pursue game

falderal /'faldə,ral/ *n* (a) folderol

'fald,stool /'fawld-/ *n* **1** a folding stool or chair; *specif* one used by a bishop **2** a folding stool or small desk at which one kneels during devotions; *specif* one used by the sovereigns of England at their coronations [ML *faldistolium*, of Gmc origin; akin to OHG *faltistuol* folding chair, fr a prehistoric WGmc compound whose first constituent is akin to OHG *faldan* to fold and whose second is represented by OHG *stuol* chair – more at [3]FOLD, STOOL]

[1]fall /fawl/ *vi* **fell** /fel/; **fallen** /'fawlən/ **1a** to descend freely by the force of gravity **b** to hang freely ⟨*her hair* ~s *over her shoulders*⟩ **c** to come as if by descending ⟨*a hush* fell *on the audience*⟩ **2a** to become less or lower in degree, level, pitch, or volume ⟨*their voices* fell *to a whisper*⟩ **b** to be uttered; issue ⟨*let* ~ *a remark*⟩ **c** to look down ⟨*her glance* fell *on me*⟩ **3a** to come down from an erect to a usu prostrate position suddenly and esp involuntarily ⟨*slipped and* fell *on the ice*⟩ **b** to enter an undesirable state, esp unavoidably or unwittingly; stumble, stray ⟨fell *into error*⟩ ⟨fell *ill*⟩ **c** to drop because wounded or dead; *esp* to die in battle – euph **d** to suffer military capture ⟨*after a long siege the city* fell⟩ **e** to lose office ⟨*the government* fell⟩ **f** to suffer ruin or defeat ⟨*we must stand or* ~ *together*⟩ **4a** to yield to temptation; sin **b** *of a woman* to lose one's virginity, esp outside marriage **5a** to move or extend in a downward direction – often + *off* or *away* ⟨*the land* ~s *away to the east*⟩ **b** to decline in quality or quantity; abate, subside – often + *off* or *away* ⟨*production* fell *off because of the strike*⟩ **c** to assume a look of disappointment or dismay ⟨*his face* fell⟩ **d** to decline in financial value ⟨*shares* fell *sharply today*⟩ **6a** to occur at a specified time or place ⟨*the accent* ~s *on the second syllable*⟩ ⟨*Christmas* ~s *on a Thursday this year*⟩ **b** to come (as if) by chance – + *in* or *into* **c** to come or pass by lot, assignment, or inheritance; devolve – usu + *on, to,* or *upon* ⟨*it* fell *to me to break the news*⟩ **7** to come within the limits, scope, or jurisdiction of sthg ⟨~s *within our borders*⟩ **8** to pass, esp involuntarily and suddenly, into a new state or condition ⟨~ *in love*⟩ ⟨*the book* fell *apart*⟩ **9** to begin heartily or actively – usu + *to* ⟨fell *to work*⟩ [ME *fallen*, fr OE *feallan*; akin to OHG *fallan* to fall, & perh to Lith *pulti*] – **fall behind** DROP BEHIND – **fall between two stools** to fail because of inability to choose between or reconcile 2 alternative or conflicting courses of action – **fall flat** to produce no response or result ⟨*the joke* fell flat⟩ – **fall for 1** to fall in love with **2** to be deceived by ⟨*he* fell for *the trick*⟩ – **fall foul of** to arouse aversion in; clash with – **fall on/upon 1** to descend upon; attack ⟨fell *hungrily* on *the pie*⟩ **2** to meet with ⟨*he* fell on *hard times*⟩ **3** to hit on – **fall over oneself** to display almost excessive eagerness – **fall short** to fail to attain a goal or target

[2]fall *n* **1** the act of falling by the force of gravity **2a** a falling out, off, or away; a dropping ⟨*a* ~ *of snow*⟩ **b** sthg or a quantity that falls or has fallen ⟨*a* ~ *of rock*⟩ **c** the quantity born – used esp with reference to lambs **3** a rope or chain for a hoisting tackle **4a** a loss of greatness or power; a collapse ⟨*the* ~ *of the Roman Empire*⟩ **b** the surrender or capture of a besieged place ⟨*the* ~ *of Troy*⟩ **c** *often cap* mankind's loss of innocence through the disobedience of Adam and Eve **5a** a downward slope **b** CATARACT 2a – usu pl with sing. meaning but sing. or pl in constr **6** a decrease in size, quantity, degree, or value **7** the distance which sthg falls **8a** an act of forcing a wrestler's shoulders to the mat for a prescribed time **b** a bout of wrestling **9** *chiefly NAm* autumn

fall about *vi* to be convulsed (with laughter) – infml

fallacy /'faləsi/ *n* **1** deceptive appearance or nature; deception, delusiveness **2** a false idea ⟨*the popular* ~ *that scientists are illiterate*⟩ **3** an argument failing to satisfy the conditions of valid inference [L *fallacia*, fr *fallac-, fallax* deceitful, fr *fallere* to deceive – more at FAIL] – **fallacious** /fə'layshəs/ *adj*, **fallaciously** *adv*, **fallaciousness** *n*

fall away *vi* **1a** to withdraw friendship or support ⟨*gradually all his friends* fell away⟩ **b** to lapse in a faith **2a** to diminish gradually in size **b** to drift off a course

fall back *vi* to retreat, recede – **fallback** /'-,-/ *n* – **fall back on/upon** to have recourse to ⟨*when facts were scarce he* fell back on *his imagination*⟩

fall down *vi* to fail to meet expectations or requirements; be inadequate ⟨*she* fell down *on the job*⟩ – infml

'fall ,guy *n* **1** one who is easily cheated or tricked **2** a scapegoat *USE* infml

fallible /'faləbl/ *adj* capable of being or likely to be wrong [ME, fr ML *fallibilis*, fr L *fallere*] – **fallibly** *adv*, **fallibility** /-'biləti/ *n*

fall in *vi* **1** to sink or collapse inwards ⟨*the roof* fell in⟩ **2** to take one's proper place in a military formation – **fall in with** to concur with ⟨*had to* fall in with *her wishes*⟩

,falling 'star *n* a meteor when falling into the earth's atmosphere and producing a bright streak of light

'fall,off /-,of/ *n* a decline, esp in quantity or quality ⟨*a* ~ *in exports*⟩

fal,lopian 'tube /fə'lohpi·ən, -pyən/ *n, often cap F* either of the pair of tubes conducting the egg from the ovary to the uterus in mammals ☞ REPRODUCTION [Gabriel *Fallopius* †1562 It anatomist]

'fall,out /-,owt/ *n* **1a** polluting particles, esp radioactive particles resulting from a nuclear explosion, descending through the atmosphere **b** descent of fallout through the atmosphere **2** secondary results or products ⟨*the war produced its own literary ~: a profusion of books – Newsweek*⟩

fall out *vi* **1** to have a disagreement; quarrel ⟨*they* fell out *with one another over money*⟩ **2** to leave one's place in the ranks of a military formation **3** to happen; COME ABOUT – fml or poetic ⟨*as it* fell out *upon a day*⟩

¹fallow /'faloh/ *adj* light yellowish brown [ME *falow*, fr OE *fealu*; akin to OHG *falo* pale, fallow, L *pallēre* to be pale, Gk *polios* grey]

²fallow *n* **1** (ploughed and harrowed) land that is allowed to lie idle during the growing season **2** (the period of) being fallow [ME *falwe, falow*, fr OE *fealg*]

³fallow *vt* to plough, harrow, etc (land) without seeding, esp so as to destroy weeds

⁴fallow *adj* **1** *of land* left unsown after ploughing **2** dormant, inactive – chiefly in *to lie fallow* – **fallowness** *n*

fallow deer *n* a small European deer with broad antlers and a pale yellow coat spotted with white in the summer

fall through *vi* to fail to be carried out

fall to *vi* to begin doing sthg (e g working or eating), esp vigorously – often imper

false /fawls/ *adj* **1** not genuine ⟨*~ documents*⟩ **2a** intentionally untrue; lying ⟨*~ testimony*⟩ **b** adjusted or made so as to deceive ⟨*a suitcase with a ~ bottom*⟩ **3** not based on reality; untrue ⟨*~ premises*⟩ ⟨*a ~ sense of security*⟩ **4** disloyal, treacherous ⟨*a ~ friend*⟩ **5a** fitting over a main part as strengthening, protection, or disguise **b** appearing forced or artificial; unconvincing **6** resembling or related to a more widely known kind ⟨*~ oats*⟩ **7** inaccurate in pitch or vowel length **8** imprudent, unwise ⟨*a ~ move*⟩ [ME *fals*, fr OF & L; OF, fr L *falsus*, fr pp of *fallere* to deceive] – **falsely** *adv*, **falseness** *n*, **falsity** *n*

,false a'larm *n* an occurrence that raises but fails to meet expectations

'falsehood /-hood/ *n* **1** an untrue statement; a lie **2** absence of truth or accuracy; falsity **3** the practice of telling lies

false pregnancy *n* a psychosomatic state in which some of the signs of pregnancy occur without conception

false rib *n* a rib whose cartilages unite indirectly or not at all with the breastbone – compare FLOATING RIB

,false 'start *n* **1** an incorrect and esp illegally early start by a competitor in a race **2** an abortive beginning to an activity or course of action

falsetto /fawl'setoh/ *n, pl* **falsettos** (a singer who uses) an artificially high voice, specif an artificially produced male singing voice that extends above the range of the singer's full voice [It, fr dim. of *falso* false, fr L *falsus*] – **falsetto** *adv*

'false,work /-,wuhk/ *n* a temporary erection on which a main work is supported during construction

falsies /'fawlsiz/ *n pl* pads of foam rubber or other material worn to enlarge the apparent size of the breasts

falsify /'fawlsi,fie/ *vt* **1** to prove or declare false **2a** to make false by fraudulent alteration ⟨*his accounts were* falsified *to conceal a theft*⟩ **b** to represent falsely; misrepresent [ME *falsifien*, fr MF *falsifier*, fr ML *falsificare*, fr L *falsus*] – **falsifier** *n*, **falsification** /-fi'kaysh(ə)n/ *n*

falter /'fawltə/ *vi* **1** to walk or move unsteadily or hesitatingly; stumble **2** to speak brokenly or weakly; stammer **3a** to hesitate in purpose or action; waver **b** to lose strength, purpose, or effectiveness; weaken ⟨*the business was ~*ing⟩ ~ *vt* to utter in a hesitant or broken manner [ME *falteren*] – **falterer** *n*, **falteringly** *adv*

fame /faym/ *n* **1** public estimation; reputation **2** popular acclaim; renown [ME, fr OF, fr L *fama* report, fame; akin to L *fari* to speak – more at ¹BAN]

famed *adj* well-known, famous

familial /fə'mili·əl, -yəl/ *adj* **1** (characteristic) of a family or its members **2** tending to occur in more members of a family than expected by chance alone ⟨*a ~ disorder*⟩ [F, fr L *familia*]

¹familiar /fə'mili·ə, -yə/ *n* **1** an intimate associate; a companion **2** FAMILIAR SPIRIT

²familiar *adj* **1** closely acquainted; intimate ⟨*a subject I am ~ with*⟩ **2a** casual, informal **b** too intimate and unrestrained; presumptuous **3** frequently seen or experienced; common [ME *familier*, fr OF, fr L *familiaris*, fr *familia*] – **familiarly** *adv*, **familiarness** *n*

familiarity /fə,mili'arəti/ *n* **1a** absence of ceremony; informality **b** an unduly informal act or expression; an impropriety **2** close acquaintance *with* or knowledge of sthg [¹FAMILIAR + -ITY]

familiar·ize, -ise /fə'mili·ə,riez, -yə,riez/ *vt* **1** to make known or familiar **2** to make well acquainted ⟨*~ yourselves with the rules*⟩ – **familiarization** /-'zaysh(ə)n/ *n*

familiar spirit *n* a spirit or demon that waits on an individual (e g a witch)

¹family /'faməli/ *n sing or pl in constr* **1** a group of people united by their common convictions (e g of religion or philosophy); a fellowship, brotherhood **2** a group of people of common ancestry or deriving from a common stock **3** a group of people living under 1 roof; *esp* a set of 2 or more adults living together and rearing their children **4a** a closely related series of elements or chemical compounds **b** a group of related languages descended from a single ancestral language **5** a category in the biological classification of living things ranking above a genus and below an order **6** a set of curves or surfaces whose equations differ only in certain constant terms [ME *familie*, fr L *familia* household (including servants as well as kin of the householder), fr *famulus* servant; perh akin to Skt *dhāman* dwelling place]

²family *adj* of or suitable for a family or all of its members ⟨*~ entertainment*⟩

,family al'lowance *n* CHILD BENEFIT

Family Division *n* a division of the High Court that deals with divorce, custody of children, etc ☞ LAW

,family 'income ,supplement *n* a social-security payment made to a family whose income is below the officially recognized minimum

'family ,man *n* **1** a man with a wife and children dependent on him **2** a man of domestic habits

,family 'name *n* a surname

,family 'planning *n* a system of achieving planned parenthood by contraception; BIRTH CONTROL

,family 'tree *n* (a diagram of) a genealogy

famine /'famin/ *n* an extreme scarcity of food; *broadly* any great shortage [ME, fr MF, fr (assumed) VL *famina*, fr L *fames* hunger]

famish /'famish/ *vt* to cause to suffer severely from hunger – usu pass ⟨*I'm* ~ed⟩ [ME *famishen*, prob alter. of *famen*, fr MF *afamer*, fr (assumed) VL *affamare*, fr L *ad-* + *fames*]

famous /'faymәs/ *adj* **1** well-known **2** excellent, first-rate ⟨~ *weather for a walk*⟩ – infml; no longer in vogue [ME, fr MF *fameux*, fr L *famosus*, fr *fama* fame] – **famously** *adv*, **famousness** *n*

famulus /'famyoolәs/ *n, pl* **famuli** /-lie, -li/ a private secretary or attendant [G, assistant to a professor, fr L, servant]

¹fan /fan/ *n* **1** a device for winnowing grain **2** an instrument for producing a current of air: e g **a** a folding circular or semicircular device that consists of material (e g paper or silk) mounted on thin slats that is waved to and fro by hand to produce a cooling current of air **b** a device, usu a series of vanes radiating from a hub rotated by a motor, for producing a current of air [ME, fr OE *fann*, fr L *vannus* – more at WINNOW] – **fanlike** *adj*

²fan *vb* **-nn-** *vt* **1a** to winnow (grain) **b** to eliminate (e g chaff) by winnowing **2** to move or impel (air) with a fan **3a** to direct or blow a current of air on (as if) with a fan **b** to stir up to activity as if by fanning a fire; stimulate ⟨*he was* ~ning *the mob's fury with an emotive speech*⟩ **4** to spread like a fan ⟨~ned *the pack of cards*⟩ **5** to fire (a revolver) by squeezing the trigger and striking the hammer to the rear with the free hand ~ *vi* **1** to move like a fan; flutter **2** to spread like a fan – often + *out* ⟨*tanks* ~ning *out across the plain*⟩

³fan *n* an enthusiastic supporter or admirer (e g of a sport, pursuit, or celebrity) ⟨*a football* ~⟩ ⟨*a Presley* ~⟩ [short for *fanatic*]

fanatic /fә'natik/ *n or adj* (one who is) excessively and often uncritically enthusiastic, esp in religion or politics [L *fanaticus* inspired by a deity, frenzied, fr *fanum* temple – more at FEAST] – **fanatical** *adj*, **fanatically** *adv*, **fanaticism** /-ti,siz(ә)m/ *n*, **fanaticize** /-ti,siez/ *vt*

'fan ,belt *n* an endless belt driving a cooling fan for a radiator ☞ CAR

fancier /'fansi·ә/ *n* one who breeds or grows a usu specified animal or plant for points of excellence ⟨*a pigeon* ~⟩

fanciful /'fansif(ә)l/ *adj* **1** given to or guided by fancy or imagination rather than by reason and experience **2** existing in fancy only; imaginary **3** marked by fancy or whim; *specif* elaborate, contrived – **fancifully** *adv*, **fancifulness** *n*

fancily /'fansәli/ *adv* in an elaborate or ornate manner ⟨~ *dressed*⟩

¹fancy /'fansi/ *n* **1** a liking based on whim rather than reason; an inclination ⟨*took a* ~ *to her*⟩ **2a** a notion, whim **b** a mental image or representation of sthg **3a** imagination, esp of a capricious or delusive sort **b** the power of mental conception and representation, used in artistic expression (e g by a poet) **4a** *sing or pl in constr the* group of fanciers or of devotees of a particular sport, esp boxing **b** sby or sthg considered likely to do well (e g in a race) – infml [ME *fantasie, fantsy* fantasy, fancy, fr MF *fantasie*, fr L *phantasia*, fr Gk, appearance, imagination, fr *phantazein* to present to the mind (middle voice, to imagine), fr *phainein* to show; akin to OE *gebōned* polished, Gk *phōs* light]

²fancy *vt* **1** to believe without knowledge or evidence ⟨*I* ~ *I've seen you somewhere before*⟩ **2a** to have a fancy for; like, desire ⟨*I really* ~ *blond men*⟩ **b** to consider likely to do well ⟨*which horse do you* ~*?*⟩ **3** to form a conception of; imagine – often imper ⟨*just* ~ *that!*⟩ *USE* (*2&3*) infml – **fanciable** *adj*

³fancy *adj* **1** based on fancy or the imagination; whimsical **2a** not plain or ordinary ⟨~ *cakes*⟩; *esp* fine, quality **b** ornamental ⟨~ *goods*⟩ **c** *of an animal or plant* bred esp for bizarre or ornamental qualities **d** parti-coloured ⟨~ *carnations*⟩ **3** extravagant, exorbitant ⟨~ *prices*⟩ – infml

,fancy 'dress *n* unusual or amusing dress (e g representing a historical or fictional character) worn for a party or other special occasion

,fancy-'free *adj* free to do what one wants, esp because not involved in a relationship – chiefly in *footloose and fancy-free*

'fancy ,man *n* a woman's lover – derog; infml

'fancy ,woman *n* **1** MISTRESS 4 – derog **2** a prostitute *USE* infml

'fancy,work *n* decorative needlework

fandango /fan'dang·goh/ *n, pl* **fandangos** (music for) a lively Spanish dance, usu performed by a couple to the accompaniment of guitar and castanets [Sp]

fanfare /'fan,feә/ *n* **1** a flourish of trumpets **2** a showy outward display [F, prob of imit origin]

fanfaronade /,fanfәrә'nahd/ *n* empty boasting; bluster – fml [F *fanfaronnade*, fr Sp *fanfarronada*, fr *fanfarrón* braggart, prob of imit origin]

fang /fang/ *n* **1a** a tooth by which an animal's prey is seized and held or torn **b** any of the long hollow or grooved teeth of a venomous snake **2** the root of a tooth or any of the prongs into which a root divides **3** a projecting tooth or prong [ME, fr OE; akin to OHG *fang* seizure, OE *fōn* to seize – more at PACT] – **fanged** *adj*

'fan-,jet *n* (an aircraft powered by) a jet engine in which some of the air drawn in bypasses the combustion chambers

'fan,light /-,liet/ *n* an esp semicircular window with radiating divisions over a door or window ☞ ARCHITECTURE

fanny /'fani/ *n* **1** *Br* the female genitals – vulg **2** *NAm* the buttocks – infml [*Fanny*, nickname for *Frances*]

'fan,tail /-,tayl/ *n* **1** a fan-shaped tail or end **2** a domestic pigeon having a broad rounded tail often with 30 or 40 feathers **3** ⁵COUNTER 2

'fan-,tan *n* **1** a Chinese gambling game in which the banker divides a pile of objects into 4's and players bet on what number will be left at the end **2** a card game in which players must build in sequence upon 7's and attempt to be the first one with no cards left [Chin *fan¹-t'an¹*]

fantasia /fan'tayzyә, -zh(y)ә/ *n* a free instrumental or literary composition not in strict form (comprising familiar tunes) [It *fantasia* & G *fantasie*, lit., fancy, fr L *phantasia* – more at FANCY]

fantas·ize, -ise /'fantә,siez/ *vb* to indulge in reverie (about); create or develop imaginative and often fantastic views or ideas (about) ⟨~d *about winning the pools*⟩ – **fantasist** *n*

fantasm /ˈfan,taz(ə)m/ *n* a phantasm

fantastic /fanˈtastik/ *adj* **1a** unreal, imaginary **b** so extreme as to challenge belief; incredible; *specif* exceedingly large or great **2** marked by extravagant fantasy or eccentricity **3** – used as a generalized term of approval ⟨*looked ~ in his velvet jacket*⟩ [ME *fantastic, fantastical*, fr MF & LL; MF *fantastique*, fr LL *phantasticus*, fr Gk *phantastikos* producing mental images, fr *phantazein* to present to the mind] – **fantastical** *adj*, **fantastically** *adv*, **fantasticalness** *n*, **fantasticality** /-ˈkaləti/ *n*

[1]**fantasy** /ˈfantəsi/ *n* **1** unrestricted creative imagination; fancy **2a** a creation of the unrestricted imagination whether expressed or merely conceived (e g a fantastic design or idea) **b** a fantasia **c** imaginative fiction or drama characterized esp by strange, unrealistic, or grotesque elements **3** (the power or process of creating) a usu extravagant mental image or daydream [ME *fantasie* – more at FANCY]

[2]**fantasy** *vb* to fantasize

Fante /ˈfanti/ *n, pl* **Fantes,** *esp collectively* **Fante** (a) Fanti

Fanti /ˈfanti/ *n, pl* **Fantis,** *esp collectively* **Fanti** (the language of) a member of an African tribe of Ghana

fantom /ˈfantəm/ *n* a phantom

ˈ**fan ˌvaulting** *n* an elaborate system of vaulting in which the ribs diverge from a single shaft to resemble the framework of a fan ☞ CHURCH

fanzine /ˈfan,zeen/ *n* a (science fiction) magazine for fans [[3]*fan* + *magazine*]

[1]**far** /fah/ *adv* **farther** /ˈfahdhə/, **further** /ˈfuhdhə/; **farthest** /ˈfahdhist/, **furthest** /ˈfuhdhist/ **1** to or at a considerable distance in space ⟨*wandered ~ into the woods*⟩ **2a** by a broad interval ⟨*the ~ distant future*⟩ **b** in total contrast – + *from* ⟨*~ from criticizing you, I'm delighted*⟩ **3** to or at an extent or degree ⟨*as ~ as I know*⟩ **4a** to or at a considerable distance or degree ⟨*a bright student will go ~*⟩ **b** MUCH 1c ⟨*~ too hot*⟩ ⟨*~ better methods*⟩ **5** to or at a considerable distance in time ⟨*worked ~ into the night*⟩ ⟨*parties are few and ~ between*⟩ [ME *fer*, fr OE *feorr*; akin to OHG *ferro* far, OE *faran* to go – more at FARE] – **by far** FAR AND AWAY – **far and away** by a considerable margin ⟨*was* far and away *the best team*⟩ – **how far** to what extent, degree, or distance ⟨*didn't know* how far *to trust him*⟩ – **so far** **1** to a certain extent, degree, or distance ⟨*when the water rose* so far, *the villagers sought higher ground*⟩ **2** up to the present ⟨*has written only one novel* so far⟩

[2]**far** *adj* **farther** /ˈfahdhə/, **further** /ˈfuhdhə/; **farthest** /ˈfahdhist/, **furthest** /ˈfuhdhist/ **1** remote in space, time, or degree ⟨*in the ~ distance*⟩ **2** long ⟨*a ~ journey*⟩ **3** being the more distant of 2 ⟨*the ~ side of the lake*⟩ **4** *of a political position* extreme ⟨*the ~ left*⟩

farad /ˈfarəd/ *n* the SI unit of electrical capacitance ☞ PHYSICS [Michael *Faraday* †1867 E physicist]

faradic /fəˈradik/ *also* **faradaic** /ˌfarəˈdayik/ *adj* of an alternating electric current produced by an induction coil

farandole /ˌfarənˈdohl (*Fr* farɑ̃dɔl)/ *n* (music for) a lively Provençal dance in which dancers hold hands and follow a leader [F, fr Prov *farandoulo*]

ˌ**far and ˈwide** *adv* in every direction; everywhere ⟨*advertised the event ~*⟩

faraway /ˌfahrəˈway/ *adj* **1** lying at a great distance; remote **2** dreamy, abstracted ⟨*a ~ look in her eyes*⟩

farce /fahs/ *n* **1** forcemeat **2** a comedy with an improbable plot that is concerned more with situation than characterization **3** the broad humour characteristic of farce **4** a ridiculous or meaningless situation or event [ME *farse*, fr MF *farce*, fr (assumed) VL *farsa*, fr L, fem of *farsus*, pp of *farcire* to stuff; akin to Gk *phrassein* to enclose] – **farcical** /ˈfahsikl/ *adj*, **farcically** *adv*, **farcicality** /-ˈkaləti/ *n*

farceur /fahˈsuh (*Fr* farsœːr)/ *n* **1** a joker, wag **2** a writer or actor of farce [F, fr MF, fr *farcer* to joke, fr OF, fr *farce*]

ˌ**far ˈcry** *n* a totally different and usu less pleasant experience or object ⟨*plastic flowers are a ~ from the real thing*⟩

farcy /ˈfahsi/ *n* **1** (cutaneous) glanders **2** an ultimately fatal bacterial infection of cattle [ME *farsin, farsi*, fr MF *farcin*, fr LL *farcimen*, fr L, sausage, fr *farcire*]

[1]**fare** /feə/ *vi* to get along; succeed, do ⟨*how did you ~ in your exam?*⟩ [ME *faren*, fr OE *faran*; akin to OHG *faran* to go, L *portare* to carry, Gk *peran* to pass through, *poros* passage, journey]

[2]**fare** *n* **1a** the price charged to transport sby **b** a paying passenger **2** food provided for a meal ⟨*good simple ~*⟩ [ME, journey, passage, supply of food, fr OE *faru, fær*; akin to OE *faran* to go]

[1]**farewell** /feəˈwel/ *interj* goodbye

[2]**farewell** *n* **1** a parting wish for good luck; a goodbye **2** an act of departure or leave-taking – **farewell** *adj*

[3]**farewell** *vt, NAm, Austr, & NZ* to bid farewell

ˌ**farˈfetched** /-ˈfecht/ *adj* not easily or naturally deduced; improbable ⟨*a ~ example*⟩ – **farfetchedness** /-ˈfechtnis, -ˈfechidnis/ *n*

ˌ**far-ˈflung** *adj* **1** widely spread or distributed **2** remote ⟨*a ~ outpost of the Empire*⟩

ˌ**far-ˈgone** *adj* in an advanced state, esp of sthg unpleasant (e g drunkenness or madness)

farina /fəˈreenə/ *n* **1** a starchy flour or fine meal of vegetable matter (e g cereal grains) used chiefly as a cereal or for making puddings **2** any of various powdery or mealy substances [L, meal, flour, fr *far* spelt – more at BARLEY] – **farinaceous** /ˌfariˈnayshəs/ *adj*

farl, farle /fahl/ *n, Scot* a small thin triangular cake or biscuit made with oatmeal [contr of Sc *fardel*, lit., fourth part, fr ME (Sc), fr *ferde del*, fr *ferde* fourth + *del* part]

[1]**farm** /fahm/ *n* **1** an area of land devoted to growing crops or raising (domestic) animals **2** FISH FARM [ME *ferme* rent, lease, fr OF, lease, fr *fermer* to fix, make a contract, fr L *firmare* to make firm, fr *firmus* firm]

[2]**farm** *vt* **1a** to collect and take the proceeds of (e g taxation or a business) on payment of a fixed sum **b** to give up the proceeds of (e g an estate or a business) to another on condition of receiving in return a fixed sum **2a** to cultivate or rear (crops or livestock) on a farm **b** to manage and cultivate (land) as farmland or as a farm **3** to attempt to receive (all the balls bowled) (e g so as to protect the other batsman from

dismissal) ~ *vi* to engage in the production of crops or livestock

farmer /'fahmə/ *n* **1** sby who pays a fixed sum for some privilege or source of income **2** sby who cultivates land or crops or raises livestock

'farm,hand /-,hand/ *n* a farm worker

'farm,house /-,hows/ *n* a dwelling house on a farm

farm out *vt* **1** to turn over for performance or use, usu on contract **2** to put (e g children) into sby's care in return for a fee /-,sted, -stid/

'farmstead /-,sted, -stid/ *n* the buildings and adjacent areas of a farm

'farm,yard /-,yahd/ *n* the area round or enclosed by farm buildings

faro /'feəroh/ *n, pl* **faros** a gambling game in which players bet on the value of the next card to be dealt [prob alter. of earlier *pharaoh*, trans of F *pharaon*]

Faroese /,feəroh'eez/ *n or adj* (a) Faeroese

,far-'off *adj* remote in time or space

farouche /fə'roohsh, fa-/ *adj* shy, unpolished; *also* wild [F, wild, shy, fr LL *forasticus* belonging outside, fr L *foras* outdoors; akin to L *fores* door – more at DOOR]

,far-'out *adj* **1** extremely unconventional; weird ⟨~ *clothes*⟩ **2** – used as a generalized term of approval ⟨~, *man!*⟩ *USE* infml; no longer in vogue – **far-outness** *n*

farrago /fə'rahgoh/ *n, pl* **farragoes** a confused collection; a hotchpotch [L *farragin-, farrago* mixed fodder, mixture, fr *far* spelt – more at BARLEY]

,far-'reaching *adj* having a wide range, influence, or effect

farrier /'fari·ə/ *n* **1** a horse doctor **2** a blacksmith who shoes horses [alter. of ME *ferrour*, fr MF *ferrour* blacksmith, fr OF *ferreor*, fr *ferrer* to fit with iron, fr (assumed) VL *ferrare*, fr L *ferrum* iron] – **farriery** *n*

¹farrow /'faroh/ *vb* to give birth to (pigs) – often + *down* [ME *farwen*, fr (assumed) OE *feargian*, fr OE *fearh* young pig; akin to OHG *farah* young pig, L *porcus* pig]

²farrow *n* (farrowing) a litter of pigs

,far'seeing /-'see·ing/ *adj* FARSIGHTED 1

Farsi /'fah,see/ *n* the modern Persian language – compare PARSI ☞ LANGUAGE [Per *fārsī*, fr *Fārs* Persia]

,far'sighted /-'sietid/ *adj* **1a** seeing or able to see to a great distance **b** having foresight or good judgment; sagacious **2** hypermetropic – **farsightedly** *adv*, **farsightedness** *n*

¹fart /faht/ *vi* to expel wind from the anus – vulg [ME *ferten, farten*; akin to OHG *ferzan* to break wind, ON *freta*, Gk *perdesthai*, Skt *pardate* he breaks wind]

²fart *n* **1** an expulsion of intestinal wind **2** an unpleasant person *USE* vulg [ME *fert, fart*, fr *ferten, farten*]

¹farther /'fahdhə/ *adv* **1** at or to a greater distance or more advanced point ⟨~ *down the corridor*⟩ **2** ¹FURTHER 3 [ME *ferther*, alter. of *further*]

²farther *adj* **1a** more distant; remoter **b** FAR 3 ⟨*the* ~ *side*⟩ **2** ²FURTHER 2

'farther,most /-,mohst/ *adj* most distant; farthest

¹farthest /'fahdhist/ *adj* most distant in space or time

²farthest *adv* **1** to or at the greatest distance in space, time, or degree **2** by the greatest degree or extent; most

farthing /'fahdhing/ *n* **1** (a coin representing) a former British money unit worth ¼ of an old penny **2** sthg of small value; a mite [ME *ferthing*, fr OE *fēorthung*; akin to MHG *vierdunc* fourth part, OE *fēortha* fourth]

farthingale /'fahdhing,gayl/ *n* a petticoat consisting of a framework of hoops, worn, esp in the 16th c, to expand a skirt at the hip line ☞ GARMENT [modif of MF *verdugale*, fr OSp *verdugado*, fr *verdugo* young shoot of a tree, fr *verde* green, fr L *viridis* – more at VERDANT]

fasces /'faseez/ *n pl but sing or pl in constr* a bundle of rods containing an axe with projecting blades carried before ancient Roman magistrates as a badge of authority and used between the 2 World Wars as the emblem of the Italian Fascist party [L, fr pl of *fascis* bundle; akin to L *fascia*]

fascia /'fayshə; *med* 'fashi·ə/ *n, pl* **fasciae** /-i,ee, -i,ie/, **fascias** **1a** a flat horizontal piece (e g of stone or board) under projecting eaves **b** a nameplate over the front of a shop **2** a broad well-defined band of colour **3** (a sheet of) connective tissue covering or binding together body structures **4** *Br* the dashboard of a motor car [It, fr L, band, bandage; akin to MIr *basc* necklace] – **fascial** *adj*

fasciated /'fashiaytid/ *adj* exhibiting fasciation

,fasci'ation /-'aysh(ə)n/ *n* a malformation of plant stems commonly manifested as enlargement and flattening as if several were fused

fascicle /'fasikl/ *n* **1** a fasciculus **2** a division of a book published in parts [L *fasciculus*, dim. of *fascis*] – **fascicled** *adj*

fasciculation /fə,sikyoo'laysh(ə)n/ *n* muscular twitching in which groups of muscle fibres contract simultaneously [NL *fasciculus* + E *-ation* (as in *fibrillation*)]

fascicule /'fasikyoohl/ *n* FASCICLE 2 [F, fr L *fasciculus*]

fasciculus /fə'sikyooləs/ *n, pl* **fasciculi** /-li, -lie/ a slender bundle of (anatomical) fibres [NL, fr L] – **fascicular** *adj*, **fasciculate** /-lət/ *adj*

fascinate /'fasinayt/ *vt* **1** to transfix by an irresistible mental power ⟨*believed that the serpent could* ~ *its prey*⟩ **2** to attract strongly, esp by arousing interest; captivate ~ *vi* to be irresistibly attractive [L *fascinatus*, pp of *fascinare*, fr *fascinum* witchcraft] – **fascinator** *n*, **fascinatingly** *adv*, **fascination** /-'naysh(ə)n/ *n*

fascine /fa'seen, fə-/ *n* a long bundle of sticks of wood bound together and used for such purposes as filling ditches and making parapets [F, fr L *fascina*, fr *fascis*]

fascism /'fashiz(ə)m/ *n* **1** a political philosophy, movement, or regime that is usu hostile to socialism, exalts nation and race, and stands for a centralized government headed by a dictatorial leader, severe regimentation, and forcible suppression of opposition **2** brutal dictatorial control [It *fascismo*, fr *fascio* bundle, fasces, group, fr L *fascis* bundle & *fasces* fasces] – **fascist** *n or adj, often cap*, **fascistic** /fa'shistik/ *adj, often cap*

Fascista /fa'shistə/ *n, pl* **Fascisti** /fa'shisti/ a member of the fascist political party under Mussolini that ruled Italy from 1922 to 1943 [It, fr *fascio*]

fash /fash/ *vt, chiefly Scot* to vex [MF *fascher*, fr (assumed) VL *fastidiare* to disgust, fr L *fastidium* disgust – more at FASTIDIOUS] – **fash** *n, chiefly Scot*

[1]**fashion** /ˈfash(ə)n/ *n* **1** the make or form of sthg **2** a manner, way ⟨*the people assembled in an orderly* ~⟩ **3a** a prevailing and often short-lived custom or style **b** the prevailing style or custom, esp in dress **c** an affluent and fashionable life style ⟨*women of* ~⟩ [ME *facioun, fasoun* shape, manner, fr OF *façon*, fr L *faction-, factio* act of making, faction, fr *factus*, pp of *facere* to make – more at [1]DO] – **after a fashion** in an approximate or rough way ⟨*became an artist* after a fashion⟩

[2]**fashion** *vt* **1** to give shape or form to, esp by using ingenuity; mould, construct **2** to mould into a particular character by influence or training; transform, adapt – **fashioner** *n*

-fashion *comb form* (*n* → *adv*) in the manner of a ⟨*wore the scarf turban*-fashion⟩

fashionable /ˈfash(ə)nəbl/ *adj* **1** conforming to the latest custom or fashion **2** of the world of fashion; used or patronized by people of fashion ⟨~ *shops*⟩ – **fashionableness** *n*, **fashionably** *adv*

[1]**fast** /fahst/ *adj* **1a** firmly fixed or attached **b** tightly closed or shut **2** firm, steadfast – chiefly in *fast friends* **3a(1)** moving or able to move rapidly; swift **(2)** taking a comparatively short time **(3)** *of a suburban train* EXPRESS 3a **(4)** accomplished quickly **(5)** quick to learn **b** conducive to rapidity of play or action or quickness of motion ⟨*a* ~ *pitch*⟩ **c** indicating in advance of what is correct ⟨*the clock was* ~⟩ **d** having or being a high photographic speed ⟨~ *film*⟩ ⟨~ *lens*⟩ **4** *of a colour* permanently dyed; not liable to fade **5a** dissipated, wild ⟨*a very* ~ *set*⟩ **b** *esp of a woman* FORWARD 3b; *also* promiscuous **6** resistant to change from destructive action, fading, etc – often in combination ⟨*colour*fast⟩ ⟨*acid*-fast *bacteria*⟩ **7** dishonest, shady; *also* acquired by dishonest means or with little effort – infml ⟨*made a* ~ *buck*⟩ [ME, fr OE *fæst*; akin to OHG *festi* firm, ON *fastr*, Arm *hast*]

[2]**fast** *adv* **1** in a firm or fixed manner **2** sound, deeply ⟨*fell* ~ *asleep*⟩ **3a** in a rapid manner; quickly **b** in quick succession ⟨*orders came in thick and* ~⟩ **4** in a reckless or dissipated manner **5** ahead of a correct time or posted schedule

[3]**fast** *vi* to abstain from some or all foods or meals ~ *vt* to deprive of food ⟨*the animals were* ~ed *for 24 hours before the experiment*⟩ [ME *fasten*, fr OE *fæstan*]

[4]**fast** *n* an act or time of fasting

ˈ**fast,back** /-ˌbak/ *n* (a motor car with) a roof sloping backwards to or nearly to the bumper

fasten /ˈfahs(ə)n/ *vt* **1** to attach or secure, esp by pinning, tying, or nailing **2** to fix or direct steadily ⟨~ed *his eyes on the awful sight*⟩ **3** to attach, impose *on* ⟨~ed *the blame on me*⟩ ~ *vi* to become fast or fixed [ME *fastnen*, fr OE *fæstnian* to make fast; akin to OHG *festinōn* to make fast, OE *fæst* fast] – **fastener** /ˈfahs(ə)nə/ *n* – **fasten on/upon/onto 1** to take a firm grip or hold on **2** to focus attention on

fastening /ˈfahs(ə)ning/ *n* a fastener

fastidious /faˈstidi·əs, -dyəs/ *adj* **1** excessively difficult to satisfy or please **2** showing or demanding great delicacy or care [ME, fr L *fastidiosus*, fr *fastidium* disgust, prob fr *fastus* arrogance + *taedium* irksomeness; akin to L *fastigium* top] – **fastidiously** *adv*, **fastidiousness** *n*

fastness /ˈfahstnis/ *n* **1a** the quality of being fixed **b** colourfast quality **2** a fortified, secure, or remote place ⟨*he spent the weekend in his mountain* ~⟩ [[1]FAST + -NESS]

ˌ**fast** ˈ**neutron** *n* a neutron with high kinetic energy

fast reactor *n* a nuclear reactor in which fast neutrons are used

fast-talk *vt or n, chiefly NAm* (to influence or persuade by) fluent, facile, and usu deceptive talk – infml

[1]**fat** /fat/ *adj* **-tt- 1** having an unusually large amount of fat: **a** plump **b** obese **c** *of a meat animal* fattened for market **2a** well filled out; thick, big ⟨*a* ~ *volume of verse*⟩ **b** prosperous, wealthy ⟨*grew* ~ *on the war – Time*⟩ **3** richly rewarding or profitable; substantial ⟨*a* ~ *part in a new play*⟩ **4** productive, fertile ⟨*a* ~ *year for crops*⟩ **5** practically nonexistent ⟨*a* ~ *chance*⟩ ⟨*a* ~ *lot of good it did him*⟩ – infml **6** foolish, thick ⟨*get that idea out of your* ~ *head*⟩ – infml [ME, fr OE *fǣtt*, pp of *fǣtan* to cram; akin to OHG *feizit* fat, L *opimus* fat, copious] – **fatly** *adv*, **fatness** *n*, **fattish** *adj*

[2]**fat** *n* **1** (animal tissue consisting chiefly of cells distended with) greasy or oily matter **2a** any of numerous compounds of carbon, hydrogen, and oxygen that are a major class of energy-rich food and are soluble in organic solvents (e g ether) but not in water **b** a solid or semisolid fat as distinguished from an oil **3** the best or richest part ⟨*the* ~ *of the land*⟩ **4** excess ⟨*we must trim the* ~ *off this budget*⟩

[3]**fat** *vt* **-tt-** to fatten

fatal /ˈfaytl/ *adj* **1** fateful, decisive **2a** of fate **b** like fate in proceeding according to a fixed sequence; inevitable **3a** causing death **b** bringing ruin **c** productive of disagreeable or contrary results – infml ⟨*it's* ~ *to offer him a drink*⟩ [ME, fr MF & L; MF, fr L *fatalis*, fr *fatum*]

ˈ**fatal,ism** /-ˌiz(ə)m/ *n* the belief that all events are predetermined and outside the control of human beings – **fatalist** *n*, **fatalistic** /-ˈistik/ *adj*, **fatalistically** *adv*

fatality /fəˈtaləti/ *n* **1** sthg established by fate **2a** the quality or state of causing death or destruction **b** the quality or condition of being destined for disaster **3** FATE 1 **4a** death resulting from a disaster **b** one who experiences or is subject to a fatal outcome

fatally /ˈfaytl·i/ *adv* **1** in a fatal manner; *esp* mortally ⟨~ *wounded*⟩ **2** as is or was fatal

fata morgana /ˌfahtə mawˈgahnə/ *n* a mirage [It, lit., Morgan the fay, sorceress of Arthurian legend]

ˌ**fat** ˈ**cat** *n, chiefly NAm* a wealthy, privileged, and usu influential person; *esp* one who contributes to a political campaign fund

[1]**fate** /fayt/ *n* **1** the power beyond human control that determines events; destiny **2a** a destiny apparently determined by fate **b** a disaster; *esp* death **3a** an outcome, end; *esp* one that is adverse and inevitable **b** the expected result of normal development ⟨*prospective* ~ *of embryonic cells*⟩ [ME, fr MF or L; MF, fr L *fatum*, lit., what has been spoken, fr neut of *fatus*, pp of *fari* to speak – more at [1]BAN]

[2]**fate** *vt* to destine; *also* to doom – usu pass ⟨*the plan was* ~d *to fail*⟩

ˈ**fateful** /-f(ə)l/ *adj* **1** having a quality of ominous prophecy ⟨*a* ~ *remark*⟩ **2a** having momentous and often unpleasant consequences; decisive ⟨*the* ~

decision to declare war⟩ **b** deadly, catastrophic **3** controlled by fate; foreordained – **fatefully** *adv,* **fatefulness** *n*

Fates /fayts/ *n pl* the 3 goddesses of classical mythology who determine the course of human life

'fat,head /-,hed/ *n* a slow-witted or stupid person; a fool – infml – **fatheaded** /,-'--/ *adj,* **fatheadedly** /,-'---/ *adv,* **fatheadedness** /,-'---/ *n*

,fat 'hen *n* a widely distributed goosefoot that is a common weed

1father /'fahdhə/ *n* **1a** a male parent of a child; *also* SIRE 3 **b** *cap* **(1)** GOD 1 **(2)** the first person of the Trinity **2** a forefather **3a** a man who relates to another in a way suggesting the relationship of father and child, esp in receiving filial respect **b** *often cap* **(1)** an old man – used as a respectful form of address **(2)** sthg personified as an old man ⟨Father *Time*⟩ ⟨Father *Thames*⟩ **4** *often cap* an early Christian writer accepted by the church as authoritative **5a** sby who originates or institutes ⟨*the ~ of radio*⟩ **b** a source, origin **6** a priest of the regular clergy – used esp as a title in the Roman Catholic church **7** any of the leading men (e g of a city) – usu pl [ME *fader,* fr OE *fæder;* akin to OHG *fater* father, L *pater,* Gk *patēr*] – **fatherhood** *n,* **fatherless** *adj,* **fatherly** *adj*

2father *vt* **1a** to beget **b** to give rise to; initiate **c** to accept responsibility for **2** to fix the paternity of *on*

,Father 'Christmas *n, Br* an old man with a white beard and red suit believed by children to deliver their presents at Christmas time

'father-in-,law *n, pl* **fathers-in-law** the father of one's spouse

'father,land /-,land/ *n* one's native land – used esp with reference to Germany

1fathom /'fadh(ə)m/ *n* a unit of length equal to 6ft (about 1.83m) used esp for measuring the depth of water ☞ UNIT [ME *fadme,* fr OE *fæthm* outstretched arms, length of the outstretched arms; akin to ON *fathmr* fathom, L *patēre* to be open, *pandere* to spread out, Gk *petannynai*]

2fathom *vt* **1** to measure by a sounding line **2** to penetrate and come to understand – often + *out* – **fathomable** *adj*

Fathometer /fə'dhomitə/ *trademark* – used for a sonic depth finder

'fathomless /-lis/ *adj* incapable of being fathomed – **fathomlessly** *adv,* **fathomlessness** *n*

fatidic /fay'tidik, fə-/, **fatidical** /-kl/ *adj* of prophecy [L *fatidicus,* fr *fatum* fate + *dicere* to say – more at DICTION]

1fatigue /fə'teeg/ *n* **1a** physical or nervous exhaustion **b** the temporary loss of power to respond induced in a sensory receptor or motor end organ by continued stimulation **2a** manual or menial military work **b** *pl* the uniform or work clothing worn on fatigue **3** the tendency of a material to break under repeated stress [F, fr MF, fr *fatiguer* to fatigue, fr L *fatigare;* akin to L af*fatim* sufficiently, & prob to L *fames* hunger]

2fatigue *vt* **1** to weary, exhaust **2** to induce a condition of fatigue in *~ vi, esp of a metal* to suffer fatigue – **fatigable** *adj,* **fatigability** /-gə'biləti/ *n,* **fatiguingly** *adv*

3fatigue *adj* being part of fatigues ⟨*a ~ cap*⟩

fatling /'fatling/ *n* a young animal fattened for slaughter

fatso /'fatsoh/ *n, pl* **fatsoes** a fat person – infml; often used as a derog form of address [prob fr *Fats,* nickname for a fat person + *-o*]

'fat,stock /-,stok/ *n* livestock that is fat and ready for market

fatten /'fat(ə)n/ *vt* **1** to make fat, fleshy, or plump; *esp* to feed (e g a stock animal) for slaughter – often + *up* **2** to make fertile *~ vi* to become fat – **fattener** *n*

1fatty /'fati/ *adj* **1** containing (large amounts of) fat; *also* corpulent **2** GREASY 2 ⟨*~ food*⟩ **3** derived from or chemically related to fat – **fattiness** *n*

2fatty *n* a fat person or animal – infml

,fatty 'acid *n* any of numerous organic acids with 1 carboxyl group (e g acetic acid) including many that occur naturally in fats, waxes, and essential oils

fatuous /'fatyoo·əs/ *adj* complacently or inanely foolish; idiotic [L *fatuus* foolish – more at BATTLE] – **fatuously** *adv,* **fatuousness** *n,* **fatuity** /fə'tyooh·əti, fə'chooh-/ *n*

faubourg /'foh,booəg/ *n* a suburb, esp of a French city [ME *fabour,* fr MF *fauxbourg,* alter. of *forsbourg,* fr OF *forsborc,* fr *fors* outside + *borc* town]

fauces /'fawseez/ *n, pl* **fauces** the narrow passage from the mouth to the pharynx situated between the soft palate and the base of the tongue – often pl with sing. meaning [L, pl, throat, fauces] – **faucial** /'fawsh(ə)l/ *adj*

faucet /'fawsit/ *n, NAm* a tap [ME, bung, faucet, fr MF *fausset* bung, fr *fausser* to damage, fr LL *falsare* to falsify, fr L *falsus* false]

faugh /faw/ *interj* – used to express contempt or disgust [imit]

1fault /fawlt/ *n* **1a** a failing **b** an imperfection, defect ⟨*a ~ in the computer*⟩ **c** an action, esp a service that does not land in the prescribed area, which loses a rally in tennis, squash, etc **2a** a misdemeanour **b** a mistake **3** responsibility for wrongdoing or failure ⟨*the accident was the driver's ~*⟩ **4** a fracture in the earth's crust accompanied by displacement (e g of the strata) along the fracture line ☞ GEOGRAPHY [ME *faute,* fr OF, fr (assumed) VL *fallita,* fr fem of *fallitus,* pp of L *fallere* to deceive, disappoint – more at FAIL] – **faultless** *adj,* **faultlessly** *adv,* **faultlessness** *n,* **faulty** *adj,* **faultily** *adv,* **faultiness** *n* – **at fault** in the wrong; liable for blame

2fault *vi* **1** to commit a fault; err **2** to produce a geological fault *~ vt* **1** to find a fault in ⟨*can't ~ his logic*⟩ **2** to produce a geological fault in

'fault,finding /-,fiending/ *adj* overinclined to criticize – **faultfinder** *n,* **faultfinding** *n*

fauna /'fawnə/ *n, pl* **faunas** *also* **faunae** /-ni, -nie/ the animals or animal life of a region, period, or special environment – compare FLORA [NL, fr LL *Fauna,* sister of Faunus, fr *Faunus,* satyr-like deity in Roman mythology] – **faunal** *adj,* **faunally** *adv,* **faunistic** /faw'nistik/ *adj*

faute de mieux /,foht də 'myuh (*Fr* foːt də mjø)/ *adv* for lack of sthg more suitable or desirable ⟨*sherry gave him a headache but he drank it ~*⟩ [F]

fauvism /'foh,viz(ə)m/ *n, often cap* a 20th-c art movement typified by the work of Matisse and characterized by pure and vivid colour and a free treatment of form [F *fauvisme,* fr *fauve* wild animal, fr *fauve* tawny, wild, of Gmc origin; akin to OHG *falo* fallow – more at 1FALLOW] – **fauvist** *n, often cap*

faux-naïf /,foh nah'eef (*Fr* foː naif)/ *n or adj* (sby) affecting a childlike innocence or simplicity [F, lit., false(ly) naive]

faux pas /ˌfoh 'pah/ *n, pl* **faux pas** /ˌfoh 'pah(z)/ an esp social blunder [F, lit., false step]

[1]**favour,** *NAm chiefly* **favor** /'fayvə/ *n* **1a(1)** friendly regard shown towards another, esp by a superior **(2)** approving consideration or attention; approbation ⟨*looked with* ~ *on our project*⟩ **b** partiality, favouritism **c** popularity **2** (an act of) kindness beyond what is expected or due **3** a token of allegiance or love (e g a ribbon or badge), usu worn conspicuously **4** consent to sexual activities, esp given by a woman – usu pl with sing. meaning; euph ⟨*granted her* ~s⟩ [ME, fr OF *favor* friendly regard, fr L, fr *favēre* to be favourable; akin to OHG *gouma* attention, OSlav *gověti* to revere] – **in favour of 1** in agreement or sympathy with; on the side of **2** to the advantage of ⟨*John gave up his rights in the house* in favour of *his wife*⟩ **3** in order to choose; out of preference for ⟨*he refused a job in industry* in favour of *an academic appointment*⟩ – **in someone's favour 1** liked or esteemed by sby ⟨*doing extra work to get back* in his boss's favour⟩ **2** to sby's advantage ⟨*the odds were* in his favour⟩ – **out of favour** unpopular, disliked

[2]**favour,** *NAm chiefly* **favor** *vt* **1a** to regard or treat with favour **b** to do a favour or kindness for; oblige – usu + *by* or *with* ⟨*Wilson* ~ed *them with a kindly smile – The Listener*⟩ **2** to show partiality towards; prefer **3a** to give support or confirmation to; sustain ⟨*this evidence* ~s *my theory*⟩ **b** to afford advantages for success to; facilitate ⟨*good weather* ~ed *the outing*⟩ **4** to look like (e g a relation) ⟨*he* ~s *his father*⟩

favourable /'fayv(ə)rəbl/ *adj* **1a** disposed to favour; partial **b** expressing or winning approval; *also* giving a result in one's favour ⟨*a* ~ *comparison*⟩ **2a** tending to promote; helpful, advantageous ⟨~ *wind*⟩ **b** successful – **favourably** *adv*

'**favoured** *adj* **1** endowed with special advantages or gifts **2** having an appearance or features of a specified kind – usu in combination ⟨*an ill-*favoured *child*⟩ **3** receiving preferential treatment

[1]**favourite** /'fayv(ə)rit/ *n* **1** sby or sthg favoured or preferred above others; *specif* one unduly favoured, esp by a person in authority ⟨*teachers should not have* ~s⟩ **2** the competitor judged most likely to win, esp by a bookmaker [It *favorito*, pp of *favorire* to favour, fr *favore* favour, fr L *favor*]

[2]**favourite** *adj* constituting a favourite

favouritism /'fayv(ə)riˌtiz(ə)m/ *n* the showing of unfair favour; partiality

[1]**fawn** /fawn/ *vi* **1** *esp of a dog* to show affection **2** to court favour by acting in a servilely flattering manner ***USE*** usu + *on* or *upon* [ME *faunen*, fr OE *fagnian* to rejoice, fr *fægen, fagan* glad – more at FAIN] – **fawner** *n*, **fawningly** *adv*

[2]**fawn** *n* **1** a young (unweaned) deer **2** light greyish brown [ME *foun*, fr MF *feon, faon* young of an animal, fr (assumed) VL *feton-, feto*, fr L *fetus* offspring – more at FOETUS]

fay /fay/ *n* a fairy – poetic [ME *faie*, fr MF *feie, fee* – more at FAIRY]

fayre /feə/ *n* [4]FAIR

faze /fayz/ *vt, chiefly NAm* to disturb the composure of; disconcert, daunt – infml [alter. of *feeze* (to drive away, frighten), fr ME *fesen*, fr OE *fēsian* to drive away]

F clef /ef/ *n* BASS CLEF ☞ MUSIC

fealty /'fee·əlti/ *n* **1** fidelity to one's feudal lord **2** allegiance, faithfulness [alter. of ME *feute*, fr OF *feelté, fealté*, fr L *fidelitat-, fidelitas* – more at FIDELITY]

[1]**fear** /fiə/ *n* **1** (an instance of) an unpleasant often strong emotion caused by anticipation or awareness of (a specified) danger; *also* a state marked by this emotion ⟨*in* ~ *of their lives*⟩ **2** anxiety, solicitude **3** profound reverence and awe, esp towards God **4** reason for alarm; danger [ME *fer*, fr OE *fǣr* sudden danger; akin to L *periculum* attempt, peril, Gk *peiran* to attempt, OE *faran* to go – more at FARE] – **fearless** *adj*, **fearlessly** *adv*, **fearlessness** *n* – **for fear of** because of anxiety about; IN CASE OF ⟨for fear of *losing electoral support*⟩

[2]**fear** *vt* **1** to have a reverential awe of ⟨~ *God*⟩ **2** to be afraid of; consider or expect with alarm ~ *vi* to be afraid or apprehensive – **fearer** *n*

'**fearful** /-f(ə)l/ *adj* **1** causing or likely to cause fear **2a** full of fear ⟨~ *of reprisals*⟩ **b** showing or arising from fear ⟨*a* ~ *glance*⟩ **c** timid, timorous ⟨*a* ~ *child*⟩ **3** extremely bad, large, or intense ⟨*a* ~ *waste*⟩ – infml – **fearfully** *adv*, **fearfulness** *n*

'**fearsome** /-s(ə)m/ *adj* FEARFUL 1, 2c – **fearsomely** *adv*, **fearsomeness** *n*

feasible /'feezəbl/ *adj* **1** capable of being done or carried out ⟨*a* ~ *plan*⟩ **2** capable of being used or dealt with successfully; suitable ⟨*our* ~ *sources of energy are limited*⟩ **3** reasonable, likely [ME *faisible*, fr MF, fr *fais-*, stem of *faire* to make, do, fr L *facere*] – **feasibleness** *n*, **feasibly** *adv*, **feasibility** /-zə'biləti/ *n*

[1]**feast** /feest/ *n* **1a** an elaborate often public meal, sometimes accompanied by a ceremony or entertainment; a banquet **b** sthg that gives abundant pleasure ⟨*a* ~ *for the eyes*⟩ **2** a periodic religious observance commemorating an event or honouring a deity, person, or thing [ME *feste* festival, feast, fr OF, festival, fr L *festa*, pl of *festum* festival, fr neut of *festus* solemn, festal; akin to L *feriae* holidays, *fanum* temple, Arm *dik'* gods]

[2]**feast** *vi* to have or take part in a feast ~ *vt* **1** to give a feast for **2** to delight, gratify ⟨~ *your eyes on her beauty*⟩ – **feaster** *n*

feat /feet/ *n* **1** a notable and esp courageous act or deed **2** an act or product of skill, endurance, or ingenuity [ME *fait* act, deed, fr MF, fr L *factum*, fr neut of *factus*, pp of *facere* to make, do – more at [1]DO]

[1]**feather** /'fedhə/ *n* **1a** any of the light horny outgrowths that form the external covering of a bird's body and consist of a shaft that bears 2 sets of barbs that interlock to form a continuous vane ☞ ANATOMY **b** the vane of an arrow **2** plumage **3** the act of feathering an oar [ME *fether*, fr OE; akin to OHG *federa* wing, L *petere* to go to, seek, Gk *petesthai* to fly, *piptein* to fall, *pteron* wing] – **feathered** *adj*, **feathery** *adj* – **a feather in one's cap** a deserved honour or mark of distinction in which one can take pride

[2]**feather** *vt* **1a** to fit (e g an arrow) with feathers **b** to cover, clothe, or adorn with feathers **2a** to turn (an oar blade) almost horizontal when lifting from the water **b** to change the angle at which (a propeller blade) meets the air so as to have the minimum wind resistance; *also* to feather the propeller blades attached to (a propeller or engine) **3** to reduce the edge of to a featheredge **4** to cut (e g air) (as if) with

a wing ~ *vi* **1** *of ink or a printed impression* to soak in and spread; blur **2** to feather an oar or an aircraft propeller blade – **feather one's nest** to provide for oneself, esp dishonestly, through a job in which one is trusted

featherbed /,--'-, '--,-/ *vt* **-dd- 1** to cushion or protect from hardship, worry, etc; to pamper **2** to assist (e g an industry) with government subsidies

,feather 'bed *n* (a bed with) a feather mattress

'feather,brain /-,brayn/ *n* a foolish scatterbrained person – **featherbrained** *adj*

'feather,edge /-,ej/ *n* (a board or plank having) a very thin sharp edge – **featheredge** *vt*

'feather,head /-,hed/ *n* a featherbrain – **featherheaded** /-'hedid/ *adj*

feathering /'fedhəring/ *n* **1a** plumage **b** the (type of) feathers of an arrow **2** a fringe of hair (e g on the legs of a dog or cart horse)

'feather,stitch /-,stich/ *n* an embroidery stitch consisting of a line of loop stitches worked in a zigzag pattern – **featherstitch** *vb*

'feather,weight /-,wayt/ *n* **1** a boxer who weighs not more than 9st (57.2kg) if professional or more than 54kg (about 8st 7lb) but not more than 57kg (about 8st 13lb) if amateur **2** sby or sthg of limited importance or effectiveness

[1]feature /'feechə/ *n* **1a** the make-up or appearance of the face or its parts ⟨*gentle of* ~⟩ **b** a part of the face ⟨*her nose was not her best* ~⟩; *also, pl* the face ⟨*an embarrassed look on his* ~*s*⟩ **2** a prominent or distinctive part or characteristic **3a** a full-length film; *esp* the main film on a cinema programme **b** a distinctive article, story, or special section in a newspaper or magazine **c** *Br* a radio documentary, often one about cultural rather than political matters – compare DOCUMENTARY [ME *feture,* fr MF, shape, form, fr L *factura* act of making, fr *factus,* pp of *facere* to make – more at [1]DO] – **featureless** /-lis/ *adj*

[2]feature *vt* **1** to give special prominence to (e g in a performance or newspaper) **2** to have as a characteristic or feature ~ *vi* to play an important part; be a feature – usu + *in*

featured /'feechəd/ *adj* having facial features of a specified kind – usu in combination ⟨*a heavy*-featured *man*⟩

febri- *comb form* fever ⟨febri*fuge*⟩ [LL, fr L *febris*]

febrifuge /'febrifyoohj/ *n* an antipyretic [F *fébrifuge,* prob fr (assumed) NL *febrifuga,* fr LL *febrifuga, febrifugia* centaury, fr *febri-* + *-fuga* -fuge] – **febrifuge** *adj*

febrile /'feebriel/ *adj* of fever; feverish [ML *febrilis,* fr L *febris* fever – more at FEVER]

February /'febrooəri, -,eri/ *n* the 2nd month of the Gregorian calendar [ME *Februarie,* fr L *Februarius,* fr *Februa,* pl, feast of purification; perh akin to L *fumus* smoke]

feces /'feeseez/ *n pl, NAm* faeces – **fecal** *adj*

feckless /'feklis/ *adj* **1** ineffectual, weak **2** worthless, irresponsible [Sc, fr *feck* effect, majority, fr ME (Sc) *fek,* alter. of ME *effect*] – **fecklessly** *adv,* **fecklessness** *n*

feculent /'fekyoolənt/ *adj* foul with impurities or excrement – fml [ME, fr L *faeculentus,* fr *faec-, faex* dregs] – **feculence** /-ləns/ *n*

fecund /'feekənd, 'fekənd/ *adj* **1** fruitful in offspring or vegetation; prolific **2** very intellectually productive or inventive to a marked degree ***USE*** fml [ME, fr MF *fecond,* fr L *fecundus* – more at FEMININE] – **fecundity** /fi'koondəti/ *n*

fecundate /'fekəndayt, 'fee-/ *vt* **1** to make fecund **2** to make fertile; impregnate ***USE*** fml [L *fecundatus,* pp of *fecundare,* fr *fecundus*] – **fecundation** /-'daysh(ə)n/ *n*

[1]fed *past of* FEED

[2]fed /fed/ *n, often cap, NAm* a federal agent or officer – infml [short for *federal*]

fedayee /fi,dah'yee, -,da'yee/ *n, pl* **fedayeen** /-'yeen/ a member of an Arab commando group operating esp against Israel [Ar *fidā'ī,* lit., one who sacrifices himself]

federal /'fed(ə)rəl/ *adj* **1a** formed by agreement between political units that surrender their individual sovereignty to a central authority but retain limited powers of government; *also* of or constituting a government so formed **b** of the central government of a federation as distinguished from those of the constituent units **2** of or loyal to the federal government of the USA in the American Civil War [L *foeder-, foedus* compact, league; akin to L *fidere* to trust – more at BIDE] – **federally** *adv*

Federal *n* a supporter or soldier of the North in the American Civil War

federal district *n* a district set apart as the seat of a federal government

federalism /'fedrəliz(ə)m/ *n, often cap* (advocacy of) the federal principle

'federalist /-list/ *n* an advocate of federalism

federate /'fedərayt/ *vt* to join in a federation – **federative** /-rətiv, -,raytiv/ *adj*

federation /,fedə'raysh(ə)n/ *n* **1** federating; *esp* the formation of a federal union **2** sthg formed by federating: e g **a** a country formed by the federation of separate states **b** a union of organizations

fedora /fi'dawrə/ *n* a low felt hat with the crown creased lengthways [*Fédora,* drama by V Sardou †1908 F dramatist]

,fed 'up *adj* discontented, bored ⟨~ *with the 9-to-5 day*⟩ – infml

[1]fee /fee/ *n* **1a** an estate in land held in feudal law from a lord **b** an inherited or heritable estate in land **2a(1)** a sum of money paid esp for entrance or for a professional service – often pl with sing. meaning **(2)** money paid for education – usu pl with sing. meaning **b** a gratuity [ME, fr OF *fé, fief,* of Gmc origin; akin to OE *feoh* cattle, property, OHG *fihu* cattle; akin to L *pecus* cattle, *pecunia* money, *pectere* to comb] – **in fee** in absolute and legal possession

[2]fee *vt* **1** to give a fee to **2** *chiefly Scot* to hire for a fee

feeble /'feebl/ *adj* **1** lacking in strength or endurance; weak ⟨*a* ~ *old man*⟩ **2** deficient in authority, force, or effect ⟨*a* ~ *joke*⟩ ⟨*a* ~ *excuse*⟩ [ME *feble,* fr OF, fr L *flebilis* lamentable, wretched, fr *flēre* to weep – more at BLEAT] – **feebleness** *n,* **feeblish** *adj,* **feebly** *adv*

,feeble'minded /-'miendid/ *adj* **1** mentally deficient **2** foolish, stupid – **feeblemindedly** *adv,* **feeblemindedness** *n*

[1]feed /feed/ *vb* **fed** /fed/ *vt* **1a** to give food to **b** to give as food **2** to provide sthg essential to the growth, sustenance, maintenance, or operation of **3** to produce or provide food for **4a** to satisfy, gratify **b** to support, encourage **5a(1)** to supply for use, consumption, or processing, esp in a continuous manner

⟨fed *the tape into the machine*⟩ **(2)** to supply material to (e g a machine), esp in a continuous manner **b** to supply (a signal or power) to an electronic circuit **6** to act as a feed for **7** to pass or throw a ball or puck to (a teammate) ~*vi* **1a** to consume food; eat **b** to prey **2** to become nourished or satisfied as if by food **3** to be moved into a machine or opening for use, processing, or storage ⟨*the grain* fed *into the silo*⟩ ***USE*** (*vi 1*) usu + *off, on,* or *upon* [ME *feden,* fr OE *fēdan*; akin to OE *fōda* food – more at FOOD]

[2]**feed** *n* **1** an act of eating **2a** (a mixture or preparation of) food for livestock **b** the amount given at each feeding **3a** material supplied (e g to a furnace) **b** a mechanism by which the action of feeding is effected **4** one who supplies cues for another esp comic performer's lines or actions **5** an esp large meal – infml

ˈ**feedˌback** /-ˌbak/ *n* **1** the return to the input of a part of the output of a machine, system, or process **2** (the return to a source of) information about the results of an action or process, usu in response to a request

feeder /ˈfeedə/ *n* **1** a device or apparatus for supplying food (e g to a caged animal) **2a** a device feeding material into or through a machine **b** a heavy wire conductor supplying electricity to a point of an electric distribution system **c** a transmission line running from a radio transmitter to an antenna **d** a road, railway, airline, or aircraft that links remote areas with the main transport system **3** an animal being fattened or suitable for fattening [[1]FEED + [2]-ER]

ˈ**feeding ˌbottle** *n* a bottle with a teat, designed to hold milk and used for feeding babies

ˈ**feedˌlot** /-ˌlot/ *n* a plot of land on which livestock are fattened for market

ˈ**feedˌstock** /-ˌstok/ *n* raw material supplied to a machine or processing plant

feed up *vt* to fatten by plentiful feeding

[1]**feel** /feel/ *vb* **felt** /felt/ *vt* **1a** to handle or touch in order to examine or explore **b** to perceive by a physical sensation coming from discrete end organs (e g of the skin or muscles) ⟨~ *a draught*⟩ **2** to experience actively or passively; be affected by ⟨*he shall* ~ *my wrath*⟩ ⟨*try to* ~ *the music*⟩ **3** to ascertain or explore by cautious trial ⟨~ing *their way*⟩ – often + *out* ⟨felt *out the opposition*⟩ **4a** to be aware of by instinct or by drawing conclusions from the evidence available ⟨felt *the presence of a stranger in the room*⟩ **b** to believe, think ⟨*is generally* felt *that such action is inadvisable*⟩ ~*vi* **1a** to (be able) to receive the sensation of touch **b** to search for sthg by using the sense of touch **2a** to be conscious of an inward impression, state of mind, or physical condition ⟨~s *much better now*⟩ **b** to believe oneself to be ⟨*I did* ~ *a fool*⟩ **3** to have sympathy or pity ⟨*really* ~s *for the underprivileged*⟩ [ME *felen,* fr OE *fēlan*; akin to OHG *fuolen* to feel, L *palpare* to caress, & perh to Gk *pallein* to brandish – more at POLEMIC] – **feel like 1** to resemble or seem to be on the evidence of touch ⟨*it* feels like *velvet*⟩ **2** to wish for; be in the mood for ⟨*do you* feel like *a drink?*⟩

[2]**feel** *n* **1** the sense of feeling; touch **2** sensation, feeling **3a** the quality of a thing as imparted through touch ⟨*the material had a velvety* ~⟩ **b** typical or peculiar quality or atmosphere ⟨*the* ~ *of an old country pub*⟩ **4** intuitive skill, knowledge, or ability – usu + *for* ⟨*a* ~ *for words*⟩

feeler /ˈfeelə/ *n* **1** a tactile appendage (e g a tentacle) of an animal **2** sthg (e g a proposal) ventured to ascertain the views of others [[1]FEEL + [2]-ER]

ˈ**feeler ˌgauge** *n* a set of thin steel strips of various known thicknesses by which small gaps may be measured

[1]**feeling** /ˈfeeling/ *n* **1a** (a sensation experienced through) the one of the 5 basic physical senses by which stimuli, esp to the skin and mucous membranes, are interpreted by the brain as touch, pressure, and temperature **b** generalized bodily consciousness, sensation, or awareness ⟨*experienced a* ~ *of safety*⟩ ⟨*a good* ~⟩ **2a** an emotional state or reaction ⟨*a* ~ *of loneliness*⟩ **b** *pl* susceptibility to impression; sensibility ⟨*the remark hurt her* ~s⟩ **3** a conscious recognition; a sense ⟨*the harsh sentence left him with a* ~ *of injustice*⟩ **4a** an opinion or belief, esp when unreasoned; a sentiment ⟨*what are your* ~s *on the matter?*⟩ **b** a presentiment ⟨*I've a* ~ *he won't come*⟩ **5** capacity to respond emotionally, esp with the higher emotions ⟨*a man of noble* ~⟩ **6** FEEL 3, 4 **7** the quality of a work of art that embodies and conveys the emotion of the artist

[2]**feeling** *adj* **1a** having the capacity to feel or respond emotionally; sensitive **b** easily moved emotionally; sympathetic **2** expressing emotion or sensitivity – **feelingly** *adv*

ˌ**fee ˈsimple** *n, pl* **fees simple** a fee without limitation to any class of heirs

feet /feet/ *pl of* [1]FOOT

fee tail *n, pl* **fees tail** a fee limited to a particular class of heirs

ˌ**feet of ˈclay** *n pl* a generally concealed but marked weakness [fr the feet of the idol in Dan 2:33]

Fehling's solution /ˈfaylingz/ *n* a blue solution of Rochelle salt and copper sulphate used as an oxidizing agent in testing for sugars and aldehydes [Hermann *Fehling* †1885 G chemist]

feign /fayn/ *vt* to give a false appearance or impression of deliberately ⟨~ *death*⟩; *also* to pretend ~*vi* to pretend, dissemble [ME *feignen,* fr OF *feign-,* stem of *feindre,* fr L *fingere* to shape, feign – more at DOUGH] – **feigner** *n*

[1]**feint** /faynt/ *n* sthg feigned; *specif* a mock blow or attack directed away from the point one really intends to attack [F *feinte,* fr OF, fr *feint,* pp of *feindre*]

[2]**feint** *vi* to make a feint ~*vt* to make a pretence of ⟨*he* ~ed *an attack and continued on his way*⟩

[3]**feint** *adj, of rulings on paper* faint, pale [alter. of [1]*faint*]

feisty /ˈfiesti/ *adj, NAm* **1** fidgety, agitated **2** touchy, quarrelsome ***USE*** infml [*feist* (small dog), by shortening & alter. fr obs *fisting hound,* fr obs *fist* (to break wind)]

feldspar /ˈfel(d)spah/, **felspar** /ˈfelspah/ *n* any of a group of minerals that consist of aluminium silicates with either potassium, sodium, calcium, or barium, and are an essential constituent of nearly all crystalline rocks [*feldspar* modif of obs G *feldspath* (now *feldspat*), fr G *feld* field + obs G *spath* (now *spat*) spar; *felspar* by alter.]

feldspathic /fel(d)ˈspathik/ *adj* of or containing feldspar [*feldspath* (var of *feldspar*), fr obs G]

felicific /ˌfeliˈsifik/ *adj* causing or intended to cause happiness – fml [L *felic-, felix*]

felicitate /fəˈlisitayt/ *vt* to offer congratulations or compliments to – usu + *on* or *upon*; fml [LL *felicitatus*, pp of *felicitare* to make happy, irreg fr L *felic-*, *felix*] – **felicitator** /-ˌtaytə/ *n*, **felicitation** /-ˈtaysh(ə)n/ *n*

felicitous /fəˈlisitəs/ *adj* **1** very well suited or expressed; apt ⟨*a ~ remark*⟩; *also* marked by or given to such expression ⟨*a ~ speaker*⟩ **2** pleasant, delightful *USE* fml – **felicitously** *adv*, **felicitousness** *n*

felicity /fəˈlisiti/ *n* **1** (sthg causing) great happiness **2** a felicitous faculty or quality, esp in art or language; aptness **3** a felicitous expression *USE* fml [ME *felicite*, fr MF *felicité*, fr L *felicitat-*, *felicitas*, fr *felic-*, *felix* fruitful, happy – more at FEMININE]

feline /ˈfeelien/ *adj* **1** of cats or the cat family **2** resembling a cat; having the characteristics generally attributed to cats, esp grace, stealth, or slyness [L *felinus*, fr *felis* cat] – **feline** *n*, **felinely** *adv*, **felinity** /feeˈlinəti/ *n*

[1]**fell** /fel/ *vt* **1** to cut, beat, or knock down ⟨*~ing trees*⟩ **2** to kill [ME *fellen*, fr OE *fellan*; akin to OE *feallan* to fall – more at FALL] – **fellable** *adj*, **feller** *n*

[2]**fell** *past of* FALL

[3]**fell** *n* a steep rugged stretch of high moorland, esp in northern England and Scotland – often pl with sing. meaning [ME, hill, mountain, fr ON *fell*, *fjall*; akin to OHG *felis* rock, MIr *all* cliff]

[4]**fell** *adj* **1** fierce, cruel **2** very destructive; deadly *USE* poetic [ME *fel*, fr OF – more at FELON] – **fellness** *n*, **felly** *adv* – **at one fell swoop** all at once; *also* with a single concentrated effort

fella /ˈfelə/ *n* FELLOW 4, 7 – infml [by alter.]

fellah /ˈfelə/ *n, pl* **fellahin, fellaheen** /-ˈheen/ a peasant or agricultural labourer in an Arab country [Ar *fallāḥ*]

fellatio /fəˈlayshioh/ *n* oral stimulation of the penis [NL *fellation-*, *fellatio*, fr L *fellatus*, pp of *felare*, *fellare*, lit., to suck – more at FEMININE] – **fellate** /ˈfelayt/ *vt*, **fellation** /feˈlaysh(ə)n/ *n*, **fellator** /ˈfelaytə/ *n*

feller /ˈfelə/ *n* FELLOW 4, 7 – infml [by alter.]

fellmonger /ˈfelˌmung·gə/ *n, Br* sby who prepares hides for leather making [*fell* (skin, hide; fr ME, fr OE) + *monger* (dealer)] – **fellmongered** *adj*, **fellmongering, fellmongery** *n*

felloe /ˈfeloh/ *n* (a segment of) the exterior rim of a spoked wheel [*ME fely*, *felive*, fr OE *felg*; akin to OHG *felga* felloe, OE *fealg* piece of ploughed land]

[1]**fellow** /ˈfeloh/ *n* **1** a comrade, associate – usu pl **2a** an equal in rank, power, or character; a peer **b** either of a pair; a mate **3** a member of an incorporated literary or scientific society **4** a man; *also* a boy **5** an incorporated member of a collegiate foundation **6** a person appointed to a salaried position allowing for advanced research **7** a boyfriend – infml [ME *felawe*, fr OE *fēolaga*, fr ON *fēlagi*, fr *fēlag* partnership, fr *fē* cattle, money + *lag* act of laying]

[2]**fellow** *adj* being a companion or associate; belonging to the same group – used before a noun ⟨*~ traveller*⟩

fellow feeling *n* a feeling of community of interest or of mutual understanding; *specif* sympathy

fellowship /-ship/ *n* **1** the condition of friendly relations between people; companionship **2a** community of interest, activity, feeling, or experience **b** the state of being a fellow or associate **3** *sing or pl in constr* a group of people with similar interests; an association **4a** the position of a fellow (e g of a university) **b** (a foundation for the provision of) the salary of a fellow

fellow traveller *n* a nonmember who sympathizes with and often furthers the ideals and programme of an organized group, esp the Communist party – chiefly derog

felo-de-se /ˌfeeloh də ˈsay, ˌfeloh, see/ *n, pl* **felones–de–se** /fəˈlohneez/, **felos–de–se** /ˈfelohz/ (sby who commits) suicide [ML *felo de se*, *fello de se*, lit., evildoer upon himself]

felon /ˈfelən/ *n* **1** sby who has committed a felony **2** a whitlow [ME, fr OF *felon*, *fel*, fr ML *fellon-*, *fello* evildoer, villain]

felonry /ˈfelənri/ *n* felons

felony /ˈfeləni/ *n* a grave crime (e g murder or arson) that was formerly regarded in law as more serious than a misdemeanour and involved forfeiture of property in addition to any other punishment – **felonious** /fəˈlohnyəs, -ni·əs/ *adj*, **feloniously** *adv*

felsite /ˈfelsiet/ *n* a dense igneous rock that consists almost entirely of feldspar and quartz [*felspar*] – **felsitic** /-ˈsitik/ *adj*

felspar /ˈfelˌspah/ *n* feldspar

[1]**felt** /felt/ *n* **1** a nonwoven cloth made by compressing wool or fur often mixed with natural or synthetic fibres **2** an article made of felt **3** a material resembling felt [ME, fr OE; akin to OHG *filz* felt, L *pellere* to drive, beat, Gk *pelas* near]

[2]**felt** *vt* **1** to make into or cover with felt **2** to cause to stick and mat together

[3]**felt** *past of* FEEL

felting /ˈfelting/ *n* **1** the process by which felt is made **2** felt

felucca /feˈlukə/ *n* a narrow lateen-rigged sailing ship, chiefly of the Mediterranean area [It *feluca*, perh deriv of Gk *epholkion* small boat]

[1]**female** /ˈfeemayl/ *n* **1** an individual that bears young or produces eggs; *esp* a woman or girl as distinguished from a man or boy ☞ SYMBOL **2** a plant or flower with an ovary but no stamens [ME, alter. of *femel*, *femelle*, fr MF & ML; MF *femelle*, fr ML *femella*, fr L, girl, dim. of *femina*]

[2]**female** *adj* **1** of or being a female **2** designed with a hole or hollow into which a corresponding male part fits ⟨*a ~ plug*⟩ – **femaleness** *n*

[1]**feminine** /ˈfemənin/ *adj* **1** of or being a female person **2** characteristic of, appropriate to, or peculiar to women; womanly **3** of or belonging to the gender that normally includes most words or grammatical forms referring to females **4a** having or occurring in an extra unstressed final syllable ⟨*~ rhyme*⟩ **b** having the final chord occurring on a weak beat [ME, fr MF *feminin*, fr L *femininus*, fr *femina* woman; akin to OE *delu* nipple, L *filius* son, *felix*, *fetus*, *fecundus* fruitful, *felare* to suck, Gk *thēlē* nipple] – **femininely** *adv*, **feminineness** *n*, **femininity** /feməˈninəti/ *n*

[2]**feminine** *n* **1** the feminine principle in human nature – esp in *eternal feminine* **2** (a word or morpheme of) the feminine gender

feminism /ˈfeminiz(ə)m/ *n* the advocacy or furtherance of women's rights, interests, and equality with men in political, economic, and social spheres – **feminist** *n or adj*, **feministic** /-ˈnistik/ *adj*

femin·ize, -ise /ˈfeminiez/ *vt* **1** to give a feminine quality to **2** to cause (a male or castrated female) to take on feminine characteristics (e g by administration of hormones) – **feminization** /-'zaysh(ə)n/ *n*

femme fatale /,fam fa'tahl, 'femi (*Fr* fam fatal)/ *n, pl* **femmes fatales** /fatahl(z) (*Fr* ~)/ a seductive and usu mysterious woman; *esp* one who lures men into dangerous or compromising situations [F, lit., disastrous woman]

femto- /'femtoh-/ *comb form* one thousand million millionth (10^{-15}) part of ⟨femto*ampere*⟩ ☞ PHYSICS [ISV, fr Dan or Norw *femten* fifteen, fr ON *fimmtān*; akin to OE *fiftēne* fifteen]

femur /'feemə/ *n, pl* **femurs, femora** /'femərə/ **1** the bone of the hind or lower limb nearest the body; the thighbone **2** the third segment of an insect's leg counting from the base *USE* ☞ ANATOMY [NL *femor-, femur,* fr L, thigh] – **femoral** /'femərəl/ *adj*

[1]**fen** /fen/ *n* an area of low wet or flooded land [ME, fr OE *fenn*; akin to OHG *fenna* fen, Skt *paṅka* mud]

[2]**fen** *n, pl* **fen** ☞ *China* at NATIONALITY [Chin (Pek) *fên*[1]]

[1]**fence** /fens/ *n* **1** a barrier (e g of wire or boards) intended to prevent escape or intrusion or to mark a boundary ⟨*a garden* ~⟩ **2a** a receiver of stolen goods **b** a place where stolen goods are bought [ME *fens,* short for *defens* defence] – **fenceless** *adj* – **on the fence** in a position of neutrality or indecision

[2]**fence** *vt* **1a** to enclose with a fence – usu + *in* **b** to separate *off* or keep *out* (as if) with a fence **2** to provide a defence for; shield, protect **3** to receive or sell (stolen goods) ~ *vi* **1a** to practise fencing **b(1)** to use tactics of attack and defence (e g thrusting and parrying) resembling those of fencing **(2)** *of a batsman* to play at and miss the ball in cricket, esp outside the off stump – usu + *at* **2** to deal in stolen goods – **fencer** *n*

'**fence-,sitting** *n* a state of often deliberate indecision or neutrality (e g in an argument), usu in an attempt to protect one's own interests – **fence sitter** *n*

fencing /'fensing/ *n* **1** the art of attack and defence with a sword (e g the foil, epée, or sabre) **2** (material used for building) fences

fend /fend/ *vi* [ME *fenden* to defend, short for *defenden*] – **fend for** to provide a livelihood for; support

fender /'fendə/ *n* a device that protects: e g **a** a cushion (e g of rope or wood) hung over the side of a ship to absorb impact **b** a low metal guard for a fire used to confine the coals **c** *NAm* a wing or mudguard

fend off *vt* to keep or ward off; repel

fenestra /fi'nestrə/ *n, pl* **fenestrae** /-stri/ **1a** an oval opening between the middle ear and the vestibule of the inner ear **b** a round opening between the middle ear and the cochlea of the inner ear **2** an opening cut in bone [NL, fr L, window] – **fenestral** *adj*

fenestrated /'fenistraytid/ *adj* **1** provided with or characterized by windows **2** *also* **fenestrate** having 1 or more openings or pores ⟨~ *blood capillaries*⟩ [L *fenestratus,* pp of *fenestrare* to provide with openings or windows]

fenestration /,feni'straysh(ə)n/ *n* **1** the arrangement of windows in a building **2** an opening in a surface (e g a wall or membrane) **3** the operation of cutting an opening in the bony labyrinth between the inner ear and tympanum as a treatment for deafness

Fenian /'feenyən/ *n* a member of a secret 19th-c Irish and Irish-American organization dedicated to the overthrow of British rule in Ireland [IrGael *Fēinne,* pl of *Fiann,* legendary band of Irish warriors] – **Fenian** *adj,* **Fenianism** *n*

fennec /'fenek/ *n* a small pale-fawn African fox with large ears [Ar *fanak*]

fennel /'fenl/ *n* a European plant of the carrot family cultivated for its aromatic seeds and foliage [ME *fenel,* fr OE *finugl,* fr (assumed) VL *fenuculum,* fr L *feniculum* fennel, dim. of *fenum* hay; perh akin to L *fetus* fruitful – more at FEMININE]

fenugreek /'fenyoo,greek/ *n* a leguminous Asiatic plant whose aromatic seeds are used as a flavouring [ME *fenugrek,* fr MF *fenugrec,* fr L *fenum Graecum,* lit., Greek hay]

feoffment /'feefmənt, 'fef-/ *n* the granting of a fief [ME *feoffement,* fr AF, fr *feoffer* to invest with a fee, fr OF *fief* fee]

-fer /-fə/ *comb form* (→ *n*) sby or sthg that bears ⟨*aqui*fer⟩ ⟨*coni*fer⟩ [F & L; F *-fère,* fr L *-fer* bearing, sby or sthg that bears, fr *ferre* to carry – more at [2]BEAR]

feral /'fiərəl/ *adj* **1** (suggestive) of a wild beast; savage **2a** not domesticated or cultivated; WILD 1a **b** having escaped from domestication and become wild ⟨~ *pigeons*⟩ [ML *feralis,* fr L *fera* wild animal, fr fem of *ferus* wild – more at FIERCE]

fer-de-lance /,feə də 'lahns/ *n, pl* **fer-de-lance** a large extremely venomous pit viper of Central and S America [F, lit., lance iron, spearhead]

ferine /'fiərien/ *adj* feral [L *ferinus,* fr *fera*]

fermata /fuh'mahtə/ *n* a prolongation at the discretion of the performer of a musical note, chord, or rest; *also* [1]PAUSE 4 [It, lit., stop, fr *fermare* to stop, fr L *firmare* to make firm]

[1]**ferment** /fə'ment/ *vb* **1** to (cause to) undergo fermentation **2** to (cause to) be in a state of agitation or intense activity – **fermentable** *adj,* **fermenter** *n*

[2]**ferment** /'fuhment/ *n* **1** an agent (e g an enzyme or organism) capable of bringing about fermentation **2a** FERMENTATION 1 **b** a state of unrest or upheaval; agitation, tumult [ME, fr L *fermentum* yeast – more at BARM]

fermentation /,fuhmen'taysh(ə)n/ *n* **1a** a chemical change with effervescence **b** an enzymatically controlled anaerobic breakdown of an energy-rich compound (e g a carbohydrate to carbon dioxide and alcohol); *broadly* an enzymatically controlled transformation of an organic compound ☞ ENERGY **2** FERMENT 2b – **fermentative** /fə'mentətiv/ *adj*

fermion /'fuhmyən, 'feə-, -mi·ən/ *n* a particle (e g an electron) that interacts with other particles in a way described by Fermi and Dirac [Enrico *Fermi* †1954 It physicist + E [2]*-on*] – **fermionic** /-mi'onik/ *adj*

fermium /'fuhmyəm, -mi·əm/ *n* an artificially produced radioactive metallic element ☞ PERIODIC TABLE [NL, fr Enrico *Fermi*]

fern /fuhn/ *n* any of a class of flowerless seedless lower plants; *esp* any of an order resembling flowering plants in having a root, stem, and leaflike fronds but differing in reproducing by spores ☞ PLANT [ME, fr OE *fearn*; akin to OHG *farn* fern, Skt *parṇa* wing, leaf] – **fernlike** *adj,* **ferny** *adj*

fernery /'fuhnəri/ *n* **1** a place or stand where ferns grow **2** a collection of growing ferns

ferocious /fə'rohshəs/ *adj* extremely fierce or violent [L *feroc-, ferox,* lit., fierce looking, fr *ferus* + *-oc-, -ox* (akin to Gk *ōps* eye) – more at EYE] – **ferociously** *adv*, **ferociousness** *n*

ferocity /fə'rosəti/ *n* the quality or state of being ferocious

-ferous /-fərəs/, **-iferous** /-'ifərəs/ *comb form* (→ *adj*) bearing; yielding; producing; containing ⟨*carboni*ferous⟩ ⟨*pesti*ferous⟩ [ME, fr L *-fer* & MF *-fere* (fr L *-fer*)]

ferrate /'ferayt/ *n* a compound of a metal with an ion that contains iron and oxygen atoms [ISV, fr L *ferrum* iron]

ferredoxin /,ferə'doksin/ *n* an iron-containing plant protein that functions as an electron carrier in photosynthetic organisms and in some bacteria [L *ferrum* iron + E *redox* + *-in*]

[1]**ferret** /'ferit/ *n* **1** a partially domesticated usu albino European polecat used esp for hunting small rodents (e g rats) **2** an active and persistent searcher [ME *furet, ferret,* fr MF *furet,* fr (assumed) VL *furittus,* lit., little thief, dim. of L *fur* thief] – **ferrety** *adj*

[2]**ferret** *vi* **1** to hunt with ferrets **2** to search *about* or *around* – infml ~ *vt* **1** to hunt (e g rats) with ferrets **2** to drive (game), esp from covert or burrows – **ferreter** *n*

ferret out *vt* to find and bring to light by searching ⟨ferret out *the answers*⟩ – infml

ferri- /feri-/ *comb form* **1** iron ⟨ferri*ferous*⟩ **2** ferric iron ⟨ferri*cyanide*⟩ [L, fr *ferrum*]

ferric /'ferik/ *adj* of, containing, or being (trivalent) iron

,ferric 'oxide *n* the red or black oxide of iron found in nature as haematite and as rust

ferrimagnetic /,ferimag'netik/ *adj* of or being a substance (e g ferrite) characterized by magnetization in which one group of magnetic ions is polarized in a direction opposite to the other – **ferrimagnetically** *adv*, **ferrimagnetism** /-'magni,tiz(ə)m/ *n*, **ferrimagnet** /'feri,magnit/ *n*

'Ferris ,wheel /'feris/ *n, NAm* BIG WHEEL [G W G *Ferris* †1896 US engineer]

ferrite /'feriet/ *n* any of several magnetic substances of high magnetic permeability consisting mainly of an iron oxide – **ferritic** /fe'ritik/ *adj*

ferritin /'feritin/ *n* an iron-containing protein that functions in the storage of iron and is found esp in the liver and spleen [*ferrite* + *-in*]

ferro- /feroh-/ *comb form* **1** (containing) iron ⟨ferro*concrete*⟩; iron and ⟨ferro*nickel*⟩ – chiefly in names of alloys **2** ferrous iron ⟨ferro*cyanide*⟩ [ML, fr L *ferrum*]

ferroelectric /ferroh·i'lektrik/ *adj* of or being a crystalline substance having spontaneous electric polarization reversible by an electric field – **ferroelectric** *n*, **ferroelectricity** /i,lek'trisəti, ,eelek/ *n*

,ferromag'netic /-mag'netik/ *adj* of or being a substance, esp iron, characterized by strong magnetization in which all the magnetic ions are polarized in the same direction – **ferromagnetic** *n*, **ferromagnetism** *n*

ferrous /'ferəs/ *adj* of, containing, or being (bivalent) iron [NL *ferrosus*, fr L *ferrum*]

ferrugineous /,ferə'jeenyəs, -ni·əs/ *adj* ferruginous

ferruginous /fə'rujinəs, fe-/ *adj* **1** of or containing iron **2** resembling iron rust in colour [L *ferrugineus, ferruginus,* fr *ferrugin-, ferrugo* iron rust, fr *ferrum*]

ferrule /'ferool, -rəl/ *n* **1** a ring or cap, usu of metal, strengthening a cane, tool handle, etc **2** a short tube or bush for making a tight joint (e g between pipes) [alter. of ME *virole,* fr MF, fr L *viriola,* dim. of *viria* bracelet, of Celtic origin; akin to OIr *fiar* oblique – more at [2]VEER]

[1]**ferry** /'feri/ *vt* **1** to carry by boat over a body of water **2** to convey (e g by car) from one place to another ~ *vi* to cross water in a boat [ME *ferien,* fr OE *ferian* to carry, convey; akin to OE *faran* to go – more at FARE]

[2]**ferry** *n* (a boat used at) a place where people or things are carried across a body of water (e g a river)

fertile /'fuhtiel/ *adj* **1a** (capable of) producing or bearing fruit (in great quantities); productive **b** characterized by great resourcefulness and activity; inventive ⟨*a* ~ *imagination*⟩ **2a(1)** capable of sustaining abundant plant growth ⟨~ *soil*⟩ **(2)** affording abundant possibilities for development ⟨*a* ~ *area for research*⟩ **b** capable of growing or developing ⟨~ *egg*⟩ **c** capable of breeding or reproducing **3** capable of being converted into fissile material [ME, fr MF & L; MF, fr L *fertilis,* fr *ferre* to carry, bear – more at [2]BEAR] – **fertilely** *adv*, **fertileness** *n*, **fertility** /fuh'tiləti/ *n*

fertil·ize, -ise /'fuhtiliez/ *vt* to make fertile: e g **a(1)** to inseminate, impregnate, or pollinate **(2)** to make (an ovule, egg, etc) capable of developing into a new individual by uniting with a male germ cell **b** to apply a fertilizer to ⟨~ *land*⟩ – **fertilizable** *adj*, **fertilization** /-'zaysh(ə)n/ *n*, **fertilizational** *adj*,

'fertil·izer, -iser /-zə/ *n* a substance (e g manure) used to make soil more fertile [FERTILIZE + [2]-ER]

ferula /'feroolə/ *n* **1** a ferule **2** any of a genus of Old World plants of the carrot family that yield various gum resins [(2) NL, genus name, fr L, giant fennel]

ferule /'ferool/ *n* a flat ruler used to punish children [L *ferula* giant fennel, ferule]

fervency /'fuhv(ə)nsi/ *n* fervour

fervent /'fuhv(ə)nt/ *adj* exhibiting deep sincere emotion; ardent ⟨*a* ~ *believer in free speech*⟩ [ME, fr MF & L; MF, fr L *fervent-, fervens,* prp of *fervēre* to boil, glow – more at [2]BURN] – **fervently** *adv*

fervid /'fuhvid/ *adj* passionately intense; ardent [L *fervidus,* fr *fervēre*] – **fervidly** *adv*, **fervidness** *n*

fervour, *NAm chiefly* **fervor** /'fuhvə/ *n* the quality or state of being fervent or fervid [ME *fervour,* fr MF & L; MF *ferveur,* fr L *fervor,* fr *fervēre*]

fescue /'feskyooh/ *n* any of a genus of tufted grasses [alter. of ME *festu* stalk, straw, fr MF, fr LL *festucum,* fr L *festuca*]

fest /fest/ *n, chiefly NAm* a meeting or occasion marked by a specified activity – often in combination ⟨*film*fest⟩ [G, celebration, fr L *festum*]

festal /'festl/ *adj* festive [L *festum* festival – more at FEAST] – **festally** *adv*

fester /'festə/ *vi* **1** to generate pus **2** to putrefy, rot **3** to rankle ~ *vt* to make inflamed or corrupt [ME *festren,* fr *fester, festre* suppurating sore, fr MF *festre,* fr L *fistula* pipe, pipe-like ulcer]

[1]**festival** /'festivl/ *adj* of, appropriate to, or set apart as a festival [ME, fr MF, fr L *festivus* festive]

[2]**festival** *n* **1a** a time marked by special (e g customary) celebration **b** FEAST 2 **2** a usu periodic pro

gramme or season of cultural events or entertainment ⟨*the Edinburgh* ~⟩ **3** gaiety, conviviality

festive /'festiv/ *adj* **1** of or suitable for a feast or festival **2** joyous, gay [L *festivus*, fr *festum*] – **festively** *adv*, **festiveness** *n*

festivity /fe'stivəti/ *n* **1** FESTIVAL 1 **2** festive activity – often pl with sing. meaning [FESTIVE + -ITY]

1festoon /fe'stoohn/ *n* a decorative chain or strip hanging between 2 points; *also* a carved, moulded, or painted ornament representing this ☞ ARCHITECTURE [F *feston*, fr It *festone*, fr *festa* festival, fr L – more at FEAST]

2festoon *vt* **1** to hang or form festoons on **2** to cover profusely and usu gaily

festschrift /'fest,shrift/ *n, pl* **festschriften** /-t(ə)n/, **festschrifts** *often cap* a volume of writings by various authors presented as a tribute or memorial, esp to a scholar [G, fr *fest* festival, celebration + *schrift* writing]

feta /'fetə, 'fetah/ *n* a firm white Greek cheese made of sheep's or goat's milk and cured in brine [NGk (*tyri*) *pheta*, fr *tyri* cheese + *pheta* slice, fr It *fetta*]

fetal /'feetl/ *adj* foetal

1fetch /fech/ *vt* **1** to go or come after and bring or take back **2a** to cause to come; bring **b** to produce as profit or return; realize **3** to reach by sailing, esp against the wind or tide and without having to tack **4** to strike or deal (a blow, slap, etc) ⟨~*ed him one in the face*⟩ – infml ~ *vi* **1** to go after sthg and bring it back **2** to take a roundabout way **3** to hold course on a body of water [ME *fecchen*, fr OE *fetian*, *feccan*; akin to OE *fōt* foot – more at FOOT] – **fetcher** *n*

2fetch *n* **1** the distance along open water or land over which the wind blows **2** the distance traversed by waves without obstruction

fetching /'feching/ *adj* attractive, becoming – **fetchingly** *adv*

fetch up *vt* **1** to bring up or out; produce **2** to bring to a stop **3** to vomit ~ *vi* to come to a specified standstill, stopping place, or result; arrive *USE* infml

1fete, fête /fayt, fet/ *n* **1** a festival **2** *Br* a usu outdoor bazaar or other entertainment held esp to raise money for a particular purpose [F *fête*, fr OF *feste* – more at FEAST]

2fete, fête *vt* to honour or commemorate (sby or sthg) with a fete or other ceremony

fête champêtre /shom'pet(rə) (*Fr* fɛt ʃãpɛːtr)/ *n, pl* **fêtes champêtres** /~/ an outdoor entertainment [F, lit., rural festival]

fetid, foetid /'feetid/ *adj* having a heavy offensive smell; stinking [ME *fetid*, fr L *foetidus*, fr *foetēre* to stink; akin to L *fumus* smoke – more at FUME] – **fetidly** *adv*, **fetidness** *n*

fetish *also* **fetich** /'fetish/ *n* **1** an object believed among a primitive people to have magical power; *broadly* a material object regarded with superstitious trust or reverence **2** an object of irrational reverence or obsessive devotion **3** an object or bodily part whose presence in reality or fantasy is psychologically necessary for sexual gratification [F & Pg; F *fétiche*, fr Pg *feitiço*, fr *feitiço* artificial, false, fr L *facticius* factitious]

fetishism *also* **fetichism** /'fetishiz(ə)m/ *n* **1** belief in magical fetishes **2** the displacement of erotic interest and satisfaction to a fetish – **fetishist** *n*, **fetishistic** /-'shistik/ *adj*

fetlock /'fet,lok/ *n* **1** a projection bearing a tuft of hair on the back of the leg above the hoof of an animal of the horse family **2** the joint of the limb or tuft of hair at the fetlock *USE* ☞ ANATOMY [ME *fitlok*, *fetlak*; akin to OE *fōt* foot]

feto- *also* **feti-** *comb form* foeto-

fetor /'feetə, -taw/ *n* a strong offensive smell; a stink – fml [ME *fetoure*, fr L *foetor*, fr *foetēre*]

1fetter /'fetə/ *n* **1** a shackle for the feet **2** sthg that confines; a restraint – usu pl with sing. meaning [ME *feter*, fr OE; akin to OE *fōt* foot]

2fetter *vt* **1** to put fetters on **2** to bind (as if) with fetters; shackle, restrain

1fettle /'fetl/ *vt* **fettling** /'fetling/ **1** to line with fettling **2** to trim the rough joints or edges of (e g unfired pottery or a metal casting) [ME *fetlen* to shape, prepare; prob akin to OE *fæt* vessel – more at VAT]

2fettle *n* a state of physical or mental fitness or order; condition ⟨*in fine* ~⟩

fettling /'fetling/ *n* loose material (e g ore or sand) thrown on the hearth of a furnace to protect it [fr gerund of *1fettle*]

fettuccine /,fetə'cheeni/ *n pl but sing or pl in constr* tagliatelle [It, pl of *fettuccina*, dim. of *fettuccia* small slice, ribbon, dim. of *fetta* slice]

fetus /'feetəs/ *n* a foetus

feu /fyooh/ *n, Scot* (land held under) a perpetual lease for a fixed rent [ME (Sc), fr MF *fé*, *fief* – more at FEE]

feud /fyoohd/ *n* a lasting state of hostilities, esp between families or clans, marked by violent attacks for the purpose of revenge [alter. of ME *feide*, fr MF, of Gmc origin; akin to OHG *fēhida* hostility, feud, OE *fāh* hostile – more at FOE] – **feud** *vi*

feudal /'fyoohdl/ *adj* of feudalism or a medieval fee; *also* suggestive of feudalism (e g in servility) [ML *feodalis*, *feudalis*, fr *feodum*, *feudum* fee, fief, of Gmc origin; akin to OHG *fihu* cattle – more at FEE] – **feudally** *adv*, **feudalize** *vt*, **feudalization** /-ie'zaysh(ə)n/ *n*

'feudal,ism /-,iz(ə)m/ *n* a medieval system of political organization involving the relationship of lord to vassal with all land held in fee, homage, the service of tenants under arms and in court, wardship, and forfeiture – **feudalist** *n*, **feudalistic** /-'istik/ *adj*

feudality /fyooh'daləti/ *n* **1** being feudal **2** a feudal holding

feudatory /'fyoohdət(ə)ri/ *adj* **1** owing feudal allegiance **2** under a foreign overlord [ML *feudatorius*, fr *feudatus*, pp of *feudare* to enfeoff, fr *feudum*]

1fever /'feevə/ *n* **1** (any of various diseases characterized by) a rise of body temperature above the normal **2a** a state of intense emotion or activity ⟨*in a* ~ *of impatience*⟩ **b** a contagious usu transient enthusiasm; a craze ⟨*football* ~ *raged throughout the world*⟩ [ME, fr OE *fēfer*, fr L *febris*; akin to L *fovēre* to warm]

2fever *vt* to throw into a fever; agitate

feverfew /'feevə,fyooh/ *n* a perennial European composite plant [ME, fr (assumed) AF *fevrefue*, fr LL *febrifugia* centaury – more at FEBRIFUGE]

feverish /'feevərish/ *also* **feverous** /-rəs/ *adj* **1a** having the symptoms of a fever **b** indicating, relating to, or caused by (a) fever **c** tending to cause or infect with fever **2** marked by intense emotion, activity, or instability – **feverishly** *adv*, **feverishness** *n*, **feverously** *adv*

'fever ,pitch *n* a state of intense excitement and agitation ⟨*raised the crowd to* ~⟩

[1]**few** /fyooh/ *adj* **1** amounting to only a small number ⟨*one of his* ~ *pleasures*⟩ **2** at least some though not many – + *a* ⟨*a good* ~ *drinks*⟩ ⟨*caught a* ~ *more fish*⟩ [ME *fewe*, pron & adj, fr OE *fēawa*; akin to OHG *fō* little, L *paucus* little, *pauper* poor, Gk *paid-*, *pais* child, Skt *putra* son] – **fewness** *n*

[2]**few** *n pl in constr* **1** not many ⟨~ *were present*⟩ ⟨*all the* ~ *that remained*⟩ ⟨~ *of his stories were true*⟩ **2** at least some though not many – + *a* ⟨*a* ~ *of them*⟩ **3** a select or exclusive group of people; an elite ⟨*the* ~⟩

[1]**fewer** /'fyooh·ə/ *n pl in constr* a smaller number of people or things

[2]**fewer** *adj, comparative of* FEW

fey /fay/ *adj* **1a** able to see into the future **b** marked by an otherworldly and irresponsible air **2** *chiefly Scot* **a** fated to die; doomed **b** marked by an excited or elated state [ME *feye* doomed, fr OE *fǣge*; akin to OHG *feigi* fey, & perh to OE *fāh* hostile, outlawed – more at FOE] – **feyness** *n*

fez /fez/ *n, pl* **-zz-** *also* **-z-** a brimless hat shaped like a truncated cone, usu red and with a tassel, which is worn by men in southern and eastern Mediterranean countries ☞ GARMENT [F, fr *Fez*, city in Morocco]

fiancé, *fem* **fiancée** /fi'onsay/ *n* sby engaged to be married [F, fr MF, fr pp of *fiancer* to promise, betroth, fr OF *fiancier*, fr *fiance* promise, trust, fr *fier* to trust, fr (assumed) VL *fidare*, alter. of L *fidere* – more at BIDE]

fiasco /fi'askoh/ *n, pl* **fiascoes** a complete and ignominious failure [F, fr It, lit., bottle, of Gmc origin; akin to OHG *flaska* bottle]

fiat /'fie·ət, -at/ *n* an authoritative and often arbitrary order; a decree ⟨*government by* ~⟩ [L, let it be done, fr *fieri* to become, be done – more at BE]

fib /fib/ *vi or n* **-bb-** (to tell) a trivial or childish lie – infml [n perh by shortening & alter. fr *fable*; vb fr n] – **fibber** *n*

Fibonacci number /feebə'nahchi/ *n* a number in the Fibonacci sequence 0, 1, 1, 2, 3, 5, 8, 13, 21, ☞ NUMBER [Leonardo *Fibonacci* †*ab* 1250 It mathematician]

,Fibo,nacci 'sequence *n* an infinite sequence of integers in which every term after the second is the sum of the 2 preceding terms ☞ NUMBER [Leonardo *Fibonacci*]

fibr- /fiebr-/, **fibro-** *comb form* fibre; fibrous tissue ⟨fibr*oid*⟩; fibrous and ⟨fibro*vascular*⟩ [L *fibra*]

fibre, *NAm chiefly* **fiber** /'fiebə/ *n* **1a** an elongated tapering supportive thick-walled plant cell **b(1)** NERVE 2 **(2)** any of the filaments composing most of the intercellular matrix of connective tissue **(3)** any of the elongated contractile cells of muscle tissue **c** a slender natural or man-made thread or filament (e g of wool, cotton, or asbestos) **2** material made of fibres **3** essential structure or character ⟨*the very* ~ *of his being*⟩; *also* strength, fortitude ⟨*a man of great moral* ~⟩ [F *fibre*, fr L *fibra*]

'fibre,board /-,bawd/ *n* a material made by compressing fibres (e g of wood) into stiff boards

'fibre,glass /-,glahs/ *n* **1** glass in fibrous form used in making various products (e g textiles and insulation materials) **2** a combination of synthetic resins and fibreglass

,fibre 'optics *n pl but sing in constr* the use of very thin (bundles of) glass or plastic fibres that transmit light throughout their length by internal reflections for bending light or seeing round corners ☞ TELECOMMUNICATION, TELEVISION – **fibre-optic** *adj*

'fibre,scope /'fiebə,skohp/ *n* a flexible instrument using fibre optics for examining inaccessible areas (e g the lining of the stomach)

fibril /'fiebril, 'fibril/ *n* a small filament or fibre [NL *fibrilla*, dim. of L *fibra*] – **fibrillar** *adj*, **fibrillose** /-lohs/ *adj*, **fibrilliform** /-'brili,fawm/ *adj*

fibrillation /,fibri'laysh(ə)n/ *n* **1** the forming of fibres or fibrils **2** very rapid irregular contractions of muscle fibres (of the heart resulting in a lack of synchronization between heartbeat and pulse) – **fibrillate** /-layt/ *vb*

fibrin /'fiebrin/ *n* a fibrous protein formed from fibrinogen by the action of thrombin, esp in the clotting of blood – **fibrinous** *adj*

fibrinogen /fie'brinəj(ə)n/ *n* a (blood plasma) protein that is produced in the liver and is converted into fibrin during clotting of blood [ISV]

fibrinolysin /,fiebrinoh'liesin, ,fiebrinl'iesin/ *n* **1** plasmin **2** streptokinase [ISV]

fibro /'fiebroh/ *n, pl* **fibros** *Austr* (a building made from) a mixture of asbestos and cement [short for *fibro-cement*]

fibroblast /'fiebrə,blast, 'fi-/ *n* a cell giving rise to connective tissue [ISV] – **fibroblastic** /-'blastik/ *adj*

[1]**fibroid** /'fiebroyd/ *adj* resembling, forming, or consisting of fibrous tissue

[2]**fibroid** *n* a benign tumour made up of fibrous and muscular tissue that occurs esp in the uterine wall

fibroin /'fiebroh·in/ *n* an insoluble protein comprising the filaments of the raw silk fibre [F *fibroïne*, fr *fibr-* + *-ine* -in]

fibroma /fie'brohmə/ *n, pl* **fibromas** *also* **fibromata** /-mətə/ a benign tumour consisting mainly of fibrous tissue – **fibromatous** /-mətəs/ *adj*

fibrosis /fie'brohsis/ *n* the abnormal increase of interstitial fibrous tissue in an organ or part of the body [NL] – **fibrotic** /-'brotik/ *adj*

fibrositis /,fiebrə'siətəs/ *n* a painful muscular condition prob resulting from inflammation of fibrous tissue (e g muscle sheaths) [NL, fr *fibrosus* fibrous, fr ISV *fibrous*]

fibrous /'fiebrəs/ *adj* **1a** containing, consisting of, or resembling fibres **b** characterized by fibrosis **c** capable of being separated into fibres ⟨*a* ~ *mineral*⟩ **2** tough, stringy [F *fibreux*, fr *fibre* fibre, fr L *fibra*] – **fibrously** *adv*, **fibrousness** *n*

fibula /'fibyoolə/ *n, pl* **fibulae** /-li/, **fibulas** **1** an ornamented clasp used esp by the ancient Greeks and Romans **2** the (smaller) outer of the 2 bones of the hind limb of higher vertebrates between the knee and ankle – compare TIBIA ☞ ANATOMY [L] – **fibular** *adj*

-fic /-fik/ *suffix* (→ *adj*) making; causing ⟨*horri*fic⟩ ⟨*paci*fic⟩ [MF & L; MF *-fique*, fr L *-ficus*, fr *facere* to make – more at [1]DO]

-fication /-fi'kaysh(ə)n/ *comb form* (→ *n*) action; production ⟨*rei*fication⟩ ⟨*jolli*fication⟩ [ME *-ficacioun*, fr MF & L; MF *-fication*, fr L *-fication-*, *-ficatio*, fr *-ficatus*, pp ending of verbs ending in *-ficare* to make, fr *-ficus*]

fiche /feesh/ *n, pl* **fiche** *also* **fiches** a microfiche

fichu /ˈfeeshooh (*Fr* fiʃy)/ *n* a woman's light triangular scarf draped over the shoulders and fastened at the bosom [F, fr pp of *ficher* to stick in, throw on, fr (assumed) VL *figicare*, fr L *figere* to fasten, pierce – more at DYKE]

ficin /ˈfies(ə)n/ *n* an enzyme that breaks down protein and is obtained from the latex of fig trees [L *ficus* fig]

fickle /ˈfikl/ *adj* lacking steadfastness or constancy; capricious [ME *fikel* deceitful, inconstant, fr OE *ficol* deceitful; akin to OE be*fician* to deceive, L *pigēre* to irk, & prob to OE *fāh* hostile – more at FOE] – **fickleness** *n*

fictile /ˈfiktiel/ *adj* **1** moulded into shape by a potter **2** of or relating to pottery [L *fictilis* moulded of clay, fr *fictus*]

fiction /ˈfiksh(ə)n/ *n* **1a** sthg invented by the imagination; *specif* an invented story ⟨*distinguish fact from* ~⟩ **b** literature (e g novels or short stories) describing imaginary people and events **2** an assumption of a possibility as a fact, irrespective of the question of its truth ⟨*a legal* ~⟩ **3** the action of feigning or creating with the imagination [ME *ficcioun*, fr MF *fiction*, fr L *fiction-*, *fictio* act of fashioning, fiction, fr *fictus*, pp of *fingere* to shape, fashion, feign – more at DOUGH] – **fictionist** *n*, **fictional** *adj*, **fictionally** *adv*, **fictionality** /-ˈaləti/ *n*, **fictionalize** *vt*, **fictionalization** /-ˈzaysh(ə)n/ *n*

fictitious /fikˈtishəs/ *adj* **1** (characteristic) of fiction **2** *of a name* false, assumed **3** not genuinely felt; feigned [L *ficticius* artificial, feigned, fr *fictus*] – **fictitiously** *adv*, **fictitiousness** *n*

fictive /ˈfiktiv/ *adj* **1** FICTITIOUS 3 **2** (capable) of imaginative creation – **fictively** *adv*

fid /fid/ *n* a tapering wooden pin used in opening the strands of a rope for splicing [origin unknown]

-fid /-fid/ *comb form* (→ *adj*) divided into (such or so many) parts ⟨*bi*fid⟩ ⟨*pinnati*fid⟩ [L *-fidus*, fr *findere* to split – more at BITE]

[1]**fiddle** /ˈfidl/ *n* **1** a violin **2** a device to keep objects from sliding off a table on board ship **3** fiddlesticks – used as an interjection; infml **4** *Br* a dishonest practice; a swindle – infml **5** *Br* an activity involving intricate manipulation ⟨*a bit of a* ~ *to get all these wires back in place*⟩ – infml [ME *fidel*, fr OE *fithele*, prob fr ML *vitula*]

[2]**fiddle** *vb* **fiddling** /ˈfidling, ˈfidl·ing/ *vi* **1** to play on a fiddle **2a** to move the hands or fingers restlessly **b** to spend time in aimless or fruitless activity – often + *about* or *around* ~ *vt* **1** *Br* to falsify (e g accounts), esp so as to gain financial advantage **2** *Br* to get or contrive by cheating or deception ⟨~d *an extra 10 pounds on his expenses*⟩ ***USE*** (*vi 2 & vt*) infml – **fiddler** *n* – **fiddle with** to tamper or meddle with – infml

ˈfiddle-ˌfaddle /ˌfadl/ *n* nonsense – often used as an interjection; infml [redupl of *fiddle* (fiddlesticks)]

ˈfiddleˌhead /-ˌhed/ *n* ornamentation on a ship's bow curved like a scroll [fr the resemblance to the scroll at the head of a violin]

ˈfiddler ˌcrab /ˈfidlə/ *n* a burrowing crab of which the male has 1 claw much enlarged [fr the position in which the enlarged claw is held, resembling the angle of a violinist's arm]

fiddlesticks /ˈfidlˌstiks/ *n pl* nonsense – used as an interjection; infml [*fiddlestick* (violin bow); fr its small value compared with the fiddle itself]

fiddling /ˈfidling/ *adj* trifling, petty ⟨*made some* ~ *excuse*⟩

fiddly /ˈfidli/ *adj, Br* **1** fiddling **2** finicky ***USE*** infml

fideism /ˈfeedayˌiz(ə)m/ *n* reliance on faith rather than reason, esp in metaphysics [prob fr F *fidéisme*, fr L *fides* faith] – **fideist** *n*, **fideistic** /-ˈistik/ *adj*

fidelity /fiˈdeləti/ *n* **1a** the quality or state of being faithful; loyalty **b** accuracy in details; exactness **2** the degree of similarity between some reproduced (e g recorded) material and its original source [ME *fidelite*, fr MF *fidelité*, fr L *fidelitat-*, *fidelitas*, fr *fidelis* faithful, fr *fides* faith]

[1]**fidget** /ˈfijit/ *n* **1** uneasiness or restlessness shown by nervous movements – usu pl with sing. meaning **2** sby who fidgets ***USE*** infml [irreg fr *fidge* to fidget, prob alter. of E dial. *fitch*, fr ME *fichen*]

[2]**fidget** *vb* to (cause to) move or act restlessly or nervously – **fidgety** *adj*

fiducial /fiˈdyoohsh(y)əl/ *adj* **1** taken as a standard of reference ⟨*a* ~ *mark*⟩ **2** founded on faith or trust **3** having the nature of a trust – **fiducially** *adv*

fiduciary /fiˈdyoohshəri/ *adj* FIDUCIAL 3 [L *fiduciarius*, fr *fiducia* confidence, trust, fr *fidere*]

fie /fie/ *interj, archaic* – used to express disgust or shock [ME *fi*, fr OF]

fief /feef/ *n* **1** a feudal estate **2** sthg over which one has rights or exercises control ⟨*a politician's* ~⟩ [F – more at FEE] – **fiefdom** /-d(ə)m/ *n*

[1]**field** /feeld/ *n* **1a** an (enclosed) area of land free of woods and buildings (used for cultivation or pasture) **b** an area of land containing a natural resource ⟨*coal* ~⟩ **c** (the place where) a battle is fought; *also* a battle **d** a large unbroken expanse (e g of ice) **2a** an area or division of an activity ⟨*a lawyer eminent in his* ~⟩ **b** the sphere of practical operation outside a place of work (e g a laboratory) ⟨*geologists working in the* ~⟩ ⟨~ *research*⟩ **c** an area in which troops are operating (e g in an exercise or theatre of war) **d(1)** an area constructed, equipped, or marked for sports **(2)** the part of a sports area enclosed by the running track and used for athletic field events **3** a space on which sthg is drawn or projected; *esp* the surface, esp a shield, on which a coat of arms is displayed **4** the participants in a sports activity, esp with the exception of the favourite or winner **5a** a set of mathematical elements that is closed under 2 binary operations, the second of which is distributive relative to the first, and that is a commutative group under the first operation and also under the second if the identity element under the first is omitted **b** a region in which a mathematical quantity (e g a scalar or vector) is associated with every point **c** a region or space in which a given effect (e g magnetism) exists **6** *also* **field of view** the area visible through the lens of an optical instrument [ME, fr OE *feld*; akin to OHG *feld* field, OE *flōr* floor]

[2]**field** *vt* **1a** to stop and pick up (a batted ball) **b** to deal with by giving an impromptu answer ⟨*the Minister* ~ed *the reporters' questions*⟩ **2** to put into the field of play or battle ⟨~ *a team*⟩ ~ *vi* to play as a fielder in cricket, baseball, etc

field artillery *n* artillery, other than antiaircraft or antitank guns, used in the field

ˈfield ˌday *n* **1a** a day for military exercises or manoeuvres **b** an outdoor meeting or social gathering **2** a time of unusual pleasure and unrestrained action ⟨*the newspaper had a* ~ *with the scandal*⟩

fielder /ˈfeeldə/ *n* any of the players whose job is to field the ball (e g in cricket) [[2]FIELD + [2]-ER]

ˈfield ˌevent *n* an athletic event (e g discus, javelin, or jumping) other than a race – compare TRACK EVENT

ˈfieldˌfare /-ˌfeə/ *n* a medium-sized Eurasian thrush with an ash-coloured head and chestnut wings [ME *feldefare,* fr OE *feldeware,* fr *feld* + *-ware* dweller]

ˈfield ˌglasses *n pl* an optical instrument usu consisting of 2 telescopes on a single frame with a focussing device

ˈfield ˌgoal *n* a goal in basketball made while the ball is in play

ˈfield ˌhockey *n, chiefly NAm* HOCKEY 1

field marshal *n* ☞ RANK

ˈfield ˌmouse *n* any of various mice or voles that inhabit fields

field mushroom *n* the common edible mushroom that is an agaric

ˈfield ˌofficer *n* a commissioned army officer of the rank of colonel, lieutenant colonel, or major

ˌfield of ˈview *n* FIELD 7

fieldsman /ˈfeeldzmən/ *n, pl* **fieldsmen** /-mən/ a fielder

field sport *n* an open-air sport (e g hunting or shooting) involving the pursuit of animals

field theory *n* a detailed mathematical description of the assumed physical properties of a region under some influence (e g gravitation)

ˈfield ˌtrip *n* a visit made by students for firsthand observation (e g to a farm or museum)

ˈfieldˌwork /-ˌwuhk/ *n* **1** a temporary fortification in the field **2** work done in the field (e g by students) to gain practical experience through firsthand observation **3** the gathering of data in anthropology, sociology, etc through the observation or interviewing of subjects in the field – **field-worker** *n*

fiend /feend/ *n* **1a** DEVIL 1 **b** a demon **c** a person of great wickedness or cruelty **2** sby excessively devoted to a specified activity or thing; a fanatic, devotee ⟨*a golf* ~⟩ ⟨*a fresh-air* ~⟩ **3** one who uses immoderate quantities of sthg (specified); an addict ⟨*a dope* ~⟩ **4** sby remarkably clever at a specified activity; WIZARD 2 ⟨*a* ~ *at arithmetic*⟩ ***USE*** *(2 & 4)* infml [ME, fr OE *fiend*; akin to OHG *fīant* enemy, Skt *pīyant* hostile (fr *pīyati* he abuses, shows hostility towards)]

fiendish /ˈfeendish/ *adj* **1** perversely diabolical **2** extremely cruel or wicked **3** excessively bad, unpleasant, or difficult – **fiendishly** *adv,* **fiendishness** *n*

fierce /fiəs/ *adj* **1** violently hostile or aggressive; combative, pugnacious **2a** lacking restraint or control; violent, heated ⟨*a* ~ *argument*⟩ **b** extremely intense or severe ⟨~ *pain*⟩ **3** furiously active or determined ⟨*make a* ~ *effort*⟩ **4** wild or menacing in appearance [ME *fiers,* fr OF, fr L *ferus* wild, savage; akin to Gk *thēr* wild animal] – **fiercely** *adv,* **fierceness** *n*

fiery /ˈfie·əri/ *adj* **1a** consisting of fire **b** burning, blazing ⟨~ *cross*⟩ **c** liable to catch fire or explode **2** very hot ⟨*a* ~ *chilli sauce*⟩ **3** of the colour of fire; *esp* red **4a** full of or exuding strong emotion or spirit; passionate ⟨*a* ~ *speech*⟩ **b** easily provoked; irascible ⟨*a* ~ *temper*⟩ **5** *of a cricket pitch* allowing the bowled ball to bounce dangerously high and fast [ME, fr *fire, fier* fire] – **fierily** *adv,* **fieriness** *n*

fiesta /fiˈestə/ *n* a saint's day in Spain and Latin America, often celebrated with processions and dances [Sp, fr L *festa* – more at FEAST]

fife /fief/ *n* a small flute used chiefly to accompany the drum [G *pfeife* pipe, fife, fr OHG *pfīfa* – more at PIPE]

fifteen /fifˈteen/ *n* **1** ☞ NUMBER **2** the fifteenth in a set or series **3** *sing or pl in constr* sthg having 15 parts or members or a denomination of 15; *esp* a Rugby Union football team [ME *fiftene,* adj, fr OE *fīftēne,* fr *fīf* five + *tīen, tēn* ten] – **fifteen** *adj or pron,* **fifteenth** /-ˈteenth/ *adj or n*

fifth /fith; *also* fifth/ *n* . **1** ☞ NUMBER **2a** (the combination of 2 notes at) a musical interval of 5 diatonic degrees **b** DOMINANT 2 [ME *fifte, fifthe,* adj & n, fr OE *fīfta* (akin to OHG *fimfto, finfto,* ON *fimmti*), fr *fīf* five + *-ta* -th – more at FIVE] – **fifth** *adj or adv,* **fifthly** *adv*

ˌfifth ˈcolumn *n* a group within a nation or faction that sympathizes with and works secretly for an enemy or rival [name applied to rebel sympathizers in Madrid in 1936 when four rebel columns were advancing on the city] – **fifth columnist** *n*

fifth wheel *n* a horizontal wheel above the front axle of a carriage enabling it to be steered without tipping; *also* a similar coupling between tractor and trailer of an articulated lorry

fifty /ˈfifti/ *n* **1** ☞ NUMBER **2** *pl* the numbers 50 to 59; *specif* a range of temperatures, ages, or dates within a century characterized by those numbers [ME, fr *fifty,* adj, fr OE *fīftig,* fr *fīftig,* n, group of 50, fr *fīf* five + *-tig* group of ten – more at EIGHTY] – **fiftieth** /-ith/ *adj or n,* **fifty** *adj or pron,* **fiftyfold** /-ˌfohld/ *adj or adv*

[1]ˌfifty-ˈfifty *adv* evenly, equally ⟨*they shared the money* ~⟩

[2]fifty-fifty *adj* half favourable and half unfavourable; even ⟨*a* ~ *chance*⟩

[1]fig /fig/ *n* **1** (any of a genus of trees that bear) a many-seeded fleshy usu pear-shaped or oblong edible fruit **2** a contemptibly worthless trifle ⟨*not worth a* ~⟩ [ME *fige,* fr OF, fr OProv *figa,* fr (assumed) VL *fica,* fr L *ficus* fig tree, fig]

[2]fig *n* dress, array ⟨*in full Regency* ~ – *The Listener*⟩ [*fig* (to adorn), var of obs *feague* (to whip), prob fr G *fegen* to sweep, burnish]

[1]fight /fiet/ *vb* **fought** /fawt/ *vi* **1a** to contend in battle or physical combat; *esp* to strive to overcome a person by blows or weapons **b** [3]BOX **2** to strive, struggle ⟨~ing *for his life*⟩ ~ *vt* **1a(1)** to contend against (as if) in battle or physical combat **(2)** to engage in a boxing match with **b** to attempt to prevent the success, effectiveness, or development of ⟨*the company* fought *the strike for months*⟩ **2a** to wage ⟨~ *a war*⟩ **b** to take part in (a boxing match) **c** to stand as a candidate for (e g a constituency) in an election **3** to struggle to endure or surmount ⟨*he* fought *his illness for a year before he died*⟩ **4a** to make (one's way) by fighting **b** to resolve or control by fighting – + *out* or *down* ⟨fought *down her fear*⟩ [ME *fighten,* fr OE *feohtan*; akin to OHG *fehtan* to fight, L *pectere* to comb – more at FEE] – **fight shy of** to avoid facing or meeting

[2]fight *n* **1a** an act of fighting; a battle, combat **b** a boxing match **c** a verbal disagreement; an argument **2** a usu protracted struggle for an objective ⟨*a* ~ *for justice*⟩ **3** strength or disposition for fighting; pugnacity ⟨*still full of* ~⟩

fight back *vi* to struggle to recover from a losing or disadvantageous position; resist – **fightback** *n*

fighter /'fietə/ *n* **1a** a pugnacious or boldly determined individual **b** [1]BOXER **2** a fast manoeuvrable aeroplane designed to destroy enemy aircraft [[1]FIGHT + [2]-ER]

fighting chance *n* a small chance that may be realized through struggle ⟨*a* ~ *of getting to the final*⟩

fight off *vt* to ward off (as if) by fighting; repel

fight out *vt* to settle (e g an argument) by fighting – esp in *fight it out*

figment /'figmənt/ *n* sthg fabricated or imagined ⟨*a* ~ *of the author's imagination*⟩ [ME, fr L *figmentum*, fr *fingere* to shape – more at DOUGH]

figural /'fig(y)ərəl/ *adj* of, concerning, or containing human or animal figures

figurant /'fig(y)ərənt/, *fem* **figurante** /-'ront/ *n* a ballet dancer who dances only in a group [F, fr prp of *figurer* to figure, represent]

figuration /,figyoo'raysh(ə)n/ *n* **1** the creation or representation of an esp allegorical or symbolic figure **2** a form, outline **3** ornamentation of a musical passage by using musical figures

figurative /'figyoorətiv/ *adj* **1a** representing by a figure or likeness; emblematic **b** representational ⟨~ *sculpture*⟩ **2** characterized by or using figures of speech, esp metaphor – **figuratively** *adv*, **figurativeness** *n*

[1]**figure** /'figə/ *n* **1a** an (Arabic) number symbol ⟨*a salary running into 6* ~s⟩ **b** *pl* arithmetical calculations ⟨*good at* ~s⟩ **c** a written or printed character **d** value, esp as expressed in numbers ⟨*the house sold at a low* ~⟩ **2** bodily shape or form, esp of a person ⟨*a slender* ~⟩ **3a** the graphic representation of an esp human form **b** a diagram or pictorial illustration in a text **c** a geometrical diagram or shape **4** an intentional deviation from the usual form or syntactic relation of words **5** the form of a syllogism with respect to the position of the middle term **6** an often repetitive pattern in a manufactured article (e g cloth) or natural substance (e g wood) **7** an appearance made; a usu favourable impression produced ⟨*the couple cut quite a* ~⟩ **8a** a series of movements in a dance **b** an outline representation of a form traced by a series of evolutions (e g by a skater on an ice surface) **9** a personage, personality ⟨*great political* ~s⟩ **10** a short musical phrase [ME, fr OF, fr L *figura*, fr *fingere*]

[2]**figure** *vt* **1** to represent (as if) by a figure or outline; portray **2a** to decorate with a pattern **b** to write figures over or under (the bass) in order to indicate the accompanying chords **3** to indicate or represent by numerals **4a** to calculate **b** *chiefly NAm* to conclude, decide ⟨*he* ~d *there was no use in further effort*⟩ **c** *chiefly NAm* to regard, consider ~ *vi* **1** to take an esp important or conspicuous part – often + *in* **2** to calculate **3** to seem reasonable or expected – infml; esp in *that figures* – **figurer** *n* – **figure on** *NAm* to take into consideration (e g in planning) ⟨figure on *$50 a month extra income*⟩

figured /'figəd/ *adj* **1** represented, portrayed **2** adorned with or formed into a figure ⟨~ *muslin*⟩ ⟨~ *wood*⟩ **3** indicated by figures

figured bass *n* a continuo

,figure 'eight *n, chiefly NAm* FIGURE OF EIGHT

'figure,head /-,hed/ *n* **1** an ornamental carved figure on a ship's bow **2** a head or chief in name only

,figure of 'eight *n* sthg (e g a skater's figure) resembling the Arabic numeral 8 in form or shape

,figure of 'speech *n* a form of expression (e g a hyperbole or metaphor) used to convey meaning or heighten effect

figure out *vt* **1** to discover, determine ⟨*try to* figure out *a solution*⟩ **2** to solve, fathom ⟨*I just can't* figure *him* out⟩

'figure ,skating *n* skating in which the skater outlines distinctive circular patterns based on the figure eight

figurine /figyoo'reen, '---/ *n* a statuette [F, fr It *figurina*, dim. of *figura* figure, fr L]

figwort /'fig,wuht/ *n* any of a genus of chiefly herbaceous plants with an irregular 2-lipped corolla [[1]*fig* (piles) + [1]*wort*; fr its supposed ability to cure piles]

Fijian /fee'jee.ən/ *n* **1** a member of the Melanesian people of the Fiji islands **2** the language of the Fijians ☞ LANGUAGE [*Fiji* Islands, SW Pacific] – **Fijian** *adj*

fil /fil/ *n* (a note or coin representing) a money unit used by various Arab countries and usu worth $^1/_{1000}$ dinar ☞ NATIONALITY [back-formation fr Ar *fils* (taken as pl)]

filament /'filəmənt/ *n* a single thread or a thin flexible threadlike object or part: e g **a** a slender conductor (e g in an electric light bulb) made incandescent by the passage of an electric current; *specif* such a conductor that heats the cathode of a thermionic device **b** an elongated thin series of attached cells or a very long thin cylindrical single cell (e g of some algae, fungi, or bacteria) **c** the anther-bearing stalk of a stamen ☞ PLANT [MF, fr ML *filamentum*, fr LL *filare* to spin – more at [5]FILE] – **filamentary** /-'mentəri/ *adj*, **filamentous** /-'mentəs/ *adj*

filaria /fi'leəri·ə/ *n, pl* **filariae** /-ri,ee/ any of numerous threadlike nematode worms that usu develop in biting insects and are parasites in the blood or tissues of mammals when adult [NL, fr L *filum*] – **filarial** *adj*, **filariid** /-ri,id/ *adj or n*

filariasis /,filə'rie·əsis, fi,leəri'aysis/ *n, pl* **filariases** /-seez/ infestation with or disease (e g elephantiasis) caused by filarial worms [NL]

filature /'filəchə/ *n* (a factory for) the reeling of silk from cocoons [F, fr LL *filatus*, pp of *filare*]

filbert /'filbət/ *n* (the sweet thick-shelled nut of) either of 2 European hazels [ME, fr AF *philber*, fr St *Philibert* †684 Frankish abbot whose feast day falls in the nutting season]

filch /filch/ *vt* to steal (sthg of small value); pilfer [ME *filchen*]

[1]**file** /fiel/ *n* a tool, usu of hardened steel, with many cutting ridges for shaping or smoothing objects or surfaces [ME, fr OE *fēol*; akin to OHG *fīla* file]

[2]**file** *vt* to rub, smooth, or cut away (as if) with a file

[3]**file** *vt* **1** to arrange in order (e g alphabetically) for preservation and reference **2** to submit or record officially ⟨~ *a lawsuit*⟩ ~ *vi* to place items, esp papers, in a file [ME *filen*, fr MF *filer* to string documents on a string or wire, fr *fil* thread, fr L *filum*]

[4]**file** *n* **1** a folder, cabinet, etc in which papers are kept in order **2** a collection of papers or publications on a subject, usu arranged or classified

[5]file *n* **1** a row of people, animals, or things arranged one behind the other **2** any of the rows of squares that extend across a chessboard from white's side to black's side [MF, fr *filer* to spin, fr LL *filare*, fr L *filum*]

[6]file *vi* to march or proceed in file

filefish /'fiel,fish/ *n* any of various bony fishes with rough granular leathery skins [[1]*file* + [1]*fish*]

[1]filet /'filit, 'filay/ *n* a lace with a square mesh and geometric designs [F, lit., net]

[2]filet *n, chiefly NAm* a fillet

fili- /fili-/, **filo-** *comb form* thread ⟨fili*form*⟩ [L *filum*]

filial /'fili·əl, -yəl/ *adj* **1** of or befitting a son or daughter, esp in his/her relationship to a parent ⟨~ *obedience*⟩ **2** having or assuming the relation of a child or offspring [ME, fr LL *filialis*, fr L *filius* son – more at FEMININE] – **filially** *adv*

filial generation *n* a generation in a breeding experiment that is successive to a parental generation

filiation /,fili'aysh(ə)n/ *n* **1a** filial relationship, esp of a son to his father **b** the adjudication of a child's paternity **2** an offshoot or branch (e g of a culture or language) **3** descent or derivation, esp from a culture or language

filibeg, fillibeg, philibeg /'filibeg/ *n* a kilt [ScGael *fēile-beag*, fr *fēileadh* kilt + *beag* little]

filibuster /'fili,bustə/ *vi or n, chiefly NAm* (to engage in) the use of extreme delaying tactics in a legislative assembly [n Sp *filibustero*, lit., freebooter; vb fr n]

filigree /'filigree/ *vt or n* (to decorate with) **a** ornamental openwork of delicate or intricate design **b** a pattern or design resembling such openwork ⟨*a ~ of frost on a window*⟩ [n F *filigrane*, fr It *filigrana*, fr L *filum* + *granum* grain; vb fr n]

filing /'fieling/ *n* a usu metal fragment rubbed off in filing – usu pl ⟨*iron* ~s⟩

filioque /'fili,ok/ *n* the affirmation, added to the Nicene Creed in the Western liturgy and rejected by the Eastern church, that the Holy Spirit proceeds from the Son as well as from the Father [LL, and from the Son]

Filipino /,fili'peenoh/ *n, pl* **Filipinos** a native or inhabitant of the Philippine islands [Sp, fr *(Islas) Filipinas* Philippine Islands] – **Filipino** *adj*

[1]fill /fil/ *vt* **1a** to put into as much as can be held or conveniently contained ⟨~ *a cup with water*⟩ **b** to supply with a full complement ⟨*the class is already* ~ed⟩ **c(1)** to cause to swell or billow ⟨*wind* ~ed *the sails*⟩ **(2)** to trim (a sail) to catch the wind **d** to repair the cavities of (a tooth) **e** to stop up; obstruct, plug **2a** to feed, satiate **b** to satisfy, fulfil ⟨~s *all requirements*⟩ **3a** to occupy the whole of ⟨*smoke* ~ed *the room*⟩ **b** to spread through **4a** to possess and perform the duties of; hold ⟨~ *an office*⟩ **b** to place a person in ⟨~ *a vacancy*⟩ ~ *vi* to become full [ME *fillen*, fr OE *fyllan*; akin to OE *full*] – **fill somebody's shoes** to take over sby's job, position, or responsibilities – **fill the bill** to suffice

[2]fill *n* **1a** the quantity needed to fill sthg ⟨*a ~ of pipe tobacco*⟩; *esp* as much as one can eat or drink ⟨*eat your* ~⟩ **b** as much as one can bear ⟨*I've had my ~ of them for today*⟩ **2** material used to fill a receptacle, cavity, passage, or low place

[1]filler /'filə/ *n* **1** a substance added to a product (e g to increase bulk or strength) **2** a composition or material used to fill holes before painting or varnishing **3** a piece (e g a plate) used to cover or fill a space between 2 parts of a structure [[1]FILL + [2]-ER]

[2]filler *n, pl* **fillers, filler** ☞ *Hungary* at NATIONALITY [Hung *fillér*]

[1]fillet, *chiefly NAm* **filet** /'filit/ *n* **1** a ribbon or narrow strip of material used esp as a headband **2a** a thin narrow strip of material **b(1)** a fleshy boneless piece of meat cut from the hind loin or upper hind leg ☞ MEAT **(2)** a long slice of boneless fish **3a** a junction in which the interior angle is rounded off or partly filled in **b** a usu triangular piece that partly fills such an interior **4** a narrow flat architectural moulding; *esp* the raised band between 2 flutes in a shaft ☞ ARCHITECTURE [ME *filet*, fr MF, dim. of *fil* thread – more at [3]FILE]

[2]fillet *vt* **1** to bind, provide, or adorn (as if) with a fillet **2a** to cut (meat or fish) into fillets **b** to remove the bones from (esp fish) **3** to remove inessential parts from

fillibeg /'fili,beg/ *n* a filibeg

fill in *vt* **1** to give necessary or recently acquired information to ⟨*friends* filled *him* in *on the latest gossip*⟩ **2** to add what is necessary to complete; MAKE OUT 2 ⟨fill in *this form, please*⟩ **3** to enrich (e g a design) with detail ~ *vi* to take sby's place, usu temporarily; substitute ⟨*he often* filled in *in emergencies*⟩

filling /'filing/ *n* **1** sthg used to fill a cavity, container, or depression ⟨*a ~ for a tooth*⟩ **2** a food mixture used to fill cakes, sandwiches, etc **3** *chiefly NAm* weft

'filling ,station *n* a retail establishment for selling fuel, oil, etc to motorists

[1]fillip /'filip/ *n* sthg that arouses or boosts; a stimulus ⟨*this should give a ~ to sales*⟩ [prob imit; orig sense, a blow or gesture made by flipping a finger away from the thumb]

[2]fillip *vt* to stimulate

fill out *vi* to put on flesh ~ *vt* , *chiefly NAm* FILL IN 2

filly /'fili/ *n* **1** a young female horse, usu of less than 4 years **2** a young woman; a girl – infml [ME *fyly*, fr ON *fylja*; akin to OE *fola* foal]

[1]film /film/ *n* **1a** a thin skin or membranous covering **b** (dimness of sight resulting from) an abnormal growth on or in the eye **2a** a thin layer or covering ⟨*a ~ of ice on the pond*⟩ **b(1)** a thin flexible transparent sheet (e g of plastic) used as a wrapping **(2)** a roll or strip of cellulose acetate or cellulose nitrate coated with a light-sensitive emulsion for taking photographs ☞ CAMERA **3a** a series of pictures recorded on film for the cinema and projected rapidly onto a screen so as to create the illusion of movement ☞ TELEVISION **b** a representation (e g of an incident or story) on film **c** CINEMA 2 – often pl with sing. meaning [ME *filme*, fr OE *filmen*; akin to Gk *pelma* sole of the foot, OE *fell* skin] – **filmic** /-mik/ *adj*, **filmically** *adv*, **filmy** *adj*, **filminess** *n*

[2]film *vt* to make a film of or from ~ *vi* **1** to be suitable for photographing **2** to make a film

filmography /fil'mogrəfi/ *n* a list of films of a prominent film figure or on a particular topic [*film* + *-ography* (as in *bibliography*)]

'film,setting /-,seting/ *n* photocomposition – **filmset** *adj*, **filmset** *vt*, **filmsetter** *n*

'film,strip /-,strip/ *n* a strip of film containing photographs, diagrams, or graphic matter for still projection

filo- – see FILI-

[1]**filter** /ˈfiltə/ *n* **1** a porous article or mass (e g of paper, sand, etc) through which a gas or liquid is passed to separate out matter in suspension **2** an apparatus containing a filter medium ⟨*a car's oil* ~⟩ **3a** a device or material for suppressing or minimizing waves or oscillations of certain frequencies (e g of electricity, light, or sound) **b** a transparent material (e g coloured glass) that absorbs light of certain colours selectively [ME *filtre*, fr ML *filtrum*, piece of felt used as a filter, of Gmc origin; akin to OHG *filz* felt – more at FELT]

[2]**filter** *vt* **1** to subject to the action of a filter **2** to remove by means of a filter ~ *vi* **1** to pass or move (as if) through a filter **2** to move gradually ⟨*the children* ~ed *out of assembly*⟩ **3** to become known over a period of time ⟨*the news soon* ~ed *through to the public*⟩ **4** *Br, of traffic* to turn left or right in the direction of the green arrow while the main lights are still red – **filterable** *also* **filtrable** *adj*, **filterability** /-rəˈbiləti/ *n*

ˈ**filter ˌbed** *n* a bed of sand or gravel for purifying water or sewage

ˈ**filter ˌfeeder** *n* an animal (e g a blue whale) adapted to filtering minute organisms or other food from water that passes through its system

ˌ**filter ˈtip** *n* (a cigar or cigarette with) a tip of porous material that filters the smoke before it enters the smoker's mouth – **filter-tipped** *adj*

filth /filth/ *n* **1** foul or putrid matter, esp dirt or refuse **2** sthg loathsome or vile; *esp* obscene or pornographic material [ME, fr OE *fȳlth*, fr *fūl* foul]

filthy /ˈfilthi/ *adj* **1** covered with or containing filth; offensively dirty **2** vile, obscene – **filthily** *adv*, **filthiness** *n*

[1]**filtrate** /ˈfiltrayt/ *vb* to filter [ML *filtratus*, pp of *filtrare*, fr *filtrum*]

[2]**filtrate** *n* material that has passed through a filter

filtration /filˈtraysh(ə)n/ *n* passing (as if) through a filter; *also* diffusion ⟨*the kidney produces urine by* ~⟩

fimbriate /ˈfimbri·ət, -ayt/, **fimbriated** /-aytid/ *adj* having the edge or extremity bordered by long slender projections; fringed [L *fimbriatus* fringed, fr *fimbria* fringe] – **fimbriation** /-ˈaysh(ə)n/ *n*

[1]**fin** /fin/ *n* **1** an external membranous part of an aquatic animal (e g a fish or whale) used in propelling or guiding the body ☞ ANATOMY **2a(1)** an appendage of a boat (e g a submarine) **(2)** a vertical aerofoil attached to an aircraft for directional stability ☞ FLIGHT **b** FLIPPER 1 **c** any of the projecting ribs on a radiator or an engine cylinder [ME *finn*, fr OE; akin to L *spina* thorn, spine] – **finlike** *adj*, **finned** *adj*

[2]**fin** *vb* **-nn-** *vi* to lash or move through the water (as if) using fins ~ *vt* to equip with fins

finagle /fiˈnaygl/ *vb* to use or obtain by devious and often dishonest methods – infml [perh alter. of E dial. *fainaigue* (to renege)] – **finagler** *n*

[1]**final** /ˈfienl/ *adj* **1** not to be altered or undone; conclusive **2** being the last; occurring at the end ⟨*the* ~ *chapter of a book*⟩ **3** of or relating to the ultimate purpose or result of a process ⟨*the* ~ *goal of life*⟩ [ME, fr MF, fr L *finalis*, fr *finis* boundary, end] – **finally** *adv*

[2]**final** *n* **1** a deciding match, game, trial, etc in a sport or competition; *also, pl* a round made up of these **2** the last examination in a course – usu pl

finale /fiˈnahli/ *n* **1** the last section of an instrumental musical composition **2** a final scene or number in (an act of) a public performance **3** the last and often climactic event or item in a sequence [It, fr *finale*, adj, final, fr L *finalis*]

finalist /ˈfienl·ist/ *n* a contestant in the finals of a competition

finality /fiˈnaləti, fie-/ *n* **1** the condition of being at an ultimate point, esp of development or authority **2** a fundamental fact, action, or belief [FINAL + -ITY]

final·ize, -ise /ˈfienl·iez/ *vt* **1** to put in final or finished form **2** to give final approval to – **finalization** /-ˈzaysh(ə)n/ *n*

ˌ**final ˈsolution** *n, often cap F&S the* deportation and extermination of the Jews by the Nazis during WW II [trans of G *endlösung*]

[1]**finance** /ˈfienans/ *n* **1** *pl* resources of money **2** the system that includes the circulation of money and involves banking, credit, and investment **3** the science of the management of funds **4** the obtaining of funds [ME, payment, ransom, fr MF, fr *finer* to end, pay, fr *fin* end – more at [1]FINE] – **financial** /fieˈnanshəl, fi-/ *adj*, **financially** *adv*

[2]**finance** *vt* to raise or provide money for

ˈ**finance ˌcompany** *n* a company that specializes in arranging or financing hire purchase

Financial Times Index /fieˈnanshəl, fi-/ *n* an index of prices on the London stock exchange based on the daily average price of selected lists of ordinary shares [fr its being published daily in the London newspaper, *The Financial Times*]

financier /fiˈnansi·ə, fie-/ *n* one skilled in dealing with finance or investment

finback /ˈfin,bak/ *n* FIN WHALE

finch /finch/ *n* any of numerous songbirds with a short stout conical beak adapted for crushing seeds [ME, fr OE *finc*; akin to OHG *fincho* finch, Gk *spiza* chaffinch]

[1]**find** /fiend/ *vb* **found** /fownd/ *vt* **1a** to come upon, esp accidentally; encounter **b** to meet with (a specified reception) ⟨*hoped to* ~ *favour*⟩ **2a** to come upon or discover by searching, effort, or experiment; obtain **b** to obtain by effort or management ⟨~ *the time to study*⟩ **c** to attain, reach ⟨*water* ~s *its own level*⟩ **3a** to experience, feel ⟨found *much pleasure in their company*⟩ **b** to perceive (oneself) to be in a specified place or condition ⟨found *himself in a dilemma*⟩ **c** to gain or regain the use or power of ⟨*trying to* ~ *his tongue*⟩ **d** to bring (oneself) to a realization of one's powers or of one's true vocation ⟨*he must be helped to* ~ *himself as an individual*⟩ **4** to provide, supply ⟨*the parents must* ~ *all the school fees themselves*⟩ **5** to determine and announce ⟨~ *a verdict*⟩ ~ *vi* to determine a case judicially by a verdict ⟨~ *for the defendant*⟩ [ME *finden*, fr OE *findan*; akin to OHG *findan* to find, L *pont-, pons* bridge, Gk *pontos* sea, Skt *patha* way, course] – **find fault** to criticize unfavourably

[2]**find** *n* **1** an act or instance of finding sthg, esp sthg valuable **2** sby or sthg found; *esp* a valuable object or talented person discovered ⟨*the new player was a real* ~⟩

finder /ˈfiendə/ *n* a small astronomical telescope

attached to a larger telescope for finding an object [[1]FIND + [2]-ER]

fin de siècle /'fan də see'eklə (*Fr* fɛ̃ də sjɛkl)/ *adj* (characteristic) of the close of the 19th c and esp its literary and artistic climate of sophisticated decadence and world-weariness [F, end of the century]

finding /'fiending/ *n* **1** FIND 2 **2a** the result of a judicial inquiry **b** the result of an investigation – usu pl with sing. meaning ⟨*the* ~s *of the welfare committee*⟩ **3** *pl, NAm* small tools and materials used by a craftsman

find out *vt* **1** to learn by study, observation, or search; discover **2a** to detect in an offence ⟨*the culprits were soon* found out⟩ **b** to ascertain the true character or identity of; unmask ~ *vi* to discover, learn, or verify sthg

[1]**fine** /fien/ *n* **1** a sum payable as punishment for an offence **2** a forfeiture or penalty paid to an injured party in a civil action [ME, end, settlement of a suit, sum paid as compensation, fr OF *fin,* fr L *finis* boundary, end] – **in fine** IN SHORT

[2]**fine** *vt* to punish by a fine

[3]**fine** *adj* **1** free from impurity **2a** very thin in gauge or texture ⟨~ *thread*⟩ ⟨~ *nib*⟩ **b** consisting of relatively small particles **c** very small ⟨~ *print*⟩ **d** keen, sharp ⟨*a knife with a* ~ *edge*⟩ **3a(1)** having a delicate or subtle quality ⟨*a wine of* ~ *bouquet*⟩ **(2)** subtle or sensitive in perception or discrimination ⟨*a* ~ *distinction*⟩ **b** performed with extreme care and accuracy ⟨~ *workmanship*⟩ **4** in, at, or through a fielding position in cricket behind the batsman and near an extension of the line between the wickets ☞ SPORT **5a** superior in quality, conception, or appearance; excellent ⟨*a* ~ *musician*⟩ **b** bright and sunny ⟨*the weather will be* ~ *in all parts of the country*⟩ **6** marked by or affecting often excessive elegance or refinement ⟨~ *manners*⟩ **7** very well ⟨*feel* ~⟩ **8** awful – used as an intensive ⟨*a* ~ *mess we're in!*⟩ [ME *fin,* fr OF, fr L *finis,* n, end, limit] – **fine** *adv,* **finely** *adv,* **fineness** *n*

[4]**fine** *vt* **1** to purify, clarify – often + *down* **2** to make finer in quality or size – often + *down* ~ *vi* **1** to become pure or clear ⟨*the ale will* ~⟩ **2** to become finer or smaller in lines or proportions; diminish – often + *away* or *down*

,fine 'art *n* (an) art (e g painting, sculpture, or music) concerned primarily with beauty rather than utility – usu pl

finery /'fienəri/ *n* dressy or showy clothing and jewels

fines *n pl* (very fine particles of) powdered material (e g ore) [[3]*fine*]

fines herbes /,feenz 'eəb (*Fr* fin zɛrb)/ *n pl* a mixture of finely chopped herbs used esp as a seasoning [F, lit., fine herbs]

finespun /'fienspun/ *adj* made or developed with extreme or excessive care or delicacy

[1]**finesse** /fi'nes/ *n* **1** refinement or delicacy of workmanship **2** skilful handling of a situation; adroitness **3** the withholding of one's highest card in the hope that a lower card will take the trick because the only opposing higher card is in the hand of an opponent who has already played [ME, fr MF, fr *fin*]

[2]**finesse** *vi* to make a finesse in playing cards ~ *vt* **1** to play (a card) in a finesse **2a** to bring about by finesse **b** to evade or trick by finesse

fine structure *n* the (electron) microscopic structure of an organism or its cells – **fine structural** *adj*

[1]**finger** /'fing·gə/ *n* **1** any of the 5 parts at the end of the hand or forelimb; *esp* one other than the thumb **2a** sthg that resembles a finger, esp in being long, narrow, and often tapering in shape ⟨*a* ~ *of toast*⟩ **b** a part of a glove into which a finger is inserted **3** the breadth of a finger ☞ UNIT [ME, fr OE; akin to OHG *fingar* finger] – **fingered** *adj,* **fingerlike** *adj* – **have a finger in the/every pie** to be involved or have an interest in sthg/everything – infml – **pull/take one's finger out** *Br* to start working hard; get cracking – slang

[2]**finger** *vt* **1a** to play (a musical instrument) with the fingers **b** to play (e g notes or chords) with a specific fingering **c** to mark fingerings on (a music score) as a guide in playing **2** to touch or feel with the fingers; handle **3** *chiefly NAm* to point out, identify ⟨~ed *his associates to the police*⟩ – infml ~ *vi* to touch or handle sthg ⟨~s *through the cards*⟩

'finger,board /-,bawd/ *n* the part of a stringed instrument against which the fingers press the strings to vary the pitch

'finger ,bowl *n* a small water bowl for rinsing the fingers at table

[1]**fingering** /'fing·gəring/ *n* (the marking indicating) the use or position of the fingers in sounding notes on an instrument

[2]**fingering** *n* a fine wool yarn for knitting, used esp in the manufacture of stockings [earlier *fingram,* prob alter. of OF *fin grain* fine grain]

'finger ,painting *n* (a picture produced by) spreading pigment on wet paper chiefly with the fingers

'finger,plate /-,playt/ *n* a protective plate fastened to a door usu near the handle to protect the door surface from finger marks

'finger,post /-,pohst/ *n* a signpost whose signs are or terminate in the shape of a pointing finger

'finger,print /-,print/ *n* **1** the impression of a fingertip on any surface; *esp* an ink impression of the lines upon the fingertip taken for purposes of identification **2** unique distinguishing characteristics (e g of a recording machine or infrared spectrum) **3** the characteristic pattern produced by chromatography or electrophoresis of a particular partially broken down protein or other macromolecule – **fingerprint** *vt,* **fingerprinting** *n*

'finger,stall /-,stawl/ *n* a protective cover for an injured finger

'finger,tip /-,tip/ *adj* readily accessible; being in close proximity

'finger,tips *n pl* – **at one's fingertips** instantly or readily available to one, esp because of a full knowledge of a subject

finial /'fieni·əl/ *n* **1** an ornament forming an upper extremity of a spire, gable, pinnacle, etc, esp in Gothic architecture ☞ ARCHITECTURE **2** a crowning ornament or detail (e g a decorative knob) [ME, fr *final, finial* final]

finical /'finikl/ *adj* finicky [prob fr [3]*fine*] – **finically** *adv,* **finicalness** *n*

finicking /'finiking/ *adj* finicky [alter. of *finical*]

finicky /'finiki/ *adj* **1** excessively exacting or meticulous in taste or standards; fussy **2** requiring delicate attention to detail ⟨*a* ~ *job*⟩ [alter. of *finicking*] – **finickiness** *n*

finis /'finis/ *n* the end, conclusion – used esp to mark the end of a book or film [ME, fr L]

[1]finish /'finish/ *vt* **1a** to end, terminate **b** to eat, drink, or use entirely – often + *off* or *up* **2a** to bring to completion or issue; complete, perfect ⟨~ed *her new novel*⟩ – often + *off* **b** to put a final coat or surface on **c** to neaten (the raw edge of a piece of sewing) to prevent fraying **d** to complete the schooling of (a girl), esp in the social graces **3a** to bring to an end the significance or effectiveness of ⟨*the scandal* ~ed *his career*⟩ **b** to bring about the death of ~ *vi* **1** to end, terminate **2a** to come to the end of a course, task, or undertaking in a specified manner ⟨~ed *with a song*⟩ **b** to come to the end of a relationship ⟨*David and I have* ~ed⟩ **3** to arrive, end, or come to rest in a specified position or manner – often + *up* ⟨*we* ~ed *up in Paris*⟩ ⟨*the car* ~ed *upside down in a ditch*⟩; *specif* to end a competition in a specified manner or position ⟨~ed *third in the race*⟩ [ME *finisshen*, fr MF *finiss-*, stem of *finir*, fr L *finire*, fr *finis*] – **finisher** *n* – **finish with** to end a relationship or affair with

[2]finish *n* **1a** the final stage; the end **b** the cause of one's ruin; downfall **2** the texture or appearance of a surface, esp after a coating has been applied **3** the result or product of a finishing process **4** the quality or state of being perfected, esp in the social graces

'finishing ,school /'finishing/ *n* a private school for girls that prepares its students esp for social activities

finite /'fieniet/ *adj* **1a** having definite or definable limits ⟨*a* ~ *number of possibilities*⟩ **b** subject to limitations, esp those imposed by the laws of nature ⟨~ *beings*⟩ **2** completely determinable in theory or in fact by counting, measurement, or thought ⟨*a* ~ *distance*⟩ ⟨*the* ~ *velocity of light*⟩ **3** neither infinite nor infinitesimal **4** *of a verb form* showing distinction of grammatical person and number [ME *finit*, fr L *finitus*, pp of *finire*] – **finite** *n*, **finitely** *adv*, **finiteness** *n*, **finitude** /'finityoohd/ *n*

fink /fingk/ *n*, *NAm* **1** an informer **2** a contemptible person *USE* infml [origin unknown]

Finn /fin/ *n* **1** a member of any people speaking Finnish or a Finnic language **2** a native or inhabitant of Finland [Sw *Finne*; akin to ON *finnr* Finn, OE *Finnas*, pl]

finnan haddie /,finən 'hadi/ *n*, *chiefly Scot* FINNAN HADDOCK

finnan haddock *n* a haddock that is split and smoked until pale yellow [*finnan* alter. of *findon*, fr *Findon*, village in Scotland]

Finnic /'finik/ *adj* of the Finns

[1]Finnish /'finish/ *adj* (characteristic) of Finland

[2]Finnish *n* a Finno-Ugric language of Finland, Karelia, and parts of Sweden and Norway ☞ LANGUAGE

Finno-Ugrian /,finoh 'yoohgri·ən/ *adj or n* Finno-Ugric

,Finno-'Ugric /'yoohgrik/ *adj* **1** of any of various peoples of N and E Europe and NW Siberia speaking related languages **2** of or constituting a subfamily of the Uralic family of languages comprising various languages spoken in Hungary, Lapland, Finland, Estonia, and the NW USSR – **Finno-Ugric** *n*

finny /'fini/ *adj* **1** having fins **2** relating to or being fish – chiefly poetic

fino /'feenoh/ *n*, *pl* **finos** a light-coloured dry sherry [Sp, fr *fino* fine, fr L *finis*, n, end, limit]

'fin ,whale *n* a large common rorqual

fiord, fjord /fjawd, 'fee,awd/ *n* a narrow inlet of the sea between cliffs (e g in Norway) [Norw *fjord*, fr ON *fjörthr* – more at FORD]

'fipple ,flute /'fipl/ *n* a tubular wind instrument characterized mainly by a whistle mouthpiece and finger holes [perh akin to ON *flipi* horse's lip]

fir /fuh/ *n* (the wood of) any of various related evergreen trees of the pine family that have flattish leaves and erect cones [ME, fr OE *fyrh*; akin to OHG *forha* fir, L *quercus* oak]

[1]fire /fie·ə/ *n* **1a** the phenomenon of combustion manifested in light, flame, and heat **b(1)** burning passion or emotion; ardour **(2)** liveliness of imagination; inspiration **2** fuel in a state of combustion (e g in a fireplace or furnace) **3a** a destructive burning (e g of a building or forest) **b** a severe trial or ordeal **4** brilliance, luminosity ⟨*the* ~ *of a diamond*⟩ **5** the discharge of firearms **6** *Br* a small usu gas or electric domestic heater [ME, fr OE *fȳr*; akin to OHG *fiur* fire, Gk *pyr*] – **fireless** *adj* – **on fire** eager, burning – **under fire** under attack

[2]fire *vt* **1a** to set on fire; kindle; *also* to ignite ⟨~ *a rocket engine*⟩ **b(1)** to give life or spirit to; inspire ⟨~d *the poet's imagination*⟩ **(2)** to fill with passion; inflame **c** to light up as if by fire **2a** to drive out or away (as if) by fire – usu + *out* **b** to dismiss from a position **3a(1)** to cause to explode **(2)** to propel (as if) from a gun ⟨~ *a rocket*⟩ **b** to throw with speed; hurl **4** to apply fire or fuel to: e g **a** to process by applying heat **b** to feed or serve the fire of ~ *vi* **1a** to catch fire; ignite **b** *of an internal-combustion engine* to undergo ignition of the explosive charge **2** to become filled with excitement or anger – often + *up* **3a** to discharge a firearm **b** to emit or let fly an object – **firer** *n*

'fire,arm /-,ahm/ *n* a weapon from which a shot is discharged by gunpowder – usu used only with reference to small arms

fire away *vi* to go ahead; begin – usu imper; infml

'fire,back /-,bak/ *n* the back lining of a furnace or fireplace

'fire,ball /-,bawl/ *n* **1** a large brilliant meteor **2** BALL LIGHTNING **3** the bright cloud of vapour and dust created by a nuclear explosion **4** a highly energetic person – infml

'fire ,blight *n* a destructive highly infectious disease of apples, pears, and related fruits caused by a bacterium

'fire,bomb /-,bom/ *n* an incendiary bomb – **firebomb** *vt*

'fire,box /-,boks/ *n* a chamber (e g of a furnace or steam boiler) that contains a fire

'fire,brand /-,brand/ *n* **1** a piece of burning material, esp wood **2** one who creates unrest or strife; an agitator, troublemaker

'fire,break /-,brayk/ *n* a strip of cleared or unplanted land intended to check a forest or grass fire

'fire,brick /-,brik/ *n* a brick that is resistant to high temperatures and is used in furnaces, fireplaces, etc

'fire bri,gade *n* an organization for preventing or extinguishing fires; *esp* one maintained in Britain by local government

'fire,bug /-,bug/ *n* a pyromaniac, fire-raiser – infml

'fire,clay /-,klay/ *n* clay that is resistant to high

temperatures and is used esp for firebricks and crucibles

'fire con,trol *n* the planning, preparation, and delivery of gunfire

'fire,crest /-,krest/ *n* a small European bird that has a red cap and conspicuous black and white stripes about the eyes [fr its bright red crest]

'fire,damp /-,damp/ *n* (the explosive mixture of air with) a combustible mine gas that consists chiefly of methane

'fire de,partment *n, NAm* FIRE BRIGADE

'fire,dog /-,dog/ *n* an andiron

'fire ,drill *n* a practice drill in extinguishing or escaping from fires

'fire-,eater *n* **1** a performer who pretends to eat fire **2** one who is quarrelsome or violent – **fire-eating** *adj*

'fire ,engine *n* a vehicle equipped with fire-fighting equipment

'fire e,scape *n* a device, esp an external staircase, for escape from a burning building

'fire ex,tinguisher *n* an apparatus for putting out fires with chemicals

'fire,fight /-,fiet/ *n* an often spontaneous exchange of fire between opposing military units

'fire ,fighter *n* sby who fights fires – **fire fighting** *n*

'fire,fly /-,flie/ *n* any of various night-flying beetles that produce a bright intermittent light

'fire,guard /-,gahd/ *n* a protective metal framework placed in front of an open fire

'fire ,irons *n pl* utensils (e g tongs, poker, and shovel) for tending a household fire

'fire,light /-,liet/ *n* the light of a fire, esp of one in a fireplace

'fire ,lighter *n* a piece of inflammable material used to help light a fire (e g in a grate)

'fire,lock /-,lok/ *n* **1** (a gun with) a gunlock in which a slow match ignites the powder charge **2a** a flintlock **b** WHEEL LOCK

'fireman /-mən/ *n, pl* **firemen** **1** sby employed to extinguish fires **2** sby who tends or feeds fires or furnaces

'fire ,opal *n* a girasol

'fire,place /-,plays/ *n* a usu framed opening made in a chimney to hold a fire; a hearth

'fire-,plug *n* a hydrant

'fire,power /-,powə/ *n* the capacity (e g of a military unit) to deliver effective fire on a target

'fire,proof /-,proohf/ *adj* proof against or resistant to fire; *also* heatproof ⟨~ *dishes*⟩ – **fireproof** *vt*, **fireproofing** *n*

'fire-,raising *n, Br* arson – **fire-raiser** *n*

'fire ,screen *n* **1** a light often ornamental screen placed in front of a fireplace as a heat shield **2** *chiefly NAm* a fireguard

'fire ,ship *n* a ship carrying combustible materials or explosives sent among the enemy's ships or works to set them on fire

'fire,side /-,sied/ *n* **1** a place near the fire or hearth **2** home – **fireside** *adj*

'fire ,station *n* a building housing fire apparatus and usu firemen

'fire,stone /-,stohn/ *n* a stone that will endure high heat

'fire ,storm *n* a huge uncontrollable fire that is started typically by bombs and that causes and is kept in being by an inrush of high winds

'fire,trap /-,trap/ *n* a building difficult to escape from in case of fire

'fire-,watcher *n* sby who watches for the outbreak of fire (e g during an air raid) – **fire-watching** *n*

'fire,water /-,wawtə/ *n* strong alcoholic drink – infml

'fire,weed /-,weed/ *n* ROSEBAY WILLOWHERB

'fire,wood /-,wood/ *n* wood cut for fuel

'fire,work /-,wuhk/ *n* **1** a device for producing a striking display (e g of light or noise) by the combustion of explosive or inflammable mixtures **2** *pl* a display of fireworks **3** *pl* **a** a display of temper or intense conflict **b** PYROTECHNICS 2

firing /'fie·əring/ *n* **1** the process of baking and fusing ceramic products by the application of heat in a kiln **2** firewood, fuel [[2]FIRE + [2]-ING]

'firing ,line *n* **1** a line from which fire is delivered against a target; *also* the troops stationed in a firing line **2** the forefront of an activity, esp one involving risk or difficulty – esp in *in the firing line*

'firing ,squad *n* a detachment detailed to fire a salute at a military burial or carry out an execution

firkin /'fuhkin/ *n* **1** a small wooden vessel or cask of usu 9 gall capacity **2** any of various British units of capacity usu equal to a quarter of a barrel (about 41l) [ME, deriv of MD *veerdel* fourth]

[1]**firm** /fuhm/ *adj* **1a** securely or solidly fixed in place **b** not weak or uncertain; vigorous ⟨*a* ~ *handshake*⟩ **c** having a solid or compact structure that resists stress or pressure **2** not subject to change, unsteadiness, or disturbance; steadfast ⟨*a* ~ *price*⟩ **3** indicating firmness or resolution ⟨*a* ~ *mouth*⟩ [ME *ferm*, fr MF, fr L *firmus*; akin to Gk *thronos* chair, throne] – **firm** *adv*, **firmish** *adj*, **firmly** *adv*, **firmness** *n*

[2]**firm** *vt* **1** to make solid, compact, or firm ⟨~ing *his grip on the racket*⟩ **2** to put into final form; settle ⟨~ *a contract*⟩ **3** to support, strengthen ⟨*help* ~ *up the franc*⟩ ~ *vi* **1** to become firm; harden **2** to recover from a decline; improve ⟨*the market* ~ed *slightly*⟩ *USE* (*vt 2 & 3, vi*) often + *up*

[3]**firm** *n* a business partnership not usu recognized as a legal person distinct from the members composing it; *broadly* any business unit or enterprise [G *firma*, fr It, signature, deriv of L *firmare* to make firm, confirm, fr *firmus*]

firmament /'fuhməmənt/ *n* the vault or arch of the sky; the heavens [ME, fr LL & L; LL *firmamentum*, fr L, support, fr *firmare*] – **firmamental** /-'mentl/ *adj*

firn /fiən/ *n* névé [G, fr G dial., relating to the previous year, fr OHG *firni* old; akin to OE *fyrn, firn* former, ancient]

[1]**first** /fuhst/ *adj* **1** preceding all others in time, order, or importance: e g **a** earliest **b** being the lowest forward gear or speed of a motor vehicle **c** relating to or having the (most prominent and) usu highest part among a group of instruments or voices **2** least, slightest ⟨*hasn't the* ~ *idea what to do*⟩ [ME, fr OE *fyrst*; akin to OHG *furist* first, OE *faran* to go – more at FARE] – **at first hand** directly from the original source

[2]**first** *adv* **1** before anything else; at the beginning ⟨*came* ~ *and left last*⟩ ⟨~ *of all we had cocktails*⟩ **2** for the first time **3** in preference to sthg else ⟨*I'll see him dead* ~⟩

[3]**first** *n, pl* (*2a*) **first,** (*2b, c, & d*) **firsts** **1** ☞ NUMBER **2** sthg or sby that is first: e g **a** the first occurrence or item of a kind ⟨*was one of the* ~ *to know*⟩ **b** the

first and lowest forward gear or speed of a motor vehicle **c** the winning place in a contest **d first, first class** *often cap* the highest level of British honours degree ⟨*got a ~ in history*⟩ **– at first** at the beginning; initially **– from the first** from the beginning

ˌfirst ˈaid *n* **1** emergency care or treatment given to an ill or injured person before proper medical aid can be obtained **2** temporary emergency measures taken to alleviate a problem before a permanent solution can be found – **first-aider** *n*

ˌfirst ˈbase *n, chiefly NAm* the first step or stage in a course of action ⟨*the plan never got to ~*⟩

ˌfirstˈborn *adj* born before all others; eldest – **firstborn** *n*

ˌfirst ˈcause *n* the self-created source of all causality – compare PRIME MOVER 1

[1]ˌfirst ˈclass *n* the first or highest group in a classification: e g **a** the highest of usu 3 classes of travel accommodation **b** FIRST 2d – **first-class** *adj*

[2]first class *adv* **1** in the highest quality of accommodation ⟨*travel ~*⟩ **2** as mail that is delivered as fast as possible ⟨*send a letter ~*⟩

ˌfirst ˌday ˈcover *n* a special envelope with a newly issued postage stamp postmarked on the first day of issue

ˌfirst-deˌgree ˈburn *n* a mild burn characterized by heat, pain, and reddening of the burned surface but without blistering or charring of tissues – compare SECOND-DEGREE BURN, THIRD-DEGREE BURN

first estate *n, often cap F&E* the 1st of the traditional political estates; *specif* the clergy

ˌfirst ˈfloor *n* **1** *Br* the floor immediately above the ground floor **2** *NAm* GROUND FLOOR

ˌfirstˈfruits *n pl* **1** agricultural produce offered to God in thanksgiving **2** the earliest products or results of an enterprise

ˌfirstˈhand *adj* of or coming directly from the original source – **firsthand** *adv*

ˌfirst ˈlady *n, often cap F&L* the wife or hostess of a US president or state governor

ˌfirst lieuˈtenant *n* ☞ RANK

firstling /ˈfuhstling/ *n* **1** the first of a class or kind **2** the first produce or result of sthg *USE* usu pl; fml

ˈfirstly /-li/ *adv* in the first place; first

first name *n* the name that stands first in a person's full name

ˌfirst ˈnight *n* the night on which a theatrical production is first performed at a given place

ˌfirst ofˈfender *n* sby convicted of an offence for the first time

ˌfirst ˈperson *n* (a member of) a set of linguistic forms (e g verb forms and pronouns) referring to the speaker or writer of the utterance in which they occur

ˌfirst ˈpost *n, Br* the first of 2 bugle calls sounded at the hour of retiring in a military camp

ˌfirst-ˈrate *adj* of the first or greatest order of size, importance, or quality – **first-rater** *n*

first reading *n* the first submitting of a bill before a legislative assembly ☞ LAW

ˌfirst reˈfusal *n* REFUSAL 2

first school *n* a primary school for children between 5 and 8

first sergeant *n* ☞ RANK

ˌfirst-ˈstring *adj* being a regular member of a team, group, etc as distinguished from a substitute

first water *n* **1** the purest lustre – used with reference to gems **2** the highest grade, degree, or quality ⟨*a fool of the ~* – Thomas Wolfe⟩

firth /fuhth/ *n* a sea inlet or estuary (e g in Scotland) [ME, fr ON *fjörthr* – more at FORD]

fisc /fisk/ *n* a state or royal treasury [L *fiscus*]

[1]fiscal /ˈfiskl/ *adj* of taxation, public revenues, or public debt ⟨*~ policy*⟩ [L *fiscalis*, fr *fiscus* basket, treasury; akin to Gk *pithos* wine jar] – **fiscally** *adv*

[2]fiscal *n* a procurator-fiscal

[1]fish /fish/ *n, pl* **fish, fishes 1a** an aquatic animal – usu in combination ⟨*star*fish⟩ ⟨*cuttle*fish⟩ **b** (the edible flesh of) any of numerous cold-blooded aquatic vertebrates that typically have an elongated scaly body, limbs, when present, in the form of fins, and gills ☞ EVOLUTION, FOOD **2** a person; *esp* a fellow – usu derog ⟨*a queer ~*⟩ [ME, fr OE *fisc*; akin to OHG *fisc* fish, L *piscis*] – **fishless** *adj*, **fishlike** *adj* – **fish out of water** a person who is out of his/her proper sphere or element

[2]fish *vi* **1** to try to catch fish **2** to seek sthg by roundabout means ⟨~ing *for compliments*⟩ **3a** to search for sthg underwater ⟨*~ for pearls*⟩ **b** to search (as if) by groping or feeling ⟨~ing *around under the bed for his shoes*⟩ ~ *vt* **1a** to (try to) catch (fish in) ⟨*~ the stream*⟩ ⟨*~ salmon*⟩ **b** to use (e g a net, type of rod, or bait) in fishing **2** to draw *out* as if fishing *USE* (*vi 2 & 3*) usu + *for*; (*vi 2 & 3b, vt 2*) infml – **fisher** *n*

[3]fish *n* a piece of wood or iron fastened alongside another member to strengthen it [*fish* (to mend), fr F *ficher* to fix, fr (assumed) VL *figicare*, fr L *figere*]

ˈfishˌbowl /-ˌbohl/ *n* a bowl for keeping live fish

fisherfolk /ˈfishəˌfohk/ *n pl in constr* people who live in a community that is dependent on fishing

ˈfisherman /-mən/ *n* **1** *fem* **ˈfisherˌwoman** one who engages in fishing as an occupation or for pleasure **2** a ship used in commercial fishing

fishery /ˈfishəri/ *n* **1** the activity or business of catching fish and other sea animals **2** a place or establishment for catching fish and other sea animals

ˈfish-ˌeye *adj* being, having, or produced by a wide-angle photographic lens that has a highly curved protruding front and covers an angle of about 180°

ˈfish ˌfarm *n* a tract of water used for the artificial cultivation of an aquatic life form (e g fishes)

ˌfish ˈfinger *n* a small oblong of fish coated with breadcrumbs

ˈfish ˌhawk *n* OSPREY 1

ˈfishˌhook /-ˌhook/ *n* a barbed hook used on the end of a line for catching fish

fishing /ˈfishing/ *n* the sport or business of or a place for catching fish

ˈfish ˌkettle *n* a usu deep long oval vessel used for cooking fish

ˈfish ˌladder *n* a series of pools arranged like steps by which fish can pass over a dam while going upstream

ˈfish ˌlouse *n* any of various small crustaceans parasitic on fish

ˈfish ˌmeal *n* ground dried fish used as fertilizer and animal food

ˈfishˌmonger /-ˌmung·gə/ *n, chiefly Br* a retail fish dealer

ˈfishˌnet /-ˌnet/ *n* a coarse open-mesh fabric

Main principles

First Aid consists of simple measures to prevent injury or illness from becoming worse until medical aid can be obtained. It aims to keep the patient in the best possible condition until responsibility is taken over by a doctor or nurse.
Treat the casualty where he/she is and move only if in dangerous surroundings, such as fumes, fire or flood.
Always handle the patient gently and reassure by talking.
Assess the general situation and establish your priorities of action.

1 Be calm, take charge, clear away a crowd, but give specific jobs to those who remain to help.
2 Diagnose what is the matter by obtaining a history of the accident, listening to the casualty's symptoms, and examining him/her for signs.
3 Render the correct first aid treatment.
4 Send the casualty to a doctor, hospital or his home.
5 Report clearly the place, type of accident, and what you have done.

Priorities

● BREATHING If breathing has stopped, make sure the mouth is clear of debris, tilt back the head to open and straighten the air passage to the lungs. Pinch the nostrils closed and blow your own breath gently through the casualty's mouth into the lungs at your own breathing rate.
● BLEEDING Blood loss must be stopped promptly, but strategy depends on the site of bleeding. Rapid blood loss is more severe in its effect than a gradual loss. Loss of large amounts deprives vital organs and produces a state of shock.

Asthma attacks
These occur when the bronchial tubes are constricted, and breathing out becomes very difficult, producing wheezing. Sit the patient up with support for the back. Loosen tight clothes which might restrict movement of the chest. Allow fresh air and ventilation. Reduce anxiety and give any medicines that have been prescribed for the emergency.

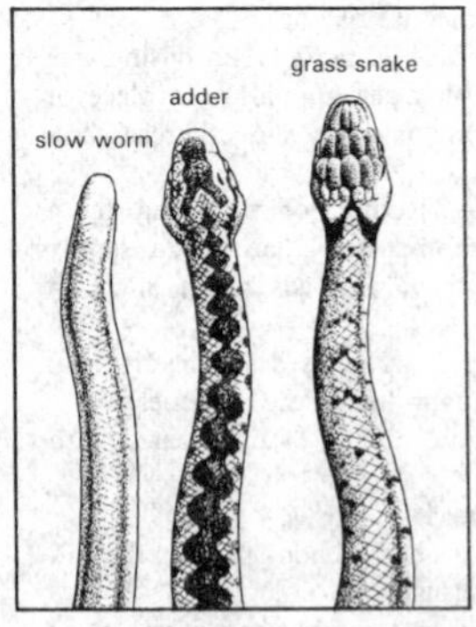

Bites and stings
If you can see it remove a bee sting gently with tweezers. Apply the tweezers as near the skin as possible, in order not to squeeze venom in. Apply an alkali or antihistamine cream to bee or wasp stings. Stings in the mouth or throat can be dangerous, and multiple stings, or a sting into a vein, should be seen by a doctor.

Snake bites
The only poisonous snake in the UK is the adder (viper).
Lay the patient down and tell him/her not to move about. Reassure him/her, and wash the wound if possible with soap and water.
Apply a dry dressing, and immobilize limb. Get the patient to hospital as quickly as possible.

Bleeding
Lay the casualty down if possible.
Elevate the injured part unless a fracture is suspected.
Loosen tight clothing, and expose the wound.

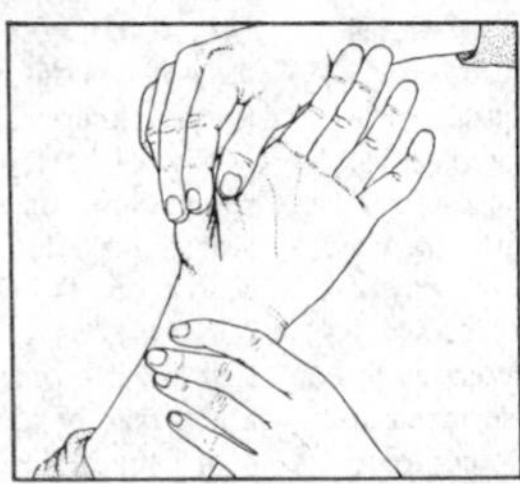

Control haemorrhage by pressure on the sides of the wound, or by direct pressure over a clean dressing.

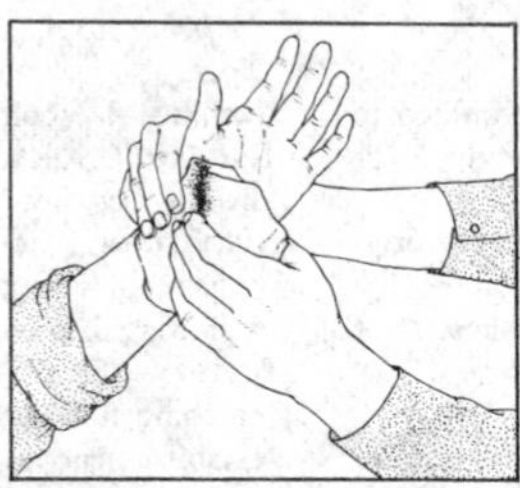

Apply sufficient sterile dressing into the depth of the wound until it projects above it, and cover with adequate padding, and bandage firmly.
If bleeding continues, add more pads, but do not disturb the original dressing, or any clots.

If a foreign body like glass is embedded in the wound, apply pads round the wound until high enough for a bandage to be applied across them so as to avoid pressing on the projecting foreign body or bone.

Apply bandages firmly enough to stop bleeding, but not so as to stop the circulation along a limb.
Immobilize the injured part, keep the casualty warm and comfortable and get him/her to hospital as quickly as possible.

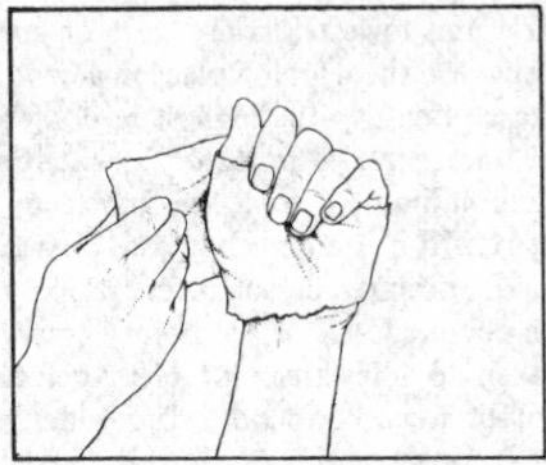

Pressure points
Pressure points are places where firm pressure upon an artery against the underlying bone will stop blood passing to a wound. This method is used when direct pressure on the wound cannot be applied.

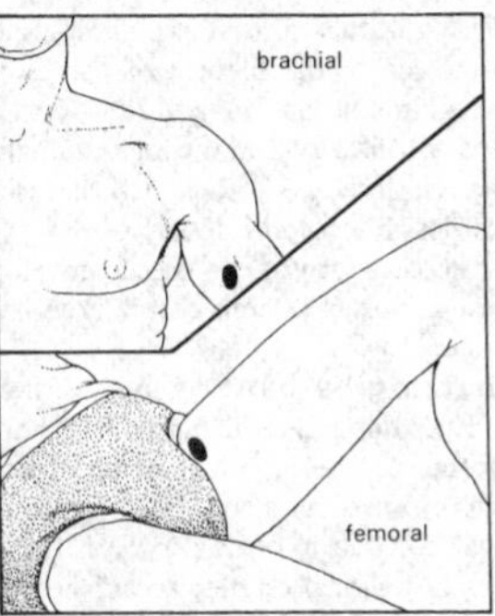

The brachial point lies in the upper arm below the belly of the biceps muscle, or where the seam of a man's jacket runs. Pressure on the underlying humerus reduces flow, if the elbow or lower arm are injured.
The femoral pressure point is found in the middle of the upper thigh and needs the pressure of both thumbs to stop haemorrhage in the lower limb.

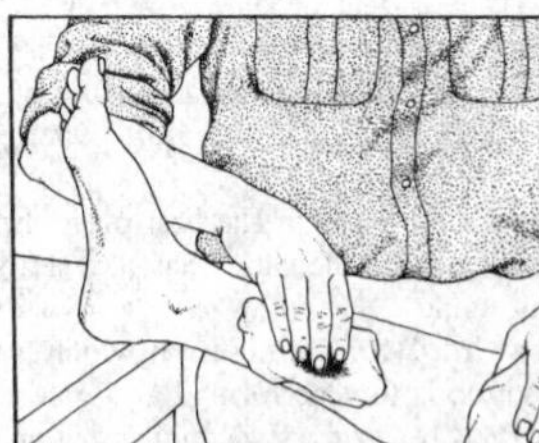

Treatment of wounds
Wash your hands if possible. Elevate the limb and protect the wound with a sterile swab. Gently clean surrounding skin and dry it with swabs of cotton wool used once only and wipe away from the wound. Then apply a sterile dressing and keep it in place with bandages or adhesive strapping.

Stop bleeding
Slight bleeding comes from injured capillary vessels and wells up as red blood. It is easily controlled by gentle pressure. Venous blood is darker, and pours from a wound, but stops immediately on elevation. Arterial bleeding is bright red and issues from a wound in jets in time with the heart beat. Elevation and firm pressure are usually effective.

Rest and keep wound elevated
This position ensures the maximal supply of blood to the brain and other vital organs while the patient is at rest.

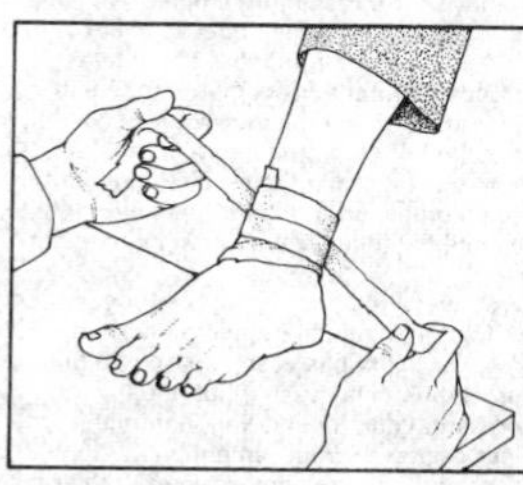

Bandage the wound
Bandages are wound with even firm pressure, and serve the purpose of keeping dressings in place and maintaining sufficient pressure to prevent further bleeding.

Nose bleeds
Sit the patient up with the head tilted slightly forward so that blood is not swallowed.
Get him to press firmly the side that is bleeding for 10 minutes, or pinch both nostrils while the patient breathes through the mouth for the same time.
Let him/her rest near an open window afterwards, with instructions not to blow the nose, or sniff.

Burns and scalds
These are wounds caused by dry or moist heat, and dangerous in proportion to their area. Danger to life arises from the greater chance of infection compared to most other wounds, and from shock through loss of plasma.

TREATMENT
1 Extinguish flames by quickest method: douse with water or smother with a blanket, coat, rug, etc.

2 Place the affected part under cold running water, or immerse in cold water.

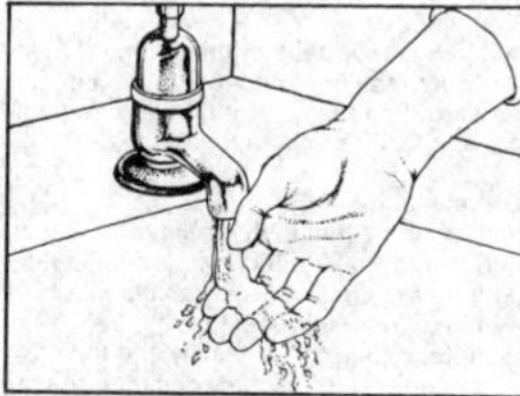

3 Do not remove burnt clothing since it is rendered sterile by heat. Do not burst blisters.

4 Remove at once rings, belts, or bangles, or anything that may cause constriction as the part begins to swell.

5 Lay the patient down, and cover the burnt area with sterile dressing, keeping the part elevated. Particular care is required not to contaminate a deep burn.

6 Guard against shock.

Chemical burns
Remove contaminated clothing, avoiding burning yourself.
Place the burned area under running water to dilute and wash off a strong acid or alkali.
Then treat according to the general treatment for burns.
Where the eye is affected:
Lead the patient to a tap or sink. Place the head under running water pulling the eyelids apart.

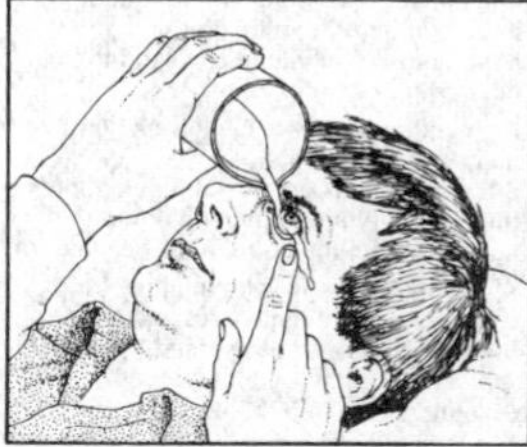

Alternatively, lay the patient down, and freely irrigate the open eye with water. Apply a pad and bandage, and seek medical aid.

Car and road accidents
Be clear about your priorities:

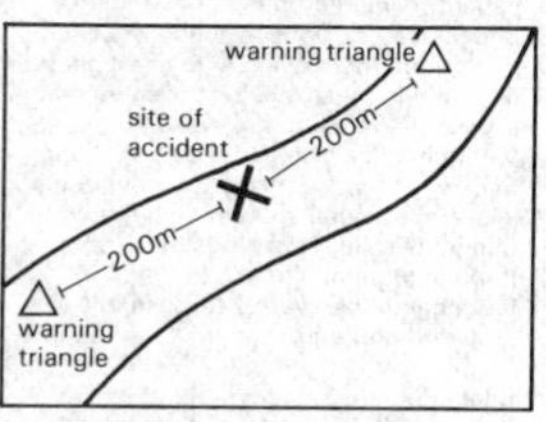

1 Warn other traffic by placing red warning triangles or similar items at a distance of 200 metres from accident in both directions. Switch on your hazard flashers.

2 Switch off engine and lights.
Disconnect battery if possible. Give a NO SMOKING order.
Try to ascertain extent of injured and injuries, including any thrown clear.
Only move occupants if car is on fire or if they are not breathing.

3 Send for ambulance service and police.
State:
Where to come
How many patients
The nature of the injuries
Whether specialist equipment is required, eg cutting gear.

ACCIDENT PROCEDURE

● **Breathing**
A crash victim is often unconscious and cannot breathe because of a bend or constriction in the airway. Open airway by extending the head backwards.
Check for obstruction of airway and relieve it, eg remove false teeth.
If still not breathing after clearing airway, pinch nose, hold head back, and inflate lungs by blowing.

● **Bleeding**
Press sides of wound together.
Elevate if possible.
Continue pressure over wound with pad and firm bandage.
Pressure point control of haemorrhage if pressure over wound impractical.

● **Unconsciousness**
Try to keep the unconscious patient breathing until ambulance arrives.
Keep the airway open and clear.
Loosen tight clothing and turn into the recovery position.

● **Shock**
Shock can result from loss of blood to the brain. In severe cases the patient will die unless he/she receives a blood transfusion. Mention a state of shock when calling for an ambulance.

● **Fractures**
Use commonsense methods of immobilization eg
Upper limb: use arm sling or pin sleeve to lapel
Lower limb: tie to sound leg, and pad between knees and ankles.

● **Wounds**
Stop bleeding and cover wound with sterile or clean dressing.
Immobilize.

● **Chest injury**
Fractured rib: if on one side only, incline patient to injured side.
Both sides: sit up with support to back.
Explosion: internal injury to chest causes difficulty in breathing. Sit patient up with support. Give oxygen if available.
Victim may be blue and cough up blood.
Sucking wound: caused by penetrating injury into pleural space.
Danger is collapse of lungs by air entering through wound.
Place hand over wound to close it, and seal with dressing.

Choking
Act immediately. Instruct patient to take a deep breath through the nose and give his strongest cough to move obstruction like a piston. Be ready to remove any obstruction (a crust, false teeth) with your finger.

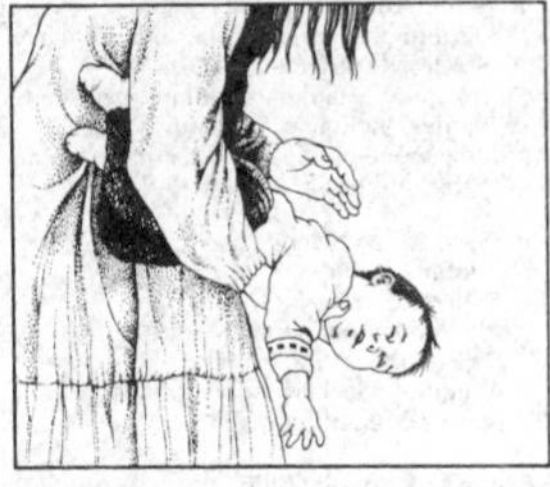

Baby: hold upside down and smack on the back to loosen a swallowed object.

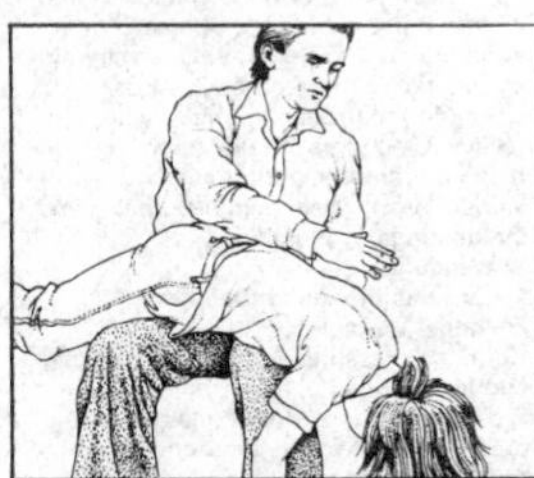

Child: place across the lap inclined down at 45 degrees, and strike smartly between the shoulder blades.

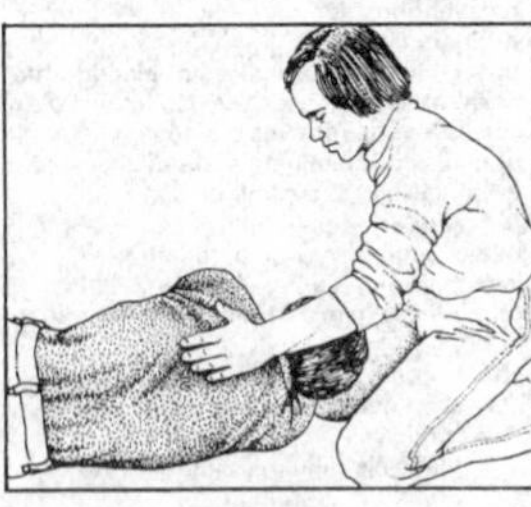

Adult: If he collapses, keep him on his side, and strike between the shoulder blades.

If obstruction remains, begin resuscitation. Remember that the tongue can obstruct the airway in unconscious patients.
If able to stand get behind him with your arms around his waist, hands gripped just below his ribs and make a firm hug inwards and upwards.

Cramp
Cramp is a painful often violent muscular contraction.
It may appear during exercise especially after sweating heavily, or after loss of body fluid through diarrhoea and vomiting. It is not dangerous except in circumstances such as swimming in cold water.
First aid is to stretch the muscle—for instance, in the back of the thigh, straighten the knee and swing the leg forward. Replacement of fluid and salt will prevent further attacks.

Diabetes
A diabetic treated with insulin may suffer from sugar deficiency:
1 if he/she does not eat within a short time after the injection.
2 if he/she exercises heavily and the sugar reserves become depleted. As the brain is deprived of sugar, behaviour may become erratic, as if drunk. The colour is pale, the patient sweats and the hands shake.

While he/she is conscious the treatment is to give the patient sugar, jam, chocolate, or honey with a little water. Repeat this after 10 minutes.
If unconscious, put the patient in the recovery position, give nothing by mouth, and send for medical help.

Ear – object in
Usually the victim is a child. Do not try to remove object, for it usually gets pushed further in.
When a small fly or insect has entered the ear, it can be floated out by olive oil or water, with the patient lying down.
Children require firm handling or they may panic.

Electric shock
Never touch the patient until the current has been switched off.
If the switch-off point is not obvious remove the patient from contact with the electric current by means of a dry non-conducting object, eg walking stick, roll of newspaper, chair, or folded garment.
The patient may require resuscitation.
Deep burns may require dressing.
Keep under observation and send to hospital.
High voltage currents may spark across a gap up to 6 metres.
If the casualty is on or near a pylon, phone the electricity authority, and do not approach until the current has been cut off.
A patient struck by lightning may be unconscious and require resuscitation.
Burns may need to be dressed.

Epileptic attack
The patient suddenly falls to the ground unconscious, sometimes emitting a high pitched cry. On the ground he/she goes rigid and holds his/her breath and may go blue. Later he/she makes regular convulsive movements, which may injure hands, feet or the tongue.

1 Remove from danger of fire, glass, bookcase, etc.
2 Protect the feet and arms with cushioning.
3 Place between the back teeth a soft gag, eg handkerchief, coat lapel, to prevent biting the tongue.
4 Control the arm and leg movements, kneeling astride the casualty, to prevent injury. Do not try and prevent these movements entirely, only reduce their force.
5 If attacks are repeated fetch medical aid.
6 After the convulsions have stopped, place in recovery position.

Eye injury
Minor Cover eye with a loose pad, and retain with sellotape. Do not insert drops or ointment. These may introduce infection.
Major Lay patient down on his back. Cover both eyes with clean material to prevent eye movements. Remove to hospital in this position, and continue to reassure the patient.

Foreign body in eye
Enquire how and what entered the eye. Low velocity particles like dust can be removed. Sit the patient in a good light. Pull down the lower lid and use the moistened corner of a handkerchief to remove the particle. If the object is under the upper lid, pull the upper lid over the lower lid twice. If this fails to remove it, stand behind the head, instruct the patient to look down and hinge the eyelid over a matchstick, and wipe away.
Particles lodged in the clear window of the eye (cornea) should be left, the eye covered with a pad until seen by a doctor.

Fractures
A fracture must be suspected when a forceful injury has been applied to a bone or joint. Pain is usually, but not always, present. Look for swelling, deformity, loss of power or movement.
A closed fracture does not break the skin.
An open fracture involves a wound so that bacteria can enter through the skin.
A complicated fracture is one where the sharp broken bone end damages other structures.
The aim of first aid is to prevent the condition becoming worse by immobilizing the fractured area.
1 Treat the patient where he is.
2 Deal first with the haemorrhage, and dress any wound temporarily.
3 Tell the patient not to move.
4 Immobilize the fracture with splints and bandages.
5 Pad between bony points, to prevent friction, and fill out hollows to prevent movement.
6 Splints should be long enough to pass beyond the joint above and below a fracture. In certain fractures of the lower limb, the uninjured limb can be used as a splint, or the trunk and leg for an arm.
7 Bandages should maintain the splint in position, and should therefore be firmly tied, but not so tight as to restrict the blood circulation.

This aspect of first aid requires special training.

Note Patients with injuries to back and neck should not be moved. Inexpert bending or twisting can complicate a spinal fracture by damaging the spinal cord. Ask the patient if he can move his fingers and toes, and feel his extremities. Note this. Maintain warmth by covering with a rug, coat, or blanket until experienced first aiders take over.

Bandages and splints
Splints may be improvised from any rigid material but they should always be padded. Neckties and belts may be used as bandages but they must not be tied so tightly as to interfere with the circulation. Never tie a bandage over the site of a fracture.

Strain
A strain is a muscle injury arising from fibres being over-stretched, so that some have torn. Treatment is by firm supporting bandaging, followed by rhythmic movement.

Sprain
This occurs near a joint. A severe sprain may be difficult to distinguish from a fracture and indeed a flake of bone may be lifted. If in doubt, treat as for a fracture. The commonest sprain is at the ankle. Swelling and pain can be reduced by applying a cold compress with the leg elevated above the horizontal. Later, apply a firm elastic bandage over a compressible pad.

Gases and fire hazards

Smoke
Smoke rapidly suffocates. Take precautions before entering smoke-filled room. If no respirator is available, take a deep breath and enter area keeping as low as possible to remove casualties who are easily accessible. Cover nose and mouth with wetted handkerchief.

Poisonous gases
Take a deep breath and hold it.
Pass quickly into room and remove casualty to safety.
If possible open doors and windows. The use of a lifeline is vital before entering a gas-filled chamber, and the help of others is usually required.

Head injuries
Blows to the head can cause fractures of the skull and/or brain damage.

Skull fracture
A fracture may not be serious unless a portion has been depressed so that it lies on or penetrates the brain underneath. A fracture of the side of the skull may cause bleeding from blood vessels which run in grooves on the inside of the skull.
Fracture of the base of the skull (the part on which the brain rests) may be suspected if there is bleeding around an eye, through an ear, or down the nose, especially if mixed with watery fluid.

Brain damage
Concussion occurs when the brain, which is soft, is shaken violently inside the rigid bones of the skull. It may last for a few seconds, or for several hours, for which time there is a subsequent loss of memory. Various degrees of disturbed consciousness may be shown.

Compression
Consciousness is gradually lost over a period of time, due to brain swelling, bleeding within the skull, or from a depressed skull fracture. This is a very serious condition which as it advances alters the size of the pupils, their reaction to light, and eventually affects the breathing which becomes thick and noisy. Such patients must not be left. Their condition should be constantly monitored, and they must be removed to special units in hospital. During transport provide and maintain a clear airway, remove dentures, clear saliva or mucus from the mouth and throat. If breathing stops, commence respiratory resuscitation at once. There are often other injuries, and these should be searched for and treated. Never attempt to give an unconscious patient any food or fluids by mouth.

Heart attack
This occurs most commonly in middle-aged men, and women over the age of 50. Severe gripping pain, often described as crushing, is felt in the centre of the chest. It may spread into the left arm, or up into the neck. The patient may be pale, with blueness of the lips, and sweating. The pulse beats quickly and rapidly, and may become irregular and faint. Breathing may be difficult, or even very wet and bubbling, with coughing and froth in the mouth. Sometimes breathlessness and collapse may be the only effects.
Keep the patient at rest. Provide a chair, loosen tight clothing, and send for medical aid. Keep crowds away, and ensure a supply of fresh air. Cover with a blanket for comfort and protection against cold.

Heat (and cold)

Heat exhaustion
Where copious sweating occurs in a hot atmosphere, the loss of fluid and minerals from the body may produce a state of weakness and collapse. The face is pale and ashen, the skin is moist, and the pulse is fast and weak. Muscles may go into cramp.
Put the patient at rest in a cool place, in light clothes, and give him/her fruit juice, to which a pinch of salt has been added, to drink slowly.

Heatstroke
Where the ambient temperature is very hot, and the usual means of regulating body temperature by sweating and breathing off water vapour are insufficient, heatstroke may occur. This is a dangerous condition. The face is red, the skin hot and dry, the pulse is rapid and bounding, and the temperature may reach abnormal heights. Urgent measures are required to bring down the temperature – strip off the clothes, place patient in a cool room, pack round wet towels, ice, fans, to reduce the temperature to around 38-39°C, and then allow the temperature to fall more slowly to normal by keeping the patient in light cotton clothes, at rest, in cool surroundings.

Cold (hypothermia)
Old people and babies are less able to maintain normal temperature. Illness, certain drugs, and unheated rooms often work in combination to produce hypothermia.
Normally warm areas of skin, eg armpits and groin, are cold to the touch.
Other symptoms are pale skin (may be deceptively pink in babies), slowness of thought and speech, which is gruff, proceeding to coma, and death.
Prevent heat loss by covering from head to foot in blanket.
Do not use hot water bottles, or give alcohol. Give warm (not hot) drinks.
Obtain medical aid.

Nose
Do not attempt to remove object placed in nose if it cannot be removed by gentle blowing. Consult a doctor.

Poisoning

Corrosive substances
All that can be done is to dilute the stomach contents by providing drinks of milk or water.
Place in the recovery position while awaiting the ambulance.
Never attempt to produce vomiting.

General management
Non-corrosive substances recently swallowed may be recovered by making the patient vomit. If he is conscious place the fingers or the back of a spoon down the throat, and repeat after giving half a tumbler of water.

Send urgently for medical aid.
Keep for identification any empty container, or sample of vomit.
Keep patient at rest, in the recovery position.
Be prepared to resuscitate if he becomes unconscious.
Remain with him until medical aid arrives.

Household poisons to be kept out of reach of children
All prescribed medicines, aspirin, alcohol, sleeping tablets, and iron tablets.
Cleaning substances, bleach, lavatory, window and general purpose cleaners.
Detergents, carpet cleaner, ammonia, perfumes and cosmetics.
Fabric cleaners, sterilizing fluids, and conditioners.
Soaps, scouring powders, liquids and creams.
Polishes, lavatory blocks, dishwashing powder.
Oven cleaning pads.
All aerosols, glues, batteries.
Cigarettes.
Garden poisons
Garden sprays, weedkillers, liquid fertilizers.
Seeds.
Flowers and berries, eg yew, laburnum, deadly nightshade.

Recovery position

The recovery position ensures that blood reaches the brain, that the patient does not swallow his/her tongue if unconscious, and that saliva, blood or vomit do not produce choking.

To place a casualty in the recovery position:

1. Loosen tight clothing, and remove hard or crushable objects from pockets.
2. Kneel beside patient and straighten the arms alongside the body, palms upwards.
3. Grasp the farther hip, and pull towards you with one hand, while protecting the face with the other.
4. Adjust limbs in flexed position, and cover with blanket.

Mouth to mouth ventilation

Pinch the casualty's nostrils as you take a deep breath.

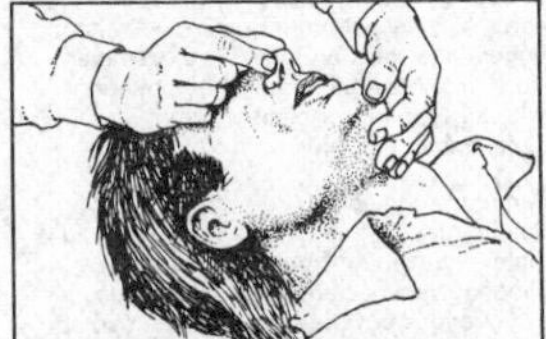

Seal your lips around the mouth and blow into it, observing from the corner of your eye that the chest rises. If the chest fails to rise, the airway is blocked and must be cleared.

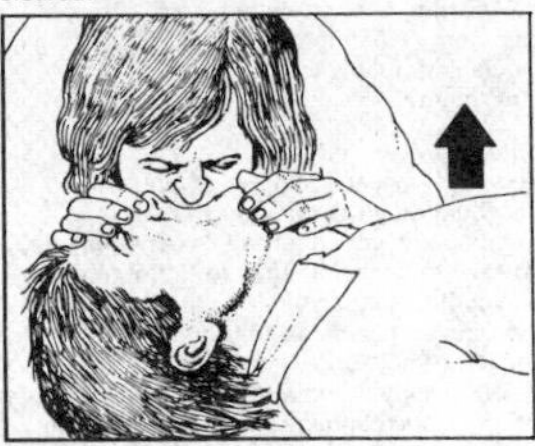

Remove your mouth to allow the chest to deflate. The escape of air is clearly audible. Inflate the lungs four times in succession rapidly, and then settle to a regular rate of one inflation every six seconds.
Continue until breathing becomes spontaneous, and do not leave the casualty until the ambulance arrives.

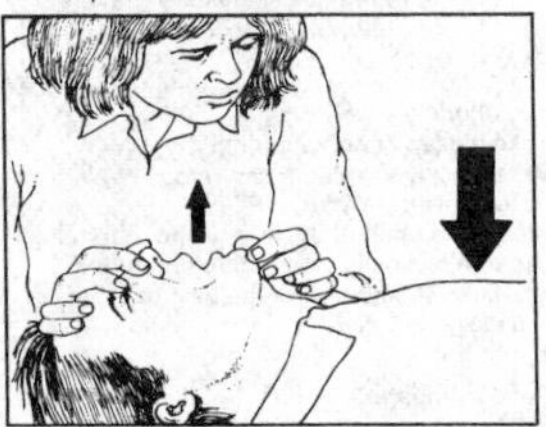

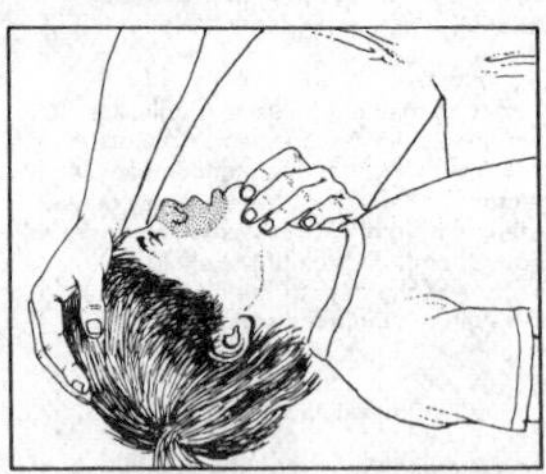

In a child Remember the greater capacity of an adult's lungs, and be guided by the rise in the child's chest which must not be filled beyond its smaller limit.
In a child breathe into the nose and mouth with your mouth.
In a baby blow gently.

Resuscitation
Where breathing has stopped the first priority is artificial respiration. When the face can be reached, and no facial injuries prevent it, the recommended method is mouth to mouth ventilation. This is an urgent procedure and seconds count.
Lay the casualty on his/her back on a firm surface.

Clearing the airway
Unless the airway is completely clear, any attempt at resuscitation will fail. Open the casualty's mouth and remove any obstructions, such as false teeth.
If the tongue has fallen back, press the chin forward.

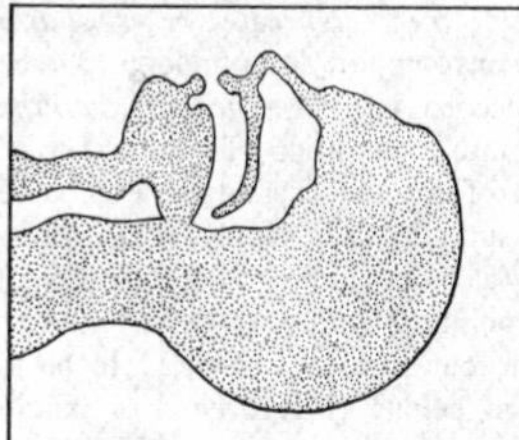

Tilt the head back fully.

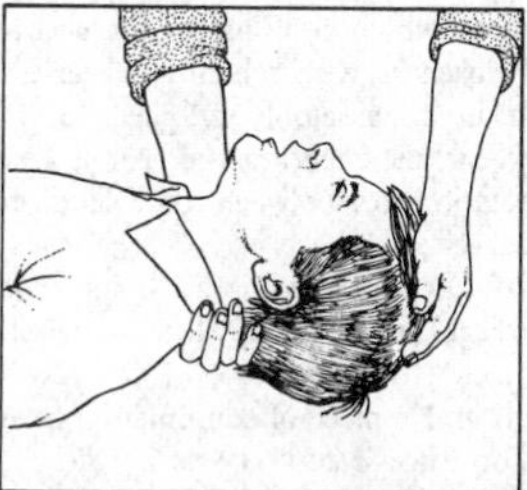

Shock and fainting
Shock results from injury, blood loss, burns, fractures, and nervous causes.
It is a dangerous condition of reduced vitality.
The casualty is pale, sweating, cold, with faint rapid pulse and shallow breathing.
Comfort, confidence and reassurance with gentle handling must be supplied by the first aider to prevent the situation from worsening.

1 Stop severe bleeding.
2 Do not move casualty.
3 Lay him/her down keeping the head low and the feet raised.
4 Loosen tight clothing.
5 Ensure fresh air.
6 Move crowd away.
7 Keep covered with blanket, but do not supply external heat.
8 Moisten the mouth and lips, but do not give anything to drink.

Fainting
This occurs as a result of nervous shock, or when standing in hot oppressive circumstances.
The pulse is slow, and the patient may become fully unconscious.
Do not try to lift him/her up, but raise the legs. Loosen tight clothing, ensure a supply of cool air.
Reassure patient as he/she recovers.
In certain circumstances, if patient is sitting, put the head down between the knees.

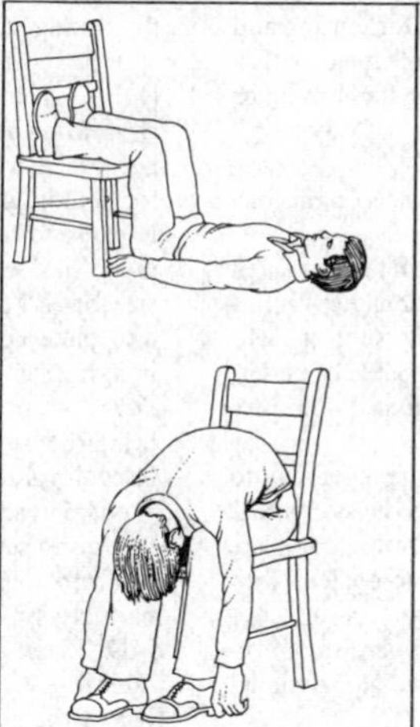

Unconsciousness
Causes of unconsciousness may not be clear – the casualty is helpless.
Priority is to protect the airway, especially when the patient is on his/her back – fish out obstructions.
Then arrest any bleeding and dress any wounds.
Consider the possibility of other injuries, eg fractures.
If he/she can be moved, turn into the recovery position, but not if back injury might be present.
Never try to pour anything into the mouth.
Be careful what you say for the patient may still be able to hear.
Treat the cause of unconsciousness if you know it.
Never leave the casualty unattended.
Remove to hospital, or ensure a medical check even if unconscious for a moment.

Safety in the home
Every year a great number of serious accidents, and millions of minor ones, take place in the home. Children are particularly vulnerable to cuts, burns, and falls – care should be taken to protect them from likely hazards.

Danger areas
Garden – always put garden tools away after use, and be especially careful when using electrical tools, eg hedge trimmers. Ponds, however shallow, constitute a danger to children.
Kitchen – electrical appliances should be wired correctly and checked often. Do not leave trailing leads, and turn saucepan handles inwards on the cooker. Knives and cleaning materials should be kept well out of reach of children.
Living room – never overload sockets with too many appliances or run cables under the carpet. Do not hang a mirror over the fireplace, and fit a fireguard when children are about.
Stairs – keep well lit and free from obstructions. Safety gates, when fitted, should be at both top and bottom.
Bathroom – keep medicine cabinets locked. Be sure that no electrical appliance can be reached by anyone in the bath.
Bedrooms – windows of children's rooms should be fitted with safety bars. Do not put portable heaters too close to furniture and curtains. Have electric blankets serviced regularly by the manufacturer.

First aid kit
scissors
tweezers
adhesive tape, or plasters
bandage, and dressings
gauze
bandages, various, including cotton and triangular
cotton wool
eye pad
lint dressing
thermometers
pocket flashlight
first aid manual
safety pins or bandage clips
eyebath
antiseptic preparations, eg alcohol
aspirin and junior aspirin
petroleum jelly
calamine lotion
sting lotion
sting reliever
indigestion remedy
antihistamine cream
nasal decongestant.

Doctor

Address

Telephone

Nearest hospital

Telephone

fish out *vt* to exhaust the supply of fish in by overfishing

'fish,plate /-,playt/ *n* a usu metal plate used to lap a butt joint [3*fish* + 1*plate*]

'fish ,slice *n* **1** a broad-bladed knife for cutting and serving fish at table **2** a kitchen implement with a broad blade and long handle used esp for turning or lifting food in frying

'fish,way /-,way/ *n* FISH LADDER

'fish,wife /-,wief/ *n* **1** a woman who sells or guts fish **2** a vulgar abusive woman

fishy /'fishi/ *adj* **1** of or like fish, esp in taste or smell **2** creating doubt or suspicion; questionable – infml

fissile /'fisiel/ *adj* **1** capable of being split or cleft; having the property of cleavage **2** capable of undergoing (nuclear) fission [L *fissilis*, fr *fissus*] – **fissility** /fi'siləti/ *n*

fission /'fish(ə)n/ *n* **1** a splitting or breaking up into parts **2** reproduction by spontaneous division into 2 or more parts each of which grows into a complete organism **3** the splitting of an atomic nucleus with the release of large amounts of energy ☞ ENERGY [L *fission-*, *fissio*, fr *fissus*, pp of *findere* to split – more at BITE] – **fission** *vb*, **fissionable** *adj*, **fissional** *adj*, **fissionability** /-ə'biləti/ *n*

'fission ,bomb *n* ATOM BOMB 1

fissiparous /fi'sipərəs/ *adj* reproducing by fission [L *fissus* + E *-parous*] – **fissiparously** *adv*, **fissiparousness** *n*

1fissure /'fishə/ *n* **1** a narrow, long, and deep opening, usu caused by breaking or parting **2** a natural cleft between body parts or in the substance of an organ (e g the brain) [ME, fr MF, fr L *fissura*, fr *fissus*]

2fissure *vb* to break into fissures

1fist /fist/ *n* **1** the hand clenched with the fingers doubled into the palm and the thumb across the fingers **2** HAND 1a ⟨*get your* ~s *off my book*⟩ **3** an attempt that meets with the specified degree of success *USE* (*2 & 3*) infml [ME, fr OE *fȳst*; akin to OHG *fūst* fist, OSlav *pęstĭ*]

2fist *vt* to hit with the fist ⟨*the goalkeeper* ~ed *the ball clear*⟩

-fisted /-fistid/ *comb form* (*adj, n* → *adj*) having (such or so many) fists ⟨*two*-fisted⟩ ⟨*tight*fisted⟩

'fist,ful /-,f(ə)l/ *n* a handful

fisticuffs /'fisti,kufs/ *n pl* the act or practice of fighting with the fists – no longer in vogue; humor [alter. of *fisty cuff*, fr obs *fisty* (related to boxing) + 4*cuff*]

fistula /'fistyoolə/ *n, pl* **fistulas, fistulae** /-li/ an abnormal or surgically made passage leading from an abscess or hollow organ to the body surface or between hollow organs [ME, fr L, pipe, fistula]

'fistulous /-ləs/ *adj* **1** (having the form or nature) of a fistula **2** hollow like a pipe or reed

1fit /fit/ *n, archaic* a division of a poem or song [ME, fr OE *fitt*; akin to OS *fittea* division of a poem, OHG *fizza* skein]

2fit *n* **1a** a sudden violent attack of a disease (e g epilepsy), esp when marked by convulsions or unconsciousness **b** a sudden but transient attack of a specified physical disturbance ⟨*a* ~ *of shivering*⟩ **2** a sudden outburst or flurry, esp of a specified activity or emotion ⟨*a* ~ *of letter-writing*⟩ [ME, fr OE *fitt* strife] – **by/in fits and starts** in a jerky, impulsive, or irregular manner

3fit *adj* **-tt- 1a(1)** adapted or suited to an end or purpose **(2)** adapted to the environment so as to be capable of surviving **b** acceptable from a particular viewpoint (e g of competence, morality, or qualifications) **2a** in a suitable state; ready **b** in such a distressing state as to be ready to do or suffer sthg specified ⟨*so tired I was* ~ *to drop*⟩ **3** HEALTHY 1 [ME; akin to ME *fitten*] – **fitly** *adv*, **fitness** *n*

4fit *vb* **fitted** *also* **fit; -tt-** *vt* **1** to be suitable for or to; harmonize with **2a** to be of the correct size or shape for **b** to insert or adjust until correctly in place **c(1)** to cause to try on (clothes) in order to make adjustments in size **(2)** to make or find clothes of the right size for ⟨*it's difficult to* ~ *him because he's so short*⟩ **d** to make a place or room for; accommodate **3** to be in agreement or accord with ⟨*the theory* ~s *all the facts*⟩ **4a** to put into a condition of readiness **b** to bring to a required form and size; adjust **c** to cause to conform to or suit sthg **5** to supply, equip –often + *out* **6** to adjust (a smooth curve of a specified type) to a given set of points **7** *archaic* to befit ~ *vi* **1** to conform to a particular shape or size **2** to be in harmony or accord; belong [ME *fitten*, fr or akin to MD *vitten* to be suitable; akin to OHG *fizza* skein]

5fit *n* **1** the manner in which clothing fits the wearer **2** the degree of closeness with which surfaces are brought together in an assembly of parts **3** the conformity between an experimental result and theoretical expectation or between data and an approximating curve

fitful /'fitf(ə)l/ *adj* having a spasmodic or intermittent character; irregular ⟨~ *sleep*⟩ [2*fit*] – **fitfully** *adv*, **fitfulness** *n*

fitment /'fitmənt/ *n* **1** a piece of equipment; *esp* an item of built-in furniture **2** *pl* FITTINGS 2 [4*fit*]

fitter /'fitə/ *n* sby who assembles or repairs machinery or appliances ⟨*a gas* ~⟩ [4FIT + 2-ER]

1fitting /'fiting/ *adj* appropriate to the situation ⟨*made a* ~ *answer*⟩ – **fittingly** *adv*, **fittingness** *n*

2fitting *n* **1** a trying on of clothes which are in the process of being made or altered **2** a small often standardized part ⟨*a plumbing* ~⟩ ⟨*an electrical* ~⟩ [4FIT + 2-ING]

fit up *vt* **1** FIX UP **2** *Br* FRAME 4a ⟨*was* fitted up *for the murder of the policeman*⟩ – slang – **fit-up** /'-,-/ *n*

five /fiev/ *n* **1** ☞ NUMBER **2** the fifth in a set or series ⟨*the* ~ *of clubs*⟩ **3** sthg having 5 parts or members or a denomination of 5 **4** *pl but sing in constr* any of several games in which players hit a ball with their hands against the front wall of a 3- or 4-walled court [ME, fr *five*, adj, fr OE *fīf*; akin to OHG *finf* five, L *quinque*, Gk *pente*] – **five** *adj or pron*, **fivefold** *adj or adv*

,five o'clock 'shadow *n* a just visible beard-growth [fr the shadow-like appearance of dark beard stubble visible on a man's face by 5 pm]

fiver /'fievə/ *n* a £5 or $5 note; *also* the sum of £5 – infml

,five-'star *adj* of the highest standard or quality ⟨*a* ~ *hotel*⟩

1fix /fiks/ *vt* **1a** to make firm, stable, or stationary **b(1)** to change into a stable compound or available form ⟨*bacteria that* ~ *nitrogen*⟩ **(2)** to kill, harden, and preserve for microscopic study **(3)** to make the image of (a photographic film) permanent by removing unused sensitive chemicals **c** to fasten, attach **2** to hold or direct steadily ⟨~es *his eyes on the* *horizon*⟩ **3a** to set or place definitely; establish **b** to assign ⟨~ *the blame*⟩ **4** to set in order; adjust **5a** to repair, mend ⟨~ *the clock*⟩ **b** to restore, cure **c** to spay, castrate **6** *chiefly NAm* to get ready or prepare (esp food or drink) ⟨*can I* ~ *you a drink?*⟩ **7a** to get even with – infml **b** to influence by illicit means ⟨*the jury had been* ~ed⟩ – infml ~ *vi* **1** to become firm, stable, or fixed **2** *chiefly NAm* to get ready; be about to ⟨*we're* ~ing *to leave soon*⟩ [ME *fixen*, fr L *fixus*, pp of *figere* to fasten – more at DYKE] – **fixable** *adj*

[2]**fix** *n* **1** a position of difficulty or embarrassment; a trying predicament **2** (a determination of) the position (e g of a ship) found by bearings, radio, etc **3** sthg influenced by illicit means ⟨*the election was a* ~⟩ – infml **4** a shot of a narcotic – slang

fixate /'fiksayt/ *vt* **1** to make fixed, stationary, or unchanging; FIX 1a **2** to direct one's gaze on **3** to arrest the psychological development of at an infantile stage ⟨*he is* ~d *at the anal stage*⟩

fixation /fik'saysh(ə)n/ *n* **1** an (obsessive or unhealthy) attachment or preoccupation **2** a concentration of the libido on infantile forms of gratification ⟨~ *at the oral stage*⟩ [FIXATE + -ION]

fixative /'fiksətiv/ *n* sthg that fixes or sets: e g **a** a substance added to a perfume, esp to prevent too rapid evaporation **b** a varnish used esp to protect crayon drawings **c** a substance used to fix living tissue – **fixative** *adj*

fixed /fikst/ *adj* **1a** securely placed or fastened; stationary **b** formed into a chemical compound ⟨~ *nitrogen*⟩ **c** not subject to or capable of change or fluctuation; settled ⟨*a* ~ *income*⟩ **d** intent; IMMOBILE 2 ⟨*a* ~ *stare*⟩ **2** supplied with sthg needed or desirable (e g money) ⟨*how are you* ~?⟩ – infml – **fixedly** /-sidli/ *adv*, **fixedness** /-sidnis/ *n* –**no fixed abode** no regular home

fixed oil *n* a nonvolatile (fatty) oil – compare ESSENTIAL OIL

'**fixed-,point** *adj* involving or being a mathematical notation (e g in a decimal system) in which the point separating whole numbers and fractions is fixed – compare FLOATING-POINT, SCIENTIFIC NOTATION

fixed star *n* any of the stars so distant that they appear to remain fixed relative to one another ☞ SYMBOL

fixer /'fiksə/ *n* sby adept at bringing about a desired result (e g by enabling sby to get round the law or officialdom) [[1]FIX + [2]-ER]

fixings /'fiksingz/ *n pl*, *NAm* trimmings ⟨*a turkey dinner with all the* ~⟩ [fr gerund of [1]*fix*]

fixity /'fiksəti/ *n* the quality or state of being fixed or stable

fixture /'fikschə/ *n* **1** fixing or being fixed **2a** sthg fixed (e g to a building) as a permanent appendage or as a structural part **b** sthg so annexed to land or a building that it is regarded as legally a part of it **3** sby or sthg invariably present in a specified setting or long associated with a specified place or activity ⟨*now a* ~ *as the England wicket keeper*⟩ **4** (an esp sporting event held on) a settled date or time [modif of LL *fixura*, fr L *fixus*]

fix up *vt* to provide *with*; make the arrangements for – infml ⟨*she* fixed *him* up *with a good job*⟩

[1]**fizz** /fiz/ *vi* to make a hissing or sputtering sound [prob imit]

[2]**fizz** *n* **1a** a fizzing sound **b** spirit, liveliness **2** an effervescent beverage (e g champagne) – infml – **fizzy** *adj*

fizzle /'fizl/ *vi or n* **fizzling** /'fizling/ (to make) a weak fizzing sound [vb prob alter. of *fist* (to break wind); n fr vb]

fizzle out *vi* to fail or end feebly, esp after a promising start – infml

fjeld /fyeld/ *n* a barren plateau of the Scandinavian upland [Dan]

fjord /fyawd, 'fee,awd/ *n* a fiord

flab /flab/ *n* soft flabby body tissue – infml [back-formation fr *flabby*]

flabbergast /'flabə,gahst/ *vt* to overwhelm with shock or astonishment – infml [prob alter. of *flabby* + *aghast*]

flabby /'flabi/ *adj* **1** (having flesh) lacking resilience or firmness **2** ineffective, feeble [alter. of *flappy*] – **flabbily** *adv*, **flabbiness** *n*

flaccid /'flaksid/ *adj* **1a** lacking normal or youthful firmness; flabby ⟨~ *muscles*⟩ **b** LIMP 1 – compare TURGID 1 **2** lacking vigour or force [L *flaccidus*, fr *flaccus* flabby] – **flaccidly** *adv*, **flaccidity** /-'sidəti/ *n*

[1]**flag** /flag/ *n* a (wild) iris or similar plant of damp ground with long leaves [ME *flagge* reed, rush]

[2]**flag** *n* a (slab of) hard evenly stratified stone that splits into flat pieces suitable for paving [ME *flagge*, fr ON *flaga* slab; akin to OE *flēan* to flay – more at FLAY]

[3]**flag** *vt* **-gg-** to lay (e g a pavement) with flags

[4]**flag** *n* **1** a usu rectangular piece of fabric of distinctive design that is used as a symbol (e g of a nation) or as a signalling device; *esp* one flown from a single vertical staff **2** NATIONALITY 3; *esp* the nationality of registration of a ship, aircraft, etc [perh fr [1]*flag*]

[5]**flag** *vt* **-gg-** **1** to put a flag on (e g for identification) **2a** to signal to (as if) with a flag **b** to signal to stop – usu + *down*

[6]**flag** *vi* **-gg-** **1** to hang loose without stiffness **2** to become feeble, less interesting, or less active; decline [perh fr obs *flag* (drooping); prob akin to *flaw* (sudden gust of wind)]

'**flag ,day** *n*, *Br* a day on which charitable contributions are solicited in exchange for small paper flags on pins or, more recently, stickers

flagellant /'flajilənt/ *n* **1** a person who scourges him-/herself as a public penance **2** a person who responds sexually to being beaten by or to beating another person [L *flagellant-*, *flagellans*, prp of *flagellare* to whip] – **flagellant** *adj*, **flagellantism** *n*

[1]**flagellate** /'flajilayt/ *vt* to whip or flog, esp as a religious punishment or for sexual gratification [L *flagellatus*, pp of *flagellare*, fr *flagellum*, dim. of *flagrum* whip; akin to ON *blaka* to wave] – **flagellation** /-'laysh(ə)n/ *n*

[2]**flagellate** /'flajilət/, **flagellated** /-laytid/ *adj* **1** having flagella **2** shaped like a flagellum [NL *flagellatus*, fr *flagellum*]

[3]**flagellate** /'flajilət/ *n* a protozoan or algal cell that has a flagellum [NL *Flagellata*, class of unicellular organisms, fr neut pl of *flagellatus*]

flagellum /flə'jeləm/ *n*, *pl* **flagella** /-lə/ *also* **flagellums** any of various elongated filament-shaped appendages of plants or animals; *esp* one that projects singly or in groups and powers the motion of a microorganism [NL, fr L, whip, shoot of a plant] – **flagellar** *adj*

[1]**flageolet** /,flajə'let/ *n* a small fipple flute [F, fr OF

flajolet, fr *flajol* flute, fr (assumed) VL *flabeolum*, fr L *flare* to blow – more at [1]BLOW]

[2]**flageolet** *n* FRENCH BEAN [F, modif of Prov *faioulet*, dim. of (assumed) OProv *faiol* kidney bean, fr (assumed) VL *fabeolus*, alter. of L *phaseolus* kidney bean]

,**flag of con'venience** *n* the flag of a country in which a ship is registered in order to avoid the taxes and regulations of the ship-owner's home country

'**flag ,officer** *n* any of the officers in the navy or coast guard above captain [fr his being entitled to display a flag with 1 or more stars indicating his rank]

,**flag of 'truce** *n* a white flag carried or displayed to an enemy as an invitation to conference or parley

flagon /'flagən/ *n* **1a** a large usu metal or pottery vessel with handle and spout and often a lid, used esp for holding liquids at table **b** a large squat short-necked bottle, often with 1 or 2 ear-shaped handles, in which cider, wine, etc are sold **2** the contents of or quantity contained in a flagon [ME, fr MF *flascon, flacon* bottle, fr LL *flascon-, flasco* – more at FLASK]

'**flag ,rank** *n* the rank of a flag officer

flagrant /'flaygrənt/ *adj* conspicuously scandalous; outrageous ⟨~ *neglect of duty*⟩ [L *flagrant-, flagrans*, prp of *flagrare* to burn – more at BLACK] – **flagrance** /-grəns/, **flagrancy** *n*, **flagrantly** *adv*

flagrante delicto /flə,granti di'liktoh/ *adv* IN FLAGRANTE DELICTO

'**flag,ship** /-,ship/ *n* **1** the ship that carries the commander of a fleet or subdivision of a fleet and flies his flag **2** the finest, largest, or most important one of a set

'**flag-,waving** *n* passionate appeal to patriotic or partisan sentiment; jingoism – **flag-waver** *n*

[1]**flail** /flayl/ *n* a threshing implement consisting of a stout short free-swinging stick attached to a wooden handle [ME *fleil, flail*, partly fr (assumed) OE *flegel* (akin to OHG *flegil* flail; both fr a prehistoric WGmc word borrowed fr LL *flagellum* flail, fr L, whip) & partly fr MF *flaiel*, fr LL *flagellum* – more at [1]FLAGELLATE]

[2]**flail** *vt* **1a** to strike (as if) with a flail **b** to swing or beat as though wielding a flail ⟨~ing *his arms to ward off the insects*⟩ **2** to thresh (grain) with a flail ~ *vi* to wave, thrash – often + *about*

flair /fleə/ *n* **1** discriminating sense; intuitive discernment, esp in a specified field ⟨*a* ~ *for style*⟩ **2** natural aptitude; talent ⟨*shows little* ~ *for the subject*⟩ **3** a uniquely attractive quality; *esp* sophistication or smartness ⟨*she has a certain* ~ *about her*⟩ *USE* (*1 & 2*) usu + *for* [F, lit., sense of smell, fr OF, odour, fr *flairier* to give off an odour, fr LL *flagrare*, fr L *fragrare* – more at FRAGRANCE]

flak /flak/ *n* **1** the fire from antiaircraft guns **2** heavy criticism or opposition – infml [G, fr *fl*iege*r*abwehr*k*anonen, fr *flieger* flyer + *abwehr* defence + *kanonen* cannons]

[1]**flake** /flayk/ *n* a platform, tray, etc for drying fish or produce [ME, hurdle, fr ON *flaki*; akin to OHG *flah* smooth, Gk *pelagos* sea, L *placēre* to please – more at PLEASE]

[2]**flake** *n* **1** a small loose mass or particle **2** a thin flattened piece or layer; a chip **3** a pipe tobacco of small irregularly cut pieces [ME, of Scand origin; akin to Norw *flak* disk]

[3]**flake** *vi* to come away in flakes – usu + *off* ~ *vt* **1** to form or separate into flakes; chip **2** to cover (as if) with flakes – **flaker** *n*

flake out *vi* to collapse or fall asleep from exhaustion – infml [perh fr obs *flake* (to become languid), var of [6]*flag*]

'**flak ,jacket** /flak/ *n* a jacket of heavy fabric containing shields (e g of metal or plastic) for protection, esp against enemy fire

flaky /'flayki/ *adj* **1** consisting of flakes **2** tending to flake – **flakiness** *n*

flam /flam/ *n* a drumbeat of 2 strokes, the first being a very quick grace note [prob imit]

[1]**flambé** /'flombay (*Fr* flɑ̃be)/ *adj, of food* sprinkled with brandy, rum, etc and ignited – used postpositively [F, fr pp of *flamber* to flame, singe, fr OF, fr *flambe* flame]

[2]**flambé** *vt* **flambéed; flambéing** to sprinkle (food) with brandy, rum, etc and ignite

flambeau /'flamboh/ *n, pl* **flambeaux, flambeaus** /-boh(z)/ a flaming torch; *broadly* TORCH 1 [F, fr MF, fr *flambe* flame]

[1]**flamboyant** /flam'boyənt/ *adj* **1** *often cap, of architecture* characterized by waving curves suggesting flames **2** ornate, florid; *also* resplendent **3** given to dashing display; ostentatious [F, fr prp of *flamboyer* to flame, fr OF, fr *flambe*] – **flamboyance** /-əns/, **flamboyancy** *n*, **flamboyantly** *adv*

[2]**flamboyant** *n* a showy tropical tree with scarlet and orange flowers

[1]**flame** /flaym/ *n* **1** (a tongue of) the glowing gaseous part of a fire **2a** a state of blazing usu destructive combustion – often pl with sing. meaning ⟨*the whole city was in* ~s⟩ **b** a condition or appearance suggesting a flame, esp in having red, orange, or yellow colour **c** bright reddish orange **d** brilliance, brightness **3** burning passion or love **4** a sweetheart – usu in *old flame* [ME *flaume, flaumbe*, fr MF *flamme* (fr L *flamma*) & *flambe*, fr OF, fr *flamble*, fr L *flammula*, dim. of *flamma*; akin to L *flagrare* to burn – more at BLACK] – **flameless** *adj*, **flameproof** /-,proohf/ *adj or vt*, **flamy** *adj*

[2]**flame** *vi* **1** to burn with a flame; blaze **2** to break out violently or passionately ⟨flaming *with indignation*⟩ **3** to shine brightly like flame; glow ~ *vt* **1** to treat or affect with flame: e g **a** to cleanse, sterilize, or destroy by fire **b** to flambé – **flamer** *n*

'**flame ,cell** *n* a hollow cell that has a tuft of cilia and is part of the excretory system of various lower invertebrates

flamenco /flə'mengkoh/ *n, pl* **flamencos** (music suitable for) a vigorous rhythmic dance (style) of the Andalusian gypsies [Sp, Flemish, like a gypsy, fr MD *Vlaminc* Fleming]

,**flame pho'tometer** *n* a spectrophotometer for determining the concentration of metals from the spectrum lines formed when the metal-containing solution is vaporized in a very hot flame – **flame photometric** *adj*, **flame photometry** *n*

'**flame,thrower** /-,throh·ə/ *n* a weapon that expels a burning stream of liquid

flaming /'flayming/ *adj* **1** being in flames or on fire; blazing **2** resembling or suggesting a flame in colour, brilliance, or shape ⟨~ *red hair*⟩ **3** ardent, passionate ⟨*had a* ~ *row with the boss*⟩ **4** BLOODY 4 – slang – **flamingly** *adv*

flamingo /flə'ming·goh/ *n, pl* **flamingos** *also* **flamingoes** any of several web-footed broad-billed aquatic birds with long legs and neck and rosy-white plumage with scarlet and black markings [Pg, fr Sp *flamenco*, prob fr OProv *flamenc*, fr *flama* flame, fr L *flamma*]

flammable /ˈflaməbl/ *adj* INFLAMMABLE 1 [L *flammare* to flame, set on fire, fr *flamma*] – **flammable** *n*, **flammability** /-məˈbiləti/ *n*

flan /flan/ *n* **1** a pastry or cake case containing a sweet or savoury filling – compare QUICHE **2** the metal disc from which a coin, medal, etc is made [F, fr OF *flaon*, fr LL *fladon-*, *flado* flat cake]

flaneur /flaˈnuh (*Fr* flanœːr)/ *n* an aimless person; an idler [F *flâneur*]

¹flange /flanj/ *n* a rib or rim for strength, for guiding, or for attachment to another object ⟨*a* ~ *on a pipe*⟩ [perh alter. of *flanch* (a curving charge on a heraldic shield)]

²flange *vt* to provide with a flange – **flanger** *n*

¹flank /flangk/ *n* **1** the (fleshy part of the) side, esp of a quadruped, between the ribs and the hip ☞ MEAT **2a** a side **b** the right or left of a formation [ME, fr OF *flanc*, of Gmc origin; akin to OHG *hlanca* loin, flank – more at LANK]

²flank *vt* **1** to protect a flank of **2** to attack or threaten the flank of **3** to be situated at the side of; border

flanker /ˈflangkə/ *n* a player (e g in rugby) positioned on the outside of the forward line [²FLANK + ²-ER]

¹flannel /ˈflanl/ *n* **1a** a twilled loosely woven wool or worsted fabric with a slightly napped surface **b** a stout cotton fabric usu napped on 1 side **2** *pl* garments of flannel; *esp* men's trousers **3** *Br* a cloth used for washing the skin, esp of the face **4** *chiefly Br* flattering talk; *also* nonsense – infml [ME *flaunneol* woollen cloth or garment] – **flannel** *adj*, **flannelly** *adj*

²flannel *vb* **-ll-** (*NAm* **-l-**, **-ll-**) /ˈflanl·ing/ *chiefly Br* *vi* to speak or write flannel, esp with intent to deceive ~ *vt* to make (one's way) or persuade (sby) to one's advantage by flannelling ***USE*** infml

flannelette /ˌflanlˈet/ *n* a napped cotton flannel

¹flap /flap/ *n* **1** a stroke with sthg broad; a slap **2** sthg broad or flat, flexible or hinged, and usu thin, that hangs loose or projects freely: e g **a** an extended part forming a closure (e g of an envelope or carton) **b** a movable control surface on an aircraft wing for increasing lift or lift and drag ☞ FLIGHT **3** the motion of sthg broad and flexible (e g a sail); *also* an instance of the up-and-down motion of a wing (e g of a bird) **4** a state of excitement or panicky confusion; an uproar – infml [ME *flappe*, prob of imit origin]

²flap *vb* **-pp-** *vt* **1** to beat (as if) with a flap **2** to (cause to) move in flaps ~ *vi* **1** to sway loosely, usu with a noise of striking and esp when moved by the wind **2a** to beat (sthg suggesting) wings **b** *esp of wings* to beat **c** to progress by flapping **d** to flutter ineffectively **3** to be in a flap or panic – infml

flapdoodle /ˈflapˌdoohdl/ *n* nonsense – infml [origin unknown]

ˈflapˌjack /-jak/ *n* **1** a thick pancake **2** a biscuit made with oats and syrup [²*flap* + *Jack* (the name)]

flapper /ˈflapə/ *n* **1a** an implement that can be flapped (e g to scare birds or swat flies) **b** FLIPPER 1 **2** a young woman; *specif* an emancipated girl of the period of WW I and the twenties – infml [²FLAP + ²-ER]

¹flare /fleə/ *vi* **1** to burn with an unsteady flame **2a** to shine or blaze with a sudden flame **b** to become suddenly and often violently excited, angry, or active **3** to open or spread outwards; *esp* to widen gradually towards the lower edge ~ *vt* **1** to cause to flare **2** to provide with a flare ⟨*a* ~d *skirt*⟩ **USE** (*vi 2*) usu + up [origin unknown]

²flare *n* **1** a (sudden) unsteady glaring light or flame **2a** (a device or substance used to produce) a fire or blaze of light used to signal, illuminate, or attract attention **b** a temporary outburst of energy **(1)** from a small area of the sun's surface **(2)** from a star **3** a sudden outburst (e g of sound, excitement, or anger) **4** a spreading outwards; *also* a place or part that spreads ⟨*jeans with wide* ~s⟩ **5** light resulting from reflection (e g between lens surfaces)

ˈflareˌstack /-ˌstak/ *n* a device (e g at an oil well) for burning unwanted material ☞ ENERGY

ˈflare-ˌup *n* an instance of sudden activity, emotion, etc ⟨*a new* ~ *of border disputes*⟩

¹flash /flash/ *vi* **1** *of flowing water* to rush, dash **2a** to burst violently into flames **b** to break forth in or like a sudden flame or flare ⟨*lightning* ~ing *in the sky*⟩ **3a** to appear suddenly ⟨*an idea* ~es *into her mind*⟩ **b** to move (as if) with great speed ⟨*the days* ~ *by*⟩ **4a** to break forth or out so as to make a sudden display ⟨*the sun* ~ed *from behind a cloud*⟩ **b** to act or speak vehemently and suddenly, esp in anger – often + *out* **5a** to give off light suddenly or in transient bursts **b** to glow or gleam, esp with animation or passion ⟨*his eyes* ~ed *in a sinister fashion*⟩ **6** to commit the offence of indecent exposure – slang ~ *vt* **1a** to cause the sudden appearance or reflection of (esp light) **b(1)** to cause (e g a mirror) to reflect light **(2)** to cause (a light) to flash **c** to convey by means of flashes of light **2a** to make known or cause to appear with great speed ⟨~ *a message on the screen*⟩ **b** to display ostentatiously ⟨*always* ~ing *his money around*⟩ **c** to expose to view suddenly and briefly ⟨~ing *a shy smile*⟩ [ME *flaschen*, of imit origin]

²flash *n* **1** a sudden burst of light ⟨*a* ~ *of lightning*⟩ **2** a sudden burst of perception, emotion, etc ⟨*had a* ~ *of intuition*⟩ **3** a short time ⟨*I'll be back in a* ~⟩ **4** an esp vulgar or ostentatious display **5** a rush of water released to permit passage of a boat **6a** a brief look; a glimpse **b** a brief news report, esp on radio or television **c** FLASHLIGHT 2; *also* flashlight photography **d** a quick-spreading flame or momentary intense outburst of radiant heat **7** a thin ridge on a cast or forged article, resulting from the hot metal, plastic, etc penetrating between the 2 parts of the mould **8** an immediate brief pleasurable feeling resulting from an intravenous injection (e g of heroin) **9** an indecent exposure of the genitals **USE** (*8 & 9*) slang

³flash *adj* **1** of sudden origin or onset and usu short duration ⟨*a* ~ *fire*⟩; *also* carried out very quickly ⟨~ *freezing*⟩ **2** flashy, showy – infml

ˈflashˌback /-ˌbak/ *n* **1** (an) interruption of chronological sequence in a literary, theatrical, or cinematic work by the evocation of earlier events **2** a burst of flame back or out to an unwanted position (e g in a furnace)

ˈflashˌbulb /-ˌbulb/ *n* an electric flash lamp in which metal foil or wire is burned

ˈflash ˌcard *n* a card bearing words, numbers, etc for brief display as a learning aid

'flash,cube /-,kyoohb/ *n* a small cube incorporating 4 flashbulbs for taking 4 photographs in succession

flasher /'flashə/ *n* **1a** a light (e g a traffic signal or car light) that catches the attention by flashing **b** a device for automatically flashing a light **2** one who commits the offence of indecent exposure – slang [[1]FLASH + [2]-ER]

flash flood *n* a brief but heavy local flood usu resulting from rainfall

'flash,gun /-,gun/ *n* a device for holding and operating a photographic flashlight

flashing /'flashing/ *n* sheet metal used in waterproofing a roof or the angle between a vertical surface and a roof [fr gerund of [1]*flash* (to cover with a thin layer)]

,flash in the 'pan *n* (sby or sthg having) a sudden success that appears promising but turns out to have no lasting significance [fr the firing of the priming in the pan of a flintlock musket without discharging the piece]

'flash ,lamp *n* **1** a portable flashing light **2** a usu electric lamp for producing flashlight for taking photographs

'flash,light /-,liet/ *n* **1** a usu regularly flashing light used for signalling (e g in a lighthouse) **2** (a photograph taken with) a sudden bright artificial light used in taking photographic pictures **3** *chiefly NAm* an electric torch

'flash,over /-,ohvə/ *n* an abnormal electrical discharge

'flash ,point *n* **1** the temperature at which vapour from a volatile substance ignites **2** a point at which sby or sthg bursts suddenly into (violent) action

'flash,tube /-,tyoohb/ *n* a gas discharge tube that produces very brief intense flashes of light and is used esp in photography

flashy /'flashi/ *adj* **1** superficially attractive; temporarily brilliant or bright **2** ostentatious or showy, esp beyond the bounds of good taste – **flashily** *adv*, **flashiness** *n*

flask /flahsk/ *n* **1** a broad flat bottle, usu of metal or leather-covered glass, used to carry alcohol or other drinks on the person **2** any of several conical, spherical, etc narrow-necked usu glass containers used in a laboratory **3** VACUUM FLASK [MF *flasque* powder flask, deriv of LL *flascon-, flasco* bottle, prob of Gmc origin; akin to OHG *flaska* bottle]

[1]flat /flat/ *adj* **-tt-** **1** having a continuous horizontal surface **2a** lying at full length or spread out on a surface; prostrate **b** resting with a surface against sthg **3** having a broad smooth surface and little thickness; *also* shallow ⟨*a ~ dish*⟩ **4a** clearly unmistakable; downright ⟨*gave a ~ denial*⟩ **b(1)** fixed, absolute ⟨*charged a ~ rate*⟩ **(2)** exact ⟨*got to work in 10 minutes ~*⟩ **5a** lacking animation; dull, monotonous; *also* inactive ⟨*trade is a bit ~ just now*⟩ **b** having lost effervescence or sparkle ⟨*~ beer*⟩ **6a** *of a tyre* lacking air; deflated **b** *of a battery* completely or partially discharged **7a** *of a musical note* lowered a semitone in pitch **b** lower than the proper musical pitch **8a** having a low trajectory ⟨*threw a fast ~ ball*⟩ **b** *of a tennis ball or shot* hit squarely without spin **9a** uniform in colour **b** *of a painting* lacking illusion of depth **c(1)** *of a photograph* lacking contrast **(2)** *of lighting for photography* not emphasizing shadows or contours **d** *esp of paint* having a matt finish [ME, fr ON *flatr*; akin to OHG *flaz* flat, Gk *platys* – more at PLACE] – **flatly** *adv*, **flatness** *n*, **flattish** *adj*

[2]flat *n* **1** an area of level ground; a plain – often pl with sing. meaning **2** a flat part or surface ⟨*the ~ of one's hand*⟩ **3** (a character indicating) a musical note 1 semitone lower than a specified or particular note ☞ MUSIC **4a** a flat piece of theatrical scenery **b** any of the sides of a nut or bolt head **5** a flat tyre **6** *often cap* the flat-racing season ⟨*the end of the ~*⟩

[3]flat *adv* **1** positively, uncompromisingly ⟨*turned the offer down ~*⟩ **2a** on or against a flat surface **b** so as to be spread out; at full length ⟨*fell ~ on the ground*⟩ **3** below the proper musical pitch **4** wholly, completely ⟨*~ broke*⟩ – infml

[4]flat *vb* **-tt-** to flatten

[5]flat *n* a self-contained set of rooms used as a dwelling [alter. of Sc *flet* floor, dwelling, fr OE; akin to ON *flatr* level, flat] – **flatlet** /-lit/ *n*

,flat 'feet *n pl but sing or pl in constr* a condition in which the arches of the insteps of the feet are flattened so that the entire sole rests on the ground

'flat,fish /-,fish/ *n* any of an order of marine fishes (e g the flounders and soles) that swim on one side of the flattened body and have both eyes on the upper side

'flat,foot /-,foot/ *n, pl* **flatfeet** /-,feet/ a policeman – slang

,flat-'footed /-'footid/ *adj* affected with flat feet – **flat-footedly** *adv*

'flat,iron /-,ie·ən/ *n* IRON 2c; *esp* one heated on a fire, stove, etc

'flat,mate /-,mayt/ *n, Br* one who shares a flat with another

,flat 'out *adv* at maximum speed, capacity, or performance – **flat-out** *adj, chiefly Br*

'flat ,race *n* a race, usu for horses, on a level course without obstacles – compare HURDLE 2b, STEEPLECHASE 1 – **flat-racing** *n*

flat spin *n* **1** an aerial manoeuvre or flight condition consisting of a spin in which the aircraft is roughly horizontal **2** a state of extreme agitation – infml

flatten /'flat(ə)n/ *vt* **1** to make flat **2** to lower in pitch, esp by a semitone **3** to beat or overcome utterly ⟨*got ~ed in the annual cricket match*⟩ – infml *~ vi* to become flat or flatter: e g **a** to extend in or into a flat position or form ⟨*hills ~ing into coastal plains*⟩ – often + *out* **b** to become uniform or stabilized, often at a new lower level – usu + *out* – **flattener** *n*

flatten out *vi, of an aircraft* to assume a position with the wings and fuselage parallel to the ground

flatter /'flatə/ *vt* **1** to praise excessively, esp from motives of self-interest or in order to gratify another's vanity **2** to raise the hope of or gratify, often groundlessly or with intent to deceive ⟨*I was ~ed by the invitation*⟩ **3a(1)** to portray or represent (too) favourably ⟨*always paints pictures that ~ his subjects*⟩ **(2)** to display to advantage ⟨*candlelight often ~s the face*⟩ **b** to judge (oneself) (too) favourably ⟨*I ~ myself I am not a fool*⟩ *~ vi* to flatter sby or sthg [ME *flateren*, fr OF *flater* to lick, flatter, of Gmc origin; akin to OHG *flaz* flat] – **flatterer** *n*, **flatteringly** *adv*, **flattery** *n*

flattie /'flati/ *n* a low-heeled usu walking shoe [[1]*flat* + *-ie*]

'flat,top /-,top/ *n, chiefly NAm* AIRCRAFT CARRIER

flatulent /'flatyoolənt/ *adj* **1** causing, marked by, or affected with accumulation of flatus 2 pretentious without real worth or substance; turgid [MF, fr L *flatus* act of blowing, act of breaking wind, fr *flatus*, pp of *flare* to blow – more at [1]BLOW] – **flatulence, flatulency** *n*, **flatulently** *adv*

flatus /'flaytəs/ *n* gas generated in the stomach or intestines [L]

'flat,ways /-,wayz/ *adv* with the flat surface presented in a specified or implied position

'flat,wise /-,wiez/ *adv, chiefly NAm* flatways

'flat,worm /-,wuhm/ *n* a platyhelminth

flaunching /'flawnching/ *n* a slope (e g of concrete) given to the top of a chimney to shed rain [*flanch, flaunch* (to slant, flare), perh fr F *flanc* flank] – **flaunch** *vb or n*

flaunt /flawnt/ *vi* **1** to wave or flutter proudly ⟨*the flag* ~s *in the breeze*⟩ **2** to parade or display oneself to public notice ~ *vt* **1** to display ostentatiously or impudently; parade ⟨~ing *his superiority*⟩ **2** to flout – nonstandard [prob of Scand origin; akin to ON *flana* to rush about – more at PLANET] – **flauntingly** *adv*, **flaunty** *adj*

flautist /'flawtist/ *n* one who plays a flute [It *flautista*, fr *flauto* flute, fr OProv *flaut*]

flavescent /flə'ves(ə)nt/ *adj* (turning) slightly yellow [L *flavescent-, flavescens*, prp of *flavescere* to turn yellow, fr *flavus*]

flavin /'flayvin/ *n* any of several yellow pigments occurring as part of the coenzymes of flavoproteins [ISV, fr L *flavus* yellow – more at BLUE]

flavine /'flayvin/ *n* acriflavine or a similar yellow dye used as an antiseptic [ISV, fr L *flavus*]

flavoprotein /,flayvoh'prohteen/ *n* an enzyme that contains a flavin and often a metal and plays a major role in biological oxidation reactions [ISV *flavin* + *-o-* + *protein*]

[1]**flavour,** *NAm chiefly* **flavor** /'flayvə/ *n* **1** the blend of taste and smell sensations evoked by a substance in the mouth; *also* a distinctive flavour ⟨*condiments give* ~ *to food*⟩ **2** characteristic or predominant quality ⟨*the newspaper retains a sporting* ~⟩ [ME *flavour*, fr (assumed) MF *flavour*, fr OF *flavor*, alter. of *flaur, flaor*, fr (assumed) VL *flator*, fr L *flare* to blow] – **flavourful** *adj*, **flavourless** *adj*, **flavoursome** /-s(ə)m/ *adj*

[2]**flavour,** *NAm chiefly* **flavor** *vt* to give or add flavour to – **flavouring** /'flayv(ə)ring/ *n*

flaw /flaw/ *n* **1** a blemish, imperfection **2** a usu hidden defect (e g a crack) that may cause failure under stress ⟨*a* ~ *in a bar of steel*⟩ **3** a weakness in sthg immaterial ⟨*a* ~ *in his argument*⟩ **4** a fault in a legal paper that may invalidate it [ME, prob of Scand origin; akin to Sw *flaga* flake, flaw; akin to OE *flēan* to flay] – **flaw** *vb*, **flawless** *adj*, **flawlessly** *adv*, **flawlessness** *n*

flax /flaks/ *n* **1** (a plant related to or resembling) a slender erect blue-flowered plant cultivated for its strong woody fibre and seed **2** the fibre of the flax plant, esp when prepared for spinning [ME, fr OE *fleax*; akin to OHG *flahs* flax, L *plectere* to braid – more at PLY]

flaxen /'flaks(ə)n/ *adj* **1** made of flax **2** resembling flax, esp in being a pale soft straw colour ⟨~ *hair*⟩

flaxseed /'flaks,seed/ *n* linseed

flay /flay/ *vt* **1** to strip off the skin or surface of; *also* to whip savagely **2a** to strip of possessions; SKIN 3 **b** to criticize or censure harshly [ME *flen*, fr OE *flēan*; akin to ON *flā* to flay, Lith *plěšti* to tear]

'F ,layer /'ef/ *n* the highest and most densely ionized layer of the ionosphere

flea /flee/ *n* **1** any of an order of wingless bloodsucking jumping insects that feed on warm-blooded animals **2** FLEA BEETLE [ME *fle*, fr OE *flēa*; akin to OHG *flōh* flea, OE *flēon* to flee] – **with a flea in one's ear** with a usu embarrassing reprimand ⟨*sent off* with a flea in his ear⟩

'flea,bag /-,bag/ *n* **1** a dirty or neglected person or animal **2** *chiefly NAm* an inferior hotel or lodging *USE* infml

'flea,bane /-,bayn/ *n* any of various composite plants that were once supposed to drive away fleas

flea beetle *n* a small jumping beetle that feeds on foliage

'flea,bite /-,biet/ *n* a trifling problem or expense – infml [*flea* + *bite*]

'flea-,bitten *adj* **1** *of a (light-coloured) horse's coat* flecked with chestnut or brown **2** shabby, run-down – infml

'flea ,market *n* a usu open-air market selling secondhand articles and antiques [trans of F *Marché aux Puces*, a market in Paris]

'flea,pit /-,pit/ *n, chiefly Br* a shabby cinema or theatre – infml or humor [*flea* + *pit*]

flèche /flesh (*Fr* flɛʃ)/ *n* a slender usu wooden spire rising from the ridge of a roof [F, lit., arrow]

fle'chette /fle'shet/ *n* a small dart-shaped projectile that can be fired from a gun or clustered in a warhead [F, fr dim. of *flèche* arrow]

[1]**fleck** /flek/ *vt* to mark or cover with flecks; streak [back-formation fr *flecked* spotted, fr ME, prob fr ON *flekkōttr*, fr *flekkr* spot]

[2]**fleck** *n* **1** a small spot or mark, esp of colour **2** a grain, particle

flection /'fleksh(ə)n/ *n* (a) flexion

fledge /flej/ *vt* **1** to rear until ready for flight or independent activity **2** to cover (as if) with feathers or down **3** to feather (esp an arrow) [*fledge* (capable of flying), fr ME *flegge*, fr OE *-flycge*; akin to OHG *flucki* capable of flying, OE *flēogan* to fly – more at [1]FLY]

fledgling, fledgeling /'flejling/ *n* **1** a young bird just fledged **2** an inexperienced person

flee /flee/ *vb* **fled** /fled/ *vi* **1** to run away from danger, evil, etc **2** to pass away swiftly; vanish ⟨*mists* ~ing *before the rising sun*⟩ ~ *vt* to run away from; shun [ME *flen*, fr OE *flēon*; akin to OHG *fliohan* to flee]

[1]**fleece** /flees/ *n* **1a** the coat of wool covering a sheep or similar animal **b** the wool obtained from a sheep at 1 shearing **2a** a soft or woolly covering like a sheep's fleece ⟨*a* ~ *of snow lay on the ground*⟩ **b** a soft bulky deep-piled fabric used chiefly for lining coats [ME *flees*, fr OE *flēos*; akin to MHG *vlius* fleece, L *pluma* feather, down] – **fleeced** *adj*, **fleecy** *adj*

[2]**fleece** *vt* to strip of money or property, usu by fraud or extortion; *esp* to overcharge – infml [[1]*fleece*; lit., to remove (a fleece) by shearing or plucking]

[1]**fleet** /fleet/ *vi* to fly swiftly; pass rapidly ⟨*clouds* ~ing *across the sky*⟩ [ME *fleten*, fr OE *flēotan* to float, swim; akin to OHG *fliozzan* to float, OE *flōwan* to flow]

[2]**fleet** *n* **1** a number of warships under a single command **2** *often cap* a country's navy – usu + *the*

3 a group of ships, aircraft, lorries, etc owned or operated under one management [ME *flete*, fr OE *flēot* ship, fr *flēotan*]

[3]**fleet** *adj* swift in motion; nimble [prob fr [1]*fleet*] – **fleetly** *adv*, **fleetness** *n*

fleet admiral *n* ☞ RANK

Fleet Air Arm *n* the branch of the Royal Navy that maintains and operates naval aircraft

,fleet ,chief petty 'officer *n* ☞ RANK

fleeting /'fleeting/ *adj* passing swiftly; transitory – **fleetingly** *adv*, **fleetingness** *n*

'Fleet ,Street *n* the national London-based press [*Fleet Street*, London, centre of the London newspaper district]

Fleming /'fleming/ *n* a member of the Germanic people inhabiting Flanders [ME, fr MD *Vlaminc*, fr *Vlam-* (as in *Vlamland* Flanders)]

[1]**Flemish** /'flemish/ *adj* of Flanders, the Flemings, or Flemish

[2]**Flemish** *n* **1** the Germanic language of the Flemings ☞ LANGUAGE **2** *pl in constr* Flemings

Flemish bond *n* a method of laying bricks in which each row consists of alternating headers and stretchers ☞ BUILDING

Flemish horse *n* a short rope suspended from the end of the yard of a sailing ship, on which a seaman stands when reefing or furling the sails ☞ SHIP

flense /flens/ *vt* to strip (e g a whale) of blubber or skin [D *flensen* or Dan & Norw *flense*]

[1]**flesh** /flesh/ *n* **1a** the soft, esp muscular, parts of the body of a (vertebrate) animal as distinguished from visceral structures, bone, hide, etc **b** excess weight; fat **2** the edible parts of an animal; *esp* the muscular tissue of any animal usu excluding fish and sometimes fowl **3a** the physical being of humans ⟨*the spirit indeed is willing, but the ~ is weak* – Mt 26:41 (AV)⟩ **b** the physical or sensual aspect of human nature ⟨*pleasures of the ~*⟩ **4a** human beings; humankind – esp in *all flesh* **b** living beings generally **c** kindred, stock ⟨*one's own ~*⟩ **5** a fleshy (edible) part of a plant or fruit [ME, fr OE *flǣsc*; akin to OHG *fleisk* flesh] – **in the flesh** in bodily form; IN PERSON

[2]**flesh** *vt* **1** to feed (e g a hawk or hound) with flesh from the kill to encourage interest in the chase; *broadly* to initiate or habituate, esp by giving a foretaste **2** to clothe or cover (as if) with flesh; *broadly* to give substance to ⟨*~ed his argument out with solid fact*⟩ – usu + *out* ~ *vi* to become (more) fleshy or substantial – usu + *out*

,flesh and 'blood *n* **1** human nature ⟨*such neglect was more than ~ could stand*⟩ **2** near kindred – chiefly in *one's own flesh and blood* **3** substance, body ⟨*attempting to give ~ to nebulous ideas*⟩

'flesh-,colour *adj or n* pinkish white with a slight yellow tint – **flesh-coloured** *adj*

-fleshed *comb form* (→ *adj*) having (such) flesh ⟨*pink*-fleshed⟩

'flesh ,fly *n* a fly whose maggots feed on flesh

fleshings /'fleshingz/ *n pl* flesh-coloured tights worn by dancers and actors

fleshly /'fleshli/ *adj* carnal

'flesh,pot /-,pot/ *n* **1** *pl* bodily comfort or good living; luxury – usu + *the* **2** a nightclub or similar place of entertainment ⟨*a tour of the city's ~s*⟩ – usu pl

'flesh ,wound *n* an injury involving penetration of body muscle without damage to bones or internal organs

fleshy /'fleshi/ *adj* **1a** consisting of or resembling flesh **b** marked by (abundant) flesh; *esp* corpulent **2** succulent, pulpy – **fleshiness** *n*

fletch /flech/ *vt* FLEDGE 3 [back-formation fr *fletcher*]

fletcher /'flechə/ *n* one who makes arrows [ME *fleccher*, fr OF *flechier*, fr *fleche* arrow]

fletton /'flet(ə)n/ *n* a type of brick [*Fletton*, district in Cambridgeshire, England]

fleur de coin /,fluh də 'kwunh (*Fr* flœr də kwɛ̃)/ *adj, of a coin* preserved in mint condition [F *à fleur de coin*, lit., with the bloom of the die]

fleur-de-lis, fleur-de-lys /,fluh də 'lee/ *n, pl* **fleurs-de-lis, fleur-de-lis, fleurs-de-lys, fleur-de-lys** /lee(z)/ **1** IRIS 2 **2** a conventionalized iris in art and heraldry [ME *flourdelis*, fr MF *flor de lis*, lit., lily flower]

fleuron /'flooəron, -rən, 'fluh-/ *n* a flower-shaped ornament used for decorative effect (e g in architecture, printing, and cooking) [F, fr MF *floron*, fr *flor, flour, flur* flower]

flew /flooh/ *past of* FLY

flews /floohz/ *n pl* the drooping side parts of the upper lip of a bloodhound or similar dog [origin unknown]

[1]**flex** /fleks/ *vt* **1** BEND 1 **2a** to bend (a limb or joint) **b** to move (a muscle or muscles) so as to flex a limb or joint [L *flexus*, pp of *flectere*]

[2]**flex** *n, chiefly Br* a length of flexible insulated electrical cable used in connecting a portable electrical appliance to a socket [short for *flexible* (*cord*)]

flexible /'fleksəbl/ *adj* **1** capable of being bent; pliant **2** yielding to influence; tractable **3** capable of changing in response to new conditions; versatile ⟨*a highly ~ curriculum*⟩ – **flexibility** /-sə'biləti/ *n*, **flexibly** *adv*

flexion *also* **flection** /'fleksh(ə)n/ *n* **1** flexing or being flexed **2** a bent part; a bend **3** a bending of (a joint between the bones of) a limb [L *flexion-, flexio*, fr *flexus*, pp of *flectere*]

flexitime /'fleksi,tiem/ *n* a system in Britain whereby employees work a set total of hours per week or month but can choose from a usu limited range of daily starting and finishing times [*flexi*ble + *time*]

flexography /flek'sogrəfi/ *n* a process of rotary letterpress printing using flexible rubber plates and quick-drying inks [*flex*ible + *-o-* + *-graphy*] – **flexographic** /,fleksə'grafik/ *adj*, **flexographically** *adv*

flexor /'fleksə/ *n* a muscle that produces flexion

flexuous /'fleksyoo·əs/ *adj* having turns or windings [L *flexuosus*, fr *flexus* bend, fr *flexus*, pp] – **flexuously** *adv*

flexure /'flekshə/ *n* **1** FLEXION 1 **2** a turn or fold – **flexural** *adj*

flibbertigibbet /,flibəti'jibit/ *n* a flighty or garrulous woman – infml [ME *flepergebet*, perh of imit origin]

[1]**flick** /flik/ *n* a light jerky movement or blow [imit]

[2]**flick** *vt* **1a** to strike lightly with a quick sharp motion **b** to remove with flicks – usu + *away* or *off* **2** to cause to move with a flick ⟨*the cow ~ed its tail from side to side*⟩ ~ *vi* **1** to move lightly or jerkily; dart **2** to direct a flick at sthg – **flick through** LEAF THROUGH

[3]flick *n* **1** FILM 4b **2** (a showing of a film at) a cinema – + *the*; usu pl *USE* infml [short for [2]*flicker*]

[1]flicker /ˈflikə/ *vi* **1** to move irregularly or unsteadily; quiver **2** to burn fitfully or with a fluctuating light **3** to appear or be present irregularly or indistinctly **4** *of a light* to fluctuate in intensity ~ *vt* to cause to flicker [ME *flikeren*, fr OE *flicorian*] – **flickeringly** /ˈflik(ə)ringli/ *adv*

[2]flicker *n* **1** a flickering (movement or light) **2** a momentary quickening or stirring ⟨*a* ~ *of interest*⟩ – **flickery** /ˈflik(ə)ri/ *adj*

ˈflick-ˌknife *n* a pocket knife with a blade that flicks open when required

flier, flyer /ˈflie·ə/ *n* **1** sby or sthg that moves very fast **2** an airman [[1]FLY + [2]-ER]

[1]flight /fliet/ *n* **1a** a passage through the air using wings **b** the ability to fly **2a(1)** a passage or journey through air or space; *specif* any such flight scheduled by an airline **(2)** the distance covered in such a flight **b** the trajectory of a struck or bowled ball; *esp* a relatively high curve imparted to a bowled ball in cricket **c** swift movement **3** a group of similar creatures or objects flying through the air **4** a brilliant, imaginative, or unrestrained exercise or display ⟨*a* ~ *of fancy*⟩ **5** (a series of locks, hurdles, etc resembling) a continuous series of stairs from one landing or floor to another **6** any of the vanes or feathers at the tail of a dart, arrow, etc that provide stability **7** a small unit of (military) aircraft or personnel in the Royal Air Force [ME, fr OE *flyht*; akin to MD *vlucht* flight, OE *flēogan* to fly] – **flightless** *adj*

[2]flight *vt* **1** [1]FLUSH 2 **2** to impart flight to (a bowled ball)

[3]flight *n* an act or instance of fleeing [ME *fluht, fliht*; akin to OHG *fluht* flight, OE *flēon* to flee]

ˈflight ˌdeck *n* **1** the deck of a ship used for the takeoff and landing of aircraft **2** the compartment housing the controls and those crew who operate them in an aircraft ☞ FLIGHT

flight lieutenant *n* ☞ RANK

ˈflight ˌpath *n* the (planned) course taken by an aircraft, spacecraft, etc

ˈflight ˌplan *n* a usu written statement of the details of an intended flight

ˈflight reˌcorder *n* a robust device fitted to an aircraft that records details of its flight, esp for use in investigating accidents

flight sergeant *n* ☞ RANK

ˌflight ˌsergeant ˈaircrew *n* ☞ RANK

flighty /ˈflieti/ *adj* **1** easily excited or upset; skittish **2** irresponsible, silly; *also* flirtatious [[1]*flight* + *-y*] – **flightily** *adv*, **flightiness** *n*

flimflam /ˈflimˌflam/ *n* **1** deception, trickery **2** nonsense, humbug *USE* infml [prob of Scand origin; akin to ON *flim* mockery] – **flimflammer** *n*

[1]flimsy /ˈflimzi/ *adj* **1a** lacking in strength or substance **b** of inferior materials or workmanship; easily destroyed or broken **2** having little worth or plausibility ⟨*a* ~ *excuse*⟩ [perh alter. of [1]*film* + *-sy* (as in *tricksy*)] – **flimsily** *adj*, **flimsiness** *n*

[2]flimsy *n* (a document printed on) a lightweight paper used esp for multiple copies

flinch /flinch/ *vi* to shrink (as if) from physical pain; *esp* to tense the muscles involuntarily in fear [MF *flenchir* to bend, turn aside] – **flinch** *n*, **flinchingly** *adv*

flinders /ˈflindəz/ *n pl* splinters, fragments [ME *flenderis*, prob of Scand origin; akin to Norw *flindra* thin piece or splinter of stone]

[1]fling /fling/ *vb* **flung** /flung/ *vi* **1** to move in a hasty or violent manner ⟨~ing *out of the room in a rage*⟩ **2** *of an animal* to kick or plunge vigorously – usu + *out* ~ *vt* **1** to throw or cast (aside), esp with force or recklessness ⟨flung *the books on the table*⟩ ⟨~ing *his arms out*⟩ ⟨flung *off all restraint*⟩ **2** to place or send suddenly and unceremoniously ⟨*the attack* flung *the enemy force into confusion*⟩ **3** to ejaculate or utter vigorously **4** to cast or direct (oneself or one's efforts) vigorously or unrestrainedly ⟨flung *herself into her work*⟩ [ME *flingen*, of Scand origin; akin to ON *flengja* to whip, *flā* to flay – more at FLAY]

[2]fling *n* **1** a period devoted to self-indulgence ⟨*determined to have one last* ~ *before settling down*⟩ **2** a casual attempt – chiefly infml

flint /flint/ *n* **1** a hard quartz found esp in chalk or limestone ☞ BUILDING **2** a flint implement used by primitive human beings **3** a material (e g an alloy of iron and cerium) used for producing a spark (e g in a cigarette lighter) [ME, fr OE; akin to OHG *flins* pebble, hard stone] – **flintlike** *adj*, **flinty** *adj*

ˈflint ˌcorn *n* a maize with hard usu rounded kernels

ˈflint ˌglass *n* heavy brilliant glass of relatively high refractive index that contains lead oxide

ˈflintˌlock /-ˌlok/ *n* (a gun having) a gunlock used in the 17th and 18th c, in which the charge is ignited by sparks struck from flint

[1]flip /flip/ *vb* **-pp-** *vt* **1** to toss or cause to move with a sharp movement, esp so as to be turned over in the air ⟨~ *a coin*⟩ **2** FLICK 1a **3** to turn *over* ~ *vi* **1** to lose one's sanity or self-control **2** to become extremely enthusiastic; go wild ⟨*I just* ~ped *over that new record*⟩ *USE* (*vi*) slang [prob imit] – **flip through** LEAF THROUGH

[2]flip *n* **1** a (motion used in) flipping or a flick **2** a somersault, esp when performed in the air **3** a mixed drink usu consisting of a sweetened spiced alcoholic drink to which beaten eggs have been added

[3]flip *adj* **-pp-** flippant, impertinent – infml

flip-flop /ˈflip ˌflop/ *n* **1** a backward handspring **2** a usu electronic device or circuit (e g in a computer) capable of assuming either of 2 stable states **3** a rubber sandal consisting of a sole and a strap fixed between the toes – **flip-flop** *vi*

flippant /ˈflip(ə)nt/ *adj* lacking proper respect or seriousness, esp in the consideration of grave matters [prob fr [1]*flip*] – **flippancy** /-si/ *n*, **flippantly** *adv*

flipper /ˈflipə/ *n* **1** a broad flat limb (e g of a seal) adapted for swimming **2** a flat rubber shoe with the front expanded into a paddle used for underwater swimming [[1]FLIP + [2]-ER]

flipping /ˈfliping/ *adj or adv*, *Br* [1]BLOODY 4, [3]BLOODY – euph [euph for *fucking*]

ˈflip ˌside *n* the side of a gramophone record which is not the principal marketing attraction [[1]*flip*]

[1]flirt /fluht/ *vi* to behave amorously without serious intent [origin unknown] – **flirty** *adj*, **flirtation** /-ˈtaysh(ə)n/ *n*, **flirtatious** /-ˈtayshəs/ *adj*, **flirtatiously** *adv*, **flirtatiousness** *n* – **flirt with** to show superficial or casual interest in or liking for

[2]flirt *n* **1** an act or instance of flirting **2** one, esp a woman, who flirts

flit /flit/ *vi* **-tt-** **1** to pass lightly and quickly or irregularly from one place or condition to another;

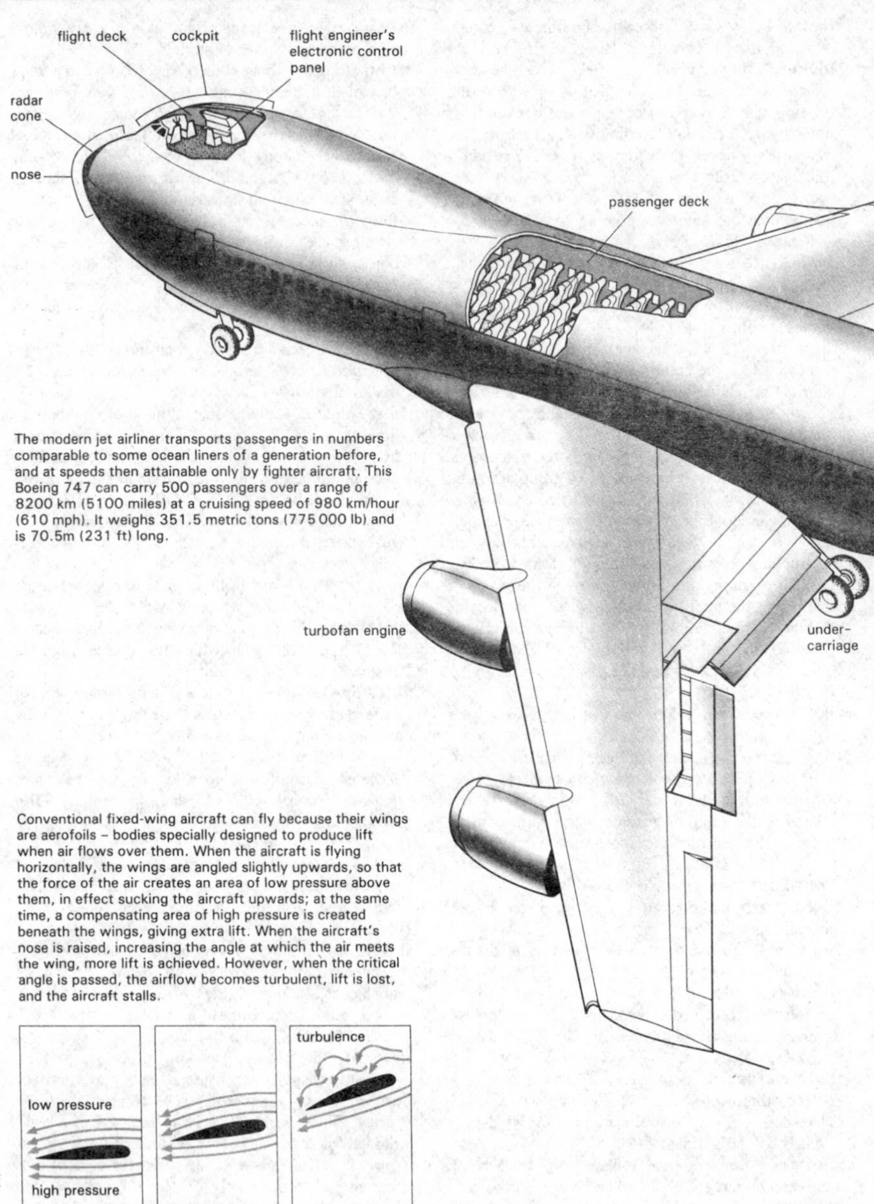

The modern jet airliner transports passengers in numbers comparable to some ocean liners of a generation before, and at speeds then attainable only by fighter aircraft. This Boeing 747 can carry 500 passengers over a range of 8200 km (5100 miles) at a cruising speed of 980 km/hour (610 mph). It weighs 351.5 metric tons (775 000 lb) and is 70.5m (231 ft) long.

Conventional fixed-wing aircraft can fly because their wings are aerofoils – bodies specially designed to produce lift when air flows over them. When the aircraft is flying horizontally, the wings are angled slightly upwards, so that the force of the air creates an area of low pressure above them, in effect sucking the aircraft upwards; at the same time, a compensating area of high pressure is created beneath the wings, giving extra lift. When the aircraft's nose is raised, increasing the angle at which the air meets the wing, more lift is achieved. However, when the critical angle is passed, the airflow becomes turbulent, lift is lost, and the aircraft stalls.

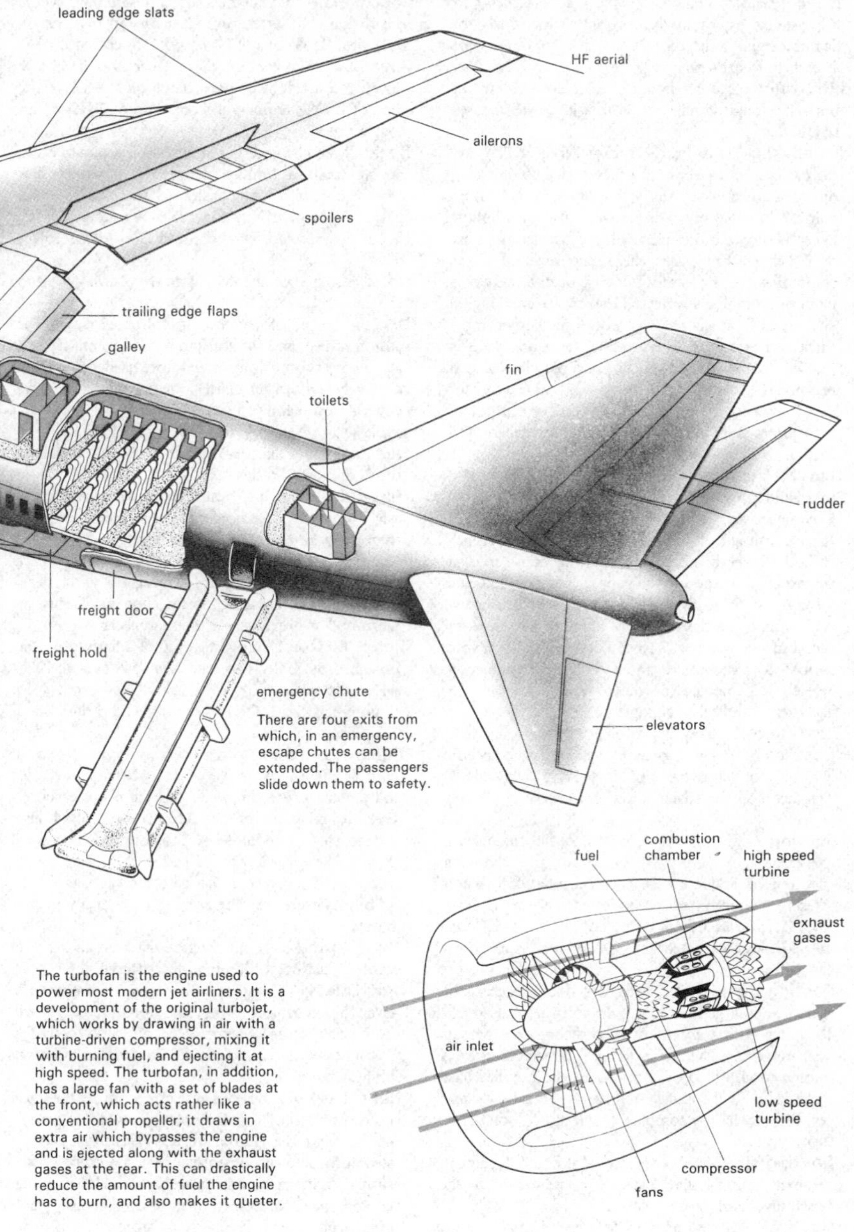

There are four exits from which, in an emergency, escape chutes can be extended. The passengers slide down them to safety.

The turbofan is the engine used to power most modern jet airliners. It is a development of the original turbojet, which works by drawing in air with a turbine-driven compressor, mixing it with burning fuel, and ejecting it at high speed. The turbofan, in addition, has a large fan with a set of blades at the front, which acts rather like a conventional propeller; it draws in extra air which bypasses the engine and is ejected along with the exhaust gases at the rear. This can drastically reduce the amount of fuel the engine has to burn, and also makes it quieter.

esp to fly in this manner **2** *chiefly Scot & NEng* to move house, esp rapidly and secretly [ME *flitten*, of Scand origin; akin to ON *flytjask* to move, OE *flēotan* to float] – **flit** *n*

flitch /flich/ *n* **1** a salted and often smoked side of pork **2** a longitudinal section of a log [ME *flicche*, fr OE *flicce*]

flitter /ˈflitə/ *vi* to flutter, flicker [freq of *flit*]

¹float /floht/ *n* **1a** a cork or other device used to keep the baited end of a fishing line afloat **b** a floating platform for swimmers or boats **c** sthg (e g a hollow ball) that floats at the end of a lever in a cistern, tank, or boiler and regulates the liquid level **d** a sac containing air or gas and buoying up the body of a plant or animal **e** a watertight structure enabling an aircraft to float on water **2** a tool for smoothing a surface of plaster, concrete, etc **3** (a vehicle with) a platform supporting an exhibit in a parade **4** a sum of money available for day-to-day use (e g for expenses or for giving change) [ME *flote* boat, float, fr OE *flota* ship; akin to OHG *flōz* raft, stream, OE *flēotan* to float – more at FLEET]

²float *vi* **1** to rest on the surface of or be suspended in a fluid **2a** to drift (as if) on or through a liquid ⟨*yellow leaves* ~ed *down*⟩ **b** to wander aimlessly **3** to lack firmness of purpose; vacillate **4** *of a currency* to find a level in the international exchange market in response to the law of supply and demand and without artificial support or control ~ *vt* **1** to cause to float in or on the surface of a liquid; *also* to carry along in this manner **2** to smooth (e g plaster) with a float **3** to present (e g an idea) for acceptance or rejection **4** to cause (currency) to float

floatage /ˈflohtij/ *n* flotage

floatation /flohˈtaysh(ə)n/ *n* flotation

ˈfloater /ˈflohtə/ *n* **1** an employee without a specific job **2** a spot before the eyes due to dead cells and cell fragments in the vitreous humour and lens [²FLOAT + ²-ER]

floating /ˈflohting/ *adj* **1** located out of the normal position ⟨*a* ~ *kidney*⟩ **2a** continually changing position or abode ⟨*a large* ~ *population*⟩ **b** not presently committed or invested ⟨~ *capital*⟩ **c** short-term and usu not funded ⟨~ *debt*⟩ **3** connected or constructed so as to operate and adjust smoothly

floating dock *n* a floating dry dock that can be partly submerged under a ship and then raised

ˈfloating-ˌpoint *adj* involving or being a mathematical notation in which a value is represented by a number multiplied by a power of the number base ⟨*the value 99.9 could be represented in a* ~ *system as .999* × 10^2⟩ – compare FIXED-POINT, SCIENTIFIC NOTATION

floating rib *n* a rib (e g any of the last 2 pairs in human beings) that has no attachment to the sternum – compare FALSE RIB

floating voter *n* one who does not always vote for the same party

floc /flok/ *n* **1** a foamy mass formed by the uniting of fine suspended particles **2** ³FLOCK 1, 2, 3 [short for *floccule*]

flocculate /ˈflokyoolayt/ *vb* to (cause to) form a flocculent mass ⟨~ *clay*⟩ – **flocculant** *n*, **flocculation** /-ˈlaysh(ə)n/ *n*

floccule /ˈflokyoohl/ *n* a small loosely united bit of material (e g ore) in or precipitated from a liquid [LL *flocculus*]

flocculent /ˈflokyoolənt/ *adj* **1** resembling wool, esp in loose fluffy texture **2** made up of flocs or floccules [L *floccus* + E *-ulent*] – **flocculence** *n*

flocculus /ˈflokyooləs/ *n*, *pl* **flocculi** /-lie/ **1** a floccule **2** a bright or dark patch on the sun [LL, dim. of L *floccus* flock of wool; akin to OHG *blaha* coarse linen]

¹flock /flok/ *n sing or pl in constr* **1** a group of birds or mammals assembled or herded together **2** a church congregation, considered in relation to its pastor **3** a large group ⟨*a whole* ~ *of tourists*⟩ [ME, fr OE *flocc* crowd, band; akin to ON *flokkr* crowd, band]

²flock *vi* to gather or move in a crowd ⟨*they* ~ed *to the beach*⟩

³flock *n* **1** a tuft of wool or cotton fibre **2** woollen or cotton refuse used for stuffing furniture, mattresses, etc **3** very short or pulverized fibre used esp to form a velvety pattern on cloth or paper or a protective covering on metal **4** FLOC 1 [ME]

⁴flock *vt* to decorate with flock – **flocking** *n*

floe /floh/ *n* (a sheet of) floating ice, esp on the sea [prob fr Norw *flo* flat layer]

flog /flog/ *vt* **-gg-** **1** to beat severely with a rod, whip, etc **2** to force into action; drive **3** to repeat (sthg) so frequently as to make uninteresting – esp in *flog something to death*; infml **4** *Br* SELL 2a – slang [perh modif of L *flagellare* to whip – more at ¹FLAGELLATE] – **flog a dead horse** to waste time or energy on worn-out or previously settled subjects

¹flood /flud/ *n* **1** an overflowing of a body of water, esp onto normally dry land **2** FLOW 2 **3** an overwhelming quantity or volume ⟨*a* ~ *of letters*⟩ **4** a floodlight [ME, fr OE *flōd*; akin to OHG *fluot* flood, OE *flōwan* to flow]

²flood *vt* **1** to cover with a flood; inundate **2a** to fill abundantly or excessively ⟨*strawberries* ~ed *the market and prices dropped*⟩ **b** to supply (a carburettor) with an excess of fuel **3** to drive *out* of a house, village, etc by flooding ~ *vi* **1** to pour forth in a flood **2** to become filled with a flood

ˈfloodˌgate /-ˌgayt/ *n* **1** a gate for shutting out or admitting water **2** sthg serving to restrain an outburst

ˈfloodˌlight /-ˌliet/ *n* (a source of) a broad beam of light for artificial illumination – **floodlight** *vt*

ˈfloodˌplain /-ˌplayn/ *n* a plain near the mouth of a river that is subject to periodic flooding and is built up by deposition of sediment ☞ GEOGRAPHY

ˈflood ˌtide *n* the tide while flowing in or at its highest point

¹floor /flaw/ *n* **1** the level base of a room **2a** the lower inside surface of a hollow structure (e g a cave or bodily part) **b** a ground surface ⟨*the ocean* ~⟩ **3** a structure between 2 storeys of a building; *also* a storey **4a** the part of an assembly in which members sit and speak **b** the members of an assembly ⟨*concluded by calling for questions from the* ~⟩ **c** the right to address an assembly ⟨*the member for Blackpool North has the* ~⟩ **5** a lower limit [ME *flor*, fr OE *flōr*; akin to OHG *fluor* meadow, L *planus* level, Gk *planasthai* to wander] – **flooring** *n*

²floor *vt* **1** to cover with a floor **2a** to knock to the floor or ground **b** to reduce to silence or defeat; nonplus *USE* (*2*) infml

floor leader *n*, *NAm* a member of a legislative body who directs his/her party's strategy in the assembly

floor manager *n* **1** a shopwalker **2** the stage manager of a television programme

'floor ,show *n* a series of acts presented in a nightclub

'floor,walker /-,wawkə/ *n, chiefly NAm* a shopwalker

floozy, floozie, floosie /'floohzi/ *n* **1** a (disreputable) woman or girl **2** a female companion – derog [perh alter. of *flossy* (showy, flashy)]

[1]flop /flop/ *vi* **-pp- 1** to swing or hang loosely but heavily **2** to fall, move, or drop in a heavy, clumsy, or relaxed manner ⟨~ped *into the chair with a sigh of relief*⟩ **3** to relax completely; slump **4** to fail completely ⟨*in spite of good reviews the play* ~ped⟩ *USE* (*3&4*) infml [alter. of [2]*flap*]

[2]flop *n* **1** (the dull sound of) a flopping motion ⟨*fell with a* ~⟩ **2** a complete failure – infml

[3]flop *adv* with a flop

floppy /'flopi/ *adj* tending to hang loosely; *esp* being both soft and flexible – **floppily** *adv*, **floppiness** *n*

,floppy 'disk *n* a flexible disk that is coated with a magnetic substance and is used to store data for a computer ☞ COMPUTER

flora /'flawrə/ *n, pl* **floras** *also* **florae** /'flawri/ **1** a treatise on, or a work used to identify, the plants of a region **2** plant life (of a region, period, or special environment) – compare FAUNA [NL, fr L *Flora*, Roman goddess of flowers]

floral /'flawrəl, 'florəl/ *adj* of flowers or a flora [L *flor-, flos* flower – more at [3]BLOW] – **florally** *adv*

floral leaf *n* a modified leaf (e g a sepal or petal) occurring as part of the inflorescence of a plant

florescence /flaw'res(ə)ns, flo-/ *n* a state or period of flourishing or flowering – fml [NL *florescentia*, fr L *florescent-, florescens*, prp of *florescere*, incho of *florēre* to blossom, flourish – more at FLOURISH] – **florescent** *adj*

floret /'flawrit, 'flo-/ *n* any of the small flowers forming the head of a (composite) plant [ME *flourette*, fr MF *flouret*, dim. of *flour* flower]

flori- /flawri-, flori-/ *comb form* flower; flowers ⟨flori culture⟩ ⟨flori*ferous*⟩ [L, fr *flor-, flos*]

floriated /'flawri,aytid, 'flori-/ *adj* decorated with or shaped like a floral motif – **floriation** /-'aysh(ə)n/ *n*

floribunda /,flori'bundə/ *n* any of various hybrid bush roses with open clusters of flowers [NL, fem of *floribundus* flowering freely]

florid /'florid/ *adj* **1** excessively flowery or ornate in style **2** tinged with red; ruddy ⟨*a* ~ *complexion*⟩ [L *floridus* blooming, flowery, fr *florēre*] – **floridly** *adv*, **floridness** *n*, **floridity** /flo'ridəti/ *n*

florilegium /,flawri'leeji·əm, ,flori-/ *n, pl* **florilegia** /-'leej(i)ə/ an anthology of writings [NL, fr L *florilegus* culling flowers, fr *flori-* + *legere* to gather – more at LEGEND]

florin /'florin/ *n* **1** any of various former gold coins of European countries **2** a former British or Commonwealth silver coin worth 2 shillings **3** ☞ *The Netherlands, Surinam* at NATIONALITY [ME, fr MF, fr OIt *fiorino*, fr *fiore* flower, fr L *flor-, flos*; fr the lily on the coins]

florist /'florist/ *n* one who deals in or grows flowers and ornamental plants for sale – **floristry** /-stri/ *n*

-florous /-flawrəs/ *comb form* (→ *adj*) having or bearing (such or so many) flowers ⟨*uni*florous⟩ [LL *-florus*, fr L *flor-, flos*]

floss /flos/ *n* **1** waste or short silk or silky fibres, esp from the outer part of a silkworm's cocoon **2** soft thread of silk or mercerized cotton for embroidery [fr or akin to D *vlos*; akin to MHG *vlus, vlius* fleece – more at [1]FLEECE] – **flossy** *adj*

flotage, floatage /'flohtij/ *n* **1** FLOTATION 1; *also* the ability to float **2** objects or material that floats; flotsam [[2]*float*]

flotation, floatation /floh'taysh(ə)n/ *n* **1** the act, process, or state of floating **2** the launching, esp by financing, of a company, enterprise, etc **3** the separation of particles of a material (e g pulverized ore) according to their relative capacity for floating on a liquid [[2]*float*]

flotilla /flə'tilə/ *n* a small fleet of ships, esp warships [Sp, dim. of *flota* fleet, fr OF *flote*, fr ON *floti*; akin to OE *flota* ship, fleet – more at FLOAT]

flotsam /'flots(ə)m/ *n* **1** floating wreckage, esp of a ship or its cargo – compare JETSAM **2** FLOTSAM AND JETSAM [AF *floteson*, fr OF *floter* to float, of Gmc origin; akin to OE *flotian* to float, *flota* ship]

,flotsam and 'jetsam /'jets(ə)m/ *n* **1** vagrants **2** unimportant miscellaneous material; ODDS AND ENDS

[1]flounce /flowns/ *vi* **1** to move in a violent or exaggerated fashion **2** to go in such a way as to attract attention, esp when angry ⟨*slapped him and* ~d *out of the room*⟩ [perh of Scand origin; akin to Norw *flunsa* to hurry] – **flounce** *n*, **flouncy** *adj*

[2]flounce *n* a wide gathered strip of fabric attached by the gathered edge (e g to the hem of a skirt or dress) [alter. of earlier *frounce*, fr ME *frouncen* to curl] – **flouncy** *adj*

[3]flounce *vt* to trim with a flounce or flounces

[1]flounder /'flowndə/ *n, pl* **flounder,** *esp for different types* **flounders** any of various flatfishes including some marine food fishes ☞ DEFENCE [ME, of Scand origin; akin to ON *flythra* flounder, *flatr* flat]

[2]flounder *vi* **1** to struggle to move or obtain footing **2** to proceed or act clumsily or ineffectually ⟨~ing *through a poor lecture*⟩ [prob alter. of *founder*] – **flounder** *n*

[1]flour /flowə/ *n* **1** finely ground meal, esp of wheat **2** a fine soft powder [ME – more at FLOWER] – **floury** /'flow(ə)ri/ *adj*

[2]flour *vt* **1** to coat (as if) with flour **2** to make (e g grain) into flour

[1]flourish /'flurish/ *vi* **1** to grow luxuriantly; thrive **2a** to achieve success; prosper **b** to be in good health **c** to reach a height of activity, development, or influence ~ *vt* to wave or wield with dramatic gestures; brandish [ME *florisshen*, fr MF *floriss-*, stem of *florir*, fr (assumed) VL *florire*, alter. of L *florēre*, fr *flor-, flos* flower]

[2]flourish *n* **1** a showy or flowery embellishment (e g in literature or handwriting) or passage (e g in music) **2a** an act of brandishing **b** an ostentatious or dramatic action

flout /flowt/ *vt* to treat with contemptuous disregard; scorn ⟨*openly* ~ing *the rules*⟩ [prob fr ME *flouten* to play the flute, fr *floute* flute] – **flouter** *n*

[1]flow /floh/ *vi* **1a** to issue or move (as if) in a stream ⟨*rivers* ~ing *to the sea*⟩ ⟨*wealth* ~ing *from the oil industry*⟩ **b** to circulate ⟨*blood* ~ing *round the body*⟩ **2** *of the tide* to rise **3** to abound ⟨~ing *with milk and honey*⟩ **4a** to proceed smoothly and readily ⟨*conversation began to* ~⟩ **b** to have a smooth graceful continuity ⟨*the* ~ing *lines of the car*⟩ **5** to hang loose or freely **6** *of a plastic solid (e g rock)* to deform under stress without cracking or rupturing [ME *flowen*, fr OE *flōwan*; akin to OHG *flouwen* to rinse, wash, L *pluere* to rain, Gk *plein* to sail, float]

²flow *n* **1** a flowing **2** the flowing in of the tide towards the land **3a** a smooth uninterrupted movement or supply ⟨*a steady* ~ *of ideas*⟩ **b** a stream or gush of fluid **c** the direction of (apparent) movement **4** the quantity that flows in a certain time **5** menstruation **6a** the motion characteristic of fluids **b** a continuous transfer of energy

'flow,chart /-,chaht/ *n* a diagram consisting of a set of symbols (e g rectangles or diamonds) and connecting lines, that shows step-by-step progression through a usu complicated procedure or system

,flow 'diagram *n* a flowchart

¹flower /'flowə/ *n* **1a** a blossom, inflorescence **b** a shoot of a higher plant bearing leaves modified for reproduction to form petals, sepals, ovaries, and anthers ☞ PLANT **c** a plant cultivated for its blossoms **2a** the finest or most perfect part or example ⟨*the* ~ *of a nation's youth destroyed in war*⟩ **b** the finest most vigorous period; prime **c** a state of blooming or flourishing – esp in *in flower* **3** *pl* a finely divided powder produced esp by condensation or sublimation ⟨~s *of sulphur*⟩ [ME *flour* flower, best of anything, flour, fr OF *flor, flour*, fr L *flor-, flos* – more at ³BLOW] – **flowered** *adj*, **flowerless** *adj*

²flower *vi* **1** to produce flowers; blossom **2** to reach a peak condition; flourish ~ *vt* **1** to cause to bear flowers **2** to decorate with a floral design – **flowerer** *n*, **flowering** *adj*

'flower ,girl *n* a girl or woman who sells flowers, esp in a market or the street

flowering plant *n* a plant that produces flowers, fruit, and seed; an angiosperm ☞ PLANT

'flower,pot /-,pot/ *n* a pot, typically the shape of a small bucket, in which to grow plants

flowery /'flowəri/ *adj* **1** of or resembling flowers **2** containing or using highly ornate language – **floweriness** *n*

flown /flohn/ *past part of* FLY

'flow ,sheet *n* a flowchart

flu /flooh/ *n* influenza

fluctuate /'fluktyoo,ayt, -choo,ayt/ *vi* **1** to rise and fall; swing back and forth **2** to change continually and irregularly; waver [L *fluctuatus*, pp of *fluctuare*, fr *fluctus* flow, wave, fr *fluctus*, pp of *fluere*] – **fluctuant** *adj*, **fluctuation** /-'aysh(ə)n/ *n*

flue /flooh/ *n* **1** a channel in a chimney for flame and smoke **2** a pipe for conveying heat (e g to water in a steam boiler) [origin unknown]

'flue-,cured *adj* cured by heat, usu from flues, without exposure to smoke or fumes ⟨~ *tobacco*⟩

fluent /'flooh·ənt/ *adj* **1** capable of flowing; fluid **2a** able to speak or write with facility; *also* spoken or written in this way ⟨*his Welsh is* ~⟩ **b** effortlessly smooth and rapid; polished ⟨*a* ~ *performance*⟩ [L *fluent-, fluens*, prp of *fluere*] – **fluency** /-si/ *n*, **fluently** *adv*

'flue ,pipe *n* an organ pipe whose tone is produced by an air current striking the lip and causing the air within to vibrate – compare REED PIPE

¹fluff /fluf/ *n* **1a** small loose bits of waste material (e g hairs and threads) that stick to clothes, carpets, etc **b** soft light fur, down, etc **2** a blunder; *esp* an actor's lapse of memory – chiefly infml [prob alter. of *flue* (fluff), fr Flem *vluwe*, fr F *velu* shaggy]

²fluff *vi* **1** to become fluffy – often + *out* or *up* **2** to make a mistake, esp in a performance ~ *vt* **1** to make fluffy – often + *out* or *up* ⟨*the bird* ~ed *out its feathers*⟩ **2a** to fail to perform or achieve successfully; bungle ⟨*he* ~ed *his exam*⟩ **b** to deliver badly or forget (one's lines) in a play *USE* (*vi 2; vt 2*) chiefly infml

fluffy /'flufi/ *adj* **1** like or covered with fluff **2** light and soft or airy ⟨*a* ~ *sponge cake*⟩ – **fluffiness** *n*

flugelhorn /'floohgl,hawn/ *n* a valved brass instrument resembling a cornet [G *flügelhorn*, fr *flügel* wing, flank + *horn* horn; fr its use to signal the outlying beaters in a shoot]

¹fluid /'flooh·id/ *adj* **1a** having particles that easily change their relative position without separation of the mass; able to flow **b** likely or tending to change or move; not fixed **2** characterized by or employing a smooth easy style ⟨*the ballerina's* ~ *movements*⟩ **3a** available for a different use **b** easily converted into cash ⟨~ *assets*⟩ [F or L; F *fluide*, fr L *fluidus*, fr *fluere* to flow; akin to Gk *phlyzein* to boil over, L *flare* to blow – more at ¹BLOW] – **fluidly** *adv*, **fluidity** /-'idəti/ *also* **fluidness** *n*

²fluid *n* **1** sthg capable of flowing to conform to the outline of its container; *specif* a liquid or gas **2** a liquid in the body of an animal or plant ⟨*cerebrospinal* ~⟩ – **fluidal** *adj*

,fluid 'drachm /dram/, *chiefly NAm* **fluidram** /,flooh·i'dram/ *n* a unit of capacity equal to ⅛fl oz (about 3.55cm³) ☞ UNIT

fluid drive *n* a device (e g an automatic car gearbox) containing fluid that transmits power from an engine to a driven unit (e g the wheels of a car)

fluidics /flooh'idiks/ *n pl but sing in constr* the use of fluid flow in shaped channels to produce devices (e g an amplifier or switch) that function like electronic components – **fluidic** *adj*

fluid·ize, -ise /'flooh·i,diez/ *vt* **1** to cause to flow like a fluid **2** to fluidize the particles of (a loose bed of material) in an upward flow (e g of a gas) to increase the rate of a chemical or physical reaction – **fluidizer** *n*, **fluidization** /-'zaysh(ə)n/ *n*

,fluid 'ounce, *NAm* **fluidounce** /,flooh·i'downs/ *n* **1** a British unit of liquid capacity equal to ¹⁄₂₀ imperial pt (about 28.41cm³) **2** a US unit of liquid capacity equal to ¹⁄₁₆ US pt (about 29.54cm³) *USE* ☞ UNIT

¹fluke /floohk/ *n* **1** a flatfish **2** a liver fluke or related trematode worm [ME, fr OE *flōc*; akin to OHG *flah* smooth – more at ¹FLAKE]

²fluke *n* **1** the part of an anchor that digs into the sea, river, etc bottom **2** a barbed end (e g of a harpoon) **3** either of the lobes of a whale's tail [perh fr ¹*fluke*; fr its flat shape]

³fluke *n* **1** an accidentally successful stroke or action **2** a stroke of luck ⟨*the discovery was a* ~⟩ [origin unknown]

fluky *also* **flukey** /'floohki/ *adj* **1** happening by or depending on chance rather than skill **2** *esp of wind* unsteady, changeable

flume /floohm/ *n* an inclined channel for conveying water (e g for power generation) [prob fr ME *flum* river, fr OF, fr L *flumen*, fr *fluere*]

flummery /'fluməri/ *n* **1** a sweet dish typically

made with flour or oatmeal, eggs, honey, and cream **2** pretentious humbug [W *llymru*]

flummox /'flumaks/ *vt* to bewilder or confuse completely [origin unknown]

flump /flump/ *vb or n* (to move or drop with) a dull heavy sound [imit]

flung /flung/ *past of* FLING

flunk /flungk/ *vb, chiefly NAm vi* **1** to fail, esp in an examination or course **2** to be turned *out* of a school or college for failure ~ *vt* **1** to give a failing mark to **2** to get a failing mark in *USE* infml [perh blend of *flinch* and *funk*]

flunky, flunkey /'flungki/ *n* **1** a liveried servant **2** a yes-man **3** *chiefly NAm* a person performing menial duties ⟨*worked as a ~ in a cookhouse*⟩ [Sc, perh fr *flanker* one who stands by sby's side]

fluor- /flooə-/, **fluoro-** *comb form* **1** fluorine ⟨fluor*ide*⟩ ⟨fluoro*carbon*⟩ **2** *also* **fluori-** fluorescence ⟨fluoro*scope*⟩ [F, fr *fluorine*]

fluorescence /flooə'res(ə)ns/ *n* the emitting of electromagnetic radiation, usu as visible light, as a result of the simultaneous absorption of radiation of shorter wavelength; *also* the radiation emitted – **fluoresce** /flooə'res/ *vi*, **fluorescer** *n*

fluorescent /flooə'res(ə)nt/ *adj* **1** of or having fluorescence **2** bright and glowing as a result of fluorescence ⟨*a ~ pink*⟩

fluo,rescent 'lamp *n* a tubular electric lamp with a coating of fluorescent material on its inner surface

fluoridate /'flooəri,dayt/ *vt* to add a fluoride to (e g drinking water) – **fluoridation** /-'daysh(ə)n/ *n*

fluoride /'flooəried/ *n* a compound of fluorine

fluorimeter /flooə'rimitə/ *n* an instrument for measuring fluorescence and related phenomena – **fluorimetry** *n*, **fluorimetric** /-ri'metrik/ *adj*

fluorinate /'flooəri,nayt/ *vt* to treat or cause to combine with (a compound of) fluorine – **fluorination** /-'naysh(ə)n/ *n*

fluorine /'flooəreen/ *n* a nonmetallic univalent halogen element that is normally a pale yellowish toxic gas ☞ PERIODIC TABLE [F, fr NL *fluor* mineral belonging to a group used as fluxes and including fluorite, fr L, flow, fr *fluere* – more at FLUID]

fluorite /'flooəriet/ *n* fluorspar [It]

fluoro- /flooəroh-/ – see FLUOR-

fluorocarbon /,flooəroh'kahb(ə)n/ *n* any of various chemically inert compounds containing carbon and fluorine, used chiefly as lubricants and refrigerants and in making resins and plastics

fluoroscope /'flooərə,skohp/ *n* an instrument used for observing the internal structure of an opaque object (e g the living body) by means of X rays [ISV] – **fluoroscopic** /-'skopik/ *adj*, **fluoroscopically** *adv*, **fluoroscopy** /flooə'roskəpi/ *n*

fluorosis /flooə'rohsis/ *n* an abnormal condition (e g mottling of the teeth) caused by excessive intake of fluorine compounds – **fluorotic** /-'rotik/ *adj*

'fluor,spar /'flooə,spah/ *n* calcium fluoride occurring as a variously coloured mineral [*fluor-* + [4]*spar*]

[1]flurry /'fluri/ *n* **1a** a gust of wind **b** a brief light fall of snow **2** a state of nervous excitement or bustle **3** a short-lived outburst of trading activity [prob fr *flurr* (to scatter, ruffle)]

[2]flurry *vb* to (cause to) become agitated and confused

[1]flush /flush/ *vi* to take wing suddenly ~ *vt* **1** to cause (a bird) to flush **2** to expose or chase from a place of concealment – often + *out* ⟨*~ out the criminals*⟩ [ME *flusshen*, perh of imit origin]

[2]flush *n* **1** (a cleansing with) a sudden flow, esp of water **2a** a sudden increase, esp of new plant growth **b** a surge of emotion ⟨*felt a ~ of anger at the insult*⟩ **3a** a tinge of red, esp in the cheeks; a blush **b** a fresh and vigorous state ⟨*in the first ~ of womanhood*⟩ **4** a transitory sensation of extreme heat; *specif* HOT FLUSH **5** *Br* a device for flushing toilets or drains [perh modif of L *fluxus* – more at FLUX]

[3]flush *vi* **1** to flow and spread suddenly and freely **2a** to glow brightly with a ruddy colour **b** to blush **3** to produce new growth ⟨*the plants* ~ed *twice during the year*⟩ ~ *vt* **1a** to cause to flow or be carried along on a stream of liquid; *specif* to dispose of thus **b** to pour liquid over or through; *esp* to cleanse (as if) with a rush of liquid ⟨*~ the toilet*⟩ **2** to inflame, excite – usu pass ⟨*was* ~ed *with victory*⟩ **3** to cause to blush

[4]flush *adj* **1** filled to overflowing **2a** having or forming a continuous edge or plane surface; not indented, recessed, or projecting ⟨*panelling ~ with the wall*⟩ **b** arranged edge to edge so as to fit snugly **3** readily available; abundant – chiefly infml **4** having a plentiful supply of money – infml – **flushness** *n*

[5]flush *adv* **1** so as to form a level or even surface or edge **2** squarely ⟨*hit him ~ on the chin*⟩

[6]flush *vt* to make flush ⟨*~ the headings on a page*⟩

[7]flush *n* a hand of playing cards, esp in a gambling game, all of the same suit [MF *flus, fluz*, fr L *fluxus* flow]

[1]fluster /'flustə/ *vb* to make or become agitated, nervous, or confused [prob of Scand origin; akin to Icel *flaustur* hurry]

[2]fluster *n* a state of agitated confusion

[1]flute /flooht/ *n* **1** a keyed woodwind instrument that consists of a cylindrical tube stopped at one end, is played by blowing air across a side hole, and has a range from middle C upwards for 3 octaves **2a** a grooved pleat **b** any of the vertical parallel grooves on the shaft of a classical column ☞ ARCHITECTURE [ME *floute*, fr MF *flahute*, fr OProv *flaut*] – **fluting** *n*

[2]flute *vi* to produce a flutelike sound ~ *vt* **1** to utter with a flutelike sound **2** to form flutes in – **fluter** *n*

flutist /'floohtist/ *n, chiefly NAm* a flautist

[1]flutter /'flutə/ *vi* **1** to flap the wings rapidly **2a** to move with quick wavering or flapping motions ⟨*flags* ~ing *in the wind*⟩ **b** to beat or vibrate in irregular spasms ⟨*his pulse* ~ed⟩ **3** to move about or behave in an agitated aimless manner ~ *vt* to cause to flutter [ME *floteren* to float, flutter, fr OE *floterian*, freq of *flotian* to float; akin to OE *flēotan* to float – more at FLEET] – **flutterer** *n*, **fluttery** *adj*

[2]flutter *n* **1** a fluttering **2a** a state of (nervous) confusion, excitement, or commotion **b** abnormal spasmodic fluttering of a body part **3** a distortion in reproduced sound similar to but at a faster rate than wow **4** an unwanted oscillation (e g of an aircraft part or bridge) set up by natural forces **5** *chiefly Br* a small gamble or bet

fluty /'floohti/ *adj* like the sound of a flute; light and clear

fluvial /'floohvi·əl, -vyəl/ *adj* of, produced by, or living in a stream or river [L *fluvialis*, fr *fluvius* river, fr *fluere*]

fluviatile /'floohvi·ə,til, -,tiel/ *adj* fluvial [MF, fr L *fluviatilis*, irreg fr *fluvius*]

[1]**flux** /fluks/ *n* **1** a continuous flow or flowing **2a** an influx **b** continual change; fluctuation ⟨*the programme was in a state of* ~⟩ **3** a substance used to promote fusion of metals (e g in soldering or brazing) **4** the rate of transfer of a fluid, particles, or energy across a given surface ☞ PHYSICS **5** *archaic* an (abnormal) flowing of fluid, esp excrement, from the body [ME, fr MF & ML; MF, fr ML *fluxus*, fr L, flow, fr *fluxus*, pp of *fluere* to flow – more at FLUID]

[2]**flux** *vt* **1** to cause to become fluid **2** to treat with a flux ~ *vi* to become fluid

fluxions /'fluksh(ə)nz/ *n pl, archaic* CALCULUS 2b [*fluxion* flow, rate of change of a varying quantity, fr MF, flow, fr L *fluxion-, fluxio*, fr *fluxus*, pp] – **fluxional** *adj*

[1]**fly** /flie/ *vb* **flew** /flooh/; **flown** /flohn/ *vi* **1a** to move in or through the air by means of wings **b** to move through the air or space **c** to float, wave, or soar in the air ⟨*flags* ~ing *at half-mast*⟩ **2a** to take flight; flee **b** to fade and disappear; vanish ⟨*the shadows have* flown⟩ **3a** to move, act, or pass swiftly ⟨*he* flew *past me*⟩ **b** to move or pass suddenly and violently into a specified state ⟨flew *into a rage*⟩ **c** to seem to pass quickly ⟨*our holiday simply* flew⟩ **4** to operate or travel in an aircraft or spacecraft **5** to depart in haste; dash – chiefly infml ~ *vt* **1a** to cause to fly ⟨~ *a kite*⟩ **b** to operate (a flying machine or spacecraft) in flight **c** to journey over by flying ⟨~ *the Atlantic*⟩ **2** to flee or escape from **3** to transport by aircraft **4** to use (a specified airline) for travelling ⟨*I always* ~ *British Airways*⟩ [ME *flien*, fr OE *flēogan*; akin to OHG *fliogan* to fly, OE *flōwan* to flow] – **flyable** *adj*, **flying** *n* – **fly at/on, fly out at** to assail suddenly and violently – **fly in the face/teeth of** to act in open defiance or disobedience of – **fly off the handle** to lose one's temper, esp suddenly

[2]**fly** *n* **1** an act or process of flying **2** *pl* the space over a stage where scenery and equipment can be hung **3a** a (garment) opening concealed by a fold of cloth extending over the fastener; *esp, pl* such an opening in the front of a pair of trousers **b** FLY SHEET 2 **c(1)** the length of an extended flag from its staff or support **(2)** the outer or loose end of a flag – compare HOIST 2b **4** *chiefly Br* a light covered horse-drawn carriage

[3]**fly** *adj, chiefly Br* keen, artful – infml [prob fr [1]*fly*]

[4]**fly** *n* **1** a winged insect – often in combination ⟨*may*fly⟩ **2** TWO-WINGED FLY **3** a natural or artificial fly attached to a fishhook for use as bait [ME *flie*, fr OE *flēoge*; akin to OHG *flioga* fly, OE *flēogan* to fly] – **fly in the ointment** a detracting factor or element

,**fly 'agaric** /'agərik, ə'garik/ *n* a poisonous toadstool with a usu bright red cap with small white scaly patches

flyaway /'flie·ə,way/ *adj* **1** lacking practical sense; flighty **2** *esp of the hair* tending not to stay in place

'**fly,back** /-,bak/ *n* the return of the spot of light on a cathode-ray tube after it has traced one image and before it begins the next

'**fly,blow** /-,bloh/ *n* (infestation, esp of meat, with) an egg or young larva deposited by a flesh fly or blowfly [[4]*fly* + *blow* (deposit of insect eggs)]

'**fly,blown** /-,blohn/ *adj* **1** infested with flyblows **2** impure, tainted; *also* not new; used

flyby /'flie,bie/ *n, pl* **flybys** /-,biez/ **1** a flypast **2** a flight of a spacecraft close to a celestial body (e g Mars), esp to obtain scientific data

[1]'**fly-by-,night** *n* **1** one who seeks to evade responsibilities or debts by flight **2** a shaky business enterprise *USE* chiefly infml

[2]'**fly-by-,night** *adj* **1** given to making a quick profit, usu by disreputable or irresponsible acts; *broadly* untrustworthy **2** transitory, passing ⟨~ *fashions*⟩ *USE* chiefly infml

'**fly,catcher** /-,kachə/ *n* any of several small birds that feed on insects caught while flying

flyer /'flie·ə/ *n* a flier

'**fly-,fishing** *n* fishing (e g for salmon or trout) using artificial flies as bait

'**fly ,front** *n* [2]FLY 3a

'**fly-,half** *n* STAND-OFF HALF [[2]*fly*]

'**fly-,in** *adj, chiefly Can* of or being a place where the only access is by aeroplane ⟨~ *communities*⟩

flying /'flie·ing/ *adj* **1a** (capable of) moving in the air **b** rapidly moving ⟨~ *feet*⟩ **c** very brief; hasty ⟨*a* ~ *visit*⟩ **2** intended for ready movement or action ⟨~ *pickets*⟩ **3** of (the operation of) or using an aircraft **4** (to be) traversed after a flying start – **with flying colours** with complete or eminent success ⟨*passed the exam* with flying colours⟩

'**flying ,boat** *n* a seaplane with a hull adapted for floating

,**flying 'bomb** *n* a pilotless aircraft carrying explosives; *esp* a V-1

,**flying 'buttress** *n* a projecting arched structure that supports a wall or building

'**flying ,fish** *n* any of numerous (tropical) fishes that have long pectoral fins and are able to glide some distance through the air

,**flying 'fox** *n* FRUIT BAT

,**flying 'lemur** *n* a tree-dwelling nocturnal mammal of E India and the Philippines that is about the size of a cat and makes long sailing leaps using a parachute-like broad fold of skin from the neck to the tail

,**flying 'mare** *n* a wrestling throw in which an opponent is seized by the wrist and thrown over the aggressor's back

'**flying ,officer** *n* ☞ RANK

,**flying 'saucer** *n* any of various unidentified flying objects reported as being saucer- or disc-shaped

'**flying ,squad** *n, often cap F&S* a standby group of people, esp police, ready to move or act swiftly in an emergency

,**flying 'squirrel** *n* any of various squirrels having folds of skin connecting the forelegs and hind legs used in making long gliding leaps

,**flying 'start** *n* **1** a start to a race in which the participants are already moving when they cross the starting line or receive the starting signal **2** a privileged or successful beginning ⟨*she got off to a* ~ *at school*⟩

'**fly,leaf** /-,leef/ *n* a blank leaf at the beginning or end of a book that is fastened to the cover [[2]*fly* + *leaf*]

'**fly,over** /-,ohvə/ *n, Br* (the upper level of) a crossing of 2 roads, railways, etc at different levels

'**fly,paper** /-,paypə/ *n* paper coated with a sticky, often poisonous, substance for killing flies

'**fly,past** /-,pahst/ *n, Br* a ceremonial usu

low-altitude flight by (an) aircraft over a person or public gathering

'fly,posting /-,pohsting/ *n* the unauthorized placing of advertising material (e g posters) in public places [2*fly*] – **flypost** *vb*

'fly ,sheet *n* **1** a small pamphlet or circular **2** an outer protective sheet covering a tent [2*fly*]

,fly 'slip *n* a fielding position in cricket behind the conventional slips and about halfway to the boundary ☞ SPORT

'fly,speck /-,spek/ *n* a speck made by fly excrement – **flyspecked** *adj*

'fly,swatter /-,swotə/ *n* a implement for killing insects that consists of a flat piece of usu rubber or plastic attached to a handle

'fly,weight /-,wayt/ *n* a boxer who weighs not more than 8st (50.8kg) if professional or more than 48kg (about 7st 7lb) but not more than 51kg (about 8st) if amateur [4*fly*]

'fly,wheel /-,weel/ *n* a wheel with a heavy rim that when revolving can either reduce speed fluctuations in the rotation of an engine or store energy [2*fly*]

FM /,ef 'em/ *adj* of or being a broadcasting or receiving system using frequency modulation and usu noted for lack of interference [*f*requency *m*odulation]

'f-,number /ef/ *n* the ratio of the focal length to the aperture in an optical system [*f*ocal length]

1foal /fohl/ *n* a young animal of the horse family [ME *fole*, fr OE *fola*; akin to L *pullus* young of an animal, Gk *pais* child – more at FEW]

2foal *vb* to give birth to (a foal)

1foam /fohm/ *n* **1a** (a substance in the form of) a light frothy mass of fine bubbles formed in or on the surface of a liquid (e g by agitation or fermentation) **b** a frothy mass formed in salivating or sweating **c** a chemical froth discharged from fire extinguishers **2** a material in a lightweight cellular form resulting from introduction of gas bubbles during manufacture **3** *the* sea – poetic [ME *fome*, fr OE *fām*; akin to OHG *feim* foam, L *spuma* foam, *pumex* pumice] – **foamless** *adj*, **foamy** *adj*, **foamily** *adv*, **foaminess** *n*

2foam *vi* **1a** to produce or form foam **b** to froth at the mouth, esp in anger; *broadly* to be angry **2** to gush out in foam **3** to become covered (as if) with foam ⟨*streets* ~ing *with life* – Thomas Wolfe⟩ ~ *vt* **1** to cause air bubbles to form in **2** to convert (e g a plastic) into a foam

,foam 'rubber *n* fine-textured spongy rubber made by introducing air bubbles before solidification

fob /fob/ *n* **1** a small pocket on or near the waistband of a man's trousers, orig for holding a watch **2** a short strap or chain attached to a watch carried in a fob or a waistcoat pocket [perh akin to G dial. *fuppe* pocket]

fob off *vt* **-bb- 1** to put off with a trick or excuse – usu + *with* **2** to pass or offer (sthg spurious or inferior) as genuine or perfect – usu + *on* [*fob* (to cheat), fr ME *fobben* – more at FOP]

fob watch *n* a large circular watch often with a cover for the face that is usu carried in a (fob) pocket

focal·ize, -ise /'fohk(ə)l,iez/ *vb* to focus – **focalization** /-'zaysh(ə)n/ *n*

focal length *n* the distance between the optical centre of a lens or mirror and the focal point ☞ CAMERA

focal plane *n* a plane that is perpendicular to the axis of a lens or mirror and passes through the focus

focal point *n* **1** the focus for a beam of incident rays parallel to the axis of a lens or mirror **2** FOCUS 5 ⟨*the fireplace was the* ~ *of the room*⟩

fo'c'sle /'fohks(ə)l/ *n* a forecastle ☞ SHIP

1focus /'fohkəs/ *n, pl* **focuses, foci** /'fohkie, -sie/ **1a** a point at which rays (e g of light, heat, or sound) converge or from which they (appear to) diverge after reflection or refraction **b** the point at which an object must be placed for an image formed by a lens or mirror to be sharp ☞ CAMERA **2a** FOCAL LENGTH **b** adjustment (e g of the eye) necessary for distinct vision **c** a state in which sthg must be placed in order to be clearly perceived ⟨*tried to bring the issues into* ~⟩ **3** a fixed point that together with a straight line forms a reference system for generating a conic section in plane geometry; *also* either of 2 fixed points used in generating an ellipse or hyperbola ☞ MATHEMATICS **4** a localized area of disease or the chief site of a generalized disease **5** a centre of activity or attention ⟨*the* ~ *of the meeting was drug abuse*⟩ **6** the place of origin of an earthquake ☞ GEOGRAPHY [NL, fr L, hearth] – **focal** *adj*, **focally** *adv* – **out of/in focus** not/having or giving the proper sharpness of outline due to good focussing

2focus *vb* **-ss-, -s-** *vt* **1** to bring to a focus **2** to cause to be concentrated ⟨~sed *their attention on the most urgent problems*⟩ **3a** to adjust the focus of **b** to bring into focus ~ *vi* **1** to come to a focus; converge **2** to bring one's eyes or a camera to a focus

fodder /'fodə/ *n* **1** (coarse) food for cattle, horses, sheep, or other domestic animals **2** sthg used to supply a constant demand ⟨*collected data which became computer* ~⟩ – compare CANNON FODDER [ME, fr OE *fōdor*; akin to OHG *fuotar* food – more at FOOD] – **fodder** *vt*

foe /foh/ *n* an enemy, adversary [ME *fo*, fr OE *fāh*, fr *fāh* hostile; akin to OHG *gifēh* hostile]

foehn /fuhn (əer føːn)/ *n* a föhn

foetid /'feetid/ *adj* fetid

foeto-, foeti-, feto-, feti- *comb form* foetus ⟨foeti*cide*⟩; foetal and ⟨foeto*placental*⟩ [NL *fetus*]

foetus, fetus /'feetəs/ *n* an unborn or unhatched vertebrate; *specif* a developing human from usu 3 months after conception to birth ☞ REPRODUCTION [NL *fetus*, fr L, act of bearing young, offspring; akin to L *fetus* fruitful] – **foetal** *adj*

1fog /fog/ *n* **1** dead or decaying grass on land in the winter **2** a second growth of grass; an aftermath [ME, rank grass]

2fog *n* **1** (a murky condition of the atmosphere caused esp by) fine particles, specif of water, suspended in the lower atmosphere **2a** a state of confusion or bewilderment **b** sthg that confuses or obscures ⟨*hid behind a* ~ *of rhetoric*⟩ **3** cloudiness on a developed photograph caused by chemical action or radiation (e g from X rays) [prob of Scand origin; akin to Dan *fog* spray, shower; akin to L *pustula* blister, pimple, Gk *physan* to blow]

3fog *vb* **-gg-** *vt* **1** to envelop or suffuse (as if) with fog **2** to make confused or confusing **3** to produce fog on (e g a photographic film) during development ~ *vi* **1** to become covered or thick with fog **2** to become blurred (as if) by a covering of fog or mist

'fog,bound /-,bownd/ *adj* **1** covered with or surrounded by fog ⟨*a* ~ *coast*⟩ **2** unable to move because of fog

'fog,bow /-,boh/ *n* a dim arc or circle of light sometimes seen in fog

fogey, fogy /'fohgi/ *n* a person with old-fashioned ideas – chiefly in *old fogey*; chiefly infml [origin unknown] – **fogeyish** *adj*, **fogeyism** *n*

foggy /'fogi/ *adj* **1a** thick with fog **b** covered or made opaque by moisture or grime **2** blurred, obscured ⟨*hadn't the* foggiest *notion what they were voting for*⟩ – **foggily** *adv*, **fogginess** *n*

'fog,horn /-,hawn/ *n* **1** a horn (e g on a ship) sounded in a fog to give warning **2** a loud hoarse voice – infml

föhn, foehn /fuhn (əer føːn)/ *n* a warm dry wind that descends the leeward side of a mountain range, esp the Alps [G, deriv of L *favonius* warm west wind]

foible /'foybl/ *n* **1** the part of a sword blade between the middle and point – compare FORTE 2 **2** a minor weakness or shortcoming in personal character or behaviour; *also* a quirk [obs F (now *faible*), fr obs *foible* weak, fr OF *feble* feeble]

foie gras /,fwah 'grah (*Fr* fwa grɑ)/ *n* the fatted liver of an animal, esp a goose, usu in the form of a pâté [F]

[1]**foil** /foyl/ *vt* **1** *esp of a hunted animal* to spoil (a trail or scent) by crossing or retracing **2** to prevent from attaining an end; frustrate, defeat [ME *foilen* to trample, full cloth, fr MF *fouler*– more at [5]FULL]

[2]**foil** *n* **1** (fencing with) a light fencing sword with a circular guard and a flexible blade tapering to a blunted point – compare ÉPÉE, SABRE 2 **2** *archaic* the track or trail of an animal

[3]**foil** *n* **1a** a curved recess between cusps (e g in Gothic tracery) **b** any of several arcs that enclose a complex design **2a** very thin sheet metal ⟨*silver* ~⟩ **b** a thin coat of tin or silver laid on the back of a mirror **3** a thin piece of metal put under a gem or inferior stone to add colour or brilliance **4** sby or sthg that serves as a contrast to another ⟨*acted as a* ~ *for a comedian*⟩ **5** a hydrofoil [ME, leaf, fr MF *foille* (fr L *folia*, pl of *folium*) & *foil*, fr L *folium* – more at BLADE]

[4]**foil** *vt* to back or cover with foil

foist /foyst/ *vt* **1a** to introduce or insert surreptitiously or without warrant – + *in* or *into* **b** to force another to accept or tolerate, esp by stealth or deceit **2** to pass off as genuine or worthy ***USE*** (*1b&2*) usu + *off on, on,* or *upon* [prob fr obs D *vuisten* to take into one's hand, fr MD *vuysten*, fr *vuyst* fist; akin to OE *fýst* fist]

[1]**fold** /fohld/ *n* **1** an enclosure for sheep; *also* a flock of sheep **2** *sing or pl in constr* a group of people adhering to a common faith, belief, or enthusiasm [ME, fr OE *falod*; akin to MLG *vālt* enclosure]

[2]**fold** *vt* **1** to pen (e g sheep) in a fold **2** to pen sheep for the fertilization of (land)

[3]**fold** *vt* **1** to lay one part of over another part **2** to reduce the length or bulk of by doubling over – often + *up* **3a** to clasp together; entwine ⟨~ed *his arms*⟩ **b** to bring (limbs) to rest close to the body ⟨*the bird* ~ed *its wings*⟩ **4a** to clasp closely; embrace **b** to wrap, envelop **5** to bend (e g a layer of rock) into folds **6** to gently incorporate (a food ingredient) into a mixture without thorough stirring or beating – usu + *in* ~ *vi* **1** to become or be capable of being folded ⟨*a* ~ing *chair*⟩ **2** to fail completely; *esp* to stop production or operation because of lack of business or capital – often + *up*; chiefly infml **3** to succumb to fatigue – infml [ME *folden*, fr OE *fealdan*; akin to OHG *faldan* to fold, Gk di*plasios* twofold] – **foldable** *adj*

[4]**fold** *n* **1** (a crease made by) a doubling or folding over **2** a part doubled or laid over another part; a pleat **3** (a hollow inside) sthg that is folded or that enfolds **4a** a bend in rock strata produced usu by compression ☞ GEOGRAPHY **b** *chiefly Br* an undulation in the landscape

-fold /-fohld/ *suffix* (→ *adj or adv*) **1** multiplied by (a specified number); times ⟨*a twelve*fold *increase*⟩ ⟨*repay you ten*fold⟩ **2** having (so many) parts ⟨*three*fold *aspect of the problem*⟩ [ME, fr OE *-feald*; akin to OHG *-falt* -fold, OE *fealdan*]

'fold,away /-ə,way/ *adj* designed to fold out of the way or out of sight ⟨*a* ~ *bed*⟩

folder /'fohldə/ *n* a folded cover or large envelope for holding or filing loose papers [[3]FOLD + [2]-ER]

folderol /'foldə,rol/ *n* **1** a useless ornament; a trifle **2** nonsense [*fol-de-rol*, a meaningless refrain in old songs]

'folding ,money *n, chiefly NAm* money in the form of bank notes – infml

'fold,out /-,owt/ *n* a folded insert in a publication larger in size than the page

foliaceous /fohli'ayshəs/ *adj* **1** of or resembling a foliage leaf **2** consisting of thin plates

foliage /'fohli·ij/ *n* **1** the leaves of a plant or clump of plants **2** (an ornamental representation of) a cluster of leaves, branches, etc [MF *fuellage*, fr *foille* leaf – more at [3]FOIL] – **foliaged** *adj*, **foliar** *adj*

'foliage ,leaf *n* an ordinary green leaf as distinguished from a floral leaf, scale, or bract

'foliage ,plant *n* a plant grown primarily for its decorative foliage

[1]**foliate** /'fohli·ət/ *adj* **1** having leaves or leaflets; *also* leaf-shaped – often in combination ⟨*tri*foliate⟩ **2** foliated [L *foliatus* leafy, fr *folium* leaf – more at BLADE]

[2]**foliate** /'fohli,ayt/ *vt* **1** to beat (metal) into a leaf or thin foil **2** to number the leaves of (e g a manuscript) – compare [4]PAGE **3** to decorate (e g an arch or pedestal) with foils ~ *vi* to divide into thin layers or leaves – **foliation** /-'aysh(ə)n/ *n*

'foli,ated *adj* composed of (easily separable) thin layers

,folic 'acid /'fohlik/ *n* a vitamin of the vitamin B complex that is found esp in green leafy vegetables and liver and whose lack in the diet results in anaemia [L *folium*]

folie à deux /,foli ah 'duh (*Fr* fɔli a dø)/ *n* the presence of the same or similar delusional ideas in 2 closely associated people [F, lit., double madness]

[1]**folio** /'fohlioh/ *n, pl* **folios** **1a** a leaf of a manuscript or book **b** a page or leaf number **2a(1)** (the size of each of the 2 leaves formed from) a sheet of paper folded once **(2)** a book printed on pages of this size **b** a book of the largest size **3** a case or folder for loose papers **4** a certain number of words taken as a unit in measuring the length of a document [ME, fr L, abl of *folium*]

[2]**folio** *vt* **folios; folioing; folioed** FOLIATE 2

[1]**folk** /fohk/ *n* **1** *pl in constr* the great proportion of a people that tends to preserve its customs, superstitions, etc **2** *pl in constr* a specified kind or class of people ⟨*old* ~⟩ – often pl with sing. meaning ⟨*just plain* ~s⟩ **3** simple music, usu song, of traditional origin or style **4** *pl in constr* people generally – infml;

often pl with sing. meaning **5** *pl* the members of one's own family; relatives – infml [ME, fr OE *folc*; akin to OHG *folc* people]

[2]**folk** *adj* **1** originating or traditional with the common people **2** of (the study of) the common people

'**folk ety,mology** *n* the transformation of words so as to bring them into an apparent relationship with other more familiar words (e g in the change of Spanish *cucaracha* to *cockroach*)

'**folk,lore** /-law/ *n* **1** traditional customs and beliefs of a people preserved by oral tradition **2** the study of the life and spirit of a people through their folklore – **folklorist** *n*, **folkloric** /-'lorik/ *adj*

folksy /'fohksi/ *adj* **1** informal or familiar in manner or style **2** having or affecting a lack of sophistication – chiefly derog *USE* infml [*folks* + *-y*] – **folksily** *adv*, **folksiness** *n*

'**folk,way** /-,way/ *n* a traditional social custom

follicle /'folikl/ *n* **1a** a small anatomical cavity or deep narrow depression **b** GRAAFIAN FOLLICLE ☞ REPRODUCTION **2** a dry 1-celled many-seeded fruit that has a single carpel and opens along 1 line only [NL *folliculus*, fr L, dim. of *follis* bag – more at FOOL] – **follicular** /fə'likyoolə/, **folliculate** /fə'likyoolət/ *also* **folliculated** /-,laytid/ *adj*

'**follicle-,stimulating ,hormone** *n* a hormone produced by the front lobe of the pituitary gland that stimulates the growth of the ovum-containing Graafian follicles and activates sperm-forming cells

follow /'foloh/ *vt* **1** to go, proceed, or come after ⟨~ed *the guide*⟩ **2a** to pursue, esp in an effort to overtake **b** to seek to attain; strive after ⟨~ *knowledge*⟩ **3a** to accept as a guide or leader **b** to obey or act in accordance with ⟨*he* ~ed *the advice*⟩ **4** to copy, imitate **5a** to walk or proceed along ⟨~ *a path*⟩ **b** to engage in as a calling or way of life; pursue (e g a course of action) **6a** to come or take place after in time or order **b** to cause to be followed – usu + *with* ⟨~ed *dinner with a liqueur*⟩ **7** to come into existence or take place as a result or consequence of **8a** to watch steadily ⟨~ed *the ball over the fence*⟩ **b** to keep the mind on ⟨~ *a speech*⟩ **c** to attend closely to; keep abreast of ⟨*she* ~ed *his career with interest*⟩ **d** to understand the logic of (e g an argument) ⟨*I don't quite* ~ *you*⟩ ~ *vi* **1** to go or come after sby or sthg in place, time, or sequence **2** to result or occur as a consequence or inference **3** *chiefly Br* to understand the logic of a line of thought [ME *folwen*, fr OE *folgian*; akin to OHG *folgēn* to follow] – **follow one's nose** to go in a straight or obvious course – **follow suit 1** to play a card of the same suit as the card led **2** to follow an example set

follower /'foloh·ə/ *n* **1a** one who follows the opinions or teachings of another **b** one who imitates another **2** [3]FAN [FOLLOW + [2]-ER]

[1]'**following** /-ing/ *adj* **1** next after; succeeding ⟨*the* ~ *day*⟩ **2** now to be stated ⟨*trains will leave at the* ~ *times*⟩ **3** *of a wind* blowing in the direction in which sthg is travelling

[2]**following** *n, pl* (*1*) **following**, (*2*) **followings 1** sthg that comes immediately after or below in writing or speech **2** *sing or pl in constr* a group of followers, adherents, or partisans

[3]**following** *prep* subsequent to ⟨~ *the lecture tea was served*⟩

,**follow-my-'leader** *n, Br* **1** a game in which the actions of a designated leader must be copied by the other players **2** the slavish following by the majority of people of an example set by an individual

follow on *vi, of a side in cricket* to bat a second time immediately after making a score that is less, by more than a predetermined limit, than that of the opposing team in its first innings – **follow-on** /'--,-/ *n*

,**follow-the-'leader** *n, NAm* follow-my-leader

follow through *vi* to continue the movement of a stroke after a cricket, golf, etc ball has been struck ~ *vt* to pursue (an activity or process), esp to a conclusion – **follow-through** /'-- ,-/ *n*

follow up *vt* **1a** to follow with sthg similar, related, or supplementary ⟨following up *his promises with action*⟩ **b** to take appropriate action about ⟨follow up *complaints and customer suggestions*⟩ **2** to maintain contact with or reexamine (a person) at usu prescribed intervals in order to evaluate a diagnosis or treatment – **follow-up** /'-- ,-/ *n*

folly /'foli/ *n* **1** lack of good sense or prudence **2** a foolish act or idea **3** (criminally or tragically) foolish actions or conduct **4** a usu fanciful structure (e g a summerhouse) built esp for scenic effect or to satisfy a whim [ME *folie*, fr OF, fr *fol* fool – more at FOOL]

foment /foh'ment/ *vt* **1** to treat with moist heat (e g for easing pain) **2** to promote the growth or development of; incite ⟨~ *a rebellion*⟩ [ME *fomenten*, fr LL *fomentare*, fr L *fomentum* fomentation, fr *fovēre* to warm, fondle, foment] – **fomenter** *n*

fomentation /,fohmen'taysh(ə)n/ *n* **1** (the application to the body of) hot moist substances **2** fomenting, instigation

fond /fond/ *adj* **1** foolish, silly ⟨~ *pride*⟩ **2** having an affection or liking for sthg specified – + *of* ⟨~ *of music*⟩ **3a** foolishly tender; indulgent **b** affectionate, loving **4** doted on; cherished ⟨*his* ~est *hopes*⟩ [ME, fr *fonne* fool] – **fondness** *n*

fondant /'fondənt (*Fr* fɔ̃dɑ̃)/ *n* (a sweet made from) a soft creamy preparation of flavoured sugar and water [F, fr prp of *fondre* to melt – more at [4]FOUND]

fondle /'fondl/ *vb* **fondling** /'fondling/ *vt* to handle tenderly or lingeringly ~ *vi* to show affection or desire by caressing [freq of obs *fond* (to be foolish, dote)]

fondly /'fondli/ *adv* **1** affectionately **2** in a willingly credulous manner ⟨*government* ~ *imagine that cutting taxes will reduce wage demands*⟩

fondue /'fond(y)ooh (*Fr* fɔ̃dy)/ *n* a dish consisting of a hot liquid (e g oil or a thick sweet or savoury sauce) into which small pieces of food are dipped for cooking or coating; *esp* one made with melted cheese and usu white wine [F *fondue*, fr fem of *fondu*, pp of *fondre*]

[1]**font** /font/ *n* **1a** a receptacle for holy water; *esp* one used in baptism ☞ CHURCH **b** a receptacle for oil in a lamp **2** *chiefly NAm* [1]FOUNT [ME, fr OE, fr LL *font-, fons*, fr L, fountain] – **fontal** *adj*

[2]**font** *n, chiefly NAm* [2]FOUNT

fontanelle, *NAm chiefly* **fontanel** /,fontə'nel/ *n* any of the spaces closed by membranous structures between the parietal bones of the skull of an infant or foetus [ME *fontinelle*, a bodily hollow or pit, fr MF *fontenele*, dim. of *fontaine* fountain]

food /foohd/ *n* **1a** (minerals, vitamins, etc together with) material consisting essentially of protein,

A **food chain** is a series of organisms existing in any natural community, or ecosystem, through which energy is transferred. Each organism in the series feeds on and obtains energy from the one preceding it and in turn is consumed by and provides energy for the one following it. Usually the number of links in the chain is 3 or 4 and each link is known as an energy or trophic level. All the food chains in a community make up the food web. The diagram shows part of a food cycle typical of organisms inhabiting the African savanna.

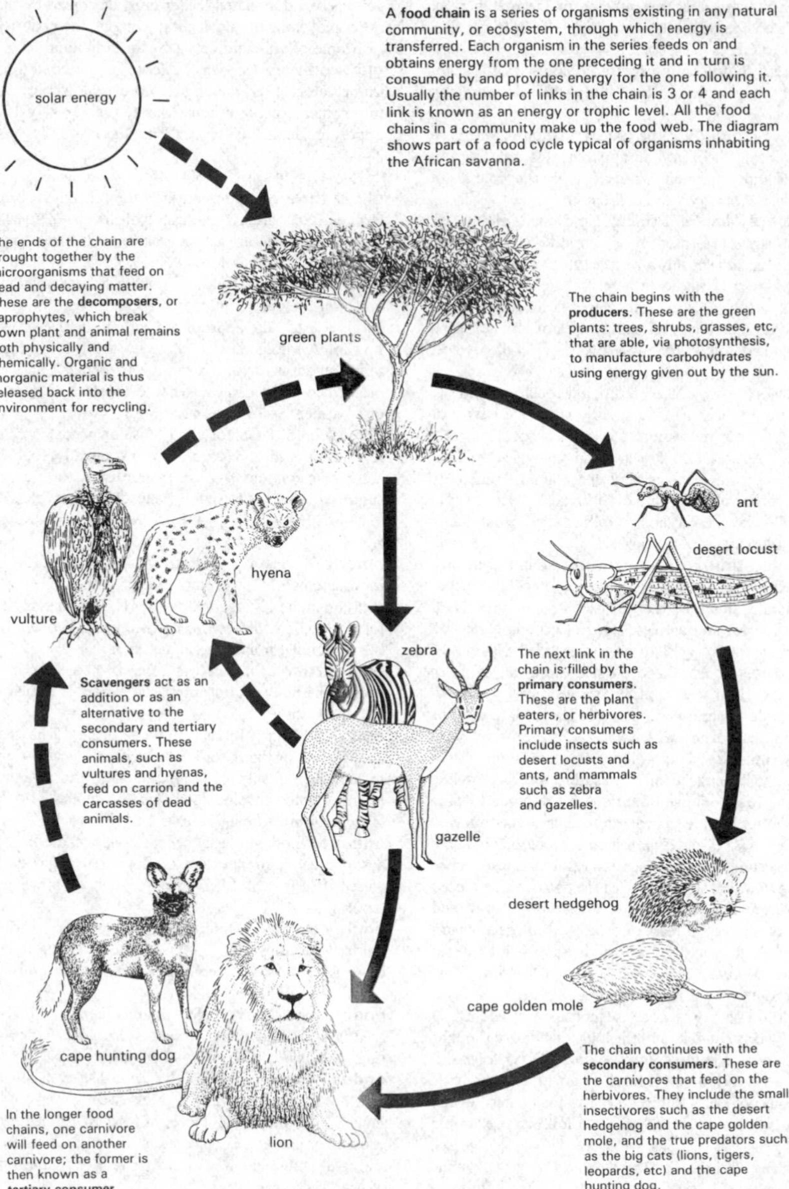

The ends of the chain are brought together by the microorganisms that feed on dead and decaying matter. These are the **decomposers**, or saprophytes, which break down plant and animal remains both physically and chemically. Organic and inorganic material is thus released back into the environment for recycling.

The chain begins with the **producers**. These are the green plants: trees, shrubs, grasses, etc, that are able, via photosynthesis, to manufacture carbohydrates using energy given out by the sun.

The next link in the chain is filled by the **primary consumers.** These are the plant eaters, or herbivores. Primary consumers include insects such as desert locusts and ants, and mammals such as zebra and gazelles.

Scavengers act as an addition or as an alternative to the secondary and tertiary consumers. These animals, such as vultures and hyenas, feed on carrion and the carcasses of dead animals.

The chain continues with the **secondary consumers.** These are the carnivores that feed on the herbivores. They include the small insectivores such as the desert hedgehog and the cape golden mole, and the true predators such as the big cats (lions, tigers, leopards, etc) and the cape hunting dog.

In the longer food chains, one carnivore will feed on another carnivore; the former is then known as a **tertiary consumer**.

carbohydrate, and fat taken into the body of a living organism and used to provide energy and sustain processes (e g growth and repair) essential for life **b** inorganic substances absorbed (e g in gaseous form or in solution) by plants **2** nutriment in solid form **3** sthg that sustains or supplies ⟨~ *for thought*⟩ [ME *fode*, fr OE *fōda*; akin to OHG *fuotar* food, fodder, L *panis* bread, *pascere* to feed]

ˈfood ˌchain *n* a hierarchical arrangement of organisms ordered according to each organism's use of the next as a food source ☞ FOOD

ˈfood ˌpoisoning *n* an acute gastrointestinal disorder caused by (the toxic products of) bacteria or by chemical residues in food

food processor *n* an electrical appliance that performs a range of operations in preparing food (e g chopping, shredding, and mixing)

ˈfoodˌstuff /-ˌstuf/ *n* a substance with food value; *esp* the raw material of food before or after processing

ˈfood ˌvacuole *n* a vacuole (e g in an amoeba) in which ingested food is digested

ˈfood ˌweb *n* all the interacting food chains in an ecological community ☞ FOOD

[1]fool /foohl/ *n* **1** a person lacking in prudence, common sense, or understanding **2a** a jester **b** a person who is victimized or made to appear foolish; a dupe **3** a cold dessert of fruit puree mixed with whipped cream or custard [ME, fr OF *fol*, fr LL *follis*, fr L, bellows, bag; akin to L *flare* to blow – more at [1]BLOW] – **foolery** /-ləri/ *n*

[2]fool *vi* **1a** to act or spend time idly or aimlessly **b(1)** to meddle, play, or trifle *with* ⟨*a dangerous man to ~ with*⟩ **(2)** to philander *with* ⟨*stop ~ing about with my wife*⟩ **2** to play or improvise a comic role; *specif* to joke ~ *vt* to make a fool of; deceive ***USE*** (*vi 1*) often + *around* or *about*

[3]fool *adj* foolish, silly ⟨*barking his ~ head off*⟩ – infml

ˈfoolˌhardy /-ˌhahdi/ *adj* foolishly adventurous and bold; rash [ME, fr OF *fol hardi*, fr *fol* foolish + *hardi* bold – more at HARDY] – **foolhardily** *adv*, **foolhardiness** *n*

foolish /ˈfoohlish/ *adj* **1** marked by or proceeding from folly **2** absurd, ridiculous – **foolishly** *adv*, **foolishness** *n*

ˈfoolˌproof /-ˌproohf/ *adj* so simple or reliable as to leave no opportunity for error, misuse, or failure ⟨*a ~ plan*⟩

foolscap /ˈfoohlskap, ˈfool-/ *n* a size of paper usu 17 × 13½in (432 × 343mm) [fr the watermark of a fool's cap formerly applied to such paper]

ˈfool's ˌerrand *n* a needless or fruitless errand

ˈfool's ˌgold *n* IRON PYRITES

ˌfool's ˈparadise *n* a state of illusory happiness

ˌfool's ˈparsley *n* a poisonous European plant of the carrot family that resembles parsley

[1]foot /foot/ *n, pl* **feet** /feet/, (*3*) **feet** *also* **foot,** (*9*) **foot** **1** the end part of the vertebrate leg on which an animal stands **2** an organ of locomotion or attachment of an invertebrate animal, esp a mollusc **3** a unit of length equal to ⅓yd (0.305m) ⟨*a 10-*foot *pole*⟩ ⟨*6* feet *tall*⟩ ☞ SYMBOL, UNIT **4** the basic unit of verse metre consisting of any of various fixed combinations of stressed and unstressed or long and short syllables **5** manner or motion of walking or running; step ⟨*fleet of ~*⟩ **6a** the lower end of the leg of a chair, table, etc **b** the piece on a sewing machine that presses the cloth against the feed **7** the lower edge or lowest part; the bottom ⟨*the ~ of a page*⟩ ⟨*the ~ of the stairs*⟩ ☞ SHIP **8a** the end that is opposite the head or top or nearest to the human feet ⟨*the ~ of the bed*⟩ **b** the part (e g of a stocking) that covers the human foot **9** *chiefly Br, sing or pl in constr* the infantry [ME *fot*, fr OE *fōt*; akin to L *ped-*, *pes* foot, Gk *pod-*, *pous*] – **footless** *adj* – **my foot** MY EYE – infml – **on foot** by walking or running ⟨*tour the city* on foot⟩ – **on one's feet** **1** standing **2** in a recovered condition (e g from illness) **3** in an impromptu manner ⟨*good debaters can think* on their feet⟩

[2]foot *vi* to dance ~ *vt* **1a** to perform the movements of (a dance) **b** to walk, run, or dance on, over, or through **2** to pay or stand credit for ⟨*agreed to ~ the bill*⟩ **3** to make or renew the foot of (e g a stocking) – **foot it** **1** to dance **2** to travel on foot

footage /ˈfootij/ *n* **1** length or quantity expressed in feet **2** (the length in feet of) exposed film

ˌfoot-and-ˈmouth, foot-and-mouth disease *n* a contagious virus disease, esp of cloven-footed animals, marked by small ulcers in the mouth, about the hoofs, and on the udder and teats

ˈfootˌball /-ˌbawl/ *n* **1** (the inflated round or oval ball used in) any of several games, esp soccer, that are played between 2 teams on a usu rectangular field having goalposts at each end and whose object is to get the ball over a goal line or between goalposts by running, passing, or kicking ☞ SPORT **2** sthg treated as a basis for contention rather than on its intrinsic merits ⟨*the bill became a political ~ in Parliament*⟩ – **footballer** *n*

ˈfootball ˌpools *n* a form of organized gambling based on forecasting the results of football matches

ˈfootˌbath /-ˌbahth/ *n* a bath for cleansing, warming, or disinfecting the feet

ˈfootˌboard /-ˌbawd/ *n* **1** a narrow platform on which to stand or brace the feet **2** a board forming the foot of a bed

ˈfoot ˌbrake *n* a brake operated by foot pressure

ˈfootˌbridge /-ˌbrij/ *n* a bridge for pedestrians

ˈfooted *adj* having a foot or feet, esp of a specified kind or number – usu in combination ⟨*a 4-*footed *animal*⟩

footer /ˈfootə/ *n, chiefly Br* soccer – infml; no longer in vogue [by shortening & alter. fr *football*]

-footer /-footə/ *comb form* (→ *n*) sby or sthg that is a (specified) number of feet in height, length, or breadth

ˈfootˌfall /-ˌfawl/ *n* the sound of a footstep

ˈfoot ˌfault *vi or n* (to make) a fault in tennis made when a server's feet are not behind the baseline

ˈfootˌhill /-ˌhil/ *n* a hill at the foot of mountains

ˈfootˌhold /-ˌhohld/ *n* **1** FOOTING 1 **2** an (established) position or basis from which to progress ⟨*secured a ~ in the plastics market*⟩

footing /ˈfooting/ *n* **1** a stable position or placing of or for the feet **2** a (condition of a) surface with respect to its suitability for walking or running on **3a** an established position; FOOTHOLD 2 **b** a position or rank in relation to others ⟨*they all started off on an equal ~*⟩ **4** an enlargement at the lower end of a foundation, wall, pier, or column to distribute the load; *also* a trench dug to accommodate this – often pl ⟨*the ~ must be excavated to a minimum depth of 4ft*⟩

footle /'foohtl/ *vi* **footling** /'foohtling/ to mess or potter *around* or *about*; *also* to waste time – infml [alter. of *footer* (to bungle), fr F *foutre* to copulate]

'foot,lights /-,liets/ *n pl* a row of lights set across the front of a stage floor

footling /'foohtling/ *adj* **1** bungling, inept ⟨~ *amateurs who understand nothing* – E R Bentley⟩ **2** unimportant, trivial; *also* pettily fussy ***USE*** infml [*footle*]

'foot,loose /-,loohs/ *adj* having no ties; free to go or do as one pleases

'footman /-mən/ *n* a servant in livery hired chiefly to wait, receive visitors, etc

footnote /-,noht/ *n* **1** a note of reference, explanation, or comment typically placed at the bottom of a printed page **2** sthg subordinately related to a larger event or work ⟨*that biography is an illuminating ~ to the history of our times*⟩ – **footnote** *vt*

[1]'foot,pad /-,pad/ *n, archaic* one who robs a pedestrian [*foot* + arch *pad* (highwayman)]

[2]footpad *n* a broad foot on the leg of a spacecraft [*foot* + [1]*pad*]

'foot,path /-,pahth/ *n* a narrow path for pedestrians; *also* PAVEMENT a

'foot,plate /-,playt/ *n, Br* the platform on which the crew stand in a locomotive

'foot,print /-,print/ *n* **1** an impression left by the foot **2** an area within which a spacecraft is intended to land

'foot ,rot *n* a progressive inflammation of the feet of sheep or cattle

,foot'rule /-'roohl/ *n* a ruler 1ft long; *also* a ruler graduated in feet and inches

foots *n pl but sing or pl in constr* material deposited, esp in aging or refining; dregs [[1]*foot* (lowest part, material at the bottom)]

footsie /'footsi/ *n* **1** surreptitious amorous caresses with the feet **2** clandestine dealings ***USE*** chiefly in *play footsie with*; infml [baby-talk dim. of [1]*foot*]

'foot,slog /-,slog/ *vi* **-gg-** to march or tramp laboriously – infml – **footslog** *n*, **footslogger** *n*

'foot ,soldier *n* an infantryman

'foot,sore /-,saw/ *adj* having sore or tender feet (e g from much walking) – **footsoreness** *n*

'foot,step /-,step/ *n* **1a** the sound of a step or tread **b** distance covered by a step **2** FOOTPRINT 1 **3** a way of life, conduct, or action – usu pl with sing. meaning ⟨*followed in his father's* ~s⟩

'foot,wear /-,weə/ *n* articles (e g shoes or boots) worn on the feet

'foot,work /-,wuhk/ *n* **1** the control and placing of the feet, esp in sport (e g in boxing or batting) **2** the activity of moving from place to place on foot ⟨*the investigation entailed a lot of* ~⟩

footy /'footi/ *n* soccer – infml [by shortening & alter. fr *football*]

fop /fop/ *n* a dandy [ME, fool; akin to ME *fobben* to deceive, MHG *voppen*] – **foppish** *adj*, **foppishly** *adv*, **foppishness** *n*

foppery /'fopəri/ *n* the behaviour, dress, or affectations (characteristic) of a fop

[1]for /fə; *strong* faw/ *prep* **1a** – used to indicate purpose ⟨*a grant ~ studying medicine*⟩ ⟨*an operation ~ cancer*⟩ ⟨*what's this knob ~?*⟩, goal or direction ⟨*left ~ home*⟩ ⟨*acted ~ the best*⟩ ⟨*getting on ~ 5*⟩, or that which is to be had or gained ⟨*now ~ a good rest*⟩ ⟨*run ~ your life*⟩ ⟨*an eye ~ a bargain*⟩ **b** to belong to ⟨*the flowers are ~ you*⟩ **2** as being or constituting ⟨*take him ~ a fool*⟩ ⟨*ate it ~ breakfast*⟩ ⟨*I ~ one don't care*⟩ – compare FOR EXAMPLE **3a** BECAUSE OF 1 ⟨*cried ~ joy*⟩ ⟨*feel better ~ a holiday*⟩ **b** because of the hindrance of ⟨*couldn't speak ~ laughing*⟩ ⟨*if it weren't ~ you I'd leave*⟩ **4a** in place of ⟨*change ~ a pound*⟩ **b** on behalf of; representing ⟨*acting ~ my client*⟩ ⟨*red ~ danger*⟩ **c** in support of; IN FAVOUR OF 1 ⟨*he played ~ England*⟩ **5** considered as; considering ⟨*tall ~ her age*⟩ ⟨*cold ~ April*⟩ **6** with respect to; concerning ⟨*famous ~ its scenery*⟩ ⟨*a stickler ~ detail*⟩ ⟨*eggs are good ~ you*⟩ **7** – used to indicate cost, payment, equivalence, or correlation ⟨*£7 ~ a hat*⟩ ⟨*all out ~ 342 runs*⟩ ⟨*punished ~ talking*⟩ ⟨*wouldn't hurt her ~ the world*⟩ ⟨*5 duds ~ every good one*⟩ **8** – used to indicate duration of time or extent of space ⟨~ *10 miles*⟩ ⟨*the worst accident ~ months*⟩ **9** on the occasion or at the time of ⟨*came home ~ Christmas*⟩ ⟨*invited them ~ 9 o'clock*⟩ **10** – used to introduce a clause with a nonfinite verb ⟨*no need ~ you to worry*⟩ ⟨*it's dangerous ~ George to hurry*⟩ **11** *chiefly NAm* AFTER 5 [ME, fr OE; akin to L *per* through, *prae* before, *pro* before, for, ahead, Gk *pro*, OE *faran* to go – more at FARE] – **for all 1** IN SPITE OF ⟨*couldn't open it* for all *their efforts*⟩ **2** to the extent that ⟨*dead* for all *I know*⟩ **3** considering how little ⟨*might as well stop talking* for all *the good it does*⟩ – **for all one is worth** with all one's might – **for it** *chiefly Br* likely to get into trouble – infml – **for what it is worth** without guarantee of wisdom or accuracy – **for you** – used after *there* or *that* in exclamations of enthusiasm or exasperation ⟨*that's country hotels* for you!⟩

[2]for *conj* **1** and the reason is that **2** BECAUSE 2

[3]for *adj* being in favour of a motion or measure

for- *prefix* **1a** so as to involve prohibition or exclusion ⟨for*bid*⟩ ⟨for*fend*⟩ **b** so as to involve omission, refraining, or neglect ⟨for*go*⟩ ⟨for*sake*⟩ ⟨for*get*⟩ ⟨for*swear*⟩ **2** destructively; detrimentally ⟨for*do*⟩ **3** completely; excessively ⟨for*spent*⟩ ⟨for*lorn*⟩ [ME, fr OE; akin to OHG *fur-* for-, OE *for*]

fora /'fawrə/ *pl of* FORUM

[1]forage /'forij/ *n* **1** food for animals, esp when taken by browsing or grazing **2** a foraging for provisions; *broadly* a search [ME, fr MF, fr OF, fr *forre* fodder, of Gmc origin; akin to OHG *fuotar* food, fodder – more at FOOD; (2) fr [2]*forage*]

[2]forage *vt* **1** to collect or take provisions or forage from **2** to secure by foraging ⟨~d *a chicken for the feast*⟩ ~ *vi* **1** to wander in search of forage or food **2** to make a search *for*; rummage – **forager** *n*

foramen /fo'raymin/ *n, pl* **foramina** /fo'raminə/, **foramens** a small anatomical opening or perforation [L *foramin-*, *foramen*, fr *forare* to bore – more at [1]BORE] – **foraminal** /fo'raminəl/ *adj*

foraminifer /,forə'minifə/, **foraminiferan** /,forəmi'nifərən/ *n, pl* **foraminifera** /,forəmi'nifərə/, **foraminifers, foraminiferans** any of an order of chiefly marine amoeba-like single-celled animals usu having hard perforated calcium-containing shells that form the bulk of chalk [NL *Foraminifera*, order name, fr L *foramin-*, *foramen* + *-fera*, neut pl of *-fer* -fer] – **foraminiferal** /-'nifərəl/, **foraminiferous** /-'nifərəs/ *adj*

foras'much as /fərəz'much/ *conj, archaic* in view of the fact that; since

[1]foray /'foray/ *vi* to make a raid or incursion [ME

forrayen, fr MF *forrer*, fr *forre* fodder – more at FORAGE] – **forayer** *n*

[2]foray *n* **1** a sudden invasion, attack, or raid **2** a brief excursion or attempt, esp outside one's accustomed sphere ⟨*the teacher's ~ into politics*⟩

[1]forbear /faw'beə/ *vb* **forbore** /faw'baw/; **forborne** /faw'bawn/ *vt* to hold oneself back from, esp with an effort of self-restraint ⟨*he* forbore *to answer the slander*⟩ ~ *vi* **1** to hold back, abstain – usu + *from* ⟨*he* forbore *from expressing his disagreement*⟩ **2** to control oneself when provoked; be patient – chiefly fml [ME *forberen*, fr OE *forberan* to endure, do without, fr *for-* + *beran* to bear]

[2]forbear /'faw,beə/ *n* a forebear

forbearance /faw'beərəns/ *n* **1** a refraining from the enforcement of sthg (e g a debt, right, or obligation) that is due **2** patience **3** leniency ['FORBEAR + -ANCE]

forbid /fə'bid/ *vt* **forbidding; forbade** /fə'bad, -'bayd, -'bed/, **forbad; forbidden /fə'bid(ə)n/** **1a** to refuse (e g by authority) to allow; command against ⟨*the law ~s shops to sell alcohol to minors*⟩ **b** to refuse access to or use of ⟨*her father* forbade *him the house*⟩ **2** to make impracticable; hinder, prevent ⟨*space ~s further treatment of the subject here*⟩ [ME *forbidden*, fr OE *forbēodan*, fr *for-* + *bēodan* to bid – more at BID] – **forbidder** *n*

for'bidden *adj, of quantum phenomena* not conforming to the usual selection principles

forbidding /fə'biding/ *adj* **1** having a menacing or dangerous appearance ⟨~ *mountains*⟩ **2** unfriendly ⟨*his father was a stern ~ figure*⟩ – **forbiddingly** *adv*, **forbiddingness** *n*

[1]force /faws/ *n* **1a** strength or energy exerted or brought to bear; active power ⟨*the ~s of nature*⟩ **b** moral or mental strength **c** capacity to persuade or convince ⟨*couldn't resist the ~ of his argument*⟩ **d** (legal) validity; operative effect ⟨*an agreement having the ~ of law*⟩ **2a(1)** a body (e g of troops or ships) assigned to a military purpose **(2)** *pl* the armed services of a nation or commander **b(1)** a body of people or things fulfilling an often specified function ⟨*a labour ~*⟩ **(2)** POLICE FORCE – often + *the* **c** an individual or group having the power of effective action ⟨*he was the driving ~ behind the passing of that bill*⟩ **3** violence, compulsion, or constraint exerted on or against a person or thing **4a** (the intensity of) an agency that if applied to a free body results chiefly in an acceleration of the body and sometimes in elastic deformation and other effects ☞ PHYSICS **b** an agency or influence analogous to a physical force ⟨*economic ~s*⟩ **5** the quality of conveying impressions intensely in writing or speech **6** *cap* a measure of wind strength as expressed by a number on the Beaufort scale ⟨*a* Force *9 gale*⟩ [ME, fr MF, fr (assumed) VL *fortia*, fr L *fortis* strong] – **in force 1** in great numbers ⟨*police were summoned* in force⟩ **2** valid, operative ⟨*the new law is now* in force⟩

[2]force *vt* **1** to compel by physical, moral, or intellectual means ⟨~d *labour*⟩ **2** to make or cause through natural or logical necessity ⟨*his arguments ~d them to admit he was right*⟩ **3a** to press, drive, or effect against resistance or inertia ⟨~ *a bill through Parliament*⟩ ⟨~d *his way through the crowd*⟩ **b** to impose or thrust urgently, importunately, or inexorably ⟨~ *unwanted attentions on a woman*⟩ **4a** to capture or penetrate by force ⟨~ *a castle*⟩ ⟨~d *the mountain passes*⟩ **b** to break open or through ⟨~ *a lock*⟩ **5a** to raise or accelerate to the utmost ⟨forcing *the pace*⟩ **b** to produce only with unnatural or unwilling effort ⟨*she ~d a smile in spite of her distress*⟩ ⟨*a ~d laugh*⟩ **6** to hasten the growth, onset of maturity, or rate of progress of ⟨forcing *rhubarb*⟩ **7** to induce (e g a particular bid from one's partner) in a card game by some conventional act, bid, etc **8** *of a batsman in cricket* to play an aggressive shot at (a delivery), esp off the back foot – **forcedly** /-sidli/ *adv*, **forcer** *n* – **force someone's hand** to cause sby to act precipitously or reveal his/her purpose or intention

'force-,feed *vt* to feed forcibly

'force ,field *n* a hypothetical invisible barrier that is impermeable to alien life forms, weaponry (e g energy beams), etc

'forceful /-f(ə)l/ *adj* possessing or filled with force; effective – **forcefully** *adv*, **forcefulness** *n*

'force-,land *vb* to land (an aircraft) involuntarily or in an emergency [back-formation fr *forced landing*] – **forced landing** *n*

,force ma'jeure /ma'zhuh (*Fr* fɔrs maʒœːr)/ *n* a disruptive event (e g war) that cannot be reasonably anticipated – compare ACT OF GOD [F, superior force]

'force,meat /-,meet/ *n* a savoury highly seasoned stuffing, esp of breadcrumbs and meat [*force* (alter. of *farce*) + *meat*]

,force of 'habit *n* behaviour made involuntary or automatic by repetition

forceps /'fawsips, -seps/ *n, pl* **forceps** an instrument used (e g in surgery and watchmaking) for grasping, holding firmly, or pulling – usu pl with sing. meaning [L, fr *formus* warm + *capere* to take – more at WARM, HEAVE]

'force ,pump *n* a pump that can force a liquid, esp water, higher than atmospheric pressure could

'force ,shield *n* FORCE FIELD

forcible /'fawsəbl/ *adj* **1** effected by force used against opposition or resistance **2** powerful, forceful ⟨*a ~ argument*⟩ – **forcibleness** *n*, **forcibly** *adv*

'forcing ,ground *n* HOTBED 2

[1]ford /fawd/ *n* a shallow part of a river or other body of water that can be crossed by wading, in a vehicle, etc [ME, fr OE; akin to ON *fjörthr* fiord, L *portus* port, OE *faran* to go – more at FARE]

[2]ford *vt* to cross (a river, stream, etc) at a ford – **fordable** *adj*

[1]fore /faw/ *adj or adv* (situated) in, towards, or adjacent to the front ☞ SHIP [ME, fr OE; akin to OE *for*]

[2]fore *n* sthg that occupies a forward position – **to the fore** in or into a position of prominence

[3]fore *interj* – used by a golfer to warn anyone in the probable line of flight of his/her ball [prob short for *before*]

fore- /faw-/ *comb form* **1** (occurring) earlier or beforehand ⟨fore*payment*⟩ ⟨foresee⟩ **2a** situated at the front; in front ⟨fore*leg*⟩ **b** front part of ⟨fore*arm*⟩ [ME *for-*, *fore-*, fr OE *fore-*, fr *fore*, adv]

,fore-and-'aft /ahft/ *adj* **1** lying, running, or acting in the general line of the length of a ship or other construction **2** having no square sails

,fore and 'aft *adv* from stem to stern

[1]forearm /faw'rahm, faw'ahm/ *vt* to arm in advance; prepare

[2]forearm /'faw,rahm/ *n* (the part in other vertebrates corresponding to) the human arm between the elbow and the wrist

forebear, forbear /'faw,beə/ *n* an ancestor, forefather [ME (Sc) *forebear*, fr *fore-* + *-bear* (fr *been* to be)]

forebode /faw'bohd, fə-/ *vt* **1** to foretell, portend **2** to have a premonition of (evil, misfortune, etc) – **foreboder** *n*

fore'boding /'bohding/ *n* an omen, prediction, or presentiment, esp of coming evil

forebrain /'faw,brayn/ *n* (the telencephalon and other parts of the adult brain that develop from) the front of the 3 primary divisions of the embryonic vertebrate brain

¹**forecast** /'faw,kahst/ *vb* **forecast, forecasted** *vt* **1** to estimate or predict (some future event or condition), esp as a result of rational study and analysis of available pertinent data **2** to serve as a forecast of; presage ⟨*such events may ~ peace*⟩ ~ *vi* to calculate or predict the future [ME *forecasten*, fr *fore-* + *casten* to cast, contrive] – **forecaster** *n*

²**forecast** *n* a prophecy, estimate, or prediction of a future happening or condition; *esp* a weather forecast

forecastle, fo'c'sle /'fohks(ə)l/ *n* **1** a short raised deck at the bow of a ship ☞ SHIP **2** a forward part of a merchant ship having the living quarters [ME *forecastel*, fr *fore-* fore- + *castel* castle]

foreclose /faw'klohz/ *vt* **1** to take away the right to redeem (e g a mortgage), usu because of nonpayment **2** to take away the right to redeem a mortgage or other debt from ~ *vi* to foreclose a mortgage or other debt [ME *forclosen*, fr OF *forclos*, pp of *forclore*, fr *fors* outside (fr L *foris*) + *clore* to close – more at FORUM] – **foreclosure** /-'klohzhə/ *n*

'**fore,court** /-,kawt/ *n* an open or paved area in front of a building; *esp* that part of a petrol station where the petrol pumps are situated

'**fore,deck** /-,dek/ *n* the forepart of a ship's main deck

'**fore-,edge** *n* the edge of a book (page) opposite the spine

'**fore,father** /-,fahdhə/ *n* **1** ANCESTOR 1a **2** a person of an earlier period and common heritage

'**fore,finger** /-,fing·gə/ *n* the finger next to the thumb

'**fore,foot** /-,foot/ *n* the forward part of a ship where the stem and keel meet

'**fore,front** /-,frunt/ *n* the foremost part or place; the vanguard ⟨*was in the ~ of the progressive movement*⟩

foregather /faw'gadhə/ *vi* to forgather

forego /fə'goh, faw-/ *vt* **foregoes; foregoing; forewent** /faw'went/; **foregone** /faw'gon/ to forgo

foregoing /'faw,goh·ing/ *adj* going before; that immediately precedes ⟨*the ~ statement is open to challenge*⟩ [fr prp of *forego* (to go before)]

,**foregone con'clusion** *n* an inevitable result; a certainty ⟨*the victory was a ~*⟩

'**fore,ground** /-,grownd/ *n* **1** the part of a picture or view nearest to and in front of the spectator **2** a position of prominence; the forefront

¹'**fore,hand** /-,hand/ *n* **1** the part of a horse in front of the rider **2** a forehand stroke in tennis, squash, etc; *also* the side or part of the court on which such strokes are made

²**forehand** *adj or adv* (made) with the palm of the hand turned in the direction of movement

forehead /'faw,hed, 'forid/ *n* the part of the face above the eyes

'**fore,hock** /-,hok/ *n* a foreleg of a bacon pig ☞ MEAT

foreign /'forən; *also* 'forin/ *adj* **1** (situated) outside a place or country; *esp* (situated) outside one's own country **2** born in, belonging to, or characteristic of some place or country other than the one under consideration **3** of or proceeding from some other person or material thing than the one under consideration **4** alien in character; not connected or pertinent *to* **5** of, concerned with, or dealing with other nations ⟨*~ affairs*⟩ ⟨*~ minister*⟩ ⟨*~ trade*⟩ **6** occurring in an abnormal situation in the living body and commonly introduced from outside [ME *forein*, fr OF, fr LL *foranus* on the outside, fr L *foris* outside – more at FORUM] – **foreignism** *n*, **foreignness** *n*

,**foreign 'aid** *n* (economic) assistance provided by one nation to another

'**foreigner** /-nə/ *n* **1** a person belonging to or owing allegiance to a foreign country; an alien **2** *chiefly dial* STRANGER 1b; *esp* a person not native to a community

,**foreign ex'change** *n* (the buying and selling of) foreign currency

,**foreign 'legion** *n* a body of foreign volunteers serving within a regular national army, esp that of France [trans of F *légion étrangère*]

'**foreign ,office** *n* the government department for foreign affairs

,**foreign 'secretary** *n* a government minister for foreign affairs

forejudge /,faw'juj/ *vt* to prejudge

fore'know *vt* **foreknew** /-'nyooh/; **foreknown** /-'nohn/ to have previous knowledge of; know beforehand, esp by paranormal means or by revelation – **foreknowledge** /-,nolij/ *n*

'**foreland** /-lənd/ *n* a promontory, headland

'**fore,leg** /-,leg/ *n* a front leg, esp of a quadruped

'**fore,limb** /-,lim/ *n* an arm, fin, wing, or leg that is (homologous to) a foreleg

'**fore,lock** /-,lok/ *n* a lock of hair growing just above the forehead ☞ ANATOMY

'**foreman** /-mən/, *fem* '**fore,woman** *n*, *pl* **foremen** /-mən/ **1** the chairman and spokesman of a jury **2** a person, often a chief worker, who supervises a group of workers, a particular operation, or a section of a plant

'**fore,mast** /-,mahst/ *n* the (lower part of the) mast nearest the bow of a ship ☞ SHIP

¹'**fore,most** /-,mohst, -məst/ *adj* **1** first in a series or progression **2** of first rank or position; preeminent [ME *formest*, fr OE, superl of *forma* first; akin to OHG *fruma* advantage, OE *fore* fore]

²**foremost** *adv* most importantly ⟨*first and ~*⟩

'**fore,name** /-,naym/ *n* a name that precedes a person's surname

'**fore,noon** /-,noohn/ *n* *the* morning – fml

forensic /fə'renzik/ *adj* **1** belonging to or used in courts of law **2** of or being the scientific investigation of crime [L *forensis* public, forensic, fr *forum*] – **forensically** *adv*

forensic medicine *n* a science that deals with the application of medical facts and methods to criminal investigations and legal problems

,**foreor'dain** /-aw'dayn/ *vt* to settle, arrange, or

appoint in advance; predestine – **foreordination** /-awdi'naysh(ə)n/ *n*

'fore,part /-,paht/ *n* the front part of sthg

'fore,play /-,play/ *n* erotic stimulation preceding sexual intercourse

'fore,quarter /-,kwawtə/ *n* the front half of a side (of the carcass) of a quadruped

'fore,runner /-,runə/ *n* **1** a premonitory sign or symptom **2a** a predecessor, forefather **b** PROTOTYPE 1

'fore,sail /-,sayl/ *n* **1** the lowest square sail on the foremast of a square-rigged ship **2** the principal fore-and-aft sail set on a schooner's foremast

foresee /faw'see/ *vt* **foreseeing; foresaw** /-'saw/; **foreseen** /-'seen/ to be aware of (e g a development) beforehand – **foreseeable** *adj*, **foreseer** /-'see·ə/ *n*

fore'shadow /-'shadoh/ *vt* to represent or typify beforehand; prefigure, suggest ⟨*present trends ~ future events*⟩ – **foreshadower** *n*

'fore,sheets /-,sheets/ *n pl* the forward part of an open boat

'fore,shore /-,shaw/ *n* **1** a strip of land bordering a body of water **2** the part of a seashore between high-tide and low-tide marks

fore'shorten /-'shawt(ə)n/ *vt* **1** to shorten (a detail in a drawing or painting) so as to create an illusion of depth **2** to make more compact

fore'show /-'shoh/ *vt* **foreshown** /-'shohn/ to foretell or foreshadow

'fore,sight /-,siet/ *n* **1** foreseeing, prescience **2** provident care; prudence ⟨*had the ~ to invest his money wisely*⟩ **3** the sight nearest the muzzle on a firearm – **foresighted** /-'sietid/ *adj*, **foresightedly** /-'sietidli/ *adv*, **foresightedness** /-'sietidnis/ *n*

'fore,skin /-,skin/ *n* a fold of skin that covers the glans of the penis

¹forest /'forist/ *n* **1** a tract of wooded land in Britain formerly owned by the sovereign and used for hunting game **2** a dense growth of trees and underbrush covering a large tract of land ☞ PLANT **3** sthg resembling a profusion of trees ⟨*a ~ of TV aerials*⟩ [ME, fr OF, fr ML *forestis*, fr L *foris* outside – more at FORUM]

²forest *vt* to cover with trees or forest – **forestation** /-'staysh(ə)n/ *n*

fore'stall /-'stawl/ *vt* **1** to exclude, hinder, or prevent by prior measures **2** to get ahead of; anticipate [ME *forstallen*, fr *forstall* act of waylaying, fr OE *foresteall*, fr *fore-* + *steall* position, stall] – **forestaller** *n*, **forestallment** *n*

'fore,stay /-,stay/ *n* a stay from the top of the foremast to the bow of a ship

forester /'foristə/ *n* **1** a person trained in forestry **2** a person, animal, moth, etc that inhabits forest land

,forest 'ranger *n* an officer charged with the patrolling and guarding of a forest

forestry /'foristri/ *n* **1** forest land **2** the scientific cultivation or management of forests

foretaste /'faw,tayst/ *n* **1** an advance indication or warning **2** a small anticipatory sample

fore'tell /-'tel/ *vt* **foretold** /-'tohld/ to tell beforehand; predict – **foreteller** *n*

'fore,thought /-,thawt/ *n* **1** a thinking or planning out in advance; premeditation **2** consideration for the future

,fore'token /-'tohkən/ *vt or n* (to indicate or warn of with) a premonitory sign

¹forever /fə'revə/ *adv* **1 forever, forevermore** for all future time; indefinitely ⟨*wants to live ~*⟩ **2** persistently, incessantly ⟨*is ~ whistling out of tune*⟩

²forever *n* a seemingly endless length of time ⟨*took her ~ to find the answer*⟩

fore'warn /-'wawn/ *vt* to warn in advance

'fore,woman /-,woomən/ *n, pl* **forewomen** /-wimin/ a woman who acts as a foreman

'fore,word /-,wuhd/ *n* a preface; *esp* one written by sby other than the author of the text

¹forfeit /'fawfit/ *n* **1** sthg lost, taken away, or imposed as a penalty **2** the loss or forfeiting of sthg, esp of civil rights **3a** an article deposited or a task performed in the game of forfeits **b** *pl but sing or pl in constr* a game in which articles are deposited (e g for making a mistake) and then redeemed by performing a silly task [ME *forfait*, fr MF, fr pp of *forfaire* to commit a crime, forfeit, prob fr *fors* outside (fr L *foris*) + *faire* to do, fr L *facere* – more at FORUM, ¹DO] – **forfeit** *adj*

²forfeit *vt* **1** to lose the right to by some error, offence, or crime **2** to subject to confiscation as a forfeit – **forfeitable** *adj*, **forfeiture** /-,fichə/ *n*

forfend /faw'fend/ *vt* to forbid – chiefly in *heaven forfend* [ME *forfenden*, fr *for-* + *fenden* to fend – more at FEND]

forgather, foregather /faw'gadhə/ *vi* to come together; assemble

¹forge /fawj/ *n* (a workshop with) an open furnace where metal, esp iron, is heated and wrought [ME, fr OF, fr L *fabrica*, fr *fabr-*, *faber* smith – more at DAFT]

²forge *vt* **1** to shape (metal or a metal object) by heating and hammering or with a press **2** to form or bring into being, esp by an expenditure of effort ⟨*made every effort to ~ party unity*⟩ **3** to counterfeit (esp a signature, document, or bank note) ~ *vi* to commit forgery – **forgeable** *adj*, **forger** *n*

³forge *vi* **1** to move forwards slowly and steadily but with effort ⟨*the great ship ~*d *through the waves*⟩ **2** to move with a sudden increase of speed and power ⟨*the horse ~*d *ahead to win the race*⟩ [prob alter. of ²*force*]

forgery /'fawjəri/ *n* **1** (the crime of) forging **2** a forged document, bank note, etc

forget /fə'get/ *vb* **forgetting; forgot** /-'got/; **forgotten** /-'got(ə)n/, *archaic or NAm* **forgot** *vt* **1** to fail to remember; lose the remembrance of ⟨*I ~ his name*⟩ **2** to fail to give attention to; disregard ⟨forgot *his old friends*⟩ **3a** to disregard intentionally; overlook ⟨*we will ~ our differences*⟩ **b** to reject the possibility of ⟨*as for going out tonight, ~ it!*⟩ ~ *vi* **1** to cease remembering or noticing ⟨*forgive and ~*⟩ **2** to fail to remember at the proper time – usu + *about* ⟨*~ about paying the bill*⟩ [ME *forgeten*, fr OE *forgietan*, fr *for-* + *-gietan* (akin to ON *geta* to get)] – **forgetter** *n* – **forget oneself** to lose one's dignity, temper, or self-control; act unsuitably or unworthily

for'getful /-f(ə)l/ *adj* **1** likely or apt to forget **2** characterized by negligent failure to remember; neglectful – usu + *of* ⟨*~ of his manners*⟩ **3** inducing oblivion ⟨*~ sleep*⟩ – poetic – **forgetfully** *adv*, **forgetfulness** *n*

for'get-me-,not *n* any of a genus of small plants of the borage family with white or bright blue flowers usu arranged in a spike

forgettable /fə'getəbl/ *adj* apt to forget or be forgotten; *esp* unworthy of remembrance ⟨*a* ~ *performance*⟩

forgive /fə'giv/ *vb* **forgave** /-'gayv/; **forgiven** /-'giv(ə)n/ *vt* **1** to cease to resent ⟨~ *an insult*⟩ ⟨~ *one's enemies*⟩ **2** to pardon ⟨~ *us our trespasses*⟩ ~ *vi* to grant forgiveness [ME *forgiven*, fr OE *forgifan*, fr *for-* + *gifan* to give] – **forgivable** *adj*, **forgivably** *adv*, **forgiver** *n*, **forgiving** *adj*, **forgivingly** *adv*

for'giveness /-nis/ *n* forgiving or being forgiven; pardon

forgo, forego /fə'goh, faw-/ *vt* **forgoes; forgoing; forwent** /faw'went/; **forgone** /faw'gon/ to abstain or refrain from ⟨~ *immediate gratification for the sake of future gains*⟩ [ME *forgon*, fr OE *forgān* to pass by, forgo, fr *for-* + *gān* to go]

forint /'fawrint/ *n* ☞ *Hungary* at NATIONALITY [Hung]

¹fork /fawk/ *n* **1** a tool or implement with 2 or more prongs set on the end of a handle: e g **a** an agricultural or gardening tool for digging, carrying, etc **b** a small implement for eating or serving food **2a** a forked part, or piece of equipment **b** a forked support for a cycle wheel – often pl with sing. meaning **3** (a part containing) a division into branches **4** any of the branches into which sthg forks **5** an attack by a chess piece (e g a knight) on 2 pieces simultaneously [ME *forke*, fr OE & ONF; OE *forca* & ONF *forque*, fr L *furca*] – **forkful** *n*

²fork *vi* **1** to divide into 2 or more branches ⟨*where the road* ~s⟩ **2** to make a turn into one of the branches of a fork ⟨*we* ~ed *left at the inn*⟩ **3** to make a payment or contribution – + *out* or *up* ~ *vt* **1** to raise, pitch, dig, or work with a fork ⟨~ *hay*⟩ **2** to attack (2 chessmen) simultaneously **3** to pay, contribute – + *out, over,* or *up* ⟨~ed *out half of his salary for a new car*⟩ *USE* (*vi 3; vt 3*) infml

forked *adj* having one end divided into 2 or more branches or points ⟨~ *lightning*⟩

'fork,lift, ,forklift 'truck *n* a vehicle for hoisting and transporting heavy objects by means of steel prongs inserted under the load

forlorn /fə'lawn/ *adj* **1a** bereft or forsaken *of* **b** sad and lonely because of isolation or desertion; desolate **2** in poor condition; miserable, wretched ⟨~ *tumbledown buildings*⟩ **3** nearly hopeless ⟨*a* ~ *attempt*⟩ [ME *forloren*, fr OE, pp of *forlēosan* to lose, fr *for-* + *lēosan* to lose] – **forlornly** *adv*

for,lorn 'hope *n* a desperate or extremely difficult enterprise [by folk etymology fr D *verloren hoop*, lit., lost troop]

¹form /fawm/ *n* **1a** the shape and structure of sthg as distinguished from its material **b** a body (e g of a person), esp in its external appearance or as distinguished from the face **2** the essential nature of a thing as distinguished from the matter in which it is embodied **3a** established or correct method of proceeding or behaving ⟨*I must ask for your name as a matter of* ~⟩ **b** a prescribed and set order of words ⟨*the* ~ *of the marriage service*⟩ **4** a printed or typed document; *esp* one with blank spaces for insertion of required or requested information ⟨*income-tax* ~s⟩ **5a** conduct regulated by external controls (e g custom or etiquette); ceremony ⟨*the rigid* ~ *of the imperial court*⟩ **b** manner or conduct of a specified sort, as tested by a prescribed or accepted standard ⟨*rudeness is simply bad* ~⟩ **6a** the bed or nest of a hare **b** a long seat; a bench **7** sthg (e g shuttering) that holds, supports, and determines shape **8a** the way in which sthg is arranged, exists, or shows itself ⟨*written in the* ~ *of a letter*⟩ **b** a kind, variety ⟨*one* ~ *of respiratory disorder*⟩ **9a** orderly method of arrangement (e g in the presentation of ideas); manner of coordinating elements (e g of an artistic production or line of reasoning) ⟨*his work lacks* ~⟩ **b** the structural element, plan, or design of a work of art – compare CONTENT 2b **10** *sing or pl in constr* a class organized for the work of a particular year, esp in a British school **11a** the past performances of a competitor considered as a guide to its future performance **b** known ability to perform ⟨*a singer at the top of his* ~⟩ **c** condition suitable for performing, esp in sports – often + *in, out of,* or *off* ⟨*was out of* ~ *all season*⟩ **12a** LINGUISTIC FORM **b** any of the ways in which a word may be written or spoken as a result of inflection or change of spelling or pronunciation ⟨*verbal* ~s⟩ **13** *NAm* a forme **14** *Br* a criminal record – slang [ME *forme*, fr OF, fr L *forma*, perh modif of Gk *morphē* form, shape] – **formless** *adj*, **formlessly** *adv*, **formlessness** *n*

²form *vt* **1** to give form, shape, or existence to; fashion ⟨~ed *from clay*⟩ ⟨~ *a judgment*⟩ **2a** to give a particular shape to; shape or mould into a certain state or after a particular model ⟨~ed *the dough into various shapes*⟩ ⟨*a state* ~ed *along the lines of the Roman Republic*⟩ **b** to arrange themselves in ⟨*the women* ~ed *a line*⟩ **c** to model or train by instruction and discipline ⟨*a mind* ~ed *by classical education*⟩ **3** to develop, acquire ⟨~ *a habit*⟩ **4** to serve to make up or constitute; be a usu essential or basic element of **5a** to produce (e g a tense) by inflection ⟨~s *the past in* -ed⟩ **b** to combine to make (a compound word) **6** to arrange in order; DRAW UP 1 ~ *vi* **1** to become formed or shaped ⟨*a scab* ~ed *over the wound*⟩ **2** to take (a definite) form; come into existence ⟨*thunderclouds were* ~ing *over the hills*⟩ – **formable** *adj*

form- *comb form* formic acid ⟨form*aldehyde*⟩ ⟨formate⟩ [*formic*]

-form /-fawm/, **-iform** *comb form* (→ *adj*) having the form or shape of; resembling ⟨*cruci*form⟩ [MF & L; MF *-forme*, fr L *-formis*, fr *forma*]

formal /'fawml/ *adj* **1a** determining or being the essential constitution or structure ⟨~ *cause*⟩ **b** of, concerned with, or being the (outward) form of sthg as distinguished from its content **2** following or according with established form, custom, or rule; conventional ⟨*lacked* ~ *qualifications for the job*⟩ **3a** based on conventional forms and rules ⟨~ *landscaping*⟩ **b** characterized by punctilious respect for correct procedure ⟨*very* ~ *in all his dealings*⟩ **c** rigidly ceremonious; prim **4** having the appearance without the substance; ostensible ⟨~ *Christians who go to church only at Easter*⟩ – **formally** *adv*

formaldehyde /faw'maldi,hied/ *n* a pungent irritating gas used chiefly as a disinfectant and preservative and in chemical synthesis [ISV *form-* + *aldehyde*]

formalin /'fawməlin/ *n* a clear aqueous solution of formaldehyde [fr *Formalin*, a trademark]

formalism /'fawml,iz(ə)m/ *n* the practice or doctrine of strict adherence to or sole consideration of prescribed or external forms (e g in mathematics, religion, or art) – **formalist** *n or adj*, **formalistic** /-'istik/ *adj*

formality /faw'maləti/ *n* **1** compliance with or observance of formal or conventional rules **2** an established form that is required or conventional

formal·ize, -ise /'fawml,iez/ *vt* **1** to make formal **2** to give formal status or approval to – **formalization** /-'zaysh(ə)n/ *n*

formant /'fawmənt/ *n* a characteristic resonance band of a vowel sound or musical instrument [G, fr L *formant-, formans*, prp of *formare*]

[1]**format** /'fawmat/ *n* **1** the shape, size, and general make-up (e g of a book) **2** the general plan of organization or arrangement [F or G; F, fr G, fr L *formatus*, pp of *formare* to form, fr *forma*]

[2]**format** *vt* **-tt-** to arrange (e g a book or data) in a particular format or style

formation /faw'maysh(ə)n/ *n* **1** giving form or shape to sthg or taking form; development **2** sthg formed ⟨*new word* ~s⟩ **3** the manner in which a thing is formed; structure **4** a body or series of rocks represented as a unit in geological mapping **5** an arrangement of a group of people or things in some prescribed manner or for a particular purpose; *also, sing or pl in constr* such a group – **formational** *adj*

[1]**formative** /'fawmətiv/ *adj* **1a** (capable of) giving form; constructive ⟨*a ~ influence*⟩ **b** used in word formation or inflection ⟨*a ~ affix*⟩ **2** capable of alteration by growth and development ⟨~ *tissues*⟩ **3** of or characterized by formative effects or formation ⟨~ *years*⟩ – **formatively** *adv*

[2]**formative** *n* a formative affix

'**form ,class** *n* a class of linguistic forms that can be used in the same position in a construction and that share 1 or more grammatical features

forme, *NAm* **form** /fawm/ *n* a frame enclosing metal type or blocks ready for printing [F *forme*, lit., form]

[1]**former** /'fawmə/ *adj* **1** of or occurring in the past ⟨*in ~ times*⟩ **2** preceding in time or order ⟨*the ~ Prime Minister*⟩ **3** first of 2 things (understood to have been) mentioned [ME, fr *forme* first, fr OE *forma* – more at FOREMOST]

[2]**former** *n, pl* **former** the first mentioned; first ⟨*of puppies and kittens the ~ are harder to train*⟩

[3]**former** *n, chiefly Br* a member of a specified school form or year ⟨*a sixth ~*⟩ – often in combination [[1]*form* + [2]*-er*]

[4]**former** *n* a frame or core on which an electrical coil is wound [[2]FORM + [2]-ER]

formerly /'fawməli/ *adv* at an earlier time; previously

Formica /faw'miekə/ *trademark* – used for any of various laminated plastics used for surfaces, esp on wood

,**formic 'acid** /'fawmik/ *n* a pungent corrosive liquid acid naturally produced by ants [L *formica* ant]

formicary /'fawmikəri/ *n* an ant nest [ML *formicarium*, fr L *formica*]

formidable /'fawmidəbl; *also* fə'midəbl/ *adj* **1** causing fear, dread, or apprehension ⟨*a ~ prospect*⟩ **2** difficult to overcome; discouraging approach **3** tending to inspire respect or awe [ME, fr L *formidabilis*, fr *formidare* to fear, fr *formido* fear; akin to Gk *mormō* she-monster] – **formidableness** *n*, **formidably** *adv*

'**form ,letter** *n* a standard letter to which pertinent details (e g address and name) are added and which is sent to a usu large number of people

,**form of 'address** *n* a correct title or expression of politeness to be used to sby

formula /'fawmyoolə/ *n, pl* **formulas, formulae** /-lee, -lie/ **1a** a set form of words for use in a ceremony or ritual **b** (a conventionalized statement intended to express) a truth, principle, or procedure, esp as a basis for negotiation or action ⟨*the 2 sides worked out a peace ~*⟩ ⟨*the ~ for a good marriage*⟩ **2** (a list of ingredients used in) a recipe **3a** a fact, rule, or principle expressed in symbols **b** a symbolic expression of the chemical composition of a substance **c** a group of numerical symbols associated to express a single concept **4** a prescribed or set form or method (e g of writing); an established rule or custom ⟨*unimaginative television programmes written to a ~*⟩ **5** a classification of racing cars specifying esp size, weight, and engine capacity [L, dim. of *forma* form] – **formulaic** /-'layik/ *adj*, **formulaically** *adv*

'**formular·ize, -ise** /-riez/ *vt* FORMULATE 1 – **formularization** /-'zaysh(ə)n/ *n*

formulary /'fawmyooləri/ *n* a book containing a list of medicinal substances and formulas

formulate /'fawmyoolayt/ *vt* **1** to state in or reduce to a formula **2** to devise or develop ⟨~ *policy*⟩ ⟨~d *a new soap*⟩ – **formulation** /-'laysh(ə)n/ *n*, **formulator** *n*

'**form,work** /-,wuhk/ *n* shuttering

formyl /'formil/ *n* the radical HCO of formic acid that is also characteristic of aldehydes [ISV]

fornicate /'fawnikayt/ *vi* to commit fornication [LL *fornicatus*, pp of *fornicare*, fr L *fornic-, fornix* arch, vault, brothel] – **fornicator** *n*

fornication /,fawni'kaysh(ə)n/ *n* voluntary sexual intercourse outside marriage

for 'nothing *adv* **1** FREE 2 **2** to no purpose; without result

forsake /fə'sayk/ *vt* **forsook** /fə'sook/ ; **forsaken** /fə'saykən/ **1** to renounce (e g sthg once cherished) without intent to recover or resume ⟨forsook *her family ties*⟩ **2** to desert, abandon ⟨*false friends ~ us in adversity*⟩ [ME *forsaken*, fr OE *forsacan*, fr *for-* + *sacan* to dispute; akin to OE *sacu* action at law – more at [1]SAKE]

forsooth /fə'soohth/ *adv* indeed, actually – now often used to imply contempt or doubt [ME *for soth*, fr OE *forsōth*, fr *for* + *sōth* truth, fr neut of *sōth* true – more at SOOTHE]

forswear /faw'sweə/ *vb* **forswear; forsworn** /-'swawn/ *vt* **1a** to reject or deny under oath **b** to (solemnly) renounce **2** to make a liar of (oneself) (as if) under oath ~ *vi* to swear falsely [ME *forsweren*, fr OE *forswerian*, fr *for-* + *swerian* to swear – more at SWEAR]

forsworn /faw'swawn/ *adj* guilty of perjury

forsythia /faw'siethi·ə, -thyə/ *n* any of a genus of ornamental shrubs of the olive family with bright yellow bell-shaped flowers appearing in early spring before the leaves [NL, genus name, fr William *Forsyth* †1804 Br botanist]

fort /fawt/ *n* a strong or fortified place [ME *forte*, fr MF *fort*, fr *fort* strong, fr L *fortis*]

fortalice /'fawtəlis/ *n, archaic* **1** a fortress **2** a small fort or outwork [ME, fr ML *fortalitia* – more at FORTRESS]

[1]**forte** /fawt; *esp sense* ' 'fawtay/ *n* **1** the area or skill in which a person excels **2** the strongest part of a sword blade being between the middle and the hilt [MF *fort*, fr *fort* strong]

[2]**forte** /'fawti, -tay/ *n, adv, or adj* (a note or passage

played) in a loud and often forceful manner – used in music [It, fr *forte* strong, fr L *fortis*]

forth /fawth/ *adv* **1** onwards in time, place, or order; forwards ⟨*from that day* ~⟩ **2** out into notice or view ⟨*put* ~ *leaves*⟩ **3** away from a centre; abroad ⟨*went* ~ *to preach*⟩ [ME, fr OE; akin to OE *for*]

forth'coming /-'kuming/ *adj* **1** approaching **2a** made available ⟨*new funds will be* ~ *next year*⟩ **b** willing to give information; responsive [obs *forth-come* (to come forth)]

'forth,right /-,riet/ *adj* going straight to the point without ambiguity or hesitation – **forthrightly** *adv*, **forthrightness** *n*

forth'with /-'widh/ *adv* immediately

fortification /,fawtifi'kaysh(ə)n/ *n* **1a** fortifying **b** the science or art of providing defensive works **2** sthg that fortifies, defends, or strengthens; *esp* works erected to defend a place or position

,fortified 'wine /'fawti,fied/ *n* a wine to which alcohol has been added during or after fermentation

fortify /'fawtifie/ *vt* to make strong: e g **a** to strengthen and secure by military defences **b** to give strength, courage, or endurance to; strengthen **c** to add material to for strengthening or enriching ~ *vi* to erect fortifications [ME *fortifien*, fr MF *fortifier*, fr LL *fortificare*, fr L *fortis* strong] – **fortifier** *n*

fortissimo /faw'tisimoh/ *adv or adj* very loud – used in music [It, superl of *forte*]

fortitude /'fawtityoohd, -choohd/ *n* patient courage in pain or adversity [ME, fr L *fortitudin-*, *fortitudo*, fr *fortis*]

fortnight /'fawt,niet/ *n*, *chiefly Br* two weeks [ME *fourtenight*, alter. of *fourtene night*, fr OE *fēowertȳne niht* fourteen nights]

[1]'fort,nightly /-li/ *adj* occurring or appearing once a fortnight

[2]fortnightly *adv*, *chiefly Br* once in a fortnight; every fortnight

[3]fortnightly *n* a publication issued fortnightly

Fortran, FORTRAN /'fawtran/ *n* a high-level computer language, primarily for mathematical and scientific applications [*for*mula *tran*slation]

fortress /'fawtris/ *n* a fortified place; *esp* a large and permanent fortification, sometimes including a town [ME *forteresse*, fr MF *forteresce*, fr ML *fortalitia*, fr L *fortis* strong]

fortuitous /faw'tyooh·itəs, -'chooh-/ *adj* **1** occurring by chance **2** fortunate, lucky [L *fortuitus*; akin to L *fort-*, *fors* chance, luck] – **fortuitously** *adv*, **fortuitousness** *n*

fortunate /'fawch(ə)nət/ *adj* **1** unexpectedly bringing some good; auspicious **2** lucky – **fortunately** *adv*, **fortunateness** *n*

fortune /'fawchoohn, -chən/ *n* **1** *often cap* a supposed (personified) power that unpredictably determines events and issues **2a** prosperity attained partly through luck **b** LUCK 1 **c** *pl* the favourable or unfavourable events that accompany the progress of an individual or thing ⟨*tracing the* ~s *of a rags-to-riches hero*⟩ ⟨*the declining* ~s *of the film industry*⟩ **3** destiny, fate ⟨*tell his* ~ *with cards*⟩ **4a** material possessions or wealth **b** a very large sum of money ⟨*won a* ~ *on the pools*⟩ – infml [ME, fr MF, fr L *fortuna*; akin to L *fort-*, *fors* chance, luck, *ferre* to carry – more at [2]BEAR]

'fortune ,hunter *n* a person who seeks wealth, esp by marriage

'fortune-,teller *n* a person who claims to foretell future events – **fortune-telling** *n or adj*

forty /'fawti/ *n* **1** ☞ NUMBER **2** *pl* the numbers 40 to 49; *specif* a range of temperatures, ages, or dates in a century characterized by those numbers [ME *fourty*, adj, fr OE *fēowertig*, fr *fēowertig* group of 40, fr *fēower* four + *-tig* group of 10 – more at EIGHTY] – **fortieth** /-ith/ *adj or n*, **forty** *adj or pron*, **fortyfold** /-,fohld/ *adj or adv*

,forty-'five *n* **1** ☞ NUMBER **2** a gramophone record that plays at 45 revolutions per minute – usu written 45 – **forty-five** *adj or pron*

,forty 'winks *n pl but sing or pl in constr* [2]NAP – infml

forum /'fawrəm/ *n*, *pl* **forums** *also* **fora** /-rə/ **1a** the marketplace or public place of an ancient Roman city forming the public centre **b** a public meeting place or medium for open discussion **2a** a public meeting or lecture involving audience discussion **b** a programme (e g on radio or television) based around the discussion of problems [L; akin to L *foris* outside, *fores* door – more at DOOR]

[1]forward /'faw·wood; *sense 1 also* 'forəd *when referring to ships and aeroplanes*/ *adj* **1a** located at or directed towards the front **b** situated in advance **2** of or occupying a fielding position in cricket in front of the batsman's wicket ☞ SPORT **3a** eager, ready **b** lacking modesty or reserve; pert **4** advanced in development; precocious **5** moving, tending, or leading towards a position in (or at the) front **6** advocating an advanced policy in the direction of what is considered progress **7** of or getting ready for the future ⟨~ *planning*⟩ [ME, fr OE *foreweard*, fr *fore-* + *-weard* -ward] – **forwardly** *adv*, **forwardness** *n*

[2]forward *adv* **1** to or towards what is ahead or in front ⟨*from that time* ~⟩ ⟨*moved slowly* ~ *through the crowd*⟩ **2** to or towards an earlier time ⟨*bring the date of the meeting* ~⟩ **3** into prominence

[3]forward /'faw·wood/ *n* a mainly attacking player in hockey, soccer, etc stationed at or near the front of his/her side or team

[4]forward *vt* **1** to help onwards; promote **2a** to send (forwards) ⟨*will* ~ *the goods on payment*⟩ **b** to send onwards from an intermediate point in transit – **forwarder** *n*

'forwards *adv* forward; *esp* forward in space

fossa /'fosə/ *n*, *pl* **fossae** /'fosi, 'fosie/ an anatomical pit or depression [NL, fr L, ditch] – **fossate** /'fosayt/ *adj*

fosse, foss /fos/ *n* a ditch, moat [ME *fosse*, fr OF, fr L *fossa*, fr fem of *fossus*]

fossick /'fosək/ *vi*, *Austr* to search for gold, esp by picking over abandoned workings ~ *vt*, *chiefly Austr* to search for (as if) by rummaging – + *out* [E dial. *fussick*, *fussock* (to potter), irreg fr E *fuss*] – **fossicker** *n*, *chiefly Austr*

[1]fossil /'fosl/ *n* **1** a relic of an animal or plant of a past geological age, preserved in the earth's crust ☞ EVOLUTION **2a** a person with outmoded views **b** sthg that has become rigidly fixed [L *fossilis* dug up, fr *fossus*, pp of *fodere* to dig – more at BED] – **fossiliferous** /,fosl'ifərəs/ *adj*

[2]fossil *adj* **1a** extracted from the earth and derived from the remains of living things ⟨*coal is a* ~ *fuel*⟩ ☞ ENERGY **b** preserved in a mineralized or petrified form from a past geological age **2** outmoded

fossil·ize, -ise /'fosl,iez/ *vt* **1** to convert into a fossil

2 to make outmoded, rigid, or fixed ~ *vi* to become fossilized – **fossilization** /-'zaysh(ə)n/ *n*

fossorial /fo'sawri·əl/ *adj* adapted to digging [ML *fossorius*, fr L *fossus*, pp]

[1]**foster** /'fostə/ *adj* giving, receiving, or sharing parental care though not related by blood ⟨*a ~ child*⟩ [ME, fr OE *fōstor-*, fr *fōstor* food, feeding; akin to OE *fōda* food – more at FOOD]

[2]**foster** *vt* **1** to give parental care to; nurture **2** to promote the growth or development of – **fosterer** *n*

'**fosterage** /-rij/ *n* **1** fostering **2** the custom of entrusting one's child to foster parents

'**foster,ling** /-,ling/ *n* a foster child

fou /fooh/ *adj, Scot* drunk [ME (Sc) *fow* full, fr ME *full*]

fouetté /fooh'etay (*Fr* fwɛte)/ *n* a quick whipping movement of the raised leg in ballet dancing [F, fr pp of *fouetter* to whip, fr MF, fr *fouet* whip, fr OF, fr *fou* beech, fr L *fagus* – more at BEECH]

fought /fawt/ *past of* FIGHT

[1]**foul** /fowl/ *adj* **1a** offensive to the senses **b** dirty, stained ⟨~ *linen*⟩ **2** notably unpleasant or distressing; detestable **3** obscene, abusive ⟨~ *language*⟩ **4a** treacherous, dishonourable ⟨*fair means or* ~⟩ **b** constituting a foul in a game or sport **5** defaced by changes ⟨~ *manuscript*⟩ **6** encrusted, clogged, or choked with a foreign substance ⟨*a ~ ship's bottom*⟩ **7** polluted ⟨~ *air*⟩ **8** entangled ⟨*a ~ anchor*⟩ [ME, fr OE *fūl*; akin to OHG *fūl* rotten, L *pus* pus, *putēre* to stink, Gk *pyon* pus] – **foulness** *n*

[2]**foul** *n* **1** an entanglement or collision in angling, sailing, etc **2** an infringement of the rules in a game or sport

[3]**foul** *vi* **1** to become or be foul; *esp* to become clogged, choked up, or entangled **2** to commit a foul in a sport or game ~ *vt* **1a** to pollute **b** to become entangled with **c** to encrust with a foreign substance **d** to obstruct, block – compare FOUL UP 3 **2** to dishonour, discredit **3** to commit a foul against

foulard /'foohlah(d)/ *n* a lightweight plain-woven or twilled silk (and cotton) fabric, usu decorated with a printed pattern [F]

'**foul,brood** /-,broohd/ *n* a bacterial disease of honeybee larvae

foully /'fowl·li/ *adv* in a foul manner

,**foul'mouthed** /-'mowdhd/ *adj* given to the use of obscene, profane, or abusive language

,**foul 'play** *n* violence; *esp* murder

'**foul-,up** *n* **1** a state of confusion caused by ineptitude, carelessness, or mismanagement **2** a mechanical difficulty *USE* infml

foul up *vt* **1** *chiefly NAm* to contaminate **2** *chiefly NAm* to spoil or confuse by making mistakes or using poor judgment **3** to entangle, block ⟨fouled up *the communications*⟩ *USE* (*2 & 3*) infml

[1]**found** /fownd/ *past of* FIND

[2]**found** *adj* having all usual, standard, or reasonably expected equipment ⟨*the boat comes fully ~, ready to go*⟩

[3]**found** *vt* **1** to take the first steps in building **2** to set or ground on sthg solid – often + *on* or *upon* **3** to establish (e g an institution), often with provision for continued financial support [ME *founden*, fr OF *fonder*, fr L *fundare*, fr *fundus* bottom – more at BOTTOM] – **founder** *n*

[4]**found** *vt* to melt (metal) and pour into a mould [MF *fondre* to pour, melt, fr L *fundere*; akin to OE *gēotan* to pour, Gk *chein*] – **founder** *n*

foundation /fown'daysh(ə)n/ *n* **1** the act of founding **2** the basis on which sthg stands or is supported **3** an organization or institution established by endowment with provision for future maintenance **4** an underlying natural or prepared base or support; *esp* the whole masonry substructure on which a building rests **5** a body or ground on which sthg is built up or overlaid **6** a cream, lotion, etc applied as a base for other facial make-up – **foundational** *adj*, **foundationally** *adv*, **foundationless** *adj*

foun'dation ,course *n* a basic general course (e g as taught in the first year at certain universities)

foun'dation ,garment *n* a girdle, corset, or other supporting undergarment

foun'dation ,stone *n* a stone in the foundation of a building, esp when laid with public ceremony

founder /'fowndə/ *vi* **1** to become disabled; *esp* to go lame **2** to collapse; GIVE WAY 3a **3** to sink **4** to come to grief; fail ~ *vt* to disable (e g a horse), esp by overwork [ME *foundren* to send to the bottom, collapse, fr MF *fondrer*, deriv of L *fundus* bottom]

,**founding 'father** *n* **1** a founder **2** *cap both Fs* a member of the American Constitutional Convention of 1787

'**foundling** /-ling/ *n* an infant found abandoned by unknown parents

found object *n* OBJET TROUVÉ

foundry /'fowndri/ *n* (a place for) casting metals [[4]*found*]

[1]**fount** /fownt/ *n* a fountain, source [MF *font*, fr L *font-, fons*]

[2]**fount,** *chiefly NAm* **font** /font/ *n, Br* a complete set of matrices of characters (e g for photocomposition) in 1 style [F *fonte*, fr MF, act of founding, fr (assumed) VL *fundita*, fem of *funditus*, pp of L *fundere* to pour – more at [4]FOUND]

[1]**fountain** /'fowntən/ *n* **1** a spring of water issuing from the earth **2** a source **3** (the structure providing) an artificially produced jet of water **4** a reservoir containing a supply of liquid (e g in a lamp or printing press) [ME, fr MF *fontaine*, fr LL *fontana*, fr L, fem of *fontanus* of a spring, fr *font-, fons*]

[2]**fountain** *vb* to (cause to) flow or spout like a fountain

'**fountain,head** /-,hed/ *n* **1** a spring that is the source of a stream **2** a principal source

'**fountain ,pen** *n* a pen containing a reservoir that automatically feeds the nib with ink

four /faw/ *n* **1** ☞ NUMBER **2** the fourth in a set or series ⟨*the ~ of hearts*⟩ **3** sthg having 4 parts or members or a denomination of 4; *esp* (the crew of) a 4-person racing rowing boat **4** a shot in cricket that crosses the boundary after having hit the ground and scores 4 runs – compare BOUNDARY 2b, SIX 3a [ME, fr *four*, adj, fr OE *fēower*; akin to OHG *fior* four, L *quattuor*, Gk *tessares, tettares*] – **four** *adj or pron*, **fourfold** /-,fohld/ *adj or adv*

,**four-di'mensional** *adj* (consisting) of elements requiring 4 coordinates to determine them

'**four ,flush** *n* a worthless hand of 4 cards of the same suit in a 5-card poker hand

,**four-'handed** *adj* **1** designed for 4 hands **2** engaged in by 4 people

,**Four 'Hundred, 400** *n, NAm the* exclusive social set of a community [arbitrary smallish number]

Fourierism /ˈfoori·ə,riz(ə)m, ˈfooriay,iz(ə)m/ *n* a system for reorganizing society into cooperative communities [F *fouriérisme*, fr F M C *Fourier* †1837 F social reformer] – **Fourierist** *n*

ˈFourier ˌseries /ˈfoori·ə, ˈfooriay/ *n* an infinite series in which the terms are constants multiplied by sine or cosine functions of integer multiples of the variable and which is used in the analysis of periodic functions (e g simple harmonic motion) [Baron J B J *Fourier* †1830 F geometrician & physicist]

ˌfour-in-ˈhand *n* (a vehicle drawn by) a team of 4 horses driven by 1 person

ˌfour-leaf ˈclover, ˌfour-leaved ˈclover *n* a clover leaf that has 4 leaflets instead of 3 and is held to bring good luck

ˌfour-letter ˈword *n* any of a group of vulgar or obscene words typically made up of 4 letters

fourpence /ˈfawp(ə)ns/ *n* the sum of 4 pence

ˈfourpenny /-p(ə)ni/ *adj* costing or worth fourpence

ˈfourpenny ˌone *n, Br* a sharp blow – infml [prob fr rhyming slang *fourpenny (bit)* hit]

ˌfour-ˈposter /ˈpohstə/ *n* a bed with 4 tall often carved corner posts designed to support curtains or a canopy

ˈfourˌscore /-ˌskaw/ *n* eighty – **fourscore** *adj*

foursome /ˈfaws(ə)m/ *n* **1** a group of 4 people or things **2** a golf match between 2 pairs of partners in which each pair plays 1 ball

¹ˌfourˈsquare /-ˈskweə/ *adj* forthright

²foursquare *adv* **1** in a solidly based and steady way **2** resolutely

ˌfour-ˈstar *adj* of a superior standard or quality ⟨*a ~ restaurant*⟩ [fr the number of asterisks used in guidebooks to denote relative excellence]

ˈfour-ˌstroke *adj* **1** of or being an internal-combustion engine with a cycle of 4 strokes (e g intake, compression, combustion, and exhaust) **2** powered by a four-stroke engine – **four-stroke** *n*

fourteen /fawˈteen/ *n* ☞ NUMBER [ME *fourtene*, fr OE *fēowertīene*, fr *fēowertīene*, adj; akin to OE *tīen* ten] – **fourteen** *adj or pron*, **fourteenth** /-ˈteenth/ *adj or n*

fourth /fawth/ *n* **1** ☞ NUMBER **2a** (the combination of 2 notes at) a musical interval of 4 diatonic degrees **b** a subdominant **3** the 4th and usu highest forward gear or speed of a motor vehicle – **fourth** *adj or adv*, **fourthly** *adv*

fourth dimension *n* **1** a dimension in addition to length, breadth, and depth; *specif* a coordinate in addition to 3 rectangular coordinates, esp when interpreted as the time coordinate in a space-time continuum **2** sthg outside the range of ordinary experience – **fourth-dimensional** *adj*

fourth estate *n, often cap F&E* PRESS 6a [fr its status as a rival to the three groups (clergy, nobility, commons) traditionally holding political power]

ˌfour-ˈway *adj* **1** allowing passage in any of 4 directions **2** including 4 participants

ˌfour-ˈwheel, ˌfour-ˈwheeled *adj* **1** having 4 wheels **2** acting on or by means of 4 wheels of an automotive vehicle ⟨*~ drive*⟩

fovea /ˈfohvi·ə, -vyə/ *n, pl* **foveae** /-viˌee, -viˌie/ a small anatomical pit; *esp* FOVEA CENTRALIS [NL, fr L, pit] – **foveal** *adj*, **foveate** /-viˌayt/ *adj*, **foveiform** /fohˈvee·iˌfawm/ *adj*

ˌfovea cenˈtralis /senˈtrahlis/ *n, pl* **foveae centrales** /-leez/ an area of the retina without rods where vision is acute [NL, central fovea]

¹fowl /fowl/ *n, pl* **fowls,** *esp collectively* **fowl** **1** BIRD 1 **2** DOMESTIC FOWL; *esp* an adult hen **3** the flesh of birds used as food [ME *foul*, fr OE *fugel*; akin to OHG *fogal* bird]

²fowl *vi* to hunt, catch, or kill wildfowl – **fowler** *n*

ˈfowling ˌpiece *n* a light gun for shooting birds or small animals

ˈfowl ˌpest *n* a fatal infectious virus disease of domestic poultry

¹fox /foks/ *n, pl* **foxes,** *esp collectively* **fox** **1** (the fur of) a red fox or related flesh-eating mammal of the dog family with a pointed muzzle, large erect ears, and a long bushy tail **2** a clever crafty person **3** *cap* a member, or the language, of an American Indian people who once lived in Wisconsin [ME, fr OE; akin to OHG *fuhs* fox, Skt *puccha* tail]

²fox *vt* **1** to outwit **2** to baffle

foxed *adj* discoloured with foxing

ˈfoxˌglove /-ˌgluv/ *n* a common tall European plant that has showy white or purple tubular flowers and is a source of digitalis ☞ PLANT

ˈfoxˌhole /-ˌhohl/ *n* a pit dug, usu hastily, for individual cover against enemy fire

ˈfoxˌhound /-ˌhownd/ *n* any of various large swift powerful hounds of great endurance used in hunting foxes

ˈfoxˌhunting /-ˌhunting/ *n* the practice of hunting foxes on horseback with a pack of hounds – **foxhunter** *n*

foxing /ˈfoksing/ *n* discoloration; *esp* brownish spots on old paper [fr its resemblance to the colour of a fox's fur]

ˈfoxˌtail /-ˌtayl/ *n* any of several grasses with spikes resembling the tail of a fox

ˌfox ˈterrier *n* a small lively smooth-haired or wire-haired terrier formerly used to dig out foxes

ˈFoxˌtrot /-ˌtrot/ – a communications code word for the letter *f*

fox-trot *vi or n* (to dance) a ballroom dance that includes slow walking and quick running steps

foxy /ˈfoksi/ *adj* **1** cunningly shrewd in conniving and contriving **2** warmly reddish brown **3** *NAm* physically attractive [¹FOX + ¹-Y] – **foxily** *adv*, **foxiness** *n*

foyer /ˈfoyˌay, -ə (*Fr* fwaje)/ *n* an anteroom or lobby (e g of a theatre); *also* an entrance hallway [F, lit., fireplace, fr ML *focarius*, fr L *focus* hearth]

Fra /frah/ *n* brother – used as a title preceding the name of an Italian monk or friar ⟨*~ Angelico*⟩ [It, short for *frate*, fr L *frater* – more at BROTHER]

fracas /ˈfrakah/ *n, pl* **fracas**/-ah(z)/, *NAm* **fracases** /-siz/ a noisy quarrel; a brawl [F, din, row, fr It *fracasso*, fr *fracassare* to shatter]

fraction /ˈfraksh(ə)n/ *n* **1a** a number (e g ¾, ⅝, 0.234) that is expressed as the quotient of 2 numbers **b** a (small) portion or section **2** an act of breaking up; *specif* the breaking of the bread by a priest in the Eucharist **3** a tiny bit; a little ⟨*a ~ closer*⟩ **4** any of several portions (e g of a distillate) separable by fractionation [ME *fraccioun*, fr LL *fraction-, fractio* act of breaking, fr L *fractus*, pp of *frangere* to break – more at BREAK]

fractional /ˈfraksh(ə)nl/ *adj* **1** of or being a fraction **2** relatively tiny or brief **3** of or being a process for separating components of a mixture through differences in physical or chemical properties ⟨~ *distillation*⟩

'fractionally /-li/ *adv* to a very small extent

'fractionate /-ayt/ *vt* to separate (e g a mixture) into different portions – **fractionation** /-'aysh(ə)n/ *n*, **fractionator** /ˌaytə/ *n*

fractious /'frakshəs/ *adj* irritable and restless; hard to control [*fraction* (discord) + *-ous*] – **fractiously** *adv*, **fractiousness** *n*

[1]**fracture** /'frakchə/ *n* **1** a break or breaking, esp of hard tissue (e g bone) **2** the appearance of a broken surface of a mineral **3a** the substitution of a diphthong for an orig simple vowel, esp under the influence of a following consonant **b** a diphthong thus substituted [ME, fr L *fractura*, fr *fractus*]

[2]**fracture** *vt* **1** to cause a fracture in **2** to damage or destroy as if by breaking apart; break up ~ *vi* to undergo fracture

frae /fray/ *prep*, *Scot* from [ME (northern) *fra*, *frae*, fr ON *frā*; akin to OE *from*]

fraenulum, **frenulum** /'frenyooləm/ *n*, *pl* **frenula** /-lə/ a fraenum [NL, dim. of L *fraenum, frenum*]

fraenum, **frenum** /'freenəm/ *n*, *pl* **frena** /-nə/ a connecting fold of membrane that supports or retains a body part (e g the tongue) [L *fraenum, frenum*, lit., bridle; akin to L *firmus* firm]

frag /frag/ *vt* **-gg-** to injure or kill (one's military leader) deliberately by means of a grenade [fr *frag*, n, short for *fragmentation (grenade)*]

fragile /'frajiel/ *adj* **1** easily shattered **2** lacking in strength; delicate [MF, fr L *fragilis* – more at FRAIL] – **fragility** /frə'jiləti/ *n*

[1]**fragment** /'fragmənt/ *n* an incomplete, broken off, or detached part [ME, fr L *fragmentum*, fr *frangere* to break – more at BREAK]

[2]**fragment** /frag'ment/ *vt* to break up or apart into fragments ~ *vi* to fall to pieces – **fragmentation** /ˌfragmən'taysh(ə)n/ *n*

fragmentary /'fragmənt(ə)ri/ *adj* consisting of fragments; incomplete – **fragmentarily** *adv*, **fragmentariness** *n*

ˌfragmen'tation ˌbomb /ˌfragmən'taysh(ə)n/ *n* a bomb or shell whose casing is thrown in fragments in all directions on exploding

fragrance /'fraygrəns/ *n* **1** (the quality or state of having) a sweet or pleasant smell **2** the smell of perfume, cologne, or toilet water [F or L; F, fr L *fragrantia*, fr *fragrant-*, *fragrans*, prp of *fragrare* to be fragrant; akin to OE *bræhen* to smell] – **fragrant** *adj*, **fragrantly** *adv*

frail /frayl/ *adj* **1** morally or physically weak **2** easily broken or destroyed **3** slight, insubstantial [ME, fr MF *fraile*, fr L *fragilis* fragile, fr *frangere*] – **frailly** *adv*, **frailness** *n*

frailty /'fraylti/ *n* a (moral) fault due to weakness [FRAIL + [2]-TY]

framboesia, *NAm* **frambesia** /fram'beezyə, -zh(y)ə/ *n* yaws [NL, fr F *framboise* raspberry; fr the appearance of the lesions]

[1]**frame** /fraym/ *vt* **1a** to plan; WORK OUT 1b, c **b** to shape, construct **2** to fit or adjust for a purpose **3** to construct by fitting and uniting the parts of **4a** to contrive evidence against (an innocent person) **b** to prearrange the outcome of (e g a contest) [ME *framen* to benefit, construct, fr OE *framian* to benefit, make progress; akin to ON *fram* forward, OE *from* from] – **framer** *n*

[2]**frame** *n* **1** sthg composed of parts fitted together and joined; *esp* the physical structure of a human body **2** a structure that gives shape or strength (e g to a building) **3a** an open case or structure made for admitting, enclosing, or supporting sthg ⟨*a window* ~⟩ ☞ ARCHITECTURE **b** a machine built on or within a framework ⟨*a spinning* ~⟩ **c** the rigid part of a bicycle **d** the outer structure of a pair of glasses that holds the lenses **4a** an enclosing border **b** the matter or area enclosed in such a border: e g **(1)** any of the squares in which scores for each round are recorded (e g in bowling) **(2)** a box of a strip cartoon **(3)** a single picture of the series on a length of film ☞ CAMERA **(4)** a single complete television picture made up of lines ☞ TELEVISION **c** a limiting, typical, or esp appropriate set of circumstances; a framework **5** a minimal unit of programmed instruction or stimulus calling for a response by the student **6** one round of play in snooker, bowling, etc **7** a frame-up – infml

[3]**frame** *adj* having a wooden frame ⟨~ *houses*⟩

ˌframe of 'mind *n* a particular mental or emotional state

ˌframe of 'reference *n* **1** an arbitrary set of axes used as a reference to describe the position or motion of sthg or to formulate physical laws **2** a set or system of facts, ideas, etc serving to orient or give particular meaning to a statement, a point of view, etc

'frame-ˌup *n* a conspiracy to frame sby or sthg – infml

'frameˌwork /-ˌwuhk/ *n* **1** a skeletal, openwork, or structural frame **2** a basic structure (e g of ideas)

franc /frangk/ *n* (a note or coin representing) the basic money unit of France, Belgium, Switzerland, and certain other French-speaking countries ☞ NATIONALITY [F]

franc C.F.A. *n* (a note or coin representing) the basic money unit of an association of French-speaking African states including Benin, Chad, the Ivory Coast, and Senegal ☞ NATIONALITY [F *communauté financière africaine* African financial community]

[1]**franchise** /'frahnchiez, 'fran-/ *n* **1** freedom from some burden or restriction **2a** a special privilege granted to an individual or group **b** a right or privilege; *specif* the right to vote **c** the right granted to an individual or group to market a company's goods or services in a particular territory; *also* the territory involved in such a right [ME, fr OF, fr *franchir* to free, fr *franc* free]

[2]**franchise** *vt* to grant a franchise to

Franciscan /fran'siskən/ *n* a member of the Order of missionary friars founded by St Francis of Assisi in 1209 [ML *Franciscus* Francis] – **Franciscan** *adj*

francium /'fransi·əm/ *n* an artificially produced radioactive element of the alkali metal group ☞ PERIODIC TABLE [NL, fr *France*]

Franco- /frangkoh-/ *comb form* **1** French nation, people, or culture ⟨Franco*phile*⟩ **2** French and ⟨Franco-*German*⟩ [ML, fr *Francus* Frenchman, fr LL, Frank]

francolin /'frangkohlin/ *n* any of numerous partridges of S Asia and Africa [F, fr It *francolino*]

francophone /'frangkəˌfohn/ *adj*, *often cap* consisting of or belonging to a French-speaking population – **Francophone** *n*

frangipane /'franjiˌpayn/ *n* a usu almond-flavoured

custardlike confection [F, frangipani (perfume), frangipane, fr It, fr Marquis Muzio *Frangipane,* 16th-c It nobleman]

frangipani /ˌfranji'pahni/ *n* **1** a perfume derived from or imitating the odour of the flower of the red jasmine **2** any of several tropical American shrubs or small trees of the periwinkle family [modif of It *frangipane*]

franglais /'frong·glay/ *n, often cap* French with a considerable number of words borrowed from English [F, blend of *français* French and *anglais* English]

[1]**frank** /frangk/ *adj* marked by free, forthright, and sincere expression ⟨*a ~ reply*⟩; *also* undisguised ⟨*~ admiration*⟩ [ME, free, generous, fr OF *franc,* fr ML *francus,* fr LL *Francus* Frank] – **frankness** *n*

[2]**frank** *vt* **1a** to send (a piece of mail) without charge **b** to put a frank on (a piece of mail) **2** to enable to pass or go freely or easily ⟨*the delegates will ~ the policy*⟩

[3]**frank** *n* **1** an official signature or sign on a piece of mail indicating exemption from postal charges **2** a mark or stamp on a piece of mail indicating postage paid **3** a franked envelope

Frank *n* a member of a W Germanic people that established themselves in the Netherlands and Gaul and on the Rhine in the 3rd and 4th c [ME; partly fr OE *Franca*; partly fr OF *Franc,* fr LL *Francus,* of Gmc origin; akin to OHG *Franko* Frank, OE *Franca*] – **Frankish** *adj*

Frankenstein /'frangkənˌstien/ *n* **1** a work or agency that ruins its originator **2** a monster in the shape of a man [Baron *Frankenstein,* hero (who constructs a human monster) of the novel *Frankenstein* by Mary Shelley †1851 E novelist]

frankfurter /'frangkˌfuhtə/ *n* a cured cooked, usu beef and pork, sausage [G *frankfurter* of Frankfurt, fr *Frankfurt am Main,* city in Germany]

frankincense /'frangkinˌsens/ *n* a fragrant gum resin chiefly from E African or Arabian trees that is burnt as incense [ME *fraunk encens,* fr *fraunk, frank* pure, free + *encens* incense]

franklin /'frangklin/ *n* a medieval English landowner of free but not noble birth [ME *frankeleyn,* fr AF *fraunclein,* fr OF *franc*]

Franklin stove *n, NAm* a freestanding metal stove resembling an open fireplace and used for heating a room [Benjamin *Franklin* †1790 US statesman & scientist, its inventor]

frankly /'frangkli/ *adv* to tell the truth; actually ⟨*~, I couldn't care less*⟩

frantic /'frantik/ *adj* **1** emotionally out of control ⟨*~ with anger and frustration*⟩ **2** marked by fast and nervous, disordered, or anxiety-driven activity [ME *frenetik, frantik* – more at FRENETIC] – **frantically** *adv,* **franticly** *adv,* **franticness** *n*

frap /frap/ *vt* **-pp-** to draw tight (e g with ropes or cables) [ME *frapen* to strike, beat, fr MF *fraper*]

frappé /'frapay (*Fr* frape)/ *n or adj* (a drink that is) chilled or partly frozen [F, fr pp of *frapper* to strike, chill, fr MF *fraper* to strike]

fraternal /frə'tuhnl/ *adj* **1a** of or involving brothers **b** of or being a fraternity or society **2** *of twins* derived from 2 ova **3** friendly, brotherly [ME, fr ML *fraternalis,* fr L *fraternus,* fr *frater* brother – more at BROTHER] – **fraternalism** *n,* **fraternally** *adv*

fraternity /frə'tuhnəti/ *n* **1** *sing or pl in constr* a group of people associated or formally organized for a common purpose, interest, or pleasure: e g **a** a fraternal order **b** a club for male students in some American universities – compare SORORITY **2** brotherliness **3** *sing or pl in constr* men of the same usu specified class, profession, character, or tastes ⟨*the racing ~*⟩

fratern·ize, -ise /'fratəˌniez/ *vi* **1** to associate or mingle on friendly terms **2** to associate on close terms with citizens or troops of a hostile country – **fraternization** /-'zaysh(ə)n/ *n*

fratricide /'fratriˌsied, 'fray-/ *n* (the act of) sby who kills his/her brother or sister [ME, fr MF or L; MF, fr L *fratricida* & *fratricidium,* fr *fratr-, frater* brother + *-cida* & *-cidium* – more at -CIDE] – **fratricidal** /-'siedl/ *adj*

Frau /frow (*ər* fraω)/ *n, pl* **Frauen** /-ən/ a German-speaking married woman – used as a title equivalent to *Mrs* [G, woman, wife, fr OHG *frouwa* mistress, lady; akin to OE *frēa* lord]

fraud /frawd/ *n* **1a** deception, esp for unlawful gain **b** a trick **2a** a person who is not what he/she pretends to be **b** sthg that is not what it seems or is represented to be [ME *fraude,* fr MF, fr L *fraud-, fraus*; akin to Skt *dhvarati* he bends, injures]

fraudulent /'frawdyooələnt/ *adj* characterized by, involving, or done by fraud – **fraudulence** *n,* **fraudulently** *adv*

fraught /frawt/ *adj* **1** filled or charged *with* sthg specified ⟨*the situation is ~ with danger*⟩ **2** *Br* characterized by anxieties and tensions ⟨*~ and complex relationships*⟩ [ME, fr pp of *fraughten* to load, fr *fraught, freight* freight – more at FREIGHT]

fräulein /'frawlien (*ər* frɔɪlaɪn)/ *n* an unmarried German-speaking woman – used as a title equivalent to *Miss* [G, dim. of *Frau*]

'Fraunhofer ˌlines /'frownˌhohfə (*ər* fraωnhofə)/ *n pl* the dark lines seen in solar and stellar spectra [Joseph von *Fraunhofer* †1826 Bavarian optician & physicist]

fraxinella /ˌfraksi'nelə/ *n* a Eurasian plant of the rue family whose flowers give off an inflammable vapour in hot weather [NL, dim. of L *fraxinus* ash tree – more at BIRCH]

[1]**fray** /fray/ *n* a brawl, fight [ME, short for *afray, affray* affray – more at AFFRAY]

[2]**fray** *vt* **1** to separate the threads at the edge of (e g fabric) **2** to strain, irritate ⟨*his temper became a bit ~ed*⟩ *~ vi* to wear out or into shreds [MF *froyer, frayer* to rub, fr L *fricare* – more at FRICTION]

[1]**frazzle** /'frazl/ *vt* to put in a state of extreme physical or nervous fatigue; upset – infml [alter. of E dial. *fazle* (to tangle, fray)]

[2]**frazzle** *n* a frazzled condition ⟨*worn to a ~*⟩ – infml

[1]**freak** /freek/ *n* **1a** a sudden and odd or seemingly pointless idea or whim **b** a seemingly capricious action or event **2** a person or animal with a physical oddity who appears in a circus, funfair, etc **3** a person seen as being highly unconventional, esp in dress or ideas **4** an ardent enthusiast ⟨*a jazz ~*⟩ **5a** a sexual pervert **b** HEAD 19 – often in combination ⟨*speed*freak⟩; slang ***USE*** (*3 & 4*) infml [origin unknown]

[2]**freak** *vb* FREAK OUT – slang

freakish /'freekish/ *adj* whimsical, capricious – **freakishly** *adv,* **freakishness** *n*

ˌfreak of 'nature *n* FREAK 2

'freak-ˌout *n* a drug-induced state of mind – slang

freak out *vt* **1** to put under the influence of a (hallucinogenic) drug **2** to put into a state of intense excitement ~ *vi* **1** to experience hallucinations or withdraw from reality, esp by taking drugs **2** to behave in an irrational, uncontrolled, or unconventional manner (as if) under the influence of drugs *USE* slang

freaky /ˈfreeki/ *adj* being a freak; characteristic of a freak

[1]**freckle** /ˈfrekl/ *n* any of the small brownish spots on the skin, esp of white people, that increase in number and intensity on exposure to sunlight [ME *freken, frekel,* of Scand origin; akin to ON *freknōttr* freckled; akin to OE *spearca* spark] – **freckly** /ˈfrekli/ *adj*

[2]**freckle** *vb* to mark or become marked with freckles or small spots

[1]**free** /free/ *adj* **1a** enjoying civil and political liberty **b** politically independent **c** not subject to the control or domination of another **2a** not determined by external influences ⟨*a ~ agent*⟩ **b** voluntary, spontaneous **3a** exempt, relieved, or released, esp from an unpleasant or unwanted condition or obligation ⟨*~ from pain*⟩ – often in combination ⟨*trouble*-free⟩ ⟨*duty*-free⟩ **b** not bound, confined, or detained by force ⟨*prisoner was now ~*⟩ **4a** having no trade restrictions **b** not subject to government regulation **5** having or taken up with no obligations or commitments ⟨*I'll be ~ this evening*⟩ **6** having an unrestricted scope ⟨*a ~ variable*⟩ **7a** not obstructed or impeded **b** not being used or occupied ⟨*used a ~ hand*⟩ **c** not hampered or restricted; unfettered ⟨*~ speech*⟩ **8** not fastened ⟨*the ~ end of the rope*⟩ **9a** lavish, unrestrained ⟨*very ~ with her praises*⟩ **b** outspoken **c** too familiar or forward **10** not costing or charging anything **11a** not (permanently) united with, attached to, or combined with sthg else; separate ⟨*~ oxygen*⟩ **b** capable of being used alone as a meaningful linguistic form ⟨hats *is a ~ form*⟩ – compare [4]BOUND 4 **12a** not literal or exact ⟨*~ translation*⟩ **b** not restricted by or conforming to conventional forms ⟨*~ jazz*⟩ **13** open to all comers [ME, fr OE *frēo*; akin to OHG *frī* free, Gk *prays* gentle] – **freely** *adv*

[2]**free** *adv* **1** in a free manner **2** without charge ⟨*admitted ~*⟩ **3** not close-hauled ⟨*sailing ~*⟩

[3]**free** *vt* **1** to cause to be free **2** to relieve or rid of sthg that restrains, confines, restricts, or embarrasses ⟨*~ her husband from debt*⟩ **3** to disentangle, clear – **freer** *n*

ˌfree and ˈeasy *adj* **1** marked by informality and lack of constraint **2** failing to observe strict standards; careless – **free and easy** *adv*

ˌfree asˌsociˈation *n* the expression of conscious thoughts, ideas, etc used esp in psychoanalysis to reveal unconscious processes; *esp* (the reporting of) the first thought, image, etc that comes to mind in response to a given stimulus (e g a word)

freebie, freebee /ˈfreebi/ *n, chiefly NAm* sthg (e g a theatre ticket) given or received without charge – infml [by alter. fr obs slang *freeby* (gratis), fr *free* + *-by*, of unknown origin]

ˈfreeˌboard /-ˌbawd/ *n* the vertical distance between the waterline and the deck of a ship

ˈfreeˌbooter /-ˌboohtə/ *n* a pirate, plunderer [D *vrijbuiter*, fr *vrijbuit* plunder, fr *vrij* free + *buit* booty]

ˈfreeˌborn /-ˌbawn/ *adj* not born in slavery

Free Church *n, chiefly Br* a British Nonconformist church

free collective bargaining *n* bargaining between trade unions and employers unhampered by government guidelines or by legal restrictions

free diving *n* SKIN DIVING

ˈfreedˌman /-man/, *fem* **ˈfreedˌwoman** *n* sby freed from slavery

freedom /ˈfreedəm/ *n* **1a** the absence of necessity or constraint in choice or action **b** liberation from slavery or restraint **c** being exempt or released *from* sthg (onerous) ⟨*~ from care*⟩ **2a** ease, facility **b** being frank, open, or outspoken **c** improper familiarity **3** boldness of conception or execution **4** unrestricted use *of* ⟨*gave him the ~ of their home*⟩ **5** a right or privilege, esp political [[1]FREE + -DOM]

ˈfreedom ˌride *n, often cap F&R* an organized ride made through states of the USA in protest against racialism and illegal segregation

free enterprise *n* an economic system that relies on private business operating competitively for profit to satisfy consumer demands and in which government action is restricted to protecting public interest and to keeping the national economy in balance

ˈfree-ˌfall *n* **1** (the condition of) unrestrained motion in a gravitational field **2** the part of a parachute jump before the parachute opens

ˌfree-ˈfloating *adj* relatively uncommitted to a particular course of action, party, etc

ˈfree-for-ˌall *n* **1** a fight or competition open to all comers and usu with no rules **2** an often vociferous quarrel or argument involving several participants

ˈfreeˌhand /-ˌhand/ *adj* done without the aid of drawing or measuring instruments – **freehand** *adv*

ˌfree ˈhand *n* freedom of action or decision ⟨*gave her a ~*⟩

ˌfreeˈhanded /-ˈhandid/ *adj* openhanded, generous – **freehandedly** *adv*

ˈfreeˌhold /-ˌhohld/ *n* a tenure in absolute possession; *also* a property held by such tenure – **freeholder** *n*

ˈfree ˌhouse *n* a public house in Britain that is entitled to sell drinks supplied by more than 1 brewery – compare TIED HOUSE

free jazz *n* jazz that is totally improvised, lacks any regular beat, and has no predetermined harmonic or melodic structure

ˌfree ˈkick *n* an unhindered kick in soccer, rugby, etc awarded because of a breach of the rules by an opponent

[1]**ˈfreeˌlance** /-ˌlahns/ *n* a person who pursues a profession without long-term contractual commitments to any one employer – **free-lance** *adj*

[2]**freelance** *vi* to act as a freelance

free lance *n* a mercenary knight

ˌfree-ˈliving *adj, of a living organism* neither parasitic nor symbiotic – **free-liver** *n*

ˈfreeˌload /-ˌlohd/ *vi* to take advantage of another's generosity or hospitality without sharing in the cost or responsibility involved – infml – **freeloader** *n*

ˌfree ˈlove *n* the concept or practice of sexual relations without legal, financial, etc commitment

ˈfreeˌman /-man/ *n* **1** sby enjoying civil or political liberty **2** sby who has the full rights of a citizen

ˌfree ˈmarket *n* an economic market operating by free competition

ˈfreeˌmartin /-ˌmahtin/ *n* a sexually imperfect usu

sterile female calf born as a twin with a male [origin unknown]

[1]**Free,mason** /-,mays(ə)n/ *n* a member of an ancient and widespread secret fraternity called Free and Accepted Masons

'**free,masonry** /-,mays(ə)nri/ *n* **1** *cap* the principles, institutions, or practices of Freemasons **2** natural or instinctive fellowship or sympathy

'**free ,port** *n* an enclosed (section of a) port where goods are received and shipped free of customs duty

,**free-'range** *adj* of, being, or produced by poultry reared in the open air rather than in a battery

,**free 'rein** *n* unrestricted liberty or scope ⟨*give ~ to one's feelings*⟩

freesia /'freezh(y)ə, -zyə/ *n* any of a genus of sweet-scented African plants of the iris family with red, white, yellow, or purple flowers [NL, genus name, fr F H T *Freese* †1876 G physician]

free skating *n* the part of a competitive figure-skating event that features artistic interpretation of steps and movements to music

,**free-'spoken** *adj* outspoken

,**free'standing** /-'standing/ *adj* standing without lateral support or attachment ⟨*a ~ column*⟩

'**free,stone** /-,stohn/ *n* **1** a stone that can be cut without splitting **2** (a fruit with) a stone to which the flesh does not cling

'**free,style** /-,stiel/ *n* **1** (a style used in) a competition in which a contestant uses a style (e g of swimming) of his/her choice **2** catch-as-catch-can **3** CRAWL 2

,**free-'swimming** *adj, of an animal that lives in water* able to swim about; not attached to a rock or other object

,**free'thinker** /-'thingkə/ *n* a person who forms opinions on the basis of reason; *esp* one who rejects religious dogma – **freethinking** *n or adj*

,**free 'thought** *n* freethinking; *specif* 18th-c deism

,**free 'trade** *n* trade based on the unrestricted international exchange of goods

free verse *n* verse without fixed metrical form

free vote *n* a vote in Parliament not subject to party instructions – compare TWO-LINE WHIP, THREE-LINE WHIP

'**free,way** /-,way/ *n, NAm* a motorway

[1],**free'wheel** /-'weel/ *n* a device fitted to a vehicle wheel allowing forward motion when the motive power is removed

[2]**freewheel** *vi* **1** *of a bicycle, cyclist, or motor car* to coast freely without power from the pedals or engine **2** to move, live, or drift along freely or irresponsibly – **freewheeler** *n*

,**free 'will** *n* the power of choosing without the constraint of divine necessity or causal law

,**free 'world** *n* the non-Communist countries of the world

[1]**freeze** /freez/ *vb* **froze** /frohz/; **frozen** /'frohz(ə)n/ *vi* **1** to become congealed into a solid (e g ice) by cold **2** to become chilled with cold ⟨*almost* froze *to death*⟩ **3** to stick solidly (as if) by freezing **4** to become clogged with ice ⟨*the water pipes* froze⟩ **5** to become fixed or motionless; *esp* to abruptly cease acting or speaking **6** to be capable of undergoing freezing for preservation ⟨*do strawberries ~ well?*⟩ ~ *vt* **1** to convert from a liquid to a solid by cold **2** to make extremely cold **3a** to act on, usu destructively, by frost **b** to anaesthetize (as if) by cold ⟨*the injection* froze *her gum*⟩ **4** to cause to become fixed, immovable, or unalterable, as if paralysed **5** to immobilize the expenditure, withdrawal, or exchange of (foreign-owned bank balances) by government regulation **6** to preserve (e g food) by freezing the water content and maintaining at a temperature below 0°C [ME *fresen*, fr OE *frēosan*; akin to OHG *friosan* to freeze, L *pruina* hoarfrost] – **freezingly** *adv*

[2]**freeze** *n* **1** freezing cold weather **2a** an act or period of freezing sthg, esp wages or prices at a certain level **b** being frozen

freeze-dry *vb* to dehydrate (sthg) while in a frozen state in a vacuum, esp for preservation – **freeze-dried** *adj*

freeze out *vt* to deliberately ignore or fail to respond to (sby) – infml

freezer /'freezə/ *n* an apparatus that freezes or keeps cool; *esp* an insulated cabinet or room for storing frozen food or for freezing food rapidly

'**freeze-,up** *n* a spell of very cold weather – infml

F region *n* the highest region of the ionosphere occurring from 145km (about 90mi) to 400km (about 250mi) above the surface of the earth

[1]**freight** /frayt/ *n* **1** the charge made for transporting goods **2** a cargo **3** a goods train [ME, fr MD or MLG *vracht, vrecht*]

[2]**freight** *vt* to load (esp a ship) with goods for transport

freighter /'fraytə/ *n* **1** a person or company that (charters and) loads a ship **2** a ship or aircraft used chiefly to carry freight

'**freight,liner** /-,lienə/ *n, Br* a train designed for carrying containerized cargo

[1]**French** /french/ *adj* of France, its people, or their language [ME, fr OE *frencisc*, fr *Franca* Frank] – **Frenchman** *n*, **Frenchness** *n*

[2]**French** *n* **1** the Romance language of the people of France and of parts of Belgium, Switzerland, and Canada ☞ LANGUAGE **2** *pl in constr* the people of France **3** language full of swear words and mild profanities – infml ⟨*I wish we'd never heard of the bugger, pardon my ~* – Alan Coren⟩

,**French 'bean** *n, chiefly Br* (the seed or pod of) a common bean often cultivated for its slender edible green pods

,**French 'bread** *n* crusty white bread made in long thin loaves

,**French Ca'nadian** *n* a French-speaking Canadian; *esp* one of French descent

,**French 'chalk** *n* a soft white granular variety of soapstone used esp for drawing lines on cloth and as a dry lubricant

,**French 'cuff** *n* a wide band turned back to make a cuff of double thickness

,**French 'curve** *n* a curved piece of flat material (e g plastic) used as an aid in drawing noncircular curves

,**French 'dressing** *n* a salad dressing of oil, vinegar, and seasonings

,**french 'fry** *n, chiefly NAm* [1]CHIP 6a – usu pl [short for *French fried (potato)*]

,**French 'horn** *n* a circular valved brass instrument with a usual range from B below the bass staff upwards for more than 3 octaves

,**French 'kiss** *n* a kiss made with open mouths and usu with tongue-to-tongue contact – **French-kiss** *vb*

ˌ**French 'knickers** *n pl* wide-legged knickers ☞ GARMENT

ˌ**French 'knot** *n* an embroidery stitch that forms a decorative knot

ˌ**French 'leave** *n* leave taken without permission [fr an 18th-c French custom of leaving a reception without taking leave of the host or hostess]

ˌ**French 'letter** *n, Br* a condom – infml

French-polish *vt* to apply French polish to (wood or furniture) in order to obtain a high gloss finish

ˌ**French 'polish** *n* a solution of shellac used as a wood polish

ˌ**French 'seam** *n* a double seam sewn on first the right, then the wrong side of a piece of fabric to enclose the raw edges

ˌ**French 'windows** *n pl* a pair of doors with full length glazing

frenetic /frə'netik/ *adj* frenzied, frantic [ME *frenetik* insane, fr MF *frenetique,* fr L *phreneticus,* modif of Gk *phrenitikos,* fr *phrenitis* inflammation of the brain, fr *phren-, phrēn* diaphragm, mind] – **frenetically** *adv*

frenulum /'frenyooləm/ *n, pl* **frenula** /-lə/ a fraenulum

frenum /'freenəm/ *n, pl* **frena** /-nə/ a fraenum

frenzied /'frenzid/ *adj* marked by frenzy ⟨*the dog's ~ barking*⟩ – **frenziedly** *adv*

frenzy /'frenzi/ *n* **1** a temporary madness **2** (a spell of) wild, compulsive, or agitated behaviour [ME *frenesie,* fr MF, fr ML *phrenesia,* alter. of L *phrenesis,* fr *phreneticus*]

Freon /'free,on/ *trademark* – used for any of various nonflammable gaseous and liquid fluorinated hydrocarbons used as refrigerants and as propellants for aerosols

frequency /'freekwənsi/ *n* **1 frequency, frequence** the fact or condition of occurring frequently **2a** the number of times that a periodic function repeats the same sequence of values during a unit variation of the independent variable **b** the number or proportion of individuals in a single class when objects are classified according to variations in a set of attributes ☞ STATISTICS **3a** the number of complete alternations per second of an alternating current **b** the number of sound waves per second produced by a sounding body **c** the number of complete oscillations per second of an electromagnetic wave ***USE*** (*3*) ☞ PHYSICS

frequency distribution *n* DISTRIBUTION 3b ☞ STATISTICS

frequency modulation *n* modulation of the frequency of a wave that is usu a radio carrier wave in accordance with the instantaneous value of some signal waveform – compare AMPLITUDE MODULATION

frequency response *n* (a graph representing) the ability of a device (e g an audio amplifier) to deal with the various frequencies applied to it

[1]**frequent** /'freekwənt/ *adj* **1** often repeated or occurring **2** habitual, persistent [ME, fr MF or L; MF, fr L *frequent-, frequens* crowded, full] – **frequently** *adv*

[2]**frequent** /fri'kwent/ *vt* to be in or visit often or habitually – **frequenter** *n,* **frequentation** /ˌfreekwen'taysh(ə)n/ *n*

frequentative /fri'kwentətiv/ *adj, of a verb aspect, form, or meaning* denoting repeated or recurrent action – **frequentative** *n*

fresco /'freskoh/ *n, pl* **frescoes, frescos** (a painting made by) the application of water colours to moist plaster – compare FRESCO SECCO [It, fr *fresco* fresh, of Gmc origin; akin to OHG *frisc* fresh]

ˌ**fresco 'secco** /'sekoh/ *n* the art of painting in water colours on dry plaster – compare FRESCO [It, dry fresco]

[1]**fresh** /fresh/ *adj* **1a** not salt ⟨~ *water*⟩ **b** free from taint; clean **c** *of wind* rather strong **d** *of weather* cool and windy **2a** *of food* not preserved **b** refreshed ⟨*rose ~ from a good night's sleep*⟩ **c** not stale, sour, or decayed **3a** (different or alternative and) new ⟨*make a ~ start*⟩ **b** newly or just come or arrived ⟨~ *from school*⟩ **4** too forward with a person of the opposite sex ⟨*slapped his face when he got ~ with me*⟩ – infml [ME, fr OF *freis,* of Gmc origin; akin to OHG *frisc* fresh; akin to OE *fersc* fresh] – **freshly** *adv,* **freshness** *n*

[2]**fresh** *adv* **1** just recently; newly ⟨*a ~ laid egg*⟩ **2** *chiefly NAm* as of a very short time ago ⟨*we're ~ out of tomatoes*⟩

fresh breeze *n* wind having a speed of 29 to 38km/h (19 to 24mph)

freshen /'fresh(ə)n/ *vi* **1** *of wind* to increase in strength **2** *of water* to lose saltiness ~ *vt* to make fresh; *also* to refresh, revive – often + *up*

freshen up *vb* to make (oneself) fresher or more comfortable, esp by washing, changing one's clothes, etc

fresher /'freshə/ *n, chiefly Br* a student in the first term at college or university – infml [by shortening & alter. fr *freshman*]

freshet /'freshit/ *n* STREAM 1 [*fresh* (a stream of fresh water) + *-et*]

fresh gale *n* wind having a speed of 62 to 74km/h (39 to 46mph)

'freshman /-mən/ *n* a fresher

ˌ**fresh'water** /-'wawtə/ *adj* of or living in fresh water

[1]**fret** /fret/ *vb* **-tt-** *vt* **1** to torment with anxiety or worry; vex **2a** to eat or gnaw into; corrode **b** to rub, chafe **c** to make (e g a channel) by wearing away **3** to agitate, ripple ~ *vi* **1** to eat into sthg; corrode **2** to chafe **3a** to become vexed or worried **b** *of running water* to become agitated [ME *freten* to devour, fret, fr OE *fretan* to devour; akin to OHG *frezzan* to devour, *ezzan* to eat – more at EAT]

[2]**fret** *n* **1** (a spot that has been subject to) wearing away **2** a state of (querulous) mental agitation or irritation

[3]**fret** *vt* **-tt- 1** to decorate with interlaced designs **2** to decorate (e g a ceiling) with embossed or carved patterns [ME *fretten,* fr MF *freter* to bind with a ferrule, fret, fr OF, fr *frete* ferrule]

[4]**fret** *n* an ornamental pattern or decoration consisting of small straight bars intersecting usu at right angles ☞ ARCHITECTURE

[5]**fret** *n* any of a series of ridges fixed across the fingerboard of a stringed musical instrument (e g a guitar) [prob fr MF *frete* ferrule]

'fretful /-f(ə)l/ *adj* **1** tending to fret; in a fret **2** *of water* having the surface agitated – **fretfully** *adv,* **fretfulness** *n*

fretsaw /'fret,saw/ *n* a narrow-bladed fine-toothed saw held under tension in a frame and used for cutting intricate patterns in thin wood

'fret,work /-,wuhk/ *n* **1** decoration consisting of

frets **2** ornamental openwork, esp in thin wood; *also* ornamental work in relief

Freudian /ˈfroydi·ən, -dyən/ *adj* of or conforming to the psychoanalytic theories or practices of S Freud [Sigmund *Freud* †1939 Austrian neurologist] – **Freudian** *n*

Freudian slip *n* a slip of the tongue that is held to reveal some unconscious aspect of the speaker's mind

friable /ˈfrie·əbl/ *adj* easily crumbled [MF or L; MF, fr L *friabilis*, fr *friare* to crumble] – **friableness** *n*, **friability** /-əˈbiləti/ *n*

friar /ˈfrie·ə/ *n* a member of a religious order combining monastic life with outside religious activity and orig owning neither personal nor community property [ME *frere, fryer*, fr OF *frere*, lit., brother, fr L *fratr-, frater* – more at BROTHER]

friary /ˈfrie·əri/ *n* (a building housing) a community of friars

fricandeau /ˈfrikəndoh/ *n, pl* **fricandeaus, fricandeaux** /-doh(z)/ (a slice of) larded veal braised or roasted and glazed in its own juices [F, fr MF, irreg fr *fricasser*]

fricassee /ˈfrikə,see, ,--ˈ-/ *n* a dish of small pieces of stewed chicken, rabbit, etc served in a white sauce [MF, fr fem of *fricassé*, pp of *fricasser* to fricassee] – **fricassee** *vt*

fricative /ˈfrikətiv/ *n* a consonant (e g /f, th, sh/) made by forcing air through a narrow opening formed by placing the tongue or lip close to another part of the mouth, or in languages other than English, esp Arabic, also by constricting the pharynx [L *fricatus*, pp of *fricare*] – **fricative** *adj*

friction /ˈfriksh(ə)n/ *n* **1a** the rubbing of one body against another **b** resistance to relative motion between 2 bodies in contact **2** disagreement between 2 people or parties of opposing views [MF or L; MF, fr L *friction-, frictio*, fr *frictus*, pp of *fricare* to rub; akin to L *friare* to crumble, Skt *brhiṇanti* they injure] – **frictional** *adj*, **frictionless** *adj*

ˈfriction ,clutch *n* a clutch in which connection is made through sliding friction

Friday /ˈfrieday, -di/ *n* the day of the week following Thursday ☞ SYMBOL [ME, fr OE *frigedæg*; akin to OHG *friatag*; both fr a prehistoric WGmc compound whose components are akin to OHG *Frīa*, goddess of love, & to OE *dæg* day] – **Fridays** *adv*

fridge /frij/ *n, chiefly Br* a refrigerator [by shortening & alter.]

friend /frend/ *n* **1a** a person whose company, interests, and attitudes one finds sympathetic and to whom one is not closely related **b** an acquaintance **2a** sby or sthg not hostile **b** sby or sthg of the same nation, party, or group **c** sby or sthg that favours or encourages sthg (e g a charity) ⟨*a ~ of the poor*⟩ **3** *cap* a Quaker [ME *frend*, fr OE *frēond*; akin to OHG *friunt* friend; both fr the prp of a prehistoric Gmc verb represented by OE *frēon* to love; akin to OE *frēo* free] – **friendless** *adj*

¹ˈfriendly /-li/ *adj* **1a** having the relationship of friends ⟨*Billy is ~ with Dave*⟩ **b** showing interest and goodwill ⟨*~ neighbours*⟩ **c** not hostile ⟨*~ nations*⟩ **d** inclined to be favourable – usu + *to* **2** cheerful, comforting **3** engaged in only for pleasure or entertainment and not hotly contested ⟨*a ~ game of poker*⟩ – **friendliness** *n*

²friendly *n, chiefly Br* a match played for practice or pleasure and not as part of a competition

ˈfriendly so,ciety *n, often cap F&S, Br* a mutual insurance association providing its subscribers with benefits during sickness, unemployment, and old age

,friendship /-ship/ *n* being friends or being friendly

frier /ˈfrie·ə/ *n* a fryer

Friesian /ˈfreezh(ə)n, -zyən/ *n, chiefly Br* any of a breed of large black-and-white dairy cattle from N Holland and Friesland [var of *Frisian*]

¹frieze /freez/ *n* a heavy coarse fabric made of wool and shoddy [ME *frise*, fr MF, fr MD *vriese*]

²frieze *n* **1** the part of an entablature between the architrave and the cornice ☞ ARCHITECTURE **2** a sculptured or ornamented band (e g on a building) [MF, perh fr ML *phrygium, frisium* embroidered cloth, fr L *phrygium*, fr neut of *Phrygius* Phrygian, fr *Phrygia*, ancient country of Asia Minor]

frig /frig/ *vi* **-gg-** **1** to masturbate **2** to have sexual intercourse *USE* vulg [prob fr E dial. *frig* (to rub), fr ME *friggen*]

frigate /ˈfrigət/ *n* **1** a square-rigged 3-masted warship next in size below a ship of the line **2** a general-purpose naval escort vessel between a corvette and a cruiser in size [MF, fr OIt *fregata*]

ˈfrigate ,bird *n* any of several strong-winged rapacious seabirds

¹fright /friet/ *n* **1** fear excited by sudden danger or shock **2** sthg unsightly, strange, ugly, or shocking ⟨*she looks a ~*⟩ – infml [ME, fr OE *fyrhto, fryhto*; akin to OHG *forhta* fear]

²fright *vt* to frighten – chiefly poetic

frighten /ˈfriet(ə)n/ *vt* **1** to make afraid; scare **2** to force by frightening ⟨*~ed them into confessing*⟩ ~ *vi* to become frightened – **frighteningly** *adv*

ˈfrightful /-f(ə)l/ *adj* **1** causing intense fear, shock, or horror **2** unpleasant, difficult ⟨*had a ~ morning*⟩ – infml – **frightfully** *adv*

frigid /ˈfrijid/ *adj* **1a** intensely cold **b** lacking warmth or intensity of feeling **2** *esp of a woman* abnormally averse to sexual contact, esp intercourse [L *frigidus*, fr *frigēre* to be cold; akin to L *frigus* frost, cold, Gk *rhigos*] – **frigidly** *adv*, **frigidness** *n*, **frigidity** /friˈjidəti/ *n*

frigid zone *n* either of 2 regions between the poles of the earth and the polar circles

¹frill /fril/ *vt* to provide or decorate with a frill

²frill *n* **1a** a gathered or pleated fabric edging used on clothing **b** a small fringed or fluted roll of paper for decorating the bone end of a chop, chicken leg, etc **2** a ruff of hair or feathers round the neck of an animal **3a** an affectation, air **b** sthg decorative but not essential *USE* (*3*) usu pl [perh fr Flem *frul*] – **frilly** *adj*

¹fringe /frinj/ *n* **1** an ornamental border (e g on a curtain or garment) consisting of straight or twisted threads or tassels **2a** sthg resembling a fringe; a border **b** the hair that falls over the forehead **c** any of the alternating light or dark bands produced by interference or diffraction of light **3a** sthg marginal, additional, or secondary **b** *sing or pl in constr* a group with marginal or extremist views **c** *often cap* a part of the British professional theatre featuring small-scale avant-garde productions [ME *frenge*, fr MF, fr (assumed) VL *frimbia*, fr L *fimbriae* (pl)]

²fringe *vt* **1** to provide or decorate with a fringe **2** to serve as a fringe for ⟨*a clearing ~d with trees*⟩

fringe benefit *n* a benefit (e g a pension) granted by

an employer to an employee that involves a money cost without affecting basic wage rates

[1]**frippery** /'fripəri/ *n* **1** nonessential ornamentation, esp of a showy or tawdry kind **2** affected elegance [MF *friperie,* deriv of ML *faluppa* piece of straw]

[2]**frippery** *adj* trifling, tawdry

Frisbee /'frizbi/ *trademark* – used for a plastic disc thrown between players by a flip of the wrist

Frisian /'freezh(ə)n, -zyən/ *n* **1** a member of a Germanic people inhabiting Friesland and the Frisian islands **2** the language of the Frisian people ☞ LANGUAGE [L *Frisii* Frisians] – **Frisian** *adj*

[1]**frisk** /frisk/ *vi* to leap, skip, or dance in a lively or playful way ~ *vt* to search (a person) for sthg, esp a hidden weapon, by passing the hands over his/her body – infml [obs *frisk* (lively)]

[2]**frisk** *n* **1** a gambol, romp **2** an act of frisking

frisky /'friski/ *adj* lively, playful – **friskiness** *n*

frisson /'freesonh (*Fr* frisɔ̃)/ *n, pl* **frissons** /'freesonh(z) (*Fr* ~)/ a shudder, thrill [F]

[1]**frit** /frit/ *n* **1** the wholly or partly fused materials of which glass is made **2** ground-up glass used as a basis for glaze or enamel [It *fritta*]

[2]**frit** *vt* **-tt- 1** to prepare (materials for glass) by heat; fuse **2** to convert into a frit

'**frit ,fly** *n* a minute fly whose larva is a pest of cereals [origin unknown]

fritillary /fri'tiləri/ *n* **1** any of numerous butterflies that are usu orange with black spots ☞ ENDANGERED **2** any of a genus of bulbous plants of the lily family with mottled or chequered flowers [NL *Fritillaria,* genus name, fr L *fritillus* dice-cup; fr the markings on the wings & petals]

fritter /'fritə/ *n* a piece of fried batter often containing fruit, meat, etc [ME *fritour,* fr MF *friture,* fr (assumed) VL *frictura,* fr *frictus,* pp of *frigere* to fry – more at [1]FRY]

fritter away *vt* to waste bit by bit ⟨fritters away *all her money on clothes*⟩ [*fritter* fr *fritters,* n pl (fragments), alter. of *fitters* (rags, fragments), fr ME *fiteres*]

Fritz /frits/ *n, Br* **1** a German **2** German soldiers collectively [G, nickname for *Friedrich* (Frederick)]

frivolous /'frivələs/ *adj* **1** lacking in seriousness; irresponsibly self-indulgent **2** lacking practicality or serious purpose; unimportant [ME, fr L *frivolus*] – **frivolity** /fri'voləti/ *n,* **frivolously** *adv,* **frivolousness** *n*

frizz /friz/ *n* (hair in) a mass of small tight curls [*frizz,* vb, fr F *friser* to shrivel up, curl, prob fr *fris-,* stem of *frire* to fry] – **frizz** *vb,* **frizzy** *adj,* **frizziness** *n*

[1]**frizzle** /'frizl/ *vb* **frizzling** /'frizling/ to frizz or curl (the hair) [prob akin to OE *frīs* curly, OFris *frīsle* curl] – **frizzle** *n,* **frizzly** /'frizli/ *adj*

[2]**frizzle** *vt* **1** to fry (e g bacon) until crisp and curled **2** to burn, scorch ~ *vi* to cook with a sizzling noise [[1]*fry* + *sizzle*]

fro /froh/ *prep, dial* from [ME, fr ON *frā*; akin to OE *from*]

frock /frok/ *n* **1** a monk's or friar's habit **2** a workman's outer shirt; *esp* SMOCK FROCK **3** a woman's dress [ME *frok,* fr MF *froc,* of Gmc origin; akin to OHG *hroch* mantle, coat]

'**frock ,coat** *n* a usu double-breasted coat with knee-length skirts worn by men, esp in the 19th c

frog /frog/ *n* **1** any of various tailless smooth-skinned web-footed largely aquatic leaping amphibians **2** the triangular horny pad in the middle of the sole of a horse's foot **3a** a loop attached to a belt to hold a weapon or tool **b** a usu ornamental fastening for the front of a garment consisting of a button and a loop **4** a device permitting the wheels on one rail of a track to cross an intersecting rail **5** a condition in the throat that produces hoarseness ⟨*had a ~ in her throat*⟩ – infml **6** *often cap* a French person – chiefly derog; infml **7** the hollow in either or both faces of a brick to take mortar ☞ BUILDING [ME *frogge,* fr OE *frogga*; akin to OHG *frosk* frog, Skt *pravate* he jumps up; (6) fr the reputation of the French for eating frogs]

'**frog,fish** /-,fish/ *n* ANGLER FISH

'**frog,hopper** /-,hopə/ *n* any of numerous leaping insects whose larvae secrete froth

'**frogman** /-mən/ *n* a person equipped with face mask, flippers, rubber suit, etc and an air supply for swimming underwater for extended periods

'**frog,march** /-,mahch/ *vt* **1** to carry (a person) face downwards by the arms and legs **2** to force (a person) to move forwards with the arms held firmly behind

'**frog,spawn** /-,spawn/ *n* (a gelatinous mass of) frog's eggs

[1]**frolic** /'frolik/ *vi* **-ck- 1** to play and run about happily **2** to make merry [D *vroolijk* merry, fr MD *vrolijc,* fr *vro* happy; akin to OHG *frō* happy, OE *frogga* frog]

[2]**frolic** *n* **1** (a) playful expression of high spirits; gaiety **2** a lighthearted entertainment or game – **frolicsome** /-s(ə)m/ *adj*

from /frəm; *strong* from/ *prep* **1** – used to indicate a starting point: e g **a** a place where a physical movement, or an action or condition suggestive of movement, begins ⟨*came here ~ the city*⟩ ⟨*shot ~ above*⟩ ⟨*translated ~ French*⟩ **b** a starting point in measuring or reckoning or in a statement of extent or limits ⟨*cost ~ £5 to £10*⟩ ⟨*lives 5 miles ~ the coast*⟩ ⟨*~ 60 to 80 people*⟩ **c** a point in time after which a period is reckoned ⟨*a week ~ today*⟩ **d** a viewpoint ⟨*seen ~ my window*⟩ ⟨*~ a practical standpoint*⟩ **2** – used to indicate separation: e g **a** physical separation ⟨*absent ~ school*⟩ ⟨*took the toy away ~ the baby*⟩ **b** removal, refraining, exclusion, release, or differentiation ⟨*protection ~ the sun*⟩ ⟨*relief ~ pain*⟩ ⟨*kept the news ~ her*⟩ ⟨*saved ~ drowning*⟩ ⟨*refrain ~ smok ing*⟩ ⟨*don't know one ~ the other*⟩ **3** – used to indicate the source, cause, agent, or basis ⟨*a call ~ my lawyer*⟩ ⟨*a friend ~ Oxford*⟩ ⟨*made ~ flour*⟩ ⟨*worked hard ~ necessity*⟩ ⟨*suffering ~ mumps*⟩ ⟨*~ what I hear, he's quite rich*⟩ [ME, fr OE; akin to OHG *fram,* adv, forth, away, OE *faran* to go – more at FARE]

frond /frond/ *n* (a shoot or thallus resembling) a leaf, esp of a palm or fern [L *frond-, frons* foliage] – **fronded** *adj*

frondeur /fron'duh (*Fr* frɔ̃dœːr)/ *n* a rebel, malcontent [F, slinger, participant in a 17th-c revolt in which the rebels were compared to schoolboys using slings only when the teacher was not looking]

[1]**front** /frunt/ *n* **1** (feigned) demeanour or bearing, esp in the face of a challenge, danger, etc ⟨*put up a brave ~*⟩ **2a** the vanguard **b** *often cap* a zone of conflict between armies **c** the lateral space occupied by a military unit **3a** a sphere of activity ⟨*progress on the educational ~*⟩ **b** a movement linking diver-

gent elements to achieve certain common objectives; *esp* a political coalition **4a** the (main) face of a building **b** the forward part or surface: e g **(1)** the part of the human body opposite to the back **(2)** the part of a garment covering the chest **c** a frontage **d** *the* beach promenade at a seaside resort **5** the boundary between 2 dissimilar air masses ☞ WEATHER **6a** a position ahead of a person or of the foremost part of a thing **b** a position of importance, leadership, or advantage **7a** a person, group, or thing used to mask the identity or true character of the actual controlling agent **b** a person who serves as the nominal head or spokesman of an enterprise or group to lend it prestige **8** the forehead – poetic [ME, fr OF, fr L *front-, frons* – more at BRINK] – **in front of 1** directly ahead of ⟨*watching the road* in front of *him*⟩ **2** in the presence of ⟨*don't swear* in front of *the children*⟩ – **out front** in the audience

²**front** *vi* **1** to face – often + *on* or *onto* ⟨*garden* ~ing *on a lake*⟩ **2** to serve as a front – often + *for* **3** *Austr & NZ* to appear; TURN UP 2 – often + *up* ~ *vt* **1** to be in front of **2** to supply a front to **3** to face towards ⟨*the house* ~s *the street*⟩ **4** to articulate (a sound) with the tongue farther forward

³**front** *adj* **1** of or situated at the front **2** articulated at or towards the front of the mouth ⟨~ *vowels*⟩ – **front** *adv*

frontage /ˈfruntij/ *n* **1a** a piece of land that fronts **b** the land between the front of a building and the street **2** (the width of) the front face of a building

¹**frontal** /ˈfruntl/ *n* a facade [²*frontal*]

²**frontal** *adj* **1** of or adjacent to the forehead ⟨~ *bone*⟩ **2a** of, situated at, or showing the front ⟨*full* ~ *nudity*⟩ **b** direct ⟨~ *assault*⟩ **3** of a meteorological front [NL *frontalis*, fr L *front-, frons*] – **frontally** *adv*

frontal lobe *n* the front lobe of either cerebral hemisphere

front bench *n* either of 2 rows of benches in Parliament on which party leaders sit

frontier /frunˈtiə/ *n* **1** a border between 2 countries **2** the boundary between the known and the unknown – often pl with sing. meaning ⟨*the* ~s *of medicine*⟩ **3** *NAm* a region that forms the margin of settled or developed territory [ME *fronter*, fr MF *frontiere*, fr *front*] – **frontier** *adj*

fronˈtiersman /-mən/ *n* a man living on the frontier

frontispiece /ˈfruntis,pees/ *n* an illustration preceding and usu facing the title page of a book or magazine [alter. of earlier *frontispice*, fr MF, fr LL *frontispicium*, lit., view of the front, fr L *front-, frons* + *-i-* + *specere* to look at – more at SPY]

front line *n* **1** a military front **2** the most advanced, responsible, or significant position in a field of activity – **front-line** *adj*

ˈfront ˌman *n* a person serving as a front or figurehead

fronto- *comb form* frontal and ⟨fronto*lateral*⟩ [ISV, fr L *front-, frons*]

ˌfront of ˈhouse *n* the parts of a theatre accessible to the public (e g the auditorium and foyer) – **front-of-house** *adj*

frontogenesis /ˌfruntohˈjenəsis/ *n* the coming together to form a distinct front of 2 dissimilar air masses, usu with the formation of cloud and precipitation [NL]

ˌfront-ˈpage *adj* very newsworthy

ˌfront ˈroom *n* a lounge; LIVING ROOM

ˈfront-ˌrunner *n* **1** a contestant who runs best when in the lead **2** a leading contestant in a competition

¹**frost** /frost/ *n* **1a** (the temperature that causes) freezing **b** a covering of minute ice crystals on a cold surface **2a** coldness of attitude or manner **b** a failure – *chiefly infml* [ME, fr OE; akin to OHG *frost*, OE *frēosan* to freeze]

²**frost** *vt* **1a** to cover (as if) with frost **b** to produce a fine-grained slightly roughened surface on (metal, glass, etc) **c** to cover (e g a cake or grapes) with sugar; *also, chiefly NAm* to ice (a cake) **2** to injure or kill (e g plants) by frost ~ *vi* to freeze – often + *over*

ˈfrostˌbite /-ˌbiet/ *n* (gangrene or other local effect of a partial) freezing of some part of the body

ˈfrostˌbitten /-ˌbit(ə)n/ *adj* afflicted with frostbite

frosting /ˈfrosting/ *n* **1** a dull or roughened finish on metal or glass **2a** *Br* thick fluffy cooked icing **b** *chiefly NAm* icing

ˈfrostˌwork /-ˌwuhk/ *n* delicate figures that moisture sometimes forms in freezing (e g on a window)

frosty /ˈfrosti/ *adj* **1** marked by or producing frost **2** (appearing as if) covered with frost **3** marked by coolness or extreme reserve in manner – **frostily** *adv*, **frostiness** *n*

¹**froth** /froth/ *n* **1a** a mass of bubbles formed on or in a liquid **b** a foamy saliva sometimes accompanying disease or exhaustion **2** sthg insubstantial or of little value [ME, fr ON *frotha*; akin to OE *āfrēothan* to froth, Gk *prēthein* to blow up]

²**froth** *vt* to cause to foam – often + *up* ~ *vi* to produce or emit froth – often + *up*

frothy /ˈfrothi/ *adj* gaily frivolous or light [¹FROTH + ¹-Y] – **frothily** *adv*, **frothiness** *n*

frottage /ˈfrotahzh/ *n* the technique or process of creating an image of an object by rubbing (e g with a pencil) on a sheet of paper placed over it [F, fr *frotter* to rub]

froufrou /ˈfrooh,frooh/ *n* **1** a rustling sound, esp of a woman's dress **2** frilly ornamentation, esp in women's clothing [F, of imit origin]

froward /ˈfroh·əd/ *adj, archaic* habitually disobedient or contrary [ME, turned away, froward, fr *fro* from + *-ward*] – **frowardly** *adv*, **frowardness** *n*

¹**frown** /frown/ *vi* **1** to contract the brow in a frown **2** to give evidence of displeasure or disapproval – often + *on* or *upon* ~ *vt* to express by frowning [ME *frounen*, fr MF *froigner* to snort, frown, of Celt origin; akin to W *ffroen* nostril] – **frowner** *n*, **frowningly** *adv*

²**frown** *n* **1** a wrinkling of the brow in displeasure, concentration, or puzzlement **2** an expression of displeasure

frowst /frowst/ *vi, chiefly Br* to remain indoors in a hot airless room [back-formation fr *frowsty*]

frowsty /ˈfrowsti/ *adj, chiefly Br* STUFFY 1a [alter. of *frowsy*]

frowsy, frowzy /ˈfrowzi/ *adj* **1** having a slovenly or uncared-for appearance **2** musty, stale [origin unknown]

froze /frohz/ *past of* FREEZE

frozen /ˈfrohz(ə)n/ *adj* **1a** treated, affected, solidified, or crusted over by freezing **b** subject to long and severe cold ⟨*the* ~ *north*⟩ **2a** drained or incapable of emotion **b** incapable of being changed, moved, or undone **c** not available for present use ⟨~ *capital*⟩ – **frozenly** *adv*, **frozenness** *n*

fructification /,fruktifi'kaysh(ə)n/ *n* **1** forming or producing fruit **2** FRUIT 1d

fructify /'fruktifie/ *vi* to bear fruit – fml ~ *vt* to make fruitful or productive ⟨*social philosophy* fructified *the political thinking of liberals – TLS*⟩ – fml [ME *fructifien*, fr MF *fructifier*, fr L *fructificare*, fr *fructus* fruit]

fructose /'fruktohz, -tohs/ *n* a (very sweet) sugar that occurs esp in fruit juices and honey

frugal /'froohg(ə)l/ *adj* economical in the expenditure of resources; sparing [MF or L; MF, fr L *frugalis* virtuous, frugal, alter. of *frugi*, fr dat of *frug-, frux* fruit, value; akin to L *frui* to enjoy] – **frugally** *adv*, **frugality** /frooh'galəti/ *n*

frugivorous /frooh'jivərəs/ *adj* feeding on fruit [L *frug-, frux* + E *-vorous*] – **frugivore** /'froohji,vaw/ *n*

[1]**fruit** /frooht/ *n* **1a** a product of plant growth (e g grain or vegetables) ⟨*the* ~s *of the field*⟩ **b(1)** the (edible) reproductive body of a flowering plant; *esp* one having a sweet pulp associated with the seed **(2)** a succulent edible plant part used chiefly in a dessert or sweet dish **c** a dish, quantity, or diet of fruits ⟨*please pass the* ~⟩ **d** the ripened fertilized ovary of a flowering plant together with its contents **2** offspring, progeny **3a** the state of bearing fruit ⟨*a tree in* ~⟩ **b** a (favourable) product or result – often pl with sing. meaning **4** *Br* a fellow – in *old fruit*; infml [ME, fr OF, fr L *fructus* fruit, use, fr *fructus*, pp of *frui* to enjoy, have the use of – more at [1]BROOK] – **fruited** *adj*

[2]**fruit** *vb* to (cause to) bear fruit

fruitarian /frooh'teəri·ən/ *n* one whose diet consists of fruit [[1]*fruit* + *-arian* (as in *vegetarian*)]

'**fruit ,bat** *n* any of various large Old World fruit-eating bats of warm regions

fruiter /'froohtə/ *n* a plant (e g a tree) producing fruit ⟨*that apple is a poor* ~⟩

fruiterer /'froohtərə/ *n* one who deals in fruit [ME, modif of MF *fruitier*, fr *fruit*]

'**fruit ,fly** *n* any of various small flies whose larvae feed on fruit or decaying vegetable matter

fruitful /'froohtf(ə)l/ *adj* **1** (conducive to) yielding or producing (abundant) fruit **2** abundantly productive – **fruitfully** *adv*, **fruitfulness** *n*

fruiting body *n* a plant organ specialized for producing spores

fruition /frooh'ish(ə)n/ *n* **1** bearing fruit **2** realization, fulfilment [ME *fruicioun*, fr MF or LL; MF *fruition*, fr LL *fruition-, fruitio*, fr L *fruitus*, alter. of *fructus*, pp]

fruitless /'froohtlis/ *adj* **1** lacking or not bearing fruit **2** useless, unsuccessful – **fruitlessly** *adv*, **fruitlessness** *n*

'**fruit ma,chine** *n, Br* a coin-operated gambling machine that pays out according to different combinations of symbols (e g different types of fruit) visible on wheels

fruity /'froohti/ *adj* **1** having the flavour of the unfermented fruit ⟨~ *wine*⟩ **2** *of a voice* marked by richness and depth **3** amusing in a sexually suggestive way ⟨*a* ~ *story*⟩ – infml [[1]FRUIT + [1]-Y] – **fruitily** *adv*, **fruitiness** *n*

frumenty /'froohmənti/ *n* wheat boiled in milk and usu flavoured with sugar and spices [ME, fr MF *frumentee*, fr *frument* grain, fr L *frumentum*, fr *frui*]

frump /frump/ *n* **1** a dowdy unattractive girl or woman **2** a staid drab old-fashioned person *USE* chiefly infml [prob fr *frumple* (to wrinkle), fr ME *fromplen*, fr MD *verrompelen*] – **frumpish** *adj*, **frumpy** *adj*

frusemide /'froohzəmied/ *n* a powerful synthetic diuretic used in the treatment of oedema and high blood pressure [alter. of *fursemide*, fr *fur*fural (a liquid aldehyde made of plant materials; fr L *furfur* bran) + *s*ulphur + *-emide*, prob alter. of *amide*]

frustrate /fru'strayt/ *vt* **1a** to balk or defeat in an endeavour; foil **b** to induce feelings of discouragement and vexation in **2** to make ineffectual; nullify [ME *frustraten*, fr L *frustratus*, pp of *frustrare* to deceive, frustrate, fr *frustra* in error, in vain; akin to L *fraus* fraud – more at FRAUD] – **frustrating** *adj*, **frustratingly** *adv*

fru'strated *adj* filled with a sense of frustration

frustration /fru'straysh(ə)n/ *n* **1a** frustrating or being frustrated **b** a deep sense of insecurity, tension, and dissatisfaction arising from unresolved problems or unfulfilled needs **2** sthg that frustrates

frustule /'frustyoohl/ *n* the hard silica-containing shell of a diatom [F, fr L *frustulum*, dim. of *frustum*]

frustum /'frustəm/ *n, pl* **frustums, frusta** /-tə/ the part of a cone or pyramid left after cutting off the top at a plane parallel to the base; *also* the part of a solid intersected between 2 usu parallel planes [NL, fr L, piece, bit]

frutescent /frooh'tes(ə)nt/ *adj* resembling a shrub [L *frut*ex shrub + E *-escent*]

[1]**fry** /frie/ *vb* to cook in hot fat [ME *frien*, fr OF *frire*, fr L *frigere*; akin to Gk *phrygein* to roast, fry, Skt *bhṛjjati* he roasts]

[2]**fry** *n* **1** a dish of fried food **2** *NAm* a social gathering (e g a picnic) at which food is fried and eaten

[3]**fry** *n, pl* **fry** **1a** recently hatched or very small (adult) fishes ☞ LIFE CYCLE **b** the young of other animals, esp when occurring in large numbers **2** a member of a group or class; *esp* a person ⟨*books for small* ~⟩ [ME, prob fr ONF *fri*, fr OF *frier, froyer* to rub, spawn – more at [2]FRAY]

fryer /'frie·ə/ *n* sthg intended for or used in frying; *esp* a deep vessel for frying foods

'**frying ,pan** *n* a shallow metal pan with a handle that is used for frying foods – **out of the frying pan into the fire** clear of one difficulty only to fall into a greater one

'**fry-,up** *n, Br* (a dish prepared by) the frying of food for a simple impromptu meal – chiefly infml

fuchsia /'fyoohshə/ *n* any of a genus of decorative shrubs with showy nodding flowers usu in deep pinks, reds, and purples [NL, genus name, fr Leonhard *Fuchs* †1566 G botanist]

fuchsine /'foohk,seen/, **fuchsin** /-sin/ *n* a brilliant bluish red dye [F *fuchsine*, prob fr NL *Fuchsia*; fr its colour]

[1]**fuck** /fuk/ *vi* **1** to have sexual intercourse **2** to mess *about* or *around* ~ *vt* to have sexual intercourse with *USE* vulg [perh of Scand origin; akin to Norw dial. *fukka* to copulate, Sw dial. *focka* to copulate, strike, push, *fock* penis; perh akin to L *pugnus* fist, *pungere* to prick, sting, Gk *pygmē* fist]

[2]**fuck** *n* **1** an act of sexual intercourse **2** the slightest amount ⟨*didn't care a* ~⟩ *USE* vulg

³fuck *interj* – used to express annoyance; vulg

ˌfuck-ˈall *n* nothing at all – vulg

fucker /ˈfukə/ *n* a fool – vulg [¹FUCK + ²-ER]

fuck off *vi* **1** to go away **2** *NAm* to fuck about *USE* vulg

fucus /ˈfyoohkəs/ *n* any of a genus of brown algae that are seaweeds used in the kelp industry [L, orchil, rouge, fr Gk *phykos* seaweed, orchil, rouge, of Sem origin; akin to Heb *pūkh* antimony used as a cosmetic] – **fucoid** /ˈfyoohˌkoyd/ *adj*

fuddle /ˈfudl/ *vt* **1** to make drunk **2** to make confused [origin unknown]

fuddy-duddy /ˈfudi ˌdudi/ *n* a person who is old-fashioned, pompous, unimaginative, or concerned about trifles – infml [perh alter. of *fussy* + *dud*] – **fuddy-duddy** *adj*

¹fudge /fuj/ *vi* to avoid commitment; hedge – usu + *on* ~ *vt* **1a** to devise or put together roughly or without adequate basis ⟨*she could always* ~ *up an excuse*⟩ **b** to falsify ⟨~d *the figures*⟩ **2** to fail to come to grips with; dodge [prob alter. of earlier *fadge* (to fit, adjust)]

²fudge *n* **1** a soft (creamy) sweet made typically of sugar, milk, butter, and flavouring **2** foolish nonsense – infml; sometimes used interjectionally

fuehrer /ˈfyooərə (əer fyrə/ *n* a führer

¹fuel /ˈfyooh·əl/ *n* **1a** a material used to produce heat or power by combustion ☞ ENERGY **b** nutritive material **c** a material from which atomic energy can be liberated, esp in a reactor **2** a source of sustenance, strength, or encouragement [ME *fewel*, fr OF *fouaille*, fr *feu* fire, fr LL *focus*, fr L, hearth]

²fuel *vb* **-ll-** (*NAm* **-l-, -ll-**) *vt* **1** to provide with fuel **2** to support, stimulate ⟨*inflation* ~led *by massive wage awards*⟩ ~ *vi* to take in fuel – often + *up*

ˈfuel ˌcell *n* a cell that continuously changes chemical energy to electrical energy

fug /fug/ *n* the stuffy atmosphere of a poorly ventilated space – chiefly infml [prob alter. of ²*fog*] – **fuggy** *adj*

fugacious /fyoohˈgayshəs/ *adj* lasting a short time – fml [L *fugac-, fugax*, fr *fugere*] – **fugacity** /fyoohˈgasəti/ *n*

fugal /ˈfyoohgl/ *adj* in the style of a musical fugue – **fugally** *adv*

-fuge /-ˌfyoohj/ *comb form* (→ *n*) sthg that drives away ⟨*in sectifuge*⟩ ⟨*febrifuge*⟩ [F, fr LL *-fuga*, fr L *fugare* to put to flight, fr *fuga* flight]

¹fugitive /ˈfyoohjətiv/ *adj* **1** running away or trying to escape **2a** elusive **b** likely to change, fade, or disappear **3** fleeting, ephemeral [ME, fr MF & L; MF *fugitif*, fr L *fugitivus*, fr *fugitus*, pp of *fugere* to flee; akin to Gk *pheugein* to flee, & prob to OHG *biogan* to bend – more at ¹BOW] – **fugitively** *adv*, **fugitiveness** *n*

²fugitive *n* a person who flees or tries to escape, esp from danger, justice, or oppression

fugleman /ˈfyoohglmən/ *n* a leader (of a group) [modif of G *flügelmann*, fr *flügel* wing + *mann* man]

fugue /fyoohg/ *n* **1** a musical composition in which 1 or 2 themes are repeated or imitated by successively entering voices and are developed in a continuous interweaving of the voice parts **2** a disturbed state in which a person performs acts of which on recovery he/she has no recollection and which usu involves disappearance from his/her usual environment [prob fr It *fuga* flight, fugue, fr L, flight, fr *fugere*] – **fuguist** *n*

führer, fuehrer /ˈfyooərə (əer fyrə)/ *n* **1** LEADER 2c(3) **2** a leader exercising tyrannical authority [G *führer* leader, guide, fr MHG *vüerer* bearer, fr *vüeren* to lead, bear, fr OHG *fuoren* to lead; akin to OE *faran* to go – more at FARE]

¹-ful /-f(ə)l/ *suffix* **1** (*n* → *adj*) full of ⟨*event*ful⟩ ⟨*colour*ful⟩ **2** (*n* → *adj*) characterized by ⟨*peace*ful⟩ ⟨*boast*ful⟩ **3** (*n* → *adj*) having the qualities of ⟨*master*ful⟩ **4** (*vb* → *adj*) tending to or able to ⟨*mourn*ful⟩ [ME, fr OE, fr *full*, adj]

²-ful *suffix* (*n* → *n*) number or amount that (a specified thing) holds or can hold ⟨*room*ful⟩ ⟨*hand*ful⟩

fulcrum /ˈfulkrəm, ˈfool-/ *n, pl* **fulcrums, fulcra** /-krə/ the support about which a lever turns [LL, fr L, bedpost, fr *fulcire* to prop – more at BALK]

fulfil, *NAm chiefly* **fulfill** /foolˈfil/ *vt* **-ll- 1a** to cause to happen as appointed or predicted – usu pass **b** to put into effect; CARRY OUT 1 **c** to measure up to; satisfy **2** to develop the full potential of [ME *fulfillen*, fr OE *fullfyllan*, fr *full* + *fyllan* to fill] – **fulfiller** *n*, **fulfilment** *n*

fulgent /ˈfulj(ə)nt/ *adj* dazzlingly bright – fml [ME, fr L *fulgent-, fulgens*, prp of *fulgēre* to shine; akin to L *flagrare* to burn – more at BLACK] – **fulgently** *adv*

fulgurite /ˈfulgyooriet/ *n* a glasslike crust produced by the fusion of sand or rock by lightning [ISV, fr L *fulgur* lightning, fr *fulgēre*]

fuliginous /fyoohˈlijinəs/ *adj* **1** sooty, murky **2** dark, dusky *USE* fml [LL *fuliginosus*, fr L *fuligin-, fuligo* soot; akin to L *fumus* smoke – more at FUME] – **fuliginously** *adv*

¹full /fool/ *adj* **1** possessing or containing a great amount or as much or as many as is possible or normal **2a** complete, esp in detail, number, or duration **b** lacking restraint, check, or qualification ⟨~ *support*⟩ **c** having all distinguishing characteristics; enjoying all authorized rights and privileges **3a** at the highest or greatest degree; maximum **b** at the height of development ⟨~ *bloom*⟩ **4** rounded in outline; *also* well filled out or plump **5a** having an abundance of material (e g in the form of gathers or folds) ⟨*a* ~ *skirt*⟩ **b** rich in experience ⟨*a* ~ *life*⟩ **6** satisfied, esp with food or drink, often to the point of discomfort – usu + *up* **7** having both parents in common ⟨~ *sisters*⟩ **8a** with the attention completely occupied by or centred on sthg ⟨*always* ~ *of his own importance*⟩ **b** filled with excited anticipation or pleasure ⟨~ *of her plans for a holiday in Fiji*⟩ **9** possessing a rich or pronounced quality **10** – used as an intensive ⟨*won by a* ~ *4 shots*⟩ [ME, fr OE; akin to OHG *fol* full, L *plenus* full, *plēre* to fill, Gk *plērēs* full, *plēthein* to be full] – **fullness** *also* **fulness** *n* – **full of oneself** bumptiously self-centred or conceited

²full *adv* exactly, squarely

³full *n* **1** the highest or fullest state, extent, or degree **2** the requisite or complete amount – chiefly in *in full*

⁴full *vi*, *of the moon* to become full ~ *vt* to make full in sewing

⁵full *vt* to cleanse and finish (woollen cloth) by moistening, heating, and pressing [ME *fullen*, fr MF *fouler*, fr (assumed) VL *fullare*, fr L *fullo* one who fulls cloth] – **fuller** *n*

fulla /'foolə/ *n, NZ* a man, fellow [prob alter. of *fellow*]

'full,back /-,bak/ *n* a primarily defensive player in soccer, rugby, etc, usu stationed nearest the defended goal ☞ SPORT

'full ,blood *n* (an individual having) descent from parents both of the same pure breed

,full-'blooded *adj* **1** of unmixed ancestry; purebred **2a** forceful, vigorous **b** virile **3** being the specified thing to a great extent ⟨*a* ~ *socialist*⟩ – **full-bloodedness** *n*

,full-'blown *adj* **1** at the height of bloom **2** fully developed or mature

,full-'bodied *adj* marked by richness and fullness, esp of flavour ⟨*a* ~ *wine*⟩

,full 'circle *adv* through a series of developments that lead back to the original source, position, or situation

,full-'dress *adj* **1** complete, full-scale **2** of or being full dress ⟨~ *uniform*⟩

full dress *n* the style of dress prescribed for ceremonial or formal social occasions

fuller /'foolə/ *n* a blacksmith's hammer for grooving and spreading iron [*fuller* (to form a groove in), perh fr the name *Fuller*]

,fuller's 'earth /'fooləz/ *n* a clayey substance used in fulling cloth and as a catalyst

,full-'fledged *adj, chiefly NAm* fully-fledged

,full 'house *n* a poker hand containing 3 of a kind and a pair

,full-'length *adj* **1** showing or adapted to the entire length, esp of the human figure **2** having a normal or standard length; unabridged

,full 'marks *n pl, Br* due credit or commendation

,full 'moon *n* the moon when its whole apparent disc is illuminated ☞ SYMBOL

,full'mouthed /-'mowdhd/ *adj* having a full complement of teeth

,full 'nelson /'nels(ə)n/ *n* a wrestling hold in which both arms are thrust under the corresponding arms of an opponent and the hands clasped behind the opponent's head – compare HALF NELSON

,full-'scale *adj* **1** identical to an original in proportion and size **2** involving full use of available resources ⟨*a* ~ *biography*⟩

,full 'stop *n* a punctuation mark . used to mark the end (e g of a sentence or abbreviation) – often used to express completion ⟨*They were just brave, clean, British success stories.* Full stop. – *Punch*⟩

,full-'term *adj* born after a pregnancy of normal length – compare PREMATURE

,full 'tilt *adv* at high speed [[2]*tilt*]

,full-'time *adj* employed for or involving full time ⟨~ *employees*⟩ – **full time** *adv*

,full 'time *n* **1** the amount of time considered the normal or standard amount for working during a given period, esp a week **2** the end of a sports, esp soccer, match

,full 'toss *n* a throw, esp a bowled ball in cricket, that has not hit the ground by the time it arrives at the point at which it was aimed

fully /'fooli/ *adv* **1** completely **2** AT LEAST 1 ⟨~ *nine tenths of us*⟩

,fully-'fashioned *adj* employing or produced by a knitting process for shaping to body lines ⟨~ *tights*⟩

,fully-'fledged, *NAm* **,full-'fledged** *adj* having attained complete status

fulmar /'foolmə/ *n* a seabird of colder regions closely related to the petrels [of Scand origin; akin to ON *fūlmār* fulmar, fr *fūll* foul + *mār* gull]

fulminant /'foolminənt, 'ful-/ *adj* FULMINATING 2

[1]'fulminate /-nayt/ *vt* to utter or thunder out with denunciation ~ *vi* **1** to thunder forth censure or invective – usu + *against* or *at* **2** to be agitated or enraged (by feelings of indignation) ⟨*he* ~d *in silence*⟩ [ME *fulminaten,* fr ML *fulminatus,* pp of *fulminare,* fr L, to flash with lightning, strike with lightning, fr *fulmin-, fulmen* lightning; akin to L *flagrare* to burn – more at BLACK] – **fulminator** *n,* **fulmination** /-'naysh(ə)n/ *n*

[2]fulminate *n* an (explosive) salt (e g of mercury) containing the radical CNO [ISV *fulmin-* (fr L *fulmin-, fulmen*) + *-ate*]

fulminating /'foolminayting, 'ful-/ *adj* **1** exploding with a vivid flash **2** coming on suddenly with great severity ⟨~ *infection*⟩

fulsome /'fools(ə)m/ *adj* **1** overabundant, copious ⟨*described in* ~ *detail*⟩ **2a** unnecessarily effusive **b** obsequious [ME *fulsom* copious, cloying, fr *full* + *-som* -some] – **fulsomely** *adv,* **fulsomeness** *n*

fulvous /'fulvəs/ *adj* dull brownish yellow [L *fulvus*; perh akin to L *flavus* yellow – more at [1]BLUE]

fu,maric 'acid /fyooh'marik/ *n* an acid that has 2 carboxyl groups in its molecular structure, is found in various plants, and is used esp in making resins [ISV, fr NL *Fumaria,* genus of herbs, fr LL, fumitory, fr L *fumus*]

fumarole /'fyoomə,rohl/ *n* a hole in a volcanic region from which hot vapours issue [It *fumarola,* modif of LL *fumariolum,* fr L *fumarium* smoke chamber for aging wine, fr *fumus* fume] – **fumarolic** /,fyoohmə'rolik/ *adj*

fumble /'fumbl/ *vb* **fumbling** /'fumbling/ *vi* **1a** to grope for or handle sthg clumsily or awkwardly **b** to make awkward attempts to do or find sthg **2** to feel one's way or move awkwardly ~ *vt* **1** to feel or handle clumsily **2** to deal with awkwardly or clumsily [prob of Scand origin; akin to Sw *fumla* to fumble] – **fumble** *n,* **fumbler** *n,* **fumblingly** *adv*

[1]fume /fyoohm/ *n* **1** an (irritating or offensive) smoke, vapour, or gas – often pl with sing. meaning **2** a state of unreasonable excited irritation or anger ⟨*in a* ~ *of impatience*⟩ [ME, fr MF *fum,* fr L *fumus*; akin to OHG *toumen* to be fragrant, Gk *thymos* mind, spirit] – **fumy** *adj*

[2]fume *vt* to expose to or treat with fumes ~ *vi* **1a** to emit fumes **b** to be in a state of excited irritation or anger ⟨*she fretted and* ~d *over the delay*⟩ **2** to rise (as if) in fumes

fumigate /'fyoohmigayt/ *vt* to apply smoke, vapour, or gas to, esp in order to disinfect or destroy pests [L *fumigatus,* pp of *fumigare,* fr *fumus* smoke + *-igare* (akin to L *agere* to drive) – more at AGENT] – **fumigator** *n,* **fumigant** *n,* **fumigation** /-'gaysh(ə)n/ *n*

fumitory /'fyoohmit(ə)ri/ *n* any of several erect or climbing plants with purple or white flowers [ME *fumeterre,* fr MF, fr ML *fumus terrae,* lit., smoke of the earth, fr L *fumus* + *terrae,* gen of *terra* earth – more at TERRACE]

[1]fun /fun/ *n* **1** (a cause of) amusement or enjoyment **2** derisive jest; ridicule ⟨*made him a figure of* ~⟩ **3** violent or excited activity or argument ⟨*let a snake loose in the classroom; then the* ~ *began*⟩ [E dial.

fun (to hoax), perh alter. of ME *fonnen*, fr *fonne* dupe]

[2]fun *adj, chiefly NAm* providing entertainment, amusement, or enjoyment ⟨*a ~ person to be with*⟩ – infml

funambulism /fyooh'nambyoo,liz(ə)m/ *n* tightrope walking – fml [L *funambulus* ropewalker, fr *funis* rope + *ambulare* to walk] – **funambulist** *n*

,fun and 'games *n pl but sing or pl in constr* high-spirited or overexcited activity

[1]function /'fungksh(ə)n/ *n* **1** an occupational duty **2** the action characteristic of a person or thing or for which a thing exists ⟨*examining the ~ of poetry in modern society*⟩ **3** any of a group of related actions contributing to a larger action **4** an impressive, elaborate, or formal ceremony or social gathering **5a** a mathematical relationship between each element of one set and at least one element of the same or another set **b** a quality, trait, or fact dependent on and varying with another **c** a facility on a computer or similar device corresponding to a mathematical function or operation [L *function-*, *functio* performance, fr *functus*, pp of *fungi* to perform; prob akin to Skt *bhuṅkte* he enjoys] – **functionless** *adj*

[2]function *vi* **1** to have a function; serve ⟨*an attributive noun ~s as an adjective*⟩ **2** to operate ⟨*a government ~s through numerous divisions*⟩

functional /'fungksh(ə)nl/ *adj* **1a** of, connected with, or being a function **b** affecting physiological or psychological functions but not organic structure ⟨*~ heart disease*⟩ – compare ORGANIC 1b **2** designed or developed for practical use without ornamentation **3** (capable of) performing a function – **functionally** *adv*

functional group *n* a characteristic reactive unit of a chemical compound

'functional,ism /-,iz(ə)m/ *n* **1** a theory that stresses the interdependence of the institutions of a society **2** a theory or practice that emphasizes practical utility or functional relations to the exclusion of ornamentation – **functionalist** *n*, **functionalist, functionalistic** /-'istik/ *adj*

functionary /'fungksh(ə)nəri/ *n* **1** sby who serves in a certain function **2** sby holding office

'function ,word *n* a word (e g a preposition or conjunction) chiefly expressing grammatical relationship

functor /'fungktə/ *n* FUNCTION WORD [[2]FUNCTION + [1]-OR]

[1]fund /fund/ *n* **1** an available quantity of material or intangible resources ⟨*~ of knowledge*⟩ **2** (an organization administering) a resource, esp a sum of money, whose principal or interest is set apart for a specific objective **3** *pl* an available supply of money [L *fundus* bottom, piece of landed property – more at BOTTOM]

[2]fund *vt* **1** to make provision of resources for discharging the interest or principal of **2** to provide funds for ⟨*research ~ed by the government*⟩

fundament /'fundəmənt/ *n* **1** the buttocks **2** the anus [ME, fr OF *fondement*, fr L *fundamentum*, fr *fundare* to found, fr *fundus*]

[1]fundamental /,fundə'mentl/ *adj* **1** serving as a basis to support existence or to determine essential structure or function – often + *to* **2** of essential structure, function, or facts ⟨*~ change*⟩ **3** of, being, or produced by the lowest component of a complex vibration **4** of central importance; principal ⟨*~ purpose*⟩ **5** belonging to one's innate or ingrained characteristics – **fundamentally** *adv*

[2]fundamental *n* **1** a minimum constituent without which a thing or system would not be what it is **2** the prime tone of a harmonic series **3** the harmonic component of a complex wave that has the lowest frequency

,funda'mentalism /-iz(ə)m/ *n* (adherence to) a belief in the literal truth of the Bible – **fundamentalist** *n or adj*

fundamental particle *n* ELEMENTARY PARTICLE

fundus /'fundəs/ *n, pl* **fundi** /-di, -die/ the bottom, or part opposite the opening, of the stomach, uterus, or other hollow organ [NL, fr L, bottom] – **fundic** *adj*

funeral /'fyoohn(ə)rəl/ *n* **1** (a procession connected with) a formal and ceremonial disposing of dead body, esp by burial or cremation; *also, NAm* a funeral service **2** a matter, esp a difficulty, that is of concern only to the specified person ⟨*if you get lost, that's your ~*⟩ – infml [ME *funerelles* (pl), fr MF *funerailles* (pl), fr LL *funeralia*, neut pl of *funeralis* (adj), fr L *funer-*, *funus* (n)]

'funeral di,rector *n* an undertaker

'funeral ,parlour *n* an undertaker's establishment

funerary /'fyoohnərəri/ *adj* of, used for, or associated with burial ⟨*a pharaoh's ~ chamber*⟩ [L *funerarius*, fr *funer-*, *funus*]

funereal /fyooh'niəri·əl/ *adj* **1** of a funeral **2** gloomy, solemn [L *funereus*, fr *funer-*, *funus*] – **funereally** *adv*

'fun ,fair *n, chiefly Br* a usu outdoor show offering amusements (e g sideshows, rides, or games of skill)

fungi- *comb form* fungus ⟨fungi*form*⟩ ⟨fungi*cide*⟩ [L *fungus*]

[1]fungible /'funjəbl/ *n* sthg fungible – usu pl

[2]fungible *adj* such that 1 specimen may be used in place of another in the satisfaction of an obligation [NL *fungibilis*, fr L *fungi* to perform – more at FUNCTION] – **fungibility** /-'biləti/ *n*

fungicide /'funjisied/ *n* a substance used for destroying or preventing fungus [ISV] – **fungicidal** /-'siedl/ *adj*, **fungicidally** *adv*

fungoid /'fung·goyd/ *adj* resembling, characteristic of, or being a fungus – **fungoid** *n*

fungous /'fung·gəs/ *adj* of, like, or caused by a fungus or fungi

fungus /'fung·gəs/ *n, pl* **fungi** /-gie, -gi/ *also* **funguses** any of a major group of often parasitic organisms lacking chlorophyll and including moulds, rusts, mildews, smuts, mushrooms, and toadstools ☞ PLANT [L] – **fungal** *adj*

[1]funicular /fyooh'nikyoolə/ *adj* **1** dependent on the tension of a cord or cable **2** (of the form) of or associated with a cord [L *funiculus* small rope, dim. of *funis* rope]

[2]funicular *n* a cable railway in which an ascending carriage counterbalances a descending carriage

[1]funk /fungk/ *n* **1a** a state of paralysing fear **b** a fit of inability to face difficulty **2** a coward *USE* infml [prob fr obs Flem *fonck*; (2) [2]*funk*]

[2]funk *vt* **1** to be afraid of **2** to avoid doing or facing (sthg) because of lack of determination *USE* infml

[3]funk *n* funky music – slang [back-formation fr *funky*]

funky /'fungki/ *adj* **1** having an offensive smell –

chiefly infml **2** having an earthy unsophisticated style and feeling (as in the blues) **3** having an earthily sexual quality **4** – used to approve sthg or sby, esp in pop culture *USE (2, 3, & 4)* slang [*funk* (offensive smell), perh fr F dial. *funquer* to emit smoke] – **funkiness** *n*

[1]**funnel** /'funl/ *n* **1** a utensil usu having the shape of a hollow cone with a tube extending from the smaller end, designed to direct liquids or powders into a small opening **2** a shaft, stack, or flue for ventilation or the escape of smoke or steam [ME *fonel*, fr OProv *fonilh*, fr ML *fundibulum*, short for L *infundibulum*, fr *infundere* to pour in, fr *in-* + *fundere* to pour – more at [4]FOUND]

[2]**funnel** *vb* **-ll-** (*NAm* **-l-**, **-ll-**) *pres part* /'funl·ing/ *vi* **1** to have or take the shape of a funnel **2** to pass (as if) through a funnel ⟨*the crowd* ~led *out of the football ground*⟩ ~ *vt* **1** to form in the shape of a funnel ⟨~led *his hands and shouted through them*⟩ **2** to move to a focal point or into a central channel ⟨*contributions were* ~led *into 1 account*⟩

funnily enough /'funl·i/ *adv* as is curious or unexpected

[1]**funny** /'funi/ *adj* **1** causing mirth and laughter; seeking or intended to amuse **2** peculiar, strange, or odd **3** involving trickery, deception, or dishonesty ⟨*told the prisoner not to try anything* ~⟩ ⟨~ *business*⟩ **4** unwilling to be helpful; difficult ⟨*at first he was a bit* ~ *about it but in the end he agreed*⟩ **5a** slightly unwell **b** slightly mad ⟨~ *in the head*⟩ **6** pleasantly amusing; nice – esp in *funny old* ⟨*look at that* ~ *old dog*⟩ *USE* (*3, 4, 5, & 6*) infml [[1]*fun* + [1]*-y*] – **funnily** /'funl·i/ *adv*, **funniness** *n*, **funny** *adv*

[2]**funny** *n* a comic strip or comic section in a periodical – usu pl

'**funny ,bone** *n* the place at the back of the elbow where the nerve supplying the hand and forearm rests against the bone [fr the tingling felt when it is struck]

'**funny ,farm** *n, chiefly NAm* a mental hospital – chiefly humor

[1]**fur** /fuh/ *vb* **-rr-** to (cause to) become coated or clogged (as if) with fur – often + *up* [ME *furren*, fr MF *fourrer*, fr OF *forrer*, fr *fuerre* sheath, of Gmc origin; akin to OHG *fuotar* sheath; akin to Gk *pōy* herd, Skt *pāti* he protects]

[2]**fur** *n* **1** a piece of the dressed pelt of an animal used to make, trim, or line garments **2** an article of clothing made of or with fur **3** the hairy coat of a mammal, esp when fine, soft, and thick; *also* such a coat with the skin **4** a coating resembling fur: e g **a** a coating of dead cells on the tongue of sby who is unwell **b** the thick pile of a fabric (e g chenille) **c** a coating formed in vessels (e g kettles or pipes) by deposition of scale from hard water **5** any of the heraldic representations of animal pelts or their colours that have a stylized pattern of tufts or patches – **furless** *adj*, **furred** *adj*

furbelow /'fuhbi,loh/ *n* **1** a pleated or gathered piece of material; *specif* a flounce on women's clothing **2** sthg that suggests a furbelow, esp in being showy or superfluous – often in *frills and furbelows* [by folk etymology fr F dial. *farbella*] – **furbelow** *vt*

furbish /'fuhbish/ *vt* **1** to polish **2** to renovate – often + *up* [ME *furbisshen*, fr MF *fourbiss-*, stem of *fourbir*, of Gmc origin; akin to OHG *furben* to polish] – **furbisher** *n*

furcula /'fuhkyoolə/ *n, pl* **furculae** /-li, -lie/ a wishbone or other forked part [NL, fr L, forked prop, dim. of *furca* fork] – **furcular** *adj*

furious /'fyooəri·əs/ *adj* **1a** exhibiting or goaded by uncontrollable anger **b** giving a stormy or turbulent appearance ⟨~ *bursts of flame from the fire*⟩ **c** marked by (violent) noise, excitement, or activity **2** INTENSE 1a [ME, fr MF *furieus*, fr L *furiosus*, fr *furia* fury] – **furiously** *adv*

furl /fuhl/ *vt* to fold or roll (e g a sail or umbrella) close to or round sthg ~ *vi* to curl or fold as in being furled [MF *ferler*, fr ONF *ferlier* to tie tightly, fr OF *fer, ferm* tight (fr L *firmus* firm) + *lier* to tie, fr L *ligare* – more at LIGATURE] – **furl** *n*

furlong /'fuhlong/ *n* a unit of length equal to 220yd (about 0.201km) ☞ UNIT [ME, fr OE *furlang*, fr *furh* furrow + *lang* long]

[1]**furlough** /'fuhloh/ *n* a leave of absence from duty granted esp to a soldier [D *verlof*, lit., permission, fr MD, fr *ver-* for- + *lof* permission; akin to OE *for-* and to MHG *loube* permission – more at FOR-, [2]LEAVE]

[2]**furlough** *vt, chiefly NAm* to grant a furlough to

furmety /'fuhməti/ *n* frumenty [by alter.]

furnace /'fuhnis/ *n* an enclosed apparatus in which heat is produced (e g for heating a building or reducing ore) [ME *furnas*, fr OF *fornaise*, fr L *fornac-, fornax*; akin to L *formus* warm – more at WARM]

furnish /'fuhnish/ *vt* to provide or supply (with what is needed); *esp* to equip with furniture [ME *furnisshen*, fr MF *fourniss-*, stem of *fournir* to complete, equip, of Gmc origin; akin to OHG *frummen* to further, *fruma* advantage – more at FOREMOST] – **furnisher** *n*

furnishing /'fuhnishing/ *n* an object that tends to increase comfort or utility; *specif* an article of furniture for the interior of a building – usu pl; compare SOFT FURNISHINGS

furniture /'fuhnichə/ *n* **1** necessary, useful, or desirable equipment: e g **a** the movable articles (e g tables, chairs, and beds) that make an area suitable for living in or use **b** accessories ⟨*door* ~⟩ **c** the whole movable equipment of a ship (e g rigging, sails, anchors, and boats) **2** pieces of wood or metal less than type high placed in printing forms to fill in blank spaces [MF *fourniture*, fr *fournir*]

'**furniture ,beetle** *n* a small beetle whose larva is a woodworm

furor /'fyooəraw/ *n, chiefly NAm* a furore [MF & L; MF, fr L, fr *furere* to rage – more at DUST]

furore /fyoo'rawri/ *n* an outburst of general excitement or indignation [It, fr L *furor*]

furphy /'fuhfi/ *n, Austr* an unlikely or absurd rumour – infml [*Furphy*, name of supplier of sanitation carts in Australia during WW I]

furrier /'furi·ə/ *n* a fur dealer [ME *furrer*, fr AF *furrere*, fr OF *forrer, fourrer* to fur]

[1]**furrow** /'furoh/ *n* **1a** a trench in the earth made by a plough **b** rural land; a field **2** sthg like the track of a plough: e g **a** a groove **b** a deep wrinkle [ME *furgh, forow*, fr OE *furh*; akin to OHG *furuh* furrow, L *porca*]

[2]**furrow** *vb* to make or form furrows, grooves, lines, etc (in)

furry /'fuhri/ *adj* like, made of, or covered with fur

[1]**further** /'fuhdhə/ *adv* **1** FARTHER 1 **2** moreover **3** to a greater degree or extent ⟨~ *annoyed by a second interruption*⟩ [ME, fr OE *furthor*; akin to OHG

furdar further; both compars fr the root of OE *forth* – more at FORTH]

[2]**further** *adj* **1** FARTHER 1 **2** extending beyond what exists or has happened; additional ⟨~ *volumes*⟩ **3** coming after the one referred to ⟨*closed until* ~ *notice*⟩

[3]**further** *vt* to help forward ⟨*this will* ~ *your chances of success*⟩ – **furtherance** /'fuhdh(ə)rəns/ *n*, **furtherer** /'fuhdh(ə)rə/ *n*

further education *n*, *Br* vocational, cultural, or recreational education for people who have left school

,further'more /-'maw/ *adv* in addition to what precedes; moreover – used esp when introducing fresh matter for consideration

'further,most /-,mohst/ *adj* most distant

'further to *prep* following up ⟨~ *your letter of the 4th July*⟩

furthest /'fuhdhist/ *adv or adj* farthest

furtive /'fuhtiv/ *adj* expressing or done by stealth [F or L; F *furtif*, fr L *furtivus*, fr *furtum* theft, fr *fur* thief; akin to Gk *phōr* thief, L *ferre* to carry – more at [2]BEAR] – **furtively** *adv*, **furtiveness** *n*

furuncle /'fyooə,rungkl/ *n* [1]BOIL [L *furunculus* petty thief, sucker, furuncle, dim. of *furon-*, *furo* ferret, thief, fr *fur*] – **furuncular** /fyoo'rungkyoolə/ *adj*, **furunculous** /-ləs/ *adj*

furunculosis /fyoo,rungkyoo'lohsis/ *n*, *pl* **furunculoses** /-seez/ a highly infectious bacterial disease of trout, salmon, and related fishes [NL, fr L *furunculus* + NL *-osis*]

fury /'fyooəri/ *n* **1** intense, disordered, and often destructive rage **2a** *cap* any of the 3 avenging deities who in Greek mythology punished crimes **b** (one who resembles) an avenging spirit **3** wild disordered force or activity **4** a frenzy [ME *furie*, fr MF & L; MF, fr L *furia*, fr *furere* to rage – more at DUST]

furze /fuhz/ *n* gorse [ME *firse*, fr OE *fyrs*] – **furzy** *adj*

fuscous /'fuskəs/ *adj* dark brownish grey [L *fuscus* – more at DUSK]

[1]**fuse** /fyoohz/ *n* **1** a combustible substance enclosed in a cord or cable for setting off an explosive charge by transmitting fire to it **2** *NAm chiefly* **fuze** the detonating device for setting off the charge in a projectile, bomb, etc [It *fuso* spindle, fr L *fusus*, of unknown origin]

[2]**fuse**, *NAm also* **fuze** *vt* to equip with a fuse

[3]**fuse** *vt* **1** to reduce to a liquid or plastic state by heat **2** to blend thoroughly (as if) by melting together **3** to cause (e g a light bulb) to fail by fusing ~ *vi* **1** to become fluid with heat **2** to become blended (as if) by melting together **3** to fail because of the melting of a fuse [L *fusus*, pp of *fundere* to pour, melt – more at [4]FOUND] – **fusible** *adj*, **fusibility** /-zə'biləti/ *n*

[4]**fuse** *n* (a device that includes) a wire or strip of fusible metal that melts and interrupts the circuit when the current exceeds a particular value

fusee, *NAm also* **fuzee** /fyooh'zee/ *n* a conical spirally grooved pulley or wheel, esp in a watch or clock [F *fusée*, lit., spindleful of yarn, fr OF, fr *fus* spindle, fr L *fusus*]

fuselage /'fyoohzi,lahzh/ *n* the central body portion of an aeroplane designed to accommodate the crew and the passengers or cargo [F, fr *fuselé* spindle-shaped, fr MF, fr *fusel*, dim. of *fus*]

fusel oil /'fyoohzl/ *n* an acrid oily poisonous liquid consisting chiefly of amyl alcohol and used esp as a source of alcohols and as a solvent [G *fusel* bad liquor]

fusi- /fyoohzi-/ *comb form* spindle ⟨fusi*form*⟩ [L *fusus*]

fusiform /'fyoohzi,fawm/ *adj* tapering towards each end ⟨~ *bacteria*⟩

fusil /'fyoohzil/ *n* a light flintlock musket [F, lit., steel for striking fire, fr OF *foisil*, fr (assumed) VL *focilis*, fr LL *focus* fire – more at FUEL]

fusilier /,fyoohzə'liə/ *n* a member of a British regiment formerly armed with fusils [F *fusilier*, fr *fusil*]

[1]**fusillade** /,fyoohzə'layd/ *n* **1** a number of shots fired simultaneously or in rapid succession **2** a spirited outburst, esp of criticism [F, fr *fusiller* to shoot, fr *fusil*]

[2]**fusillade** *vt* to attack or shoot down by a fusillade

fusion /'fyoohzh(ə)n/ *n* **1** fusing or rendering plastic by heat **2** a union (as if) by melting: e g **a** a merging of diverse elements into a unified whole **b** the union of light atomic nuclei to form heavier nuclei resulting in the release of enormous quantities of energy [L *fusion-*, *fusio*, fr *fusus*, pp]

[1]**fuss** /fus/ *n* **1a** needless or useless bustle or excitement **b** a show of (affectionate) attention – often in *make a fuss of* **2a** a state of agitation, esp over a trivial matter **b** an objection, protest ⟨*kicked up a* ~ *about the new regulations*⟩ [perh imit]

[2]**fuss** *vi* **1a** to create or be in a state of restless activity; *specif* to shower affectionate attentions **b** to pay close or undue attention to small details ⟨~ed *with her hair*⟩ **2** to become upset; worry ~ *vt* to agitate, upset – **fusser** *n*

'fuss,budget /-,bujit/ *n* a fusspot – infml – **fussbudgety** *adj*

'fuss,pot /-,pot/ *n* a person who fusses about trifles – infml

fussy /'fusi/ *adj* **1** nervous and excitable (about small matters) **2a** showing too much concern over details **b** fastidious ⟨*not* ~ *about food*⟩ **3** having too much or too detailed ornamentation – **fussily** *adv*, **fussiness** *n*

fustian /'fusti·ən, 'fuschən/ *n* **1** a strong cotton or linen fabric (e g corduroy or velveteen), usu having a pile face and twill weave **2** pretentious and banal writing or speech [ME, fr OF *fustaine*, fr ML *fustaneum*, prob fr *fustis* tree trunk, fr L, club] – **fustian** *adj*

fustic /'fustik/ *n* (any of various esp tropical American trees with) wood that yields a yellow dye [ME *fustik*, fr MF *fustoc*, fr Ar *fustuq*, fr Gk *pistakē* pistachio tree – more at PISTACHIO]

fusty /'fusti/ *adj* **1** stale or musty from being left undisturbed for a long time **2** out-of-date **3** rigidly old-fashioned or reactionary [ME, fr *fust* wine cask, fr MF, club, cask, fr L *fustis*] – **fustily** *adv*, **fustiness** *n*

fut /fut/ *adv* phut

futile /'fyoohtiel/ *adj* **1** completely ineffective **2** *of a person* ineffectual [MF or L; MF, fr L *futilis* that pours out easily, useless, fr *fut-* (akin to *fundere* to pour) – more at [4]FOUND] – **futilely** *adv*, **futileness** *n*, **futility** /fyooh'tiləti/ *n*

futtock /'futək/ *n* any of the usu 4 or 5 curved timbers joined together to form the lower part of the compound ribs of a ship ☞ SHIP [prob alter. of *foothook* (futtock)]

futtock shroud *n* a short rope or iron rod connecting the topmast rigging with the lower mast ☞ SHIP

[1]**future** /ˈfyoohchə/ *adj* **1** that is to be; *specif* existing after death **2** of or constituting the verb tense that expresses action or state in future time [ME, fr OF & L; OF *futur*, fr L *futurus* about to be – more at BE]

[2]**future** *n* **1a** time that is to come **b** that which is going to occur **2** likelihood of success ⟨*not much ~ in trying to sell furs in a hot country*⟩ **3** sthg (e g a bulk commodity) bought for future acceptance or sold for future delivery – usu pl **4** (a verb form in) the future tense of a language – **futureless** *adj*

ˌ**future ˈperfect** *adj* of or constituting a verb tense (e g *will have finished*) expressing completion of an action at or before a future time – **future perfect** *n*

futurism /ˈfyoohchəˌriz(ə)m/ *n* **1** *often cap* a movement in art, music, and literature begun in Italy about 1910 and seeking to express the dynamic energy and movement of mechanical processes **2** a point of view that finds meaning or fulfilment in the future rather than in the past or present – **futurist** *n or adj*

futuristic /ˌfyoohchəˈristik/ *adj* of the future or futurism; *esp* bearing no relation to known or traditional forms; ultramodern – **futuristically** *adv*

futurity /fyoohˈtyooərəti, -ˈchooə-/ *n* **1** FUTURE 1a **2** *pl* future events or prospects **3** *chiefly NAm* a competition, esp a horse race, for which entries are made well in advance of the event [[1]FUTURE + -ITY]

futurology /ˌfyoohchəˈroləji/ *n* the forecasting of the future from current trends in society [G *futurologie*, fr *futur* future + *-o-* + *-logie* -logy] – **futurologist** *n*

fu-yung /ˌfooh ˈyung/ *n* (a dish containing) a mixture of egg white, cornflour, and sometimes minced chicken [Chin (Pek) *fu*[2] *yung*[2], lit., hibiscus]

fuze /fyoohz/ *n or vt, NAm* [1]FUSE 2, [2]FUSE

fuzee /fyoohˈzee/ *n, NAm* a fusee

[1]**fuzz** /fuz/ *n* fine light particles or fibres (e g of down or fluff) [prob back-formation fr *fuzzy*]

[2]**fuzz** *n sing or pl in constr* the police – slang [origin unknown]

fuzzy /ˈfuzi/ *adj* **1** marked by or giving a suggestion of fuzz ⟨*a ~ covering of felt*⟩ **2** not clear; indistinct [perh fr LG *fussig* loose, spongy; akin to OHG *fūl* rotten – more at FOUL] – **fuzzily** *adv*, **fuzziness** *n*

ˈ**fuzzy-ˌwuzzy** /-ˌwuzi/ *n, Br* a Sudanese soldier; *broadly* any African Negro – chiefly derog [redupl of *fuzzy*; fr the appearance of his hair]

-fy /-fie/, **-ify** *suffix* (→ *vb*) **1** become or cause to be ⟨*pur*ify⟩ ⟨*molli*fy⟩ ⟨*solidi*fy⟩ **2** fill with ⟨*stupe*fy⟩ ⟨*horri*fy⟩ **3** give the characteristics of; make similar to ⟨*countr*ify⟩ ⟨*dandi*fy⟩ **4** engage in (a specified activity) ⟨*argu*fy⟩ ⟨*speechi*fy⟩ – often humor or derog [ME *-fien*, fr OF *-fier*, fr L *-ficare*, fr *-ficus* -fic]

fylfot /ˈfilˌfot/ *n* a swastika [ME, device used to fill the lower part of a painted glass window, fr *fillen* to fill + *fot* foot]

G

g /jee/ *n, pl* **g's, gs** *often cap* **1** (a graphic representation of or device for reproducing) the 7th letter of the English alphabet **2** the 5th note of a C-major scale **3** a unit of force equal to the force exerted by gravity on a body at rest and used to indicate the force to which a body is subjected when accelerated **4** *chiefly NAm* a sum of $1000 – slang [(3) *g*ravity; (4) *g*rand]

[1]**gab** /gab/ *vi* **-bb-** to chatter, blab – infml [prob short for *gabble*] – **gabber** *n*

[2]**gab** *n* (idle) talk – infml

gabardine /ˌgabəˈdeen, ˈ--ˌ-/ *n* **1** GABERDINE 1 **2a** a firm durable fabric (e g of wool or rayon) twilled with diagonal ribs on the right side **b** *chiefly Br* a waterproof coat made of gabardine

gabble /ˈgabl/ *vb* **gabbling** /ˈgabl·ing, ˈgabling/ to talk or utter rapidly or unintelligibly [prob imit] – **gabble** *n*, **gabbler** *n*

gabbro /ˈgabroh/ *n, pl* **gabbros** a granular igneous rock composed of a calcium-containing feldspar and an iron and magnesium silicates [It] – **gabbroic** /gaˈbroh·ik/ *adj*

gabby /ˈgabi/ *adj* talkative, garrulous – infml

gabelle /gaˈbel/ *n* a tax on salt levied in France before 1790 [ME, fr MF, fr OIt *gabella* tax, fr Ar *qabālah*]

gaberdine /ˈgabəˌdeen, ˌ--ˈ-/ *n* **1** a coarse long coat or smock worn chiefly by Jews in medieval times **2** GABARDINE 2 [MF *gaverdine*]

gabion /ˈgaybi·ən, -byən/ *n* a hollow cylinder of wickerwork, iron, etc filled with earth and used esp in building fieldworks or as a support in mining [MF, fr OIt *gabbione*, lit., large cage, aug of *gabbia* cage, fr L *cavea* – more at CAGE]

gable /ˈgaybl/ *n* the vertical triangular section of wall between 2 slopes of a pitched roof ☞ ARCHITECTURE [ME, fr MF, of Gmc origin; akin to ON *gafl* gable – more at CEPHALIC] – **gabled** *adj*

[1]**gad** /gad/ *vi* **-dd-** to go or travel in an aimless or restless manner or in search of pleasure – usu + *about* [ME *gadden*, prob back-formation fr *gadling* companion, fr OE *gædeling*] – **gadder** *n*

[2]**gad** *interj, archaic* – used as a mild oath [euphemism for *God*]

gadarene /ˈgadəˌreen/ *adj, often cap* headlong, precipitate ⟨*a ~ rush to the cities*⟩ [fr the demon-possessed *Gadarene* swine (Mt 8:28) that rushed into the sea]

ˈgadˌfly /-ˌflie/ *n* **1** any of various flies (e g a horsefly or botfly) that bite or annoy livestock **2** a usu intentionally annoying person who stimulates or provokes others, esp by persistent irritating criticism [*gad* (metal spike, goad, rod), fr ON *gaddr* spike, sting]

gadget /ˈgajit/ *n* a usu small and often novel mechanical or electronic device, esp on a piece of machinery [perh fr F *gâchette* catch of a lock, trigger, dim. of *gâche* staple, hook] – **gadgetry** /-tri/ *n*

gadoid /ˈgaydoyd/ *adj* resembling or related to the cods [NL *Gadus*, genus of fishes, fr Gk *gados*, a fish] – **gadoid** *n*

gadolinite /ˈgadəliˌniet/ *n* a black or brown mineral that is a silicate of iron, beryllium, yttrium, and cerium [G *gadolinit*, fr Johann *Gadolin* †1852 Finn chemist]

gadolinium /ˌgadəˈlinyəm, -ni·əm/ *n* a magnetic metallic element of the rare-earth group ☞ PERIODIC TABLE [NL, fr J *Gadolin*]

gadroon /gəˈdroohn/ *n* **1** an elaborately notched or indented convex moulding in architecture **2** a convex or concave fluting used in decorating silverware, glassware, etc [F *godron* round plait, gadroon, fr MF *goderon*, perh dim. of OF *godet* drinking cup] – **gadrooning** *n*

gadwall /ˈgadwawl/ *n, pl* **gadwalls,** *esp collectively* **gadwall** a greyish brown duck about the size of a mallard [origin unknown]

Gael /gayl, gahl/ *n* **1** a Scottish Highlander **2** a Gaelic-speaking inhabitant of Scotland or Ireland [ScGael *Gāidheal* & IrGael *Gaedheal*]

Gaelic /ˈgaylik; *Scots* ˈgahlik; *Irish* ˈgalik/ *adj* of or being (the Goidelic language of) the Celts in Ireland, the Isle of Man, and the Scottish Highlands ☞ LANGUAGE – **Gaelic** *n*

ˌGaelic ˈcoffee *n* IRISH COFFEE

[1]**gaff** /gaf/ *n* **1a** a spear or spearhead for killing fish or turtles **b** a pole with a hook for holding or landing heavy fish **2** a spar on which the head of a fore-and-aft sail is extended ☞ SHIP [F *gaffe*, fr Prov *gaf*, fr *gafar* to seize]

[2]**gaff** *vt* to strike or secure (e g a fish) with a gaff

gaffe /gaf/ *n* a social blunder; FAUX PAS [F, lit., gaff]

gaffer /ˈgafə/ *n* **1** the chief lighting electrician in a film or television studio **2** *Br* a foreman or overseer **3** *dial* an old man – compare GAMMER [prob alter. of *godfather*]

[1]**gag** /gag/ *vb* **-gg-** *vt* **1** to apply a gag to or put a gag in the mouth of (to prevent speech) **2** to cause to retch **3** to obstruct, choke ⟨*~ a valve*⟩ **4** to prevent from having free speech or expression – chiefly journ *~ vi* **1** to heave, retch **2** to tell jokes [ME *gaggen* to strangle, of imit origin]

[2]**gag** *n* **1** sthg thrust into the mouth to keep it open or prevent speech or outcry **2** JOKE 1a **3** a hoax, trick **4** a check to free speech – chiefly journ

gaga /ˈgahˌgah/ *adj* **1a** senile **b** slightly mad **2** infatuated – often + *about* *USE* infml [F, fr *gaga* fool, of imit origin]

[1]**gage** /gayj/ *n* **1** a token of defiance; *specif* a glove, cap, etc thrown on the ground in former times as a challenge to a fight **2** sthg deposited as a pledge of

performance [ME, fr MF, of Gmc origin; akin to OHG *wetti* pledge – more at WED]

[2]**gage** *n* **1** GAUGE 3 **2** *NAm* GAUGE 1, 2, 4, 5, 6

[3]**gage** *vt, NAm* to gauge

[4]**gage** *n* a greengage

gaggle /ˈgagl/ *n* **1** a flock (of geese) **2** *sing or pl in constr* a typically noisy or talkative group or cluster – chiefly infml [ME *gagyll*, fr *gagelen* to cackle]

gaiety /ˈgayəti/ *n* **1** merrymaking; *also* festive activity **2** gay quality, spirits, manner, or appearance [F *gaieté*, fr OF, fr *gai* gay]

gaily /ˈgayli/ *adv* in a gay manner

[1]**gain** /gayn/ *n* **1** resources or advantage acquired or increased; a profit **2** the obtaining of profit or possessions **3a** an increase in amount, magnitude, or degree ⟨*a ~ in efficiency*⟩ **b** the ratio of output power to input power in an amplifier [ME *gayne*, fr MF *gaigne, gain*, fr OF *gaaigne, gaaing*, fr *gaaignier* to till, earn, gain, of Gmc origin; akin to OHG *weidanōn* to hunt for food, L *vis* power – more at VIM]

[2]**gain** *vt* **1a(1)** to get possession of or win, usu by industry, merit, or craft **(2)** to increase a lead over or catch up a rival by (esp time or distance) ⟨~ed *35yd on the third lap*⟩ **b** to get by a natural development or process ⟨~ *strength*⟩ **c** to acquire ⟨~ *a friend*⟩ **d** to arrive at ⟨~ed *the river that night*⟩ **2** to increase in ⟨~ *momentum*⟩ **3** *of a timepiece* to run fast by the amount of ⟨*the clock* ~s *a minute a day*⟩ ~ *vi* **1** to get advantage; profit ⟨*hoped to ~ from his crime*⟩ **2** to increase, specif in weight **3** *of a timepiece* to run fast – **gainer** *n* – **gain ground** to make progress

ˈ**gainful** /-f(ə)l/ *adj* profitable ⟨~ *employment*⟩ [[1]GAIN + [1]-FUL] – **gainfully** *adv*

gainsay /gaynˈsay/ *vt* **gainsays** /-ˈsez/; **gainsaid** /-ˈsed/ **1** to deny, dispute ⟨*couldn't ~ the statistics*⟩ **2** to oppose, resist [ME *gainsayen*, fr *gain-* against (fr OE *gēan-*) + *sayen* to say – more at AGAIN] – **gainsayer** *n*

gait /gayt/ *n* **1** a manner of walking or moving on foot **2** a sequence of foot movements (e g a walk, trot, or canter) by which a horse moves forwards [ME *gait, gate* gate, way]

gaited /ˈgaytid/ *adj* having a specified gait – usu in combination ⟨*slow*-gaited⟩

gaiter /ˈgaytə/ *n* a cloth or leather covering reaching from the instep to ankle, mid-calf, or knee [F *guêtre*, fr MF *guestre, guiestre*, prob of Gmc origin; akin to OE *wrist* wrist]

gal /gal/ *n* a girl – used in writing to represent esp a US or upper-class pronunciation [by alter.]

gala /ˈgahlə/ *n* **1** a festive gathering (that constitutes or marks a special occasion) **2** *Br* a gala sports meeting ⟨*a swimming ~*⟩ [It, fr MF *gale* merrymaking, festivity, pleasure]

galact- /gəlakt-/, **galacto-** *comb form* **1** milk ⟨galac*topoiesis*⟩ **2** containing galactose in the molecular structure ⟨galact*uronic acid*⟩ [L *galact-*, fr Gk *galakt-, galakto-*, fr *galakt-, gala*]

galactic /gəˈlaktik/ *adj* of a galaxy, esp the Milky Way galaxy

galactose /gəˈlaktohz, -tohs/ *n* a sugar that is less soluble and less sweet than glucose [F, fr *galact-*]

galago /gəˈlaygoh/ *n, pl* **galagos** BUSH BABY [NL, genus name, perh fr Wolof *golokh* monkey]

galah /gəˈlah/ *n* **1** an Australian cockatoo with a rose-coloured breast and a grey back **2** *Austr* a fool, simpleton [native name in Australia]

galantine /ˈgalənteen/ *n* a cold dish of boned and usu stuffed cooked meat glazed with aspic [F, fr OF *galentine, galatine* fish sauce, fr ML *galatina*, prob fr L *gelatus*, pp of *gelare* to freeze, congeal]

Galatians /gəˈlaysh(i)ənz/ *n pl but sing in constr* a book of the New Testament ascribed to St Paul and addressed to the Christians of Galatia

galaxy /ˈgaləksi/ *n* **1a** *often cap* MILKY WAY **b** any of many independent systems composed chiefly of stars, dust, and gases and separated from each other in the universe by vast distances ☞ ASTRONOMY **2** an assemblage of brilliant or notable people or things [ME *galaxie, galaxias*, fr LL *galaxias*, fr Gk, fr *galakt-, gala* milk; akin to L *lac* milk]

gale /gayl/ *n* **1** a strong wind; *specif* a moderate gale, strong gale, or esp fresh gale **2** a noisy outburst ⟨~s *of laughter*⟩ [origin unknown]

galea /ˈgayli·ə/ *n* an anatomical part suggesting a helmet [NL, fr L, helmet] – **galeate** /-ˌayt/ *also* **galeated** *adj*

galena /gəˈleenə/ *n* lead sulphide occurring as a bluish grey mineral [L, lead ore]

Galenic /gəˈlenik/, **Galenical** /-kl/ *adj* of or being the medical methods or principles of Galen [*Galen* †*ab* 200 Gk physician & writer] – **Galenical** *n*, **Galenism** /ˈgayliˌniz(ə)m/ *n*

Galibi /gəˈleebi/ *n, pl* **Galibis**, *esp collectively* **Galibi** a member, or the language, of a Carib people of French Guiana

Galilean /ˌgaləˈlayən, -ˈlee·ən/ *adj* of or developed by Galileo Galilei, the founder of experimental physics and astronomy [*Galileo* Galilei †1642 It physicist & astronomer]

galilee /ˈgaləˌlee/ *n* a chapel or porch at the entrance of a church [AF, fr ML *galilaea*]

galingale /ˈgalingˌgayl/ *n* (a plant related to) an Old World sedge with an aromatic root used in cooking [ME, a kind of ginger, fr MF *galingal*, fr Ar *khalanjān*]

galipot /ˈgaliˌpot/ *n* a crude turpentine oleoresin obtained from a S European pine [F]

[1]**gall** /gawl/ *n* **1a** BILE 1 **b** sthg bitter to endure **c** rancour **2** brazen and insolent audacity [ME, fr OE *gealla*; akin to Gk *cholē, cholos* gall, wrath, OE *geolu* yellow – more at YELLOW]

[2]**gall** *n* a skin sore caused by rubbing [ME *galle*, fr OE *gealla*, fr L *galla* gallnut]

[3]**gall** *vt* **1a** to wear (away) by rubbing; chafe **b** to cause feelings of mortification and irritation in; vex acutely **2** to harass ⟨~ed *by enemy fire*⟩ ~ *vi* to become sore or worn by rubbing – **gallingly** *adv*

[4]**gall** *n* a diseased swelling of plant tissue produced by infection with fungi, insect parasites, etc [ME *galle*, fr MF, fr L *galla*; perh akin to Skt *glau* round lump]

Galla /ˈgalə/ *n, pl* **Gallas**, *esp collectively* **Galla** a member or the Cushitic language of any of several peoples of Kenya and S Ethiopia ☞ LANGUAGE

[1]**gallant** /ˈgalənt, gəˈlahnt, gəˈlant/ *n* a (young) man of fashion (who is particularly attentive to women)

[2]**gallant** /*sense* 1 ˈgalənt; *sense 2* ˈgalənt, gəˈlahnt, gəˈlant/ *adj* **1a** splendid, stately ⟨*a ~ ship*⟩ **b** nobly chivalrous and brave **2** courteously and elaborately attentive, esp to ladies [ME *galaunt*, fr MF *galant*, fr prp of *galer* to have a good time, fr *gale* pleasure,

of Gmc origin; akin to OE *wela* weal – more at WEALTH] – **gallantly** *adv*

gallantry /ˈgaləntri/ *n* **1a** an act of marked courtesy **b** courteous attention to a lady **2** spirited and conspicuous bravery

ˈgall ˌbladder *n* a membranous muscular sac in which bile from the liver is stored ☞ DIGESTION

galleon /ˈgali·ən/ *n* a heavy square-rigged sailing ship of the 15th to early 18th c used (by the Spanish) for war or commerce [OSp *galeón*, fr MF *galion*, fr OF *galie* galley]

gallery /ˈgaləri/ *n* **1** a covered passage for walking; a colonnade **2** an outdoor balcony **3a** a long and narrow passage, room, or corridor ⟨*a shooting* ~⟩ **b** a horizontal subterranean passage in a cave or (military) mining system **c** a passage, esp in the ground or wood, made by a mole or insect **4a** (a collection worthy of being displayed as if in) a room or building devoted to the exhibition of works of art ⟨*the National* Gallery⟩ ⟨*the novel contained a rich* ~ *of characters*⟩ **b** an institution or business exhibiting or dealing in works of art **5** *sing or pl in constr* **a** (the occupants of) a balcony projecting from 1 or more interior walls of a hall, auditorium, or church, to accommodate additional people, or reserved for musicians, singers, etc ☞ CHURCH **b** the undiscriminating general public ⟨*a politician who always plays to the* ~⟩ **c** the spectators at a tennis, golf, etc match [MF *galerie*, fr ML *galeria*, prob alter. of *galilea, galilaea* galilee] – **galleried** *adj*

galley /ˈgali/ *n* **1** a large low usu single-decked ship propelled by oars and sails and used esp in the Mediterranean in the Middle Ages and in classical antiquity **2** a kitchen on a ship or aircraft ☞ FLIGHT **3a** a long oblong tray with upright sides for holding set type **b galley, galley proof** a proof in the form of a long sheet (taken from type on a galley) [ME *galeie*, fr OF *galie*, deriv of MGk *galea*]

ˈgalley ˌslave *n* a drudge

galliard /ˈgalyəd/ *n* a quick and lively dance that was popular in the 16th and 17th c [MF *gaillarde*, fem of *gaillard*, adj, lively, valiant, fr OF, prob of Celt origin; akin to OIr *gal* bravery]

Gallic /ˈgalik/ *adj* (characteristic) of Gaul or France [L *Gallicus*, fr *Gallia* Gaul]

ˌgallic ˈacid /ˈgalik/ *n* an acid found widely in plants and used esp in dyes, inks, and as a photographic developer [F *gallique*, fr *galle* gall]

gallicism /ˈgalisiz(ə)m/ *n, often cap* a characteristic French word or expression (occurring in another language)

ˈgallic·ize, -ise /-siez/ *vb* to (cause to) conform to a French mode or idiom – **gallicization** /-ˈzaysh(ə)n/ *n*

gallimaufry /ˌgaliˈmawfri/ *n* a medley, jumble – chiefly humor [MF *galimafree* hash]

gallinaceous /ˌgaliˈnayshəs/ *adj* of an order of (ground-living) birds including the pheasants, turkeys, grouse, and the common domestic fowl [L *gallinaceus* of domestic fowl, fr *gallina* hen, fr *gallus* cock]

gallinule /ˈgali,nyoohl/ *n* any of several aquatic birds of the rail family [NL *Gallinula*, genus of birds, fr L, pullet, dim. of *gallina*]

gallipot /ˈgali,pot/ *n* a small usu ceramic vessel formerly used to hold medicines (e g ointments) [ME *galy pott*, prob fr *galy, galeie* galley + *pott* pot; fr its being imported in galleys]

gallium /ˈgali·əm/ *n* a rare trivalent metallic element that melts at just above room temperature ☞ PERIODIC TABLE [NL, fr L *gallus* cock (intended as trans of Paul *Lecoq* de Boisbaudran †1912 F chemist)]

gallivant /ˈgalivant/ *vi* to travel energetically or roam about for pleasure [perh alter. of *gallant* (to act like a gallant, flirt)]

gallon /ˈgalən/ *n* either of 2 units of liquid capacity equal to 8pt: **a** a British unit equal to about 4.546l **b** WINE GALLON *USE* ☞ UNIT [ME *galon*, a liquid measure, fr ONF, fr ML *galeta* pail, a liquid measure] – **gallonage** /-nij/ *n*

galloon /gəˈloohn/ *n* a narrow lace, braid, etc trimming for dresses [F *galon*, fr MF, fr OF *galonner* to adorn with braid] – **gallooned** *adj*

[1]gallop /ˈgaləp/ *n* **1** a fast bounding gait of a quadruped; *specif* the fastest natural 3-beat gait of the horse **2** a ride or run at a gallop **3** a rapid or hasty progression ⟨*rushed through the reports at a* ~ ⟩ [MF *galop*, fr OF]

[2]gallop *vb* to (cause to) progress or ride at a gallop – **galloper** *n*

galloping /ˈgaləping/ *adj* increasing rapidly; accelerating ⟨~ *inflation*⟩

Galloway /ˈgaləway/ *n* (any of) a breed of hardy chiefly black beef cattle native to SW Scotland [*Galloway*, district of Scotland]

gallows /ˈgalohz/ *n, pl* **gallows** *also* **gallowses 1 gallows, gallows tree** a frame, usu of 2 upright posts and a crosspiece, for hanging criminals **2** *the* punishment of hanging [ME *galwes*, pl of *galwe*, fr OE *gealga*; akin to OHG *galgo* gallows, Arm *jatk* twig]

gallows humour *n* grim humour that makes fun of a very serious or terrifying situation

gallstone /ˈgawl,stohn/ *n* a calculus formed in the gall bladder or bile ducts

ˈGallup ˌpoll /ˈgaləp/ *n* a survey of public opinion frequently used as a means of forecasting sthg (e g an election result) [George *Gallup* b1901 US public opinion statistician]

ˈgall ˌwasp *n* any of several wasps whose larvae produce plant galls in which they feed

galop /ˈgaləp/ *n* (music for) a lively dance in duple time [F – more at GALLOP]

galore /gəˈlaw/ *adj* abundant, plentiful – used after a noun ⟨*bargains* ~⟩ [IrGael *go leor* enough]

galosh /gəˈlosh/ *n* a rubber overshoe [ME *galoche* clog, patten, fr MF] – **galoshed** *adj*

galumph /gəˈlum(p)f/ *vi* to move with a clumsy heavy tread – infml [prob alter. of [2]*gallop*]

galvanic /galˈvanik/ *adj* **1** of, being, or producing a direct current of electricity resulting from chemical action ⟨*a* ~ *cell*⟩ **2** having an electric effect; stimulating vigorous activity or vitality – **galvanically** *adv*

galvanism /ˈgalvən,iz(ə)m/ *n* **1** (the therapeutic use of) direct electric current produced by chemical action **2** vital or forceful activity [F or It; F *galvanisme*, fr It *galvanismo*, fr Luigi *Galvani* †1798 It physician & physicist who first described it]

ˈgalvan·ize, -ise /-iez/ *vt* **1** to subject to or stimulate, rouse, or excite (as if) by the action of an electric current ⟨~ *a muscle*⟩ ⟨*the candidate* ~d *his supporters into action*⟩ **2** to coat (iron or steel) with zinc as a protection from rust – **galvanizer** *n*, **galvanization** /ˈzaysh(ə)n/ *n*

galvanometer /ˌgalvə'nomitə/ *n* an instrument for measuring a small electric current by using the electromagnetic effect of the current – **galvanometric** /-nə'metrik/ *adj*

gam- /gam-/, **gamo-** *comb form* **1** united; joined ⟨gamo*sepalous*⟩ **2** sexual ⟨gam*ic*⟩ ⟨gamo*genesis*⟩ [NL, fr Gk, marriage, fr *gamos* – more at BIGAMY]

gambier /'gambiə/ *n* an astringent substance from a Malayan woody climbing plant, used esp in tanning [Malay *gambir*]

gambit /'gambit/ *n* **1** a chess opening, esp in which a player risks (several) minor pieces to gain an advantage **2a** a remark intended to start a conversation or make a telling point **b** a calculated move; a stratagem [It *gambetto*, lit., act of tripping someone, fr *gamba* leg, fr LL *gamba, camba*, modif of Gk *kampē* bend – more at [1]CAMP]

[1]gamble /'gambl/ *vb* **gambling** /'gambling/ *vi* **1a** to play a game (of chance) for money or property **b** to bet or risk sthg on an uncertain outcome **2** SPECULATE 2 ~ *vt* **1** to risk by gambling; wager **2** to venture, hazard [prob back-formation fr *gambler*, prob alter. of obs *gamner*, fr obs *gamen* (to play)] – **gambler** *n*

[2]gamble *n* **1** the playing of a game (of chance) for stakes **2** (sthg involving) an element of risk

gamboge /gam'bohj, -'boozh/ *n* **1** a gum resin from some SE Asian trees that is used as a yellow pigment **2** a strong yellow [NL *gambogium*, alter. of *cambugium*, irreg fr *Cambodia*, country of SE Asia]

gambol /'gambl/ *vb or n* **-ll-** (*NAm* **-l-, -ll-**); **gambolling** /'gambl·ing, 'gambling/ (to engage in) skipping or leaping about in play [modif of MF *gambade* spring of a horse, gambol, prob fr OProv *camba* leg, fr LL *gamba, camba*]

gambrel /'gambrəl/, **gambrel roof** *n* a roof like a mansard but with 2 opposite vertical ends ☞ ARCHITECTURE [ONF *gamberel* crooked stick, hock, fr *gambe* leg, fr LL *gamba*]

[1]game /gaym/ *n* **1a(1)** activity engaged in for diversion or amusement; play **(2)** the equipment for a particular esp indoor game **b** often derisive or mocking jesting ⟨*make ~ of a nervous player*⟩ **2a** a course or plan consisting of (secret) manoeuvres directed towards some end ⟨*playing a waiting ~*⟩ **b** a specified type of activity seen as competitive or governed by rules (and pursued for financial gain) ⟨*the newspaper ~*⟩ **3a(1)** (the quality of play in) a physical or mental competition conducted according to rules with the participants in direct opposition to each other; a match **(2)** a division of a larger contest **(3)** the number of points necessary to win a game **b** *pl* organized sports, esp athletics **c** a situation that involves contest, rivalry, or struggle ⟨*got into microelectronics early in the ~*⟩ **4a** animals under pursuit or taken in hunting; *specif* (the edible flesh of) certain wild mammals, birds, and fish (e g deer and pheasant), hunted for sport or food **b** an object of ridicule or attack – often in *fair game* **5** prostitution – slang; often in *on the game* [ME, fr OE *gamen*; akin to OHG *gaman* amusement]

[2]game *vi* GAMBLE 1 ~ *vt archaic* to lose or squander by gambling

[3]game *adj* **1** having a resolute unyielding spirit ⟨~ *to the end*⟩ **2** ready to take risks or try sthg new [[1]*game*] – **gamely** *adv*, **gameness** *n*

[4]game *adj* injured, crippled, or lame ⟨*a ~ leg*⟩ [perh fr [3]*game*]

'gameˌbook /-ˌbook/ *n* a book for recording game killed

'gameˌkeeper /-ˌkeepə/ *n* one who has charge of the breeding and protection of game animals or birds on a private preserve

gamelan /'gamiˌlan/ *n* **1** a SE Asian instrument like the xylophone **2** a flute, string, and percussion orchestra of SE Asia [Jav]

'game ˌpoint *n* a situation in tennis, badminton, etc in which 1 player or side will win the game by winning the next point

gamesmanship /'gaymzmənˌship/ *n* the art or practice of winning games by means other than superior skill without actually violating the rules

gamesome /'gayms(ə)m/ *adj* merry, frolicsome – **gamesomely** *adv*, **gamesomeness** *n*

gamester /'gaymstə/ *n* one who plays games; *esp* a gambler

gamet-, **gameto-** *comb form* gamete ⟨gameto*phore*⟩ [NL, fr *gameta*]

gametangium /ˌgami'tanji·əm/ *n, pl* **gametangia** /-ji·ə/ a (plant) organ in which gametes are developed [NL, fr *gamet-* + Gk *angeion* vessel – more at ANGI-]

gamete /'gameet, gə'meet/ *n* a mature germ cell with a single set of chromosomes capable of fusing with another gamete of the other sex to form a zygote from which a new organism develops [NL *gameta*, fr Gk *gametēs* husband, fr *gamein* to marry, fr *gamos* marriage – more at BIGAMY] – **gametic** /gə'metik/ *adj*, **gametically** *adv*

game theory *n* the strategic analysis of a business, military, social, etc conflict

gametophyte /gə'meetohˌfiet/ *n* (a member of) the generation that bears sex organs, of a plant with alternation of generations – compare SPOROPHYTE [ISV] – **gametophytic** /ˌgamitoh'fitik/ *adj*

gamine /'gameen (*Fr* gamĩn)/ *n or adj* (a girl or woman) having an elfin impish appeal [F, fem of *gamin* urchin]

gamma /'gamə/ *n* **1** the 3rd letter of the Greek alphabet **2** C 4 [ME, fr LL, fr Gk, of Sem origin; akin to Heb *gimel*, 3rd letter of the Heb alphabet]

gamma globulin *n* any of several immunoglobulins in blood or serum including most antibodies

'gamma ˌray *n* (a quantum of) electromagnetic radiation of shorter wavelength than X rays emitted in some radioactive decay processes – usu pl ☞ PHYSICS

gammer /'gamə/ *n, dial* an old woman – compare GAFFER 3 [prob alter. of *godmother*]

[1]gammon /'gamən/ *n* (the meat of) the lower end including the hind leg of a side of bacon removed from the carcass after curing with salt – compare HAM 2 ☞ MEAT [ONF *gambon* ham, aug of *gambe* leg, fr LL *gamba*]

[2]gammon *n* the winning of a backgammon game before the loser removes any men from the board [perh alter. of ME *gamen* game] – **gammon** *vt*

[3]gammon *n* nonsense, humbug – not now in vogue [obs *gammon* (talk)]

gammy /'gami/ *adj, Br* [4]GAME – infml [prob irreg fr [4]*game* + *-y*]

ˌgamo'petalous /ˌgamoh'petələs/ *adj, of a flower* having the corolla composed of united petals [NL *gamopetalus*, fr *gam-* + *petalus* petalous]

ˌgamo'sepalous /-'sepələs/ *adj, of a flower* having the calyx composed of united sepals [prob fr (assumed) NL *gamosepalus*, fr *gam-* + *sepalus* sepalous]

gamp /gamp/ *n, Br* a large, esp loosely tied, umbrella – infml [Sarah *Gamp*, nurse with a large umbrella in the novel *Martin Chuzzlewit* by Charles Dickens †1870 E writer]

gamut /'gamət/ *n* **1** the whole series of recognized musical notes **2** an entire range or series [ML *gamma ut*, lowest note in medieval scale of music, fr *gamma*, applied to the lowest note G on the bass clef + *ut*, applied to the first note of a hexachord, the notes of which were named after the first syllables of 6 lines of a Latin hymn, *ut, re, mi, fa, sol, la*]

gamy, gamey /'gaymi/ *adj* having the strong flavour or smell of game (that has been hung until high) – **gamily** *adv*, **gaminess** *n*

-gamy /-gəmi/ *comb form* (→ *n*) **1** marriage ⟨*polygamy*⟩ **2** possession of (such) reproductive organs or (such) a mode of fertilization ⟨*apogamy*⟩ [ME *-gamie*, fr LL *-gamia*, fr Gk – more at BIGAMY] – **-gamic** /-gamik/, **-gamous** *comb form* (→ *adj*)

¹gander /'gandə/ *n* **1** an adult male goose **2** a simpleton [ME, fr OE *gandra*; akin to OE *gōs* goose]

²gander *n* a look, glance – infml ⟨*talking and taking* ~*s at the girls – Life*⟩ [prob fr ¹*gander*; fr the outstretched neck of a person craning to look at sthg]

Gandhian /'gandi·ən/ *adj* of the Indian leader Mahatma Gandhi (†1948) or his principle of nonviolent protest

¹gang /gang/ *n* **1** a combination of similar implements or devices arranged to act together **2** *sing or pl in constr* a group of people **a** working together **b** associating for criminal, disreputable, etc ends; *esp* a group of adolescents who (disreputably) spend leisure time together **c** that have informal and usu close social relations ⟨*have the* ~ *over for a party*⟩ [ME, fr OE; akin to OHG *gang* act of going, Skt *jaṅghā* shank]

²gang *vt vt* to assemble or operate (e g mechanical parts) simultaneously as a group ~ *vi* to move or act as a gang ⟨*the children* ~ed *together*⟩

³gang *vi, Scot* to go [ME *gangen*, fr OE *gangan*; akin to OE *gang*]

'gang-,bang *n* sexual intercourse usu between 1 woman and a succession of men on 1 occasion; *esp* collective rape – slang [¹*gang* 2 + ²*bang* 4]

ganger /'gang·ə/ *n, Br* the foreman of a gang of workmen

'gang,land /-,land/ *n* UNDERWORLD 2

gangling /'gang·gling/, **gangly** /-gli/ *adj* tall, thin, and awkward in movement ⟨*a* ~ *gawky child*⟩ [perh irreg fr Sc *gangrel* vagrant, lanky person]

ganglion /'gang·glion, -ən/ *n, pl* **ganglia** /-gli·ə/ *also* **ganglions** **1a** a small cyst on a joint membrane or tendon sheath **b** a mass of nerve cells outside the brain or spinal cord; *also* NUCLEUS 2b **2** a focus of strength, energy, or activity [LL, fr Gk] – **ganglionated** /-ə,naytid/ *adj*, **ganglionic** /-'onik/ *adj*

gangplank /'gang,plangk/ *n* a movable board, plank, etc used to board a ship from a quay or another ship

¹gangrene /'gang,green/ *n* **1** local death of the body's soft tissues due to loss of blood supply **2** a pervasive moral evil [L *gangraena*, fr Gk *gangraina*; akin to Gk *gran* to gnaw] – **gangrenous** /-grinəs/ *adj*

²gangrene *vb* to make or become gangrenous

gangster /'gangstə/ *n* a member of a criminal gang – **gangsterism** *n*

gangue /gang/ *n* the worthless part of an ore [F, fr G *gang* vein of metal, fr OHG, act of going]

gang up *vi* **1** to combine as a group for a specific (disreputable) purpose **2** to make a joint assault *on*

'gang,way /-,way/ *n* **1** a (temporary) passageway (constructed of planks) **2a** the opening in a ship's side or rail through which it is boarded **b** a gangplank **3** a clear passage through a crowd – often used interjectionally **4** *Br* a narrow passage between sections of seats in a theatre, storage bays in a warehouse, etc

ganister, gannister /'ganistə/ *n* a (mixture containing) fine-grained quartz used for furnace linings [origin unknown]

ganja /'ganjə/ *n, WI* potent cannabis used esp for smoking [Hindi *g ajā*, fr Skt *gañjā*]

gannet /'ganit/ *n* **1** any of several related large fish-eating seabirds that breed in large colonies chiefly on offshore islands **2** a greedy person; a scavenger [ME *ganet*, fr OE *ganot*; akin to OE *gōs* goose] – **gannetry** /-tri/ *n*

gantlet /'gantlit, 'gawn-/ *n, chiefly NAm* a gauntlet

gantry /'gantri/ *n* **1** a frame for supporting barrels **2** a frame structure raised on side supports that spans over or round sthg and is used for railway signals, as a travelling crane, for servicing a rocket before launching, etc [perh modif of ONF *gantier*, fr L *cantherius* trellis]

gaol /jay(ə)l/ *vb or n, chiefly Br* (to) jail

gap /gap/ *n* **1** a break in a barrier (e g a wall or hedge) **2a** a mountain pass **b** a ravine **3** an empty space between 2 objects or 2 parts of an object **4** a break in continuity ⟨*unexplained* ~s *in his story*⟩ **5** a disparity or difference ⟨*the* ~ *between imports and exports*⟩ **6** a wide difference in character or attitude ⟨*the generation* ~⟩ [ME, fr ON, chasm, hole; akin to ON *gapa* to gape] – **gappy, gapped** *adj*

¹gape /gayp/ *vi* **1a** to open the mouth wide **b** to open or part widely ⟨*holes* ~d *in the pavement*⟩ **2** to gaze stupidly or in openmouthed surprise or wonder **3** to yawn [ME *gapen*, fr ON *gapa*; akin to L *hiare* to gape, yawn – more at YAWN] – **gapingly** *adv*

²gape *n* **1** an act of gaping; *esp* an openmouthed stare **2** the average width of the open mouth or beak **3** a fit of yawning **4** *pl* a disease of young birds characterized by constant gaping and caused by gapeworms infesting the windpipe

gaper /'gaypə/ *n* any of several large (edible) burrowing clams [¹GAPE + ²-ER]

'gape,worm /-,wuhm/ *n* a nematode worm that causes gapes in birds

gar /gah/ *n* a (fish resembling a) garfish

¹garage /'garahzh, 'garij/ *n* **1** a building for the shelter of motor vehicles **2** an establishment for providing essential services (e g the supply of petrol or repair work) to motor vehicles [F, act of docking, garage, fr *garer* to dock, fr MF, to take care, of Gmc origin; akin to OHG bi*warōn* to protect – more at ¹WARE]

²garage *vt* to keep or put in a garage

garam masala /,garəm mah'sahlə/ *n* an aromatic mixture of ground coriander, cumin, cinnamon, etc used esp in curries [Hindi *garam masālā*, fr *garam* hot, pungent + *masālā* spice]

garb /gahb/ *n* **1** a style of clothing; dress ⟨*arranged themselves in priestly* ~⟩ **2** an outward form; appearance [MF or OIt; MF *garbe* graceful contour, grace, fr OIt *garbo* grace] – **garb** *vt*

garbage /'gahbij/ *n* **1** worthless writing or speech **2** *chiefly NAm* RUBBISH 1 [ME, animal entrails; akin to OF *garbe* tax paid in sheaves]

garble /'gahbl/ *vt* **garbling** /'gahbling/ to distort or confuse, giving a false impression of the facts ⟨*a* ~d *message*⟩ [ME *garbelen* to sift, select, fr OIt *garbellare* to sift, fr Ar *gharbala*, fr *ghirbāl* sieve, fr LL *cribellum*; akin to L *cernere* to sift – more at CERTAIN] – **garbler** *n*

garboard /'gah,bawd/ *n* the plank next to a ship's keel [obs D *gaarboord*]

garçon /gah'sonh (*Fr* garsɔ̃)/ *n, pl* **garçons** /-'sonh(z) (*Fr* ~)/ a waiter, esp in a French restaurant [F, boy, servant]

garda /'gahdə/ *n, pl* **gardai** /'gahdi, -die/ **1** the Irish police **2** a member of the garda [IrGael]

[1]**garden** /'gahd(ə)n/ *n* **1a** a plot of ground where herbs, fruits, vegetables, or typically flowers are cultivated **b** a rich well-cultivated region ⟨*the* ~ *of England*⟩ **2a** a public recreation area or park ⟨*a botanical* ~⟩ **b** an open-air eating or drinking place ⟨*beer* ~⟩ [ME *gardin*, fr ONF, of Gmc origin; akin to OHG *gart* enclosure – more at [2]YARD] – **gardenful** *n*

[2]**garden** *vi* to work in, cultivate, or lay out a garden – **gardener** *n*

[3]**garden** *adj* of a cultivated as distinguished from a wild kind grown in the open ⟨*a* ~ *plant*⟩

garden city *n* a planned town with spacious residential areas including public parks and considerable garden space

gardenia /gah'deenyə, -ni·ə/ *n* any of a genus of Old World tropical trees and shrubs with showy fragrant white or yellow flowers [NL, genus name, fr Alexander *Garden* †1791 Sc naturalist]

'garden ,party *n* a usu formal party held on the lawns of a garden

garderobe /'gahd,rohb/ *n* (a part of a medieval building used as) a privy [ME, fr MF; akin to ONF *warderobe* wardrobe]

garfish /'gah,fish/ *n* a European and N Atlantic fish with a long body and elongated jaws [ME *garfysshe*, prob fr OE *gār* spear + *fysshe* fish]

garganey /'gahgəni/ *n* a small European duck of which the male has a broad white stripe over the eye [It dial. *garganei*, of imit origin]

gargantuan /gah'gantyoo·ən/ *adj, often cap* gigantic, colossal ⟨*a* ~ *meal*⟩ [*Gargantua*, gigantic king in the novel *Gargantua* by François Rabelais †1553 F humorist & satirist]

garget /'gahgit/ *n* mastitis (occurring chronically in cows) [prob fr ME, throat, fr MF *gargate*; akin to MF *gargouiller* to gurgle] – **gargety** *adj*

[1]**gargle** /'gahgl/ *vb* **gargling** /'gahgling, 'gahgl·ing/ *vt* **1** to blow air from the lungs through (a liquid) held in the mouth or throat **2** to cleanse (the mouth or throat) in this manner ~ *vi* **1** to use a gargle **2** to speak or sing as if gargling [MF *gargouiller*, of imit origin]

[2]**gargle** *n* **1** a liquid used in gargling **2** a bubbling liquid sound produced by gargling

gargoyle /'gah,goyl/ *n* a spout in the form of a grotesque human or animal figure projecting from a roof gutter to throw rainwater clear of a building ☞ CHURCH [ME *gargoyl*, fr MF *gargouille*; akin to MF *gargouiller*] – **gargoyled** *adj*

garibaldi /,gari'bawldi/ *n* **1** a woman's loose long-sleeved orig bright red blouse **2** *Br* a biscuit with a layer of currants in it [Giuseppe *Garibaldi* †1882 It patriot]

garish /'geərish/ *adj* **1** excessively and gaudily bright or vivid **2** tastelessly showy [origin unknown] – **garishly** *adv*, **garishness** *n*

[1]**garland** /'gahlənd/ *n* **1** a wreath of flowers or leaves worn as an ornament or sign of distinction **2** an anthology or collection [ME, fr MF *garlande*, fr OF]

[2]**garland** *vt* to form into or deck with a garland

garlic /'gahlik/ *n* (the pungent compound bulb, much used as a flavouring in cookery, of) a European plant of the lily family [ME *garlek*, fr OE *gārlēac*, fr *gār* spear + *lēac* leek – more at [2]GORE] – **garlicky** *adj*

garlic mustard *n* a common European plant of the mustard family with small white flowers and a garlic-like smell

garment /'gahmənt/ *n* an article of clothing [ME, fr MF *garnement*, fr OF, fr *garnir* to equip – more at GARNISH]

[1]**garner** /'gahnə/ *n* **1** a granary **2** a grain bin *USE* fml or poetic [ME, fr OF *gernier, grenier*, fr L *granarium*, fr *granum* grain]

[2]**garner** *vt* to gather, store – fml or poetic

garnet /'gahnit/ *n* **1** a hard brittle silicate mineral used as an abrasive and in its transparent deep red form as a gem **2** a dark red [ME *grenat*, fr MF, fr *grenat*, adj, red like a pomegranate, fr (*pomme*) *grenate* pomegranate]

[1]**garnish** /'gahnish/ *vt* **1a** to decorate, embellish **b** to add decorative or savoury touches to (food) **2** to garnishee [ME *garnishen*, fr MF *garniss-*, stem of *garnir* to warn, equip, garnish, of Gmc origin; akin to OHG *warnōn* to take heed – more at WARN]

[2]**garnish** *n* **1** an embellishment, ornament **2** an edible savoury or decorative addition (e g watercress) to a dish

[1]**garnishee** /,gahni'shee/ *n* sby served with a garnishment

[2]**garnishee** *vt* **garnisheeing** **1** to serve with a garnishment **2** to take (money owed) by legal authority following a garnishment

'garnishment /-mənt/ *n* a judicial warning to a debtor not to pay his/her debt to anyone other than the appropriate third party [[1]GARNISH + -MENT]

garniture /'gahnichə/ *n* an embellishment, trimming [MF, equipment, alter. of OF *garnesture*, fr *garnir*]

garpike /'gah,piek/ *n* a garfish

garret /'garit/ *n* a small room just under the roof of a house [ME *garette* watchtower, fr MF *garite*, perh fr OProv *garida*, fr *garir* to protect, of Gmc origin; akin to OHG *werien*]

[1]**garrison** /'garis(ə)n/ *n* **1** a (fortified) town or place in which troops are stationed **2** *sing or pl in constr* the troops stationed at a garrison [ME *garisoun* protection, fr OF *garison*, fr *garir* to protect, of Gmc origin; akin to OHG *werien* to defend – more at WEIR]

[2]**garrison** *vt* **1** to station troops in **2a** to assign (troops) as a garrison **b** to occupy with troops

Historical clothes
ca 100 BC
ca 1400
ca 1600
ca 1850
codpiece
Roman toga
doublet and hose
farthingale and ruff
crinoline

Ethnic clothes
caftan
sari and choli
turban
poncho
lederhosen

Shirts and trousers/skirts
safari shirt
Bermuda shorts
jodhpurs
culottes
smock
O.K.
bellbottoms
drainpipe
dirndl skirt
T-shirt
cravat
kilt and sporran
leg-warmers
miniskirt

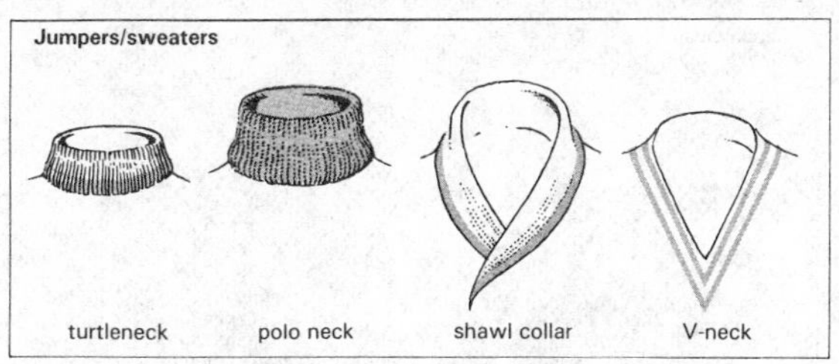
Jumpers/sweaters
turtleneck
polo neck
shawl collar
V-neck

Jackets
hacking jacket
Norfolk jacket
donkey jacket
anorak (parka)

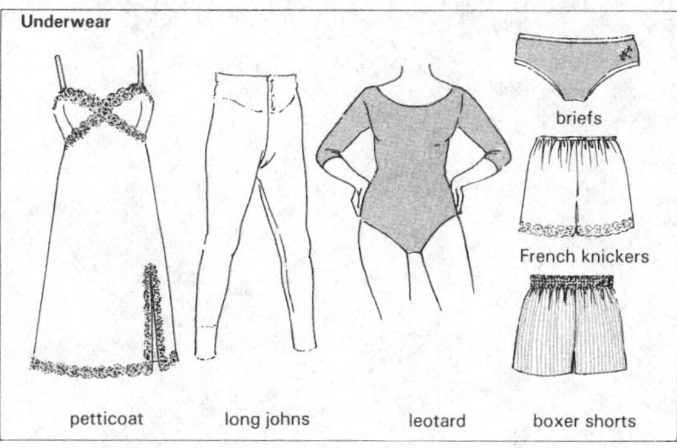
Underwear
petticoat
long johns
leotard
briefs
French knickers
boxer shorts

Suits and dresses
morning dress
double-breasted suit
pinafore dress
Empire line evening dress

Footwear
platform soled
court shoe
spat
brogue
espadrille
moccasin
mule
T-strap
slingback
winkle-picker
cowboy boot

Vestments
crosier
mitre
amice
lappet
pallium
chasuble
maniple
dalmatic
tunicle
stole
alb
apparel on alb

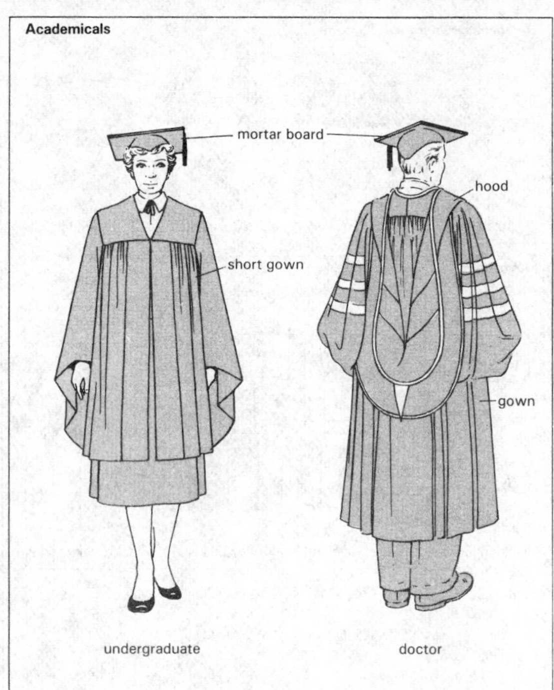
Academicals
mortar board
hood
short gown
gown
undergraduate
doctor

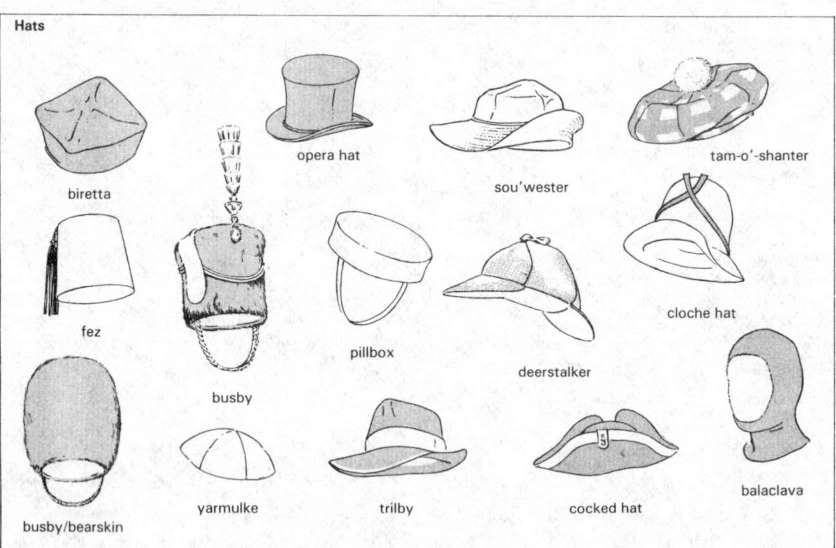
Hats
biretta
opera hat
sou'wester
tam-o'-shanter
fez
busby
pillbox
deerstalker
cloche hat
busby/bearskin
yarmulke
trilby
cocked hat
balaclava

garrison cap *n* a visorless folding cap worn as part of a military uniform – compare SERVICE CAP

[1]garrotte, garotte, *chiefly NAm* **garrote** /gə'rot/ *n* **1** (a Spanish method of execution using) an iron collar for strangling sby **2** strangling, esp with robbery as the motive [Sp *garrote* cudgel, garrotte, prob fr MF *garrot* heavy wooden projectile]

[2]garrotte, garotte, *chiefly NAm* **garrote** *vt* **1** to execute with a garrotte **2** to strangle and rob – **garrotter** *n*

garrulous /'gar(y)ooləs/ *adj* excessively talkative, esp about trivial things [L *garrulus,* fr *garrire* to chatter – more at CARE] – **garrulously** *adv,* **garrulousness** *n,* **garrulity** /ga'roohləti/ *n*

garter /'gahtə/ *n* **1** a band, usu of elastic, worn to hold up a stocking or sock **2** *cap* (the blue velvet garter that is the badge of) the Order of the Garter; *also* membership of the Order [ME, fr ONF *gartier,* fr *garet* bend of the knee, of Celt origin; akin to OIr *gairri* calves of the legs]

'garter ,snake *n* any of numerous harmless longitudinally striped American snakes

'garter ,stitch *n* (the ribbed pattern formed by using only) a plain knit stitch

[1]gas /gas/ *n, pl* **-s-** *also* **-ss- 1** a fluid (e g air) that has neither independent shape nor volume and tends to expand indefinitely **2a** a gas or gaseous mixture used to produce general anaesthesia, as a fuel, etc ☞ ENERGY **b** a substance (e g tear gas or mustard gas) that can be used to produce a poisonous, asphyxiating, or irritant atmosphere **3** *NAm* petrol **4** empty talk – chiefly infml [NL, alter. of L *chaos* space, chaos; (3) short for *gasoline*] – **gaseous** /'gasi·əs, 'gay-/ *adj,* **gaseousness** *n*

[2]gas *vb* **-ss-** *vt* **1** to treat chemically with a gas **2** to poison or otherwise affect adversely with gas ~ *vi* **1** to give off gas **2** to talk idly – chiefly infml

'gas,bag /-,bag/ *n* an idle talker – infml

'gas ,chamber *n* a chamber in which prisoners are executed or animals killed by poison gas

gascon /'gaskən/ *n* **1** *cap* a native of Gascony **2** a braggart [ME *Gascoun,* fr MF *gascon*] – **Gascon** *adj*

gas gangrene *n* often rapidly progressive gangrene marked by impregnation of the (dying) tissue with gas and caused by infection with a clostridial bacterium

[1]gash /gash/ *vt or n* (to injure with) a deep long cut or cleft, esp in flesh [vb ME *garsen,* fr ONF *garser,* fr (assumed) VL *charissare,* fr Gk *charassein* to scratch, engrave – more at CHARACTER; n fr vb]

[2]gash *n* sthg, specif rubbish on board ship, superfluous or extra – infml [origin unknown]

gasholder /'gas,hohldə/ *n* a gasometer

gasify /'gasifie, 'gay-/ *vb* to change into gas ⟨~ *coal*⟩ – **gasifier** *n,* **gasification** /-fi'kaysh(ə)n/ *n*

gasket /'gaskit/ *n* (a specially shaped piece of) sealing material for ensuring that a joint, esp between metal surfaces, does not leak liquid or gas [prob alter. of F *garcette* thin rope, fr OF, girl, dim. of *garce* girl, fem of *gars* boy]

gaskin /'gaskin/ *n* a part of the hind leg of a quadruped between the stifle and the hock ☞ ANATOMY [obs *gaskin* (hose, breeches), prob short for *galligaskins* (loose trousers, leggings)]

gaslight /'gas,liet/ *n* (light from) a gas flame or gas lighting fixture

'gas ,mask *n* a mask connected to a chemical air filter and used as a protection against noxious fumes or gases

gasoline, gasolene /,gasə'leen, '--,-/ *n, NAm* petrol ['*gas* + *-ol* + *-ine* or *-ene*] – **gasolinic** /-'linik/ *adj*

gasometer /ga'somitə/ *n* a (large cylindrical storage) container for gas [F *gazomètre,* fr *gaz* + *-o-* + *-mètre* -meter]

'gas-,operated *adj, of an automatic firearm* using gases produced by the burning of the powder to operate the mechanism

gasp /gahsp/ *vi* **1** to catch the breath suddenly and audibly (e g with shock) **2** to breathe laboriously ~ *vt* to utter with gasps – usu + *out* ⟨*he* ~*ed out his message*⟩ [ME *gaspen*; akin to ON *geispa* to yawn] – **gasp** *n*

gasper /'gahspə/ *n, Br* a cigarette – not now in vogue [GASP + [2]-ER]

'gas ,ring *n* a hollow metal perforated ring through which jets of gas issue and over which food is cooked

gasser /'gasə/ *n* an oil well that yields gas [[2]GAS + [2]-ER]

gassy /'gasi/ *adj* full of, containing, or like gas ⟨~ *beer*⟩ – **gassiness** *n*

gastarbeiter /'gast,ahbietə/ *n* a foreign worker, esp in a German-speaking country [G]

gasteropod /'gast(ə)rə,pod/ *n* a gastropod

gastr- /gastr-/, **gastro-** *also* **gastri-** *comb form* **1** belly ⟨gastro*pod*⟩; stomach ⟨gastr*itis*⟩ ⟨gastr*ectomy*⟩ **2** gastric and ⟨gastro*intestinal*⟩ [Gk, fr *gastr-, gastēr*]

gastric /'gastrik/ *adj* of the stomach [Gk *gastr-, gastēr,* alter. of (assumed) Gk *grastēr,* fr Gk *gran* to gnaw, eat]

gastric juice *n* a thin acidic digestive liquid secreted by glands in the lining of the stomach

gastrin /'gastrin/ *n* a polypeptide hormone secreted by the stomach lining that induces secretion of gastric juice

gastroenteritis /,gastroh,entə'rietəs/ *n* inflammation of the lining of the stomach and the intestines, usu causing painful diarrhoea [NL]

gastronome /'gastrə,nohm/, **gastronomist** /ga'stronəmist/ *n* an epicure, gourmet [F, back-formation fr *gastronomie*]

gastronomy /ga'stronəmi/ *n* the art or science of good eating [F *gastronomie,* fr Gk *Gastronomia,* title of a 4th-c BC poem, fr *gastro-* belly + *-nomia* -nomy] – **gastronomic** /,gastrə'nomik/ *also* **gastronomical** *adj,* **gastronomically** *adv*

gastropod /'gastrə,pod/ *n* any of a large class of molluscs (e g snails) usu with a distinct head bearing sensory organs ☞ EVOLUTION [NL *Gastropoda,* class name, fr Gk *gastr-* + *pod-, pous* foot] – **gastropod** *adj,* **gastropodan** /ga'stropədən; *also* ,gastrə'pohdən/ *adj or n*

gastrula /'gastroolə/ *n, pl* **gastrulas, gastrulae** /-li/ the embryo of a metazoan animal at the stage in its development succeeding the blastula stage and consisting of a hollow 2-layered cellular cup – compare BLASTULA, MORULA [NL, fr *gastr-*] – **gastrular** *adj*

gastrulate /'gastroo,layt/ *vi* to become or form a gastrula – **gastrulation** /-'laysh(ə)n/ *n*

gas turbine *n* an internal-combustion engine in which turbine blades are driven by hot gases whose pressure and velocity are intensified by compressed air introduced into the combustion chamber

'gas,works /-,wuhks/ *n, pl* **gasworks** a plant for manufacturing gas – often pl with sing. meaning

[1]**gat** /gat/ *archaic past of* GET

[2]**gat** *n* a firearm – slang [short for *Gatling (gun)*]

[1]**gate** /gayt/ *n* **1** (the usu hinged frame or door that closes) an opening in a wall or fence **2** a city or castle entrance, often with defensive structures **3a** a means of entrance or exit **b** a mountain pass **c** a space between 2 markers through which a skier, canoeist, etc must pass in a slalom race **d** a mechanically operated barrier used as a starting device for a race **e** either of a pair of barriers that **(1)** let water in and out of a lock **(2)** close a road at a level crossing **4** an (electronic) device (e g in a computer) that produces a signal when specified input conditions are met ⟨*a logic* ~⟩ **5** the set of notches in a manually worked gearbox into which the gear lever is pushed to select the gears **6** the total admission receipts or the number of spectators at a sporting event [ME, fr OE *geat*; akin to ON *gat* opening, Gk *chezein* to defecate]

[2]**gate** *vt, Br* to punish by confinement to the premises of a school or college

gateau /'gatoh/ *n, pl* **gateaux, gateaus** /-tohz/ any of various rich often filled elaborate (cream) cakes [F *gâteau* cake, fr OF *gastel*, prob of Gmc origin]

'gate-,crasher *n* one who enters, attends, or participates without a ticket or invitation – **gate-crash** *vb*

'gate,fold /-,fohld/ *n, chiefly NAm* a foldout

'gate,house /-,hows/ *n* **1** a structure above or beside a gate (e g of a city wall or castle) often used in former times as a guardroom or prison ☞ CHURCH **2** a lodge at the entrance to the grounds of a large house **3** a building at a dam or lock from which the sluices or gates are controlled

'gate,keeper /-,keepə/ *n* sby who or sthg that tends or guards a gate

,gateleg 'table /'gaytleg/ *n* a table with drop leaves supported by 2 movable legs

'gate,post /-,pohst/ *n* the post on which a gate is hung or against which it closes

'gate,way /-,way/ *n* **1** an opening for a gate **2** GATE 3a

[1]**gather** /'gadhə/ *vt* **1** to bring together; collect (*up*) **2** to pick, harvest **3a** to summon up ⟨~ed *his courage*⟩ **b** to accumulate ⟨~ *speed*⟩ **c** to prepare (e g oneself) for an effort **4a** to bring together the parts of **b** to draw about or close to sthg ⟨~ing *her cloak about her*⟩ **c** to pull (fabric) together, esp along a line of stitching, to create small tucks **5** to reach a conclusion (intuitively from hints or through inferences) ⟨*I* ~ *you're ready to leave*⟩ ~ *vi* to come together in a body ⟨*a crowd had* ~ed⟩ [ME *gaderen*, fr OE *gaderian*; akin to OFris *gaderia* to gather, MLG *gadderen*, MHG *gatern* to unite] – **gatherer** *n*

[2]**gather** *n* sthg gathered; *esp* a tuck in cloth made by gathering

'gathering /-ring/ *n* **1** an assembly, meeting; *also* a compilation **2** an abscess **3** a gather or series of gathers in cloth **4** SECTION 11

'Gatling ,gun /'gatling/ *n* an early machine gun with a revolving cluster of barrels fired once each per revolution [R J *Gatling* †1903 US inventor]

gauche /gohsh/ *adj* lacking social experience or grace [F, lit., left, fr *gauchir* to turn aside] – **gauchely** *adv*, **gaucheness** *n*

gaucherie /'gohsh(ə)ri/ *n* (an instance of) tactless or awkward manner or behaviour [F, fr *gauche*]

gaucho /'gowchoh/ *n, pl* **gauchos** a cowboy of the pampas [AmerSp, prob fr Quechua *wáhcha* poor person, orphan]

gaud /gawd/ *n, archaic* a gaudy ornament or trinket [ME *gaude* trick, toy, prob fr OF *gaudir* to enjoy, rejoice, fr L *gaudēre* to rejoice]

[1]**gaudy** /'gawdi/ *adj* ostentatiously or tastelessly (and brightly) ornamented – **gaudily** *adv*, **gaudiness** *n*

[2]**gaudy** *n* a feast, esp a dinner for ex-students, in some British universities [prob fr L *gaudium* joy – more at JOY]

[1]**gauge,** *NAm also* **gage** /gayj/ *n* **1a** measurement according to some standard or system **b** dimensions, size **2** an instrument for or a means of measuring or testing sthg (e g a dimension or quantity) **3 gauge, gage** relative position of a ship with reference to another ship and the wind **4** the distance between the rails of a railway, wheels on an axle, etc **5** a measure of the size of the bore of a shotgun **6a** the thickness of a thin sheet of metal, plastic, film, etc **b** the diameter of wire, a hypodermic needle, a screw, etc **c** (a measure of) the fineness of a knitted fabric [ME *gauge*, fr ONF]

[2]**gauge,** *NAm also* **gage** *vt* **1a** to measure (exactly) the size, dimensions, capacity, or contents of **b** to estimate, judge ⟨*can you* ~ *his reaction?*⟩ **2** to check for conformity to specifications or limits – **gaugeable** *adj*, **gaugeably** *adv*

gauger /'gayjə/ *n, chiefly Scot* an exciseman who inspects dutiable bulk goods (e g whisky) [[2]GAUGE + [2]-ER]

Gaul /gawl/ *n* a Celt of ancient Gaul [*Gaul*, ancient region of Europe including most of what is now France, fr F *Gaule*, fr L *Gallia*]

gauleiter /'gow,lietə/ *n* **1** *often cap* an official in charge of a district in Nazi Germany **2** an arrogant henchman [G, fr *gau* district, region + *leiter* leader]

Gaulish /'gawlish/ *adj or n* (of or being Gaul, the Gauls, or) the Celtic language of the ancient Gauls

Gaullism /'gaw,liz(ə)m/ *n* the political principles and policies of the French political leader Charles de Gaulle (†1970) – **Gaullist** *adj or n*

gaunt /gawnt/ *adj* **1** excessively thin and angular as if from suffering **2** barren, desolate [ME, perh of Scand origin] – **gauntly** *adv*, **gauntness** *n*

[1]**gauntlet** /'gawntlit/ *n* **1** a glove to protect the hand, worn with medieval armour **2** a strong protective glove with a wide extension above the wrist, used esp for sports and in industry **3** a challenge to combat – esp in *take up/throw down the gauntlet* [ME, fr MF *gantelet*, dim. of *gant* glove, of Gmc origin; akin to MD *want* mitten, ON *vöttr* gloves] – **gauntleted** *adj*

[2]**gauntlet** *n* a double file of men armed with weapons with which to strike at sby made to run between them; *broadly* criticism or an ordeal or test – usu in *run the gauntlet* [by folk etymology fr *gantelope*, modif of Sw *gatlopp*, fr OSw *gatulop*, fr *gata* road, lane + *lop* course, run]

gaur /'gowə/ *n* a large E Indian wild ox [Hindi, fr Skt *gaura*; akin to Skt *go* bull, cow – more at [1]COW]

gauss /gows/ *n, pl* **gauss** *also* **gausses** the cgs unit of magnetic induction [K F *Gauss* †1855 G mathematician & astronomer]

Gaussian distribution /ˈgowsi·ən/ *n* NORMAL DISTRIBUTION [K F *Gauss*]

gauze /gawz/ *n* **1a** a thin often transparent fabric used chiefly for clothing or draperies **b** a loosely woven cotton surgical dressing **c** a fine mesh of metal or plastic filaments **2** a thin haze or mist [MF *gaze*, prob fr *Gaza*, town in Palestine] – **gauzily** *adv*, **gauziness** *n*, **gauzy** *adj*

gavage /ˈgavahzh, ˈgavij/ *n* introduction of material, esp food, into the stomach by a tube [F, fr *gaver* to stuff, feed forcibly]

gave /gayv/ *past of* GIVE

gavel /ˈgavl/ *n* a small mallet with which a chairman, judge, or auctioneer commands attention or confirms a vote, sale, etc [origin unknown]

ˈgavel,kind /-ˌkiend/ *n* a former system of land tenure, esp in Kent, providing for equal division of the estate of sby who died without making a will, among the heirs [ME *gavelkynde*, fr *gavel* rent, tribute (fr OE *gafol*) + *kinde* kind]

gavial /ˈgayvi·əl, -vyəl/ *n* a large Indian crocodile [F, modif of Hindi *ghaṛiyāl*]

gavotte /gəˈvot/ *n* **1** an 18th-c dance in which the feet are raised rather than slid **2** a composition or movement of music in moderately quick $\frac{4}{4}$ time [F, fr MF, fr OProv *gavoto*, fr *gavot* inhabitant of the Alps] – **gavotte** *vi*

Gawd /gawd/ *n* God – used in writing to represent a substandard pronunciation

[1]**gawk** /gawk/ *vi* to gawp – infml [perh alter. of obs *gaw* (to stare), fr ME *gawen*, fr ON *gā* to heed, mark] – **gawker** *n*

[2]**gawk** *n* a clumsy awkward person [prob fr E dial. *gawk* (left-handed)] – **gawkish** *adj*, **gawkishly** *adv*, **gawkishness** *n*

gawky /ˈgawki/ *adj* awkward and usu lanky ⟨*a* ~ *child*⟩ [[2]*gawk* + *-y*] – **gawkily** *adv*, **gawky** *n*

gawp /gawp/ *vi* to gape or stare stupidly – infml [alter. of ME *galpen* to yawn, gape; akin to OE *gielpan* to boast, praise – more at YELP]

[1]**gay** /gay/ *adj* **1** happily excited **2** bright, attractive ⟨~ *sunny meadows*⟩ **3** given to social pleasures ⟨*the* ~ *life*⟩ **4** homosexual [ME, fr MF *gai*] – **gay** *adv*, **gayness** *n*

[2]**gay** *n* a homosexual

gaze /gayz/ *vi or n* (to fix the eyes in) a steady and intent look [vb ME *gazen*, prob of Scand origin; akin to Sw dial. *gasa* to stare; n fr vb] – **gazer** *n*

gazebo /gəˈzeeboh/ *n, pl* **gazebos** a freestanding structure placed to command a view; *also* a belvedere [perh fr *gaze* + L *-ebo* (as in *videbo* I shall see)]

gazelle /gəˈzel/ *n, pl* **gazelles,** *esp collectively* **gazelle** any of numerous small, graceful, and swift African and Asian antelopes noted for their soft lustrous eyes ☞ FOOD [F, fr MF, fr Ar *ghazāl*]

[1]**gazette** /gəˈzet/ *n* **1** a newspaper – usu in newspaper titles **2** an official journal containing announcements of honours and government appointments [F, fr It *gazzetta*, fr It dial. *gazeta*, fr *gazeta* small copper coin (the price of the newspaper)]

[2]**gazette** *vt, Br* to announce (the appointment or status of) in an official gazette ⟨*he was* ~d *major*⟩

gazetteer /ˌgazəˈtiə/ *n* a dictionary of place names [*The Gazetteer's: or, Newsman's Interpreter*, a geographical index edited by Laurence Echard †1730 E historian]

gazpacho /gəzˈpachoh, gəs-/ *n, pl* **gazpachos** a Spanish cold soup containing tomatoes, olive oil, garlic, peppers, and usu breadcrumbs [Sp]

gazump /gəˈzump/ *vb, Br* to thwart (a would-be house purchaser) by raising the price after agreeing to sell at a certain price [earlier *gezumph, gazoomph, gazumph* to swindle, perh fr Yiddish] – **gazumper** *n*

G clef /jee/ *n* TREBLE CLEF ☞ MUSIC

G-cramp *n* a cramp shaped like a letter G

ge-, geo- *comb form* **1a** ground; soil ⟨geo*phyte*⟩ ⟨geo*phagia*⟩ **b** earth; earth's surface ⟨geo*physics*⟩ ⟨geo*desic*⟩ **2** geographical; geography and ⟨geo*politics*⟩ [ME *geo-*, fr MF & L; MF, fr L, fr Gk *gē-*, *geō-*, fr *gē*]

gean /jeen/ *n, chiefly Br* (the fruit of) a wild sweet cherry [MF *guisne, guine*]

[1]**gear** /giə/ *n* **1a** clothing, garments **b** movable property; goods **2** a set of equipment usu for a particular purpose ⟨*fishing* ~⟩ **3a(1)** a mechanism that performs a specific function in a complete machine ⟨*the steering* ~⟩ **(2)** a toothed wheel (that is one of a set of interlocking wheels) **(3)** working relation, position, or adjustment ⟨*out of* ~⟩ ⟨*put the car in* ~⟩ **b** any of 2 or more adjustments of a transmission (e g of a bicycle or motor vehicle) that determine direction of travel or ratio of engine speed to vehicle speed [ME *gere*, fr OE *gearwe*; akin to OHG *garuwi* equipment, clothing, OE *gearu* ready] – **gearless** *adj*

[2]**gear** *vt* **1a** to provide with or connect by gearing **b** to put into gear **2** to adjust *to* so as to match, blend with, or satisfy sthg ⟨*an institution* ~ed *to the needs of the blind*⟩

ˈgear,box /-ˌboks/ *n* (a protective casing enclosing) a set of (car) gears ☞ CAR

gearing /ˈgiəring/ *n* **1** a series of gear wheels **2** *Br* (the advantage gained by) the use of extra capital (e g borrowed money) to increase the returns on invested equity capital

ˈgear ˌlever *n* a control, esp a rod, on a gear-changing mechanism (e g a gearbox) used to engage the different gears ☞ CAR

ˈgear,shift /-ˌshift/ *n, NAm* GEAR LEVER

gear up *vt* to make ready for effective operation; *also* to put (e g oneself) into a state of anxious excitement or nervous anticipation

ˈgear ˌwheel *n* GEAR 3a(2)

gecko /ˈgekoh/ *n, pl* **geckos, geckoes** any of numerous small chiefly tropical lizards able to walk on vertical or overhanging surfaces [Malay *geˈkok*, of imit origin]

gee /jee/ *interj, chiefly NAm* – used as an introductory expletive or to express surprise or enthusiasm [euphemism for *Jesus*]

gee-gee /ˈjee-ˌjee/ *n* a horse – used esp by or to children or in racing slang [redupl of *gee* (as in *gee-up*)]

geese /gees/ *pl of* GOOSE

ˌgee-ˈup *interj* – used as a direction, esp to a horse, to move ahead [origin unknown]

ˌgee ˈwhiz /wiz/ *interj, chiefly NAm* gee [euphemism for *Jesus Christ*]

geezer /ˈgeezə/ *n* a man (who is thought a little odd or peculiar) – chiefly infml; esp in *old geezer* [prob alter. of Sc *guiser* (one in disguise, mummer)]

gegenschein /'gaygən,shien/ *n, often cap* a faint light usu in the ecliptic opposite the sun [G, fr *gegen* against, counter- + *schein* shine]

Gehenna /gə'henə/ *n* HELL 1c, 2a [LL, fr Gk *Geenna*, fr Heb *Gê' Hinnōm*, lit., valley of Hinnom]

[1]**'Geiger ,counter** /'geigə/ *n* an electronic instrument for detecting the presence and intensity of ionizing radiations (e g cosmic rays or particles from a radioactive substance)

Geiger-Müller counter /'moolə/ *n* GEIGER COUNTER [Hans *Geiger* †1945 G physicist & W *Müller*, 20th-c G physicist]

geisha /'gayshə/, **'geisha ,girl** *n, pl* **geisha, geishas** a Japanese girl who is trained to provide entertaining and lighthearted company, esp for a man or a group of men [Jap, fr *gei* art + *-sha* person]

[1]**gel** /jel/ *n* **1** a colloid in a more solid form than a sol **2** JELLY 3 [*gelatin*]

[2]**gel,** *chiefly NAm* **jell** *vb* **-ll- 1** to change (from a sol) into a gel **2** to (cause to) take shape or become definite – **gelable** *adj*, **gelation** /ji'laysh(ə)n/ *n*

[3]**gel** /gel/ *n* a girl – used in writing to represent an upper-class pronunciation [by alter.]

gelate /'jelayt/ *vi* to gel

gelatin, gelatine /'jelətin, -teen/ *n* **1** a glutinous material obtained from animal tissues by boiling; *esp* a protein used esp in food (e g to set jellies) and photography **2** a thin coloured transparent sheet used to colour a stage light [F *gélatine* edible jelly, gelatin, fr It *gelatina*, fr *gelato*, pp of *gelare* to freeze, fr L – more at COLD] – **gelatinize** /ji'latiniez/ *vb*, **gelatinization** /-'zaysh(ə)n/ *n*

gelatinous /ji'latinəs/ *adj* resembling gelatin or jelly, esp in consistency; viscous – **gelatinously** *adv*, **gelatinousness** *n*

gelation /ji'laysh(ə)n/ *n* the action or process of freezing [L *gelation-*, *gelatio*, fr *gelatus*, pp of *gelare*]

geld /geld/ *vt* to castrate – used esp with reference to male animals [ME *gelden*, fr ON *gelda*; akin to OE *gelte* young sow, Gk *gallos* eunuch, priest of Cybele]

gelding /'gelding/ *n* a castrated male horse [ME, fr ON *geldingr*, fr *gelda*]

gelid /'jelid/ *adj* extremely cold; icy [L *gelidus*, fr *gelu* frost, cold – more at COLD] – **gelidly** *adv*, **gelidity** /ji'lidəti/ *n*

gelignite /'jeligniet/ *n* a dynamite in which the adsorbent base is a mixture of potassium or sodium nitrate usu with wood pulp [*gel*atin + L *ign*is fire + E *-ite* – more at IGNEOUS]

[1]**gem** /jem/ *n* **1** a precious or sometimes semiprecious stone, esp when cut and polished for use in jewellery **2** sby or sthg highly prized or much beloved [ME *gemme*, fr MF, fr L *gemma* bud, gem] – **gemmy** *adj*

[2]**gem** *vt* **-mm-** to adorn (as if) with gems

Gemara /ge'mahrə/ *n* a commentary on the Mishnah forming most of the Talmud [Aram *gĕmārā* completion] – **Gemaric** /-rik/ *adj*, **Gemarist** *n*

gemeinschaft /gə'mien,shaft/ *n* a social relationship or community characterized by solidarity based on loyalty and kinship – compare GESELLSCHAFT [G, community, fr *gemein* common, general + *-schaft* -ship]

[1]**'geminate** /'jeminət/ *adj* arranged in pairs [L *geminatus*, pp of *geminare* to double, fr *geminus* twin; akin to Skt *yama* twin] – **geminately** *adv*

[2]**'geminate** /-,nayt/ *vb* to make or become paired or doubled – **gemination** /-'naysh(ə)n/ *n*

Gemini /'jemini, -nie/ *n* (sby born under) the 3rd sign of the zodiac in astrology, which is pictured as twins ☞ SYMBOL [L, lit., the twins (Castor and Pollux)] – **Geminian** /-'nee·ən, -'nie·ən/ *adj or n*

gemma /'jemə/ *n, pl* **gemmae** /-mee/ a bud; *broadly* an asexual plant reproductive body [L] – **gemmate** /'jemayt/, **gemmaceous** /je'mayshəs/ *adj*, **gemmation** /-sh(ə)n/ *n*

gemmule /'jemyoohl/ *n* an internal reproductive bud (e g of a sponge) with a resistant case [F, fr L *gemmula*, dim. of *gemma* bud] – **gemmulation** /-yoo'laysh(ə)n/ *n*, **gemmuliferous** /-'lif(ə)rəs/ *adj*

gemstone /'jem,stohn/ *n* a mineral or petrified material used as a gem

gen /jen/ *n, Br* the correct or complete information – infml [short for *general (information)*]

[1]**gen-, geno-** *comb form* **1** race ⟨geno*cide*⟩ **2** genus; kind ⟨geno*type*⟩ [Gk *genos* birth, race, kind – more at KIN]

[2]**gen-, geno-** *comb form* gene ⟨genome⟩

-gen /-jən/ *also* **-gene** /-jeen/ *comb form* (*n* → *n*) **1** sthg that produces ⟨*andro*gen⟩ ⟨*carcino*gen⟩ **2** sthg that is (so) produced ⟨*phos*gene⟩ [F *-gène*, fr Gk *-genēs* born; akin to Gk *genos* birth]

gendarme /'zhon,dahm (*Fr* ʒɑ̃darm)/ *n* **1** a member of a corps of armed police, esp in France **2** a policeman – chiefly humor [F, fr MF, back-formation fr *gensdarmes*, pl of *gent d'armes*, lit., armed men]

'gen,darmerie, gendarmery /-məri (*Fr* -məri)/ *n, sing or pl in constr* a body of gendarmes [MF *gendarmerie*, fr *gendarme*]

gender /'jendə/ *n* **1** sex **2a** a system of subdivision within a grammatical class of a language (e g noun or verb), partly based on sexual characteristics, that determines agreement with and selection of other words or grammatical forms **b** (membership of) a subclass within such a system [ME *gendre*, fr MF *genre*, *gendre*, fr L *gener-*, *genus* birth, race, kind, gender – more at KIN]

gene /jeen/ *n* a unit of inheritance that is carried on a chromosome, controls transmission of hereditary characters, and consists of DNA or, in some viruses, RNA [G *gen*, short for *pangen*, fr *pan-* + *-gen*] – **genic** /'jenik/ *adj*, **genically** *adv*

genealogy /jeeni'aləji/ *n* **1** (an account of) the descent of a person, family, or group from an ancestor or from older forms **2** the study of family pedigrees [ME *genealogie*, fr MF, fr LL *genealogia*, fr Gk, fr *genea* race, family + *-logia* -logy; akin to Gk *genos* race] – **genealogist** *n*, **genealogical** /-ə'lojikl/ *adj*, **genealogically** *adv*

genera /'jenərə/ *pl of* GENUS

[1]**general** /'jen(ə)rəl/ *adj* **1** involving or applicable to the whole **2** of, involving, or applicable to (what is common to) every member of a class, kind, or group **3a** applicable to or characteristic of the majority of individuals involved; prevalent **b** concerned or dealing with universal rather than particular aspects **4** approximate rather than strictly accurate **5** not confined by specialization or careful limitation **6** holding superior rank or taking precedence over others similarly titled ⟨*the* ~ *manager*⟩ [ME, fr

MF, fr L *generalis*, fr *gener-*, *genus* kind, class – more at KIN] – **in general** usually; FOR THE MOST PART

[2]**general** *n* **1** the chief of a religious order or congregation **2** ☞ RANK

ˌ**General A'merican** *n* nonregional American pronunciation

ˌ**general as'sembly** *n, often cap G&A* the highest governing body of a religious denomination (e g the Presbyterian church)

General Certificate of Education *n* a British secondary-school examination taken at 3 levels

ˌ**general e'lection** *n* an election in which candidates are elected in all constituencies of a nation or state

generalissimo /ˌjen(ə)rə'lisimoh/ *n, pl* **generalissimos** the supreme commander of several armies acting together or of a nation's armed forces [It, fr *generale* general + *-issimo*, superl suffix]

generalist /'jen(ə)rəlist/ *n* one whose skills, interests, etc extend to several different fields or activities

generality /ˌjenə'raləti/ *n* **1** total applicability **2** generalization **3** *the* greatest part; *the* bulk

general·ization, -isation /ˌjen(ə)rəlie'zaysh(ə)n/ *n* **1** generalizing **2** a general statement, law, principle, or proposition (that does not take adequate account of the facts) **3** the occurring of a response to a stimulus similar but not identical to a reference stimulus

general·ize, -ise /'jen(ə)rəˌliez/ *vt* **1** to give a general form to **2** to derive or induce (a general conception or principle) from particulars **3** to give general applicability to ⟨~ *a law*⟩ ~ *vi* to make generalizations or vague or indefinite statements – **generalizable** *adj*, **generalizer** *n*

generally /'jen(ə)rəli/ *adv* **1** without regard to specific instances ⟨~ *speaking*⟩ **2** usually; AS A RULE ⟨*he* ~ *drinks tea*⟩ **3** collectively; AS A WHOLE ⟨*of interest to children* ~⟩

general of the air force *n* ☞ RANK

general of the army *n* ☞ RANK

general paralysis of the insane *n* GENERAL PARESIS

general paresis *n* the insanity and paralysis caused by tertiary syphilis

general practitioner *n* a medical doctor who treats all types of disease and is usu the first doctor consulted by a patient

generalship /'jen(ə)rəlship/ *n* **1** the (tenure of) office of a general **2** military skill in a high commander

general staff *n* a group of officers who aid a commander in administration, training, supply, etc

ˌ**general 'strike** *n* a strike in all or many of the industries of a region or country

general studies *n pl* school courses designed to give subject specialists some education outside their subject

general theory of relativity *n* RELATIVITY 2b

generate /'jenəˌrayt/ *vt* **1** to bring into existence or originate (e g by a life-giving, physical, or chemical process); produce ⟨~ *electricity*⟩ **2** to define (a linguistic, mathematical, etc structure (e g a curve or surface)) by the application of 1 or more rules or operations to given quantities **3** to be the cause of (a situation, action, or state of mind) [L *generatus*, pp of *generare*, fr *gener-*, *genus* birth – more at KIN]

generation /ˌjenə'raysh(ə)n/ *n* **1** *sing or pl in constr* **a** a group of living organisms constituting a single step in the line of descent from an ancestor **b** a group of individuals born and living at the same time **c** a group of individuals sharing a usu specified status for a limited period ⟨*the next* ~ *of students*⟩ **d** a type or class of objects usu developed from an earlier type ⟨*a new* ~ *of computers*⟩ **2** the average time between the birth of parents and that of their offspring **3a** the producing of offspring; procreation **b** the process of coming or bringing into being ⟨~ *of income*⟩ ⟨~ *of electricity*⟩ [ME *generacioun*, fr MF *generation*, fr L *generation-*, *generatio*, fr *generatus*] – **generational** *adj*

generative /'jen(ə)rətiv/ *adj* having the power or function of generating, originating, producing, reproducing, etc

ˌ**generative 'grammar** *n* **1** an ordered set of rules for producing the grammatical sentences of a language **2** TRANSFORMATIONAL GRAMMAR

generator /'jenəˌraytə/ *n* **1** an apparatus for producing a vapour or gas **2** DYNAMO 1; *also* an alternator ☞ ENERGY [GENERATE + [1]-OR]

generic /ji'nerik/ *adj* **1** (characteristic) of or applied to (members of) a whole group or class **2** (having the rank) of a biological genus [F *générique*, fr L *gener-*, *genus* birth, kind, class] – **generically** *adv*

generous /'jen(ə)rəs/ *adj* **1** magnanimous, kindly **2** liberal in giving (e g of money or help) **3** marked by abundance, ample proportions, or richness [MF or L; MF *genereus*, fr L *generosus*, fr *gener-*, *genus* birth, family] – **generously** *adv*, **generousness** *n*, **generosity** /ˌjenə'rosəti/ *n*

genesis /'jenəsis/ *n, pl* **geneses** /-ˌseez/ the origin or coming into being of sthg [L, fr Gk, fr *gignesthai* to be born – more at KIN]

Genesis *n* the first book of the Old Testament [Gk]

genet /'jenit/ *n* any of several small Old World flesh-eating mammals related to the civets [ME *genete*, fr MF, fr Ar *jarnayṭ*]

genetic /jə'netik/ *adj* **1** of or determined by the origin or development of sthg **2a** of or involving genetics **b** genic [*genesis*] – **genetically** *adv*

-genetic /-jə'netik/ *comb form* (→ *adj*) -GENIC 1, 2 ⟨*psycho*genetic⟩ ⟨*spermato*genetic⟩

genetic code *n* the sequence of bases in DNA or RNA strands that forms the biochemical basis of heredity and determines the specific amino acid sequence in proteins

ge'netics *n pl but sing in constr* **1** the biology of (the mechanisms and structures involved in) the heredity and variation of organisms **2** the genetic make-up of an organism, type, group, or condition – **geneticist** /-sist/ *n*

Geneva bands /je'neevə/ *n pl* two strips of white cloth suspended from the front of the collar of some Protestant clergymen [*Geneva*, city in Switzerland; fr their use by the Calvinist clergy of Geneva]

Geneva convention *n* any of a series of agreements, first made at Geneva, concerning the treatment of prisoners of war and of the sick, wounded, and dead in battle

Genevan /jə'neev(ə)n/ *adj or n* (of Calvinism or) a Calvinist

[1]**genial** /'jeenyəl, ni·əl/ *adj* **1** favourable to growth or comfort; mild ⟨~ *sunshine*⟩ **2** cheerfully good-tempered; kindly [L *genialis*, fr *genius*] – **genially** *adv*, **genialness** *n*, **geniality** /-ni'aləti/ *n*

[2]**genial** /jə'nee·əl/ *adj* of the chin [Gk *geneion* chin, fr *genys* jaw – more at CHIN]

-genic /-jenik/ *comb form* (→ *adj*) **1** producing; forming ⟨*erotogenic*⟩ **2** produced by; formed from ⟨*phytogenic*⟩ **3** well-suited to production or reproduction by (a specified medium) ⟨*photogenic*⟩ ⟨*telegenic*⟩ [ISV *-gen* & *-geny* + *-ic*]

genie /'jeeni/ *n, pl* **genies** *also* **genii** /-ni,ie/ a jinn [F *génie*, fr Ar *jinnīy*]

genital /'jenitl/ *adj* **1** of or being the genitalia or another sexual organ **2** of or characterized by the final stage of sexual development in which oral and anal impulses are replaced by gratification obtained from (sexual) relationships – compare ANAL, ORAL [ME, fr L *genitalis*, fr *genitus*, pp of *gignere* to beget – more at KIN] – **genitally** *adv*

genitalia /jeni'tayli·ə, -lyə/ *n pl* the (external) reproductive and sexual organs [L, fr neut pl of *genitalis*]

genitals /'jenitlz/ *n pl* the genitalia

genitive /'jenitiv/ *adj or n* (of or in) a grammatical case expressing typically a relationship of possessor or source; *also* sthg in this case – compare POSSESSIVE [adj ME, fr L *genetivus, genitivus*, lit., of birth, fr *genitus*; n fr adj] – **genitival** /-'tievl/ *adj*, **genitivally** *adv*

genito- /jenitoh-/ *comb form* genital and ⟨genito*urinary*⟩ [*genital*]

,genito'urinary /-'yooərin(ə)ri/ *adj* of the (functions of the) genital and urinary organs

genius /'jeenyəs, -ni·əs/ *n, pl* (*1a*) **genii** /-ni,ie/, (*1b & 3*) **genii** *also* **geniuses**, (*4*) **geniuses** *also* **genii** **1a** an attendant spirit of a person or place **b** one who influences another for good or bad **2a** a peculiar, distinctive, or identifying character or spirit ⟨*optimism was the ~ of the Victorian era*⟩ **b** the associations and traditions of a place **3** a spirit or jinn **4a** a single strongly marked capacity or aptitude ⟨*had a ~ for teaching maths*⟩ **b** (a person endowed with) extraordinary intellectual power (as manifested in creative activity) [L, tutelary spirit, fondness for social enjoyment, fr *gignere* to beget]

,genius 'loci /'lohsie/ *n, pl* **genii loci** /'jeeni,ee/ the pervading spirit of a place [L]

geno- – see GEN-

genoa /'jenoh·ə/ *n* a large jib which partly overlaps a ship's mainsail [*Genoa*, city in Italy]

genocide /'jenə,sied/ *n* the deliberate murder of a racial or cultural group ['*gen-* + *-cide*] – **genocidal** /-'siedl/ *adj*

genome /'jee,nohm/ *n* a single set of an organism's chromosomes with the genes they contain [G *genom*, fr *gen-* [2]gen- + chromos*om* chromosome] – **genomic** /ji'nomik/ *adj*

genotype /'jenoh,tiep/ *n* the genetic constitution of an individual or group – compare PHENOTYPE – **genotypic** /-'tipik/ *also* **genotypical** *adj*, **genotypically** *adv*

-genous /-jənəs/ *comb form* (→ *adj*) **1** producing; yielding ⟨*alkaligenous*⟩ **2** produced by; originating in ⟨*endogenous*⟩ [*-gen* + *-ous*]

genre /'zhonh·rə (*Fr* ʒɑ̃ːr)/ *n* **1** a sort, type **2** a category of artistic, musical, or literary composition characterized by a particular style, form, or content [F, fr MF *genre* kind, gender – more at GENDER]

gens /jenz/ *n, pl* **gentes** /'jenteez/ a clan formed through the male line of descent [L *gent-, gens* – more at GENTLE]

gent /jent/ *n* a gentleman – nonstandard or humor

gentamicin /jentə'miesin/ *n* a broad-spectrum antibiotic used esp to treat serious infections [alter. of earlier *gentamycin*, fr *genta-* (prob irreg fr *gentian violet*; fr the colour of the organism from which it is produced) + *-mycin*]

genteel /jen'teel/ *adj* **1a** of or appropriate to (the status or manners of) the gentry or upper class **b** free from vulgarity or rudeness; polite **2a** maintaining or striving to maintain the appearance of superior social status or respectability **b** marked by false delicacy, prudery, or affectation [MF *gentil* gentle] – **genteelly** *adv*, **genteelness** *n*

genteelism /jen'tee,liz(ə)m/ *n* a word believed by its user to be more genteel than another (e g *stomach* for *belly*)

gentian /'jensh(ə)n/ *n* any of several related esp mountain plants with showy usu blue flowers [ME *gencian*, fr MF *gentiane*, fr L *gentiana*, perh fr *Gentius*, 2nd-c BC Illyrian king said to have discovered its virtues]

gentian violet *n, often cap G&V* a violet dye used as a biological stain and as a skin disinfectant in the treatment of boils, ulcers, etc

gentile /'jentiel/ *adj or n, often cap* (of) a non-Jewish person [ME, fr LL *gentilis*, fr L *gent-, gens* nation]

gentility /jen'tiləti/ *n* **1** *sing or pl in constr* the members of the upper class **2a** genteel attitudes, behaviour, or activity **b** superior social status or prestige indicated by manners, possessions, etc [ME *gentilete*, fr MF *gentileté*, fr L *gentilitat-, gentilitas* state of belonging to the same clan, fr *gentilis*]

[1]**gentle** /'jentl/ *adj* **1a** honourable, distinguished; *specif* of or belonging to a gentleman ⟨*of ~ birth*⟩ **b** kind, amiable ⟨*bear with me, ~ reader*⟩ **2** free from harshness, sternness, or violence; mild, soft; *also* tractable **3** MODERATE 1, 2a [ME *gentil*, fr OF, fr L *gentilis* of a clan, of the same clan, fr *gent-, gens* clan, nation; akin to L *gignere* to beget – more at KIN] – **gentleness** *n*, **gently** /'jentli/ *adv*

[2]**gentle** *n* a maggot, esp when used as bait for fish ['*gentle* (soft)]

[3]**gentle** *vt* to make mild, docile, soft, or moderate

gentle breeze *n* wind having a speed of 12 to 19km/h (8 to 12mph)

'gentle,folk /-,fohk/ *also* **gentlefolks** *n pl* people of good family and breeding

gentleman /'jentlmən/ *n, pl* **gentlemen** /~/ **1a** a man belonging to the landed gentry or nobility **b** a man who is chivalrous, well-mannered, and honourable (and of good birth or rank) **c** a man of independent wealth who does not work for gain **2** a valet – usu in *gentleman's gentleman* **3** a man of any social class or condition ⟨*ladies and* gentlemen⟩ – often as a courteous reference ⟨*show this ~ to a seat*⟩ – **gentlemanlike** *adj*

,gentleman-at-'arms *n, pl* **gentlemen-at-arms** any of a bodyguard of 40 gentlemen who attend the British sovereign on state occasions

'gentlemanly /-li/ *adj* characteristic of or having the character of a gentleman – **gentlemanliness** *n*

gentleman's agreement gentlemen's agreement *n* an unwritten agreement secured only by the honour of the participants

'gentle ,sex *n* the female sex

'gentle,woman *n, pl* **gentlewomen** /-,wimin/ **1a** a woman of noble or gentle birth **b** a woman attendant on a lady of rank **2** a lady

gentry /'jentri/ *n, sing or pl in constr* **1** the upper class **2** a class whose members are (landed proprietors) entitled to bear a coat of arms though not of noble rank [ME *gentrie*, alter. of *gentrise*, fr OF *genterise, gentelise*, fr *gentil* gentle]

gents /jents/ *n, pl* **gents** *often cap, Br* a public lavatory for men – chiefly infml [short for *gentlemen's*]

genuflect /'jenyoo,flekt/ *vi* to bend the knee, esp in worship or as a gesture of respect (to sacred objects) [LL *genuflectere*, fr L *genu* knee + *flectere* to bend – more at KNEE] – **genuflector** *n*, **genuflection, genuflexion** /-'flekshj(ə)n/ *n*

genuine /'jenyooin/ *adj* **1** actually produced by or proceeding from the alleged source or author or having the reputed qualities or character ⟨*the signature is* ~⟩ ⟨*this is a* ~ *antique*⟩ **2** free from pretence; sincere [L *genuinus* native, genuine; akin to L *gignere* to beget – more at KIN] – **genuinely** *adv*, **genuineness** *n*

genus /'jeenəs/ *n, pl* **genera** /'jenərə/ **1** a category in the classification of living things ranking between the family and the species **2** a class divided into several subordinate classes [L *gener-, genus* birth, race, kind – more at KIN]

-geny /-jəni/ *comb form* (→ *n*) origin; development; mode of production of ⟨*bio*geny⟩ ⟨*onto*geny⟩ [Gk *-geneia* act of being born, fr *-genēs* born – more at -GEN]

geo- – see GE-

geocentric /jeeoh'sentrik/ *adj* **1** measured from or observed as if from the earth's centre **2** having or relating to the earth as centre – compare HELIOCENTRIC – **geocentrically** *adv*

,geochro'nology /-krə'noləji/ *n* the chronology of the past as indicated by geological data – **geochronologic** /-krohnə'lojik/, **geochronological** *adj*, **geochronologically** *adv*, **geochronologist** /-krə'noləjist/ *n*

geode /'jee,ohd/ *n* (a rounded stone having) a cavity lined with crystals or mineral matter [L *geodes*, a gem, fr Gk *geōdēs* earthlike, fr *gē* earth] – **geodic** /ji'odik/ *adj*

[1]**,geo'desic** /-'desik, -'deesik/ *adj* **1** geodetic **2** made of light straight structural elements mostly in tension ⟨*a* ~ *dome*⟩

[2]**geodesic** *n* the shortest line on a given surface between 2 points

geodesy /ji'odəsi/ *n* a branch of applied mathematics that determines the exact positions of points and the shape and area of (large portions of) the earth's surface [Gk *geōdaisia*, fr *geō-* ge- + *daiesthai* to divide – more at TIDE] – **geodesist** *n*, **geodetic** /jeeoh'detik/ *adj*, **geodetically** *adv*

geography /ji'ogrəfi/ *n* **1** a science that deals with the earth and its life; *esp* the description of land, sea, air, and the distribution of plant and animal life including human beings and their industries 👁 **2** the geographical features of an area [L *geographia*, fr Gk *geōgraphia*, fr *geographein* to describe the earth's surface, fr *geō-* + *graphein* to write – more at CARVE] – **geographer** *n*, **geographic** /jee-ə'grafik/, **geographical** *adj*, **geographically** *adv*

geoid /'jeeoyd/ *n* (the shape of) the surface that the earth would have if all parts of the earth had the same height as the mean sea level of the oceans [G, fr Gk *geoeidēs* earthlike, fr *gē*] – **geoidal** /-'oydl/ *adj*

geological time /jee-ə'lojikl/ *n* the time occupied by the earth's geological history

geology /ji'oləji/ *n* **1a** a science that deals with the history of the earth's crust, esp as recorded in rocks **b** a study of the solid matter of a celestial body (e g the moon) **2** the geological features of an area [NL *geologia*, fr *ge-* + *-logia* -logy] – **geologist** *n*, **geologize** *vi*, **geological** /jee-ə'lojikl/, **geologic** *adj*, **geologically** *adv*

geomagnetic /jeeohmag'netik/ *adj* of the earth's magnetism – **geomagnetically** *adv*, **geomagnetism** /-'magnitiz(ə)m/ *n*, **geomagnetist** /-'magnitist/ *n*

geometer /ji'omitə/ *n* **1** a specialist in geometry **2** a geometrid

geometric /ji-ə'metrik/, **geometrical** /-kl/ *adj* **1a** of or according to (the laws of) geometry **b** increasing in a geometric progression ⟨~ *population growth*⟩ **2a** *cap* of or being (a style of) ancient Greek pottery decorated with geometric patterns **b** using, being, or decorated with patterns formed from straight and curved lines – **geometrically** *adv*

geometric mean *n* the nth root of the product of *n* numbers (e g the square root of 2 numbers) ⟨*the* ~ *of 9 and 4 is 6*⟩

geometric progression *n* a sequence (e g 1, ½, ¼) in which the ratio of any term to its predecessor is constant

geometrid /ji'omətrid/ *n* any of a family of moths with large wings and larvae that are inchworms [deriv of Gk *geōmetrēs* geometer, fr *geōmetrein*] – **geometrid** *adj*

geometry /ji'omətri/ *n* **1a** a branch of mathematics that deals with the measurement, properties, and relationships of points, lines, angles, surfaces, and solids **b** a particular type or system of geometry **2** (surface) shape **3** an arrangement of objects or parts that suggests geometrical figures [ME *geometrie*, fr MF, fr L *geometria*, fr Gk *geōmetria*, fr *geōmetrein* to measure the earth, fr *geō-* ge- + *metron* measure – more at MEASURE]

geomorphic /jeeoh'mawfik/ *adj* of or concerned with the form or solid surface features of the earth, moon, etc

,geomor'phology /-maw'foləji/ *n* (the geology of) the structure and formation of the features of the surface of the earth or other celestial body [ISV] – **geomorphologist** *n*, **geomorphologic** /-,mawfə'lojik/, **geomorphological** *adj*, **geomorphologically** *adv*,

geophysics /-'fiziks/ *n pl but sing or pl in constr* the physics of the earth including meteorology, oceanography, seismology, etc [ISV] – **geophysical** *adj*, **geophysically** *adv*, **geophysicist** *n*

,geo'politics /-'politiks/ *n pl but sing in constr* the study of the influence of geography, economics, and demography on politics – **geopolitical** *adj*, **geopolitically** *adv*

Geordie /'jawdi/ *n* (the dialect of) a native or inhabitant of Tyneside [Sc *Geordie*, nickname for *George*] – **Geordie** *adj*

georgette /jaw'jet/ *n* a thin strong clothing crepe of silk or of other material with a dull pebbly surface [fr *Georgette*, a trademark]

[1]**Georgian** /'jawj(ə)n/ *n or adj* (a native or inhabitant or the language) of Georgia in the Caucasus ☞ LANGUAGE

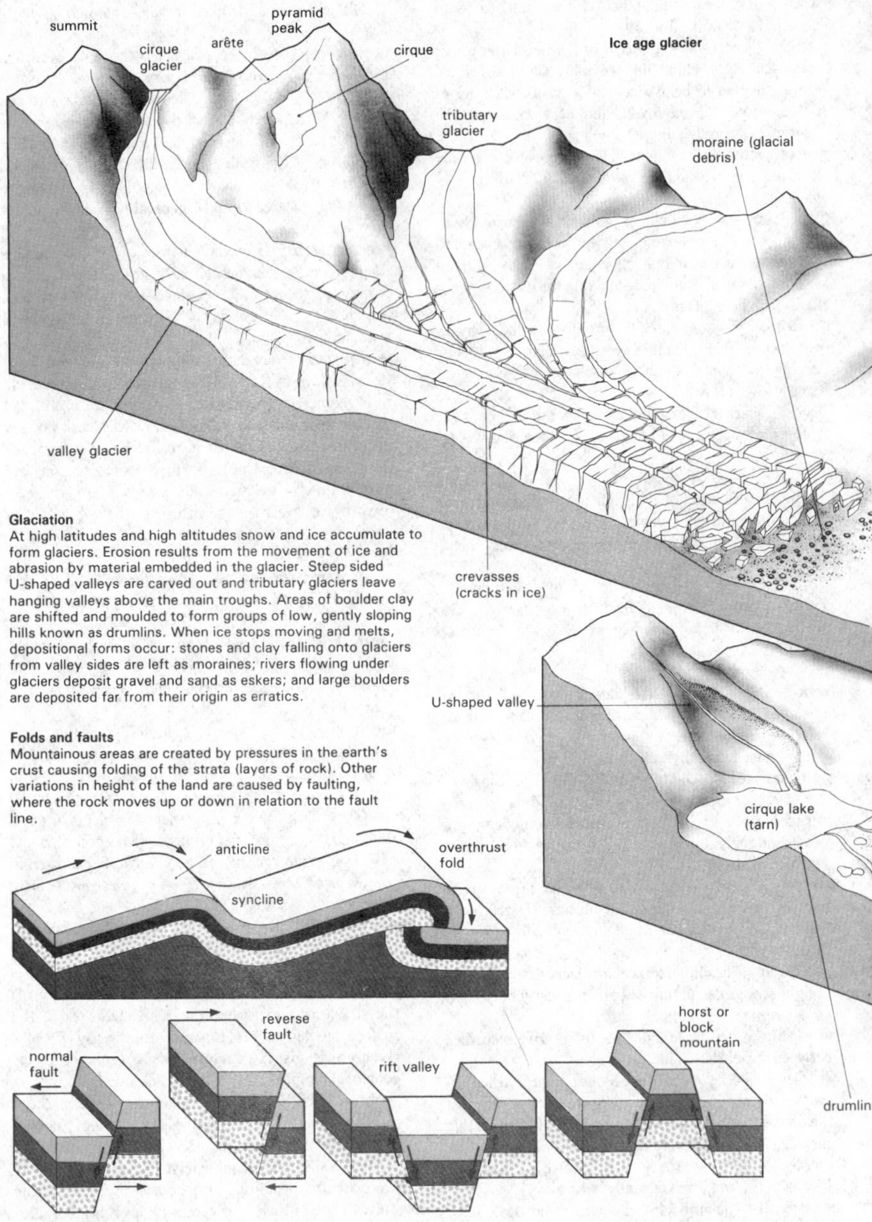

Glaciation
At high latitudes and high altitudes snow and ice accumulate to form glaciers. Erosion results from the movement of ice and abrasion by material embedded in the glacier. Steep sided U-shaped valleys are carved out and tributary glaciers leave hanging valleys above the main troughs. Areas of boulder clay are shifted and moulded to form groups of low, gently sloping hills known as drumlins. When ice stops moving and melts, depositional forms occur: stones and clay falling onto glaciers from valley sides are left as moraines; rivers flowing under glaciers deposit gravel and sand as eskers; and large boulders are deposited far from their origin as erratics.

Folds and faults
Mountainous areas are created by pressures in the earth's crust causing folding of the strata (layers of rock). Other variations in height of the land are caused by faulting, where the rock moves up or down in relation to the fault line.

☞ EVOLUTION

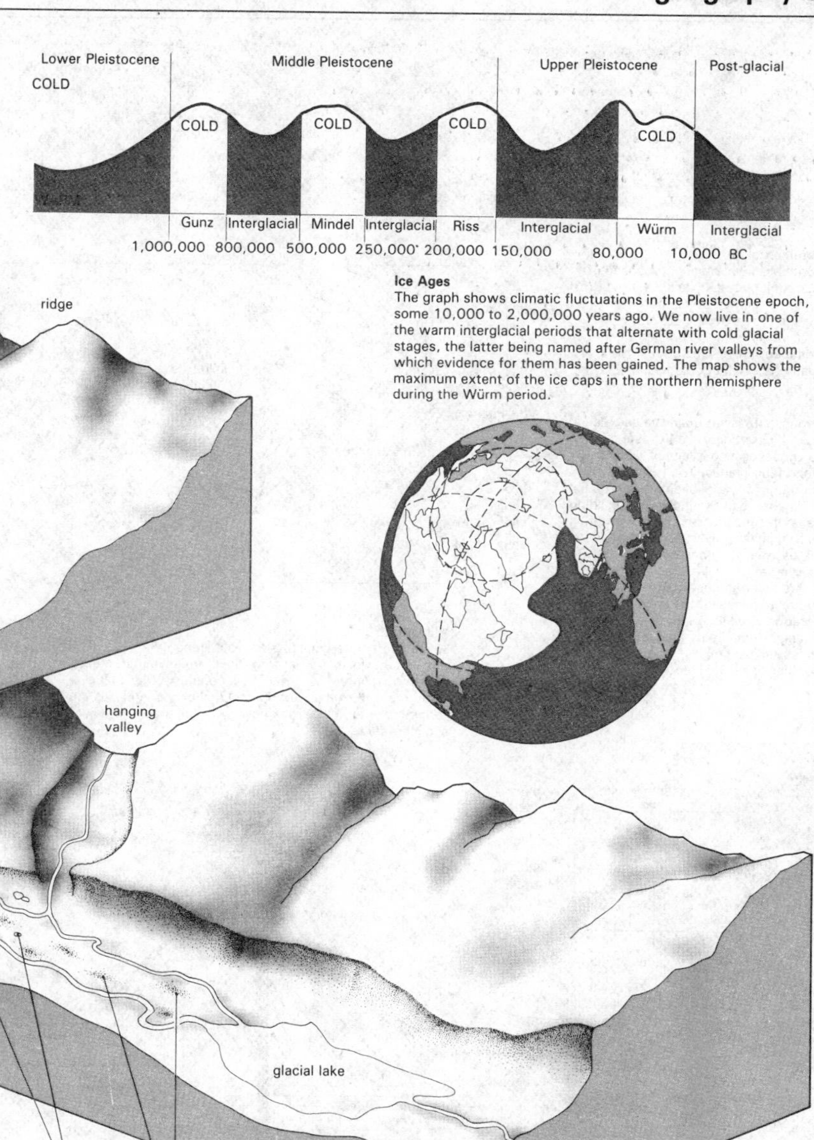

Ice Ages
The graph shows climatic fluctuations in the Pleistocene epoch, some 10,000 to 2,000,000 years ago. We now live in one of the warm interglacial periods that alternate with cold glacial stages, the latter being named after German river valleys from which evidence for them has been gained. The map shows the maximum extent of the ice caps in the northern hemisphere during the Würm period.

After the glacier

PANGAEA

200 million years ago

LAURASIA

GONDWANA

180 million years ago

NORTH AMERICA

EURASIA

AFRICA

SOUTH AMERICA

INDIA

ANTARCTICA

65 million years ago

Continental drift

Continents, which are composed of rigid rock plates, glide slowly over the semi-molten mantle beneath the earth's crust. Geologists can work backwards from the present positions of the continents to suggest their positions in past geological eras.

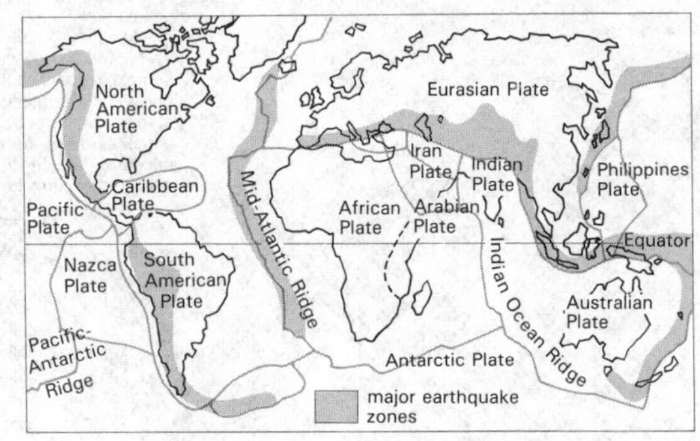

Intense stress set up in the earth's crust by continental drift results in earthquakes as movement occurs along fault planes. The Himalaya range is thought to have been thrown up by the pressure of the Indian plate sliding beneath the Eurasian plate. Along the Pacific coast of North America two plates are sliding past each other, causing earthquakes as the stress builds up at an obstruction and is suddenly released. Seismologists can determine the location, or epicentre, of an earthquake by analyzing the shockwaves it emits, recorded at a number of seismic stations.

Volcanoes

A volcano erupts when molten rock (magma) forces its way through the earth's crust from the mantle. A characteristic volcanic mountain is formed by a cone of ash and lava thrown out from the vent. Laccoliths, dykes, and sills are formed where molten rock flows into the cracks in adjacent sedimentary rocks.

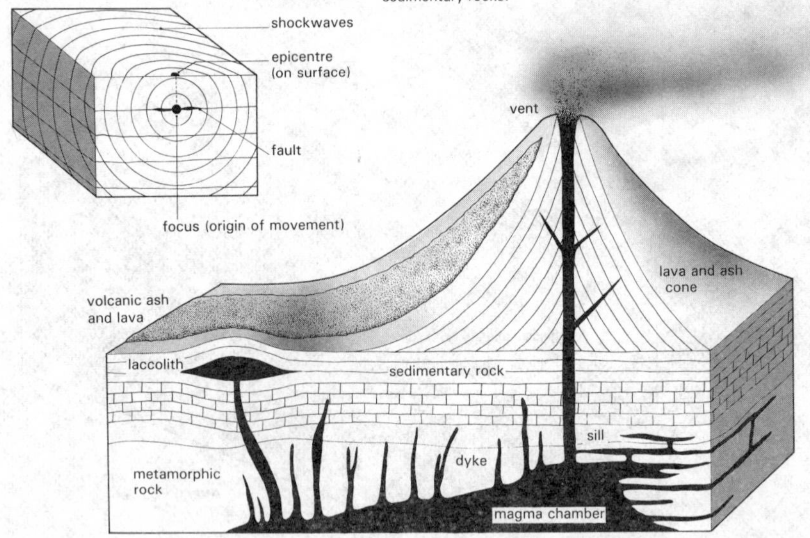

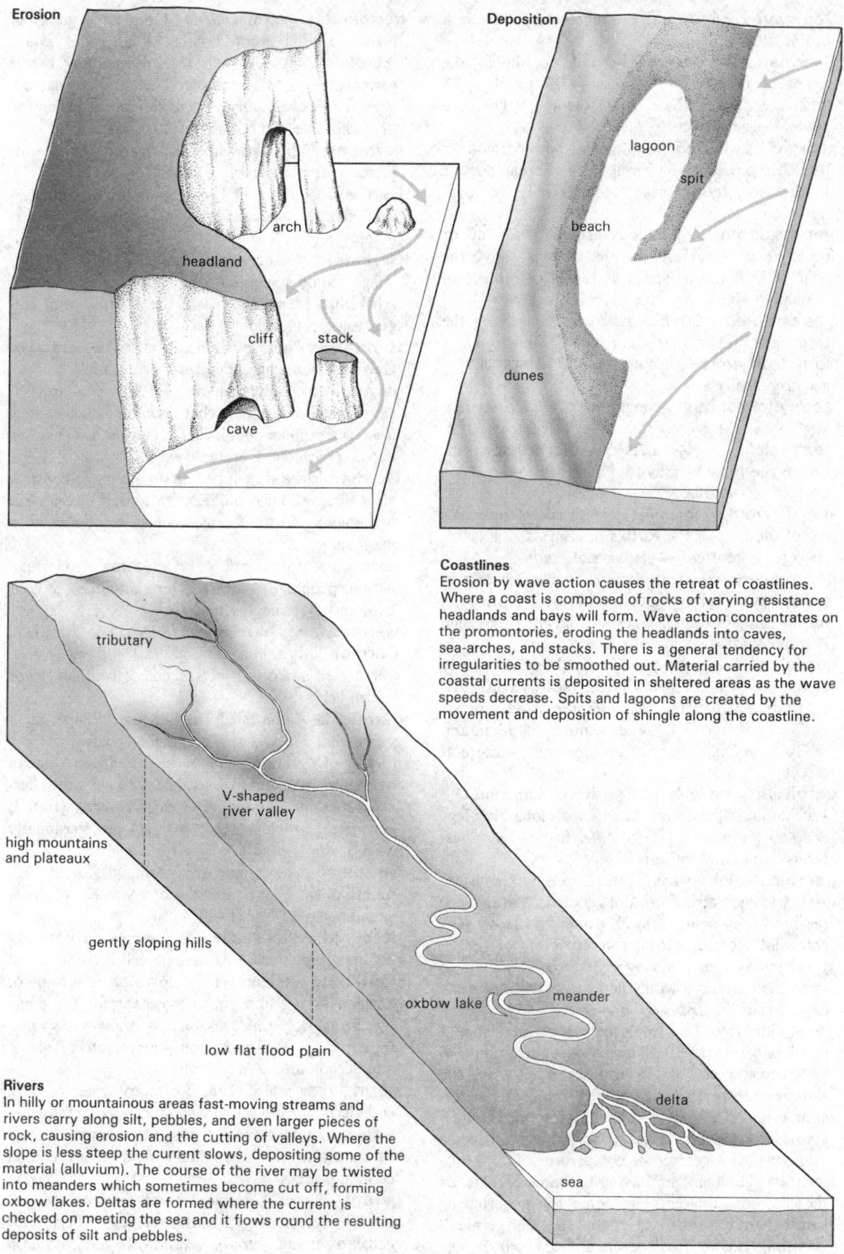

Coastlines
Erosion by wave action causes the retreat of coastlines. Where a coast is composed of rocks of varying resistance headlands and bays will form. Wave action concentrates on the promontories, eroding the headlands into caves, sea-arches, and stacks. There is a general tendency for irregularities to be smoothed out. Material carried by the coastal currents is deposited in sheltered areas as the wave speeds decrease. Spits and lagoons are created by the movement and deposition of shingle along the coastline.

Rivers
In hilly or mountainous areas fast-moving streams and rivers carry along silt, pebbles, and even larger pieces of rock, causing erosion and the cutting of valleys. Where the slope is less steep the current slows, depositing some of the material (alluvium). The course of the river may be twisted into meanders which sometimes become cut off, forming oxbow lakes. Deltas are formed where the current is checked on meeting the sea and it flows round the resulting deposits of silt and pebbles.

[2]**Georgian** *n or adj* (a native or inhabitant) of Georgia in the USA

[3]**Georgian** *adj* **1** (characteristic) of (the time of) the reigns of the first 4 Georges (1714 to 1830) **2** (characteristic) of the reign of George V (1910 to 1936) – **Georgian** *n*

georgic /'jawjik/ *n* a poem dealing with agriculture [the *Georgics*, poem by Virgil †19 BC Roman poet, fr L *Georgica*, fr Gk *geōrgika* lands under cultivation]

,geo'stationary /,jeeoh'stayshən(ə)ri/ *adj* of or being an artificial satellite that travels above the equator at the same speed as the earth rotates, so remaining above the same place

,geo'strophic /-'strofik/ *adj* of or caused by the rotation of the earth ⟨~ *wind*⟩ [*ge-* + Gk *strophikos* turned, fr *strophē* turning – more at STROPHE] – **geostrophically** *adv*

,geo'synchronous /-'singkrənəs/ *adj* geostationary

,geo'taxis /-'taksis/ *n* a response of a cell or organism to the force of gravity [NL, fr *ge-* + *-taxis*] – **geotactic** /-'taktik/ *adj*

,geo'thermal /-'thuhml/, **geothermic** /'thuhmik/ *adj* of the heat of the earth's interior ☞ ENERGY [ISV *ge-* + *thermal*] – **geothermally** *adv*

geotropism /jee·ə'troh,piz(ə)m/ *n* tropism (e g in the downward growth of roots) in which gravity is the orienting factor [ISV *ge-* + *-tropism*] – **geotropic** /-'tropik/ *adj*, **geotropically** *adv*

geranium /jə'raynyəm, -nyi·əm/ *n* **1** any of a widely distributed genus of plants having radially symmetrical flowers with glands that alternate with the petals **2** a pelargonium [NL, genus name, fr L, geranium, fr Gk *geranion*, fr dim. of *geranos* crane – more at CRANE]

gerbil *also* **gerbille** /'juh,bil/ *n* any of numerous Old World mouselike desert rodents with long hind legs adapted for leaping [F *gerbille*, fr NL *Gerbillus*, genus name, dim. of *jerboa*]

ger'falcon /juh'fawkən, -'falkən/ *n* a gyrfalcon

geriatric /jeri'atrik/ *adj* **1** of geriatrics, the aged, or the process of aging **2** aged, decrepit – derog [Gk *gēras* old age + E *-iatric*] – **geriatric** *n*

,geri'atrics *n pl but sing in constr* a branch of medicine that deals with (the diseases of) old age – **geriatrician** /-ə'trish(ə)n/ *n*

germ /juhm/ *n* **1a** a small mass of cells capable of developing into (a part of) an organism **b** the embryo of a cereal grain that is usu separated from the starchy endosperm during milling **2** sthg that serves as an origin **3** a (disease-causing) microorganism [F *germe*, fr L *germin-*, *germen*, fr *gignere* to beget – more at KIN] – **germproof** *adj*, **germy** *adj*

german /'juhmən/ *adj* having the same parents, or the same grandparents, on either the maternal or paternal side – usu in comb ⟨*brother*-german⟩ ⟨*cousin*-german⟩ [ME *germain*, fr MF, fr L *germanus* having the same parents, irreg fr *germen*]

[1]**German** *n* **1a** a native or inhabitant of Germany **b** one (e g a Swiss German) who speaks German as his/her native language outside Germany **2** the Germanic language of the people of Germany, Austria, and parts of Switzerland ☞ LANGUAGE [ML *Germanus*, fr L, any member of the Germanic peoples]

[2]**German** *adj* (characteristic) of Germany, the Germans, or German

germander /juh'mandə/ *n* **1** any of a genus of plants of the mint family **2** any of several (blue-flowered) speedwells [ME *germaunder*, fr MF *germandree*, fr ML *germandrea*, alter. of L *chamaedrys*, fr Gk *chamaidrys*, fr *chamai* on the ground + *drys* oak, tree – more at HUMBLE, TREE]

germane /juh'mayn/ *adj* both relevant and appropriate [var of *german*] – **germanely** *adv*

[1]**Germanic** /juh'manik/ *adj* **1** German **2** (characteristic) of the Germanic-speaking peoples **3** of Germanic

[2]**Germanic** *n* a branch of the Indo-European language family containing English, German, Dutch, Afrikaans, Flemish, Frisian, the Scandinavian languages, and Gothic

Germanist /'juhmənist/ *n* a specialist in German or Germanic language, literature, or culture

germanium /juh'maynyəm, -ni·əm/ *n* a greyish-white metalloid element that resembles silicon and is used as a semiconductor ☞ PERIODIC TABLE [NL, fr ML *Germania* Germany]

,German 'measles *n pl but sing or pl in constr* a virus disease that is milder than typical measles but is damaging to the foetus when occurring early in pregnancy

Germano- /juhmanoh-/ *comb form* **1** German nation, people, or culture ⟨Germano*phile*⟩ **2** German and ⟨Germano-*Russian*⟩

,German 'shepherd *n, chiefly NAm* an Alsatian

,German 'silver *n* NICKEL SILVER

'germ ,cell *n* (a cell from which is derived) an egg or sperm cell

germicide /'juhmi,sied/ *n* sthg that kills germs – **germicidal** /-'siedl/ *adj*, **germicidally** *adv*

germinal /'juhminl/ *adj* **1a** in the earliest stage of development **b** creative, seminal **2** (having the characteristics) of a germ cell or early embryo [F, fr L *germin-*, *germen* – more at GERM] – **germinally** /-nəli/ *adv*

Germinal /zheəminahl (*Fr* ʒerminal)/ *n* the 7th month of the French Revolutionary calendar corresponding to 22 March–20 April

germinal vesicle *n* the enlarged nucleus of the egg before completion of its meiotic cell division

germinate /'juhminayt/ *vt* to cause to sprout or develop ~ *vi* **1** to begin to grow; sprout **2** to come into being [L *germinatus*, pp of *germinare* to sprout, fr *germin-*, *germen* bud, germ] – **germinative** /-nətiv/ *adj*, **germination** /-'naysh(ə)n/ *n*

'germ ,layer *n* any of the 3 primary layers of cells, endoderm, ectoderm, or mesoderm, differentiated early in the development of most embryos

'germ ,plasm *n* the hereditary material of the germ cells; the genes

geront- /jeront-/, **geronto-** *comb form* old person; old age ⟨geronto*logy*⟩ ⟨geronto*cracy*⟩ [F *géront-*, *géronto-*, fr Gk *geront-*, *geronto-*, fr *geront-*, *gerōn* old man; akin to Gk *gēras* old age]

gerontocracy /jeron'tokrəsi/ *n* rule by old men [F *gérontocratie*, fr *géront-* geront- + *-cratie* -cracy] – **gerontocrat** /jə'rontəkrat/ *n*, **gerontocratic** /-'kratik/ *adj*

gerontology /jeron'toləji/ *n* the biology and medicine of aging and the problems of the aged [ISV] – **gerontologist** *n*, **gerontological** /jerontə'lojikl/, **gerontologic** *adj*

-gerous /-jərəs/ *comb form* (→ *adj*) bearing; producing ⟨*denti*gerous⟩ [L *-ger,* fr *gerere* to bear – more at CAST]

[1]**gerrymander** /'jeri,mandə/ *n* (a pattern of districts resulting from) gerrymandering [Elbridge *Gerry* †1814 US statesman + sala*mander,* fr the shape of an election district formed during Gerry's governorship of Massachusetts]

[2]**gerrymander** *vt* to divide (an area) into election districts to give one political party an electoral advantage – **gerrymandering** *n*

gerund /'jerənd/ *n* a verbal noun in Latin that expresses generalized or uncompleted action [LL *gerundium,* fr L *gerundus,* gerundive of *gerere* to bear, carry on – more at CAST]

[1]**gerundive** /ji'rundiv/ *adj or n* (of or like) the Latin future passive participle that expresses the desirability or necessity of an action and has the same suffix as the gerund – **gerundively** *adv,* **gerundival** /jerən'dievl/ *adj*

[2]**gerundive** *adj* of or similar to the gerund

gesellschaft /gə'zel,shahft/ *n* a social relationship or society characterized by mechanistic associations based on division of labour, utility, and self-interest – compare GEMEINSCHAFT [G, companionship, society, fr *gesell* companion + *-schaft* -ship]

gesso /'jesoh/ *n, pl* **gessoes** **1** plaster of paris or gypsum mixed with glue for use in painting or making bas-reliefs **2** a paste used as a basis for painting or gilding on wood or occas canvas [It, lit., gypsum, fr L *gypsum*]

gest, geste /jest/ *n* a tale of adventures; *esp* a romance in verse [ME *geste* – more at JEST]

gestalt /gə'shtalt/ *n, pl* **gestalten** /-tn/, **gestalts** a structure, pattern, etc (e g a melody) that as an object of perception constitutes a functional unit with properties not derivable from the sum of its parts [G, lit., shape, form]

Gestalt psychology *n* the study of perception and behaviour using the theory that perceptions, reactions, etc are gestalts

gestapo /gə's(h)tahpoh/ *n, pl* **gestapos** a secret-police organization operating esp against suspected traitors; *specif, cap* that of Nazi Germany [G, fr *Ge*heime *Sta*ats*po*lizei secret state police]

gestate /'jestayt/ *vt* to carry in gestation ~ *vi* to be in the process of gestation [back-formation fr *gestation*]

gestation /je'staysh(ə)n/ *n* **1** the carrying of young in the uterus; pregnancy **2** conception and development, esp in the mind [L *gestation-, gestatio,* fr *gestatus,* pp of *gestare* to bear, fr *gestus,* pp of *gerere* to bear] – **gestational** *adj*

gesticulate /je'stikyoo,layt/ *vi* to make expressive gestures, esp when speaking ⟨~d *to the waiter for the bill* – Rebecca West⟩ [L *gesticulatus,* pp of *gesticulari,* fr (assumed) L *gesticulus,* dim. of L *gestus*] – **gesticulator** *n,* **gesticulative** /-lətiv/ *adj,* **gesticulatory** /-lətri/ *adj,* **gesticulation** /-'laysh(ə)n/ *n*

[1]**gesture** /'jeschə/ *n* **1a** a movement, usu of the body or limbs, that expresses or emphasizes an idea, sentiment, or attitude **b** the use of gestures **2** sthg said or done for its effect on the attitudes of others or to convey a feeling (e g friendliness) [ML *gestura* mode of action, fr L *gestus,* pp] – **gestural** *adj*

[2]**gesture** *vb* to make or express (by) a gesture

[1]**get** /get/ *vb* **-tt-; got; got** /got/, *NAm also* **gotten** /'gotn/; *nonstandard pres pl & 1 & 2 sing* **got** *vt* **1** to gain possession of: e g **a** to obtain by way of benefit or advantage ⟨~ *the better of an enemy*⟩ ⟨got *little for his trouble*⟩ **b** to obtain by concession or entreaty ⟨~ *your mother's permission to go*⟩ **c** to seek out and fetch or provide ⟨~ *blackberries in the wood*⟩ ⟨~ *you a present*⟩ **d** to acquire by memorizing or calculation ⟨~ *the verse by heart*⟩ ⟨~ *the answer to a problem*⟩ **e** to seize **2a** to receive as a return; earn ⟨*he* got *a bad reputation for carelessness*⟩ **b** to become affected by; catch ⟨got *measles from his sister*⟩ **c** to be subjected to ⟨~ *the sack*⟩ **3** to beget **4a** to cause to come, go, or move ⟨*quickly* ~ *his luggage through customs*⟩ ⟨*grumbling won't* ~ *you anywhere*⟩ **b** to bring into a specified condition by direct action ⟨~ *my shoes mended*⟩ ⟨*let me* ~ *this clear*⟩ **c** to prevail on; induce ⟨~ *the Russians to give an English broadcast* – *SEU S*⟩ **5** to make ready; prepare ⟨~ *dinner*⟩ **6a** to overcome ⟨*I'll* ~ *him on that point*⟩ **b** to take vengeance on; *specif* to kill ⟨*out to* ~ *his man*⟩ **7a** to have – used in the present perfect tense form with present meaning ⟨*I've* got *no money*⟩ **b** to have as an obligation or necessity – used in the present perfect tense form with present meaning; + *to* and an understood or expressed infinitive ⟨*he has* got *to come*⟩ ⟨*I won't if I haven't* got *to*⟩ **8a** to hear ⟨*I didn't quite* ~ *that for the noise*⟩ **b** to establish communication with ⟨~ *her on the telephone*⟩ **9a** to puzzle ⟨*you've really* got *me there*⟩ **b** to irritate ⟨*his superior attitude really* ~s *me*⟩ **10** to hit ⟨~ *him on the ear with a potato*⟩ **11** to understand ⟨*don't* ~ *me wrong*⟩ **12** to affect emotionally ⟨*the sight of her tears* got *him*⟩ ~ *vi* **1** to reach or enter into the specified condition or activity ⟨~ *drunk*⟩ ⟨*food's* ~ting *cold*⟩ ⟨~ *moving*⟩ ⟨*you're* ~ting *a big girl now*⟩ ⟨*they* got *married last week*⟩ – used as a verbal auxiliary instead of *be* to form the passive ⟨*wouldn't take the slightest risk of* ~ting *trapped inside* – *SEU W*⟩ **2a** to reach, arrive ⟨*where's my pen* got *to?*⟩ **b** to succeed in coming or going ⟨~ *into my jeans*⟩ ⟨*at last we're* ~ting *somewhere*⟩ ⟨~ *to sleep after midnight*⟩ **c** to contrive by effort, luck, or permission – + *to* and an infinitive ⟨*when you* ~ *to know him*⟩ ⟨*she never* ~s *to drive the car*⟩ ***USE*** (*vt* 9a, 9b, 10, 11, & 12) infml [ME *geten,* fr ON *geta* to get, beget; akin to OE bi*gietan* to beget, L pre*hendere* to seize, grasp, Gk *chandanein* to hold, contain] – **get ahead** to achieve success ⟨*determined to* get ahead *in life*⟩ – **get a move on** to hurry up – **get at 1** to reach effectively ⟨get at *the truth*⟩ **2** to influence corruptly; bribe **3** to nag, tease **4** to mean, imply ⟨*what's he* getting at?⟩ – **get away with** to do (a reprehensible act) without criticism or penalty – **get cracking/weaving** to make a start; get going ⟨*ought to* get cracking *on the washing up*⟩ – infml – **get even with** to repay in kind; revenge oneself on – **get into** to possess, dominate ⟨*what's* got into *you?*⟩ – **get it** CATCH IT – **get off one's bike** *Austr* to become annoyed – infml – **get one's eye in** *chiefly Br* to get into practice; *specif* to gain ability to judge the speed and direction of a moving ball – **get one's goat** to make one angry or annoyed – infml – **get one's own back** to revenge oneself – **get on one's high horse** to adopt an unyielding and usu arrogant attitude – **get outside** to eat (sthg) – infml – **get over 1** to overcome, surmount **2** to recover from **3** to accept calmly ⟨*can't* get over *your beard*⟩ – **get rid of** to rid oneself of; disencumber oneself of by eliminating,

dismissing, or clearing away – **get round** **1** to circumvent, evade **2** to cajole, persuade – **get the better of** to overcome – **get there** **1** to be successful **2** to understand what is meant – **get the wind up** to become frightened – infml – **get the wrong end of the stick** to misunderstand sthg – **get through** **1** to reach the end of; complete **2a** USE UP 1 ⟨got through *a lot of money*⟩ **b** WHILE AWAY ⟨*hardly knew how to* get through *his days*⟩ – **get under one's skin** to cause one persistent and often troublesome irritation, stimulation, or excitement – **get up someone's nose** to irritate sby intensely – infml – **get wind of** to become aware of

[2]**get** *n* **1** sthg begotten **2** a successful return of a difficult shot in tennis, squash, etc **3** *Br* a git – slang

get about *vi* **1** to be up and about; be well enough to walk **2** to become circulated, esp orally ⟨*the news soon* got about⟩

get across *vb* to make or become clear or convincing

get along *vi* **1** to move away; leave for another destination **2** to manage **3** to be or remain on congenial terms

getaway /ˈgetə,way/ *n* a departure, escape

get back *vi* to return, revert – **get back at** to gain revenge on; retaliate against

get by *vi* **1** to manage, survive ⟨*we'll* get by *without your help*⟩ **2** to succeed by a narrow margin; be just about acceptable

get down *vi* to leave or descend (e g from a vehicle) ~ *vt* **1** to depress ⟨*the weather was* getting *her* down⟩ **2** to swallow ⟨get *this medicine* down⟩ **3** to record in writing ⟨get down *the details*⟩ – **get down to** to apply serious attention or consideration to; concentrate one's efforts on

get off *vi* **1** to start, leave **2** to escape from a dangerous situation or from punishment ⟨*won't* get off *lightly*⟩ **3** to leave work with permission **4** *Br* to start an amorous or sexual relationship – often + *with*; slang ~ *vt* **1** to secure the release of or procure a modified penalty for ⟨*his lawyers* got *him* off *with little difficulty*⟩ **2** to send, post

get on *vi* **1** GET ALONG **2** to become late or old – **get on for** to come near; approach ⟨*he's* getting on for *90*⟩

get out *vi* **1** to emerge, escape ⟨*doubted that he would* get out *alive*⟩ **2** to become known; LEAK 2 ⟨*their secret* got out⟩ ~ *vt* **1** to cause to emerge or escape **2** to bring before the public; *esp* to publish ⟨get *a new book* out⟩

get round *vi* GET ABOUT 2 – **get round to** to give esp overdue attention or consideration

getter /ˈgetə/ *n* a substance introduced into a vacuum tube, electric lamp, etc to remove traces of gas [[1]GET + [2]-ER]

ˈ**get-to,gether** *n* an (informal social) gathering or meeting

get together *vt* to bring together; accumulate ~ *vi* **1** to come together; assemble **2** to unite in discussion or promotion of a project

getup /ˈget,up/ *n* the outer appearance; *specif* an outfit, clothing – infml

get up *vi* **1a** to arise from bed **b** to rise to one's feet **2** to go ahead or faster – used in the imperative as a command, esp to driven animals ~ *vt* **1** to organize ⟨got up *a party for the newcomers*⟩ **2** to arrange the external appearance of; dress **3** to acquire a knowledge of **4** to create in oneself ⟨*can't* get up *an atom of sympathy for them*⟩

geum /ˈjee·əm/ *n* an avens [NL, fr L *gaeum, geum* herb bennet]

gewgaw /ˈgyooh,gaw/ *n* a bauble, trinket [origin unknown]

gey /gay/ *adv, chiefly Scot* very, quite [alter. of *gay*, adv]

geyser /ˈgeezə; *sense* ˈ *also* ˈgiezə/ *n* **1** a spring that intermittently throws out jets of heated water and steam **2** *Br* an apparatus with a boiler in which water (e g for a bath) is rapidly heated by a gas flame and may be stored [Icel *Geysir*, name of a hot spring in Iceland, fr *geysir* gusher, fr *geysa* to rush forth, fr ON; akin to OE *gēotan* to pour – more at [4]FOUND]

gharial /ˈgeəri·əl/ *n* a gavial [Hindi *ghaṛiyāl*]

gharry /gari/ *n* a usu horse-drawn Indian taxi [Hindi *gāṛī*]

ghastly /ˈgahstli/ *adj* **1a** (terrifyingly) horrible ⟨*a* ~ *crime*⟩ **b** intensely unpleasant, disagreeable, or objectionable ⟨*such a life seems* ~ *in its emptiness and sterility* – Aldous Huxley⟩ **2** pale, wan [ME *gastly*, fr *gasten* to terrify] – **ghastliness** *n*

ghat /gawt/ *n* a broad flight of steps providing access to an Indian river [Hindi *ghāṭ*]

Ghazi /ˈgahzi/ *n* a Muslim soldier fighting a non-Muslim adversary [Ar *ghāzī*]

ghee, ghi /gee/ *n* a semifluid clarified butter made, esp in India, from cow's or buffalo's milk [Hindi *ghī*, fr Skt *ghṛta*; akin to MIr *gert* milk]

gherkin /ˈguhkin/ *n* **1** (a slender annual climbing plant of the cucumber family that bears) a small prickly fruit used for pickling **2** the small immature fruit of the cucumber used for pickling [D *gurken*, pl of *gurk* cucumber, fr *augurk*, fr LG *augurke*, fr MLG, fr Pol *ogurek*, fr MGk *agouros* watermelon, cucumber]

ghetto /ˈgetoh/ *n, pl* **ghettos, ghettoes** **1** part of a city in which Jews formerly lived **2** an often slum area of a city in which a minority group live, esp because of social, legal, or economic pressures; *broadly* an area with 1 predominant type of resident [It]

Ghibelline /ˈgibi,lien/ *n* a member of a political party in medieval Italy supporting the German emperors – compare GUELF [It *Ghibellino*, fr OIt, fr MHG *Wibeling* name of the Salian emperors, fr *Wibeling* castle in Franconia, Germany]

ghillie /ˈgili/ *n* a gillie

[1]**ghost** /gohst/ *n* **1** the seat of life or intelligence ⟨*give up the* ~⟩ **2** a disembodied soul; *esp* the soul of a dead person haunting the living **3a** a faint shadowy trace ⟨*a* ~ *of a smile*⟩ **b** the least bit ⟨*didn't have a* ~ *of a chance*⟩ **4** a false image in a photographic negative or on a television screen **5** a ghost-writer **6** a red blood cell that has lost its haemoglobin [ME *gost, gast*, fr OE *gāst*; akin to OHG *geist* spirit, Skt *heḍa* anger] – **ghostlike** *adj*

[2]**ghost** *vb* to ghostwrite

ˈ**ghostly** /-li/ *adj* of, like, or being a ghost; spectral – **ghostliness** *n*

ˈ**ghost ,town** *n* a once-flourishing but now deserted town

ˈ**ghost,write** /-,riet/ *vb* **ghostwrote** /-,roht/, **ghostwritten** /-,rit(ə)n/ to write (e g a speech) for another who is the presumed author [back-formation fr *ghost-writer*] – **ghost-writer** *n*

ghoul /goohl/ *n* **1** a evil being of Arabic legend that robs graves and feeds on corpses **2** one who enjoys the macabre [Ar *ghūl*, fr *ghāla* to seize] – **ghoulish** *adj*, **ghoulishly** *adv*, **ghoulishness** *n*

ghyll /gil/ *n* [3]GILL

[1]GI /jee 'ie/ *adj* (characteristic) of US military personnel or equipment [*g*alvanized *i*ron; fr abbr used in listing articles such as rubbish bins, but taken as abbr for *government issue* or *general issue*]

[2]GI *n, pl* **GI's, GIs** a member of the US army, esp a private

[1]giant /'jie·ənt/ *n* **1** *fem* **giantess** /-tis/ a legendary humanoid being of great stature and strength **2** sby or sthg extraordinarily large **3** a person of extraordinary powers ⟨*a literary* ~⟩ [ME *giaunt*, fr MF *geant*, fr L *gigant-*, *gigas*, fr Gk] – **giantlike** *adj*

[2]giant *adj* extremely large

giant anteater *n* a large S American anteater ☞ ENDANGERED

giant hogweed *n* a plant that is a close relative of cow parsnip but grows to more than 3m (10ft) tall

giantism /'jie·əntiz(ə)m/ *n* gigantism

,giant 'panda *n* PANDA 2 ☞ ENDANGERED

,giant se'quoia *n* BIG TREE

giaour /'jow·ə/ *n* one outside the Muslim faith; INFIDEL 1a [Turk *gâvur*]

[1]gibber /'jibə/ *vi* to make rapid, inarticulate, and usu incomprehensible utterances ⟨*a* ~ing *idiot*⟩ [imit]

[2]gibber *n, Austr* a small stone; a pebble; *also* a boulder, rock [prob native name in Australia]

gibberellin /jibə'relin/ *n* any of several plant hormones that promote shoot growth [NL *Gibberella fujikoroi*, fungus from which it was first isolated]

gibberish /'jibərish/ *n* unintelligible or meaningless language [prob fr [1]*gibber*]

gibbet /'jibit/ *vt or n* (to execute or expose on) an upright post with an arm for hanging the bodies of executed criminals [n ME *gibet*, fr OF; vb fr n]

gibbon /'gib(ə)n/ *n* any of several tailless Asian anthropoid tree-dwelling apes [F]

gibbous /'gibəs/ *adj* **1a** *of the moon or a planet* seen with more than half but not all of the apparent disc illuminated **b** swollen on 1 side; convex, protuberant **2** having a hump; humpbacked [ME, fr MF *gibbeux*, fr LL *gibbosus* humpbacked, fr L *gibbus* hump] – **gibbously** *adv*, **gibbousness** *n*, **gibbosity** /gi'bosəti/ *n*

gibe, jibe /jieb/ *vb* to jeer (at) [perh fr MF *giber* to shake, handle roughly] – **gibe** *n*, **giber** *n*

giblets /'jiblits/ *n pl* a fowl's heart, liver, or other edible internal organs – compare HASLET [ME *gibelet* entrails, garbage, fr MF, stew of wildfowl]

gid /gid/ *n* a disease, esp of sheep, caused by the larva of a tapeworm developing in the brain [back-formation fr *giddy*]

giddap /gi'dup/ *interj* gee-up [alter. of *get up*]

giddy /'gidi/ *adj* **1** lightheartedly frivolous **2a** feeling, or causing to feel, a sensation of unsteadiness and lack of balance as if everything is whirling round **b** whirling rapidly [ME *gidy* mad, foolish, fr OE *gydig* possessed, mad; akin to OE *god*] – **giddily** *adv*, **giddiness** *n*

gie /gee/ *vb, chiefly Scot* to give [by alter.]

[1]gift /gift/ *n* **1** a natural capacity or talent **2** sthg freely given by one person to another **3** the act, right, or power of giving ⟨*the regional fund is not in M Pompidou's* ~ *– The Times*⟩ [ME, fr ON, something given, talent; akin to OE *giefan* to give] – **gift of the gab** the ability to talk glibly and persuasively – infml

[2]gift *vt* to present

'gifted *adj* **1** having or revealing great natural ability **2** highly intelligent ⟨~ *children*⟩ – **giftedly** *adv*, **giftedness** *n*

,Gift of 'Tongues *n* inspired ecstatic speaking; *specif* that occurring among the followers of Jesus at Pentecost

'gift ,token *n* a certified statement redeemable for merchandise to the amount stated thereon – compare TOKEN 5

'gift ,wrap *vt* to wrap (merchandise intended as a gift) decoratively

[1]gig /gig/ *n* **1** a long light ship's boat propelled by oars, sails, etc **2** a light 2-wheeled one-horse carriage [ME *gigg* top, perh of Scand origin; akin to ON *geiga* to turn aside; akin to OE *geonian, ginian* to yawn – more at YAWN]

[2]gig *n* a pronged spear for catching fish [short for earlier *fizgig, fishgig*, of unknown origin]

[3]gig *n* a musician's engagement for a specified time; *esp* such an engagement for 1 performance [origin unknown]

giga- /jigə-, gigə-/ *comb form* one thousand million (10^9) ⟨giga*volt*⟩ ☞ PHYSICS [ISV, fr Gk *gigas* giant]

'giga,hertz /-,huhts/ *n* a unit of frequency equal to 1,000,000,000 hertz [ISV *giga-* + *hertz*]

gigant- /jiegant-/, **giganto-** *comb form* giant ⟨gigan*tism*⟩ [Gk, fr *gigant-*, *gigas*]

gigantic /jie'gantik/ *adj* unusually great or enormous – **gigantically** *adv*

gigantism /'jiegan,tiz(ə)m, -'-,--/ *n* development of a plant or animal to abnormally large size

[1]giggle /'gigl/ *vi* **giggling** /'gigl·ing, 'gigling/ to laugh with repeated short catches of the breath (and in a silly manner) [imit] – **giggler** *n*, **gigglingly** *adv*

[2]giggle *n* **1** an act or instance of giggling **2** *chiefly Br* sthg that amuses or diverts – chiefly infml ⟨*did it for a* ~⟩ – **giggly** *adj*

gigolo /'zhigəloh/ *n, pl* **gigolos** **1** a man paid by a usu older woman for companionship or sex **2** a professional dancing partner or male escort [F, back-formation fr *gigolette* girl who frequents public dances, prostitute, fr *giguer* to dance – more at JIG]

gigot /'zhigoh, 'jigət/ *n* a (cooked) leg of meat (e g lamb) [MF, dim. of *gigue* fiddle – more at JIG; fr its shape]

'gigot ,sleeve *n* a leg-of-mutton sleeve

gigue /zheeg/ *n* a lively dance movement having compound triple rhythm and consisting of 2 sections, each of which is repeated – compare JIG [F – more at JIG]

'Gila ,monster /'heelə/ *n* a large orange and black venomous lizard of SW USA [*Gila*, river in Arizona, USA]

[1]gild /gild/ *vt* **gilded, gilt** /gilt/ **1** to overlay (as if) with a thin covering of gold **2** to give an attractive but often deceptive appearance to [ME *gilden*, fr OE *gyldan*; akin to OE *gold*] – **gilder** *n*, **gilding** *n* – **gild the lily** to add unnecessary ornamentation to sthg beautiful in its own right

[2]gild *n* a guild

gilet /'zheelay/ *n* **1** a bodice or part of a bodice styled like a waistcoat **2** a loose waistcoat [F, fr Sp *gileco, jaleco*, fr Ar *jalīkah*, a garment worn by slaves, fr Turk *yelek* waistcoat]

[1]**gill** /jil/ *n* ☞ UNIT [ME *gille*, perh fr MF *gille, gelle* vat, tub, fr L *gerulus* bearer, carrier, fr *gerere* to bear – more at CAST]

[2]**gill** /gil/ *n* **1** an organ, esp of a fish, for oxygenating blood using the oxygen dissolved in water **2** the flesh under or about the chin or jaws – usu pl with sing. meaning **3** any of the radiating plates forming the undersurface of the cap of some fungi (e g mushrooms) [ME *gile, gille*, prob of Scand origin; akin to OSw *gel, geel* gill, jaw, ON *gjilnar* lips] – **gilled** *adj*

[3]**gill, ghyll** /gil/ *n, Br* **1** a ravine **2** a narrow mountain stream or rivulet [ME *gille*, fr ON *gil*]

'gill ,cover /gil/ *n* the operculum

gillie, gilly, ghillie /'gili/ *n* an attendant to sby who is hunting or fishing in Scotland [ScGael *gille* & IrGael *giolla* boy, servant]

gillion /'gilyən/ *n, Br* a thousand millions – compare BILLION ☞ NUMBER [*giga-* + *million*] – **gillion** *adj*, **gillionth** *adj or n*

'gill ,net *n* a flat net suspended vertically in the water with meshes for entangling fishes' gills – **gillnet** *vt*

gillyflower /'jili,flowə/ *n* any of several plants having clove-scented flowers: e g **a** an Old World pink **b** a wallflower [by folk etymology fr ME *gilofre* clove, fr MF *girofle, gilofre*, fr L *caryophyllum*, fr Gk *karyophyllon*, fr *karyon* nut + *phyllon* leaf – more at CAREEN, BLADE]

[1]**gilt** /gilt/ *adj* covered with gold or gilt; of the colour of gold [ME, fr pp of *gilden* to gild]

[2]**gilt** *n* **1** (sthg that resembles) gold laid on a surface **2** superficial brilliance; surface attraction **3** a gilt-edged security – usu pl

[3]**gilt** *n* a young female pig [ME *gylte*, fr ON *gyltr*; akin to OE *gelte* young sow – more at GELD]

,gilt-'edged, gilt-edge *adj* **1** of the highest quality or reliability **2** *of government securities* having a guaranteed fixed interest rate and redeemable at face value

gimbal /'jimbl, 'gimbl/ *n* a device that allows a ship's compass, stove, etc to remain level when its support is tipped – usu pl with sing. meaning [alter. of obs *gemel, gimmal* (double ring), deriv of L *geminus* twin]

gimcrack /'jim,krak/ *n* a showy unsubstantial object of little use or value [perh alter. of ME *gibecrake*, of uncertain meaning] – **gimcrack** *adj*, **gimcrackery** *n*

[1]**gimlet** /'gimlit/ *n* **1** a tool for boring small holes in wood, usu consisting of a crosswise handle fitted to a tapered screw – compare AUGER **2** a cocktail consisting of lime juice, gin or vodka, and soda water [ME, fr MF *guimbelet*]

[2]**gimlet** *adj, of eyes* piercing, penetrating ⟨*give him a* gimlet-*eyed stare*⟩

gimmick /'gimik/ *n* a scheme, device, or object devised to gain attention or publicity [origin unknown] – **gimmickry** *n*, **gimmicky** *adj*

[1]**gin** /jin/ *n* any of various tools or mechanical devices: e g **a** a snare or trap for game **b** a machine for raising or moving heavy weights **c** COTTON GIN [ME *gin*, modif of OF *engin* – more at ENGINE]

[2]**gin** *vt* **-nn- 1** to snare **2** to separate (cotton fibre) from seeds and waste material – **ginner** *n*, **ginning** *n*

[3]**gin** *n* a spirit made by distilling a mash of grain with juniper berries [by shortening & alter. fr *geneva*, modif of obs D *genever* (now *jenever*), lit., juniper, fr L *juniperus*]

[4]**gin** *n, Austr* a female aborigine – derog; compare LUBRA [native name in Australia]

,gin and 'it *n, Br* a drink that consists of gin and Italian vermouth [*it*, short for *Italian (vermouth)*]

ginger /'jinjə/ *n* **1a** (any of several cultivated tropical plants with) a thickened pungent aromatic underground stem used (dried and ground) as a spice, or candied as a sweet **b** the spice usu prepared by drying and grinding ginger **2** a strong brown colour [ME, fr OF *gimgibre*, fr ML *gingiber*, alter. of L *zingiber*, fr Gk *zingiberis*, prob modif of Skt *śṛngavera*] – **gingery** *adj*

,ginger 'ale *n* a sweet yellowish carbonated nonalcoholic drink flavoured with ginger

,ginger 'beer *n* a weak alcoholic effervescent drink of milky appearance, made by the fermentation of ginger and syrup; *also* a similar nonalcoholic commercial preparation

'ginger,bread /-,bred/ *n* a thick biscuit or cake made with treacle or syrup and flavoured with ginger [ME *gingerbreed*, by folk etymology fr *gingebras* ginger paste, fr OF *gingembraz*, fr *gimgibre*]

'ginger ,group *n, Br* a pressure group (e g within a political party) urging stronger action

gingerly /'jinjəli/ *adj* very cautious or careful [perh fr MF *gensor, genzor*, compar of *gent* well-born, dainty, delicate] – **gingerliness** *n*, **gingerly** *adv*

'ginger ,nut *n* a hard brittle biscuit flavoured with ginger

'ginger ,snap *n* GINGER NUT

ginger up *vt* to stir to activity; vitalize ⟨ginger up *boardroom attitudes – Punch*⟩ [fr the practice of stimulating a horse with ginger]

gingham /'ging·əm/ *n* a plain-weave often checked clothing fabric usu of yarn-dyed cotton [modif of Malay *genggang* checkered cloth]

gingiv-, gingivo- *comb form* gum; gums ⟨gingiv*itis*⟩ [L *gingiva*]

gingiva /jin'jievə/ *n, pl* **gingivae** /-vi/ [1]GUM [L – more at CONGER] – **gingival** *adj*

ginkgo /'gingk,goh, 'ging,koh/, **gingko** /'ging,koh/ *n, pl* **ginkgoes, gingkoes** a showy (ornamental) Chinese gymnospermous tree with fan-shaped leaves and yellow fruit ☞ PLANT [NL *Ginkgo*, genus name, fr Jap *ginkyo*]

'gin ,palace *n* a gaudy public house – derog

,gin 'rummy *n, Br* a form of rummy in which each of 2 players is dealt 10 cards and each may end play when the value of his/her unmatched cards is less than 10 [[3]*gin*]

ginseng /'jin,seng/ *n* (the aromatic root, widely valued as a tonic, of) a Chinese or American plant of the ivy family [Chin (Pek) *jen*[2]*-shen*[1]]

,gippy 'tummy /'jipi/ *n* indigestion and diarrhoea (affecting visitors to hot countries) – infml [*gippy* by shortening & alter. fr *Egyptian*]

gipsy, *NAm* **gypsy** /'jipsi/ *n* **1** *often cap* a member of a dark Caucasian people coming orig from India to Europe in the 14th or 15th c and leading a migratory way of life **2** a person who moves from place to place; a wanderer [by shortening & alter. fr *Egyptian*]

'gipsy ,moth *n* an Old World tussock moth whose hairy caterpillar is a destructive defoliator of trees

giraffe /ji'raf, ji'rahf/ *n, pl* **giraffes,** *esp collectively* **giraffe** a large African ruminant mammal with a very long neck and a beige coat marked with brown or black patches ☞ LIFE CYCLE [It *giraffa*, fr Ar *zirāfah*]

girandole /'jirən,dohl/ *n* **1** a radiating and showy composition (of skyrockets fired together) **2** an ornamental branched candle holder [F & It; F, fr It *girandola*, fr *girare* to turn, fr LL *gyrare*, fr L *gyrus* circle, spiral]

girasol, girasole /'jirə,sol, -,sohl/ *n* an opal that gives out fiery reflections in bright light [It *girasole*, fr *girare* + *sole* sun, fr L *sol* – more at [1]SOLAR]

gird /guhd/ *vb* **girded, girt** /guht/ *vt* **1a** to encircle or bind with a flexible band (e g a belt) **b** to surround **2** to provide or equip with a sword **3** to prepare (oneself) for action ~ *vi* to prepare for action [ME *girden*, fr OE *gyrdan*; akin to OE *geard* yard – more at [2]YARD] – **gird one's loins, gird up one's loins** to prepare for action; muster one's resources

girder /'guhdə/ *n* a horizontal main supporting beam [*gird* + [2]*-er*]

[1]girdle /'guhdl/ *n* **1** sthg that encircles or confines: e g **a** a belt or cord encircling the body, usu at the waist **b** a woman's tightly fitting undergarment that extends from the waist to below the hips **c** a bony ring at the front and rear end of the trunk of vertebrates supporting the arms or legs **d** a ring made by the removal of the bark and cambium round a plant stem or tree trunk **2** the edge of a cut gem that is grasped by the setting [ME *girdel*, fr OE *gyrdel*; akin to OHG *gurtil* girdle, OE *gyrdan* to gird]

[2]girdle *vt* **girdling** /'guhdling/ **1** to encircle (as if) with a girdle **2** to cut a girdle round (esp a tree), usu in order to kill

[3]girdle *n, Scot & dial Eng* a griddle [ME (Sc) *girdill, girdil*, alter. of ME *gredil* – more at GRIDDLE]

girl /guhl/ *n* **1a** a female child **b** a young unmarried woman **2a** a sweetheart, girlfriend **b** a daughter **3** a woman – chiefly infml [ME *gurle, girle* young person of either sex] – **girlhood** *n*, **girlish** *adj*, **girlishness** *n*

,girl 'Friday *n* a female general assistant, esp in an office [*girl* + *Friday* as in *man Friday*, character in the novel *Robinson Crusoe* by Daniel Defoe †1731 E writer]

'girl,friend /-,frend/ *n* **1** a frequent or regular female companion of a boy or man; *esp* one with whom he is romantically involved **2** a female friend

,girl 'guide *n, chiefly Br* GUIDE 3 – not now used technically

girlie, girly /'guhli/ *adj* featuring nude or scantily clothed young women ⟨~ *magazines*⟩

,girl 'scout *n, NAm* GUIDE 3

girn /giən/ *vi, Scot & N Eng* to be peevish or fretful [ME *girnen*, alter. of *grinnen* to grin, snarl] – **girn** *n*

giro /'jie(ə)roh/ *n* a computerized low-cost system of money transfer comparable to a current account that is one of the national post office services in many European countries [G, fr It, turn, transfer, fr L *gyrus* circle, spiral]

girt /guht/ *vb* to gird [ME *girten*, alter. of *girden* to gird]

[1]girth /guhth/ *n* **1** a strap that passes under the body of a horse or other animal to fasten esp a saddle on its back **2** a measurement of thickness round a body [ME, fr ON *gjörth*; akin to OE *gyrdan* to gird]

[2]girth *vt* **1** to encircle **2** to bind or fasten with a girth

gismo /'gizmoh/ *n, pl* **gismos** a gizmo

gist /jist/ *n* *the* main point of a matter; *the* essence [AF, it lies, fr MF, fr *gesir* to lie, fr L *jacēre* – more at ADJACENT]

git /git/ *n, chiefly Br* a worthless, contemptible, or foolish person – slang [var of *get* (offspring, bastard), fr [1]*get*]

gittern /'gituhn/ *n* a medieval guitar [ME *giterne*, fr MF *guiterne*, modif of OSp *guitarra* guitar]

[1]give /giv/ *vb* **gave** /gayv/; **given** /'giv(ə)n/ *vt* **1** to make a present of ⟨~ *a doll to a child*⟩ **2a** to grant, bestow, or allot (by formal action) **b** to accord or yield to another ⟨~ *blood*⟩ ⟨~ *him her confidence*⟩ **3a** to administer as a sacrament or medicine **b** to commit to another as a trust or responsibility ⟨gave *her his coat to hold*⟩ **c** to convey or express to another ⟨~ *an order*⟩ ⟨~ *my regards to your family*⟩ **4a** to proffer, present (for another to use or act on) ⟨gave *his hand to the visitor*⟩ **b** to surrender (oneself) to a partner in sexual intercourse **5** to present to view or observation ⟨gave *a signal*⟩ ⟨gave *no sign of life*⟩ **6a** to present for, or provide by way of, entertainment ⟨~ *a party*⟩ **b** to present, perform, or deliver in public ⟨~ *a lecture*⟩ ⟨~ *a piano recital*⟩ **7** to propose as a toast ⟨*I* ~ *you the Queen*⟩ **8** to attribute, ascribe ⟨gave *all the glory to God*⟩ **9** to yield as a product or effect ⟨*cows* ~ *milk*⟩ ⟨*84 divided by 12* ~s *7*⟩ ⟨*she* gave *him two sons*⟩ **10** to make known; show ⟨*the thermometer* ~s *the temperature*⟩ **11** to yield possession of by way of exchange; pay **12** to make, execute, or deliver (e g by some bodily action) ⟨gave *him a push*⟩ ⟨*the ship* gave *a lurch*⟩ ⟨gave *a hollow laugh*⟩ **13a** to inflict as punishment ⟨gave *the boy a whipping*⟩ **b** to cause to undergo; impose ⟨~ *them a spelling test*⟩ ⟨~ *it a try*⟩ **14a** to award by formal verdict ⟨~ *judgment against the plaintiff*⟩ **b** to make a specified ruling on the status of (a player) ⟨*Bowles was* ~n *offside*⟩ **15a** to offer for consideration, acceptance, or use ⟨*don't* ~ *me that old line*⟩ **b** to agree to act in accordance with ⟨*I* ~ *you my word*⟩ ⟨~ *a legal undertaking*⟩ **16a** to cause to have or receive ⟨*mountains always* gave *him pleasure*⟩ **b** to cause to catch or contract ⟨*digging* ~s *me backache*⟩ **c** to cause (sby) (to think or wonder) ⟨*I was* given *to understand that he was ill*⟩ **17** to apply freely or fully; devote ⟨~ *one's time to the service of others*⟩ **18** to allow, concede ⟨*it's late, I* ~ *you that*⟩ **19** to care to the extent of ⟨*didn't* ~ *a hang*⟩ ~ *vi* **1** to make gifts **2** to yield or collapse in response to pressure ⟨*the fence* gave *under his weight*⟩ **3** to afford a view or passage; open ⟨*the door* ~s *directly upon the garden*⟩ **4** *of weather* to become mild **5** to impart information; talk – infml **6** to happen; GO ON 3 – slang ⟨*what* ~s?⟩ [ME *given*, of Scand origin; akin to OSw *giva* to give; akin to OE *giefan, gifan* to give, L *habēre* to have, hold] – **giver** *n* – **give a dog a bad name** to implant prejudice by slander – **give a good account of** to acquit (oneself) well – **give a miss** *chiefly Br* to avoid, bypass ⟨*language learners* give *Russian* a miss – *TES*⟩ – **give as good as one gets** to counterattack with equal vigour – **give birth to** **1** to bring forth as a mother **2** to be the cause or origin of – **give chase** to go in pursuit – **give ground** to withdraw before superior force; retreat – **give me** I prefer ⟨give me *London any day!*⟩ – **give or take** allowing for a specified imprecision ⟨*three hours,* give or take *a few minutes either way*⟩ – **give place** to yield by way of being superseded ⟨*valves* give place *to transistors*⟩ – **give someone a wide berth** to stay at a safe distance from sby – **give someone best** *Br* to acknowledge sby's superiority – **give someone/something his/her/its head** **1** to give sby or sthg greater freedom and responsibility **2** to allow (a horse) to gallop – **give someone rope** to give sby free scope – **give the lie to** to belie – **give way 1a** to retreat; GIVE GROUND **b** to yield the right of way ⟨gave way *to oncoming traffic*⟩ **2** to yield oneself without restraint or control ⟨give way *to tears*⟩ **3a** to yield (as if) to physical stress ⟨*the wind caused the roof to* give way⟩ **b** to yield to entreaty or insistence **4** GIVE PLACE

²give *n* the capacity or tendency to yield to pressure; resilience, elasticity ⟨*there's no* ~ *in this mattress*⟩ ⟨*there's no* ~ *in her political opinions*⟩

,give-and-'take *n* **1** the practice of making mutual concessions **2** the good-natured exchange of ideas or words

'give,away /-ə,way/ *n* **1** an unintentional revelation or betrayal **2** sthg given free or at a reduced price

give away *vt* **1** to make a present of **2** to hand over (a bride) to the bridegroom at a wedding **3a** to betray **b** to disclose, reveal – esp in **give the game/show away** **4** to be at a disadvantage in a sporting contest by (e g a weight or age) compared with an opponent ⟨giving away *4 years to the junior champion*⟩

give in *vt* to hand in; deliver ⟨gave in *the money he'd found*⟩ ~ *vi* to yield under insistence or entreaty

given /'giv(ə)n/ *adj* **1** prone, disposed ⟨~ *to swearing*⟩ **2** *of an official document* executed on the date specified **3a** fixed, specified ⟨*at a* ~ *time*⟩ **b** assumed as actual or hypothetical ⟨~ *that all men are equal before the law*⟩ [ME, fr pp of *given* to give] – **given** *n*

'given ,name *n, chiefly NAm* CHRISTIAN NAME

give off *vt* to emit ⟨gave off *an unpleasant smell*⟩

give out *vt* **1** to declare, publish ⟨giving out *that the doctor required a few days of complete rest* – Charles Dickens⟩ **2** to emit ⟨gave out *a constant hum*⟩ **3** to issue, distribute ⟨gave out *new uniforms*⟩ ~ *vi* to come to an end; fail ⟨*finally their patience* gave out *and they came to blows*⟩

give over *vt* **1** to set apart for a particular purpose or use **2** to deliver to sby's care ~ *vi* to bring an activity to an end ⟨*told him to* give over *and let me alone* – Brendan Behan⟩ – infml

give up *vt* **1** to surrender, esp as a prisoner ⟨*he* gave *himself* up⟩ **2** to desist from ⟨*refused to* give up *trying*⟩ **3a** to abandon (oneself) to a particular feeling, influence, or activity ⟨gave *himself* up *to despair*⟩ **b** to renounce ⟨*I must* give up *sugar*⟩ **4** to declare incurable or insoluble ⟨*the doctors* gave *her* up *for dead*⟩ **5** to stop having a relationship with ⟨*she's* given *me* up⟩ ~ *vi* to abandon an activity or course of action; *esp* to stop trying – **give up the ghost** to die

gizmo, gismo /'gizmoh/ *n, pl* **gizmos, gismos** *chiefly NAm* a gadget [origin unknown]

gizzard /'gizəd/ *n* **1** a muscular enlargement of the alimentary canal of birds that immediately follows the crop and has a tough horny lining for grinding food **2** a thickened part of the alimentary canal of some animals (e g an earthworm) similar in function to the crop of a bird [alter. of ME *giser*, fr ONF *guisier*, fr L *gigeria* (pl) giblets]

glabella /glə'belə/ *n, pl* **glabellae** /-li/ the smooth part of the forehead between the eyebrows [NL, fr L, fem of *glabellus* hairless, dim. of *glaber*] – **glabellar** *adj*

glabrous /'glabrəs/ *adj* smooth; *esp* having a surface without hairs or projections [L *glabr-, glaber* smooth, bald – more at GLAD] – **glabrousness** *n*

glacé /'glasay/ *adj* **1** made or finished so as to have a smooth glossy surface ⟨~ *silk*⟩ **2** coated with a glaze; candied ⟨~ *cherries*⟩ [F, fr pp of *glacer* to freeze, ice, glaze, fr L *glaciare*, fr *glacies* ice]

glacial /'glays(h)yəl/ *adj* **1a** extremely cold ⟨*a* ~ *wind*⟩ **b** devoid of warmth and cordiality ⟨*a* ~ *smile*⟩ **2a** of or produced by glaciers **b** of or being any of those parts of geological time when much of the earth was covered by glaciers **3** resembling ice in appearance, esp when frozen ⟨~ *acetic acid*⟩ [L *glacialis*, fr *glacies*] – **glacially** *adv*

glaciate /'glays(h)i,ayt/ *vt* **1** to freeze **2a** to cover with ice or a glacier **b** to subject to glacial action – **glaciation** /-'aysh(ə)n/ *n*

glacier /'glasi·ə, 'glay-/ *n* a large body of ice moving slowly down a slope or spreading outwards on a land surface ☞ GEOGRAPHY [F dial., fr MF dial., fr MF *glace* ice, fr L *glacies*; akin to L *gelu* frost – more at COLD]

glacio- *comb form* **1** glacier ⟨glacio*logy*⟩ **2** glacial and ⟨glacio*fluvial*⟩

glaciology /glasi'oləji, glay-/ *n* a science dealing with glacial action and effects [ISV *glacier* + *-o-* + *-logy*] – **glaciologist** *n*, **glaciologic** /-si·ə'lojik/, **glaciological** *adj*

glacis /'glasi, 'glasis, 'glay-/ *n, pl* **glacis** /-siz, -seez/ a slope with no cover for attackers that runs downwards from a fortification [F, fr *glacer* to freeze, slide]

¹glad /glad/ *adj* **-dd-** **1** expressing or experiencing pleasure, joy, or delight **2** very willing ⟨~ *to do it*⟩ **3** causing happiness and joy ⟨~ *tidings*⟩ [ME, shining, glad, fr OE *glæd*; akin to OHG *glat* shining, smooth, L *glaber* smooth, bald] – **gladden** *vt*, **gladly** *adv*, **gladness** *n*

²glad *n* a gladiolus – infml

glade /glayd/ *n* an open space within a wood or forest [perh fr ¹*glad*]

glad eye *n* an amorous or sexually inviting look ⟨*he gave her the* ~⟩ – infml

glad hand *n* a warm welcome or greeting often prompted by ulterior motives – infml – **glad hand** *vt*

gladiator /'gladi,aytə/ *n* **1** sby trained to fight in the arena for the entertainment of ancient Romans **2** sby engaging in a public fight or controversy [L, fr *gladius* sword, of Celt origin; akin to W *cleddyf* sword; akin to L *clades* destruction, Gk *klados* sprout, branch – more at ¹HALT] – **gladiatorial** /,gladi·ə'tawri·əl/ *adj*

gladiolus /gladi'ohləs/ *n, pl* **gladioli** /-lie/ any of a genus of (African) plants of the iris family with spikes of brilliantly coloured irregular flowers [NL, genus name, fr L, gladiolus, fr dim. of *gladius*]

'glad ,rags *n pl* smart clothes – infml

gladsome /'glads(ə)m/ *adj* giving or showing joy; cheerful – chiefly poetic – **gladsomely** *adv*, **gladsomeness** *n*

Gladstone bag /'gladstən/ *n* a travelling bag with flexible sides on a rigid frame that opens flat into 2 equal compartments [W E Gladstone †1898 E statesman]

glaikit /ˈglaykit/ *adj, chiefly Scot* foolish, giddy [ME (Sc)]

glair, glaire /gleə/ *n* **1** (a sizing liquid made from) egg white **2** any substance similar to an egg white [ME *gleyre* egg white, fr MF *glaire,* modif of (assumed) VL *claria,* fr L *clarus* clear – more at CLEAR]

glaive /glayv/ *n, archaic* a sword [ME, fr MF, javelin, sword, modif of L *gladius* sword]

glamor·ize, -ise *also* **glamour·ize, -ise** /ˈglaməˌriez/ *vt* **1** to make glamorous ⟨~ *the living room*⟩ **2** to romanticize ⟨*the novel* ~s *war*⟩

glamour, *NAm also* **glamor** /ˈglamə/ *n* a romantic, exciting, and often illusory attractiveness; *esp* alluring or fascinating personal attraction [Sc *glamour,* alter. of E *grammar;* fr the popular association of erudition with occult practices] – **glamorous** *also* **glamourous** *adj,* **glamorously** *also* **glamourously** *adv*

[1]**glance** /glahns/ *vi* **1** to strike a surface obliquely so as to go off at an angle ⟨*the bullet* ~d *off the wall*⟩ – often + *off* **2a** to flash or gleam with intermittent rays of reflected light ⟨*brooks* glancing *in the sun*⟩ **b** to make sudden quick movements ⟨*dragonflies* glancing *over the pond*⟩ **3** to touch on a subject or refer to it briefly or indirectly ⟨*the work* ~s *at the customs of ancient cultures*⟩ **4a** *of the eyes* to move swiftly from one thing to another **b** to take a quick look at sthg ⟨~d *at his watch*⟩ ~ *vt* **1a** to cause to glance off a surface by throwing or shooting **b** to play a glance in cricket at (a ball) or at the bowling of (a bowler) **2** *archaic* to catch a glimpse of [ME *glencen, glenchen,* perh alter. of *glenten* to move quickly – more at GLINT]

[2]**glance** *n* **1** a quick intermittent flash or gleam **2** a deflected impact or blow **3a** a swift movement of the eyes **b** a quick or cursory look **4** an allusion **5** a stroke in cricket that barely deflects the ball from its line of flight – **at first glance** on first consideration ⟨at first glance *the subject seems harmless enough*⟩

[3]**glance** *n* any of several usu dark mineral sulphides with a metallic lustre [G *glanz* lustre, glance; akin to OHG *glanz* bright – more at GLINT]

glancing /ˈglahnsing/ *adj* having a slanting direction ⟨*a* ~ *blow*⟩ – **glancingly** *adv*

[1]**gland** /gland/ *n* **1** (an animal structure that does not secrete but resembles) an organ that selectively removes materials from the blood, alters them, and secretes them esp for further use in the body or for elimination **2** any of various secreting organs (e g a nectary) of plants [F *glande,* fr OF, glandular swelling on the neck, gland, modif of L *gland-, glans* acorn; akin to Gk *balanos* acorn] – **glandless** *adj*

[2]**gland** *n* **1** a device for preventing leakage of fluid past a joint in machinery **2** the movable part of a stuffing box by which the packing is compressed [origin unknown]

glanders /ˈglandəz/ *n pl but sing or pl in constr* a contagious bacterial disease, esp of horses, in which mucus is discharged profusely from the nostrils [MF *glandre* glandular swelling on the neck, fr L *glandulae,* fr pl of *glandula,* dim. of *gland-, glans*] – **glandered** /-dəd/ *adj*

glandular /ˈglandyoolə/ *adj* of, involving, or being (the cells or products of) glands – **glandularly** *adv*

ˌ**glandular ˈfever** *n* INFECTIOUS MONONUCLEOSIS

glans /glanz/ *n, pl* **glandes** /ˈglanˌdeez/ a conical vascular part at the end of the penis or clitoris [L *gland-, glans,* lit., acorn]

[1]**glare** /gleə/ *vi* **1** to shine with a harsh uncomfortably brilliant light **2** to stare angrily or fiercely ~ *vt* to express (e g hostility) by staring fiercely [ME *glaren;* akin to OE *glæs* glass]

[2]**glare** *n* **1a** a harsh uncomfortably bright light; *specif* painfully bright sunlight **b** garishness **2** an angry or fierce stare

glaring /ˈgleəring/ *adj* painfully and obtrusively evident ⟨*a* ~ *error*⟩ – **glaringly** *adv,* **glaringness** *n*

[1]**glass** /glahs/ *n* **1a** a hard brittle usu transparent or translucent inorganic substance formed by fusing a mixture of silica sand, metallic oxides, and other ingredients **b** a substance resembling glass, esp in hardness and transparency **c** a substance (e g pumice) produced by the quick cooling of molten rock from the earth's core **2a** sthg made of glass: e g **(1)** a glass drinking vessel (e g a tumbler or wineglass) **(2)** a mirror; LOOKING GLASS **(3)** a barometer **b(1)** an optical instrument (e g a magnifying glass) for viewing objects not readily seen **(2)** *pl* a pair of lenses together with a frame to hold them in place for correcting defects of vision or protecting the eyes **3** the quantity held by a glass container or drinking vessel **4** glassware [ME *glas,* fr OE *glæs;* akin to OE *geolu* yellow – more at YELLOW] – **glassful** *n,* **glassless** *adj*

[2]**glass** *vt* to enclose, case, or wall with glass ⟨*the sun porch was* ~ed *in*⟩

ˈ**glass,blowing** /-ˌbloh·ing/ *n* the art of shaping a mass of semimolten glass by blowing air into it through a tube – **glassblower** *n*

ˈ**glass ˌcloth** *n* a usu linen cloth for drying glasses; *broadly* TEA TOWEL

ˌ**glass ˈfibre** *n* fibreglass

ˈ**glass,house** /-ˌhows/ *n, chiefly Br* **1** a greenhouse **2** a military prison – slang

glassine /ˈglaseen/ *n* a transparent paper highly resistant to air and grease [[1]*glass* + *-ine*]

ˈ**glass,paper** /-ˌpaypə/ *n* paper to which a thin layer of powdered glass has been glued for use as an abrasive – **glasspaper** *vt*

ˈ**glass ˌsnake** *n* (an Old World lizard similar to) a limbless lizard of the S USA with a fragile tail

ˈ**glass,ware** /-ˌweə/ *n* articles made of glass

ˌ**glass ˈwool** *n* glass fibres in a mass resembling wool used esp for thermal insulation

ˈ**glass,works** /-ˌwuhks/ *n, pl* **glassworks** a place where glass is made – often pl with sing. meaning

ˈ**glass,wort** /-ˌwuht/ *n* any of a genus of salt-marsh plants with woody jointed succulent stems and leaves reduced to fleshy sheaths [fr its former use in the manufacture of glass]

glassy /ˈglahsi/ *adj* dull, lifeless ⟨~ *eyes*⟩ [[1]GLASS + [1]-Y] – **glassily** *adv,* **glassiness** *n*

Glaswegian /glazˈweejən, glahz-/ *n or adj* (a native or inhabitant) of Glasgow [irreg fr *Glasgow,* city in Scotland]

Glauber's salt /ˈglowbəz/ *n* hydrated sodium sulphate, esp when used as a purgative – sometimes pl with sing. meaning [Johann *Glauber* †1668 G chemist]

glaucoma /glawˈkohmə/ *n* increased pressure

within the eyeball (leading to damage to the retina and gradual loss of vision) [L, cataract, fr Gk *glaukōma*, fr *glaukos*]

glaucous /'glawkəs/ *adj* **1a** pale yellowy green **b** *esp of plants or plant parts* of a dull blue or bluish-green colour **2** *of a plant or fruit* having a powdery or waxy coating giving a frosted appearance [L *glaucus* gleaming, grey, fr Gk *glaukos*] – **glaucousness** *n*

glaur /glaw/ *n, chiefly Scot* mud, mire [origin unknown]

[1]**glaze** /glayz/ *vt* **1** to provide or fit with glass **2** to coat (as if) with a glaze ⟨~ *apple tarts*⟩ **3** to give a smooth glossy surface to ~ *vi* **1** to become glazed or glassy ⟨*his eyes* ~d *over*⟩ **2** to form a glaze [ME *glasen*, fr *glas* glass] – **glazer** *n*

[2]**glaze** *n* **1a** a liquid preparation that gives a glossy coating to food **b** a mixture predominantly of oxides (e g silica and alumina) applied to the surface of ceramic wares as decoration and to make them nonporous **c** a transparent or translucent colour applied to a printed surface to modify its tone **d** a smooth glossy or lustrous surface or finish **2** a glassy film (e g of ice)

glazier /'glayzi·ə, -zyə/ *n* one who fits glass, esp into windows, as an occupation – **glaziery** /-ri/ *n*

[1]**gleam** /gleem/ *n* **1a** a transient appearance of subdued or partly obscured light **b** a glint ⟨*a* ~ *of anticipation in his eyes*⟩ **2** a brief or faint appearance or occurrence ⟨*a* ~ *of hope*⟩ [ME *gleem*, fr OE *glǣm*; akin to OE *geolu* yellow – more at YELLOW] – **gleamy** *adj*

[2]**gleam** *vi* **1** to shine with subdued steady light or moderate brightness **2** to appear briefly or faintly

glean /gleen/ *vi* **1** to gather produce, esp grain, left by reapers **2** to gather material (e g information) bit by bit ~ *vt* **1a** to pick up (e g grain) after a reaper **b** to strip (e g a field) by gleaning **2a** to gather (e g information) bit by bit **b** to pick over in search of relevant material [ME *glenen*, fr MF *glener*, fr LL *glennare*; akin to MIr di*gliunn* I glean, OHG *glanz* bright – more at GLINT] – **gleanable** *adj*, **gleaner** *n*

gleanings /'gleenings/ *n pl* things acquired by gleaning

glebe /gleeb/ *n* **1** land belonging to an ecclesiastical benefice **2** *archaic* (a plot of cultivated) land [L *gleba* clod, land – more at [1]CLIP]

glee /glee/ *n* **1** a feeling of merry high-spirited joy or delight **2** an unaccompanied song for 3 or more usu male solo voices [ME, fr OE *glēo* entertainment, music; akin to ON *glý* joy, Gk *chleuē* joke] – **gleeful** *adj*, **gleefully** *adv*, **gleefulness** *n*

'**glee ,club** *n* a chorus, esp in the USA, organized for singing usu short secular pieces

glen /glen/ *n* a secluded narrow valley [ME (Sc), valley, fr (assumed) ScGael *glenn*; akin to MIr *glend* valley]

glengarry /glen'gari/ *n, often cap* a straight-sided woollen cap coming to a rounded point over the brow and having 2 short ribbons hanging down behind, worn esp as part of Highland military uniform [*Glengarry*, valley in Scotland]

gley /glay/ *n* a sticky clay formed under the surface of some waterlogged soils [Russ *gleĭ* clay; akin to OE *clǣg* clay – more at CLAY]

glial /'glie·əl, 'glee·əl/ *adj* of or being neuroglia [NL *glia* neuroglia, fr MGk, glue]

glib /glib/ *adj* **-bb- 1** showing little forethought or preparation; lacking depth and substance ⟨~ *solutions to problems*⟩ **2** marked by (superficial or dishonest) ease and fluency in speaking or writing [prob modif of LG *glibberig* slippery] – **glibly** *adv*, **glibness** *n*

[1]**glide** /glied/ *vi* **1** to move noiselessly in a smooth, continuous, and effortless manner **2** to pass gradually and imperceptibly **3a** *of an aircraft* to fly without the use of engines **b** to fly in a glider ~ *vt* to cause to glide [ME *gliden*, fr OE *glīdan*; akin to OHG *glītan* to glide]

[2]**glide** *n* **1** the act or action of gliding **2a** a portamento **b** a transitional sound produced by the vocal organs passing from one articulatory position to another

'**glide ,path** *n* the path of descent of an aircraft in landing, esp as marked by ground radar or radio

glider /'gliedə/ *n* an aircraft similar to an aeroplane but without an engine ['GLIDE + [2]-ER]

[1]**glimmer** /'glimə/ *vi* **1** to shine faintly or unsteadily **2** to appear indistinctly with a faintly luminous quality [ME *glimeren*; akin to OE *glǣm* gleam]

[2]**glimmer** *n* **1** a feeble or unsteady light **2a** a dim perception or faint idea **b** a small sign or amount ⟨*a* ~ *of intelligence*⟩

glimmering /'glimәring/ *n* a glimmer

[1]**glimpse** /glimps/ *vt* to get a brief look at [ME *glimsen*; akin to MHG *glimsen* to glimmer, OE *glǣm* gleam]

[2]**glimpse** *n* a brief fleeting view or look

[1]**glint** /glint/ *vi* **1** *of rays of light* to strike a reflecting surface obliquely and dart out at an angle **2** to shine with tiny bright flashes; sparkle or glitter, esp by reflection ~ *vt* to cause to glint [ME *glinten* to dart obliquely, glint, alter. of *glenten*, of Scand origin; akin to Sw dial. *glänta* to clear up; akin to OHG *glanz* bright, OE *geolu* yellow – more at YELLOW]

[2]**glint** *n* **1** a tiny bright flash of light; a sparkle **2** a brief or faint manifestation ⟨*detected a* ~ *of recognition in her expression*⟩

[1]**glissade** /gli'sahd, -'sayd/ *vi* to slide usu in a standing or squatting position down a slope, esp one that is snow-covered [F, n, slide, glissade, fr *glisser* to slide, fr OF *glicier*, alter. of *glier*, of Gmc origin; akin to OHG *glītan* to glide]

[2]**glissade** *n* **1** the action of glissading **2** a gliding step in ballet

glissando /gli'sandoh/ *n, pl* **glissandi** /-di/, **glissandos** a rapid sliding up or down the musical scale [prob modif of F *glissade*]

glisten /'glis(ə)n/ *vi* to shine, usu by reflection, with a sparkling radiance or with the lustre of a wet or oiled surface [ME *glistnen*, fr OE *glisnian*; akin to OE *glisian* to glitter, *geolu* yellow – more at YELLOW]

glister /'glistə/ *vi* to glitter – chiefly poetic [ME *glistren*; akin to OE *glisian*] – **glister** *n*

glitch /glich/ *n* a false or misleading electronic signal [prob fr G *glitschen* to slide, slip; akin to OHG *glītan* to glide – more at GLIDE]

[1]**glitter** /'glitə/ *vi* **1a** to shine by reflection with a brilliant or metallic lustre ⟨~ing *sequins*⟩ **b** to shine with a hard cold glassy brilliance ⟨~ing *eyes*⟩ **2** to be brilliantly attractive in a superficial or deceptive way ⟨*the chance of success* ~ed *before them*⟩ [ME *gliteren*, fr ON *glitra*; akin to OE *geolu* yellow] – **glitteringly** *adv*

[2]**glitter** *n* **1** sparkling brilliance, showiness, or attrac-

tiveness 2 small glittering particles used for ornamentation – **glittery** *adj*

gloaming /'glohming/ *n* *the* twilight, dusk [ME (Sc) *gloming*, fr OE *glōmung*, fr *glōm* twilight; akin to OE *glōwan* to glow]

[1]**gloat** /gloht/ *vi* to observe or think about sthg with great and often malicious satisfaction, gratification, or relish [prob of Scand origin; akin to ON *glotta* to grin scornfully; akin to OE *geolu* yellow] – **gloater** *n*, **gloatingly** *adv*

[2]**gloat** *n* a gloating feeling

glob /glob/ *n* a blob, dollop – chiefly infml [perh blend of *globe* and *blob*]

global /'glohbl/ *adj* 1 spherical 2 of or involving the entire world 3 general, comprehensive – **globally** *adv*

global·ize, -ise /'glohbl,iez/ *vt* to make worldwide in scope or application – **globalization** /-'zaysh(ə)n/ *n*

,global 'village *n* the world viewed as a totally integrated system of which all parts are interdependent

globe /glohb/ *n* sthg spherical or rounded: e g **a** a spherical representation of the earth, a heavenly body, or the heavens **b** EARTH 4 [MF, fr L *globus* – more at [1]CLIP]

globe artichoke *n* ARTICHOKE 1b

'globe,fish /-,fish/ *n* any of a family of (tropical) poisonous marine fishes which can distend themselves to a globular form

'globe,flower /-,flowə/ *n* any of a genus of plants of the buttercup family with spherical yellow flowers

'globe-,trotter *n* one who travels widely – **globe-trotting** *n or adj*

globin /'glohbin/ *n* a colourless protein obtained by removal of haem from esp haemoglobin [ISV, back-formation fr *haemoglobin*]

globular /'globyoolə/ *adj* 1 globe- or globule-shaped ⟨~ *proteins*⟩ 2 having or consisting of globules [partly fr L *glob*us + E *-ular*; partly fr L *globul*us + E *-ar*] – **globularly** *adv*, **globularness** *n*

globule /'globyoohl/ *n* a tiny globe or ball (e g of liquid or melted solid) [F, fr L *globulus*, dim. of *globus*]

globulin /'globyoolin/ *n* any of a class of widely occurring proteins that are soluble in dilute salt solutions

glockenspiel /'glokən,speel, -,shpeel/ *n* a percussion instrument consisting of a series of graduated metal bars played with 2 hammers [G, fr *glocke* bell + *spiel* play]

glomerule /'glomə,roohl/ *n* a compact clustered flower head like that of a composite plant [NL *glomerulus*]

glomerulus /glo'meryooləs/ *n, pl* **glomeruli** /-lie/ a small coiled or intertwined mass; *specif* the compact mass of capillaries at the end of each nephron of the kidneys of vertebrates [NL, glomerulus, glomerule, dim. of L *glomer-, glomus* ball] – **glomerular** *adj*

[1]**gloom** /gloohm/ *vi* 1 to mope 2 to loom up dimly or sombrely ⟨*the castle* ~ed *before them*⟩ ~ *vt* to make dark, murky, or sombre [ME *gloumen*; akin to OE *geolu* yellow – more at YELLOW]

[2]**gloom** *n* 1 partial or total darkness **2a** lowness of spirits **b** an atmosphere of despondency ⟨*a* ~ *fell over the household*⟩

gloomy /'gloohmi/ *adj* **1a** partially or totally dark; *esp* dismally and depressingly dark ⟨~ *weather*⟩ **b** low in spirits 2 causing gloom ⟨*a* ~ *story*⟩ – **gloomily** *adv*, **gloominess** *n*

Gloria /'glawri·ə, -riah/ *n* 1 GLORIA IN EXCELSIS 2 GLORIA PATRI [L, glory]

Gloria in Excelsis /,glawri·ə in ek'selsis, -'chel-/ *n* a Christian liturgical hymn modelled on the Psalms [LL, glory (be to God) on high; fr its opening words]

,Gloria 'Patri /'patri/ *n* a 2-verse doxology to the Trinity [LL, glory (be) to the Father; fr its opening words]

glorify /'glawri,fie/ *vt* **1a** to make glorious by bestowing honour, praise, or admiration **b** to elevate to celestial glory 2 to shed radiance or splendour on 3 to cause to appear better, more appealing, or more important than in reality 4 to give glory to (e g in worship) – **glorifier** *n*, **glorification** /-fi'kaysh(ə)n/ *n*

glorious /'glawri·əs/ *adj* **1a** possessing or deserving glory **b** conferring glory 2 marked by great beauty or splendour 3 delightful, wonderful ⟨*had a* ~ *weekend*⟩ – **gloriously** *adv*, **gloriousness** *n*

[1]**glory** /'glawri/ *n* **1a** (sthg that secures) praise or renown **b** worshipful praise, honour, and thanksgiving ⟨*giving* ~ *to God*⟩ 2 a (most) commendable asset ⟨*her hair was her crowning* ~⟩ **3a** (sthg marked by) resplendence or magnificence ⟨*the* ~ *that was Greece and the grandeur that was Rome* – E A Poe⟩ **b** the splendour, blessedness, and happiness of heaven; *broadly* eternity 4 a state of great gratification or exaltation 5 a ring or spot of light: e g **a** an aureole **b** CORONA 2a, b [ME *glorie*, fr MF & L; MF *glorie, gloire*, fr L *gloria*]

[2]**glory** *vi* to rejoice proudly ⟨~ing *in their youth and vigour*⟩

'glory ,box *n, Austr & NZ* BOTTOM DRAWER

[1]**gloss** /glos/ *n* 1 (sthg that gives) surface lustre or brightness 2 a deceptively attractive outer appearance 3 paint to which varnish has been added to give a gloss finish [prob of Scand origin; akin to Icel *glossa* to glow; akin to OE *geolu* yellow]

[2]**gloss** *n* **1a** a brief explanation (e g in the margin of a text) of a difficult word or expression **b** a false interpretation (e g of a text) **2a** a glossary **b** an interlinear translation **c** a continuous commentary accompanying a text [ME *glose*, fr OF, fr L *glossa* unusual word requiring explanation, fr Gk *glōssa, glōtta* tongue, language, unusual word; akin to Gk *glōchis* projecting point]

[3]**gloss** *vt* to supply glosses for

gloss- /glos-/, **glosso-** *comb form* 1 tongue ⟨gloss*al*⟩ ⟨gloss*itis*⟩; tongue and ⟨glosso*pharyngeal*⟩ 2 language ⟨glosso*logy*⟩ [L, fr Gk *glōss-, glōsso-*, fr *glōssa*]

glossa /'glosə/ *n, pl* **glossae** /-si/ *also* **glossas** a (structure like a) tongue, esp in (the labium of) an insect [NL, fr Gk *glōssa*]

glossary /'glosəri/ *n* a list of terms (e g those used in a particular text or in a specialized field), usu with their meanings [ME, fr ML *glossarium*, fr L *glossa*]

glossolalia /,glosoh'layli·ə, -lyə/ *n* the practice of ecstatic speaking, esp in evangelical Christianity; GIFT OF TONGUES [NL, fr Gk *gloss-* + *lalia* chatter, fr *lalein* to chatter, talk]

gloss over *vt* 1 to make appear right and acceptable 2 to veil or hide by treating rapidly or superficially

⟨glossing over *humiliations, gilding small moments of glory – TLS*⟩ [[1]*gloss*]

[1]**glossy** /ˈglosi/ *adj* **1** having a surface lustre or brightness **2** attractive in an artificially opulent, sophisticated, or smoothly captivating manner ⟨*a ~ musical*⟩ – **glossily** *adv*, **glossiness** *n*

[2]**glossy** *n, chiefly Br* a magazine expensively produced on glossy paper and often having a fashionable or sophisticated content

-glot /-ˌglot/ *comb form* (→ *n*) person who speaks a (specified) number of languages ⟨*a mono*glot⟩ [Gk *-glōttos, -glōssos*, fr *glōtta, glōssa* language, tongue]

glott- /glot-/, **glotto-** *comb form* language ⟨glotto*chronology*⟩ [Gk *glōtt-, glōtto-*, fr *glōtta, glōssa*]

ˌ**glottal ˈstop** /ˈglotl/ *n* a speech sound produced by sudden closure of the glottis

glottis /ˈglotis/ *n, pl* **glottises, glottides** /-tiˌdeez/ (the structures surrounding) the elongated space between the vocal cords – compare EPIGLOTTIS [Gk *glōttid-, glōttis*, fr *glōtta* tongue – more at [2]GLOSS] – **glottal** *adj*

[1]**glove** /gluv/ *n* **1** a covering for the hand having separate sections for each of the fingers and the thumb and often extending part way up the arm **2** BOXING GLOVE [ME, fr OE *glōf*; akin to ON *glōfi* glove]

[2]**glove** *vt* to cover (as if) with a glove

ˈ**glove ˌbox** *n, chiefly Br* GLOVE COMPARTMENT

ˈ**glove comˌpartment** *n* a small storage compartment in the dashboard of a motor vehicle

[1]**glow** /gloh/ *vi* **1** to shine (as if) with an intense heat **2a** to experience a sensation (as if) of heat; show a ruddy colour (as if) from being too warm ⟨~ing *with rage*⟩ **b** to show satisfaction or elation ⟨~ *with pride*⟩ [ME *glowen*, fr OE *glōwan*; akin to OE *geolu* yellow – more at YELLOW] – **glowingly** *adv*

[2]**glow** *n* **1** brightness or warmth of colour ⟨*the ~ of his cheeks*⟩ **2a** warmth of feeling or emotion **b** a sensation of warmth ⟨*the drug produces a sustained ~*⟩ **3a** the state of glowing with heat and light **b** light (as if) from sthg burning without flames or smoke

glower /ˈglowə/ *vi* to look or stare with sullen annoyance or anger [ME (Sc) *glowren*, perh of Scand origin; akin to Norw dial. *glȳra* to look askance, Icel *glossa* to glow – more at [1]GLOSS] – **glower** *n*

ˈ**glowˌworm** /-ˌwuhm/ *n* a luminescent wingless insect; *esp* a larva or wingless female of a firefly that emits light from the abdomen

gloxinia /glokˈsinyə, -ni·ə/ *n* any of a genus of Brazilian tuberous plants including one cultivated for its showy bell-shaped flowers [NL, genus name, fr B P *Gloxin* 18th-c G botanist]

gluc- /gloohk-/, **gluco-** *comb form* **1** glucose ⟨gluco*neogenesis*⟩ **2** chemically related to or containing a glucose molecule in the molecular structure ⟨gluc*uronic acid*⟩ [ISV]

glucagon /ˈgloohkəˌgon, -gən/ *n* a protein hormone produced esp by the pancreatic islets of Langerhans that promotes an increase in the sugar content of the blood by increasing the rate of breakdown of glycogen in the liver [*gluc-* + *-agon* (perh fr Gk *agōn*, prp of *agein* to lead, drive) – more at AGENT]

glucocorticoid /ˌgloohkohˈkawtiˌkoyd/ *n* any of several corticosteroids (e g cortisol) that affect metabolic processes and are used in medicine (e g in treating rheumatoid arthritis) because they suppress inflammation and inhibit the activity of the immune system

gluconeogenesis /ˌgloohkəˌnee·əˈjenəsis/ *n* formation of glucose within the (liver of the) animal body from substances (e g fats) other than carbohydrates [NL] – **gluconeogenic** /-ˈjenik/ *adj*

glucose /ˈgloohkohz, -kohs/ *n* a sweet (dextrorotatory form of a) sugar that occurs widely in nature and is the usual form in which carbohydrate is assimilated by animals [F, modif of Gk *gleukos* must, sweet wine; akin to Gk *glykys* sweet]

glucoside /ˈgloohkəˌsied, -koh-/ *n* a glycoside (that yields glucose on hydrolysis) – **glucosidic** /-ˈsidik/ *adj*, **glucosidically** *adv*

[1]**glue** /glooh/ *n* **1** any of various strong adhesives; *esp* a gelatinous protein substance that forms a strongly adhesive solution and is obtained by boiling hides, bones, etc **2** a solution of glue used for sticking things together [ME *glu*, fr MF, fr LL *glut-, glus* –more at CLAY] – **gluey** *adj*, **gluily** *adv*

[2]**glue** *vt* **gluing** *also* **glueing** **1** to cause to stick tightly with glue ⟨~ *the wings onto the model aeroplane*⟩ **2** to fix (e g the eyes) on an object steadily or with deep concentration ⟨*kept her eyes* ~d *to the TV*⟩

ˈ**glue-ˌsniffing** *n* the (habitual) inhalation of the vapour of various glues to produce intoxication – **glue-sniffer** *n*

glum /glum/ *adj* **-mm- 1** broodingly morose **2** dreary, gloomy [prob akin to ME *gloumen* to gloom] – **glumly** *adv*, **glumness** *n*

glume /gloohm/ *n* a chaffy bract, specif in the spikelet of grasses [NL *gluma*, fr L, hull, husk; akin to L *glubere* to peel – more at [2]CLEAVE] – **glumaceous** /-ˈmayshəs/ *adj*

[1]**glut** /glut/ *vt* **-tt- 1** to fill, esp with food, to beyond capacity **2** to flood (the market) with goods so that supply exceeds demand [ME *glouten, glotten*, prob fr MF *glotir, gloutir* to swallow, fr L *gluttire* – more at GLUTTON]

[2]**glut** *n* an excessive supply (e g of a harvested crop) which exceeds market demand

glutamate /ˈgloohtəmayt/ *n* a salt or ester of glutamic acid

gluˌtamic ˈacid /ˈgloohˈtamik/ *n* an acidic amino acid found in most proteins [ISV *glut*en + *am*ino + *-ic*]

glutamine /ˈgloohtəmeen, -min/ *n* an amino acid that is a chemical base and is found in nearly all proteins [ISV *glut*en + *amine*]

glutaraldehyde /ˌgloohtəˈraldihied/ *n* a compound containing 2 aldehyde groups which is used esp in leather tanning and fixation of biological tissues for microscopy [*glutar*ic acid (a crystalline acid) + *aldehyde*]

glutathione /ˌgloohtəˈthie·ohn/ *n* a sulphur-containing peptide important in biological chemical reactions involving an oxidation or a reduction [ISV *gluta-* (fr *glutamic acid*) + *thi-* + *-one*]

gluten /ˈgloohtin/ *n* an elastic protein substance, esp of wheat flour, that gives cohesiveness to dough [L *glutin-, gluten* glue; akin to LL *glut-, glus* glue – more at CLAY] – **glutenous** *adj*

gluteus /ˈgloohti·əs, gloohˈtee·əs/ *n, pl* **glutei** /ˈgloohtiˌie, gloohˈteeˌie/ any of the large muscles of the buttocks [NL *glutaeus, gluteus*, fr Gk *gloutos* buttock – more at CLOUD] – **gluteal** *adj*

glutinous /ˈgloohtinəs/ *adj* (thick and) sticky;

gummy [MF or L; MF *glutineux*, fr L *glutinosus*, fr *glutin-*, *gluten*] – **glutinously** *adv*, **glutinousness** *n*

glutton /'glut(ə)n/ *n* **1a** one given habitually to greedy and voracious eating and drinking **b** one who has a great capacity for accepting or enduring sthg ⟨*he's a ~ for punishment*⟩ **2** the wolverine [ME *glotoun*, fr OF *gloton*, fr L *glutton-*, *glutto*; akin to L *gluttire* to swallow, *gula* throat, OE *ceole*] – **gluttonous** *adj*, **gluttonousness** *n*

gluttony /'glut(ə)n·i/ *n* excess in eating or drinking

glyc-, **glyco-** *comb form* sugar; *specif* glucose ⟨gly*caemia*⟩ [ISV, fr Gk *glyk-* sweet, fr *glykys*]

glycan /'gliekan/ *n* a polysaccharide

glycer-, **glycero-** *comb form* related to glycerol ⟨glycer*aldehyde*⟩ [ISV, fr *glycerin*]

glyceraldehyde /,glisə'raldihied/ *n* a sweet compound formed as an intermediate in carbohydrate metabolism

glyceride /'glisəried/ *n* an ester of glycerol, esp with fatty acids – **glyceridic** /-'ridik/ *adj*

glycerin /'glisərin/, **glycerine** /'glisəreen, --'-/ *n* glycerol [F *glycérine*, fr Gk *glykeros* sweet; akin to Gk *glykys* sweet]

glycerol /'glisərol/ *n* a sweet syrupy alcohol usu obtained from fats and used esp as a solvent and plasticizer [*glycer*in + *-ol*]

glycine /'glieseen, -'-/ *n* a sweet amino acid found in most proteins

glycogen /'gliekohjen/ *n* a polysaccharide that is the chief storage carbohydrate of animals

glycogenesis /,gliekoh'jenəsis/ *n* the formation of (sugar from) glycogen [NL] – **glycogenetic** /-jə'netik/ *adj*

glycol /'gliekol/ *n* ETHYLENE GLYCOL [ISV *glyc-* + *-ol*]

glycolysis /glie'koləsis/ *n* the enzymatic breakdown of a carbohydrate with the production of energy for storage in the cell [NL] – **glycolytic** /-kə'litik/ *adj* **glycolytically** *adv*

glycopeptide /,gliekoh'peptied/ *n* a glycoprotein

glycoprotein /-'prohteen/ *n* a protein combined with 1 or more carbohydrate groups

glycoside /'gliekə,sied, -koh-/ *n* any of numerous sugar derivatives in which a nonsugar group is attached by an oxygen or nitrogen atom and that on hydrolysis yield a sugar – **glycosidic** /-'sidik/ *adj*, **glycosidically** *adv*

glycosuria /,gliekoh'syooəri·ə/ *n* the presence of abnormal amounts of sugar in the urine [NL] – **glycosuric** /-rik/ *adj*

glyph /glif/ *n* a carved symbolic figure or character; *esp* a symbol (e g a curved arrow on a road sign) that conveys information without using words [Gk *glyphē* carved work, fr *glyphein* to carve – more at ²CLEAVE] – **glyphic** *adj*

glyptic /'gliptik/ *adj* of carving, esp on gems [prob fr F *glyptique*, fr Gk *glyptikē*, fr *glyphein*]

gnarled /nahld/ *adj* **1** full of or covered with knots or protuberances **2** crabbed in disposition, aspect, or character [prob alter. of *knurled*]

gnash /nash/ *vt* to strike or grind (esp the teeth) together [alter. of ME *gnasten*, prob of imit origin] – **gnash** *n*

gnat /nat/ *n* any of various small usu biting 2-winged flies [ME, fr OE *gnætt*; akin to OE *gnagan* to gnaw] – **gnatty** *adj*

gnath-, **gnatho-** *comb form* jaw ⟨gnath*ic*⟩ [NL, fr Gk *gnath-*, fr *gnathos*; akin to Gk *genys* jaw – more at CHIN]

-gnathous *comb form* (→ *adj*) having (such) a jaw ⟨*opistho*gnathous⟩ [NL *-gnathus*, fr Gk *gnathos*]

gnaw /naw/ *vt* **1a** to bite or chew on with the teeth; *esp* to wear away by persistent biting or nibbling ⟨*a dog ~ing a bone*⟩ **b** to make by gnawing ⟨*rats ~ed a hole*⟩ **2** to affect as if by continuous eating away; plague **3** to erode, corrode *~ vi* **1** to bite or nibble persistently **2** to destroy or reduce sthg (as if) by gnawing ⟨*waves ~ing away at the cliffs*⟩ [ME *gnawen*, fr OE *gnagan*; akin to OHG *gnagan* to gnaw, ON *gnaga*] – **gnawer** *n*

gneiss /nies/ *n* a metamorphic rock usu composed of light bands of feldspar and quartz and dark bands of mica or hornblende [G *gneis*, prob alter. of MHG *gneiste*, *ganeiste* spark, fr OHG *gneisto*] – **gneissic** /-,sik/ *adj*, **gneissoid** /-,soyd/ *adj*, **gneissose** /-sohs/ *adj*

gnocchi /'noki, gə'noki/ *n pl* small dumplings made from flour, semolina, potatoes, or choux pastry [It, pl of *gnocco*, alter. of *nocchio* knot in wood]

gnome /nohm/ *n* a dwarf of folklore who lives under the earth and guards treasure [F, fr NL *gnomus*] – **gnomish** *adj*

,Gnome of 'Zurich /'zyooərikh/ *n, pl* **Gnomes of Zurich** an international banker usu considered to have great power over the financial sector of national economies – infml; usu pl [*Zurich*, city in Switzerland famous for banking]

gnomic /'nohmik, 'nomik/ *adj* characterized by aphorism ⟨*~ poetry*⟩ [LL *gnomicus*, fr Gk *gnōmikos*, fr *gnōmē* maxim, fr *gignōskein* to know]

gnomon /'nohmon/ *n* an object that by the position or length of its shadow serves as an indicator of esp the hour of the day: e g **a** the shadow-producing part of a sundial **b** a column or shaft erected perpendicular to the horizon [L, fr Gk *gnōmōn* interpreter, pointer on a sundial, fr *gignōskein*] – **gnomonic** /noh'monik/ *adj*

-gnosis /-g'nohsis/ *comb form* (→ *n*), *pl* **-gnoses** /-,seez/ knowledge; recognition ⟨*pro*gnosis⟩ [L, fr Gk *gnōsis*]

gnosticism /'nosti,siz(ə)m/ *n, often cap* a religious outlook or system, esp of various cults of late pre-Christian and early Christian centuries, distinguished by the conviction that matter is evil and that emancipation comes through esoteric spiritual knowledge [LL *gnosticus*, fr Gk *gnōstikos* of knowledge, fr *gignōskein*] – **Gnostic** /'nostik/ *n*

gnu /nooh/ *n, pl* **gnus**, *esp collectively* **gnu** any of several large horned African antelopes with an oxlike head, a short mane, and a long tail [modif of Bushman *nqu*]

¹go /goh/ *vb* **went** /went/; **gone** /gon/ *vi* **1** to proceed on a course ⟨*~ slow*⟩ ⟨went *by train*⟩ ⟨went *to France*⟩ – compare STOP **2a** to move out of or away from a place; leave ⟨*I must ~*⟩ ⟨*the ferry ~es every hour*⟩ – sometimes used with a further verb to express purpose ⟨*I* went *to see them*⟩ ⟨*I'll ~ and look*⟩ **b** to make an expedition for a specified activity ⟨*~ shopping*⟩ ⟨*~ skydiving*⟩ **3a** to pass by means of a specified process or according to a specified procedure ⟨*your suggestion will ~ before the committee*⟩ **b(1)** to proceed in a thoughtless or reckless manner – used to intensify a complementary verb ⟨*don't ~ saying that*⟩ ⟨*why did she have to ~ and spoil everything?*⟩ ⟨*he's been* and gone *and* told *her*⟩

(2) to proceed to do sthg surprising – used with *and* to intensify a complementary verb ⟨*she* went *and won first prize*⟩ **c(1)** to extend ⟨*it's true as far as it* ~es⟩ ⟨*the field* ~es *as far as the stream*⟩ **(2)** to speak, proceed, or develop in a specified direction or up to a specified limit ⟨*you've* gone *too far*⟩ ⟨*don't let's* ~ *into details*⟩ **4** to travel on foot or by moving the feet **5** to be, esp habitually ⟨~ *bareheaded*⟩ ⟨~ *barefoot*⟩ **6a** to become lost, consumed, or spent ⟨*my pen's* gone⟩ ⟨*half their income* ~es *in rent*⟩ **b** to die **c** to elapse ⟨*only three weeks to* ~⟩ ⟨*the evening* went *pleasantly enough*⟩ **d** to be got rid of (e g by sale or removal) ⟨*these slums must* ~⟩ ⟨~ing *cheap*⟩ **e** to fail ⟨*his hearing started to* ~⟩ **f** to succumb; GIVE WAY ⟨*at last the dam* went⟩ **7a** to happen, progress – often + *on* ⟨*what's* ~ing *on*⟩ ⟨*how are things* ~ing*?*⟩ **b** to be in general or on an average ⟨*cheap, as yachts* ~⟩ **c** to pass or be granted by award, assignment, or lot ⟨*the prize* went *to a French girl*⟩ **d** to turn out (well) ⟨*worked hard to make the party* ~⟩ **8** to put or subject oneself ⟨went *to unnecessary expense*⟩ **9a** to begin an action, motion, or process ⟨*here* ~es⟩ ⟨*ready, steady,* ~*!*⟩ ⟨~ *to court to recover damages*⟩ **b** to maintain or perform an action or motion ⟨*his tongue* went *nineteen to the dozen*⟩ ⟨went *like this with her eyebrows*⟩ **c** to function in a proper or specified way ⟨*trying to get the motor to* ~⟩ ⟨*felt ill, but tried to keep* ~ing⟩ **d** to make a characteristic noise ⟨*the telephone* went⟩ **e** to perform a demonstrated action ⟨~ *like this with your left foot*⟩ **10a** to be known or identified as specified ⟨*now* ~es *by another name*⟩ **b(1)** to be in phrasing or content ⟨*as the saying* ~es⟩ ⟨*the story* ~es *that the expedition was a failure*⟩ **(2)** to be sung or played in a specified manner ⟨*the song* ~es *to the tune of 'Greensleeves'*⟩ **11a** to act or occur in accordance or harmony ⟨*a good rule to* ~ *by*⟩ **b** to contribute to a total or result ⟨*taxes that* ~ *for education*⟩ **12** to be about, intending, or destined – + *to* and an infinitive ⟨*is* ~ing *to leave town*⟩ ⟨*is it* ~ing *to rain?*⟩ **13a** to come or arrive at a specified state or condition ⟨~ *to sleep*⟩ ⟨~ *to waste*⟩ **b** to join a specified institution professionally or attend it habitually ⟨*to* ~ *on the stage*⟩ ⟨*does she* ~ *to school?*⟩ **c** to come to be; turn ⟨*the tyre* went *flat*⟩ ⟨*he* went *broke*⟩ – compare COME 3 **d(1)** to become voluntarily ⟨~ *bail for his friend*⟩ **(2)** to change to a specified system or tendency ⟨~ *supersonic*⟩ ⟨*the company* went *public*⟩ ⟨~ *comprehensive*⟩ **e** to continue to be; remain ⟨~ *hungry*⟩ ⟨~ *without sugar*⟩ ⟨*jobs* went *unfilled*⟩ **14** to be compatible *with*, harmonize ⟨*claret* ~es *with beef*⟩ **15a** to be capable of passing, extending, or being contained or inserted ⟨*it won't* ~ *round my waist*⟩ ⟨*3 into 2 won't* ~⟩ **b** to belong ⟨*these books* ~ *on the top shelf*⟩ **16a** to carry authority ⟨*what she said* went⟩ **b** to be acceptable, satisfactory, or adequate ⟨*anything* ~es *here*⟩ **c** to be the case; be valid ⟨*and that* ~es *for you too*⟩ **17** to empty the bladder or bowels ⟨*always* ~ *after breakfast*⟩ – euph ~ *vt* **1** to proceed along or according to ⟨~ *one's own way*⟩ **2** to traverse ⟨~ *ten miles*⟩ **3** to undertake by travelling ⟨~ *errands*⟩ **4** to emit (a sound) ⟨*the bell* ~es *ding dong*⟩ **5** to participate to the extent of ⟨~ *shares*⟩ ⟨~ *halves*⟩ **6** to perform, effect ⟨~ *the limit*⟩ **7** to change to; adopt ⟨*you* ~ *wheels or you go bust* – R A Keith⟩ **8** *Br* to say – nonstandard; used in direct speech ⟨*so she* ~es *'Don't you ever do that again!'*⟩ [ME *gon*, fr OE *gān*; akin to OHG *gān* to go, Gk *kichanein* to reach, attain] – **go about** to undertake; SET ABOUT – **go after** to seek, pursue – **go against 1** to act in opposition to; offend **2** to turn out unfavourably to – **go ahead 1** to begin **2** to continue, advance – **go all the way 1** to enter into complete agreement **2** to engage in actual sexual intercourse – **go along with 1** to occur as a natural accompaniment of **2** to agree with; support – **go ape** to run amok; lose control – **go at 1** to attack, assail **2** to undertake energetically – **go back on 1** to fail to keep (e g a promise) **2** to be disloyal to; betray – **go begging** to be available but in little demand – **go by the board** to be discarded – **go crook** *Aust & NZ* to lose one's temper – **go for 1** to serve or be accounted as ⟨*pigs that* go for *pork*⟩ ⟨*it all* went for *nothing*⟩ **2** to try to secure ⟨*he* went for *the biggest mango*⟩ **3a** to favour, accept ⟨*cannot* go for *your idea*⟩ **b** to have an interest in or liking for ⟨*she* went for *him in a big way*⟩ **4** to attack, assail ⟨went for *him when his back was turned*⟩ – **go for a burton** *Br* to get lost, broken, or killed – slang – **go great guns** to achieve great success – **go hang** to cease to be of interest or concern – **go into 1** to be contained in ⟨*5* goes into *60 12 times*⟩ **2** to investigate **3** to explain in depth ⟨*the book doesn't* go into *the moral aspects*⟩ – **go it 1** to behave in a reckless, excited, or impromptu manner **2** to proceed rapidly or furiously **3** to conduct one's affairs; act ⟨*insists on* going it *alone*⟩ – **go missing** *chiefly Br* to disappear – **go off the deep end 1** to enter recklessly on a course of action **2** to become very excited or perturbed – **go on** to be enthusiastic about ⟨*we don't* go *much* on *cars* – Len Deighton⟩ – compare GO ON *vi* – **go one better** to outdo or surpass another – **go out of one's way** to take extra trouble – **go over 1** EXAMINE 1 **2a** REPEAT 1 **b** to study, revise – **go phut** *chiefly Br* to stop functioning – infml – **go places** to be on the way to success – **go slow** to hold a go-slow – **go steady** to be the constant and exclusive boyfriend or girl friend of another or each other – **go straight** to abandon a life of crime – **go the way of all flesh** to die – **go through 1** to subject to thorough examination, study, or discussion; GO OVER **2** to experience, undergo **3** to perform ⟨went through *his work in a daze*⟩ – compare GO THROUGH *vi* – **go to bed with** to have sexual intercourse with – **go to one's head 1** to make one confused, excited, or dizzy **2** to make one conceited or overconfident – **go to pieces** to become shattered (e g in nerves or health) – **go to pot** to deteriorate, collapse – infml ⟨*the office* went to pot *while his secretary was away*⟩ – **go to sleep** to lose sensation; become numb ⟨*my foot has* gone to sleep⟩ – **go to town 1** to work or act rapidly or efficiently **2** to indulge oneself ostentatiously ⟨*the papers* went to town *on the hidden life of Leroy* – *Sunday Times*⟩ – **go walkabout 1** *Austr* to go on a walkabout **2** *Br* to meet and hold a conversation informally with members of the public during an official engagement or tour ⟨*the Queen* going walkabout *in Milton Keynes*⟩ – **go west** to die or become destroyed or expended – humor – **go with 1** GO ALONG WITH 1 ⟨*the responsibility that* goes with *parenthood*⟩ **2** to be the social or esp sexual companion of

[2]**go** *n, pl* **goes 1** the act or manner of going **2** energy, vigour ⟨*full of get up and* ~⟩ **3a** a turn in an activity (e g a game) **b** an attempt, try ⟨*have a* ~ *at paint-*

ing⟩ **c** chance, opportunity ⟨*a fair* ~ *at work for everyone* – *The Listener*⟩ **4** a spell of activity ⟨*finished the job at one* ~⟩ **5** a success ⟨*made a* ~ *of the business*⟩ **6** *the* height of fashion; *the* rage ⟨*shawls are all the* ~ *at the moment*⟩ – chiefly infml **7** an often unexpected or awkward turn of affairs – chiefly infml ⟨*it's a rum* ~⟩ – **on the go** constantly or restlessly active – infml

[3]**go** *adj* functioning properly ⟨*declared all systems* ~ *for the rocket launch*⟩

[4]**go** *n* an Oriental game of capture and territorial domination played by 2 players with counters on a board covered in a grid [Jap]

goa /'goh·ə/ *n* a common gazelle of Tibet [Tibetan *dgoba*]

go about *vi* to change tack when sailing

[1]**goad** /gohd/ *n* **1** a pointed rod used to urge on an animal **2** sthg that pricks, urges, or stimulates (into action) [ME *gode*, fr OE *gād* spear, goad; akin to Langobardic *gaida* spear, Skt *hinoti* he urges on]

[2]**goad** *vt* **1** to drive (e g cattle) with a goad **2** to incite or rouse by nagging or persistent annoyance

[1]**,go-a'head** *adj* energetic and progressive

[2]**'go-a,head** *n* a sign, signal, or authority to proceed

goal /gohl/ *n* **1** an end towards which effort is directed **2a** an area or object through or into which players in various games attempt to put a ball or puck against the defence of the opposing side ☞ SPORT **b** (the points gained by) the act of putting a ball or puck through or into a goal [ME *gol* boundary, limit; perh akin to OE *gǣlen* to hinder, impede]

'goal ,area *n* a rectangular area 18.3m by 5.5m (20yd by 6yd) immediately in front of each goal on a soccer pitch ☞ SPORT

goalie /'gohli/ *n* a goalkeeper – infml

'goal,keeper /-,keepə/ *n* a player who defends the goal in soccer, hockey, lacrosse, etc ☞ SPORT – **goalkeeping** *n*

'goal ,kick *n* a free kick in soccer awarded to the defending side when the ball is sent over the goal line by an opposing player

'goal ,line *n* a line at either end and usu running the width of a playing area on which a goal or goal post is situated ☞ SPORT

'goal,mouth /-,mowth/ *n* the area of a playing field directly in front of the goal

go along *vi* **1** to move along; proceed **2** to go or travel as a companion **3** to agree, cooperate ⟨*I'd* go along *with your suggestion*⟩

'goal,post /-,pohst/ *n* either of usu 2 vertical posts that with or without a crossbar constitute the goal in soccer, rugby, etc

goanna /goh'anə/ *n* a large Australian lizard [alter. of *iguana*]

go around *vi* **1** to go here and there, esp in company ⟨*the friends she* goes around *with*⟩ **2** GO ROUND 1, 2

goat /goht/ *n* **1** any of various long-legged (horned) ruminant mammals smaller than cattle and related to the sheep **2** a lecherous man **3** a foolish person – infml; compare GET ONE'S GOAT [ME *gote*, fr OE *gāt*; akin to OHG *geiz* goat, L *haedus* kid] – **goatish** *adj*, **goatlike** *adj*

goatee /'goh,tee/ *n* a small pointed beard [fr its resemblance to the beard of a he-goat]

'goat,fish /-,fish/ *n* MULLET b

'goat's ,beard *n* a Eurasian composite plant whose yellow flower heads close at about midday

'goat,skin /-,skin/ *n* (leather made from) the skin of a goat

'goat,sucker /-,sukə/ *n* a nightjar [fr the belief that it sucks the milk from goats]

[1]**gob** /gob/ *n* a shapeless or sticky lump [ME *gobbe*, fr MF *gobe* large piece of food, back-formation fr *gobet*]

[2]**gob** *n, Br* MOUTH 1a – slang [IrGael & ScGael, beak, protruding mouth]

gobbet /'gobit/ *n* a piece, portion [ME *gobet*, fr MF, mouthful, piece]

[1]**gobble** /'gobl/ *vt* **gobbling** /'gobling, 'gobl·ing/ **1** to swallow or eat greedily or noisily **2** to take, accept, or read eagerly – often + *up* [prob irreg fr [1]*gob*]

[2]**gobble** *vi* to make the guttural sound of a male turkey or a similar sound [imit] – **gobble** *n*

gobbledygook, gobbledegook /'gobldi,goohk/ *n* wordy and generally unintelligible jargon [irreg fr *gobble*, n]

gobbler /'goblə/ *n* a male turkey – infml

'go-be,tween *n* an intermediate agent

goblet /'goblit/ *n* **1** a drinking vessel that has a usu rounded bowl, a foot, and a stem and is used esp for wine **2** the part of a liquidizer in which food is liquidized or ground by means of rotating blades [ME *gobelet*, fr MF]

'goblet ,cell *n* a mucus-secreting epithelial cell shaped like a goblet and found in mucous membranes (e g of the intestines)

goblin /'goblin/ *n* a grotesque mischievous elf [ME *gobelin*, fr MF, fr ML *gobelinus*, perh deriv of Gk *kobalos* rogue]

gobstopper /'gob,stopə/ *n* a large round hard sweet [[2]*gob*]

goby /'gohbi/ *n, pl* **gobies**, *esp collectively* **goby** any of numerous spiny-finned fishes with the pelvic fins often united to form a sucking disc [L *gobius* gudgeon, fr Gk *kōbios*]

go-by /'goh ,bie/ *n* an act of avoidance; a miss ⟨*give them the* ~⟩

go by *vi* to pass ⟨*as time* goes by⟩

god /god/ *n* **1** *cap* the supreme or ultimate reality; the being perfect in power, wisdom, and goodness whom human beings worship as creator and ruler of the universe **2** a being or object believed to have more than natural attributes and powers (e g the control of a particular aspect of reality) and to require human beings' worship **3** sby or sthg of supreme value **4** a very influential person **5** *pl* the highest gallery in a theatre, usu with the cheapest seats [ME, fr OE; akin to OHG *got* god] – **godlike** *adj*

,god-'awful *adj* extremely unpleasant – infml ⟨~ *explosions of violence* – *Playboy*⟩ [*god*damned + *awful*]

'god,child /-,chield/ *n* sby for whom sby else becomes sponsor at baptism

[1]**goddamn, goddam** /go(d)'dam/ *n, often cap* a damn ⟨*he doesn't give a* ~ *about anything*⟩

[2]**goddamn, goddam** /go(d)'dam/ *vb, often cap* to damn ⟨*I'll be* ~*ed*⟩ ⟨*you feel like swearing and* ~*ing worse and worse* – Ernest Hemingway⟩

goddamned /go(d)'damd, '-,-/, **goddamn, goddam** /go(d)'dam, '-,-/ *adj or adv* damned

'god,daughter /-,dawtə/ *n* a female godchild

goddess /'godes, -dis/ *n* **1** a female deity **2** a woman whose great charm or beauty arouses adoration

godet /goh'det, 'goh,day/ *n* an esp triangular inset, inserted into a garment to give fullness or flare (e g at the bottom of a skirt) [F, lit., drinking cup, mug, prob of Gmc origin]

godetia /gə'deeshə/ *n* any of several American plants of the evening primrose family widely grown as hardy annuals for their showy white, pink, or red flowers [NL, fr C H *Godet* †1879 Swiss botanist]

'god,father /-,fahdhə/ *n* **1** a male godparent at baptism **2** one having a relation to sby or sthg like that of a godfather to his godchild ⟨*the ~ of a whole generation of rebels – TLS*⟩

'God-,fearing *adj* devout

'godfor,saken /-fə,saykən/ *adj* **1** remote, desolate **2** neglected, dismal

'god,head /-,hed/ *n* **1** divine nature or essence **2** *cap* **a** GOD 1 – usu + *the* **b** *the* nature of God, esp as existing in 3 persons [ME *godhed*, fr *god* + *-hed* -hood; akin to ME *-hod* -hood]

'godless /-lis/ *adj* not acknowledging a deity; impious – **godlessness** *n*

'godly /-li/ *adj* **1** divine **2** pious, devout – **godliness** *n*

'god,mother /-,mudhə/ *n* a female godparent

godown /'goh,down/ *n* a warehouse in an Asian country, esp India [Malay *gudang*]

go down *vi* **1a** to fall (as if) to the ground ⟨*the plane* went down *in flames*⟩ **b** to go below the horizon ⟨*the sun* went down⟩ **c** to sink ⟨*the ship* went down *with all hands*⟩ **2** to be capable of being swallowed ⟨*the medicine* went down *easily*⟩ **3** to undergo defeat **4a** to find acceptance ⟨*will the plan* go down *well with the farmers?*⟩ **b** to come to be remembered, esp by posterity ⟨*he will* go down *in history as a great general*⟩ **5a** to undergo a decline or decrease ⟨*the market is* going down⟩ **b** *esp of a computer system or program* to crash **6** to become ill – usu + *with* ⟨*he* went down *with flu*⟩ **7** *Br* to leave a university – compare COME DOWN, GO UP **8** to be sent to prison – slang **– go down on** to perform fellatio or cunnilingus on – vulg

'god,parent /-,peərənt/ *n* a sponsor at baptism

,God's 'acre *n* a churchyard – euph

godsend /'god,send/ *n* a desirable or needed thing or event that comes unexpectedly [back-formation fr *god-sent*]

'god,son /-,sun/ *n* a male godchild

,God'speed /-'speed/ *n* a prosperous journey; success ⟨*bade him ~*⟩ [ME *god speid*, fr the phrase *God spede you* God prosper you]

godwit /'god,wit/ *n* any of a genus of long-billed wading birds resembling curlews [origin unknown]

goer /'goh·ə/ *n* **1** a regular attender – usu in combination ⟨*a theatre*goer⟩ **2** sby or sthg that moves or does things fast or actively; *esp* a swinger – infml [[1]GO + [2]-ER]

goffer /'gohfə/ *vt* to crimp, wave, or flute (e g linen or a lace edging), esp with a heated iron [F *gaufrer*] – **goffer** *n*

,go-'getter *n* an aggressively enterprising person – **go-getting** *adj or n*

goggle /'gogl/ *vi* **goggling** /'gogling/ to stare with wide or protuberant eyes [ME *gogelen* to squint] – **goggler** *n*

'goggle-,box *n, Br* a television set – infml

,goggle-'eyed *adj or adv* with the eyes wide or bulging (in amazement or fascination)

goggles /'goglz/ *n pl* protective glasses set in a flexible frame that fits snugly against the face

go-go /'goh ,goh/ *adj* of or being the music or a style of dance performed or a dancer performing at a disco [*a-go-go* disco, fr *Whisky à Gogo*, cafe & disco in Paris, fr F *à gogo* galore]

[1]Goidelic /goy'delik/ *adj* **1** of the Gaels **2** of or constituting Goidelic [MIr *Gōidel* Gael]

[2]Goidelic *n* the group of Celtic languages comprising Irish Gaelic, Scots Gaelic, and Manx

go in *vi* **1** to enter **2** *of a celestial body* to become obscured by a cloud ⟨*the sun* went in *for 5 minutes*⟩ **3** to form a union or alliance – often + *with* ⟨*asked the rest of us to* go in *with them on the project*⟩ – **go in for 1** to engage in, esp as a hobby or for enjoyment **2** to enter and compete in (e g a test or race) ⟨*decided not to* go in for *her A-levels until the following year*⟩

[1]going /'goh·ing/ *n* **1** an act or instance of going – often in combination ⟨*theatre*going⟩ **2** the condition of the ground (e g for horse racing) **3** advance, progress ⟨*found the ~ too slow and gave up the job*⟩ **4** the depth of the tread of a stair

[2]going *adj* **1a** living, existing ⟨*the best novelist ~*⟩ **b** available for use or enjoyment ⟨*asked if there were any jobs ~*⟩ **2a** current, prevailing ⟨*~ price*⟩ **b** profitable, thriving ⟨*~ concern*⟩ **– going for** favourable to ⟨*had everything* going for *me*⟩

,going-'over *n, pl* **goings-over 1** a thorough examination or investigation **2** a severe scolding

,goings-'on *n pl* **1** actions, events ⟨*coming-out parties and sundry ~*⟩ **2** reprehensible happenings or conduct ⟨*tales of scandalous ~ in high circles*⟩

goitre, *NAm chiefly* **goiter** /'goytə/ *n* an abnormal enlargement of the thyroid gland visible as a swelling of the front of the neck [F *goitre*, fr MF, back-formation fr *goitron* throat, fr (assumed) VL *guttrion-*, *guttrio*, fr L *guttur* throat, crop of a bird]

goitrogen /'goytrəjən/ *n* a substance that induces goitre formation – **goitrogenic** /-'jenik/ *adj*

go-kart /'goh ,kaht/ *n* a tiny racing car with small wheels [*go* + *kart*, alter. of *cart*]

Golconda /gol'kondə/ *n* a rich mine; *broadly* a source of great wealth [*Golconda*, city in India, famous for its diamonds]

gold /gohld/ *n* **1** a malleable ductile yellow metallic element that occurs chiefly free or in a few minerals and is used esp in coins and jewellery and as a currency reserve ☞ PERIODIC TABLE **2a(1)** gold coins **(2)** GOLD MEDAL ⟨*won a ~ in the 100m*⟩ **b** money **c** GOLD STANDARD **d** gold as a commodity **3** a deep metallic yellow **4** sthg valued as excellent or the finest of its kind ⟨*a heart of ~*⟩ **5** (a shot hitting) the golden or yellow centre spot of an archery target [ME, fr OE; akin to OE *geolu* yellow – more at YELLOW]

'gold,beater /-,beetə/ *n* sby who beats gold into gold leaf – **goldbeating** *n*

'gold,brick /-,brik/ *n* sthg that appears to be valuable but is actually worthless – infml

'gold,crest /-,krest/ *n* a very small olive-green European bird that has a bright yellow crown

'gold ,digger *n* a woman who uses charm to extract money or gifts from men – infml

golden /'gohld(ə)n/ *adj* **1** consisting of, relating to, or containing gold **2a** of the colour of gold **b** BLOND 1a **3** prosperous, flourishing ⟨~ *days*⟩ **4** highly favoured and promising (worldly) success – often in *golden boy/girl* **5** favourable, advantageous ⟨*a ~ opportunity*⟩ **6** of or marking a 50th anniversary ⟨~ *wedding*⟩ – **goldenly** *adv*, **goldenness** *n*

'golden ,age *n* a period of great happiness, prosperity, and achievement

,golden 'eagle *n* a large eagle of the northern hemisphere with brownish yellow tips on the head and neck feathers

'golden,eye /-,ie/ *n* a large-headed swift-flying diving duck of which the male is strikingly marked in black and white

,golden 'hamster *n* a small tawny hamster widely kept as a pet

,golden 'hand,shake *n* a large ex gratia money payment given by a company to an employee, esp on retirement

,Golden 'Horde /hawd/ *n sing or pl in constr* a body of Mongol Tartars who overran E Europe in the 13th c [fr the golden tent of the Mongol ruler]

,golden 'mean *n* the medium between extremes; moderation

,golden 'number *n* a number marking a year in the Metonic cycle of 19 years and used in calculating the date of Easter

,golden 'oriole *n* an Old World oriole of which the male is brilliant yellow

,golden 'plover *n* either of 2 kinds of plover whose upper parts are speckled golden yellow and white in summer

,golden re'triever *n* a medium-sized golden-coated retriever

,golden'rod /-'rod/ *n* any of numerous composite plants with (loosely clustered) heads of small usu yellow flowers

,golden 'rule *n* **1** a rule of ethical conduct, recorded in Mt 7:12 and Lk 6:31, requiring one to treat others as one would wish to be treated by them **2** a guiding principle

'golden ,section *n* the proportion of a geometrical figure or of a divided line such that the smaller dimension is to the greater as the greater is to the whole ☞ MATHEMATICS

,golden 'syrup *n* the pale yellow syrup derived from cane sugar refining and used in cooking

'gold,finch /-,finch/ *n* a small red, black, yellow, and white European finch

'gold,fish /-,fish/ *n* a small (golden yellow) fish related to the carps and widely kept in aquariums and ponds

,gold 'leaf *n* gold beaten into very thin sheets and used esp for gilding

,gold 'medal *n* a medal of gold awarded to sby who comes first in a competition

'gold ,mine *n* a rich source of sthg desired (e g information)

'gold ,rush *n* a rush to newly discovered goldfields in pursuit of riches

'gold,smith /-,smith/ *n* one who works in gold or deals in articles of gold

'gold ,standard *n* a standard of money under which the basic unit of currency is defined by a stated quantity of gold of a fixed fineness

golem /'gohlem/ *n* a clay figure of Hebrew folklore endowed with life [Yiddish *goylem*, fr Heb *gōlem* shapeless mass]

golf /golf/ *n* a game in which a player using special clubs attempts to hit a ball into each of the 9 or 18 successive holes on a course with as few strokes as possible [ME (Sc), perh modif of MD *colf, colve* club, bat] – **golf** *vi*

Golf – a communications code word for the letter *g*

'golf ,ball *n* a spherical ball that carries the characters in an electric typewriter

'golf ,course *n* an area of land laid out for playing golf consisting of a series of 9 or 18 holes each with a tee, fairway, and putting green

golfer /'golfə/ *n* sby who plays golf

'golf ,links *n* a golf course, esp near the sea – often pl with sing. meaning

Golgi /'golji, 'golgi/ *adj* of the Golgi apparatus or bodies ⟨~ *vesicles*⟩

'Golgi ,appa,ratus *n* a cytoplasmic organelle that appears in electron microscopy as a series of parallel (vesicular) membranes and is concerned with secretion of cell products [Camillo *Golgi* †1926 It physician]

'Golgi ,body *n* (a discrete particle of) the Golgi apparatus

Goliath /gə'lie·əth/ *n* a giant [Heb *Golyath*, biblical giant of the Philistines slain by David (1 Sam 17)]

Go'liath ,beetle *n* a very large African beetle that has a black body marked with white stripes

golliwog, gollywog /'goli,wog/ *n* a child's doll made from soft material that is dressed as a man and has a black face and black hair standing out round its head [*Golliwogg*, an animated doll in children's fiction by Bertha Upton †1912 US writer]

gollop /'goləp/ *vt or n* (to) gulp – infml [by alter.]

[1]**golly** /'goli/ *interj* – used to express surprise [euphemism for *God*]

[2]**golly** *n* a golliwog [by shortening & alter.]

golosh /gə'losh/ *n, chiefly Br* a galosh

gon-, gono- *comb form* sexual; reproductive; gonad ⟨gon*idium*⟩ [Gk, fr *gonos* procreation, seed, fr *gignesthai* to be born – more at KIN]

-gon /-gon, -gən/ *comb form* (→ *n*) geometrical figure having (so many) angles ⟨*deca*gon⟩ [NL *-gonum*, fr Gk *-gōnon*, fr *gōnia* angle; akin to Gk *gony* knee – more at KNEE]

gonad /'gohnad; *also* 'go-/ *n* any of the primary sex glands (e g the ovaries or testes) [NL *gonad-, gonas*, fr Gk *gonos*] – **gonadal** /-'nadl/ *adj*

gonadotrophic /,gonədə'trohfik, gə,nadə-/, **gonadotropic** /-'tropik/ *adj* acting on or stimulating the gonads [ISV]

gonadotrophin /,gonə'dotrəfin, go,nadoh'trohfin/, **gonadotropin** /,gonə'dotrəpin, go,nadoh'trohpin/ *n* a gonadotrophic hormone (e g follicle-stimulating hormone)

gondola /'gondələ/ *n* **1** a long narrow flat-bottomed boat used on the canals of Venice **2a** an enclosure suspended from a balloon for carrying passengers or instruments **b** a cabin suspended from a cable and used for transporting passengers (e g up a ski slope) **3** a fixture approachable from all sides used in self-service retail shops to display merchandise [It, fr ML *gondula*, dim. of (assumed) VL *condua*]

gondolier /,gondə'liə/ *n* a boatman who propels a gondola [F, fr It *gondoliere*, fr *gondola*]

[1]**gone** /gon/ *adj* **1a** involved, absorbed ⟨*far ~ in hysteria*⟩ **b** pregnant by a specified length of time

⟨*she's 6 months* ~⟩ **c** infatuated – often + *on*; infml ⟨*was real* ~ *on that man*⟩ **2** dead – euph [fr pp of *go*]

²gone *adv, Br* past, turned ⟨*it's* ~ *3 o'clock*⟩

goner /'gonə/ *n* one whose case or state is hopeless or lost – infml

gonfalon /'gonfələn/ *n* a gonfanon [It *gonfalone*, fr OIt, fr OF *gonfanon, gonfalon*]

gonfanon /'gonfə,non, -nən/ *n* a flag that hangs from a crosspiece or frame [ME *gonfanoun*, fr MF *gonfanon*, fr OF, of Gmc origin; akin to OHG *gundfano* war flag, fr *gund-* battle, war + *-fano* cloth]

gong /gong/ *n* **1** a disc-shaped percussion instrument that produces a resounding tone when struck with a usu padded hammer **2** a flat saucer-shaped bell **3** a medal or decoration – slang [Malay & Jav, of imit origin] – **gong** *vi*

goni-, gonio- *comb form* corner; angle ⟨gonio*meter*⟩ [Gk *gōnia*]

gonidium /go'nidi·əm/ *n, pl* **gonidia** /-di·ə/ an asexual reproductive cell or group of cells in or on a gametophyte [NL, fr *gon-* + *-idium*] – **gonidial** *adj*

goniometer /,gohni'omitə/ *n* an instrument for measuring angles – **goniometry** /-'omətri/ *n*, **goniometric** /-ni·ə'metrik/ *adj*

gonna /'gonə, gənə/ *verbal auxiliary pres* to be going to ⟨*I'm* ~ *wash that man right out of my hair* – Oscar Hammerstein⟩ – nonstandard [alter. of *going to*]

gono- – see GON-

gonococcus /,gonoh'kokəs/ *n, pl* **gonococci** /-'kok(s)ie, -'kok(s)i/ the pus-producing bacterium that causes gonorrhoea [NL] – **gonococcal, gonococcic** /-'kok(s)ik/ *adj*

gonorrhoea, *chiefly NAm* **gonorrhea** /,gonə'riə/ *n* a venereal disease in which there is inflammation of the mucous membranes of the genital tracts caused by gonococcal bacteria [NL, fr LL, morbid loss of semen, fr Gk *gonorrhoia*, fr *gon-* + *-rrhoia* -rrhoea] – **gonorrhoeal** *adj*

-gony /-g(ə)ni/ *comb form* (→ *n*) origin; reproduction; manner of coming into being ⟨*sporo*gony⟩ ⟨*cosmo*gony⟩ [L *-gonia*, fr Gk, fr *gonos*]

goo /gooh/ *n* **1** sticky matter **2** cloying sentimentality *USE* infml [perh alter. of *glue*] – **gooey** *adj*

¹good /good/ *adj* **better** /'betə/; **best** /best/ **1a(1)** of a favourable character or tendency ⟨~ *news*⟩ **(2)** bountiful, fertile ⟨~ *land*⟩ **(3)** handsome, attractive ⟨~ *looks*⟩ **b(1)** suitable, fit ⟨*it's a* ~ *day for planting roses*⟩ **(2)** free from injury or disease; whole ⟨*1* ~ *arm*⟩ **(3)** not depreciated ⟨*bad money drives out* ~⟩ **(4)** commercially sound ⟨*a* ~ *risk*⟩ **(5)** certain to last or live ⟨~ *for another year*⟩ **(6)** certain to pay or contribute ⟨~ *for a few quid*⟩ **(7)** certain to elicit a specified result ⟨*always* ~ *for a laugh*⟩ **c(1)** agreeable, pleasant; *specif* amusing **(2)** beneficial to the health or character ⟨*spinach is* ~ *for you*⟩ **(3)** not rotten; fresh ⟨*the beef is still* ~⟩ **d** ample, full **e(1)** well-founded, true ⟨~ *reasons*⟩ **(2)** deserving of respect; honourable ⟨*in* ~ *standing*⟩ **(3)** legally valid ⟨~ *title*⟩ **f(1)** adequate, satisfactory; *also* strong, robust **(2)** conforming to a standard ⟨~ *English*⟩ **(3)** choice, discriminating ⟨~ *taste*⟩ **2a(1)** morally commendable; virtuous ⟨*a* ~ *man*⟩ **(2)** correct; *specif* well-behaved **(3)** kind, benevolent ⟨~ *intentions*⟩ **b** reputable; *specif* wellborn ⟨*a* ~ *family*⟩ **c** competent, skilful ⟨*a* ~ *doctor*⟩ **d** loyal ⟨*a* ~ *Catholic*⟩ [ME, fr OE *gōd*; akin to OHG *guot* good, Skt *gadh* to hold fast] – **goodish** *adj* – **as good as** virtually; IN EFFECT ⟨as good as *dead*⟩ – **as good as gold** extremely well-behaved ⟨*the child was* as good as gold⟩ – **good and** very, entirely – infml ⟨*should be* good and *ready by Tuesday*⟩ – **in someone's good books** in sby's favour

²good *n* **1a** sthg good ⟨*it's no* ~ *complaining*⟩ **b** the quality of being good ⟨*to know* ~ *from evil*⟩ **c** a good element or portion ⟨*recognized the* ~ *in him*⟩ **2** prosperity, benefit ⟨*for the* ~ *of the community*⟩ **3a** sthg that has economic utility or satisfies an economic want – usu pl **b** *pl* personal property having intrinsic value but usu excluding money, securities, and negotiable instruments **c** *pl* wares, merchandise ⟨*tinned* ~s ⟩ **4** *pl but sing or pl in constr* the desired or necessary article ⟨*came up with the* ~s⟩ – infml **5** *pl* proof of wrongdoing – slang ⟨*the police have got the* ~s *on him*⟩ – **for good** forever, permanently – **to the good 1** for the best; beneficial ⟨*this rain is all* to the good⟩ **2** in a position of net gain or profit ⟨*he ended the game £10* to the good⟩

³good *adv* well – infml

,good 'book *n, often cap G&B* the Bible

¹goodbye, *NAm also* **goodby** /good'bie/ *interj* – used to express farewell [alter. of *God be with you*]

²goodbye, *NAm also* **goodby** *n* a concluding remark or gesture at parting ⟨*time to say our* ~s⟩

¹'good-for-,nothing *adj* of no value; worthless

²good-for-nothing *n* an idle worthless person

,Good 'Friday *n* the Friday before Easter, observed in churches as the anniversary of the crucifixion of Christ [fr its special sanctity]

,good-'hearted *adj* having a kindly generous disposition – **good-heartedly** *adv*, **good-heartedness** *n*

,good-'humoured *adj* good-natured, cheerful – **good-humouredly** *adv*

goodie /'goodi/ *n* a goody

'good ,life *n* a life marked by a high standard of living

,good-'looking *adj* having a pleasing or attractive appearance – **good-looker** *n*

goodly /'goodli/ *adj* **1** significantly large in amount; considerable ⟨*a* ~ *number*⟩ **2** *archaic* pleasantly attractive; handsome

,good-'natured *adj* of a cheerful and cooperative disposition – **goodnaturedly** *adv*, **good-naturedness** *n*

goodness /'goodnis/ *n* the nutritious or beneficial part of sthg ⟨*boil all the* ~ *out of the meat*⟩ [¹GOOD + -NESS]

,good 'o, good oh /oh/ *interj* – used as an expression of approval or pleasure

,good 'offices *n pl* power or action that helps sby out of a difficulty – often in *through the good offices of*

,Good Sa'maritan /sə'marit(ə)n/ *n* SAMARITAN 2a

'goods ,train *n, chiefly Br* a train of wagons for carrying goods

,good-'tempered *adj* having an even temper; not easily annoyed – **good-temperedly** *adv*, **good-temperedness** *n*

'good-,time ,girl *n* a female prostitute – euph

,good'will /-'wil/ *n* **1a** a kindly feeling of approval and support; benevolent interest or concern **b** the favour or prestige that a business has acquired beyond the mere value of what it sells **2a** cheerful consent **b** willing effort – **goodwilled** *adj*

ˌgood ˈword *n* a favourable statement ⟨*put in a ~ for me*⟩

goody, goodie /ˈgoodi/ *n* **1** sthg particularly attractive, pleasurable, or desirable **2** a good person or hero *USE* infml

ˈgoody-ˌgoody *n or adj* (sby) affectedly or ingratiatingly prim or virtuous – infml

¹goof /goohf/ *n* **1** a ridiculous stupid person **2** *chiefly NAm* a blunder *USE* infml [prob alter. of E dial. *goff* (simpleton)]

²goof *vb, chiefly NAm vi* to make a goof; blunder ~ *vt* to make a mess of; bungle – often + *up* *USE* infml

ˈgoofˌball /-ˌbawl/ *n, NAm* a mentally abnormal person – slang

go off *vi* **1** to explode **2** to go forth or away; depart **3** to undergo decline or deterioration; *specif, of food or drink* to become rotten or sour **4** to follow a specified course; proceed ⟨*the party* went off *well*⟩ **5** to make a characteristic noise; sound ⟨*the alarm* went off⟩ – compare GO OFF THE DEEP END

goofy /ˈgoohfi/ *adj* silly, daft – infml – **goofily** *adv*, **goofiness** *n*

googly /ˈgoohgli/ *n* a usu slow delivery by a right-handed bowler in cricket that is an off break as viewed by a right-handed batsman although apparently delivered with a leg-break action [origin unknown]

googol /ˈgoohgol/ *n* ten raised to the power 100 [coined by a child]

ˈgoogolˌplex /-ˌpleks/ *n* ten raised to the power of a googol [*googol* + *-plex* (as in *duplex*)]

goo-goo /ˈgooh gooh/ *adj* loving, enticing – infml; chiefly in *goo-goo eyes* ⟨*make ~ eyes at each other – New Republic*⟩ [prob alter. of *goggle*, adj, staring]

goon /goohn/ *n* **1** *NAm* a man hired to terrorize or eliminate opponents **2** an idiot, dope – slang [partly short for E dial. *gooney* (simpleton); partly fr Alice the *Goon*, subhuman comic-strip creature by E C Segar †1938 US cartoonist] – **goony** *adj*

go on *vi* **1** to continue; CARRY ON 2 **2a** to proceed (as if) by a logical step ⟨*he* went on *to explain why*⟩ **b** *of time* to pass **3** to take place; happen ⟨*what's* going on*?*⟩ **4** to be capable of being put on ⟨*her gloves wouldn't* go on⟩ **5a** to talk, esp in an effusive manner ⟨*the way people* go on *about pollution*⟩ **b** to criticize constantly; nag ⟨*you're always* going on *at me*⟩ **6a** to come into operation, action, or production ⟨*the lights* went on *at sunset*⟩ **b** to appear on the stage **7** *Br* to manage; GET ALONG ⟨*how did you* go on *for money?*⟩

goosander /goohˈsandə/ *n* a sawbill duck of the northern hemisphere [alter. of earlier *gossander*, prob fr *gos-* (as in *gosling*) + berg*ander* (sheldrake)]

¹goose /goohs/ *n, pl* (*1 & 2*) **geese** /gees/, (*3*) **gooses** **1** (the female of) any of numerous large long-necked web-footed waterfowl **2** a simpleton, dolt **3** a tailor's smoothing iron with a gooseneck handle [ME *gos*, fr OE *gōs*; akin to OHG *gans* goose, L *anser*] – **goosey** *adj*

²goose *vt, chiefly NAm* to poke between the buttocks – vulg

gooseberry /ˈgoozb(ə)ri/ *n* **1** (the shrub that bears) an edible acid usu prickly green or yellow fruit **2** an unwanted companion to 2 lovers – chiefly in *to play gooseberry* [perh fr ¹*goose* + *berry*]

ˈgoose ˌbumps *n pl, chiefly NAm* gooseflesh

ˈgooseˌflesh /-ˌflesh/ *n* a bristling roughness of the skin produced by erection of its papillae, usu from cold or fear [prob fr the resemblance to a plucked fowl]

ˈgooseˌfoot /-ˌfoot/ *n, pl* **goosefoots** any of several plants with small green flowers that grow esp on disturbed or cultivated land

goosegog /ˈgoozˌgog/ *n, Br* a gooseberry – infml [*goose*berry + *gog*, of unknown origin]

ˈgoose ˌgrass *n* cleavers

ˈgooseˌneck /-ˌnek/ *n* sthg (e g a flexible jointed metal pipe) curved like the neck of a goose or U-shaped – **goosenecked** *adj*

ˈgoose ˌpimples *n pl* gooseflesh

ˈgoose ˌstep *n* a straight-legged marching step – **goose-stepper** *n*

go out *vi* **1a** to leave a room, house, country, etc **b** to fight in a duel **c** to travel to a distant place ⟨*they* went out *to Africa*⟩ **d** to work away from home ⟨*she* went out *charring*⟩ **2a** to become extinguished ⟨*the hall light* went out⟩ **b** to become obsolete or unfashionable **c** to play the last card of one's hand **3** to spend time regularly *with* sby of esp the opposite sex **4** to be broadcast ⟨*the programme* went out *at 9 o'clock*⟩

go over *vi* **1** to become converted (e g to a religion or political party) **2** to receive approval; succeed ⟨*my play should* go over *well in Scotland*⟩

gopher /ˈgohfə/ *n* **1** any of several American burrowing rodents that are the size of a large rat and have large cheek pouches **2** any of numerous small N American ground squirrels closely related to the chipmunks [origin unknown]

goral /ˈgawrəl/ *n* either of 2 E Asian mammals that resemble small antelopes [perh deriv of Skt *gaura* gaur]

¹gorblimey /gawˈbliemi/ *interj, Br* – used to express surprise and indignation; slang [euphemism for *God blind me*]

²gorblimey *adj, Br* common, vulgar ⟨*spoke with a ~ accent*⟩ – no longer in vogue

ˈGordian ˌknot /ˈgawdi·ən, -dyən/ *n* an intricate problem; *esp* one insoluble in its own terms [*Gordius*, King of Phrygia, who tied an intricate knot which supposedly could be undone only by the future ruler of Asia, and which Alexander the Great cut with his sword]

¹gore /gaw/ *n* (clotted) blood [ME, filth, fr OE *gor*; akin to OE *wearm* warm]

²gore *n* a tapering or triangular piece of material (e g cloth) used to give shape to sthg (e g a garment or sail) [ME, fr OE *gāra*; akin to OE *gār* spear, Gk *chaios* shepherd's staff] – **gored** *adj*

³gore *vt* to pierce or wound with a horn or tusk [ME *goren*, prob fr *gore, gare* spear, fr OE *gār*]

¹gorge /gawj/ *n* **1** the throat **2** the (contents of the) stomach or belly **3** the entrance into an outwork of a fort **4** a narrow steep-walled valley, often with a stream flowing through it ☞ GEOGRAPHY [ME, fr MF, fr LL *gurga*, alter. of L *gurges* throat, whirlpool – more at VORACIOUS]

²gorge *vi* to eat greedily or until full ~ *vt* **1** to fill completely or to the point of making distended ⟨*veins* ~d *with blood*⟩ **2** to swallow greedily – **gorger** *n*

gorgeous /'gawjəs/ *adj* **1** splendidly beautiful or magnificent **2** very fine; pleasant ⟨*it was a ~ day for a picnic*⟩ [ME *gorgayse*, fr MF *gorgias* elegant, fr *gorgias* neckerchief, fr *gorge*] – **gorgeously** *adv*, **gorgeousness** *n*

gorget /'gawjit/ *n* a piece of armour protecting the throat [ME, fr MF, fr *gorge*]

gorgon /'gawgən/ *n* **1** *cap* any of 3 sisters in Greek mythology who had live snakes in place of hair and whose glance turned the beholder to stone **2** an ugly or repulsive woman [L *Gorgon-*, *Gorgo*, fr Gk *Gorgōn*] – **Gorgonian** /gaw'gohnyən, -ni·ən/ *adj*

gorgonian /gaw'gohnyən, -ni·ən/ *n* any of an order of colonial anthozoan polyps [deriv of L *gorgonia* coral, fr *Gorgon-*, *Gorgo*] – **gorgonian** *adj*

Gorgonzola /,gawgən'zohlə/ *n* a blue-veined strongly flavoured cheese of Italian origin [It, fr *Gorgonzola*, town in Italy]

gorilla /gə'rilə/ *n* **1** an anthropoid ape of western equatorial Africa related to the chimpanzee but less erect and much larger ☞ ENDANGERED **2** an ugly or brutal man [deriv of Gk *Gorillai*, a mythical African tribe of hairy women]

gormand·ize, -ise /'gawmən,diez/ *vb* to eat voraciously; gorge [*gormand*, alter. of *gourmand*] – **gormandizer** *n*

gormless /'gawmlis/ *adj*, *Br* lacking understanding and intelligence; stupid – infml [alter. of E dial. *gaumless*, fr *gaum* attention, understanding (fr ME *gome*, fr ON *gaum*, *gaumr*) + *-less*]

go round *vi* **1** to spread, circulate ⟨*there's a rumour* going round⟩ **2** to satisfy demand; meet the need ⟨*not enough jobs to* go round⟩ **3** GO AROUND 1

gorse /gaws/ *n* a spiny yellow-flowered evergreen leguminous European shrub [ME *gorst*, fr OE – more at HORROR] – **gorsy** *adj*

Gorsedd /'gawsedh/ *n* a mock druidical institution that assembles twice a year to confer bardic degrees and titles [W, lit., mound, court, throne]

gory /'gawri/ *adj* **1** covered with gore; bloodstained **2** full of violence; bloodcurdling ⟨*a ~ film*⟩

gosh /gosh/ *interj* – used to express surprise [euphemism for *God*]

goshawk /'gos,hawk/ *n* any of several long-tailed hawks with short rounded wings [ME *goshawke*, fr OE *gōshafoc*, fr *gōs* goose + *hafoc* hawk]

gosling /'gozling/ *n* a young goose [ME, fr *gos* goose]

,go-'slow *n*, *Br* a deliberate slowing down of production by workers as a means of forcing management's compliance with their demands

¹gospel /'gospl/ *n* **1** *often cap* the message of the life, death, and resurrection of Jesus Christ; *esp* any of the first 4 books of the New Testament, or any similar apocryphal book, relating this **2** *cap* a liturgical reading from any of the New Testament Gospels **3** the message or teachings of a religious teacher or movement **4a** sthg accepted as a guiding principle ⟨*the ~ of hard work*⟩ **b** sthg so authoritative as not to be questioned ⟨*they took his word as ~*⟩ [ME, fr OE *gōdspel*, fr *gōd* good + *spell* tale – more at SPELL]

²gospel *adj* **1** of the Christian gospel; evangelical **2** of or being usu evangelistic religious songs of American origin

'gospel ,side *n*, *often cap G* the left side of an altar or chancel as one faces it [fr the custom of reading the Gospel from this side]

gossamer /'gosəmə/ *n* **1** a film of cobwebs floating in air in calm clear weather **2** sthg light, insubstantial, or tenuous [ME *gossomer*, fr *gos* goose + *somer* summer] – **gossamer** *adj*, **gossamery** *adj*

¹gossip /'gosip/ *n* **1** sby who habitually reveals usu sensational facts concerning other people's actions or lives **2a** (rumour or report of) the facts related by a gossip **b** a chatty talk [ME *gossib* godparent, crony, fr OE *godsibb*, fr *god* + *sibb* kinsman, fr *sibb* related] – **gossipry** /-pri/ *n*, **gossipy** *adj*

²gossip *vi* to relate gossip – **gossiper** *n*

got /got/ **1** *past of* GET **2** *pres pl & 1&2 sing of* GET ⟨*I ~ news for you*⟩ ⟨*we ~ to go*⟩ – nonstandard; compare GOTCHA, GOTTA

gotcha /'gochə/ *interj* **1** – used to indicate that one has understood **2** – used as a shout of triumph when seizing sthg or succeeding in an attempt *USE* infml [alter. of *got you*]

Goth /goth/ *n* a member of a Germanic people that invaded parts of the Roman Empire between the 3rd and 5th c AD [LL *Gothi*, pl, of Gmc origin]

¹Gothic /'gothik/ *adj* **1** of the Goths, their culture, or Gothic **2** of a style of architecture prevalent from the middle of the 12th c to the early 16th c characterized by vaulting and pointed arches **3** *often not cap* of or like a class of novels of the late 18th and early 19th c dealing with macabre or mysterious events – **gothically** *adv*, **Gothicism** /-,siz(ə)m/ *n*, **gothicize** /-,siez/ *vt*

²Gothic *n* **1** the E Germanic language of the Goths **2** Gothic architectural style **3a** BLACK LETTER **b** SANS SERIF *USE* (*3*) ☞ ALPHABET

,Gothic Re'vival *n* an artistic and architectural style of the 18th and 19th c largely imitative of Gothic style

go through *vi* **1** to continue firmly or obstinately to the end – often + *with* ⟨*can't* go through *with the wedding*⟩ **2a** to receive approval or sanction **b** to come to a desired or satisfactory conclusion

¹gotta /'gotə/ *vt pres* to have a ⟨*I ~ horse*⟩ – nonstandard [alter. of *got a*]

²gotta *verbal auxiliary pres* to have to; must ⟨*we ~ go*⟩ – nonstandard [alter. of *got to*]

gotten /'gotn/ *NAm past part of* GET

götterdämmerung /,guhtə'deməroong/ *n*, *often cap* the final destruction of the gods and the world in Germanic mythology [G, twilight of the gods]

gouache /goo'ahsh (*Fr* gwaʃ)/ *n* a method of painting with opaque watercolours that have been ground in water and mixed with a gum preparation [F, deriv of L *aquatio* act of fetching water, fr *aquatus*, pp of *aquari* to fetch water, fr *aqua* water – more at ISLAND]

Gouda /'gowdə/ *n* a mild cheese of Dutch origin that is similar to Edam but contains more fat [*Gouda*, town in the Netherlands]

¹gouge /gowj/ *n* **1** a chisel with a curved cross section and bevel on the concave side of the blade **2** *chiefly NAm* overcharging, extortion – infml [ME *gowge*, fr MF *gouge*, fr LL *gulbia*, of Celt origin; akin to OIr *gulban* sting]

²gouge *vt* **1** to scoop out (as if) with a gouge **2** to force *out* (an eye), esp with the thumb **3** *chiefly NAm* to subject to extortion; overcharge – infml – **gouger** *n*

goulash /'goohlash/ *n* **1** a meat stew made usu with veal or beef and highly seasoned with paprika **2** a round in bridge played with hands dealt in lots of 5,

5, and 3 cards consecutively from a pack formed by the unshuffled arranged hands from a previous deal [Hung *gulyás* herdsman's stew]

go under *vi* to be destroyed or defeated; fail ⟨*empty order books and high interest charges forced the company to* go under⟩

go up *vi, Br* to enter or return to a university

gourd /gooəd/ *n* (the fruit of) any of the cucumber family of typically tendril-bearing climbing plants (e g the melon, squash, and pumpkin); *esp* any of various hard-rinded inedible fruits used for ornament or for vessels and utensils [ME *gourde*, fr MF, fr L *cucurbita*]

gourde /gooəd/ *n* ☞ *Haiti* at NATIONALITY [AmerF, fr F, fem of *gourd* numb, dull, heavy, fr L *gurdus* dull, stupid]

gourmand /ˈgawmənd, ˈgooə- (*Fr* gurmɑ̃)/ *n* one who is excessively fond of or heartily interested in food and drink [MF *gourmant*] – **gourmandism** *n*

gourmet /ˈgawmay, ˈgooə- (*Fr* gurmɛ)/ *n* a connoisseur of food and drink [F, fr MF, alter. of *gromet* boy servant, vintner's assistant, fr ME *grom* groom] – **gourmet** *adj*

gout /gowt/ *n* **1** painful inflammation of the joints, esp that of the big toe, resulting from a metabolic disorder in which there is an excessive amount of uric acid in the blood **2** a sticky blob [ME *goute*, fr OF, gout, drop, fr L *gutta* drop] – **gouty** *adj*

govern /ˈguv(ə)n/ *vt* **1** to exercise continuous sovereign authority over **2a** to control, determine, or strongly influence ⟨*availability often* ~s *choice*⟩ **b** to hold in check; restrain **3** to require (a word) to be in a usu specified case ⟨*in English a transitive verb* ~s *a pronoun in the accusative*⟩ **4** to serve as a precedent or deciding principle for ⟨*habits and customs that* ~ *human decisions*⟩ ~ *vi* **1** to prevail **2** to exercise authority [ME *governen*, fr OF *governer*, fr L *gubernare* to steer, govern, fr Gk *kybernan*] – **governable** *adj*

governance /ˈguv(ə)nəns/ *n* governing or being governed – fml

governess /ˈguv(ə)nis/ *n* a woman entrusted with the private teaching and often supervision of a child

government /ˈguv(ə)nmənt, ˈguvəmənt/ *n* **1** governing; *specif* authoritative direction or control **2** the office, authority, or function of governing **3** policy making as distinguished from administration **4** the machinery through which political authority is exercised **5** *sing or pl in constr* the body of people that constitutes a governing authority – **governmental** /-ˈmentl/ *adj*, **governmentally** *adv*

governor /ˈguv(ə)nə/ *n* **1a** a ruler, chief executive, or nominal head of a political unit **b** a commanding officer **c** the managing director and usu the principal officer of an institution or organization **d** a member of a group (e g the governing body of a school) that controls an institution **2** a device giving automatic control of pressure, fuel, steam, etc, esp to regulate speed **3a** sby (e g a father, guardian, or employer) looked on as governing – slang **b** Mister, Sir – slang; used as a familiar form of address [[1]GOVERN + [1]-OR] – **governorate** /-rət, -rayt/ *n*, **governorship** *n*

ˌgovernor-ˈgeneral *n, pl* **governors-general, governor-generals** a governor of high rank; *esp* one representing the Crown in a Commonwealth country – **governor-generalship** *n*

gowan /ˈgowən/ *n, chiefly Scot* OXEYE DAISY; *broadly* any white or yellow meadow flower [prob alter. of ME *gollan*]

gown /gown/ *n* **1a** a loose flowing robe worn esp by a professional or academic person when acting in an official capacity ☞ GARMENT **b** a woman's dress, esp one that is elegant or for formal wear **c** an outer garment worn in an operating theatre **2** the body of students and staff of a college or university ⟨*riots between town and* ~⟩ [ME, fr MF *goune*, fr LL *gunna*, a fur or leather garment]

gownsman /ˈgownzmən/ *n* a professional or academic person

goy /goy/ *n, pl* **goyim** /-əm, -eem/, **goys** a gentile – chiefly derog [Yiddish, fr Heb *gōy* people, nation] – **goyish** *adj*

ˌGraafian ˈfollicle /ˈgrahfi·ən/ *n* a vesicle in the ovary of a mammal enclosing a developing egg [Regnier de *Graaf* †1673 D anatomist]

[1]grab /grab/ *vb* **-bb-** *vt* **1** to take or seize hastily or by a sudden motion or grasp **2** to obtain unscrupulously **3** to forcefully engage the attention of – infml ⟨*he* ~s *an audience*⟩ ~ *vi* to make a grab; snatch [obs D or LG *grabben*; akin to ME *graspen* to grasp, Skt *gṛbhṇāti* he seizes] – **grabber** *n*

[2]grab *n* **1a** a sudden snatch **b** an unlawful or unscrupulous seizure **c** sthg intended to be grabbed – often in combination ⟨*a grab-rail*⟩ **2a** a mechanical device for clutching an object – **up for grabs** available for anyone to take or win – infml

ˈgrab ˌbag *n, chiefly NAm* LUCKY DIP

grabby /ˈgrabi/ *adj* grasping, greedy – infml

graben /ˈgrahb(ə)n/ *n* RIFT VALLEY [G, ditch]

[1]grace /grays/ *n* **1a** unmerited divine assistance given to human beings for their regeneration or sanctification **b** a state of being pleasing to God **2** a short prayer at a meal asking a blessing or giving thanks **3a** disposition to or an act or instance of kindness or clemency **b** a special favour ⟨*each in his place, by right, not* ~, *shall rule his heritage* – Rudyard Kipling⟩ **c** a temporary exemption; a reprieve **d** approval, favour **4a** a charming trait or accomplishment **b** an elegant appearance or effect; charm **c** ease and suppleness of movement or bearing **5** – used as a title for a duke, duchess, or archbishop **6** consideration, decency ⟨*had the* ~ *to blush*⟩ [ME, fr OF, fr L *gratia* favour, charm, thanks, fr *gratus* pleasing, grateful; akin to OHG *queran* to sigh, Skt *gṛṇāti* he praises] – **with bad/good grace** (un)willingly or (un)happily ⟨*took his defeat* with good grace⟩

[2]grace *vt* **1** to confer dignity or honour on **2** to adorn, embellish

graceful /ˈgraysf(ə)l/ *adj* displaying grace in form, action, or movement – **gracefully** *adv*, **gracefulness** *n*

graceless /ˈgrayslis/ *adj* **1** lacking a sense of propriety **2** devoid of elegance; awkward [[1]GRACE + -LESS] – **gracelessly** *adv*, **gracelessness** *n*

ˈgrace ˌnote *n* a musical note added as an ornament ☞ MUSIC

Graces /ˈgraysiz/ *n pl* the 3 beautiful sister goddesses in Greek mythology who are the givers of charm and beauty

gracile /ˈgrasiel/ *adj* **1** slender, slight **2** graceful [L *gracilis*] – **gracileness, gracility** /graˈsiləti/ *n*

gracious /ˈgrayshəs/ *adj* **1a** marked by kindness and courtesy **b** marked by tact and delicacy **c** having those qualities (e g comfort, elegance, and freedom from hard work) made possible by wealth ⟨~ *living*⟩ **2** merciful, compassionate – used conventionally of royalty and high nobility [ME, fr MF *gracieus*, fr L *gratiosus* enjoying favour, agreeable, fr *gratia*] – **graciously** *adv*, **graciousness** *n*

grackle /ˈgrakl/ *n* any of various Old World starlings [deriv of L *graculus* jackdaw]

gradable, gradeable /ˈgraydəbl/ *adj* capable of grammatical comparison or intensification ⟨*beautiful is a ~ adjective, but* atomic *is not*⟩ [[2]GRADE + -ABLE] – **gradability** /-ˈbiləti/ *n*

gradate /grəˈdayt/ *vi* to shade into the next colour, note, or stage ~ *vt* to arrange in a progression, scale, or series [back-formation fr *gradation*]

gradation /grəˈdaysh(ə)n/ *n* **1** (a step or place in) a series forming successive stages **2** a gradual passing from one tint or shade to another (e g in a painting) **3** ablaut [[2]GRADE + -ATION] – **gradational** *adj*, **gradationally** *adv*

[1]**grade** /grayd/ *n* **1a(1)** a stage in a process **(2)** a position in a scale of ranks or qualities **b** a degree of severity of illness **2** a class of things of the same stage or degree **3** a gradient **4** a domestic animal with one parent purebred and the other of inferior breeding **5** *NAm* a school form; a class **6** *NAm* a mark indicating a degree of accomplishment at school [F, fr L *gradus* step, degree; akin to L *gradi* to step, go, Lith *gridyti* to go, wander] – **gradeless** *adj*

[2]**grade** *vt* **1a** to arrange in grades; sort **b** to arrange in a scale or series **2** to improve (e g cattle) by breeding with purebred animals – often + *up* **3** *NAm* to assign a mark to – **grader** *n*

-grade /-grayd/ *comb form* (→ *adj*) walking ⟨*planti*grade⟩; moving ⟨*retro*grade⟩ [F, fr L *-gradus*, fr *gradi*]

ˈ**grade ˌcrossing** *n, chiefly NAm* LEVEL CROSSING

gradient /ˈgraydi·ənt, -dyənt/ *n* **1** the degree of inclination of a road or slope; *also* a sloping road or railway **2** change in the value of a (specified) quantity with change in a given variable, esp distance ⟨*a vertical temperature ~*⟩ ⟨*a concentration ~*⟩ [L *gradient-, gradiens*, prp of *gradi*]

gradual /ˈgradyooəl, -jooəl, -jəl/ *adj* proceeding or happening by steps or degrees [ML *gradualis*, fr *gradus*] – **gradually** *adv*, **gradualness** *n*

graduand /ˈgradyooˌand, -joo-/ *n, Br* one about to graduate [ML *graduandus*, gerundive of *graduare*]

[1]**graduate** /ˈgradyoo·ət, -joo-/ *n* **1** the holder of an academic degree **2** a graduated cup, cylinder, or flask for measuring **3** *chiefly NAm* one who has completed a course of study [ME *graduat*, fr ML *graduatus*, fr pp of *graduare* to graduate, fr *gradus*]

[2]**graduate** *adj* **1** holding an academic degree or diploma ⟨*a ~ secretary*⟩ **2** postgraduate

[3]**graduate** /ˈgradyooˌayt, -joo-/ *vt* **1** to mark with degrees of measurement **2** to divide into grades or intervals ~ *vi* **1** to receive an academic degree **2** to move up to a usu higher stage of experience, proficiency, or prestige **3** to change gradually **4** *NAm* to complete a course of study – **graduator** *n*

graduation /ˌgradyooˈaysh(ə)n, -joo-/ *n* **1** a mark (e g on an instrument or vessel) indicating degrees or quantity **2** the award of an academic degree

graec·ize, -ise /ˈgreeˌsiez/ *vt, often cap* to make Greek or Hellenistic in character

Graeco-, *chiefly NAm* **Greco-** /greekoh-/ *comb form* **1** Greek nation, people, or culture ⟨Graeco-*mania*⟩ **2** Greek and ⟨Graeco-*Roman*⟩ [L *Graeco-*, fr *Graecus*]

ˌ**Graeco-ˈRoman** /ˌgreekoh/ *n* a style of wrestling resembling catch-as-catch-can but in which holds on the legs are disallowed

Graf /grahf/ *fem* **Gräfin** /ˈgrayfin/ *n, pl* **Grafen** /ˈgrahfn/ a German, Austrian, or Swedish count – usu used as a title [G]

graffito /grəˈfeetoh, gra-/ *n, pl* **graffiti** /-ti/ an inscription or drawing, usu of a crude or political nature, made on a wall, rock, etc – usu pl [It, dim. of *graffio* scratch, fr *graffiare* to scratch]

[1]**graft** /grahft/ *vt* **1a** to cause (a plant scion) to unite with a stock; *also* to unite (plants or scion and stock) to form a graft **b** to propagate (a plant) by grafting **2** to attach, add **3** to implant (living tissue) surgically ~ *vi* **1** to become grafted **2** to perform grafting **3** *NAm* to practise graft [ME *graften*, alter. of *graffen*, fr *graffe* graft, fr MF *grafe*, fr ML *graphium*, fr L, stylus, fr Gk *grapheion*, fr *graphein* to write – more at CARVE] – **grafter** *n*

[2]**graft** *n* **1a** a grafted plant **b** (the point of insertion upon a stock of) a scion **2** (living tissue used in) grafting **3a** the improper use of one's position (e g public office) to one's private, esp financial, advantage **b** sthg acquired by graft

[3]**graft** *vi, Br* to work hard – slang [E dial. *graft* (to dig), alter. of [1]*grave*] – **graft** *n*

Grail /grayl/ *n* HOLY GRAIL [ME *graal*, fr MF, bowl, grail, fr ML *gradalis*]

[1]**grain** /grayn/ *n* **1** a seed or fruit of a cereal grass; *also* (the seeds or fruits collectively of) the cereal grasses or similar food plants **2a** a discrete (small hard) particle or crystal (e g of sand, salt, or a metal) **b** the least amount possible ⟨*not a ~ of truth in what he said*⟩ **c** fine crystallization (e g of sugar) **3** a fast dye **4a** a granular surface, nature, or appearance **b** the outer or hair side of a skin or hide (from which the hair has been removed) **5** ☞ UNIT **6a** the arrangement of the fibres in wood **b** the direction, alignment, or texture of the constituent particles, fibres, or threads ⟨*the ~ of a rock*⟩ ⟨*the ~ of a fabric*⟩ **7** tactile quality **8** natural disposition or character; temper **9** (a brilliant scarlet dye made from) either kermes or cochineal – not now used technically [ME; partly fr MF *grain* cereal grain, fr L *granum*; partly fr MF *graine* seed, kermes, fr L *grana*, pl of *granum* – more at [1]CORN] – **grained** *adj*, **grainy** *adj*, **graininess** *n* – **against the grain** counter to one's inclination, disposition, or feeling

[2]**grain** *vt* **1** to form into grains; granulate **2** to paint in imitation of the grain of wood or stone ~ *vi* to become granular; granulate – **grainer** *n*

grain whisky *n* whisky distilled from barley and maize in continuous stills and used chiefly in producing blended whiskies

[1]**gralloch** /ˈgraləkh/ *n, Br* the entrails of a dead animal, esp a deer killed in a hunt [ScGael *greallach*]

[2]**gralloch** *vt, Br* to remove the entrails from (e g a deer)

[1]**gram** /gram/ *n* a leguminous plant (e g the chick-pea) grown esp for its seed [obs Pg (now *grão*), grain, fr L *granum*]

[2]**gram, gramme** *n* one thousandth of a kilogram (about 0.04oz) ☞ UNIT [F *gramme*, fr LL *gramma*, a small weight, fr Gk *grammat-, gramma*

letter, writing, a small weight, fr *graphein* to write – more at CARVE]

-gram /-gram/ *comb form* (→ *n*) drawing; writing; record ⟨*ideo*gram⟩ ⟨*tele*gram⟩ ⟨*chrono*gram⟩ [L *-gramma*, fr Gk, fr *gramma*]

gram atom *n* a quantity of an element in grams with a weight numerically equal to its atomic weight

gramineous /grə'mini·əs/, **graminaceous** /,grami'nayshəs/ *adj* of a grass [L *gramineus*, fr *gramin-*, *gramen* grass] – **gramineousness** *n*

grammalogue /'gramə,log/ *n* a logogram [Gk *gramma* letter + E *-logue*]

¹grammar /'gramə/ *n* **1** the study of the classes of words, their inflections, and their functions and relations in the sentence; *broadly* this study when taken to include that of phonology and sometimes of usage **2** the characteristic system of inflections and syntax of a language **3a** a grammar textbook **b** speech or writing evaluated according to its conformity to grammatical rules **4** the principles or rules of an art, science, or technique [ME *gramere*, fr MF *gramaire*, modif of L *grammatica*, fr Gk *grammatikē*, fr fem of *grammatikos* of letters, fr *grammat-*, *gramma*] – **grammarian** /grə'meəri·ən/ *n*

²grammar *adj* of the type of education provided at a grammar school ⟨*the ~ stream*⟩

'grammar ,school *n* **1** a secondary school that emphasized the study of the classics **2** *Br* a secondary school providing an academic type of education from the age of 11 to 18

grammatical /grə'matikl/ *adj* **1** of grammar **2** conforming to the rules of grammar – **grammatically** *adv*, **grammaticalness** *n*, **grammaticality** /-'kaləti/ *n*

gram-molecular weight *n* ⁵MOLE

'gram ,molecule *n* ⁵MOLE

,gram-'negative *adj* not holding the purple dye when stained by Gram's method

gramophone /'graməfohn/ *n* a device for reproducing sounds from the vibrations of a stylus resting in a spiral groove on a rotating disc; *specif, chiefly Br* RECORD PLAYER [alter. of *phonogram*]

,gram-'positive *adj* holding the purple dye when stained by Gram's method

grampus /'grampəs/ *n* any of various (dolphinlike) small whales (e g the killer whale) [alter. of ME *graspey*, *grapay*, fr MF *graspeis*, fr *gras* fat (fr L *crassus*) + *peis* fish (fr L *piscis*) – more at ¹FISH]

'Gram's ,method /gramz/ *n* the treatment of bacteria with a solution of iodine and potassium iodide after staining with gentian violet so that some species are decolorized and some remain coloured [Hans *Gram* †1938 Dan physician]

gran /gran/ *n, chiefly Br* a grandmother – infml

grana /'graynə/ *pl of* GRANUM

granadilla /,granə'dilə/ *n* the oblong fruit of various (tropical American) passionflowers used as a dessert [Sp, dim. of *granada* pomegranate]

granary /'granəri/ *n* **1** a storehouse for threshed grain **2** a region producing grain in abundance [L *granarium*, fr *granum* grain]

¹grand /grand/ *adj* **1** having more importance than others; foremost **2** complete, comprehensive ⟨*the ~ total of all money paid out*⟩ **3** main, principal **4** large and striking in size, extent, or conception ⟨*a ~ design*⟩ **5a** lavish, sumptuous ⟨*a ~ celebration*⟩ **b** marked by regal form and dignity; imposing **c** lofty, sublime ⟨*writing in the ~ style*⟩ **6** intended to impress ⟨*a man of ~ gestures and pretentious statements*⟩ **7** very good; wonderful – infml ⟨*a ~ time*⟩ [MF, large, great, grand, fr L *grandis*] – **grandly** *adv*, **grandness** *n*

²grand *n* **1** GRAND PIANO **2a** *Br* a thousand pounds **b** *NAm* a thousand dollars *USE* (*2*) slang

,grand'aunt /-'ahnt/ *n* a great-aunt

grandchild /'gran,chield/ *n* a child of one's son or daughter

granddad, grandad /'gran,dad/ *n* a grandfather – infml

granddaughter /'gran,dawtə/ *n* a daughter of one's son or daughter

,grand 'duchess *n* **1** the wife or widow of a grand duke **2** a woman having in her own right the rank of a grand duke

,grand 'duchy *n* the territory of a grand duke or grand duchess

,grand 'duke *n* the sovereign ruler of any of various European states

grande dame /,grond 'dahm (*Fr* grɑ̃d dam)/ *n* a usu elderly dignified woman of high rank or standing [F, lit., great lady]

grandee /gran'dee/ *n* a Spanish or Portuguese nobleman of the highest rank [Sp *grande*, fr *grande*, adj, large, great, fr L *grandis*]

grandeur /'granjə, -dyə/ *n* **1** the quality of being large or impressive; magnificence **2** personal greatness marked by nobility, dignity, or power [ME, fr MF, fr *grand*]

grandfather /'gran(d),fahdhə/ *n* the father of one's father or mother; *broadly* a male ancestor – **grandfatherly** *adj*

,grand,father 'clock *n* a tall pendulum clock standing directly on the floor [fr the song *My Grandfather's Clock* by Henry C Work †1884 US songwriter]

grandiloquence /gran'diləkwəns/ *n* lofty or pompous eloquence; bombast [prob fr MF, fr L *grandiloquus* using lofty language, fr *grandis* + *loqui* to speak] – **grandiloquent** *adj*, **grandiloquently** *adv*

grandiose /'grandiohs, -ohz/ *adj* **1** impressive because of uncommon largeness, scope, or grandeur **2** characterized by affectation of grandeur or by absurd exaggeration [F, fr It *grandioso*, fr *grande* great, fr L *grandis*] – **grandiosely** *adv*, **grandioseness**, **grandiosity** /-'osəti/ *n*

,grand 'jury *n* a jury in the USA that examines accusations and if the evidence warrants makes formal charges

grandma /'gran,mah, 'gram,mah/ *n* a grandmother – infml

grand mal /,gronh'mal (*Fr* grɑ̃ mal)/ *n* (an attack of) the severe form of epilepsy – compare PETIT MAL [F, lit., great illness]

,grand 'master *n* a chess player who has consistently scored higher than a standardized score in international competition

grandmother /'gran,mudhə, 'grand-, 'gram-/ *n* the mother of one's father or mother; *broadly* a female ancestor – **grandmotherly** *adj*

,grand,mother 'clock *n* a smaller version of a grandfather clock

,Grand 'National *n* the major British steeplechase for horses that is run annually at Aintree near Liverpool

grandnephew /'grand,nefyooh/ *n* a great-nephew

'grand,niece /-,nees/ *n* a great-niece

ˌ**grand 'opera** *n* opera with a serious dramatic plot and no spoken dialogue

grandpa /'granˌpah, 'gram-/ *n* a grandfather – infml

grandparent /'gran(d)ˌpeərənt/ *n* the parent of one's father or mother – **grandparenthood** *n*, **grandparental** /-pə'rentl/ *adj*

ˌ**grand pi'ano** *n* a piano with horizontal frame and strings

grand prix /ˌgronh 'pree (*Fr* grɑ̃ pri)/ *n, pl* **grand prix** *often cap G&P* any of a series of long-distance races for formula cars, held consecutively in different countries [F *Grand Prix de Paris*, an international horse race established 1863, lit., grand prize of Paris]

ˌ**grand 'slam** *n* **1** the winning of all the tricks in 1 hand of a card game, specif bridge **2** a clean sweep or total success, esp in a sport

grandson /'gran(d)ˌsun/ *n* a son of one's son or daughter

1'**grandˌstand** /-ˌstand/ *n* a usu roofed stand for spectators at a racecourse, stadium, etc in an advantageous position for viewing the contest

2**grandstand** *vi, NAm* to play or act so as to impress onlookers – infml – **grandstander** *n*

ˌ**grand 'tour** *n* **1** an extended tour of the Continent, formerly a usual part of the education of young British gentlemen – usu + *the* **2** an extensive and usu educational tour

'**grandˌuncle** /-ˌungkl/ *n* a great-uncle

grange /graynj/ *n* a farm; *esp* a farmhouse with outbuildings [ME, granary, farmhouse, fr MF, fr ML *granica*, fr L *granum* grain]

grani- *comb form* grain; seeds ⟨grani*vorous*⟩ [L, fr *granum*]

granite /'granit/ *n* **1** a very hard granular igneous rock formed of quartz, feldspar, and mica and used esp for building **2** unyielding firmness or endurance [It *granito*, fr pp of *granire* to granulate, fr *grano* grain, fr L *granum*] – **granitelike** *adj*, **granitoid** /-ˌtoyd/ *adj*, **granitic** /gra'nitik/ *adj*

'**graniteˌware** /-ˌweə/ *n* ironware with mottled enamel usu in 2 tones of grey; *also* pottery with a speckled granitelike appearance

1**granny, grannie** /'grani/ *n* a grandmother – infml [by shortening & alter.]

2**granny, grannie** *adj* designed for use by an older relative – infml ⟨~ *flat*⟩

'**granny ˌbond** *n, Br* a savings bond, available only to those over a certain age, which is guaranteed to maintain its value in line with the rate of inflation

'**granny ˌknot** *n* a wrongly tied insecure reef knot

ˌ**Granny 'Smith** /smith/ *n* a large green variety of (cooking) apple [Maria Ann ('Granny") *Smith* †1870 Austr gardener]

granolith /'granəlith/ *n* an artificial stone of crushed granite and cement [*grano-* granite (fr G) + *-lith*] – **granolithic** /-'lithik/ *adj*

1**grant** /grahnt/ *vt* **1a** to consent to carry out or fulfil (e g a wish or request) ⟨~ *a child his wish*⟩ **b** to permit as a right, privilege, or favour ⟨*luggage allowances* ~ed *to passengers*⟩ **2** to bestow or transfer formally **3a** to be willing to concede **b** to assume to be true [ME *granten*, fr OF *creanter, graanter*, fr (assumed) VL *credentare*, fr L *credent-, credens*, prp of *credere* to believe – more at CREED] – **grantable** *adj*, **granter** *n*, **grantor** /ˌgrahn'taw/ *n*

2**grant** *n* **1** sthg granted; *esp* a gift for a particular purpose **2** a transfer of property; *also* the property so transferred

ˌ**grant-in-'aid** *n, pl* **grants-in-aid** **1** a grant or subsidy paid by a central to a local government in aid of a public undertaking **2** a grant to a school or individual for a project

granul- /granyool-/, **granuli-, granulo-** *comb form* granule ⟨granul*ose*⟩ [LL *granulum*]

granular /'granyoolə/ *adj* (apparently) consisting of granules; having a grainy texture – **granularly** *adv*, **granularity** /-'larəti/ *n*

granulate /'granyooˌlayt/ *vt* to form or crystallize into grains or granules ⟨~d *sugar*⟩ ~ *vi , esp of a wound* (to form minute granules of new capillaries while beginning) to heal – **granulator** *n*, **granulation** /-'laysh(ə)n/ *n*, **granulative** /-ˌlaytiv, -lə-/ *adj*

granule /'granyoohl/ *n* a small grain [LL *granulum*, dim. of L *granum* grain]

granulocyte /'granyooləˌsiet/ *n* any of various white blood cells that have cytoplasm containing large numbers of conspicuous stainable granules and a nucleus with many lobes – compare AGRANULOCYTE, BASOPHIL, EOSINOPHIL [ISV] – **granulocytic** /-'sitik/ *adj*

granum /'graynəm/ *n, pl* **grana** /-nə/ any of the stacks of thin layers of chlorophyll-containing material in plant chloroplasts [NL, fr L, grain]

grape /grayp/ *n* **1** (any of a genus of widely cultivated woody vines that bear, in clusters,) a smooth-skinned juicy greenish white to deep red or purple berry eaten as a fruit or fermented to produce wine **2** grapeshot [ME, fr OF *crape, grape* hook, grape stalk, bunch of grapes, grape, of Gmc origin; akin to OHG *krāpfo* hook – more at CRAVE] – **grapy** *adj*

'**grapeˌfruit** /-ˌfrooht/ *n* (a small tree that bears) a large round citrus fruit with a bitter yellow rind and a somewhat acid juicy pulp

ˌ**grape 'hyacinth** *n* any of several small plants of the lily family with many usu blue flowers

'**grapeˌshot** /-ˌshot/ *n* a cluster of small iron balls used as a charge for a cannon

'**grapeˌvine** /-ˌvien/ *n* a secret or unofficial means of circulating information or gossip

1**graph** /grahf, graf/ *n* **1** a diagram (e g a series of points, a line, a curve, or an area) expressing a relation between quantities or variables **2** the collection of all points whose coordinates satisfy a given relation (e g the equation of a function) [short for *graphic formula*]

2**graph** *vt* to plot on or represent by a graph

-graph /-ˌgrahf, -ˌgraf/ *comb form* (→ *n*) **1** sthg written or represented ⟨*mono*graph⟩ ⟨*picto*graph⟩ **2** instrument for recording or transmitting (sthg specified or by a specified means) ⟨*seismo*graph⟩ ⟨*tele*graph⟩ [(1) MF *-graphe*, fr L *-graphum*, fr Gk *-graphon*, fr neut of *-graphos* written, fr *graphein* to write; (2) F *-graphe*, fr LL *-graphus* writer, fr Gk *-graphos*]

grapheme /'grafeem/ *n* the set of units of a writing system that represent a phoneme ⟨*the* f *of* fin, *the* ph *of* phantom, *and the* gh *of* laugh *are members of one* ~⟩ – **graphemic** /-'feemik/ *adj*, **graphemically** *adv*

1**graphic** /'grafik/ *also* **graphical** /-kl/ *adj* **1** formed by writing, drawing, or engraving **2** marked by clear and vivid description; sharply outlined **3a** of the pictorial arts **b** of or employing engraving, etching, lithography, photography, or other methods of reproducing material in the graphic arts **c** of or according to graphics **4** *of a rock or mineral surface* having marks resembling written characters **5** of or represented by a graph **6** of writing [L *graphicus*, fr Gk *graphikos*, fr *graphein*] – **graphically** *adv*, **graphicness** *n*

[2]**graphic** *n* **1** a product of graphic art **2** a picture, map, or graph used for illustration or demonstration **3** a graphic representation displayed by a computer (e g on a VDU)

-graphic /-'grafik/, **-graphical** /-kl/ *comb form* (→ *adj*) **1** written, represented, or transmitted in (such) a way ⟨*stylo*graphic⟩ ⟨*ideo*graphic⟩ **2** of writing on a (specified) subject ⟨*autobio*graphic⟩ [LL *-graphicus*, fr Gk *-graphikos*, fr *graphikos*]

ˌgraphic 'arts *n pl* the fine and applied arts of representation, decoration, and writing or printing on flat surfaces

'graphics *n pl but sing or pl in constr* **1a** the art or science of drawing an object on a 2-dimensional surface according to mathematical rules of projection **b** GRAPHIC ARTS **c** (the art or technique of making) designs (e g advertising posters) containing both typographic and pictorial elements **2** the process whereby a computer displays graphics on a VDU and an operator can manipulate them (e g with a light pen)

graphite /'grafiet/ *n* a soft black lustrous form of carbon that conducts electricity and is used esp in lead pencils and as a lubricant [G *graphit*, fr Gk *graphein* to write] – **graphitize** /-fitiez, -fietiez/ *vt*, **graphitic** /gra'fitik/ *adj*

grapho- *comb form* writing ⟨grapho*logist*⟩ [F, fr MF, fr Gk, fr *graphē*, fr *graphein*]

graphology /gra'foləji/ *n* the study of handwriting, esp for the purpose of character analysis [F *graphologie*, fr *grapho-* + *-logie* -logy] – **graphologist** *n*, **graphological** /-fə'lojikl/ *adj*

'graph ˌpaper *n* paper ruled for drawing graphs

-graphy /-grəfi/ *comb form* (→ *n*) **1** writing or representation in (such) a manner or on (a specified subject) or by (a specified means) ⟨*photo*graphy⟩ ⟨*calli*graphy⟩ ⟨*bio*graphy⟩ **2** art or science of ⟨*organo*graphy⟩ ⟨*choreo*graphy⟩ [L *-graphia*, fr Gk, fr *graphein*] – **-grapher** *comb form* (→ *n*)

grapnel /'grapnəl/ *n* an instrument with several claws that is hurled with a line attached in order to hook onto a ship, the top of a wall, etc [ME *grapenel*, fr (assumed) MF *grapinel*, dim. of *grapin*, dim. of *grape* hook – more at GRAPE]

grappa /'grapə/ *n* an Italian spirit distilled from the fermented remains of grapes after the juice has been extracted for making wine [It]

[1]**grapple** /'grapl/ *n* **1** a grapnel **2** a hand-to-hand struggle [MF *grappelle*, dim. of *grape* hook – more at GRAPE]

[2]**grapple** *vb* **grappling** /'grapling, 'grapl·ing/ *vt* to seize (as if) with a grapple ~ *vi* to come to grips *with*; wrestle – **grappler** *n*

graptolite /'graptəˌliet/ *n* any of numerous extinct fossil Palaeozoic marine animals [Gk *graptos* painted (fr *graphein* to write, paint) + E *-lite*]

[1]**grasp** /grahsp/ *vi* to make the motion of seizing; clutch ~ *vt* **1** to take, seize, or clasp eagerly (as if) with the fingers or arms **2** to succeed in understanding; comprehend [ME *graspen* – more at GRAB] – **graspable** *adj*, **grasper** *n*

[2]**grasp** *n* **1** a firm hold **2** control, power ⟨*he is in her* ~⟩ **3** the power of seizing and holding or attaining ⟨*success was just beyond his* ~⟩ **4** comprehension ⟨*showed a firm* ~ *of her subject*⟩

grasping /'grahsping/ *adj* eager for material possessions; avaricious – **graspingly** *adv*, **graspingness** *n*

[1]**grass** /grahs/ *n* **1a** herbage suitable or used for grazing animals **b** pasture, grazing **2** any of a large family of plants with slender leaves and (green) flowers in small spikes or clusters, that includes bamboo, wheat, rye, corn, etc **3** land on which grass is grown ⟨*keep off the* ~⟩ **4** grass leaves or plants **5** cannabis; *specif* marijuana – slang **6** *Br* a police informer – slang [ME *gras*, fr OE *græs*; akin to OHG *gras* grass, OE *grōwan* to grow; (6) rhyming slang *grass(hopper)* copper (policeman)] – **grasslike** *adj* – **put/send out to grass** to cause (sby) to enter usu enforced retirement

[2]**grass** *vt* **1** to feed (livestock) on grass **2** to cover or seed with grass – often + *down* ~ *vi*, *Br* to inform the police; *esp* to betray sby to the police – slang

'grassˌhopper /-ˌhopə/ *n* any of numerous plant-eating insects with hind legs adapted for leaping – compare LOCUST ☞ LIFE CYCLE

'grassland /-lənd, -ˌland/ *n* **1** farmland used for grazing **2** land on which the natural dominant plant forms are grasses ☞ PLANT

ˌgrass of Par'nassus /pah'nasəs/ *n* any of a genus of perennial (marsh) plants with single small whitish flowers [*Parnassus*, mountain in Greece]

ˌgrass 'roots *n pl but sing or pl in constr* **1** society at the local level as distinguished from the centres of political leadership **2** the fundamental level or source – **grass-roots** *adj*

'grass ˌsnake *n* a nonpoisonous European snake with 2 yellow or orange patches forming a collar behind its head ☞ DEFENCE

ˌgrass 'widow *n* a woman whose husband is temporarily away from her

ˌgrass 'widower *n* a man whose wife is temporarily away from him

grassy /'grahsi/ *adj* **1** consisting of or covered with grass **2** (having a smell) like grass

grat /grat/ *past of* [2]GREET

[1]**grate** /grayt/ *n* **1** a frame or bed of metal bars to hold the fuel in a fireplace, stove, or furnace **2** a fireplace [ME, fr ML *crata, grata* hurdle, modif of L *cratis* – more at HURDLE]

[2]**grate** *vt* **1** to reduce to small particles by rubbing on sthg rough ⟨~ *cheese*⟩ **2a** to gnash or grind noisily **b** to cause to make a rasping sound ~ *vi* **1** to rub or rasp noisily **2** to cause irritation; jar ⟨*his manner of talking* ~s *on my nerves*⟩ [ME *graten*, fr MF *grater* to scratch, of Gmc origin; akin to OHG *krazzōn* to scratch] – **grater** *n*

grateful /'graytf(ə)l/ *adj* **1** feeling or expressing thanks **2** pleasing, comforting [obs *grate* (pleasing, thankful), fr L *gratus* – more at GRACE] – **gratefully** *adv*, **gratefulness** *n*

graticule /'gratikyoohl/ *n* **1** a network or scale visible when using a telescope, microscope, etc and used in locating or measuring objects **2** the network of latitude and longitude lines on which a map is drawn [F, fr L *craticula* fine latticework, dim. of *cratis*]

gratification /ˌgratifi'kaysh(ə)n/ *n* **1** gratifying or being gratified **2** a source of satisfaction or pleasure

gratify /'grati,fie/ *vt* **1** to be a source of or give pleasure or satisfaction to **2** to give in to; satisfy ⟨~ *a whim*⟩ [MF *gratifier*, fr L *gratificari*, lit., to make oneself pleasing, fr *gratus* + *-ificari*, passive of *-ificare* -ify] – **gratifyingly** *adv*

grating /'grayting/ *n* **1** a partition, covering, or frame of parallel bars or crossbars **2** a lattice used to close or floor any of various openings **3** a set of close parallel lines or bars ruled on a polished surface to produce (optical) spectra by diffraction

gratis /'gratis, 'grah-, 'gray-/ *adv or adj* without charge or recompense; free [ME, fr L *gratiis, gratis*, fr abl pl of *gratia* favour – more at GRACE]

gratitude /'grati,tyoohd/ *n* the state or feeling of being grateful; thankfulness [ME, fr MF or ML; MF, fr ML *gratitudo*, fr L *gratus* grateful]

gratuitous /grə'tyooh·itəs/ *adj* **1a** costing nothing; free **b** not involving a return benefit or compensation **2** not called for by the circumstances; unwarranted ⟨*the film contained scenes of ~ violence*⟩ [L *gratuitus*, fr *gratus*] – **gratuitously** *adv*, **gratuitousness** *n*

gratuity /grə'tyooh·əti/ *n* sthg given voluntarily, usu in return for or in anticipation of some service; *esp* a tip

gravamen /grə'vaymen, -mən/ *n, pl* **gravamens, gravamina** /-'vaminə/ the material part of a legal grievance [LL, burden, fr L *gravare* to burden, fr *gravis*]

[1]**grave** /grayv/ *vt* **graven, graved** to engrave [ME *graven* to dig, bury, engrave, fr OE *grafan*; akin to OHG *graban* to dig, OSlav *pogreti* to bury]

[2]**grave** *n* an excavation for burial of a body; *broadly* a tomb [ME, fr OE *græf*; akin to OHG *grab* grave, OE *grafan* to dig]

[3]**grave** *vt* to clean and then tar (e g a ship's bottom) [ME *graven*]

[4]**grave** /grayv/ *adj* **1a** requiring serious consideration; important ⟨~ *problems*⟩ **b** likely to produce great harm or danger ⟨*a ~ mistake*⟩ **2** serious, dignified **3** drab in colour; sombre **4** *of a sound* low in pitch [MF, fr L *gravis* heavy, grave – more at [1]GRIEVE] – **gravely** *adv*, **graveness** *n*

[5]**grave** /grahv/ *adj or n* (being or marked with) an accent ` × used to show that a vowel is pronounced with a fall of pitch (e g in ancient Greek) or has a certain quality (e g è in French) ☞ SYMBOL

[1]**gravel** /'gravl/ *n* **1** (a stratum or surface of) loose rounded fragments of rock mixed with sand **2** a sandy deposit of small stones in the kidneys and urinary bladder [ME, fr MF *gravele*, fr OF, dim. of *grave, greve* pebbly ground, beach]

[2]**gravel** *adj* GRAVELLY 2

[3]**gravel** *vt* **-ll-** (*NAm* **-l-, -ll-**), /'gravl·ing/ **1** to cover or spread with gravel **2** to perplex, confound

'gravel-,blind *adj* having very weak vision [suggested by *sand-blind*]

gravelly /'gravl·i/ *adj* **1** of, containing, or covered with gravel **2** harsh, grating ⟨*a ~ voice*⟩

,graven 'image /'grayv(ə)n/ *n* an idol, usu carved from wood or stone

graver /'grayvə/ *n* any of various tools (e g a burin) used in engraving [[1]GRAVE + [2]-ER]

Graves /grahv/ *n, pl* **Graves** /~/ a dry white or occas red Bordeaux produced in the Graves district

Graves' disease /grayvz/ *n* hyperthyroidism accompanied by enlargement of the thyroid gland and abnormal protrusion of the eyeball [Robert J *Graves* †1853 Ir physician]

'grave,stone /-,stohn/ *n* a stone over or at one end of a grave, usu inscribed with the name and details of the dead person

'grave,yard /-,yahd/ *n* **1** a cemetery **2** a condition of final disappointment or failure ⟨*the ~ of their hopes*⟩

gravi- *comb form* heavy; weight ⟨grav*imeter*⟩ [MF, fr L, fr *gravis*]

gravid /'gravid/ *adj* pregnant [L *gravidus*, fr *gravis* heavy] – **gravidly** *adv*, **gravidity** /gra'vidəti/ *n*

gravimeter /gra'vimitə, 'gravi,meetə/ *n* a weighing instrument for measuring variations in gravity on the earth, moon, etc [F *gravimètre*, fr *gravi-* + *-mètre* -meter]

gravimetric /,gravi'metrik/ *adj* of the measurement **a** of density or weight **b** of a gravitational field using a gravimeter – **gravimetrically** *adv*, **gravimety** /gra'vimətri/ *n*

graving dock /'grayving/ *n* DRY DOCK

gravitas /'gravitas/ *n* a solemn and serious quality or manner [L, lit., heaviness, fr *gravis*]

gravitate /'gravitayt/ *vb* to (cause to) move under the influence of gravitation – **gravitate towards** to move or be compulsively drawn towards

gravitation /,gravi'taysh(ə)n/ *n* (movement resulting from) the natural force of mutual attraction between bodies or particles ☞ PHYSICS [GRAVITATE + -ION] – **gravitational** *adj*, **gravitationally** *adv*, **gravitative** /-,taytiv/ *adj*

gravitational wave /,gravi'taysh(ə)nl/ *n* a hypothetical wave by means of which gravitational attraction is effected

gravity /'gravəti/ *n* **1a** dignity or sobriety of bearing **b** significance; *esp* seriousness ⟨*he couldn't comprehend the ~ of the situation*⟩ **2** (the quality of having) weight **3** (the attraction of a celestial body for bodies at or near its surface resulting from) gravitation ☞ PHYSICS [MF or L; MF *gravité*, fr L *gravitat-, gravitas*, fr *gravis*] – **gravity** *adj*

'gravity ,feed *n* (a mechanism for) the supplying of material by the action of gravity alone

gravure /grə'vyooə/ *n* **1** the process of printing from an intaglio plate of copper or wood **2** photogravure [F, fr *graver* to grave, of Gmc origin; akin to OHG *graban* to dig, engrave – more at [1] [2]GRAVE]

gravy /'grayvi/ *n* the (thickened and seasoned) fat and juices from cooked meat used as a sauce [ME *gravey*, fr MF *gravé*]

'gravy ,train *n* a much exploited source of easy money – infml

gray /gray/ *vb, n, or adj, chiefly NAm* (to) grey

grayling /'grayling/ *n, pl* **graylings,** *esp collectively* **grayling** any of several freshwater (food and sport) fishes of the salmon family [ME, fr *gray* + *-ling*]

[1]**graze** /grayz/ *vi* to feed on growing herbage ~ *vt* **1a** to crop and eat (growing herbage) **b** to feed on the herbage of (e g a pasture) **2** to put to graze ⟨~d *the cows on the meadow*⟩ [ME *grasen*, fr OE *grasian*, fr *græs* grass] – **grazable** *adj*, **grazer** *n*

[2]**graze** *vt* **1** to touch lightly in passing **2** to abrade, scratch ⟨~d *her elbow*⟩ ~ *vi* to touch or rub against sthg in passing ⟨*our bumpers just* ~d⟩ [perh fr [1]*graze*]

³graze *n* (an abrasion, esp of the skin, made by) a scraping along a surface

grazier /ˈgrayzyə, -zi·ə/ *n* **1** one who grazes cattle, usu for beef production **2** *Austr* a sheep farmer

¹grease /grees/ *n* **1a** melted down animal fat **b** oily matter **c** a thick lubricant **2** oily wool as it comes from the sheep [ME *grese*, fr OF *craisse, graisse*, fr (assumed) VL *crassia*, fr L *crassus* fat] – **greaseless** *adj*, **greaseproof** *adj* – **in the grease** *of wool or fur* in the natural uncleaned condition

²grease *vt* **1** to smear, lubricate, or soil with grease **2** to hasten or ease the process or progress of – **greaser** *n* – **grease the palm of** to bribe

grease monkey *n* a mechanic – infml

ˈgrease,paint /-,paynt/ *n* theatrical make-up

greasy /ˈgreesi/ *adj* **1a** smeared or soiled with grease **b** oily in appearance, texture, or manner ⟨*his ~ smile* – Jack London⟩ **c** slippery **2** containing an unusual amount of grease ⟨*~ food*⟩ – **greasily** *adv*, **greasiness** *n*

¹great /grayt/ *adj* **1a** notably large in size or number **b** of a relatively large kind – in plant and animal names **c** elaborate, ample ⟨*~ detail*⟩ **2a** extreme in amount, degree, or effectiveness ⟨*~ bloodshed*⟩ **b** of importance; significant ⟨*a ~ day in European history*⟩ **3** full of emotion ⟨*~ with anger*⟩ **4a** eminent, distinguished ⟨*a ~ poet*⟩ **b** aristocratic, grand ⟨*~ ladies*⟩ **5** main, principal ⟨*a reception in the ~ hall*⟩ **6** removed in a family relationship by at least 3 stages directly or 2 stages indirectly – chiefly in combination ⟨*great-grandfather*⟩ **7** markedly superior in character or quality; *esp* noble **8a** remarkably skilled **b** enthusiastic, keen ⟨*she was a ~ film-goer*⟩ **9** *archaic* pregnant ⟨*~ with child*⟩ **10** – used as a generalized term of approval ⟨*had a ~ time*⟩; infml [ME *grete*, fr OE *grēat*; akin to OHG *grōz* large] – **great** *adv*, **greatly** *adv*, **greatness** *n* – **no great shakes** not very good, skilful, effective, etc ⟨*he's* no great shakes *as a boss*⟩

²great *n, pl* **great, greats** one who is great – usu pl ⟨*the ~s of the stage*⟩

,great-ˈaunt *n* an aunt of one's father or mother

,Great ˈBear *n* URSA MAJOR

great circle *n* a circle formed on the surface of a sphere, specif the earth, by the intersection of a plane that passes through the centre of the sphere

ˈgreat,coat /-,koht/ *n* a heavy overcoat

great crested grebe *n* a large Old World grebe that has black projecting ear tufts in the breeding season

,Great ˈDane /dayn/ *n* any of a breed of massive powerful smooth-coated dogs

,great diˈvide *n* **1** a significant point of division **2** death – euph; + *the* [the *Great Divide*, NAm watershed]

greater /ˈgraytə/ *adj, often cap* consisting of a central city together with adjacent areas that are geographically or administratively connected with it ⟨Greater *London*⟩ [compar of *great*]

greater celandine *n* CELANDINE 1

,greatˈhearted /-ˈhahtid/ *adj* generous, magnanimous – **greatheartedly** *adv*, **greatheartedness** *n*

ˈgreat-,nephew *n* a grandson of one's brother or sister

ˈgreat-,niece *n* a granddaughter of one's brother or sister

great organ *n* the principal division of an organ including the loudest stops

,great ˈpower *n, often cap G&P* any of the nations that figure most decisively in international affairs

,Great ˈRussian *n or adj* (a member) of the Russian-speaking people of the central and NE USSR

Greats *n pl* the course and final BA examination in classics at Oxford

,great ˈtit *n* a large common black, white, and yellow Eurasian and N African tit

ˈgreat-,uncle *n* an uncle of one's father or mother

,Great ˈWar *n* *the* first World War of 1914 to 1918

greave /greev/ *n* a piece of armour for the leg below the knee [ME *greve*, fr MF]

grebe /greeb/ *n* any of a family of swimming and diving birds closely related to the loons but having lobed instead of webbed toes [F *grèbe*]

Grecian /ˈgreesh(ə)n/ *adj* Greek [L *Graecia* Greece] – **Grecian** *n*, **grecianize** *vt, often cap*

Greco- /greekoh-, grekoh-/ *comb form, chiefly NAm* Graeco-

greed /greed/ *n* **1** excessive acquisitiveness; avarice **2** excessive desire for or consumption of food [back-formation fr *greedy*]

greedy /ˈgreedi/ *adj* **1** having a usu excessive desire for sthg, esp food or money **2** having a great need *for* ⟨*plants ~ for water*⟩ [ME *gredy*, fr OE *grǣdig*; akin to OHG *grātag* greedy] – **greedily** *adv*, **greediness** *n*

ˈgreedy-,guts *n, pl* **greedy-guts** *chiefly Br* one who eats too much; a glutton – infml

¹Greek /greek/ *n* **1** a native or inhabitant of Greece **2** the Indo-European language used by the Greeks ☞ ALPHABET, LANGUAGE **3** *not cap* sthg unintelligible ⟨*it's all ~ to me*⟩ – infml [ME *Greke*, fr OE *Grēca*, fr L *Graecus*, fr Gk *Graikos*; (3) trans of L *Graecum* (in the medieval phrase *Graecum est; non potest legi* It is Greek; it cannot be read)]

²Greek *adj* **1** of Greece, the Greeks, or Greek **2** **Greek, Greek Orthodox** **a** ORTHODOX 2a **b** of an Eastern church, esp the established Orthodox church of Greece using the Byzantine rite in Greek

Greek cross *n* a cross with 4 equal arms intersecting at right angles ☞ SYMBOL

Greek fire *n* an incendiary composition used in ancient sea warfare and said to have burst into flame on contact with water

¹green /green/ *adj* **1** of the colour green **2a** covered by green growth or foliage ⟨*~ fields*⟩ **b** consisting of green (edible) plants ⟨*a ~ salad*⟩ **3a** youthful, vigorous **b** not ripened or matured; immature ⟨*~ apples*⟩ **c** fresh, new **4** appearing pale, sickly, or nauseated **5** affected by intense envy or jealousy **6a** not aged ⟨*a ~ ham*⟩ **b** not dressed or tanned ⟨*~ hides*⟩ **c** *of wood* freshly sawn; unseasoned **7a** deficient in training, knowledge, or experience **b** lacking sophistication; naive **8** being an exchange unit that has a differential rate of exchange in relation to the specified currency and is used for paying agricultural producers in the European economic community ⟨*the ~ pound*⟩ [ME *grene*, fr OE *grēne*; akin to OE *grōwan* to grow – more at GROW] – **greenly** *adv*, **greenness** *n*

²green *vi* to become green

³green *n* **1** a colour whose hue resembles that of growing fresh grass or the emerald and lies between blue and yellow in the spectrum **2** sthg of a green colour **3** *pl* green leafy vegetables (e g spinach and cabbage) the leaves and stems of which are often cooked **4a** a common or park in the centre of a town or village **b** a smooth area of grass for a special purpose (e g bowling or putting) – **greeny** *adj*

ˌgreen alga *n* an alga in which the chlorophyll is not masked by other pigments

ˈgreenˌback /-ˌbak/ *n, NAm* a legal-tender note issued by the US government – infml

green bacon *n* unsmoked bacon

green belt *n* a belt of parks, farmland, etc encircling an urban area and usu subject to restrictions on new building

green card *n* an international certificate of motor insurance

green cross code *n* a British code of safety for the use of people, esp children, crossing roads

greenery /ˈgreenəri/ *n* green foliage or plants

ˌgreen-ˈeyed *adj* jealous

ˌgreen-eyed ˈmonster *n* jealousy – + *the*

ˈgreenˌfinch /-ˌfinch/ *n* a common green and yellow Old World finch

ˌgreen ˈfingers *n pl* an unusual ability to make plants grow – **green-fingered** *adj*

ˈgreenˌfly /-ˌflie/ *n, pl* **greenflies,** *esp collectively* **greenfly** *Br* (an infestation by) any of various green aphids that are destructive to plants

ˈgreenˌgage /-ˌgayj/ *n* any of several small rounded greenish cultivated plums [*green* + Sir William *Gage* †1820 E botanist]

ˈgreenˌgrocer /-ˌgrohsə/ *n, chiefly Br* a retailer of fresh vegetables and fruit – **greengrocery** *n*

ˈgreenˌheart /-ˌhaht/ *n* (the hard greenish wood of) a tropical S American evergreen tree

ˈgreenˌhorn /-ˌhawn/ *n* **1** an inexperienced or unsophisticated (easily cheated) person **2** *chiefly NAm* a newcomer (e g to a country) unacquainted with local manners and customs [obs *greenhorn* (animal with young horns)]

ˈgreenˌhouse /-ˌhows/ *n* a glassed enclosure for the cultivation or protection of tender plants ☞ ENERGY

greenhouse effect *n* the warming of the lower layers of the atmosphere by absorption and reradiation of solar radiation

greening /ˈgreening/ *n* any of several apples having a green skin when ripe

greenish /ˈgreenish/ *adj* rather green – **greenishness** *n*

green light *n* authority or permission to undertake a project [fr the green traffic light which signals permission to proceed]

green manure *n* a herbaceous crop (e g clover) ploughed under while green to enrich the soil

green monkey disease *n* an often fatal virus disease that causes high fever and internal bleeding and is transmitted to humans by a species of W African monkey

Green Paper *n, chiefly Br* a set of proposals issued by the government for public comment [fr colour of cover]

green pepper *n* SWEET PEPPER

green revolution *n* high crop yields due to extensive use of artificial fertilizers and high-yielding plant strains

ˈgreenroom /-room, -ˌroohm/ *n* a room in a theatre or concert hall where performers can relax when not on stage [prob fr its orig being painted green]

ˈgreenˌsand /-ˌsand/ *n* a (stratum of) sand or sandstone coloured by the dull green silicates of iron and potassium

ˈgreenˌshank /-ˌshangk/ *n* an Old World wading bird with olive-green legs and feet

ˈgreenˌsick /-ˌsik/ *adj* (suffering from) chlorosis [back-formation fr *greensickness*] – **greensickness** *n*

ˈgreenˌstick ˌfracture /-ˌstik/ *n* a fracture in a young individual in which the bone is partly broken and partly bent

ˈgreenˌstone /-ˌstohn/ *n* any of numerous dark green compact rocks (e g diorite)

ˈgreenˌstuff /-ˌstuf/ *n* green vegetation; greens

ˈgreenˌsward /-ˌswawd/ *n* turf that is green with growing grass

ˌgreen ˈtea *n* tea that is light in colour from incomplete fermentation of the leaf before firing

ˌgreen ˈthumb *n, NAm* GREEN FINGERS – **green-thumbed** *adj*

ˌgreen ˈturtle *n* a large edible sea turtle ☞ ENDANGERED

Greenwich Mean Time /ˈgrenich, ˈgrinij, -nich/ *n* the mean solar time of the meridian of Greenwich used as the primary point of reference for standard time throughout the world [*Greenwich*, borough of London]

ˈgreenˌwood /-ˌwood/ *n* a forest green with foliage

[1]greet /greet/ *vt* **1** to welcome with gestures or words **2** to meet or react to in a specified manner ⟨*the candidate was* ~ed *with catcalls*⟩ **3** to be perceived by ⟨*a surprising sight* ~ed *her eyes*⟩ [ME *greten*, fr OE *grētan*; akin to OE *grǣtan* to weep] – **greeter** *n*

[2]greet *vi* **grat** /grat/; **grutten** /ˈgrutn/ *Scot* to weep, lament [ME *greten*, fr OE *grǣtan*; akin to ON *grāta* to weep]

greeting /ˈgreeting/ *n* **1** a salutation at meeting **2** an expression of good wishes; regards – usu pl with sing. meaning ⟨*birthday* ~s⟩

ˈgreetings ˌcard *n* a card containing a message of good will usu sent or given on some special occasion (e g an anniversary)

gregarious /griˈgeəri·əs/ *adj* **1a** tending to associate with others of the same kind ⟨*a* ~ *gull*⟩ **b** marked by or indicating a liking for companionship; sociable **c** of a crowd, flock, or other group of people, animals, etc **2** *of a plant* growing in a cluster or a colony [L *gregarius* of a flock or herd, fr *greg-, grex* flock, herd; akin to Gk *ageirein* to collect, *agora* assembly] – **gregariously** *adv*, **gregariousness** *n*

Gregorian /griˈgawri·ən/ *adj* of Pope Gregory XIII or the Gregorian calendar

Gregorian calendar *n* a revision of the Julian Calendar now in general use, that was introduced in 1582 by Pope Gregory XIII and adopted in Britain and the American colonies in 1752 and that restricts leap years to every 4th year except for those centenary years not divisible by 400

Gregorian chant *n* a rhythmically free liturgical chant in unison practised in the Roman Catholic church [*Gregorian* fr Pope *Gregory* I †604]

greisen /ˈgriez(ə)n/ *n* a rock consisting chiefly of quartz and mica that is common in Cornwall and Saxony [G]

gremlin /ˈgremlin/ *n* a mischievous creature said to cause malfunctioning of machinery or equipment

[perh modif of IrGael *gruaimin* ill-humoured little fellow]

grenade /grə'nayd/ *n* **1** a small missile that contains explosive, gas, incendiary chemicals, etc and is thrown by hand or launcher **2** a glass container of chemicals that bursts when thrown, releasing a fire extinguishing agent, tear gas, etc [MF, pomegranate, fr LL *granata*, fr L, fem of *granatus* seedy, fr *granum* grain – more at ¹CORN]

grenadier /,grenə'diə/ *n* a member of a regiment or corps formerly specially trained in the use of grenades

grenadine /,grenə'deen, '---/ *n* a syrup flavoured with pomegranates and used in mixed drinks [F, fr *grenade*]

Gresham's law /'gresh(ə)mz/ *n* an observation in economics: when 2 coins are equal in debt-paying value but unequal in intrinsic value, the one having the lesser intrinsic value tends to remain in circulation and the other to be hoarded or exported as bullion [Sir Thomas *Gresham* †1579 E financier]

grew /grooh/ *past of* GROW

¹**grey,** *NAm chiefly* **gray** /gray/ *adj* **1** of the colour grey **2a** dull in colour **b** having grey hair **3a** lacking cheer or brightness; dismal ⟨*a ~ day*⟩ **b** intermediate or unclear in position, condition, or character ⟨*a ~ area*⟩ **4** *of a textile* being in an unbleached undyed state as taken from the loom **5** *of a horse* having white hair but dark skin [ME, fr OE *grǣg*; akin to OHG *grāo* grey, OSlav *zĭrěti* to see] – **greyly** *adv*, **greyness** *n*

²**grey,** *NAm chiefly* **gray** *n* **1** any of a series of neutral colours ranging between black and white **2** sthg grey; *esp* grey clothes, paint, or horses

³**grey,** *NAm chiefly* **gray** *vb* to make or become grey

'**grey,beard** /-,biəd/ *n* an old man

grey eminence *n* ÉMINENCE GRISE

Grey Friar *n* a Franciscan friar [fr the colour of his habit]

'**greyhound** /-hownd/ *n* (any of) a tall slender smooth-coated breed of dogs characterized by swiftness and keen sight and used for coursing game and racing [ME *grehound*, fr OE *grighund*, fr *grig-* (akin to ON *grey* bitch) + *hund* hound]

'**greyish** /-ish/ *adj, of a colour* low in saturation [¹GREY + -ISH]

'**grey,lag** /-,lag/, **greylag goose** *n* a common grey Eurasian wild goose with pink legs [*grey* + ²*lag* (one who lags or is last); prob fr its late migration]

grey matter *n* **1** brownish-grey nerve tissue, esp in the brain and spinal cord, containing nerve-cell bodies as well as nerve fibres **2** brains, intellect – infml

grey squirrel *n* a common light grey to black orig American squirrel that causes severe damage to deciduous trees

'**grey,wacke** /-,wakə/ *n* a coarse usu dark grey sandstone or conglomerate of cemented rock fragments [part trans of G *grauwacke*]

grid /grid/ *n* **1** a grating **2a** a network of conductors for distribution of electric power **b** (sthg resembling) a network of uniformly spaced horizontal and perpendicular lines for locating points on a map **3** the starting positions of vehicles on a racetrack **4** GRILL 1 [back-formation fr *gridiron*] – **gridded** *adj*

griddle /'gridl/ *n* a flat metal surface on which food is cooked by dry heat [ME *gredil* gridiron, fr ONF, fr LL *craticulum*, alter. of L *craticula*, dim. of *cratis* wickerwork – more at HURDLE]

'**grid,iron** /-,ie·ən/ *n* GRILL 1 [ME *gredire*, perh alter. of *gredil*]

grief /greef/ *n* (a cause of) deep and poignant distress (e g due to bereavement) [ME *gref*, fr OF, heavy, grave, fr (assumed) VL *grevis*, alter. of L *gravis*] – **griefless** *adj*

grievance /'greev(ə)ns/ *n* **1** a cause of distress (e g unsatisfactory working conditions) felt to afford reason for complaint or resistance **2** the formal expression of a grievance; a complaint

¹**grieve** /greev/ *vt* to cause to suffer grief ~ *vi* to suffer from grief, esp over a bereavement – often + *for* [ME *greven*, fr OF *grever*, fr L *gravare* to burden, fr *gravis* heavy, grave; akin to Goth *kaurjos*, pl, heavy, Gk *barys*, Skt *guru*] – **griever** *n*

²**grieve** *n, Scot* a farm or estate manager or overseer [ME *greif*, fr OE *grǣfa* governor, sheriff; akin to OE *gerēfa* reeve – more at ¹REEVE]

grievous /'greevəs/ *adj* **1** causing or characterized by severe pain, suffering, or sorrow ⟨*a ~ loss*⟩ **2** serious, grave ⟨*~ fault*⟩ – **grievously** *adv*, **grievousness** *n*

griffin /'grifin/, **griffon, gryphon** /-fən/ *n* a mythical animal with the head and wings of an eagle and the body and tail of a lion [ME *griffon*, fr MF *grifon*, fr *grif*, fr L *gryphus*, fr Gk *gryp-*, *gryps*, fr *grypos* curved; akin to OE *cradol* cradle]

griffon /'grifən/ *n* (any of) a breed of **a** (Belgian) toy dogs **b** (Dutch) sporting dogs [F, lit., griffin]

griffon vulture *n* any of a genus of large Old World vultures

grift /grift/ *vi, NAm* ¹GRAFT 3 – slang [*grift*, n, perh alter. of *graft*] – **grift** *n*, **grifter** *n*

grigri /'gree,gree/ *n, pl* **grigris** a gris-gris

grike, gryke /griek/ *n* a cleft developed in a horizontal limestone surface by solution [alter. of ME *crike*, fr ON *criki* crack, bend]

¹**grill** /gril/ *vt* **1** to cook on or under a grill by radiant heat **2a** to torture (as if) with great heat **b** to subject to intense and usu long periods of questioning – infml ~ *vi* to become grilled – **griller** *n*

²**grill** *n* **1** a cooking utensil of parallel bars on which food is exposed to heat (e g from burning charcoal) **2** an article or dish of grilled food **3 grill, grillroom** a usu informal restaurant or dining room, esp in a hotel **4** *Br* an apparatus on a cooker under which food is cooked or browned by radiant heat [F *gril*, fr LL *craticulum* – more at GRIDDLE]

grillage /'grilij/ *n* a framework for support in building on marshy or treacherous soil [F, fr *griller* to supply with grilles, fr *grille*]

grille, grill /gril/ *n* **1** a grating forming a barrier or screen; *specif* an ornamental metal one at the front end of a motor vehicle **2** an opening covered with a grille [F *grille*, alter. of OF *greille*, fr L *craticula*, dim. of *cratis* wickerwork – more at HURDLE]

grilse /grils/ *n, pl* **grilse** a young mature (Atlantic) salmon returning from the sea to spawn for the first time [ME *grills*, perh fr MF *grisel*, *grisle* grey]

grim /grim/ *adj* **-mm- 1** fierce or forbidding in disposition, action, or appearance **2** unflinching, unyielding ⟨*~ determination*⟩ **3** ghastly or sinister in character **4** unpleasant, nasty ⟨*had a pretty ~ afternoon at the dentist's*⟩ – infml [ME, fr OE *grimm*; akin to OHG *grimm* fierce, Gk *chromados* action of gnashing] – **grimly** *adv*, **grimness** *n*

grimace /'griməs, gri'mays/ *n* a distorted facial expression, usu of disgust, anger, or pain [F, fr MF, alter. of *grimache*, of Gmc origin; akin to OE *grīma* mask] – **grimace** *vi*, **grimacer** *n*

grimalkin /gri'malkin/ *n* – used in stories as a name for a (female elderly) cat [alter. of *grey malkin*, fr *grey* + E dial. *malkin* (female cat), fr ME *malkyn*, fr *Malkyn*, female forename]

grime /griem/ *n* soot or dirt, esp when sticking to or embedded in a surface [Flem *grijm*, fr MD *grime* soot, mask; akin to OE *grīma* mask, Gk *chriein* to anoint – more at CHRISM] – **grime** *vt*, **grimy** *adj*, **griminess** *n*

Grimm's law /grimz/ *n* a statement in historical linguistics: the Germanic languages are related to those of Proto-Indo-European by a regular system of consonantal changes [Jacob *Grimm* †1863 G philologist]

grin /grin/ *vi* **-nn-** to smile so as to show the teeth [ME *grennen*, fr OE *grennian*; akin to OHG *grennen* to snarl] – **grin** *n*, **grinner** *n*

[1]**grind** /griend/ *vb* **ground** /grownd/ *vt* **1** to reduce to powder or small fragments by crushing between hard surfaces **2** to wear down, polish, or sharpen by friction; whet ⟨~ *an axe*⟩ **3a** to rub, press, or twist harshly ⟨ground *the cigarette out with a heel*⟩ ⟨ground *his fist into his opponent's stomach*⟩ **b** to press together with a rotating motion ⟨~ *the teeth*⟩ **4** to operate or produce by turning a crank ⟨~ *a hand organ*⟩ ~ *vi* **1** to perform the operation of grinding **2** to become pulverized, polished, or sharpened by friction **3** to move with difficulty or friction, esp so as to make a grating noise ⟨~ing *gears*⟩ **4** to work monotonously; *esp* to study hard ⟨~ *for an exam*⟩ **5** to rotate the hips in an erotic manner [ME *grinden*, fr OE *grindan*; akin to L *frendere* to crush, grind, Gk *chondros* grain, OE *grēot* grit] – **grindingly** *adv* – **grind into** to instil (knowledge, facts, etc) into (sby) with great difficulty

[2]**grind** *n* **1** dreary monotonous labour or routine **2** the result of grinding; *esp* material obtained by grinding to a particular degree of fineness **3a** the act of rotating the hips in an erotic manner – compare BUMP 3 **b** *Br* an act of sexual intercourse – vulg **4** *chiefly NAm* a swot – infml

grind down *vt* to oppress, harass

grinder /'griendə/ *n* a molar tooth ['GRIND + [2]-ER]

grind out *vt* to produce in a mechanical way ⟨grind out *best-sellers*⟩ – derog

'**grind,stone** /-,stohn/ *n* **1** MILLSTONE 1 **2** a flat circular stone that revolves on an axle and is used for grinding, shaping, etc

gringo /'gring·goh/ *n, pl* **gringos** an (English-speaking) foreigner in Spain or Latin America [Sp, prob alter. of *griego* Greek, stranger, fr L *Graecus* Greek]

[1]**grip** /grip/ *vb* **-pp-** *vt* **1** to seize or hold firmly **2** to attract and hold the interest of ⟨*a story that* ~s *the reader*⟩ ~ *vi* to take firm hold [ME *grippen*, fr OE *grippan*; akin to OE *grīpan*] – **gripper** *n*, **grippingly** *adv*

[2]**grip** *n* **1a** a strong or tenacious grasp **b** manner or style of gripping **2a** control, mastery, power ⟨*he kept a good* ~ *on his pupils*⟩ **b** (power of) understanding or doing ⟨*she has a good* ~ *of the situation*⟩ **3** a part or device that grips ⟨*a hair* ~⟩ **4** a part by which sthg is grasped; *esp* a handle **5** one who handles scenery, properties, lighting, or camera equipment in a theatre or film or television studio **6** a travelling bag

[1]**gripe** /griep/ *vt* to cause intestinal gripes in ~ *vi* **1** to experience intestinal gripes **2** to complain persistently – infml [ME *gripen* to grasp, seize, fr OE *grīpan*; akin to OHG *grīfan* to grasp, Lith *griebti*] – **griper** *n*

[2]**gripe** *n* **1** a stabbing spasmodic intestinal pain – usu pl **2** a grievance, complaint – infml

grippe /grip/ *n* influenza [F, lit., seizure, fr *gripper* to seize] – **grippy** *adj*

griseofulvin /,grizioh'foolvin, -'ful-/ *n* an antibiotic given orally to treat fungal infections [NL *griseofulvum*, specific epithet of *Penicillium griseofulvum*, mould from which it is obtained]

grisette /gri'zet/ *n* a young French working-class woman [F, fr *grisette* (dress made of) cheap grey cloth, fr *gris* grey]

gris-gris /'gree ,gree/ *n, pl* **gris-gris** /'gree ,greez/ an African amulet or spell [F, of African origin; akin to Balante *grigri* amulet]

grisly /'grizli/ *adj* inspiring horror, intense fear, or disgust; forbidding ⟨*houses that were dark and* ~ *under the blank, cold sky* – D H Lawrence⟩ [ME, fr OE *grislic*, fr *gris-* (akin to OE *āgrīsan* to fear); akin to OHG *grīsenlīh* terrible] – **grisliness** *n*

grison /'gries(ə)n, 'griz(ə)n/ *n* any of various S American flesh-eating mammals that resemble large weasels [F, fr *grison* grey, fr MF, fr *gris* – more at GRIZZLED]

grist /grist/ *n* **1** (a batch of) grain for grinding **2** the product obtained from grinding grain [ME, fr OE *grīst*; akin to OE *grindan* to grind] – **grist to the mill** sthg that can be put to use or profit

gristle /'grisl/ *n* cartilage; *broadly* tough cartilaginous or fibrous matter, esp in cooked meat [ME *gristil*, fr OE *gristle*; akin to MLG *gristel* gristle] – **gristly** /'grisli/ *adj*, **gristliness** *n*

[1]**grit** /grit/ *n* **1** a hard sharp granule (e g of sand or stone); *also* material composed of such granules **2** the structure or texture of a stone that adapts it to grinding **3** firmness of mind or spirit; unyielding courage – infml [ME *grete*, fr OE *grēot*; akin to OHG *grioz* sand, L *furfur* bran, Gk *chrōs* skin]

[2]**grit** *vb* **-tt-** *vi* to give forth a grating sound ~ *vt* **1** to cover or spread with grit **2** to cause (esp one's teeth) to grind or grate

grits /grits/ *n pl but sing or pl in constr* grain, esp oats, husked and usu coarsely ground [ME *gryt*, fr OE *grytt*; akin to OE *grēot*]

gritty /'griti/ *adj* **1** courageously persistent or determined **2** caustic, incisive ⟨~ *realism*⟩ ['GRIT + [1]-Y] – **grittily** *adv*, **grittiness** *n*

grizzle /'grizl/ *vi* **grizzling** /'grizling, 'grizl·ing/ *Br* **1** *of a child* to cry quietly and fretfully **2** to complain in a self-pitying way – often + *about* *USE* infml [origin unknown]

'**grizzled** *adj* sprinkled or streaked with grey ⟨*a* ~ *beard*⟩ [ME *griseled*, fr MF *grisel* grey, fr OF, fr *gris* grey, of Gmc origin; akin to OHG *grīs* grey]

[1]'**grizzly** /-li/ *adj* grizzled [ME *grisel* grey, fr MF]

[2]**grizzly, grizzly bear** *n* a very large typically brownish yellow bear that lives in the highlands of western N America [prob var of *grisly*]

groan /grohn/ *vi* **1** to utter a deep moan **2** to creak under strain ⟨*the boards* ~ed *under our weight*⟩ ~ *vt* to utter with groaning [ME *gronen*, fr OE *grānian*; akin to OHG *grīnan* to growl] – **groan** *n*, **groaner** *n*

[1]**groat** /groht/ *n* hulled grain (broken into fragments larger than grits) – usu pl with sing. meaning but sing. or pl in constr [ME *grotes*, pl, fr OE *grotan*; akin to OE *grēot*]

[2]**groat** *n* a former British coin worth 4 old pence [ME *groot*, fr MD]

grocer /ˈgrohsə/ *n* a dealer in (packaged or tinned) staple foodstuffs, household supplies, and usu fruit, vegetables, and dairy products [ME, fr MF *grossier* wholesaler, fr *gros* coarse, wholesale – more at GROSS]

grocery /ˈgrohs(ə)ri/ *n* **1** *pl* commodities sold by a grocer **2** a grocer's shop

grog /grog/ *n* alcoholic drink; *specif* spirits (e g rum) mixed with water [*Old Grog*, nickname of Edward Vernon †1757 E admiral responsible for diluting the sailors' rum]

groggy /ˈgrogi/ *adj* weak and dazed, esp owing to illness or tiredness [*grog* + *-y*] – **groggily** *adv*, **grogginess** *n*

grogram /ˈgrogrəm/ *n* a coarse loosely woven fabric of silk, silk and mohair, or silk and wool – compare GROSGRAIN [MF *gros grain* coarse texture]

groin /groyn/ *n* **1a** the fold marking the join between the lower abdomen and the inner part of the thigh **b** the male genitals – euph **2** the line along which 2 intersecting vaults meet ☞ CHURCH **3** *chiefly NAm* a groyne [alter. of ME *grynde*, fr OE, abyss; akin to OE *grund* ground]

grommet /ˈgromit/ *n* **1** a ring, usu of twisted rope **2** an eyelet of firm material to strengthen or protect an opening [perh fr obs F *gormette* curb of a bridle]

gromwell /ˈgromwəl/ *n* any of a genus of hard-seeded plants of the borage family [ME *gromil*, fr MF]

[1]**groom** /groohm/ *n* **1** one who is in charge of the feeding, care, and stabling of horses **2** a bridegroom **3** *archaic* a manservant [ME *grom* boy, man, manservant]

[2]**groom** *vt* **1** to clean and care for (e g a horse) **2** to make neat or attractive ⟨*an impeccably* ~ed *woman*⟩ **3** to get into readiness for a specific objective; prepare ⟨*was being* ~ed *as a Tory candidate*⟩ ~ *vi* to groom oneself – **groomer** *n*

[1]**groove** /groohv/ *n* **1a** a long narrow channel or depression **b** the continuous spiral track on a gramophone record whose irregularities correspond to the recorded sounds **2** a fixed routine; a rut **3** top form – infml ⟨*a great talker when he is in the* ~⟩ **4** an enjoyable or exciting experience – infml; no longer in vogue [ME *groof*; akin to OE *grafan* to dig – more at [1] [2]GRAVE]

[2]**groove** *vt* **1** to make a groove in **2** to excite pleasurably – infml; no longer in vogue ~ *vi* **1** to form a groove **2** to enjoy oneself intensely; *also* to get on well – infml; no longer in vogue – **groover** *n*

groovy /ˈgroohvi/ *adj* fashionably attractive or exciting – infml; no longer in vogue

grope /grohp/ *vi* **1** to feel about blindly or uncertainly *for* **2** to search blindly or uncertainly *for* or *after* ⟨groping *for the right words*⟩ ~ *vt* **1** to touch or fondle the body of (a person) for sexual pleasure **2** to find (e g one's way) by groping [ME *gropen*, fr OE *grāpian*; akin to OE *gripan* to seize] – **grope** *n*, **groper** *n*

groschen /ˈgrohsh(ə)n/ *n*, *pl* **groschen** *often cap* **1** ☞ *Austria* at NATIONALITY **2** a German coin worth 10 pfennigs [G]

grosgrain /ˈgroh,grayn/ *n* a strong closely woven corded fabric, usu of silk or rayon and with crosswise ribs – compare GROGRAM [F *gros grain* coarse texture]

gros point /ˈgroh ,poynt/ *n* a large cross-stitch or tent stitch; *also* needlepoint embroidery worked on canvas across double threads in gros point – compare PETIT POINT [F, lit., large point]

[1]**gross** /grohs/ *adj* **1** glaringly noticeable, usu because excessively bad or objectionable; flagrant ⟨~ *error*⟩ **2a** big, bulky; *esp* excessively fat **b** *of vegetation* dense, luxuriant **3** consisting of an overall total before deductions (e g for taxes) are made ⟨~ *income*⟩ – compare NET 1a **4** made up of material or perceptible elements; corporal ⟨*the* ~er *part of human nature*⟩ **5** coarse in nature or behaviour; *specif* crudely vulgar [ME, fr MF *gros* thick, coarse, fr L *grossus*] – **grossly** *adv*, **grossness** *n*

[2]**gross** *n* an overall total exclusive of deductions

[3]**gross** *vt* to earn or bring in (an overall total) exclusive of deductions – **grosser** *n*

[4]**gross** *n*, *pl* **gross** a group of 12 dozen things ⟨*a* ~ *of pencils*⟩ [ME *groce*, fr MF *grosse*, fr fem of *gros*]

gross domestic product *n* the total volume of the goods and services produced in a country during a specified period, usu a year, excluding income from possessions and investments abroad – compare GROSS NATIONAL PRODUCT

gross national product *n* the total value of the goods and services produced in a country during a specified period, usu a year – compare GROSS DOMESTIC PRODUCT

grosso modo /,grosoh ˈmodoh/ *adv* as an approximation; roughly – fml [It]

grosz /grosh/ *n*, *pl* **groszy** /-shi/ ☞ *Poland* at NATIONALITY [Pol]

grot /grot/ *n* (unpleasant) dirt, soot, etc – infml [back-formation fr *grotty*]

[1]**grotesque** /grohˈtesk/ *n* **1** a style of decorative art in which incongruous or fantastic human and animal forms are interwoven with natural motifs (e g foliage) **2** sby grotesque **3** SANS SERIF [MF & OIt; MF, fr OIt (*pittura*) *grottesca*, lit., cave painting, fem of *grottesco* of a cave, fr *grotta*]

[2]**grotesque** *adj* (having the characteristics) of the grotesque: e g **a** fanciful, bizarre **b** absurdly incongruous **c** departing markedly from the natural, expected, or typical – **grotesquely** *adv*, **grotesqueness** *n*

groˈtesquerie *also* **grotesquery** /-kəri/ *n* **1** sthg grotesque **2** grotesqueness [*grotesque* + *-erie* -ery]

grotto /ˈgrotoh/ *n*, *pl* **grottoes** *also* **grottos** **1** an esp picturesque cave **2** an excavation or structure made to resemble a natural cave [It *grotta*, *grotto*, fr L *crypta* cavern, crypt]

grotty /ˈgroti/ *adj*, *Br* nasty, unpleasant – slang [by shortening & alter. fr *grotesque*] – **grottily** *adv*

grouch /growch/ *n* **1** a bad-tempered complaint **2** a habitually irritable or complaining person; a grumbler [prob alter. of *grutch* (grudge)] – **grouch** *vi*, **grouchy** *adj*

[1]**ground** /grownd/ *n* **1a** the bottom of a body of water **b** *pl* **(1)** SEDIMENT 1 **(2)** ground coffee beans after brewing **2** a basis for belief, action, or argument – often pl with sing. meaning ⟨~s *for complaint*⟩ **3a**

a surrounding area; a background **b** (material that serves as) a substratum **4a** the surface of the earth **b** an area used for a particular purpose ⟨*parade* ~⟩ ⟨*football* ~⟩ **c** *pl* the area round and belonging to a house or other building **d** an area to be won or defended (as if) in battle **e** an area of knowledge or special interest ⟨*covered a lot of* ~ *in his lecture*⟩ **5a** [3]SOIL 2b **b** *chiefly NAm* EARTH 8 [ME, fr OE *grund*; akin to OHG *grunt* ground, Gk *chrainein* to touch slightly] – **off the ground** started and in progress ⟨*the programme never got* off the ground⟩ – **to ground** into hiding

[2]**ground** *vt* **1** to bring to or place on the ground **2a** to provide a reason or justification for **b** to instruct in fundamentals (e g of a subject) **3** to restrict (e g a pilot or aircraft) to the ground **4** *chiefly NAm* to earth ~ *vi* to run aground

[3]**ground** *past of* GRIND

'**ground,bait** /-,bayt/ *n* bait scattered on the water so as to attract fish

'**ground ,bass** /bays/ *n* a short bass passage continually repeated below constantly changing melody and harmony

'**ground ,cover** *n* (all the) low-growing plants (in a forest except young trees)

'**ground ef,fect** *n* an aircraft's gaining of added buoyancy when close to the ground; *also* a similar but intentionally produced effect (e g in a hovercraft) – **ground-effect** *adj*

,**ground 'floor** *n* the floor of a house on a level with the ground – compare FIRST FLOOR

grounding /'grownding/ *n* fundamental training in a field of knowledge

ground ivy *n* a trailing plant of the mint family with bluish-purple flowers

'**groundless** /-lis/ *adj* having no foundation ⟨~ *fears*⟩ – **groundlessly** *adv*, **groundlessness** *n*

'**groundling** /-ling/ *n* **1** a spectator who stood in the pit of an Elizabethan theatre **2** sby of low status

'**ground,nut** /-,nut/ *n* **1** (a N American leguminous plant with) an edible tuberous root **2** *chiefly Br* the peanut

ground pine *n* **1** a European yellow-flowered bugle with a resinous smell **2** any of several club mosses with long creeping stems

ground plan *n* **1** a plan of the ground floor of a building **2** a first or basic plan

ground rent *n* the rent paid by a lessee for the use of land, esp for building

ground rule *n* a basic rule of procedure

groundsel /'grown(d)zl, -sl/ *n* a (plant related to a) European composite plant that is a common weed and has small yellow flower heads [ME *groundeswele*, fr OE *grundeswelge*, fr *grund* ground + *swelgan* to swallow – more at [2]SWALLOW]

'**ground,sheet** /-,sheet/ *n* a waterproof sheet placed on the ground (e g in a tent)

'**groundsman** /-mən/ *n* sby who tends a playing field, esp a cricket pitch

ground speed *n* the speed (e g of an aircraft) relative to the ground

ground squirrel *n* any of various burrowing N American rodents; *esp* a chipmunk

'**ground,staff** /-,stahf/ *n* the people who maintain a sports ground

ground state *n* the lowest possible energy level of a system of interacting elementary particles

ground stroke *n* a stroke made (e g in tennis) by hitting a ball that has rebounded from the ground – compare VOLLEY 1c(1)

ground swell *n* a sea swell caused by an often distant gale or ground tremor

'**ground,work** /-,wuhk/ *n* (work done to provide) a foundation or basis

[1]**group** /groohp/ *n* **1** two or more figures or objects forming a complete unit in a composition **2** *sing or pl in constr* **a** a number of individuals or objects assembled together or having some unifying relationship **b** an operational and administrative unit belonging to a command of an air force **3a** an assemblage of atoms forming part of a molecule; a radical ⟨*a methyl* ~⟩ **b** all the (similar) chemical elements forming one of the vertical columns of the periodic table **4** a mathematical set that is closed under a binary associative operation, has an identity element, and has an inverse for every element [F *groupe*, fr It *gruppo*, of Gmc origin; akin to OHG *kropf* craw – more at CROP]

[2]**group** *vt* **1** to combine in a group **2** to assign to a group; classify ~ *vi* to form or belong to a group – **groupable** *adj*

group captain *n* ☞ RANK

grouper /'groohpə/ *n, pl* **groupers,** *esp collectively* **grouper** any of numerous (large bottom-dwelling) fishes usu of warm seas [Pg *garoupa*]

groupie /'groohpi/ *n* an ardent (female) fan of a famous person, esp a rock star, who follows the object of admiration on tour [[1]*group* + *-ie*]

grouping /'groohping/ *n* a set of individuals or objects combined in a group

group practice *n* a practice run by a group of associated medical general practitioners

group therapy *n* the treatment of several individuals (with similar psychological problems) simultaneously through group discussion and mutual aid

[1]**grouse** /grows/ *n, pl* **grouse** any of several (important game) birds with a plump body and strong feathered legs [origin unknown]

[2]**grouse** *vi or n* (to) grumble – infml [origin unknown] – **grouser** *n*

[1]**grout** /growt/ *n* **1** sediment (e g tea leaves) at the bottom of a vessel – usu pl with sing. meaning **2** **grout, grouting** a thin mortar used for filling spaces (e g the joints in masonry) [ME, fr OE *grūt* coarse meal; akin to OE *grytt* grit]

[2]**grout** *vt* to fill up or finish with grout – **grouter** *n*

grove /grohv/ *n* a small wood, group, or planting of trees [ME, fr OE *grāf*]

grovel /'grovl/ *vi* **-ll-** (*NAm* **-l-, -ll-**) /'grovl·ing/ **1** to lie or creep with the body prostrate in token of subservience or abasement **2** to abase or humble oneself [back-formation fr *groveling* prone, fr *groveling*, adv, fr ME, fr *gruf*, adv, on the face (fr ON *ā grūfu*) + *-ling*; akin to OE *crēopan* to creep] – **groveller** *n*, **grovellingly** *adv*

grow /groh/ *vb* **grew** /grooh/; **grown** /grohn/ *vi* **1a** to spring up and develop to maturity (in a specified place or situation) **b** to assume some relation (as if) through a process of natural growth ⟨*2 tree trunks* grown *together*⟩ **2a** to increase in size by addition of material (e g by assimilation into a living organism or by crystallization) **b** to increase, expand **3** to develop from a parent source ⟨*the book* grew *out of a series of lectures*⟩ **4** to become gradually ⟨grew pale⟩ ~ *vt* **1** to cause to grow; produce ⟨~ *roses*⟩ **2** DEVELOP 5 ⟨~ *wings*⟩ [ME *growen*, fr OE *grōwan*; akin to OHG *gruowan* to grow] – **grower** *n*, **growingly** *adv* – **grow on** to have an increasing influence on; *esp* to become more pleasing to

'growing ˌpains *n pl* **1** pains in the legs of growing children that have no known cause **2** the early problems attending a new project or development

[1]**growl** /growl/ *vi* **1a** to rumble **b** to utter a growl **2** to complain angrily [prob imit]

[2]**growl** *n* a deep guttural inarticulate sound

growler /'growlə/ *n* a small iceberg [[1]GROWL + [2]-ER]

grown /grohn/ *adj* **1** fully grown; mature ⟨~ *men*⟩ **2** overgrown or covered (*with*)

'grown-ˌup *n or adj* (an) adult

growth /grohth/ *n* **1a** (a stage in the process of) growing **b** progressive development **c** an increase, expansion **2a** sthg that grows or has grown **b** a tumour or other abnormal growth of tissue **3** the result of growth; a product

'growth ˌfactor *n* a substance (e g a vitamin) necessary for the growth of an organism

'growth ˌhormone *n* **1** a polypeptide growth-regulating hormone of vertebrates that is secreted by the front lobe of the pituitary gland **2** any of various plant substances (e g an auxin or gibberellin) that promote growth

grow up *vi* **1** *of a person* to develop towards or arrive at a mature state **2** to arise and develop ⟨*the movement* grew up *in the 60s*⟩ **3** to begin to act sensibly – usu imper

groyne, *chiefly NAm* **groin** /groyn/ *n* a rigid structure built out from a shore, esp to check erosion of the beach [*groyne* prob alter. of *groin*]

[1]**grub** /grub/ *vb* **-bb-** *vt* **1** to clear by digging up roots and stumps **2** to dig *up* or *out* (as if) by the roots ~ *vi* **1** to dig in the ground, esp for sthg that is difficult to find or extract **2** to search about; rummage [ME *grubben*; akin to OE *grafan* to dig – more at [1] [2]GRAVE] – **grubber** *n*

[2]**grub** *n* **1** a soft thick wormlike larva of an insect **2** food – infml [ME *grubbe*, prob fr *grubben*]

grubby /'grubi/ *adj* dirty, grimy ⟨~ *hands*⟩ [[2]GRUB + [1]-Y] – **grubbily** *adv*, **grubbiness** *n*

'grub-ˌscrew *n* a headless screw-bolt

'grubˌstake /-ˌstayk/ *n*, *NAm* supplies or funds given to a mining prospector in return for a share in his/her discoveries; *broadly* any material assistance provided to an organization or individual [[2]*grub* + *stake*]

'Grub ˌStreet *n* the world or life-style of needy literary hacks [*Grub Street*, London, formerly inhabited by literary hacks]

[1]**grudge** /gruj/ *vt* to be unwilling or reluctant to give or admit; begrudge ⟨~d *the money to pay taxes*⟩ [ME *grucchen*, *grudgen* to grumble, complain, fr OF *groucier*, of Gmc origin; akin to MHG *grogezen* to howl] – **grudger** *n*

[2]**grudge** *n* a feeling of deep-seated resentment or ill will

grudging /'grujing/ *adj* unwilling, reluctant – **grudgingly** *adv*

gruel /'grooh·əl/ *n* a thin porridge [ME *grewel*, fr MF *gruel*, of Gmc origin; akin to OE *grūt* grout]

gruelling, *NAm chiefly* **grueling** /'grooh·əling/ *adj* trying or taxing to the point of causing exhaustion; punishing ⟨*a* ~ *race*⟩ [fr prp of obs *gruel* (to punish)]

gruesome /'groohs(ə)m/ *adj* inspiring horror or repulsion; ⟨~ *scenes of torture*⟩ [alter. of earlier *growsome*, fr E dial. *grow*, *grue* (to shiver), fr ME *gruen*, prob fr MD *grūwen*; akin to OHG in*grūēn* to shiver] – **gruesomely** *adv*, **gruesomeness** *n*

gruff /gruf/ *adj* **1** brusque or stern in manner, speech, or aspect ⟨*a* ~ *reply*⟩ **2** deep and harsh ⟨*a* ~ *voice*⟩ [D *grof*; akin to OHG *grob* coarse, *hruf* scurf – more at DANDRUFF] – **gruffly** *adv*, **gruffness** *n*

grumble /'grumbl/ *vb* **grumbling** /'grumbling/ *vi* **1** to mutter in discontent **2** to rumble ~ *vt* to express in a moaning or discontented way [prob fr MF *grommeler*, deriv of MD *grommen*; akin to OHG *grimm* grim] – **grumble** *n*, **grumbler** *n*, **grumblingly** *adv*, **grumbly** *adj*

grumbling /'grumbling/ *adj* causing intermittent pain or discomfort ⟨*a* ~ *appendix*⟩

grummet /'grumit/ *n* a grommet

grump /grump/ *n* **1** *pl* a fit of ill humour or sulkiness **2** a grumpy person [obs *grumps* (snubs, slights), prob of imit origin]

grumpy /'grumpi/ *adj* moodily cross; surly – **grumpily** *adv*, **grumpiness** *n*

Grundyism /'grundiˌiz(ə)m/ *n* prudery [*Mrs Grundy*]

[1]**grunt** /grunt/ *vb* to utter (with) a grunt [ME *grunten*, fr OE *grunnettan*, freq of *grunian*, of imit origin] – **grunter** *n*

[2]**grunt** *n* the deep short guttural sound of a pig; *also* a similar sound

gruntled /'gruntld/ *adj* (made) contented or satisfied – infml [back-formation fr *disgruntled*]

grutten /'grutn/ *past part of* [2]GREET

Gruyère /'grooh·yeə (*Fr* gryjɛːr)/ *n* a Swiss cheese with smaller holes and a slightly fuller flavour than Emmenthal [*Gruyère*, district of Switzerland]

gryke /griek/ *n* a grike

gryphon /'grifən/ *n* a griffin

'G-ˌstring *n* a small piece of cloth, leather, etc covering the genitalia and held in place by thongs, elastic, etc that is passed round the hips and between the buttocks [origin unknown]

guaiac /'g(w)ieˌak/ *n* guaiacum [NL *Guaiacum*]

guaiacum /'g(w)ie·əkəm/ *n* (a resin with a faint balsamic smell or the hard greenish brown wood of) any of several tropical American trees [NL, genus name, fr Sp *guayaco*, fr Taino *guayacan*]

guanaco /gwah'nahkoh/ *n*, *pl* **guanacos,** *esp collectively* **guanaco** a S American mammal that has a soft thick fawn-coloured coat and is related to the camel [Sp, fr Quechua *huanacu*]

guanine /'gwahneen/ *n* a purine base that is one of the 4 bases whose order in a DNA or RNA chain codes genetic information – compare ADENINE, CYTOSINE, THYMINE, URACIL [*guano* + *-ine*; fr its being found esp in guano]

guano /'gwahnoh/ *n* (an artificial fertilizer similar to) a phosphate-rich substance consisting chiefly of the excrement of seabirds and used as a fertilizer [Sp, fr Quechua *huanu* dung]

guanosine /'gwahnəseen/ *n* a nucleoside containing guanine [blend of *guanine* and *ribose*]

guarani /ˌgwahrə'nee/ *n*, *pl* *(1)* **guarani, guaranis,** *(2)* **guaranis, guaranies** **1** *cap* a member or the language of a people inhabiting Bolivia, Paraguay, and S Brazil ☞ LANGUAGE 2 ☞ *Paraguay* at NATIONALITY [Sp *guaraní*] – **guaranian** /-ˈnee·ən/ *n or adj*

[1]**guarantee** /ˌgarənˈtee/ *n* **1** one who guarantees **2** a written undertaking to answer for the payment of a debt or the performance of a duty of another in case of the other's default **3a** an agreement by which one person accepts responsibility for another's obligations, esp debts, in case of default **b** an assurance of the quality of or of the length of use to be expected from a product offered for sale, accompanied by a promise to replace it or pay the customer back **4** sthg given as security; a pledge [prob alter. of [1]*guaranty*]

[2]**guarantee** *vt* **guaranteed; guaranteeing 1** to undertake to answer for the debt or default of **2a** to undertake to do or secure (sthg) ⟨*she* ~d *delivery of the goods*⟩ **b** to engage for the existence, permanence, or nature of **3** to give security to

guarantor /ˌgarənˈtaw/ *n* **1** one who guarantees **2** one who makes or gives a guarantee [*guaranty* + [1]*-or*]

guaranty /ˈgarənti/ *n* GUARANTEE 2 [MF *garantie*, fr OF, fr *garantir* to guarantee, fr *garant* warrant, of Gmc origin; akin to OHG *werēnto* guarantor – more at [1]WARRANT]

[1]**guard** /gahd/ *n* **1** a defensive position in boxing, fencing, etc **2** the act or duty of protecting or defending **3** a person or a body of men on sentinel duty **4a** a person or group whose duty is to protect a place, people, etc **b** *pl* HOUSEHOLD TROOPS **5** a protective or safety device; *esp* a device on a machine for protecting against injury **6** *Br* the person in charge of a railway train [ME *garde*, fr MF, fr OF, fr *garder* to guard, defend, of Gmc origin; akin to OHG *wartēn* to watch, take care – more at WARD OFF]

[2]**guard** *vt* **1** to protect from danger, esp by watchful attention; make secure ⟨*policemen* ~ing *our cities*⟩ **2** to watch over so as to prevent escape, entry, theft, etc; *also* to keep in check ⟨~ *your tongue*⟩ ~ *vi* to watch by way of caution or defence; stand guard – **guarder** *n* – **guard against** to attempt to prevent (sthg) by taking precautions

ˈ**guard ˌcell** *n* either of the 2 crescent-shaped cells that border and open and close a plant stoma

guarded /ˈgahdid/ *adj* marked by caution ⟨*a* ~ *reply*⟩ ⟨*a* ~ *look*⟩ – **guardedly** *adv*, **guardedness** *n*

ˈ**guardˌhouse** /-ˌhows/ *n* a building used by soldiers on guard duty or as a prison

guardian /ˈgahdi·ən, -dyən/ *n* **1** one who or that which guards or protects **2** sby who has the care of the person or property of another; *specif* sby entrusted by law with the care of sby who is of unsound mind, not of age, etc – **guardianship** *n*

ˈ**guardˌrail** /-ˌrayl/ *n* a railing for guarding against danger or trespass

ˈ**guardroom** /-room, -ˌroohm/ *n* a room serving as a guardhouse ☞ CHURCH

ˈ**guardsman** /-mən/ *n* a member of a military body called *guard* or *guards*

ˈ**guard's ˌvan** *n*, *Br* a railway wagon or carriage attached usu at the rear of a train for the use of the guard

guava /ˈgwahvə/ *n* (the sweet acid yellow edible fruit of) a shrubby tropical American tree [modif of Sp *guayaba*, of Arawakan origin; akin to Tupi *guayava* guava]

gubbins /ˈgubinz/ *n pl but sing in constr, pl* **gubbins** *Br* **1** the inner workings of a machine; gadgetry **2** a thingamajig **3** a group or collection of objects associated with sthg specified ⟨*he received the catalogue and all the* ~ *that goes with it*⟩ *USE* infml [pl of *gubbin* (fragment, scrap), alter. of obs *gobone* (gobbet, portion), fr ME *gobyn, goboun*]

gubernatorial /ˌgyoohbənəˈtawri·əl/ *adj* of a governor [L *gubernator* governor, fr *gubernatus*, pp of *gubernare* to govern – more at GOVERN]

guddle /ˈgudl/ *vb*, *chiefly Scot* to catch (fish) by groping with the hands (e g under stones or banks of streams) [prob imit]

[1]**gudgeon** /ˈguj(ə)n/ *n* **1** a pivot or journal **2** a socket for a rudder pintle [ME *gudyon*, fr MF *goujon*]

[2]**gudgeon** *n, pl* **gudgeons,** *esp collectively* **gudgeon** a small European freshwater fish used esp for food or bait [ME *gojune*, fr MF *gouvion, gougon*, fr L *gobion-, gobio*, alter. of *gobius* – more at GOBY]

ˈ**gudgeon ˌpin** *n* a metal pin linking the piston and connecting rod in an internal-combustion engine

guelder rose /ˈgeldə/ *n* a (cultivated) shrub of the honeysuckle family with clusters of white flowers [*Guelderland, Gelderland*, province of the Netherlands]

Guelf, Guelph /gwelf/ *n* a member of a political party in medieval Italy opposing the German emperors – compare GHIBELLINE [It *Guelfo*]

guenon /gəˈnon (*Fr* gənɔ̃/ *n, pl* **guenons,** *esp collectively* **guenon** any of various long-tailed (tree-dwelling) African monkeys [F, fr MF]

guernsey /ˈguhnzi/ *n, often cap* **1** (any of) a breed of fawn and white dairy cattle larger than the jersey **2** a thick knitted tunic or jersey traditionally worn by sailors [*Guernsey*, Channel islands]

guerrilla, guerilla /gəˈrilə/ *n* a member of a small independent fighting force which engages in sabotage, unexpected assaults, etc [Sp *guerrilla*, fr dim. of *guerra* war, of Gmc origin; akin to OHG *werra* strife – more at WAR]

[1]**guess** /ges/ *vt* **1** to form an opinion of with little or no consideration of the facts **2** to arrive at a correct conclusion about by conjecture, chance, or intuition ⟨~ed *the answer*⟩ **3** *chiefly NAm* to believe, suppose ⟨*I* ~ *you're right*⟩ – infml ~ *vi* to make a guess [ME *gessen*, prob of Scand origin; akin to ON *geta* to get, guess – more at GET] – **guesser** *n*

[2]**guess** *n* a surmise, estimate

guesstimate /ˈgestimət/ *n* an estimate made without adequate information – infml [blend of *guess* and *estimate*] – **guesstimate** /-ˌmayt/ *vt*

ˈ**guessˌwork** /-ˌwuhk/ *n* (judgment based on) the act of guessing

[1]**guest** /gest/ *n* **1a** a person entertained in one's home **b** a person taken out, entertained, and paid for by another **c** a person who pays for the services of an establishment (e g a hotel) **2** one who is present by invitation ⟨*a* ~ *star on a TV programme*⟩ [ME *gest*, fr ON *gestr*; akin to OE *gæst* guest, stranger, L *hostis* stranger, enemy]

[2]**guest** *vi* to appear as a guest

ˈ**guestˌhouse** /-ˌhows/ *n* a private house used to accommodate paying guests

ˈ**guest ˌworker** *n* an immigrant worker who is a temporary resident of a country, esp in the Common

Market, and is usu employed in an unskilled job [trans of G *gastarbeiter*]

guff /guf/ *n* humbug, nonsense – infml [prob imit]

guffaw /'gufaw, gə'faw/ *vi or n* (to utter) a loud or boisterous laugh [imit]

guidance /'gied(ə)ns/ *n* **1** help, advice **2** the process of controlling the course of a projectile by a built-in mechanism [²GUIDE + -ANCE]

¹guide /gied/ *n* **1a** one who leads or directs another **b** one who shows and explains places of interest to travellers, tourists, etc **c** sthg, esp a guidebook, that provides sby with information about a place, activity, etc **d** sthg or sby that directs a person in his/her conduct or course of life **2** a bar, rod, etc for steadying or directing the motion of sthg **3** *often cap, chiefly Br* a member of a worldwide movement of girls and young women founded with the aim of forming character and teaching good citizenship through outdoor activities and domestic skills; *specif* a member of the intermediate section for girls aged from 10 to 15 [ME, fr MF, fr OProv *guida*, of Gmc origin; akin to OE *wītan* to look after, *witan* to know – more at WIT]

²guide *vt* **1** to act as a guide to; direct in a way or course **2** to direct or supervise, usu to a particular end; *also* to supervise the training of ~ *vi* to act or work as a guide; give guidance – **guider** *n*, **guidable** *adj*

'guide,book /-,book/ *n* a handbook; *esp* a book of information for travellers

'guide ,dog *n* a dog trained to lead a blind person

'guide,line /-,lien/ *n* a line by which one is guided; *esp* an indication of policy or conduct

'guide,post /-,pohst/ *n* a signpost

'guide,way /-,way/ *n* a channel or track

guiding /'gieding/ *n, chiefly Br* the activities of the Guide movement

guidon /'gied(ə)n/ *n* a triangular or forked pennant (e g a standard of a regiment of dragoons) [MF]

guild /gild/ *n sing or pl in constr* an association of people with similar interests or pursuits; *esp* a medieval association of merchants or craftsmen [ME *gilde*, fr ON *gildi* payment, guild; akin to OE *gield* tribute, guild – more at DANEGELD] – **guildship** *n*

guilder /'gildə/ *n* a gulden [modif of D *gulden*]

,guild'hall /-'hawl/ *n* a hall where a guild or corporation usu assembles; *esp* TOWN HALL

'guildsman /-mən/ *n* a guild member

guild socialism *n* an early socialist theory advocating state ownership of industry with control by guilds of workers

guile /giel/ *n* deceitful cunning; duplicity [ME, fr OF] – **guileful** *adj*, **guilefully** *adv*, **guileless** *adj*, **guilelessly** *adv*

guillemot /'gili,mot/ *n, pl* **guillemots,** *esp collectively* **guillemot** any of several narrow-billed auks of northern seas [F, fr MF, dim. of *Guillaume* William]

guillotine /'giləteen/ *n* **1** a machine for beheading consisting of a heavy blade that slides down between grooved posts **2** an instrument (e g a paper cutter) that works like a guillotine **3** limitation of the discussion of legislative business by the imposition of a time limit – compare CLOSURE [F, fr Joseph *Guillotin* †1814 F physician] – **guillotine** *vt*

guilt /gilt/ *n* **1** the fact of having committed a breach of conduct, esp one that violates law **2a** responsibility for a criminal or other offence **b** feelings of being at fault or to blame, esp for imagined offences or from a sense of inadequacy [ME, delinquency, guilt, fr OE *gylt*]

guilty /'gilti/ *adj* **1** justly answerable for an offence **2a** suggesting or involving guilt ⟨*a ~ deed*⟩ **b** feeling guilt ⟨*their ~ consciences*⟩ – **guiltily** *adv*, **guiltiness** *n*

guinea /'gini/ *n* **1** a former British gold coin worth 21 shillings **2** a money unit worth £1 and 5 new pence [*Guinea*, region of W Africa, supposed source of the gold from which it was made]

'guinea ,fowl /'gini/ *n* a W African bird with white-speckled slaty plumage that is related to the pheasants and is widely kept for food

'guinea ,pig *n* **1** a small stout-bodied short-eared nearly tailless rodent often kept as a pet **2** sby or sthg used as a subject of (scientific) research or experimentation

'guinea ,worm *n* a very long slender nematode worm of warm climates that lives under the skin of human beings and other mammals

guipure /gi'pyooə/ *n* a heavy large-patterned decorative lace on a fabric foundation [F]

guise /giez/ *n* **1** external appearance; aspect **2** assumed appearance; semblance [ME, fr OF, of Gmc origin; akin to OHG *wīsa* manner – more at ¹WISE] – **in the guise of** masquerading as

guitar /gi'tah/ *n* a flat-bodied stringed instrument with a long fretted neck, plucked with a plectrum or the fingers [F *guitare*, fr Sp *guitarra*, fr Ar, *qītār*, fr Gk *kithara* cithara] – **guitarist** *n*

Gujarati, Gujerati /,goojə'rahti/ *n or adj, pl* **Gujarati, Gujerati** (the language or a member of a people) of the state of Gujarat in W India ☞ LANGUAGE [Hindi *gujarātī*, fr *Gujarāt* Gujarat]

gulch /gulch/ *n, chiefly NAm* a ravine, esp with a torrent flowing through it [perh fr E dial. *gulch* (to gulp), fr ME *gulchen*]

gulden /'goold(ə)n/ *n, pl* **guldens, gulden** ☞ *The Netherlands, Netherlands Antilles, Surinam* at NATIONALITY [ME (Sc), fr MD *gulden florijn* golden florin]

gules /gyoohlz/ *n* red – used in heraldry [ME *goules*, fr MF]

¹gulf /gulf/ *n* **1** a partially landlocked part of the sea, usu larger than a bay **2** a deep chasm; an abyss **3** an unbridgeable gap ⟨*the ~ between theory and practice*⟩ [ME *goulf*, fr MF *golfe*, fr It *golfo*, fr LL *colpus*, fr Gk *kolpos* bosom, gulf; akin to OE *hwealf* vault, OHG *walbo*]

²gulf *vt* to engulf

'gulf,weed /-,weed/ *n* a sargassum [*Gulf* of Mexico]

¹gull /gul/ *n* any of numerous related long-winged web-footed largely white, grey, or black aquatic birds [ME, of Celt origin; akin to W *gwylan* gull]

²gull *vt* to trick, cheat, or deceive ⟨~ed *into a bad purchase*⟩ [obs *gull* (gullet), fr ME *golle*, fr MF *goule*]

Gullah /'gulə; *also* 'goolə/ *n* a member or the English dialect of a group of Negroes of the sea islands and coast of S Carolina, Georgia, and NE Florida

gullet /'gulit/ *n* the oesophagus; *broadly* the throat ☞ DIGESTION [ME *golet*, fr MF *goulet*, dim. of *goule* throat, fr L *gula* – more at GLUTTON]

gullible /'guləbl/ *adj* easily deceived or cheated – **gullibility** /-'biləti/ *n*

[1]**gully** *also* **gulley** /'guli/ *n* **1** a trench worn in the earth by running water after rain **2** a deep gutter or drain **3** a fielding position in cricket close to the batsman on the off side and between point and the slips ☞ SPORT [obs *gully* (gullet), prob alter. of ME *golet*]

[2]**gully** *vt vt* to make gullies in

gulp /gulp/ *vt* to swallow hurriedly, greedily, or in 1 swallow – often + *down* ~ *vi* to make a sudden swallowing movement as if surprised or nervous [ME *gulpen*, fr a MD or MLG word akin to D & Fris *gulpen* to bubble forth, drink deep; akin to OE *gielpan* to boast – more at YELP] – **gulp** *n*, **gulper** *n*

gulp back *vt* to keep back (as if) by swallowing; suppress ⟨gulped back *his tears*⟩

[1]**gum** /gum/ *n* (the tissue that surrounds the teeth and covers) the parts of the jaws from which the teeth grow ☞ DIGESTION [ME *gome*, fr OE *gōma* palate; akin to OHG *guomo* palate, Gk *chaos* abyss]

[2]**gum** *n* **1a** any of numerous polysaccharide plant substances that are gelatinous when moist but harden on drying – compare MUCILAGE **b** any of various substances (e g a mucilage or gum resin) that exude from plants **2** a substance or deposit resembling a plant gum (e g in adhesive quality) **3** *Austr* a eucalyptus [ME *gomme*, fr OF, fr L *cummi, gummi*, fr Gk *kommi*, fr Egypt *qmy.t*] – **gummy** *adj*

[3]**gum** *vb* **-mm-** *vt* to smear or stick (as if) with gum ~ *vi* to exude or form gum – **gummer** *n*

[4]**gum** *n* God – esp in *by gum* as a mild oath [euphemism]

,gum 'arabic *n* a water-soluble gum obtained from several acacias and used esp in the manufacture of adhesives and in pharmacy

gumbo /'gumboh/ *n* **1** a (meat and vegetable) soup thickened with okra pods **2** *often cap* a patois used by Negroes and Creoles, esp in Louisiana **3** *NAm* OKRA 1 [AmerF *gombo*, of Bantu origin; akin to Umbundu *ochinggômbo* okra] – **gumbo** *adj*

gumboil /'gum,boyl/ *n* an abscess in the gum

'gum,boot /-,booht/ *n* a strong waterproof rubber boot reaching usu to the knee

gumma /'gumə/ *n, pl* **gummas** *also* **gummata** /'gumətə/ a rubbery tumour characteristic of tertiary syphilis [NL *gummat-, gumma*, fr LL, gum, alter. of L *gummi*] – **gummatous** *adj*

gumption /'gumpsh(ə)n/ *n* **1** shrewd practical common sense **2** initiative; *specif* boldness [origin unknown]

'gum ,resin *n* a mixture of gum and resin (e g myrrh), usu obtained by making an incision in a plant and allowing the juice which exudes to solidify

gumshoe /'gum,shooh/ *n, chiefly NAm* a detective – infml [*gumshoe* (rubber shoe, sby who walks stealthily)]

'gum ,tree *n* a eucalyptus

gum up *vt* to prevent or impede the proper working or carrying out of – esp in *gum up the works*; infml

[1]**gun** /gun/ *n* **1a** a piece of ordnance, usu with a high muzzle velocity and a comparatively flat trajectory **b** a rifle, pistol, etc **c** a device that throws a projectile **2** a discharge of a gun **3a** sby who carries a gun in a shooting party **b** *NAm* one who is skilled with a gun; *esp* a gunman [ME *gonne, gunne*] – **gunned** *adj*

[2]**gun** *vt* **-nn- 1** to fire on **2** to shoot – often + *down* – **gun for** to search for in order to attack – infml

[1]**'gun,boat** /-,boht/ *n* a relatively heavily armed ship of shallow draught

[2]**gunboat** *adj* of or employing the high-handed use of naval or military power ⟨~ *diplomacy*⟩

'gun,cotton /-,kot(ə)n/ *n* (an explosive highly nitrated with) cellulose nitrate

'gun,dog /-,dog/ *n* a dog trained to locate or retrieve game for hunters

'gun,fire /-,fie·ə/ *n* the (noise of) firing of guns

gunge /gunj/ *n, Br* an unpleasant, dirty, or sticky substance – slang [origin unknown] – **gungy** *adj*

gung ho /,gung 'hoh/ *adj, chiefly NAm* extremely or excessively enthusiastic [*Gung ho!*, motto (interpreted as meaning 'work together'') of certain US marine raiders in **WW II**, fr Chin (Pek) *kung*[1]*-ho*[2], short for *chung*[1]*-kuo*[2] *kung*[1]*-yeh*[4] *ho*[2]*-tso*[4] *she*[4] Chinese Industrial Cooperatives Society]

gunk /gungk/ *n, chiefly NAm* gunge – slang [prob imit]

gunlayer /'gun,layə/ *n* sby who aims a large gun

'gun,lock /-,lok/ *n* the mechanism for igniting the charge of a firearm

'gunman /-mən/ *n* a man armed with a gun; *esp* a professional killer

'gun,metal /-,metl/ *n* (a metal treated to imitate) a bronze formerly used for cannon – **gunmetal** *adj*

gunnel /'gunl/ *n* a gunwale

gunner /'gunə/ *n* **1** a soldier or airman who operates a gun; *specif* a private in the Royal Artillery **2** sby who hunts with a gun **3** a warrant officer who supervises naval ordnance and ordnance stores

gunnery /'gunəri/ *n* the use of guns; *specif* the science of the flight of projectiles and of the effective use of guns

gunnery sergeant *n* ☞ RANK

gunny /'guni/ *n* a coarse heavy material, usu of jute, used esp for sacking [Hindi *gani*]

gunpoint /'gun,poynt/ *n* – **at gunpoint** under threat of death

'gun,powder /-,powdə/ *n* an explosive mixture of potassium nitrate, charcoal, and sulphur used in gunnery and blasting

'gun ,room *n* quarters on a British warship used by junior officers

'gun,runner /-,runə/ *n* one who carries or deals in contraband arms and ammunition – **gunrunning** *n*

'gun,ship /-,ship/ *n* a heavily armed relatively slow aircraft (e g a helicopter or converted transport aeroplane) used to suppress ground fire; *also* an antitank helicopter

'gun,shot /-,shot/ *n* **1** a shot or projectile fired from a gun **2** the range of a gun ⟨*out of* ~⟩

'gun-,shy *adj, esp of a dog* afraid of the sound of a gun

'gun,slinger /-,sling·ə/ *n* a gunman – slang

'gun,smith /-,smith/ *n* sby who designs, makes, or repairs firearms

gunwale, gunnel /'gunl/ *n* the upper edge of a ship's or boat's side [ME *gonnewale*, fr *gonne* gun + *wale*; fr its former use as a support for guns]

guppy /'gupi/ *n, pl* **guppies**, *esp collectively* **guppy** a small (aquarium) fish native to the W Indies and S America [R J L *Guppy* †1916 Trinidadian naturalist]

gurgle /ˈguhgl/ *vb* **gurgling** /ˈguhgling/ *vi* to make the sound (as if) of unevenly flowing water; *also* to flow or move with such a sound ~ *vt* to utter with a gurgling sound [prob imit] – **gurgle** *n*

Gurkha /ˈguhkə/ *n* a member of the dominant race in Nepal (serving in the British or Indian army)

gurnard /ˈguhnəd/ *n, pl* **gurnards,** *esp collectively* **gurnard** any of various fishes with large armoured heads and 3 pairs of pectoral fins [ME, fr MF *gornart,* irreg fr *grognier* to grunt, fr L *grunnire,* of imit origin]

guru /ˈgoohrooh, ˈgoo-/ *n, pl* **gurus** **1** a personal religious teacher and spiritual guide (e g in Hinduism) **2a** a spiritual and intellectual guide; a mentor **b** an acknowledged leader or chief proponent (e g of a cult or idea) – infml ⟨*the* ~ *of modern philosophical thought*⟩ [Hindi *gurū,* fr Skt *guru,* fr *guru,* adj, heavy, venerable – more at [1]GRIEVE]

[1]**gush** /gush/ *vi* **1** to issue copiously or violently **2** to emit a sudden copious flow **3** to make an effusive often affected display of sentiment or enthusiasm ⟨*women* ~ing *over the baby*⟩ ~ *vt* to emit in a copious free flow [ME *guschen*] – **gushy** *adj,* **gushing** *adj*

[2]**gush** *n* **1** (sthg emitted in) a sudden outpouring **2** an effusive and usu affected display of sentiment or enthusiasm

gusher /ˈgushə/ *n* an oil well with a copious natural flow [[1]GUSH + [2]-ER]

gusset /ˈgusit/ *n* **1** a piece of material inserted in a seam (e g the crotch of an undergarment) to provide expansion or reinforcement **2** a plate or bracket for strengthening an angle in framework [ME, piece of armour covering the joints in a suit of armour, fr MF *gouchet*] – **gusset** *vt*

[1]**gust** /gust/ *n* **1** a sudden brief rush of (rain carried by the) wind **2** a sudden outburst; a surge ⟨*a* ~ *of emotion*⟩ [prob fr ON *gustr;* akin to OHG *gussa* flood, OE *gēotan* to pour – more at [4]FOUND] – **gustily** *adv,* **gustiness** *n,* **gusty** *adj*

[2]**gust** *vi* to blow in gusts ⟨*winds* ~ing *up to 40 mph*⟩

gustatory /ˈgustət(ə)ri/, **gustative** /-tiv/ *adj* of, associated with, or being the sense of taste [L *gustatus,* pp of *gustare* to taste; akin to L *gustus* taste, liking] – **gustatorily** *adv,* **gustation** /guˈstaysh(ə)n/ *n*

gusto /ˈgustoh/ *n* enthusiastic and vigorous enjoyment or vitality ⟨*he sang with great* ~⟩ [Sp, fr L *gustus*]

[1]**gut** /gut/ *n* **1a** the basic emotionally or instinctively responding part of a person ⟨*a* ~ *feeling*⟩ **b** (a part of) the alimentary canal **c** the belly or abdomen **d** catgut **2** a narrow (water) passage **3** the sac of silk taken from a silkworm and drawn out into a thread for use in attaching a fish hook to a fishing line **4** *pl* the inner essential parts ⟨*the* ~s *of a car*⟩ – infml **5** *pl* courage, determination – infml [ME, fr OE *guttas,* pl; akin to OE *gēotan* to pour]

[2]**gut** *vt* **-tt-** **1** to eviscerate, disembowel **2a** to destroy the inside of ⟨*fire* ~ted *the building*⟩ **b** to destroy the essential power or effectiveness of ⟨*inflation* ~ting *the economy of a country*⟩ **3** to extract the essentials of ⟨~ *a novel*⟩

[3]**gut** *adj* arising from or concerning one's strongest emotions or instincts ⟨*her* ~ *reaction to their behaviour was one of disgust*⟩

ˈ**gutless** /-lis/ *adj* lacking courage; cowardly – infml – **gutlessness** *n*

ˈ**gutsy** /-si/ *adj* **1** courageous **2** expressing or appealing strongly to the physical passions; lusty ⟨*belting out* ~ *rock*⟩ *USE* infml – **gutsiness** *n*

gutta-percha /ˌgutə ˈpuhchə/ *n* a tough plastic substance obtained from the latex of several Malaysian trees and used esp for electrical insulation [Malay *gĕtah-pĕrcha,* fr *gĕtah* sap, latex + *pĕrcha,* tree producing gutta-percha]

guttate /ˈgutayt/ *adj* having small (coloured) spots or drops [L *guttatus,* fr *gutta*]

[1]**gutter** /ˈgutə/ *n* **1** a trough just below the eaves or at the side of a street to catch and carry off rainwater, surface water, etc **2** a white space between 2 pages of a book, 2 postage stamps on a sheet, etc **3** *the* lowest or most vulgar level or condition of human life [ME *goter,* fr OF *goutiere,* fr *goute* drop, fr L *gutta*]

[2]**gutter** *vt* to cut or wear gutters in ~ *vi* **1** to flow in rivulets **2a** *of a candle* to burn unevenly so that melted wax runs down one side **b** *of a flame* to burn fitfully or feebly; be on the point of going out

[3]**gutter** *adj* (characteristic) of the gutter; *esp* marked by extreme vulgarity or cheapness ⟨*the* ~ *press*⟩

guttering /ˈgutəring/ *n* a length or section of a gutter

ˈ**gutter,snipe** /-ˌsniep/ *n* a deprived child living in poverty and usu dressed in ragged clothes [[1]*gutter* + *snipe* (wretched person), fr [1]*snipe*]

guttural /ˈgut(ə)rəl/ *adj* **1** of the throat **2a** formed or pronounced in the throat ⟨~ *sounds*⟩ **b** velar or palatal [MF, prob fr ML *gutturalis,* fr L *guttur* throat – more at [1]COT] – **gutturally** *adv,* **gutturalize** *vt,* **gutturalization** /-ˈzaysh(ə)n/ *n*

guv /guv/ *n, Br* GOVERNOR 3 – slang

guvnor /ˈguvnə/ *n, Br* GOVERNOR 3 – slang [by alter.]

[1]**guy** /gie/ *vt or n* (to steady or reinforce with) a rope, chain, rod, etc attached to sthg as a brace or guide [prob fr D *gei* brail]

[2]**guy** *n* **1** *often cap* a humorous effigy of a man burnt in Britain on Guy Fawkes Night **2** a man, fellow – infml [*Guy* Fawkes †1606 E conspirator]

[3]**guy** *vt* to make fun of; ridicule

ˈ**Guy ˌFawkes ˌNight** /ˌgie ˈfawks/ *n* November 5 observed in Britain with fireworks and bonfires in commemoration of the arrest of Guy Fawkes in 1605 for attempting to blow up the Houses of Parliament

guzzle /ˈguzl/ *vb* **guzzling** /ˈguzling, ˈguzl·ing/ to consume (sthg) greedily, continually, or habitually [origin unknown] – **guzzler** *n*

gwyniad /ˈgwiniad/ *n* a whitefish found in Bala Lake in N Wales [W, fr *gwyn* white]

gybe, *NAm chiefly* **jibe** /jieb/ *vi vi* **1** *of a fore-and-aft sail* to swing (suddenly and violently) from one side to another when running before the wind **2** to change a ship's course so that the sail gybes ~ *vt* to cause to gybe [perh modif of D *gijben*]

gym /jim/ *n* **1** a gymnasium **2** development of the body by games, exercises, etc, esp in school

gymkhana /jimˈkahnə/ *n* a sporting event featuring competitions and displays; *specif* a meeting involving competition in horse riding and carriage driving [prob modif of Hindi *gend-khāna* racket court]

gymn- /jimn-/, **gymno-** *comb form* naked; bare

⟨gymno*sperm*⟩ [NL, fr Gk, fr *gymnos* – more at NAKED]

gymnasium /jim'nayzi·əm, -zyəm/ *n, pl* **gymnasiums, gymnasia** /-zi·ə/ **1** a large room or separate building used for indoor sports and gymnastic activities **2** a German or Scandinavian secondary school that prepares pupils for university [L, exercise ground, school, fr Gk *gymnasion*, fr *gymnazein* to exercise naked, fr *gymnos*; (2) G, fr L, school]

gymnast /'jimnast/ *n* sby trained in gymnastics [MF *gymnaste*, fr Gk *gymnastēs* trainer, fr *gymnazein*] – **gymnastic** /-'nastik/ *adj*

gymnastics /jim'nastiks/ *n pl but sing or pl in constr* **1** physical exercises developing or displaying bodily strength and coordination, often performed in competition **2** an exercise in intellectual or physical dexterity ⟨*verbal* ~⟩

gymnosperm /'jimnoh,spuhm/ *n* any of a class of woody vascular seed plants (e g conifers) that produce naked seeds not enclosed in an ovary – compare ANGIOSPERM ☞ PLANT [deriv of NL *gymn-* + Gk *sperma* seed – more at SPERM] – **gymnospermy** *n*, **gymnospermous** /-'spuhməs/ *adj*

[1]**gymslip** /'jim,slip/ *n, chiefly Br* a girl's tunic or pinafore dress that is worn usu with a belt as part of a school uniform

[2]**gymslip** *adj, chiefly Br* of a schoolgirl or a girl of school age ⟨*a ~ pregnancy*⟩ – infml

gyn-, gyno- *comb form* **1** woman ⟨gyno*cracy*⟩ **2** female reproductive organ; ovary ⟨gyno*phore*⟩; pistil ⟨gyno*ecium*⟩ [Gk *gyn-*, fr *gynē* – more at QUEEN]

gynaec-, gynaeco-, *NAm chiefly* **gynec-, gyneco-** woman; reproductive organs of women ⟨gynae*cology*⟩ [GK *gynaik-*, *gynaiko-*, fr *gynaik-*, *gynē* woman]

gynaecology /,gienə'koləji, ,jie-/ *n* a branch of medicine that deals with diseases and disorders (of the reproductive system) of women [ISV] – **gynaecologist** *n*, **gynaecologic** /-kə'lojik/, **gynaecological** *adj*

gynandromorph /jie'nandrə,mawf, /-ji-, gie-, -droh-/ *n* an (abnormal) individual having characters of both sexes in different parts of the body [ISV] – **gynandromorphy** *n*, **gynandromorphic** /-'mawfik/ *adj*, **gynandromorphism** *n*, **gynandromorphous** *adj*

gynandrous /ji'nandrəs, jie-, gie-/ *adj, of a flower, esp an orchid* having the male and female parts united in a column [Gk *gynandros* of doubtful sex, fr *gynē* woman + *andr-*, *anēr* man – more at ANDR-]

-gyne /-jien/ *comb form* (→ *n*) woman; female ⟨*pseudo*gyne⟩ [Gk *gynē*]

gynoecium /jie'neesi·əm, gie-/ *n, pl* **gynoecia** /-si·ə/ all the female parts of a flower [NL, alter. of L *gynaeceum* women's apartments, fr Gk *gynaikeion*, fr *gynaik-*, *gynē*]

-gynous /-jənəs/ *comb form* (→ *adj*) having (such or so many) females or female parts or organs ⟨*hetero*gynous⟩ [NL *-gynus*, fr Gk *-gynos*, fr *gynē*] – **-gyny** *comb form* (→ *n*)

[1]**gyp** /jip/ *n* **1** *Br* a college servant at Cambridge university – compare BEDDER, SCOUT **2** *NAm* **a** a cheat, swindler **b** a fraud, swindle *USE* (*2*) infml [prob short for *gypsy*]

[2]**gyp** *vb* **-pp-** *NAm* to cheat – infml

[3]**gyp** *n* sharp pain – chiefly in *give one gyp*; infml [origin unknown]

gypsophila /jip'sofilə; *often* ,jipsə'fili·ə/ *n* any of a genus of Old World plants of the pink family with many small delicate flowers [NL, genus name, fr L *gypsum* + *-phila* -phil]

gypsum /'jipsəm/ *n* hydrated calcium sulphate occurring as a mineral and used esp in plaster of paris [L, fr Gk *gypsos*, of Sem origin; akin to Ar *jibs* plaster] – **gypseous** /-si·əs/ *adj*, **gypsiferous** /-'sif(ə)rəs/ *adj*

gypsy /'jipsi/ *n, chiefly NAm* a gipsy

gyr-, gyro- *comb form* **1** ring; circle; spiral; rotation ⟨gyro*magnetic*⟩ **2** gyroscope ⟨gyro*compass*⟩ [prob fr MF, fr L, fr Gk, fr *gyros*]

gyrate /jie'rayt, ji/ *vb* **1** to revolve round a point or axis **2** to (cause to) move with a circular or spiral motion – **gyrator** *n*, **gyration** /-'raysh(ə)n/ *n*, **gyrational** *adj*, **gyratory** /'jierət(ə)ri, -'ray-/ *adj*

gyrfalcon /'juh,faw(l)kən/ *n* a large powerful arctic falcon [ME *gerfaucun*, fr MF *girfaucon*]

gyro /'jie·(ə)roh/ *n, pl* **gyros** **1** a gyroscope **2** a gyrocompass *USE* infml

gyrocompass /'jie·əroh,kumpəs/ *n* a compass in which the horizontal axis of a constantly spinning gyroscope always points to true north

,gyromag'netic /-mag'netik/ *adj* of the magnetic properties of a rotating electrical particle

gyroplane /jie·ərə,playn/ *n* an aircraft supported by rapidly rotating horizontal aerofoils [ISV]

'gyro,scope /-,skohp/ *n* a wheel that is mounted to spin rapidly about an axis and is free to turn in various directions but that maintains constant orientation while spinning in the absence of applied forces [F, fr *gyr-* + *-scope*; fr its original use to illustrate the rotation of the earth] – **gyroscopic** /-'skopik/ *adj*, **gyroscopically** *adv*

h /aych/ *n, pl* **h's, hs** *often cap* **1** (a graphic representation of or device for reproducing) the 8th letter of the English alphabet **2** a speech counterpart of orthographic *h*

ha /hah/ *interj* – used esp to express surprise, joy, triumph, etc [ME]

haar /hah/ *n* a cold fog on the E coast of Britain [prob fr a LG or D dial. word; akin to ON *hārr* grey, hoary]

Habakkuk /'habəkook/ *n* (a book of the Old Testament attributed to) a Hebrew prophet of 7th-c Judah [Heb *Hăbhaqqūq*]

habanera /,habə'nyeərə/ *n* (music for) a Cuban dance in slow duple time [Sp (*danza*) *habanera*, lit., Havanan dance, fr La *Habana* (Havana), capital city of Cuba]

habdalah /,hahvdə'lah, hahv'dawlə/ *n, often cap* a Jewish domestic ceremony marking the close of a Sabbath or holy day [Heb *habhdālāh* separation]

habeas corpus /,haybi·əs 'kawpəs, -byəs/ *n* a judicial writ requiring a detained person to be brought before a court so that the legality of his/her detention may be examined [ME, fr ML, lit., you should have the body (the opening words of the writ)]

haberdasher /'habə,dashə/ *n* **1** *Br* a dealer in buttons, thread, ribbon, etc used in making clothes **2** *NAm* a dealer in shirts, ties, and other minor articles of menswear [ME *haberdassher*, prob fr modif of AF *hapertas* petty merchandise]

'haber,dashery /-ri/ *n* **1** goods sold by a haberdasher **2** a haberdasher's shop

habergeon /'habəjən/ *n* (a sleeveless mail jacket shorter than) a hauberk [ME *haubergeoun*, fr MF *haubergeon*, dim. of *hauberc* hauberk]

habiliment /hə'bilimənt/ *n* an article of clothing (characteristic of an occupation or occasion) – usu pl; fml [MF *habillement*, fr *habiller* to dress a log, dress, fr *bille* log – more at [3]BILLET]

[1]habit /'habit/ *n* **1** a costume characteristic of a calling, rank, or function ⟨*riding* ~⟩ ⟨*monk's* ~⟩ **2** bodily or mental make-up ⟨*a cheerful* ~ *of mind*⟩ **3a** a settled tendency or usual manner of behaviour **b** an acquired pattern or mode of behaviour **4** addiction ⟨*a drug* ~⟩ **5** characteristic mode of growth, occurrence, or appearance (e g of a plant or crystal) [ME, fr OF, fr L *habitus* condition, character, fr *habitus*, pp of *habēre* to have, hold – more at GIVE]

[2]habit *vt* to clothe, dress – fml

habitable /'habitəbl/ *adj* capable of being lived in – **habitableness** *n*, **habitably** *adv*, **habitability** /-'biləti/ *n*

habitant /'habitənt/ *n* **1** an inhabitant, resident **2** (a descendant of) a settler of French origin

habitat /'habitat/ *n* **1** the (type of) place where a plant or animal naturally grows or lives **2** HABITATION 2 [L, it inhabits, fr *habitare*]

habitation /,habi'taysh(ə)n/ *n* **1** the act of inhabiting; occupancy **2** a dwelling place; a residence, home [ME *habitacioun*, fr MF *habitation*, fr L *habitation-, habitatio*, fr *habitatus*, pp of *habitare* to inhabit, fr *habitus*, pp]

'habit-,forming *adj* inducing the formation of an addiction

habitual /hə'bityooəl, -chooəl/ *adj* **1** having the nature of a habit ⟨~ *smoking*⟩ **2** by force of habit ⟨~ *drunkard*⟩ **3** in accordance with habit; customary ⟨*gave his* ~ *end of term speech*⟩ – **habitually** *adv*, **habitualness** *n*

habituate /hə'bityooayt, -choo-/ *vt* to make used *to* ~ *vi* to cause habituation

habituation /hə,bityoo'aysh(ə)n, -choo-/ *n* psychological need for a drug after a period of use [HABITUATE + -ION]

habitué /hə'bityoo,ay, -choo,ay/ *n* one who frequents a specified place ⟨~s *of the theatre*⟩ [F, fr pp of *habituer* to frequent, fr LL *habituare* to habituate, fr L *habitus*]

haboob /hə'boohb/ *n* a sandstorm in N Africa [Ar *habūb* violent wind]

Habsburg /'hapsbuhg/ *n or adj* (a) Hapsburg

hacek /'hah·chek/ *n* an inverted circumflex accent (e g in *č*) ☞ SYMBOL [Czech *háček*, lit., little hook]

hachure /ha'shyooə/ *n* a line used on a map to shade and denote hills, valleys, etc [F]

hacienda /,hasi'endə/ *n* (the main house of) a large estate or plantation, esp in a Spanish-speaking country [Sp, fr L *facienda*, neut pl of *faciendus*, gerundive of *facere* to make, do]

[1]hack /hak/ *vt* **1a** to cut (as if) with repeated irregular or unskilful blows **b** to sever with repeated blows *vt* **2** to clear by cutting away vegetation ⟨~ *a path*⟩ **3** to kick (an opposing player or the ball in football) **4** *chiefly NAm* to bear, tolerate – slang ~ *vi* **1** to make cutting blows or rough cuts **2** to cough in a short dry manner ⟨*a* ~*ing cough*⟩ [ME *hakken*, fr OE *-haccian*; akin to OHG *hacchōn* to hack, OE *hōc* hook] – **hacker** *n*

[2]hack *n* **1** a mattock, pick, etc **2** (a wound from) a kick in football **3** a hacking blow

[3]hack *n* **1** the board on which a falcon's meat is served **2** the state of partial liberty in which a young hawk is kept before training – usu + *at* [blend of [1]*hatch* and *heck* (hatch, rack)]

[4]hack *n* **1a** a riding horse let out for hire **b** [1]JADE 1 **c** a light easy saddle horse **2** an act of hacking; a ride **3** one who produces mediocre work for financial gain; *esp* a commercial writer **4** *NAm* a taxi [short for *hackney*]

[5]hack *adj* **1** performed by, suited to, or characteristic of a hack ⟨~ *writing*⟩ **2** hackneyed, trite

[6]hack *vb* to ride (a horse) at an ordinary pace, esp over roads – **hacker** *n*

hackamore /ˈhakə,maw/ *n* a bridle with a loop capable of being tightened about the nose and used in place of a bit on a horse not used to one [by folk etymology fr Sp *jáquima*]

ˈhacking ˌjacket /ˈhaking/ *n* a waisted riding coat with slits in the skirt and slanting flapped pockets ☞ GARMENT [[6]*hack*]

hackle /ˈhakl/ *n* **1** a steel comb with long teeth for dressing flax or hemp **2a** any of the long narrow feathers on the neck of a domestic cock or other bird **b** *pl* the erectile hairs along the neck and back of esp a dog **3** an artificial fishing fly made from a cock's hackles [ME *hakell*; akin to OHG *hāko* hook – more at HOOK]

[1]**hackney** /ˈhakni/ *n* any of an English breed of rather compact English horses with a conspicuously high leg action [ME *hakeney*, prob fr *Hakeneye* Hackney, borough of London]

[2]**hackney** *adj* kept for public hire ⟨*a ~ cab*⟩

hackneyed /ˈhaknid/ *adj* lacking in freshness or originality; meaningless because used or done too often

hacksaw /ˈhak,saw/ *n* a fine-toothed saw, esp for cutting metal – **hacksaw** *vt*

had /d, əd, həd; *strong* had/ *past of* HAVE

hadal /ˈhaydl/ *adj* of or being the parts of the ocean below 6000m (about 6562yd) [F, fr *Hadès* Hades]

haddock /ˈhadək/ *n, pl* **haddocks,** *esp collectively* **haddock** an important Atlantic food fish, usu smaller than the related common cod [ME *haddok*]

hade /hayd/ *n* the angle made by the plane of a rock fault or vein with the vertical [*hade* (to incline from the vertical), of unknown origin]

Hades /ˈhaydeez/ *n* **1** the underground abode of the dead in Greek mythology **2** *often not cap* hell – euph [Gk *Haidēs*]

hadith /həˈdeeth/ *n, often cap* the body of traditions relating to Muhammad and his companions [Ar *ḥadīth*]

hadj /haj/ *n* the hajj

hadji /ˈhaji/ *n* a hajji

hadn't /ˈhadnt/ had not

hadron /ˈhadron/ *n* a pion or heavier elementary particle that takes part in strong interactions [ISV *hadr-* thick, heavy (fr Gk *hadros*) + [2]*-on*] – **hadronic** /haˈdronik/ *adj*

hadst /hadst/ *archaic past 2nd sing of* HAVE

haem, *chiefly NAm* **heme** /heem/ *n* a deep red iron-containing compound that occurs esp as the oxygen-carrying part of haemoglobin [ISV, fr *haematin*]

haem-, haema-, haemo-, *NAm* **hem-, hema-, hemo-** *comb form* blood ⟨haemo*flagellate*⟩ ⟨haemo*philia*⟩ [MF *hemo-*, fr L *haem-, haemo-*, fr Gk *haim-, haimo-*, fr *haima*]

haemagglutinate /ˌheeməˈgloohtinayt, ˌhemə-/ *vt* to cause agglutination of (red blood cells) – **haemagglutination** /-ˈnaysh(ə)n/ *n*

haemal /ˈheeml/ *adj* **1** of the blood (vessels) **2** of or situated on the same side of the spinal cord as that on which the heart is placed

haemat-, haemato-, *NAm* **hemat-, hemato-** *comb form* haem- ⟨haemato*id*⟩ ⟨haemato*genous*⟩ [L *haemat-, haemato-*, fr Gk *haimat-, haimato-*, fr *haimat-, haima*]

haematic /heeˈmatik/ *adj* of, containing, or affecting the blood

haematin /ˈhemətin, ˈhee-/ *n* (a brownish or bluish black derivative of oxidized) haem

haematite /ˈhemətiet, ˈhee-/ *n* iron oxide occurring as a crystalline or red earthy mineral

haematocrit /ˈheemətoh,krit, ˈhemə-, hiˈmatə-/ *n* (an instrument for determining) the ratio of the volume of red blood cells to volume of whole blood [ISV *haemat-* + Gk *kritēs* judge, fr *krinein* to judge – more at CERTAIN]

haemaˈtology /ˌheeməˈtoləji/ *n* the biology and medicine of (diseases of) the blood and blood-forming organs – **haematologic** /-təˈlojik/, **haematological** *adj*

haematoma /ˌheeeməˈtohmə, ˌhemə-/ *n* a tumour or swelling containing blood; BRUISE 1a

haemin /ˈheemin/ *n* a red-brown to blue-black salt derived from oxidized haem [ISV]

haemo- – see HAEM-

haemocoele, haemocoel /ˈheemə,seel/ *n* a body cavity in arthropods or some other invertebrates that normally contains blood and functions as part of the circulatory system

haemocyanin /ˌheemohˈsie·ənin/ *n* a colourless copper-containing respiratory pigment found in the blood of various arthropods and molluscs that is analogous to the haemoglobin of higher animals [ISV]

haemocyte /ˈheemoh,siet, ˈhemoh-/ *n* a blood cell, esp of an invertebrate animal [ISV]

ˌhaemocyˈtometer /-sieˈtomitə/ *n* an instrument for counting (blood) cells suspended in a liquid, usu when viewed under a microscope [ISV]

ˌhaemodiˈalysis /-dieˈaləsis/ *n* purification of the blood (of sby whose kidneys have failed) by dialysis

ˌhaemoˈglobin /-ˈglohbin/ *n* an iron-containing protein that occurs in the red blood cells of vertebrates and is the means of oxygen transport from the lungs to the body tissues [ISV, short for earlier *haematoglobulin*] – **haemoglobinous** *adj,* **haemoglobinic** /-glohˈbinik/ *adj*

ˈhaemoˌlymph /-,limf/ *n* a circulatory fluid of various invertebrate animals that is functionally comparable to the blood and lymph of vertebrates

haemolysis /hiˈmolisis/ *n* dissolution of red blood cells with release of haemoglobin [NL] – **haemolytic** /ˌheemohˈlitik, hemoh-/ *adj,* **haemolyse** /ˈheemohliez, ˈhemoh-/ *vt*

haemophilia /ˌheemohˈfili·ə, -mə-/ *n* delayed clotting of the blood with consequent difficulty in controlling bleeding even after minor injuries, occurring as a hereditary defect, usu in males [NL] – **haemophilic** /-ˈfilik/ *adj*

ˌhaemoˈphiliac /-liak/ *n or adj* (sby) suffering from haemophilia

haemopoiesis /ˌheemohpoyˈeesis, ˌhemoh-/ *n* the formation of blood cells in the bone marrow and lymphoid tissue [NL] – **haemopoietic** /-poyˈetik/ *adj,* **haemopoietically** *adv*

haemorrhage /ˈhemərij/ *n* a (copious) loss of blood from the blood vessels [F & L; F *hémorrhagie*, fr L *haemorrhagia*, fr Gk *haimorrhagia*, fr *haimo-* haem- + *-rrhagia*] – **haemorrhage** *vi,* **haemorrhagic** /ˌheməˈrajik/ *adj*

haemorrhoid /ˈheməroyd/ *n* a mass of dilated veins in swollen tissue round or near the anus – usu pl with sing. meaning [MF *hemorrhoides*, pl, fr L *haemorrhoidae*, fr Gk *haimorrhoides*, fr *haimorrhoos* flowing with blood, fr *haimo-* + *rhein* to flow] – **haemorrhoidal** /-'roydl/ *adj*

haemostasis /,heemoh'staysis, ,hemoh-/ *n* arrest of bleeding [NL, fr Gk *haimostasis* styptic, fr *haimo-* haem- + *-stasis*] – **haemostatic** /-'statik/ *adj*

hafnium /'hafnyəm, -ni·əm/ *n* a metallic transition element chemically resembling zirconium ☞ PERIODIC TABLE [NL, fr *Hafnia* Copenhagen, city in Denmark]

[1]**haft** /hahft/ *n* the handle of a weapon or tool [ME, fr OE *hæft*; akin to OE *hebban* to lift – more at HEAVE]

[2]**haft** *vt* to fit with a haft

[1]**hag** /hag/ *n* **1** a witch **2** an ugly and usu ill-natured old woman [ME *hagge*] – **haggish** *adj*

[2]**hag** *n, Scot & NEng* (a firm spot in) a bog [E dial. *hag* (felled timber), of Scand origin; akin to ON *högg* stroke, blow; akin to OE *hēawan* to hew]

'hag,fish /-,fish/ *n* any of several marine vertebrates that are related to the lampreys, resemble eels, and feed on fishes by boring into their bodies

haggadah /hə'gahdə/ *n* **1** *often cap* ancient Jewish lore forming the nonlegal part of the Talmud – compare HALAKAH **2** *cap* the narrative read at the Passover seder [Heb *haggādhāh*]

Haggai /'hagay,ie/ *n* (a book of the Old Testament attributed to) a Hebrew prophet who flourished about 500 BC and advocated the rebuilding of the Temple at Jerusalem [Heb]

[1]**haggard** /'hagəd/ *adj* **1** *of a hawk* not tamed **2** having a worn or emaciated appearance, esp through anxiety or lack of sleep [MF *hagard*] – **haggardly** *adv*, **haggardness** *n*

[2]**haggard** *n* an adult hawk caught wild

haggis /'hagis/ *n* a traditionally Scottish dish that consists of the heart, liver, and lungs of a sheep, calf, etc minced with suet, oatmeal, and seasonings and traditionally boiled in the stomach of the animal [ME *hagese*, perh fr *haggen* to hack, chop]

haggle /'hagl/ *vi* **haggling** /'hagling/ to bargain, wrangle [freq of E dial. *hag* (to hew)] – **haggler** *n*

hagi- /hagi-/, **hagio-** *comb form* **1** holy ⟨hagio*scope*⟩ **2** saints ⟨hagio*graphy*⟩ [LL, fr Gk, fr *hagios*]

hagiography /,hagi'ografi/ *n* **1** biography of saints or venerated people **2** idealizing or idolizing biography – **hagiographer** *n*, **hagiographic** /-ə'grafik/ *adj*, **hagiographical** *adj*, **hagiographically** *adv*

hagioscope /'hagi·ə,skohp/ *n* a narrow opening in an inside wall or pillar of a church giving a view of the main altar to those in a side aisle or transept

hah /hah/ *interj* ha

[1]**ha-ha** /hah 'hah/ *interj* – used to express or represent laughter or derision [ME, fr OE *ha ha*]

[2]**ha-ha** /'hah ,hah/ *n* a fence or retaining wall sunk into a ditch and used as a boundary (e g of a park or grounds) so as to give an uninterrupted view [F *haha*, prob fr *haha*, interj of surprise]

haiku /'hie,kooh/ *n, pl* **haiku** (a poem in) an unrhymed Japanese verse form of 3 lines containing 5, 7, and 5 syllables respectively – compare TANKA [Jap]

[1]**hail** /hayl/ *n* **1** (precipitation in the form of) small particles of clear ice or compacted snow **2** a group of things directed at sby or sthg and intended to cause pain, damage, or distress ⟨*a ~ of bullets*⟩ ⟨*a ~ of obscenities*⟩ [ME, fr OE *hægl*; akin to OHG *hagal* hail, Gk *kachlēx* pebble]

[2]**hail** *vi* **1** to precipitate hail **2** to pour down or strike like hail

[3]**hail** *interj* **1** – used to express acclamation ⟨*~ to the chief* – Sir Walter Scott⟩ **2** *archaic* – used as a salutation [ME, fr ON *heill*, fr *heill* healthy – more at WHOLE]

[4]**hail** *vt* **1a** to salute, greet **b** to greet with enthusiastic approval; acclaim *as* **2** to greet or summon by calling ⟨*~ a taxi*⟩ *~ vi* to call (a greeting to a passing ship) – **hailer** *n* – **hail from** to be or have been a native or resident of

[5]**hail** *n* **1** a call to attract attention **2** hearing distance ⟨*stayed within ~*⟩ **3** *archaic* an exclamation of greeting or acclamation

hail-fellow-well-met *adj* heartily and often excessively informal from the first moment of meeting [fr the archaic greeting 'Hail, fellow! Well met!']

,Hail 'Mary /'meəri/ *n* a Roman Catholic prayer to the Virgin Mary that consists of salutations and a plea for her intercession [trans of ML *Ave, Maria*]

'hail,stone /-,stohn/ *n* a pellet of hail

hair /heə/ *n* **1a** (a structure resembling) a slender threadlike outgrowth on the surface of an animal; *esp* (any of) the many usu pigmented hairs that form the characteristic coat of a mammal **b** the coating of hairs, esp on the human head or other body part **2** haircloth **3** HAIR'S BREADTH ⟨*won by a ~*⟩ [ME, fr OE *hær*; akin to OHG *hār* hair] – **hairless** *adj*, **hairlessness** *n*, **hairlike** *adj*

'hair,breadth /-,bret·th, -,bredth/ *n* HAIR'S BREADTH

'hair,brush /-,brush/ *n* a brush for the hair

'hair,cloth /-,kloth/ *n* any of various stiff wiry fabrics, esp of horsehair or camel hair, used for upholstery or for stiffening in garments

'hair,cut /-,kut/ *n* (the result of) cutting and shaping of the hair – **haircutter** *n*, **haircutting** *n*

'hair,do /-,dooh/ *n, pl* **hairdos** a hairstyle

'hair,dresser /-,dresə/ *n* sby whose occupation is cutting, dressing, and styling the hair – **hairdressing** *n*

haired /heəd/ *adj* having hair (of a specified kind) ⟨*fair*-haired⟩

'hair,grip /-,grip/ *n, Br* a flat hairpin with prongs that close together

'hair,line /-,lien/ *n* **1** a very slender line; *esp* a tiny line or crack on a surface **2** (a fabric with) a design consisting of lengthways or widthways lines usu 1 thread wide **3** the line above the forehead beyond which hair grows – **hairline** *adj*

'hair,piece /-,pees/ *n* a section of false hair worn to enhance a hairstyle or make a person's natural hair seem thicker or more plentiful

[1]**'hair,pin** /-,pin/ *n* **1** a 2-pronged U-shaped pin of thin wire for holding the hair in place **2** a sharp bend in a road

[2]**hairpin** *adj* having the shape of a hairpin ⟨*a ~ bend*⟩

'hair-,raiser *n* a thriller

'hair-,raising *adj* causing terror or astonishment – **hair-raisingly** *adv*

'hair's ,breadth *n* a very small distance or margin

'hair ,shirt *n* a rough shirt worn next to the skin as a penance

'hair-,slide *n, Br* a (decorative) clip for the hair

¹**hair,space** *n* a very thin space between (the letters of) words

¹**hair,splitting** /-,spliting/ *n* argument over unimportant differences and points of detail; quibbling – **hairsplitting** *adj*, **hairsplitter** *n*

¹**hair,spring** /-,spring/ *n* a slender spiral spring that regulates the motion of the balance wheel of a timepiece

¹**hair,style** /-,stiel/ *n* a way of wearing or arranging the hair – **hairstyling** *n*, **hairstylist** *n*

¹**hair-,trigger** *adj* immediately responsive to or disrupted by the slightest stimulus ⟨*a ~ temper*⟩

hair trigger *n* a trigger so adjusted that very slight pressure will fire the gun

hairy /'heəri/ *adj* **1** covered with (material like) hair **2** made of or resembling hair **3** frighteningly dangerous ⟨*a ~ crossing through mountainous waves*⟩ – infml – **hairiness** *n*

hajj, hadj /haj/ *n* the pilgrimage to Mecca prescribed as a religious duty for Muslims [Ar *ḥajj*]

hajji, hadji /'haji/ *n* one who has made a pilgrimage to Mecca – used as a title [Ar *ḥajjī*, fr *ḥajj*]

haka /'hahkah/ *n* a ceremonial Maori war dance [Maori]

hake /hayk/ *n, pl* **hakes,** *esp collectively* **hake** any of several marine food fishes related to the common Atlantic cod [ME]

hakenkreuz /'hahkən,kroyts/ *n, often cap* the swastika used as a symbol of German anti-Semitism or of Nazi Germany [G, fr *haken* hook + *kreuz* cross]

¹**hakim** /'hakeem/ *n* a Muslim physician [Ar *ḥakīm*, lit., wise one]

²**hakim** *n* a Muslim ruler, governor, or judge [Ar *ḥākim*]

hal-, halo- *comb form* salt ⟨halo*phyte*⟩ [F, fr Gk, fr *hals* – more at SALT]

halakah /,hahlə'khah, hə'lahkə/ *n, often cap* the body of Jewish law supplementing the scriptural law and forming the legal part of the Talmud – compare HAGGADAH 1 [Heb *halākhāh*, lit., way] – **halakic** /hə'lakik, -'lah-/ *adj, often cap*

halala *also* **halalah** /hə'lahlə/ *n, pl* **halala, halalas** ☞ *Saudi Arabia* at NATIONALITY [Ar]

halation /hə'laysh(ə)n/ *n* the spreading of light beyond its proper boundaries (e g in a faulty photographic image) [*halo* + *-ation*]

halberd /'halbəd/ *n* a long-handled weapon combining a spear and battle-axe, used esp in the 15th and 16th c [ME *halberd*, fr MF *hallebarde*, fr MHG *helmbarte*, fr *helm* handle + *barte* axe] – **halberdier** /-'diə/ *n*

halbert /'halbət/ *n* a halberd

¹**halcyon** /'halsi·ən/ *n*, a kingfisher – poetic [ME *alceon* bird believed to breed at sea and calm the waves, fr L *halcyon*, fr Gk *alkyōn, halkyōn*]

²**halcyon** *adj* calm, peaceful – esp in *halcyon days*

hale /hayl/ *adj* free from defect, disease, or infirmity; sound ⟨*a ~ and hearty old man*⟩ [partly fr ME (northern) *hale*, fr OE *hāl*; partly fr ME *hail*, fr ON *heill* – more at WHOLE]

haler /'hahlə/ *n, pl* **halers, haleru** /-lə,rooh/ ☞ *Czechoslovakia* at NATIONALITY [Czech]

¹**half** /hahf/ *n, pl* **halves** /hahvz/ **1a** either of 2 equal parts into which sthg is divisible; *also* a part of a thing approximately equal to a half **b** half an hour – used in designation of time **2** either of a pair: e g **a** a partner ⟨*my other ~*⟩ **b** a school term – used esp at some British public schools **3** sthg of (approximately) half the value or quantity: e g **a** half a pint **b** a child's ticket **c** HALFPENNY 1 [ME, fr OE *healf*; akin to L *scalpere* to cut, OE *sciell* shell] – **and a half** of remarkable quality – infml ⟨*that was a party* and a half!⟩ – **by half** by a great deal – **by halves** half heartedly – **in half** into 2 (nearly) equal parts

²**half** *adj* **1a** being one of 2 equal parts ⟨*a ~ share*⟩ ⟨*~ a dozen*⟩ **b(1)** amounting to approximately half ⟨*~ the class*⟩ ⟨*a ~ mile*⟩ ⟨*~ my life*⟩ **(2)** falling short of the full or complete thing ⟨*~ measures*⟩ ⟨*a ~ smile*⟩ **2** extending over or covering only half ⟨*a ~ door*⟩ ⟨*~ sleeves*⟩ **3** *Br* half past ⟨*~ seven*⟩ – **halfness** *n*

³**half** *adv* **1** in an equal part or degree ⟨*she was ~ crying, ~ laughing*⟩ **2** nearly but not completely ⟨*~ cooked*⟩ ⟨half-*remembered stories from her childhood*⟩ – compare NOT HALF – **half as much again** one-and-a-half times as much

,**half-a-'crown** *n* HALF CROWN

,**half a 'dozen** *n* a set of 6; *also* several

,**half-and-'half** *n* sthg that is approximately half one thing and half another; *specif* a mixture of 2 beers (e g mild and bitter) – **half-and-half** *adj or adv*

'**half,back** /-,bak/ *n* a player in rugby, soccer, hockey, etc positioned immediately behind the forward line – **halfback** *adj*

,**half-'baked** *adj* marked by or showing a lack of forethought or judgment; foolish ⟨*a ~ scheme for making money*⟩

'**half,beak** /,beek/ *n* any of a family of marine fishes with a long protruding lower jaw

half blood *n* **1a** the relation between people having only 1 parent in common **b** a person so related to another **2** a half-breed **3** GRADE 4 – **half-blooded** *adj*

half blue *n* (the colours awarded to) one who represents either Oxford or Cambridge in a minor sport against the other university

,**half-'board** *n* provision of bed, breakfast, and evening meal (e g by a hotel)

'**half-,bound** *adj, of a book* bound in 2 materials with the better quality material (e g leather) on the spine and corners – **half binding** *n*

'**half-,bred** *adj* having 1 purebred parent – **half-bred** *n*

'**half-,breed** *n* the offspring of parents of different races – **half-breed** *adj*

half brother *n* a brother related through 1 parent only

'**half-,caste** *n* a half-breed – **half-caste** *adj*

half cock *n* **1** the position of the hammer of a firearm when about half retracted and held by the safety catch so that it cannot be operated by a pull on the trigger **2** a state of inadequate preparation – esp in *go off at half cock*

,**half-'cocked** *adj* lacking adequate preparation or forethought

half-court line *n* a line down the middle of the floor of a squash court, from the short line to the back wall, which separates the backhand and forehand courts ☞ SPORT

,**half 'crown** *n* (a former British silver coin worth) 2 shillings and sixpence

,**half-'hardy** *adj, of a plant* able to withstand a moderately low temperature but injured by severe frost

,**half'hearted** /-'hahtid/ *adj* lacking enthusiasm or

effort ⟨~ *attempts to start a conversation*⟩ – **half-heartedly** *adv*, **halfheartedness** *n*

ˈhalf ˌhitch *n* a type of simple knot made so as to be easily unfastened

ˌhalf-ˈholiday *n* a holiday of half a day, esp an afternoon

ˌhalf ˈhour *n* **1** a period of 30 minutes **2** the middle point of an hour – **half-hourly** *adv or adj*

ˌhalf-ˈinch *vt, chiefly Br* to steal – infml [rhyming slang *half inch* pinch]

ˈhalf-ˌknot *n* a knot joining the ends of 2 cords together, often used as the basis of other knots (e g a reef knot)

ˈhalf-ˌlength *n* a portrait showing only the upper half of the body

ˈhalf-ˌlife *n* the time required for half of **a** the atoms of a radioactive substance to become disintegrated **b** a drug or other substance to be eliminated from an organism by natural processes

ˈhalf-ˌlight *n* dim greyish light (e g at dusk)

ˌhalf-ˈmast *n* the position of a flag lowered halfway down the staff as a mark of mourning

ˌhalf-ˈmoon *n* (sthg shaped like) the figure of the moon when half its disc is illuminated – **half-moon** *adj*

ˌhalf ˈnelson /ˈnels(ə)n/ *n* a wrestling hold in which one arm is thrust under the corresponding arm of an opponent and the hand placed on the back of the opponent's neck – compare FULL NELSON

ˈhalf ˌnote *n, NAm* a minim

halfpenny /ˈhaypni/ *n* **1** (a British bronze coin representing) one half of a penny **2** a small amount – **halfpenny** *adj*

halfpennyworth /ˈhaypəth/ *n* as much as can be bought for 1 halfpenny; *broadly* a small amount

¹ˈhalf-ˌpint *n* a small or inconsequential person – infml

²ˈhalf-ˌpint *adj* of less than average size; diminutive – infml

ˌhalf-ˈround *adj* having a cross section that is a semicircle ⟨*a ~ file*⟩

half sister *n* a sister related through 1 parent only

ˌhalf ˈsovereign *n* a former British gold coin worth 10 shillings

ˈhalf ˌstep *n, NAm* a semitone

ˌhalf ˈterm *n, chiefly Br* (a short holiday taken at) a period about halfway through a school term

ˌhalf-ˈtimbered *adj* constructed of timber framework with spaces filled in by brickwork or plaster – **half-timbering** *n*

ˌhalfˈtime /-ˈtiem/ *n* (an intermission marking) the completion of half of a game or contest

ˈhalf-ˌtitle *n* the title of a book standing alone on a right-hand page immediately preceding the title page

ˈhalfˌtone /-ˌtohn/ *n* **1** any of the shades of grey between the darkest and the lightest parts of a photographic image **2** a photoengraving made from an image photographed through a screen and then etched so that the details of the image are reproduced in dots – **halftone** *adj*

ˈhalf-ˌtrack *n* (a vehicle with) a drive system of an endless chain or track at the back and wheels at the front – **half-track, half-tracked** *adj*

ˈhalf-ˌtruth *n* a statement that is only partially true; *esp* one deliberately intended to deceive

ˌhalf-ˈvolley *n* **1** a shot in tennis made at a ball just after it has bounced **2** an easily-hit delivery of the ball in cricket that bounces closer than intended to the batsman

ˌhalfˈway /-ˈway/ *adj or adv* **1** midway between 2 points **2** (done or formed) partially – **halfway** *adv*

ˌhalfway ˈhouse *n* **1** a place (e g an inn) to stop midway on a journey **2** a halfway point or place; *esp* a compromise **3** a house, hostel, etc for former residents (e g psychiatric patients) of institutions, that is designed to help them readjust to living in the community

ˈhalf-ˌwit *n* a foolish or mentally deficient person – derog – **half-witted** /-ˈwitid/ *adj*, **half-wittedness** *n*

halibut /ˈhalibət/ *n, pl* **halibuts,** *esp collectively* **halibut** a large marine food flatfish [ME *halybutte*, fr *haly, holy* holy + *butte* flatfish, fr MD or MLG *but*; fr its being eaten on holy days]

halide /ˈhalied/ *n* a binary compound of a halogen and another element or radical

halite /ˈhaliet/ *n* ROCK SALT

halitosis /ˌhaliˈtohsis/ *n* (a condition of having) offensively smelling breath [NL, fr L *halitus* breath, fr *halare* to breathe – more at EXHALE] – **halitotic** /-ˈtotik/ *adj*

hall /hawl/ *n* **1a** the house of a medieval king or noble **b** the chief living room in a medieval house or castle **2** the manor house of a landed proprietor **3a** a building used by a college or university for some special purpose ⟨*a ~ of residence*⟩ **b** (a division of) a college at some universities **c** (a meal served in) the common dining room of an English college **4** the entrance room or passage of a building **5** a large room for public assembly or entertainment **6** *NAm* a corridor or passage in a building [ME *halle*, fr OE *heall*; akin to L *cella* small room, *celare* to conceal – more at HELL]

hallelujah /ˌhaliˈloohyə/ *n or interj* (a shout, song, etc) used to express praise, joy, or thanks [Heb *halălūyāh* praise (ye) the Lord]

halliard /ˈhalyəd/ *n* a halyard

¹hallmark /ˈhawlˌmahk/ *n* **1** an official mark stamped on gold and silver articles in Britain after an assay test to testify to their purity **2** a distinguishing characteristic or object ⟨*the dramatic speeches which are the ~ of a barrister*⟩ [Goldsmiths' *Hall*, London, where gold and silver articles were assayed and stamped]

²hallmark *vt* to stamp with a hallmark

¹hallo /haˈloh, hə-/, **halloa** /-ˈloh(ə)/ *vb, interj, or n* **halloing; halloed; halloaing; halloaed;** *pl* **hallos; halloas** (to) hollo

²hallo *n or interj, pl* **hallos** *chiefly Br* (a) hello

ˌHall of ˈFame *n, chiefly NAm* (a structure housing memorials to) a group of famous or illustrious individuals

halloo /həˈlooh/ *vb, interj, or n* **hallooing; hallooed;** *pl* **halloos** (to) hollo

hallow /ˈhaloh/ *vt* **1** to make holy or set apart for holy use **2** to respect and honour greatly; venerate [ME *halowen*, fr OE *hālgian*, fr *hālig* holy – more at HOLY]

Halloween, Hallowe'en /ˌhalohˈeen/ *n* October 31, the eve of All Saints' Day, observed by dressing up in disguise, party turns, etc [short for *All Hallow Even* All Saints' Eve]

hallstand /ˈhawl,stand/ *n* a piece of furniture with pegs for holding coats, hats, and umbrellas

hallucinate /həˈloohsinayt/ *vt* to perceive or experience as a hallucination ~ *vi* to have hallucinations [L *hallucinatus*, pp of *hallucinari* to prate, dream]

hallucination /hə,loohsiˈnaysh(ə)n/ *n* **1** the perception of sthg apparently real to the perceiver but which has no objective reality, *also* the image, object, etc perceived **2** a completely unfounded or mistaken impression or belief – **hallucinational** *adj*, **hallucinative** /ˈloohsinətiv/ *adj*

hallucinatory /həˈloohsinət(ə)ri/ *adj* **1** tending to produce hallucination ⟨~ *drugs*⟩ **2** resembling or being a hallucination

hallucinogen /həˈloohsinəjən/ *n* a substance (e g LSD) that induces hallucinations [*hallucin*ation + *-o-* + *-gen*] – **hallucinogenic** /-nəˈjenik/ *adj*

hallux /ˈhaləks/ *n, pl* **halluces** /ˈhaləseez/ the innermost digit (e g the big toe) of the hind or lower limb [NL, fr L *hallus, hallux*]

hallway /ˈhawl,way/ *n* an entrance hall or corridor

[1]**halo** /ˈhayloh/ *n, pl* **halos, haloes 1** a circle of light appearing to surround the sun or moon and resulting from refraction or reflection of light by ice particles in the earth's atmosphere **2a** NIMBUS 1, 2 **b** a differentiated zone surrounding a central object **3** the aura of glory or veneration surrounding an idealized person or thing [L *halos*, fr Gk *halōs* threshing floor, disc, halo]

[2]**halo** *vt* **haloing; haloed** to form into or surround with a halo

halo- – see HAL-

halogen /ˈhaləjen/ *n* any of the 5 elements fluorine, chlorine, bromine, iodine, and astatine that form part of group VII A of the periodic table [Sw] – **halogenate** /-jə,nayt/ *vt*, **halogenation** /-ˈnaysh(ə)n/ *n*, **halogenous** /həˈlojənəs/ *adj*

halothane /ˈhaləthayn/ *n* a nonexplosive general anaesthetic that is inhaled [*halo-* + *ethane*]

[1]**halt** /hawlt/ *adj, archaic* lame [ME, fr OE *healt*; akin to OHG *halz* lame, L *clades* destruction, Gk *klan* to break]

[2]**halt** *vi* **1** to hesitate between alternative courses; waver **2** to display weakness or imperfection (e g in speech or reasoning); falter

[3]**halt** *n* **1** a (temporary) stop or interruption **2** *Br* a railway stopping place, without normal station facilities, for local trains [G, fr MHG, fr *halt*, imper of *halten* to hold, fr OHG *haltan* – more at [1]HOLD]

[4]**halt** *vi* to come to a halt ~ *vt* **1** to bring to a stop ⟨*the strike has* ~ed *tubes and buses*⟩ **2** to cause to stop; end ⟨~ *the slaughter of seals*⟩

[1]**halter** /ˈhawltə/ *n* **1a** a rope or strap for leading or tying an animal **b** a band round an animal's head to which a lead may be attached **2** a noose for hanging criminals [ME, fr OE *hælftre*; akin to OHG *halftra* halter, OE *hielfe* helve]

[2]**halter** *vt* to put a halter on or catch (as if) with a halter

ˈ**halter,break** /-,brayk/ *vt* **halterbroke** /-,brohk/; **halterbroken** /-,brohkən/ to accustom (e g a colt) to wearing a halter

haltere /ˈhaltiə/ *also* **halter** /ˈhaltə/ *n, pl* **halteres** /halˈtiəreez/ either of a pair of club-shaped sensory organs in a two-winged fly that maintain equilibrium in flight [NL *halter*, fr L, jumping weight, fr Gk *haltēr*, fr *hallesthai* to leap – more at SALLY]

ˈ**halter ,neck** *n* (a garment having) a neckline formed by a strap passing from the front of a garment round the neck and leaving the shoulders and upper back bare

halting /ˈhawlting/ *adj* hesitant, faltering ⟨*the witness spoke in a* ~ *manner*⟩ – **haltingly** *adv*

halvah, halva /ˈhalvah/ *n* a sweet confection of crushed sesame seeds mixed with a syrup (e g honey) [Yiddish *halva*, fr Romanian, fr Turk *helva*, fr Ar *ḥalwā* sweetmeat]

halve /hahv/ *vt* **1a** to divide into 2 equal parts **b** to reduce to a half ⟨halving *the present cost*⟩ **2** to play (e g a hole or match in golf) in the same number of strokes as one's opponent [ME *halven*, fr *half*]

[1]**halves** /hahvz/ *pl of* HALF

[2]**halves** *adv* with equal half shares ⟨*let's go* ~⟩

halyard, halliard /ˈhalyəd/ *n* a rope or tackle for hoisting or lowering [alter. of ME *halier*, fr *halen* to pull – more at HAUL]

[1]**ham** /ham/ *n* **1** a buttock with its associated thigh – usu pl **2** (the meat of) the rear end of a bacon pig, esp the thigh, when removed from the carcass before curing with salt – compare GAMMON ☞ MEAT **3a** an inexpert but showy performer; *also* an actor performing in an exaggerated theatrical style **b** an operator of an amateur radio station [ME *hamme*, fr OE *hamm*; akin to OHG *hamma* ham, Gk *knēmē* shinbone; (3) short for *hamfatter*, fr 'The *Ham-fat* Man,' Negro minstrel song] – **ham** *adj*

[2]**ham** *vb* **-mm-** *vt* to execute with exaggerated speech or gestures; overact ~ *vi* to overplay a part

hamadryad /,haməˈdrie·ad, -əd/ *n* **1** a dryad **2a** KING COBRA **b** a baboon worshipped by the ancient Egyptians [L *hamadryad-, hamadryas*, fr Gk, fr *hama* together with + *dryad-, dryas* dryad – more at SAME]

hamburger /ˈhambuhgə/ *n* a round flat cake of minced beef; *also* a sandwich of a fried hamburger in a bread roll [G *Hamburger* of Hamburg, fr *Hamburg*, city in Germany]

[1]**hame** /haym/ *n* either of 2 curved projections on the collar of a draught horse to which the traces are attached [ME, fr MD]

[2]**hame** *n, Scot* home [ME (Sc & northern), var of *home*]

,**ham-ˈfisted** *adj, chiefly Br* lacking dexterity with the hands; clumsy – infml

,**ham-ˈhanded** *adj* ham-fisted – infml

Hamitic /haˈmitik, hə-/ *adj* belonging or relating to the Berber, Cushitic, and sometimes Egyptian branches of the Afro-Asiatic languages [*Hamite* a member of a group of African peoples, fr *Ham*, son of Noah & supposed ancestor of the Egyptians & other African people]

hamlet /ˈhamlit/ *n* a small village [ME, fr MF *hamelet*, dim. of *ham* village, of Gmc origin; akin to OE *hām* village, home]

hammam /ˈhahmahm/ *n* TURKISH BATH [Ar *ḥammām* bath]

[1]**hammer** /ˈhamə/ *n* **1a** a hand tool that consists of a solid head set crosswise on a handle and is used to strike a blow (e g to drive in a nail) **b** a power tool that substitutes a metal block or a drill for the hammerhead **2a** a lever with a striking head for ringing a bell or striking a gong **b** the part of the mechanism of a modern gun whose action ignites the cartridge **c** the malleus ☞ NERVE **d** a gavel **e(1)** a padded mallet in a piano action for striking a string

(2) a hand mallet for playing various percussion instruments **3** (an athletic field event using) a metal sphere weighing 16lb (about 7.3kg) attached by a wire to a handle and thrown for distance [ME *hamer*, fr OE *hamor*; akin to OHG *hamar* hammer, Gk *akmē* point, edge – more at EDGE] – **under the hammer** for sale at auction

[2]**hammer** *vi* **1** to strike blows, esp repeatedly, (as if) with a hammer; pound **2** to make repeated efforts *at*; *esp* to reiterate an opinion or attitude ⟨*the lectures all* ~ed *away at the same points*⟩ ~ *vt* **1** to beat, drive, or shape (as if) with repeated blows of a hammer **2** to force as if by hitting repeatedly ⟨*wanted to* ~ *him into submission*⟩ **3** to declare formally that (a member of the Stock Exchange) is insolvent and is therefore forbidden to trade **4** to beat decisively – infml ⟨*we* ~ed *them at football*⟩ – **hammerer** *n* – **hammer into** to cause (sby) to learn or remember (sthg) by continual repetition

ˌhammer and ˈsickle *n* an emblem consisting of a crossed hammer and sickle used chiefly as a symbol of Communism

ˌhammer and ˈtongs *adv* with great force, vigour, or violence ⟨*went at each other* ~⟩

ˈhammer ˌbeam *n* either of the short horizontal beams or cantilevers to support either end of an arch or principal rafter in a roof truss

ˈhammerˌhead *n* **1** the striking part of a hammer **2** any of various medium-sized sharks with eyes at the ends of bulging projections on each side of the flattened head

hammering /ˈhaməring/ *n* a decisive defeat – infml

ˈhammerˌlock *n* a wrestling hold in which an opponent's arm is held bent behind his back

hammer out *vt* to produce or bring about through lengthy discussion ⟨hammered out *a new policy*⟩

ˈhammerˌtoe *n* a toe that is bent permanently downwards

hammock /ˈhamək/ *n* a hanging bed, usu made of netting or canvas and suspended by cords at each end [Sp *hamaca*, fr Taino]

hammy /ˈhami/ *adj* (characteristic) of ham actors – chiefly infml – **hammily** *adv*, **hamminess** *n*

[1]**hamper** /ˈhampə/ *vt* **1** to restrict the movement or operation of by bonds or obstacles; hinder **2** to interfere with; encumber [ME *hamperen*]

[2]**hamper** *n* a large basket with a cover for packing, storing, or transporting crockery, food, etc ⟨*picnic* ~⟩ [ME *hampere*, alter. of *hanaper*, lit., case to hold goblets, fr MF *hanapier*, fr *hanap* goblet, of Gmc origin; akin to OE *hnæpp* bowl]

hamster /ˈhamstə/ *n* any of numerous small Old World rodents with very large cheek pouches [G, fr OHG *hamustro*, of Slav origin; akin to OSlav *chomĕstorŭ* hamster]

[1]**hamstring** /ˈhamˌstring/ *n* **1** either of 2 groups of tendons at the back of the human knee **2** a large tendon above and behind the hock of a quadruped ☞ ANATOMY

[2]**hamstring** *vt* **hamstrung** /-strung/ **1** to cripple by cutting the leg tendons **2** to make ineffective or powerless; cripple

Han /han/ *n* the Chinese people; ethnic Chinese [*Han*, Chin dynasty 207 BC–AD 220]

[1]**hand** /hand/ *n* **1a** (the segment of the forelimb of vertebrate animals corresponding to) the end of the forelimb of human beings, monkeys, etc when modified as a grasping organ **b** a part (e g the chela of a crustacean) serving the function of or resembling a hand **c** sthg resembling a hand: e g **(1)** a stylized figure of a hand used as a pointer or marker **(2)** a group of usu large leaves (e g of tobacco) reaped or tied together or of bananas growing together **d** a forehock of pork ☞ MEAT **e** an indicator or pointer on a dial **2a** possession – usu pl with sing. meaning ⟨*the documents fell into the* ~s *of the enemy*⟩ **b** control, supervision – usu pl with sing. meaning ⟨*I'll leave the matter in your capable* ~s⟩ **3a** a side, direction ⟨*men fighting on either* ~⟩ **b** either of 2 sides or aspects of an issue or argument ⟨*on the one* ~ *we can appeal for peace, on the other declare war*⟩ **4** a pledge, esp of betrothal or marriage **5** handwriting **6a** skill, ability ⟨*tried her* ~ *at sailing*⟩ **b** an instrumental part ⟨*had a* ~ *in the crime*⟩ **7** a unit of measure equal to 4in (about 102mm) used esp for the height of a horse ☞ UNIT **8a** assistance or aid, esp when involving physical effort ⟨*lend a* ~⟩ **b** a round of applause **9a** (the cards or pieces held by) a player in a card or board game **b** a single round in a game **c** the force or solidity of one's position (e g in negotiations) **d** a turn to serve in a game (e g squash) in which only the server may score points and which lasts as long as the server can win points **10a** one who performs or executes a particular work ⟨*2 portraits by the same* ~⟩ **b** a worker, employee ⟨*employed over 100* ~s⟩; *esp* one employed at manual labour or general tasks ⟨*a field* ~⟩ **c** a member of a ship's crew ⟨*all* ~s *on deck*⟩ **d** one skilled in a particular action or pursuit ⟨*she's an old* ~ *at this job*⟩ **11a** handiwork **b** style of execution; workmanship ⟨*the* ~ *of a master*⟩ [ME, fr OE; akin to OHG *hant* hand] – **at hand** near in time or place – **at the hands of, at the hand of** by the act or instrumentality of – **by hand** with the hands, usu as opposed to mechanically – **in hand 1** not used up or lost and at one's disposal ⟨*they have a game* in hand⟩ **2** *of a horse* being led rather than being ridden **3** UNDER WAY ⟨*put the work* in hand⟩ – **off one's hands** out of one's care or charge – **on hand 1** ready to use **2** in attendance; present – **on one's hands** in one's possession, care, or management – **out of hand 1** without delay; without reflection or consideration ⟨*refused it* out of hand⟩ **2** out of control ⟨*that child has got quite* out of hand⟩ – **to hand** available and ready for use; *esp* within reach

[2]**hand** *vt* **1** to lead or assist with the hand ⟨*he* ~ed *her out of the car*⟩ **2** to give or pass (as if) with the hand ⟨~ *a letter to her*⟩ – **hand it to** to give credit to

ˌhand and ˈfoot *adv* totally, assiduously ⟨*waited on him* ~⟩

ˌhand and ˈspring *n* a cut of pork consisting of the hand, jowl, knuckle, trotter, and a few ribs ☞ MEAT [*spring* (the belly or lower part of the forequarter of pork)]

handbag /ˈhandˌbag/ *n* a bag designed for carrying small personal articles and money, carried usu by women

ˈhandˌball *n* **1** (the small rubber ball used in) a game resembling fives and played in a walled court or against a single wall **2** an amateur indoor or outdoor game between 2 teams of 7 or 11 players whose object is to direct a soccer ball into the opponent's goal by throwing and catching

'hand,barrow *n* a flat rectangular frame with handles at both ends for carrying loads

'hand,bill *n* a small printed sheet to be distributed (e g for advertising) by hand

'hand,book *n* a short reference book, esp on a particular subject

[1]**'hand,craft** *n* (a) handicraft

[2]**handcraft** *vt* to fashion by handicraft

handcuff /'hand,kuf/ *vt* to apply handcuffs to; manacle

handcuffs *n pl* a pair of metal rings, usu connected by a chain or bar, for locking round prisoners' wrists

hand down *vt* **1** to transmit in succession (e g from father to son); bequeath **2** to give (an outgrown article of clothing) to a younger member of one's family **3** to deliver in court ⟨hand down *a judgment*⟩

-handed /handid/ *comb form* (*adj* → *adj*) having or using a specified (kind of) hand or (number of) hands ⟨*a large*-handed *man*⟩ ⟨*right*-handed⟩ – **hander** *comb form* (*adj* → *n*)

handedness /'handidnis/ *n* **1** a tendency to use one hand rather than the other **2** the quality of existing in one or both of a pair of mirror images

hander /'handə/ *n* a play, film, etc having a specified number of leading roles – usu in combination ⟨*the new musical was a spectacular two*-hander⟩

handful /'handf(ə)l/ *n, pl* **handfuls** *also* **handsful** /'handzf(ə)l/ **1** as much or as many as the hand will grasp **2** a small quantity or number **3** sby or sthg (e g a child or animal) that is difficult to control – infml ⟨*that boy is a real* ~⟩

'hand,grip *n* a handle

'hand,gun *n* a firearm held and fired with 1 hand

'hand,hold *n* sthg to hold on to for support (e g in mountain climbing)

[1]**handicap** /'handi,kap/ *n* **1** (a race or contest with) an artificial advantage or disadvantage given to contestants so that all have a more equal chance of winning **2** a (physical) disability or disadvantage that makes achievement unusually difficult [obs *handicap* (a game in which forfeits were held in a cap), fr *hand in cap*]

[2]**handicap** *vt* **-pp- 1** to assign handicaps to; impose handicaps on **2** to put at a disadvantage

handicapper /'handi,kappə/ *n* **1** sby who assigns handicaps **2** sby who competes, esp in golf, with a specified handicap – usu in combination ⟨*a 5*-handicapper⟩

handicraft /'handi,krahft/ *n* **1** (an occupation requiring) manual skill **2** articles fashioned by handicraft [ME *handi-crafte*, alter. of *handcraft*] – **handicrafter** *n*

'hand-,in *n* the server in a game (e g squash or badminton) in which only the server may score points

,hand in 'glove *adv* in extremely close relationship or agreement, esp in sthg underhand ⟨*were found to be working* ~ *with the racketeers*⟩

,hand in 'hand *adv* **1** clasping one another's hands (e g in intimacy or affection) **2** in close association

handiwork /'handi,wuhk/ *n* **1** (the product of) work done by the hands **2** work done personally [ME *handiwerk*, fr OE *handgeweorc*, fr *hand* + *geweorc*, fr *ge-* (collective prefix) + *weorc* work]

handkerchief /'hangkə,cheef, -chif/ *n, pl* **handkerchiefs** *also* **handkerchieves** /-,cheevz/ a small piece of cloth used for various usu personal purposes (e g blowing the nose or wiping the eyes) or as a clothing accessory

[1]**handle** /'handl/ *n* **1** a part that is designed to be grasped by the hand **2** the feel of a textile **3** a title; *also* an esp aristocratic or double-barrelled name – infml [ME *handel*, fr OE *handle*; akin to OE *hand*] – **handled** *adj*, **handleless** *adj* – **off the handle** into a state of sudden and violent anger

[2]**handle** *vb* **handling** /'handling, 'handl·ing/ *vt* **1a** to try or examine (e g by touching or moving) with the hand ⟨~ *silk to judge its weight*⟩ **b** to manage with the hands ⟨~ *a horse*⟩ **2a** to deal with (e g a subject or idea) in speech or writing, or as a work of art **b** to manage, direct ⟨*a solicitor* ~s *all my affairs*⟩ **3** to deal with, act on, or dispose of ⟨~d *the clients very well*⟩ **4** to engage in the buying, selling, or distributing of (a commodity) ~ *vi* to respond to controlling movements in a specified way ⟨*car that* ~s *well*⟩ – **handleable** *adj*

'handle,bar *n* a bar, esp on a cycle or scooter, for steering – often pl with sing. meaning

,handlebar mou'stache *n* a long heavy moustache that curves upwards at each end

handler /'handlə/ *n* one who is in immediate physical charge of an animal ⟨*a police dog* ~⟩ [[2]HANDLE + [2]-ER]

handling /'handling/ *n* **1** the packaging and shipping of an object or material (e g to a consumer) **2** the manner in which sthg is treated (e g in a stage production) **3** *Br* the offence of dealing with stolen goods [[2]HANDLE + [2]-ING]

,hand'made *adj* made by hand rather than by machine

'hand,maid *n* a handmaiden

'hand,maiden *n* a personal maid or female servant

'hand-me-,down *n* a reach-me-down

hand off *vt* to push off (an opposing player) with the palm of the hand so as to avoid a tackle in rugby – **handoff** /'-,-/ *n*

hand on *vt* HAND DOWN

'hand,out *n* **1** sthg (e g food, clothing, or money) distributed free, esp to people in need **2** a folder or circular of information for free distribution

'hand-,out *n* a player (e g in squash or badminton) who is not hand-in

hand out *vt* **1** to give freely or without charge **2** to administer ⟨hand out *a severe punishment*⟩

hand over *vb* to yield control or possession (of)

,hand'pick *vt* **1** to pick by hand rather than by machine **2** to select personally and carefully

'hand,rail *n* a narrow rail for grasping with the hand as a support, esp near stairs ☞ ARCHITECTURE

'hand,saw *n* a saw, usu operated with 1 hand

,hands 'down *adv* without much effort; easily ⟨*they won* ~⟩

'hand,set *n* RECEIVER 3b

'hand,shake *n* a clasping and shaking of each other's usu right hand by 2 people (e g in greeting or farewell)

handsome /'hansəm/ *adj* **1** considerable, sizable ⟨*a painting that commanded a* ~ *price*⟩ **2** marked by graciousness or generosity; liberal ⟨~ *contributions to charity*⟩ **3a** *of a man* having a pleasing appearance; good-looking **b** *of a woman* attractive in a dignified statuesque way **4** *NAm* marked by skill or cleverness; adroit [ME *handsom* easy to manipulate, fr [1]*hand* + [1]*-some*] – **handsomely** *adv*, **handsomeness** *n*

'hand,spike *n* a bar used as a lever, chiefly by sailors and gunners [by folk etymology fr D *handspaak*, fr *hand* + *spaak* pole]

'hand,spring *n* an acrobatic movement in which the body turns forwards or backwards in a full circle from a standing position and lands first on the hands and then on the feet

'hand,stand *n* an act of supporting and balancing the body on only the hands with the legs in the air

,hand-to-'hand *adj* involving physical contact; very close ⟨~ *fighting*⟩ – **hand to hand** *adv*

,hand-to-'mouth *adj* having or providing only just enough to live on; precarious ⟨*a* ~ *existence*⟩

'hand,work *n* work done with the hands and not by machine – **handworker** *n*

,hand'woven *adj* produced on a hand-operated loom

'hand,writing *n* writing done by hand; *esp* the style of writing peculiar to a particular person

,hand'wrought *adj* fashioned by hand or without complex machinery

handy /'handi/ *adj* **1a** convenient for use; useful **b** *of a vessel or vehicle* easily handled **2** clever in using the hands, esp in a variety of practical ways **3** conveniently near – infml [[1]*hand* + *-y*] – **handily** *adv*, **handiness** *n*

'handyman /-mən, -,man/ *n* **1** sby who does odd jobs **2** sby competent in a variety of skills or repair work

[1]**hang** /hang/ *vb* **hung** /hung/, (*1b*) **hanged** *vt* **1a** to fasten to some elevated point by the top so that the lower part is free; suspend **b** to suspend by the neck until dead – often used as a mild oath ⟨*I'll be* ~ed⟩ **c** to fasten on a point of suspension so as to allow free motion within given limits ⟨~ *a door*⟩ ⟨~ *a pendulum*⟩ **d** to suspend (meat, esp game) before cooking to make the flesh tender and develop the flavour **2** to decorate, furnish, or cover by hanging sthg up (e g flags or bunting) ⟨*a room* hung *with tapestries*⟩ **3** to hold or bear in a suspended or inclined position ⟨hung *his head in shame*⟩ **4** to fasten (sthg, esp wallpaper) to a wall (e g with paste) **5** to display (pictures) in a gallery ~ *vi* **1a** to remain fastened at the top so that the lower part is free; dangle **b** to die by hanging **2** to remain poised or stationary in the air **3** to stay on; persist ⟨*the smell of the explosion* hung *in the afternoon air*⟩ **4** to be imminent; impend ⟨*doom* hung *over the nation*⟩ **5** to fall or droop from a usu tense or taut position ⟨*his mouth* hung *open*⟩ **6** to depend ⟨*election* ~s *on one vote*⟩ **7** to lean, incline, or jut over or downwards **8** to fall in flowing lines ⟨*the coat* ~s *well*⟩ [partly fr ME *hon*, fr OE *hōn*, vt; partly fr ME *hangen*, fr OE *hangian*, vi & vt; both akin to OHG *hāhan*, vt, to hang, *hangēn*, vi] – **hangable** *adj* – **hang fire 1** to be slow in the explosion of a charge after its primer has been discharged **2** to be delayed or held up – **hang in the balance** to be uncertain or at stake – **hang on 1** to pay close attention to ⟨hangs on *her every word*⟩ **2** to depend on ⟨*the success of the whole enterprise* hangs on *your cooperation*⟩ **3** to be burdensome or oppressive ⟨*time* hangs on *his hands*⟩

[2]**hang** *n* **1** the manner in which a thing hangs **2** a downward slope; *also* a droop **3** the special method of doing, using, or dealing with sthg; the knack – chiefly in *get the hang of* **4** *Austr & NZ* an impressive amount ⟨*they got down in a* ~ *of a hurry* – Frank Sargeson⟩

hang about *vi*, *Br* **1** to wait or stay, usu without purpose or activity **2** to delay or move slowly *USE* infml

hangar /'hangə/ *n* a shed; *esp* a large shed for housing aircraft [F]

hang around *vi* HANG ABOUT 1

hang back *vi* to be reluctant to move or act; hesitate

hangdog /'hang,dog/ *adj* ashamed; *also* abject

[1]**hanger** /'hangə/ *n* a wood growing on a steeply sloping hillside [OE *hangra*, fr *hangian* to hang]

[2]**hanger** *n* a device (e g a loop or strap) by which or to which sthg is hung or hangs; *esp* a hook and crosspiece to fit inside the shoulders of a dress, coat, etc to keep the shape of the garment when hung up [[1]HANG + [2]-ER]

,hanger-'on *n*, *pl* **hangers-on** one who attempts to associate with a person, group, etc, esp for personal gain; a dependant [*hang on* + *-er*]

'hang-,glider *n* (sby who flies) a glider that resembles a kite and is controlled by the body movements of the harnessed person suspended beneath it – **hang-glide** *vi*

hang in *vi*, *chiefly NAm* to refuse to be discouraged or intimidated; persist – infml

[1]**hanging** /'hang·ing/ *n* **1** (an) execution by suspension from a noose **2a** a curtain **b** a covering (e g a tapestry) for a wall

[2]**hanging** *adj* **1** situated or lying on steeply sloping ground ⟨~ *gardens*⟩ **2** jutting out; overhanging ⟨*a* ~ *rock*⟩ **3** adapted for sustaining a hanging object ⟨*a* ~ *rail*⟩ **4** deserving or liable to inflict hanging ⟨*a* ~ *matter*⟩ ⟨*a* ~ *judge*⟩ [(1, 2) fr prp of [1]*hang*; (3, 4) fr gerund of [1]*hang*]

hanging valley *n* a valley ending in a steeply descending cliff face ☞ GEOGRAPHY

'hangman /-mən/ *n* one who hangs a condemned person; a public executioner

hangnail /'hang,nayl/ *n* a bit of skin hanging loose at the side or root of a fingernail [by folk etymology fr *agnail*]

hang on *vi* **1** to keep hold; hold onto sthg **2** to persist tenaciously ⟨*a cold that* hung on *all spring*⟩ **3** to wait for a short time ⟨hang on *a second*⟩ **4** to remain on the telephone ⟨*could you* hang on *please and I'll connect you*⟩ – **hang on to** to hold or keep tenaciously ⟨*learned to* hang on to *his money*⟩

'hang,out *n* a place where one is often to be seen – slang

hang out *vi* **1** to protrude, esp downwards **2** to live or spend much time – slang ⟨*the kids* hang out *on street corners*⟩

hangover /'hang·ohvə/ *n* **1** sthg (e g a custom) that remains from the past **2** the disagreeable physical effects following heavy consumption of alcohol or use of other drugs

'hang-,up *n* a source of mental or emotional difficulty – infml

hang up *vt* **1** to place on a hook or hanger ⟨*told the child to* hang up *his coat*⟩ **2** to delay, suspend ⟨*the negotiations were* hung up *for a week*⟩ ~ *vi* to terminate a telephone conversation, often abruptly

hank /hangk/ *n* **1** a coil, loop; *specif* a coiled or looped bundle (e g of yarn, rope, or wire) usu containing a definite length **2** a ring attaching a jib or staysail to a stay [ME, of Scand origin; akin to ON *hönk* hank; akin to OE *hangian* to hang]

hanker /ˈhangkə/ *vi* to desire strongly or persistently – usu + *after* or *for* [prob fr Flem *hankeren*, freq of *hangen* to hang; akin to OE *hangian*] – **hankering** *n*

hankie, hanky /ˈhangki/ *n* a handkerchief – infml [*handk*erchief + *-ie, -y*]

ˌhanky-ˈpanky /ˈpangki/ *n* mildly improper or deceitful behaviour – infml [prob alter. of *hocus-pocus*]

Hanoverian /ˌhanəˈviəri·ən/ *adj* of or supporting the British royal house that reigned from 1714 to 1901 [*Hanover*, former province of Germany] – **Hanoverian** *n*

Hansa /ˈhansə, ˈhahnzah/, **Hanse** /hans/ *n* **1** a medieval merchant guild **2** a medieval league of (merchants of) various free German cities trading abroad **3** the entrance fee to a Hansa *USE* (1 & 2) sing. or pl in constr [*Hansa* fr ML, fr MLG *hanse*; *Hanse* fr ME, fr MF, fr MLG] – **Hanseatic** /ˌhansiˈatik/ *n or adj*

Hansard /ˈhansahd/ *n* the official report of Parliamentary proceedings [Luke *Hansard* †1828 E printer]

hansom /ˈhansəm/, **hansom cab** *n* a light 2-wheeled covered carriage with the driver's seat high up at the back [Joseph *Hansom* †1882 E architect]

Hanukkah, Chanukah /ˈhahnook(h)ah/ *n* an 8-day Jewish holiday falling in December and commemorating the rededication of the Temple of Jerusalem after its defilement by Antiochus of Syria [Heb *ḥănukkāh* dedication]

hanuman /ˌhunooˈmahn/ *n* **1** *cap* the Hindu monkey-god, noted for his devotion to Rama **2** a long-tailed Asian monkey considered sacred by Hindus [Hindi *Hanumān*, fr Skt *hanumant*, lit., possessing (large) jaws, fr *hanu* jaw]

hào *n* ☞ *Vietnam* at NATIONALITY [Vietnamese]

hapax legomenon /ˌhapaks liˈgomənon, -nən/ *n, pl* **hapax legomena** /-nə/ a word or form which occurs only once [Gk, something said only once]

ha'penny /ˈhaypni/ *n* a halfpenny

haphazard /hapˈhazəd/ *adj* marked by lack of plan or order; aimless [*haphazard*, n (chance, accident), fr *hap* (event, chance) + *hazard*] – **haphazard** *adv*, **haphazardly** *adv*, **haphazardness** *n*

hapl-, haplo- *comb form* **1** single; simple **2** of the haploid generation or condition ⟨haplo*sis*⟩ [NL, fr Gk, fr *haploos*, fr *ha-* one + *-ploos* multiplied by; akin to Gk *homos* same – more at SAME, DOUBLE; (2) *haploid*]

hapless /ˈhaplis/ *adj* having no luck; unfortunate [*hap* (event, chance) + *-less*] – **haplessly** *adv*, **haplessness** *n*

haplography /hapˈlogrəfi/ *n* a written haplology

haploid /ˈhaployd/ *adj* having half the number of chromosomes characteristic of somatic cells ⟨*gametes are usually* ~⟩ – compare DIPLOID, POLYPLOID [ISV, fr Gk *haploeidēs* single, fr *haploos*] – **haploid** *n*, **haploidy** *n*

haplology /hapˈloləji/ *n* contraction of a word by the omission of 1 or more similar sounds or syllables in pronunciation (e g /ˈliebri/ for 'library") [ISV *hapl-* + *-logy*]

hap'orth, ha'porth, ha'p'orth /ˈhaypəth/ *n* a halfpennyworth ⟨*doesn't make a* ~ *of difference*⟩ [by contr]

happen /ˈhapn/ *vi* **happening** /ˈhapn·ing, ˈhapning/ **1** to occur by chance – often + *it* ⟨*it so* ~s *I'm going your way*⟩ **2** to come into being as an event; occur **3** to have the luck or fortune *to*; chance ⟨*he* ~ed *to overhear the plotters*⟩ [ME *happenen*, fr *hap* event, chance, fortune, fr ON *happ* good luck; akin to OE *gehæp* suitable] – **happen on/upon** to see or meet (sthg or sby) by chance ⟨happened upon *an old acquaintance last week*⟩

happening /ˈhapn·ing, ˈhapning/ *n* **1** sthg that happens; an occurrence **2a** the creation or presentation of a nonobjective work of art (e g an action painting) **b** a usu unscripted or improvised often multimedia public performance in which the audience participates

happenstance /ˈhapnˌstahns, -stəns/ *n, NAm* a circumstance regarded as due to chance [*happen* + circum*stance*]

happily /ˈhapəli/ *adv* **1** by good fortune; luckily ⟨~, *he never knew*⟩ **2** in a happy manner or state ⟨*lived* ~ *ever after*⟩ **3** in an adequate or fitting manner; successfully ⟨*white wine goes* ~ *with fish*⟩

happy /ˈhapi/ *adj* **1** favoured by luck or fortune; fortunate **2** well adapted or fitting; felicitous ⟨*a* ~ *choice*⟩ **3a** enjoying or expressing pleasure and contentment **b** glad, pleased ⟨*I was very* ~ *to hear from you*⟩ **4** characterized by a dazed irresponsible state – usu in combination ⟨*a punch*-happy *boxer*⟩ **5** impulsively quick or overinclined to use sthg – usu in combination ⟨*trigger*-happy⟩ **6** having or marked by an atmosphere of good fellowship; friendly **7** satisfied as to the fact; confident, sure ⟨*we're now quite* ~ *that the murder occurred at about 5.30*⟩ **8** tipsy – euph [ME, fr *hap*] – **happiness** *n*

ˈhappy-go-ˈlucky *adj* blithely unconcerned; carefree

happy hour *n* a limited period of the day during which drinks are sold in a bar, pub, etc at reduced prices

ˌhappy ˈhunting ˌground *n* a choice or profitable area of activity – infml

Hapsburg /ˈhapsbuhg/ *n or adj* (a member, esp a monarch) of a princely German house that reigned in Austria from 1278 to 1918 and in Spain from 1516 to 1700 [*Habsburg*, castle in Aargau, Switzerland]

hapten /ˈhapt(ə)n/ *n* a small (separable) part of an antigen that reacts specifically with an antibody [G *hapten*]

haptic /ˈhaptik/, **haptical** /-kl/ *adj* relating to or based on the sense of touch [ISV, fr Gk *haptesthai* to touch]

hara-kiri /ˌharə ˈkiri/ *n* suicide by ritual disembowelment practised by the Japanese samurai, esp when disgraced or found guilty of a crime carrying the death penalty for commoners [Jap *harakiri*]

¹harangue /həˈrang/ *n* **1** a speech addressed to a public assembly **2** a lengthy, ranting, and usu censorious speech or piece of writing [ME *arang*, fr MF *arenge*, fr OIt *aringa*]

²harangue *vb* to make or address in a harangue

harass /ˈharəs/ *vt* **1** to worry and impede by repeated raids ⟨~ed *the enemy*⟩ **2** to annoy or worry persistently [F *harasser*, fr MF, fr *harer* to set a dog on, fr OF *hare*, interj used to incite dogs, of Gmc origin; akin to OHG *hier* here – more at HERE] – **harasser** *n*, **harassment** *n*

harbinger /ˈhahbinjə/ *n* **1** one who pioneers or initiates a major change; a precursor **2** sthg that presages or foreshadows what is to come [ME *herbergere*, fr OF, host, fr *herberge* hostelry, of Gmc origin; akin to OHG *heriberga*] – **harbinger** *vt*

[1]**harbour,** *NAm chiefly* **harbor** /ˈhahbə/ *n* **1** a place of security and comfort; a refuge **2** a part of a body of water providing protection and anchorage for ships ⟨*the ship came into* ~⟩ [ME *herberge*; akin to OHG *heriberga* army encampment, hostelry; both fr a prehistoric WGmc–NGmc compound whose constituents are akin respectively to OHG *heri* army & to OHG *bergan* to shelter– more at HARRY, BURY]

[2]**harbour,** *NAm chiefly* **harbor** *vt* **1** to give shelter or refuge to **2** to be the home or habitat of; contain ⟨*these cracks can* ~ *dangerous bacteria*⟩ **3** to have or keep (e g thoughts or feelings) in the mind ⟨~ed *a grudge*⟩ ~ *vi* to take shelter (as if) in a harbour

harbourage /ˈhahbərij/ *n* shelter, harbour

ˈ**harbour,master** *n* the officer who regulates the use of a harbour

[1]**hard** /hahd/ *adj* **1** not easily penetrated or yielding to pressure; firm **2a** *of alcoholic drink* having a high percentage of alcohol **b** *of water* containing salts of calcium, magnesium, etc that inhibit lathering with soap **3a** of or being radiation of relatively high penetrating power ⟨~ *X rays*⟩ **b** having or producing relatively great photographic contrast ⟨*a* ~ *negative*⟩ **4a** metal as distinct from paper ⟨~ *money*⟩ **b** *of currency* stable in value; *also* soundly backed and readily convertible into foreign currencies without large discounts **c** being high and firm ⟨~ *prices*⟩ **d** available to borrowers in limited supply and at high interest rates **5** firmly and closely twisted ⟨~ *yarns*⟩ **6a** physically fit or resistant to stress ⟨*the* ~ *men ran 100mi a week*⟩ **b** free of weakness or defects **7a(1)** firm, definite ⟨*reached a* ~ *agreement*⟩ **(2)** not speculative or conjectural; factual ⟨~ *evidence*⟩ **b** close, searching ⟨*gave a* ~ *look*⟩ **8a(1)** difficult to endure ⟨~ *times*⟩ **(2)** oppressive, inequitable ⟨*indirect taxes are* ~ *on the poor*⟩ **b** lacking consideration or compassion; ⟨*a* ~ *heart*⟩ **c(1)** harsh, severe ⟨*said some* ~ *things*⟩ **(2)** resentful ⟨~ *feelings*⟩ **d** inclement ⟨~ *winter*⟩ **e(1)** forceful, violent ⟨~ *blows*⟩ **(2)** demanding energy or stamina ⟨~ *work*⟩ **(3)** using or performing with great energy or effort ⟨*a* ~ *worker*⟩ **9a** sharply defined; stark ⟨*a* ~ *outline*⟩ **b** *of c and g* pronounced /k/ and /g/ respectively – not used technically **10a** difficult to do, understand, or explain ⟨~ *problems*⟩ **b** having difficulty in doing sthg ⟨~ *of hearing*⟩ **c** difficult to magnetize or demagnetize **11a** *of a drug* addictive and gravely detrimental to health ⟨*such* ~ *drugs as heroin*⟩ **b** *of pornography* HARD-CORE 2 **12** PERSISTENT 2b [ME, fr OE *heard*; akin to OHG *hart* hard, Gk *kratos* strength] – **hardness** *n*

[2]**hard** *adv* **1a** with great or maximum effort or energy; strenuously ⟨*were* ~ *at work*⟩ **b** in a violent manner; fiercely **c** to the full extent – used in nautical directions ⟨*steer* ~ *aport*⟩ **d** in a searching or concentrated manner ⟨*stared* ~ *at him*⟩ **2a** in such a manner as to cause hardship, difficulty, or pain; severely **b** with bitterness or grief ⟨*took his defeat* ~⟩ **3** in a firm manner; tightly **4** to the point of hardness ⟨*the water froze* ~⟩ **5** close in time or space ⟨*the house stood* ~ *by the river*⟩ – **hard done by** unfairly treated

[3]**hard** *n, chiefly Br* a firm usu artificial foreshore or landing place [[1]*hard*]

ˌ**hard-and-ˈfast** *adj* fixed, strict ⟨*a* ~ *rule*⟩

ˈ**hard,back** *n* a book bound in stiff covers – compare PAPERBACK – **hardback** *adj*

ˌ**hard-ˈbitten** *adj* steeled by difficult experience; tough

ˈ**hard,board** *n* (a) composition board made by compressing shredded wood chips

ˌ**hard-ˈboil** *vt* to cook (an egg) in the shell until both white and yolk have solidified [back-formation fr *hard-boiled*]

ˌ**hard-ˈboiled** *adj* devoid of sentimentality; tough

ˌ**hard ˈcase** *n* a tough or hardened person

ˌ**hard ˈcash** *n* money in the form of coin or bank notes as opposed to cheques or credit

ˌ**hard ˈcheese** *n, chiefly Br* HARD LUCK – often used as an interjection expressing mild sympathy; infml

hard coal *n* anthracite

hard copy *n* copy (e g produced in connection with a computer or from microfilm) that is readable without the use of a special device

ˈ**hard,core** *n, Br* compacted rubble or clinker used esp as a foundation for roads, paving, or floors

ˌ**hard-ˈcore** *adj* **1** of or constituting a hard core ⟨~ *Conservative supporters*⟩ **2** *of pornography* extremely explicit; *specif* showing real rather than simulated sexual acts

ˌ**hard ˈcore** *n sing or pl in constr* the unyielding or uncompromising members that form the nucleus of a group

harden /ˈhahdn/ *vt* **1** to make hard or harder **2** to confirm in disposition, feelings, or action; *esp* to make callous ⟨~ed *his heart*⟩ **3a** to toughen, inure ⟨~ *troops*⟩ **b** to inure (e g plants) to cold or other unfavourable environmental conditions – often + *off* **4** to protect from blast or heat ⟨~ *a missile emplacement*⟩ ~ *vi* **1** to become hard or harder **2a** to become confirmed or strengthened ⟨*opposition began to* ~⟩ **b** to assume an appearance of harshness ⟨*her face* ~ed *at the word*⟩ **3** to become higher or less subject to fluctuations downwards ⟨*prices* ~ed *quickly*⟩ – **hardener** *n*

hardening /ˈhahdn·ing, ˈhahdning/ *n* **1** sthg that hardens **2** sclerosis ⟨~ *of the arteries*⟩

ˈ**hard ,hat** *n* **1** a protective hat made of rigid material (e g metal or fibreglass) and worn esp by construction workers **2** *chiefly NAm* a construction worker

ˈ**hard,head** *n* a hardheaded person

ˌ**hardˈheaded** *adj* **1** stubborn **2** sober, realistic ⟨~ *common sense*⟩ – **hardheadedly** *adv*, **hardheadedness** *n*

ˈ**hard,heads** *n, pl* **hardheads** any of several knapweeds

ˌ**hardˈhearted** *adj* lacking in sympathetic understanding; unfeeling – **hardheartedly** *adv*, **hardheartedness** *n*

ˌ**hard-ˈhitting** *adj* vigorous, effective ⟨*a* ~ *series of articles*⟩

ˌ**hard ˈlabour** *n* compulsory labour as part of prison discipline

ˌ**hard-ˈline** *adj* advocating or involving a persistently firm course of action; unyielding ⟨*a* ~ *policy on unemployment*⟩ – **hard-liner** *n*

ˌ**hard ˈlines** *n pl, chiefly Br* HARD LUCK – often used as an interjection expressing mild sympathy; infml

ˌhard ˈluck *n, chiefly Br* bad luck – often used as an interjection expressing mild sympathy

hardly /ˈhahdli/ *adv* **1** in a severe manner; harshly **2** with difficulty; painfully **3** only just; barely ⟨*I ~ knew her*⟩ **4** scarcely ⟨*that news is ~ surprising*⟩

ˌhard-ˈnosed *adj* **1** hard-bitten, stubborn **2** HARD-HEADED 2 ⟨*~ budgeting*⟩

ˌhard-of-ˈhearing *adj* partially deaf

ˈhard-ˌon *n, pl* **hard-ons** ERECTION 1 – vulg

ˈhard ˌpad *n* a frequently fatal virus disease of dogs related to distemper

hard palate *n* the bony front part of the palate forming the roof of the mouth

ˈhardˌpan *n* a hard compact soil layer

hard-paste porcelain, ˈhard ˌpaste *n* PORCELAIN 1a

ˌhard ˈput *adj* barely able; faced with difficulty ⟨*was ~ to find an explanation*⟩

hard rock *n* basic rock music played in its original style

hard rubber *n* ebonite

hard sauce *n* a creamed mixture of butter and sugar usu flavoured with brandy or rum and served esp with hot rich puddings

hard sell *n* aggressive high-pressure salesmanship – compare SOFT SELL

ˌhard-ˈset *adj* rigid, fixed

hardship /ˈhahdship/ *n* (an instance of) suffering, privation

ˌhard ˈshoulder *n* either of 2 surfaced strips of land along a road, esp a motorway, on which stopping is allowed only in an emergency

ˈhardˌstanding *n* a hard-surfaced area on which vehicles (e g cars or aeroplanes) may park

ˈhardˌtack *n* SHIP'S BISCUIT

ˈhardˌtop *n* a motor car with a rigid top

ˌhard ˈup *adj* short of sthg, esp money ⟨*I'm very ~ for summer clothes*⟩ – infml

ˈhardˌware *n* **1** items sold by an ironmonger **2** the physical components (e g electronic and electrical devices) of a vehicle (e g a spacecraft) or an apparatus (e g a computer) **3** tape recorders, closed-circuit television, etc used as instructional equipment

ˌhardˈwearing *adj* durable

ˈhard ˌwheat *n* a wheat (e g durum) with hard kernels that are high in gluten and yield a strong flour suitable for making bread and pasta

ˈhardˌwood *n* (the wood of) a broad-leaved as distinguished from a coniferous tree – **hardwood** *adj*

hardy /ˈhahdi/ *adj* **1** bold, audacious **2a** inured to fatigue or hardships; robust **b** capable of withstanding adverse conditions; *esp* capable of living outdoors over winter without artificial protection ⟨*~ plants*⟩ [ME *hardi,* fr OF, fr (assumed) OF *hardir* to make hard, of Gmc origin; akin to OE *heard* hard] – **hardiness** *n*

¹hare /heə/ *n, pl* **hares,** *esp collectively* **hare** **1** any of various swift timid long-eared mammals like large rabbits with long hind legs **2** a figure of a hare moved mechanically along a dog track for the dogs to chase [ME, fr OE *hara*; akin to OHG *haso* hare, L *canus* hoary, grey]

²hare *vi* to run fast – infml

ˌhare and ˈhounds *n* PAPER CHASE

ˈhareˌbell *n* a slender plant with blue bell-shaped flowers that grows esp on heaths and in open woodlands

ˈhareˌbrained *adj* flighty, foolish – infml

ˌhareˈlip *n* a split in the upper lip like that of a hare occurring as a congenital deformity – **harelipped** *adj*

harem /ˈheərəm, hahˈreem/ *n* **1a** a usu secluded (part of a) house allotted to women in a Muslim household **b** *sing or pl in constr* the women occupying a harem **2** a group of females associated with 1 male – used with reference to polygamous animals [Ar *ḥarīm*, lit., something forbidden & *ḥaram*, lit., sanctuary]

haricot /ˈharikoh/, **ˌharicot ˈbean** *n* FRENCH BEAN [F]

harijan /ˌhahriˈjahn, ˈharijən/ *n, often cap* an Indian untouchable [Skt *harijana* one belonging to the god Vishnu, fr *Hari* Vishnu + *jana* person]

hari-kari /ˌhari ˈkahri/ *n* hara-kiri

hark /hahk/ *vi* to listen closely [ME *herken*; akin to OHG *hōrechen* to listen]

hark back *vi* to return *to* an earlier topic or circumstance

harken /ˈhahkən/ to hearken

harlequin /ˈhahlikwin/ *n* **1a** *cap* a stock character in comedy and pantomime **b** a buffoon **2** a variegated pattern (e g of a textile) [It *arlecchino*, fr MF *Helquin*, a demon]

harlequinade /ˌhahlikwiˈnayd/ *n* a part of a play or pantomime in which Harlequin has a leading role

harlequin duck *n* a small N American and Icelandic diving sea duck the male of which is bluish with black, white, and chestnut markings

harlot /ˈhahlət/ *n, archaic* a woman prostitute [ME, fr OF *herlot* rogue] – **harlotry** *n*

¹harm /hahm/ *n* **1** physical or mental damage; injury **2** mischief, wrong [ME, fr OE *hearm*; akin to OHG *harm* injury, OSlav *sramŭ* shame] – **harmful** *adj,* **harmfully** *adv,* **harmfulness** *n* – **out of harm's way** safe from danger

²harm *vt* to cause harm to

harmattan /hahˈmat(ə)n/ *n* a dry dust-laden wind that blows off the desert onto the Atlantic coast of Africa from December to February [Twi *haramata*]

harmless /ˈhahmlis/ *adj* **1** free from harm, liability, or loss **2** lacking capacity or intent to injure – **harmlessly** *adv,* **harmlessness** *n*

¹harmonic /hahˈmonik/ *adj* **1** of musical harmony, a harmonic, or harmonics **2** pleasing to the ear; harmonious **3** expressible in terms of sine or cosine functions ⟨*~ function*⟩ – **harmonically** *adv,* **harmonicalness** *n*

²harmonic *n* **1a** a tone in a harmonic series **b** a flutelike tone produced on a stringed instrument by touching a vibrating string at a point (e g the midpoint) which divides it into halves, thirds, etc **2** a component frequency of a harmonic motion that is an integral multiple of the fundamental frequency

harmonica /hahˈmonikə/ *n* a small rectangular wind instrument with free reeds recessed in air slots from which notes are sounded by breathing out and in [It *armonica*, fem of *armonico* harmonious]

harˈmonics *n pl but sing or pl in constr* the study of the physical characteristics of musical sounds

harmonic series *n* a set of tones consisting of a fundamental and all the overtones whose frequency ratio to it can be expressed in whole numbers

harmonious /hahˈmonyəs, -ni·əs/ *adj* **1** musically concordant **2** having the parts arranged so as to produce a pleasing effect ⟨*the patterns blended into a ~ whole*⟩ 3 marked by agreement – **harmoniously** *adv*, **harmoniousness** *n*

harmonist /'hahmənist/ *n* one who is skilled in musical harmony – **harmonistic** /,hahmə'nistik/ *adj*, **harmonistically** *adv*

harmonium /hah'mohni·əm, -nyəm/ *n* a reed organ in which pedals operate a bellows that forces air through free reeds [F, fr MF *harmonie, armonie*]

harmon·ize, -ise /'hahməniez/ *vi* **1** to be in harmony **2** to play or sing in harmony ~ *vt* **1** to bring into consonance or accord **2** to provide or accompany with harmony – **harmonizer** *n*, **harmonization** /,hah mənie'zaysh(ə)n/ *n*

harmony /'hahməni/ *n* **1a** the (pleasant-sounding) combination of simultaneous musical notes in a chord **b** (the science of) the structure of music with respect to the composition and progression of chords **2a** pleasing or congruent arrangement of parts ⟨*a painting exhibiting ~ of colour and line*⟩ **b** agreement, accord ⟨*lives in ~ with her neighbours*⟩ **3** an arrangement of parallel literary passages (e g of the Gospels) [ME *armony*, fr MF *armonie*, fr L *harmonia*, fr Gk, joint, harmony, fr *harmos* joint – more at [1]ARM]

[1]**harness** /'hahnis/ *n* **1a** the gear of a draught animal other than a yoke **b** (military) equipment (for a knight) **2** sthg that resembles a harness (e g in holding or fastening sthg) ⟨*a safety ~*⟩ **3** a part of a loom which holds and controls the heddles [ME *herneis* baggage, gear, fr OF] – **in harness 1** in one's usual work, surroundings, or routine ⟨*back* in harness *after a long illness*⟩ **2** in close association ⟨*working* in harness *with his colleagues*⟩

[2]**harness** *vt* **1a** to put a harness on (e g a horse) **b** to attach (e g a wagon) by means of a harness **2** to tie together; yoke **3** to utilize; *esp* to convert (a natural force) into energy

'**harness ,racing** *n* the sport of trotting

[1]**harp** /hahp/ *n* a musical instrument that has strings stretched across an open triangular frame, plucked with the fingers [ME, fr OE *hearpe*; akin to OHG *harpha* harp, Gk *karphos* dry stalk] – **harpist** *n*

[2]**harp** *vi* – **harp on** to dwell on or return to (a subject) tediously or monotonously

harper /'hahpə/ *n* a harp player

harpoon /hah'poohn/ *n* a barbed spear used esp in hunting large fish or whales [prob fr D *harpoen*, fr OF *harpon* brooch, fr *harper* to grapple] – **harpoon** *vt*, **harpooner** *n*

'**harp ,seal** *n* an arctic seal with a black saddle-shaped mark on the back

harpsichord /'hahpsi,kawd/ *n* a chromatic keyboard instrument having a horizontal frame and strings and producing notes by the action of quills or leather points plucking the strings [modif of It *arpicordo*, fr *arpa* harp + *corda* string] – **harpsichordist** *n*

harpy /'hahpi/ *n* **1** *cap* a rapacious creature of Greek mythology with the head of a woman and the body of a bird **2** a predatory person; *esp* a rapacious woman – derog [L *Harpyia*, fr Gk]

harquebus /'hahkwibəs/ *n* an arquebus

harridan /'harid(ə)n/ *n* an ill-tempered unpleasant woman [perh modif of F *haridelle* old horse, gaunt woman]

harried /'harid/ *adj* beset by worrying problems; harassed

[1]**harrier** /'hari·ə/ *n* **1** a hunting dog resembling a small foxhound and used esp for hunting hares **2** a runner in a cross-country team [irreg fr [1]*hare*]

[2]**harrier** *n* any of various slender hawks with long angled wings [alter. of earlier *harrower*, fr arch *harrow* (to rob, plunder), var of *harry*]

,**Harris 'tweed** /'haris/ *trademark* – used for a loosely woven tweed made in the Outer Hebrides

Harrovian /hə'rohvi·ən, -vyən/ *n or adj* (a pupil) of Harrow School [NL *Harrovia* Harrow, district of London]

[1]**harrow** /'haroh/ *n* a cultivating implement set with spikes, spring teeth, or discs and drawn over the ground esp to pulverize and smooth the soil [ME *harwe*]

[2]**harrow** *vt* **1** to cultivate (ground or land) with a harrow **2** to cause distress to; agonize – **harrower** *n*

harrumph /hə'rum(p)f/ *vi or n* (to make) a guttural sound as if clearing the throat, esp as a sign of disapproval [imit]

harry /'hari/ *vt* **1** to make a destructive raid on; ravage **2** to torment (as if) by constant attack; harass [ME *harien*, fr OE *hergian*; akin to OHG *heriōn* to lay waste, *heri* army, Gk *koiranos* commander]

harsh /hahsh/ *adj* **1** having a coarse uneven surface; rough **2** disagreeable or painful to the senses ⟨*a ~ light*⟩ **3** unduly exacting; severe **4** lacking in aesthetic appeal or refinement; crude [ME *harsk*, of Scand origin; akin to Norw *harsk* harsh] – **harshen** *vb*, **harshly** *adv*, **harshness** *n*

hart /haht/ *n, chiefly Br* the male of the (red) deer, esp when over 5 years old – compare HIND [ME *hert*, fr OE *heort*; akin to L *cervus* hart, Gk *keras* horn – more at HORN]

hartebeest /'hahti,beest/ *n* any of several large African antelopes with ridged horns that project upwards and outwards [obs Afrik (now *hartbees*), fr D, fr *hart* deer + *beest* beast]

hartshorn /'hahts,hawn/ *n* ammonium carbonate – not now used technically [fr the earlier use of hart's horns as the chief source of ammonia]

'**hart's-,tongue** *n* a Eurasian fern with undivided fronds

harum-scarum /,heərəm 'skeərəm/ *adj* reckless, irresponsible – infml [perh alter. of *helter-skelter*] – **harum-scarum** *adv*

haruspex /hə'ruspeks/ *n, pl* **haruspices** /-spi,seez/ a diviner in ancient Rome basing his predictions on the entrails of animals [L]

[1]**harvest** /'hahvist/ *n* **1** (the season for) the gathering in of agricultural crops **2** (the yield of) a mature crop of grain, fruit, etc **3** the product or reward of exertion [ME *hervest*, fr OE *hærfest*; akin to L *carpere* to pluck, gather, Gk *karpos* fruit, *keirein* to cut – more at SHEAR]

[2]**harvest** *vt* **1** to gather in (a crop); reap **2** to gather (a natural product) as if by harvesting ⟨*~ bacteria*⟩ ~ *vi* to gather in a food crop – **harvestable** *adj*, **harvester** *n*

,**Harvest 'Festival** *n* a festival of thanksgiving for the harvest celebrated on a Sunday in September or October in British churches

,**harvest 'home** *n* **1** the gathering or the time of harvest **2** a festival at the close of harvest

'**harvestman** /-mən/ *n* an arachnid with a small rounded body and very long slender legs

ˈharvest ˌmite *n* a 6-legged mite larva that sucks the blood of vertebrates and causes intense irritation

ˌharvest ˈmoon *n* the full moon nearest the time of the September equinox

has /haz/ *pres 3rd sing of* HAVE

ˈhas-ˌbeen *n* sby or sthg that has passed the peak of effectiveness, success, or popularity – infml

¹hash /hash/ *vt* to chop (e g meat and potatoes) into small pieces [F *hacher*, fr OF *hachier*, fr *hache* battle-axe, of Gmc origin; akin to OHG *hāppa* sickle; akin to Gk *koptein* to cut – more at CAPON]

²hash *n* **1** (a dish consisting chiefly of reheated cooked) chopped food, esp meat **2** a rehash **3** a muddle, mess ⟨*made a* ~ *of things*⟩ ***USE***(2 & 3) infml

³hash *n* hashish – infml

hashish /ˈhashish, -sheesh/ *n* the resin from the flowering tops of the female hemp plant that is smoked, chewed, etc for its intoxicating effect – compare BHANG, MARIJUANA, CANNABIS [Ar *ḥashīsh*]

haslet /ˈhazlit/ *n* the edible entrails (e g the liver) of an animal, esp a pig (cooked and compressed into a meat loaf) – compare GIBLETS [ME *hastelet*, fr MF, piece of meat roasted on a spit]

hasn't /ˈhaznt/ has not

hasp /hahsp/ *n* a device for fastening; *esp* a hinged metal strap that fits over a staple and is secured by a pin or padlock [ME, fr OE *hæsp*; akin to MHG *haspe* hasp] – **hasp** *vt*

¹hassle /ˈhasl/ *n* **1** a heated often protracted argument; a wrangle **2** a trying problem; a struggle ⟨*it's such a* ~ *getting across London*⟩ ***USE*** infml [perh fr ²*haggle* + ²*tussle*]

²hassle *vb* **hassling** /ˈhasling/ *vi* to argue, fight ⟨~d *with the referee*⟩ ~ *vt* to subject to usu persistent harassment ***USE*** infml

hassock /ˈhasək/ *n* **1** a tussock **2** a cushion for kneeling on, esp in church [ME, sedge, fr OE *hassuc*]

hast /hast/ *archaic pres 2 sing of* HAVE

hastate /ˈhastayt/ *adj* shaped like (the triangular head of) a spear ⟨*a* ~ *leaf*⟩ ☞ PLANT [NL *hastatus*, fr L *hasta* spear – more at ¹YARD] – **hastately** *adv*

¹haste /hayst/ *n* **1** rapidity of motion; swiftness **2** rash or headlong action; precipitateness ⟨*marry in* ~, *repent at leisure*⟩ [ME, fr OF, of Gmc origin; akin to OE *hǣst* violence] – **make haste** to act quickly; hasten

²haste *vi* to move or act swiftly – fml

hasten /ˈhays(ə)n/ *vt* **1** to cause to hurry ⟨~ed *her to the door* – A J Cronin⟩ **2** to accelerate ⟨~ *the completion of the project*⟩ ~ *vi* to move or act quickly; hurry – **hastener** *n*

hasty /ˈhaysti/ *adj* **1** done or made in a hurry **2** precipitate, rash **3** prone to or showing anger; irritable – **hastily** *adv*, **hastiness** *n*

hat /hat/ *n* **1** a covering for the head usu having a shaped crown and brim ☞ GARMENT **2** a role, position – infml ⟨*wearing his ministerial* ~⟩ [ME, fr OE *hæt*; akin to OHG *huot* head covering – more at HOOD] – **hatless** *adj*

ˈhatˌband *n* a fabric, leather, etc band round the crown of a hat just above the brim

¹hatch /hach/ *n* **1** a small door or opening (e g in a wall or aircraft) **2a** (the covering for) an opening in the deck of a ship or in the floor or roof of a building **b** a hatchway [ME *hache*, fr OE *hæc*; akin to MD *hecke* trapdoor]

²hatch *vi* **1** to emerge from an egg or pupa **2** to incubate eggs; brood **3** to give forth young ⟨*the egg* ~ed⟩ ~ *vt* **1** to produce (young) from an egg by applying heat **2** to devise, esp secretly; originate [ME *hacchen*; akin to MHG *hecken* to mate] – **hatchable** *adj*, **hatcher** *n*

³hatch *n* (a brood of young produced by) hatching

⁴hatch *vt* to mark (e g a drawing, map, or engraving) with fine closely spaced parallel lines [ME *hachen*, fr MF *hacher* to inlay, chop up] – **hatching** *n*

ˈhatchˌback *n* (a usu small motor car with) an upward-opening hatch giving entry to the luggage and passenger compartment

hatchery /ˈhachəri/ *n* a place for hatching (esp fish) eggs

hatchet /ˈhachit/ *n* a short-handled axe [ME *hachet*, fr MF *hachette*, dim. of *hache* battle-axe – more at HASH]

ˈhatchet ˌman *n* one hired for murder, coercion, or attack – slang

hatchling /ˈhachling/ *n* a recently hatched animal

hatchment /ˈhachmənt/ *n* a square panel set cornerwise bearing the coat of arms of a deceased person for display outside a house or in a church ☞ CHURCH [perh alter. of *achievement*]

ˈhatchˌway *n* a passage giving access (e g to a lower deck in a ship); *also* ¹HATCH 2a

¹hate /hayt/ *n* **1** intense hostility or dislike; loathing **2** an object of hatred – infml ⟨*one of my pet* ~s⟩ [ME, fr OE *hete*; akin to OHG *haz* hate, Gk *kēdos* grief]

²hate *vb* to feel extreme enmity or aversion (towards) – **hater** *n* – **hate someone's guts** to hate sby with great intensity

ˈhateful /-f(ə)l/ *adj* **1** full of hate; malicious **2** deserving of or arousing hate – **hatefully** *adv*, **hatefulness** *n*

hath /hath/ *archaic pres 3 sing of* HAVE

ˌhatha ˈyoga /ˈhatə, ˈhathə, ˈhahthə/ *n* a yoga consisting of physical and breathing exercises for the body in order to keep it healthy and thus leave the mind free from its demands [Skt *haṭha* force, persistence + *yoga* – more at YOGA]

ˌhat in ˈhand *adv* CAP IN HAND

hatred /ˈhaytrid/ *n* hate [ME, fr *hate* + OE *rǣden* condition – more at KINDRED]

ˈhat ˌtrick *n* three successes by 1 person or side in a usu sporting activity; *specif* the dismissing of 3 batsmen with 3 consecutive balls by a bowler in cricket [prob fr a former practice of rewarding the feat by the gift of a hat]

hauberk /ˈhawˌbuhk/ *n* a tunic of chain mail worn as defensive armour, esp from the 12th to the 14th c [ME, fr OF *hauberc*, of Gmc origin; akin to OE *healsbeorg* neck armour]

haughty /ˈhawti/ *adj* disdainfully proud; arrogant [obs *haught*, fr ME *haute*, fr MF *haut*, lit., high, fr L *altus* – more at OLD] – **haughtily** *adv*, **haughtiness** *n*

¹haul /hawl/ *vt* **1a** to pull with effort; drag **b** to transport in a vehicle, esp a cart **2** to bring *up* (e g before an authority for judgment) – infml ⟨~ed *up before the magistrate for a traffic offence*⟩ ~ *vi* **1** to pull, drag ⟨~ed *on the rope*⟩ **2** *of the wind* to shift [ME *halen* to pull, fr OF *haler*, of Gmc origin; akin to MD *halen* to pull; akin to OE ge*holian* to obtain] – **haulage** /-lij/ *n*

[2]**haul** *n* **1** the act or process of hauling **2a** an amount gathered or acquired; a take ⟨*the burglar's* ~⟩ **b** the fish taken in a single draught of a net **3a** transport by hauling or the load transported **b** the distance or route over which a load is transported ⟨*a long* ~⟩

haulier /'hawli·ə/, *NAm* **hauler** /'hawlə/ *n* a person or commercial establishment whose business is transport by lorry [[1]HAUL + -IER, [2]-ER]

haulm /hawm/ *n* **1** the stems or tops of potatoes, peas, beans, etc (after the crop has been gathered) **2** *Br* an individual plant stem [ME *halm*, fr OE *healm*; akin to OHG *halm* stem, L *culmus* stalk, Gk *kalamos* reed]

haunch /hawnch/ *n* **1** [2]HIP 1a **2a** HINDQUARTER 2 – usu pl **b** HINDQUARTER 1 **3** the lower half of either of the sides of an arch [ME *haunche*, fr OF *hanche*, of Gmc origin; akin to MD *hanke* haunch] – **on one's haunches** in a squatting position

[1]**haunt** /hawnt/ *vt* **1a** to visit often; frequent **b** to continually seek the company of (a person) **2a** to recur constantly and spontaneously to ⟨*the tune* ~ed *her all day*⟩ **b** to reappear continually in; pervade ⟨*a sense of tension that* ~s *his writing*⟩ **3** to visit or inhabit as a ghost ~ *vi* **1** to stay around or persist; linger **2** to appear habitually as a ghost [ME *haunten*, fr OF *hanter*] – **haunter** *n*, **hauntingly** *adv*

[2]**haunt** *n* a place habitually frequented ⟨*the bar was a favourite* ~ *of criminals*⟩

Hausa /'howsə/ *n, pl* **Hausa,** *esp collectively* **Hausas** **1** a member of a Negroid people of N Nigeria and S Niger **2** the Chad language of the Hausa people widely used in W Africa ☞ LANGUAGE

hausfrau /'hows,frow/ *n* a housewife [G, fr *haus* house + *frau* woman, wife]

hau'stellum /haw'steləm/ *n, pl* **haustella** /-lə/ a mouth part (e g of an insect) adapted to suck blood, plant juices, etc [NL, fr L *haustus*, pp of *haurire* to drink, draw – more at EXHAUST] – **haustellate** /-layt/ *adj*

hautboy, hautbois /'ohboy/ *n, archaic* an oboe [MF *hautbois*, fr *haut* high + *bois* wood]

haute couture /,oht kooh'tyooə (*Fr* ot kuty:r)/ *n* (the houses or designers that create) exclusive and often trend-setting fashions for women [F, lit., high sewing]

,**haute cui'sine** /kwi'zeen (*Fr* k izin)/ *n* elaborate cookery that reaches a high standard [F, lit., high cooking]

,**haute é'cole** /ay'kol (*Fr* ekɔl)/ *n* a highly stylized form of classical riding [F, lit., high school]

hauteur /oh'tuh (*Fr* otœ:r)/ *n* arrogance, haughtiness [F, fr *haut* high – more at HAUGHTY]

haut monde /,oh 'mon(h)d (*Fr* o mɔ̃d)/ *n* high society [F]

Havana /hə'vanə/ *n* (a cigar made in Cuba or from) tobacco (of the type) grown in Cuba [prob fr Sp *habano*, fr *habano* of Havana, fr La *Habana* (Havana), capital city of Cuba]

[1]**have** /v, əv, həv; *strong* hav/ *vb* **has** /s, z, əz, həz; *strong* haz/; **had** /d, əd, həd; *strong* had/ *vt* **1a** to hold in one's possession or at one's disposal ⟨~ *a car*⟩ ⟨has *only a little French*⟩ **b** to contain as a constituent or be characterized by ⟨~ *red hair*⟩ ⟨*coat* has *no pockets*⟩ ⟨has *it in him to win*⟩ **2** to own as an obligation or necessity – + *to* and an expressed or understood infinitive ⟨~ *to go*⟩ ⟨*don't* ~ *to if you don't want to*⟩ **3** to stand in relationship to ⟨~ *enemies*⟩ ⟨~ *2 sisters*⟩ **4a** to get, obtain ⟨*these shoes are the best to be* had⟩ **b** to receive ⟨had *news*⟩ **c** to accept; *specif* to accept in marriage **d** to have sexual intercourse with (a woman or passive partner) **5** to display, show ⟨had *the impudence to refuse*⟩ ⟨~ *mercy on us*⟩ **6a** to experience, esp by undergoing or suffering ⟨~ *a cold*⟩ ⟨~ *my watch stolen*⟩ **b** to undertake and make or perform ⟨~ *a bath*⟩ ⟨~ *a look at that*⟩ **c** to entertain in the mind ⟨~ *an opinion*⟩ ⟨~ *a down on him*⟩ **d** to engage in; CARRY ON ⟨~ *sex*⟩ ⟨~ *a meeting*⟩ **7a** to cause to by persuasive or forceful means ⟨~ *the children stay*⟩ ⟨*so he would* ~ *us believe*⟩ **b** *chiefly Br* to bring into a specified condition by the action of another ⟨~ *my shoes mended*⟩ **c** to cause to be ⟨*soon* ~ *it finished*⟩ **d** to invite as a guest ⟨~ *them over for drinks*⟩ **8** to allow, permit ⟨*I'm not* having *any more of that*⟩ **9a** to hold in a position of disadvantage or certain defeat ⟨*we* ~ *him now*⟩ **b** to perplex, floor ⟨*you* ~ *me there*⟩ **10** to be able to exercise; be entitled to ⟨*I* ~ *my rights*⟩ **11a** to be pregnant with or be the prospective parents of ⟨*they're* having *a baby in August*⟩ **b** to give birth to ⟨*the cat's just* had *kittens*⟩ **12** to partake of; consume ⟨~ *dinner*⟩ ⟨~ *a cigar*⟩ **13** to take advantage of; fool ⟨*been* had *by his partner*⟩ – infml ~ *va* **1** – used with the past participle to form the present perfect ⟨has *gone home*⟩, the past perfect ⟨had *already eaten*⟩, the future perfect ⟨*will* ~ *finished dinner by then*⟩, or nonfinite perfective forms ⟨having *gone*⟩ ⟨*silly not to* ~ *gone*⟩; used with *got* to express obligation or necessity ⟨~ *got to go*⟩; used in the past tense with the past participle as a rather literary expression of the conditional ⟨had *I known*⟩ **2** WOULD 1b ⟨*I* had *as soon not*⟩ ***USE*** British speakers in particular often express the idea of ***momentary as opposed to habitual possession or experience with*** *have got* ⟨have *you* got *a cold?*⟩ ⟨*do you* have *many colds?*⟩ [ME *haven*, fr OE *habban*; akin to OHG *haben* to have, *hevan* to lift – more at HEAVE] – **have a lot/enough on one's plate** to be (fully) occupied, often with a variety of tasks, problems, etc – **have an ear to the ground** to be in receipt of information not generally known – **have a screw/slate loose** to be slightly cracked, feebleminded, or eccentric – **have a way with** to be good at dealing with ⟨*he* has a way with *old ladies*⟩ – **have a way with one** to be charming, esp persuasively – **have been around** to be sophisticated or well-informed – **have coming** to deserve or merit what one gets, benefits by, or suffers ⟨*he* had *that* coming *to him*⟩ – **have done with** to bring to an end; have no further concern with ⟨*let us* have done with *name-calling*⟩ – **have had it** **1** to have had and missed one's chance – infml **2** to have passed one's prime; be obsolete, smashed, or dead ⟨*I'm afraid the car's* had it⟩ – infml – **have it** **1** to maintain, affirm ⟨*as rumour* has it⟩ **2** to live in the specified conditions ⟨*never* had it *so good*⟩ – **have it both ways** to exploit or profit from each of a pair of contradictory positions, circumstances, etc; *also* to maintain 2 contradictory views simultaneously – **have it coming to one** to deserve what one is going to get – **have it in for** to intend to do harm to – **have it off/away** to copulate *with* – slang – **have it out** to settle a matter of contention by discussion or a fight – **have no time for** to be unable or reluctant to spend time

on; dislike – infml **– have one's eye on 1** to watch, esp constantly and attentively **2** to have as an objective **– have one's hands full** to be fully occupied ⟨*what with the triplets, 6 goldfish, 3 dogs, and the mushroom farm, he's* got his hands full *most days*⟩ **– have one's head screwed on** to be sensible, practical, or provident **– have one's work cut out** to be hard put to it **– have taped** to have the measure of; be in command or control of ⟨*soon have the problem* taped⟩ **– have the advantage of** to have superiority over; *specif* to have personal unreciprocated knowledge of – often used as an ironic disclaimer of acquaintanceship ⟨*I'm afraid you* have the advantage *of me*⟩ **– have the wind of** to be to windward of **– have to do with 1** to deal with **2** to have in the way of connection or relation with or effect on ⟨*the lawyer would* have *nothing* to do with *the case*⟩ – compare TO DO WITH **– have up one's sleeve** to have as an undeclared resource ⟨*he's* got *some new ideas* up his sleeve⟩ **– not have a clue** to know nothing; not to know **– what have you** any of various other things that might also be mentioned ⟨*paper clips, pins, and* what have you⟩

[2]**have** *n* a wealthy person – usu pl; esp in *the haves and have-nots*

haven /'hayv(ə)n/ *n* **1** a harbour, port **2** a place of safety or refuge [ME, fr OE *hæfen*; akin to MHG *habene* harbour, OE *hebban* to lift – more at HEAVE]

'have-,not *n* a poor person – usu pl; compare [2]HAVE

haven't /'havnt/ have not

,have 'on *vt* **1** to be wearing ⟨have *a new suit* on⟩ **2** to have plans for ⟨*what do you* have on *for tomorrow?*⟩ **3** *chiefly Br* to deceive, tease – infml

haver /'hayvə/ *vi, chiefly Br* to be indecisive; hesitate [origin unknown]

havers /'hayvəz/ *n pl, chiefly Scot* nonsense, poppycock [*haver*]

haversack /'havə,sak/ *n* a knapsack [F *havresac*, fr G *habersack* bag for oats, fr *haber* oats + *sack* bag]

,have 'up *vt* to bring before the authorities ⟨*he was* had up *in court for dangerous driving*⟩ – infml

havoc /'havək/ *n* **1** widespread destruction; devastation **2** great confusion and disorder ⟨*several small children can create* ~ *in a house*⟩ [ME *havok*, fr AF, modif of OF *havot* plunder]

[1]**haw** /haw/ *n* (a berry of) hawthorn [ME *hawe*, fr OE *haga* – more at HEDGE]

[2]**haw** *n* (a domestic animal's inflamed) nictitating membrane [origin unknown]

[3]**haw** *vi* to utter a sound resembling *haw*, esp in hesitation ⟨*hummed and* ~ed *before answering*⟩ – compare HUM [imit]

[4]**haw** *interj* – often used to indicate hesitation

Hawaiian /hə'wie·ən/ *n or adj* (a native or inhabitant) of Hawaii [*Hawaii*, group of islands in Pacific Ocean]

Ha,waiian gui'tar *n* STEEL GUITAR

hawfinch /'haw,finch/ *n* a large Eurasian finch with a large heavy bill [[1]*haw*]

haw-'haw *interj* ha-ha

[1]**hawk** /hawk/ *n* **1** any of numerous medium-sized birds of prey that have (short) rounded wings and long tails and that hunt during the day **2** a small board with a handle on the underside for holding mortar or plaster **3** one who takes a militant attitude; a supporter of a warlike policy – usu contrasted with *dove* [ME *hauk*, fr OE *hafoc*; akin to OHG *habuh* hawk, Russ *kobets*, a falcon] – **hawkish** *adj*, **hawkishly** *adv*, **hawkishness** *n*

[2]**hawk** *vi* **1** to hunt game with a trained hawk **2** to soar and strike like a hawk ⟨*birds* ~ ing *after insects*⟩ ~ *vt* to hunt on the wing like a hawk

[3]**hawk** *vt* to offer for sale in the street ⟨~ing *newspapers*⟩ [back-formation fr [2]*hawker*]

[4]**hawk** *vi* to utter a harsh guttural sound (as if) in clearing the throat ~ *vt* to raise by hawking ⟨~ *up phlegm*⟩ [imit]

[5]**hawk** *n* an audible effort to force up phlegm from the throat

[1]**hawker** /'hawkə/ *n* a falconer

[2]**hawker** *n* sby who hawks wares [by folk etymology fr LG *höker*, fr MLG *höker*, fr *hōken* to peddle; akin to OE *hēah* high]

'hawk,moth *n* any of numerous stout-bodied moths with long strong narrow fore wings ☞ DEFENCE

hawksbill /'hawks,bil/ *n* a flesh-eating sea turtle whose shell yields a valuable tortoiseshell

'hawk,weed *n* any of several red, orange, or yellow composite plants

hawse /hawz/ *n* **1** a hawsehole **2** the part of a ship's bow that contains the hawseholes [ME *halse*, fr ON *hals* neck, hawse – more at COLLAR]

hawsehole /'hawz,hohl/ *n* a hole in the bow of a ship through which a cable passes

hawser /'hawzə/ *n* a large rope [ME, fr AF *hauceour*, fr MF *haucier* to hoist, fr (assumed) VL *altiare*, fr L *altus* high – more at OLD]

'hawser-,laid *adj* cable-laid

hawthorn /'haw,thawn/ *n* any of a genus of spring-flowering spiny shrubs of the rose family with white or pink flowers and small red fruits [ME *hawethorn*, fr OE *hagathorn*, fr *haga* hawthorn + *thorn* – more at HEDGE]

[1]**hay** /hay/ *n* herbage, esp grass, mowed and cured for fodder [ME *hey*, fr OE *hieg*; akin to OHG *hewi* hay, OE *hēawan* to hew]

[2]**hay** *vi* to cut, cure, and store grass for hay

[3]**hay, hey** *n* a rustic dance featuring winding and interweaving dance figures [MF *haye*]

'hay,box *n* a well-insulated airtight box used to keep a previously heated vessel hot and allow slow cooking to continue

'hay,cock *n* a small conical pile of hay in a field

'hay ,fever *n* nasal catarrh and conjunctivitis occurring usu in the spring and summer through allergy to pollen

'hay,maker *n* **1** one who tosses and spreads hay to dry after cutting **2** *chiefly NAm* a powerful blow – **haymaking** *n*

'hay,rick /-,rik/ *n* a haystack

'hay,stack *n* a relatively large sometimes thatched outdoor pile of hay

'hay,wire *adj* **1** out of order ⟨*the radio went* ~⟩ **2** emotionally or mentally upset; crazy ⟨*went completely* ~ *after the accident*⟩ *USE* infml [fr the use of baling wire for makeshift repairs]

[1]**hazard** /'hazəd/ *n* **1** a game of chance played with 2 dice **2a** a risk, peril **b** a source of danger **3** a golf-course obstacle (e g a bunker) [ME, fr MF *hasard*, fr Ar *az-zahr* the die]

[2]**hazard** *vt* **1** to expose to danger ⟨*a captain guilty of* ~ing *his ship*⟩ **2** to venture, risk ⟨~ *a guess*⟩

hazardous /'hazədəs/ *adj* **1** depending on hazard or

chance **2** involving or exposing one to risk (e g of loss or harm) ⟨*a ~ occupation*⟩ – **hazardously** *adv*, **hazardousness** *n*

[1]**haze** /hayz/ *vb* to make or become hazy or cloudy [prob back-formation fr *hazy*]

[2]**haze** *n* **1** vapour, dust, smoke, etc causing a slight decrease in the air's transparency **2** vagueness or confusion of mental perception [prob back-formation fr *hazy*]

[3]**haze** *vt, chiefly NAm* to harass (a new student) with ridicule, criticism, etc [origin unknown] – **hazer** *n*, **hazing** *n*

hazel /ˈhayzl/ *n* **1** (the wood or nut of) any of a genus of shrubs or small trees bearing nuts **2** a yellowish light to strong brown [ME *hasel*, fr OE *hæsel*; akin to OHG *hasal* hazel, L *corulus*] – **hazel** *adj*

ˌ**hazel** ˈ**hen** *n* a European woodland grouse

ˈ**hazel,nut** *n* the nut of a hazel

hazy /ˈhayzi/ *adj* **1** obscured, cloudy ⟨*a ~ view of the mountains*⟩ **2** vague, indefinite ⟨*had only a ~ recollection of what happened*⟩ [origin unknown] – **hazily** *adv*, **haziness** *n*

ˈ**H-,bomb** *n* HYDROGEN BOMB

[1]**he** /(h)i, ee; *strong* hee/ *pron* **1** that male person or creature who is neither speaker nor hearer ⟨*~ is my father*⟩ – + cap in reference to God; compare SHE, HIM, HIS, IT, THEY **2** – used in a generic sense or when the sex of the person is unspecified ⟨*~ that hath ears to hear, let him hear* –Mt 11:15 (AV)⟩ [ME, fr OE *hē*; akin to OE *hēo* she, *hit* it, OHG *hē* he, L *cis, citra* on this side, Gk *ekeinos* that person]

[2]**he** *n* **1** a male person or creature ⟨*is the baby a ~ or a she?*⟩ ⟨*a he-goat*⟩ **2** [2]IT 1

[1]**head** /hed/ *n, pl* **heads**, (*4b*) **head** **1** the upper or foremost division of the body containing the brain, the chief sense organs, and the mouth **2a** the seat of the intellect; the mind ⟨*2 ~s are better than 1*⟩ **b** natural aptitude or talent ⟨*a good ~ for figures*⟩ **c** mental or emotional control; composure ⟨*a level ~*⟩ **d** a headache **3** the obverse of a coin – usu pl with sing. meaning; compare TAIL 5 **4a** a person, individual ⟨*a ~ count*⟩ **b** a single individual (domestic animal) out of a number – usu pl ⟨*500 ~ of cattle*⟩ **5a** the end that is upper, higher, or opposite the foot ⟨*the ~ of the table*⟩ ☞ SHIP **b** the source of a stream, river, etc **c** either end of sthg (e g a cask or drum) whose 2 ends need not be distinguished **d** DRIFT 5 **6** a director, leader: e g **a** a school principal **b** one in charge of a department in an institution ⟨*the ~ of the English department*⟩ **7a** a capitulum **b** the foliaged part of a plant, esp when consisting of a compact mass of leaves or fruits **8** the leading part of a military column, procession, etc **9a** the uppermost extremity or projecting part of an object; the top ☞ ARCHITECTURE **b** the striking part of a weapon, tool, implement, etc **10a** a body of water kept in reserve at a height **b** a mass of water in motion **11a** (the pressure resulting from) the difference in height between 2 points in a body of liquid **b** the pressure of a fluid ⟨*a good ~ of steam*⟩ **12a** (parts adjacent to) the bow of a ship **b** a (ship's) toilet – usu pl with sing. meaning in British English **13** a measure of length equivalent to a head ⟨*the horse won by a ~*⟩ **14** the place of leadership, honour, or command ⟨*at the ~ of his class*⟩ **15a** a word often in larger letters placed above a passage in order to introduce or categorize **b** a separate part or topic **16** the foam or froth that rises on a fermenting or effervescing liquid **17a** the part of a boil, pimple, etc at which it is likely to break **b** a culminating point; a crisis – esp in *come to a head* **18a** a part of a machine or machine tool containing a device (e g a cutter or drill); *also* the part of an apparatus that performs the chief or a particular function **b** any of at least 2 electromagnetic components which bear on the magnetic tape in a tape recorder, such that one can erase recorded material if desired and another may either record or play back **19** one who uses LSD, cannabis, etc habitually or excessively – often in combination; slang [ME *hed*, fr OE *hēafod*; akin to OHG *houbit* head, L *caput*] – **headless** *adj*, **headlessness** *n* – **off one's head** crazy, mad – **over someone's head** **1** beyond sby's comprehension ⟨*I understand the gist but the technical language is* over my head⟩ **2** so as to pass over sby's superior standing or authority ⟨*went* over his *supervisor's* head *to complain*⟩

[2]**head** *adj* **1** principal, chief ⟨*~ cook*⟩ ⟨*~ office*⟩ **2** situated at the head

[3]**head** *vt* **1** to cut back or off the upper growth of (a plant) **2a** to provide with a head **b** to form the head or top of ⟨*tower ~ed by a spire*⟩ **3** to be at the head of; lead ⟨*~ a revolt*⟩ **4** to go round the head of (a stream) **5a** to put sthg at the head of (e g a list); *also* to provide with a heading **b** to stand as the first or leading member of ⟨*~s the list of heroes*⟩ **6** to set the course of ⟨*~ a ship northwards*⟩ **7** to drive (e g a soccer ball) with the head ~ *vi* **1** to form a head ⟨*this cabbage ~s early*⟩ **2** to point or proceed in a specified direction ⟨*~ing for disaster*⟩

headache /ˈhedayk/ *n* **1** pain in the head **2** a difficult situation or problem – **headachy** *adj*

ˌ**head and** ˈ**shoulders** *adv* to a great degree; considerably ⟨*stood ~ above the rest in character and ability*⟩

ˈ**head,band** *n* a band worn round the head, esp to keep hair out of the eyes

ˈ**head,board** *n* a board forming the head (e g of a bed)

ˈ**head ,case** *n* a mad person; a lunatic – infml

ˈ**head,cheese** *n* BRAWN 2

ˈ**head,dress** *n* an often elaborate covering for the head

headed /ˈhedid/ *adj* **1** having a head or a heading ⟨*~ notepaper*⟩ **2** having a head or heads of a specified kind or number – in combination ⟨*a cool-*headed *businessman*⟩ ⟨*a round*headed *screw*⟩

header /ˈhedə/ *n* **1** a brick or stone laid in a wall with its end towards the face of the wall – compare STRETCHER ☞ BUILDING **2** a headfirst fall or dive **3** a shot or pass in soccer made by heading the ball

ˌ**head**ˈ**first** *adv* with the head foremost; headlong ⟨*dived ~ into the waves*⟩ – **headfirst** *adj*

ˌ**head**ˈ**foremost** *adv* headfirst

ˈ**head-,hunting** *n* **1** decapitating and preserving the heads of enemies as trophies **2** searching for and recruitment of personnel, esp at the executive level and often from other firms – **headhunter** *n*

heading /ˈheding/ *n* **1** the compass direction in which a ship or aircraft points **2a** an inscription, headline, or title standing at the top or beginning (e g of a letter or chapter) **b** a piece used in making either of the flat ends of a barrel **3** DRIFT 5

ˈheadˌlamp *n* a headlight

headland /ˈhedlənd/ *n* **1** unploughed land near an edge of a field **2** a point of usu high land jutting out into a body of water ☞ GEOGRAPHY

ˈheadˌlight *n* (the beam cast by) the main light mounted on the front of a motor vehicle

ˈheadˌline *n* a title printed in large type above a newspaper story or article; *also, pl, Br* a summary given at the beginning or end of a news broadcast

ˈheadˌlong *adv or adj* **1** headfirst **2** without deliberation **3** without pause or delay [ME *hedlong,* alter. of *hedling,* fr *hed* head]

ˈheadman /-mən/ *n* a chief of a primitive community

ˌheadˈmaster, *fem* **ˌheadˈmistress** *n* one who heads the staff of a school – **headmastership** *n*

ˈheadˌmost *adj* most advanced; leading

head off *vt* to stop the progress of or turn aside by taking preventive action; block ⟨head *them* off *at the pass*⟩

ˌhead of ˈstate *n, often cap H&S* the titular head of a state (e g a monarch) as distinguished from the head of government (e g a prime minister)

ˌhead-ˈon *adv or adj* **1** with the head or front making the initial contact ⟨*the cars collided* ~⟩ ⟨*a* ~ *collision*⟩ **2** in direct opposition ⟨*what happens when primitive and civilized man meet* ~*?*⟩ ⟨*a* ~ *confrontation*⟩

ˌhead over ˈheels *adv* **1** turning (as if) in a somersault **2** very much; completely ⟨~ *in love*⟩

ˈheadˌphone *n* an earphone held over the ear by a band worn on the head – usu pl

ˈheadˌpiece *n* an ornamental printed device esp at the beginning of a chapter

ˌheadˈquarters *n, pl* **headquarters** **1** a place from which a commander exercises command **2** the administrative centre of an enterprise *USE* often pl with sing. meaning

ˈheadˌrace *n* a channel taking water to a mill wheel or turbine

ˈheadˌrest *n* a support for the head; *esp* a cushioned pad supporting the head in a vehicle

ˈheadroom /-room, -roohm/ *n* vertical space (e g beneath a bridge) sufficient to allow passage or unrestricted movement

ˈheadˌset *n* an attachment for holding earphones and a microphone to one's head

ˈheadship /-ship/ *n* the position or office of a head (e g a headmaster); leadership

ˈheadˌshrinker *n* **1** a headhunter who shrinks the heads of his/her victims **2** a psychoanalyst or psychiatrist – humor

headsman /ˈhedzmən/ *n* an executioner

ˈheadˌspring *n* a fountainhead, source

ˈheadˌstall *n* the part of a bridle or halter that encircles the head

ˌhead ˈstart *n* **1** an advantage granted or achieved at the beginning of a race, competition, etc **2** an advantageous or favourable beginning

ˈheadˌstock *n* a bearing or pedestal for a revolving or moving part (e g in a lathe)

ˈheadˌstone *n* a memorial stone placed at the head of a grave

ˈheadˌstrong *adj* wilful, obstinate ⟨*violent* ~ *actions*⟩

ˌhead ˈteacher *n* a headmaster or headmistress

ˌhead-ˈup *adj, of an instrument display* visible without the eyes having to look down from the view ahead

ˌheadˈwaiter *n* the head of the dining-room staff of a restaurant or hotel

ˈheadˌwater /-ˌwawtə/ *n* the upper part or source of a river – usu pl with sing. meaning ☞ GEOGRAPHY

ˈheadˌway *n* **1a** (rate of) motion in a forward direction **b** advance, progress **2** headroom **3** the time interval between 2 vehicles travelling in the same direction on the same route

ˈheadˌwind /-ˌwind/ *n* a wind blowing in a direction opposite to a course, esp of a ship or aircraft

ˈheadˌword *n* a word or term placed at the beginning (e g of a chapter or encyclopedia entry)

ˈheadˌwork *n* mental effort; thinking

heady /ˈhedi/ *adj* **1** violent, impetuous **2a** tending to make giddy or exhilarated; intoxicating **b** giddy, exhilarated ⟨~ *with his success*⟩ – **headily** *adv,* **headiness** *n*

heal /heel/ *vt* **1a** to make sound or whole ⟨~ *a wound*⟩ **b** to restore to health **2** to restore to a sound or normal state; mend ⟨~ *a breach between friends*⟩ ~ *vi* to return to a sound or healthy state [ME *helen,* fr OE *hǣlan;* akin to OHG *heilen* to heal, OE *hāl* whole – more at WHOLE] – **healer** *n*

health /helth/ *n* **1a** soundness of body, mind, or spirit **b** the general condition of the body ⟨*in poor* ~⟩ **2** condition ⟨*the economic* ~ *of the country is not good*⟩; *esp* a sound or flourishing condition; well-being **3** a toast to sby's health or prosperity [ME *helthe,* fr OE *hǣlth,* fr *hāl*]

ˈhealth ˌfarm *n* a usu rural residential establishment that caters for people wishing to lose weight

ˈhealth ˌfood *n* organically grown untreated food (e g live yoghourt) containing no synthetic ingredients and eaten for the health-giving properties credited to it – compare WHOLEFOOD, JUNK FOOD

ˈhealthful /-f(ə)l/ *adj* **1** beneficial to health of body or mind **2** HEALTHY 1

ˈhealth ˌvisitor *n* sby employed by a local authority in Britain to visit old people, nursing mothers, etc and advise them on health matters

healthy /ˈhelthi/ *adj* **1** enjoying or showing health and vigour of body, mind, or spirit **2** conducive to good health **3** prosperous, flourishing – **healthily** *adv,* **healthiness** *n*

[1]heap /heep/ *n* **1** a collection of things lying one on top of another; a pile **2** a great number or large quantity; a lot – infml; often pl with sing. meaning ⟨~s *more to say*⟩ [ME *heep,* fr OE *hēap;* akin to OE *hēah* high]

[2]heap *vt* **1a** to throw or lay in a heap; pile *up* ⟨*his sole object was to* ~ *up riches*⟩ **b** to form or round into a heap ⟨~ed *the earth into a mound*⟩ **2** to supply abundantly *with; also* to bestow lavishly or in large quantities *upon*

hear /hiə/ *vb* **heard** /huhd/ *vt* **1** to perceive (sound) with the ear **2** to learn by hearing ⟨*I* ~d *you were leaving*⟩ **3a** to listen to with attention; heed ⟨~ *me out*⟩ **b** to attend ⟨~ *mass*⟩ **4** to give a legal hearing to ~ *vi* **1** to have the capacity of perceiving sound **2** to gain information; learn ⟨*I've* ~d *about what you did*⟩ **3** – often in the expression *Hear! Hear!* indicating approval (e g during a speech) [ME *heren,* fr OE *hīeran;* akin to OHG *hōren* to hear, L *cavēre* to be on guard, Gk *akouein* to hear] – **hearer** *n* – **hear from**

to receive a communication from – **hear of** to entertain the idea of – usu neg ⟨*wouldn't* hear of *it*⟩

hearing /ˈhiəring/ *n* **1a** the one of the 5 basic physical senses by which waves received by the ear are interpreted by the brain as sounds varying in pitch, intensity, and timbre **b** earshot **2a** an opportunity to be heard **b** a trial in court

ˈhearing ˌaid *n* an electronic device worn by a deaf person for amplifying sound before it reaches the ears

hearken /ˈhahkən/ *vi* to listen *to*; *also* to heed – poetic [ME *herknen*, fr OE *heorcnian*; akin to OHG *hōrechen* to listen]

hearsay /ˈhiəˌsay/ *n* sthg heard from another; rumour

ˈhearˌsay ˌevidence *n* evidence based not on a witness's personal knowledge but on matters told him/her by another

hearse /huhs/ *n* a vehicle for transporting a dead body in its coffin [ME *herse* candelabrum, catafalque, fr MF *herce* harrow, frame for holding candles, fr L *hirpic-, hirpex* harrow]

¹heart /haht/ *n* **1a** a hollow muscular organ that by its rhythmic contraction acts as a force pump maintaining the circulation of the blood ☞ ANATOMY **b** the breast, bosom **c** sthg resembling a heart in shape; *specif* a conventionalized representation of a heart **2a** a playing card marked with 1 or more red heart-shaped figures **b** *pl but sing or pl in constr* the suit comprising cards identified by this figure **c** *pl but sing in constr* a card game in which the object is to avoid taking tricks containing a heart or the queen of spades **3a** humane disposition; compassion ⟨*have you no* ~*?*⟩ **b** love, affections ⟨*lost his* ~ *to her*⟩ **c** courage, spirit ⟨*had no* ~ *for the task*⟩ **4** one's innermost character or feelings ⟨*a man after my own* ~⟩ **5a** the central or innermost part (of a lettuce, cabbage, etc) **b** the essential or most vital part ⟨*the* ~ *of the matter*⟩ [ME *hert*, fr OE *heorte*; akin to OHG *herza* heart, L *cord-, cor*, Gk *kardia*] – **by heart** by rote or from memory

²heart *vt, of a cabbage, lettuce, etc* to form a heart

ˈheartˌache *n* mental anguish; sorrow

ˈheart atˌtack *n* an instance of abnormal functioning of the heart; *esp* CORONARY THROMBOSIS

ˈheartˌbeat *n* a single complete pulsation of the heart

ˈheart ˌblock *n* incoordination of the beating of the atria and ventricles of the heart resulting in a decreased output of blood

ˈheartˌbreak *n* intense grief or distress

ˈheartˌbreaking *adj* **1** causing intense sorrow or distress ⟨*a* ~ *waste of talent*⟩ **2** extremely trying or difficult ⟨*a* ~ *task*⟩ – **heartbreakingly** *adv*

ˈheartˌbroken *adj* overcome by sorrow

ˈheartˌburn *n* a burning pain behind the lower part of the breastbone usu resulting from spasm of the stomach or throat muscles

hearted /ˈhahtid/ *adj* having a heart, esp of a specified kind – usu in combination ⟨*a faint*hearted *leader*⟩ ⟨*a broken*hearted *lover*⟩

hearten /ˈhahtn/ *vt* to cheer, encourage – **hearteningly** *adv*

ˈheart ˌfailure *n* (inability of the heart to perform adequately often leading to) cessation of the heartbeat and death

ˈheartˌfelt *adj* deeply felt; earnest

hearth /hahth/ *n* **1a** a brick, stone, or cement area in front of the floor of a fireplace **b** the lowest section of a metal-processing furnace **2** home, fireside ⟨*the comforts of* ~ *and home*⟩ [ME *herth*, fr OE *heorth*; akin to OHG *herd* hearth, Skt *kūḍayāti* he singes]

ˈhearthˌstone *n* a soft stone or composition of powdered stone and pipe clay used to whiten or scour hearths and doorsteps

heartily /ˈhahtəli/ *adv* **1a** with all sincerity; wholeheartedly ⟨*I* ~ *recommend it*⟩ **b** with zest; vigorously ⟨*ate* ~⟩ **2** quite, thoroughly ⟨~ *sick of all this talk*⟩ [HEARTY + ²-LY]

ˈheartland /-ˌland, -lənd/ *n* a central and vital area

ˈheartless /-lis/ *adj* unfeeling, cruel – **heartlessly** *adv*, **heartlessness** *n*

ˌheart-ˈlung maˌchine *n* a mechanical pump that shunts the body's blood away from the heart and maintains the circulation and respiration during heart surgery

ˈheartˌrending *adj* HEARTBREAKING 1 – **heartrendingly** *adv*

ˈheart-ˌsearching *n* close examination of one's motives or feelings ⟨*reached the decision after much* ~⟩

ˈheartsˌease *n* any of various violas; *esp* the wild pansy

ˈheartˌsick *adj* very despondent; depressed – **heartsickness** *n*

ˈheartˌsore *adj* heartsick

ˈheartˌstrings *n pl* the deepest emotions or affections ⟨*pulled at his* ~⟩

ˈheartˌthrob *n* one who is the object of or arouses infatuation

¹ˌheart-to-ˈheart *adj* sincere and intimate ⟨~ *confidences*⟩

²heart-to-heart *n* a frank or intimate talk – infml

ˈheartˌwarming *adj* inspiring sympathetic feeling; cheering

ˈheartˌwood *n* the older harder nonliving central wood in a tree, usu darker and denser than the surrounding sapwood

¹hearty /ˈhahti/ *adj* **1a** enthusiastically or exuberantly friendly; jovial **b** unrestrained, vigorous ⟨*a* ~ *laugh*⟩ **2a** robustly healthy ⟨*hale and* ~⟩ **b** substantial, abundant ⟨*a* ~ *meal*⟩ – **heartiness** *n*

²hearty *n* **1** a sailor **2** *chiefly Br* a sporty outgoing person ⟨*rugger* hearties⟩

¹heat /heet/ *vb* to make or become warm or hot – often + *up* [ME *heten*, fr OE *hǣtan*; akin to OE *hāt* hot] – **heatable** *adj*, **heatedly** *adv*

²heat *n* **1a** the condition of being hot; warmth; *also* a marked degree of this **b** excessively high bodily temperature **c** the form of energy associated with the random motions of the molecules, atoms, etc of which matter is composed, transmitted by conduction, convection, or radiation **d** an esp high temperature ⟨*at melting* ~⟩ **e** any of a series of degrees of heating ⟨*this iron has 4* ~s⟩ **2a** intensity of feeling or reaction ⟨*the* ~ *of passion*⟩ **b** the height or stress of an action or condition ⟨*in the* ~ *of battle*⟩ **c** readiness for sexual intercourse in a female mammal; *specif* oestrus – usu in *on heat* or (*chiefly NAm*) *in heat* **3** pungency of flavour **4a** a single round of a contest that has 2 or more rounds for each contestant **b** any of several preliminary contests whose winners go into the final **5** pressure, coercion ⟨*his enemies turned the* ~ *on him*⟩ – slang – **heatless** *adj*, **heatproof** /ˈheetˌproohf/ *adj*

heated /ˈheetid/ *adj* marked by anger ⟨*a ~ argument*⟩

ˈ**heat ˌengine** *n* a mechanism (e g an internal-combustion engine) for converting heat energy into mechanical energy

heater /ˈheetə/ *n* a device that gives off heat or holds sthg to be heated [[1]HEAT + [2]-ER]

ˈ**heat exˌchanger** *n* a device (e g in a nuclear power station) that transfers heat from one liquid or gas to another without their mixing ☞ ENERGY

heath /heeth/ *n* **1** any of various related evergreen plants that thrive on barren usu acid soil, with whorls of needlelike leaves and clusters of small flowers **2a** a tract of wasteland **b** a large area of level uncultivated land usu with poor peaty soil and bad drainage [ME *heth*, fr OE *hǣth*; akin to OHG *heida* heather, OW *coit* forest] – **heathless** *adj*, **heathlike** *adj*, **heathy** *adj*

heathen /ˈheedh(ə)n/ *n, pl* **heathens, heathen 1** an unconverted member of a people or nation that does not acknowledge the God of the Bible – often pl + *the* ⟨*the ~ say there is no God*⟩ **2** an uncivilized or irreligious person [ME *hethen*, fr OE *hǣthen*; akin to OHG *heidan* heathen] – **heathen** *adj*, **heathenish** *adj*, **heathenism** *n*, **heathendom** /-dəm/ *n*, **heathenize** /ˈheedhnˌiez/ *vt*

heather /ˈhedhə/ *n* a (common usu purplish-pink flowered northern) heath [ME (northern) *hather*] – **heather** *adj*

heathery /ˈhedhəri/ *adj* having flecks of various colours ⟨*a soft ~ tweed*⟩ [HEATHER + [1]-Y]

Heath Robinson /ˌheeth ˈrobins(ə)n/ *adj, Br* impractically complex and ingenious – infml [W *Heath Robinson* †1944 E cartoonist famous for his drawings of absurdly ingenious machines]

ˈ**heat ˌpump** *n* an apparatus for transferring heat by mechanical means to a place of higher temperature (e g for heating or cooling a building) ☞ ENERGY

ˈ**heat ˌrash** *n* PRICKLY HEAT

ˈ**heat ˌsink** *n* a means of absorbing or dissipating unwanted heat

ˈ**heatˌstroke** *n* overheating of the body resulting from prolonged exposure to high temperature and leading to (fatal) collapse

ˈ**heat ˌwave** *n* a period of unusually hot weather

[1]**heave** /heev/ *vb* **heaved, hove** /hohv/ *vt* **1** to lift upwards or forwards, esp with effort **2** to throw, cast **3** to utter with obvious effort ⟨~d *a sigh*⟩ **4** to cause to swell or rise **5** to haul, draw ~ *vi* **1** to rise or become thrown or raised up **2a** to rise and fall rhythmically ⟨*his chest* ~ing *with sobs*⟩ **b** to pant **3** to vomit **4** to pull [ME *heven*, fr OE *hebban*; akin to OHG *hevan* to lift, L *capere* to take] – **heaver** *n* – **heave in/into sight** to come into view

[2]**heave** *n* **1a** an effort to heave or raise **b** a throw, cast **2** an upward motion; *esp* a rhythmical rising ⟨*the ~ of the sea*⟩ **3** *pl but sing or pl in constr* BROKEN WIND

heaven /ˈhev(ə)n/ *n* **1** (any of the spheres of) the expanse of space that surrounds the earth like a dome; the firmament – usu pl with sing. meaning **2** *often cap* the dwelling place of God, his angels, and the spirits of those who have received salvation; Paradise **3** *cap* GOD 1 **4** a place or condition of utmost happiness [ME *heven*, fr OE *heofon*; akin to OHG *himil* heaven]

ˈ**heavenly** /-li/ *adj* **1** of heaven or the heavens; celestial ⟨*the ~ choirs*⟩ **2a** suggesting the blessed state of heaven; divine ⟨*~ peace*⟩ **b** delightful ⟨*what a ~ idea*⟩ – infml – **heavenliness** *n*

ˌ**heaven-ˈsent** *adj* providential

ˈ**heavenward** /-wood/ *adj* directed towards heaven or the heavens – **heavenwards,** *NAm chiefly* **heavenward** *adv*

ˌ**heave ˈto** *vb* to bring (a ship) to a stop with head to wind

ˌ**heavier-than-ˈair** /ˈhevi·ə/ *adj* of greater weight than the air displaced

heavily /ˈhevəli/ *adv* **1** slowly and laboriously; dully **2** to a great degree; severely [HEAVY + [2]-LY]

Heaviside layer /ˈhevisied/ *n* E LAYER [Oliver *Heaviside* †1925 E physicist]

[1]**heavy** /ˈhevi/ *adj* **1a** having great weight **b** having great weight in proportion to size **c** *of an isotope or compound* having, being, or containing atoms of greater than normal mass ⟨*~ hydrogen*⟩ **2** hard to bear; *specif* grievous ⟨*a ~ sorrow*⟩ **3** of weighty import; serious ⟨*a ~ book*⟩ **4** emotionally intense; profound ⟨*a ~ silence*⟩ **5a** oppressed; burdened ⟨*returned with ~ spirit from the meeting*⟩ **b** pregnant; *esp* approaching parturition – often + *with* **6a** slow, sluggish ⟨*~ movements*⟩ **b** lacking sparkle or vivacity; dull ⟨*the book made ~ reading*⟩ **7** dulled with weariness; drowsy ⟨*his eyelids felt ~ with sleep*⟩ **8a** of an unusually large amount ⟨*~ traffic*⟩ **b** of great force ⟨*~ seas*⟩ **c** overcast ⟨*a ~ sky*⟩ **d** *of ground or soil* full of clay and inclined to hold water; impeding motion **e** loud and deep ⟨*the ~ roll of thunder*⟩ **f** laborious, difficult ⟨*made ~ going of it*⟩ **g** of large capacity or output **h** consuming in large quantities – usu + *on* ⟨*this car is ~ on petrol*⟩ **9a** digested with difficulty, usu because of excessive richness ⟨*~ fruit cake*⟩ **b** *esp of bread* not sufficiently raised or leavened **10** producing heavy usu large goods (e g coal, steel, or machinery) often used in the production of other goods ⟨*~ industry*⟩ **11a** of the larger variety ⟨*a ~ howitzer*⟩ **b** heavily armoured, armed, or equipped ⟨*the ~ cavalry*⟩ **12** *of rock music* loud and strongly rhythmic – slang **13** *chiefly NAm* frighteningly serious; *specif* threatening – slang; often used as an interjection [ME *hevy*, fr OE *hefig*; akin to OHG *hebic* heavy, OE *hebban* to lift – more at HEAVE] – **heaviness** *n* – **with a heavy hand 1** with little mercy; sternly **2** without grace; clumsily

[2]**heavy** *adv* in a heavy manner; heavily ⟨*time hangs ~ on us*⟩

[3]**heavy** *n* **1** *pl* units (e g of bombers, artillery, or cavalry) of the heavy sort **2a** (an actor playing) a villain **b** sby of importance or significance – infml **3** a serious newspaper – usu pl; infml **4** one hired to compel or deter by means of threats or physical violence ⟨*set a gang of* heavies *on him*⟩ – slang

ˌ**heavy-ˈduty** *adj* able or designed to withstand unusual strain or wear

ˌ**heavy-ˈfooted** *adj* heavy and slow in movement; dull

ˌ**heavy-ˈhanded** *adj* **1** clumsy, awkward **2** oppressive, harsh – **heavy-handedly** *adv*, **heavy-handedness** *n*

ˌ**heavyˈhearted** *adj* despondent, melancholy – **heavyheartedly** *adv*, **heavyheartedness** *n*

ˈ**heavy ˌspar** *n* barytes

ˈ**heavy ˌwater** *n* water enriched esp with deuterium

'heavy,weight *n* **1** sby or sthg above average weight **2** one in the usu heaviest class of contestants: e g **a** a boxer whose weight is not limited if he is professional or is more than 81kg (about 12st 10lb) if he is amateur **b** a wrestler weighing over 100kg (about 15st 10lb) **c** a weight-lifter weighing over 110kg (about 17st 4lb) **3** an important or influential person ⟨*an intellectual* ~⟩

hebdomad /'hebdəmad/ *n* a week – fml [L *hebdomad-, hebdomas*, fr Gk, fr *hebdomos* seventh, fr *hepta* seven – more at SEVEN]

hebdomadal /heb'domədl/ *adj* weekly – fml – **hebdomadally** *adv*

hebephrenia /,heebi'freenyə, -ni·ə/ *n* schizophrenia characterized esp by silliness and regression to a childish state [NL, fr Gk *hēbē* youth] – **hebephrenic** /-'frenik/ *adj*

Hebraic /hi'brayik/, **Hebraistic** /,heebray'istik/ *adj* of the Hebrews, their culture, or Hebrew [ME *Ebrayke*, fr LL *Hebraicus*, fr Gk *Hebraikos*, fr *Hebraios*] – **Hebraically** *adv*, **Hebraistically** *adv*

Hebraist /'heebray,ist/ *n* a specialist in Hebrew and Hebraic studies

Hebrew /'heebrooh/ *n* **1** a member or descendant of any of a group of N Semitic peoples including the Israelites; *esp* an Israelite **2** the Semitic language of the ancient Hebrews; *also* a later form of Hebrew ☞ ALPHABET, LANGUAGE [ME *Ebreu*, fr OF, fr LL *Hebraeus*, fr L, adj, fr Gk *Hebraios*, fr Aram *'Ebrai*] – **Hebrew** *adj*

'Hebrews *n pl but sing in constr* a theological treatise addressed to early Christians and included as a book in the New Testament

hecatomb /'hekətoohm, -tohm/ *n* **1** an ancient Greek and Roman sacrifice of 100 oxen or cattle **2** the sacrifice or slaughter of many victims [L *hecatombe*, fr Gk *hekatombē*, fr *hekaton* hundred + *bous* cow – more at HUNDRED, COW]

heck /hek/ *n* HELL 2a – used as an interjection or intensive ⟨*what the* ~!⟩ ⟨*a* ~ *of a lot of money*⟩ [euphemism]

heckle /'hekl/ *vt* **heckling** /'hekling/ to harass and try to disconcert (e g a speaker) with questions, challenges, or gibes [ME *hekelen*, fr *heckele* hackle; akin to OHG *hāko* hook – more at HOOK] – **heckler** *n*

hect- /hekt-/, **hecto-** *comb form* hundred (10^2) ⟨*hectograph*⟩ ☞ PHYSICS [F, irreg fr Gk *hekaton*]

hectare /'hektah/ *n* ☞ UNIT [F, fr *hect-* + *are*]

hectic /'hektik/ *adj* **1** of, being, or suffering from a fluctuating fever (e g in tuberculosis) **2** filled with excitement or feverish activity ⟨*the* ~ *days before Christmas*⟩ [ME *etyk*, fr MF *etique*, fr LL *hecticus*, fr Gk *hektikos* habitual, consumptive, fr *echein* to have – more at SCHEME] – **hectically** *adv*

hector /'hektə/ *vi* to play the bully; swagger ~ *vt* to intimidate by bullying or blustering [*Hector*, a Trojan warrior in Homer's *Iliad*] – **hectoringly** *adv*

he'd /eed, id, hid; *strong* heed/ he had; he would

heddle /'hedl/ *n* any of the sets of parallel cords or wires that with their mounting compose the harness used to guide warp threads in a loom [prob alter. of ME *helde*, fr OE *hefeld*; akin to ON *hafald* heddle, OE *hebban* to lift – more at HEAVE]

¹hedge /hej/ *n* **1a** a boundary formed by a dense row of shrubs or low trees **b** a barrier, limit **2** a means of protection or defence (e g against financial loss) **3** a calculatedly noncommittal or evasive statement [ME *hegge*, fr OE *hecg*; akin to OE *haga* hedge, hawthorn, L *colum* sieve]

²hedge *vt* **1** to enclose or protect (as if) with a hedge **2** to hem in or obstruct (as if) with a barrier; hinder **3** to protect oneself against losing (e g a bet), esp by making counterbalancing transactions ~ *vi* **1** to plant, form, or trim a hedge **2** to avoid committing oneself to a definite course of action, esp by making evasive statements **3** to protect oneself financially: e g **a** to buy or sell commodity futures as a protection against loss due to price fluctuation – often + *against* **b** to minimize the risk of a bet – **hedger** *n*, **hedgingly** *adv*

hedgehog /'hej,hog/ *n* any of a genus of small Old World spine-covered insect-eating mammals that are active at night ☞ FOOD

'hedge,hop *vi* **-pp-** to fly an aircraft close to the ground and rise over obstacles as they appear [back-formation fr *hedgehopper*] – **hedgehopper** *n*

'hedge,row /-,roh/ *n* a row of shrubs or trees surrounding a field

'hedge ,sparrow *n* a dunnock

hedonic /hee'donik, hi-/ *adj* **1** of or characterized by pleasure **2** hedonistic – **hedonically** *adv*

hedonism /'hedə,niz(ə)m, 'hee-/ *n* (conduct based on) the doctrine that personal pleasure is the sole or chief good [Gk *hēdonē* pleasure; akin to Gk *hēdys* sweet – more at SWEET] – **hedonist** *n*, **hedonistic** /,hedə'nistik, ,hee-/ *adj*, **hedonistically** *adv*

-hedral /-heedrəl/ *comb form* (→ *adj*) having (such) a surface or (such or so many) surfaces ⟨*di*hedral⟩ [NL *-hedron*]

-hedron /-heedr(ə)n/ *comb form*, (→ *n*), *pl* **-hedrons, -hedra** /-rə/ crystal or geometrical figure having (such or so many) surfaces ⟨*penta* hedron⟩ ⟨*trapezo*hedron⟩ [NL, fr Gk *-edron*, fr *hedra* seat – more at SIT]

heebie-jeebies /,heebi 'jeebiz/ *n pl the* jitters, willies – infml [coined by Billy DeBeck †1942 US cartoonist]

¹heed /heed/ *vb* to pay attention (to) [ME *heeden*, fr OE *hēdan*; akin to OHG *huota* guard]

²heed *n* attention, notice ⟨*take* ~⟩

'heedful /-f(ə)l/ *adj* attentive, mindful *of* – **heedfully** *adv*, **heedfulness** *n*

'heedless /-lis/ *adj* inconsiderate, thoughtless – **heedlessly** *adv*, **heedlessness** *n*

hee-haw /'hee ,haw/ *n* **1** the bray of a donkey **2** a loud rude laugh; a guffaw [imit] – **hee-haw** *vi*

¹heel /heel/ *n* **1** (the back part of the hind limb of a vertebrate corresponding to) the back of the human foot below the ankle and behind the arch or an anatomical structure resembling this **2** either of the crusty ends of a loaf of bread **3** the part of a garment or an article of footwear that covers or supports the human heel **4a** the lower end of a mast **b** the base of a tuber or cutting of a plant used for propagation **5** a backward kick with the heel in rugby, esp from a set scrum **6** a contemptible person – slang [ME, fr OE *hēla*; akin to ON *hæll* heel, OE *hōh* – more at ¹HOCK] – **heeled** *adj*, **heelless** *adj* – **down at (the) heel** in or into a run-down or shabby condition – **on the heels of** immediately following; closely behind – **to heel** **1** close behind – usu used in training a dog **2** into agreement or line; under control

²heel *vt* **1** to supply with a heel; *esp* to renew the heel of ⟨~ *a sock*⟩ **2** to exert pressure on, propel, or strike (as if) with the heel; *specif* to kick (a rugby ball) with the heel, esp out of a scrum ~ *vi* to move along at the heels of sby or close behind sthg ⟨*a dog that* ~s *well*⟩ – **heeler** *n*

[3]**heel** *vi* to tilt to one side ~ *vt* to cause (a boat) to heel [alter. of ME *heelden*, fr OE *hieldan*; akin to OHG *hald* inclined, Lith *šalis* side, region]

[4]**heel** *n* (the extent of) a tilt to one side

,heel-and-'toe *adj* with a stride in which the heel of one foot touches the ground before the toe of the other foot leaves it

'heel,ball *n* a mixture of wax and lampblack used to polish the heels of footwear and to take brass or stone rubbings

heel in *vt* to plant (cuttings or plants) temporarily before setting in the final growing position [*heel*, alter. of E dial. *hele, heal* to cover over, fr ME *helen* to hide, conceal, fr OE *helian*]

[1]**heft** /heft/ *n, dial Br & NAm* weight, heaviness [irreg fr *heave*]

[2]**heft** *vt* **1** to test the weight of by lifting **2** *dial* to heave up; hoist

hefty /'hefti/ *adj* **1** large or bulky and usu heavy **2** powerful, mighty ⟨*a* ~ *blow*⟩ **3** impressively large ⟨*a* ~ *price to pay*⟩ – **heftily** *adv*, **heftiness** *n*

Hegelian /hay'geeli·ən, -lyən/ *adj* of Hegel, his philosophy, or his dialectical method [Georg *Hegel* †1831 G philosopher] – **Hegelian** *n*, **Hegelianism** /-,niz(ə)m/ *n*

hegemony /hi'geməni/ *n* domination by one nation, group, etc over others [Gk *hēgemonia*, fr *hēgemōn* leader, fr *hēgeisthai* to lead – more at SEEK]

hegira *also* **hejira** /'hejirə/ *n* a journey, esp when undertaken to escape from a dangerous or undesirable situation; *specif, cap* the flight of Muhammad from Mecca to Medina in 622 AD, the event marking the beginning of the Muhammadan era [ML *hegira*, fr Ar *hijrah*, lit., flight]

heifer /'hefə/ *n* a young cow (that has at most 1 calf) [ME *hayfare*, fr OE *hēahfore*]

heigh-ho /'hay ,hoh/ *interj* – used to express boredom, weariness, or sadness [*heigh* (var of *hey*) + *ho*]

height /hiet/ *n* **1** the highest or most extreme point; the zenith ⟨*at the* ~ *of his powers*⟩ **2a** the distance from the bottom to the top of sthg standing upright ☞ UNIT **b** the elevation above a level **3** the condition of being tall or high **4a** a piece of land (e g a hill or plateau) rising to a considerable degree above the surrounding country – usu pl with sing. meaning **b** a high point or position [ME *heighthe*, fr OE *hīehthu*; akin to OHG *hōhida* height, OE *hēah* high]

heighten /'hiet(ə)n/ *vt* **1a** to increase the amount or degree of; augment ⟨~ed *his awareness of the problem*⟩ **b** to deepen, intensify ⟨*her colour was* ~ed *by emotion*⟩ **2** to raise high or higher; elevate ⟨*the building was* ~ed *by another storey*⟩ ~ *vi* **1** to become great or greater in amount, degree, or extent **2** to intensify

,height-to-'paper *n* the height of printing type measured from foot to face and standardized at 0.9186in (about 23.33mm) in English-speaking countries

heinous /'haynəs, 'heenəs/ *adj* hatefully or shockingly evil; abominable ⟨*a* ~ *crime*⟩ [ME, fr MF *haineus*, fr *haine* hate, fr *hair* to hate, of Gmc origin; akin to OHG *haz* hate – more at HATE] – **heinously** *adv*, **heinousness** *n*

heir /eə/ *n* **1** sby who inherits or is entitled to succeed to an estate or rank **2** sby who receives or is entitled to receive some position, role, or quality passed on from a parent or predecessor [ME, fr OF, fr L *hered-, heres*; akin to Gk *chēros* bereaved, OE *gān* to go] – **heirless** *adj*, **heirship** *n*

,heir ap'parent *n, pl* **heirs apparent** **1** an heir who cannot be displaced so long as he/she outlives the person from whom he/she is to inherit **2** one whose succession, esp to a position or role, appears certain under existing circumstances

heiress /'eəris/ *n* a female heir, esp to great wealth

'heir,loom /-loohm/ *n* **1** a piece of valuable property handed down within a family for generations **2** sthg of special value handed on from one generation to another [ME *heirlome*, fr *heir* + *lome* implement – more at [1]LOOM]

,heir pre'sumptive *n, pl* **heirs presumptive** an heir who can be displaced only by the birth of a child with a superior claim

heist /hiest/ *vt, NAm* **1** to commit armed robbery on **2** to steal *USE* slang [alter. of [1]*hoist*] – **heist** *n*

hejira /'hejirə/ *n* a hegira

HeLa /'heelə/ *adj* of, derived from, or being a particular strain of human cells kept continuously in tissue culture [*He*nrietta *La*cks *fl* 1951, whose cervical cancer provided the original cells]

held /held/ *past of* HOLD

heldentenor /'heldn,tenə/ *n, often cap* a tenor with a dramatic voice suited to heroic roles [G, fr *held* hero + *tenor*]

[1]**heli-, helio-** *comb form* sun ⟨*helio*centric⟩ [L, fr Gk *hēli-, hēlio-*, fr *hēlios* – more at [1]SOLAR]

[2]**heli-** *comb form* helicopter ⟨*heli*port⟩

heliacal /hi'lie·əkl/ *adj* relating to or near the sun – used esp of the last setting of a star before and its first rising after invisibility due to nearness to the sun [LL *heliacus*, fr Gk *hēliakos*, fr *hēlios*]

helic-, helico- *comb form* helix; spiral ⟨*helical*⟩ [Gk *helik-, heliko-*, fr *helik-, helix* spiral – more at HELIX]

helical /'helikl/ *adj* (having the form) of a helix; *broadly* SPIRAL 1a – **helically** *adv*

helicoid /'helikoyd/, **helicoidal** /-'koydl/ *adj* forming or arranged in a spiral

helicon /'helikən/ *n* a large circular tuba similar to a sousaphone [prob fr Gk *helik-, helix* + E *-on* (as in *bombardon* bass tuba); from its tube's forming a spiral encircling the player's body]

helicopter /'heli,koptə/ *n* an aircraft which derives both lift and propulsive power from a set of horizontally rotating rotors or vanes and is capable of vertical takeoff and landing [F *hélicoptère*, fr Gk *heliko-* + *pteron* wing – more at FEATHER]

heliocentric /,heelioh'sentrik/ *adj* **1** referred to, measured from, or as if observed from the sun's centre **2** having or relating to the sun as a centre – compare GEOCENTRIC

heliograph /'heeli·ə,grahf, -,graf/ *n* **1** a photoheliograph **2** an apparatus for signalling using the sun's rays reflected from a mirror [ISV]

,helio'graphic /-'grafik/ *adj* of heliography or a heliograph

heliography /,heeli'ogrəfi/ *n* the system or practice of signalling with a heliograph

heliostat /'heelioh,stat/ *n* an instrument consisting of a mirror moved on an axis so as to reflect a sunbeam steadily in one direction [NL *heliostata,* fr *heli-* + Gk *-statēs* -stat]

heliotaxis /ˌheelioh'taksis/ *n* the response of a cell or organism to the stimulus of sunlight [NL]

heliotrope /'heeli·əˌtrohp/ *n* **1** any of a genus of plants of the borage family **2** (a) bloodstone **3** light purple [L *heliotropium,* fr Gk *hēliotropion,* fr *hēlio-* heli- + *tropos* turn – more at TROPE; fr its flowers' turning towards the sun]

heliotropism /ˌheeli'otrəpiz(ə)m/ *n* a tropism in which sunlight is the orienting stimulus – **heliotropic** /-lioh'tropik/ *adj,* **heliotropically** *adv*

heliport /'heliˌpawt/ *n* a place for helicopters to take off and land [*heli*copter + *port*]

helium /'heeli·əm, -lyəm/ *n* a noble gaseous element found in natural gases and used esp for inflating balloons and in low-temperature research ☞ PERIODIC TABLE [NL, fr Gk *hēlios*]

helix /'heeliks/ *n, pl* **helices** /'heliˌseez/ *also* **helixes** **1** sthg spiral in form (e g a coil formed by winding wire round a uniform tube) **2** the rim curved inwards of the external ear ☞ NERVE **3** a curve traced on a cylinder by the rotation of a point moving up the cylinder at a constant rate; *broadly* SPIRAL 1b [L, fr Gk; akin to Gk *eilyein* to roll, wrap – more at VOLUBLE]

hell /hel/ *n* **1a** a nether world (e g Hades or Sheol) inhabited by the spirits of the dead **b** the nether realm of the devil in which the souls of those excluded from Paradise undergo perpetual torment **c** the home of the devil and demons in which the damned suffer punishment **2a** a place or state of torment, misery, or wickedness – often as an interjection, an intensive, or as a generalized term of abuse ⟨*one* ~ *of a mess*⟩ ⟨*go to* ~⟩ **b** a place or state of chaos or destruction ⟨*all* ~ *broke loose*⟩ **c** a severe scolding ⟨*got* ~ *for coming in late*⟩ [ME, fr OE; akin to OHG *helan* to conceal, L *celare,* Gk *kalyptein*] – **for the hell of it** for the intrinsic amusement or satisfaction of an activity – **hell to pay** serious trouble ⟨*if he's late there'll be* hell to pay⟩ – **like hell** **1** very hard or much ⟨*worked* like hell *to get the job done on time*⟩ **2** – used to intensify denial of a statement; slang ⟨*'I did 4 hours overtime.'* 'Like hell *you did!'*⟩ – **what the hell** it doesn't matter

he'll /hil, eel, il; *strong* heel/ he will; he shall

ˌhell-'bent *adj* stubbornly and often recklessly determined ⟨*civilization is* ~ *on self-destruction* – R F Delderfield⟩

'hellˌcat *n* a spiteful ill-tempered woman

hellebore /'helibaw/ *n* any of a genus of showy-flowered plants of the buttercup family [L *helleborus,* fr Gk *helleboros*]

helleborine /'helibərin, -brien/ *n* any of various plants of the orchid family [L, a kind of hellebore, fr Gk *helleborinē,* fr *helleboros*]

Hellene /'heleen/ *n* GREEK 1 [Gk *Hellēn*]

Hellenic /he'lenik, -'leenik, hə-/ *adj* of Greece, its people, or its language

Hellenism /'heliˌniz(ə)m/ *n* **1** devotion to or imitation of ancient Greek culture **2** Greek civilization, esp as later modified by oriental influences **3** a body of humanistic and classical ideals associated with ancient Greece – **hellenize** *vb, often cap*

Hellenist /'helinist/ *n* **1** sby living in ancient times who was Greek in language, outlook, and way of life but not in ancestry **2** a specialist in the language or culture of ancient Greece

Hellenistic /ˌheli'nistik/ *adj* of Greek history, culture, or art after Alexander the Great

ˌhell-for-'leather *adv or adj* at full speed ⟨*pelted* ~ *down the street*⟩ – infml [perh alter. of *all of a lather*]

'hellˌhole *n* **1** the pit of hell **2** a place of extreme discomfort, squalor, or evil – infml

'hellˌhound *n* a fiendish person

hellion /'heli·ən, 'helyən/ *n, NAm* a troublesome or mischievous person – infml [prob alter. of *hallion* (scamp)]

[1]hellish /'helish/ *adj* of, resembling, or befitting hell; diabolical – **hellishly** *adv,* **hellishness** *n*

[2]hellish *adv* extremely, damnably ⟨*a* ~ *cold day*⟩

hello /he'loh, 'heloh, hə-/ *n, pl* **hellos** an expression or gesture of greeting – used interjectionally in greeting, in answering the telephone, to express surprise, or to attract attention [alter. of *hollo*]

ˌhell's 'angel *n, often cap H* a member of a reckless and often violent gang who wear leather clothing and ride motorcycles – compare ROCKER 3

ˌhell's 'bells *interj* – used esp to express irritation or impatience

helluva /'heləvə/ *adj* great, terrific – slang; often used as an intensive ⟨*a* ~ *din*⟩ [alter. of *hell of a*]

[1]helm /helm/ *n* HELMET 1 [ME, fr OE]

[2]helm *n* **1** a tiller or wheel controlling the steering of a ship **2** the position of control; the head ⟨*a new dean is at the* ~ *of the medical school*⟩ [ME *helme,* fr OE *helma;* akin to OHG *helmo* tiller]

[3]helm *vt* to steer (as if) with a helm

helmet /'helmit/ *n* **1** a covering or enclosing headpiece of ancient or medieval armour **2** any of various protective head coverings, esp made of a hard material to resist impact **3** sthg, esp a hood-shaped petal or sepal, resembling a helmet [MF, dim. of *helme* helmet, of Gmc origin; akin to OE *helm* helmet, OHG *helan* to conceal – more at HELL] – **helmeted** *adj,* **helmetlike** *adj*

helminth /'helminth/ *n* an (intestinal) worm – used technically [Gk *helminth-, helmis;* akin to Gk *eilyein* to roll – more at VOLUBLE] – **helminthic** /hel'minthik/ *adj*

helminth-, helmintho- *comb form* helminth ⟨helmintho*logy*⟩ [NL, fr Gk *helminth-, helmis*]

helmsman /'helmzmən/ *n* the person at the helm – **helmsmanship** *n*

helot /'helət/ *n* **1** *cap* a serf in ancient Sparta **2** a serf, slave [L *Helotes,* pl, fr Gk *Heilōtes*] – **helotry** /-tri/ *n*

[1]help /help/ *vt* **1** to give assistance or support to ⟨~ *a child to understand his lesson*⟩ **2** to remedy, relieve ⟨*took an aspirin to* ~ *her headache*⟩ **3a** to be of use to; benefit **b** to further the advancement of; promote ⟨~ing *industry with loans*⟩ **4a** to refrain from ⟨*couldn't* ~ *laughing*⟩ **b** to keep from occurring; prevent ⟨*they couldn't* ~ *the accident*⟩ **c** to restrain (oneself) from taking action ⟨*tried not to say anything, but couldn't* ~ *myself*⟩ **5** to serve with food or drink, esp at a meal ⟨*let me* ~ *you to some salad*⟩ **6** to appropriate sthg for (oneself), esp dishonestly ⟨~ed *himself to my pen*⟩ ~ *vi* to be of use or benefit ⟨*every little* ~s⟩ [ME *helpen,* fr OE *helpan;* akin to OHG *helfan* to help, Lith *šelpti*] – **helper** *n* – **help somebody on/off with** to help sby take off/put on (an article of clothing)

[2]help *n* **1** aid, assistance **2** remedy, relief ⟨*there was* *no ~ for it*⟩ **3a** sby, esp a woman, hired to do work, esp housework ⟨*a mother's ~*⟩ **b** the services of a paid worker; *also, chiefly NAm* the workers providing such services ⟨*~ wanted*⟩

'helpful /-f(ə)l/ *adj* of service or assistance; useful – **helpfully** *adv*, **helpfulness** *n*

helping /'helping/ *n* a serving of food

'helpless /-lis/ *adj* **1** lacking protection or support; defenceless **2** lacking strength or effectiveness; powerless – **helplessly** *adv*, **helplessness** *n*

'help,mate *n* one who is a companion and helper; *esp* a spouse [by folk etymology fr *helpmeet*]

'help,meet *n, archaic* a helpmate [[2]*help* + *meet*, adj]

help out *vb* to give assistance or aid (to), esp when in great difficulty ⟨*she* helped *me* out *when I was in hospital*⟩

[1]**helter-skelter** /,heltə 'skeltə/ *adj or adv* (done) in a hurried and disorderly manner ⟨*ran ~ down the stairs*⟩ [imit]

[2]**,helter-'skelter** *n* a spiral slide at a fairground

helve /helv/ *n* a haft [ME, fr OE *hielfe*; akin to OE *healf* half]

Helvetian /hel'veesh(y)ən/ *adj* Swiss [NL *Helvetia* land of the Helvetii, Switzerland, fr L *Helvetii*, ancient people of Switzerland] – **Helvetian** *n*

[1]**hem** /hem/ *n* **1** the border of a cloth article when turned back and stitched down; *esp* the bottom edge of a garment finished in this manner **2** a similar border on an article of plastic, leather, etc [ME, fr OE; akin to MHG *hemmen* to hem in, Arm *kamel* to press]

[2]**hem** *vb* **-mm-** *vt* **1a** to finish (e g a skirt) with a hem **b** to border, edge **2** to enclose, confine – usu + *in* or *about* ⟨*~*med *in by enemy troops*⟩ *~ vi* to make a hem in sewing – **hemmer** *n*

[3]**hem** *interj* – often used to indicate a pause in speaking [imit]

hem-, hema-, hemo- *comb form, NAm* haem-

'he-,man /'hee/ *n* a strong virile man – infml

hemat-, hemato- *comb form, NAm* haemat-

heme /heem/ *n, chiefly NAm* haem

hemi- /hemi-/ *prefix* half ⟨hemisphere⟩ [ME, fr L, fr Gk *hēmi-* – more at SEMI-]

hemicellulose /,hemi'selyoolohs, -lohz/ *n* any of various polysaccharides of plant cell walls that are less complex than cellulose [ISV]

hemichordate /,hemi'kawdət, -dayt/ *n* any of a division of marine chordate animals with an outgrowth of the pharyngeal wall prob homologous with the notochord of higher chordates [NL *Hemichordata*, group name, fr *hemi-* + *Chordata* chordates]

hemidemisemiquaver /,hemi,demi,semi'kwayvə/ *n* a musical note with the time value of ½ of a demisemiquaver

,hemi'hedral /-'heedrəl/ *adj, of a crystal* having half the faces required for complete symmetry – compare HOLOHEDRAL [*hemi-* + *-hedron*]

hemiola /,hemi'ohlə/ *n* a musical rhythmic alteration consisting of 3 beats in place of 2 or 2 beats in place of 3 [LL *hemiolia*, fr Gk *hēmiolia* ratio of 1½ to 1, fr *hēmi-* + *holos* whole – more at SAFE]

,hemi'plegia /-'pleej(y)ə/ *n* paralysis of (part of) 1 lateral half of the body [NL, fr MGk *hēmiplēgia* paralysis, fr Gk *hēmi-* + *-plēgia* -plegia] – **hemiplegic** /-jik/ *adj or n*

hemisphere /'hemi,sfiə/ *n* **1a** a half of the celestial sphere when divided into 2 halves by the horizon, the celestial equator, or the ecliptic **b** the northern or southern half of the earth divided by the equator or the eastern or western half divided by a meridian **2** either of the 2 half spheres formed by a plane that passes through the sphere's centre **3** CEREBRAL HEMISPHERE [ME *hemispere*, fr L *hemisphaerium*, fr Gk *hēmisphairion*, fr *hēmi-* + *sphairion*, dim. of *sphaira* sphere] – **hemispheric** /,hemi'sferik/, **hemispherical** *adj*

hemistich /'hemi,stik/ *n* half of a line of verse usu divided from the other half by a caesura [L *hemistichium*, fr Gk *hēmistichion*, fr *hēmi-* + *stichos* line, verse; akin to Gk *steichein* to go, walk – more at STAIR]

hemline /'hem,lien/ *n* the line formed by the lower hemmed edge of a garment, esp a dress

hemlock /'hemlok/ *n* **1** (a poison obtained from) a very tall plant of the carrot family or a related very poisonous plant **2** (the soft light wood of) any of a genus of evergreen coniferous trees of the pine family [ME *hemlok*, fr OE *hemlic*]

hemo- – see HEM-

hemp /hemp/ *n* **1** (marijuana, hashish, or a similar drug obtained from) a tall widely cultivated plant from which a tough fibre used esp for making rope is prepared **2** the fibre of hemp or (a plant yielding) a similar fibre (e g jute) [ME, fr OE *hænep*; akin to OHG *hanaf* hemp; both prob fr the source of Gk *kannabis* hemp] – **hempen** *adj*

'hemp ,nettle *n* any of a genus of hairy Old World plants of the mint family

'hem,stitch *vt or n* (to decorate with) drawnwork that consists of open spaces and embroidered groups of cross threads and is used esp on or next to the stitching line of hems

[1]**hen** /hen/ *n* **1a** a female bird, specif a domestic fowl (over a year old) **b** a female lobster, crab, fish, or other aquatic animal **2** an esp fussy woman – infml **3** *chiefly Scot* DEAR 1b – used to girls and women [ME, fr OE *henn*; akin to OE *hana* cock – more at CHANT]

[2]**hen** *adj* relating to or intended for women only ⟨*a ~ party*⟩

,hen and 'chickens *n* any of several plants with offsets, runners, or proliferous flowers

'hen,bane /-,bayn/ *n* a poisonous fetid Old World plant of the nightshade family that contains hyoscyamine and scopolamine [[1]*hen* + *bane*; fr its poison being fatal esp to fowl]

hence /hens/ *adv* **1** from this time; later than now **2** because of a preceding fact or premise ⟨*born at Christmas; ~ the name Noel*⟩ **3** from here; away – fml ⟨*go ~*⟩; sometimes + *from* ⟨*depart from ~*⟩; sometimes used as an interjection ⟨*~! Depart!*⟩ [ME *hennes, henne*, fr OE *heonan*; akin to OHG *hinnan* away, OE *hēr* here]

,hence'forth *adv* from this time or point on ⟨*promise never to get drunk ~*⟩

,hence'forward *adv* henceforth

henchman /'henchmən/ *n* **1** a trusted follower; a right-hand man **2** a follower whose support is chiefly for personal advantage [ME *hengestman* groom, fr *hengest* stallion (fr OE) + *man*; akin to OHG *hengist* gelding]

hendecasyllabic /,hendekəsi'labik/ *adj* consisting of (metrical lines of) 11 syllables [L *hendecasyllabus*, fr Gk *hendeka* eleven (fr *hen-*, *heis* one + *deka* ten)

+ *syllabē* syllable – more at SAME, TEN] – **hendecasyllabic** *n*, **hendecasyllable** /'hendekə,siləbl/ *n*

hendiadys /hen'die·ədis/ *n* the expression of an idea by the use of 2 independent words connected by *and* (e g *nice and warm* instead of *nicely warm*) [LL *hendiadys, hendiadyoin*, modif of Gk *hen dia dyoin* one through two]

henequen /'henikin/ *n* (a strong hard fibre obtained from the leaves of) a tropical American agave plant [Sp *henequén*]

henge /henj/ *n* a prehistoric monument consisting of a circular structure made of wood or stones [back-formation fr *Stonehenge*, a prehistoric stone monument near Salisbury in England]

'hen ,harrier *n* a common Eurasian hawk

¹henna /'henə/ *n* **1** an Old World tropical shrub or small tree with fragrant white flowers **2** a reddish brown dye obtained from the leaves of the henna plant and used esp on hair [Ar *ḥinnā'*]

²henna *vt* **hennaing; hennaed** to dye or tint (esp hair) with henna

henpecked /'hen,pekt/ *adj* cowed by persistent nagging ⟨~ *husband*⟩

henry /'henri/ *n, pl* **henrys, henries** the SI unit of electrical inductance ☞ PHYSICS [Joseph *Henry* †1878 US physicist]

,hen-'toed *adj* having the toes turned in

hep /hep/ *adj* **-pp-** ⁴HIP

heparin /'hepərin/ *n* a polysaccharide that is found esp in liver and is injected to slow the clotting of blood, esp in the treatment of thrombosis [ISV, fr Gk *hēpar* liver] – **heparinize** /-,niez/ *vt*

hepat-, hepato- *comb form* **1** liver ⟨hep *atoma*⟩ ⟨hepato*toxic*⟩ ⟨hepat*ectomy*⟩ **2** hepatic and ⟨hepato*biliary*⟩ [L, fr Gk *hēpat-, hēpato-*, fr *hēpat-, hēpar*]

hepatic /hi'patik/ *adj* of or resembling the liver [L *hepaticus*, fr Gk *hēpatikos*, fr *hēpat-, hēpar*; akin to L *jecur* liver]

hepatica /hi'patikə/ *n* any of a genus of plants of the buttercup family with lobed leaves and delicate flowers [NL, genus name, fr ML, liverwort, fr L, fem of *hepaticus*]

hepatitis /,hepə'tietəs/ *n, pl* **hepatitides** /-'titədeez/ (a condition marked by) inflammation of the liver: **a** INFECTIOUS HEPATITIS **b** SERUM HEPATITIS [NL]

Hepplewhite /'hepl,wiet/ *adj* of or being a late 18th-c English furniture style characterized by lightness, elegance, and graceful curves [George *Hepplewhite* †1786 E cabinet-maker]

hepta-, hept- *comb form* **1** seven ⟨hepta*meter*⟩ **2** containing 7 atoms, groups, or chemical equivalents in the molecular structure ⟨hept*ane*⟩ [Gk, fr *hepta* – more at SEVEN]

heptad /'heptad/ *n* a group or series of 7 [Gk *heptad-, heptas*, fr *hepta*]

heptagon /'heptəgən/ *n* a polygon of 7 angles and 7 sides ☞ MATHEMATICS [Gk *heptagōnos* heptagonal, fr *hepta* + *gōnia* angle – more at -GON] – **heptagonal** /hep'tagənl/ *adj*

heptameter /hep'tamitə/ *n* a line of verse consisting of 7 metrical feet

heptane /'heptayn/ *n* a hydrocarbon of the alkane series that occurs in petroleum and is used esp as a solvent and in determining octane numbers

heptarchy /'hep,tahki/ *n* a supposed confederacy of 7 Anglo-Saxon kingdoms of the 7th and 8th c

¹her /hə, ə; *strong* huh/ *adj* of her or herself, esp as possessor ⟨~ *house*⟩ ⟨~ *fuselage*⟩, agent ⟨~ *research*⟩, or object of an action ⟨~ *rescue*⟩ – used in titles of females ⟨~ *Majesty*⟩ [ME *hire*, fr OE *hiere*, gen of *hēo* she – more at HE]

²her *pron, objective case of* SHE – compare phrases at ME 1

herald /'herəld/ *n* **1a** an officer whose original duties of officiating at tournaments gave rise to other duties (e g recording names, pedigrees, and armorial bearings or tracing genealogies) **b** an official messenger between leaders, esp in war **c** an officer of arms ranking above a pursuivant and below a king of arms **2a** an official crier or messenger **b** sby or sthg that conveys news or proclaims ⟨*it was the lark, the* ~ *of the morn* – Shak⟩ **3** a harbinger, forerunner [ME, fr MF *hiraut*, fr an (assumed) Gmc compound whose first component is akin to OHG *heri* army, and whose second is akin to OHG *waltan* to rule – more at HARRY, WIELD] – **herald** *vt*

heraldic /hi'raldik/ *adj* of a herald or heraldry – **heraldically** *adv*

heraldry /'herəldri/ *n* **1** the system, originating in medieval times, of identifying individuals by hereditary insignia; *also* the practice of granting, classifying, and creating these **2** the study of the history, display, and description of heraldry and heraldic insignia **3** pageantry

herb /huhb/ *n* **1** a seed plant that does not develop permanent woody tissue and dies down at the end of a growing season **2** a plant (part) valued for its medicinal, savoury, or aromatic qualities ⟨*cultivated her* ~ *garden*⟩ [ME *herbe*, fr OF, fr L *herba*] – **herbal** *adj*

herbaceous /huh'bayshəs/ *adj* of, being, or having the characteristics of a (part of a) herb

herbaceous border *n* a permanent flower border of hardy, usu perennial, herbaceous plants

herbage /'huhbij/ *n* (the succulent parts of) herbaceous plants (e g grass), esp when used for grazing

herbal /'huhbl/ *n* a book about (the medicinal properties of) plants

'herbalist /-ist/ *n* sby who grows or sells herbs, esp for medicines

herbarium /huh'beəri·əm/ *n, pl* **herbaria** /-ri·ə/ (a place containing) a collection of dried plant specimens usu mounted and systematically arranged for reference

herbicide /'huhbi,sied/ *n* sthg used to destroy or inhibit plant growth [L *herba* + ISV *-cide*] – **herbicidal** /,huhbi'siedl/ *adj*

herbivore /'huhbivaw/ *n* a plant-eating animal ☞ FOOD [NL *Herbivora*, group of mammals, fr neut pl of *herbivorus* plant-eating, fr L *herba* + *-vorus* -vorous] – **herbivorous** /huh'bivərəs/ *adj*

herb Robert /'robət/ *n* a common geranium with small reddish purple flowers [prob fr *Robertus* (St Robert) †1067 F ecclesiastic]

herculean /,huhkyoo'lee·ən/ *adj* of extraordinary strength, size, or difficulty ⟨*a* ~ *task*⟩ [*Hercules*, Greco-Roman mythological hero, fr L, fr Gk *Hēraklēs*]

'Hercules ,beetle /'huhkyooleez/ *n* a very large S American beetle

¹herd /huhd/ *n* **1** a number of animals of 1 kind kept together or living as a group **2a** *sing or pl in constr* a group of people usu having a common bond – often derog ⟨*the* ~ *instinct*⟩ **b** *the* masses – derog ⟨*the*

common ~⟩ [ME, fr OE *heord*; akin to OHG *herta* herd, Gk *korthys* heap] – **herdlike** *adj*

[2]**herd** *vi* to assemble or move in a herd or group ~ *vt* **1** to keep or move (animals) together **2** to gather, lead, or drive as if in a herd ⟨~ed *his pupils into the hall*⟩

'herdsman /-mən/ *n* a manager, breeder, or tender of livestock

[1]**here** /hiə/ *adv* **1** in or at this place ⟨*turn* ~⟩ – often interjectional, esp in answering a roll call **2** at or in this point or particular ⟨~ *we agree*⟩ **3** to this place or position ⟨*come* ~⟩ **4** – used when introducing, offering, or drawing attention ⟨~ *she comes*⟩ ⟨~ *is the news*⟩ ⟨~, *take it*⟩ **5** – used interjectionally to attract attention ⟨~, *what's all this?*⟩ [ME, fr OE *hēr*; akin to OHG *hier* here, OE *hē* he] – **here goes** – used to express resolution at the outset of a bold act; infml – **here's to** – used when drinking a toast – **here, there, and everywhere** scattered lavishly about – **here we go again** the same distressing events are repeating themselves – **here you are** **1** here is what you wanted **2** you have arrived – **neither here nor there** of no consequence; irrelevant

[2]**here** *adj* **1** – used for emphasis, esp after a demonstrative ⟨*this book* ~⟩ ⟨*ask my son* ~⟩ **2** – used for emphasis between a demonstrative and the following noun; substandard ⟨*this* ~ *book*⟩

[3]**here** *n* this place or point ⟨*full up to* ~⟩

'herea,bouts /-ə,bowts/ *adv* in this vicinity

[1]**,here'after** /-'ahftə/ *adv* **1** after this **2** in some future time or state

[2]**,here'after** *n, often cap* **1** *the* future **2** an existence beyond earthly life

,here and 'now *n* *the* immediate present ⟨*lived in the* ~ *without regard for the future*⟩

,here and 'there *adv* **1** in one place and another **2** FROM TIME TO TIME

hereby /hiə'bie, 'hiə-/ *adv* by this means or pronouncement ⟨*I* ~ *declare her elected*⟩

hereditament /,heri'ditəmənt/ *n* (real) property that can be inherited [ML *hereditamentum*, fr LL *hereditare*, fr L *hered-, heres*]

hereditary /hi'redit(ə)ri/ *adj* **1a** genetically transmitted or transmissible from parent to offspring **b** characteristic of one's predecessors; ancestral ⟨~ *pride*⟩ **2a** received or passing by inheritance **b** having title through inheritance ⟨~ *peer*⟩ **3** traditional ⟨~ *enemy*⟩ **4** of inheritance or heredity – **hereditarily** *adv*

heredity /hi'rediti/ *n* **1** the sum of the qualities and potentialities genetically derived from one's ancestors **2** the transmission of qualities from ancestor to descendant through a mechanism lying primarily in the chromosomes [MF *heredité*, fr L *hereditat-, hereditas*, fr *hered-, heres* heir – more at HEIR]

Hereford /'herifəd/ *n* any of an English breed of red hardy beef cattle with white faces and markings [*Hereford*, county of England]

herein /hiə'rin/ *adv* in this – fml

,herein'after /-'ahftə/ *adv* in the following part of this writing or document – fml

hereof /hiə'rov/ *adv* of this – fml

hereon /hiə'ron/ *adv* on this – fml

heresiarch /hi'reezi,ahk/ *n* an originator or chief advocate of a heresy [LL *haeresiarcha*, fr LGk *hairesiarchēs*, fr *hairesis* + Gk *-archēs* -arch]

heresy /'herəsi/ *n* **1** (adherence to) a religious belief or doctrine contrary to or incompatible with an explicit church dogma **2** an opinion or doctrine contrary to generally accepted belief [ME *heresie*, fr OF, fr LL *haeresis*, fr LGk *hairesis*, fr Gk, action of taking, choice, sect, fr *hairein* to take]

heretic /'herətik/ *n* **1** a dissenter from established church dogma; *esp* a baptized member of the Roman Catholic church who disavows a revealed truth **2** one who dissents from an accepted belief or doctrine [ME *(h)eretik*, fr MF *(h)eretique*, fr LL *haereticus*, fr LGk *hairetikos*, fr Gk, able to choose, fr *hairein*] – **heretic, heretical** /hi'retikl/ *adj*, **heretically** *adv*

hereto /hiə'tooh/ *adv* to this matter or document – fml

heretofore /,hiətooh'faw/ *adv* up to this time; hitherto – fml

hereunder /hiə'rundə/ *adv* under or in accordance with this writing or document – fml

hereunto /,hiərun'tooh/ *adv* to this – fml

hereupon /,hiərə'pon/ *adv* **1** on this matter ⟨*if all are agreed* ~⟩ **2** immediately after this ⟨*let us* ~ *adjourn*⟩

herewith /hiə'widh/ *adv* **1** hereby **2** with this; enclosed in this – fml

heritable /'heritəbl/ *adj* **1** capable of being inherited **2** HEREDITARY 1a, 2a – **heritability** /,heritə'biləti/ *n*

heritage /'heritij/ *n* **1** sthg transmitted by or acquired from a predecessor; a legacy ⟨*a rich* ~ *of folklore*⟩ **2** a birthright ⟨*the* ~ *of natural freedom*⟩ [ME, fr MF, fr *heriter* to inherit, fr LL *hereditare*, fr L *hered-, heres* heir – more at HEIR]

heritor /'heritə/ *n* an inheritor

herl /huhl/ *n* a barb of a feather used in tying an artificial fishing fly [ME *herle*]

hermaphrodite /huh'mafrədiet/ *n* **1** an animal or plant having both male and female reproductive organs **2** sthg that is a combination of 2 usu opposing elements [ME *hermofrodite*, fr L *hermaphroditus*, fr Gk *hermaphroditos*, fr *Hermaphroditos*, mythological son of Hermes and Aphrodite who became joined in body with the nymph Salmacis] – **hermaphrodite** *adj*, **hermaphroditism** *n*, **hermaphroditic** /-,mafrə'dietik/ *adj*, **hermaphroditically** *adv*

hermaphrodite brig *n* a 2-masted vessel with square sails on the foremast and fore-and-aft sails on the after mast

hermeneutics /,huhmə'nyoohtiks/ *n pl but sing or pl in constr* (the study of) the principles and methodology of Biblical interpretation [Gk *hermēneutikē*, fr fem of *hermēneutikos* interpretative, fr *hermēneuein* to interpret, fr *hermēneus* interpreter] – **hermeneutic, hermeneutical** *adj*

hermetic /huh'metik/ *also* **hermetical** /-kl/ *adj* **1** *often cap* of or relating to the Gnostic and alchemical writings attributed to Hermes Trismegistus **2a** airtight ⟨~ *seal*⟩ **b** impervious to external influences **3** *often cap* abstruse, recondite – infml [NL *hermeticus*, fr *Hermet-, Hermes Trismegistus* (fr Gk *Hermēs trismegistos*, lit., Hermes thrice-greatest), legendary author of mystical & alchemical works; (2) fr the belief that Hermes Trismegistus invented a magic seal to keep vessels airtight] – **hermetically** *adv*

hermeticism /huh'metə,siz(ə)m/ *n, often cap* (adherence to) a system of ideas based on hermetic teachings – **hermeticist** *n*

hermetism /'huhmə,tiz(ə)m/ *n, often cap* hermeticism – **hermetist** *n*

hermit /'huhmit/ *n* **1** one who retires from society and lives in solitude, esp for religious reasons **2** a recluse [ME *eremite*, fr OF, fr LL *eremita*, fr LGk *erēmitēs*, fr Gk, adj, living in the desert, fr *erēmia* desert, fr *erēmos* lonely – more at RETINA] – **hermitism** *n*, **hermitic** /huh'mitik/ *adj*

'hermitage /-tij/ *n* **1** the habitation of one or more hermits **2** a secluded residence or private retreat; a hideaway

'hermit ˌcrab *n* any of numerous chiefly marine 10-legged crustaceans that have soft abdomens and occupy the empty shells of gastropod molluscs ☞ DEFENCE

hernia /'huhni·ə, -nyə/ *n, pl* **hernias, herniae** /-ni,ee/ a protrusion of (part of) an organ through a wall of its enclosing cavity (e g the abdomen) [L – more at YARN] – **hernial** *adj*, **herniated** /-ni,aytid/ *adj*

hero /'hiəroh/ *n, pl* **heroes 1a** a mythological or legendary figure often of divine descent endowed with great strength or ability **b** an illustrious warrior **c** a person, esp a man, admired for noble achievements and qualities (e g courage) **2** the principal male character in a literary or dramatic work [L *heros*, fr Gk *hērōs*] – **heroize** *vt*

heroic /hi'roh·ik/ *also* **heroical** /-kl/ *adj* **1** of or befitting heroes **2a** showing or marked by courage **b** grand, noble **3** of impressive size, power, or effect; potent **4** of heroic verse – **heroically** *adv*

heˌroic 'couplet *n* a rhyming couplet in iambic pentameter

heroics *n pl* **1** HEROIC VERSE **2** extravagantly grand behaviour or language

heˌroic 'verse *n* the verse form employed in epic poetry (e g the heroic couplet in English)

heroin /'heroh·in/ *n* a strongly physiologically addictive narcotic made from, but more potent than, morphine [fr *Heroin*, a trademark] – **heroinism** *n*

heroine /'heroh·in/ *n* **1a** a mythological or legendary woman having the qualities of a hero **b** a woman admired for her noble achievements and qualities, esp courage **2** the principal female character in a literary or dramatic work [L *heroina*, fr Gk *hērōinē*, fem of *hērōs*]

heroism /'heroh,iz(ə)m/ *n* heroic conduct or qualities; *esp* extreme courage

heron /'herən/ *n, pl* **herons,** *esp collectively* **heron** any of various long-necked long-legged wading birds with a long tapering bill, large wings, and soft plumage [ME *heiroun*, fr MF *hairon*, of Gmc origin; akin to OHG *heigaro* heron, Gk *krizein* to creak, OHG *scrīan* to scream]

'heronry /-ri/ *n* a place where herons breed

'hero ˌworship *n* **1** veneration of a hero **2** foolish or excessive admiration for sby – **hero-worship** *vt*, **hero-worshipper** *n*

herpes /'huhpeez/ *n* herpes simplex or a similar inflammatory virus disease of the skin [L, fr Gk *herpēs*, fr *herpein* to creep – more at SERPENT] – **herpetic** /-'petik/ *adj*

herpes simplex /'simpleks/ *n* a virus disease marked by groups of watery blisters on the skin or mucous membranes (e g of the mouth, lips, or genitals) [NL, lit., simple herpes]

herpes zoster /'zostə/ *n* shingles [NL, lit., girdle herpes]

herpet-, herpeto- *comb form* **1** reptile; reptiles ⟨herpeto*fauna*⟩ ⟨herpeto*logy*⟩ **2** herpes ⟨herpet*iform*⟩ [Gk *herpeton*, fr neut of *herpetos* creeping, fr *herpein*; (2) L *herpet-, herpes*]

herpetology /ˌhuhpi'toləji/ *n* zoology dealing with reptiles and amphibians – **herpetologist** *n*, **herpetologic** /-tə'lojik/, **herpetological** *adj*, **herpetologically** *adv*

Herr /heə/ *n, pl* **Herren** /'heərən, 'herən/ – used of a German-speaking man as a title equivalent to *Mr* [G]

herrenvolk /'herən,folk/ *n, often cap* a master race; *specif* the German people according to the Nazis [G]

herring /'hering/ *n, pl* **herring,** *esp for different types* **herrings** a N Atlantic food fish that is preserved in the adult state by smoking or salting [ME *hering*, fr OE *hæring*; akin to OHG *hārinc* herring]

¹'herringˌbone /-ˌbohn/ *n* (sthg arranged in) a pattern made up of rows of parallel lines with any 2 adjacent rows slanting in opposite directions; *esp* a twilled fabric decorated with this pattern

²herringbone *vt* to make a herringbone pattern on ~ *vi* to ascend a (snow) slope by pointing the toes of the skis out

'herringˌbone ˌstitch *n* a needlework stitch that forms a zigzag pattern

'herring ˌgull *n* a large gull of the northern hemisphere that as an adult is largely white with a blue-grey mantle and dark wing tips ☞ LIFE CYCLE

hers /huhz/ *pron, pl* **hers** that which or the one who belongs to her – used without a following noun as a pronoun equivalent in meaning to the adjective *her*; compare phrases at MINE 2

herself /hə'self; *medially often* ə-/ *pron* **1** that identical female person or creature – compare SHE 1, ONESELF; used reflexively ⟨*she considers* ~ *lucky*⟩, for emphasis ⟨*she* ~ *did it*⟩ ⟨*Britain* ~⟩, or in absolute constructions ⟨~ *an orphan, she understood the situation*⟩ **2** her normal self ⟨*isn't quite* ~⟩

hertz /huhts/ *n, pl* **hertz** the SI unit of frequency equal to 1 cycle per second ☞ PHYSICS [Heinrich *Hertz* †1894 G physicist]

Hertzian wave /'huhtsi·ən, -syən/ *n* a radio wave of wavelength ranging from less than 1mm to more than 1km [Heinrich *Hertz*]

he's /hiz, eez, iz; *strong* heez/ he is; he has

hesitant /'hezit(ə)nt/ *adj* tending to hesitate; irresolute – **hesitance, hesitancy** *n*, **hesitantly** *adv*

hesitate /'hezitayt/ *vi* **1** to hold back, esp in doubt or indecision **2** to be reluctant or unwilling *to* **3** to stammer [L *haesitatus*, pp of *haesitare* to stick fast, hesitate, fr *haesus*, pp of *haerēre* to stick; akin to Lith *gaišti* to loiter] – **hesitater** *n*, **hesitatingly** *adv*, **hesitative** *adj*, **hesitation** /ˌhezi'taysh(ə)n/ *n*

Hesperian /hes'piəri·ən/ *adj* western, occidental – poetic [L *Hesperia*, the west, fr Gk, fr fem of *hesperios* of the evening, western, fr *hesperos* evening – more at WEST]

hesperidium /ˌhespə'ridi·əm/ *n, pl* **hesperidia** /-di·ə/ an orange or similar fruit with a leathery rind and a pulp divided into sections [NL, orange, fr L *Hesperides*, mythological nymphs guarding a garden where golden apples grow, fr Gk]

Hesperus /'hespərəs/ *n* EVENING STAR [L, fr Gk *Hesperos*]

hessian /'hesi·ən/ *n* **1** a coarse heavy plain-weave

fabric, usu of jute or hemp, used esp for sacking **2** a lightweight material resembling hessian and used chiefly in interior decoration [*Hesse*, region or state in SW Germany]

'Hessian ˌfly *n* a small fly that is destructive to wheat in America

hetaera /hi'tee·ərə/ *n, pl* **hetaeras, hetaerae** /-'tiəˌree/ a courtesan, esp in ancient Greece [Gk *hetaira*, lit., companion, fem of *hetairos*] – **hetaerism** *n*

heter-, hetero- *comb form* other; different; abnormal ⟨hetero*morphic*⟩ [MF or LL; MF, fr LL, fr Gk, fr *heteros*; akin to Gk *heis* one – more at SAME]

hetero /'hetəroh/ *n, pl* **heteros** a heterosexual

ˌheterochro'matic /-kroh'matik/ *adj* **1** of or having different colours **2** made up of various wavelengths or frequencies **3** of heterochromatin – **heterochromatism** /-'krohmətiz(ə)m/ *n*

ˌhetero'chromatin /-'krohmətin/ *n* densely staining chromatin that appears as nodules in or along chromosomes and contains relatively few genes [G]

'heteroˌclite /-ˌkliet/ *adj* **1** deviating from common forms or rules **2** *of a noun* irregular in declension [MF or LL; MF, fr LL *heteroclitus*, fr Gk *heteroklitos*, fr *heter-* + *klinein* to lean, inflect – more at [1]LEAN] – **heteroclite** *n*

ˌhetero'cyclic /-'siklik, -'sie-/ *adj* of, characterized by, or being a ring composed of atoms of more than 1 kind [ISV] – **heterocyclic** *n*, **heterocycle** /'hetərohˌsiekl/ *n*

'heteroˌdox /-ˌdoks/ *adj* **1** contrary to or different from established doctrines or opinions, esp in matters of religion ⟨*a ~ sermon*⟩ **2** holding opinions or doctrines which are not orthodox [LL *heterodoxus*, fr Gk *heterodoxos*, fr *heter-* + *doxa* opinion – more at DOXOLOGY] – **heterodoxy** *n*

'heteroˌdyne /-ˌdien/ *adj, of a radio signal, receiver, etc* combining 2 similar radio frequencies to produce a lower frequency or beat – **heterodyne** *vt*

ˌheteroga'metic /-gə'metik/ *adj* forming 2 kinds of germ cells of which one produces male offspring and the other female offspring – **heterogamete** /ˌhetəroh'gameet/ *n*

heterogamy /ˌhetə'rogəmi/ *n* (the condition of having) sexual reproduction involving fusion of unlike gametes – **heterogamous** *adj*

heterogeneous /ˌhetərə'jeeni·əs, -nyəs/ *adj* consisting of dissimilar ingredients or constituents; disparate [ML *heterogeneus*, *heterogenus*, fr Gk *heterogenēs*, fr *heter-* + *genos* kind – more at KIN] – **heterogeneously** *adv*, **heterogeneousness** *n*, **heterogeneity** /-rohjə'nee·əti/ *n*

ˌhetero'genesis /-'jenəsis/ *n* ALTERNATION OF GENERATIONS [NL] – **heterogenetic** /-jə'netik/ *adj*

heterogony /ˌhetə'rogəni/ *n* ALTERNATION OF GENERATIONS

heterograft /'hetərohˌgrahft/ *n* a graft of tissue taken from a donor of one species and grafted into a recipient of another species

heterologous /ˌhetə'roləgəs/ *adj* derived from a different species ⟨*~ transplants*⟩ – **heterologously** *adv*

heteromorphic /ˌhetəroh'mawfik/, **heteromorphous** /-fəs/ *adj* exhibiting diversity of form or forms ⟨*~ pairs of chromosomes*⟩ [ISV] – **heteromorphism** *n*

heteronomy /ˌhetə'ronəmi/ *n* subjection to the law or domination of another; *esp* a lack of moral freedom or self-determination – compare AUTONOMY [*heter-* + *-nomy* (as in *autonomy*)] – **heteronomous** *adj*

heteronym /'hetərohˌnim/ *n* any of 2 or more words spelt alike but different in meaning and pronunciation (e g *sow* the noun and *sow* the verb) – **heteronymous** /ˌhetə'ronimәs/ *adj*

ˌhetero'sexual /-'seksyoo(ə)l, -sh(ə)l/ *adj or n* (of or being) sby having a sexual preference for members of the opposite sex – compare HOMOSEXUAL [ISV] – **heterosexually** *adv*, **heterosexuality** /-ˌseksyoo'aləti, -ˌsekshoo-/ *n*

heterosis /ˌhetə'rohsis/ *n* a marked vigour or capacity for growth often shown by crossbred animals or plants [NL] – **heterotic** /-'rotik/ *adj*

heterotrophic /ˌhetəroh'trohfik/ *adj* needing complex organic compounds for essential metabolic processes – compare AUTOTROPHIC – **heterotrophically** *adv*, **heterotroph** /'hetərohˌtrohf/ *n*

ˌhetero'zygote /-'ziegoht, -'zigoht/ *n* an animal, plant, or cell having dissimilar alleles (e g 1 dominant and 1 recessive) of a particular gene – compare HOMOZYGOTE – **heterozygous** /-'zigəs/ *adj*, **heterozygosis** /-zie'gohsis/ *n*, **heterozygosity** /-zie'gosəti/ *n*

ˌhet 'up *adj* highly excited; upset – infml [*het*, dial. past of *heat*]

[1]heuristic /ˌhyooə'ristik, hoy-/ *adj* **1** furthering investigation but otherwise unproved or unjustified ⟨*a ~ assumption*⟩ **2** of problem-solving techniques that proceed by trial and error ⟨*a ~ computer program*⟩ [G *heuristisch*, fr NL *heuristicus*, fr Gk *heuriskein* to discover; akin to OIr *fūar* I have found] – **heuristically** *adv*

[2]heuristic *n* the study or practice of heuristic method

hew /hyooh/ *vb* **hewed; hewed, hewn** /hyoohn/ *vt* **1** to strike, chop, or esp fell with blows of a heavy cutting instrument ⟨~ed *off a branch*⟩ ⟨~ed *down the tree*⟩ **2** to give form or shape to (as if) with heavy cutting blows – often + *out* ⟨*she* ~ed *out a career for herself*⟩ ~ *vi* to make cutting blows [ME *hewen*, fr OE *hēawan*; akin to OHG *houwan* to hew, L *cudere* to beat] – **hewer** *n*

[1]hex /heks/ *vb, NAm vi* to practise witchcraft ~ *vt* to affect as if by an evil spell; jinx [PaG *hexe*, fr G *hexen*, fr *hexe* witch] – **hexer** *n*

[2]hex *n, NAm* **1** a spell, jinx **2** a witch

hexa-, hex- *comb form* **1** six ⟨hexamerous⟩ **2** containing 6 atoms, groups, or chemical equivalents in the molecular structure ⟨hexane⟩ ⟨hexa*valent*⟩ [Gk, fr *hex* six – more at SIX]

hexad /'heksad/ *n* a group or series of 6 [LL *hexad-*, *hexas*, fr Gk, fr *hex*] – **hexadic** /hek'sadik/ *adj*

hexadecimal /ˌheksə'desiml/ *adj* of or being a number system with a base of 16

hexagon /'heksəgən/ *n* a polygon of 6 angles and 6 sides ☞ MATHEMATICS [Gk *hexagōnon*, neut of *hexagōnos* hexagonal, fr *hexa-* + *gōnia* angle – more at -GON] – **hexagonal** /hek'sagənl/ *adj*, **hexagonally** *adv*

hexagram /'heksəgram/ *n* a 6-pointed star drawn by extending the sides of a regular hexagon [ISV]

ˌhexa'hedron /-'heedrən/ *n, pl* **hexahedrons** *also* **hexahedra** /-rə/ a polyhedron of 6 faces [LL, fr Gk *hexaedron*, fr neut of *hexaedros* of six surfaces, fr *hexa-* + *hedra* seat – more at SIT]

hexameter /hek'samitə/ *n* a line of verse consisting of 6 metrical feet [L, fr Gk *hexametron*, fr neut of *hexametros* having six measures, fr *hexa-* + *metron* measure – more at MEASURE]

hexane /'heksayn/ *n* a volatile liquid hydrocarbon of the alkane series, found in petroleum [ISV]

hexapod /'heksə,pod/ *n or adj* (an insect) having 6 feet [Gk *hexapod-, hexapous* having six feet, fr *hexa-* + *pod-, pous* foot – more at FOOT]

hexose /'heksohs, -sohz/ *n* a monosaccharide (e g glucose) containing 6 carbon atoms in the molecule [ISV]

hexyl /'heks(ə)l/ *n* an alkyl radical C_6H_{13} derived from a hexane [ISV]

[1]**hey** /hay/ *interj* – used esp to call attention or to express inquiry, surprise, or exultation [ME]

[2]**hey** *n* [3]HAY

heyday /'hay,day/ *n* the period of one's greatest vigour, prosperity, or fame [*heyday*, interj expressing usu joy or exultation, fr earlier *heyda*, alter. of [1]*hey*]

hey presto /,hay 'prestoh/ *interj* – used as an expression of triumph or satisfaction on completing or demonstrating sthg; *esp* used by conjurers about to reveal the outcome of a trick

hi /hie/ *interj* – used esp to attract attention or, esp in the USA, as a greeting [ME *hy*]

[1]**hiatus** /hie'aytəs/ *n* **1a** a break, gap **b** an (abnormal) anatomical gap or passage **2a** a lapse in continuity **b** the occurrence of 2 vowel sounds together without pause or intervening consonantal sound [L, fr *hiatus*, pp of *hiare* to yawn – more at YAWN]

[2]**hiatus** *adj* **1** involving a hiatus **2** *of a hernia* having a part that protrudes through the oesophageal opening of the diaphragm

hibernal /hie'buhnl/ *adj* of or occurring in winter

hibernate /'hiebənayt/ *vi* **1** to pass the winter in a torpid or resting state – compare AESTIVATE **2** to be or become inactive or dormant [L *hibernatus*, pp of *hibernare* to pass the winter, fr *hibernus* of winter; akin to L *hiems* winter, Gk *cheimōn*] – **hibernator** *n*, **hibernation** /,hiebə'naysh(ə)n/ *n*

Hibernian /hie'buhni·ən, -nyən/ *adj* (characteristic) of Ireland – chiefly poetic [L *Hibernia* Ireland] – **Hibernian** *n*

hibiscus /hie'biskəs/ *n* any of a genus of herbaceous plants, shrubs, or small trees of the mallow family with large showy flowers [NL, genus name, fr L, marshmallow]

[1]**hiccup** *also* **hiccough** /'hikup/ *n* **1** a spasmodic involuntary inhalation with closure of the glottis accompanied by a characteristic sharp sound **2** an attack of hiccuping – usu pl but sing. or pl in constr **3** *chiefly Br* a brief interruption or breakdown; a hitch ⟨*a mistake due to a* ~ *in the computer*⟩ – infml [imit]

[2]**hiccup** *also* **hiccough** *vi* **-p-, -pp-** to make a hiccup or hiccups

hick /hik/ *n, chiefly NAm* an unsophisticated provincial person [*Hick*, nickname for *Richard*] – **hick** *adj*

[1]**hickey** /'hiki/ *n, chiefly NAm* a gadget, object [origin unknown]

[2]**hickey** *n, chiefly NAm* a lovebite [origin unknown]

hickory /'hikəri/ *n* (the usu tough pale wood of) any of a genus of N American hardwood trees of the walnut family that often have sweet edible nuts [short for obs *pokahickory*, fr *pawcohiccora* food prepared from pounded nuts (in some Algonquian language of Virginia)] – **hickory** *adj*

hidalgo /hi'dalgoh/ *n, pl* **hidalgos** *often cap* a member of the lower nobility of Spain [Sp]

hidden /'hid(ə)n/ *adj* **1** out of sight; concealed **2** obscure, unexplained

[1]**hide** /hied/ *n* any of various former English units of land area based on the amount of land that would support 1 free family and dependants [ME, fr OE *higid*]

[2]**hide** *vb* **hid** /hid/; **hidden** /hid(ə)n/, **hid** *vt* **1** to put out of sight; conceal **2** to keep secret ⟨hid *the news from his parents*⟩ **3** to screen from view ⟨*house* hidden *by trees*⟩ ~ *vi* **1** to conceal oneself **2** to remain out of sight – often + *out* [ME *hiden*, fr OE *hȳdan*; akin to Gk *keuthein* to conceal, OE *hȳd* hide, skin] – **hider** *n*

[3]**hide** *n, chiefly Br* a camouflaged hut or other shelter used for observation, esp of wildlife or game

[4]**hide** *n* the raw or dressed skin of an animal – used esp with reference to large heavy skins [ME, fr OE *hȳd*; akin to OHG *hūt* hide, L *cutis* skin, Gk *kytos* hollow vessel] – **hide or/nor hair** the least vestige or trace – infml ⟨*hadn't seen* hide or hair *of his wife for 20 years*⟩

'hide-and-,seek *n* a children's game in which one player covers his/her eyes and then hunts for the other players who have hidden themselves

'hide,away /-ə,way/ *n* a retreat, hideout

'hide,bound /-,bownd/ *adj* narrow or inflexible in character

hideous /'hidi·əs/ *adj* **1** offensive to the senses, esp the sight; exceedingly ugly **2** morally offensive; shocking [alter. of ME *hidous*, fr OF, fr *hisde, hide* terror] – **hideously** *adv*, **hideousness** *n*

hideout /'hied,owt/ *n* a place of refuge or concealment

'hidey-,hole, hidy-hole /'hiedi/ *n* a hideout – infml [alter. of earlier *hiding-hole*]

[1]**hiding** /'hieding/ *n* a state or place of concealment ⟨*go into* ~⟩

[2]**hiding** *n* a beating, thrashing ⟨*gave him a good* ~⟩; *also* a severe defeat – infml [fr gerund of *hide* (to flog), fr [4]*hide*]

hidrosis /hi'drohsis/ *n* sweating [NL, fr Gk *hidrōsis*, fr *hidroun* to sweat, fr *hidrōs* sweat] – **hidrotic** /-'drotik/ *adj*

hie /hie/ *vb* **hying, hieing** *archaic* to hurry [ME *hien*, fr OE *hīgian* to strive, hasten; akin to OSw *hikka* to pant, Skt *śīghra* quick]

hier-, hiero- *comb form* sacred; holy ⟨hiero*logy*⟩ [LL, fr Gk, fr *hieros* – more at IRE]

hierarchical /,hie·ə'rahkikl, ,hiə-/, **hierarchic** *adj* of or arranged in a hierarchy – **hierarchically** *adv*

hierarchy /'hie·ərahki, 'hiə-/ *n* **1** (church government by) a body of clergy organized according to rank, specif the bishops of a province or nation **2** a graded or ranked series [ME *ierarchie*, fr MF *ierarchie, hierarchie*, fr ML *hierarchia*, fr LGk, fr Gk *hierarchēs* high priest]

,hie'ratic /-'ratik/ *adj* **1** of or written in a simplified form of ancient Egyptian hieroglyphics **2** (characteristic) of a priest, esp in dignity or stateliness of manner [L *hieraticus* priestly, fr Gk *hieratikos*, deriv of *hieros*] – **hieratically** *adv*

hieroglyph /'hie·ərə,glif, 'hiərə-/ *n* a pictorial character used in hieroglyphics – compare IDEOGRAM [F *hiéroglyphe,* fr MF, back-formation fr *hiéroglyphique*]

ˌhiero'glyphic /-fik/, **hieroglyphical** /-kl/ *adj* **1** written in, constituting, belonging to, or inscribed with a system of writing mainly in hieroglyphs **2** difficult to decipher [MF *hieroglyphique,* fr LL *hieroglyphicus,* fr Gk *hieroglyphikos,* fr *hier-* + *glyphein* to carve – more at [2]CLEAVE] – **hieroglyphically** *adv*

hieroglyphics *n pl but sing or pl in constr* **1** a system of hieroglyphic writing; *specif* the picture script of various ancient peoples (e g the Egyptians) **2** sthg like hieroglyphics, esp in being difficult to decipher

hierophant /'hie·ərə,fant/ *n* **1** a priest in ancient Greece responsible for initiation rites, esp to Eleusis **2** an expositor, interpreter – fml [LL *hierophanta,* fr Gk *hierophantēs,* fr *hier-* + *phainein* to show] – **hierophantic** /ˌhie·ərə'fantik/ *adj*

hi-fi /'hie ˌfie, ˌhie 'fie/ *n* **1** HIGH FIDELITY **2** equipment for the high-fidelity reproduction of sound *USE* infml

higgledy-piggledy /ˌhigldi 'pigldi/ *adv* in confusion; topsy-turvy – infml [origin unknown] – **higgledy-piggledy** *adj*

[1]high /hie/ *adj* **1a** extending upwards for a considerable or above average distance ⟨*rooms with ~ ceilings*⟩ **b** situated at a considerable height above a base (e g the ground) ⟨*a ~ plateau*⟩ **c** *of physical activity* extending to or from, or taking place at a considerable height above, a base (e g the ground or water) ⟨*~ diving*⟩ **d** having a specified elevation; tall ⟨*6 feet ~*⟩ – often in combination ⟨*sky*-high⟩ **2** at the period of culmination or fullest development ⟨*~ summer*⟩ ⟨*~ Gothic*⟩ **3** elevated in pitch ⟨*a ~ note*⟩ **4** relatively far from the equator ⟨*~ latitudes*⟩ **5** *of meat, esp game* slightly decomposed or tainted **6a** exalted in character; noble ⟨*~ principles*⟩ **b** good, favourable ⟨*has a very ~ opinion of her*⟩ **7** of greater degree, amount, cost, value, or content than average ⟨*~ prices*⟩ ⟨*food ~ in iron*⟩ **8a** foremost in rank, dignity, or standing ⟨*~ officials*⟩ **b** critical, climactic ⟨*the ~ point of the novel is the escape*⟩ **c** marked by sublime or heroic events or subject matter ⟨*~ tragedy*⟩ **9** forcible, strong ⟨*~ winds*⟩ **10a** showing elation or excitement ⟨*feelings ran ~*⟩ **b** intoxicated by alcohol or a drug **11** advanced in complexity, development, or elaboration ⟨*~er nerve centres*⟩ ⟨*~er mathematics*⟩ ⟨*~ technology*⟩ **12** *of a vowel* CLOSE 2b **13** *of a gear* designed for fast speed **14** *of words* expressive of anger **15** rigidly traditionalist ⟨*a ~ Tory*⟩; *specif* HIGH CHURCH [ME, fr OE *hēah*; akin to OHG *hoh* high, L *cacumen* point, top] – **highly** *adv* – **on one's high horse** stubbornly or disdainfully proud ⟨*gave up trying to reason with him when he got* on his high horse⟩

[2]high *adv* at or to a high place, altitude, or degree ⟨*threw the ball ~ in the air*⟩

[3]high *n* **1** a region of high atmospheric pressure **2** a high point or level; a height ⟨*sales have reached a new ~*⟩ **3** *NAm* TOP 4 – **on high** in or to a high place, esp heaven

high altar *n* the principal altar in a church

ˌhigh and 'dry *adv* **1** out of the water **2** in a helpless or abandoned situation; without recourse

ˌhigh and 'low *adv* everywhere ⟨*hunted ~ but could not find the ring*⟩

ˌhigh-and-'mighty *adj* arrogant, imperious

highball /'hie,bawl/ *n* a drink of spirits (e g whisky) and water or a carbonated beverage, served with ice in a tall glass

ˌhigh'born /-'bawn/ *adj* of noble birth

'highˌboy /-ˌboy/ *n, NAm* TALLBOY 1

'highˌbrow /-ˌbrow/ *adj* dealing with, possessing, or having pretensions to superior intellectual and cultural interests or activities ⟨*a ~ radio programme*⟩ – **highbrow** *n,* **highbrowed** *adj,* **highbrowism** *n*

high camp *adj or n* (marked by) a sophisticated form of camp style or behaviour

'high ˌchair *n* a child's chair with long legs, a footrest, and usu a feeding tray

ˌHigh 'Church *adj* tending, in the Anglican church, towards Roman Catholicism in liturgy, ceremonial, and dogma – **High Churchman** *n*

ˌhigh-'class *adj* superior, first-class

ˌhigh-'coloured *adj* FLORID 2

ˌhigh com'mand *n* the supreme headquarters of a military force

ˌhigh com'missioner *n* a principal commissioner; *esp* an ambassadorial representative of one Commonwealth country stationed in another

ˌHigh 'Court *n* the lower branch of the Supreme Court of Judicature of England and Wales ☞ LAW

High Court of Justiciary *n* the superior criminal court of Scotland dealing with treason, murder, rape, and all cases involving heavy penalties, and with appeal to the Court of Criminal Appeal ☞ LAW

ˌHigh 'Dutch *n* **1** HIGH GERMAN **2** Dutch of the Netherlands rather than Afrikaans

ˌhigh-'energy *adj* yielding a relatively large amount of energy when undergoing hydrolysis ⟨*~ phosphate bonds in ATP*⟩

higher criticism *n* the critical study of biblical writings, esp to determine their sources – compare LOWER CRITICISM – **higher critic** *n*

ˌhigher edu'cation *n* education beyond the secondary level, at a college or university

ˌhigher-'up *n* a person occupying a superior rank or position – infml; compare HIGH-UP

highest common factor *n* the largest integer or the polynomial of highest degree that is an exact divisor of each of 2 or more integers or polynomials

high explosive *n* an explosive (e g TNT) that explodes with extreme rapidity and has a shattering effect

ˌhighfa'lutin /-fə'loohtin/ *adj* pretentious, pompous ⟨*written in a ~ style*⟩ – infml [perh fr *high* + alter. of *fluting,* prp of *flute*]

ˌhigh 'fashion *n* **1** the latest in fashion or design **2** HAUTE COUTURE

high fidelity *n* the faithful reproduction of sound – **high-fidelity** *adj*

ˌhigh 'finance *n* (the major financial institutions engaged in) large and complex financial operations

ˌhigh-'flier, high-flyer *n* a person who shows extreme ambition or outstanding promise

ˌhigh-'flown *adj* **1** excessively ambitious or extravagant **2** excessively elaborate or inflated; pretentious ⟨*~ rhetoric*⟩

ˌhigh-'flying *adj* **1** rising to considerable height **2** marked by extravagance, pretension, or excessive ambition

ˌhigh 'gear *n* TOP GEAR 2

,High 'German *n* German as used in S and central Germany

,high-'grade *adj* **1** of superior grade or quality ⟨~ *bonds*⟩ **2** being near the upper or most favourable extreme of a specified range

,high-'handed *adj* overbearingly arbitrary – **high-handedly** *adv*, **high-handedness** *n*

,High 'Holiday *n* either of 2 important Jewish holidays: **a** ROSH HASHANAH **b** YOM KIPPUR

,high 'jinks /jingks/ *n pl* high-spirited fun and games

'high ,jump *n* (an athletic field event consisting of) a jump for height over a bar suspended between uprights – **high jumper** *n*, **high jumping** *n* – **for the high jump** about to receive a severe reprimand or punishment

highland /'hieland/ *n* high or mountainous land – usu pl with sing. meaning – **highland** *adj*, **highlander** *n*

Highland *adj* **1** of the Highlands of Scotland **2** relating to or being a member of a shaggy long-haired breed of hardy beef cattle – **Highlander** *n*

,Highland 'fling *n* a lively solo Scottish folk dance

'Highlands *n pl* *the* northwest mountainous part of Scotland

,high-'level *adj* **1** occurring, done, or placed at a high level **2** of high importance or rank ⟨~ *diplomats*⟩ **3** *of a computer language* having each word equal to several machine code instructions and being easily understandable to humans

'high ,life *n* luxurious living associated with the rich

¹'high,light /-,liet/ *n* **1** the lightest spot or area (e g in a painting or photograph) **2** an event or detail of special significance or interest ⟨~s *from the week's news*⟩ **3** a contrasting brighter part in the hair or on the face that reflects or gives the appearance of reflecting light

²'high,light *vt* **1a** to focus attention on; emphasize **b** to emphasize (e g a figure) with light tones in painting, photography, etc **2** to give highlights to – **highlighter** *n*

highly /'hieli/ *adv* **1** to a high degree; extremely ⟨~ *delighted*⟩ **2** with approval; favourably ⟨*speak ~ of someone*⟩

,highly-'strung, high-strung *adj* extremely nervous or sensitive

,high 'mass *n, often cap H&M* an elaborate sung mass

,high-'minded *adj* having or marked by elevated principles and feelings – **high-mindedly** *adv*, **high-mindedness** *n*

Highness /'hienis/ *n* – used as a title for a person of exalted rank (e g a king or prince) ['HIGH + -NESS]

,high-'octane *adj* having a high octane number and hence good antiknock properties ⟨~ *petrol*⟩

,high-'pitched *adj* **1** having a high pitch ⟨*a ~ voice*⟩ **2** marked by or exhibiting strong feeling; agitated ⟨*a ~ election campaign*⟩

high polymer *n* a polymer (e g polystyrene) of high molecular weight

,high-'powered *also* **high-power** *adj* having great drive, energy, or capacity; dynamic ⟨~ *executives*⟩

,high-'pressure *adj* **1** having or involving a (comparatively) high pressure, esp greatly exceeding that of the atmosphere **2a** using, involving, or being aggressive and insistent sales techniques ⟨~ *selling*⟩ **b** imposing or involving severe strain or tension ⟨~ *occupations*⟩

,high 'priest *n* **1** a chief priest, esp of the ancient Jewish Levitical priesthood **2** the head or chief exponent of a movement – **high priesthood** *n*

,high 'priestess *n* **1** a chief priestess **2** the female head or chief exponent of a movement

,high re'lief *n* sculptural relief in which at least half of the circumference of the design stands out from the surrounding surface – compare BAS-RELIEF

,high-'rise *adj* (situated in a building) constructed with a large number of storeys ⟨~ *flats*⟩ ⟨~ *blocks*⟩ – **high rise** *n*

'high,road /-,rohd/ *n* **1** *the* easiest course *to* ⟨*the ~ to success*⟩ **2** *chiefly Br* a main road

'high ,school *n* **1** *chiefly Br* secondary school; *esp* GRAMMAR SCHOOL 2 – now chiefly in names **2** *NAm* a school usu for pupils aged about 15-18

,high 'sea *n* the part of a sea or ocean outside territorial waters – usu pl with sing. meaning

,high-'sounding *adj* pompous, but meaningless

,high-'speed *adj* **1** (adapted to be) operated at high speed **2** relating to the production of photographs by very short exposures

,high-'spirited *adj* characterized by a bold or lively spirit; *also* highly-strung ⟨*a ~ horse*⟩ – **high-spiritedly** *adv*, **high-spiritedness** *n*

'high,spot /-,spot/ *n* the most important or enjoyable feature of sthg ⟨*the ~ of his political career*⟩

'high-,stepping *adj, of a horse* lifting the feet high – **high-stepper** *n*

'high ,street *n, Br* a main or principal street, esp containing shops

,high-'strung *adj* highly-strung

high table *n, often cap H&T* a dining-room table, usu on a platform, used by the masters and fellows of a British college, or at a formal dinner or reception (e g by distinguished guests)

'high,tail /-,tayl/ *vi, chiefly NAm* to move away at full speed – often + *it*

,high 'tea *n, Br* a fairly substantial early evening meal (at which tea is served) – compare TEA 4b

,high 'tech /tek/ *n* **1** a style of interior decoration involving the use of industrial building materials, fittings, etc **2** high technology – **high tech** *adj*

,high-'tension *adj* having a high voltage; *also* relating to apparatus to be used at high voltage

,high 'tide *n* **1** (the time of) the tide when the water reaches its highest level **2** the culminating point; the climax

,high-'toned *adj* high in social, moral, or intellectual quality; dignified

,high 'treason *n* TREASON 2

,high-'up *n* a person of high rank or status – infml; compare HIGHER-UP – **high-up** *adj*

,high 'water *n* HIGH TIDE 1

,high-'water ,mark *n* **1** a mark showing the highest level reached by the surface of a body of water **2** the highest point or stage

'high,way /-,way/ *n* **1** a public way; *esp* a main direct road **2** a busbar

,highway 'code *n, often cap H&C, Br* the official code of rules and advice for the safe use of roads

'highwayman /-mən/ *n* a (mounted) robber of travellers on a road, esp in former times

hijack, high-jack /'hiejak/ *vt* **1a** to stop and steal from (a vehicle in transit) **b** to seize control of, and often divert, (a means of transport) by force ⟨*gunmen* ~ed *a plane bound for Frankfurt*⟩ **2** to steal, rob, or kidnap as if by hijacking [origin unknown] – **hijack** *n*, **hijacker** *n*

[1]**hike** /hiek/ *vi* to go on a hike [*hike*, vt, to jerk, pull, perh akin to [1]*hitch*] – **hiker** *n*

[2]**hike** *n* **1** a long walk in the country, esp for pleasure or exercise **2** *chiefly NAm* an increase or rise ⟨*a new wage* ~⟩

hike up *vt, chiefly NAm* to move, pull, or raise with a sudden movement ⟨hiked *himself* up *on the wall*⟩ – infml

hilar /'hielə/ *adj* of, relating to, or located near a hilum

hilarious /hi'leəri·əs/ *adj* marked by or causing hilarity [irreg fr L *hilarus, hilaris* cheerful, fr Gk *hilaros*] – **hilariously** *adv*, **hilariousness** *n*

hilarity /hi'larəti/ *n* mirth, merriment

Hilary term /'hiləri/ *n* the Oxford university term beginning in January [St *Hilary* †367 F bishop, whose feast day is 13 January]

[1]**hill** /hil/ *n* **1** a usu rounded natural rise of land lower than a mountain **2** an artificial heap or mound (e g of earth) **3** an esp steep slope [ME, fr OE *hyll*; akin to L *collis* hill, *culmen* top] – **hilly** *adj* – **over the hill** past one's prime; too old

[2]**hill** *vt* to draw earth round the roots or base of (plants)

hillbilly /'hil,bili/ *n, chiefly NAm* a person from a remote or culturally unsophisticated area [[1]*hill* + *Billy*, nickname for *William*]

hill climb *n* a race for cars, motorcycles, etc up a hill side

'**hill,fort** /-,fawt/ *n* a fortified hilltop characteristic of Iron Age settlements in W Europe

hillock /'hilək/ *n* a small hill – **hillocky** *adj*

hilt /hilt/ *n* a handle, esp of a sword or dagger [ME, fr OE; akin to OE *healt* lame – more at [1]HALT] – **to the hilt** completely

hilum /'hieləm/ *n, pl* **hila** /-lə/ **1a** a scar on a seed (e g a bean) marking the point of attachment of the ovule to its stalk **b** the nucleus of a starch grain **2** a notch, opening, etc in a bodily part, usu where a vessel, nerve, etc enters [NL, fr L, trifle]

him /him/ *pron, objective case of* HE – compare phrases at ME 1 [ME, fr OE, dat of *hē* he – more at HE]

himation /hi'mati,on/ *n* an ancient Greek rectangular garment of cloth draped about the body and over the left shoulder [Gk, fr *hennynai* to clothe – more at WEAR]

himself /him'self; *medially often* im-/ *pron* **1a** that identical male person or creature – compare HE 1, ONESELF; used reflexively ⟨*he considers* ~ *lucky*⟩, for emphasis ⟨*he* ~ *did it*⟩, or in absolute constructions ⟨~ *unhappy, he understood the situation*⟩ **b** – used reflexively when the sex of the antecedent is unspecified ⟨*everyone must fend for* ~⟩ **2** his normal self ⟨*isn't quite* ~ *today*⟩ **3** *chiefly NAm* oneself – used with *one* ⟨*one should wash* ~⟩

Hinayana /,heenə'yahnə/ *n* Theravada [Skt *hīnayāna*, lit., lesser vehicle] – **Hinayanist** *n*, **Hinayanistic** /-yah'nistik/ *adj*

[1]**hind** /hiend/ *n, pl* **hinds** *also* **hind** a female (red) deer – compare HART [ME, fr OE; akin to OHG *hinta* hind, Gk *kemas* young deer]

[2]**hind** *adj* situated at the back or behind; rear [ME, prob back-formation fr OE *hinder*, adv, behind; akin to OHG *hintar*, prep, behind]

'**hind,brain** /-,brayn/ *n* (the cerebellum, pons, and other parts of the adult brain that develop from) the rear of the 3 primary divisions of the embryonic vertebrate brain

[1]**hinder** /'hində/ *vt* **1** to retard or obstruct the progress of; hamper **2** to restrain, prevent – often + *from* [ME *hindren*, fr OE *hindrian*; akin to OE *hinder* behind] – **hinderer** *n*

[2]**hinder** /'hiendə/ *adj* situated behind or at the rear; posterior [ME, fr OE *hinder*, adv]

Hindi /'hindi/ *n* **1** a literary and official Indic language of N India **2** a complex of Indic dialects of N India *USE* ☞ ALPHABET, LANGUAGE [Hindi *hindī*, fr *Hind* India, fr Per] – **Hindi** *adj*

hindmost /'hiend,mohst/ *adj* furthest to the rear; last

hindquarter /,heind'kwawtə, 'heind,kwawtə/ *n* **1** the back half of a side (of the carcass) of a quadruped **2** *pl* the hind legs (and adjoining structures) of a quadruped

hindrance /'hindrəns/ *n* **1** the action of hindering **2** an impediment, obstacle

hindsight /'hiend,siet/ *n* the grasp or picture of a situation that one has after it has occurred – compare FORESIGHT

Hindu, *archaic* **Hindoo** /'hindooh, hin'dooh/ *n* an adherent of Hinduism [Per *Hindū* inhabitant of India, fr *Hind* India] – **Hindu** *adj*

'**Hindu,ism** /-,iz(ə)m/ *n* the dominant religion of India which involves belief in the illusory nature of the physical universe and in cycles of reincarnation, and is associated with a caste system of social organization

[1]**Hindustani** /,hindooh'stahni, -'stani/ *n* **1** a group of Indic dialects of N India and Pakistan of which Hindi and Urdu are considered the main written forms **2** a form of speech allied to Urdu but less divergent from Hindi [Hindi *Hindūstānī*, fr Per *Hindūstān* India]

[2]**Hindustani** *adj* of Hindustan, its people, or Hindustani

[1]**hinge** /'hinj/ *n* **1a** a jointed or flexible device on which a swinging part (e g a door or lid) turns **b** a flexible joint in which bones are held together by ligaments **c** a small piece of thin gummed paper used in fastening a postage stamp in an album **2** a point or principle on which sthg turns or depends [ME *heng*; akin to MD *henge* hook, OE *hangian* to hang]

[2]**hinge** *vt* to attach by or provide with hinges ~ *vi* **1** to hang or turn (as if) on a hinge ⟨*door* ~s *outwards*⟩ **2** to depend or turn *on* a single consideration or point

[1]**hinny** /'hini/ *n* a hybrid offspring of a stallion and a female ass – compare MULE [L *hinnus*]

[2]**hinny, hinnie** *n, Scot & N Eng* DEAR 1b [E dial., var of *honey*]

[1]**hint** /hint/ *n* **1** a brief practical suggestion or piece of advice ⟨~s *for home decorators*⟩ **2** an indirect or veiled statement; an insinuation **3** a slight indication or trace; a suggestion – usu + *of* ⟨*a* ~ *of irony in her voice*⟩ [prob alter. of obs *hent* (act of seizing), fr *hent* (to seize)]

[2]**hint** *vt* to indicate indirectly or by allusion ⟨~ed *that something was up*⟩ ~ *vi* to give a hint – **hint at** to imply or allude to (sthg)

hinterland /'hintə,land/ *n* **1** a region lying inland from a coast **2** a region remote from urban or cultural centres [G, fr *hinter* hinder + *land*]

[1]**hip** /hip/ *n* the ripened fruit of a rose [ME *hipe*, fr OE *hēope*; akin to OHG *hiafo* hip]

[2]**hip** *n* **1a** the projecting region at each side of the lower or rear part of the mammalian trunk formed by the pelvis and upper part of the thigh **b** HIP JOINT **2** an external angle between 2 adjacent sloping sides of a roof ☞ ARCHITECTURE [ME, fr OE *hype*; akin to OHG *huf* hip, L *cubitum* elbow, *cubare* to lie, Gk *kybos* cube, die, OE *hēah* high – more at HIGH]

[3]**hip** *interj* – usu used to begin a cheer ⟨~ ~ *hooray*⟩ [origin unknown]

[4]**hip** *adj* **-pp-** keenly aware of or interested in the newest developments; *broadly* trendy – infml [alter. of *hep*, of unknown origin] – **hipness** /-nis/ *n*

'**hip,bone** /-,bohn/ *n* INNOMINATE BONE ☞ ANATOMY

'**hip ,flask** *n* a flat flask, usu for holding spirits, carried in a hip pocket

'**hip ,joint** *n* the joint between the femur and the hipbone ☞ ANATOMY

hipp-, hippo- *comb form* horse ⟨hippo*phagous*⟩ [L, fr Gk, fr *hippos* – more at EQUINE]

hipped /hipt/ *adj* having hips, esp of a specified kind – often in combination ⟨*broad*-hipped⟩

hippie, hippy /'hipi/ *n* a usu young person, esp during the 1960s, who rejected established mores, advocated a nonviolent ethic, and, in many cases, used psychedelic drugs; *broadly* a long-haired unconventionally dressed young person [[4]*hip* + *-ie*] – **hippiehood** *n*, **hippie** *adj*, **hippiedom** /-d(ə)m/ *n*

hippo /'hipoh/ *n, pl* **hippos** a hippopotamus – infml

hippocampus /,hipoh'kampəs/ *n, pl* **hippocampi** /-pie/ a curved elongated ridge of nervous tissue inside each hemisphere of the brain [NL, fr Gk *hippokampos* sea horse, fr *hipp-* + *kampos* sea monster] – **hippocampal** *adj*

Hippocratic oath /,hipə'kratik/ *n* an oath embodying a code of medical ethics [*Hippocratic* fr LL *Hippocraticus*, fr *Hippocrates* †*ab*377 BC Gk physician]

hippodrome /'hipədrohm/ *n* **1** an arena for equestrian performances or circuses **2** a music hall, theatre, etc – esp in names [MF, fr L *hippodromos*, fr Gk, fr *hipp-* + *dromos* racecourse – more at DROMEDARY]

hippopotamus /,hipə'potəməs/ *n, pl* **hippopotamuses, hippopotami** /-mie/ any of several large plant-eating 4-toed chiefly aquatic mammals, with an extremely large head and mouth, very thick hairless skin, and short legs [L, fr Gk *hippopotamos*, fr *hipp-* + *potamos* river, fr *petesthai* to fly, rush – more at FEATHER]

-hippus /-hipəs/ *comb form* (→ *n*) horse – in generic names, esp of extinct ancestors of the horse ⟨*Eo*hippus⟩ [NL, fr Gk *hippos* – more at EQUINE]

hipster /'hipstə/ *n* **1** sby who is unusually aware of and interested in new and unconventional patterns, esp in jazz **2** *pl* trousers that start from the hips rather than the waist [(1) [4]*hip*; (2) [2]*hip*]

hircine /'huhsien/ *adj* goatlike [L *hircinus*, fr *hircus* he-goat]

[1]**hire** /hie·ə/ *n* **1** payment for the temporary use of sthg **2** hiring or being hired [ME, fr OE *hȳr*; akin to MD *hūre* hire]

[2]**hire** *vt* **1a** to engage the services of for a set sum ⟨~ *a new crew*⟩ **b** to engage the temporary use of for an agreed sum ⟨~ *a hall*⟩ **2** to grant the services of or temporary use of for a fixed sum ⟨~ *themselves out*⟩ – **hirer** *n*

'**hireling** /-ling/ *n* a person who works for payment, esp for purely mercenary motives – derog

,**hire 'purchase** *n, chiefly Br* a system of paying for goods by instalments ⟨*bought their car on* ~⟩ ⟨*signed a* ~ *agreement*⟩

hirsute /huh'syooht/ *adj* covered with (coarse stiff) hairs [L *hirsutus*; akin to L *horrēre* to bristle, tremble – more at HORROR] – **hirsuteness** *n*

hir'su,tism /-,tiz(ə)m/ *n* excessive growth of hair

[1]**his** /iz; *strong* hiz/ *adj* **1** of him or himself, esp as possessor ⟨~ *house*⟩ ⟨~ *tail*⟩, agent ⟨~ *writings*⟩, or object of an action ⟨~ *confirmation*⟩ – used in titles of males ⟨~ *Majesty*⟩ **2** *chiefly NAm* one's – used with *one* ⟨*one's duty to* ~ *public*⟩ [ME, fr OE, gen of *hē* he]

[2]**his** /hiz/ *pron, pl* **his** that which or the one who belongs to him – used without a following noun as a pronoun equivalent in meaning to the adjective *his*; compare phrases at MINE 2

Hispanic /hi'spanik/ *adj* (characteristic) of Spain, Portugal, or Latin America [L *hispanicus*, fr *Hispania* Iberian peninsula, Spain] – **Hispanicism** /-ni,siz(ə)m/ *n*, **Hispanicist** /-ni,sist/ *n*, **Hispanicize** /-ni,siez/ *vt*

hispid /'hispid/ *adj* covered with bristles, stiff hairs, etc ⟨*a* ~ *plant*⟩ – compare PUBESCENT 2 [L *hispidus*; prob akin to L *horrēre*] – **hispidity** /hi'spidəti/ *n*

hiss /his/ *vi* to make a sharp voiceless sound like a prolonged *s*, esp in disapproval ~ *vt* **1** to show disapproval of by hissing **2** to utter with a hiss [ME *hissen*, of imit origin] – **hiss** *n*

hist /hist/ *interj* – used to attract attention [origin unknown]

hist- /hist-/, **histo-** *comb form* tissue ⟨histo*logy*⟩ [F, fr Gk *histos* mast, loom beam, web, fr *histanai* to cause to stand]

histamine /'histəmin/ *n* an amine that is a neurotransmitter in the autonomic nervous system and whose release under certain conditions causes an allergic reaction [ISV] – **histaminic** /,histə'minik/ *adj*

histidine /'histədeen, -din/ *n* an amino acid that is a chemical base and is found in most proteins [ISV]

histiocyte /'histi·əsiet/ *n* a macrophage (that is not capable of independent movement) [Gk *histion* web (dim. of *histos*) + ISV *-cyte*] – **histiocytic** /,histi·ə'sitik/ *adj*

histochemistry /,histoh'kemistri/ *n* histology in which chemical techniques are used in preparing tissues for microscopy [ISV] – **histochemical** /-'kemikl/ *adj*

,**histocom,pati'bility** /-kəm,patə'biləti/ *n* a state of mutual tolerance that allows some tissues to be grafted effectively onto others

histogram /'histəgram/ *n* a diagram consisting of a series of adjacent rectangles, the height and width of each rectangle being varied to represent each of 2 variables ☞ STATISTICS [*histo*ry + *-gram*]

histology /his'toləji/ *n* (anatomy that deals with) the organization and microscopic structure of animal and plant tissues [F *histologie*, fr *hist-* + *-logie* -logy]

– **histologist** *n*, **histological** /ˌhistəˈlojikl/ *adj*, **histologic** *adj*, **histologically** *adv*

histone /ˈhistohn/ *n* any of various proteins found associated with DNA in chromosomes [ISV]

histopathology /ˌhistohpəˈtholəji/ *n* (pathology concerned with) the tissue changes accompanying disease [ISV] – **histopathologist** *n*

historian /hiˈstawri·ən/ *n* a student or writer of history

historic /hiˈstorik/ *adj* **1** (likely to be) famous or important in history ⟨*a* ~ *occasion*⟩ **2** *of a tense* expressive of past time

hiˈstorical /-kl/ *adj* **1a** of or based on history **b** used in the past **2** famous in history **3** diachronic ⟨~ *linguistics*⟩ **4** dealing with or representing the events of history ⟨*a* ~ *novel*⟩ – **historically** *adv*

historicism /hiˈstorisiz(ə)m/ *n* a theory that emphasizes the importance of history as a standard of value or determiner of events – **historicist** *adj or n*

historicity /ˌhistəˈrisəti/ *n* historical authenticity

historico- *comb form* historical; historical and ⟨*historicosocial*⟩

historic present *n* the present tense used to relate past events

historiographer /ˌhistoriˈogrəfə/ *n* a usu official writer of history [MF *historiographeur*, fr LL *historiographus*, fr Gk *historiographos*, fr *historia* + *graphein* to write – more at CARVE]

ˌhistoriˈography /-fi/ *n* **1** the writing of history **2** the principles of historical writing – **historiographic** /hiˌstawri·əˈgrafik/ *adj*, **historiographical** *adj*

history /ˈhistəri/ *n* **1** (a chronological record of) significant past events BRITISH **2a** a treatise presenting systematically related natural phenomena ⟨*a* ~ *of British birds*⟩ **b** an account of sby's medical, sociological, etc background **3** a branch of knowledge that records the past **4a** past events ⟨*that's all* ~ *now*⟩ **b** an unusual or interesting past ⟨*this goblet has a* ~⟩ **c** previous treatment, handling, or experience [L *historia*, fr Gk, inquiry, history, fr *histōr*, *istōr* knowing, learned; akin to Gk *eidenai* to know – more at WIT]

histrionic /ˌhistriˈonik/ *adj* **1** of actors, acting, or the theatre **2** deliberately affected; theatrical [LL *histrionicus*, fr L *histrion-*, *histrio* actor, alter. of *hister*, fr Etruscan] – **histrionically** *adv*

histrionics *n pl but sing or pl in constr* deliberate display of emotion for effect

1hit /hit/ *vb* **-tt-; hit** *vt* **1a** to reach (as if) with a blow; strike ⟨~ *the ball*⟩ ⟨~ *by an attack of flu*⟩ **b** to make sudden forceful contact with ⟨*the car* ~ *the tree*⟩ **2a** to bring into contact ⟨~ *the stick against the railings*⟩ **b** to deliver, inflict ⟨~ *a severe blow*⟩ **3** to have a usu detrimental effect or impact on ⟨~ *hard by the drought*⟩ **4** to discover or meet, esp by chance ⟨*I seem to have* ~ *a snag*⟩ **5a** to reach, attain ⟨*prices* ~ *a new high*⟩ **b** to cause a propelled object to strike (e g a target), esp for a score in a contest **c** *of a batsman* to score (runs) in cricket; *also* to score runs off a ball bowled by (a bowler) **6** to indulge in, esp excessively ⟨~ *the bottle*⟩ **7** to arrive at or in ⟨~ *town*⟩ **8** to rob **9** *chiefly NAm* to kill ~ *vi* **1** to strike a blow **2a** to come into forceful contact with sthg **b** to attack ⟨*wondered where the enemy would* ~ *next*⟩ **c** to happen or arrive, esp with sudden or destructive force ⟨*the epidemic* ~ *that summer*⟩ **3** to come, esp by chance; arrive at or find sthg – + *on* or *upon* ⟨~ *on a solution*⟩ *USE* (*vt 6 & 7*) infml; (*vt 8 & 9*) slang [ME *hitten*, fr ON *hitta* to meet with, hit] – **hit it off** to get along well – infml – **hit the jackpot** to be or become notably and unexpectedly successful – **hit the nail on the head** to be exactly right – **hit the road** to start on a journey – infml – **hit the roof** to give vent to a burst of anger or angry protest – infml

2hit *n* **1** a blow; *esp* one that strikes its target **2a** a stroke of luck **b** sthg (e g a popular tune) that enjoys great success ⟨*the song was a big* ~⟩ **3** a telling remark **4** a robbery **5** *chiefly NAm* an act of murder *USE* (*4 & 5*) slang

ˌhit-and-ˈmiss *adj* hit-or-miss

ˌhit-and-ˈrun *adj* **1** being or involving a driver who does not stop after causing damage or injury **2** involving rapid action and immediate withdrawal ⟨~ *raids on coastal towns*⟩

1hitch /hich/ *vt* **1** to move by jerks **2** to catch or fasten (as if) by a hook or knot ⟨~ed *his horse to the top rail of the fence*⟩ – often + *up* **3** to solicit and obtain (a free lift) in a passing vehicle ~ *vi* to hitch-hike – infml [ME *hytchen*] – **hitcher** *n*

2hitch *n* **1** a sudden movement or pull; a jerk ⟨*gave his trousers a* ~⟩ **2** a sudden halt or obstruction; a stoppage ⟨*a* ~ *in the proceedings*⟩ **3** a knot used for a temporary fastening **4** *NAm* a period usu of military service – slang

ˈhitchˌhike /-ˌhiek/ *vi* to travel by obtaining free lifts in passing vehicles – **hitchhiker** *n*

1hither /ˈhidhə/ *adv* to or towards this place – fml [ME *hider*, *hither*, fr OE *hider*; akin to Goth *hidre* hither, L *citra* on this side – more at HE]

2hither *adj* NEAR 3a ⟨*the* ~ *side of the hill*⟩ – fml

ˌhither and ˈthither *adv* in all directions

ˌhitherˈto /-ˈtooh/ *adv* up to this time; until now – fml

Hitlerian /hitˈliəri·ən/ *adj* of Adolf Hitler or his regime in Germany [Adolf *Hitler* †1945 G political leader]

Hitlerism /ˈhitləriz(ə)m/ *n* the nationalistic and totalitarian principles and policies of Adolf Hitler – **Hitlerite** /-iet/ *n or adj*

hit off *vt* to represent or imitate accurately

ˌhit-or-ˈmiss *adj* showing a lack of planning or forethought; haphazard

hit out *vi* **1** to aim violent blows *at* **2** to aim angry verbal attacks *at*; speak violently *against*

ˈhit paˌrade *n* a group or listing of popular songs ranked in order of the number of records of each sold

Hittite /ˈhitiet/ *n* a member of a people that established an empire in Asia Minor and Syria in the 2nd millennium BC; *also* their language [Heb *Ḥittī*, fr Hitt *hatti*] – **Hittite** *adj*

1hive /hiev/ *n* **1** (a structure for housing) a colony of bees **2** a place full of busy occupants ⟨*a* ~ *of industry*⟩ [ME, fr OE *hȳf*; akin to Gk *kypellon* cup, OE *hēah* high – more at HIGH]

2hive *vt* to collect into a hive ~ *vi*, *of bees* to enter and take possession of a hive

hive off *vt* to separate from a group or larger unit; *specif* to assign (e g assets or responsibilities) to a subsidiary company or agency ~ *vi* **1** to become separated from a group; form a separate or subsidiary unit **2** to leave without warning ⟨hived off *at 4.30*⟩ – infml

hives /hievz/ *n pl but sing or pl in constr* urticaria [origin unknown]

ho /hoh/ *interj* **1** – used esp to attract attention to sthg specified ⟨*land* ~⟩ **2** – used to express surprise or triumph; compare HO-HO [ME]

¹hoar /haw/ *adj* hoary – fml [ME *hor*, fr OE *hār*; akin to OHG *hēr* hoary]

²hoar *n* FROST 1b [ME, hoariness, fr *hor*, adj]

¹hoard /hawd/ *n* **1** an often secret supply (e g of money or food) stored up for preservation or future use **2** a cache of valuable archaeological remains [ME *hord*, fr OE; akin to Gk *kysthos* vulva, OE *hȳdan* to hide]

²hoard *vb* to lay up a hoard (of)

hoarding /ˈhawding/ *n* **1** a temporary fence put round a building site **2** *Br* a large board designed to carry outdoor advertising [earlier *hourd, hoard*, prob deriv of OF *hourt* scaffold, platform]

ˈhoar,frost /-,frost/ *n* FROST 1b

hoarse /haws/ *adj* **1** rough or harsh in sound; grating ⟨~ *voice*⟩ **2** having a hoarse voice ⟨~ *with shouting*⟩ [ME *hos, hors*, fr OE *hās*; akin to OE *hāt* hot – more at HOT] – **hoarsely** *adv*, **hoarseness** *n*, **hoarsen** /ˈhaws(ə)n/ *vb*

hoary /ˈhawri/ *adj* **1a** grey or white with age; *also* grey-haired **b** having greyish or whitish hair, down, or leaves **2** impressively or venerably old; ancient **3** hackneyed ⟨*a* ~ *old joke*⟩ – **hoariness** *n*

¹hoax /hohks/ *vt* to play a trick on; deceive [prob contr of *hocus*] – **hoaxer** *n*

²hoax *n* an act of deception; a trick ⟨*the warning about the bomb was a* ~⟩

¹hob /hob/ *n, dial Br* a goblin, elf [ME *hobbe*, fr *Hobbe*, nickname for *Robert*]

²hob *n* **1** a ledge near a fireplace on which sthg may be kept warm **2** a horizontal surface either on a cooker or installed as a separate unit that contains heating areas on which pans are placed [origin unknown]

hobbit /ˈhobit/ *n* a member of an imaginary race of genial hole-dwellers that resemble small human beings [figure in novels by J R R Tolkien †1973 E writer]

¹hobble /ˈhobl/ *vi* to move along unsteadily or with difficulty; *esp* to limp ~ *vt* **1** to cause to limp **2** to fasten together the legs of (e g a horse) to prevent straying; fetter [ME *hoblen*; akin to MD *hobbelen* to turn, roll; (2) prob alter. of earlier *hopple*]

²hobble *n* **1** a hobbling movement **2** sthg (e g a rope) used to hobble an animal

hobbledehoy /,hobldiˈhoy/ *n* an awkward gawky youth [origin unknown]

¹hobby /ˈhobi/ *n* a leisure activity or pastime engaged in for interest or recreation [short for *hobbyhorse*] – **hobbyist** *n*

²hobby *n* a small Old World falcon that catches small birds while in flight [ME *hoby*, fr MF *hobé*]

ˈhobby,horse /-,haws/ *n* **1** a figure of a horse fastened round the waist of a performer in a morris dance **2a** a toy consisting of an imitation horse's head attached to one end of a stick on which a child can pretend to ride **b** a toy horse on a merry-go-round **c** ROCKING HORSE **3** a topic to which one constantly returns [arch *hobby* (small light horse), fr ME *hoby, hobyn*, prob fr *Hobbin*, nickname for *Robin*]

hobgoblin /,hobˈgoblin/ *n* **1** a goblin **2** a bugbear; BOGEY 2

hobnail /ˈhob,nayl/ *n* a short large-headed nail for studding shoe soles [arch *hob* (peg or stake used as a target in games)] – **hobnailed** *adj*

hobnob /ˈhob,nob/ *vi* **-bb-** **1** to associate familiarly **2** to talk informally ***USE*** usu + *with*; infml [fr the obs phrase *drink hobnob* (to drink alternately to one another)]

hobo /ˈhoh,boh/ *n, pl* **hoboes** *also* **hobos** **1** *chiefly NAm* a migratory worker **2** *NAm* TRAMP 1 [perh fr *ho, bo* (assumed to be form of greeting between tramps)]

Hobson's choice /ˈhobs(ə)nz/ *n* an apparently free choice which offers no real alternative [prob fr Thomas *Hobson* †1631 E liveryman, who required every customer to take the horse nearest the door]

¹hock /hok/ *n* the tarsal joint of the hind limb of a horse or related quadruped that corresponds to the ankle in human beings ☞ ANATOMY [ME *hoch, hough*, fr OE *hōh* heel; akin to ON *hāsin* hock, Skt *kaṅkāla* skeleton]

²hock *n, often cap, chiefly Br* a dry to medium-dry or sometimes sweet white table wine produced in the Rhine valley [modif of G *hochheimer*, fr *Hochheim*, town in Germany]

³hock *n* **1** ¹PAWN 2 ⟨*got her watch out of* ~⟩ **2** DEBT 1 ⟨*in* ~ *to the bank*⟩ **USE** infml [D *hok* pen, prison]

⁴hock *vt* to pawn – infml

hockey /ˈhoki/ *n* **1** a game played on grass between 2 teams of usu 11 players whose object is to direct a ball into the opponents' goal with a stick that has a flat-faced blade **2** *NAm* ICE HOCKEY [perh fr MF *hoquet* shepherd's crook, dim. of *hoc* hook, of Gmc origin; akin to OE *hōc* hook]

hocus /ˈhohkəs/ *vt* **-ss-** (*NAm* **-s-, -ss-**) to drug (e g an animal or its drink) [obs *hocus*, n, short for *hocus-pocus*]

,hocus-ˈpocus /ˈpohkəs/ *n* **1** SLEIGHT OF HAND **2** pointless activity or words, usu intended to obscure or deceive [prob fr *hocus pocus*, imitation Latin phrase used by jugglers]

hod /hod/ *n* **1** a trough mounted on a pole handle for carrying mortar, bricks, etc **2** a coal scuttle; *specif* a tall one used to shovel fuel directly onto a fire [prob fr MD *hodde*; akin to MHG *hotte* cradle, ME *schuderen* to shudder]

hodgepodge /ˈhoj,poj/ *n, chiefly NAm* a hotchpotch [by alter.]

ˈHodgkin's di,sease /ˈhojkinz/ *n* a malignant disease characterized by progressive anaemia with enlargement of the lymph glands, spleen, and liver [Thomas *Hodgkin* †1866 E physician]

¹hoe /hoh/ *n* any of various implements, esp one with a long handle and flat blade, used for tilling, weeding, etc [ME *howe*, fr MF *houe*, of Gmc origin; akin to OHG *houwa* mattock, *houwan* to hew – more at HEW]

²hoe *vi* to work with a hoe ~ *vt* **1** to weed or cultivate (land or a crop) with a hoe **2** to remove (weeds) by hoeing

ˈhoe,down /-,down/ *n, chiefly NAm* a gathering featuring square dances

¹hog /hog/ *n* **1** a hogg **2** a warthog or other wild pig **3** *Br* a castrated male pig raised for slaughter **4** *chiefly NAm* a domestic (fully grown) pig **5** a selfish, gluttonous, or filthy person – slang; compare ROAD HOG [ME *hogge*, fr OE *hogg*]

²hog *vt* **-gg-** **1** to cut (a horse's mane) off or short **2**

A TABLE OF MAJOR EVENTS IN WORLD HISTORY

	EUROPE	NEAR EAST AND NORTH AFRICA	ASIA	AFRICA, AMERICAS AND PACIFIC
	10,000 BC Last great Ice Age ends. **6000–4000** *Farming spreads using 'slash and burn' techniques to farm in forests.*	**9000–8000** *Domestication of animals and cultivation of crops.* **8350–7350** *Foundation of Jericho – 1st walled town.* c.**7000** *Copper ores used in Anatolia.* c.**6000** *1st known pottery and woollen textiles.* c.**5000** *Agricultural settlements in Mesopotamia and Egypt.* c.**4000** *Bronze casting; 1st use of plough.* *Irrigation allows surplus of crops – prosperity – basis of civilization.*	**6000** *Rice cultivation (Thailand).*	**10,000** Last Ice Age ends. **9000** Hunters spread south through the Americas.
3500	c.**3200–2000** Early Cycladic civilization in the Aegean.	c.**3500** *Invention of sail (Egypt).* *Invention of plough and wheel (Mesopotamia).* c.**3200** Beginning of Old Kingdom in Egypt. c.**3100** Menes unites Egypt – 1st dynasty. *Lunar calendar – Sumer.* *Pictographic writing – Sumer.*	**3500** *Earliest Chinese city (Lung-shan culture).* c.**3400** *Cart developed in Caucasus.*	
3000		c.**3000** *Development of major cities – Sumer.* *Solar calendar.* Gilgamesh, legendary Sumerian king. *Cuneiform writing – Sumer.*	**3000** *Bronze used in Thailand.* c.**2750** Growth of civilizations in the Indus valley.	c.**3000** *Arable farming in central Africa.* *Pottery develops in America.*
2500	c.**2500–1550** *Minoan Bronze Age culture in Crete.* *Use of sail on seagoing vessels.* c.**2400** *Stonehenge.*	**2371–2230** Akkadian Empire – 1st empire in world history. *Use of plough spreads to rain-watered lands, bringing civilization to Turkey, Canaan.* c.**2200** Babylonian Empire. Middle Kingdom begins in Egypt. Hebrews first go to Canaan.	c.**2500** *Domestication of horse (steppes).* *Farming in Yellow Valley.*	c.**2500** Sahara begins to dry out. *Maize cultivation in Mexico.*
2000	c.**1600–1300** *Mycenean Greece.*	**1800** Assyrian state founded. **1750** Hammurabi founds Babylonian Empire; issues 1st code of laws. c.**1600** Hyksos invaders rule Egypt. **1567–1090** New Kingdom in Egypt.	c.**2000** *Cities at Mohenjo-Daro, Harappa.* c.**1600** Shang Dynasty in China. *Chinese calligraphy develops.*	c.**2000** *Metalworking in Peru.* Settlement of Melanesia by Indonesians.
1500	c.**1350** Sack of Troy. c.**1100** Dorians invade Greece with iron weapons. **1090** Etruscans enter Italy.	c.**1370** Akhnaton tries to develop worship of one God, the Sun, in Egypt. c.**1200** Jewish Exodus from Egypt; beginning of Jewish religion. c.**1100** *Alphabetic writing developed by Phoenicians.* Solomon – height of Israel's power.	**1500–1200** *Rig Veda and other Vedic Hymns composed.* **1027** Chou overthrows Shang Dynasty in China. *Silk weaving and astronomy develop under Chou – also use of copper coins.*	c.**1150** *Olmec civilization in Mexico.*
1000		c.**840** Rise of Urartu – rival of Assyria. **814** Phoenician colony at Carthage.	**850** *First Upanishads written.* *Integers and '0' invented in India.*	c.**900** Kingdom of Kush (Nubia).
800	**776** *1st Olympic Games in Greece.* **753** Traditional date for foundation of Rome. c.**750** Greek cities found colonies around Mediterranean. *Iliad and Odyssey.* *Hesiod's poetry first written down.*	**750** Amos, 1st great prophet in Israel. **721–705** Assyrian Empire at military height.	c.**800** Aryans expand southwards in India. Kingdoms on Ganges. **771** Collapse of Chou Dynasty.	

☞ BRITISH

EUROPE	NEAR EAST AND NORTH AFRICA	ASIA	AFRICA, AMERICAS AND PACIFIC	
c.**700** *Architects build in stone.* c.**700–450** *Hallstatt culture in Western Europe – iron tools, mixed farming.* **650** Rise of 'tyrants' in Greek cities. *Coins used in Greece.* *Greek lyric poetry develops.* **621** Draco's legal code.	c.**700** Scythian horsemen spread to east Europe. **663** Assyrian conquest of Egypt – *iron-working spreads.* **650** *1st coins used in Lydia (modern Turkey).* **612** Sack of Nineveh by Babylonians. Collapse of Assyrian power.	**650** *Iron technology in China.*		700
594 *Thales of Miletus – beginning of Greek philosophy.* **510** Roman Republic. c.**505** Democracy fully established in Athens.	**586** Fall of Jerusalem – Jews taken to Babylon. **550** Cyrus the Great ends Babylonian Empire – founds Persian Empire. Zoroastrianism becomes official religion. **540** Deutero-Isaiah, prophet of exile. **521** Darius the Great rules from Nile to Indus.	**528** Death of Mahavira founder of Jain Sect. **520** Death of Lao-Tzu founder of Taoism.		600
c.**500** Solon's legal code. **500–100** *La Tène Celtic culture in Europe.* **490–480** Battles of Marathon, Salamis, and Plataea prevent Persian domination of Greece. **479–338** *Height of 'classical' culture in Greece.* *Drama: Aeschylus, Sophocles.* *Medicine: Hippocrates.* *Philosophy: Socrates, Plato, Aristotle.* **449** Twelve Tables of Roman law first written. **431–404** Pelopponesian War between Athens and Sparta.	**486–465** Xerxes, son of Darius I, rules Persian Empire.	c.**500** Sinhalese (Aryans) reach Ceylon – caste system in India. **500–200** *Bhagavad Gita written.* **486** Death of Buddha. **479** *Death of Confucius.* **403–221** 'Warring States' in China.	c.**500** *First hieroglyphics in Mexico.* *Iron making spreads to sub-Saharan Africa.* *Beginning of Nok culture in Nigeria.*	500
356 Philip II king of Macedon. **338** Battle of Chaeronaea: Macedon controls Greece.	Alexander the Great conquers Asia Minor and Egypt (**332**) Persia (**330**) reaches India (**329**) dies (**323**). Empire divided into 4 sections: Macedon, Egypt, Syria, Pergamum. **312–64** Seleucids rule area extending from Thrace to India. **304** Ptolemy I, Governor of Egypt, founds independent dynasty.	Cavalry techniques spread to Asia. **350–200** Great period of Chinese thought, Taoist, Confucian, Legalist schools; scientific discoveries. **322** Beginning of Mauryan Empire in India. 1st sections of Great Wall of China.		400
290 Rome completes conquest of central Italy. **264** 1st Punic War against Carthage – Rome conquers Sicily (ends **214**). **218–201** 2nd Punic War – Hannibal invades Italy and is defeated. **206** Rome conquers Spain.	**290** *Foundation of Alexandrian Library.*	**262** Asoka, Emperor converted to Buddhism. **247** Arasces I founds kingdom of Parthia. **221–206** Ch'in Dynasty strengthens Great Wall. *'Ramayana' completed by this date.* **206**– AD **221** Han Dynasty in China.		300
168 Rome conquers Macedonia. **146** Rome conquers Greece. **133–132** Tiberius and Caius Gracchus fail in their reform movement.	**149–146** Rome destroys Carthage in 3rd Punic War and creates province of Africa **149**.	**185** Kings of Bactria conquer north-west India. **138** Chang Chien explores central Asia. **112** *Silk road opens across central Asia.*		200
89 All Italy receives Roman Citizenship. **49** Julius Caesar conquers Gaul. **47–45** Civil War. **44** Caesar assassinated. **31** Battle of Actium: Octavian dominates Rome. **27** Beginning of Roman Empire – Octavian becomes Augustus.	**30** Deaths of Antony and Cleopatra – Egypt becomes Roman province. c.**3** Birth of Christ.	Extension of Great Wall. **9** Wang Mang deposes Han Dynasty in China.	c.**100** Camel introduced to Sahara.	100

	EUROPE	NEAR EAST AND NORTH AFRICA	ASIA	AFRICA, AMERICAS AND PACIFIC
AD1	**43** Roman invasion of Britain. **46–47** Missionary journeys of Paul. **64** Nero's persecution of Christians. **79** Vesuvius eruption, Pompeii buried.	c.**30** Christ's crucifixion. **44** Rome conquers Mauritania (Morocco). **53** Parthia defeats Rome.	**25** Restoration of Han Dynasty; capital at Lo-Yang. **91** Chinese defeat Huns from Mongolia.	c.**50** Ethiopian kingdom expands.
100	**117** Roman Empire at its greatest extent. **117–38** Hadrian – Roman Emperor. **161–80** Marcus Aurelius – Roman Emperor.	**116** Trajan conquers Mesopotamia. **132** Jewish revolt crushed. Jews dispersed.	**105** *1st use of paper in China.* c.**150** Buddhism reaches China. *Earliest surviving Sanskrit inscription.* **184** 'Yellow Turban' rebellions.	c.**150** Berber and Mandingo tribes dominate Niger Basin.
200	**212** Roman citizenship given to all free people in Empire. **234** War on Rhine frontier. **238** Goths raid frontier. **293** Emperor Diocletian reorganizes Roman Empire into East and West.	c.**200** Mishnah (Jewish law) compiled. **200–50** *Development of Christian theology – Tertullian, Clement, Origen.* **224** Foundation of Sassanian Dynasty in Persia.	**221** End of Han Dynasty: China splits into three states. **245** Chinese envoys visit Funan (Cambodia). **285** Confucianism introduced into Japan.	
300	**313** Edict of Milan published by Constantine. Toleration of Christianity. **370** Huns appear in Europe. **378** Visigoths defeat and kill Roman Emperor.	**325** Nicene creed. **330** Capital of Roman Empire transferred to Constantinople.	c.**300** *Foot stirrup used.* **304** Huns invade China, which becomes fragmented until **589**. **320** Gupta Empire begins in India. **350** Huns invade Persia and India.	**300** *Hopewell Indians in North America.* *Mayan civilization in Mexico.* Settlement of Eastern Polynesia. **325** Ethiopia conquers Nubia.
400	**410** Visigoths sack Rome, overrun Spain. **449** Angles, Saxons, Jutes begin conquest of Britain. **476** Last Roman emperor in West deposed. **486** Frankish kingdom founded by Clovis. **493** Ostrogoths take power in Italy. **497** Franks converted to Christianity.	**426** *St Augustine of Hippo writes 'The City of God'.* **429** Vandal kingdom in North Africa.	**480** Gupta Empire overthrown.	
500	**529** Rule of St Benedict regulates Western monasteries. **542** Bubonic Plague ravages Europe. **568** Lombards conquer North Italy. **590** Gregory the Great extends Papal power.	**527–65** Justinian – Emperor of Eastern Roman Empire. **534** Justinian's legal code. **553** Justinian brings Italy and North Africa back into Eastern Roman Empire control.	**531** Sassanian Empire spreads from Persia. **550** Buddhism enters Japan from Korea. **589** China briefly reunified by Sui Dynasty.	
600	**680** Bulgars invade Balkans.	**610–41** Heraclius defends East Roman Empire, now called Byzantine, from Persians and Arabs. **611** Persian armies capture Jerusalem and Antioch and overrun Asia Minor. **622** Hegira of Muhammad – *beginning of Islamic calendar.* **632** Death of Muhammad: Arab expansion begins.	**607** Tibet unified. **624** China united under T'ang Dynasty. **645** Buddhism reaches Tibet. *Japanese society remodelled on Chinese lines.*	c.**600** *Apogee of Mayan civilization in Mexico.*
700	**711** Muslim invasion of Spain. **732** Battle of Poitiers keeps Arabs out of France. **751** Lombards overrun Ravenna, last Byzantine stronghold. **793** Viking raids begin.	**717** Emperor Leo III prevents Arab conquest of Constantinople. **750** Abbasid Caliphate established. **751** *Muslims learn papermaking from Chinese.*	**712** Arabs conquer Sind, Samarkand. **745** Uighur Empire starts in Mongolia. **757** Battle of Talas River. Sets boundary of China and Abbasid Caliphate.	c.**700** Rise of Empire of Ghana.
800	**800** Charlemagne crowned Emperor in Rome. Later became Holy Roman Emperor. **843** Treaty of Verdun, divided Frankish Empire. **871** Alfred, King of Wessex, halts Danes.	**809** Death of Haroun-al-Rashid, Abbasid Caliph, protagonist of 1001 nights.	**802** Angkor kingdom established in Cambodia. **833** *1st printed book in China.* **842** Tibetan Empire disintegrates. **890** *Japanese cultural renaissance.*	**800** Settlers reach Easter Island from Polynesia. **836** Struggle for Indian Deccan. **850** Settlers reach New Zealand. Collapse of Mayan Civilization in Mexico.

	EUROPE	NEAR EAST AND NORTH AFRICA	ASIA	AFRICA, AMERICAS AND PACIFIC
900	**911** Vikings obtain Duchy of Normandy. **937** Magyar raids from Hungary. **955** Otto I (German) defeats Magyars, who accept Christianity. **959** Unification of England (Eadgar). **960** Poland founded. **962** Otto I becomes Holy Roman Emperor. **972** Hungary founded. **983** Slavs rebel against Germans. **987** Capetians rule France.	**935** *Text of Koran finalized.* **936** Caliphs of Baghdad lose power. **969** Fatimids conquer Egypt and found Cairo.	**907** Last T'ang Emperor deposed. **916** Khitan kingdom in Mongolia. **939** Vietnam becomes independent. **947** Khitans overrun North China. Liao Dynasty established; capital at Peking. **967** Fujiwara rule Japan. **979** Sung Dynasty reunites China.	**990** Expansion of Inca Empire (Peru).
1000	**1014** Battle of Clontarf. Vikings defeated in Ireland. **1016** Canute the Great rules England, Denmark, and Norway. **1031** Caliphate of Cordova collapses. **1054** Division between Orthodox and Western Christianity. **1066** Normans conquer England. **1071** Normans conquer southern Italy. **1073** Gregory VII becomes Pope – start of conflict between Popes and Holy Roman Emperors. **1095** First Crusade begins.	**1037** *Death of Avicenna, Persian philosopher.* **1055** Seljuk Turks take Baghdad. **1071** Battle of Manzikert – Seljuk Turks take Byzantium. **1096** Europeans found crusader states in Holy Land.	**1000** *Great Age of Chinese painting and ceramics under Sung Dynasty.* **1018** Muslims break power of Hindu states. **1020** *'Tale of Genji' written in Japan.* **1044** First Burmese state. **1045** *Movable type invented in China.*	c.**1000** Vikings colonize Greenland and discover Vinland (America). c.**1000** *First Iron Age culture at Zimbabwe.* **1076** Arabs destroy kingdom of Ghana.
1100	**1100** *First European universities at Salerno and Bologna.* **1125** Germans renew eastward expansion. **1154** *Chartres Cathedral begins spread of Gothic architecture.* Henry II becomes King of England and Northern France. **1198** Innocent III becomes Pope – height of Papal power.	**1100** *Omar Khayyam writes 'The Rubaiyat'.* **1135** Almohads dominate North Africa and Muslim Spain. **1147–49** Second Crusade. **1171** Saladin (a Turk) conquers Egypt. **1189–92** Third Crusade. Richard I fails to recapture Jerusalem from Saladin. **1198** *Death of Averröes, scientist.*	**1126** Chin overrun North China, Sung kept in South. **1150** *Hindu temple of Angkor Wat built in Cambodia.* **1175** First Muslim Empire in India. **1185** Minamoto warlords in Japan. **1193** *Zen Buddhists begin in Japan.*	**1100** *Toltecs build their first capital in Mexico.* **1150** *Beginnings of Yoruba city-states in Nigeria.*
1200	**1206** Albigensian crusades. **1215** Magna Carta. King John concedes to English barons. **1226** *St Francis of Assisi dies.* **1236** Mongols invade Russia. **1241** Mongols invade Poland, Hungary, and Bohemia. **1242** Alexander Nevsky defeats Germans. **1291** Swiss confederation begins.	**1204** Fourth Crusade. Europeans capture Jerusalem. **1250–1919** Ottoman Empire – Turkish empire in Europe, Asia and Africa. **1258** Mongols invade Baghdad. **1261** Greeks resume rule in Constantinople. **1299** Ottoman Turks begin expansion in Anatolia.	**1206** Turkish Sultanate of Delhi rules North India. Genghis Khan starts conquest of Asia. **1234** Mongols destroy Chin in China **1264** Kublai Khan starts Yüan Dynasty in China. **1275** *Marco Polo visits China.* **1279** Mongols conquer southern China.	**1250** *Mayapan becomes dominant Maya city of Yucatán.*
1300	**1309** Papacy moves from Rome to Avignon. **1314** Battle of Bannockburn. Scotland defeats England. **1325** Ivan I begins recovery of Moscow. **1337** Hundred Years War between France and England begins. **1348** Black Death in Europe. **1360** Treaty of Brétigny. **1378–1429** Great Schism – division in the Church leads to two Popes – one in Avignon, one in Rome. **1389** Battle of Kosovo: Ottomans gain control in Balkans. **1397** Union of Kalmar unites Sweden, Norway, and Denmark into a single monarchy.	**1361** Ottomans capture Adrianople, entering Balkans. c.**1369** Timur (Tamburlaine) rules area of Iraq, Iran, and Afghanistan from Samarkand.	**1333** End of Minamoto in Japan. c.**1341** Black Death starts in Asia. **1349** Chinese expand into south-east Asia. **1368** Ming Dynasty in China. End of Mongol rule. c.**1390** Sack of Delhi. **1392** Korea becomes independent.	**1300** *Empire of Benin in Nigeria.* **1325** *Rise of Aztecs in Mexico – city of Tenochtitlán founded.*

	EUROPE	NEAR EAST AND NORTH AFRICA	ASIA	AFRICA, AMERICAS AND PACIFIC
1400	**1415** Battle of Agincourt. Henry V resumes war against France. **1428** Joan of Arc. Beginning of French revival. **1478** Ivan III, 1st Russian Tzar, throws off Mongol rule. **1492** Spaniards expel Arabs and Jews and invade North Africa. **1494** Italian wars. Beginning of struggle between Hapsburgs and French kings.	**1402** Timur defeats Ottoman Turks at Ankara. **1453** Ottoman Turks capture Constantinople. End of Byzantine Empire.	**1428** Vietnam expels Chinese. **1498** *Vasco Da Gama reaches India.*	**1415** Beginning of Portugal's African Empire under Henry the Navigator. c.**1450** Height of Songhai Empire in south Sahara. *University at Timbuktu.* Monomotapa Empire founded in Zimbabwe. c.**1470** Incas conquer Chimú kingdom. **1492** *Columbus reaches America.* **1493** Treaty of Tordesillas – Pope divides New World between Spanish and Portuguese.
1500	**1500** *Italian Renaissance.* **1519** Charles V, King of Spain and Netherlands, becomes Holy Roman Emperor. **1521** Martin Luther outlawed by the Diet of Worms. *Protestant Reformation.* **1534** Henry VIII breaks with the Church at Rome. **1556** Ivan IV conquers Volga Basin. **1572** Dutch revolt against Spain. **1581** Russian conquest of Siberia begins. **1588** English defeat Spanish Armada.	**1500** Shah Ismail founds Dynasty in Persia. **1516** Ottomans conquer Syria, Egypt, Arabia.	**1511** Portuguese take Malacca, Malaysia. **1526** Moghul Dynasty (Islamic) in North India founded by Babur, descended from Timur. **1557** Portuguese colony at Macao, Southern China. **1565** Akbar extends rule halfway down India. *Important cultural period.* **1571** Spanish conquer Philippines.	**1505** Portuguese have trading posts in East Africa. **1510** African slaves go to America. **1519** Cortez begins conquest of Aztecs. *Magellan crosses Pacific.* **1532** Pizzaro begins conquest of Incas. **1546** Songhai Empire destroys Mali Empire. **1571** Portuguese colony in Angola. **1578** Moroccans defeat Portuguese. **1591** Moroccans destroy Songhai Empire.
1600	**1600** Foundation of English and Dutch (1602) East India Companies. **1642–1649** English Civil War. **1683** Hapsburgs break the Ottoman seige of Vienna, and establish basis of Austrian Empire. **1688** 'Glorious Revolution' in England. **1689** 'Grand Alliance' surrounds and checks Louis XIV of France. **1699** Hapsburgs obtain Hungary from Turks.	**1600**'s and **1700**'s Barbary pirates raid from North African coast.	**1609** Tokugawa shogunate in Japan. **1619** Beginning of Dutch East Indian Empire. **1641** Dutch take Malacca. **1644** New Manchu Dynasty. **1650** *Cultural developments in Japan – kabuki, puppet theatre, the novel.* **1674** Hindu Maharatha kingdom. **1689** Treaty between Russia and China. **1690** English found Calcutta. **1697** Chinese occupy Outer Mongolia.	**1600** Height of Oyo Empire in Africa. **1607** English found Jamestown, Virginia, U.S.A. **1608** French found Quebec. **1620** Mayflower sails to New England. **1628** Portuguese destroy Monomotapa Empire in Zimbabwe. **1652** Dutch found Cape Colony in South Africa. **1662** Portuguese destroy Kongo kingdom in Africa.
1700	**1700–20** Great Northern War. **1703** Foundation of St. Petersburg. Peter the Great westernizes Russia. **1707** Union of England and Scotland. **1709** Peter the Great defeats Swedes at Poltava. **1713** Treaty of Utrecht ends war of Spanish succession, apportions colonization rights. **1740** Frederick the Great begins to strengthen Prussia. **1748** Maria Theresa secures Austrian throne, but has to give up Silesia to Prussia (war of Austrian succession). **1756–63** Seven Years War (England and Prussia against France, Austria, Russia). **1760** *Industrial Revolution begins in Britain; leads to mechanization, steam power, factory system, and improved transport and communications.* **1762** Catherine the Great of Russia withdraws from war. **1763** Peace of Paris. England and Prussia victorious. **1772, 1793, 1795** Partitions of Poland. **1783** Russia takes Crimea. **1789 – 99** French Revolution.	c.**1735** *Wahabite movement to purify Islam starts in Arabia.* **1736** Nadir Shah takes power in Persia. **1798** Napoleon attacks Egypt.	**1707** Death of Aurungzebe – decline of Moghul power. **1747** Afghanistan founded. **1751** French control Deccan and Carnatic in India. China overruns Tibet. **1757** Battle of Plassey: British destroy French power in India. **1796** British conquer Ceylon.	**1700** Rise of Asante power (Gold Coast). **1728** *Bering begins Russian exploration of Alaska.* **1730** Rise of Ancient Empire of Bornu. **1760** British take French colonies at Quebec, Montreal. **1768** *Cook explores Pacific.* **1775–81** American War of Independence. **1789** U.S. Constitution adopted – George Washington first President.

1800

EUROPE

1804 Napoleon defeats Austria and Prussia.

1805 Nelson defeats French at Trafalgar.

1812 Napoleon invades Russia.

1815 Wellington defeats Napoleon at Waterloo. Congress of Vienna.

1830 Revolutionary movements in France, Germany, Poland, Italy; Belgium becomes independent.

1845 Famine in Ireland.

1848 Revolutionary movements in Europe; French Second Republic proclaimed.
Karl Marx 'Communist Manifesto.

1854–56 Crimean War.

1860 Unification of Italy.

1861 Emancipation of serfs in Russia.

1864 Suppression of Polish revolt.

1870 Franco-Prussian war.

1871 Proclamation of German Empire and French Third Republic.

1878 Treaty of Berlin – Balkan countries independent of Turks.

1879 Dual alliance: Germany and Austria-Hungary.

1894 Franco-Russian alliance.

ASIA AND MIDDLE EAST

1818 Britain defeats Marathas and rules India – beginning of the British Raj.

1819 Britain founds Singapore.

1825–30 Indonesians rebel against Dutch.

1830 Russia begins conquest of Kazakhstan.

1842 Britain annexes Hong Kong after Opium War.

1850–64 T'ai-p'ing rebellion causes much suffering.

1853 *Railway and telegraph in India.*

1854 Perry, U.S. naval officer, opens Japan to U.S. trade.

1857 Indian mutiny.

1863 Indo-China becomes French Protectorate.

1868 End of Tokugawa Shogunate – Meiji restoration in Japan. *Modernization begins.*

1879 Britain controls Afghanistan after Afghan War.

1885 Indian National Congress formed.

1886 British annex Burma.

1894–95 War between China and Japan. Japan takes Formosa.

AFRICA

1804 Fulani conquer Hausa.

1806 British control Cape Colony.

1807 Slave Trade abolished in British Empire.

1811 Mohammed Ali controls Egypt.

1818 Shaka forms Zulu kingdom in south east Africa.

1822 Liberia founded: colony for freed slaves.

1830 French begin conquest of Algeria.

1835 'Great Trek' of Boers leads to foundation of Natal, Orange Free State, Transvaal.

1853 *Livingstone's explorations begin.*

1860 French expand in West Africa.

1869 *Suez Canal opens.*

1875 Disraeli buys Suez Canal Company to ensure British control.

1880 – 1900 Peak period of partition and colonization of Africa by Europe.

1899 Boer War begins.

AMERICAS AND PACIFIC

1803 Purchase of Louisiana doubles size of U.S.

1808–26 Central and South American states become independent from Spain and Portugal.

1819 U.S. purchases Florida from Spain.

1823 Monroe doctrine – U.S. intends to keep Europe out of Western Hemisphere.

1840 Britain annexes New Zealand.

1845 U.S. annexes Texas.

1846 Oregon treaty sets U.S.–Canadian boundary.

1846–48 Mexican war. U.S. annexes New Mexico and California.

1849 California gold rush.

1850 Australia and New Zealand granted responsible government.

1861–65 Civil War in U.S.

1863 Slavery abolished in U.S.

1865 President Lincoln assassinated.

1867 Dominion of Canada established.

1898 Spanish American war: U.S. annexes Guam, Puerto Rico, Philippines.

1900

EUROPE

1904 Anglo-French entente.

1905 Norway independent of Sweden. Revolution in Russia, followed by reforms.

1907 Anglo-Russian entente.

1912–13 Balkan wars.

1914–18 First World War.

1917 Russian Revolution. Communists take control.

1918–21 Civil War in Russia.

1920 League of Nations founded.

1922 Mussolini controls Italy.
Eire created.

1933 Hitler becomes Chancellor of Germany.

1936 Spanish Civil War.

1938 Stalin's purges.

1939 German-Soviet non-aggression pact.

1939–45 Second World War.

1945 Yalta. Russia lays basis for domination of Eastern Europe.

1947 Marshall plan to rebuild Europe.

1948 Communist governments take over in East Europe. Berlin airlift.

1955 Warsaw Pact.

1956 Polish, Hungarian revolts crushed.

1957 Treaty of Rome. EEC formed.

1961 Berlin Wall built.

1968 Russians stop liberalization in Czechoslovakia.

1969 Violence in Northern Ireland starts.

1973 Britain, Eire, Denmark join EEC.

1974 Turkey invades Cyprus.

1975 End of dictatorship in Spain.

ASIA AND MIDDLE EAST

1900 Boxer Rebellion in China against foreign influences.

1904–05 Russo-Japanese war. Japanese win.

1910 Japan takes Korea.

1911 Chinese Revolution. Sun Yat-sen president of new republic.

1926 Chiang Kai-Shek leads China.

1931 Japan occupies Manchuria.

1934 Long March of Mao.

1945 Japan – 1st atom bombs dropped by U.S.

1947 India and Pakistan independent.

1948 Israel independent.

1949 Indonesia independent.
Mao Tse-Tung's communists take over in China.

1950 Korean War begins.

1954 Laos, Cambodia, Vietnam granted independence. Vietnam divided – war begins.

1965–71 War between India and Pakistan. Bangladesh formed.

1966 Chinese cultural revolution.

1967 3rd Arab-Israeli war.

1973 4th Arab-Israeli war.
U.S. withdraws from Vietnam.

1975 Communists rule in Laos, Cambodia, Vietnam.

1978 Camp David Summit between Israel and Egypt.

1978–79 Iranian revolution.

1979 Russia invades Afghanistan.

1984 Indira Gandhi, prime minister of India, assassinated.

AFRICA

1908 Belgium takes over Congo.

1910 Union of South Africa formed.

1911 Italy conquers Libya.

1914 Britain proclaims protectorate over Egypt.

1935 Italy invades Ethiopia.

1942 Battle of El Alamein: British gain advantage in North Africa.
Allied landings in Morocco and Algeria.

1949 Apartheid policy begins in South Africa.

1952 Mau-Mau rebellion in Kenya.
Nasser throws off British rule in Egypt.

1956 Suez canal crisis.

1957–61 Many African states achieve independence.

1962 Algeria becomes independent.

1965 Rhodesia declares U.D.I.

1967 Civil War in Nigeria.

1975 Portugal gives independence to Mozambique, Angola.

1980 Zimbabwe granted independence.

1981 President Sadat of Egypt assassinated.

AMERICAS AND PACIFIC

1901 Unification of Australia.

1903 *Wright Brothers' first flight.*

1907 New Zealand becomes dominion.

1911 Mexican revolution.

1914 *Panama canal opens.*

1920 U.S. refuses to join League of Nations.

1929 Wall Street Crash of stock market.

1933 Roosevelt introduces New Deal.

1941 Attack on Pearl Harbor by Japanese – U.S. enters World War II against Germany and Japan.

1942 *Fermi builds 1st nuclear reactor.*

1945 United Nations founded.

1948 Nato founded.

1949 Organization of American states.

1952 *Contraceptive pill developed in U.S.*

1959 Cuban revolution.

1963 President Kennedy assassinated.

1966 Rise of black protest movements in U.S.

1968 Student protest movement.

1969 *First man on the moon.*

1970 Allende – President of Chile (killed 1973).

1971 Nixon and Kissinger start detente with China and U.S.S.R.

1973 First steep rise in oil prices jolts western economies.

1974 Nixon resigns after Watergate.

1982 Falkland Islands crisis.

to appropriate a selfish or excessive share of; monopolize ⟨~ged *the discussion*⟩ – infml

'hog,back /-,bak/ *n, chiefly NAm* a hogsback

hogg /hog/ *n, Br* a young unshorn sheep [var of *hog*]

hogget /'hogit/ *n, Br* a hogg

hoggish /'hogish/ *adj* grossly selfish, gluttonous, or filthy

Hogmanay /'hogmənay, ,hogmə'nay/ *n, Scot* the eve of New Year's Day [origin unknown]

'hogs,back /-,bak/ *n* a ridge with a sharp summit and steeply sloping sides

'hogs,head /-,hed/ *n* **1** a large cask or barrel **2** any of several measures of capacity; *esp* a measure of 52½ imperial gallons (about 238l)

'hog,wash /-,wosh/ *n* **1** SWILL 1, SLOP 3a **2** sthg worthless; *specif* meaningless talk – slang

'hog,weed /-,weed/ *n, Br* a tall foul-smelling Old World plant of the carrot family, with large leaves and broad heads of white or pinkish flowers

ho-ho /hoh 'hoh/ *interj* – used to express hearty amusement

ho hum /'hoh ,hum/ *interj* – used to express weariness, boredom, or disdain [imit]

hoick /hoyk/ *vt* to lift or pull abruptly; yank – infml ⟨~ed *my case out of the rack*⟩ [prob alter. of [1]*hike*]

hoi polloi /,hoy pə'loy/ *n pl* *the* common people; *the* masses [Gk, the many]

[1]hoist /hoyst/ *vt* to raise into position (as if) by means of tackle; *broadly* to raise [alter. of earlier *hoise*, perh fr MD *hischen*]

[2]hoist *n* **1** an apparatus for hoisting **2a** the distance a flag extends along its staff or support **b** the end of a flag next to the staff – compare [2]FLY 3c(2)

[3]hoist *adj* – **hoist with one's own petard** made a victim of or hurt by one's own usu malicious scheme

hoity-toity /,hoyti 'toyti/ *adj* having an air of assumed importance; haughty – infml [irreg redupl of E dial. *hoit* (to play the fool)]

hokey /'hohki/ *adj, chiefly NAm* corny; *also* contrived, phoney [irreg fr *hokum* + *-y*]

hokum /'hohkəm/ *n, chiefly NAm* **1** a crude device, esp sentimental or comic, designed to appeal to an audience **2** pretentious nonsense; bunkum [prob fr *ho*cus-pocus + bun*kum*]

hol-, holo- *comb form* **1** complete; total ⟨holo*metabolism*⟩ **2** completely; totally ⟨holo*graphic*⟩ [ME, fr OF, fr L, fr Gk, fr *holos* whole – more at SAFE]

Holarctic /ho'lahktik/ *adj* of or being the biogeographical area that includes the northern parts of the Old World and New World

[1]hold /hohld/ *vb* **held** /held/ *vt* **1a** to have in one's keeping; possess ⟨~s *the title to the property*⟩ **b** to retain by force ⟨*troops* ~ing *the ridge*⟩ **c** to keep by way of threat or coercion ⟨~ing *the child for ransom*⟩ **2a** to keep under control; check ⟨held *her tongue*⟩ **b** to stop the action of temporarily; delay ⟨held *the presses to insert a late story*⟩ **c** to keep from advancing or from attacking successfully ⟨held *their opponents to a draw*⟩ **d** to restrict, limit ⟨~ *price increases to a minimum*⟩ **e** to bind legally or morally ⟨~ *a man to his word*⟩ **3a** to have, keep, or support in the hands or arms; grasp ⟨held *her to him*⟩ **b** to keep in a specified situation, position, or state ⟨~ *the ladder steady*⟩ **c** to support, sustain ⟨*the roof won't* ~ *much weight*⟩ **d** to retain ⟨*houses should* ~ *their value*⟩ **e** to keep in custody **f** to set aside; reserve ⟨~ *a room*⟩ **4** to bear, carry ⟨*the soldierly way he* ~s *himself*⟩ **5a** to keep up without interruption; continue ⟨*ship* held *its course*⟩ **b** to keep the uninterrupted interest or attention of ⟨held *the audience in suspense*⟩ **6a** to contain or be capable of containing ⟨*the can* ~s *5 gallons*⟩ **b** to have in store ⟨*what the future* ~s⟩ **7a** to consider to be true; believe **b** to have in regard ⟨*she* held *the matter to be of little importance*⟩ **8a** to engage in with sby else or with others ⟨~ *a conference*⟩ **b** to cause to be conducted; convene ⟨~ *a meeting of the council*⟩ **9a** to occupy as a result of appointment or election ⟨~s *a captaincy in the navy*⟩ **b** to have earned or been awarded ⟨~s *a PhD*⟩ ~ *vi* **1a** to maintain position ⟨*the defensive line is* ~ing⟩ **b** to continue unchanged; last ⟨*hopes the weather will* ~⟩ **2** to withstand strain without breaking or giving way ⟨*the anchor* held *in the rough sea*⟩ **3** to bear or carry oneself ⟨*asked her to* ~ *still*⟩ **4** to be or remain valid; apply ⟨*the rule* ~s *in most cases*⟩ **5** to maintain a course; continue ⟨held *south for several miles*⟩ [ME *holden*, fr OE *healdan*; akin to OHG *haltan* to hold, L *celer* rapid] – **hold a brief for** to be retained as counsel for – **hold forth** to speak at great length – **hold good** to be true or valid – **hold one's own** to maintain one's ground, position, or strength in the face of competition or adversity – **hold the fort** to cope with problems for or look after the work of sby who is absent – **hold to 1** to remain steadfast or faithful to; ABIDE BY **2** to cause to hold to ⟨held *him to his promise*⟩ – **hold water** to stand up under criticism or analysis – **hold with** to agree with or approve of ⟨*don't* hold with *such practices*⟩ – **not hold a candle to** to be much inferior to; not qualify for comparison with

[2]hold *n* **1a** a manner of grasping an opponent in wrestling **b** influence, control ⟨*his father had a strong* ~ *over him*⟩ **c** possession ⟨*tried to get* ~ *of a road map*⟩ **2** sthg that may be grasped as a support **3** a temporary stoppage of a countdown (e g in launching a spacecraft)

[3]hold *n* **1** a space below a ship's deck in which cargo is stored ☞ SHIP **2** the cargo compartment of a plane [alter. of *hole*]

'hold,all /-,awl/ *n* a bag or case for miscellaneous articles

hold back *vt* **1** to hinder the progress of; restrain **2** to retain in one's keeping ~ *vi* to keep oneself in check

hold down *vt* **1** to keep within limits; *specif* to keep at a low level ⟨*try to* hold *prices* down⟩ **2** to hold and keep (a position of responsibility) ⟨holding down *2 jobs*⟩

holder /'hohldə/ *n* **1** a device that holds an often specified object ⟨*cigarette* ~⟩ **2a** an owner **b** a tenant **c** a person in possession of and legally entitled to receive payment of a bill, note, or cheque [[1]HOLD + [2]-ER]

holdfast /'hohld,fahst/ *n* a part by which an alga or other organism clings to a (flat) surface

holding /'hohlding/ *n* **1** land held **2** property (e g land or securities) owned – usu pl with sing. meaning

'holding ,company *n* a company whose primary business is holding a controlling interest in the shares of other companies – compare INVESTMENT COMPANY, SUBSIDIARY

hold off *vt* **1** to keep at a distance ⟨hold *the dogs* off⟩ **2** to resist successfully; withstand ⟨hold off *the enemy attack*⟩ **3** to defer action on; postpone ~ *vi* **1** to keep off or at a distance ⟨*hope the rain* holds off⟩ **2** to defer action; delay

hold on *vi* **1** to persevere in difficult circumstances **2** to wait; HANG ON ⟨hold on *a minute!*⟩ – **hold on to** to keep possession of

hold out *vt* to present as likely or realizable; proffer ⟨*the doctors* hold out *every hope of her recovery*⟩ ~ *vi* **1** LAST 2 ⟨*hope the car* holds out *till we get home*⟩ **2** to refuse to yield or give way ⟨*the garrison* held out *against the enemy attack*⟩ – **hold out for** to insist on as the price for an agreement – **hold out on** to withhold sthg (e g information) from – infml

hold over *vt* **1** to postpone **2** to prolong the engagement or tenure of ⟨*the show was* held over *for another week by popular demand*⟩

'hold,up /-,up/ *n* **1** an armed robbery **2** a delay

hold up *vt* **1** to delay, impede ⟨*got* held up *in the traffic*⟩ **2** to rob at gunpoint **3** to present, esp as an example ⟨*her work was* held up *as a model*⟩ ~ *vi* to endure a test; HOLD OUT

[1]**hole** /hohl/ *n* **1** an opening into or through a thing **2a** a hollow place; *esp* a pit or cavity **b** a deep place in a body of water **c** a place in the crystal structure of a semiconductor, equivalent to a positively charged particle, where an electron has left its normal position **3** an animal's burrow **4** a serious discrepancy or flaw ⟨*picked* ~s *in his story*⟩ **5a** the unit of play from the tee to the hole in golf **b** a cavity in a putting green into which the ball is to be played in golf **6** a dirty or dingy place ⟨*lives in a dreadful* ~⟩ **7** an awkward position; a fix *USE* (*6 & 7*) infml [ME, fr OE *hol* (fr neut of *hol*, adj, hollow) & *holh*; akin to OHG *hol*, adj, hollow, L *caulis* stalk, stem, Gk *kaulos*] – **holey** *adj*

[2]**hole** *vt* **1** to make a hole in **2** to drive into a hole ~ *vi* **1** to make a hole in sthg **2** to play one's ball into the hole in golf – usu + *out*

,hole-and-'corner *adj* clandestine, underhand

hole up *vi* to take refuge or shelter *in* ~ *vt* to place (as if) in a refuge or hiding place *USE* infml

[1]**holiday** /'holiday, -di/ *n* **1** a day, often in commemoration of some event, on which no paid employment is carried out ⟨*Christmas Day is a public* ~⟩ **2** a period of relaxation or recreation spent away from home or work ⟨*went on* ~ *for a fortnight*⟩ – often pl with sing. meaning [ME, fr OE *hāligdæg*, fr *hālig* holy + *dæg* day]

[2]**holiday** *vi* to take or spend a holiday

'holiday,maker /-,maykə/ *n* a person who is on holiday

,holier-than-'thou /'hohli·ə/ *adj* having an air of superior piety or morality

holiness /'hohlinis/ *n* **1** *cap* – used as a title for various high religious dignitaries ⟨*His* Holiness *Pope John Paul II*⟩ **2** sanctification [HOLY + -NESS]

holism /'hoh,liz(ə)m/ *n* a view of the universe, and esp living nature, as being composed of interacting wholes that are more than simply the sum of their parts [*hol-* + *-ism*] – **holistic** /hoh'listik/ *adj*

holla /'holə/ *vb, n, or interj* (to) hollo

holland /'holənd/ *n, often cap* a cotton or linen fabric in plain weave, usu heavily sized or glazed, that is used for window blinds, bookbinding, and clothing [ME *holand*, fr *Holand* Holland, province of the Netherlands, fr MD *Holland*]

hollandaise sauce /holən'dayz/ *n* a rich sauce made with butter, egg yolks, and lemon juice or vinegar [F *sauce hollandaise*, lit., Dutch sauce]

holler /'holə/ *vb, chiefly NAm* to call out or shout (sthg) [alter. of *hollo*] – **holler** *n*

[1]**hollo** *also* **holloa** /ho'loh, 'ho-/ *interj* **1** – used to attract attention **2** – used as a call of encouragement or jubilation [origin unknown]

[2]**hollo** *also* **holloa** *vi or n* **hollos; holloing; holloed;** *pl* **hollos** (to utter) an exclamation or call of *hollo*

[1]**hollow** /'holoh/ *adj* **1a** having a recessed surface; sunken **b** curved inwards; concave **2** having a cavity within ⟨~ *tree*⟩ **3** echoing like a sound made in or by beating on an empty container; muffled **4a** deceptively lacking in real value or significance ⟨*a* ~ *victory*⟩ **b** lacking in truth or substance; deceitful ⟨~ *promises*⟩ [ME *holw, holh*, fr *holh* hole, den, fr OE *holh* hole, hollow – more at HOLE] – **hollowly** *adv*, **hollowness** *n*

[2]**hollow** *vb* to make or become hollow

[3]**hollow** *n* **1** a depressed or hollow part of a surface; *esp* a small valley or basin **2** an unfilled space; a cavity

[4]**hollow** *adv* **1** in a hollow manner ⟨*his laughter rang* ~⟩ **2** completely, totally – infml ⟨*she beat me* ~⟩

hollow out *vt* to form a cavity or hole in; *also* to make in this way

'hollow,ware, holloware /-,weə/ *n* domestic vessels that have a significant depth and volume; *specif* metal pots, pans, etc

holly /'holi/ *n* (the foliage of) any of a genus of trees and shrubs with thick glossy spiny-edged leaves and usu bright red berries [ME *holin, holly*, fr OE *holegn*; akin to OHG *hulis* holly, MIr *cuilenn*]

hollyhock /'holi,hok/ *n* a tall orig Chinese plant of the mallow family with large coarse rounded leaves and tall spikes of showy flowers [ME *holihoc*, fr *holi* holy + *hoc* mallow, fr OE]

'Holly,wood /-,wood/ *n* the American film industry [*Hollywood*, district of Los Angeles, California, USA]

holm /hohlm, hohm/ *n, Br* a small inland or inshore island; *also* flat low-lying land near a river [ME, fr OE, fr ON *hōlmr*; akin to OE *hyll* hill]

holmium /'holmi·əm/ *n* a metallic element of the rare-earth group that forms highly magnetic compounds ☞ PERIODIC TABLE [NL, fr *Holmia* Stockholm, city in Sweden]

holm oak *n* a S European evergreen oak [ME *holm* holly, alter. of *holin*]

holo- – see HOL-

holocaust /'holə,kawst/ *n* **1** a sacrificial offering consumed by fire **2** an instance of wholesale destruction or loss of life **3** *often cap the* genocidal persecution of European Jewry by Hitler and the Nazi party during WW II [ME, fr OF *holocauste*, fr LL *holocaustum*, fr Gk *holokauston*, fr neut of *holokaustos* burnt whole, fr *hol-* + *kaustos* burnt, fr *kaiein* to burn – more at CAUSTIC]

Holocene /'holəseen/ *adj* RECENT 2 ☞ EVOLUTION [ISV] – **Holocene** *n*

hologram /'holəgram/ *n* a pattern produced by the interference between one part of a split beam of coherent light (e g from a laser) and the other part of the same beam reflected off an object; *also* a photographic reproduction of this pattern that when suitably illuminated produces a three-dimensional picture

¹holograph /-grahf, -graf/ *n* a document wholly in the handwriting of its author; *also* the handwriting itself [LL *holographus*, fr LGk *holographos*, fr Gk *hol-* + *graphein* to write – more at CARVE] – **holograph** *adj*, **holographic** /-ˈgrafik/ *adj*

holography /hoˈlogrəfi/ *n* the technique of making or using a hologram – **holograph** /ˈholəgrahf, -graf/ *vt*, **holographic** /ˌholəˈgrafik/ *adj*, **holographically** *adv*

holohedral /ˌholəˈheedrəl/ *adj, of a crystal* having all the faces required for complete symmetry – compare HEMIHEDRAL [*hol-* + Gk *hedra* seat – more at SIT]

holometabolous /ˌhohlohməˈtabələs, ˌholoh-/ *adj, of an insect* having undergone complete metamorphosis – **holometabolism** *n*

holophrastic /ˌholəˈfrastik/ *adj* expressing a complex of ideas in a single word or in a fixed phrase [ISV *hol-* + *-phrastic* (fr Gk *phrazein* to point out, declare)]

holophytic /ˌholohˈfitik/ *adj* obtaining food in the manner of a green plant by photosynthetic activity

holothurian /ˌholəˈthyooəri·ən/ *n* a sea cucumber or related echinoderm [deriv of Gk *holothourion* water polyp] – **holothurian** *adj*

holozoic /ˌholohˈzoh·ik/ *adj* obtaining food in the manner of most animals by ingesting complex organic matter

hols /holz/ *n pl, chiefly Br* holidays – infml [by shortening]

holstein /ˈholstein/ *n, chiefly NAm* a Friesian [short for *holstein-friesian*, fr *Holstein*, region of Germany + *Friesian*]

holster /ˈhohlstə, ˈhol-/ *n* a usu leather holder for a pistol [D; akin to OE *heolstor* cover, *helan* to conceal – more at HELL]

holt /hohlt/ *n* a den or lair, esp of an otter [ME, alter. of ²*hold*]

holy /ˈhohli/ *adj* **1** set apart to the service of God or a god; sacred **2a** characterized by perfection and transcendence; commanding absolute adoration and reverence ⟨*the ~ Trinity*⟩ **b** spiritually pure; godly **3** evoking or worthy of religious veneration or awe ⟨*the ~ cross*⟩ **4** terrible, awful – used as an intensive ⟨*a ~ terror*⟩ [ME, fr OE *hālig*; akin to OE *hāl* whole – more at WHOLE]

ˌHoly Comˈmunion *n* COMMUNION 1

ˈholy ˌday *n* a day set aside for special religious observance

ˌHoly ˈFather *n* POPE 1

ˌHoly ˈGhost *n* HOLY SPIRIT

ˌHoly ˈGrail *n* *the* cup or platter that according to medieval legend was used by Christ at the Last Supper and became the object of knightly quests

ˈholy ˌhour *n* an afternoon period during which public houses close in Ireland

Holy Innocents' Day *n* December 28 kept by churches in memory of the children killed by Herod according to Mt 2:16

ˌHoly ˈJoe /joh/ *n* a parson, chaplain; *also* a pious person – infml [*Joe*, nickname for *Joseph*]

ˈHoly ˌLand *n* *the* territory containing sites associated with the ministry and death of Christ

ˌholy of ˈholies *n* the innermost and most sacred chamber of the Jewish tabernacle and temple; *broadly* any place or thing considered sacred [trans of LL *sanctum sanctorum*, trans of Heb *gōdhesh hag- gŏdhāshīm*]

holy orders *n pl, often cap H&O* the office of a Christian minister

ˌHoly ˈRoller /ˈrohlə/ *n* a member of any of several ecstatic Protestant fundamentalist sects – often derog

Holy Roman Empire *n* a loose confederation of mainly German and Italian territories under an emperor, that existed from the 9th or 10th c to 1806

ˌHoly ˈSaturday *n* the Saturday before Easter

ˌHoly ˈSee *n* *the* papacy

ˌHoly ˈSpirit *n* *the* 3rd person of the Trinity

ˈholyˌstone /-ˌstohn/ *vt or n* (to clean with) a soft sandstone used for scrubbing a ship's decks

ˌHoly ˈThursday *n* **1** ASCENSION DAY **2** MAUNDY THURSDAY

ˈHoly ˌWeek *n* the week before Easter during which the last days of Christ's life are commemorated

ˌholy ˈwrit *n, often cap H&W* a writing or utterance of unquestionable authority

hom-, homo- *comb form* **1** one and the same; similar; alike ⟨homo*graph*⟩ ⟨homo*sexual*⟩ **2** containing one more CH_2 group than (the specified compound) ⟨homo*cysteine*⟩ [L, fr Gk, fr *homos* – more at SAME]

homage /ˈhomij/ *n* **1a** a ceremony by which a man acknowledges himself the vassal of a lord **b** an act done or payment made by a vassal **2a** reverential regard; deference **b** flattering attention; tribute [ME, fr OF *hommage*, fr *homme* man, vassal, fr L *homin-*, *homo* man; akin to OE *guma* man, L *humus* earth – more at HUMBLE]

homburg /ˈhombuhg/ *n* a felt hat with a stiff curled brim and a high crown creased lengthways [*Homburg*, town in Germany]

¹home /hohm/ *n* **1a** a family's place of residence; a domicile **b** a house **2** the social unit formed by a family living together ⟨*comes from a broken ~*⟩ **3a** a congenial environment ⟨*the theatre is my spiritual ~*⟩ **b** a habitat **4a** a place of origin; *also* one's native country **b** the place where sthg originates or is based ⟨*Lord's, ~ of cricket*⟩ **5** an establishment providing residence and often care for children, convalescents, etc [ME *hom*, fr OE *hām* village, home; akin to Gk *kōmē* village, L *civis* citizen, Gk *koiman* to put to sleep – more at CEMETERY] – **homeless** *adj*, **homelessness** *n* – **at home** **1** relaxed and comfortable; AT EASE 2 ⟨*felt completely* at home *on the stage*⟩ **2** on familiar ground; knowledgeable ⟨*teachers* at home *in their subjects*⟩

²home *adv* **1** to or at home ⟨*wrote ~*⟩ **2** to a final, closed, or standard position ⟨*drive a nail ~*⟩ **3** to an ultimate objective (e g a finishing line) **4** to a vital sensitive core ⟨*the truth struck ~*⟩ **5** HOME AND DRY

³home *adj* **1** of or being a home, place of origin, or base of operations **2** prepared, carried out, or designed for use in the home ⟨*~ cooking*⟩ **3** operating or occurring in a home area ⟨*the ~ team*⟩

⁴home *vi* **1** to go or return home **2** *of an animal* to return accurately to one's home or birthplace from a distance – **home in on** to be directed at or head towards (a specified goal, target, etc)

home-, homeo- *comb form, chiefly NAm* homoe-

ˌhome and ˈdry *adv* having safely or successfully achieved one's purpose

ˈhomeˌbird /-ˌbuhd/ *n* a homebody – infml

'home,body /-,bodi/ *n* one whose life centres round the home

'home,bound /-,bownd/ *adj* confined to the home ⟨~ *invalids*⟩ [*home* + [4]*bound*]

,home'bred /-'bred/ *adj* produced at home; indigenous

'home ,brew *n* an alcoholic drink (e g beer) made at home

'home,coming /-,kuming/ *n* a returning home

,home eco'nomics *n pl but sing or pl in constr* DOMESTIC SCIENCE – **home economist** *n*

,home from 'home *n, Br* a place as comfortable or congenial as one's own home

,home 'front *n* the sphere of civilian activity in war

,home'grown /-'grohn/ *adj* produced in, coming from, or characteristic of the home country or region ⟨~ *vegetables*⟩ ⟨~ *politicians*⟩

,home 'help *n, Br* a person employed by a local authority to carry out household chores for the sick, elderly, or disabled

'homeland /-lənd/ *n* **1** one's native land **2** a Bantustan

'home,like /-,liek/ *adj* characteristic of one's own home, esp in being cheerful or cosy

'homely /-li/ *adj* **1** commonplace, familiar ⟨*explained the problem in ~ terms*⟩ **2** of a sympathetic character; kindly **3** simple, unpretentious ⟨*a ~ meal of bacon and eggs*⟩ **4** *chiefly NAm* not good-looking; plain [[1]HOME + [1]-LY] – **homeliness** *n*

,home'made /-'mayd/ *adj* made in the home, on the premises, or by one's own efforts ⟨~ *cakes*⟩

'home ,office *n, often cap H&O the* government office concerned with internal affairs

'home ,plate *n* a rubber slab at which a baseball batter stands

homer /'hohmə/ *n* HOMING PIGEON

Homeric /hoh'merik/ *adj* **1** (characteristic) of Homer, his age, or his writings **2** of epic proportions; heroic ⟨*a ~ feat of endurance*⟩ [L *Homericus*, fr Gk *Homērikos*, fr *Homēros* Homer *fl ab* 850 BC Gk epic poet]

,home 'rule *n* limited self-government by the people of a dependent political unit – compare SELF-GOVERNMENT

,home 'run *n* a hit in baseball that enables the batter to make a complete circuit of the bases and score a run

,home 'secretary *n, often cap H&S* a government minister for internal affairs

'home,sick /-,sik/ *adj* longing for home and family while absent from them [back-formation fr *homesickness*] – **homesickness** *n*

'home ,signal *n* a railway signal that controls the movement of trains into a section of track

[1]**'home,spun** /-,spun/ *adj* **1** made of homespun **2** lacking sophistication; simple ⟨~ *prose*⟩

[2]**homespun** *n* a loosely woven usu woollen or linen fabric orig made from yarn spun at home

'homestead /-stid/ *n* **1** a house and adjoining land occupied by a family **2** *Austr & NZ* the owner's living quarters on a sheep or cattle station – **homesteader** /-,stedə/ *n*

'homestead ,law *n* any of several US legislative acts authorizing the sale of public lands to settlers

'home ,straight *n* *the* straight final part of a racecourse usu opposite the grandstand

'home,stretch /-,strech/ *n* *the* final stage (e g of a project)

,home 'truth *n* an unpleasant but true fact about a person's character or situation – often pl

'homeward /-wood/ *adj* being or going towards home

'homewards, *chiefly NAm* **homeward** *adv* towards home

'home,work /-,wuhk/ *n* **1** work done in one's own home for pay **2** an assignment given to a pupil to be completed esp away from school **3** preparatory reading or research (e g for a discussion) ⟨*she's done her ~ on the subject*⟩ – **homeworker** *n*

homey /'hohmi/ *adj* homy

homicide /'homisied/ *n* (the act of) sby who kills another [ME, fr MF, fr L *homicida & homicidium*, fr *homo* man + *-cida & -cidium* – more at -CIDE] – **homicidal** /,homi'siedl/ *adj*

homiletic /,homi'letik/, **homiletical** /-kl/ *adj* **1** of or resembling a homily **2** relating to homiletics [LL *homileticus*, fr Gk *homilētikos* of conversation, fr *homilein*]

,homi'letics *n pl but sing in constr* the art of preaching

homily /'homili/ *n* **1** a sermon **2** a lecture on moral conduct [ME *omelie*, fr MF, fr LL *homilia*, fr LGk, fr Gk, conversation, discourse, fr *homilein* to consort with, address, fr *homilos* crowd, assembly]

'homing ,pigeon /'hohming/ *n* a domesticated pigeon trained to return home

hominid /'hominid/ *n* any of a family of biped primate mammals comprising recent man and his immediate ancestors [deriv of L *homin-, homo* man] – **hominid** *adj*

hominoid /'hominoyd/ *adj* resembling or related to man – **hominoid** *n*

hominy /'homini/ *n* crushed or coarsely ground husked maize, esp when boiled with water or milk [prob of Algonquian origin; akin to Natick *-minne* grain]

[1]**homo** /hohmoh/ *n, pl* **homos** any of a genus of primate mammals including recent man and various extinct ancestors [NL *Homin-, Homo*, genus name, fr L, man]

[2]**homo** *n, pl* **homos** a homosexual – chiefly derog [by shortening]

homoe-, homoeo-, *chiefly NAm* **home-, homeo-** *comb form* like; similar ⟨homoeo*stasis*⟩ [L & Gk; L *homoeo-*, fr Gk *homoi-, homoio-*, fr *homoios*, fr *homos* same – more at SAME]

homoeopath /'homi·ə,path/ *n* a practitioner of a system of disease treatment relying on the administration of minute doses of a remedy that produces symptoms like those of the disease [G *homöopath*, fr *homöo-* homoe- + *-path*] – **homoeopathic** /-mi·ə'pathik/ *adj,* **homoeopathy** /,homi'opəthi/ *n*

homoeostasis /,homioh'staysis/ *n* the physiological maintenance of relatively constant conditions (e g constant internal temperature) within the body in the face of changing external conditions [NL] – **homoeostatic** /-'statik/ *adj,* **homoeostatically** *adv*

homogenate /hoh'mojinayt, ho-/ *n* a product of homogenizing

homogeneity /,homəjə'nee·əti, -'nay-, ,hohmoh-/ *n* the quality or state of being homogeneous

homogeneous /,homə'jeenyəs, -ni·əs/ *adj* **1** of the same or a similar kind or nature **2** of uniform structure or composition throughout ⟨*a culturally ~*

neighbourhood⟩ **3** *of an equation, fraction, etc* having each term of the same degree when all variables are taken into account ⟨$x^2 + xy + y^2 = 0$ *is a ~ equation*⟩ **4** HOMOGENOUS 1 [ML *homogeneus, homogenus*, fr Gk *homogenēs*, fr *hom-* + *genos* kind – more at KIN] – **homogeneously** *adv*, **homogeneousness** *n*

homogen·ize, -ise /ho'mojəniez, hə-/ *vt* **1** to make homogeneous **2** to reduce the particles of so that they are uniformly small and evenly distributed; *esp* to break up the fat globules of (milk) into very fine particles ~ *vi* to become homogenized – **homogenizer** *n*, **homogenization** /-'zaysh(ə)n/ *n*

homogenous /ho'mojənəs, hə-/ *adj* **1** of or exhibiting homogeny **2** HOMOGENEOUS 1, 2, 3

homogeny /ho'mojəni, hə-/ *n* correspondence between parts or organs due to descent from the same ancestral type

homograft /'hohmə,grahft, 'homə-/ *n* a graft of tissue taken from a donor of the same species as the recipient

homograph /'homəgrahf, -,graf, 'hoh-/ *n* any of 2 or more words spelt alike but different in meaning, derivation, or pronunciation (e g the noun *conduct* and the verb *conduct*) – **homographic** /,homə'grafik, ,hohmə-/ *adj*

homoi-, homoio- *comb form* homoe-

homoiotherm /hə'moyoh,thuhm/ *n* a warm-blooded organism – **homoiothermy** *n*, **homoiothermic** /hə,moyoh'thuhmik/, **homoiothermal** *adj*

homologate /ho'moləgayt/ *vt* to sanction or allow, esp officially [ML *homologatus*, pp of *homologare* to agree, fr Gk *homologein*, fr *homologos*] – **homologation** /ho,molə'gaysh(ə)n/ *n*

homologous /ho'moləgəs/ *adj* **1a** having the same relative position, value, or structure **b(1)** exhibiting biological homology **(2)** *of chromosomes* joining together with each other in pairs at meiotic cell division and having the same or corresponding genes **c** belonging to or consisting of a chemical series (e g the alkanes) whose members exhibit homology **2** derived from an organism of the same species ⟨*a ~ tissue graft*⟩ [Gk *homologos* agreeing, fr *hom-* + *legein* to say – more at LEGEND] – **homologize** /-jiez/ *vb*

homologue, *NAm also* **homolog** /'homəlog/ *n* a chemical compound, chromosome, etc that exhibits homology

homology /ho'moləji/ *n* **1** correspondence in structure but not necessarily in function **a** between different parts of the same individual **b** between parts of different organisms due to evolutionary differentiation from a common ancestor **2** the relation existing **a** between chemical compounds in a series whose successive members have a regular difference in composition **b** between elements in the same group of the periodic table **3** a similarity often attributable to common origin – chiefly fml

homomorphy /'homə,mawfi/ *n* similarity of form (with different fundamental structure or origin) [ISV] – **homomorphism** *n*, **homomorphic** /-'mawfik/ *adj*

homonym /'homənim/ *n* **1a** a homophone **b** a homograph **c** any of 2 or more words that are both spelt and pronounced alike **2** a namesake – chiefly fml [L *homonymum*, fr Gk *homōnymon*, fr neut of *homōnymos* having the same name, fr *hom-* + *onyma, onoma* name – more at NAME] – **homonymic** /,homə'nimik, ,hoh-/, **homonymous** /ho'moniməs, hoh-/ *adj*, **homonymously** *adv*, **homonymy** *n*

homophone /'homəfohn/ *n* **1** any of 2 or more words pronounced alike but different in meaning, derivation, or spelling (e g *to, too,* and *two*) **2** a character or group of characters pronounced the same as another [ISV] – **homophonous** /ho'mofənəs/ *adj*

homophonic /,homə'fonik/ *adj* of or being music consisting of a single accompanied melodic line – compare POLYPHONIC [Gk *homophōnos* being in unison, fr *hom-* + *phōnē* sound – more at [1]BAN] – **homophony** /ho'mofəni/ *n*

homopterous /hoh'moptərəs/ *adj* of a large suborder of true bugs that have sucking mouthparts and include the aphids and cicadas [deriv of Gk *hom-* + *pteron* wing – more at FEATHER] – **homopteran** /-rən/ *n or adj*

Homo sapiens /,hohmoh 'sapi·enz, 'homoh-/ *n* mankind ☞ EVOLUTION [NL, species name, fr *Homo*, genus name + *sapiens*, specific epithet, fr L, wise, intelligent – more at [1]HOMO, SAPIENT]

homosexual /,homə'seksyoo(ə)l, -'seksh(ə)l/ *adj or n* (of, for, or being) sby having a sexual preference for members of his/her own sex – compare HETEROSEXUAL – **homosexually** *adj*, **homosexuality** /-,seksyoo'aləti, -shoo-/ *n*

homozygote /,hohmoh'ziegoht, ,homoh-, -'zigoht/ *n* an animal, plant, or cell having identical alleles of a particular gene and so breeding true for that gene – compare HETEROZYGOTE [ISV] – **homozygosity** /-'gosəti/, **homozygosis** /-'gohsis/ *n*, **homozygous** /-'ziegəs/ *adj*

homunculus /ho'mungkyooləs/ *n, pl* **homunculi** /-,lie/ a little man; a manikin [L, dim. of *homin-, homo* man – more at HOMAGE]

homy, homey /'hohmi/ *adj* homelike – chiefly infml

hone /hohn/ *vt or n* (to sharpen or make more keen or effective with or as if with) a stone for sharpening a cutting tool ⟨*finely ~d sarcasm*⟩ [n ME, fr OE *hān* stone; akin to ON *hein* whetstone, L *cot-, cos*, Gk *kōnos* cone; vb fr n]

honest /'onist/ *adj* **1** free from fraud or deception; legitimate, truthful **2** respectable or worthy **3a** marked by integrity **b** frank, sincere ⟨*an ~ answer*⟩ [ME, fr OF *honeste*, fr L *honestus* honourable, fr *honos, honor* honour]

,honest 'broker *n* a neutral mediator

'honestly /-li/ *adv* to speak in an honest way ⟨~, *I don't know why I bother*⟩ [HONEST + [2]-LY]

honesty /'onisti/ *n* **1a** upright and straightforward conduct; integrity **b** sincerity, truthfulness **2** any of a genus of European plants of the mustard family with large broad smooth semitransparent seed pods

honey /'huni/ *n* **1a** (a pale golden colour like that typical of) a sweet viscous sticky liquid formed from the nectar of flowers in the honey sac of various bees **b** a sweet liquid resembling honey that is collected or produced by various insects **2** sthg sweet or agreeable; sweetness **3** *chiefly NAm* sweetheart, dear **4** a superlative example ⟨*a ~ of a girl* – Philip Roth⟩ – chiefly infml [ME *hony*, fr OE *hunig*; akin to OHG *honag* honey, L *canicae* bran]

'honey ,badger *n* a ratel

'honey,bee /-,bee/ *n* (a social honey-producing bee

related to) a European bee kept for its honey and wax ☞ DEFENCE

'honey ,buzzard *n* a Eurasian and African hawk that feeds on the larvae of wasps and bees

[1]'honey,comb /-,kohm/ *n* **1** (sthg resembling in shape or structure) a mass of 6-sided wax cells built by honeybees in their nest to contain their brood and stores of honey **2** (tripe from) the second stomach of a cow or other ruminant mammal

[2]honeycomb *vt* **1** to cause to be chequered or full of cavities like a honeycomb **2** to penetrate into every part; riddle ⟨*the government is* ~ed *with spies* – T H White⟩

'honey,dew /-,dyooh/ *n* a sweet deposit secreted on the leaves of plants usu by aphids

,honeydew 'melon *n* a pale smooth-skinned muskmelon with greenish sweet flesh

'honey ,eater *n* any of several chiefly S Pacific songbirds with a long tongue for extracting nectar and small insects from flowers

honeyed *also* **honied** /'hunid/ *adj* sweetened (as if) with honey ⟨~ *words*⟩

'honey ,guide *n* any of several small plainly coloured birds that inhabit Africa, the Himalayas, and the E Indies and are supposed to lead people or animals to the nests of bees

'honey,moon /-,moohn/ *n* **1** the period immediately following marriage, esp when taken as a holiday by the married couple **2** a period of unusual harmony following the establishment of a new relationship ⟨*the government's* ~ *with the public*⟩ [*honey* + [1]*moon* 2] – **honeymoon** *vi*, **honeymooner** *n*

'honey ,sac *n* a distension of the oesophagus of a bee in which honey is produced

'honey,suckle /-,sukl/ *n* any of a genus of (climbing) shrubs usu with showy sweet-smelling flowers rich in nectar [ME *honysoukel*, alter. of *honysouke*, fr OE *hunisūce*, fr *hunig* honey + *sūcan* to suck]

[1]honk /hongk/ *n* (a sound made by a car's electric horn like) the short loud unmusical tone that is the characteristic cry of the goose [imit]

[2]honk *vb* to (cause to) make a honk ⟨*the driver* ~ed *his horn*⟩ – **honker** *n*

honkie, honky /'hongki/ *n, chiefly NAm* a white man – derog; used by Blacks [origin unknown]

honky-tonk /'hongki ,tongk/ *n* **1** a form of ragtime piano playing **2** a cheap nightclub or dance hall – chiefly infml [origin unknown] – **honky-tonk** *adj*

honorarium /,onə'reəri·əm/ *n, pl* **honorariums, honoraria** /-ri·ə/ a payment in recognition of professional services on which no price is set [L, fr neut of *honorarius*]

honorary /'on(ə)rəri/ *adj* **1a** conferred or elected in recognition of achievement, without the usual obligations ⟨*an* ~ *degree*⟩ **b** unpaid, voluntary ⟨*an* ~ *chairman*⟩ **2** depending on honour for fulfilment ⟨*an* ~ *obligation*⟩ [L *honorarius*, fr *honor*] – **honorarily** *adv*

[1]honorific /,onə'rifik/ *adj* **1** conferring or conveying honour ⟨~ *titles*⟩ **2** belonging to or constituting a class of grammatical forms (e g in Chinese) used in speaking to or about a social superior – **honorifically** *adv*

[2]honorific *n* an honorific expression

[1]honour, *NAm chiefly* **honor** /'onə/ *n* **1a** good name or public esteem ⟨*his* ~ *was at stake*⟩ **b** outward respect; recognition **2** a privilege ⟨*I have the* ~ *to welcome you*⟩ **3** *cap* a person of superior social standing – now used esp as a title for a holder of high office (e g a judge in court) ⟨*if Your* Honour *pleases*⟩ **4** one who brings respect or fame ⟨*was an* ~ *to his profession*⟩ **5** a mark or symbol of distinction: e g **a** an exalted title or rank **b** a ceremonial rite or observance – usu pl ⟨*buried with full military* ~s⟩ **6** *pl* a course of study for a university degree more exacting and specialized than that leading to a pass degree **7** (a woman's) chastity or purity **8a** a high standard of ethical conduct; integrity **b** one's word given as a pledge ⟨~ *bound*⟩ **9** *pl* social courtesies or civilities extended by a host ⟨*did the* ~s *at the table*⟩ **10a** an ace, king, queen, or jack of the trump suit in whist; *also* these cards and the 10 in bridge or the 4 aces when the contract is no trumps **b** the privilege of playing first from the tee in golf awarded to the player who won the previous hole [ME, fr OF *honor*, fr L *honos, honor*]

[2]honour, *NAm chiefly* **honor** *vt* **1a** to regard or treat with honour or respect **b** to confer honour on **2a** to live up to or fulfil the terms of ⟨~ *a commitment*⟩ **b** to accept and pay when due ⟨~ *a cheque*⟩ **3** to salute (e g one's partner) with a bow in a country dance

honourable, *NAm chiefly* **honorable** /'on(ə)rəbl/ *adj* **1** worthy of honour **2** performed or accompanied with marks of honour or respect **3** entitled to honour – used as a title for the children of certain British noblemen and for various government officials **4a** bringing credit to the possessor or doer ⟨*an* ~ *performance*⟩ **b** consistent with an untarnished reputation ⟨*an* ~ *discharge from the army*⟩ **5** characterized by (moral) integrity ⟨*his intentions were* ~⟩

'honours ,list *n* a twice-yearly produced list of people who are to be honoured by the British sovereign in recognition of their public service

hooch /hoohch/ *n, NAm* spirits, esp when inferior or illicitly made or obtained – slang [short for *hoochinoo* (spirits made by the Hoochinoo Indians of Alaska)]

[1]hood /hood/ *n* **1a** a loose often protective covering for the top and back of the head and neck that is usu attached to the neckline of a garment **b** a usu leather covering for a hawk's head and eyes **2a** an ornamental scarf worn over an academic gown that indicates by its colour the wearer's university and degree ☞ GARMENT **b** a hoodlike marking, crest, or expansion on the head of an animal (e g a cobra or seal) **3a** a folding waterproof top cover for an open car, pram, etc **b** a cover or canopy for carrying off fumes, smoke, etc **4** *NAm* BONNET 2 [ME, fr OE *hōd*; akin to OHG *huot* head covering] – **hood** *vt*

[2]hood *n* a hoodlum or gangster – infml

-hood /-hood/ *suffix* (*adj or n* → *n*) **1** state or condition of ⟨*priest*hood⟩ ⟨*man*hood⟩ **2** quality or character of ⟨*likeli*hood⟩ **3** time or period of ⟨*child*hood⟩ **4** instance of (a specified quality or condition) ⟨*a false*hood⟩ **5** *sing or pl in constr* body or class of people sharing (a specified character or state) ⟨*brother*hood⟩ ⟨*priest*hood⟩ [ME *-hod*, fr OE *-hād*; akin to OHG *-heit* state, condition, *heitar* bright, clear]

'hooded *adj* **1** covered (as if) by a hood ⟨~ *eyes*⟩ **2** shaped like a hood

,hooded 'crow *n* a black and grey Eurasian crow closely related to the carrion crow

hoodie /'hoodi/, **hoodie crow** *n, chiefly Scot* HOODED CROW

hoodlum /'hoohdləm/ *n* **1** a (violent) thug **2** a young rowdy [origin unknown] – **hoodlumish** *adj*

[1]**hoodoo** /'hooh,dooh/ *n, pl* **hoodoos** *chiefly NAm* voodoo [of African origin; akin to Hausa *hu*[3]*'du*[3]*'ba*[1] to arouse resentment] – **hoodooism** *n*

[2]**hoodoo** *vt, chiefly NAm* to cast an evil spell on; *broadly* to bring bad luck to

hoodwink /'hood,wingk/ *vt* to deceive, delude – chiefly infml [[1]*hood* + [1]*wink*] – **hoodwinker** *n*

hooey /'hooh·i/ *n* nonsense – slang [origin unknown]

[1]**hoof** /hoohf, hoof/ *n, pl* **hooves** /hoohvz/, **hoofs** (a foot with) a curved horny casing that protects the ends of the digits of a horse, cow, or similar mammal and that corresponds to a nail or claw ☞ ANATOMY [ME, fr OE *hōf*; akin to OHG *huof* hoof, Skt *śapha*] – **hoofed** *adj* – **on the hoof** *of a meat animal* before being butchered; while still alive ⟨*50p a pound* on the hoof⟩

[2]**hoof** *vt* to kick ~ *vi* to go on foot – usu + *it* *USE* infml

'**hoof,beat** /-,beet/ *n* the sound of a hoof striking a hard surface

hoofer /'hoohfə, 'hoofə/ *n, NAm* a professional dancer – slang

hoo-ha /'hooh ,hah/ *n* a fuss, to-do – chiefly infml [prob imit]

[1]**hook** /hook/ *n* **1** (sthg shaped like) a curved or bent device for catching, holding, or pulling **2a** (a flight of) a ball in golf that deviates from a straight course in a direction opposite to the dominant hand of the player propelling it – compare SLICE **b** an attacking stroke in cricket played with a horizontal bat aimed at a ball of higher than waist height and intended to send the ball on the leg side **3** a short blow delivered in boxing with a circular motion while the elbow remains bent and rigid [ME, fr OE *hōc*; akin to MD *hoec* fishhook, corner, OHG *hāko* hook, Lith *kengė*] – **by hook or by crook** by any possible means – **hook, line, and sinker** completely ⟨*swallowed all the lies* hook, line, and sinker⟩

[2]**hook** *vt* **1** to form into a hook (shape) **2** to seize, make fast, or connect (as if) by a hook **3** to make (e g a rug) by drawing loops of yarn, thread, or cloth through a coarse fabric with a hook **4a** to hit or throw (a ball) so that a hook results **b** to play a hook in cricket at (a ball) or at the bowling of (a bowler) **5** to steal – infml ~ *vi* **1** to form a hook; curve **2** to become hooked **3** to play a hook in cricket or golf

hookah /'hookə, -kah/ *n* a water pipe (with a single flexible tube by which smoke is drawn through water and into the mouth) – compare NARGHILE [Ar *ḥuqqah* bottle of a water pipe]

,**hook and** '**eye** *n* a fastening device used chiefly on garments that consists of a hook that links with a loop

hooked *adj* **1** (shaped) like or provided with a hook **2** made by hooking ⟨*a* ~ *rug*⟩ **3a** addicted to drugs – slang **b** very enthusiastic or compulsively attached (to sthg specified) ⟨~ *on skiing*⟩ – infml

hooker /'hookə/ *n* **1** (the position of) a player in rugby stationed in the middle of the front row of the scrum ☞ SPORT **2** *chiefly NAm* a woman prostitute – slang [[2]HOOK + [2]-ER]

'**hook,up** /-,up/ *n* (the plan of) a combination (e g of electronic circuits) used for a specific often temporary purpose (e g radio transmission)

'**hook,worm** /-,wuhm/ *n* (infestation with or disease caused by) any of several parasitic nematode worms that have strong mouth hooks for attaching to the host's intestinal lining

hooky, hookey /'hooki/ *n, chiefly NAm* truant – chiefly in *play hooky*; infml [prob fr slang *hook, hook it* (to make off)]

hooligan /'hoohligən/ *n* a young ruffian or hoodlum [perh fr Patrick *Hooligan fl* 1898 Irish criminal in London] – **hooliganism** *n*

[1]**hoop** /hoohp/ *n* **1** a large (rigid) circular strip used esp for holding together the staves of containers, as a child's toy, or to expand a woman's skirt **2** a circular figure or object **3** an arch through which balls must be hit in croquet [ME, fr OE *hōp*; akin to MD *hoep* ring, hoop, Lith *kabė* hook]

[2]**hoop** *vt* to bind or fasten (as if) with a hoop – **hooper** *n*

hoop-la /'hoohp ,lah/ *n* a (fairground) game in which prizes are won by tossing rings over them [partly fr [1]*hoop*; partly fr *hoopla* (commotion, excitement, nonsense), fr F *houp-là*, interj]

hoopoe /'hoohpooh, -poh/ *n* (any of several birds related to) a Eurasian and N African bird with pale pinkish brown plumage, a long erectile crest, and a slender downward-curving bill [alter. of obs *hoop*, fr MF *huppe*, fr L *upupa*, of imit origin]

hooray /hoo'ray/ *interj* hurray

[1]**hoot** /hooht/ *vi* **1** to utter a loud shout, usu in contempt **2a** to make (a sound similar to) the long-drawn-out throat noise of an owl **b** to sound the horn, whistle, etc of a motor car or other vehicle ⟨*the driver* ~ed *at me as he passed*⟩ **3** to laugh loudly – infml ~ *vt* **1** to assail or drive out by hooting ⟨~ed *down the speaker*⟩ **2** to express in or by hooting ⟨~ed *their disapproval*⟩ [ME *houten*, of imit origin]

[2]**hoot** *n* **1** a sound of hooting **2** DAMN 2 ⟨*I couldn't care 2* ~s⟩ **3** a source of laughter or amusement ⟨*the play was an absolute* ~⟩ *USE* (*2, 3*) infml

hooter /'hoohtə/ *n, chiefly Br* **1** a device (e g the horn of a car) for producing a loud hooting noise **2** the nose – infml [[1]HOOT + [2]-ER]

hoots *interj, chiefly Scot* – used to express impatience, dissatisfaction, or objection [origin unknown]

hoover /'hoohvə/ *vb* to clean using a vacuum cleaner

Hoover *trademark* – used for a vacuum cleaner

[1]**hop** /hop/ *vb* **-pp-** *vi* **1** to move by a quick springy leap or in a series of leaps; *esp* to jump on 1 foot **2** to make a quick trip, esp by air **3** to board or leave a vehicle ⟨~ *onto a bus*⟩ ~ *vt* **1** to jump over ⟨~ *a fence*⟩ **2** *NAm* to ride on, esp without authorization ⟨~ *a train*⟩ *USE* (*vi 2, 3*) infml [ME *hoppen*, fr OE *hoppian*; akin to OE *hype* hip] – **hop it** *Br* go away! – infml

[2]**hop** *n* **1a** a short leap, esp on 1 leg **b** a bounce, a rebound **2** a short or long flight between 2 landings ⟨*flew to Bangkok in 3* ~s⟩ **3** DANCE 2 – infml

[3]**hop** *n* **1** a climbing plant of the hemp family with inconspicuous green flowers of which the female ones are in cone-shaped catkins **2** *pl* the ripe dried catkins of a hop used esp to impart a bitter flavour to beer [ME *hoppe*, fr MD; akin to OHG *hopfo* hop, OE *scēaf* sheaf – more at SHEAF]

[4]**hop** *vt* **-pp-** to impregnate (esp beer) with hops

[1]**hope** /hohp/ *vi* to wish with expectation of fulfilment ~ *vt* **1** to long for with expectation of obtainment **2** to expect with desire; trust [ME *hopen*, fr OE *hopian*; akin to MHG *hoffen* to hope] – **hoper** *n* – **hope against hope** to hope without any basis for expecting fulfilment

[2]**hope** *n* **1** trust, reliance ⟨*all my ~ is in the Lord*⟩ **2a** desire accompanied by expectation of or belief in fulfilment ⟨*has high ~s of an early recovery*⟩ **b** sby or sthg on which hopes are centred **c** sthg hoped for

'**hope ,chest** *n*, *NAm* BOTTOM DRAWER

[1]'**hopeful** /-f(ə)l/ *adj* **1** full of hope ⟨*I'm ~ he'll come*⟩ **2** inspiring hope ⟨*the situation looks ~*⟩ – **hopefulness** *n*

[2]**hopeful** *n* a person who aspires to or is likely to succeed ⟨*young ~s*⟩

'**hopefully** /-f(ə)l·i/ *adv* **1** in a hopeful manner **2** it is hoped ⟨*~ he will arrive in time*⟩ – disapproved of by some speakers

'**hopeless** /-lis/ *adj* **1** having no expectation of success **2a** giving no grounds for hope ⟨*a ~ case*⟩ **b** incapable of solution, management, or accomplishment ⟨*a ~ task*⟩ **3** incompetent, useless – chiefly infml ⟨*I'm ~ at sums*⟩ – **hopelessly** *adv*, **hopelessness** *n*

hoplite /'hoplit/ *n* a heavily armed infantry soldier of ancient Greece [Gk *hoplitēs*, fr *hoplon* tool, weapon, fr *hepein* to care for, work at – more at SEPULCHRE]

hopper /'hopə/ *n* **1** a leaping insect; *specif* an immature hopping form of an insect **2a** a (funnel-shaped) receptacle for the discharging or temporary storage of grain, coal, etc **b** a goods wagon with a floor through which bulk materials may be discharged **c** a barge that can discharge dredged material through an opening bottom [[1]HOP + [2]-ER; (2) fr the shaking motion of hoppers used to feed grain into a mill]

hopping /'hoping/ *adv* – **hopping mad** extremely annoyed – infml

hopsack /'hop,sak/ *n* **1** a coarse sacking material **2** a firm rough-surfaced clothing fabric woven in basket weave [ME *hopsak* sack for hops, fr *hoppe* hop + *sak* sack]

'**hop,scotch** /-,skoch/ *n* a children's game in which a player tosses an object (e g a stone) into areas of a figure outlined on the ground and hops through the figure and back to regain the object [[1]*hop* + [2]*scotch* slight cut, scratch, scratched line]

,**hop, ,skip, and 'jump** *n* a short distance – infml

Horatian /hə'raysh(y)ən, ho-/ *adj* (characteristic) of Horace or his poetry [L *Horatianus*, fr *Horatius* Horace (Quintus Horatius Flaccus) †8 BC Roman poet]

horde /hawd/ *n* **1** a (Mongolian) nomadic people or tribe **2** a crowd, swarm [MF, G, & Pol; MF & G, fr Pol *horda*, of Mongolic origin; akin to Mongolian *orda* camp, horde]

horehound /'haw,hownd/ *n* (a plant resembling or related to) a plant of the mint family with hoary downy leaves and bitter juice [ME *horhoune*, fr OE *hārhūne*, fr *hār* hoary + *hūne* horehound – more at HOAR]

horizon /hə'riez(ə)n/ *n* **1a** the apparent junction of earth and sky **b(1)** the plane that is tangent to the earth's surface at an observer's position **(2)** (the great circle formed by the intersection with the celestial sphere of) the plane parallel to such a plane but passing through the earth's centre **c** range of perception, experience, or knowledge **2a** the geological deposit of a particular time, usu identified by distinctive fossils **b** any of the reasonably distinct soil or subsoil layers in a vertical section of land [ME *orizon*, fr LL *horizont-*, *horizon*, fr Gk *horizont-*, *horizōn*, fr prp of *horizein* to bound, define, fr *horos* boundary; akin to L *urvus* circumference of a city] – **horizonal** *adj*

horizontal /,hori'zontl/ *adj* **1a** near the horizon **b** in the plane of or (operating in a plane) parallel to the horizon or a base line; level ⟨*~ distance*⟩ ⟨*a ~ engine*⟩ **2** of or concerning relationships between people of the same rank in different hierarchies – compare VERTICAL 4 – **horizontally** *adv*

hormone /'hawmohn/ *n* (a synthetic substance with the action of) a product of living cells that usu circulates in body liquids (e g the blood or sap) and produces a specific effect on the activity of cells remote from its point of origin [Gk *hormōn*, prp of *horman* to stir up, fr *hormē* impulse, assault – more at SERUM] – **hormonal** /haw'mohnl/ *adj*, **hormonally** *adv*

horn /hawn/ *n* **1a(1)** any of the usu paired bony projecting parts on the head of cattle, giraffes, deer, and similar hoofed mammals and some extinct mammals and reptiles **(2)** a permanent solid pointed part consisting of keratin that is attached to the nasal bone of a rhinoceros **b** a natural projection from an animal (e g a snail or owl) resembling or suggestive of a horn **c** the tough fibrous material consisting chiefly of keratin that covers or forms the horns and hooves of cattle and related animals, or other hard parts (e g claws or nails) **d** a hollow horn used as a container **2** sthg resembling or suggestive of a horn: e g **a** either of the curved ends of a crescent **b** a horn-shaped body of land or water **3a** an animal's horn used as a wind instrument **b(1)** HUNTING HORN **(2)** FRENCH HORN **c** a wind instrument used in a jazz band; *esp* a trumpet **d** a device (e g on a motor car) for making loud warning noises ⟨*a fog ~*⟩ [ME, fr OE; akin to OHG *horn*, L *cornu*, Gk *keras*] – **horn** *adj*, **horned** *adj*, **hornless** *adj*, **hornlike** *adj*

hornbeam /'hawn,beem/ *n* any of a genus of trees of the hazel family with smooth grey bark and hard white wood [*horn* + [1]*beam*; fr its hard smooth wood]

'**horn,bill** /-,bil/ *n* any of a family of large Old World birds with enormous bills

hornblende /'hawn,blend/ *n* a dark mineral that consists chiefly of silicates of calcium, magnesium, and iron and is a major constituent of many igneous and metamorphic rocks [G] – **hornblendic** /hawn'blendik/ *adj*

'**horn,book** /-,book/ *n* a child's primer that consisted of a sheet of parchment or paper protected by a sheet of transparent horn

,**horned 'toad** *n* any of several small insect-eating lizards of W USA and Mexico with hornlike spines

hornet /'hawnit/ *n* a large wasp with a black and yellow banded abdomen and a powerful sting [ME *hernet*, fr OE *hyrnet*; akin to OHG *hornaz* hornet, L *crabro*]

'**hornet's ,nest** *n* an angry or hostile reaction – esp in *stir up a hornet's nest*

horn in *vi* to intrude – slang; often + *on*

ˌhorn of ˈplenty *n* a cornucopia

ˈhornˌpipe /-ˌpiep/ *n* (a piece of music for) a lively British folk dance typically associated with sailors [ME, wind instrument made partly of horn]

ˈhorn-ˌrims *n pl* glasses with horn rims – **horn-rimmed** *adj*

ˈhornˌswoggle /-ˌswogl/ *vt* to bamboozle, hoax – slang [origin unknown]

horny /ˈhawni/ *adj* **1** (made) of horn **2** sexually aroused – slang [(2) *horn* (erect penis) + *-y*]

horology /hoˈroləji/ *n* **1** the science of measuring time **2** the art of constructing instruments for indicating time [Gk *hōra* hour + E *-logy*] – **horologer** *n*, **horologist** *n*, **horologic** /ˌhorəˈlojik/, **horological** *adj*

horoscope /ˈhorəˌskohp/ *n* (an astrological forecast based on) a diagram of the relative positions of planets and signs of the zodiac at a specific time, esp sby's birth, used by astrologers to infer individual character and personality traits and to foretell events in a person's life [MF, fr L *horoscopus*, fr Gk *hōroskopos*, fr *hōra* + *skopein* to look at – more at SPY]

horrendous /həˈrendəs/ *adj* dreadful, horrible [L *horrendus*, fr gerundive of *horrēre* to bristle, tremble] – **horrendously** *adv*

horrible /ˈhorəbl/ *adj* **1** marked by or arousing horror ⟨*a ~ accident*⟩ **2** extremely unpleasant or disagreeable – chiefly infml ⟨*~ weather*⟩ [ME, fr MF, fr L *horribilis*, fr *horrēre*] – **horribleness** *n*, **horribly** /ˈhoribli/ *adv*

horrid /ˈhorid/ *adj* **1** horrible, shocking **2** repulsive, nasty ⟨*a ~ little boy*⟩ [L *horridus* rough, shaggy, bristling, fr *horrēre*] – **horridly** *adv*, **horridness** *n*

horrific /həˈrifik/ *adj* arousing horror; horrifying ⟨*a ~ account of the tragedy*⟩ – **horrifically** *adv*

horrify /ˈhorifie/ *vt* **1** to cause to feel horror **2** to fill with distaste; shock – **horrifyingly** *adv*

horror /ˈhorə/ *n* **1a** intense fear, dread, or dismay **b** intense aversion or repugnance **2** (sby or sthg that has) the quality of inspiring horror ⟨*contemplating the ~ of their lives* – Liam O'Flaherty⟩ ⟨*that child is a perfect ~*⟩ **3** *pl* a state of horror, depression, or apprehension – chiefly infml [ME *horrour*, fr MF *horror*, fr L, action of trembling, fr *horrēre* to tremble; akin to OE *gorst* gorse, Gk *chersos* dry land]

ˈhorror-ˌstruck, ˈhorror-ˌstricken *adj* filled with horror

hors de combat /ˌaw də ˈkombah (*Fr* ɔːr də kɔ̃ba)/ *adv or adj* out of the fight; disabled [F]

hors d'oeuvre /ˌaw ˈduhv (*Fr* ɔːr dœvr)/ *n, pl* **hors d'oeuvres** *also* **hors d'oeuvre** /ˈduhv(z) (*Fr* ~)/ any of various savoury foods usu served as appetizers [F *hors-d'œuvre*, lit., outside of work]

¹horse /haws/ *n, pl* **horses,** (*3*) **horse** **1a(1)** a large solid-hoofed plant-eating quadruped mammal domesticated by humans since prehistoric times and used as a beast of burden, a draught animal, or for riding ☞ ANATOMY **(2)** a racehorse ⟨*play the ~s*⟩ **b** a male horse; a stallion or gelding **2a** a usu 4-legged frame for supporting sthg (e g planks) **b(1)** POMMEL HORSE **(2)** VAULTING HORSE **3** *sing or pl in constr* the cavalry **4** a mass of wall rock occurring in a vein **5** a rope suspended from the yard of a sailing ship, on which the seamen stand when working on the sails ☞ SHIP **6** heroin – slang [ME *hors*, fr OE; akin to OHG *hros* horse] – **from the horse's mouth** from the original source

²horse *vi* to engage in horseplay ⟨horsing *around*⟩ ~ *vt* to provide (e g a person or vehicle) with a horse

¹ˈhorseˌback /-bak/ *n* – **on horseback** mounted on a horse

²horseback *adv, chiefly NAm* ON HORSEBACK

ˈhorseˌbean /-ˌbeen/ *n* BROAD BEAN [*horse* (large, coarse; in names of plants & animals), fr ¹*horse*]

ˈhorseˌbox /-ˌboks/ *n* a lorry or closed trailer for transporting horses

ˈhorse ˌbrass *n* a brass ornament worn orig on a horse's harness

ˈhorseˌbreaker /-ˌbraykə/ *n* one who breaks in or trains horses

ˌhorse ˈchestnut *n* (the large glossy brown seed of) a large tree with 5-lobed leaves and erect conical clusters of showy flowers ☞ PLANT

ˈhorseˌfly /-ˌflie/ *n* any of a family of swift usu large flies with bloodsucking females – compare CLEG

ˈhorseˌhair /-ˌheə/ *n* hair (from the mane or tail) of a horse; *also* cloth made from this

horse latitudes *n pl* either of 2 belts in the region of latitudes 30°N and 30°S with weather characterized by calms and light changeable winds

ˈhorseˌlaugh /-ˌlahf/ *n* a loud boisterous laugh

ˈhorse ˌmackerel *n* any of various large (food) fishes

ˈhorseman /-mən/, *fem* **ˈhorseˌwoman** *n* **1** a rider on horseback **2** a (skilled) breeder, tender, or manager of horses – **horsemanship** *n*

ˈhorseˌplay /-ˌplay/ *n* rough or boisterous play

ˈhorseˌpower /-ˌpowə/ *n* an imperial unit of power equal to about 746W

ˈhorseˌradish /-ˌradish/ *n* **1** a tall coarse white-flowered plant of the mustard family **2** (a condiment prepared from) the pungent root of the horseradish

ˈhorse ˌsense *n* COMMON SENSE

ˈhorseˌshit /-ˌshit/ *n, chiefly NAm* bullshit – vulg

ˈhorseˌshoe /-ˌshooh/ *n* (sthg with a shape resembling) a shoe for horses, usu consisting of a narrow U-shaped plate of iron fitting the rim of the hoof ☞ ARCHITECTURE – **horseshoe** *vt*, **horseshoer** /-ˌshooh·ə/ *n*

horseshoe bat *n* any of several Old World bats with a horseshoe-shaped pad on the muzzle

horseshoe crab *n, NAm* KING CRAB

ˈhorseˌtail /-ˌtayl/ *n* any of a genus of flowerless plants related to the ferns ☞ PLANT

ˈhorse-ˌtrading *n* negotiation accompanied by hard bargaining and reciprocal concessions

ˈhorseˌwhip /-ˌwip/ *vt* to flog (as if) with a whip for horses

ˈhorseˌwoman /-ˌwoomən/ *n* a female horseman

horsey, horsy /ˈhawsi/ *adj* **1** of or resembling a horse **2** very interested in horses, horse riding, or horse racing **3** characteristic of horsemen – **horsily** *adv*, **horsiness** *n*

horsie /ˈhawsi/ *n* – used as a pet name for a horse

horst /hawst/ *n* a block of the earth's crust higher than and separated by faults from adjacent blocks ☞ GEOGRAPHY [G]

hortative /ˈhawtətiv/, **hortatory** /ˈhawtət(ə)ri/ *adj* giving encouragement – fml [LL *hortativus*, fr L *hortatus*, pp of *hortari* to urge – more at YEARN] – **hortatively** *adv*

horticulture /'hawti,kulchə/ *n* the science and art of growing fruits, vegetables, and flowers [L *hortus* garden + E *-i-* + *culture* – more at ²YARD] – **horticultural** /,hawti'kulch(ə)rəl/ *adj*, **horticulturally** *adv*, **horticulturist** *n*

hosanna /hoh'zanə/ *interj or n* (used as) a cry of acclamation and adoration [ME *osanna*, fr LL, fr Gk *hōsanna*, fr Heb *hōshī'āh-nnā* pray, save (us)!]

¹**hose** /hohz/ *n, pl* (*1*) **hose,** (*2*) **hoses** **1** a leg covering that sometimes covers the foot: e g **a** short breeches reaching to the knee ⟨*doublet and* ~⟩ ☞ GARMENT **b** *pl, chiefly NAm* stockings; *also* tights **2** a flexible tube for conveying fluids (e g from a tap or in a car engine) [ME, fr OE *hosa* stocking, husk; akin to OHG *hosa* leg covering, Gk *kystis* bladder, OE *hȳd* hide]

²**hose** *vt* to spray, water, or wash with a hose ⟨~ *down a stable floor*⟩

Hosea /hoh'zee·ə/ *n* (an Old Testament book ascribed to) a Hebrew prophet of the 8th c BC [Heb *Hōshēa'*]

hosepipe /'hohz,piep/ *n* a length of hose for conveying water (e g for watering plants or putting out fires)

hosiery /'hohzyəri/ *n* socks, stockings, and tights in general

hospice /'hospis/ *n* **1** a place of shelter for travellers or the destitute (run by a religious order) **2** *Br* a nursing home, esp for terminally ill patients [F, fr L *hospitium*, fr *hospit-, hospes* host – more at ²HOST]

hospitable /ho'spitəbl, 'hos-/ *adj* **1a** offering a generous and cordial welcome (to guests or strangers) **b** offering a pleasant or sustaining environment ⟨*a* ~ *climate*⟩ **2** readily receptive ⟨~ *to new ideas*⟩ – **hospitably** *adv*

hospital /'hospitl/ *n* **1** an institution where the sick or injured are given medical care – often used in British English without an article ⟨*the injured were taken to* ~⟩ **2** a repair shop for specified small objects ⟨*a doll's* ~⟩ [ME, fr OF, fr ML *hospitale*, fr LL, hospice, fr L, guest room, fr neut of *hospitalis* of a guest, fr *hospit-, hospes*]

hospitality /,hospi'taləti/ *n* hospitable treatment or reception

hospital·ize, -ise /'hospitl·iez/ *vt* to place in a hospital as a patient – **hospitalization** /,hospitl·ie'zaysh(ə)n/ *n*

Hospitaller, *NAm* **Hospitaler** /'hospitl·ə/ *n* a member of a charitable, orig military, religious order established in Jerusalem in the 12th c [ME *hospitalier*, fr MF, fr ML *hospitalarius*, fr LL *hospitale*]

¹**host** /hohst/ *n* **1** a very large number; a multitude **2** an army – chiefly poetic or archaic [ME, fr OF, fr LL *hostis*, fr L, stranger, enemy – more at GUEST]

²**host** *n* **1a** an innkeeper ⟨*mine* ~⟩ **b** one who receives or entertains guests socially or officially **c** sby or sthg that provides facilities for an event or function ⟨*our college served as* ~ *for the chess tournament*⟩ **2a** a living animal or plant on or in which a parasite or smaller organism lives **b** an individual into which a tissue or part is transplanted from another **3** a compere on a radio or television programme [ME *hoste* host, guest, fr OF, fr L *hospit-, hospes*, fr *hostis*]

³**host** *vt* to act as host at or of ⟨~ed *a series of TV programmes*⟩

⁴**host** *n, often cap* the bread consecrated in the Eucharist [ME *hoste*, fr MF *hoiste*, fr LL & L; LL *hostia* Eucharist, fr L, sacrifice]

hostage /'hostij/ *n* a person held by one party as a pledge that promises will be kept or terms met by another party ⟨*hijackers took 3* ~s⟩ [ME, fr OF, fr *hoste* host, guest]

hostel /'hostl/ *n* **1** *chiefly Br* a supervised residential home: e g **a** an establishment providing accommodation for nurses, students, etc **b** an institution for junior offenders, ex-offenders, etc, encouraging social adaptation **2** YOUTH HOSTEL **3** an inn – chiefly poetic or archaic [ME, lodging, inn, fr OF, fr LL *hospitale* hospice] – **hosteller** *n*

'hostelry /-ri/ *n* an inn, hotel

hostess /hoh'stes/ *n* **1** a woman who entertains socially or acts as host **2a** a female employee on a ship, aeroplane, etc who manages the provisioning of food and attends to the needs of passengers **b** a woman who acts as a companion to male patrons, esp in a nightclub; *also* a prostitute

hostile /'hostiel/ *adj* **1** of or constituting an enemy **2** antagonistic, unfriendly **3** not hospitable ⟨*a* ~ *environment*⟩ [MF or L; MF, fr L *hostilis*, fr *hostis*] – **hostile** *n*, **hostilely** *adv*

hostility /ho'stiləti/ *n* **1** *pl* overt acts of warfare **2** antagonism, opposition, or resistance [HOSTILE + -ITY]

hostler /'oslə/ *n, chiefly NAm* an ostler

¹**hot** /hot/ *adj* **-tt-** **1a** having a relatively high temperature **b** capable of giving a sensation of heat or of burning, searing, or scalding **c** having a temperature higher than normal body temperature **2a** vehement, fiery ⟨*a* ~ *temper*⟩ **b** sexually excited; *also* sexually arousing **c** eager, enthusiastic ⟨~ *on the idea*⟩ **d** of or being an exciting style of jazz with strong rhythms – compare ¹COOL 2c **3** severe, stringent – usu + *on* ⟨*police are* ~ *on drunken drivers*⟩ **4** having or causing the sensation of an uncomfortable degree of body heat ⟨*felt too* ~⟩ **5a** very recent; fresh ⟨~ *off the press*⟩ **b** close to sthg sought ⟨*guess again, you're getting* ~⟩ **6a** suggestive of heat or of burning objects ⟨~ *colours*⟩ **b** pungent, peppery ⟨*a* ~ *curry*⟩ **7a** of intense and immediate interest; sensational **b** performing well or strongly fancied to win (e g in a sport) ⟨~ *favourite*⟩ **c** currently popular; selling very well **d** very good – used as a generalized term of approval ⟨*his English is not so* ~⟩ **8** (of, being, or for material that is) radioactive **9a** recently and illegally obtained ⟨~ *jewels*⟩ **b** wanted by the police *USE* (*2b, 2c, & 7d*) infml, (*9*) slang [ME, fr OE *hāt*; akin to OHG *heiz* hot, Lith *kaĩsti* to get hot] – **hottish** *adj*, **hotness** *n*

²**hot** *adv* hotly

,hot 'air *n* empty talk – chiefly infml

'hot,bed /-,bed/ *n* **1** a bed of soil heated esp by fermenting manure and used for forcing or raising seedlings **2** an environment that favours rapid growth or development, esp of sthg specified ⟨*a* ~ *of crime*⟩

,hot-'blooded *adj* excitable, ardent – **hot-bloodedness** *n*

hotchpotch /hoch,poch/ *n* a mixture composed of many usu unrelated parts; a jumble [ME *hochepot*, fr MF, fr OF, fr *hochier* to shake + *pot*]

,hot ,cross 'bun *n* a yeast-leavened spicy bun marked with a cross and eaten esp on Good Friday

'hot,dog *n* a frankfurter or other sausage (heated and served in a bread roll)

hotel /(h)oh'tel/ *n* a usu large establishment that provides meals and (temporary) accommodation for the public, esp for people travelling away from home [F *hôtel*, fr OF *hostel*]

Hotel – a communications code word for the letter *h*

hotelier /(h)oh·telyə, -yay/ *n* a proprietor or manager of a hotel [F *hôtelier*, fr OF *hostelier*, fr *hostel*]

,hot 'flash *n, NAm* HOT FLUSH

,hot 'flush *n* a sudden brief flushing and sensation of heat, usu associated with an imbalance of endocrine hormones occurring esp at the menopause

'hot,foot /-,foot/ *vi or adv* (to go) in haste – **hotfoot it** to hotfoot

'hot,head /-,hed/ *n* a hotheaded person

,hot'headed /-'hedid/ *adj* fiery, impetuous – **hotheadedly** *adv*, **hotheadedness** *n*

¹'hot,house /-,hows/ *n* a heated greenhouse, esp for tropical plants

²hothouse *adj* delicate, overprotected

'hot ,line *n* a direct telephone line kept in constant readiness for immediate communication (e g between heads of state)

'hotly /-li/ *adv* in a hot or fiery manner ⟨*a ~ debated issue*⟩

,hot 'metal *n* a method of printing using type cast directly from molten metal

,hot 'pepper *n* (a plant bearing) any of various small usu thin-walled pungent capsicum fruits

'hot ,plate *n* a metal plate or spiral, usu on an electric cooker, on which food can be heated and cooked

'hot ,pot *n* a (mutton, lamb, or beef and potato) stew cooked esp in a covered pot

,hot po'tato *n* a controversial or sensitive question or issue – infml

'hot ,rod *n* a motor vehicle rebuilt or modified for high speed and fast acceleration – **hot-rodder** *n*

'hot ,seat *n* **1** a position involving risk, embarrassment, or responsibility for decision-making ⟨*in the ~ at the interview*⟩ – infml **2** ELECTRIC CHAIR – slang

'hot,shot /-,shot/ *n* a showily successful or important person – infml – **hotshot** *adj*

,hot 'spring *n* a spring of naturally hot water ☞ ENERGY

,hot 'stuff *n* **1** sby or sthg of outstanding ability or quality **2** sby or sthg sexually exciting ⟨*she's really ~*⟩ *USE* infml

Hottentot /'hot(ə)n,tot/ *n* a member, or the language, of a people of southern Africa apparently of mixed Bushman and Bantu origin [Afrik]

hot up *vi* to become hot; increase in activity, intensity, liveliness, excitement, etc ⟨*air raids began to* hot up *about the beginning of February* – George Orwell⟩ ~ *vt* to make hotter, livelier, or faster

,hot 'water *n* a distressing predicament (likely to lead to punishment); trouble – infml

,hot-'water ,bottle *n* a usu flat rubber container that is filled with hot water and used esp to warm a (person in) bed

¹hound /hownd/ *n* **1** a dog; *esp* one of any of various hunting breeds typically with large drooping ears and a deep bark that track their prey by scent **2** a mean or despicable person **3** one who is devoted to the pursuit of sthg specified [ME, fr OE *hund*; akin to OHG *hunt* dog, L *canis*, Gk *kyōn*]

²hound *vt* **1** to pursue (as if) with hounds **2** to harass persistently – **hounder** *n*

'hound's-,tongue *n* any of various coarse plants of the borage family with tongue-shaped leaves (and dull reddish-purple flowers)

,hounds,tooth 'check /-,toohth/, **hound's-tooth check** *n* a small broken-check textile pattern

hour /owə/ *n* **1** (any of the 7 times of day set aside for) a daily liturgical devotion **2** the 24th part of a day; a period of 60 minutes **3a** *the* the time of day reckoned in hours and minutes by the clock; *esp* the beginning of each full hour measured by the clock ⟨*the train leaves on the ~*⟩ **b** *pl* the time reckoned in one 24-hour period from midnight to midnight ⟨*attack at 0900 ~s*⟩ **4a** a fixed or customary period of time set aside for a usu specified purpose ⟨*the lunch ~*⟩ – often pl ⟨*during office ~s*⟩ **b** a particular, usu momentous, period or point of time ⟨*in his ~ of need*⟩ **c** *the* present ⟨*the story of the ~*⟩ **5** *pl* one's regular time of getting up or going to bed ⟨*kept late ~s*⟩ **6** the work done or distance travelled at normal rate in an hour ⟨*the city was 2 ~s away*⟩ **7** *NAm* a unit of educational credit [ME, fr OF *heure*, fr LL & L; LL *hora* canonical hour, fr L, hour of the day, fr Gk *hōra*]

¹'hour,glass /-,glahs/ *n* a glass or perspex instrument for measuring time consisting of 2 bulbs joined by a narrow neck from the uppermost of which a quantity of sand, water, etc runs into the lower in the space of an hour

²hourglass *adj* shapely with a narrow waist ⟨*an ~ figure*⟩

'hour ,hand *n* the short hand that marks the hours on the face of a watch or clock

houri /'hooəri/ *n, pl* **houris** **1** any of the female virgin attendants of the blessed in the Muslim paradise **2** a voluptuously beautiful young woman [F, fr Per *hūri*, fr Ar *ḥūriyah*]

¹hourly /'owəli/ *adv* **1** at or during every hour; *also* continually ⟨*we're expecting him ~*⟩ **2** by the hour ⟨*~ paid workers*⟩

²hourly *adj* **1** occurring or done every hour; *also* continual **2** reckoned by the hour

¹house /hows/ *n, pl* **houses** /'howziz/ **1** a building designed for people to live in **2a** an animal's shelter or refuge (e g a nest or den) **b** a building in which sthg is housed or stored ⟨*a hen ~*⟩ **c** a building used for a particular purpose, esp eating, drinking, or entertainment ⟨*a public ~*⟩ **3** any of the 12 equal sectors into which the celestial sphere is divided in astrology **4a** *sing or pl in constr* the occupants of a house ⟨*you'll wake the whole ~*⟩ **b** a family including ancestors, descendants, and kindred ⟨*the ~ of Tudor*⟩ **5a** (a residence of) a religious community **b** any of several groups into which a British school may be divided for social purposes or games **6** (the chamber of) a legislative or deliberative assembly; *esp* a division of a body consisting of 2 chambers **7a** a business organization or establishment ⟨*a publishing ~*⟩ ⟨*~ style*⟩ **b** *cap* a large building used by a business or institution – used in names ⟨*Transport* House⟩ **c** (the audience in) a theatre or concert hall ⟨*a full ~*⟩ [ME *hous*, fr OE *hūs*; akin to OHG *hūs* house] – **houseful** *n*, **houseless** *adj* – **on the house** at the expense of an establishment or its management ⟨*have a drink* on the house⟩

²**house** /howz/ *vt* **1** to provide with accommodation or storage space **2** to serve as shelter for; contain ⟨*a library* ~s *thousands of books*⟩

'**house ar,rest** *n* confinement to one's place of residence instead of prison

'**house,boat** /-,boht/ *n* an often permanently moored boat that is fitted out as a home

'**house,bound** /-,bownd/ *adj* confined to the house (e g because of illness)

'**house,breaking** /-,brayking/ *n* an act of breaking into and entering the house of another with a criminal purpose – **housebreaker** *n*

'**house,broken** /-,brohkən/ *adj, chiefly NAm* housetrained

'**house,carl** /-,kahl/ *n* a member of the bodyguard of a Danish or early English king or noble [OE *hūscarl*, fr ON *hūskarl*, fr *hūs* house + *karl* man]

'**house,coat** /-,koht/ *n* a woman's light dressing gown for wear round the house; *also* a short overall

'**house,craft** /-,krahft/ *n* **1** DOMESTIC SCIENCE **2** skill in running a household

'**house,father** /-,fahdhə/, *fem* '**house,mother** /-,mudhə/ *n* sby in charge of a group of young people living in care (e g in a children's home)

'**house,fly** /-,flie/ *n* a fly found in most parts of the world that frequents houses and carries disease

'**house,guest** /-,gest/ *n* GUEST 1a

¹'**house,hold** /-,hohld/ *n sing or pl in constr* all the people who live together in a dwelling

²**household** *adj* **1** domestic **2** familiar, common ⟨*a* ~ *name*⟩

household cavalry *n* a cavalry regiment appointed to guard a sovereign or his/her residence

'**house,holder** /-,hohldə/ *n* a person who occupies a dwelling as owner or tenant

household troops *n pl* troops appointed to guard a sovereign or his/her residence

'**house,keeper** /-,keepə/ *n* sby, esp a woman, employed to take charge of the running of a house

'**house,keeping** /-,keeping/ *n* **1** (money used for) the day-to-day running of a house and household affairs **2** the general management of an organization which ensures its smooth running (e g the provision of equipment, keeping of records, etc) **3** the routine tasks that have to be done in order for sthg to function properly

'**house,leek** /-,leek/ *n* a pink-flowered Eurasian plant which grows esp on walls and roofs

'**house,lights** /-,liets/ *n pl* the lights that illuminate the auditorium of a theatre

'**house,maid** /-,mayd/ *n* a female servant employed to do housework

house,maid's knee *n* a swelling over the knee due to an enlargement of the bursa in the front of the kneecap [fr its frequent occurrence among servants who often work on their knees]

'**houseman** /-mən/ *n* (one holding) the most junior grade of British hospital doctor

'**house ,martin** *n* a European martin with blue-black plumage and white rump that nests on cliffs and under the eaves of houses

'**house,master** /-,mahstə/, *fem* '**house,mistress** *n* a teacher in charge of a school house

'**house,mother** /-,mudhə/, *masc* '**house,father** *n* sby in charge of a group of young people living in care (e g in a children's home)

'**house ,mouse** *n* a common usu grey mouse that lives and breeds in and around buildings and is found in most parts of the world

house of cards *n* a precarious structure or situation

,**House of 'Commons** *n* the lower house of the British and Canadian parliaments ☞ LAW

house of ill repute *n* a brothel – euph

,**House of 'Lords** *n* **1** the upper house of Parliament **2** the body of Law Lords that constitutes the highest British court of appeal *USE* ☞ LAW

House of Representatives *n* the lower house of the US Congress or Australian Parliament

'**houseparent** /-,peərənt/ *n* a housemother or housefather

'**house ,party** *n* a party lasting for a day or more held at a large, usu country, house

'**house,plant** /-,plahnt/ *n* a plant grown or kept indoors

'**house-,proud** *adj* (excessively) careful about the management and appearance of one's house

'**house ,sparrow** *n* a brown Eurasian sparrow that lives esp in or near human settlements

,**house-to-'house** *adj* DOOR-TO-DOOR 1

'**house,top** /-,top/ *n* a roof – **from the housetops** for all to hear; IN PUBLIC ⟨*shouting their grievances* from the housetops⟩

'**house,train** /-,trayn/ *vt* **1** *chiefly Br* to train (e g a pet) to defecate and urinate outdoors **2** to teach (e g a person) to behave acceptably – humor

'**house,warming** /-,wawming/ *n* a party to celebrate moving into a new house or premises

housewife /'hows,wief; *sense 2* 'huzif/ *n* **1** a usu married woman who runs a house **2** a small container for needlework articles (e g thread) – **housewifely** /'hows,wiefli/ *adj*, **housewifery** /-,wif(ə)ri/ *n*

'**house,work** /-,wuhk/ *n* the work (e g cleaning) involved in maintaining a house

housing /'howzing/ *n* **1** (the provision of) houses or dwelling-places collectively **2** a protective cover for machinery, sensitive instruments, etc

housing association *n* a nonprofitmaking society that constructs, renovates, and helps tenants to rent or buy housing

hove /hohv/ *past of* HEAVE

hovel /'hovl/ *n* a small, wretched, and often dirty house or abode [ME]

hover /'hovə/ *vi* **1** to hang in the air or on the wing **2a** to linger or wait restlessly around a place **b** to be in a state of uncertainty, irresolution, or suspense [ME *hoveren*, freq of *hoven* to hover] – **hover** *n*, **hoverer** *n*

'**hover,craft** /-,krahft/ *n, pl* **hovercraft** a vehicle supported on a cushion of air provided by fans and designed to travel over both land and sea

'**hover,fly** /-,flie/ *n* any of various brightly coloured flies that hover in the air ☞ DEFENCE

'**hover,port** /-,pawt/ *n* a place where passengers embark on and disembark from hovercraft [*hover*craft + *port*]

'**hover,train** /-,trayn/ *n* a train that travels on a cushion of air along a special usu concrete track

¹**how** /how/ *adv* **1a** in what manner or way ⟨~ *do you spell it?*⟩ ⟨*know* ~ *it works*⟩ **b** with what meaning; to what effect ⟨~ *can you explain it?*⟩ **c** for what reason; why ⟨~ *could you do it?*⟩ **2** by what measure or quantity ⟨~ *much does it cost?*⟩ – often used in an exclamation as an intensive ⟨~ *nice*

of you to come!⟩ **3** in what state or condition (e g of health) ⟨~ *are you?*⟩ ⟨~ *is the market today?*⟩ [ME, fr OE *hū*; akin to OHG *hwuo* how, OE *hwā* who – more at WHO] – **how about** what do you say to or think of ⟨how about *going to London for the day?*⟩ – **how come** how does it happen; why is it ⟨how come *we never meet?*⟩ – infml – **how do you do** – used as a formal greeting between people meeting for the first time – **how's that** **1** – used to call attention to and invite comment on sthg ⟨how's that *for enterprise?*⟩ **2** please repeat **3** – used in cricket as an appeal to the umpire to give the batsman out

[2]**how** *conj* **1a** the way, manner, or state in which ⟨*remember* ~ *they fought*⟩ ⟨*asked* ~ *he felt*⟩ **b** that ⟨*do you remember* ~ *he arrived right at the end*⟩ **2** however, as ⟨*do it* ~ *you like*⟩

[3]**how** *n* the manner in which sthg is done ⟨*the* ~ *and the why of it*⟩

howdah /'howdə/ *n* a usu canopied seat on the back of an elephant or camel [Hindi *hauda*]

,how-do-you-'do, how d'ye do /dyə/ *n* a confused or embarrassing situation – infml [fr the phrase *how do you do?*]

howdy /'howdi/ *n, chiefly NAm* hello – infml [alter. of *how do (you do)*]

howe /how, hoh/ *n, Scot* a hollow, valley [ME (northern) *how, holl*, fr OE *hol*, fr *hol*, adj, hollow – more at HOLE]

[1]**however** /how'evə/ *conj* in whatever manner or way ⟨*can go* ~ *he likes*⟩

[2]**however** *adv* **1** to whatever degree or extent; no matter how ⟨~ *fast I eat*⟩ **2** in spite of that; nevertheless ⟨*would like to go;* ~, *I think I'd better not*⟩ **3** how in the world ⟨~ *did you manage it?*⟩ – infml

howff, howf /howf, hohf/ *n, Scot* a haunt, resort; *esp* a pub [D *hof* enclosure; akin to OE *hof* enclosure, *hȳf* hive]

howitzer /'how·itzə/ *n* a short cannon usu with a medium muzzle velocity and a relatively high trajectory [D *houwitser*, deriv of Czech *houfnice* ballista]

howl /howl/ *vi* **1a** *esp of dogs, wolves, etc* to make a loud sustained doleful cry **b** *of wind* to make a sustained wailing sound **2** to cry loudly and without restraint (e g with pain or laughter) ~ *vt* to utter with a loud sustained cry [ME *houlen*; akin to MHG *hiulen* to howl, Gk *kōkyein* to shriek] – **howl** *n*

howl down *vt* to express one's disapproval of (e g a speaker or his/her views), esp by shouting in order to prevent from being heard

howler /'howlə/ *n* a stupid and comic blunder – infml [HOWL + [2]-ER]

'howler ,monkey *n* any of a genus of S and Central American monkeys that have a long prehensile tail and a loud howling cry

howling /'howling/ *adj* very great, extreme, or severe ⟨*a* ~ *success*⟩ – infml

howzat /how'zat/ *interj* HOW'S THAT 3 [by alter.]

[1]**hoy** /hoy/ *interj* – used in attracting attention or in driving animals [ME]

[2]**hoy** *n* a small usu fore-and-aft rigged coaster [ME, fr MD *hoei*]

hoyden /'hoydn/ *n* a boisterous girl [perh fr obs D *heiden* country lout, fr MD, heathen; akin to OE *hǣthen* heathen – more at HEATHEN] – **hoydenish** *adj*

hub /hub/ *n* **1** the central part of a wheel, propeller, or fan through which the axle passes **2** the centre of activity or importance [prob alter. of [2]*hob*]

hubble-bubble /'hubl ,bubl/ *n* **1** WATER PIPE 2 **2** a flurry of noise or activity; a commotion [redupl of *bubble*]

hubbub /'hubub/ *n* a noisy confusion; uproar [prob of Celt origin; akin to ScGael *ub ub*, interj of contempt]

hubby /'hubi/ *n* a husband – infml [by alter.]

hubcap /'hub,kap/ *n* a removable metal cap placed over the hub of a wheel

hubris /'hyoohbris/ *n* overweening pride, usu leading to retribution [Gk *hybris* – more at OUT] – **hubristic** /hyooh'bristik/ *adj*

huckaback /'hukə,bak/ *n* an absorbent durable fabric of cotton, linen, or both, used chiefly for towels [origin unknown]

huckleberry /'huklb(ə)ri, -,beri/ *n* **1** (an edible dark blue or black berry of) any of a genus of American shrubs of the heath family **2** a blueberry [perh alter. of *hurtleberry* (whortleberry, huckleberry)]

[1]**huckster** /'hukstə/ *n* **1** a hawker, pedlar **2** *chiefly NAm* one who writes advertising material, esp for radio or television [ME *hukster*, fr MD *hokester*, fr *hoeken* to peddle; akin to MLG *hōken* to peddle – more at HAWKER]

[2]**huckster** *vi* to haggle ~ *vt* **1** to deal in or bargain over **2** to promote or advertise, esp in an aggressive or underhand manner

[1]**huddle** /'hudl/ *vb* **huddling** /'hudling, 'hudl·ing/ *vt* **1** to crowd together **2** to draw or curl (oneself) up ~ *vi* **1** to gather in a closely-packed group **2** to curl up; crouch [prob fr or akin to ME *hoderen* to huddle]

[2]**huddle** *n* **1** a closely-packed group; a bunch **2** a secretive or conspiratorial meeting ⟨*went into a* ~ *with his colleagues*⟩

hue /hyooh/ *n* **1** a complexion, aspect ⟨*political factions of every* ~⟩ **2** the attribute of colours that permits them to be classed as red, yellow, green, blue, or an intermediate between any adjacent pair of these colours; *also* a colour having this attribute – compare LIGHTNESS, SATURATION [ME *hewe*, fr OE *hīw*; akin to OE *hār* hoary – more at HOAR]

,hue and 'cry *n* **1** a cry formerly used when in pursuit of a criminal **2** a clamour of alarm or protest [*hue* (shout, outcry), fr ME *hew, hu*, fr OF *hue*, fr *huer* to shout, fr *hu*, interj]

hued *adj* coloured – usu in combination ⟨*green*-hued⟩

[1]**huff** /huf/ *vi* **1** to emit loud puffs (e g of breath or steam) **2** to make empty threats ⟨*management* ~ed *and puffed about the chances of a lockout*⟩ [imit]

[2]**huff** *n* – **huffily** *adv*, **huffiness** *n*, **huffish** *adj*, **huffy** *adj* – **in a huff** in a piqued and resentful mood

[1]**hug** /hug/ *vt* **-gg-** **1** to hold or press tightly, esp in the arms **2a** to feel very pleased with (oneself) **b** to cling to; cherish ⟨~ged *his miseries like a sulky child* – John Buchan⟩ **3** to stay close to ⟨*thick smoke* ~ged *the ground*⟩ [perh of Scand origin; akin to ON *hugga* to soothe] – **huggable** *adj*

[2]**hug** *n* a tight clasp or embrace

huge /hyoohj/ *adj* great in size, scale, degree, or scope; enormous ⟨~ *mountains*⟩ ⟨*a* ~ *success*⟩ [ME, fr OF *ahuge*] – **hugely** *adv*, **hugeness** *n*

'hugely /-li/ *adv* very much; enormously ⟨*was* ~ *excited*⟩

hugger-mugger /'hugə ,mugə/ *n* **1** secrecy **2** confusion, muddle [origin unknown] – **hugger-mugger** *adj or adv*

huh /huh, hah/ *interj* – used to express surprise, disapproval, or inquiry

hula *also* **,hula-'hula** /'hoolə/ *n* a Polynesian dance involving swaying of the hips [Hawaiian]

'hula ,hoop *n* a light usu cane or plastic hoop that can be made to spin round the waist by gyrating the body [*hula*]

hulk /hulk/ *n* **1a** the hull of a ship that is no longer seaworthy and is used as a storehouse or, esp formerly, as a prison **b** an abandoned wreck or shell, esp of a vessel **2** a person, creature, or thing that is bulky or unwieldy ⟨*a big ~ of a man*⟩ [ME *hulke*, fr OE *hulc*, fr ML *holcas*, fr Gk *holkas*, fr *helkein* to pull – more at SULCUS]

hulking /'hulking/ *adj* bulky, massive

¹hull /hul/ *n* **1a** the outer covering of a fruit or seed **b** the calyx that surrounds some fruits (e g the strawberry) **2** the main frame or body of a ship, flying boat, airship, etc **3** a covering, casing [ME, fr OE *hulu*; akin to OHG *hala* hull, OE *helan* to conceal – more at HELL]

²hull *vt* **1** to remove the hulls of **2** to hit or pierce the hull of (e g a ship) – **huller** *n*

hullabaloo /,huləbə'looh/ *n, pl* **hullabaloos** a confused noise; uproar – infml [perh irreg fr *hallo* + Sc *balloo*, interj used to hush children]

hullo /hu'loh/ *interj or n, chiefly Br* hello

¹hum /hum/ *vb* **-mm-** *vi* **1a** to utter a prolonged /m/ sound **b** to make the characteristic droning noise of an insect in motion or a similar sound **2** to be lively or active – infml **3** to have an offensive smell – slang ~ *vt* **1** to sing with the lips closed and without articulation **2** to affect or express by humming [ME *hummen*; akin to MHG *hummen* to hum, MD *hommel* bumblebee] – **hum** *n* – **hum and ha** *also* **hum and haw** to equivocate

²hum *interj* – used to express hesitation, uncertainty, disagreement, etc

¹human /'hyoohmən/ *adj* **1** (characteristic) of humans ⟨~ *voice*⟩ **2** consisting of men and women ⟨*the ~ race*⟩ ⟨*a ~ barrier*⟩ **3a** having the esp good attributes (e g kindness and compassion) thought to be characteristic of humans ⟨*is really very ~*⟩ **b** having, showing, or concerned with qualities or feelings characteristic of mankind ⟨*to err is ~*⟩ ⟨~ *interest*⟩ [ME *humain*, fr MF, fr L *humanus*; akin to L *homo* man – more at HOMAGE] – **humanness** *n*

²human, **,human 'being** *n* a man, woman, or child; a person

humane /hyooh'mayn/ *adj* **1a** marked by compassion or consideration for other human beings or animals **b** causing the minimum pain possible ⟨~ *killing of animals*⟩ **2** characterized by broad humanistic culture; liberal ⟨~ *studies*⟩ [ME *humain*] – **humanely** *adv*, **humaneness** *n*

human engineering *n, chiefly NAm* ergonomics

humanism /'hyoohmə,niz(ə)m/ *n* **1** a cultural movement dominant during the Renaissance that was characterized by a revival of classical learning and a shift of emphasis from religious to secular concerns; *broadly* literary culture **2** humanitarianism **3** a doctrine, attitude, or way of life based on human interests or values; *esp* a philosophy that asserts the intrinsic worth of man and that usu rejects religious belief – **humanist** *n or adj*, **humanistic** /,hyoohmə'nistik/ *adj*, **humanistically** *adv*

humanitarian /hyooh,mani'teəri·ən/ *n* one who promotes human welfare and social reform; a philanthropist – **humanitarian** *adj*, **humanitarianism** /-,niz(ə)m/ *n*

humanity /hyooh'manəti/ *n* **1** the quality of being humane **2** the quality or state of being human **3** *pl the* cultural branches of learning **4** mankind

human·ize, -ise /'hyoomə,niez/ *vt* **1** to cause to be or seem human **2** to make humane – **humanization** /,hyoohmənie'zaysh(ə)n/ *n*

,human'kind /-'kiend/ *n sing or pl in constr* human beings collectively

'humanly /-li/ *adv* **1a** from a human viewpoint **b** within the range of human capacity ⟨*as perfectly as is ~ possible*⟩ **2a** in a manner characteristic of humans, esp in showing emotion or weakness **b** with humaneness

humanoid /'hyoohmə,noyd/ *adj* having human form or characteristics – **humanoid** *n*

¹humble /'humbl/ *adj* **1** having a low opinion of oneself; unassertive **2** marked by deference or submission ⟨*a ~ apology*⟩ **3a** ranking low in a hierarchy or scale ⟨*man of ~ origins*⟩ **b** modest, unpretentious ⟨*a ~ dwelling*⟩ [ME, fr OF, fr L *humilis* low, humble, fr *humus* earth; akin to Gk *chthōn* earth, *chamai* on the ground] – **humbleness** *n*, **humbly** *adv*

²humble *vt* **1** to make humble in spirit or manner; humiliate **2** to destroy the power, independence, or prestige of

'humble-,bee *n* a bumblebee [ME *humbylbee*, fr *humbyl-* (akin to MD *hommel* bumblebee) + *bee* – more at HUM]

¹humbug /'hum,bug/ *n* **1a** sthg designed to deceive and mislead **b** an impostor, sham **2** pretence, deception **3** drivel, nonsense **4** a hard usu peppermint-flavoured striped sweet made from boiled sugar [origin unknown] – **humbuggery** *n*

²humbug *vb* **-gg-** to deceive with a hoax

humdinger /'hum,dingə/ *n* an excellent or remarkable person or thing – infml [origin unknown]

humdrum /'hum,drum/ *adj* monotonous, dull [irreg redupl of *hum*] – **humdrum** *n*

humeral /'hyoohmərəl/ *adj* (situated in the region) of the humerus or shoulder

humerus /'hyoohmərəs/ *n, pl* **humeri** /-,rie/ the long bone of the upper arm or forelimb extending from the shoulder to the elbow ☞ ANATOMY [NL, fr L, upper arm, shoulder; akin to Goth *ams* shoulder, Gk *ōmos*]

humid /'hyoohmid/ *adj* containing or characterized by perceptible moisture ⟨*a ~ climate*⟩ [F or L; F *humide*, fr L *humidus*, fr *humēre* to be moist] – **humidly** *adv*

humidifier /hyooh'midi,fie·ə/ *n* a device for supplying or maintaining humidity (e g in a centrally heated room)

humidify /hyooh'midifie/ *vt* to make humid – **humidification** /-,midifi'kaysh(ə)n/ *n*

humidity /hyooh'midəti/ *n* (the degree of) moisture or dampness, esp in the atmosphere – compare RELATIVE HUMIDITY

humidor /'hyoohmidaw/ *n* a case or room in which cigars or tobacco can be kept moist [*humid* + *-or* (as in *cuspidor*)]

humify /'hyoohmifie/ *vb* to convert into or form humus – **humification** /,hyoohmifi'kaysh(ə)n/ *n*

humiliate /hyooh'miliayt/ *vt* to cause to feel humble; lower the dignity or self-respect of [LL *humiliatus*, pp of *humiliare*, fr L *humilis* low – more at HUMBLE] – **humiliation** /-,mili'aysh(ə)n/ *n*

humility /hyooh'miləti/ *n* the quality or state of being humble

hummingbird /'huming,buhd/ *n* any of numerous tiny brightly coloured usu tropical American birds related to the swifts, having a slender bill and narrow wings that beat rapidly making a humming sound

hummock /'humək/ *n* **1** a hillock **2** a ridge of ice [alter. of earlier *hammock*, of unknown origin] – **hummocky** *adj*

hummus, houmous /'hoohməs, 'hooməs/ *n* a puree made from chick-peas and sesame seed paste, served as an appetizer or salad [Turk *humus* mashed chick-peas]

humoral /'hyoohmərəl/ *adj* of or relating to a bodily fluid or secretion (e g an endocrine hormone)

humoresque /,hyoomə'resk/ *n* a musical composition that is whimsical or fanciful in character [G *humoreske*, fr *humor*, fr E *humour*]

humorist /'hyoohmərist/ *n* a person specializing in or noted for humour in speech, writing, or acting – **humoristic** /,hyoohmə'ristik/ *adj*

humorous /'hyoohmərəs/ *adj* full of, characterized by, or expressing humour – **humorously** *adv*, **humorousness** *n*

¹humour, *NAm chiefly* **humor** /'hyoohmə/ *n* **1** any of the 4 fluids of the body (blood, phlegm, and yellow and black bile) formerly held to determine, by their relative proportions, a person's health and temperament **2** characteristic or habitual disposition ⟨*a man of cheerful* ~⟩ **3** a state of mind; a mood **4** a sudden inclination; a caprice **5a** (sthg having) the quality of causing amusement **b** the faculty of expressing or appreciating what is comic or amusing [ME *humour*, fr MF *humeur*, fr ML & L; ML *humor* humour of the body, fr L, moisture; akin to ON *vökr* damp, L *humēre* to be moist, Gk *hygros* wet] – **humourless** *adj*, **humourlessness** *n* – **out of humour** in a bad temper

²humour, *NAm chiefly* **humor** *vt* to comply with the mood or wishes of; indulge

¹hump /hump/ *n* **1** a rounded protuberance: e g **a** a humped or crooked back **b** a fleshy protuberance on the back of a camel, bison, etc **c** a mound, knoll **2** a difficult, trying, or critical phase ⟨*we're over the* ~ *now*⟩ **3** *Br* a fit of depression or sulking – infml; + *the* ⟨*he's got the* ~⟩ [akin to MLG *hump* bump, L *incumbere* to lie down, Gk *kymbē* bowl, OE *hype* hip] – **humped** *adj*

²hump *vt* **1** to form or curve into a hump **2** *chiefly Br* to carry with difficulty ⟨~*ing suitcases around*⟩ **3** to have sexual intercourse with ~ *vi* **1** to rise in a hump **2** *Austr* to travel around or go on foot **3** to have sexual intercourse *USE* (*vt2; vi2*) infml; (*vt3; vi3*) slang

'hump,back /-,bak/ *n* **1** a hunchback **2** *also* **humpback whale** a large whale related to the rorquals but having very long flippers – **humpbacked** *adj*

,humpback 'bridge *n* a usu narrow bridge rising and falling steeply from a central hump

humph /hum(p)f/ *vi or interj* (to utter) a gruntlike sound used to express doubt or contempt [imit]

¹humpy /'humpi/ *adj* **1** full of or covered in humps **2** having the form of a hump **3** irritable, irascible – infml

²humpy *n*, *Austr* a small or primitive hut [native name in Australia]

humus /'hyoohməs/ *n* a brown or black organic soil material resulting from partial decomposition of plant or animal matter [NL, fr L, earth – more at HUMBLE] – **humic** /-mik/ *adj*

Hun /hun/ *n, pl* **Huns** (*2b*) **Huns**, *esp collectively* **Hun** **1** a member of a nomadic Mongolian people who overran a large part of central and E Europe under Attila during the 4th and 5th c AD **2a** *often not cap* a person who is wantonly destructive **b** a German; *esp* a German soldier in WW I or II – derog [LL *Hunni*, pl] – **Hunnish** *adj*

¹hunch /hunch/ *vi* to assume a bent or crooked posture ~ *vt* to bend into a hump or arch ⟨~*ed his shoulders*⟩ [origin unknown]

²hunch *n* **1** HUMP 1 **2** a strong intuitive feeling

'hunch,back /-,bak/ *n* (sby with) a humped back – **hunchbacked** *adj*

hundred /'hundrəd/ *n, pl* **hundreds, hundred** **1** ☞ NUMBER **2** the number occupying the position 3 to the left of the decimal point in Arabic notation; *also, pl* this position **3** 100 units or digits; *specif* £100 ⟨*must have cost* ~s⟩ **4** *pl the* numbers 100 to 999 **5** a score of 100 or more runs made by a batsman in cricket **6** *pl the* 100 years of a specified century ⟨*the 19* ~s⟩ **7** a historical subdivision of a county **8** an indefinitely large number – infml; often pl with sing. meaning [ME, fr OE; akin to ON *hundrath* hundred; both fr a prehistoric WGmc-NGmc compound whose constituents were akin respectively to OE *hund* hundred & to Goth *garathjan* to count; akin to L *centum* hundred, Gk *hekaton*, Av *satəm*, OE *tīen* ten – more at TEN, REASON] – **hundred** *adj*, **hundredth** /-dth/ *adj or n*

,hundreds and 'thousands *n pl* tiny strips of sugar of assorted bright colours, used esp for cake decoration

'hundred,weight /-,wayt/ *n, pl* **hundredweight, hundredweights** **1** a British unit of weight equal to 112lb (about 50.80kg) **2** *chiefly NAm* a US unit of weight equal to 100lb (about 45.36kg) *USE* ☞ UNIT

hung /hung/ *past of* HANG

Hungarian /hung'geəri·ən/ *n* **1** a native or inhabitant of Hungary; a Magyar **2** the Finno-Ugric language of Hungary [*Hungary*, country in central Europe] – **Hungarian** *adj*

¹hunger /'hung·gə/ *n* **1** (a weakened condition or unpleasant sensation arising from) a craving or urgent need for food **2** a strong desire; a craving [ME, fr OE *hungor*; akin to OHG *hungar* hunger, Skt *kāṅkṣati* he desires]

²hunger *vi* **1** to feel or suffer hunger **2** to have an eager desire – usu + *for* or *after*

'hunger ,strike *n* refusal, as an act of protest, to eat enough to sustain life – **hunger striker** *n*

,hung 'jury *n* a jury that fails to reach a verdict

,hung 'over *adj* suffering from a hangover

hungry /'hung·gri/ *adj* **1a** feeling hunger **b** characterized by or indicating hunger or appetite ⟨*a* ~ *look*⟩ **2** eager, avid ⟨~ *for power*⟩ **3** not rich or fertile; barren – **hungrily** *adv*, **hungriness** *n*

hunk /hungk/ *n* **1** a large lump or piece **2** a usu muscular sexually attractive man – infml [Flem *hunke*]

hunkers /'hungkəz/ *n pl* the haunches – infml [*hunker* (to crouch, squat), perh of Scand origin]

hunky-dory /,hungki 'dawri/ *adj* excellent, fine – infml [obs E dial. *hunk* (home base) + *-dory* (origin unknown)]

¹hunt /hunt/ *vt* **1a** to pursue for food or enjoyment ⟨~ *foxes*⟩ **b** to use (e g hounds) in the search for game **2a** to pursue with intent to capture ⟨~ed *the escaped prisoner*⟩ **b** to search out; seek **3** to persecute or chase, esp by harrying **4** to traverse in search of prey ~*vi* **1** to take part in a hunt, esp regularly **2** to attempt to find sthg **3** *of a device, machine, etc* to run alternately fast and slowly [ME *hunten*, fr OE *huntian*; akin to OHG heri*hunda* battle spoils, ON *henda* to grasp]

²hunt *n* **1** the act, the practice, or an instance of hunting **2a** *sing or pl in constr* a group of usu mounted hunters and their hounds **b** the area hunted

hunter /'huntə/, *fem* (*1a&2*) **huntress** /-tris/ *n* **1a** sby who hunts game, esp with hounds **b** a usu fast strong horse used in hunting **2** a person who hunts or seeks sthg, esp overeagerly ⟨*a fortune* ~⟩ **3** a watch with a hinged metal cover to protect it

'hunter's ,moon *n* the first full moon after harvest moon

hunting /'hunting/ *n* the pursuit of game on horseback with hounds

'hunting ,ground *n* an area of usu fruitful search or exploitation ⟨*the British Empire is now a favourite* ~ *for historians*⟩

'hunting ,horn *n* a signal horn used in the chase, usu consisting of a long coiled tube with a flared bell

,hunting 'pink *adj or n* (of) the red colour of the coats worn by fox-hunters

,Huntington's cho'rea /'huntingtənz/ *n* a hereditary fatal brain disorder that develops usu in middle age and is characterized by chorea and nervous degeneration [George *Huntington* †1916 US neurologist]

'huntsman /-mən/ *n* **1** HUNTER 1a **2** sby who looks after the hounds of a hunt

¹hurdle /'huhdl/ *n* **1a** a portable framework, usu of interlaced branches and stakes, used esp for enclosing land or livestock **b** a frame formerly used for dragging traitors to execution **2a** a light barrier jumped by men, horses, dogs, etc in certain races **b** *pl* any of various races over hurdles **3** a barrier, obstacle [ME *hurdel*, fr OE *hyrdel*; akin to OHG *hurd* hurdle, L *cratis* wickerwork, hurdle]

²hurdle *vb* **hurdling** /'huhdling/ *vt* **1** to jump over, esp while running **2** to overcome, surmount ~*vi* to run in hurdle races – **hurdler** *n*

hurdy-gurdy /,huhdi 'guhdi/ *n* a musical instrument in which the sound is produced by turning a crank; *esp* BARREL ORGAN [prob imit]

hurl /huhl/ *vt* **1** to drive or thrust violently **2** to throw forcefully **3** to utter or shout violently ⟨~ed *insults at him*⟩ ~*vi* to rush, hurtle [ME *hurlen*, prob of imit origin] – **hurl** *n*, **hurler** *n*

hurling /'huhling/ *n* an Irish game resembling hockey played between 2 teams of 15 players each [fr gerund of *hurl*]

hurly-burly /,huhli 'buhli/ *n* (an) uproar, commotion [prob alter. & redupl of *hurling*, gerund of *hurl*]

hurrah /hoo'rah/ *interj* hurray

hurray /hoo'ray/ *interj* – used to express joy, approval, or encouragement [perh fr G *hurra*]

hurricane /'hurikən/ *n* (a usu tropical cyclone with) a wind of a velocity greater than 117km/h (73 to 136mph) [Sp *huracán*, fr Taino *hurakán*]

'hurricane ,deck *n* an upper deck of a ship

'hurricane ,lamp *n* a candlestick or oil lamp equipped with a glass chimney to protect the flame

hurried /'hurid/ *adj* done in a hurry – **hurriedly** *adv*

¹hurry /'huri/ *vt* **1a** to transport or cause to go with haste; rush ⟨~ *him to hospital*⟩ **b** to cause to move or act with (greater) haste **2** to hasten the progress or completion of ⟨*don't* ~ *this passage of the music*⟩ ~*vi* to move or act with haste – often + *up* [perh fr ME *horyen*]

²hurry *n* **1** flurried and often bustling haste **2** a need for haste; urgency ⟨*there's no* ~ *for it*⟩ – **in a hurry** **1** without delay; hastily **2** eager ⟨*never* in a hurry *to get up*⟩ **3** without difficulty; easily ⟨*won't manage that* in a hurry⟩ – infml

¹hurt /huht/ *vb* **hurt** *vt* **1a** to afflict with physical pain; wound **b** to cause mental distress to; offend **2** to be detrimental to ⟨~ *his chances of success*⟩ ~*vi* **1** to feel pain; suffer **2** to cause damage, distress, or pain [ME *hurten, hirten* to strike, injure, prob fr OF *hurter* to collide with, prob of Gmc origin; akin to ON *hrūtr* ram (male sheep)]

²hurt *n* **1** a bodily injury or wound **2** (a cause of) mental distress **3** wrong, harm – **hurtful** *adj*, **hurtfully** *adv*, **hurtfulness** *n*

hurtle /hurtl/ *vb* **hurtling** /'huhtling/ *vi* to move rapidly or precipitately ~*vt* to hurl, fling [ME *hurtlen* to collide, freq of *hurten*]

¹husband /'huzbənd/ *n* a married man, esp in relation to his wife [ME *husbonde*, fr OE *hūsbonda* master of a house, fr ON *hūsbōndi*, fr *hūs* house + *bōndi* householder] – **husbandly** *adj*

²husband *vt* to make the most economical use of; conserve ⟨~ *one's strength*⟩

husbandry /'huzbəndri/ *n* **1** the judicious management of resources **2** farming, esp of domestic animals

¹hush /hush/ *vb* to make or become quiet or calm [back-formation fr *husht* (hushed), fr ME *hussht*, fr *huissht*, interj used to enjoin silence]

²hush *n* a silence or calm, esp following noise

,hush-'hush *adj* secret, confidential – infml

'hush ,money *n* money paid secretly to prevent disclosure of damaging information

hush up *vt* to keep secret; suppress ⟨hush *the story* up⟩

¹husk /husk/ *n* **1** a dry or membranous outer covering (e g a shell or pod) of a seed or fruit **2** a useless outer layer of sthg [ME *husk, huske*, prob modif of MD *huuskijn*, dim. of *huus* house, cover]

²husk *vt* to strip the husk from

¹husky /'huski/ *adj* of, resembling, or containing husks

²husky *adj* hoarse, breathy ⟨*a* ~ *voice*⟩ [prob fr *husk* (huskiness), fr obs *husk* (to have a dry cough), prob of imit origin] – **huskily** *adv*, **huskiness** *n*

³husky *adj* burly, hefty – infml [prob fr ¹*husk*]

⁴husky *n* ESKIMO DOG [prob by shortening & alter. fr *Eskimo*]

huss /hus/ *n* dogfish [alter. of ME *husk*]

hussar /hoo'zah/ *n* **1** a Hungarian horseman of the

15th c **2** *often cap* a member of any of various European cavalry regiments [Hung *huszár* hussar, (obs) highway robber, fr Serb *husar* pirate, fr ML *cursarius* – more at CORSAIR]

Hussite /'husiet/ *n* a member of the Bohemian religious and nationalist movement led by John Huss [NL *Hussita*, fr John *Huss* †1415 Bohemian religious reformer] – **Hussite** *adj*, **Hussitism** *n*

hussy /'husi/ *n* an impudent or promiscuous woman or girl [alter. of *housewife*]

hustings /'hustingz/ *n pl but sing or pl in constr* **1** a raised platform used until 1872 for the nomination of candidates for Parliament and for election speeches **2** a place where election speeches are made **3** the proceedings of an election campaign [ME, local court, fr OE *hūsting* deliberative assembly, fr ON *hūsthing*, fr *hūs* house + *thing* assembly]

hustle /'husl/ *vb* **hustling** /'husling/ *vt* **1a** to push or convey roughly, forcibly, or hurriedly ⟨~d *him into a taxi*⟩ **b** to impel, force ⟨~d *her into accepting*⟩ **2** to swindle, cheat *out of* – infml ~*vi* **1** to hasten, hurry **2** *chiefly NAm* to make strenuous, often dishonest, efforts to secure money or business **3** *chiefly NAm* to engage in prostitution; solicit [D *husselen* to shake, fr MD *hutselen*, freq of *hutsen*; akin to MD *hodde* hod] – **hustle** *n*, **hustler** *n*

hut /hut/ *n* a small often temporary dwelling of simple construction [MF *hutte*, of Gmc origin; akin to OHG *hutta* hut; akin to OE *hȳd* skin, hide]

hutch /huch/ *n* **1** a pen or cage for a small animal (e g a rabbit) **2** a shack, shanty – infml; derog [ME *huche*, fr OF]

hutment /'hutmənt/ *n* an encampment of huts

hyacinth /'hie·ə,sinth/ *n* **1** a jacinth **2** a common garden plant with fragrant usu blue, pink, or white flowers that grow in spikes; *also* any of various related bulbous plants of the lily family **3** a colour varying from light violet to mid-purple [L *hyacinthus*, a precious stone, a flowering plant, fr Gk *hyakinthos*] – **hyacinth** *adj*, **hyacinthine** /,hie·ə'sinthien/ *adj*

Hyades /'hie·ədeez/ *n pl* a cluster of stars in the constellation Taurus held by the ancients to indicate rainy weather when they rise with the sun [L, fr Gk]

hyaena /hie'eenə/ *n* a hyena

hyal-, hyalo- *comb form* glass; glassy; hyaline ⟨hyal*escent*⟩ ⟨hyalo*gen*⟩ [LL, glass, fr Gk, fr *hyalos*]

[1]**hyaline** /'hie·əlin/ *adj* **1** of or relating to glass **2a** *of biological materials or structures* (nearly) transparent **b** *of a mineral* glassy, vitreous [LL *hyalinus*, fr Gk *hyalinos*, fr *hyalos*]

[2]**hyaline** *n* sthg glassy or transparent (e g a clear sky or sea) – poetic

hyaline cartilage *n* translucent bluish white cartilage that is present in joints and respiratory passages and forms most of the foetal skeleton

hyalite /'hie·əliet/ *n* a colourless or translucent opal [G *hyalit*, fr Gk *hyalos*]

hyaloid /'hie·əloyd/ *adj*, *of biological materials or structures* glassy, transparent [Gk *hyaloeidēs*, fr *hyalos*]

hyaloplasm /'hie·əloh,plaz(ə)m/ *n* the clear, fluid, apparently homogeneous basic substance of cytoplasm [prob fr G *hyaloplasma*, fr *hyal-* + *-plasma* -plasm]

hybrid /'hiebrid/ *n* **1** an offspring of 2 animals or plants of different races, breeds, varieties, etc ☞ SYMBOL **2** a person of mixed cultural background **3a** sthg heterogeneous in origin or composition **b** a word (e g *television*) made up of elements from different languages [L *hybrida*] – **hybrid** *adj*, **hybridism** *n*, **hybridist** *n*, **hybridize** *vb*, **hybridizable** /-,diezəbl/ *adj*, **hybridization** /-'zaysh(ə)n/ *n*, **hybridity** /hie'bridəti/ *n*

hybrid vigour *n* heterosis

hydatid /'hiedətid/ *n* (a fluid-filled sac produced by and containing) a tapeworm larva [Gk *hydatid-*, *hydatis* watery cyst, fr *hydat-*, *hydōr*]

hydr-, hydro- *comb form* **1a** water ⟨hydr*ous*⟩ ⟨hydro*electricity*⟩ **b** liquid ⟨hydro*kinetics*⟩ ⟨hydro*meter*⟩ **2** hydrogen; containing or combined with hydrogen ⟨hydro*carbon*⟩ ⟨hydro*chloric*⟩ [ME *ydr-*, *ydro-*, fr OF, fr L *hydr-*, *hydro-*, fr Gk, fr *hydōr* – more at WATER]

hydra /'hiedrə/ *n* **1** a persistent evil that is not easily overcome **2** any of numerous small tubular freshwater polyps having a mouth surrounded by tentacles [*Hydra*, a serpent in Gk mythology with many heads which regrew when cut off, fr L, fr Gk; (2) NL, genus name, fr L, Hydra]

hydrangea /hie'draynjə/ *n* any of a genus of shrubs which produce large clusters of white, pink, or pale blue flowers [NL, genus name, fr *hydr-* + Gk *angeion* vessel – more at ANGI-]

hydrant /'hiedrənt/ *n* a discharge pipe with a valve and nozzle from which water may be drawn from a main

[1]**hydrate** /'hiedrayt/ *n* a compound or complex ion formed by the union of water with another substance

[2]**hydrate** /'hiedrayt, hie'drayt/ *vt* to cause to take up or combine with (the elements of) water – **hydrator** *n*, **hydration** /hie'draysh(ə)n/ *n*

hydraulic /hie'drolik/ *adj* **1** operated, moved, or effected by means of liquid, esp liquid moving through pipes **2** of hydraulics ⟨~ *engineer*⟩ **3** hardening or setting under water ⟨~ *cement*⟩ [L *hydraulicus*, fr Gk *hydraulikos*, fr *hydraulis* hydraulic organ, fr *hydr-* + *aulos* reed instrument – more at ALVEOLUS] – **hydraulically** *adv*

hy,draulic 'ram *n* a pump that forces running water to a higher level by using the kinetic energy of a descending flow

hy'draulics *n pl but sing in constr* a branch of physics that deals with the practical applications of liquid in motion

hydrazine /'hiedrəzeen, -zin/ *n* a colourless liquid that acts as a reducing agent and is used esp in rocket fuels [ISV]

-hydric /-hiedrik/ *suffix* (→ *adj*) **1** containing (so many) acid hydrogens ⟨*mono*hydric⟩ **2** containing (so many) hydroxyl groups ⟨*hexa*hydric *alcohols*⟩

hydride /'hiedried/ *n* a compound of hydrogen usu with a more electropositive element or radical

,hydri,odic 'acid /,hiedri'odik/ *n* a solution of hydrogen iodide in water that is a strong acid and reducing agent [ISV]

hydro /'hiedroh/ *n*, *pl* **hydros** *Br* a hotel or establishment providing facilities for hydropathic treatment [short for *hydropathic establishment*]

hydro- *comb form* – see HYDR-

,hydro,bromic 'acid /,hiedroh'brohmik/ *n* a solution of hydrogen bromide in water that is a strong acid and a weak reducing agent [ISV]

hydrocarbon /,hiedroh'kahb(ə)n/ *n* an organic compound (e g benzene) containing only carbon and hydrogen – **hydrocarbonous, hydrocarbonaceous** /-,kahbə'nayshəs/, **hydrocarbonic** /-kah'bonik/, *adj*

hydrocele /'hiedroh,seel/ *n* an accumulation of watery liquid in a body cavity (e g the scrotum) [L, fr Gk *hydrokēlē*, fr *hydr-* + *kēlē* tumour – more at -CELE]

hydrocephalus /,hiedroh'sefələs/ *also* **hydrocephaly** /-li/ *n* an abnormal increase in the amount of cerebrospinal fluid within the brain cavity accompanied by enlargement of the skull and brain atrophy [NL *hydrocephalus*, fr LL, hydrocephalic, fr Gk *hydrokephalos*, fr *hydr-* + *kephalē* head – more at CEPHALIC] – **hydrocephalic** /-se'falik/ *adj*

,hydro,chloric 'acid /,hiedrə'klorik/ *n* a solution of hydrogen chloride in water that is a strong corrosive acid and is naturally present in the gastric juice [ISV]

hydrochloride /,hiedrə'klawried/ *n* a compound of hydrochloric acid, esp with an organic chemical base (e g an alkaloid)

hydrocortisone /,hiedroh'kawtizohn, -sohn/ *n* a steroid hormone that is produced by the cortex of the adrenal gland and used esp in the treatment of rheumatoid arthritis

,hydrocy,anic 'acid /,hiedrohsie'anik/ *n* a solution of hydrogen cyanide in water that is a highly poisonous weak acid [ISV]

hydrodynamics /,hiedrohdie'namiks, -di-/ *n pl but sing in constr* a science that deals with the motion of fluids and the forces acting on solid bodies immersed in them [NL *hydrodynamica*, fr neut pl of *hydrodynamicus*, adj, fr *hydr-* + *dynamicus* dynamic] – **hydrodynamic** *adj*, **hydrodynamicist** /-die'naməsist/ *n*

,hydroe'lectric /-i'lektrik/ *adj* of or being the production of electricity by waterpower ☞ ENERGY [ISV] – **hydroelectrically** *adv*, **hydroelectricity** /-lek'trisəti/ *n*

,hydroflu,oric 'acid /,hiedrohflooh'orik/ *n* a solution of hydrogen fluoride in water that is a poisonous weak acid used esp in etching glass [ISV]

hydrofoil /'hiedrə,foyl/ *n* (a ship or boat fitted with) an aerofoil-like device that, when attached to a ship, lifts the hull out of the water at speed

hydrogen /'hiedrəj(ə)n/ *n* the simplest and lightest of the elements that is normally a highly inflammable gas – compare DEUTERIUM, TRITIUM ☞ PERIODIC TABLE [F *hydrogène*, fr *hydr-* + *-gène* -gen; fr the fact that water is generated by its combustion] – **hydrogenous** /hie'drojinəs/ *adj*

hydrogenate /hie'drojinayt/ *vt* to combine or treat (esp an unsaturated organic compound) with hydrogen – **hydrogenation** /hie ,droji'naysh(ə)n/ *n*

'hydrogen ,bomb *n* a bomb whose violent explosive power is due to the sudden release of atomic energy resulting from the nuclear fusion of hydrogen initiated by the explosion of an atom bomb

'hydrogen ,bond *n* a weak electrostatic chemical bond consisting of a hydrogen atom bonded to 2 electronegative atoms (e g oxygen or nitrogen)

,hydrogen 'cyanide *n* **1** a poisonous usu gaseous compound that has the smell of bitter almonds **2** HYDROCYANIC ACID

,hydrogen pe'roxide *n* an unstable compound used esp as an oxidizing and bleaching agent, an antiseptic, and a rocket propellant

,hydrogen 'sulphide *n* an inflammable poisonous gas that has a smell of rotten eggs and is formed in putrefying matter

hydrography /hie'drogrəfi/ *n* (the description, measurement, and mapping of) bodies of water (e g seas) [MF *hydrographie*, fr *hydr-* + *-graphie* -graphy] – **hydrographer** *n*, **hydrographic** /,hiedrə'grafik/ *adj*, **hydrographically** *adv*

hydroid /'hiedroyd/ *n* a hydrozoan (polyp) [NL *Hydroida*, order name, fr *Hydra*] – **hydroid** *adj*

hydrology /hie'droləji/ *n* a science dealing with the properties, distribution, and circulation of the water of the earth and atmosphere [NL *hydrologia*, fr L *hydr-* + *-logia* -logy] – **hydrologist** *n*, **hydrologic** /,hiedrə'lojik/, **hydrological** *adj*, **hydrologically** *adv*

hydrolyse, *NAm* **hydrolyze** /'hiedrəliez/ *vb* to undergo or subject to hydrolysis ⟨~d *protein*⟩ [ISV, fr NL *hydrolysis*] – **hydrolysable** *adj*

hydrolysis /hie'droləsis/ *n* chemical breakdown involving splitting of a bond and addition of the elements of water [NL] – **hydrolytic** /,hiedrə'litik/ *adj*, **hydrolytically** *adv*

hydrometer /hie'dromitə/ *n* an instrument for determining specific gravities of solutions and hence their strength – **hydrometry** *n*, **hydrometric** /,hiedroh'metrik/, **hydrometrical** *adj*

hydronium /hie'drohni·əm, -nyəm/ *n* a hydrated hydrogen ion H_3O^+ [ISV *hydr-* + *-onium*]

hydropathy /hie'dropəthi/ *n* hydrotherapy [ISV] – **hydropathic** /,hiedroh'pathik/ *adj*, **hydropathically** *adv*

hydrophane /'hiedrə,fayn/ *n* a semitranslucent opal that becomes transparent in water

hydrophilic /,hiedrə'filik/ *adj* of or having a strong affinity for water [NL *hydrophilus*, fr Gk *hydr-* + *-philos* -philous] – **hydrophilicity** /-fə'lisəti/ *adv*

hydrophobia /,hiedrə'fohbi·ə/ *n* **1** abnormal dread of water **2** rabies [LL, fr Gk, fr *hydr-* + *-phobia* fear of something – more at PHOBIA]

,hydro'phobic /-'fohbik/ *adj* **1** characteristic of or suffering from hydrophobia **2** lacking affinity for water – **hydrophobicity** /-fə 'bisəti/ *n*

'hydro,phone /-,fohn/ *n* an instrument for listening to sound transmitted through water

hydrophyte /'hiedroh,fiet/ *n* a plant that grows in water or waterlogged soil [ISV] – **hydrophytic** /,hiedroh'fitik/ *adj*

hydroplane /'hiedroh,playn, -drə-/ *n* **1** a speedboat fitted with hydrofoils or a stepped bottom so that the hull is raised wholly or partly out of the water when moving at speed **2** a horizontal surface on a submarine's hull, used to control movement upwards or downwards

hydroponics /,hiedroh'poniks, -drə-/ *n pl but sing in constr* the growing of plants in (a mechanically supporting medium containing) nutrient solutions rather than soil [*hydr-* + Gk *-ponikos* cultural (in *geōponikos* agricultural, fr *geōponein* to plough, fr *gē* earth + *ponein* to toil)] – **hydroponic** *adj*, **hydroponically** *adv*

hydroquinone /,hiedrohkwi'nohn/ *n* a phenol that is a reducing agent and is used esp as a photographic developer [ISV]

hydrosphere /'hiedrə,sfiə/ *n* the waters and watery vapour of the earth's surface and atmosphere [ISV] – **hydrospheric** /,hiedrə'sferik/ *adj*

,hydro'static /-'statik/, **hydrostatical** /-kl/ *adj* of or being (the pressures exerted by) liquids at rest [prob fr NL *hydrostaticus*, fr *hydr-* + *staticus* static] – **hydrostatically** *adv*

ˌhydroˈstatics *n pl but sing in constr* physics dealing with the characteristics of liquids at rest, esp the pressure in or exerted by a liquid

hydrotherapy /ˌhiedroˈtherəpi/ *n* the use of water in the treatment of disease; *esp* treatment using exercise in heated water [ISV]

hydrothermal /ˌhiedrəˈthuhml/ *adj* relating to or caused by the action of hot water, esp on the earth's crust [ISV] – **hydrothermally** *adv*

ˌhydroˈthorax /-ˈthawraks/ *n* an excess of watery fluid in the pleural cavity, usu resulting from failing circulation [NL]

hydrotropism /hieˈdrotrəpiz(ə)m/ *n* a tropism (e g in plant roots) in which water (vapour) is the orienting factor [ISV] – **hydrotropic** /ˌhiedrohˈtropik/ *adj*, **hydrotropically** *adv*

hydrous /ˈhiedrəs/ *adj* containing water (chemically combined with other atoms or molecules)

hydroxide /hieˈdroksied/ *n* a compound of hydroxyl with an element or radical [ISV]

hydroxy /hieˈdroksi/ *adj* hydroxyl; *esp* containing hydroxyl, esp in place of hydrogen – often in combination ⟨hydroxy*acetic acid*⟩ [ISV, fr *hydroxyl*]

hydroxyl /hieˈdroksil, -siel/ *n* the univalent group or radical OH consisting of 1 hydrogen atom and 1 oxygen atom that is characteristic of hydroxides, alcohols, etc [*hydr-* + *ox-* + *-yl*] – **hydroxylate** /-layt/ *vt*, **hydroxylic** /ˌhiedrokˈsilik/ *adj*

hydroxytryptamine /hieˌdroksiˈtriptəmeen/ *n* serotonin

hydrozoan /ˌhiedrəˈzoh·ən/ *n* any of a class of coelenterates that includes simple and compound polyps and jellyfishes [deriv of Gk *hydr-* + *zōion* animal – more at ZO-] – **hydrozoan** *adj*

hyena, hyaena /hieˈeenə/ *n* any of several large strong nocturnal flesh-eating Old World mammals that usu feed as scavengers ☞ FOOD [L *hyaena*, fr Gk *hyaina*, fr *hys* hog – more at [1]SOW]

hyet-, hyeto- *comb form* rain ⟨hyeto*logy*⟩ [Gk, fr *hyetos*, fr *hyein* to rain – more at SUCK]

hygiene /ˈhieˌjeen/ *n* (conditions or practices, esp cleanliness, conducive to) the establishment and maintenance of health [F *hygiène* & NL *hygieina*, fr Gk, neut pl of *hygieinos* healthful, fr *hygiēs* healthy; akin to Skt *su* well, & to L *vivus* living – more at [1]QUICK] – **hygienist** *n*, **hygienic** /hieˈjeenik/ *adj*, **hygenics** *n pl but sing in constr*, **hygienically** *adv*

hygr- *also* **hygro-** *comb form* humidity; moisture ⟨hy groscope⟩ ⟨hygro*meter*⟩ [Gk, fr *hygros* wet – more at HUMOUR]

hygrometer /hieˈgromitə/ *n* an instrument for measuring the humidity of the atmosphere [prob fr F *hygromètre*, fr *hygr-* + *-mètre* -meter] – **hygrometry** *n*, **hygrometric** /ˌhiegrəˈmetrik/ *adj*

hygrophilous /hieˈgrofiləs/ *adj* living or growing in moist places

hygroscope /ˈhiegrəˌskohp/ *n* an instrument that shows changes in humidity (e g of the atmosphere)

ˌhygroˈscopic /-ˈskopik/ *adj* readily taking up and retaining moisture [fr the use of such materials in the hygroscope] – **hygroscopically** *adv*, **hygroscopicity** /-skoˈpisəti/ *n*

hying /ˈhie·ing/ *pres part of* HIE

hyl-, hylo- *comb form* **1** matter; material ⟨hylozo*ism*⟩ **2** wood ⟨hylo*phagous*⟩ [Gk, fr *hylē*, lit., wood]

hymen /ˈhiemen/ *n* a fold of mucous membrane partly closing the opening of the vagina in virgins [LL, fr Gk *hymēn* membrane] – **hymenal** *adj*

hymeneal /ˌhiemeˈnee·əl/ *adj* nuptial – poetic [L *hymenaeus* wedding song, wedding, fr Gk *hymenaios*, fr *Hymēn*, god of marriage]

hymenium /hieˈmeeni·əm/ *n, pl* **hymenia** /-ni·ə/, **hymeniums** a spore-bearing layer in fungi [NL, fr Gk *hymēn* membrane] – **hymenial** *adj*

hymenopteran, hymenopteron /ˌhiemiˈnoptərən/ *n* any of an order of highly specialized usu stinging insects (e g bees, wasps, or ants) that often associate in large colonies and have usu 4 membranous wings [NL *hymenopteron*, fr Gk, neut of *hymenopteros* membrane-winged, fr *hymēn* + *pteron* wing – more at FEATHER] – **hymenopteran** *adj*

[1]hymn /him/ *n* **1** a song of praise to God; *esp* a metrical composition that can be included in a religious service **2** a song of praise or joy [ME *ymne*, fr OF, fr L *hymnus* song of praise, fr Gk *hymnos*]

[2]hymn *vt* to praise or worship in hymns ~ *vi* to sing a hymn

hymnal /ˈhimnəl/ *n* (a book containing) a collection of church hymns [ME *hymnale*, fr ML, fr L *hymnus*]

hymnary /ˈhimnəri/ *n* a hymnal

ˈhymnˌbook /-ˌbook/ *n* a hymnal

hyoid /ˈhieˌoyd/ *adj* of the hyoid bone

hyoid bone *n* a complex of joined bones situated at the base of the tongue and supporting the tongue and its muscles [NL *hyoides*, fr Gk *hyoeidēs* shaped like the letter upsilon (Υ, υ), being the hyoid bone, fr *y*, *hy* upsilon]

hyoscine /ˈhie·əˌseen/ *n* an alkaloid found in various plants of the nightshade family that has effects on the nervous system similar to those of atropine [ISV *hyos*cyamine + *-ine*]

hyoscyamine /ˌhie·əˈsie·əmeen, -min/ *n* the laevorotatory form of atropine found esp in deadly nightshade and henbane [G *hyoscyamin*, fr NL *Hyoscyamus*, genus of herbs, fr L, henbane, fr Gk *hyoskyamos*, lit., swine's bean, fr *hyos* (gen of *hys* swine) + *kyamos* bean – more at [1]SOW]

hyp- – see HYPO-

hypabyssal /ˌhipəˈbisl/ *adj* of or being igneous rock formed at a moderate depth below the earth's surface [ISV]

hypaethral /hieˈpeethrəl, hi-/ *adj* open to the sky ⟨*a ~ temple*⟩ [L *hypaethrus* exposed to the open air, fr Gk *hypaithros*, fr *hypo-* + *aithēr* ether, air – more at ETHER]

hype /hiep/ *n* **1** extravagant and esp false publicity ⟨*media ~*⟩ **2** a deceit, swindle – slang [origin unknown]

ˌhyped-ˈup *adj* keyed up – slang [*hype* (to stimulate), short for *hypodermic*]

hyper /ˈhiepə/ *adj* overexcited, overwrought – slang [*hyper-*]

hyper- *prefix* **1** above; beyond; super- ⟨hy per*physical*⟩ **2a** excessively ⟨hyper*sensitive*⟩ ⟨hyper*critical*⟩ ⟨hyper*active*⟩ **b** excessive ⟨hy per*aemia*⟩ ⟨hyper*tension*⟩ **3** that exists in or is a space of more than 3 dimensions ⟨hyper*cube*⟩ ⟨hyper*space*⟩ [ME *iper-*, fr L *hyper-*, fr Gk, fr *hyper* – more at OVER]

hyperaemia /ˌhiepəˈreemi·ə, -myə/ *n* excess of blood in a body part [NL]

hyperaesthesia /-eesˈtheezyə, -zh(y)ə/ *n* a pathologically increased sensitivity to sensory stimuli (e g touch) [NL, fr *hyper-* + *aesthesia* (as in *anaesthesia*)]

hyper'baric /,hiepə'barik/ *adj* of or using greater than normal pressure, esp of oxygen ⟨~ *oxygen chambers*⟩ [*hyper-* + *bar-* + *-ic*] – **hyperbarically** *adv*

hyperbola /hie'puhbələ/ *n, pl* **hyperbolas, hyperbolae** /-,lee/ a plane curve generated by a point so moving that the difference of its distances from 2 fixed points is a constant; the intersection of a double right circular cone with a plane that cuts both halves of the cone – compare ELLIPSE, PARABOLA ☞ MATHEMATICS [NL, fr Gk *hyperbolē*]

hyperbole /hie'puhbəli/ *n* a figure of speech based on extravagant exaggeration [L, fr Gk *hyperbolē* excess, hyperbole, hyperbola, fr *hyperballein* to exceed, fr *hyper-* + *ballein* to throw – more at DEVIL] – **hyperbolist** *n*, **hyperbolize** /-,liez/ *vb*

[1]**hyperbolic** /,hiepə'bolik/ *also* **hyperbolical** /-kl/ *adj* of, characterized by, or given to hyperbole – **hyperbolically** *adv*

[2]**hyperbolic** *also* **hyperbolical** *adj* of or analogous to a hyperbola

hyperbolic function *n* any of a set of 6 functions related to the hyperbola in a way similar to that in which the trigonometric functions are related to a circle

hyperboloid /hie'puhbə,loyd/ *n* a surface, some plane sections of which are hyperbolas and no plane sections of which are parabolas – compare ELLIPSOID, PARABOLOID ☞ MATHEMATICS – **hyperboloidal** /-'loydl/ *adj*

[1]**hyperborean** /,hiepə'bawri·ən/ *adj* **1** of an extreme northern region **2** of any of the Arctic peoples

[2]**hyperborean** *n* an inhabitant of a cool northern climate [L *Hyperborei* (pl), fr Gk *Hyperboreoi*, fr *hyper-* beyond + *Boreas* (god of the) north wind]

,hyper'conscious /-'konshəs/ *adj* acutely aware or sensitive

'hyper,fine /-,fien/ *adj* of or being very closely spaced **a** energy levels in an atom **b** spectral lines

,hyper'focal ,distance /-'fohkl/ *n* the limit of the region of sharp focus for a lens focussed at infinity [ISV]

,hypergly'caemia /-glie'seemiy, -mi·ə/ *n* excess of sugar in the blood (e g in diabetes mellitus) [NL]

,hyperin'flation /-in'flaysh(ə)n/ *n* very rapid inflation of an economy – **hyperinflationary** *adj*

,hyperki'netic /-ki'netik/ *adj* of or marked by abnormally increased, usu uncontrollable, muscular movement – **hyperkinesis** /-ki'neesis/

'hyper,market /-,mahkit/ *n* a very large self-service retail store selling a wide range of household and consumer goods and usu situated on the outskirts of a major town or city

,hyperme'tropia /-me'trohpi·ə, -pyə/ *n* a condition in which visual images come to a focus behind the retina of the eye and vision is better for distant than for near objects; longsightedness – compare MYOPIA [NL, fr Gk *hypermetros* beyond measure (fr *hyper-* + *metron* measure, metre) + NL *-opia*] – **hypermetropic** /-'tropik/, **hypermetropical** *adj*

hyperon /'hiepəron/ *n* any of a group of unstable elementary particles that belong to the baryon group [prob fr *hyper-* + *-on*]

hyperopia /,hiepə'rohpi·ə, -pyə/ *n* hypermetropia [NL] – **hyperopic** /-'ropik/ *adj*

,hyper'physical /-'fizikl/ *adj* supernatural – **hyperphysically** *adv*

,hyper'plasia /-playzyə, -zh(y)ə/ *n* an abnormal or unusual increase in the elements (e g the cells of a tissue) composing a body part ⟨*cervical* ~⟩ [NL] – **hyperplastic** /-'plastik/ *adj*

,hyper'sensitive /-'sensətiv/ *adj* abnormally susceptible (e g to a drug or antigen) – **hypersensitiveness** *n*, **hypersensitivity** /-,sensə'tivəti/ *n*

,hyper'sonic /-'sonik/ *adj* of or being a speed (over) 5 times that of the speed of sound – compare SONIC [ISV] – **hypersonically** *adv*

'hyper,space /-,spays/ *n* **1** space of more than 3 dimensions **2** space other than ordinary Euclidean space

hypersthene /'hiepəs,theen/ *n* iron magnesium silicate occurring as a green to black mineral in igneous rocks [F *hypersthène*, fr Gk *hyper-* + *sthenos* strength] – **hypersthenic** /,hiepəs'thenik/ *adj*

,hyper'tension /-'tensh(ə)n/ *n* (the systemic condition accompanying) abnormally high (arterial) blood pressure [ISV] – **hypertensive** /-'tensiv/ *adj or n*

,hyper'thermia /-thuhmi·ə/ *n* very high body temperature [NL, fr *hyper-* + *therm-* + *-ia*] – **hyperthermic** /-mik/ *adj*

,hyper'thyroi,dism /-'thieroy,diz(ə)m/ *n* (the condition of increased metabolic and heart rate, enlargement of the thyroid gland, nervousness, etc resulting from) excessive activity of the thyroid gland – compare HYPOTHYROIDISM [ISV] – **hyperthyroid** *adj*

,hyper'tonic /-'tonik/ *adj* **1** having excessive muscular tone or tension **2** having a higher concentration than a surrounding medium or a liquid under comparison – compare HYPOTONIC, ISOTONIC [ISV] – **hypertonicity** /-toh'nisəti/ *n*

hypertrophy /hie'puhtrəfi/ *n* excessive increase in bulk of an organ or part [prob fr NL *hypertrophia*, fr *hyper-* + *-trophia* -trophy] – **hypertrophied** *adj*, **hypertrophic** /,hiepə'trofik/ *adj*

,hyper,venti'lation /-,venti'laysh(ə)n/ *n* excessive breathing leading to abnormal loss of carbon dioxide from the blood

hypha /'hiefə/ *n, pl* **hyphae** /-,fee/ any of the threads that make up the mycelium of a fungus [NL, fr Gk *hyphē* web; akin to Gk *hyphos* web – more at [1]WEAVE] – **hyphal** *adj*

[1]**hyphen** /'hief(ə)n/ *n* a punctuation mark - used to divide or to join together words, word elements, or numbers [LL & Gk; LL, fr Gk, fr *hyph' hen* under one, fr *hypo* under + *hen*, neut of *heis* one – more at UP, SAME]

[2]**hyphen** *vt* to hyphenate

'hyphen,ate /-ayt/ *vt* to join or separate with a hyphen – **hyphenation** /,hief(ə)n'aysh(ə)n/ *n*

hypn-, hypno- *comb form* **1** sleep ⟨hypno*phobia*⟩ **2** hypnotism ⟨hypno*genesis*⟩ [F, fr LL, fr Gk, fr *hypnos* – more at SOMNOLENT]

hypnagogic, hypnogogic /,hipnə'gojik/ *adj* of or associated with the drowsiness preceding sleep – compare HYPNOPOMPIC [F *hypnagogique*, fr Gk *hypn-* + *-agōgos* leading, inducing, fr *agein* to lead – more at AGENT]

,hypno'genesis /-'jenəsis/ *n* the induction of a hypnotic state [NL] – **hypnogenetic** /-jə'netik/ *adj*, **hypnogenetically** *adv*

,hypno'pompic /-'pompik/ *adj* of or associated with the semiconsciousness preceding waking – compare

HYPNAGOGIC [*hypn-* + Gk *pompē* act of sending – more at POMP]

hypnosis /hip'nohsis/ *n, pl* **hypnoses** /-seez/ **1** any of various conditions that (superficially) resemble sleep; *specif* one induced by a person to whose suggestions the subject is then markedly susceptible **2** HYPNOTISM 1 [NL]

hypnotherapy /,hipnoh'therəpi/ *n* the (psychotherapeutic) treatment of mental or physical disease, compulsive behaviour, etc using hypnosis

[1]**hypnotic** /hip'notik/ *adj* **1** tending to produce sleep; soporific **2** of hypnosis or hypnotism [F or LL; F *hypnotique*, fr LL *hypnoticus*, fr Gk *hypnōtikos*, fr *hypnoun* to put to sleep, fr *hypnos*] – **hypnotically** *adv*

[2]**hypnotic** *n* **1** sthg (e g a drug) that induces sleep **2** a person or animal that is or can be hypnotized

hypnotism /'hipnə,tiz(ə)m/ *n* **1** the induction of hypnosis **2** HYPNOSIS 1 – **hypnotist** *n*

hypnot·ize, -ise /'hipnətiez/ *vt* **1** to induce hypnosis in **2** to dazzle or overcome (as if) by suggestion; mesmerize ⟨*drivers* ~d *by speed*⟩ – **hypnotizable** *adj*, **hypnotization** /,hipnətie'zaysh(ə)n/ *n*

[1]**hypo** /'hiepoh/ *n, pl* **hypos** sodium thiosulphate used as a fixing agent in photography [short for *hyposulphite*]

[2]**hypo** *n, pl* **hypos** a hypodermic

hypo-, hyp- *prefix* **1** under; beneath ⟨hypo*blast*⟩ ⟨hypo*dermic*⟩ **2** less than normal or normally ⟨hyp*aesthesia*⟩ ⟨hypo*tension*⟩ **3** in a lower state of oxidation ⟨hypo*chlorous acid*⟩ [ME *ypo-*, fr OF, fr LL *hypo-*, *hyp-*, fr Gk, fr *hypo* – more at UP]

hypoblast /'hiepə,blast/ *n* the endoderm of an embryo – **hypoblastic** /,hiepə'blastik/ *adj*

hypocaust /'hiepə,kawst/ *n* an ancient Roman central heating system with an underground furnace and flues [L *hypocaustum*, fr Gk *hypokauston*, fr *hypokaiein* to light a fire under, fr *hypo-* + *kaiein* to burn – more at CAUSTIC]

hypochlorite /,hiepə'klawriet/ *n* a salt or ester of hypochlorous acid

,hypo,chlorous 'acid /,hiepə'klawrəs/ *n* an unstable weak acid that is a strong oxidizing agent and is used esp as a bleach, disinfectant, and chlorinating agent [ISV]

,hypo'chondria /-'kondri·ə/ *also* **hypochondriasis** /-kond'rie·əsis/ *n* morbid concern about one's health [NL, fr LL, pl, upper abdomen (formerly regarded as the seat of hypochondria), fr Gk, lit., the parts under the cartilage (of the breastbone), fr *hypo-* + *chondros* cartilage, granule, grain – more at GRIND]

hypochondriac /,hiepə'kondriak/ *n or adj* (sby) affected by hypochondria [F *hypochondriaque*, fr Gk *hypochondriakos*, fr *hypochondria*]

hypocorism /hie'pokəriz(ə)m/ *n* (the use of) a pet name [LL *hypocorisma*, fr Gk *hypokorisma*, fr *hypokorizesthai* to call by pet names, fr *hypo-* + *korizesthai* to caress, fr *koros* boy, *korē* girl] – **hypocoristic** /,hiepəkaw'ristik/ *adj*

hypocotyl /,hiepə'kotil/ *n* the part of a plant embryo or seedling below the cotyledon [ISV]

hypocrisy /hi'pokrəsi/ *n* the feigning of virtues, beliefs, or standards, esp in matters of religion or morality [ME *ypocrisie*, fr OF, fr LL *hypocrisis*, fr Gk *hypokrisis* act of playing a part on the stage, hypocrisy, fr *hypokrinesthai* to answer, act on the stage, fr *hypo-* + *krinein* to decide – more at CERTAIN]

hypocrite /'hipəkrit/ *n* one given to hypocrisy [ME *ypocrite*, fr OF, fr LL *hypocrita*, fr Gk *hypokritēs* actor, hypocrite, fr *hypokrinesthai*] – **hypocritical** /,hipə'kritikl/ *adj*, **hypocritically** *adv*

hypocycloid /,hiepə'siekloyd/ *n* a curve traced by a point on the circumference of a circle that rolls internally on a fixed circle

[1]**,hypo'dermic** /-'duhmik/ *adj* **1** of the parts beneath the skin **2** adapted for use in or administered by injection beneath the skin [ISV] – **hypodermically** *adv*

[2]**hypodermic** *n* **1** a hypodermic injection **2** HYPODERMIC SYRINGE

hypodermic syringe *n* a small syringe used with a hollow needle for injection or withdrawal of material beneath the skin

hypogeal /,hiepə'jee·əl/, **hypogeous** /-əs/, **hypogean** /-ən/ *adj* growing, remaining, or occurring below the surface of the ground ⟨~ *cotyledons*⟩ – compare EPIGEAL [LL *hypogeus* subterranean, fr Gk *hypogaios*, fr *hypo-* + *gē* earth]

hypogene /'hiepəjeen/ *adj, of rock* formed or occurring at depths below the earth's surface – compare EPIGENE [*hypo-* + Gk *-genēs* born, produced – more at -GEN]

hypoglossal nerve /,hiepə'glosl/ *n* either of the 12th and final pair of cranial nerves that supply muscles of the tongue in higher vertebrates

hypoglycaemia /,hiepohglie'seemyə, -mi·ə/ *n* abnormally low amount of sugar in the blood [NL] – **hypoglycaemic** /-mik/ *adj*

hypogynous /hie'pojinəs/ *adj* (having floral organs) attached to the receptacle or axis below the ovary and free from it – compare EPIGYNOUS, PERIGYNOUS – **hypogyny** *n*

hypolimnion /,hiepoh'limni·ən/ *n, pl* **hypolimnia** /-ni·ə/ the (oxygen-deficient nutrient-rich) water below the thermocline of a lake – compare EPILIMNION [NL, fr *hypo-* + Gk *limnion*, dim. of *limnē* lake]

hypomania /,hiepə'maynyə/ *n* a mild form of mania [NL] – **hypomanic** /-'manik/ *adj*

hypophysis /hie'pofəsis/ *n, pl* **hypophyses** /-seez/ PITUITARY GLAND [NL, fr Gk, attachment underneath, fr *hypophyein* to grow beneath, fr *hypo-* + *phyein* to grow, produce – more at BE] – **hypophyseal, hypophysial** /,hiepə'fizi·əl/ *adj*, **hypophysectomy** /hie,pofə'sektəmi/ *n*, **hypophysectomize** /-miez/ *vt*

hypoplasia /,hiepə'playzyə, -zh(y)ə/ *n* arrested development in which an organ or part remains below the normal size or in an immature state [NL] – **hypoplastic** /-'plastik/ *adj*

,hypo'sensit·ize, -ise /-'sensətiez/ *vt* to reduce the sensitivity of, esp to sthg that causes an allergic reaction; desensitize – **hyposensitization** /-,sensətie'zaysh(ə)n/ *n*

hypostasis /hie'postəsis/ *n, pl* **hypostases** /-seez/ **1** the settling of blood in the lower parts of an organ or body, esp due to impaired circulation **2** the substance or essential nature of an individual [LL, substance, sediment, fr Gk, support, foundation, substance, sediment, fr *hyphistasthai* to stand under, support, fr *hypo-* + *histasthai* to be standing – more at STAND] – **hypostatic** /,hiepoh'statik/, **hypostatical** *adj*, **hypostatically** *adv*

hypostat·ize, -ise /hie'postə,tiez/ *vt* to reify [Gk

hypostatos substantially existing, fr *hyphistasthai*] – **hypostatization** /-,pos tətie'zaysh(ə)n/ *n*

hyposulphite /,hiepoh'sulfiet/ *n* thiosulphate, esp as used as a fixing agent in photography

,hypo'taxis /-'taksis/ *n* syntactic subordination (e g by a conjunction) [NL, fr Gk, subjection, fr *hypotassein* to arrange under, fr *hypo-* + *tassein* to arrange – more at TACTICS] – **hypotactic** /-'taktik/ *adj*

,hypo'tension /'tensh(ə)n/ /-poh-/ *n* abnormally low blood pressure [ISV] – **hypotensive** /-siv/ *adj or n*

hypotenuse /hie'pot(ə)n,yoohz/ *n* the side of a right-angled triangle that is opposite the right angle ☞ MATHEMATICS [L *hypotenusa*, fr Gk *hypoteinousa*, fr fem of *hypoteinōn*, prp of *hypoteinein* to subtend, fr *hypo-* + *teinein* to stretch – more at THIN]

hypothalamus /,hiepə'thaləməs/ *n* a part of the brain that lies beneath the thalamus and includes centres that regulate body temperature, appetite, and other autonomic functions [NL] – **hypothalamic** /-mik/ *adj*

hypothec /hie'pothik/ *n* legal right in favour of a creditor over the property of his/her debtor – used in Roman and Scots law [F & LL; F *hypothèque*, fr MF, fr LL *hypotheca*, fr Gk *hypothēkē* deposit, pledge, fr *hypotithenai* to deposit as a pledge]

hypothermia /,hiepoh'thuhmi·ə/ *n* abnormally low body temperature [NL, fr *hypo-* + *therm-* + *-ia*] – **hypothermic** /-mik/ *adj*

hypothesis /hie'pothəsis/ *n, pl* **hypotheses** /-seez/ **1** a provisional assumption made in order to investigate its logical or empirical consequences **2** a proposition assumed for the sake of argument [Gk, fr *hypotithenai* to put under, suppose, fr *hypo-* + *tithenai* to put – more at DO]

hypothes·ize, -ise /hie'pothə,siez/ *vb* to form or adopt as a hypothesis

hypothetical /,hiepə'thetikl/ *adj* **1** involving logical hypothesis **2** of or depending on supposition; conjectural – **hypothetically** *adv*

hypothyroidism /,hiepoh'thieroy,diz(ə)m/ *n* (the condition of lowered metabolic rate, lethargy, etc resulting from) deficient activity of the thyroid gland – compare HYPERTHYROIDISM [ISV] – **hypothyroid** *adj*

hypotonic /,hiepə'tonik/ *adj* **1** having deficient muscular tone or tension **2** having a lower concentration than a surrounding medium or a liquid under comparison – compare HYPERTONIC, ISOTONIC [ISV] – **hypotonically** *adv*, **hypotonicity** /-tə'nisəti/ *n*

hypoxia /hie'poksi·ə, hi-/ *n* a deficiency of oxygen reaching the tissues of the body [NL, fr *hypo-* + *ox-* + *-ia*] – **hypoxic** /-sik/ *adj*

hyps-, hypsi-, hypso- *comb form* height; altitude ⟨hypso*graphy*⟩ [Gk, fr *hypsos* height; akin to OE *ūp* up]

hypsography /hip'sogrəfi/ *n* the measurement and mapping of the earth's surface with reference to elevation [ISV]

hyrax /'hieraks/ *n, pl* **hyraxes** *also* **hyraces** /-rə,seez/ any of several small thickset short-legged mammals with feet with soft pads and broad nails [Gk *hyrak-*, *hyrax* shrewmouse]

hyssop /'hisəp/ *n* **1** a plant used in purificatory rites by the ancient Hebrews **2** a Eurasian plant of the mint family with aromatic leaves [ME *ysop*, fr OE *ysope*, fr L *hyssopus*, fr Gk *hyssōpos*, of Sem origin; akin to Heb *ēzōbh* hyssop]

hyster-, hystero- *comb form* **1** womb ⟨hystero*tomy*⟩ **2** hysteria ⟨hystero*genic*⟩; hysteria and ⟨hystero*neurasthenia*⟩ [F or L; F *hystér-*, fr L *hyster-*, fr Gk, fr *hystera*; (2) NL, fr *hysteria*]

hysterectomy /,histə'rektəmi/ *n* surgical removal of the uterus – **hysterectomize** *vt*

hysteresis /,histə'reesis/ *n* a delay in the production of an effect by a cause; *esp* an apparent lag in the values of resulting magnetization in a magnetic material due to a changing magnetizing force [NL, fr Gk *hysterēsis* shortcoming, fr *hysterein* to be late, fall short, fr *hysteros* later – more at OUT] – **hysteretic** /-'retik/ *adj*

hysteria /hi'stiəri·ə/ *n* **1** a mental disorder marked by emotional excitability and disturbances (e g paralysis) of the normal bodily processes **2** unmanageable emotional excess [NL, fr E *hysteric*, adj, fr L *hystericus*, fr Gk *hysterikos*, fr *hystera* womb; fr the former notion that hysteric women were suffering from disturbances of the womb] – **hysteric** /-'sterik/ *n*, **hysteric, hysterical** *adj*, **hysterically** *adv*

hysterics /hi'steriks/ *n pl but sing or pl in constr* a fit of uncontrollable laughter or crying; hysteria

hysteron proteron /,histərɒn 'protərɒn/ *n* a figure of speech consisting of the reversal of a natural or rational order (e g in *thunder and lightning*) [LL, fr Gk, lit., (the) later earlier, (the) latter first]

I

i /ie/ *n, pl* **i's, is** *often cap* **1** (a graphic representation of or device for reproducing) the 9th letter of the English alphabet **2** one ☞ NUMBER **3** – used as a symbol for the imaginary unit

I /ie/ *pron* the one who is speaking or writing ⟨~ *feel fine*⟩ ⟨*my wife and* ~⟩ – compare ME, MINE, MY, WE [ME, fr OE *ic*; akin to OHG *ih* I, L *ego*, Gk *egō*]

-i- – used as a connective vowel to join word elements, esp of Latin origin ⟨*matri*linear⟩ ⟨*rat*icide⟩ [ME, fr OF, fr L, stem vowel of most nouns and adjectives in combination]

¹-ia *suffix* (→ *n*) **1** pathological condition of ⟨*hyster*ia⟩ ⟨*anaem*ia⟩ **2** genus of (specified plant or animal) ⟨*Fuchs*ia⟩ **3** territory, world, or society of ⟨*suburb*ia⟩ ⟨*Austral*ia⟩ [NL, fr L & Gk, suffix forming feminine nouns]

²-ia *suffix* (→ *n pl*) **1** higher taxon (e g class or order) consisting of (specified plants or animals) ⟨*Saur*ia⟩ **2** things derived from or relating to ⟨*regal*ia⟩ ⟨*juvenil*ia⟩ [NL, fr L (neut pl of *-ius*, adj ending) & Gk, neut pl of *-ios*, adj ending]

³-ia *pl of* -IUM

-ial – see ¹-AL ⟨*manor*ial⟩ [ME, fr MF, fr L *-ialis*, fr *-i-* + *-alis* -al]

iamb /ˈie·am(b)/ *n* a metrical foot consisting of 1 short or unstressed syllable followed by 1 long or stressed syllable [L *iambus*, fr Gk *iambos*] – **iambic** /ieˈambik/ *adj or n*

iambus /ieˈambəs/ *n* an iamb [L]

-ian – see -AN

-iana /-iˈahnə/ – see -ANA

-iasis /-ie·əsis/ *suffix* (→ *n*), *pl* **-iases** disease having the characteristics of or produced by ⟨*hypochondr*iasis⟩ ⟨*psor*iasis⟩ [NL, fr L, fr Gk, suffix of action, fr denominative verbs in *-ian, -iazein*]

-iatric /-iˈatrik/ *also* **-iatrical** /-kl/ *comb form* (→ *adj*) of or relating to (a specified medical treatment) ⟨*paed*iatric⟩ [NL *-iatria*]

-iatrics *comb form* (→ *n pl but sing or pl in constr*) medical treatment ⟨*paed*iatrics⟩

iatro- *comb form* medical; healing ⟨iatro*genic*⟩ ⟨iatro*chemistry*⟩ [NL, fr Gk, fr *iatros* physician]

iatrogenic /ie,atrohˈjenik/ *adj* induced inadvertently by (the treatment of) a medical doctor ⟨*an* ~ *rash*⟩ [Gk *iatros* + E *-genic*] – **iatrogenically** *adv*

-iatry /-ˈie·ətri/ *comb form* (→ *n*) medical treatment ⟨*psych*iatry⟩ [F *-iatrie*, fr NL *-iatria*, fr Gk *iatreia* art of healing, fr *iatros*]

¹Iberian /ieˈbiəri·ən/ *n* a member of any of the ancient peoples inhabiting the Caucasus between the Black and Caspian seas [*Iberia*, ancient region of the Caucasus] – **Iberian** *adj*

²Iberian *n* **1a** a member of any of the Caucasian peoples that in ancient times inhabited Spain and Portugal **b** a native or inhabitant of Spain or Portugal **2** any of the languages of the ancient Iberians [*Iberia*, peninsula in Europe] – **Iberian** *adj*

ibex /ˈiebeks/ *n, pl* **ibexes,** *esp collectively* **ibex** any of several wild goats living chiefly in high mountain areas of the Old World and having large ridged backward-curving horns [L]

ibidem /iˈbiedem/ *adv* in the same book, chapter, passage, etc as previously mentioned [L, in the same place]

-ibility /-əˈbiləti/ – see -ABILITY

ibis /ˈiebis/ *n, pl* **ibises,** *esp collectively* **ibis** any of several wading birds related to the herons but distinguished by a long slender downward-curving bill [L, fr Gk, fr Egypt *hby*]

-ible /-ibl, -əbl/ – see -ABLE

Ibo /ˈeeboh/ *n, pl* **Ibos,** *esp collectively* **Ibo** **1** a member of a Negro people of the area round the lower Niger **2** a Kwa language widely used in S Nigeria ☞ LANGUAGE

IC *n* INTEGRATED CIRCUIT

¹-ic /-ik/ *suffix* (*n* → *adj*) **1** having the character or form of; being ⟨*panoram*ic⟩ ⟨*run*ic⟩ **2a** (characteristic) of or associated with ⟨*Homer*ic⟩ ⟨*quixot*ic⟩ **b** related to, derived from, or containing ⟨*alcohol*ic⟩ ⟨*ole*ic⟩ **3** utilizing ⟨*electron*ic⟩ ⟨*atom*ic⟩ **4** exhibiting ⟨*nostalg*ic⟩; affected with ⟨*allerg*ic⟩ **5** characterized by; producing ⟨*analges*ic⟩ **6** having a valency relatively higher than in (specified compounds or ions named with an adjective ending in *-ous*) ⟨*ferr*ic *iron*⟩ ⟨*mercur*ic⟩ [ME, fr OF & L; OF *-ique*, fr L *-icus* – more at ¹-Y]

²-ic *suffix* (→ *n*) **1** one having the character or nature of ⟨*fanat*ic⟩ **2** one belonging to or associated with ⟨*ep*ic⟩ **3** one affected by ⟨*alcohol*ic⟩ **4** one that produces ⟨*emet*ic⟩

-ical /-ikl/ *suffix* (*n* → *adj*) -ic ⟨*symmetr*ical⟩ ⟨*geolog*ical⟩ [ME, fr LL *-icalis* (as in *clericalis* clerical, *radicalis* radical)]

ICBM *n, pl* **ICBM's, ICBMs** an intercontinental ballistic missile

¹ice /ies/ *n* **1a** frozen water **b** a sheet or stretch of ice **2** a substance reduced to the solid state by cold ⟨*ammonia* ~ *in the rings of Saturn*⟩ **3** (a serving of) a frozen dessert: e g **a** ICE CREAM **b** WATER ICE **4** *NAm* diamonds – slang [ME *is*, fr OE *is*; akin to OHG *is* ice, Av *isu-* icy] – **iceless** *adj* – **on ice** in abeyance; in reserve for later use ⟨*kept their plans* on ice *for the time being*⟩

²ice *vt* **1a** to coat with or convert into ice **b** to supply or chill with ice **2** to cover (as if) with icing ~ *vi* **1** to become ice-cold **2** to become covered or clogged with ice ⟨*the carburettor* ~d *up*⟩

ˈice ˌage *n* **1** a time of widespread glaciation **2** *cap I&A* the Pleistocene glacial epoch ☞ GEOGRAPHY

ˈice ˌaxe *n* a combination pick and adze with a spiked handle used in climbing on snow or ice

'ice ˌbag *n* a bag of ice for application of cold to a part of the body

'iceˌberg /-ˌbuhg/ *n* **1** a large floating mass of ice detached from a glacier **2** an emotionally cold person [prob part trans of Dan or Norw *isberg*, fr *is* ice + *berg* mountain]

'iceˌblink /-ˌblingk/ *n* a glare in the sky over a sheet of ice, caused by the reflection of light

'iceˌboat /-ˌboht/ *n* a boat or frame on runners propelled on ice, usu by sails

'iceˌbox /-ˌboks/ *n* **1** *Br* the freezing compartment of a refrigerator **2** *NAm* a refrigerator

'iceˌbreaker /-ˌbraykə/ *n* a ship equipped to make and maintain a channel through ice

'ice ˌcap /-ˌkap/ *n* a lasting (extensive) cover of ice ☞ GEOGRAPHY

ice cream /ˌies 'kreem, 'ies ˌkreem/ *n* a sweet flavoured frozen food containing cream (substitute) and often eggs

'ice ˌhockey *n* a game played on an ice rink by 2 teams of 6 players on skates whose object is to drive a puck into the opponent's goal with a hockey stick

Icelander /'iesˌlandə, -ləndə/ *n* a native or inhabitant of Iceland [Dan *Islænder*, fr *Island* Iceland, island between the Arctic & Atlantic]

[1]**Icelandic** /ies'landik/ *adj* (characteristic) of Iceland

[2]**Icelandic** *n* the N Germanic language of the Icelandic people ☞ LANGUAGE

Iceland moss *n* an edible lichen of mountainous and arctic regions that yields an extract used esp as a sizing agent

Iceland poppy *n* any of various cultivated poppies with usu pastel-coloured smallish single or double flowers

Iceland spar *n* a doubly refracting transparent form of calcite

ice lolly /ˌies 'loli, 'ies ˌloli/ *n* an ice cream or esp a flavoured piece of ice on a stick

'iceˌman /-ˌman/ *n* **1** a man skilled in travelling on ice **2** one who sells or delivers ice, esp in the USA

Iceni /ie'seenie/ *n pl* an ancient British people who revolted against the Romans in AD 61 under Boadicea [L] – **Icenian** /-ni·ən/, **Icenic** /-nik/ *adj*

'ice ˌpack *n* **1** an expanse of pack ice **2** ICE BAG

'ice ˌpick *n* a hand tool ending in a spike for chipping ice

'ice ˌshow *n* an entertainment consisting of various acrobatic, dance, etc routines, esp to music, by ice skaters

'ice ˌskate *n* a shoe with a metal runner attached for skating on ice – **ice-skate** *vi*, **ice skater** *n*

I Ching /ching/ *n* an ancient Chinese book that is a source of Confucian and Taoist philosophy and presents 64 symbolic 6-line figures each containing information relevant to daily life and future events, and accompanied by an explanatory text which advises on the possible courses of action and their outcome [Chin, lit., classic (book) of changes]

ichn-, ichno- *comb form* footprint; track ⟨ichno*logy*⟩ [Gk, fr *ichnos*]

ichneumon /ik'nyoohmən/ *n* **1** a mongoose **2** **ichneumon, ichneumon fly** any of various related 4-winged insects whose larvae are usu internal parasites of other insect larvae, esp caterpillars [L, fr Gk *ichneumōn*, lit., tracker, fr *ichneuein* to track, fr *ichnos*]

ichor /'iekaw/ *n* **1** a fluid that took the place of blood in the veins of the ancient Greek gods **2** a thin watery or blood-tinged discharge [Gk *ichōr*] – **ichorous** *adj*

ichthy-, ichthyo- *comb form* fish ⟨ichthyo*logy*⟩ [L, fr Gk, fr *ichthys*; akin to Arm *jukn* fish]

ichthyophagous /ˌikthi'ofəgəs/ *adj* eating or subsisting on fish [Gk *ichthyophagos*, fr *ichthy-* + *-phagos* -phagous]

ichthyosaur /'ikthi·əˌsaw/ *n* any of an order of extinct marine reptiles with fish-shaped bodies and long snouts [deriv of Gk *ichthy-* + *sauros* lizard – more at SAURIAN] – **ichthyosaurian** /ˌikthi·ə'sawri·ən/ *adj or n*

-ician /-ish(ə)n/ *suffix* (→ *n*) specialist in or practitioner of ⟨*beaut*ician⟩ ⟨*techn*ician⟩ [ME, fr OF *-icien*, fr L *-ica* (as in *rhetorica* rhetoric) + OF *-ien* -ian]

icicle /'iesikl/ *n* a hanging tapering mass of ice formed by the freezing of dripping water [ME *isikel*, fr *is* ice + *ikel* icicle, fr OE *gicel*; akin to OHG *ihilla* icicle, MIr *aig* ice]

icing /'iesing/ *n* a sweet (creamy) coating for cakes or other baked goods

'icing ˌsugar *n* finely powdered sugar used in making cake icings and sweets

icky /'iki/ *adj* cloying, sentimental – infml [perh baby-talk alter. of *sticky*]

icon, ikon /'iekon/ *n* **1** a usu pictorial representation; an image **2** a conventional religious image typically painted on a small wooden panel and used in worship by the Eastern Christian Church [L, fr Gk *eikōn*, fr *eikenai* to resemble] – **iconic** /ie'konik/ *adj*, **iconically** *adv*, **iconicity** /ˌiekon'nisəti/ *n*

icon-, icono- *comb form* image; likeness ⟨icono*later*⟩ ⟨icono*grapher*⟩ [Gk *eikon-*, *eikono-*, fr *eikon-*, *eikōn*]

iconoclasm /ie'konəˌklaz(ə)m/ *n* the doctrine, practice, or attitude of an iconoclast [fr *iconoclast*, by analogy to *enthusiast/enthusiasm*]

i'conoˌclast /-ˌklast/ *n* **1** a person who destroys religious images or opposes their veneration **2** one who attacks established beliefs or institutions [ML *iconoclastes*, fr MGk *eikonoklastēs*, lit., image destroyer, fr Gk *eikono-* + *klan* to break – more at [1]HALT] – **iconoclastic** /-ˌkonə'klastik/ *adj*, **iconoclastically** *adv*

iconographer /ˌiekə'nogrəfə/ *n* a student of iconography

iconography /ˌiekə'nogrəfi/ *n* **1** pictorial material relating to or illustrating a subject; a pictorial record of a subject **2** the traditional or conventional images or symbols associated with a subject, esp a religious or legendary subject **3** the imagery or symbolism of a work of art, an artist, or a body of art **4** iconology **5** a published work dealing with or featuring iconography [Gk *eikonographia* sketch, description, fr *eikonographein* to describe, fr *eikon-* + *graphein* to write – more at CARVE] – **iconographic** /ieˌkonə'grafik/, **iconographical** *adj*, **iconographically** *adv*

iconology /ˌiekə'noləji/ *n* the study of icons or of artistic symbolism [F *iconologie*, fr *icono-* icon- + *-logie* -logy] – **iconological** /ieˌkonə'lojik(ə)l/ *adj*

iconostasis /ˌiekə'nostəsis/ *n, pl* **iconostases** /-ˌseez/ a screen or partition with doors and tiers of icons separating the sanctuary from the nave in Eastern churches [MGk *eikonostasi*]

icosahedron /ˌiekəsəˈheedrən/ *n, pl* **icosahedrons, icosehedra** /-drə/ a polyhedron of 20 faces ☞ MATHEMATICS [Gk *eikosaedron*, fr *eikosi* twenty + *-edron* -hedron – more at VIGESIMAL] – **icosahedral** *adj*

-ics /-iks/ *suffix* (→ *n pl but sing or pl in constr*) **1** study, knowledge, skill, or practice of ⟨*linguistics*⟩ ⟨*electronics*⟩ **2** actions, activities, or mode of behaviour characteristic of (a specified person or thing) ⟨*histrionics*⟩ ⟨*acrobatics*⟩ **3** qualities, operations, or phenomena relating to ⟨*mechanics*⟩ ⟨*acoustics*⟩ [*-ic* + *-s*; trans of Gk *-ika*, fr neut pl of *-ikos* -ic]

icterus /ˈiktərəs/ *n* JAUNDICE 1 [NL, fr Gk *ikteros*; akin to Gk *iktis*, a yellow bird] – **icteric** /ikˈterik/ *adj*

ictus /ˈiktəs/ *n* rhythmic or metrical stress [L, fr *ictus*, pp of *icere* to strike; akin to Gk *aichmē* lance]

icy /ˈiesi/ *adj* **1a** covered with, full of, or consisting of ice **b** intensely cold **2** characterized by personal coldness ⟨*an ~ stare*⟩ – **icily** *adv*, **iciness** *n*

id /id/ *n* the one of the 3 divisions of the mind in psychoanalytic theory that is completely unconscious and is the source of psychic energy derived from instinctual needs and drives – compare EGO, SUPEREGO [NL, fr L, it]

[1]**-id** /-id, -əd/ *suffix* (→ *n*) **1** member of (a specified zoological family) ⟨*arachnid*⟩ **2** meteor associated with or radiating from (a specified constellation or comet) ⟨*Perseid*⟩ [(1) L *-ides*, masc patronymic suffix, fr Gk *-idēs*; (2) It *-ide*, fr L *-id-*, *is*, fem patronymic suffix, fr Gk]

[2]**-id** *suffix* (→ *n*) (such) a body, particle, or structure ⟨*energid*⟩ ⟨*pyramid*⟩ [prob fr L *-id-*, *-is*, fem patronymic suffix, fr Gk]

[3]**-id** *suffix* (→ *n*) -ide

I'd /ied/ I had; I should; I would

-idae /-idee/ *suffix* (→ *n pl*) members of (a specified zoological family) ⟨*Felidae*⟩ [NL, fr L, fr Gk *-idai*, pl of *-idēs*]

ID card /ˌie ˈdee/ *n* IDENTITY CARD

ide /ied/ *n* a European freshwater food fish of the carp family [Sw *id*]

-ide /-ied/ *suffix* (→ *n*) **1** binary chemical compound – added to the contracted name of the nonmetallic or more electronegative element ⟨*hydrogen sulphide*⟩ or radical ⟨*cyanide*⟩ **2** chemical compound derived from or related to (a specified compound) ⟨*glucoside*⟩ ⟨*lanthanide*⟩ [G & F; G *-id*, fr F *-ide* (as in *oxide*)]

idea /ieˈdiə/ *n* **1a** a transcendent entity of which existing things are imperfect representations **b** a plan of action **2a** an indefinite or vague impression ⟨*I'd an ~ you were coming*⟩ **b** sthg (e g a thought, concept, or image) actually or potentially present in the mind ⟨*the ~ of death never occurred to him*⟩ **3** a formulated thought or opinion **4** whatever is known or supposed about sthg **5** an individual's conception of the perfect or typical example of sthg specified ⟨*not my ~ of a good time*⟩ **6** the central meaning or aim of a particular action or situation ⟨*the ~ of the game is to score goals*⟩ [L, fr Gk, fr *idein* to see – more at WIT] – **idealess** *adj*

[1]**ideal** /ieˈdeel/ *adj* **1a** existing only in the mind; *broadly* lacking practicality **b** relating to or constituting mental images, ideas, or conceptions **2** of or embodying an ideal; perfect ⟨*an ~ spot for a picnic*⟩ [F or LL; F *idéal*, fr LL *idealis*, fr L *idea*]

[2]**ideal** *n* **1** a standard of perfection, beauty, or excellence **2** one looked up to as embodying an ideal or as a model for imitation **3** an ultimate object or aim – **idealless** *adj*

idealism /ieˈdeeˌliz(ə)m/ *n* **1a** a theory that the essential nature of reality lies in consciousness or reason **b** a theory that only what is immediately perceived (e g sensations or ideas) is real **2** the practice of living according to one's ideals **3** a literary or artistic theory or practice that affirms the preeminent value of imagination and representation of ideal types as compared with faithful copying of nature

iˈdealist /-list/ *n* **1** one who advocates or practises idealism in art or writing **2** sby guided by ideals; *esp* one who places ideals before practical considerations – **idealist, idealistic** /-ˌdeeˈlistik/ *adj*, **idealistically** *adv*

ideality /ˌiediˈaləti/ *n* **1** the quality or state of being ideal **2** sthg imaginary or idealized

ideal·ize, -ise /ieˈdeeliez/ *vt* **1** to attribute qualities of excellence or perfection to **2** to represent in an ideal form ~ *vi* to form ideals – **idealizer** *n*, **idealization** /-ˌdeelieˈzaysh(ə)n/ *n*

iˈdeally /-li/ *adv* **1** in accordance with an ideal; perfectly ⟨*~ suited for the job*⟩ **2** for best results ⟨*~, we should eat less sugar*⟩

ideate /ˈiediˌayt/ *vb* to form an idea (of) – **ideation** /ˌiediˈaysh(ə)n/ *n*, **ideational** *adj*

idée fixe /ˌeeday ˈfeeks (*Fr* ide fiks)/ *n, pl* **idées fixes** /~/ a fixed or obsessive idea [F]

idem /ˈidem, ˈiedem/ *pron* the same as previously mentioned [L, same – more at IDENTITY]

identical /ieˈdentikl/ *adj* **1** being the same ⟨*the ~ place we stopped before*⟩ **2** being very similar or exactly alike ⟨*the copy was ~ with the original*⟩ **3** *of twins, triplets, etc* derived from a single egg [prob fr ML *identicus*, fr LL *identitas*]

identification /ieˌdentifiˈkaysh(ə)n/ *n* **1a** identifying or being identified **b** evidence of identity ⟨*employees must carry ~ at all times*⟩ **2a** the putting of oneself mentally in the position of another **b** the (unconscious) attribution of the characteristics of another to oneself in order to attain gratification, emotional support, etc

identification parade *n, chiefly Br* a line-up of people arranged by the police to allow a witness to identify a suspect

identify /ieˈdentifie/ *vt* **1a** to cause to be or become identical **b** to associate or link closely ⟨*groups that are identified with conservation*⟩ **2** to establish the identity of ~ *vi* to experience psychological identification ⟨*~ with the hero of a novel*⟩ – **identifiable** *adj*, **identifiably** *adv*, **identifier** *n*

[1]**identikit** /ieˈdentikit/ *n, often cap* a set of alternative facial characteristics used by the police to build up a likeness, esp of a suspect; *also* a likeness constructed in this way [fr *Identi-kit*, a trademark]

[2]**identikit** *adj, often cap* **1** of or produced by identikit **2** like many others of the same type ⟨*a middlebrow ~ novel*⟩

identity /ieˈdentəti/ *n* **1** the condition of being exactly alike **2** the distinguishing character or personality of an individual **3** the condition of being the same as sthg or sby known or supposed to exist ⟨*establish the ~ of the stolen goods*⟩ **4** an algebraic equation that remains true whatever values are substituted for the symbols ⟨$(x+y)^2 = x^2 + 2xy + y^2$ *is an* ~⟩ **5** IDENTITY ELEMENT **6** *Austr & NZ* a person, character [MF *identité*, fr LL *identitat-, identitas*, irreg fr L *idem* same, fr *is* that – more at ITERATE]

i'dentity ˌcard *n* a card bearing information that establishes the identity of the holder

identity element *n* an element that leaves any element of the set to which it belongs unchanged when combined with it by a specified mathematical operation ⟨*0 is the* ~ *in the group of numbers under addition*⟩

i'dentity paˌrade *n* IDENTIFICATION PARADE

ideo- *comb form* idea ⟨ideogram⟩ [F *idéo-*, fr Gk *idea*]

ideogram /'idi·əˌgram/ *n* **1** a stylized picture or symbol used instead of a word or sound to represent a thing or idea – compare HIEROGLYPH **2** a logogram – compare PICTOGRAPH – **ideogramic, ideogrammic** /ˌidi·ə'gramik/ *adj*, **ideogrammatic** /ˌidi·əgrə'matik/ *adj*

ideograph /'idi·əˌgrahf, -ˌgraf/ *n* an ideogram – **ideographic** /ˌidi·ə'grafik/ *adj*, **ideographically** *adv*

ideography /ˌidi'ogrəfi/ *n* the use of ideograms

ideologue /'iedee·əˌlog/ *n* **1** an (unpractical) theorist **2** an advocate or adherent of a particular ideology [F *idéologue*, back-formation fr *idéologie*]

ideology /ˌiedi'oləji/ *n* **1** a systematic body of concepts **2** a manner of thinking characteristic of an individual, group, or culture ⟨*medical* ~⟩ **3** the ideas behind a social, political, or cultural programme [F *idéologie*, fr *idéo-* ideo- + *-logie* -logy] – **ideologist** *n*, **ideological** /ˌiedee·ə'lojikl, -ˌ--'---/ *also* **ideologic** *adj*, **ideologically** *adv*

ides /iedz/ *n pl but sing or pl in constr* (the week preceding) the 15th day of March, May, July, or October or the 13th day of any other month in the ancient Roman calendar [MF, fr L *idus*]

-idine /-ədeen/ *suffix* (→ *n*) nitrogen-containing chemical compound related in origin or structure to (a specified compound) ⟨*tolu*idine⟩ ⟨*pyrrol*idine⟩ [ISV *-ide* + *-ine*]

idio- *comb form* one's own; personal; distinct ⟨idiolect⟩ [Gk, fr *idios* – more at IDIOT]

idiocy /'idi·əsi/ *n* **1** extreme mental deficiency **2** sthg notably stupid or foolish

idiolect /'idi·əˌlekt/ *n* the language or speech pattern of an individual [*idio-* + *-lect* (as in *dialect*)] – **idiolectal** /-'lektl/, **idiolectic** /-'lektik/ *adj*

idiom /'idi·əm/ *n* **1a** the language peculiar to a people or to a district, community, or class **b** the syntactic, grammatical, or structural form peculiar to a language **2** an expression in the usage of a language that has a meaning that cannot be derived from the sum of the meanings of its elements **3** a characteristic style or form of artistic expression ⟨*the modern jazz* ~⟩ [MF & LL; MF *idiome*, fr LL *idioma* individual peculiarity of language, fr Gk *idiōmat-, idiōma*, fr *idiousthai* to appropriate, fr *idios*]

idiomatic /ˌidi·ə'matik/ *adj* of or conforming to idiom – **idiomatically** *adv*, **idiomaticity** /-mə'tisəti/ *n*

idiopathic /ˌidi·ə'pathik/ *adj, of a disease* arising spontaneously or from an unknown cause – **idiopathically** *adv*

idiosyncrasy /ˌidioh'singkrəsi/ *n* **1** characteristic peculiarity of habit or structure **2** a characteristic of thought or behaviour peculiar to an individual or group; *esp* an eccentricity [Gk *idiosynkrasia*, fr *idio-* + *synkerannynai* to blend, fr *syn-* + *kerannynai* to mingle, mix – more at CRATER] – **idiosyncratic** /-sing'kratik/ *adj*, **idiosyncratically** *adv*

idiot /'idi·ət/ *n* **1** an (ineducable) person afflicted with idiocy, esp from birth **2** a silly or foolish person [ME, fr L *idiota* ignorant person, fr Gk *idiōtēs* one in a private station, layman, ignorant person, fr *idios* one's own, private; akin to L *sed, se* without, *sui* of oneself] – **idiot** *adj*, **idiotic** /ˌidi'otik/ *adj*, **idiotically** *adv*

'idiot ˌboard *n* a device that is used to prompt a performer on television – infml

-idium /-idi·əm/ *suffix* (→ *n*) *pl* **-idiums, -idia** /-idi·ə/ small or lesser kind of ⟨*anther*idium⟩ [NL, fr Gk *-idion*, dim. suffix]

¹idle /'iedl/ *adj* **1** having no particular purpose or value ⟨~ *curiosity*⟩ **2** groundless ⟨~ *rumour*⟩ **3** not occupied or employed: e g **a** not in use or operation ⟨*machines lying* ~⟩ **b** not turned to appropriate use ⟨~ *funds*⟩ **4** lazy [ME *idel*, fr OE *īdel*; akin to OHG *ītal* worthless] – **idleness** *n*, **idly** /'iedli/ *adv*

²idle *vb* **idling** /'iedling/ *vi* **1a** to spend time in idleness **b** to move idly **2** *esp of an engine* to run without being connected to the part (e g the wheels of a car) that is driven, so that no useful work is done ~ *vt* **1** to pass in idleness **2** to cause to idle – **idler** *n*

'idler ˌwheel *n* a wheel, gear, or roller used to transfer motion or to guide or support sthg

Ido /'eedoh/ *n* an artificial international language based on Esperanto [Esperanto, offspring, fr Gk *-idēs*, patronymic suffix]

idol /'iedl/ *n* **1** an image or symbol used as an object of worship; *broadly* a false god **2** an object of passionate or excessive devotion ⟨*a pop* ~⟩ [ME, fr OF *idole*, fr LL *idolum*, fr Gk *eidōlon* phantom, idol; akin to Gk *eidos* form – more at IDYLL]

idolater /ie'dolətə/ *n* **1** a worshipper of idols **2** a passionate and often uncritical admirer [ME *idolatrer*, fr MF *idolatre*, fr LL *idololatres*, fr Gk *eidōlolatrēs*, fr *eidōlon* + *-latrēs* -later]

idolatry /ie'dolətri/ *n* **1** the worship of a physical object as a god **2** excessive attachment or devotion to sthg – **idolatrous** *adj*, **idolatrously** *adv*, **idolatrousness** *n*

idol·ize, -ise /'ied(ə)lˌiez/ *vt* to worship idolatrously; *broadly* to love or admire to excess ~ *vi* to practise idolatry – **idolizer** *n*, **idolization** /-'zaysh(ə)n/ *n*

idyll, idyl /'idil/ *n* **1** a simple work in poetry or prose describing peaceful rustic life or pastoral scenes **2** an episode suitable for an idyll **3** a pastoral or romantic musical composition [L *idyllium*, fr Gk *eidyllion*, fr dim. of *eidos* form; akin to Gk *idein* to see – more at WIT] – **idyllic** /i'dilik/ *adj*, **idyllically** *adv*

-ie /-ee/ *suffix* (*n* → *n*) ⁴-Y [ME]

-ier /-iə/ – see ²-ER

¹if /if/ *conj* **1a** in the event that ⟨~ *she should telephone, let me know*⟩ **b** supposing ⟨~ *you'd listened, you'd know*⟩ **c** on condition that **2** whether ⟨*asked* ~ *the mail had come*⟩ **3** – used to introduce an exclamation expressing a wish ⟨~ *it would only rain*⟩ **4** even if; although ⟨*an interesting* ~ *irrelevant point*⟩ **5** that – used after expressions of emotion ⟨*I don't care* ~ *she's cross*⟩ ⟨*it's not surprising* ~ *you're annoyed*⟩ **6** – used with a negative when an expletive introduces startling news ⟨*blow me ~ he didn't hit her!*⟩ [ME, fr OE *gif*; akin to OHG *ibu* if] – **if anything** on the contrary even; perhaps even ⟨if anything, *you ought to apologize*⟩

²if *n* **1** a condition, stipulation ⟨*the question depends on too many* ~s⟩ **2** a supposition ⟨*a theory full of* ~s⟩

-iferous /-if(ə)rəs/ – see -FEROUS [ME, fr L *-ifer*, fr *-i-* + *-fer* -ferous]

-iform /-ifawm/ – see -FORM ⟨*rami*form⟩ [MF & L; MF *-iforme*, fr L *-iformis*, fr *-i-* + *-formis* -form]

-ify /-ifie, -əfie/ – see -FY [ME *-ifien*, fr OF *-ifier*, fr L *-ificare*, fr *-i-* + *-ficare* -fy]

Igbo /'igboh/ *n pl* **Igbos**, *esp collectively* **Igbo** (an) Ibo

igloo /'iglooh/ *n, pl* **igloos** **1** an Eskimo dwelling, usu made of snow blocks and in the shape of a dome **2** a structure shaped like a dome [Esk *iglu, igdlu* house]

igneous /'igni·əs/ *adj* **1** fiery **2** relating to or formed by the flow or solidification of molten rock from the earth's core ⟨~ *rocks*⟩ [L *igneus*, fr *ignis* fire; akin to Skt *agni* fire]

igni- *comb form* fire; burning ⟨igni*tron*⟩ [L, fr *ignis*]

ignis fatuus /,ignis 'fatyoo·əs/ *n, pl* **ignes fatui** /,igneez 'fatyoo,ie/ a will-o'-the-wisp [ML, lit., foolish fire]

ignite /ig'niet/ *vt* **1a** to set fire to; *also* to kindle **b** to cause (a fuel mixture) to burn **2** to spark off; excite, esp suddenly ~ *vi* **1** to catch fire **2** to begin to glow **3** to burst forth suddenly into violence or conflict [L *ignitus*, pp of *ignire* to ignite, fr *ignis*] – **ignitable** *also* **ignitible** *adj*, **igniter, ignitor** *n*

ignition /ig'nish(ə)n/ *n* **1** the act or action of igniting **2** the process or means (e g an electric spark) of igniting a fuel mixture ☞ CAR

ignoble /ig'nohbl/ *adj* **1** of low birth or humble origin **2** base, dishonourable [L *ignobilis*, fr *in-* + *nobilis* noble] – **ignobleness** *n*, **ignobly** *adv*, **ignobility** /,ignoh'biləti/ *n*

ignominious /,ignə'mini·əs/ *adj* **1** marked by or causing disgrace or discredit **2** humiliating, degrading ⟨*suffered an ~ defeat*⟩ – **ignominiously** *adv*, **ignominiousness** *n*

ignominy /'ignəmini/ *n* **1** deep personal humiliation and disgrace **2** disgraceful or dishonourable conduct or quality [MF or L; MF *ignominie*, fr L *ignominia*, fr *ig-* (as in *ignorare* to be ignorant of, ignore) + *nomin-, nomen* name, repute – more at NAME]

ignoramus /,ignə'rayməs, -'rahməs/ *n* an ignorant person [*Ignoramus*, ignorant lawyer in *Ignoramus*, play by George Ruggle †1622 E dramatist, fr NL *ignoramus* endorsement by a Grand Jury on a bill of indictment giving insufficient evidence for prosecution, fr L, we do not know, fr *ignorare*]

ignorance /'ignərəns/ *n* the state of being ignorant

ignorant /'ignərənt/ *adj* **1** lacking knowledge, education, or comprehension (of sthg specified) **2** caused by or showing lack of knowledge **3** lacking social training; impolite – chiefly infml – **ignorantly** *adv*

ignore /ig'naw/ *vt* to refuse to take notice of; disregard [obs *ignore* (to be ignorant of), fr F *ignorer*, fr L *ignorare*, fr *ignarus* ignorant, unknown, fr *in-* + *gnoscere, noscere* to know – more at KNOW] – **ignorable** *adj*, **ignorer** *n*

iguana /,igyoo'ahnə, i'gwahnə/ *n* any of various large lizards; *esp* a plant-eating (dark-coloured) tropical American lizard with a serrated crest on its back [Sp, fr Arawak *iwana*]

iguanodon /,igyoo'ahnədon, i'gwah-/ *n* a very large plant-eating dinosaur [NL *Iguanodont-, Iguanodon*, genus name, fr Sp *iguana* + NL *-odon* (as in *mastodon*)]

IHS – used as a Christian symbol and monogram for *Jesus* [LL, part transliteration of Gk ΙΗΣ, abbreviation for ΙΗΣΟΥΣ *Iēsous* Jesus]

ikebana /,ikay'bahnə, ,iki-, ,eek-/ *n* the Japanese art of flower arranging that emphasizes form and balance [Jap, fr *ikeru* to keep alive, arrange + *hana* flower]

ikon /'iekon/ *n* an icon

il- /il-/ – see IN-

ilang-ilang /,eelang 'eelang/ *n* ylang-ylang

ile- *also* **ileo-** *comb form* **1** ileum ⟨*ile*itis⟩ **2** ileal and ⟨ileo*caecal*⟩ [NL *ileum*]

¹-ile /-iel/ *suffix* (→ *adj*) (capable) of (such action) ⟨*prehen*sile⟩; liable to (so act or be acted on) ⟨*vola*tile⟩ ⟨*frag*ile⟩ [ME, fr MF, fr L *-ilis*]

²-ile *suffix* (→ *n*) segment of (a specified size) in a frequency distribution ⟨*dec*ile⟩ [prob fr *-ile* (as in *quartile*, n)]

ileum /'ili·əm/ *n, pl* **ilea** /'ili·ə/ the last division of the small intestine extending between the jejunum and the large intestine [NL, fr L, groin, viscera] – **ileal** *adj*

ileus /'ili·əs/ *n* obstruction of the bowel [L, fr Gk *eileos*, fr *eilyein* to roll – more at VOLUBLE]

ilex /'ieleks/ *n* **1** HOLM OAK **2** the holly [L]

iliac /'iliak/ *also* **ilial** /'ili·əl/ *adj* of or located near the ilium [LL *iliacus*, fr L *ilium*]

ilio- *comb form* iliac and ⟨ilio*lumbar*⟩ [NL *ilium*]

ilium /'ili·əm/ *n, pl* **ilia** /'ili·ə/ the upper and largest of the 3 principal bones composing either half of the pelvis [NL, fr L *ilium, ileum*]

¹ilk /ilk/ *pron, chiefly Scot that* same – esp in the names of landed families [ME, fr OE *ilca*, fr a prehistoric compound whose constituents are akin respectively to Goth *is* he (akin to L *is* he, that) and OE *gelic* like – more at ³LIKE]

²ilk *n* sort, kind ⟨*politicians and others of that* ~⟩

³ilk *adj, chiefly Scot* each, every [ME, adj & pron, fr OE *ylc, ælc* – more at EACH]

ilka /'ilkə/ *adj, chiefly Scot* ilk [ME, fr *ilk* + *a* (indef article)]

¹ill /il/ *adj* **worse** /wuhs/; **worst** /wuhst/ **1** bad: e g **a** morally evil ⟨~ *deeds*⟩ **b** malevolent, hostile ⟨~ *feeling*⟩ **c** attributing evil or an objectionable quality ⟨*held an ~ opinion of his neighbours*⟩ **2a** causing discomfort or inconvenience; disagreeable ⟨~ *effects*⟩ **b(1)** not normal or sound ⟨~ *health*⟩ **(2)** not in good health; *also* nauseated **(3)** *chiefly Br* hurt, wounded ⟨*still very ~ after the accident*⟩ **3** unlucky, disadvantageous ⟨*an ~ omen*⟩ ⟨~ *fortune*⟩ **4** socially improper ⟨~ *breeding*⟩ **5a** unfriendly, hostile ⟨~ *feeling*⟩ ⟨~ *will*⟩ **b** harsh ⟨~ *treatment*⟩ [ME, fr ON *illr*]

²ill *adv* **worse; worst** **1a** with displeasure or hostility **b** in a harsh manner ⟨*used him* ~⟩ **c** so as to reflect unfavourably ⟨*spoke ~ of his neighbours*⟩ **2** in a reprehensible, harsh, or deficient manner ⟨*fared* ~⟩ ⟨ill-*adapted to city life*⟩ **3** hardly, scarcely ⟨~ *at* *ease*⟩ ⟨*can* ~ *afford such extravagances*⟩ **4a** in an unfortunate manner; badly, unluckily ⟨ill-*fated*⟩ **b** in a faulty, imperfect, or unpleasant manner ⟨ill-*equipped*⟩ ***USE*** often in combination

³ill *n* **1** the opposite of good; evil **2a** (a) misfortune, trouble ⟨*hope no more* ~s *befall him*⟩ **b(1)** an ailment **(2)** sthg that disturbs or afflicts ⟨*economic and social* ~s⟩ **3** sthg that reflects unfavourably ⟨*spoke no* ~ *of him*⟩

I'll /iel/ I will; I shall

,ill-ad'vised *adj* showing lack of proper consideration or sound advice – **ill-advisedly** /əd'viezidli/ *adv*

,ill at 'ease *adj* uneasy, uncomfortable

illative /i'laytiv/ *adj* inferential [LL *illativus*, fr L *illatus*, suppletive pp of *inferre* to bring in, infer, fr *in-* in- + *latus*, suppletive pp of *ferre* to bear] – **illatively** *adv*

,ill-'bred *adj* having or showing bad upbringing; impolite

illegal /i'leegl/ *adj* not authorized by law [F or ML; F *illégal*, fr ML *illegalis*, fr L *in-* + *legalis* legal] – **illegally** *adv*, **illegality** /,ili'galəti/ *n*

illegible /i'lejəbl/ *adj* not legible – **illegibly** *adv*, **illegibility** /i,lejə'biləti/ *n*

illegitimate /,ili'jitimət/ *adj* **1** not recognized as lawful offspring; *specif* born out of wedlock **2** wrongly deduced or inferred **3** departing from the regular; abnormal **4** illegal – **illegitimately** *adv*, **illegitimacy** /-məsi/ *n*

,ill-'favoured *adj* **1** unattractive in physical appearance **2** offensive, objectionable

,ill-'gotten *adj* acquired by illicit or improper means – esp in *ill-gotten gains*

,ill-'humoured *adj* surly, irritable

illiberal /,i'librəl/ *adj* not liberal: e g **a** lacking culture and refinement **b** not broad-minded; bigoted **c** opposed to liberalism [MF or L; MF, fr L *illiberalis* ignoble, stingy, fr L *in-* + *liberalis* liberal] – **illiberalism** *n*, **illiberally** *adv*, **illiberalness, illiberality** /-,libə'raləti/ *n*

illicit /i'lisit/ *adj* not permitted; unlawful ⟨~ *love affairs*⟩ [L *illicitus*, fr *in-* + *licitus* lawful – more at LICIT] – **illicitly** *adv*

illiterate /i'lit(ə)rət/ *adj* **1** unable to read or write **2** showing lack of education [L *illiteratus*, fr *in-* + *litteratus* literate] – **illiterate** *n*, **illiterately** *adv*, **illiterateness, illiteracy** /-rəsi/ *n*

,ill-'mannered *adj* having bad manners

,ill-'natured *adj* having a disagreeable disposition; surly – **ill-naturedly** *adv*

illness /'ilnis/ *n* an unhealthy condition of body or mind

illogical /i'lojikl/ *adj* **1** contrary to the principles of logic **2** devoid of logic; senseless – **illogically** *adv*, **illogicalness, illogicality** /i,loji'kaləti/ *n*

,ill-'tempered *adj* ill-natured – **ill-temperedly** *adv*

,ill-'timed *adj* badly timed; *esp* inopportune

,ill-'treat *vt* to treat cruelly or improperly – **ill-treatment** *n*

illume /i'lyoohm/ *vt* to illuminate – poetic [short for *illumine*]

illuminate /i'l(y)oohminayt/ *vt* **1a(1)** to cast light on; fill with light **(2)** to brighten **b** to enlighten spiritually or intellectually **2** to elucidate **3** to decorate (a manuscript) with elaborate initial letters or marginal designs in gold, silver, and brilliant colours [L *illuminatus*, pp of *illuminare*, fr *in-* + *luminare* to light up, fr *lumin-*, *lumen* light – more at LUMINARY] – **illuminatingly** *adv*, **illuminator** *n*, **illuminative** /-nətiv/ *adj*

illuminati /i,l(y)oohmi'nahti/ *n pl* **1** *cap* any of various groups claiming special religious enlightenment **2** people who are or claim to be unusually enlightened [It & NL; It, fr NL, fr L, pl of *illuminatus*]

illumination /i,loohmi'naysh(ə)n, i,lyooh-/ *n* **1** illuminating or being illuminated: e g **a** spiritual or intellectual enlightenment **b** decorative lighting or lighting effects ⟨*the Blackpool* ~s⟩ **c** decoration of a manuscript by the art of illuminating **2** the amount of light per unit area of a surface on which it falls ☞ PHYSICS **3** any of the decorative features used in the art of illuminating or in decorative lighting

illumine /i'l(y)oohmin/ *vt* to illuminate – poetic [ME *illuminen*, fr MF or L; MF *illuminer*, fr L *illuminare*] – **illuminable** *adj*

,ill-'use *vt* to treat harshly or unkindly – **ill-usage** *n*

illusion /i'l(y)oohzh(ə)n/ *n* **1** a false impression or notion ⟨*I have no* ~s *about my ability*⟩ **2a(1)** a misleading image presented to the vision **(2)** sthg that deceives or misleads intellectually **b(1)** perception of an object in such a way that it presents a misleading image ⟨*an optical* ~⟩ **(2)** HALLUCINATION 1 [ME, fr MF, fr LL *illusion-*, *illusio*, fr L, action of mocking, fr *illusus*, pp of *illudere* to mock at, fr *in-* + *ludere* to play, mock – more at LUDICROUS] – **illusional** *adj*, **illusionist** *n*

illusory /i'l(y)oohsəri, -zəri/ *adj* deceptive, unreal ⟨~ *hopes*⟩ – **illusorily** *adv*, **illusoriness** *n*

illustrate /'iləstrayt/ *vt* **1a** to clarify (by giving or serving as an example or instance) **b** to provide (e g a book) with visual material **2** to show clearly; demonstrate ~ *vi* to give an example or instance [L *illustratus*, pp of *illustrare*, fr *in-* + *lustrare* to purify, make bright, shine] – **illustrator** *n*

illustration /,ilə'straysh(ə)n/ *n* **1** illustrating or being illustrated **2** sthg that serves to illustrate: e g **a** an example that explains or clarifies sthg **b** a picture or diagram that helps to make sthg clear or attractive – **illustrational** *adj*

illustrative /'iləstrətiv, -stray-/ *adj* serving or intended to illustrate ⟨~ *examples*⟩ – **illustratively** *adv*

illustrious /i'lustri·əs/ *adj* marked by distinction or renown [L *illustris*, prob back-formation fr *illustrare*] – **illustriously** *adv*, **illustriousness** *n*

,ill 'will *n* unfriendly feeling

im- /im-/ – see IN-

I'm /iem/ I am

image /'imij/ *n* **1** a reproduction (e g a portrait or statue) of the form of a person or thing **2a** the optical counterpart of an object produced by a lens, mirror, etc or an electronic device **b** a likeness of an object produced on a photographic material **3a** exact likeness ⟨*God created man in his own* ~ – Gen 1:27 (RSV)⟩ **b** a person who strikingly resembles another specified person ⟨*he's the* ~ *of his father*⟩ **4** a typical example or embodiment (e g of a quality) ⟨*he's the* ~ *of goodness*⟩ **5a** a mental picture of sthg (not actually present) **b** an idea, concept **6** a figure of speech, esp a metaphor or simile **7** a conception created in the minds of people, esp the general public ⟨*worried about his public* ~⟩ **8** an element in the range of a mathematical function that corresponds to a particular element in the domain ***USE*** (2) ☞

CAMERA [ME, fr OF, short for *imagene*, fr L *imagin-*, *imago*; akin to L *imitari* to imitate]

imagery /'imij(ə)ri/ *n* **1** (the art of making) images **2** figurative language **3** mental images; *esp* the products of imagination

imaginable /i'majinəbl/ *adj* capable of being imagined – **imaginableness** *n*, **imaginably** *adv*

[1]**imaginal** /i'majinl/ *adj* of imagination, images, or imagery [*imagine* + *-al*]

[2]**imaginal** *adj* of the insect imago [NL *imagin-*, *imago*]

imaginary /i'majin(ə)ri/ *adj* **1** existing only in imagination; lacking factual reality **2** containing or relating to (a multiple of) the positive square root of minus 1 – **imaginarily** *adv*, **imaginariness** *n*

imaginary number *n* COMPLEX NUMBER

imaginary part *n* the part of a complex number (e g *3i* in *2+3i*) that has the imaginary unit as a factor

imaginary unit *n* the positive square root of minus 1; $+\sqrt{1}$

imagination /i,maji'naysh(ə)n/ *n* **1** the act or power of forming a mental image of sthg not present to the senses or never before wholly perceived in reality **2** creative ability **3** a fanciful or empty notion

imaginative /i'maj(i)nətiv/ *adj* **1** of or characterized by imagination **2** given to imagining; having a lively imagination **3** of images; *esp* showing a command of imagery – **imaginatively** *adv*, **imaginativeness** *n*

imagine /i'maj(ə)n/ *vt* **1** to form a mental image of (sthg not present) **2** to suppose, think ⟨*I* ~ *it will rain*⟩ **3** to believe without sufficient basis ⟨~s *himself to be indispensable*⟩ ~ *vi* to use the imagination [ME *imaginen*, fr MF *imaginer*, fr L *imaginari*, fr *imagin-*, *imago* image]

imagism /'imi,jiz(ə)m/ *n*, *often cap* a 20th-c movement in poetry advocating the expression of ideas and emotions through clear precise images – **imagist** *n*, **imagist, imagistic** /,imi'jistik/ *adj*, **imagistically** *adv*

imago /i'maygoh/ *n*, *pl* **imagoes, imagines** /i'mahginayz, -'may-, -ji-, -neez/ **1** an insect in its final mature (winged) state ☞ LIFE CYCLE **2** a subconscious idealized mental image of a person, esp a parent [NL, fr L, image]

imam /i'mahm, '--/ *n* **1** the leader of prayer in a mosque **2** *cap* a Shiite leader held to be the divinely appointed successor of Muhammad **3** a caliph; *also* any of various Islamic doctors of law or theology [Ar *imām*] – **imamate** /-mət, -mayt/ *n*

imbalance /im'baləns/ *n* lack of balance: e g **a** lack of functional balance in a physiological system ⟨*hormonal* ~⟩ **b** lack of balance between segments of a country's economy **c** numerical disproportion

imbecile /'imbəseel, -siel/ *n* **1** MENTAL DEFECTIVE **2** a fool, idiot [F *imbécile*, fr *imbécile* weak, weak-minded, fr L *imbecillus*] – **imbecile, imbecilic** /,imbə'silik/ *adj*

imbecility /,imbə'siləti/ *n* **1** being (an) imbecile **2** (an instance of) utter foolishness or nonsense

imbed /im'bed/ *vb* **-dd-** to embed

imbibe /im'bieb/ *vt* **1** to drink **2** to take in or up; absorb, assimilate ~ *vi* DRINK 2 [L *imbibere* to drink in, conceive, fr *in-* + *bibere* to drink] – **imbiber** *n*

[1]**imbricate** /'imbrikət, -kayt/ *adj* (having scales, sepals, etc) lying lapped over each other in regular order [LL *imbricatus*, pp of *imbricare* to cover with pantiles, fr L *imbric-*, *imbrex* pantile, fr *imbr-*, *imber* rain; akin to Gk *ombros* rain] – **imbricately** *adv*

[2]**imbricate** /'imbrikayt/ *vb* to overlap, esp in regular order – **imbrication** /,imbri'kaysh(ə)n/ *n*

imbroglio /im'brohlioh/ *n*, *pl* **imbroglios** **1** a confused mass **2a** an intricate or complicated situation (e g in a drama) **b** a confused or complicated misunderstanding or disagreement [It, fr *imbrogliare* to entangle, fr MF *embrouiller*, fr *en-* + *brouiller* to broil]

imbrue /im'brooh/ *vt* to stain, drench – chiefly fml [ME *enbrewen*, prob fr MF *abrevrer*, *embevrer* to soak, drench, deriv of L *bibere* to drink]

imbue /im'byooh/ *vt* **1** to tinge or dye deeply **2** to cause to become permeated ⟨*a man* ~d *with a strong sense of duty*⟩ [L *imbuere*]

imidazole /,imi'dazohl, -'day-, ,imidə'zohl/ *n* (any of various derivatives of) an organic compound that is a chemical base with a characteristic heterocyclic structure [ISV]

imide /'imied/ *n* a compound that is derived from ammonia by replacement of 2 hydrogen atoms by a metal or by acid radicals [ISV, alter. of *amide*] – **imidic** /i'midik/ *adj*

imitate /'imitayt/ *vt* **1** to follow as a pattern, model, or example **2** to reproduce **3** to resemble **4** to mimic; TAKE OFF [L *imitatus*, pp of *imitari* – more at IMAGE] – **imitable** *adj*, **imitator** *n*

[1]**imitation** /,imi'taysh(ə)n/ *n* **1** an act or instance of imitating **2** sthg produced as a copy; a counterfeit **3** the repetition in one musical part of the melodic theme, phrase, or motive previously found in another musical part – compare OSTINATO, SEQUENCE 1c – **imitational** *adj*

[2]**imitation** *adj* made in imitation of sthg else that is usu genuine and of better quality

imitative /'imitətiv/ *adj* **1a** marked by or given to imitation ⟨*acting is an* ~ *art*⟩ **b** onomatopoeic **2** imitating sthg superior – **imitatively** *adv*, **imitativeness** *n*

immaculate /i'makyoolət/ *adj* **1** without blemish; pure **2** free from flaw or error **3** spotlessly clean [ME *immaculat*, fr L *immaculatus*, fr *in-* + *maculatus*, pp of *maculare* to stain, fr *macula* spot, stain] – **immaculately** *adv*, **immaculateness, immaculacy** /-ləsi/ *n*

Immaculate Conception *n* the conception of the Virgin Mary held in Roman Catholic dogma to have freed her from original sin

immanent /'imənənt/ *adj* **1** indwelling; *esp* having existence only in the mind **2** pervading nature or the souls of men ⟨*belief in an* ~ *God*⟩ – compare TRANSCENDENT [LL *immanent-*, *immanens*, prp of *immanēre* to remain in place, fr L *in-* + *manēre* to remain – more at MANSION] – **immanence, immanency** *n*, **immanently** *adv*

immaterial /,imə'tiəri·əl/ *adj* **1** not consisting of matter; incorporeal **2** unimportant [ME *immateriel*, fr MF, fr LL *immaterialis*, fr L *in-* + LL *materialis* material] – **immaterially** *adv*, **immaterialness, immateriality** /-,tiəri'aləti/ *n*, **immaterialize** /-'tiəriə,liez/ *vt*

immature /,imə'tyooə/ *adj* **1** lacking complete growth, differentiation, or development **2a** not having arrived at a definitive form or state ⟨*a vigorous but* ~ *school of art*⟩ **b** exhibiting less than an expected degree of maturity ⟨*emotionally* ~ *adults*⟩

[L *immaturus,* fr *in-* + *maturus* mature] – **immature** *n,* **immaturely** *adv,* **immatureness, immaturity** *n*
immeasurable /iˈmezh(ə)rəbl/ *adj* indefinitely extensive [IM- + MEASURABLE] – **immeasurableness** *n,* **immeasurably** *adv*
immediacy /iˈmeedi·əsi/ *n* **1** the quality or state of being immediate **2** sthg requiring immediate attention – usu pl ⟨*the* immediacies *of life*⟩
immediate /iˈmeedi·ət, -dyət/ *adj* **1a** acting or being without any intervening agency or factor ⟨*the* ~ *cause of death*⟩ **b** involving or derived from a single premise ⟨*an* ~ *inference*⟩ **2** next in line or relationship ⟨*only the* ~ *family was present*⟩ **3** occurring at once or very shortly **4** in close or direct physical proximity ⟨*the* ~ *neighbourhood*⟩ **5** directly touching or concerning a person or thing [LL *immediatus,* fr L *in-* + LL *mediatus* intermediate – more at MEDIATE] – **immediateness** *n*
[1]**imˈmediately** /-li/ *adv* **1** in direct relation or proximity; directly ⟨*the parties* ~ *involved in the case*⟩ **2** without delay
[2]**immediately** *conj* AS SOON AS
immedicable /iˈmedikəbl/ *adj* incurable – chiefly fml [L *immedicabilis,* fr *in-* + *medicabilis* medicable] – **immedicably** *adv*
immemorial /ˌimiˈmawri·əl/ *adj* extending beyond the reach of memory, record, or tradition ⟨*existing from time* ~⟩ [prob fr F *immémorial,* fr MF, fr *in-* + *memorial*] – **immemorially** *adv*
immense /iˈmens/ *adj* very great, esp in size, degree, or extent [MF, fr L *immensus* immeasurable, fr *in-* + *mensus,* pp of *metiri* to measure – more at MEASURE] – **immensely** *adv,* **immenseness, immensity** *n*
immerse /iˈmuhs/ *vt* **1** to plunge into sthg, esp a fluid, that surrounds or covers **2** to baptize by complete submergence **3** to engross, absorb ⟨*completely* ~d *in his work*⟩ [L *immersus,* pp of *immergere,* fr *in-* + *mergere* to merge] – **immersible** *adj*
imˈmersed *adj, of a plant* growing wholly under water
immersion /iˈmuhsh(ə)n/ *n* disappearance of a celestial body behind or into the shadow of another [IMMERSE + -ION]
imˈmersion ˌheater *n* an electrical apparatus for heating a liquid in which it is immersed; *esp* an electric water-heater fixed inside a domestic hot-water storage tank
immigrant /ˈimigrənt/ *n* **1** one who comes to a country to take up permanent residence **2** a plant or animal that becomes established in an area where it was previously unknown [IMMIGRATE + -ANT] – **immigrant** *adj*
immigrate /ˈimigrayt/ *vi* to come into a country of which one is not a native for permanent residence ~ *vt* to bring in or send as immigrants [L *immigratus,* pp of *immigrare* to remove, go in, fr *in-* + *migrare* to migrate] – **immigration** /ˌimiˈgraysh(ə)n/ *n,* **immigrational** *adj*
imminent /ˈiminənt/ *adj* about to take place; *esp* impending, threatening [L *imminent-, imminens,* prp of *imminēre* to project, threaten, fr *in-* + *-minēre* (akin to L *mont-, mons* mountain)] – **imminently** *adv,* **imminentness, imminence** /-nəns/ *n*
immiscible /iˈmisəbl/ *adj* incapable of being mixed – used technically – **immiscibly** *adv,* **immiscibility** /iˌmisəˈbiləti/ *n*
immitigable /iˈmitigəbl/ *adj* incapable of being mitigated – chiefly fml [LL *immitigabilis,* fr L *in-* + *mitigare* to mitigate] – **immitigableness** *n,* **immitigably** *adv*
immobile /iˈmohbiel/ *adj* **1** incapable of being moved **2** motionless ⟨*keep the patient* ~⟩ [ME *in-mobill,* fr L *immobilis,* fr *in-* + *mobilis* mobile] – **immobility** /ˌimohˈbiləti/ *n*
immobil·ize, -ise /iˈmohbiliez/ *vt* **1** to prevent freedom of movement or effective use of **2** to reduce or eliminate motion of (sby or a body part) by mechanical means or by strict bed rest [IMMOBILE + -IZE] – **immobilizer** *n,* **immobilization** /iˌmohbilieˈzaysh(ə)n/ *n*
immoderate /iˈmod(ə)rət/ *adj* lacking in moderation; excessive [ME *immoderat,* fr L *immoderatus,* fr *in-* + *moderatus,* pp of *moderare* to moderate] – **immoderately** *adv,* **immoderacy** /-rəsi/, **immoderateness, immoderation** /-ˌmodəˈraysh(ə)n/ *n*
immodest /iˈmodist/ *adj* not conforming to standards of sexual propriety [L *immodestus,* fr *in-* + *modestus* modest] – **immodestly** *adv,* **immodesty** *n*
immolate /ˈimohlayt/ *vt* **1** to kill as a sacrificial victim **2** to kill, destroy [L *immolatus,* pp of *immolare,* fr *in-* + *mola* meal; fr the custom of sprinkling victims with sacrificial meal] – **immolator** *n,* **immolation** /ˌimohˈlaysh(ə)n/ *n*
immoral /iˈmorəl/ *adj* not conforming to conventional moral standards, esp in sexual matters – **immorally** *adv,* **immorality** /ˌiməˈraləti/ *n*
[1]**immortal** /iˈmawtl/ *adj* **1** exempt from death ⟨*the* ~ *gods*⟩ **2** enduring forever; imperishable ⟨~ *fame*⟩ [ME, fr L *immortalis,* fr *in-* + *mortalis* mortal] – **immortally** *adv,* **immortalize** *vt,* **immortality** /ˌimawˈtaləti/ *n*
[2]**immortal** *n* **1a** one exempt from death **b** *pl, often cap* the gods of classical antiquity **2** a person of lasting fame
immortelle /ˌimawˈtel/ *n* an everlasting flower [F, fr fem of *immortel* immortal, fr L *immortalis*]
immovable /iˈmoohvəbl/ *adj* **1** not moving or not intended to be moved **2a** steadfast, unyielding **b** incapable of being moved emotionally – **immovably** *adv,* **immovableness, immovability** /iˌmoohvəˈbiləti/ *n*
imˈmovables *n pl* real property
immune /iˈmyoohn/ *adj* **1** free, exempt ⟨~ *from prosecution*⟩ **2** having a high degree of resistance to a disease ⟨~ *to diphtheria*⟩ **3a** having or producing antibodies to a corresponding antigen ⟨*an* ~ *serum*⟩ **b** concerned with or involving immunity ⟨*an* ~ *response*⟩ [L *immunis,* fr *in-* + *munia* services, obligations; akin to L *munus* service] – **immune** *n,* **immunize** /ˈimyooniez/ *vt,* **immunization** /ˌimyoonieˈzaysh(ə)n/ *n*
immunity /iˈmyoohnəti/ *n* being immune; *specif* the ability to resist the effects or development of a disease-causing parasite, esp a microorganism
immuno- *comb form* immunity; immunology and ⟨im muno*genesis*⟩ ⟨immuno*chemistry*⟩ [ISV, fr *immune*]
immunoassay /ˌimyoonoh·əˈsay, ˌimyoonohˈasay/ *n* the identification and measurement of the concentration of a substance (e g a protein) through its capacity to act as an antigen in the presence of specific antibodies that react with it – **immunoassayable** *adj*
immunoglobulin /ˌimyoonohˈglobyoolin/ *n* a protein (e g an antibody) that is made up of light and

heavy amino acid chains and usu binds specifically to a particular antigen

immunology /ˌimyooˈnoləji/ *n* biology that deals with the phenomena and causes of immunity [ISV] – **immunologist** *n*, **immunologic** /ˌimyoonəˈlojik/, **immunological** *adj*, **immunologically** *adv*

immunosuppression /ˌimyoonohsəˈpresh(ə)n/ *n* suppression (e g by drugs) of natural immune responses – **immunosuppress** *vt*, **immunosuppressant** *n or adj*, **immunosuppressive** /-siv/ *adj*

ˌimmunoˈtherapy /-ˈtherəpi/ *n* treatment of or preventive measures against disease by administering (preparations of) antigens [ISV]

immure /iˈmyooə/ *vt* **1** to enclose (as if) within walls; imprison **2** to build into, or esp entomb in, a wall [ML *immurare*, fr L *in-* + *murus* wall] – **immurement** *n*

immutable /iˈmyoohtəbl/ *adj* not capable of or susceptible to change [ME, fr L *immutabilis*, fr *in-* + *mutabilis* mutable] – **immutably** *adv*, **immutableness, immutability** /iˌmyoohtəˈbiləti/ *n*

¹imp /imp/ *n* **1** a small demon **2** a mischievous child; a scamp [ME *impe*, fr OE *impa*, fr *impian* to imp]

²imp *vt, archaic* to graft or repair (e g a falcon's wing or tail) with a feather to improve flight [ME *impen*, fr OE *impian*; akin to OHG *impfōn* to graft; both from a prehistoric WGmc word borrowed fr (assumed) VL *imputare*, fr L *in-* + *putare* to prune – more at PAVE]

¹impact /imˈpakt/ *vt* to fix or press firmly (as if) by packing or wedging ~ *vi* to impinge or make contact, esp forcefully [L *impactus*, pp of *impingere* to push against – more at IMPINGE] – **impactive** /-tiv/ *adj*

²impact /ˈimpakt/ *n* **1a** an impinging or striking, esp of one body against another **b** (the impetus produced by or as if by) a violent contact or collision **2** a strong or powerful effect or impression ⟨*the ~ of modern science on our society*⟩

imˈpacted *adj, of a tooth* not erupted as a result of lack of space in the jaw or of obstruction by bone or other teeth

impaction /imˈpaksh(ə)n/ *n* becoming or being impacted; *esp* the lodging of sthg (e g faeces) in a body passage

impair /imˈpeə/ *vt* to diminish in quality, strength, or amount [ME *empeiren*, fr MF *empeirer*, fr (assumed) VL *impejorare*, fr L *in-* + LL *pejorare* to make worse – more at PEJORATIVE] – **impairer** *n*, **impairment** *n*

imˈpaired *adj, Can, of a driver or driving* under the influence of alcohol or narcotics

impala /imˈpahlə/ *n* a large brownish African antelope [Zulu]

impale /imˈpayl/ *vt* **1** to pierce (as if) with sthg pointed; *esp* to torture or kill by fixing on a stake **2** to join (coats of arms) on a heraldic shield divided in half vertically [MF & ML; MF *empaler*, fr ML *impalare*, fr L *in-* + *palus* stake – more at ¹POLE] – **impalement** *n*

impalpable /imˈpalpəbl/ *adj* **1** incapable of being sensed by the touch; intangible **2** not easily discerned or grasped by the mind – **impalpably** *adv*, **impalpability** /imˌpalpəˈbiləti/ *n*

impanel /imˈpanl/ *vt* to empanel

impart /imˈpaht/ *vt* **1** to convey, transmit ⟨*the flavour ~ed by herbs*⟩ **2** to make known; disclose [MF & L; MF *impartir*, fr L *impartire*, fr *in-* + *partire* to divide, part] – **impartable** *adj*, **impartment, impartation** /ˌimpahˈtaysh(ə)n/ *n*

impartial /imˈpahsh(ə)l/ *adj* not biased – **impartially** *adv*, **impartiality** /imˌpahshiˈaləti/ *n*

impartible /imˈpahtəbl/ *adj* not divisible ⟨*an ~ inheritance*⟩ [LL *impartibilis*, fr L *in-* + LL *partibilis* divisible, fr L *partire*] – **impartibly** *adv*

impassable /imˈpahsəbl/ *adj* incapable of being passed, traversed, or surmounted – **impassably** *adv*, **impassableness, impassability** /imˌpahsəˈbiləti/ *n*

impasse /ˈamˌpas (*Fr* ɛ̃pɑːs)/ *n* **1** a predicament from which there is no obvious escape **2** DEADLOCK 2 [F, fr *in-* + *passer* to pass]

impassible /imˈpasəbl/ *adj* incapable of suffering, of feeling emotion, or of experiencing pain or injury – chiefly fml [ME, fr MF or LL; MF, fr LL *impassibilis*, fr L *in-* + LL *passibilis* capable of feeling, fr L *passus*, pp of *pati* to suffer – more at PATIENT] – **impassibly** *adv*, **impassibility** /imˌpasəˈbiləti/ *n*

impassion /imˈpash(ə)n/ *vt* to arouse the feelings or passions of [prob fr It *impassionare*, fr *in-* (fr L) + *passione* passion, fr LL *passion-*, *passio*] – **impassioned** *adj*

impassive /imˈpasiv/ *adj* **1** incapable of or not susceptible to emotion **2** showing no feeling or emotion – **impassively** *adv*, **impassiveness, impassivity** /ˌimpaˈsivəti/ *n*

impasto /imˈpastoh/ *n* (the technique of) applying pigment thickly in painting [It, fr *impastare* to make into a paste, fr *in-* (fr L) + *pasta* paste, fr LL] – **impastoed** *adj*

impatient /imˈpaysh(ə)nt/ *adj* **1a** restless or quickly roused to anger or exasperation **b** intolerant ⟨*~ of delay*⟩ **2** showing or caused by a lack of patience ⟨*an ~ reply*⟩ **3** eagerly desirous; anxious ⟨*~ to see her boyfriend*⟩ [ME *impacient*, fr MF, fr L *impatient-*, *impatiens*, fr *in-* + *patient-*, *patiens* patient] – **impatience** *n*, **impatiently** *adv*

impeach /imˈpeech/ *vt* **1a** to bring an accusation against **b** to charge with a usu serious crime; *specif, chiefly NAm* to charge (a public official) with misconduct in office **2** to cast doubt on; *esp* to challenge the credibility or validity of ⟨*~ the testimony of a witness*⟩ [ME *empechen*, fr MF *empeechier* to hinder, fr LL *impedicare* to fetter, fr L *in-* + *pedica* fetter, fr *ped-*, *pes* foot – more at FOOT] – **impeachable** *adj*, **impeachment** *n*

impeccable /imˈpekəbl/ *adj* **1** incapable of sinning **2** free from fault or blame; flawless [L *impeccabilis*, fr *in-* + *peccare* to sin] – **impeccably** *adv*, **impeccability** /imˌpekəˈbiləti/ *n*

impecunious /ˌimpiˈkyoohnyəs, -ni·əs/ *adj* having very little or no money – chiefly fml [*in-* + obs *pecunious* (rich), fr ME, fr L *pecuniosus*, fr *pecunia* money – more at FEE] – **impecuniously** *adv*, **impecuniousness, impecuniosity** /-iˈosəti/ *n*

impedance /imˈpeed(ə)ns/ *n* sthg that impedes; *esp* the opposition in an electrical circuit to the flow of an alternating current that is analogous to the opposition of an electrical resistance to the flow of a direct current

impede /imˈpeed/ *vt* to interfere with or retard the progress of [L *impedire*, fr *in-* + *ped-*, *pes* foot – more at FOOT] – **impeder** *n*

impediment /imˈpedimənt/ *n* **1** sthg that impedes; *esp* a physiological speech defect **2** a hindrance to lawful marriage

impedimenta /imˌpediˈmentə/ *n pl* **1** unwieldy

baggage or equipment **2** things that impede; encumbrances [L, pl of *impedimentum* impediment, fr *impedire*]

impel /im'pel/ *vt* **-ll-** **1** to urge forward or force into action ⟨*felt* ~led *to speak his mind*⟩ **2** to propel [L *impellere*, fr *in-* + *pellere* to drive – more at FELT]

impeller *also* **impellor** /im'pelə/ *n* (a blade of) a rotor [IMPEL + ²-ER]

impend /im'pend/ *vi* **1a** to hover threateningly; menace **b** to be about to happen **2** *archaic* to be suspended; hang [L *impendēre*, fr *in-* + *pendēre* to hang – more at PENDANT]

impenetrability /im,penitrə'biləti/ *n* the inability of 2 portions of matter to occupy the same space at the same time [IMPENETRABLE + -ITY]

impenetrable im'penitrəbl/ *adj* **1a** incapable of being penetrated or pierced **b** inaccessible to intellectual influences or ideas **2** incapable of being comprehended **3** having the property of impenetrability [ME *impenetrabel*, fr MF *impenetrable*, fr L *impenetrabilis*, fr *in-* + *penetrabilis* penetrable] – **impenetrableness** *n*, **impenetrably** *adv*

¹**imperative** /im'perətiv/ *adj* **1a** of or being the grammatical mood that expresses command **b** expressive of a command, entreaty, or exhortation **c** having power to restrain, control, and direct **2** urgent ⟨*an* ~ *duty*⟩ [LL *imperativus*, fr L *imperatus*, pp of *imperare* to command – more at EMPEROR] – **imperatively** *adv*, **imperativeness** *n*

²**imperative** *n* **1** (a verb form expressing) the imperative mood **2** sthg imperative: e g **a** a command, order **b** an obligatory act or duty **c** an imperative judgment or proposition

imperator /,impə'rahtaw/ *n* a commander in chief or emperor of the ancient Romans [L – more at EMPEROR] – **imperatorial** /im,perə'tawri·əl/ *adj*

imperceptible /impə'septəbl/ *adj* **1** not perceptible by the mind or senses **2** extremely slight, gradual, or subtle ⟨*an* ~ *change in attitude*⟩ [MF, fr ML *imperceptibilis*, fr L *in-* + LL *perceptibilis* perceptible] – **imperceptibly** *adv*, **imperceptibility** /-'biləti/ *n*

impercipient /,impə'sipi·ənt/ *adj* not perceptive – **impercipience** *n*

¹**imperfect** /im'puhfikt/ *adj* **1** not perfect: e g **a** defective **b** not having the stamens and carpels in the same flower **2** of or being a verb tense expressing a continuing state or an incomplete action, esp in the past **3** *of a cadence* passing to a dominant chord from a tonic chord [ME *imperfit*, fr MF *imparfait*, fr L *imperfectus*, fr *in-* + *perfectus* perfect] – **imperfectly** *adv*, **imperfectness** *n*

²**imperfect** *n* (a verb form expressing) the imperfect tense

imperfection /,impə'feksh(ə)n/ *n* the quality or state of being imperfect; *also* a fault, blemish

imperfective /,impə'fektiv/ *adj, of a form of a verb* expressing action as incomplete or repeated – compare PERFECTIVE – **imperfective** *n*

imperforate /im'puhf(ə)rət/ *adj* **1** having no (normal anatomical) opening **2** *of a stamp or a sheet of stamps* lacking perforations

¹**imperial** /im'piəri·əl/ *adj* **1a** of or befitting an empire, emperor, or empress **b** of the British Empire **2a** sovereign, royal **b** regal, imperious **3** belonging to an official nonmetric British series of weights and measures [ME, fr MF, fr LL *imperialis*, fr L *imperium* command, empire] – **imperially** *adv*

²**imperial** *n* a size of paper usu 30 × 22in (762 × 559mm)

imperialism /im'piəri·ə,liz(ə)m/ *n* **1** government by an emperor **2** the policy, practice, or advocacy of extending the power and dominion of a nation, esp by territorial acquisition – **imperialist** *n or adj*, **imperialistic** /-'listik/ *adj*, **imperialistically** *adv*

imperil /im'perəl/ *vt* **-ll-** (*NAm* **-l-**, **-ll-**) to endanger – **imperilment** *n*

imperious /im'piəri·əs/ *adj* marked by arrogant assurance; domineering ⟨*his* ~ *arbitrariness*⟩ [L *imperiosus*, fr *imperium*] – **imperiously** *adv*, **imperiousness** *n*

imperishable /im'perishəbl/ *adj* **1** not perishable or subject to decay **2** enduring permanently ⟨~ *fame*⟩ – **imperishable** *n*, **imperishably** *adv*, **imperishableness**, **imperishability** /-shə'biləti/ *n*

imperium /im'piəri·əm/ *n* supreme power; sovereignty [L – more at EMPIRE]

impermanent /im'puhmənənt/ *adj* transient – **impermanence**, **impermanency** *n*, **impermanently** *adv*

impermeable /im'puhmi·əbl/ *adj* not permitting passage, esp of a fluid [LL *impermeabilis*, fr L *in-* + LL *permeabilis* permeable] – **impermeably** *adv*, **impermeability** /-ə'biləti/ *n*

impersonal /-'puhs(ə)nl/ *adj* **1a** denoting verbal action with no expressed subject (e g *methinks*) or with a merely formal subject (e g *rained* in *it rained*) **b** *of a pronoun* indefinite **2a** having no personal reference or connection; objective **b** not involving or reflecting the human personality or emotions ⟨*spoke in a flat* ~ *tone*⟩ **c** not having personality ⟨*an* ~ *deity*⟩ [LL *impersonalis*, fr L *in-* + LL *personalis* personal] – **impersonalize** *vt*, **impersonally** *adv*, **impersonality** /-,puhsə'naləti/ *n*

impersonate /im'puhsənayt/ *vt* to assume or act the character of – **impersonator** *n*, **impersonation** /-'naysh(ə)n/ *n*

impertinent /im'puhtinənt/ *adj* **1** not restrained within due or proper bounds ⟨~ *curiosity*⟩; *also* rude, insolent **2** irrelevant – chiefly fml [ME, fr MF, fr LL *impertinent-*, *impertinens*, fr L *in-* + *pertinent-*, *pertinens*, prp of *pertinēre* to pertain] – **impertinence** *n*, **impertinently** *adv*

imperturbable /,impə'tuhbəbl, -puh-/ *adj* marked by extreme calm and composure [ME, fr LL *imperturbabilis*, fr L *in-* + *perturbare* to perturb] – **imperturbably** *adv*, **imperturbability** /-bə'biləti/ *n*

impervious /im'puhvi·əs/ *adj* **1** impenetrable ⟨*a coat* ~ *to rain*⟩ **2** not capable of being affected or disturbed ⟨~ *to criticism*⟩ ***USE*** usu + *to* [L *impervius*, fr *in-* + *pervius* pervious] – **imperviously** *adv*, **imperviousness** *n*

impetigo /,impə'tiegoh/ *n* a contagious skin disease characterized by blisters and pustules [L, fr *impetere* to attack – more at IMPETUS] – **impetiginous** /-'tijinəs/ *adj*

impetuous /im'petyoo·əs/ *adj* **1** marked by impulsive vehemence ⟨*an* ~ *temperament*⟩ **2** marked by forceful and violent movement – chiefly poetic [ME, fr MF *impetueux*, fr LL *impetuosus*, fr L *impetus*] – **impetuousness** *n*, **impetuously** *adv*, **impetuosity** /im,petyoo'osəti/ *n*

impetus /'impitəs/ *n* **1a** a driving force **b** an incentive, stimulus ⟨*gave a new* ~ *to the ailing economy*⟩ **2** the energy possessed by a moving body [L, assault, impetus, fr *impetere* to attack, fr *in-* + *petere* to go to, seek – more at FEATHER]

impi /ˈimpi/ *n, pl* **impis** *SAfr* an armed usu organized band of Africans [Zulu]

impiety /imˈpie·əti/ *n* (an act showing) a lack of reverence

impinge /imˈpinj/ *vi* **1** to strike, dash **2** to make an impression **3** to encroach, infringe ⟨~ *on other people's rights*⟩ *USE* usu + *on* or *upon* [L *impingere*, fr *in-* + *pangere* to fasten, drive in – more at PACT] – **impingement** *n*

impious /ˈimpi·əs/ *adj* lacking in reverence or proper respect (e g for God); irreverent [L *impius*, fr *in-* + *pius* pious] – **impiously** *adv*

impish /ˈimpish/ *adj* mischievous [¹IMP + -ISH] – **impishly** *adv*, **impishness** *n*

implacable /imˈplakəbl/ *adj* not capable of being appeased or pacified ⟨*an* ~ *enemy*⟩ [MF or L; MF, fr L *implacabilis*, fr *in-* + *placabilis* easily placated] – **implacableness** *n*, **implacably** *adv*, **implacability** /-kəˈbiləti/ *n*

¹**implant** /imˈplahnt/ *vt* **1a** to fix or set securely or deeply **b** to set permanently in the consciousness or habit patterns **2** to insert in the tissue of a living organism – **implantable** *adj*, **implanter** *n*, **implantation** /ˌimplahnˈtaysh(ə)n/ *n*

²**implant** /ˈimˌplahnt/ *n* sthg (e g a graft or hormone pellet) implanted in tissue

implausible /imˈplawzəbl/ *adj* provoking disbelief – **implausibly** *adv*, **implausibility** /-zəˈbiləti/ *n*

implead /imˈpleed/ *vt* to take legal action against [ME *empleden*, fr MF *emplaider*, fr OF *emplaidier*, fr *en-* + *plaidier* to plead]

¹**implement** /ˈimplimənt/ *n* **1** an article serving to equip ⟨*the* ~s *of religious worship*⟩ **2** (sby or sthg that serves as) a utensil or tool [ME, fr LL *implementum* action of filling up, fr L *implēre* to fill up, fr *in-* + *plēre* to fill – more at ¹FULL]

²**implement** /ˈimpliment, -mənt/ *vt* CARRY OUT; *esp* to give practical effect to ⟨*plans not yet* ~ed *due to lack of funds*⟩ – **implementation** /ˌimpliməntˈtaysh(ə)n/ *n*

implicate /ˈimplikayt/ *vt* **1** to involve as a consequence, corollary, or inference; imply **2a** to bring into (incriminating) connection **b** to involve in the nature or operation of sthg; affect **3** *archaic* to entwine [L *implicatus*, pp of *implicare* – more at EMPLOY]

implication /ˌimpliˈkaysh(ə)n/ *n* **1a** implicating or being implicated **b** incriminating involvement **2a** implying or being implied **b** a logical relation between 2 propositions such that if the first is true the second must be true **3** sthg implied – **implicative** /imˈplikətiv/ *adj*

implicit /imˈplisit/ *adj* **1a** implied rather than directly stated ⟨*an* ~ *assumption*⟩ **b** potentially present though not realized or visible **2** unquestioning, absolute ⟨~ *obedience*⟩ [L *implicitus*, pp of *implicare*] – **implicitly** *adv*, **implicitness** *n*

implode /imˈplohd/ *vb* to collapse inwards suddenly [*in-* + *-plode* (as in *explode*)]

implore /imˈplaw/ *vt* **1** to call on in supplication; beseech **2** to call or beg for earnestly; entreat [MF or L; MF *implorer*, fr L *implorare*, fr *in-* + *plorare* to cry out]

implosion /imˈplohzh(ə)n/ *n* **1** imploding **2** the release of obstructed breath inwards that occurs in the articulation of one kind of stop consonant **3** the act or action of coming (as if) to a centre [*in-* + *-plosion* (as in *explosion*)] – **implosive** /-ziv, -siv/ *adj or n*

imply /imˈplie/ *vt* **1** to involve or indicate as a necessary or potential though not expressly stated consequence **2** to express indirectly; hint at ⟨*his silence* implied *consent*⟩ [ME *emplien*, fr MF *emplier*, fr L *implicare*]

impolite /ˌimpəˈliet/ *adj* not polite; rude – **impolitely** *adv*, **impoliteness** *n*

impolitic /imˈpolətik/ *adj* unwise, ill-advised – chiefly fml – **impoliticly** *adv*

imponderable /imˈpond(ə)rəbl/ *n or adj* (sthg) incapable of being precisely weighed or evaluated [ML *imponderabilis*, fr L *in-* + LL *ponderabilis* appreciable, fr L *ponderare* to weigh, ponder] – **imponderably** *adv*, **imponderability** /-rəˈbiləti/ *n*

¹**import** /imˈpawt/ *vt* **1** to bring from a foreign or external source; *esp* to bring (e g merchandise) into a place or country from another country **2** to convey as meaning or portent; signify – chiefly fml [ME *importen*, fr L *importare* to bring into, fr *in-* + *portare* to carry – more at ¹FARE] – **importable** *adj*, **importer** *n*, **importation** /ˌimpawˈtaysh(ə)n/ *n*

²**import** /ˈimpawt/ *n* **1** sthg imported **2** importing, esp of merchandise **3** purport, meaning **4** (relative) importance ⟨*it is hard to determine the* ~ *of this decision*⟩ *USE* (*3 & 4*) fml

importance /imˈpawt(ə)ns/ *n* consequence, significance

important /imˈpawt(ə)nt/ *adj* of considerable significance or consequence [MF, fr OIt *importante*, fr L *important-, importans*, prp of *importare*] – **importantly** *adv*

importunate /imˈpawtyoonət, -chənət/ *adj* troublesomely urgent; extremely persistent in request or demand – chiefly fml – **importunately** *adv*, **importunity** /ˌimpawˈtyoohnəti, -ˈchoohn-/ *n*

importune /imˈpawtyoohn, -choohn/ *vt* **1** to press or urge with repeated requests; solicit with troublesome persistence **2** to solicit for purposes of prostitution ~ *vi* to beg, urge, or solicit importunately *USE* chiefly fml [MF or ML; MF *importuner*, fr ML *importunare*, fr L *importunus* unfit, troublesome, fr *in-* + *-portunus* (as in *opportunus* fit) – more at OPPORTUNE] – **importuner** *n*

impose /imˈpohz/ *vt* **1a** to establish or apply as compulsory **b** to establish or make prevail by force **2** to arrange (typeset or plated pages) in order for printing **3** PALM OFF ⟨~ *fake antiques on the public*⟩ **4** to force into the company or on the attention of another ⟨~ *oneself on others*⟩ ~ *vi* to take unwarranted advantage ⟨~d *on his good nature*⟩; *also* to be an excessive requirement or burden *USE* (*except vt 1 & 2*) + *on* or *upon* [MF *imposer*, fr L *imponere*, lit., to put upon (perf indic *imposui*), fr *in-* + *ponere* to put – more at POSITION] – **imposer** *n*

imposing /imˈpohzing/ *adj* impressive because of size, bearing, dignity, or grandeur – **imposingly** *adv*

imposition /ˌimpəˈzish(ə)n/ *n* **1** the act of imposing **2** sthg imposed: e g **a** a levy, tax **b** an excessive or unwarranted requirement or burden

impossible /imˈposəbl/ *adj* **1a** incapable of being or occurring; not possible **b** seemingly incapable of being done, attained, or fulfilled; insuperably difficult **c** difficult to believe ⟨*an* ~ *story*⟩ **2** extremely undesirable or difficult to put up with ⟨*life became*

~ *because of lack of money*⟩ [ME, fr MF & L; MF, fr L *impossibilis,* fr *in-* + *possibilis* possible] – **impossibly** *adv,* **impossibility** /im,posəˈbiləti, ,---ˈ---/ *n*

[1]**impost** /ˈimpohst/ *n* a tax [MF, fr ML *impositum,* fr L, neut of *impositus,* pp of *imponere*]

[2]**impost** *n* a bracket, top part of a pillar, or moulding that supports an arch ☞ ARCHITECTURE [F *imposte,* deriv of L *impositus*]

impostor, imposter /imˈpostə/ *n* one who assumes a false identity or title for fraudulent purposes [LL *impostor,* fr *impostus,* pp]

imposture /imˈposchə/ *n* (an instance of) fraud, deception [LL *impostura,* fr L *impositus, impostus,* pp of *imponere*]

impotent /ˈimpət(ə)nt/ *adj* **1** lacking in efficacy, strength, or vigour **2a** unable to copulate through an inability to maintain an erection of the penis **b** *of a male* STERILE 1 – not used technically [ME, fr MF & L; MF, fr L *impotent-, impotens,* fr *in-* + *potent-, potens* potent] – **impotence, impotency** *n,* **impotent** *n,* **impotently** *adv*

impound /imˈpownd/ *vt* **1a** to shut up (as if) in a pound; confine **b** to take and hold in legal custody **2** to collect and confine (water) (as if) in a reservoir – **impoundment** *n*

impoverish /imˈpov(ə)rish/ *vt* **1** to make poor **2** to deprive of strength, richness, or fertility [ME *enpoverisen,* fr MF *empovriss-,* stem of *empovrir,* fr *en-* + *povre* poor – more at POOR] – **impoverisher** *n,* **impoverishment** *n*

impracticable /imˈpraktikəbl/ *adj* **1** incapable of being put into effect or carried out **2** impassable ⟨*an* ~ *road*⟩ – **impracticably** *adv,* **impracticableness, impracticability** /-kəˈbiləti/ *n*

impractical /imˈpraktikl/ *adj* not practical: e g **a** incapable of dealing sensibly with practical matters **b** impracticable ⟨*economically* ~⟩ – **impracticality** /-tiˈkaləti/ *n,* **impractically** *adv*

imprecate /ˈimprikayt/ *vb* to invoke evil (on); curse [L *imprecatus,* pp of *imprecari,* fr *in-* + *precari* to pray – more at PRAY] – **imprecatory** *adj,* **imprecation** /,impriˈkaysh(ə)n/ *n*

impregnable /imˈpregnəbl/ *adj* **1** incapable of being taken by assault ⟨*an* ~ *fortress*⟩ **2** beyond criticism or question ⟨*an* ~ *social position*⟩ [ME *imprenable,* fr MF, fr *in-* + *prenable* vulnerable to capture, fr *prendre* to take – more at [4]PRIZE] – **impregnably** *adv,* **impregnability** /-nəˈbiləti/ *n*

[1]**impregnate** /ˈimpregnayt/ *adj* filled, saturated

[2]**impregnate** *vt* **1a** to introduce sperm cells into **b** to make pregnant; fertilize **2a** to cause to be imbued, permeated, or saturated **b** to permeate thoroughly [LL *impraegnatus,* pp of *impraegnare,* fr L *in-* + *praegnas* pregnant] – **impregnable** /imˈpregnəbl/ *adj,* **impregnation** /,impregˈnaysh(ə)n/ *n,* **impregnator** /imˈpregnaytə/ *n*

impresario /,impriˈsahrioh/ *n, pl* **impresarios** one who organizes, puts on, or sponsors a public entertainment (e g a sports event); *esp* the manager or conductor of an opera or concert company [It, fr *impresa* undertaking, fr *imprendere* to undertake, fr (assumed) VL *imprehendere,* fr L *in-* + *prehendere* to seize – more at PREHENSILE]

imprescriptible /,impriˈskriptəbl/ *adj* that cannot be taken away or revoked; inalienable [MF, fr *in-* [1]in- + *prescriptible* subject to prescription, fr ML *praescriptibilis,* fr *praescriptus,* pp of *praescribere* to claim by right of prescription – more at PRESCRIBE]

[1]**impress** /imˈpres/ *vt* **1a** to apply with pressure so as to imprint **b** to mark (as if) by pressure or stamping **2a** to fix strongly or deeply (e g in the mind or memory) **b** to produce a deep and usu favourable impression on **3** to transmit (force or motion) by pressure ~ *vi* to produce a (favourable) impression ⟨*performances that failed to* ~⟩ [ME *impressen,* fr L *impressus,* pp of *imprimere,* fr *in-* + *premere* to press – more at [2]PRESS] – **impressible** *adj*

[2]**impress** /ˈimpres/ *n* **1** the act of impressing **2** a mark made by pressure **3** an impression, effect

[3]**imˈpress** *vt* **1** to force into naval service **2** to procure or enlist by forcible persuasion [*in-* + *press*] – **impressment** *n*

impression /imˈpresh(ə)n/ *n* **1** the act or process of impressing **2** the effect produced by impressing: e g **a** a stamp, form, or figure produced by physical contact **b** a (marked) influence or effect on the mind or senses; *esp* a favourable impression **3a** an effect of alteration or improvement ⟨*the settlement left little* ~ *on the wilderness*⟩ **b** a telling image impressed on the mind or senses ⟨*first* ~s *of Greece*⟩ **4a** the amount of pressure with which an inked printing surface deposits its ink on the paper **b** (a print or copy made from) the contact of a printing surface and the material being printed **c** all the copies of a publication (e g a book) printed in 1 continuous operation **5** a usu indistinct or imprecise notion or recollection **6** an imitation or representation of salient features in an artistic or theatrical medium; *esp* an imitation in caricature of a noted personality as a form of theatrical entertainment

imˈpressionable /-əbl/ *adj* **1** easily influenced **2** easily moulded – **impressionability** /-əˈbiləti/ *n*

impressionism /-iz(ə)m/ *n* **1** *often cap* an art movement, esp in late 19th-c France, that tries to convey the effects of actual reflected light on natural usu outdoor subjects **2** literary depiction that seeks to convey a general subjective impression rather than a detailed re-creation of reality – **impressionist** *n or adj, often cap*

im,pressionˈistic /-ˈistik/ *adj* **1** of or being impressionism **2** based on or involving subjective impression as distinct from knowledge, fact, or systematic thought – **impressionistically** *adv*

impressive /imˈpresiv/ *adj* making a marked impression; stirring deep feelings, esp of awe or admiration – **impressively** *adv,* **impressiveness** *n*

imprimatur /,impriˈmahtə, -ˈmaytə/ *n* **1** a licence granted, esp by Roman Catholic episcopal authority, to print or publish **2** sanction, approval [NL, let it be printed, fr *imprimere* to print, fr L, to imprint, impress – more at [1]IMPRESS]

imprimis /imˈpriemis/ *adv* in the first place – used to introduce a list of items [ME *inprimis,* fr L *in primis* among the first (things)]

[1]**imprint** /imˈprint/ *vt* **1** to mark (as if) by pressure **2** to fix indelibly or permanently (e g on the memory)

[2]**imprint** /ˈimprint/ *n* **1** a mark or depression made by pressure ⟨*the fossil* ~ *of a dinosaur's foot*⟩ **2** a publisher's name printed at the foot of a title-page **3** an indelible distinguishing effect or influence ⟨*their work bears a sort of regional* ~ – Malcolm Cowley⟩ [MF *empreinte,* fr fem of *empreint,* pp of *empreindre* to imprint, fr L *imprimere*]

imprinting /im'printing/ *n* a behaviour pattern rapidly established early in the life of an animal that involves attachment to an object or other animal, esp the animal's mother, seen just after birth

imprison /im'priz(ə)n/ *vt* to put (as if) in prison [ME *imprisonen*, fr OF *emprisoner*, fr *en-* + *prison*] – **imprisonment** *n*

improbable /im'probəbl/ *adj* unlikely to be true or to occur [MF or L; MF, fr L *improbabilis*, fr *in-* + *probabilis* probable] – **improbably** *adv*, **improbability** /-bə'biləti, ,improb-/ *n*

improbity /im'prohbəti/ *n* lack of integrity; dishonesty – chiefly fml [MF or L; MF *improbité*, fr L *improbitas*, fr *improbus* bad, dishonest, fr *in-* [1]in- + *probus* good, honest – more at PROVE]

[1]**impromptu** /im'promptyooh/ *adj* made, done, composed, or uttered (as if) on the spur of the moment ⟨*an ~ change of plan*⟩ [F, fr *impromptu* extemporaneously, fr L *in promptu* in readiness] – **impromptu** *adv*

[2]**impromptu** *n* **1** sthg impromptu **2** a musical composition suggesting improvisation

improper /im'propə/ *adj* **1** not in accordance with fact, truth, or correct procedure ⟨*~ inference*⟩ **2** not suitable or appropriate **3** not in accordance with propriety or modesty; indecent [MF *impropre*, fr L *improprius*, fr *in-* + *proprius* proper] – **improperly** *adv*

improper fraction *n* a fraction whose numerator is equal to, larger than, or of equal or higher degree than the denominator

impropriety /,imprə'prie·əti/ *n* **1** being improper **2** an improper act or remark; *esp* an unacceptable use of a word [F or LL; F *impropriété*, fr LL *improprietat-*, *improprietas*, fr L *improprius*]

improvable /im'proohvəbl/ *adj* capable of improving or being improved – **improvability** /-və'biləti/ *n*

improve /im'proohv/ *vt* **1a** to enhance in value or quality; make better **b** to increase the value of (land or property) by making better (e g by cultivation or the erection of buildings) **2** to use to good purpose ~ *vi* **1** to advance or make progress in what is desirable **2** to make useful additions or amendments ⟨*the new version* ~s *on the original*⟩ [AF *emprouer* to invest profitably, fr OF *en-* + *prou* advantage, fr LL *prode* – more at PROUD]

im'provement /-mənt/ *n* **1** improving or being improved **2** (sthg that gives) increased value or excellence ⟨~s *to an old house*⟩

improver /im'proohvə/ *n, chiefly Br* one who works for low wages in order to gain instruction and experience in a trade or occupation, esp while serving an apprenticeship [IMPROVE + [2]-ER]

improvident /im'provid(ə)nt/ *adj* lacking foresight; not providing for the future [LL *improvident-*, *improvidens*, fr L *in-* + *provident-*, *providens* provident] – **improvidence** *n*, **improvidently** *adv*

improvise /'imprəviez/ *vb* **1** to compose, recite, or perform impromptu or without a set script, musical score, etc **2** to make, devise, or provide (sthg) without preparation (from what is conveniently to hand) [F *improviser*, fr It *improvvisare*, fr *improvviso* sudden, fr L *improvisus*, lit., unforeseen, fr *in-* + *provisus*, pp of *providēre* to see ahead – more at PROVIDE] – **improviser** *n*, **improvisation** /-'zaysh(ə)n/ *n*, **improvisatory** /,imprəvie'zaytəri, im'provizətri, ,imprə'viezətri/ *adj*

imprudent /im'proohd(ə)nt/ *adj* lacking discretion or caution [ME, fr L *imprudent-*, *imprudens*, fr *in-* + *prudent-*, *prudens* prudent] – **imprudence** *n*, **imprudently** *adv*

impudent /'impyood(ə)nt/ *adj* marked by contemptuous or cocky boldness or disregard of others [ME, fr L *impudent-*, *impudens*, fr *in-* + *pudent-*, *pudens*, prp of *pudēre* to feel shame] – **impudence** *n*, **impudently** *adv*

impugn /im'pyoohn/ *vt* to assail by words or arguments; call into question the validity or integrity of [ME *impugnen*, fr MF *impugner*, fr L *impugnare*, fr *in-* + *pugnare* to fight] – **impugnable** *adj*, **impugner** *n*

impulse /'impuls/ *n* **1a** (motion produced by) the act of driving onwards with sudden force **b** a wave of excitation transmitted through a nerve that results in physiological (e g muscular) activity or inhibition **2a** a force so communicated as to produce motion suddenly **b** inspiration, stimulus ⟨*the creative ~*⟩ **3a** a sudden spontaneous inclination or incitement to some usu unpremeditated action **b** a propensity or natural tendency, usu other than rational **4a** the change in momentum produced by a (large) force **b** PULSE 4a [L *impulsus*, fr *impulsus*, pp of *impellere* to impel]

impulsion /im'pulsh(ə)n/ *n* **1a** impelling or being impelled **b** an impelling force **c** an impetus **2** IMPULSE 3

impulsive /im'pulsiv/ *adj* **1** having the power of driving or impelling **2** actuated by or prone to act on impulse **3** acting momentarily – **impulsively** *adv*, **impulsiveness** *n*

impunity /im'pyoohnəti/ *n* exemption or freedom from punishment, harm, or loss ⟨*trespassing with ~*⟩ [MF or L; MF *impunité*, fr L *impunitat-*, *impunitas*, fr *impune* without punishment, fr *in-* + *poena* pain]

impure /im'pyooə/ *adj* not pure: e g **a** not chaste **b** containing sthg unclean ⟨*~ water*⟩ **c** ritually unclean **d** mixed; *esp* adulterated [F & L; F, fr L *impurus*, fr *in-* + *purus* pure] – **impurely** *adv*, **impurity** *n*

impute /im'pyooht/ *vt* **1** to lay the responsibility or blame for, often unjustly **2** to credit to a person or a cause; *esp* to attribute unjustly [ME *inputen*, fr L *imputare*, fr *in-* + *putare* to think, consider – more at PAVE] – **imputable** *adj*, **imputative** /-tətiv/ *adj*, **imputation** /,im pyoo'taysh(ə)n/ *n*

[1]**in** /in/ *prep* **1a(1)** – used to indicate location within or inside sthg three-dimensional ⟨*swimming ~ the lake*⟩ **(2)** – used to indicate location within or not beyond limits ⟨*~ reach*⟩ ⟨*~ sight*⟩ ⟨*wounded ~ the leg*⟩ **(3)** at – used with the names of cities, countries, and seas ⟨*~ London*⟩ **(4)** during ⟨*~ the summer*⟩ ⟨*~ 1959*⟩ ⟨*lost ~ transit*⟩ **(5)** by or before the end of ⟨*wrote it ~ a week*⟩ ⟨*will come ~ an hour*⟩ **b** INTO 1a ⟨*went ~ the house*⟩ **2a** – used to indicate means, instrumentality, or medium of expression ⟨*drawn ~ pencil*⟩ ⟨*written ~ French*⟩ ⟨*drink your health ~ cider*⟩ **b** – used to describe costume ⟨*a child ~ gumboots*⟩ ⟨*a girl ~ red*⟩ **3a** – used to indicate qualification, manner, circumstance, or condition ⟨*~ fun*⟩ ⟨*~ public*⟩ ⟨*~ step*⟩ ⟨*~ his sleep*⟩ ⟨*~ a hurry*⟩ ⟨*~ pain*⟩ **b** so as to be ⟨*broke ~ pieces*⟩ – compare INTO 1b **c** – used to indicate occupation or membership ⟨*a job ~ insurance*⟩ ⟨*everyone ~ the team*⟩ **4a** as regards

⟨*equal* ~ *distance*⟩ ⟨*weak* ~ *arithmetic*⟩ **b** by way of ⟨*said* ~ *reply*⟩ ⟨*the latest thing* ~ *shoes*⟩ **5a** – used to indicate division, arrangement, or quantity ⟨*standing* ~ *a circle*⟩ ⟨*arrived* ~ *their thousands*⟩ **b** – used to indicate the larger member of a ratio ⟨*one* ~ *six is eligible*⟩ ⟨*a tax of 40p* ~ *the £*⟩ **6** *of an animal* pregnant with ⟨~ *calf*⟩ **7** – used to introduce indirect objects ⟨*rejoice* ~⟩ or to form adverbial phrases; compare IN FACT, IN RETURN [ME, fr OE; akin to OHG *in* in, L *in*, Gk *en*] – **in it** of advantage (e g between competitors or alternatives) ⟨*there's not much* in it *between them*⟩ ⟨*what's* in it *for me?*⟩

[2]in *adv* **1a** to or towards the inside or centre ⟨*come* ~ *out of the rain*⟩ **b** so as to incorporate ⟨*mix* ~ *the flour*⟩ **c** to or towards home, the shore, or one's destination ⟨*3 ships came sailing* ~⟩ **d** at a particular place, esp at one's home or business ⟨*be* ~ *for lunch*⟩ **e** into concealment ⟨*the sun went* ~⟩ **2a** so as to be added or included ⟨*fit a piece* ~⟩ ⟨*write a paragraph* ~⟩ **b** in or into political power ⟨*voted them* ~⟩ **c(1)** on good terms ⟨~ *with the boss*⟩ **(2)** in a position of assured success **(3)** into a state of efficiency or proficiency ⟨*work a horse* ~⟩ **d** in or into vogue or fashion **e** in or into a centre, esp a central point of control ⟨*letters pouring* ~⟩ ⟨*after harvests are* ~⟩ ⟨*went* ~ *to bat*⟩ – **in for** certain to experience ⟨in for *trouble*⟩ – compare LET IN FOR – **in on** having a share in

[3]in *adj* **1a** located inside **b** being in operation or power ⟨*the fire's still* ~⟩ **c** shared by a select group ⟨*an* ~ *joke*⟩ **2** directed or serving to direct inwards ⟨*the* ~ *tray*⟩ **3** extremely fashionable ⟨*the* ~ *place to go*⟩

[1]in- /in-/, **il-** /il-/, **im-** /im-/, **ir-** /ir-/ *prefix* not; non-; un- – usu *il-* before *l* ⟨il*logical*⟩, *im-* before *b,m,* or *p* ⟨im*balance*⟩ ⟨im*moral*⟩ ⟨im*practical*⟩, *ir-* before *r* ⟨ir*reducible*⟩, and *in-* before other sounds ⟨in*conclusive*⟩ [ME, fr MF, fr L; akin to OE *un-*]

[2]in-, il-, im-, ir- *prefix* **1** in; within; into; towards; on ⟨in*flux*⟩ ⟨im*merse*⟩ ⟨ir*radiance*⟩ – usu *il-* before *l, im-* before *b,m,* or *p, ir-* before *r,* and *in-* before other sounds **2** [1]EN- ⟨im*peril*⟩ ⟨in*spirit*⟩ [ME, fr MF, fr L, fr *in* in, into]

[1]-in /-in/ *suffix* (→ *n*) chemical compound: e g **a** hydrolytic enzyme ⟨*peps*in⟩ **b** antibiotic ⟨*streptomyc*in⟩ **c** [2]-INE ⟨*glycer*in⟩ [F *-ine*, fr L *-ina*, fem of *-īnus* of or belonging to – more at [1]-EN]

[2]-in *comb form* (→ *n*) **1** organized public protest by means of or in favour of; demonstration ⟨*teach*-in⟩ ⟨*love*-in⟩ **2** public group activity ⟨*sing*-in⟩ [[2]*in* (as in *sit-in*)]

inability /,inə'biləti/ *n* lack of sufficient power, resources, or capacity ⟨*his* ~ *to do maths*⟩ [ME *inabilite*, fr MF *inhabilité*, fr *in-* + *habilité* ability]

in absentia /,in ab'sentiah, -shiah/ *adv* in absence [L]

inaccessible *adj*

inaccuracy /in'akyoorəsi/ *n* **1** being inaccurate **2** a mistake, error

inaccurate /in'akyoorət/ *adj* faulty [[1]IN- + ACCURATE] – **inaccurately** *adv*

inaction /in'aksh(ə)n/ *n* lack of action or activity

inactive /in'aktiv/ *adj* **1** not given to action or effort **2** out of use; not functioning **3** relating to members of the armed forces who are not performing or available for military duties **4** *of a disease* quiescent **5** chemically or biologically inert, esp because of the loss of some quality – **inactively** *adv*, **inactivate** /-,vayt/ *vt*, **inactivity** /,inak'tivəti/ *n*

inadequate /in'adikwət/ *adj* not adequate: e g **a** insufficient **b** characteristically unable to cope – **inadequacy** *n*, **inadequately** *adv*, **inadequateness** *n*

inadmissible *adj*

inadvertence /,inəd'vuht(ə)ns/, **inadvertency** /-si/ *n* (a result of) inattention [ML *inadvertentia*, fr L *in-* + *advertent-*, *advertens*, prp of *advertere* to advert]

inadvertent /,inəd'vuht(ə)nt/ *adj* **1** heedless, inattentive **2** unintentional [back-formation fr *inadvertence*] – **inadvertently** *adv*

inadvisable *adj*

-inae /-inee/ *suffix* (→ *n pl*) members of the subfamily of – in all names of zoological subfamilies in recent classifications ⟨*Fel*inae⟩ [NL *-īnae*, fr L, fem pl of *-īnus*]

inalienable /in'aylyənəbl/ *adj* incapable of being alienated [prob fr F *inaliénable*, fr *in-* + *aliénable* alienable] – **inalienably** *adv*, **inalienability** /-nə'biləti/ *n*

inamorata /,inamə'rahtə, in,amə-/ *n* a woman with whom one is in love or is having a sexual relationship [It *innamorata*, fr fem of *innamorato*, pp of *innamorare* to inspire with love, fr *in-* (fr L) + *amore* love, fr L *amor*, fr *amare* to love]

inane /i'nayn/ *adj* lacking significance, meaning, or point [L *inanis* empty, insubstantial] – **inanely** *adv*, **inaneness, inanity** /i'nanəti/ *n*

inanimate /in'animət/ *adj* **1** not endowed with life or spirit **2** lacking consciousness or power of motion [LL *inanimatus*, fr L *in-* + *animatus*, pp of *animare* to animate] – **inanimately** *adv*, **inanimateness** *n*

inanition /,inə'nish(ə)n/ *n* **1** the quality of being empty **2** the absence or loss of social, moral, or intellectual vitality or vigour *USE* fml [ME *in-anisioun*, fr ML *inanition-*, *inanitio*, fr *inanitus*, pp of *inanire* to make empty, fr *inanis*]

inapplicable *adj*

inapposite *adj*

inappreciable /,inə'preesh(y)əbl/ *adj* too small or slight to be perceived [prob fr F *inappréciable*, fr MF *inappreciable*, fr *in-* + *appreciable*] – **inappreciably** *adv*

inappropriate *adj*

inapt /in'apt/ *adj* not suitable or appropriate [[1]IN- + APT] – **inaptly** *adv*, **inaptness** *n*

inaptitude /in'aptityoohd/ *n* lack of aptitude

inarticulate /,inah'tikyoolət/ *adj* **1a** not understandable as spoken words ⟨~ *cries*⟩ **b** incapable of (being expressed by) speech, esp under stress of emotion **2a** not giving or not able to give coherent, clear, or effective expression to one's ideas or feelings **b** not coherently, clearly, or effectively expressed ⟨*an* ~ *speech*⟩ **3** not jointed or hinged [LL *inarticulatus*, fr L *in-* + *articulatus*, pp of *articulare* to utter distinctly; (3) NL *inarticulatus*, fr L *in-* + *articulatus* articulate] – **inarticulately** *adv*, **inarticulateness** *n*

inartistic /,inah'tistik/ *adj* **1** not conforming to the principles of art **2** not appreciative of art – **inartistically** *adv*

inasmuch as /inəz'much əz/ *conj* **1** INSOFAR AS **2** in view of the fact that; because

inattention /,inə'tensh(ə)n/ *n* failure to pay attention; disregard

inattentive *adj*

inaudible *adj*

[1]**inaugural** /in'awgyoorəl/ *adj* marking a beginning; first in a projected series [F, fr *inaugurer* to inaugurate, fr L *inaugurare*]

[2]**inaugural** *n* an address at inauguration

inaugurate /in'awgyoorayt/ *vt* **1** to induct ceremonially into office **2** to observe formally, or bring about, the beginning of [L *inauguratus*, pp of *inaugurare*, lit., to practise augury, fr *in-* + *augurare* to augur; fr the rites connected with augury] – **inaugurator** *n*, **inauguration** /-,awgyoo'raysh(ə)n/ *n*

Inauguration Day *n* January 20 following a presidential election, on which the president of the USA is inaugurated

inauspicious *adj*

in between *adv or prep* between – **in-between** *adj*

inboard /in'bawd/ *adv* **1** towards the centre line of a vessel **2** in a position closer or closest to the long axis of an aircraft – **inboard** /in'bawd, '-,-/ *adj*

in'born /-'bawn/ *adj* **1** born in or with one; forming part of one's natural make-up **2** hereditary, inherited

,in'bred /-'bred/ *adj* **1** rooted and deeply ingrained in one's nature **2** subjected to or produced by inbreeding

'in,breeding /-,breeding/ *n* **1** the interbreeding of closely related individuals, esp to preserve and fix desirable characters **2** confinement to a narrow range or a local or limited field of choice – **inbreed** *vt*, **inbreeder** *n*

,in'built /-'bilt/ *adj* built-in; *esp* inherent

Inca /'ingkə/ *n* **1** a king or member of the ruling family of an empire existing in Peru before the Spanish conquest **2** a member of the Quechuan peoples inhabiting the Inca empire [Sp, fr Quechua *inka* king, prince] – **Incan** *adj*, **Incaic** /ing'kayik/ *adj*

incalculable /in'kalkyooləbl/ *adj* **1** too large or numerous to be calculated **2** unpredictable, uncertain – **incalculably** *adv*, **incalculability** /-lə'biləti/ *n*

in 'camera *adv* in private [NL, lit., in a chamber]

incandescent /,inkan'des(ə)nt/ *adj* **1a** white, glowing, or luminous with intense heat **b** strikingly bright, radiant, or clear **2** of or being visible light produced by a (white) hot body [prob fr F, fr L *incandescent-*, *incandescens*, prp of *incandescere* to become hot, fr *in-* + *candescere* to become hot, fr *candēre* to glow – more at CANDID] – **incandesce** *vb*, **incandescence** *n*, **incandescently** *adv*

incandescent lamp *n* an electric lamp in which an electrically-heated filament gives off light

incantation /,inkan'taysh(ə)n/ *n* the use of spoken or sung spells in magic ritual; *also* a formula so used [ME *incantacioun*, fr MF *incantation*, fr LL *incantation-*, *incantatio*, fr L *incantatus*, pp of *incantare* to enchant – more at ENCHANT] – **incantatory** /in'kantət(ə)ri/ *adj*

incapable /in'kaypəbl/ *adj* lacking capacity, ability, or qualification for the purpose or end in view: e g **a** not in a state or of a kind to admit *of* **b** not able or fit for the doing or performance *of* [MF, fr *in-* + *capable*] – **incapableness** *n*, **incapably** *adv*, **incapability** /-pə'biləti/ *n*

incapacitate /,inkə'pasitayt/ *vt* **1** to deprive of capacity or natural power; disable **2** to disqualify legally – **incapacitation** /-'taysh(ə)n/ *n*

incapacity /,inkə'pasəti/ *n* lack of ability or power or of natural or legal qualifications [F *incapacité*, fr MF, fr *in-* + *capacité* capacity]

incarcerate /in'kahsərayt/ *vt* to imprison, confine [L *incarceratus*, pp of *incarcerare*, fr *in-* + *carcer* prison] – **incarceration** /-'raysh(ə)n/ *n*

[1]**incarnadine** /in'kahnədien/ *adj* **1** flesh-coloured **2** blood red *USE* poetic [MF *incarnadin*, fr OIt *incarnadino*, fr *incarnato* flesh-coloured, fr LL *incarnatus*]

[2]**incarnadine** *vt* to make incarnadine

[1]**incarnate** /in'kahnət, -nayt/ *adj* **1** invested with bodily, esp human, nature and form **2** that is the essence of; typified ⟨*evil* ~⟩ [ME *incarnat*, fr LL *incarnatus*, pp of *incarnare* to incarnate, fr L *in-* + *carn-*, *caro* flesh – more at CARNAL]

[2]**incarnate** /'inkah,nayt/ *vt* to make incarnate

incarnation /,inkah'naysh(ə)n/ *n* **1** making or being incarnate **2a(1)** the embodiment of a deity or spirit in an earthly form **(2)** *cap* Christ's human manifestation **b** a quality or concept typified or made concrete, esp in a person **3** any of several successive bodily manifestations or lives

[1]**incendiary** /in'sendyəri/ *n* **1a** one who deliberately sets fire to property **b** an incendiary agent (e g a bomb) **2** one who inflames or stirs up factions, quarrels, or sedition [L *incendiarius*, fr *incendium* conflagration, fr *incendere*] – **incendiarism** /-,riz(ə)m/ *n*

[2]**incendiary** *adj* **1** of the deliberate burning of property **2** tending to inflame or stir up trouble **3** (of, being, or involving the use of a missile containing a chemical) that ignites spontaneously on contact

[1]**incense** /'insens/ *n* **1** material used to produce a fragrant smell when burned **2** the perfume given off by some spices and gums when burned; *broadly* a pleasing scent [ME *encens*, fr OF, fr LL *incensum*, fr L, neut of *incensus*, pp of *incendere* to set on fire, fr *in-* + *-cendere* to burn; akin to L *candēre* to glow – more at CANDID]

[2]**incense** /in'sens/ *vt* to arouse the extreme anger or indignation of [ME *encensen*, fr MF *incenser*, fr L *incensus*]

incentive /in'sentiv/ *n* sthg that motivates or spurs one on (e g to action or effort) [ME, fr LL *incentivum*, fr neut of *incentivus* stimulating, fr L, setting the tune, fr *incentus*, pp of *incinere* to set the tune, fr *in-* + *canere* to sing – more at CHANT] – **incentive** *adj*

incept /in'sept/ *vt* to take in; *esp* to ingest [L *in-* + *-ceptus*, fr *captus*, pp of *capere* to take] – **inceptor** *n*

inception /in'sepsh(ə)n/ *n* an act, process, or instance of beginning [L *inception-*, *inceptio*, fr *inceptus*, pp of *incipere* to begin, fr *in-* + *capere* to take – more at HEAVE]

inceptive /in'septiv/ *adj* inchoative – **inceptive** *n*, **inceptively** *adv*

incertitude /in'suhtityoohd/ *n* uncertainty, doubt [MF, fr LL *incertitudo*, fr L *in-* + LL *certitudo* certitude]

incessant /in'ses(ə)nt/ *adj* continuing without interruption [ME *incessaunt*, fr LL *incessant-*, *incessans*, fr L *in-* + *cessant-*, *cessans*, prp of *cessare* to delay – more at CEASE] – **incessancy** *n*, **incessantly** *adv*

incest /'insest/ *n* sexual intercourse between people so closely related that they are forbidden by law to marry [ME, fr L *incestum*, fr neut of *incestus* impure, fr *in-* + *castus* pure – more at CASTE]

incestuous /in'sestyoo·əs/ *adj* **1** being, guilty of, or involving incest **2** unhealthily closed to outside influences – **incestuously** *adv*, **incestuousness** *n*

[1]**inch** /inch/ *n* **1** a unit of length equal to ⅓₆yd (about 25.4mm) ☞ SYMBOL, UNIT **2** a small amount, distance, or degree **3** *pl* stature, height **4** a fall of rain, snow, etc enough to cover a surface to the depth of 1in [ME, fr OE *ynce*, fr L *uncia* twelth part, ounce, inch – more at [1]OUNCE] – **every inch** to the utmost degree ⟨*looks* every inch *a winner*⟩ – **within an inch of one's life** very thoroughly; soundly ⟨*thrashed him* within an inch of his *life*⟩

[2]**inch** *vb* to move by small degrees

[3]**inch** *n, chiefly Scot* an island – usu in place-names [ME, fr ScGael *innis*]

inchoate /'inkoh·ayt/ *adj* only partly in existence or operation; *esp* imperfectly formed or formulated ⟨*an* ~ *longing*⟩ – fml [L *inchoatus*, pp of *inchoare*, lit., to hitch up, fr *in-* + *cohum* strap fastening a plough beam to the yoke] – **inchoately** *adv*, **inchoateness** *n*

inchoative /in'koh·ətiv/ *adj, of a verb* denoting the beginning of an action or state – **inchoative** *n*, **inchoatively** *adv*

inchworm /'inch,wuhm/ *n* a rather small hairless caterpillar that is the larva of a moth, specif a geometrid moth, and moves with a looping movement

incidence /'insid(ə)ns/ *n* **1a** an occurrence **b** the rate of occurrence or influence ⟨*a high* ~ *of crime*⟩ **2** the meeting of sthg (e g a projectile or a ray of light) with a surface

[1]**incident** /'insid(ə)nt/ *n* **1** an occurrence of an action or situation that is a separate unit of experience **2** an occurrence that is a cause of conflict or disagreement ⟨*a serious border* ~⟩ **3** an event occurring as part of a series or as dependent on or subordinate to sthg else [ME, fr MF, fr ML *incident-*, *incidens*, fr L, prp of *incidere* to fall into, fr *in-* + *cadere* to fall – more at CHANCE]

[2]**incident** *adj* **1** that is a usual accompaniment or consequence ⟨*the confusion* ~ *to moving house*⟩ **2** dependent on another thing in law **3** falling or striking on sthg ⟨~ *light rays*⟩

[1]**incidental** /,insi'dentl/ *adj* **1** occurring merely by chance **2** likely to ensue as a chance or minor consequence

[2]**incidental** *n* **1** sthg incidental **2** *pl* minor items (e g of expenses)

incidentally /,insi'dentl·i/ *adv* **1** by chance **2** BY THE WAY

incidental music *n* descriptive music played during a play to project a mood or to accompany stage action

incinerate /in'sinərayt/ *vt* to cause to burn to ashes [ML *incineratus*, pp of *incinerare*, fr L *in-* + *ciner-*, *cinis* ashes; akin to Gk *konis* dust, ashes] – **incineration** /-'raysh(ə)n/ *n*

incinerator /in'sinəraytə/ *n* a furnace or container for incinerating waste materials [INCINERATE + [1]-OR]

incipient /in'sipi·ənt/ *adj* beginning to come into being or to become apparent [L *incipient-*, *incipiens*, prp of *incipere* to begin – more at INCEPTION] – **incipience, incipiency** *n*, **incipiently** *adv*

incise /in'siez/ *vt* **1** to cut into **2a** to carve letters, figures, etc into; engrave **b** to carve (e g an inscription) into a surface [MF or L; MF *inciser*, fr L *incisus*, pp of *incidere*, fr *in-* + *caedere* to cut – more at CONCISE]

in'cised *adj, of a wound* (as if) made with a sharp knife

incision /in'sizh(ə)n/ *n* **1a** a (marginal) notch **b** a cut or gash; *specif* one made, esp in surgery, into the body **2** an incising

incisive /in'siesiv/ *adj* impressively direct and decisive (e g in manner or presentation) – **incisively** *adv*, **incisiveness** *n*

incisor /in'siezə/ *n* a cutting tooth; *specif* any of the cutting teeth in mammals in front of the canines ☞ DIGESTION

incite /in'siet/ *vt* to move to action; stir up [MF *inciter*, fr L *incitare*, fr *in-* + *citare* to put in motion – more at CITE] – **inciter** *n*, **incitement, incitation** /,insie'taysh(ə)n/ *n*

incivility /,insi'viləti/ *n* **1** being uncivil **2** a rude or discourteous act [MF *incivilité*, fr LL *incivilitat-*, *incivilitas*, fr *incivilis*, fr L *in-* + *civilis* civil]

inclement /in'klemənt/ *adj* physically severe; stormy [L *inclement-*, *inclemens*, fr *in-* + *clement-*, *clemens* clement] – **inclemency** *n*, **inclemently** *adv*

inclination /,inkli'naysh(ə)n/ *n* **1a** a bow, nod **b** a tilting of sthg **2** a particular tendency or propensity; *esp* a liking **3a** (the degree of) a deviation from the vertical or horizontal **b** a slope **c** the angle between 2 lines or planes ⟨*the* ~ *of 2 rays of light*⟩ [[1]INCLINE + -ATION] – **inclinational** *adj*

[1]**incline** /in'klien/ *vb* **1** to (cause to) lean, tend, or become drawn towards an opinion or course of conduct **2** to (cause to) deviate or move from a line, direction, or course, esp from the vertical or horizontal [ME *inclinen*, fr MF *incliner*, fr L *inclinare*, fr *in-* + *clinare* to lean – more at LEAN]

[2]**incline** /'inklien/ *n* an inclined surface; a slope

inclined plane *n* a plane surface that makes an angle with the plane of the horizon

inclinometer /,inkli'nomitə/ *n* **1** an apparatus for determining the direction of the earth's magnetic field with reference to the plane of the horizon **2** an instrument for indicating the inclination to the horizontal of an axis of a ship or aircraft

inclose /in'klohz/ *vt* to enclose – **inclosure** /-zhə/ *n*

include /in'kloohd/ *vt* **1** to contain, enclose **2** to take in or comprise as a part of a larger group, set, or principle [ME *includen*, fr L *includere*, fr *in-* + *claudere* to close – more at [4]CLOSE] – **includable, includible** *adj*

inclusion /in'kloohzh(ə)n/ *n* **1** including or being included **2** sthg included: e g **a** a gaseous, liquid, or solid foreign body enclosed in a mass, esp a mineral **b** sthg (e g a starch grain) taken up by, or stored within, a living cell [L *inclusion-*, *inclusio*, fr *inclusus*, pp of *includere*]

inclusive /in'kloohsiv, -ziv/ *adj* **1a** broad in orientation or scope **b** covering or intended to cover all or the specified items, costs, or services ⟨~ *of VAT*⟩ **2** including the stated limits or extremes ⟨*Monday to Friday* ~⟩ – **inclusively** *adv*, **inclusiveness** *n*

inclusive disjunction *n* a complex sentence in logic that is true when either or both of its constituent sentences are true

[1]**incognito** /,inkog'neetoh/ *adv or adj* with one's identity concealed [It, fr L *incognitus* unknown, fr

in- + *cognitus,* pp of *cognoscere* to know – more at COGNITION]

[2]**incognito** *n, pl* **incognitos** the state or disguise of one who is incognito

incognizant /in'kogniz(ə)nt/ *adj* lacking awareness or consciousness *of* – **incognizance** *n*

incoherent /,inkoh'hiərənt/ *adj* lacking in logical connection or clarity of expression; unintelligible [[1]IN- + COHERENT] – **incoherence, incoherency** *n,* **incoherently** *adv*

incombustible /,inkəm'bustəbl/ *adj* incapable of being ignited or burned [ME, prob fr MF, fr *in-* + *combustible*] – **incombustibility** /-'biləti/ *n*

income /'inkum, 'inkəm/ *n* **1** a coming in; an input, influx **2** (the amount of) a usu periodic gain or recurrent benefit usu measured in money that derives from one's work, property, or investment

'**income ,tax** *n* a tax on income

[1]**incoming** /'in,kuming/ *n* **1** a coming in, arrival **2** *pl* INCOME 2

[2]**incoming** *adj* **1** arriving or coming in ⟨*an ~ ship*⟩ ⟨*the ~ tide*⟩ **2** just starting, beginning, or succeeding ⟨*the ~ president*⟩

incommensurable /,inkə'mensh(ə)rəbl/ *adj* lacking a common basis of comparison in respect to a quality normally subject to comparison; incapable of being compared [[1]IN- + COMMENSURABLE] – **incommensurably** *adv,* **incommensurability** /-rə'biləti/ *n*

incommensurate /,inkə'menshərət/ *adj* not adequate (in proportion) – **incommensurately** *adv*

incommode /,inkə'mohd/ *vt* to inconvenience, trouble – fml [MF *incommoder,* fr L *incommodare,* fr *incommodus* inconvenient, fr *in-* + *commodus* convenient – more at COMMODE]

incommodious /,inkə'mohdi·əs/ *adj* inconvenient or uncomfortable, esp because of being too small – fml [[1]IN- + COMMODIOUS] – **incommodiously** *adv,* **incommodiousness** *n*

incommunicado /,inkə,myoohni'kahdoh/ *adv or adj* without means of communication; *also* in solitary confinement [Sp *incomunicado,* fr pp of *incomunicar* to deprive of communication, fr *in-* (fr L) + *comunicar* to communicate, fr L *communicare*]

incommutable /,inkə'myoohtəbl/ *adj* **1** not interchangeable **2** unchangeable [ME, fr L *incommutabilis,* fr *in-* + *commutabilis* commutable] – **incommutably** *adv*

incomparable /in'komp(ə)rəbl/ *adj* **1** matchless **2** not suitable for comparison [ME, fr MF, fr L *incomparabilis,* fr *in-* + *comparabilis* comparable] – **incomparableness** *n,* **incomparably** *adv,* **incomparability** /-rə'biləti/ *n*

incompatible /,inkəm'patəbl/ *adj* **1** (incapable of association because) incongruous, discordant, or disagreeing **2** unsuitable for use together because of undesirable chemical or physiological effects ⟨*~ drugs*⟩ [MF & ML; MF, fr ML *incompatibilis,* fr L *in-* + ML *compatibilis* compatible] – **incompatibly** *adv,* **incompatibility** /-ə'biləti/ *n*

incompetent /in'kompit(ə)nt/ *adj* **1** lacking the qualities needed for effective action **2** not legally qualified ⟨*an ~ witness*⟩ **3** inadequate to or unsuitable for a particular purpose [MF *incompétent,* fr *in-* + *compétent* competent] – **incompetence, incompetency** *n,* **incompetent** *n,* **incompetently** *adv*

incomplete /,inkəm'pleet/ *adj* **1** unfinished **2** lacking a part [ME *incompleet,* fr LL *incompletus,* fr L *in-* + *completus* complete] – **incompletely** *adv,* **incompleteness** *n*

incomprehensible /,inkompri'hensəbl, -,--'---/ *adj* impossible to comprehend or understand [ME, fr L *incomprehensibilis,* fr *in-* + *comprehensibilis* comprehensible] – **incomprehensibleness** *n,* **incomprehensibly** *adv,* **incomprehensibility** /-sə'biləti/ *n*

incomprehension /,inkompri'hensh(ə)n/ *n* lack of comprehension or understanding

incompressible /,inkəm'presəbl/ *adj* resistant to compression – **incompressibly** *adv,* **incompressibility** /-,presə'biləti/ *n*

inconceivable /,inkən'seevəbl/ *adj* **1** beyond comprehension; unimaginable **2** unbelievable [[1]IN- + CONCEIVABLE] – **inconceivableness** *n,* **inconceivably** *adv,* **inconceivability** /-və'biləti/ *n*

inconclusive /,inkən'kloohsiv/ *adj* leading to no conclusion or definite result – **inconclusively** *adv,* **inconclusiveness** *n*

incongruous /in'kong·groo·əs/ *adj* out of place; discordant or disagreeing [LL *incongruus,* fr L *in-* + *congruus* congruous] – **incongruously** *adv,* **incongruousness, incongruity** /,inkong'groohəti/ *n*

inconsequent /in'konsikwənt/ *adj* **1** lacking reasonable sequence; illogical **2** irrelevant [LL *inconsequent-, inconsequens,* fr L *in-* + *consequent-, consequens* consequent] – **inconsequence** *n,* **inconsequently** *adv*

inconsequential /,inkonsi'kwensh(ə)l/ *adj* **1** irrelevant **2** of no significance – **inconsequentially** *adv,* **inconsequentiality** /-shi'aləti/ *n*

inconsiderable /,inkən'sid(ə)rəbl/ *adj* trivial ⟨*exercised no ~ influence*⟩ [MF, fr *in-* + *considerable,* fr ML *considerabilis* considerable] – **inconsiderableness** *n,* **inconsiderably** *adv*

inconsiderate /,inkən'sid(ə)rət/ *adj* careless of the rights or feelings of others; thoughtless [L *inconsideratus,* fr *in-* + *consideratus* considerate] – **inconsiderately** *adv,* **inconsiderateness, inconsideration** /-,sidə 'raysh(ə)n/ *n*

inconsistent /,inkən'sist(ə)nt/ *adj* **1** not compatible; containing incompatible elements ⟨*an ~ argument*⟩ **2** not consistent or logical in thought or actions – **inconsistency, inconsistence** *n,* **inconsistently** *adv*

inconsolable /,inkən'sohləbl/ *adj* incapable of being consoled; brokenhearted [L *inconsolabilis,* fr *in-* + *consolabilis* consolable] – **inconsolably** *adv*

inconsonant /in'kons(ə)nənt/ *adj* not harmonious [[1]IN- + [2]CONSONANT] – **inconsonance** *n*

,incon'spicuous /,inkən'spikyoo·əs/ *adj* not readily noticeable [L *inconspicuus,* fr *in-* + *conspicuus* conspicuous] – **inconspicuously** *adv,* **inconspicuousness** *n*

inconstant /in'konst(ə)nt/ *adj* **1** likely to change frequently without apparent reason **2** unfaithful ⟨*an ~ lover*⟩ [ME, fr MF, fr L *inconstant-, inconstans,* fr *in-* + *constant-, constans* constant] – **inconstancy** *n,* **inconstantly** *adv*

incontestable /,inkən'testəbl/ *adj* not contestable; indisputable ⟨*~ proof*⟩ [F, fr *in-* + *contestable,* fr *contester* to contest] – **incontestably** *adv,* **incontestability** /-'biləti/ *n*

incontinent /in'kontinənt/ *adj* **1** lacking self-restraint (e g in sexual appetite) **2** suffering from lack of control of urination or defecation **3** not under control or restraint [ME, fr MF or L; MF, fr L *incontinent-, incontinens*, fr *in-* + *continent-, continens* continent] – **incontinence** *n*, **incontinently** *adv*

incontrovertible /,inkontrə'vuhtəbl, in,kon-/ *adj* indisputable – **incontrovertibly** *adv*

inconvenience /,inkən'veenyəns, -ni·əns/ *vt or n* (to subject to) difficulty or discomfort or sthg that is inconvenient

inconvenient /,inkən'veenyənt, -ni·ənt/ *adj* not convenient, esp in causing difficulty, discomfort, or annoyance [ME, fr MF, fr L *inconvenient-, inconveniens*, fr *in-* + *convenient-, conveniens* convenient] – **inconveniently** *adv*

inconvertible /,inkən'vuhtəbl/ *adj, of a currency* not exchangeable for a foreign currency – **inconvertibly** *adv*, **inconvertibility** /-tə'biləti/ *n*

incoordination /,inkoh,awdi'naysh(ə)n/ *n* lack of (muscular) coordination

incorporate /in'kawpərayt/ *vt* **1a** to unite thoroughly with or work indistinguishably into sthg **b** to admit to membership in a corporate body **2a** to combine thoroughly to form a consistent whole **b** to form into a legal corporation ~ *vi* **1** to unite in or as 1 body **2** to form a legal corporation [ME *incorporaten*, fr LL *incorporatus*, pp of *incorporare*, fr L *in-* + *corpor-, corpus* body] – **incorporator** *n*, **incorporable** /-rəbl/ *adj*, **incorporation** /-'raysh(ə)n/ *n*

in'corporated *also* **incorporate** *adj* **1** united in 1 body **2** formed into a legal corporation – compare LIMITED COMPANY

incorporeal /,inkaw'pawri·əl/ *adj* **1** having no material body or form **2** based upon property (e g bonds or patents) which has no intrinsic value [L *incorporeus*, fr *in-* + *corporeus* corporeal] – **incorporeally** *adv*, **incorporeity** /in,kawpə'rayəti, ,inkaw-, -'ree·əti/ *n*

incorrect /,inkə'rekt/ *adj* **1** inaccurate; factually wrong **2** not in accordance with an established norm; improper [ME, fr MF or L; MF, fr L *incorrectus*, fr *in-* + *correctus* correct] – **incorrectly** *adv*, **incorrectness** *n*

incorrigible /in'korijəbl/ *adj* **1** incapable of being corrected or amended; *esp* incurably bad **2** unwilling or unlikely to change [ME, fr LL *incorrigibilis*, fr L *in-* + *corrigere* to correct – more at CORRECT] – **incorrigibly** *adv*, **incorrigibility** /-jə'biləti/ *also* **incorrigibleness** *n*

incorruptible /,inkə'ruptəbl/ *adj* **1** not subject to decay or dissolution **2** incapable of being bribed or morally corrupted [[1]IN- + CORRUPTIBLE] – **incorruptibly** *adv*, **incorruptibility** /-tə'biləti/ *n*

[1]**increase** /in'krees/ *vi* **1** to become progressively greater (e g in size, amount, quality, number, or intensity) **2** to multiply by the production of young ~ *vt* to make greater [ME *encresen*, fr MF *encreistre*, fr L *increscere*, fr *in-* + *crescere* to grow – more at CRESCENT] – **increasable** *adj*, **increasingly** *adv*

[2]**increase** /'inkrees/ *n* **1** (an) addition or enlargement in size, extent, quantity, etc **2** sthg (e g offspring, produce, or profit) added to an original stock by addition or growth

incredible /in'kredəbl/ *adj* **1** too extraordinary and improbable to be believed; *also* hard to believe **2** – used as a generalized term of approval [ME, fr L *incredibilis*, fr *in-* + *credibilis* credible] – **incredibly** *adv*, **incredibility** /-də'biləti/ *n*

incredulous /in'kredyooləs/ *adj* **1** unwilling to admit or accept what is offered as true **2** expressing disbelief [L *incredulus*, fr *in-* + *credulus* credulous] – **incredulously** *adv*, **incredulity** /,inkri'dyoohləti/ *n*

increment /'ingkrimənt, in-/ *n* **1** (the amount of) an increase, esp in quantity or value **2a** any of a series of regular consecutive additions **b** a minute increase in the value of a variable (e g velocity) ☞ SYMBOL **3** a regular increase in pay resulting from an additional year's service [ME, fr L *incrementum*, fr *increscere*] – **incremental** /-'mentl/ *adj*, **incrementally** *adv*

incriminate /in'kriminayt/ *vt* to involve in or demonstrate involvement in a crime or fault [LL *incriminatus*, pp of *incriminare*, fr L *in-* + *crimin-, crimen* crime] – **incriminatory** /-nətri/ *adj*, **incrimination** /-'naysh(ə)n/ *n*

incrust /in'krust/ *vb* to encrust

incrustation /,inkru'staysh(ə)n/ *n* **1** encrusting or being encrusted **2** (a growth or accumulation resembling) a crust or hard coating [L *incrustation-, incrustatio*, fr *incrustatus*, pp of *incrustare* to encrust]

incubate /'ingkyoobayt, 'in-/ *vt* **1** to sit on so as to hatch (eggs) by the warmth of the body; *also* to maintain (e g an embryo or a chemically active system) under conditions favourable for hatching, development, or reaction **2** to cause (e g an idea) to develop ~ *vi* **1** to sit on eggs **2** to undergo incubation [L *incubatus*, pp of *incubare*, fr *in-* + *cubare* to lie – more at [2]HIP] – **incubative** /-,baytiv/, **incubatory** /'ingkyoo,baytəri, -bətri, 'in-/ *adj*

incubation /,ingkyoo'baysh(ə)n, ,in-/ *n* **1** incubating **2** the period between infection by a disease-causing agent and the manifestation of the disease

incubator /'ingkyoo,baytə, 'in-/ *n* **1** an apparatus in which eggs are hatched artificially **2** an apparatus that maintains controlled conditions, esp for the housing of premature or sick babies or the cultivation of microorganisms [INCUBATE + [1]-OR]

incubus /'ingkyoobəs, 'in-/ *n, pl* **incubuses, incubi** /-,bie/ **1** a male demon believed to have sexual intercourse with women in their sleep – compare SUCCUBUS **2** (one who or that which oppresses or burdens like) a nightmare [ME, fr LL, fr L *incubare*]

inculcate /'inkulkayt/ *vt* to teach or instil by frequent repetition or warning ⟨~d *a sense of social responsibility in her children*⟩ ⟨*students* ~d *with a desire for knowledge*⟩ [L *inculcatus*, pp of *inculcare*, lit., to tread on, fr *in-* + *calcare* to trample, fr *calc-, calx* heel] – **inculcator** *n*, **inculcation** /,inkul'kaysh(ə)n/ *n*

inculpable /in'kulpəpl/ *adj* free from guilt

inculpate /'inkulpayt/ *vt* to incriminate [LL *inculpatus*, fr L *in-* + *culpatus*, pp of *culpare* to blame – more at CULPABLE] – **inculpatory** /in'kulpət(ə)ri/ *adj*, **inculpation** /,inkul'paysh(ə)n/ *n*

incumbency /in'kumb(ə)nsi/ *n* the sphere of action or period of office of an incumbent

[1]**incumbent** /in'kumb(ə)nt/ *n* the holder of an office or Anglican benefice [ME, fr L *incumbent-, incumbens*, prp of *incumbere* to lie down on, fr *in-* + *-cumbere* to lie down; akin to L *cubare* to lie – more at [2]HIP]

[2]**incumbent** *adj* **1** imposed as a duty or obligation – usu + *on* or *upon* **2** occupying a specified office ⟨*the* ~ *caretaker*⟩

incunable /in'kyoohnəbl/ *n* an incunabulum [F, fr NL *incunabulum*]

incunabulum /,inkyoo'nabyooləm/ *n, pl* **incunabula** /-lə/ **1** a book printed before 1501 **2** an artefact from an early period [NL, fr L *incunabula*, pl, swaddling clothes, cradle, source, fr *in-* + *cunae* cradle – more at CEMETERY]

incur /in'kuh/ *vt* **-rr-** to become liable or subject to; bring upon oneself ⟨*she* ~red *several debts*⟩ [L *incurrere*, lit., to run into, fr *in-* + *currere* to run – more at CURRENT] – **incurrable** *adj*, **incurrence** *n*

incurable *adj*

incurious /in'kyooəri·əs/ *adj* lacking a normal or usual curiosity ⟨*a blank* ~ *stare*⟩ [L *incuriosus*, fr *in-* + *curiosus* curious] – **incuriously** *adv*, **incuriosity** /-,kyooəri'osəti/ *n*

incursion /in'kuhsh(ə)n/ *n* an unexpected or sudden usu brief invasion or entrance, esp into another's territory [ME, fr MF or L; MF, fr L *incursion-, incursio*, fr *incursus*, pp of *incurrere*] – **incursive** /-siv/ *adj*

incus /'ingkəs/ *n, pl* **incudes** /in'kyoohdeez/ the middle bone of a chain of 3 small bones in the ear of a mammal; the anvil ☞ NERVE [NL, fr L, anvil, fr *incudere*]

incuse /in'kyoohz/ *adj, esp of (designs on) old coins* formed by stamping or punching in [L *incusus*, pp of *incudere* to stamp, strike, fr *in-* + *cudere* to beat – more at HEW]

ind-, indi-, indo- *comb form* (resembling) indigo ⟨indo*le*⟩ [ISV, fr L *indicum* – more at INDIGO]

Ind-, Indo- *comb form* **1** Indian ⟨Indo-*British*⟩; Indian and ⟨Indo-*African*⟩ **2** Indo-European ⟨Indo-*Hittite*⟩ [Gk, fr *Indos* India]

indaba /in'dahbə/ *n, chiefly SAfr* a conference, parley [Zulu *in-daba* affair]

indebted /in'detid/ *adj* **1** owing money **2** owing gratitude or recognition to another [ME *indetted*, fr OF *endeté*, pp of *endeter* to involve in debt, fr *en-* + *dete* debt] – **indebtedness** *n*

in'decent /in'dees(ə)nt/ *adj* **1** hardly suitable; unseemly ⟨*he remarried with* ~ *haste*⟩ **2** morally offensive [MF or L; MF *indécent*, fr L *indecent-, indecens*, fr *in-* + *decent-, decens* decent] – **indecency** *n*, **indecently** *adv*

indecent assault *n* a sexual assault exclusive of rape

indecent exposure *n* intentional public exposure of part of one's body (e g the genitals) in violation of generally accepted standards of decency

indecision /,indi'sizh(ə)n/ *n* a wavering between 2 or more possible courses of action [F *indécision*, fr *indécis* undecided, fr LL *indecisus*, fr L *in-* + *decisus*, pp of *decidere* to decide]

indecisive /,indi'siesiv/ *adj* **1** giving an uncertain result ⟨*an* ~ *battle*⟩ **2** marked by or prone to indecision – **indecisively** *adv*, **indecisiveness** *n*

indeclinable /,indi'klienəbl/ *adj* having no grammatical inflections [MF, fr LL *indeclinabilis*, fr L *in-* + LL *declinabilis* capable of being inflected, fr L *declinare* to inflect – more at DECLINE]

indecorous *adj*

indecorum /,indi'kawrəm/ *n* impropriety [L, neut of *indecorus* improper, fr *in-* + *decorus* proper]

indeed /in'deed/ *adv* **1** without any question; truly ⟨*it is* ~ *remarkable*⟩ – often used in agreement ⟨~ *I will*⟩ **2** – used for emphasis after *very* and an adjective or adverb ⟨*very cold* ~⟩ **3** in point of fact; actually ⟨*I don't mind;* ~, *I'm pleased*⟩ ⟨*if* ~ *they come at all*⟩ **4** – expressing irony, disbelief, or surprise ⟨*'she wants to marry him.'* 'Indeed?' *'Does she* ~*!'*⟩ [ME *in dede*, fr *in* + *dede* deed]

indefatigable /,indi'fatigəbl/ *adj* tireless [MF, fr L *indefatigabilis*, fr *in-* + *defatigare* to fatigue, fr *de* down + *fatigare* to fatigue] – **indefatigably** *adv*, **indefatigability** /-gə'biləti/ *n*

,inde'feasible /-di'feezəbl/ *adj* not capable of being annulled or forfeited ⟨*an* ~ *right*⟩ – **indefeasibly** *adv*, **indefeasibility** /-zə'biləti/ *n*

,inde'fensible /-di'fensəbl/ *adj* incapable of being defended or justified – **indefensibly** *adv*, **indefensibility** /-sə'biləti/ *n*

,inde'finable /-di'fienəbl/ *adj* incapable of being precisely described or analysed – **indefinable** *n*, **indefinably** *adv*

in'definite /-'definət/ *adj* **1** designating an unidentified or not immediately identifiable person or thing ⟨*the* ~ *articles* a *and* an⟩ **2** not precise; vague **3** having no exact limits [L *indefinitus*, fr *in-* + *definitus* definite] – **indefinite** *n*, **indefinitely** *adv*, **indefiniteness** *n*

indefinite integral *n* a function whose derivative is a given function ☞ SYMBOL

indehiscent /,indi'his(ə)nt/ *adj* remaining closed at maturity ⟨~ *fruits*⟩ – **indehiscence** *n*

indelible /in'deləbl/ *adj* (making marks difficult to remove or) incapable of being removed or erased [ML *indelibilis*, alter. of L *indelebilis*, fr *in-* + *delēre* to delete] – **indelibly** *adv*, **indelibility** /-lə'biləti/ *n*

indelicate /in'delikət/ *adj* offensive to good manners or refined taste [[1]IN- + DELICATE] – **indelicacy** *n*, **indelicately** *adv*

indemnify /in'demnifie/ *vt* **1** to secure against harm, loss, or damage **2** to make compensation to for incurred harm, loss, or damage [L *indemnis* unharmed, fr *in-* + *damnum* damage] – **indemnification** /-fi'kaysh(ə)n/ *n*

indemnity /in'demnəti/ *n* security against harm, loss, or damage [ME *indempnyte*, fr MF *indemnité*, fr L *indemnitat-, indemnitas*, fr *indemnis*]

indemonstrable /,indi'monstrəbl/ *adj* not subject to proof [[1]IN- + DEMONSTRABLE] – **indemonstrably** *adv*

[1]**indent** /in'dent/ *vt* **1a** to cut or divide (a document) to produce sections with edges that can be matched for authentication **b** to draw up (e g a deed) in 2 or more exact copies **2** to notch the edge of **3** to set (e g a line of a paragraph) in from the margin **4** *chiefly Br* to requisition officially ~ *vi* **1** to form an indentation **2** *chiefly Br* to make out an official requisition [ME *indenten*, fr MF *endenter*, fr OF, fr *en-* + *dent* tooth, fr L *dent-, dens* – more at TOOTH] – **indenter** *n*

[2]**indent** /'indent/ *n* **1** an indenture **2** an indention **3** *chiefly Br* an official requisition

[3]**indent** /-'-/ *vt* (to force inwards so as) to form a depression in [ME *endenten*, fr *en-* + *denten* to dent] – **indenter** *n*

[4]**indent** /'--/ *n* (an) indentation

indentation /,inden'taysh(ə)n/ *n* **1a** an angular cut in an edge **b** a usu deep recess (e g in a coastline) **2** indention

indention /in'densh(ə)n/ *n* **1** indenting or being indented **2** the blank space produced by indenting

[1]**indenture** /in'denchə/ *n* **1a** an indented document **b** a contract binding sby to work for another – usu

pl with sing. meaning **2a** a formal certificate (e g an inventory or voucher) prepared for purposes of control **b** a document stating the terms under which a security (e g a bond) is issued

[2]**indenture** *vt* to bind (e g an apprentice) by indentures

independence /ˌindiˈpend(ə)ns/ *n* being independent

Independence Day *n* a day set aside for public celebration of the achievement of national independence; *esp* the public holiday observed in the USA on July 4 commemorating the Declaration of Independence in 1776

[1]**independent** /ˌindiˈpend(ə)nt/ *adj* **1** not dependent: e g **a(1)** self-governing **(2)** not affiliated with a larger controlling unit **b(1)** not relying on sthg else ⟨*an ~ conclusion*⟩ **(2)** not committed to a political party **c(1)** not requiring or relying on, or allowing oneself to be controlled by, others (e g for guidance or care) **(2)** having or providing enough money to live on, esp without working ⟨*a woman of ~ means*⟩ **2a** MAIN 4 ⟨*the ~ clause*⟩ **b** neither deducible from nor incompatible with another statement ⟨*~ postulates*⟩ – **independently** *adv*

[2]**independent** *n, often cap* sby not bound by a political party

independent school *n* a school providing full-time education without support from public funds

ˌin-ˈdepth *adj* having detailed thoroughness; searching ⟨*~ questions*⟩ ⟨*an ~ study*⟩

indescribable /ˌindiˈskriebəbl/ *adj* **1** that cannot be described ⟨*an ~ sensation*⟩ **2** surpassing description ⟨*~ joy*⟩ – **indescribably** *adv*

indestructible *adj*

indeterminable /ˌindiˈtuhminəbl/ *adj* incapable of being definitely decided or ascertained

indeterminate /ˌindiˈtuhminət/ *adj* **1** not definitely or precisely determined or fixed **2** having an infinite number of solutions ⟨*a system of ~ equations*⟩ [ME *indeterminat*, fr LL *indeterminatus*, fr L *in-* + *determinatus*, pp of *determinare* to determine] – **indeterminacy** *n*, **indeterminately** *adv*, **indeterminateness**, **indetermination** /-ˈnaysh(ə)n/ *n*

ˌindeˈtermiˌnism /-diˈtuhmiˌniz(ə)m/ *n* a theory that actions and choices are not determined by previous physical or mental events – **indeterminist** *n*, **indeterministic** /-ˈnistik/ *adj*

[1]**index** /ˈindeks/ *n, pl* **indexes, indices** /ˈindiseez/, (4) *usu* **indices 1** a guide or list to aid reference: e g **a** an alphabetical list of items (e g topics or names) treated in a printed work that gives with each item the page number where it appears **b** CARD INDEX **2** sthg that points towards or demonstrates a particular state of affairs ⟨*the fertility of the land is an ~ of the country's wealth*⟩ **3** a list of restricted or prohibited material; *specif, cap the* list of books banned by the Roman Catholic church **4** a mathematical figure, letter, or expression; *esp* an exponent **5** a character ☞ used to direct attention (e g to a note or paragraph) **6** a number derived from a series of observations and used as an indicator or measure (e g of change in prices); *specif* INDEX NUMBER [L *indic-*, *index* forefinger, informer, guide, fr *indicare* to indicate] – **indexical** /inˈdeksikl/ *adj*

[2]**index** *vt* **1** to provide with or list in an index **2** to serve as an index of **3** to cause to be index-linked ~ *vi* to prepare an index – **indexer** *n*

indexation /ˌindekˈsaysh(ə)n/ *n* the act or process of making sthg (e g a pension) index-linked

ˈindex ˌfinger *n* the forefinger

ˌindex-ˈlinked *adj* increasing or decreasing proportionately to a rise or fall in an index, esp the cost-of-living index

ˈindex ˌnumber *n* a number used to indicate change in value (e g of cost or price) as compared with the value, usu taken to be 100, at some earlier time

indi- – see IND-

India /ˈindi·ə/ – a communications code word for the letter *i* [*India*, subcontinent of Asia]

ˌindia ˈink *n, often cap 1st I, NAm* INDIAN INK

Indiaman /ˈindi·əmən/ *n, pl* **Indiamen** /-mən/ a (sailing) ship used in trade with India or the E Indies in former times

Indian /ˈindi·ən/ *n* **1** a native or inhabitant of India **2a** a member of any of the indigenous peoples of N, Central, or S America excluding the Eskimos **b** any of the native languages of American Indians [*India*, subcontinent of Asia, fr L, fr Gk, fr *Indos* India, Indus (river in NW India), fr OPer *Hindu* India; akin to Skt *sindhu* river, esp (river or region of) Indus; (2) fr the belief held by Columbus that the lands he discovered were part of Asia] – **Indian** *adj*

Indian club *n* a club shaped like a large bottle that is swung for gymnastic exercise

Indian corn *n, chiefly NAm* maize

ˈIndian ˌfile *n* SINGLE FILE [fr the (American) Indian practice of going through woods in single file]

Indian hemp *n* HEMP 1

ˌindian ˈink *n, often cap 1st I, Br* (an ink made from) a solid black pigment used in drawing and lettering [fr a belief that it was made in India]

ˌIndian ˈsummer *n* **1** a period of warm weather in late autumn or early winter **2** a happy or flourishing period occurring towards the end of sthg, esp of a person's life

Indian wrestling *n, NAm* ARM WRESTLING

ˌindia ˈrubber *n, often cap I* [1]RUBBER 1b

Indic /ˈindik/ *adj* **1** of India **2** of or constituting the Indian branch of the Indo-European languages – **Indic** *n*

indicate /ˈindikayt/ *vt* **1a(1)** to point to; point out **(2)** to show or demonstrate as or by means of a sign or pointer **b** to be a sign or symptom of **c** to demonstrate or suggest the necessity or advisability of – chiefly pass **2** to state or express briefly; suggest [L *indicatus*, pp of *indicare*, fr *in-* + *dicare* to proclaim, dedicate – more at DICTION]

indication /ˌindiˈkaysh(ə)n/ *n* **1** the action of indicating **2a** sthg (e g a sign or suggestion) that serves to indicate **b** sthg indicated as advisable or necessary **3** the degree indicated on a graduated instrument

[1]**indicative** /inˈdikətiv/ *adj* **1** of or constituting the grammatical mood that represents the denoted act or state as an objective fact **2** serving to indicate ⟨*actions ~ of fear*⟩ – **indicatively** *adv*

[2]**indicative** *n* the indicative mood; *also* a verb form expressing it

indicator /ˈindikaytə/ *n* **1a** a hand or needle on an instrument (e g a dial) **b** an instrument for giving visual readings attached to a machine or apparatus **c** a device (e g a flashing light) on a vehicle that indicates an intention to change direction **2a** a substance (e g litmus) that shows, esp by change of colour, the condition (e g acidity or alkalinity) of a solution **b** TRACER 2 **3** a statistic (e g the level of industrial production) that gives an indication of the state of a national economy [INDICATE + [1]-OR] – **indicatory** /in'dikət(ə)ri/ *adj*

indices /'indiseez/ *pl of* INDEX

indicia /in'dishi·ə/ *n pl* distinctive marks; indications [L, pl of *indicium* sign, fr *indicare*]

indict /in'diet/ *vt* **1** to charge with an offence **2** to charge with a crime [alter. of earlier *indite*, fr ME *inditen*, fr AF *enditer*, fr OF, to write down – more at INDITE] – **indicter, indictor** *n*

indictable /in'dietəbl/ *adj* (making one) liable to indictment

indictable offence *n* a serious crime triable in the Crown Court ☞ LAW

indictment /in'dietmənt/ *n* **1** indicting **2** a formal written accusation by a prosecuting authority **3** grounds for severe censure; condemnation – usu + *of* ⟨*a searing ~ of contemporary society*⟩

indifference /in'dif(ə)rəns/ *n* **1** the quality, state, or fact of being indifferent **2** absence of interest or importance ⟨*it's a matter of complete ~ to me*⟩

indifferent /in'difrənt/ *adj* **1** that does not matter one way or the other **2** not interested in or concerned about sthg ⟨*completely ~ to the outcome*⟩ **3a** neither good nor bad; mediocre ⟨*does ~ work at the office*⟩ **b** not very good; inferior ⟨*a very ~ wine*⟩ **4** chemically, magnetically, etc neutral [ME, fr MF or L; MF, regarded as neither good nor bad, fr L *indifferent-, indifferens*, fr *in-* + *different-, differens*, prp of *differre* to be different – more at DIFFERENT] – **indifferently** *adv*

indigenous /in'dij(ə)nəs/ *adj* **1** originating, growing, or living naturally in a particular region or environment ⟨*~ to Australia*⟩ **2** innate, inborn [LL *indigenus*, fr L *indigena*, n, native, fr OL *indu, endo* in, within (akin to L *in* & to L *de* down) + L *gignere* to beget – more at DE-, KIN] – **indigenously** *adv*, **indigenize** *vt*

indigent /'indij(ə)nt/ *adj* needy, poor – fml [ME, fr MF, fr L *indigent-, indigens*, prp of *indigēre* to need, fr OL *indu* + L *egēre* to need; akin to OHG *ekrōdi* thin] – **indigence** *n*, **indigent** *n*

indigestible /,indi'jestəbl/ *adj* not (easily) digested [LL *indigestibilis*, fr L *in-* + LL *digestibilis* digestible] – **indigestibility** /-'biləti/ *n*

indigestion /,indi'jeschən/ *n* (pain in the digestive system usu resulting from) difficulty in digesting sthg

indignant /in'dignənt/ *adj* filled with or marked by indignation [L *indignant-, indignans*, prp of *indignari* to be indignant, fr *indignus* unworthy, fr *in-* + *dignus* worthy – more at DECENT] – **indignantly** *adv*

indignation /,indig'naysh(ə)n/ *n* anger aroused by sthg judged unjust, unworthy, or mean

indignity /in'dignəti/ *n* **1** an act that offends against a person's dignity or self-respect **2** humiliating treatment [L *indignitat-, indignitas*, fr *indignus*]

indigo /'indigoh/ *n, pl* **indigos, indigoes 1** (any of several dyes related to) a blue dye with a coppery lustre formerly obtained from a plant and now made artificially **2** a dark greyish blue colour whose hue lies between violet and blue in the spectrum **3** a (leguminous) plant that yields indigo [It dial., fr L *indicum*, fr Gk *indikon*, fr neut of *indikos* Indic, fr *Indos* India]

indirect /,indi'rekt, -die-/ *adj* **1a** deviating from a direct line or course **b** not going straight to the point **2** not straightforward or open **3** not directly aimed at ⟨*~ consequences*⟩ **4** stating what a real or supposed original speaker said but with changes of tense, person, etc ⟨*~ speech*⟩ – compare DIRECT 5 [ME, fr ML *indirectus*, fr L *in-* + *directus* direct] – **indirectly** *adv*, **indirectness** *n*

indirect object *n* a grammatical object representing the secondary goal of the action of its verb (e g *her* in *I gave her the book*)

indirect tax *n* a tax levied on goods, services, etc and paid indirectly by a person or organization purchasing these goods or services at an increased price – compare DIRECT TAX

indiscernible /,indi'suhnəbl/ *adj* **1** that cannot be perceived or recognized **2** not recognizable as separate or distinct

indiscipline /in'disiplin/ *n* lack of discipline – **indisciplined** *adj*

indiscreet /,indi'skreet/ *adj* not discreet; imprudent [ME *indiscrete*, fr MF & LL; MF *indiscret*, fr LL *indiscretus*, fr L, indistinguishable, fr *in-* + *discretus*, pp of *discernere* to separate – more at DISCERN] – **indiscreetly** *adv*

,indi'screte /-di'skreet/ *adj* not separated into distinct parts [L *indiscretus*]

,indi'scretion /-di'skresh(ə)n/ *n* (an act or remark showing) lack of discretion

,indi'scriminate /-di'skriminət/ *adj* **1** not marked by careful distinction; lacking in discrimination and discernment **2** not differentiated; confused – **indiscriminately** *adv*, **indiscriminateness** *n*

,indi'spensable /-di'spensəbl/ *adj* that cannot be done without – **indispensable** *n*, **indispensableness** *n*, **indispensably** *adv*, **indispensability** /-sə'biləti/ *n*

,indi'spose /-di'spohz/ *vt* **1** to make unfit **2** to make averse [prob back-formation fr *indisposed*]

,indi'sposed *adj* **1** slightly ill **2** averse [ME, not prepared for, unfitted, fr *in-* + *disposed*]

,indispo'sition /-dispə'zish(ə)n/ *n* **1** disinclination **2** (a) slight illness

,indi'sputable /-di'spyoohtəbl/ *adj* incontestable [LL *indisputabilis*, fr L *in-* + *disputabilis* disputable] – **indisputableness** *n*, **indisputably** *adv*

,indis'soluble /-di'solyoobl/ *adj* incapable of being dissolved, decomposed, undone, or annulled – **indissolubility** *n*, **indissolubly** *adv*

,indi'stinct /-di'stingkt/ *adj* not distinct: e g **a** not sharply outlined or separable; not clearly seen **b** not clearly recognizable or understandable [L *indistinctus*, fr *in-* + *distinctus* distinct] – **indistinctly** *adv*, **indistinctness** *n*

,indi'stinctive /-di'stingktiv/ *adj* lacking distinctive qualities or features

,indi'stinguishable /-di'sting·gwishəbl/ *adj* incapable of being **a** clearly perceived **b** discriminated – **indistinguishably** *adv*

indite /in'diet/ *vt* to give expression to; *esp* to write – fml [ME *enditen*, fr OF *enditer* to write down, proclaim, fr (assumed) VL *indictare* to proclaim, fr L *indictus*, pp of *indicere* to proclaim, fr *in-* + *dicere* to say – more at DICTION]

indium /'indi·əm/ *n* a rare silvery (trivalent) metallic element ☞ PERIODIC TABLE [NL, fr ISV *ind-* + NL *-ium*; fr the 2 indigo-blue lines in its spectrum]

[1]**individual** /,indi'vidyooəl, -jəl/ *adj* **1a** of or being an individual **b** intended for 1 person ⟨*an ~ serving*⟩ **2** existing as a distinct entity; separate **3** having

marked individuality ⟨*an ~ style*⟩ [ML *individualis*, fr L *individuus* indivisible, fr *in-* + *dividuus* divided, fr *dividere* to divide] – **individually** *adv*

[2]**individual** *n* **1** a particular person, being, or thing (as distinguished from a class, species, or collection) **2** a person ⟨*an odd ~*⟩

individualism /,indi'vidyooə,liz(ə)m, -jəliz(ə)m/ *n* (conduct guided by) **a** a doctrine that bases morality on the interests of the individual **b** a theory maintaining the independence of the individual and stressing individual initiative

individualist /,indi'vidyooə,list, -jəlist/ *n* one who shows marked individuality or independence in thought or behaviour – **individualist, individualistic** *adj*

individuality /,individyoo'aləti, -joo-/ *n* **1** the total character peculiar to and distinguishing an individual from others **2** the tendency to pursue one's course with marked independence or self-reliance [[1]INDIVIDUAL + -ITY]

individual·ize, -ise /,indi'vidyooə,liez, -jəliez/ *vt* **1** to make individual in character **2** to treat or notice individually **3** to adjust or adapt to suit a particular individual – **individualization** /-lie'zaysh(ə)n/ *n*

individuate /,indi'vidyoo,ayt, -joo-/ *vt* to give individuality or individual form to – **individuation** /-'aysh(ə)n/ *n*

indivisible *adj*

indo- /indoh-/ – see IND-

Indo- – see IND-

,Indo-'Aryan *n* **1** a member of any of the peoples of India of Indo-European language and Caucasian physique **2** the Indo-Iranian languages of India and Pakistan – **Indo-Aryan** *adj*

,Indo-Chi'nese *n* **1** a native or inhabitant of Indochina **2** Sino-Tibetan [(1) *Indochina*, former region of SE Asia; (2) *Ind-* + *Chinese*] – **Indo-Chinese** *adj*

indoctrinate /in'doktrinayt/ *vt* to imbue with a usu partisan or sectarian opinion, point of view, or ideology [prob fr ME *endoctrinen*, fr MF *endoctriner*, fr OF, fr *en-* + *doctrine* teaching, sthg taught] – **indoctrinator** *n*, **indoctrination** /-'naysh(ə)n/ *n*

,Indo-Euro'pean *adj or n* (of or belonging to) a family of languages spoken in most of Europe, Asia as far east as N India, and N and S America

,Indo-Ger'manic *adj or n* Indo-European

,Indo-I'ranian *adj or n* (of or constituting) a subfamily of the Indo-European languages comprising the Indic and the Iranian branches

indole /'indohl/ *n* (a derivative of) a compound that is a decomposition product of some proteins and is formed from indigo [ISV *ind-* + *-ole*]

,indolea,cetic 'acid /,indohlə'setik/ *n* a plant hormone that promotes growth and rooting of plants

indolent /'indələnt/ *adj* **1a** causing little or no pain **b** slow to develop or heal ⟨*an ~ ulcer*⟩ **2a** averse to activity, effort, or movement **b** conducive to or exhibiting laziness [LL *indolent-*, *indolens* insensitive to pain, fr L *in-* + *dolent-*, *dolens*, prp of *dolēre* to feel pain – more at CONDOLE] – **indolence** *n*, **indolently** *adv*

indomethacin /,indoh'methəsin/ *n* a synthetic drug used esp to relieve (arthritic) pain and inflammation [*indole* + *meth-* + *acetic acid* + *-in*]

indomitable /in'domitəbl/ *adj* incapable of being subdued [LL *indomitabilis*, fr L *in-* + *domitare* to tame – more at DAUNT] – **indomitably** *adv*, **indomitability** /-tə'biləti/ *n*

Indonesian /,ində'neezh(ə)n, -zyən/ *n* **1** a native or inhabitant of Indonesia or the Malay archipelago **2** BAHASA INDONESIA [*Indonesia*, country in SE Asia] – **Indonesian** *adj*

indoor /in'daw/ *adj* **1** of the interior of a building **2** done, living, or belonging indoors ⟨*an ~ sport*⟩ [alter. (influenced by *in*) of obs *within-door*, adj, fr the phrase *within door* in a building]

indoors /in'dawz/ *adv* in or into a building

indorse /in'daws/ *vt* to endorse

indraught /'indrahft/ *n* **1** a drawing or pulling in **2** an inward flow or current (e g of air or water)

indrawn /in'drawn/ *adj* **1** drawn in **2** aloof, reserved

indri /'indri/ *n* a large Madagascan lemur with black and white markings [F, fr Malagasy *indry* look!]

indubitable /in'dyoohbitəbl/ *adj* too evident to be doubted [F or L; F, fr L *indubitabilis*, fr *in-* + *dubitabilis* open to doubt, fr *dubitare* to doubt] – **indubitably** *adv*, **indubitability** /-tə'biləti/ *n*

induce /in'dyoohs/ *vt* **1** to lead on to do sthg; move by persuasion or influence **2a** to cause to appear or to happen; BRING ON; *specif* to cause (labour) to begin by the use of drugs **b** to cause the formation of **c** to produce (e g an electric current) by induction **3** to establish by logical induction; *specif* to infer from particulars – compare DEDUCE [ME *inducen*, fr L *inducere*, fr *in-* + *ducere* to lead – more at [1]TOW] – **inducer** *n*, **inducible** *adj*

in'ducement /-mənt/ *n* sthg that induces; *esp* a motive or consideration that encourages one to do sthg

induct /in'dukt/ *vt* **1** to place formally in office **2a** to introduce, initiate **b** *NAm* to enrol for military training or service [ME *inducten*, fr ML *inductus*, pp of *inducere*, fr L]

inductance /in'dukt(ə)ns/ *n* **1a** a property of an electric circuit by which an electromotive force is induced in it by a variation of current either in the circuit itself or in a neighbouring circuit **b** the amount of inductance of an electric circuit **2** a circuit or device possessing inductance *USE* ☞ PHYSICS

induction /in'duksh(ə)n/ *n* **1a** the act or process of inducting (e g into office) **b** an initial experience; an initiation **2a** the act or an instance of reasoning from particular premises to a general conclusion; *also* a conclusion reached by such reasoning **b** mathematical demonstration of the validity of a law concerning all the positive integers, by proving that the law holds for the first integer and that if it holds for all the integers preceding a given integer it must hold for the given integer **3a** the act of causing or bringing on or about **b** the process by which an electrical conductor becomes electrified when near a charged body, by which a magnetizable body becomes magnetized when in a magnetic field or in the magnetic flux set up by a magnetomotive force, or by which an electromotive force is produced in a circuit by varying the magnetic field linked with the circuit **c** the drawing of the fuel-air mixture from the carburettor into the combustion chamber of an internal-combustion engine

inductive /in'duktiv/ *adj* **1** of or employing mathematical or logical induction **2** of inductance or electrical induction **3** introductory – **inductively** *adv*, **inductiveness** *n*

inductor /in'duktə/ *n* a component that is included in an electrical circuit to provide inductance and that usu consists of a coiled conductor [INDUCT + [1]-OR]

indue /in'dyooh/ *vt* to endue

indulge /in'dulj/ *vt* **1a** to give free rein to (e g a taste) **b** to allow (oneself) to do sthg pleasurable or gratifying **2** to treat with great or excessive leniency, generosity, or consideration ~ *vi* to indulge oneself [L *indulgēre* to be complaisant] – **indulger** *n*

indulgence /in'dulj(ə)ns/ *n* **1** a remission of (part of) the purgatorial atonement for confessed sin in the Roman Catholic church **2** indulging or being indulgent **3** an indulgent act **4** sthg indulged in

indulgent /in'dulj(ə)nt/ *adj* indulging or characterized by indulgence [L *indulgent-, indulgens,* prp of *indulgēre*] – **indulgently** *adv*

indurate /'indyooərayt/ *vt* **1** to make unfeeling or obdurate **2** to make hardy **3** to make hard ~ *vi* to grow hard [L *induratus,* pp of *indurare,* fr *in-* + *durare* to harden, fr *durus* hard – more at DURING] – **induration** /-'raysh(ə)n/ *n*, **indurative** /in'dyooərətiv/ *adj*

indusium /in'dyoohzi·əm/ *n, pl* **indusia** a covering outgrowth or membrane (e g of a cluster of fern spores) [NL, fr L, tunic]

[1]**industrial** /in'dustri·əl/ *adj* **1** of, involved in, or derived from industry **2** characterized by highly developed industries ⟨*an ~ nation*⟩ **3** used in industry ⟨*~ diamonds*⟩ – **industrially** *adv*

[2]**industrial** *n* a share or bond issued by an industrial enterprise – usu pl

in,dustrial 'action *n* action (e g a strike or go-slow) taken by a body of workers to force an employer to comply with demands

industrial archaeology *n* the scientific study of the products and remains of past industrial activity

in'dustrial e,state *n* an area, usu at a distance from the centre of a city or town, designed esp for a community of industries and businesses

industrialism /in'dustri·ə,liz(ə)m/ *n* social organization in which industries, esp large-scale industries, are dominant

industrialist /in'dustri·əlist/ *n* one who is engaged in the management of an industry

industrial·ize, -ise /in'dustri·ə,liez/ *vb* to make or become industrial; introduce industry (to) ⟨*~ an agricultural region*⟩ – **industrialization** /-'zaysh(ə)n/ *n*

industrial melanism *n* genetically determined darkening, esp in insects that occur in areas blackened by industrial pollutants

in,dustrial re'lations *n pl* the dealings or relationships between a usu large business or industrial enterprise and the employees, esp the trade unions, operating within it

in,dustrial revo'lution *n* a rapid major development of an economy (e g in England in the late 18th c) marked by the general introduction of mechanized techniques and large-scale production

in'dustrial ,school *n* a school specializing in the teaching of manual skills, esp to juvenile delinquents

industrious /in'dustri·əs/ *adj* **1** persistently diligent **2** constantly, regularly, or habitually occupied – **industriously** *adv*, **industriousness** *n*

industry /'indəstri/ *n* **1** diligence in an employment or pursuit **2a** systematic work, esp for the creation of value **b(1)** a usu specified group of productive or profit-making enterprises ⟨*the car ~*⟩ **(2)** an organized field of activity regarded in its commercial aspects ⟨*the Shakespeare ~*⟩ **c** manufacturing activity as a whole ⟨*the nation's ~*⟩ [MF *industrie* skill, employment involving skill, fr L *industria* diligence, fr *industrius* diligent, fr OL *indostruus,* fr *indu* in + *-struus* (akin to L *struere* to build) – more at INDIGENOUS, STRUCTURE]

indwell /,in'dwel/ *vb* to exist within as an activating spirit, force, or principle – **indweller** /'---/ *n*

[1]**-ine** /-ien, -een, -in/ *suffix* (→ *adj*) **1** of or resembling ⟨*equine*⟩ ⟨*feminine*⟩ **2** made of; like ⟨*opaline*⟩ ⟨*crystalline*⟩ [ME *-in, -ine,* fr MF & L; (1) MF *-in,* fr L *-īnus;* (2) MF *-in,* fr L *-inus,* fr Gk *-inos* – more at [1]-EN]

[2]**-ine** *suffix* (→ *n*) **1** chemical compound: e g **a** carbon compound (e g an amino acid or alkaloid) that is a chemical base and contains nitrogen ⟨*atropine*⟩ ⟨*morphine*⟩ ⟨*leucine*⟩ ⟨*glycine*⟩ **b** mixture of compounds (e g of hydrocarbons) ⟨*kerosine*⟩ **c** usu gaseous hydride ⟨*arsine*⟩ **2** [1]-IN a,b [ME *-ine, -in,* fr MF & L; MF *-ine,* fr L *-īna,* fr fem of *-īnus,* adj suffix]

inebriate /in'eebriayt/ *vt* to exhilarate or stupefy (as if) by liquor; intoxicate [L *inebriatus,* pp of *inebriare,* fr *in-* + *ebriare* to intoxicate, fr *ebrius* drunk – more at SOBER] – **inebriant** *adj or n*, **inebriate** *adj or n*, **inebriation** /-'aysh(ə)n/, **inebriety** /,ini'brie·əti/ *n*

inedible /in'edəbl/ *adj* not fit to be eaten

ineffable /in'efəbl/ *adj* **1** unutterable **2** not to be uttered; taboo ⟨*the ~ name of Jehovah*⟩ [ME, fr MF, fr L *ineffabilis,* fr *in-* + *effabilis* capable of being expressed, fr *effari* to speak out, fr *ex-* + *fari* to speak – more at [1]BAN] – **ineffably** *adv*

ineffective /,ini'fektiv/ *adj* **1** not producing an intended effect **2** not capable of performing efficiently or achieving results – **ineffectively** *adv*, **ineffectiveness** *n*

ineffectual /,ini'fektyooəl, -chooəl/ *adj* **1** not producing or not able to give the proper or intended effect **2** unable to get things done; weak in character ⟨*a very ~ person*⟩ – **ineffectually** *adv*, **ineffectualness** *n*

inefficacy /in'efikəsi/ *n* lack of power to produce a desired effect [LL *inefficacia,* fr L *inefficac-, inefficax* ineffective, fr *in-* + *efficac-, efficax* effective]

inefficient /,ini'fish(ə)nt/ *adj* not producing the effect intended or desired, esp in a capable or economical way [[1]IN- + EFFICIENT] – **inefficiency** *n*, **inefficiently** *adv*

inelastic /,ini'lastik/ *adj* **1** slow to react or respond to changing conditions **2** inflexible, unyielding [[1]IN- + ELASTIC] – **inelasticity** /,inila'stisəti/ *n*

inelegant /in'eligənt/ *adj* lacking in refinement, grace, or good taste [MF, fr L *inelegant-, inelegans,* fr *in-* + *elegant-, elegans* elegant] – **inelegance** *n*, **inelegantly** *adv*

ineligible /in'elijəbl/ *adj* not qualified or not worthy to be chosen or preferred [F *inéligible,* fr *in-* + *éligible* eligible] – **ineligibility** /-jə'biləti/ *n*

ineluctable /,ini'luktəbl/ *adj* not to be avoided, changed, or resisted – fml [L *ineluctabilis,* fr *in-* + *eluctari* to struggle out, fr *ex-* + *luctari* to struggle – more at LOCK] – **ineluctably** *adv*

inept /i'nept/ *adj* **1** not suitable or apt to the time, place, or occasion **2** lacking sense or reason **3** generally incompetent [F *inepte*, fr L *ineptus*, fr *in-* + *aptus* apt] – **ineptitude** *n*, **ineptly** *adv*, **ineptness** *n*

inequality /,ini'kwoləti/ *n* **1a** social disparity **b** disparity of distribution or opportunity **2** an instance of being unequal **3** a formal statement of inequality between 2 expressions, usu with a sign of inequality (e g ⟨, ⟩, or ≠ signifying respectively *is less than, is greater than,* and *is not equal to*) between them [MF *inequalité*, fr L *inaequalitat-, inaequalitas*, fr *inaequalis* unequal, fr *in-* + *aequalis* equal]

inequitable /in'ekwitəbl/ *adj* unfair – **inequitably** *adv*

inequity /in'ekwiti/ *n* (an instance of) injustice or unfairness

ineradicable /,ini'radikəbl/ *adj* incapable of being eradicated – **ineradicably** *adv*

inert /i'nuht/ *adj* **1** lacking the power to move **2** deficient in active (chemical or biological) properties **3** not moving; inactive, indolent [L *inert-, iners* unskilled, idle, fr *in-* + *art-, ars* skill – more at ARM] – **inertly** *adv*, **inertness** *n*

inert gas *n* NOBLE GAS

inertia /i'nuhshə/ *n* **1** a property of matter by which it remains at rest or in uniform motion in the same straight line unless acted on by some external force **2** indisposition to motion, exertion, or change [NL, fr L, lack of skill, fr *inert-, iners*] – **inertial** *adj*, **inertially** *adv*

inertial guidance *n* guidance (e g of an aircraft or spacecraft) by comparison of preprogrammed data with data collected by measurement of inertial forces within the craft

inertia reel *n* a device allowing automatic adjustment to accommodate slow body movements ⟨~ *safety belts*⟩

inertia selling *n, chiefly Br* the practice of sending unrequested goods to people with the intention of demanding payment if the goods are not returned

inescapable /,ini'skaypəbl/ *adj* unavoidable – **inescapably** *adv*

inessential /,ini'sensh(ə)l/ *n or adj* (sthg) that is not essential

inestimable /in'estiməbl/ *adj* **1** too great to be estimated **2** too valuable or excellent to be measured [ME, fr MF, fr L *inaestimabilis*, fr *in-* + *aestimabilis* estimable] – **inestimably** *adv*

inevitable /in'evitəbl/ *adj* incapable of being avoided or evaded; bound to happen or to confront one [ME, fr L *inevitabilis*, fr *in-* + *evitabilis* avoidable] – **inevitableness** *n*, **inevitably** *adv*, **inevitability** /-tə'biləti/ *n*

inexact /,inig'zakt/ *adj* not precisely correct or true [F, fr *in-* + *exact*] – **inexactitude** *n*, **inexactly** *adv*, **inexactness** *n*

inexcusable /,iniks'kyoohzəbl/ *adj* without excuse or justification [L *inexcusabilis*, fr *in-* + *excusabilis* excusable] – **inexcusableness** *n*, **inexcusably** *adv*

inexhaustible /,inig'zawstəbl/ *adj* incapable of being used up or worn out – **inexhaustibly** *adv*, **inexhaustibility** /-stə'biləti/ *n*

inexorable /in'eks(ə)rəbl/ *adj* **1** not to be persuaded or moved by entreaty **2** continuing inevitably; that cannot be averted [L *inexorabilis*, fr *in-* + *exorabilis* pliant, fr *exorare* to prevail upon, fr *ex-* + *orare* to speak – more at ORATION] – **inexorably** *adv*, **inexorability** /-rə'biləti/ *n*

inexpedient *adj*

inexpensive /,inik'spensiv/ *adj* reasonable in price; cheap – **inexpensively** *adv*, **inexpensiveness** *n*

inexperience /,inik'spiəri·əns/ *n* **1** lack of (the skill gained from) experience **2** lack of knowledge of the ways of the world [MF, fr LL *inexperientia*, fr L *in-* + *experientia* experience] – **inexperienced** *adj*

inexpert /in'ekspuht/ *adj* unskilled [ME, fr MF, fr L *inexpertus*, fr *in-* + *expertus* expert] – **inexpertly** *adv*, **inexpertness** *n*

inexplicable /,inik'splikəbl, in'eksplikəbl/ *adj* incapable of being explained, interpreted, or accounted for [MF, fr L *inexplicabilis*, fr *in-* + *explicabilis* explicable] – **inexplicableness** *n*, **inexplicably** *adv*, **inexplicability** /-kə'biləti/ *n*

inexpressible /,inik'spresəbl/ *adj* beyond one's power to express – **inexpressibly** *adv*, **inexpressibility** /-sə'biləti/ *n*

inexpressive /,inik'spresiv/ *adj* lacking expression or meaning – **inexpressively** *adv*, **inexpressiveness** *n*

in extenso /,in ik'stensoh/ *adv* at full length [ML]

inextinguishable /,inik'sting·gwishəbl/ *adj* unquenchable – **inextinguishably** *adv*

in extremis /,in ik'streemis/ *adv* in extreme circumstances; *esp* at the point of death [L]

inextricable /in'ekstrikəbl/ *adj* **1** from which one cannot extricate oneself **2** incapable of being disentangled or untied ⟨*an* ~ *knot*⟩ [MF or L; MF, fr L *inextricabilis*, fr *in-* + *extricabilis* extricable] – **inextricably** *adv*

infallible /in'faləbl/ *adj* **1** incapable of error; *esp, of the Pope* incapable of error in defining dogma **2** not liable to fail [ML *infallibilis*, fr L *in-* + LL *fallibilis* fallible] – **infallibly** *adv*, **infallibility** /-lə'biləti/ *n*

infamous /'infəməs/ *adj* **1** having a reputation of the worst kind; notorious **2** disgraceful [ME, fr L *infamis*, fr *in-* + *fama* fame] – **infamously** *adv*

infamy /'infəmi/ *n* **1** evil reputation brought about by sthg grossly criminal, shocking, or brutal **2** an extreme and publicly known criminal or evil act

infancy /'inf(ə)nsi/ *n* **1** early childhood **2** a beginning or early period of existence ⟨*when sociology was in its* ~⟩ **3** the legal status of an infant

[1]**infant** /'inf(ə)nt/ *n* **1** a child in the first period of life **2** a minor [ME *enfaunt*, fr MF *enfant*, fr L *infant-, infans*, fr *infant-, infans* incapable of speech, young, fr *in-* + *fant-, fans*, prp of *fari* to speak – more at BAN]

[2]**infant** *adj* **1** in an early stage of development **2** concerned with or intended for young children, esp those aged from 5 to 7 or 8 ⟨*an* ~ *teacher*⟩

infanta /in'fantə/ *n* a daughter of a Spanish or Portuguese monarch [Sp & Pg, fem of *infante*]

infante /in'fanti/ *n* a younger son of a Spanish or Portuguese monarch [Sp & Pg, lit., infant, fr L *infant-, infans*]

infanticide /in'fantisied/ *n* (the act of) sby who kills an infant [LL *infanticidium* & *infanticida*, fr L *infant-, infans* + *-i-* + *-cidium* & *-cida* -cide – more at -CIDE]

infantile /'inf(ə)ntiel/ *adj* (suggestive) of infants or infancy ⟨~ *behaviour*⟩

infantile paralysis *n* poliomyelitis

infantilism /in'fanti,liz(ə)m/ *n* **1** retention of childish physical, mental, or emotional qualities in adult life **2** an act or expression that indicates lack of maturity – used technically

infantry /'inf(ə)ntri/ *n sing or pl in constr* (a branch of an army containing) soldiers trained, armed, and equipped to fight on foot [MF & OIt; MF *infanterie*, fr OIt *infanteria*, fr *infante* boy, foot soldier, fr L *infant-, infans*]

'infantryman /-mən/ *n* an infantry soldier

'infant ,school *n, Br* a kindergarten for children aged from 5 to 7 or 8

infarct /in'fahkt/ *n* an area of death in a tissue or organ resulting from obstruction of the local blood circulation [L *infarctus*, pp of *infarcire* to stuff, fr *in-* + *farcire* to stuff – more at FARCE] – **infarcted** *adj*, **infarction** *n*

infatuate /in'fatyooayt/ *vt* **1** to affect with folly **2** to inspire with powerful but superficial or short-lived feelings of love and desire [L *infatuatus*, pp of *infatuare*, fr *in-* + *fatuus* fatuous] – **infatuated** *adj*, **infatuation** /-'aysh(ə)n/ *n*

infect /in'fekt/ *vt* **1** to contaminate (e g air or food) with a disease-causing agent **2a** to pass on a disease or a disease-causing agent to **b** to invade (an individual or organ), usu by penetration – used with reference to a pathogenic organism **3** to transmit or pass on sthg (e g an emotion) to [ME *infecten*, fr L *infectus*, pp of *inficere*, fr *in-* + *facere* to make, do – more at DO] – **infector** *n*

infection /in'feksh(ə)n/ *n* **1** infecting **2** (an agent that causes) a contagious or infectious disease **3** the communication of emotions or qualities through example or contact

infectious /in'fekshəs/ *adj* **1a infectious, infective** capable of causing infection **b** communicable by infection – compare CONTAGIOUS **2** readily spread or communicated to others ⟨~ *excitement*⟩ – **infectiously** *adv*, **infectiousness** *n*

infectious hepatitis *n* a highly infectious liver inflammation caused by a virus

infectious mononucleosis *n* an acute infectious disease characterized by fever and swelling of lymph glands

infelicitous /,infə'lisitəs/ *adj* not apt; not suitably chosen for the occasion – **infelicitously** *adv*

infelicity /,infə'lisəti/ *n* **1** being infelicitous **2** sthg infelicitous [ME *infelicite*, fr L *infelicitas*, fr *infelic-, infelix* unhappy, fr *in-* + *felic-, felix* fruitful – more at FEMININE]

infer /in'fuh/ *vb* **-rr-** *vt* **1** to derive as a conclusion from facts or premises – compare IMPLY **2** to suggest, imply – disapproved of by some speakers ~ *vi* to draw inferences [MF or L; MF *inferer*, fr L *inferre*, lit., to carry or bring into, fr *in-* + *ferre* to carry – more at ²BEAR] – **inferable** *adj*

inference /'inf(ə)rəns/ *n* **1a** the act of inferring **b** the act of passing from statistical sample data to generalizations (e g of the value of population parameters), usu with calculated degrees of certainty **2** sthg inferred; *esp* a proposition arrived at by inference

inferential /,infə'rensh(ə)l/ *adj* deduced or deducible by inference [ML *inferentia* inference, fr L *inferent-, inferens*, prp of *inferre*]

inferior /in'fiəri·ə/ *adj* **1** situated lower down **2** of low or lower degree or rank **3** of little or less importance, value, or merit **4a** *of an animal or plant part* situated below or at the base of another (corresponding) part **b(1)** *of a calyx* lying below the ovary **(2)** *of an ovary* lying below the petals or sepals **5** of or being a subscript **6** *of a planet* nearer the sun than the earth is [ME, fr L, compar of *inferus* – more at UNDER] – **inferior** *n*, **inferiorly** *adv*, **inferiority** /-ri'orəti/ *n*

inferi'ority ,complex *n* a sense of personal inferiority often resulting either in timidity or, through overcompensation, in exaggerated aggressiveness

infernal /in'fuhnl/ *adj* **1** of hell **2** hellish, diabolical **3** damned – infml ⟨*an* ~ *nuisance*⟩ [ME, fr OF, fr LL *infernalis*, fr *infernus* hell, fr L, lower; akin to L *inferus* inferior] – **infernally** *adv*

inferno /in'fuhnoh/ *n, pl* **infernos** a place or a state that resembles or suggests hell, esp in intense heat or raging fire [It, hell, fr LL *infernus*]

infertile /in'fuhtiel/ *adj* not fertile or productive ⟨~ *eggs*⟩ ⟨~ *fields*⟩ [MF, fr LL *infertilis*, fr L *in-* + *fertilis* fertile] – **infertility** /,infə'tiləti/ *n*

infest /in'fest/ *vt* **1** to spread or swarm in or over in a troublesome manner ⟨*shark-*infested *waters*⟩ **2** to live in or on as a parasite [MF *infester*, fr L *infestare*, fr *infestus* hostile] – **infestation** /,infe'staysh(ə)n/ *n*

infidel /'infidl/ *n* **1a** an unbeliever in or opponent of a particular religion, esp of Christianity or Islam **b** sby who acknowledges no religious belief **2** a disbeliever in sthg specified or understood [MF *infidele*, fr LL *infidelis* unbelieving, fr L, unfaithful, fr *in-* + *fidelis* faithful, fr *fides* faith] – **infidel** *adj*

infidelity /,infi'deləti/ *n* **1** lack of belief in a religion **2a** unfaithfulness, disloyalty **b** marital unfaithfulness

¹infield /'infeeld/ *n* (the fielding positions in) the area of a cricket or baseball field relatively near the wickets or bounded by the bases – **infielder** *n*

²infield /-'-/ *adv* away from the edge of a playing field

infighting /'in,fieting/ *n* **1** fighting or boxing at close quarters **2** prolonged and often bitter dissension among members of a group or organization – **infighter** *n*

infill /'infil/ *vt* to fill in (a gap); *esp* to build houses in between (houses already standing) ☞ BUILDING – **infilling** *n*

infiltrate /'infiltrayt/ *vt* **1** to cause (e g a liquid) to permeate sthg (e g by penetrating its pores or interstices) **2** to pass into or through (a substance) by filtering or permeating **3** to enter or become established in gradually or unobtrusively ~ *vi* to enter, permeate, or pass through a substance or area by filtering or by insinuating gradually – **infiltrative** *adj*, **infiltrator** *n*, **infiltration** /-'traysh(ə)n/ *n*

¹infinite /'infinət/ *adj* **1** subject to no limitation or external determination **2** extending indefinitely **3** immeasurably or inconceivably great or extensive **4a** extending beyond, lying beyond, or being greater than any arbitrarily chosen finite value, however large ⟨*there are an* ~ *number of positive integers*⟩ **b** extending to infinity ⟨~ *plane surface*⟩ [ME *infinit*, fr MF or L; MF, fr L *infinitus*, fr *in-* + *finitus* finite] – **infinitely** *adv*, **infiniteness** *n*

²infinite *n* **1** divineness, sublimity – + *the* **2** an incalculable or very great number **3** an infinite quantity or magnitude

¹infinitesimal /,infini'tesiml/ *n* an infinitesimal variable or quantity [NL *infinitesimus* infinite in rank, fr L *infinitus*]

²infinitesimal *adj* **1** taking on values arbitrarily

close to zero **2** immeasurably or incalculably small – **infinitesimally** *adv*

infinitive /in'finətiv/ *adj or n* (using) a verb form that performs some functions of a noun and that in English is used with *to* (e g *go* in *I asked him to go*) except with auxiliary and various other verbs (e g *go* in *I must go*) [adj LL *infinitivus*, fr L *infinitus*; n fr adj] – **infinitival** /,infini'tievl/ *adj or n*

infinitude /in'finityoohd/ *n* **1** the quality or state of being infinite **2** sthg infinite, esp in extent **3** an infinite number or quantity

infinity /in'finəti/ *n* **1a** the quality of being infinite **b** unlimited extent of time, space, or quantity **2** an indefinitely great number or amount **3** a distance so great that the rays of light from a point source at that distance may be regarded as parallel *USE* ☞ SYMBOL

infirm /in'fuhm/ *adj* **1** physically feeble, esp from age **2** weak in mind, will, or character [ME, fr L *infirmus*, fr *in-* + *firmus* firm] – **infirmly** *adv*

infirmary /in'fuhməri/ *n* HOSPITAL 1

infirmity /in'fuhməti/ *n* **1** being infirm or frail **2** a disease, malady

[1]**infix** /in'fiks/ *vt* **1** to fasten or fix by piercing or thrusting in **2** to instil, inculcate **3** to insert (e g a sound or letter) as an infix [L *infixus*, pp of *infigere*, fr *in-* + *figere* to fasten – more at DYKE]

[2]**infix** /'infiks/ *n* an affix inserted in the body of a word or root – compare PREFIX, SUFFIX

in flagrante delicto /,in flə'granti di'liktoh/ *adv* in the very act of committing a misdeed [ML, lit., in blazing crime]

inflame /in'flaym/ *vt* **1** to set on fire **2a** to excite or arouse passion or excessive action or feeling in **b** to make more heated or violent **3** to cause to redden or grow hot **4** to cause inflammation in (bodily tissue) ~ *vi* **1** to burst into flame **2** to become excited or angered **3** to become affected with inflammation [ME *enflamen*, fr MF *enflamer*, fr L *inflammare*, fr *in-* + *flamma* flame] – **inflamer** *n*

inflammable /in'flaməbl/ *adj* **1** capable of being easily ignited and of burning rapidly ☞ SYMBOL **2** easily inflamed, excited, or angered [F, fr ML *inflammabilis*, fr L *inflammare* to inflame] – **inflammable** *n*, **inflammableness, inflammability** /-mə'biləti/ *n*

inflammation /,inflə'maysh(ə)n/ *n* **1** inflaming or being inflamed **2** a response to cellular injury marked by local redness, heat, and pain

inflammatory /in'flamət(ə)ri/ *adj* **1** tending to inflame ⟨~ *speeches*⟩ **2** accompanied by or tending to cause inflammation

inflatable /in'flaytəbl/ *n* an inflatable boat, toy, etc

inflate /in'flayt/ *vt* **1** to swell or distend (with air or gas) **2** to increase (a price level) or cause (a volume of credit or the economy) to expand ~ *vi* to become inflated [L *inflatus*, pp of *inflare*, fr *in-* + *flare* to blow – more at [1]BLOW] – **inflatable** *adj*, **inflator, inflater** *n*

in'flated *adj* **1** bombastic, exaggerated **2** expanded to an abnormal or unjustifiable volume or level ⟨~ *prices*⟩ **3** swelled out; distended

inflation /in'flaysh(ə)n/ *n* inflating or being inflated; *esp* a substantial and continuing rise in the general level of prices, caused by or causing an increase in the volume of money and credit or an expansion of the economy – **inflationary** *adj*

inflect /in'flekt/ *vt* **1** to vary (a word) by inflection **2** to change or vary the pitch of (a voice or note) ~ *vi* to become modified by inflection [ME *inflecten*, fr L *inflectere* to bend, modulate, fr *in-* + *flectere* to bend] – **inflective** *adj*

inflection, *Br also* **inflexion** /in'fleksh(ə)n/ *n* **1** change in pitch or loudness of the voice **2a** the change in the form of a word showing its case, gender, number, tense, etc **b** an element (e g a suffix) showing such variation **3** (a point on a curve of) change of curvature with respect to a fixed line from concave to convex or conversely ☞ MATHEMATICS – **inflectional** *adj*

inflexed /in'flekst/ *adj* bent or turned abruptly inwards, downwards, or towards the axis [L *inflexus*, pp of *inflectere*]

inflexible /in'fleksəbl/ *adj* rigidly firm: e g **a** lacking or deficient in suppleness **b** UNYIELDING 2 **c** incapable of change [ME, fr L *inflexibilis*, fr *in-* + *flexibilis* flexible] – **inflexibly** *adv*, **inflexibility** /-sə'biləti/ *n*

inflict /in'flikt/ *vt* to force or impose (sthg damaging or painful) on sby [L *inflictus*, pp of *infligere*, fr *in-* + *fligere* to strike – more at PROFLIGATE] – **inflicter, inflictor** *n*, **infliction** *n*

,in-'flight *adj* made, carried out, or provided in flight ⟨~ *refuelling*⟩ ⟨~ *meals*⟩

inflorescence /,inflaw'res(ə)ns, -flə-/ *n* **1a** (the arrangement of flowers on) a floral axis ☞ PLANT **b** a flower cluster; *also* a solitary flower **2** the budding and unfolding of blossoms; flowering [NL *inflorescentia*, fr LL *inflorescent-*, *inflorescens*, prp of *inflorescere* to begin to bloom, fr L *in-* + *florescere* to begin to bloom – more at FLORESCENCE] – **inflorescent** *adj*

inflow /'infloh/ *n* a flowing in ⟨*a pipe taking the maximum rate of* ~⟩

[1]**influence** /'infloo·əns/ *n* **1** an ethereal fluid supposed to flow from the stars and to affect the actions of human beings **2** the power to achieve sthg desired by using wealth or position **3** the act, power, or capacity of causing or producing an effect in indirect or intangible ways **4** sby or sthg that exerts influence; *esp* sby or sthg that tends to produce a moral or immoral effect on another [ME, fr MF, fr ML *influentia*, fr L *influent-*, *influens*, prp of *influere* to flow in, fr *in-* + *fluere* to flow – more at FLUID] – **under the influence** affected by alcohol; drunk ⟨*was arrested for driving* under the influence⟩

[2]**influence** *vt* to affect, alter, or modify by indirect or intangible means

influent /'in,flooh·ənt, -'--/ *n* a tributary stream [ME, fr *influent* flowing in, fr L *influent-*, *influens*, prp of *influere*]

influential /,infloo'ensh(ə)l/ *adj* exerting or possessing influence – **influentially** *adv*

influenza /,infloo'enzə/ *n* **1** a highly infectious virus disease characterized by sudden onset, fever, severe aches and pains, and inflammation of the respiratory mucous membranes **2** any of numerous feverish usu virus diseases of domestic animals marked by respiratory symptoms [It, lit., influence, fr ML *influentia*; fr the belief that epidemics were due to the influence of the stars]

influx /'influks/ *n* a usu sudden increase in flowing in; the arrival of large amounts [LL *influxus*, fr L, pp of *influere*]

info /'infoh/ *n* information – infml

infold /in'fohld/ *vt* to enfold

inform /in'fawm/ *vt* **1** to impart an essential quality or character to **2** to communicate knowledge to ~ *vi* **1** to give information or knowledge **2** to act as an informer *against* or *on* [ME *informen*, fr MF *enformer*, fr L *informare* to give shape to, fr *in-* + *forma* form] – **informant** *n*

informal /in'fawml/ *adj* marked by an absence of formality or ceremony; everyday – **informally** *adv*, **informality** /,infaw'maləti/ *n*

information /,infə'maysh(ə)n/ *n* **1** the communication or reception of facts or ideas **2a** knowledge obtained from investigation, study, or instruction **b** news **c** (significant) facts or data **d** a signal or character (e g in a radio transmission or computer) representing data **e** a quantitative measure of the content of information; *specif* a numerical quantity that measures the uncertainty in the outcome of an experiment to be performed **3** a formal accusation presented to a magistrate – **informational** *adj*

information science *n* the collection, classification, storage, retrieval, and distribution of recorded knowledge

information technology *n* the gathering, processing, and circulation of information by a combination of computing and telecommunications

information theory *n* a theory that deals statistically with the efficiency of communication of information

informative /in'fawmətiv/, **informatory** /in'fawmət(ə)ri/ *adj* conveying facts or ideas; instructive – **informatively** *adv*, **informativeness** *n*

informed /in'fawmd/ *adj* **1** possessing or based on possession of information **2** knowledgeable about matters of contemporary interest

informer /in'fawmə/ *n* one who informs against another, esp to the police for a financial reward

infra /'infrə/ *adv* lower on the same or a following page [L]

infra- /infrə-/ *prefix* **1** below ⟨infra*renal*⟩ ⟨infra*structure*⟩; less than ⟨infra*human*⟩ **2** within ⟨infra*specific*⟩ ⟨infra*territorial*⟩ **3** below in a scale or series ⟨infra*red*⟩ [L *infra* – more at UNDER]

infraction /in'fraksh(ə)n/ *n* a violation, infringement [L *infraction-, infractio*, fr *infractus*, pp of *infringere*]

,infra 'dig *adj* beneath one's dignity – infml [short for L *infra dignitatem*]

infrangible /in'franjəbl/ *adj* **1** not capable of being broken or separated **2** not to be infringed or violated [MF, fr LL *infrangibilis*, fr L *in-* + *frangere* to break – more at BREAK] – **infrangibly** *adv*, **infrangibility** /-jə'biləti/ *n*

infrared /,infrə'red/ *adj or n* (being, using, producing, or sensitive to) electromagnetic radiation with a wavelength between the red end of the visible spectrum and microwaves, that is commonly perceived as heat ☞ PHYSICS

,infra'sonic /-'sonik/ *adj* (of, being, using, or produced by waves or vibrations) having a frequency below the lower threshold of human hearing

'infra,structure /-,strukchə/ *n* **1** an underlying foundation or basic framework **2** the permanent installations required for military purposes

infrequent /in'freekwənt/ *adj* **1** rare **2** not habitual or persistent [L *infrequent-, infrequens*, fr *in-* + *frequent-, frequens* frequent] – **infrequency** *n*, **infrequently** *adv*

infringe /in'frinj/ *vt* to encroach on; violate ~ *vi* to encroach, trespass [L *infringere*, lit., to break off, fr *in-* + *frangere* to break – more at BREAK] – **infringement** *n*

infundibular /,infun'dibyoolə/, **infundibulate** /-lət/ *adj* **1** funnel-shaped **2** of or having an infundibulum

infundibulum /,infun'dibyooləm/ *n, pl* **infundibula** /-lə/ the funnel-shaped mass of grey matter that connects the pituitary gland to the brain [NL, fr L, funnel – more at FUNNEL]

infuriate /in'fyooəriayt/ *vt* to make furious [ML *infuriatus*, pp of *infuriare*, fr L *in-* + *furia* fury] – **infuriate** *adj*, **infuriatingly** *adv*

infuse /in'fyoohz/ *vt* **1** to inspire, imbue **2** to steep in liquid without boiling so as to extract the soluble properties or constituents [ME *infusen*, fr MF & L; MF *infuser*, fr L *infusus*, pp of *infundere* to pour in, fr *in-* + *fundere* to pour – more at ^{4}FOUND] – **infuser** *n*

infusible /in'fyoohzəbl/ *adj* very difficult or impossible to fuse or melt – **infusibility** /-zə'biləti/ *n*

infusion /in'fyoohzh(ə)n/ *n* **1** infusing **2** the continuous slow introduction of a solution, esp into a vein **3** an extract obtained by infusing

infusorian /,infyooh'zawri·ən/ *n* any of a group composed of different types of minute living organisms found esp in decomposing organic matter; *esp* a cilia-bearing protozoan – not now used technically [deriv of L *infusus*] – **infusorial** *adj*, **infusorian** *adj*

^{1}**-ing** /-ing/ *suffix* (→ *vb or adj*) – used to form the present participle ⟨*sail*ing⟩ and sometimes to form an adjective resembling a present participle but not derived from a verb ⟨*swashbuckl*ing⟩ [ME, alter. of *-ende*, fr OE, fr *-e-*, verb stem vowel + *-nde*, prp suffix – more at -ANT]

^{2}**-ing** *suffix* (→ *n*) **1** action or process of ⟨*runn*ing⟩ ⟨*sleep*ing⟩; *also* instance of (a specified action or process) ⟨*a meet*ing⟩ – sometimes used to form a noun resembling a gerund but not derived from a verb ⟨*skydiv*ing⟩ **2** product or result of (a specified action or process) ⟨*an engrav*ing⟩ – often pl with sing. meaning ⟨*earn*ings⟩ **3** activity or occupation connected with ⟨*boat*ing⟩ ⟨*bank*ing⟩ **4a** collection or aggregate of ⟨*shipp*ing⟩ ⟨*hous*ing⟩ **b** sthg connected with, consisting of, or used in making ⟨*scaffold*ing⟩ ⟨*shirt*ing⟩ **5** sthg related to (a specified concept) ⟨*off*ing⟩ [ME, fr OE, suffix forming nouns from verbs; akin to OHG *-ung*, suffix forming nouns from verbs]

ingenious /in'jeeni·əs/ *adj* marked by originality, resourcefulness, and cleverness [MF *ingenieux*, fr L *ingeniosus*, fr *ingenium* natural capacity – more at ENGINE] – **ingeniously** *adv*

ingenue, ingénue /,anzhay'nooh (*Fr* ɛ̃ʒeny)/ *n* **1** a naive or artless young woman **2** (an actress playing) the stage role of an ingenue [F *ingénue*, fem of *ingénu* ingenuous, fr L *ingenuus*]

ingenuity /,inji'nyooh·əti/ *n* (resourceful) cleverness; inventiveness [L *ingenuitas* ingenuousness, fr *ingenuus* ingenuous; afterwards influenced in meaning by *ingenious*]

ingenuous /in'jenyoo·əs/ *adj* showing innocent or childlike simplicity; frank, candid [L *ingenuus* native, free born, fr *in-* + *gignere* to beget – more at KIN] – **ingenuously** *adv*, **ingenuousness** *n*

ingest /in'jest/ *vt* to take in (as if) for digestion; absorb [L *ingestus*, pp of *ingerere* to carry in, fr *in-*

+ *gerere* to bear – more at CAST] – **ingestible** *adj*, **ingestion** *n*, **ingestive** *adj*

inglenook /ˈing·gl,nook/ *n* (a seat in) an alcove by a large open fireplace [ScGael *aingeal* light, fire + E *nook*]

inglorious /inˈglawri·əs/ *adj* shameful, ignominious [L *inglorius*, fr *in-* + *gloria* glory] – **ingloriously** *adv*

,in-ˈgoal *n* a rectangular area behind the goal line in rugby, extending completely across the field, in which the ball must be touched down to score a try ☞ SPORT

ingoing /ˈingoh·ing/ *adj* entering

ingot /ˈing·gət/ *n* a (bar-shaped) mass of cast metal [ME, mould for casting metal, prob fr OE *in* + *goten*, pp of *gēotan* to pour, cast in metal]

¹ingrain /inˈgrayn/ *vt* to work (sthg) indelibly into a natural texture or mental or moral constitution

²ingrain /ˈin·grayn/ *n or adj* (an article) made of fibres that are dyed to various colours before being spun into yarn, or made of the resultant yarn

ˈin,grained *adj* firmly and deeply implanted; deep-rooted – **ingrainedly** *adv*

ingratiate /inˈgrayshi,ayt/ *vt* to gain favour for (e g oneself) by deliberate effort ⟨~ *themselves with the public*⟩ [*in-* + L *gratia* grace] – **ingratiatingly** *adv*, **ingratiatory** /-shi·ət(ə)ri/ *adj*, **ingratiation** /-ˈaysh(ə)n/ *n*

ingratitude /inˈgratityoohd/ *n* forgetfulness or scant recognition of kindness received [ME, fr MF, fr ML *ingratitudo*, fr L *in-* + LL *gratitudo* gratitude]

ingredient /inˈgreedi·ənt/ *n* sthg that forms a component part of a compound, combination, or mixture [ME, fr L *ingredient-*, *ingrediens*, prp of *ingredi* to go into, fr *in-* + *gradi* to go – more at GRADE]

ingress /ˈin·gres/ *n* **1** the act of entering; *specif* that of a celestial body into eclipse, occultation, or transit **2** the right of entrance or access [ME, fr L *ingressus*, fr *ingressus*, pp of *ingredi*]

ingrowing /ˈin,groh·ing/, *NAm chiefly* **ingrown** /-grohn/ *adj* growing inwards; *specif* having the free tip or edge embedded in the flesh ⟨*an* ~ *toenail*⟩

ingrowth /ˈin,grohth/ *n* **1** a growing inwards **2** sthg that grows in or into a space

inguinal /ˈing·gwinl/ *adj* of or situated in the groin region [L *inguinalis*, fr *inguin-*, *inguen* groin – more at ADEN-]

ingurgitate /inˈguhjitayt/ *vt* to swallow greedily or in large quantities [L *ingurgitatus*, pp of *ingurgitare*, fr *in-* + *gurgit-*, *gurges* whirlpool – more at VORACIOUS] – **ingurgitation** /-ˈtaysh(ə)n/ *n*

inhabit /inˈhabit/ *vt* to occupy or be present in ⟨*the hopes and fears that* ~ *the human mind*⟩ [ME *enhabiten*, fr MF & L; MF *enhabiter*, fr L *inhabitare*, fr *in-* + *habitare* to dwell, fr *habitus*, pp of *habēre* to have – more at GIVE] – **inhabitable** *adj*, **inhabitancy** *n*, **inhabitant** *n*, **inhabitation** /-ˈtaysh(ə)n/ *n*

inhalant /inˈhaylənt/ *n* sthg (e g a medication) that is inhaled

inhalation /,inhəˈlaysh(ə)n/ *n* (material for) inhaling

inhale /inˈhayl/ *vb* to breathe in [*in-* + *-hale* (as in *exhale*)]

inhaler /inˈhaylə/ *n* a device used for inhaling a medication [INHALE + ²-ER]

inharmonious /,inhahˈmohnyəs, -ni·əs/ *adj* **1** not harmonious **2** not congenial or compatible – **inharmoniously** *adv*

inhere /inˈhiə/ *vi* to be inherent; belong ⟨*power to make laws* ~s *in the state*⟩ [L *inhaerēre*, fr *in-* + *haerēre* to adhere – more at HESITATE]

inherent /inˈherənt, -ˈhiə-/ *adj* intrinsic to the constitution or essence of sthg [L *inhaerent-*, *inhaerens*, prp of *inhaerēre*] – **inherence** *n*, **inherently** *adv*

inherit /inˈherit/ *vt* **1** to receive **a** by right **b** from an ancestor at his/her death **2** to receive by genetic transmission ⟨~ *a strong constitution*⟩ ~ *vi* to receive sthg by inheritance [ME *enheriten* to make heir, inherit, fr MF *enheriter* to make heir, fr LL *inhereditare*, fr L *in-* + *hereditas* inheritance – more at HEREDITY] – **inheritor** *n*, **inheritress** /-tris/, **inheritrix** /-triks/ *n*

inheritable /inˈheritəbl/ *adj* **1** capable of being inherited **2** capable of inheriting – **inheritability** /-təˈbiləti/ *n*

inheritance /inˈherit(ə)ns/ *n* **1a** inheriting property **b** the transmission of genetic qualities from parent to offspring **c** the acquisition of a possession, condition, or trait from past generations **2a** sthg that is or may be inherited **b** sthg acquired or derived from the past

inhesion /inˈheezh(ə)n/ *n* inherence [L *inhaesus*, pp of *inhaerēre*]

inhibit /inˈhibit/ *vt* **1** to prohibit *from* doing sthg **2a** to restrain **b** to discourage from free or spontaneous activity, esp by psychological or social controls ~ *vi* to cause inhibition [ME *inhibiten*, fr L *inhibitus*, pp of *inhibēre*, fr *in-* + *habēre* to have – more at GIVE] – **inhibitive** *adj*, **inhibitory** *adj*

inhibition /,inhiˈbish(ə)n/ *n* **1a** inhibiting or being inhibited **b** sthg that forbids, debars, or restricts **2a** a psychological restraint on another psychological or physical activity ⟨*sexual* ~s⟩ **b** a restraining of a function (e g of a bodily organ or enzyme)

inhibitor, inhibiter /inˈhibitə/ *n* sthg that slows or interferes with a chemical action [INHIBIT + ¹-OR, ²-ER]

inhomogeneous /,inhoməˈjeenyəs, -ni·əs/ *adj* not homogeneous – **inhomogeneity** /,inhoməjəˈnay·əti, -ˈnee-, -hohmoh-/ *n*

inhospitable /,inhoˈspitəbl/ *adj* **1** not friendly or welcoming **2** providing no shelter or means of support – **inhospitableness** *n*, **inhospitably** *adv*

inhospitality /,inhospiˈtaləti/ *n* being inhospitable

inhuman /inˈhyoohmən/ *adj* **1a** inhumane **b** failing to conform to basic human needs **2** being other than human [MF & L; MF *inhumain*, fr L *inhumanus*, fr *in-* + *humanus* human] – **inhumanly** *adv*

inhumane /,inhyoohˈmayn/ *adj* lacking in kindness or compassion [MF *inhumain* & L *inhumanus*] – **inhumanely** *adv*

inhumanity /,inhyoohˈmanəti/ *n* **1** being pitiless or cruel **2** a cruel or barbarous act

inhume /inˈhyoohm/ *vt* to bury, inter – fml [prob fr F *inhumer*, fr L *inhumare*, fr *in-* + *humus* earth – more at HUMBLE] – **inhumation** /,inhyoohˈmaysh(ə)n/ *n*

inimical /iˈnimik(ə)l/ *adj* **1** hostile or indicating hostility **2** adverse in tendency, influence, or effects [LL *inimicalis*, fr L *inimicus* enemy – more at ENEMY] – **inimically** *adv*

inimitable /iˈnimitəbl/ *adj* defying imitation [MF or L; MF, fr L *inimitabilis*, fr *in-* + *imitabilis* imitable] – **inimitableness** *n*, **inimitably** *adv*

iniquity /i'nikwəti/ *n* **1** gross injustice **2** a sin [ME *iniquite*, fr MF *iniquité*, fr L *iniquitat-, iniquitas*, fr *iniquus* uneven, fr *in-* + *aequus* equal] – **iniquitous** *adj*

[1]**initial** /i'nish(ə)l/ *adj* **1** of the beginning ⟨*the ~ symptoms of a disease*⟩ **2** first ⟨*the ~ number of a code*⟩ [MF & L; MF, fr L *initialis*, fr *initium* beginning, fr *initus*, pp of *inire* to go into, fr *in-* + *ire* to go – more at ISSUE] – **initially** *adv*

[2]**initial** *n* **1** the first letter of a name **2** *pl* the first letter of each word in a full name

[3]**initial** *vt* **-ll-** (*NAm* **-l-, -ll-**) to put initials (indicating ownership or authorization) on

initial teaching alphabet *n* a 44-character phonetic alphabet designed for teaching children to read English

[1]**initiate** /i'nishiayt/ *vt* **1** to cause or enable the beginning of; start **2** to instil with rudiments or principles (of sthg complex or obscure) **3** to induct into membership (as if) by formal rites [LL *initiatus*, pp of *initiare*, fr L, to induct, fr *initium*] – **initiator** *n*, **initiatory** *adj*

[2]**initiate** /i'nishi·ət/ *adj* **1** initiated or properly admitted (e g to membership or an office) **2** instructed in some secret knowledge

[3]**i'nitiate** /-ət/ *n* **1** sby who is undergoing or has undergone initiation **2** sby who is instructed or proficient in a complex or specialized field

initiation /i,nishi'aysh(ə)n/ *n* **1** initiating or being initiated **2** the ceremony or formal procedure with which sby is made a member of a sect or society

[1]**initiative** /i'nish(y)ətiv/ *adj* introductory, preliminary

[2]**initiative** *n* **1** a first step, esp in the attainment of an end or goal **2** energy or resourcefulness displayed in initiation of action **3** a procedure enabling voters to propose a law by petition – compare REFERENDUM – **on one's own initiative** without being prompted; independently of outside influence or control

inject /in'jekt/ *vt* **1a** to throw, drive, or force into sthg ⟨*~ fuel into an engine*⟩ **b** to force a fluid into **2** to introduce as an element or factor [L *injectus*, pp of *inicere*, fr *in-* + *jacere* to throw – more at [2]JET] – **injector** *n*

injection /in'jeksh(ə)n/ *n* **1a** injecting **b** the placing of an artificial satellite or a spacecraft into an orbit or on a trajectory **2** sthg (e g a medication) that is injected

injection moulding *n* the manufacture of rubber or plastic articles by injecting heated material into a mould – **injection-moulded** *adj*

injudicious /,injooh'dishəs/ *adj* indiscreet, unwise – **injudiciously** *adv*, **injudiciousness** *n*

Injun /'injən/ *n* a N American Indian – infml [alter. of *Indian*]

injunction /in'jungksh(ə)n/ *n* **1** an order, warning **2** a writ requiring sby to do or refrain from doing a particular act [MF & LL; MF *injonction*, fr LL *injunction-, injunctio*, fr L *injunctus*, pp of *injungere* to enjoin – more at ENJOIN] – **injunctive** *adj*

injure /'injə/ *vt* **1** to do injustice to **2a** to inflict bodily hurt on **b** to impair the soundness of **c** to inflict damage or loss on [back-formation fr *injury*]

injurious /in'jooəri·əs/ *adj* inflicting or tending to inflict injury – **injuriously** *adv*, **injuriousness** *n*

injury /'injəri/ *n* **1** a wrong **2** hurt, damage, or loss sustained [ME *injurie*, fr L *injuria*, fr *injurus* injurious, fr *in-* + *jur-, jus* right – more at JUST]

'**injury-,time** *n* time added on to the end of a match in soccer, rugby, etc to compensate for time lost through injuries to players

injustice /in'justis/ *n* (an act or state of) unfairness [ME, fr MF, fr L *injustitia*, fr *injustus* unjust, fr *in-* + *justus* just]

[1]**ink** /ingk/ *n* **1** a coloured liquid used for writing and printing **2** the black secretion of a squid or similar cephalopod mollusc that hides it from a predator or prey [ME *enke*, fr OF, fr LL *encaustum*, fr neut of L *encaustus* burned in, fr Gk *enkaustos*, verbal of *enkaiein* to burn in – more at ENCAUSTIC] – **inky** *adj*

[2]**ink** *vt* to apply ink to

inkblot test /'ingkblot/ *n* RORSCHACH TEST

'**ink ,cap** *n* any of several toadstools whose cap melts into an inky fluid after the spores have matured

inked /ingkt/ *adj, Austr & NZ* drunk, incapacitated – infml [*ink* (cheap wine), fr [1]*ink*]

[1]'**ink,horn** /-,hawn/ *n* a small portable bottle (e g of horn) for holding ink

[2]**inkhorn** *adj* ostentatiously pedantic ⟨*~ terms*⟩

inkling /'ingkling/ *n* **1** a faint indication **2** a slight knowledge or vague idea [ME *yngkiling*, prob fr *inclen* to hint at; akin to OE *inca* suspicion, Lith *ingis* sluggard]

'**ink,stand** /-,stand/ *n* a stand with fittings for holding ink and often pens

'**ink,well** /-,wel/ *n* a container (e g in a school desk) for ink

inlaid /in'layd/ *adj* **1** set into a surface in a decorative design ⟨*tables with ~ marble*⟩ **2** decorated with a design or material set into a surface ⟨*a table with an ~ top*⟩

[1]**inland** /'in,land, -lənd/ *adv or n* (into or towards) the interior part of a country

[2]**inland** /'inlənd/ *adj* **1** of the interior of a country **2** *chiefly Br* not foreign; domestic

inlander /'inləndə/ *n* one who lives inland

,**Inland 'Revenue** *n* the government department responsible for collecting taxes in Britain

'**in-,law** *n* a relative by marriage – infml ⟨*all her ~s turned up*⟩ [back-formation fr *mother-in-law*, etc]

[1]**inlay** /in'lay/ *vt* **inlaid** /-'layd/ **1** to set into a surface or ground material for decoration or reinforcement **2** to decorate with inlaid material

[2]**inlay** /'inlay/ *n* **1** inlaid work or a decorative inlaid pattern **2** a dental filling shaped to fit a cavity

inlet /'inlet, -lit/ *n* **1** a (long and narrow) recess in a shoreline or a water passage between 2 land areas **2** a means of entry; *esp* an opening for intake ⟨*a fuel ~*⟩ [fr its letting water in]

inlier /'in,lie·ə/ *n* an outcrop of rock surrounded by rock of younger age [[3]*in* + *-lier* (as in *outlier*)]

in loco parentis /in ,lohkoh pə'rentis/ *adv* in the place of and esp having the responsibilities of a parent [L]

inly /'inli/ *adv* inwardly, intimately – poetic

inmate /'inmayt/ *n* any of a group occupying a place of residence, esp a prison or hospital

in medias res /in ,meedias 'rayz/ *adv* in or into the middle of a narrative or plot [L, lit., into the middle of things]

in memoriam /,in mi'mawri·əm, -am/ *prep* in memory of [L]

inmost /'inmohst/ *adj* **1** furthest within **2** most intimate [ME, fr OE *innemest*, superl of *inne*, adv, in, within, fr *in*, adv]

inn /in/ *n* **1a** an establishment (e g a small hotel) providing lodging and food, esp for travellers **b** PUBLIC HOUSE **2** a residence formerly provided for students in London [ME, fr OE; akin to ON *inni* dwelling, inn, OE *in*, adv]

innards /ˈinədz/ *n pl* **1** the internal organs of a human being or animal; *esp* the viscera **2** the internal parts of a structure or mechanism *USE* infml [alter. of *inwards*]

innate /iˈnayt/ *adj* **1a** existing in or belonging to an individual from birth **b** inherent **c** originating in the intellect **2** ENDOGENOUS 2 [ME *innat*, fr L *innatus*, pp of *innasci* to be born in, fr *in-* + *nasci* to be born – more at NATION] – **innately** *adv*, **innateness** *n*

inner /ˈinə/ *adj* **1a** situated within; internal ⟨*an* ~ *chamber*⟩ **b** situated near to a centre, esp of influence ⟨*an* ~ *circle of government ministers*⟩ **2** of the mind or soul ⟨*the* ~ *life of man*⟩ [ME, fr OE *innera*, compar of *inne* within – more at INMOST] – **inner** *n*, **innermost** *adj*

inner city *n* a usu older and more densely populated central section of a city; *esp* such an area characterized by social problems – **inner-city** *adj*

inner ear *n* the innermost part of the ear from which sound waves are transmitted to the brain as nerve impulses ☞ NERVE

ˌinner ˈlight *n, often cap I&L* a divine influence held, esp in Quaker doctrine, to enlighten and guide the soul

inner man *n* **1** the soul, mind **2** the stomach, appetite

inner planet *n* any of the planets Mercury, Venus, Earth, and Mars that as a group have orbits nearer the sun than the outer planets

inner space *n* space at or near the earth's surface or under the sea

ˈinner ˌtube *n* an inflatable tube inside the casing of a pneumatic tyre

innervate /ˈinəvayt/ *vt* to supply with nerves – **innervation** /-ˈvaysh(ə)n/ *n*

inning /ˈining/ *n* a baseball team's turn at batting or a division of a baseball game consisting of a turn at batting for each team [[2]*in* + [2]*-ing*]

ˈinnings *n, pl* **innings** **1a** any of the alternating divisions of a cricket match during which one side bats and the other bowls **b** the (runs scored in or quality of the) turn of 1 player to bat **c** an unplayed innings of a side ⟨*won by an* ~ *and 32 runs*⟩ **2a** a period in which sby has opportunity for action or achievements **b** *chiefly Br* the duration of sby's life ⟨*he had a good* ~⟩

innkeeper /ˈinˌkeepə/ *n* the landlord of an inn

innocent /ˈinəs(ə)nt/ *adj* **1a** free from guilt or sin; pure **b** harmless in effect or intention ⟨*an* ~ *conversation*⟩ **c** free from legal guilt **2** lacking or deprived of sthg ⟨*a face* ~ *of make-up*⟩ **3a** artless, ingenuous **b** ignorant, unaware [ME, fr MF, fr L *innocent-*, *innocens*, fr *in-* + *nocent-*, *nocens* wicked, fr prp of *nocēre* to harm – more at NOXIOUS] – **innocence, innocency** *n*, **innocent** *n*, **innocently** *adv*

innocuous /iˈnokyoo·əs/ *adj* **1** having no harmful effects **2** inoffensive, insipid [L *innocuus*, fr *in-* + *nocēre*] – **innocuously** *adv*, **innocuousness** *n*

innominate /iˈnominət/ *adj* having no name; *also* anonymous – chiefly fml [LL *innominatus*, fr L *in-* + *nominatus*, pp of *nominare* to nominate]

innominate bone *n* the large bone composed of the ilium, ischium, and pubis that forms half of the pelvis in mammals; the hipbone

innovate /ˈinəvayt/ *vi* to make changes; introduce sthg new [L *innovatus*, pp of *innovare*, fr *in-* + *novus* new – more at NEW] – **innovative** *adj*, **innovator** *n*, **innovatory** *adj*, **innovation** /-ˈvaysh(ə)n/ *n*

ˌInns of ˈCourt *n pl* (4 buildings housing) 4 societies of students and barristers in London which have the exclusive right of admission to the English Bar

innuendo /ˌinyooˈendoh/ *n, pl* **innuendos, innuendoes** an oblique allusion; *esp* a veiled slight on sby's character or reputation [L, by hinting, fr *innuere* to hint, fr *in-* + *nuere* to nod – more at NUMEN]

innumerable /iˈnyoohmərəbl/ *adj* countless [ME, fr L *innumerabilis*, fr *in-* + *numerabilis* numerable] – **innumerably** *adv*

innumerate /iˈnyoohmərət/ *adj, Br* lacking understanding of the mathematical approach; not numerate – **innumerate** *n*, **innumeracy** *n*

inobservance /ˌinəbˈzuhvəns/ *n* **1** lack of attention **2** failure to observe a custom, rule, etc [F & L; F, fr L *inobservantia*, fr *in-* + *observantia* observance] – **inobservant** *adj*

inoculate /iˈnokyoolayt/ *vt* **1a** to introduce a microorganism into ⟨~ *mice with anthrax*⟩ **b** to introduce (e g a microorganism) into a culture, animal, etc for growth **c** VACCINATE 2 **2** to imbue [ME *inoculaten* to insert a bud in a plant, fr L *inoculatus*, pp of *inoculare*, fr *in-* + *oculus* eye, bud – more at EYE] – **inoculative** /-laytiv/ *adj*, **inoculator** *n*, **inoculation** /-ˈlaysh(ə)n/ *n*

inoculum /iˈnokyooləm/ *n, pl* **inocula** /-lə/ material used for inoculation [NL, fr L *inoculare*]

ˌin-ˈoff *n* the potting of one ball after it has touched another in billiards, snooker, etc [fr the phrase *in off (the red ball* or *the white ball)*]

inoffensive /ˌinəˈfensiv/ *adj* **1** not causing any harm; innocuous **2** not objectionable to the senses – **inoffensively** *adv*, **inoffensiveness** *n*

inoperable /inˈop(ə)rəbl/ *adj* **1** not suitable for surgery **2** impracticable [prob fr F *inopérable*]

inoperative /inˈop(ə)rətiv/ *adj* not functioning; having no effect

inopportune /ˌinopəˈtyoohn/ *adj* inconvenient, unseasonable [L *inopportunus*, fr *in-* + *opportunus* opportune] – **inopportunely** *adv*, **inopportuneness** *n*

in ˈorder that *conj* THAT 2(1)

inordinate /inˈawdinət/ *adj* exceeding reasonable limits [ME *inordinat*, fr L *inordinatus*, fr *in-* + *ordinatus*, pp of *ordinare* to put in order, arrange – more at ORDAIN] – **inordinately** *adv*

inorganic /ˌinawˈganik/ *adj* **1a** being or composed of matter other than plant or animal; mineral **b** of, being, or dealt with by a branch of chemistry concerned with inorganic substances **2** not arising through natural growth – **inorganically** *adv*

inosculate /iˈnoskyoolayt/ *vb* to unite by apposition or contact; blend [deriv of L *osculare* to provide with a mouth or outlet, fr *osculum*, dim. of *os* mouth] – **inosculation** /-ˈlaysh(ə)n/ *n*

inotropic /ˌienəˈtrohpik, ˌeenə-, -ˈtropik/ *adj* of or influencing the force of contraction of heart muscle [ISV *ino-* (fr Gk *in-*, *is* sinew) + *-tropic*]

inpatient /ˈinˌpaysh(ə)nt/ *n* a hospital patient who

receives lodging and food as well as treatment – compare OUTPATIENT

¹input /ˈinpoot/ *n* **1a** an amount coming or put in **b** sthg (e g energy, material, or data) supplied to a machine or system **c** a component of production (e g land, labour, or raw materials) **2** the point at which an input (e g of energy, material, or data) is made

²input *vt* **-tt-** to enter (e g data) into a computer or data-processing system ☞ COMPUTER

inquest /ˈin(g)kwest/ *n* **1** a judicial inquiry, esp by a coroner, into the cause of a death **2** an inquiry or investigation, esp into sthg that has failed [ME, fr OF *enqueste*, fr (assumed) VL *inquaestus*, pp of *inquaerere* to inquire]

inquietude /inˈkwie·ətyoohd/ *n* uneasiness, restlessness [ME, fr MF or LL; MF, fr LL *inquietudo*, fr L *inquietus* disturbed, fr *in-* + *quietus* quiet]

inquiline /ˈinkwilien/ *n* an animal (e g the cuckoo) that lives habitually in the abode of some other species [L *inquilinus* tenant, lodger, fr *in-* + *colere* to cultivate, dwell – more at WHEEL] – **inquiline** *adj*, **inquilinism** /-liniz(ə)m/ *n*, **inquilinous** /-ˈlienəs/ *adj*

inquire /inˈkwie·ə/ *vt* to ask about; ask to be told ~ *vi* **1** to seek information by questioning **2** to make a search or inquiry [ME *enquiren*, fr OF *enquerre*, fr (assumed) VL *inquaerere*, alter. of L *inquirere*, fr *in-* + *quaerere* to seek] – **inquirer** *n*, **inquiringly** *adv* – **inquire after** to ask about the health of

inquiry /inˈkwie·əri/ *n* **1** a request for information **2** a systematic investigation

inˈquiry ˌagent *n, Br* PRIVATE DETECTIVE

inquisition /ˌinkwiˈzish(ə)n/ *n* **1** the act of inquiring **2** a judicial or official inquiry **3a** *cap* a former Roman Catholic tribunal for the discovery and punishment of heresy **b** a ruthless investigation or examination [ME *inquisicioun*, fr MF *inquisition*, fr L *inquisition-*, *inquisitio*, fr *inquisitus*, pp of *inquirere*] – **inquisitional** *adj*

inquisitive /inˈkwizətiv/ *adj* **1** eager for knowledge or understanding **2** fond of making inquiries; *esp* unduly curious about the affairs of others – **inquisitively** *adv*, **inquisitiveness** *n*

inquisitor /inˈkwizitə/ *n* one who inquires or conducts an inquisition (harshly or with hostility)

inquisitorial /inˌkwiziˈtawri·əl/ *adj* of a system of criminal procedure in which the judge is also the prosecutor – compare ACCUSATORIAL – **inquisitorially** *adv*

in re /in ˈray/ *prep* in the matter of [L]

inroad /ˈinˌrohd/ *n* **1** a raid **2** a serious or forcible encroachment or advance ⟨*an illness made* ~s *on his savings*⟩

inrush /ˈinˌrush/ *n* a crowding or flooding in

insalubrious /ˌinsəˈl(y)oohbri·əs/ *adj* unhealthy ⟨*an* ~ *climate*⟩ [L *insalubris*, fr *in-* + *salubris* healthful – more at SAFE] – **insalubriously** *adv*, **insalubrity** *n*

ˌins and ˈouts *n pl* characteristic peculiarities and complexities; ramifications

insane /inˈsayn/ *adj* **1** mentally disordered; exhibiting insanity **2** typical of or intended for insane people ⟨*an* ~ *asylum*⟩ **3** utterly absurd [L *insanus*, fr *in-* + *sanus* sane] – **insanely** *adv*, **insanity** /inˈsanəti/ *n*

insanitary /inˈsanit(ə)ri/ *adj* unclean enough to endanger health; filthy, contaminated

insatiable /inˈsaysh(y)əbl/ *adj* incapable of being satisfied [ME *insaciable*, fr MF, fr L *insatiabilis*, fr *in-* + *satiare* to satisfy – more at SATIATE] – **insatiably** *adv*, **insatiability** /-ˈbiləti/ *n*

insatiate /inˈsayshi·ət/ *adj* insatiable

inscape /ˈinskayp/ *n* a unity perceived in natural objects that is expressed in literature [*in-* + *-scape* (as in *landscape*)]

inscribe /inˈskrieb/ *vt* **1a** to write, engrave, or print (as a lasting record) **b** to enter on a list; enrol **2** to address or dedicate to sby, esp by a handwritten note **3** to draw within a figure so as to touch at as many points as possible ⟨*a regular polygon* ~d *in a circle*⟩ [L *inscribere*, fr *in-* + *scribere* to write – more at SCRIBE] – **inscriber** *n*

inscription /inˈskripsh(ə)n/ *n* **1a** a title, superscription **b** EPIGRAPH 2 **c** LEGEND 2a **2** a handwritten dedication in a book or on a work of art **3a** the act of inscribing **b** the enrolment of a name (as if) on a list [ME *inscripcioun*, fr L *inscription-*, *inscriptio*, fr *inscriptus*, pp of *inscribere*] – **inscriptional** *adj*, **inscriptive** *adj*

inscrutable /inˈskroohtəbl/ *adj* hard to interpret or understand; enigmatic [ME, fr LL *inscrutabilis*, fr L *in-* + *scrutari* to search – more at SCRUTINY] – **inscrutableness** *n*, **inscrutably** *adv*, **inscrutability** /-təˈbiləti/ *n*

insect /ˈinsekt/ *n* **1** any of a class of arthropods with a well-defined head, thorax, and abdomen, only 3 pairs of legs, and typically 1 or 2 pairs of wings **2** any of various small invertebrate animals (e g woodlice and spiders) – not used technically **3** a worthless or insignificant person [L *insectum*, fr neut of *insectus*, pp of *insecare* to cut into, fr *in-* + *secare* to cut – more at ²SAW]

insectarium /ˌinsekˈteəri·əm/ *n, pl* **insectariums**, **insectaria** /-ri·ə/ an insectary

insectary /inˈsektəri/ *n* a place where insects are kept or reared

insecticide /inˈsektisied/ *n* sthg that destroys insects [ISV] – **insecticidal** /-ˈsiedl/ *adj*

insectivore /inˈsektiˌvaw/ *n* **1** any of an order of mammals including moles, shrews, and hedgehogs that are mostly small, nocturnal, and eat insects **2** an insect-eating plant or animal ☞ FOOD [deriv of L *insectum* + *-vorus* -vorous]

insecure /ˌinsiˈkyooə/ *adj* **1** lacking adequate protection or guarantee ⟨*an* ~ *job*⟩ **2** not firmly fixed or supported ⟨*the hinge is* ~⟩ **3a** not stable or well-adjusted ⟨*an* ~ *marriage*⟩ **b** deficient in assurance; beset by fear and anxiety [ML *insecurus*, fr L *in-* + *securus* secure] – **insecurely** *adv*, **insecurity** *n*

inseminate /inˈseminayt/ *vt* **1** sow 1b, 1c **2** to introduce semen into the genital tract of (a female) [L *inseminatus*, pp of *inseminare*, fr *in-* + *semin-*, *semen* seed – more at SEMEN] – **inseminator** *n*, **insemination** /-ˈnaysh(ə)n/ *n*

insensate /inˈsensayt, -sət/ *adj* **1** insentient **2** lacking in human feeling [LL *insensatus*, fr L *in-* + LL *sensatus* having sense, fr L *sensus* sense] – **insensately** *adv*

insensible /inˈsensəbl/ *adj* **1** incapable or bereft of feeling or sensation: e g **a** having lost consciousness **b** lacking or deprived of sensory perception ⟨~ *to pain*⟩ **2** incapable of being felt or sensed **3** lacking concern or awareness [ME, fr MF & L; MF, fr L *insensibilis*, fr *in-* + *sensibilis* sensible] – **insensibly** *adv*, **insensibility** /-səˈbiləti/ *n*

insensitive /inˈsensətiv/ *adj* **1** lacking the ability to respond to or sympathize with the needs or feelings of others **2** not physically or chemically sensitive ⟨~ *to light*⟩ – **insensitively** *adv*, **insensitiveness, insensitivity** /-'tivəti/ *n*

insentient /in'senshi·ənt/ *adj* not endowed with the capacity to perceive – **insentience** *n*

inseparable /in'sep(ə)rəbl/ *adj* incapable of being separated [ME, fr L *inseparabilis*, fr *in-* + *separabilis* separable] – **inseparable** *n*, **inseparably** *adv*, **inseparability** /-rə'biləti/ *n*

[1]**insert** /in'zuht, -'suht/ *vt* **1** to put or thrust in ⟨~ *a coin in a slot machine*⟩ **2** to put or introduce into the body of sthg ⟨~ *an advertisement in a newspaper*⟩ **3** to set in and make fast; *esp* to insert by sewing between 2 cut edges ~ *vi*, *of a muscle* to be in attachment to a specified part ⟨*muscles* ~ *on bone*⟩ [L *insertus*, pp of *inserere*, fr *in-* + *serere* to join – more at SERIES] – **inserter** *n*

[2]**insert** /'--/ *n* sthg (esp written or printed) inserted

insertion /in'zuhsh(ə)n, -'suh-/ *n* **1** the mode or place of attachment of an organ or part **2** embroidery or needlework inserted as ornament between 2 pieces of fabric **3** a single appearance of an advertisement (e g in a newspaper) [[1]INSERT + -ION] – **insertional** *adj*

,in-'service *adj*, *of training* undertaken in mid-career

[1]**inset** /'inset/ *n* sthg set in: e g **a** a small illustration set within a larger one **b** a piece of cloth set into a garment for decoration, shaping, etc

[2]**in'set** *vt* **-tt-; inset, insetted** to insert as an inset

inshore /in'shaw/ *adj or adv* (near or moving) towards the shore

[1]**inside** /in'sied/ *n* **1** an inner side or surface **2a** an interior or internal part ⟨*fire destroyed the* ~ *of the house*⟩ **b** inward nature, thoughts, or feeling **c** the middle or main part of a division of time ⟨*the* ~ *of a week*⟩ **d** viscera, entrails – usu pl with sing. meaning **3** a position of confidence or of access to confidential information **4** the middle portion of a playing area **5** the side of a pavement nearer the wall

[2]**inside** *adj* **1** of, on, near, or towards the inside ⟨*an* ~ *toilet*⟩ **2** of or being the inner side of a curve or being near the side of the road nearest the kerb or hard shoulder ⟨*driving on the* ~ *lane*⟩

[3]**inside** *prep* **1a** in or into the interior of **b** on the inner side of **2** within ⟨~ *an hour*⟩

[4]**inside** *adv* **1** to or on the inner side **2** in or into the interior **3** indoors **4** *chiefly Br* in or into prison – slang

inside job *n* a crime, esp a robbery, committed by or with the help of sby associated with (e g employed by) the victim – infml

,inside-'left *n* an attacking player to the left of the centre-forward in a traditional soccer lineup ☞ SPORT

in'side of *prep* **1** in less time than **2** *chiefly NAm* inside *USE* infml

,inside 'out *adv* **1** with the inner surface on the outside ⟨*turned his socks* ~⟩ **2** in a very thorough manner – infml ⟨*knows his subject* ~⟩

insider /in'siedə/ *n* sby recognized or accepted as a member of a group, category, or organization; *esp* one who has access to confidential information or is in a position of power

,inside-'right *n* an attacking player to the right of the centre-forward in a traditional soccer lineup ☞ SPORT

inside track *n* the inner lane of a curved racetrack

insidious /in'sidi·əs/ *adj* **1** harmful but enticing **2a** acting gradually and imperceptibly but with grave consequences **b** *of a disease* developing so gradually as to be well established before becoming apparent [L *insidiosus*, fr *insidiae* ambush, fr *insidēre* to sit in, sit on, fr *in-* + *sedēre* to sit – more at SIT] – **insidiously** *adv*, **insidiousness** *n*

insight /'in,siet/ *n* the power of or an act or result of discerning the true or underlying nature of sthg – **insightful** *adj*

insigne /in'signi/ *n*, *pl* **insignia** /in'signi·ə/ a badge of authority or honour [L, mark, badge, fr neut of *insignis* marked, distinguished, fr *in-* + *signum* mark, sign]

insignia /in'signi·ə/ *n pl in constr*, *pl* **insignia, insignias** badges of authority or honour – sometimes treated as sing. in American English

insignificant /,insig'nifikənt/ *adj* **1** lacking meaning or import; inconsequential **2** very small in size, amount, or number – **insignificance, insignificancy** *n*, **insignificantly** *adv*

insincere /,insin'siə/ *adj* hypocritical [L *insincerus*, fr *in-* + *sincerus* sincere] – **insincerely** *adv*, **insincerity** /-'serəti/ *n*

insinuate /in'sinyoo,ayt/ *vt* **1** to introduce (an idea) or suggest (sthg unpleasant) in a subtle or oblique manner **2** to gain acceptance for (e g oneself) by craft or stealth [L *insinuatus*, pp of *insinuare*, fr *in-* + *sinuare* to bend, curve, fr *sinus* curve] – **insinuative** *adj*, **insinuator** *n*

insinuation /in,sinyoo'aysh(ə)n/ *n* a sly and usu derogatory reference [INSINUATE + -ION]

insipid /in'sipid/ *adj* **1** devoid of any definite flavour **2** devoid of interesting or stimulating qualities [F & LL; F *insipide*, fr LL *insipidus*, fr L *in-* + *sapidus* savoury, fr *sapere* to taste – more at SAGE] – **insipidly** *adv*, **insipidity** /-si'pidəti/ *n*

insist /in'sist/ *vi* **1** to take a resolute stand **2** to place great emphasis or importance *on* sthg ~ *vt* to maintain persistently [MF or L; MF *insister*, fr L *insistere* to stand upon, persist, fr *in-* + *sistere* to stand; akin to L *stare* to stand – more at STAND]

insistent /in'sist(ə)nt/ *adj* **1** insisting forcefully or repeatedly; emphatic **2** demanding attention [L *insistent-*, *insistens*, prp of *insistere*] – **insistence** *n*, **insistently** *adv*

in situ /in 'sityooh/ *adv or adj* in the natural or original position [L, in position]

insobriety /,insə'brie·əti/ *n* intemperance, esp in drinking

,inso'far as /insə'fah, insoh'fah/ *conj* to the extent or degree that ⟨*I'll help you* ~ *I can*⟩

insolation /,insə'laysh(ə)n/ *n* solar radiation that has been received on a given surface [F or L; F, exposure to the sun, fr MF, fr L *insolation-*, *insolatio*, fr *insolatus*, pp of *insolare* to place in the sunlight, fr *in-* + *sol* sun – more at [1]SOLAR]

insole /'in,sohl/ *n* **1** an inside sole of a shoe **2** a strip the shape of the sole that is placed inside a shoe for warmth or comfort

insolent /'insələnt/ *adj* showing disrespectful rudeness; impudent [ME, fr L *insolent-*, *insolens*; akin to L *insolescere* to grow haughty] – **insolence** *n*, **insolently** *adv*

insoluble /in'solyoobl/ *adj* **1** having or admitting of no solution or explanation **2** (practically) incapable of being dissolved in liquid [ME *insolible*, fr L *insolubilis*, fr *in-* + *solvere* to free, dissolve – more at SOLVE] – **insoluble** *n*, **insolubleness** *n*, **insolubly** *adv*, **insolubility** /-'biləti/ *n*

insolvable /in'solvəbl/ *adj, chiefly NAm* impossible to solve ⟨*an apparently ~ problem*⟩ – **insolvably** *adv*

insolvent /in'solvənt/ *adj* **1** unable to pay debts as they fall due; *specif* having liabilities in excess of the value of assets held **2** relating to or for the relief of insolvents – **insolvency** *n*, **insolvent** *n*

insomnia /in'somni·ə/ *n* prolonged (abnormal) inability to obtain adequate sleep [L, fr *insomnis* sleepless, fr *in-* + *somnus* sleep – more at SOMNOLENT] – **insomniac** /-ak/ *adj or n*

inso'much that /insə'much, insoh'much/ *conj* to such a degree that

insouciance /in'soohsyəns (*Fr* ɛ̃suːsjɑ̃ːs)/ *n* lighthearted unconcern [F, fr *in-* + *soucier* to trouble, disturb, fr L *sollicitare*] – **insouciant** *adj*, **insouciantly** *adv*

inspect /in'spekt/ *vt* **1** to examine closely and critically; scrutinize **2** to view or examine officially [L *inspectus*, pp of *inspicere*, fr *in-* + *specere* to look – more at SPY] – **inspection** *n*, **inspective** *adj*

inspector /in'spektə/ *n* a police officer ranking immediately above a sergeant [INSPECT + [1]-OR] – **inspectorate** /-rət/ *n*, **inspectorship** *n*

inspiration /,inspi'raysh(ə)n/ *n* **1a** a divine influence or action on a person which qualifies him/her to receive and communicate sacred revelation **b** the action or power of stimulating the intellect or emotions **2** the drawing of air into the lungs **3a** being inspired **b** an inspired idea ⟨*I've had an ~, let's go to the seaside*⟩ **4** an inspiring agent or influence – **inspirational** *adj*, **inspirationally** *adv*, **inspiratory** *adj*

inspirator /'inspi,raytə/ *n* an injector, respirator, etc by which gas, vapour, etc is drawn in [INSPIRE + -ATOR]

inspire /in'spie·ə/ *vt* **1** to inhale **2a** to influence or guide by divine inspiration **b** to exert an animating or exalting influence on ⟨*was particularly* ~d *by the Impressionists*⟩ ⟨inspiring *music*⟩ **c** to act as a stimulus for ⟨*threats don't necessarily ~ people to work harder*⟩ ⟨*music* ~d *by a trip to Venice*⟩ **d** to affect – usu + *with* ⟨*seeing the old room again* ~d *him with nostalgia*⟩ **3** to communicate to an agent supernaturally ⟨*writings* ~d *by God*⟩ ~ *vi* to breathe in [ME *inspiren*, fr MF & L; MF *inspirer*, fr L *inspirare* to blow or breathe upon, fr *in-* + *spirare* to breathe – more at SPIRIT] – **inspirer** *n*

in'spired *adj* outstanding or brilliant in a way that suggests divine inspiration ⟨*gave an ~ rendering of the piano sonata*⟩

inspirit /in'spirit/ *vt* to animate, encourage

inspissate /in'spisayt/ *vt* to make thick or thicker, esp by condensation [LL *inspissatus*, pp of *inspissare*, fr L *in-* + *spissare* to thicken, fr *spissus* thick; akin to Gk *spidios* extended, L *spatium* space] – **inspissation** /-'saysh(ə)n/ *n*

instability /,instə'biləti/ *n* lack of (emotional or mental) stability

install /in'stawl/ *vt* **1** to induct into an office, rank, or order, esp with ceremonies or formalities ⟨~ed *the new department chairman*⟩ **2** to establish in a specified place, condition, or status **3** to place in usu permanent position for use or service ⟨*had a shower* ~ed *in the bathroom*⟩ [MF *installer*, fr ML *installare*, fr L *in-* + ML *stallum* stall, fr OHG *stal*] – **installer** *n*

installation /,instə'laysh(ə)n/ *n* **1** a device, apparatus, or piece of machinery fixed or fitted in place to perform some specified function ⟨*a new gas central-heating ~*⟩ **2** a military base or establishment ⟨*US ~*s *in Europe*⟩ [INSTALL + -ATION]

instalment, *NAm chiefly* **installment** /in'stawlmənt/ *n* **1** any of the parts into which a debt is divided when payment is made at intervals **2a** any of several parts (e g of a publication) presented at intervals **b** a single part of a serial story [alter. of earlier *estallment* payment by instalment, deriv of OF *estaler* to place, fix, fr *estal* place, of Gmc origin; akin to OHG *stal* place, stall]

[1]**instance** /'inst(ə)ns/ *n* **1** an example cited as an illustration or proof **2** the institution of a legal action ⟨*a court of first ~*⟩ **3** a situation viewed as 1 stage in a process or series of events ⟨*prefers, in this ~, to remain anonymous – TLS*⟩ **4** a solicitation, request – fml ⟨*am writing to you at the ~ of my client*⟩ [ME *instaunce*, fr MF *instance* act of urging, motive, instant, fr L *instantia* presence, urgency, fr *instant-, instans*] – **for instance** as an example

[2]**instance** *vt* **1** to exemplify by an instance **2** to put forward as a case or example; cite

instancy /'inst(ə)nsi/ *n* urgency, insistence

[1]**instant** /'inst(ə)nt/ *n* **1** an infinitesimal space of time; *esp* a point in time separating 2 states ⟨*at the ~ of death*⟩ **2** the present or current month [ME, fr ML *instant-, instans*, fr *instant-, instans*, adj, instant, fr L]

[2]**instant** *adj* **1a** present, current ⟨*previous felonies not related to the ~ crime*⟩ **b** of or occurring in the present month – used in commercial communications **2** immediate ⟨*the play was an ~ success*⟩ **3a(1)** premixed or precooked for easy final preparation ⟨*~ mashed potatoes*⟩ **(2)** appearing (as if) in ready-to-use form ⟨*updating your image with ~ beards, moustaches, and sideburns – Playboy*⟩ **b** immediately soluble in water ⟨*~ coffee*⟩ **4** demanding, urgent – fml [ME, fr MF or L; MF, fr L *instant-, instans*, fr prp of *instare* to stand upon, urge, fr *in-* + *stare* to stand – more at STAND]

instantaneous /,inst(ə)n'tayni·əs/ *adj* **1** done, occurring, or acting in an instant or instantly; IMMEDIATE 3 ⟨*death was ~*⟩ **2** occurring or present at a particular instant ⟨*~ velocity*⟩ [ML *instantaneus*, fr *instant-, instans*, n] – **instantaneously** *adv*, **instantaneousness, instantaneity** /,instantə'nayəti, -'nee·əti/ *n*

instanter /in'stantə/ *adv* instantly – fml [ML, fr L, earnestly, vehemently, fr *instant-, instans*]

instantiate /in'stanshiayt/ *vt* to represent (an abstraction) by a concrete instance – **instantiation** /-'aysh(ə)n/ *n*

instantly /'inst(ə)ntli/ *adv* immediately; AT ONCE

instar /'in,stah/ *n* (an insect or similar arthropod in) a (particular) stage between successive moults [NL, fr L, equivalent, figure; akin to L *instare* to stand upon]

instate /in'stayt/ *vt* to set or establish in a rank or office

instauration /,instaw'raysh(ə)n/ *n* restoration after decay or a lapse – fml [L *instauration-, instauratio*, fr *instauratus*, pp of *instaurare* to renew, restore – more at STORE]

instead /in'sted/ *adv* as a substitute or alternative ⟨*was going to write but called* ~⟩ ⟨*sent his son* ~⟩ – compare STEAD

in'stead of *prep* as a substitute for or alternative to [ME *in sted of*]

instep /'in,step/ *n* **1** (the upper surface of) the arched middle portion of the human foot **2** the part of a shoe or stocking over the instep [perh fr *in* + *step*]

instigate /'instigayt/ *vt* **1** to goad or urge forwards; provoke, incite **2** to initiate (a course of action or procedure, e g a legal investigation) [L *instigatus*, pp of *instigare* – more at ³STICK] – **instigator** *n*, **instigation** /-'gaysh(ə)n/ *n*

instil, *NAm chiefly* **instill** /in'stil/ *vt* **-ll- 1** to cause to enter drop by drop ⟨~ *medication into the infected eye*⟩ **2** to impart gradually ⟨~ling *in children a love of learning*⟩ – + *in* or *into* [MF & L; MF *instiller*, fr L *instillare*, fr *in-* + *stillare* to drip, trickle – more at DISTIL] – **instillment, instillation** /,insti'laysh(ə)n/ *n*

¹instinct /'instingkt/ *n* **1** a natural or inherent aptitude, impulse, or capacity ⟨*had an* ~ *for the right word*⟩ **2** (a largely inheritable tendency of an organism to make a complex and specific) response to environmental stimuli without involving reason [ME, fr L *instinctus* impulse, fr *instinctus*, pp of *instinguere* to incite; akin to L *instigare* to instigate] – **instinctive** *adj*, **instinctively** *adv*, **instinctual** *adj*

²instinct *adj* imbued, infused – fml ⟨~ *with patriotism*⟩

¹institute /'instityooht/ *vt* **1** to instate **2** to originate and establish; inaugurate ⟨~d *many social reforms*⟩ [ME *instituten*, fr L *institutus*, pp of *instituere*, fr *in-* + *statuere* to set up – more at STATUTE]

²institute *n* sthg instituted: e g **a(1)** an elementary principle recognized as authoritative **(2)** *pl* a (legal) compendium **b** (the premises used by) an organization for the promotion of a cause ⟨*an* ~ *for the blind*⟩ **c** an educational institution

institute of education *n, often cap I&E* any of 20 institutions that oversee teacher training in England and Wales

institution /,insti'tyoohsh(ə)n/ *n* **1** an established practice in a culture ⟨*the* ~ *of marriage*⟩; *also* a familiar object **2** an established organization or (public) body (e g a university or hospital) [¹INSTITUTE + -ION] – **institutional** *adj*

institutionalism /insti'tyoohsh(ə)nl,iz(ə)m/ *n* emphasis on organization (e g in religion) at the expense of other factors

institutional·ize, -ise /insti'tyoohsh(ə)nl,iez/ *vt* **1** to make into an institution ⟨~d *phrases*⟩ **2a** to put or keep in an institution **b** to allow to acquire personality traits typical of people in an institution – **institutionalization** /-'zaysh(ə)n/ *n*

instruct /in'strukt/ *vt* **1** to teach **2a** to direct authoritatively **b** COMMAND 1 **3** to engage (a lawyer, specif a barrister) for a case [ME *instructen*, fr L *instructus*, pp of *instruere*, fr *in-* + *struere* to build – more at STRUCTURE]

instruction /in'struksh(ə)n/ *n* **1a** ORDER 7b, COMMAND 1 – often pl with sing. meaning ⟨*had* ~s *not to admit strangers*⟩ **b** *pl* an outline or manual of technical procedure **c** a code that tells a computer to perform a particular operation **2** teaching – **instructional** *adj*

instructive /in'struktiv/ *adj* carrying a lesson; enlightening – **instructively** *adv*, **instructiveness** *n*

instructor /in'struktə/, *fem* **instructress** /-tris/ *n* a teacher: e g **a** a teacher of a technical or practical subject ⟨*a swimming* ~⟩ **b** *NAm* a college teacher below professorial rank [INSTRUCT + ¹-OR] – **instructorship** *n*

¹instrument /'instrəmənt/ *n* **1a** a means whereby sthg is achieved, performed, or furthered **b** a dupe; TOOL 3 **2** an implement, tool, or device designed esp for delicate work or measurement ⟨*scientific* ~s⟩ **3** a device used to produce music **4** a formal legal document **5** an electrical or mechanical device used in navigating an aircraft [ME, fr L *instrumentum*, fr *instruere* to arrange, instruct]

²instrument *vt* to orchestrate

¹instrumental /,instrə'mentl/ *adj* **1a** serving as an instrument, means, agent, or tool ⟨*was* ~ *in organizing the strike*⟩ **b** of or done with an instrument or tool **2** relating to, composed for, or performed on a musical instrument **3** of or being a grammatical case or form expressing means or agency – **instrumentally** *adv*

²instrumental *n* a musical composition or passage for instruments but not voice

instrumentalist /,instrə'mentl,ist/ *n* a player on a musical instrument

instrumentality /,instrəmen'taləti/ *n* a means, agency [¹INSTRUMENTAL + -ITY]

instrumentation /,instrəmən'taysh(ə)n, -men-/ *n* the arrangement or composition of music for instruments

'instrument ,panel *n* a panel on which instruments are mounted; *esp* a dashboard

insubordinate /,insə'bawdinət/ *adj* unwilling to submit to authority – **insubordinately** *adv*, **insubordination** /-'naysh(ə)n/ *n*

insubstantial /,insəb'stansh(ə)l/ *adj* **1** lacking substance or material nature; unreal **2** lacking firmness or solidity; flimsy [prob fr F *insubstantiel*, fr LL *insubstantialis*, fr L *in-* + LL *substantialis* substantial] – **insubstantiality** /-shi'aləti/ *n*

insufferable /in'suf(ə)rəbl/ *adj* intolerable ⟨*an* ~ *bore*⟩ – **insufferably** *adv*

insufficiency /,insə'fish(ə)nsi/ *n* being insufficient; *specif* inability of an organ or body part (e g the heart or kidneys) to function normally

insufficient /,insə'fish(ə)nt/ *adj* deficient in power, capacity, or competence [ME, fr MF, fr LL *insufficient-*, *insufficiens*, fr L *in-* + *sufficient-*, *sufficiens* sufficient] – **insufficiently** *adv*

insufflate /'insu,flayt/ *vt* **1** to blow on or into **2** to blow (e g a powder or gas), esp into a cavity *USE* fml [LL *insufflatus*, pp of *insufflare*, fr L *in-* + *sufflare* to blow up, fr *sub-* up + *flare* to blow – more at SUB-, ¹BLOW] – **insufflator** *n*, **insufflation** /-'flaysh(ə)n/ *n*

insular /'insyoolə/ *adj* **1** of or being an island **2a** of island people **b** that results (as if) from lack of contact with other peoples or cultures; narrow-minded **3** of an island of cells or tissue [LL *insularis*, fr L *insula* island] – **insularism** *n*, **insularly** *adv*, **insularity** /-'larəti/ *n*

insulate /'insyoolayt/ *vt* to place in a detached situation; *esp* to separate from conducting bodies by means of nonconductors so as to prevent transfer of electricity, heat, or sound [L *insula* island]

insulation /,insyoo'laysh(ə)n/ *n* **1** insulating or being insulated ☞ ENERGY **2** material used in insulating [INSULATE + -ION]
insulator /'insyoo,laytə/ *n* (a device made from) a material that is a poor conductor of electricity and is used for separating or supporting conductors to prevent undesired flow of electricity [INSULATE + [1]-OR]
insulin /'insyoo,lin/ *n* a protein pancreatic hormone secreted by the islets of Langerhans that is essential esp for the metabolism of carbohydrates and is used in the treatment of diabetes mellitus [NL *insula* islet (of Langerhans), fr L, island]
[1]**insult** /in'sult/ *vt* to treat with insolence, indignity, or contempt; *also* to cause offence or damage to ⟨*arguments that ~ the reader's intelligence*⟩ [MF or L; MF *insulter*, fr L *insultare*, lit., to spring upon, fr *in-* + *saltare* to leap – more at SALTIRE] – **insultingly** *adv*
[2]**insult** /'insult/ *n* **1** an act of insulting; sthg that insults **2** (sthg that causes) injury to the body or 1 of its parts ⟨*pollution and other environmental ~s*⟩
insuperable /in's(y)oohprəbl/ *adj* incapable of being surmounted, overcome, or passed over ⟨*~ difficulties*⟩ [ME, fr MF & L; MF, fr L *insuperabilis*, fr *in-* + *superare* to surmount, fr *super* over – more at OVER] – **insuperably** *adv*
insupportable /,insə'pawtəbl/ *adj* **1** unendurable ⟨*~ pain*⟩ **2** incapable of being sustained ⟨*~ charges*⟩ [MF or LL; MF, fr LL *insupportabilis*, fr L *in-* + *supportare* to support] – **insupportably** *adv*
insurance /in'shooərəns, -'shaw-/ *n* **1** insuring or being insured **2a** the business of insuring people or property **b** (the protection offered by) a contract whereby one party undertakes to indemnify or guarantee another against loss by a particular contingency or risk **c(1)** the premium demanded under such a contract **(2)** the sum for which sthg is insured
insure /in'shooə, in'shaw/ *vt* **1** to give, take, or procure insurance on or for **2** *chiefly NAm* to ensure ~ *vi* to contract to give or take insurance; *specif* to underwrite [ME *insuren*, prob alter. of *assuren* to assure] – **insurable** *adj*, **insurer** *n*
in'sured *n, pl* **insured** sby whose life or property is insured
insurgent /in'suhj(ə)nt/ *n* a rebel [L *insurgent-*, *insurgens*, prp of *insurgere* to rise up, fr *in-* + *surgere* to rise – more at SURGE] – **insurgence, insurgency** *n*, **insurgent** *adj*
insurmountable /,insə'mowntəbl/ *adj* insuperable ⟨*~ problems*⟩ – **insurmountably** *adv*
insurrection /,insə'reksh(ə)n/ *n* (a) revolt against civil authority or established government [ME, fr MF, fr LL *insurrection-*, *insurrectio*, fr *insurrectus*, pp of *insurgere*] – **insurrectional** *adj*, **insurrectionary** *adj or n*, **insurrectionist** *n*
inswing /'in,swing/ *n* the swing of a bowled cricket ball from the off to the leg side – compare OUTSWING – **inswinger** *n*
intact /in'takt/ *adj* **1** untouched, esp by anything that harms or diminishes; whole, uninjured **2a** being a virgin **b** not castrated [ME *intacte*, fr L *intactus*, fr *in-* + *tactus*, pp of *tangere* to touch – more at TANGENT]
intaglio /in'tahlioh/ *n, pl* **intaglios** **1a** (the act or process of producing) an incised or engraved design made in hard material, esp stone, and sunk below the surface of the material **b** printing done from a plate engraved in intaglio **2** sthg (e g a gem) carved in intaglio [It, fr *intagliare* to engrave, cut, fr ML *intaliare*, fr L *in-* + LL *taliare* to cut – more at TAILOR]
intake /'in,tayk/ *n* **1** an opening through which liquid or gas enters an enclosure or system **2a** a taking in **b(1)** *sing or pl in constr* an amount or number taken in **(2)** sthg taken in
Intal /'intal/ *trademark* – used for sodium cromoglycate
intangible /in'tanjəbl/ *n or adj* (sthg) not tangible [adj F or ML; F, fr ML *intangibilis*, fr L *in-* + LL *tangibilis* tangible; n fr adj] – **intangibly** *adv*, **intangibility** /-jə'biləti/ *n*
intarsia /in'tahsi·ə/ *n* inlaid mosaic work of wood [G, modif of It *intarsio*]
integer /'intijə/ *n* the number 1 or any number (e g 6, 0, -23) obtainable by once or repeatedly adding 1 to or subtracting 1 from the number 1 [L, adj, whole, entire – more at ENTIRE]
integrable /'intigrəbl/ *adj* capable of being integrated – **integrability** /-'biləti/ *n*
[1]**integral** /'intigrəl; *esp in maths* in'tegrəl/ *adj* **1a** essential to completeness; constituent – chiefly in *integral part* **b** of a mathematical integer, integral, or integration **c** formed as a unit with another part **2** composed of integral parts **3** lacking nothing essential; whole – **integrally** *adv*, **integrality** /,inti'graləti/ *n*
[2]**integral** *n* **1** a mathematical expression denoting a definite integral or an indefinite integral ☞ SYMBOL **2** a solution of a differential equation
integral calculus *n* a branch of mathematics dealing with methods of finding indefinite integrals and with their applications (e g to the determination of lengths, areas, and volumes and to the solution of differential equations)
integrand /'inti,grand/ *n* a mathematical expression to be integrated [L *integrandus*, gerundive of *integrare*]
integrate /'intigrayt/ *vt* **1** to form or blend into a whole **2a** to combine together or with sthg else **b** to incorporate into a larger unit – usu + *into* **3** to find the integral of (e g a function or differential equation) **4** to end the segregation of or in ~ *vi* **1** to become integrated **2** to calculate an integral [L *integratus*, pp of *integrare*, fr *integr-*, *integer*] – **integrative** *adj*
,integrated 'circuit *n* an electronic circuit formed in or on a single tiny slice of semiconductor material (e g silicon) – **integrated circuitry** *n*
integration /,inti'graysh(ə)n/ *n* **1a** ending of segregation **b** coordination of mental processes **2a** the operation of finding a function whose differential is known **b** the operation of solving a differential equation [INTEGRATE + -ION]
,inte'grationist /-ist/ *n* an advocate of social integration
integrator /'intigraytə/ *n* a device (e g in a computer) whose output corresponds to a mathematical integral [INTEGRATE + [1]-OR]
integrity /in'tegrəti/ *n* **1** an unimpaired condition **2** uncompromising adherence to a code of esp moral or artistic values **3** the quality or state of being com-

plete or undivided ⟨*the ~ of the Empire was threatened*⟩

integument /in'tegyoomənt/ *n* a skin, membrane, husk, or other covering or enclosure, esp of (part of) a living organism [L *integumentum*, fr *integere* to cover, fr *in-* + *tegere* to cover – more at THATCH] – **integumental** /-'mentl/ *adj*, **integumentary** /-'ment(ə)ri/ *adj*

intellect /'int(ə)lekt/ *n* the capacity for intelligent thought, esp when highly developed [ME, fr MF or L; MF, fr L *intellectus*, fr *intellectus*, pp of *intellegere* to understand – more at INTELLIGENT]

intellection /,int(ə)l'eksh(ə)n/ *n* thought, reasoning – **intellective** *adj*

[1]**intellectual** /,int(ə)l'ektyoo·əl, -chəl/ *adj* **1a** of the intellect **b** developed or chiefly guided by the intellect rather than by emotion or experience ⟨*a coldly ~ artist*⟩ **2** given to or requiring the use of the intellect – **intellectualize** *vb*, **intellectually** *adv*, **intellectuality** /-'aləti/ *n*

[2]**intellectual** *n* an intellectual person

,**intell'ectual,ism** /-,iz(ə)m/ *n* (excessive) devotion to the exercise of intellect or to intellectual pursuits – **intellectualist** *n*

intelligence /in'telij(ə)ns/ *n* **1** the ability to learn, apply knowledge, or think abstractly, esp in allowing one to deal with new or trying situations; *also* the skilled use of intelligence or reason **2** the act of understanding **3a** news; INFORMATION 2a, c **b** (a group of people who gather) information concerning an enemy [ME, fr MF, fr L *intelligentia*, fr *intelligent-, intelligens* intelligent]

intelligence quotient *n* a number expressing the ratio of sby's intelligence as determined by a test to the average for his/her age

intelligencer /in'telij(ə)nsə/ *n* a bringer of news; REPORTER b

intelligence test *n* a test designed to determine relative mental capacity

intelligent /in'telij(ə)nt/ *adj* having or indicating esp high intelligence [L *intelligent-, intelligens*, prp of *intelligere, intellegere* to understand, fr *inter-* + *legere* to gather, select – more at LEGEND] – **intelligently** *adv*

intelligentsia /in,teli'jentsi·ə/ *n sing or pl in constr* the intellectuals who form an artistic, social, or political vanguard [Russ *intelligentsiya*, fr L *intelligentia* intelligence]

intelligible /in'telijəbl/ *adj* **1** capable of being understood **2** able to be apprehended by the intellect only [ME, fr L *intelligibilis*, fr *intelligere*] – **intelligibly** *adv*, **intelligibility** /-jə'biləti/ *n*

intemperate /in'temp(ə)rət/ *adj* not temperate; *esp* going beyond the bounds of reasonable behaviour [ME *intemperat*, fr L *intemperatus*, fr *in-* + *temperatus*, pp of *temperare* to temper] – **intemperately** *adv*, **intemperateness** *n*

intend /in'tend/ *vt* **1** to mean, signify **2a** to have in mind as a purpose or goal **b** to design for a specified use or future ⟨*poems ~ed for reading aloud*⟩ [ME *entenden, intenden*, fr MF *entendre* to purpose, fr L *intendere* to stretch out, to purpose, fr *in-* + *tendere* to stretch – more at THIN]

intendant /in'tend(ə)nt/ *n* an administrative official, esp under the French, Spanish, or Portuguese monarchies [F, fr MF, fr L *intendent-, intendens*, prp of *intendere* to intend, attend]

in'tended *n* one's future spouse ⟨*she was his ~*⟩ – infml

intendment /in'tendmənt/ *n* the true (legal) intention

intense /in'tens/ *adj* **1a** existing or occurring in an extreme degree **b** having or showing a usual characteristic in extreme degree **2** INTENSIVE a **3a** feeling emotion deeply, esp by nature or temperament **b** deeply felt [ME, fr MF, fr L *intensus*, fr pp of *intendere* to stretch out] – **intensely** *adv*, **intenseness** *n*

intensifier /in'tensi,fie·ə/ *n* a linguistic element (e g *very*) that gives force or emphasis [INTENSIFY + [2]-ER]

intensify /in'tensi,fie/ *vb* to make or become (more) intense – **intensification** /-fi'kaysh(ə)n/ *n*

intension /in'tensh(ə)n/ *n* **1** intensity **2** a connotation – **intensional** *adj*

intensity /in'tensəti/ *n* **1** extreme degree of strength, force, or energy **2** the magnitude of force or energy per unit (e g of surface, charge, or mass) **3** SATURATION 1 [INTENSE + -ITY]

[1]**intensive** /in'tensiv/ *adj* of or marked by intensity or intensification: e g **a** highly concentrated **b** constituting or relating to a method designed to increase productivity by the expenditure of more capital and labour rather than by increase in the land or raw materials used ⟨*~ farming*⟩ – **intensively** *adv*

[2]**intensive** *n* an intensifier

[1]**intent** /in'tent/ *n* **1a** the act or fact of intending **b** the state of mind with which an act is done **2** criminal intention ⟨*loitering with ~*⟩ **3** meaning, significance [ME *entent*, fr OF, fr LL *intentus*, fr L, act of stretching out, fr *intentus*, pp of *intendere*] – **to all intents and purposes** in every practical or important respect; virtually

[2]**intent** *adj* **1** directed with strained or eager attention; concentrated **2** having the mind, attention, or will concentrated *on* sthg or some end or purpose ⟨*~ on his work*⟩ [L *intentus*, fr pp of *intendere*] – **intently** *adv*, **intentness** *n*

intention /in'tensh(ə)n/ *n* **1** a determination to act in a certain way; a resolve **2** *pl* purpose with respect to proposal of marriage **3a** what one intends to do or bring about; an aim **b** the object for which religious devotion is offered **4** a concept

intentional /in'tensh(ə)nl/ *adj* done by intention or design – **intentionally** *adv*

[1]**inter** /in'tuh/ *vt* **-rr-** to deposit (a dead body) in the earth or a tomb [ME *enteren*, fr OF *enterrer*, fr (assumed) VL *interrare*, fr *in-* + L *terra* earth – more at TERRACE]

[2]**inter** *n* any of various intermediate examinations – infml [short for *intermediate*]

inter- /intə-/ *prefix* **1** between; among; in the midst ⟨inter*city*⟩ ⟨inter*penetrate*⟩ ⟨inter*stellar*⟩ **2a** reciprocal ⟨inter*relation*⟩ **b** reciprocally ⟨inter*marry*⟩ **3** located between ⟨inter*face*⟩ **4** carried on between ⟨inter*national*⟩ **5** occurring between ⟨inter*glacial*⟩ ⟨inter*lunar*⟩ [ME *inter-, enter-*, fr MF & L; MF *inter-, entre-*, fr L *inter-*, fr *inter*; akin to OHG *untar* between, among, Gk *enteron* intestine, OE *in* in]

interact /,intə'rakt/ *vi* to act upon each other – **interactant** *n*, **interaction** *n*

interactive /,intə'raktiv/ *adj* characterized by interaction, specif by the exchange of information between a computer and user while a program is being run

inter alia /ˌintə ˈrayli·ə/ *adv* among other things [L]

ˌinteraˈtomic /-əˈtomik/ *adj* existing or acting between atoms

ˌinterˈbreed /-ˈbreed/ *vb* **interbred** /-ˈbred/ *vi* **1** to crossbreed **2** to breed within a closed population ~ *vt* to cause to interbreed

intercalary /inˈtuhkəl(ə)ri/ *adj* **1a** inserted in a calendar to resynchronize it with some objective time-measure (e g the solar year) **b** *of a year* containing an intercalary period **2** inserted between other elements or layers; interpolated [L *intercalarius*, fr *intercalare*]

intercalate /inˈtuhkəˌlayt/ *vt* to insert between or among existing items, elements, or layers [L *intercalatus*, pp of *intercalare*, fr *inter-* + *calare* to call, summon – more at [1]LOW] – **intercalation** /-ˈlaysh(ə)n/ *n*

intercede /ˌintəˈseed/ *vi* to beg or plead on behalf of another with a view to reconciling differences [L *intercedere*, fr *inter-* + *cedere* to go – more at CEDE]

ˌinterˈcellular /-ˈselyoolə/ *adj* occurring between cells ⟨~ *spaces*⟩

[1]**ˌinterˈcept** /-ˈsept/ *vt* **1** to stop, seize, or interrupt in progress, course, or movement, esp from one place to another **2** to intersect [L *interceptus*, pp of *intercipere*, fr *inter-* + *capere* to take, seize – more at HEAVE] – **interception** *n*

[2]**ˈinterˌcept** *n* **1** the distance from the origin to a point where a graph crosses a coordinate axis **2** an interception

ˈinterˌceptor, intercepter /-ˌseptə/ *n* a high-speed fast-climbing fighter plane or missile designed for defence against raiding bombers or missiles [[1]INTERCEPT + [1]-OR, [2]-ER]

ˌinterˈcession /-ˈsesh(ə)n/ *n* the act of interceding, esp by prayer, petition, or entreaty [MF or L; MF, fr L *intercession-*, *intercessio*, fr *intercessus*, pp of *intercedere*] – **intercessional** *adj*, **intercessor** *n*, **intercessory** *adj*

[1]**ˌinterˈchange** /-ˈchaynj/ *vt* **1** to put each of (2 things) in the place of the other **2** EXCHANGE 1 ~ *vi* to change places reciprocally [ME *entrechaungen*, fr MF *entrechangier*, fr OF, fr *entre-* inter- + *changier* to change] – **interchangeable** *adj*, **interchangeably** *adv*, **interchangeability** /-jəˈbiləti/ *n*

[2]**ˈinterˌchange** *n* **1** (an) interchanging **2** a junction of 2 or more roads having a system of separate levels that permit traffic to pass from one to another without the crossing of traffic streams

ˌinterˈcity /-ˈsiti/ *adj* existing or travelling (quickly) between cities

ˌintercolˈlegiate /-kəˈleeji·ət/ *adj* between colleges ⟨~ *athletics*⟩

ˈinterˌcom /-ˌkom/ *n* a local communication system (e g in a ship or building) with a microphone and loudspeaker at each station [short for *intercommunication (system)*]

ˌinterconˈnect /-kəˈnekt/ *vb* to connect with one another – **interconnection** *n*

ˌinterˌcontiˈnental /-ˌkontiˈnentl/ *adj* extending among continents; *also* carried on or (capable of) travelling between continents ⟨~ *ballistic missile*⟩

ˌinterˈcostal /-ˈkostl/ *adj* (of a part) situated between the ribs [NL *intercostalis*, fr L *inter-* + *costa* rib] – **intercostal** *n*

ˈinterˌcourse /-ˌkaws/ *n* **1** connection or dealings between people or groups **2** exchange, esp of thoughts or feelings **3** physical sexual contact between individuals that involves the genitals of at least 1 person ⟨*oral* ~⟩; *esp* SEXUAL INTERCOURSE a [ME *intercurse*, prob fr MF *entrecours*, fr ML *intercursus*, fr L, act of running between, fr *intercursus*, pp of *intercurrere* to run between, fr *inter-* + *currere* to run – more at CURRENT]

ˈinterˌcrop /-ˌkrop/ *vb* **-pp-** *vt* to grow a crop in between rows, plots, etc of (another crop) ~ *vi* to grow 2 or more crops simultaneously on the same plot – **intercrop** *n*

ˈinterˌcross /-ˌkros/ *n* (a product of) crossbreeding – **intercross** /--ˈ-/ *vb*

ˌinterˈcurrent /-ˈkurənt/ *adj* intervening; *esp* occurring during the course of another disease [L *intercurrent-*, *intercurrens*, prp of *intercurrere*] – **intercurrently** *adv*

ˌinterˈcut /-ˈkut/ *vb* **-tt-; intercut** *vt* **1** to insert a contrasting camera shot into (a film sequence) by cutting; *broadly* to insert contrasting matter into **2** to insert (a contrasting camera shot) into a film sequence by cutting; *broadly* to insert (contrasting matter) into a narrative ~ *vi* to alternate contrasting camera shots by cutting

ˌinterˌdepartˈmental /-ˌdeepahtˈmentl/ *adj* carried on between or involving different departments (e g of a firm or an educational institution) – **interdepartmentally** *adv*

ˌinterdeˈpend /-diˈpend/ *vi* to depend on each other – **interdependence, interdependency** *n*, **interdependent** *adj*

[1]**ˈinterˌdict** /-ˌdikt/ *n* **1** a Roman Catholic disciplinary measure withdrawing most sacraments and Christian burial from a person or district **2** a prohibition [ME *entredit*, fr OF, fr L *interdictum* prohibition, praetorian interdict, fr neut of *interdictus*, pp of *interdicere* to interpose, forbid, fr *inter-* + *dicere* to say – more at DICTION]

[2]**ˌinterˈdict** *vt* to forbid in a usu formal or authoritative manner – **interdiction** /-ˈdiksh(ə)n/ *n*, **interdictory** /-ˈdiktəri/ *adj*

ˌinterˈdisciplinary /-ˈdisiplinəri/ *adj* involving 2 or more disciplines or fields of study

[1]**interest** /ˈint(ə)rest, -rəst/ *n* **1a(1)** right, title, or legal share in sthg **(2)** participation in advantage and responsibility **b** a business in which one has an interest **2** benefit; ADVANTAGE 2; *specif* self-interest ⟨*it is to your* ~ *to speak first*⟩ **3a** a charge for borrowed money, generally a percentage of the amount borrowed **b** sthg added above what is due **4** a financially interested group **5a** readiness to be concerned with, moved by, or have one's attention attracted by sthg; curiosity **b** (the quality in) a thing that arouses interest ⟨*sport doesn't hold much* ~ *for me*⟩ ⟨*has many* ~*s*⟩ [ME, prob alter. of earlier *interesse*, fr AF & ML; AF, fr ML, fr L, to be between, make a difference, concern, fr *inter-* + *esse* to be – more at IS]

[2]**interest** *vt* **1** to induce or persuade to participate or engage, esp in an enterprise **2** to concern or engage (sby, esp oneself) *in* an activity or cause **3** to engage the attention or arouse the interest of

ˈinterested *adj* **1** having the interest aroused or

attention engaged **2** affected or involved; not impartial – **interestedly** *adv*

interesting /ˈint(ə)resting/ *adj* holding the attention – **interestingly** *adv*

1'inter,face /-ˌfays/ *n* **1** a surface forming a common boundary of 2 bodies, regions, or phases ⟨*an oil-water* ~⟩ **2** the place at which (diverse) independent systems meet and act on or communicate with each other ⟨*the man-machine* ~⟩ – **interfacial** /-ˈfaysh(ə)l/ *adj*

2,inter'face *vt* **1** to connect by means of an interface ⟨~ *a machine with a computer*⟩ **2** to serve as an interface for ~ *vi* **1** to become interfaced **2** to serve as an interface

'inter,facing /-ˌfaysing/ *n* stiffening material attached between 2 layers of fabric

,inter'fere /-ˈfiə/ *vi* **1** to get in the way of, hinder, or impede another – + *with* ⟨*noise* ~s *with my work*⟩ **2** to enter into or take a part in matters that do not concern one **3** *of sound, light, etc waves* to act so as to augment, diminish, or otherwise affect one another **4** to claim priority for an invention **5** to hinder illegally an attempt of a player to catch or hit a ball or puck – usu + *with* [MF *(s')entreferir* to strike one another, fr OF, fr *entre-* inter- + *ferir* to strike, fr L *ferire* – more at ¹BORE]

,inter'ference /-ˈfiərəns/ *n* **1** the phenomenon resulting from the meeting of 2 wave trains (e g of light or sound) with an increase in intensity at some points and a decrease at others **2** the illegal hindering of an opponent in hockey, ice hockey, etc **3** (sthg that produces) the confusion of received radio signals by unwanted signals or noise [INTERFERE + -ENCE] – **interferential** /-fəˈrensh(ə)l/ *adj*

,interfe'rometer /-fəˈromitə/ *n* an instrument that uses light interference phenomena for precise determination of wavelength, distance, etc [ISV] – **interferometric** /-ˌfiərəˈmetrik/ *adj*, **interferometry** /-fəˈromitri, -fiə-/ *n*

,inter'feron /-ˈfiəron/ *n* a protein that inhibits the development of viruses and is produced by cells in response to infection by a virus [*interfer*ence + *-on*]

,inter'file /-ˈfiel/ *vt* ³FILE 1 ~ *vi* ³FILE; *also* to fit in with an existing file

,inter'fuse /-ˈfyoohz/ *vt* to blend, infuse [L *interfusus*, pp of *interfundere* to pour between, fr *inter-* + *fundere* to pour – more at ⁴FOUND] – **interfusion** /-zh(ə)n/ *n*

1,inter'grade /-ˈgrayd/ *vi* to merge gradually one with another through a continuous series of intermediate forms – **intergradation** /-grəˈdaysh(ə)n/ *n*

2'inter,grade *n* an intermediate or transitional form

'inter,growth /-ˌgrohth/ *n* (the product of) a growing between or together

1interim /ˈintərim/ *n* an intervening time ⟨*in the* ~⟩ [L, adv, meanwhile, fr *inter* between – more at INTER-]

2interim *adj* temporary, provisional

1interior /inˈtiəri·ə/ *adj* **1** lying, occurring, or functioning within the limits or interior **2** away from the border or shore **3** of the mind or soul [MF & L; MF, fr L, compar of (assumed) OL *interus* inward, on the inside; akin to L *inter*] – **interiorize** *vt*, **interiorly** *adv*, **interiority** /-ˈorəti/ *n*

2interior *n* **1** the internal or inner part of a thing; *also* *the* inland **2** internal affairs ⟨*the minister of the* ~⟩ **3** a representation of the interior of a building or room

interior angle *n* **1** the angle between two sides of a polygon **2** an angle between a line crossing two parallel lines and either of the latter and lying inside the parallel lines ☞ MATHEMATICS

interior decoration *n* (the art or practice of planning) the decorating and furnishing of the interiors of rooms – **interior decorator** *n*

interior design *n* INTERIOR DECORATION – **interior designer** *n*

interior monologue *n* a literary device presenting a character's thoughts and feelings in the form of a monologue

in,terior-'sprung *adj* having (coil) springs within a padded casing ⟨~ *mattress*⟩

interject /ˌintəˈjekt/ *vt* to throw in (e g a remark) abruptly among or between other things [L *interjectus*, pp of *intericere*, fr *inter-* + *jacere* to throw – more at ²JET] – **interjector** *n*, **interjectory** /-t(ə)ri/ *adj*

,inter'jection /-ˈjeksh(ə)n/ *n* an ejaculatory word (e g *Wonderful*) or utterance (e g *ah* or *good heavens*) usu expressing emotion [INTERJECT + -ION] – **interjectional** *adj*, **interjectionally** *adv*

,inter'lace /-ˈlays/ *vt* **1** to unite (as if) by lacing together **2** to mingle, blend, or intersperse ⟨*narrative* ~d *with anecdotes*⟩ ~ *vi* to cross one another intricately [ME *entrelacen*, fr MF *entrelacer*, fr OF *entrelacier*, fr *entre-* inter- + *lacier* to lace] – **interlacement** *n*

,inter'lard /-ˈlahd/ *vt* to intersperse, esp *with* sthg foreign or irrelevant [MF *entrelarder*, fr OF, fr *entre* inter- + *larder* to lard, fr *lard*, n]

'inter,leaf /-ˌleef/ *n* a usu blank leaf inserted between 2 leaves of a book

,inter'leave /-ˈleev/ *vt* to provide with interleaves

,inter'line /-ˈlien/ *vt* to provide (a garment) with an interlining [ME *interlinen*, fr *inter-* + *linen* to line]

,inter'linear /-ˈlini·ə/ *adj* inserted between lines already written or printed [ME *interliniare*, fr ML *interlinearis*, fr L *inter-* + *linea* line]

'inter,lining /-ˌliening/ *n* a lining (e g of a coat) sewn between the ordinary lining and the outside fabric to give additional warmth or bulk

,inter'lock /-ˈlok/ *vi* to become engaged, interrelated, or interlocked ~ *vt* **1** to lock together **2** to connect so that motion of any part is constrained by another – **interlock** /ˈ--ˌ-/ *n or adj*

,inter'locutor /-ˈlokyootə/, *fem* **interlocutress** /-tris/ *n* one who takes part in dialogue or conversation [L *interlocutus*, pp of *interloqui* to speak between, fr *inter-* + *loqui* to speak] – **interlocution** /-lo ˈkyoohsh(ə)n/ *n*

,inter'locutory /-ˈlokyoot(ə)ri/ *adj* pronounced during a legal action and only provisional ⟨~ *decree*⟩ [ML *interlocutorius*, fr LL *interlocutus*, pp of *interloqui* to pronounce a provisional sentence, fr L, to speak between]

'inter,loper /-ˌlohpə/ *n* sby who interferes or encroaches; an intruder [*inter-* + *-loper* (akin to MD *lopen* to run, OE *hlēapan* to leap) – more at LEAP] – **interlope** /ˌ--ˈ-, ˈ--ˌ-/ *vi*

'inter,lude /-ˌloohd/ *n* **1** an intervening or interruptive period, space, or event, esp of a contrasting character; an interval **2** a musical composition inserted between the parts of a longer composition, a drama, or a religious service [ME *enterlude*, fr ML *interludium*, fr L *inter-* + *ludus* play – more at LUDICROUS]

ˌinterˈmarriage /-ˈmarij/ *n* **1** marriage between members of different families, tribes, etc **2** endogamy

ˌinterˈmarry /-ˈmari/ *vi* **1** to marry each other or sby from the the same group **2** to become connected by marriage with another group or with each other ⟨*the different races ~ freely*⟩

ˌinterˈmediary /-ˈmeedi·əri/ *n or adj* (sby or sthg) acting as a mediator or go-between

¹ˌinterˈmediate /-ˈmeedi·ət/ *adj* being or occurring at or near the middle place, stage, or degree or between 2 others or extremes [ML *intermediatus*, fr L *intermedius*, fr *inter-* + *medius* mid, middle – more at MID] – **intermediately** *adv*, **intermediacy** /-əsi/ *n*

²intermediate *n* a chemical compound formed as an intermediate step in a reaction

interment /inˈtuhmənt/ *n* burial [¹INTER + -MENT]

intermezzo /ˌintəˈmetsoh/ *n, pl* **intermezzi** /-see/, **intermezzos 1** a movement coming between the major sections of an extended musical work (e g an opera) **2** a short independent instrumental composition [It, deriv of L *intermedius* intermediate]

interminable /inˈtuhminəbl/ *adj* having or seeming to have no end; *esp* wearisomely long [ME, fr LL *interminabilis*, fr L *in-* + *terminare* to terminate] – **interminableness** *n*, **interminably** *adv*, **interminability** /-ˈbiləti/ *n*

ˌinterˈmingle /-ˈming·gl/ *vb* to mix or mingle together or with sthg else

ˌinterˈmission /-ˈmish(ə)n/ *n* **1** intermitting or being intermitted **2** an intervening period of time (e g between acts of a performance or attacks of a disease) [L *intermission-*, *intermissio*, fr *intermissus*, pp of *intermittere*]

ˌinterˈmit /-ˈmit/ *vb* **-tt-** to (cause to) cease for a time or at intervals [L *intermittere*, fr *inter-* + *mittere* to send – more at SMITE]

ˌinterˈmittent /-ˈmit(ə)nt/ *adj* coming and going at intervals; not continuous ⟨*~ rain*⟩ [L *intermittent-*, *intermittens*, prp of *intermittere*] – **intermittence** *n*, **intermittently** *adv*

ˌintermoˈlecular /-məˈlekyoolə/ *adj* existing or acting between molecules – **intermolecularly** *adv*

¹intern /inˈtuhn/ *vt* to confine, esp during a war ⟨*~ enemy aliens*⟩ [F *interner*, fr *interne* internal, fr MF, fr L *internus*] – **internee** /ˌintuhˈnee/ *n*, **internment** *n*

²intern, interne /ˈintuhn/ *n, NAm* an advanced student or graduate in medicine, teaching, etc gaining supervised practical experience (e g in a hospital or classroom) [F *interne*, fr *interne*, adj] – **intern** *vi*, **internship** *n*

internal /inˈtuhnl/ *adj* **1** existing or situated within the limits or surface of sthg **2** applied through the stomach by swallowing ⟨*an ~ medicine*⟩ **3** of or existing within the mind **4** depending only on the properties of the thing under consideration without reference to things outside it ⟨*~ evidence of forgery in a document*⟩ **5** (present or arising) within (a part of) the body or an organism ⟨*an ~ organ*⟩ ⟨*an ~ stimulus*⟩ **6** within a state ⟨*~ strife*⟩ ⟨*~ affairs*⟩ [L *internus*; akin to L *inter* between] – **internally** *adv*, **internality** /ˌintuhˈnaləti/ *n*

inˌternal-comˈbustion ˌengine *n* a heat engine in which the combustion that generates the heat energy takes place inside the engine (e g in a cylinder)

internal·ize, -ise /inˈtuhnl·ˌiez/ *vt* to make internal; *specif* to incorporate (e g learnt values) within the self as guiding principles – **internalization** /-ˈzaysh(ə)n/ *n*

internal rhyme *n* rhyme between a word within a line and another either at the end of the same line or within another line

¹ˌinterˈnational /-ˈnash(ə)nl/ *adj* **1** affecting or involving 2 or more nations ⟨*~ trade*⟩ ⟨*an ~ movement*⟩ **2** known, recognized, or renowned in more than 1 country ⟨*an ~ celebrity*⟩ – **internationally** *adv*, **internationality** /-ˈaləti/ *n*

²international *n* **1** (sby who plays or has played in) a sports, games, etc match between 2 national teams **2** *also* **internationale** *often cap* any of several socialist or communist organizations of international scope [(2) F *internationale*, fr fem of *international*, adj, fr E]

international date line *n, often cap I, D, & L* an arbitrary line approximately along the 180th meridian, east and west of which the date differs by 1 calendar day

ˌinterˈnationalˌism /-ˌiz(ə)m/ *n* **1** international character, interests, or outlook **2** (an attitude favouring) cooperation among nations – **internationalist** *n or adj*

ˌinterˈnational·ˌize, -ise /-ˌiez/ *vb* to make or become international; *esp* to place under international control – **internationalization** /-ie ˈzaysh(ə)n/ *n*

international law *n* a body of rules accepted as governing relations between nations

International Phonetic Alphabet *n* an alphabet designed to represent each human speech sound with a unique symbol

International Scientific Vocabulary *n* a set of international specialized or technical terms adapted to the structure of the individual languages in which they are used – abbr *ISV*

international unit *n* an internationally agreed unit of a vitamin, hormone, etc that produces a standard biological effect

interne /ˈintuhn/ *n* an intern

internecine /ˌintəˈneesien/ *adj* **1** mutually destructive **2** of or involving conflict within a group [L *internecinus* deadly, fr *internecare* to destroy, kill, fr *inter-* + *necare* to kill, fr *nec-*, *nex* violent death – more at NOXIOUS]

ˈinterˌnode /-ˌnohd/ *n* an interval or part between 2 nodes (e g of a plant stem) [L *internodium*, fr *inter-* + *nodus* knot] – **internodal** /-ˈnohdl/ *adj*

ˌinterˈnuclear /-ˈnyoohkli·ə/ *adj* situated or occurring between atomic or biological nuclei

ˌinterˈnuncial /-ˈnunshl/ *adj* serving to link sensory and motor neurons [It *internunzio* conveyer of messages, go-between, fr L *internuntius*, *internuncius*, fr *inter-* + *nuntius*, *nuncius* messenger] – **internuncially** *adv*

ˌinteroˈceptive /-rohˈseptiv/ *adj* of or being stimuli arising within the body, esp in the viscera [*inter-* (as in *interior*) + *-o-* + *-ceptive* (as in *receptive*)]

interpellate /inˈtuhpilayt/ *vt* to question (e g a minister) formally concerning an action or policy [L *interpellatus*, pp of *interpellare* to interrupt, fr *inter-* + *-pellare* (fr *pellere* to drive)] – **interpellator** *n*, **interpellation** /-ˈlaysh(ə)n/ *n*

interpenetrate /,intə'penitrayt/ *vt* to penetrate thoroughly ~ *vi* to penetrate mutually – **interpenetration** /-'traysh(ə)n/ *n*

'inter,phase /-,fayz/ *n* the interval between the end of one mitotic or meiotic division and the beginning of another

,inter'planetary /-'planit(ə)ri/ *adj* existing, carried on, or operating between planets

'inter,play /-,play/ *n* interaction – **interplay** /,--'-, '--,-/ *vi*

,inter'pleader /-'pleedə/ *n* a legal proceeding by which 2 parties making the same claim against a third party determine between themselves which is the rightful claimant [AF *enterpleder*, fr *enterpleder*, vb]

'Inter,pol /-,pol/ *n* an international police organization for liaison between national police forces [*international police*]

interpolate /in'tuhpəlayt/ *vt* **1** to alter or corrupt (e g a text) by inserting new or foreign matter **2** to insert between other things or parts; *esp* to insert (words) into a text or conversation **3** to estimate values of (a function) between 2 known values [L *interpolatus*, pp of *interpolare* to refurbish, alter, interpolate, fr *inter-* + *-polare* (fr *polire* to polish)] – **interpolative** /-lətiv/ *adj*, **interpolator** /-laytə/ *n*, **interpolation** /-'laysh(ə)n/ *n*

interpose /,intə'pohz/ *vt* **1** to place between 2 things or in an intervening position **2** to put forth by way of interference or intervention ⟨*prevented a decision by* interposing *a veto*⟩ **3** to interrupt with (words) during a conversation or argument ~ *vi* **1** to be or come in an intervening position **2** INTERVENE 3 **3** to interrupt [MF *interposer*, fr L *interponere* (perf indic *interposui*), fr *inter-* + *ponere* to put – more at POSITION] – **interposer** *n*, **interposition** /-pə'zish(ə)n/ *n*

interpret /in'tuhprit/ *vt* **1** to expound the meaning of ⟨~ *a dream*⟩ **2** to conceive of in the light of one's beliefs, judgments, or circumstances; construe **3** to represent by means of art; bring to realization by performance ⟨~s *a role*⟩ ~ *vi* to act as an interpreter [ME *interpreten*, fr MF & L; MF *interpreter*, fr L *interpretari*, fr *interpret-*, *interpres* agent, negotiator, interpreter] – **interpretable** *adj*, **interpretive** /-tiv/, **interpretative** /-tətiv/ *adj*, **interpretatively** *adv*

interpretation /in,tuhpri'taysh(ə)n/ *n* an instance of artistic interpreting in performance or adaptation [INTERPRET + -ATION] – **interpretational** *adj*

interpreter /in'tuhpritə/ *n* **1** one who translates orally for people speaking in different languages **2** a computer program that translates an instruction into machine language for immediate execution [INTERPRET + ²-ER]

interred /in'tuhd/ *past of* INTER

interregnum /,intə'regnəm/ *n, pl* **interregnums, interregna** /-'regnə/ **1** the time during which **a** a throne is vacant between reigns **b** the normal functions of government are suspended **2** a lapse or pause in a continuous series [L, fr *inter-* + *regnum* reign – more at REIGN]

,interre'late /-ri'layt/ *vb* to bring into or be in a relationship where each one depends upon or is acting upon the other – **interrelation** /-ri'laysh(ə)n/, **interrelationship** *n*

interring /in'tuhring/ *pres part of* INTER

interrobang /in'terə,bang/ *n* a punctuation mark for use at the end of an exclamatory question [*interrogation mark* + *bang* (printers' slang for exclamation mark)]

interrogate /in'terəgayt/ *vt* **1** to question formally **2** to give or send out a signal to (e g a computer) to trigger a response [L *interrogatus*, pp of *interrogare*, fr *inter-* + *rogare* to ask – more at RIGHT] – **interrogator** *n*, **interrogation** /-'gaysh(ə)n/ *n*

interrogation mark *n* QUESTION MARK

¹interrogative /,intə'rogətiv/, **interrogatory** /-t(ə)ri/ *adj* **1a** of or being the grammatical mood that expresses a question **b** used in a question **2** questioning – **interrogatively** *adv*

²interrogative *n* **1** an interrogative utterance **2** a word, esp a pronoun, used in asking questions **3** the interrogative mood of a language

interrogatory /,intə'rogət(ə)ri/ *n* a formal question; *esp* a written question to be answered under direction of a court

¹interrupt /,intə'rupt/ *vt* **1** to break the flow or action of (a speaker or speech) **2** to break the uniformity or continuity of (sthg) ~ *vi* to interrupt an action; *esp* to interrupt another's utterance with one's own [ME *interrupten*, fr L *interruptus*, pp of *interrumpere*, fr *inter-* + *rumpere* to break – more at BEREAVE] – **interrupter** *n*, **interruptible** *adj*, **interruption** /-sh(ə)n/ *n*, **interruptive** /-tiv/ *adj*

²interrupt *n* (a circuit that conveys) a signal to a computer that halts a program while a higher-priority program is carried out

inter se /,intə 'say/ *adv or adj* among or between themselves [L]

,inter'sect /-'sekt/ *vt* to pierce or divide (e g a line or area) by passing through or across ~ *vi* to meet and cross at a point [L *intersectus*, pp of *intersecare*, fr *inter-* + *secare* to cut – more at ²SAW]

intersection /'intə,seksh(ə)n, ,--'--/ *n* **1** a place where 2 or more things (e g streets) intersect **2** the set of elements common to 2 sets; *esp* the set of points common to 2 geometric configurations ☞ SYMBOL [INTERSECT + -ION]

'inter,sex /-,seks/ *n* (the condition of being) an intersexual individual [ISV]

,inter'sexual /-'seksyooəl, -sh(ə)l/ *adj* intermediate in sexual characters between a typical male and a typical female [ISV] – **intersexually** *adv*, **intersexuality** /-syoo'aləti, -shoo'aləti/ *n*

,inter'space /-'spays/ *vt* to separate (e g printed letters) by spaces

,inter'species /-'speeshiz/ *adj* interspecific

,interspe'cific /-spə'sifik/ *adj* existing or arising between different species

,inter'sperse /-'spuhs/ *vt* **1** to insert at intervals among other things ⟨interspersing *drawings throughout the text*⟩ **2** to diversify or vary with scattered things ⟨interspersing *the text with drawings*⟩ [L *interspersus* interspersed, fr *inter-* + *sparsus*, pp of *spargere* to scatter – more at SPARK] – **interspersion** /-sh(ə)n/ *n*

¹,inter'state /-'stayt/ *adj* between 2 or more states, esp of the USA or of Australia ⟨*an* ~ *highway*⟩

²interstate *adv, Austr* to or in another state ⟨*went* ~ *to live*⟩

,inter'stellar /-'stelə/ *adj* located or taking place among the stars

interstice /in'tuhstis/ *n* a small space between adjacent things – fml [F, fr LL *interstitium*, fr L *interstitus*, pp of *intersistere* to stand still in the middle, fr *inter-* + *sistere* to come to a stand; akin to L *stare* to stand]

interstitial /,intə'stishl/ *adj* **1** of or situated in interstices **2** of or being a crystalline compound in which (small) atoms or ions occupy holes between larger metal atoms or ions in the crystal lattice – **interstitially** *adv*

,inter'tidal /-'tiedl/ *adj* of or being the part of a seashore between high and low watermarks – **intertidally** *adv*

,inter'twine /-'twien/ *vt* to twine together ~ *vi* to twine about one another – **intertwinement** *n*

interval /'intəv(ə)l/ *n* **1** an intervening space: e g **a** a time between events or states; a pause **b** a distance or gap between objects, units, or states ⟨*lamp posts placed at regular* ~s⟩ **c** the difference in pitch between 2 notes **2** a set of real numbers between 2 numbers; *also* the set of real numbers greater or less than some number **3** *Br* a break in the presentation of an entertainment (e g a play) [ME *intervalle*, fr MF, fr L *intervallum* space between ramparts, interval, fr *inter-* + *vallum* rampart – more at WALL]

,inter'vene /-'veen/ *vi* **1** to enter or appear as sthg irrelevant or extraneous **2** to occur or come between 2 things, esp points of time or events **3** to come in or between so as to hinder or modify **4a** to enter a lawsuit as a third party **b** to interfere in another nation's internal affairs [L *intervenire* to come between, fr *inter-* + *venire* to come – more at COME] – **intervenor** *n*, **intervention** /-'vensh(ə)n/ *n*

,inter'vention /-'vensh(ə)n/ *adj*, *of a commodity* purchased from the producer by the European economic community when the market price falls to a specified level ⟨~ *butter*⟩

,inter'vention,ism /-,iz(ə)m/ *n* intervening; *specif* interference in the political affairs of another country – **interventionist** *n or adj*

intervertebral disc /intə'vuhtibrəl/ *n* any of the tough elastic discs between the bodies of adjoining vertebrae

'inter,view /-vyooh/ *n* **1** a formal consultation usu to evaluate qualifications (e g of a prospective student or employee) **2** (a report of) a meeting at which information is obtained (e g by a journalist) from sby [MF *entrevue*, fr (*s'*)*entrevoir* to see one another, meet, fr *entre-* inter- + *voir* to see – more at VIEW] – **interview** *vt*, **interviewer** *n*, **interviewee** /-vyooh'ee/ *n*

inter vivos /,intə 'veevos/ *adv or adj* between living people ⟨*property transferred* ~⟩ [LL]

,inter'war /-'waw/ *adj* occurring or falling between wars, esp WW I and II

,inter'weave /-'weev/ *vb* **interwove** /-'wohv/ *also* **interweaved; interwoven** /-'wohv(ə)n/ *also* **interweaved** **1** to weave together **2** to intermingle, blend – **interwoven** *adj*, **interweave** /'intə,weev/ *n*

[1]**intestate** /in'testayt, -tət/ *adj* having made no valid will ⟨*he died* ~⟩ [ME, fr L *intestatus*, fr *in-* + *testatus* testate] – **intestacy** /-stəsi/ *n*

[2]**intestate** *n* sby who dies intestate

intestinal /in'testinl/ *adj* of, being, affecting, or occurring in the intestine – **intestinally** *adv*

[1]**intestine** /in'testin/ *adj* of the internal affairs of a state or country [MF or L; MF *intestin* internal, fr L *intestinus*, fr *intus* within – more at ENT-]

[2]**intestine** *n* the tubular part of the alimentary canal that extends from the stomach to the anus [MF *intestin*, fr L *intestinum*, fr neut of *intestinus*]

intimacy /'intiməsi/ *n* **1** familiarity **2** SEXUAL INTERCOURSE – euph [[2]INTIMATE + -CY]

[1]**intimate** /'intimayt/ *vt* to make known: e g **a** to announce **b** to hint; IMPLY 2 [LL *intimatus*, pp of *intimare* to put in, announce, fr L *intimus* innermost, superl of (assumed) OL *interus* inward – more at INTERIOR] – **intimation** /-'maysh(ə)n/ *n*

[2]**intimate** /'intimət/ *adj* **1a** intrinsic, essential **b** belonging to or characterizing one's deepest nature **2** marked by very close association, contact, or familiarity **3a** marked by a warm friendship developing through long association **b** suggesting informal warmth or privacy **4** of a very personal or private nature **5** involved in a sexual relationship; *specif* engaging in an act of sexual intercourse ⟨*in six months they were* ~ *six times in the car and twice on a mountainside – News of the World*⟩ – euph [alter. of obs *intime*, fr L *intimus*] – **intimately** *adv*

[3]**intimate** *n* a close friend or confidant

intimidate /in'timidayt/ *vt* to frighten; *esp* to compel or deter (as if) by threats [ML *intimidatus*, pp of *intimidare*, fr L *in-* + *timidus* timid] – **intimidator** *n*, **intimidatory** /-t(ə)ri/ *adj*, **intimidation** /-'daysh(ə)n/ *n*

intitule /in'tityoohl/ *vt*, *Br* to supply (e g a legislative act) with a title [MF *intituler*, fr LL *intitulare*, fr L *in-* + *titulus* title]

into /'intə *before consonants; otherwise* 'intooh/ *prep* **1a** so as to be inside ⟨*come* ~ *the house*⟩ **b** so as to be ⟨*grow* ~ *a woman*⟩ ⟨*divide it* ~ *sections*⟩ ⟨*roll it* ~ *a ball*⟩ **c** so as to be in (a state) ⟨*get* ~ *trouble*⟩ ⟨*shocked* ~ *silence*⟩ **d** so as to be expressed in ⟨*translate it* ~ *French*⟩, dressed in ⟨*changed* ~ *his uniform*⟩, engaged in ⟨*go* ~ *farming*⟩, or a member of ⟨*enter* ~ *an alliance*⟩ – compare COME INTO **e** – used in division as the inverse of *by* or *divided by* ⟨*divide 35* ~ *70*⟩ **2** – used to indicate a partly elapsed period of time or a partly traversed extent of space ⟨*far* ~ *the night*⟩ ⟨*deep* ~ *the jungle*⟩ **3** in the direction of; *esp* towards the centre of ⟨*look* ~ *the sun*⟩ ⟨*inquire* ~ *the matter*⟩ **4** to a position of contact with; against ⟨*ran* ~ *a wall*⟩ **5** involved with ⟨*they were* ~ *hard drugs*⟩; *esp* keen on ⟨*are you* ~ *meditation?*⟩ – infml [ME, fr OE *intō*, fr [2]*in* + *tō* to]

intolerable /in'tol(ə)rəbl/ *adj* unbearable [ME, fr L *intolerabilis*, fr *in-* + *tolerabilis* tolerable] – **intolerableness** *n*, **intolerably** *adv*

in'tolerant /-'tolərənt/ *adj* **1** unable or unwilling to endure ⟨*a plant* ~ *of direct sunlight*⟩ **2** unwilling to grant or share social, professional, political, or religious rights; bigoted – **intolerance** *n*, **intolerantly** *adv*

intonate /'intohnayt/ *vt* to intone, utter

intonation /,intə'naysh(ə)n/ *n* **1** sthg that is intoned; *specif* the opening notes of a Gregorian chant **2** performance of music with respect to correctness of pitch and harmony **3** the rise and fall in pitch of the voice in speech [INTONE + -ATION]

intone /in'tohn/ *vb* to utter (sthg) in musical or prolonged tones; recite in singing tones or in a monotone [ME *entonen*, fr MF *entoner*, fr ML *intonare*, fr L *in-* + *tonus* tone] – **intoner** *n*

in toto /in 'tohtoh/ *adv* totally, entirely [L]

intoxicate /in'toksikayt/ *vt* **1** POISON 1a **2a** to excite or stupefy by alcohol or a drug, esp to the point where physical and mental control is markedly diminished **b** to cause to lose self-control through excitement or elation [ML *intoxicatus*, pp of *intoxicare*, fr L *in-* + *toxicum* poison – more at TOXIC] – **intoxicant** *n or adj*, **intoxicatedly** *adv*, **intoxication** /-ˈkaysh(ə)n/ *n*

intra- /intrə-/ *prefix* **1** within; inside ⟨intra*uterine*⟩ **2** intro- ⟨*an* intra*muscular injection*⟩ [LL, fr L *intra*, fr (assumed) OL *interus*, adj, inward – more at INTERIOR]

intracellular /ˌintrəˈselyoolə/ *adj* situated, occurring, or functioning within a living cell ⟨~ *enzymes*⟩

ˌintraˈcranial /-ˈkraynyəl, -ni·əl/ *adj* (affecting or involving structures) within the skull – **intracranially** *adv*

intractable /inˈtraktəbl/ *adj* **1** not easily managed or directed; OBSTINATE 1 **2** not easily manipulated, wrought, or solved **3** not easily relieved or cured ⟨~ *pain*⟩ [L *intractabilis*, fr *in-* + *tractabilis* tractable] – **intractableness** *n*, **intractably** *adv*, **intractability** /-ˈbiləti/ *n*

intrados /inˈtraydos/ *n, pl* **intrados, intradoses** the underside of an arch – compare EXTRADOS ☞ ARCHITECTURE [F, fr L *intra* within + F *dos* back – more at DOSSIER]

intramural /ˌintrəˈmyooərəl/ *adj* within the limits of a community or institution (e g a university) – **intramurally** *adv*

ˌintraˈmuscular /-ˈmuskyoolə/ *adj* in or going into a muscle [ISV] – **intramuscularly** *adv*

intransigent /inˈtransij(ə)nt, -ˈtranzi-/ *adj* refusing to compromise or to abandon an extreme position or attitude, esp in politics; uncompromising [Sp *intransigente*, fr *in-* + *transigente*, prp of *transigir* to compromise, fr L *transigere* to transact – more at TRANSACT] – **intransigence** *n*, **intransigent** *n*, **intransigently** *adv*

inˈtransitive /-ˈtransitiv, -ˈtrahn-, -zitiv/ *adj* characterized by not having a direct object ⟨*an* ~ *verb*⟩ [LL *intransitivus*, fr L *in-* + LL *transitivus* transitive] – **intransitive** *n*, **intransitively** *adv*

intraspecific /ˌintrəspəˈsifik/ *adj* occurring within a species; involving members of 1 species – **intraspecifically** *adv*

ˌintraˈuterine /-ˈyoohtərin, -rien/ *adj* situated, used, or occurring in the uterus [ISV]

intrauterine device, intrauterine contraceptive device *n* a device inserted and left in the uterus to prevent conception

ˌintraˈvascular /-ˈvaskyoolə/ *adj* situated or occurring in a (blood) vessel – **intravascularly** *adv*

ˌintraˈvenous /-ˈveenəs/ *adj* situated or occurring in, or entering by way of a vein; *also* used in intravenous procedures [ISV] – **intravenously** *adv*

intrench /inˈtrench/ *vb* to entrench

intrepid /inˈtrepid/ *adj* fearless, bold, and resolute [L *intrepidus*, fr *in-* + *trepidus* alarmed – more at TREPIDATION] – **intrepidly** *adv*, **intrepidity** /-ˈpidəti/ *n*

intricate /ˈintrikət/ *adj* **1** having many complexly interrelating parts or elements **2** difficult to resolve or analyse [ME, fr L *intricatus*, pp of *intricare* to entangle, fr *in-* + *tricae* trifles, impediments] – **intricacy** /-kəsi/ *n*, **intricately** *adv*

¹intrigue /inˈtreeg/ *vt* **1** to arouse the interest or curiosity of **2** to captivate; FASCINATE 2 ⟨*her beauty* ~s *me*⟩ ~ *vi* to carry on an intrigue; *esp* to plot, scheme [F *intriguer*, fr It *intrigare*, fr L *intricare* to entangle, perplex] – **intriguer** *n*

²intrigue /ˈintreeg, -ˈ-/ *n* **1a** a secret scheme or plot **b** the practice of engaging in or using scheming or underhand plots **2** a clandestine love affair

intriguing /inˈtreeging/ *adj* engaging the interest to a marked degree; fascinating – **intriguingly** *adv*

intrinsic /inˈtrinzik/ *adj* **1** belonging to the essential nature or constitution of sthg ⟨*an ornament of no* ~ *worth but of great sentimental value*⟩ **2** originating or situated within the body [MF *intrinsèque* internal, fr LL *intrinsecus*, fr L, adv, inwardly; akin to L *intra* within – more at INTRA-] – **intrinsically** *adv*

intrinsic factor *n* a substance produced by the lining of the intestines that is required for the absorption of vitamin B_{12} – compare EXTRINSIC FACTOR

intro /ˈintroh/ *n, pl* **intros** INTRODUCTION 1 – infml

intro- *prefix* **1** in; into ⟨intro*jection*⟩ **2** inwards; within ⟨intro*vert*⟩ – compare EXTRO- [ME, fr MF, fr L, fr *intro* inside, to the inside, fr (assumed) OL *interus*, adj, inward]

introduce /ˌintrəˈdyoohs/ *vt* **1** to lead or bring in, esp for the first time ⟨~ *a rare plant species into the country*⟩ **2a** to bring into play ⟨~ *a new line of approach into the argument*⟩ **b** to bring into practice or use; institute **3** to lead to or make known by a formal act, announcement, or recommendation: e g **a** to cause to be acquainted; make (oneself or sby) known to another **b** to present formally (e g at court or into society) **c** to announce formally or by an official reading **d** to make preliminary explanatory or laudatory remarks about (e g a speaker) **4** PLACE 2a, INSERT 2 ⟨*the risk of* introducing *harmful substances into the body*⟩ **5** to bring to a knowledge or discovery of sthg ⟨~ *her to the works of Byron*⟩ [L *introducere*, fr *intro-* + *ducere* to lead – more at ¹TOW]

introduction /ˌintrəˈduksh(ə)n/ *n* **1a** a preliminary treatise or course of study **b** a short introductory musical passage **2** sthg introduced; *specif* a plant or animal new to an area [ME *introduccioun* act of introducing, fr MF *introduction*, fr L *introduction-, introductio*, fr *introductus*, pp of *introducere*]

introductory /ˌintrəˈdukt(ə)ri/ *adj* of or being a first step that sets sthg going or in proper perspective; preliminary – **introductorily** *adv*

introit /ˈintroyt/ *n* a piece of music sung or played at the beginning of a church service; *specif, often cap* the antiphon or psalm sung as the priest approaches the altar to celebrate the Eucharist [MF *introite*, fr ML *introitus*, fr L, entrance, fr *introitus*, pp of *introire* to go in, fr *intro-* + *ire* to go – more at ISSUE]

introject /ˌintrəˈjekt/ *vt* to incorporate (attitudes or ideas) unconsciously into one's personality [*intro-* + *-ject* (as in *project*, vb)] – **introjection** /-ˈjeksh(ə)n/ *n*

ˌintroˈmission /-ˈmish(ə)n/ *n* intromitting; *esp* the (period of) insertion of the penis in the vagina in copulation [F, fr MF, fr L *intromissus*, pp of *intromittere*]

ˌintroˈmit /-ˈmit/ *vt* **-tt-** to put in, insert [L *intromittere*, fr *intro-* + *mittere* to send] – **intromittent** *adj*

introspect /-ˈspekt/ *vi* to examine one's own mind or its contents reflectively [L *introspectus*, pp of *introspicere* to look inside, fr *intro-* + *specere* to look

– more at SPY] – **introspection** /-'speksh(ə)n/ *n*, **introspective** /-tiv/ *adj*

[1]**,intro'vert** /-'vuht/ *vt* to turn inwards or in on itself or oneself: e g **a** to draw in (a tubular part) usu by invagination **b** to concentrate or direct (the mind, thoughts, or emotions) on oneself [*intro-* + *-vert* (as in *divert*)] – **introversion** /-'vuhsh(ə)n/ *n*

[2]**'intro,vert** *n* **1** sthg (e g the eyestalk of a snail) that is or can be drawn in **2** one whose attention and interests are directed towards his/her own mental life – compare EXTROVERT

intrude /in'troohd/ *vi* **1** to thrust oneself in without invitation, permission, or welcome **2** to enter as a geological intrusion ~ *vt* **1** to thrust or force in or on, esp without permission, welcome, or suitable reason **2** to cause (e g rock) to intrude [L *intrudere* to thrust in, fr *in-* + *trudere* to thrust – more at THREAT] – **intruder** *n*

intrusion /in'troohzh(ə)n/ *n* **1** intruding or being intruded; *specif* wrongfully entering upon the property of another **2** (the forcible entry of) rock or magma forced while molten into or between other rock formations [ME, fr MF, fr ML *intrusion-*, *intrusio*, fr L *intrusus*, pp of *intrudere*]

intrusive /in'troohsiv, -ziv/ *adj* **1** characterized by (a tendency to) intrusion **2** *of a rock* being an intrusion – **intrusively** *adv*

intrust /in'trust/ *vt* to entrust

intubation /,intyoo'baysh(ə)n/ *n* the introduction of a tube into a hollow organ (e g the windpipe) – **intubate** /'intyoo,bayt/ *vt*

intuit /in'tyooh·it/ *vt* to apprehend by intuition – **intuitable** *adj*

intuition /,intyooh'ish(ə)n/ *n* **1a** (knowledge gained by) immediate apprehension or cognition **b** the power of attaining direct knowledge without evident rational thought and the drawing of conclusions from evidence available **2** quick and ready insight [LL *intuition-*, *intuitio* act of contemplating, fr L *intuitus*, pp of *intueri* to look at, contemplate, fr *in-* + *tueri* to look at] – **intuitional** *adj*, **intuitive** /in'tyooh·itiv/ *adj*, **intuitively** *adv*

intumesce /,intyoo'mes/ *vi* ENLARGE 1, SWELL 1b [L *intumescere* to swell up, fr *in-* + *tumescere*, incho of *tumēre* to swell – more at THUMB] – **intumescence** *n*, **intumescent** *adj*

intussusception /'intəsə'sepsh(ə)n/ *n* a drawing in of sthg from without; *esp* the slipping of a length of intestine into an adjacent portion, usu producing obstruction [prob fr (assumed) NL *intussusception-*, *intussusceptio*, fr (assumed) NL *intussusceptus*, pp of (assumed) NL *intussuscipere* to cause to turn inwards, fr L *intus* within + *suscipere* to take up – more at ENT-, SUSCEPTIBLE] – **intussuscept** /-'sept/ *vb*, **intussusceptive** /-'septiv/ *adj*

inundate /'inundayt/ *vt* to cover or overwhelm (as if) with a flood [L *inundatus*, pp of *inundare*, fr *in-* + *unda* wave – more at WATER] – **inundation** /-'daysh(ə)n/ *n*

inure /i'nyooə/ *vt* to accustom *to* sthg undesirable [ME *enuren*, fr *en-* + *ure*, n, use, custom, fr MF *uevre* work, practice, fr L *opera* work – more at OPERA] – **inurement** *n*

inurn /i'nuhn/ *vt* to place (e g cremated remains) in an urn

in utero /in 'yoohtəroh/ *adv* in the uterus [L]

inutile /in'yoohtiel/ *adj* useless, unusable – fml [ME, fr MF, fr L *inutilis*, fr *in-* + *utilis* useful – more at UTILITY] – **inutility** /-'tiləti/ *n*

in vacuo /in 'vakyoo,oh/ *adv* in a vacuum; *esp* without being related to practical application, relevant facts, etc [NL]

invade /in'vayd/ *vt* **1** to enter (e g a country) for hostile purposes **2** to encroach on ⟨*a noise* ~d *his privacy*⟩ **3a** to spread over or into as if invading **b** to affect injuriously and progressively ⟨*gangrene* ~s *healthy tissue*⟩ [ME *invaden*, fr L *invadere*, fr *in-* + *vadere* to go – more at WADE] – **invader** *n*

invaginate /in'vajinayt/ *vt* **1** to enclose, sheathe **2** to fold in so that an outer becomes an inner surface ~ *vi* to undergo invagination [ML *invaginatus*, pp of *invaginare*, fr L *in-* + *vagina* sheath]

invagination /in,vaji'naysh(ə)n/ *n* **1** invaginating **2** an invaginated part

[1]**invalid** /in'valid/ *adj* **1** without legal force **2** logically inconsistent [L *invalidus* weak, fr *in-* + *validus* strong – more at VALID] – **invalidly** *adv*, **invalidity** /,invə'lidəti, -va-/ *n*

[2]**invalid** /'invəlid; *also* -,leed/ *adj* **1** suffering from disease or disability **2** of or suited to an invalid [L & F; F *invalide*, fr L *invalidus*]

[3]**invalid** /'invəlid/ *n* one who is sickly or disabled

[4]**invalid** /'invəlid, ,invə'leed/ *vt* to remove from active duty by reason of sickness or disability ⟨*he was* ~ed *out of the army*⟩

invalidate /in'validayt/ *vt* to make invalid; *esp* to weaken or destroy the convincingness of (e g an argument or claim) – **invalidation** /-'daysh(ə)n/ *n*

invaluable /in'valyooəbl/ *adj* valuable beyond estimation; priceless [[1]*in-* + [2]*value* + *-able*] – **invaluably** *adv*

Invar /'invah/ *trademark* – used for an alloy of iron and nickel with a low coefficient of thermal expansion

invariable /in'veəri·əbl/ *adj* not (capable of) changing; constant – **invariable** *n*, **invariableness** *n*, **invariably** *adv*, **invariability** /-ə'biləti/ *n*

in'variant /-'veəri·ənt/ *adj* unchanging; *specif* unaffected by a particular mathematical operation ⟨~ *under rotation of the coordinate axes*⟩ – **invariance** *n*, **invariant** *n*

invasion /in'vayzh(ə)n/ *n* **1** an invading, esp by an army **2** the incoming or spread of sthg usu harmful [ME *invasioune*, fr MF *invasion*, fr LL *invasion-*, *invasio*, fr L *invasus*, pp of *invadere*] – **invasive** /-siv, -ziv/ *adj*

invective /in'vektiv/ *n* abusive or insulting (use of) language; denunciation [ME *invectif*, adj, fr MF, fr L *invectivus*, fr *invectus*, pp of *invehere*] – **invective** *adj*, **invectively** *adv*

inveigh /in'vay/ *vi* to speak or protest bitterly or vehemently *against* [L *invehi* to attack, inveigh, passive of *invehere* to carry in, fr *in-* + *vehere* to carry – more at WAY]

inveigle /in'vaygl/ *vt* **inveigling** / in'vaygling/ to win (sby or sthg) over by ingenuity or flattery [modif of MF *aveugler* to blind, hoodwink, fr OF *avogler*, fr *avogle* blind, fr ML *ab oculis*, lit., lacking eyes] – **inveiglement** *n*

invent /in'vent/ *vt* **1** to think up ⟨~ *an excuse*⟩ **2** to produce (e g sthg useful) for the first time [ME *inventen* to find, discover, fr L *inventus*, pp of *invenire* to come upon, find, fr *in-* + *venire* to come – more at COME] – **inventor** *n*, **inventress** *n*

invention /in'vensh(ə)n/ *n* **1** productive imagination; inventiveness **2a** sthg invented: e g **(1)** a (misleading) product of the imagination **(2)** a contrivance or process devised after study and experiment **b** a short keyboard composition, usu in double counterpoint [INVENT + -ION]

inventive /in'ventiv/ *adj* **1** creative **2** characterized by invention – **inventively** *adv*, **inventiveness** *n*

[1]**inventory** /'invəntri/ *n* **1a** an itemized list (e g of the property of an individual or estate) **b** a list of traits, preferences, attitudes, etc used to evaluate personal characteristics or skills **2a** the items listed in an inventory **b** *NAm* the quantity of goods, components, or raw materials on hand; STOCK 5b **3** the taking of an inventory [ML *inventorium*, alter. of LL *inventarium*, fr *inventus*]

[2]**inventory** *vt* to make an inventory of; catalogue

[1]**inverse** /in'vuhs, '--/ *adj* **1** opposite in order, direction, nature, or effect **2** *of a mathematical function* expressing the same relationship as another function but from the opposite viewpoint **3** being or relating to an inverse function ⟨~ *sine*⟩ [L *inversus*, fr pp of *invertere*] – **inversely** *adv*

[2]**inverse** *n* **1** a direct opposite **2** an inverse function or operation in mathematics ⟨*addition is the* ~ *of subtraction*⟩

inverse proportion *n* the relation between 2 quantities, one of which varies directly as the reciprocal of the other – **inversely proportional** *adj*

inversion /in'vuhsh(ə)n/ *n* **1** the act or process of inverting **2** a reversal of position, order, form, or relationship: e g **a(1)** a change in normal word order; *esp* the placement of a verb before its subject **(2)** the process or result of changing, converting, or reversing the relative positions of the elements of a musical interval, chord, or phrase **b** being turned inwards or inside out **3** the operation of forming the inverse of a magnitude, operation, or element **4** homosexuality **5** a conversion of a substance showing dextrorotation into one showing laevorotation or vice versa ⟨~ *of sucrose*⟩ **6** a conversion of direct current into alternating current **7** a reversal of the normal atmospheric temperature gradient – **inversive** /-siv/ *adj*

[1]**invert** /in'vuht/ *vt* **1a** to turn inside out or upside down **b** to turn (e g a foot) inwards **2a** to reverse in position, order, or relationship **b** to subject to musical inversion **c** to subject to chemical inversion **d** to express the mathematical inverse, esp the reciprocal, of [L *invertere*, fr *in-* + *vertere* to turn – more at [1]WORTH] – **invertible** *adj*

[2]**invert** /'invuht/ *n* sby or sthg characterized by inversion; *esp* a homosexual

invertase /in'vuhtayz, -tays/ *n* an enzyme capable of converting sucrose into invert sugar [ISV]

invertebrate /in'vuhtibrət, -brayt/ *adj* **1** (of animals) lacking a spinal column or notochord **2** lacking in strength or vitality of character [NL *invertebratus*, fr L *in-* + NL *vertebratus* vertebrate] – **invertebrate** *n*

in,verted 'comma *n* **1** a comma in type printed upside down at the top of the line **2** *chiefly Br* QUOTATION MARK

in,verted 'pleat *n* a pleat made by forming 2 folded edges which are secured to face each other on the right side of the fabric – compare BOX PLEAT

inverter /in'vuhtə/ *n* a device for converting direct current into alternating current [[1]INVERT + [2]-ER]

invert sugar *n* a mixture of glucose and fructose found in fruits or produced artificially from sucrose

[1]**invest** /in'vest/ *vt* **1** to confer (the symbols of) authority, office, or rank on **2** to clothe, endow, or cover (as if) *with* sthg ⟨~ed *with an air of mystery*⟩ **3** to surround with troops or ships so as to prevent escape or entry [L *investire* to clothe, surround, fr *in-* + *vestis* garment; (1) ML *investire*, fr L, to clothe; (3) MF *investir*, fr OIt *investire*, fr L, to surround]

[2]**invest** *vt* **1** to commit (money) to a particular use (e g buying shares or new capital outlay) in order to earn a financial return **2** to devote (e g time or effort) to sthg for future advantages ~ *vi* to make an investment ⟨~ *in a new car*⟩ [It *investire* to clothe, invest money, fr L, to clothe] – **investable** *adj*, **investor** *n*

investigate /in'vestigayt/ *vb* **1** to make a systematic examination or study (of) **2** to conduct an official inquiry (into) [L *investigatus*, pp of *investigare* to track, investigate, fr *in-* + *vestigium* footprint, track] – **investigational** *adj*, **investigative** /-gətiv/ *adj*, **investigator** *n*, **investigatory** /-t(ə)ri/ *adj*, **investigation** /-'gaysh(ə)n/ *n*

investiture /in'vestichə/ *n* a formal ceremony conferring an office or honour on sby [ME, fr ML *investitura*, fr *investitus*, pp of *investire*]

[1]**investment** /in'vestmənt/ *n* a siege or blockade [[1]*invest*]

[2]**investment** *n* (a sum of) money invested for income or profit; *also* the asset (e g property) purchased [[2]*invest*]

in'vestment ,company *n* a company whose primary business is acquiring shares or securities of other companies purely for investment purposes – compare HOLDING COMPANY

investment trust *n* an investment company that purchases securities on behalf of its investors – compare UNIT TRUST

inveterate /in'vet(ə)rət/ *adj* **1** firmly, obstinately, and persistently established **2** habitual ⟨*an* ~ *liar*⟩ [L *inveteratus*, fr pp of *inveterare* to age (vt), fr *in-* + *veter-*, *vetus* old – more at WETHER] – **inveteracy** /-si/ *n*, **inveterately** *adv*

invidious /in'vidi·əs/ *adj* **1** tending to cause discontent, ill will, or envy **2** of an unpleasant or objectionable nature; of a kind causing or likely to cause harm or resentment [L *invidiosus* envious, invidious, fr *invidia* envy – more at ENVY] – **invidiously** *adv*, **invidiousness** *n*

invigilate /in'vijilayt/ *vb* to keep watch (over); *specif, Br* to supervise (candidates) at (an examination) [L *invigilatus*, pp of *invigilare* to keep watch, fr *in-* + *vigilare* to keep watch – more at VIGILANT] – **invigilator** *n*, **invigilation** /-'laysh(ə)n/ *n*

invigorate /in'vigərayt/ *vt* to give fresh life and energy to [prob fr *in-* + *vigour*] – **invigoratingly** *adv*, **invigorator** *n*, **invigoration** /-'raysh(ə)n/ *n*

invincible /in'vinsəbl/ *adj* incapable of being conquered or subdued [ME, fr MF, fr LL *invincibilis*, fr L *in-* + *vincere* to conquer – more at VICTOR] – **invincibleness** *n*, **invincibly** *adv*, **invincibility** /-'biləti/ *n*

inviolable /in'vie·ələbl/ *adj* (to be kept) secure from violation, profanation, or assault [MF or L; MF, fr L *inviolabilis*, fr *in-* + *violare* to violate] – **inviolably** *adv*, **inviolability** /-'biləti/ *n*

inviolate /in'vie·ələt, -,layt/ *adj* not violated or profaned – **inviolacy** /-ləsi/ *n*, **inviolately** /-lətli/ *adv*, **inviolateness** *n*

invisible /in'vizəbl/ *adj* **1** incapable (by nature or circumstances) of being seen **2a** not appearing in published financial statements ⟨~ *assets*⟩ **b** not reflected in statistics ⟨~ *earnings*⟩ **c** of or being trade in services (e g insurance or tourism) rather than goods – compare VISIBLE **3** too small or unobtrusive to be seen or noticed; inconspicuous [ME, fr MF, fr L *invisibilis*, fr *in-* + *visibilis* visible] – **invisible** *n*, **invisibleness** *n*, **invisibly** *adv*, **invisibility** /-zə'biləti/ *n*

in,visible 'ink *n* an ink that remains invisible on paper until it is given some special treatment

invitation /,invi'taysh(ə)n/ *n* **1** an often formal request to be present or participate **2** an incentive, inducement [[1]INVITE + -ATION] – **invitational** *adj*

[1]invite /in'viet/ *vt* **1a** to offer an incentive or inducement to **b** to (unintentionally) increase the likelihood of ⟨*his actions ~ trouble*⟩ **2** to request (the presence of) formally or politely [MF or L; MF *inviter*, fr L *invitare*] – **invitatory** /-tət(ə)ri/ *adj*, **inviter** *n*, **invitee** /-'tee/ *n*

[2]invite /'inviet/ *n* an invitation – infml

inviting /in'vieting/ *adj* attractive, tempting – **invitingly** *adv*

in vitro /in 'veetroh, 'vitroh/ *adv or adj* outside the living body and in an artificial environment [NL, lit., in glass]

in vivo /in 'veevoh/ *adv or adj* in the living body of a plant or animal [NL, lit., in the living]

invocation /,invə'kaysh(ə)n/ *n* **1** the act or process of petitioning for help or support; *specif, often cap* an invocatory prayer, esp at the beginning of a church service **2** the performing of magical rites in order to summon spirits [ME *invocacioun*, fr MF *invocation*, fr L *invocation-*, *invocatio*, fr *invocatus*, pp of *invocare*] – **invocational** *adj*, **invocatory** /in'vokət(ə)ri/ *adj*

[1]invoice /'invoys/ *n* **1** [4]BILL 3a; *specif* an itemized list of goods shipped, usu specifying the price and the terms of sale **2** a consignment of merchandise [modif of MF *envois*, pl of *envoi* message – more at [1]ENVOY]

[2]invoice *vt* to submit an invoice for or to

invoke /in'vohk/ *vt* **1a** to petition (e g a deity) for help or support **b** to appeal to or cite as an authority **2** to call forth (e g a spirit) by uttering a spell or magical formula **3** to make an earnest request for; SOLICIT 3 **4** to put into effect ⟨~ *economic sanctions*⟩ [ME *invoken*, fr MF *invoquer*, fr L *invocare*, fr *in-* + *vocare* to call – more at VOICE] – **invoker** *n*

involucre /,invə'loohkə/ *n* 1 or more whorls of bracts situated below and close to a flower (cluster) or fruit [F, fr NL *involucrum*, fr L, sheath, fr *involvere* to wrap] – **involucral** /-krəl/ *adj*

involuntary /in'volənt(ə)ri/ *adj* **1** done contrary to or without choice **2** not subject to conscious control; reflex ⟨~ *muscle*⟩ [LL *involuntarius*, fr L *in-* + *voluntarius* voluntary] – **involuntarily** *adv*, **involuntariness** *n*

[1]involute /'invəlooht/ *adj* **1a** curled spirally **b** curled or curved inwards, esp at the edge ⟨*an ~ leaf*⟩ **c** having the form of an involute ⟨*a gear with ~ teeth*⟩ **2** CONVOLUTED 1 [L *involutus* involved, fr pp of *involvere*] – **involutely** *adv*

[2]involute *n* a curve traced by a point on a thread kept taut as it is unwound from another curve

[3]involute /,invə'looht/ *vi* to return to a former condition ⟨*after pregnancy the uterus ~s*⟩

involution /,invə'loohsh(ə)n/ *n* **1** a (part) curving inwards **2** a shrinking or return to a former size [L *involution-*, *involutio*, fr *involutus*, pp of *involvere*]

involve /in'volv/ *vt* **1a** to cause to be associated or take part **b** to occupy (oneself) absorbingly; *esp* to commit (oneself) emotionally **2** to envelop **3** to relate closely **4a** to have within or as part of itself **b** to require as a necessary accompaniment [ME *involven* to roll up, wrap, fr L *involvere*, fr *in-* + *volvere* to roll – more at VOLUBLE] – **involvement** *n*, **involver** *n*

in'volved *adj* **1** (needlessly or excessively) complex **2** taking part *in* ⟨*workers ~ in building a dam*⟩ – **involvedly** /-vidli/ *adv*

invulnerable /in'vulnərəbl/ *adj* **1** incapable of being injured or harmed **2** immune to or proof against attack [L *invulnerabilis*, fr *in-* + *vulnerare* to wound – more at VULNERABLE] – **invulnerableness** *n*, **invulnerably** *adv*, **invulnerability** /-rə'biləti/ *n*

inward /'inwood/ *adj* **1** situated within or directed towards the inside **2** of or relating to the mind or spirit ⟨*struggled to achieve ~ peace*⟩ [ME, fr OE *inweard*; akin to OHG *inwert* inward; both fr a prehistoric WGmc compound whose constituents are represented by OE *in* & OE *-weard* -ward] – **inwardness** *n*

'inwardly /-li/ *adv* **1** beneath the surface; internally **2** to oneself; in one's private thoughts

'inwards, *NAm chiefly* **inward** *adv* **1** towards the inside, centre, or interior **2** towards the inner being

,in-'wrought *adj* **1** *of a fabric* decorated with a pattern woven or worked in **2** *of a pattern* woven or worked in (e g to a fabric)

inyala /in'yahlə/ *n, pl* **inyalas,** *esp collectively* **inyala** a nyala [Zulu *inxala*]

iod-, iodo- *comb form* iodine ⟨iodize⟩ ⟨iodo*form*⟩ [F *iode*]

iodic /ie'odik/ *adj* of or containing (pentavalent) iodine [F *iodique*, fr *iode*] – **iodate** /'ie·ə,dayt/ *n*

iodide /'ie·ə,died/ *n* a compound of iodine with an element or radical; *esp* a salt or ester of hydriodic acid [ISV]

iodine /'ie·ə,deen/ *n* a (solid blackish grey) halogen element ☞ PERIODIC TABLE [F *iode*, fr Gk *ioeidēs* violet-coloured, fr *ion* violet] – **iodinate** /ie'odinayt/ *vt*, **iodination** /-'naysh(ə)n/ *n*

iod·ize, -ise /'ie·ə,diez/ *vt* to treat with iodine or an iodide ⟨~d *salt*⟩

iodoform /ie'odə,fawm/ *n* a yellow solid compound with a penetrating smell that is a mild disinfectant [ISV *iod-* + *-form* (as in *chloroform*)]

iodopsin /,ie·ə'dopsin/ *n* a light-sensitive pigment in the retinal cones that is important in the perception of colour, esp in daylight vision [*iod-* (fr Gk *ioeidēs* violet-coloured) + Gk *opsis* sight, vision + E *-in* – more at OPTIC]

iodous /ie'odəs/ *adj* of or containing (trivalent) iodine [ISV]

ion /'ie·ən/ *n* **1** an atom or group of atoms that carries a positive or negative electric charge as a result of having lost or gained 1 or more electrons **2** a free electron or other charged subatomic particle

[Gk, neut of *iōn*, prp of *ienai* to go – more at ISSUE]

-ion /-i·ən/ *suffix* (*vb* → *n*) **1a** act or process of ⟨valida*tion*⟩ **b** result of (a specified act or process) ⟨regula*tion*⟩ **2** quality or condition of ⟨hydra*tion*⟩ ⟨ambi*tion*⟩ [ME *-ioun, -ion*, fr OF *-ion*, fr L *-ion-, -io*]

ion exchange *n* a reversible reaction, used esp for softening or removing dissolved substances from water, in which one kind of ion is interchanged with another of like charge – **ion-exchanger** *n*

ionic /ie'onik/ *adj* **1** of, existing as, or characterized by ions ⟨~ *gases*⟩ **2** functioning by means of ions ⟨~ *conduction*⟩ [ISV] – **ionicity** /,ie·ə'nisəti/ *n*

[1]**Ionic** *adj* **1** (characteristic) of Ionia **2** of that 1 of the 3 Greek orders of architecture that is characterized esp by the scroll-shaped ornament of its capital ☞ ARCHITECTURE [L & MF; MF *ionique*, fr L *ionicus*, fr Gk *iōnikos*, fr *Iōnia* Ionia, ancient region of Asia Minor]

[2]**Ionic** *n* a dialect of ancient Greek used in Ionia

ionic bond *n* an electrovalent chemical bond

ionium /ie'ohni·əm/ *n* a natural radioactive isotope of thorium with a mass number of 230 [*ion*; fr its ionizing action]

ion·ize, -ise /'ie·ə,niez/ *vb* to convert or become converted wholly or partly into ions [ISV] – **ionizable** *adj*, **ionizer** *n*, **ionization** /-'zaysh(ə)n/ *n*

ionophore /ie'onə,faw/ *n* a compound that increases the transport of a (metal) ion across a lipid barrier (e g a cell membrane) by reversibly combining with the ion and by increasing the permeability of the barrier to it

ionosphere /ie'onə,sfiə/ *n* the part of the earth's atmosphere that extends from an altitude above that of the stratosphere out to at least 480km (about 300mi) and consists of several distinct regions containing free ions; *also* a comparable region surrounding another planet – **ionospheric** /-'sferik/ *adj*, **ionospherically** *adv*

iota /ie'ohtə/ *n* **1** the 9th letter of the Greek alphabet **2** an infinitesimal amount [L, fr Gk *iōta*, of Sem origin; akin to Heb *yōdh*, 10th letter of the Heb alphabet]

IOU /,ie oh 'yooh/ *n* (a written acknowledgment of) a debt [prob fr the pronunciation of *I owe you*]

-ious /-i·əs/ *suffix* (*n* → *adj*) -ous ⟨cap*tious*⟩ [ME; partly fr OF *-ious, -ieux*, fr L *-iosus*, fr *-i-* (penultimate vowel of some noun stems) + *-osus* -ous; partly fr L *-ius*, adj suffix]

IPA *n* INTERNATIONAL PHONETIC ALPHABET

ipecac /'ipi,kak/ *n* ipecacuanha

ipecacuanha /,ipi,kakyoo'ahnə/ *n* (a tropical S American creeping plant of the madder family with) an underground stem and root formerly used dried as a purgative and emetic [Pg *ipecacuanha*, fr Tupi *ipekaaguéne*]

ipse dixit /,ipsay 'diksit/ *n* an arbitrary dogmatic assertion [L, he himself said it]

ipsilateral /,ipsi'lat(ə)rəl/ *adj* situated or appearing on or affecting the same side of the body – compare CONTRALATERAL [ISV, fr L *ipse* self, himself + *later-, latus* side] – **ipsilaterally** *adv*

ipso facto /,ipsoh 'faktoh/ *adv* by the very nature of the case [NL, lit., by the fact itself]

IQ *n* INTELLIGENCE QUOTIENT

ir- – see [1]IN-

Iranian /i'rayni·ən, i'rahni·ən/ *n* **1** a native or inhabitant of Iran **2** a branch of the Indo-European family of languages that includes Persian [*Iran*, country in SW Asia] – **Iranian** *adj*

Iraqi /i'rahki, i'raki/ *n* **1** a native or inhabitant of Iraq **2** the dialect of Modern Arabic spoken in Iraq [Ar *'irāqīy*, fr *'Irāq* Iraq, country in SW Asia] – **Iraqi** *adj*

irascible /i'rasibl/ *adj* having an easily provoked temper [MF, fr LL *irascibilis*, fr L *irasci* to become angry, be angry, fr *ira* anger] – **irascibleness** *n*, **irascibly** *adv*, **irascibility** /-'biləti/ *n*

irate /ie'rayt/ *adj* roused to or arising from anger [L *iratus*, fr *ira*] – **irately** *adv*, **irateness** *n*

ire /ie·ə/ *n* intense and usu openly displayed anger [ME, fr OF, fr L *ira*; akin to OE *ofost* haste, zeal, Gk *hieros* holy, *oistros* gadfly, frenzy] – **ireful** *adj*

irid-, irido- *comb form* **1** rainbow ⟨irid*escent*⟩ **2** iris of the eye ⟨irid*ectomy*⟩ **3** iridium ⟨irid*ic*⟩; iridium and ⟨irid*osmium*⟩ [(1) L *irid-, iris*; (2) NL *irid-, iris*; (3) ML *iridium*]

iridaceous /iri'dayshəs/ *adj* of the iris family

iridescence /iri'des(ə)ns/ *n* (a display or effect suggestive of) a play of changing colours in a soap bubble, bird's plumage, etc – **iridescent** *adj*, **iridescently** *adv*

iridium /i'ridi·əm/ *n* a silver-white hard brittle very heavy (tetravalent) metallic element of the platinum group ☞ PERIODIC TABLE [NL, fr L *irid-, iris*; fr the colours produced by its dissolving in hydrochloric acid] – **iridic** /-dik/ *adj*

iris /'ieris/ *n, pl* (*1*) **irises, irides** /'ierideez/, (*2*) **irises, irides**, *esp collectively* **iris** **1a** the opaque contractile diaphragm perforated by the pupil that forms the coloured portion of the eye ☞ NERVE **b iris, iris diaphragm** an adjustable diaphragm of thin opaque plates that can be moved to control the size of an aperture **2** any of a large genus of plants with long straight leaves and large showy flowers ☞ PLANT [(2) NL *Irid-, Iris*, genus name, fr L *irid-, iris* rainbow, iris plant, fr Gk, rainbow, iris plant, iris of the eye; (1) NL *irid-, iris*, fr Gk]

[1]**Irish** /'ierish/ *adj* **1** of Ireland or the Irish (language) **2** amusingly illogical [ME, fr OE *Īras* Irishmen, of Celtic origin; akin to OIr *Ēriu* Ireland] – **Irishman** /-mən/ *n*

[2]**Irish** *n* **1** *pl in constr* the people of Ireland **2 Irish, Irish Gaelic** the Celtic language of Ireland, esp as used since the end of the medieval period ☞ ALPHABET

,Irish 'coffee *n* hot sugared coffee with Irish whiskey and whipped cream

,Irish 'moss *n* carrageen

,Irish 'setter *n* (any of) a breed of chestnut-brown or mahogany-red gundogs

,Irish 'terrier *n* (any of) a breed of active medium-sized terriers with a dense usu reddish wiry coat

,Irish 'whiskey *n* whisky made in Ireland, chiefly of barley

,Irish 'wolf,hound *n* (any of) a breed of very large tall hounds of the general form of a greyhound but much larger and stronger

irk /uhk/ *vt* to make weary, irritated, or bored [ME *irken*]

'irksome /-s(ə)m/ *adj* troublesome, annoying – **irksomely** *adv*, **irksomeness** *n*

[1]**iron** /'ie·ən/ *n* **1** a heavy malleable ductile magnetic silver-white metallic element that readily rusts in

moist air, occurs in most igneous rocks, and is vital to biological processes ☞ PERIODIC TABLE **2** sthg (orig) made of iron: e g **a** sthg used to bind or restrain – usu pl **b** a heated metal implement used for branding or cauterizing **c** a metal implement with a smooth flat typically triangular base that is heated (e g by electricity) and used to smooth or press clothing **d** a stirrup **e** any of a numbered series of usu 9 golf clubs with metal heads of varying angles for hitting the ball to various heights and lengths **3** great strength or hardness [ME, fr OE *īsern, īren*; akin to OHG *īsarn* iron] – **iron in the fire** a prospective course of action; a plan not yet realized ⟨*got several* irons in the fire *and I'm hoping to land something before very long* – W S Maugham⟩

[2]**iron** *adj* **1** (made) of iron **2** resembling iron (e g in appearance, strength, solidity, or durability) – **ironness** *n*

[3]**iron** *vt* **1** to smooth (as if) with a heated iron ⟨~ed *his shirt*⟩ **2** to remove (e g wrinkles) by ironing – often + *out* ~ *vi* to be capable of being ironed ⟨*this skirt* ~s *well*⟩ ***USE*** ☞ SYMBOL

Iron Age *n* the period of human culture characterized by the widespread use of iron for making tools and weapons and dating from before 1000 BC

,iron'bound /-'bownd/ *adj* bound (as if) with iron: e g **a** rugged or harsh ⟨~ *coast*⟩ **b** stern, rigorous

[1]**,iron'clad** /-'klad/ *adj* sheathed in iron or steel armour

[2]**'iron,clad** *n* an ironclad naval vessel, esp in the 19th c

,iron 'curtain *n, often cap I&C* an esp political and ideological barrier between the Communist countries of E Europe and the non-Communist countries of (and those friendly to) W Europe

,iron 'grey *adj or n* dark greenish grey

ironic /ie'ronik/, **ironical** /-kl/ *adj* **1** of, containing, or constituting irony **2** given to irony – **ironically** *adv*, **ironicalness** *n*

ironing /'ie·əning/ *n* clothes and cloth articles (e g towels and tablecloths) that are (to be) ironed

'ironing ,board *n* a narrow flat board, on which clothes are ironed, mounted on collapsible and adjustable legs

ironist /'ierənist/ *n* one who uses irony, esp in the development of a literary work or theme

,iron 'lung *n* a device for artificial respiration that fits over the patient's chest and forces air into and out of the lungs

'iron,monger /-,mung·gə/ *n, Br* a dealer in esp household hardware – **ironmongery** *n*

iron out *vt* to put right or correct (e g a problem or defect); resolve (e g difficulties)

,iron 'pyrites *n* iron disulphide occurring as a lustrous pale brass-yellow mineral

'iron ,ration *n* an emergency food ration, esp for a soldier [fr its orig consisting mainly of tinned food]

'iron,stone /-,stohn/ *n* a hard sedimentary iron ore, esp a siderite

'iron,ware /-,weə/ *n* articles, esp vessels and implements for domestic use, made of iron

'iron,works /-,wuhks/ *n, pl* **ironworks** a mill or building where iron or steel is smelted or heavy iron or steel products are made – often pl with sing. meaning

irony /'ierəni/ *n* **1a** the use of words to express a meaning other than and esp the opposite of the literal meaning **b** an expression or utterance using irony **2a** (an event or situation showing) incongruity between actual circumstances and the normal, appropriate, or expected result **b** DRAMATIC IRONY **3** an attitude of detached awareness of incongruity ⟨*viewed with* ~ *the craze for individuality*⟩ [L *ironia*, fr Gk *eirōneia*, fr *eirōn* dissembler]

Iroquoian /,irə'kwoyən/ *n* a language family of eastern N America including Cherokee, Erie, and Mohawk ☞ LANGUAGE – **Iroquoian** *adj*

Iroquois /'irəkwoy(z)/ *n pl in constr* a confederation of N American Indian tribes of the W USA [F, fr Algonquin *Irinakhoiw*, lit., real adders]

irradiate /i'raydiayt/ *vt* **1a** to cast rays (of light) upon **b** to give intellectual or spiritual insight to **c** to affect or treat by (exposure to) radiant energy (e g heat) **2** to emit like rays (of light); RADIATE 2 [L *irradiatus*, pp of *irradiare*, fr *in-* + *radius* ray] – **irradiance** *n*, **irradiative** *adj*, **irradiator** *n*

irradiation /i,raydi'aysh(ə)n/ *n* **1** an irradiating **2** exposure to radiation (e g X rays or alpha rays)

[1]**irrational** /i'rash(ə)nl/ *adj* not rational: e g **a** not governed by or according to reason **b** being or having a value that is an irrational number ⟨*an* ~ *root of an equation*⟩ [ME, fr L *irrationalis*, fr *in-* + *rationalis* rational] – **irrationalism** *n*, **irrationalist** *n*, **irrationally** *adv*, **irrationality** /-'aləti/ *n*

[2]**irrational, irrational number** *n* a number (e g π) that cannot be expressed as the result of dividing 1 integer by another – compare RATIONAL NUMBER, SURD ☞ NUMBER

[1]**irreconcilable** /i'rekən,sieləbl/ *adj* impossible to reconcile: e g **a** resolutely opposed **b** INCOMPATIBLE 1 – **irreconcilableness** *n*, **irreconcilably** *adv*, **irreconcilability** /-lə'biləti/ *n*

[2]**irreconcilable** *n* an opponent of compromise or collaboration

irrecoverable /,iri'kuv(ə)rəbl/ *adj* not capable of being recovered or retrieved – **irrecoverably** *adv*

irredeemable /,iri'deeməbl/ *adj* not redeemable; *esp* beyond remedy; hopeless – **irredeemably** *adv*

irredentism /,iri'den,tiz(ə)m/ *n* advocacy of the restoration of territories to the countries to which they are historically or ethnically related [It *irredentismo*, fr *(Italia) irredenta* Italian-speaking territory not incorporated in Italy, lit., unredeemed Italy] – **irredentist** *n or adj*

irreducible /,iri'dyoohsəbl/ *adj* impossible to bring into a desired, normal, or simpler state ⟨*an* ~ *matrix*⟩ – **irreducibly** *adv*, **irreducibility** /-sə'biləti/ *n*

irrefrangible /,iri'franjəbl/ *adj* not capable of being refracted

irrefutable /,iri'fyoohtəbl, i'refyootəbl/ *adj* incontrovertible [LL *irrefutabilis*, fr L *in-* + *refutare* to refute] – **irrefutably** *adv*, **irrefutability** /-'biləti/ *n*

[1]**irregular** /i'regyoolə/ *adj* **1a** contrary to rule, custom, or moral principles **b** not inflected in the normal manner; *specif* STRONG 14 **c** inadequate because of failure to conform **d** *of troops* not belonging to the regular army organization **2** lacking symmetry or evenness **3** lacking continuity or regularity, esp of occurrence or activity [ME *irreguler*, fr MF, fr LL *irregularis* not in accordance with rule, fr L *in-* + *regularis* regular] – **irregularly** *adv*

[2]**irregular** *n* an irregular soldier

irregularity /i,regyoo'larəti/ *n* sthg irregular (e g

contrary to accepted professional or ethical standards) [¹IRREGULAR + -ITY]

irrelevant /i'reliv(ə)nt/ *adj* not relevant; inapplicable – **irrelevance** *n*, **irrelevancy** *n*, **irrelevantly** *adv*

irreligion /ˌiri'lij(ə)n/ *n* hostility to or disregard of religion [MF or L; MF, fr L *irreligion-, irreligio*, fr *in-* + *religion-, religio* religion] – **irreligionist** *n*, **irreligious** *adj*, **irreligiously** *adv*

irremediable /ˌiri'meedi·əbl, -dyəbl/ *adj* not remediable; *specif* incurable [L *irremediabilis*, fr *in-* + *remediabilis* remediable] – **irremediableness** *n*, **irremediably** *adv*

irreparable /i'rep(ə)rəbl/ *adj* not able to be restored to a previous condition [ME, fr MF, fr L *irreparabilis*, fr *in-* + *reparabilis* reparable] – **irreparableness** *n*, **irreparably** *adv*

irreplaceable /ˌiri'playsəbl/ *adj* having no adequate substitute [IR- + REPLACEABLE] – **irreplaceably** *adv*

irrepressible /ˌiri'presəbl/ *adj* impossible to restrain or control [IR- + REPRESSIBLE] – **irrepressibly** *adv*, **irrepressibility** /-sə'biləti/ *n*

irreproachable /ˌiri'prohchəbl/ *adj* offering no foundation for blame or criticism [IR- + REPROACHABLE] – **irreproachably** *adv*, **irreproachability** /-chə'biləti/ *n*

irresistible /ˌiri'zistəbl/ *adj* impossible to resist successfully; highly attractive or enticing – **irresistibleness** *n*, **irresistibly** *adv*, **irresistibility** /-'biləti/ *n*

irresolute /i'rezəl(y)ooht/ *adj* lacking decision or a firm aim and purpose – **irresolutely** *adv*, **irresoluteness** *n*, **irresolution** /-'l(y)oohsh(ə)n/ *n*

ˌirre'spective of /ˌiri'spektiv/ *prep* without regard or reference to; IN SPITE OF

irresponsible /ˌiri'sponsəbl/ *adj* **1** showing no regard for the consequences of one's actions **2** unable to bear responsibility [IR- + RESPONSIBLE] – **irresponsibly** *adv*, **irresponsibility** /-sə'biləti/ *n*

irreverence /i'rev(ə)rəns/ *n* (an act or utterance showing) lack of reverence – **irreverent** *adj*, **irreverently** *adv*

irreversible /ˌiri'vuhsəbl/ *adj* unable to be changed back into a previous state or condition [IR- + ¹REVERSIBLE] – **irreversibly** *adv*, **irreversibility** /sə'biləti/ *n*

irrevocable /i'revəkəbl/ *adj* incapable of being revoked or altered [ME, fr L *irrevocabilis*, fr *in-* + *revocabilis* revocable] – **irrevocably** *adv*, **irrevocability** /-'biləti/ *n*

irrigate /'irigayt/ *vt* to wet, moisten: e g **a** to supply (e g land) with water by artificial means **b** to flush (e g an eye or wound) with a stream of liquid ~ *vi* to practise irrigation [L *irrigatus*, pp of *irrigare*, fr *in-* + *rigare* to water] – **irrigator** *n*, **irrigation** /-'gaysh(ə)n/ *n*

irritable /'iritəbl/ *adj* capable of being irritated: e g **a** easily exasperated or excited **b** (excessively) responsive to stimuli – **irritableness** *n*, **irritably** *adv*, **irritability** /-'biləti/ *n*

irritant /'irit(ə)nt/ *n* sthg that irritates or excites – **irritant** *adj*

irritate /'iritayt/ *vt* **1** to excite impatience, anger, or displeasure in **2** to induce a response to a stimulus in or of ~ *vi* to cause or induce displeasure or anger [L *irritatus*, pp of *irritare*] – **irritatingly** *adv*, **irritative** /-tətiv/ *adj*, **irritation** /-'taysh(ə)n/ *n*

irrupt /i'rupt/ *vi* to rush in forcibly or violently [L *irruptus*, pp of *irrumpere*, lit., to break in, fr *in-* + *rumpere* to break – more at BEREAVE] – **irruption** /-sh(ə)n/ *n*, **irruptive** /-tiv/ *adj*, **irruptively** *adv*

is /z; *strong* iz/ *pres 3 sing of* BE, *dial pres 1&2 sing of* BE, *substandard pres pl of* BE [ME, fr OE; akin to OHG *ist* is (fr *sīn* to be), L *est* (fr *esse* to be), Gk *esti* (fr *einai* to be)]

is-, iso- *comb form* **1** equal; homogeneous; uniform ⟨is*acoustic*⟩ **2** isomeric with (a specified compound or radical) ⟨iso*propyl*⟩ [LL, fr Gk, fr *isos* equal]

Isaiah /ie'zie·ə/ *n* (a book of the Old Testament attributed to) a major Hebrew prophet active about 720 BC [Heb *Yĕshaʿyāhū*]

ischaemia /is'keemi·ə/ *n* local deficiency of blood due to decreased arterial flow [NL, fr *ischaemus* styptic, fr Gk *ischaimos*, fr *ischein* to restrain + *haima* blood; akin to Gk *echein* to hold – more at SCHEME]

ischium /'iski·əm/ *n, pl* **ischia** /'iski·ə/ the rearmost and lowest of the 3 principal bones composing either half of the pelvis [L, hip joint, fr Gk *ischion*] – **ischial** *adj*

-ise /-iez/ – see -IZE

isentropic /ˌiesen'tropik/ *adj* of equal or constant entropy – **isentropically** *adv*

-ish /-ish/ *suffix* **1** (*n* → *adj*) of or belonging to (a specified country or ethnic group) ⟨*Finn*ish⟩ **2a(1)** (*adj, n* → *adj*) having a trace of ⟨*summer*ish⟩; slightly ⟨*purpl*ish⟩ ⟨*bigg*ish⟩ **(2)** (*n* → *adj*) having the approximate age of ⟨*forty*ish⟩ **(3)** (*n* → *adj*) being or occurring at the approximate time of ⟨*eight*ish⟩ **b** (*n* → *adj*) having the characteristics of ⟨*boy*ish⟩ ⟨*mul*ish⟩ – often derog ⟨*child*ish⟩ ⟨*book*ish⟩ [ME, fr OE *-isc*; akin to OHG *-isc* -ish, Gk *-iskos*, dim. suffix]

isinglass /'iezingˌglahs/ *n* a very pure gelatin prepared from the air bladders of sturgeons and other fishes and used esp in jellies and glue [prob by folk etymology fr obs D *huizenblas*, fr MD *huusblase*, fr *huus* sturgeon + *blase* bladder]

Islam /'izlahm, -lam/ *n* **1** the religious faith of Muslims including belief in Allah as the sole deity and in Muhammad as his prophet **2a** the civilization or culture accompanying Islamic faith **b** the group of modern nations in which Islam is the dominant religion [Ar *islām* submission (to the will of God)] – **Islamic** /-mik/ *n or adj*, **Islamize** /'izləmiez/ *vt*, **Islamization** /-'zaysh(ə)n/ *n*

island /'ielənd/ *n* **1** an area of land surrounded by water and smaller than a continent **2** sthg like an island (e g in being isolated or surrounded) **3** TRAFFIC ISLAND **4** an isolated superstructure on the deck of a ship, esp an aircraft carrier [alter. of earlier *iland*, fr ME, fr OE *īgland*; akin to ON *eyland* island; both fr a prehistoric NGmc-WGmc compound whose first constituent is represented by OE *īg* island (akin to OE *ēa* river, L *aqua* water) and whose second is represented by OE *land*] – **islander** *n*

isle /iel/ *n* a (small) island – used in some names [ME, fr OF, fr L *insula*]

islet /'ielit/ *n* **1** a little island **2** a small isolated mass of 1 type of tissue

ˌislet of 'Langerhans /'lang·əˌhanz/ *n* any of the groups of endocrine cells in the pancreas that secrete insulin [Paul *Langerhans* †1888 G physician]

ism /'iz(ə)m/ *n* a distinctive doctrine, cause, theory, or practice – often derog [*-ism*]

-ism /-iz(ə)m/ *suffix* (*n, adj* → *n*) **1a** act, practice, or process of ⟨*plagiar*ism⟩ **b** mode of behaviour characteristic of (sby or sthg specified) ⟨*cannibal*ism⟩ **2a** state, condition, or property of ⟨*magnet*ism⟩ **b** pathological state or condition resulting from excessive use of (a specified drug) ⟨*alcohol*ism⟩ or marked by resemblance to (a specified person or thing) ⟨*gigant*ism⟩ **3a** doctrine, theory, or cult of ⟨*Buddh*ism⟩ **b** adherence to (a specified doctrine or system) ⟨*stoic*ism⟩ **c** prejudice on grounds of ⟨*sex*ism⟩ **4** characteristic or peculiar feature of (a specified language or variety of language) ⟨*colloquial*ism⟩ ⟨*Anglic*ism⟩ [ME *-isme*, fr MF & L; MF, partly fr L *-isma* (fr Gk) & partly fr L *-ismus*, fr Gk *-ismos*; Gk *-isma* & *-ismos*, fr verbs in *-izein* -ize]

isn't /'iznt/ is not

iso- – see IS-

isobar /'iesohbah, 'iesə-/ *n* **1** a line on a chart connecting places where the atmospheric pressure is the same **2** any of 2 or more atoms or elements having the same atomic weights or mass numbers but different atomic numbers [ISV *is-* + *-bar* (fr Gk *baros* weight); akin to Gk *barys* heavy – more at [1]GRIEVE] – **isobaric** /-'barik/ *adj*

isochron /'iesə,kron/ *n* a line on a chart connecting points at which an event occurs simultaneously or which represents the same time or time difference [ISV *is-* + *-chron* (fr Gk *chronos* time)]

isochronal /ie'sokrənl/, **isochronous** /-nəs/ *adj* having equal duration; recurring at regular intervals [Gk *isochronos*, fr *is-* + *chronos* time] – **isochronally** *adv*, **isochronism** *n*

isocline /'iesoh,klien/ *n* a fold of rock so closely compressed that the 2 sides are (nearly) parallel – **isoclinal** /-'klienl/, **isoclinic** /-'klinik/ *adj*

isodynamic /,iesohdie'namik/ *adj* connecting points at which the magnetic intensity is the same ⟨~ *line*⟩ [ISV]

,isoe'lectric /-i'lektrik/ *adj* having or representing no difference of electric potential [ISV]

,iso'enzyme /-'enziem/ *n* an isozyme – **isoenzymatic** /-enzi'matik/ *adj*, **isoenzymic** /-en'ziemik/ *adj*

,iso'genic /-'jenik/ *adj* characterized by essentially identical genes ⟨*identical twins are* ~⟩ [*is-* + *gene* + *-ic*]

'iso,gloss /-,glos/ *n* (a representation of) an imaginary line dividing places or regions that differ in a particular linguistic feature [ISV *is-* + Gk *glōssa* language – more at [2]GLOSS] – **isoglossal** /-'glosl/ *adj*

[1]isogonic /,iesə'gonik/, **isogonal** /ie'sogənl/ *adj* of or having equal angles [ISV *is-* + Gk *gōnia* angle – more at -GON]

[2]isogonic *adj* of, having, or indicating equality of magnetic dip

isohel /'iesoh,hel, 'iesə-/ *n* a line on a chart connecting places of equal duration of sunshine [*is-* + Gk *hēlios* sun – more at [1]SOLAR]

isohyet /,iesoh'hie·ət/ *n* a line on a chart connecting areas of equal rainfall [ISV *is-* + Gk *hyetos* rain – more at HYET-] – **isohyetal** /-'hie·ətl/ *adj*

isolate /'ies(ə)layt/ *vt* **1** to set apart from others; *also* to quarantine **2** to separate from another substance so as to obtain in a pure form **3** to insulate [back-formation fr *isolated* set apart, fr F *isolé*, fr It *isolato*, fr *isola* island, fr L *insula*] – **isolatable** *adj*, **isolator** *n*, **isolable** *adj*, **isolation** /-'laysh(ə)n/ *n*

isolationism /,iesə'layshən,iz(ə)m/ *n* a policy of national isolation by refraining from engaging in international relations – **isolationist** *n or adj*

isoleucine /,iesoh'loohseen, -sin, ,iesə-/ *n* an essential amino acid found in most proteins and essential to the diet of human beings [ISV]

isomer /'iesəmə/ *n* a compound, radical, ion, or nuclide isomeric with 1 or more others [ISV, back-formation fr *isomeric*, fr Gk *isomerēs* equally divided, fr *is-* + *meros* part – more at MERIT]

isomerism /ie'somə,riz(ə)m/ *n* **1** the relation of 2 or more chemical compounds, radicals, or ions that contain the same numbers of atoms of the same elements but differ in structural arrangement and properties **2** the relation of 2 or more types of atom with the same mass number and atomic number but different energy states and rates of radioactive decay **3** the condition of being isomerous – **isomerize** *vb*, **isomerization** /-rie'zaysh(ə)n/ *n*, **isomeric** /,iesoh'merik/ *adj*

isomerous /ie'somərəs/ *adj* having an equal number of parts (e g ridges or markings); *esp, of a flower* having the members of each floral whorl equal in number

isometric /,iesoh'metrik, ,iesə-/ *also* **isometrical** /-kl/ *adj* **1** of or characterized by equality of measure **2** CUBIC 2 **3** of or involving isometrics **4** being a representation of an object in which 3 mutually perpendicular axes are equally inclined to the drawing surface – **isometrically** *adv*

isometric line *n* a line representing changes of pressure or temperature under conditions of constant volume

,iso'metrics *n pl but sing or pl in constr* (a system of) exercises in which opposing muscles are contracted so that there is little shortening but great increase in tone of muscle fibres involved

isomorphic /,iesə'mawfik, ,iesoh-/ *adj* having or involving structural similarity or identity – **isomorph** *n*, **isomorphically** *adv*, **isomorphism** *n*, **isomorphous** *adj*

isophote /'iesə,foht, 'iesoh-/ *n* a line on a chart joining points of equal light intensity from a given source [ISV *is-* + *-phote* (fr Gk *phōt-*, *phōs* light) – more at FANCY] – **isophotal** /-'fohtl/ *adj*

isopleth /'iesoh,pleth, 'iesə-/ *n* a line on a map connecting points at which a given variable (e g humidity) has a constant value [ISV *is-* + Gk *plēthos* quantity; akin to Gk *plēthein* to be full – more at FULL] – **isoplethic** /-'plethik/ *adj*

isopod /'iesə,pod/ *n* any of a large order of small crustaceans with eyes not borne on stalks and having 7 pairs of similar legs [deriv of Gk *is-* + *pod-*, *pous* foot – more at FOOT] – **isopod** *adj*, **isopodan** /ie'sopədən, ,iesə'pohdən/ *adj or n*

'iso,prene /-,preen/ *n* an inflammable liquid compound used esp in synthetic rubber [prob fr *is-* + *propyl* + *-ene*]

isosceles /ie'sosəleez/ *adj, of a triangle* having 2 equal sides ☞ MATHEMATICS [LL, fr Gk *isoskelēs*, fr *is-* + *skelos* leg – more at CYLINDER]

isoseismal /,iesoh'siezməl, ,iesə-/ *adj* relating to, having, or indicating equal intensity of earthquake shock

isostasy /ie'sostəsi/ *n* the condition of equilibrium in the earth's crust maintained by a yielding flow of sub-surface rock material under gravitational stress [ISV *is-* + Gk *-stasia* condition of standing, fr *his-*

tanai to cause to stand – more at STAND] – **isostatic** /,iesoh'statik, ,iesə-/ *adj*

isotherm /'iesoh,thuhm, 'iesə-/ *n* **1** a line on a chart connecting points having the same temperature at a given time or the same mean temperature for a given period **2** a line on a chart representing changes of volume or pressure under conditions of constant temperature [F *isotherme* isothermal, fr *is-* + Gk *thermos* hot – more at WARM] – **isothermal** /-'thuhml/ *adj*

isotonic /,iesə'tonik/ *adj* having the same concentration as a surrounding medium or a liquid under comparison – compare HYPERTONIC, HYPOTONIC [ISV] – **isotonicity** /-toh'nisəti/ *n*

isotope /'iesə,tohp/ *n* any of 2 or more species of atoms of a chemical element that have the same atomic number and nearly identical chemical behaviour but differ in atomic mass or mass number and physical properties [*is-* + Gk *topos* place – more at TOPIC] – **isotopic** /-'topik/ *adj*, **isotopically** *adv*, **isotopy** /ie'sotəpi; *also* 'iesə,tohpi/ *n*

isotropic /iesoh'tropik, ,iesə-/ *adj* having physical properties with the same values in all directions ⟨*an ~ crystal*⟩ [ISV] – **isotropy** /ie'sotrəpi/ *n*

'iso,zyme /-,ziem/ *n* any of 2 or more chemically distinct but functionally similar enzymes – **isozymic** /-'ziemik/ *adj*

I-spy /ie 'spie/ *n* a children's game in which a visible object is guessed from the initial letter of its name

Israel /'izrayəl, 'izrie·əl/ *n* **1** the Jewish people **2** a people chosen by God ⟨*Christians claim to be the true ~*⟩ [ME, fr OE, fr LL, fr Gk *Israēl*, fr Heb *Yiśrā'ēl*]

Israeli /iz'rayli/ *adj* (characteristic) of modern Israel [NHeb *yiśrĕ'ēlī*, fr Heb, Israelite, n & adj, fr *Yiśrā'ēl*] – **Israeli** *n*

Israelite /'izrəliet/ *n* any of the descendants of the Hebrew patriarch Jacob; *specif* a member of any of the 10 Hebrew tribes occupying northern Palestine in biblical times [ME, fr LL *Israelita*, fr Gk *Israēlitēs*, fr *Israēl*] – **Israelite** *adj*

[1]**issue** /'ish(y)ooh, 'isyooh/ *n* **1** the action of going, coming, or flowing out **2** a means or place of going out **3** offspring ⟨*died without ~*⟩ **4** an outcome that usu resolves or decides a problem **5** a matter that is in dispute between 2 or more parties; a controversial topic **6** sthg coming out from a usu specified source **7a** the act of publishing, giving out, or making available ⟨*the next ~ of commemorative stamps*⟩ **b** the thing or the whole quantity of things given out, published, or distributed at 1 time ⟨*read the latest ~*⟩ [ME, exit, proceeds, fr MF, fr OF, fr *issir* to come out, go out, fr L *exire* to go out, fr *ex-* + *ire* to go; akin to Goth *iddja* he went, Gk *ienai* to go, Skt *eti* he goes] – **issueless** *adj* – **at issue** under discussion or consideration; in dispute – **join/take issue** to take an opposing or conflicting stand; disagree or engage in argument on a point of dispute

[2]**issue** *vi* **1a** to go, come, or flow out **b** to emerge **2** to descend from a specified parent or ancestor **3** to be a consequence – + *in* **4** to appear or become available through being given out, published, or distributed ~ *vt* **1** to cause to come out **2a** to give out, distribute, or provide officially **b** to send out for sale or circulation – **issuer** *n*

[1]**-ist** /-ist/ *suffix* (→ *n*) **1a** one who performs (a specified action) ⟨*cyclist*⟩ **b** one who makes or produces (a specified thing) ⟨*novelist*⟩ **c** one who plays (a specified musical instrument) ⟨*harpist*⟩ **d** one who operates (a specified mechanical instrument or device) ⟨*motorist*⟩ **2** one who specializes in or practises (a specified art, science, skill, or profession) ⟨*geologist*⟩ ⟨*ventriloquist*⟩ **3** one who adheres to or advocates (a specified doctrine, system, or code of behaviour) ⟨*socialist*⟩ ⟨*royalist*⟩ ⟨*hedonist*⟩ ⟨*Calvinist*⟩ **4** one who is prejudiced on grounds of ⟨*sexist*⟩ [ME *-iste*, fr OF & L; OF *-iste*, fr L *-ista*, *-istes*, fr Gk *-istēs*, fr verbs in *-izein* -ize]

[2]**-ist** *suffix* (→ *adj*) **1** relating to, or characteristic of ⟨*dilettantist*⟩ ⟨*obscurantist*⟩ **2** showing prejudice on grounds of ⟨*racist*⟩

isthmian /'isthmi·ən/ *adj* of or occurring on or near an isthmus; *esp, often cap* of the Isthmus of Corinth in Greece or the games held there in ancient times

isthmus /'isməs; *also* 'isthməs/ *n* **1** a narrow strip of land connecting 2 larger land areas **2** a narrow anatomical part connecting 2 larger parts [L, fr Gk *isthmos*]

istle /'istli/ *n* a strong fibre (e g for cordage or basketry) made from various tropical American plants [AmerSp *ixtle*, fr Nahuatl *ichtli*]

[1]**it** /it/ *pron* **1a** that thing, creature, or group – used as subject or object ⟨*saw the house and noticed that ~ was very old*⟩ ⟨*had a baby but lost ~*⟩; compare HE, ITS, THEY, THERE 2 **b** the person in question ⟨*who is ~? It's me*⟩ **2** – used as subject of an impersonal verb ⟨*~'s raining*⟩ ⟨*~'s not far to London*⟩ **3a** – used as anticipatory subject or object of a verb ⟨*~'s no fun being a secretary*⟩ ⟨*I take ~ that you refuse*⟩ **b** – used to highlight part of a sentence ⟨*~ was the President who arrived yesterday*⟩ ⟨*~ was yesterday that he arrived*⟩ **c** – used with many verbs and prepositions as a meaningless object ⟨*run for ~*⟩ ⟨*footed ~ back to camp*⟩ **4a** this, that – used to refer to previous or following information ⟨*She failed.* It's *a shame*⟩ **b** – used to refer to an explicit or implicit state of affairs ⟨*how's ~ going?*⟩ **5** that which is available ⟨*one boiled egg and that's ~*⟩, important ⟨*yes, that's just ~*⟩, or appropriate ⟨*a bit tighter; that's ~*⟩ [ME, fr OE *hit* – more at HE]

[2]**it** *n* **1** the player in a usu children's game who performs a unique role (e g trying to catch others in a game of tag) **2** SEX APPEAL; *also* SEXUAL INTERCOURSE – infml

Italian /i'tali·ən/ *n* **1** a native or inhabitant of Italy **2** the Romance language of the Italians ☞ LANGUAGE [ME, fr L *Italia* Italy, country of S Europe, fr Gk *Italia*] – **Italian** *adj*, **Italianate** /-nət, -nayt/ *adj*

[1]**italic** /i'talik/ *adj* **1** *cap* (characteristic) of ancient Italy or of Italic **2** of a type style with characters that slant upwards to the right (e g in '*these words are italic*')

[2]**italic** *n* **1** (a character in) an italic type style **2** *cap* the Italic branch of the Indo-European language family that includes Latin, ancient Italian languages, and the Romance languages descended from Latin

italic·ize, -ise /i'tali,siez/ *vt* to print in italics – **italicization** /-'zaysh(ə)n/ *n*

Italo- /italoh-/ *comb form* Italian; Italian and ⟨Italo-*Austrian*⟩

[1]**itch** /ich/ *vi* **1** to have or produce an itch **2** to have a restless desire ⟨*were ~ing to go outside*⟩~ – infml ~ *vt* to cause to itch [ME *icchen*, fr OE *giccan*; akin to OHG *jucchen* to itch]

[2]**itch** *n* **1a** an irritating sensation in the upper surface

of the skin that makes one want to scratch **b** a skin disorder characterized by such a sensation **2** a restless desire – infml – **itchiness** *n*, **itchy** *adj*

it'd /'itəd/ it had; it would

[1]**-ite** /-iet/ *suffix* (→ *n*) **1a** one who belongs to (a specified place, group, etc) ⟨*Israel*ite⟩ ⟨*social*ite⟩ ⟨*Hitt*ite⟩ **b** adherent or follower of (a specified doctrine or movement) ⟨*Pre-Raphael*ite⟩ ⟨*Thatcher*ite⟩ **2a(1)** product of ⟨*metabol*ite⟩ ⟨*catabol*ite⟩ **(2)** commercially manufactured product ⟨*ebon*ite⟩ **b** -itol ⟨*inos*ite⟩ **3** fossil ⟨*ammon*ite⟩ **4** mineral ⟨*baux* ite⟩ ⟨*benton*ite⟩ **5** segment or constituent part of (a specified body or organ) ⟨*som*ite⟩ ⟨*dendr*ite⟩ [ME, fr OF & L; OF, fr L *-ita, -ites*, fr Gk *-itēs*; (3) NL *-ites*, fr L; (5) F, fr L *-ita, -ites*]

[2]**-ite** *suffix* (→ *n*) salt or ester of (a specified acid with a name ending in *-ous*) ⟨*sulph*ite⟩ [F, alter. of *-ate* -ate, fr NL *-atum*]

[1]**item** /'ietəm/ *adv* and in addition – used to introduce each article in a list or enumeration [ME, fr L, fr *ita* thus]

[2]**item** *n* **1** a separate unit in an account or series **2** a separate piece of news or information

item·ize, -ise /'ietəmiez/ *vt* to list ⟨~d *all expenses*⟩ – **itemization** /-'zaysh(ə)n/ *n*

iterate /'itərayt/ *vt* to say or do again or repetitively [L *iteratus*, pp of *iterare*, fr *iterum* again; akin to L *is* he, that, *ita* thus, Skt *itara* the other, *iti* thus] – **iteration** /-'raysh(ə)n/ *n*

iterative /'itərətiv/ *adj* **1** frequentative **2** relating to or being a computational procedure in which each repetition of a cycle of operations produces a result that approximates more closely to the desired result – **iteratively** *adv*

ithyphallic /,ithi'falik/ *adj* having an erect penis – used of figures in pictures or statues [LL *ithyphallicus*, fr Gk *ithyphallikos*, fr *ithyphallos* erect phallus, fr *ithys* straight + *phallos* phallus]

itinerancy /ie'tinərənsi, i'ti-/ *n* a system (e g in the Methodist Church) of rotating ministers among several congregations [ITINERANT + -CY]

itinerant /ie'tinərənt, i'ti-/ *adj* travelling from place to place; *esp* covering a circuit ⟨~ *preacher*⟩ [LL *itinerant-, itinerans*, prp of *itinerari* to journey, fr L *itiner-, iter* journey, way, fr *ire* to go – more at ISSUE] – **itinerant** *n*

i'tinerary /ie'tinərəri, i'ti-/ *n* **1** the (proposed) route of a journey **2** a travel diary **3** a traveller's guidebook

itinerate /ie'tinərayt, i'ti-/ *vi* to travel from place to place, esp on a preaching or judicial circuit – **itineration** /-'raysh(ə)n/ *n*

-itious /-ishəs/ *suffix* (→ *adj*) relating to or having the characteristics of ⟨*fict*itious⟩ ⟨*superst*itious⟩ [L *-icius, -itius*]

-itis /-ietəs/ *suffix* (→ *n*), *pl* **-itises** *also* **-itides** /-ietədeez/ **1** disease or inflammation of ⟨*bronch*itis⟩ **2a** suffering caused by a surfeit or excess of ⟨*election*itis⟩ **b** infatuation or obsession with ⟨*jazz*itis⟩ *USE* (2) humor [NL, fr L & Gk; L, fr Gk, fr fem of *-itēs* -ite]

it'll /'itl/ it will; it shall

-itol /-itol/ *suffix* (→ *n*) polyhydroxy alcohol, usu related to a sugar ⟨*mann*itol⟩ [ISV *-ite* (fr [1]*-ite*) + *-ol*]

its /its/ *adj* relating to it or itself, esp as possessor ⟨~ *climate*⟩ ⟨*going to* ~ *kennel*⟩, agent ⟨*a child proud of* ~ *first drawings*⟩, or object of an action ⟨~ *final enactment into law*⟩

it's /its/ it is; it has

itself /it'self/ *pron* **1** that identical thing, creature, or group – compare [1]IT 1; used reflexively ⟨*a cat washing* ~⟩ or for emphasis ⟨*the letter* ~ *was missing*⟩; compare ONESELF **2** its normal self – **in itself** intrinsically considered ⟨*not dangerous* in itself⟩

itsy-bitsy /,itsi 'bitsi/ *adj* tiny – infml [prob fr baby talk for *little bit*]

-ity /-əti/ *suffix* (→ *n*) **1** quality or state of ⟨*author*ity⟩ ⟨*theatrical*ity⟩; *also* instance of (a specified quality or state) ⟨*an obscen*ity⟩ **2** amount or degree of ⟨*humid*ity⟩ ⟨*salin*ity⟩ [ME *-ite*, fr OF or L; OF *-ité*, fr L *-itat-, -itas*, fr *-i-* (stem vowel of adjs) + *-tat-, -tas* -ity; akin to Gk *-tēt-, -tēs* -ity]

IUD *n* INTRAUTERINE DEVICE

-ium /-i·əm/ *suffix* (→ *n*), *pl* **-iums, -ia** /-i·ə/ **1a** chemical element ⟨*sod*ium⟩ **b** positive ion ⟨*imidazol*ium⟩ ⟨*ammon*ium⟩ **2** small kind of; mass of – esp in botanical terms ⟨*pollin*ium⟩ **3** biological part; part or region of body ⟨*epithel*ium⟩ ⟨*hypogastr*ium⟩ [(1) NL, fr L, ending of some neut nouns; (2, 3) NL, fr L, fr Gk *-ion*]

[1]**-ive** /-iv/ *suffix* (→ *adj*) **1** tending to; disposed to ⟨*correct*ive⟩ ⟨*sport*ive⟩ **2** performing (a specified function) ⟨*descript*ive⟩ ⟨*generat*ive⟩ [ME *-if, -ive*, fr MF & L; MF *-if*, fr L *-ivus*]

[2]**-ive** *suffix* (→ *n*) **1** sby or sthg that performs or serves to accomplish (a specified action) ⟨*sedat*ive⟩ ⟨*detect*ive⟩ **2** sby who is in or affected by (a specified state or condition) ⟨*capt*ive⟩ ⟨*consumpt*ive⟩

I've /iev/ I have

ivied /'ievid/ *adj* overgrown with ivy ⟨~ *walls*⟩

ivory /'ievəri/ *n* **1** the hard creamy-white form of dentine of which the tusks of elephants and other tusked mammals are made **2** a creamy slightly yellowish white colour **3** *pl* things (e g dice or piano keys) made of (sthg resembling) ivory – infml [ME *ivorie*, fr OF *ivoire*, fr L *eboreus* of ivory, fr *ebor-, ebur* ivory, fr Egypt *b*, *bw* elephant, ivory] – **ivory** *adj*

,ivory 'black *n* a fine black pigment made by calcining ivory

'ivory ,nut *n* the nutlike seed of a S American palm that is the source of vegetable ivory

,ivory 'tower *n* aloofness from practical concerns; *also* a place encouraging such an attitude [trans of F *tour d'ivoire*]

ivy /'ievi/ *n* a very common and widely cultivated Eurasian woody climbing plant with evergreen leaves, small yellowish flowers, and black berries [ME, fr OE *īfig*; akin to OHG *ebah* ivy]

'Ivy ,League *adj*, *NAm* (characteristic) of a group of long-established prestigious eastern US colleges (e g Harvard)

izard /'izəd/ *n* a chamois found in the Pyrenees [F]

-ize, -ise /-iez/ *suffix* (→ *vb*) **1a(1)** cause to be, conform to, or resemble ⟨*liquid*ize⟩ ⟨*popular*ize⟩ **(2)** subject to (a specified action) ⟨*plagiar*ize⟩ ⟨*critic*ize⟩ **(3)** impregnate, treat, or combine with ⟨*albumin*ize⟩ ⟨*oxid*ize⟩ **b** treat like; make into ⟨*lion*ize⟩ ⟨*proselyt*ize⟩ **c** treat according to the method of ⟨*bowdler*ize⟩ **2a** become; become like ⟨*crystal*ize⟩ **b** engage in (a specified activity) ⟨*phil-*

osophize⟩ [ME *-isen*, fr OF *-iser*, fr LL *-izare*, fr Gk *-izein*]

J

j /jay/ *n, pl* **j's, js** *often cap* (a graphic representation of or device for reproducing) the 10th letter of the English alphabet

[1]**jab** /jab/ *vb* **-bb-** *vt* **1a** to pierce (as if) with a sharp object **b** to poke quickly or abruptly **2** to strike with a short straight blow ~ *vi* **1** to make quick or abrupt thrusts (as if) with a sharp or pointed object **2** to strike sby with a short straight blow [alter. of *job* (to strike)]

[2]**jab** *n* **1** a short straight punch in boxing delivered with the leading hand **2** a hypodermic injection – infml

jabber /'jabə/ *vi or n* (to engage in) rapid or unintelligible talk or chatter [vb ME *jaberen*, of imit origin; n fr vb] – **jabberer** *n*

jaborandi /jabə'randi/ *n* the dried leaves of either of 2 S American shrubs that contain an alkaloid with actions similar to those of acetylcholine [Pg, fr Tupi *yaborandí*]

jabot /'zhaboh/ *n* a pleated frill of lace or cloth attached down the centre front of a woman's bodice [F]

jacaranda /jakə'randə/ *n* any of a genus of tropical American trees with showy blue flowers [NL, genus name, fr Pg, a tree of this genus]

jacinth /'jasinth/ *n* a reddish orange transparent zircon used as a gem [ME *iacinct*, fr OF *jacinthe*, fr L *hyacinthus*, a flowering plant, a gem]

jacinthe /'jasinth, zhah'sant/ *n* a medium orange colour [F]

[1]**jack** /jak/ *n* **1a** MAN 1a(1), e, 3 – usu as an intensive in such phrases as *every man jack* **b** a labourer, lumberjack, or steeplejack **2** any of various portable mechanisms for exerting pressure or lifting a heavy object a short distance **3** a male donkey **4a** a small white target ball in lawn bowling **b(1)** *pl but sing in constr* a game in which players toss and pick up small bone or metal objects in a variety of shapes in between throws of a ball **(2)** a small 6-pointed metal object used in the game of jacks **5** a playing card carrying the figure of a soldier or servant and ranking usu below the queen **6a** JACK PLUG **b** JACK SOCKET [ME *jacke*, fr *Jacke*, nickname for *Johan* John]

[2]**jack** *vt* **1** to move or lift (as if) by a jack **2** to raise the level or quality of **3** GIVE UP – usu + *in*; infml ⟨*I was fed up with my job so I* ~ed *it in*⟩ *USE* (*1&2*) usu + *up*

jackal /'jakl/ *n* **1** any of several Old World wild dogs smaller than the related wolves **2** sby who collaborates with another in committing immoral acts [Turk *çakal*, fr Per *shagāl*, fr Skt *sṛgāla*]

jackanapes /'jakə,nayps/ *n* **1** a monkey, ape **2a** an impudent or conceited person **b** a mischievous child [perh alter. of (assumed) *Jack Ape*, name given to a pet ape]

jackaroo, jackeroo /jakə'rooh/ *n, Austr* a young inexperienced worker on a cattle or sheep station [[1]*jack* + *-aroo* (as in *kangaroo*)]

jackass /'jak,as/ *n* **1** a male ass **2** a stupid person; a fool

'jack,boot /-,booht/ *n* **1** a heavy military leather boot extending above the knee and worn esp during the 17th and 18th c **2a** a laceless military boot reaching to the calf **b** political repression effected by military or paramilitary force – + *the* – **jackbooted** *adj*

,Jack-by-the-'hedge *n* GARLIC MUSTARD

jackdaw /'jak,daw/ *n* a common black and grey Eurasian bird that is related to but smaller than the common crow

[1]**jacket** /'jakit/ *n* **1** an outer garment for the upper body opening down the full length of the centre front ☞ GARMENT **2a** the natural coat of an animal **b** the skin of a (baked) potato **3a** a thermally insulating cover (e g for a hot water tank) **b(1)** DUST JACKET **(2)** the cover of a paperback book [ME *jaket*, fr MF *jaquet*, dim. of *jaque* short jacket, fr *jacque* peasant, fr the name *Jacques* James]

[2]**jacket** *vt* to put a jacket on; enclose in or with a jacket

,Jack 'Frost *n* frost or frosty weather personified

'jack,hammer /-,hamə/ *n, NAm* PNEUMATIC DRILL

'jack-in-,office *n* a self-important minor official

'jack-in-the-,box *n, pl* **jack-in-the-boxes, jacks-in-the-box** a toy consisting of a small box out of which a figure springs when the lid is raised

[1]**'jack,knife** /-,nief/ *n* **1** a large clasp knife for the pocket **2** a dive in which the diver bends from the waist, touches the ankles with straight knees, and straightens out before hitting the water

[2]**jackknife** *vt* to cause to double up like a jackknife ~ *vi* **1** to double up like a jackknife **2** *esp of an articulated lorry* to turn or rise and form an angle of 90 degrees or less

,jack-of-'all-,trades *n, pl* **jacks-of-all-trades** a handy versatile person – sometimes derog

'jack-o'-,lantern *n* **1** a will-o'-the-wisp **2** a lantern made from a hollowed-out pumpkin cut to look like a human face

'jack ,plane *n* a plane used in the first stages of smoothing wood

'jack ,plug *n* a single-pronged electrical plug for insertion into a jack socket

'jack,pot /-,pot/ *n* **1** (a combination that wins) a top prize on a fruit machine **2** a large prize (e g in a lottery), often made up of several accumulated prizes that have not been previously won [[1]*jack* 5 + [1]*pot* 4; fr a form of poker in which a player requires 2 jacks or better to open]

Jack Russell terrier /'rusl/ *n* any of a breed of small pugnacious terriers orig bred to hunt rats

[*Jack* (John) *Russell* †1883 E clergyman & dog-fancier]

'jack,snipe /-,sniep/ *n* a small Old World true snipe

'jack ,socket *n* an electrical socket that is designed to receive a jack plug

,jack 'tar *n* a sailor – infml

'jack ,towel *n, dial Br* ROLLER TOWEL

jack up *vt, NZ* to settle, fix

Jacobean /jakə'bee·ən/ *adj* of (the age of) James I [NL *Jacobaeus*, fr *Jacobus* James]

Jacobin /'jakəbin/ *n* a member of a radical democratic political group engaging in terrorist activities during the French Revolution; *broadly* an extremist radical [F, fr *Jacobin* Dominican; fr the group's founding in the Dominican convent in the Rue St-Jacques in Paris] – **Jacobinism** *n*

Jacobite /'jakəbiet/ *n* a supporter of James II or of the Stuarts after 1688 [*Jacobus* (James II)] – **Jacobitism** /jakə'bitiz(ə)m/ *n*

,Jacob's 'ladder /'jaykəbz/ *n* **1** any of a genus of plants of the phlox family that have bell-shaped flowers **2** a ship's rope or wire ladder [fr the ladder seen in a dream by Jacob in Gen 28:12]

jacquard /'jakahd/ *n, often cap* **1** a loom apparatus or head for weaving figured fabrics **2** a fabric of intricate variegated weave or pattern [Joseph *Jacquard* †1834 F inventor]

jacquerie /'zhakəri (*Fr* ʒakri)/ *n, often cap* a peasants' revolt [F, fr the French peasant revolt in 1358, fr MF, fr *jacque* peasant – more at JACKET]

jactitation /jakti'taysh(ə)n/ *n* a tossing to and fro or jerking and twitching of (a part of) the body [LL *jactitation-, jactitatio*, fr *jactitatus*, pp of *jactitare*, freq of *jactare* to throw – more at [2]JET]

[1]jade /jayd/ *n* **1** a vicious or worn-out old horse **2** *archaic* a flirtatious or disreputable woman [ME]

[2]jade *n* either of 2 typically green hard gemstones: **a** jadeite **b** nephrite [F, fr obs Sp (*piedra de la*) *ijada*, lit., loin stone; fr the belief that jade cures renal colic]

'jaded *adj* fatigued (as if) by overwork or dissipation [fr pp of *jade* (to wear out by overwork), fr [1]*jade*]

,jade 'green *n or adj* (a) light bluish green

jadeite /'jaydiet/ *n* the rarer more valuable usu white to green jade that is a silicate of sodium and aluminium [F]

jaeger /'yaygə/ *n* a skua [G *jäger* hunter]

jaffa /'jafə/ *n, often cap* a large type of orange grown esp in Israel [*Jaffa*, former port in Israel]

[1]jag /jag/ *vt* **-gg-** **1** to cut or tear unevenly or raggedly **2** to cut indentations into [ME *jaggen* to stab, slash]

[2]jag *n* a sharp projecting part – **jaggy** *adj*

[3]jag *n* a period of indulgence ⟨*a crying* ~⟩; *esp* a drinking bout – slang [origin unknown]

jagged /'jagid/ *adj* having a sharply uneven edge or surface – **jaggedly** *adv*, **jaggedness** *n*

jaguar /'jagyoo·ə/ *n* a big cat of tropical America that is typically brownish yellow or buff with black spots [Sp *yaguar* & Pg *jaguar*, fr Guarani *yaguara* & Tupi *jaguara*]

jaguarundi /jagwə'roondi/ *n, pl* **jaguarundis** a slender long-tailed greyish wildcat of Central and S America [AmerSp & Pg, fr Tupi *jaguarundi* & Guarani *yaguarundi*]

jai alai /,khay ah'lay/ *n* a court game for 2 or 4 players who use a long curved wicker basket strapped to the wrist to catch and hurl a ball against a wall [Sp, fr Basque, fr *jai* festival + *alai* merry]

[1]jail, *Br also* **gaol** /jayl/ *n* a prison [ME *jaiole*, fr OF, fr (assumed) VL *caveola*, dim. of L *cavea* cage – more at CAGE]

[2]jail, *Br also* **gaol** *vt* to confine (as if) in a jail

'jail,bird /-,buhd/ *n* a person who has been (habitually) confined in jail

'jail,break /-,brayk/ *n* an escape from jail

'jail de,livery *n* the clearing of a jail by bringing the prisoners to trial

jailer, jailor /'jaylə/ *n* **1** a keeper of a jail **2** sby or sthg that restricts another's liberty (as if) by imprisonment

Jain /jayn, jien/ *n* an adherent of a Hindu sect whose religion resembles Buddhism [Hindi, fr Skt *Jaina*] – **Jainism** *n*

jakes /jayks/ *n, pl* **jakes** a privy – infml [perh fr F *Jacques* James]

jalap /'jaləp/ *n* (a drastic purgative prepared from the root of) a Mexican plant [F & Sp; F *jalap*, fr Sp *jalapa*, fr *Jalapa*, city in Mexico]

jalopy /jə'lopi/ *n* a dilapidated old vehicle or aircraft – infml [origin unknown]

jalousie /'zhaləzi, 'zhaloo,zee/ *n* a blind with adjustable horizontal slats for admitting light and air while excluding sun and rain [F, lit., jealousy, fr OF *jelous* jealous]

[1]jam /jam/ *vb* **-mm-** *vt* **1a** to press, squeeze, or crush into a close or tight position **b** to cause to become wedged so as to be unworkable ⟨~ *the typewriter keys*⟩ **c** to block passage of or along ⟨*crowds* ~ming *the streets*⟩ **d** to fill (to excess) ⟨*a book* ~med *with facts*⟩ **2** CRUSH 1; *also* to bruise by crushing **3** to send out interfering signals or cause reflections so as to make **a** (a radio signal) unintelligible **b** (a radio device) ineffective ~ *vi* **1a** to become blocked or wedged **b** to become unworkable through the jamming of a movable part **2** to crowd or squash tightly together ⟨*they all* ~med *into the room*⟩ **3** to take part in a jam session – slang [perh imit]

[2]jam *n* **1** a crowded mass that impedes or blocks ⟨*traffic* ~⟩ **2** the pressure or congestion of a crowd **3** a difficult state of affairs – infml

[3]jam *n* a preserve made by boiling fruit and sugar to a thick consistency [prob fr [1]*jam*]

jamb /jam/ *n* a straight vertical member or surface forming the side of an opening for a door, window, etc [ME *jambe*, fr MF, lit., leg, fr LL *gamba* – more at GAMBIT]

jamboree /jambə'ree/ *n* **1** a large festive gathering **2** a large gathering of scouts or guides in a camp [origin unknown]

James /jaymz/ *n* (a book of the New Testament attributed to) a brother of Jesus [F, fr LL *Jacobus*]

jammy /'jami/ *adj, Br* **1** lucky **2** easy *USE* infml [[3]*jam* + [1]*-y*]

jam on *vt* to apply (brakes) suddenly and forcibly

,jam-'packed *adj* full to overflowing

'jam ,session *n* an impromptu jazz performance that features group improvisation [[2]*jam*]

jandal /'jandl/ *n, NZ* a flip-flop [prob alter. of *sandal*]

jangle /'jang·gl/ *vi* **1** *of the nerves* to be in a state of tense irritation **2** to make a harsh or discordant often ringing noise ~ *vt* **1** to utter or cause to sound in a jangling way **2** to excite (e g nerves) to tense irritation [ME *janglen*, fr OF *jangler*, of Gmc origin; akin to MD *jangelen* to grumble] – **jangle** *n*, **jangly** *adj*

janissary /ˈjanisəri/ *n* **1** *often cap* a soldier of an élite corps of Turkish troops organized in the 14th c and abolished in 1826 **2** a loyal or subservient official or supporter [It *gianizzero*, fr Turk *yeniçeri*]

janitor /ˈjanitə/, *fem* **janitress** /-tris/ *n* **1** a doorkeeper; [1]PORTER **2** *NAm* a caretaker [L, fr *janua* door, fr *janus* arch, gate] – **janitorial** /-ˈtawri·əl/ *adj*

janizary /ˈjanizəri/ *n* a janissary

January /ˈjanyoo(ə)ri/ *n* the 1st month of the Gregorian calendar [ME *Januarie*, fr L *Januarius*, 1st month of the ancient Roman year, fr *Janus*, god of doors, gates, & beginnings, fr *janus*]

Jap /jap/ *n* a Japanese – infml

[1]**japan** /jəˈpan/ *n* **1** a varnish giving a hard brilliant finish **2** work (e g lacquer ware) finished and decorated in the Japanese manner [*Japan*, country in E Asia]

[2]**japan** *vt* **-nn- 1** to cover with a coat of japan **2** to give a high gloss to

Japanese /japəˈneez/ *n, pl* **Japanese 1** a native or inhabitant of Japan **2** the language of the Japanese ☞ ALPHABET, LANGUAGE – **Japanese** *adj*

Japanese quince *n* the japonica

jape /jayp/ *vi or n* (to) jest, joke [vb ME *japen* to trick, copulate with, jest; n fr vb]

japonica /jəˈponikə/ *n* a hardy ornamental shrub of the rose family with clusters of scarlet, white, or pink flowers [NL, fr fem of *Japonicus* Japanese, fr *Japonia* Japan]

[1]**jar** /jah/ *vb* **-rr-** *vi* **1a** to make a harsh or discordant noise **b** to be out of harmony *with* **c** to have a harshly disagreeable effect – + *on* or *upon* **2** to vibrate ~ *vt* to cause to jar, esp by shaking or causing a shock to [prob imit] – **jarringly** *adv*

[2]**jar** *n* **1** a jarring noise **2a** a sudden or unexpected shake **b** an unsettling shock (e g to nerves or feelings)

[3]**jar** *n* **1a** a usu cylindrical short-necked and wide-mouthed container, made esp of glass **b** the contents of or quantity contained in a jar **2** a glass of an alcoholic drink, esp beer – infml [MF *jarre*, fr OProv *jarra*, fr Ar *jarrah* earthen water vessel] – **jarful** *n*

jardiniere /ˌzhahdiˈnyeə (*Fr* ʒardinjɛːr)/ *n* **1** an ornamental stand or large pot for plants or flowers **2** a garnish consisting of several vegetables arranged in groups round meat [F *jardinière*, lit., female gardener]

jargon /ˈjahgən/ *n* **1a** confused unintelligible language **b** outlandish or barbarous language **2** the terminology or idiom of a particular activity or group ⟨*scientific* ~⟩ **3** obscure and often pretentious language [ME, fr MF] – **jargonize** *vb*, **jargonistic** /-ˈnistik/ *adj*

jargoon /jahˈgoohn/ *n* a colourless, pale yellow, or smoky zircon [F *jargon* – more at ZIRCON]

jarl /yahl/ *n* a Scandinavian noble ranking immediately below the king [ON – more at EARL]

jarrah, jarra /ˈjarə/ *n* (the wood of) an Australian eucalyptus [native name in Australia]

jasmine /ˈjasmin, ˈjaz-/ *n* **1** any of numerous often climbing shrubs that usu have extremely fragrant flowers; *esp* a high-climbing half-evergreen Asian shrub with fragrant white flowers **2** a light yellow [F *jasmin*, fr Ar *yāsamīn*, fr Per]

jasper /ˈjaspə/ *n* an opaque quartz which is usu red brown, yellow, or dark green [ME *jaspre*, fr MF, fr L *jaspis*, fr Gk *iaspis*, of Sem origin; akin to Heb *yāshĕpheh* jasper] – **jaspery** *adj*

Jat /jaht/ *n* a member of an Indo-Aryan people living esp in the Punjab and Uttar Pradesh [Hindi *Jāṭ*]

jaundice /ˈjawndis/ *n* **1** an abnormal condition marked by yellowish pigmentation of the skin, tissues, and body fluids caused by the deposition of bile pigments **2** a state of prejudice inspired by bitterness, envy, or disillusionment [ME *jaundis*, fr MF *jaunisse*, fr *jaune* yellow, fr L *galbinus* yellowish green, fr *galbus* yellow]

ˈ**jaundiced** *adj* **1** affected with jaundice **2** mistrustful or prejudiced, esp because of bitterness, envy, or disillusionment

jaunt /jawnt/ *vi or n* (to make) a short journey for pleasure [origin unknown]

ˈ**jaunting ˌcar** /ˈjawnting/ *n* a light open 2-wheeled horse-drawn vehicle used formerly in Ireland

jaunty /ˈjawnti/ *adj* having or showing airy self-confidence; sprightly [modif of F *gentil* genteel, elegant] – **jauntily** *adv*, **jauntiness** *n*

ˌ**Java ˈman** /ˈjahvə/ *n* pithecanthropus [*Java*, island in Indonesia, where skulls of pithecanthropus were found]

Javanese /jahvəˈneez/ *n, pl* **Javanese 1** a member of an Indonesian people inhabiting the island of Java **2** the Austronesian language of the inhabitants of Java ☞ LANGUAGE [*Java* + *-nese* (as in *Japanese*)] – **Javanese** *adj*

javelin /ˈjav(ə)lin/ *n* a light spear thrown as a weapon or in an athletic field event; *also* the sport of throwing the javelin [MF *javeline*, alter. of *javelot*, of Celt origin; akin to OIr *gabul* forked stick]

Jaˈvelle ˌwater /zhəˈvel, zha-/ *n* an aqueous solution of sodium hypochlorite used in disinfecting, bleaching, etc [*Javel*, former village in France]

[1]**jaw** /jaw/ *n* **1a** either of 2 cartilaginous or bony structures that in most vertebrates form a framework above and below the mouth in which the teeth are set **b** any of various organs of invertebrates that perform the function of the vertebrate jaws **2** *pl* **a** the entrance of a narrow pass or channel **b** the 2 parts of a machine, tool, etc between which sthg may be clamped or crushed ⟨*the* ~s *of a vice*⟩ **c** a position or situation of imminent danger ⟨*stared into the* ~s *of death*⟩ **3a** continual and esp impudent or offensive talk – infml **b** a friendly chat – infml [ME]

[2]**jaw** *vi* to talk or gossip for a long time or long-windedly – infml

ˈ**jawˌbone** /-ˌbohn/ *n* the bone of an esp lower jaw

ˈ**jawˌbreaker** /-ˌbraykə/ *n* a word which is difficult to pronounce – infml

jawed /jawd/ *adj* having jaws, esp of a specified type or shape – usu in combination ⟨*square*-jawed⟩

jay /jay/ *n* an Old World bird of the crow family with a dull pink body, black, white, and blue wings, and a black-and-white crest [ME, fr MF *jai*, fr LL *gaius*]

ˈ**jayˌwalk** /-ˌwawk/ *vi* to cross a street carelessly so as to be endangered by traffic [*jay* (simpleton, yokel) + *walk*] – **jaywalker** *n*

jazz /jaz/ *n* **1** music developed esp from ragtime and blues and characterized by syncopated rhythms and individual or group improvisation around a basic theme or melody **2** empty pretentious talk ⟨*spouted a lot of scientific* ~⟩ – infml **3** similar but unspecified things ⟨*planting, weeding, cropping, and all that* ~ – *Evening Argus* (Brighton)⟩ – infml [prob fr NAm Negro slang *jazz* copulation, frenzy, prob of W African origin]

jazz up *vt* **1** to play (e g a piece of music) in the style of jazz **2** to enliven **3** to make bright, esp in a vivid or garish way *USE* infml

jazzy /'jazi/ *adj* **1** having the characteristics of jazz **2** garish, gaudy – infml – **jazzily** *adv*, **jazziness** *n*

jealous /'jeləs/ *adj* **1a** intolerant of rivalry or unfaithfulness ⟨*the Lord your God is a* ~ *God* – Ex 20:5(AV)⟩ **b** apprehensive of and hostile towards a (supposed) rival **2** resentful, envious *of* **3** vigilant in guarding a possession, right, etc ⟨~ *of his honour*⟩ **4** distrustfully watchful ⟨*kept a* ~ *eye on her husband*⟩ [ME *jelous*, fr OF, fr (assumed) VL *zelosus*, fr LL *zelus* zeal – more at ZEAL] – **jealously** *adv*, **jealousness** *n*, **jealousy** *n*

jean /jeen/ *n* a durable twilled cotton cloth used esp for work clothes [short for *jean fustian*, fr ME *Gene* Genoa, city in Italy + *fustian*]

jeans /jeenz/ *n pl in constr, pl* **jeans** casual usu close-fitting trousers, made esp of blue denim

jeep /jeep/ *n* a small rugged general-purpose motor vehicle with 4-wheel drive, used esp by the armed forces [alter. of *gee pee*, fr *g*eneral-*p*urpose]

[1]**jeer** /jiə/ *vb* to laugh mockingly or scoff (at) [origin unknown] – **jeerer** *n*, **jeeringly** *adv*

[2]**jeer** *n* a jeering remark; a taunt

Jehovah /ji'hohvə/ *n* GOD 1 ⟨*in the Lord* ~ *is everlasting strength* – Isaiah 26:4 (AV)⟩ [NL, false reading (as *Yĕhōwāh*) of Heb *Yahweh*]

Je,hovah's 'Witness *n* a member of a fundamentalist sect practising personal evangelism, rejecting the authority of the secular state, and preaching that the end of the present world is imminent

jejun- /jijoohn-/, **jejuno-** *comb form* jejunum ⟨*jejunectomy*⟩ [L *jejunum*]

jejune /ji'joohn/ *adj* **1** lacking nutritive value or substance; *also* barren **2** lacking interest or significance **3** lacking maturity; puerile [L *jejunus*] – **jejunely** *adv*, **jejuneness** *n*

jejunum /ji'joohnəm/ *n* the section of the small intestine between the duodenum and the ileum [L, fr neut of *jejunus*] – **jejunal** *adj*

Jekyll and Hyde /jekəl ənd 'hied/ *n* a person having a split personality, one side of which is good and the other evil [Dr *Jekyll* & Mr *Hyde*, the 2 sides of the split personality of the protagonist of *The Strange Case of Dr Jekyll and Mr Hyde* by R L Stevenson †1894 Sc writer] – **Jekyll-and-Hyde** *adj*

jell /jel/ *vb, chiefly NAm* to gel

jellaba /jə'lahbə/ *n* a djellaba

[1]**jelly** /'jeli/ *n* **1a** a soft fruit-flavoured transparent dessert set with gelatin **b** a savoury food product of similar consistency, made esp from meat stock and gelatin **2** a clear fruit preserve made by boiling sugar and the juice of fruit **3** a substance resembling jelly in consistency [ME *gelly*, fr MF *gelee*, fr fem of *gelé*, pp of *geler* to freeze, congeal, fr L *gelare* – more at COLD]

[2]**jelly** *vi* to jell ~ *vt* **1** to bring to the consistency of jelly; cause to set **2** to set in a jelly ⟨jellied *beef*⟩

'jelly ,baby *n* a small soft gelatinous sweet in the shape of a person

'jelly,fish /-,fish/ *n* **1** a free-swimming marine coelenterate that has a nearly transparent saucer-shaped body and extendable tentacles covered with stinging cells **2** a person lacking firmness of character

jemmy /'jemi/ *vt or n, Br* (to force open with) a steel crowbar, used esp by burglars [*Jemmy*, nickname for *James*]

je ne sais quoi /,zhə nə say 'kwah (*Fr* ʒə nə sɛ kwa)/ *n* a quality that cannot be adequately described or expressed [F, lit., I know not what]

jennet /'jenit/ *n* **1** a small Spanish riding horse **2** a female donkey [ME *genett*, fr MF *genet*, fr Catal, Zenete (member of a Berber people), horse]

jenny /'jeni/ *n* **1** a female donkey **2** SPINNING JENNY [fr the name *Jenny*]

jeon /jun/ *n* ☞ *Korea (North), Korea (South)* at NATIONALITY [Korean]

jeopard·ize, -ise /'jepədiez/ *vt* to put in jeopardy

jeopardy /'jepədi/ *n* **1** exposure to or risk of death, loss, injury, etc; danger **2** liability to conviction faced by a defendant in a criminal trial [ME *jeopardie*, fr AF *juparti*, fr OF *jeu parti* alternative, lit., divided game]

jequirity bean /ji'kwirəti/ *n* (the poisonous scarlet and black seed of) the rosary pea [Pg *jequiriti*]

jerboa /juh'boh·ə/ *n* any of several nocturnal Old World desert rodents with long legs adapted for jumping [Ar *yarbū'*]

jeremiad /,jerə'mie·əd/ *n* a prolonged lamentation or complaint [F *jérémiade*, fr *Jérémie* Jeremiah, fr LL *Jeremias*]

Jeremiah /,jerə'mie·ə/ *n* **1** (a book of the Old Testament attributed to) a Hebrew prophet of the 6th and 7th c BC **2** sby who is mournfully pessimistic about the present and foretells a calamitous future [LL *Jeremias*, fr Gk *Hieremias*, fr Heb *Yirmĕyāh*]

[1]**jerk** /juhk/ *vt* **1** to give a quick suddenly arrested push, pull, twist, or jolt to **2** to propel with short abrupt motions **3** to utter in an abrupt or snappy manner ~ *vi* **1** to make a sudden spasmodic motion **2** to move in short abrupt motions [prob alter. of E dial. *yerk* (to thrash, attack, excite), fr ME *yerken* to bind tightly] – **jerker** *n*

[2]**jerk** *n* **1** a single quick motion (e g a pull, twist, or jolt) **2a** an involuntary spasmodic muscular movement due to reflex action **b** *pl* spasmodic movements due to nervous excitement **3** *chiefly NAm* a stupid, foolish, or naive person – infml

[3]**jerk** *vt* to preserve (e g beef or venison) by cutting into long slices or strips and drying in the sun [back-formation fr *jerky* (preserved meat), modif of AmerSp *charqui*]

jerkin /'juhkin/ *n* **1** a close-fitting hip-length sleeveless jacket, made esp of leather and worn by men in the 16th and 17th c **2** a man's or woman's sleeveless jacket [origin unknown]

jerk off *vb, chiefly NAm* to masturbate – vulg

jerky /'juhki/ *adj* **1** marked by irregular or spasmodic movements **2** marked by abrupt or awkward changes – **jerkily** *adv*, **jerkiness** *n*

jeroboam /,jerə'boh·əm, -əm/ *n* a wine bottle holding 4 to 6 times the usual amount [*Jeroboam* I † *ab* 912 BC king of the northern kingdom of Israel]

Jerry /'jeri/ *n, chiefly Br* **1** a German; *esp* a German soldier in WW II 2 *sing or pl in constr* the German armed forces in WW II [by shortening & alter.]

'jerry-,build /'jeri-/ *vt* **jerry-built** /bilt/ to build (e g houses) cheaply and flimsily [back-formation fr *jerry-built,* of unknown origin] – **jerry-builder** *n,* **jerry-built** *adj*

jerry can, jerrican /'jeri,kan/ *n* a narrow flat-sided container for carrying liquids, esp petrol or water, with a capacity of about 25l (about 5gal) [*Jerry* + *can*; fr its German design]

jersey /'juhzi/ *n* **1** a plain weft-knitted fabric made of wool, nylon, etc and used esp for clothing **2** [2]JUMPER 1 **3** *often cap* any of a breed of small short-horned cattle noted for their rich milk [*Jersey,* one of the Channel islands]

Jerusalem artichoke /jə'roohsələm/ *n* (an edible sweet-tasting tuber of) a perennial N American sunflower [*Jerusalem* by folk etymology fr It *girasole* girasol]

jess /jes/ *n* a short strap made esp of leather which is secured to the leg of a hawk and usu has a ring on the other end for attaching a leash [ME *ges,* fr MF *gies,* fr pl of *jet* throw, fr *jeter* to throw – more at [2]JET] – **jess** *vt*

[1]jest /jest/ *n* **1** an amusing or mocking act or utterance; a joke **2** a frivolous mood or manner ⟨*was just said in* ~⟩ [ME *geste* deed, exploit, prank, fr OF, fr L *gesta* deeds, fr neut pl of *gestus,* pp of *gerere* to bear, wage – more at CAST]

[2]jest *vi* **1** to speak or act without seriousness **2** to make a witty remark

jester /'jestə/ *n* a retainer formerly kept in great households to provide casual amusement and commonly dressed in a brightly coloured costume [[2]JEST + [2]-ER]

Jesu /'jeezyooh/ *n* Jesus – poetic

Jesuit /'jezyoo·it/ *n* **1** a member of the Society of Jesus, a Roman Catholic order founded by St Ignatius Loyola in 1534 which is devoted to missionary and educational work **2** one given to intrigue or equivocation [NL *Jesuita,* fr LL *Jesus*] – **jesuitism, jesuitry** /-tri/ *n, often cap,* **jesuitize** *vb, often cap,* **jesuitic** /-'itik/, **jesuitical** *adj, often cap,* **jesuitically** *adv, often cap*

Jesus /'jeezəs/, **,Jesus 'Christ** *n* **1** the Jewish religious teacher whose life, death, and resurrection as reported by the Evangelists in the New Testament are the basis of the Christian message of salvation **2** – used interjectionally as an expression of surprise, dismay, annoyance, etc; slang [LL, fr Gk *Iēsous,* fr Heb *Yēshūa'*]

'Jesus ,freak *n* a usu young member of any of various evangelical Christian groups characterized by a simple, usu communal way of life – infml

[1]jet /jet/ *n* **1** a hard velvet-black form of coal that is often polished and used for jewellery **2** an intense black [ME, fr MF *jaiet,* fr L *gagates,* fr Gk *gagatēs,* fr *Gagas,* town & river in Asia Minor]

[2]jet *vb* **-tt-** *vi* to spout forth in a jet or jets ~ *vt* **1** to emit in a jet or jets **2** to direct a jet of liquid or gas at [MF *jeter,* lit., to throw, fr L *jactare* to throw, fr *jactus,* pp of *jacere* to throw; akin to Gk *hienai* to send]

[3]jet *n* **1a** a forceful stream of fluid discharged from a narrow opening or a nozzle **b** a nozzle or other narrow opening for emitting a jet of fluid **2** (an aircraft powered by) a jet engine

[4]jet *vi* **-tt-** to travel by jet aircraft

,jet-'black *adj* of a very dark black

jeté /zhə'tay (*Fr* ʒəte)/ *n* a high arching leap in ballet in which the dancer has one leg stretched forwards and the other backwards [F, fr pp of *jeter*]

'jet ,engine *n* an engine that produces motion in one direction as a result of the discharge of a jet of fluid in the opposite direction; *specif* an aircraft engine that discharges the hot air and gases produced by the combustion of a fuel to produce propulsion or lift

'jet ,lag *n* a temporary disruption of normal bodily rhythms after a long flight, esp due to differences in local time

,jet-pro'pelled *adj* moving (as if) by jet propulsion

jet propulsion *n* propulsion of a body produced by the forwardly directed forces resulting from the backward discharge of a jet of fluid; *specif* propulsion of an aeroplane by jet engines

jetsam /'jetsəm/ *n* **1** goods thrown overboard to lighten a ship in distress; *esp* such goods when washed ashore **2** FLOTSAM AND JETSAM [alter. of *jettison*]

'jet ,set *n sing or pl in constr* an international wealthy elite who frequent fashionable resorts [[3]*jet*] – **jet-set** *adj,* **jetsetter** *n*

'jet ,stream *n* a current of strong winds high in the atmosphere usu blowing from a westerly direction and often exceeding a speed of 400km/hour (250mi per hour)

[1]jettison /'jetis(ə)n/ *n* **1** the act of jettisoning cargo **2** abandonment [ME *jetteson,* fr AF *getteson,* fr OF *getaison* action of throwing, fr L *jactation-, jactatio,* fr *jactatus,* pp of *jactare* – more at [2]JET]

[2]jettison *vt* **1** to throw (e g goods or cargo) overboard to lighten the load of a ship in distress **2** to cast off as superfluous or encumbering; abandon **3** to drop (e g unwanted material) from an aircraft or spacecraft in flight – **jettisonable** *adj*

jetty /'jeti/ *n* **1** a structure (e g a pier or breakwater) extending into a sea, lake, or river to influence the current or tide or to protect a harbour **2** a small landing pier [ME *jette,* fr MF *jetee,* fr fem of *jeté,* pp of *jeter* to throw – more at [2]JET]

jeu d'esprit /,zhuh de'spree (*Fr* ʒø dɛspri)/ *n, pl* **jeux d'esprit** /~/ a witty comment or composition [F, lit., play of the mind]

jeunesse dorée /zhuh,nes daw'ray (*Fr* ʒønɛs dɔre)/ *n* young people of wealth and fashion [F, gilded youth]

jew /jooh/ *vt* to get the better of financially, esp by hard bargaining – often + *out of;* derog

Jew, *fem* **Jewess** /-'es, -is/ *n* **1** a member of a Semitic people existing as a nation in Palestine from the 6th c BC to the 1st c AD, some of whom now live in Israel and others in various countries throughout the world **2** a person whose religion is Judaism **3** sby given to hard financial bargaining – derog [ME, fr OF *gyu,* fr L *Judaeus,* fr Gk *Ioudaios,* fr Heb *Yĕhūdhī,* fr *Yĕhūdhāh* Judah, Jewish kingdom] – **Jewish** *adj*

jewel /'jooh·əl/ *n* **1** an ornament of precious metal often set with stones and worn as an accessory **2** sby or sthg highly esteemed **3** a precious stone **4** a bearing for a pivot (e g in a watch or compass) made of crystal, precious stone, or glass [ME *juel,* fr OF, dim. of *jeu* game, play, fr L *jocus* game, joke – more at JOKE] – **jewelled** *adj*

jeweller, *NAm chiefly* **jeweler** /'jooh·ələ/ *n* sby who deals in, makes, or repairs jewellery and often watches, silverware, etc

'jewellery, *NAm chiefly* **jewelry** /-ri/ *n* jewels, esp as worn for personal adornment

jewfish /'jooh,fish/ *n* any of various large groupers living esp in southern seas

'Jewry /-ri/ *n* **1** a Jewish quarter (e g of a town); a ghetto **2** the Jewish people collectively

,Jew's 'harp, Jews' harp *n* a small lyre-shaped instrument that is placed between the teeth and sounded by striking a metal tongue with the finger

jezail /jə'ziel, -'zayl/ *n* a long heavy Afghan rifle [Per *jazā'il*]

Jezebel /'jezəbel, -bl/ *n, often not cap* a shameless or immoral woman [*Jezebel,* wife of a King of Israel, known for her wicked conduct (1 Kings 16:31 ff)]

JHVH *n* YHWH

jiao /jow/ *n* ☞ *China* at NATIONALITY [Chin]

[1]**jib** /jib/ *n* a triangular sail set on a stay extending from the top of the foremast to the bow or the bowsprit ☞ SHIP [origin unknown]

[2]**jib** *vb* **-bb-** *chiefly NAm* to gybe

[3]**jib** *n* the projecting arm of a crane [prob by shortening & alter. fr *gibbet*]

[4]**jib** *vi* **-bb-** *esp of a horse* to refuse to proceed further [prob fr [2]*jib*] – **jibber** *n* – **jib at** to recoil or baulk at

[1]**jibe** /jieb/ *vb* to gibe

[2]**jibe** *vb, chiefly NAm* to gybe

jiff /jif/ *n* a jiffy [by shortening]

jiffy /'jifi/ *n* a moment, instant ⟨*ready in a* ~⟩ – infml [origin unknown]

[1]**jig** /jig/ *n* **1** (a piece of music for) any of several lively springy dances in triple time – compare GIGUE **2a** any of several fishing lures that jerk up and down in the water **b** a device used to hold a piece of work in position (e g during machining or assembly) and to guide the tools working on it **c** a device in which crushed ore or coal is separated from waste by agitating in water [prob fr MF *giguer* to dance, fr *gigue* fiddle, of Gmc origin; akin to OHG *gīga* fiddle; akin to ON *geiga* to turn aside – more at [1]GIG]

[2]**jig** *vb* **-gg-** *vt* **1** to dance in the rapid lively manner of a jig **2a** to cause to make a rapid jerky movement **b** to separate (a mineral from waste) with a jig **3** to catch (a fish) with a jig **4** to machine by using a jig ~ *vi* **1a** to dance a jig **b** to move with rapid jerky motions **2** to fish with a jig **3** to work with or operate a jig

jigger /'jigə/ *n* **1** (a glass container holding) a variable measure of spirits used esp in mixing drinks **2** *chiefly NAm* sthg, esp a gadget or small piece of apparatus, which one is (temporarily) unable to designate accurately – infml [[2]JIG + [2]-ER]

jiggered /'jigəd/ *adj* **1** blowed, damned ⟨*well I'll be* ~⟩ – infml **2** *N Eng* tired out; exhausted [perh euphemism for *buggered*]

jiggery-pokery /jigəri 'pohkəri/ *n, Br* dishonest underhand dealings or scheming – infml [alter. of Sc *joukery-pawkery,* fr *jouk* to cheat + *pawk* trick]

jiggle /'jigl/ *vb* **jiggling** /'jigl·ing, 'jigling/ to (cause to) move with quick short jerks – infml [freq of [2]*jig*] – **jiggle** *n*

jigsaw /'jig,saw/ *n* **1** a power-driven fretsaw **2** **jigsaw, jigsaw puzzle** a puzzle consisting of small irregularly cut pieces, esp of wood or card, that are fitted together to form a picture for amusement; *broadly* sthg composed of many disparate parts or elements

jihad /ji'had/ *n* **1** a holy war waged on behalf of Islam as a religious duty **2** a crusade for a principle or belief [Ar *jihād*]

jilt /jilt/ *vt* to cast off (e g one's lover) capriciously or unfeelingly [*jilt* (flirtatious woman), prob alter. of earlier *jillet,* fr *Jill* (nickname for *Gillian*) + *-et*]

,jim 'crow /jim/ *n, often cap J&C, NAm* **1** racial discrimination, esp against black Americans ⟨~ *laws*⟩ **2** a Negro – derog ⟨~ *schools*⟩ [*Jim Crow,* stereotype Negro in a 19th-c song-and-dance act]

jimjams /'jim,jamz/ *n pl* **1** DELIRIUM TREMENS **2** JITTERS 1 *USE* infml; + *the* [perh alter. of *delirium tremens*]

jimsonweed /'jims(ə)n,weed/ *n, often cap, NAm* THORN APPLE [*jimson* alter. of *jamestown,* fr *Jamestown,* site of first permanent E settlement in USA]

[1]**jingle** /'jing·gl/ *vb* **jingling** /'jing·gling, 'jing·gl·ing/ to (cause to) make a light clinking or tinkling sound [ME *ginglen,* of imit origin]

[2]**jingle** *n* **1** a light, esp metallic clinking or tinkling sound **2** a short catchy song or rhyme characterized by repetition of phrases and used esp in advertising – **jingly** *adj*

jingo /'jing·goh/ *interj* – used as a mild oath in *by jingo* [prob euphemism for *Jesus*]

'jingo,ism /-,iz(ə)m/ *n* belligerent patriotism; chauvinism [fr the occurrence of *by jingo* in the refrain of a 19th-c E chauvinistic song] – **jingoist** *n,* **jingoistic** /-'istik/ *adj,* **jingoistically** *adv*

[1]**jink** /jingk/ *n* **1** a quick evasive turn **2** *pl* pranks, frolics – esp in *high jinks* [origin unknown]

[2]**jink** *vi* to move quickly with sudden turns and shifts (e g in dodging)

jinn, djinn /jin/ *n, pl* **jinns, jinn** **1** any of a class of spirits that according to Muslim demonology inhabit the earth, assume various forms, and exercise supernatural power **2** a spirit, often in human form, which serves whoever summons it [Ar *jinnīy* demon]

jinni, jinnee /ji'nee, 'jini/ *n* a jinn

jinx /jingks/ *n* sby or sthg (e g a force or curse) which brings bad luck – infml [prob alter. of *jynx* (wryneck); fr the use of wrynecks in witchcraft] – **jinx** *vt*

jitney /'jitni/ *n, NAm* NICKEL 2 – slang [origin unknown]

[1]**jitter** /'jitə/ *vi* **1** to be nervous or act in a nervous way **2** to make continuous fast repetitive movements [origin unknown]

[2]**jitter** *n* **1** *pl* panic or extreme nervousness – usu + *the* **2** an irregular random movement – **jittery** *adj*

'jitter,bug /-,bug/ *n* (one who dances) a jazz variation of the two-step in which couples swing, balance, and twirl

jiu-jitsu /jooh 'jitsooh/ *n* ju-jitsu

[1]**jive** /jiev/ *n* **1** (dancing or *the* energetic dance performed to) swing music **2** *NAm* **a** glib or deceptive talk **b** a type of jargon used esp by jazz musicians [origin unknown]

[2]**jive** *vi* **1** to dance to or play jive **2** *NAm* to kid ~ *vt NAm* to cajole; TEASE 2b

jo /joh/ *n, pl* **joes** *chiefly Scot* a sweetheart, dear [alter. of *joy*]

joanna /joh'anə/ *n, Br* a piano – infml [rhyming slang]

[1]**job** /job/ *n* **1a** a piece of work; *esp* a small piece of work undertaken at a stated rate **b** sthg produced by work **2a(1)** a task **(2)** sthg requiring unusual exertion ⟨*it was a real* ~ *to talk over that noise*⟩ **b** a

specific duty, role, or function **c** a regular paid position or occupation **d** *chiefly Br* a state of affairs – + *bad* or *good* ⟨*make the best of a bad* ~⟩ **3** an object of a usu specified type ⟨*bought myself a brand-new V-8 sports* ~⟩ **4a** a plan or scheme designed or carried out for private advantage ⟨*suspected the whole incident was a put-up* ~⟩ **b** a crime; *specif* a robbery ***USE*** (*3&4*) infml [perh fr obs *job* (lump), fr ME *jobbe*, perh alter. of *gobbe* gob – more at [1]GOB] – **jobless** *adj* – **on the job 1** engaged in one's occupation; AT WORK 1 ⟨*this burglar is known to wear black woollen gloves when he is* on the job⟩ **2** in the act of copulation – vulg

[2]**job** *vb* **-bb-** *vi* **1** to do odd or occasional pieces of work, usu at a stated rate ⟨*a* ~bing *gardener*⟩ **2** to carry on public business for private gain **3a** to carry on the business of a middleman or wholesaler **b** to work as a stockjobber ~ *vt* **1** to buy and sell (e g shares) for profit **2** to hire or let for a definite job or period of service **3** to get, deal with, or effect by jobbery **4** to subcontract – usu + *out*

Job /johb/ *n* (a narrative and poetic book of the Old Testament which tells of) a Jewish patriarch who endured afflictions with fortitude and faith – usu in *the patience of Job* [L, fr Gk *Iōb*, fr Heb *Iyyōbh*]

jobber /'jobə/ *n* a stockjobber

jobbery /'jobəri/ *n* corruption in public office

'Job ˌCentre *n* a government office where unemployed people can look at job vacancies on display and arrange interviews with prospective employers

ˌjob 'lot *n* a miscellaneous collection of goods sold as a lot; *broadly* any miscellaneous collection of articles

ˌJob's 'comforter /johbz/ *n* sby whose attempts to encourage or comfort have the opposite effect [fr the tone of the speeches made to Job by his friends]

ˌJob's 'tears *n pl but sing in constr* an Asiatic grass whose seeds are often used as beads

jock /jok/ *n* a jockey – infml

Jock *n, Br* a Scotsman; *esp* a Scottish soldier – infml [Sc nickname for *John*]

[1]**jockey** /'joki/ *n* **1** sby who rides a horse, esp as a professional in races **2** *NAm* sby who operates a specified vehicle, device, or object ⟨*a truck* ~⟩ [*Jockey*, Sc nickname for *John*]

[2]**jockey** *vt* **1** to ride (a horse) as a jockey **2** to manoeuvre or manipulate by adroit or devious means ⟨~ed *me into handing over the money*⟩ **3** *chiefly NAm* to drive or operate; *also* to manoeuvre ~ *vi* **1** to act as a jockey **2** to manoeuvre for advantage ⟨~ed *for position*⟩

jockstrap /'jokˌstrap/ *n* a support for the genitals worn by men taking part in strenuous esp sporting activities [*jock* (penis) + *strap*]

jocose /jə'kohs/ *adj* **1** given to joking **2** jocular ***USE*** fml or poetic [L *jocosus*, fr *jocus* joke] – **jocosely** *adv*, **jocoseness** *n*, **jocosity** /jə'kosəti/ *n*

jocular /'jokyoolə/ *adj* **1** habitually jolly **2** characterized by joking [L *jocularis*, fr *joculus*, dim. of *jocus*] – **jocularly** /-'larəti/ *adv*, **jocularity** *n*

jocund /'jokənd/ *adj* marked by or suggestive of high spirits; merry – fml or poetic [ME, fr LL *jocundus*, alter. of L *jucundus* pleasant, fr *juvare* to help] – **jocundly** *adv*, **jocundity** /joh'kundəti, jə-/ *n*

jodhpurs /'jodpəz/ *n pl in constr, pl* **jodhpurs** riding trousers cut full at the hips and close-fitting from knee to ankle ☞ GARMENT [*Jodhpur*, city in India]

Joel /'joh·əl/ *n* a narrative and prophetic book of the Old Testament [L, fr Gk *Iōēl*, fr Heb *Yō'ēl*]

joey /'joh·i/ *n, Austr* a young kangaroo [native name in Australia]

[1]**jog** /jog/ *vb* **-gg-** *vt* **1** to give a slight shake or push to; nudge **2** to rouse (the memory) ~ *vi* **1** to move up and down or about with a short heavy motion **2a** to run or ride at a slow trot **b** to go at a slow or monotonous pace [perh alter. of *shog* (to shake, shove), fr ME *shoggen*]

[2]**jog** *n* **1** a slight shake **2a** a jogging movement or pace **b** a slow trot

jogger /'jogə/ *n* sby who regularly jogs to keep fit

joggle /'jogl/ *vb* **joggling** /'jogling, 'jogl·ing/ to (cause to) move or shake slightly – infml [freq of [1]*jog*] – **joggle** *n*

'jog ˌtrot *n* **1** a slow regular trot (e g of a horse) **2** a routine or monotonous progression

Johannine /joh'hanien/ *adj* (characteristic) of the apostle John or the New Testament books ascribed to him [LL *Johannes* John]

john /jon/ *n* **1** *NAm* TOILET 2 – infml **2** *chiefly NAm* a prostitute's client – slang [fr the name *John*]

John *n* **1** the 4th Gospel in the New Testament **2** any of 3 short didactic letters addressed to early Christians and included in the New Testament [LL *Johannes*, fr Gk *Iōannēs*, fr Heb *Yōḥānān*]

ˌJohn 'Barleyˌcorn /'bahliˌkawn/ *n* alcoholic liquor personified

ˌJohn 'Bull /bool/ *n* **1** the English nation personified **2** a typical Englishman, esp regarded as truculently insular [*John Bull*, character typifying the English nation in *The History of John Bull* by John Arbuthnot †1735 Sc physician & writer] – **John Bullish** *adj*, **John Bullishness** *n*, **John Bullism** *n*

ˌJohn 'Dory /'dawri/ *n* a common yellow to olive European food fish [earlier *dory*, fr ME *dorre*, fr MF *doree*, lit., gilded one]

johnny /'joni/ *n, often cap* a fellow, guy – infml [fr the name *Johnny*]

ˌJohnny-ˌcome-'lately *n, pl* **Johnny-come-latelies, Johnnies-come-lately** a late or recent arrival

Johnsonian /jon'sohnyən, -ni·ən/ *adj* (characteristic) of Samuel Johnson, his works, or his style of writing; *esp* having balanced phraseology and Latinate diction [Samuel *Johnson* †1784 E lexicographer & writer] – **Johnsonese** /jonsə'neez/ *n*

ˌJohn 'Thomas /'toməs/ *n, Br* a penis – euph [fr the names *John & Thomas*]

joie de vivre /ˌzhwah də 'veev (*Fr* ʒwa də viːvr)/ *n* keen enjoyment of life [F, lit., joy of living]

[1]**join** /joyn/ *vt* **1a** to put or bring together so as to form a unit **b** to connect (e g points) by a line **c** to adjoin; MEET 1c ⟨*where the river* ~ s *the sea*⟩ **2** to put or bring into close association or relationship ⟨~ed *in marriage*⟩ **3a** to come into the company of ⟨~ed *us for lunch*⟩ **b** to become a member of ⟨~ed *the sports club*⟩ ~ *vi* **1** to come together so as to be connected **2** to come into close association: e g **a** to form an alliance **b** to become a member of a group **c** to take part in a collective activity – usu + *in* [ME *joinen*, fr OF *joindre*, fr L *jungere* – more at YOKE] – **joinable** *adj* – **join battle** to engage in battle or conflict

[2]**join** *n* JOINT 2a

joinder /'joyndə/ *n* a joining in a legal action [F *joindre* to join]

joiner /'joynə/ *n* **1** one who constructs or repairs wooden articles, esp furniture or fittings – compare CARPENTER **2** a gregarious person who joins many organizations – infml [[1]JOIN + [2]-ER]

joinery /'joynəri/ *n* **1** the craft or trade of a joiner **2** woodwork done or made by a joiner

[1]**joint** /joynt/ *n* **1a(1)** a point of contact between 2 or more bones of an animal skeleton together with the parts that surround and support it **(2)** NODE 3a **b** a part or space included between 2 articulations, knots, or nodes **c** a large piece of meat (for roasting) cut from a carcass ☞ MEAT **2a** a place where 2 things or parts are joined **b** an area at which 2 ends, surfaces, or edges are attached **c** a crack in rock not accompanied by dislocation **d** the hinge of the binding of a book along the back edge of each cover **3** a shabby or disreputable place of entertainment – infml **4** a marijuana cigarette – slang [ME *jointe*, fr OF, fr *joindre*] – **jointed** *adj*, **jointedly** *adv*, **jointedness** *n* – **out of joint 1** *of a bone* dislocated **2** disordered, disorganized

[2]**joint** *adj* **1** united, combined ⟨*a ~ effort*⟩ **2** common to 2 or more: e g **a** involving the united activity of 2 or more **b** held by, shared by, or affecting 2 or more **3** sharing with another ⟨*~ heirs*⟩ **4** being a function of or involving 2 or more random variables ⟨*a ~ probability density function*⟩ [ME, fr MF, fr pp of *joindre*]

[3]**joint** *vt* **1** to fit together **2** to provide with a joint **3** to prepare (e g a board) for joining by planing the edge **4** to separate the joints of (e g meat) [[1]*joint*]

jointer /'joyntə/ *n* any of various tools used in making joints [[3]JOINT + [2]-ER]

'jointly /-li/ *adv* together

joint stock *n* capital held jointly and usu divided into shares between the owners

joint-stock company *n* a company consisting of individuals who own shares representing a joint stock of capital

jointure /'joynchə/ *n* property settled on a wife as provision for her widowhood [ME, joint, jointure, fr MF, fr L *junctura*, fr *junctus*, pp of *jungere* to join]

join up *vi* to enlist in an armed service

joist /joyst/ *n* any of the parallel small timbers or metal beams that support a floor or ceiling [ME *giste*, fr MF, fr (assumed) VL *jacitum*, fr L *jacēre* to lie – more at ADJACENT]

jojoba /hə'hohbə/ *n* a shrub or small tree of the box family, native to N America, having edible seeds that yield a valuable wax similar in properties to sperm oil [MexSp]

[1]**joke** /johk/ *n* **1a** sthg said or done to provoke laughter; *esp* a brief oral narrative with a humorous twist – compare PRACTICAL JOKE **b** the humorous or ridiculous element in sthg **c** an instance of joking or making fun ⟨*can't take a ~*⟩ **d** a laughingstock **2** sthg of little difficulty or seriousness; a trifling matter ⟨*that exam was a ~*⟩ – often in neg constructions ⟨*no ~ to be lost in the desert*⟩ [L *jocus*; akin to OHG *gehan* to say, Skt *yācati* he implores] – **jokey, joky** *adj*

[2]**joke** *vi* to make jokes – **jokingly** *adv*

joker /'johkə/ *n* **1** sby given to joking **2** a playing card added to a pack usu as a wild card **3a** sthg (e g an expedient or stratagem) held in reserve to gain an end or escape from a predicament **b** *chiefly NAm* an unsuspected or misunderstood clause in a document that greatly alters it **c** *chiefly NAm* a not readily apparent factor or condition that nullifies a seeming advantage **4** a fellow; *esp* an insignificant, obnoxious, or incompetent person – infml

jolie laide /,zholi 'led (*Fr* ʒɔli lɛd)/ *n, pl* **jolies laides** /,zholi 'led(z) (*Fr* ~)/ a woman whose looks are decidedly plain, but whose manner and charm make her highly attractive [F, lit., pretty ugly woman]

jollification /jolifi'kaysh(ə)n/ *n* (an instance of) merrymaking

[1]**jolly** /'joli/ *adj* **1a** full of high spirits **b** given to conviviality **c** expressing, suggesting, or inspiring gaiety **2** extremely pleasant or agreeable – infml **3** *Br* slightly drunk – euph [ME *jolif, joli*, fr OF] – **jolliness** *n*, **jollity** *n*

[2]**jolly** *adv* very – infml ⟨*~ cold for the time of year*⟩

[3]**jolly** *vt* **1** to (try to) put in good humour, esp to gain an end – usu + *along* **2** to make cheerful or bright – + *up*; infml

'jolly ,boat *n* a ship's boat of medium size used for general work [origin unknown]

,Jolly 'Roger /'rojə/ *n* a pirate's black flag with a white skull and crossbones [prob fr [1]*jolly* + the name *Roger*]

[1]**jolt** /johlt/ *vt* **1** to cause to move with a sudden jerky motion **2** to give a (sudden) knock or blow to **3** to abruptly disturb the composure of ⟨*crudely* ~ed *out of that mood* – Virginia Woolf⟩ ~ *vi* to move with a jerky motion [prob blend of obs *joll* (to strike) and *jot* (to bump)]

[2]**jolt** *n* an unsettling blow, movement, or shock – **jolty** *adj*

Jonah /'johnə/ *n* (a narrative book of the Old Testament telling of) an Israelite prophet who resisted a divine call to preach repentance to the people of Nineveh, was swallowed and vomited by a great fish, and eventually carried out his mission [Heb *Yōnāh*]

jongleur /,zhong'gluh (*Fr* ʒɔ̃glœːr)/ *n* a wandering medieval minstrel [F, fr OF *jogleour* – more at JUGGLER]

jonquil /'jongkwil/ *n* a Mediterranean plant of the daffodil family that is widely cultivated for its yellow or white fragrant flowers [F *jonquille*, fr Sp *junquillo*, dim. of *junco* reed, fr L *juncus*; akin to ON *einir* juniper, L *juniperus*]

Joshua /'josh(y)oo·ə/ *n* (a mainly narrative book of the Old Testament telling of) the divinely commissioned successor of Moses and military leader of the Israelites during the conquest of Canaan [Heb *Yehōshūa'*]

joss /jos/ *n* a Chinese idol or cult image [Pidgin E, fr Pg *deus* god, fr L – more at DEITY]

'joss ,house *n* a Chinese temple or shrine

'joss ,stick *n* a slender stick of incense (e g for burning in front of a joss)

jostle /'josl/ *vb* **jostling** /'josling, 'josl·ing/ **1a** to come in contact or into collision (with) **b** to make (one's way) by pushing **2** to vie (with) in gaining an objective [alter. of *justle*, freq of [1]*joust*] – **jostle** *n*

[1]**jot** /jot/ *n* the least bit ⟨*not a ~ of evidence*⟩ [L *iota, jota* iota]

[2]**jot** *vt* **-tt-** to write briefly or hurriedly – **jotting** *n*

jotter /'jotə/ *n* a small book or pad for notes or memoranda

joule /joohl/ *n* the SI unit of work or energy equal to the work done when a force of 1N moves its point of application through a distance of 1m ☞ PHYSICS, UNIT [James *Joule* †1889 E physicist]

journal /'juhnl/ *n* **1** a record of current transactions: e g **a** an account of day-to-day events **b** a private record of experiences, ideas, or reflections kept regularly **c** a record of the transactions of a public body, learned society, etc **d** LOG 3, 4 **2a** a daily newspaper **b** a periodical dealing esp with matters of current interest or specialist subjects **3** the part of a rotating shaft, axle, roll, or spindle that turns in a bearing [ME, service book containing the day hours, fr MF, fr *journal* daily, fr L *diurnalis*, fr *diurnus* of the day, fr *dies* day – more at DEITY]

'journal ,box *n* a metal housing to support and protect a journal bearing

,journal'ese /-'eez/ *n* a style of writing supposed to be characteristic of newspapers; *specif* loose or cliché-ridden writing

'journal,ism /-,iz(ə)m/ *n* **1** (the profession of) the collecting and editing of material of current interest for presentation through news media **2a** writing designed for publication in a newspaper or popular magazine **b** writing characterized by a direct presentation of facts or description of events without an attempt at interpretation

'journalist /-ist/ *n* a person engaged in journalism, esp one working for a news medium – **journalistic** /-'istik/ *adj*

'journal·ize, -ise /-iez/ *vb* to record in or keep a journal – **journalizer** *n*

journey /'juhni/ *n* **1** travel from one place to another, esp by land and over a considerable distance **2** the distance involved in a journey, or the time taken to cover it [ME, fr OF *journee* day's journey, fr *jour* day, fr LL *diurnum*, fr L, neut of *diurnus*] – **journey** *vi*, **journeyer** *n*

'journeyman /-mən/ *n* **1** a worker who has learned a trade and is employed by another person, usu by the day **2** an experienced reliable worker or performer, as distinguished from one who is outstanding [ME, fr *journey* journey, a day's labour + *man*]

¹joust /jowst/ *vi* to fight in a joust or tournament [ME *jousten*, fr OF *juster*, fr (assumed) VL *juxtare*, fr L *juxta* near; akin to L *jungere* to join – more at YOKE] – **jouster** *n*

²joust *n* a combat on horseback between 2 knights or men-at-arms with lances

Jove /johv/ *n* Jupiter, the chief Roman god – often used interjectionally to express surprise or agreement ⟨*by ~!*⟩ [L *Jov-*, *Juppiter*]

jovial /'johvi·əl/ *adj* markedly good-humoured [MF & LL; MF, fr LL *jovialis* Jovian, fr *Jov-*, *Juppiter*] – **jovially** *adj*, **joviality** /-'aləti/ *n*

Jovian /'johvi·ən/ *adj* (characteristic) of the god or planet Jupiter

¹jowl /jowl/ *n* **1** the jaw; *esp* a mandible **2** CHEEK 1 [alter. of ME *chavel*, fr OE *ceafl*; akin to MHG *kivel* jaw, Av *zafar-* mouth]

²jowl *n* usu slack flesh associated with the lower jaw or throat – often pl with sing. meaning [ME *cholle*, prob fr OE *ceole* throat]

joy /joy/ *n* **1** (the expression of) an emotion or state of great happiness, pleasure, or delight **2** a source or cause of delight **3** *Br* success, satisfaction ⟨*had no ~ at the first shop he went into*⟩ – infml [ME, fr OF *joie*, fr L *gaudia*, pl of *gaudium*, fr *gaudēre* to rejoice; akin to Gk *gēthein* to rejoice] – **joyless** *adj*, **joylessly** *adv*, **joylessness** *n*

'joyful /-f(ə)l/ *adj* filled with, causing, or expressing joy – **joyfully** *adv*, **joyfulness** *n*

'joyous /-əs/ *adj* joyful – **joyously** *adv*, **joyousness** *n*

'joy,ride /-,ried/ *n* **1** a ride in a motor car taken for pleasure and often without the owner's consent **2** a short pleasure flight in an aircraft – **joyrider** *n*, **joyriding** *n*

'joy,stick /-,stik/ *n* **1** a hand-operated lever that controls an aeroplane's elevators and ailerons **2** a control for any of various devices that resembles an aeroplane's joystick, esp in being capable of motion in 2 or more directions [perh fr slang *joystick* (penis)]

jubilant /'joohbilənt/ *adj* filled with or expressing great joy [L *jubilant-*, *jubilans*, prp of *jubilare* to rejoice] – **jubilance** *n*, **jubilantly** *adv*

Jubilate /joohbi'lahti/ *n* the 100th Psalm sung liturgically in Catholic and Anglican churches [L, 2 pl imper of *jubilare*; fr its opening word]

jubilation /joohbi'laysh(ə)n/ *n* being jubilant; rejoicing [ME *jubilacioun*, fr L *jubilation-*, *jubilatio*, fr *jubilatus*, pp of *jubilare*]

jubilee /joohbi'lee, '--,-/ *n* **1** *often cap* a year of emancipation and restoration provided by ancient Hebrew law to be kept every 50 years **2** (a celebration of) a special anniversary (e g of a sovereign's accession) ⟨*remembered Queen Victoria's diamond ~*⟩ **3** a period of time, proclaimed by the Pope ordinarily every 25 years, during which a special plenary indulgence is granted to Catholics who perform certain works of repentance and piety **4** a season or occasion of celebration [ME, fr MF & LL; MF *jubilé*, fr LL *jubilaeus*, modif of LGk *iōbēlaios*, fr Heb *yōbhēl* ram's horn, jubilee]

Judaism /'joohday,iz(ə)m/ *n* **1** a religion developed among the ancient Hebrews and characterized by belief in 1 transcendent God and by a religious life in accordance with Scriptures and rabbinic traditions **2** (conformity with) the cultural, social, and religious beliefs and practices of the Jews [LL *judaismus*, fr Gk *ioudaismos*, fr *Ioudaios* Jew] – **Judaize** *vt*, **Judaizer** *n*, **Judaic** /-'day·ik/ *adj*

Judas /'joohdəs/ *n* **1** one who betrays, esp under the guise of friendship **2 judas, judas hole** a peephole in a door [*Judas* Iscariot, the apostle who betrayed Christ]

'Judas ,tree *n* any of a genus of trees and shrubs that are often cultivated for their showy esp purplish flowers [fr the belief that Judas Iscariot hanged himself from such a tree]

judder /'judə/ *vi*, *chiefly Br* to vibrate jerkily [prob alter. of *shudder*] – **judder** *n*

Jude /joohd/ *n* a short epistle addressed to early Christians included as a book in the New Testament [LL *Judas*]

¹judge /juj/ *vt* **1** to form an opinion about through careful weighing of evidence **2** to sit in judgment on **3** to determine or pronounce after deliberation **4** to decide the result of (a competition or contest) **5** to form an estimate or evaluation of **6** to hold as an opinion ~ *vi* **1** to form a judgment or opinion **2** to act as a judge ⟨*to ~ between us*⟩ [ME *juggen*, fr OF *jugier*, fr L *judicare*, fr *judic-*, *judex* judge, fr *jus* right, law + *dicere* to decide, say – more at JUST, DICTION]

²judge *n* sby who judges: e g **a** a public official authorized to decide questions brought before a court ☞ LAW **b** *often cap* a Hebrew tribal leader in the period after the death of Joshua **c** sby appointed to decide in a competition or (sporting) contest (e g diving) **d** sby who gives an (authoritative) opinion ⟨*a good ~ of character*⟩ ⟨*a good ~ of modern art*⟩ [ME *juge*, fr MF, fr L *judex*] – **judgeship** *n*

ˌjudge ˈadvocate *n* an officer appointed to superintend the trial and advise on law at a court martial

ˌjudge ˌadvocate ˈgeneral *n* the senior civil legal officer in control of courts martial

Judges /ˈjujiz/ *n pl but sing in constr* a narrative and historical book of the Old Testament

judgment, judgement /ˈjujmənt/ *n* **1** (a formal utterance of) an authoritative opinion **2a** a formal decision by a court **b** an obligation (e g a debt) created by a court decision **3a Judgment, Last Judgment** *the* the final judging of mankind by God **b** a calamity held to be sent by God as a punishment **4** (the process of forming) an opinion or evaluation based on discerning and comparing **5** the capacity for judging – **judgmental** /-ˈmentl/ *adj*

ˈJudgment ˌDay *n* the day of God's judgment of mankind at the end of the world, according to various theologies

judicature /ˈjoohdikəchə/ *n* **1** the administration of justice **2** a court of justice **3** JUDICIARY 1 **4** (the duration of) a judge's office [MF, fr ML *judicatura*, fr L *judicatus*, pp of *judicare*]

judicial /joohˈdish(ə)l/ *adj* **1** of a judgment, judging, justice, or the judiciary **2** ordered by a court ⟨*~ separation*⟩ **3** of, characterized by, or expressing judgment; CRITICAL 1c [ME, fr L *judicialis*, fr *judicium* judgment, fr *judex*] – **judicially** *adv*

judiciary /joohˈdishəri/ *n* **1a** a system of courts of law **b** the judges of these courts **2** a judicial branch of the US government [*judiciary*, adj, fr L *judiciarius* judicial, fr *judicium*] – **judiciary** *adj*

judicious /joohˈdishəs/ *adj* having, exercising, or characterized by sound judgment – **judiciously** *adv*, **judiciousness** *n*

judo /ˈjoohdoh/ *n* a martial art developed from ju-jitsu and emphasizing the use of quick movement and leverage to throw an opponent [Jap *jūdō*, fr *jū* weakness, gentleness + *dō* art] – **judoist** *n*

judy /ˈjoohdi/ *n, often cap* a girl – slang [*Judy*, nickname for *Judith*]

¹jug /jug/ *n* **1a(1)** *chiefly Br* a vessel for holding and pouring liquids that typically has a handle and a lip or spout **(2)** *chiefly NAm* a large deep earthenware or glass vessel for liquids that usu has a handle and a narrow mouth often fitted with a cork; FLAGON 1b **b** the contents of or quantity contained in a jug; a jugful **2** prison – infml [perh fr *Jug*, nickname for *Joan*] – **jugful** *n*

²jug *vt* **-gg-** **1** to stew (e g a hare) in an earthenware vessel **2** to imprison – infml

juggernaut /ˈjugəˌnawt/ *n* **1** an inexorable force or object that crushes anything in its path **2** *chiefly Br* a very large, usu articulated, lorry; *esp* one considered too large for safety [Hindi *Jagannāth*, title of Vishnu, lit., lord of the world; fr a former belief that devotees of Vishnu threw themselves beneath the wheels of a cart bearing his image in procession]

¹juggle /ˈjugl/ *vb* **juggling** /ˈjugling/ *vi* **1** to perform the tricks of a juggler **2** to engage in manipulation, esp in order to achieve a desired end ~ *vt* **1** to manipulate, esp in order to achieve a desired end ⟨*~ an account to hide a loss*⟩ **2** to hold or balance precariously **3** to toss in the manner of a juggler [ME *jogelen*, fr MF *jogler* to joke, fr L *joculari*, fr *joculus*, dim. of *jocus* joke]

²juggle *n* an act or instance of juggling

juggler /ˈjuglə/ *n* one skilled in keeping several objects in motion in the air at the same time by alternately tossing and catching them [ME *jogelour*, fr OE *geogelere*, fr OF *jogleour*, fr L *joculator*, fr *joculatus*, pp of *joculari*] – **jugglery** *n*

jugular /ˈjugyoolə/ *adj* **1a** of the throat or neck **b** of the jugular vein **2** *of a ventral fin of a fish* located on the throat [LL *jugularis*, fr L *jugulum* collarbone, throat; akin to L *jungere* to join – more at YOKE]

jugular vein, jugular *n* any of several veins of each side of the neck that return blood from the head

juice /joohs/ *n* **1** the extractable fluid contents of cells or tissues **2a** *pl* the natural fluids of an animal body **b** the liquid or moisture contained in sthg **3** the inherent quality of sthg; *esp* the basic force or strength of sthg **4** a medium (e g electricity or petrol) that supplies power – infml [ME *jus*, fr OF, broth, juice, fr L; akin to Skt *yūṣa* broth] – **juiceless** *adj*

juicy /ˈjoohsi/ *adj* **1** succulent **2** financially rewarding or profitable – infml **3** rich in interest ⟨*a ~ problem*⟩; *esp* interesting because of titillating content ⟨*~ scandal*⟩ – infml – **juicily** *adv*, **juiciness** *n*

ju-jitsu, jiu-jitsu /jooh ˈjitsooh/ *n* a martial art employing holds, throws, and paralysing blows to subdue or disable an opponent [Jap *jūjutsu*, fr *jū* weakness, gentleness + *jutsu* art]

juju /ˈjoohˌjooh/ *n* (a magic attributed to) a fetish or charm of W African peoples [of W African origin; akin to Hausa *djudju* fetish]

jujube /ˈjoohˌjoohb/ *n* **1** (the edible fruit of) any of several trees of the buckthorn family **2** a fruit-flavoured gum or lozenge [ME, fr ML *jujuba*, alter. of L *zizyphum*, fr Gk *zizyphon*]

jukebox /ˈjoohkˌboks/ *n* a coin-operated record player that automatically plays records chosen from a restricted list [Gullah *juke* disorderly, of W African origin; akin to Bambara *dzugu* wicked]

julep /ˈjoohlip/ *n, chiefly NAm* a drink consisting of a spirit and sugar poured over crushed ice and garnished with mint [ME, syrupy liquid, fr MF, fr Ar *julāb*, fr Per *gulāb*, fr *gul* rose + *āb* water]

Julian calendar /ˈjoohlyən, -li·ən/ *n* a calendar introduced in Rome in 46 BC establishing the 12-month year of 365 days with an extra day every fourth year – compare GREGORIAN CALENDAR [L *julianus*, fr Gaius *Julius* Caesar †44 BC Roman general & statesman]

¹julienne /joohliˈen/ *n* a clear soup containing julienne vegetables [F, prob fr the name *Jules*, *Julien*]

²julienne *adj* cut into long thin strips ⟨*~ potatoes*⟩ ⟨*green beans ~*⟩

ˈjuliet ˌcap /ˈjoohli·ət, -et/ *n* a woman's small close-fitting brimless cap worn esp by brides [fr the name *Juliet*]

Juliett /joohliˈet/ – a communications code word for the letter *j* [prob irreg fr *Juliet*]

July /jooˈlie/ *n* the 7th month of the Gregorian calendar [ME *Julie*, fr OE *Julius*, fr L, fr Gaius *Julius* Caesar]

[1]**jumble** /ˈjumbl/ *vt* **jumbling** /ˈjumbling/ to mix *up* in a confused or disordered mass [perh imit]

[2]**jumble** *n* **1** a mass of things mingled together without order or plan **2** *Br* articles for a jumble sale

ˈ**jumble ˌsale** *n, Br* a sale of donated secondhand articles, usu conducted to raise money for some charitable purpose

jumbo /ˈjumboh/ *n, pl* **jumbos** a very large specimen of its kind [prob fr *mumbo-jumbo*] – **jumbo** *adj*

ˈ**jumbo ˌjet** *n* a large jet aeroplane capable of carrying several hundred passengers

jumbuck /ˈjumˌbuk/ *n, Austr* a sheep [native name in Australia]

[1]**jump** /jump/ *vi* **1a** to spring into the air, esp using the muscular power of feet and legs **b** to move suddenly or involuntarily from shock, surprise, etc **c** to move quickly or energetically (as if) with a jump; *also* to act with alacrity **2** to pass rapidly, suddenly, or abruptly (as if) over some intervening thing: e g **a** to skip ⟨~ed *to the end of the book*⟩ **b** to rise suddenly in rank or status ⟨~ed *from captain to colonel*⟩ **c** to make a mental leap **d** to come to or arrive at a position or judgment without due deliberation ⟨~ *to conclusions*⟩ **e** to undergo a sudden sharp increase ⟨*prices* ~ed *sky-high*⟩ **3** to move haphazardly or aimlessly **4** to make a sudden verbal or physical attack – usu + *on* or *upon* **5** *NAm* to bustle with activity ⟨*by midnight the place was really* ~ing⟩ ~ *vt* **1a** to (cause to) leap over ⟨~ *a hurdle*⟩ ⟨~ed *his horse over the fence*⟩ **b** to pass over, esp to a point beyond; skip, bypass **c** to act, move, or begin before (e g a signal) **2a** to escape or run away from **b** to leave hastily or in violation of an undertaking ⟨~ed *bail*⟩ **c** to depart from (a normal course) ⟨*the train* ~ed *the rails*⟩ **3a** to make a sudden or surprise attack on **b** to occupy without proper legal rights ⟨~ *a mining claim*⟩ **4** *chiefly NAm* to leap aboard, esp so as to travel illegally [prob akin to LG *gumpen* to jump] – **jump at** to accept eagerly ⟨jump at *the chance*⟩ – **jump the gun 1** to start in a race before the starting signal **2** to act, move, or begin sthg before the proper time – **jump the queue 1** to move in front of others in a queue **2** to obtain an unfair advantage over others who have been waiting longer – **jump to it 1** to make an enthusiastic start **2** to hurry

[2]**jump** *n* **1a(1)** an act of jumping; a leap **(2)** a sports contest (e g the long jump) including a jump **(3)** a space, height, or distance cleared by a jump **(4)** an obstacle to be jumped over (e g in a horse race) **b** a sudden involuntary movement; a start **2a** a sharp sudden increase (e g in amount, price, or value) **b** a sudden change or transition; *esp* one that leaves a break in continuity **c** any of a series of moves from one place or position to another; a move **3** *pl the* fidgets – infml

ˌ**jumped-ˈup** *adj* recently risen in wealth, rank, or status – derog

[1]**jumper** /ˈjumpə/ *n* **1** a short wire used to close a break in or cut out part of a circuit **2** a jumping animal; *esp* a horse trained to jump obstacles [[1]JUMP + [2]-ER]

[2]**jumper** *n* **1** *Br* a knitted or crocheted garment worn on the upper body ☞ GARMENT **2** *NAm* PINAFORE 2 [prob fr E dial. *jump* (loose jacket), perh alter. of *jupe* (coat, jacket), fr OF, fr Ar *jubbah*]

ˈ**jumping ˌbean** /ˈjumping/ *n* a seed of any of several Mexican shrubs of the spurge family that tumbles about because of the movements inside it of the larva of a small moth

ˌ**jumping ˈjack** *n* a firework that jumps about when lit

ˌ**jumping-ˈoff** *adj* – **jumping-off place/point** a place or point from which an enterprise is launched

ˈ**jump-ˌjet** *n, chiefly Br* a jet aircraft able to take off and land vertically

ˈ**jump ˌlead** /leed/ *n* a length of thick electric cable for starting the engine of a motor vehicle with a flat battery, by using a second battery

ˈ**jump-ˌoff** *n* the final round of a showjumping competition – **jump off** *vi*

ˈ**jump ˌseat** *n* a folding seat for temporary use in a vehicle or aircraft

ˈ**jump ˌstart** *n* the starting of a motor vehicle's engine using jump leads – **jump start** *vt*

ˈ**jumpˌsuit** /-ˌs(y)ooht/ *n* a 1-piece garment combining top and trousers or shorts

jumpy /ˈjumpi/ *adj* **1** having jumps or sudden variations **2** nervous, jittery – **jumpiness** *n*

junction /ˈjungksh(ə)n/ *n* **1** joining or being joined **2a** a place of meeting **b** an intersection of roads, esp where 1 terminates **c** a point of contact or interface between dissimilar metals or semiconductor regions (e g in a transistor) **3** sthg that joins [L *junction-, junctio*, fr *junctus*, pp of *jungere* to join – more at YOKE] – **junctional** *adj*

juncture /ˈjungkchə/ *n* **1** an instance or place of joining; a connection or joining part **2** a point of time (made critical by a concurrence of circumstances)

June /joohn/ *n* the 6th month of the Gregorian calendar [ME, fr MF & L; MF *Juin*, fr L *Junius*]

ˈ**june ˌbug** *n* a chafer

Jungian /ˈyoong·i·ən/ *adj* (characteristic) of the psychoanalytical psychology of Carl Jung [Carl *Jung* †1961 Swiss psychologist] – **Jungian** *n*

jungle /ˈjung·gl/ *n* **1** an area overgrown with thickets or masses of (tropical) trees and other vegetation **2a** a confused, disordered, or complex mass ⟨*the* ~ *of tax laws*⟩ **b** a place of ruthless struggle for survival ⟨*the blackboard* ~⟩ [Hindi *jaṅgal*] – **jungly** /ˈjung·gli/ *adj*

ˈ**jungle ˌfowl** *n* any of several Asian wild birds from which domestic fowls have prob descended

[1]**junior** /ˈjoohnyə/ *n* **1** a person who is younger than another ⟨*she is my* ~⟩ **2a** a person holding a lower or subordinate position in a hierarchy of ranks **b** a member of a younger form in a school **3** *NAm* a student in the next-to-the-last year before graduating **4** *NAm* a male child; a son – infml [L, n & adj]

[2]**junior** *adj* **1** younger – used, esp in the USA, to distinguish a son with the same name as his father **2** lower in standing or rank **3** for children aged from 7 to 11 ⟨*a* ~ *school*⟩ [L, compar of *juvenis* young – more at YOUNG]

juniorate /ˈjoohnyərayt, -rət/ *n* (a seminary providing) a course of higher study (preparatory to that in philosophy) for candidates for the priesthood, brotherhood, or sisterhood

ˈ**junior ˌcollege** *n* a US college that offers 2 years of studies corresponding to the first 2 years of a 4-year college course

ˌ**Junior ˈCommon ˌRoom** *n* a common room for students, pupils, etc

ˈ**junior ˌschool** *n* **1** a primary school for children aged esp from 7 to 11 **2** a junior department for preparing intended pupils of a fee-paying secondary school

,junior 'seaman *n* ☞ RANK

,junior tech'nician *n* ☞ RANK

juniper /'joohnipə/ *n* any of several evergreen shrubs or trees of the cypress family [ME *junipere*, fr L *juniperus* – more at JONQUIL]

'juniper ,oil *n* an oil obtained from the fruit of the common juniper and used esp in gin and liqueurs

¹junk /jungk/ *n* **1** pieces of old cable or rope used for mats, swabs, or oakum **2a** secondhand or discarded articles or material; *broadly* RUBBISH 1 **b** sthg of little value or inferior quality **3** narcotics; *esp* heroin – slang [ME *jonke*] – **junky** *adj*

²junk *vt* to get rid of as worthless – infml

³junk *n* a sailing ship used in the Far East with a high poop and overhanging stem, little or no keel, and lugsails often stiffened with horizontal battens [Pg *junco*, fr Jav *joṅ*]

Junker /'yoongkə/ *n* a member of the Prussian landed aristocracy [G, fr OHG *junchērro*, lit., young lord] – **Junkerdom** /-d(ə)m/ *n*, **Junkerism** *n*

¹junket /'jungkit/ *n* **1** a dessert of sweetened flavoured milk curdled with rennet **2** a festive social affair (at public or a firm's expense) – chiefly infml [ME *ioncate*, deriv of (assumed) VL *juncata*, fr L *juncus* rush]

²junket *vi* to feast, banquet – infml – **junketer** *n*, **junketeer** /-'tiə/ *n*

'junk ,food *n* processed food (e g hot dogs or candy floss) that typically has a high carbohydrate content but overall low nutritional value – compare WHOLEFOOD, HEALTHFOOD

junkie, junky /'jungki/ *n* a drug peddler or addict – infml ['*junk* 3 + *-ie*, ¹*-y*]

Junoesque /joohnoh'esk/ *adj*, *of a woman* having stately beauty [*Juno*, ancient It goddess, wife of Jupiter]

junta /'juntə, 'hoontə/ *n sing or pl in constr* **1** a political council or committee; *esp* a group controlling a government after a revolution **2** a junto [Sp, fr fem of *junto* joined, fr L *junctus*, pp of *jungere* to join – more at YOKE]

junto /'juntoh/ *n sing or pl in constr, pl* **juntos** a group of people joined for a common purpose [prob alter. of *junta*]

Jupiter /'joohpitə/ *n* the largest of the planets and 5th in order from the sun ☞ ASTRONOMY, SYMBOL [L, supreme deity of the Roman pantheon]

jural /'jooərəl/ *adj* of law, rights, or obligations [L *jur-, jus* law] – **jurally** *adv*

Jurassic /joo'rasik/ *adj or n* (of or being) the middle period of the Mesozoic era between the Cretaceous and the Triassic ☞ EVOLUTION [F *jurassique*, fr *Jura* mountain range between France & Switzerland]

juridical /joo'ridikl/ *also* **juridic** /joo'ridik/ *adj* **1** JUDICIAL 1 **2** of or being jurisprudence; legal ⟨~ *terms*⟩ [L *juridicus*, fr *jur-, jus* + *dicere* to say – more at DICTION] – **juridically** *adv*

jurisconsult /jooəris'konsult/ *n* a jurist [L *jurisconsultus*, fr *juris* (gen of *jus*) + *consultus*, pp of *consulere* to consult]

,juris'diction /-'diksh(ə)n/ *n* **1** the power, right, or authority to apply the law **2** the authority of a sovereign power **3** the limits within which authority may be exercised [ME *jurisdiccioun*, fr OF & L; OF *juridiction*, fr L *jurisdiction-, jurisdictio*, fr *juris* + *diction-, dictio* act of saying – more at DICTION] – **jurisdictional** *adj*, **jurisdictionally** *adv*

,juris'prudence /-'proohd(ə)ns/ *n* (the science or philosophy of) a body or branch of law ⟨*criminal* ~⟩ [F & LL; F, fr MF, fr LL *jurisprudentia*, fr L *prudentia juris*] – **jurisprudential** /-prooh'densh(ə)l/ *adj*

jurist /'jooərist/ *n* **1** sby with a thorough knowledge of law **2** *NAm* a lawyer; *specif* a judge [MF *juriste*, fr ML *jurista*, fr L *jur-, jus*]

juristic /joo'ristik/, **juristical** /-kl/ *adj* of a jurist, jurisprudence, or law – **juristically** *adv*

juror /'jooərə/ *n* **1** a member of a jury **2** one who takes an oath

¹jury /'jooəri/ *n* **1** a body of usu 12 people who hear evidence in court and are sworn to give an honest verdict, esp of guilty or not guilty, based on this evidence **2** a committee for judging a contest or exhibition [ME *jure*, fr AF *juree*, fr OF *jurer* to swear, fr L *jurare*, fr *jur-, jus*]

²jury *adj* improvised for temporary use (in an emergency) ⟨*a* ~ *rig for a sailing boat*⟩ [origin unknown]

'juryman /-mən/, *fem* **'jury,woman** *n* JUROR 1

jussive /jusiv/ *n* a word, form, case, or mood expressing command [L *jussus*, pp of *jubēre* to order; akin to Gk *hysminē* battle] – **jussive** *adj*

¹just /just/ *adj* **1a** conforming (rigidly) to fact or reason ⟨*a* ~ *but not a generous decision*⟩ **b** conforming to a standard of correctness; proper **2a(1)** acting or being in conformity with what is morally upright or equitable **(2)** being what is merited; deserved **b** legally correct [ME, fr MF & L; MF *juste*, fr L *justus*, fr *jus* right, law; akin to Skt *yos* welfare] – **justly** *adv*, **justness** *n*

²just *adv* **1a** exactly, precisely – not following *not* ⟨~ *right*⟩ ⟨~ *the thing for your cold*⟩ **b** at this moment and not sooner ⟨*he's only* ~ *arrived*⟩ – sometimes used with the past tense ⟨*the bell* ~ *rang*⟩ **c** only at this moment and not later ⟨*I'm* ~ *coming*⟩ **2a** by a very small margin; immediately, barely ⟨~ *too late*⟩ ⟨*only* ~ *possible*⟩ **b** only, simply ⟨~ *a short note*⟩ **3** quite ⟨*not* ~ *yet*⟩ ⟨~ *as well I asked*⟩ **4** perhaps, possibly **5** very, completely ⟨~ *wonderful*⟩ **6** indeed – sometimes expressing irony ⟨*didn't he* ~*!*⟩ *USE (5, 6)* infml – **just about 1** almost **2** not more than ⟨just about *room to cook*⟩ – **just in case** as a precaution – **just now 1** at this moment **2** a moment ago – **just on** almost exactly – used with reference to numbers and quantities – **just so 1** tidily arranged **2** – used to express agreement – **just the same** nevertheless; EVEN SO

justice /'justis/ *n* **1a** the maintenance or administration of what is just **b** the administration of law ⟨*court of* ~⟩ **c** JUSTICE OF THE PEACE **2a** the quality of being just, impartial, or fair **b** (conformity to) the principle or ideal of just dealing or right action **3** conformity to truth, fact, or reason **4** *Br* – used as a title for a judge ⟨*Mr* Justice *Smith*⟩ [ME, fr OF, fr L *justitia*, fr *justus*]

,justice of the 'peace *n* a lay magistrate empowered chiefly to administer summary justice in minor cases and to commit for trial

justiciable /ju'stishi·əbl/ *adj* **1** liable to trial ⟨*a* ~ *offence*⟩ **2** capable of legal decision ⟨*a* ~ *issue*⟩ – **justiciability** /-'biləti/ *n*

justify /'justifie/ *vt* **1** to prove or show to be just, right, or reasonable **2** to extend freedom from the consequences of sin to, by Christ's righteousness or by grace **3** to space out (e g a line of printed text) so as to be flush with a margin [ME *justifien*, fr MF or LL; MF *justifier*, fr LL *justificare*, fr L *justus*] – **justifier** *n*, **justifiable** *adj*, **justifiably** *adv*, **justificatory** /justifi'kayt(ə)ri/ *adj*, **justification** /-'kaysh(ə)n/ *n*

[1]**jut** /jut/ *vi* **-tt-** to extend out, up, or forwards; project, protrude – often + *out* [partly var of [2]*jet* (to project); partly short for obs *jutty* (to project), fr ME *jutteyen*]

[2]**jut** *n* sthg that juts (out)

jute /jooht/ *n* the glossy fibre of either of 2 E Indian plants of the linden family used chiefly for sacking, burlap, and twine [Hindi & Beng *jūṭ*]

Jute *n* a member of a Germanic people that invaded England and esp Kent along with the Angles and Saxons in the 5th c AD [ME, fr ML *Jutae* Jutes, of Gmc origin] – **Jutish** *adj*

[1]**juvenile** /'joovəniel/ *adj* **1** physiologically immature or undeveloped **2** (characteristic) of or suitable for children or young people [F or L; F *juvénile*, fr L *juvenilis*, fr *juvenis* young person – more at YOUNG] – **juvenilely** *adv*, **juvenility** /-'niləti/ *n*

[2]**juvenile** *n* **1a** a young person **b** a book for young people **2** a young individual resembling an adult of its kind except in size and reproductive activity **3** an actor who plays youthful parts

juvenile court *n* a court with special jurisdiction over delinquent and dependent young people

juvenile hormone *n* an insect hormone that controls maturation to the imago and plays a role in reproduction

juvenilia /joohvə'nili·ə/ *n pl* artistic or literary works produced in an artist's or author's youth [L, neut pl of *juvenilis*]

juxta- /jukstə-/ *comb form* situated near ⟨juxta*glomerular cells*⟩; beside ⟨juxta*pose*⟩ [L *juxta* near]

juxtapose /jukstə'pohz/ *vt* to place side by side [prob back-formation fr *juxtaposition*] – **juxtaposition** /-pə'zish(ə)n/ *n*, **juxtapositional** *adj*

K

k /kay/ *n, pl* **k's, ks,** *often cap* **1** (a graphic representation of or device for reproducing) the 11th letter of the English alphabet **2** a unit of computer storage capacity equal to 1024 bytes ⟨*a memory of 64*K⟩ [(2) *k*ilo-]

ka /kah/ *n* the personality double believed in ancient Egypt to be born with, and survive, an individual [Egypt]

Kaaba /ˈkahbə/ *n* a small building in the court of the Great Mosque at Mecca containing a sacred black stone which is the goal of Islamic pilgrimage [Ar *ka'bah,* lit., square building]

kabala, kabbala, kabbalah /kəˈbahlə/ *n* the cabala – **kabalism** *n,* **kabalist** /ˈkabəlist/ *n,* **kabalistic** /-ˈlistik/ *adj*

Kabuki /kəˈboohki/ *n* traditional Japanese popular drama performed in a highly stylized manner by males only [Jap, lit., art of singing and dancing]

Kabyle /kəˈbiel/ *n* a member or the language of a Berber people of the mountainous coastal area E of Algiers [Ar *qabā'il,* pl of *qabīlah* tribe]

kaddish /ˈkadish/ *n, often cap* a Jewish prayer recited in the daily ritual of the synagogue and by mourners after the death of a close relative [Aram *qaddīsh* holy]

kadi /ˈkahdi, ˈkaydi/ *n* a qadi

Kaffir, Kafir /ˈkafə/ *n* **1** a member of a group of southern African Bantu-speaking peoples **2** *often not cap, chiefly SAfr* a S African Black – derog [Ar *kāfir* infidel]

Kafkaesque /ˌkafkəˈesk/ *adj* suggestive of the writings of Franz Kafka, esp in expressing the anxieties and alienation of 20th-c man [Franz *Kafka* †1924 Austrian writer]

kaftan /ˈkafˌtan/ *n* a caftan

kailyard, kaleyard, kailyard school /ˈkaylˌyahd/ *n* a late 19th-c literary movement specializing in a parochial and sentimentalized depiction of Scottish Lowland life [Sc, lit., cabbage garden]

kainite /ˈkieniet, ˈkay-/ *also* **kainit** /kieˈneet/ *n* a naturally occurring hydrated sulphate and chloride of magnesium and potassium used as a fertilizer [G *kainit,* fr Gk *kainos* new – more at RECENT]

kaiser /ˈkiezə/ *n* an emperor of Germany during the period 1871 to 1918 [G, fr OHG *keisur* emperor, fr a prehistoric Gmc word borrowed fr L *Caesar,* cognomen of Gaius Julius *Caesar* †44 BC Roman general & statesman] – **kaiserdom** /-d(ə)m/ *n*

ˈ**kaiserin** /-rin/ *n* the wife of a kaiser [G, fem of *kaiser*]

kaka /ˈkahkə/ *n* an olive brown New Zealand parrot [Maori]

kakapo /ˈkahkəˌpoh/ *n, pl* **kakapos** a chiefly nocturnal burrowing New Zealand parrot ☞ ENDANGERED [Maori]

kakemono /ˌkakiˈmohnoh/ *n, pl* **kakemonos** a Japanese painting or inscription on a silk or paper scroll designed to be hung on a wall [Jap]

kala-azar /ˌkahlə əˈzah, ˌkalə/ *n* a severe infectious disease, chiefly of Asia, marked esp by fever and enlargement of the spleen and liver and caused by a protozoan transmitted by the bite of sand flies [Hindi *kālā-āzār* black disease, fr *kālā* black + Per *āzār* disease]

kale, kail /kayl/ *n* **1** a hardy cabbage with curled often finely cut leaves that do not form a dense head **2** *Scot* a broth of cabbage, esp kale [Sc, fr ME (northern) *cal,* fr OE *cāl* – more at COLE]

kaleidoscope /kəˈliedəˌskohp/ *n* **1** a tubular instrument containing loose chips of coloured glass between mirrors so placed that an endless variety of symmetrical patterns is produced as the instrument is rotated and the chips of glass change position **2** sthg that is continually changing; *esp* a variegated changing pattern, scene, or succession of events [Gk *kalos* beautiful + *eidos* form + E *-scope* – more at CALLIGRAPHY, IDOL] – **kaleidoscopic** /-ˈskopik/, **kaleidoscopical** *adj,* **kaleidoscopically** *adv*

kalends /ˈkaləndz/ *n pl but sing or pl in constr* calends

Kalmuck, Kalmuk /ˈkalmək/, **Kalmyk** /ˈkalmik/ *n* a member or the language of a group of Mongolian peoples inhabiting a region stretching from W China to the Caspian Sea ☞ LANGUAGE [Russ *Kalmyk,* fr Kazan Tartar]

kalpa /ˈkahlpə, ˈkal-/ *n* a period in which, according to Hindu cosmology, the universe undergoes a cycle of creation and destruction [Skt]

Kama /ˈkahmə/ *n* the Hindu god of love [Skt *Kāma,* fr *kāma* love]

kame /kaym/ *n* a mound of sand and gravel deposited by water from a melting glacier ☞ GEOGRAPHY [Sc, kame, comb, fr ME (northern) *camb* comb, fr OE]

[1]**kamikaze** /ˌkamiˈkahzi/ *n* (the volunteer Japanese pilot of) an explosive-packed aircraft crashed on a target by its pilot [Jap, lit., divine wind]

[2]**kamikaze** *adj* suicidal ⟨*the city's ~ taxi drivers*⟩ – humor

kampong, campong /ˈkampong, -ˈ-/ *n* a hamlet or village in a Malay-speaking country [Malay]

Kampuchean /ˌkampooˈchee·ən/ *n or adj* (a native or inhabitant) of Kampuchea [*Kampuchea* (formerly Khmer Republic, formerly Cambodia), country in SE Asia]

kanaka /kəˈnakə, ˈkanəkə/ *n, often cap* a South Sea islander [Hawaiian, person, human being]

Kanarese /ˌkanəˈreez/ *n, pl* **Kanarese** **1** a member of a Kannada-speaking people of Mysore in S India **2** Kannada [*Kanara,* district of India]

kangaroo /ˌkang·gəˈrooh/ *n, pl* **kangaroos** any of various plant-eating marsupial mammals of Australia, New Guinea, and adjacent islands that hop on their long powerful hind legs ☞ LIFE CYCLE [prob native name in Australia]

kangaroo court *n* an unauthorized or irresponsible court in which justice is perverted

kangaroo rat *n* any of numerous nocturnal burrowing rodents of dry parts of W USA

Kannada /'kanədə/ *n* the major Dravidian language of Mysore in S India ☞ LANGUAGE [Kannada *kannaḍa*]

Kantian /'kanti·ən, 'kahn-/ *adj* of Kant or his philosophy [Immanuel *Kant* †1804 G philosopher] – **Kantian** *n*, **Kantianism** *n*

kaolin /'kayəlin/ *n* a fine usu white clay formed from decomposed feldspar and used esp in ceramics [F *kaolin*, fr *Kao-ling*, hill in SE China, where it was originally obtained]

kaon /'kay,on/ *n* an unstable heavy elementary particle of the meson family that exists in positive, negative, and neutral forms [ISV *ka* K (fr *K-meson*, its earlier name) + [2]*-on*]

kapok /'kaypok/ *n* a mass of silky fibres that surround the seeds of a tropical tree and are used esp as a soft (insulating) filling for mattresses, cushions, sleeping bags, etc [Malay]

kappa /'kapə/ *n* the 10th letter of the Greek alphabet [Gk, of Sem origin; akin to Heb *kaph*, 11th letter of the Heb alphabet]

kaput /kə'poot/ *adj* no longer able to function; broken, exhausted – infml [G, fr F *capot* not having made a trick at piquet]

karabiner /,karə'beenə/ *n* a carabiner

karakul, caracul /'karəkl/ *n* **1** *often cap* any of a breed of hardy fat-tailed sheep from Bukhara **2** the tightly curled glossy black coat of karakul lambs valued as fur [*Karakul*, village in Bukhara, USSR]

karat /'karət/ *n*, *NAm* CARAT 2

karate /kə'rahti/ *n* a martial art in which opponents use their hands and feet to deliver crippling blows [Jap, lit., empty hand]

karma /'kahmə/ *n*, *often cap* the force generated by a person's actions, held in Hinduism and Buddhism to determine his/her destiny in his/her next existence [Skt *karman* (nom *karma*), lit., work] – **karmic** /-mik/ *adj*, *often cap*

karoo, karroo /kə'rooh/ *n*, *pl* **karoos, karroos** a dry tableland of S Africa [Afrik *karo*]

karst /kahst/ *n* an irregular limestone region with underground streams, caverns, and potholes [G] – **karstic** *adj*

kart /kaht/ *n* a go-kart – **karting** *n*

kary- /kari-/, **karyo-** *comb form* nucleus of a cell ⟨karyo*kinesis*⟩ [NL, fr Gk *karyon* nut – more at CAREEN]

karyokinesis /,kariohkineesis, -kie-/ *n*, *pl* **karyokineses** /-seez/ (the division of the nucleus that occurs in) mitotic cell division [NL, fr *kary-* + Gk *kinēsis* motion, fr *kinein* to move] – **karyokinetic** /-'netik/ *adj*

karyotype /'karioh,tiep/ *n* (the sum of the specific characteristics of) the chromosomes of a cell [ISV] – **karyotypic** /-'tipik/ *adj*

karzy /'kahzi/ *n*, *Br* TOILET 2 – slang [modif of It *casa* house]

Kasbah /'kaz,bah/ *n* a Casbah

Kashmiri /kash'miəri/ *n*, *pl* **Kashmiris**, *esp collectively* **Kashmiri 1** a native or inhabitant of Kashmir **2** the Indic language of Kashmir ☞ LANGUAGE [*Kashmir*, region of the Indian subcontinent]

kashruth, kashrut /'kash,root/ *n* the Jewish dietary laws [Heb *kashrūth*, lit., fitness]

kat, khat /kaht, kat/ *n* a shrub of the spindle tree family cultivated by the Arabs for its leaves and buds that are the source of a habit-forming drug similar to amphetamine when chewed or used as a tea [Ar *qāt*]

kata /'kahtah/ *n* a formal training exercise in an Oriental martial art (e g karate) [Jap]

katabatic /,katə'batik/ *adj* moving downwards ⟨*a ~ wind*⟩ [LGk *katabatikos* of descent, fr Gk *katabatos* descending, fr *katabainein* to descend, fr *kata-* cata- + *bainein* to go]

katydid /'kaytidid/ *n* any of several large green N American long-horned grasshoppers [imit]

kauri /'kowəri/ *n* (the fine white straight-grained wood of) a tall New Zealand timber tree of the pine family [Maori *kawri*]

kava /'kahvə/ *n* (an intoxicating beverage made from the crushed root of) an Australasian shrubby pepper plant [Tongan & Marquesan, lit., bitter]

kayak /'kie(y)ak/ *n* an Eskimo canoe made of a frame covered with skins; *also* a similar canvas-covered or fibreglass canoe [Esk *qajaq*]

[1]**kayo, KO** /kay'oh/ *n*, *pl* **kayos** KNOCKOUT 1 – infml [*k*nock*o*ut]

[2]**kayo, KO** *vt* **kayoes, kayos; kayoing; kayoed** to knock out – infml

Kazan /kə'zan, kə'zahn/ *adj* of or from the city of Kazan in the USSR ⟨*the ~ Tartar language*⟩

kazoo /kə'zooh/ *n*, *pl* **kazoos** a musical instrument consisting of a tube into which one sings or hums to vibrate a membrane covering a side hole [imit]

kea /'kayə/ *n* a large green New Zealand parrot that normally eats insects but sometimes destroys sheep by slashing the back to feed on the kidney fat [Maori]

kebab /ki'bab/ *n* cubes of (marinated) meat cooked with onions, mushrooms, etc, usu on a skewer [Per, Hindi, Ar, & Turk; Per & Hindi *kabāb*, fr Ar, fr Turk *kebap*]

ked /ked/ *n* SHEEP KED

[1]**kedge** /kej/ *vb* to pull (a ship) along by means of a line attached to an anchor [ME *caggen*]

[2]**kedge** *n* a small anchor used esp in kedging

kedgeree /,kejə'ree, '---/ *n* a dish containing rice, flaked fish, and chopped hard-boiled eggs [Hindi *khicaṛī*, fr Skt *khiccā*]

keek /keek/ *vi or n*, *chiefly Scot* (to) peep, look [vb ME *kiken*, prob fr MD *kīken*; akin to MLG *kīken* to look; n fr vb] – **keeker** *n*

[1]**keel** /keel/ *n* a flat-bottomed ship; *esp* a barge used on the river Tyne to carry coal [ME *kele*, fr MD *kiel*; akin to OE *cēol* ship, *cot* small house – more at [1]COT]

[2]**keel** *n* **1a** a timber or plate which extends along the centre of the bottom of a vessel and usu projects somewhat from the bottom ☞ SHIP **b** the main load-bearing member (e g in an airship) **2** a projection (e g the breastbone of a bird) suggesting a keel **3** a ship – poetic [ME *kele*, fr ON *kjölr*; akin to OE *ceole* throat, beak of a ship – more at GLUTTON] – **keeled** *adj*, **keelless** *adj*

[3]**keel** *vt* to cause to turn over ~ *vi* **1** to turn over **2** to fall *over* (as if) in a faint

'**keel,haul** /-,hawl/ *vt* **1** to drag (a person) under the keel of a ship as punishment **2** to rebuke severely [D *kielhalen*, fr *kiel* keel + *halen* to haul]

keelson /'kelsən, 'keel-/, **kelson** /'kelsən/ *n* a structural beam fastened to the keel of a ship for strength and to support the flooring [prob of Scand origin; akin to Sw *kölsvin* keelson]

[1]**keen** /keen/ *adj* **1a** having or being a fine edge or point; sharp **b** affecting one as if by cutting or piercing ⟨*a ~ wind*⟩ **2a** enthusiastic, eager ⟨*a ~ swimmer*⟩ **b** *of emotion or feeling* intense ⟨*took a ~ interest*⟩ **3a** intellectually alert; *also* shrewdly astute ⟨*a ~ awareness of the problem*⟩ **b** sharply contested; competitive; *specif, Br, of prices* low in order to be competitive **c** extremely sensitive in perception ⟨*~ eyesight*⟩ **4** *NAm* wonderful, excellent [ME *kene* brave, sharp, fr OE *cēne* brave; akin to OHG *kuoni* brave, OE *cnāwan* to know – more at KNOW] – **keenly** *adv*, **keenness** *n* – **keen on** interested in; attracted to

[2]**keen** *vi or n* (to utter) a loud wailing lamentation for the dead, typically at Irish funerals [IrGael *caoinim* I lament] – **keener** *n*

[1]**keep** /keep/ *vb* **kept** /kept/ *vt* **1a** to take notice of by appropriate conduct; fulfil (the obligations of) ⟨*~ a promise*⟩ ⟨*~ the law*⟩ **b** to act fittingly in relation to (a feast or ceremony) ⟨*~ the Sabbath*⟩ **c** to conform to in habits or conduct ⟨*~ late hours*⟩ **d** to stay in accord with (a beat) ⟨*~ time*⟩ ⟨*~ step*⟩ **2a** to watch over and defend; guard ⟨*~ us from harm*⟩ ⟨*~s goal for the local team*⟩ **b(1)** to take care of, esp as an owner; tend ⟨*~s a dog*⟩ **(2)** to support ⟨*earns enough to ~ himself*⟩ **(3)** to maintain in a specified condition – often in combination ⟨*a well-*kept *garden*⟩ **c** to continue to maintain ⟨*~ order*⟩ ⟨*~ a lookout*⟩ **d(1)** to cause to remain in a specified place, situation, or condition ⟨*~ him waiting*⟩ ⟨kept *him up all night*⟩ ⟨*a net to ~ the birds out*⟩ **(2)** to store habitually for use ⟨*where do you ~ the butter?*⟩ **(3)** to preserve (food) in an unspoilt condition ⟨*how long can you ~ fish in a freezer?*⟩ **e** to have or maintain in one's service, employment, or possession or at one's disposal ⟨*~ a car*⟩ ⟨*~ a mistress*⟩ – often + *on* ⟨*~ the cook on for another month*⟩ ⟨*~ the flat on over the summer*⟩ **f** to record by entries in a book ⟨*~ accounts*⟩ ⟨*~ a diary*⟩ **g** to have customarily in stock for sale **3a** to delay, detain ⟨*what* kept *you?*⟩ ⟨*~ children in after school*⟩ **b** to hold back; restrain ⟨*~ him from going*⟩ ⟨kept *him back with difficulty*⟩ **c** to save, reserve ⟨*~ some for later*⟩ **d** to refrain from revealing or releasing ⟨*~ a secret*⟩ ⟨kept *the news back*⟩ **4** to retain possession or control of ⟨kept *the money he found*⟩ ⟨*~ a copy of the letter*⟩ ⟨*~ your temper*⟩ **5a** to continue to follow ⟨*~ the path*⟩ **b** to stay or remain on or in, often against opposition ⟨kept *his ground*⟩ ⟨*~ your seat*⟩ **6** to manage, run ⟨*~s a shop*⟩ *~ vi* **1a** to maintain a course ⟨*~ right*⟩ **b** to continue, usu without interruption ⟨*~ talking*⟩ ⟨*~ on smiling*⟩ **c** to persist in a practice ⟨kept *bothering them*⟩ ⟨kept *on smoking in spite of warnings*⟩ **2a** to stay or remain in a specified desired place, situation, or condition ⟨*~ warm*⟩ ⟨*~ out of the way*⟩ ⟨*~ off the grass*⟩ **b** to remain in good condition ⟨*meat will ~ in the freezer*⟩ **c** to be or remain with regard to health ⟨*how are you ~*ing*?*⟩ ⟨*she ~s well*⟩ **d** to call for no immediate action ⟨*the matter will ~ till morning*⟩ **3** to act as wicketkeeper or goalkeeper – infml [ME *kepen*, fr OE *cēpan*; akin to OHG *chapfēn* to look] – **keep an/one's eye on** to watch over – **keep at** to persist in doing or concerning oneself with – **keep cave** *Br* to act as a lookout at school – **keep company** to provide with companionship ⟨*won't anyone stay and* keep *me* company*?*⟩ – **keep from** to refrain from; help ⟨*can't* keep from *laughing*⟩ – **keep one's eye in** *chiefly Br* to keep in practice; *specif* to retain ability to judge the speed and direction of a moving ball – **keep one's eyes open/peeled,** *Br* **keep one's eyes skinned** to be on the alert; be watchful – **keep one's feet** to avoid overbalancing – **keep one's fingers crossed** to hope for the best – **keep one's hand in** to remain in practice – **keep one's head above water** to remain solvent; *broadly* to stay out of difficulty – **keep one's nose clean** to keep one's record untarnished by playing safe – **keep one's shirt on,** *Br* **keep one's hair on** to remain calm; keep one's temper – infml – **keep the ball rolling** to play one's part (e g in conversation) – **keep to 1** to stay in or on ⟨keep to *the path*⟩ **2** not to deviate from; ABIDE BY ⟨keep to *the rules*⟩ – **keep to oneself 1** to keep secret ⟨kept *the facts* to himself⟩ **2** *also* **keep oneself to oneself** to remain solitary or apart from other people – **keep warm** to occupy (a position) temporarily for another

[2]**keep** *n* **1** a castle, fortress, or fortified tower ☞ CHURCH **2** the means (e g food) by which one is kept ⟨*earned his ~*⟩ – **for keeps 1** with the provision that one keeps as one's own what one wins or receives ⟨*he gave it to me* for keeps⟩ – infml **2** FOR GOOD ⟨*came home* for keeps⟩ – infml

keeper /'keepə/ *n* **1a** a protector, guardian **b** a gamekeeper **c** a custodian **d** a curator **2** any of various devices (e g a latch or guard ring) for keeping sthg in position **3a** a goalkeeper **b** a wicketkeeper *USE* (*3*) chiefly infml [[1]KEEP + [2]-ER]

,keep 'fit *n* physical exercises designed to keep one healthy and supple

keeping /'keeping/ *n* custody, care [[1]KEEP + [2]-ING] – **out of/in keeping** not/conforming or agreeing with sthg implied or specified – usu + *with*

'keep,net /-,net/ *n* a large net suspended in the water in which an angler keeps caught fish alive

keep on *vi* to talk continuously; *esp* to nag ⟨kept on *at him to buy her a fur coat*⟩

'keep,sake /-'sayk/ *n* sthg (given, to be) kept as a memento, esp of the giver [[1]*keep* + *-sake* (as in *namesake*)]

keep up *vt* **1** to persist or persevere in; continue ⟨keep up *the good work*⟩ **2** to preserve from decline ⟨keep up *appearances*⟩ *~ vi* **1** to maintain an equal pace or level of activity, progress, or knowledge (e g with another) **2** to continue without interruption ⟨*rain* kept up *all night*⟩

keeshond /'kays,hond, 'kees-/ *n* (any of) a breed of small heavy-coated dogs with pointed muzzle and erect ears [D, prob fr *Kees* (nickname for *Cornelis* Cornelius) + *hond* dog, fr MD; akin to OE *hund* hound]

keg /keg/ *n, Br* **1** a small barrel having a capacity of (less than) 10gal (about 45.5l); *specif* a metal beer barrel from which beer is pumped by pressurized gas **2** beer from a keg [ME *kag*, of Scand origin; akin to ON *kaggi* keg]

kelp /kelp/ *n* **1** any of various large brown seaweeds **2** the ashes of seaweed used esp as a source of iodine [ME *culp*]

kelpie /'kelpi/ *n* a water sprite of Scottish folklore

said to delight in drowning travellers [prob of Celt origin; akin to ScGael *caipeach* colt]

kelson /'kelsən/ *n* a keelson

kelt /kelt/ *n* a salmon or sea trout after spawning [ME (northern), prob fr ScGael *cealt*]

Kelt *n* a Celt – **Keltic** *adj*

kelter /'keltə/ *n, chiefly Br* kilter

kelvin /'kelvin/ *n* the SI unit of temperature defined by the Kelvin scale ☞ PHYSICS

Kelvin *adj* of, conforming to, or being a scale of temperature on which absolute zero is at 0 and water freezes at 273.16K under standard conditions [William Thomson, Lord *Kelvin* †1907 Sc physicist]

[1]**ken** /ken/ *vb* **-nn-** *chiefly Scot* to have knowledge (of); know [ME *kennen*, fr OE *cennan* to make known & ON *kenna* to perceive; both akin to OE *can* know – more at [1]CAN]

[2]**ken** *n* the range of perception, understanding, or knowledge – usu + *beyond, outside*

kenaf /kə'naf/ *n* (the fibre, used esp for ropes, of) an E Indian hibiscus [Per]

kendo /'kendoh/ *n* the Japanese martial art of fencing with bamboo staves [Jap *kendō*, fr *ken* sword + *dō* art]

[1]**kennel** /'kenl/ *n* **1a** a shelter for a dog **b** an establishment for the breeding or boarding of dogs – often pl with sing. meaning but sing. or pl in constr ⟨*runs a* ~s *in the country*⟩ **2** a pack of dogs [ME *kenel*, deriv of (assumed) VL *canile*, fr L *canis* dog – more at HOUND]

[2]**kennel** *vt* **-ll-** (*NAm* **-l-**, **-ll-**), /'kenl·ing/ to put or keep (as if) in a kennel

Kennelly-Heaviside layer /'kenəli 'hevisied/ *n* E LAYER [Arthur *Kennelly* †1939 US electrical engineer & Oliver *Heaviside* †1925 E physicist]

kenning /'kening/ *n* a metaphorical compound word or phrase used esp in Old English and Old Norse poetry (e g *swan-road* for *ocean*) [ON, fr *kenna*]

Kentishman /'kentishmən/ *n* a native or inhabitant of Kent; *specif* one from west of the river Medway – compare MAN OF KENT

kentledge /'kentlij/ *n* pig iron or scrap metal used as permanent ballast in a ship [prob fr F *quintelage* ballast]

kepi /'kaypee (*Fr* kepi)/ *n* a round French military cap with a flat top and a horizontal peak [F *képi*, fr G dial. *käppi*, dim. of *kappe* cap, fr OHG *kappa* cloak, cape, fr LL *cappa* head covering, cloak]

Keplerian /kep'liəri·ən/ *adj* of the astronomer Kepler or his laws concerning the motions of the planets in their orbits [Johannes *Kepler* †1630 G astronomer]

kept /kept/ *past of* KEEP

keramic /ki'ramik/ *adj or n* ceramic

kerat-, kerato- *comb form* **1** cornea ⟨kerat*itis*⟩ **2** – see CERAT-

keratin /'kerətin/ *n* any of various fibrous proteins that form the chemical basis of nails, claws, and other horny tissue and hair [ISV] – **keratinous** /ki'ratinəs/ *adj*, **keratinize** /ki'ratiniez, 'kerətiniez/ *vb*

kerb /kuhb/ *n, Br* **1** the edging, esp of stone, to a pavement, path, etc **2** a market for trading in securities not listed on a stock exchange [alter. of *curb*; (2) fr its orig trading on the street]

'kerb ,drill *n, Br* a sequence of actions, esp looking to right and left, performed before crossing a road

'kerb,stone *n, Br* a block of stone forming a kerb

kerchief /'kuhchif/ *n, pl* **kerchiefs** /-chivz/ *also* **kerchieves** /~, -cheevz/ **1** a square or triangle of cloth used as a head covering or worn as a scarf around the neck **2** a handkerchief [ME *courchef*, fr OF *cuevrechief*, fr *covrir* to cover + *chief* head – more at CHIEF]

kerf /kuhf/ *n* a slit or notch made by a saw or cutting torch [ME, fr OE *cyrf* action of cutting; akin to OE *ceorfan* to carve – more at CARVE]

kerfuffle /kə'fufl/ *n, chiefly Br* a fuss, commotion – infml [Sc *curfuffle* disorder, agitation]

kermes /'kuhmiz/ *n* the dried bodies of the females of various scale insects that are found on the kermes oak and constitute a red dyestuff [F *kermès*, fr Ar *qirmiz*]

,kermes 'oak *n* a dwarf often shrubby Mediterranean oak

kern, kerne /kuhn/ *n* a lightly-armed medieval Irish foot soldier [ME *kerne*, fr MIr *cethern* band of soldiers]

kernel /'kuhnl/ *n* **1** the inner softer often edible part of a seed, fruit stone, or nut **2** a whole seed of a cereal **3** a central or essential part; CORE 2 [ME, fr OE *cyrnel*, dim. of *corn*]

kerosine, kerosene /'kerəseen/ *n, chiefly NAm* PARAFFIN 3 [Gk *kēros* wax + E *-ene* (as in *camphene*)]

kerry /'keri/ *n, often cap* any of an Irish breed of small black dairy cattle [County *Kerry*, Eire]

,Kerry 'blue, Kerry blue terrier *n* any of an Irish breed of terrier with a silky bluish coat

kersey /'kuhzi/ *n* a heavy compact ribbed or twilled woollen cloth with a short nap [ME, prob fr *Kersey*, village in Suffolk, England]

'kersey,mere /-miə/ *n* a fine woollen fabric with a close nap made in fancy twill weaves [alter. (influenced by *kersey*) of *cassimere* (cashmere), fr obs *Cassimere* (Kashmir)]

Kesp /kesp/ *trademark* – used for a textured vegetable protein woven from spun fibres and used as a meat substitute

kestrel /'kestrəl/ *n* a small common Eurasian and N African falcon that is noted for its habit of hovering in the air against a wind [ME *castrel*, fr MF *crecerelle*, fr *crecelle* rattle, prob of imit origin]

ket-, keto- *comb form* ketone ⟨ket*osis*⟩ [ISV]

ketch /kech/ *n* a fore-and-aft rigged ship with the mizzenmast stepped forward of the rudder [ME *cache*, prob fr *cacchen* to chase, catch]

ketchup /'kechəp, -up/, *NAm chiefly* **catchup** /~, 'kachəp/ *n* any of several sauces made with vinegar and seasonings and used as a relish; *esp* a sauce made from seasoned tomato puree [Malay *kĕchap* spiced fish sauce]

ketone /'keetohn/ *n* an organic compound (e g acetone) with a carbonyl group attached to 2 carbon atoms [G *keton*, alter. of *aceton* acetone] – **ketonic** /ki'tonik/ *adj*

ketone body *n* a ketone or related compound found in the blood and urine in abnormal amounts in conditions of impaired metabolism (e g diabetes mellitus)

ketosis /ki'tohsis/ *n* an abnormal increase of ketone bodies in the body [NL] – **ketotic** /ki'totik/ *adj*

kettle /'ketl/ *n* **1** a metal vessel used esp for boiling liquids; *esp* one with a lid, handle, and spout that is placed on top of a stove or cooker or contains an electric heating-element and is used to boil water **2** a steep-sided hollow in a deposit of glacial drift, caused by the melting of a mass of underlying ice ☞ GEOGRAPHY [ME *ketel,* fr ON *ketill*; akin to OE *cietel* kettle; both fr a prehistoric Gmc word borrowed fr L *catillus,* dim. of *catinus* bowl]

'kettle,drum /-,drum/ *n* a percussion instrument that consists of a hollow brass or copper hemisphere with a parchment head whose tension can be changed to vary the pitch

,kettle of 'fish *n* a (muddled or awkward) state of affairs – infml

¹key /kee/ *n* **1a** a usu metal instrument by which the bolt of a lock is turned **b** sthg having the form or function of such a key ⟨*a ~ for a clock*⟩ **2a** a means of gaining or preventing entrance, possession, or control **b** an instrumental or deciding factor **3a** sthg that gives an explanation or identification or provides a solution **b** a list of words or phrases explaining symbols or abbreviations **c** an arrangement of the important characteristics of a group of plants or animals used for identification **4** a small piece of wood or metal used as a wedge or for preventing motion between parts **5a** any of the levers of a keyboard musical instrument that is pressed by a finger or foot to actuate the mechanism and produce the notes **b** a lever that controls a vent in the side of a woodwind instrument or a valve in a brass instrument **c** a small button or knob on a keyboard (e g of a typewriter) designed to be pushed down by the fingers **6** a (particular) system of 7 notes based on their relationship to a tonic **7** characteristic style or tone **8** a small switch for opening or closing an electric circuit **9** a dry usu single-seeded fruit (e g of an ash or elm tree) **10** the indentation, roughness, or roughening of a surface to improve adhesion of plaster, paint, etc [ME, fr OE *cǣg*; akin to MLG *keige* spear] – **keyed** *adj,* **keyless** *adj*

²key *vt* **1** to secure or fasten by a key **2** to roughen (a surface) to provide a key for plaster, paint, etc **3** to bring into harmony or conformity; make appropriate **4** to make nervous, tense, or excited – usu + *up* ⟨*was ~ed up over her impending operation*⟩ **5** to keyboard

³key *adj* of basic importance; fundamental

⁴key *n* a low island or reef, esp in the Caribbean area [Sp *cayo,* fr Lucayo]

¹'key,board /-,bawd/ *n* **1a** a bank of keys on a musical instrument (e g a piano) typically having 7 usu white and 5 raised usu black keys to the octave **b** any instrument having such a keyboard, esp when forming part of a pop or jazz ensemble **2** a set of systematically arranged keys by which a machine is operated

²keyboard *vi* to operate a machine (e g for typesetting) by means of a keyboard ~ *vt* to capture or set (e g data or text) by means of a keyboard – **keyboarder** *n*

'key,button /-,but(ə)n/ *n* ¹KEY 5c

key grip *n* the chief grip in a film or television studio

'key,hole /-,hohl/ *n* a hole in a lock into which the key is put

'key ,money *n* a payment made by a tenant to secure occupancy of a rented property

Keynesianism /'kaynzi·əniz(ə)m/ *n* the economic theories ascribed to J M Keynes and his followers; *specif* the theory that government should regulate effective demand, inflation, and employment through its monetary and fiscal policies [J M *Keynes* †1946 E economist] – **Keynesian** *adj*

¹keynote /'key,noht/ *n* **1** the first and harmonically fundamental note of a scale **2** the fundamental or central fact, principle, idea, or mood

²keynote *adj* being or delivered by a speaker who presents the issues of primary interest to an assembly ⟨*a ~ speech*⟩

'key,punch /-,punch/ *n* a machine with a keyboard used to cut holes or notches in punched cards – **keypunch** *vt,* **keypuncher** *n*

key signature *n* the sharps or flats placed on the musical staff to indicate the key ☞ MUSIC

'key,stone /-,stohn/ *n* **1** the wedge-shaped piece at the apex of an arch that locks the other pieces in place – compare VOUSSOIR ☞ ARCHITECTURE **2** sthg on which associated things depend for support

khaki /'kahki/ *n* **1** a dull yellowish brown **2** a khaki-coloured cloth made usu of cotton or wool and used esp for military uniforms [Hindi *khākī* dust-coloured, fr *khāk* dust, fr Per] – **khaki** *adj*

Khalka /'kalkə/ *n* the official language of the Mongolian People's Republic

khamsin /'kamsin, kam'seen/ *n* a hot southerly Egyptian wind coming from the Sahara [Ar *rīḥ al-khamsīn* the wind of the fifty (days between Easter and Pentecost)]

khan /kahn/ *n* a medieval supreme ruler over the Turkish, Tartar, and Mongol tribes [ME *caan,* fr MF, of Turkic origin; akin to Turk *han* prince] – **khanate** /'kahnayt/ *n*

khat /kaht, kat/ *n* kat

khedive /ki'deev/ *n* a ruler of Egypt during the period 1867 to 1914, governing as a viceroy of the sultan of Turkey [F *khédive,* fr Turk *hidiv*] – **khedivial** /-vi·əl/, **khedival** *adj*

Khmer /kmeə/ *n, pl* **Khmers,** *esp collectively* **Khmer** **1** a member of one of the main ethnic groups of Kampuchea; *broadly* a Kampuchean **2** the official language of Kampuchea ☞ LANGUAGE – **Khmerian** /-ri·ən/ *adj*

Khoisan /'koysahn, -'-/ *n* a group of African languages comprising Hottentot and the Bushman languages

khoum /khoom/ *n* ☞ *Mauritania* at NATIONALITY [of Ar origin]

khyber /'kiebə/ *n, Br* the buttocks, arse – slang [rhyming slang *Khyber (Pass)* arse, fr the *Khyber Pass* between Afghanistan & Pakistan]

kiang /ki'ang/ *n* an Asiatic wild ass usu with a reddish back and sides and white underparts, muzzle, and legs [Tibetan *rkyaṅ*]

kibble /kibl/ *vt* to grind coarsely [origin unknown]

kibbutz /ki'boots/ *n, pl* **kibbutzim** /-'tseem/ a collective farm or settlement in Israel [NHeb *qibbūṣ,* fr Heb, gathering]

kib'butznik /-nik/ *n* a member of a kibbutz [Yiddish, fr *kibbutz* + *-nik*]

kibe /kieb/ *n* an ulcerated chilblain, esp on the heel [ME, prob fr W *cibi, cibwst*]

kibitzer /'kibitsə/ *n* sby who looks on and often offers unwanted advice or comment, esp at a card game [Yiddish *kibitser,* fr *kibitsen* to kibitz, fr G *kiebitzen,* fr *kiebitz* lapwing, busybody, fr MHG *gībitz* lapwing, of imit origin] – **kibitz** *vb*

kibosh /ˈkie,bosh/ *n* sthg that serves as a check or stop ⟨*put the* ~ *on that*⟩ – infml [origin unknown] – **kibosh** *vt*

[1]**kick** /kik/ *vi* **1a** to strike out with the foot or feet **b** to make a kick in football **2** to show opposition; rebel **3** *of a firearm* to recoil when fired ~ *vt* **1** to strike suddenly and forcefully (as if) with the foot **2** to score by kicking a ball **3** to free oneself of (a drug or drug habit) – infml [ME *kiken*] – **kick oneself** to reprove oneself for some stupidity or omission – **kick one's heels 1** to be kept waiting **2** to be idle – **kick over the traces** to cast off restraint, authority, or control – **kick the bucket** DIE 1 – infml, humor – **kick upstairs** to promote to a higher but less desirable position

[2]**kick** *n* **1a** a blow or sudden forceful thrust with the foot; *specif* one causing the propulsion of an object **b** the power to kick **c** a repeated motion of the legs used in swimming **d** a sudden burst of speed, esp in a footrace **2** the recoil of a gun **3** power or strength to resist; *broadly* resilience ⟨*still has some* ~ *in him*⟩ **4a** a stimulating effect or quality ⟨*this drink has quite a* ~⟩ **b** a stimulating or pleasurable experience or feeling – often pl ⟨*he did it for* ~s⟩ **c** an absorbing or obsessive new interest ⟨*on a health food* ~ *at present*⟩

[3]**kick** *n* an indentation in the base of a glass vessel, esp a bottle [origin unknown]

kick about *vb* KICK AROUND

kick around *vt* **1** to treat inconsiderately or high-handedly **2** to consider (a problem) from various angles, esp in an unsystematic or experimental way ~ *vi* **1** to wander aimlessly or idly **2** to lie unused or unwanted ⟨*there's a spare blanket* kicking around *in one of these rooms*⟩ *USE* (*vt & vi*) infml

ˈ**kick,back** /-,bak/ *n* **1** a sharp violent reaction **2** a money return received usu because of help or favours given or sometimes because of confidential agreement or coercion

kicker /ˈkikə/ *n* a horse with a habit of kicking [[1]KICK + [2]-ER]

ˈ**kick,off** /-,of/ *n* **1** a kick that puts the ball into play in soccer, rugby, etc **2** an act or instance of starting or beginning

kick off *vi* **1** to start or resume play with a kickoff **2** to start or begin proceedings – infml

kick out *vt* to dismiss or eject forcefully or summarily – infml

ˈ**kick ,pleat** *n* a short pleat consisting of a layer of fabric sewn under an opening at the lower edge of a narrow skirt to allow freedom of movement

kickshaw /ˈkikshaw/ *n* **1** a fancy dish **2** a bauble, gewgaw [modif of F *quelque chose* something]

ˈ**kick,stand** /-,stand/ *n* a swivelling stand for a 2-wheeled vehicle when not in use [fr its being put in position by a kick]

kick-starter *n* a foot-operated starter (e g for a motorcycle) – **kick-start** *vt*

kick up *vt* **1** to cause to rise upwards; raise ⟨*clouds of dust* kicked up *by passing cars*⟩ **2** to stir up (a row, a fuss, trouble, etc) – infml

[1]**kid** /kid/ *n* **1** the young of a goat or related animal **2** the flesh, fur, or skin of a kid **3** a child; *also* a young person (e g a teenager) – infml [ME *kide*, of Scand origin; akin to ON *kith* kid] – **kiddish** *adj* – **with kid gloves** with special consideration

[2]**kid** *vi* **-dd-** *of a goat or antelope* to bring forth young

[3]**kid** *vb* **-dd-** *vt* **1a** to mislead as a joke ⟨*it's the truth; I wouldn't* ~ *you*⟩ **b** to convince (oneself) of sthg untrue or improbable **2** to make fun of ~ *vi* to engage in good-humoured fooling *USE* (*vt & vi*) infml [prob fr [1]*kid*] – **kidder** *n*, **kiddingly** *adv*

Kidderminster /ˈkidə,minstə/ *n* a type of ingrain carpet [*Kidderminster*, town in England]

kiddie, kiddy /kidi/ *n* a small child – infml [[1]*kid* + *-ie*]

ˈ**kiddi,wink** /-wingk/ *n* a kiddie [*kiddie* + *wink* (of unknown origin), perh after *kiddlywink* (beerhouse, building)]

kiddush /ˈkidəsh, kiˈdoohsh/ *n* a ceremonial blessing pronounced over wine or bread in a Jewish home or synagogue on a sabbath or other holy day [LHeb *qiddūsh* sanctification]

,**kid-ˈglove** *adj* using or involving especially considerate or tactful methods

kidnap /ˈkidnap/ *vt* **-pp-, -p-** to seize and detain (a person) by force and often for ransom [prob back-formation fr *kidnapper*, fr *kid* + obs *napper* (thief)] – **kidnapper, kidnaper** *n*

kidney /ˈkidni/ *n* **1a** either of a pair of organs situated in the body cavity near the spinal column that excrete waste products of metabolism in the form of urine ☞ DIGESTION **b** an excretory organ of an invertebrate **2** the kidney of an animal eaten as food **3** sort, kind, or type, esp with regard to temperament [ME]

ˈ**kidney ,bean** *n* (any of the kidney-shaped seeds of) the French bean

kidskin /ˈkid,skin/ *n* (a soft pliant leather made from) the skin of a kid

kieselguhr, kieselgur /ˈkeezl,gooə/ *n* loose or porous earth consisting of the fossil remains of diatoms, used for polishing, filtering, and as an absorbent in the manufacture of dynamite [G *kieselgur*]

kike /kiek/ *n, chiefly NAm* a Jew – derog [prob alter. of *kiki*, redupl of *-ki*, common ending of names of Jews who lived in Slavonic countries]

Kikuyu /kiˈkooh·yooh/ *n, pl* **Kikuyus**, *esp collectively* **Kikuyu 1** a member of a Bantu-speaking people of Kenya **2** the Bantu language of the Kikuyu people

kilderkin /ˈkildəkin/ *n* a small cask having a capacity of 16 or 18gal (about 73 or 82l) [ME, fr MD *kindekijn*, fr ML *quintale* quintal]

[1]**kill** /kil/ *vt* **1** to deprive of life **2a** to put an end to **b** to defeat, veto **3a** to destroy the vital, active, or essential quality of ⟨~ed *the pain with drugs*⟩ **b** to spoil, subdue, or neutralize the effect of ⟨*that colour* ~s *the room*⟩ **c(1)** to turn off (studio or stage lighting) **(2)** to remove (a shadow) by adjusting lighting or moving a camera **4** to cause (time) to pass (e g while waiting) **5** to hit (a shot) so hard in a racket game that a return is impossible **6** to cause (e g an engine) to stop **7** to cause extreme pain to ⟨*my feet are* ~ing *me*⟩ **8** to overwhelm with admiration or amusement **9** to discard or abandon further investigation of (a story) – journ ~ *vi* to destroy life *USE* (*6, 7, 8*) infml [ME *killen, cullen* to strike, beat, kill; perh akin to OE *cwellan* to kill– more at QUELL] – **killer** *n* – **to kill** TO THE NINES ⟨*dressed* to kill⟩

[2]**kill** *n* **1** a killing or being killed ⟨*moved in for the* ~⟩ **2** sthg killed: e g **a** animals killed in a shoot, hunt, season, or particular period of time **b** an enemy

aircraft, submarine, etc destroyed by military action

killdeer /'kil,diə/ *n, pl* **killdeers,** *esp collectively* **killdeer** a plover of temperate N America [imit]

'killer ,whale /'kilə/ *n* a flesh-eating gregarious black-and-white toothed whale found in most seas of the world

killick /kilik/ *n* an anchor [origin unknown]

killifish /'kili,fish/ *n* a topminnow [*killie, killy* (killifish; fr *kill* channel, river, stream – fr D *kil,* fr MD *kille* – + *-ie, -y*) + *fish*]

[1]**killing** /'kiling/ *n* a sudden notable gain or profit – infml [[1]KILL + [2]-ING]

[2]**killing** *adj* **1** extremely exhausting or difficult to endure **2** highly amusing *USE* infml – **killingly** *adv*

'kill,joy /-,joy/ *n* one who spoils the pleasure of others

kill off *vt* to destroy totally or in large numbers

kiln /kiln/ *n* an oven, furnace, or heated enclosure used for processing a substance by burning, firing, or drying [ME *kilne,* fr OE *cyln,* fr L *culina* kitchen, fr *coquere* to cook – more at COOK] – **kiln** *vt*

kilo /'keeloh/ *n, pl* **kilos** **1** a kilogram **2** a kilometre

Kilo – a communications code word for the letter *k*

kilo- *comb form* thousand ⟨kilo*ton*⟩ ☞ PHYSICS [F, modif of Gk *chilioi* – more at MILE]

kilobit /'kiləbit/ *n* either of 2 units of information: **a** one equal to 1000 bits **b** one equal to 1024 bits [ISV]

'kilo,byte /-,biet/ *n* either of 2 units of computer storage: **a** one equal to 1000 bytes **b** one equal to 1024 bytes [ISV]

'kilo,calorie /-,kaləri/ *n* the quantity of heat required to raise the temperature of 1kg of water 1°C under standard conditions [ISV]

'kilo,cycle /-,siekl/ *n* a kilohertz [ISV]

'kilo,gram /-,gram/ *n* **1** the SI unit of mass and weight equal to the mass of a platinum-iridium cylinder kept near Paris, and approximately equal to the weight of a litre of water **2** a unit of force equal to the weight of a kilogram mass under the earth's gravitational attraction *USE* ☞ PHYSICS, UNIT [F *kilogramme,* fr *kilo-* + *gramme* gram]

'kilo,hertz /-,huhts/ *n* a unit of frequency equal to 1000 hertz [ISV]

kilometre /'kilə,meetə, ki'lomitə/ *n* 1000 metres ☞ UNIT [F *kilomètre,* fr *kilo-* + *mètre* metre]

'kilo,ton /-,tun/ *n* an explosive force equivalent to that of 1000 tons of TNT

'kilo,watt /-,wot/ *n* 1000 watts [ISV]

,kilowatt-'hour *n* a unit of work or energy equal to that expended by 1kW in 1hr ☞ UNIT

kilt /kilt/ *n* a skirt traditionally worn by Scotsmen that is formed usu from a length of tartan, is pleated at the back and sides, and is wrapped round the body and fastened at the front ☞ GARMENT [ME *kilten* to gather up (a skirt), of Scand origin; akin to ON *kjalta* fold of a gathered skirt]

kilter /'kiltə/ *n* adjustment; (good) working order – chiefly in *out of kilter* [origin unknown]

kimono /ki'mohnoh/ *n, pl* **kimonos** a loose robe with wide sleeves and a broad sash traditionally worn by the Japanese [Jap, clothes]

[1]**kin** /kin/ *n* **1** a group of people of common ancestry **2** *sing or pl in constr* one's relatives **3** *archaic* kinship [ME, fr OE *cyn*; akin to OHG *chunni* race, L *genus* birth, race, kind, Gk *genos,* L *gignere* to beget, Gk *gignesthai* to be born]

[2]**kin** *adj* kindred, related

-kin /-kin/ *also* **-kins** *suffix* (→ *n*) small kind of ⟨*cat*kin⟩ ⟨*manni*kin⟩ [ME, fr MD *-kin*; akin to OHG *-chīn,* dim. suffix]

kina /'keenə/ *n* ☞ *Papua New Guinea* at NATIONALITY [native name in Papua]

kinaesthesia, *NAm chiefly* **kinesthesia** /,kinəs'theezi·ə, -zh(y)ə, ,kie-/ *n* the sense of the position and movement of the joints of the body [NL, fr Gk *kinein* + *aisthēsis* perception – more at ANAESTHESIA] – **kinaesthetic** /-'thetik/ *adj,* **kiaesthetically** *adv*

kinaesthesis, *NAm chiefly* **kinesthesis** /,kinəs'theesis/ *n* kinaesthesia

[1]**kind** /kiend/ *n* **1** fundamental nature or quality **2a** a group united by common traits or interests **b** a specific or recognized variety – often in combination ⟨*how delinquents differ from the rest of juvenile-*kind – *TLS*⟩ **c** a doubtful or barely admissible member of a category ⟨*a* ~ *of grey*⟩ [ME *kinde,* fr OE *cynd*; akin to OE *cyn* kin] – **in kind** **1** in goods, commodities, or natural produce as distinguished from money **2** in a similar way or with the equivalent of what has been offered or received ⟨*repayed his generosity* in kind⟩

[2]**kind** *adj* **1** disposed to be helpful and benevolent **2** forbearing, considerate, or compassionate **3** showing sympathy, benevolence, or forbearance **4** cordial, friendly **5** not harmful; mild, gentle – **kindness** *n*

kinda /'kiendə/ *adv* KIND OF – used in writing to suggest casual speech [by alter.]

kindergarten /'kində,gahtn/ *n* a school or class for small children [G, fr *kinder* children + *garten* garden]

kindhearted /,kiend'hahtid/ *adj* marked by a sympathetic nature – **kindheartedly** *adv,* **kindheartedness** *n*

kindle /'kindl/ *vb* **kindling** /'kindling/ *vt* **1** to set (a fire, wood, etc) burning **2** to stir up (e g emotion) ~ *vi* **1** to catch fire **2** to become animated or aroused [ME *kindlen,* fr ON *kynda*; akin to OHG *cunte*sal fire]

kindling /'kindling/ *n* material (e g dry wood and leaves) for starting a fire

[1]**kindly** /'kiendli/ *adj* **1** agreeable, beneficial **2** sympathetic, generous – **kindliness** *n*

[2]**kindly** *adv* **1** in an appreciative or sincere manner ⟨*I'd take it* ~ *if you'd put in a good word for the boy*⟩ **2** – used (1) to add politeness or emphasis to a request ⟨~ *fill in the attached questionnaire*⟩ (2) to convey irritation or anger in a command ⟨*will you* ~ *shut that door*⟩

'kind of *adv* **1** to a moderate degree; somewhat ⟨*it's* ~ *late to begin*⟩ **2** in a manner of speaking ⟨*all you can do is* ~ *nurse it – SEU S*⟩ **3** roughly, approximately *USE* infml

[1]**kindred** /'kindrid/ *n* **1** *sing or pl in constr* (one's) relatives **2** family relationship [ME, fr *kin* + OE *rǣden* condition, fr *rǣdan* to advise, read]

[2]**kindred** *adj* similar in nature or character

kine /kien/ *archaic pl of* cow

kinematics /,kini'matiks, ,kie-/ *n pl but sing in constr* a branch of physics that deals with aspects of motion without consideration of mass or force [F *cinématique,* fr Gk *kinēmat-, kinēma* motion – more at CINEMATOGRAPH] – **kinematic, kinematical** *adj*, **kinematically** *adv*

kinesics /ki'neesiks, kie-/ *n pl but sing in constr* a systematic study of the relationship between bodily cues or movements (e g eye movement, blushes, or shrugs) and communication [Gk *kinēsis* + E *-ics*]

-kinesis /-ki'neesis/ *comb form* (→ *n*), *pl* **-kineses** /-seez/ **1** movement ⟨*tele*kinesis⟩ ⟨*psycho*kinesis⟩ **2** division ⟨*karyo*kinesis⟩ [NL, fr Gk *kinēsis* motion, fr *kinein* to move]

kinesthesia /,kinəs'theezi·ə, -zh(y)ə, ,kie-/ *n, chiefly NAm* kinaesthesia – **kinesthetic** /-'thetik/ *adj*, **kinesthetically** *adv*

kinesthesis /,kinəs'theesis/ *n, chiefly NAm* kinaesthesis

kinet-, kineto- *comb form* movement; motion ⟨ki netogenic⟩ ⟨kinetoscope⟩ [Gk *kinētos* moving]

kinetic /ki'netik/ *adj* of motion [Gk *kinētikos*, fr *kinētos* moving, fr *kinein*]

kinetic art *n* art (e g sculpture) depending for its effect on the movement of surfaces or volumes – **kinetic artist** *n*

kinetic energy *n* energy that a body or system has by virtue of its motion

ki'netics *n pl but sing or pl in constr* **1** science that deals with the effects of forces on the motions of material bodies or with changes in a physical or chemical system **2** the mechanism by which a physical or chemical change is effected

kinetic theory *n* any of several theories in physics based on the fact that constituent particles of a substance are in vigorous motion

king /king/ *n* **1** a male monarch of a major territorial unit; *esp* one who inherits his position and rules for life **2** the holder of a preeminent position **3** the principal piece of each colour in a set of chessmen that has the power to move 1 square in any direction and must be protected against check **4** a playing card marked with a stylized figure of a king and ranking usu below the ace **5** a draughtsman that has reached the opposite side of the board and is empowered to move both forwards and backwards [ME, fr OE *cyning*; akin to OHG *kuning* king, OE *cyn* kin] – **kingship** *n*

'king,bolt /-,bohlt/ *n* a large or major bolt

,king 'cobra *n* a large venomous cobra of southeastern Asia and the Philippines

king crab *n* any of several closely related marine arthropods that have a broad crescent-shaped cephalothorax

'king,craft /-,krahft/ *n* the art of governing as a king

'king,cup /-,kup/ *n* MARSH MARIGOLD

'kingdom /-d(ə)m/ *n* **1** a territorial unit with a monarchical form of government **2** *often cap* the eternal kingship of God **3** an area or sphere in which sby or sthg holds a preeminent position **4** any of the 3 primary divisions into which natural objects are commonly classified – compare ANIMAL KINGDOM, MINERAL KINGDOM, PLANT KINGDOM

'king,fish /-,fish/ *n* the opah

'king,fisher /-,fishə/ *n* any of numerous small brightly-coloured fish-eating birds with a short tail and a long stout sharp bill

,King 'James ,Version /jaymz/ *n* AUTHORIZED VERSION [*King James* I †1625 who commissioned this translation of the Bible]

'king,klip /-,klip/ an edible eel-like marine fish [short for *kingklipfish*, trans of Afrik *koningklipvis*]

'king,maker /-,maykə/ *n* sby having influence over the choice of candidates for office

king penguin *n* a large antarctic penguin

'king,pin /-,pin; *also sense* ' ,-'-/ *n* **1** the key person or thing in a group or undertaking **2** a kingbolt

'king ,post *n* a vertical supporting post connecting the apex of a triangular truss (e g of a roof) with the base – compare QUEEN POST ☞ ARCHITECTURE

Kings /kingz/ *n pl but sing in constr* any of 2 or, in the Roman Catholic canon, 4 narrative and historical books of the Old Testament

,King's 'Bench *n* QUEEN'S BENCH – used when the British monarch is a man

,King's 'Counsel *n* QUEEN'S COUNSEL – used when the British monarch is a man

,King's 'English *n* standard or correct S British English speech or usage – used when the monarch is a man

,king's 'evil *n, often cap K&E* scrofula [fr the former belief that it could be healed by a king's touch]

kingship /'kingship/ *n* the position, office, or dignity of a king

'king-,size, 'king-,sized *adj* larger or longer than the regular or standard size

kinin /'kienin/ *n* any of various polypeptide hormones that are formed locally in the tissues and chiefly affect smooth muscle [Gk *kinein* to move, stimulate + E *-in*]

kink /kingk/ *n* **1** a short tight twist or curl caused by sthg doubling or winding on itself **2** an eccentricity or mental peculiarity; *esp* such eccentricity in sexual behaviour or preferences [D; akin to MLG *kinke* kink] – **kink** *vb*

kinkajou /'kingkə,jooh/ *n* a slender nocturnal tree-dwelling fruit-eating mammal of Mexico and Central and S America [F, of Algonquian origin; akin to Ojibwa *qwingwâage* wolverine]

kinky /'kingki/ *adj* **1** closely twisted or curled **2a** offbeat **b** titillatingly unusual or bizarre; *esp* sexually perverted ***USE*** (2) infml [*kink* + *-y*] – **kinkiness** *n*

kinsfolk /'kinz,fohk/ *n pl* relatives

kinship /'kinship/ *n* **1** blood relationship **2** similarity

kinsman /'kinzmən/, *fem* **'kins,woman** *n* a (male) relative

kiosk /'kee,osk/ *n* **1** an open summerhouse or pavilion common in Turkey or Iran **2** a small stall or stand used esp for the sale of newspapers, cigarettes, and sweets **3** *Br* a public telephone box [Turk *köşk*, fr Per *kūshk* portico; (2, 3) F *kiosque*, fr Turk *köşk*]

¹kip /kip/ *n, pl* **kip, kips** ☞ *Laos* at NATIONALITY [Thai]

²kip *n, chiefly Br* **1** a place to sleep **2** a period of sleep ***USE*** infml [perh fr Dan *kippe* cheap tavern]

³kip *vi* **-pp-** *chiefly Br* **1** to sleep **2** to lie down to sleep – often + *down* ***USE*** infml

¹kipper /'kipə/ *n* a kippered fish, esp a herring – compare BUCKLING [ME *kypre* male salmon, fr OE *cypera*; akin to OE *coper* copper]

²kipper *vt* to cure (split dressed fish) by salting and drying, usu by smoking

Kirghiz /'kuhgiz/ *n, pl* **Kirghiz, Kirghizes** a member of a Mongolian people inhabiting chiefly the Central Asian steppes; *also* the language of this people ☞ LANGUAGE [Kirghiz *Kyrghyz*]

kirk /kuhk/ *n* **1** *cap the* national Church of Scotland as distinguished from the Church of England or the Episcopal Church in Scotland **2** *chiefly Scot* a church [ME (northern), fr ON *kirkja,* fr OE *cirice* – more at CHURCH]

kirsch /kiəsh/ *n* a dry colourless spirit distilled from the fermented juice of the black morello cherry [G, short for *kirschwasser,* fr *kirsche* cherry + *wasser* water]

kirtle /'kuhtl/ *n* a man's tunic or coat or a woman's dress worn esp in the Middle Ages [ME *kirtel,* fr OE *cyrtel,* fr (assumed) OE *curt* short, fr L *curtus* shortened – more at SHEAR]

kismet /'kizmet, 'kis-/ *n, often cap* FATE 1, 2a [Turk, fr Ar *qismah* portion, lot]

[1]**kiss** /kis/ *vt* **1a** to touch with the lips, esp as a mark of affection or greeting **b** to express or effect by kissing ⟨~ed *her good night*⟩ **2** to touch gently or lightly ⟨*wind gently* ~ing *the trees*⟩ ~ *vi* **1** to touch one another with the lips, esp as a mark of love or sexual desire **2** to come into gentle contact [ME *kissen,* fr OE *cyssan;* akin to OHG *kussen* to kiss] – **kissable** *adj*

[2]**kiss** *n* an act or instance of kissing

'kiss-,curl *n* a small curl of hair falling on the forehead or cheek

kisser /'kisə/ *n* the mouth or face – slang [[1]KISS + [2]-ER]

,kiss of 'death *n* an act or association bound to cause ruin or failure – infml [fr the kiss with which Judas betrayed Jesus (Mk 14:44-46)]

,kiss of 'life *n* artificial respiration in which the rescuer blows air into the victim's lungs by mouth-to-mouth contact

,kiss of 'peace *n* a ceremonial kiss, embrace, or clasping of hands used in Christian liturgies, esp the Eucharist

[1]**kit** /kit/ *n* **1** a set of tools or implements **2** a set of parts ready to be assembled ⟨*a model aeroplane* ~⟩ **3** a set of clothes and equipment for use in a specified situation; *esp* the equipment carried by a member of the armed forces [ME *kitt, kyt* wooden tub, prob fr MD *kitte, kit* jug, vessel]

[2]**kit** *vt* **-tt-** *chiefly Br* to equip, outfit; *esp* to clothe – usu + *out* or *up* ⟨*all* ~ted *out for camping*⟩

[3]**kit** *n* a kitten

'kit,bag /-,bag/ *n* a large cylindrical bag carried over the shoulder and used for holding the kit, esp of a member of the armed forces

kitchen /'kichin/ *n* a place (e g a room in a house or hotel) where food is prepared [ME *kichene,* fr OE *cycene;* akin to OHG *chuhhina* kitchen; both fr a prehistoric WGmc word borrowed fr LL *coquina,* fr L *coquere* to cook – more at COOK]

kitchenette /,kichi'net/ *n* a small kitchen or alcove containing cooking facilities

,kitchen 'garden *n* a garden in which vegetables are grown

,kitchen-'sink *adj, Br, esp of drama* portraying modern daily life in a realistic and often sordid manner

kite /kiet/ *n* **1** any of various hawks with long narrow wings, a deeply forked tail, and feet adapted for taking insects and small reptiles as prey **2** a light frame covered with thin material (e g paper or cloth), designed to be flown in the air at the end of a long string [ME, fr OE *cȳta;* akin to MHG *kūze* owl, Gk *goan* to lament]

'Kite-,mark *n* a kite-shaped mark on goods approved by the British Standards Institution ☞ SYMBOL

kith /kith/ *n* friends or neighbours ⟨~ *and kin*⟩ [ME, fr OE *cȳthth,* fr *cūth* known – more at UNCOUTH]

kitsch /kich/ *n* artistic or literary material that is pretentious or inferior and is usu designed to appeal to popular or sentimental taste [G] – **kitschy** *adj*

[1]**kitten** /'kitn/ *n* the young of a cat or other small mammal [ME *kitoun,* fr (assumed) ONF *caton,* dim. of *cat,* fr LL *cattus*]

[2]**kitten** *vi* to give birth to kittens

kittenish /'kitn·ish/ *adj* coyly playful or flirtatious [[1]KITTEN + -ISH]

kittiwake /'kiti,wayk/ *n* any of various gulls that have a short or rudimentary hind toe [imit]

[1]**kittle** /'kitl/ *vt, chiefly Scot* to tickle [ME (northern) *kytyllen,* prob fr ON *kitla*]

[2]**kittle** *adj, Scot* difficult or risky to deal with

[1]**kitty** /'kiti/ *n* CAT 1a; *esp* a kitten – used chiefly as a pet name or calling name

[2]**kitty** *n* a jointly held fund of money (e g for household expenses) [[1]*kit*]

kiwi /'keewi/ *n* **1** a flightless New Zealand bird with hairlike plumage **2** *cap* a New Zealander [Maori, of imit origin]

Klan /klan/ *n* KU KLUX KLAN – **Klanism** /'kla,niz(ə)m/ *n,* **Klansman** /-mən/ *n*

Klaxon /'klaks(ə)n/ *trademark* – used for a powerful electrically operated horn or warning signal

Kleenex /'kleeneks/ *trademark* – used for a paper handkerchief

'Klein ,bottle /klien/ *n* a 1-sided surface that is formed by passing the narrow end of a tapered tube through the side of the tube and flaring this end out to join the other end [Felix *Klein* †1925 G mathematician]

klepht /kleft/ *n, often cap* a Greek belonging to any of several independent guerrilla communities after the Turkish conquest of Greece in the 15th c [NGk *klephtēs,* lit., robber, fr Gk *kleptēs,* fr *kleptein* to steal; akin to Goth *hlifan* to steal, L *clepere*] – **klephtic** /-tik/ *adj, often cap*

kleptomania /,kleptə'maynyə/ *n* an irresistible desire to steal, esp when not accompanied by economic motives or desire for financial gain [NL, fr Gk *kleptein* to steal + LL *mania*] – **kleptomaniac** /-ni,ak/ *n*

'klieg ,light, kleig light /kleeg/ *n* a powerful arc lamp used in film studios [John H *Kliegl* †1959 & Anton T *Kliegl* †1927 German-born US lighting experts]

'Kline,felter's ,syndrome /'klien,feltəz/ *n* an abnormal condition in a man characterized by 2 X and 1 Y chromosomes, infertility, and smallness of the testicles [Harry F *Klinefelter* b 1912 US physician]

klipspringer /'klip,spring·ə/ *n* a small African antelope [Afrik, fr *klip* cliff, rock + *springer* springer, leaper]

klystron /'klistron, 'klie-/ *n* an electron tube in which bunching of electrons is produced by electric fields and which is used for the generation and amplification of uhf current [fr *Klystron,* a trademark]

knack /nak/ *n* a special ability, capacity, or skill that enables sthg, esp of a difficult or unusual nature, to be done with ease ⟨*skating is easy once you've got the ~*⟩; *broadly* APTITUDE 1 ⟨*has a ~ for saying the wrong thing*⟩ [ME *knak, knakke* trick, prob fr *knak* sharp blow or sound, of imit origin]

[1]**knacker** /ˈnakə/ *n, Br* **1** sby who buys and slaughters worn-out horses for use esp as animal food or fertilizer ⟨*a ~'s yard*⟩ **2** a buyer of old ships, houses, or other structures for their constituent materials [prob fr E dial. (saddlemaker)] – **knackery** *n*

[2]**knacker** *vt, chiefly Br* to exhaust – infml ⟨*after working all night I felt ~*ed⟩

knap /nap/ *vt* **-pp-** to break with a quick blow; *esp* to shape (flints) by breaking off pieces [ME *knappen*, of imit origin] – **knapper** *n*

knapsack /ˈnap,sak/ *n* a (soldier's) bag (e g of canvas or leather) strapped on the back and used for carrying supplies or personal belongings [LG *knappsack* or D *knapzak*, fr LG & D *knappen* to make a snapping noise, eat + LG *sack* or D *zak* sack]

ˈ**knap,weed** /-,weed/ *n* a widely naturalized European perennial with tough wiry stems and knobby heads of purple flowers [ME *knopwed*, fr *knop* knob + *wed* weed]

knave /nayv/ *n* **1** an unprincipled deceitful fellow **2** JACK 5 **3** *archaic* a male servant [ME, fr OE *cnafa* boy, male servant; akin to OHG *knabo* boy] – **knavery** /ˈnayv(ə)ri/ *n*, **knavish** *adj*, **knavishly** *adv*

knead /need/ *vt* **1** to work and press into a mass (as if) with the hands ⟨*~ing dough*⟩ **2** to manipulate (as if) by kneading ⟨*~ the idea into shape*⟩ [ME *kneden*, fr OE *cnedan*; akin to OHG *knetan* to knead, OE *cnotta* knot] – **kneadable** *adj*, **kneader** *n*

[1]**knee** /nee/ *n* **1a** (the part of the leg that includes) a joint in the middle part of the human leg that is the articulation between the femur, tibia, and kneecap **b** a corresponding joint in an animal, bird, or insect **2** sthg (e g a piece of wood or iron) shaped like the human knee [ME, fr OE *cnēow*; akin to OHG *kneo* knee, L *genu*, Gk *gony*] – **kneed** *adj*

[2]**knee** *vt* to strike with the knee

[1]**kneecap** /ˈnee,kap/ *n* a thick flat triangular movable bone that forms the front point of the knee and protects the front of the joint ☞ ANATOMY

[2]**kneecap** *vt* to smash the kneecap of, as a punishment or torture

,**knee-ˈdeep** *adj* **1** knee-high **2** immersed *in* (as if) up to the knees ⟨*~ in work*⟩

,**knee-ˈhigh** *adj* high or deep enough to reach up to the knees

ˈ**knee ,jerk** *n* an involuntary forward kick produced by a light blow on the tendon below the kneecap

kneel /neel/ *vi* **knelt** /nelt/, **kneeled** to fall or rest on the knee or knees [ME *knelen*, fr OE *cnēowlian*; akin to OE *cnēow* knee] – **kneeler** *n*

ˈ**knees-,up** *n, pl* **knees-ups** *chiefly Br* **1** an exhausting party dance in which alternate knees are raised in time with the increasing tempo of the music **2** a boisterous celebration, usu with dancing *USE* infml

[1]**knell** /nel/ *vi* **1** *of a bell* to ring, esp for a death, funeral, etc **2** to sound ominously ~ *vt* to summon, announce, or proclaim (as if) by a knell [ME *knellen*, fr OE *cnyllan*; akin to MHG er*knellen* to toll]

[2]**knell** *n* **1** (the sound of) a bell rung slowly (e g for a funeral or disaster) **2** an indication of the end or failure of sthg

Knesset /ˈknesit/ *n* the legislative assembly of Israel [NHeb, *kĕneseth*, lit., gathering, assembly, fr Heb *kānas* to gather]

knew /nyooh/ *past of* KNOW

Knickerbocker /ˈnikə,bokə/ *n* a descendant of the early Dutch settlers of New York [Diedrich *Knickerbocker*, fictitious author of *History of New York* by Washington Irving †1859 US writer]

,**knicker,bocker ˈglory** *n* an elaborate dessert, typically consisting of layers of fruit, jelly, ice cream, and cream served in a tall glass

ˈ**knicker,bockers** *n pl* short baggy trousers gathered on a band at the knee [fr the resemblance of the garment to the knee-breeches of the Dutchman, *Knickerbocker*, in Cruikshank's illustrations to Irving's *History of New York*]

knickers /ˈnikəz/ *n pl* **1** *Br* women's pants **2** *NAm* knickerbockers [short for *knickerbockers*]

ˈ**knick-,knack** /ˈnik,nak/ *n* a small trivial ornament or trinket – infml [redupl of *knack*]

[1]**knife** /nief/ *n, pl* **knives** /nievz/ **1a** a cutting implement consisting of a more or less sharp blade fastened to a handle **b** such an instrument used as a weapon **2** a sharp cutting blade or tool in a machine [ME *knif*, fr OE *cnif*; akin to MLG *knīf* knife, OE *cnotta* knot] – **knifelike** /ˈnief,liek/ *adj* – **at knifepoint** under a threat of death by being knifed

[2]**knife** *vt* **1** to cut, slash, or wound with a knife **2** to cut, mark, or spread with a knife **3** *chiefly NAm* to try to defeat by underhand means – infml

ˈ**knife-,edge** *n* **1** a sharp wedge of hard material (e g steel) used as a fulcrum or pivot in a pair of scales, a pendulum, etc **2** sthg sharp and narrow (e g a ridge of rock) resembling the edge of a knife **3** an uncertain or precarious position or condition

ˈ**knife ,pleat** *n* a narrow flat pleat; *esp* any of a series of such pleats that overlap and fall in the same direction

[1]**knight** /niet/ *n* **1a(1)** a mounted man-at-arms serving a feudal superior; *esp* a man ceremonially inducted into special rank after service as page and squire **(2)** a man honoured by a sovereign for merit, ranking below a baronet **(3)** sby equivalent to a knight in rank **b** a man devoted to the service of a lady (e g as her champion) **2** either of 2 pieces of each colour in a set of chessmen that move from 1 corner to the diagonally opposite corner of a rectangle of 3 by 2 squares over squares that may be occupied [ME, fr OE *cniht*; akin to OHG *kneht* youth, military follower, OE *cnotta* knot] – **knightly** *adj or adv*, **knighthood** /ˈniet·hood/ *n*

[2]**knight** *vt* to make a knight of

,**knight-ˈerrant** *n, pl* **knights-errant** **1** a knight travelling in search of chivalrous adventures **2** a quixotic or chivalrous person

,**knight-ˈerrantry** *n, pl* **knight-errantries** quixotic conduct

,**Knight ˈTemplar** /ˈtemplə/ *n, pl* **Knights Templars, Knights Templar** a templar

[1]**knit** /nit/ *vb* **knit, knitted; -tt-** *vt* **1a** to link firmly or closely **b** to unite intimately **2a** to cause to grow together ⟨*time and rest will ~ a fractured bone*⟩ **b** to contract into wrinkles ⟨*~ted her brow in thought*⟩ **3a** to form (e g a fabric, garment, or design) by working 1 or more yarns into a series of

interlocking loops using 2 or more needles or a knitting machine **b** to work (e g a specified number of rows) using a knitting stitch, specif knit stitch ⟨~ *1, purl 1*⟩ ~ *vi* **1a** to make knitted fabrics or articles **b** to work yarn or thread in a knitting stitch, specif knit stitch **2a** to become compact **b** to grow together **c** to become joined or drawn together [ME *knitten*, fr OE *cnyttan*; akin to OE *cnotta* knot] – **knitter** *n*

[2]**knit, knit stitch** *n* a basic knitting stitch that produces a raised pattern on the front of the work – compare PURL 2

knitting /ˈniting/ *n* work that has been or is being knitted

knob /nob/ *n* **1a** a rounded protuberance **b** a small rounded ornament, handle, or control (for pushing, pulling, or turning) **2** a small piece or lump (e g of coal or butter) [ME *knobbe*; akin to MLG *knubbe* knob, OE *-cnoppa*] – **knobbed** *adj*, **knobby** *adj* – **with knobs on** to an even greater degree – infml

knobble /ˈnobl/ *n* a small rounded irregularity [ME *knoble*, fr *knobbe* + *-le* (dim. suffix)] – **knobbly** *adj*

knobkerrie /ˈnob,keri/ *n* a short wooden club with a knobbed head used esp by S African tribesmen [Afrik *knopkierie*, fr *knop* knob + *kierie* club]

[1]**knock** /nok/ *vi* **1** to strike sthg with a sharp (audible) blow; *esp* to strike a door seeking admittance **2** to collide with sthg **3** to be in a place, often without any clearly defined aim or purpose – usu + *about* or *around* **4a** to make a sharp pounding noise **b** *of an internal-combustion engine* to make a metallic rapping noise because of a mechanical defect; *also* [7]PINK 3 **5** to find fault ~ *vt* **1a(1)** to strike sharply **(2)** to drive, force, make, or take (as if) by so striking ⟨~ed *a hole in the wall*⟩ ⟨*her earnings would be* ~ed *off her mother's benefit – The Times*⟩ **b** to set forcibly in motion with a blow **2** to cause to collide (with each other) ⟨~ed *their heads together*⟩ **3** to find fault with ⟨*always* ~ing *those in authority*⟩ ***USE*** (*vi 5; vt 3*) infml [ME *knoken*, fr OE *cnocian*; akin to MHG *knochen* to press] – **knock together** to make or assemble, esp hurriedly or shoddily

[2]**knock** *n* **1a** (the sound of) a knocking or a sharp blow or rap ⟨*the engine has a* ~⟩ **b** a piece of bad luck or misfortune **2** a harsh and often petty criticism **3** INNINGS 1b – infml

knockabout /ˈnokə,bowt/ *adj* **1** suitable for rough use ⟨~ *clothes*⟩ **2** (characterized by antics that are) boisterous ⟨*a* ~ *comedy*⟩

knock about *vt* to treat roughly or with physical violence

knock back *vt, chiefly Br* **1** to drink (an alcoholic beverage) rapidly **2** to cost; SET BACK 2 **3** to surprise, disconcert ***USE*** infml

[1]ˈ**knock,down** /-,down/ *n* sthg (e g a piece of furniture) that can be easily assembled or dismantled

[2]**knockdown** *adj* **1** having such force as to strike down or overwhelm **2** easily assembled or dismantled ⟨*a* ~ *table*⟩ **3** *of a price* very low or substantially reduced; *esp* being the lowest acceptable to the seller

knock down *vt* **1** to strike to the ground (as if) with a sharp blow **2** to dispose of (an item for sale at an auction) *to* a bidder **3** to take apart; disassemble **4** to make a reduction in ⟨knock *the price* down *to £4*⟩

knocker /ˈnokə/ *n* a metal ring, bar, or hammer hinged to a door for use in knocking [KNOCK + [2]-ER]

ˈ**knockers** *n pl* a woman's breasts – vulg

,**knock-for-ˈknock** *adj* of or being an agreement between insurance companies whereby each company indemnifies its own policyholder regardless of legal liability

ˈ**knocking ,shop** /ˈnoking/ *n, Br* a brothel – vulg [*knock* (to copulate with), fr [1]*knock*]

,**knock-ˈknee** *n* a condition in which the legs curve inwards at the knees – often pl with sing. meaning but sing. or pl in constr – **knock-kneed** *adj*

knock off *vi* to stop doing sthg, esp one's work ~ *vt* **1** to do hurriedly or routinely ⟨knocked off *one painting after another*⟩ **2** to discontinue, stop ⟨knocked off *work at 5*⟩ **3** to deduct ⟨knocked off *a pound to make the price more attractive*⟩ **4** to kill; *esp* to murder **5** to steal **6** *Br* to have sexual intercourse with ***USE*** (*4&5*) infml, (*6*) slang

ˈ**knock-,on** *n* (an instance of) the knocking of the ball forwards on the ground with the hand or arm in rugby in violation of the rules – **knock on** *vt*

knockout, knock-out /ˈnok,owt/ *n* **1a** knocking out or being knocked out **b** a blow that knocks out an opponent (or knocks him down for longer than a particular time, usu 10s, and results in the termination of a boxing match) **c** TECHNICAL KNOCKOUT **2** a competition or tournament with successive rounds in which losing competitors are eliminated until a winner emerges in the final **3** sby or sthg that is sensationally striking or attractive – infml – **knockout** *adj*

knock out *vt* **1** to empty (a tobacco pipe) by striking on or with sthg **2** KNOCK UP 1 **3a** to defeat (a boxing opponent) by a knockout **b** to make unconscious **4** to tire out; exhaust **5** to eliminate (an opponent) from a knockout competition **6** to overwhelm with amazement or pleasure – infml

ˈ**knock,out ,drops** *n pl* drops containing a drug (e g chloral hydrate) put into a drink, esp surreptitiously, to produce unconsciousness or stupefaction

knock up *vt* **1** to make, prepare, or arrange hastily **2** KNOCK OUT 4 **3** to achieve a total of ⟨knocked up *300mi in the first day of travelling*⟩ **4** *Br* to rouse, awaken **5** *chiefly NAm* to make pregnant – infml ~ *vi* to practise informally before a tennis, squash, etc match

knoll /nol/ *n* a small round hill; a mound [ME *knol*, fr OE *cnoll*; akin to ON *knollr* mountaintop, OE *cnotta* knot]

[1]**knot** /not/ *n* **1a** an interlacing of (parts of) 1 or more strings, threads, etc that forms a lump or knob **b** a piece of ribbon, braid etc tied as an ornament **c** a (sense of) tight constriction ⟨*his stomach was all in* ~s⟩ **2** sthg hard to solve **3** a bond of union; *esp* the marriage bond **4a** a protuberant lump or swelling in tissue **b** (a rounded cross-section in timber of) the base of a woody branch enclosed in the stem from which it arises **5** a cluster of people or things **6a** a speed of 1 nautical mile per hour ☞ UNIT **b** 1 nautical mile – not used technically [ME, fr OE *cnotta*; akin to OHG *knoto* knot, Lith *gniusti* to press]

[2]**knot** *vb* **-tt-** *vt* **1** to tie in or with a knot **2** to unite closely or intricately ~ *vi* to form a knot or knots – **knotter** *n*

[3]**knot** *n, pl* **knots,** *esp collectively* **knot** (a bird of) a species of migratory sandpiper [ME *knott*]

'knot,grass /-,grahs/ *n* a widely occurring weed of the dock family with jointed stems and minute flowers

'knot,hole /-,hohl/ *n* a hole in a board or tree trunk where a knot or branch has come out

knotty /'noti/ *adj* complicated or difficult (to solve) ⟨*a ~ problem*⟩ [¹KNOT + ¹-Y] – **knottiness** *n*

knout /nowt/ *n* a whip formerly used in Russia for flogging criminals [Russ *knut*, of Scand origin; akin to ON *knūtr* knot; akin to OE *cnotta*] – **knout** *vt*

¹know /noh/ *vb* **knew** /nyooh/; **known** /nohn/ *vt* **1a(1)** to perceive directly; have direct cognition of **(2)** to have understanding of **(3)** to recognize or identify ⟨*would ~ him again*⟩ **b(1)** to be acquainted or familiar with **(2)** to have experience of **2a** to be aware of the truth or factual nature of; be convinced or certain of **b** to have a practical understanding of ⟨*~s how to write*⟩ **3** *archaic* to have sexual intercourse with ~*vi* to (come to) have knowledge (of sthg) [ME *knowen*, fr OE *cnāwan*; akin to OHG bi*chnāan* to recognize, L *gnoscere, noscere* to come to know, Gk *gignōskein*] – **knowable** *adj*, **knower** *n* – **be to know** be expected to discern; have any knowledge of ⟨*how* was *I* to know *it wouldn't bite?*⟩ – **not know someone from Adam** have no idea who sby is – **you know** – used for adding emphasis to a statement ⟨*you'll have to try harder,* you know, *if you want to succeed*⟩

²know *n* – **in the know** in possession of confidential or otherwise exclusive knowledge or information

'know-,all *n* one who behaves as if he/she knows everything

'know-,how *n* (practical) expertise

knowing /'noh·ing/ *adj* **1** having or reflecting knowledge, information, or intelligence **2** shrewd or astute; *esp* implying (that one has) knowledge of a secret **3** deliberate, conscious – **knowingly** *adv*

'know-it-,all *n* a know-all – **know-it-all** *adj*

knowledge /'nolij/ *n* **1a** the fact or condition of knowing sthg or sby through experience or association **b** acquaintance with, or understanding or awareness of, sthg ⟨*some ~ of Newtonian physics*⟩ **2a** the range of a person's information, perception, or understanding ⟨*is it true? Not to my ~*⟩ **b** the fact or condition of having information or of being learned ⟨*a man of little ~*⟩ **3** the sum of what is known; the body of truth, information, and principles acquired by mankind (on some subject) [ME *knowlege*, fr *knowlechen* to acknowledge, irreg fr *knowen*]

knowledgeable /'nolijəbl/ *adj* having or exhibiting knowledge or intelligence; well-informed – **knowledgeably** *adv*

known /nohn/ *adj* generally recognized ⟨*a ~ authority on this topic*⟩

¹knuckle /'nukl/ *n* **1** the rounded prominence formed by the ends of the 2 bones at a joint; *specif* any of the joints between the hand and the fingers or the finger joints closest to these **2** a cut of meat consisting of the lowest leg joint of a pig, sheep, etc with the adjoining flesh ☞ MEAT [ME *knokel*; akin to MHG *knöchel* knuckle, OE *cnotta* knot] – **near the knuckle** almost improper or indecent

²knuckle *vi* **knuckling** /'nukling/ to place the knuckles on the ground in shooting a marble

'knuckle,bone /-,bohn/ *n* either of the bones forming a knuckle; *esp* a metacarpal or metatarsal bone of a sheep formerly used in gaming or divination

knuckle down *vi* to apply oneself earnestly

'knuckle-,duster *n* a metal device worn over the front of the doubled fist for protection and use as a weapon

knuckle under *vi* to give in, submit ⟨*refused to* knuckle under *to any dictatorship*⟩

knur, *Br also* **knurr** /nuh/ *n* a hard lump or knot (e g on a tree trunk) [ME *knorre*; akin to OE *cnotta* knot]

knurl /nuhl/ *n* a small knob or protuberance; *esp* any of a series of small ridges, beads, etc on a surface to aid in gripping [prob alter. of *knur*] – **knurled** *adj*

¹KO /,kay'oh/ *n, pl* **KOs** a kayo – infml [*k*nock *o*ut]

²KO *vt* **KO's; KO'ing; KO'd** to kayo – infml

koa /'koh·ə/ *n* a (Hawaiian tree with) fine-grained red wood [Hawaiian]

koala /koh'ahlə/, **ko,ala 'bear** *n* an Australian tree-dwelling marsupial mammal that has large hairy ears, grey fur, and sharp claws and feeds on eucalyptus leaves [native name in Australia]

koan /'koh,ahn/ *n* a paradox to be meditated upon, used by Zen Buddhist monks to gain enlightenment [Jap *kōan*, fr *kō* public + *an* proposition]

kobo /'koh,boh/ *n, pl* **kobo** ☞ *Nigeria* at NATIONALITY [native name in Nigeria]

kobold /'kobohld/ *n* **1** a gnome in German folklore that inhabits underground places **2** a domestic spirit of German folklore [G – more at COBALT]

'Köchel ,number /'kuhkh(ə)l/ *n* any of a group of numbers used as a cataloguing system for Mozart's works [Ludwig von *Köchel* †1877 Austrian naturalist & cataloguer of Mozart's works]

kodiak bear /'kohdi,ak/ *n* a brown bear of Alaska [*Kodiak* Island, S Alaska]

kohl /kohl/ *n* (a cosmetic preparation made with) a black powder used, orig chiefly by Asian women, to darken the eyelids [Ar *kuḥl*]

kohlrabi /'kohl,rahbi/ *n, pl* **kohlrabies** a cabbage with a greatly enlarged fleshy turnip-shaped edible stem [G, modif (influenced by G *kohl* cabbage) of It *cavoli rape*, pl of *cavolo rapa* kohlrabi, fr *cavolo* cabbage + *rapa* turnip]

koine /'koyni/ *n* **1** *cap* the Greek language as used in E Mediterranean countries in the Hellenistic and Roman periods **2** a language of a region that has become the lingua franca of a larger area [Gk *koinē*, fr fem of *koinos* common]

kola /'kohlə/ *n* ²COLA

'kola ,nut, cola nut *n* the bitter caffeine-containing seed of any of several trees that is chewed esp as a stimulant and used in beverages [*kola*, of African origin (akin to Temne *K'ola* kola nut, Mandingo *kolo*) + *nut*]

kolinsky /kə'linski/ *n* (the fur of) any of several Asiatic minks [Russ *kolinskiĭ* of Kola, fr *Kola*, town and peninsula in USSR]

kolkhoz /kol'hawz, kol'khawz/ *n, pl* **kolkhozy** /-zi/, **kolkhozes** a collective farm of the USSR [Russ, fr *kol*lektivnoe *khoz*yaĭstvo collective farm]

Kol Nidre /,kol 'nidri, -rə/ *n* a formula for the annulment of private vows chanted in the synagogue on the eve of Yom Kippur [Aram *kol nidhrē* all the vows; fr the opening phrase of the prayer]

komodo dragon /kə'mohdoh/ *n* an Indonesian monitor lizard that is the largest of all known lizards ☞ ENDANGERED [*Komodo* Island, Indonesia]

Komsomol /,komso'mol/ *n* the Communist youth

organization of the USSR [Russ, fr *Kom*munisticheskiĭ *So*yuz *Mol*odezhi Communist Union of Youth]

Kongo /ˈkong·goh/ *n, pl* **Kongos,** *esp collectively* **Kongo** a member, or the Bantu language, of a people of the lower Congo

koodoo /ˈkooh,dooh/ *n* a kudu

kook /koohk/ *n, NAm* a nut, loony – infml [by shortening & alter. fr *cuckoo*] – **kookie, kooky** *adj,* **kookiness** *n*

kookaburra /ˈkookə,burə/ *n* a large Australian kingfisher that has a call resembling loud laughter [native name in Australia]

kopeck, copeck *also* **kopek** /ˈkohpek/ *n* ☞ *Union of Soviet Socialist Republics* at NATIONALITY [Russ *kopeĭka*]

kopje, koppie /ˈkopi/ *n* a small hill on the S African veld; *broadly, SAfr* a small hill [Afrik *koppie*]

Koran, Qur'an /kawˈrahn/ *n* the book composed of writings accepted by Muslims as revelations made to Muhammad by Allah through the angel Gabriel [Ar *qur'ān,* fr *qara'a* to read, recite] – **Koranic** /-nik/ *adj*

Korean /kəˈree·ən/ *n or adj* (a native or inhabitant or the language) of Korea ☞ LANGUAGE [*Korea,* peninsula in E Asia]

koruna /koˈroohnə/ *n, pl* **koruny, korunas** ☞ *Czechoslovakia* at NATIONALITY [Czech, lit., crown, fr L *corona*]

[1]**kosher** /ˈkohshə/ *adj* **1a** *of food* prepared according to Jewish law **b** selling kosher food ⟨*a ~ butcher*⟩ **2** proper, legitimate – infml [Yiddish, fr Heb *kāshēr* fit, proper] – **kosher** *n*

[2]**kosher** *vt* to make (food) kosher

koto /ˈkoh,toh/ *n, pl* **kotos** a long Japanese musical instrument with a rectangular wooden body and 13 silk strings [Jap]

koumiss, kumiss /ˈkoohmis/ *n* an alcoholic drink of fermented (mare's) milk made orig by the nomadic peoples of central Asia [Russ *kumys*]

kowhai /ˈkoh,wie/ *n* a golden-flowered shrub or small tree of Australasia and Chile [Maori]

[1]**kowtow** /ˈkow,tow, ˈkoh-/ *n* a (Chinese) gesture of deep respect in which one kneels and touches the ground with one's forehead [Chin (Pek) *k'o*[1] *t'ou*[2], fr *k'o*[1] to bump + *t'ou*[2] head]

[2]**kowtow** /,-ˈ-/ *vi* **1** to make a kowtow **2** to show obsequious deference

[1]**kraal** /krahl/ *n* **1** a village of S African tribesmen **2** an enclosure for domestic animals in S Africa [Afrik, fr Pg *curral* pen for cattle, enclosure, fr (assumed) VL *currale* enclosure for vehicles – more at CORRAL]

[2]**kraal** *vt* to pen in a kraal

kragdadige /ˈkrahkh,dahdikh·ə/ *n, SAfr* an advocate of hard-line policies – compare VERLIGTE, VERKRAMPTE [Afrik *kragdadig* firm, determined, fr D *krachtdadig*]

kragdadigheid /ˈkrakh,dahdikh,hiet/ *n, SAfr* uncompromising toughness (e g by government in response to demands for liberalization) [Afrik, fr *kragdadig* + *-heid* -ness]

krait /kriet/ *n* any of several extremely venomous E Asian snakes that are active at night [Hindi *karait*]

kraken /ˈkrahkən/ *n* a mythical Scandinavian sea monster [Norw dial.]

kraut /krowt/ *n, often cap* a German – chiefly derog [G, cabbage]

ˈ**Krebs ,cycle** /krebz/ *n* a sequence of reactions in the living organism which provide energy stored in phosphate bonds [Sir Hans (Adolf) *Krebs* †1981 Brit (German-born) biochemist]

kremlin /ˈkremlin/ *n* **1** a citadel within a Russian town or city **2** *cap the* government of the USSR [prob fr obs G *kremelin,* fr Russ *kreml'*; (2) the *Kremlin,* citadel of Moscow and governing centre of the USSR]

kremlinology /,kremliˈnoləji/ *n, often cap* the study of Soviet policies and practices – **kremlinologist** *n, often cap*

krill /kril/ *n* planktonic crustaceans and larvae that are the principal food of whalebone whales [Norw *kril* fry of fish]

kris /krees/ *n* a Malay or Indonesian dagger with a wavy blade [Malay *kĕris*]

Krishna /ˈkrishnə/ *n* a deity of later Hinduism worshipped as an incarnation of Vishnu [Skt *Kṛṣṇa*]

krona /ˈkrohnə/ *n, pl* **kronor** /~/ ☞ *Sweden* at NATIONALITY [Sw, lit., crown]

króna /ˈkrohnə/ *n, pl* **kronur** /~/ ☞ *Iceland* at NATIONALITY [Icel *krōna,* lit., crown]

krone /ˈkrohnə/ *n, pl* **kroner** /~/ ☞ *Denmark, Norway* at NATIONALITY [Dan, lit., crown]

Kru /krooh/ *n, pl* **Krus,** *esp collectively* **Kru** a member, or the language, of a Negro people of Liberia

Krugerrand /ˈkroohgə,rahnt, -,rand/ *n* a 1-ounce (28.35g) gold coin of S Africa [SJP *Kruger* †1904 SAfr statesman + *rand*]

krummhorn /ˈkroom,hawn/ *n* a crumhorn

krypton /ˈkript(ə)n/ *n* a noble gaseous element found in very small amounts in air ☞ PERIODIC TABLE [Gk, neut of *kryptos* hidden – more at CRYPT]

Kshatriya /ˈkshatri·ə/ *n* a Hindu of an upper military caste [Skt *kṣatriya*]

kudos /ˈk(y)oohdos/ *n* fame and renown, esp resulting from an act or achievement [Gk *kydos*; akin to Gk *akouein* to hear – more at HEAR]

kudu, koodoo /ˈkooh,dooh/ *n, pl* **kudus,** *esp collectively* **kudu** a large greyish brown African antelope with large spirally twisted horns [Afrik *koedoe*]

Ku Klux Klan /,k(y)ooh ,kluks ˈklan/ *n* **1** a secret society opposing the right of blacks to vote after the US Civil War **2** a secret political organization in the USA that confines its membership to American-born Protestant whites and is hostile to blacks [perh fr Gk *kyklos* circle + E *clan*]

kukri /ˈkookri/ *n* a short curved knife used esp by Gurkhas [Hindi *kukṛī*]

kulak /ˈkooh,lak/ *n* **1** a prosperous peasant farmer in prerevolutionary Russia **2** a member of a class of peasant-proprietors working for individual profit – used technically in Marxist literature [Russ, lit., fist]

kultur /koolˈtooə/ *n, often cap* **1** CULTURE 4 **2** German culture as conceived by militant Nazis and Hohenzollern expansionists, esp emphasizing individual subordination to the state and practical efficiency – often derog [G, fr L *cultura* culture]

Kulˈtur,kampf /-,kampf/ *n* conflict between civil and religious authorities, esp over control of education; *specif* the conflict between the German government and the Papacy in the late 19th c [G, fr *kultur* + *kampf* conflict]

kumiss /'koohmis/ *n* koumiss

kümmel /'kooml/ *n* a colourless aromatic liqueur flavoured with caraway seeds [G, lit., caraway seed, fr OHG *kumin* cumin]

kumquat, cumquat /'kumkwot/ *n* (any of several trees that bear) any of several small citrus fruits that are used chiefly for preserves [Chin (Cant) *kam kwat,* fr *kam* gold + *kwat* orange]

kung fu /,kung 'fooh, ,koong/ *n* a Chinese martial art resembling karate [Chin dial., alter. of Pek *ch*^{1}*üan*^{2}*fa*^{3}, lit., boxing principles]

Kurd /kuhd/ *n* a member of a pastoral and agricultural people who inhabit adjoining parts of Turkey, Iran, Iraq, and Syria and the Armenian and Azerbaijan sectors of the Soviet Caucasus – **Kurdish** *adj*

Kurdish /'kuhdish/ *n* the Iranian language of the Kurds ☞ LANGUAGE

kurrajong /'kurə,jong/ *n* any of several Australian trees or shrubs having strong bast fibre [native name in Australia]

kurtosis /kuh'tohsis/ *n* the peakedness or flatness of the graph of a frequency distribution [Gk *kyrtōsis* convexity, fr *kyrtos* convex; akin to L *curvus* curved – more at CROWN]

kuru /'koorooh/ *n* a fatal disease of the nervous system that occurs among tribesmen in eastern New Guinea [native name in New Guinea, lit., trembling]

kurus /koo'roohsh/ *n, pl* **kurus** ☞ *Turkey* at NATIONALITY [Turk *kuruş*]

kvass /k'vahs/ *n* a slightly alcoholic beverage made in E Europe usu by fermenting mixed cereals and adding flavouring [Russ *kvas*]

Kwa /kwah/ *n* a branch of the Niger-Congo language family that includes Ibo and Yoruba

kwacha /'kwahchə/ *n, pl* **kwacha** ☞ *Malawi, Zambia* at NATIONALITY [native name in Zambia, lit., dawn]

kwanza /'kwanzə/ *n* ☞ *Angola* at NATIONALITY [of Bantu origin]

kwashiorkor /,kwashi'awkə/ *n* severe malnutrition in infants and children that is caused by a diet high in carbohydrate and low in protein [native name in Ghana, lit., red boy]

kyanite /'kie·əniet/ *n* aluminium silicate occurring as blue (aggregate of) crystals and sometimes used as a gemstone [deriv of Gk *kyanos* dark blue enamel, lapis lazuli]

kyat /ki'aht/ *n* ☞ *Burma* at NATIONALITY [Burmese]

kye, ky /kie/ *n pl, dial* cattle [ME *ky,* fr OE *cȳ,* pl of *cū* cow]

kyphosis /kie'fohsis/ *n* abnormal backward curvature of the spine – compare LORDOSIS, SCOLIOSIS [NL, fr Gk *kyphōsis,* fr *kyphos* humpbacked; akin to OE *hēah* high] – **kyphotic** /-'fotik/ *adj*

kyrie /'kiri,ay/, **kyrie eleison** /e'lay(i)son/ *n, often cap* a short liturgical prayer, often set to music, that begins with or consists of the words 'Lord, have mercy" [NL, fr LL *kyrie eleison,* transliteration of Gk *kyrie eleēson* Lord, have mercy]

L

l /el/ *n, pl* **l's, ls** *often cap* **1a** (a graphic representation of or device for reproducing) the 12th letter of the English alphabet **b** sthg shaped like the letter L **2** fifty ☞ NUMBER **3** *NAm* an elevated railway; an el

l- /el-/ *prefix* **1** laevorotatory ⟨l-*tartaric acid*⟩ **2** having a similar configuration at an optically active carbon atom to the configuration of laevorotatory glyceraldehyde – usu printed as a small capital ⟨L-*fructose*⟩ [ISV, fr *laev-*]

la /lah/ *n* the 6th note of the diatonic scale in solmization [ME, fr ML – more at GAMUT]

laager /'lahgə/ *n* a camp; *esp* an encampment protected by a circle of wagons or armoured vehicles [obs Afrik *lager* (now *laer*), fr G] – **laager** *vi*

lab /lab/ *n* a laboratory

labdanum /'labdənəm/ *n* a fragrant oleoresin derived from various rockroses and used in perfumery [ML *lapdanum*, fr L *ladanum, ledanum*, fr Gk *ladanon, lēdanon*, fr *lēdon* rockrose]

[1]**label** /'laybl/ *n* **1** a slip (e g of paper or cloth), inscribed and fastened to sthg to give information (e g identification or directions) **2** a descriptive or identifying word or phrase: e g **a** an epithet **b** a word or phrase used with a dictionary definition to provide additional information (e g level of usage) **3** an adhesive stamp **4** TRADE NAME 1b, 2; *specif* a name used by a company producing commercial recordings ⟨*several new record* ~s⟩ [ME, narrow band, strip, fr MF]

[2]**label** *vt* **-ll-** (*NAm* **-l-, -ll-**), /'laybl·ing/ **1a** to fasten a label to **b** to describe or categorize (as if) with a label **2** to make (e g an element) traceable, by substitution of a radioactive or other special isotope – **labellable** /'laybl·əbl/ *adj*, **labeller** *n*

[1]**labial** /'laybi·əl/ *adj* **1** of the lips or labia **2** articulated using 1 or both lips [ML *labialis*, fr L *labium* lip] – **labially** *adv*, **labialize** /-,liez/ *vt*, **labialization** /-lie'zaysh(ə)n/ *n*

[2]**labial** *n* a labial consonant (e g /f/ and /p/)

labia majora /,laybi·ə mə'jawrə/ *n pl* the outer fatty folds bounding the vulva [NL, lit., larger lips]

,labia mi'nora /mi'nawrə/ *n pl* the inner highly vascular largely connective-tissue folds bounding the vulva [NL, lit., smaller lips]

labiate /'laybiayt, -ət/ *adj, of a plant corolla or calyx* having 2 unequal portions resembling lips [NL *labiatus*, fr L *labium*]

labile /'laybil, -biel/ *adj* **1** readily open to change ⟨*an emotionally* ~ *person*⟩ **2** unstable ⟨*a* ~ *mineral*⟩ [F, fr MF, prone to err, fr LL *labilis*, fr L *labi* to slip – more at SLEEP] – **lability** /lə'biləti/ *n*

labio- *comb form* labial and ⟨labio*dental*⟩ [L *labium*]

labium /'laybi·əm/ *n, pl* **labia** /-bi·ə/ **1** any of the folds at the margin of the vulva – compare LABIA MAJORA, LABIA MINORA ☞ REPRODUCTION **2** the (lower) lip of a flower divided into 2 lip-like parts **3a** a lower mouthpart of an insect **b** a liplike part of various invertebrates [NL, fr L, lip – more at LIP]

laboratory /lə'borətri/ *n* a place equipped for scientific experiment, testing, or analysis; *broadly* a place providing opportunity for research in a field of study [ML *laboratorium*, fr L *laboratus*, pp of *laborare* to labour, fr *labor*]

laborious /lə'bawri·əs/ *adj* involving or characterized by effort [ME, fr MF or L; MF *laborieux*, fr L *laboriosus*, fr *labor*] – **laboriously** *adv*, **laboriousness** *n*

'labor ,union *n, NAm* TRADE UNION

[1]**labour,** *NAm chiefly* **labor** /'laybə/ *n* **1a** expenditure of effort, esp when difficult or compulsory; toil **b** human activity that provides the goods or services in an economy **c** (the period of) the physical activities involved in the birth of young **2** an act or process requiring labour; a task **3a** *sing or pl in constr* an economic group comprising those who do manual work or work for wages **b** workers ⟨*local* ~ *isn't suitable*⟩ **4** *sing or pl in constr, cap* the Labour party [ME, fr OF, fr L *labor*]

[2]**labour,** *NAm chiefly* **labor** *vi* **1** to exert one's powers of body or mind, esp with great effort; work, strive **2** to move with great effort ⟨*a fat man* ~ing *up the stairs*⟩ **3** to be in labour when giving birth **4** to suffer from some disadvantage or distress ⟨~ *under a delusion*⟩ **5** *of a ship* to pitch or roll heavily ~ *vt* **1** to treat in laborious detail ⟨~ *the obvious*⟩ **2** *archaic* to spend labour on or produce by labour

Labour *adj* of or being a political party, specif one in the UK, advocating a planned socialist economy and associated with working-class interests

'Labour ,Day *n* a day set aside for special recognition of working people: e g **a** the first Monday in September observed in the USA and Canada as a public holiday **b** MAY DAY

'laboured *adj* bearing marks of labour and effort; *esp* lacking ease of expression ⟨*a* ~ *speech*⟩

labourer /'layb(ə)rə/ *n* one who does unskilled manual work, esp outdoors [[2]LABOUR + [2]-ER]

'labour ex,change *n, often cap L&E* a government office that seeks to match unemployed people and vacant jobs and that is responsible for paying out unemployment benefit

,labour-in'tensive *adj* **1** using proportionately more labour than capital or land in the process of production – compare CAPITAL-INTENSIVE **2** employing or made by a high proportion of people (rather than machinery)

labourite /'laybəriet/ *n, often cap* a member or supporter of the Labour party

,labour of 'love *n* a task performed for the pleasure it yields rather than for personal gain

'labour,saving /-,sayving/ *adj* adapted to replace or

decrease (manual) labour ⟨~ *domestic appliances*⟩

labrador /ˈlabrədaw/ *n, often cap* LABRADOR RETRIEVER

labradorite /ˌlabrəˈdawriet/ *n* a feldspar showing a play of several colours due to light diffraction [*Labrador* peninsula, Canada]

ˌLabrador reˈtriever *n* a retriever characterized by a dense black or golden coat [*Labrador*, Newfoundland]

labrum /ˈlabrəm, ˈlay-/ *n, pl* **labra** /-brə/ an upper or front mouthpart of an arthropod [NL, fr L, lip, edge – more at LIP]

laburnum /ləˈbuhnəm/ *n* any of a small genus of Eurasian leguminous shrubs and trees with bright yellow flowers and poisonous seeds [NL, genus name, fr L, laburnum]

labyrinth /ˈlabərinth/ *n* **1** a place that is a network of intricate passageways, tunnels, blind alleys, etc **2** sthg perplexingly complex or tortuous in structure, arrangement, or character **3** (the tortuous anatomical structure in) the ear or its bony or membranous part [ME *laborintus*, fr L *labyrinthus*, fr Gk *labyrinthos*] – **labyrinthine** /ˌlabəˈrinˌthien/ *adj*

[1]lac /lak/ *n* a resinous substance secreted by a scale insect [Per *lak* & Hindi *lākh*, fr Skt *lākṣā*]

[2]lac *n* a lakh

laccolith /ˈlakəlith/ *n* a mass of intrusive igneous rock having a domed top that produces bulging of the overlying strata ☞ GEOGRAPHY [Gk *lakkos* cistern + E *-lith*]

[1]lace /lays/ *n* **1** a cord or string used for drawing together 2 edges (e g of a garment or shoe) **2** an ornamental braid for trimming coats or uniforms **3** an openwork usu figured fabric made of thread, yarn, etc, used for trimmings, household furnishings, garments, etc [ME, fr OF *laz*, fr L *laqueus* snare – more at DELIGHT]

[2]lace *vt* **1** to draw together the edges of (as if) by means of a lace passed through eyelets **2** to draw or pass (e g a lace) through sthg **3** to confine or compress by tightening laces, esp of a corset **4** to adorn (as if) with lace **5** to beat, lash **6a** to add a dash of an alcoholic drink to **b** to give savour or variety to ⟨*a mundane story line* ~d *with witty repartee*⟩ ~ *vi* to be fastened or tied *up* with a lace [ME *lacen*, fr OF *lacier*, fr L *laqueare* to ensnare, fr *laqueus*]

lacerate /ˈlasəˌrayt/ *vt* **1** to tear or rend roughly **2** to cause sharp mental or emotional pain to [L *laceratus*, pp of *lacerare* to tear; akin to L *lacer* mangled, Gk *lakis* rent]

laceration /ˌlasəˈraysh(ə)n/ *n* a torn and ragged wound [LACERATE + -ION]

ˈlace-ˌup *n, chiefly Br* a shoe or boot that is fastened with laces

ˈlaceˌwing /-ˌwing/ *n* any of various insects having wings with a fine network of veins

laches /ˈlachiz/ *n, pl* **laches** /-ˌcheez/ negligence in carrying out a legal duty or undue delay in asserting a legal claim [ME *lachesse*, fr MF *laschesse*, fr OF *lasche* lax]

lachrymal, lacrimal /ˈlakriməl/ *adj* **1** of or constituting the glands that produce tears **2** of or marked by tears [MF or ML; MF *lacrymal*, fr ML *lacrimalis, lachrymalis*, fr L *lacrima* tear – more at [1]TEAR]

lachrymation, lacrimation /ˌlakriˈmaysh(ə)n/ *n* the (abnormal or excessive) secretion of tears [L *lacrimation-, lacrimatio*, fr *lacrimatus*, pp of *lacrimare* to weep, fr *lacrima* tear]

lachrymator /ˈlakriˌmaytə/ *n* a tear-producing substance (e g a tear gas)

lachrymatory /ˈlakrimətri/ *adj* of or prompting tears [ML *lachrymatorius*, fr LL *lacrimatorius*, fr L *lacrimatus*, pp]

lachrymose /ˈlakrimohs/ *adj* **1** given to weeping **2** tending to cause tears – **lachrymosely** *adv*

lacing /ˈlaysing/ *n* **1** lace **2** a trace or sprinkling that adds savour or variety **3** BEATING 1

laciniate /laˈsiniayt, -ət/ *adj* bordered with a fringe ⟨*a* ~ *petal*⟩ [L *lacinia* flap; akin to L *lacer* mangled] – **laciniation** /-ˈaysh(ə)n/ *n*

[1]lack /lak/ *vi* **1** to be deficient or missing **2** to be short or have need of sthg – usu + *for* ⟨*she will not* ~ *for advisers*⟩ ~ *vt* to stand in need of; suffer from the absence or deficiency of [ME *laken*, fr MD; akin to ON *leka* to leak]

[2]lack *n* **1** the fact or state of being wanting or deficient **2** sthg lacking

lackadaisical /ˌlakəˈdayzikl/ *adj* lacking life or zest; *also* (reprehensibly) casual or negligent [árch *lackadaisy* (exclamation of regret), alter. of *lackaday, alack the day* + *-ical*] – **lackadaisically** *adv*

lackey /ˈlaki/ *n* **1** a usu liveried retainer **2** a servile follower [MF *laquais*]

ˈlackˌlustre /-ˌlustə/ *adj* lacking in sheen, radiance, or vitality; dull

laconic /ləˈkonik/ *adj* using, or involving the use of, a minimum of words; terse [L *laconicus* Spartan, fr Gk *lakōnikos*; fr the Spartan reputation for terseness of speech] – **laconically** *adv*, **laconicism** /-niˌsiz(ə)m/ *n*

[1]lacquer /ˈlakə/ *n* **1** a clear or coloured varnish obtained by dissolving a substance (e g shellac) in a solvent (e g alcohol) **2** a durable natural varnish; *esp* one obtained from an Asian shrub of the sumach family [Pg *lacré* sealing wax, fr *laca* lac, fr Ar *lakk*, fr Per *lak*]

[2]lacquer *vt* to coat with lacquer – **lacquerer** *n*

lacrimal /ˈlakriml/ *adj* lachrymal

lacrimation /ˌlakriˈmaysh(ə)n/ *n* lachrymation

lacrosse /ləˈkros/ *n* a game played on grass by 2 teams of 10 players, whose object is to throw a ball into the opponents' goal, using a long-handled stick that has a triangular head with a loose mesh pouch for catching and carrying the ball [CanF *la crosse*, lit., the crosier]

lact- /lakt-/, **lacti-, lacto-** *comb form* **1** milk ⟨lacto*flavin*⟩ **2a** lactic acid ⟨lact*ate*⟩ **b** lactose ⟨lactase⟩ [F & L; F, fr L, fr *lact-, lac* – more at GALAXY]

lactate /ˈlakˌtayt/ *vi* to secrete milk [L *lactatus*, pp of *lactare*, fr *lact-, lac*]

lactation /lakˈtaysh(ə)n/ *n* (the period of time given to) the secretion of milk by a mammal – **lactational** *adj*, **lactationally** *adv*

[1]lacteal /ˈlakti-əl/ *adj* **1** consisting of, producing, or resembling milk **2a** conveying or containing a milky fluid **b** of the lacteals [L *lacteus* of milk, fr *lact-, lac*]

[2]lacteal *n* any of the lymphatic vessels conveying chyle to the thoracic duct

lactic /ˈlaktik/ *adj* of milk

ˌlactic ˈacid *n* an organic acid, normally present in living tissue, and used esp in food and medicine and in industry

lactiferous /lakˈtifərəs/ *adj* **1** secreting or conveying milk 2 yielding a milky juice [F or LL; F *lactifère*, fr LL *lactifer*, fr L *lact-*, *lac* + *-fer*] – **lactiferousness** *n*

lactose /'laktohz, -tohs/ *n* a sugar that is present in milk [ISV]

,lacto-,vege'tarianism /laktoh/ *n* vegetarianism that allows the inclusion of certain animal products (e g milk, cheese, and sometimes eggs) – **lacto-vegetarian** *n*

lacuna /lə'kyoohnə/ *n, pl* **lacunae** /-ni/, **lacunas** 1 a blank space or a missing part 2 a small cavity in an anatomical structure [L, pool, pit, gap – more at LAGOON] – **lacunal** *adj*, **lacunar** *adj*, **lacunary** *adj*, **lacunate** /-nayt/ *adj*

lacustrine /lə'kustrien/ *adj* of or occurring in lakes [prob fr F or It *lacustre*, fr L *lacus* lake]

lacy /'laysi/ *adj* resembling or consisting of lace

lad /lad/ *n* 1 a male person between early boyhood and maturity 2 a fellow, chap 3 *Br* STABLE LAD [ME *ladde*]

ladanum /'ladənəm/ *n* labdanum

[1]**ladder** /'ladə/ *n* 1 a structure for climbing up or down that has 2 long sidepieces of metal, wood, rope, etc joined at intervals by crosspieces on which one may step 2a sthg that resembles or suggests a ladder in form or use b *chiefly Br* a vertical line in hosiery or knitting caused by stitches becoming unravelled 3 a series of ascending steps or stages 4 a means of rising or climbing (e g to a higher status or social position) [ME, fr OE *hlǣder*; akin to OHG *leitara* ladder, OE *hlinian, hleonian* to lean – more at [1]LEAN]

[2]**ladder** *vb, chiefly Br* to develop a ladder (in) ⟨*she* ~ed *her tights*⟩ ⟨*her tights have* ~ed⟩

laddie /'ladi/ *n* a (young) lad

lade /layd/ *vt* **laded, laden** /'laydn/ 1 to put a load or burden on or in (e g a ship); load 2 to put or place as a load, esp for shipment 3 to weigh down with sthg [ME *laden*, fr OE *hladan*; akin to OHG *hladan* to load, OSlav *klasti*]

la-di-da, lah-di-dah /,lah di 'dah/ *adj* affectedly refined, esp in voice and pronunciation – infml [perh alter. of *lardy-dardy* (foppish)]

ladies /'laydiz/ *n pl but sing in constr, often cap, chiefly Br* a public lavatory for women – infml [short for *ladies' room, ladies' lavatory*, etc]

'ladies' ,man, lady's man *n* a man who likes to please or to be with women

'ladies' ,room *n* a room equipped with toilets for use by women

ladies' tresses *n pl but sing or pl in constr* any of a widely distributed genus of terrestrial orchids

Ladin /la'deen/ *n* (one whose mother tongue is) Romansh [Rhaeto-Romanic, fr L *Latinum* Latin]

lading /'layding/ *n* cargo, freight [fr gerund of *lade*]

ladino /lə'deenoh/ *n, pl* **ladinos** 1 Judeo-Spanish 2 *often cap* a Spanish-American of mixed descent [Sp, fr *ladino* cunning, learned, lit., Latin, fr L *latinus*; (2) AmerSp, fr Sp]

[1]**ladle** /'laydl/ *n* 1 a deep-bowled long-handled spoon used esp for taking up and conveying liquids or semiliquid foods (e g soup) 2 a vessel for carrying molten metal [ME *ladel*, fr OE *hlædel*, fr *hladan*]

[2]**ladle** *vt* **ladling** /'laydl·ing/ to take up and convey (as if) in a ladle

lady /'laydi/ *n* 1a a woman with authority, esp as a feudal superior b a woman receiving the homage or devotion of a knight or lover 2a a woman of refinement or superior social position b a woman – often in courteous reference ⟨*show the* ~ *to a seat*⟩ or usu pl in address ⟨ladies *and gentlemen*⟩ 3 a wife ⟨*the captain and his* ~⟩ – compare OLD LADY 4a *cap* any of various titled women in Britain – used as a title b *cap* a female member of an order of knighthood – compare DAME [ME, fr OE *hlǣfdīge*, fr *hlāf* bread + *-dīge* (akin to *dǣge* kneader of bread) – more at [1]LOAF, DAIRY]

'lady,bird /-,buhd/ *n* any of numerous small beetles of temperate and tropical regions; *esp* any of several ladybirds that have red wing cases with black spots [Our *Lady*, the Virgin Mary]

'lady,bug /-,bug/ *n, NAm* a ladybird

'lady ,chapel *n, often cap L&C* a chapel dedicated to the Virgin Mary that is usu part of a larger church

'Lady ,Day *n* March 25 observed as the feast of the Annunciation

,lady-in-'waiting *n, pl* **ladies-in-waiting** a lady of a queen's or princess's household appointed to wait on her

'lady-,killer *n* a man who captivates women

'lady,like /-,liek/ *adj* 1 resembling a lady, esp in manners; well-bred 2 becoming or suitable to a lady

,lady's 'bed,straw /'bed,straw/ *n* a common Eurasian bedstraw with bright yellow flowers [Our *Lady*, the Virgin Mary]

'ladyship /-ship/ *n* – used as a title for a woman having the rank of lady [LADY + -SHIP]

,lady's 'slipper *n* any of several temperate-zone orchids having flowers whose shape suggests a slipper

'lady's-,smock *n* CUCKOOFLOWER 1

Laetrile /'laytriel/ *trademark* – used for a drug derived from amygdalin that is held to be of use in the treatment of cancer

laev-, laevo-, *NAm* **lev-, levo-** 1 laevorotatory ⟨laev*ulose*⟩ 2 to the left ⟨laevo*rotatory*⟩ [L *laevus* left; akin to Gk *laios* left]

laevorotary /,leevoh'rohtəri/ *adj* laevorotatory

,laevo'rotatory /-'rohtət(ə)ri, -roh'tayt(ə)ri/ *adj* turning towards the left or anticlockwise; *esp* rotating the plane of polarization of light to the left – compare DEXTROROTATORY – **laevorotation** /-roh'taysh(ə)n/ *n*

laevulose /'levyoolohs, -lohz/ *n* FRUCTOSE 2 [ISV, irreg fr *laev-* + *-ose*]

[1]**lag** /lag/ *vi* **-gg-** 1a to stay or fall behind; fail to keep pace – often + *behind* b to become retarded in attaining maximum value 2 to slacken or weaken gradually [prob of Scand origin; akin to Norw *lagga* to go slowly]

[2]**lag** *n* 1 the act or an instance of lagging 2 comparative slowness or retardation 3 an interval between related events; *specif* TIME LAG

[3]**lag** *vt* **-gg-** 1 to send to prison 2 to arrest *USE* slang [origin unknown]

[4]**lag** *n* 1 a convict 2 an ex-convict

[5]**lag** *n* lagging [orig sense, stave of a barrel, wooden covering or casing; prob of Scand origin; akin to ON *lögg* rim of a barrel]

[6]**lag** *vt* **-gg-** to cover or provide with lagging – **lagger** *n*

lagan /'lagən/ *n* goods thrown into the sea with a buoy attached so that they may be found again; *also* goods lying on the seabed [MF *lagan* or ML *laganum* debris washed up from the sea, prob of Gmc origin; akin to ON *lög* law]

lager /'lahgə/ *n* a light beer brewed by slow fermentation [G *lagerbier* beer made for storage, fr *lager* storehouse + *bier* beer]

laggard /'lagəd/ *n* sby who or sthg that lags or lingers – **laggardly** *adv or adj*

lagging /'laging/ *n* material for thermal insulation (e g wrapped round a boiler or laid in a roof) [[5]*lag* + *-ing*]

lagomorph /'lagə,mawf/ *n* any of an order of gnawing mammals comprising the rabbits and hares [deriv of Gk *lagōs* hare + *morphē* form] – **lagomorphic** /-'mawfik/ *adj*, **lagomorphous** *adj*

lagoon /lə'goohn/ *n* a shallow channel or pool usu separated from a larger body of water by a sand bank, reef, etc ☞ GEOGRAPHY [F & It; F *lagune*, fr It *laguna*, fr L *lacuna* pit, pool, fr *lacus* lake]

lah-di-dah /,lah di 'dah/ *adj* la-di-da

laic /'layik/, **laical** /'layikl/ *adj* of the laity [LL *laicus*, fr LGk *laïkos*, fr Gk, of the people, fr *laos* people] – **laically** *adv*

laicism /'layi,siz(ə)m/ *n* a political movement or programme having secularization as its principal aim

laic·ize, -ise /'layi,siez/ *vt* to secularize – **laicization** /-'zaysh(ə)n/ *n*

[1]**laid** /layd/ *past of* LAY

[2]**laid** *n* paper watermarked with fine lines running across the grain – compare WOVE [*laid (paper)*, fr pp of [1]*lay*]

,laid-'back *adj* relaxed, casual – infml

lain /layn/ *past part of* LIE

[1]**lair** /leə/ *n* **1** the resting or living place of a wild animal **2** a refuge or place for hiding [ME, fr OE *leger*, akin to OHG *legar* bed, OE *licgan* to lie – more at [1]LIE]

[2]**lair** *n, Austr* a showily dressed young man – chiefly derog [*leary, lairy* (artful, flash in dress or manners); akin to OE *læran* to teach, *leornian* to learn] – **lairy** *adj*

laird /leəd/ *n, Scot* a member of the landed gentry [ME (northern) *lord, lard* lord]

laissez-aller /,lesay 'alay (*Fr* lese ale)/ *n* lack of constraint [F *laissez aller* let (someone) go]

laissez-faire, *Br also* **laisser-faire** /,lesay 'feə (*Fr* lese fɛːr)/ *n* a doctrine opposing government interference in economic affairs [F *laissez faire*, imper of *laisser faire* to let (people) do (as they choose)] – **laissez-faire** *adj*

laity /'layəti/ *n sing or pl in constr* **1** the people of a religion other than its clergy **2** the mass of the people as distinguished from those of a particular profession [[5]*lay*]

[1]**lake** /layk/ *n* a large inland body of water; *also* a pool of oil, pitch, or other liquid ☞ GEOGRAPHY [ME, fr OF *lac* lake, fr L *lacus*; akin to OE *lagu* sea, Gk *lakkos* pond]

[2]**lake** *n* **1a** a deep purplish red pigment orig prepared from lac or cochineal **b** any of numerous usu bright pigments composed essentially of a soluble dye absorbed in or combined with an inorganic carrier **2** CARMINE 2 [F *laque* lac, fr OProv *laca*, fr Ar *lakk* – more at LACQUER]

'lake ,dwelling *n* a (prehistoric) dwelling built on piles in a lake

,Lakeland 'terrier /'laykland/ *n* any of an English breed of small wirehaired terriers [*Lakeland* (Lake District), area in NW England where the breed was developed]

lakh /lak/ *n, chiefly Ind* **1** one hundred thousand ⟨*50 ~s of rupees*⟩ **2** a great number [Hindi *lākh*, fr Skt *lakṣa*, lit., mark, sign] – **lakh** *adj*

-lalia /-'laylyə/ *comb form* (→ *n*) speech disorder (of a specified type) ⟨*echo*lalia⟩ [NL, fr Gk *lalia* chatter, fr *lalein* to chat]

Lallans /'lalənz/ *n* Lowland Scots dialect [Sc, var of *Lowlands*]

[1]**lam** /lam/ *vt* **-mm-** to beat soundly – infml [of Scand origin; akin to ON *lemja* to thrash; akin to OE *lama* lame]

[2]**lam** *n, NAm* sudden or hurried flight, esp from the law – infml [[1]*lam* (to depart hurriedly)]

lama /'lahmə/ *n* a Lamaist monk [Tibetan *blama*]

Lamaism /'lahmə,iz(ə)m/ *n* the Buddhism of Tibet, marked by a dominant monastic hierarchy headed by the Dalai Lama – **Lamaist** *n or adj*, **Lamaistic** /-'istik/ *adj*

Lamarckism /lah'mah,kiz(ə)m/ *n* a theory of organic evolution asserting that changes in the environment of plants and animals cause changes in their structure that are transmitted to their offspring [J B de Monet *Lamarck* †1829 F botanist & zoologist] – **Lamarckian** *adj*

lamasery /'lahməsəri/ *n* a monastery of lamas [F *lamaserie*, fr *lama* + Per *sarāī* palace]

[1]**lamb** /lam/ *n* **1a** a young sheep, esp one that is less than a year old or without permanent teeth **b** the young of various animals (e g the smaller antelopes) other than sheep **2a** a gentle, meek, or innocent person **b** a dear, pet **3** the flesh of a lamb used as food ☞ MEAT [ME, fr OE; akin to OHG *lamb* lamb, *elaho* elk – more at ELK]

[2]**lamb** *vi* to give birth to a lamb ~ *vt* to tend (ewes) at lambing time – **lamber** /'lamə/ *n*

lambaste, lambast /lam'bast/ *vt* **1** to beat, thrash **2** to attack verbally; censure [prob fr [1]*lam* + *baste*]

lambda /'lamdə/ *n* **1** the 11th letter of the Greek alphabet **2** an unstable elementary particle of the hyperon family that exists in a neutral form with a mass 2183 times that of an electron [Gk, of Sem origin; akin to Heb *lāmedh*, 12th letter of the Heb alphabet]

lambent /'lamb(ə)nt/ *adj* **1** playing lightly on or over a surface; flickering ⟨*~ flames*⟩ **2** softly bright or radiant ⟨*eyes ~ with love*⟩ **3** marked by lightness or brilliance, esp of expression ⟨*a ~ wit*⟩ ***USE*** fml [L *lambent-, lambens*, prp of *lambere* to lick – more at [4]LAP] – **lambently** *adv*, **lambency** /-b(ə)nsi/ *n*

lambert /'lambət/ *n* the cgs unit of brightness [Johann Heinrich *Lambert* †1777 G physicist & philosopher]

lambrequin /'lamb(r)ə,kin/ *n, chiefly NAm* a short decorative piece of drapery (e g for the top of a window or door) [F]

lambskin /'lam,skin/ *n* **1** (leather made from) the skin of a lamb or small sheep **2** the skin of a lamb dressed with the wool on

[1]**lame** /laym/ *adj* **1** having a body part, esp a leg, so disabled as to impair freedom of movement; *esp* having a limp caused by a disabled leg **2** weak, unconvincing ⟨*a ~ excuse*⟩ [ME, fr OE *lama*; akin to OHG *lam* lame, Lith *limti* to break down] – **lamely** *adv*, **lameness** *n*

[2]lame *vt* **1** to make lame **2** to make weak or ineffective

lamé /'lahmay/ *n* a brocaded clothing fabric made from any of various fibres combined with tinsel weft threads often of gold or silver [F]

'lame,brain /-,brayn/ *n, NAm* a dull-witted or erratic person – **lamebrain, lamebrained** *adj*

,lame 'duck *n* sby or sthg (e g a person or business) that is weak or incapable

lamell-, lamelli- *comb form* lamella ⟨lamelli*form*⟩ ⟨lamell*ose*⟩ [NL, fr *lamella*]

lamella /lə'melə/ *n, pl* **lamellae** /-li/ *also* **lamellas** a thin flat scale, membrane, or part (e g a gill of a mushroom) [NL, fr L, dim. of *lamina* thin plate] – **lamellar** *adj,* **lamellate** /'lamilayt, lə'melayt, -lət/ *adj,* **lamellation** /,lamə'laysh(ə)n/ *n*

lamellibranch /lə'meli,brangk/ *n, pl* **lamellibranchs** any of a class of bivalve molluscs (e g clams, oysters, and mussels) [NL *Lamellibranchia*, classname, fr *lamell-* + L *branchia* gill – more at BRANCHIA] – **lamellibranch** *adj,* **lamellibranchiate** /-'brangkiayt/ *adj or n*

lamellicorn /lə'meli,kawn/ *adj* of or belonging to a group of large beetles (e g the stag beetle) [NL *Lamellicornia*, superfamily name, fr *lamell-* + L *-cornia*, neut pl of *-cornis* of horn] – **lamellicorn** *n*

[1]lament /lə'ment/ *vi* to feel or express grief or deep regret; mourn aloud – often + *for* or *over* ~ *vt* to lament or mourn (demonstratively) for [MF & L; MF *lamenter*, fr L *lamentari*, fr *lamentum*, n, lament; akin to ON *lōmr* loon, L *latrare* to bark, Gk *lēros* nonsense] – **lamentation** /,lamən'taysh(ə)n/ *n*

[2]lament *n* **1** an expression of grief **2** a dirge, elegy

lamentable /'lamәntəbl/ *adj* that is to be regretted; deplorable – **lamentableness** *n,* **lamentably** *adv*

,Lamen'tations /,lamən'taysh(ə)nz/ *n pl but sing in constr* a poetic book of the Old Testament, attributed to Jeremiah, on the fall of Jerusalem

lamin-, lamini-, lamino- *comb form* lamina; laminae ⟨lam inar⟩ ⟨lamin*itis*⟩

lamina /'laminə/ *n, pl* **laminae** /-ni/, **laminas** a thin plate, scale, layer, or flake [L]

laminar /'laminə/ *adj* arranged in, consisting of, or resembling laminae

,laminar 'flow *n* streamline flow in a viscous fluid near a solid boundary – compare TURBULENT FLOW

[1]laminate /'lami,nayt/ *vt* **1** to roll or compress (e g metal) into a thin plate or plates **2** to separate into laminae **3** to make by uniting superimposed layers of 1 or more materials **4** to overlay with a thin sheet or sheets of material (e g metal or plastic) ~ *vi* to separate into laminae

[2]laminate /'laminət, -nayt/ *adj* covered with or consisting of laminae

[3]laminate /'laminət, -nayt/ *n* a product made by laminating

lamination /,lami'naysh(ə)n/ *n* **1** a laminate structure **2** a lamina [[1]LAMINATE + -ION]

laminitis /,lami'nietəs/ *n* painful inflammation of the lining of a horse's hoof [NL]

Lammas /'laməs/ *n* **1** August 1 formerly celebrated in England as a harvest festival **2** *also* **Lammastide** the time of the year around Lammas [ME *Lammasse*, fr OE *hlāfmæsse*, fr *hlāf* loaf, bread + *mæsse* mass; fr the fact that formerly loaves from the first ripe grain were consecrated on this day]

lammergeier, lammergeyer /'lamə,gie·ə/ *n* a large vulture that lives in mountain regions from the Pyrenees to northern China [G *lämmergeier*, fr *lämmer* (pl of *lamm* lamb) + *geier* vulture]

lamp /lamp/ *n* **1** any of various devices for producing visible light: e g **a** a vessel containing an inflammable substance (e g oil or gas) that is burnt to give out artificial light **b** a usu portable electric device containing a light bulb **2** any of various light-emitting devices (e g a sunlamp) which produce electromagnetic radiation (e g heat radiation) **3** a source of intellectual or spiritual illumination [ME, fr OF *lampe*, fr L *lampas*, fr Gk, fr *lampein* to shine; akin to ON *leiptr* lightning]

'lamp,black /-,blak/ *n* a pigment made from finely powdered black soot [fr the black soot deposited by the flame of a smoking oil lamp]

'lamp,lighter /-,lietə/ *n* one whose occupation was to light and extinguish street gas lamps

lampoon /lam'poohn/ *vt or n* (to make the subject of) a harsh vitriolic satire [n F *lampon*, perh fr *lampons* let us drink, fr *lamper* to guzzle; vb fr n] – **lampooner, lampoonist** *n,* **lampoonery** *n*

'lamp ,post *n* a post, usu of metal or concrete, that supports a light which illuminates a street or other public area (e g a park)

lamprey /'lampri/ *n* any of several eel-like aquatic vertebrates that have a large sucking mouth with no jaws [ME, fr OF *lampreie*, fr ML *lampreda*]

'lamp,shade /-,shayd/ *n* a decorative translucent cover placed round an electric light bulb to reduce glare

'lamp ,standard *n* LAMP POST

Lancastrian /lang'kastri·ən/ *n or adj* **1** (a native or inhabitant) of Lancashire **2** (an adherent) of the English royal house of Lancaster that ruled from 1399 to 1461 [John of Gaunt, Duke of *Lancaster* †1399]

[1]lance /lahns/ *n* **1** a weapon having a long shaft with a sharp steel head carried by horsemen for use when charging **2a** LANCET 1 **b** a spear or harpoon for killing whales **3** LANCER 1 [ME, fr OF, fr L *lancea*]

[2]lance *vt* **1** to pierce (as if) with a lance **2** to open (as if) with a lancet ⟨~ *a boil*⟩ [ME *launcen*, fr MF *lancer*, fr LL *lanceare*, fr L *lancea*]

,lance 'corporal *n* ☞ RANK [*lance* (as in obs *lancepesade* lance corporal, fr MF *lancepessade*, fr OIt *lancia spezzata* battle-trained or seasoned soldier, lit., broken lance)]

lancelet /'lahnslit/ *n* any of various small translucent marine animals

lanceolate /'lahnsi·əlayt, -lət/ *adj* shaped like a lance head; *specif* tapering to a point at the apex and sometimes at the base ⟨~ *leaves*⟩ ☞ PLANT [LL *lanceolatus*, fr L *lanceola*, dim. of *lancea*]

lancer /'lahnsə/ *n* **1** a member of a light-cavalry unit (formerly) armed with lances **2** *pl but sing in constr* (the music for) a set of 5 quadrilles each in a different metre

lancet /'lahnsit/ *n* **1** a sharp-pointed and usu 2-edged surgical instrument used to make small incisions **2a** *also* **lancet window** a high narrow window with an acutely pointed head ☞ CHURCH **b** *also* **lancet arch** an acutely pointed arch ***USE*** *(2)* ☞ ARCHITECTURE [ME *lancette*, fr MF, dim. of *lance*]

lancewood /'lahns,wood/ *n* (a tree yielding) a tough elastic wood used esp for carriage shafts, fishing rods, and bows

¹land /land/ *n* **1a** the solid part of the surface of a celestial body, esp the earth **b** ground or soil of a specified situation, nature, or quality ⟨*wet* ~⟩ **2** (*the* way of life in) *the* rural and esp agricultural regions of a country ⟨*going back to the* ~⟩ **3** (the people of) a country, region, etc **4** a realm, domain ⟨*in the* ~ *of dreams*⟩ **5** ground owned as property – often pl with sing. meaning [ME, fr OE; akin to OHG *lant* land, OIr *land* open space] – **landless** *adj*

²land *vt* **1** to set or put on shore from a ship **2a** to set down (e g passengers or goods) after conveying **b** to bring to or cause to reach a specified place, position, or condition ⟨*his carelessness* ~ed *him in trouble*⟩ **c** to bring (e g an aeroplane) to a surface from the air **3a** to catch and bring in (e g a fish) **b** to gain, secure ⟨~ *a job*⟩ – infml **4** to strike, hit ⟨~ed *him one on the nose*⟩ – infml **5** to present or burden *with* sthg unwanted – infml ~*vi* **1a** to go ashore from a ship; disembark **b** *of a boat, ship, etc* to come to shore; *also* to arrive on shore in a boat, ship, etc **2a** to end up – usu + *up* ⟨*took the wrong bus and* ~ed *up on the other side of town*⟩ **b** to strike or come to rest on a surface (e g after a fall) ⟨~ed *on his head*⟩ **c** *of an aircraft, spacecraft, etc* to alight on a surface; *also* to arrive in an aircraft, spacecraft, etc which has alighted on a surface

'land ,agent *n* ESTATE AGENT

landau /'landaw/ *n* a 4-wheeled carriage with a folding top divided into 2 sections [*Landau*, town in Rhineland-Palatinate (pre-1945 Bavaria), Germany, where first made]

landaulet /,landə'let/ *n* a small landau

'land ,breeze *n* a breeze blowing seawards from the land, generally at night

'land ,crab *n* any of various crabs that live mostly on land and breed in the sea

landed /'landid/ *adj* **1** owning land ⟨~ *proprietors*⟩ **2** consisting of land ⟨~ *property*⟩

'land,fall /-,fawl/ *n* an act or instance of sighting or reaching land after a voyage or flight

'land,form /-,fawm/ *n* a natural feature of the earth's surface (e g a mountain)

'land,holder /-,hohldə/ *n* a holder or owner of land – **landholding** *adj or n*

landing /'landing/ *n* **1** the act of going or bringing to a surface from the air or to shore from the water ☞ SPACE **2** a place for discharging and taking on passengers and cargo **3** a level space at the end of a flight of stairs or between 2 flights of stairs

'landing ,craft *n* any of numerous naval craft designed for putting troops and equipment ashore

'landing ,stage *n* a sometimes floating platform for landing passengers or cargo

'landing ,strip *n* a runway without normal airfield or airport facilities

'land,lady /-,laydi/ *n* **1** a female landlord **2** the female proprietor of a guesthouse or lodging house

'land-,line *n* a telecommunications link using cables as opposed to radio transmission

'land,locked /-,lokt/ *adj* (nearly) enclosed by land

'land,lord /-,lawd/ *n* **1** sby who owns land, buildings, or accommodation for lease or rent **2** sby who owns or keeps an inn; an innkeeper

'land,lubber /-,lubə/ *n* a person unacquainted with the sea or seamanship – **landlubberly** *adj*

'land,mark /-mahk/ *n* **1a** an object (e g a stone) that marks a boundary **b** a conspicuous object that can be used to identify a locality **2** an event that marks a turning point or new development ⟨*a* ~ *in the history of aviation*⟩

'land,mass /-,mas/ *n* a large area of land

'land ,rail *n* a corncrake

¹'land,scape /-,skayp/ *n* **1** natural, esp inland scenery **2a** a picture, drawing, etc of landscape **b** the art of depicting landscape [D *landschap*, fr *land* + *-schap* -ship]

²landscape *vt* to improve or modify the natural beauties of ~*vi* to engage in the occupation of landscape gardening – **landscaper** *n*

landscape architect *n* LANDSCAPE GARDENER – **landscape architecture** *n*

,landscape 'gardener *n* one who designs and arranges the layout of gardens and grounds – **landscape gardening** *n*

'land,slide /-,slied/ *n* **1** a usu rapid movement of rock, earth, etc down a slope; *also* the moving mass **2** an overwhelming victory, esp in an election

'land,slip /-,slip/ *n* a small landslide

¹lane /layn/ *n* **1** a narrow passageway, road, or street **2a** a fixed ocean route used by ships **b** a strip of road for a single line of vehicles **c** AIR LANE **d** any of several marked parallel courses to which a competitor must keep during a race (e g in running or swimming) **e** a narrow hardwood surface down which the ball is sent towards the pins in tenpin bowling [ME, fr OE *lanu*; akin to MD *lane* lane]

²lane *adj, Scot* lone [ME (Sc), var of *lone*]

'lane,way /-,way/ *n, chiefly Can* a lane or mews running between or behind houses

Langobardic /,lang·gə'bahdik, -goh-/ *n* the W Germanic language of the Lombard people [L *Langobardus* Lombard]

lang syne /,lang 'sien; *often* 'zien/ *n or adv, Scot* (times) long ago [ME (Sc), fr *lang* long + *syne* since]

language /'lang·gwij/ *n* **1a** those words, their pronunciation, and the methods of combining them used by a particular people, nation, etc ⟨*the English* ~⟩ 👁 **b(1)** (the faculty of making and using) audible articulate meaningful sound **(2)** a systematic means of communicating using conventionalized signs, sounds, gestures, or marks ☞ ALPHABET **(3)** the suggestion by objects, actions, or conditions of associated ideas or feelings ⟨*body* ~⟩ **(4)** a formal system of signs and symbols (e g a logical calculus or one for use with a computer) together with rules for the formation and transformation of admissible expressions **2a** a particular style or manner of verbal expression **b** the specialized vocabulary and phraseology belonging to a particular group or profession ⟨*legal* ~⟩ [ME, fr OF, fr *langue* tongue, language, fr L *lingua* – more at TONGUE]

'language la,boratory *n* a room, usu divided into booths each equipped with a tape recorder, where foreign languages are learnt by listening and speaking

langue /long·g (*Fr* lɑ̃ːg)/ *n* language regarded as a system of elements or a set of habits common to a community of speakers – compare PAROLE; COMPETENCE 2 [F, lit., language]

langue d'oc /'long·gə ,dok (*Fr* lɑ̃ːg dɔk)/ *n* (the medieval dialects of S France including medieval Provençal, which formed the basis of) Provençal [F, fr OF, lit., language of *oc*; fr the Provençal use of the word *oc* for 'yes'']

langue d'oïl /do'eel (*Fr* dɔil)/ *n* (the medieval

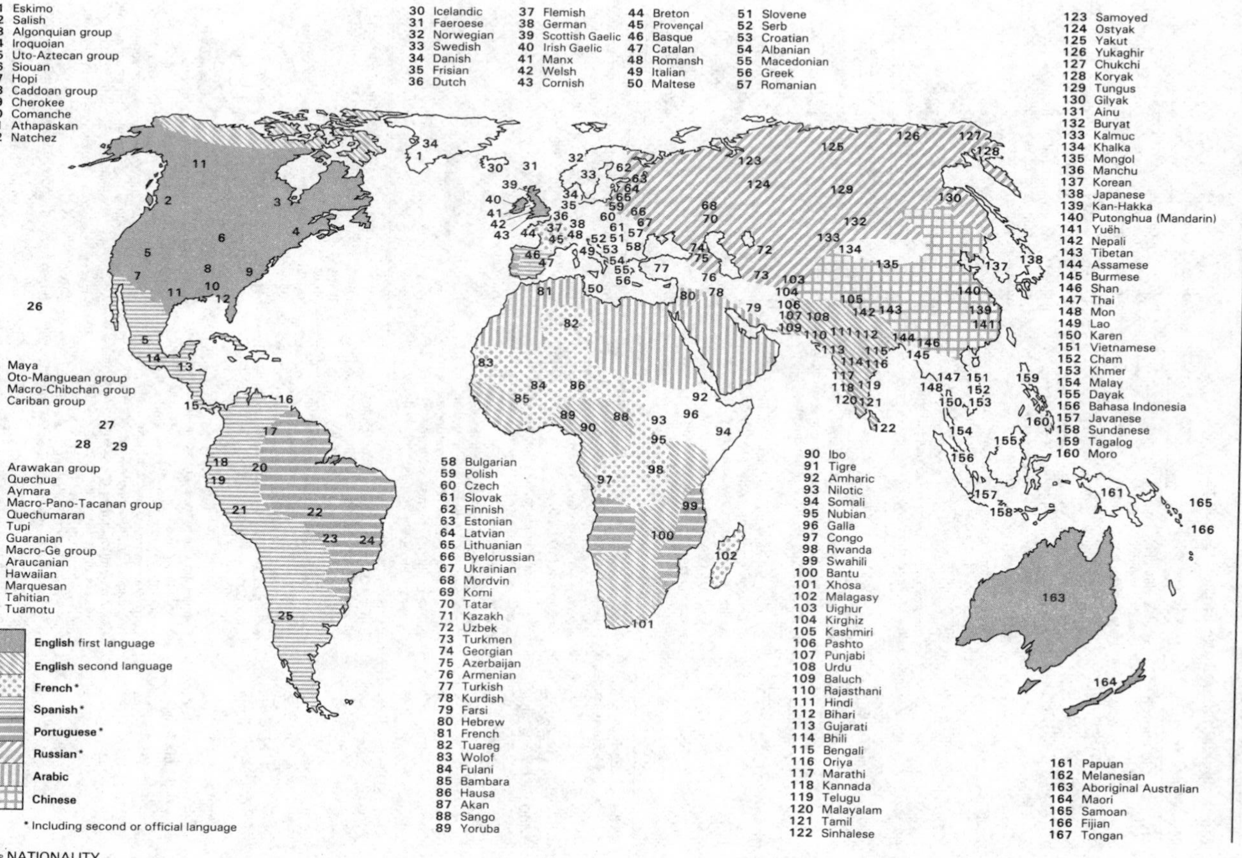

☞ NATIONALITY

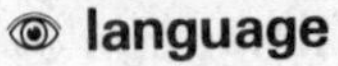

Chronological table of the English language

date and period	historical development	extracts from period texts
AD 450 **Old English** Gēse, ic sprece Englisc	English develops from the languages of the West Germanic tribes (Angles, Saxons, and Jutes) who invade Britain in the 5th and 6th centuries and drive the Celtic-speaking population north and west.	Hwæt, wē Gār-Dena in gēardagum *Hear: We the Spear-Danes in days of yore* þēodcvninga þrym gefrūnon *the people's kings' glory have heard tell of* hū þā æþelingas ellen fremedon *how those princes deed of bravery performed* (Hear! We have heard tell of the glory of the Danish kings in days of yore, and of how those princes performed deeds of bravery!)
597	Arrival of St Augustine and his missionaries marks beginning of the conversion of the English to Christianity. Many religious terms are borrowed from Latin.	
900	The invasions by the Danes and Norwegians in the 9th and 10th centuries introduce a large number of Norse words into English. The West Saxon dialect emerges as the main form of Old English and is used in the literature of the period.	*Beowulf* (mainly W Saxon) 8th century, written down late 10th century 
1100 **Middle English** Yis, I speke Englyssh	After the Norman Conquest French is used as the language of government, business, and the ruling classes for 200 years. The grammatical endings of nouns, verbs, and adjectives in Old English become simplified.	Whan that Aprill with his shoures soote *When showers sweet* The droghte of March hath perced to the roote, *drought pierced* And bathed every veyne in swich licour *vein such moisture* Of which vertu engendred is the flour *By power flower*
1300	By the 14th century the East Midland dialect of London emerges as the standard form of English and is used as the literary language.	Chaucer, *Canterbury Tales*, General Prologue (SE Midland late 14th century)
1400	Henry IV (1399–1413) is the first English-speaking king to rule since 1066.	
1500 **Early Modern English** Yes, I speake English	The spread of printing (1475 onwards) helps stabilize the written language so that it becomes suitable for serious literary works (eg Tyndale's translation of the New Testament in 1525).	To be, or not to be, that is the question, Whether tis nobler in the minde to suffer The slings and arrowes of outragious fortune, Or to take Armes against a sea of troubles, And by opposing, end them.
1600	The revival of interest in Classical Latin and Greek leads to many learned words being introduced. The 'great vowel shift' that began in Chaucer's day brings about major changes in pronunciation (Chaucer's pronunciation of *house* probably rhymed with *goose*, Shakespeare's with *gross*).	Shakespeare *Hamlet* (2nd Quarto 1604) 
1700 **Later Modern English** Yes, I speak English	Samuel Johnson's first major English dictionary (published 1755) attempts to fix and refine the language further.	I have protracted my work till most of those whom I wished to please, have sunk into the grave, and success and miscarriage are empty sounds: I therefore dismiss it with frigid tranquillity, having little to fear or hope from censure or from praise.
1800	The growth of British colonial power up to the late 19th century leads to the spread of English as a world language and the emergence of distinct varieties of English in countries like North America, South Africa, and Australia.	Samuel Johnson, Preface to *A Dictionary of the English Language* (mid 18th century)
1900 **Present-day English**	Present-day English is almost an international language, spoken, either as a first or second language, in most parts of the world. It has borrowed words from countless other languages, and the boom in science and technology has led to the creation of large numbers of new words, many of them derived from Latin and Greek. English today is richer than ever before, but, like all living languages, it is still in the process of changing.	British Airways is considering introducing gambling, such as bingo and fruit machines, on long-haul flights in an attempt to win passengers. As the fight for passengers and financial survival hots up among international airlines, the company has commissioned market research on various forms of in-flight entertainment. (From a news report, 1981; the passage contains at least 12 words, or senses of words, unknown in Shakespeare's time)

English imported

English contains words derived, directly and indirectly, from over 100 languages, besides owing a great deal to Latin, German, French and Greek. Sources of some of these borrowings are shown with approximate dates of their introduction into English.

EUROPE

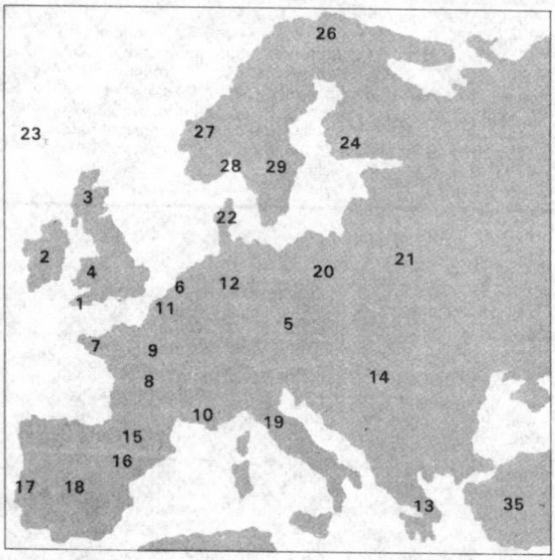

BRITISH ISLES

1 Cornish
wrasse 1670
porbeagle 1760

2 Irish Gaelic
shamrock 1570
brogue 1590
tory 1640
galore 1670
whisky 1710
smithereens 1840

3 Scottish Gaelic
clan 1420
slogan 1510
cairn 1530
trousers 1610

4 Welsh
coracle 1550
flummery 1620
cwm 1850
corgi 1920

5 Czech
pistol 1570
howitzer 1700
robot 1920

6 Dutch
frolic 1540
yatch 1560
landscape 1600
brandy 1620
easel 1630
cruise 1650
sleigh 1700
spook 1800
boss (*chief*) 1820
dope 1850

FRANCE

7 Breton
bijou 1840
menhir 1840
dolmen 1860

8 French
capon 1000
proud 1050
juggler 1100
prison 1120
duke 1130
justice 1140
market 1150
standard 1150
grace 1170
catch 1200
boil (*vb*) 1220
city 1220
judge 1220
face 1290
manor 1290
parliament 1290
pork 1290
voice 1290
beef 1300
tailor 1300
carpenter 1320
due 1340
scent 1370
village 1380
kestrel 14??
guardian 1420
attainder 1470

FRANCE

serviette 1490
fricassee 1570
role 1600
cadet 1610
cajole 1640
entre nous 1690
glacier 1740
bidet 1760
brochure 1760
frisson 1780
aspic 1790
séance 1800
gourmet 1820
communism 1840
cancan 1850
hangar 1850
monocle 1860
frappé 1890
garage 1900
camouflage 1910
discotheque 1950

9 Gaulish
andiron 1300
bracket 1580

10 Provençal
nutmeg 1360
funnel 1400
cocoon 1700
nougat 1830

11 Flemish
grime 1470
hunk 1810

12 German
plunder 1630
spanner 1640
zinc 1650
quartz 1760
poodle 1820
dachshund 1880
seminar 1890

GREECE

13 Ancient Greek
priest 600
church 700
devil 700
angel 950
hypocrisy 1220
allegory 1380
diaphragm 1400
idea 1430
alphabet 1510
drama 1520
anemone 1550
rhythm 1560
bulb 1570
larynx 1580
pathos 1580
cosmos 1650

Modern Greek
moussaka 1940
enosis 1950

14 Hungarian
hussar 1530
coach 1560
goulash 1870
paprika 1900

IBERIAN PENINSULA

15 Basque
chaparral 1850
jai alai 1910

16 Catalan
brocade 1560
barrack 1690
aubergine 1790

17 Portuguese
marmalade 1530
caste 1550
molasses 1580
tank 1620
albino 1780

IBERIAN PENINSULA

18 Spanish
cask 1530
galleon 1530
mosquito 1580
sherry 1610
cargo 1660
stevedore 1790
ranch 1810
silo 1830

ITALIAN PENINSULA

19 Etruscan
histrionic 1560
mantissa 1640

Italian
cupola 1550
squadron 1560
stanza 1590
macaroni 1600
umbrella 1610
balcony 1620
regatta 1650
sonata 1690
portfolio 1720
influenza 1740
mozzarella 1910

Latin
candle 700
dish 700
street 700
wine 700
temple 820
anchor 880
port (*harbour*) 890
rose 890
mile 970
altar 1000
cheese 1000
cup 1000
fever 1000
pear 1000

ITALIAN PENINSULA

capital (*adj*) 1220
minor 1300
translate 1300
necessary 1340
create 1380
tradition 1380
cancer 1390
respect 1390
cadaver 1400
ligament 1400
major 1400
neuter 1400
punctual 1400
provide 1410
minute (*adj*) 1420
separate 1430
spine 1430
frustrate 1450
aggravate 1470
legal 1500
pauper 1510
enormous 1530
item 1530
segregate 1540
fusion 1550
section 1560
select 1570
strict 1590
radius 1600
specimen 1610
insomnia 1620
curt 1630
onus 1640
data 1650
simulate 1650
rabies 1660
fulcrum 1670
lens 1690
momentum 1700
calix 1710
propaganda 1720
alibi 1730
prospectus 1780
hibernate 1800
omnibus 1830
sanatorium 1870
referendum 1880

20 Polish
mazurka 1820

21 Russian
muzhik 1570
tsar 1670
vodka 1800
samovar 1830
pogrom 1880
cosmonaut 1960

SCANDINAVIA

22 Danish
troll 1610

23 Faroese
skua 1680

24 Finnish
sauna 1950

25 Icelandic
eider 1740
geyser 1780

26 Lapp
tundra 1840

27 Norwegian
lemming 1600
fiord 1670
kraken 1750
floe 1820
ski 1850
slalom 1920

28 Old Norse
egg (*n*) 800
call 1000
law 1000
fellow 1010
take 1100
die (*vb*) 1130
root 1150
crook 1170
anger 1200
raise 1200
seat 1200
they 1200
want 1200
sky 1220
window 1220
loan 1240
leg 1270
dirt 1300
weak 1300
flat 1320
odd 1330
snub 1340

29 Swedish
gauntlet (as in *run the gauntlet*) 1660
tungsten 1770
moped 1950
ombudsman 1950

NEAR EAST

30 Akkadian
ziggurat 1880

31 Arabic
alkali 1390
syrup 1390
lemon 1400
algebra 1540
magazine 1580
monsoon 1580
sash 1590
emir 1620
sofa 1620
harem 1630
alcove 1680
ghoul 1790

32 Aramaic
abbot 880
dragoman 13??

33 Hebrew
rabbi 1000
shibboleth 1380

34 Persian
spinach 1530
turban 1560
bazaar 1600
sherbet 1600
shawl 1660

35 Turkish
divan 1590
coffee 1600
cossack 1600
jackal 1600
kiosk 1620
yoghourt 1620
bosh 1830

NORTH AMERICA

36 Abnaki
skunk 1630
wigwam 1630
37 Algonquian
moccasin 1610
toboggan 1830
38 Cree
pemmican 1800
39 Eskimo
kayak 1760
igloo 1850
40 Greenland Eskimo
anorak 1920
41 Narraganset
papoose 1630
squash (*vegetable*) 1640
wampum 1640
42 Ojibwa
totem 1770

ASIA

43 Balti
polo 1870
44 Bengali
dinghy 1800
45 Burmese
chindit 1940
46 Chinese
silk 1000
tea 1650
kowtow 1800
tycoon 1860
yen 1870
47 Hindi
bungalow 1680
dungaree 1700
shampoo 1760
jungle 1780
pyjamas 1800
loot 1840
gymkhana 1860
khaki 1860
48 Japanese
kimono 1890
rickshaw 1890
dan 1940
kamikaze 1940
49 Javanese
junk (*ship*) 1550
palanquin 1590
gong 1600
50 Maldive islands
atoll 1620
51 Malay
sago 1550
bamboo 1600
gingham 1610
amok 1660
ketchup 1710
caddy 1790
52 Malayalam
copra 1580
teak 1700
53 Mongolian
horde 1560
mogul 1590
54 Sanskrit
sugar 1290
lingam 1720
avatar 1780
suttee 1790
yoga 1820
nirvana 1840
swastika 1870
55 Sinhalese
tourmaline 1760
anaconda 1770
beriberi 1880
56 Tamil
pariah 1620
cheroot 1670
catamaran 1700
mulligatawny 1780
57 Tibetan
lama 1650
yak 1800
58 Tungus
shaman 1700

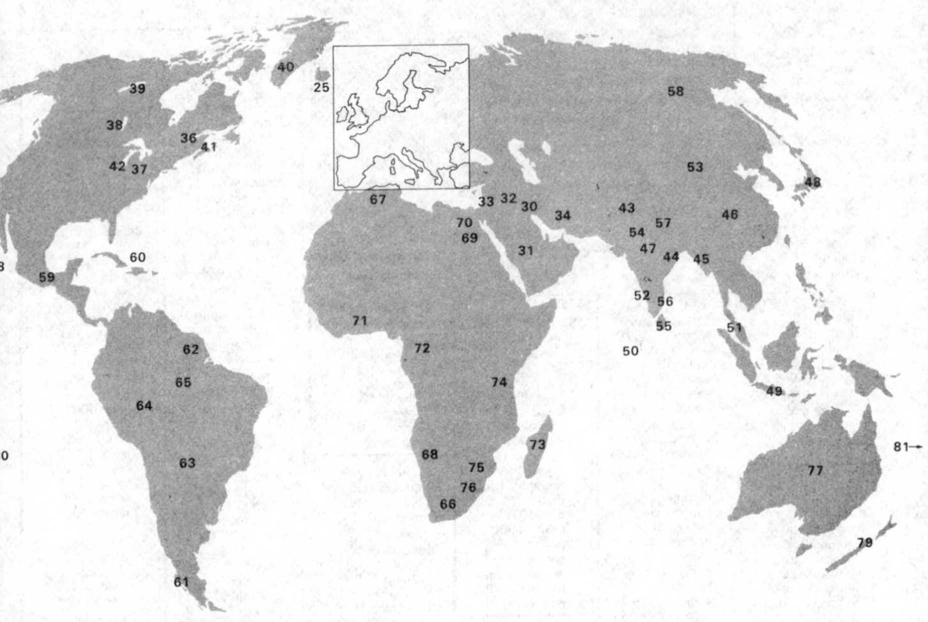

CENTRAL AMERICA

59 Nahuatl
chocolate 1600
tomato 1600
coyote 1850
60 Taino
hammock 1550
hurricane 1550
maize 1550
potato 1560
tobacco 1580
barbecue 1660

SOUTH AMERICA

61 Araucanian
poncho 1750
62 Arawakan
iguana 1550
canoe 1560
63 Guarani
jaguar 1600
64 Quechua
condor 1600
llama 1600
puma 1780
quinine 1830
65 Tupi
toucan 1570
tapioca 1710
cougar 1770
petunia 1820

AFRICA

66 Afrikaans
spoor 1820
commando 1830
trek 1850
apartheid 1950
67 Berber
zouave 1850
68 Bushman
gnu 1780
69 Coptic
adobe 1830
70 Egyptian
pharoah 890
ivory 1300
gum 1390
nitre 1400
71 Ewe
voodoo 1880
72 Kongo
chimpanzee 1740
zombie 1930
73 Malagasy
raffia 1880
74 Swahili
bwana 1880
75 Tswana
tsetse 1850
76 Zulu
mamba 1890
impala 1900

AUSTRALASIA

77 Australian native languages
kangaroo 1770
dingo 1790
wombat 1800
boomerang 1830
wallaby 1830
budgerigar 1850
78 Hawaiian
lei 1840
ukulele 1900
79 Maori
kiwi 1830
moa 1840
80 Tahitian
tattoo 1770
81 Tongan
taboo 1780
kava 1820

French dialects of N France which formed the basis of) modern French [F, fr OF, lit., language of *oïl*; fr the French use of the word *oïl* for 'yes']

languid /'lang·gwid/ *adj* **1** drooping or flagging (as if) from exhaustion; weak **2a** spiritless or apathetic in character **b** *esp of literary style* lacking colour; uninteresting **3** lacking force or quickness, esp of movement; sluggish [MF *languide*, fr L *languidus*, fr *languēre* to languish – more at SLACK] – **languidly** *adv*, **languidness** *n*

languish /'lang·gwish/ *vi* **1** to be or become feeble or enervated **2a** to become dispirited or depressed; pine – often + *for* **b** to lose intensity or urgency ⟨*his interest* ~ed⟩ **c** to suffer hardship or neglect ⟨~ed *in prison for 2 years*⟩ **3** to assume an expression of emotion appealing for sympathy [ME *languishen*, fr MF *languiss-*, stem of *languir*, fr (assumed) VL *languire*, fr L *languēre*] – **languishingly** *adv*, **languishment** *n*

languor /'lang·gə/ *n* **1** weakness or weariness of body or mind **2** a feeling or mood of wistfulness or dreaminess **3** heavy or soporific stillness [ME, fr OF, fr L, fr *languēre*] – **languorous** *adj*, **languorously** *adv*

langur /lung'gooə/ *n* any of various Asiatic slender long-tailed monkeys [Hindi *lāgūr*]

lank /langk/ *adj* **1** lean, gaunt **2** straight, limp, and usu greasy ⟨~ *hair*⟩ [(assumed) ME, fr OE *hlanc*; akin to OHG *hlanca* loin, L *clingere* to girdle] – **lankly** *adv*, **lankness** *n*

lanky /'langki/ *adj* ungracefully tall and thin – **lankily** *adv*, **lankiness** *n*

lanner /'lanə/ *n* (the female of) a falcon of S Europe, SW Asia, and Africa [ME *laner*, fr MF *lanier*]

lanneret /'lanə,ret/ *n* a male lanner

lanolin, lanoline /'lanəlin/ *n* wool grease, esp when refined for use in ointments and cosmetics [L *lana* wool + ISV *-ol* + *-in*]

lantern /'lantən/ *n* **1** a portable protective case with transparent windows that houses a light (e g a candle) **2a** the chamber in a lighthouse containing the light **b** a structure above an opening in a roof which has glazed or open sides for light or ventilation **3** MAGIC LANTERN [ME *lanterne*, fr MF, fr L *lanterna*, fr Gk *lamptēr*, fr *lampein* to shine – more at LAMP]

'lantern ,fly *n* any of several large brightly marked insects having a hollow structure at the front of the head once thought to emit light

lanthanide /'lanthənied/ *n* any one of a series of elements of increasing atomic numbers beginning with lanthanum (57) or cerium (58) and ending with lutetium (71) [ISV]

lanthanum /'lanthənəm/ *n* a white soft malleable metallic element that occurs in rare-earth minerals ☞ PERIODIC TABLE [NL, fr Gk *lanthanein* to escape notice]

lanugo /lə'nyoohgoh/ *n* soft downy hair; *esp* that covering the foetus of some mammals, including humans [L, down – more at WOOL]

lanyard /'lanyəd/ *n* **1** a piece of rope or line for fastening sthg on board ship ☞ SHIP **2** a cord worn round the neck as a decoration or to hold sthg (e g a knife) **3** a cord used in firing certain types of cannon [alter. of ME *lanyer*, fr MF *laniere*]

Lao /low/ *n or adj, pl* **Laos,** *esp collectively* **Lao** (a member or the language) of a Tai people living in Laos and adjacent parts of NE Thailand ☞ LANGUAGE

Laodicean /,layohdi'see·ən/ *n or adj* (one who is) lukewarm or indifferent with regard to religion or politics [*Laodicea* (now Latakia), ancient city in Asia Minor; fr the reproach to the church of the Laodiceans in Rev 3:15-16]

Laotian /lay'ohsh(ə)n, 'lowsh(ə)n/ *n* a Lao [prob fr F *laotien*, adj & n, irreg fr *Lao*] – **Laotian** *adj*

[1]**lap** /lap/ *n* (the clothing covering) the front part of the lower trunk and thighs of a seated person [ME *lappe*, fr OE *læppa*; akin to OHG *lappa* flap, L *labi* to slide – more at SLEEP] – **lapful** *n* – **drop/land (sthg) in someone's lap** to (cause to) become sby's responsibility – **in the lap of luxury** in an environment of great ease, comfort, and wealth – **in the lap of the gods** beyond human influence or control

[2]**lap** *vb* **-pp-** *vt* **1a** to fold or wrap over or round **b** to envelop entirely; swathe **2** to surround or hold protectively (as if) in the lap **3a** to place or lie so as to (partly) cover (one another) ⟨~ *tiles on a roof*⟩ **b** to unite (e g beams or timbers) so as to preserve the same breadth and depth throughout **4a** to dress, smooth, or polish (e g a metal surface) to a high degree of refinement or accuracy **b** to work (2 surfaces) together with or without abrasives until a very close fit is produced **5a** to overtake and thereby lead or increase the lead over (another contestant) by a full circuit of a racetrack **b** to complete a circuit of (a racetrack) ~ *vi* **1** to overlap **2** to traverse or complete a circuit of a course

[3]**lap** *n* **1a** the amount by which one object overlaps another **b** the part of an object that overlaps another **2** a smoothing and polishing tool (e g for metal or precious stones), usu consisting of a rotating disc covered with abrasive **3** a layer of a flexible substance (e g fibres or paper) wound round sthg, esp a roller **4a** (the distance covered during) the act or an instance of moving once round a closed course or track **b** one stage or segment of a larger unit (e g a journey) **c** one complete turn (e g of a rope round a drum)

[4]**lap** *vb* **-pp-** *vi* **1** to take in liquid with the tongue **2** to move in little waves, usu making a gentle splashing sound ⟨*the sea* ~ped *gently against the edge of the quay*⟩ ~ *vt* **1a** to take in (liquid) with the tongue **b** to take in eagerly or quickly – usu + *up* ⟨*the crowd* ~ped *up every word he said*⟩ **2** to flow or splash against in little waves [ME *lapen*, fr OE *lapian*; akin to OHG *laffan* to lick, L *lambere*, Gk *laphyssein* to devour]

[5]**lap** *n* **1** an act or instance of lapping **2** a thin or weak beverage or food **3** a gentle splashing sound

laparotomy /,lapə'rotəmi/ *n* surgical incision through the abdominal wall [Gk *lapara* flank + ISV *-tomy*]

lapdog /'lap,dog/ *n* a small dog that may be held in the lap

lapel /lə'pel/ *n* a fold of the top front edge of a coat or jacket that is continuous with the collar [dim. of [1]*lap*]

[1]**lapidary** /'lapidəri/ *n* sby who cuts, polishes, or engraves precious stones

[2]**lapidary** *adj* **1a** sculptured in or engraved on stone **b** of or relating to (the cutting of) gems **2** *of literary style* having the elegance and dignity associated with monumental inscriptions [L *lapidarius* of stone, fr *lapid-*, *lapis* stone; akin to Gk *lepas* crag]

lapillus /lə'piləs/ *n, pl* **lapilli** /-lie/ a small fragment of lava ejected in a volcanic eruption – usu pl [L, dim. of *lapis*]

lapis lazuli /,lapis 'lazyoolie, -li/ *n* (the colour of) a rich blue semiprecious stone [ME, fr ML, fr L *lapis* + ML *lazuli*, gen of *lazulum* lapis lazuli, fr Ar *lāzaward* – more at AZURE]

'**lap ,joint** *n* a joint made by overlapping 2 ends or edges and fastening them together – **lap-jointed** *adj*

Laplander /'lap,landə/ *n* LAPP 1

Lapp /lap/ *n* **1** a member of a nomadic people of N Scandinavia and the Kola peninsula of N Russia **2** *also* **Lappish** any or all of the Finno-Ugric languages of the Lapps [Sw; perh akin to MHG *lappe* simpleton] – **Lapp** *adj*, **Lappish** *adj*

lappet /'lapit/ *n* **1** a fold or flap on a garment or headdress **2** a flat overlapping or hanging piece, esp of flesh or membrane (e g the wattle of a bird) ['*lap* + *-et*]

[1]**lapse** /laps/ *n* **1** a slight error (e g of memory or in manners) **2a** a drop; *specif* a drop in temperature, humidity, or pressure with increasing height **b** an esp moral fall or decline ⟨*a* ~ *from grace*⟩ **3a(1)** the legal termination of a right or privilege through failure to exercise it **(2)** the termination of insurance coverage for nonpayment of premiums **b** a decline into disuse **4** an abandonment of religious faith **5** a continuous passage or elapsed period ⟨*returned after a* ~ *of several years*⟩ [L *lapsus*, fr *lapsus*, pp of *labi* to slip – more at SLEEP]

[2]**lapse** *vi* **1a** to fall or depart from an attained or accepted standard or level (e g of morals) – usu + *from* **b** to sink or slip gradually ⟨*the guests* ~d *into silence when the speech began*⟩ **2** to go out of existence or use **3** to pass to another proprietor by omission or negligence **4** *of time* to run its course; pass

'**lapse ,rate** *n* the rate of change of temperature, humidity, or pressure with changing height

lapsus linguae /,lapsəs 'ling·gwi/ *n* a slip of the tongue [L]

lapwing /'lap,wing/ *n* a crested Old World plover noted for its shrill wailing cry [ME, by folk etymology fr OE *hlēapewince*; akin to OE *hlēapan* to leap, *wincian* to wink]

larboard /'lahbəd/ *n, archaic* [4]PORT [ME *ladeborde*] – **larboard** *adj*

larceny /'lahsəni/ *n* theft [ME, fr MF *larcin* theft, fr L *latrocinium* robbery, fr *latron-*, *latro* mercenary soldier; akin to OE un*lǣd* poor, Gk *latron* pay]

larch /lahch/ *n* (the wood of) any of a genus of trees of the pine family with short deciduous leaves [prob fr G *lärche*, fr L *laric-*, *larix*]

[1]**lard** /lahd/ *vt* **1a** to dress (e g meat) for cooking by inserting or covering with fat, bacon, etc **b** to cover with grease **2** to intersperse or embellish (e g speech or writing) *with* sthg

[2]**lard** *n* a soft white solid fat obtained by rendering the esp abdominal fat of a pig [ME, fr OF, fr L *lardum*; akin to L *laetus* glad, *largus* abundant, Gk *larinos* fat] – **lardy** *adj*

larder /'lahdə/ *n* a place where food is stored; a pantry [ME, fr MF *lardier*, fr OF, fr *lard*]

lardon /'lahd(ə)n/ *n* a strip (e g of pork fat or bacon) with which meat is larded – compare BARD [F, piece of fat pork, fr OF, fr *lard*]

lardoon /lah'doohn/ *n* a lardon

'**lardy ,cake** /'lahdi/ *n* a sweet cake made with yeast dough, dried fruit, and lard

lares and penates /,lahreez ənd pe'nahteez/ *n pl* **1** the Ancient Roman household gods **2** the goods of a household [*lares* fr L, pl of *lar*, a Roman household god; *penates* fr L, Roman household gods]

Largactil /lah'gaktil/ *trademark* – used for chlorpromazine

[1]**large** /lahj/ *adj* **1** having more than usual power, capacity, or scope **2** exceeding most other things of like kind (in quantity or size) **3** dealing in great numbers or quantities; operating on an extensive scale ⟨*a* ~ *and highly profitable business*⟩ [ME, fr OF, fr L *largus*] – **largeness** *n*, **largish** *adj*

[2]**large** *n* – **at large 1** without restraint or confinement; AT LIBERTY ⟨*the escaped prisoner is still* at large⟩ **2** AS A WHOLE ⟨*society* at large⟩

large calorie *n* a kilocalorie

large intestine *n* the rear division of the vertebrate intestine that is divided into caecum, colon, and rectum, and concerned esp with the resorption of water and formation of faeces

'**largely** /'lahjli/ *adv* to a large extent

,**large-'scale** *adj* **1** involving great numbers or quantities **2** *of a map* showing much detail

largess, largesse /lah'jes/ *n* **1** liberal giving, esp to an inferior **2** sthg (e g money) given generously as a gift [ME *largesse*, fr OF, fr *large*]

,**large 'white** *n* any of a British breed of large long-bodied white pigs

larghetto /lah'getoh/ *n, adv, or adj, pl* **larghettos** (a movement that is) slower than andante but not as slow as largo – used in music [adj It, somewhat slow, dim. of *largo*; n & adv fr adj]

largo /'lahgoh/ *n, adv, or adj, pl* **largos** (a movement to be) played in a very slow and broad manner – used in music [adj It, slow, broad, fr L *largus* abundant; n & adv fr adj]

lari /'lahri/ *n* ☞ *Maldive Islands* at NATIONALITY [Per *lārī*]

lariat /'lari·ət/ *n, chiefly NAm* a lasso [AmerSp *la reata* the lasso, fr Sp *la* the (fem of *el*, fr L *ille* that) + AmerSp *reata* lasso, fr Sp *reatar* to tie again, fr *re-* + *atar* to tie, fr L *aptare* to fit – more at ADAPT]

[1]**lark** /lahk/ *n* any of numerous brown singing birds mostly of Europe, Asia, and northern Africa; *esp* a skylark [ME, fr OE *lāwerce*; akin to OHG *lērihha* lark]

[2]**lark** *vi* to have fun – usu + *about* or *around* [prob alter. of E dial. *lake* (to frolic), fr ME *laiken*, fr ON *leika* to play, dance]

[3]**lark** *n* **1** a lighthearted adventure; *also* a prank **2** *Br* a type of activity; *esp* a business, job ⟨*it's a good* ~: *80 quid a week, own car, and no questions asked*⟩ *USE* infml

larkspur /'lahk,spuh/ *n* a delphinium; *esp* a cultivated annual delphinium grown for its bright irregular flowers [fr the spur-shaped calyx]

larrikin /'larikin/ *n, Austr* a hooligan [perh fr *Larry* (nickname for *Lawrence*) + *-kin*]

larrup /'larəp/ *vt, Br dial* to beat soundly – infml [perh imit]

larva /'lahvə/ *n, pl* **larvae** /-vi/ **1** the immature, wingless, and often wormlike feeding form that hatches from the egg of many insects and is transformed into a pupa or chrysalis from which the adult emerges ☞ LIFE CYCLE **2** the early form (e g a tadpole) of an animal (e g a frog) that undergoes metamorphosis before becoming an adult [NL, fr L, spectre, mask; akin to L *lar*, Roman household deity] – **larval** *adj*

larvi- *comb form* larva ⟨larv*icide*⟩ [NL, fr *larva*]

larvicide /ˈlahvi,sied/ *n* an agent for killing larval pests

laryng-, laryngo- *comb form* **1** larynx ⟨laryng*itis*⟩ **2** laryngeal and ⟨laryngo*pharyngeal*⟩ [NL, fr Gk, fr *laryng-, larynx*]

laryngeal /,larinˈjee·əl, ləˈrinji·əl/ *n* a nerve, artery, etc that supplies or is associated with the larynx

laryngectomy /,laringˈgektəmi/ *n* surgical removal of (part of) the larynx

laryngitis /,larinˈjietəs/ *n* inflammation of the larynx [NL] – **laryngitic** /-ˈjitik/ *adj*

larynx /ˈlaringks/ *n, pl* **larynges** /ləˈrin,jeez/, **larynxes** the modified upper part of the trachea of air-breathing vertebrates that contains the vocal cords in human beings, most other mammals, and a few lower forms ☞ DIGESTION [NL *laryng-, larynx*, fr Gk] – **laryngeal** /,larinˈjee·əl, ləˈrinji·əl/

lasagne /ləˈzanyə/ *n* (a baked dish of minced meat, sauce, and) pasta in the form of broad flat sheets [It, pl of *lasagna*, fr (assumed) VL *lasania*, fr L *lasanum* cooking-pot, fr Gk *lasanon* chamber pot]

lascar /ˈlaskə/ *n, often cap* an E Indian sailor, army servant, or artilleryman [Hindi *lashkar* army; E *lascar* influenced in meaning by Hindi *lashkarī* soldier, sailor]

lascivious /ləˈsivi·əs/ *adj* inclined or inciting to lechery or lewdness [L *lascivia* wantonness, fr *lascivus* wanton – more at LUST] – **lasciviously** *adv*, **lasciviousness** *n*

lase /layz/ *vi* to function as a laser by emitting coherent light [back-formation fr *laser*]

laser /ˈlayzə/ *n* a device that generates an intense beam of coherent light or other electromagnetic radiation of a single wavelength by using the natural oscillations of atoms or molecules [*l*ight *a*mplification by *s*timulated *e*mission of *r*adiation]

[1]**lash** /lash/ *vi* **1** to move violently or suddenly **2** to beat, pour ⟨*rain* ~ed *down*⟩ **3** to attack physically or verbally, (as if) with a whip – often + *at, against,* or *out* ~ *vt* **1** to strike quickly and forcibly (as if) with a lash **2a** to drive (as if) with a whip; rouse ⟨~ed *the crowd into a frenzy*⟩ **b** to cause to lash [ME *lashen*, perh of imit origin]

[2]**lash** *n* **1a(1)** a stroke (as if) with a whip **(2)** (the flexible part of) a whip **b** a sudden swinging movement or blow **2** violent beating ⟨*the* ~ *of a north wind*⟩ **3** an eyelash **4** *Austr & NZ* an attempt, go – infml

[3]**lash** *vt* to bind or fasten with a cord, rope, etc [ME *lasschen* to lace, fr MF *lacier* – more at [2]LACE] – **lasher** *n*

[1]**lashing** /ˈlashing/ *n* a physical or verbal beating [[1]*lash*]

[2]**lashing** *n* sthg used for binding, wrapping, or fastening [[3]*lash*]

ˈlashings *n pl* an abundance – usu + *of* ⟨~ *of hot water*⟩; infml [fr gerund of [1]*lash*]

lash out *vi* **1** to make a sudden violent physical or verbal attack – usu + *at* or *against* **2** *Br* to spend unrestrainedly – often + *on*; infml

lass /las/, **lassie** /ˈlasi/ *n* a young woman; a girl [ME *las*]

lassa fever /ˈlasə/ *n* an acute severe often fatal virus disease of tropical countries [*Lassa*, village in northern Nigeria]

lassitude /ˈlasityoohd/ *n* **1** fatigue, weariness **2** languor, listlessness [MF, fr L *lassitudo*, fr *lassus* weary – more at [2]LET]

[1]**lasso** /laˈsooh, ˈlasoh/ *n, pl* **lassos, lassoes** a rope or long thong of leather with a running noose that is used esp for catching horses and cattle [Sp *lazo*, fr L *laqueus* snare – more at DELIGHT]

[2]**lasso** *vt* **lassos, lassoes; lassoed; lassoing** to catch (as if) with a lasso – **lassoer** *n*

[1]**last** /lahst/ *vi* **1** to continue in time **2a** to remain in good or adequate condition, use, or effectiveness **b** to manage to continue (e g in a course of action) **c** to continue to live ⟨*he won't* ~ *much longer*⟩ ~ *vt* **1** to continue in existence or action as long as or longer than – often + *out* ⟨*couldn't* ~ *out the training*⟩ **2** to be enough for the needs of ⟨*the supplies will* ~ *them a week*⟩ [ME *lasten*, fr OE *lǣstan* to last, follow; akin to OE *lāst* footprint] – **laster** *n*

[2]**last** *adj* **1** following all the rest: e g **a** final, latest **b** being the only remaining ⟨*his* ~ *pound*⟩ **2** of the final stage of life ⟨~ *rites*⟩ **3** next before the present; most recent ⟨~ *week*⟩ ⟨*this is better than his* ~ *book*⟩ **4a** lowest in rank or standing; *also* worst **b** least suitable or likely ⟨*he'd be the* ~ *person to fall for flattery*⟩ **5a** conclusive, definitive ⟨*the* ~ *word on the subject*⟩ **b** single – used as an intensive ⟨*ate every* ~ *scrap*⟩ [ME, fr OE *latost*, superl of *læt* late] – **lastly** *adv* – **last but one 1** second most recent **2** penultimate

[3]**last** *adv* **1** after all others; at the end ⟨*came* ~ *and left first*⟩ **2** on the most recent occasion ⟨*when we* ~ *met*⟩ **3** in conclusion; lastly ⟨*and* ~, *the economic aspect*⟩

[4]**last** *n* sby or sthg last – **at last/at long last** after everything; finally; *esp* after much delay – **to the last** till the end

[5]**last** *n* a form (e g of metal) shaped like the human foot, over which a shoe is shaped or repaired [ME, fr OE *lǣste*, fr *lāst* footprint; akin to OHG *leist* shoemaker's last, L *lira* furrow – more at LEARN]

,last-ˈditch *adj* made as a final effort, esp to avert disaster ⟨*a* ~ *attempt*⟩

lasting /ˈlahsting/ *adj* existing or continuing for a long while [prp of [1]*last*] – **lastingly** *adv*, **lastingness** *n*

,last ˈpost *n* the second of 2 bugle calls sounded at the hour for retiring in a military camp; *also* such a bugle call sounded at a military funeral or tattoo

,last ˈstraw *n* the last of a series (e g of events or indignities) stretching one's patience beyond its limit [fr the fable of the last straw that broke the camel's back when added to his burden]

,Last ˈSupper *n* the supper eaten by Jesus and his disciples on the night of his betrayal in which he requested them to celebrate the Eucharist in his memory

,last ˈthing *adv* as the final action, esp before going to bed ⟨*always has a cup of cocoa* ~ *at night*⟩

,Last ˈThings *n pl* events (e g the resurrection and divine judgment of all mankind) marking the end of the world; *specif* death, judgment, Heaven, and Hell in Catholic theology [trans of ML *Novissima*]

,last ˈword *n* **1** the final remark in a verbal exchange **2** the power of final decision **3** the most up-to-date or fashionable example of its kind ⟨*the ~ in sports cars*⟩

latakia /ˌlatəˈkiə/ *n, often cap* a highly aromatic oriental smoking tobacco [*Latakia*, seaport in Syria]

[1]**latch** /lach/ *vi* **1** to attach oneself ⟨~ed *onto a rich widow*⟩ **2** to gain understanding or comprehension *USE* + *on* or *onto* [ME *lachen*, fr OE *læccan*; akin to Gk *lambanein* to take, seize]

[2]**latch** *n* **1** a fastener (e g for a door) with a pivoted bar that falls into a notch on the door post **2** a fastener (e g for a door) in which a spring slides a bolt into a hole when the door is shut – **latch** *vt*

ˈlatchˌkey /-ˌkee/ *n* a key to an outside (front) door

ˈlatchˌkey ˌchild *n, chiefly Br* a child whose mother is regularly out on his/her return from school; *specif* one given a key to let him-/herself in

[1]**late** /layt/ *adj* **1a** occurring or arriving after the expected time ⟨*a ~ spring*⟩ **b** of the end of a specified time span ⟨*the ~ Middle Ages*⟩ **2a** (recently) deceased – used with reference to names, positions or specified relationships ⟨*the ~ James Scott*⟩ ⟨*his ~ wife*⟩ ⟨*the ~ chairman*⟩ **b** just prior to the present, esp as the most recent of a succession ⟨*the ~ government*⟩ ⟨*some ~ news has just arrived*⟩ **3** far on in the day or night ⟨*it's too ~ to go now*⟩ [ME, late, slow, fr OE *læt*; akin to OHG *laz* slow, OE *lǣtan* to let] – **lateness** *n*

[2]**late** *adv* **1a** after the usual or proper time ⟨*stayed up ~*⟩ **b** at or near the end of a period of time or of a process – often + *on* ⟨*~ on in the experiment*⟩ **2** until lately ⟨*Dr Evans, ~ of Birmingham, now lectures at Durham*⟩ – **of late** in the period shortly or immediately before; recently ⟨*have not seen him* of late⟩

lateen /ləˈteen/ *adj* of or being a rig characterized by a triangular sail hung from a long spar set obliquely on a low mast [F (*voile*) *latine* lateen sail, fr MF, fem of *latin*, lit., Latin, fr L *latinus*; fr its use in the Mediterranean]

lately /ˈlaytli/ *adv* recently; OF LATE ⟨*has been friendlier ~*⟩

ˈlatency ˌperiod, latency /ˈlayt(ə)nsi/ *n* a stage of personality development observed in W Europe, N America, and some other cultures, that extends from about the age of 5 to puberty, and during which sexual urges appear to lie dormant

La Tène /lah ˈten (*Fr* la tɛn)/ *adj* of the later period of the Iron Age in Europe dating from the 5th c BC to the Roman conquests [*La Tène*, shallows of the Lake of Neuchâtel, Switzerland, where remains of it were first discovered]

latent /ˈlayt(ə)nt/ *adj* present but not manifest ⟨*a ~ infection*⟩ ⟨*his desire for success remained ~*⟩ [L *latent-*, *latens*, fr prp of *latēre* to lie hidden; akin to OHG *luog* den, Gk *lanthanein* to escape notice] – **latency** /-si/ *n*, **latently** *adj*

ˌlatent ˈheat *n* heat given off or absorbed in a change of phase without a change in temperature

ˈlatent ˌperiod *n* **1** the incubation period of a disease **2** the interval between stimulation and response

[1]**lateral** /ˈlat(ə)rəl/ *adj* **1** of the side; situated on, directed towards, or coming from the side **2** made by allowing air to escape on either or both sides of the tongue ⟨*l is a ~ consonant*⟩ [L *lateralis*, fr *later-*, *latus* side] – **laterally** *adv*

[2]**lateral** *n* a lateral consonant

lateral line *n* a sense organ along the side of a fish sensitive to low vibrations ☞ ANATOMY

ˌlateral ˈthinking *n* thinking that concentrates on unexpected aspects of a problem or proceeds by seemingly illogical methods

laterite /ˈlatəˌriet/ *n* a usu red clay formed from rock decay and consisting esp of iron oxides and aluminium hydroxides [L *later* brick] – **lateritic** /-ˈritik/ *adj*

latest /ˈlaytist/ *n* **1** *the* most recent or currently fashionable style or development ⟨*the ~ in diving techniques*⟩ **2** *the* latest acceptable time ⟨*be home by one at the ~*⟩ [*latest*, adj, superl of *late*]

latex /ˈlayteks/ *n, pl* **latices** /ˈlatəˌseez/, **latexes** **1** a milky usu white fluid that is produced by various flowering plants (e g of the spurge and poppy families) and is the source of rubber, gutta-percha, chicle, and balata **2** a water emulsion of a synthetic rubber or plastic [NL *latic-*, *latex*, fr L, fluid] – **laticiferous** /ˌlatiˈsifərəs/ *adj*

[1]**lath** /lahth/ *n, pl* **laths,** /lahths, lahdhz/ **lath** a thin narrow strip of wood, esp for nailing to woodwork (e g rafters or studding) as a support (e g for tiles or plaster) ☞ BUILDING [ME, fr OE *lætt*; akin to OHG *latta* lath, W *llath* yard]

[2]**lath** *vt* to cover or line with laths – **lathing** *n*

[1]**lathe** /laydh/ *n* a former administrative district of Kent [ME, fr OE *læth* estate; akin to ON *lāth* landed property]

[2]**lathe** *n* a machine in which work is rotated about a horizontal axis and shaped by a fixed tool [prob fr ME *lath* supporting stand, prob of Scand origin; akin to Dan *-lad* supporting structure; akin to ON *hlatha* to load]

[1]**lather** /ˈlahdhə/ *n* **1a** a foam or froth formed when a detergent (e g soap) is agitated in water **b** foam or froth from profuse sweating (e g on a horse) **2** an agitated or overwrought state [(assumed) ME, fr OE *lēathor*; akin to OE *lēag* lye – more at LYE] – **lathery** *adj*

[2]**lather** *vt* **1** to spread lather over **2** to beat severely – infml ~ *vi* to form a (froth like) lather – **latherer** *n*

latices /ˈlatəseez/ *pl of* LATEX

latifundium /ˌlatiˈfundi·əm/ *n, pl* **latifundia** /-di·ə/ a great landed estate [L, fr *latus* wide + *fundus* piece of landed property – more at BOTTOM]

latimeria /ˌlatiˈmiəri·ə/ *n* any of a genus of living coelacanth fishes of deep seas off southern Africa [NL, genus name, fr Marjorie Courtenay-*Latimer* *b*1907 SAfr museum director]

[1]**Latin** /ˈlatin/ *adj* **1** of Latium or the Latins **2a** of or composed in Latin **b** Romance **3** of the part of the Christian church using a Latin liturgy; *broadly* ROMAN CATHOLIC **4** of the peoples or countries using Romance languages **5** *chiefly NAm* of the peoples or countries of Latin America [ME, fr OE, fr L *Latinus*, fr *Latium*, ancient country of Italy] – **Latinize** *vb*

[2]**Latin** *n* **1** the Italic language of ancient Latium and of Rome ☞ LANGUAGE **2** a member of the people of ancient Latium **3** a member of any of the Latin peoples **4** *chiefly NAm* a native or inhabitant of Latin America

Latinate /ˈlatinət, -nayt/ *adj* of, resembling, or derived from Latin

ˌLatin ˈcross *n* a cross consisting of a long upright

bar crossed near the top by a shorter transverse bar ☞ SYMBOL

Latinism /'latiniz(ə)m/ *n* **1** a characteristic feature of Latin occurring in another language **2** Latin quality, character, or mode of thought

latin·ize, -ise /'latiniez/ *vt* **1** to give a Latin form or character to **2** ROMANIZE 2 – **latinization** /-'zaysh(ə)n/ *n*

'Latin ,Quarter *n* a section of the Left Bank in Paris frequented by students and artists [trans of F *Quartier Latin*]

latitude /'latityoohd/ *n* **1a** the angular distance of a point on the surface of a celestial body, esp the earth, measured N or S from the equator – compare LONGITUDE **b** the angular distance of a celestial body from the ecliptic **2** a region as marked by its latitude – often pl with sing. meaning **3** (permitted) freedom of action or choice [ME, fr L *latitudin-, latitudo,* fr *latus* wide; akin to Arm *lain* wide] – **latitudinal** /,lati'tyoohdinl/ *adj,* **latitudinally** *adv*

latitudinarian /,lati,tyoohdi'neəri·ən/ *n or adj* (a person) liberal in standards of religious belief and conduct; *specif* a member of the Church of England favouring freedom of doctrine and practice within it – **latitudinarianism** *n*

latrine /lə'treen/ *n* a small pit used as a toilet, esp in a military camp, barracks, etc; *broadly* a toilet [F, fr L *latrina,* contr of *lavatrina,* fr *lavere* to wash – more at LYE]

-latry /-lətri/ *comb form* (→ *n*) worship ⟨*helio*latry⟩ ⟨*ido*latry⟩ [ME *-latrie,* fr OF, fr LL *-latria,* fr Gk, fr *latreia*] – **-later** /-lətə/ *comb form* (→ *n*)

[1]latter /'latə/ *adj* **1** of the end; later, final ⟨*the ~ stages of a process*⟩ **2** recent, present ⟨*in ~ years*⟩ **3** second of 2 things, or last of several things mentioned or understood ⟨*of ham and beef the ~ meat is cheaper today*⟩ [ME, fr OE *lætra,* compar of *læt* late]

[2]latter *n, pl* **latter** the second or last mentioned

'latter-,day *adj* of present or recent times

,Latter-,Day 'Saint *n* a Mormon [fr Mormons' name for themselves, the Church of Jesus Christ of *Latter-Day Saints*]

'latterly /-li/ *adv* **1** towards the end or latter part of a period **2** lately

lattice /'latis/ *n* **1** (a window, door, etc having) a framework or structure of crossed wooden or metal strips with open spaces between **2** a network or design like a lattice **3a** a regular geometrical arrangement of points or objects over an area or in space **b** the geometrical arrangement of the atoms or ions in a crystal [ME *latis,* fr MF *lattis*] – **lattice** *vt,* **latticed** *adj*

'lattice,work /-,wuhk/ *n* a lattice or work made of lattices

Latvian /'latvi·ən/ *n* **1** a native or inhabitant of Latvia; *specif* a Lett **2** the Baltic language of the Latvians ☞ LANGUAGE [*Latvia,* country in N central Europe, since 1940 a constituent republic of USSR] – **Latvian** *adj*

[1]laud /lawd/ *n* **1** *pl but sing or pl in constr, often cap* an office usu immediately following matins and forming with it the first of the canonical hours **2** praise – used esp in hymns [ME *laudes* (pl), fr ML, fr L, pl of *laud-, laus* praise; akin to OHG *liod* song; (2) ME *laude,* fr *laudes* (pl)]

[2]laud *vt* to praise, esp with hymns [L *laudare,* fr *laud-, laus*]

laudable /'lawdəbl/ *adj* worthy of praise; commendable – **laudableness** *n,* **laudably** *adv,* **laudability** /,lawdə'biləti/ *n*

laudanum /'lawdənəm/ *n* **1** any of various preparations of opium formerly used in medicine **2** a tincture of opium [NL]

laudatory /'lawdət(ə)ri/, **laudative** /-dətiv/ *adj* of or expressing praise

[1]laugh /lahf/ *vi* **1a** to make the explosive vocal sounds characteristically expressing amusement, mirth, joy, or derision **b** to experience amusement, mirth, joy, or derision ⟨~ed *inwardly though her face remained grave*⟩ **2** to produce a sound of or like laughter – chiefly poetic ⟨*a* ~ing *brook*⟩ ~ *vt* **1** to influence or bring to a specified state by laughter ⟨~ed *him out of his fears*⟩ **2** to utter (as if) with a laugh ⟨~ed *her consent*⟩ **3** to dismiss as trivial – + *off* or *away* ⟨*you can't ~ off a royal commission* – Alan Villiers⟩ [ME *laughen,* fr OE *hliehhan;* akin to OHG *lachēn* to laugh, OE *hlōwan* to moo – more at [1]LOW] – **laugher** *n,* **laughingly** *adv* – **laugh up one's sleeve** to be secretly amused

[2]laugh *n* **1** the act or sound of laughing **2** an expression of mirth or scorn **3** a means of entertainment; a diversion – often pl with sing. meaning **4** a cause for derision or merriment; a joke – infml ⟨*swim in that current? That's a* ~ ⟩

laughable /'lahfəbl/ *adj* of a kind to provoke laughter or derision; ridiculous – **laughableness** *n,* **laughably** *adv*

'laughing ,gas *n* NITROUS OXIDE

,laughing 'jack,ass *n* the kookaburra [fr its call, which resembles loud laughter]

'laughing,stock /-,stok/ *n* an object of ridicule

laughter /'lahftə/ *n* **1** a sound (as if) of laughing **2** the action of laughing [ME, fr OE *hleahtor;* akin to OE *hliehhan*]

[1]launch /lawnch/ *vt* **1a** to throw forward; hurl **b** to release or send off (e g a self-propelled object) ⟨~ *a rocket*⟩ **2a** to set (an esp newly built boat or ship) afloat **b** to start or set in motion (e g on a course or career) **c** to introduce (a new product) onto the market ⟨*a party to ~ a new book*⟩ ~ *vi* **1** to throw oneself energetically – + *into* or *out into* ⟨~ed *into a brilliant harangue*⟩ **2** to make a start – usu + *out* or *forth* ⟨~ed *forth on a long-winded explanation*⟩ [ME *launchen,* fr ONF *lancher,* fr LL *lanceare* to wield a lance – more at LANCE]

[2]launch *n* an act or instance of launching

[3]launch *n* **1** the largest boat carried by a warship **2** a large open or half-decked motorboat [Sp or Pg; Sp *lancha,* fr Pg]

launcher /'lawnchə/ *n* a device for launching rockets, missiles, etc [[1]LAUNCH + [2]-ER]

'launching ,pad /'lawnching/ *n* a noninflammable platform from which a rocket can be launched

'launch ,pad *n* **1** LAUNCHING PAD **2** a base from which sthg is set in motion ⟨*the project is still on the* ~⟩

'launch ,vehicle *n* the rocket power source or sources used to launch a spacecraft

launder /'lawndə/ *vt* **1** to wash (e g clothes) in water **2** to make ready for use by washing, sometimes starching, and ironing **3** to give (sthg, esp money, obtained illegally) the appearance of being respectable or legal ~ *vi* to become clean by washing, ironing, etc ⟨*clothes that ~ well*⟩ [ME *launder* launderer, contr of *lavender,* fr MF *lavandier,* fr ML *lavandarius,* fr L *lavandus,* gerundive of *lavare* to wash] – **launderer** *n,* **laundress** /-dris/ *n*

launderette /ˌlawnd(ə)'ret/ *n* a self-service laundry [fr *Launderette,* a trademark]

Laundromat /'lawndrəˌmat/ *trademark* – used for a self-service laundry

laundry /'lawndri/ *n* **1** clothes or cloth articles that have been or are to be laundered, esp by being sent to a laundry **2** a place where laundering is done; *esp* a commercial laundering establishment

laureate /'lawri·ət/ *n* a person specially honoured for achievement in an art or science [L *laureatus* crowned with laurel, fr *laurea* laurel wreath, fr fem of *laureus* of laurel, fr *laurus*] – **laureate** *adj,* **laureateship** *n*

laurel /'lorəl/ *n* **1** any of a genus of trees or shrubs that have alternate entire leaves, small flowers, and fruits that are ovoid berries **2** a tree or shrub that resembles the true laurel **3** a crown of laurel awarded as a token of victory or preeminence; distinction, honour – usu pl with sing. meaning [ME *lorel,* fr OF *lorier,* fr *lor* laurel, fr L *laurus*]

lav /lav/ *n* a lavatory – infml

lava /'lahvə/ *n* (solidified) molten rock that issues from a volcano ☞ GEOGRAPHY [It, fr L *labes* fall; akin to L *labi* to slide – more at SLEEP] – **lavalike** *adj*

lavabo /lə'vayboh/ *n, pl* **lavabos** *often cap* the celebrant's ritual hand-washing and saying of Psalm 25: 6–12 after the offertory at Mass [L, I shall wash, fr *lavare*]

lavage /'lavij (*Fr* lava:ʒ)/ *n* the therapeutic washing of an organ [F, fr MF, fr *laver* to wash, fr L *lavare*]

lavation /la'vaysh(ə)n/ *n* washing, cleansing – fml [L *lavation-, lavatio,* fr *lavatus*] – **lavational** *adj*

lavatorial /ˌlavə'tawri·əl/ *adj* characterized by excessive reference to lavatories and (the bodily functions associated with) their use; *broadly;* vulgar ⟨~ *humour*⟩

lavatory /'lavətri/ *n* **1** a toilet **2** *NAm* a room with facilities for washing and usu with 1 or more toilets [ME *lavatorie* washbasin, fr ML *lavatorium,* fr L *lavatus,* pp of *lavare* to wash – more at LYE] – **lavatory** *adj*

'lavatory ˌpaper *n* TOILET PAPER

lave /layv/ *vt* to wash; BATHE 1 – poetic [ME *laven,* fr OE *lafian;* akin to OHG *labōn* to wash; both fr a prehistoric WGmc word borrowed fr L *lavare*]

lavender /'lavində/ *n* **1** a Mediterranean plant of the mint family widely cultivated for its narrow aromatic leaves and spikes of lilac-purple flowers which are dried and used in perfume sachets **2** pale purple [ME *lavendre,* fr AF, fr ML *lavandula*]

¹laver /'layvə/ *n* a large basin used for ceremonial ablutions in ancient Jewish worship [ME *lavour,* fr MF *lavoir*]

²laver *n* any of several mostly edible seaweeds [NL, fr L, a water plant]

¹lavish /'lavish/ *adj* **1** expending or bestowing profusely **2** expended, bestowed, or produced in abundance [ME *lavas* abundance, fr MF *lavasse* downpour of rain, fr *laver* to wash, fr L *lavare*] – **lavishly** *adj,* **lavishness** *n*

²lavish *vt* to expend or bestow with profusion

law /law/ *n* **1a(1)** a rule of conduct formally recognized as binding or enforced by authority **(2)** the whole body of such rules ⟨*the* ~ *of the land*⟩ 👁 **(3)** COMMON LAW **b** the control brought about by such law – esp in *law and order* **c** litigation ⟨*ready to go to* ~⟩ **2a** a rule one should observe **b** control, authority **3a** *often cap* the revelation of the will of God set out in the Old Testament **b** *cap* the first part of the Jewish scriptures; the Pentateuch **4** a rule of action, construction, or procedure ⟨*the* ~*s of poetry*⟩ **5** the law relating to one subject ⟨*company* ~⟩ **6** *often cap the* legal profession **7** jurisprudence **8a** a statement of an order or relation of natural phenomena ⟨*the first* ~ *of thermodynamics*⟩ ⟨*Boyle's* ~⟩ **b** a necessary relation between mathematical or logical expressions **9** *sing or pl in constr, often cap the* police – infml [ME, fr OE *lagu,* of Scand origin; akin to ON *lög* law, pl of *lag* layer, due place, order; akin to OE *licgan* to lie – more at ¹LIE] – **in/at law** according to the law – **law unto him-/her-/itself** sby or sthg that does not follow accepted conventions

'law-aˌbiding *adj* abiding by or obedient to the law

'lawˌbreaker /-ˌbraykə/ *n* one who violates the law – **lawbreaking** *adj or n*

lawful /'lawf(ə)l/ *adj* **1** allowed by law **2** rightful ⟨*your* ~ *Queen*⟩ – **lawfully** *adv,* **lawfulness** *n*

'lawˌgiver /-ˌgivə/ *n* sby who gives a code of laws to a people

lawks /lawks/ *interj, dial or archaic, Br* – used to express surprise [euphemism for *Lord*]

lawless /'lawlis/ *adj* **1** not regulated by or based on law **2** not restrained or controlled by law – **lawlessly** *adv,* **lawlessness** *n*

'Law ˌLord *n* a member of the House of Lords qualified to take part in its judicial proceedings

'lawˌmaker /-ˌmaykə/ *n* a legislator – **lawmaking** *n*

lawman /'lawˌman, -mən/ *n, NAm* a law-enforcement officer

lawmerchant *n, pl* **laws merchant** the legal rules formerly applied to commercial transactions [ME *lawe marchaund* (trans of ML *lex mercatoria*), fr *lawe* law + *marchaund, marchant,* adj, merchant]

¹lawn /lawn/ *n* a fine sheer linen or cotton fabric of plain weave that is thinner than cambric [ME, fr *Laon,* town in France] – **lawny** *adj*

²lawn *n* an area of ground (e g around a house or in a garden or park) that is covered with grass and is kept mowed [ME *launde,* fr MF *lande* heath, of Celt origin; akin to OIr *land* open space – more at LAND]

'lawn ˌmower *n* a machine for cutting grass on lawns

ˌlawn 'tennis *n* tennis played on a grass court ☞ SPORT

ˌlaw of 'averages *n the* principle that one extreme will be cancelled out by its opposite, and the balance redressed

'law ˌofficer *n* an official appointed to administer and interpret the law; *specif* a British attorney general or solicitor general

ˌlaw of 'nations *n* INTERNATIONAL LAW

ˌlaw of 'war *n* a code that governs the duties of belligerents

lawrencium /law'rensi·əm, lo-/ *n* a short-lived radioactive artificial element ☞ PERIODIC TABLE [NL, fr Ernest O *Lawrence* †1958 US physicist]

'lawˌsuit /-ˌs(y)ooht/ *n* a noncriminal case in a court of law

lawyer /'lawyə, 'loyə/ *n* sby whose profession is to conduct lawsuits or to advise on legal matters

lax /laks/ *adj* **1** *of the bowels* loose, open **2** not strict or stringent; negligent ⟨*~ morals*⟩ ⟨*~ in his duties*⟩; *also* deficient in firmness or precision ⟨*his ideas are a bit ~*⟩ **3a** not tense, firm, or rigid; slack ⟨*a ~ rope*⟩ **b** not compact or exhibiting close cohesion; loose ⟨*a ~ flower cluster*⟩ **4** *of a speech sound* articulated with the muscles in a relatively relaxed state (e g the vowel /i/ in contrast with the vowel /ee/) [ME, fr L *laxus* loose – more at SLACK] – **laxity, laxness** *n,* **laxly** *adv,* **laxation** /lak'saysh(ə)n/ *n*

laxative /'laksətiv/ *n or adj* (a usu mild purgative) having a tendency to loosen or relax the bowels (to relieve constipation) [adj ME *laxatif,* fr ML *laxativus,* fr L *laxatus,* pp of *laxare* to loosen, fr *laxus;* n fr adj] – **laxativeness** *n*

[1]**lay** /lay/ *vb* **laid** /layd/ *vt* **1** to beat or strike down with force ⟨*a blow that* laid *him to the ground*⟩ ⟨*wheat* laid *flat by the wind and rain*⟩ **2a** to put or set down **b** to place for rest or sleep; *esp* to bury **3** *of a bird* to produce (an egg) **4** to calm, allay ⟨*~ the dust*⟩ ⟨*~ a ghost*⟩ **5** to bet, wager ⟨*~ odds on the favourite*⟩ ⟨*~ my life on it*⟩ **6** to press down giving a smooth and even surface ⟨laid *tarmac on the road*⟩ **7a** to dispose or spread over or on a surface ⟨*~ a cloth on the table*⟩ **b** to set in order or position ⟨*~ a table for dinner*⟩ ⟨*~ bricks*⟩ **c** to put (strands) in place and twist to form a rope, hawser, or cable **8a** to put or impose as a duty, burden, or punishment – esp + *on* or *upon* **b** to put as a burden of reproach ⟨laid *the blame on him*⟩ **c** to advance as an accusation; impute ⟨*the disaster was* laid *to faulty inspection*⟩ ⟨laid *a charge of manslaughter*⟩ **9** to place (sthg immaterial) on sthg ⟨*~ stress on grammar*⟩ **10** to prepare, contrive ⟨*a well-*laid *plan*⟩ **11a** to bring into position or against or into contact with sthg ⟨laid *the watch to his ear*⟩ ⟨*the horse* laid *his ears back*⟩ **b** to prepare or position for action or operation ⟨*~ a fire in the fireplace*⟩ **c** to adjust (a gun) to the proper direction and elevation **12** to bring to a specified condition ⟨*~ waste the land*⟩ **13a** to assert, allege ⟨*~ claim to an estate*⟩ **b** to submit for examination and judgment ⟨laid *his case before the tribunal*⟩ **14** to place fictitiously; locate ⟨*the scene is* laid *in wartime London*⟩ **15** to put aside for future use; store, reserve – + *aside, by, in,* or *up* **16** to put out of use or consideration – + *aside* or *by* **17** to copulate with – slang *~ vi* **1** *esp of a hen* to produce eggs **2** to wager, bet **3** to apply oneself vigorously ⟨laid *to his oars*⟩ **4** [1]LIE – nonstandard [ME *leyen,* fr OE *lecgan;* akin to OE *licgan* to lie – more at [1]LIE] – **lay about one** to deal blows indiscriminately; lash out on all sides – **lay hands on 1** to seize forcibly **2** to find – **lay into** to attack with words or blows – **lay it on 1** to exaggerate, esp in order to flatter or impress ⟨*that was really* laying it on *a bit thick*⟩ **2** to charge an exorbitant price – **lay on the table** to make public; disclose – **lay low 1** to knock or bring down; *esp* destroy **2** to cause to be ill or physically weakened – **lay open** to expose: e g **a** to cut ⟨*a blow that* laid *his head* open⟩ **b** to explain or make known; UNCOVER 1 ⟨*the facts of the case were* laid *wide* open⟩ – **lay siege to 1** to besiege militarily **2** to attempt to conquer or persuade diligently or persistently

[2]**lay** *n* **1** (a partner in) sexual intercourse – slang **2** *chiefly NAm* the position or situation in which sthg lies, esp relative to sthg else ⟨*the ~ of the land*⟩ – **in lay** *esp of a hen* in condition to lay eggs

[3]**lay** *past of* LIE

[4]**lay** *n* a simple narrative poem intended to be sung; a ballad [ME, fr OF *lai*]

[5]**lay** *adj* **1** of or performed by the laity **2** of domestic or manual workers in a religious community ⟨*a ~ brother*⟩ **3** not belonging to a particular profession [ME, fr OF *lai,* fr LL *laicus,* fr Gk *laikos* of the people, fr *laos* people]

layabout /'layəbowt/ *n, chiefly Br* a lazy shiftless person

'lay-,by *n, pl* **lay-bys** *Br* a branch from or widening of a road to permit vehicles to stop without obstructing traffic

'lay ,day *n* a day allowed for loading or unloading a vessel

lay down *vt* **1** to surrender; GIVE UP ⟨laid down *her life for the cause*⟩ **2a** to begin to construct (e g a ship or railway) **b** to establish, prescribe; *esp* to dictate ⟨*~ the law*⟩ **3** to store; *specif* to store (wine) in a cellar

[1]**layer** /'layə/ *n* **1a** a single thickness of some substance spread or lying over or under another (as part of a series) **b** any of a series of gradations or depths ⟨*~s of meaning*⟩ **2a** a branch or shoot of a plant treated to induce rooting while still attached to the parent plant **b** a plant developed by layering [[1]LAY + [2]-ER]

[2]**layer** *vt* **1** to propagate (a plant) by means of layers **2** to cut (hair) in layers **3** to arrange or form (as if) in layers ⟨*potato slices ~ed with cheese*⟩ **4** to form out of or with layers *~ vi , of a plant* to form roots where a stem comes in contact with the ground

layette /lay'et/ *n* a complete outfit of clothing and equipment for a newborn infant [F, fr MF, dim. of *laye* box, fr MD *lade;* akin to MHG *lade* box, OE *hladan* to load – more at LADE]

lay figure *n* **1** a jointed model of the human body used by artists, esp to show the arrangement of drapery **2** a person likened to a dummy or puppet [obs *layman* (lay figure), fr D *leeman,* fr *lid* limb + *man* man]

layman /'laymən/, *fem* **'lay,woman** *n* **1** a person not of the clergy **2** a person without special (e g professional) knowledge of some field

'lay,off /-,of/ *n* **1** the laying off of an employee or work force **2** a period of unemployment, inactivity, or idleness

lay off *vt* **1** to cease to employ (a worker), usu temporarily **2a** to let alone **b** to avoid ⟨lay off *pastry and pud – The Times*⟩ *~ vi* to stop or desist, specif from an activity causing annoyance *USE* (*vt 2; vi*) infml

lay on *vt, chiefly Br* **1** to supply (e g water or gas) to a building **2** to supply; organize ⟨*cars were* laid on⟩ ⟨*they* laid on *a good meal*⟩

'lay,out /-,owt/ *n* **1** arranging or laying out **2** the plan, design, or arrangement of sthg (e g rooms in a building or matter to be printed) laid out **3** sthg laid out ⟨*a model train ~*⟩

lay out *vt* **1** to prepare (a corpse) for a funeral **2** to arrange according to a plan ⟨*flower beds and lawns were* laid out *in a formal pattern*⟩ **3** to knock flat or unconscious **4** to spend **5** to exert (oneself) for a purpose *USE* (*except 1 & 2*) infml

Making Laws

In the UK law is made by legislation or by case law.

Legislation
Supreme legislative authority is vested in Parliament and Bills must go through both houses and have the Royal Assent before they can become Acts of Parliament. Bills can be presented in either House, but usually start in the Commons. They may be presented on behalf of the government or by a private member, though fewer of the latter reach the statute book.
In the case of Public General Acts, the procedure is as follows:

COMMONS

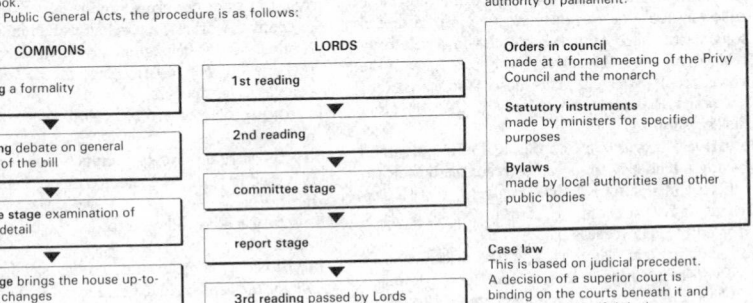

- **1st reading** a formality
- **2nd reading** debate on general principles of the bill
- **committee stage** examination of the bill in detail
- **report stage** brings the house up-to-date with changes
- **3rd reading** allows for minor changes only

LORDS

- **1st reading**
- **2nd reading**
- **committee stage**
- **report stage**
- **3rd reading** passed by Lords

Royal Assent the bill is now law as an Act of Parliament

Delegated legislation is made by subordinate authorities acting under the authority of parliament.

Orders in council
made at a formal meeting of the Privy Council and the monarch

Statutory instruments
made by ministers for specified purposes

Bylaws
made by local authorities and other public bodies

Case law
This is based on judicial precedent. A decision of a superior court is binding on the courts beneath it and sometimes on itself. It is the principle behind the decison which constitutes the binding precedent.

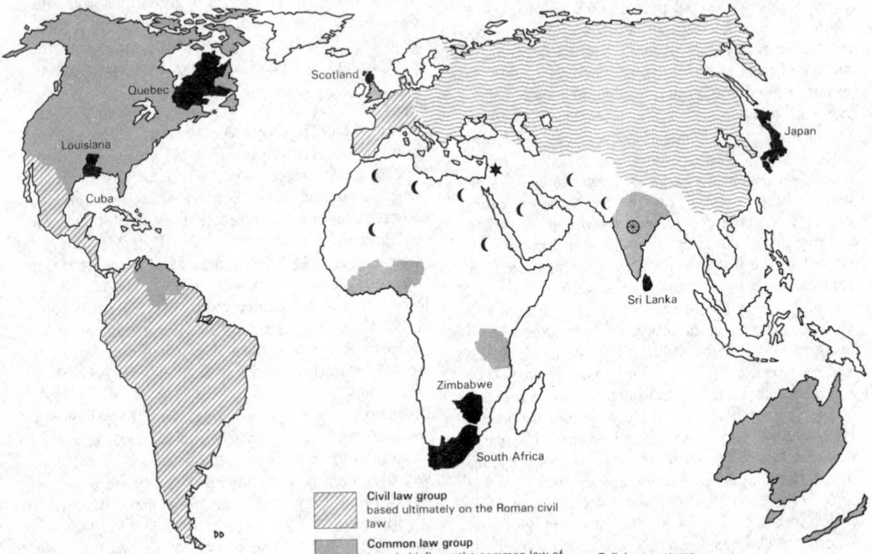

Civil law group
based ultimately on the Roman civil law

Common law group
based chiefly on the common law of England

Socialist group
new legal codes based upon Marxist philosophy, but with traces of civil law

Hybrid systems
basically civil law, but heavily influenced by common law ideas and rules

Religious systems
Religious systems may be influenced by the common law, civil law and/or socialist law.

- Islamic law
- Hindu law
- Jewish law

Systems of law
Comparative law studies have grouped the main world legal systems into families, whose members resemble each other in institutions and methods, usually as a result of a common history or borrowing.

Principal criminal courts

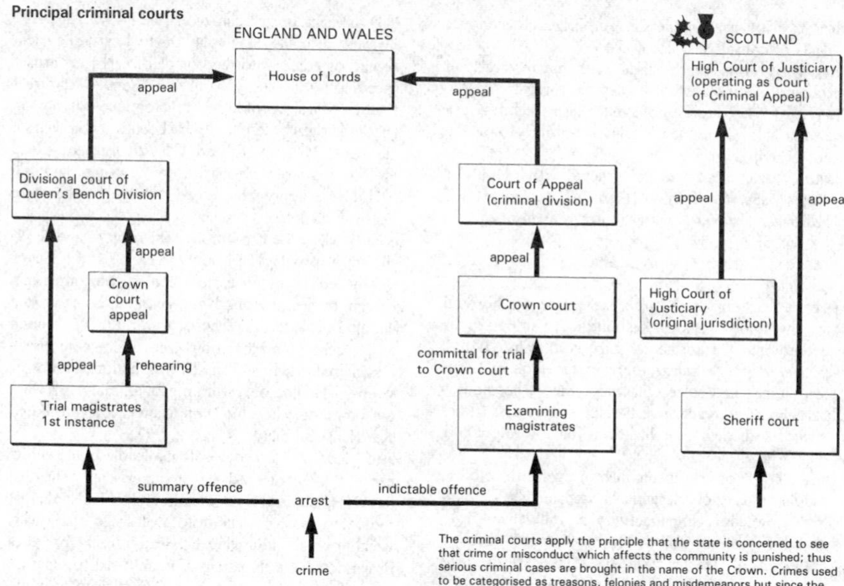

The criminal courts apply the principle that the state is concerned to see that crime or misconduct which affects the community is punished; thus serious criminal cases are brought in the name of the Crown. Crimes used to be categorised as treasons, felonies and misdemeanors but since the 1967 Criminal Law Act they have been divided only into arrestable and non-arrestable offences.

Principal civil courts

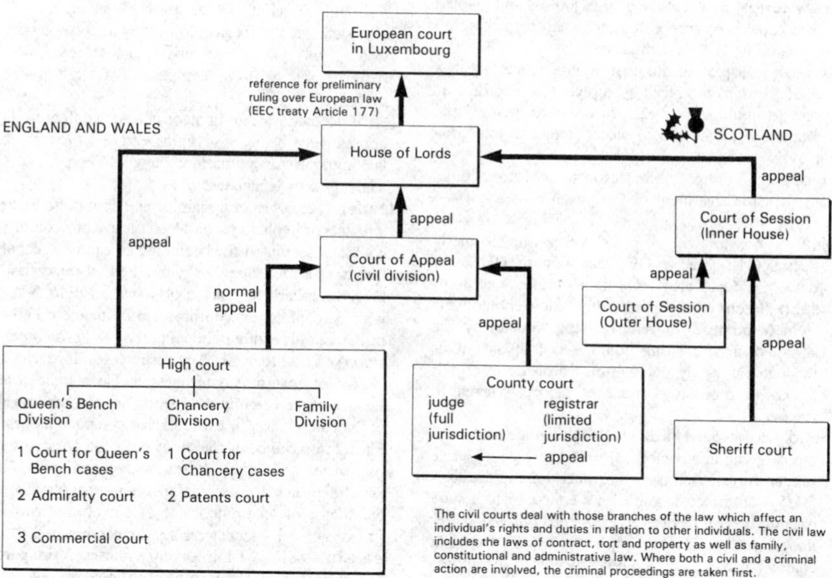

The civil courts deal with those branches of the law which affect an individual's rights and duties in relation to other individuals. The civil law includes the laws of contract, tort and property as well as family, constitutional and administrative law. Where both a civil and a criminal action are involved, the criminal proceedings are taken first.

lay reader *n* a lay person authorized to conduct parts of church services

lay shaft *n* an intermediate shaft that receives and transmits power, esp in a gearbox [prob fr [1]*lay*]

lay up *vt* **1** to store up; have or keep for future use **2** to disable or confine with illness or injury **3** to take out of active service

lazar /'lazə/ *n, archaic* one afflicted with a repulsive disease; *specif* a leper [ME, fr ML *lazarus,* fr LL *Lazarus,* beggar with sores mentioned in Lk 16:20]

lazaret /,lazə'ret/ *n* a lazaretto [F, fr It dial. *lazareto*]

lazaretto /,lazə'retoh/ *n, pl* **lazarettos** **1** a hospital for contagious diseases **2** a building or ship used for detention in quarantine **3** a ship's storeroom [It dial. *lazareto,* alter. of *nazareto,* fr *Santa Maria di Nazaret,* church in Venice that maintained a hospital]

laze /layz/ *vi* to act or rest lazily ~ *vt* to pass (time) *away* in idleness or relaxation [back-formation fr *lazy*] – **laze** *n*

lazy /'layzi/ *adj* **1a** disinclined or averse to activity; indolent; *also* not energetic or vigorous ⟨*a* ~ *manner*⟩ **b** encouraging inactivity or indolence ⟨*a* ~ *afternoon*⟩ **2** moving slowly ⟨*a* ~ *river*⟩ [perh fr MLG *lasich* feeble; akin to MHG *erleswen* to become weak, ON *lasinn* dilapidated] – **lazily** *adv,* **laziness** *n*

'lazy,bones /-,bohnz/ *n, pl* **lazybones** a lazy person – infml

lazy tongs *n* an arrangement of jointed and pivoted bars capable of great extension, used for picking up or handling sthg at a distance

LCD *n* a display of numbers, symbols, etc (e g in a digital watch) produced by applying an electric current to liquid crystal cells in order to increase the amount of light they reflect [*l*iquid *c*rystal *d*isplay]

L-dopa /,el 'dohpə/ *n* the laevorotatory form of dopa used in the treatment of Parkinson's disease [*l-* + *dopa*]

lea /lee/ *n* (an area of) grassland, pasture – chiefly poetic [ME *leye,* fr OE *lēah;* akin to OHG *lōh* thicket, L *lucus* grove, *lux* light – more at LIGHT]

leach /leech/ *vt* to separate the soluble components from (a mixture) or remove (sthg soluble) by the action of a percolating liquid ~ *vi* to pass out or through (as if) by percolation [prob deriv of OE *leccan* to moisten – more at LEAK] – **leach** *n,* **leacher** *n*

[1]**lead** /leed/ *vb* **led** /led/ *vt* **1a(1)** to guide on a way, esp by going in advance **(2)** to cause to go with one (under duress) ⟨led *the condemned man to the scaffold*⟩ **b** to direct or guide on a course or to a state or condition; influence ⟨*reflection* led *him to a better understanding of the problem*⟩ **c** to serve as a channel or route for ⟨*a pipe* ~s *water to the house*⟩ ⟨*the road* led *her to a small village*⟩ **2** to go through; live ⟨~ *a quiet life*⟩ **3a(1)** to direct the operations, activity, or performance of; have charge of ⟨led *a safari into little known territory*⟩ **(2)** to act as or be a leader in or of ⟨~ *fashion*⟩ ⟨~ *an orchestra*⟩ **b** to go or be at the head or ahead of **4** to begin play, esp at a card game, with ~ *vi* **1a(1)** to guide sby or sthg along a way **(2)** to act as or be a leader **b(1)** to lie or run in a specified place or direction ⟨*the path* ~s *uphill*⟩ **(2)** to serve as an entrance or passage ⟨*this door* ~s *to the garden*⟩ **2a** to be first or ahead **b(1)** to begin, open – usu + *off* ⟨led *off with a speech by the chairman*⟩ **(2)** to play the first card of a trick, round, or game **3** to tend or be directed towards a specified result ⟨*study* ~ing *to a degree*⟩ **4** to direct the first of a series of blows at an opponent in boxing (*with* the right or left hand) [ME *leden,* fr OE *lǣdan;* akin to OHG *leiten* to lead, OE *līthan* to go] – **lead up to** to prepare the way for, esp by using a gradual or indirect approach – **lead someone a dance** to cause sby a lot of trouble

[2]**lead** /leed/ *n* **1a(1)** position at the front or ahead **(2)** the act or privilege of leading in cards; *also* the card or suit led **b** guidance, direction; (an) example **c** a margin or position of advantage or superiority **2a** a channel of water **(1)** leading to a mill **(2)** through an ice field **b** an indication, clue **c** (one who plays) a principal role in a dramatic production **d** a line or strap for leading or restraining an animal (e g a dog) **e** a news story of chief importance **3** an insulated electrical conductor **4** [4]PITCH 2b(2)

[3]**lead** /led/ *n* **1** a heavy soft malleable bluish-white metallic element used esp in pipes, cable sheaths, batteries, solder, type metal, and shields against radioactivity ☞ PERIODIC TABLE **2a** the (lead) weight on a sounding line **b** *pl* lead framing for panes in windows **c** a thin strip of metal used to separate lines of type in printing **3a** a thin stick of graphite or crayon in or for a pencil **b** WHITE LEAD **4** bullets, projectiles ⟨*the* ~ *was flying*⟩ **5** *pl, Br* (a usu flat roof covered with) thin lead sheets [ME *leed,* fr OE *lēad;* akin to MHG *lōt* lead] – **leadless** *adj*

[4]**lead** /led/ *vt* **1** to fix (window glass) in position with leads **2** to separate lines of (type) with leads **3** to treat or mix with (a compound of) lead ⟨~ed *petrol*⟩

leaden /'led(ə)n/ *adj* **1a** made of lead **b** dull grey **2a** oppressively heavy ⟨~ *limbs*⟩ ⟨*a* ~ *silence*⟩ **b** lacking spirit or animation; sluggish ⟨~ *prose*⟩ – **leadenly** *adv,* **leadenness** *n*

leader /'leedə/ *n* **1a** a main or end shoot of a plant **b** *pl* dots or hyphens used to lead the eye horizontally **c** a blank section at the beginning or end of a reel of film or recorded tape **2a** sby or sthg that ranks first, precedes others, or holds a principal position **b** sby who has commanding authority or influence **c(1)** the principal officer of a political party ⟨~ *of the opposition*⟩ **(2)** either of 2 government ministers in charge of government business in Parliament ⟨*the* Leader *of the Commons*⟩ **(3)** the principal member of the ruling party in a totalitarian system **3** a horse placed in advance of the other horse or horses of a pair or team **4** *chiefly Br* a newspaper editorial **5a** *Br* the principal first violinist and usu assistant conductor of an orchestra **b** *NAm* CONDUCTOR 2 [[1]LEAD + [2]-ER] – **leaderless** *adj,* **leadership** *n*

'lead-,in /leed/ *n* **1** introductory matter **2** the part of the groove on a record before the recording

[1]**leading** /'leeding/ *adj* coming or ranking first; foremost, principal ⟨*the* ~ *role*⟩

[2]**leading** /'leding/ *n* [3]LEAD 2c; *also* a space between printed lines made (as if) with a lead

leading aircraftman /'leeding/ *n* ☞ RANK

leading article *n, chiefly Br* LEADER 4

leading case *n* a legal case which establishes a precedent

leading edge *n* the foremost edge of an aerofoil (e g a propeller blade or wing)

ˌleading ˈlady, *masc* **leading man** *n* an actress who plays the female lead in a film, play, etc

ˌleading ˈlight *n* a prominent and influential person in a particular sphere

leading note *n* the seventh note of a diatonic scale

ˌleading ˈquestion *n* a question so phrased as to suggest the expected answer

ˈleading ˌreins *n pl* straps by which children are supported when beginning to walk

ˌleading ˈseaman *n* ☞ RANK

ˈleading ˌstrings *n pl* **1** LEADING REINS **2** a state of unnecessary or prolonged dependence – chiefly in *in leading strings*

ˈlead-ˌoff /leed/ *n* a beginning or leading action; a start

lead on *vt* **1** to entice or induce to proceed in a (mistaken or unwise) course **2** to cause to believe sthg that is untrue

ˌlead ˈpencil /led/ *n* a pencil containing a graphite lead

leadscrew /ˈleed,skrooh/ *n* a screw that moves the carriage of a lathe

leadsman /ˈledzmən/ *n* a man who uses a sounding lead to determine depth of water

ˈlead ˌtime /leed/ *n* the period between the initiation and the completion of a new production process

[1]leaf /leef/ *n, pl* **leaves** /leevz/ **1a(1)** any of the usu green flat and typically broad-bladed outgrowths from the stem of a plant that function primarily in food manufacture by photosynthesis ☞ PLANT **(2)** a modified leaf (e g a petal or sepal) **b(1)** (the state of having) foliage ⟨*in* ~⟩ **(2)** the leaves of a plant (e g tobacco) as an article of commerce **2a** a part of a book or folded sheet of paper containing a page on each side **b(1)** a part (e g of a window shutter, folding door, or table) that slides or is hinged – compare DROP LEAF **(2)** a section that can be inserted into a tabletop to extend it **c(1)** a thin sheet of metal, marble, etc **(2)** metal (e g gold or silver) in sheets, usu thinner than foil [ME *leef*, fr OE *lēaf*; akin to OHG *loub* leaf, L *liber* bast, book, Skt *lumpati* he injures, robs] – **leafless** *adj*, **leaflike** *adj*

[2]leaf *vi* to shoot out or produce leaves – **leaf through** to turn over the pages of (e g a book) quickly while only glancing at the contents

leafage /ˈleefij/ *n* FOLIAGE 1

ˈleaf ˌcurl *n* a plant disease characterized by curling of the leaves

-leafed *comb form* (*adj* → *adj*) -leaved

ˈleafˌhopper /-ˌhopə/ *n* any of numerous small leaping insects that suck the juices of plants

leaflet /ˈleeflit/ *n* **1a** any of the divisions of a compound leaf **b** a small or young foliage leaf **2** a single sheet of paper or small loose-leaf pamphlet containing printed matter (e g advertising)

ˈleaf ˌminer *n* any of various small insects that as larvae burrow in and eat the internal tissues of leaves

ˈleaf ˌmould *n* a compost or soil layer composed chiefly of decayed vegetable matter

leaf shutter *n* a shutter for a camera made of usu 5 thin metallic leaves that swing out of the light path when a picture is taken

ˈleaf ˌspring *n* a spring made of superimposed metal strips

ˈleafˌstalk /-ˌstawk/ *n* a petiole

leafy /ˈleefi/ *adj* **1** having or thick with leaves ⟨~ *woodlands*⟩ **2** consisting chiefly of leaves ⟨*green* ~ *vegetables*⟩ – **leafiness** *n*

[1]league /leeg/ *n* any of various units of distance of about 3mi (5km) ☞ UNIT [ME *leuge, lege*, fr LL *leuga, leuca*, of Gaulish origin]

[2]league *n* **1a** an association of nations, groups, or people for a common purpose or to promote a common interest **b** (a competition for an overall title, in which each person or team plays all the others at least once, held by) an association of people or sports clubs **2** a class, category ⟨*the top* ~⟩ [ME (Sc) *ligg*, fr MF *ligue*, fr OIt *liga*, fr *ligare* to bind, fr L – more at LIGATURE] – **leaguer** *n* – **in league** in alliance

[3]league *vb* to form into a league

leaguer /ˈleegə/ *n* a laager [D *leger*; akin to OHG *legar* act of lying down, bed – more at [1]LAIR]

league table *n* a table showing the relative positions of competitors in a league; *broadly* a list in order of merit

[1]leak /leek/ *vi* **1** to (let a substance) enter or escape through a crack or hole **2** to become known despite efforts at concealment – often + *out* ~ *vt* **1** to permit to enter or escape (as if) through a leak **2** to give out (information) surreptitiously ⟨~ed *the story to the press*⟩ [ME *leken*, fr ON *leka*; akin to OE *leccan* to moisten, OIr *legaim* I melt] – **leakage** *n*

[2]leak *n* **1a** a crack or hole through which sthg (e g a fluid) is admitted or escapes, usu by mistake **b** a means by which sthg (e g secret information) is admitted or escapes, usu with prejudicial effect **c** a loss of electricity due to faulty insulation **2** a leaking or that which is leaked; *esp* a disclosure **3** an act of urinating – slang

leaky /ˈleeki/ *adj* permitting fluid, information, etc to leak in or out; *broadly* not watertight ⟨*a* ~ *argument*⟩ – **leakiness** *n*

leal /leel/ *adj, chiefly Scot* loyal, true [ME *leel*, fr OF *leial, leel* – more at LOYAL] – **leally** *adv*

[1]lean /leen/ *vb* **leant** /lent/, **leaned** /leend, lent/ *vi* **1a** to incline or bend from a vertical position ⟨~t *forward to look*⟩ **b** to rest supported *on/against* sthg **2** to rely for support or inspiration – + *on* or *upon* **3** to incline in opinion, taste, etc **4** to exert pressure; use coercion – + *on*; infml ~ *vt* to place *on/against* for support [ME *lenen*, fr OE *hleonian*; akin to OHG *hlinēn* to lean, Gk *klinein*, L *clinare*] – **lean** *n*

[2]lean *adj* **1a** lacking or deficient in flesh or bulk **b** *of meat* containing little or no fat **2** lacking richness, sufficiency, or value **3a** deficient in an essential or important quality or ingredient **b** *esp of a fuel mixture* low in the combustible component [ME *lene*, fr OE *hlǣne*] – **leanly** *adv*, **leanness** *n*

[3]lean *n* the part of meat that consists principally of fat-free muscular tissue

leaning /ˈleening/ *n* a definite but weak attraction, tendency, or partiality

ˈlean-ˌto *n, pl* **lean-tos** a small building having a roof that rests on the side of a larger building or wall

[1]leap /leep/ *vb* **leapt** /lept/, **leaped** /leept, lept/ *vi* **1** to jump in or through the air **2a** to pass abruptly from one state or topic to another; *esp* to rise quickly ⟨*the idea* ~t *into his mind*⟩ **b** to seize eagerly *at* an opportunity, offer, etc ~ *vt* to pass over by leaping [ME *lepen*, fr OE *hlēapan*; akin to OHG *hlouffan* to run, ON *hlaupa* to jump, leap] – **leaper** *n*

[2]leap *n* **1a** (the distance covered by) a jump **b** a place leapt over or from **2** a sudden transition, esp a rise or increase

[1]**'leap,frog** /-,frog/ *n* a game in which one player bends down and another leaps over him/her

[2]**leapfrog** *vb* **-gg-** **1** to leap (over) (as if) in leapfrog **2** to go ahead of (each other) in turn

'leap ,year *n* a year with an extra day added to make it coincide with the solar year; *esp* a year in the Gregorian calendar with February 29 as the 366th day [prob fr the 'leap" made by any date after February in a leap year over the weekday on which it would normally fall]

learn /luhn/ *vb* **learnt** /luhnt/, **learned** /luhnd, luhnt/ *vt* **1a(1)** to gain knowledge of or skill in ⟨~ *a trade*⟩ **(2)** to memorize ⟨~ *the lines of a play*⟩ **b** to come to be able – + infinitive ⟨~ *to dance*⟩ **c** to come to realize or know ⟨*we* ~ed *that he was ill*⟩ **2** to teach – substandard ~ *vi* to acquire knowledge or skill [ME *lernen*, fr OE *leornian*; akin to OHG *lernēn* to learn, L *lira* furrow, track] – **learnable** *adj*, **learner** *n*

learned /'luhnid; *sense 2* luhnd/ *adj* **1** characterized by or associated with learning; erudite **2** acquired by learning ⟨~ *versus innate behaviour patterns*⟩ – **learnedly** /-nidli/ *adv*, **learnedness** /-nidnis/ *n*

learning /'luhning/ *n* **1** acquired knowledge or skill **2** modification of a behavioural tendency by experience (e g exposure to conditioning)

[1]**lease** /lees/ *n* **1** a contract putting the land or property of one party at the disposal of another, usu for a stated period and rent **2** a (prospect of) continuance – chiefly in *lease of life*

[2]**lease** *vt* to grant by or hold under lease [AF *lesser*, fr OF *laissier* to let go, fr L *laxare* to loosen, fr *laxus* slack – more at SLACK]

'lease,hold /-,hohld/ *n* tenure by or property held by lease – **leaseholder** *n*

leash /leesh/ *n* **1a** [2]LEAD 2d **b** a restraint, check **2** a set of 3 animals (e g greyhounds, foxes, or hares) [ME *lees, leshe*, fr OF *laisse*, fr *laissier*] – **leash** *vt*

[1]**least** /leest/ *adj* **1** lowest in rank, degree, or importance **2a** smallest in quantity or extent **b** being (of) a kind distinguished by small size ⟨~ *bittern*⟩ **c** smallest possible; slightest ⟨*haven't the* ~ *idea*⟩ [ME *leest*, fr OE *lǣst*, superl of *lǣssa* less] – **at least** **1** as a minimum; if not more ⟨*costs* at least *£5*⟩ **2** if nothing else; IN ANY CASE ⟨at least *it is legal*⟩

[2]**least** *n* the smallest quantity, number, or amount ⟨*it's the* ~ *I can do*⟩ ⟨*to say the* ~⟩ – **least of all** especially not ⟨*no one,* least of all *the children paid attention*⟩

[3]**least** *adv* to the smallest degree or extent ⟨least-*known*⟩ ⟨*when we* ~ *expected it*⟩

least squares *n pl* a method of fitting a curve to a set of points representing statistical data in such a way that the sum of the squares of the distances of the points from the curve is a minimum

'least,ways /-,wayz/, **leastwise** /-wiez/ *adv, chiefly dial* AT LEAST 2

[1]**leather** /'ledhə/ *n* **1** animal skin dressed for use **2** sthg wholly or partly made of leather; *esp* a piece of chamois, used esp for polishing metal or glass [ME *lether*, fr OE *lether-*; akin to OHG *leder* leather]

[2]**leather** *vt* to beat with a strap; thrash

Leatherette /,ledhə'ret/ *trademark* – used for an imitation leather

'leather,jacket /-jakit/ *n, chiefly Br* the larva of the crane fly

leathern /'ledhən/ *adj* made of or resembling leather

'leather,neck /-,nek/ *n* MARINE 2 – slang; used esp by sailors [fr the leather neckband formerly part of the uniform]

leathery /'ledhəri/ *adj* resembling leather in appearance or consistency; *esp* tough

[1]**leave** /leev/ *vb* **left** /left/ *vt* **1a(1)** to bequeath **(2)** to have (esp members of one's family) remaining after one's death **b** to cause to remain as an aftereffect **2a** to cause or allow to be or remain in a specified or unaltered condition ⟨*his manner* left *me cold*⟩ ⟨~ *the washing-up for tomorrow*⟩ **b** to fail to include, use, or take along ⟨left *his notes at home*⟩ – sometimes + *off* or *out* ⟨left *his name off the list*⟩ **c** to have remaining or as a remainder ⟨*10 from 12* ~s *2*⟩ **d** to permit to be or remain subject to the action or control of a specified person or thing ⟨*just* ~ *everything to me*⟩ ⟨*nothing* left *to chance*⟩ **e** to allow to do or continue sthg without interference ⟨~ *you to take care of things*⟩ **3a** to go away from ⟨*told him to* ~ *the room*⟩ **b** to desert, abandon ⟨left *his wife*⟩ **c** to withdraw from ⟨left *school at 15*⟩ **4** to put, station, deposit, or deliver, esp before departing ⟨*the postman* left *a package for you*⟩ ⟨~ *your name with the receptionist*⟩ ~ *vi* to depart; SET OUT [ME *leven*, fr OE *lǣfan*; akin to OHG ver*leiben* to leave, OE be*līfan* to be left over, Gk *lipos* fat] – **leaver** *n* – **leave alone/be** LET ALONE/BE – **leave go** LET GO – **leave well alone** to avoid meddling

[2]**leave** *n* **1** permission to do sthg **2** authorized (extended) absence (e g from employment) [ME *leve*, fr OE *lēaf*; akin to MHG *loube* permission, OE a*lȳfan* to allow – more at BELIEVE]

-leaved /-leevd/ *comb form* (*adj* → *adj*) having (such or so many) leaves ⟨*palmate*-leaved⟩ ⟨*4*-leaved *clover*⟩

[1]**leaven** /'lev(ə)n/ *n* **1** a substance (e g yeast) used to produce fermentation or a gas in dough, batter, etc to lighten it; *esp* a mass of fermenting dough reserved for this purpose **2** sthg that modifies or lightens [ME *levain*, fr MF, fr (assumed) VL *levamen*, fr L *levare* to raise – more at LEVER]

[2]**leaven** *vt* to raise or make lighter (as if) with a leaven

leave off *vb* to stop, cease

leaves /leevs/ *pl of* leaf

'leave-,taking *n* a departure, farewell

leavings /'leevingz/ *n pl* remains, residue

Lebanese /,lebə'neez/ *n or adj, pl* **Lebanese** /~/ (a native or inhabitant) of the Lebanon [*Lebanon*, country in SW Asia]

lebensraum /'layb(ə)nz,rowm/ *n, often cap* territory necessary for national existence or self-sufficiency – used chiefly with reference to land Nazi Germany attempted to take in WW II [G, fr *leben* living, life + *raum* space]

lecher /'lechə/ *n* a man who engages in lechery [ME *lechour*, fr OF *lecheor*, fr *lechier* to lick, live in debauchery, of Gmc origin; akin to OHG *leckōn* to lick – more at LICK]

lechery /'lechəri/ *n* inordinate indulgence in sexual activity; debauchery, lasciviousness – **lecherous** *adj*, **lecherously** *adv*

lecithin /'lesəthin/ *n* any of several waxy compounds that are widely distributed in animals and plants and have emulsifying, wetting, and antioxidant properties [ISV, fr Gk *lekithos* yolk of an egg]

lectern /ˈlekˌtuhn/ *n* a reading desk; *esp* one from which the Bible is read in church [ME *lettorne*, fr MF *letrun*, fr ML *lectorinum*, fr L *lector* reader, fr *lectus*, pp of *legere* to read – more at LEGEND]

lection /ˈleksh(ə)n/ *n* a variant reading in a particular copy or edition of a text [NL *lection-*, *lectio*, fr L, act of reading, fr *lectus*]

lectionary /ˈleksh(ə)nri/ *n* a book or list of scriptural texts proper to each day of the church year [ML *lectionarium*, fr LL *lection-*, *lectio* liturgical lesson for a particular day, fr L, act of reading]

lector /ˈlektaw/ *n* the reader of a lesson in a church service [LL, fr L, reader]

¹lecture /ˈlekchə/ *n* **1** a discourse given to an audience, esp for instruction **2** a reproof delivered at length; a reprimand [ME, act of reading, fr MF, fr LL *lectura*, fr L *lectus*, pp]

²lecture *vi* to deliver a lecture or series of lectures ~ *vt* **1** to deliver a lecture to **2** to reprove at length or severely – **lecturer** *n*

ˈlectureship /-ship/ *n* the office of an academic lecturer

led /led/ *past of* LEAD

LED /ˌel ˌee ˈdee; *also* led/ *n* a diode that emits light when an electric current is passed through it and that is used esp to display numbers, symbols, etc on a screen (e g in a pocket calculator) ☞ TELECOMMUNICATION [*l*ight-*e*mitting *d*iode]

lederhosen /ˈlaydəˌhohz(ə)n/ *n pl in constr, pl* **lederhosen** traditional leather shorts that often have braces and are worn esp in Bavaria ☞ GARMENT [G, fr MHG *lederhose*, fr *leder* leather + *hose* trousers]

ledge /lej/ *n* **1** a (narrow) horizontal surface that projects from a vertical or steep surface (e g a wall or rock face) **2** an underwater ridge or reef **3** a mineral-bearing lode or vein [ME *legge* bar of a gate, prob fr *leggen* to lay] – **ledgy** *adj*

¹ledger /ˈlejə/ *n* **1** a book containing (the complete record of all) accounts **2** a horizontal piece of timber secured to the uprights of scaffolding [ME *legger*, prob fr *leyen*, *leggen* to lay]

²ledger *vi* to fish with ledger tackle

ˈledger ˌline, leger line *n* a short line added above or below a musical staff to extend its range ☞ MUSIC

ˈledger ˌtackle *n* fishing tackle arranged so that the weight and bait rest on the bottom

lee /lee/ *n* **1** protecting shelter **2 lee, lee side** the side (e g of a ship) sheltered from the wind [ME, fr OE *hlēo*; akin to OFris *hlī* protection, shelter, OHG *lāo* lukewarm, L *calēre* to be warm]

ˈleeˌboard /-ˌbawd/ *n* either of 2 movable flat surfaces attached to the outside of the hull of a sailing vessel that reduce leeway when lowered

¹leech /leech/ *n* **1** any of numerous flesh-eating or bloodsucking usu freshwater worms **2** one who gains or seeks to gain profit or advantage from another, esp by clinging persistently **3** *archaic* a physician, surgeon [ME *leche* physician, fr OE *lǣce*; akin to OHG *lāhhi* physician; (1) prob fr its former use by physicians for bleeding patients]

²leech *vt* to bleed by the use of leeches

³leech *n* **1** either vertical edge of a square sail **2** the rear edge of a fore-and-aft sail *USE* ☞ SHIP [ME *leche*, fr MLG *līk* boltrope; akin to MHG ge*leich* joint – more at LIGATURE]

Lee-Enfield /ˌlee ˈenfeeld/ *n* a magazine-fed British military rifle [James P *Lee* †1904 US (Sc-born) designer + *Enfield*, district of London]

leek /leek/ *n* a biennial plant of the lily family grown for its mildly pungent leaves and esp for its thick edible stalk [ME, fr OE *lēac*; akin to OHG *louh* leek, ON *laukr* leek, garlic]

leer /liə/ *vi or n* (to give) a lascivious, knowing, or sly look [prob fr obs *leer* (cheek), fr ME *ler*, *lere*, fr OE *hlēor*; akin to OS *hleor* cheek, ON *hlȳr*]

lees /leez/ *n pl* the sediment of a liquor (e g wine) during fermentation and aging [ME *lie*, fr MF, fr ML *lia*]

lee shore *n* a shore lying off a ship's lee side

lee side *n* LEE 2

¹leeward /ˈleewood; *naut* ˈlooh·əd/ *adj or adv* in or facing the direction towards which the wind is blowing – compare WINDWARD

²leeward *n* LEE 2

ˈleeˌway /-ˌway/ *n* **1** off-course sideways movement of a ship in the direction of the wind **2a** an allowable margin of freedom or variation; tolerance **b** a margin of shortcoming in performance ⟨*she has a lot of ~ to make up after her absence*⟩

¹left /left/ *adj* **1a** of, situated on, or being the side of the body in which most of the heart is located **b(1)** located nearer to the left hand than to the right; *esp* located on the left hand when facing in the same direction as an observer ⟨*the ~ wing of an army*⟩ **(2)** located on the left when facing downstream ⟨*the ~ bank of a river*⟩ **2** *often cap* of the Left in politics [ME, fr OE, weak; akin to MLG *lucht* left; fr the left hand's being the weaker in most people] – **left** *adv*

²left *n* **1a** (a blow struck with) the left hand **b** the location or direction of the left side **c** the part on the left side **2** *sing or pl in constr, often cap* the members of a European legislative body occupying the left of a legislative chamber as a result of holding more radical political views than other members **3** *sing or pl in constr* **a** *cap* those professing socialist or radical political views **b** *often cap* LEFT WING 1

³left *past of* LEAVE

left atrioventricular valve /ˌaytriohvenˈtrikyoolə/ *n* BICUSPID VALVE

ˈleft-ˌback *n* a fullback playing on the left side of the pitch in a traditional soccer lineup ☞ SPORT

ˌLeft ˈBank *n* the bohemian district of Paris situated on the left bank of the Seine [trans of F *Rive Gauche*]

ˌleft-ˈhalf *n* a halfback playing on the left side of the pitch in a traditional soccer lineup ☞ SPORT

ˌleft-ˈhand *adj* **1** situated on the left **2** left-handed

ˌleft-ˈhanded *adj* **1** using the left hand habitually or more easily than the right; *also* swinging from left to right ⟨*a ~ batsman*⟩ **2** of, designed for, or done with the left hand **3** morganatic **4** clumsy, awkward **5** ambiguous, double-edged ⟨*a ~ compliment*⟩ **6** anticlockwise – used of a twist, rotary motion, or spiral curve as viewed from a given direction with respect to the axis of rotation – **left-handed, left-handedly** *adv*, **left-handedness** *n*

ˌleft-ˈhander *n* **1** a left-handed person **2** a blow struck with the left hand

leftism /ˈlefˌtiz(ə)m/ *n, often cap* (advocacy of) the principles and policy of the Left – **leftist** *n or adj*

,left-'luggage *adj, Br* of or for the storing of luggage for safekeeping

'left,over /-,ohvə/ *n* an unused or unconsumed residue; *esp* leftover food – often pl – **leftover** *adj*

leftward /'leftwood/ *adj* towards or on the left

'leftwards, *chiefly NAm* **leftward** *adv* towards the left

,left 'wing *n sing or pl in constr* **1** *often cap L&W* the more socialist division of a group or party **2** *cap L&W* LEFT 3a – **left-wing** *adj,* **left-winger** *n*

lefty /'lefti/ *n* a left-winger – infml

[1]**leg** /leg/ *n* **1** a limb of an animal used esp for supporting the body and for walking: e g **a** (an artificial replacement for) either of the lower limbs of a human **b** a (hind) leg of a meat animal, esp above the hock ☞ MEAT **c** any of the appendages on each segment of an arthropod (e g an insect or spider) used in walking and crawling **2a** a pole or bar serving as a support or prop ⟨*the* ~s *of a tripod*⟩⟨*a table* ~⟩ **b** a branch of a forked or jointed object ⟨*the* ~s *of a compass*⟩ **3** the part of a garment that covers (part of) the leg **4** either side of a triangle as distinguished from the base or hypotenuse **5a** LEG SIDE **b** a fielding position in cricket on the leg side of the pitch – usu in combination ⟨*fine* ~⟩⟨*short* ~⟩ ☞ SPORT **6a** the course and distance sailed on a single tack **b** a portion of a trip; a stage **c** the part of a relay race run by 1 competitor **d** any of a set of events or games that must all be won to decide a competition [ME, fr ON *leggr*; akin to OE *līra* muscle, calf, L *lacertus* muscle, upper arm] – **a leg to stand on** the least support or basis for one's position, esp in a controversy – **on one's last legs** at or near the end of one's resources; on the verge of failure, exhaustion, or ruin

[2]**leg** *vi* **-gg-** – **leg it** to walk or run fast; *esp* to hurry

[3]**leg** *adj* **1** *esp of a ball bowled in cricket* moving or tending to move in the direction of the off side ⟨*a* ~ *break*⟩ **2** in, on, through, or towards the leg side of a cricket field ⟨*the* ~ *stump*⟩

legacy /'legəsi/ *n* **1** a gift by will; a bequest **2** sthg passed on or remaining from an ancestor or predecessor or from the past ⟨*the bitter* ~ *of 2 world wars*⟩ [ME *legacie* office of a legate, bequest, fr MF or ML; MF, office of a legate, fr ML *legatia*, fr L *legatus*]

legal /'leegl/ *adj* **1** of law **2a** deriving authority from law **b** established by or having a formal status derived from law **3** permitted by law **4** recognized in common law as distinguished from equity [ME, fr MF, fr L *legalis*, fr *leg-*, *lex* law] – **legalize** *vt,* **legally** *adv,* **legalization** /-ie'zaysh(ə)n/ *n*

,legal 'aid *n* payments from public funds to those who cannot afford legal advice or representation

,legal 'fiction *n* an assertion recognized by the law as fictitious but accepted for convenience as true

'legal,ism /-,iz(ə)m/ *n* strict or excessive conformity to the law or to a (moral) code – **legalist** *n,* **legalistic** /-'istik/ *adj,* **legalistically** *adv*

legality /li'galəti/ *n* **1** lawfulness **2** *pl* the requirements and procedures of the law

,legal 'tender *n* currency which a creditor is bound by law to accept as payment of a money debt

legate /'legət/ *n* an official delegate or representative [ME, fr OF & L; OF *legat*, fr L *legatus* deputy, emissary, fr pp of *legare* to depute, send as emissary, bequeath, fr *leg-*, *lex*] – **legateship** *n,* **legatine** /'legə,tien, ,-teen/ *adj*

legatee /,legə'tee/ *n* one to whom a legacy is bequeathed

legation /li'gaysh(ə)n/ *n* (the official residence of) a diplomatic mission in a foreign country headed by a minister [ME *legacioun*, fr MF & L; MF *legation*, fr L *legation-*, *legatio*, fr *legatus*]

legato /li'gahtoh/ *n, adv, or adj, pl* **legatos** (a manner of performing or passage of music performed) in a smooth and connected manner [It, lit., tied]

,leg before 'wicket *adj, of a batsman in cricket* out because of having obstructed with a part of the body, esp the legs, a ball that would otherwise have hit the wicket

'leg ,bye *n* a run scored in cricket after the ball has touched a part of the batsman's body but not his bat or hands – compare BYE, EXTRA

legend /'lej(ə)nd/ *n* **1a(1)** a story coming down from the past; *esp* one popularly regarded as historical **(2)** a body of such stories ⟨*a character in Celtic* ~⟩ **b** a person, act, or thing that inspires legends ⟨*a* ~ *in her own lifetime*⟩ **2a** an inscription or title on an object (e g a coin) **b** CAPTION 2 **c** the key to a map, chart, etc [ME *legende*, fr MF & ML; MF *legende*, fr ML *legenda*, fr L, fem of *legendus*, gerundive of *legere* to gather, select, read; akin to Gk *legein* to gather, say, *logos* speech, word, reason] – **legendry** /-dri/ *n*

legendary /'lejənd(ə)ri/ *adj* (characteristic) of (a) legend; *esp* told of in legend

legerdemain /,lejədə'man, -'mayn/ *n* **1** SLEIGHT OF HAND **2** a display of artful skill, trickery, or adroitness ⟨*political* ~⟩ [ME, fr MF *leger de main* light of hand]

'leger ,line /'lejə/ *n* LEDGER LINE

-legged /-'legid; *also* -'legd/ *comb form* (*adj* → *adj*) having (such or so many) legs ⟨*a 4-legged animal*⟩

legging /'leging/ *n* a closely fitting covering (e g of leather) that reaches from the ankle to the knee or thigh

leggy /'legi/ *adj* **1** having disproportionately long legs ⟨*a* ~ *colt*⟩ **2** *esp of a woman* having attractively long legs **3** *of a plant* spindly

leghorn /'leg,hawn; *sense 2* le'gawn/ *n* **1** (a hat of) fine plaited straw made from an Italian wheat **2** *cap* any of a Mediterranean breed of small hardy domestic fowls [*Leghorn* (Livorno), port in Italy from where the straw was exported]

legible /'lejəbl/ *adj* capable of being read or deciphered ⟨~ *handwriting*⟩ [ME, fr LL *legibilis*, fr L *legere* to read] – **legibly** *adv,* **legibility** /,lejə'biləti/ *n*

[1]**legion** /'leej(ə)n/ *n sing or pl in constr* **1** the principal unit of the ancient Roman army comprising 3000 to 6000 foot soldiers with cavalry **2** a very large number; a multitude **3** a national association of ex-servicemen ⟨*the Royal British* Legion⟩ [ME, fr OF, fr L *legion-*, *legio*, fr *legere* to gather – more at LEGEND]

[2]**legion** *adj* many, numerous ⟨*the problems are* ~⟩

[1]**legionary** /'leejən(ə)ri/ *adj* of or being a legion [L *legionarius*, fr *legion-*, *legio*]

[2]**legionary** *n* a legionnaire

legionnaire /,leejə'neə/ *n* a member of a (foreign) legion [F *légionnaire*, fr L *legionarius*]

legion'naire's di,sease *n* a serious sometimes fatal infectious disease like pneumonia that is caused by a bacterium and often affects groups of closely associated people [fr its outbreak among a group of US ex-servicemen in 1976]

legislate /'leji,slayt/ *vi* to make or enact laws [back-formation fr *legislator*]

legislation /,leji'slaysh(ə)n/ *n* **1** (the making of) laws **2** a prospective law [LEGISLATE + -ION] – **legislative** /'lejislətiv/ *adj*, **legislatively** *adv*

legislator /'leji,slaytə/ *n* a maker of laws [L *legis lator*, lit., proposer of a law, fr *legis*, gen of *lex* law + *lator* proposer, fr *latus*, suppletive pp of *ferre* to carry, propose – more at TOLERATE, [2]BEAR] – **legislatress** /-tris/, **legislatrix** /-triks/ *n*, **legislatorial** /-slə'tawri·əl/ *adj*

legislature /'lejisləchə/ *n* a body of people having the power to legislate

legit /lə'jit/ *adj* LEGITIMATE 2, 3a, 4, 5 – infml

[1]**legitimate** /lə'jitimət/ *adj* **1** lawfully begotten; *specif* born in wedlock **2** neither spurious nor false; genuine ⟨~ *grievance*⟩ **3a** in accordance with law ⟨*a* ~ *government*⟩ **b** ruling by or based on the strict principle of hereditary right ⟨*a* ~ *king*⟩ **4** conforming to recognized principles or accepted rules and standards **5** relating to plays acted by professional actors but not including revues, music hall, or some forms of musical comedy **6** in accord with reason or logic; following logically ⟨*a* ~ *deduction*⟩ [ML *legitimatus*, pp of *legitimare* to legitimate, fr L *legitimus* legitimate, fr *leg-*, *lex* law] – **legitimately** *adv*, **legitimacy** /-si/ *n*

[2]**legitimate** /-,mayt/, **legitimat·ize, -ise** /lə'jitimə,teiz/ **legitim·ize, -ise** /-,meiz/ *vt* **1a** to give legal status to **b** JUSTIFY 1 **2** to give (an illegitimate child) the legal status of one legitimately born – **legitimation** /lə'jiti'maysh(ə)n/, **legitimatization** /-mətie'zaysh(ə)n/, **legitimization** /-mie'zaysh(ə)n/ *n*

legitimism /lə'jiti,miz(ə)m/ *n, often cap* adherence to the principles of political legitimacy or to sby claiming a throne by descent – **legitimist** *n, often cap*, **legitimist** *adj*

legless /'leglis/ *adj, chiefly Br* DRUNK 1 – infml ['LEG + -LESS]

,leg-of-'mutton, leg-o'-mutton *adj* having an approximately triangular shape ⟨~ *sleeves*⟩

'leg-,pull *n* a playful trick or hoax intended to deceive sby [fr the phrase *pull somebody's leg*]

legroom /'legroohm, -,room/ *n* space in which to extend the legs while seated

'leg ,side, leg *n* the part of a cricket field on the side of a line joining the middle stumps in which the batsman stands when playing a ball – compare OFF SIDE ☞ SPORT

legume /'legyoohm/ *n* **1** the (edible) pod or seed of a leguminous plant **2** any of a large family of plants, shrubs, and trees having pods containing 1 or many seeds and including important food and forage plants (e g peas, beans, or clovers) [F *légume*, fr L *legumin-*, *legumen* leguminous plant, fr *legere* to gather – more at LEGEND] – **leguminous** /lə'gyoohminəs/ *adj*

'leg-,up *n* **1** assistance in mounting an object **2** a helping hand; a boost *USE* infml

'leg-,warmer *n* a knitted legging ☞ GARMENT

'leg,work /-,wuhk/ *n* work involving physical activity and forming the basis of more creative or mentally exacting work

[1]**lei** /lay/ *n* a wreath or necklace usu of flowers or leaves that is a symbol of affection in Polynesia [Hawaiian]

[2]**lei** *pl of* LEU

leishmaniasis /,leeshmə'nie·əsis/ *n* any of various diseases (e g kala-azar) caused by any of a genus of parasitic protozoan organisms [NL, fr Sir William *Leishman* †1926 Br physician]

leisure /'lezhə/ *n* **1** freedom provided by the cessation of activities; *esp* time free from work or duties **2** unhurried ease [ME *leiser*, fr OF *leisir*, fr *leisir* to be permitted, fr L *licēre* – more at LICENCE] – **leisureless** *adj* – **at leisure, at one's leisure** **1** at an unhurried pace **2** at one's convenience

'leisured *adj* **1** having plenty of free time, esp because of not needing to work **2** leisurely

[1]**'leisurely** /-li/ *adv* without haste; deliberately

[2]**leisurely** *adj* characterized by leisure; unhurried – **leisureliness** *n*

leitmotiv, leitmotif /'lietmoh,teef/ *n* **1** a musical phrase that accompanies the reappearance of an idea, person, or situation **2** a (dominant) recurring theme, esp in a literary work [G *leitmotiv*, fr *leiten* to lead + *motiv* motive, fr F *motif*]

[1]**lek** /lek/ *n* ☞ *Albania* at NATIONALITY [Alb]

[2]**lek** *n* an area where black grouse or other social birds congregate to carry on display and courtship behaviour [prob fr Sw, sport, play]

lekker /'lekə/ *adj, SAfr* pleasant, nice – infml [Afrik, fr D]

lemma /'lemə/ *n, pl* **lemmas, lemmata** /'lemətə/ **1** a proposition accepted as true for the sake of demonstrating another proposition **2** the argument or theme of a composition prefixed as a title or introduction; *broadly* (a subsidiary part of) a heading or introduction [L, fr Gk *lēmma* thing taken, assumption, fr *lambanein* to take – more at LATCH]

lemming /'leming/ *n* any of several small short-tailed furry-footed northern voles; *esp* one of northern mountains that undergoes recurrent mass migrations [Norw; akin to ON *lōmr* guillemot, L *latrare* to bark – more at LAMENT]

lemon /'lemən/ *n* **1** (a stout thorny tree that bears) an oval yellow acid citrus fruit **2** a pale yellow colour **3** one who or that which is unsatisfactory or worthless; a dud – infml [ME *lymon*, fr MF *limon*, fr ML *limon-*, *limo*, fr Ar *laymūn*] – **lemony** *adj*

lemonade /,lemə'nayd/ *n* a (carbonated) soft drink made or flavoured with lemon

lemon balm *n* a bushy perennial Old World plant of the mint family often cultivated for its fragrant lemon-flavoured leaves

'lemon,grass /-,grahs/ *n* a robust grass that grows in tropical regions and is the source of an essential oil with an odour of lemon or verbena

,lemon 'sole *n* a flatfish that is found in N Atlantic and European waters and is highly valued for food [*lemon* fr F *limande*, a flatfish]

'lemon ,squeezer *n* a device for pressing the juice from citrus fruits

lempira /'lempirə/ *n* ☞ *Honduras* at NATIONALITY [AmerSp, fr *Lempira*, 16th-c Indian chief]

lemur /'leemə/ *n* any of numerous tree-dwelling chiefly nocturnal mammals, esp of Madagascar, typically having a muzzle like a fox, large eyes, very soft woolly fur, and a long furry tail [NL, fr L *lemures*, pl, ghosts; akin to Gk *lamia* devouring monster]

lend /lend/ *vb* **lent** /lent/ *vt* **1a** to give for temporary use on condition that the same or its equivalent be returned **b** to let out (money) for temporary use on condition of repayment with interest **2a** to give the assistance or support of; afford, contribute ⟨*a dispassionate and scholarly manner which* ~s *great force to his criticisms – TLS*⟩ **b** to adapt or apply (oneself); accommodate ⟨*a topic that* ~s *itself admirably to class discussion*⟩ ~ *vi* to make a loan [ME *lenen, lenden*, fr OE *lǣnan*, fr *lǣn* loan – more at LOAN] – **lender** *n*

,lend-'lease *n* the transfer of goods and services to an ally in a common cause – used esp with reference to the system by which the USA gave material aid to the Allies in WW II – **lend-lease** *vt*

length /leng(k)th/ *n* **1a(1)** the longer or longest dimension of an object ☞ PHYSICS, UNIT **(2)** the extent from end to end ⟨*walked the* ~ *of the street*⟩ **b** a measured distance or dimension ⟨*a 2m* ~ *of tube*⟩ **c** the quality or state of being long **2a** duration or extent in or with regard to time ⟨*the* ~ *of a broadcast*⟩ **b** relative duration or stress of a sound **3a** distance or extent in space ⟨*an arm's* ~ *apart*⟩ **b** the length of sthg taken as a unit of measure ⟨*his horse led by a* ~⟩ **4** the degree to which sthg (e g a course of action or a line of thought) is carried; a limit, extreme – often pl with sing. meaning ⟨*went to great* ~s *to learn the truth*⟩ **5a** a long expanse or stretch ⟨~s *of hair*⟩ **b** a piece, esp of a certain length (being or usable as part of a whole or of a connected series) ⟨*a* ~ *of pipe*⟩ **6** the (ideal) distance down a cricket pitch which the bowled ball travels before pitching **7** the vertical extent of sthg (e g an article of clothing), esp with reference to the position it reaches on the body – usu in combination ⟨*shoulder-length hair*⟩ [ME *lengthe*, fr OE *lengthu*, fr *lang* long] – **at length 1** fully, comprehensively **2** for a long time **3** finally; AT LAST

lengthen /'length(ə)n, 'lengkth(ə)n/ *vb* to make or become longer

'length,ways /-,wayz/, **lengthwise** /-,wiez/ *adv or adj* in the direction of the length ⟨*bricks are generally laid* ~⟩

lengthy /'leng(k)thi/ *adj* of great or unusual length; long; *also* excessively or tediously protracted – **lengthily** *adv*, **lengthiness** *n*

lenient /'leenyənt, 'leeni·ənt/ *adj* **1** of a mild or merciful nature; not severe ⟨~ *laws*⟩ **2** *archaic* exerting a soothing or easing influence [L *lenient-, leniens*, prp of *lenire* to soften, soothe, fr *lenis* soft, mild – more at ²LET] – **lenience, leniency** *n*, **leniently** *adv*

Leninism /'leni,niz(ə)m/ *n* the (communist) principles and policies advocated by Lenin [V I *Lenin* (Ulyanov) †1924 Russ political leader] – **Leninist, Leninite** /-,niet/ *n or adj*

lenitive /'lenətiv/ *adj* relieving pain or stress [MF *lenitif*, fr ML *lenitivus*, fr L *lenitus*, pp of *lenire*] – **lenitive** *n*

lenity /'lenəti/ *n* gentleness, mercy – fml [F & L; F *lénité*, fr L *lenitat-, lenitas*, fr *lenis*]

lens /lenz/ *n* **1a** a piece of glass or other transparent material with 2 opposite regular surfaces, at least 1 of which is curved, that is used either singly or combined in an optical instrument to form an image by focussing rays of light ☞ CAMERA **b** a combination of 2 or more simple lenses **2** a device for directing or focussing radiation other than light (e g sound waves or electrons) **3** sthg shaped like an optical lens with both sides convex **4** a transparent lens-shaped or nearly spherical body in the eye that focuses light rays (e g on the retina) ☞ NERVE [NL *lent-, lens*, fr L, lentil; fr its shape] – **lensed** *adj*, **lensless** *adj*

lensman /'lenzmən/ *n* a photographer or cameraman – infml

Lent /lent/ *n* the 40 weekdays from Ash Wednesday to Easter observed by Christians as a period of penitence and fasting [ME *lente* springtime, Lent, fr OE *lengten*; akin to OHG *lenzin* spring] – **Lenten** *adj*

Lenten fare /'lent(ə)n/ *n* food or a diet without meat

lenticel /'lenti,sel, -s(ə)l/ *n* a pore in the stems of woody plants through which gases are exchanged between the atmosphere and the stem tissues [NL *lenticella*, dim. of L *lent-, lens* lentil]

lenticular /len'tikyoolə/ *adj* **1** having the shape of a lens with both sides convex **2** of a lens [L *lenticularis* lentil-shaped, fr *lenticula* lentil]

lentil /'lentl/ *n* (the small round edible seed of) a widely cultivated Eurasian leguminous plant [ME, fr OF *lentille*, fr L *lenticula*, dim. of *lent-, lens*; akin to Gk *lathyros* vetch]

lento /'lentoh/ *adv or adj* in a slow manner – used in music [It, fr *lento*, adj, slow, fr L *lentus* pliant, sluggish, slow – more at LITHE]

Leo /'lee·oh/ *n* (sby born under) the 5th sign of the zodiac in astrology, pictured as a lion ☞ SYMBOL [L, lit., lion – more at LION]

leone /li'ohni/ *n* ☞ *Sierra Leone* at NATIONALITY [*Sierra Leone*]

leonine /'lee·ənien/ *adj* resembling a lion; having the characteristics (e g courage) popularly ascribed to a lion [ME, prob fr OF *léonin*, fr L *leoninus*, fr *leon-, leo*]

leopard /'lepəd/, *fem* **leopardess** /-'des/ *n* **1** a big cat of southern Asia and Africa that is usu tawny or buff with black spots arranged in broken rings or rosettes ☞ ENDANGERED **2** a heraldic charge that is a lion with the farther forepaw raised and its head turned towards the observer [ME, fr OF *leupart*, fr LL *leopardus*, fr Gk *leopardos*, fr *leōn* lion + *pardos* leopard]

leotard /'lee·ə,tahd/ *n* a close-fitting one-piece garment worn by dancers or others performing physical exercises ☞ GARMENT [Jules *Léotard* †1870 F trapeze performer]

leper /'lepə/ *n* **1** sby suffering from leprosy **2** a person shunned for moral or social reasons; an outcast [ME, fr *lepre* leprosy, fr OF, fr LL *lepra*, fr Gk, fr *lepein* to peel; akin to OE *læfer* reed]

lepid- /lepid-/, **lepido-** *comb form* flake; scale ⟨*Lepidoptera*⟩ [NL, fr Gk, fr *lepid-, lepis* scale, fr *lepein*]

lepidolite /le'pidəliet/ *n* a violet-coloured mica containing lithium [G *lepidolith*, fr *lepid-* + *-lith*]

lepidopteran /,lepi'doptərən/ *n* any of a large order of insects comprising the butterflies, moths, and skippers that are caterpillars in the larval stage and have 4 wings usu covered with minute overlapping and often brightly coloured scales when adult [NL *Lepidoptera*, order of insects, fr *lepid-* + Gk *pteron* wing – more at FEATHER] – **lepidopteran** *adj*, **lepidopterous** *adj*

lepidopterist /,lepi'doptərist/ *n* a specialist in the study of lepidopterans

lepidopteron /,lepi'doptərən/ *n, pl* **lepidoptera**

/-rə/ *also* **lepidopterons** a lepidopteran [NL, sing. of *Lepidoptera*]

leporine /ˈlepərien/ *adj* of or resembling the hare [L *leporinus*, fr *lepor-*, *lepus* hare]

leprechaun /ˈleprik(h)awn/ *n* a mischievous elf of Irish folklore [IrGael *leipreachān*, fr MIr *lūchorpān*, fr *lū* small + *corpān* body, dim. of *corp*, fr L *corpus*]

leprosy /ˈleprəsi/ *n* a long-lasting bacterial disease characterized by loss of sensation with eventual paralysis, wasting of muscle, and production of deformities and mutilations [*leprous* + *-y*] – **leprotic** /leˈprotik/ *adj*

leprous /ˈleprəs/ *adj* of, resembling, or suffering from leprosy [ME, fr LL *leprosus* leprous, fr *lepra* leprosy]

-lepsy /-ˌlepsi/ *comb form* (→ *n*) attack; seizure ⟨cata*lepsy*⟩ [MF *-lepsie*, fr LL *-lepsia*, fr Gk *-lēpsia*, fr *lēpsis*, fr *lambanein* to take, seize – more at LATCH]

lepto- *comb form* narrow; slender ⟨lepto*cephalous*⟩ [Gk, fr *leptos*, lit., peeled, husked, fr *lepein* to peel]

[1]**lepton** /ˈlepˌton/ *n* any of a group of elementary particles (e g an electron or muon) that take part in weak interactions with other elementary particles and weigh less than mesons and baryons [Gk *leptos* + E [2]*-on*] – **leptonic** /lepˈtonik/ *adj*

[2]**lepton** *n, pl* **lepta** /ˈleptah/ ☞ *Greece* at NATIONALITY [NGk, fr Gk, small bronze coin, fr neut of *leptos* small]

leptospirosis /ˌleptohspie·əˈrohsis/ *n, pl* **leptospiroses** /-ˌseez/ any of several diseases in human beings and domestic animals caused by any of various spirochaetal bacteria [NL]

lesbian /ˈlezbi·ən/ *n, often cap* a female homosexual [L *lesbius* of Lesbos, fr Gk *Lesbios*, fr *Lesbos*, island in the Aegean Sea, home of Sappho *fl ab* 600 BC Gk poetess & reputed homosexual] – **lesbian** *adj*, **lesbianism** *n*

ˌlese ˈmajesty /leez, lez/, **lèse majesté** /(*Fr* lɛz maʒɛste)/ *n* **1a** a crime (e g treason) committed against a sovereign power **b** an offence violating the dignity of a ruler **2** an affront to dignity or importance [MF *lese majesté*, fr L *laesa majestas*, lit., injured majesty]

lesion /ˈleezh(ə)n/ *n* **1** injury, harm **2** abnormal change in the structure of an organ or part due to injury or disease [ME, fr MF, fr L *laesion-*, *laesio*, fr *laesus*, pp of *laedere* to injure]

[1]**less** /les/ *adj* **1** fewer ⟨*~ than 3*⟩ ⟨*a call for ~ government controls*⟩ – disapproved of by some speakers **2** lower in rank, degree, or importance ⟨*James the* Less⟩ ⟨*no ~ a person than the president himself*⟩ **3** smaller in quantity or extent ⟨*of ~ importance*⟩ ⟨*in ~ time*⟩ ⟨*weighs 3 pounds ~*⟩ [ME, fr OE *lǣs*, adv & n, and *lǣssa*, adj; akin to OS & OFris *lēs* less, Gk *limos* hunger]

[2]**less** *adv* to a lesser degree or extent ⟨*sleeps ~ in summer*⟩ ⟨*much ~ angrily*⟩ – **less and less** to a progressively smaller size or extent – **less than** by no means; not at all ⟨*was being* less than *honest in her replies*⟩

[3]**less** *prep* diminished by; minus ⟨*£100 ~ tax*⟩

[4]**less** *n, pl* **less** a smaller portion or quantity – **less of** **1** not so truly ⟨*he's* less of *a fool than I thought*⟩ **2** enough of ⟨less of *your cheek!*⟩ – infml

-less /-lis/ *suffix* (→ *adj*) **1a** destitute of; not having ⟨*brain* less⟩ ⟨*child*less⟩ ⟨*hope*less⟩ **b** free from ⟨*pain*less⟩ ⟨*care*less⟩ **2** unable to (so act or be acted on) ⟨*tire*less⟩ ⟨*stain*less⟩ [ME *-les*, *-lesse*, fr OE *-lēas*, fr *lēas* devoid, false; akin to OHG *lōs* loose, OE *losian* to get lost – more at LOSE]

lessee /leˈsee/ *n* sby who holds property under a lease [ME, fr AF, fr *lessé*, pp of *lesser* to lease – more at LEASE]

lessen /ˈles(ə)n/ *vb* to reduce in size, extent, etc; diminish, decrease

lesser /ˈlesə/ *adj or adv* less in size, quality, or significance ⟨lesser-*known*⟩ ⟨*the ~ of 2 evils*⟩ – not used in comparatives

lesser black-backed gull *n* a common Eurasian gull that is about the size of a herring gull and has a greyish black back

ˌlesser ˈcelandine /ˈseləndien/ *n* CELANDINE 2

lesson /ˈles(ə)n/ *n* **1** a passage from sacred writings read in a service of worship **2a** a reading or exercise to be studied **b** a period of instruction **3a** sthg, esp a piece of wisdom, learned by study or experience ⟨*her years of travel had taught her valuable ~*s⟩ **b** an instructive or warning example ⟨*the ~*s *history holds for us*⟩ [ME, fr OF *leçon*, fr LL *lection-*, *lectio*, fr L, act of reading, fr *lectus*, pp of *legere* to read – more at LEGEND]

lessor /ˈlesaw, -ˈ-/ *n* sby who conveys property by lease [ME *lessour*, fr AF, fr *lesser* to lease]

lest /lest/ *conj* **1** so that not; IN CASE ⟨*obeyed her ~ she should be angry*⟩ **2** that – used after an expression of fear ⟨*afraid ~ she be angry*⟩ [ME *les the*, *leste*, fr OE *thȳ lǣs the*, fr *thȳ* (instrumental of *thæt* that) + *lǣs* + *the*, relative particle]

[1]**let** /let/ *n* **1** a serve or rally in tennis, squash, etc that does not count and must be replayed **2** sthg that impedes; an obstruction – fml ⟨*without ~ or hindrance*⟩ [ME, obstruction, fr *letten* to hinder, fr OE *lettan*; akin to OHG *lezzen* to delay, hurt, OE *lǣt* late]

[2]**let** *vt* **let; -tt-** **1** to cause to; make ⟨*~ it be known*⟩ **2a** to offer or grant for rent or lease ⟨*~ rooms*⟩ **b** to assign, esp after bids ⟨*~ a contract*⟩ **3a** to give opportunity to, whether by positive action or by failure to prevent; allow to ⟨*he ~ his beard grow*⟩ ⟨*please ~ me know*⟩ ⟨*~ the prisoner go*⟩ **b** to allow to escape, enter, or pass ⟨*~ the dogs loose*⟩ ⟨*~ them through*⟩ ⟨*she ~ out a scream*⟩ **4** – used in the imperative to introduce a request or proposal ⟨*~ us pray*⟩ ⟨*~ me see*⟩, a challenge ⟨*just ~ him try*⟩, a command ⟨*~ it be known*⟩, or sthg to be supposed for the sake of argument ⟨*~ AB be equal to BC*⟩; compare LET'S [ME *leten*, fr OE *lǣtan*; akin to OHG *lāzzan* to permit, L *lassus* weary, *lenis* soft, mild] – **let alone/be** to stop or refrain from molesting, disturbing, or interrupting ⟨*please* let *the cat* alone⟩ – **let fall/drop** to mention casually as if by accident – **let fly** to aim a blow – **let go** to stop holding ⟨let go *of the handle*⟩ – **let in for** to involve (sby, esp oneself) in sthg undesirable ⟨let *myself* in for *a lot of work*⟩ – **let into** to insert into (a surface) ⟨*a tablet* let into *the wall*⟩ – **let loose on** to give freedom of access to or of action with respect to ⟨*can't* let *him* loose on *the files just yet*⟩ – **let oneself go** **1** to behave with relaxed ease or abandonment **2** to allow one's appearance to deteriorate – **let rip** to proceed with abandon ⟨*lost his temper and really* let rip⟩ – infml – **let slip** **1** LET FALL **2** to fail

to take ⟨let slip *a chance*⟩ – **let up on** to become less severe towards

[3]let *n, Br* **1** an act or period of letting premises (e g a flat or bed-sitter) **2** premises rented or for rent

-let /-lit/ *suffix* (→ *n*) **1** -ETTE 1 ⟨*book*let⟩ ⟨*star*let⟩ **2** article worn on (a specified part of the body) ⟨*ank*let⟩ [ME, fr MF *-elet*, fr *-el*, dim. suffix (fr L *-ellus*) + *-et*]

,let a'lone *prep* to say nothing of; *esp* still less ⟨*can't walk*, let alone *run*⟩

'let,down /-,down/ *n* a disappointment, disillusionment – infml

let down *vt* **1** to make (a garment) longer **2** to fail in loyalty or support; disappoint ⟨let *her friend* down *badly*⟩

lethal /'leeth(ə)l/ *adj* relating to or (capable of) causing death [L *letalis, lethalis*, fr *letum* death] – **lethally** *adv*, **lethality** /lee'thaləti/ *n*

lethargic /lə'thahjik/ *adj* **1** sluggish **2** indifferent, apathetic [LETHARGY + [1]-IC] – **lethargically** /-kli/ *adv*

lethargy /'lethəji/ *n* **1** abnormal drowsiness **2** lack of energy or interest [ME *litargie*, fr ML *litargia*, fr LL *lethargia*, fr Gk *lēthargia*, fr *lēthargos* forgetful, lethargic, fr *lēthē* + *argos* lazy – more at ARGON]

Lethe /'leethi/ *n* the river in Hades in Greek mythology whose waters caused drinkers to forget their past [L, fr Gk *Lēthē*, fr *lēthē* forgetfulness; akin to Gk *lanthanein* to escape notice, *lanthanesthai* to forget – more at LATENT] – **Lethean** /'leethi·ən/ *adj*

let off *vt* **1** to cause to explode ⟨let *the fireworks* off⟩ **2** to excuse from punishment **3** *chiefly Br* to offer (part of a building) for rent

let on *vi* **1** to reveal or admit sthg; *esp* to divulge secret information ⟨*nobody* let on *about the surprise party*⟩ **2** to pretend ⟨*she* let on *that she was a stranger*⟩ – infml

'let-,out *n* sthg (e g an exclusion clause in a contract) that provides an opportunity to escape or be released from an obligation – infml

let out *vt* **1** to make (a garment) wider (e g by inserting an inset) – compare TAKE IN **2** to excuse from an obligation or responsibility **3** *chiefly Br* to express publicly; *esp* to blab **4** *chiefly Br* to rent out (e g property)

let's /lets/ let us – used of a group that includes the one addressed ⟨~ *face it*⟩ ⟨~ *dance, Mary*⟩ ⟨~ *not have lunch yet*⟩; compare [2]LET 4

Lett /let/ *n* a member of a people mainly inhabiting Latvia [G *Lette*, fr Latvian *Latvi*]

[1]letter /'letə/ *n* **1** a symbol, usu written or printed, representing a speech sound and constituting a unit of an alphabet ☞ ALPHABET **2a** a written or printed message addressed to a person or organization and usu sent through the post **b** a formal written communication containing a grant or authorization – usu pl with sing. meaning **3** *pl but sing or pl in constr* **a** literature; BELLES LETTRES **b** learning; *esp* scholarly knowledge of or achievement in literature ⟨*a man of* ~s⟩ **4** the precise wording; the strict or literal meaning ⟨*obeyed the instructions to the* ~⟩ **5a** a single piece of type **b** a style of type [ME, fr OF *lettre*, fr L *littera* letter of the alphabet, *litterae*, pl, epistle, literature]

[2]letter *vt* to set down in or mark with letters

'letter ,bomb *n* an explosive device concealed in an envelope or package and sent through the post to the intended victim

'letter ,box *n, Br* a hole or box (e g in a door) to receive material delivered by post

'lettered *adj* learned, educated

'letter,head /-,hed/ *n* stationery printed with a heading; *also* the heading itself

lettering /'letəring/ *n* the letters used in an inscription, esp as regards their style or quality

'letter,press /-,pres/ *n* **1** (work produced by) printing from an inked raised surface **2** *chiefly Br* text (e g of a book) as distinct from pictorial illustrations

,letters of 'credence *n pl* a formal document authorizing the power of a diplomatic agent to act for his/her government

letters patent *n pl* a formal document (e g from a sovereign) conferring on sby the sole right to exploit his/her invention

letting /'leting/ *n, chiefly Br* [3]LET

Lettish /'letish/ *n* LATVIAN 2

lettre de cachet /,let(rə) də ka'shay (*Fr* lɛtr də kaʃɛ)/ *n, pl* **lettres de cachet** /~/ an official order usu authorizing imprisonment without trial of a named person [F, lit., letter with a seal]

lettuce /'letis/ *n* a common garden vegetable whose succulent edible leaves are used esp in salads [ME *letuse*, fr OF *laitues*, pl of *laitue*, fr L *lactuca*, fr *lact-*, *lac* milk – more at GALAXY; fr its milky juice]

letup /'letup/ *n* a cessation or lessening of effort, activity, or intensity

let up *vi* **1a** to diminish, slow down, or cease **b** to relax or cease one's efforts or activities **2** to become less severe – usu + *on*; infml

leu /'layooh/ *n, pl* **lei** /lay/ ☞ *Romania* at NATIONALITY [Romanian, lit., lion, fr L *leo* – more at LION]

leuc-, leuco-, leuk-, leuko- *comb form* **1** white; colourless ⟨leuco*cyte*⟩ ⟨leuco*rrhoea*⟩ **2** white matter of the brain ⟨leuco*tomy*⟩ [NL *leuc-, leuco-*, fr Gk *leuk-, leuko-*, fr *leukos* – more at [1]LIGHT]

leucine /'lyoohseen/ *n* an amino acid found in most proteins and essential to the diet of human beings [ISV *leuc-* + *-ine*]

leucocyte /'l(y)oohkə,siet/ *n* WHITE BLOOD CELL

leucoma /l(y)ooh'kohmə/ *n* a dense white opaque part in the cornea of the eye [LL, fr Gk *leukōma*, fr *leukos* white]

leucorrhoea /,l(y)oohkə'riə/ *n* a thick whitish discharge from the vagina resulting from inflammation or congestion of the mucous membrane [NL]

leucotomy /l(y)ooh'kotəmi/ *n* a lobotomy

leukaemia /l(y)ooh'keemyə, -mi·ə/ *n* any of several usu fatal types of cancer that are characterized by an abnormal increase in the number of white blood cells in the body tissues, esp the blood, and occur in acute or chronic form [NL]

lev /lef/ *n, pl* **leva** /'levə/ ☞ *Bulgaria* at NATIONALITY [Bulg, lit., lion]

lev-, levo- *comb form, chiefly NAm* laev- [F *lévo-*, fr L *laevus* left; akin to Gk *laios* left]

levanter /lə'vantə/ *n* a strong easterly Mediterranean wind [*Levant*, the countries of the eastern Mediterranean, fr F *levant*, prp of *lever* to rise]

levator /li'vaytə, 'levətaw/ *n, pl* **levatores** /,levə'tawreez, 'levətə,reez/, **levators** a muscle that serves to raise a part of the body – compare DEPRESSOR [NL, fr L *levatus*, pp of *levare* to raise – more at LEVER]

[1]**levee** /'levi/ *n* **1** a reception of visitors formerly held by a person of rank on rising from bed **2** a reception, usu in honour of a particular person [F *lever*, fr MF, act of arising, fr (*se*) *lever* to rise, fr L *levare*]

[2]**levee** *n, NAm* **1** an embankment for preventing or confining flooding **2** a river landing place [F *levée*, fr OF, act of raising, fr *lever* to raise – more at LEVER]

[1]**level** /'levəl/ *n* **1** a device (e g a spirit level) for establishing a horizontal line or plane **2a** a horizontal state or condition **b** the equilibrium of a fluid marked by a horizontal surface of even altitude ⟨*water seeks its own* ~⟩ **c** an (approximately) horizontal line, plane, or surface **3a** a position of height in relation to the ground; height ⟨*eye* ~⟩ **b** a practically horizontal or flat area, esp of land **4** a position or place in a scale or rank (e g of value or importance) ⟨*a high* ~ *of academic excellence*⟩ **5** (a passage in) an interconnecting series of regularly worked horizontal mine passages **6** the (often measurable) size or amount of sthg specified ⟨*noise* ~⟩ [ME, fr MF *livel*, fr (assumed) VL *libellum*, alter. of L *libella*, fr dim. of *libra* weight, balance] – **on the level** honest; BONA FIDE

[2]**level** *vb* **-ll-** (*NAm* **-l-**, **-ll-**), /'levl·ing/ *vt* **1a** to make (a line or surface) horizontal; make level, even, or uniform **b** to raise or lower to the same height – often + *up* ⟨~ up *the picture with the one next to it*⟩ **2a** to bring to a horizontal aiming position **b** to aim, direct – + *at* or *against* ⟨~led *a charge of fraud at her*⟩ **3** to bring to a common level, plane, or standard; equalize ⟨*love* ~s *all ranks* – W S Gilbert⟩ **4** to lay level with the ground; raze **5** to find the heights of different points in (a land area) ~ *vi* **1** to attain or come to a level – usu + *out* or *off* ⟨*the plane* ~led *off at 10,000ft*⟩ **2** to aim a gun or other weapon horizontally **3** to deal frankly and openly – infml

[3]**level** *adj* **1a** having no part higher than another **b** parallel with the plane of the horizon; conforming to the curvature of the liquid parts of the earth's surface **2a** even, unvarying ⟨*a* ~ *temperature*⟩ **b** equal in advantage, progression, or standing ⟨*drew* ~ *with the leaders*⟩ **c** steady, unwavering ⟨*spoke in* ~ *tones*⟩ **3** distributed evenly; uniform ⟨~ *stress*⟩ – **levelly** *adv*, **levelness** *n* – **level best** very best ⟨*she did her* level best⟩

,**level 'crossing** *n, Br* the crossing of railway and road or 2 railways on the same level

,**level'headed** /-'hedid/ *adj* having sound judgment; sensible – **levelheadedness** *n*

leveller, *NAm chiefly* **leveler** /'levələ/ *n* **1** *cap* a member of a radical group during the English Civil War who advocated legal equality and religious tolerance **2** an advocate of equality **3** sthg that tends to reduce human differences [[2]LEVEL + [2]-ER]

[1]**lever** /'leevə/ *n* **1a** a bar used for prizing up or dislodging sthg **b** an inducing or compelling force; a tool ⟨*attempts to use food as a political* ~ – *Time*⟩ **2a** a rigid bar used to exert a pressure or sustain a weight at one end by applying force at the other and turning it on a fulcrum **b** a projecting part by which a mechanism is operated or adjusted [ME, fr OF *levier*, fr *lever* to raise, fr L *levare*; akin to L *levis* light in weight – more at [4]LIGHT]

[2]**lever** *vt* to prize, raise, or move (as if) with a lever

leverage /'leevərij/ *n* **1** the action of a lever or the mechanical advantage gained by it **2** power, influence

leveret /'lev(ə)rit/ *n* a hare in its first year [ME, fr (assumed) MF *levret*, fr MF *levre* hare, fr L *lepor-*, *lepus*]

leviathan /lə'vie·əthən/ *n* **1** *often cap* a biblical sea monster **2** sthg large or formidable [ME, fr LL, fr Heb *liwyāthān*] – **leviathan** *adj*

levigate /'levi,gayt/ *vt* to grind to a fine smooth powder while in a moist condition [L *levigatus*, pp of *levigare*, fr *levis* smooth + *-igare* (akin to *agere* to drive) – more at [1]LIME, AGENT] – **levigation** /-'gaysh(ə)n/ *n*

levitate /'levi,tayt/ *vb* to (cause to) rise or float in the air, esp in apparent defiance of gravity [*levity*] – **levitation** /,levi'taysh(ə)n/ *n*, **levitational** *adj*

Levite /'leeviet/ *n* a member of the priestly Hebrew tribe of Levi [ME, fr LL *Levita*, *Levites*, fr Gk *Leuitēs*, fr *Leui* Levi, third son of Jacob, fr Heb]

Levitical /lə'vitikl/ *adj* of the Levites or Leviticus [LL *Leviticus*]

Leviticus /lə'vitikəs/ *n* the third book of the Old Testament [LL, lit., of the Levites]

levity /'levəti/ *n* lack of seriousness; *esp* excessive or unseemly frivolity [L *levitat-*, *levitas* lightness, frivolity, fr *levis* light in weight – more at [4]LIGHT]

[1]**levy** /'levi/ *n* **1a** the imposing or collection of a tax, fine, etc **b** an amount levied **2a** the enlistment or conscription of men for military service **b** *sing or pl in constr* troops raised by levy [ME, fr MF *levee*, fr OF, act of raising – more at [2]LEVEE]

[2]**levy** *vt* **1** to impose, collect, or demand by legal authority ⟨~ *a tax*⟩ **2** to enlist or conscript for military service **3** to prepare for and make (war) – usu + *on* or *upon* – **leviable** *adj*

lewd /l(y)oohd/ *adj* **1** sexually coarse or suggestive **2** obscene, salacious ⟨~ *songs*⟩ [ME *lewed* vulgar, fr OE *lǣwede* of the laity, ignorant] – **lewdly** *adv*, **lewdness** *n*

lewis /'looh·is/ *n* a device consisting of wedges or curved metal bars used to grip and hoist large stones or blocks [prob fr the name *Lewis*]

lewisite /'looh·i,siet/ *n* a blister-inducing liquid developed as a poison gas for war use [Winford *Lewis* †1943 US chemist]

lexical /'leksikl/ *adj* **1** of words or the vocabulary of a language as distinguished from its grammar and construction **2** of a lexicon – **lexically** *adv*, **lexicality** /,leksi'kaləti/ *n*

lexicography /,leksi'kogrəfi/ *n* (the principles of) the editing or making of a dictionary – **lexicographer** *n*, **lexicographic** /,leksikə'grafik/, **lexicographical** *adj*

lexicology /,leksi'koləji/ *n* a branch of linguistics concerned with the meaning and use of words [F *lexicologie*, fr *lexico-* (fr LGk *lexiko-*, fr *lexikon*) + *-logie* -logy] – **lexicologist** *n*

lexicon /'leksikən/ *n, pl* **lexica** /-kə/, **lexicons** **1** a dictionary, esp of Greek, Latin, or Hebrew **2** the vocabulary of a language, individual, or subject [LGk *lexikon*, fr neut of *lexikos* of words, fr Gk *lexis* word, speech, fr *legein* to say – more at LEGEND]

lexis /'leksis/ *n, pl* **lexes** /-seez/ LEXICON 2 [Gk, speech, word]

[1]**ley** /lee, lay/ *n* arable land used temporarily for hay or grazing [var of *lea*]

[2]**ley** *n* an alignment of landmarks held to mark the course of a prehistoric trackway [var of *lea* (tract of open ground)]

liability /,lie·ə'biləti/ *n* **1** being liable **2** sthg for which one is liable; *esp, pl* debts **3** a hindrance, drawback – infml

liable /'lie·əbl/ *adj* **1** legally responsible **2** exposed or subject *to* ⟨*~ to a fine*⟩ ⟨*~ to hurt yourself*⟩ **3** habitually likely *to* ⟨*she's ~ to get annoyed*⟩ [(assumed) AF, fr OF *lier* to bind, fr L *ligare* – more at LIGATURE]

liaise /lee'ayz/ *vi* **1** to establish a connection and cooperate **2** to act as a liaison officer [back-formation fr *liaison*]

liaison /lee'ayzon, -z(ə)n, -zonh/ *n* **1** a substance or mixture used in cooking to thicken or bind liquids **2a** a close bond or connection **b** an illicit sexual relationship; AFFAIR 3a **3** the pronunciation (e g in the French *est-il*) of an otherwise silent consonant before a word beginning with a vowel sound **4** communication, esp between parts of an armed force [F, fr MF, fr *lier*]

liana /li'ahnə/ *n* a climbing plant, esp of tropical rain forests, that roots in the ground ☞ PLANT [F *liane*] – **lianoid** /'lee·ə,noyd/ *adj*

liar /'lie·ə/ *n* one who (habitually) tells lies [ME, fr OE *lēogere*, fr *lēogan* to lie – more at [3]LIE]

Lias /'lie·əs/ *adj or n* (of or being) the earliest subdivision of the Jurassic (rocks) [n F, fr E (a limestone rock); adj fr n] – **Liassic** /,lie'asik, li-/ *adj*

lib /lib/ *n, often cap* LIBERATION 2 – infml ⟨*women's ~*⟩ – **libber** *n*

libation /lie'baysh(ə)n/ *n* **1** (an act of pouring) a liquid used in a sacrifice to a god **2a** an act or instance of drinking **b** a beverage, esp alcoholic *USE* (2) fml or humor [L *libation-, libatio*, fr *libatus*, pp of *libare* to pour as an offering; akin to Gk *leibein* to pour]

[1]libel /'liebl/ *n* **1** (a) defamation of sby by published writing or pictorial representation as distinguished from spoken words or gestures – compare SLANDER **2** a false insulting statement [ME, written declaration, fr MF, fr L *libellus*, dim. of *liber* book – more at LEAF] – **libellous** *adj*

[2]libel *vb* **-ll-** (*NAm* **-l-, -ll-**), /'liebl·ing/ to make or publish a libel (against) – **libeller** *n*, **libellist** *n*

[1]liberal /'librəl/ *adj* **1** of or in liberal studies ⟨*~ education*⟩ **2a** generous, openhanded ⟨*a ~ giver*⟩ **b** abundant, ample ⟨*a ~ helping*⟩ **3** broad-minded, tolerant; *esp* not bound by authoritarianism, orthodoxy, or tradition **4** *cap* based on or advocating (political) liberalism; *specif* of a political party in the UK advocating economic freedom and moderate reform [ME, fr MF, fr L *liberalis* suitable for a freeman, generous, fr *liber* free; akin to OE *lēodan* to grow, Gk *eleutheros* free] – **liberally** *adv*, **liberalness**, **liberality** /libə'raləti/ *n*

[2]liberal *n* **1** one who is not strict in the observance of orthodox ways (e g in politics or religion) **2** *cap* a supporter of a Liberal party **3** a champion of individual rights

,liberal 'arts *n pl* the medieval studies comprising the trivium and quadrivium

liberalism /'librəliz(ə)m/ *n* **1** breadth of mind; tolerance, understanding **2a** a political philosophy based on belief in progress and the protection of political and civil liberties **b** *cap* Liberal principles and policies – **liberalist** *n or adj*, **liberalistic** /,librə'listik/ *adj*

liberal·ize, -ise /'librə,liez/ *vb* to make or become (more) liberal – **liberalization** /-'zaysh(ə)n/ *n*

,Liberal 'Juda,ism *n* REFORM JUDAISM

,liberal 'studies *n pl* studies (e g language, history, etc) intended to provide general knowledge rather than professional or vocational skills

liberate /'libə,rayt/ *vt* **1** to set free; *specif* to free (e g a country) from foreign domination **2** to free (a molecule, ion, etc) from combination **3** to steal – euph or humor [L *liberatus*, pp of *liberare*, fr *liber* free] – **liberator** *n*

liberation /,libə'raysh(ə)n/ *n* **1** liberating or being liberated **2** the seeking of equal rights and status ⟨*gay ~*⟩ – **liberationist** *n*

libertarian /,libə'teəri·ən/ *n* **1** a believer in free will **2** an advocate of liberty – **libertarian** *adj*, **libertarianism** *n*

libertine /'libəteen/ *n* a person who is unrestrained by convention or morality; *specif* one leading a dissolute life [ME *libertyn* freedman, fr L *libertinus*, fr *libertinus*, adj, of a freedman, fr *libertus* freedman, fr *liber*] – **libertinage** /-tinij/, **libertinism** /-ti,niz(ə)m/ *n*

liberty /'libəti/ *n* **1a** the power to do as one pleases **b** freedom from physical restraint or dictatorial control **c** the enjoyment of various rights and privileges ⟨*civil ~*⟩ **d** the power of choice **2** a right or immunity awarded or granted; a privilege **3a** a breach of etiquette or propriety **b** a risk, chance ⟨*took foolish* liberties *with her health*⟩ [ME, fr MF *liberté*, fr L *libertat-, libertas*, fr *liber* free – more at LIBERAL] – **at liberty 1** free **2** at leisure; unoccupied

'liberty ,cap *n* a close-fitting conical cap used as a symbol of liberty (e g by the French revolutionaries)

'liberty ,horse *n* a circus horse that performs without a rider

libidinous /li'bidinəs/ *adj* having or marked by strong sexual desire; lascivious [ME, fr MF *libidineus*, fr L *libidinosus*, fr *libidin-, libido*] – **libidinously** *adv*, **libidinousness** *n*

libido /li'beedoh/ *n, pl* **libidos 1** emotional or mental energy derived in psychoanalytic theory from primitive biological urges **2** sexual drive [NL *libidin-, libido*, fr L, desire, lust, fr *libēre* to please – more at LOVE] – **libidinal** /li'bid(ə)nəl/ *adj*

Lib-Lab /,lib 'lab/ *adj* involving both the Labour and Liberal parties ⟨*the ~ pact*⟩ [*Lib*eral + *Lab*our]

Libra /'leebrə, 'lie-/ *n* (sby born under) the 7th sign of the zodiac in astrology, pictured as a pair of scales ☞ SYMBOL [ME, fr L, lit., scales, pound] – **Libran** *n or adj*

librarian /lie'breəri·ən/ *n* sby who manages or assists in a library – **librarianship** *n*

library /'liebrəri/ *n* **1a** a place in which books, recordings, films, etc are kept for reference or for borrowing by the public **b** a collection of such books, recordings, etc **2** a series of related books issued by a publisher [ME, fr ML *librarium*, fr L, neut of *librarius* of books, fr *libr-, liber* book – more at LEAF]

library science *n, chiefly NAm* the study or the principles and practices of librarianship

librate /lie'brayt/ *vi* **1** to oscillate, vibrate **2** to stay poised [L *libratus*, pp of *librare* to balance, fr *libra* scales]

libration /lie'braysh(ə)n/ *n* an apparent oscillation of the moon or other celestial body that causes parts at the edge of the disc to become alternately visible and invisible [L *libration-, libratio*, fr *libratus*] – **librational, libratory** /'liebrət(ə)ri/ *adj*

libretto /li'bretoh/ *n, pl* **librettos, libretti** /-ti/ (the book containing) the text of a work (e g an opera) that is both theatrical and musical [It, dim. of *libro* book, fr L *libr-, liber*] – **librettist** *n*

Librium /'libri·əm/ *trademark* – used for chlordiazepoxide

Libyan /'libi·ən/ *n* **1** a native or inhabitant of Libya **2** a Berber language of ancient N Africa [*Libya*, country in N Africa, fr L *Libye, Libya*, fr Gk *Libyē*] – **Libyan** *adj*

lice /lies/ *pl of* LOUSE

licence, *NAm chiefly* **license** /'lies(ə)ns/ *n* **1a** permission to act **b** freedom of action **2** (a certificate giving evidence of) permission granted by authority to engage in an otherwise unlawful activity, esp the sale of alcoholic drink **3a** freedom that allows or is used with irresponsibility **b** disregard for rules of propriety or personal conduct **4** freedom claimed by an artist or writer to alter facts or deviate from the rules of an art, esp for the sake of the effect gained ⟨*poetic* ~⟩ [ME, fr MF *licence*, fr L *licentia*, fr *licent-, licens*, prp of *licēre* to be permitted; akin to Latvian *līkt* to come to terms]

license, licence /'lies(ə)ns/ *vt* to give official permission to or for (esp the sale of alcoholic drink)

ˌlicensed 'victualler *n, Br* a publican holding a licence to sell food and alcoholic drink on the premises

licensee /ˌlies(ə)n'see/ *n* the holder of a licence; *esp, Br* a publican

'license ˌplate *n, NAm* a renewable number plate showing that the vehicle to which it is attached is licensed

licentiate /lie'sens(h)i·ət, -ayt/ *n* **1** one licensed to practise a profession **2** an academic degree awarded by some European universities [ML *licentiatus*, fr pp of *licentiare* to allow, fr L *licentia*]

licentious /lie'senshəs/ *adj* behaving in a sexually uncontrolled manner [L *licentiosus*, fr *licentia*] – **licentiously** *adv*, **licentiousness** *n*

lichee /'liechee, -'-/ *n* a litchi

lichen /'liekən, 'lichin/ *n* **1** any of numerous complex plants made up of an alga and a fungus growing in symbiotic association on a solid surface (e g a rock or tree trunk) ☞ PLANT **2** any of several skin diseases characterized by raised spots [L, fr Gk *leichēn, lichēn*] – **lichenous** *adj*, **lichenoid** /-ˌnoyd/ *adj*

'lich-ˌgate /lich/ *n* a lych-gate

licit /'lisit/ *adj* not forbidden (by law); permissible [MF *licite*, fr L *licitus*, fr pp of *licēre* to be permitted – more at LICENCE] – **licitly** *adv*

¹lick /lik/ *vt* **1a(1)** to draw the tongue over, esp in order to taste, moisten, or clean ⟨~ *a stamp*⟩ **(2)** to flicker or play over like a tongue **b** to take into the mouth with the tongue; lap – usu + *up* **2a** to strike repeatedly; thrash **b** to get the better of; overcome ⟨*has* ~ed *every problem*⟩ ~ *vi* to lap (as if) with the tongue; *also* to dart like a tongue ⟨*flames* ~ing *at the windows*⟩ ***USE*** (*vt 2*) infml [ME *licken*, fr OE *liccian*; akin to OHG *leckōn* to lick, L *lingere*, Gk *leichein*] – **lick into shape** to put into proper form or condition

²lick *n* **1a** an act or instance of licking **b** a small amount; a touch ⟨*a* ~ *of paint*⟩ **2** ⁵BLOW 1 **3** a place to which animals regularly go to lick a salt deposit **4** speed, pace ⟨*the car was travelling at a good* ~⟩ – infml – **a lick and a promise** sthg hastily and not thoroughly done; *esp* a quick wash

licking /'liking/ *n* **1** a sound thrashing; a beating **2** a severe setback; a defeat ***USE*** infml

licorice /'likərish, -ris/ *n* liquorice

lictor /'liktə/ *n* an officer of ancient Rome who carried the fasces and accompanied the chief magistrates in public appearances [L; perh akin to L *ligare* to bind]

lid /lid/ *n* **1** a hinged or detachable cover (for a receptacle) **2** the operculum in mosses [ME, fr OE *hlid*; akin to OHG *hlit* cover, OE *hlinian, hleonian* to lean – more at ¹LEAN] – **lidded** *adj*

lido /'liedoh, 'lee-/ *n, pl* **lidos 1** a fashionable beach resort **2** a public open-air swimming pool [*Lido*, resort near Venice in Italy, fr L *litus* shore]

¹lie /lie/ *vi* **lying; lay** /lay/; **lain** /layn/ **1a** to be or to stay at rest in a horizontal position; rest, recline ⟨~ *motionless*⟩ ⟨~ *asleep*⟩ **b** to assume a horizontal position – often + *down* **c** to be or remain in a specified state or condition ⟨~ *in wait*⟩ ⟨*machinery* lying *idle*⟩ **2a** *of sthg inanimate* to be or remain in a flat or horizontal position on a surface ⟨*books* lying *on the table*⟩ **b** *of snow* to remain on the ground without melting **3** to have as a direction; ¹LEAD 1b(1) ⟨*the route* lay *to the west*⟩ **4a** to occupy a specified place or position ⟨*hills* ~ *behind us*⟩ ⟨*the responsibility* ~s *with us*⟩ **b** to have an adverse or disheartening effect; weigh ⟨*remorse* lay *heavily on her*⟩ **c** *of an action, claim, etc in a court of law* to be sustainable or admissible **5** to remain at anchor or becalmed [ME *lien*, fr OE *licgan*; akin to OHG *ligen* to lie, L *lectus* bed, Gk *lechos*] – **lie low 1** to stay in hiding; strive to avoid notice **2** to bide one's time

²lie *n* **1** the way, position, or situation in which sthg lies ⟨*the* ~ *of the land*⟩ **2** a haunt of an animal or fish

³lie *vi* **lying** /'lie·ing/ **1** to make an untrue statement with intent to deceive; speak falsely **2** to create a false or misleading impression ⟨*the camera never* ~s⟩ [ME *lien*, fr OE *lēogan;* akin to OHG *liogan* to lie, OSlav *lŭgati*]

⁴lie *n* **1** an untrue or false statement, esp when made with intent to deceive **2** sthg that misleads or deceives

liebfraumilch /'leebfrowˌmilkh/ *n, often cap* a dry Hock [G, alter. of *liebfrauenmilch*, fr *Liebfrauenstift*, religious foundation in Worms, Germany + *milch* milk]

lied /leed (*Ger* liːt)/ *n, pl* **lieder** /'leedə, (*Ger* liːdər)/ a German song; *esp* a 19th-c setting of a lyrical poem [G, song, fr OHG *liod* – more at LAUD]

'lie deˌtector *n* an instrument for detecting physical evidence of the mental tension that accompanies telling lies

'lie-ˌdown *n, chiefly Br* a brief rest, esp on a bed – infml

lie down *vi* to submit meekly or abjectly to defeat, disappointment, or insult ⟨*won't take that criticism* lying down⟩

lief /leef/ *adv, archaic* soon, gladly ⟨*I'd as* ~ *go as not*⟩ [ME *lef, leif*, fr OE *lēof*, adj; akin to OE *lufu* love – more at LOVE]

¹liege /leej/ *adj* **1a** entitled to feudal allegiance **b** owing feudal allegiance **2** faithful, loyal [ME, fr OF, fr LL *laeticus*, fr *laetus* serf, of Gmc origin; akin to OFris *let* serf]

[2]**liege** *n* **1a** a feudal vassal **b** a loyal subject **2** a feudal superior

ˈ**liege ˌman** *n* **1** LIEGE 1a **2** a devoted follower

lie in *vi* **1** to be confined to give birth to a child **2** *chiefly Br* to stay in bed until later than usual in the morning – **lie-in** *n*

lien /ˈlee·ən, leen/ *n* the legal right to hold another's property until a claim is met [MF, tie, band, fr L *ligamen*, fr *ligare* to bind – more at LIGATURE]

lie off *vi, of a ship* to keep a little distance away from the shore or another ship

lie over *vi* to await attention at a later time ⟨*several jobs* lying over *from last week*⟩

lierne /liˈuhn, liˈeən/ *n* a nonstructural rib in a vault ☞ CHURCH [F, fr MF, fr *lier* to bind, tie –more at LIABLE]

lie to *vi, of a ship* to stay stationary with head to windward

lieu /l(y)ooh/ *n* [MF, place, fr L *locus* – more at [1]STALL] – **in lieu** in substitution; instead ⟨*I'm sending this message* in lieu *of a letter*⟩

lie up *vi* **1** to stay in bed, esp for a long period **2** *of a ship* to remain in dock or out of commission **3** to remain inactive or at rest

lieutenancy /lefˈtenənsi; *NAm* looh-/ *n* the office, rank, or commission of a lieutenant

lieutenant /lefˈtenənt; *Royal Navy* ləˈtenənt; *NAm* loohˈtenənt/ *n* **1** an official empowered to act for a higher official; a deputy or representative **2** ☞ RANK [ME, fr MF, fr *lieu* + *tenant* holding, fr *tenir* to hold, fr L *tenēre* – more at THIN]

lieutenant colonel *n* ☞ RANK

lieutenant commander *n* ☞ RANK

lieutenant general *n* ☞ RANK

lieutenant governor *n* a deputy or subordinate governor

lieutenant junior grade *n, pl* **lieutenants junior grade** ☞ RANK

[1]**life** /lief/ *n, pl* **lives** /lievz/ **1a** the quality that distinguishes a vital and functional being from a dead body **b** a principle or force considered to underlie the distinctive quality of animate beings – compare VITALISM 1 **c** a state of matter (e g a cell or an organism) characterized by capacity for metabolism, growth, reaction to stimuli, and reproduction **2a** the sequence of physical and mental experiences that make up the existence of an individual **b** an aspect of the process of living ⟨*the sex* ~ *of the frog*⟩ **3** BIOGRAPHY 1 **4** a state or condition of existence ⟨~ *after death*⟩ **5a** the period from birth to death or to the present time ⟨*I have lived here all my* ~⟩ **b** a specific phase of earthly existence ⟨*adult* ~⟩ **c** the period from an event or the present time until death ⟨*a member for* ~⟩ **d** a sentence of imprisonment for life ⟨*got* ~ *for the murder*⟩ **6** a way or manner of living ⟨*a holy* ~⟩ ⟨*a full* ~⟩ **7** a person ⟨*many* lives *were lost in the disaster*⟩ **8** the source of pleasure, interest, or enjoyment in living; the reason for living ⟨*his work was his whole* ~⟩ **9** the living form considered as a model ⟨*painted from* ~⟩ **10** the period of usefulness, effectiveness, or functioning of sthg inanimate ⟨*the expected* ~ *of torch batteries*⟩ **11** a period of existence (e g of a subatomic particle) – compare HALF-LIFE **12** living beings (e g of a specified kind or environment) ⟨*forest* ~⟩ **13a** the active part of human existence, esp in a wide range of circumstances or experiences ⟨*left home to see* ~⟩ **b** activity from living things; movement ⟨*stirrings of* ~⟩ **c** the activities of a specified sphere, area, or time ⟨*the political* ~ *of the country*⟩ **14** (one who provides) interest, animation, or vigour ⟨*the* ~ *and soul of the party*⟩ **15** any of several chances to participate given to a contestant in some games, 1 of which is forfeited each time he/she loses; *also* a failed chance to get a batsman out ⟨*dropped a catch and gave the batsman a* ~⟩ [ME *lif*, fr OE *līf*; akin to OE *libban* to live – more at LIVE]

[2]**life** *adj* **1** using a living model ⟨*a* ~ *class*⟩ **2** of, being, or provided by life insurance ⟨*a* ~ *policy*⟩

ˌ**life-and-ˈdeath** *adj* involving death or risk to life; vitally important

ˈ**life ˌbelt** *n* a buoyant belt for keeping a person afloat

ˈ**lifeˌblood** /-ˌblud, ˌ-ˈ-/ *n* **1** the blood necessary to life **2** a vital or life-giving force

ˈ**lifeˌboat** /-ˌboht/ *n* a robust buoyant boat for use in saving lives at sea

ˈ**life ˌbuoy** /boy/ *n* a buoyant often ring-shaped float to which a person may cling in the water

ˈ**life ˌcycle** *n* the series of stages in form and functional activity through which an organism, group, culture, etc passes during its lifetime

ˌ**life exˈpectancy** *n* the expected length of sby's or sthg's life, based on statistical probability

ˈ**life-ˌforce** *n* ÉLAN VITAL

ˈ**life-ˌgiving** *adj* giving or having power to give life or spirit; invigorating

ˈ**lifeˌguard** /-ˌgahd/ *n* a usu expert swimmer employed to safeguard other swimmers – **lifeguard** *vi*

ˌ**life ˈhistory** *n* the changes through which an organism passes in its development from the primary stage to its natural death

ˈ**life inˌsurance** *n* insurance providing for payment of a stipulated sum to a beneficiary on the death of the insured person or to the insured person on reaching a certain age

ˈ**life ˌjacket** *n* a buoyant device that is designed to keep a person afloat and can be worn continuously as a precaution against drowning

ˈ**lifeless** /-lis/ *adj* **1a** dead **b** inanimate **2** having no living beings ⟨*a* ~ *planet*⟩ **3** lacking qualities expressive of life and vigour; dull ⟨*a* ~ *voice*⟩ [[1]LIFE + -LESS] – **lifelessly** *adv*, **lifelessness** *n*

ˈ**lifeˌlike** /-ˌliek/ *adj* accurately representing or imitating (the appearance of objects in) real life

ˈ**lifeˌline** /-ˌlien/ *n* **1a** a rope for saving or safeguarding life: e g **(1)** one stretched along the deck of a ship in rough weather **(2)** one fired to a ship in distress by means of a rocket **b** the line by which a diver is lowered and raised **2** sthg, esp the sole means of communication, regarded as indispensable for the maintenance or protection of life

ˈ**lifeˌlong** /-ˌlong/ *adj* lasting or continuing throughout life

ˌ**life of ˈRiley** /ˈrieli/ *n* a carefree comfortable way of living – esp in *live the life of Riley* [fr the name *Riley* or *Reilly*]

ˌ**life ˈpeer,** *fem* **life peeress** /ˈpiəris/ *n* a British peer whose title is not hereditary – **life peerage** *n*

ˈ**life preˌserver** *n* **1** *chiefly Br* a small weighted club **2** *chiefly NAm* a life jacket, life buoy, etc

lifer /ˈliefə/ *n* one sentenced to life imprisonment – infml

ˈ**life ˌraft** *n* a raft for use by people forced into the water (e g in a shipwreck)

'life,saver /-,sayvə/ *n* sby or sthg timely and effective in the prevention or relief of distress or difficulty – **lifesaving** *adj or n*

,life 'science *n* a science (e g biology, medicine, anthropology, or sociology) that deals with living organisms and life processes – **life scientist** *n*

'life-,size, life-sized *adj* of natural size; of the size of the original ⟨*a ~ statue*⟩

'life-,style *n* an individual's way of life

'life ,table *n* a table of life based on the mortality statistics for several years

'life,time /-,tiem/ *n* the length of time for which a person, living thing, subatomic particle, etc exists

,life'work /-'wuhk/ *n* the entire or principal work (filling the whole) of one's lifetime

[1]lift /lift/ *vt* **1a** to raise from a lower to a higher position; elevate **b** to raise in rank or condition **2** to put an end to (a blockade or siege) by withdrawing the surrounding forces **3** to revoke, rescind ⟨*~ an embargo*⟩ **4a** to plagiarize **b** to take out of normal setting ⟨*~ a word out of context*⟩ **5** to take up (e g a root crop) from the ground **6** to hit (e g a cricket ball) or to hit the bowling of (a bowler) into the air **7** to steal ⟨*had her purse ~*ed⟩ – infml *~ vi* **1** to ascend, rise **2a** to disperse upwards ⟨*until the fog ~*s ⟩ **b** *of bad weather* to cease temporarily ⟨*the rain finally ~*ed⟩ **3** *of a bowled ball in cricket* to rise at a sharper angle than expected after pitching [ME *liften*, fr ON *lypta*; akin to OE *lyft* air – more at LOFT] – **liftable** *adj*, **lifter** *n*

[2]lift *n* **1a** (a device for) lifting or (the amount) being lifted **b** the lifting up of a dancer or skater usu by her partner **2** a usu free ride as a passenger in a motor vehicle **3** a slight rise or elevation of ground **4** the distance or extent to which sthg (e g water in a canal lock) rises **5** a usu temporary feeling of cheerfulness, pleasure, or encouragement ⟨*her new haircut gave her a real ~*⟩ **6** the upward part of the aerodynamic force acting on an aircraft or aerofoil that opposes the pull of gravity ☞ FLIGHT **7** an organized transport of men, equipment, or supplies; *esp* an airlift **8** any of the ropes by which the yard is suspended from the mast on a square-rigged ship ☞ SHIP **9** *chiefly Br* a device for conveying people or objects from one level to another, esp in a building

'lift-,off *n* a vertical takeoff by an aircraft, rocket vehicle, or missile ☞ SPACE – **lift off** *vi*

ligament /'ligəmənt/ *n* a tough band of connective tissue forming the capsule round a joint or supporting an organ (e g the womb) ☞ ANATOMY [ME, fr ML & L; ML *ligamentum*, fr L, band, tie, fr *ligare*] – **ligamentary** /-'ment(ə)ri/, **ligamentous** /-'mentəs/ *adj*

ligand /'ligənd, 'lie-/ *n* an ion, molecule, etc joined by many bonds to a central atom, ion, etc (e g in a coordination complex) [L *ligandus*, gerundive of *ligare*]

ligate /'lie,gayt, -'-/ *vt* to tie with a ligature [L *ligatus*, pp of *ligare*] – **ligation** /lie'gaysh(ə)n/ *n*

ligature /'ligəchə/ *n* **1a** sthg that is used to bind; *specif* a thread used in surgery **b** sthg that unites or connects **2** the action of binding or tying **3** [2]SLUR 1 **4** a character consisting of 2 or more letters or characters joined together; *esp* one (e g) other than a diphthong [ME, fr MF, fr LL *ligatura*, fr L *ligatus*, pp of *ligare* to bind, tie; akin to MHG ge*leich* joint, Alb *lith* I tie]

[1]light /liet/ *n* **1a** (the sensation aroused by) sthg that makes vision possible by stimulating the sense of sight **b** an electromagnetic radiation in the wavelength range including infrared, visible, ultraviolet, and X rays; *specif* the part of this range that is visible to the human eye ☞ PHYSICS **2** daylight **3** a source of light: e g **a** a celestial body **b** a burning candle **c** an electric light **4a** spiritual illumination **b** INNER LIGHT **c** understanding, knowledge **d** *the* truth ⟨*see the ~*⟩ **5a** public knowledge ⟨*facts brought to ~*⟩ **b** a particular aspect or appearance in which sthg is viewed ⟨*now saw the matter in a different ~*⟩ **6** a particular illumination in a place ⟨*studio with a north ~*⟩ **7** (enlightening) information or explanation ⟨*he shed some ~ on the problem*⟩ **8** a medium (e g a window) through which light is admitted **9** *pl* a set of principles, standards, or opinions ⟨*true by your ~*s⟩ **10** LEADING LIGHT **11** a specified expression, perceived as being in sby's eyes ⟨*the ~ of love in his eyes*⟩ **12a** a lighthouse **b** TRAFFIC LIGHT **13** the representation in art of the effect of light on objects or scenes **14** a flame or spark for lighting sthg (e g a cigarette) **15** *Br* the answer to 1 of the clues of a crossword [ME, fr OE *lēoht*; akin to OHG *lioht* light, L *luc-*, *lux* light, *lucēre* to shine, Gk *leukos* white] – **lightless** *adj*, **lightproof** /-,proohf/ *adj* – **in the light of** with the insight provided by

[2]light *adj* **1** having plenty of light; bright ⟨*a ~ airy room*⟩ **2a** pale in colour or colouring **b** *of colours* medium in saturation and high in lightness

[3]light *vb* **lit** /lit/, **lighted** /'lietid/ *vi* **1** LIGHT UP 1 **2** to catch fire *~ vt* **1** to set fire to **2a** to conduct (sby) with a light; guide **b** to illuminate ⟨*a room* lit *by a bay window*⟩

[4]light *adj* **1a** having little weight; not heavy **b** designed to carry a comparatively small load ⟨*a ~ van*⟩ **c** of the smaller variety ⟨*a ~ gun*⟩ **d** (made of materials) having relatively little weight in proportion to bulk ⟨*aluminium is a ~ metal*⟩ **e** containing less than the legal, standard, or usual weight ⟨*a ~ coin*⟩ **2a** of little importance; trivial **b** not abundant ⟨*~ rain*⟩ ⟨*a ~ crop of wheat*⟩ **3a** *of sleep or a sleeper* easily disturbed **b** exerting a minimum of force or pressure; gentle, soft ⟨*a ~ touch*⟩ ⟨*a ~ breeze*⟩ ⟨*a ~ voice*⟩ **c** faint ⟨*~ print*⟩ **4a** easily endurable ⟨*~ taxation*⟩ **b** requiring little effort ⟨*~ work*⟩ **5** nimble ⟨*~ on his feet*⟩ **6** lacking seriousness; frivolous **7** free from care; cheerful ⟨*a ~ heart*⟩ **8** intending or intended chiefly to entertain ⟨*~ reading*⟩ **9** *of a drink* having a comparatively low alcoholic content or a mild flavour ⟨*a ~ white wine*⟩ **10a** easily digested ⟨*a ~ dessert*⟩ **b** well leavened ⟨*a ~ cake*⟩ **11** lightly armoured, armed, or equipped ⟨*~ cavalry*⟩ **12** easily pulverized; crumbly ⟨*~ soil*⟩ **13** dizzy, giddy ⟨*felt ~ in the head*⟩ **14a** carrying little or no cargo ⟨*the ship returned ~*⟩ **b** producing light usu small goods often for direct consumption ⟨*~ industry*⟩ [ME, fr OE *lēoht*; akin to OHG *līhti* light, L *levis*, Gk *elachys* small] – **lightish** *adj*, **lightly** *adv*, **lightness** *n*

[5]light *adv* **1** lightly **2** with the minimum of luggage ⟨*travel ~*⟩

[6]light *vi* **lighted, lit** /lit/ **1** to settle, alight ⟨*a bird* lit *on the lawn*⟩ **2** to arrive by chance; happen ⟨lit *upon a solution*⟩ [ME *lighten*, fr OE *līhtan*; akin to OE *lēoht* light in weight]

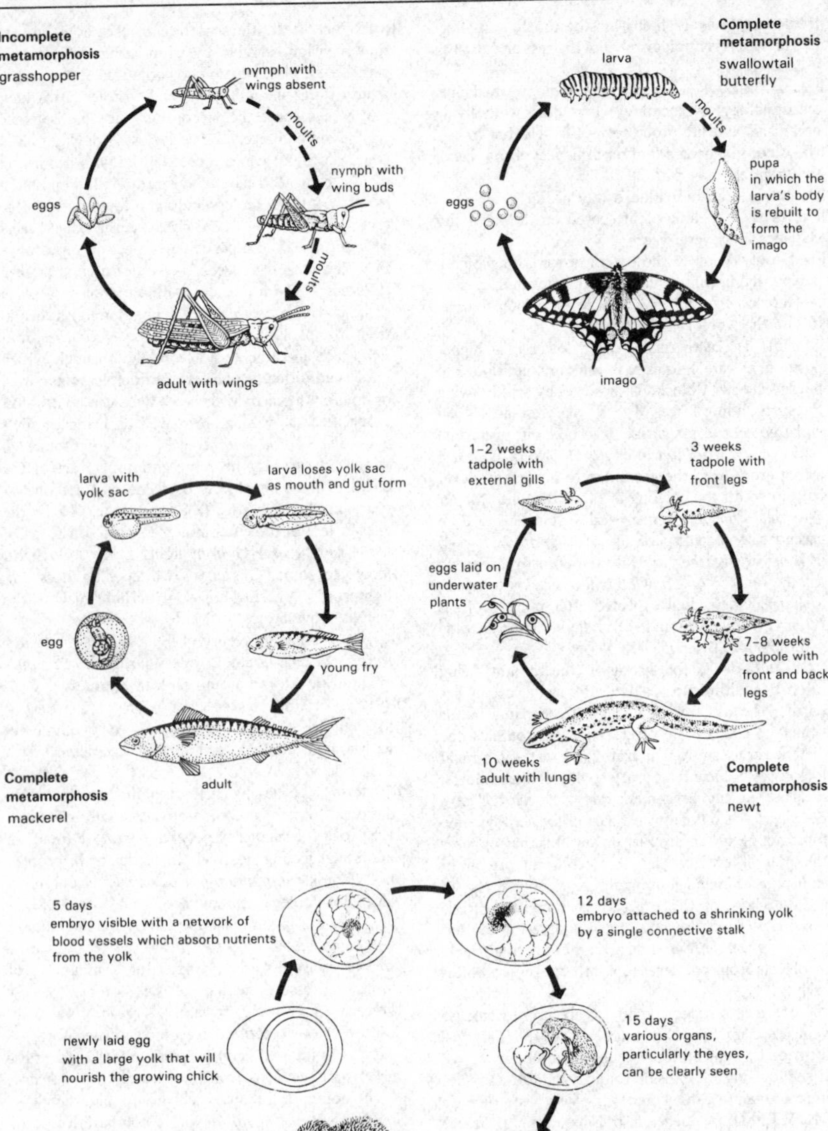
Incomplete metamorphosis
grasshopper
nymph with wings absent
moults
nymph with wing buds
moults
eggs
adult with wings
Complete metamorphosis
swallowtail butterfly
larva
moults
pupa in which the larva's body is rebuilt to form the imago
eggs
imago
larva with yolk sac
larva loses yolk sac as mouth and gut form
young fry
egg
adult
Complete metamorphosis
mackerel
1–2 weeks tadpole with external gills
3 weeks tadpole with front legs
eggs laid on underwater plants
7–8 weeks tadpole with front and back legs
10 weeks adult with lungs
Complete metamorphosis
newt
5 days
embryo visible with a network of blood vessels which absorb nutrients from the yolk
12 days
embryo attached to a shrinking yolk by a single connective stalk
newly laid egg
with a large yolk that will nourish the growing chick
15 days
various organs, particularly the eyes, can be clearly seen
29 days
newly hatched chick
23 days
chick is fully formed and absorbs the remaining yolk into its abdomen
Development of the avian egg
turkey

Development of a marsupial mammal

After a six-week gestation, the kangaroo gives birth to a tiny undeveloped offspring, which crawls to its mother's pouch and attaches itself to a nipple. When sufficiently developed the young kangaroo makes excursions from the pouch, but will return to suckle until it is a year old.

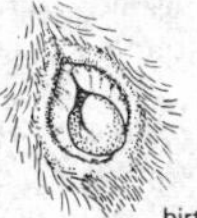
birth

young kangaroo crawls to pouch

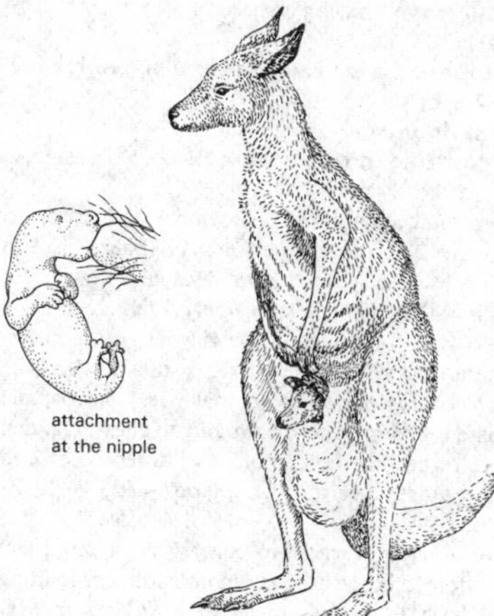
attachment at the nipple

Development of a placental mammal

The young of placental mammals are nurtured and protected inside the mother during early development. Continuous nourishment and oxygen pass from the mother to the embryo via the placenta. As a result, the offspring are born at a more advanced stage of development than marsupial offspring. ☞ REPRODUCTION

Oviparity

Birds and many reptiles are oviparous: the young develop and hatch from eggs outside the mother's body. In general, oviparous species lay large numbers of eggs in order that some of their offspring might survive.

Ovoviviparity

Some lizards and snakes are ovoviviparous: the young develop in eggs inside the mother's body and hatch at, or just after, laying. Offspring produced ovoviviparously are less vulnerable to climatic variations and predation than those produced oviparously.

Viviparity

Most mammals, some reptiles, and a few fish are viviparous: the young develop inside the mother and are born in an active state. A giraffe is well-developed at birth as it must run with the herd, soon after, in order to survive. Rabbits, on the other hand, are born blind, naked, and helpless in the protection of the burrow.

crocodile hatching from egg

puff adder and young

herring gull chicks in nest

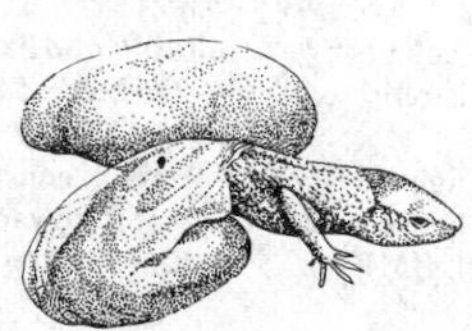
common lizard hatching from newly-laid soft membranous egg

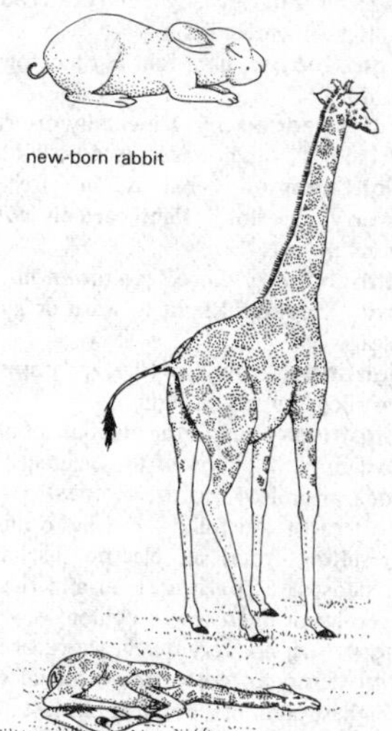
new-born rabbit

new-born giraffe

light air *n* wind having a speed of 1 to 5km/h (1 to 3mph)

light breeze *n* wind having a speed of 6 to 11km/h (4 to 7mph)

'light ,bulb *n* INCANDESCENT LAMP

light-emitting diode *n* an LED ☞ TELECOMMUNICATION

[1]**lighten** /'liet(ə)n/ *vt* **1** to make (more) light or clear; illuminate **2** to make (e g a colour) lighter ~ *vi* **1** to grow lighter; brighten **2** to discharge flashes of lightning [ME *lightenen*, fr *light*] – **lightener** *n*

[2]**lighten** *vt* **1** to reduce the weight of ⟨~ *the lorry*⟩ ⟨~ *her duties*⟩ **2** to relieve (partly) of a burden ⟨*the news* ~ed *his mind*⟩ **3** to make less wearisome; alleviate ⟨~ed *his gloom*⟩; *broadly* to cheer, gladden ~ *vi* **1** to become lighter or less burdensome **2** to become more cheerful ⟨*his mood* ~ed⟩ – **lightener** *n*

[1]**lighter** /'lietə/ *vt or n* (to convey by) a large usu flat-bottomed barge used esp in unloading or loading ships [n ME, fr (assumed) MD *lichter*, fr MD *lichten* to unload; akin to OE *lēoht* light in weight; vb fr n]

[2]**lighter** *n* a device for lighting (a cigar, cigarette, etc) [[3]LIGHT + [2]-ER]

lighterage /'lietərij/ *n* (the charge for) the loading, unloading, or transport of goods by means of a lighter

,lighter-than-'air *adj*, *of an aircraft* of less weight than the air displaced

,light-'fingered *adj* **1** adroit in stealing, esp picking pockets **2** having a light and dexterous touch; nimble – **light-fingeredness** *n*

,light-'footed, light-foot *adj* moving gracefully and nimbly

,light-'headed *adj* **1** mentally disoriented; dizzy **2** frivolous – **light-headedly** *adv*, **light-headedness** *n*

,light'hearted /-'hahtid/ *adj* free from care or worry; cheerful – **lightheartedly** *adv*, **lightheartedness** *n*

'light,house /-,hows/ *n* a tower, mast, etc equipped with a powerful light to warn or guide shipping at sea

lighting /'lieting/ *n* (the apparatus providing) an artificial supply of light

'lightness /-nis/ *n* the attribute of object colours by which more or less of the incident light is reflected or transmitted [[2]LIGHT + -NESS]

[1]**lightning** /'lietning/ *n* (the brilliant light flash resulting from) an electric discharge between 2 clouds or between a cloud and the earth [ME, fr gerund of *lightenen* to lighten]

[2]**lightning** *adj* very quick, short, or sudden

'lightning con,ductor *n* a metal rod fixed to the highest point of a building or mast and connected to the earth or water below as a protection against lightning

,light 'opera *n* an operetta

light out *vi*, *NAm* to leave in a hurry – infml ⟨lit out *for home as soon as he could*⟩ [[6]*light*]

'light ,pen *n* a pen-shaped photoelectric device that is pointed at a VDU to create or identify characters, symbols, etc for input into a computer

lights /liets/ *n pl* the lungs, esp of a slaughtered sheep, pig, etc [ME *lightes*, fr *light* light in weight]

'light,ship /-,ship/ *n* a moored vessel equipped with a powerful light to warn or guide shipping at sea

'light ,show *n* an entertainment of ever-changing coloured light

'lights-,out *n* **1** a command or signal for putting out lights **2** a prescribed bedtime for people living in an institution (e g boarding school)

light up *vb* **1** to illuminate or become illuminated or lit (in a sudden or conspicuous manner) ⟨*fireworks* lit up *the night sky*⟩ ⟨*her face* lit up⟩ **2** to ignite (a cigarette, pipe, etc)

'light,weight /-,wayt/ *n or adj* **1** (a boxer) weighing not more than 9st 9lb (61.2kg) if professional or more than 57kg (about 8st 13lb) but not more than 60kg (about 9st 6lb) if amateur **2** (sby) of little ability or importance

'light-,year *n* a unit of length in astronomy equal to the distance that light travels in 1 year in a vacuum; 9,460 thousand million km (about 5,878 thousand million mi) ☞ ASTRONOMY, UNIT

lign-, ligni-, ligno- *comb form* **1** wood ⟨lignin⟩ ⟨ligneous⟩ **2** lignin and ⟨lignocellulose⟩ [L *lign-*, *ligni-*, fr *lignum*, fr *legere* to gather – more at LEGEND]

lignify /'lignifie/ *vb* to convert into or become wood or woody tissue [F *lignifier*, fr L *lignum*] – **lignification** /-fi'kaysh(ə)n/ *n*

lignin /'lignin/ *n* a substance that forms the (cementing material between the) woody cell walls of plants

lignite /'ligniet/ *n* a brownish black coal that is harder than peat but usu retains the texture of the original wood [F, fr L *lignum*] – **lignitic** /-'nitik/ *adj*

lignocaine /'lignə,kayn/ *n* a synthetic local anaesthetic

lignum vitae /,lignəm 'vieti/ *n*, *pl* **lignum vitaes** (the very hard heavy dark wood of) any of several tropical American trees [NL, lit., wood of life]

ligulate /'ligyoolət, -layt/ *adj* **1** shaped like a strap ⟨*the* ~ *corolla of a ray flower of a composite plant*⟩ ☞ PLANT **2** having ligules

ligule /'ligyoohl/ *n* an appendage on a foliage leaf and esp on the part of a blade of grass that forms a sheath round the stem [NL *ligula*, fr L, small tongue, strap; akin to L *lingere* to lick – more at LICK]

likable *also* **likeable** /'liekəbl/ *adj* pleasant, agreeable – **likableness** *n*, **likability** /-'biləti/ *n*

[1]**like** /liek/ *vt* **1a** to find agreeable, acceptable, or pleasant; enjoy ⟨~s *games*⟩ ⟨~s *playing games*⟩ **b** to feel towards; regard ⟨*how would you* ~ *a change?*⟩ **2** to wish or choose to have, be, or do; want ⟨~s *to help*⟩ ⟨~s *us to come early*⟩ ~ *vi* to feel inclined; choose ⟨*you can leave any time you* ~⟩ [ME *liken*, fr OE *līcian*; akin to OE *gelīc* alike] – **if you like** SO TO SPEAK

[2]**like** *n* a liking, preference ⟨*one's* ~s *and dislikes*⟩

[3]**like** *adj* **1a** alike in appearance, character, or quantity ⟨*suits of* ~ *design*⟩ **b** bearing a close resemblance; *esp* faithful ⟨*his portrait is very* ~⟩ **2** likely [ME, alter. of *ilich*, fr OE *gelīc* like, alike; akin to OHG *gilīh* like, alike; both fr a prehistoric Gmc compound whose first constituent is represented by OE *ge-* (associative prefix) and whose second is represented by OE *līc* body; akin to Lith *lygus* like – more at co-]

[4]**like** *prep* **1a** having the characteristics of; similar to ⟨*his house is* ~ *a barn*⟩ **b** typical of ⟨*was* ~ *her to do that*⟩ **2a** in the manner of; similarly to ⟨*act* ~ *a*

fool⟩ **b** to the same degree as ⟨*fits* ~ *a glove*⟩ **c** close to ⟨*cost something* ~ *£5*⟩ **3** appearing to be, threaten, or promise ⟨*you seem* ~ *a sensible man*⟩ **4** – used to introduce an example ⟨*a subject* ~ *physics*⟩ – **like that 1** in that way ⟨*don't eat* like that⟩ **2** without demur or hesitation ⟨*can't change jobs just* like that⟩ – **like anything/crazy** – used to emphasize a verb; infml ⟨*run* like anything⟩

[5]**like** *n* one who or that which is like another, esp in high value; a counterpart ⟨*never saw the* ~ *of it*⟩ ⟨*had no use for the* ~s *of him*⟩ ⟨*her* ~ *will never be seen again*⟩ – **the like** similar things ⟨*football, tennis, and* the like⟩

[6]**like** *adv* **1** likely, probably ⟨*he'll come as* ~ *as not*⟩ **2** SO TO SPEAK ⟨*went up to her casually,* ~⟩ – nonstandard

[7]**like** *conj* **1** in the same way as ⟨*if she can sing* ~ *she can dance*⟩ **2** *chiefly NAm* as if ⟨*acts* ~ *he knows what he's doing*⟩

-like /-liek/ *comb form* (*n* → *adj*) resembling or characteristic of ⟨*bell*-like⟩ ⟨*lady*like⟩

likelihood /'liekli,hood/ *n* probability ⟨*in all* ~ *it will rain*⟩

[1]**likely** /'liekli/ *adj* **1** having a high probability of being or occurring ⟨~ *to succeed*⟩ ⟨*the* ~ *result*⟩ **2a** reliable, credible ⟨*a* ~ *enough story*⟩ **b** incredible – used ironically ⟨*a* ~ *tale!*⟩ **3** seeming appropriate; suitable ⟨*a* ~ *spot*⟩ **4** promising ⟨~ *lads*⟩ [ME, fr ON *glīkligr*, fr *glīkr* like; akin to OE *gelīc*]

[2]**likely** *adv* probably – often in *most/very/more/quite likely* ⟨*he most* ~ *will give up*⟩

,**like-'minded** *adj* having a similar outlook or disposition – **like-mindedly** *adv*, **like-mindedness** *n*

liken /'liekən/ *vt* to find or point out similarities in; compare

'**likeness** /-nis/ *n* **1** resemblance **2** a copy, portrait ⟨*a good* ~ *of her*⟩ **3** *archaic* an appearance, semblance [[3]LIKE + -NESS]

'**like,wise** /-,wiez/ *adv* **1** in like manner; similarly ⟨*go and do* ~⟩ **2** moreover; IN ADDITION **3** similarly so with me ⟨*answered '*~*' to 'Pleased to meet you'*⟩

liking /'lieking/ *n* favourable regard; fondness, taste ⟨*took a* ~ *to the newcomer*⟩ ⟨*things were not to his* ~⟩

likuta /li'k(y)oohtə/ *n, pl* **makuta** /mah-/ ☞ *Zaire* at NATIONALITY [of Niger-Congo origin; prob akin to obs Nupe *kuta* stone]

lilac /'lielək, -lak/ *n* **1** a European shrub of the olive family with heart-shaped leaves and large clusters of fragrant white or (pale pinkish) purple flowers **2** pale pinkish purple [obs F (now *lilas*), fr Ar *līlak*, fr Per *nīlak* bluish, fr *nīl* blue, fr Skt *nīla* dark blue]

lilangeni /,lilang'geni/ *n, pl* **emalangeni** /,eemahlang'geni/ ☞ *Swaziland* at NATIONALITY [of Bantu origin]

lilliputian /,lili'pyoohsh(y)ən/ *n or adj, often cap* (sby or sthg) remarkably tiny or diminutive [*Lilliput*, imaginary country of tiny people in *Gulliver's Travels* by Jonathan Swift †1745 Ir satirist]

Li-Lo /'lie ,loh/ *trademark* – used for an airbed

[1]**lilt** /lilt/ *vb* to sing or speak rhythmically and with varying pitch [ME *lulten*] – **liltingly** *adv*

[2]**lilt** *n* **1** (a song or tune with) a rhythmic swing, flow, or rising and falling inflection **2** a light springy motion ⟨*a* ~ *in her step*⟩

lily /'lili/ *n* **1** any of a genus of plants that grow from bulbs and are widely cultivated for their variously coloured showy flowers; *also* any of various other plants of the lily or the related daffodil or iris families **2** WATER LILY **3** a calla **4** FLEUR-DE-LIS 2 **5** one resembling a lily in fairness, purity, or fragility – poetic [ME *lilie*, fr OE, fr L *lilium*] – **liliaceous** /-'ayshəs/ *adj*

,**lily-'livered** /'livəd/ *adj* lacking courage; cowardly

,**lily of the 'valley** *n* a low perennial plant of the lily family that has usu 2 large leaves and a stalk of fragrant drooping bell-shaped white flowers

'**lily ,pad** *n* a large flat floating leaf of a water lily

,**lily-'white** *adj* **1** pure white **2** irreproachable, pure

'**lima ,bean** /'liemə/ *n* (the flat edible seed of) any of various widely cultivated bushy or tall-growing orig tropical American beans [*Lima*, capital city of Peru]

[1]**limb** /lim/ *n* **1** any of the projecting paired appendages of an animal body used esp for movement and grasping but sometimes modified into sensory or sexual organs; *esp* a leg or arm of a human being **2** a large primary branch of a tree **3** an active member or agent ⟨~s *of the law*⟩ **4** an extension, branch; *specif* any of the 4 branches or arms of a cross **5** *archaic* a mischievous child [ME *lim*, fr OE; akin to ON *limr* limb, L *limes* limit, *limen* threshold, Gk *leimōn* meadow] – **limbless** *adj* – **out on a limb** in an exposed and unsupported position

[2]**limb** *vt* to dismember; *esp* to cut off the limbs of (a felled tree)

[3]**limb** *n* **1** the graduated edge of a quadrant, levelling staff, etc **2** the outer edge of the apparent disc of a celestial body **3** the broad flat part of a petal or sepal furthest from its base [L *limbus* border – more at [1]LIMP]

limbed /limd/ *adj* having (a specified kind or number of) limbs – usu in combination ⟨*strong*-limbed⟩

[1]**limber** /'limbə/ *n* a 2-wheeled (ammunition-carrying) vehicle to which a gun may be attached [ME *lymour*]

[2]**limber** *adj* supple in mind or body; flexible [origin unknown] – **limberly** *adv*, **limberness** *n*

limber up *vb* to (cause to) become supple, flexible, or prepared for physical action ⟨limbered up *before the match*⟩

limbic /'limbik/ *adj* of or being a group of structures in the brain, including the hypothalamus and hippocampus, that are concerned esp with emotion and motivation [NL *limbicus* of a border or margin, fr L *limbus*]

[1]**limbo** /'limboh/ *n, pl* **limbos 1** *often cap* an abode of souls that are according to Roman Catholic theology barred from heaven because of not having received Christian baptism **2a** a place or state of restraint or confinement, or of neglect or oblivion **b** an intermediate or transitional place or state [ME, fr ML, abl of *limbus* limbo, fr L, border – more at [1]LIMP]

[2]**limbo** *n, pl* **limbos** a W Indian acrobatic dance that involves bending over backwards and passing under a low horizontal pole [native name in W Indies]

[1]**lime** /liem/ *n* **1** birdlime **2a** a caustic solid consisting of calcium (and some magnesium) oxide, obtained by heating calcium carbonate (e g in the form of shells or limestone) to a high temperature, and used in building (e g in plaster) and in agriculture ☞ BUILDING **b** calcium hydroxide (occurring as a dry

white powder), made by treating caustic lime with water **c** calcium ⟨*carbonate of* ~⟩ – not now used technically [ME, fr OE *līm*; akin to OHG *līm* birdlime, L *lima* file, *linere* to smear, *levis* smooth, Gk *leios*] – **limy** *adj*

[2]**lime** *vt* to treat or cover with lime ⟨~ *the soil in the spring*⟩

[3]**lime** *n* (the light fine-grained wood of) any of a genus of widely planted (ornamental) trees that usu have heart-shaped leaves [alter. of ME *lind*, fr OE; akin to OHG *linta* linden]

[4]**lime** *n* a (spiny tropical citrus tree cultivated for its) small spherical greenish-yellow fruit [F, fr Prov *limo*, fr Ar *līm*]

'lime,juicer /'joohsə/ *n, NAm* a British ship or sailor – slang [fr the former use of lime juice on British ships as a drink to prevent scurvy]

'lime,light /-,liet/ *n* **1** (the white light produced by) a stage lighting instrument producing illumination by means of an intense flame directed on a cylinder of lime **2** *the* centre of public attention ⟨*she's in the* ~ *again*⟩

limen /'liemən, -men/ *n* THRESHOLD 3 [L *limin-, limen* – more at [1]LIMB]

limerick /'limərik/ *n* a humorous and often epigrammatic or indecent verse form of 5 lines with a rhyme scheme of aabba [*Limerick*, city & county in Eire]

'lime,stone /-,stohn/ *n* a widely-occurring rock consisting mainly of calcium carbonate

'lime,wash /-,wash/ *n* a mixture of lime and water used as a coating (e g for walls)

'lime,water /-,wawtə/ *n* an alkaline solution of calcium hydroxide in water used esp as an antacid

limey /'liemi/ *n, often cap, NAm* a British person, esp a sailor – slang [*lime*-juicer + *-y*]

liminal /'liminəl/ *adj* **1** of or at a sensory threshold **2** barely perceptible [L *limin-, limen* threshold]

[1]**limit** /'limit/ *n* **1a** a boundary **b** *pl* the place enclosed within a boundary ⟨*must not go off* ~s⟩ **2a** sthg that bounds, restrains, or confines ⟨*worked within the* ~s *of his knowledge*⟩ ⟨*set a* ~ *on his spending*⟩ **b** a line or point that cannot or should not be passed **3** a prescribed maximum or minimum amount, quantity, or number ⟨*a speed* ~⟩ **4** a number which is approached but not reached by the value of **a** a function when the independent variable is made to approach a prescribed number or to increase or decrease indefinitely **b** the sum of a series as the number of terms is increased indefinitely **5** sby or sthg exasperating or intolerable – + *the*; infml [ME, fr MF *limite*, fr L *limit-, limes* boundary – more at [1]LIMB] – **limitless** *adj*, **limitlessly** *adv*, **limitlessness** *n*

[2]**limit** *vt* **1** to restrict to specific bounds or limits ⟨*the specialist can no longer* ~ *himself to his speciality*⟩ **2** to curtail or reduce in quantity or extent; curb ⟨*we must* ~ *the power of aggressors*⟩ – **limitable** *adj*, **limiter** *n*, **limitative** /'limitətiv/ *adj*

limitation /,limi'taysh(ə)n/ *n* **1** (sthg that is) limiting; *esp* a limit of capability **2** a period defined by statute after which a claimant is barred from bringing a legal action [[2]LIMIT + -ATION] – **limitational** *adj*

limited /'limitid/ *adj* **1** confined within limits; restricted ⟨~ *success*⟩ **2** restricted as to the scope of powers ⟨*a* ~ *monarchy*⟩ **3** lacking the ability to grow or do better ⟨*a bit* ~; *a bit thick in the head* – Virginia Woolf⟩ **4** *Br* being a limited company – **limitedly** *adv*, **limitedness** *n*

limited company *n* a company in which the responsibility of an individual shareholder for the company's debts is limited according to the amount of his/her personal interest – compare INCORPORATED

limnology /lim'noləji/ *n* the scientific study of physical, chemical, biological, etc conditions in fresh waters (e g lakes) [Gk *limnē* pool, marshy lake + ISV *-logy*] – **limnologist** *n*, **limnological** /,limnə'lojəkl/ *adj*, **limnologically** *adv*

limo /'limoh/ *n, pl* **limos** a limousine – infml

limousine /,limə'zeen, '---/ *n* a luxurious motor car (with a glass partition separating the driver from the passengers) [F, lit., cloak, fr *Limousin*, former province of France]

[1]**limp** /limp/ *vi* **1** to walk in a manner that avoids putting the full weight of the body on 1 (injured) leg **2** to proceed slowly or with difficulty ⟨*the plane* ~ed *home*⟩ [prob fr ME *lympen* to fall short; akin to OE *limpan* to happen, L *limbus* border, *labi* to slide – more at SLEEP] – **limper** *n*

[2]**limp** *n* a limping movement or gait

[3]**limp** *adj* **1a** lacking firmness and body; drooping or shapeless **b** not stiff or rigid ⟨*a* ~ *cover for a book*⟩ **2** lacking energy [akin to [1]*limp*] – **limply** *adv*, **limpness** *n*

limpet /'limpit/ *n* **1** a marine gastropod mollusc with a low conical shell broadly open beneath, that clings very tightly to rock when disturbed **2** sby or sthg that clings tenaciously **3** an explosive device designed to cling to the hull of a ship, tank, etc ⟨*a* ~ *mine*⟩ [ME *lempet*, fr OE *lempedu*, fr ML *lampreda*]

limpid /'limpid/ *adj* **1** transparent, pellucid ⟨~ *streams*⟩ **2** clear and simple in style ⟨~ *prose*⟩ [F or L; F *limpide*, fr L *limpidus*, fr *lympha*, *limpa* water – more at LYMPH] – **limpidly** *adv*, **limpidness**, **limpidity** /lim'pidəti/ *n*

limulus /'limyooləs/ *n, pl* **limuli** /-lie/ any of a genus of king crabs [NL, genus name, fr L *limus* sidelong]

linage /'lienij/ *n* the number of lines of printed or written matter

linchpin, lynchpin /'linch,pin/ *n* **1** a locking pin inserted crosswise (e g through the end of an axle or shaft) **2** sby or sthg regarded as a vital or coordinating factor ⟨*the* ~ *of the organization*⟩ [ME *lynspin*, fr *lyns* linchpin (fr OE *lynis*) + *pin*]

linctus /'lingktəs/ *n* any of various syrupy usu medicated liquids used to relieve throat irritation and coughing [NL, fr L, pp of *lingere* to lick – more at LICK]

lindane /'lindayn/ *n* a type of benzene hexachloride used as an insecticide that persists in the environment [T van der *Linden* b1884 D chemist]

linden /'lind(ə)n/ *n* [3]LIME [ME, made of linden wood, fr OE, fr *lind* linden tree]

[1]**line** /lien/ *vt* **1** to cover the inner surface of; provide with a lining ⟨~ *a cloak with silk*⟩ **2** to fill ⟨lining *his pockets with other people's money*⟩ **3** to serve as the lining of ⟨*tapestries* ~d *the walls*⟩ [ME *linen*, fr *line* flax, fr OE *līn* – more at LINEN]

[2]**line** *n* **1a(1)** a (comparatively strong slender) cord or rope **(2)** a rope used on shipboard **b(1)** a device for catching fish consisting of a usu single-filament cord with hooks, floats, a reel, etc **(2)** scope for activity **c** a length of material (e g cord) used in measuring

and levelling ⟨*a plumb* ~⟩ **d** piping for conveying a fluid (e g steam or compressed air) **e(1)** (a connection for communication by means of) a set of wires connecting one telephone or telegraph (exchange) with another **(2)** the principal circuits of an electric power distribution system **2a** a horizontal row of written or printed characters **b** a single row of words in a poem **c** a short letter; a note **d** a short sequence of words spoken by an actor playing a particular role; *also, pl* all of the sequences making up a particular role **3a** sthg (e g a ridge, seam, or crease) that is distinct, elongated, and narrow **b** a wrinkle (e g on the face) **c(1)** the course or direction of sthg in motion ⟨*the* ~ *of march*⟩ **(2)** the trail of scent left by a hunted animal **d** a real or imaginary straight line ⟨*lies on a* ~ *between London and Glasgow*⟩ **e** a boundary or limit (of an area) ⟨*the state* ~⟩ ⟨*there's a very fine* ~ *between punishment and cruelty*⟩ **f** (a single set of rails forming) a railway track **4a** a course of conduct, action, or thought **b** a field of activity or interest ⟨*what's your* ~*?*⟩ **c** a specified way or theme of talking or writing **5a(1)** a related series of people or things coming one after the other in time; a family, lineage **(2)** a strain produced and maintained by selective breeding **b** a linked series of trenches and fortifications, esp facing the enemy – usu pl with sing. meaning **c** a military formation in which men, companies, etc are abreast of each other **d** naval ships arranged in a regular order ⟨*the fleet changed from* ~ *ahead to* ~ *abreast*⟩ **e** the regular and numbered infantry regiments of the army as opposed to auxiliary forces or household troops **f** a rank of objects of 1 kind; a row **g** (the company owning or operating) a group of vehicles, ships, aeroplanes, etc carrying passengers or goods regularly over a route ⟨*a shipping* ~⟩ **h** an arrangement of operations in manufacturing allowing ordered occurrence of various stages of production **6** a narrow elongated mark drawn, projected, or imagined (e g on a map): e g **a** a boundary, contour, circle of latitude or longitude, etc **b** *the* equator **c** any of the horizontal parallel strokes on a music staff on or between which notes are placed – compare SPACE 3 **d** a mark (e g in pencil) that forms part of the formal design of a picture; *also* an artist's use of such lines ⟨*purity of* ~⟩ **e** (a single passage of the scanning spot tracing) a horizontal line on a television screen – compare FRAME 4b(4) ☞ TELEVISION **f** a narrow part of a spectrum (e g of light from the sun) distinguished by being noticeably more or less bright than neighbouring areas ⟨*the sodium* ~s *occur in the yellow part of the spectrum*⟩ **g** a demarcation of a limit with reference to which the playing of some game or sport is regulated – usu in combination ⟨*a touch*line⟩ **7** a straight or curved geometric element, generated by a moving point (continually satisfying a particular condition), that has length but no breadth **8a** a defining outline; a contour ⟨*the* ~ *of a building*⟩ ⟨*the clean* ~s *of a ship*⟩ **b** a general plan; a model – usu pl with sing. meaning ⟨*writing sthg on the* ~s *of a guidebook*⟩ **9** merchandise or services of the same general class for sale or regularly available **10** an indication (e g of intention) based on insight or investigation ⟨*got a* ~ *on their plans*⟩ **11** *pl, Br* a row of tents or huts in a military camp **12** *chiefly Br* a pica **13** *pl, Br* a (specified) number of lines of writing, esp to be copied as a school punishment [ME; partly fr OF *ligne*, fr L *linea*, fr fem of *lineus* made of flax, fr *linum* flax; partly fr OE *līne*; akin to OE *līn*] – **liny** *also* **liney** /ˈlieni/ *adj* – **between the lines 1** by concealed implication **2** by way of inference ⟨*if you read* between the lines, *the meaning is different*⟩ – **in line for** due or in a position to receive – **into line** into a state of agreement or obedience – **on the line** at risk ⟨*put his job* on the line *because of his principles*⟩

³line *vt* **1** to mark or cover with a line or lines **2** to place or form a line along ⟨*pedestrians* ~ *the streets*⟩ **3** to form into a line or lines; LINE UP

lineage /ˈlini·ij/ *n* a (group of organisms belonging to the same) line of descent from a common ancestor or source [ME *linage*, fr MF *linage, lignage*, fr OF, fr *ligne*]

lineal /ˈlini·əl/ *adj* **1** composed of or arranged in lines **2** consisting of or being in a direct line of ancestry or descent – usu contrasted with *collateral* **3** of, being, or dealing with a lineage – **lineally** *adv*, **lineality** /ˌliniˈaləti/ *n*

lineament /ˈlini·əmənt/ *n* a distinctive outline, feature, or contour of a body or figure, esp a face – usu pl [ME, fr L *lineamentum*, fr *linea*] – **lineamental** /-ˈmentl/ *adj*

linear /ˈlini·ə/ *adj* **1a(1)** of, being, or resembling a line **(2)** involving a single dimension **b** *of an equation, function, etc* containing any number of variables, all of the first degree, and represented graphically by a straight line **c(1)** characterized by an emphasis on line; *esp* having clearly defined outlines **(2)** *esp of writing* composed of simply drawn lines with little attempt at pictorial representation **d** consisting of a straight chain of atoms **2** having or being a response or output that is directly proportional to the input ⟨*a good amplifier is* ~⟩ – **linearly** *adv*, **linearity** /-ˈarəti/ *n*

ˌLinear ˈA *n* a linear form of writing used in Crete from the 18th to the 15th c BC

linear accelerator *n* a device in which charged particles are accelerated in a straight line by successive impulses from a series of electric fields

ˌLinear ˈB *n* a linear form of writing used in Crete and on the Greek mainland from the 15th to the 12th c BC ☞ ALPHABET

linear motor *n* an electric motor that produces thrust in a straight line by direct induction(e g between a track and a vehicle running on it)

linear perspective *n* representation in a drawing or painting of parallel lines as converging in order to give the illusion of depth and distance

ˌlinear ˈprogramming *n* a mathematical method of solving practical problems (e g the allocation of resources) by means of the interaction of many separate linear functions

lineation /ˌliniˈaysh(ə)n/ *n* **1** the action of marking with lines; delineation **2** an arrangement of lines [ME *lineacion* outline, fr L *lineation-, lineatio*, fr *lineatus*, pp of *lineare* to make straight, fr *linea*]

ˈline enˌgraving *n* **1** (a plate or print produced by) a method of engraving in metal using incised lines of varying width and closeness **2** a linocut – **line engraver** *n*

linen /ˈlinin/ *n* **1** cloth or yarn made from flax **2** clothing or household articles (e g sheets and tablecloths) made of a usu washable cloth, esp linen [ME, fr *linen* (adj) flaxen, fr OE *līnen*, fr *līn* flax; akin to OHG *līn* flax; both fr a prehistoric Gmc word borrowed fr L *linum* flax]

,line of 'duty *n* all that is authorized, required, or normally associated with some field of responsibility

,line of 'force *n* a line in a (magnetic, electric, etc) field of force whose tangent at any point gives the direction of the field at that point

,line of 'sight *n* a straight line from an observer's eye to a distant point towards which he/she is looking

'line-,out *n* (a method in Rugby Union of returning the ball to play after it has crossed a touchline which involves throwing it in between) a line of forwards from each team [*line out* to line up]

'line ,printer *n* a high-speed printing device (e g for a computer) that prints each line as a unit rather than character by character ☞ COMPUTER – **line printing** *n*

[1]liner /'lienə/ *n* a passenger ship belonging to a shipping company and usu sailing scheduled routes [[2,3]LINE + [2]-ER]

[2]liner *n* a replaceable (metal) lining (for reducing the wear of a mechanism) [[1]LINE + [2]-ER] – **linerless** *adj*

linesman /'lienzmən/ *n* an official who assists the referee or umpire in various games, esp in determining if a ball or player is out of the prescribed playing area

'line,up /-,up/ *n* (a list of) the players playing for usu 1 side in a game ☞ SPORT

'line-,up *n* **1** a line of people arranged esp for inspection or as a means of identifying a suspect **2** a group of people or items assembled for a particular purpose ⟨*the ~ for tonight's show*⟩

line up *vi* to assume an orderly arrangement in a line ⟨line up *for inspection*⟩ ~ *vt* **1** to put into alignment **2** to assemble or organize

[1]ling /ling/ *n* a large food fish of shallow seas off Greenland and Europe [ME; akin to D *leng* ling, G *länge*]

[2]ling *n* the commonest British heather [ME, fr ON *lyng*; akin to Lith *lenkti* to bend – more at [2]-LING]

[1]-ling /-ling/ *suffix* (*adj or n* → *n*) **1** one connected with ⟨*hire* ling⟩ ⟨*sib*ling⟩ **2** young, small, or lesser kind of ⟨*duck*ling⟩ ⟨*prince*ling⟩ **3** one having (a specified quality or attribute) ⟨*under*ling⟩ ⟨*dar*ling⟩ [ME, fr OE; akin to OE *-ing*]

[2]-ling *suffix* (*n or adj* → *adj or adv*) of or in (such) a state, direction, or manner ⟨*dark*ling⟩ [ME *-ling* (fr OE), *-linges* (fr *-ling* + *-es* -s); akin to OHG *-lingūn* -ling, Lith *lenkti* to bend]

linga /'ling·gə/ *n* a phallus symbolic of the masculine cosmic principle and of the Hindu god Siva – compare YONI [Skt *liṅga* (nom *liṅgam*), lit., characteristic]

Lingala /ling'gahlə/ *n* a Bantu language of the Congo

lingam /'ling·gəm/ *n* a linga

linger /'ling·gə/ *vi* **1a** to delay going, esp because of reluctance to leave; tarry **b** to dwell on a subject – usu + *over, on,* or *upon* **2** to continue unduly or unhappily in a failing or moribund state – often + *on* **3** to be slow to act; procrastinate **4** to be protracted or slow in disappearing [ME (northern) *lengeren* to dwell, freq of *lengen* to prolong, fr OE *lengan*; akin to OE *lang* long] – **lingerer** *n*, **lingeringly** *adv*

lingerie /'lonh·zhəri, 'lan(h)- (*Fr* lɛ̃ʒri)/ *n* women's underwear and nightclothes [F, fr MF, fr *linge* linen, fr L *lineus* made of flax – more at [2]LINE]

lingo /'ling·goh/ *n, pl* **lingoes** **1** a foreign language **2** JARGON 2 *USE* infml [prob fr Prov, tongue, fr L *lingua* – more at TONGUE]

lingu-, lingui-, linguo- *comb form* **1** language ⟨lin*guist*⟩ **2** tongue ⟨lingui*form*⟩ [L *lingu-*, fr *lingua*]

lingua franca /,ling·gwə 'frangkə/ *n, pl* **lingua francas, linguae francae** /,ling·gwie 'frangkie/ **1** a language spoken in Mediterranean ports that consists of a mixture of Italian with French, Spanish, Greek, and Arabic **2** a language used as a common or commercial tongue among people not speaking the same native language **3** sthg resembling a common language [It, lit., Frankish language]

lingual /'ling·gwəl/ *adj* **1a** of or resembling the tongue **b** lying near or next to the tongue **c** articulated with the tongue **2** linguistic – **lingually** *adv*

linguist /'ling·gwist/ *n* **1** sby accomplished in languages; *esp* POLYGLOT 1 **2** sby who specializes in linguistics

linguistic /ling'gwistik/ *adj* of language or linguistics – **linguistically** *adv*

linguistic form *n* a meaningful unit of speech (e g a morpheme, word, or sentence)

linguistics /ling'gwistiks/ *n pl but sing in constr* the study of human language with regard to its nature, structure, and modification – compare PHILOLOGY

liniment /'linimənt/ *n* a liquid preparation that is applied to the skin, esp to allay pain or irritation [ME, fr LL *linimentum*, fr L *linere* to smear – more at [1]LIME]

lining /'liening/ *n* **1** (a piece of) material used to line sthg (e g a garment). **2** providing sthg with a lining

[1]link /lingk/ *n* **1** a connecting structure: e g **a(1)** a single ring or division of a chain **(2)** a unit of length formerly used in surveying equal to 7.92in (about 20.12cm) ☞ UNIT **b** the fusible part of an electrical fuse **2** sthg analogous to a link of chain: e g **a** a connecting element ⟨*sought a ~ between smoking and cancer*⟩ **b** a unit in a communications system [ME, of Scand origin; akin to ON *hlekkr* chain; akin to OE *hlanc* lank] – **linker** *n*

[2]link *vt* to join, connect ⟨*road that ~*s *2 towns*⟩ ~ *vi* to become connected by a link – often + *up*

linkage /'lingkij/ *n* **1** the manner or style of being joined; *specif* BOND 3a **2** the relationship between genes on the same chromosome that causes them to be inherited together **3a** a system of links **b** the degree of electromagnetic interaction expressed as the product of the number of turns of a coil and the magnetic flux linked by the coil [[2]LINK + -AGE]

linkman /'lingkmən/ *n* a broadcaster whose function is to link and introduce separate items, esp in a news programme

links /lingks/ *n pl* **1** GOLF COURSE – often pl with sing. meaning **2** *Scot* sand hills, esp along the seashore [ME, rising ground, sand hills, fr OE *hlincas*, pl of *hlinc* ridge; akin to OE *hlanc*]

'link,up /-,up/ *n* **1** the establishment of contact; a meeting ⟨*the ~ of 2 spacecraft*⟩ **2a** sthg that serves as a linking device or factor **b** a functional whole that is the result of a linkup

Linnaean, Linnean /li'nee·ən/ *adj* of or following the systematic methods of the Swedish botanist Linné who established the system of binomial nomenclature for all living things [NL Carolus *Linnaeus* (Carl von Linné) †1778 Sw botanist]

linnet /'linit/ *n* a common small Old World finch

having variable reddish brown plumage [MF *linette*, fr *lin* flax, fr L *linum*; fr its feeding on linseed]

lino /'lienoh/ *n, pl* **linos** *chiefly Br* linoleum

'lino,cut /-,kut/ *n* (a print made from) a design cut in relief on a piece of linoleum

linoleate /li'nohli,ayt/ *n* a salt or ester of linoleic acid

,lino,leic 'acid /,linə'layik, -'lee-/ *n* a liquid unsaturated fatty acid found in oils obtained from plants (e g linseed or peanut oil) and essential for mammalian nutrition [Gk *lin*on flax + ISV *oleic* (*acid*)]

linolenate /,linə'laynayt, -'lee-/ *n* a salt or ester of linolenic acid

linolenic acid /linə'laynik, -'lee-/ *n* a liquid unsaturated fatty acid found esp in drying oils (e g linseed oil) and essential for mammalian nutrition [ISV, irreg fr *linoleic*]

linoleum /li'nohli·əm/ *n* a floor covering with a canvas back and a coloured or patterned surface of hardened linseed oil and a filler (e g cork dust) [L *lin*um flax + *oleum* oil – more at OIL]

Linotype /'lienə,tiep, -noh-/ *trademark* – used for a keyboard-operated typesetting machine that produces each line of type in the form of a solid metal slug

linsang /'linsang/ *n* any of various Asiatic mammals that are related to the civets and genets [Malay]

linseed /'linseed/ *n* the seed of flax used esp as a source of linseed oil [ME, fr OE *līnsǣd*, fr *līn* flax + *sǣd* seed – more at LINEN]

'linseed ,oil *n* a yellowish drying oil obtained from flaxseed and used esp in paint, varnish, printing ink, and linoleum and for conditioning cricket bats

linsey-woolsey /,linzi 'woolzi/ *n* a coarse sturdy fabric of wool and linen or cotton [ME *lynsy wolsye*, prob fr *Lindsey*, village in Suffolk, England + *wolle* wool + *-sy*, arbitrary suffix]

linstock /'lin,stok/ *n* a staff formerly used to hold a lighted match for firing cannon [D *lontstok*, fr *lont* match + *stok* stick]

lint /lint/ *n* **1** a soft absorbent material with a fleecy surface that is made from linen and is used chiefly for surgical dressings **2** *chiefly NAm* FLUFF 1a [ME] – **linty** *adj*

lintel /'lintl/ *n* a horizontal architectural member spanning and usu carrying the load above an opening ☞ ARCHITECTURE [ME, fr MF, fr LL *limitaris* threshold, fr L, constituting a boundary, fr *limit-, limes* boundary – more at [1]LIMB]

linter /'lintə/ *n, NAm* **1** *pl* the fuzz of short fibres that sticks to cottonseed after the ginning process **2** a machine for removing linters

lion /'lie·ən/, *fem* **lioness** /'lie·ənes/ *n, pl* **lions,** (*1a*) **lions,** *esp collectively* **lion** **1a** a flesh-eating big cat of open or rocky areas of Africa and formerly southern Asia that has a tawny body with a tufted tail and in the male a shaggy blackish or dark brown mane ☞ FOOD **b** *cap* Leo **2** a person of interest or importance ⟨*literary* ~s⟩ [ME, fr OF, fr L *leon-, leo*, fr Gk *leōn*]

,lion'hearted /-'hahtid/ *adj* courageous, brave

lion·ize, -ise /'lie·ə,niez/ *vt* to treat as an object of great interest or importance – **lionizer** *n*, **lionization** /-'zaysh(ə)n/ *n*

lion's mouth *n* a place of great danger

'lion's ,share *n* the largest or best portion

lip /lip/ *n* **1** either of the 2 fleshy folds that surround the mouth **2a** a fleshy edge or margin (e g of a wound) **b** a labium **3** the edge of a hollow vessel or cavity; *esp* one shaped to make pouring easy **4** an embouchure **5** impudent or insolent talk, esp in reply – slang [ME, fr OE *lippa*; akin to OHG *leffur* lip, & prob to L *labium, labrum* lip] – **lipless** *adj*, **liplike** *adj*

lip-, lipo- *comb form* fat; fatty tissue; fatty ⟨*lipoma*⟩ ⟨lipo*protein*⟩ [NL, fr Gk, fr *lipos* – more at [1]LEAVE]

lipase /'lipayz, -ays, 'lie-/ *n* an enzyme that accelerates the hydrolysis or synthesis of fats or the breakdown of lipoproteins [ISV]

'lip ,gloss *n* a cosmetic for giving a gloss to the lips

lipid /'lipid, 'lie-/ *n* any of various substances that with proteins and carbohydrates form the principal structural components of living cells and that include fats, waxes, and related and derived compounds [ISV] – **lipidic** /-'pidik/ *adj*

Lipizzaner, Lippizaner /,lipit'sahnə/ *n* (any of) a breed of horses developed in Austria and used esp in dressage displays [G, fr *Lipizza, Lippiza*, stud in Yugoslavia (formerly the Austrian Imperial Stud)]

lipogenesis /,liepə'jenəsis/ *n* the formation of fatty acids in the living body [NL]

lipophilic /,lipə'filik, lie-/ *adj* having an affinity for lipids (e g fats)

,lipo'protein /,lipoh-, ,liepoh-/ *n* a conjugated protein that is a complex of protein and lipid

lipped /lipt/ *adj* having a lip or lips, esp of a specified kind or number – often in combination ⟨*tight*-lipped⟩

lipping /'liping/ *n* an embouchure

'lip,reading /-,reeding/ *n* the interpreting of a speaker's words (e g by the deaf) by watching the movements of the lips – **lip-read** *vb*, **lip-reader** *n*

'lip ,service *n* support in words but not in deeds ⟨*paid ~ to racial equality but still employed only whites*⟩

lipstick /'lip,stik/ *n* (a cased stick of) a waxy solid cosmetic for colouring the lips

'lip ,strap *n* a strap that passes under a horse's chin to hold the bit in position

liquate /'liekwayt/ *vt* to separate (esp a metal) from an ore, alloy, etc by selective melting [L *liquatus*, pp of *liquare*; akin to L *liquēre*] – **liquation** /lie'kwaysh(ə)n/ *n*

liquefacient /,likwi'faysh(ə)nt/ *n* sthg that liquefies a substance or promotes liquefaction

,lique'faction /-'faksh(ə)n/ *n* **1** the process of making or becoming liquid **2** the state of being liquid [ME, fr LL *liquefaction-, liquefactio*, fr L *liquefactus*, pp of *liquefacere*, fr *liquēre* to be fluid + *facere* to make – more at [1]DO]

liquefy *also* **liquify** /'likwifie/ *vt* to reduce to a liquid state ~ *vi* to become liquid [MF *liquefier*, fr L *liquefacere*] – **liquefiable** /-,fie·əbl/ *adj*, **liquefier** /-fie·'ə/ *n*, **liquefiability** /-fie·əbiləti/ *n*

liquescent /li'kwes(ə)nt/ *adj* being or tending to become liquid [L *liquescent-, liquescens*, prp of *liquescere* to become fluid, incho of *liquēre*]

liqueur /li'kyooə/ *n* any of several usu sweetened alcoholic drinks variously flavoured (e g with fruit or aromatics) [F, fr OF *licour* liquid – more at LIQUOR]

liquid /'likwid/ *adj* **1** flowing freely like water **2** neither solid nor gaseous; characterized by free movement of the constituent molecules among themselves but without the tendency to separate like those of gases ⟨~ *mercury*⟩ **3a** shining and clear ⟨*large ~ eyes*⟩ **b** *of a sound* flowing, pure, and free of harshness **c** smooth and unconstrained in movement **d** *of a consonant (e g /r/ or /l/)* articulated without friction and capable of being prolonged like a vowel **4** consisting of or capable of ready conversion into cash ⟨~ *assets*⟩ [ME, fr MF *liquide*, fr L *liquidus*, fr *liquēre* to be fluid; akin to L *lixa* water, lye, OIr *fliuch* damp] – **liquid** *n*, **liquidly** *adv*, **liquidness** *n*, **liquidity** /li'kwidəti/ *n*

,liquid 'air *n* air in the liquid state that is intensely cold and used chiefly as a refrigerant

liquidambar /,likwi'dambə/ *n* (a resin from) the sweet gum tree [NL, genus name, fr L *liquidus* + ML *ambar, ambra* amber]

liquidate /'likwidayt/ *vt* **1a** to settle (a debt), esp by payment **b** to settle the accounts of (e g a business) and use the assets towards paying off the debts **2** to get rid of; *specif* to kill **3** to convert (assets) into cash ~ *vi* **1** to liquidate debts, damages, or accounts **2** to be or become liquidated [LL *liquidatus*, pp of *liquidare* to melt, fr L *liquidus*] – **liquidation** /-'daysh(ə)n/ *n*

liquidator /'likwi,daytə/ *n* a person appointed by law to liquidate a company [LIQUIDATE + [1]-OR]

,liquid 'crystal *n* a liquid having certain physical, esp optical, properties shown by crystalline solids but not by ordinary liquids

,liquid ,crystal di'splay *n* an LCD

liquid·ize, -ise /'likwidiez/ *vt* to cause to be liquid; *esp* to pulverize (e g fruit or vegetables) into a liquid

liquid·izer, -iser /'likwidiezə/ *n, chiefly Br* a domestic electric appliance for grinding, puréeing, liquidizing, or blending foods

liquidus /'likwidəs/ *n* a curve, usu on a temperature and composition graph for a mixture, above which only the liquid phase can exist – compare SOLIDUS [L *liquidus* liquid]

[1]liquor /'likə/ *n* a liquid substance: e g **a** a solution of a drug in water **b** BATH 2c **c** a liquid, esp water, in which food has been cooked **d** *chiefly NAm* a usu distilled rather than fermented alcoholic drink [ME *licour*, fr OF, fr L *liquor*, fr *liquēre*]

[2]liquor *vt* **1** to dress (e g leather) with oil or grease **2** to make drunk with alcoholic drink – usu + *up* ~ *vi* to drink alcoholic drink, esp to excess – usu + *up*

liquorice /'likərish, -ris/ *n* **1** a European leguminous plant having spikes of blue flowers and grown for its roots **2** the dried root of liquorice; *also* an extract of this used esp in medicine, brewing, and confectionery [ME *licorice*, fr OF, fr LL *liquiritia*, alter. of L *glycyrrhiza*, fr Gk *glykyrrhiza*, fr *glykys* sweet + *rhiza* root – more at [1]ROOT]

lira /'liərə/ *n, pl (1)* **lire** *also* **liras**, *(2)* **liras** *also* **lire** **1** ☞ *Italy* at NATIONALITY **2** ☞ *Turkey* at NATIONALITY [fr L *libra*, a unit of weight]

lisente /li'sente/ *n* ☞ *Lesotho* at NATIONALITY [of Bantu origin]

lisle /liel/ *n* a smooth tightly twisted thread usu made of long-staple cotton [*Lisle*, former name of Lille, city in N France]

[1]lisp /lisp/ *vi* **1** to pronounce /s/ and /z/ imperfectly, esp by giving them the sounds of /th/ and /dh/ **2** to speak with a lisp [ME *lispen*, fr OE *-wlyspian*; akin to OHG *lispen* to lisp] – **lisper** *n*

[2]lisp *n* a speech defect or affectation characterized by lisping

lissom, lissome /'lis(ə)m/ *adj* easily flexed; lithe, nimble [alter. of *lithesome*, fr *lithe* + *-some*]

[1]list /list/ *n* **1** a band or strip of material; *esp* a selvage **2** *pl but sing or pl in constr* **a** (the fence surrounding) a tiltyard **b** a scene of competition [ME, fr OE *liste*; akin to OHG *līsta* edge, Alb *leth*]

[2]list *n* a roll or catalogue of words or numbers (e g representing people or objects belonging to a class), usu arranged in order so as to be easily found ⟨*a guest* ~⟩ ⟨*a shopping* ~⟩ [F *liste*, fr It *lista*, of Gmc origin; akin to OHG *lista*]

[3]list *vt* **1** to make a list of **2** to include on a list; *specif, Br* to include (a building) in an official list as being of architectural or historical importance and hence protected from demolition

[4]list *vb* to (cause to) lean to one side ⟨*the ship was* ~ing *badly*⟩ [origin unknown] – **list** *n*

[1]listen /'lis(ə)n/ *vi* **1** to pay attention to sound ⟨~ *to music*⟩ **2** to hear or consider with thoughtful attention; heed ⟨~ *to a plea*⟩ **3** to be alert to catch an expected sound ⟨~ *for his step*⟩ [ME *listnen*, fr OE *hlysnan*; akin to Skt *śroṣati* he hears, OE *hlūd* loud] – **listener** /'lisn·ə/ *n*

[2]listen *n* an act of listening – infml

listen in *vi* to tune in to or monitor a broadcast – **listener-in** *n*

listing /'listing/ *n* **1** an act or instance of making or including in a list **2** sthg listed

listless /'listlis/ *adj* characterized by indifference, lack of energy, and disinclination for exertion; languid [ME *listles*, fr *list* desire (fr *lysten* to wish, fr OE *lystan* to be pleasing) + *-les* -less] – **listlessly** *adv*, **listlessness** *n*

lit /lit/ *past of* LIGHT

litany /'lit(ə)n·i/ *n* a prayer consisting of a series of petitions by the leader with alternate responses by the congregation [ME *letanie*, fr OF, fr LL *litania*, fr LGk *litaneia*, fr Gk, entreaty, fr *litanos* entreating; akin to OE *līm* lime]

litchi, lichee /'liechee, -'-/ *n* (a Chinese tree that bears) an oval fruit that has a hard scaly outer covering and a small hard seed surrounded by edible pulp [Chin (Pek) *li[4] chih[1]*]

-lite /-liet/ *comb form* (→ *n*) mineral ⟨*rhodo*lite⟩; rock ⟨*aero*lite⟩; fossil ⟨*ichno*lite⟩ [F, alter. of *-lithe*, fr Gk *lithos* stone]

liter /'leetə/ *n, NAm* a litre

literacy /'lit(ə)rəsi/ *n* the quality or state of being literate

[1]literal /'lit(ə)rəl/ *adj* **1a** according with the exact letter of a written text; *specif* according with the letter of the scriptures **b** having the factual or ordinary construction or primary meaning of a term or expression; actual **c** characterized by a lack of imagination; prosaic ⟨*a very* ~ *approach to the subject*⟩ **2** of or expressed in letters **3** reproduced word for word; exact, verbatim ⟨*a* ~ *translation*⟩ [ME, fr MF, fr ML *litteralis*, fr L, of a letter, fr *littera* letter] – **literalness, literality** /,litə'raləti/ *n*

[2]literal *n* a misprint involving a single letter

literalism /'litrəliz(ə)m/ *n* the rejection of allegorical or metaphorical interpretations of esp biblical texts – **literalist** *n*, **literalistic** /-'listik/ *adj*

literally /'litrəli/ *adv* **1** in the literal sense; without metaphor or exaggeration **2** with exact equivalence; verbatim ⟨*follow the instructions* ~⟩ **3** – used to intensify a metaphorical or hyperbolic expression ⟨*she was ~ tearing her hair out*⟩; disapproved of by some speakers

literary /'lit(ə)rəri/ *adj* **1a** of, being, or concerning literature ⟨~ *criticism*⟩ **b** characteristic of or being in a formal, rather than colloquial, style **2a** well-read **b** producing, well versed in, or connected with literature – **literarily** *adv*, **literariness** *n*

¹literate /'lit(ə)rət/ *adj* **1a** educated, cultured **b** able to read and write **2** versed in literature or creative writing [ME *literat*, fr L *litteratus* marked with letters, literate, fr *litterae* letters, literature, fr pl of *littera*] – **literately** *adv*, **literateness** *n*

²literate *n* a literate person

literati /,litə'rahti/ *n pl* the educated class; the intelligentsia [obs It *litterati*, fr L, pl of *litteratus*]

literation /,litə'raysh(ə)n/ *n* the representation of sounds or words by letters [L *littera* + E *-ation*]

literature /'lit(ə)rəchə/ *n* **1a** writings in prose or verse; *esp* writings having artistic value or expression and expressing ideas of permanent or universal interest **b** the body of writings on a particular subject ⟨*scientific* ~⟩ **c** printed matter (e g leaflets or circulars) **2** the body of musical compositions ⟨*the piano ~ of Brahms*⟩

lith-, litho- *comb form* **1** stone ⟨litho*graph*⟩ ⟨litho*tomy*⟩ **2** lithium ⟨lith*ic*⟩ [(1) L, fr Gk, fr *lithos*; (2) NL *lithium*]

-lith /-lith/ *comb form* (→ *n*) **1a** structure or implement of stone ⟨*mega*lith⟩ ⟨*eo*lith⟩ **b** (artificial) stone ⟨*grano*lith⟩ **2** stone in (a specified body cavity) ⟨*uro*lith⟩ **3** -lite ⟨*lacco*lith⟩ [NL *-lithus* & F *-lithe*, fr Gk *lithos*]

litharge /'lithahj/ *n* a fused lead monoxide – compare MASSICOT [ME, fr MF, fr L *lithargyrus*, fr Gk *lithargyros*, fr *lithos* + *argyros* silver – more at ARGENT]

lithe /liedh/ *adj* flexible, supple [ME, fr OE *lithe* gentle; akin to OHG *lindi* gentle, L *lentus* slow] – **lithely** *adv*, **litheness** *n*

lithia /'lithi·ə/ *n* a white oxide of lithium [NL, fr Gk *lithos*]

lithic /'lithik/ *adj* **1** (made) of stone **2** of lithium [Gk *lithikos*, fr *lithos*] – **lithically** *adv*

-lithic /-'lithik/ *comb form* (→ *adj*) relating to or characteristic of (a specified stage) in human beings' use of stone implements ⟨*Neo*lithic⟩ [*lithic*]

lithium /'lithi·əm/ *n* a soft silver-white element of the alkali metal group that is the lightest metal known ☞ PERIODIC TABLE [NL, fr *lithia*]

,lithium 'carbonate *n* a lithium salt used in the glass and ceramic industries and to treat manic-depressive psychosis

litho /'liethoh/ *n, pl* **lithos** **1** a lithograph **2** lithography

lithograph /'lithə,grahf, -,graf/ *vt or n* (to produce or copy in the form of) a print made by lithography – **lithographic** /-'grafik/ *adj*, **lithographically** *adv*

lithography /li'thogrəfi/ *n* the process of printing from a surface (e g a stone or a metal plate) on which the image to be printed is ink-receptive and the blank area ink-repellent [G *lithographie*, fr *lith-* + *-graphie* -graphy]

lithology /li'tholəji/ *n* (the study of) the composition, shape, etc of (a) rock – **lithologic** /,lithə'lojik/ *also* **lithological** *adj*, **lithologically** *adv*

lithophyte /'lithə,fiet/ *n* a plant that grows on rock [F, fr *lith-* + *-phyte*] – **lithophytic** /-'fitik/ *adj*

lithopone /'lithə,pohn/ *n* a white pigment consisting essentially of zinc sulphide and barium sulphate [ISV *lith-* + Gk *ponos* work]

'litho,sphere /-,sfiə/ *n* the solid rocky crust of the earth or another celestial body [ISV]

lithotomy /li'thotəmi/ *n* surgical incision of the urinary bladder for removal of a stone [LL *lithotomia*, fr Gk, fr *lithotomein* to perform a lithotomy, fr *lith-* + *temnein* to cut – more at TOME]

Lithuanian /,lithyoo'aynyən, -ni·ən/ *n* **1** a native or inhabitant of Lithuania **2** the Baltic language of the Lithuanians ☞ LANGUAGE [*Lithuania*, country in E Europe, now a republic of the USSR] – **Lithuanian** *adj*

litigate /'litigayt/ *vi* to carry on a lawsuit ~ *vt* to contest (an issue) at law [L *litigatus*, pp of *litigare*, fr *lit-*, *lis* lawsuit + *agere* to drive – more at AGENT] – **litigable** /'litigəbl/ *adj*, **litigant** /-gənt/ *n or adj*, **litigation** /-'gaysh(ə)n/ *n*

litigious /li'tijəs/ *adj* **1** (excessively) inclined to engage in lawsuits **2** subject to litigation **3** tending to argue; disputatious – fml [ME, fr MF *litigieux*, fr L *litigiosus*, fr *litigium* dispute, fr *litigare*] – **litigiously** *adv*, **litigiousness** *n*

litmus /'litməs/ *n* a colouring matter from lichens that turns red in acid solutions and blue in alkaline solutions and is used as an acid-alkali indicator [of Scand origin; akin to ON *litmosi* herbs used in dyeing, fr *litr* colour (akin to OHG ant*lizzi* face, L *vultus*) + *mosi* moss (akin to OE *mōs* moss)]

'litmus ,paper *n* absorbent paper coloured with litmus and used as an indicator

litotes /'lietə,teez, 'li-, lie'tohteez/ *n, pl* **litotes** /~/ understatement in which an affirmative is expressed by the negative of its opposite (e g in 'not a bad singer'') [Gk *litotēs*, fr *litos* simple; akin to Gk *leios* smooth – more at ¹LIME]

litre, *NAm chiefly* **liter** /'leetə/ *n* a metric unit of capacity equal to 1.000 028dm³ (about 0.220gal) ☞ UNIT [F *litre*, fr ML *litra*, a measure, fr Gk, a weight]

¹litter /'litə/ *n* **1a** a covered and curtained couch carried by people or animals **b** a stretcher or other device for carrying a sick or injured person **2a** material used as bedding for animals **b** the uppermost slightly decayed layer of organic matter on the forest floor **3** a group of offspring of an animal, born at 1 birth **4a** rubbish or waste products, esp in a public place **b** an untidy accumulation of objects (e g papers) [ME, fr OF *litiere*, fr *lit* bed, fr L *lectus* – more at ¹LIE] – **littery** *adj*

²litter *vt* **1** to provide (e g a horse) with litter as a bed **2** to give birth to (young) **3a** to strew with litter, esp scattered articles ⟨~ *the horse's stall*⟩ ⟨~ *the desk-top with papers*⟩ **b** to scatter about in disorder ~ *vi* **1** to give birth to a litter **2** to strew litter

litterae humaniores /,litəri hyooh,mani'awreez/ *n pl* classics as a university subject [ML, lit., more humane letters]

litterateur *also* **littérateur** /,litərə'tuh (*Fr* literatœːr)/ *n* a literary man; *esp* a professional writer [F *littérateur*, fr L *litterator* critic, fr *litteratus* literate]

litterbug /'litə,bug/ *n* a litterlout

'litter,lout /-,lowt/ *n* one who carelessly drops rubbish in public places – infml

¹little /'litl/ *adj* **littler** /'litlə/, **less** /les/, **lesser** /'lesə/; **littlest** /'litlist/, **least** /leest/ **1a** amounting to only a small quantity ⟨*had ~ or no time*⟩ **b** *of a plant or animal* small in comparison with related forms – used in vernacular names **c** small in condition, distinction, or scope **d** narrow, mean ⟨*the pettiness of ~ minds*⟩ **2** not much: e g **a** existing only in a small amount or to a slight degree ⟨*unfortunately he has ~ money*⟩ **b** short in duration; brief ⟨*wait a ~ while*⟩ **c** existing to an appreciable though not extensive degree or amount – + *a* ⟨*fortunately she had a ~ money in the bank*⟩ **3** small in importance or interest; trivial [ME *littel*, fr OE *lȳtel*; akin to OHG *luzzil* little, Lith *liūsti* to be sad] – **littleness** *n*

[2]**little** *adv* **less** /les/; **least** /leest/ **1** to no great degree or extent; not much ⟨little-*known*⟩ **2** not at all ⟨*cared ~ for his neighbours*⟩

[3]**little** *n* **1a** only a small portion or quantity; not much ⟨*understood ~ of his speech*⟩ ⟨*do what ~ I can*⟩ **b** at least some, though not much – + *a* ⟨*have a ~ of this cake*⟩ **2** a short time or distance ⟨*walk for a ~*⟩ – **a little** somewhat, rather ⟨a little *over 50 years*⟩ ⟨*found the play* a little *boring*⟩

,Little 'Bear *n* URSA MINOR

,little by 'little *adv* by small degrees or amounts; gradually

,Little 'Dipper /'dipə/ *n, chiefly NAm* URSA MINOR

,little 'englander /'ingləndə/ *n, often cap L&E* an opponent of British imperial expansion, esp in the 19th c

,little 'finger *n* the fourth and smallest finger of the hand counting the index finger as the first

'little ,leaf *n* any of several plant disorders characterized by small and often discoloured and distorted leaves

Little Office *n* a short office in honour of the Virgin Mary

,little 'owl *n* an Old World insect-eating owl that is distinguished by its small size and squat flat-headed appearance

'little ,people *n pl* imaginary beings (e g fairies, elves, etc) of folklore – + *the*

,little 'toe *n* the outermost and smallest digit of the foot

,little 'woman *n* one's wife – humor; often derog

[1]**littoral** /'litərəl/ *adj* of or occurring on or near a (sea) shore [L *litoralis*, fr *litor-, litus* seashore]

[2]**littoral** *n* a coastal region; *esp* the intertidal zone

liturgical /li'tuhjikl/ *adj* **1** (having the characteristics) of liturgy **2** using or favouring the use of liturgy – **liturgically** *adv*

liturgist /'litəjist/ *n* **1** a person who follows, compiles, or leads a liturgy **2** a specialist in the study of formal public worship

liturgy /'litəji/ *n* **1** *often cap* the form of service used in the celebration of Communion, esp in the Orthodox church **2** a prescribed form of public worship [LL *liturgia*, fr Gk *leitourgia*, fr (assumed) Gk (Attic) *leïtos* public (fr Gk *laos* – Attic *leōs* – people) + *-ourgia* -urgy]

livable *also* **liveable** /'livəbl/ *adj* **1** suitable for living in or with **2** endurable – **livableness** *n*

[1]**live** /liv/ *vi* **1** to be alive; have the life of an animal or plant **2** to continue alive ⟨*his illness is so serious, he is lucky to ~*⟩ **3** to maintain oneself; subsist ⟨*she ~*d *by writing*⟩ ⟨*he ~*d *by his wits*⟩ **4** to conduct or pass one's life ⟨*~*d *only for her work*⟩ **5** to occupy a home; dwell ⟨*they had always ~*d *in the country*⟩ **6** to attain eternal life ⟨*though he were dead, yet shall he ~* – Jn 11:25 (AV)⟩ **7** to have a life rich in experience ⟨*the right to ~, not merely to exist*⟩ **8** to cohabit – + *together* or *with* **9** *chiefly Br, of a thing* to be found in a specified place, esp normally or usually – infml *~ vt* **1** to pass, spend, or experience **2** to enact, practise ⟨*~ a lie*⟩ ⟨*really ~*s *her faith*⟩ [ME *liven*, fr OE *libban*; akin to OHG *lebēn* to live, L *caelebs* unmarried] – **live in sin** to cohabit – **live it up** to enjoy an exciting or extravagant social life or social occasion ⟨lived it up *with wine and song – Newsweek*⟩ – **live up to** to act or be in accordance with (esp a standard expected by sby)

[2]**live** /liev/ *adj* **1** having life **2** containing living organisms ⟨*~ yoghourt*⟩ **3** exerting force or containing energy: e g **a** glowing ⟨*~ coals*⟩ **b** connected to electric power **c** *of ammunition, bombs, etc* unexploded, unfired **d** driven by or imparting motion or power **e** *of a nuclear reactor or nuclear bomb* charged with material capable of undergoing fission **4** of continuing or current interest ⟨*~ issues*⟩ **5** *esp of a rock* not quarried or cut; native **6** in play in a game ⟨*a ~ ball*⟩ **7a** of or involving the presence or participation of real people ⟨*a ~ audience*⟩ ⟨*~ music*⟩ **b** broadcast while happening ⟨*a ~ television programme*⟩ [short for *alive*]

[3]**live** /liev/ *adv* during, from, or at a live production

live down /liv/ *vt* to cause (e g a crime or mistake) to be forgotten, esp by future good behaviour ⟨*made a mistake and couldn't* live *it* down⟩

live in /liv/ *vi* to live in one's place of work ⟨*the housekeeper is required to* live in⟩

livelihood /'lievli,hood/ *n* a means of support or sustenance [alter. of ME *livelode* course of life, fr OE *līflād*, fr *līf* + *lād* course – more at LODE]

livelong /'liv,long/ *adj* whole, entire – chiefly poetic ⟨*the ~ day*⟩ [ME *lef long*, fr *lef* dear + *long* – more at LIEF]

lively /'lievli/ *adj* **1** briskly alert and energetic; vigorous, animated ⟨*a ~ discussion*⟩ ⟨*~ children racing home from school*⟩ **2** brilliant, vivid ⟨*a ~ flashing wit*⟩ ⟨*a ~ colour*⟩ **3** quick to rebound; resilient **4** responding readily to the helm ⟨*a ~ boat*⟩ **5** full of life, movement, or incident ⟨*the crowded streets made a ~ scene*⟩ **6** full of possibly disagreeable or dangerous action – humor ⟨*given a ~ time by enemy artillery*⟩ [ME, fr OE *līflīc*, fr *līf* life] – **livelily** *adv*, **liveliness** *n*, **lively** *adv*

liven /'liev(ə)n/ *vb* to make or become lively – often + *up*

,live 'oak /liev/ *n* any of several N American evergreen oaks

live out /liv/ *vi* to live outside one's place of work ⟨*owing to the shortage of college rooms, some students must* live out⟩ *~ vt* to live till the end of ⟨*will the sick man* live out *the month?*⟩

[1]**liver** /'livə/ *n* **1a** a large vascular glandular organ of vertebrates that secretes bile and causes changes in the blood (e g by converting blood sugar into glycogen) ☞ DIGESTION **b** any of various large digestive glands of invertebrates **2** the liver of an animal (e g a calf or pig) eaten as food **3** a greyish reddish brown **4** *archaic* the seat of the emotions [ME, fr OE *lifer*, akin to OHG *lebra* liver]

[2]**liver** *n* one who lives, esp in a specified way ⟨*a clean ~*⟩

'liver ,fluke *n* any of various worms that invade and damage the liver of mammals, esp sheep

liverish /'livərish/ *adj* **1** suffering from liver disorder; bilious **2** peevish, irascible; *also* glum – **liverishness** *n*

Liverpudlian /,livə'pudli·ən/ *n* (the dialect of) a native or inhabitant of Liverpool [*Liverpudl-* (alter. – influenced by *puddle* – of *Liverpool,* city in England) + E *-ian*] – **Liverpudlian** *adj*

'liver ,sausage *n* a sausage consisting chiefly of cooked minced liver often with pork trimmings

'liver,wort /-,wuht/ *n* a plant of a class related to and resembling the mosses but differing in reproduction and development ☞ PLANT

[1]**livery** /'livəri/ *n* **1a** the distinctive clothing worn by a member of a livery company or guild **b** the uniform of servants employed by an individual or a single household **c** distinctive colouring or marking; *also* distinctive dress **d** a distinctive colour scheme (e g on aircraft) distinguishing an organization or group **2** the legal delivering of property **3** *chiefly NAm* LIVERY STABLE [ME, fr OF *livree,* lit., delivery, fr *livrer* to deliver, fr L *liberare* to free – more at LIBERATE] – **liveried** /'livərid/ *adj*

[2]**livery** *adj* liverish

'livery ,company *n* any of various London craft or trade associations that are descended from medieval guilds

'liveryman /-mən/ *n* a freeman of the City of London who is a member of a livery company

'livery ,stable *n* an establishment where horses are stabled and fed for their owners

lives /lievz/ *pl of* LIFE

,live 'steam /liev/ *n* steam direct from a boiler and under full pressure

'live,stock /-,stok/ *n* **1** animals kept or raised for use or pleasure; *esp* farm animals kept for use and profit **2** *Br* small verminous creatures (e g lice or fleas) – chiefly humor

,live 'wire /'liev/ *n* an alert, active, or aggressive person

livid /'livid/ *adj* **1** discoloured by bruising **2** ashen, pallid ⟨*this cross, thy* ~ *face, thy pierced hands and feet* – Walt Whitman⟩ **3** reddish **4** very angry; enraged ⟨*was* ~ *at his son's disobedience*⟩ [F *livide,* fr L *lividus,* fr *livēre* to be blue; akin to OE *slāh* sloe, Russ *sliva* plum] – **lividness** *n,* **lividity** /li'vidəti/ *n*

[1]**living** /'living/ *adj* **1a** having life; alive **b** existing in use ⟨*a* ~ *language*⟩ **2** [2]LIVE 3a **3a** true to life; exact – esp in *the living image of* **b** suited for living ⟨*the* ~ *area*⟩ **4** – used as an intensive ⟨*scared the* ~ *daylights out of him*⟩ **5** *of feelings, ideas, etc* full of power and force ⟨*in* ~ *colour*⟩ – **livingness** *n*

[2]**living** *n* **1** the condition of being alive **2** a manner of life **3a** means of subsistence; a livelihood ⟨*earning a* ~⟩ **b** *Br* a benefice

,living 'death *n* a life so full of misery that death would be preferable

'living ,room *n* a room in a residence used for everyday activities

'living ,space *n* lebensraum

'living ,standard *n* STANDARD OF LIVING

,living 'wage *n* **1** a subsistence wage **2** a wage sufficient to provide an acceptable standard of living

livre /'leevrə, (*Fr* livr)/ *n* (a coin representing) a former French money unit worth 20 sols [F, fr L *libra,* a unit of weight]

lixiviate /lik'siviayt/ *vt* to extract a soluble constituent from (a solid mixture) by washing or percolation [LL *lixivium* lye, fr L *lixivius* made of lye, fr *lixa* lye – more at LIQUID] – **lixiviation** /-'aysh(ə)n/ *n*

lizard /'lizəd/ *n* any of a suborder of reptiles distinguished from the snakes by 2 pairs of well differentiated functional limbs (which may be lacking in burrowing forms), external ears, and eyes with movable lids ☞ LIFE CYCLE [ME *liserd,* fr MF *laisarde,* fr L *lacerta;* akin to L *lacertus* muscle – more at LEG]

'll /-l/ *vb* will, shall ⟨*you'll be late*⟩

llama /'lahmə/ *n* any of several wild and domesticated S American ruminant mammals related to the camels but smaller and without a hump; *esp* the domesticated guanaco [Sp, fr Quechua]

llano /'l(y)ahnoh/ *n, pl* **llanos** an open grassy plain, esp in Spanish America [Sp, plain, fr L *planum* – more at PLAIN]

Lloyd's /loydz/ *n* an association of London underwriters specializing in marine insurance and shipping news and insuring against losses of almost every kind [Edward *Lloyd* †*ab* 1730 E coffee-house keeper whose premises in London became the centre of shipbroking & marine insurance business]

lo /loh/ *interj, archaic* – used to call attention or to express wonder or surprise [ME, fr OE *lā*]

loach /lohch/ *n* any of a family of small Old World freshwater fishes related to the carps [ME *loche,* fr MF]

[1]**load** /lohd/ *n* **1a** an amount, esp large or heavy, that is (to be) carried, supported, or borne; a burden **b** the quantity that can be carried at 1 time by a specified means – often in combination ⟨*a boat*load *of tourists*⟩ **2** the forces to which a structure is subjected ⟨*the* ~ *on the arch*⟩ **3** a burden of responsibility, anxiety, etc ⟨*took a* ~ *off her mind*⟩ **4** external resistance overcome by a machine or other source of power **5a** power output (e g of a power plant) **b** a device to which power is delivered **6** the amount of work to be performed by a person, machine, etc **7** a large quantity or amount; a lot – usu pl with sing. meaning; infml ⟨*there's* ~s *of room on the back seat*⟩ [ME *lod,* fr OE *lād* support, carrying – more at LODE] – **get a load of** to pay attention to (sthg surprising) – slang

[2]**load** *vt* **1a** to put a load in or on ⟨~ *a van with furniture*⟩ **b** to place in or on a means of conveyance ⟨~ *cargo*⟩ **2** to encumber or oppress with sthg heavy, laborious, or disheartening; burden ⟨*a company* ~ed *down with debts*⟩ **3a** to weight or shape (dice) to fall unfairly **b** to charge with one-sided or prejudicial influences; bias **c** to charge with emotional associations or hidden implications ⟨*a* ~ed *statement*⟩ **4a** to put a load or charge in (a device or piece of equipment) ⟨~ *a gun*⟩ **b** to place or insert in a device or piece of equipment ⟨~ *a film in a camera*⟩ **5** to affect, often adversely, (the output of a preceding stage of an electrical circuit) ~ *vi* **1** to receive a load **2** to put a load on or in a carrier, device, or container; *esp* to insert the charge in a firearm – **loader** *n*

'loaded *adj* having a large amount of money – infml

loading /'lohding/ *n* **1** a cargo, weight, or stress placed on sthg **2** a surcharge

'loading ,gauge *n, Br* a bar suspended over railway tracks to show how high a train may be loaded

'load ,line *n* PLIMSOLL LINE

'load,star /-,stah/ *n* a lodestar

'load,stone /-,stohn/ *n* (a) lodestone

¹loaf /lohf/ *n, pl* **loaves** /lohvz/ **1** a mass of bread often having a regular shape and standard weight **2** a shaped or moulded often symmetrical mass of food (e g sugar or chopped cooked meat) **3** *Br* head, brains – slang; esp in *use one's loaf* [ME *lof,* fr OE *hlāf;* akin to OHG *hleib* loaf; (3) rhyming slang *loaf (of bread)* head]

²loaf *vi* to spend time in idleness [prob back-formation fr *loafer* (idler), perh short for *landloafer,* fr G *landläufer* tramp, fr *land* + *läufer* runner]

loafer /'lohfə/ *n* **1** one who loafs **2** *chiefly NAm* a low leather shoe similar to a moccasin but with a broad flat heel [(2) fr *Loafer,* a trademark]

loam /lohm/ *n* ³SOIL 2a; *specif* crumbly soil consisting of a mixture of clay, silt, and sand [ME *lom* clay, clayey mixture, fr OE *lām;* akin to OE *līm* lime] – **loamy** *adj*

¹loan /lohn/ *n* **1a** money lent at interest **b** sthg lent, usu for the borrower's temporary use **2** the grant of temporary use [ME *lon,* fr ON *lān;* akin to OE *lǣn* loan, *lēon* to lend, L *linquere* to leave, Gk *leipein*]

²loan *vt* to lend ⟨~ed *to the gallery by an unnamed owner*⟩ – **loanable** *adj*

,lo and be'hold /loh/ *interj* – used to express wonder or surprise

'loan trans,lation *n* a word or phrase introduced into a language through translation of the elements of a term in another language (e g *superman* from German *Übermensch*)

'loan,word /-,wuhd/ *n* a word taken from another language and at least partly naturalized

loath, loth /lohth/ *also* **loathe** /lohdh/ *adj* unwilling *to* do sthg disliked; reluctant [ME *loth* loathsome, fr OE *lāth;* akin to OHG *leid* loathsome, OIr *liuss* aversion]

loathe /lohdh/ *vt* to dislike greatly, often with disgust or intolerance; detest [ME *lothen,* fr OE *lāthian,* fr *lāth*] – **loather** *n*

loathing /'lohdhing/ *n* extreme disgust; detestation

loathsome /'lohdhs(ə)m, 'lohth-/ *adj* giving rise to loathing; disgusting [ME *lothsum,* fr *loth* evil, fr OE *lāth,* fr *lāth,* adj] – **loathsomely** *adv,* **loathsomeness** *n*

loaves /lohvz/ *pl of* LOAF

¹lob /lob/ *vb* **-bb-** *vt* **1** to throw, hit, or propel easily or in a high arc **2** to hit a lob against (an opponent, esp in tennis) ~ *vi* to hit a ball easily in a high arc, esp in tennis, squash, etc [*lob* (a loosely hanging object), prob of LG or Flem origin]

²lob *n* a ball that is lobbed

lob-, lobo- *comb form* lobe ⟨lobar⟩ ⟨lobotomy⟩

lobation /loh'baysh(ə)n/ *n* **1** the condition of having lobes **2** a lobed part

¹lobby /'lobi/ *n* **1** a porch or small entrance hall **2** an anteroom of a legislative chamber to which members go to vote during a division **3** *sing or pl in constr* a group of people engaged in lobbying [ML *lobium* gallery, of Gmc origin; akin to OHG *louba* porch]

²lobby *vi* to try to influence members of a legislative body towards an action ~ *vt* **1** to secure the passage of (legislation) by influencing public officials **2** to try to influence (e g a member of a legislative body) towards an action – **lobbyer** *n,* **lobbyist** *n*

lobe /lohb/ *n* a curved or rounded projection or division; *esp* such a projection or division of a bodily organ or part [MF, fr LL *lobus,* fr Gk *lobos*] – **lobed** /lohbd/ *adj,* **lobar** /'lohbə/ *adj,* **lobate** /'lohbayt/, **lobated** *adj*

lobectomy /loh'bektəmi/ *n* surgical removal of a lobe of an organ (e g a lung) or gland (e g the thyroid) [ISV]

'lobe-,fin *n* any of a large group of mostly extinct fishes that have paired fins resembling limbs and that may be ancestral to the ground-living vertebrates – **lobe-finned** *adj*

lobelia /loh'beelyə/ *n* any of a genus of widely distributed herbaceous plants often cultivated for their clusters of small showy flowers [NL, genus name, fr Matthias de *Lobel* †1616 Flem botanist]

lobotomy /lə'botəmi, loh-/ *n* a brain operation used, esp formerly, in the treatment of some mental disorders (e g violent psychoses) in which nerve fibres in the cerebral cortex are cut in order to change behaviour [ISV] – **lobotomize** /loh'botomiez, lə-/ *vt*

lobscouse /'lob,skows/ *n* a (sailors') dish prepared by stewing or baking meat with vegetables and ship biscuit [origin unknown]

lobster /'lobstə/ *n, pl* **lobsters,** *esp collectively* **lobster** any of a family of large edible 10-legged marine crustaceans that have stalked eyes, a pair of large claws, and a long abdomen [ME, fr OE *loppestre,* modif (prob influenced by OE *loppe* spider) of L *locusta* crustacean, lobster]

'lobster ,pot *n* (a basket used as) a trap for catching lobsters

lobule /'lobyoohl/ *n* (a subdivision of) a small lobe – **lobulate** /-layt/ *adj,* **lobulose** /-lohs, -lohz/ *adj*

¹local /'lohk(ə)l/ *adj* **1** characterized by or relating to position in space **2** (characteristic) of or belonging to a particular place; not general or widespread ⟨~ *news*⟩ **3a** primarily serving the needs of a particular limited district ⟨~ *government*⟩ **b** *of a public conveyance* making all the stops on a route **4** involving or affecting only a restricted part of a living organism [ME *localle,* fr MF *local,* fr LL *localis,* fr L *locus* place – more at ¹STALL] – **locally** *adv*

²local *n* a local person or thing ⟨*spoke to the friendly* ~s⟩: e g **a** *Br the* neighbourhood pub **b** *NAm* a local public conveyance (e g a train or bus)

,local au'thority *n sing or pl in constr* the body of elected and salaried people who administer British local government

,local 'colour *n* the description in a literary work of the features and peculiarities of a particular locality and its inhabitants

locale /loh'kahl/ *n* a place or locality, esp when viewed in relation to a particular event or characteristic; a scene [modif of F *local,* fr *local,* adj]

,local 'government *n* the government of a specific local subdivision of a major political unit

localism /'lohk(ə)l,iz(ə)m/ *n* **1** affection or partiality for a particular place, esp to the exclusion of others **2** a local idiom or custom

locality /loh'kaləti/ *n* **1** the fact or condition of having a location in space or time **2** a particular place, situation, or location

local·ize, -ise /'lok(ə)l,iez/ *vt* **1** to give local characteristics to **2** to assign to or keep within a definite locality ~ *vi* to collect in a specific or limited area – **localization** /-ie'zaysh(ə)n/ *n*

locate /loh'kayt/ *vt* **1** to determine or indicate the place, site, or limits of **2** to set or establish in a particular spot [L *locatus*, pp of *locare* to place, fr *locus*] – **locatable** *adj*, **locater** *n*

location /loh'kaysh(ə)n/ *n* **1** a particular place or position **2** a place outside a studio where a (part of a) picture is filmed – usu in *on location* [LOCATE + -ION] – **locational** *adj*, **locationally** *adv*

locative /'lokətiv/ *n* (a form in) a grammatical case expressing place where or wherein [L *locus* + E *-ative* (as in *vocative*)] – **locative** *adj*

loch /lokh/ *n* a lake or (nearly landlocked) arm of the sea in Scotland [ME (Sc) *louch*, fr ScGael *loch*; akin to L *lacus* lake]

loci /'lohsi; *also* lohki/ *pl of* LOCUS

[1]**lock** /lok/ *n* **1** a curl, tuft, etc of hair **2** *pl* the hair of the head [ME *lok*, fr OE *locc*; akin to OHG *loc* lock, L *luctari* to struggle, *luxus* dislocated]

[2]**lock** *n* **1a** a fastening that can be opened and often closed only by means of a particular key or combination **b** a gunlock **2a** an enclosed section of waterway (e g a canal) which has gates at each end and in which the water level can be raised or lowered to move boats from one level to another **b** AIR LOCK **3a** a locking or fastening together **b** a hold in wrestling secured on a usu specified body part **4** *chiefly Br* the (maximum) extent to which the front wheels of a vehicle are turned to change the direction of travel ⟨*from* ~ *to* ~ *is 3⅝ turns of the steering wheel*⟩ [ME *lok*, fr OE *loc*; akin to OHG *loh* enclosure, OE *locc* lock of hair]

[3]**lock** *vt* **1a** to fasten the lock of **b** to make fast (as if) with a lock ⟨~ *up the house*⟩ **2a** to shut in or out or make secure or inaccessible (as if) by means of locks ⟨~ed *himself away from the curious world*⟩ ⟨~ed *her husband out*⟩ **b** to hold fast or inactive; fix in a particular situation or method of operation **3a** to make fast by the interlacing or interlocking of parts **b** to hold in a close embrace **c** to grapple in combat; *also* to bind closely – often pass ⟨*administration and students were* ~ed *in conflict*⟩ **4** to move or permit (e g a ship) to pass by raising or lowering in a lock ~ *vi* to become locked – **lockable** *adj*

lockage /'lokij/ *n* **1** an act or process of passing through a lock **2** a system of locks **3** the tariff charged for passing through a lock

locker /'lokə/ *n* **1** a cupboard or compartment that may be closed with a lock; *esp* one for individual storage use **2** a chest or compartment on board ship [[3]LOCK + [2]-ER]

locket /'lokit/ *n* a small case usu of precious metal that has space for a memento (e g a small picture) and is usu worn on a chain round the neck [MF *loquet* latch, fr MD *loke*; akin to OE *loc*]

,**lock 'forward** *n* either of two players positioned inside the second row of the scrum in rugby ☞ SPORT

lockjaw /'lok,jaw/ *n* an early symptom of tetanus characterized by spasm of the jaw muscles and inability to open the jaws; *also* tetanus

'lock,keeper /-,keepə/ *n* sby who looks after a canal or river lock

'lock,nut /-,nut/ *n* **1** a nut screwed hard up against another to prevent either of them from moving **2** a nut so constructed that it locks itself when screwed up tight

lock on *vt* to sight and follow automatically by means of a radar beam or sensor

'lock,out /-,owt/ *n* a whole or partial closing of a business by an employer in order to gain concessions from or resist demands of employees

lock out *vt* to subject (a body of employees) to a lockout

'lock,smith /-,smith/ *n* sby who makes or mends locks as an occupation

'lock,step /-,step/ *n* a mode of marching in step as closely as possible

'lock,stitch /-,stich/ *n* a sewing machine stitch formed by the looping together of 2 threads, 1 on each side of the material being sewn – **lock-stitch** *vb*

,**lock, ,stock, and 'barrel** *adv* wholly, completely [fr the principal parts of a flintlock]

'lock,up /-,up/ *n* **1** (the time of) locking; the state of being locked **2** a (small local) prison **3** *Br* a lock-up shop or garage

'lock-,up *adj*, *Br*, *of a building* (able to be) locked up and left when not in use

[1]**loco** /'lohkoh/ *n*, *pl* **locos** a locomotive

[2]**loco** *adj*, *chiefly NAm* out of one's mind – slang [Sp]

locomotion /,lohkə'mohsh(ə)n/ *n* **1** an act or the power of moving from place to place **2** TRAVEL 1, 2a [L *locus* + E *motion*]

[1]**locomotive** /,lohkə'mohtiv/ *adj* **1** of or functioning in locomotion **2** of travel **3** moving, or able to move, by self-propulsion

[2],**loco'motive** *n* an engine that moves under its own power; *esp* one that moves railway carriages and wagons

,**loco'motor** /-'mohtə/ *adj* **1** LOCOMOTIVE 1 **2** affecting or involving the locomotive organs

,**loco,motor a'taxia** /ə'taksi·ə/ *n* a tertiary syphilitic disorder of the nervous system marked esp by disturbances of gait and difficulty in coordinating voluntary movements

locoweed /'lohkoh,weed/ *n* any of several leguminous plants of western N America that cause madness in livestock

loculus /'lokyooləs/ *n*, *pl* **loculi** /'lokyoo,lee/ a small chamber or cavity, esp in a plant or animal body [NL, fr L, dim. of *locus*] – **locular** /lokyoolə/ *adj*, **loculate** /lokyoolayt/ *adj*

locum /'lohkəm/ *n* sby filling an office for a time or temporarily taking the place of another – used esp with reference to a doctor or clergyman [short for *locum tenens*]

,**locum 'tenens** /'tenenz/ *n*, *pl* **locum tenentes** /te'nenteez, -tiz/ a locum – fml [ML, lit., one holding a place]

locus /'lohkəs, 'lokəs/ *n*, *pl* **loci** /'lohsie, 'lohsi; *also* 'lohkie, 'lohki/ *also* **locuses** **1** a place, locality **2** the set of all points whose location is determined by stated conditions **3** the position on a chromosome of a particular gene or allele [L – more at [1]STALL]

,**locus 'classicus** /'klasikəs/ *n*, *pl* **loci classici** /'klasiki, -kie/ the best-known and most authoritative passage or work on a particular subject [NL]

,**locus 'standi** /'standie/ *n* the right to appear in court or be heard on any question [L, lit., place to stand]

locust /'lohkəst/ *n* **1** a migratory grasshopper that often travels in vast swarms stripping the areas passed of all vegetation ☞ FOOD **2** any of various hard-wooded leguminous trees; *esp* a carob [ME, fr L *locusta*]

'**locust ,bean** *n* the fruit of the carob

locution /loh'kyoohsh(ə)n, lə-/ *n* **1** a word or expression characteristic of a region, group, or cultural level **2** phraseology [ME *locucioun*, fr L *locution-, locutio*, fr *locutus*, pp of *loqui* to speak]

lode /lohd/ *n* an ore deposit [ME, fr OE *lād* course, support; akin to OE *līthan* to go – more at [1]LEAD]

loden /'lohd(ə)n/ *n* a dull greyish green; *also* a thick woollen cloth (e g for coats) typically of this colour [G, fr OHG *lodo* coarse cloth]

lodestar, loadstar /'lohd,stah/ *n* **1** a star that guides; *esp* POLE STAR **2** sthg that serves as a guiding star [ME *lode sterre*, fr *lode* course, fr OE *lād*]

'**lode,stone, loadstone** /-,stohn/ *n* **1** (a piece of) magnetized mineral iron oxide **2** sthg that strongly attracts; a magnet [obs *lode* (course), fr ME]

[1]**lodge** /loj/ *vt* **1a** to provide temporary, esp rented, accommodation for **b** to establish or settle in a place **2** to serve as a receptacle for; contain, house **3** to beat (e g a crop) flat to the ground **4** to fix in place **5** to deposit for safeguard or preservation ⟨~ *your money in the nearest bank*⟩ **6** to place or vest (e g power), esp in a source, means, or agent **7** to lay (e g a complaint) before authority ~ *vi* **1a** to occupy a place, esp temporarily **b** to be a lodger **2** to come to rest; settle ⟨*the bullet* ~d *in his chest*⟩ **3** *esp of hay or grain crops* to fall or lie down

[2]**lodge** *n* **1** the meeting place of a branch of an esp fraternal organization **2** a house set apart for residence in a particular season (e g the hunting season) **3a** a house orig for the use of a gamekeeper, caretaker, porter, etc **b** a porter's room (e g at the entrance to a college, block of flats, etc) **c** the house where the head of a university college lives, esp in Cambridge **4** a den or lair of an animal or a group of animals (e g beavers or otters) **5** a wigwam [ME *loge*, fr OF, of Gmc origin; akin to OHG *louba* porch]

lodger /'lojə/ *n* one who occupies a rented room in another's house [[1]LODGE + [2]-ER]

lodging /'lojing/ *n* **1** a place to live; a dwelling **2a** a temporary place to stay ⟨*a* ~ *for the night*⟩ **b** a rented room or rooms for residing in, usu in a private house rather than a hotel – usu pl with sing. meaning

'**lodging ,house** *n* a house where lodgings are provided and let

loess /'loh·is, les/ *n* a usu yellowish brown loamy deposit found in Europe, Asia, and N America and believed to be chiefly deposited by the wind [G *löss*] – **loessial** /loh'esi·əl, 'lesi·əl/

[1]**loft** /loft/ *n* **1** an attic **2a** a gallery in a church or hall **b** an upper floor in a barn or warehouse used for storage – sometimes in combination ⟨*a hay*loft⟩ **c** a shed or coop for pigeons **3** the backward slant of the face of a golf-club head **4** *NAm* an upper room or floor [ME, fr OE, fr ON *lopt* air; akin to OE *lyft* air, OHG *luft*]

[2]**loft** *vt* to propel through the air or into space ⟨~ed *the ball over midwicket*⟩

lofty /'lofti/ *adj* **1** having a haughty overbearing manner; supercilious **2a** elevated in character and spirit; noble **b** elevated in position; superior **3** rising to a great height; impressively high ⟨~ *mountains*⟩ – **loftily** *adv*, **loftiness** *n*

[1]**log** /log/ *n* **1** a usu bulky piece or length of unshaped timber (ready for sawing or for use as firewood) **2** an apparatus for measuring the rate of a ship's motion through the water **3a** the record of the rate of a ship's speed or of her daily progress; *also* the full nautical record of a ship's voyage **b** the full record of a flight by an aircraft **4** any of various records of performance ⟨*a computer* ~⟩ [ME *logge*, prob of Scand origin; akin to ON *lāg* fallen tree; akin to OE *licgan* to lie – more at [1]LIE]

[2]**log** *vb* **-gg-** *vt* **1** to cut (trees) for timber **2** to enter details of or about in a log **3a** to move or attain (e g an indicated distance, speed, or time) as noted in a log **b(1)** to sail a ship or fly an aircraft for (an indicated distance or period of time) **(2)** to have (an indicated record) to one's credit; achieve ⟨~ged *about 30,000 miles a year in his car*⟩ ~ *vi* to cut logs for timber

[3]**log** *n* a logarithm

log-, logo- *comb form* thought; speech ⟨logo*gram*⟩ ⟨logo*rrhoea*⟩ [Gk, fr *logos* – more at LEGEND]

-log /-log/ *comb form* (→ *n*), *chiefly NAm* -logue

loganberry /'lohgənb(ə)ri, -,beri/ *n* (the red sweet edible berry of) an upright-growing raspberry hybrid [James H *Logan* †1928 US lawyer + E *berry*]

logarithm /'logə,ridh(ə)m/ *n* the exponent that indicates the power to which a number is raised to produce a given number ⟨*the* ~ *of 100 to the base 10 is 2*⟩ [NL *logarithmus*, fr *log-* + Gk *arithmos* number – more at ARITHMETIC] – **logarithmic** /-'ridhmik/ *adj*, **logarithmically** *adv*

'**log,book** /-,book/ *n* **1** LOG 3, 4 **2** *Br* a document held with a motor vehicle that gives the vehicle's registration number, make, engine size, etc and a list of its owners – not now used technically; compare REGISTRATION DOCUMENT

loge /lohzh/ *n* a box in a theatre [F – more at LODGE]

logger /'logə/ *n, NAm* a lumberjack

loggerhead /'logə,hed/ *n* **1** any of various very large marine turtles **2** an iron tool consisting of a long handle ending in a ball or bulb that is heated and used to melt tar or to heat liquids [prob fr E dial. *logger* (block of wood) + *head*] – **at loggerheads** in or into a state of quarrelsome disagreement

loggia /'loj(i)ə/ *n, pl* **loggias** *also* **loggie** /'lojie/ a roofed open gallery behind a colonnade or arcade [It, fr F *loge*]

logic /'lojik/ *n* **1a(1)** a science that deals with the formal principles and structure of thought and reasoning **(2)** a specified branch or system of logic **b** a particular mode of reasoning viewed as valid or faulty ⟨*couldn't follow his* ~⟩ **c** the interrelation or sequence of facts or events when seen as inevitable or predictable **d** the fundamental principles and the connection of circuit elements for performing Boolean operations (e g those needed for arithmetical computation) in a computer; *also* the circuits themselves **2** sthg that forces a decision apart from or in opposition to reason ⟨*the* ~ *of war*⟩ [ME *logik*, fr MF *logique*, fr L *logica*, fr Gk *logikē*, fr fem of *logikos* of reason, fr *logos* reason – more at LEGEND] – **logician** /lo'jish(ə)n, lə-/ *n*

logical /'lojikl/ *adj* **1** of or conforming with logic ⟨*a* ~ *argument*⟩ **2** capable of reasoning or of using reason in an orderly fashion ⟨*a* ~ *thinker*⟩ – **logically** *adv*, **logicalness, logicality** /loji'kaləti/ *n*

,logical 'positi,vism *n* a 20th-c philosophical movement stressing linguistic analysis and rejecting metaphysical theories – **logical positivist** *n*

logico- /lojikoh-/ *comb form* logical;logical and ⟨logico- *mathematical*⟩

logistics /lo'jistiks, lə-/ *n pl but sing or pl in constr* **1** the aspect of military science dealing with the transportation, quartering, and supplying of troops in military operations **2** the handling of the details of an operation [F *logistique* art of calculating, logistics, fr Gk *logistikē* art of calculating, fr fem of *logistikos* of calculation, fr *logizein* to calculate, fr *logos* reason] – **logistic** *adj,* **logistically** *adv*

logjam /'log,jam/ *n, chiefly NAm* a deadlock, impasse

logo /'logoh/ *n, pl* **logos** LOGOTYPE 2

logo- – see LOG-

logogram /'logə,gram/ *n* a character or sign used (e g in shorthand) to represent an entire word – **logogrammatic** /-grə'matik/ *adj*

logograph /'logə,grahf, -,graf/ *n* a logogram

'logo,griph /-,grif/ *n* a word puzzle (e g an anagram) [*log-* + Gk *griphos* reed basket, riddle – more at CRIB]

logorrhoea /,logə'riə/ *n* excessive and often incoherent talkativeness or wordiness [NL]

Logos /'logos/ *n, pl* **Logoi** /'logoy/ WORD 4 [Gk, speech, word, reason – more at LEGEND]

logotype /'logə,tiep/ *n* **1** a single block or piece of type that prints a whole word (e g the name of a newspaper) **2** an identifying symbol (e g for advertising)

logrolling /'log,rohling/ *n, chiefly NAm* the trading of votes by members of a legislature to secure favourable action on projects of mutual interest [fr a former US custom of neighbours assisting one another in rolling logs]

-logue, *NAm chiefly* **-log** /-log/ *comb form* (→ *n*) **1** conversation; talk ⟨*duo*logue⟩ **2** student; specialist ⟨*sino*logue⟩ [ME *-logue,* fr OF, fr L *-logus,* fr Gk *-logos,* fr *legein* to speak – more at LEGEND]

-logy /-ləji/ *comb form* (→ *n*) **1** oral or written expression ⟨*phraseo*logy⟩; *esp* body of writings of (a specified kind) or on (a specified subject) ⟨*tri*logy⟩ ⟨*hagio*logy⟩ **2** doctrine; theory; science ⟨*eth* nology⟩ ⟨*semio*logy⟩ [ME *-logie,* fr OF, fr L *-logia,* fr Gk, fr *logos* word]

loin /loyn/ *n* **1a** the part of a human being or quadruped on each side of the spinal column between the hipbone and the lower ribs **b** a cut of meat comprising this part of one or both sides of a carcass with the adjoining half of the vertebrae included ☞ MEAT **2** *pl* **a** the upper and lower abdominal regions and the region about the hips **b(1)** the pubic region **(2)** the genitals [ME *loyne,* fr MF *loigne,* fr (assumed) VL *lumbea,* fr L *lumbus;* akin to OE *lendenu* loins]

'loin,cloth /-,kloth/ *n* a cloth worn about the hips and covering the genitals

loiter /'loytə/ *vi* **1** to remain in an area for no obvious reason; HANG ABOUT **2** to make frequent pauses while travelling; dawdle [ME *loiteren,* prob fr MD *loteren* to waggle, be loose] – **loiterer** *n*

loll /lol/ *vi* **1** to hang down loosely ⟨*his tongue* ~ed *out*⟩ **2** to recline, lean, or move in a lazy or excessively relaxed manner; lounge [ME *lollen,* prob of imit origin]

lollipop, lollypop /'loli,pop/ *n* a large often round flat sweet of boiled sugar on the end of a stick [prob fr E dial. *lolly* (tongue) + *pop*]

'lollipop ,man, *fem* **'lollipop ,lady** *n, Br* sby controlling traffic to allow (school) children to cross busy roads [fr the round warning sign on a pole carried by him/her]

lollop /'loləp/ *vi* to move or proceed with an ungainly loping motion [¹*loll* + *-op* (as in *gallop*)]

lolly /'loli/ *n* **1** a lollipop or ice lolly **2** *Br* money – infml [short for *lollipop*]

Lombard /'lombahd, -bəd/ *n* **1** a member of a Teutonic people that invaded Italy and settled in the Po valley in the 6th c AD **2** a native or inhabitant of Lombardy [ME *Lumbarde,* fr MF *lombard,* fr OIt *lombardo,* fr L *Langobardus*] – **Lombardian** /lom'bardi·ən/ *adj,* **Lombardic** /lom'bardik/ *adj*

,Lombardy 'poplar /'lombədi, 'lum-/ *n* a much planted tall narrow European poplar [*Lombardy,* district of Italy]

loment /'lohment/ *n* a dry 1-celled fruit that breaks transversely into numerous usu 1-seeded segments at maturity [NL *lomentum,* fr L, wash made of bean meal, fr *lotus,* pp of *lavare* to wash – more at LYE]

Lomotil /'lohmə,til/ *trademark* – used for diphenoxylate hydrochloride

,London 'plane /'lundən/ *n* a fast-growing smoke-resistant hybrid plane tree that is often planted in streets of towns [*London,* capital city of England]

lone /lohn/ *adj* **1** only, sole **2** situated alone or separately; isolated **3** having no company; solitary – fml [ME, short for *alone*] – **loneness** *n*

lonely /'lohnli/ *adj* **1** cut off from others; solitary **2** not frequented by people; desolate **3** sad from being alone or without friends – **lonelily** *adv,* **loneliness** *n*

,lonely 'hearts *adj* of or for lonely people seeking companions or spouses ⟨*a* ~ *club*⟩

loner /'lohnə/ *n* a person or animal that prefers solitude

¹lonesome /'lohns(ə)m/ *adj* **1** lonely **2** LONE 2 ⟨*on the trail of the* ~ *pine* – Ballard Macdonald⟩ – **lonesomely** *adv,* **lonesomeness** *n*

²lonesome *n* self – infml ⟨*sat all on his* ~⟩

,lone 'wolf *n* a person who prefers to work, act, or live alone

¹long /long/ *adj* **1a** extending for a considerable distance **b** having greater length or height than usual **2a** having a specified length ⟨*6ft* ~⟩ **b** forming the chief linear dimension ⟨*the* ~ *side of the room*⟩ **3** extending over a considerable or specified time ⟨*a* ~ *friendship*⟩ ⟨*2 hours* ~⟩ **4** containing a large or specified number of items or units ⟨*a* ~ *list*⟩ ⟨*300 pages* ~⟩ **5a** *of a speech sound or syllable* of relatively long duration **b** being one of a pair of similarly spelt vowel sounds that is longer in duration ⟨~ a *in* fate⟩ **c** bearing a stress or accent **6a** having the capacity to reach or extend a considerable distance ⟨*a* ~ *left jab*⟩ **b** hit for a considerable distance ⟨*a* ~ *drive from the tee*⟩ **7** *of betting odds* greatly differing in the amounts wagered on each side **8** subject to great odds ⟨*a* ~ *chance*⟩ **9** owning or accumulating securities or goods, esp in anticipation of an advance in prices ⟨*they are now* ~ *on wheat*⟩ [ME *long, lang,* fr OE; akin to OHG *lang* long, L *longus,* Gk *dolichos*] – **longish** *adj,* **longness** *n* – **before long** in a short time; soon – **in the long run** in the course of sufficiently prolonged time, trial, or experience – compare IN THE SHORT RUN – **long in the tooth** past one's best days; old – **not by a long chalk** not at all

[2]**long** *adv* **1** for or during a long or specified time ⟨*not ~ returned*⟩ **2** at a point of time far before or after a specified moment or event ⟨*was excited ~ before the big day*⟩ **3** after or beyond a specified time ⟨*said it was no ~er possible*⟩ – **so long** goodbye – infml

[3]**long** *n* a long syllable – **the long and (the) short** the gist; the outline ⟨the long and the short *of it was that we had to walk home*⟩

[4]**long** *vi* to feel a strong desire or craving, esp *for* sthg not likely to be attained [ME *longen*, fr OE *langian*; akin to OHG *langēn* to long, OE *lang* long]

ˌlong aˈgo *n* the distant past – **long-ago** *adj*

ˈlongˌboat /-ˌboht/ *n* the largest boat carried by a sailing vessel

ˈlongˌbow /-ˌboh/ *n* a long wooden bow for shooting arrows, specif that used in medieval England that was about 6ft (1.8m) long, was made of yew or ash, and was drawn by hand

ˌlong-ˈchain *adj* having a relatively long chain of (carbon) atoms in the molecule

[1]**ˌlong-ˈdistance** *adj* **1** covering or effective over a long distance **2** *of telephone communication* between points a long distance apart

[2]**long-distance** *adv* by long-distance telephone

ˌlong diˈvision *n* arithmetical division in which the calculations corresponding to the division of parts of the dividend by the divisor are written out

ˌlong-ˌdrawn-ˈout *adj* extended to a great length; protracted

ˌlong-ˌeared ˈowl *n* a medium-sized European owl with long ear tufts

longeron /ˈlonjərən/ *n* a fore-and-aft framing member of an aircraft fuselage [F, fr *allonger* to make long]

longevity /lonˈjevəti; *also* longˈgevəti/ *n* (great) length of life ⟨*a study of ~*⟩ [LL *longaevitas*, fr L *longaevus* long-lived, fr *longus* long + *aevum* age – more at [1]AYE]

ˈlongˌhair /-ˌheə/ *n* a person with, or usu thought of as having, long hair: e g **a** a hippie **b** sby of an artistic, esp avant-garde, temperament **c** an unworldly intellectual [back-formation fr *long-haired*] – **long-hair, long-haired** *adj*

ˈlongˌhand /-ˌhand/ *n* ordinary writing; handwriting

ˌlong ˈhaul *n* **1** a lengthy usu difficult period of time ⟨*the ~ back to health*⟩ **2** the transport of goods over long distances – **long-haul** *adj*

ˌlongˈheaded /-ˈhedid/ *adj* **1** having unusual foresight or wisdom **2** dolichocephalic

ˈlong ˌhop *n* an easily hit short-pitched delivery of a cricket ball

ˈlongˌhorn /-ˌhawn/ *n* any of a breed of long-horned cattle of Spanish derivation

ˌlong-ˌhorned ˈbeetle, longhorn beetle *n* any of various beetles usu distinguished by their very long antennae

ˌlong-ˌhorned ˈgrassˌhopper *n* any of various grasshoppers distinguished by their very long antennae

longi- *comb form* long ⟨longi*pennate*⟩ ⟨longi*tude*⟩ [ME, fr L, fr *longus*]

longicorn /ˈlonjiˌkawn/ *adj* of or being long-horned beetles [deriv of *longi-* + L *cornu* horn – more at HORN] – **longicorn** *n*

longing /ˈlong·ing/ *n* a strong desire, esp for sthg difficult to attain – **longingly** *adv*

longitude /ˈlonjityoohd; *also* ˈlong·giˌtyoohd/ *n* the (time difference corresponding to) angular distance of a point on the surface of a celestial body, esp the earth, measured E or W from a prime meridian (e g that of Greenwich) – compare LATITUDE 1a [ME, fr L *longitudin-, longitudo* length, fr *longus*]

ˌlongiˈtudinal /-ˈtyoohdinl/ *adj* **1** of length or the lengthways dimension **2** placed or running lengthways – **longitudinally** *adv*

ˌlongiˌtudinal ˈwave *n* a wave (e g a sound wave) in which the particles of the medium vibrate in the direction of the line of advance of the wave – compare TRANSVERSE WAVE

ˈlong ˌjohns /jonz/ *n pl* underpants with legs extending usu down to the ankles – infml ☞ GARMENT [fr the name *John* + *-s*]

ˈlong ˌjump *n* (an athletic field event consisting of) a jump for distance from a running start – **long jumper** *n*

ˌlong ˈleg *n* a fielding position in cricket near the boundary behind the batsman on the leg side of the pitch ☞ SPORT

ˌlong-ˈlife *adj* (processed so as to be) long-lasting

ˌlong-ˈlived /livd/ *adj* **1** characterized by long life ⟨*a ~ family*⟩ **2** long-lasting, enduring – **long-livedness** *n* /-ˈliv(e)dnis/

ˌlong ˈoff *n* a fielding position in cricket near the boundary behind the bowler on the off side of the pitch ☞ SPORT

ˌlong ˈon *n* a fielding position in cricket near the boundary behind the bowler on the leg side of the pitch ☞ SPORT

ˌlong-ˈrange *adj* **1** involving or taking into account a long period of time ⟨*~ planning*⟩ **2** relating to or fit for long distances ⟨*~ rockets*⟩

ˈlong ˌrun *n* a relatively long period of time – usu in *in the long run* – **long-run** *adj*

ˈlongˌship /-ˌship/ *n* a long open ship propelled by oars and a sail and used by the Vikings principally to carry warriors

ˈlongˌshoreman /-ˌshawmən/ *n, chiefly NAm* a docker [*longshore*, short for *alongshore*]

ˈlong ˌshot *n* **1** (a bet at long odds on) a competitor given little chance of winning **2** a venture that involves considerable risk and has little chance of success – **by a long shot** by a great deal

ˌlongˈsighted /-ˈsietid/ *adj* hypermetropic – **longsightedness** *n*

ˌlong-ˈstanding *adj* of long duration

ˈlong ˌstop *n* a now little-used fielding position in cricket near the boundary and directly behind the wicketkeeper ☞ SPORT

ˌlong-ˈsuffering *n or adj* (the quality of) patiently enduring pain, difficulty, or provocation – **long-sufferingly** *adv*

ˈlong ˌsuit *n* the activity or quality in which a person excels

ˌlong-ˈterm *adj* occurring over or involving a relatively long period of time

ˌlong ˈton *n* a British unit of weight equal to 2240lb (about 1016.05kg)

longueur /longˈguh (*Fr* lɔ̃gœːr)/ *n, pl* **longueurs** /longˈguh(z) (*Fr* ~)/ a dull and tedious part or period [F, lit., length]

ˌlong vaˈcation *n* the long summer holiday of British law courts and universities

ˌlong-ˈwaisted *adj* of more than average length from the shoulders to the waist

ˈlong ˌwave *n* a band of radio waves typically used for sound broadcasting and covering wavelengths of 1000m or more

ˈlongˌways /-ˌwayz, wiz/ *adv* lengthways

ˌlong weekˈend *n* a short holiday including a weekend

ˌlong-ˈwinded /-ˈwindid/ *adj* tediously long in speaking or writing – **long-windedly** *adv*, **long-windedness** *n*

longwise /ˈlong,wiez, -wiz/ *adv* lengthways

[1]loo /looh/ *n* (money staked at) an old card game in which the winner of each trick takes a portion of the pool while losing players have to contribute to the next pool [short for obs *lanterloo*, fr F *lanturelu* piffle]

[2]loo *n, chiefly Br* TOILET 2 – infml [perh modif of F *lieu (d'aisance)* toilet or *l'eau* the water]

loofah /ˈloohfə/ *n* a dried seed pod of any of several plants of the cucumber family that is used as a bath sponge [NL *Luffa*, genus name, fr Ar *lūf*]

[1]look /look/ *vt* **1** to find out or learn by the use of one's eyes ⟨~ *what time it starts*⟩ ⟨~ *what you've done!*⟩ **2** to regard intensely; examine ⟨~ *him in the eye*⟩ ⟨~ *a gift horse in the mouth*⟩ **3** to express by the eyes or facial expression ⟨~ed *daggers at him*⟩ **4** to have an appearance that befits or accords with ⟨*really* ~ed *the part*⟩ ~ *vi* **1a** to use the power of sight; *esp* to make a visual search *for* **b** to direct one's attention ⟨~ *into the matter*⟩ **c** to direct the eyes ⟨~ *at him!*⟩ **2** to have the appearance of being; appear, seem ⟨~s *very ill*⟩ ⟨~ed *to be crying* – Colin MacInnes⟩ **3** to have a specified outlook ⟨*the house* ~ed *east*⟩ [ME *looken*, fr OE *lōcian*; akin to OS *lōcōn* to look] – **look after** to take care of – **look sharp** to be quick; hurry

[2]look *n* **1a** the act of looking **b** [2]GLANCE 3 **2a** a facial expression ⟨*she had a funny* ~ *on her face*⟩ **b** (attractive) physical appearance – usu pl with sing. meaning **3** the state or form in which sthg appears ⟨*a new* ~ *in knitwear*⟩ ⟨*has the* ~ *of a loser about him*⟩

ˈlook-aˌlike *n* sby or sthg that looks like another; a double

look back *vi* **1** to remember – often + *to, on* **2** to fail to make successful progress – in *never look back* ⟨*after his initial success, he never* looked back⟩

look down *vi* to have an attitude of superiority or contempt – + *on* or *upon* ⟨*snobbishly* looks down *on the poor*⟩

looker /ˈlookə/ *n* **1** one having an appearance of a specified kind – often in combination ⟨*a good*-looker⟩ **2** an attractive person, esp a woman – infml [[1]LOOK + [2]-ER]

ˈlook-ˌin *n* a chance to take part; *also* a chance of success – infml

look in *vi, Br* to pay a short visit ⟨*will* look in *on the party*⟩

ˈlooking ˌglass /ˈlooking/ *n* a mirror

look on *vi* to be a spectator

ˈlookˌout /-ˌowt/ *n* **1** one engaged in keeping watch **2** a place or structure affording a wide view for observation **3** a careful looking or watching **4** a matter of care or concern ⟨*it's your* ~ *if you do such a silly thing*⟩ **5** *chiefly Br* a future possibility; a prospect

look out *vi* **1** to take care – often imper **2** to keep watching ⟨look out *for your parents*⟩ ~ *vt*, *chiefly Br* to choose by inspection; select ⟨look out *a suit for the interview*⟩

look over *vt* to examine (quickly) – **lookover** *n* /ˈlook,ohvə/

look up *vi* to improve in prospects or conditions ⟨*business is* looking up⟩ ~ *vt* **1** to search for (as if) in a reference work ⟨look up *a phone number in the directory*⟩ **2** to pay a usu short visit to ⟨looked up *my friend while I was there*⟩ **3** to have an attitude of respect – + *to* ⟨*always* looked up *to their parents*⟩

[1]loom /loohm/ *n* a frame or machine for weaving together yarns or threads into cloth [ME *lome* tool, loom, fr OE *gelōma* tool; akin to MD al*lame* tool]

[2]loom *vi* **1** to come into sight indistinctly, in enlarged or distorted and menacing form, often as a result of atmospheric conditions **2a** to appear in an impressively great or exaggerated form **b** to take shape as an impending occurrence ⟨*exams* ~ed *large*⟩ [origin unknown]

[1]loon /loohn/ *n* a mad or silly person [ME *loun* rogue, idler]

[2]loon *n* any of several large fish-eating diving birds that have the legs placed far back under the body [of Scand origin; akin to ON *lōmr* loon – more at LAMENT]

loony, looney /ˈloohni/ *adj* crazy, foolish – infml [by shortening & alter. fr *lunatic*] – **looniness** *n*, **loony** *n*

ˈloony ˌbin *n* MADHOUSE 1 – humor

[1]loop /loohp/ *n* **1** a (partially) closed figure that has a curved outline surrounding a central opening **2a** sthg shaped like a loop **b** a manoeuvre in which an aircraft passes successively through a climb, inverted flight, and a dive, and then returns to normal flight **c** a zigzag-shaped intrauterine contraceptive device **3** a ring or curved piece used to form a fastening or handle **4** a piece of film or magnetic tape whose ends are spliced together so as to reproduce the same material continuously **5** a series of instructions (e g for a computer) that is repeated until a terminating condition is reached [ME *loupe*, of unknown origin]

[2]loop *vi* **1** to make, form, or move in a loop or loops **2** to execute a loop in an aircraft ~ *vt* **1a** to make a loop in, on, or about **b** to fasten with a loop **2** to join (2 courses of loops) in knitting **3** to form a loop with ⟨~ed *the wool round the knitting needle*⟩ – **loop the loop** to perform a loop in an aircraft

looper /ˈloohpə/ *n* **1** an inchworm **2** a device on a sewing machine for making loops [[2]LOOP + [2]-ER]

[1]loophole /ˈloohp,hohl/ *n* **1** a small opening through which missiles, firearms, etc may be discharged or light and air admitted **2** a means of escape; *esp* an ambiguity or omission in a text through which its intent may be evaded [arch *loop*, fr ME *loupe*; perh akin to MD *lupen* to watch, peer]

[2]loophole *vt* to make loopholes in

ˈloop ˌline *n* a railway line that leaves and later rejoins a main line

ˌloop of ˈHenle /ˈhenli/ *n* a part of each nephron in a kidney that plays a part in water resorption [F G J *Henle* †1885 G pathologist]

ˈloop ˌstitch *n* a needlework stitch consisting of a series of interlocking loops

loopy /ˈloohpi/ *adj* slightly crazy or foolish – infml [[2]LOOP + [1]-Y]

[1]**loose** /loohs/ *adj* **1a** not rigidly fastened or securely attached **b** having worked partly free from attachments ⟨*the masonry is ~ at the base of the wall*⟩ **c** *of a cough* produced freely and accompanied by rising of mucus **d** not tight-fitting ⟨*a ~ cardigan*⟩ **2a** free from a state of confinement, restraint, or obligation ⟨*a lion ~ in the streets*⟩ **b** not brought together in a bundle, container, or binding ⟨*~ hair*⟩ **3** not dense, close, or compact in structure or arrangement **4a** lacking in (power of) restraint ⟨*a ~ tongue*⟩ ⟨*~ bowels*⟩ **b** dissolute, promiscuous ⟨*~ living*⟩ **5** not tightly drawn or stretched; slack **6a** lacking in precision, exactness, or care ⟨*a ~ translation*⟩ **b** permitting freedom of interpretation ⟨*the wording of the document is very ~*⟩ [ME *lous*, fr ON *lauss*; akin to OHG *lōs* loose – more at -LESS] – **loosely** *adv*, **loosen** /ˈloohs(ə)n/ *vb*, **looseness** *n*

[2]**loose** *vt* **1a** to let loose; release **b** to free from restraint **2** to make loose; untie ⟨*~ a knot*⟩ **3** to cast loose; detach **4** to let fly; discharge (e g a bullet)

[3]**loose** *adv* in a loose manner; loosely ⟨*the rope hung ~*⟩

ˈloose ˌbox *n, Br* an individual enclosure within a barn or stable in which an animal may move about freely

ˌloose ˈcover *n, chiefly Br* a removable protective usu cloth cover for an article of furniture (e g an upholstered chair)

ˌloose ˈend *n* – **at a loose end** having nothing to do

ˌloose-ˈleaf *adj* bound so that individual leaves can be detached or inserted ⟨*a ~ photograph album*⟩

ˌloose-ˈlimbed /limd/ *adj* having flexible or supple limbs

loosestrife /ˈloohs,strief/ *n* **1** any of a genus of plants of the primrose family with leafy stems and yellow or white flowers **2** any of a genus of plants including some with showy spikes of purple flowers [intended as trans of Gk *lysimacheios* loosestrife (as if fr *lysis* act of loosing + *machesthai* to fight) – more at LYSIS]

[1]**loot** /looht/ *n* **1** goods, usu of considerable value, taken in war; spoils **2** sthg taken illegally (e g by force or deception) ⟨*the robbers' ~*⟩ [Hindi *lūṭ*, fr Skt *luṇṭati* he robs]

[2]**loot** *vb* **1** to plunder or sack (a place) in war **2** to seize and carry away (sthg) by force or illegally, esp in war or public disturbance – **looter** *n*

[1]**lop** /lop/ *n* small branches and twigs cut from a tree [ME *loppe*]

[2]**lop** *vt* **-pp- 1a** to cut off branches or twigs from **b** to cut from a person **2** to remove or do away with as unnecessary or undesirable – usu + *off* or *away* ⟨*~ped several thousand off the annual budget*⟩ – **lopper** *n*

[1]**lope** /lohp/ *n* an easy bounding gait capable of being sustained for a long time [ME *loup, lope* leap, fr ON *hlaup*; akin to OE *hlēapan* to leap – more at LEAP]

[2]**lope** *vi* to go, move, or ride at a lope – **loper** *n*

ˌlop-ˈeared *adj* having ears that droop [*lop* (to hang down, droop), perh of imit origin]

lophophore /ˈlohfə,faw/ *n* a circular or horseshoe-shaped organ about the mouth, esp of a brachiopod or bryozoan, that bears tentacles and functions esp in food collecting [Gk *lophos* crest + E *-phore*]

lopsided /ˌlopˈsiedid/ *adj* **1** having one side heavier or lower than the other **2** lacking in balance, symmetry, or proportion [*lop* (to hang down, droop)] – **lopsidedly** *adv*, **lopsidedness** *n*

loquacious /ləˈkwayshəs/ *adj* talkative – fml [L *loquac-, loquax*, fr *loqui* to speak] – **loquaciously** *adv*, **loquaciousness** *n*, **loquacity** /ləˈkwasəti/ *n*

loquat /ˈlohkwət, -kwot/ *n* (the yellow edible fruit of) an often cultivated Asiatic evergreen tree of the rose family [Chin (Cant) *lō-kwat*, fr *lō* rush + *kwat* orange]

loran /ˈlawrən/ *n* a system of navigation using pulsed signals sent out by 2 pairs of radio stations [*lo*ng-*ra*nge *n*avigation]

[1]**lord** /lawd/ *n* **1** one having power and authority over others: e g **a** a (hereditary) ruler **b** sby from whom a feudal fee or estate is held **c** BARON 3 **2** *cap* **a** GOD 1 **b** Jesus – often + *Our* **3** a man of rank or high position: e g **a** a feudal tenant holding land directly from the king **b** a British nobleman: e g **(1)** BARON 2a **(2)** a marquess, earl, or viscount **(3)** the son of a duke or marquess or the eldest son of an earl **(4)** a bishop of the Church of England **4** *pl, cap* HOUSE OF LORDS – often + *the* ☞ LAW **5** – used as the title of a lord or as an official title ⟨Lord *Advocate*⟩ [ME *loverd, lord*, fr OE *hlāford*, fr *hlāf* loaf + *weard* keeper – more at [1]LOAF]

[2]**lord** *vi* to act like a lord; *esp* to put on airs – usu + *it* ⟨*~s it over his friends*⟩

Lord *interj* – used to express surprise, amazement, or dismay; esp in *Oh Lord!, Good Lord!*, etc

ˌlord ˈadvocate *n, often cap L&A* the chief law officer of the Crown in Scotland

ˌLord ˈChamberlain *n* the chief officer of the British royal household

ˌlord ˈchancellor *n, often cap L&C* an officer of state who presides over the House of Lords, serves as head of the judiciary, and is usu a member of the cabinet

ˌLord ˌChief ˈJustice *n, pl* **Lords Chief Justice** the president of the Queen's Bench Division of the High Court

Lord Justice of Appeal *n, pl* **Lords Justices of Appeal** a judge of the Court of Appeal

ˌLord Lieuˈtenant *n, pl* **Lords Lieutenant, Lord Lieutenants** an official representative of a sovereign in a British county

lordly /ˈlawdli/ *adj* **1a** (having the characteristics) of a lord; dignified **b** grand, noble **2** disdainful and arrogant – **lordliness** *n*, **lordly** *adv*

Lord of Appeal in Ordinary *n, pl* **Lords of Appeal in Ordinary** an eminent lawyer appointed a life peer to hear appeals in the Lords

lordosis /lawˈdohsis/ *n* abnormal forward curvature of the spine – compare KYPHOSIS, SCOLIOSIS [NL, fr Gk *lordōsis*, fr *lordos* curving forwards; akin to OE *belyrtan* to deceive] – **lordotic** /lawˈdotik/ *adj*

ˌLord ˌPresident of the ˈCouncil *n, pl* **Lord Presidents of the Council** the president of the Privy Council

ˌLord ˌPrivy ˈSeal /ˈprivi/ *n, pl* **Lords Privy Seal** a member of the British Cabinet with no departmental duties

ˌlords and ˈladies *n pl but sing in constr* cuckoopint

Lord's day *n, often cap D* Sunday – usu + *the* [fr

the Christian belief that Christ rose from the dead on Sunday]

'lordship /-ship/ *n* **1** – used as a title for a lord **2** the authority of a lord

,Lord's 'Prayer *n* *the* prayer taught by Jesus beginning 'Our Father''

,Lord's 'table *n, often cap T* ALTAR 2

[1]**lore** /law/ *n* a specified body of knowledge or tradition ⟨*bird* ~⟩ ⟨*ghost* ~⟩ [ME, learning, doctrine, lesson, fr OE *lār*; akin to OHG *lēra* doctrine, OE *leornian* to learn]

[2]**lore** *n* the space between the eye and bill in a bird or the corresponding region in a reptile or fish [NL *lorum*, fr L, thong, rein; akin to Gk *eulēra* reins] – **loreal** /'lawri·əl/ *adj*

lorgnette /law'nyet/ (*Fr* lɔrɲɛt)/ *n* a pair of glasses or opera glasses with a handle [F, fr *lorgner* to take a sidelong look at, fr MF, fr *lorgne* cross-eyed]

lorgnon /law'nyon (*Fr* lɔrɲɔ̃)/ *n* a lorgnette [F, fr *lorgner*]

lorica /lo'riekə/ *n, pl* **loricae** /-ki/ a hard protective case or shell [NL, fr L, breastplate, fr *lorum*] – **loricate** /'lorikayt/, **loricated** *adj*

lorikeet /'lorikeet, --'-/ *n* any of numerous small tree-dwelling parrots mostly of Australasia [*lory* (parrot; fr Malay *nuri, luri*) + *-keet* (as in *parakeet*)]

lorimer /'lorimə/ *n* a maker of the metal parts of bridles and saddles [ME *lorimer, loriner*, fr OF *lormier, lorenier*, fr *lorain* strap holding a horse's saddle, fr LL *loramentum* harness, straps, fr L *lorum* strap]

loriner /'lorinə/ *n* a lorimer

loris /'lawris/ *n* any of several small nocturnal slow-moving tree-dwelling primates [F, perh fr obs D *loeris* simpleton] – **lorisiform** /law'risi,fawm/ *adj*

lorry /'lori/ *n, Br* a large motor vehicle for carrying loads by road [perh fr E dial. *lurry* (to pull, drag)]

lose /loohz/ *vb* **lost** /lost/ *vt* **1a** to bring to destruction; perish – usu pass ⟨*the ship was* lost *on the reef*⟩ **b** to damn ⟨lost *souls*⟩ **2** to miss from one's possession or from a customary or supposed place; *also* to fail to find ⟨lost *her glasses*⟩ **3** to suffer deprivation of; part with, esp in an unforeseen or accidental manner ⟨lost *his leg in an accident*⟩ **4** to suffer loss through the death of or final separation from (sby) ⟨lost *a son in the war*⟩ **5a** to fail to use; let slip by ⟨*he* lost *his chance of a place in the team*⟩ **b(1)** to be defeated in (a contest for) ⟨~ *a battle*⟩ ⟨~ *a prize*⟩ **(2)** to have less of ⟨*the aircraft began to* ~ *height*⟩ **c** to fail to catch with the senses or the mind ⟨lost *part of what was said*⟩ **6** to cause the loss of ⟨*one careless statement* lost *her the election*⟩ **7** to fail to keep or maintain ⟨lost *her balance*⟩ **8a** to cause to miss one's way ⟨lost *themselves in the maze of streets*⟩ **b** to withdraw (oneself) from immediate reality ⟨lost *himself in a book*⟩ **9** to fail to keep in sight or in mind ⟨*I* lost *track of his reasoning*⟩ **10** to free oneself from; get rid of ⟨*dieting to* ~ *some weight*⟩ **11** to run slow by the amount of – used with reference to a timepiece ⟨*my watch* ~s *a minute each day*⟩ ~ *vi* **1** to undergo deprivation of sthg of value **2** to undergo defeat **3** *of a timepiece* to run slow [ME *losen*, fr OE *losian* to perish, lose, fr *los* destruction; akin to OE *lēosan* to lose; akin to ON *losa* to loosen, L *luere* to release, atone for, Gk *lyein* to loosen, dissolve, destroy] – **lose one's head** to lose self-control (e g in anger or panic)

lose out *vi* **1** to make a loss **2** to be the loser, esp unluckily *USE* often + *on*

loser /'loohzə/ *n* **1** one who loses, esp consistently **2** one who does poorly; a failure

'losing ,hazard /'loohzing/ *n* the pocketing of the cue ball after it strikes an object ball in billiards

loss /los/ *n* **1a** the act or an instance of losing possession **b** the harm or privation resulting from loss or separation **2** a person, thing, or amount lost ⟨*the woman who retired is a great* ~ *to her firm*⟩: e g **a** *pl* killed, wounded, or captured soldiers **b** the power diminution of a circuit element corresponding to conversion of electric power into heat **3a** failure to gain, win, obtain, or use sthg **b** an amount by which cost exceeds revenue **4** decrease in amount, size, or degree **5** destruction, ruin ⟨*the ship went down with the* ~ *of many lives*⟩ [ME *los*, prob back-formation fr *lost*, pp of *losen* to lose] – **at a loss** uncertain, puzzled

loss leader *n* an article sold at a loss in order to draw customers

lossy /'losi/ *adj* causing diminution or dissipation of electrical energy

lost /lost/ *adj* **1a** unable to find the way **b** no longer visible **c** bewildered, helpless **2** ruined or destroyed physically or morally **3a** no longer possessed ⟨*one's* ~ *youth*⟩ **b** no longer known ⟨*the* ~ *art of letter-writing*⟩ **4a** taken away or beyond reach or attainment; denied **b** insensible, hardened ⟨~ *to shame*⟩ **5** rapt, absorbed ⟨~ *in reverie*⟩ [pp of *lose*]

,lost 'cause *n* a cause that has lost all prospect of success

lost wax *n* CIRE PERDUE

[1]**lot** /lot/ *n* **1** an object used as a counter in deciding a question by chance ⟨*they drew* ~s *for who was to go*⟩ **2** (the use of lots as a means of making) a choice **3a** sthg that falls to sby by lot; a share **b** one's way of life or worldly fate; fortune ⟨*it's my* ~ *to be misunderstood*⟩ **4a** a portion of land; *esp* one with fixed boundaries designated on a plot or survey **b** a film studio and its adjoining property **5** an article or a number of articles offered as 1 item (e g in an auction sale) ⟨*what am I bid for* ~ *16?*⟩ **6a** *sing or pl in constr* a number of associated people; a set ⟨*hello you* ~ – Margaret Drabble⟩ **b** a kind, sort – chiefly in *a bad lot* **7** a considerable amount or number ⟨*a* ~ *of illness*⟩ ⟨*has* ~s *of friends*⟩ – often pl with sing. meaning **8** *chiefly Br* the whole amount or number ⟨*ate up the whole* ~⟩ *USE* (*6a&8*) infml [ME, fr OE *hlot*; akin to OHG *hlōz*, Lith *kliudyti* to hook on] – **a lot 1** lots ⟨*drove* a lot *faster*⟩ – chiefly infml **2** often, frequently ⟨*goes there* a lot⟩ – chiefly infml

[2]**lot** *vt* **-tt- 1** to form or divide into lots **2** to allot, apportion

loth /lohth/ *adj* loath

lothario /lə'thahrioh/ *n, pl* **lotharios** *often cap* a man whose chief interest is seducing women [*Lothario*, seducer in the play *The Fair Penitent* by Nicholas Rowe †1718 E dramatist]

loti /'lohti/ *n, pl* **maloti** /ma'lohti/ ☞ *Lesotho* at NATIONALITY [of Bantu origin]

lotion /'lohsh(ə)n/ *n* a medicinal or cosmetic liquid for external use [L *lotion-, lotio* act of washing, fr *lotus*, pp of *lavere* to wash – more at LYE]

lots /lots/ *adv* much, considerably ⟨*is ~ older than me*⟩ – infml [pl of [1]*lot*]
lottery /'lot(ə)ri/ *n* **1** (a way of raising money by the sale or) the distribution of numbered tickets some of which are later randomly selected to entitle the holder to a prize **2** an event or affair whose outcome is (apparently) decided by chance ⟨*buying a second-hand car is a ~*⟩ [MF *loterie*, fr MD, fr *lot* lot; akin to OE *hlot* lot]
lotto /'lotoh/ *n* bingo [It, lottery, lotto, fr F *lot* lot, of Gmc origin; akin to OE *hlot* lot]
lotus /'lohtəs/ *n* **1** a fruit considered in Greek legend to cause indolence and dreamy contentment **2** any of various water lilies including several represented in ancient Egyptian and Hindu art and religious symbolism **3** any of a genus of widely distributed upright herbaceous plants (e g bird's-foot trefoil) [L & Gk; L *lotus*, fr Gk *lōtos*, fr Heb *lōt* myrrh; (3) NL, genus name, fr L]
'lotus-,eater *n* sby who lives in dreamy indolence [*lotus-eaters*, a mythical people living in indolence caused by lotus fruit, trans of Gk *Lōtophagoi*]
'lotus po,sition *n* a yoga position in which one sits with legs folded and the arms resting on the knees [trans of Skt *padmāsana*, fr *padma* lotus (symbolizing transcendence of external impulse and sensation) + *āsana* seat, posture]
louche /loohsh/ *adj* morally dubious; disreputable, seedy [F, lit., cross-eyed, fr L *luscus* one-eyed]
loud /lowd/ *adj* **1** marked by or producing a high volume of sound **2** clamorous, noisy **3** obtrusive or offensive in appearance; flashy ⟨*a ~ checked suit*⟩ [ME, fr OE *hlūd*; akin to OHG *hlūt* loud, L in*clutus* famous, Gk *klytos*, Skt *śṛṇoti* he hears] – **loud** *adv*, **louden** *vb*, **loudly** *adv*, **loudness** *n*
,loud-'hailer *n, chiefly Br* a megaphone
'loud,mouth /-,mowth/ *n* a person given to much loud offensive talk – infml – **loudmouthed** /-,mowdhd/ *adj*
loudspeaker /,lowd'speekə/ *n* (a cabinet that contains) an electromechanical device that converts electrical energy into acoustic energy and that is used to reproduce audible sounds in a room, hall, etc
lough /lokh/ *n* a loch in Ireland [ME, of Celt origin; akin to OIr *loch* lake; akin to L *lacus* lake]
louis d'or /,looh·i 'daw (*Fr* lwi dɔr)/ *n, pl* **louis d'or** /~/ **1** a French gold coin first struck in 1640 and issued until the Revolution **2** the French 20-franc gold piece issued after the Revolution [F, fr *Louis* XIII †1643 King of France + *d'or* of gold]
Louis Quatorze /,looh·i ka'tawz (*Fr* ~ katɔrz/ *adj* (characteristic) of the architecture or furniture of the reign of Louis XIV of France [F, Louis XIV †1715 King of France]
Louis Quinze /kanhz (*Fr* kɛ̃z)/ *adj* (characteristic) of the architecture or furniture of the reign of Louis XV of France [F, Louis XV †1774 King of France]
Louis Seize /sez (*Fr* sɛz)/ *adj* (characteristic) of the architecture or furniture of the reign of Louis XVI of France [F, Louis XVI †1793 King of France]
Louis Treize /trez (*Fr* trɛz)/ *adj* (characteristic) of the furniture or architecture of the reign of Louis XIII of France [F, Louis XIII]
[1]**lounge** /lownj/ *vi* to act or move idly or lazily; loll [origin unknown] – **lounger** *n*
[2]**lounge** *n* **1** a room in a private house for sitting in; SITTING ROOM **2** a room in a public building providing comfortable seating; *also* a waiting room (e g at an airport)
lounge bar *n, Br* SALOON BAR
'lounge ,suit *n* a man's suit for wear during the day and on informal occasions
loupe /loohp/ *n* a small optical magnifying instrument used esp by jewellers and watchmakers [F, gem of imperfect brilliancy, loupe]
loup-garou /,looh ga'rooh (*Fr* lu garu/ *n, pl* **loups-garous** a werewolf [MF]
lour /'lowə/ *vi or n, chiefly Br* [1] [2]LOWER – **loury** /'lowəri/ *adj*, **louring** /lowring/ *adj*
louse /lows/ *n, pl* **lice**, /lies/; *sense 2* **louses** **1a** any of various small wingless usu flattened insects parasitic on warm-blooded animals **b** any of several small arthropods that are not parasitic – usu in combination ⟨*book ~*⟩ ⟨*wood ~*⟩ **2** a contemptible person – infml [ME *lous*, fr OE *lūs*; akin to OHG *lūs* louse, W *llau* lice]
louse up /lows, lowz/ *vt* to make a mess of; spoil – infml
'louse,wort /-,wuht/ *n* any of a genus of plants of the figwort family
lousy /'lowzi/ *adj* **1** infested with lice **2a** very mean; despicable ⟨*a ~ trick to play*⟩ **b** very bad, unpleasant, useless, etc **c** amply or excessively supplied ⟨*~ with money*⟩ ⟨*the place was ~ with police*⟩ *USE* (*2*) infml – **lousily** *adv*, **lousiness** *n*
lout /lowt/ *n* a rough ill-mannered man or youth [perh fr ON *lūtr* bent down, fr *lūta* to bow down] – **loutish** /-tish/ *adj*
louvre, louver /'loohvə/ *n* **1** a roof lantern or turret with slatted apertures for the escape of smoke or admission of light **2** an opening provided with 1 or more slanted fixed or movable strips of metal, wood, glass, etc to allow flow of air or sound (e g in a bell louvre) but to exclude rain or sun or to provide privacy ☞ CHURCH [ME *lover*, fr MF *lovier*] – **louvered, louvred** /'loohvəd/ *adj*
lovable *also* **loveable** /'luvəbl/ *adj* having qualities that deserve love; worthy of love – **lovableness** *n*, **lovably** *adv*
lovage /'luvij/ *n* any of several aromatic perennial plants of the carrot family; *esp* a European plant sometimes cultivated as a herb or flavouring agent [ME *lovache*, fr AF, fr LL *levisticum*, alter. of L *ligusticum*, fr neut of *ligusticus* of Liguria (ancient country in SW Europe, now part of Italy), fr *Ligur-*, *Ligus*, n, inhabitant of Liguria]
[1]**love** /luv/ *n* **1a**(**1**) strong affection for another ⟨*maternal ~ for a child*⟩ (**2**) attraction based on sexual desire; strong affection and tenderness felt by lovers **b** an assurance of love ⟨*give her my ~*⟩ **2** warm interest in, enjoyment of, or attraction to sthg ⟨*~ of music*⟩ **3a** the object of interest and enjoyment ⟨*music was his first ~*⟩ **b** a person who is loved; DEAR 1a; *also* DEAR 1b **4a** unselfish loyal and benevolent concern for the good of another **b**(**1**) the fatherly concern of God for man (**2**) a person's adoration of God **5** a god or personification of love **6** an amorous episode; LOVE AFFAIR ⟨*My Life and* Loves – Frank Harris⟩ **7** a score of zero in tennis, squash, etc **8** SEXUAL INTERCOURSE – euph [ME, fr OE *lufu*; akin to OHG *lupa* love, OE *lēof* dear, L *lubēre*, *libēre* to please; (7) fr the phrase *to play for love* to play for nothing (i e without stakes)] – **for love or money** in any possible way – usu neg ⟨*couldn't get a ticket for love or money*⟩

[2]**love** *vt* **1** to hold dear; cherish **2a** to feel a lover's passion, devotion, or tenderness for **b(1)** to caress (2) to have sexual intercourse with **3** to like or desire actively; take pleasure in ⟨~d *to play the violin*⟩ **4** to thrive in ⟨*the rose* ~s *sunlight*⟩ ~ *vi* to feel love or affection or experience desire

'love af,fair *n* **1** an often temporary romantic attachment between lovers, esp a man and a woman **2** a lively enthusiasm

'love ,apple *n, archaic* the tomato [prob trans of F *pomme d'amour*]

'love,bird /-,buhd/ *n* any of various small usu grey or green parrots that show great affection for their mates

'love,bite /-,biet/ *n* a temporary red mark produced by biting or sucking an area of one's partner's skin, esp the neck, in sexual play

'love ,child *n* an illegitimate child – euph

'love ,feast *n* a meal eaten together by a Christian congregation in token of brotherly love

,love-in-a-'mist *n* a European garden plant of the buttercup family

'love ,knot *n* a stylized knot sometimes used as an emblem of love

'loveless /-lis/ *adj* **1** without love ⟨*a* ~ *marriage*⟩ **2** unloving **3** unloved – **lovelessly** *adv*, **lovelessness** *n*

,love-lies-'bleeding *n* any of various plants of the amaranth family widely cultivated for their drooping clusters of small usu scarlet or purple flowers

'love,lock /-,lok/ *n* a long lock of hair worn over the shoulder by men in the 17th and 18th c

'love,lorn /-,lawn/ *adj* sad because of unrequited love [*lorn* (forsaken), fr ME, fr *loren*, pp of *lesen* to lose, fr OE *lēosan*] – **lovelornness** *n*

[1]**lovely** /'luvli/ *adj* **1** delicately or delightfully beautiful **2** very pleasing; fine ⟨*a* ~ *view*⟩ [ME, fr OE *luflīc* loving, lovable, fr *lufu* love + *-līc* [1]-ly] – **lovelily** *adv*, **loveliness** *n*, **lovely** *adv*

[2]**lovely** *n* a beautiful woman – infml ⟨*hello, my* ~⟩

'love,making /-,mayking/ *n* **1** courtship **2** sexual activity; *esp* SEXUAL INTERCOURSE

'love ,match *n* a marriage or engagement undertaken for love rather than financial or other advantages

'love ,nest *n* a small secret flat, foom, or house used for conducting a usu illicit sexual relationship

lover /'luvə/ *n* **1a** a person in love **b** a man with whom a woman has sexual relations, esp outside marriage **c** *pl* 2 people in love with each other; *esp* 2 people who habitually have sexual relations **2** DEVOTEE 2 ⟨*a* ~ *of the theatre*⟩

loverly /'luvəli/ *adj, Br* lovely – nonstandard or humor

'love ,seat *n* an S-shaped double chair or settee that allows 2 people to sit side by side though facing in opposite directions

'love,sick /-,sik/ *adj* languishing with love – **lovesickness** *n*

lovey /'luvi/ *n, chiefly Br* LOVE 3b – infml

loving /'luving/ *adj* feeling or showing love; affectionate ⟨~ *care*⟩ ⟨*a* ~ *glance*⟩ – **lovingly** *adv*

'loving ,cup *n* a large ornamental drinking vessel with 2 or more handles that is passed among a group of people for all to drink from

[1]**low** /loh/ *vi or n* (to make) the deep sustained throat sound characteristic of esp a cow [vb ME *loowen*, fr OE *hlōwan*; akin to OHG *hluoen* to moo, L *calare* to call, summon, Gk *kalein*; n fr vb]

[2]**low** *adj* **1a** not measuring much from the base to the top; not high ⟨*a* ~ *wall*⟩ **b** situated or passing little above a reference line, point, or plane ⟨~ *bridges*⟩ ⟨*his work was* ~ *on his list of priorities*⟩ **c** low-necked **2a** situated or passing below the normal level or below the base of measurement ⟨~ *ground*⟩ **b** marking a nadir or bottom ⟨*the* ~ *point of her career*⟩ **3a** *of sound* not shrill or loud; soft **b** depressed in pitch ⟨*a* ~ *note*⟩ **4** near the horizon ⟨*it was evening, and the sun was* ~⟩ **5** humble in character or status ⟨*people of* ~ *birth*⟩ **6a** lacking strength, health, or vitality; weak ⟨*he's been very* ~ *with pneumonia*⟩ **b** lacking spirit or vivacity; depressed ⟨~ *spirits*⟩ **7** of less than usual degree, size, amount, or value ⟨~ *pressure*⟩ ⟨*prices are* ~ *at the moment*⟩ **8a** lacking dignity or formality ⟨*a* ~ *style of writing*⟩ **b** morally reprehensible ⟨*played a* ~ *trick on her*⟩ **c** coarse, vulgar ⟨~ *language*⟩ **9** unfavourable, disparaging ⟨*had a* ~ *opinion of him*⟩ **10** *of a gear* designed for slow speed **11** *of a vowel* open [ME *lah, low*, fr ON *lāgr*; akin to MHG *læge* low, flat] – **lowness** *n*

[3]**low** *n* **1** sthg low: e g **a** a depth, nadir ⟨*sales have reached a new* ~⟩ **b** a region of low atmospheric pressure ☞ WEATHER **2** *NAm* BOTTOM 4c

[4]**low** *adv* at or to a low place, altitude, or degree

low 'blood ,pressure *n* hypotension

,low'born /-'bawn/ *adj* born to parents of low social rank

'low,boy /-,boy/ *n, NAm* a low chest or side table that is supported on short legs

,low'bred /-'bred/ *adj* rude, vulgar

'low,brow /-,brow/ *adj* dealing with, possessing, or having unsophisticated or unintellectual tastes, esp in the arts – often derog – **lowbrow** *n*

,Low 'Church *adj* tending, esp in the Anglican church, to minimize emphasis on the priesthood, sacraments, and ceremonial and often to emphasize evangelical principles – **Low Churchman** *n*

,low 'cloud *n* cloud with an average height of less than 2000m (about 6500ft)

,low 'comedy *n* comedy bordering on farce and depending on physical action and situation rather than wit and characterization

,low-'cut *adj* fashioned so as to leave the cleavage or breasts exposed ⟨*she wore a very* ~ *dress to the party*⟩

'low,down /-,down/ *n* inside information – usu + *the*; infml

,low-'down *adj* contemptible, base – infml

[1]**lower**, *Br chiefly* **lour** /'lowə/ *vi* **1** to look sullen; frown **2** to become dark, gloomy, and threatening [ME *louren*; akin to MHG *lūren* to lie in wait] – **lowering** *adj*

[2]**lower**, *Br chiefly* **lour** *n* **1** a lowering look; a frown **2** a gloomy sky or aspect of weather – **lowery** *adj*

[3]**lower** /'loh·ə/ *adj* **1** relatively low in position, rank, or order **2** less advanced in the scale of evolutionary development ⟨~ *organisms*⟩ **3** constituting the popular, more representative, and often (e g in Britain) more powerful branch of a legislative body consisting of 2 houses ⟨*the* ~ *chamber*⟩ **4a** beneath the earth's surface **b** *often cap* being an earlier division of the named geological period or series ⟨Lower *Carboniferous*⟩

[4]**lower** /'loh·ə/ *vi* to move down; drop; *also* to dimin-

ish ~ *vt* **1a** to cause to descend; let down in height ⟨~ed *the boat over the side of the ship*⟩ ⟨~ *your aim*⟩ **b** to reduce the height of ⟨~ed *the ceiling*⟩ **2a** to reduce in value, amount, degree, strength, or pitch ⟨~ *the price*⟩ ⟨~ *your voice*⟩ **b** to bring down; degrade; *also* to humble ⟨*I wouldn't* ~ *myself to speak to them*⟩ **c** to reduce the objective of ⟨~ed *their sights and accepted less*⟩

,lower 'bound *n* a number less than or equal to every element of a given set

,lower-'case *adj, of a letter* of or conforming to the series (e g a, b, c rather than A, B, C) typically used elsewhere than at the beginning of sentences or proper names [fr the compositor's practice of keeping such letters in the lower of a pair of type cases]

lower case *n* **1** a type case containing lower-case letters and usu spaces and quads **2** lower-case letters ☞ ALPHABET

,lower'classman *n, NAm* a member of the freshman or sophomore class in a college or secondary school [fr the phrase *lower class* 'freshman or sophomore class' + *man*]

,lower 'criticism *n* criticism aimed at the restoration of (biblical) texts by comparison of extant manuscripts – compare HIGHER CRITICISM

,lower 'deck *n* **1** a deck below the main deck of a ship ☞ SHIP **2** *sing or pl in constr, chiefly Br* the petty officers and men of a ship or navy as distinguished from the officers – compare QUARTERDECK

,Lower ,Forty-'eight *n pl, NAm* the 48 states of the USA excluding Alaska

,lower 'fungus *n* a fungus with absent or rudimentary filaments

'lower,most /-,mohst, -məst/ *adj* lowest

'lower ,regions *n pl* hell – euph

,lower 'school *n* a school or part of a school for younger pupils

,lower 'sixth *n, often cap L&S* the first year of a school sixth form

,lowest ,common de'nominator *n* **1** the lowest common multiple of 2 or more denominators **2** sthg (e g a level of taste) that typifies or is common, acceptable, or comprehensible to all or the greatest possible number of people – chiefly derog

,lowest ,common 'multiple *n* the smallest number that is a multiple of each of 2 or more numbers

,lowest 'terms *n pl* the numerator and denominator of a fraction that have no factors in common ⟨*reduce a fraction to* ~⟩

,low 'frequency *n* a radio frequency in the range between 30 and 300kHz

,Low 'German *n* **1** Plattdeutsch **2** the W Germanic languages (e g Dutch) other than High German

,low-'grade *adj* **1** of inferior grade or quality ⟨~ *bonds*⟩ **2** being near the lower or least favourable extreme of a range

,low-'key *also* **low-keyed** /keed/ *adj* of low intensity; restrained

Lowland /'lohlənd/ *adj* of the Lowlands of Scotland – **Lowlander** /-ləndə/ *n*

,Low 'Latin *n* the Latin language in its later stages (e g Vulgar or Medieval Latin)

,low-'level *adj* **1** occurring, done, or placed at a low level **2** *of a computer language* having each word, symbol, etc equal to one machine code instruction and being easily understandable to machines

,low-'loader *n* a vehicle with a low load-carrying platform

¹lowly /'lohli/ *adv* **1** in a humble or meek manner **2** in a low position, manner, or degree

²lowly *adj* **1** humble and modest in manner or spirit **2** low in the scale of biological or cultural evolution **3** ranking low in a social or economic hierarchy – **lowliness** *n*

,low-'lying *adj* lying below the normal level or surface or below the base of measurement or mean elevation ⟨~ *clouds*⟩

,low 'mass *n, often cap L&M* a mass recited by a single celebrant – compare HIGH MASS

,low-'necked, low-neck *adj* having a low-cut neckline

,low-'paid *adj* receiving a low wage

,low-'pitched *adj* **1** *of sound* not shrill; deep **2** *of a roof* sloping gently

,low 'profile *n* an inconspicuous mode of operation or behaviour (intended to attract little attention) ⟨*the Government has been keeping a* ~ *over the disturbances – The Guardian*⟩

,low re'lief *n* bas-relief

'low-,rise *adj, chiefly NAm* constructed with only 1 or 2 storeys ⟨*a* ~ *classroom building*⟩

,low silhou'ette *n* LOW PROFILE

,low-'spirited *adj* dejected, depressed – **low-spiritedly** *adv*, **low-spiritedness** *n*

,Low 'Sunday /'sunday, -di/ *n* the Sunday following Easter

,low-'tension *adj* having a low voltage; *also* relating to apparatus for use at low voltages

,low 'tide *n* (the time of) the tide when the water reaches its lowest level

,low 'water *n* LOW TIDE

lox /loks/ *n* liquid oxygen [*l*iquid *ox*ygen]

loxodrome /'loksə,drohm/ *n* RHUMB LINE [ISV, back-formation fr *loxodromic*, prob fr (assumed) NL *loxodromicus*, fr Gk *loxos* oblique + *dromos* course] – **loxodromic** /-'dromik/ *adj*, **loxodromically** *adv*

loyal /'loyəl/ *adj* **1** unswerving in allegiance (e g to a person, country, or cause); faithful **2** showing such allegiance ⟨*her* ~ *determination to help the party*⟩ [MF, fr OF *leial, leel*, fr L *legalis* legal] – **loyally** *adv*, **loyalty** /-ti/ *n*

loyalist /'loyəlist/ *n* sby loyal to a government or sovereign, esp in time of revolt

lozenge /'lozinj/ *n* **1** (sthg shaped like) a figure with 4 equal sides and 2 acute and 2 obtuse angles **2** a small often medicated sweet [ME *losenge*, fr MF *losange*, fr OF]

LP /,el 'pee/ *n* a gramophone record designed to be played at 33⅓ revolutions per minute and typically having a diameter of 12in (30.5cm) and a playing time of 20–25min [*l*ong *p*laying]

LSD /,el es 'dee/ *n* a drug taken illegally for its potent action in producing hallucinations and altered perceptions [*l*ysergic acid *d*iethylamide]

lubber /'lubə/ *n* **1** a big clumsy fellow **2** a clumsy seaman [ME *lobre, lobur*] – **lubberliness** *n*, **lubberly** *adj or adv*

lubra /'loohbrah, -brə/ *n, Austr* an Australian aboriginal woman – compare ⁴GIN [native name in Tasmania]

lubricant /'loohbrikənt/ *n* **1** a substance (e g grease or oil) capable of reducing friction, heat, and wear when introduced as a film between solid surfaces **2**

sthg that lessens or prevents difficulty – **lubricant** *adj*

lubricate /'loohbrikayt/ *vt* **1** to make smooth or slippery **2** to apply a lubricant to ~ *vi* to act as a lubricant [L *lubricatus*, pp of *lubricare*, fr *lubricus* slippery – more at SLEEVE] – **lubricator** *n*, **lubricative** /-,kaytiv, -kətiv/ *adj*, **lubrication** /-'kaysh(ə)n/ *n*

lubricious /looh'brishəs/ *adj* **1** lecherous, salacious **2** slippery, smooth *USE* fml [(1) ML *lubricus*, fr L, slippery, easily led astray; (2) L *lubricus*] – **lubriciously** *adv*, **lubricity** /looh'brisəti/ *n*

lubricous /'loohbrikəs/ *adj* lubricious

Lucan, Lukan /'loohkən/ *adj* of (the Gospel of) Luke [LL *lucanus*, fr *Lucas* Luke, fr Gk *Loukas*]

Lucayo /looh'kie·oh/ *n* (the language of) an extinct Arawakan tribe of the Bahamas

lucent /'loohs(ə)nt/ *adj* **1** glowing with light; luminous **2** clear, translucent [L *lucent-*, *lucens*, prp of *lucēre* to shine – more at [1]LIGHT] – **lucently** *adv*, **lucency** /'loohs(ə)nsi/ *n*

lucerne *also* **lucern** /looh'suhn/ *n*, *chiefly Br* a deep-rooted European leguminous plant widely grown for fodder [F *luzerne*, fr Prov *luserno*]

lucid /'loohsid/ *adj* **1** having full use of one's faculties; sane **2** clear to the understanding; plain [L *lucidus*; akin to L *lucēre*] – **lucidly** *adv*, **lucidness**, **lucidity** /looh'sidəti/ *n*

Lucifer /'loohsifə/ *n* **1** – used as a name of the devil **2** the planet Venus when appearing as the morning star [ME, the morning star, a fallen rebel archangel, the Devil, fr OE, fr L, the morning star, fr *lucifer* light-bearing, fr *luc-*, *lux* light + *-fer* -ferous – more at [1]LIGHT]

luciferase /looh'sifə,rayz, -,rays/ *n* an enzyme that catalyses the oxidation of luciferin [ISV, fr *luciferin*]

luciferin /looh'sifərin/ *n* a protein in some organisms (e g fireflies and glowworms) that gives out practically heatless light when undergoing oxidation [ISV, fr L *lucifer* light-bearing]

luck /luk/ *n* **1** whatever good or bad events happen to a person by chance **2** the tendency for a person to be consistently fortunate or unfortunate **3** success as a result of good fortune [ME *lucke*, fr MD *luc*; akin to MHG *gelücke* luck]

lucky /'luki/ *adj* having, resulting from, or bringing good luck – **luckily** *adv*, **luckiness** *n*

,lucky 'dip *n*, *Br* an attraction (e g at a fair) in which articles can be drawn unseen from a receptacle

lucrative /'loohkrətiv/ *adj* producing wealth; profitable [ME *lucratif*, fr MF, fr L *lucrativus*, fr *lucratus*, pp of *lucrari* to gain, fr *lucrum*] – **lucratively** *adv*, **lucrativeness** *n*

lucre /'loohkə/ *n* financial gain; profit; *also* money – esp in *filthy lucre* [ME, fr L *lucrum*; akin to OE *lēan* reward, OHG *lōn*, Gk *leia* booty]

lucubration /,loohkyoo'braysh(ə)n/ *n* **1** laborious study or meditation, esp when done at night **2** studied or pretentious expression in speech or writing USE fml [L *lucubration-*, *lucubratio* study by night, work produced at night, fr *lucubratus*, pp of *lucubrare* to work by lamplight; akin to L *luc-*, *lux* light] – **lucubrate** /'loohkyoo,brayt/ *vi*

Luddite /'ludiet/ *n* a member of a group of early 19th-c English workmen who destroyed laboursaving machinery as a protest against unemployment; *broadly* sby opposed to change, esp automation [Ned *Ludd* *fl* 1779 half-witted Leicestershire villager]

ludicrous /'loohdikrəs/ *adj* **1** amusing because of obvious absurdity or incongruity **2** meriting derision [L *ludicrus*, fr *ludus* play, sport; akin to L *ludere* to play, Gk *loidoros* abusive] – **ludicrously** *adv*, **ludicrousness** *n*

ludo /'loohdoh/ *n* a simple game played on a square board with counters and dice in which the first to reach the home square wins [L, I play, fr *ludere*]

lues /'looh·eez/ *n*, *pl* **lues** syphilis [NL, fr L, plague; akin to Gk *lyein* to loosen, destroy – more at LOSE] – **luetic** /looh'etik/ *adj*, **luetically** /-'etikli/ *adv*

[1]**luff** /luf/ *n* the forward edge of a fore-and-aft sail ☞ SHIP [ME, weather side of a ship, luff, fr MF *lof* weather side of ship]

[2]**luff** *vi* to sail nearer the wind – often + *up*

luffa /'lufə/ *n* a loofah

Luftwaffe /'looft,vahfə/ *n* the German Air Force just before and during WW II [G, fr *luft* air + *waffe* weapon]

[1]**lug** /lug/ *vt* **-gg-** to drag, pull, or carry with great effort – infml [ME *luggen* to pull by the hair or ear, drag, prob of Scand origin; akin to Norw *lugga* to pull by the hair]

[2]**lug** *n* a lugsail

[3]**lug** *n* **1** sthg (e g a handle) that projects like an ear **2** [1]EAR 1a – chiefly dial. or humor [ME (Sc) *lugge* ear, perh fr ME *luggen*]

luge /loohzh/ *n* a small toboggan that is ridden in a supine position and used esp in racing [F]

luggage /'lugij/ *n* (cases, bags, etc containing) the belongings that accompany a traveller [[1]LUG + -AGE]

lugger /'lugə/ *n* a small fishing or coasting boat that carries 1 or more lugsails [*lugsail*]

lughole /'lug,hohl/ *n*, *Br* [1]EAR 1a – chiefly dial or humor

lugsail /'lug,sayl, -səl/ *n* a 4-sided fore-and-aft sail attached to an obliquely hanging yard [perh fr [3]*lug*]

lugubrious /looh'goohbri·əs, lə-/ *adj* (exaggeratedly or affectedly) mournful [L *lugubris*, fr *lugēre* to mourn; akin to Gk *lygros* mournful] – **lugubriously** *adv*, **lugubriousness** *n*

lugworm /'lug,wuhm/ *n* any of a genus of marine worms that are used for bait [origin unknown]

Lukan /'loohkən/ *adj* Lucan

Luke /loohk/ *n* the 3rd Gospel in the New Testament [L *Lucas*, fr Gk *Loukas*]

lukewarm /,loohk'wawm/ *adj* **1** moderately warm; tepid **2** lacking conviction; indifferent [ME, fr *luke* tepid + *warm*; akin to OHG *lāo* lukewarm – more at LEE] – **lukewarmly** *adv*, **lukewarmness** *n*

[1]**lull** /lul/ *vt* **1** to cause to sleep or rest; soothe **2** to cause to relax vigilance, esp by deception [ME *lullen*, prob of imit origin]

[2]**lull** *n* a temporary pause or decline in activity

lullaby /'luləbie/ *n* a song to quieten children or lull them to sleep [obs *lulla*, interj used to lull a child (fr ME) + *bye*, interj used to lull a child, fr ME *by*]

lulu /'looh,looh/ *n*, *chiefly NAm* sby or sthg that is remarkable or wonderful [prob fr *Lulu*, nickname for *Louise*]

lum /lum/ *n*, *chiefly Scot* a chimney [origin unknown]

lumb-, lumbo- *comb form* lumbar and ⟨lumbo*sacral*⟩ [L *lumbus* loin – more at LOIN]

lumbago /lum'baygoh/ *n* muscular pain of the lumbar region of the back [L, fr *lumbus*]
lumbar /'lumbə/ *adj* of or constituting the loins or the vertebrae between the thoracic vertebrae and sacrum ⟨*the* ~ *region*⟩ [NL *lumbaris*, fr L *lumbus*]
[1]**lumber** /'lumbə/ *vi* to move heavily or clumsily [ME *lomeren*]
[2]**lumber** *n* **1** surplus or disused articles (e g furniture) that are stored away **2** *NAm* timber or logs, esp when dressed for use [perh fr *Lombard* (banker, moneylender, pawnshop; fr the prominence of Lombards as moneylenders); fr the use of pawnshops as storehouses of disused property] – **lumber** *adj*
[3]**lumber** *vt* **1** to clutter (as if) with lumber; encumber, saddle ⟨*parents,* ~ed *with the unenviable task of guiding choice – The Economist*⟩ **2** *NAm* to cut down and saw the timber of – **lumberer** /'lumb(ə)rə/ *n*
'**lumber,jack** /-jak/ *n* a person engaged in logging
lumen /'loohmin/ *n, pl* **lumina** /'loohminə/, **lumens** **1** the cavity of a tubular organ ⟨*the* ~ *of a blood vessel*⟩ **2** the SI unit of luminous flux ☞ PHYSICS [NL *lumin-, lumen*, fr L, light, air shaft, opening] – **luminal** *also* **lumenal** /'loohminəl/ *adj*
lumin-, lumini-, lumino- *comb form* light ⟨lumini*ferous*⟩ [ME *lumin-*, fr L *lumin-, lumen*]
luminance /'loohminəns/ *n* the luminous intensity of a surface in a given direction per unit of projected area
luminary /'loohmin(ə)ri/ *n* a source of light or illumination: e g **a** a natural body that gives light (e g the sun or moon) **b** a person brilliantly outstanding in some respect [ME *luminarye*, fr MF & LL; MF *luminaire* lamp, fr LL *luminaria*, pl of *luminare* lamp, heavenly body, fr L, window, fr *lumin-, lumen* light; akin to L *lucēre* to shine – more at [1]LIGHT] – **luminary** *adj*
luminesce /,loohmi'nes/ *vi* to exhibit luminescence [back-formation fr *luminescent*]
luminescence /,loohmi'nes(ə)ns/ *n* (an emission of) light that occurs at low temperatures and that is produced by physiological processes (e g in the firefly), by chemical action, by friction, or by electrical action – **luminescent** /-sənt/ *adj*
luminiferous /,loohmi'nifərəs/ *adj* transmitting, producing, or yielding light
luminosity /,loohmi'nosəti/ *n* **1a** being luminous **b** sthg luminous **2a** the relative quantity of light **b** relative brightness of sthg
luminous /'loohminəs/ *adj* **1a** emitting or full of light; bright **b** of light or luminous flux **2** easily understood; *also* explaining clearly [ME, fr L *luminosus*, fr *lumin-, lumen*] – **luminously** *adv*, **luminousness** *n*
luminous flux *n* radiant flux in the visible-wavelength range ☞ PHYSICS
luminous paint *n* paint containing a phosphorescent compound causing it to glow in the dark
lumme /'lumi/ *interj, Br* – used to express surprise; infml [contr of *love me* (in the expression *Lord love me!*)]
lummox /'luməks/ *n* a clumsy person – infml [origin unknown]
[1]**lump** /lump/ *n* **1** a usu compact piece or mass of indefinite size and shape ⟨*a* ~ *of coal or sugar*⟩ **2a** an abnormal swelling **b** BRUISE 1 **3** a heavy thickset person; *specif* one who is stupid or dull **4** *Br the* whole group of casual nonunion building workers [ME]
[2]**lump** *vt* **1** to group without discrimination **2** to make lumps on, in, or of ~ *vi* to become formed into lumps
[3]**lump** *adj* not divided into parts; entire ⟨*a* ~ *sum*⟩
[4]**lump** *vt* to put up with – chiefly in *like it or lump it*; infml [*lump* (to be sulky, dislike), of imit origin]
lumpen /'loompən/ *adj* cut off from the economic and social class with which they might normally be identified ⟨~ *proletariat*⟩ [G *lumpenproletariat* lowest section of the proletariat, fr *lump* contemptible person (fr *lumpen* rags) + *proletariat*]
lumpish /'lumpish/ *adj* **1** dull, sluggish **2** heavy, awkward – **lumpishly** *adv*, **lumpishness** *n*
lumpy /'lumpi/ *adj* **1a** filled or covered with lumps **b** characterized by choppy waves **2** having a thickset clumsy appearance – **lumpily** *adv*, **lumpiness** *n*
lunacy /'loohnəsi/ *n* **1a** insanity (interrupted by lucid intervals) – not now in technical use **b** insanity amounting to lack of capability or responsibility in law **2** wild foolishness; extravagant folly **3** a foolish act [*lunatic*]
'**luna ,moth** /'loohnə/ *n* a large N American moth with crescent-shaped markings and long tails on the hind wings [NL *luna* (specific epithet of *Actias luna*, the luna moth), fr L, moon]
lunar /'loohnə/ *adj* **1a** of the moon **b** designed for use on the moon ⟨~ *vehicles*⟩ **2 lunar, lunate** shaped like a crescent **3** measured by the moon's revolution ⟨~ *month*⟩ [L *lunaris*, fr *luna* moon; akin to L *lucēre* to shine – more at [1]LIGHT]
lunar eclipse *n* an eclipse in which the moon passes partly or wholly through the earth's shadow
lunar month *n* the period of time, averaging 29½ days, between 2 successive new moons
lunatic /'loohnətik/ *adj* **1a** insane **b** of or designed for the care of insane people ⟨*a* ~ *asylum*⟩ **2** wildly foolish [ME *lunatik*, fr OF or LL; OF *lunatique*, fr LL *lunaticus*, fr L *luna*; fr the belief that lunacy fluctuated with the phases of the moon] – **lunatic** *n*
lunatic fringe *n* the extremist or fanatical members of a political or social movement
lunation /looh'naysh(ə)n/ *n* LUNAR MONTH [ME *lunacioun*, fr ML *lunation-, lunatio*, fr L *luna*]
[1]**lunch** /lunch/ *n* (the food prepared for) a light midday meal; *broadly, NAm* a light meal [prob short for *luncheon*, fr E dial. *luncheon* (a large lump), alter. of earlier *lunch* (lump, piece, esp of food), prob alter. of *lump*]
[2]**lunch** *vi* to eat lunch
luncheon /'lunch(ə)n/ *n* **1** a midday social gathering at which a formal, usu relatively large, meal is eaten **2** lunch – fml
'**luncheon ,meat** *n* a precooked mixture of meat (e g pork) and cereal shaped in a loaf
'**luncheon ,voucher** *n* a voucher given to an employee as a benefit additional to pay and exchangeable for food in some British restaurants or shops
lune /loohn/ *n* a crescent-shaped figure on a plane surface or sphere formed by 2 intersecting arcs [L *luna* moon – more at LUNAR]
lunette /looh'net (*Fr* lynɛt)/ *n* sthg (e g a window, space above a door, or fortification) shaped like a

crescent [F, fr OF *lunete* small object shaped like the moon, fr *lune* moon]

lung /lung/ *n* **1** either of the usu paired compound saclike organs in the chest that constitute the basic respiratory organ of air-breathing vertebrates ☞ DIGESTION **2** any of various respiratory organs of invertebrates [ME *lunge*, fr OE *lungen*; akin to OHG *lungun* lung, *līhti* light in weight – more at ⁴LIGHT]

¹lunge /lunj/ *vb* to make a lunge (with) [by shortening & alter. fr obs *allonge* (to make a thrust with a sword), fr F *allonger* to lengthen]

²lunge *n* **1** a sudden thrust or forceful forward movement **2** the act of plunging forward

³lunge *n* a long rein used to hold and guide a horse in breaking and training [F *longe*, fr OF, fr fem of *lonc* long, fr L *longus*]

⁴lunge *vt* to guide (a horse) on a lunge in a circular course round the trainer

-lunged /-lungd/ *comb form* (→ *adj*) having a lung or lungs of a specified kind or number ⟨*one*-lunged⟩

ˈlungˌfish /-ˌfish/ *n* any of various fishes that breathe by a modified air bladder as well as gills

lungi /ˈloong·gi/ *n* a usu cotton cloth worn variously as a loincloth, turban, or sash, esp by Indians [Hindi *lungī*, fr Per]

ˈlungˌwort /-ˌwuht/ *n* a European plant of the borage family with usu white-spotted leaves covered in rough hairs, and bluish flowers [fr its being formerly used to treat lung diseases]

lunisolar /ˌloohniˈsohlə/ *adj* of or attributed to the moon and the sun [L *luna* moon + E *-i-* + *solar*]

lunule /ˈloohnyoohl/ *n* a crescent-shaped body part or marking (e g the whitish mark at the base of a fingernail) [NL *lunula*, fr L, crescent-shaped ornament, fr dim. of *luna* moon]

Lupercalia /ˌloohpuhˈkaylyə/ *n* an ancient Roman festival celebrated on February 15 to ensure fertility for the people, fields, and flocks [L, pl, fr *Lupercus*, god of flocks] – **Lupercalian** /-ˈkaylyən/ *adj*

lupin *also* **lupine** /ˈloohpin/ *n* **1** any of a genus of leguminous plants some of which are cultivated for fertiliser, fodder, their edible seeds, or their long spikes of variously coloured flowers **2** an edible lupin seed [ME *lupine*, fr L *lupinus, lupinum*, fr *lupinus*, adj]

lupine /ˈloohpien/ *adj* of or resembling a wolf [L *lupinus*, fr *lupus* wolf – more at WOLF]

lupus /ˈloohpəs/ *n* any of several diseases characterized by skin disorders [ML, fr L, wolf]

ˌlupus ˌeryˌthemaˈtosus /ˌerəˌtheeməˈtohsəs/ *n* a slowly progressive systemic disease that is marked by degenerative changes of connective tissue, reddish skin lesions, arthritic changes, lesions of internal organs, and wasting [NL, lit., erythematous lupus]

ˌlupus vulˈgaris /voolˈgahris, vul-/ *n* a tuberculous disease of the skin marked by ulceration and scarring [NL, lit., common lupus]

¹lurch /luhch/ *n* [obs *lurch* (game like backgammon, decisive defeat in this game), fr MF *lourche* deceived] – **in the lurch** in a vulnerable and unsupported position; deserted – infml

²lurch *vi* **1** to roll or tip abruptly; pitch **2** to stagger [origin unknown] – **lurch** *n*

lurcher /ˈluhchə/ *n* any of several types of swift-running dogs that are crosses between greyhound or whippet and another breed (e g the collie or terrier) [E dial. *lurch* (to prowl), fr ME *lorchen*, prob alter. of *lurken* to lurk]

¹lure /lyooə, looə/ *n* **1** a bunch of feathers and often meat attached to a long cord and used by a falconer to recall his/her bird **2a** sby or sthg used to entice or decoy **b** the power to appeal or attract ⟨*the ~ of success*⟩ **3** a decoy for attracting animals to capture [ME, fr MF *loire*, of Gmc origin; akin to MHG *luoder* bait; akin to OE *lathian* to invite, OHG *ladōn*]

²lure *vt* **1** to recall (a hawk) by means of a lure **2** to tempt with a promise of pleasure or gain

Lurex /ˈlyooəreks/ *trademark* – used for a type of thread which is (partly) coated so as to give a metallic appearance

lurid /ˈl(y)ooərid/ *adj* **1** wan and ghastly pale in appearance **2a** causing horror or revulsion; gruesome **b** sensational ⟨~ *newspaper reports of the crime*⟩ **c** highly coloured; gaudy [L *luridus* pale yellow, sallow] – **luridly** *adv*, **luridness** *n*

lurk /luhk/ *vi* **1a** to lie hidden in wait, esp with evil intent **b** to move furtively or inconspicuously **2** to lie hidden; *esp* to be a hidden threat [ME *lurken*; akin to MHG *lūren* to lie in wait – more at LOWER] – **lurker** *n*

luscious /ˈlushəs/ *adj* **1** having a delicious taste or smell **2** having sensual appeal; seductive **3** richly luxurious or appealing to the senses; *also* excessively ornate [ME *lucius*, perh alter. of *licius*, short for *delicious*] – **lusciously** *adv*, **lusciousness** *n*

¹lush /lush/ *adj* **1** producing or covered by luxuriant growth ⟨~ *grass*⟩ ⟨~ *pastures*⟩ **2** opulent, sumptuous [ME *lusch* soft, tender] – **lushly** *adv*

²lush *n, chiefly NAm* a heavy drinker; an alcoholic [origin unknown]

¹lust /lust/ *n* **1** strong sexual desire, esp as opposed to love **2** an intense longing; a craving [ME, pleasure, appetite, sexual desire, fr OE; akin to OHG *lust* pleasure, L *lascivus* wanton] – **lustful** *adj*

²lust *vi* to have an intense (sexual) desire or craving

lustral /ˈlustrəl/ *adj* purificatory [L *lustralis*, fr *lustrum*]

lustrate /ˈlustrayt/ *vt* to purify ceremonially [L *lustratus*, pp of *lustrare* to brighten, purify] – **lustration** /luˈstraysh(ə)n/ *n*

¹lustre, *NAm chiefly* **luster** /ˈlustə/ *n* a lustrum

²lustre, *NAm chiefly* **luster** *n* **1** (the quality of) the glow of reflected light from a surface (e g of a mineral) **2a** a glow of light (as if) from within **b** radiant beauty **3** glory, distinction **4** a glass pendant used esp to ornament a chandelier **5** a lustrous fabric with cotton warp and a wool, mohair, or alpaca weft [MF, fr OIt *lustro*, fr *lustrare* to shine, fr L] – **lustreless** *adj*

³lustre, *NAm chiefly* **luster** *vt* to give lustre or distinction to – **lustring** *n*

ˈlustreˌware /-ˌweə/ *n* ceramic ware decorated with an iridescent glaze

lustrous /ˈlustrəs/ *adj* evenly shining ⟨*a ~ satin*⟩ ⟨*the ~ glow of an opal*⟩ – **lustrously** *adv*

lustrum /ˈlustrəm/ *n, pl* **lustrums, lustra** /ˈlustrə/ a period of 5 years [L, purification of the Roman people made every 5 years after the census; akin to L *lustrare* to brighten, purify]

lusty /ˈlusti/ *adj* **1** full of vitality; healthy **2** full of strength; vigorous [[1]*lust* + [1]*-y*] – **lustily** *adv*, **lustiness** *n*

lute /looht/ *n* a stringed instrument with a large pear-shaped body, a neck with a fretted fingerboard, and pairs of strings tuned in unison [ME, fr MF *lut*, fr OProv *laut*, fr Ar *al-'ūd*, lit., the wood]

[1]lute-, luteo- *comb form* yellowish ⟨luteo*lin*⟩ [L *luteus*]

[2]lute-, luteo- *comb form* corpus luteum ⟨luteo*trophic*⟩ [NL (*corpus*) *luteum*]

luteal /'loohti·əl/ *adj* of or involving the corpus luteum

lutein·ize /'loohti·i,niez, -teeniez/, **-ise** *vb* to produce or become corpora lutea – **luteinization** /,loohti·inie'zaysh(ə)n, -teen-/

'lutei,nizing ,hormone *n* a hormone from the front lobe of the pituitary gland that in the female stimulates the development esp of corpora lutea and in the male interstitial tissue of the testis

lutenist /'loohtinist/, **lutanist** /-tən-/ *n* a lute player [ML *lutanista*, fr *lutana* lute, prob fr MF *lut*]

luteotrophic /,loohtioh'trofik, -'trohfik/ *adj* promoting the growth of corpora lutea

luteotrophic hormone *n* prolactin

,luteo'trophin /-'trohfin/ *n* prolactin [*luteotroph*ic + *-in*]

,luteo'tropin /-'trohpin/ *n* prolactin

luteous /'loohti·əs/ *adj* greenish or brownish yellow [L *luteus* yellowish, fr *lutum*, a plant used for dyeing yellow]

lutetium *also* **lutecium** /looh'teesh(y)əm/ *n* a metallic element of the rare-earth group ☞ PERIODIC TABLE [NL, fr L *Lutetia*, ancient name of Paris, city in France]

[1]Lutheran /'loohthərən/ *n* a member of a Lutheran church

[2]Lutheran *adj* relating to religious doctrines (e g justification by faith alone) or Protestant churches derived from Martin Luther or his followers [Martin *Luther* †1546 G religious reformer] – **Lutheranism** *n*

lutz /loots/ *n* a jump in ice-skating from one skate with a complete turn in the air and a return to the other skate [prob irreg fr Gustave *Lussi b* 1898 Swiss figure skater, its inventor]

lux /luks/ *n, pl* **lux, luxes** the SI unit of illumination ☞ PHYSICS [L, light – more at [1]LIGHT]

luxate /'luksayt/ *vt* to dislocate [L *luxatus*, pp of *luxare*, fr *luxus* dislocated – more at [1]LOCK] – **luxation** /luk'saysh(ə)n/ *n*

luxuriant /lug'zhooəri·ənt/ *adj* **1** characterized by abundant growth **2a** exuberantly rich and varied; prolific **b** richly or excessively ornamented ⟨~ *prose*⟩ – **luxuriance** *n*, **luxuriantly** *adv*

luxuriate /lug'zhooəriayt/ *vi* to enjoy oneself consciously; revel – often + *in* [L *luxuriatus*, pp of *luxuriare*, fr *luxuria*]

luxurious /lug'zhooəri·əs/ *adj* **1** fond of luxury or self-indulgence; *also* voluptuous **2** characterized by opulence and rich abundance – **luxuriously** *adv*, **luxuriousness** *n*

luxury /'lukshəri/ *n* **1** great ease or comfort based on habitual or liberal use of expensive items without regard to cost ⟨*lived in* ~⟩ **2a** sthg desirable but costly or difficult to obtain **b** sthg relatively expensive adding to pleasure or comfort but not indispensable [ME *luxurie*, fr MF, fr L *luxuria* rankness, luxury, excess; akin to L *luxus* luxury, excess]

lwei /lway/ *n* ☞ *Angola* at NATIONALITY [of Bantu origin]

[1]-ly /-li/ *suffix* (→ *adj*) **1** like in appearance, manner, or nature; having the characteristics of ⟨*queen*ly⟩ ⟨*father*ly⟩ **2** recurring regularly at intervals of; every ⟨*hour*ly⟩ ⟨*dai*ly⟩ [ME, fr OE *-līc, -lic*; akin to OHG *-līh*; both fr a prehistoric Gmc noun represented by OE *līc* body – more at [1]LIKE]

[2]-ly *suffix* (→ *adv*) **1** in (such) a manner ⟨*slow*ly⟩; like ⟨*king*ly⟩ **2** from (such) a point of view ⟨*musical*ly *speaking*⟩ **3** with respect to ⟨*part*ly⟩ **4** as is (specified); it is (specified) that ⟨*natural*ly⟩ ⟨*regrettab*ly⟩ **5** speaking (in a specified way) ⟨*frank*ly⟩ ⟨*brief*ly⟩ [ME, fr OE *-līce, -lice*, fr *-līc*, adj suffix]

lycaenid /lie'seenid/ *n* any of a family of medium-sized often brilliantly coloured butterflies (e g the blues or coppers) [deriv of NL *Lycaena*, genus of butterflies, fr Gk *lykaina*, fem of *lykos* wolf]

lycanthrope /'liekən,throhp, lie'kanthrohp/ *n* **1** a person displaying lycanthropy **2** a werewolf [NL *lycanthropus*, fr Gk *lykanthrōpos* werewolf, fr *lykos* wolf + *anthrōpos* man – more at WOLF]

lycanthropy /lie'kanthrəpi/ *n* **1** a delusion that one has become a wolf **2** the change from a human being into a wolf, held to be possible by witchcraft or magic – **lycanthropic** /,liekan'thropik/ *adj*

lycée /'leesay (*Fr* lise)/ *n* a French public secondary school [F, fr MF, hall for public lectures, fr L *Lyceum*, gymnasium near Athens where Aristotle taught, fr Gk *Lykeion*, fr neut of *lykeios*, epithet of Apollo, god of poetry]

lychee /'liechi/ *n* a litchi

'lych-,gate /lich/ *n* a roofed gate in a churchyard traditionally used as resting place for a coffin during part of a burial service [ME *lycheyate*, fr *lich* body, corpse (fr OE *līc*) + *gate, yate* gate]

lychnis /'liknis/ *n* any of a genus of plants of the pink family [NL, genus name, fr L, a red flower, fr Gk; akin to Gk *lychnos* lamp, L *lux* light – more at [1]LIGHT]

lycopod /'liekə,pod/ *n* LYCOPODIUM 1; *broadly* CLUB MOSS [NL *Lycopodium*]

lycopodium /,liekə'pohdi·əm/ *n* **1** any of a large genus of erect or creeping club mosses with evergreen 1-nerved leaves **2** a fine yellowish powder of lycopodium spores used in pharmacy and as a component of fireworks and flashlight powders [NL, genus name, fr Gk *lykos* wolf + *podion*, dim. of *pod-, pous* foot – more at FOOT]

Lycra /'liekrə/ *trademark* – used for a synthetic stretchy yarn made from polyurethane and used chiefly in corsetry and swimwear

lyddite /'lidiet/ *n* a high explosive composed chiefly of picric acid [*Lydd*, town in England]

lye /lie/ *n* a strong alkaline liquid rich in potassium carbonate, leached from wood ashes, and used esp in making soap; *broadly* a strong alkaline solution [ME, fr OE *lēag*; akin to OHG *louga* lye, L *lavare, lavere* to wash, Gk *louein*]

,lying-'in /'lie·ing/ *n, pl* **lyings-in, lying-ins** confinement for childbirth

lying in state *n* (the period of) the ceremonial display of (a coffin containing) the dead body of sby of high rank to which people may pay their last respects

lymph /limf/ *n* a pale fluid resembling blood plasma that contains white blood cells but normally no red blood cells, that circulates in the lymphatic vessels, and bathes the cells of the body [L *lympha* water goddess, water, fr Gk *nymphē* nymph – more at NUPTIAL]

lymph-, lympho- *comb form* lymph; lymphatic tissue ⟨lympho*cyte*⟩ [NL *lympha*]

[1]**lymphatic** /lim'fatik/ *adj* **1** of, involving, or produced by lymph, lymphoid tissue, or lymphocytes **2** conveying lymph ⟨~ *vessels*⟩

[2]**lymphatic** *n* a vessel that contains or conveys lymph

'**lymph ,gland** *n* LYMPH NODE

'**lymph ,node** *n* any of the rounded masses of lymphoid tissue that occur along the course of the lymphatic vessels and in which lymphocytes are formed

lymphocyte /'limfəsiet/ *n* a white blood cell that is present in large numbers in lymph and blood and defends the body by immunological responses to invading or foreign matter (e g by producing antibodies) – compare MONOCYTE ☞ ANATOMY [ISV] – **lymphocytic** /,limfə'sitik/ *adj*

lymphoid /'limfoyd/ *adj* **1** of or resembling lymph **2** of or constituting the tissue characteristic of the lymph nodes

lymphoma /lim'fohmə/ *n, pl* **lymphomas, lymphomata** /lim'fohmətə, ,limfə'mahtə/ a tumour of lymphoid tissue [NL] – **lymphomatous** *adj*, **lymphomatoid** /-,toyd/ *adj*

lynch /linch/ *vt* to put to death illegally by mob action [*lynch law*] – **lyncher** *n*

lynchet /'linchit/ *n, Br* a terrace formed on a hillside by prehistoric cultivation [*lynch* (alter. of *link* ridge of land) + *-et* – more at LINKS]

'**lynch ,law** *n* the punishment of presumed crimes or offences usu by death without due process of law [prob fr William *Lynch* †1820 US citizen who organized extralegal tribunals in Virginia]

'**lynch,pin** /-,pin/ *n* a linchpin

lynx /lingks/ *n, pl* **lynx, lynxes** any of various wildcats with relatively long legs, a short stubby tail, mottled coat, and often tufted ears [L, fr Gk; akin to OE *lox* lynx, Gk *leukos* white – more at [1]LIGHT]

'**lynx-,eyed** *adj* having keen eyesight

lyo- *comb form* dispersed state; dispersion ⟨lyo*philic*⟩ [prob fr NL, fr Gk *lyein* to loosen, dissolve – more at LOSE]

lyophilic /,lie·ə'filik/ *adj* marked by strong affinity between a dispersed substance and the substance in which it is dispersed ⟨*a* ~ *colloid*⟩ – compare LYOPHOBIC

lyophil·ize, -ise /lie'ofiliez/ *vt* to freeze-dry – **lyophilization** /lie,ofilie'zaysh(ə)n/ *n*

lyophobic /,lie·ə'fohbik/ *adj* marked by lack of strong affinity between a dispersed substance and the substance in which it is dispersed ⟨*a* ~ *colloid*⟩ – compare LYOPHILIC

lyrate /'lie·ərət/ *adj* shaped like a lyre ☞ PLANT

lyre /'lie·ə/ *n* a stringed instrument of the harp family used by the ancient Greeks esp to accompany song and recitation [ME *lire*, fr OF, fr L *lyra*, fr Gk]

'**lyre,bird** /-,buhd/ *n* either of 2 Australian birds the male of which displays tail feathers in the shape of a lyre during courtship

[1]**lyric** /'lirik/ *adj* **1** suitable for being set to music and sung **2** expressing direct personal emotion ⟨~ *poetry*⟩ [MF or L; MF *lyrique* of a lyre, fr L *lyricus*, fr Gk *lyrikos*, fr *lyra*]

[2]**lyric** *n* **1** a lyric poem **2** *pl* the words of a popular song – **lyricist** /'lirisist/, **lyrist** /'lie·ərist/ *n*

'**lyrical** /'lirikl/ *adj* **1** lyric **2** full of admiration or enthusiasm – esp in *wax lyrical* – **lyrically** *adv*

lyricism /'lirisiz(ə)m/ *n* **1** a directly personal and intense style or quality in an art **2** great enthusiasm or exuberance [[1]LYRIC + -ISM]

lys-, lysi-, lyso- *comb form* lysis ⟨lys*in*⟩ [NL, fr Gk *lys-, lysi-* loosening, fr *lysis*]

lysate /'liesayt/ *n* a product of lysis

lyse /lies, liez/ *vb* to (cause to) undergo lysis [back-formation fr NL *lysis*]

-lyse, *NAm chiefly* **-lyze** /-liez/ *comb form* (→ *vb*) produce or undergo lytic disintegration or dissolution ⟨*electro*lyse⟩ [ISV, prob irreg fr NL *-lysis*]

ly,sergic 'acid /lie'suhjik/ *n* an acid obtained from alkaloids that occur in ergot [*lys-* + *erg*ot]

lysergic acid diethylamide /die,eethi'laymied, ,die·ə'thieləmied/ *n* LSD

lysin /'liesin/ *n* a substance capable of causing lysis; *esp* an antibody capable of causing disintegration of red blood cells or microorganisms

lysine /'lieseen, -sin/ *n* a basic amino acid that is essential to nutrition in humans

lysis /'liesis/ *n, pl* **lyses** /-seez/ **1** the gradual decline of a disease process (e g fever) **2** a process of disintegration or dissolution (e g of cells) [NL, fr Gk, act of loosening, dissolution, remission of fever, fr *lyein* to loosen – more at LOSE] – **lytic** /'litik/ *adj*, **lytically** *adv*

-lysis /-ləsis/ *comb form,* (→ *n*) *pl* **-lyses** /-seez/ decomposition; disintegration; breaking down ⟨*electro*lysis⟩ ⟨*auto*lysis⟩ [NL, fr L & Gk; L, loosening, fr Gk, fr *lysis*] – **-lytic** /-'litik/ *comb form* (→ *adj*)

Lysol /'liesol, -sohl/ *n* a mildly corrosive solution of cresol and soap, formerly used as a disinfectant [*lys-* + [1]*-ol*]

lysolecithin /,liesə'lesəthin, -soh-/ *n* a hydrolytic substance formed by the enzymatic hydrolysis of a lecithin (e g by some snake venoms)

lysosome /'liesə,sohm/ *n* a vesicle surrounded by a membrane that occurs in cell cytoplasm and contains enzymes capable of breaking down unwanted material or causing autolysis [ISV *lys-* + [3]*-some*] – **lysosomal** /,liesə'sohml/ *adj*

lysozyme /'liesə,ziem/ *n* an enzyme present in egg white and in human tears and saliva that destroys the capsules of various bacteria

-lyte /-liet/ *comb form* (→ *n*) substance capable of undergoing (a specified process or change) ⟨*electro*lyte⟩ [Gk *lytos* that may be untied, soluble, fr *lyein*]

lythe /liedh/ *n, Br* the pollack [origin unknown]

-lytic /-'litik/ *suffix* (→ *adj*) of or effecting (such) decomposition ⟨*hydro*lytic *enzymes*⟩ [Gk *lytikos* able to loosen, fr *lyein*]

-lyze /-liez/ *comb form* (→ *vb*), *NAm* -lyse

M

m /em/ *n, pl* **m's, ms** *often cap* **1** (a graphic representation of or device for reproducing) the 13th letter of the English alphabet **2** one thousand ☞ NUMBER **3** sthg shaped like the letter M **4** an em

'm /-m/ *vb* am ⟨*I'm going*⟩

ma /mah/ *n* MOTHER 1a – chiefly as a term of address; infml [short for *mama*]

ma'am /mam, mahm; *unstressed* məm/ *n* madam – used widely in the USA and in Britain, esp by servants and when addressing the Queen or a royal princess

mac, mack /mak/ *n, Br* a raincoat – infml [short for *mackintosh*]

Mac *n* – used informally to address **a** a Scotsman **b** *NAm* an unknown man [*Mac-, Mc-*, common Sc & Ir patronymic prefix]

macabre /mə'kahb(r)ə/ *adj* **1** having death as a subject **2** dwelling on the gruesome **3** tending to produce horror in an onlooker [F, fr (*danse*) *macabre* dance of death, fr MF (*danse de*) *Macabré*]

macadam /mə'kadəm/ *n* material used in making a macadamized road [John *McAdam* †1836 Sc engineer]

macadam·ize /mə'kadəmiez/, **-ise** *vt* to construct or finish (a road) by compacting into a solid mass successive layers of small broken stones

macaque /mə'kahk/ *n* any of numerous short-tailed Old World monkeys [F, fr Pg *macaco*]

macaroni /makə'rohni/ *n, pl* (2) **macaronis, macaronies** **1** pasta made from durum wheat and shaped in hollow tubes that are wider in diameter than spaghetti **2** an English dandy of the late 18th and early 19th c who affected continental ways [It *maccheroni*, pl of *maccherone*, fr It dial. *maccarone* dumpling, macaroni]

macaronic /,makə'ronik/ *adj* characterized by a mixture of Latin with vernacular words that sometimes have Latin endings [NL *macaronicus*, fr It dial. *maccarone* macaroni]

macaroon /,makə'roohn/ *n* a small cake or biscuit composed chiefly of egg whites, sugar, and ground almonds or occasionally coconut [F *macaron*, fr It dial. *maccarone*]

ma'cassar ,oil /mə'kasə/ *n, often cap M* a preparation containing oil formerly used for dressing the hair [*Macassar* (Makassar), city in Indonesia]

macaw /mə'kaw/ *n* any of numerous parrots including some of the largest and showiest [Pg *macau*]

Maccabees /'makə,beez/ *n pl* **1** a priestly family who led a Jewish revolt against Seleucid rule and reigned over Palestine from 142 to 63 BC **2** *sing in constr* either of 2 narrative and historical books included in the Roman Catholic canon of the Old Testament and in the Protestant Apocrypha [Gk *Makkabaioi*, fr pl of *Makkabaios*, surname of Judas Maccabaeus 2nd-c BC Jewish patriot] – **Maccabean** /-,bee·ən/ *adj*

McCarthyism /mə'kahthi,iz(ə)m/ *n* fanatical opposition to (Communist) elements held to be subversive, accompanied by indiscriminate and unsubstantiated charges against individuals [Joseph R *McCarthy* †1957 US politician] – **McCarthyist** *n*

McCoy /mə'koy/ *n* sthg that is neither imitation nor substitute – usu in *the real McCoy* [alter. of *Mackay* (in the phrase *the real MacKay* the true chief of the MacKay clan, a position often disputed)]

[1]**mace** /mays/ *n* **1** a medieval heavy spiked staff or club **2** an ornamental staff used as a symbol of authority [ME, fr MF, fr (assumed) VL *mattia*; akin to OHG *medela* plough, L *mateola* mallet]

[2]**mace** *n* an aromatic spice consisting of the dried external fibrous covering of a nutmeg [ME, fr MF *macis*, fr L *macir*, an East Indian spice, fr Gk *makir*]

Mace *trademark* – used for a riot control agent containing tear gas

macédoine /,masə'dwahn, 'masədoyn/ *n* a mixture of fruits or vegetables served sometimes in jelly as a salad, cocktail, or garnish [F, fr *Macédoine* Macedonia, region of S Europe; perh fr the mixture of races in Macedonia]

macerate /'masərayt/ *vt* **1** to cause to waste away (as if) by excessive fasting **2** to cause to become soft or separated into constituent elements (as if) by steeping in fluid ~ *vi* to soften and wear away, esp as a result of being wetted [L *maceratus*, pp of *macerare* to soften, steep] – **macerator** *n*, **maceration** /,masə'raysh(ə)n/ *n*

Mach /mak, mahk/ *n* MACH NUMBER ⟨*an aeroplane flying at ~ 2*⟩

machete /mə'sheti, -'chayti/ *n* a large heavy knife used for cutting vegetation and as a weapon [Sp]

Machiavellian /,maki·ə'veli·ən/ *adj* cunning and deceitful [Niccolò *Machiavelli* †1527 It statesman & political theorist]

,Machia'vellia,nism /-,niz(ə)m/ *n* the political theory of Machiavelli; *esp* the view that the necessities of the State transcend individual morality

ma,chico'lation /ma,chikə'laysh(ə)n/ *n* an opening between the corbels of a projecting parapet or in the floor of a gallery or roof of a portal for discharging missiles upon assailants below ☞ CHURCH [ML *machicolatus*, pp of *machicolare* to furnish with machicolations, fr OF *machicoller*, fr *machicoleis* machicolation, fr *macher* to crush + *col* neck, fr L *collum* – more at COLLAR] – **machicolate** /-'chikəlayt/ *vt*

machinate /'makinayt/ *vi* to plan or plot, esp to do harm [L *machinatus*, pp of *machinari*, fr *machina* machine, contrivance] – **machinator** *n*

machination /,maki'naysh(ə)n/ *n* a scheming or

crafty action or plan intended to accomplish some usu evil end [MACHINATE + -ION]

[1]**machine** /mə'sheen/ *n* **1a** a combination of parts that transmit forces, motion, and energy one to another in a predetermined manner ⟨*a sewing* ~⟩ **b** an instrument (e g a lever or pulley) designed to transmit or modify the application of power, force, or motion **c** a combination of mechanically, electrically, or electronically operated parts for performing a task **d** a coin-operated device **e** machinery – + *the* or in pl ⟨*humanity must not become the servant of the* ~⟩ **2a** a person or organization that acts like a machine **b** the (controlling or inner) organization (e g of a group or activity) ⟨*the war* ~⟩ **c** a highly organized political group [MF, structure, fabric, fr L *machina*, fr Gk *mēchanē* (Doric dial. *machana*), fr *mēchos* means, expedient – more at MAY]

[2]**machine** *vt* **1** to shape, finish, or operate on by a machine **2** to act on, produce, or perform a particular operation or activity on, using a machine; *esp* to sew using a sewing machine ⟨~ *the zip in place*⟩ – **machinable** *also* **machineable** *adj*

machine code *n* a system of symbols and rules for coding information in a form usable by a machine (e g a computer); *also* information so coded

ma'chine ,gun *n* an automatic gun for rapid continuous fire – **machine-gun** *vb*, **machine gunner** *n*

ma,chine-'readable *adj* directly usable by a computer ⟨~ *text*⟩

machinery /mə'sheen(ə)ri/ *n* **1a** machines in general or as a functioning unit **b** the working parts of a machine **2** the means by which sthg is kept in action or a desired result is obtained **3** the system or organization by which an activity or process is controlled

ma'chine ,tool *n* a usu power-driven machine designed for cutting or shaping wood, metal, etc

machinist /mə'sheenist/ *n* **1** a craftsman skilled in the use of machine tools **2** one who operates a machine, esp a sewing machine

machismo /mə'kizmoh, -'chiz-/ *n* an exaggerated awareness and assertion of masculinity [MexSp, fr Sp *macho* male]

'Mach ,number, Mach *n* a number representing the ratio of the speed of a body to the speed of sound in the surrounding atmosphere ⟨*a* ~ *of 2 indicates a speed that is twice that of sound*⟩ [Ernst *Mach* †1916 Austrian physicist]

macho /'machoh, 'mahchoh, -koh/ *adj* aggressively virile [Sp, male, fr L *masculus* – more at MALE]

mack /mak/ *n, Br* a raincoat – infml [short for *mackintosh*]

mackerel /'mak(ə)rəl/ *n, pl* **mackerels,** *esp collectively* **mackerel** a fish of the N Atlantic that is green with dark blue bars above and silvery below and is one of the most important food fishes; *also* any of various usu small or medium-sized related fishes ☞ LIFE CYCLE [ME *makerel*, fr OF]

'mackerel ,shark *n* the porbeagle

mackerel sky *n* a sky covered with rows of altocumulus or cirrocumulus clouds

mackintosh *also* **macintosh** /'makintosh/ *n, chiefly Br* a raincoat [Charles *Macintosh* †1843 Sc chemist & inventor]

mackle /'makl/ *vb* to blur [F *macule* spot, stain, fr L *macula*]

macle /'makl/ *n* TWIN 3 [F, wide-meshed net, lozenge, macle, fr OF, mesh, lozenge, of Gmc origin; akin to OHG *masca* mesh – more at MESH]

macr-, macro- *comb form* **1** long ⟨macro*diagonal*⟩ ⟨macro*biotic*⟩ **2** large ⟨macro*spore*⟩ **3** including or more comprehensive than ⟨*Macro-Ge*⟩ – used of a language group [F & L, fr Gk *makr-, makro-* long, fr *makros* – more at MEAGRE]

macrame, macramé /mə'krahmi/ *n* (the act of making) a coarse lace or fringe made by knotting threads or cords in a geometrical pattern [F or It; F *macramé*, fr It *macramè*, fr Turk *makrama* napkin, towel, fr Ar *migramah* embroidered veil]

macro /'makroh/ *n, pl* **macros** a single computer instruction that stands for a sequence of operations [short for *macroinstruction*]

macrobiotic /,makrəbie'otik, -kroh-/ *adj* of or being a restricted diet, esp one consisting chiefly of whole grains or whole grains and vegetables, that is usu undertaken with the intention of promoting health and prolonging life

macrocephalous /,makroh'sefələs/, **macrocephalic** /-si'falik/ *adj* having or being an exceptionally large head or cranium [F *macrocéphale*, fr Gk *makrokephalos* having a long head, fr *makr-* + *kephalē* head – more at CEPHALIC] – **macrocephaly** *n*

macroclimate /'makroh,kliemət/ *n* the predominant or normal climate of a large region

macrocosm /'makrə,koz(ə)m/ *n* **1** the universe **2** a complex that is a large-scale reproduction of 1 of its constituents [F *macrocosme*, fr ML *macrocosmos*, fr L *macr-* + Gk *kosmos* order, universe] – **macrocosmic** /,makrə'kozmik/ *adj*, **macrocosmically** *adv*

macroeconomics /,makroh·ekə'nomiks, -eekə-/ *n pl but sing in constr* a study of large-scale economics (e g of a nation) – compare MICROECONOMICS – **macroeconomic** *adj*

,macro'molecule /-'molikyoohl/ *n* a large molecule (e g of a protein or rubber) built up from smaller chemical structures [ISV] – **macromolecular** /-mə'lekyoolə/ *adj*

macron /'makron/ *n* a mark ¯ × used over a vowel or syllable to indicate a long or stressed sound ☞ SYMBOL [Gk *makron*, neut of *makros* long]

macronutrient /,makroh'nyoohtri·ənt/ *n* a nutrient element of which relatively large quantities are essential to the growth and welfare of a plant – compare TRACE ELEMENT

'macro,phage /-,fayj, -,fahzh/ *n* any of various large cells that are distributed throughout the body tissues, ingest foreign matter and debris, and may be attached to the fibres of a tissue or mobile [F, fr *macr-* + *-phage*] – **macrophagic** /-'fajik/ *adj*

,macro'scopic /-'skopik/ *also* **macroscopical** /-kl/ *adj* **1** large enough to be observed by the naked eye **2** considered in terms of large units or elements [ISV *macr-* + *-scopic* (as in *microscopic*)] – **macroscopically** *adv*

'macro,structure /-,strukchə/ *n* the structure of a metal, body part, the soil, etc revealed by visual examination with little or no magnification – **macrostructural** /-strukch(ə)rəl/ *adj*

macula /'makyoolə/ *n, pl* **maculae** /-li/ *also* **maculas** **1** a blotch, spot; *esp* a macule **2** an anatomical structure (e g the macula lutea) having the form of a spot differentiated from surrounding tissues [L] – **macular** *adj*

macula lutea /'loohti·ə/ *n, pl* **maculae luteae**

/-ti,ee/ a small yellowish area lying slightly to the side of the centre of the retina that constitutes the region of best vision [NL, lit., yellow spot]

maculation /,makyoo'laysh(ə)n/ *n* the arrangement of spots and markings on an animal or plant

macule /'makyoohl/ *n* a patch of skin altered in colour but usu not raised that is a characteristic feature of various diseases (e g smallpox) [F, fr L *macula*]

mad /mad/ *adj* **1** mentally disordered; insane – not now used technically **2** utterly foolish; senseless **3** carried away by intense anger **4** carried away by enthusiasm or desire **5** affected with rabies **6** intensely excited or distraught; frantic **7** marked by intense and often chaotic activity ⟨*made a* ~ *dash for cover*⟩ [ME *medd, madd,* fr OE *gemǣd,* pp of (assumed) *gemǣdan* to madden, fr *gemād* silly, mad; akin to OHG *gimeit* foolish, crazy, Skt *methati* he hurts] – **like mad** very hard, fast, loud, etc ⟨*shouted* like mad⟩

madam /'madəm/ *n, pl* **madams,** (1) **mesdames** /'may,dam/ **1** a lady – used without a name as a form of respectful or polite address to a woman **2** a mistress – used as a title formerly with the Christian name but now with the surname or esp with a designation of rank or office ⟨Madam *Chairman*⟩ ⟨Madam *President*⟩ **3** a female brothel keeper **4** *Br* a conceited pert young lady or girl ⟨*a little* ~⟩ [ME, fr OF *ma dame,* lit., my lady]

madame /'madəm; (*Fr* madam)/ *n, pl* **mesdames** /'may,dam/, (2) **madames** – used as a title equivalent to *Mrs* preceding the name of a married woman not of English-speaking nationality or used without a name as a generalized term of direct address [F, fr OF *ma dame*]

madcap /'mad,kap/ *adj* marked by impulsiveness or recklessness – **madcap** *n*

madden /'madn/ *vt* **1** to drive mad; craze **2** to exasperate, enrage

madder /'madə/ *n* **1** a Eurasian plant with whorled leaves and small yellowish flowers **2** (a dye prepared from) the root of the madder [ME, fr OE *mædere;* akin to OHG *matara* madder]

made /mayd/ *adj* **1** assembled or prepared, esp by putting together various ingredients ⟨~ *mustard*⟩ **2** assured of success ⟨*you've got it* ~⟩ – infml [ME, fr pp of *maken* to make]

Madeira /mə'diərə/ *n* any of several fortified wines from Madeira [Pg, fr *Madeira* Islands in E Atlantic]

madeira cake *n, often cap, Br* a very rich sponge cake

mademoiselle /,madmwə'zel (*Fr* madmwazɛl)/ *n, pl* **mademoiselles, mesdemoiselles** /,maydmwə'zel (*Fr* mɛdmwazɛl/ **1** an unmarried French-speaking girl or woman – used as a title equivalent to *Miss* for an unmarried woman not of English-speaking nationality **2** a French governess or female language teacher [F, fr OF *ma damoisele,* lit., my (young) lady]

,made-to-'measure *adj, of a garment* made according to an individual's measurements in order to achieve a good fit – compare OFF-THE-PEG

,made-'up *adj* **1** wearing make-up **2** fancifully conceived or falsely devised; fictional **3** fully assembled **4** *of a road* covered in tarmac

madhouse /'mad,hows/ *n* **1** a lunatic asylum – not used technically **2** a place of uproar or confusion

'madly /-li/ *adv* to a degree suggestive of madness: e g **a** with great energy; frantically **b** without restraint; passionately

'madman /-mən/, *fem* **'mad,woman** *n* a person who is or acts insane

'madness /-nis/ *n* **1a** insanity **b** extreme folly **2** any of several ailments of animals marked by frenzied behaviour; *specif* rabies [MAD + -NESS]

Madonna /mə'donə/ *n* VIRGIN MARY [It, fr OIt *ma donna,* lit., my lady]

Ma'donna ,lily *n* a white lily with trumpet-shaped flowers

madras /mə'dras, -'drahs/ *n* a fine usu cotton plain-woven shirting and dress fabric, usu in brightly coloured checked or striped designs [*Madras,* city in India]

madrepore /,madri'paw/ *n* any of various reef-building corals of tropical seas [F *madrépore,* fr It *madrepora,* fr *madre* mother (fr L *mater*) + *poro* pore (fr L *porus*) – more at ¹MOTHER] – **madreporian** /-'pawri·ən/ *adj or n,* **madreporic** /-'porik/ *adj*

madrigal /'madrig(ə)l/ *n* **1** a short medieval love poem **2** an unaccompanied and often complex secular song for several voices [It *madrigale,* fr ML *matricale,* fr neut of (assumed) *matricalis* simple, fr LL, of the womb, fr L *matric-, matrix* womb] – **madrigalian** /,madri'gali·ən/ *adj*

maduro /mə'dyooəroh/ *n, pl* **maduros** a dark-coloured relatively strong cigar [Sp, fr *maduro* ripe, fr L *maturus* – more at MATURE]

Maecenas /mie'seenəs/ *n* a generous patron, esp of literature or art [L, fr Gaius *Maecenas* †8 BC Roman statesman & patron of literature]

maelstrom /'maylstrohm/ *n* **1** a powerful whirlpool **2** sthg resembling a maelstrom in turbulence and violence [obs D (now *maalstroom*), fr *malen* to grind + *strom* stream; akin to OHG *malan* to grind, *stroum* stream – more at STREAM]

maenad /'meenad/ *n* **1** a female participant in ritual orgies in honour of Dionysus **2** a distraught woman [L *maenad-, maenas,* fr Gk *mainad-, mainas,* fr *mainesthai* to be mad; akin to Gk *menos* spirit – more at MIND] – **maenadic** /,mee'nadik/ *adj*

maestro /'miestroh/ *n, pl* **maestros, maestri** /-tri/ a master in an art; *esp* an eminent composer, conductor, or teacher of music [It, lit., master, fr L *magister* – more at MASTER]

Mae West /,may 'west/ *n* an inflatable life jacket [*Mae West* †1980 US actress noted for her full figure]

Mafia /'mafi·ə/ *n sing or pl in constr* **1** a secret society of Sicilian political terrorists **2** an organized secret body originating in Sicily and prevalent esp in the USA that controls illicit activities (e g vice and narcotics) **3** *often not cap* an excessively influential coterie of a usu specified kind ⟨*the literary* ~⟩ [It, fr It dial., boldness, bragging]

mafioso /,mafi'ohzoh/ *n, pl* **mafiosi** /-si/ a member of the Mafia [It, fr *Mafia*]

mag /mag/ *n* a magazine – infml

magazine /,magə'zeen, '---/ *n* **1** a storeroom for arms, ammunition, or explosives (e g gunpowder) **2a** a usu illustrated periodical, bound in paper covers, containing miscellaneous pieces by different authors **b** a television or radio programme containing a number of usu topical items, often without a common theme **3** a supply chamber: e g **a** a holder from which cartridges can be fed into a gun chamber automatically **b** a lightproof chamber for films or plates in a camera or for film in a film projector [MF, fr OProv, fr Ar *makhāzin*, pl of *makhzan* storehouse]

magdalen /'magdələn/ *n, often cap* **1** a reformed prostitute **2** a home for reformed prostitutes [Mary *Magdalen* or *Magdalene*, woman healed by Jesus of evil spirits (Lk 8:2), identified with a reformed prostitute (Lk 7:36–50)]

Magdalenian /,magdə'leenyən, -ni·ən/ *adj* of the latest Palaeolithic culture in Europe characterized by implements of flint, bone, and ivory and by cave paintings [F *magdalénien*, fr *La Madeleine*, rock shelter in SW France]

magenta /mə'jentə/ *n* **1** fuchsine **2a** a deep purplish red **b** a pinkish red – used in photography with reference to one of the primary colours [*Magenta*, town in Italy]

maggot /'magət/ *n* a soft-bodied legless grub that is the larva of a 2-winged fly (e g the housefly) [ME *mathek, maddok, magotte*, of Scand origin; akin to ON *mathkr* maggot; akin to OE *matha* maggot] – **maggoty** *adj*

magi /'mayjie/ *pl of* MAGUS

[1]**magic** /'majik/ *n* **1** (rites, incantations, etc used in) the art of invoking supernatural powers to control natural forces by means of charms, spells, etc **2a** an extraordinary power or influence producing results which defy explanation **b** sthg that seems to cast a spell ⟨*the ~ of the voice*⟩ **3** the art of producing illusions by sleight of hand [ME *magik*, fr MF *magique*, fr L *magice*, fr Gk *magikē*, fem of *magikos* of the Magi, magical, fr *magos* magus, sorcerer, of Iranian origin; akin to OPer *mogush* sorcerer]

[2]**magic** *adj* **1** of, being, or used in magic **2** having seemingly supernatural qualities **3** – used as a general term of approval; infml ⟨*this new record is really ~*⟩ – **magical** *adj*, **magically** *adv*

[3]**magic** *vt* **-ck-** to affect, influence, or take *away* (as if) by magic

,magic 'eye *n* PHOTOELECTRIC CELL

magician /mə'jish(ə)n/ *n* **1** one skilled in magic **2** a conjurer

,magic 'lantern *n* an early device for the projection of still pictures from slides

,magic 'square *n* a square array of numbers in which the sum of each vertical, horizontal, or diagonal row is the same

'Maginot ,Line /'mazhinoh; (*Fr* maʒino)/ *n* a line of defensive fortifications built in NE France before WW II [André *Maginot* †1932 F minister of war]

magisterial /,maji'stiəri·əl/ *adj* **1a** of, being, or having the characteristics of a master or teacher **b** having masterly skill **2** of a magistrate [LL *magisterialis* of authority, fr *magisterium* office of a master, fr *magister*] – **magisterially** *adv*

magistral /'majistrəl/ *adj* (characteristic) of a master; MAGISTERIAL 1a [LL *magistralis*, fr *magistr-, magister*] – **magistrally** *adv*

magistrate /'majistrayt, -strət/ *n* a civil legislative or executive official: e g **a** a principal official exercising governmental powers **b** a paid or unpaid local judicial officer who presides in a magistrates' court ☞ LAW [ME *magistrat*, fr L *magistratus* magistracy, magistrate, fr *magistr-, magister* master, political superior – more at MASTER] – **magistracy** /-strəsi/ *n*, **magistrature** /-strə,chə/ *n*, **magistratical** /,maji'stratikl/ *adj*

magistrate's court *n* a court of summary jurisdiction for minor criminal cases and preliminary hearings ☞ LAW

Maglemosian /,magli'mohsi·ən, -sh(ə)n/ *adj or n* (of) an early Mesolithic culture characterized by lakeside settlements and fishing implements [*Maglemose*, site in Denmark]

magma /'magmə/ *n* **1** a thin pasty suspension (e g of a precipitate in water) **2** molten rock material within the earth from which an igneous rock results by cooling ☞ GEOGRAPHY [L *magmat-, magma* dregs, fr Gk, thick unguent, fr *massein* to knead – more at MINGLE] – **magmatic** /mag'matik/ *adj*

Magna Carta *also* **Magna Charta** /,magnə 'kahtə/ *n* **1** a charter of liberties to which the English barons forced King John to assent in 1215 **2** a document constituting a fundamental guarantee of rights and privileges [ML, lit., great charter]

magnanimous /mag'nanimas/ *adj* **1** showing or suggesting a lofty and courageous spirit **2** showing or suggesting nobility of feeling and generosity of mind; not subject to petty feelings [L *magnanimus*, fr *magnus* great + *animus* spirit – more at MUCH, ANIMATE] – **magnanimously** *adv*, **magnanimity** /,magnə'niməti/ *n*

magnate /'magnayt/ *n* a person of wealth or influence, often in a specified area of business or industry [ME *magnates*, pl, fr LL, fr L *magnus*]

magnesia /mag'neezh(y)ə, -zyə/ *n* **1** a white oxide of magnesium used esp in making cements, insulation, fertilizers, and rubber, and in medicine as an antacid and mild laxative **2** magnesium [NL, fr *magnes carneus*, a white earth, lit., flesh magnet] – **magnesian** *adj*

magnesite /'magnəsiet/ *n* magnesium carbonate occurring as a mineral and used esp as a refractory

magnesium /mag'neezyəm/ *n* a silver-white bivalent metallic element that burns with an intense white light, is lighter than aluminium, and is used in making light alloys ☞ PERIODIC TABLE [NL, fr *magnesia*]

magnet /'magnit/ *n* **1a** LODESTONE 1 **b** a body (of iron, steel, etc) that has an (artificially imparted) magnetic field external to itself and attracts iron **2** sthg that attracts [ME *magnete*, fr MF, fr L *magnet-, magnes*, fr Gk *magnēs* (*lithos*), lit., stone of Magnesia, ancient city in Asia Minor]

magnet-, magneto- *comb form* magnetic force; magnetism; magnetic ⟨magneto*electric*⟩ ⟨magnet*on*⟩ [L *magnet-, magnes*]

magnetic /mag'netik/ *adj* **1a** of magnetism or a magnet **b** (capable of being) magnetized **c** working by magnetic attraction **2** possessing an extraordinary power or ability to attract or charm – **magnetically** *adv*

magnetic equator *n* ACLINIC LINE

magnetic field *n* a region of space (near a body possessing magnetism or carrying an electric current) in which magnetic forces can be detected

mag,netic 'flux *n* lines of force used to represent magnetic induction ☞ PHYSICS

magnetic needle *n* a slender bar of magnetized iron, steel, etc that when freely suspended indicates the direction of a magnetic field in which it is placed and that is the essential part of a magnetic compass

magnetic north *n* the northerly direction in the

earth's magnetic field as indicated by a horizontal magnetic needle

magnetic pole *n* either of 2 small nonstationary regions in the N and S geographical polar areas of the earth or another celestial body towards which a magnetic needle points from any direction

magnetic resonance *n* the resonant vibration of electrons, atoms, molecules, or nuclei when in a magnetic field in response to radio waves at particular frequencies

magnetic storm *n* a marked local disturbance of the earth's magnetic field, prob related to sunspot activity

magnetic tape *n* a ribbon of thin paper or plastic with a magnetizable coating for use in recording sound, video, etc signals ☞ COMPUTER, SYMBOL

magnetism /'magni,tiz(ə)m/ *n* **1** (physics dealing with) a class of physical forces and interactions that includes the attraction for iron shown by a permanent magnet or an electromagnet and is believed to be produced by moving electric charges **2** an ability to attract or charm

magnetite /'magni,tiet/ *n* iron oxide occurring as a black mineral strongly attracted by a magnet – **magnetitic** /,magni'titik/ *adj*

'magnet·ize, -ise /-tiez/ *vt* **1** to attract like a magnet **2** to cause to be a magnet – **magnetizable** *adj*, **magnetizer** *n*, **magnetization** /-'zaysh(ə)n/ *n*

magneto /mag'neetoh/ *n, pl* **magnetos** an alternator with permanent magnets (formerly) used to generate a high voltage for the ignition in an internal-combustion engine [short for *magnetoelectric machine*]

magneto- – see MAGNET-

magnetohydrodynamic /mag,neetoh·hiedrohdie'namik/ *adj* of or being phenomena arising from the motion of electrically conducting fluids in the presence of electric and magnetic fields – **magnetohydrodynamics** *n pl but sing or pl in constr*

magnetometer /,magni'tomitə/ *n* an instrument for measuring magnetic intensity, esp of the earth's magnetic field – **magnetometry** /-tri/ *n*, **magnetometric** /-toh'metrik/ *adj*

magneton /'magniton, mag'nieton/ *n* a unit in which the magnetic moment of a particle (e g an atom) is measured [ISV *magnet-* + [2]*-on*]

magnetopause /mag'neetoh,pawz/ *n* the outer boundary of a magnetosphere [*magneto*sphere + L *pausa* stop – more at PAUSE]

mag'neto,sphere /-,sfiə/ *n* a region surrounding a celestial body, specif the earth, in which charged particles are trapped by its magnetic field – **magnetospheric** /-'sferik/ *adj*

mag,neto'striction /-'striksh(ə)n/ *n* the change in the dimensions of a ferromagnetic body caused by magnetization or demagnetization [ISV *magnet-* + *-striction* (as in *constriction*)] – **magnetostrictive** /-'striktiv/ *adj*, **magnetostrictively** *adv*

magnetron /'magnitron/ *n* a thermionic diode that is used with an externally applied magnetic field as a high-power microwave oscillator (e g for a radar transmitter) [blend of *magnet* and *-tron*]

Magnificat /mag'nifikat/ *n* (a musical setting of) the canticle of the Virgin Mary in Luke 1:46–55 [ME, fr L, (it) magnifies, fr *magnificare* to magnify; fr the first word of the canticle]

magnification /,magnifi'kaysh(ə)n/ *n* **1** a magnifying or being magnified **2** the apparent enlargement of an object by a microscope, telescope, etc

magnificent /mag'nifis(ə)nt/ *adj* **1** marked by stately grandeur and splendour **2a** sumptuous in structure and adornment **b** strikingly beautiful or impressive **3** sublime ⟨*her ~ prose*⟩ **4** exceptionally fine or excellent ⟨*a ~ day*⟩ [L *magnificent-*, irreg fr *magnificus* noble, splendid, fr *magnus* great – more at MUCH] – **magnificence** *n*, **magnificently** *adv*

magnify /'magnifie/ *vt* **1** to (falsely) increase in significance **2** to enlarge in fact or in appearance ⟨*a telescope* magnifies *distant objects*⟩ ~ *vi* to have the power of causing objects to appear larger than they are [ME *magnifien*, fr MF *magnifier*, fr L *magnificare*, fr *magnificus*] – **magnifier** *n*

'magnifying ,glass *n* a single optical lens for magnifying

magniloquent /mag'niləkwənt/ *adj* grandiloquent [back-formation fr *magniloquence*, fr L *magniloquentia*, fr *magniloquus* magniloquent, fr *magnus* + *loqui* to speak] – **magniloquence** *n*, **magniloquently** *adv*

magnitude /'magnityoohd/ *n* **1a** (great) size or extent **b** a quantity, number **2** the importance or quality of sthg **3** the apparent brightness of a celestial body, esp a star, measured on a logarithmic scale in which a difference of 5 units corresponds to the multiplication or division of the brightness of light by 100 [ME, fr L *magnitudo*, fr *magnus*]

magnolia /mag'nohli·ə, -lyə/ *n* any of a genus of shrubs and trees with evergreen or deciduous leaves and usu large white, yellow, rose, or purple flowers [NL, genus name, fr Pierre *Magnol* †1715 F botanist]

magnum /'magnəm/ *n* a wine bottle holding twice the usual amount (about 1.5l) [L, neut of *magnus* great]

,magnum 'opus /'ohpəs/ *n* the greatest achievement of an artist, writer, etc [L, great work]

magpie /'magpie/ *n* **1** any of numerous birds of the crow family with a very long tail and black-and-white plumage **2** one who chatters noisily **3** one who collects objects in a random fashion [*Mag* (nickname for *Margaret*) + *pie*]

maguey /'magway/ *n* (a hard fibre obtained from) any of various fleshy-leaved agave plants [Sp, fr Taino]

magus /'maygəs/ *n, pl* **magi** /-jie/ **1a** a member of a Zoroastrian hereditary priestly class in ancient Persia **b** *often cap* any of the traditionally 3 wise men from the East who paid homage to the infant Jesus **2** a magician, sorcerer [ME, fr L, fr Gk *magos* – more at MAGIC]

Magyar /'magyah/ *n* (the language of) a member of the Finno-Ugric people of Hungary [Hung] – **Magyar** *adj*

maharajah, maharaja /,mah·hah'rahjə/ *n* a Hindu prince ranking above a rajah [Skt *mahārāja*, fr *mahat* great + *rājan* raja; akin to Gk *megas* great – more at MUCH]

maharani, maharanee /,mah·hah'rahnee/ *n* **1** the wife of a maharaja **2** a Hindu princess ranking above a rani [Hindi *mahārānī*, fr *mahā* great (fr Skt *mahat*) + *rānī* rani]

maharishi /,mah·hah'rishi/ *n* a Hindu teacher of mystical knowledge [Skt *mahārṣi*, fr *mahat* + *ṛṣi* sage and poet]

mahatma /mah'hatmə/ *n* a person revered for outstanding moral and spiritual qualities – used as a title of honour, esp by Hindus [Skt *mahātman*, fr *mahātman* great-souled, fr *mahat* + *ātman* soul – more at ATMAN]

Mahayana /ˌmah·həˈyahnə/ *n* a liberal and theistic branch of Buddhism prevalent in Tibet, China, and Japan that teaches social concern and universal salvation – compare THERAVADA [Skt *mahāyāna*, lit., great vehicle] – **Mahayanist** *n*, **Mahayanistic** /ˌmah·həyahˈnistik/ *adj*

Mahdi /ˈmahdi/ *n* (a leader claiming to be) the expected messiah of Muslim tradition [Ar *mahdīy*, lit., one rightly guided] – **Mahdism** *n*, **Mahdist** *n*

mah-jong, mah-jongg /ˌmah ˈjong/ *n* a game of Chinese origin usu played by 4 people with 144 tiles that are drawn and discarded until one player secures a winning hand [Chin *ma-ch'iao*, lit., sparrows]

mahlstick /ˈmawlˌstik/ *n* a maulstick

mahogany /məˈhog(ə)ni/ *n* **1** (any of various tropical, esp W Indian, trees that yield) a durable usu reddish-brown moderately hard and heavy wood, widely used for fine cabinetwork **2** the reddish-brown colour of mahogany [origin unknown]

mahout /məˈhowt/ *n* a keeper and driver of an elephant [Hindi *mahāwat, mahāut*]

Mahratta /məˈrahtə/ *n* a Maratha

maid /mayd/ *n* **1** an unmarried girl or woman; *also* a female virgin **2** a female servant [ME *maide*, short for *maiden*]

maidan /mieˈdahn/ *n* a parade ground or esplanade in Asia [Hindi *maidān*, fr Ar]

[1]**maiden** /ˈmayd(ə)n/ *n* **1** an unmarried girl or woman **2** a former Scottish beheading device like a guillotine **3** a horse that has never won a race **4 maiden, maiden over** an over in cricket in which no runs are credited to the batsman [ME, fr OE *mægden, mæden*, dim. of *mægeth*; akin to OHG *magad* maiden, OIr *mug* serf, *macc* son] – **maidenly** *adj*, **maidenliness** *n*, **maidenhood** /-hood/ *n*

[2]**maiden** *adj* **1a(1)** not married **(2)** VIRGIN 2, 3 **b** *of a female animal* never having borne young or been mated **c** that has not been altered from its original state **2** being the first or earliest of its kind ⟨*the ship's ~ voyage*⟩

ˈmaidenˌhair /-ˌheə/ *n* any of a genus of ferns with fronds that have delicate spreading branches

ˈmaidenhair ˌtree *n* a ginkgo

ˈmaidenˌhead /-ˌhed/ *n* **1** virginity **2** the hymen [ME *maidenhed*, fr *maiden* + *-hed* -hood; akin to ME *-hod* -hood]

ˈmaiden ˌname *n* the surname of a woman prior to marriage

ˌmaid of ˈhonour *n, pl* **maids of honour** **1** a bride's principal unmarried wedding attendant **2** a puff pastry tartlet filled with custard

ˈmaidˌservant /-ˌsuhv(ə)nt/ *n* a female servant

maieutic /mayˈyoohtik/ *adj* of or resembling the Socratic method of eliciting ideas latent in the mind of another [Gk *maieutikos* of midwifery]

maigre /ˈmaygə/ *adj* **1** *of days in the calendar of the Roman Catholic church* prescribed for fasting or for not eating meat **2** suitable for eating on maigre days; *specif* not containing meat (juices) [F, lit., meagre, fr MF]

[1]**mail** /mayl/ *n* **1a** a bag of posted items conveyed from one post office to another **b** the postal matter that makes up 1 particular consignment **c** a conveyance that transports mail **2** a postal system [ME *male* pack, bag, fr OF, of Gmc origin; akin to OHG *malaha* bag]

[2]**mail** *vt* [4]POST 1 – **mailable** *adj*

[3]**mail** *n* **1** armour made of interlocking metal rings, chains, or sometimes plates **2** a hard enclosing covering of an animal [ME *maille*, fr MF, fr L *macula* spot, mesh] – **mailed** *adj*

[4]**mail** *vt* to clothe (as if) with mail

ˈmailˌbag /-ˌbag/ *n* a bag used to carry mail

ˈmailˌbox /-ˌboks/ *n, NAm* a letter box

ˈmailing ˌlist /ˈmayling/ *n* an organization's list of the names and addresses to which it regularly sends information

ˈmailˌman /-ˌman/ *n, NAm* a postman

ˈmail ˌorder *n* an order for goods that is received and fulfilled by post – **mail-order** *adj*

maim /maym/ *vt* to mutilate, disfigure, or wound seriously; cripple [ME *maynhen, maymen*, fr OF *maynier*] – **maimer** *n*

[1]**main** /mayn/ *n* **1** physical strength – in *with might and main* **2** the chief or essential part – chiefly in *in the main* **3** the chief pipe, duct, or cable of a public service (e g gas, electricity, or water) – often pl with sing. meaning ⟨*turned the electricity off at the ~s*⟩ **4a** a mainland **b** the high sea ***USE*** (*4*) chiefly poetic or archaic [(1) ME, fr OE *mægen*; akin to OHG *magan* strength, OE *magan* to be able; (2, 3, 4) [2]*main* or by shortening – more at MAY]

[2]**main** *adj* **1** chief, principal **2** fully exerted ⟨*used ~ force*⟩ **3** connected with or located near the mainmast or mainsail ☞ SHIP **4** *of a clause* able to stand alone (e g *he laughed* in *he laughed when he heard*) [ME, fr OE *maegen-*, fr *mægen* strength]

[3]**main** *n* a number from 4 to 9 inclusive called by a player before throwing the dice in the game of hazard [prob fr [2]*main*]

main chance *n* *the* chance that promises most advantage or profit – esp in *have an eye for the main chance*

ˌmain ˈdeck *n* **1** the highest deck that extends the full width and length of a naval vessel **2** the upper deck of a merchant vessel between the poop and forecastle ***USE*** ☞ SHIP

ˈmainˌframe /-ˌfraym/ *n* a large computer (installation) that is bigger than a minicomputer

ˈmainland /-lənd/ *n* the largest land area of a continent, country, etc, considered in relation to smaller offshore islands – **mainlander** *n*

ˈmainˌline /-ˌlien/ *vb* to inject (a narcotic or other drug of abuse) into a vein – slang – **mainliner** *n*

ˌmain ˈline *n* a principal railway line

ˈmainly /-li/ *adv* in most cases or for the most part; chiefly

ˈmainˌmast /-ˌmahst; *naut* -məst/ *n* (the lowest section of) a sailing vessel's principal mast ☞ SHIP

mains /maynz/ *adj* of or (suitable to be) powered by electricity from the mains ⟨*a ~ razor*⟩

ˈmainˌsail /-ˌsayl; *naut* -s(ə)l/ *n* **1** the lowest square sail on the mainmast of a square-rigged ship ☞ SHIP **2** the principal fore-and-aft sail on the mainmast of a fore-and-aft rigged ship

ˈmain-ˌsequence *adj* of or being a dwarf star, similar to the sun, which is the quiet middle phase of a star's development

ˈmainˌspring /-ˌspring/ *n* **1** the chief spring, esp of a watch or clock **2** the chief motive, agent, or cause

'main,stay /-,stay/ *n* **1** a rope that stretches forwards from a sailing ship's maintop, usu to the foot of the foremast, and provides the chief support of the mainmast **2** a chief support

'main,stream /-,streem/ *n* a prevailing current or direction of activity or influence – **mainstream** *adj*

'Main ,Street *n* (a place where people hold) materialistic self-satisfied ideals [*Main Street*, novel by Sinclair Lewis †1951 US novelist] – **Main Streeter** *n*

maintain /mayn'tayn/ *vt* **1** to keep in an existing state (e g of operation, repair, efficiency, or validity) **2** to sustain against opposition or danger **3** to continue or persevere in **4** to support, sustain, or provide for ⟨*has a family to* ~⟩ **5** to affirm (as if) in argument [ME *mainteinen*, fr OF *maintenir*, fr ML *manutenēre*, fr L *manu tenēre* to hold in the hand] – **maintainable** *adj*, **maintainer** *n*

maintained school *n* a school provided, controlled, or aided by a British local education authority

maintenance /'mayntinəns/ *n* **1** maintaining or being maintained **2** (payment for) the upkeep of property or equipment **3** *chiefly Br* payments for the support of one spouse by another, esp of a woman by a man, pending or following legal separation or divorce [ME, fr MF, fr OF, fr *maintenir*]

maintop /'mayn,top/ *n* a platform at the top of the mainmast of a square-rigged ship ☞ SHIP

maisonette /,mays(ə)n'et/ *n* **1** a small house **2** a part of a house, usu on 2 floors, let or sold separately [F *maisonnette*, fr OF, dim. of *maison* house, fr L *mansion-*, *mansio* dwelling place – more at MANSION]

[1]maître d'hôtel /,metrə doh'tel/ *n, pl* **maîtres d'hôtel** /~/ **1** a majordomo **2** a headwaiter [F, lit., master of house]

[2]maître d'hôtel *adj* containing or cooked with butter, parsley, and lemon juice ⟨~ *butter*⟩

maize /mayz/ *n* (the ears or edible seeds of) a tall widely cultivated cereal grass bearing seeds on elongated ears [Sp *maíz*, fr Taino *mahiz*]

majesty /'majəsti/ *n* **1** sovereign power **2** – used in addressing or referring to a king or queen ⟨*Your* Majesty⟩ **3a** impressive bearing or aspect **b** greatness or splendour of quality or character [ME *maieste*, fr OF *majesté*, fr L *majestat-*, *majestas*; akin to L *major* greater] – **majestic** /mə'jestik/ *adj*, **majestically** *adv*

majolica /mə'jolikə, -'yol-/ *n* a type of early Italian tin-glazed earthenware [It *maiolica*, fr ML *Majolica* Majorca, largest of the Balearic Islands, fr LL *Majorica*]

[1]major /'mayjə/ *adj* **1a** greater in importance, size, rank, or degree ⟨*one of our* ~ *poets*⟩ **b** of considerable importance ⟨*a* ~ *improvement*⟩ **2** having attained the age of majority **3** notable or conspicuous in effect or scope **4** involving serious risk to life; serious ⟨*a* ~ *operation*⟩ **5a** *esp of a scale or mode* having semitones between the third and fourth and the seventh and eighth degrees **b** being or based on a (specified) major scale ⟨*in a* ~ *key*⟩ ⟨*a piece in D* ~⟩ **c** being an interval (equivalent to that) between the first and the second, third, sixth, or seventh degree of a major scale **d** *of a chord* having an interval of a major third between the root and the next note above it [ME *maiour*, fr L *major*, compar of *magnus* great, large – more at MUCH]

[2]major *n* **1** one who has attained the age of majority **2** a major musical interval, scale, key, or mode **3** ☞ RANK

major axis *n* the chord of an ellipse passing through its focuses ☞ MATHEMATICS

majordomo /,mayjə'dohmoh/ *n, pl* **majordomos** **1** a man having charge of a large household (e g a palace) **2** a butler or steward [Sp *mayordomo* or obs It *maiordomo*, fr ML *major domus*, lit., chief of the house]

majorette /,mayjə'ret/ *n* a girl or woman who twirls a baton and accompanies a marching band [short for *drum majorette*, fem of *drum major* leader of a marching band]

,major 'general *n* ☞ RANK [F *major général*, fr *major*, n + *général*, adj, general]

majority /mə'jorəti/ *n* **1** the (status of one who has attained the) age at which full legal rights and responsibilities are acquired **2a** a number greater than half of a total **b** the amount by which such a greater number exceeds the remaining smaller number **3** the greatest in number of 2 or more groups constituting a whole; *specif* (the excess of votes over its rival obtained by) a group having sufficient votes to obtain control **4** the military office, rank, or commission of a major [1MAJOR + -ITY]

major league *n* a league of highest classification in US sport, esp baseball

major order *n* **1** the priesthood in the Roman Catholic church **2** the offices of bishop, priest, or deacon in the Orthodox or Anglican church ***USE*** usu pl

'major ,suit *n* either of the suits of hearts or spades that are of superior scoring value in bridge – compare MINOR SUIT

majuscule /'majiskyoohl/ *n* (a letter in) a style of handwriting employing only capital or uncial letters – compare MINUSCULE [F, fr L *majusculus* rather large, dim. of *major*] – **majuscule** *adj*, **majuscular** /mə'juskyoolə/ *adj*

makar /'mahkə, 'may-/ *n*, *Scot* a poet [ME *maker* maker, poet]

[1]make /mayk/ *vb* **made** /mayd/ *vt* **1a** to create or produce (for someone) by work or action ⟨~ *a dress*⟩ ⟨made *in Korea*⟩ ⟨*she* made *herself a cup of coffee*⟩ **b** to cause; BRING ABOUT ⟨~ *a disturbance*⟩ ⟨~ *peace*⟩ **2** to formulate in the mind ⟨~ *plans*⟩ ⟨~ *no doubt about it*⟩ **3** to put together from ingredients or components ⟨*butter is* made *from milk*⟩ – often + *up* **4** to compute or estimate to be ⟨*what time do you* ~ *it?*⟩ **5a** to assemble and set alight the materials for (a fire) **b** to renew or straighten the bedclothes on (a bed) **c** to shuffle (a pack of cards) in preparation for dealing **6a** to cause to be or become ⟨made *him bishop*⟩ ⟨*couldn't* ~ *himself heard*⟩ **b** to cause (sthg) to appear or seem to; represent as ⟨*in the film they* ~ *the battle take place in winter*⟩ **c(1)** to change, transform ⟨~ *the material into a skirt*⟩ **(2)** to produce as an end product ⟨*the navy will* ~ *a man of you*⟩ **d** to carry on right through (a period) ⟨*take sandwiches and* ~ *a day of it*⟩ **7a** to enact, establish ⟨~ *laws*⟩ **b** to draft or produce a version of ⟨~ *a will*⟩ **8** to cause (an electric circuit) to be completed **9a** to perform; CARRY OUT ⟨~ *a speech*⟩ ⟨~ *a discovery*⟩ ⟨~ *a sweeping gesture*⟩ ⟨~ *a detour*⟩ **b** to eat ⟨~ *a good breakfast*⟩ **c** to put forward for acceptance ⟨~ *an offer*⟩ ⟨~ *a promise*⟩ **10** to cause to act in a specified way; compel ⟨*rain* ~s *the flowers grow*⟩ ⟨*she was* made *to give in*⟩ **11a** to amount to; count as ⟨*4 and 4* ~ *8*⟩ ⟨~s *a great difference*⟩ **b** to be integral or essential to the existence or success of ⟨*it* made *my day*⟩ **c** to combine to form ⟨*hydrogen and oxygen* ~ *water*⟩ **12** to be capable of becoming or of serving as ⟨*you'll* ~ *a lexicographer yet*⟩ **13** to reach, attain ⟨*never* ~ *the airfield*⟩ ⟨*the story* made *the papers*⟩ – often + *it* ⟨*you'll never* ~ *it that far*⟩ **14** to gain (e g money) by working, trading, dealing, etc **15a** to act so as to acquire ⟨~ *enemies*⟩ **b** to score (points, runs, etc) in a game or sport **16a** to fulfil (a contract) in bridge or another card game **b** to win a trick with (a card) **17** to persuade to consent to sexual intercourse – infml ~ *vi* **1a** to behave so as to seem ⟨made *as though he were angry*⟩ **b** to behave as if beginning a specified action ⟨made *as if to hand it over*⟩ **c** to act so as to be ⟨~ *ready to leave*⟩ **2** to set out or go (in a specified direction) ⟨made *towards the door*⟩ ⟨*we're* making *for the coast*⟩ **3** to undergo manufacture or processing – usu + *up* ⟨*the silk* ~s *up beautifully*⟩ [ME *maken*, fr OE *macian*; akin to OHG *mahhōn* to prepare, make, OSlav *mazati* to anoint] – **maker** *n* – **as near as makes no difference** almost exactly – **make a book** to take bets *on* – **make a meal of** *Br* to make more of than is necessary or tactful – **make an exhibition of oneself** to behave foolishly in public – **make away with 1** MAKE OFF WITH ⟨*the thief* made away with *her handbag*⟩ **2** to destroy – **make believe** to pretend, feign – **make bold** to venture, dare ⟨made *so* bold *as to ask for more*⟩ – **make certain/sure 1** to ascertain by enquiry **2** to take measures to ensure ⟨make certain *of a seat*⟩ – **make do** to get along or manage with the means at hand – **make ends meet** to live within one's income – **make eyes** to ogle – + *at* – **make fast** to tie or attach firmly – **make for** to be conducive to ⟨*courtesy* makes for *safer driving*⟩ – **make free with** to take excessive or disrespectful liberties with – **make friends 1** to acquire friends **2** to become friendly ⟨make friends *with a neighbour*⟩ – **make fun of** to make an object of amusement or ridicule – **make good 1** MAKE UP *vt* 4 **2** to be successful in life **3** *chiefly Br* to repair ⟨make good *the brickwork under the window*⟩ – **make head or tail of** to understand in the least ⟨*I can't make* head or tail of *it*⟩ – **make it 1** to be successful ⟨*actors trying to* make it *in the big time*⟩ – infml **2** to achieve sexual intercourse – slang – **make like** to act the part of; imitate – slang – **make love 1** to woo, court; *also* to pet, neck **2** to engage in sexual intercourse – **make no bones** to have no hesitation or shame ⟨makes no bones *about giving her opinion*⟩ – **make of 1** to attribute a specified degree of significance to ⟨*tends to* make *too much* of *his problems*⟩ **2** to understand by; conclude as to the meaning of ⟨*could* make *nothing* of *the play*⟩ – **make oneself scarce** to hide or avoid sby or sthg unobtrusively – **make public** to disclose – **make the grade** MAKE IT 1 – **make tracks** to leave ⟨*its getting late; we'll have to* make tracks⟩ – infml – **make water** to urinate – euph – **make way** to give room ⟨*the crowd* made way *for the ambulance*⟩ – **make with** *chiefly NAm* to produce, perform – usu + *the*; slang

[2]**make** *n* **1a** the manner or style in which sthg is constructed **b** a place or origin of manufacture; BRAND 3a **2** the physical, mental, or moral constitution of a person **3** the type or process of making or manufacturing – **on the make 1** rising or attempting to rise to a higher social or financial status **2** *NAm* in search of a sexual partner or sexual adventure

'make-be,lieve *n or adj* (sthg) imaginary or pretended

make off *vi* to leave in haste – **make off with** to take away; steal

make out *vt* **1** to draw up in writing **2** to complete (e g a printed form or document) by writing information in appropriate spaces **3** to find or grasp the meaning of ⟨*tried to* make out *what had happened*⟩ **4** to claim or pretend to be true ⟨made out *that he had never heard of me*⟩ **5** to identify (e g by sight or hearing) with difficulty or effort ~ *vi* **1** to fare, manage ⟨*how is he* making out *in his new job?*⟩ **2** *chiefly NAm* to engage in sexual intercourse – slang

make over *vt* **1** to transfer the title of (property) ⟨made over *the estate to his eldest son*⟩ **2** *chiefly NAm* to remake, remodel ⟨made *the whole house* over⟩

Maker /'maykə/ *n* GOD 1 [[1]MAKE + [2]-ER]

'make,ready /-,redi/ *n* final preparation for printing

'make,shift /-,shift/ *adj or n* (being) a crude and temporary expedient

'make-,up *n* **1a** the way in which the parts of sthg are put together **b** physical, mental, and moral constitution **2a** cosmetics (e g lipstick and mascara) applied, esp to the face, to give colour or emphasis **b** the effect achieved by the application of make-up **c** materials (e g wigs and cosmetics) used for special costuming (e g for a play)

make up *vt* **1a** to invent (e g a story), esp in order to deceive **b** to set (an account) in order **2a** to arrange typeset matter into (columns or pages) for printing **b** to produce (e g clothes) by cutting and sewing **c** PREPARE 3a ⟨make up *a prescription*⟩ **3** to wrap or fasten up ⟨make *the books* up *into a parcel*⟩ **4** to compensate for (a deficiency); *esp* to make (e g a required amount or number) complete **5** to settle, decide ⟨made up *his mind to leave*⟩ ⟨made up *their differences*⟩ **6a** to prepare in physical appearance for a role **b** to apply cosmetics to ~ *vi* **1** to become reconciled **2** to compensate *for* ⟨*we* made up *for lost time*⟩ **3** to put on costumes or make-up (e g for a play) **4** to assemble a finished article; *esp* to complete a garment by sewing together

'make,weight /-,wayt/ *n* **1** sthg added to bring a weight to a desired value **2** sthg of little intrinsic value thrown in to fill a gap

making /'mayking/ *n* **1** a process or means of advancement or success **2a** the essential qualities for becoming – often pl with sing. meaning ⟨*had the* ~s *of a great artist*⟩ **b** *pl, chiefly NAm & Austr* paper and tobacco used for rolling one's own cigarettes [[1]MAKE + [2]-ING] – **in the making** in the process of becoming, forming, or developing

mako /'mahkoh/, **mako shark** *n, pl* **makos** either of 2 species of shark that are notable sport fish [Maori]

makuta /mah'koohtə/ *pl of* LIKUTA

mal- *comb form* **1a** bad ⟨mal*practice*⟩; faulty ⟨mal*function*⟩ **b** badly ⟨mal*odorous*⟩; deficiently ⟨mal*nourished*⟩ **2a** abnormal ⟨mal*formation*⟩ **b** abnormally ⟨mal*formed*⟩ **3** not ⟨mal*content*⟩ ⟨mal*adroit*⟩ [ME, fr MF, fr OF, fr *mal* bad (fr L *malus*) & *mal* badly, fr L *male*, fr *malus* – more at SMALL]

malabsorption /maləb'zawpsh(ə)n; *also* -əb'saw-/ *n* the deficient absorption of food substances, vitamins, etc (e g vitamin B_{12}) from the stomach and intestines

malac-, malaco- *comb form* soft ⟨malacoid⟩ [L, fr Gk *malak-, malako-*, fr *malakos*; akin to L *molere* to grind]

ma'lacca ,cane /mə'lakə/ *n* an often mottled cane from an Asiatic rattan palm used esp for walking sticks [*Malacca*, city & state in Malaya]

Malachi /'malə,kie/ *n* a prophetic book of the Old Testament [Heb *Mal'ākhī*]

malachite /'malə,kiet/ *n* hydrated copper carbonate occurring as a green mineral and used esp for ornaments [ME *melochites*, fr L *molochites*, fr Gk *molochitēs*, fr *molochē* mallow]

malacology /,malə'koləji/ *n* a branch of zoology dealing with molluscs [F *malacologie*, contr of *malacozoologie*, fr NL *Malacozoa*, zoological group including soft-bodied animals (fr *malac-* + *-zoa*) + F *-logie* -logy] – **malacologist** *n*, **malacological** /-kə'lojikl/ *adj*

malacostracan /,malə'kostrəkən/ *n* any of a major subclass of crustaceans including the crabs, woodlice, lobsters, shrimps, etc [deriv of Gk *malakostrakos* soft-shelled, fr *malak-* + *ostrakon* shell – more at OYSTER] – **malacostracan** *adj*

maladjusted /,malə'justid/ *adj* poorly or inadequately adjusted, specif to one's social environment and conditions of life – **maladjustment** *n*

maladministration /,malədmini'straysh(ə)n/ *n* incompetent or corrupt administration, esp in public office – **maladminister** /-'ministə/ *vt*

maladroit /malə'droyt/ *adj* clumsy, inept [F, fr MF, fr *mal-* + *adroit*]

malady /'malədi/ *n* an animal disease or disorder [ME *maladie*, fr OF, fr *malade* sick, fr L *male habitus* in bad condition]

Malaga /'maləgə/ *n* a usu sweet fortified wine from the Málaga region of Spain

Malagasy /,malə'gasi/ *n, pl* **Malagasy** *also* **Malagasies** (the language of) a native or inhabitant of the Malagasy Republic ☞ LANGUAGE [*Malagasy* Republic (Madagascar), island in Indian Ocean] – **Malagasy** *adj*

malaise /ma'lez, -'layz/ *n* **1** an indeterminate feeling of debility or lack of health, often accompanying the start of an illness **2** a vague sense of mental or moral unease [F *malaise*, fr OF, fr *mal-* + *aise* comfort – more at EASE]

malapropism /'malәpro,piz(ә)m/ *n* (an instance of) an incongruous misapplication of a word (e g in 'always said 'polobears' and 'neonstockings' ' – *Time*) [Mrs *Malaprop*, character often misusing words in *The Rivals*, comedy by R B Sheridan †1816 Ir dramatist]

malaria /mə'leəri·ə/ *n* a disease caused by protozoan parasites in the red blood cells, transmitted by the bite of mosquitoes, and characterized by periodic attacks of chills and fever [It, fr *mala aria* bad air] – **malarious** *adj*, **malarial** *adj*, **malarian** *adj*

malarkey /mə'lahki/ *n* foolishness; *esp* insincere or foolish talk – infml [origin unknown]

malate /'malayt, 'may-/ *n* a salt or ester of malic acid

malathion /,malə'thie,on, -ən/ *n* an insecticide less poisonous to mammals than parathion [fr *Malathion*, a trademark]

Malay /mə'lay/ *n* (the language of) a member of a people of the Malay peninsula and adjacent islands ☞ LANGUAGE [obs D *Malayo* (now *Maleier*), fr Malay *Mĕlayu*] – **Malay** *adj*, **Malayan** *n or adj*

Malayalam /mə'layəlam, ,mali'ahləm/ *n* a Dravidian language of SW India ☞ LANGUAGE

Malayo- /məlayoh-/ *comb form* Malayan and ⟨Malayo-*Indonesian*⟩

[1]**malcontent** /,malkən'tent/ *n* a discontented person; *esp* sby violently opposed to a government or regime

[2]**malcontent, malcontented** *adj* dissatisfied with the existing state of affairs [MF, fr OF, fr *mal-* + *content*]

mal de mer /,mal də 'meə/ *n* seasickness [F]

[1]**male** /mayl/ *adj* **1a(1)** of or being the sex that produces relatively small sperms, spermatozoids, or spermatozoa by which the eggs of a female are made fertile **(2)** *of a plant or flower* having stamens but no ovaries **b(1)** (characteristic) of the male sex **(2)** made up of male individuals **2** designed for fitting into a corresponding hollow part [ME, fr MF *masle, male*, adj & n, fr L *masculus*, dim. of *mar-, mas* male] – **maleness** *n*

[2]**male** *n* a male person, animal, or plant ☞ SYMBOL

,male 'chauvinist *n* a man who believes in the inherent superiority of men over women and is excessively loyal to his own sex – **male chauvinism** *n*

,male ,chauvinist 'pig *n* MALE CHAUVINIST – derog

malediction /,malə'diksh(ə)n/ *n* a curse – fml [ME *malediccioun*, fr LL *malediction-, maledictio*, fr *maledictus*, pp of *maledicere* to curse, fr L, to speak evil of, fr *male* badly + *dicere* to speak, say – more at MAL-, DICTION] – **maledictory** /-'dikt(ə)ri/ *adj*

malefaction /,mali'faksh(ə)n/ *n* an evil deed – fml

malefactor /'mali,faktə/ *n* **1** a criminal; *esp* a felon **2** one who does evil – fml [ME, fr L, fr *malefactus*, pp of *malefacere* to do evil, fr *male* + *facere* to do – more at [1]DO]

male fern *n* a fern from which an extract is obtained that is used to treat tapeworm infestation

malefic /mə'lefik/ *adj* **1** having malignant influence **2** harmful, malicious *USE* fml [L *maleficus* wicked, mischievous, fr *male*] – **maleficence** /-fis(ə)ns/ *n*, **maleficent** /-fis(ə)nt/ *adj*

malevolent /mə'levələnt/ *adj* having, showing, or arising from an often intense desire to do harm [L *malevolent-, malevolens*, fr *male* badly + *volent-, volens*, prp of *velle* to wish – more at MAL-, [1]WILL] – **malevolence** *n*, **malevolently** *adv*

malfeasance /mal'feez(ə)ns/ *n* (official) misconduct [*mal-* + obs *feasance* (doing, execution)]

malformation /,malfaw'maysh(ə)n/ *n* anomalous, abnormal, or faulty formation or structure – **malformed** *adj*

,mal'function /-'fungksh(ə)n/ *vi* to fail to operate in the normal manner – **malfunction** *n*

,malic 'acid /'malik/ *n* an acid found in the juices of certain fruits (e g apples) and other plants [F *acide malique*, fr L *malum* apple, fr Gk *mēlon, malon*]

malice /'malis/ *n* conscious desire to harm; *esp* a premeditated desire to commit a crime [ME, fr OF, fr L *malitia*, fr *malus* bad – more at SMALL] – **malicious** /mə'lishəs/ *adj*, **maliciously** *adv*, **maliciousness** *n*

,malice a'forethought *n* that which is said to accompany the doing of any act known in advance to be capable of causing serious harm; *specif* that which must be proved in order to make a killing an act of murder

[1]**malign** /mə'lien/ *adj* **1a** harmful in nature, influence, or effect **b** *of a disease* malignant, virulent **2** bearing or showing (vicious) ill will or hostility [ME *maligne*, fr MF, fr L *malignus*, fr *male* badly + *gignere* to beget – more at MAL-, KIN]

[2]**malign** *vt* to utter injuriously (false) reports about; speak ill of [ME *malignen*, fr MF *maligner* to act maliciously, fr LL *malignari*, fr L *malignus*]

malignant /mə'lignənt/ *adj* **1a** harmful in nature, influence, or effect **b** passionately and relentlessly malevolent **2** *of a disease* very severe or deadly ⟨~ *malaria*⟩; *specif, of a tumour* tending to infiltrate, spread, and cause death [LL *malignant-, malignans*, prp of *malignari*] – **malignantly** *adv*, **malignancy** /-nənsi/ *n*

malinger /mə'ling·gə/ *vi* to pretend illness or incapacity so as to avoid duty or work [F *malingre* sickly] – **malingerer** *n*

mall /mawl, mal/ *n* **1** a public promenade, often bordered by trees **2** *NAm* a shopping precinct, usu with associated parking space [The *Mall*, promenade in London, orig an alley used for playing pall-mall (an old game played with balls & mallets)]

mallard /'malahd, -ləd/ *n, pl* **mallards**, *esp collectively* **mallard** a common large wild duck that is the ancestor of the domestic ducks [ME, fr MF *mallart*]

malleable /'mali·əbl/ *adj* **1** *esp of metals* capable of being beaten or rolled into a desired shape **2** easily shaped by outside forces or influences [ME *malliable*, fr MF or ML; MF *malleable*, fr ML *malleabilis*, fr *malleare* to hammer, fr L *malleus* hammer; akin to L *molere* to grind – more at [2]MEAL] – **malleableness** *n*, **malleability** /,mali·ə'biləti/ *n*

mallee /'mali/ *n* (a dense thicket or growth of) any of several low-growing shrubby Australian eucalyptuses [native name in Australia]

mallet /'malit/ *n* **1** a hammer with a usu large head of wood, plastic, etc **2** an implement with a large usu cylindrical wooden head for striking the ball in croquet, polo, etc **3** a light hammer with a small rounded or spherical usu padded head used in playing certain musical instruments (e g a vibraphone) [ME *maillet*, fr MF, fr OF, dim. of *mail* hammer, fr L *malleus*]

malleus /'mali·əs/ *n, pl* **mallei** /-li,ie/ the outermost of the chain of 3 small bones that transmit sound to the inner ear of mammals; the hammer ☞ NERVE [NL, fr L, hammer]

mallow /'maloh/ *n* any of various related plants with usu deeply cut lobed leaves and showy flowers [ME *malwe*, fr OE *mealwe*, fr L *malva*]

malm /mahm/ *n* a soft crumbly limestone (soil) [ME *malme*, fr OE *mealm-*; akin to OE *melu* meal – more at [2]MEAL]

malmsey /'mahmzi/ *n, often cap* the sweetest variety of Madeira [ME *malmesey*, fr ML *Malmasia* Monemvasia, village in Greece where it was orig produced]

malnutrition /,malnyooh'trish(ə)n/ *n* faulty or inadequate nutrition

,mal'odorous /-'ohd(ə)rəs/ *adj* smelling bad – fml

Malpighian tubule /mal'pigi·ən/ *n* any of a group of long vessels that open into the alimentary canal in insects and other arthropods and function esp as excretory organs [Marcello *Malpighi* †1694 It anatomist]

malpractice /mal'praktis/ *n* **1** failure to exercise due professional skill or care **2** an instance of improper conduct; malfeasance – **malpractitioner** /,malprak'tish(ə)nə/ *n*

[1]**malt** /mawlt/ *n* **1** grain softened in water, allowed to germinate, then roasted and used esp in brewing and distilling **2** unblended malt whisky produced in a particular area ⟨*the finest Highland* ~s⟩ [ME, fr OE *mealt*; akin to OHG *malz* malt, OE *meltan* to melt] – **malty** *adj*

[2]**malt** *vt* **1** to convert into malt **2** to make or treat with malt or malt extract ~ *vi* to become malt

Maltese /mawl'teez/ *n, pl* **Maltese** (the language of) a native or inhabitant of Malta ☞ LANGUAGE [*Malta*, island in the Mediterranean] – **Maltese** *adj*

,Maltese 'cross *n* a cross consisting of 4 equal arms that widen out from the centre and have their outer ends indented by a V ☞ SYMBOL

Malthusian /mal'thyoohzh(ə)n, -zi·ən/ *adj* of Malthus or his theory that population tends to increase faster than its means of subsistence and that widespread poverty inevitably results unless population growth is checked [Thomas *Malthus* †1834 E economist] – **Malthusian** *n*

maltings /'mawltingz/ *n, pl* **maltings** an establishment where malt is prepared and stored

maltose /'mawltohz, -tohs/ *n* a sugar formed esp from starch by amylase [F, fr E [1]*malt*]

maltreat /,mal'treet/ *vt* to treat cruelly or roughly [F *maltraiter*, fr MF, fr *mal-* + *traiter* to treat, fr OF *traitier* – more at TREAT] – **maltreatment** *n*

,malt 'whisky *n* whisky distilled from malted barley

malversation /,malvuh'saysh(ə)n/ *n* corruption in office – fml [MF, fr *malverser* to be corrupt, fr *mal* + *verser* to turn, handle, fr L *versare*, fr *versus*, pp of *vertere* to turn – more at [1]WORTH]

mam /mam/ *n, dial Br* [1]MOTHER 1a [short for *mama*]

[1]**mama, mamma** /mə'mah/ *n* [1]MOTHER 1a – formerly used in address [baby talk]

[2]**mama, mamma** /'mumə; *NAm* 'mahmə/ *n* mummy – used informally and by children

mamba /'mambə/ *n* any of several (tropical) African venomous snakes related to the cobras but with no hood [Zulu *im-amba*]

mambo /'mamboh/ *n, pl* **mambos** (the music for) a ballroom dance of Haitian origin that resembles the rumba [AmerSp] – **mambo** *vi*

Mameluke /'mami,look/ *n* a member of a politically powerful Egyptian military class occupying the sultanate from 1250 to 1517 [F *mameluk*, fr Ar *mamlūk*, lit., slave]

mamillary, *NAm* **mammillary** /'mamil(ə)ri/ *adj* of or resembling the breasts [L *mamilla, mammilla* breast, nipple] – **mamillate** /-layt/ *adj*, **mamillated** *adj*

mamma /'mamə/ *n, pl* **mammae** /-mi/ a mammary

gland with its accessory parts [L, mother, breast, of baby-talk origin] – **mammate** /-mayt/ *adj*

mammal /ˈmaməl/ *n* any of a class of higher vertebrates comprising humans and all other animals that have mammary glands and nourish their young with milk ☞ EVOLUTION [deriv of LL *mammalis* of the breast, fr L *mamma* breast] – **mammalian** /maˈmayli·ən/ *adj or n*, **mammalogy** /ˌmamәˈloləji/ *n*

mammary /ˈmaməri/ *adj* of, lying near, or affecting the mammary glands

ˈ**mammary** ˌ**gland** *n* the breasts or other large compound modified skin glands in female mammals that secrete milk and are situated on the front of the body in pairs

Mammon /ˈmamən/ *n* material wealth or possessions, esp considered as an evil [LL *mammona*, Gk *mamōna*, fr Aram *māmōnā* riches]

[1]**mammoth** /ˈmaməth/ *n* any of numerous large hairy long-tailed extinct Pleistocene elephants [Russ *mamont, mamot*]

[2]**mammoth** *adj* of very great size

mammy /ˈmami/ *n* **1** mamma, mummy – used esp by children **2** *NAm* a Negro nanny of white children, esp formerly in the southern USA [alter. of *mamma*]

[1]**man** /man/ *n, pl* **men** /men/ **1a(1)** a human being; *esp* an adult male as distinguished from a woman or child **(2)** a man belonging to a usu specified category – usu in combination ⟨*business*man⟩ ⟨*horse*man⟩ **(3)** a husband – esp in *man and wife* **(4)** a male sexual partner **b** the human race **c** a member of a family of biped primate mammals anatomically related to the great apes but distinguished esp by greater brain development and a capacity for articulate speech and abstract reasoning; *broadly* any ancestor of modern man ☞ EVOLUTION **d** one possessing the qualities associated with manhood (e g courage and strength) **e** a fellow, chap – used interjectionally **2a** a feudal vassal **b** *pl* the members of (the ranks of) a military force **c** *pl* the working force as distinguished from the employer and usu the management **d** *pl* the members of a team **3a** an individual, person ⟨*what can a* ~ *do in this situation?*⟩ **b** the most suitable man ⟨*he's your* ~ *for the job*⟩ **4** any of the pieces moved by each player in chess, draughts, etc **5** *often cap, NAm the* police **6** *often cap, NAm the* white establishment – used by Negroes **7** – used interjectionally to express intensity of feeling ⟨~, *what a party!*⟩ *USE* (*5, 6 & 7*) slang [ME, fr OE; akin to OHG *man* man, Skt *manu*] – **manless** *adj*, **manlike** *adj* – **to a man** without exception

[2]**man** *vt* **-nn- 1** to supply with the man or men necessary **2** to take up station by ⟨~ *the pumps*⟩ **3** to serve in the force or complement of

mana /ˈmahnə/ *n* the power of elemental forces embodied in an object or person [of Melanesian & Polynesian origin; akin to Hawaiian & Maori *mana*]

ˌ**man-about-ˈtown** *n, pl* **men-about-town** /men/ a worldly and socially active man

[1]**manacle** /ˈmanəkl/ *n* **1** a shackle or handcuff **2** a restraint *USE* usu pl [ME *manicle*, fr MF, fr L *manicula*, dim. of *manus* hand – more at MANUAL]

[2]**manacle** *vt* **1** to confine (the hands) with manacles **2** to subject to a restraint

manage /ˈmanij/ *vt* **1a** to make and keep submissive **b** to use (e g money) economically **2** to succeed in handling (e g a difficult situation or person) **3** to succeed in accomplishing ⟨*she could only* ~ *a smile*⟩ ⟨*always* ~s *to win*⟩ **4** to conduct the running of (esp a business); *also* to have charge of (e g a sports team or athlete) ~ *vi* to be able to cope with difficulties; *esp* to use one's finances to the best advantage [It *maneggiare*, fr *mano* hand, fr L *manus*] – **manageable** *adj*

ˈ**management** /-mənt/ *n* **1** the act or art of managing **2** *sing or pl in constr* the collective body of those who manage or direct an enterprise

manager /ˈmanijə/, *fem* **manageress** /-jəˌres/ *n* **1** one who conducts business or household affairs **2** sby who directs a sports team, player, entertainer, etc [MANAGE + [2]-ER] – **managership** *n*, **managerial** /ˌmaniˈjiəri·əl/ *adj*

ˌ**managing diˈrector** *n* the chief director of a company, responsible for the overall management of the company's business

mañana /manˈyahnə/ *adv or n* (at) an indefinite time in the future [Sp, lit., tomorrow, fr earlier *cras mañana* early tomorrow, fr *cras* tomorrow (fr L) + *mañana* early, fr L *mane* early in the morning]

ˈ**man** ˌ**ape** *n* an ape-man

ˌ**man-at-ˈarms** *n, pl* **men-at-arms** a (heavily armed and usu mounted) soldier

manatee /ˌmanəˈtee/ *n* any of several (tropical) aquatic plant-eating mammals with broad tails [Sp *manatí*]

Manchu /manˈchooh/ *n, pl* **Manchus,** *esp collectively* **Manchu** (the language of) a member of the orig nomadic native Mongolian race of Manchuria who established a dynasty in China in 1644 ☞ LANGUAGE – **Manchu** *adj*

manciple /ˈmansipl/ *n* a steward or caterer, esp in a college or monastery [ME, fr ML *mancipium* office of steward, fr L, act of purchase, fr *mancip-, manceps* purchaser – more at EMANCIPATE]

Mancunian /mangˈkyoohni·ən/ *n or adj* (a native or inhabitant) of Manchester [LL *Mancunium* Manchester, city in England]

-mancy /-mənsi/ *comb form* (→ *n*) divination ⟨*necro*mancy⟩ [ME *-mancie*, fr OF, fr L *-mantia*, fr Gk *-manteia*, fr *manteia*, fr *mantis* diviner, prophet – more at MANTIS]

mandala /ˈmahndələ/ *n* a Hindu or Buddhist graphic symbol used in ritual and meditation; *specif* a circle enclosing a square with a deity on each of its 4 sides used to represent the universe [Skt *maṇḍala* circle]

mandamus /manˈdayməs/ *n* a judicial writ requiring sthg to be carried out [L, we enjoin, fr *mandare*]

mandarin /ˈmandərin, ˌ--ˈ-/ *n* **1a** a public official in the Chinese Empire ranked according to any of 9 grades **b** a person of position and influence, esp in literary or bureaucratic circles; *esp* an elder and often reactionary member of such a circle **2** *cap* **a** the primarily northern dialect of Chinese used by the court and officials under the Empire **b** the chief dialect of Chinese that has a standard variety spoken in the Peking area **3 mandarin, mandarin orange** (a small spiny Chinese orange tree that bears) a yellow to reddish orange fruit [Pg *mandarim*, fr Malay *mĕntĕri*, fr Skt *mantrin* counsellor, fr *mantra* counsel – more at MANTRA]

ˌ**mandarin ˈcollar** *n* a narrow stand-up collar

ˌ**mandarin** ˈ**duck** *n* a brightly marked crested Asian duck, often found domesticated

[1]**mandate** /ˈmandayt, -dət/ *n* **1** an authoritative command from a superior **2** an authorization to act on the behalf of another; *specif* the political authority given by electors to parliament ⟨*the ~ of the people*⟩ **3a** an order granted by the League of Nations to a member nation for the establishment of a responsible government over a conquered territory **b** a mandated territory [MF & L; MF *mandat*, fr L *mandatum*, fr neut of *mandatus*, pp of *mandare* to entrust, enjoin, prob irreg fr *manus* hand + *-dere* to put – more at MANUAL, [1]DO]

[2]**mandate** /ˈmandayt/ *vt* to administer or assign under a mandate

[1]**mandatory** /ˈmandət(ə)ri/ *adj* **1** containing or constituting a command **2** compulsory, obligatory

[2]**mandatory** *n* a nation or person holding a mandate

mandible /ˈmandibl/ *n* **1a** JAW 1a **b** a lower jaw together with its surrounding soft parts **c** the upper or lower part of a bird's bill **2** any of various mouth parts in insects or other invertebrates for holding or biting food [MF, fr LL *mandibula*, fr L *mandere* to chew – more at MOUTH] – **mandibular** /manˈdibyoolə/ *adj*, **mandibulate** /-ˌlayt/ *adj or n*

mandolin *also* **mandoline** /ˌmandəˈlin/ *n* a musical instrument of the lute family with a fretted neck [It *mandolino*, dim. of *mandola* lute, fr F *mandore*, modif of LL *pandura* 3-stringed lute, fr Gk *pandoura*]

mandragora /manˈdragərə/ *n* mandrake [ME]

mandrake /ˈmandrayk/ *n* (the root of) a Mediterranean plant of the nightshade family with whitish or purple flowers and a large forked supposedly man-shaped root formerly used in medicine [ME, prob alter. of *mandragora*, fr OE, fr L *mandragoras*, fr Gk]

mandrel *also* **mandril** /ˈmandrəl/ *n* **1** an axle or spindle inserted into a hole in a workpiece to support it during machining **2** a metal bar round which material (e g metal) may be cast, shaped, etc [prob modif of F *mandrin*]

mandrill /ˈmandril/ *n* a large gregarious baboon found in W Africa, the male of which has red and blue striped cheeks [prob fr [1]*man* + *drill* (W African baboon), prob native name in W Africa]

mane /mayn/ *n* **1** long thick hair growing about the neck of a horse, male lion, etc ☞ ANATOMY **2** long thick hair on a person's head [ME, fr OE *manu*; akin to OHG *mana* mane, L *monile* necklace]

ˈ**man-ˌeater** *n* a person or animal that eats human flesh – **man-eating** *adj*

manege *also* **manège** /maˈnezh/ *n* **1** a school for training horses and teaching horsemanship **2** the movements or paces of a trained horse [F *manège*, fr It *maneggio* training of a horse, fr *maneggiare* to manage]

manes /ˈmahnayz/ *n pl, often cap* the spirits of the ancient Roman dead to which graveside sacrifices were made [L]

maneuver /məˈnoohvə/ *vb or n, NAm* (to) manoeuvre

manful /ˈmanf(ə)l/ *adj* having courage and resolution – **manfully** *adv*

mangabey /ˈmang·gəbi/ *n* any of a genus of long-tailed African monkeys [*Mangaby*, region of Malagasy Republic]

mangan-, **mangano-** *comb form* manganese ⟨*manganous*⟩ [G *mangan*, fr F *manganèse*]

manganese /ˌmang·gəˈneez/ *n* a greyish white hard divalent or hexavalent metallic element ☞ PERIODIC TABLE [F *manganèse*, fr It *manganese* magnesia, manganese, fr ML *magnesia*] – **manganic** /mangˈganik/ *adj*, **manganous** /ˈmang·gənəs/ *adj*

ˌ**manganese diˈoxide** *n* a dark insoluble compound used esp as an oxidizing agent and in making glass and ceramics

manganin /ˈmang·gənin/ *n* an alloy of copper, manganese, and nickel used esp for electrical resistors

mange /manj, maynj/ *n* any of various contagious skin diseases affecting domestic animals or sometimes human beings, marked by inflammation and loss of hair and caused by a minute parasitic mite [ME *manjewe*, fr MF *mangene* itching, fr *mangier* to eat]

mangel-wurzel /ˈmang·gl ˌwuhzl/, **mangel** *n* a large yellow to orange type of beet grown as food for livestock [G *mangoldwurzel, mangelwurzel*, fr *mangold* beet + *wurzel* root]

manger /ˈmaynjə/ *n* a trough or open box in a stable for holding feed [ME *mangeour, manger*, fr MF *maingeure*, fr *mangier* to eat, fr L *manducare* to chew, devour, fr *manducus* glutton, fr *mandere* to chew – more at MOUTH]

[1]**mangle** /ˈmang·gl/ *vt* **1** to hack or crush (as if) by repeated blows **2** to spoil by poor work, errors, etc [ME *manglen*, fr AF *mangler*, freq of OF *maynier* to maim]

[2]**mangle** *vt or n* (to pass through) a machine with rollers for squeezing water from and pressing laundry [n D *mangel*, fr G, fr MHG, dim. of *mange* mangonel, mangle, fr L *manganum*; vb fr n]

mango /ˈmang·goh/ *n, pl* **mangoes, mangos** (a tropical evergreen tree that bears) a yellowish red fruit with a firm skin, large stone, and juicy edible slightly acid pulp [Pg *manga*, fr Tamil *mān-kāy*]

mangold /ˈmang·gohld, -gəld/ *n* a mangel-wurzel

mangonel /ˈmang·gəˌnel/ *n* a military engine formerly used to throw rocks, stones, etc [ME, fr MF, prob fr ML *manganellus*, dim. of LL *manganum* philtre, mangonel, fr Gk *manganon*; akin to MIr *meng* deception]

mangosteen /ˈmang·gohˌsteen/ *n* (an E Indian tree that bears) a dark reddish brown fruit with thick rind and edible flesh [Malay *mangustan*]

mangrove /ˈmangˌgrohv/ *n* any of a genus of tropical maritime trees or shrubs with prop roots that form dense masses [prob fr Pg *mangue* mangrove (fr Sp *mangle*, fr Taino) + E *grove*]

mangy /ˈmanji, ˈmaynji/ *adj* **1** suffering or resulting from mange **2** having many worn or bare spots

manhandle /manˈhandl, ˈ-ˌ--/ *vt* **1** to move or manage by human force **2** to handle roughly

manhattan /manˈhatn/ *n, often cap* a cocktail consisting of vermouth, whisky, and sometimes a dash of bitters [*Manhattan*, borough of New York City, USA]

manhole /ˈmanˌhohl/ *n* a covered opening through which a person may go, esp to gain access to an underground or enclosed structure (e g a sewer)

ˈ**manhood** /-hood/ *n* **1** manly qualities **2** the condition of being an adult male as distinguished from a child or female **3** *sing or pl in constr* adult males collectively [[1]MAN + -HOOD]

ˈ**man-ˌhour** *n* a unit of 1 hour's work by 1 person,

used esp as a basis for cost accounting and wage calculation

'man,hunt /-,hunt/ *n* an organized hunt for sby, esp a criminal

mania /'maynyə/ *n* **1** abnormal excitement and euphoria marked by mental and physical hyperactivity and disorganization of behaviour **2** excessive or unreasonable enthusiasm – often in combination ⟨*Beatle*mania⟩ [ME, fr LL, fr Gk, fr *mainesthai* to be mad; akin to Gk *menos* spirit – more at MIND]

maniac /'mayniak/ *n* one who is or acts as if (violently) insane; a lunatic – not used technically [LL *maniacus* maniacal, fr Gk *maniakos*, fr *mania*]

maniacal /mə'nie·əkl/ *also* **maniac** /'mayniak/ *adj* **1** affected with or suggestive of madness **2** characterized by ungovernable frenzy

manic /'manik/ *adj* affected by, relating to, or resembling mania – **manic** *n*, **manically** *adv*

,manic-de'pressive *adj* of or affected by a mental disorder characterized by alternating mania and (extreme) depression – **manic-depressive** *n*

Manichaean, Manichean /,mani'kee·ən/, **Manichee** /'mani,kee/ *n* **1** a believer in a religious dualism originating in Persia in the 3rd c AD and teaching the release of the spirit from matter through austere living **2** a believer in religious or philosophical dualism [LL *manichaeus*, fr LGk *manichaios*, fr *Manichaios* Manes † *ab* 276 AD Per founder of the sect] – **Manichaean** *adj*, **Manichaeanism** *n*, **Manichaeism** /'manikee,iz(ə)m/ *n*

¹manicure /'manikyooə/ *n* **1** (a) treatment for the care of the hands and fingernails **2** a manicurist [F, fr L *manus* hand + F *-icure* (as in *pédicure* pedicure) – more at MANUAL]

²manicure *vt* **1** to give a manicure to **2** to trim closely and evenly – **manicurist** *n*

¹manifest /'manifest/ *adj* readily perceived by the senses (e g sight) or mind; obvious [ME, fr MF or L; MF *manifeste*, fr L *manifestus*, lit., hit by the hand, fr *manus* + *-festus* (akin to L in*festus* hostile) – more at DARE] – **manifestly** *adv*

²manifest *vt* to make evident or certain by showing or displaying ~ *vi of a spirit, ghost, etc* to appear in visible form – **manifester** *n*

³manifest *n* a list of passengers or an invoice of cargo, esp for a ship

manifestation /,manife'staysh(ə)n/ *n* a sign (e g materialization) of the presence of a spirit [²MANIFEST + -ATION]

manifesto /,mani'festoh/ *n, pl* **manifestos, manifestoes** a public declaration of intentions, esp by a political party before an election [It, denunciation, indication, fr *manifestare* to manifest, fr L, fr *manifestus*]

¹manifold /'manifohld/ *adj* many and varied [ME, fr OE *manigfeald*, fr *manig* many + *-feald* -fold] – **manifoldly** *adv*, **manifoldness** *n*

²manifold *n* **1** a whole that unites or consists of many diverse elements **2** a hollow fitting (e g connecting the cylinders of an internal combustion engine with the exhaust pipe) with several outlets or inlets for connecting 1 pipe with several other pipes ☞ CAR

³manifold *vt* to make (many) copies of

Manihot /'mani,hot/ *n* a genus of tropical American herbs or shrubs economically important for their fruit (e g cassava) [NL, fr F, cassava, of Tupian origin]

manikin, mannikin /'manikin/ *n* **1** a mannequin **2** a little man [D *mannekijn* little man, fr MD, dim. of *man*; akin to OE *man*]

manila *also* **manilla** /mə'nilə/ *adj, often cap* made of Manila paper or hemp – **manila** *n*

Manila hemp *n* abaca [*Manila*, city in the Philippine Islands]

manila paper *n, often cap M* a strong paper of a brownish or buff colour with a smooth finish, made orig from Manila hemp

manilla /mə'nilə/ *n* a horseshoe-shaped metal bracelet used as money by some peoples of W Africa [Pg *manilha* or Sp *manilla*]

manille /mə'nil/ *n* the second highest trump in various card games (e g ombre) [modif of Sp *malilla*]

,man in the 'street *n* an average or typical person, esp for statistical purposes

manioc /'mani,ok/ *n* cassava [F *manioc* & Sp & Pg *mandioca*, of Tupian origin; akin to Tupi *manioca* cassava]

maniple /'manipl/ *n* **1** a long narrow strip of silk worn at mass over the left arm by clerics of or above the order of subdeacon ☞ GARMENT **2** a subdivision of the ancient Roman legion consisting of either 120 or 60 men [(1) ML *manipulus*, fr L, handful, fr *manus* hand + *-pulus* (akin to L *plēre* to fill); fr its having been originally held in the hand; (2) L *manipulus*, fr *manipulus* handful; fr the custom of using a handful of hay on the end of a pole as a military standard]

manipulate /mə'nipyoolayt/ *vt* **1** to handle or operate, esp skilfully **2a** to manage or use skilfully **b** to control or influence by artful, unfair, or insidious means, esp to one's own advantage **3** to examine and treat (a fracture, sprain, etc) by moving bones into the proper position manually [back-formation fr *manipulation*, fr F, fr *manipule* handful, fr L *manipulus*] – **manipulatable** *adj*, **manipulator** *n*, **manipulative** /-lətiv/ *adj*, **manipulatory** /-'lət(ə)ri/ *adj*, **manipulation** /-'laysh(ə)n/ *n*

,man 'jack *n* individual man ⟨*every* ~⟩

mankind /man'kiend/ *n sing but sing or pl in constr* the human race

'man,like /-,liek/ *adj* resembling or characteristic of **a** a man rather than an animal **b** a man rather than a woman or child

manly /-li/ *adj* (marked by the good qualities) befitting a man – **manliness** *n*

,man-'made *adj* made or produced by human beings rather than nature; *also* synthetic

manna /'manə/ *n* **1** food miraculously supplied to the Israelites in their journey through the wilderness **2** a sudden source of benefit [ME, fr OE, fr LL, fr Gk, fr Heb *mān*]

manned /mand/ *adj* **1** equipped with men **2** *of a spacecraft* carrying a human crew

mannequin /'manikin/ *n* **1** an artist's, tailor's, or dressmaker's model of the human figure; *also* such a model used esp for displaying clothes **2** a woman who models clothing [F, fr D *mannekijn* little man – more at MANIKIN]

manner /'manə/ *n* **1** a kind, sort; *also* sorts ⟨*all ~ of information*⟩ **2a** the mode or method in which sthg is done or happens **b** a method of artistic execution; a style **3** *pl* **a** (rules of) social conduct **b**

social behaviour evaluated as to politeness; *esp* conduct indicating good background ⟨*mind your* ~s!⟩ **4** characteristic or distinctive bearing, air, or deportment [ME *manere*, fr OF *maniere* way of acting, fr (assumed) VL *manuaria*, fr L, fem of *manuarius* of the hand, fr *manus* hand – more at MANUAL] – **mannerless** *adj*

mannered /'manəd/ *adj* **1** having manners of a specified kind – usu in combination ⟨*well*-mannered⟩ **2** having an artificial or stilted character

mannerism /'manə,riz(ə)m/ *n* **1a** exaggerated or affected adherence to a particular style in art or literature **b** *often cap* a style of art in late 16th-c Europe characterized by distortion of the human figure **2** a characteristic (unconscious) gesture or trait; an idiosyncrasy – **mannerist** *n*, **manneristic** /,manə'ristik/ *adj*

¹mannerly /-li/ *adj* showing or having good manners – **mannerliness** *n*, **mannerly** *adv*

mannikin /'manikin/ *n* a manikin

mannish /'manish/ *adj* resembling, befitting, or typical of a man rather than a woman – **mannishly** *adv*, **mannishness** *n*

¹manoeuvre, *NAm chiefly* **maneuver** /mə'noohvə/ *n* **1a** a military or naval movement **b** a (large-scale) training exercise for the armed forces **2** an intended and controlled deviation from a straight and level flight path in the operation of an aircraft **3** a skilful or dexterous movement **4** an adroit and clever management of affairs, often using deception [F *manœuvre*, fr OF *maneuvre* work done by hand, fr ML *manuopera*, fr L *manu operare* to work by hand]

²manoeuvre, *NAm chiefly* **maneuver** *vi* **1** to perform a military or naval manoeuvre (to secure an advantage) **2** to perform a manoeuvre **3** to use stratagems ~ *vt* **1** to cause (e g troops) to execute manoeuvres **2** to manipulate with adroitness **3** to bring about or secure as a result of contriving – **manoeuvrable** *adj*, **manoeuvrer** *n*, **manoeuvrability** /mə,noohv(ə)rə'biləti/ *n*

,Man of 'Kent /kent/ *n* a native or inhabitant of Kent; *specif* one from east of the river Medway – compare KENTISHMAN

,man of 'letters *n* **1** a scholar **2** a reputable author

,man of 'straw *n* **1a** weak or imaginary opposition (e g an argument or adversary) set up only to be easily countered **b** a person set up to serve as a cover for a (questionable) transaction **2** a weak and irresolute person

,man of the 'house *n* the chief male in a household

,man of the 'world *n* a man of wide experience

,man-of-'war *n, pl* **men-of-war** /men/ a warship (of the days of sail)

manometer /mə'nomitə/ *n* an instrument for measuring the pressure of gases and vapours [F *manomètre*, fr Gk *manos* sparse, loose, rare + F *-mètre* – more at MONK] – **manometry** /-tri/ *n*, **manometric** /,manoh'metrik/, **manometrical** *adj*, **manometrically** *adv*

manor /'manə/ *n* **1** a landed estate **2a** a medieval estate under a lord who held a variety of rights over land and tenants, including the right to hold court **b manor, manor house** the house of the lord of a manor **3** a district of police administration – slang [ME *maner*, fr OF *manoir*, fr *manoir* to sojourn, dwell, fr L *manēre* – more at MANSION] – **manorial** /mə'nawri·əl/ *adj*, **manorialism** *n*

'man,power /-,powə/ *n* the total supply of people available for work or service

manqué /'mong,kay (*Fr* mɑ̃ke)/ *adj* that could have been but failed to be – used after the noun modified ⟨*a poet* ~⟩ [F, fr pp of *manquer* to lack, fail]

mansard /'mansahd, -səd/, **mansard roof** *n* a roof with a lower steeper slope and a higher shallower one on all 4 sides ☞ ARCHITECTURE [F *mansarde*, fr François *Mansart* †1666 F architect]

manse /mans/ *n* the residence of an esp Presbyterian or Baptist clergyman [ME *manss* mansion house, fr ML *mansa, mansus, mansum*, fr L *mansus*, pp of *manēre*]

manservant /'man,suhv(ə)nt/ *n, pl* **manservants** a male servant, esp a valet

-manship /-mənship/ *suffix* (→ *n*) art or skill of one who practises ⟨*horse*manship⟩ ⟨*games*manship⟩

mansion /'mansh(ə)n/ *n* **1a** the house of the lord of a manor **b** a large imposing residence **2** a separate apartment in a large structure **3** *archaic* a dwelling [ME, fr MF, fr L *mansion-, mansio*, fr *mansus*, pp of *manēre* to remain, dwell; akin to Gk *menein* to remain]

manslaughter /'man,slawtə/ *n* the unlawful killing of sby without malicious intent

'manta ,ray /'mantə/, **manta** *n* any of several extremely large rays of warm seas [AmerSp *manta*, fr Sp, blanket; fr its being caught in traps resembling large blankets]

mantelet /'manti,let, 'mantlit/ *n* **1** a short loose cape **2** a movable shield or shelter: e g **a** a movable shelter formerly used by besiegers when attacking **b** the movable frontal plate of the turret of an armoured fighting vehicle [ME, fr MF, dim. of *mantel, manteau* mantle]

mantelpiece /'mantl,pees/, **mantel** *n* an ornamental structure round a fireplace; *also* a mantelshelf [MF *mantel*]

'mantel,shelf /-,shelf/, **mantel** *n* a shelf forming part of or above a mantelpiece

mantic /'mantik/ *adj* of divination [Gk *mantikos*, fr *mantis*]

mantilla /man'tilə/ *n* a light scarf worn over the head and shoulders esp by Spanish and Latin-American women [Sp, dim. of *manta*]

mantis /'mantis/ *n, pl* **mantises, mantes** /-teez/ any of several insects that feed on other insects; *esp* PRAYING MANTIS [NL, fr Gk, lit., diviner, prophet; akin to Gk *mainesthai* to be mad – more at MANIA]

mantissa /man'tisə/ *n* the part of a common logarithm following the decimal point [L *mantisa, mantissa* makeweight, fr Etruscan]

¹mantle /'mantl/ *n* **1a** a loose sleeveless garment worn over other clothes; a cloak **b** a mantle regarded as a symbol of preeminence or authority **2a** sthg that covers, envelops, or conceals **b** a fold of a tunicate's, barnacle's, or mollusc's body wall (lining the shell) **3** the feathers covering the back, shoulders,and wings of a bird **4** a lacelike sheath of some reflecting material that gives light by incandescence when placed over a flame **5** the part of the earth or a similar planet that lies between the crust and central core [ME *mantel*, fr OF, fr L *mantellum*]

²mantle *vt* to cover (as if) with a mantle

mantlet /'mantlit/ *n* a mantelet

,man-to-'man *adj* **1** characterized by frankness and honesty **2** of or being a defensive system in soccer, basketball, etc in which each player marks 1 specific opponent

mantra /'mantrə/ *n* a devotional incantation (e g in Hinduism or Buddhism) [Skt, sacred counsel, formula, fr *manyate* he thinks; akin to L *mens* mind – more at MIND]

'man,trap /-,trap/ *n* a trap for catching people

¹manual /'manyooəl/ *adj* **1** of or involving the hands **2** requiring or using physical skill and energy **3** worked or done by hand and not by machine or automatically [ME *manuel*, fr MF, fr L *manualis*, fr *manus* hand; akin to OE *mund* hand, Gk *marē*] – **manually** *adv*

²manual *n* **1** a book of instructions; a handbook **2** the set movements in the handling of a weapon during a military drill or ceremony **3** a keyboard for the hands; *specif* any of the several keyboards of an organ that control separate divisions of the instrument

manubrium /mə'nyoohbri·əm/ *n, pl* **manubria** /-bri·ə/ *also* **manubriums** the section of the sternum nearest the head of human beings and many other mammals [NL, fr L, handle, fr *manus*]

manufactory /,manyoo'fakt(ə)ri/ *n* a factory

¹manufacture /,manyoo'fakchə/ *n* **1** the esp large-scale making of wares by hand or by machinery **2** an industry using mechanical power and machinery **3** the act or process of producing sthg [MF, fr L *manu factus* made by hand]

²manufacture *vt* **1** to make (materials) into a product suitable for use **2** to make (wares) from raw materials by hand or by machinery, esp on a large scale **3** to invent, fabricate **4** to produce as if by manufacturing ⟨*writers who ~ stories for television*⟩ – **manufacturing** *n*

manufacturer /,manyoo'fakchərə/ *n* an employer in a manufacturing industry [²MANUFACTURE + ²-ER]

manuka /'mahnookə/ *n* an evergreen New Zealand shrub of the myrtle family that forms large areas of scrub [Maori]

manumit /,manyoo'mit/ *vt* **-tt-** to release from slavery [ME *manumitten*, fr MF *manumitter*, fr L *manumittere*, fr *manus* hand + *mittere* to let go, send – more at SMITE] – **manumission** /-'mish(ə)n/ *n*

¹manure /mə'nyooə/ *vt* to enrich (land) by the application of manure [ME *manouren* to till, cultivate, fr MF *manouvrer*, lit., to do work by hand, fr L *manu operare*] – **manurer** *n*

²manure *n* material that fertilizes land; *esp* the faeces of domestic animals – **manurial** /-ri·əl/ *adj*

manuscript /'manyoo,skript/ *n or adj* (a composition or document) written by hand or typed as distinguished from a printed copy [adj L *manu scriptus* written by hand; n ML *manuscriptum*, fr neut of L *manu scriptus*]

¹Manx /mangks/ *adj* (characteristic) of the Isle of Man [alter. of earlier *Maniske*, fr (assumed) ON *manskr*, fr *Mana* Isle of Man]

²Manx *n* **1** *pl in constr* the people of the Isle of Man **2** the almost extinct Celtic language of the Manx people ☞ LANGUAGE

,Manx 'cat *n* (any of) a breed of short-haired domestic cats some of which have no external tail

'Manxman /-mən/, *fem* **'Manx,woman** *n* a native or inhabitant of the Isle of Man

Manx shearwater /'shiə,wawtə/ *n* a small black-and-white N Atlantic shearwater

¹many /'meni/ *adj* **more** /maw/; **most** /mohst/ **1** consisting of or amounting to a large but unspecified number ⟨*worked for ~ years*⟩ ⟨many-*sided*⟩ **2** being one of a large number ⟨*~ a man*⟩ ⟨*~ is the time I've wondered*⟩ [ME, fr OE *manig*; akin to OHG *manag* many, OSlav *mŭnogŭ* much] – **as many** the same in number ⟨*saw 3 plays in* as many *days*⟩

²many *pron pl in constr* a large number of people or things ⟨*~ prefer to stay at home*⟩ ⟨*I haven't got as ~ as you*⟩

³many *n pl in constr* **1** a large but indefinite number ⟨*a good ~ of them have already left*⟩ **2** *the* the great majority

⁴many *adv* to a considerable degree or amount; far – with plurals ⟨*~ more cars than usual*⟩

,many-'sided *adj* **1** having many sides or aspects **2** having many interests or aptitudes – **many-sidedness** *n*

Manzanilla /,manzə'nilə/ *n* a pale very dry sherry [Sp, dim. of *manzana* apple]

Maoism /'mow,iz(ə)m/ *n* Marxism-Leninism as developed in China chiefly by Mao Tse-tung [*Mao Tse-tung* †1976 Chin political leader] – **Maoist** *n or adj*

Maori /'mowri, 'mahri/ *n, pl* **Maoris,** *esp collectively* **Maori** **1** a member of the indigenous people of New Zealand **2** the Austronesian language of the Maori ☞ LANGUAGE

Maoritanga /,mowri'tahng·ə/ *n, NZ* Maori culture [Maori]

¹map /map/ *n* **1** a representation, usu on a flat surface, of (part of) the earth's surface, the celestial sphere, etc 👁 **2** sthg that represents with a clarity suggestive of a map [ML *mappa*, fr L, napkin, towel]

²map *vt* **-pp-** **1a** to make a map of **b** to delineate as if on a map **c** to survey in order to make a map **2** to assign to every element of (a mathematical set) an element of the same or another set **3** to plan in detail – often + *out* ⟨*~ out a programme*⟩ – **mappable** *adj*, **mapper** *n*

maple /'maypl/ *n* (the hard light-coloured close-grained wood, used esp for furniture, of) any of a genus of widely planted trees or shrubs [ME, fr OE *mapul-*; akin to ON *möpurr* maple]

maple sugar *n* sugar made by boiling maple syrup

maple syrup *n* syrup made by concentrating the sap of (sugar) maple trees

maquette /ma'ket/ *n* a small preliminary model of a sculpture (e g in wax or clay) [F, fr It *macchietta*, dim. of *macchia* sketch, deriv of L *macula* spot]

maquis /'maki/ *n, pl* **maquis** /~/ **1** (an area of) thick scrubby underbrush of Mediterranean shores ☞ PLANT **2a** *often cap* a member of the French Resistance during WW II **b** *sing or pl in constr* a band of maquis [F, fr It *macchie*, pl of *macchia* thicket, spot, fr L *macula*]

mar /mah/ *vt* **-rr-** to detract from the perfection or wholeness of [ME *marren*, fr OE *mierran* to obstruct, waste; akin to OHG *merren* to obstruct]

marabou, marabout /'marəbooh/ *n* a large African stork [F *marabout*, lit., marabout]

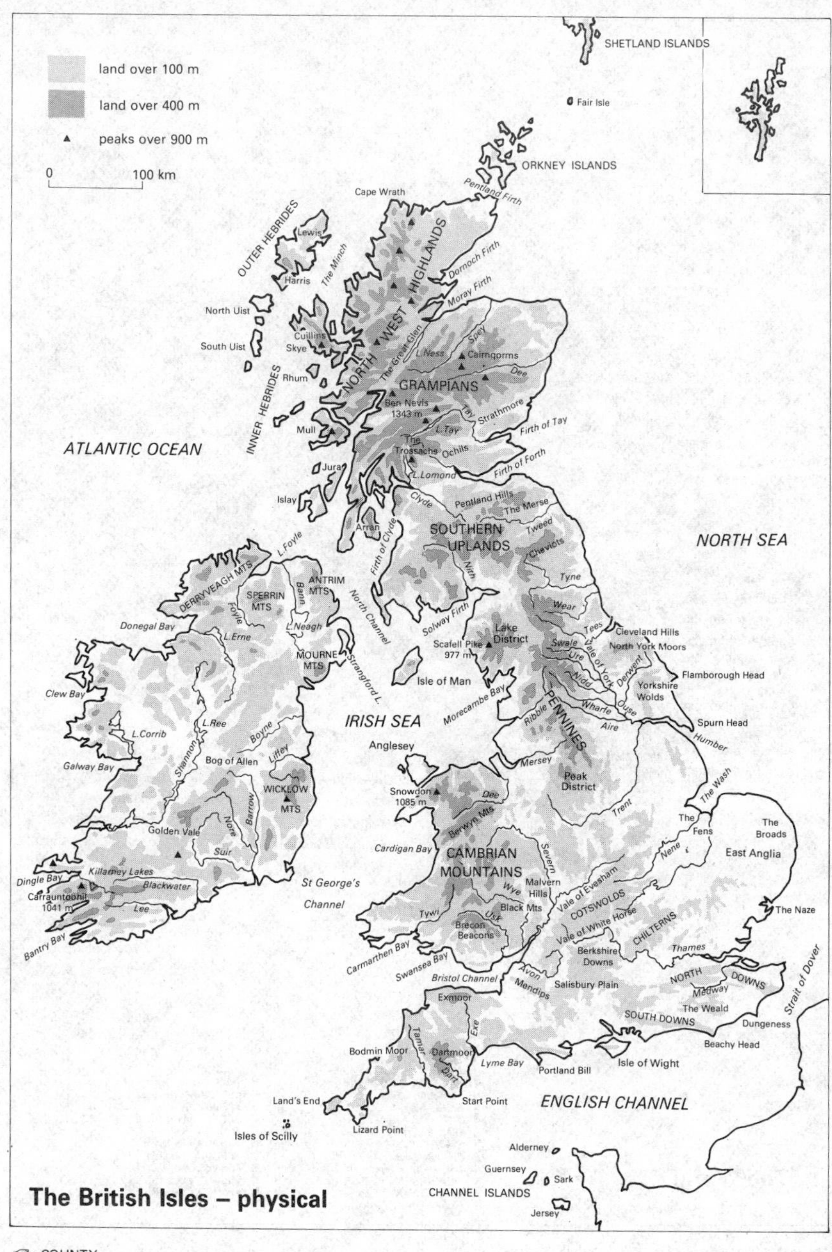

The British Isles – physical

☞ COUNTY

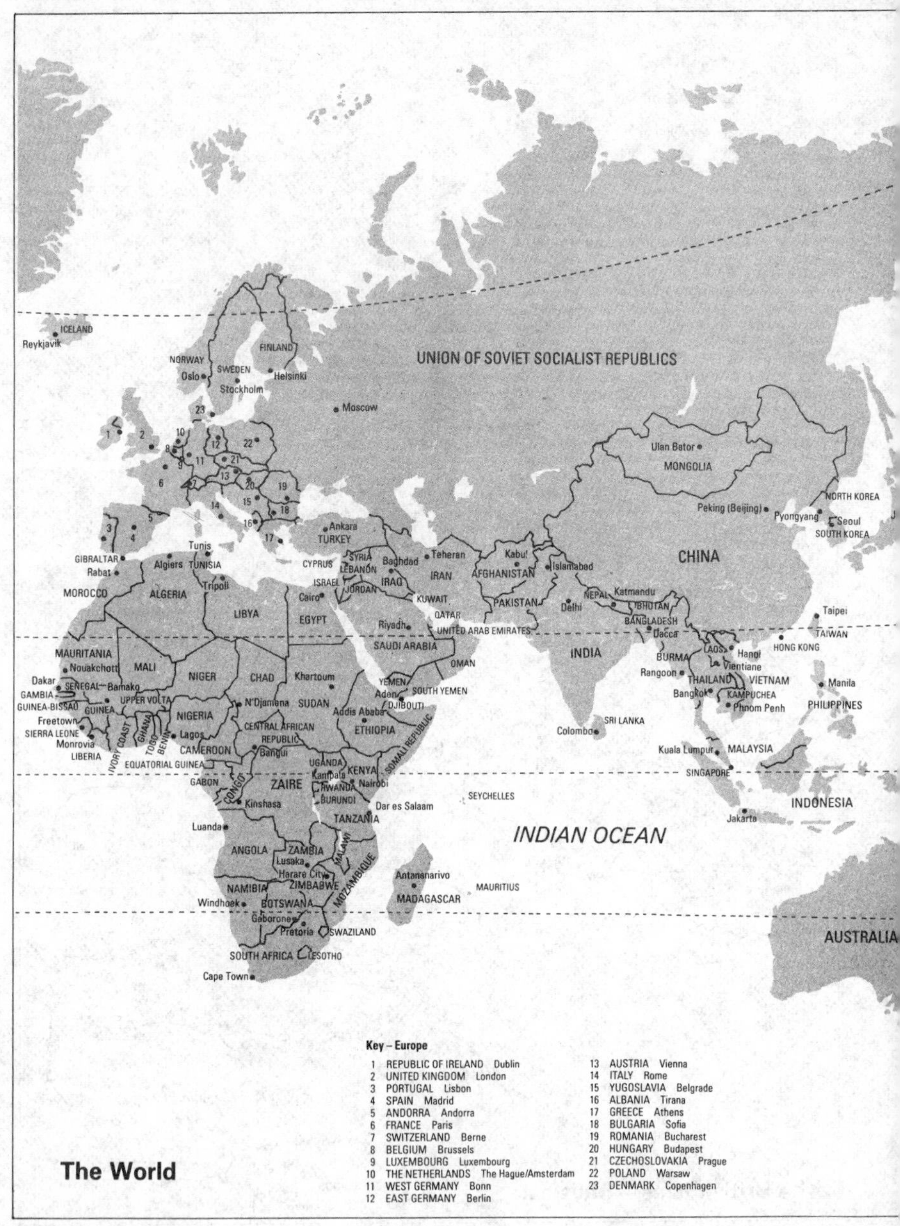

Key – Europe

1 REPUBLIC OF IRELAND Dublin
2 UNITED KINGDOM London
3 PORTUGAL Lisbon
4 SPAIN Madrid
5 ANDORRA Andorra
6 FRANCE Paris
7 SWITZERLAND Berne
8 BELGIUM Brussels
9 LUXEMBOURG Luxembourg
10 THE NETHERLANDS The Hague/Amsterdam
11 WEST GERMANY Bonn
12 EAST GERMANY Berlin
13 AUSTRIA Vienna
14 ITALY Rome
15 YUGOSLAVIA Belgrade
16 ALBANIA Tirana
17 GREECE Athens
18 BULGARIA Sofia
19 ROMANIA Bucharest
20 HUNGARY Budapest
21 CZECHOSLOVAKIA Prague
22 POLAND Warsaw
23 DENMARK Copenhagen

The World

☞ NATIONALITY, LANGUAGE

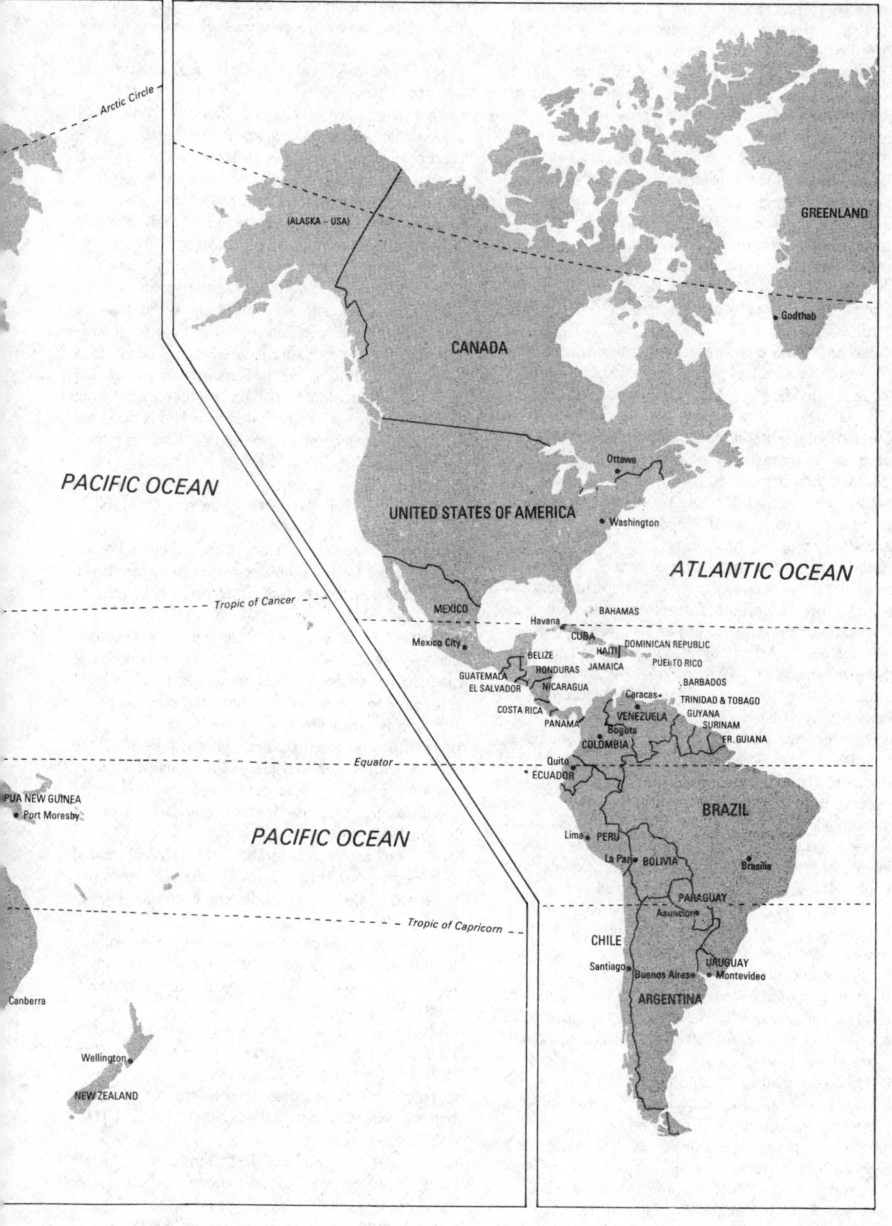
Arctic Circle
(ALASKA - USA)
GREENLAND
Godthab
CANADA
Ottawa
PACIFIC OCEAN
UNITED STATES OF AMERICA
Washington
ATLANTIC OCEAN
Tropic of Cancer
MEXICO
BAHAMAS
Havana
CUBA
Mexico City
HAITI
DOMINICAN REPUBLIC
BELIZE
JAMAICA
PUERTO RICO
HONDURAS
GUATEMALA
EL SALVADOR
NICARAGUA
BARBADOS
Caracas
TRINIDAD & TOBAGO
COSTA RICA
VENEZUELA
GUYANA
PANAMA
Bogota
SURINAM
COLOMBIA
FR. GUIANA
Equator
Quito
ECUADOR
PUA NEW GUINEA
Port Moresby
BRAZIL
PACIFIC OCEAN
Lima
PERU
La Paz
BOLIVIA
Brasilia
PARAGUAY
Asuncion
Tropic of Capricorn
CHILE
URUGUAY
Santiago
Buenos Aires
Montevideo
ARGENTINA
Canberra
Wellington
NEW ZEALAND

marabout /'marəbooh/ *n, often cap* (a shrine marking the grave of) a Muslim holy man of N Africa [F, fr Pg *marabuto*, fr Ar *murābiṭ*]

maraca /mə'rakə/ *n* a dried gourd or a rattle like a gourd that is used as a rhythm instrument and is usu played as one of a pair [Pg *maracá*]

maraschino /,marə'sheenoh, -'skeenoh/ *n, pl* **maraschinos** *often cap* **1** a sweet liqueur distilled from the fermented juice of a bitter wild cherry **2** a usu large cherry preserved in true or imitation maraschino [It, fr *marasca* bitter wild cherry]

marasmus /mə'razməs/ *n* progressive emaciation, esp in the young, due usu to faulty digestion and absorption of food [LL, fr Gk *marasmos*, fr *marainein* to waste away – more at SMART] – **marasmic** /-mik/ *adj or n*

Maratha, Mahratta /mə'rahtə/ *n* a member of a people of the S central part of India [Marathi *Marāṭhā* & Hindi *Marhaṭṭā*, fr Skt *Mahārāṣṭra* Maharashtra]

Marathi /mə'rahti/ *n* the chief Indic language of the state of Maharashtra in India ☞ LANGUAGE [Marathi *marāṭhī*]

marathon /'marəth(ə)n/ *n* **1** a long-distance race; *specif* a foot race of 26mi 385yd (about 42.2km) that is contested on an open course in major athletics championships **2a** an endurance contest **b** an event or activity characterized by great length or concentrated effort [*Marathon*, Greece, site of a victory of Greeks over Persians in 490 BC, the news of which was carried to Athens by a long-distance runner]

maraud /mə'rawd/ *vi* to roam about in search of plunder ~ *vt* to raid, pillage [F *marauder*] – **marauder** *n*

maravedi /,marə'vaydi/ *n, pl* **maravedis** a medieval Spanish copper coin unit worth $\frac{1}{34}$ real [Sp *maravedí*, fr Ar *Murābiṭīn* 11th- & 12th- c Muslim dynasty in N Africa & Spain]

[1]**marble** /'mahbl/ *n* **1a** (more or less) crystallized limestone that can be highly polished and is used esp in building and sculpture **b** a sculpture or carving made of marble **2a** a little ball made of a hard substance, esp glass, and used in children's games **b** *pl but sing in constr* any of several games played with marbles, the object of which is to hit a mark or hole, to hit another player's marble, or to knock as many marbles as possible out of a ring **3** marbling **4** *pl* elements of common sense; *esp* sanity – infml ⟨*he's lost his* ~!⟩ [ME, fr OF *marbre*, fr L *marmor*, fr Gk *marmaros*]

[2]**marble** *vt* **marbling** /'mahbl·ing, 'mahbling/ to give a veined or mottled appearance to (e g the edges of a book) – **marbling** /-b(ə)ling/ *n*

'**marbled** *adj* **1a** made of or veneered with marble **b** marked by an extensive use of marble as an architectural or decorative feature ⟨*ancient* ~ *cities*⟩ **2** *of meat* marked by a mixture of fat and lean

marc /mahk/ *n* **1** the organic residue remaining after an extraction process (e g the pressing of grapes) **2** brandy made from the residue of grapes after pressing [F, fr MF, fr *marchier* to trample]

marcasite /,mahkə'seet, 'mahkə,siet/ *n* (a piece of) crystallized iron pyrites or a similar mineral, used esp for jewellery [ME *marchasite*, fr ML *marcasita*, fr Ar *marqashīthā*]

marcel /mah'sel/ *n* a deep soft wave made in the hair by a heated curling iron [*Marcel* Grateau †1936 F hairdresser] – **marcel** *vt*

[1]**march** /mahch/ *n, often cap* a border region; *esp* a tract of land between 2 countries whose ownership is disputed – usu pl ⟨*the Welsh* ~es⟩ [ME *marche*, fr OF, of Gmc origin; akin to OHG *marha* boundary – more at [1]MARK]

[2]**march** *vi* to have common borders or frontiers ⟨*a region that* ~es *with Canada in the north*⟩

[3]**march** *vi* **1** to move along steadily, usu in step with others **2a** to move in a direct purposeful manner **b** to make steady progress ⟨*time* ~es *on*⟩ ~ *vt* **1** to cause to march ⟨~ed *him off to the police station*⟩ **2** to cover by marching ⟨~ed *30 miles*⟩ [MF *marchier* to trample, march, fr OF, to trample, prob of Gmc origin; akin to OHG *marcōn* to mark]

[4]**march** *n* **1a** the action of marching **b** the distance covered within a specified period of time by marching **c** a regular measured stride or rhythmic step used in marching **d** steady forward movement **2** a musical composition, usu in duple or quadruple time, that has a strongly accentuated beat and is designed or suitable to accompany marching – **on the march** moving steadily; advancing

March *n* the 3rd month of the Gregorian calendar [ME, fr OF, fr L *martius*, fr *martius* of Mars, fr *Mart-, Mars*]

[1]**marcher** /'mahchə/ *n* **1** one who inhabits a border region **2** the lord of a border region in former times ⟨*the King's authority was constantly challenged by the* ~ *lords*⟩

[2]**marcher** *n* one who marches, esp for a specified cause ⟨*a peace* ~⟩

'**marching ,orders** /'mahching/ *n pl* **1** official notice for troops to move **2** notice of dismissal ⟨*the player was given his* ~ *after the brutal foul*⟩

marchioness /,mahshə'nes, 'mahshənis/ *n* **1** the wife or widow of a marquess **2** a woman having in her own right the rank of a marquess [ML *marchionissa*, fr *marchion-, marchio* marquess, fr *marca* border region]

Mardi Gras /,mahdi 'grah/ *n* (a carnival period culminating on) Shrove Tuesday often observed (e g in New Orleans) with parades and festivities [F, lit., fat Tuesday]

[1]**mare** /meə/ *n* a female equine animal, esp when fully mature or of breeding age; *esp* a female horse [ME, fr OE *mere*; akin to OHG *merha* mare, OE *mearh* horse, W *march*]

[2]**mare** /'mahray/ *n, pl* **maria** /-ri·ə/ any of several large dark areas on the surface of the moon or Mars [NL, fr L, sea – more at MARINE]

mare clausum /,mahray 'klows(ə)m/ *n* a navigable body of water under the jurisdiction of 1 nation [NL, lit., closed sea]

mare liberum /,mahray 'leebərəm/ *n* a navigable body of water open to all nations [NL, lit., free sea]

'**mare's ,nest** /meəz/ *n, pl* **mare's nests, mares' nests** a false discovery, illusion, or deliberate hoax

'**mare's ,tail** *n, pl* **mare's tails, mares' tails** **1** a common aquatic plant with long shoots covered with narrow leaves **2** a long streak of cirrus cloud

margarine /,mahjə'reen; *also* ,mahgə'reen, '---/ *n* a substitute for butter made usu from vegetable oils churned with ripened skimmed milk to a smooth emulsion [F, fr Gk *margaron* pearl]

margay /'mahgay/ *n* a small American spotted cat resembling the ocelot [F, fr Tupi *maracaja*]

[1]**marge** /mahj/ *n* MARGIN 1,2 – poetic [MF, fr L *margo*]

[2]**marge** *n* margarine – infml [by shortening & alter.]

[1]**margin** /'mahjin/ *n* **1** the part of a page outside the main body of printed or written text **2** the outside limit and adjoining surface of sthg **3a** a spare amount or measure or degree allowed (e g in case of error) **b(1)** a bare minimum below which or an extreme limit beyond which sthg becomes impossible or is no longer desirable **(2)** the limit below which economic activity cannot be continued under normal conditions **4** the difference between net sales and the cost of merchandise sold **5** measure or degree of difference [ME, fr L *margin-, margo* border – more at [1]MARK] – **margined** *adj*

[2]**margin** *vt* to provide with a border

[1]**marginal** /'mahjinl/ *adj* **1** written or printed in the margin **2** of or situated at a margin or border **3** close to the lower limit of qualification, acceptability, or function **4** of or providing a nominal profit margin **5** being a constituency where the Member of Parliament was elected with only a small majority – compare SAFE 6 [ML *marginalis*, fr L *margin-, margo*] – **marginally** *adv*, **marginality** /,mahji'naləti/ *n*

[2]**marginal** *n* a marginal constituency

marginalia /,mahji'naylyə/ *n pl* marginal notes (e g in a book) [NL, fr ML, neut pl of *marginalis*]

margrave /'mahgrayv/ *n* **1** the hereditary title of some princes of the Holy Roman Empire **2** a member of the German nobility corresponding in rank to a British marquess [D *markgraaf*, fr MD *marcgrave*; akin to OHG *marcgrāvo*; both fr a prehistoric D-G compound whose constituents are akin to OHG *marha* boundary & to OHG *grāvo* count – more at [1]MARK] – **margravial** /mah'grayvi·əl/ *adj*

margravine /'mahgrə,veen/ *n* the wife of a margrave

marguerite /,mahgə'reet/ *n* (a single-flowered chrysanthemum like) an oxeye daisy [F, fr MF *margarite* pearl, daisy, fr L *margarita* pearl, fr Gk *margaritēs*, fr *margaron*]

Marian /'meəri·ən/ *adj* of the Virgin Mary

mariculture /'mari,kulchə/ *n* the cultivation of marine organisms by exploiting their natural environment [L *mare* sea + E *-culture* (as in *agriculture*)]

marigold /'marigohld/ *n* any of a genus of composite plants with showy yellow or red flower heads [ME, fr *Mary*, mother of Jesus + ME *gold*]

marijuana, marihuana /,marə'(h)wahnə, -yoo'ahnə/ *n* **1** HEMP 1 **2** a usu mild form of cannabis [MexSp *mariguana, marihuana*]

marimba /mə'rimbə/ *n* a percussion instrument resembling a large xylophone [of African origin; akin to Kimbundu *marimba* xylophone]

marina /mə'reenə/ *n* a dock or basin providing secure moorings for motorboats, yachts, etc [It & Sp, seashore, fr fem of *marino*, adj, marine, fr L *marinus*]

marinade /,mari'nayd/ *vt or n* (to soak in) a blend of oil, wine or vinegar, herbs, and spices in which meat, fish, etc is soaked, esp to enrich its flavour [n F, fr Sp *marinada*, fr *marinar* to pickle in brine, fr *marino*; vb fr n]

marinate /'marinayt/ *vt* to marinade [prob fr It *marinato*, pp of *marinare* to marinade, fr *marino*]

[1]**marine** /mə'reen/ *adj* **1** of or (living) in the sea **2** of or used in the navigation or commerce of the sea ⟨*a ~ chart*⟩ ⟨*~ law*⟩ [ME, fr L *marinus*, fr *mare* sea; akin to OE *mere* sea, pool, OHG *meri* sea, OSlav *morje*]

[2]**marine** *n* **1** seagoing ships (of a specified nationality or class) ⟨*the mercantile ~*⟩ **2a** any of a class of soldiers serving on shipboard or in close association with a naval force **b** ☞ RANK **3** a seascape

mariner /'marinə/ *n* a seaman, sailor [ME, fr AF, fr OF *marinier*, fr ML *marinarius*, fr L *marinus*]

Mariolatry /,meəri'olətri/ *n* excessive veneration of the Virgin Mary – **Mariolater** *n*

marionette /,mari·ə'net/ *n* a small-scale usu wooden figure with jointed limbs that is moved from above by attached strings or wires [F *marionnette*, fr MF *maryonete*, fr *Marion*, dim. of *Marie* Mary]

marital /'maritl/ *adj* of marriage [L *maritalis*, fr *maritus* married] – **maritally** *adv*

maritime /'mari,tiem/ *adj* **1** MARINE 2 **2** of or bordering on the sea [L *maritimus*, fr *mare*]

marjoram /'mahjəram, -rəm/ *n* any of various plants of the mint family used as herbs; *also* oregano [alter. of ME *majorane*, fr MF, fr ML *majorana*]

[1]**mark** /mahk/ *n* **1a(1)** a conspicuous object serving as a guide for travellers **(2)** sthg (e g a line, notch, or fixed object) designed to record position **b** any of the points on a sounding line that correspond to a depth in whole fathoms **c** TARGET 2a **d** the starting line or position in a track event **e** a goal or desired object **f** the point under discussion ⟨*that comment was rather off the ~*⟩ **g** an established or accepted standard of performance, quality, or condition ⟨*his singing was hardly up to the ~*⟩ **2a(1)** a sign or token ⟨*a ~ of his esteem*⟩ **(2)** an impression on the surface of sthg; *esp* a scratch, stain, etc that spoils the appearance of a surface **(3)** a distinguishing characteristic ⟨*bears the ~ of an educated woman*⟩ **b(1)** a symbol used for identification or indication of ownership **(2)** a symbol, esp a cross, made in place of a signature **c** a written or printed symbol ⟨*punctuation ~s*⟩ **d** *cap* – used with a numeral to designate a particular model of a weapon or machine ⟨Mark *II*⟩ **e** a symbol representing a judgment of merit, esp one used by a teacher **f** a point or level (reached) ⟨*passed the halfway ~*⟩ **3a** attention, notice ⟨*nothing worthy of ~ occurred*⟩ **b** importance, distinction ⟨*a person of little ~*⟩ **c** a lasting or strong impression ⟨*years of warfare have left their ~ on the country*⟩ **d** an assessment of merits ⟨*got high ~s for honesty*⟩ **4** an object of attack; *specif* a victim of a swindle – infml [ME, fr OE *mearc* boundary, march, sign; akin to OHG *marha* boundary, L *margo*]

[2]**mark** *vt* **1a(1)** to fix or trace *out* the limits of **(2)** to plot the course of **b** to set apart (as if) by a line or boundary – usu + *off* **2a(1)** to designate or identify (as if) by a mark ⟨*~ed for greatness*⟩ **(2)** to make or leave a mark on **(3)** to label (merchandise) so as to indicate price or quality **(4)** to add appropriate symbols, characters, or other marks to or on ⟨*~ the manuscript for the printer*⟩ – usu + *up* **b(1)** to indicate by a mark ⟨*X ~s the spot*⟩ **(2)** to register, record ⟨*~ the date in your diary*⟩ **(3)** to evaluate by marks ⟨*~ examination papers*⟩ **c(1)** to characterize, distinguish ⟨*the flamboyance that ~s her stage appearance*⟩ **(2)** to be the occasion of (sthg notable); to indicate as a particular time ⟨*this year ~s the 50th anniversary of the organization*⟩ **3** to take notice of

⟨~ *what I say*⟩ **4** *Br* to stay close to (an opposing player) in hockey, soccer, etc so as to hinder the getting or play of the ball ~ *vi* **1** to become or make sthg stained, scratched, etc ⟨*it won't ~ will it?*⟩ **2** to evaluate sthg by marks [ME *marken*, fr OE *mearcian*; akin to OHG *marcōn* to determine the boundaries of, OE *mearc* boundary] – **marker** *n* – **mark time 1** to keep the time of a marching step by moving the feet alternately without advancing **2** to function listlessly or unproductively while waiting to progress or advance

[3]**mark** *n* **1** *often cap* (a note or coin representing) the basic money unit of either East or West Germany ☞ *Germany (Democratic Republic), Germany (Federal Republic)* at NATIONALITY **2** a markka [ME, fr OE *marc*, prob of Scand origin; akin to ON *mörk* mark; akin to OE *mearc* sign]

Mark *n* the 2nd Gospel in the New Testament [L *Marcus*]

Mark der Deutschen Demokratischen Republik /ˌmahk deə ˌdoychən demohˌkratishən repoo'bleek (əer mark deːr dɔɪtʃən demokraːtɪʃən republiːk)/ *n* ☞ *Germany (Democratic Republic)* at NATIONALITY [G, mark of the German Democratic Republic]

'mark,down /-ˌdown/ *n* (the amount of) a reduction in price – **mark down** *vt*

marked /mahkt/ *adj* **1a** having natural marks (of a specified type) ⟨*wings ~ with white*⟩ **b** made identifiable by marking ⟨*a ~ card*⟩ **2** having a distinctive or emphasized character ⟨*a ~ American accent*⟩ **3** being an object of attack, suspicion, or vengeance ⟨*a ~ man*⟩ **4** distinguished from a basic form (e g the singular) by the presence of a particular linguistic feature (e g *s* indicating the plural form) – **markedly** /'mahkidli/ *adv*

[1]**market** /'mahkit/ *n* **1a** a meeting together of people for the purpose of trade, by private purchase and sale **b** an open space, building, etc where a market (e g for trading in provisions or livestock) is held **2a** (a geographical area or section of the community in which there is) demand for commodities ⟨*the foreign ~*⟩ **b** commercial activity; extent of trading **c** an opportunity for selling ⟨*create new ~s for our product*⟩ **d** the area of economic activity in which the forces of supply and demand affect prices ⟨*~ value*⟩ [ME, fr ONF, fr L *mercatus* trade, marketplace, fr *mercatus*, pp of *mercari* to trade, fr *merc-*, *merx* merchandise; akin to Oscan *amiricadut* without remuneration] – **in the market** interested in buying ⟨in the market *for a house*⟩ – **on the market** available for purchase

[2]**market** *vi* to deal in a market ~ *vt* to sell – **marketable** *adj*, **marketability** /ˌmahkitə'biləti/ *n*

market cross *n* a cross orig erected in a market place

,market 'garden *n* a plot in which vegetables are grown for market – **market gardener** *n*, **market gardening** *n*

marketing /'mahkiting/ *n* the skills and functions, including packaging, promotion, and distribution, involved in selling goods

'market,place /-ˌplays/ *n* **1** an open place in a town where markets are held **2** MARKET 2c, d

,market 'research *n* research (e g the collection and analysis of information about consumer preferences) dealing with the patterns or state of demand (for a particular product) in a market

marking /'mahking/ *n* **1** (the giving of) a mark or marks **2** arrangement, pattern, or disposition of marks

'marking ,ink *n* indelible ink for marking fabric

markka /'mahkə/ *n, pl* **markkaa** /-ˌkah/, **markkas** ☞ *Finland* at NATIONALITY [Finn, fr Sw *mark*, a unit of value; akin to ON *mörk*]

'Markov ,chain /'mahkof/ *n* a random sequence of states in which the probability of occurrence of a future state depends only on the present state and not on the path by which it was reached [A A *Markov* †1922 Russ mathematician]

marksman /'mahksmən/, *fem* **'marks,woman** *n, pl* **marksmen**, *fem* **markswomen** a person skilled in hitting a mark or target – **marksmanship** *n*

'mark,up /-ˌup/ *n* (the amount of) an increase in price – **mark up** *vt*

marl /mahl/ *vt or n* (to fertilize with) a crumbly earthy deposit (e g of silt or clay) that contains calcium carbonate and is used esp as a fertilizer for lime-deficient soils [n ME, fr MF *marle*, fr ML *margila*, dim. of L *marga* marl, fr Gaulish; vb fr n] – **marly** *adj*

marlin /'mahlin/ *n* any of several large oceanic game fishes [short for *marlinspike*; fr the appearance of its beak]

marline, marlin /'mahlin/ *n* a thin 2-stranded usu tarred rope used on board ship [D *marlijn*, alter. of *marling*, fr *meren, marren* to tie, moor, fr MD *meren, maren* – more at [2]MOOR]

'marline,spike, marlinspike /-ˌspiek/ *n* a pointed steel tool used to separate strands of rope or wire

marlite /'mah(rə)ˌliet/ *n* a marl resistant to the action of air

[1]**marmalade** /'mahməˌlayd/ *n* a clear sweetened preserve made from oranges, lemons, etc and usu containing pieces of fruit peel [Pg *marmelada* quince conserve, fr *marmelo* quince, fr L *melimelum*, a sweet apple, fr Gk *melimēlon*, fr *meli* honey + *mēlon* apple – more at MELLIFLUOUS]

[2]**marmalade** *adj, esp of cats* brownish orange

Marmite /'mahmiet/ *trademark* – used for a concentrated yeast extract used esp as a savoury spread

marmoreal /mah'mawri·əl/, *also* **marmorean** /-ri·ən/ *adj* of or like marble or a marble statue – chiefly poetic [L *marmoreus*, fr *marmor* marble, fr Gk *marmaros*]

marmoset /'mahməzet/ *n* any of numerous soft-furred S and Central American monkeys [ME *marmusette*, fr MF *marmoset* grotesque figure, fr *marmouser* to mumble, of imit origin]

marmot /'mahmət/ *n* any of several stout-bodied short-legged small-eared burrowing rodents [F *marmotte*]

Maronite /'marəniet/ *n* a member of a Syrian Christian church now existing chiefly in the Lebanon [ML *maronita*, fr *Maron-, Maro* 5th-c AD Syrian monk]

[1]**maroon** /mə'roohn/ *vt* **1** to abandon on a desolate island or coast **2** to isolate in a helpless state [*Maroon*]

[2]**maroon** *n* **1** a dark brownish red **2** an explosive rocket used esp as a distress signal [F *marron* Spanish chestnut]

Maroon /mə'roohn/ *n* (a descendant of) a fugitive Negro slave of the W Indies and Guiana in the 17th and 18th c [modif of AmerSp *cimarrón*, fr *cimarrón* wild, savage, lit., living on mountaintops, fr Sp *cima* peak, fr L *cyma* young sprout of cabbage]

marque /mahk/ *n* a brand or model of a product, esp a car [F, mark, brand, fr *marquer* to mark, of Gmc origin; akin to OHG *marcōn* to mark]

marquee /mah'kee/ *n* **1** a large tent (e g for an outdoor party or exhibition) **2** *NAm* a permanent canopy projecting over an entrance (e g of a hotel or theatre) [modif of F *marquise*, lit., marchioness]

Marquesan /mah'kayz(ə)n/ *adj or n* (of) an inhabitant, or the Austronesian language, of the Marquesas islands ☞ LANGUAGE

marquess, marquis /'mahkwis/ *n, pl* **marquesses, marquises, marquis** (a European nobleman equivalent in rank to) a member of the British peerage ranking below a duke and above an earl [ME *marquis, markis*, fr MF *marquis*, alter. of *marchis*, fr *marche* march] – **marquessate** /-kwisit/, **marquisate** /-kwizit, -sit/ *n*

marquetry *also* **marqueterie** /'mahkətri/ *n* decorative work of pieces of wood, ivory, etc inlaid in a wood veneer that is then applied to a surface (e g of a piece of furniture) [MF *marqueterie*, fr *marqueter* to chequer, inlay, fr *marque* mark]

marquise /mah'keez/ *n* **1** a marchioness **2** a gem or ring setting shaped like an oval with pointed ends [F, fem of *marquis*]

'marram ,grass /'marəm/ *n* any of several strong wiry grasses that grow on sandy shores and prevent erosion [of Scand origin; akin to ON *maralmr*, a beach grass]

marriage /'marij/ *n* **1a** the state of being or mutual relation of husband and wife **b** the institution whereby a man and a woman are joined in a special kind of social and legal dependence **2** an act or the rite of marrying; *esp* the wedding ceremony **3** an intimate or close union [ME *mariage*, fr MF, fr *marier* to marry] – **marriageable** *adj*

,marriage of con'venience *n* a marriage contracted for advantage rather than for love

[1]**married** /'marid/ *adj* **1a** joined in marriage **b** of married people **2** united, joined

[2]**married** *n* a married person ⟨*young* ~s⟩

marrons glacés /,maronh 'glasay/ *n pl* chestnuts candied or preserved in syrup [F]

marrow /'maroh/ *n* **1a** a soft tissue that fills the cavities and porous part of most bones and contains many blood vessels **b** the substance of the spinal cord **2** the inmost, best, or essential part; the core **3** *chiefly Br* VEGETABLE MARROW [ME *marowe*, fr OE *mearg*; akin to OHG *marag* marrow, Skt *majjan*] – **marrowless** *adj*, **marrowy** *adj*

marrowbone /'marə,bohn, -roh-/ *n* a bone rich in marrow

marrowfat /'marə,fat, -roh-/ *n* any of several types of large pea

[1]**marry** /'mari/ *vt* **1a** to give in marriage **b** to take as spouse **c** to perform the ceremony of marriage for **d** to obtain by marriage ⟨*she* married *money*⟩ **2** to bring together closely, harmoniously, and usu permanently ~ *vi* **1a** to take a spouse **b** to become husband and wife **2** to join in a close or harmonious relationship [ME *marien*, fr OF *marier*, fr L *maritare*, fr *maritus* married] – **marry into** to become a member of or obtain by marriage ⟨married into *a prominent family*⟩

[2]**marry** *interj, archaic* – used for emphasis, esp to express amused or surprised agreement [ME *marie*, fr *Marie*, the Virgin Mary]

Mars /mahz/ *n* the planet 4th in order from the sun and conspicuous for its red colour ☞ ASTRONOMY, SYMBOL [L *Mart-, Mars*, Roman god of war]

Marsala /mah'sahlə/ *n* a (sweet) fortified wine from Sicily [*Marsala*, town in Sicily]

marsh /mahsh/ *n* (an area of) soft wet land usu covered with sedges, rushes, etc [ME *mersh*, fr OE *merisc, mersc*; akin to MD *mersch* marsh, OE *mere* sea, pool – more at MARINE] – **marshy** *adj*, **marshiness** *n*

[1]**marshal** /'mahsh(ə)l/ *n* **1a** a high official in a medieval royal household **b** one who arranges and directs a ceremony **c** one who arranges the procedure at races **2a** FIELD MARSHAL **b** an officer of the highest military rank **3a** a chief officer in the USA responsible for court processes in a district **b** the head of a US police or fire department [ME, fr OF *mareschal*, of Gmc origin; akin to OHG *marahscalc* marshal, fr *marah* horse + *scalc* servant] – **marshalcy** /-si/, **marshalship** *n*

[2]**marshal** *vb* **-ll-** (*NAm* **-l-, -ll-**), /'mahshl·ing/ *vt* **1** to place in proper rank or position **2** to bring together and order in an effective way ⟨~ *one's thoughts*⟩ **3** to lead ceremoniously or solicitously; usher ~ *vi* to form or collect together (in a proper order)

'marshalling ,yard *n, chiefly Br* a place where railway vehicles are shunted and assembled into trains

marshal of the Royal Air Force *n* ☞ RANK

'marsh ,gas *n* methane

'marsh ,harrier *n* an Old World hawk

marshmallow /,mahsh'maloh/ *n* **1** a pink-flowered Eurasian marsh plant of the mallow family **2** a light spongy confection made from the root of the marshmallow or from sugar, albumen, and gelatin – **marshmallowy** *adj*

,marsh 'mari,gold /'mari,gohld/ *n* a European and N American marsh plant of the buttercup family with large bright yellow flowers

[1]**marsupial** /mah'syoohpi·əl, -'sooh-/ *adj* **1** of or being a marsupial **2** of or forming a marsupium or pouch

[2]**marsupial** *n* any of an order of lower mammals including the kangaroos, wombats, and opossums that have a pouch on the abdomen of the female for carrying young, and do not develop a placenta ☞ LIFE CYCLE [deriv of NL *marsupium*]

mar'supium /-pi·əm/ *n, pl* **marsupia** /-pi·ə/ the abdominal pouch of a marsupial, formed by a fold of the skin and enclosing the mammary glands [NL, fr L, purse, pouch, fr Gk *marsypion*, dim. of *marsypos* pouch]

mart /maht/ *n* a place of trade (e g an auction room or market) [ME, fr MD *marct, mart*, prob fr ONF *market*]

Martello /mah'teloh/, **Mar'tello ,tower** *n* a circular masonry fort or blockhouse formerly used (e g in Britain) for coastal defence [alter. of Cape *Mortella*, Corsica, where such a tower was captured by a British fleet in 1794]

marten /'mahtin/ *n, pl* **martens,** *esp collectively* **marten** any of several slender-bodied flesh-eating tree-dwelling mammals larger than the related weasels [ME *martryn*, fr MF *martrine* marten fur, fr

OF, fr fem of *martrin* of a marten, fr *martre* marten, of Gmc origin; akin to OE *mearth* marten]

martensite /'mahtin,ziet/ *n* the chief constituent of steel hardened by rapid cooling [Adolf *Martens* †1914 G metallurgist] – **martensitic** /,mahtin'zitik/ *adj*

martial /'mahsh(ə)l/ *adj* of or suited to war or a warrior; *also* warlike [ME, fr L *martialis* of (the god) Mars, fr *Mart-, Mars*] – **martially** *adv*

,martial 'art *n* an Oriental art of combat (e g judo or karate) practised as a sport

,martial 'law *n* the law administered by military forces in occupied territory or in an emergency

Martian /'mahsh(ə)n/ *adj* of or coming from the planet Mars [ME, fr OF *martien*, fr L *Mart-, Mars* (the planet) Mars] – **Martian** *n*

martin /'mahtin/ *n* any of various birds of the swallow family: e g **a** a house martin **b** a sand martin [MF, fr St *Martin*; prob fr the migration of martins around Martinmas]

martinet /,mahti'net/ *n* a strict disciplinarian [Jean *Martinet* †1672 F army officer]

martingale /'mahtin,gayl/ *n* **1** one or more straps fastened to the girth of a horse's harness, passed between the forelegs, and attached to the reins, noseband, or bit, for checking the upward movement of the horse's head **2** any of several systems of betting in which the stake is doubled every time a bet is lost [MF]

martini /mah'teeni/ *n* a cocktail made of gin and dry vermouth [prob fr *Martini* & Rossi, It firm selling vermouth]

Martinmas /'mahtinməs, -,mas/ *n* November 11 celebrated as the feast of St Martin [ME *martinmasse*, fr St *Martin* + ME *masse* mass]

martlet /'mahtlit/ *n* a bird used in heraldry that resembles a martin but has no feet [MF, prob alter. of *martinet*, dim. of *martin*]

[1]**martyr** /'mahtə/ *n* **1** one who is put to death for adherence to a cause, esp a religion **2** a victim, esp of constant (self-inflicted) suffering [ME, fr OE, fr LL, fr Gk *martyr-, martys*, lit., witness; akin to L *memor* mindful] – **martyrize** *vt*, **martyrdom** /-tədəm/ *n*, **martyrization** /,mahtərie'zaysh(ə)n/ *n*

[2]**martyr** *vt* **1** to put to death as a martyr **2** to inflict agonizing pain on

martyrology /,mahtə'roləji/ *n* ecclesiastical history concerned with the lives and sufferings of martyrs – **martyrologist** *n*, **martyrological** /-rə'lojikl/ *adj*

[1]**marvel** /'mahv(ə)l/ *n* one who or that which is marvellous [ME *mervel*, fr OF *merveille*, fr LL *mirabilia* marvels, fr L, neut pl of *mirabilis* wonderful, fr *mirari* to wonder – more at SMILE]

[2]**marvel** *vi* **-ll-** (*NAm* **-l-, -ll-**), /'mahvl·ing/ to become filled with surprise, wonder, or amazed curiosity

marvellous, *NAm chiefly* **marvelous** /'mahvl·əs/ *adj* **1** causing wonder **2** of the highest kind or quality – **marvellously** *adv*, **marvellousness** *n*

Marxism /'mahksiz(ə)m/ *n* the political and economic principles and policies advocated by Karl Marx, that stress the importance of human labour in determining economic value, the struggle between classes as an instrument of social change, and dictatorship of the proletariat [Karl *Marx* †1883 G political philosopher] – **Marxist** *n or adj*, **Marxian** /-si·ən/ *adj*

,Marxism-'Leninism /'leniniz(ə)m/ *n* a theory and practice of communism developed by Lenin from the doctrines of Marx – **Marxist-Leninist** *n or adj*

marzipan /'mahzi,pan/ *n* a paste made from ground almonds, sugar, and egg whites, used for coating cakes or shaped into small sweets [G, fr It *marzapane*, a medieval coin, marzipan, fr Ar *mawthabān*, a medieval coin]

Masai /'masie/ *n, pl* **Masais,** *esp collectively* **Masai** a member or the language of a pastoral and hunting people of Kenya and Tanzania

mascara /ma'skahrə/ *n* a cosmetic for colouring, esp darkening, the eyelashes [It *maschera* mask]

mascon /'maskon/ *n* any of the concentrations of mass that are situated just under the surface of the moon and have strong gravitational pull [[2]*mass* + *concentration*]

mascot /'maskot, -kət/ *n* a person, animal, or object adopted as a (good luck) symbol [F *mascotte*, fr Prov *mascoto*, fr *masco* witch, fr ML *masca*]

[1]**masculine** /'maskyoolin/ *adj* **1a** male **b** having qualities appropriate to a man ⟨*her deep* ~ *voice*⟩ **2** of, belonging to, or being the gender that normally includes most words or grammatical forms referring to males **3** having or occurring in a stressed final syllable [ME *masculin*, fr MF, fr L *masculinus*, fr *masculus*, n, male, dim. of *mas* male] – **masculinely** *adv*, **masculineness** *n*, **masculinize** /-,niez/ *vt*, **masculinity** /,mas kyoo'linəti/ *n*

[2]**masculine** *n* (a word or morpheme of) the masculine gender

maser /'mayzə/ *n* a device that works like a laser for amplifying or generating (microwave) radiation [*m*icrowave *a*mplification by *s*timulated *e*mission of *r*adiation]

[1]**mash** /mash/ *n* **1** crushed malt or grain meal steeped and stirred in hot water to convert starch to sugar **2** a mixture of bran or similar feeds and usu hot water for livestock **3** a soft pulpy mass **4** *Br* mashed potatoes – infml [ME, fr OE *māx-*; akin to MHG *meisch* mash]

[2]**mash** *vt* **1** to crush, pound, etc to a soft pulpy state **2** to heat and stir (e g crushed malt) in water to prepare wort – **masher** *n*

[1]**mask** /mahsk/ *n* **1a** a (partial) cover for the face used for disguise or protection **b(1)** a figure of a head worn on the stage in ancient times to identify the character **(2)** a grotesque false face worn at carnivals or in rituals **c** a copy of a face made by sculpting or by means of a mould – compare DEATH MASK **2a** sthg that disguises or conceals; *esp* a pretence, facade **b** a translucent or opaque screen to cover part of the sensitive surface in taking or printing a photograph **3** a device covering the mouth and nose used **a** to promote breathing (e g by connection to an oxygen supply) **b** to remove noxious gas from air **c** to prevent exhalation of infective material (e g during surgery) **4** a face-pack **5** the head or face of a fox, dog, etc [MF *masque*, fr OIt *maschera*]

[2]**mask** *vt* **1** to provide, cover, or conceal (as if) with a mask: e g **a** to make indistinct or imperceptible ⟨~s *the strong flavour*⟩ **b** to cover up ⟨~ed *his real purpose*⟩ **2** to cover for protection **3** to modify the shape of (e g a photograph) by means of a mask

,masked 'ball *n* a ball at which the participants wear masks

masochism /'masə,kiz(ə)m/ *n* **1** a sexual perversion in which pleasure is experienced from being physically or mentally abused – compare SADISM **2**

pleasure from sthg tiresome or painful – not used technically [ISV, fr Leopold von Sacher-*Masoch* †1895 Austrian novelist] – **masochist** *n*, **masochistic** /ˌmasəˈkistik/ *adj*, **masochistically** *adv*

mason /ˈmays(ə)n/ *n* **1** a skilled worker with stone **2** *cap* a freemason [ME, fr OF *maçon*, prob of Gmc origin; akin to OE *macian* to make]

ˌMason-ˈDixon ˌline /ˈdiks(ə)n/ *n* the S boundary line of Pennsylvania; *also* the boundary line between the free N and slave-owning S states of the USA [Charles *Mason* †1787 and Jeremiah *Dixon fl* 1767 E surveyors]

Masonic /məˈsonik/ *adj* (characteristic) of Freemasons or Freemasonry

masonry /ˈmays(ə)nri/ *n* **1** work done with or sthg constructed of stone; *also* a brick construction ☞ ARCHITECTURE **2** *cap* FREEMASONRY 1

Masora, Masorah /məˈsawrə/ *n* a body of notes on the text of the Hebrew Old Testament [NHeb *měsōrāh*, fr LHeb *māsōreth* tradition, fr Heb, bond] – **Masoretic** /ˌmasəˈretik/ *adj*

masque /mahsk/ *n* **1** MASQUERADE 1 **2** a short allegorical dramatic entertainment of the 16th and 17th c performed by masked actors [MF *masque*, fr OIt *maschera* mask]

[1]**masquerade** /ˌmaskəˈrayd/ *n* **1** a social gathering of people wearing masks and often fantastic costumes **2** sthg that is merely show [MF, fr OIt dial. *mascardada*, fr OIt *maschera*]

[2]**masquerade** *vi* **1** to disguise oneself; *also* to wear a disguise **2** to assume the appearance of sthg that one is not – usu + *as* – **masquerader** *n*

[1]**mass** /mas/ *n* **1** *cap* the liturgy or a celebration of the Eucharist, esp in Roman Catholic and Anglo-Catholic churches **2** a musical setting for the ordinary of the Mass [ME, fr OE *mæsse*, modif of (assumed) VL *messa*, lit., dismissal at the end of a religious service, fr LL *missa*, fr L, fem of *missus*, pp of *mittere* to send – more at SMITE]

[2]**mass** *n* **1a** a quantity of matter or the form of matter that holds together in 1 body **b(1)** an (unbroken) expanse ⟨*a mountain* ~⟩ ⟨*a* ~ *of colour*⟩ **(2)** the principal part or main body **(3)** a total, whole – esp in *in the mass* **c** the property of a body that is a measure of its inertia, causes it to have weight in a gravitational field, and is commonly taken as a measure of the amount of material it contains ☞ PHYSICS **2** a large quantity, amount, or number – often pl with sing. meaning ⟨*there was* ~es *of food left*⟩ **3** *pl* the body of ordinary people as contrasted with the élite [ME *masse*, fr MF, fr L *massa*, fr Gk *maza*; akin to Gk *massein* to knead – more at MINGLE] – **massless** *adj*

[3]**mass** *vb* to assemble in or collect into a mass

[4]**mass** *adj* **1a** of, designed for, or consisting of the mass of the people ⟨*a* ~ *market*⟩ **b** participated in by or affecting a large number of individuals ⟨~ *murder*⟩ **c** large scale **2** viewed as a whole; total

Massachuset /ˌmasəˈchoohsit/ *n, pl* **Massachusets** *also* **Massachusetts,** *esp collectively* **Massachuset** a member, or the Algonquian language, of an American Indian people of Massachusetts [Massachuset *Massa-ad-chu-es-et*, a locality, lit., about the big hill]

[1]**massacre** /ˈmasəkə/ *vt* **1** to kill (as if) in a massacre **2** to defeat severely; *also* MANGLE 2 – infml – **massacrer** /-krə/ *n*

[2]**massacre** *n* **1** the ruthless and indiscriminate killing of large numbers **2** complete defeat or destruction [MF]

massage /ˈmasahj, -sahzh/ *n* (an act of) kneading, rubbing, etc of the body in order to relieve aches, tone muscles, give relaxation, etc [F, fr *masser* to massage, fr Ar *massa* to stroke] – **massage** *vt*, **massager** *n*

ˌmass ˈdefect /ˈdeefekt/ *n* the difference between the mass of an isotope and its mass number

massé /ˈmasi/ *n* a shot in billiards, snooker, etc made with a (nearly) vertical cue so as to drive the cue ball in a curved path [F, fr pp of *masser* to make a massé shot, fr *masse* sledgehammer, fr MF *mace* mace]

masseter /maˈseetə/ *n* a large muscle that raises the lower jaw and assists in chewing [NL, fr Gk *masētēr*, fr *masasthai* to chew]

masseur /maˈsuh/, *fem* **masseuse** /masˈsuhz/ *n* one who practises massage and physiotherapy [F, fr *masser*]

massicot /ˈmasiˌkot/ *n* yellow lead monoxide used esp as a pigment – compare LITHARGE [ME *masticot*, fr MF *massicot, masticot*, fr OIt *massicotto* pottery glaze]

massif /ˈmaseef/ *n* **1** a principal mountain mass **2** a mountainous block bounded by faults or folds and displaced as a unit [F, fr *massif*, adj]

massive /ˈmasiv/ *adj* **1a** large, solid, or heavy **b** impressively large or ponderous **c** *of a mineral* not obviously crystalline **2a** large or impressive in scope or degree **b** large in comparison to what is typical ⟨*a* ~ *dose of penicillin*⟩ **c** extensive and severe ⟨~ *haemorrhage*⟩ [ME *massiffe*, fr MF *massif*, fr *masse* mass] – **massively** *adv*, **massiveness** *n*

ˌmass ˈmedia *n pl* broadcasting, newspapers, and other means of communication designed to reach large numbers of people

mass number *n* the number (of protons and neutrons in the nucleus) that expresses the mass of an isotope

mass observation *n, Br* the study and reporting of everyday human behaviour, habits, and opinions

ˌmass-proˈduce /prəˈdyoohs/ *vt* to produce (goods) in large quantities by standardized mechanical processes [back-formation fr *mass production*] – **mass production** /prəˈduksh(ə)n/ *n*

mass spectrograph *n* an apparatus that separates a stream of charged particles (e g electrons or fragments of a molecule) according to mass, usu with photographic recording of the data

mass spectrometer *n* an apparatus similar to a mass spectrograph but usu adapted for the electrical measurement of data – **mass spectrometry** /-mətri/ *n*

mass spectrum *n* the spectrum of a stream of charged particles produced by a mass spectrograph or mass spectrometer

massy /ˈmasi/ *adj* massive, heavy – fml

[1]**mast** /mahst/ *n* **1** a tall pole or structure rising from the keel or deck of a ship, esp for carrying sails **2** a vertical pole or lattice supporting a radio or television aerial [ME, fr OE *mæst*; akin to OHG *mast*, L *malus*] – **before the mast** as an ordinary sailor, not an officer

[2]**mast** *vt* to give a mast to

[3]**mast** *n* beechnuts, acorns, etc accumulated on the forest floor and often serving as food for animals (e g

pigs) [ME, fr OE *mæst*; akin to OHG *mast* food, mast, OE *mete* food – more at MEAT]

mastaba /'mastəbə/ *n* an Egyptian tomb that is oblong in shape with sloping sides and a flat roof [Ar *maṣṭabah* stone bench]

mastectomy /ma'stektəmi/ *n* excision or amputation of a breast [Gk *mastos* breast]

-masted /-mahstid/ *comb form* (*adj* → *adj*) having (such or so many) masts

[1]**master** /'mahstə/ *n* **1a(1)** a male teacher **(2)** a person holding an academic degree higher than a bachelor's but lower than a doctor's **b** *often cap* a revered religious leader **c** a workman qualified to teach apprentices ⟨*a ~ carpenter*⟩ **d** an artist, performer, player, etc of consummate skill **2a** one having control or authority over another **b** one who or that which conquers or masters; a victor **c** a person qualified to command a merchant ship **d(1)** an owner, esp of a slave or animal **(2)** *often cap* one who directs a hunt and has overall control of the pack of hounds **e** an employer **f** the male head of a household **3** *cap* a youth or boy too young to be called *mister* – used as a title **4** a presiding officer in an institution or society (e g a Masonic lodge) or at a function **5a** a mechanism or device that controls the operation of another **b** an original from which copies (e g of film or gramophone records) can be made **6** *archaic* Mr [ME, fr OE *magister* & OF *maistre*, both fr L *magister*; akin to L *magnus* great – more at MUCH] – **mastership** *n*

[2]**master** *vt* **1** to become master of; overcome **2a** to become skilled or proficient in the use of **b** to gain a thorough understanding of

[3]**master** *adj* **1** having chief authority; controlling **2** principal, main ⟨*the ~ bedroom*⟩

master aircrew *n* ☞ RANK

,**master-at-'arms** *n, pl* **masters-at-arms** a petty officer responsible for maintaining discipline aboard ship

master chief petty officer *n* ☞ RANK

'**master ,class** *n* a class in which an eminent musician listens to and corrects advanced pupils

'**masterful** /-f(ə)l/ *adj* **1** inclined to take control and dominate **2** having or showing the technical, artistic, or intellectual skill of a master – **masterfully** *adv*, **masterfulness** *n*

master gunnery sergeant *n* ☞ RANK

'**master ,key** *n* a key designed to open several different locks

'**masterly** /-li/ *adj* showing superior knowledge or skill [[1]MASTER + [1]-LY] – **masterliness** *n*

[1]'**master,mind** /-,miend/ *n* **1** one who masterminds a project **2** a person of outstanding intellect

[2]'**master,mind** *vt* to be the intellectual force behind (a project)

,**master of 'arts** *n, often cap M&A* the recipient of a master's degree, usu in an arts subject

,**master of 'ceremonies**, *fem* ,**mistress of 'ceremonies** /'mistris/ *n* **1** one who determines the procedure to be observed on a state or public occasion **2** one who acts as host, esp by introducing speakers, performers, etc, at an event

,**master of 'science** *n, often cap M&S* the recipient of a master's degree in a scientific subject

,**Master of the 'Rolls** *n* the presiding judge of the Court of Appeal

'**master,piece** /-,pees/ *n* a work done with extraordinary skill; *esp* the supreme creation of a type, period, or person [prob trans of D *meesterstuk* or G *meisterstück* (orig, a piece of work qualifying a craftsman for the rank of master)]

'**master ,sergeant** *n* ☞ RANK

'**master,stroke** /-,strohk/ *n* a masterly performance or move

mastery /'mahstəri/ *n* **1a** the authority of a master **b** the upper hand in a contest or competition **2a** possession or display of great skill or technique **b** skill or knowledge that makes one master of a subject [ME *maistrie*, fr OF, fr *maistre* master]

masthead /'mahst,hed/ *n* **1** the top of a mast **2** the name of a newspaper displayed on the top of the first page

mastic /'mastik/ *n* **1** an aromatic resin that exudes from mastic trees and is used esp in varnishes **2** a pasty substance used as a protective coating or cement [ME *mastik*, fr L *mastiche*, fr Gk *mastichē*; akin to Gk *mastichan*]

masticate /'mastikayt/ *vt* **1** to grind or crush (food) before swallowing, (as if) with the teeth; to chew **2** to soften or reduce to pulp (e g by crushing) ~ *vi* to chew [LL *masticatus*, pp of *masticare*, fr Gk *mastichan* to gnash the teeth; akin to Gk *masasthai* to chew – more at MOUTH] – **masticator** *n*, **masticatory** /-kət(ə)ri/ *adj or n*, **mastication** /,mas ti'kaysh(ə)n/ *n*

'**mastic ,tree** *n* a small S European tree of the sumach family that yields mastic

mastiff /'mastif/ *n* any of a breed of very large powerful deep-chested smooth-coated dogs used chiefly as guard dogs [ME *mastif*, modif of MF *mastin*, fr (assumed) VL *mansuetinus*, fr L *mansuetus* tame, fr pp of *mansuescere* to tame, fr *manus* hand + *suescere* to accustom]

mastitis /ma'stietəs/ *n* inflammation of the breast or udder, usu caused by infection [NL] – **mastitic** /ma'stitik/ *adj*

mastodon /'mastə,don/ *n* any of numerous extinct mammals similar to the related mammoths and elephants [NL *mastodont-*, *mastodon*, fr Gk *mastos* breast, nipple + *odont-*, *odōn*, *odous* tooth – more at TOOTH; fr the nipple-shaped projections on the molar teeth] – **mastodont** /-,dont/ *adj or n*, **mastodontic** /-'dontik/ *adj*

mastoid /'mastoyd/ *adj or n* (of, near, or being) a somewhat conical part of the temporal bone lying behind the ear [NL *mastoides* resembling a nipple, mastoid, fr Gk *mastoeidēs*, fr *mastos* breast – more at MEAT] – **mastoiditis** /,mastoy'dietəs/ *n*

masturbation /,mastə'baysh(ə)n/ *n* stimulation of the genitals commonly resulting in orgasm and accomplished by any means except sexual intercourse [prob fr (assumed) NL *masturbation-*, *masturbatio*, fr L *masturbatus*, pp of *masturbari* to masturbate] – **masturbate** /'mastəbayt/ *vb*, **masturbatory** /'mastə,baytəri/ *adj*

[1]**mat** /mat/ *n* **1a** a piece of coarse usu woven, felted, or plaited fabric (e g of rushes or rope) used esp as a floor covering; *also* RUG 1 **b** DOORMAT 1 **c** an often decorative piece of material used to protect a surface from heat, moisture, etc caused by an object placed on it **d** a large thick pad used as a protective surface for wrestling, tumbling, gymnastics, etc **2** sthg made up of many intertwined or tangled strands [ME, fr OE *meatte*, fr LL *matta*, of Sem origin; akin to Heb *miṭṭāh* bed]

[2]**mat** *vb* **-tt-** *vt* **1** to provide with a mat or matting **2**

to form into a tangled or compact mass ~*vi* to become tangled or intertwined

[3]**mat** *vt, adj, or n* **-tt-** (to) matt

matador /'matədaw/ *n* one who has the principal role and who kills the bull in a bullfight [Sp, fr *matar* to kill]

[1]**match** /mach/ *n* **1a** one who or that which is equal to or able to contend with another **b** a person or thing exactly like another **2** two people, animals, or things that go well together **3** a contest between 2 or more teams or individuals **4a** a marriage union **b** a prospective partner in marriage [ME *macche,* fr OE *mæcca;* akin to OE *macian* to make – more at MAKE]

[2]**match** *vt* **1a** to be equal to (an opponent) **b** to set in competition, opposition, or comparison **2a** to cause to correspond ⟨~ing *life-style to income*⟩ **b(1)** to be, find, or provide the exact counterpart or equal of or for **(2)** to harmonize with **c** to provide funds complementary to **3** *archaic* to join or give in marriage ~*vi* **1** to be a counterpart or equal **2** to harmonize – **matcher** *n*

[3]**match** *n* **1** a chemically prepared wick or cord formerly used in firing firearms or powder **2** a short slender piece of wood, cardboard, etc tipped with a mixture that ignites when subjected to friction [ME *macche,* fr MF *meiche*]

matchboard /'mach,bawd/ *n* a board with a groove cut along one edge and a tongue along the other so as to fit snugly with the edges of similarly cut boards

'matchless /-lis/ *adj* having no equal – **matchlessly** *adv*

matchlock /'mach,lok/ *n* (a musket with) a gunlock with a match for igniting the charge

matchmaker /'mach,maykə/ *n* one who arranges marriages; *also* one who derives vicarious pleasure from contriving to arrange marriages – **matchmaking** *n*

'match ,play *n* a golf competition scored by number of holes won rather than strokes played – compare STROKE PLAY

'match ,point *n* a situation in tennis, badminton, etc in which a player will win the match by winning the next point

matchstick /'mach,stik/ *n* [3]MATCH 2; *specif* one made of wood

matchwood /'mach,wood/ *n* wood suitable for matches; *also* wood splinters

[1]**mate** /mayt/ *vt* CHECKMATE 2 [ME *maten,* fr MF *mater,* fr OF *mat,* n, checkmate, fr Ar *māt* (in *shāh māt*)]

[2]**mate** *n* CHECKMATE 1

[3]**mate** *n* **1a** an associate, companion – usu in combination ⟨*flat*mate⟩ ⟨*play*mate⟩ **b** an assistant to a more skilled workman ⟨*plumber's* ~⟩ **c** a friend, chum – often used in familiar address, esp to a man by a man **2** a deck officer on a merchant ship ranking below the captain **3a** either of a pair: e g **(1)** either member of a breeding pair of animals **(2)** either of 2 matched objects **b** a marriage partner [ME, prob fr MLG *māt;* akin to OE *gemetta* guest at one's table, *mete* food – more at MEAT]

[4]**mate** *vt* **1** to join or fit together; couple **2a** to join together as mates **b** to provide a mate for ~*vi* **1** to become mated ⟨*gears that* ~ *well*⟩ **2** to copulate

maté, mate /'matay, 'mahtay/ *n* **1** a tealike aromatic beverage used chiefly in S America **2** (the leaves and shoots, used in making maté, of) a S American holly [F & AmerSp; F *maté,* fr AmerSp *mate,* fr Quechua]

matelot /'mat(ə)loh/ *n, Br* SAILOR 1b – infml [F, fr MF, fr MD *mattenoot,* fr *matte* mat, bed + *noot* companion]

mater /'maytə/ *n, chiefly Br* a mother – now usu humor [L]

materfamilias /,maytəfə'mili·əs/ *n* a female head of a household [L, fr *mater* + *familias,* arch gen of *familia* household – more at FAMILY]

[1]**material** /mə'tiəri·əl/ *adj* **1a(1)** of, derived from, or consisting of matter; *esp* physical **(2)** bodily **b** of matter rather than form ⟨~ *cause*⟩ **2** important, significant ⟨*facts* ~ *to the investigation*⟩ **3** of or concerned with physical rather than spiritual things [ME *materiel,* fr MF & LL; MF, fr LL *materialis,* fr L *materia* matter – more at MATTER] – **materially** *adv,* **materiality** /mə,tiəri'aləti/ *n*

[2]**material** *n* **1a(1)** the elements, constituents, or substances of which sthg is composed or can be made **(2)** matter that has usu specified qualities which give it individuality ⟨*sticky* ~⟩ **b(1)** data that may be worked into a more finished form – compare RAW MATERIAL **(2)** a person considered with a view to his/her potential for successful training ⟨*I don't think he's officer* ~⟩ **c** cloth **2** *pl* apparatus necessary for doing or making sthg

ma'teria,lism /-,liz(ə)m/ *n* **1a** a theory that only physical matter is real and that all processes and phenomena can be explained by reference to matter **b** a doctrine that the highest values lie in material well-being and material progress **2** a preoccupation with or stress on material rather than spiritual things – **materialist** *n or adj,* **materialistic** /-'listik/ *adj*

materialize, -ise /mə'tiəri·ə,liez/ *vb* **1** to (cause to) have existence or tangibility ⟨~ *an idea in words*⟩ **2** to (cause to) appear in or assume bodily form – **materialization** /-lie'zaysh(ə)n/ *n*

matériel, materiel /mə,tieri'el/ *n* equipment, apparatus, and supplies used by an organization, the armed forces, etc [F *matériel,* fr *matériel,* adj]

maternal /mə'tuhnl/ *adj* **1** (characteristic) of a mother **2** related through a mother [ME, fr MF *maternel,* fr L *maternus,* fr *mater* mother – more at [1]MOTHER] – **maternally** *adv*

[1]**maternity** /mə'tuhnəti/ *n* **1a** motherhood **b** motherliness **2** a hospital department for the care of women before and during childbirth

[2]**maternity** *adj* designed for wear during pregnancy ⟨*a* ~ *dress*⟩

[1]**matey** /'mayti/ *n, chiefly Br* [3]MATE 1c – chiefly in familiar address [[3]*mate* + [4]*-y*]

[2]**matey** *adj, chiefly Br* friendly – infml [[3]*mate* + [1]*-y*] – **mateyness, matiness** *n*

math /math/ *n, NAm* mathematics

mathematical /,mathə'matikl/ *also* **mathematic** /-tik/ *adj* **1** of, used in, using, or according with mathematics **2** rigorously exact [L *mathematicus,* fr Gk *mathēmatikos,* fr *mathēmat-, mathēma* mathematics, fr *manthanein* to learn; akin to Goth *mundon* to pay attention, Skt *medhā* intelligence] – **mathematically** *adv*

mathematics /,mathə'matiks/ *n pl but sing or pl in constr* **1** the science of numbers and their operations, interrelations, and combinations and of space configurations and their structure, measurement, etc **2** the mathematics or mathematical operations

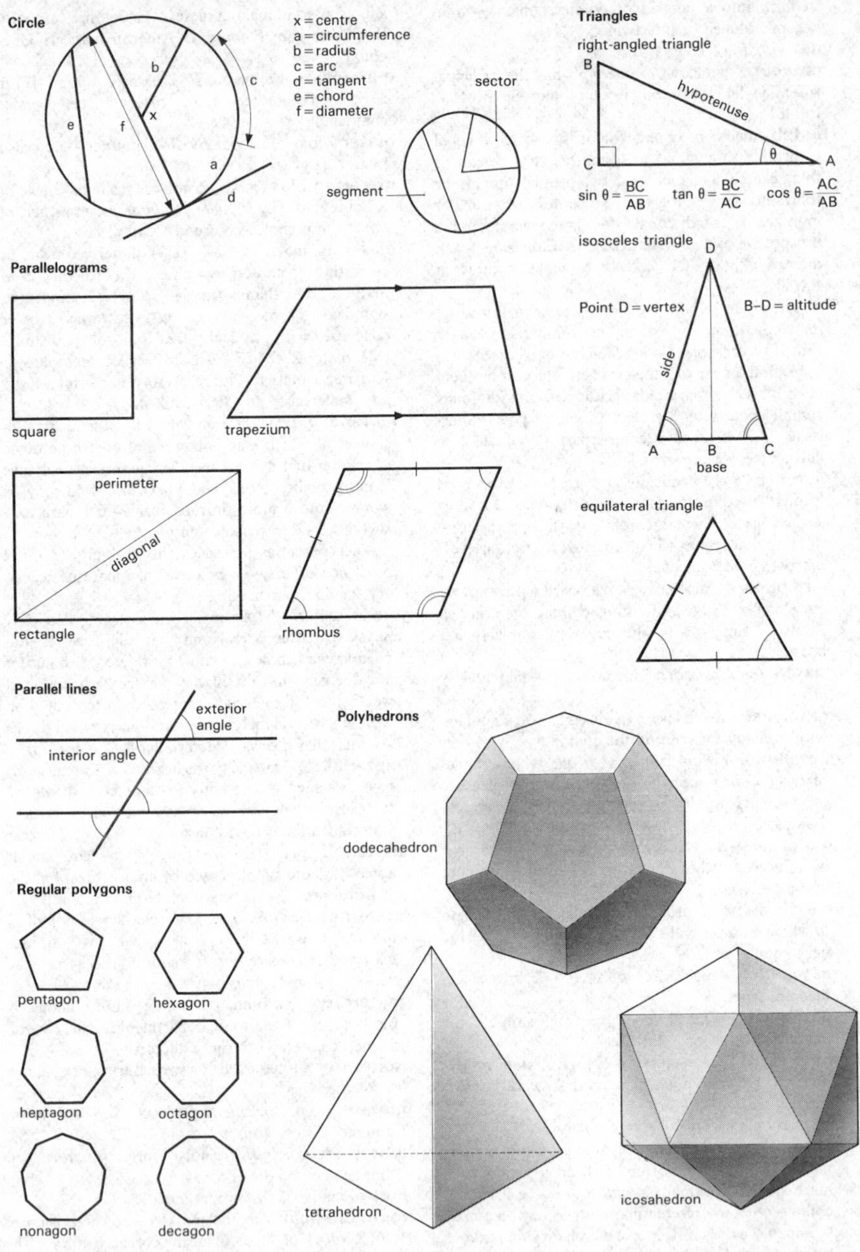
Circle
x = centre
a = circumference
b = radius
c = arc
d = tangent
e = chord
f = diameter
b
c
x
e
f
a
d
sector
segment
Triangles
right-angled triangle
B
hypotenuse
θ
C
A
sin θ = BC/AB
tan θ = BC/AC
cos θ = AC/AB
isosceles triangle
D
Point D = vertex
B–D = altitude
side
A
B
C
base
equilateral triangle
Parallelograms
square
trapezium
perimeter
diagonal
rectangle
rhombus
Parallel lines
exterior angle
interior angle
Polyhedrons
dodecahedron
Regular polygons
pentagon
hexagon
heptagon
octagon
nonagon
decagon
tetrahedron
icosahedron

☞ SYMBOL

Conic sections

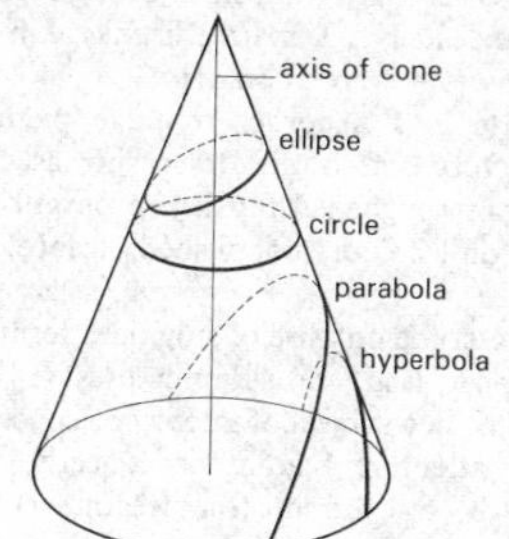

Hyperbola

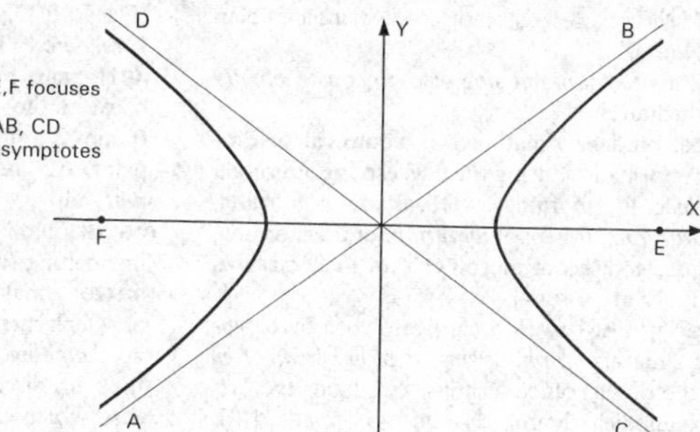

Ellipse

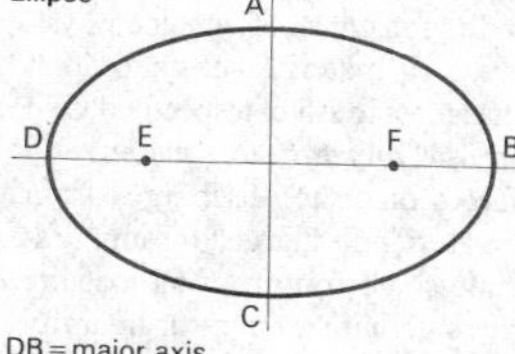

DB = major axis
AC = minor axis
E,F = focuses

Parabola

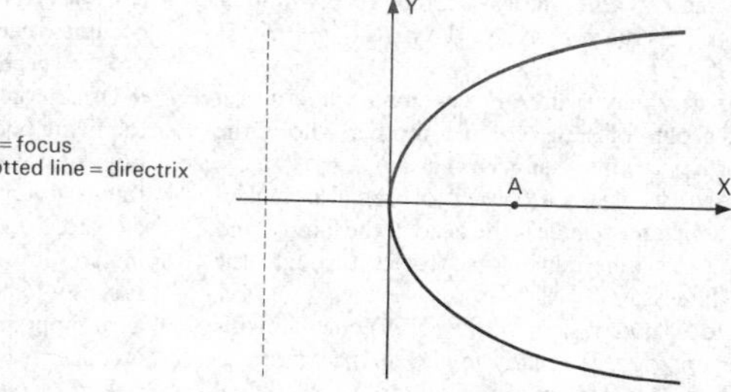

Golden section

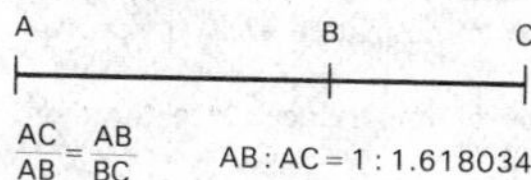

$\frac{AC}{AB} = \frac{AB}{BC}$ AB : AC = 1 : 1.618034

Trigonometric functions sine and cosine

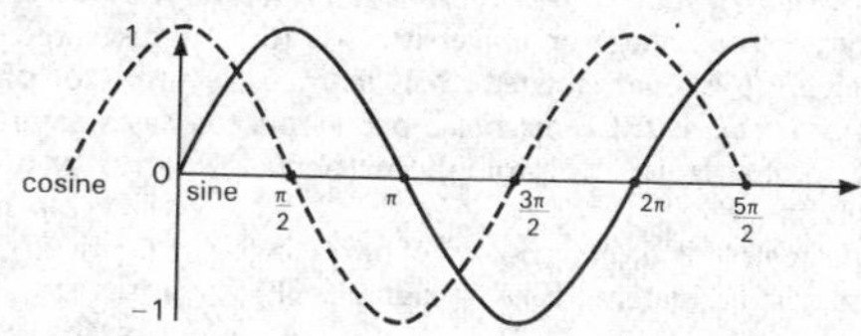

Hyperboloid

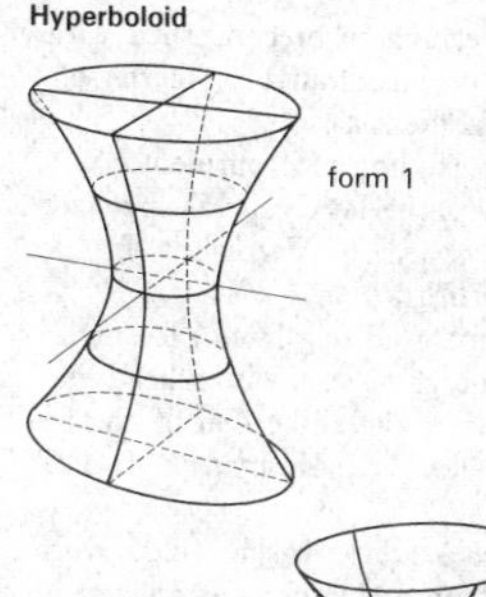

tangent

A, B, C, D = points of inflection ----- = asymptotes

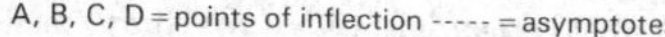

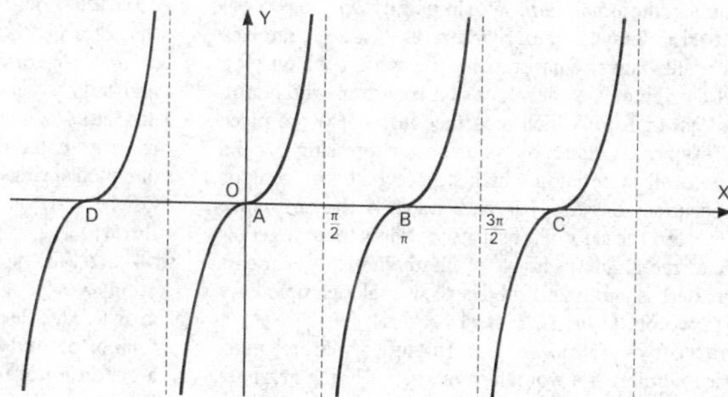

involved in a particular problem, field of study, etc *USE* (eye symbol) (hand symbol) SYMBOL – **mathematician** /-mə'tish(ə)n/ *n*

maths /maths/ *n pl but sing or pl in constr, chiefly Br* mathematics

matinée, matinee /'matinay/ *n* a musical or dramatic performance during the day, esp the afternoon [F *matinée,* lit., morning, fr OF, fr *matin* morning, fr L *matutinum,* fr neut of *matutinus* of the morning, fr *Matuta,* goddess of morning; akin to L *maturus* ripe – more at MATURE]

'matinee ,jacket *n, Br* a cardigan worn by babies

matins /'matinz/ *n pl but sing or pl in constr often cap* **1** the (night) office forming with lauds the first of the canonical hours **2** MORNING PRAYER [ME *matines,* fr OF, fr LL *matutinae,* fr L, fem pl of *matutinus*]

matr-, matri- *also* **matro-** *comb form* mother ⟨*matri*arch⟩ ⟨*matro*nymic⟩ [L *matr-, matri-,* fr *matr-, mater*]

matriarch /'maytri,ahk/ *n* a woman who rules a family, group, or state; *specif* a mother who is the head of her family – **matriarchal** *adj*

'matri,archy /-ki/ *n* a (system of) social organization in which the female is the head of the family, and descent and inheritance are traced through the female line

matricide /'maytri,sied/ *n* (the act of) one who kills his/her mother [L *matricida* & *matricidium,* fr *matr-* + *-cida* & *-cidium* – more at -CIDE] – **matricidal** /,maytri'siedl/ *adj*

matriculate /mə'trikyoolayt/ *vt* to enrol as a member of a body, esp a college or university ~ *vi* (to become eligible) to be matriculated [ML *matriculatus,* pp of *matriculare,* fr LL *matricula* public roll, dim. of *matric-, matrix* list, fr L, womb] – **matriculation** /-'laysh(ə)n/ *n*

matrilineal /,matri'lini·əl, ,maytri-/ *adj* of or tracing descent through the maternal line – **matrilineally** *adv*

matrimony /'matriməni/ *n* MARRIAGE 1 [ME, fr MF *matremoine,* fr L *matrimonium,* fr *matr-, mater* mother, matron – more at [1]MOTHER] – **matrimonial** /,matri'mohni·əl/ *adj,* **matrimonially** *adv*

matrix /'maytriks/ *n, pl* **matrices** /-,seez/, **matrixes** **1** a substance, environment, etc within which sthg else originates or develops **2** a mould in which sthg is cast or from which a surface in relief (e g a piece of type) is made by pouring or pressing **3** the (natural) material in which sthg (e g a fossil, gem, or specimen for study) is embedded **4** the substance between the cells of a tissue that holds them together **5** a rectangular array of mathematical elements treated as a unit and subject to special algebraic laws [L, womb, fr *matr-, mater*]

matron /'maytrən/ *n* **1a** a (dignified mature) married woman **b** a woman in charge of living arrangements in a school, residential home, etc **2** *Br* a woman in charge of the nursing in a hospital – not now used technically [ME *matrone,* fr MF, fr L *matrona,* fr *matr-, mater*] – **matronly** *adj*

,matron of 'honour *n* a bride's principal married wedding attendant

matronymic /,matrə'nimik/ *n* a metronymic [*matr-* + *-onymic* (as in *patronymic*)]

[1]matt, mat, matte /mat/ *vt* to make (e g metal or colour) matt

[2]matt, mat, matte *adj* lacking lustre or gloss; *esp* having an even surface free from shine or highlights [F *mat,* fr OF, defeated, fr L *mattus* drunk; akin to L *madēre* to be wet – more at MEAT]

[3]matt, mat, matte *n* **1** a border round a picture between the picture and frame or serving as the frame **2** a dull or roughened finish (e g on gilt or paint) [F *mat* dull colour, unpolished surface, fr *mat,* adj]

matte /mat/ *n* a crude mixture of sulphides formed in smelting (copper, lead, etc) sulphide ores [F]

[1]matter /'matə/ *n* **1a** a subject of interest or concern or which merits attention **b** an affair, concern ⟨*it's no laughing* ~⟩ **c** material (for treatment) in thought, discourse, or writing **d** that part of a legal case which deals with facts rather than law **e** a condition (unfavourably) affecting a person or thing ⟨*what's the* ~*?*⟩ **2a** the substance of which a physical object is composed **b** material substance that occupies space and has mass **c** sth of a specified kind or for a specified purpose ⟨*mineral* ~⟩ ⟨*reading* ~⟩ **d(1)** material (e g faeces or urine) discharged from the living body **(2)** material discharged by suppuration; pus **3** the formless substratum of all existing things **4** a more or less definite amount or quantity ⟨*a* ~ *of 10 years*⟩ [ME *matere,* fr OF, fr L *materia* matter, physical substance, fr *mater*] – **as a matter of fact** as it happens; actually – often used in correcting a misapprehension – **for that matter** so far as that is concerned – **no matter** it does not matter; irrespective of ⟨*would be calm* no matter *what the provocation*⟩

[2]matter *vi* **1** to be of importance **2** to form or discharge pus

,matter of 'course *n* sthg routine or to be expected as a natural consequence

,matter-of-'fact *adj* keeping to or concerned with fact; *esp* not fanciful or imaginative – **matter-of-factly** *adv,* **matter-of-factness** *n*

mattery /'matəri/ *adj* exuding pus; purulent

Matthew /'mathyooh/ *n* the 1st Gospel in the New Testament [F *Mathieu,* fr LL *Matthaeus,* fr Gk *Matthaios,* fr Heb *Mattithyāh*]

matting /'mating/ *n* material (e g hemp) for mats

mattock /'matək/ *n* a digging tool with a head like that of a pick and often a blade like that of an axe or adze – compare [5]PICK 1 [ME *mattok,* fr OE *mattuc*]

mattress /'matris/ *n* a fabric casing filled with resilient material (e g foam rubber or an arrangement of coiled springs) used esp on a bed [ME *materas,* fr OF, fr Ar *maṭraḥ* place where something is thrown]

[1]mature /mə'tyooə/ *adj* **1** based on careful consideration ⟨*a* ~ *judgment*⟩ **2a** having completed natural growth and development; ripe **b** having attained a final or desired state **3a** (characteristic) of or having a condition of full or adult development **b** older or more experienced than others of his/her kind ⟨*a* ~ *student*⟩ **4** due for payment ⟨*a* ~ *loan*⟩ [ME, fr L *maturus* ripe; akin to L *mane* in the morning, *manus* good] – **maturely** *adv,* **matureness, maturity** *n*

[2]mature *vt* to bring to full development or completion ~ *vi* **1** to become mature **2** to become due for payment – **maturation** /,matyoo'raysh(ə)n/ *n,* **maturational** *adj*

matutinal /,matyoo'tienl/ *adj* of or occurring in the morning – fml [LL *matutinalis,* fr L *matutinus* – more at MATINÉE]

matzo /'matsoh/ *n, pl* **matzoth** /-soht(h)/, **matzos** /-sohs/ (a wafer of) unleavened bread eaten esp at the Passover [Yiddish *matse*, fr Heb *maṣṣāh*]

maudlin /'mawdlin/ *adj* **1** weakly and effusively sentimental **2** drunk enough to be emotionally silly [alter. of Mary *Magdalen*; fr the practice of depicting her as a weeping, penitent sinner]

[1]**maul** /mawl/ *vt* **1** *esp of an animal* to attack and tear the flesh of **2** to handle roughly [ME *mallen*, fr OF *maillier*, fr *mail* hammer, fr L *malleus*; akin to L *molere* to grind – more at [2]MEAL] – **mauler** *n*

[2]**maul** *n* **1** a situation in Rugby Union in which 1 or more players from each team close round the player carrying the ball who tries to get the ball out to his own team – compare RUCK **2** a confused and noisy struggle

maulstick, mahlstick /'mawl,stik/ *n* a stick used by painters to support and steady the hand while working [part trans of D *maalstok*, fr obs D *malen* to paint + D *stok* stick]

Mau Mau /'mow ,mow/ *n* a political terrorist organization founded in 1952 with the aim of driving Europeans out of Kenya [origin unknown]

maun /mawn/ *verbal auxiliary, Scot* must [ME *man*, fr ON, will, shall]

maunder /'mawndə/ *vi* **1** to act or wander idly **2** to speak in a rambling or indistinct manner; *also, Br* to grumble [prob imit] – **maunderer** /-dərə/ *n*

maundy /'mawndi/ *n, often cap* (the distribution of) maundy money

'**maundy ,money** *n, often cap 1st or 1st&2nd M* specially minted coins given to selected poor people by the British Sovereign in a ceremony on Maundy Thursday

,**Maundy 'Thursday** *n* the Thursday before Easter observed in commemoration of the Last Supper [ME *maunde* ceremony of washing the feet of the poor on Maundy Thursday, fr OF *mandé*, fr L *mandatum* command; fr Jesus' words in John 13:34 – more at MANDATE]

mausoleum /,mawsə'lee·əm/ *n, pl* **mausoleums** *also* **mausolea** /-'lee·ə/ a large and elaborate tomb [L, fr Gk *mausōleion*, fr *Mausōlos* Mausolus † *ab* 353 BC, ruler of Caria in Asia Minor]

mauve /mohv/ *n or adj* bluish purple [n F, mallow, fr L *malva*; adj fr n]

maverick /'mav(ə)rik/ *n* **1** an independent and nonconformist individual **2** *NAm* an unbranded range animal; *esp* a motherless calf [Samuel A *Maverick* †1870 US pioneer who did not brand his calves]

mavis /'mayvis/ *n* SONG THRUSH – chiefly poetic [ME, fr MF *mauvis*]

mavourneen /mə'vooəneen/ *n, Irish* my darling [IrGael *mo mhuirnīn*, fr *mo* my + *muirnīn* darling]

maw /maw/ *n* **1a** an animal's stomach or crop **b** the throat, gullet, or jaws, esp of a voracious flesh-eating animal **2** sthg resembling a maw, esp in gaping or tending to swallow things up [ME, fr OE *maga*; akin to OHG *mago* stomach, Lith *makas* purse]

mawkish /'mawkish/ *adj* **1** having an insipid often unpleasant taste **2** sickly or feebly sentimental [ME *mawke* maggot, fr ON *mathkr* – more at MAGGOT] – **mawkishly** *adv*, **mawkishness** *n*

maxi /'maksi/ *n, pl* **maxis** a floor-length woman's coat, skirt, etc [*maxi-*]

maxi- *comb form* **1** extra long ⟨maxi-*skirt*⟩ **2** extra large ⟨maxi-*budget*⟩ [fr *maximum*, by analogy to *minimum* : *mini-*]

maxilla /mak'silə/ *n, pl* **maxillae** /-li/, **maxillas** **1a** JAW 1a **b** (either of 2 bones of) the upper jaw of a human or other higher vertebrate **2** any of the (1 or 2 pairs of) mouthparts behind the mandibles in insects and other arthropods [L, dim. of *mala* jaw] – **maxillary** /-ləri/ *adj or n*

maxim /'maksim/ *n* (a succinct expression of) a general truth, fundamental principle, or rule of conduct [ME *maxime*, fr MF, fr ML *maxima*, fr L, fem of *maximus*, superl of *magnus* great – more at MUCH]

maximal /'maksiml/ *adj* **1** greatest; most comprehensive **2** being an upper limit – **maximally** *adv*

maximalist /'maksiml,ist/ *n* one who seeks to secure immediate acceptance of his/her demands without compromise

maxim·ize, ise /'maksi,miez/ *vt* to increase to a maximum or to the highest possible degree – **maximization** /-'zaysh(ə)n/ *n*

maximum /'maksiməm/ *n, pl* **maxima** /-mə/, **maximums** **1** the greatest quantity or value attainable or attained **2** the period of highest or most extreme development [L, neut of *maximus*] – **maximum** *adj*

maxwell /'makswəl, -wel/ *n* the cgs unit of magnetic flux [James Clerk *Maxwell* †1879 Sc physicist]

may /may/ *verbal auxiliary, pres sing & pl* **may**; *past* **might** /miet/ *va* **1a** have permission to ⟨*you ~ go now*⟩; have liberty to ⟨*what's this, ~ I ask?*⟩ **b** be in some degree likely to ⟨*you ~ be right*⟩ ⟨*the road ~ well be closed*⟩ – compare AS WELL 3 **2** – used to express a wish or desire, esp in prayer, curse, or benediction ⟨*long ~ he reign*⟩ **3** – used to express purpose or expectation ⟨*sit here so I ~ see you better*⟩, contingency ⟨*he'll do his duty come what ~*⟩, or concession ⟨*he ~ be slow but he is thorough*⟩; used in questions to emphasize ironic uncertainty ⟨*and who ~ you be?*⟩ [ME (1 & 3 sing. pres indic), fr OE *mæg*; akin to OHG *mag* (1 & 3 sing. pres indic) have power, am able (infinitive *magan*), Gk *mēchos* means, expedient]

May *n* **1** the 5th month of the Gregorian calendar **2** *not cap* (the blossom of) hawthorn [ME, fr OF & L; OF *mai*, fr L *Maius*, fr *Maia*, Roman goddess]

maya /'mie·ə/ *n* the diverse world as perceived by the senses, held in Hinduism to conceal the unity of absolute being; *broadly* deceptive appearance or illusion [Skt *māyā*]

Maya /'mie·ə/ *n, pl* **Mayas**, *esp collectively* **Maya** a member or the language of a group of American Indian peoples inhabiting the Yucatán peninsula until the 15th c ☞ LANGUAGE [Sp] – **Mayan** *n or adj*

mayapple /'may,apl/ *n* (a N American plant that bears) an edible egg-shaped yellow fruit [*May*]

maybe /'may,bee/ *adv* perhaps [ME, fr (it) *may be*]

maybug /'may,bug/ *n* a cockchafer

Mayday /'may,day/ – used for an international radiotelephone signal word used as a distress call [F *m'aider* help me]

'**May ,Day** *n* May 1 celebrated as a springtime festival and in many countries as a public holiday in honour of working people

mayest /'mayist/, **mayst** /mayst/ *archaic pres 2 sing of* MAY

'may,flower /-,flowə/ *n* any of various spring-blooming plants

'may,fly /-,flie/ *n* any of an order of insects with an aquatic nymph and a short-lived fragile adult with membranous wings

mayhem /'mayhem/ *n* **1** needless or wilful damage **2** a state of great confusion or disorder [ME *mayme*, fr AF *mahaim*, fr OF, loss of a limb, fr *maynier* to maim]

maying /'maying/ *n, often cap* the celebrating of May Day [ME, fr gerund of *mayen* to may, celebrate May Day]

mayn't /maynt/ may not

mayonnaise /,mayə'nayz/ *n* a thick dressing (e g for salad) made with egg yolks, vegetable oil, and vinegar or lemon juice [F]

mayor /meə/ *n* the chief executive or nominal head of a city or borough [ME *maire*, fr OF, fr L *major* greater – more at MAJOR] – **mayoral** /'meərəl/ *adj*

mayoralty /'meərəlti/ *n* the (term of) office of a mayor [ME *mairaltee*, fr MF *mairalté*, fr OF, fr *maire*]

mayoress /'meəris/ *n* **1** the wife or hostess of a mayor **2** a female mayor

maypole /'may,pohl/ *n* a tall ribbon-wreathed pole forming a centre for dances, esp on May Day

mayst /mayst/ mayest

'May ,Week *n* a Cambridge university festival period in June with boat races between the colleges, balls, etc – compare EIGHTS WEEK

¹maze /mayz/ *vt, archaic* to bewilder, perplex [ME *mazen*, prob fr (assumed) OE *masian* to confuse; perh akin to Sw *masa* to be sluggish]

²maze *n* **1a** (a drawn representation of) a network of paths designed to confuse and puzzle those who attempt to walk through it **b** sthg intricately or confusingly complicated **2** *archaic* a state of bewilderment – **mazy** *adj*

mazer /'mayzə/ *n* a large drinking bowl orig of a hard wood [ME, fr OF *mazere*, of Gmc origin; akin to OHG *masar* gnarled excrescence on a tree]

mazurka *also* **mazourka** /mə'zuhkə/ *n* (music for, or in the rhythm of) a Polish folk dance in moderate triple time [F, fr Pol *mazurka* woman of province Mazovia]

mazzard /'mazəd/ *n* a (wild) sweet cherry (used as a rootstock for grafting) [origin unknown]

MC *n* MASTER OF CEREMONIES

¹me /mee/ *pron, objective case of* I ⟨*looked at* ~⟩ ⟨*fatter than* ~⟩ ⟨*it's* ~⟩ [ME, fr OE *mē*; akin to OHG *mih* me, L *me*, Gk *me*, Skt *mā*]

²me *n* sthg suitable for me ⟨*that dress isn't really* ~⟩

³me *n* the 3rd note of the diatonic scale in solmization [ML *mi* – more at GAMUT]

mea culpa /,mayah 'koolpah/ *n or interj* (a formal acknowledgment) used to admit personal fault [L, through my fault]

¹mead /meed/ *n* a fermented alcoholic drink made of water, honey, malt, and yeast [ME *mede*, fr OE *medu*; akin to OHG *metu* mead, Gk *methy* wine, Skt *madhu* sweet, honey, mead]

²mead *n* a meadow – archaic or poetic [ME *mede*, fr OE *mǣd*]

meadow /'medoh/ *n* (an area of moist low-lying usu level) grassland [ME *medwe*, fr OE *mǣdwe*, oblique case form of *mǣd*; akin to OE *māwan* to mow – more at ²MOW]

'meadow ,grass *n* any of various grasses that thrive in moist areas

'meadow ,pipit *n* a common olive and white Old World pipit

'meadow ,saffron *n* a (lilac-flowered European) colchicum

'meadow,sweet *n* a tall Eurasian plant of the rose family with creamy-white fragrant flowers

meagre, *NAm chiefly* **meager** /'meegə/ *adj* **1** having little flesh **2** deficient in quality or quantity [ME *megre*, fr MF *maigre*, fr L *macr-*, *macer* lean; akin to OE *mæger* lean, Gk *makros* long] – **meagrely** *adv*, **meagreness** *n*

¹meal /meel, miəl/ *n* **1** the portion of food taken or provided at 1 time to satisfy appetite **2** (the time of) eating a meal [ME *meel* appointed time, meal, fr OE *mǣl*; akin to OHG *māl* time, L *metiri* to measure – more at MEASURE]

²meal *n* (a product resembling, esp in texture) the usu coarsely ground seeds of a cereal grass or pulse [ME *mele*, fr OE *melu*; akin to OHG *melo* meal, L *molere* to grind, Gk *mylē* mill]

mealie /'meeli/ *n, SAfr* (an ear of) maize [Afrik *mielie*, fr Pg *milho* millet, fr L *milium* – more at MILLET]

,meals on 'wheels *n* a service whereby meals are brought to the housebound

'meal,time *n* the usual time for a meal

'meal,worm *n* the larva of various beetles that infest grain products; *esp* one raised as food for insect-eating animals, bait for fishing, etc

mealy /'meeli/ *adj* **1** soft, dry, and crumbly **2** containing meal **3a** covered with meal or fine granules **b** *esp of a horse* flecked with another colour

'mealy,bug /-,bug/ *n* any of numerous scale insects with a white powdery covering that are pests, esp of fruit trees

,mealy-'mouthed *adj* unwilling to speak plainly or directly, esp when this may offend

¹mean /meen/ *adj* **1** lacking distinction or eminence; merely ordinary or inferior ⟨*a man of* ~ *estate*⟩ ⟨*no* ~ *feat*⟩ **2** of poor shabby inferior quality or status **3** not honourable or worthy; base; *esp* small-minded **4a** not generous **b** characterized by petty malice; spiteful **c** *chiefly NAm* particularly bad-tempered, unpleasant, or disagreeable **d** excellent, impressive – infml ⟨*blows a* ~ *trumpet – Globe & Mail* (Toronto)⟩ [ME *mene*, fr *imene*, fr OE *gemǣne*; akin to OHG *gimeini* common, L *communis* common, *munus* service, gift] – **meanly** *adv*, **meanness** *n*

²mean *vb* **meant** /ment/ *vt* **1** to have in mind as a purpose; intend ⟨*she* ~t *no offence*⟩ ⟨*I* ~ *to leave soon*⟩ **2** to serve or intend to convey, produce, or indicate; signify ⟨*red* ~s *danger*⟩ ⟨*this action will* ~ *war*⟩ **3** to intend for a particular use or purpose ⟨*it is* ~t *to relieve pain*⟩ ⟨*I* ~t *it as a warning*⟩ **4** to have significance or importance to the extent or degree of ⟨*health* ~s *everything*⟩ ~ *vi* to have an intended purpose – chiefly in *to mean well/ill* [ME *menen*, fr OE *mǣnan*; akin to OHG *meinen* to have in mind, OSlav *měniti* to mention] – **I mean** – used to introduce and emphasize a clause or sentence or when hesitating ⟨*it wasn't too bad.* I mean *it didn't even hurt*⟩ – **mean business** to be in earnest

³mean *n* **1a** a middle point between extremes **b** a value that lies within a range of values and is computed according to a prescribed law; *esp* ARITHMETIC

MEAN ☞ STATISTICS **2** *pl but sing or pl in constr* that which enables a desired purpose to be achieved; *also* the method used to attain an end **3** *pl* resources available for disposal; *esp* wealth ⟨*a man of* ∼s⟩ [ME *mene*, fr MF *meien*, fr *meien*, adj]

⁴mean *adj* **1** occupying a middle position; intermediate in space, order, time, kind, or degree **2** being the mean of a set of values ⟨∼ *temperature*⟩ [ME *mene*, fr MF *meien*, fr L *medianus* – more at MEDIAN]

¹meander /mi'andə/ *n* a turn or winding of a stream – usu pl ☞ GEOGRAPHY [L *maeander*, fr Gk *maiandros*, fr *Maiandros* (now *Menderes*), river in Asia Minor]

²meander *vi* **1** to follow a winding course **2** to wander aimlessly without urgent destination

mean free path *n* the average distance travelled in a gas by a molecule between collisions with other molecules

meanie /'meeni/ *n* a narrow-minded or ungenerous person – infml [¹*mean* + *-ie*]

¹meaning /'meening/ *n* **1** that which is conveyed or which one intends to convey, esp by language **2** significant quality; value ⟨*this has no* ∼ *in law*⟩ **3** implication of a hidden or special significance ⟨*a glance full of* ∼⟩ – **meaningful** *adj*, **meaningfully** *adv*, **meaningfulness** *n*, **meaningless** *adj*, **meaninglessly** *adv*, **meaninglessness** *n*

²meaning *adj* significant, expressive – **meaningly** *adv*

'means ,test *n* an examination into sby's financial state to determine his/her eligibility for public assistance, for a student grant, etc

'mean ,sun *n* a fictitious sun used for timekeeping that moves at a constant rate along the celestial equator

meant /ment/ *adj*, *past of* MEAN *Br* expected, supposed ⟨*to get a mature student's place you are* ∼ *to have a minimum of five O-levels – Observer Magazine*⟩ [fr pp of ²*mean*]

¹meantime /'meen,tiem/ *n* the intervening time ⟨*in the* ∼⟩ [⁴*mean*]

²meantime *adv* meanwhile

'mean ,time *n* time that is based on the motion of the mean sun and that has the mean solar second as its unit

¹meanwhile /'meen,wiel/ *n* the meantime

²meanwhile *adv* **1** during the intervening time **2** during the same period ⟨∼, *down on the farm*⟩

measles /'meezlz/ *n pl but sing or pl in constr* **1** (German measles or another disease similar to) an infectious virus disease marked by a rash of distinct red circular spots **2** infestation with larval tapeworms, esp in pigs or pork [(1) ME *meseles*, pl of *mesel* measles, spot characteristic of measles, alter. (influenced by *mesel* leper) of *masel*; akin to MD *masel* spot characteristic of measles, & prob to OHG *masar* gnarled excrescence on tree – more at MAZER; (2) ME *mesel* infested with tapeworms, lit., leprous, fr OF, fr ML *misellus* leper, fr L, wretch, fr *misellus*, dim. of *miser* miserable]

measly /'meezli/ *adj* **1** infected with measles **2** containing larval tapeworms ⟨∼ *pork*⟩ **3** contemptibly small; *also* worthless – infml

¹measure /'mezhə/ *n* **1a(1)** an appropriate or due portion ⟨*had their* ∼ *of luck*⟩ **(2)** a (moderate) extent, amount, or degree ⟨*a* ∼ *of respectability*⟩ **(3)** a fixed, suitable, or conceivable limit ⟨*wisdom beyond* ∼⟩ **b(1)** the dimensions, capacity, or amount of sthg ascertained by measuring **(2)** the character, nature, or capacity of sby or sthg ascertained by assessment – esp in *get the measure of* **(3)** the width of a full line of type **c** a measured quantity ⟨*a* ∼ *of whisky*⟩ ⟨*short* ∼⟩ **2a** an instrument or utensil for measuring **b(1)** a standard or unit of measurement ⟨*the metre is a* ∼ *of length*⟩ **(2)** a system of standard units of measure ⟨*metric* ∼⟩ ⟨*liquid* ∼⟩ ☞ UNIT **3a** a (slow and stately) dance **b(1)** poetic rhythm measured by quantity or accent; *specif* ²METRE 1 **(2)** musical time **c(1)** the notes and rests that form a bar of music **(2)** a metrical unit; FOOT 4 **4** an exact divisor or factor of a quantity **5** a basis or standard of comparison **6a** a step planned or taken to achieve an end ⟨*we must take* ∼s *to improve sales*⟩ **b** a proposed legislative act ⟨∼s *to combat unemployment*⟩ [ME *mesure*, fr OF, fr L *mensura*, fr *mensus*, pp of *metiri* to measure; akin to OE *mǣth* measure, Gk *metron* metre, measure, Skt *māti* he measures]

²measure *vt* **1** to choose or control with cautious restraint; regulate ⟨∼d *his words to suit the occasion*⟩ **2** to take or allot in measured amounts – usu + *out* ⟨∼ *out 60g of flour*⟩ **3** to mark off by making measurements – often + *off* **4** to ascertain the measurements of **5** to estimate or appraise by a criterion – usu + *against* or *by* **6** to serve as a measure of ⟨*a thermometer* ∼s *temperature*⟩ ∼ *vi* **1** to take or make a measurement **2** to have a specified measurement ⟨∼s *2ft from end to end*⟩ – **measurable** *adj*, **measurably** *adv*

'measured *adj* **1** rhythmical; *esp* slow and regular **2** carefully thought out ⟨*a* ∼ *remark*⟩ – **measuredly** *adv*

'measureless /-lis/ *adj* having no observable limit; immeasurable

'measurement /-mənt/ *n* **1** measuring **2** a figure, extent, or amount obtained by measuring **3** MEASURE 2b

measure up *vi* to have necessary or fitting qualifications – often + *to*

'measuring ,worm /'mezhəring/ *n* an inchworm

meat /meet/ *n* **1a** food; *esp* solid food as distinguished from drink **b** the edible part of sthg as distinguished from a husk, shell, or other covering **2** animal tissue used as food; *esp* FLESH 2 ◉ **3** the core or essence of sthg **4** *archaic* a meal; *esp* dinner [ME *mete*, fr OE; akin to OHG *maz* food, L *madēre* to be wet, Gk *madaros* wet, *mastos* breast, Skt *madati* he is drunk]

meatus /mi'aytəs/ *n*, *pl* **meatuses, meatus** (the opening on the outside of) a natural body passage [LL, fr L, going, passage, fr *meatus*, pp of *meare* to go – more at PERMEATE]

meaty /'meeti/ *adj* **1** full of meat; fleshy **2** rich in matter for thought **3** of or like meat – **meatiness** *n*

mecca /'mekə/ *n*, *often cap* a place regarded as a goal (by a specified group of people) [*Mecca*, city in Saudi Arabia, birthplace of Muhammad and holy city of Islam]

Meccano /mi'kahnoh/ *trademark* – used for a toy construction set, esp of perforated strips of metal or plastic

mechanic /mi'kanik/ *n* a skilled worker who repairs or maintains machinery ⟨*a motor* ∼⟩ [prob fr MF *mechanique*, *mecanique*, adj & n, fr L *mechanicus*,

Lamb

Frozen lamb from New Zealand is available all year round in Britain. Home-produced lamb is sold fresh in early summer. Mutton is meat from the more mature sheep and has a coarser and fattier texture.

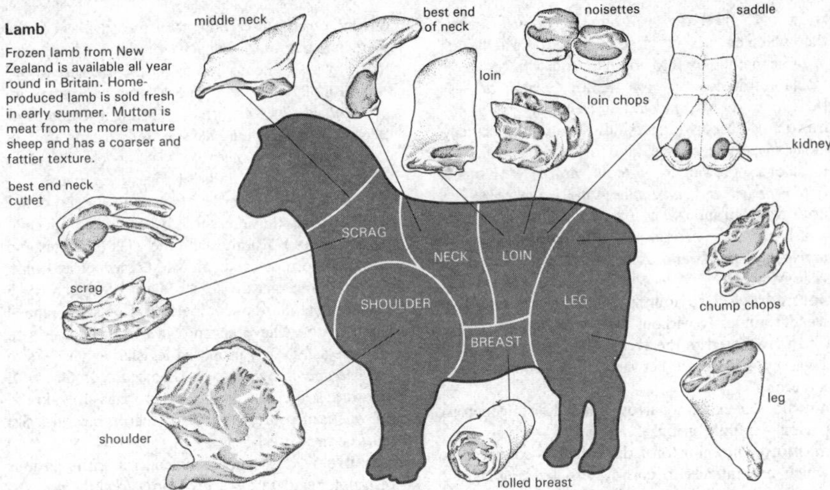

Pork

Pork should be moist and pink – it is sold all year round. Fillet or tenderloin is taken from a larger pig than most butchers use and may not always be available. Pork steak is taken from the chump and leg.

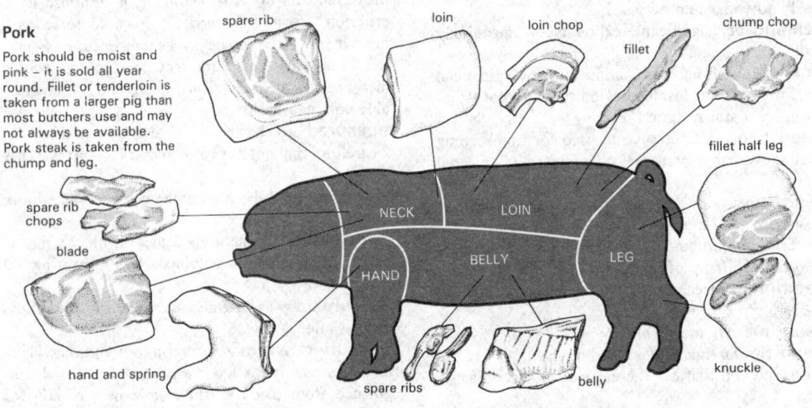

Bacon and ham

Ham is cured in a different way from bacon, though shoulder bacon is often sold as ham. True ham consists of the gammon only. Bacon is cured by salting and may also be smoked.

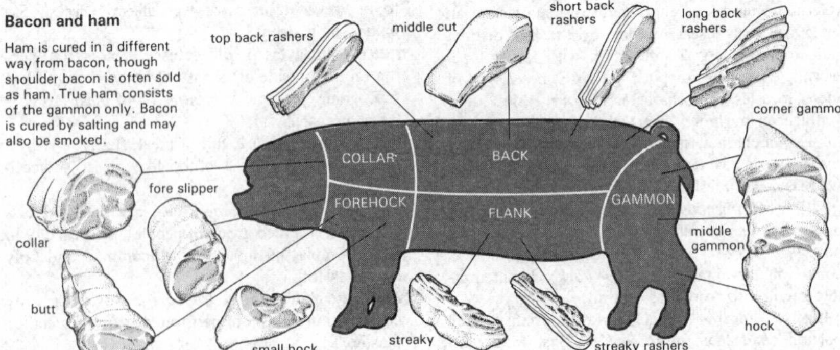

Beef

Cuts of meat from each animal vary from country to country and are subject to variation within Britain. Beef should be dark red in colour with a layer of creamy yellow fat. Joints which are to be roasted may require extra fat to keep the meat moist as it is cooking.

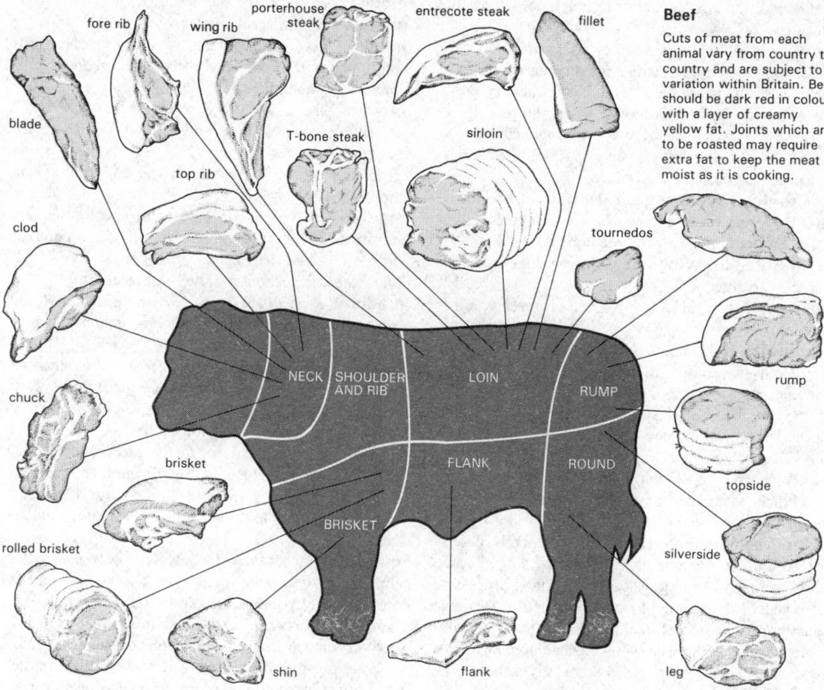

fore rib
wing rib
porterhouse steak
entrecote steak
fillet
blade
T-bone steak
sirloin
top rib
clod
tournedos
NECK
SHOULDER AND RIB
LOIN
RUMP
rump
chuck
FLANK
ROUND
topside
brisket
BRISKET
silverside
rolled brisket
shin
flank
leg

Veal

Veal is a pale soft meat which requires careful cooking to prevent it from becoming too dry.

best end cutlets
loin chop
fillet
middle neck
best end of neck
loin
escalopes
scrag
leg
NECK AND SHOULDER
BEST END NECK AND LOIN
shoulder
BREAST
LEG
knuckle
rolled breast

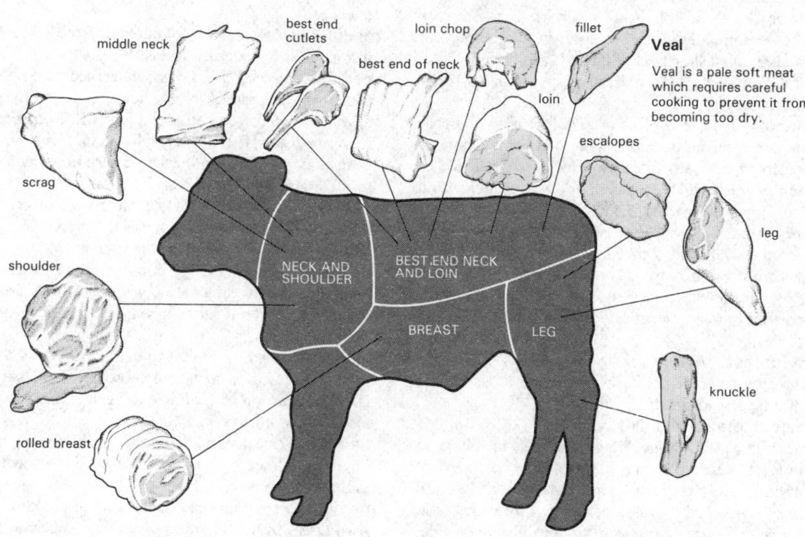

fr Gk *mēchanikos*, fr *mēchanē* machine – more at MACHINE]

me'chanical /-kl/ *adj* **1a** of or using machinery **b** made, operated by, or being a machine or machinery **2** done as if by machine; lacking in spontaneity **3** of, dealing with, or in accordance with (the principles of) mechanics ⟨~ *energy*⟩ ⟨~ *engineering*⟩ **4** caused by or being a physical as opposed to a chemical process – **mechanically** *adv*

mechanical advantage *n* the ratio of the force that performs the useful work of a machine to the force that is applied to the machine

mechanical drawing *n* (a) drawing done with the aid of instruments

mechanician /,mekə'nish(ə)n/ *n* a mechanic or machinist

mechanics /mi'kaniks/ *n pl but sing or pl in constr* **1** the physics and mathematics of (the effect on moving and stationary bodies of) energy and forces **2** the practical application of mechanics to the design, construction, or operation of machines or tools **3** mechanical or functional details

mechanism /'mekəniz(ə)m/ *n* **1a** a piece of machinery **b** a process or technique for achieving a result **2** mechanical operation or action **3** a theory that all natural processes are mechanically determined and can be explained by the laws of physics and chemistry **4** the physical or chemical processes involved in a natural phenomenon (e g an action, reaction, or biological evolution) [LL *mechanisma* contrivance, fr Gk *mēchanē*] – **mechanist** *n*, **mechanistic** /,mekə'nistik/ *adj*, **mechanistically** *adv*

mechan·ize, -ise /'mekəniez/ *vt* **1** to make mechanical or automatic **2a** to equip with machinery, esp in order to replace human or animal labour **b** to equip with (armed and armoured) motor vehicles – **mechanization** /-'zaysh(ə)n/ *n*

meconium /mi'kohni·əm/ *n* a dark greenish mass that accumulates in the bowels during foetal life and is discharged shortly after birth [L, lit., poppy juice, fr Gk *mēkōnion*, fr *mēkōn* poppy; akin to OHG *mago* poppy]

medal /'medl/ *n* a piece of metal with a (stamped) design, emblem, inscription, etc that commemorates a person or event or is awarded for excellence or achievement [MF *medaille*, fr OIt *medaglia* coin worth half a denarius, medal, fr (assumed) VL *medalis* half, fr LL *medialis* middle, fr L *medius* – more at MID] – **medallic** /mi'dalik/ *adj*

medallion /mi'dalyən/ *n* **1** a large medal **2** a decorative tablet, panel, etc, often bearing a figure or portrait in relief [F *médaillon*, fr It *medaglione*, aug of *medaglia*]

'medallist, *NAm chiefly* **medalist** /-ist/ **1** a designer, engraver, or maker of medals **2** a recipient of a (specified) medal as an award

'medal ,play *n* STROKE PLAY

meddle /'medl/ *vi* **meddling** /'medling, 'medl·ing/ to interest oneself in what is not one's concern; interfere unduly – usu + *in* or *with* [ME *medlen*, fr OF *mesler, medler*, fr (assumed) VL *misculare*, fr L *miscēre* to mix – more at MIX] – **meddler** *n*, **meddlesome** /'medl·səm/ *adj*

Mede /meed/ *n* a native or inhabitant of ancient Media in Persia [ME, fr L *Medus*, fr Gk *Mēdos*]

¹media /'meedi·ə/ *n, pl* **mediae** /-di,ee/ the middle muscular part of the wall of a blood or lymph vessel [NL, fr L, fem of *medius* middle]

²media *pl of* MEDIUM

mediaeval /,medi'eevl/ *adj* medieval

medial /'meedi·əl/ *adj* being, occurring in, or extending towards the middle; median [LL *medialis*, fr L *medius*] – **medially** *adv*

¹median /'meedi·ən/ *n* **1** a median vein, nerve, etc **2** a value in a series above and below which there are an equal number of values ☞ STATISTICS **3** a line from a vertex of a triangle to the midpoint of the opposite side

²median *adj* **1** in the middle or in an intermediate position **2** lying in the plane that divides an animal into right and left halves [MF or L; MF, fr L *medianus*, fr *medius* middle – more at MID]

mediant /'meedi·ənt/ *n* the 3rd note of a diatonic scale [It *mediante*, fr LL *mediant-*, *medians*, prp of *mediare* to be in the middle]

mediastinum /,meedi·ə'stienəm/ *n, pl* **mediastina** /-nə/ (the contents or walls of) the space in the chest between the coverings of the lungs, containing all the chest organs except the lungs [NL, fr L, neut of *mediastinus* medial, fr *medius*] – **mediastinal** *adj*

¹mediate /'meedi·ət/ *adj* acting through an intervening agent or agency [ME, fr LL *mediatus* intermediate, fr pp of *mediare*] – **mediacy** /-di·əsi/ *n*, **mediately** *adv*

²mediate /'meedi,ayt/ *vi* to intervene between parties in order to reconcile them ~ *vt* **1** to bring about (a settlement) by mediation **2a** to act as intermediary agent in or between **b** to transmit or effect by acting as an intermediate mechanism or agency [ML *mediatus*, pp of *mediare*, fr LL, to be in the middle, fr L *medius* middle – more at MID] – **mediator** *n*, **mediatory** /di·ət(ə)ri/ *adj*, **mediative** /-di·ətiv/ *adj*, **mediation** /,meedi'aysh(ə)n/ *n*

¹medic /'medik/ *n* a medick

²medic *n* a medical doctor or student – infml [L *medicus*]

medicable /'medikəbl/ *adj* curable, remediable [L *medicabilis*, fr *medicare* to heal]

¹medical /'medikl/ *adj* **1** of or concerned with physicians or the practice of medicine **2** requiring or devoted to medical treatment [F or LL; F *médical*, fr LL *medicalis*, fr L *medicus* physician, fr *mederi* to heal; akin to Av vī-*mad*- healer, & perh to L *meditari* to meditate] – **medically** *adv*

²medical /'medikl/, **medical examination** *n* an examination to determine sby's physical fitness

medicament /mi'dikəmənt/ *n* MEDICINE 1

medicare /'medi,keə/ *n* comprehensive medical insurance, esp for the aged, sponsored by the US and Canadian governments [blend of *medical* and *care*]

medicate /'medikayt/ *vt* **1** to treat medicinally **2** to impregnate with a medicinal substance ⟨~d *soap*⟩ [L *medicatus*, pp of *medicare* to heal, fr *medicus*] – **medication** /,medi'kaysh(ə)n/ *n*

medicinal /mə'dis(ə)nl/ *n or adj* (a substance) tending or used to cure disease or relieve pain – **medicinally** *adv*

medicine /'medəsin/ *n* **1** a substance or preparation used (as if) in treating disease **2** the science and art of the maintenance of health and the prevention and treatment of disease (using nonsurgical methods) [ME, fr OF, fr L *medicina*, fr fem of *medicinus* of a physician, fr *medicus*]

'medicine ,ball *n* a heavy ball that is usu thrown between people for exercise

'medicine ,man *n* a healer or sorcerer, esp among the N American Indians – compare WITCH DOCTOR

medick, medic /'medik/ *n* any of a genus of leguminous plants that includes lucerne [ME *medike*, fr L *medica*, fr Gk *mēdikē*, fr fem of *mēdikos* Median, fr *Mēdia* Media, ancient country of Persian empire]

medico /'medikoh/ *n, pl* **medicos** ²MEDIC – infml [It *medico* or Sp *médico*, both fr L *medicus*]

medico- *comb form* medical ⟨medico*psychology*⟩; medical and ⟨medico*legal*⟩ [NL, fr L *medicus*]

medieval, mediaeval /,medi'eevl/ *adj* of or like the Middle Ages [L *medius* middle + *aevum* age – more at ¹AYE] – **medievalism** *n*, **medievalist** *n*, **medievally** *adv*

Medieval Latin *n* liturgical and literary Latin of the 7th–15th c

mediocre /,meedi'ohkə/ *adj* **1** neither good nor bad; indifferent; *esp* conspicuously lacking distinction or imagination **2** not good enough; fairly bad [MF, fr L *mediocris*, lit., halfway up a mountain, fr *medius* + *ocris* stony mountain; akin to L *acer* sharp – more at EDGE] – **mediocrity** /,meedi'okrəti/ *n*

meditate /'meditayt/ *vt* to focus one's thoughts on; consider or plan in the mind ~ *vi* **1** to engage in deep or serious reflection **2** to empty the mind of thoughts and fix the attention on 1 matter, esp as a religious exercise [L *meditatus*, pp of *meditari* – more at METE] – **meditator** *n*, **meditative** /-tətiv/ *adj*, **meditatively** *adv*, **meditation** /,medi 'taysh(ə)n/ *n*

Mediterranean /,meditə'raynyən, -ni·ən/ *adj* **1** of or characteristic of (the region round) the Mediterranean sea **2** of or resembling a physical type of the Caucasian race characterized by medium or short stature, slender build, and dark complexion [*Mediterranean* Sea, between Europe & Africa, fr L *mediterraneus* inland, landlocked, fr *medius* + *terra* land]

¹**medium** /'meedi·əm/ *n, pl* **mediums, media** /-di·ə/, *(2b(2))* **media**, *(2e)* **mediums**, *(3b)* **media** *also* **mediums** **1** (sthg in) a middle position or state **2** a means of effecting or conveying sthg: e g **a(1)** a substance regarded as the means of transmission of a force or effect ⟨*air is the ~ that conveys sound*⟩ **(2)** a surrounding or enveloping substance; *esp* MATRIX 3 **b(1)** a channel of communication **(2)** *pl but sing or pl in constr* MASS MEDIA **c** a mode of artistic expression or communication ⟨*discovered his true ~ as a writer*⟩ **d** an intermediary, go-between **e** one through whom others seek to communicate with the spirits of the dead **f** a material or technical means of artistic expression ⟨*found watercolour a satisfying ~*⟩ **3a** a condition or environment in which sthg may function or flourish **b** a nutrient for the artificial cultivation of bacteria and other (single-celled) organisms **c** a liquid with which dry pigment can be mixed [L, fr neut of *medius* middle – more at MID]

²**medium** *adj* intermediate in amount, quality, position, or degree

'medium ,wave *n* a band of radio waves, typically used for sound broadcasting, covering wavelengths between about 180m and 600m – sometimes pl with sing. meaning

medlar /'medlə/ *n* (a small Eurasian tree of the rose family that bears) a fruit like a crab apple used in preserves [ME *medeler*, fr MF *meslier*, *medlier*, fr *mesle*, *medle* medlar fruit, fr L *mespilum*, fr Gk *mespilon*]

medley /'medli/ *n* **1** a (confused) mixture **2** a musical composition made up of a series of songs or short musical pieces [ME *medle*, fr MF *medlee*, fr fem of *medlé*, pp of *medler* to mix – more at MEDDLE]

medulla /mi'dulə/ *n, pl (1)* **medullae** /-li/, *(2)* **medullas** *also* **medullae** **1a** MARROW 1 **b** MEDULLA OBLONGATA **2a** the inner or deep part of an animal or plant structure ⟨*the adrenal ~*⟩ **b** the myelin sheath that surrounds some nerves [L]

me,dulla oblon'gata /oblong'gahtə/ *n, pl* **medulla oblongatas, medullae oblongatae** /-ti/ the (pyramid-shaped) part of the brain of vertebrates whose back part merges with the spinal cord [NL, lit., oblong medulla]

medullary /mi'duləri/ *adj* **1** of or located in a medulla, esp the medulla oblongata **2** of or located in the pith of a plant

me,dullary 'ray *n* a wedge of tissue that is composed of parenchyma cells, joins the vascular bundles in the stems of many plants, and connects the pith with the cortex

medullated /'med(ə)l,aytid, mi'dul-/ *adj* myelinated

medusa /mi'dyoohzə/ *n, pl* **medusae** /-zi/, **medusas** a (small hydrozoan) jellyfish [NL, fr *Medusa*, one of the 3 Gorgons with snakes for hair, fr L, fr Gk *Medousa*; fr the resemblance of some species to a head with snake-like curls] – **medusan** *adj or n*, **medusoid** /-zoyd/ *adj*

meek /meek/ *adj* **1** patient and without resentment **2** lacking spirit and courage; timid [ME, of Scand origin; akin to ON *mjūkr* gentle; akin to L *mucus* nasal mucus] – **meekly** *adv*, **meekness** *n*

meerkat /'miə,kat/ *n* any of several small flesh-eating S African mammals related to the mongooses [Afrik, fr D, a kind of monkey, fr MD *meercatte* monkey, fr *meer* sea + *catte* cat; fr the fact that monkeys came to Europe from overseas]

meerschaum /'miəshəm/ *n* **1** hydrated magnesium silicate occurring, chiefly in Asia Minor, as a white clayey mineral and used esp for tobacco pipes **2** a tobacco pipe with a bowl made of meerschaum [G, fr *meer* sea + *schaum* foam]

¹**meet** /meet/ *vb* **met** /met/ *vt* **1a** to come into the presence of by accident or design **b** to be present to greet the arrival of ⟨met *the London train*⟩ **c** to come into contact or conjunction with ⟨*where the river ~s the sea*⟩ **d** to appear to the perception of ⟨*hazy sunshine ~s the eye*⟩ **2** to encounter as antagonist or foe **3** to answer, esp in opposition ⟨*his speech was* met *by loud catcalls*⟩ **4** to conform to, esp exactly and precisely; satisfy ⟨*this should ~ your requirements*⟩ **5** to pay fully ⟨*~ the cost*⟩ **6** to become acquainted with **7** to experience during the course of sthg ⟨met *his death during the war*⟩ ~ *vi* **1** to come together **a** from different directions **b** for a common purpose **c** as contestants, opponents, or enemies **2** to join at a fastening ⟨*the waistcoat won't ~*⟩ **3** to become acquainted [ME *meten*, fr OE *mētan*; akin to OHG *muoz* meeting, Arm *matčim* I approach] – **meet someone halfway** to make concessions to; compromise with

²**meet** *n* the assembling of participants for a hunt or for competitive sports

³**meet** *adj* suitable, proper – fml [ME *mete*, fr OE *gemǣte*; akin to OE *metan* to mete] – **meetly** *adv*

meeting /'meeting/ *n* **1** a coming together: e g **a** an assembly of people for a common purpose **b** a session of horse or greyhound racing **2** a permanent organizational unit of the Quakers **3** an intersection, junction

'meeting,house *n* a building used for Protestant worship

mega- /megə-/, **meg-** *comb form* **1a** great; large ⟨mega*lith*⟩ ⟨mega*spore*⟩ **b** having (a specified part) of large size ⟨mega*cephalic*⟩ **2** million (10^6) ⟨mega*watt*⟩ ⟨meg*ohm*⟩ ☞ PHYSICS [Gk, fr *megas* large – more at MUCH]

megabit /'mega,bit/ *n* a unit of computer information **a** equal to 1,000,000 bits **b** equal to 2^{20} bits

'mega,byte /-,biet/ *n* a unit of computer storage **a** equal to 1,000,000 bytes **b** equal to 2^{20} bytes

'mega,cycle /-,siekl/ *n* a megahertz

'mega,death /-,deth/ *n* one million deaths – used as a unit esp in reference to atomic warfare

'mega,hertz /-,huhts/ *n* a unit of frequency equal to 1,000,000 hertz [ISV]

megal- /meg(ə)l-/, **megalo-** *comb form* **1** large; of giant size ⟨megalo*polis*⟩ ⟨megalo*blast*⟩ **2** grandiose ⟨megalo*mania*⟩ [NL, fr Gk, fr *megal-, megas* – more at MUCH]

megalith /'megəlith/ *n* a huge undressed block of stone used in prehistoric monuments – **megalithic** /,megə'lithik/ *adj*

megalomania /,meg(ə)lə'mayny·ə/ *n* **1** a mania for grandiose things **2** feelings of personal omnipotence and grandeur occurring as a delusional mental disorder – compare SUPERIORITY COMPLEX [NL] – **megalomaniac** /-ni·ak/ *adj or n*, **megalomaniacal** /-mə'nie·əkl/ *adj*

,mega'lopolis /,meg(ə)l'opəlis/ *n* **1** a very large city **2** a densely populated urban region embracing 1 or several metropolises – **megalopolitan** /-lə'polit(ə)n/ *n or adj*

megaphone /'megə,fohn/ *n* a hand-held device used to amplify or direct the voice – **megaphonic** /,mega'fonik/ *adj*

'mega,ton /-tun/ *n* an explosive force (of an atom or hydrogen bomb) equivalent to that of 1,000,000 tons of TNT

[1]megrim /'meegrəm/ *n* **1** migraine **2** vertigo, dizziness – usu pl with sing. meaning [ME *migreime*, fr MF *migraine*]

[2]megrim *n* any of several small flounders or other flatfishes [origin unknown]

meiosis /mie'ohsis/ *n, pl* **meioses** /-,seez/ **1** understatement **2** a specialized cellular process of division in gamete-producing cells by which 1 of each pair of chromosomes passes to each resulting gametic cell which thus has half the number of chromosomes of the original cell – compare MITOSIS [NL, fr Gk *meiōsis* diminution, fr *meioun* to diminish, fr *meiōn* less – more at MINOR] – **meiotic** /-'otik/ *adj*, **meiotically** *adv*

Meissen /'mies(ə)n/ *n* a type of European hard-paste porcelain developed in the 18th c at Meissen near Dresden

melamine /'meləmin, -,meen/ *n* (an organic compound used esp to make) a melamine resin or a derived plastic [G *melamin*]

,melamine 'resin *n* any of various plastics used esp in moulded products and coatings

melan-, melano- *comb form* **1** black; dark ⟨melan*in*⟩ **2** melanin ⟨melano*id*⟩ ⟨melano*cyte*⟩ [ME, fr MF, fr LL, fr Gk, fr *melan-, melas* – more at MULLET]

melancholia /,melən'kohli·ə/ *n* feelings of extreme depression and worthlessness occurring as an abnormal mental condition [NL, fr LL, melancholy] – **melancholiac** /-'koli,ak/ *n*

[1]melancholy /'melənkəli, -koli/ *n* **1a** (a tendency to) irascibility or depression; melancholia **b** BLACK BILE **2a** depression of mind or spirits **b** a sad pensive mood [ME *malencolie*, fr MF *melancolie*, fr LL *melancholia*, fr Gk, fr *melan-* + *cholē* bile – more at [1]GALL] – **melancholic** /-'kolik/ *adj or n*, **melancholically** *adv*

[2]melancholy *adj* **1** depressed in spirits; dejected **2** causing, tending to cause, or expressing sadness or depression

Melanesian /,melə'neezh(y)ən, -zyən/ *n* **1** a member of the dominant indigenous group of Melanesia **2** a language group consisting of the Austronesian languages of Melanesia ☞ LANGUAGE [*Melanesia*, island group in Pacific, fr Gk *melas* + *nēsos* island] – **Melanesian** *adj*

mélange /'maylonhzh (*Fr* melɑ̃:ʒ)/ *n* a mixture (of incongruous elements) [F, fr MF, fr *mesler, meler* to mix – more at MEDDLE]

melanin /'melənin/ *n* a dark brown or black animal and plant pigment (e g of skin or hair)

melanism /'melə,niz(ə)m/ *n* an increased amount of (nearly) black pigmentation of skin, feathers, hair, etc – **melanic** /mi'lanik/ *adj*

melan·ize /'meləniez/, **-ise** *vt* **1** to convert into or increase the amount of melanin in **2** to make dark or black – **melanization** /,melə nie'zaysh(ə)n/ *n*

melanocyte-stimulating hormone /mi'lanəsiet, 'melənoh-/ *n* a hormone of the pituitary gland in vertebrates that produces darkening of the skin – compare MELATONIN

melanoma /,melə'nohmə/ *n, pl* **melanomas** *also* **melanomata** /-mətə/ a usu malignant tumour, esp of the skin, containing dark pigment [NL]

melanophore /mi'lanoh,faw, 'melənoh-/ *n* a melanin-containing chromatophore, esp of fishes, amphibians, and reptiles

melanosis /,melə'nohsis/ *n* the (abnormal) deposition of pigments, esp melanin, in the tissues of the body [NL] – **melanotic** /,melə'notik/ *adj*

melatonin /,melə'tohnin/ *n* a hormone of the pineal gland in vertebrates that produces lightening of the skin – compare MELANOCYTE-STIMULATING HORMONE [prob fr *mela*nocyte + sero*tonin*]

,Melba 'toast /'melbə/ *n* very thin crisp toast [Dame Nellie *Melba* †1931 Austr operatic soprano]

[1]meld /meld/ *vb* to declare (a card or combination of cards) for a score in a card game, esp by placing face up on the table [G *melden* to announce, fr OHG *meldōn*; akin to OE *meldian* to announce, OSlav *moliti* to ask for]

[2]meld *n* a card or combination of cards that is or can be melded

mêlée, melee /'melay/ *n* a confused or riotous struggle; *esp* a general hand-to-hand fight [F *mêlée*, fr OF *meslee*, fr *mesler* to mix – more at MEDDLE]

melic /'melik/ *adj, of poetry* intended to be sung [L *melicus*, fr Gk *melikos*, fr *melos* song – more at MELODY]

melilot /'melilot/ *n* any of a genus of leguminous plants widely cultivated to enrich the soil and for hay [ME *mellilot*, fr MF *melilot*, fr L *melilotos*, fr Gk *melilōtos,* fr *meli* honey + *lōtos* clover, lotus – more at MELLIFLUOUS]

meliorate /'meeli·ə,rayt/ *vb* to ameliorate [LL *melioratus,* pp of *meliorare,* fr L *melior* better; akin to L *multus* much, Gk *mala* very] – **meliorative** /-rətiv/ *adj,* **melioration** /,meeli·ə'raysh(ə)n/ *n*

melisma /mə'lizmə/ *n, pl* **melismata** /-mətə/ a group of notes or tones sung on 1 syllable, esp in plainsong [NL, fr Gk, song, melody, fr *melizein* to sing, fr *melos* song] – **melismatic** /,meliz'matik/ *adj*

melliferous /mə'lifərəs/ *adj* producing or yielding honey [L *mellifer,* fr *mell-, mel* + *-fer* -ferous]

mellifluous /mə'lifloo·əs/, **mellifluent** /-ənt/ *adj* smoothly or sweetly flowing ⟨*a ~ voice*⟩ [LL *mellifluus,* fr L *mell-, mel* honey + *fluere* to flow; akin to Goth *milith* honey, Gk *melit-, meli*] – **mellifluously, mellifluently** *adv,* **mellifluousness, mellifluence** *n*

mellophone /'melə,fohn/ *n* a circular valved brass instrument with a range similar to that of the French horn [*mellow* + *-phone*]

Mellotron /'melə,tron/ *trademark* – used for an electronic keyboard instrument in which the sound source is a prerecorded tape

mellow /'meloh/ *adj* **1a** *of a fruit* tender and sweet because ripe **b** *of a wine* well aged and pleasingly mild **2a** made gentle by age or experience **b** rich and full but free from harshness ⟨*~ lighting*⟩ **c** pleasantly intoxicated [ME *melowe*] – **mellow** *vb,* **mellowly** *adv,* **mellowness** *n*

melodeon, melodion /mə'lohdi·ən/ *n* a reed organ in which the air is drawn through the reeds by suction bellows [G *melodion,* fr *melodie* melody, fr OF]

melodic /mə'lodik/ *adj* **1** of or forming melody **2** melodious – **melodically** *adv*

melodious /mə'lohdi·əs/ *adj* of or producing (a pleasing) melody – **melodiously** *adv,* **melodiousness** *n*

melodist /'melədist/ *n* **1** a singer **2** a composer of melodies

melodrama /'melə,drahmə/ *n* **1a** a work (e g a film or play) characterized by crude emotional appeal and by the predominance of plot and action over characterization **b** the dramatic genre comprising such works **2** sensational or sensationalized events or behaviour [modif of F *mélodrame,* fr Gk *melos* + F *drame* drama, fr LL *drama*] – **melodramatic** /,melədrə'matik/ *adj,* **melodramatically** *adv,* **melodramatist** /,melə 'dramətist/ *n,* **melodramatize** /,meloh'dramə,tiez, -'drahmə-/ *vt*

melodramatics /,melədrə'matiks/ *n pl* MELODRAMA 2

melody /'melədi/ *n* **1** an agreeable succession or arrangement of sounds **2a** a rhythmic succession of single notes organized as an aesthetic whole **b** the chief part in a harmonic composition [ME *melodie,* fr OF, fr LL *melodia,* fr Gk *melōidia* chanting, music, fr *melos* limb, musical phrase, song (akin to Bret *mell* joint) + *aeidein* to sing – more at ODE]

melon /'melən/ *n* (any of various plants of the cucumber family having) a fruit (e g a watermelon) containing sweet edible flesh and usu eaten raw [ME, fr MF, fr LL *melon-, melo,* short for L *melopepon-, melopepo,* fr Gk *mēlopepōn,* fr *mēlon* apple + *pepōn,* an edible gourd – more at PUMPKIN]

¹melt /melt/ *vi* **1** to become altered from a solid to a liquid state, usu by heating **2a** to dissolve, disintegrate ⟨*food that ~s in the mouth*⟩ **b** to disappear as if by dissolving ⟨*his anger ~ed*⟩ **3** to be or become mild, tender, or gentle **4** to lose distinct outline; blend ⟨*tried to ~ into the background*⟩ *~ vt* **1** to reduce from a solid to a liquid state, usu by heating **2** to cause to disappear or disperse **3** to make tender or gentle [ME *melten,* fr OE *meltan*; akin to L *mollis* soft, *molere* to grind – more at ²MEAL] – **meltable** *adj,* **meltingly** *adv*

²melt *n* **1a** molten material **b** the mass melted at a single operation **2** (the period of) melting or being melted ⟨*the river overflowed during the Spring ~*⟩

³melt *n* the spleen, esp when used as food [ME *milte,* fr OE; akin to OHG *miltzi* spleen]

'melting ,point /'melting/ *n* the temperature at which a solid melts

'melting ,pot *n* a place, a situation, or the result of mixing diverse ideas, peoples, traditions, etc

'melt,water *n* water from the melting of (glacial) ice or snow

member /'membə/ *n* **1** a part or organ of the body: e g **a** a limb **b** the penis – euph **2a** an individual or unit belonging to or forming part of a group or organization **b** *often cap* one who is entitled to sit in a legislative body; *esp* a member of Parliament **3a** a constituent part of a whole **b** a beam or similar (load-bearing) structure, esp in a building **c** either of the expressions on either side of a mathematical equation or inequality [ME *membre,* fr OF, fr L *membrum*; akin to Goth *mimz* flesh, Gk *mēros* thigh, *mēninx* membrane, Skt *māṁsa* flesh]

'membership /-ship/ *n sing or pl in constr* the body of members ⟨*an organization with a large ~*⟩ [MEMBER + -SHIP]

membrane /'membrayn/ *n* a thin pliable sheet or layer, esp in an animal or plant [L *membrana* skin, parchment, fr *membrum*] – **membranous** /-brənəs/ *adj*

memento /mə'mentoh/ *n, pl* **mementos, mementoes** sthg (e g a souvenir) that serves as a reminder of past events, people, etc [ME, fr L, remember, imper of *meminisse* to remember; akin to L *ment-, mens* mind]

me,mento 'mori /'mawri/ *n, pl* **memento mori** a reminder of mortality; *esp* a death's-head [L, remember that you must die]

memo /'memoh/ *n, pl* **memos** a memorandum

memoir /'memwah/ *n* **1a** a narrative written from personal experience **b** an autobiography – usu pl with sing. meaning **c** a biography **2** a learned essay on a particular topic *USE* (*1a&1c*) often pl with sing. meaning [F *mémoire,* lit., memory, fr L *memoria*] – **memoirist** *n*

memorabilia /,mem(ə)rə'bili·ə/ *n pl* (records of) memorable events [L, fr neut pl of *memorabilis*]

memorable /'mem(ə)rəbl/ *adj* worth remembering; notable [ME, fr L *memorabilis,* fr *memorare* to remind, mention, fr *memor* mindful] – **memorability** /,mem(ə)rə'biləti/ *n,* **memorably** *adv*

memorandum /,memə'randəm/ *n, pl* **memorandums, memoranda** /-də/ **1** an often unsigned informal record or communication; *also* a written reminder **2** a document recording the terms of an agreement, the formation of a company, etc **3** a usu brief communication for internal circulation (e g within an office) [ME, fr L, neut of *memorandus* to be remembered, gerundive of *memorare*]

¹memorial /mə'mawri·əl/ *adj* serving to commemorate a person or event [MEMORY + [1]-AL] – **memorially** *adv*, **memorialize** /-liez/ *vt*

[2]**memorial** *n* **1** sthg, esp a monument, that commemorates a person or event **2** a historical record – often pl

memor·ize, -ise /'meməriez/ *vt* to commit to memory; learn by heart – **memorizable** *adj*, **memorization** /,memərie'zaysh(ə)n/ *n*

memory /'mem(ə)ri/ *n* **1** (the power or process of recalling or realizing) the store of things learned and retained from an organism's experience ⟨*good visual* ~⟩ **2** commemorative remembrance ⟨*a statue in* ~ *of the hero*⟩ **3a** (the object of) recall or recollection ⟨*had no* ~ *of the incident*⟩ ⟨*left many happy* memories⟩ **b** (posthumous) image or impression ⟨*his* ~ *will stay with us*⟩ **c** the time within which past events can be or are remembered **4** (the capacity of) a device in which information, esp for a computer, can be inserted and stored, and from which it may be extracted when wanted **5** a capacity of a metal, plastic, etc for retaining effects as the result of past treatment, or for returning to a former condition [ME *memorie*, fr MF *memoire*, fr L *memoria*, fr *memor* mindful; akin to OE *mimorian* to remember, L *mora* delay, Gk *mermēra* care, Skt *smarati* he remembers]

memsahib /'mem,sah·hib/ *n* a white foreign woman of high social status living in India; *broadly* any woman of rank in India [Hindi *memṣāḥib*, fr E *ma'am* + Hindi *ṣāḥib* sahib, fr Ar *ṣāḥib* friend, lord]

men /men/ *pl of* MAN

men-, meno- *comb form* menstruation ⟨menor*rhagia*⟩ [NL, fr Gk *mēn* month – more at MOON]

[1]**menace** /'menis/ *n* **1** a show of intention to inflict harm; a threat **2a** a source of danger **b** a person who causes annoyance [ME, fr MF, fr L *minacia*, fr *minac-*, *minax* threatening, fr *minari* to threaten – more at [1]MOUNT]

[2]**menace** *vb* to threaten or show intent to harm – **menacingly** *adv*

ménage /me'nahzh, '--/ *n* a household [F, fr OF *mesnage* dwelling, fr (assumed) VL *mansionaticum*, fr L *mansion-*, *mansio* mansion]

,ménage à 'trois /ah trwah/ *n* a relationship in which 3 people, esp a married couple and the lover of 1, live together [F, lit., household for three]

menagerie /mə'najəri/ *n* a place where animals are kept and trained, esp for exhibition; *also* a zoo [F *ménagerie*, fr MF, management of a household or farm, fr *menage*]

menarche /'menahki/ *n* (the onset of the menstrual function marked by) the first menstrual period [NL, fr *men-* + Gk *archē* beginning] – **menarcheal** /,menah'kee·əl/ *adj*

[1]**mend** /mend/ *vt* **1** to improve or rectify ⟨~ *one's ways*⟩ ⟨*attempt to* ~ *matters*⟩ **2a** to restore to sound condition or working order; repair **b** to restore to health; cure ~ *vi* **1** to undergo improvement **2** to improve in health; *also* to heal [ME *menden*, short for *amenden* – more at AMEND] – **mendable** *adj*, **mender** *n*

[2]**mend** *n* a mended place or part – **on the mend** improving, esp in health

mendacity /men'dasəti/ *n* (sthg marked by) untruthfulness – fml [LL *mendacitas*, fr L *mendac-*, *mendax* lying, false – more at AMEND] – **mendacious** /-'dayshəs/ *adj*, **mendaciously** *adv*

mendelevium /,mendə'leevi·əm/ *n* an artificially produced radioactive metallic element ☞ PERIODIC TABLE [NL, fr Dmitri *Mendeleev* †1907 Russ chemist]

Mendelian /men'deeli·ən/ *adj* of or according with the genetic principle that genes occur in pairs, each gamete receives 1 member of each pair, and that an organism thus has 1 gene of each pair randomly selected from each of its parents [Gregor *Mendel* †1884 Austrian botanist] – **Mendelian** *n*, **Mendelism** *n*

mendicant /'mendikənt/ *n* **1** BEGGAR 1 **2** *often cap* a friar living off alms [L *mendicant-*, *mendicans*, prp of *mendicare* to beg, fr *mendicus* beggar – more at AMEND] – **mendicant** *adj*, **mendicancy, mendicity** /men'disəti/ *n*

menfolk /'men,fohk/ *n pl in constr* **1** men in general **2** the men of a family or community

menhir /'menhiə/ *n* a single upright roughly-shaped monolith, usu of prehistoric origin [F, fr Bret, fr *men* stone (akin to W *maen* stone, Corn *mēn*) + *hir* long; akin to OIr *sīr* long, L *serus* late – more at SINCE]

[1]**menial** /'meenyəl, -ni·əl/ *adj* **1** of servants; lowly **2a** degrading; *also* servile **b** lacking in interest or status ⟨*a boring* ~ *job*⟩ [ME *meynial*, fr *meynie* household, retinue, fr OF *mesnie*, fr (assumed) VL *mansionata*, fr L *mansion-*, *mansio* dwelling] – **menially** *adv*

[2]**menial** *n* a domestic servant or retainer

Mé'nière's di,sease /mə'nyeəz/ *n* recurrent attacks of dizziness, ringing in the ears, and deafness occurring as a disorder of the inner ear [Émile A *Ménière* †1905 F physician]

mening-, meningo- *also* **meningi-** *comb form* meninges ⟨mening*itis*⟩; meninges and ⟨meningo*encephalitis*⟩ [NL, fr *mening-*, *meninx*]

meninges /mə'ninjeez/ *pl of* MENINX – **meningeal** /-ji·əl/ *adj*

meningitis /,menin'jietəs/ *n* bacterial, fungal, or viral inflammation of the meninges [NL] – **meningitic** /-'jitik/ *adj*

meninx /'meningks, 'mee-/ *n, pl* **meninges** /mə'ninjeez/ any of the 3 membranes (the dura mater, pia mater, and arachnoid) that envelop the brain and spinal cord – usu pl [NL, fr Gk *mēning-*, *mēninx* membrane; akin to L *membrana* membrane]

meniscus /mə'niskəs/ *n, pl* **menisci** /-'nisie/ *also* **meniscuses** **1** a crescent-shaped body or figure **2** a lens that is concave on one side and convex on the other **3** the curved concave or convex upper surface of a column of liquid [NL, fr Gk *mēniskos*, fr dim. of *mēnē* moon, crescent – more at MOON]

Mennonite /'menəniet/ *n* a member of any of various Protestant groups derived from the Anabaptist movement in Holland and characterized by congregational autonomy and rejection of military service [G *Mennonit*, fr *Menno* Simons †1561 Frisian religious reformer]

meno- – see MEN-

menopause /'menə,pawz/ *n* (the time of) the natural cessation of menstruation occurring usu between the ages of 45 and 50 [F *ménopause*, fr *méno-* men- + *pause*] – **menopausal** /,menə'pawzl/ *adj*

menorah /mi'nawrə/ *n* a many-branched candelabrum used in Jewish worship [Heb *mĕnōrāh* candlestick]

menorrhagia /,menaw'rayjyə/ *n* abnormally profuse menstrual flow [NL] – **menorrhagic** /-nə'rajik/ *adj*

menorrhoea /menə'riə/ *n* normal menstrual flow [NL]

menses /'menseez/ *n pl but sing or pl in constr* the menstrual flow [L, lit., months, pl of *mensis* month – more at MOON]

Menshevik /'menshəvik/ *n* a member of the less radical wing of the Russian Social Democratic party before and during the Russian Revolution [Russ *men'shevik*, fr *men'she* less; fr their forming the minority group of the party] – **Menshevism** *n*, **Menshevist** *n*

mens rea /,menz 'ree·ə/ *n* criminal intent [NL, lit., guilty mind]

'men's ,room *n, chiefly NAm* a men's toilet

menstruation /,menstroo'aysh(ə)n/ *n* the discharging of blood, secretions, and tissue debris from the uterus that recurs in nonpregnant primate females of breeding age at approximately monthly intervals; *also* a single occurrence of this ☞ REPRODUCTION [LL *menstruatus*, pp of *menstruari* to menstruate, fr L *menstrua* menses, fr neut pl of *menstruus* monthly, fr *mensis*] – **menstruous** *adj*, **menstruate** /-stroo,ayt/ *vi*, **menstrual** /'menstroo(ə)l/ *adj*

menstruum /'menstroo·əm/ *n, pl* **menstruums, menstrua** /-stroo·ə/ a solvent – used in alchemy [ML, lit., menses, alter. of L *menstrua*; fr the comparison made by alchemists of a base metal in a solvent undergoing transmutation into gold with an ovum in the womb being (supposedly) transformed by menstrual blood]

mensuration /,menshə'raysh(ə)n/ *n* **1** measurement **2** geometry applied to the computation of lengths, areas, or volumes [LL *mensuration-, mensuratio*, fr *mensuratus*, pp of *mensurare* to measure, fr *mensura* measure] – **mensurable** /'menshərəbl/ *adj*, **mensural** *adj*

-ment /-mənt/ *suffix* (*vb* → *n*) **1a** concrete result, object, or agent of a (specified) action ⟨*embank*ment⟩ ⟨*entangle*ment⟩ **b** concrete means or instrument of a (specified) action ⟨*entertain*ment⟩ **2a** action; process ⟨*encircle*ment⟩ ⟨*develop*ment⟩ **b** place of a (specified) action ⟨*encamp*ment⟩ [ME, fr OF, fr L *-mentum*; akin to L *-men*, suffix denoting concrete result, Gk *-mat-, -ma*]

mental /'mentl/ *adj* **1a** of the mind or its activity ⟨~ *health*⟩ ⟨~ *processes*⟩ **b** of intellectual as contrasted with emotional or physical activity ⟨~ *ability*⟩ ⟨*a* ~ *age of 3*⟩ **c** (performed or experienced) in the mind ⟨~ *arithmetic*⟩ ⟨~ *anguish*⟩ **2** of, being, or (intended for the care of people) suffering from a psychiatric disorder ⟨*a* ~ *patient*⟩ ⟨~ *illness*⟩ **3** crazy; *also* stupid – infml [ME, fr MF, fr LL *mentalis*, fr L *ment-, mens* mind – more at MIND] – **mentally** *adv*

,mental de'fective *n* one who is mentally deficient

,mental de'ficiency *n* failure in development of the mind resulting in a need for continuing parental or institutional care

'mental,ism /-,iz(ə)m/ *n* a doctrine that only individual minds and their subjective states are real – **mentalist** /-ist/ *n*

mentality /men'taləti/ *n* **1** mental power or capacity; intelligence **2** a mode of thought; mental disposition or outlook

mentation /men'taysh(ə)n/ *n* mental activity – fml [L *ment-, mens* + E *-ation*]

menthol /'menthol/ *n* an alcohol that occurs esp in mint oils and has the smell and cooling properties of peppermint [G, deriv of L *mentha* mint] – **mentholated** /-thə,laytid/ *adj*

¹mention /'mensh(ə)n/ *n* **1** a brief reference to sthg; a passing remark **2** a formal citation for outstanding achievement [ME *mencioun*, fr OF *mention*, fr L *mention-, mentio*, fr *ment-, mens*]

²mention *vt* to make mention of; refer to; *also* to cite for outstanding achievement – **mentionable** *adj*

mentor /'mentaw/ *n* a wise and trusted adviser [*Mentor*, tutor of Odysseus' son Telemachus in Homer's *Odyssey*, fr L, fr Gk *Mentōr*]

menu /'menyooh/ *n, pl* **menus** (a list of) the dishes that may be ordered (e g in a restaurant) or that are to be served (e g at a banquet) [F, fr *menu* small, detailed, fr L *minutus* minute (adj)]

meow /mee'ow/ *vi or n* (to) miaow [imit]

Mephistopheles /,mefis'tofəleez/ *n* a diabolical or fiendish person [G, name for the devil in various versions of the Faust legend] – **Mephistophelean** /-fistə'feeli·ən/, **Mephistophelian** *adj*

-mer *comb form* (→ *n*) **1** sthg that is (a specified type) of polymer or isomer ⟨*tauto*mer⟩ **2** sthg that has (such or so many) parts ⟨*pento*mer⟩ [ISV, fr Gk *meros* part – more at MERIT] – **merism** *comb form* (→ *n*), **merous** *comb form* (→ *adj*)

mercantile /'muhkəntiel/ *adj* **1** of or concerned with merchants or trading ⟨~ *law*⟩ **2** of mercantilism [F, fr It, fr *mercante* merchant, fr L *mercant-, mercans*, fr prp of *mercari* to trade – more at MARKET]

mercantilism /'muhkəntl,iz(ə)m, -,tiel,iz(ə)m/ *n* an economic system first prominent in the 17th c that was intended to increase the power and wealth of a nation by strict governmental regulation of the national economy – **mercantilist** *n or adj*

mercapt-, mercapto- *comb form* containing the –SH group in the molecular structure ⟨mercapto*purine*⟩ [ISV, fr *mercaptan*]

mercaptan /muh'kaptan/ *n* any of various (organic) compounds analogous to alcohols but containing sulphur in place of oxygen [G, fr Dan, fr ML *mercurium captans*, lit., seizing mercury]

Mercator's projection /muh'kaytəz/ *n* a map projection showing the lines of longitude as parallel evenly-spaced straight lines and the lines of latitude as parallel straight lines whose distance from each other increases with their distance from the equator [Gerhardus *Mercator* (Gerhard Kremer) †1594 Flem geographer]

¹mercenary /'muhs(ə)nri/ *n* a hired soldier in foreign service [ME, fr L *mercenarius*, fr *merced-, merces* wages – more at MERCY]

²mercenary *adj* **1** serving merely for (financial) reward **2** hired for service in the army of a foreign country – **mercenariness** *n*, **mercenarily** /,muhsə'neərəli/ *adv*

mercer /'muhsə/ *n, Br* a dealer in (fine quality) textile fabrics [ME, fr OF *mercier* merchant, fr *mers* merchandise, fr L *merc-, merx* – more at MARKET] – **mercery** *n*

mercer·ize, -ise /'muhsə,riez/ *vt* to give (e g cotton or fabrics) lustre and strength by chemical treatment [John *Mercer* †1866 E calico printer] – **mercerization** /,muhsərie'zaysh(ə)n/ *n*

¹merchandise /ˈmuhchən,dies/ *n* **1** the commodities that are bought and sold in commerce **2** wares for sale [ME *marchaundise*, fr OF *marcheandise*, fr *marcheant*]

²merchandise /ˈmuhchən,diez/ *vb* to buy and sell in business; trade (in) – **merchandiser** *n*

¹merchant /ˈmuhchənt/ *n* **1** a wholesaler; *also, chiefly NAm* a shopkeeper **2** a person who is given to a specified activity – chiefly derog ⟨*a speed* ~⟩ [ME *marchant*, fr OF *marcheant*, fr (assumed) VL *mercatant-*, *mercatans*, fr prp of *mercatare* to trade, fr L *mercatus*, pp of *mercari* – more at MARKET]

²merchant *adj* of or used in commerce; *esp* of a merchant navy

merchantable /ˈmuhchəntəbl/ *adj* marketable, salable

,merchant ˈbank *n* a firm of private bankers that handle bills of exchange and guarantee new issues of securities – **merchant banker** *n*

ˈmerchantman /-mən/ *n, pl* **merchantmen** /-mən/ a ship used in commerce

,merchant maˈrine *n, chiefly NAm* MERCHANT NAVY

,merchant ˈnavy *n, Br* (the personnel of) the privately or publicly owned commercial ships of a nation

mercur-, mercuro- *comb form* mercury ⟨mercur*ous*⟩ ⟨mercur*ic*⟩ [ISV, fr *mercury*]

¹mercurial /muhˈkyooəri·əl/ *adj* **1** of or born under the planet Mercury **2** having qualities of eloquence, ingenuity, or thievishness attributed to Mercury **3** characterized by rapid and unpredictable changes of mood **4** of, containing, or caused by mercury – **mercurially** *adv*

²mercurial *n* a drug or chemical containing mercury

,mercurous ˈchloride /ˈmuhkyərəs/ *n* an insoluble compound formerly used as a purgative

mercury /ˈmuhkyoori/ *n* **1** a heavy silver-white poisonous univalent or bivalent metallic element that is liquid at ordinary temperatures and used in thermometers, barometers, etc ☞ PERIODIC TABLE **2** *cap* the planet nearest the sun ☞ ASTRONOMY, SYMBOL [ME *mercurie*, fr ML *mercurius*, fr L *Mercurius* Mercury, god of commerce, travel, etc (fr *merc-*, *merx*), & the planet Mercury] – **mercuric** *adj*, **mercurous** *adj*

mercy /ˈmuhsi/ *n* **1** compassion or forbearance shown esp to an offender **2a** an act of divine compassion; a blessing **b** a fortunate circumstance ⟨*it was a* ~ *they found her before she froze*⟩ **3** compassionate treatment of those in distress [ME, fr OF *merci*, fr ML *merced-*, *merces*, fr L, price paid, wages, fr *merc-*, *merx* merchandise – more at MARKET] – **merciful** *adj*, **mercifully** *adv*, **mercifulness** *n*, **merciless** *adj*, **mercilessly** *adv*, **mercilessness** *n* – **at the mercy of** wholly in the power of; with no way to protect oneself against

ˈmercy ,killing *n* euthanasia

ˈmercy ,seat *n* **1** the gold plate resting on the ancient Jewish ark according to the account in Exodus **2** the throne of God

¹mere /miə/ *n* a (small) lake [ME, fr OE – more at MARINE]

²mere *adj* being what is specified and nothing else; nothing more than ⟨*a* ~ *child*⟩ [ME, fr L *merus* pure, unmixed – more at MORN] – **merely** *adv*

³mere *n* a ceremonial Maori hand weapon made of bone or greenstone [Maori]

-mere /-miə/ *comb form* (→ *n*) part; segment ⟨*blastomere*⟩ [F *-mère*, fr Gk *meros* part – more at MERIT]

meretricious /,merəˈtrishəs/ *adj* **1** tawdrily and falsely attractive **2** based on pretence or insincerity; specious [L *meretricius*, fr *meretric-*, *meretrix* prostitute, fr *merēre* to earn – more at MERIT] – **meretriciously** *adv*, **meretriciousness** *n*

merganser /muhˈgansə/ *n* any of various usu crested fish-eating and diving sawbill ducks [NL, fr L *mergus*, a waterfowl (fr *mergere*) + *anser* goose – more at GOOSE]

merge /muhj/ *vb* **1** to (cause to) combine or unite **2** to blend or (cause to) come together gradually without abrupt change [L *mergere* to dip, plunge; akin to Skt *majjati* he dives] – **mergence** *n*

merger /ˈmuhjə/ *n* **1** the absorption of an estate, contract, or interest in another – used in law **2** a combining or combination, esp of 2 organizations (e g business concerns) [*merge* + *-er* (as in *waiver*)]

meridian /məˈridi·ən/ *n* **1** a great circle passing through the poles of the celestial sphere and the zenith of a given place **2** a high point, esp of success or greatness **3** (a representation on a map or globe of) a circle on the surface of the earth or other celestial body passing through both poles [ME, fr MF *meridien*, fr *meridien* of noon, fr L *meridianus*, fr *meridies* noon, south, irreg fr *medius* mid + *dies* day – more at MID, DEITY] – **meridian** *adj*

meridional /məˈridi·ənl/ *adj* **1** of, characteristic of, or (being people) situated in the south, esp of France **2** of a meridian [ME, fr MF *meridionel*, fr LL *meridionalis*, irreg fr L *meridies*] – **meridional** *n*, **meridionally** *adv*

meringue /məˈrang/ *n* (a small cake, cream-filled shell, etc made with) a mixture of stiffly beaten egg whites and sugar baked until crisp [F]

merino /məˈreenoh/ *n, pl* **merinos** **1** (any of) a breed of fine-woolled white orig Spanish sheep **2** a soft wool or wool and cotton clothing fabric resembling cashmere **3** a fine wool and cotton yarn used for hosiery and knitwear [Sp]

meristem /ˈmeristem/ *n* a plant tissue that is the major area of growth and is made up of small cells capable of dividing indefinitely [Gk *meristos* divided (fr *merizein* to divide, fr *meros*) + E *-em* (as in *system*)] – **meristematic** /mə,ristəˈmatik/ *adj*, **meristematically** *adv*

¹merit /ˈmerit/ *n* **1a** the quality of deserving well or ill ⟨*payment by* ~⟩ **b** a praiseworthy quality; virtue **c** worth, excellence **2** spiritual credit held to be earned by performance of righteous acts and to ensure future benefits **3** *pl* the intrinsic rights and wrongs of a (legal) case [ME, fr OF *merite*, fr L *meritum*, fr neut of *meritus*, pp of *merēre* to deserve, earn; akin to Gk *meros* part, L *memor* mindful – more at MEMORY]

²merit *vt* to be worthy of or entitled to

meritocracy /,meriˈtokrəsi/ *n* (a social system based on) leadership by the talented [¹*merit* + *-o-* + *-cracy*] – **meritocratic** /-təˈkratik/ *adj*

meritorious /,meriˈtawri·əs/ *adj* deserving of reward or honour [ME, fr ML *meritorius*, fr L, that brings in money, fr *meritus*] – **meritoriously** *adv*, **meritoriousness** *n*

merlin /'muhlin/ *n* a small N American and European falcon with pointed wings [ME *meriloun*, fr AF *merilun*, fr OF *esmerillon*, aug of *esmeril*, of Gmc origin; akin to OHG *smiril* merlin]

merlon /'muhlən/ *n* any of the solid intervals between indentations of a battlemented parapet ☞ CHURCH [F, fr It *merlone*, aug of *merlo* battlement, fr ML *merulus*, fr L, blackbird]

mermaid /'muh,mayd/, *masc* **merman** /-,man/ *n, pl masc* **mermen** /-,men/ a mythical sea creature usu represented with a woman's body to the waist and a fish's tail [ME *mermaide*, fr *mere* sea, lake + *maide* maid]

,mermaid's 'purse *n* the leathery egg case of the skate or a related fish

Merovingian /,meroh'vinji·ən/ *n or adj* (a member) of the first Frankish dynasty reigning from about AD 500 to 751 [F *mérovingien*, fr ML *Merovingi* Merovingians, fr *Merovaeus* Merowig †458 Frankish founder of the dynasty]

merriment /'merimənt/ *n* lighthearted gaiety or fun

merry /'meri/ *adj* **1** full of gaiety or high spirits **2** marked by festivity **3** slightly drunk; tipsy – infml [ME *mery*, fr OE *myrge, merge*; akin to OHG *murg* short – more at [1]BRIEF] – **merrily** *adv*, **merriness** *n*

'merry-go-,round *n* a fairground machine with seats, often shaped like horses, that revolve about a fixed centre

'merry,making *n* gay or festive activity – **merrymaker** *n*

mes-, meso- *comb form* **1** mid; in the middle ⟨Meso*lithic*⟩ **2** intermediate (e g in size or type) ⟨meso*morph*⟩ ⟨mes*on*⟩ [L, fr Gk, fr *mesos* – more at MID]

mesa /'maysə/ *n* a usu isolated hill, esp in SW USA, with steeply sloping sides and a level top [Sp, lit., table, fr L *mensa*]

mésalliance /me'zali·əns/ *n* a marriage with sby of inferior social position [F, fr *més-* mis- + *alliance*]

mescal /me'skal/ *n* **1** a small cactus with rounded stems covered with mescaline-containing jointed protuberances used as a hallucinogen, esp among the Mexican Indians **2** (a usu colourless Mexican spirit made esp from) the maguey plant [Sp *mezcal, mescal*, fr Nahuatl *mexcalli* mescal liquor]

me'scal ,button *n* any of the dried disc-shaped tops of the mescal

mescaline /'meskəlin, -leen/ *n* a hallucinogenic alkaloid found in mescal buttons

mesdames /may'dam/ *pl of* MADAM *or of* MADAME *or of* MRS

mesdemoiselles /,maydəmwah'zel/ *pl of* MADEMOISELLE

mesembryanthemum /,mezembri'anthiməm, mi,-zembri-/ *n* any of a genus of chiefly S African fleshy-leaved herbaceous plants or undershrubs [NL, genus name, fr Gk *mesēmbria* midday (fr *mes-* + *hēmera* day) + *anthemon* flower, fr *anthos* – more at ANTHOLOGY]

mesencephalon /,mesen'sef(ə)lon/ *n* the midbrain [NL] – **mesencephalic** /-si'falik/ *adj*

mesentery /'mez(ə)n,teri, 'mes-/ *n* any of several membranous double folds of the peritoneum of vertebrates, that envelop the intestines and connected organs and join them with the rear wall of the abdominal cavity [NL *mesenterium*, fr MF & Gk; MF *mesentere*, fr Gk *mesenterion*, fr *mes-* + *enteron* intestine – more at INTER-] – **mesenteric** /,mez(ə)n'terik, ,mes-/ *adj*

[1]mesh /mesh/ *n* **1** an open space in a net, network, etc **2a** the cords, wires, etc that make up a net; NETWORK 1 ⟨*wire* ~⟩ **b** a woven, knitted, or knotted fabric with evenly spaced small holes **3a** an interlocking or intertwining arrangement or construction **b** a web, snare – usu pl with sing. meaning **4** working contact (e g of the teeth of gears) ⟨*in* ~⟩ [prob fr obs D *maesche*; akin to OHG *masca* mesh, Lith *mazgos* knot]

[2]mesh *vt* **1** to catch or entangle (as if) in the openings of a net **2** to cause to engage ~ *vi* **1** *esp of gears* to be in or come into mesh **2** to fit or work together properly or successfully

mesial /'meezi·əl/ *adj* (in or directed towards the) middle; *esp, of a plane* dividing an animal into right and left halves [*mes-* + *-ial*] – **mesially** *adv*

mesio- /meezioh-, meesioh-/ *comb form* mesial and ⟨mesio *distal*⟩ ⟨mesio*buccal*⟩ [*mesi*al + *-o-*]

mesmerism /'mezmə,riz(ə)m/ *n* hypnotism [F A *Mesmer* †1815 Austrian physician & hypnotist] – **mesmerist** *n*, **mesmeric** /mez'merik/ *adj*

mesmer·ize, -ise /'mezməriez/ *vt* **1** to hypnotize **2** to fascinate, rivet – **mesmerizer** *n*

meso- – see MES-

mesoblast /'meezə,blast, 'mesoh-/ *n* (the embryonic cells that give rise to) mesoderm – **mesoblastic** /,meezə'blastik, ,mesoh-/ *adj*

'meso,derm /-,duhm/ *n* (tissue derived from) the middle of the 3 primary germ layers of an embryo that is the source of bone, muscle, connective tissue, and the inner layer of the skin in the adult – compare ENDODERM, ECTODERM 2 [ISV] – **mesodermal** /-'duhml/, **mesodermic** /-mik/ *adj*

Mesolithic /,mesoh'lithik/ *adj or n* (of or being) a transitional period of the Stone Age between the Palaeolithic and the Neolithic [ISV]

mesomorphic /,mesoh'mawfik/ *adj* having a muscular body build [*meso*derm + *-morphic*; fr the predominance in such types of structures developed from the mesoderm] – **mesomorphism, mesomorph** /'mesoh,mawf/ *n*, **mesomorphy** *n*

meson /'meezon/ *n* any of a group of unstable elementary particles including the pions and kaons that are bosons and have a mass between that of an electron and a proton [ISV *mes-* + [2]*-on*] – **mesonic** /mee'zonik, mi-, -'so-/ *adj*

mesophyll /'mesoh,fil/ *n* the parenchymatous tissue between the epidermal surface layers of a foliage leaf [NL *mesophyllum*, fr *mes-* + Gk *phyllon* leaf – more at BLADE] – **mesophyllic** /-'filik/ *adj*, **mesophyllous** *adj*

'meso,phyte /-,fiet/ *n* a plant that grows under medium conditions of moisture [ISV] – **mesophytic** /-'fitik/ *adj*

'meso,sphere /-,sfiə/ *n* a layer of the upper atmosphere which extends from the top of the stratosphere to an altitude of about 80km (about 50mi) and in which photochemical reactions take place – **mesospheric** /-'sferik/ *adj*

,mesotheli'oma /-theeli'ohmə/ *n, pl* **mesotheliomas, mesotheliomata** /-mətə/ a tumour of the lining of the peritoneum, lungs, heart, etc, often occurring after prolonged contact with blue asbestos dust [NL, fr *mesothelium* epithelium derived from mesoderm, fr *mes-* + epi*thelium*]

Mesozoic /,mezoh'zoh·ik/ *adj or n* (of or being) an

era of geological history that extends from the end of the Permian to the Tertiary ☞ EVOLUTION

mesquite /me'skeet/ *n* a spiny leguminous tree or shrub that forms extensive thickets in the SW USA and Mexico and bears sugar-rich pods used as a livestock feed [Sp, fr Nahuatl *mizquitl*]

1**mess** /mes/ *n* **1** a prepared dish of soft or liquid food; *also* a usu unappetizing mixture of ingredients eaten together **2a(1)** *sing or pl in constr* a group of people (e g servicemen or servicewomen) who regularly take their meals together **(2)** a meal so taken **b** a place where meals are regularly served to a group ⟨*the officers' ~*⟩ **3a** a confused, dirty, or offensive state or condition **b** a disordered situation resulting from misunderstanding, blundering, or misconduct [ME *mes*, fr OF, fr LL *missus* course at a meal, fr *missus*, pp of *mittere* to put, fr L, to send – more at SMITE]

2**mess** *vi* **1** to take meals with a mess **2** to make a mess **3a** to dabble, potter **b** to handle or play *with* sthg, esp carelessly **c** to interfere, meddle *USE* (*3*) often + *about* or *around*

mess about *vb, chiefly Br vi* **1a** to waste time **b** to work according to one's whim or mood ⟨messing about *in boats*⟩ **2** to conduct an affair *with* ⟨messing about *with someone else's husband*⟩ ~*vt* to treat roughly or without due consideration ⟨*he shouldn't* mess *the men* about *too much, they know their job – The Lorry Driver*⟩

message /'mesij/ *n* **1** a communication in writing, in speech, or by signals **2** a messenger's errand or function **3** a central theme or idea intended to inspire, urge, warn, enlighten, advise, etc [ME, fr OF, fr ML *missaticum*, fr L *missus*, pp of *mittere*]

messenger /'mesinjə/ *n* one who bears a message or does an errand: e g **a** a dispatch bearer in government or military service **b** an employee who carries messages [ME *messangere*, fr OF *messagier*, fr *message*]

messenger RNA *n* an RNA that carries the code for the synthesis of a particular protein and acts as a template for its formation – compare TRANSFER RNA

messiah /mə'sie·ə/ *n* **1** *often cap* **a** *the* expected king and deliverer of the Jews **b** Jesus **2** a professed leader of some cause [Heb *māshīaḥ* & Aram *mĕshīḥā*, lit., anointed] – **messiahship** *n*

messianic /,mesi'anik/ *adj* **1** of a messiah **2** marked by idealistic enthusiasm for a cherished cause **3** of a time of blessedness and peace associated with the Jewish and Christian concept of the end of the world [(assumed) NL *messianicus*, fr LL *Messias* + L *-anicus* (as in *romanicus* Romanic)] – **messianism** /mə'sie·ə,niz(ə)m, 'mesi·ə,niz(ə)m/ *n*

Messias /mə'sie·əs/ *n* MESSIAH 1 [ME, fr LL, fr Gk, fr Aram *mĕshīḥā*]

Messidor /'mesidaw (*Fr* mesidɔːr)/ *n* the 10th month of the French Revolutionary calendar, corresponding to 20June–19 July [F, fr L *messis* harvest + Gk *dōron* gift]

messieurs /'mesyuh, 'mesəz (*Fr* mɛsjø)/ *pl of* MONSIEUR

'**mess ,jacket** *n* a short fitted man's jacket reaching to the waist and worn as part of a uniform on formal occasions in the mess

'**mess ,kit** *n* a compact kit of cooking and eating utensils for soldiers, campers, etc

'**mess,mate** /-,mayt/ *n* a member of a (ship's) mess

Messrs /'mesəz/ *pl of* MR ⟨*~ Jones, Brown, and Robinson*⟩

messuage /'meswij/ *n* a dwelling house with its outbuildings and land [ME, fr AF, prob alter. of OF *mesnage* – more at MÉNAGE]

mess up *vt* to make a mess of; spoil – infml

messy /'mesi/ *adj* **1** marked by confusion, disorder, or dirt **2** lacking neatness or precision; slovenly **3** unpleasantly or tryingly difficult to conclude – **messily** *adv*, **messiness** *n*

mestiza /me'steezə/, *masc* **mestizo** /-zoh/ *n, pl* **mestizas,** *masc* **mestizos** a person of mixed European and American Indian ancestry [Sp, fem of *mestizo* mixed, fr LL *mixticius*, fr L *mixtus*, pp of *miscēre* to mix – more at MIX]

1**met** /met/ *past of* MEET

2**met** *adj* meteorological ⟨*the ~ office forecast*⟩

meta- /metə-/, **met-** *prefix* **1a** situated behind or beyond ⟨meta*carpus*⟩ ⟨meta*galaxy*⟩ **b** later or more highly organized or specialized form of ⟨meta*xylem*⟩ **2** change; transformation ⟨meta *morphosis*⟩ ⟨meta*bolism*⟩ **3** more comprehensive; transcending; of a higher or second order ⟨meta*psychology*⟩ – used with the name of a discipline to designate a new but related discipline designed to deal critically with the original one ⟨meta*language*⟩ **4a** related to ⟨meta*aldehyde*⟩ **b** involving substitution at 2 positions in the benzene ring that are separated by 1 carbon atom – compare ORTHO-, PARA- [NL & ML, fr L or Gk; L, change, fr Gk, among, with, after, change, fr *meta* among, with, after; akin to OE *mid, mith* with, OHG *mit*]

metabolism /mə'tabl,iz(ə)m/ *n* all the processes (by which a specified substance is dealt with) in the building up and destruction of living tissue; *specif* the chemical changes in living cells by which energy is provided and new material is assimilated [ISV, fr Gk *metabolē* change, fr *metaballein* to change, fr *meta-* + *ballein* to throw – more at DEVIL] – **metabolize** *vb*, **metabolic** /,metə'bolik/ *adj*

metabolite /mə'tabl,iet/ *n* **1** a product of metabolism **2** a substance essential to the metabolism of a particular organism or to a particular metabolic process

metacarpal /,metə'kahpl/ *n* a metacarpal bone ☞ ANATOMY

,**meta'carpus** /-'kahpəs/ *n* the part of the hand or forefoot between the wrist and fingers or the ankle and toes [NL] – **metacarpal** *adj*

'**meta,centre** /-,sentə/ *n* the point of intersection of the vertical line through the centre of buoyancy of a floating body with the vertical line through the new centre of buoyancy when the body is displaced (e g by being heeled over) – **metacentric** /-'sentrik/ *adj or n*

,**meta'genesis** /-'jenəsis/ *n* ALTERNATION OF GENERATIONS [NL] – **metagenetic** /-jə'netik/ *adj*, **metagenetically** *adv*

metal /'metl/ *n* **1** any of various opaque, fusible, ductile, and typically lustrous substances (e g iron, copper, or mercury), esp chemical elements, that are good conductors of electricity and heat, form positive ions by loss of electrons, and yield basic oxides and hydroxides **2** glass in its molten state **3** either of the heraldic colours gold or silver **4** *chiefly Br* ROAD METAL [ME, fr OF, fr L *metallum* mine, metal, fr Gk *metallon*] – **metalliferous** /ˌmetlˈifərəs/ *adj*

metalanguage /ˈmetəˌlang·gwij/ *n* a language used to talk about language

metalled /ˈmetld/, *NAm chiefly* **metaled** *adj, chiefly Br, of a road* covered with a surface of broken stones

metallic /miˈtalik/ *adj* **1** of, containing, like, or being (a) metal **2** yielding metal **3** having an acrid quality – **metallically** *adv*

metall·ize, -ise, *NAm also* **metalize** /ˈmetl·iez/ *vt* to treat, combine, or coat with a metal – **metallization** /-ˈzaysh(ə)n/ *n*

metallography /ˌmetlˈogrəfi/ *n* the study of the (microscopic) structure of metals [F *métallographie,* fr L *metallum* + F *-graphie* -graphy] – **metallographer** *n,* **metallographic** /miˌtaləˈgrafik/ *adj,* **metallographically** *adv*

[1]**metalloid** /ˈmetl·oyd/ *n* an element (e g arsenic) having some properties of typical metals and some properties of typical nonmetals

[2]**metalloid** *also* **metalloidal** /ˌmetlˈoydl/ *adj* **1** resembling a metal **2** of or being a metalloid

metallurgy /məˈtaləji, ˈmetlˌuhji/ *n* the science and technology of metals [NL *metallurgia,* fr Gk *metallon* + NL *-urgia* -urgy] – **metallurgist** *n,* **metallurgical** /ˌmetlˈuhjikl/ *adj,* **metallurgically** *adv*

ˈ**metalˌwork** /-ˌwuhk/ *n* the craft or product of shaping things out of metal – **metalworker** *n*

metamere /ˈmetəˌmiə/ *n* a somite [ISV] – **metameric** /-ˈmerik/ *adj,* **metamerically** *adv,* **metamerism** /məˈtaməˌriz(ə)m/ *n*

metamorphic /ˌmetəˈmawfik/ *adj* **1** of or involving metamorphosis **2** *of a rock* of or produced by metamorphism – **metamorphically** *adv*

metamorphism /ˌmetəˈmawfiz(ə)m/ *n* a change in rock effected esp by heat and pressure and resulting in a more compact and crystalline structure

metamorphose /metəˈmawfohz, ˌ---ˈ-/ *vt* **1a** to change into a different physical form **b** to change strikingly the appearance or character of; transform **2** to cause (rock) to undergo metamorphism ~ *vi* to undergo metamorphosis [prob fr MF *metamorphoser,* fr *metamorphose* metamorphosis, fr L *metamorphosis*]

ˌ**metaˈmorphosis** /-ˈmawfəsis/ *n, pl* **metamorphoses** /-seez/ **1a** change of form, structure, or substance, esp by supernatural means **b** a striking alteration (e g in appearance or character) **2** a marked (abrupt) change in the form or structure of a butterfly, frog, etc occurring in the course of development ☞ LIFE CYCLE [L, fr Gk *metamorphōsis,* fr *metamorphoun* to transform, fr *meta-* + *morphē* form]

ˈ**metaˌphase** /-ˌfayz/ *n* the stage of mitotic or meiotic cell division in which the chromosomes become arranged in the equatorial plane of the spindle [ISV]

metaphor /ˈmetəfə, -ˌfaw/ *n* (an instance of) a figure of speech in which a word or phrase literally denoting one kind of object or idea is applied to another to suggest a likeness or analogy between them (e g in *the ship ploughs the sea*) – compare SIMILE [MF or L; MF *metaphore,* fr L *metaphora,* fr Gk, fr *metapherein* to transfer, fr *meta-* + *pherein* to bear – more at [2]BEAR] – **metaphoric** /-ˈforik/, **metaphorical** *adj,* **metaphorically** *adv*

ˌ**metaˈphysic** /-ˈfizik/ *n* a particular system of metaphysics [ME *metaphesyk,* fr ML *Metaphysica*] – **metaphysic** *adj*

ˌ**metaˈphysical** /-ˈfizikl/ *adj* **1** of metaphysics **2** *often cap* of or being poetry, esp of the early 17th c, marked by elaborate subtleties of thought and expression – **metaphysically** *adv*

ˌ**metaˈphysics** *n pl but sing in constr* **1** a division of philosophy concerned with ultimate causes and the underlying nature of things; *esp* ontology **2** pure or speculative philosophy [ML *Metaphysica,* title of Aristotle's treatise on the subject, fr Gk *(ta) meta (ta) physika,* lit., the (works) after the physical (works); fr its position in his collected works] – **metaphysician** /-fiˈzish(ə)n/ *n*

ˌ**metaˈplasia** /-ˈplayzi·ə, -zh(y)ə/ *n* (abnormal) replacement of cells of one type by cells of another [NL] – **metaplastic** /-ˈplastik/ *adj*

ˌ**metaˈstable** /-ˈstaybl/ *adj* having or characterized by only a slight margin of (chemical) stability ⟨*a ~ compound*⟩ [ISV] – **metastably** *adv,* **metastability** /-stəˈbiləti/ *n*

metastasis /miˈtastəsis/ *n, pl* **metastases** /-seez/ change of position, state, or form; *specif* a secondary growth of a malignant tumour at a site distant from the primary growth [NL, fr LL, transition, fr Gk, fr *methistanai* to change, fr *meta-* + *histanai* to set – more at STAND] – **metastatic** /ˌmetəˈstatik/ *adj,* **metastatically** *adv,* **metastasize** /miˈtastəsiez/ *vi*

metatarsal /ˌmetəˈtahsl/ *n* a metatarsal bone ☞ ANATOMY

ˌ**metaˈtarsus** /-ˈtahsəs/ *n* the part of the foot in human beings or of the hind foot in 4-legged animals between the ankle and toes [NL] – **metatarsal** *adj*

metathesis /məˈtathəsis/ *n, pl* **metatheses** /-seez/ a change of place or condition: e g **a** transposition of 2 phonemes in a word (e g in Old English *bridd,* Modern English *bird*) **b** DOUBLE DECOMPOSITION [Gk, fr *metatithenai* to transpose, fr *meta-* + *tithenai* to place – more at [1]DO] – **metathetical** /ˌmetəˈthetikl/, **metathetic** *adj,* **metathetically** *adv*

ˌ**metaˈthorax** /-ˈthawraks/ *n* the rear segment of the thorax of an insect [NL] – **metathoracic** /-thawˈrasik/ *adj*

ˌ**metaˈzoan** /-ˈzoh·ən/ *n* any of a kingdom or subkingdom of animals that comprises all those with multicellular bodies differentiated into tissues [NL *Metazoa,* group name, fr *meta-* + *-zoa*] – **metazoal** *adj,* **metazoan** *adj*

mete /meet/ *vt* to assign by measure; allot – usu + *out* [ME *meten,* fr OE *metan;* akin to OHG *mezzan* to measure, L *modus* measure, *meditari* to meditate]

metempsychosis /ˌmetempsieˈkohsis/ *n* the passing of the soul at death into another body [LL, fr Gk *metempsychōsis,* fr *metempsychousthai* to undergo metempsychosis, fr *meta-* + *empsychos* animate, fr *en-* + *psychē* soul – more at PSYCH-]

meteor /ˈmeeti·ə, -ˌaw/ *n* a phenomenon in the atmosphere; *esp* (the streak of light produced by the passage of) any of many small particles of matter in the solar system observable only when heated by friction so that they glow as they fall into the earth's atmosphere [ME, fr MF *meteore,* fr ML *meteorum,* fr Gk *meteōron* phenomenon in the sky, fr neut of *meteōros* high in air, fr *meta-* + *-eōros* (akin to Gk *aeirein* to lift)]

meteoric /ˌmeetiˈorik/ *adj* **1** of a meteor **2** resembling a meteor in speed or in sudden and temporary brilliance ⟨~ *rise to fame*⟩ – **meteorically** *adv*

meteorite /ˈmeeti·ə,riet/ *n* a meteor that reaches the surface of the earth without being completely vaporized – **meteoritic** /-ˈritik/, **meteoritical** *adj*

meteoroid /ˈmeeti·ə,royd/ *n* a particle in orbit round the sun that becomes a meteor when it meets the earth's atmosphere – **meteoroidal** /-ˈroydl/ *adj*

meteorology /,meeti·əˈroləji/ *n* **1** the science of the atmosphere and its phenomena, esp weather and weather forecasting ☞ WEATHER **2** the weather or atmospheric phenomena of a region [F or Gk; F *météorologie*, fr MF, fr Gk *meteōrologia*, fr *meteōron* + *-logia* -logy] – **meteorologist** *n*, **meteorologic** /-rəˈlojik/, **meteorological** *adj*, **meteorologically** *adv*

[1]**meter** /ˈmeetə/ *n*, *NAm* a metre

[2]**meter** *n* an instrument for measuring (and recording) the amount of sthg (e g gas, electricity, or parking time) used [[2]*-meter*]

[3]**meter** *vt* **1** to measure by means of a meter **2** to supply in a measured or regulated amount

[1]**-meter** /-mətə/ *comb form* (→ *n*) measure or unit of metrical verse ⟨*penta*meter⟩ – compare FOOT 4 [[2]*metre*]

[2]**-meter** *comb form* (→ *n*) instrument or means for measuring ⟨*baro*meter⟩ [F *-mètre*, fr Gk *metron* measure]

meth-, **metho-** *comb form* methyl ⟨meth*acrylic*⟩ [ISV, fr *methyl*]

methadon /ˈmethə,don/ *n* methadone

methadone /ˈmethə,dohn/ *n* a synthetic narcotic drug used esp as a substitute narcotic in the treatment of heroin addiction and as a painkiller [6-di-*meth*ylamino-4, 4-*d*iphenyl-3-heptan*one*]

methamphetamine /,methamˈfetəmin/ *n* an amphetamine drug [*meth-* + *amphetamine*]

methane /ˈmee,thayn/ *n* an inflammable gaseous hydrocarbon of the alkane series used as a fuel and as a raw material in chemical synthesis ☞ ENERGY [ISV]

methanol /ˈmethənol/ *n* a volatile inflammable poisonous liquid alcohol that is added to ethyl alcohol to make it unfit to drink and is used as a solvent and as a raw material in chemical synthesis [ISV]

Methedrine /ˈmethədrin/ *trademark* – used for methamphetamine

metheglin /məˈtheglin/ *n* [1]MEAD [W *meddyglyn*]

methinks /miˈthingks/ *vb impersonal* **methought** /miˈthawt/ *archaic* it seems to me [ME *me thinketh*, fr OE *mē thincth*, fr *mē* (dat of *ic* I) + *thincth* (it) seems, fr *thyncan* to seem]

methionine /miˈthie·ə,neen, -,nien/ *n* a sulphur-containing amino acid that is found in most proteins and is an essential constituent of human diet [ISV, fr methyl + *thion-* + *-ine*]

method /ˈmethəd/ *n* **1a** a systematic procedure for doing sthg **b** a regular way of doing sthg **2a** an orderly arrangement or system **b** the habitual practice of orderliness and regularity **3** *cap* a dramatic technique by which an actor seeks to identify closely with the inner personality of the character being portrayed – usu + *the* [MF or L; MF *methode*, fr L *methodus*, fr Gk *methodos*, fr *meta-* + *hodos* way – more at CEDE]

methodical /məˈthodikl/, *NAm also* **methodic** *adj* **1** arranged, characterized by, or performed with method or order **2** habitually proceeding according to method; systematic – **methodically** *adv*, **methodicalness** *n*

Methodism /ˈmethədiz(ə)m/ *n* (the doctrines and practice of) the Methodist churches

Methodist /ˈmethədist/ *n or adj* (a member) of any of the denominations deriving from the Wesleyan revival in the Church of England [*method* + *-ist*; orig sense, one devoted to a particular method] – **Methodistic** /-ˈdistik/ *adj*

method·ize, **-ise** /ˈmethədiez/ *vt* to reduce to method; systematize

methodology /,methəˈdoləji/ *n* (the analysis of) the body of methods and rules employed by a science or discipline [NL *methodologia*, fr L *methodus* + *-logia* -logy] – **methodologist** *n*, **methodological** /-dəˈlojikl/ *adj*

methotrexate /,methəˈtreksayt/ *n* a synthetic anticancer drug used esp to treat lymphomas and some forms of leukaemia [*meth-* + *-trexate*, of unknown origin]

meths /meths/ *n pl but sing in constr, Br* METHYLATED SPIRITS – infml [by contr]

Methuselah /miˈthyoohzələ/ *n* a champagne bottle holding 8 times the usual amount [*Methuselah*, a biblical patriarch said to have lived 969 years (Gen 5:27), fr Heb *Měthūshāʼēl*]

methyl /ˈmethil, ˈmeethil, -thiel/ *n* a univalent hydrocarbon radical CH_3 derived from methane [ISV, back-formation fr *methylene*] – **methylic** /məˈthilik/ *adj*

methyl alcohol *n* methanol

methylate /ˈmethilayt/ *vt* **1** to impregnate or mix with methanol **2** to introduce the methyl group into – **methylator** *n*, **methylation** /-ˈlaysh(ə)n/ *n*

,**methylated ˈspirits** *n pl but sing or pl in constr* alcohol mixed with an adulterant, esp methanol, to make it undrinkable and therefore exempt from duty

methylene /ˈmethə,leen/ *n* a bivalent hydrocarbon radical CH_2 derived from methane [F *méthylène*, fr Gk *methy* wine + *hylē* wood – more at [1]MEAD]

,**methylene ˈblue** *n* a dye used esp to stain biological specimens, and as an antidote in cyanide poisoning

metical /metiˈkal/ *n*, *pl* **meticaes** /metiˈkiesh/ ☞ *Mozambique* at NATIONALITY [Pg, fr Ar *mithqāl*, a unit of weight]

meticulous /məˈtikyooləs/ *adj* marked by extreme or excessive care over detail [L *meticulosus* timid, fr *metus* fear + *-iculosus* (as in *periculosus* dangerous)] – **meticulously** *adv*, **meticulousness** *n*

métier /ˈmaytyay/ *n* one's trade; *also* sthg (e g an activity) in which one is expert or successful [F, fr (assumed) VL *misterium*, alter. of L *ministerium* work, ministry]

metif /mayˈteef/ *n* an octoroon [F *métif*, alter. of *métis*]

métis /meˈtees/ *n*, *pl* **métis** one of mixed blood: **a** a half-breed **b** a crossbred animal [F, fr LL *mixticius* mixed – more at MESTIZA]

metoestrus /meˈteestrəs/ *n* the period of regression that follows oestrus in a mammal's sexual cycle [NL]

Metonic cycle /miˈtonik/ *n* a period of 19 years covering all the phases of the moon, after which the new moons occur again on the same cycle of dates [*Meton*, 5th-c BC Gk astronomer]

metonym /'metənim/ *n* a word used in metonymy [back-formation fr *metonymy*]

metonymy /mi'tonəmi/ *n* a figure of speech in which the name of an attribute of a thing is used in place of the thing itself (e g lands belonging to the *crown*) [L *metonymia*, fr Gk *metōnymia*, fr *meta-* + *-ōnymia* -onymy]

metope /'metohp, 'metəpi/ *n* the space between 2 triglyphs of a Doric frieze [Gk *metopē*, fr *meta-* + *opē* opening; akin to Gk *ōps* eye, face – more at EYE]

metr-, metro- *comb form* uterus ⟨metro*rrhagia*⟩ [NL, fr Gk *mētr-*, fr *mētra*, fr *mētr-*, *mētēr* mother – more at [1]MOTHER]

[1]**metre,** *NAm chiefly* **meter** /'meetə/ *n* the SI unit of length equal to a certain number of wavelengths of a specific radiation of the krypton isotope $_{36}Kr^{86}$ (about 1.094yd) ☞ PHYSICS, UNIT [F *mètre*, fr Gk *metron* measure]

[2]**metre,** *NAm chiefly* **meter** *n* **1** systematically arranged and measured rhythm in verse ⟨*iambic* ~⟩ **2** a basic recurrent rhythmical pattern of accents and beats per bar in music [ME, fr OE & MF; OE *mēter*, fr L *metrum*, fr Gk *metron* measure, metre; MF *metre*, fr OF, fr L *metrum* – more at MEASURE] – **metrist** /'metrist/ *n*

metre-kilogram-second *adj* of or being a system of units based on the metre, the kilogram, and the second – compare SI

metric /'metrik/ *adj* **1 metric, metrical** (using or being units) based on the metre, litre, and kilogram as standard of measurement – compare SI **2** metrical – **metrically** *adv*

-metric /-'metrik/, **-metrical** /-kl/ *comb form* (→ *adj*) **1** of, employing, or obtained by (a specified meter) ⟨*galvano*metric⟩ **2** of or relating to the art, process, or science of measuring (sthg specified) ⟨*chron* ometric⟩ ⟨*gravi*metrical⟩

metrical /'metrikl/, **metric** *adj* **1** of or composed in metre **2** of measurement – **metrically** *adv*

metricate /'metrikayt/ *vt* to change into or express in the metric system ~ *vi* to adopt the metric system – **metrication** /-'kaysh(ə)n/ *n*

metrics /metriks/ *n pl but sing or pl in constr* a part of prosody that deals with metrical structure

metric ton *n* a tonne

metro /'metroh/ *n, pl* **metros** an underground railway system in a city ⟨*the Leningrad* ~⟩ [F *métro*, short for (*chemin de fer*) *métropolitain* metropolitan railway]

Metro *adj, Can* of or relating to the inner urban area of a Canadian city, esp of Toronto [short for *Metropolitan*]

metro- – see METR-

metronidazole /,metrə'niedə,zohl/ *n* a synthetic drug used to treat infections, esp vaginal trichomoniasis, produced by protozoans [*me*thyl + *-tron-* (prob fr *nitro*) + im*ide* + *azole*]

metronome /'metrə,nohm/ *n* an instrument designed to mark exact time by a regularly repeated tick [Gk *metron* + *-nomos* controlling, fr *nomos* law – more at NIMBLE] – **metronomic** /,metrə'nomik/ *adj*

metronymic /,metrə'nimik/ *n* a name derived from a mother or maternal ancestor (e g by suffixation) [MGk *mētrōnymikos*, adj, named after one's mother, fr Gk *mētr-*, *mētēr* mother + *onyma*, *onoma* name] – **metronymic** *adj*

metropolis /mi'tropəlis/ *n* **1** the chief city of a country, state, or region **2** a centre of a usu specified activity **3** a large or important city [LL, fr Gk *mētropolis*, fr *mētr-*, *mētēr* mother + *polis* city – more at [1]MOTHER, POLICE]

[1]**metropolitan** /,metrə'polit(ə)n/ *n* **1** the primate of an ecclesiastical province **2** one who lives in a metropolis

[2]**metropolitan** *adj* **1** of or constituting a metropolitan or his see **2** (characteristic) of a metropolis **3** of or constituting a mother country [LL *metropolitanus* of the see of a metropolitan, fr *metropolita*, n, metropolitan, fr LGk *mētropolitēs*, fr *mētropolis* see of a metropolitan, fr Gk, chief city]

metropolitan area *n* a large urban area in Britain governed by a single local authority

metrorrhagia /,meetrə'rayji·ə, ,met-, -raw-/ *n* profuse bleeding from the uterus, esp between menstrual periods [NL] – **metrorrhagic** /-jik/ *adj*

-metry /-mətri/ *comb form* (→ *n*) art, process, or science of measuring (sthg specified) ⟨*chrono*metry⟩ ⟨*photo*metry⟩ [ME *-metrie*, fr MF, fr L *-metria*, fr Gk, fr *metrein* to measure, fr *metron* – more at MEASURE]

mettle /'metl/ *n* **1** strength of spirit or temperament **2** staying quality; stamina [alter. of *metal*] – **on one's mettle** aroused to do one's best

'mettlesome /-s(ə)m/ *adj* spirited [METTLE + [1]-SOME]

meuniere /muh'nyeə (*Fr* mønjɛ:r)/ *adj* with a sauce of melted butter, parsley, and lemon juice ⟨*sole* ~⟩ [F (*à la*) *meunière*, lit., in the manner of a miller's wife, fr *meunière* miller's wife, fem of *meunier* miller, fr LL *molinarius*, fr *molina* mill]

[1]**mew** /myooh/ *vi* to utter a miaow or similar sound ⟨*gulls* ~*ed over the bay*⟩ ~ *vt* to miaow [ME *mewen*, of imit origin] – **mew** *n*

[2]**mew** *vt* to shut up; confine – often + *up* [ME *mewen*, fr *mewe*, n – more at MEWS]

mewl /myoohl/ *vi* to cry weakly; whimper [imit]

mews /myoohz/ *n pl but sing or pl in constr, pl* **mews** *chiefly Br* (living accommodation adapted from) stables built round an open courtyard [ME *mewe* cage for moulting hawks, coop, fr MF *mue*, fr *muer* to moult, fr L *mutare* to change]

Mexican /'meksikən/ *n* **1** a native or inhabitant of Mexico **2** NAHUATL 2 [Sp *mexicano*, *mejicano*, fr *Mexico*, a country in Southern North America] – **Mexican** *adj*

mezereon /mə'ziəri·ən/ *n* a small European shrub with fragrant lilac purple flowers [ME *mizerion*, fr ML *mezereon*, fr Ar *māzariyūn*, fr Per]

mezuzah, mezuza /mə'zoohzə/ *n* a small oblong case containing a parchment inscribed with religious texts, fixed to the doorpost by some Jewish families as a sign and reminder of their faith [Heb *mĕzūzāh* doorpost]

mezzanine /'mezəneen/ *n* a low-ceilinged storey between 2 main storeys, esp the ground and first floors, of a building [F, fr It *mezzanino*, fr *mezzano* middle, fr L *medianus* middle, median]

mezza voce /,metsə 'vohchi/ *adv or adj* with medium or half volume of tone – used in music [It, lit., half voice]

mezzo /'metsoh/, **mezzo-soprano** *n, pl* **mezzos, mezzo-sopranos** (a singer with) a woman's voice with a range between that of the soprano and contralto [It *mezzosoprano,* fr *mezzo* middle, moderate, half + *soprano*]

mezzo forte /'fawtay/ *adj or adv* moderately loud – used in music [It]

mezzo piano /pi'ahnoh/ *adj or adv* moderately soft – used in music [It]

mezzo-rilievo /ri'leevoh, ree'lyayvoh/ *n* sculptural relief which is halfway between bas-relief and high relief and in which about half of the circumference of the design stands out from the surrounding area [It, fr *mezzo* + *rilievo* relief]

mezzotint /'metsoh,tint/ *n* (a print produced by) a method of engraving on copper or steel by scraping or burnishing a roughened surface to produce light and shade [modif of It *mezzatinta,* fr *mezza* (fem of *mezzo*) + *tinta* tint]

mi /mee/ *n* the 3rd note of the diatonic scale in solmization [ML – more at GAMUT]

mi-, mio- *comb form* less ⟨Miocene⟩ [prob fr NL *meio-,* fr Gk, fr *meiōn* – more at MINOR]

MI5 *n* the security service of British Military Intelligence – not now in official use [*m*ilitary *i*ntelligence]

MI6 *n* the espionage service of British Military Intelligence – not now in official use

miaow, meow /mi'ow, myow/ *vi or n* (to make) the characteristic cry of a cat [imit]

miasma /mi'azmə/ *n, pl* **miasmas** *also* **miasmata** /-mətə/ **1** a heavy vapour (e g from a swamp) formerly believed to cause disease; *broadly* any heavy or malodorous vapour **2** a pervasive influence that tends to weaken or corrupt [NL, fr Gk, defilement, fr *miainein* to pollute] – **miasmal** *adj,* **miasmatic** /,mee·əz'matik/ *adj,* **miasmic** /mi'azmik/ *adj*

mica /'miekə/ *n* any of various coloured or transparent silicate materials occurring as crystals that readily separate into very thin flexible leaves [NL, fr L, grain, crumb; akin to Gk *mikros* small] – **micaceous** /mie'kayshəs/ *adj*

Micah /'miekə/ *n* (a book of the Old Testament attributed to) a Hebrew prophet of the 8th c BC [Heb *Mīkhāh,* short for *Mīkhāyāh*]

mice /mies/ *pl of* MOUSE

micelle /mi'sel/ *n* a body of molecules or ions that forms a colloidal particle [NL *micella,* fr L *mica*] – **micellar** /mi'selə/ *adj*

Michaelmas /'mik(ə)lməs/ *n* September 29 celebrated as the feast of St Michael the Archangel [ME *mychelmesse,* fr OE *Michaeles mæsse* Michael's mass]

Michaelmas daisy *n* any of several (Autumn-blooming) asters widely grown as garden plants

Michaelmas term *n* the university term beginning in October

mick /mik/ *n* an Irishman – chiefly derog [*Mick,* nickname for *Michael,* common Irish forename]

mickey /miki/ *n* [origin unknown] – **take the mickey** to make sby an object of amusement by humorous or playful ridicule – infml

,Mickey 'Finn /fin/ *n* an alcoholic drink doctored usu with a hypnotic drug [prob fr the name *Mickey Finn*]

,Mickey 'Mouse *adj* trivial, petty – infml [*Mickey Mouse,* cartoon character created by Walt Disney †1966 US film producer]

mickle /'mikl/ *adj, chiefly Scot* great, much [ME *mikel,* fr OE *micel* – more at MUCH] – **mickle** *adv, chiefly Scot*

Micmac /'mik,mak/ *n, pl* **Micmacs,** *esp collectively* **Micmac** a member, or the Algonquian language, of an American Indian people of E Canada [Micmac *Migmac,* lit., allies]

micr-, micro- *comb form* **1a** small; minute ⟨micro*cosm*⟩ **b** used for or involving minute quantities or variations ⟨micro*barograph*⟩ ⟨micro*calorimeter*⟩ **c** microscopic ⟨micro*organism*⟩ **2** one millionth (10^{-6}) part of (a specified unit) ⟨micro*second*⟩ ⟨micro*gram*⟩ ⟨micro*hm*⟩ ☞ PHYSICS **3** enlarging; magnifying; amplifying ⟨micro*phone*⟩ **4a** used in or involving microscopy ⟨micro*dissection*⟩ **b** used in or connected with microphotography ⟨micro*copy*⟩ ⟨micro*film*⟩ **5** of a small or localized area ⟨micro*climate*⟩ ⟨micro*habitat*⟩ [ME *micro-,* fr L, fr Gk *mikr-, mikro-,* fr *mikros, smikros* small, short; akin to OE *smēalīc* careful, exquisite]

micro /'miekroh/ *adj* very small; *esp* microscopic [*micr-*]

microbe /'miekrohb/ *n* a microorganism, germ [ISV *micr-* + Gk *bios* life – more at ¹QUICK] – **microbial** /mie'krohbi·əl/, **microbic** /-bik/ *adj*

microbiology /,miekrəbie'oləji, -kroh-/ *n* the biology of bacteria and other microscopic forms of life [ISV] – **microbiologist** *n,* **microbiological** /-bie·ə'lojikl/, **microbiologic** *adj*

microcephalic /,miekrohsi'falik/ *n or adj* (sby) having an abnormally small head and usu mental defects [adj NL *microcephalus,* fr *micr-* + Gk *kephalē* head – more at CEPHALIC; n fr adj] – **microcephaly** /-'sefəli/ *n*

'micro,circuit /-,suhkit/ *n* a compact electronic circuit; *esp* INTEGRATED CIRCUIT – **microcircuitry** *n*

'micro,climate /-,kliemət/ *n* the essentially uniform local climate of a small site or habitat [ISV] – **microclimatic** *adj,* **microclimatology** *n*

'microcom,puter /-kəm,pyoohtə/ *n* a small self-contained computer that is based on one or more microprocessors and that typically has a keyboard and a visual display unit ☞ COMPUTER

'micro,copy /-,kopi/ *n* a photographic copy in which graphic matter is greatly reduced in size [ISV] – **microcopy** *vb*

microcosm /'miekrə,koz(ə)m/ *n* **1** a little world; *esp* an individual human being or human nature seen as an epitome of the world or universe **2** a whole (e g a community) that is an epitome of a larger whole [ME, fr ML *microcosmus,* modif of Gk *mikros kosmos*] – **microcosmic** /-'kozmik/ *adj*

microcrystal /'miekroh,kristl/ *n* a crystal visible only under the microscope – **microcrystalline** /-'krist(ə)l,ien/ *adj,* **microcrystallinity** /-'inəti/ *n*

microdot /'miekrə,dot/ *n* a photographic reproduction of printed matter reduced to the size of a single dot for security or ease of transmission

microeconomics /,miekroh-eekə'nomiks, -ekə-/ *n pl but sing in constr* a study of economics in terms of individual areas of activity (e g a firm, household, or prices) – compare MACROECONOMICS – **microeconomic** *adj*

,microelec'tronics /-i,lek'troniks, -,elek-/ *n pl but sing in constr* a branch of electronics that deals with or produces miniaturized electronic circuits and components – **microelectronic** *adj*

'micro,fiche /-,feesh/ *n, pl* **microfiche, microfiches** /-shiz/ a sheet of microfilm containing rows of very small images of pages of printed matter [F, fr *micr-* + *fiche* peg, tag, slide, fr OF, fr *ficher* to stick in – more at FICHU]

microfilm /ˈmiekrə͵film/ *n* a film bearing a photographic record on a reduced scale of graphic matter (e g printing) [ISV] – **microfilm** *vb*, **microfilmable** /-ˈfilməbl/ *adj*

microhabitat /͵miekrohˈhabitat/ *n* a small usu specialized and isolated habitat (e g a decaying tree stump)

͵microinˈstruction /-inˈstruksh(ə)n/ *n* a computer instruction corresponding to several machine instructions

ˈmicro͵lith /-͵lith/ *n* a tiny flint blade tool often set in a bone or wooden haft [ISV]

͵microma͵nipuˈlation /-mə͵nipyooˈlaysh(ə)n/ *n* dissection and injection of tissue or cells under the microscope using fine needles controlled by a series of levers

micrometer /mieˈkromitə/ *n* **1** an instrument for measuring distances between objects seen through a microscope or telescope **2** a gauge for making precise measurements of length by means of a spindle moved by a finely threaded screw [F *micromètre*, fr *micr-* + *-mètre* -meter]

micron /ˈmiekron/ *n, pl* **microns** *also* **micra** /-krə/ one millionth (10^{-6}) part of a metre – not now recommended for technical use [NL, fr Gk *mikron*, neut of *mikros* small – more at MICR-]

Micronesian /͵miekrəˈneezh(y)ən, -zi·ən/ *n* **1** a native or inhabitant of Micronesia **2** a group of Austronesian languages spoken in the Micronesian islands [ISV, fr NL *Micronesia*, islands of the Western Pacific ocean east of the Philippines] – **Micronesian** *adj*

micronutrient /͵miekrohˈnyoohtri·ənt/ *n* a nutrient (e g a trace element) required in small quantities

͵microˈorganism /-ˈawgəniz(ə)m/ *n* an organism of (smaller than) microscopic size [ISV]

microphage /ˈmiekrə͵fayj, -͵fahzh/ *n* a small phagocyte [ISV]

microphone /ˈmiekrə͵fohn/ *n* a device that converts sounds into electrical signals, esp for transmission or recording [ISV] – **microphonic** /-ˈfonik/ *adj*

microphotograph /͵miekrohˈfohtəgrahf, -graf/ *n* a reduced photograph that must be magnified for viewing; a microcopy [ISV] – **microphotograph** *vt*, **microphotographic** /-fohtəˈgrafik/ *adj*, **microphotography** /-fəˈtogrəfi/ *n*

͵microˈprocessor /-ˈprohsesə/ *n* a very small computer composed of 1 or more integrated circuits functioning as a unit ☞ COMPUTER [ISV]

ˈmicro͵pyle /-piel/ *n* **1** a differentiated area of the surface of an egg through which the sperm enters **2** an opening in the surface of an ovule of a flowering plant through which the pollen tube penetrates [ISV *micr-* + Gk *pylē* gate] – **micropylar** /-ˈpielə/ *adj*

microscope /ˈmiekrə͵skohp/ *n* an instrument consisting of (a combination of) lenses for making enlarged images of minute objects using light or other radiations [NL *microscopium*, fr *micr-* + *-scopium* -scope]

͵microˈscopic /-ˈskopik/ *also* **microscopical** /-kl/ *adj* **1** of or conducted with the microscope or microscopy **2** resembling a microscope, esp in perception **3a** invisible or indistinguishable without the use of a microscope **b** very small, fine, or precise – **microscopically** *adv*

microscopy /mieˈkroskəpi/ *n* the use of or investigation with the microscope – **microscopist** *n*

microsome /ˈmiekroh͵sohm/ *n* a minute particle **a** seen in the cytoplasm of a cell viewed through a light microscope **b** seen in a fraction obtained by heavy centrifugation of broken cells viewed through an electron microscope [G *mikrosom*, fr *mikr-* micr- + *-som* -some] – **microsomal** /-ˈsohml/ *adj*

ˈmicro͵structure /-͵strukchə/ *n* the microscopic structure of a mineral, alloy, living cell, etc [ISV] – **microstructural** *adj*

͵microˈsurgery /-ˈsuhjəri/ *n* minute (surgical) dissection or manipulation of living tissue, usu under a microscope (e g in eye surgery) – **microsurgical** *adj*

ˈmicro͵switch /-͵swich/ *n* an electrical switch that can be operated by a small usu delicate movement

ˈmicro-͵teaching *n* the teaching of a small group for a short time, esp as practice for a trainee teacher

ˈmicro͵tome /-͵tohm/ *n* an instrument for cutting sections (e g of plant or animal tissues) for microscopic examination [ISV]

ˈmicro͵tone /-͵tohn/ *n* a musical interval smaller than a semitone – **microtonally** *adv*, **microtonal** /-ˈtohnl/ *adj*, **microtonality** /-tohˈnaləti/ *n*

͵microˈtubule /-ˈtyoohbyoohl/ *n* any of the minute cylindrical structures in cells that are widely distributed in cytoplasm and are made up of protein subunits – **microtubular** /-ˈtyoohbyoolə/ *adj*

microwave /ˈmiekrə͵wayv/ *n* a band of very short electromagnetic waves of between 1m and 0.1m in wavelength

microwave oven *n* an oven in which food is cooked by the heat produced as a result of the interaction between penetrating microwaves and the substance of the food

micturate /ˈmiktyoorayt/ *vi* to (want to) urinate – fml; sometimes used technically [L *micturire*, fr *mictus*, pp of *mingere*; akin to OE *mīgan* to urinate, Gk *omeichein*] – **micturition** /-ˈrish(ə)n/ *n*

[1]**mid** /mid/ *adj* **1** being the part in the middle or midst ⟨*in ~ ocean*⟩ – often in combination ⟨mid-*August*⟩ ⟨*in* mid-*sentence*⟩ **2** occupying a middle position **3** *of a vowel* articulated with the tongue midway between the upper and lower areas of the mouth [ME, fr OE *midde*; akin to OHG *mitti* middle, L *medius*, Gk *mesos*] – **mid** *adv*

[2]**mid** *prep* amid – poetic

͵midˈair /-ˈeə/ *n* a point or region in the air not immediately near the ground

͵mid-Atˈlantic *adj or n* (of) a dialect halfway between American and British English

ˈmid͵brain /-͵brayn/ *n* (the parts of the adult brain that develop from) the middle of the 3 primary divisions of the embryonic vertebrate brain

͵midˈday /-ˈday/ *n* the middle part of the day; noon

midden /ˈmid(ə)n/ *n* **1** a dunghill **2** a refuse heap; *esp* a heap or stratum of domestic rubbish found on the site of an ancient settlement [ME *midding*, of Scand origin; akin to ON *myki* dung, *dyngja* manure pile – more at MUCUS, DUNG]

[1]**middle** /ˈmidl/ *adj* **1** equally distant from the extremes; central **2** at neither extreme **3** *cap* **a** constituting a division intermediate between those prior and later or upper and lower ⟨Middle *Palaeozoic*⟩ **b** belonging to a period of a language intermediate between Old and New or Modern forms

⟨Middle *Dutch*⟩ [ME *middel*, fr OE; akin to L *medius*]

[2]**middle** *n* **1** a middle part, point, or position **2** the waist **3** the position of being among or in the midst of sthg **4** sthg intermediate between extremes; a mean

[3]**middle** *vt* to hit (a shot) correctly with the middle of the bat in cricket

ˌ**middle 'age** *n* the period of life from about 40 to about 60 – **middle-aged** *adj*

ˌ**middle-ˌaged 'spread** *n* an increase in girth, esp round the waist, associated with middle age

'**Middle ˌAges** *n pl* the period of European history from about AD 500 to about 1500

ˌ**Middle A'merica** *n* the US middle class – **Middle American** *n*

'**middleˌbrow** /-ˌbrow/ *adj* dealing with or having conventional and often bourgeois intellectual and cultural interests and activities – often derog – **middlebrow** *n*

middle C *n* the note designated by the first ledger line below the treble staff and the first above the bass staff

ˌ**middle 'class** *n* a class occupying a position between upper and lower; *esp* a fluid heterogeneous grouping of business and professional people, bureaucrats, and some farmers and skilled workers – often pl with sing. meaning – **middle-class** *adj*

ˌ**middle-'distance** *adj* of or being a footrace over a distance between 400m and 1mi

middle distance *n* the part of a picture or view between the foreground and the background

middle ear *n* a cavity through which sound waves are transmitted by a chain of tiny bones from the eardrum to the inner ear ☞ NERVE

Middle English *n* English of the 12th to 15th c ☞ LANGUAGE

middle game *n* the part of a chess game following the opening moves when players attempt to gain and exploit positional and material superiority – compare END GAME, OPENING 3a

middle ground *n* a standpoint midway between extremes

'**middleˌman** /-ˌman/ *n* an intermediary between 2 parties; *esp* a dealer intermediate between the producer of goods and the retailer or consumer

middle name *n* **1** a name between one's first name and surname **2** a quality of character for which sby is well known ⟨*generosity is her* ~⟩

ˌ**middle-of-the-'road** *adj* conforming to the majority in taste, attitude, or conduct; *also* neither right-wing nor left-wing in political conviction – **middle-of-the-roader** *n*, **middle-of-the-roadism** *n*

middle school *n* (part of) a school for pupils aged 8–12 or 9–13

'**middleˌweight** /-ˌwayt/ *n* a boxer who weighs not more than 11st 6lb (72.6kg) if professional or more than 71kg (about 11st 2lb) but not more than 75kg (about 11st 11lb) if amateur

middling /'midling/ *adj* **1** of middle or moderate size, degree, or quality **2** mediocre, second-rate [ME (Sc) *mydlyn*, prob fr *mid, midde* mid + *-ling*] – **middling** *adv*, **middlingly** *adv*

'**middlings** *n pl but sing or pl in constr* a granular product or by-product of grain, esp wheat, milling usu used in animal feeds

middy /'midi/ *n* a midshipman – infml; no longer in vogue [by shortening & alter.]

midfield /'midˌfeeld, -'-/ *n* (the players who normally play in) the part of a pitch or playing field midway between the goals ☞ SPORT

midge /mij/ *n* a tiny two-winged fly [ME *migge*, fr OE *mycg*; akin to OHG *mucka* midge, Gk *myia* fly, L *musca*]

midget /'mijit/ *n* **1** a very small person; a dwarf **2** sthg (e g an animal) much smaller than usual [*midge* + *-et*] – **midget** *adj*

midi /'midi/ *n* a woman's garment that extends to the mid-calf [[1]*mid* + *-i* (as in *mini*)]

midland /'midlənd/ *n, often cap* the central region of a country – usu pl with sing. meaning – **midland** *adj, often cap*

midline /mid'lien, '-ˌ-/ *n* the middle line or plane, esp of (a part of) the body

'**midˌmost** /-ˌmohst/ *adj* in or near the middle – **midmost** *adv or n*

midnight /'midˌniet/ *n* the middle of the night; *specif* 12 o'clock at night – **midnight** *adj*, **midnightly** *adv or adj*

ˌ**midnight 'sun** *n* the sun visible at midnight in the arctic or antarctic summer

ˌ**mid-'off** *n* a fielding position in cricket near the bowler on the off side of the pitch ☞ SPORT

ˌ**mid-'on** *n* a fielding position in cricket near the bowler on the leg side of the pitch ☞ SPORT

'**midˌpoint** /-ˌpoynt/ *n* a point midway between the beginning and end of sthg

midrash /'midrash/ *n, pl* **midrashim** /-'rashim/ a Jewish work of commentary and exegesis on a biblical text [Heb *midhrāsh* exposition, explanation] – **midrashic** /-'rashik/ *adj, often cap*

'**midˌrib** /-ˌrib/ *n* the central vein of a leaf

midriff /'midrif/ *n* **1** DIAPHRAGM 1 **2** the middle part of the human torso [ME *midrif*, fr OE *midhrif*, fr *midde* mid + *hrif* belly; akin to OHG *href* body, L *corpus*]

midshipman /'midˌshipmən/ *n* (the rank of) a young person training to become a naval officer ☞ RANK

'**midˌships** /-ˌships/ *adv* amidships ☞ SHIP

midst /midst/ *n* **1** the inner or central part or point; the middle **2** a position near to the members of a group ⟨*a traitor in our* ~⟩ **3** the condition of being surrounded or beset (e g by problems) **4** a period of time about the middle of a continuing act or state ⟨*in the* ~ *of the celebrations*⟩ [ME *middest*, alter. of *middes*, back-formation fr *amiddes* amid] – **midst** *prep*

ˌ**mid'stream** /-'streem/ *n* **1** the part of a stream towards the middle **2** the middle part of a process

ˌ**mid'summer** /-'sumə/ *n* the summer solstice

ˌ**Midsummer 'Day** *n* June 24 celebrated as the feast of the nativity of John the Baptist

ˌ**mid'way** /-'way/ *adv* halfway

ˌ**mid'week** /-'week/ *n* the middle of the week – **midweek** *adj*, **midweekly** *adj or adv*

ˌ**mid-'wicket** *n* a fielding position in cricket on the leg side equidistant from each wicket ☞ SPORT

midwife /'midˌwief/ *n* **1** a woman who assists other women in childbirth **2** sby or sthg that helps to produce or bring forth sthg [ME *midwif*, fr *mid* with (fr OE) + *wif* woman]

midwifery /'midˌwifəri/ *n* (the art of) assisting at childbirth; *also* obstetrics

ˌ**mid'winter** /-'wintə/ *n* the winter solstice

mien /meen/ *n* air or bearing, esp as expressive of

mood or personality – fml [by shortening & alter. fr [2]*demean*]

[1]**miff** /mif/ *n* **1** a brief outburst of bad temper **2** a trivial quarrel ***USE*** infml [origin unknown]

[2]**miff** *vt* to make cross or peeved – infml

[1]**might** /miet/ *past of* MAY – used to express permission or liberty in the past ⟨*asked whether he ~ come*⟩ ⟨*the king ~ do nothing without parliament's consent*⟩, a past or present possibility contrary to fact ⟨*I ~ well have been killed*⟩ ⟨*if he were older he ~ understand*⟩, purpose or expectation in the past ⟨*wrote it down so that I ~ not forget it*⟩, less probability or possibility than *may* ⟨*~ get there before it rains*⟩, a polite request ⟨*you ~ post this letter for me*⟩, or as a polite or ironic alternative to *may* ⟨*who ~ you be?*⟩ or to *ought* or *should* ⟨*you ~ at least apologize*⟩ ⟨*he ~ have offered to help*⟩ [ME, fr OE *meahte, mihte*; akin to OHG *mahta, mohta* could]

[2]**might** *n* **1** power, authority, or resources wielded individually or collectively **2a** physical strength **b** all the power or effort one is capable of [ME, fr OE *miht*; akin to OHG *maht* might, *magan* to be able – more at MAY]

mightily /ˈmiet(ə)l·i/ *adv* very much ⟨*it amused us ~* – Charles Dickens⟩ [[1]MIGHTY + [2]-LY]

mightn't /ˈmietnt/ might not

[1]**mighty** /ˈmieti/ *adj* **1** powerful **2** accomplished or characterized by might ⟨*a ~ thrust*⟩ **3** imposingly great ⟨*the ~ mountains*⟩ – **mightiness** *n*

[2]**mighty** *adv* to a great degree; extremely ⟨*a ~ big man*⟩

mignonette /ˌminyəˈnet/ *n* an annual garden plant with fragrant greenish yellow flowers or any of various related plants [F *mignonnette*, fr obs F, fem of *mignonnet* dainty, fr MF, fr *mignon* darling]

migraine /ˈmeegrayn/ *n* recurrent severe headache usu associated with disturbances of vision, sensation, and movement often on only 1 side of the body [F, fr LL *hemicrania* pain in one side of the head, fr Gk *hēmikrania*, fr *hēmi-* hemi- + *kranion* cranium] – **migrainous** *adj*

migrant /ˈmiegrənt/ *n* **1** a person who moves regularly in order to find work, esp in harvesting crops **2** an animal that moves from one habitat to another [MIGRATE + [1]-ANT] – **migrant** *adj*

migrate /mieˈgrayt/ *vi* **1** to move from one country or locality to another **2** *of an animal* to pass usu periodically from one region or climate to another for feeding or breeding [L *migratus*, pp of *migrare*; akin to Gk *ameibein* to change] – **migration** /-sh(ə)n/ *n*, **migrational** *adj*, **migrator** *n*

migratory /ˈmiegrət(ə)ri/ *adj* wandering, roving [MIGRATE + [2]-ORY]

mikado /miˈkahdoh/ *n, pl* **mikados** – formerly used as a title for the emperor of Japan [Jap]

mike /miek/ *n* a microphone – infml [by shortening & alter.]

Mike – a communications code word for the letter *m*

mil /mil/ *n* **1** a unit of length equal to $^1/_{1000}$in (about 0.0254mm) used esp for the diameter of wire and formerly in precision engineering **2** ☞ *Cyprus, Malta* at NATIONALITY [L *mille* thousand – more at MILE]

milady /miˈlaydi/ *n* an Englishwoman of noble or gentle birth – often used as a term of address or reference [F, fr E *my lady*]

milch /milch/ *adj, of a domestic animal* bred or used primarily for milk production [ME *milche*, fr OE *-milce*; akin to OE *melcan* to milk – more at EMULSION]

[1]**mild** /mield/ *adj* **1** gentle in nature or manner **2a** not strong in flavour or effect **b** not being or involving what is extreme **3** not severe; temperate ⟨*a ~ climate*⟩ **4** easily worked; malleable ⟨*~ steel*⟩ [ME, fr OE *milde*; akin to Gk *malthakos* soft, OE *melu* meal – more at [2]MEAL] – **mildly** *adv*, **mildness** *n*

[2]**mild** *n, Br* a dark-coloured beer not flavoured with hops

[1]**mildew** /ˈmildyooh/ *n* (a fungus producing) a usu whitish growth on the surface of organic matter (e g paper or leather) or living plants [ME, fr OE *meledēaw*; akin to OHG *militou* honeydew] – **mildewy** *adj*

[2]**mildew** *vb* to affect or become affected (as if) with mildew

mile /miel/ *n* **1** any of various units of distance: e g **a** a unit equal to 1760yd (about 1.61km) ☞ UNIT **b** NAUTICAL MILE ☞ UNIT **2** a large distance or amount – often pl with sing. meaning [ME, fr OE *mīl*; akin to OHG *mīla* mile; both fr a prehistoric WGmc word borrowed fr L *milia* miles, fr *milia passuum*, lit., thousands of paces, fr *milia*, pl of *mille* thousand, perh fr a prehistoric compound whose constituents are akin to Gk *mia* (fem of *heis* one) and to Gk *chilioi* thousand, Skt sa*hasra* – more at SAME] – **miles from nowhere** in an extremely remote place

mileage /ˈmielij/ *n* **1** an allowance for travelling expenses at a certain rate per mile **2** total length or distance in miles: e g **a** the number of miles travelled over a period of time **b** the distance, or distance covered, in miles **c** the average distance in miles a vehicle will travel for an amount of fuel

ˈ**mileˌpost** /-ˌpohst/ *n* a post indicating the distance in miles from or to a given point

miler /ˈmielə/ *n* a person or horse that competes in mile races

miles *adv* very much ⟨*worked ~ better when oiled*⟩ – infml

milestone /ˈmielˌstohn/ *n* **1** a stone serving as a milepost **2** a crucial stage in sthg's development

milfoil /ˈmilˌfoyl/ *n* **1** yarrow **2** any of a genus of water plants with submersed leaves divided into very narrow segments [ME, fr OF, fr L *millefolium*, fr *mille* + *folium* leaf – more at BLADE]

miliary /ˈmilyəri/ *adj* having, made up of, or accompanied by many small projections, blisters, or nodules [L *miliarius* of millet, fr *milium* millet – more at MILLET]

milieu /ˈmeelyuh (*Fr* miljø)/ *n, pl* **milieus, milieux** /-lyuh(z) (*Fr* ~)/ an environment, setting ⟨*three studies of women, each from a different ~* – Edmund Wilson⟩ [F, fr OF, midst, fr *mi* middle (fr L *medius*) + *lieu* place, fr L *locus*]

militant /ˈmilit(ə)nt/ *adj* **1** engaged in warfare or combat **2** aggressively active (e g in a cause); combative [ME, fr MF, fr L *militant-, militans*, prp of *militare* to engage in warfare] – **militancy** *n*, **militant** *n*, **militantly** *adv*, **militantness** *n*

militarism /ˈmilitəˌriz(ə)m/ *n* **1** exaltation of military virtues and ideals **2** a policy of aggressive military preparedness – **militarist** *n*, **militaristic** /-ˈristik/ *adj*, **militaristically** *adv*

militar·ize, -ise /ˈmilitəˌriez/ *vt* **1** to equip with military forces and defences **2** to give a military character to – **militarization** /-ˈzaysh(ə)n/ *n*

[1]**military** /ˈmilit(ə)ri/ *adj* **1** (characteristic) of soldiers, arms, or war **2** carried on or supported by armed force ⟨*a ~ dictatorship*⟩ **3** of the army or armed forces [MF *militaire*, fr L *militaris*, fr *milit-*, *miles* soldier] – **militarily** *adv*

[2]**military** *n* **1** *pl in constr* soldiers **2** *sing or pl in constr the* army (as opposed to civilians or police) ☞ RANK

military police *n* a branch of an army that carries out police functions within the army

militate /ˈmilitayt/ *vi* to have significant weight or effect – often + *against* [L *militatus*, pp of *militare* to engage in warfare, fr *milit-*, *miles* soldier]

militia /miˈlish(y)ə/ *n sing or pl in constr* a body of citizens with some military training who are called on to fight only in an emergency [L, military service, fr *milit-*, *miles*] – **militiaman** /-mən/ *n*

[1]**milk** /milk/ *n* **1** a (white or creamy) liquid secreted by the mammary glands of females for the nourishment of their young (and used as a food by humans) **2** a milklike liquid: e g **a** the latex of a plant **b** the juice of a coconut **c** a cosmetic lotion, esp a cleanser [ME, fr OE *meolc*, *milc*; akin to OHG *miluh* milk] – **milky** *adj*, **milkiness** *n*

[2]**milk** *vt* **1** to draw milk from the breasts or udder of **2** to draw sthg from as if by milking: e g **a** to induce (a snake) to eject venom **b** to compel or persuade to yield illicit or excessive profit or advantage ⟨*opera stars who ~ their audience for applause*⟩ – **milker** *n*

ˌmilk-and-ˈwater *adj* weak, insipid

ˈmilk ˌfever *n* **1** a feverish disorder following childbirth **2** a disease of cows, sheep, goats, etc that have recently given birth, caused by a drain on the body's mineral reserves during the establishment of the milk flow

ˈmilk ˌfloat *n*, *Br* a light usu electrically-propelled vehicle for carrying esp milk for domestic delivery

ˌmilk ˈleg *n* a painful swelling of the leg after childbirth caused by thrombosis in the veins

ˈmilkˌmaid /-ˌmayd/ *n* a female who works in a dairy

ˈmilkman /-mən/ *n* one who sells or delivers milk

ˌmilk of magˈnesia *n* a white suspension of magnesium hydroxide in water, used as an antacid and mild laxative

ˌmilk ˈpudding *n* a pudding consisting of rice, tapioca, sago, etc boiled or baked in (sweetened) milk

ˈmilk ˌrun *n* a regular journey or course [fr the resemblance in regularity & uneventfulness to the morning delivery of milk]

milk shake *n* a thoroughly shaken or blended beverage made of milk and a flavouring syrup

ˈmilkˌsop /-ˌsop/ *n* a weak and unmanly male [ME, fr *milk* + *sop*]

milk sugar *n* lactose

milk tooth *n* a tooth of a mammal, esp a child, that is replaced later in life

ˈmilkˌweed /-ˌweed/ *n* any of various plants that secrete milky latex

ˈmilkˌwort /-ˌwuht/ *n* any of a genus of herbaceous plants and shrubs with many-coloured showy flowers

ˌMilky ˈWay /ˈmilki/ *n* a broad irregular band of faint light that stretches completely round the celestial sphere and is caused by the light of the many stars forming the galaxy of which the sun and the solar system are a part [ME, trans of L *via lactea*]

[1]**mill** /mil/ *n* **1** a building provided with machinery for grinding grain into flour **2a** a machine or apparatus for grinding grain **b** a machine or hand-operated device for crushing or grinding a solid substance (e g coffee beans or peppercorns) **3** a building or collection of buildings with machinery for manufacturing **4** MILLING MACHINE **5** an experience that has a hardening effect on the character – usu in *through the mill* [ME *mille*, fr OE *mylen*; akin to OHG *muli* mill; both fr a prehistoric NGmc-WGmc word borrowed fr LL *molina*, *molinum*, fr fem and neut of *molinus* of a mill, of a millstone, fr L *mola* mill, millstone; akin to L *molere* to grind – more at [2]MEAL]

[2]**mill** *vt* **1** to subject to an operation or process in a mill: e g **a** to grind into flour, meal, or powder **b** to shape or dress by means of a rotary cutter **2** to give a raised rim or a ridged edge to (a coin) **3** to cut grooves in the metal surface of (e g a knob) ~ *vi* **1** to move in a confused swirling mass – usu + *about* or *around* **2** to undergo milling

ˈmillˌboard /-ˌbawd/ *n* strong cardboard suitable for book covers and for panelling in furniture [alter. of *milled board*]

ˈmillˌdam /-ˌdam/ *n* a dam to make a millpond

millenarian /ˌmiliˈneəri·ən/ *adj* **1** of or relating to 1000 years **2** of or having belief in the millennium – **millenarian** *n*, **millenarianism** *n*

[1]**millenary** /miˈlenəri/ *n* **1** a group of 1000 units or things **2** 1000 years [LL *millenarium*, fr neut of *millenarius* of a thousand, fr L *milleni* one thousand each, fr *mille*]

[2]**millenary** *adj* **1** relating to or consisting of 1000 **2** suggesting a millennium [L *millenarius*]

millennium /miˈleni·əm/ *n*, *pl* **millennia** /-ni·ə/, **millenniums 1a** a period of 1000 years **b** (the celebration of) a 1000th anniversary **2a** *the* thousand years mentioned in Revelation 20 during which holiness is to prevail and Christ is to reign on earth **b** a (future) golden age [NL, fr L *mille* thousand + NL *-ennium* (as in *biennium* period of two years)] – **millennial** *adj*

millepede /ˈmiliˌpeed/ *n* a millipede

millepore /ˈmiliˌpaw/ *n* any of an order of often large stony reef-building corals [deriv of L *mille* thousand + *porus* pore]

miller /ˈmilə/ *n* sby who owns or works a mill, esp for corn [[2]MILL + [2]-ER]

ˌmiller's-ˈthumb *n* any of several small freshwater fishes

millesimal /miˈlesim(ə)l/ *n* the quotient of a unit divided by 1000; any of 1000 equal parts of anything [L *millesimus*, adj, thousandth, fr *mille*] – **millesimal** *adj*, **millesimally** *adv*

millet /ˈmilit/ *n* (the seed of) any of various small-seeded annual cereal and forage grasses cultivated for their grain, used as food [ME *milet*, fr MF, dim. of *mil*, fr L *milium*; akin to Gk *melinē* millet]

milli- /mili-/ *comb form* one thousandth (10^{-3}) part of (a specified unit) ⟨milli*ampere*⟩ ☞ PHYSICS, UNIT [F, fr L *milli-* thousand, fr *mille* – more at MILE]

milliard /ˈmiliˌahd, ˈmilyahd/ *n* a thousand millions

(10^9) [F, fr MF *miliart*, fr *mili-* (fr *milion* million)]

millibar /'mili,bah/ *n* a unit of pressure equal to $^1/_{1000}$ bar [ISV]

milligram /'mili,gram/ *n* one thousandth of a gram (about 0.015 grain) ☞ UNIT [F *milligramme*, fr *milli-* + *gramme* gram]

millilitre *n* a thousandth of a litre (.002pt) ☞ UNIT

millime /mə'leem/ *n* ☞ *Sudan, Tunisia* at NATIONALITY [modif of Ar *mallim*, fr F *millième*]

millimetre /'mili,meetə/ *n* one thousandth of a metre (about 0.039in) [F *millimètre*, fr *milli-* + *mètre* metre]

millimicro- *comb form* nano-

milliner /'milinə/ *n* sby who designs, makes, trims, or sells women's hats [irreg fr *Milan*, city in Italy; fr the importation of women's finery from Italy in the 16th c] – **millinery** *n*

'milling ma,chine /'miling/ *n* a machine tool for shaping metal against rotating milling cutters

million /'milyən/ *n, pl* **millions, million 1** ☞ NUMBER **2** an indefinitely large number – infml; often pl with sing. meaning ⟨~s *of cars in that traffic jam*⟩ **3** *pl* [1]MASS 3 ⟨*appealing to the* ~s⟩ [ME *milioun*, fr MF *milion*, fr OIt *milione*, aug of *mille* thousand, fr L – more at MILE] – **million** *adj*, **millionth** *adj or n*

millionaire /,milyə'neə/ *n* sby whose wealth is estimated at a million or more money units [F *millionnaire*, fr *million*, fr MF *milion*]

,millio'nairess /-ris/ *n* a woman who is (the wife of) a millionaire

millipede, millepede /'mili,peed/ *n* any of numerous myriopods usu with a cylindrical segmented body and 2 pairs of legs on each segment [L *millepeda*, a small crawling animal, fr *mille* thousand + *ped-*, *pes* foot – more at FOOT]

millpond /'mil,pond/ *n* a pond produced by damming a stream to produce a head of water for operating a mill

'mill,race /-,rays/ *n* (the current in) a channel in which water flows to and from a mill wheel [ME *milnras*, fr *miln, mille* mill + *ras* race, current]

'mill,stone /-,stohn/ *n* **1** either of a pair of circular stones that rotate against each other and are used for grinding (grain) **2** a heavy or crushing burden

'mill ,wheel *n* a waterwheel that drives a mill

'mill,wright /-,riet/ *n* sby who plans, builds, or maintains mills

milometer /mie'lomitə/ *n* an odometer calibrated in miles

milord /mi'lawd/ *n* an Englishman of noble or gentle birth – often used in imitation of foreigners [F, fr E *my lord*]

milt /milt/ *n* the male reproductive glands of fishes when filled with secretion; *also* the secretion of these glands [prob fr MD *milte* milt of fish, spleen; akin to OE *milte* spleen – more at [3]MELT] – **milty** *adj*

milter /'miltə/ *n* a male fish in breeding condition

[1]mime /miem/ *n* **1** an ancient dramatic entertainment representing scenes from life usu in a ridiculous manner **2** the art of portraying a character or telling a story by body movement [L *mimus*, fr Gk *mimos* imitator, actor; akin to Gk *mimeisthai* to imitate]

[2]mime *vi* to act a part with mimic gesture and action, usu without words ~ *vt* **1** to mimic **2** to act out in the manner of a mime – **mimer** *n*

mimesis /mi'meesis/ *n* imitation, mimicry [LL, fr Gk *mimēsis*, fr *mimeisthai*]

mimetic /mi'metik/ *adj* **1** imitative **2** relating to, characterized by, or exhibiting mimicry [LL *mimeticus*, fr Gk *mimētikos*, fr *mimeisthai*] – **mimetically** *adv*

[1]mimic /'mimik/ *adj* **1a** IMITATIVE 1 **b** imitation, mock ⟨*a* ~ *battle*⟩ **2** of mime or mimicry [L *mimicus*, fr Gk *mimikos*, fr *mimos*] – **mimical** *adj*

[2]mimic *vt* **-ck- 1** to imitate slavishly; ape **2** to ridicule by imitation **3** to simulate **4** to resemble by biological mimicry – **mimic** *n*

mimicry /'mimikri/ *n* **1** the act or an instance of mimicking **2** resemblance of one organism to another that secures it an advantage (e g protection from predation) ☞ DEFENCE

mimosa /mi'mohzə, -sə/ *n* any of a genus of leguminous trees, shrubs, and herbaceous plants of warm regions with globular heads of small white, pink, or esp yellow flowers [NL, genus name, fr L *mimus* mime; fr its apparent imitation of animal sensitivity in drooping & closing its leaves when touched]

mina /'mienə/ *n* a myna

minacious /mi'nayshəs/ *adj* minatory [L *minac-, minax* threatening, fr *minari*]

minaret /,minə'ret/ *n* a slender tower attached to a mosque and surrounded by 1 or more projecting balconies from which the summons to prayer is made [F, fr Turk *minare*, fr Ar *manārah* lighthouse]

minatory /'minət(ə)ri/ *adj* menacing, threatening – fml [LL *minatorius*, fr L *minatus*, pp of *minari* to threaten – more at [1]MOUNT]

[1]mince /mins/ *vt* **1** to cut or chop into very small pieces **2** to keep (one's words) within the bounds of decorum ⟨*doesn't* ~ *his words*⟩ ~ *vi* to walk with short affected steps [ME *mincen*, fr MF *mincer*, fr (assumed) VL *minutiare*, fr L *minutia* smallness – more at MINUTIA] – **mincer** *n*

[2]mince *n* minced meat

'mince,meat /-,meet/ *n* a finely chopped mixture of raisins, apples, suet, spices, etc (with brandy) which traditionally used to contain meat

,mince 'pie *n* a sweet usu small and round pie filled with mincemeat

mincing /'minsing/ *adj* affectedly dainty or delicate ⟨*trying to speak in a small* ~ *treble* – George Eliot⟩ – **mincingly** *adv*

[1]mind /miend/ *n* **1** the (capabilities of the) organized conscious and unconscious mental processes of an organism that result in reasoning, thinking, perceiving, etc **2a** recollection, memory ⟨*keep that in* ~⟩ **b** attention, concentration ⟨*can't keep her* ~ *on her work*⟩ **3** the normal condition of the mental faculties ⟨*lost his* ~⟩ **4a** an intention, desire ⟨*he changed his* ~⟩ ⟨*doesn't know his own* ~⟩ ⟨*I've a good* ~ *to box his ears*⟩ ⟨*had half a* ~ *to leave early*⟩ **b** an opinion, view ⟨*unwilling to speak his* ~⟩ ⟨*they were of the same* ~⟩ ⟨*though she's just a child, she has a* ~ *of her own*⟩ ⟨*in two* ~s *about the problem*⟩ **5** a disposition, mood ⟨*her state of* ~ *was calm*⟩ ⟨*always has good peace of* ~⟩ **6** the mental attributes of a usu specified group ⟨*the scientific* ~⟩ **7** a person considered as an intellectual being ⟨*one of the finest* ~s *of the academic world*⟩ **8a** the intellect and rational faculties as contrasted with the emotions **b** the human spirit and intellect as opposed to the body and the material world ⟨~ *over matter*⟩

[ME, fr OE *gemynd*; akin to OHG *gimunt* memory; both fr a prehistoric EGmc-WGmc compound whose first constituent is represented by OE *ge-* (perfective prefix) and whose second is akin to L *ment-, mens* mind, *monēre* to remind, warn, Gk *menos* spirit, *mnasthai, mimnēskesthai* to remember – more at co-] – **bear/keep in mind** to think of, esp at the appropriate time; not forget – **on one's mind** as a preoccupation; troubling one's thoughts ⟨*she can't work with the problem of the mortgage* on her mind⟩

²**mind** *vt* **1** to attend to closely ⟨~ *how you behave*⟩ ⟨~ *your manners*⟩ ⟨~ *your own business*⟩ **2** to pay attention to or follow (advice, instructions, or orders) **3a** to be concerned about; care ⟨*I don't* ~ *what we do*⟩ ⟨*Never* ~ *the hole in your tights: no one will notice*⟩ **b** to object to ⟨*do you* ~ *going?*⟩ ⟨*I don't* ~ *the noise*⟩ **4a** to be careful ⟨~ *you finish your homework!*⟩ **b** to be cautious about ⟨~ *the step*⟩ **5** to give protective care to; look after ⟨~ed *the children while their parents were out*⟩ ~ *vi* **1** to be attentive or wary – often + *out* **2** to be or become concerned; care ⟨*would you prefer tea or coffee? I don't* ~⟩ ⟨*I'm sorry, I've spilt my coffee. Never* ~*!*⟩ – **minder** *n* – **mind you** take this fact into account; notice this ⟨mind you, *I don't blame him*⟩

'**mind,bending** /-,bending/ *adj* at the limits of understanding or credibility – infml – **mindbendingly** *adv*, **mindbender** *n*

'**mind-,blowing** *adj* **1** of or causing a psychic state similar to that produced by a psychedelic drug **2** mentally or emotionally exhilarating *USE* infml – **mindblower** *n*

'**mind-,boggling** *adj* causing great surprise or wonder – infml

'**minded** *adj* **1** having a (specified kind of) mind – usu in combination ⟨*narrow*-minded⟩ **2** inclined, disposed ⟨*was not* ~ *to report his losses – Herts & Essex Observer*⟩ – **mindedness** *n*

'**mind-ex,panding** *adj* PSYCHEDELIC 1b – infml

'**mindful** /-f(ə)l/ *adj* keeping in mind; aware *of* – **mindfully** *adv*, **mindfulness** *n*

'**mindless** /-lis/ *adj* **1** devoid of thought or intelligence; senseless ⟨~ *violence*⟩ **2** involving or requiring little thought or concentration ⟨*the work is routine and fairly* ~⟩ **3** inattentive, heedless – usu + *of* ⟨*dashed into the burning house* ~ *of the danger*⟩ – **mindlessly** *adv*, **mindlessness** *n*

'**mind ,reader** *n* sby who can, or is thought to be able to, perceive another's thought directly – **mind reading** *n*

,**mind's 'eye** *n* the faculty of visual memory or imagination

¹**mine** /mien/ *adj, archaic* my – used before a vowel or *h* ⟨~ *host*⟩ or sometimes to modify a preceding noun ⟨*mistress* ~⟩ [ME *min*, fr OE *mīn* – more at MY]

²**mine** *pron, pl* **mine** that which or the one who belongs to me – used without a following noun as a pronoun equivalent in meaning to the adjective *my* ⟨*children younger than* ~⟩ ⟨*that brother of* ~⟩ ⟨*the house became* ~⟩ – **me and mine** I and my family and possessions

³**mine** *n* **1a** an excavation from which mineral substances are taken **b** an ore deposit **2** an underground passage beneath an enemy position **3** an encased explosive designed to destroy enemy personnel, vehicles, or ships **4** a rich source *of* ⟨*a* ~ *of information*⟩ [ME, fr MF, fr (assumed) VL *mina*, prob of Celt origin; akin to W *mwyn* ore]

⁴**mine** *vt* **1a** to dig an underground passage to gain access to or cause the collapse of (an enemy position) **b** UNDERMINE 2 **2** to obtain from a mine **3** to place military mines in, on, or under ⟨~ *a harbour*⟩ **4** to dig into for ore, coal, etc **5** to seek valuable material in ~ *vi* to dig a mine – **miner** *n*, **mining** *n*

'**mine,layer** /-,layə/ *n* a vessel or aircraft for laying mines

mineral /'min(ə)rəl/ *n* **1** (a synthetic substance resembling) a solid homogeneous crystalline material that results from the inorganic processes of nature; *broadly* any of various naturally occurring substances (e g stone, coal, and petroleum) obtained by drilling, mining, etc **2** sthg neither animal nor vegetable **3** *Br* MINERAL WATER – usu pl [ME, fr ML *minerale*, fr neut of *mineralis*, adj, fr *minera* mine, ore, fr OF *miniere*, fr *mine*] – **mineral** *adj*

mineral·ize, -ise /'min(ə)rə,liez/ *vt* **1** to impregnate with or convert into a mineral or inorganic compound **2** to petrify – **mineralization** /-'zaysh(ə)n/ *n*

mineral kingdom *n* the one of the 3 basic groups of natural objects that includes inorganic objects – compare ANIMAL KINGDOM, PLANT KINGDOM

mineralogy /,minə'raləji/ *n* a science dealing with the structure, properties, and classification of minerals [prob fr (assumed) NL *mineralogia*, irreg fr ML *minerale* + L *-logia* -logy] – **mineralogist** *n*, **mineralogical** /-rə'lojikl/ *adj*

'**mineral ,oil** *n* an oil of mineral as opposed to vegetable origin

'**mineral ,water** *n* water naturally or artificially impregnated with mineral salts or gases (e g carbon dioxide); *broadly* any effervescent nonalcoholic beverage

minestrone /,mini'strohni/ *n* a rich thick vegetable soup usu containing pasta (e g macaroni) [It, aug of *minestra*, fr *minestrare* to serve, dish up, fr L *ministrare*, fr *minister* servant – more at MINISTER]

minesweeper /'mien,sweepə/ *n* a ship designed for removing or neutralizing mines – **minesweeping** *n*

Ming /ming/ *n* a Chinese dynasty dated from AD 1368 to 1644 [Chin (Pek) *ming*² luminous]

mingle /'ming·gl/ *vb* **mingling** /'ming·gling/ *vt* to bring or mix together or with sthg else ~ *vi* **1** to become mingled **2** to mix with or go among a group of people ⟨*simply will not* ~ *at parties*⟩ ⟨~d *with the crowd*⟩ [ME *menglen*, freq of *mengen* to mix, fr OE *mengan*; akin to MHG *mengen* to mix, Gk *massein* to knead]

mingy /'minji/ *adv* mean, stingy – infml [perh blend of ¹*mean* and *stingy*]

mini /'mini/ *n, pl* **minis** **1** sthg small of its kind (e g a motor car) **2** a woman's skirt or dress with the hemline several inches above the knee [*mini-*] – **mini** *adj*

mini- /mini-/ *comb form* miniature; of small dimensions ⟨mini*computer*⟩; *specif* having a hemline several inches above the knee ⟨mini*skirt*⟩ ☞ GARMENT [*miniature*]

¹**miniature** /'minəchə/ *n* **1a** a copy or representation on a much reduced scale **b** sthg small of its kind **2** a painting in an illuminated manuscript **3** the art of painting miniatures **4** a very small painting (e g a portrait on ivory or metal) [It *miniatura* art of illuminating a manuscript, fr ML, fr L *miniatus*, pp

of *miniare* to colour with minium, fr *minium* cinnabar, red lead] – **miniaturist** /-,chooərist/ *n*

[2]**miniature** *adj* **1** (represented) on a small or reduced scale **2** of still photography using film 35mm wide or smaller

miniatur·ize, -ise /'minəchə,riez/ *vt* to design or construct as a small copy; reduce in scale – **miniaturization** /-'zaysh(ə)n/ *n*

minibus /'mini,bus/ *n* a small bus for carrying usu between 5 and 10 passengers

'mini,cab /-,kab/ *n* a motor car that serves as a taxicab when hired by telephone but that cannot cruise in search of passengers

'minicom,puter /-kəm,pyoohtə/ *n* a small digital computer

minim /'minim/ *n* **1** a musical note with the time value of 2 crotchets or ½ of a semibreve ☞ MUSIC **2** a unit of capacity equal to $^1/_{60}$ fluid drachm (about 59.19mm³) ☞ UNIT [L *minimus* least] – **minim** *adj*

minimal /'miniml/ *adj* of or being a minimum; constituting the least possible – **minimalize** *vt*, **minimally** *adv*

minimal art *n* abstract art, esp sculpture, consisting of simple geometric forms executed in an impersonal style

'minimalist /-ist/ *n* one who favours restricting the powers of a political organization or is content with minimum achievement

minim·ize, -ise /'minimiez/ *vt* **1** to reduce to a minimum **2** to represent (sby or sthg) at less than true value; PLAY DOWN – **minimizer** *n*, **minimization** /-'zaysh(ə)n/ *n*

minimum /'miniməm/ *n, pl* **minima** /-mə/, **minimums** **1** the least quantity or value assignable, admissible, or possible **2** the lowest degree or amount reached or recorded [L, neut of *minimus* smallest; akin to L *minor* smaller] – **minimum** *adj*

minimum lending rate *n* the discount rate fixed by a country's central bank (e g the Bank of England)

minimum wage *n* a wage fixed by legal authority or by contract as the least that may be paid either to employees generally or to a particular category of employees

minion /'minyən/ *n* **1** a servile attendant **2** FAVOURITE 1 **3** a minor official – derog [MF *mignon* darling]

minipill /'mini,pil/ *n* an oral contraceptive in the form of a pill taken daily by a woman over a monthly cycle and containing only progesterone

miniscule /'miniskyoohl/ *adj* minuscule [by alter.]

[1]**minister** /'ministə/ *n* **1** AGENT 1a, 2 **2a** one officiating or assisting the officiant in Christian worship **b** a clergyman, esp of a Protestant or nonconformist church **c** the superior of any of several religious orders **3** a high officer of state managing a division of government **4** a diplomatic representative accredited to a foreign state [ME *ministre*, fr OF, fr L *minister* servant; akin to L *minor* smaller] – **ministerial** /-'stiəri·əl/ *adj*, **ministerially** *adv*

[2]**minister** *vi* **1** to perform the functions of a minister of religion **2** to give aid or service ⟨~ *to the sick*⟩ – **ministrant** *n or adj*

,minister-'general *n* MINISTER 2c

,minister of 'state *n* a government minister ranking below a head of department

,minister wi,thout port'folio *n* a government minister with no specific departmental responsibilities

ministration /,mini'straysh(ə)n/ *n* the act or process of ministering, esp in religious matters

ministry /'ministri/ *n* **1** service, ministration **2** the office, duties, or functions of a minister **3** the body of ministers of religion or government **4** the period of service or office of a minister or ministry **5** a government department presided over by a minister

minium /'mini·əm/ *n, archaic* RED LEAD [ME, fr L, cinnabar, red lead, of Iberian origin; akin to Basque *arminéa* cinnabar]

miniver /'minivə/ *n* a white fur used chiefly for robes of state [ME *meniver*, fr OF *menu vair* small vair]

mink /mingk/ *n, pl* **mink, minks** **1** any of several semiaquatic flesh-eating mammals that resemble weasels and have partially webbed feet and a soft thick coat **2** the soft fur or pelt of the mink [ME]

minke whale /'mingkə/ a small rorqual of northern seas [prob fr (the name) *Meincke*, reputedly a Norw whaling gunner]

minnesinger /'mini,sing·ə/ *n* a member of a class of German lyric poets and musicians of the 12th to the 14th c [G, fr MHG, fr *minne* love + *singer*]

minnow /'minoh/ *n, pl* **minnows,** *esp collectively* **minnow** **1** a small dark-coloured freshwater fish or any of various small fishes ☞ ANATOMY **2** sthg small or insignificant of its kind [ME *menawe*; akin to OE *myne* minnow, Russ *men'* eelpout]

[1]**Minoan** /mi'noh·ən/ *adj* of the Bronze Age culture of Crete (3000–1100 BC) [L *minous* of Minos, fr Gk *minōios*, fr *Minōs* Minos, legendary king of Crete]

[2]**Minoan** *n* a native or inhabitant of ancient Crete

[1]**minor** /'mienə/ *adj* **1a** inferior in importance, size, rank, or degree ⟨*a* ~ *poet*⟩ **b** comparatively unimportant ⟨*a* ~ *alteration*⟩ **2** not having attained majority **3a** *esp of a scale or mode* having semitones between the second and third, fifth and sixth, and sometimes seventh and eighth steps **b** being or based on a (specified) minor scale ⟨*in a* ~ *key*⟩ ⟨*a piece in A* ~⟩ **c** being an interval less by a semitone than a corresponding major interval **d** *of a chord* having an interval of a minor third between the root and the next note above it **4** not serious or involving risk to life ⟨*a* ~ *illness*⟩ [ME, fr L, smaller, inferior; akin to OHG *minniro* smaller, L *minuere* to lessen, Gk *meiōn* less]

[2]**minor** *n* **1** sby who has not attained majority **2** a minor musical interval, scale, key, or mode

minor axis *n* the chord of an ellipse passing through the centre and perpendicular to the major axis ☞ MATHEMATICS

minor canon *n* a canon in the Church of England usu having liturgical duties but no vote in the chapter

minority /mie'norəti, mi-/ *n* **1a** the period before attainment of majority **b** the state of being a legal minor **2** the smaller of 2 groups constituting a whole; *specif* a group with less than the number of votes necessary for control **3** *sing or pl in constr* a group of people who share common characteristics or interests differing from those of the majority of a population

minor order *n* any of the Roman Catholic or

Eastern clerical orders that are lower in rank than major orders – usu pl

minor planet *n* an asteroid

minor suit *n* either of the suits of clubs or diamonds that in bridge are of inferior scoring value – compare MAJOR SUIT

Minotaur /'mienə,taw/ *n* a mythological monster shaped half like a man and half like a bull and confined in the labyrinth at Crete [ME, fr MF, fr L *Minotaurus*, fr Gk *Minōtauros*, fr *Minōs* Minos, legendary king of Crete + *tauros* bull]

minster /'minstə/ *n* a large or important church often having cathedral status [ME, monastery, church attached to a monastery, fr OE *mynster*, fr LL *monasterium* monastery]

minstrel /'minstrəl/ *n* **1** a medieval singer, poet, or musical entertainer **2** any of a troupe of performers usu with blackened faces giving a performance of supposedly Negro singing, jokes, dancing, etc [ME *menestrel*, fr OF, official, servant, minstrel, fr LL *ministerialis* imperial household officer, fr L *ministerium* service, fr *minister* servant – more at MINISTER]

'minstrelsy /-si/ *n* **1** the singing and playing of a minstrel **2** *sing or pl in constr* a body of minstrels **3** songs or poems (composed or performed by minstrels) [ME *minstralcie*, fr MF *menestralsie*, fr *menestrel*]

¹mint /mint/ *n* **1** a place where money is made **2** a vast sum or amount – infml [ME *mynt* coin, money, fr OE *mynet*; akin to OHG *munizza* coin; both fr a prehistoric WGmc word borrowed fr L *moneta* mint, coin, fr *Moneta*, epithet of Juno; fr the fact that the Romans coined money in the temple of Juno Moneta]

²mint *vt* **1** to make (e g coins) by stamping metal **2** to fabricate, invent ⟨~ *a new word*⟩ – **minter** *n*

³mint *adj* unspoilt as if fresh from a mint; pristine ⟨*in ~ condition*⟩

⁴mint *n* **1** any of a genus of plants that have whorled leaves and foliage with a characteristic strong taste and smell, used esp as a flavouring **2** a sweet, chocolate, etc flavoured with mint [ME *minte*, fr OE; akin to OHG *minza*; both fr a prehistoric WGmc compound borrowed fr L *mentha* mint]

mintage /'mintij/ *n* **1** the action, process, or cost of minting coins **2** coins produced in a single period of minting

'mint ,mark *n* an official mark stamped on a coin to indicate its origin

minuend /'minyoo,end/ *n* a number from which another is to be subtracted [L *minuendum*, neut of *minuendus*, gerundive of *minuere* to lessen – more at MINOR]

minuet /,minyoo'et/ *n* (music for or in the rhythm of) a slow graceful dance in ¾ time [F *menuet*, fr obs F, tiny, fr OF, fr *menu* small, fr L *minutus*]

¹minus /'mienəs/ *prep* **1** diminished by ⟨*seven ~ four is three*⟩ ☞ SYMBOL **2** without ⟨~ *his hat*⟩ [ME, fr L *minus*, adv, less, fr neut of *minor* smaller – more at MINOR]

²minus *n* **1** a negative quantity **2** a deficiency, defect

³minus *adj* **1** negative ⟨*a ~ quantity*⟩ ⟨*a temperature of ~ 10°C*⟩ **2** having negative qualities; *esp* involving a disadvantage ⟨*a ~ factor*⟩ **3** falling low in a specified range ⟨*a mark of B ~*⟩

¹minuscule /'minə,skyoohl/ *n* (a lower-case letter in) a style of small flowing handwriting – compare MAJUSCULE ☞ ALPHABET [F, fr L *minusculus* rather small, dim. of *minor* smaller]

²minuscule *adj* **1** written in minuscules **2** very small

'minus ,sign *n* a sign – denoting subtraction or a negative quantity ☞ SYMBOL

¹minute /'minit/ *n* **1** the 60th part of an hour of time or of a degree **2** the distance one can cover in a minute ⟨*lived 5 ~s from the station*⟩ **3** a short space of time; a moment **4a** MEMORANDUM 3 **b** *pl* the official record of the proceedings of a meeting [ME, fr MF, fr LL *minuta*, fr L *minutus* small, fr pp of *minuere* to lessen – more at MINOR]

²minute *vb* to make notes or a brief summary (of)

³minute /mie'nyooht/ *adj* **1** extremely small **2** of minor importance; petty **3** marked by painstaking attention to detail [L *minutus*] – **minutely** *adv*, **minuteness** *n*

'minute ,hand *n* the long hand that marks the minutes on the face of a watch or clock

'minute,man /-,man/ *n* a member of a group of armed men pledged to take the field at a minute's notice during and immediately before the American Revolution

minutia /mi'nyoohshyə, mie-/ *n, pl* **minutiae** /-shi,ee/ a minor detail – usu pl [L *minutiae* trifles, details, fr pl of *minutia* smallness, fr *minutus*]

minx /mingks/ *n* a flirtatious girl [origin unknown]

mio- – see MI-

Miocene /'mie·ə,seen/ *adj or n* (of or being) an epoch of the Tertiary between the Pliocene and the Oligocene ☞ EVOLUTION

miosis, myosis /mie'ohsis/ *n, pl* **mioses** /-seez/ excessive smallness or contraction of the pupil of the eye [NL, fr Gk *myein* to be closed (of the eyes) + NL *-osis*] – **miotic** /mie'otik/ *adj or n*

mir /miə/ *n* a village community in tsarist Russia [Russ]

miracle /'mirəkl/ *n* **1** an extraordinary event manifesting divine intervention in human affairs **2** an astonishing or unusual event, thing, or accomplishment **3** a person or thing that is a remarkable example or instance of sthg ⟨*this watch is a ~ of precision*⟩ [ME, fr OF, fr L *miraculum*, fr *mirari* to wonder at – more at SMILE]

'miracle ,play *n* a medieval drama based on episodes from the Bible or the life of a saint; *also* MYSTERY PLAY

miraculous /mi'rakyooləs/ *adj* **1** of the nature of a miracle; supernatural **2** evoking wonder like a miracle; marvellous **3** (capable of) working miracles [MF *miraculeux*, fr ML *miraculosus*, fr L *miraculum*] – **miraculously** *adv*, **miraculousness** *n*

mirage /'mirahzh/ *n* **1** an optical illusion appearing esp as a pool of water or as the reflection of distant objects caused by the reflection of rays of light by a layer of heated air (near the ground) **2** sthg illusory and unattainable [F, fr *mirer* to look at, fr L *mirari*]

¹mire /'mie·ə/ *n* **1** a tract of soft waterlogged ground; a marsh, bog **2** (deep) mud or slush [ME, fr ON *mȳrr*; akin to OE *mōs* bog – more at MOSS] – **miry** *adj*

²mire *vt* to cause to stick fast (as if) in mire; BOG DOWN

mirepoix /miə'pwah/ *n, pl* **mirepoix** a mixture of

diced vegetables sautéed and used in brown sauces or as a bed for braising meat on [F, prob fr Charles de Lévis, Duc de *Mirepoix* †1757 F diplomat & general]

mirk /muhk/ *n* murk – **mirky** *adj*

¹mirror /'mirə/ *n* **1** a smooth surface (e g of metal or silvered glass) that forms images by reflection **2** sthg that gives a true representation [ME *mirour*, fr OF, fr *mirer* to look at, fr L *mirari* to wonder at – more at SMILE] – **mirrorlike** *adj*

²mirror *vt* to reflect (as if) in a mirror

mirror carp *n* a domesticated variety of the carp with large shiny scales

,mirror 'image *n* sthg that has its parts reversely arranged in comparison with another similar thing

mirth /muhth/ *n* happiness or amusement accompanied with laughter [ME, fr OE *myrgth*, fr *myrge* merry – more at MERRY] – **mirthful** *adj*, **mirthfully** *adv*, **mirthfulness** *n*, **mirthless** *adj*

MIRV /muhv/ *n* an intercontinental missile having multiple warheads which may be directed to separate targets [*m*ultiple *i*ndependently targeted *r*eentry *v*ehicle]

¹mis- /mis-/ *prefix* **1** badly; wrongly; unfavourably ⟨mis *judge*⟩ ⟨mis*behave*⟩ **2** suspicious; apprehensive ⟨mis*giving*⟩ **3** bad; wrong ⟨mis*deed*⟩ ⟨mis*fit*⟩ **4** opposite or lack of ⟨mis*trust*⟩ ⟨mis*fortune*⟩ **5** not ⟨mis*understand*⟩ [partly fr ME, fr OE; partly fr ME *mes-*, *mis-*, fr OF *mes-*, of Gmc origin; akin to OE *mis-*; akin to OE *missan* to miss]

²mis-, miso- *comb form* hatred ⟨miso*gamy*⟩ [Gk, fr *misein* to hate]

misadventure /,misəd'venchə/ *n* a misfortune, mishap [ME *mesaventure*, fr OF, fr *mesavenir* to chance badly, fr *mis-* ¹mis- + *avenir* to chance, happen, fr L *advenire* – more at ADVENTURE]

,misa'ligned /-ə'liend/ *adj* not correctly aligned – **misalignment** *n*

,misal'liance /-ə'lie·əns/ *n* an improper or unsuitable alliance; *esp* a mésalliance [modif of F *mésalliance*]

misanthrope /'miz(ə)n,throhp/, **misanthropist** /mi'zanthrəpist/ *n* one who hates or distrusts people [Gk *misanthrōpos* hating mankind, fr *mis-* ²mis- + *anthrōpos* man] – **misanthropic** /,miz(ə)n'thropik/ *adj*, **misanthropy** /mi'zanthrəpi/ *n*

misapply /,misə'plie/ *vt* to apply wrongly – **misapplication** /-,apli'kaysh(ə)n/ *n*

,misappre'hend /-apri'hend/ *vt* to misunderstand – **misapprehension** /-,hensh(ə)n/ *n*

,misap'propriate /-ə'prohpriayt/ *vt* to appropriate wrongly (e g by theft or embezzlement) – **misappropriation** /-'aysh(ə)n/ *n*

,misbe'gotten /-bi'gotn/ *adj* **1** having a disreputable or improper origin **2** wretched, contemptible ⟨*a ~ scoundrel*⟩ **3** *archaic* illegitimate, bastard

,misbe'have /-bi'hayv/ *vi* to behave badly – **misbehaviour** *n*

,mis'calculate /-'kalkyoolayt/ *vb* to calculate wrongly – **miscalculation** /-'laysh(ə)n/ *n*

'mis,carriage /-,karij/ *n* **1** a failure in administration ⟨*~ of justice*⟩ **2** the expulsion of a human foetus before it is viable, esp after the 12th week of gestation

,mis'carry /-'kari/ *vi* **1** to suffer miscarriage of a foetus **2** to fail to achieve an intended purpose

,mis'cast /-'kahst/ *vt* **miscast** to cast in an unsuitable role

miscegenation /,mis,eji'naysh(ə)n, ,misijə-/ *n* interbreeding of races, esp between sby white and sby nonwhite [L *miscēre* to mix + *genus* race – more at MIX, KIN] – **miscegenational** *adj*

miscellanea /,misə'laynyə, -ni·ə/ *n pl* a miscellaneous collection, esp of literary works [L, fr neut pl of *miscellaneus*]

miscellaneous /-nyəs, -ni·əs/ *adj* **1** consisting of diverse items or members **2** having various characteristics or capabilities [L *miscellaneus*, fr *miscellus* mixed, prob fr *miscēre* to mix] – **miscellaneously** *adv*, **miscellaneousness** *n*

miscellany /mi'seləni/ *n* **1** a mixture of various things **2** a book containing miscellaneous literary pieces [prob modif of F *miscellanées*, pl, fr L *miscellanea*] – **miscellanist** *n*

mischance /,mis'chahns/ *n* (a piece of) bad luck [ME *mischaunce*, fr OF *meschance*, fr *mis-* ¹mis- + *chance*]

mischief /'mischif/ *n* **1** a specific injury or damage from a particular agent ⟨*did himself a ~ on the barbed wire*⟩ **2** sthg or esp sby that causes harm or annoyance **3** often playful action that annoys or irritates, usu without causing or intending serious harm **4** the quality or state of being mischievous [ME *meschief*, fr OF, calamity, fr *mes-* + *chief* head, end – more at CHIEF]

mischievous /'mischivəs/ *adj* **1** harmful, malicious **2** able or tending to cause annoyance, unrest, or minor injury **3a** playfully provocative; arch **b** disruptively playful – **mischievously** *adv*, **mischievousness** *n*

'misch ,metal /mish/ *n* an alloy of rare-earth metals used esp in tracer bullets and as a flint in lighters [G *mischmetall*, fr *mischen* to mix + *metall* metal]

miscible /'misibl/ *adj*, *esp of a liquid* capable of being mixed (*with* another liquid in any proportion without separating) [ML *miscibilis*, fr L *miscēre* to mix – more at MIX] – **miscibility** /-'biləti/ *n*

misconceive /,miskən'seev/ *vt* to interpret wrongly; misunderstand – **misconception** /-kən'sepsh(ə)n/ *n*

mis'conduct /-'kondukt/ *n* **1** mismanagement of responsibilities **2** adultery – **misconduct** /,miskən'dukt/ *vt*

,miscon'strue /-kən'strooh/ *vt* to construe wrongly; misinterpret – **misconstruction** /-kən 'struksh(ə)n/ *n*

mis'count /-'kownt/ *vt* to count wrongly ~ *vi* to make a wrong count [ME *misconten*, fr MF *mesconter*, fr *mes-* ¹mis- + *conter* to count] – **miscount** /'--/ *n*

miscreant /'miskri·ənt/ *adj or n* (of) one who behaves criminally or maliciously [ME *miscreaunt* disbeliever, heretic, fr MF *mescreant*, prp of *mescroire* to disbelieve, fr *mes-* ¹mis- + *croire* to believe, fr L *credere* – more at CREED]

,miscre'ate /-kri'ayt/ *vt* to create badly or incorrectly ⟨*a higher image, a legitimate hope: she had ~d and deformed it, but it had been there* – Margaret Drabble⟩

,mis'cue /-'kyooh/ *vi or n* (to make) a faulty stroke in billiards or snooker in which the cue slips

,mis'date /-'dayt/ *vt* to date (e g a letter) wrongly

,mis'deal /-'deel/ *vb* to deal (cards) incorrectly – **misdeal** *n*

,mis'deed /-'deed/ *n* a wrong deed; an offence

,misde'meanour /-di'meenə/ *n* **1** a minor crime

formerly technically distinguished from a felony **2** a misdeed

,misdi'rect /-di'rekt, -die-/ *vt* **1** to give a wrong direction to **2** to address (mail) wrongly – **misdirection** *n*

mise-en-scène /,meez onh 'sen (*Fr* miz ɑ̃ sɛn)/ *n, pl* **mise-en-scènes** /sen(z) (*Fr* ~)/ **1** the arrangement of actors, props, and scenery on a stage in a theatrical production **2** the environment or setting in which sthg takes place [F *mise en scène*, lit., (action of) putting on stage]

miser /'miezə/ *n* a mean grasping person; *esp* one who hoards wealth [L *miser* miserable, wretched] – **miserly** *adj*, **miserliness** *n*

miserable /'miz(ə)rəbl/ *adj* **1a** wretchedly inadequate or meagre **b** causing extreme discomfort or unhappiness **2** in a pitiable state of distress or unhappiness **3** shameful, contemptible ⟨*a ~ failure*⟩ [ME, fr MF, fr L *miserabilis* wretched, pitiable, fr *miserari* to pity, fr *miser*] – **miserableness** *n*, **miserably** *adv*

miserere /,mizə'reəri/ *n* **1** *cap* the 51st Psalm **2** a misericord [L, be merciful, fr *misereri* to be merciful, fr *miser* wretched; fr the first word of the Psalm]

misericord, misericorde /mi'zeri,kawd/ *n* a ledge on the underside of the hinged seat of a choir stall, on which, when the seat is turned up, the occupant can support him-/herself while standing [ML *misericordia* seat in church, fr L, mercy, fr *misericord-*, *misericors* merciful, fr *misereri* + *cord-*, *cor* heart – more at HEART]

misery /'mizəri/ *n* **1** (a cause of) physical or mental suffering or discomfort **2** great unhappiness and distress **3** *chiefly Br* a grumpy or querulous person; *esp* a killjoy – infml [ME *miserie*, *misere*, fr MF, fr L *miseria*, fr *miser*]

misfeasance /mis'feez(ə)ns/ *n* the wrongful exercise of lawful authority [MF *mesfaisance*, fr *mesfaire* to do wrong, fr *mes-* [1]mis- + *faire* to make, do, fr L *facere* – more at [1]DO] – **misfeasor** *n*

,mis'field /-'feeld/ *vb* to make a mistake in fielding (the ball) in cricket, baseball, etc – **misfield** *n*

,mis'fire /-'fie·ə/ *vi* **1** *of a motor vehicle, engine, etc* to have the explosive or propulsive charge fail to ignite at the proper time ⟨*the engine* ~d⟩ **2** *esp of a firearm* to fail to fire **3** to fail to have an intended effect – **misfire** /'--/ *n*

'mis,fit /-,fit/ *n* **1** sthg that fits badly **2** a person poorly adjusted to his/her environment

,mis'fortune /-'fawchoohn, -chən/ *n* **1** bad luck **2** a distressing or unfortunate incident or event; *also* the resultant unhappy situation ⟨*feared that some ~ would befall her*⟩ ⟨*sympathized with her in her ~*⟩

,mis'give /-'giv/ *vb* **misgave** /-'gayv/; **misgiven** /-'giv(ə)n/ to (cause to) be fearful or apprehensive

,mis'giving /-'giving/ *n* a feeling of doubt, suspicion, or apprehension, esp concerning a future event

,mis'govern /-'guvən/ *vt* to govern badly – **misgovernment** /-'guv(ə)nmənt, -'guvəmənt/ *n*

,mis'guide /-'gied/ *vt* to lead astray – **misguidance** *n*

,mis'guided *adj* directed by mistaken ideas, principles, or motives – **misguidedly** *adv*, **misguidedness** *n*

,mis'handle /-'handl/ *vt* **1** to treat roughly; maltreat **2** to mismanage (a situation, crisis, etc)

mishap /'mis,hap/ *n* an unfortunate accident [ME, fr [1]*mis-* + *hap* (happening, chance), fr ON *happ* good luck]

,mis'hear /-'hiə/ *vb* **misheard** /-'huhd/ to hear wrongly

,mis'hit /-'hit/ *vt* **mishit; -tt-** to hit (a ball or stroke) faultily – **mishit** /'mis,hit/ *n*

mishmash /'mish,mash/ *n* a hotchpotch, jumble – infml [partly fr MHG *misch-masch*, redupl of *mischen* to mix; partly fr Yiddish *mish mash*, fr MHG *mischmasch*]

Mishnah, Mishna /'mishnə/ *n* the collection of Jewish traditions compiled about AD 200 to form the basis of the Talmud [Heb *mishnāh* instruction, oral law, fr *shānāh* to repeat, learn] – **Mishnaic** /-'nayik/ *adj*

misinform /,misin'fawm/ *vt* to give untrue or misleading information to – **misinformation** /-infə'maysh(ə)n/ *n*

,misin'terpret /-in'tuhprit/ *vt* to understand or explain wrongly – **misinterpretation** /-in,tuhpri'taysh(ə)n/ *n*

,mis'judge /-'juj/ *vt* **1** to estimate wrongly **2** to have an unjust opinion of ~ *vi* to make a mistaken judgment – **misjudgment** *n*

Miskito /mi'skeetoh/ *n, pl* **Miskitos,** *esp collectively* **Miskito** a member, or the language, of a people of Nicaragua and Honduras

mislay /mis'lay/ *vt* **mislaid** /-'layd/ to leave in an unremembered place

,mis'lead /-'leed/ *vt* **misled** /-'led/ to lead in a wrong direction or into a mistaken action or belief – **misleadingly** *adv*

,mis'manage /-'manij/ *vt* to manage wrongly or incompetently – **mismanagement** *n*

,mis'match /-'mach/ *vt* to match incorrectly or unsuitably, esp in marriage – **mismatch** /'-,-/ *n*

,mis'name /-'naym/ *vt* to call by the wrong name

,mis'nomer /-'nohmə/ *n* (a use of) a wrong name or designation [ME *misnoumer*, fr MF *mesnommer* to misname, fr *mes-* [1]mis- + *nommer* to name, fr L *nominare* – more at NOMINATE]

miso- – see [2]MIS-

misogamist /mi'sogəmist, mie-/ *n* one who hates marriage [Gk *mis-* [2]mis- + *gamos* marriage] – **misogamy** *n*

misogynist /mi'soj(ə)n·ist, mie-/ *n* one who hates women [Gk *misogynēs*, fr *mis-* [2]mis- + *gynē* woman] – **misogynous** *adj*, **misogyny** *n*, **misogynistic** /-'istik/ *adj*

misology /mi'soləji, mie-/ *n* a hatred of argument, reasoning, or knowledge [Gk *misologia*, fr *mis-* [2]mis- + *-logia* -logy]

misplace /mis'plays/ *vt* **1a** to put in the wrong place **b** to mislay **2** to direct towards a wrong object or outcome ⟨~d *affections*⟩ ⟨~d *enthusiasm*⟩ **3** to fail to suit to the occasion ⟨~d *humour*⟩ – **misplacement** *n*

,mis'print /-'print/ *vt* to print wrongly – **misprint** /'-,-/ *n*

misprision /mis'prizh(ə)n/ *n* **1** misconduct or neglect of (public) duty **2** concealment of treason or felony by sby not actually a participant [ME, fr MF *mesprison* error, wrongdoing, fr OF, fr *mespris*, pp of *mesprendre* to make a mistake, fr *mes-* [1]mis- + *prendre* to take, fr L *prehendere* to seize – more at PREHENSILE]

,mispro'nounce /-prə'nowns/ *vt* to pronounce wrongly

,mispro,nunci'ation /-prə,nunsi'aysh(ə)n/ *n* (an instance of) mispronouncing

,mis'quote /-'kwoht/ *vt* to quote incorrectly – **misquotation** /-kwoh'taysh(ə)n/ *n*

,mis'read /-'reed/ *vt* **misread** /-'red/ to read or interpret incorrectly

,misre'port /-ri'pawt/ *vt* to report falsely – **misreport** *n*

,misrepre'sent /-repri'zent/ *vt* to represent falsely; give an untrue or misleading account of – **misrepresentation** /-'taysh(ə)n/ *n*

[1]**,mis'rule** /-'roohl/ *vt* to rule incompetently

[2]**,mis'rule** *n* **1** misruling or being misruled **2** disorder, anarchy

[1]**miss** /mis/ *vt* **1** to fail to hit, reach, contact, or attain ⟨~ed *the train*⟩ ⟨*his arrow* ~ed *the mark*⟩ ⟨~ed *her step and fell heavily*⟩ **2** to discover or feel the absence of, esp with regret ⟨*didn't* ~ *his cheque book for several days*⟩ ⟨~ed *his wife desperately*⟩ **3** to escape, avoid ⟨*narrowly* ~ed *being run over*⟩ **4** to leave out; omit – often + *out* **5** to fail to understand, sense, or experience ⟨*he* ~ed *the point of the speech*⟩ **6** to fail to perform or attend ⟨~ed *his appointment*⟩ **7** to fail to take advantage of ⟨*never* ~es *an opportunity of playing golf*⟩ ~ *vi* **1** to fail to hit sthg **2** to misfire ⟨*the engine* ~ed⟩ [ME *missen*, fr OE *missan*; akin to OHG *missan* to miss, L *mutare* to change] – **miss out on** to lose or not to have had (a good opportunity) ⟨*people who* missed out on *further education*⟩ – **miss the boat** to fail to take advantage of an opportunity

[2]**miss** *n* **1** a failure to hit **2** a failure to attain a desired result **3** a deliberate avoidance or omission of sthg ⟨*felt so full he gave the dessert a* ~⟩

[3]**miss** *n* **1a** – used as a title preceding the name of an unmarried woman or girl **b** – used before the name of a place or of a line of activity or before some epithet to form a title for a usu young unmarried female who is representative of the thing indicated ⟨Miss *World*⟩ **2** young lady – used without a name as a conventional term of address to a young woman **3** a young unmarried woman or girl – chiefly infml [short for *mistress*]

missal /'misl/ *n* a book containing the order of service of the mass for the whole year [ME *messel*, fr MF & ML; MF, fr ML *missale*, fr neut of *missalis* of the mass, fr LL *missa* mass – more at [1]MASS]

'missel ,thrush /'misl/ *n* MISTLE THRUSH

misshape /,mis'shayp/ *vt* to shape badly; deform – **misshapen** *adj*, **misshapenly** *adv*

missile /'misiel; *NAm* 'misl/ *n* an object thrown or projected, usu so as to strike sthg at a distance; *also* a self-propelled weapon that travels through the air [L, fr neut of *missilis* capable of being thrown, fr *missus*, pp of *mittere* to throw, send – more at SMITE]

missilery /'mislri/ *n* (the science dealing with the design, manufacture, and use of guided) missiles

missing /'mising/ *adj* absent; *also* lost ⟨~ *in action*⟩

,missing 'link *n* **1** an item needed to complete a continuous series **2** a supposed intermediate form between man and his anthropoid ancestors

mission /'mish(ə)n/ *n* **1a** a ministry commissioned by a religious organization to propagate its faith or carry on humanitarian work, usu abroad **b** assignment to or work in a field of missionary enterprise **c** a mission establishment **d** *pl* organized missionary work **e** a campaign to increase church membership or strengthen Christian faith **2a** a group sent to a foreign country to negotiate, advise, etc **b** a permanent embassy or legation **3** a specific task with which a person or group is charged **4a** a definite military, naval, or aerospace task ⟨*a bombing* ~⟩ ⟨*a space* ~⟩ **b** a flight operation of an aircraft or spacecraft in the performance of a mission ⟨*a* ~ *to Mars*⟩ **5** a calling, vocation [NL, ML, & L; NL *mission-, missio* religious mission, fr ML, task assigned, fr L, act of sending, fr *missus*, pp of *mittere*]

[1]**missionary** /'mishən(ə)ri/ *adj* **1** relating to, engaged in, or devoted to missions **2** characteristic of a missionary

[2]**missionary** *n* a person undertaking a mission; *esp* one in charge of a religious mission in some remote part of the world

missionary position *n* a position for sexual intercourse in which the woman lies on her back with the man above and facing her, regarded as the conventional position [fr its being reputedly advocated as the proper position by missionaries to primitive peoples]

missioner /'mishənə/ *n* a person engaged in parochial missionary work

missive /'misiv/ *n* a written communication; a letter – fml [MF *lettre missive*, lit., letter intended to be sent]

misspell /,mis'spel/ *vt* **misspelt**, *Nam chiefly* **misspelled** to spell incorrectly

,mis'spend /-'spend/ *vt* **misspent** /-'spent/ to spend wrongly or foolishly; squander ⟨*regretted his* misspent *youth*⟩

,mis'state /-'stayt/ *vt* to state incorrectly; give a false account of – **misstatement** *n*

,mis'step /-'step/ *n* **1** a wrong step **2** a blunder

missus, missis /'misiz/ *n* **1** a wife – infml or humor ⟨*have you met the* ~*?*⟩ **2** *chiefly Br* – used to address a married woman; infml [alter. of *mistress*]

missy /'misi/ *n* a young girl; miss – infml

[1]**mist** /mist/ *n* **1** water in the form of diffuse particles in the atmosphere, esp near the earth's surface **2** sthg that dims or obscures ⟨*the* ~s *of time*⟩ **3** a film, esp of tears, before the eyes **4a** a cloud of small particles suggestive of a mist **b** a suspension of a finely divided liquid in a gas [ME, fr OE; akin to MD *mist* mist, Gk *omichlē*]

[2]**mist** *vi* to be or become misty ~ *vt* to cover (as if) with mist

[1]**mistake** /mi'stayk/ *vt* **mistook** /mi'stook/; **mistaken** /mi'staykən/ **1** to choose wrongly ⟨mistook *her way in the dark*⟩ **2a** to misunderstand the meaning, intention, or significance of **b** to estimate wrongly **3** to identify wrongly; confuse with another ⟨*I* mistook *him for his brother*⟩ [ME *mistaken*, fr ON *mistaka* to take by mistake, fr *mis-* [1]mis- + *taka* to take – more at TAKE]

[2]**mistake** *n* **1** a misunderstanding of the meaning or significance of sthg **2** a wrong action or statement arising from faulty judgment, inadequate knowledge, or carelessness

mistaken /mi'staykən/ *adj* **1** *of a person* wrong in opinion ⟨*if you think he's honest, you're* ~⟩ **2** *of an action, idea, etc* based on wrong thinking; incorrect ⟨*trusted him in the* ~ *belief that he was honest*⟩ – **mistakenly** *adv*

mister /'mistə/ *n* **1** – used sometimes in writing

instead of the usual *Mr* **2** sir – used without a name as a generalized infml term of direct address of a man who is a stranger **3** a man not entitled to a title of rank or an honorific or professional title [alter. of [1]*master*]

mistime /,mis'tiem/ *vt* to time badly

'mistle ,thrush, missel thrush /'misl/ *n* a large Eurasian thrush with larger spots on its underparts than the song thrush [obs *mistle, missel* (mistletoe), fr ME *mistel*, fr OE; fr its feeding on mistletoe berries]

mistletoe /'misl,toh/ *n* a European shrub that grows as a parasite on the branches of trees and has thick leaves and waxy white glutinous berries [ME *mistilto* basil, fr OE *misteltān*, fr *mistel* mistletoe, basil + *tān* twig; akin to OHG & OS *mistil* mistletoe, OHG *zein* twig]

mistral /'mistrəl, mi'strahl (*Fr* mistral)/ *n* a strong cold dry northerly wind of S France [F, fr Prov, fr *mistral* masterful, fr L *magistralis* – more at MAGISTRAL]

mistreat /,mis'treet/ *vt* to treat badly [ME *mistreten*, prob fr MF *mestraitier*, fr OF, fr *mis-* [1]mis- + *traitier* to treat – more at TREAT] – **mistreatment** *n*

mistress /'mistris/ *n* **1a** a woman in a position of power or authority **b** the female head of a household **2** a woman who has achieved mastery of a subject or skill **3** sthg personified as female that rules or directs **4** a woman with whom a man has a continuing sexual relationship outside marriage **5** *chiefly Br* a schoolmistress ⟨*thoroughly disliked the maths* ~⟩ **6** *archaic* a sweetheart **7** – used archaically as a title preceding the name of a woman and now superseded by *Mrs, Miss*, and *Ms* [ME *maistresse*, fr MF, fr OF, fem of *maistre* master – more at MASTER]

mistrial /,mis'trie·əl/ *n* a trial declared void because of some error in the proceedings

,mis'trust /-'trust/ *vt* **1** to have little trust in; be suspicious of **2** to doubt the reliability or effectiveness of – **mistrust** *n*, **mistrusted** *adj*, **mistrustful** *adj*, **mistrustfully** *adv*

misty /'misti/ *adj* **1** obscured by mist **2** not clear to the mind or understanding; indistinct – **mistily** *adv*, **mistiness** *n*

misunderstand /,misundə'stand/ *vt* **1** to fail to understand **2** to interpret incorrectly

,misunder'standing /-'standing/ *n* **1** a failure to understand; a misinterpretation **2** a disagreement, dispute

,mis'usage /-'yoohsij/ *n* **1** bad treatment; abuse **2** wrong or improper use (e g of words) [MF *mesusage*, fr *mis-* + *usage*]

,mis'use /-'yoohz/ *vt* **1** to put to wrong or improper use **2** to abuse or maltreat [ME *misusen*; partly fr *mis-* + *usen* to use; partly fr MF *mesuser* to abuse, fr OF, fr *mis-* + *user* to use] – **misuse** /,mis'yoohs/ *n*

mite /miet/ *n* **1** any of numerous (extremely) small arachnids that often infest animals, plants, and stored foods **2** a small coin or sum of money ⟨*a widow's* ~⟩ **3** a very small object or creature; *esp* a small child [ME, fr OE *mīte*; akin to MD *mite* mite, small copper coin, OHG *meizan* to cut, OE *gemād* silly; (2) ME, fr MF, small Flemish copper coin, fr MD] – **a mite** to a small extent – infml

Mithras /'mithras/ *n* an ancient Persian god whose cult flourished in the late Roman empire and had as its central ceremony the sacrifice of a bull [L, fr Gk, fr OPer *Mithra*] – **Mithraic** /mi'thrayik/ *adj*, **Mithraist** *n*, **Mithraism** /'mithrə,iz(ə)m/ *n*

mithridate /'mithridayt/ *n* a sweetened medicinal preparation formerly held to be a universal antidote to poison [ML *mithridatum*, fr LL *mithridatium*, fr L, dogtooth violet (used as an antidote), fr Gk *mithridation*, fr *Mithridatēs* Mithridates VI †63 BC King of Pontus, who reputedly inured himself to poisons]

mitigate /'mitigayt/ *vt* **1** to cause to become less harsh or hostile **2a** to make less severe or painful; alleviate **b** to extenuate ⟨mitigating *circumstances*⟩ [ME *mitigaten*, fr L *mitigatus*, pp of *mitigare* to soften, fr *mitis* soft + *-igare* (akin to L *agere* to drive); akin to OIr *mōith* soft – more at AGENT] – **mitigatory** /'miti,gaytəri, -gət(ə)ri/ *adj*, **mitigation** /-'gaysh(ə)n/ *n*

mitochondrion /,mietoh'kondri·ən/ *n, pl* **mitochondria** /-dri·ə/ any of several organelles in a cell that are rich in fats, proteins, and enzymes and produce energy through cellular respiration [NL, fr Gk *mitos* thread + *chondrion*, dim. of *chondros* grain – more at GRIND] – **mitochondrial** *adj*, **mitochondrially** *adv*

mitosis /mie'tohsis/ *n, pl* **mitoses** /-seez/ the formation of 2 new nuclei from an original nucleus, each having the same number of chromosomes as the original nucleus, during cell division; *also* cell division in which this occurs – compare MEIOSIS [NL, fr Gk *mitos* thread] – **mitotic** /mie'totik/ *adj*

mitrailleuse /,meetrie'uhz/ *n* a machine gun (with several bar rels) [F]

mitral /'mietrəl/ *adj* relating to, being, or adjoining a bicuspid valve [[1]MITRE + [1]-AL]

'mitral ,valve *n* BICUSPID VALVE

[1]**mitre,** *NAm chiefly* **miter** /'mietə/ *n* **1** a tall pointed divided headdress with 2 bands hanging down at the back worn by bishops and abbots on ceremonial occasions ☞ GARMENT **2** MITRE JOINT **3** a seam joining 2 parts of a sail whose fabric runs in different directions ☞ SHIP [ME *mitre*, fr MF, fr OF, fr L *mitra* headband, turban, fr Gk; akin to Skt *mitra* friend]

[2]**mitre,** *NAm chiefly* **miter** *vt* **1** to bevel the ends of to make a mitre joint **2** to match or fit together in a mitre joint

'mitre ,box *n* a device for guiding a handsaw at the proper angle in making a mitre joint in wood

'mitre ,gear *n* either of a pair of bevel gears with axes at right angles

'mitre ,joint *n* a joint made by cutting the ends of 2 pieces of wood at an oblique angle so that they form a right angle when fitted together

mitt /mit/ *n* **1a** a glove that leaves the (ends of the) fingers uncovered **b** MITTEN 1 **c** a baseball catcher's protective glove made in the style of a mitten **2** a hand or paw; *specif* a person's hand – infml [short for *mitten*]

mitten /'mit(ə)n/ *n* **1** a glove that is divided into one part covering the fingers and another part covering the thumb **2** MITT 1a [ME *mitain*, fr MF *mitaine*, fr OF, fr *mite* mitten]

mitzvah /'mitsvah/ *n, pl* **mitzvoth** /'mitsvoht, -vohth, -vohs/, **mitzvahs** **1** a commandment of the Jewish law **2** a charitable act considered in Judaism to be specially praiseworthy [Heb *miṣwāh*]

[1]**mix** /miks/ *vt* **1a(1)** to combine or blend into a mass

(2) to combine with another – often + *in* ⟨*prepare the soup and* ~ *in the herbs*⟩ **b** to bring into close association ⟨~ *business with pleasure*⟩ **2** to prepare by mixing different components or ingredients ⟨~ *a drink*⟩ **3** to control the balance of (various sounds), esp during the recording of a film, broadcast, record, etc ~ *vi* **1a** to become mixed **b** to be capable of mixing **2** to seek or enjoy the society of others **3** to crossbreed **4** to become actively involved ⟨*decided not to* ~ *in politics*⟩ [ME *mixen*, back-formation fr *mixte* mixed, fr MF, fr L *mixtus*, pp of *miscēre* to mix; akin to Gk *mignynai* to mix] – **mix it** to fight, brawl – infml

[2]**mix** *n* **1** an act or process of mixing **2** a product of mixing; *specif* a commercially prepared mixture of food ingredients **3** a combination ⟨*the right* ~ *of jobs, people, and amenities – The Times*⟩ **4** a combination in definite proportions of 2 or more recordings (e g of a singer and an accompaniment)

mixed /mikst/ *adj* **1** combining diverse elements **2** made up of or involving people of different races, national origins, religions, classes, or sexes **3** including or accompanied by conflicting or dissimilar elements ⟨~ *feelings*⟩ **4** deriving from 2 or more races or breeds ⟨*a person of* ~ *blood*⟩ [ME *mixte*]

,mixed 'bag *n* a miscellaneous collection; an assortment

,mixed e'conomy *n* an economic system in which free enterprise and nationalized industries coexist

,mixed 'farming *n* the growing of food crops and the rearing of livestock on the same farm

,mixed 'grill *n* a dish of several meats and vegetables grilled together

,mixed 'metaphor *n* a combination of incongruous metaphors (e g in *iron out bottlenecks*)

,mixed 'number *n* a number (e g 5⅔) composed of an integer and a fraction

,mixed-'up *adj* marked by perplexity, uncertainty, or disorder; confused – infml

mixer /'miksə/ *n* **1a** a set of adjustable electrical resistances or attenuators used to combine signals, esp sound signals, from a number of sources in variable proportions for recording, broadcasting, etc; *also* one who operates such a device **b** a container, device, or machine for mixing sthg (e g food or concrete) **2a** a person considered with respect to his/her sociability ⟨*was shy and a poor* ~⟩ **b** a nonalcoholic beverage intended to be drunk mixed with spirits [[1]MIX + [2]-ER]

mixture /'mikschə/ *n* **1a** mixing or being mixed **b** the relative proportions of constituents; *specif* the proportion of fuel to air produced in a carburettor **2a** (a portion of) matter consisting of 2 or more components in varying proportions that retain their own properties **b** a fabric woven of different coloured threads **c** a combination of several different kinds; a blend [MF, fr OF *misture*, fr L *mixtura*, fr *mixtus*]

'mix-,up *n* a state or instance of confusion

mix up *vt* **1** to make untidy or disordered **2** to mistake or confuse ⟨*it's easy to* mix *her* up *with her sister*⟩

mizzen, **mizen** /'miz(ə)n/ *n* (the principal fore-and-aft sail set on) a mizzenmast ☞ SHIP [ME *meson*, fr MF *misaine*, prob deriv of Ar *mazzān* mast]

'mizzen,mast /-,mahst/ *n* the mast behind the mainmast in a sailing vessel ☞ SHIP

mizzle /'mizl/ *vi* **mizzling** /'mizling, 'mizl·ing/ to drizzle [ME *misellen*; akin to Flem *mizzelen* to drizzle, MD *mist* fog, mist] – **mizzle** *n*, **mizzly** *adj*

[1]**mnemonic** /ni'monik, nee-/ *adj* **1** assisting or intended to assist the memory **2** of memory [Gk *mnēmonikos*, fr *mnēmōn* mindful, fr *mimnēskesthai* to remember – more at MIND] – **mnemonically** *adv*

[2]**mnemonic** *n* a mnemonic device or code

mne'monics *n pl but sing in constr* the art of improving the memory

mo, mo' /moh/ *n, chiefly Br* a very short space of time; a moment – infml; often in *half a mo* [short for *moment*]

moa /'moh·ə/ *n* a very large extinct flightless bird of New Zealand [Maori]

[1]**moan** /mohn/ *n* **1** a complaint ⟨*the unflagging stream of* ~s *and queries – Honey Magazine*⟩ **2** a low prolonged sound of pain or grief [ME *mone*, fr (assumed) OE *mān*]

[2]**moan** *vt* **1** to lament **2** to utter with moans ~ *vi* **1** to produce (a sound like) a moan **2** to complain, grumble ⟨*always* ~ing *on about something*⟩ – **moaner** *n*

[1]**moat** /moht/ *n* a deep wide trench round a castle, fortified home, etc that is usu filled with water ☞ CHURCH [ME *mote*, prob fr MF *motte* bank, mound, fr OF *mote*]

[2]**moat** *vt* to surround (as if) with a moat ⟨*a* ~ed *grange*⟩

[1]**mob** /mob/ *n* **1** *the* masses, populace **2** a disorderly riotous crowd **3** a criminal gang **4** *chiefly Austr* a flock, drove, or herd of animals **5** *sing or pl in constr, chiefly Br* a crowd, bunch – infml [short for earlier *mobile*, fr L *mobile vulgus* fickle crowd] – **mobbish** *adj*, **mobocracy** *n*

[2]**mob** *vt* **-bb-** **1** to attack in a large crowd or group **2** to crowd round, esp out of curiosity or admiration

'mob ,cap *n* a woman's full soft cap with a frill round the edge [*mob* (woman's cap; perh modif of obs D *mop*) + *cap*]

[1]**mobile** /'mohbiel/ *adj* **1** capable of moving or being moved **2** changing quickly in expression or mood **3** (capable of) undergoing movement into a different social class **4** marked by movement ⟨~ *warfare*⟩ [MF, fr L *mobilis*, fr *movēre* to move] – **mobility** /moh'biləti, mə-/ *n*

[2]**mobile** *n* a structure (e g of cardboard or metal) with usu suspended parts that are moved in different planes by air currents or machinery

mobil·ize, -ise /'mohbiliez/ *vt* **1a** to put into movement or circulation **b** to release (sthg stored in the body) for use in an organism **2a** to assemble and make ready (e g troops) for active service **b** to marshal (e g resources) for action ~ *vi* to undergo mobilization – **mobilization** /-'zaysh(ə)n/ *n*

Möbius strip /'muhbi·əs/ *n* a one-sided surface that is constructed from a rectangle by holding one end fixed, rotating the opposite end through 180°, and joining it to the first end [August *Möbius* †1868 G mathematician]

mobster /'mobstə/ *n, chiefly NAm* a member of a criminal gang

moccasin /'mokəsin/ *n* a soft leather heelless shoe with the sole brought up the sides of the foot and joined to the upper by a puckered seam ☞ GAR-

MENT [of Algonquian origin; akin to Natick *mokkussin* shoe]

mocha /'mokə, 'mohkə/ *n* **1** a coffee of superior quality, specif grown in Arabia **2** a flavouring obtained from a (mixture of cocoa or chocolate with a) strong coffee infusion [*Mocha*, town in Arabia]

[1]**mock** /mok/ *vt* **1** to treat with contempt or ridicule **2** to disappoint the hopes of **3** to mimic in fun or derision ~*vi* to jeer, scoff [ME *mocken*, fr MF *mocquer*, fr OF *moquier*] – **mocker** *n*, **mockingly** *adv*

[2]**mock** *n* a school examination used as a rehearsal for an official one

[3]**mock** *adj* (having the character) of an imitation or simulation ⟨~ *cream*⟩ ⟨*a* ~ *battle*⟩

[4]**mock** *adv* in an insincere or pretended manner – usu in combination ⟨mock-*serious*⟩

mockery /'mokəri/ *n* **1** jeering or contemptuous behaviour or words **2** an object of laughter or derision **3** a deceitful or contemptible imitation; a travesty **4** sthg insultingly or ridiculously inappropriate

mockingbird /'moking,buhd/ *n* a common bird of esp the southern USA that imitates the calls of other birds

,mock 'orange *n* an ornamental shrub of the hydrangea family with showy aromatic white flowers

mock turtle soup *n* a soup made from a calf's head in imitation of green turtle soup

'mock-,up *n* a full-sized structural model built accurately to scale

[1]**mod** /mod/ *n* a Gaelic competitive festival of the arts, esp singing and recitation, held in Scotland [ScGael *mōd*, fr ON *mōt* meeting; akin to OE *mōt* assembly – more at MOOT]

[2]**mod** *n, often cap* a member of a group of young people in Britain, esp in the 1960s, noted for their neat and distinctive style of dress – compare ROCKER 3 [short for *modern*] – **mod** *adj, often cap*

modal /'mohdl/ *adj* **1** of modality in logic **2** of or being (in) a mode (e g in music); *specif* being in one of the church modes rather than a major or minor key **3** of general form or structure as opposed to particular substance or content **4** of or being a form or category indicating grammatical mood [ML *modalis*, fr L *modus*] – **modally** *adv*

modal auxiliary *n* an auxiliary verb (e g *can, must, may*) expressing a distinction of mood

modality /moh'daləti/ *n* **1** a modal quality or attribute; a form **2** the classification of logical propositions according to the possibility, impossibility, contingency, or necessity of their content **3** a procedure (e g massage) or apparatus used in (physical) therapy **4** [2]MOOD [MODAL + -ITY]

mod con /,mod 'kon/ *n, Br* a modern convenience; *esp* a household fitting or device designed to increase comfort or save time – infml; often in *all mod cons*

[1]**mode** /mohd/ *n* **1a** an arrangement of the 8 diatonic musical notes of an octave in any of several fixed schemes which use different patterns of whole tones and semitones between successive notes **b** a rhythmical scheme, esp in 13th and 14th-c music **2** [2]MOOD **3** MODALITY 2 **4a** a particular form or variety of sthg **b** a form or manner of expression; a style **5** a way of doing or carrying out sthg **6** a particular functional arrangement or condition ⟨*a spacecraft in orbiting* ~⟩ **7** the most frequently occurring value in a set of data ☞ STATISTICS **8** any of various stationary vibration patterns of which an elastic body or oscillatory system is capable ⟨*the vibration* ~s *of a propeller blade*⟩ [ME *moede*, fr L *modus* measure, manner, musical mode – more at METE; (3) LL *modus*, fr L]

[2]**mode** *n* a prevailing fashion or style (e g of dress or behaviour) – fml [F, fr L *modus*]

[1]**model** /'modl/ *n* **1** structural design ⟨*built his home on the* ~ *of an old farmhouse*⟩ **2** a replica of sthg in relief or 3 dimensions; *also* a representation of sthg to be constructed **3** an example worthy of imitation or emulation ⟨*this essay is a* ~ *of clarity*⟩ **4** sby or sthg that serves as a pattern for an artist; *esp* one who poses for an artist **5** one who is employed to wear merchandise, esp clothing, in order to display it ⟨*a fashion* ~⟩ **6** a type or design of an article or product (e g a garment or car) **7** a (simplified) description or analogy used to help visualize sthg (e g an atom) that cannot be directly observed **8** a system of postulates, data, and inferences presented as a mathematical description of an entity or state of affairs **9** a prostitute – euph [MF *modelle*, fr OIt *modello*, fr (assumed) VL *modellus*, fr L *modulus* small measure, fr *modus*]

[2]**model** *vb* **-ll-** (*NAm* **-l-, -ll-**), /'modl·ing/ *vt* **1** to plan or form after a pattern **2** to shape in a mouldable material; *broadly* to produce a representation or simulation of ⟨*using a computer to* ~ *a problem*⟩ **3** to construct or fashion in imitation of a particular model **4** to display, esp by wearing ⟨~led *hats for a living*⟩ ~*vi* **1** to design or imitate forms **2** to work or act as a fashion model – **modeller** *n*

[3]**model** *adj* **1** (worthy of) being a pattern for others ⟨*a* ~ *student*⟩ **2** being a miniature representation of sthg ⟨*a* ~ *aeroplane*⟩

modem /'mohdem/ *n* an electronic device that converts data from a form understandable by a computer into a form that can be transmitted via a telephone line, radio signal, etc and that reconverts data so received (e g to allow communication between distant computers) [*mo*dulator + *dem*odulator]

[1]**moderate** /'mod(ə)rət/ *adj* **1a** avoiding extremes of behaviour or expression **b** not violent; temperate **2a** being (somewhat less than) average in quality, amount, or degree **b** (done or kept) within reasonable limits ⟨~ *wage demands*⟩ [ME, fr L *moderatus*, fr pp of *moderare* to moderate; akin to L *modus* measure] – **moderately** *adv*, **moderateness** *n*

[2]**moderate** /'modərayt/ *vt* **1** to lessen the intensity or extremeness of **2** to preside over ~*vi* **1** to act as a moderator **2** to decrease in violence, severity, intensity, or volume – **moderation** /-'raysh(ə)n/ *n*

[3]**moderate** /'mod(ə)rət/ *n* one who holds moderate views or favours a moderate course [[1]*moderate*]

moderate breeze *n* wind having a speed of 20 to 28km/h (13 to 18mph)

moderate gale *n* wind having a speed of 50 to 61km/h (32 to 38mph)

Moderations /,modə'raysh(ə)ns/ *n pl* the first honours examination at Oxford in some subjects [*moderator* (university official presiding over examinations)]

moderato /,modə'rahtoh/ *adv or adj* in a moderate tempo – used in music [It, fr L *moderatus*]

moderator /'modəraytə/ *n* **1** a mediator **2** the presiding officer of a Presbyterian governing body **3**

a substance (e g graphite) used for slowing down neutrons in a nuclear reactor – **moderatorship** *n*

modern /'modən/ *adj* **1a** (characteristic) of a period extending from a particular point in the past to the present time **b** (characteristic) of the present or the immediate past; contemporary **2** involving recent techniques, styles, or ideas **3** *cap* constituting the present or most recent period of a language [LL *modernus*, fr L *modo* just now, fr *modus* measure – more at METE] – **modernness, modernity** /mo'duhnəti, mə-/ *n*

,Modern 'English *n* English since the late 15th c ☞ LANGUAGE

modernism /'modəniz(ə)m/ *n* **1** a practice, usage, or expression characteristic of modern times **2** *often cap* a tendency in theology to adapt traditional doctrine to contemporary thought by minimizing the role of the supernatural **3** the theory and practices of modern art; *esp* a search for new forms of expression involving a deliberate break with the past – **modernist** *n or adj*, **modernistic** /-'nistik/ *adj*

modern·ize, -ise /'modəniez/ *vt* to adapt to modern needs, style, or standards ~ *vi* to adopt modern views, habits, or techniques – **modernization** /-'zaysh(ə)n/ *n*

,modern 'languages *n pl but sing or pl in constr* contemporary foreign languages as a subject of academic study

,modern 'maths /maths/ *n pl but sing or pl in constr* mathematics that is based on set theory, esp as taught in primary and secondary schools

modern pentathlon *n* a contest in which all contestants compete in a 300-m freestyle swimming race, a 4000-m cross-country run, a 5000-m 30-jump equestrian steeplechase, épée fencing, and target shooting at 25m

modest /'modist/ *adj* **1** having a moderate estimate of one's abilities or worth; not boastful or self-assertive **2** (characteristic) of a modest nature **3** carefully observant of proprieties of dress and behaviour **4** small or limited in size, amount, or aim [L *modestus* moderate; akin to L *modus* measure] – **modestly** *adv*, **modesty** *n*

modicum /'modikəm/ *n* a small or limited amount [ME, fr L, neut of *modicus* moderate, fr *modus* measure]

modification /,modifi'kaysh(ə)n/ *n* **1** the limiting of a statement **2** the making of a limited change to sthg

modifier /'modifie·ə/ *n* a word or word group that modifies another [MODIFY + ²-ER]

modify /'modifie/ *vt* **1** to make less extreme **2** to limit in meaning; qualify **3a** to make minor changes in **b** to make basic changes in, often for a specific purpose ~ *vi* to undergo change [ME *modifien*, fr MF *modifier*, fr L *modificare* to measure, moderate, fr *modus*] – **modifiable** *adj*

modish /'mohdish/ *adj* fashionable, stylish – **modishly** *adv*, **modishness** *n*

Mods /modz/ *n pl* Moderations – infml

modular /'modyoolə/ *adj* of or based on a module or modulus – **modularly** *adv*, **modularity** /-'larəti/ *n*

modular arithmetic *n* arithmetic that deals with whole numbers that have been replaced by the remainders left after division by a fixed number ⟨*in a ~ with modulus 5, 3 multiplied by 4 would be 2*⟩

modulate /'modyoolayt/ *vt* **1** to vary in tone; make tuneful ⟨*~ one's voice*⟩ **2** to adjust to or keep in proper measure or proportion **3** to vary the amplitude, frequency, or phase of (a carrier wave or signal) by combining with a wave of a different frequency, so as to transmit a radio, television, etc signal ~ *vi* to pass by regular chord or melodic progression from one musical key or tonality into another [L *modulatus*, pp of *modulari* to play, sing, fr *modulus* small measure, rhythm, dim. of *modus* measure – more at METE] – **modulator** *n*, **modulatory** /'modyoolət(ə)ri/ *adj*, **modulation** /-'laysh(ə)n/ *n*

module /'modyoohl/ *n* **1** a standard or unit of measure; *esp* one by which the proportions of an architectural composition are regulated **2** a standardized or independent unit used in construction (e g of buildings, electronic systems, or spacecraft) ☞ SPACE [L *modulus*]

modulo /'modyooloh/ *prep* with respect to a modulus of ⟨*19 and 54 give the same value ~ 7*⟩ [NL, abl of *modulus*]

modulus /'modyooləs/ *n, pl* **moduli** /-lie/ **1** a constant or coefficient that expresses the degree in which a property is possessed by a substance or body **2a** the positive square root of the sum of the positive values of the squares of the real and imaginary parts of a complex number **b** a number that is used to divide another number in order to find out the remainder (e g in modular arithmetic) **c** the factor by which a logarithm of a number to one base is multiplied to obtain the logarithm of the number to a new base [NL, fr L, small measure]

modus operandi /,mohdəs opə'randi/ *n, pl* **modi operandi** /'mohdie/ a method of procedure [NL]

,modus vi'vendi /vi'vendi/ *n, pl* **modi vivendi** **1** a practical compromise, esp between opposed or quarrelling parties **2** a manner of living; a way of life [NL, manner of living]

mofette, moffette /moh'fet (*Fr* mɔfɛt)/ *n* a vent in the earth from which carbon dioxide and some nitrogen and oxygen escape [F *mofette* gaseous exhalation]

Mogadon /'mogə,don/ *trademark* – used for nitrazepam

moggie, moggy /'mogi/ *n, Br* CAT 1a – infml [prob fr *Mog*, nickname for *Margaret*]

mogul /'mohg(ə)l/ *n* **1 Mogul, Moghul** a member of a Muslim dynasty of Turkish and Mongolian origin ruling India from the 16th to the 18th c **2** a great or prominent (business) person [Per *Mughul*, fr Mongolian *Mongol*]

mohair /'moh,heə/ *n* a fabric or yarn made (partly) from the long silky hair of the Angora goat – compare ANGORA 2 [modif of obs It *mocaiarro*, fr Ar *mukhayyar*, lit., choice]

Mohammedan /mə'hamid(ə)n/ *adj* Muhammadan

Mohawk /'moh,hawk/ *n, pl* **Mohawks**, *esp collectively* **Mohawk** **1** (the language of) a member of a N American Indian people of the Mohawk river valley in New York State **2** *often not cap* a turn in ice-skating from an edge of one foot to the same edge of the other foot in the opposite direction – compare CHOCTAW [of Algonquian origin; akin to Narraganset *Mohowaùuck*]

Mohican /moh'heekən, mə-/ *n, pl* **Mohicans**, *esp collectively* **Mohican** (the language of) a member of a N American Indian people of the upper Hudson river valley

Moho /ˈmoh,hoh/ *n* *the* point of transition between the earth's crust and mantle [short for *Mohorovicic discontinuity*, fr Andrija *Mohorovičić* †1936 Yugoslav geologist]

Mohock /ˈmoh,hok/ *n* a member of a gang of aristocratic ruffians who molested people in London streets in the 18th c [alter. of *Mohawk*]

Mohorovicic discontinuity /,moh·həˈrohvəchich/ *n* the Moho

ˈMohs' ,scale /mohz/ *n* a scale of hardness for minerals [Friedrich *Mohs* †1839 G mineralogist]

moidore /ˈmoydaw/ *n* a former Portuguese gold coin [modif of Pg *moeda de ouro*, lit., coin of gold]

moiety /ˈmoyəti/ *n* **1** either of 2 (approximately) equal parts **2** any of the portions into which sthg is divided [ME *moite*, fr MF *moité*, fr LL *medietat-, medietas*, fr L *medius* middle – more at MID]

moiré /ˈmwahray (*Fr* mware)/, **moire** /ˈmwahray; *also* mwah/ *n* an irregular wavy sheen on a fabric or metal [F *moiré*, fr *moiré* like watered mohair, fr E *mohair*] – **moiré** *adj*

moist /moyst/ *adj* **1** slightly wet; damp **2** highly humid [ME *moiste*, fr MF, fr (assumed) VL *muscidus*, alter. of L *mucidus* slimy, fr *mucus*] – **moistly** *adv*, **moistness** *n*, **moisten** /ˈmoysn/ *vb*

moisture /ˈmoyschə/ *n* liquid diffused, condensed, or absorbed in relatively small amounts [ME, modif of MF *moistour*, fr *moiste*]

moistur·ize, -ise /ˈmoyschə,riez/ *vt* to add or restore moisture to (e g the skin) – **moisturizer** *n*

moke /mohk/ *n* **1** *Br* a donkey **2** *Austr* a horse, esp of poor appearance ***USE*** slang [origin unknown]

mol /mohl/ *n* [5]MOLE

molal /ˈmohləl/ *adj* of or containing 1 gram molecule (of solute) in 1kg of solvent – not now used technically [[5]*mole*] – **molality** /moh ˈlaləti/ *n*

[1]**molar** /ˈmohlə/ *n* a grinding tooth with a rounded or flattened surface; *specif* one lying behind the incisors and canines of a mammal ☞ DIGESTION [L *molaris*, fr *molaris* of a mill, fr *mola* millstone – more at MILL]

[2]**molar** *adj* of or located near the molar teeth

[3]**molar** *adj* **1** of a mass of matter as distinguished from the properties of individual molecules or atoms **2** of or containing 1 gram molecule (of solute) in 1 litre of solution ⟨*a ~ solution*⟩ [(1) L *moles* mass – more at [3]MOLE; (2) [5]*mole*] – **molarity** /mohˈlarəti/ *n*

molasses /məˈlasiz/ *n* the darkest most viscous syrup remaining after all sugar that can be separated by crystallization has been removed during the refining of raw sugar [Pg *melaço*, fr LL *mellaceum* grape juice, fr L *mell-, mel* honey – more at MELLIFLUOUS]

mold /mohld/ *vt or n, NAm* (to) mould

[1]**mole** /mohl/ *n* a pigmented spot, mark, or lump on the human body; *esp* a naevus [ME, fr OE *māl*; akin to OHG *meil* spot]

[2]**mole** *n* **1** any of numerous small burrowing insect-eating mammals with minute eyes, concealed ears, and soft fur ☞ FOOD **2** one who works subversively within an organization, esp to secretly further the interests of a rival organization or government [ME; akin to MLG *mol*]

[3]**mole** *n* (a harbour formed by) a massive work of masonry, large stones, etc laid in the sea as a pier or breakwater [MF, fr OIt *molo*, fr LGk *mōlos*, fr L *moles*, lit., mass, exertion; akin to OHG *muodi* weary, Gk *mōlos* exertion]

[4]**mole** *n* an abnormal mass in the womb, esp when containing foetal tissues [F *môle*, fr L *mola* mole, lit., mill, millstone – more at MILL]

[5]**mole** *also* **mol** /mohl/ *n* the basic SI unit of substance; the amount of substance that contains the same number of atoms, molecules, ions, etc as there are atoms in 0.012kg of carbon-12 ☞ PHYSICS [G *mol*, short for *molekulargewicht* molecular weight, fr *molekular* molecular + *gewicht* weight]

ˈmole ,cricket /mohl/ *n* any of several large crickets whose front legs are extensively developed for use in digging

molecular /məˈlekyoolə/ *adj* of, produced by, or consisting of molecules ⟨*~ oxygen*⟩ – **molecularly** *adv*, **molecularity** /-ˈlarəti/ *n*

molecular biology *n* the study of the basic molecular organization and functioning of living matter

molecular weight *n* the sum of the atomic weights of the constituent atoms of a molecule

molecule /ˈmolikyoohl/ *n* the smallest particle of a substance that retains its characteristic properties, consisting of 1 or more atoms [F *molécule*, fr NL *molecula*, dim. of L *moles* mass]

ˈmole ,drain *n* a drainage channel just below the surface used esp for draining heavy soils on farms

ˈmole,hill /-,hil/ *n* a mound of earth thrown up by a burrowing mole

molest /məˈlest/ *vt* to annoy, disturb, or attack; *specif* to annoy or attack (esp a child or woman) sexually [ME *molesten*, fr MF *molester*, fr L *molestare*, fr *molestus* burdensome, annoying, fr *moles* mass] – **molester** *n*, **molestation** /,moleˈstaysh(ə)n, ,moh-/ *n*

moll /mol/ *n* **1** a prostitute **2** a gangster's girl friend ***USE*** infml [prob fr *Moll*, nickname for *Mary*]

mollie *also* **molly** /ˈmoli/ *n* any of a genus of brightly coloured topminnows often kept in aquariums [short for NL *Mollienisia*, genus name, fr François *Mollien* †1850 F statesman]

mollify /ˈmolifie/ *vt* **1** to lessen the anger or hostility of **2** to reduce in intensity [ME *mollifien*, fr MF *mollifier*, fr LL *mollificare*, fr L *mollis* soft – more at [1]MELT] – **mollification** /-fiˈkaysh(ə)n/ *n*

mollusc, *NAm chiefly* **mollusk** /ˈmoləsk/ *n* any of a large phylum of invertebrate animals with soft bodies not divided into segments and usu enclosed in a shell, including the snails, shellfish, octopuses, and squids [F *mollusque*, fr NL *Mollusca*, phylum name, fr L, neut pl of *molluscus* soft, fr *mollis*] – **molluscan** /moˈluskən/ *adj*

mollycoddle /ˈmoli,kodl/ *vt* **mollycoddling** /ˈmoli,kodling, -,kodl·ing/ to treat with excessive indulgence and attention [*Molly*, nickname for *Mary*]

,Molotov ˈcocktail /ˈmolətof/ *n* a crude hand grenade made from a bottle filled with petrol or other inflammable liquid with usu a saturated rag for a wick [Vyacheslav M *Molotov b* 1890 Russ statesman]

molt /mohlt/ *vb or n, NAm* (to) moult

molten /ˈmohlt(ə)n/ *adj* melted by heat [ME, fr pp of *melten* to melt]

molto /ˈmoltoh/ *adv* much, very – used in music ⟨~ *sostenuto*⟩ [It, fr L *multum*, fr neut of *multus* much]

molybdenite /mə'libd(ə)n,iet/ *n* molybdenum disulphide occurring as a blue-grey mineral [NL *molybdena*]

molybdenum /mə'libd(ə)nəm/ *n* a metallic element resembling chromium and tungsten and used esp in strengthening and hardening steel ☞ PERIODIC TABLE [NL, fr *molybdena*, a lead ore, molybdenite, molybdenum, fr L *molybdaena* galena, fr Gk *molybdaina*, fr *molybdos* lead]

mom /mom/ *n, NAm* ²MUM

moment /'mohmənt/ *n* **1** a very brief interval or point of time **2a** present time ⟨*at the* ~⟩ **b** a time of excellence or prominence ⟨*she has her* ~s⟩ **3** importance in influence or effect **4** a stage in historical or logical development **5** (a measure of) the tendency of a force to produce turning motion **6** the product of a force and the distance from its line of action to a particular axis [ME, fr MF, fr L *momentum* movement, particle sufficient to turn the scales, moment, fr *movēre* to move]

momentarily /'mohmənt(ə)rəli, ,mohmən'terəli/ *adv* **1** for a moment **2** *chiefly NAm* instantly

momentary /'mohmənt(ə)ri/ *adj* lasting a very short time – **momentariness** *n*

,moment of i'nertia *n* the ratio of the turning force applied to a body free to rotate about a particular axis to the acceleration thus produced

,moment of 'truth *n* **1** the moment of the final sword thrust in a bullfight **2** a moment of crisis on whose outcome everything depends

momentous /mə'mentəs, moh-/ *adj* of great consequence or significance – **momentousness** *n*

momentum /mə'mentəm, moh-/ *n, pl* **momenta** /-tə/, **momentums** the product of the mass of a body and its velocity [NL, fr L, movement]

momma /'momə, 'mumə/ *n, NAm* ²MUM

Mon /mohn/ *n* a member, or the language of, the dominant ethnic group of Burma and Thailand

mon-, mono- *comb form* **1** one; single; alone ⟨mon*oplane*⟩ ⟨mono*drama*⟩ ⟨mono*phobia*⟩ **2a** containing 1 (specified) atom, radical, or group ⟨mono*hydrate*⟩ ⟨mon*oxide*⟩ **b** monomolecular ⟨mono*layer*⟩ [ME, fr MF & L; MF, fr L, fr Gk, fr *monos* alone, single – more at MONK]

monad /'mohnad, 'mo-/ *n* **1** a unit; one **2** ATOM 1 [LL *monad-, monas*, fr Gk, fr *monos*] – **monadism** *n*, **monadic** /mə'nadik/ *adj*

monadelphous /,monə'delfəs/ *adj, of stamens* united by the filaments into 1 group usu forming a tube around the carpels [*mon-* + *-adelphous* having groups of stamens, deriv of Gk *adelphos* brother]

monandrous /mo'nandrəs/ *adj* **1** having (flowers with) a single stamen **2** of or based on monandry [(2)Gk *monandros*, fr *mon-* + *-andros* having (so many) men – more at -ANDROUS]

monandry /mo'nandri/ *n* **1** the state or custom of having only 1 husband at a time **2** a monandrous condition of a plant or flower

monarch /'monək/ *n* **1** sby who reigns over a kingdom or empire **2** sby or sthg occupying a commanding or preeminent position **3** a large American butterfly with orange-brown wings with black veins and borders ☞ DEFENCE [LL *monarcha*, fr Gk *monarchos*, fr *mon-* + *-archos* -arch] – **monarchal** /mə'nahkl/, **monarchial** /-ki·əl/, **monarchic** /-kik/, **monarchical** *adj*

monarchism /'monə,kiz(ə)m/ *n* government by or the principles of monarchy – **monarchist** *n or adj*, **monarchistic** /-'kistik/ *adj*

monarchy /'monəki/ *n* (a government or state with) undivided rule by a monarch

monastery /'monəst(ə)ri/ *n* a residence occupied by a religious community, esp of monks [ME *monasterie*, fr LL *monasterium*, fr LGk *monastērion*, fr Gk, hermit's cell, fr *monazein* to live alone, fr *monos* single – more at MONK]

monastic /mə'nastik/ *adj* of or being monasteries, monks, or nuns – **monastic** *n*, **monastically** *adv*, **monasticism** /-sti,siz(ə)m/ *n*

monatomic /monə'tomik/ *adj* **1** consisting of (molecules containing) 1 atom **2** having 1 replaceable atom or radical ⟨~ *alcohols*⟩ – **monatomically** *adv*

monazite /'monəziet/ *n* a mineral that is a phosphate of cerium and lanthanum and often contains thorium [G *monazit*, fr Gk *monazein*]

Monday /'munday, -di/ *n* the day of the week following Sunday ☞ SYMBOL [ME, fr OE *mōnandæg*; akin to OHG *mānatag* Monday; both fr a prehistoric WGmc compound whose components are represented by OE *mōna* moon and by OE *dæg* day] – **Mondays** *adv*

monecious /mə'neeshəs, mo-/ *adj, NAm* monoecious

monetarism /'munitə,riz(ə)m/ *n* an economic theory that the most effective way of controlling the economy is by controlling only the supply of money – **monetarist** *n or adj*

monetary /'munit(ə)ri/ *adj* of money or its behaviour in an economy [LL *monetarius* of a mint, of money, fr L *moneta*] – **monetarily** /'munit(ə)rəli/ *adv*

money /'muni/ *n, pl* **moneys, monies** **1** sthg generally accepted as a means of payment; *esp* officially printed, coined, or stamped currency ☞ NATIONALITY **2** (one who has) wealth reckoned in terms of money ⟨*she refused to marry* ~⟩ **3** a form or denomination of coin or paper money **4** the first, second, and third places in a race on whose result money is betted – usu in *in/out of the money* [ME *moneye*, fr MF *moneie*, fr L *moneta* mint, money – more at ¹MINT]

moneybags /'muni,bagz/ *n, pl* **moneybags** a wealthy person – derog

'money ,box *n* a container for small personal savings, usu with a slot for the insertion of coins

'money ,changer *n* one whose occupation is the exchanging of kinds or denominations of currency

moneyed, monied /'munid/ *adj* **1** having much money **2** consisting of or derived from money

moneyer /'muni·ə/ *n* a minter [ME, fr OF *monier*, fr LL *monetarius* master of a mint, coiner, fr *monetarius* of a mint]

'money ,grubber *n* a person sordidly bent on accumulating money – infml – **money-grubbing** *adj or n*

'money,lender /-,lendə/ *n* one whose business is lending money and charging interest on it

'money-,maker *n* a product or enterprise that produces much profit – **moneymaking** *adj or n*

'money ,spider *n* a small spider supposed to bring luck to the person on whom it crawls

'money-,spinner *n, chiefly Br* a money-maker – infml – **money-spinning** *adj or n*

'money,wort /-,wuht/ *n* CREEPING JENNY

monger /ˈmung·gə/ *n* **1** a trader or dealer ⟨*ale*-monger⟩ **2** one who attempts to stir up or spread sthg petty or discreditable ⟨*gossip*monger⟩ ⟨*war*monger⟩ *USE* usu in combination [ME *mongere*, fr OE *mangere*, fr L *mangon-, mango*, of Gk origin; akin to Gk *manganon* charm, philtre – more at MANGONEL]

mongo /ˈmong·goh/ *n, pl* **mongo** ☞ *Mongolia* at NATIONALITY [Mongolian]

Mongol /ˈmong,gol, ˈmong·gl/ *n* **1** a member of any of the chiefly pastoral peoples of Mongolia **2** MONGOLIAN 2 **3** a person of Mongoloid racial stock **4** *often not cap* a sufferer from Down's syndrome [Mongolian *Mongol*] – **Mongol** *adj*

Mongolian /mongˈgohlyən, -li·ən/ *n* **1a** MONGOL 1, 3 **b** a native or inhabitant of Mongolia or of the Mongolian People's Republic **2** the language of the Mongol people ☞ ALPHABET, LANGUAGE – **Mongolian** *adj*

mongolism /ˈmong·g(ə)l,iz(ə)m/ *n* DOWN'S SYNDROME

Mongoloid /ˈmong·g(ə)loyd/, **Mongolic** /mongˈgolik/ *adj* **1** (characteristic) of or constituting a major racial stock including peoples of N and E Asia, Malaysians, Eskimos, and often American Indians **2** *not cap* of or suffering from Down's syndrome – **Mongoloid** *n*

mongoose /ˈmong,goohs/ *n, pl* **mongooses** *also* **mongeese** /-,gees/ an agile ferret-sized esp Indian mammal that feeds on snakes and rodents and is related to the civets [Hindi *māgūs*, fr Prakrit *maṅguso*]

mongrel /ˈmong·grəl, ˈmung-/ *n* a dog or other individual (of unknown ancestry) resulting from the interbreeding of diverse breeds [prob fr ME *mong* mixture, short for *ymong*, fr OE *gemong* crowd – more at AMONG] – **mongrel, mongrelly** *adj*, **mongrelize** *vt*, **mongrelization** /-lie ˈzaysh(ə)n/ *n*

monied /ˈmunid/ *adj* moneyed

monies /ˈmuniz/ *pl of* MONEY

moniker, monicker /ˈmunikə/ *n* a name, nickname – slang [origin unknown]

moniliasis /,mohniˈlie·əsis, ,mo-/ *n, pl* **moniliases** /-seez/ candidiasis; *specif* thrush [NL, fr *Monilia*, genus of fungi, fr L *monile* necklace]

moniliform /moˈnili,fawm/ *adj* shaped like a string of beads ⟨~ *insect antennae*⟩ [L *monile* necklace – more at MANE] – **moniliformly** *adv*

monism /ˈmoh,niz(ə)m, ˈmo-/ *n* **1** a doctrine that a complex entity (e g the universe) is basically a single unit **2** a doctrine that asserts the identity of mind and matter [G *monismus*, fr *mon-* + *-ismus* -ism] – **monist** *n*, **monistic** /-ˈnistik/, **monistical** *adj*

[1]**monitor** /ˈmonitə/, *fem* **monitress** /ˈmonitris/ *n* **1a** a pupil appointed to help a teacher **b** sby or sthg that monitors or is used in monitoring: e g **(1)** a receiver used to view the picture being picked up by a television camera **(2)** a device for observing a biological condition or function ⟨*a heart* ~⟩ **2** any of various large tropical Old World lizards closely related to the iguanas **3** a small warship with guns heavy in relation to its size [L, one who warns, overseer, fr *monitus*, pp of *monēre* to warn – more at MIND; (3) *Monitor*, first ship of the type] – **monitorship** *n*, **monitorial** /,moniˈtawri·əl/ *adj*

[2]**monitor** *vt* **1** to keep (a broadcast) under surveillance by means of a receiver, in order to check the quality or fidelity to a frequency or to investigate the content (e g for political significance) **2** to observe or inspect, esp for a special purpose **3** to regulate or control the operation of (e g a machine or process)

monitory /ˈmonit(ə)ri/ *adj* warning, admonitory – fml [L *monitorius*, fr *monitus*]

monk /mungk/ *n* a male member of a religious order, living apart from the world under vows of poverty, chastity, etc [ME, fr OE *munuc*, fr LL *monachus*, fr LGk *monachos*, fr Gk, adj, single, fr *monos* single, alone; akin to OHG *mengen* to lack, Gk *manos* sparse] – **monkhood** /-hood/ *n*

[1]**monkey** /ˈmungki/ *n* **1** any (small long-tailed) primate mammal with the exception of the human beings and usu also the lemurs and tarsiers ☞ EVOLUTION **2** the falling weight of a pile driver **3a** a mischievous child; a scamp **b** a ludicrous figure; a fool ⟨*made a* ~ *of him*⟩ **4** £500 or $500 – slang *USE* (*3*) infml [prob of LG origin; akin to *Moneke*, name of an ape, prob of Romance origin; akin to OSp *mona* monkey]

[2]**monkey** *vi* **1** to act in an absurd or mischievous manner **2** TAMPER 2 – usu + *with USE* infml; often + *about* or *around*

ˈ**monkey ,business** *n* mischievous or underhand activity – infml

ˈ**monkey ,jacket** *n* a short fitted uniform jacket reaching to the waist

ˈ**monkey ,nut** *n* PEANUT 1

ˈ**monkey-,puzzle** *n* a commonly planted S American evergreen gymnospermous tree with intertwined branches and stiff sharp leaves

ˈ**monkey ,wrench** *n* a large spanner with one fixed and one adjustable jaw

monkfish /ˈmungk,fish/ *n* any of various flat fishes closely related to the sharks and rays

monkish /ˈmungkish/ *adj* practising strict self-denial; ascetic – often derog [MONK + -ISH]

monkshood /ˈmungks,hood/ *n* a very poisonous Eurasian plant often cultivated for its showy spikes of white or purplish flowers

mono /ˈmonoh/ *adj or n* monophonic (sound reproduction)

mono- – see MON-

monobasic /,monohˈbaysik/ *adj* having only 1 replaceable hydrogen atom in each molecule [ISV]

monocarpic /,monohˈkahpik/ *adj, of a plant* bearing fruit only once and then dying [prob fr (assumed) NL *monocarpicus*, fr NL *mon-* + *-carpicus* -carpic]

monochord /ˈmonə,kawd/ *n* an instrument that is used for measuring and demonstrating the mathematical relations of musical notes [ME *monocorde*, fr MF, fr ML *monochordum*, fr Gk *monochordon*, fr *mon-* + *chordē* string – more at YARN]

monochromatic /,monəkrəˈmatik/ *adj* **1** having or consisting of 1 colour or hue **2** consisting of radiation of a single wavelength [L *monochromatos*, fr Gk *monochrōmatos*, fr *mon-* + *chrōmat-, chrōma* colour – more at CHROMATIC] – **monochromatically** *adv*, **monochromaticity** /,monə,krohməˈtisəti/ *n*

monochrome /ˈmonə,krohm/ *adj or n* (of, using, or being) reproduction or execution in 1 colour, black and white, or shades of grey [ML *monochroma*, fr L, fem of *monochromos* of one colour, fr Gk *monochrōmos*, fr *mon-* + *-chrōmos* -chrome] – **monochromist** /-,krohmist/ *n*, **monochromic** /-ˈkrohmik/ *adj*

monocle /'monəkl/ *n* an eyeglass for 1 eye [F, fr LL *monoculus* having one eye, fr L *mon-* + *oculus* eye – more at EYE] – **monocled** /'monək(ə)ld/ *adj*

monoclinal /,monoh'klienl/ *adj* (relating to strata, a fold, etc) having a single oblique inclination – **monoclinal** *n*

monocline /'monə,klien/ *n* a monoclinal geological fold

monoclinic /,monə'klinik/ *adj* having or being a system of crystal structure characterized by 3 unequal axes only 2 of which are at right angles to each other [ISV]

monocoque /'monə,kok/ *n* **1** a type of construction (e g of a fuselage) in which the outer skin carries (nearly) all the stresses **2** a type of vehicle construction in which the body is integral with the chassis [F, fr *mon-* + *coque* shell, fr L *coccum* excrescence on a tree, fr Gk *kokkos* berry]

monocot /'monə,kot/ *n* a monocotyledon

monocotyledon /,monə,koti'leedn/ *n* any of various plants of a group comprising all those with a single cotyledon and usu parallel-veined leaves (e g the grasses, orchids, and lilies) ☞ PLANT [deriv of NL *mon-* + *cotyledon*] – **monocotyledonous** *adj*

monocular /mo'nokyoolə/ *adj* of, involving, affecting, or suitable for use with only 1 eye [LL *monoculus* having one eye] – **monocularly** *adv*

monoculture /'monə,kulchə/ *n* the cultivation of a single agricultural product to the exclusion of other uses of the land – **monocultural** /-'kulchərəl/ *adj*

monocyte /'monə,siet/ *n* a large white blood cell that is present in small numbers in the blood and defends the body by engulfing and digesting invading or unwanted matter – compare LYMPHOCYTE ☞ ANATOMY [ISV] – **monocytic** /-'sitik/ *adj*

monody /'monədi/ *n* **1** an ode sung by 1 voice, esp in a Greek tragedy **2** a poem lamenting sby's death [ML *monodia*, fr Gk *monōidia*, fr *monōidos* singing alone, fr *mon-* + *aidein* to sing – more at ODE] – **monodist** *n*, **monodic** /mə'nodik/, **monodical** *adj*, **monodically** *adv*

monoecious, *NAm also* **monecious** /mə'neeshəs, mo-/ *adj* hermaphroditic; *esp* having female and male flowers on the same plant – compare DIOECIOUS [deriv of Gk *mon-* + *oikos* house – more at VICINITY] – **monoeciously** *adv*, **monoecism** /mə'nee,siz(ə)m/ *n*

monoestrous /mə'neestrəs, mo-/ *n* experiencing oestrus once each year; having a single annual breeding period

monofilament /,monə'filəmənt/ *n* a single untwisted synthetic filament (e g of nylon)

monogamy /mə'nogəmi/ *n* the state or custom of being married to 1 person at a time [F *monogamie*, fr LL *monogamia*, fr Gk, fr *monogamos* monogamous, fr *mon-* + *gamos* marriage – more at BIGAMY] – **monogamist** *n*, **monogamous** *adj*, **monogamously** *adv*, **monogamic** /,monə'gamik/ *adj*

monogenesis /,monə'jenəsis/ *n* unity of origin (e g of all languages from an original language) [NL] – **monogenetic** /-jə'netik/ *adj*, **monogeny** /mə'nojəni/ *n*

monogerm /'monə,juhm/ *adj* producing or being a fruit that gives rise to a single plant ⟨*a ~ variety of sugar beet*⟩ [*mon-* + *germ*inate] – **monogermity** /-'juhməti/ *n*

monogram /'monə,gram/ *vt or n* (to mark with) a character usu formed of the interwoven initials of a name [n LL *monogramma*, fr Gk *mon-* + *gramma* letter – more at ²GRAM; vb fr n] – **monogrammatic** /-grə'matik/ *adj*

monograph /'monə,grahf, -,graf/ *n* a treatise on a small area of learning – **monographic** /-'grafik/ *adj*

monogyny /mə'nojəni/ *n* the state or custom of having only 1 wife at a time [ISV] – **monogynous** *adj*

monohybrid /,monoh'hiebrid/ *n or adj* (an organism, cell, etc) having 2 different versions of 1 gene

monohydric /,monoh'hiedrik/ *adj* containing 1 atom of acid hydrogen or 1 hydroxyl group in the molecular structure

monolayer /'monoh,layə/ *n* a single continuous layer 1 cell or molecule in thickness

monolingual /,monoh'ling·gwəl/ *adj* knowing or using only 1 language – **monolingual** *n*

monolith /'monə,lith/ *n* **1** a single large block of stone, often in the form of an obelisk or column **2** a massive structure **3** an organized whole that acts as a single powerful force [F *monolithe*, fr *monolithe* consisting of a single stone, fr L *monolithus*, fr Gk *monolithos*, fr *mon-* + *lithos* stone]

monolithic /,monə'lithik/ *adj* **1** formed from or produced in or on a single crystal ⟨*a ~ silicon chip*⟩ **2** constituting a massive uniform whole ⟨*the ~ totalitarian state*⟩ [MONOLITH + ¹-IC] – **monolithically** *adv*

monologue, *NAm also* **monolog** /'monə,log/ *n* **1** a dramatic or literary soliloquy; *also* a dramatic sketch performed by 1 speaker **2** a long speech monopolizing conversation [F *monologue*, fr *mon-* + *-logue* (as in *dialogue*)] – **monologuist** /mə'noləgist/, **monologist** /-jist, -gist/ *n*

monomania /,monoh'maynyə/ *n* obsessional concentration on a single object or idea [NL] – **monomaniac** /-'mayniak/ *n or adj*

monomer /'monəmə/ *n* a chemical compound that can undergo polymerization; a single unit of a polymer [ISV *mon-* + *-mer* (as in *polymer*)] – **monomeric** /,monə'merik/ *adj*

monomial /mo'nohmi·əl/ *n or adj* (a mathematical expression) consisting of a single term [blend of *mon-* and *-nomial* (as in *binomial*)]

monomolecular /,monohmə'lekyoolə/ *adj* (of a layer) only 1 molecule thick ⟨*a ~ film*⟩ – **monomolecularly** *adv*

mononucleosis /,monoh,nyoohkli'ohsis/ *n* INFECTIOUS MONONUCLEOSIS

mononucleotide /,monoh'nyoohkli·ə,tied/ *n* a nucleotide, esp as contrasted with a polynucleotide

monophonic /,monoh'fonik/ *adj* of or being a system for sound reproduction in which the sound signal is not split into 2 or more different channels between the source and the point of use – **monophonically** *adv*

monophthong /'monəf,thong/ *n* a simple nongliding vowel sound (e g /i/ in *bid*) [LGk *monophthongos* single vowel, fr Gk *mon-* + *phthongos* sound] – **monophthongal** /-'thong·gl/ *adj*

monoplane /'monə,playn/ *n* an aeroplane with only 1 main pair of wings

monopole /'monə,pohl/ *n* a radio aerial consisting of a single usu straight radiating element

monopolist /mo'nopəlist/ *n* one who has or favours a monopoly – **monopolistic** /-'listik/ *adj*

monopol·ize, -ise /mə'nopəliez/ *vt* to get a monopoly of; assume complete possession or control of – **monopolizer** *n*, **monopolization** /-'zaysh(ə)n/ *n*

monopoly /mə'nopəli/ *n* **1** (a person or group having) exclusive ownership or control (through legal privilege, command of the supply of a commodity, concerted action, etc) **2** sthg, esp a commodity, controlled by one party [L *monopolium*, fr Gk *monopōlion*, fr *mon-* + *pōlein* to sell]

monorail /'monoh,rayl/ *n* (a vehicle running on) a single rail serving as a track for a wheeled vehicle

monosaccharide /,monoh'sakəried/ *n* a sugar (e g glucose) not decomposable to simpler sugars [ISV]

monosodium glutamate /,monə,sohdi·əm 'gloohtəmayt/ *n* a salt of glutamic acid used for seasoning foods

monosyllable /'monə,siləbl/ *n* a word of 1 syllable; *specif* one used by sby intending to be pointedly brief in answering or commenting [modif of MF or LL; MF *monosyllabe*, fr LL *monosyllabon*, fr Gk, fr neut of *monosyllabos* having one syllable, fr *mon-* + *syllabē* syllable] – **monosyllabic** /-si'labik/ *adj*, **monosyllabically** *adv*

monotheism /'monohthee,iz(ə)m/ *n* the doctrine or belief that there is only 1 God – **monotheist** /-,thee·ist/ *n*, **monotheistic** /-'istik/ *adj*

[1]**monotone** /'monə,tohn/ *n* **1** a succession of speech sounds in 1 unvarying pitch **2** a single unvaried musical note **3** a tedious sameness or repetition [Gk *monotonos* monotonous]

[2]**monotone** *adj* **1** having a uniform colour **2** MONOTONIC 2

monotonic /,monə'tonik/ *adj* **1** uttered in a monotone **2** *of a mathematical function* increasing continuously or decreasing continuously as the independent variable increases – **monotonically** *adv*

monotonous /mə'not(ə)nəs/ *adj* **1** uttered or sounded in 1 unvarying tone **2** tediously uniform or repetitive [Gk *monotonos*, fr *mon-* + *tonos* tone] – **monotonously** *adv*, **monotonousness, monotony** *n*

monotreme /'monoh,treem/ *n* any of an order of lower mammals comprising the platypus and echidna [NL *Monotremata*, group name, fr Gk *mon-* + *trēmat-*, *trēma* hole – more at TREMATODE] – **monotrematous** /-'treemətəs, -'tremətəs/ *adj*

monotype /'monə,tiep/ *n* an impression on paper taken from a painting on glass or metal

Monotype *trademark* – used for a keyboard-operated typesetting machine that casts and sets metal type in separate characters

monovalent /,monoh'vaylənt/ *adj* UNIVALENT 1 [ISV]

monozygotic /,monohzie'gotik/ *adj* IDENTICAL 3

Mon'roe ,Doctrine /mən'roh, mun-/ *n* a statement of US foreign policy expressing opposition to extension of European influence in the western hemisphere [James *Monroe* †1831 US President]

monsieur /mə'syuh/ *n, pl* **messieurs** /me'syuh, mə'syuhz/ – used by or to a French-speaking man as a title equivalent to Mr or without a name as a term of direct address [MF, lit., my lord]

monsignor /,monsin'yaw/ *n, pl* **monsignors, monsignori** /-ri/ – used as a title for certain Roman Catholic prelates and officers of the papal court [It *monsignore*, fr F *monseigneur*] – **monsignorial** /-ri·əl/ *adj*

monsoon /mon'soohn/ *n* **1** a seasonal wind of S Asia blowing from the SW in summer and the NE in winter **2** the season of the SW monsoon, marked by very heavy rains [obs D *monssoen*, fr Pg *monção*, fr Ar *mawsim* time, season] – **monsoonal** *adj*

monster /'monstə/ *n* **1a** an animal or plant of (grotesquely) abnormal form or structure **b** an (imaginary) animal of incredible shape or form that is usu dangerous or horrifying **2** one exceptionally large for its kind ⟨~ *tomatoes*⟩ **3** sthg monstrous; *esp* a person of appalling ugliness, wickedness, or cruelty [ME *monstre*, fr MF, fr L *monstrum* omen, monster, prob fr *monēre* to warn, remind]

monstrance /'monstrəns/ *n* a vessel in which the consecrated Host is exposed for veneration, esp in a Catholic church [MF, fr ML *monstrantia*, fr L *monstrant-*, *monstrans*, prp of *monstrare* to show – more at MUSTER]

monstrosity /mon'strosəti/ *n* **1** MONSTER 1a **2** (the quality or state of being) sthg monstrous

monstrous /'monstrəs/ *adj* **1** having the qualities or appearance of a monster; extraordinarily large **2a** extraordinarily ugly or vicious **b** outrageously wrong or ridiculous – **monstrously** *adv*, **monstrousness** *n*

mons veneris /,monz 'venəris/ *n, pl* **montes veneris** /'monteez/ a rounded raised mass of fatty tissue over the pubic bone and above the vulva of the human female [NL, lit., hill of Venus or of venery]

montage /monh'tahzh/ *n* **1a** a picture made by combining or overlapping several separate pictures **b** an artistic composition made from different materials combined or juxtaposed **2** (a film sequence using) a method of film editing in which the chronological sequence of events is interrupted by juxtaposed or rapidly succeeding shots [F, fr *monter* to mount]

montane /'montayn/ *adj* of, being, or growing or living in the area of cool slopes just below the tree line on mountains [L *montanus* of a mountain – more at MOUNTAIN]

montbretia /mon(t)'breesh(y)ə/ *n* a widely grown hybrid plant of the iris family with bright yellow or orange flowers [NL, fr A F E Coquebert de *Montbret* †1801 F naturalist]

Montessorian /,monti'sawri·ən/ *adj* of or being a system of teaching young children through play [Maria *Montessori* †1952 It physician & educator]

month /munth/ *n* **1a** any of the 12 divisions of the year in the Julian or Gregorian calendars corresponding roughly with the period of the moon's rotation; *also* any similar division of the year in other calendars **b** 28 days or 4 weeks; *also* the interval between the same date in adjacent months **2** *pl* an indefinite usu protracted period of time ⟨*he's been gone for* ~s⟩ **3** a ninth of the typical duration of human pregnancy ⟨*in her 8th* ~⟩ [ME, fr OE *mōnath*; akin to OHG *mānōd* month, OE *mōna* moon] – **monthly** *adv or adj*

[2]**monthly** /-li/ *n* **1** a monthly periodical **2** *pl* a menstrual period – infml

monticule /'montikyoohl/ *n* a small elevation or prominence; *esp* a subordinate cone of a volcano [F, fr LL *monticulus*, dim. of L *mont-*, *mons* mountain – more at [1]MOUNT]

Montilla /mon'tilə/ *n* a typically dry unfortified white wine made in the Córdoba area of Spain that resembles sherry [Sp, fr *Montilla*, town in Spain]

monument /'monyoomənt/ *n* **1** a written record **2a** a lasting evidence or reminder of sby or sthg notable or influential **b** a memorial stone, sculpture, or structure erected to commemorate a person or event **3** a structure or site of historical or archaeological importance [ME, fr L *monumentum*, lit., memorial, fr *monēre* to remind – more at MIND]

monumental /ˌmonyooˈmentl/ *adj* **1a** of, serving as, or resembling a monument **b** occurring or used on a monument ⟨*a ~ inscription*⟩ **2** very great in degree; imposing, outstanding ⟨*their ~ arrogance*⟩ ⟨*a ~ work*⟩ – **monumentally** *adv*

moo /mooh/ *vi or n* [1]LOW [imit]

mooch /moohch/ *vi* **1** to wander aimlessly or disconsolately – usu + *around, about*, or *along* **2** *NAm* to sponge, cadge ~ *vt*, *NAm* **1** to steal; MAKE OFF WITH **2** to cadge, beg *USE* infml [prob fr F dial. *muchier* to hide, lurk] – **moocher** *n*

[1]**mood** /moohd/ *n* **1a** (the evocation, esp in art or literature, of) a predominant emotion, feeling, or frame of mind **b** the right frame of mind ⟨*you must be in the ~, or you'll fall asleep – The Listener*⟩ **2** a fit of often silent anger or bad temper **3** a prevailing attitude [ME, fr OE *mōd*; akin to OHG *muot* mood, L *mos* will, custom]

[2]**mood** *n* a distinct form or set of inflectional forms of a verb indicating whether the action or state it denotes is considered a fact, wish, possibility, etc ⟨*the subjunctive ~*⟩ [alter. of [1]*mode*]

moody /ˈmoohdi/ *adj* **1** sullen or gloomy **2** temperamental – **moodily** *adv*, **moodiness** *n*

Moog /moohg/, **Moog synthesizer** *trademark* – used for a musical synthesizer

[1]**moon** /moohn/ *n* **1a** (the appearance or visibility from the earth of) the earth's natural satellite that shines by reflecting the sun's light ⟨*there is a ~ tonight*⟩ ☞ SYMBOL **b** a satellite **2** LUNAR MONTH – poetic *USE* (*1*) ☞ ASTRONOMY [ME *mone*, fr OE *mōna*; akin to OHG *māno* moon, L *mensis* month, Gk *mēn* month, *mēnē* moon] – **moonless** *adj*, **moonlet** *n*, **moonlike** *adj* – **over the moon** absolutely delighted

[2]**moon** *vi* **1** to move about listlessly **2** to spend time in idle gazing or daydreaming *USE* often + *around* or *about*; infml

ˈmoonˌbeam /-ˌbeem/ *n* a ray of light from the moon

ˈmoonˌcalf /-ˌkahf/ *n* MONSTER 1a

ˈmoonˌfish /-ˌfish/ *n, pl* **moonfish, moonfishes** an opah

moonie /ˈmoohni/ *n, often cap* a member of a religious sect, founded in 1954 by Sun Myung Moon, whose adherents live in communes, donate all their possessions to the movement, and believe that the founder has been given a divine mission to complete the task, orig given to Adam and then to Christ, of uniting the whole world in a perfect sinless family [Sun Myung *Moon b* 1920 Korean industrialist & religious leader]

ˈmoonˌlight /-ˌliet/ *vi* **moonlighted** to hold a second job in addition to a regular one [back-formation fr *moonlighter* one whose activities are done at night] – **moonlighter** *n*

ˈmoonˌlit /-ˌlit/ *adj* lighted (as if) by the moon

ˈmoonˌquake /-ˌkwayk/ *n* a ground tremor on the moon

ˈmoonˌrat /-ˌrat/ *n* an insect-eating mammal of SE Asia

ˈmoonˌshine /-ˌshien/ *n* **1** the light of the moon **2** empty talk; nonsense **3** (illegally distilled) spirits, esp whisky – infml

ˈmoonˌshiner /-ˌshienə/ *n, NAm* a maker or seller of illicit spirits

ˈmoonˌstone /-ˌstohn/ *n* a transparent or translucent opalescent feldspar used as a gem

ˈmoonˌstruck /-ˌstruk/ *adj* affected (as if) by the moon; *specif* mentally unbalanced

moony /ˈmoohni/ *adj* inanely dreamy; moonstruck – infml [[1]MOON + [1]-Y]

[1]**moor** /maw, mooə/ *n, chiefly Br* an expanse of open peaty infertile usu heath-covered upland [ME *mor*, fr OE *mōr*; akin to OHG *meri* sea – more at MARINE]

[2]**moor** *vt* to make (e g a boat or buoy) fast with cables, lines, or anchors ~ *vi* **1** to secure a vessel by mooring **2** to be made fast [ME *moren*; akin to MD *meren*, *maren* to tie, moor]

Moor *n* a member of the mixed Arab and Berber people that conquered Spain in the 8th c AD [ME *More*, fr MF, fr L *Maurus* inhabitant of Mauretania, ancient country of N Africa] – **Moorish** *adj*

moorage /ˈmawrij, ˈmooərij/ *n* a place to moor [[2]MOOR + -AGE]

moorhen /ˈmawˌhen, ˈmooə-/ *n* a common red-billed blackish bird of the rail family that nests near fresh water

mooring /ˈmawring, ˈmooəring/ *n* **1** a place where or an object to which a ship, boat, etc can be made fast **2** the lines, chains, anchors, etc used to make a ship, boat, etc fast ⟨*she may have dragged her* ~s⟩ **3** moral principles used as a guide to behaviour ⟨*lose one's* ~s⟩ *USE* usu pl with sing. meaning [[2]MOOR + [2]-ING]

moose /moohs/ *n, pl* **moose 1** a large N American ruminant mammal of the deer family with very large flattened antlers **2** the European elk [of Algonquian origin; akin to Natick *moos* moose]

[1]**moot** /mooht/ *n* **1** an early English assembly to decide points of community and political interest **2** a mock court in which law students argue hypothetical cases [ME, fr OE *mōt*; akin to OE *mētan* to meet – more at [1]MEET]

[2]**moot** *vt* to put forward for discussion ⟨*the idea was first* ~ed *years ago*⟩

[3]**moot** *adj* open to question; debatable – usu in *moot point*

[1]**mop** /mop/ *n* **1** an implement consisting of a head made of absorbent material fastened to a long handle and used esp for cleaning floors **2** (sthg like) a shock of untidy hair [ME *mappe*, perh deriv of L *mappa* napkin, towel]

[2]**mop** *vt* **-pp- 1** to clean (a floor or other surface) with a mop **2** to wipe (as if) with a mop ⟨~ped *his brow with a handkerchief*⟩ – **mopper** *n*

mope /mohp/ *vi* to give oneself up to brooding; become listless or dejected [prob fr obs *mop, mope* (fool)] – **moper** *n*

moped /ˈmohped/ *n* a low-powered motorcycle whose engine can be pedal-assisted (e g for starting) [Sw, fr *mo*tor motor + *ped*al pedal]

mopes /mohps/ *n pl but sing or pl in constr* the blues or low spirits

moppet /ˈmopit/ *n* a young child; *esp* a little girl – chiefly infml; apprec [obs *mop* (fool, child)]

mop up *vt* **1** to eliminate remaining resistance in (e g a previously occupied area in a war) **2** to absorb, take up, or deal with (esp a remnant or remainder) ~ *vi* to complete a project or transaction – **mop-up** /'-,-/ *n*

moquette /mo'ket/ *n* a carpet or upholstery fabric with a velvety pile [F]

mor /maw/ *n* a humus usu in forests that forms a distinct layer above the underlying soil [Dan]

moraine /mo'rayn/ *n* an accumulation of earth and stones carried and deposited by a glacier ☞ GEOGRAPHY [F] – **morainal, morainic** *adj*

[1]**moral** /'morəl/ *adj* **1a** of or being principles of right and wrong in conduct; ethical **b** expressing or teaching a conception of right conduct ⟨*a ~ poem*⟩ **c** conforming to a standard of right conduct ⟨*a ~ person*⟩ **d** sanctioned by, resulting from, or operative on one's conscience or (correct) moral judgment ⟨*a ~ obligation*⟩ ⟨*a ~ right*⟩ **e** capable of distinguishing right and wrong ⟨*man is a ~ being*⟩ **2** very probable though not proved ⟨*a ~ certainty*⟩ **3** of, occurring in, or acting on the mind, emotions, or will ⟨*a ~ victory*⟩ ⟨*~ support*⟩ [ME, fr MF, fr L *moralis*, fr *mor-*, *mos* custom – more at [1]MOOD] – **morally** *adv*

[2]**moral** *n* **1** (a concluding passage pointing out) the moral significance or practical lesson **2** *pl* **a** moral practices or teachings; standards of esp sexual conduct ⟨*a man of loose ~*s⟩ **b** ethics

morale /mə'rahl/ *n* the mental and emotional condition (e g of enthusiasm or loyalty) of an individual or group with regard to the function or tasks at hand [modif of F *moral*, fr *moral*, adj]

moralism /'morə,liz(ə)m/ *n* **1** a conventional moral attitude or saying **2** an often exaggerated emphasis on moral rectitude

moralist /'morəlist/ *n* **1** one concerned with moral principles and problems **2** one concerned with regulating the morals of others – often derog – **moralistic** /-'listik/ *adj*, **moralistically** *adv*

morality /mə'raləti/ *n* **1** a system or sphere of moral conduct ⟨*Christian ~*⟩ **2** (degree of conformity to standards of) right conduct or moral correctness ⟨*questioned the ~ of his act*⟩

mo'rality ,play *n* a form of allegorical drama popular esp in the 15th and 16th c in which the characters personify moral or abstract qualities (e g pride or youth)

moral·ize, -ise /'morəliez/ *vt* **1** to interpret morally; draw a moral from **2** to make moral or morally better ~ *vi* to make moral reflections – **moralizer** *n*, **moralization** /-lie'zaysh(ə)n/ *n*

,moral phi'losophy *n* ethics

morass /mə'ras/ *n* **1** a marsh, swamp **2** sthg that ensnares, confuses, or impedes [D *moeras*, modif of OF *maresc*, of Gmc origin; akin to OE *mersc* marsh – more at MARSH] – **morassy** *adj*

moratorium /,morə'tawri·əm/ *n, pl* **moratoriums, moratoria** /-ri·ə/ **1** a legally authorized delay in the performance of an obligation or the payment of a debt **2** a suspension of (a specified) activity – usu + *on* [NL, fr LL, neut of *moratorius* dilatory, fr L *moratus*, pp of *morari* to delay, fr *mora* delay]

Moravian /mə'rayvi·ən/ *n* **1** a member of a Protestant denomination derived from the Hussite movement for religious reform in Bohemia and Moravia **2a** a native or inhabitant of Moravia **b** the group of Czech dialects spoken by the Moravians [*Moravia*, former province of Czechoslovakia] – **Moravian** *adj*

morbid /'mawbid/ *adj* **1** of, affected with, induced by, or characteristic of disease ⟨*~ anatomy*⟩ **2** abnormally susceptible to or characterized by gloomy feelings; *esp* having an unnatural preoccupation with death **3** grisly, gruesome ⟨*~ curiosity*⟩ [L *morbidus* diseased, fr *morbus* disease; akin to Gk *marainein* to waste away – more at SMART] – **morbidly** *adv*, **morbidness** *n*

morbidity /maw'bidəti/ *n* the relative incidence of (a) disease [MORBID + -ITY]

mordacious /maw'dayshəs/ *adj* **1** MORDANT 1 **2** given to biting *USE* fml [L *mordac-*, *mordax* biting, fr *mordēre* to bite – more at SMART] – **mordacity** /maw'dasəti/ *n*

[1]**mordant** /'mawd(ə)nt/ *adj* **1** caustic or sharply critical in thought, manner, or style ⟨*~ wit*⟩ **2** acting as a mordant **3** burning, pungent [MF, prp of *mordre* to bite, fr L *mordēre*] – **mordancy** *n*, **mordantly** *adv*

[2]**mordant** *n* **1** a chemical that fixes a dye by combining with it to form an insoluble compound **2** a corroding substance used in etching

mordent /'mawd(ə)nt/ *n* a musical ornament made by a quick alternation of a principal note with either of the immediately adjacent notes ☞ MUSIC [It *mordente*, fr L *mordent-*, *mordens*, prp of *mordēre*]

[1]**more** /maw/ *adj* **1** greater in quantity or number ⟨*something ~ than she expected*⟩ ⟨*7 is 2 ~ than 5*⟩ **2** additional, further ⟨*three ~ guests arrived*⟩ ⟨*have some ~ tea*⟩ ⟨*what ~ do you want?*⟩ [ME, fr OE *māra*; akin to OE *mā*, adv, more, OHG *mēr*, OIr *mōr* large] – **neither/nothing more or/nor less than** simply, plainly

[2]**more** *adv* **1a** as an additional amount ⟨*not much ~ to do*⟩ **b** moreover, again ⟨*summer is here once ~*⟩ **2** to a greater degree or extent ⟨*you should practise ~*⟩ ⟨*~ sad than angry*⟩ ⟨*costs ~ than making your own beer – SEU S*⟩ – often used with an adjective or adverb to form the comparative ⟨*much ~ evenly matched*⟩ – **more often than not** at most times; usually

[3]**more** *n, pl* **more** **1** a greater or additional quantity, amount, or part ⟨*hope to see ~ of her*⟩ ⟨*tell me ~*⟩ ⟨*~ than meets the eye*⟩ **2** *pl* additional ones ⟨*many ~ were found as the search continued*⟩ – **more of** nearer to being (sthg specified) ⟨*it's* more of *a sofa than a bed*⟩

,more and 'more *adv* to a progressively increasing degree

moreish *also* **more-ish** /'mawrish/ *adj* so tasty as to cause a desire for more – chiefly infml

morel /mo'rel/ *n* (a fungus related to) a large edible fungus with a light yellowish brown cap [F *morille*, of Gmc origin; akin to OHG *morhila* morel]

morello /mə'reloh/ *n, pl* **morellos** a cultivated red-skinned sour cherry used esp in jams [prob modif of Flem *amarelle*, *marelle*, fr ML *amarellum*, a cultivated cherry, fr L *amarus* sour]

,more or 'less *adv* **1** to some extent or degree; somewhat **2** almost, nearly

moreover /maw'rohvə/ *adv* in addition to what has been said – used to introduce new matter

mores /'mawreez/ *n pl* the (morally binding) customs or conventions of a particular group [L, pl of *mor-*, *mos* custom – more at [1]MOOD]

moresque /maw'resk/ *adj, often cap* typical of Moorish art or architecture [F, fr Sp *morisco*, fr *moro* Moor, fr L *Maurus*]

more than *adv* very, exceedingly ⟨*was ~ happy*⟩

morganatic /ˌmawgəˈnatik/ *adj* of or being a marriage between people of different rank in which the rank of the inferior partner remains unchanged and the children do not succeed to the titles or property of the parent of higher rank [NL *matrimonium ad morganaticam*, lit., marriage with morning gift] – **morganatically** *adv*

morganite /ˈmawgəniet/ *n* a rose-coloured beryl [J P *Morgan* †1913 US financier]

morgue /mawg/ *n* **1a** a mortuary **b** a gloomy dispiriting place **2** a collection of reference works and files in a newspaper office [F]

moribund /ˈmoriˌbund/ *adj* dying [L *moribundus*, fr *mori* to die – more at MURDER] – **moribundity** /-ˈbundəti/ *n*

morion /ˈmawri·ən/ *n* a high-crested helmet with no visor [MF]

Morisco /məˈriskoh/ *n, pl* **Moriscos, Moriscoes** a (Spanish) Moor [Sp, fr *morisco*, adj, fr *moro* Moor] – **Morisco** *adj*

Mormon /ˈmawmən/ *n* a member of the Church of Jesus Christ of Latter-Day Saints, founded in 1830 in the USA by Joseph Smith, and following precepts contained in the Book of Mormon, a sacred text that he discovered – **Mormonism** *n*

morn /mawn/ *n* the morning – chiefly poetic [ME, fr OE *morgen*; akin to OHG *morgan* morning, L *merus* pure, unmixed]

ˌmornay ˈsauce /ˈmawnay/ *n* a rich creamy cheese sauce [perh fr Philippe de *Mornay* †1623 F Huguenot leader]

morning /ˈmawning/ *n* **1a** the dawn **b** the time from midnight or sunrise to noon **2** an early period (e g of time or life); the beginning [ME, fr *morn* + *-ing* (as in *evening*)] – **in the morning** tomorrow morning

ˈmorning ˌcoat *n* a man's tailcoat that is worn on formal occasions during the day

ˈmorning ˌdress *n* men's dress for formal occasions (e g a wedding) during the day ☞ GARMENT

ˌmorning ˈglory *n* any of various usu twining plants of the bindweed family with showy trumpet-shaped flowers

ˌMorning ˈPrayer *n* a daily morning office of the Anglican church

ˈmornings *adv, chiefly NAm* in the morning; on any morning

ˈmorning ˌsickness *n* nausea and vomiting occurring esp in the morning during the earlier months of a woman's pregnancy

ˌmorning ˈstar *n* a bright planet, specif Venus, seen in the eastern sky before or at sunrise

Moro /ˈmawroh/ *n, pl* **Moros,** *esp collectively* **Moro** **1** a member of any of several Muslim peoples of the S Philippines **2** an Austronesian language of the Moro peoples ☞ LANGUAGE [Sp, lit., Moor, fr L *Maurus*]

morocco /məˈrokoh/ *n* a fine leather made from goatskin tanned with sumach [*Morocco*, country in N Africa]

moron /ˈmawron/ *n* **1** MENTAL DEFECTIVE **2** a very stupid person – infml [irreg fr Gk *mōros* foolish, stupid; akin to Skt *mūra* foolish] – **moronism** *n*, **moronic** /məˈronik/ *adj*

morose /məˈrohs/ *adj* (having a disposition) marked by or expressive of gloom [L *morosus*, lit., capricious, fr *mor-*, *mos* will – more at [1]MOOD] – **morosely** *adv*, **moroseness** *n*

morph /mawf/ *n* [2]ALLOMORPH [back-formation fr *morpheme*]

morph- /mawf-/, **morpho-** *comb form* form ⟨*morphogenesis*⟩ [G, fr Gk, fr *morphē*]

-morph /-mawf/ *comb form* (→ *n*) one having (such) a form ⟨*iso*morph⟩ [ISV, fr *-morphous*] – **-morphic, -morphous** *comb form* (→ *adj*), **-morphy** *comb form* (→ *n*)

morpheme /ˈmawfeem/ *n* a meaningful linguistic unit that contains no smaller meaningful parts and can be either a free form (e g *pin*) or a bound form (e g the *-s* of *pins*) ☞ ALPHABET [F *morphème*, fr Gk *morphē* form] – **morphemic** /mawˈfeemik/ *adj*

morphemics /mawˈfeemiks/ *n pl but sing in constr* the study of morphemes and esp of word structure

morphia /ˈmawfi·ə/ *n* morphine [NL, fr *Morpheus* Roman god of dreams & sleep]

morphine /ˈmawfeen/ *n* the principal alkaloid of opium that is an addictive narcotic drug used esp as a powerful painkiller [F, fr *Morpheus*] – **morphinism** *n*, **morphinic** /-ˈfeenik, -ˈfinik/ *adj*

-morphism /-ˈmawfiz(ə)m/ *comb form* (→ *n*) **1** quality or state of having (such) a form ⟨*hetero*morphism⟩ **2** conceptualization in (such) a form ⟨*anthropo*morphism⟩ [LL *-morphus* -morphous, fr Gk *-mor phos*]

morphogenesis /ˌmawfohˈjenəsis/ *n* the formation and differentiation of tissues and organs (during embryonic development) [NL] – **morphogenetic** /-jəˈnetik/ *adj*

morphology /mawˈfoləji/ *n* **1** (the biology of) the form and structure of animals and plants **2a** a study and description of word formation in a language including inflection, derivation, and compounding **b** the system of word-forming elements and processes in a language **3** (a study of) the structure or form of sthg [G *morphologie*, fr *morph-* + *-logie* -logy] – **morphologist** *n*, **morphological** /ˌmawfəˈlojikl/ *adj*

ˈmorris ˌdance /ˈmoris/ *n* any of several traditional English dances that are performed by groups of people wearing costumes to which small bells are attached [ME *moreys daunce*, fr *moreys* Moorish (fr *More* Moor) + *daunce* dance] – **morris dancer** *n*

morrow /ˈmoroh/ *n* **1** the next day – fml **2** *archaic* the morning [ME *morn, morwen* morn]

Morse /maws/, **ˌMorse ˈcode** *n* a signalling code consisting of dots and dashes used to send messages by light or by sound signals or esp by radio [Samuel *Morse* †1872 US artist & inventor] – **morse** *vb*

morsel /ˈmawsl/ *n* **1** a small piece of food **2** a small quantity; a scrap [ME, fr OF, dim. of *mors* bite, fr L *morsus*, fr *morsus*, pp of *mordēre* to bite – more at SMART]

mort /mawt/ *n* a note sounded on a hunting horn when a deer is killed [prob alter. of ME *mot* horn note, fr MF, word, horn note – more at MOT]

[1]**mortal** /ˈmawtl/ *adj* **1** causing or about to cause death; fatal **2a** not living forever; subject to death **b** humanly conceivable ⟨*every ~ thing*⟩ **3** marked by relentless hostility ⟨*a ~ enemy*⟩ **4** very great, intense, or severe **5** of or connected with death **6** very tedious and prolonged ⟨*waited 3 ~ hours*⟩ – infml [ME, fr MF, fr L *mortalis*, fr *mort-*, *mors* death – more at MURDER]

[2]**mortal** *n* **1** a human being **2** a person of a specified kind

mortality /maw'taləti/ *n* **1** being mortal **2** the death of large numbers of people, animals, etc **3** the human race ⟨*take these tears,* ~ *'s relief* – Alexander Pope⟩ **4a** the number of deaths in a given time or place **b** the ratio of deaths in a given time to population **c** the number lost, or the rate of loss or failure

mor'tality ,table *n* LIFE TABLE

mortally /'mawtl·i/ *adv* **1** in a deadly or fatal manner **2** to an extreme degree; intensely

,mortal 'sin *n* a sin (e g murder) of such gravity that it totally debars the soul from divine grace – compare VENIAL SIN – **mortal sinner** *n*

[1]**mortar** /'mawtə/ *n* **1** a strong usu bowl-shaped vessel (e g of stone) in which substances are pounded or ground with a pestle **2** a usu muzzle-loading artillery gun having a tube short in relation to its calibre, a low muzzle velocity, and a high trajectory [(1) ME *morter,* fr OE *mortere* & MF *mortier,* fr L *mortarium;* akin to Gk *marainein* to waste away – more at SMART; (2) MF *mortier*]

[2]**mortar** *n* a mixture of cement, lime, gypsum plaster, etc with sand and water, that hardens and is used to join bricks, stones, etc or for plastering ☞ BUILDING [ME *morter,* fr OF *mortier,* fr L *mortarium*]

[3]**mortar** *vt* to plaster or make fast with mortar

'mortar,board /-,bawd/ *n* **1** [1]HAWK 2 **2** an academic cap consisting of a close-fitting crown with a stiff flat square attached on top

[1]**mortgage** /'mawgij/ *n* **1** a transfer of the ownership of property (e g for security on a loan) on condition that the transfer becomes void on payment **2** the state of the property whose ownership is transferred by a mortgage [ME *morgage,* fr MF, fr OF, fr *mort* dead (fr L *mortuus,* fr pp of *mori* to die) + *gage* – more at MURDER]

[2]**mortgage** *vt* **1** to transfer the ownership of (property) by a mortgage **2** to make subject to a claim or obligation

mortgagee /,mawgi'jee/ *n* sby to whom property is mortgaged

mortgagor /'mawgijə, ,mawgi'jaw/ *also* **mortgager** /'mawgijə/ *n* sby who mortgages his/her property

mortician /maw'tish(ə)n/ *n, chiefly NAm* an undertaker [L *mort-, mors* death]

mortify /'mawtifie/ *vt* **1** to subdue (e g bodily needs and desires), esp by abstinence or self-inflicted suffering **2** to subject to feelings of shame or acute embarrassment ~ *vi* to become necrotic or gangrenous [ME *mortifien* to kill, subdue, fr MF *mortifier,* fr LL *mortificare,* fr L *mort-, mors*] – **mortification** /-fi'kaysh(ə)n/ *n*

[1]**mortise** *also* **mortice** /'mawtis/ *n* a usu rectangular cavity cut into a piece of material (e g wood) to receive a protrusion, esp a tenon, of another piece [ME *mortays,* fr MF *mortaise*]

[2]**mortise** *also* **mortice** *vt* **1** to join or fasten securely, specif by a mortise and tenon joint **2** to cut or make a mortise in

'mortise ,lock *n* a lock that is designed to be fitted into a mortise in the edge of a door

mortmain /'mawt,mayn/ *n* **1** a nontransferable possession of lands or buildings by an ecclesiastical or other corporation **2** (the condition of) property or other gifts nontransferably bequeathed to a church or corporation [ME *morte-mayne,* fr MF *mortemain,* fr OF, fr *morte* (fem of *mort* dead) + *main* hand, fr L *manus* – more at MANUAL]

[1]**mortuary** /'mawtyooəri, -chəri/ *n* a room or building in which dead bodies are kept before burial or cremation [ME *mortuarie,* fr ML *mortuarium,* fr L, neut of *mortuarius* of the dead, fr *mortuus,* pp]

[2]**mortuary** *adj* of death or the burial of the dead

morula /'moroolə/ *n, pl* **morulae** /-li/ the embryo of a metazoan animal at a (very early) stage in its development preceding the blastula stage, consisting of a solid globular mass of cells – compare BLASTULA, GASTRULA [NL, fr L *morum* mulberry]

mosaic /mə'zayik, moh-/ *n* **1** (a piece of) decorative work made from small pieces of different coloured material (e g glass or stone) inlaid to form pictures or patterns **2** sthg like a mosaic **3a** (a part of) an organism composed of cells with different genetic make-up; CHIMERA 3 **b** a virus disease of plants (e g tobacco) characterized esp by diffuse yellow and green mottling of the foliage [ME *musycke,* fr MF *mosaique,* fr OIt *mosaico,* fr ML *musaicum,* alter. of LL *musivum,* fr neut of *musivus* of a muse, artistic, fr L *Musa* muse] – **mosaic** *adj,* **mosaicism** /moh 'zayi,siz(ə)m/ *n,* **mosaicist** /-,sist/ *n*

Mosaic *adj* of Moses or the institutions or writings attributed to him [NL *Mosaicus,* fr *Moses,* biblical prophet & lawgiver]

Moselle, Mosel /moh'zel/ *n* a typically light-bodied white table wine made in the valley of the Moselle [G *moselwein,* fr *Mosel* Moselle, river in Germany + G *wein* wine]

mosey /'mohzi/ *vi, NAm* to saunter – infml [origin unknown]

Moslem /'moozlim/ *n or adj* (a) Muslim

mosque /mosk/ *n* a building used for public worship by Muslims [MF *mosquee,* fr OIt *moschea,* fr OSp *mezquita,* fr Ar *masjid* temple, fr *sajada* to prostrate oneself]

mosquito /mo'skeetoh/ *n, pl* **mosquitoes** *also* **mosquitos** any of numerous 2-winged flies with females that suck the blood of animals and often transmit diseases (e g malaria) to them [Sp, fr *mosca* fly, fr L *musca* – more at MIDGE] – **mosquitoey** *adj*

mo'squito ,boat *n, NAm* MOTOR TORPEDO BOAT

mo'squito ,net *n* a net or screen for keeping out mosquitoes

moss /mos/ *n* **1** (any of various plants resembling) any of a class of primitive plants with small leafy stems bearing sex organs at the tip; *also* many of these plants growing together and covering a surface ☞ PLANT **2** *chiefly Scot* a (peat) bog [ME, fr OE *mōs* bog; akin to OHG *mos* moss, L *muscus*] – **mosslike** *adj,* **mossy** *adj*

moss agate *n* an agate containing brown, black, or green mosslike markings

moss animal *n* a bryozoan

'moss,back /-,bak/ *n, NAm* an extremely conservative person; a fogey – infml [*mossback* (old turtle with mossy growth on its back, large sluggish fish)]

'moss ,rose *n* an older variety of garden rose with a glandular mossy growth on the calyx and flower stalk

'moss-,trooper *n* any of a class of 17th-c raiders in the Scottish Border – **moss-trooping** *adj*

[1]**most** /mohst/ *adj* **1** the majority of ⟨~ *men*⟩ **2** greatest in quantity or extent ⟨*the* ~ *ability*⟩ [ME, fr OE *mǣst;* akin to OHG *meist* most, OE *māra* more – more at MORE]

[2]**most** *adv* **1** to the greatest degree or extent ⟨*what I like* ~ *about him*⟩ – often used with an adjective or

adverb to form the superlative ⟨*the* ~ *challenging job he ever had*⟩ **2** very ⟨*shall* ~ *certainly come*⟩ ⟨*her argument was* ~ *persuasive*⟩

[3]**most** *n, pl* **most** the greatest quantity, number, or amount ⟨*it's the* ~ *I can do*⟩ ⟨*spends* ~ *of her time in bed*⟩ ⟨~ *became discouraged and left*⟩ ⟨*she made the* ~ *of the fine weather*⟩ – **at most, at the most** **1** as a maximum limit ⟨*took him an hour* at most *to finish the job*⟩ **2** AT BEST

[4]**most** *adv, archiac, dial, or NAm* almost

-most /-mohst/ *suffix* (→ *adj*) **1** most; to the highest possible degree ⟨*inner*most⟩ ⟨*ut*most⟩ **2** most towards ⟨*top*most⟩ ⟨*hind*most⟩ [ME, alter. of *-mest* (as in *formest* foremost)]

mostly /ˈmohstli/ *adv* for the greatest part; mainly; *also* in most cases; usually

mot /moh/ *n, pl* **mots** /moh(z)/ a pithy or witty saying [F, word, saying, fr L *muttum* grunt – more at MOTTO]

MOT *also* **MoT** *n* a compulsory annual roadworthiness test in Britain for motor vehicles older than a certain age [*M*inistry *O*f *T*ransport]

mote /moht/ *n* a small particle; *esp* a particle of dust suspended in the air [ME *mot*, fr OE; akin to MD & Fris *mot* sand]

motel /mohˈtel/ *n* an establishment which provides accommodation and parking and in which the rooms are usu accessible from an outdoor parking area [blend of *motor* and *hotel*]

motet /mohˈtet/ *n* a choral composition on a sacred text [ME, fr MF, dim. of *mot*]

moth /moth/ *n* **1** CLOTHES MOTH **2** a usu night-flying insect with feathery antennae and a stouter body and duller colouring than the butterflies [ME *mothe*, fr OE *moththe*; akin to MHG *motte* moth]

ˈmoth,ball /-ˌbawl/ *n* **1** a naphthalene or (formerly) camphor ball used to keep moths from clothing **2** *pl* a state of indefinitely long protective storage; *also* a state of having been rejected as of no further use or interest – **mothball** *vt*

ˈmoth ˌbean *n* (the yellowish brown edible seed of) a bean cultivated, esp in India, for food, forage, and soil conditioning [prob by folk etymology fr Marathi *maṭh*]

ˈmoth-ˌeaten *adj* **1** eaten into by moth larvae ⟨~ *clothes*⟩ **2a** very worn-out or shabby in appearance **b** antiquated, outmoded

[1]**mother** /ˈmudhə/ *n* **1a** a female parent **b** an old or elderly woman **2** a source, origin ⟨*necessity is the* ~ *of invention*⟩ [ME *moder*, fr OE *mōdor*; akin to OHG *muoter* mother, L *mater*, Gk *mētēr*, Skt *mātṛ*] – **motherhood** *n*, **motherless** *adj*

[2]**mother** *adj* **1a** of or being a mother **b** bearing the relation of a mother **2** derived (as if) from one's mother **3** acting as or providing a parental stock – used without reference to sex

[3]**mother** *vt* **1a** to give birth to **b** to give rise to; initiate, produce **2** to care for or protect like a mother – often derog

[4]**mother, mother of vinegar** *n* a slimy membrane of yeast and bacterial cells that develops on the surface of alcoholic liquids undergoing vinegar-producing fermentation and is added to wine or cider to produce vinegar [akin to MD *modder* mud, lees, dregs, MLG *mudde* mud]

ˌMother ˌCarey's ˈchicken /ˈkeəriz/ *n* STORM PETREL [origin unknown]

ˌMother ˈGoose ˌrhyme *n, chiefly NAm* NURSERY RHYME [*Mother Goose*, fictional author of *Mother Goose's Melodies*, collection of nursery rhymes published in London *ab* 1760]

Mothering Sunday /ˈmudhəring/ *n* the fourth Sunday in Lent observed in Britain in honour of motherhood

ˈmother-in-ˌlaw *n, pl* **mothers-in-law** the mother of one's spouse

ˈmother,land /-ˌland/ *n* one's fatherland

ˈmotherly /-li/ *adj* **1** (characteristic) of a mother **2** like a mother; maternal – **motherliness** *n*

ˌmother-ˈnaked *adj* stark naked

ˌmother-of-ˈpearl *n* the hard pearly iridescent substance forming the inner layer of a mollusc shell

ˈMother's ˌDay *n* MOTHERING SUNDAY

ˌmother suˈperior *n, often cap M&S* the head of a religious community of women

ˈmother ˌtongue *n* **1** one's native language **2** a language from which another language derives

mothproof /ˈmoth,proohf/ *vt or adj* (to make) resistant to attack by the larvae of (clothes) moths

motif /mohˈteef/ *n* **1** a recurring element forming a theme in a work of art or literature; *esp* a dominant idea or central theme **2** a single or repeated design or colour **3** a leitmotiv [F, motive, motif]

motile /ˈmohtiel/ *adj* exhibiting or capable of movement [L *motus*, pp] – **motility** /mohˈtiləti/ *n*

[1]**motion** /ˈmohsh(ə)n/ *n* **1a** a formal proposal made in a deliberative assembly **b** an application to a court or judge for an order, ruling, or direction **2a** an act, process, or instance of changing position; movement **b** an active or functioning state or condition **3a** an act or instance of moving the body or its parts; a gesture **b** *pl* actions, movements; *esp* merely simulated or mechanical actions – often in *go through the motions* **4** melodic change of pitch **5a** an evacuation of the bowels – usu pl with sing. meaning **b** the matter evacuated [ME *mocioun*, fr MF *motion*, fr L *motion-*, *motio* movement, fr *motus*, pp of *movēre* to move] – **motional** *adj*, **motionless** *adj*, **motionlessness** *n*

[2]**motion** *vt* to direct by a gesture ⟨~ed *me to a seat*⟩

ˈmotion ˌpicture *n, chiefly NAm* a film, movie

motivate /ˈmohtivayt/ *vt* to provide with a motive or incentive; impel ⟨~d *by fear*⟩ – **motivation** /-ˈvaysh(ə)n/ *n*

[1]**motive** /ˈmohtiv/ *n* **1** a need, desire, etc that causes sby to act **2** a recurrent phrase or figure that is developed through the course of a musical composition [ME, fr MF *motif*, fr *motif*, adj, moving] – **motiveless** *adj*

[2]**motive** *adj* **1** moving or tending to move to action **2** of (the causing of) motion ⟨~ *energy*⟩ [MF or ML; MF *motif*, fr ML *motivus*, fr L *motus*, pp]

motive power *n* sthg (e g water or steam) whose energy is used to impart motion to machinery

motivity /mohˈtivəti/ *n* the power of (producing) movement

mot juste /ˌmoh ˈzhoohst (*Fr* mo ʒyst)/ *n, pl* **mots justes** /~/ the exactly right word or phrasing [F]

[1]**motley** /ˈmotli/ *adj* **1** multicoloured **2** composed of varied (disreputable or unsightly) elements [ME, perh fr *mot* mote, speck]

[2]**motley** *n* **1** a woollen fabric of mixed colours made in England between the 14th and 17th c **2** a haphaz-

ard mixture (of incompatible elements) [ME, prob fr [1]*motley*]

moto-cross /'mohtoh ˌkros/ *n* the sport of racing motorcycles across country on a rugged usu hilly closed course [*motor* + *cross (country)*]

[1]**motor** /'mohtə/ *n* **1** sthg or sby that imparts motion **2** any of various power units that develop energy or impart motion: e g **a** a small compact engine **b** INTERNAL-COMBUSTION ENGINE **c** a rotating machine that transforms electrical energy into mechanical energy **3** MOTOR VEHICLE; *esp* MOTOR CAR [L, fr *motus*, pp of *movēre* to move] – **motorless** *adj*

[2]**motor** *adj* **1a** causing or imparting motion **b** of or being a nerve (fibre) that conducts an impulse causing the movement of a muscle ☞ NERVE **c** of or involving muscular movement **2a** equipped with or driven by a motor **b** of or involving motor vehicles ⟨*the ~ trade*⟩

[3]**motor** *vi* to travel by motor car; *esp* DRIVE 2

Motorail /'mohtəˌrayl/ *trademark* – used for a railway system in which a passenger train also carries the passengers' cars

'motor ˌbike *n* a motorcycle – infml

'motorˌboat /-ˌboht/ *n* a usu small boat propelled by a motor

'motorˌcade /-ˌkayd/ *n* a procession of motor vehicles

'motor ˌcar *n* a usu 4-wheeled motor vehicle designed for transporting a small number of people and typically propelled by an internal-combustion engine

'motorˌcycle /-ˌsiekl/ *n* a 2-wheeled motor vehicle that can carry 1 or sometimes 2 people astride the engine – **motorcycle** *vi*, **motorcyclist** /-ˌsieklist/ *n*

motorist /'mohtərist/ *n* sby who drives a car

motor·ize, -ise /'mohtəriez/ *vt* **1** to equip (e g a vehicle) with a motor **2** to provide with motor-driven equipment (e g for transport) – **motorization** /-rie'zaysh(ə)n/ *n*

'motorman /-mən/ *n* a driver of a motor-driven vehicle (e g a bus or underground train)

'motor ˌscooter *n* a usu 2-wheeled motor vehicle having a seat so that the driver sits in front of rather than astride the engine

motor torpedo boat *n* a high-speed motorboat whose principal offensive armament is torpedoes

'motor ˌvehicle *also* **motor** *n* an automotive vehicle not operated on rails; *esp* one with rubber tyres for use on roads

'motorˌway /-ˌway/ *n, Br* a major road designed for high-speed traffic that has separate carriageways for different directions and certain restrictions on the types of vehicle and driver allowed on it

motte /mot/ *n* the fortified mound of a (Norman) castle ☞ CHURCH [F – more at MOAT]

[1]**mottle** /'motl/ *n* **1** a coloured spot or blotch **2** an irregular pattern of spots or blotches on a surface [prob back-formation fr *motley*] – **mottled** *adj*

[2]**mottle** *vt* **mottling** /'motl·ing/ to mark with mottles

motto /'motoh/ *n, pl* **mottoes** *also* **mottos** **1** a sentence, phrase, or word inscribed on sthg as appropriate to or indicative of its character or use **2** a short expression of a guiding principle; a maxim **3** (a piece of paper printed with) a usu humorous or sentimental saying [It, fr L *muttum* grunt, fr *muttire* to mutter]

moue /mooh/ *n* a little grimace; a pout [F, fr MF, of Gmc origin; akin to MD *mouwe* protruding lip]

mouflon, moufflon /'moohflonh/ *n* (any of) a wild race of the domestic sheep found on European mountains [F *mouflon*, fr It dial. *movrone*, fr LL *mufron-*, *mufro*]

mouillé /'mwee·ay/ *adj* pronounced palatally [F, lit., moistened]

moujik /'moohzhik/ *n* a muzhik

[1]**mould,** *NAm chiefly* **mold** /mohld/ *n* crumbling soft (humus-rich) soil suited to plant growth [ME *mold, molde*, fr OE *molda, molde*; akin to OHG *molta* soil, L *molere* to grind – more at [2]MEAL]

[2]**mould,** *NAm chiefly* **mold** *n* **1** distinctive character or type ⟨*need to recruit more men of his ~*⟩ **2** the frame on or round which an object is constructed **3** a cavity or form in which a substance (e g a jelly or a metal casting) is shaped **4** a moulding **5** a fixed pattern or form [ME *mold, molde*, fr OF *modle*, fr L *modulus*, dim. of *modus* measure – more at METE]

[3]**mould,** *NAm chiefly* **mold** *vt* **1** to give shape to **2** to form in a mould **3** to exert a steady formative influence on **4** to fit closely to the contours of **5** to ornament with moulding or carving ⟨*~ed picture frames*⟩

[4]**mould,** *NAm chiefly* **mold** *n* (a fungus producing) an often woolly growth on the surface of damp or decaying organic matter [ME *mowlde*]

'mouldˌboard /-ˌbawd/ *n* a curved plate on a ploughshare for lifting and turning the soil

moulder, *NAm chiefly* **molder** /'mohldə/ *vi* to crumble into dust or decayed fragments, esp gradually [freq of *mould* (to become mouldy), fr [4]*mould*]

moulding /'mohlding/ *n* **1** an article produced by moulding **2** a decorative recessed or embossed surface **3** a decorative band or strip used for ornamentation or finishing (e g on a cornice) ☞ ARCHITECTURE

mouldy /'mohldi/ *adj* **1** of, resembling, or covered with a mould-producing fungus **2** old and mouldering; fusty, crumbling **3a** miserable, nasty **b** stingy ***USE*** (*3*) infml

moulin /'moohlanh (*Fr* mulɛ̃)/ *n* a nearly cylindrical vertical shaft worn in a glacier by water from melting snow and ice [F, lit., mill, fr LL *molinum* – more at MILL]

[1]**moult,** *NAm chiefly* **molt** /mohlt/ *vb* to shed or cast off (hair, feathers, shell, horns, or an outer layer) periodically [alter. of ME *mouten*, fr OE *-mūtian* to change, fr L *mutare*]

[2]**moult,** *NAm chiefly* **molt** *n* moulting; *specif* ecdysis

mound /mownd/ *n* **1a(1)** an artificial bank of earth or stones **(2)** the slightly elevated ground on which a baseball pitcher stands **b** a knoll, hill **2** a heap, pile [origin unknown]

[1]**mount** /mownt/ *n* a high hill; a mountain – usu before a name ⟨Mount *Everest*⟩ [ME, fr OE *munt* & OF *mont*, fr L *mont-, mons*; akin to ON *mœna* to project, L *minari* to project, threaten]

[2]**mount** *vi* **1** to increase in amount, extent, or degree **2** to rise, ascend **3** to get up on or into sthg above ground level; *esp* to seat oneself (e g on a horse) for riding *~ vt* **1a** to go up; climb **b(1)** to seat or place oneself on ⟨*the speaker ~ed the platform*⟩ **(2)** COVER 6a **2a** to lift up; raise, erect **b** to place (e g

artillery) in position **c** to initiate and carry out (e g an assault or strike) **3a** to set (sby) on a means of conveyance ⟨~ed *his little daughter on a donkey*⟩ **b** to provide with animals for riding **4** to station for defence or observation or as an escort ⟨~ *guard over the palace*⟩ **5a** to attach to a support **b** to arrange or assemble for use or display **6a** to prepare (e g a specimen) for examination or display **b** to organize and present for public viewing or performance; stage ⟨~ed *a sumptuous opera*⟩ [ME *mounten*, fr MF *monter*, fr (assumed) VL *montare*, fr L *mont-, mons*]

[3]**mount** *n* **1** an opportunity to ride a horse, esp in a race **2** sthg on which sby or sthg is mounted: e g **a** the material (e g cardboard) on which a picture is mounted **b** a jewellery setting **c** an attachment for an accessory **d** a hinge, card, etc for mounting a stamp in a stamp collection **3** a horse for riding

mountain /'mownt(ə)n, -tayn/ *n* **1** a landmass that projects conspicuously above its surroundings and is higher than a hill **2a** a vast amount or quantity – often pl with sing. meaning **b** a supply, esp of a specified usu agricultural commodity, in excess of demand ⟨*a butter* ~⟩ [ME, fr OF *montaigne*, fr (assumed) VL *montanea*, fr fem of *montaneus* of a mountain, alter. of L *montanus*, fr *mont-, mons*]

,mountain 'ash *n* a rowan or related tree of the rose family usu with small red fruits

mountaineering /,mowntə'niəring/ *n* the pastime or technique of climbing mountains and rock faces – **mountaineer** /-'niə/ *n*

mountain lion *n* a puma

mountainous /'mownt(ə)nəs/ *adj* **1** containing many mountains **2** resembling a mountain; huge – **mountainously** *adv*

'mountain ,sickness *n* sickness caused by insufficient oxygen in the air at heights, esp above 3,500m (about 10,000ft)

mountebank /'mownti,bangk/ *n* **1** sby who sells quack medicines from a platform **2** a charlatan [It *montimbanco*, fr *montare* to mount + *in* in, on + *banco, banca* bench – more at [4]BANK] – **mountebankery** /-kəri/ *n*

Mountie /'mownti/ *n* a member of the Royal Canadian Mounted Police [*mount*ed policeman]

mounting /'mownting/ *n* [3]MOUNT 2

mourn /mawn/ *vi* to feel or express (e g in a conventional manner) grief or sorrow, esp for a death ~ *vt* to feel or express grief or sorrow for [ME *mournen*, fr OE *murnan*; akin to OHG *mornēn* to mourn, Gk *mermēra* care – more at MEMORY] – **mourner** *n*

'mournful /-f(ə)l/ *adj* expressing, causing, or filled with sorrow – **mournfully** *adv*, **mournfulness** *n*

mourning /'mawning/ *n* **1** the act or state of one who mourns **2a** an outward sign (e g black clothes or an armband) of grief for a person's death ⟨*is wearing* ~⟩ **b** a period of time during which signs of grief are shown

[1]**mouse** /mows/ *n, pl* **mice** /mies/ **1** any of numerous small rodents with a pointed snout, rather small ears, and slender tail **2** a timid person [ME, fr OE *mūs*; akin to OHG *mūs* mouse, L *mus*, Gk *mys* mouse, muscle]

[2]**mouse** *vi* to hunt for mice ~ *vt*, *chiefly NAm* to search for carefully – usu + *out* – **mouser** *n*

'mouse ,deer *n* a chevrotain

'mouse-,ear *n* any of several plants (e g hawkweed) with soft hairy leaves

mouse-ear chickweed *n* any of several related usu hairy chickweeds

'mouse,trap /-,trap/ *n* a trap for mice

moussaka, mousaka /mooh'sahkə/ *n* a Greek dish consisting of layers of minced meat (e g lamb), aubergine or potato, tomato, and cheese with cheese or savoury custard topping [NGk *mousakas*]

mousse /moohs/ *n* a light sweet or savoury cold dish usu containing cream, gelatin, and whipped egg whites [F, lit., froth, fr LL *mulsa* mixture of honey and water; akin to L *mel* honey – more at MELLIFLUOUS]

mousseline /'moohsleen/ *n* a fine sheer fabric (e g of rayon) that resembles muslin [F, lit., muslin – more at MUSLIN]

moustache, *NAm chiefly* **mustache** /mə'stahsh, mə'stash/ *n* **1** the hair growing or allowed to grow on sby's upper lip **2** hair or bristles round the mouth of a mammal [MF *moustache*, fr OIt *mustaccio*, fr MGk *moustaki*, dim. of Gk *mystak-, mystax* upper lip, moustache]

Mousterian /mooh'stiəri·ən/ *adj* of a Lower Palaeolithic culture characterized by well-made flint tools [F *moustérien*, fr Le *Moustier*, cave in Dordogne, France]

mousy, mousey /'mowsi/ *adj* **1** of or resembling a mouse: e g **a** quiet, stealthy **b** timid; *also* colourless **2** *of hair* light greyish brown

[1]**mouth** /mowth/ *n, pl* **mouths** /mowdhz/ **1a** the opening through which food passes into an animal's body; *also* the cavity in the head of the typical vertebrate animal bounded externally by the lips that encloses the tongue, gums, and teeth **b** a grimace made with the lips **c** a horse's response to pressure on the bit **d** an individual, esp a child, requiring food ⟨*too many* ~s *to feed*⟩ **2a** utterance ⟨*finally gave* ~ *to his feelings*⟩ **b** MOUTHPIECE 3 **3** sthg like a mouth, esp in affording entrance or exit: e g **a** the place where a river enters a sea, lake, etc **b** the opening of a cave, volcano, etc **c** the opening of a container **4a** a tendency to talk too much **b** impertinent language – compare [1]LIP 2 *USE* (*4*) infml [ME, fr OE *mūth*; akin to OHG *mund* mouth, L *mandere* to chew, Gk *masasthai* to chew, *mastax* mouth, jaws] – **mouthed** /mowdhd/ *adj*, **mouthlike** *adj* – **down in the mouth** dejected, sulky

[2]**mouth** /mowdh/ *vt* **1** to utter pompously **2** to repeat without comprehension or sincerity **3** to form (words) soundlessly with the lips ~ *vi* to talk pompously

mouthful /'mowthf(ə)l/ *n* **1a** a quantity that fills the mouth **b** the amount (of food) put into the mouth at 1 time **2** a small quantity **3a** a word or phrase that is very long or difficult to pronounce **b** *chiefly NAm* a very apt or significant comment or statement – chiefly in *say a mouthful USE* (*3*) infml

'mouth ,organ *n* a harmonica

'mouth,part /-,paht/ *n* a structure or appendage near or forming part of the mouth

'mouth,piece /-,pees/ *n* **1** sthg placed at or forming a mouth **2** a part (e g of a musical instrument or a telephone) that goes in the mouth or is put next to the mouth **3** sby or sthg that expresses or interprets another's views

'mouth-,watering *adj* stimulating or appealing to the appetite; appetizing – **mouth-wateringly** *adv*

mouthy /'mowdhi/ *adj* garrulous

movable, moveable /'moohvəbl/ *n or adj* (property)

able to be removed – often used to distinguish personal property from buildings, land, etc; usu pl [[1]MOVE + -ABLE]

,movable 'feast *n* an annual church festival (e g Easter) not celebrated on the same date each year

[1]**move** /moohv/ *vi* **1a(1)** to go or pass with a continuous motion **(2)** to proceed or progress towards a (specified) place or condition ⟨moving *up the executive ladder*⟩ – often + *on* ⟨~ *on to the next item*⟩ **b** to go away ⟨*it's time we were* moving⟩ **c(1)** to transfer a piece in a board game (e g in chess) from one position to another ⟨*it's your turn to* ~⟩ **(2)** *of a piece in board games* to travel or be capable of travelling to another position ⟨*the bishop* ~s *diagonally*⟩ **d(1)** to change one's residence **(2)** to change one's (official) location **2** to pass one's life in a specified environment ⟨~s *in fashionable circles*⟩ **3** to change position or posture **4** to take action; act **5** to make a formal request, application, or appeal **6** to change hands by being sold or rented – often + *quickly* or *slowly* **7** *of the bowels* to evacuate **8a** to operate or function, esp mechanically **b** to show marked activity or speed – infml ⟨*after a brief lull things really began to* ~⟩ ~ *vt* **1a** to change the place or position of **b** to transfer (e g a piece in chess) from one position to another **2a(1)** to cause to go or pass with a continuous motion **(2)** to take (furniture and possessions) from one residence or location to another **b** to cause to operate or function ⟨*this button* ~s *the whole machine*⟩ **3** to cause (the body or part of the body) to change position or posture **4** to prompt to action **5** to affect in such a way as to lead to a show of emotion or of a specified emotion **6** to propose formally in a deliberative assembly **7** to cause (the bowels) to evacuate [ME *moven*, fr MF *movoir*, fr L *movēre*] – **mover** *n*

[2]**move** *n* **1a** the act of moving a piece (e g in chess) **b** the turn of a player to move **2a** a step taken so as to gain an objective **b** a movement **c** a change of residence or official location – **on the move 1** in a state of moving about from place to place ⟨*a salesman is constantly* on the move⟩ **2** in a state of moving ahead or making progress ⟨*said that civilization is always* on the move⟩

move in *vi* **1** to take up occupation of a dwelling or place of work **2** to advance aggressively in order to gain control – often + *on* ⟨*police* moved in *on the criminals hiding in the house*⟩

'movement /-mənt/ *n* **1a** the act or process of moving; *esp* change of place, position, or posture **b** a particular instance or manner of moving **c** an action, activity – usu pl with sing. meaning ⟨*troop* ~s⟩ **2a** a trend, specif in prices **b** an organized effort to promote an end ⟨*the civil rights* ~⟩ **3** the moving parts of a mechanism that transmit motion **4** a unit or division having its own key, rhythmic structure, and themes and forming a separate part of an extended musical composition **5a** the development of the action in a work of literature **b** the quality of a book, play, etc of having a quickly moving plot **6** MOTION 5

move on *vi* to change one's residence or location for another ~ *vt* to cause to depart ⟨*the squatters were* moved on *by the police*⟩

move out *vi* to leave a dwelling or place of work

move over *vi* to make room

movie /'moohvi/ *n* FILM 3a, b [*moving picture*]

moving /'moohving/ *adj* **1a** marked by or capable of movement **b** of a change of residence **2a** producing or transferring motion or action ⟨*the* ~ *spirit behind the scheme*⟩ **b** evoking a deep emotional response – **movingly** *adv*

,moving 'picture *n, chiefly NAm* a film, movie

[1]**mow** /mow/ *n* **1** a stack of hay, grain, fodder, etc (in a barn) **2** the part of a barn where hay or straw is stored [ME, heap, stack, fr OE *mūga*; akin to ON *mūgi* heap, Gk *mykōn*]

[2]**mow** /moh/ *vb* **mowed; mowed, mown** /mohn/ *vt* **1** to cut down (a crop, esp grass) **2** to cut down the standing herbage, esp grass, of (e g a field) ~ *vi* to cut down standing herbage, esp grass [ME *mowen*, fr OE *māwan*; akin to OHG *māen* to mow, L *metere* to reap, mow, Gk *aman*] – **mower** *n*

mow down *vt* **1** to kill, destroy, or knock down, esp in great numbers or mercilessly **2** to overcome swiftly and decisively; rout

moxie /'moksi/ *n, NAm* courage – infml [fr *Moxie*, a trademark for a soft drink]

mozzarella /,motsə'relə/ *n* a moist white unsalted unripened curd cheese [It]

mozzetta /moh(t)'zetə/ *n* a short cape with a small ornamental hood worn over the rochet by Roman Catholic prelates [It]

Mr /'mistə/ *n, pl* **Messrs** /'mesəz/ **1** – used as a conventional title of courtesy before a man's surname, except when usage requires the substitution of a title of rank or an honorary or professional title **2** – used in direct address before a man's title of office ⟨*may I ask one more question,* ~ *Chairman?*⟩ **3** – used before the name of a place or of a profession or activity or before some epithet (e g *clever*) to form a title applied to a male viewed or recognized as representative of the thing indicated ⟨~ *Football*⟩ [*Mr* fr ME, abbr of *maister* master; *Messrs* abbr of *Messieurs*, fr F, pl of *Monsieur*]

mRNA *n* MESSENGER RNA

Mrs /'misiz/ *n, pl* **Mesdames** /may'dahm/ **1a** – used as a conventional title of courtesy before a married woman's surname, except when usage requires the substitution of a title of rank or an honorary or professional title ⟨*spoke to* ~ *Smith*⟩ **b** – used before the name of a place (e g a country or city) or of a profession or activity (e g a sport) or before some epithet (e g *clever*) to form a title applied to a married woman viewed or recognized as representative of the thing indicated ⟨~ *Tennis 1982*⟩ **2** a wife ⟨*took the* ~ *along to the pub*⟩ – infml [*Mrs* abbr of [1]*mistress; Mesdames* fr F, pl of *Madame*]

,Mrs 'Grundy /'grundi/ *n* sby marked by prudish conventionality in personal conduct [*Mrs Grundy*, offstage character personifying prudery in the play *Speed the Plough* by Thomas Morton †1838 E dramatist]

Ms /məz, miz/ *n* – used instead of Mrs or Miss, esp when marital status is unknown or irrelevant

MSH *n* MELANOCYTE-STIMULATING HORMONE

mu /m(y)ooh/ *n* the 12th letter of the Greek alphabet [Gk *my*]

muc-, muci-, muco- *comb form* **1** mucus ⟨muco*protein*⟩ **2** mucous and ⟨muco*purulent*⟩ [L *muc-*, fr *mucus*]

[1]**much** /much/ *adj* **more** /maw/; **most** /mohst/ **1** great in quantity or extent ⟨*not* ~ *money*⟩ ⟨*nothing* ~ *to do*⟩ ⟨*how* ~ *milk is there?*⟩ – compare SO MUCH **2** excessive, immoderate ⟨*it's a bit* ~ *having to work so late*⟩ [ME *muche* large, much, fr *michel*,

muchel, fr OE *micel, mycel*; akin to OHG *mihhil* great, large, L *magnus*, Gk *megas*] – **too much 1** wonderful, exciting **2** terrible, awful

[2]**much** *adv* **more; most 1a(1)** to a great degree or extent; considerably ⟨~ *happier*⟩ ⟨*don't* ~ *like it*⟩ ⟨~ *to my surprise*⟩ ⟨*how* ~ *did it cost?*⟩ – compare SO MUCH (2) very – with verbal adjectives ⟨*was* ~ *amused*⟩ **b** frequently, often ⟨~ *married*⟩ **c** by far ⟨~ *the fatter*⟩ ⟨*I'd* ~ *rather not*⟩ ⟨~ *the brightest student*⟩ **2** nearly, approximately ⟨*looks* ~ *the way his father did*⟩ – **as much 1** the same quantity **2** that, so ⟨*I thought* as much⟩ – **much less** and certainly not ⟨*can't even walk,* much less *run*⟩

[3]**much** *n* **1** a great quantity, amount, or part ⟨*gave away* ~⟩ ⟨~ *of the night*⟩ ⟨*got too* ~ *to do*⟩ – compare SO MUCH **2** sthg considerable or impressive ⟨*wasn't* ~ *to look at*⟩ ⟨*the film wasn't up to* ~⟩ ⟨*I don't think* ~ *of that idea*⟩ **3** a relative quantity or part ⟨*I'll say this* ~ *for him*⟩ – **too much for 1** more than a match for **2** beyond the endurance of

'much as *conj* however much; even though

muchness /'muchnis/ *n* [[1]MUCH + -NESS] – **much of a muchness** very much the same

mucilage /'myoohsilij/ *n* a gelatinous substance obtained esp from seaweeds and similar to plant gums [ME *muscilage*, fr LL *mucilago* mucus, musty juice, fr L *mucus*]

mucilaginous /,myoohsi'lajinəs/ *adj* **1** sticky, viscid **2** of, full of, or secreting mucilage [LL *mucilaginosus*, fr *mucilagin-, mucilago*]

muck /muk/ *n* **1** soft moist farmyard manure **2** slimy dirt or filth **3** mire, mud **4a** a worthless or useless thing; rubbish – infml **b** *Br* – used in *Lord Muck* and *Lady Muck* to designate an arrogantly patronizing person [ME *muk*, perh fr OE *-moc*; akin to ON *myki* dung – more at MUCUS] – **mucky** *adj*

muck about *vb, chiefly Br* MESS ABOUT – infml

mucker /'mukə/ *n* a friend, pal – infml [*muck (in)* + [2]*-er*]

muck in *vi, Br* to share or join in esp a task ⟨*all* mucked in *together*⟩; *also* to share sleeping accommodation – infml

muck out *vi* to remove manure or filth, esp from an animal's quarters ~*vt* to clear (e g a stable) of manure

'muck,rake /-,rayk/ *vi* to search out and publicly expose real or apparent misconduct of prominent individuals [obs *muckrake*, n (rake for dung)] – **muckraker** *n*

muck sweat *n* – **in a muck sweat** sweating profusely, esp through fear or haste

muck up *vt, chiefly Br* **1** to dirty (as if) with muck; soil **2** to bungle, spoil *USE* infml

muco- – see MUC-

mucosa /myooh'kohzə/ *n, pl* **mucosae** /-zi/, **mucosas** MUCOUS MEMBRANE [NL, fr L, fem of *mucosus* mucous]

mucous /'myoohkəs/ *adj* of, like, secreting, or covered (as if) with mucus [L *mucosus*, fr *mucus*]

,mucous 'membrane /'membrayn/ *n* a membrane rich in mucous glands, specif lining body passages and cavities (e g the mouth) with openings to the exterior

mucro /'myoohkroh/ *n, pl* **mucrones** /-neez/ a sharp end point or part (e g of a leaf) ☞ PLANT [NL *mucron-, mucro*, fr L, point, edge; akin to Gk *amyssein* to scratch, sting] – **mucronate** /'myoohkrə,nayt/ *adj*

mucus /'myoohkəs/ *n* a thick slippery secretion produced by mucous membranes (e g in the nose) which it moistens and protects [L, nasal mucus; akin to ON *myki* dung, Gk *myxa* mucus]

mud /mud/ *n* **1** (a sticky mixture of a solid and a liquid resembling) soft wet earth **2** abusive and malicious remarks or charges [ME *mudde*, prob fr MLG; akin to OE *mōs* bog – more at MOSS]

[1]**muddle** /'mudl/ *vb* **muddling** /'mudling, 'mudl·ing/ *vt* **1** to stupefy, esp with alcohol **2** to mix confusedly in one's mind – often + *up* **3** to cause confusion to ~*vi* to proceed or get along in a confused aimless way – + *along* or *on* [prob fr obs D *moddelen*, fr MD, fr *modde* mud; akin to MLG *mudde*] – **muddler** *n*

[2]**muddle** *n* **1** a state of (mental) confusion **2** a confused mess

,muddle'headed /-'hedid/ *adj* **1** mentally confused **2** inept, bungling – **muddleheadedness** *n*

muddle through *vi* to succeed in spite of incompetence or lack of method and planning

[1]**muddy** /'mudi/ *adj* **1** lacking in clarity or brightness **2** obscure in meaning; muddled, confused [MUD + [1]-Y] – **muddily** *adv*, **muddiness** *n*

[2]**muddy** *vt* to make cloudy, dull, or confused

mudflap /'mud,flap/ *n* a flap suspended behind the wheel of a vehicle to prevent mud, splashes, etc being thrown up

'mud,flat /-,flat/ *n* a muddy area of ground covered at high tide – often pl with sing. meaning

'mud,guard /-,gahd/ *n* a metal or plastic guard over the wheel of a bicycle, motorcycle, etc to deflect or catch mud

'mud,lark /-,lahk/ *n* a destitute child in Victorian London; *esp* one who tried to find useful or salable objects in the tidal mud of the Thames

'mud,pack /-,pak/ *n* a face-pack containing fuller's earth

'mud ,puppy *n* any of several large American salamanders

'mud,stone /-,stohn/ *n* a hardened shale produced by the consolidation of mud

muesli /'m(y)oohzli, 'mwayzli/ *n* a (breakfast) dish of Swiss origin consisting of rolled oats, dried fruit, nuts, grated apple, etc [G *müsli*, fr *mus* soft food, pulp, fr OHG *muos*; akin to OE *mōs* food]

muezzin /mooh'ezin/ *n* a mosque official who calls the faithful to prayer at fixed daily times, usu from a minaret [Ar *mu'adhdhin*]

[1]**muff** /muf/ *n* a warm cylindrical wrap in which both hands are placed [D *mof*, fr MF *moufle* mitten, fr ML *muffula*]

[2]**muff** *n* **1** a failure to hold a ball in attempting a catch **2** a timid awkward person, esp in sports – infml ⟨*a hopeless* ~ *at tennis*⟩ [perh fr [1]*muff*]

[3]**muff** *vt* **1** to handle awkwardly; bungle **2** to fail to hold (a ball) when attempting a catch

muffin /'mufin/ *n* a light round yeast-leavened bun usu served hot [prob fr LG *muffen*, pl of *muffe* cake]

[1]**muffle** /'mufl/ *vt* **muffling** /'mufling/ **1** to wrap up so as to conceal or protect **2a** to wrap or pad with sthg to dull the sound **b** to deaden the sound of **3** to keep down; suppress ⟨~d *laughter*⟩ [ME *muflen*]

[2]**muffle** *n* a chamber in a furnace or kiln where

articles can be heated without direct contact with flames or combustion products [F *moufle*, lit., mitten, fr MF]

muffler /'muflə/ *n* **1** a warm scarf worn round the neck **2** *NAm* a silencer for a motor vehicle

[1]**mufti** /'mufti/ *n* a professional Muslim jurist [Ar *mufti*]

[2]**mufti** *n* civilian or ordinary clothes worn by one who is usually in uniform [prob fr [1]*mufti*]

[1]**mug** /mug/ *n* **1** a large usu cylindrical drinking cup **2** the face or mouth of sby **3** *Br* sby easily deceived; a sucker *USE* (*2 & 3*) infml [origin unknown]

[2]**mug** *vt* **-gg-** to assault, esp in the street with intent to rob [back-formation fr *mugger*, prob fr obs *mug* (to punch in the face), fr [1]*mug*] – **mugger** *n*

muggins /'muginz/ *n, pl* **mugginses, muggins** a fool, simpleton – slang; often used in address ⟨~ *here lost her passport*⟩ [prob fr the name *Muggins*]

muggy /'mugi/ *adj, of weather* warm, damp, and close [E dial. *mug* (drizzle), prob of Scand origin] – **muggily** *adv*, **mugginess** *n*

'mug's ,game *n, chiefly Br* a profitless activity – infml [[1]*mug* 3]

'mug ,shot *n* a photograph of a suspect's face – slang [[1]*mug* 2]

mug up *vb, Br* to study hard – infml [*mug* (to study), of unknown origin]

'mug,wort /-,wuht/ *n* a tall Eurasian composite plant with small brownish flower heads [ME, fr OE *mucgwyrt*, fr *mucg-* (perh akin to OE *mycg* midge) + *wyrt* wort – more at MIDGE, [1]WORT]

'mug,wump /-,wump/ *n, chiefly NAm* an independent in politics [obs slang *mugwump* (important person), fr Natick *mugwomp* captain]

Muhammadan /mə'hamid(ə)n/ *adj* of Muhammad or Islam [*Muhammad* †632 Arabian prophet & founder of Islam] – **Muhammadan** *n*, **Muhammadanism** *n*

mulatto /myooh'latoh/ *n, pl* **mulattoes, mulattos** the first-generation offspring of a Negro and a white person [Sp *mulato*, fr *mulo* mule, fr L *mulus*]

mulberry /'mulb(ə)ri/ *n* (any of a genus of trees of the fig family bearing) an edible usu purple multiple fruit [ME *murberie, mulberie*, fr OF *moure* mulberry (fr L *morum*, fr Gk *moron*) + ME *berie* berry]

mulch /mulch/ *n* a protective covering (e g of compost) spread on the ground to control weeds, enrich the soil, etc [perh irreg fr E dial. *melch* (soft, mild)] – **mulch** *vt*

[1]**mulct** /mulkt/ *n* a fine, penalty [L *multa, mulcta*]

[2]**mulct** *vt* **1** to punish by a fine **2a** to swindle **b** to obtain by swindling

[1]**mule** /myoohl/ *n* **1** the offspring of a mating between a (female) horse and an ass **2** a very stubborn person **3** a machine for simultaneously drawing and twisting fibre into yarn or thread and winding it onto spindles [ME, fr OF *mul*, fr L *mulus*]

[2]**mule** *n* a backless shoe or slipper ☞ GARMENT [MF, a kind of slipper, fr L *mulleus* shoe worn by magistrates]

muleta /m(y)ooh'laytə/ *n* a small cape attached to a stick that is used by a matador during the final stage of a bullfight [Sp, crutch, muleta, dim. of *mula* she-mule, fr L, fem of *mulus*]

muleteer /,myoohlə'tiə/ *n* sby who drives mules [F *muletier*, fr *mulet*, fr OF, dim. of *mul* mule]

muley /'myoohli/ *adj, of an animal of a type that normally has horns* polled or (naturally) hornless [of Celtic origin; akin to IrGael & ScGael *maol* bald, hornless, W *moel*]

mulish /'myoohlish/ *adj* unreasonably and inflexibly obstinate [[1]*mule*] – **mulishly** *adv*, **mulishness** *n*

[1]**mull** /mul/ *vt* to heat, sweeten, and flavour (e g wine or beer) with spices [origin unknown]

[2]**mull** *n* crumbly soil humus forming a layer of mixed organic matter and mineral soil and merging into the underlying mineral soil [G, fr Dan *muld*, fr ON *mold* dust, soil; akin to OHG *molta* dust, soil – more at [1]MOULD]

[3]**mull** *n* a headland or peninsula in Scotland [ME (Sc) *mole*, prob fr ON *mūli* projecting crag, snout, muzzle; akin to OHG *mūla, mūl* mouth (of an animal), Gk *myllon* lip, L *mutus* mute – more at [1]MUTE]

mullah /'mulə, 'moolə/ *n* a Muslim of a quasi-clerical class trained in traditional law and doctrine [Turk *molla* & Per & Hindi *mulla*, fr Ar *mawlā*] – **mullahism** /-,iz(ə)m/ *n*

mullein *also* **mullen** /'mulən/ *n* any of a genus of plants of the figwort family with spikes of usu yellow flowers [ME *moleyne*, fr AF *moleine*, prob fr OF *mol* soft, fr L *mollis*]

muller /'mulə/ *n* a pestle usu for grinding substances on a slab [alter. of ME *molour*, prob fr *mullen* to grind, fr *mul, mol* dust, prob fr MD]

Müllerian /moo'liəri·ən, myooh-/ *adj* of or being mimicry between 2 or more inedible or dangerous species, considered to reduce the difficulties of recognition by potential predators [Fritz *Müller* †1897 G zoologist]

mullet /'mulit/ *n, pl* **mullet,** *esp for different types* **mullets** any of a family of **a** food fishes with elongated bodies **b** red or golden fishes with 2 barbels on the chin [ME *molet*, fr MF *mulet*, fr L *mullus* red mullet, fr Gk *myllos*; akin to Gk *melas* black, Skt *malina* dirty, black]

mulligatawny /,muligə'tawni/ *n* a rich meat soup of Indian origin seasoned with curry [Tamil *miḷakutaṇṇi*, a strongly seasoned soup, fr *miḷaku* pepper + *taṇṇi* water]

mullion /'muli·ən/ *n* a slender vertical bar placed esp between panes or panels (e g of windows or doors) ☞ ARCHITECTURE [prob alter. of *monial* (mullion), fr ME *moynel, moniel*, fr MF *moinel*, perh fr *moyen* middle] – **mullion** *vt*

mullock /'mulək/ *n, Austr* mining refuse [ME *mullok* rubbish, refuse, fr *mul, mol dust*]

mull over *vt* to consider at length [*mull* (to grind, ponder), fr ME *mullen* – more at MULLER]

multi- /multi-/ *comb form* **1a** many; multiple; much ⟨multi-*storey*⟩ **b** more than 2 ⟨multi*lateral*⟩ ⟨multi*valent*⟩ **c** more than 1 ⟨multi*parous*⟩ **2** many times over ⟨multi*millionaire*⟩ [ME, fr MF or L; MF, fr L, fr *multus* much, many – more at MELIORATE]

'multi,coloured /-,kuləd/ *adj* of various colours

,multi'dentate /-'dentayt/ *adj* having many teeth

,multi'farious /-'feəri·əs/ *adj* having or occurring in great variety; diverse [L *multifarius*, fr *multi-* + *-farius* (akin to *facere* to make, do)] – **multifariously** *adv*, **multifariousness** *n*

'multi,form /-,fawm/ *adj* having many forms or appearances [F *multiforme*, fr L *multiformis*, fr *multi-* + *-formis* -form] – **multiformity** /-'fawməti/ *n*

,multi'lateral /-'lat(ə)rəl/ *adj* **1** having many sides **2** participated in by more than 2 parties **3** *of a school* divided into more than 2 separately organized sides offering different curricula – **multilaterally** *adv*

,multi'layered /-'layəd/, **multilayer** *adj* having or involving several distinct layers, strata, or levels ⟨~ *tropical rain forest*⟩

,multi'lingual /-'ling·gwəl/ *adj* **1** POLYGLOT 2 **2** using or able to use several languages ⟨*a* ~ *stewardess*⟩ – **multilingualism** *n*, **multilingually** *adv*

,multi'media /-'meedi·ə/ *adj* using or involving several media

,multi,millio'naire /-,milyə'neə/ *n* sby whose wealth is estimated at many millions of money units

,multi'national /-'nash(ə)nl/ *adj* **1** of more than 2 nations ⟨*a* ~ *alliance*⟩ ⟨*a* ~ *society*⟩ **2** having divisions in more than 2 countries ⟨*a* ~ *company*⟩ – **multinational** *n*

multiparous /mul'tipərəs/ *adj* **1** producing many or more than 1 offspring at a birth **2** having given birth 1 or more times previously [NL *multiparus*, fr *multi-* + L *-parus* -parous]

,multi'partite /-'pahtiet/ *adj* multilateral [L *multipartitus*, fr *multi-* + *partitus*, pp of *partire* to divide, fr *part-*, *pars* part]

,multi'phasic /-'fayzik/ *adj* having various phases or elements ⟨*a* ~ *test*⟩

[1]**multiple** /'multipl/ *adj* **1** consisting of, including, or involving more than 1 **2** many, manifold ⟨~ *achievements*⟩ **3** shared by many ⟨~ *ownership*⟩ **4** *of a fruit* formed by coalescence of the ripening ovaries of several flowers [F, fr L *multiplex*, fr *multi-* + *-plex* -fold – more at SIMPLE]

[2]**multiple** *n* **1** the product of a quantity by an integer ⟨*35 is a* ~ *of 7*⟩ **2 multiple, multiple store** *chiefly Br* CHAIN STORE

,multiple-'choice *adj* having several answers from which 1 is to be chosen ⟨*a* ~ *exam question*⟩

,multiple scle'rosis *n* progressively developing partial or complete paralysis and jerking muscle tremor resulting from the formation of patches of hardened nerve tissue in nerves of the brain and spinal cord that have lost their myelin

,multiple 'unit *n* a train that has 1 or more carriages containing motors for propulsion and is used mainly for local services

,multiple 'voting *n* illegal voting by 1 person in 2 or more constituencies

[1]**multiplex** /'multi,pleks/ *adj* **1** manifold, multiple **2** being or relating to a system allowing several messages to be transmitted simultaneously by the same circuit or channel [L]

[2]**multiplex** *vb* to send (messages or signals) by a multiplex system – **multiplexer, multiplexor** *n*

multiplicable /,multi'plikəbl/ *adj* capable of being multiplied

multiplicand /,multipli'kand/ *n* a number that is to be multiplied by another [L *multiplicandus*, gerundive of *multiplicare*]

multiplication /,multipli'kaysh(ə)n/ *n* **1** multiplying or being multiplied **2** a mathematical operation that at its simplest is an abbreviated process of adding an integer to itself a specified number of times and that is extended to other numbers in accordance with laws that are valid for integers [ME *multiplicacioun*, fr MF *multiplication*, fr L *multiplication-*, *multiplicatio*, fr *multiplicatus*, pp of *multiplicare* to multiply] – **multiplicative** /,multi'plikətiv/ *adj*, **multiplicatively** *adv*

,multipli'cation ,sign *n* the symbol × denoting multiplication ☞ SYMBOL

multiplicity /,multi'plisəti/ *n* **1** the quality or state of being multiple or various **2** a great number ⟨*a* ~ *of errors*⟩ [MF *multiplicité*, fr LL *multiplicitat-*, *multiplicitas*, fr L *multiplic-*, *multiplex*]

multiplier /'multi,plie·ə/ *n* **1** a number by which another number is multiplied **2** an instrument or device for multiplying or intensifying some effect **3** a key-operated machine or mechanism or circuit on a machine that multiplies figures and records the products [MULTIPLY + [2]-ER]

multiply /'multiplie/ *vt* **1** to increase in number, esp greatly or in multiples; augment **2a** to combine by multiplication ⟨~ *7 and 8*⟩ **b** to combine with (another number) by multiplication – usu pass ⟨*7 multiplied by 8 is 56*⟩ ~ *vi* **1a** to become greater in number; spread **b** to breed or propagate **2** to perform multiplication *USE* (*vt 2; vi 2*) ☞ SYMBOL [ME *multiplien*, fr OF *multiplier*, fr L *multiplicare*, fr *multiplic-*, *multiplex* multiple] – **multipliable** *adj*

,multi'pronged /-'prongd/ *adj* having several distinct aspects or elements

,multi'purpose /-'puhpəs/ *adj* serving several purposes

,multi'racial /-'raysh(ə)l/ *adj* composed of, involving, or representing various races – **multiracialism** *n*

'multi,stage /-,stayj/ *adj* **1** having successive operating stages; *esp* having propulsion units that operate in turn ⟨~ *rockets*⟩ **2** conducted in stages ⟨*a* ~ *investigation*⟩

,multi-'storey /-'stawri/ *n or adj* (a building, esp a car park) having several storeys

multitude /'multityoohd/ *n* **1** the state of being many **2** a great number; a host **3** a crowd – chiefly fml **4** *the* populace, masses [ME, fr MF or L; MF, fr L *multitudin-*, *multitudo*, fr *multus* much – more at MELIORATE]

multitudinous /,multi'tyoohdinəs/ *adj* **1** comprising a multitude of individuals; populous **2** existing in a great multitude **3** existing in or consisting of innumerable elements or aspects *USE* fml – **multitudinously** *adv*, **multitudinousness** *n*

multiversity /,multi'vuhsəti/ *n* a very large university with many component divisions [*multi-* + *-versity* (as in *university*)]

[1]**mum** /mum/ *adj* silent ⟨*keep* ~⟩ – infml [prob imit of a sound made with closed lips]

[2]**mum** *n*, *chiefly Br* MOTHER 1a – infml [short for *mummy*]

mumble /'mumbl/ *vb* **mumbling** /'mumbling, 'mumbl·ing/ to say (words) in an inarticulate usu subdued voice [ME *momelen*, of imit origin] – **mumble** *n*, **mumbler** /'mumblə/ *n*

mumbo jumbo /,mumboh 'jumboh/ *n* **1** elaborate but meaningless ritual **2** involved activity or language that obscures and confuses [*Mumbo Jumbo*, an idol or deity held to have been worshipped in Africa]

mumetal /'myooh,metl/ *n* a nickel-containing alloy that has a high magnetic permeability [μ (*mu*), symbol for permeability]

mummery /'muməri/ *n* **1** a performance of mumming **2** an absurd or pretentious ceremony or performance

mummify /'mumifie/ *vt* **1** to embalm and dry (the body of an animal or human being) **2** to cause to dry up and shrivel ~ *vi* to dry up and shrivel like a mummy – **mummification** /,mumifi'kaysh(ə)n/ *n*

mumming /'muming/ *n* **1** the practice of performing in a traditional pantomime **2** the custom of going about merrymaking in disguise during festivals [ME *mommyng*, fr gerund of *mommen* to perform in a pantomime, fr MF *momer* to go masked] – **mummer** *n*

[1]**mummy** /'mumi/ *n* **1** a body embalmed for burial in the manner of the ancient Egyptians **2** an unusually well-preserved dead body [ME *mummie* powdered parts of a mummified body used as a drug, fr MF *momie*, fr ML *mumia* mummy, powdered mummy, fr Ar *mūmiyah* bitumen, mummy, fr Per *mūm* wax]

[2]**mummy** *n, chiefly Br* MOTHER 1a – used esp by or to children [baby talk, var of *mama, mamma*]

mumps /mumps/ *n pl but sing or pl in constr* an infectious virus disease marked by gross swelling of esp the parotid glands [fr pl of obs *mump* (grimace)]

mun /mən; *strong* mun/ *verbal auxiliary, dial Br* **1** must **2** may [ME *mun, mon* must, shall, fr ON *mon* shall (1 & 3 sing. pres indic; infinitive *munu, monu*); akin to OE *man, mon* he remembers, thinks of, L *ment-, mens* mind]

munch /munch/ *vb* to chew (food) with a crunching sound and visible movement of the jaws [ME *monchen*, prob of imit origin] – **muncher** *n*

mundane /mun'dayn/ *adj* **1** (characteristic) of this world in contrast to heaven **2** practical and ordinary, esp to the point of dull familiarity [ME *mondeyne*, fr MF *mondain*, fr LL *mundanus*, fr L *mundus* world] – **mundanely** *adv*, **mundaneness** *n*

'**mung ,bean** /mung/ *n* (the edible green or yellow seeds of) an erect bushy bean grown in warm regions, esp as the chief source of bean sprouts [Hindi *m ug*, fr Skt *mudga*]

mungo /'mung·goh/ *n, pl* **mungos** reclaimed wool of poor quality; shoddy [origin unknown]

municipal /myooh'nisipl/ *adj* **1a** of a municipality **b** having local self-government **2** restricted to 1 locality [L *municipalis* of a municipality, fr *municip- municeps* inhabitant of a municipality, lit., undertaker of duties, fr *munus* duty, service + *capere* to take – more at [1]MEAN, HEAVE] – **municipally** *adv*

municipality /myooh,nisi'paləti/ *n* (the governing body of) a primarily urban political unit having corporate status and some self-government

municipal·ize, -ise /myooh'nisip(ə)l,iez/ *vt* to invest control of in a municipality – **municipalization** /-ie'zaysh(ə)n/ *n*

munificent /myooh'nifis(ə)nt/ *adj* **1** giving or bestowing with great generosity **2** characterized by great liberality *USE* fml [back-formation fr *munificence*, fr L *munificentia*, fr *munificus* generous, fr *munus* service, gift] – **munificence** *n*, **munificently** *adv*

muniment /'myoohnimənt/ *n* a document kept as evidence of title or privilege – usu pl [AF, fr MF, defence, fr L *munimentum*, fr *munire* to fortify]

munition /myooh'nish(ə)n/ *n* armament, ammunition – usu pl with sing. meaning [MF, fr L *munition- munitio*, fr *munitus*, pp of *munire* to fortify, fr *moena* walls; akin to OE *mǣre* boundary, L *murus* wall] – **munition** *vt*

muntin /'muntin/ *n* a strip separating panes of glass in a sash window or panels in a door ☞ ARCHITECTURE [alter. of *montant* (vertical dividing bar), fr F, fr prp of *monter* to rise – more at [2]MOUNT]

muntjac *also* **muntjak** /'munt,jak/ *n* any of several small deer of SE Asia and the E Indies [prob modif. of Jav *mindjangan* deer]

'**Muntz ,metal** /munts/ *n* a widely used brass zinc alloy [George *Muntz* †1857 E metal manufacturer]

muon /'myooh·on/ *n* an unstable elementary particle similar to but heavier than the electron, that occurs esp in cosmic rays [contr of earlier *mu-meson*, fr *mu* (taken as a symbol for *meson*, and used to distinguish it from the short-lived pi-meson, i e pion)] – **muonic** /myooh'onik/ *adj*

[1]**mural** /'myooərəl/ *adj* of, resembling, or applied to a wall [L *muralis*, fr *murus* wall – more at MUNITION]

[2]**mural** *n* a mural work of art (e g a painting) – **muralist** *n*

[1]**murder** /'muhdə/ *n* **1** the crime of unlawfully and intentionally killing sby **2** sthg very difficult, dangerous, or disagreeable – infml ⟨*it was ~ trying to park*⟩ [partly fr ME *murther*, fr OE *morthor*; partly fr ME *murdre*, fr OF, of Gmc origin; akin to OE *morthor*; akin to OHG *mord* murder, L *mort-, mors* death, *mori* to die, Gk *brotos* mortal]

[2]**murder** *vt* **1** to kill (sby) unlawfully and intentionally **2** to slaughter brutally **3a** to put an end to **b** to mutilate, mangle ⟨*~ a sonata*⟩ ~ *vi* to commit murder – **murderer,** *fem* **murderess** /-ris/ *n*

murderous /'muhd(ə)rəs/ *adj* **1a** having the purpose or capability of murder **b** characterized by or causing murder or bloodshed **2** capable of overwhelming ⟨*~ heat*⟩ – **murderously** *adv*, **murderousness** *n*

murex /'myooəreks/ *n, pl* **murices** /'myooəriseez/, **murexes** any of a genus of tropical marine gastropod molluscs with a rough (spiny) shell that yield a purple dye [NL, genus name, fr L, purple shell; akin to Gk *myak-, myax* sea-mussel]

muriate /'myooəri·ət, -ayt/ *n* a chloride [F, back-formation fr (*acide*) *muriatique* muriatic acid (hydrochloric acid), fr L *muriaticus* pickled in brine, fr *muria* brine]

murine /'myooərien, -rin/ *adj* of or being a common domestic rat or esp (house) mouse [deriv of L *mur-, mus* mouse – more at MOUSE] – **murine** *n*

murk /muhk/ *n* gloom, darkness; *also* fog [ME *mirke*, prob fr ON *myrkr*]

murky /'muhki/ *adj* dark and gloomy – **murkily** *adv*, **murkiness** *n*

[1]**murmur** /'muhmə/ *n* **1** a half-suppressed or muttered complaint **2a** a low indistinct (continuous) sound **b** a subdued or gentle utterance **3** an atypical sound of the heart indicating an abnormality [ME *murmure*, fr MF, fr L *murmur* murmur, roar, of imit origin]

[2]**murmur** *vi* **1** to make a murmur **2** to complain, grumble ~ *vt* to say in a murmur ⟨~ed *an apology for being late*⟩ – **murmurer** *n*

murmuration /,muhmə'raysh(ə)n/ *n* a flock – used with reference to starlings [[2]MURMUR + -ATION]

murmurous /'muhmərəs/ *adj* **1** filled with or making murmurs **2** low and indistinct – **murmurously** *adv*

muscadine /'muskədien, -din/ *n* a grape of the

southern USA with musky fruits borne in small clusters [prob alter. of *muscatel*]

muscarine /'muskəreen/ *n* an alkaloid orig found in fly agaric that gives the effect of stimulation of the parasympathetic nervous system (e g in stimulating smooth muscle and dilating blood vessels) [G *muskarin*, fr NL *muscaria*, specific epithet of *Amanita muscaria* fly agaric] – **muscarinic** /-'rinik/ *adj*

muscat /'muskət, -kat/ *n* any of several cultivated grapes used in making wine and raisins [F, fr Prov, fr *muscat* musky, fr *musc* musk, fr LL *muscus*]

muscatel /,muskə'tel/ *n* **1** a sweet dessert wine made from muscat grapes **2** a raisin made from muscat grapes [ME *muskadelle*, fr MF *muscadel*, fr OProv, fr *muscadel* resembling musk, fr *muscat*]

muscle /'musl/ *n* **1** (an organ that moves a body part, consisting of) a tissue made of modified elongated cells that contract when stimulated to produce motion ANATOMY **2** muscular strength; brawn [MF, fr L *musculus*, fr dim. of *mus* mouse – more at MOUSE] – **muscled** *adj*

'muscle-,bound /-,bownd/ *adj* **1** having enlarged muscles with impaired elasticity, often as a result of excessive exercise **2** lacking flexibility; rigid

muscle in *vi* **muscling** /'musl·ing, 'musling/ to interfere forcibly – infml; often + *on*

muscovado /,muskə'vahdoh/ *n* the unrefined sugar obtained as crystals after sugarcane juice has been evaporated and the molasses drained off [Sp or Pg; Sp *(azúcar) mascabado*, fr Pg *(açúcar) mascavado*, fr *açúcar* sugar + *mascavado*, pp of *mascavar* to adulterate, separate raw sugar (from molasses), fr (assumed) VL *minuscapare*, fr L *minus* less + *caput* head]

muscovite /'muskə,viet/ *n* **1** *cap* a native or inhabitant of (the ancient principality of) Moscow **2** a colourless to pale brown potassium mica [ML or NL *Muscovia, Moscovia* Moscow, principality & city of Russia] – **Muscovite** *adj*

Muscovy duck /'muskəvi/ *n* a large S American crested duck widely kept in domestication [prob alter. of *musk duck*]

muscul-, musculo- *comb form* **1** muscle ⟨muscular⟩ **2** muscular and ⟨musculo*skeletal*⟩ [LL *muscul-*, fr L *musculus*]

muscular /'muskyoolə/ *adj* **1a** of, constituting, or performed by muscle or the muscles **b** having well-developed musculature **2** having strength of expression or character; vigorous – **muscularly** *adv*, **muscularity** /-'larəti/ *n*

,muscular 'dystrophy *n* progressive wasting of muscles occurring as a hereditary disease

musculature /'muskyooləchə/ *n* the system of muscles of (part of) the body [F, fr L *musculus*]

[1]**muse** /myoohz/ *vi* to become absorbed in thought; *esp* to engage in daydreaming ~ *vt* to think or say reflectively [ME *musen*, fr MF *muser* to gape, idle, muse, fr *muse* mouth of an animal, fr ML *musus*] – **muser** *n*

[2]**muse** *n* **1** *cap* any of the 9 sister goddesses in Greek mythology who were the patrons of the arts and sciences **2** a source of inspiration; *esp* a woman who influences a creative artist [ME, fr MF, fr L *Musa*, fr Gk *Mousa*; prob akin to Gk *mnasthai* to remember]

museum /myooh'zee·əm/ *n* an institution devoted to the acquiring, care, study, and display of objects of interest or value; *also* a place exhibiting such objects [L *Museum* library, study, fr Gk *Mouseion*, fr neut of *Mouseios* of the Muses, fr *Mousa*]

mu'seum ,piece *n* **1** an object interesting enough for a museum to display **2** sthg absurdly old-fashioned

mush /mush/ *n* **1** a soft mass of semiliquid material **2** mawkish sentimentality [prob alter. of *mash*]

[1]**mushroom** /'mushroohm, -room/ *n* **1** the enlarged, esp edible, fleshy fruiting body of a class of fungus, consisting typically of a stem bearing a flattened cap **2** a fungus [ME *musseroun*, fr MF *mousseron*, fr LL *mussirion-, mussirio*]

[2]**mushroom** *vi* **1** to spring up suddenly or multiply rapidly **2** to flatten at the end on impact **3** to pick wild mushrooms ⟨*go* ~ing⟩

mushy /'mushi/ *adj* **1** having the consistency of mush **2** mawkishly sentimental – **mushily** *adv*, **mushiness** *n*

music /'myoohzik/ *n* **1a** the science or art of ordering tones or sounds in succession and combination to produce a composition having unity and continuity **b** vocal, instrumental, or mechanical sounds having rhythm, melody, or harmony **2** an agreeable sound **3** the score of a musical composition set down on paper ***USE*** [ME *musik*, fr OF *musique*, fr L *musica*, fr Gk *mousikē* any art presided over by the Muses, esp music, fr fem of *mousikos* of the Muses, fr *Mousa* Muse]

[1]**musical** /'myoohzikl/ *adj* **1** having the pleasing harmonious qualities of music **2** having an interest in or talent for music **3** set to or accompanied by music **4** of music, musicians, or music lovers – **musically** *adv*, **musicality** /-'kaləti/ *n*

[2]**musical** *n* a film or theatrical production that consists of songs, dances, and dialogue based on a unifying plot

'musical ,box, *chiefly NAm* **music box** *n* a container enclosing an apparatus that reproduces music mechanically when activated

,musical 'chairs *n pl but sing in constr* a game in which players march to music round a row of chairs numbering 1 less than the players and scramble for seats when the music stops

,musical 'comedy *n* a musical; *esp* one of a sentimental or humorous nature

'music ,centre *n, Br* a usu stereophonic system that houses a record player, a radio, and a cassette tape recorder in a single unit

'music ,hall *n* (a theatre formerly presenting) entertainments consisting of a variety of unrelated acts (e g acrobats, comedians, or singers)

musician /myooh'zish(ə)n/ *n* a composer, conductor, or performer of music; *esp* an instrumentalist – **musicianship** *n*

musicology /,myoohzi'koləji/ *n* the study of music as a branch of knowledge or field of research [It *musicologia*, fr L *musica* music + *-logia* -logy] – **musicologist** *n*, **musicological** /,myoohzikə'lojikl/ *adj*

'music ,stool *n* a stool usu having an adjustable height and used by a pianist

musing /'myoohzing/ *n* meditation, reflection – **musingly** *adv*

musique concrète /mooh,zeek kong'kret (*Fr* myzik kɔ̃krɛt/ *n* a montage of recorded natural sounds (e g voices, traffic noise, and bird calls) arbitrarily modified and arranged [F, lit., concrete music]

Clefs

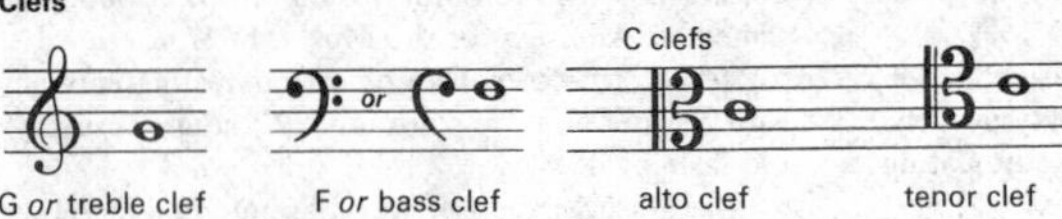

The C clef is called the alto clef or the tenor clef, depending on where it is placed on the staff. The positions of middle C on the alto and tenor clefs are shown.

Notes and rests, and their values

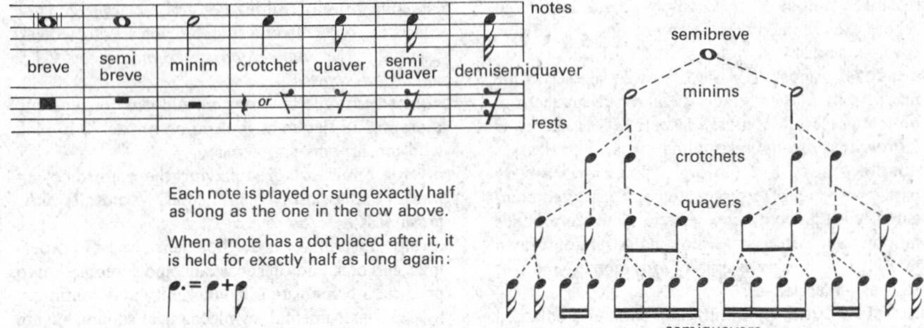

Each note is played or sung exactly half as long as the one in the row above.

When a note has a dot placed after it, it is held for exactly half as long again:

Accidentals

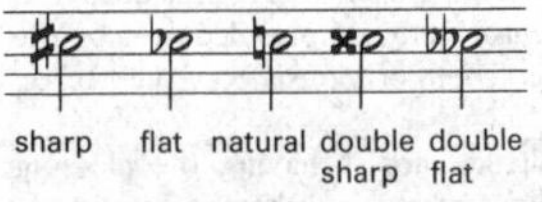

Accidentals are notes that are outside the key indicated by the key signature.

Grace notes are decorative notes before a main note; if they have a stroke across the tail (acciaccaturas) they are played as quickly as possible, but if not (appoggiaturas) they take half the length of the main note.

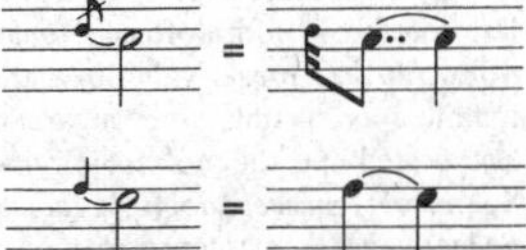

Playing instructions

First bars of Schubert's *Gute Nacht*

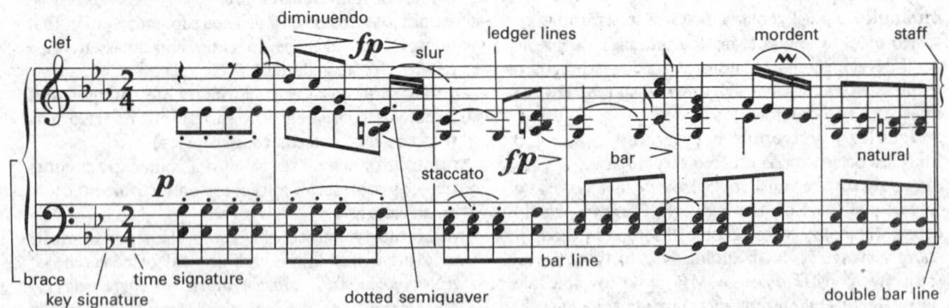

musk /musk/ *n* **1a** (a synthetic substitute for) a substance with a penetrating persistent smell that is obtained from a gland of the male musk deer and used as a perfume fixative; *also* a similar substance from another animal **b** the odour of musk **2** any of various plants with musky smells [ME *muske,* fr MF *musc,* fr LL *muscus,* fr Gk *moschos,* fr Per *mushk,* fr Skt *muṣka* testicle, fr dim. of *mūṣ* mouse; akin to OE *mūs* mouse] – **musky** *adj*

'musk ,deer *n* a small heavy-limbed hornless deer of central Asia, the male of which produces musk

muskeg /'mus,keg/ *n* **1** a sphagnum bog of northern N America, often with tussocks **2** a usu thick deposit of partially decayed vegetable matter of wet northern regions [of Algonquian origin; akin to Ojibwa *mŭskeg* grassy bog]

musket /'muskit/ *n* a heavy large-calibre shoulder firearm with a smooth bore [MF *mousquet,* fr OIt *moschetto* arrow for a crossbow, musket, fr dim. of *mosca* fly, fr L *musca* – more at MIDGE]

musketeer /,muskə'tiə/ *n* a soldier armed with a musket [modif of MF *mousquetaire,* fr *mousquet*]

musketry /'muskitri/ *n* **1** (troops armed with) muskets **2** musket fire

muskmelon /'musk,melən/ *n* (an Asiatic plant that bears) a usu sweet musky-smelling edible melon

'musk-,ox *n* a thickset shaggy-coated wild ox of Greenland and northern N America ☞ DEFENCE

'musk,rat /-,rat/ *n, pl* **muskrats,** *esp collectively* **muskrat** an aquatic rodent of N America with a long scaly tail and webbed hind feet [prob by folk etymology fr a word of Algonquian origin; akin to Natick *musquash* muskrat]

'musk ,rose *n* a rose of the Mediterranean region with musky flowers

'musk ,thistle *n* a Eurasian thistle with drooping musky flower heads

Muslim /'moozlim, 'muz-/ *n* an adherent of Islam [Ar *muslim,* lit., one who surrenders (to God)] – **Muslim** *adj*

muslin /'muzlin/ *n* a plain-woven sheer to coarse cotton fabric [F *mousseline,* fr It *mussolina,* fr Ar *mawṣilīy* of Mosul, fr al-*Mawṣil* Mosul, city in Iraq]

musquash /'muskwosh/ *n* (the dark glossy brown fur or pelt of) the muskrat [of Algonquian origin; akin to Natick *musquash* muskrat]

[1]**muss** /mus/ *n, NAm* a state of disorder; mess – infml [origin unknown] – **mussy** *adj*

[2]**muss** *vt, NAm* to make untidy; disarrange, dishevel – infml

mussel /'musl/ *n* **1** a marine bivalve mollusc with a dark elongated shell **2** a freshwater bivalve mollusc whose shell has a lustrous mother-of-pearl lining [ME *muscle,* fr OE *muscelle*; akin to OHG *muscula* mussel; both fr a prehistoric WGmc word borrowed fr (assumed) VL *muscula,* fr L *musculus* muscle, mussel]

Mussulman /'muslmən, 'moos-/ *n, pl* **Mussulmen** /-mən, -men/, **Mussulmans** *archaic* a Muslim [Turk *müslüman* & Per *musulmān,* modif of Ar *muslim*]

[1]**must** /məs(t); *strong* must/ *verbal auxiliary, pres & past all persons* **must 1a** be commanded or requested to ⟨*you ~ stop*⟩ **b** certainly should; ought by all means to ⟨*I ~ read that book*⟩ ⟨*we* mustn*'t despair*⟩ **2** be compelled by physical, social, or legal necessity to ⟨*man ~ eat to live*⟩ ⟨*I ~ say you're looking much better*⟩; be required by need or purpose to ⟨*we ~ hurry if we want to catch the bus*⟩ – past often replaced by *had to* except in reported speech; used in the negative to express the idea of prohibition ⟨*we ~ not park here*⟩ **3** [1]WILL 6 ⟨*if you ~ go at least wait till morning*⟩; *esp* be unreasonably or perversely compelled to ⟨*why ~ you be so stubborn?*⟩ ⟨*in spite of my advice, she ~ go and do the opposite*⟩ **4** be logically inferred or supposed to ⟨*it ~ be time*⟩ ⟨*they* mustn*'t have arrived*⟩ – compare [1]CAN 1d **5** was presumably certain to; was or were bound to ⟨*if he really was there I ~ have seen him*⟩ [ME *moste,* fr OE *mōste,* past indic & subj of *mōtan* to be allowed to, have to; akin to OHG *muozan* to be allowed to, have to, OE *metan* to measure – more at METE]

[2]**must** /must/ *n* an essential or prerequisite

[3]**must** /must/ *n* grape juice before and during fermentation [ME, fr OE, fr L *mustum,* fr neut of *mustus* young, fresh, new]

mustache /mə'stahsh, mə'stash/ *n, chiefly NAm* a moustache

mustachio /mə'stahshioh, mə'stashioh/ *n, pl* **mustachios** a (large) moustache [Sp & It; Sp *mostacho,* fr It *mustaccio*] – **mustachioed** *adj*

mustang /'mustang/ *n* the small hardy naturalized horse of the western plains of the USA [MexSp *mestengo,* fr Sp, stray, fr *mesteño* strayed, fr *mesta* annual roundup of cattle that disposed of strays, fr ML (*animalia*) *mixta* mixed animals]

mustard /'mustəd/ *n* (a pungent yellow powder used as a condiment or in medicine, esp as an emetic or counterirritant, and ground from the seeds of) any of several related plants with lobed leaves, yellow flowers, and straight seed pods [ME, fr OF *mostarde,* fr *moust* must, fr L *mustum*] – **mustardy** *adj*

'mustard ,gas *n* an irritant and blister-inducing oily liquid used as a poison gas

[1]**muster** /'mustə/ *vt* **1a** to assemble, convene **b** to call the roll of **2** to summon in response to a need ⟨*all the courage he could ~*⟩ ~ *vi* to come together; congregate [ME *mustren* to show, muster, fr OF *monstrer,* fr L *monstrare* to show, fr *monstrum* evil omen, monster – more at MONSTER]

[2]**muster** *n* **1a** assembling (for military inspection) **b** an assembled group; a collection **2** a critical examination ⟨*slipshod work that would never pass ~*⟩

'muster ,roll *n* a register of the officers and men in a military unit or ship's company

musth, must /must/ *n* a periodic state of frenzy in the male elephant, usu connected with the rutting season [Hindi *mast* intoxicated, fr Per; akin to OE *mete* meat]

mustn't /'musnt/ must not

musty /'musti/ *adj* **1** affected by mould, damp, or mildew **2** tasting or smelling of damp and decay [*must* (musk, mould; fr MF, alter. of *musc* musk) + [1]*-y*] – **mustily** *adv,* **mustiness** *n*

mutable /'myoohtəbl/ *adj* **1** capable of or liable to change or alteration **2** capable of or subject to mutation [L *mutabilis,* fr *mutare* to change – more at MISS] – **mutableness** *n,* **mutably** *adv,* **mutability** /,myoohtə'biləti/ *n*

mutagen /'myoohtəjən/ *n* sthg (e g mustard gas) that increases the frequency of mutation [ISV *mutation* + *-gen*] – **mutagenesis** /-'jenəsis/ *n,* **mutagenic** /-'jenik/ *adj,* **mutagenically** *adv,* **mutagenicity** /-jə'nisəti/ *n*

mutation /myooh'taysh(ə)n/ *n* **1** (a) significant and fundamental alteration **2** sandhi; *specif* umlaut **3** (an individual or strain differing from others of its type and resulting from) a relatively permanent change in an organism's hereditary material [ME *mutacioun*, fr MF *mutation*, fr L *mutation-*, *mutatio*, fr *mutatus*, pp of *mutare*] – **mutational** *adj*, **mutationally** *adv*, **mutant** /'myooht(ə)nt/ *n*, **mutate** /myooh'tayt/ *vb*

mutatis mutandis /mooh,tahtis mooh'tandis/ *adv* with the necessary changes having been made or respective differences considered [NL]

[1]**mute** /myooht/ *adj* **1** unable to speak; dumb **2a** felt but not expressed ⟨~ *sympathy*⟩ **b** refusing to plead ⟨*the prisoner stands* ~⟩ **3** *of letters* (*e g the* b *in* plumb) not pronounced [ME *muet*, fr MF, fr OF *mu*, fr L *mutus*; akin to OHG *māwen* to cry out, Gk *mytēs* mute] – **mutely** *adv*, **muteness** *n*

[2]**mute** *n* **1** one who cannot or does not speak **2** STOP 7 **3** a device attached to a musical instrument to reduce, soften, or muffle its tone

[3]**mute** *vt* **1** to muffle or reduce the sound of **2** to tone down (a colour)

[4]**mute** *vi*, *of a bird* to pass waste matter from the body [ME *muten*, fr MF *meutir*, short for *esmeutir*, fr OF *esmeltir*, of Gmc origin]

'**muted** *adj* **1** silent, subdued **2** provided with or produced or modified by the use of a mute – **mutedly** *adv*

mute swan *n* the common white swan of Europe and W Asia that produces no loud notes

mutilate /'myoohtilayt/ *vt* **1** to cut off or permanently destroy or damage a limb or essential part of **2** to damage or deface ⟨*the censors had* ~d *the script*⟩ [L *mutilatus*, pp of *mutilare*, fr *mutilus* mutilated; akin to L *muticus* curtailed, docked, OIr *mut* short] – **mutilator** *n*, **mutilation** /-'laysh(ə)n/ *n*

mutineer /,myoohti'niə/ *n* sby who mutinies

mutinous /'myoohtinəs/ *adj* **1** tending to mutiny; rebellious **2** of or constituting mutiny – **mutinously** *adv*, **mutinousness** *n*

mutiny /'myoohtini/ *n* open resistance to lawful authority; *esp* concerted revolt (e g of a naval crew) against discipline or a superior officer [obs *mutine* (to rebel), fr MF (*se*) *mutiner*, fr *mutin* mutinous, fr *meute* revolt, fr (assumed) VL *movita*, fr fem of *movitus*, alter. of L *motus*, pp of *movēre* to move] – **mutiny** *vi*

mutt /mut/ *n* **1** a dull or stupid person **2** a (mongrel) dog [short for *muttonhead* (dull-witted person)]

mutter /'mutə/ *vi* **1** to utter sounds or words in a low or indistinct voice **2** to utter muffled threats or complaints ~ *vt* to utter, esp in a low or indistinct voice [ME *muteren*; akin to L *muttire* to mutter, *mutus* mute] – **mutter** *n*, **mutterer** *n*

mutton /'mutn/ *n* the flesh of a mature sheep used as food ☞ MEAT [ME *motoun*, fr OF *moton* ram, wether, of Celt origin; akin to MBret *mout* wether] – **muttony** *adj*

'**mutton,chops** /-,chops/ *n pl* side-whiskers that are narrow at the temple and broad by the lower jaws

mutual /'myoohtyooəl, -chəl/ *adj* **1a** directed by each towards the other ⟨~ *affection*⟩ **b** having the same specified feeling for each other ⟨*they had long been* ~ *enemies*⟩ **2** shared by 2 or more in common [ME, fr MF *mutuel*, fr L *mutuus* lent, borrowed, mutual; akin to L *mutare* to change – more at MISS] – **mutualize** *vb*, **mutually** *adv*, **mutuality** /-'aləti/ *n*

mutualism /'myoohtyooə,liz(ə)m, -chəliz(ə)m/ *n* **1** the doctrine or practice of mutual dependence as essential for social welfare **2** symbiosis for mutual benefit – **mutualist** *n*, **mutualistic** /-'listik/ *adj*

Muzak /'myoohzak/ *trademark* – used for recorded background music played in public places

muzhik /'moohzhik/ *n*, *pl* **muzhiks** *also* **muzhiki** /-ki/ a Russian peasant [Russ]

[1]**muzzle** /'muzl/ *n* **1a** the projecting jaws and nose of a dog or other animal **b** a covering for the mouth of an animal used to prevent biting, barking, etc **2** the discharging end of a pistol, rifle, etc [ME *musell*, fr MF *musel*, fr dim. of *muse* mouth of an animal, fr ML *musus*]

[2]**muzzle** *vt* **muzzling** /'muzl·ing, 'muzling/ **1** to fit with a muzzle **2** to restrain from free expression; gag – **muzzler** *n*

'**muzzle-,loader** *n* a firearm that is loaded through the muzzle

muzzy /'muzi/ *adj* mentally confused; befuddled [perh blend of *muddled* and *fuzzy*] – **muzzily** *adv*, **muzziness** *n*

my /mie/ *adj* **1** of me or myself, esp as possessor ⟨~ *car*⟩, agent ⟨~ *promise*⟩, or object of an action ⟨~ *injuries*⟩ – sometimes used with vocatives ⟨~ *child*⟩ ⟨~ *lord*⟩ and in the opening of a letter ⟨My *dear Mrs Jones*⟩ **2** – used interjectionally to express surprise and sometimes reduplicated ⟨~ *oh* ~!⟩, in certain fixed exclamations ⟨~ *God!*⟩, and with names of certain parts of the body to express doubt or disapproval ⟨~ *foot!*⟩ [ME, fr OE *mīn*, fr *mīn*, suppletive gen of *ic* I; akin to OE *mē* me]

my- /mie-/, **myo-** *comb form* muscul- ⟨my*ograph*⟩ ⟨my*oneural*⟩ [NL, fr Gk, fr *mys* mouse, muscle – more at MOUSE]

myasthenia /,mie·əs'theenyə, -ni·ə/ *n* muscular weakness [NL] – **myasthenic** *adj*

,**myas,thenia 'gravis** /'grahvis/ *n* a disease characterized by progressive weakness and exhaustibility of voluntary muscles without wasting [NL, lit., grave myasthenia]

myc-, **myco-** *comb form* fungus ⟨myco*logy*⟩ ⟨my*cosis*⟩ [NL, fr Gk *mykēt-*, *mykēs*; akin to Gk *myxa* nasal mucus]

mycelium /mie'seelyəm/ *n*, *pl* **mycelia** /-lyə/ the mass of interwoven filamentous hyphae that forms the body of a fungus and is usu submerged in another body (e g of soil or the tissues of a host) [NL, fr *myc-* + Gk *hēlos* nail, wart, callus] – **mycelial** *adj*

Mycenaean *also* **Mycenian** /,miesi'nee·ən/ *adj* (characteristic) of the Bronze Age culture of Mycenae and the Eastern Mediterranean area, esp from 1400 BC to 1100 BC [*Mycenae*, ancient city of Greece, fr L, fr Gk *Mykēnai*] – **Mycenaean** *n*

mycetozoan /mie,setə'zoh·ən/ *n* SLIME MOULD [NL *Mycetozoa*, order of protozoans, fr Gk *mykēt-*, *mykēs* + NL *-zoa*] – **mycetozoan** *adj*

mycoflora /,miekə'flawrə/ *n* the fungi characteristic of a region or special environment [NL]

mycology /mie'koləji/ *n* (the biology of) fungal life or fungi [NL *mycologia*, fr *myc-* + L *-logia* -logy] – **mycologist** *n*, **mycological** /,miekə'lojikl/ *also* **mycologic** *adj*, **mycologically** *adv*

mycoplasma /,miekoh'plazmə/ *n*, *pl* **mycoplasmas**, **mycoplasmata** /-mətə/ any of a genus of minute microorganisms without cell walls that are intermediate in some respects between viruses and bacteria and are mostly parasitic, usu in mammals [NL, genus name, fr *myc-* + *plasma*] – **mycoplasmal** *adj*

mycorrhiza /ˌmiekəˈriezə/ *n, pl* **mycorrhizae** /-zi/, **mycorrhizas** the symbiotic association of the mycelium of a fungus with the roots of a flowering plant (e g an orchid) [NL, fr *myc-* + Gk *rhiza* root – more at [1]ROOT] – **mycorrhizal** *adj*

mycosis /mieˈkohsis/ *n, pl* **mycoses** /-seez/ infection with or disease caused by a fungus [NL] – **mycotic** /mieˈkotik/ *adj*

mycotoxin /ˌmiekəˈtoksin/ *n* a toxic substance produced by a fungus, esp a mould

mydriasis /mieˈdrie·əsis/ *n* a long-continued (excessive) dilation of the pupil of the eye [L, fr Gk] – **mydriatic** /ˌmidriˈatik/ *adj or n*

myel-, myelo- *comb form* marrow; spinal cord ⟨myelencephalon⟩ [NL, fr Gk, fr *myelos*, fr *mys* mouse, muscle – more at MOUSE]

myelin /ˈmie·əlin/ *n* a soft white fatty material that forms a thick sheath about the cytoplasmic core of nerve cells adapted for fast conduction of nervous impulses [ISV] – **myelinic** /-ˈlinik/ *adj*

myelinated /ˈmie·əliˌnaytid/ *adj, of a nerve fibre* having a sheath of myelin

myelitis /ˌmie·əˈlietəs/ *n* inflammation of the bone marrow [NL]

myelogenous /ˌmie·əˈlojinəs/, **myelogenic** /ˌmie·əlohˈjenik/ *adj* of, originating in, or produced by the bone marrow [ISV]

myeloid /ˈmie·əˌloyd/ *adj* myelogenous [ISV]

myeloma /ˌmie·əˈlohmə/ *n* a tumour of the bone marrow [NL] – **myelomatous** /-mətəs/ *adj*

myna, mynah *also* **mina** /ˈmienə/ *n* any of various Asian starlings; *esp* a largely black one easily taught to pronounce words [Hindi *mainā*, fr Skt *madana*]

myo- – see MY-

myocardium /ˌmie·ohˈkahdi·əm/ *n* the middle muscular layer of the heart wall [NL, fr *my-* + Gk *kardia* heart – more at HEART] – **myocardial** *adj*, **myocarditis** /-kahˈdietəs/ *n*

myofibril /ˌmie·ohˈfiebril, -ˈfibril/ *n* any of the long thin parallel contractile filaments of a muscle cell [NL *myofibrilla*, fr *my-* + *fibrilla* fibril] – **myofibrillar** *adj*

myoglobin /ˌmie·əˈglohbin, ˈ--ˌ--/ *n* a red iron-containing protein pigment in muscles, similar to haemoglobin [ISV]

myope /ˈmieˌohp/ *n* a myopic person [F, fr LL *myops* myopic, fr Gk *myōps*, fr *myein* to be closed + *ōps* eye, face – more at MYSTERY, EYE]

myopia /mieˈohpi·ə/ *n* defective vision of distant objects resulting from the focussing of the visual images in front of the retina; shortsightedness – compare HYPERMETROPIA [NL, fr Gk *myōpia*, fr *myōp-*, *myōps*] – **myopic** /mieˈopik, -ˈohpik/ *adj*, **myopically** *adv*

myosin /ˈmie·əsin/ *n* a fibrous muscle protein that reacts with actin to produce muscular movement [ISV *myos-* (fr Gk *myos*, gen of *mys* mouse, muscle) + *-in*]

myosis /mieˈohsis/ *n* miosis – **myotic** /mieˈotik/ *adj*

[1]**myriad** /ˈmiri·əd/ *n* **1** ten thousand **2** an indefinitely large number – often pl with sing. meaning [Gk *myriad-*, *myrias*, fr *myrioi* countless, ten thousand]

[2]**myriad** *adj* innumerable, countless

myriapod, myriopod /ˈmiri·əˌpod/ *n* a millipede, centipede, or related arthropod with a body made up of numerous similar segments bearing jointed legs [deriv of Gk *myrioi* + *pod-*, *pous* foot – more at FOOT]

myrmec-, myrmeco- *comb form* ant ⟨myrmecophagous⟩ [Gk *myrmēk-*, *myrmēko-*, fr *myrmēk-*, *myrmēx* – more at PISMIRE]

myrmidon /ˈmuhmid(ə)n/ *n* a subordinate who carries out orders unquestioningly [L *Myrmidon-*, *Myrmido*, fr Gk *Myrmidōn*, one of the legendary Thessalian people accompanying Achilles to the Trojan War]

myrobalan /mieˈrobələn, mi-/ *n* **1** the dried astringent fruit of an E Indian tree used chiefly in tanning and in inks **2** an Asian plum tree much used in Europe as grafting stock [MF *mirobolan*, fr L *myrobalanus*, fr Gk *myrobalanos*, fr *myron* unguent + *balanos* acorn – more at SMEAR, GLAND]

myrrh /muh/ *n* (a mixture of labdanum with) brown bitter aromatic gum resin obtained from any of several African and Asian trees [ME *myrre*, fr OE, fr L *myrrha*, fr Gk, of Sem origin; akin to Ar *murr* myrrh]

myrtle /ˈmuhtl/ *n* **1** an evergreen S European bushy shrub with shiny leaves, fragrant white or rosy flowers, and black berries, or a related tropical shrub or tree **2** *NAm* [1]PERIWINKLE [ME *mirtille*, fr MF, fr ML *myrtillus*, fr L *myrtus*, fr Gk *myrtos*, prob of Sem origin]

myself /mieˈself/ *pron* **1** that identical one that is I – used reflexively ⟨*I got ~ a new suit*⟩, for emphasis ⟨*I ~ will go*⟩, or in absolute constructions ⟨*~ a tourist, I nevertheless avoided other tourists*⟩ **2** my normal self ⟨*I'm not quite ~ today*⟩ – compare ONESELF [ME, alter. of *meself*]

mysterious /miˈstiəri·əs/ *adj* **1** difficult to comprehend **2** containing, suggesting, or implying mystery – **mysteriously** *adv*, **mysteriousness** *n*

mystery /ˈmist(ə)ri/ *n* **1a** a religious truth disclosed by revelation alone **b(1)** any of the 15 events (e g the Nativity, the Crucifixion, or the Assumption) serving as a subject for meditation during the saying of the rosary **(2)** *cap* a Christian sacrament; *specif* the Eucharist **c** a secret religious rite (e g of Eleusinian or Mithraic cults) **2a** sthg not understood or beyond understanding ⟨*his disappearance remains a ~*⟩ ⟨*a ~ illness*⟩ **b** a fictional work dealing usu with the solution of a mysterious crime **3** an enigmatic or secretive quality [ME *mysterie*, fr L *mysterium*, fr Gk *mystērion*, fr (assumed) *mystos* keeping silence, fr Gk *myein* to be closed (of the eyes or lips)]

ˈmystery ˌplay, mystery *n* a medieval religious drama based on episodes from the Scriptures [F *mystère*, fr L *mysterium*]

mystic /ˈmistik/ *n* a person who believes that God or ultimate reality can only be apprehended by direct personal experience (and who orders his/her life towards this goal)

mystical /ˈmistikl/, **mystic** *adj* **1** having a sacred or spiritual meaning not given by normal modes of thought or feeling **2** of or resulting from a person's direct experience of communion with God or ultimate reality **3** of mysteries or esoteric rites **4** of mysticism or mystics **5a** mysterious, incomprehensible **b** obscure, esoteric **c** arousing awe and wonder [ME *mistik*, fr L *mysticus* of mysteries, fr Gk *mys-*

tikos, fr (assumed) *mystos*] – **mystically** *adv*, **mysticism** /-,siz(ə)m/ *n*

mystification /,mistifi'kaysh(ə)n/ *n* mystifying or being mystified

mystify /'mistifie/ *vt* **1** to perplex, bewilder **2** to cause to appear mysterious or obscure [F *mistifier*, fr *mystère* mystery, fr L *mysterium*] – **mystifier** *n*, **mystifyingly** *adv*

mystique /mi'steek/ *n* **1** a mystical reverential atmosphere or quality associated with a person or thing **2** an esoteric skill peculiar to an occupation or activity [F, fr *mystique*, adj, mystic, fr L *mysticus*]

myth /mith/ *n* **1** a traditional story that embodies popular beliefs or explains a practice, belief, or natural phenomenon **2** a parable, allegory **3a** a person or thing having a fictitious existence **b** a belief subscribed to uncritically by an (interested) group [Gk *mythos* tale, speech, myth]

mythical /'mithikl/ *also* **mythic** *adj* **1** based on or described in a myth **2** invented or imagined – **mythically** *adv*

mythic·ize, -ise /'mithi,siez/ *vt* to treat as or make the basis of a myth – **mythicizer** *n*

mythological /,mithə'lojikl/ *adj* **1** of or dealt with in mythology or myths **2** lacking factual or historical basis – **mythologically** *adv*

mytholog·ize, -ise /mi'tholəjiez/ *vt* to build a myth round ~ *vi* to relate, classify, and explain myths – **mythologizer** *n*

mythology /mi'tholəji/ *n* **1** a body of myths, esp those dealing with the gods and heroes of a particular people **2** a branch of knowledge that deals with myth **3** a body of beliefs, usu with little factual foundation, lending glamour or mystique to sby or sthg [F or LL; F *mythologie*, fr LL *mythologia* interpretation of myths, fr Gk, legend, myth, fr *mythologein* to relate myths, fr *mythos* + *logos* speech – more at LEGEND] – **mythologist** *n*

,my 'word *interj* – used to express surprise or astonishment

myxoedema /,miksə'deemə/ *n* thickening and dryness of the skin and loss of vigour resulting from severe hypothyroidism [NL, fr Gk *myxa* lamp wick, mucus + NL *oedema* swelling]

myxoma /mik'sohmə/ *n, pl* **myxomas, myxomata** /-mətə/ a soft tumour made up of gelatinous connective tissue [NL, fr Gk *myxa*] – **myxomatous** /-mətəs/ *adj*

myxomatosis /,miksəmə'tohsis/ *n* a severe flea-transmitted virus disease of rabbits that is characterized by the formation of myxomas in the body, and that has been used in their biological control [NL, fr *myxomat-*, *myxoma*]

myxomycete /,miksoh'mieseet, ,---'-/ *n* SLIME MOULD [deriv of Gk *myxa* + *mykēt-*, *mykēs* fungus – more at MYC-] – **myxomycetous** /,---'--/ *adj*

N

n /en/ *n, pl* **n's, ns** *often cap* **1** (a graphic representation of or device for reproducing) the 14th letter of the English alphabet **2** an indefinite number **3** the haploid or gametic number of chromosomes **4** an en

-n – see [1]-EN

'n' *also* **'n** /(ə)n/ *conj* and ⟨*fish ~ chips*⟩

na /nə/ *adv, Scot* no [ME (northern), fr OE *nā* – more at NO]

Naafi /'nafi/ *n* the organization which runs shops and canteens in British military establishments; *also* any of these shops or canteens [*N*avy, *A*rmy, and *A*ir *F*orce *I*nstitutes]

nab /nab/ *vt* **-bb-** **1** to arrest; apprehend **2** to catch hold of; grab *USE* infml [perh alter. of E dial. *nap*, prob of Scand origin]

nabob /'naybob/ *n* **1** a provincial governor of the Mogul empire in India **2** a man of great wealth – used orig of an Englishman grown rich in India [Hindi & Urdu *nawwāb*, fr Ar *nuwwāb*, pl of *nā'ib* governor] – **nabobess** /-'bes/ *n*

nacelle /na'sel/ *n* a housing for an aircraft engine [F, lit., small boat, fr LL *navicella*, dim. of L *navis* ship – more at [2]NAVE]

nacre /'naykə/ *n* mother-of-pearl [MF, fr OIt *naccara* drum, nacre, fr Ar *naqqārah* drum] – **nacred** *adj*, **nacreous** /'naykri·əs/ *adj*

NAD *n* a widely occurring compound that is a cofactor of numerous enzymes that catalyse oxidation or reduction reactions [*n*icotinamide-*a*denine *d*inucleotide]

Na-dene /nə 'deen/ *also* **Na-déné** /~, nah 'deni/ *n* a group of related American Indian languages spoken in parts of NW USA [*na-* (fr an Athapaskan word-stem basically meaning 'people") + *Déné* (a member or the language of an Athapaskan people living in Alaska & NW Canada), fr F, fr Déné]

nadir /'naydiə, 'nah-/ *n* **1** the point of the celestial sphere that is directly opposite the zenith and vertically downwards from the observer **2** the lowest point [ME, fr MF, fr Ar *naẓīr* opposite]

naevus /'neevəs/ *n* a congenital pigmented area on the skin; a birthmark [NL, fr L]

,naff 'off /naf/ *vi, Br* FUCK OFF 1 – euph; slang [*naff* perh alter. of *eff*]

[1]**nag** /nag/ *n* a horse; *esp* one that is old or in poor condition [ME *nagge*; akin to D *negge* small horse]

[2]**nag** *vb* **-gg-** *vi* **1** to find fault incessantly **2** to be a persistent source of annoyance or discomfort ~ *vt* to subject to constant scolding or urging [prob of Scand origin; akin to ON *gnaga* to gnaw; akin to OE *gnagan* to gnaw] – **nagger** *n*, **nagging** *adj*, **naggingly** *adv*

[3]**nag** *n* a person, esp a woman, who nags habitually

Naga /'nahgə/ *n, pl* **Nagas,** *esp collectively* **Naga** a member of a group of Tibeto-Burman peoples in Assam and adjoining parts of Burma

nagana /nə'gahnə/ *n* a fatal disease of domestic animals in tropical Africa caused by a trypanosome and transmitted by tsetse flies [Zulu *u-nakane, ulu-nakane*]

Nahuatl /'nah,wahtl, -,wo-/ *n, pl* **Nahuatls,** *esp collectively* **Nahuatl** **1** a group of American Indian peoples of S Mexico and Central America **2** the language of the Nahuatl people [Sp, fr Nahuatl] – **Nahuatlan** /nah'wahtlən, -'wotlən/ *adj or n*

Nahum /'nayhəm/ *n* (an Old Testament book attributed to) a Hebrew prophet of the 7th c BC [Heb *Naḥūm*]

naiad /'niead/ *n, pl* **naiads, naiades** /'nie·ə,deez/ **1** *often cap* a nymph in classical mythology living in lakes, rivers, etc **2** the aquatic larva of a mayfly, dragonfly, damselfly, etc [F or L; F *naïade*, fr L *naiad-, naias*, fr Gk, fr *nan* to flow – more at NOURISH]

naice /nays/ *adj* affectedly proper or polite – humor or derog [alter. of *nice*]

naïf /nah'eef/ *adj* naive [F] – **naïf** *n*

[1]**nail** /nayl/ *n* **1** (a claw or other structure corresponding to) a horny sheath protecting the upper end of each finger and toe of human beings and other primates **2** a slender usu pointed and headed spike designed to be driven in, esp with a hammer, to join materials, act as a support, etc [ME, fr OE *nægl*; akin to OHG *nagal* nail, fingernail, L *unguis* fingernail, toenail, claw, Gk *onyx*]

[2]**nail** *vt* **1** to fasten (as if) with a nail **2** to fix steadily **3** to catch, trap **4** to detect and expose (e g a lie or scandal) so as to discredit **5** *chiefly NAm* to hit, strike *USE* (*except 1*) infml – **nailer** *n*

nail down *vt* **1** to define or establish clearly **2** to secure a definite promise or decision from

nainsook /'nayn,sook/ *n* a soft lightweight cotton cloth [Hindi *nainsukh*, fr *nain* eye + *sukh* delight]

naira /'nierə/ *n* ☞ *Nigeria* at NATIONALITY [native name in Nigeria]

naive, naïve /nah'eev, nie-/ *adj* **1** ingenuous, unsophisticated **2** lacking in worldly wisdom or informed judgment; *esp* credulous **3** PRIMITIVE 3d [F *naïve*, fem of *naïf*, fr OF, inborn, natural, fr L *nativus* native] – **naively** *adv*, **naiveness** *n*

naiveté, naïveté, naivete /nah'eevəti, nie-/ *n* naivety [F *naïveté*, fr OF, inborn character, fr *naïf*]

naivety *also* **naïvety** /nah'eev'ti, nie-/ *n* **1** being naive **2** a naive remark or action

naked /'naykid/ *adj* **1** having no clothes on **2a** *of a knife or sword* not enclosed in a sheath or scabbard **b** exposed to the air or to full view ⟨*a ~ light*⟩ **c** *of (part of) a plant or animal* lacking hairs or other covering or enveloping parts (e g a shell or feathers) **d** lacking foliage or vegetation **3** without furnishings or ornamentation ⟨*a ~ room*⟩ **4** unarmed, defenceless **5** lacking factual confirmation or support ⟨~

faith⟩ **6** not concealed or disguised ⟨*the ~ truth*⟩ **7** unaided by any optical device ⟨*visible to the ~ eye*⟩ [ME, fr OE *nacod*; akin to OHG *nackot* naked, L *nudus*, Gk *gymnos*] – **nakedly** *adv*, **nakedness** *n*

namby-pamby /,nambi 'pambi/ *adj* **1** insipidly sentimental **2** lacking resolution or firmness; soft [*Namby Pamby*, satirical nickname given to Ambrose Philips †1749 E poet] – **namby-pamby** *n*, **namby-pambyism** *n*

[1]**name** /naym/ *n* **1** a word or phrase designating an individual person or thing **2** a descriptive usu disparaging epithet ⟨*called him ~*s⟩ **3a** reputation ⟨*gave the town a bad ~*⟩ **b** a famous or notorious person or thing **4** family, kindred ⟨*was a disgrace to his ~*⟩ **5** semblance as opposed to reality ⟨*a friend in ~ only*⟩ [ME, fr OE *nama*; akin to OHG *namo* name, L *nomen*, Gk *onoma, onyma*] – **one's name is mud** one is in disgrace

[2]**name** *vt* **1** to give a name to; call **2** to identify by name **3** to nominate, appoint **4** to decide on; choose ⟨*~ the day for the wedding*⟩ **5** to mention explicitly; specify – **nameable** *adj*, **namer** *n*

'name-,calling *n* the use of abusive language, esp when resorted to in place of reasoned argument

'name ,day *n* the feast day of the saint whose name one has taken at baptism

'name-,dropping *n* seeking to impress others by the apparently casual mention of prominent people as friends – **name-dropper** *n*

'nameless /-lis/ *adj* **1** obscure, undistinguished **2** not known by name; anonymous **3** having no legal right to a name; illegitimate **4a** having no name ⟨*a ~ species of moth*⟩ **b** left purposely unnamed ⟨*a certain person who shall remain ~*⟩ **5** not marked with a name ⟨*a ~ grave*⟩ **6a** not capable of being described; indefinable ⟨*~ fears*⟩ **b** too terrible or distressing to describe ⟨*a ~ horror*⟩ – **namelessly** *adv*, **namelessness** *n*

'namely /-li/ *adv* that is to say

,name of the 'game *n* *the* essence or true purpose of an activity ⟨*in dieting perseverance is the ~*⟩

'name,plate /-,playt/ *n* a plate or plaque bearing a name

'name,sake /-,sayk/ *n* sby or sthg that has the same name as another [prob fr *name's sake* (i e one named for the sake of another's name)]

nancy /'nansi/ *n* an effeminate male (homosexual) – derog [fr the female name *Nancy*]

nankeen /,nang'keen/ *n* a durable brownish yellow cotton fabric orig made in China [*Nanking*, city in China]

nanna /'nanə/ *n, Br* a granny – used by or to children [prob baby-talk]

nanny *also* **nannie** /'nani/ *n, chiefly Br* a child's nurse; a nursemaid [prob baby-talk]

'nanny ,goat *n* a female domestic goat – infml [*Nanny*, nickname for *Anne*]

nano- *comb form* one thousand millionth (10^{-9}) part of ⟨nanosecond⟩ ☞ PHYSICS [ISV, fr Gk *nanos* dwarf]

[1]**nap** /nap/ *vi* **-pp-** **1** to take a short sleep, esp during the day **2** to be off one's guard ⟨*caught his opponent ~ping*⟩ [ME *nappen*, fr OE *hnappian*; akin to OHG *hnaffezen* to doze]

[2]**nap** *n* a short sleep, esp during the day

[3]**nap** *n* a hairy or downy surface (e g on a woven fabric); a pile [ME *noppe*, fr MD, flock of wool, nap; akin to OE *hnoppian* to pluck, Gk *konis* ashes – more at INCINERATE] – **napless** *adj*, **napped** *adj*

[4]**nap** *vt* **-pp-** to raise a nap on (fabric or leather)

[5]**nap** *n* NAPOLEON 2

[6]**nap** *vt* **-pp-** to recommend (a horse) as a possible winner – **nap** *n*

[1]**napalm** /'nay,pahm/ *n* **1** a thickener consisting of a mixture of aluminium soaps **2** petrol jellied with napalm and used esp in incendiary bombs and flamethrowers [*na*phthenate (a salt of naphthene) + *palm*itate]

[2]**napalm** *vt* to attack with napalm

nape /nayp/ *n* the back of the neck [ME]

napery /'naypəri/ *n* household linen; *esp* table linen [ME, fr MF *naperie*, fr *nappe, nape* tablecloth – more at NAPKIN]

naphth-, naphtho- *comb form* naphthalene ⟨naphtho*quinone*⟩ [ISV, fr *naphtha* & *naphthalene*]

naphtha /'nafthə/ *n* **1** petroleum **2** any of various liquid hydrocarbon mixtures used chiefly as solvents [L, fr Gk, of Iranian origin; akin to Per *neft* naphtha]

naphthalene /'nafthəleen/ *n* a hydrocarbon usu obtained by distillation of coal tar and used esp in the synthesis of organic chemicals [alter. of earlier *naphthaline*, irreg fr *naphtha*] – **naphthalenic** /-'lenik/ *adj*

Napierian logarithm /nə,piəri·ən/ *n* NATURAL LOGARITHM [John *Napier* †1617 Sc mathematician]

napkin /'napkin/ *n* **1** a usu square piece of material (e g linen or paper) used at table to wipe the lips or fingers and protect the clothes **2** *chiefly Br* a nappy – fml [ME *nappekin*, fr *nappe* tablecloth, fr MF, fr L *mappa* napkin]

napoleon /nə'pohli·ən/ *n* **1** a French 20-franc gold coin **2** (a bid to win all 5 tricks at) a card game played with hands of 5 cards in which players bid to name the numbers of tricks they will take [F *napoléon*, fr *Napoléon* Napoleon I †1821 Emperor of France]

Napoleonic /nə,pohli'onik/ *adj* of or resembling Napoleon I ⟨*~ ambitions*⟩

nappy /'napi/ *n, chiefly Br* a square piece of cloth or paper worn by babies to absorb and retain excreta and usu drawn up between the legs and fastened at the waist [*nap*kin + *-y*]

'nappy ,rash *n* a rash on the part of a baby's body covered by its nappy caused esp by contact with ammonia from its urine

narcissism /'nahsi,siz(ə)m/ *n* love of or sexual desire for one's own body [G *narzissismus*, fr *Narziss* Narcissus, a youth in Gk mythology who died for love of his own reflection & was turned into a narcissus, fr L *Narcissus*, fr Gk *Narkissos*] – **narcissist** *n or adj*, **narcissistic** /-'sistik/ *adj*

narcissus /nah'sisəs/ *n* a daffodil; *esp* one whose flowers are borne separately and have a short corona [NL, genus name, fr L, fr Gk *narkissos*]

narcolepsy /'nahkə,lepsi/ *n* brief attacks of deep sleep occurring as an abnormal condition [ISV, fr Gk *narkē*] – **narcoleptic** /-'leptik/ *n or adj*

narcosis /nah'kohsis/ *n, pl* **narcoses** /-seez/ stupor or unconsciousness produced by narcotics or other chemicals [NL, fr Gk *narkōsis* action of benumbing, fr *narkoun*]

[1]**narcotic** /nah'kotik/ *n* a usu addictive drug, esp (a derivative of) morphine, that dulls the senses, induces prolonged sleep, and relieves pain – compare

HEROIN [ME *narkotik*, fr MF *narcotique*, fr *narcotique*, adj, fr ML *narcoticus*, fr Gk *narkōtikos*, fr *narkoun* to benumb, fr *narkē* numbness – more at SNARE] – **narcotize** /'nahkə,tiez/ *vb*

²**narcotic** *adj* **1a** like, being, or yielding a narcotic **b** inducing mental lethargy; soporific **2** of (addiction to) narcotics – **narcotically** *adv*

nard /nahd/ *n* the spikenard plant [ME *narde*, fr MF or L; MF, fr L *nardus*, fr Gk *nardos*, of Sem origin; akin to Heb *nērd* nard]

narghile, nargileh /'nahgili/ *n* a water pipe (with several flexible tubes for drawing the smoke through water) – compare HOOKAH [Per *nārgīla*, fr *nārgīl* coconut (of which the bowls were orig made)]

naris /'naris, 'neə-/ *n, pl* **nares** /-reez/ the opening of the nose or nasal cavity of a vertebrate [L; akin to L *nasus* nose – more at NOSE]

¹**nark** /nahk/ *n* **1** *Br* a police informer **2** *chiefly Austr* an annoying person or thing ***USE*** slang [prob fr Romany *nak* nose]

²**nark** *vb, Br vi* to act as an informer – slang; often + *on* ~ *vt* to offend, affront – infml

Narraganset /,narə'gansit/ *n, pl* **Narragansets,** *esp collectively* **Narraganset** a member, or the Algonquian language, of an American Indian people of Rhode Island

narrate /nə'rayt/ *vt* to recite the details of (a story) [L *narratus*, pp of *narrare*, fr L *gnarus* knowing; akin to L *gnoscere, noscere* to know – more at KNOW] – **narrator** /nə'raytə, 'narətə/ *n*

narration /nə'raysh(ə)n/ *n* **1** (a) narrating **2** a story, narrative – **narrational** *adj*

narrative /'narətiv/ *n* **1** sthg (e g a story) that is narrated **2** the art or practice of narration – **narrative** *adj*, **narratively** *adv*

¹**narrow** /'naroh/ *adj* **1** of little width, esp in comparison with height or length **2** limited in size or scope; restricted **3** inflexible, hidebound **4** only just sufficient or successful ⟨*a* ~ *escape*⟩ **5** TENSE 3 [ME *narowe*, fr OE *nearu*; akin to OHG *narwa* scar, *snuor* cord, Gk *narnax* box] – **narrowly** *adv*, **narrowness** *n*

²**narrow** *n* a narrow part or (water) passage; *specif* STRAIT 1 – usu pl with sing. meaning

³**narrow** *vt* **1** to make narrow or narrower **2** to restrict the scope or sphere of ~ *vi* to become narrow or narrower

'**narrow ,boat** *n* a canal barge with a beam of 2.1m (7ft) or less

,**narrow 'gauge** /gayj/ *n* a railway gauge narrower than standard gauge

,**narrow-'minded** /-'miendid/ *adj* lacking tolerance or breadth of vision; bigoted – **narrow-mindedly** *adv*, **narrow-mindedness** *n*

narthex /'nahtheks/ *n* **1** the portico of an early church **2** a vestibule at the west end of a church [LGk *narthēx*, fr Gk, giant fennel, cane, casket]

narwhal *also* **narwal** /'nahwəl/ *n* a small arctic whale, the male of which has a long twisted ivory tusk [Norw & Dan *narhval* & Sw *narval*, prob modif of Icel *náhvalur*, fr ON *nāhvalr*, fr *nār* corpse + *hvalr* whale; fr its colour]

nary /'nari, 'neəri/ *adj, chiefly dial* not one single [alter. of *ne'er a*]

nas-, naso- *also* **nasi-** *comb form* **1** nose ⟨naso*sinusitis*⟩ **2** nasal; nasal and ⟨naso*labial*⟩ [L *nasus* nose – more at NOSE]

¹**nasal** /'nayzl/ *n* a nasal speech sound [MF, nosepiece, fr OF, fr *nes* nose, fr L *nasus*]

²**nasal** *adj* **1** of the nose **2a** uttered through the nose with the mouth passage closed (as in English /m, n, ng/) **b** uttered with both the mouth and nose passage open (as in French *en*) **c** characterized by resonance produced through the nose – **nasally** *adv*, **nasality** /nay'zaləti/ *n*

nasal,ize, -ise /'nayzl,iez/ *vb* to speak or say in a nasal manner – **nasalization** /-ie'zaysh(ə)n/ *n*

nascent /'nas(ə)nt, 'nay-/ *adj* in the process of being born; just beginning to develop – fml [L *nascent-, nascens*, prp of *nasci* to be born – more at NATION] – **nascence** *n*, **nascency** *n*

nastic /'nastik/ *adj* of or being a movement of a plant part caused by the disproportionate growth of 1 surface [Gk *nastos* close-pressed, fr *nassein* to press]

nasturtium /nə'stuhsh(ə)m/ *n* (any of a genus of plants related to) a widely cultivated plant with showy spurred flowers and pungent seeds [L, a cress, perh fr *nasus* nose + *-turtium, -turcium* (fr *torquēre* to twist); fr its strong smell]

nasty /'nahsti/ *adj* **1a** disgustingly filthy **b** repugnant, esp to smell or taste **2** obscene, indecent **3** mean, tawdry ⟨*cheap and* ~ *furniture*⟩ **4a** harmful, dangerous ⟨*a* ~ *accident*⟩ **b** disagreeable, dirty ⟨~ *weather*⟩ **5** giving cause for concern or anxiety ⟨*a* ~ *suspicion*⟩ **6** spiteful, vicious ⟨*trespassers who turn* ~ *when challenged*⟩ [ME] – **nastily** *adv*, **nastiness** *n*

natal /'naytl/ *adj* of, present at, or associated with (one's) birth ⟨*a* ~ *star*⟩ [ME, fr L *natalis*, fr *natus*, pp of *nasci* to be born – more at NATION]

natality /nə'taləti/ *n* the birthrate

natation /nay'taysh(ə)n/ *n* the action or art of swimming – fml [L *natation-, natatio*, fr *natatus*, pp of *natare* to swim, float]

natatorial /,naytə'tawri·əl/, **natatory** /'naytət(ə)ri/ *adj* (adapted to) swimming

natch /nach/ *adv* NATURALLY 2 – infml; usu used interjectionally [by shortening & alter.]

nates /'nayteez/ *n pl* the buttocks [L, pl of *natis* buttock; akin to Gk *nōtos, nōton* back]

Natick /'naytik/ *n* a dialect of Massachuset

nation /'naysh(ə)n/ *n* **1** *sing or pl in constr* **a** a people with a common origin, tradition, and language (capable of) constituting a nation-state **b** a community of people possessing a more or less defined territory and government **2** a tribe or federation of tribes (e g of American Indians) [ME *nacioun*, fr MF *nation*, fr L *nation-, natio* birth, race, nation, fr *natus*, pp of *nasci* to be born; akin to L *gignere* to beget – more at KIN] – **nationhood** *n*

¹**national** /'nash(ə)nl/ *adj* **1** of a nation **2** belonging to or maintained by the central government **3** of or being a coalition government – **nationally** *adv*

²**national** *n* **1** a citizen of a specified nation **2** a competition that is national in scope – usu pl

,**national as'sistance** *n, Br, often cap N&A* SUPPLEMENTARY BENEFIT – not now used technically

,**National Cer'tificate** *n* a British technician's qualification obtained at either of 2 levels by part-time study

,**national 'debt** *n* the amount of money owed by the government of a country

,**National Di'ploma** *n* an advanced British qualification, usu in a technical or applied subject, obtained

at either of 2 levels typically by part-time or sandwich-course study
ˌNational ˈFront *n* an extreme right-wing political party of Britain asserting the racial superiority of the indigenous British population over immigrants (e g blacks)
ˌnational ˈgrid *n, Br* **1** a country-wide network of high-voltage cables between major power stations ☞ ENERGY **2** the system of coordinates used for map reference by the Ordnance Survey
ˌNational ˈGuard *n* a militia force recruited by each state of the USA and equipped by the federal government that can be called up by either
ˌNational ˈHealth ˌService, National Health *n* the British system of medical care, started in 1948, by which every person receives free medical treatment paid for by taxation
ˌnational inˈsurance *n, often cap N&I* a compulsory social-security scheme in Britain funded by contributions from employers, employees, and the government which insures the individual against sickness, retirement, and unemployment
nationalism /ˈnash(ə)nl,iz(ə)m/ *n* loyalty and devotion to a nation; *esp* the exalting of one nation above all others
ˈnationalˌist /-ˌist/ *n* **1** an advocate of nationalism **2** *cap* a member of a political group advocating national independence or strong national government – **nationalist, nationalistic** /-ˈistik/ *adj,* **nationalistically** *adv*
nationality /ˌnash(ə)nˈaləti/ *n* **1** national character **2** national status **3** citizenship of a particular nation **4** existence as a separate nation **5a** NATION 1a **b** an ethnic group within a larger unit ***USE*** 0
national·ize, -ise /ˈnash(ə)nl,iez/ *vt* **1** to make national **2** to invest control or ownership of in the national government – **nationalizer** *n,* **nationalization** /-ieˈzaysh(ə)n/ *n*
ˌnational ˈpark *n* an area of special scenic, historical, or scientific importance preserved and maintained by the government
ˌnational ˈproduct *n* the value of the goods and services produced in a nation during a year
ˌnational ˈservice *n* conscripted service in the British armed forces – **national serviceman** /-mən/ *n*
ˌnational ˈsocialism *n* Nazism – **national socialist** *adj*
nation-state /ˌ-- ˈ-, ˈ-- ˌ-/ *n* a sovereign state inhabited by a relatively homogeneous people as opposed to several nationalities
[1]native /ˈnaytiv/ *adj* **1** inborn, innate ⟨~ *talents*⟩ **2** belonging to a particular place by birth ⟨~ *to Yorkshire*⟩ **3a** belonging to or being the place of one's birth ⟨*my ~ language*⟩ **b** of or being one's first language or sby using his/her first language ⟨*a ~ speaker*⟩ ⟨~ *fluency*⟩ **4** living (naturally), grown, or produced in a particular place; indigenous **5** found in nature, esp in a pure form ⟨*mining ~ silver*⟩ **6** *chiefly Austr* (superficially) resembling a specified British plant or animal [ME *natif,* fr MF, fr L *nativus,* fr *natus,* pp of *nasci* to be born – more at NATION] – **natively** *adv,* **nativeness** *n*
[2]native *n* **1** one born or reared in a particular place ⟨*a ~ of London*⟩ **2a** an original or indigenous (non-European) inhabitant **b** a plant, animal, etc indigenous to a particular locality **3** a local resident
nativity /nəˈtivəti/ *n* **1** birth; *specif, cap* the birth of Jesus **2** a horoscope [ME *nativite,* fr MF *nativité,* fr ML *nativitat-, nativitas,* fr LL, birth, fr L *nativus*]
natron /ˈnay,tron, -trən/ *n* hydrated sodium carbonate occurring as a mineral and used in ancient times in embalming [F, fr Sp *natrón,* fr Ar *naṭrūn,* fr Gk *nitron*]
natter /ˈnatə/ *vi or n, chiefly Br* (to) chatter, gossip – infml [prob imit]
natterjack /ˈnatəjak/ *n* a common brownish yellow W European toad with short hind legs which runs rather than hops [origin unknown]
natty /ˈnati/ *adj* neat and trim; spruce [perh alter. of earlier *netty,* fr obs *net* (neat, clean)] – **nattily** *adv,* **nattiness** *n*
[1]natural /ˈnachərəl/ *adj* **1** based on an inherent moral sense ⟨~ *justice*⟩ ⟨~ *law*⟩ **2** in accordance with or determined by nature **3** related by blood rather than by adoption ⟨*his ~ parents*⟩ **4** innate, inherent ⟨*a ~ talent for art*⟩ **5** of nature as an object of study **6** having a specified character or attribute by nature ⟨*a ~ athlete*⟩ **7** happening in accordance with the ordinary course of nature ⟨*death from ~ causes*⟩ **8** normal or expected ⟨*events followed their ~ course*⟩ **9** existing in or produced by nature without human intervention ⟨~ *scenery*⟩ **10** (as if) in a state unenlightened by culture or morality ⟨~ *man*⟩ **11a** having a physical or real existence **b** of the physical as opposed to the spiritual world **12a** true to nature; lifelike **b** free from affectation or constraint **c** not disguised or altered in appearance or form **13a** (containing only notes that are) neither sharp nor flat **b** having the pitch modified by the natural sign [ME, fr MF, fr L *naturalis* of nature, fr *natura* nature] – **naturalness** *n*
[2]natural *n* **1** one born mentally defective **2** (a note affected by) a sign placed on the musical staff to nullify the effect of a preceding sharp or flat ☞ MUSIC **3** one having natural skills or talents ⟨*as an actor, he was a ~*⟩ **4** one who is likely to be particularly suitable or successful ***USE*** *(3 & 4)* infml
ˌnatural ˈgas *n* gas from the earth's crust; *specif* a combustible mixture of methane and other hydrocarbons used chiefly as a fuel and as raw material in industry ☞ ENERGY
ˌnatural ˈhistory *n* **1** a treatise on some aspect of nature **2** the natural development of an organism, disease, etc over a period of time **3** the usu amateur study, esp in the field, of natural objects (e g plants and animals), often in a particular area
naturalism /ˈnachərə,liz(ə)m/ *n* **1** action or thought based on natural desires and instincts **2** a theory discounting supernatural explanations of the origin and meaning of the universe **3** realism in art or literature, esp when emphasizing scientific observation of life without idealization of the ugly – **naturalist** *adj,* **naturalistic** /ˈ-listik/ *adj,* **naturalistically** *adv*
naturalist /ˈnachərə,list/ *n* **1** a follower or advocate of naturalism **2** a student of natural history
natural·ize, -ise /ˈnachərə,liez/ *vt* **1a** to introduce into common use or into the vernacular **b** to cause (e g a plant) to become established as if native **2** to make natural **3** to admit to citizenship ~ *vi* to become naturalized – **naturalization** /-lieˈzaysh(ə)n/ *n*
ˌnatural ˈlogarithm *n* a logarithm with *e* as base
ˈnaturally /-li/ *adv* **1** by nature ⟨~ *timid*⟩ **2** as

might be expected ⟨~, *we shall be there*⟩ **3** in a natural manner

ˌnatural ˈnumber *n* the number 1 or any number (e g 3, 12, 432) obtained by repeatedly adding 1 to the number 1

ˌnatural reˈsources *n pl* industrial materials and capacities (e g mineral deposits and waterpower) supplied by nature

ˌnatural ˈscience *n* any of the sciences (e g physics or biology) that deal with objectively measurable phenomena – **natural scientist** *n*

ˌnatural seˈlection *n* a natural process that tends to result in the survival of organisms best adapted to their environment and the elimination of (mutant) organisms carrying undesirable traits

ˌnatural theˈology *n* deism

nature /ˈnaychə/ *n* **1a** the inherent character or constitution of a person or thing **b** disposition, temperament **2a** a creative and controlling force in the universe **b** the inner forces in an individual **3** a kind, class ⟨*documents of a confidential* ~⟩ **4** the physical constitution of an organism **5** the external world in its entirety **6** (a way of life resembling) mankind's original or natural condition **7** natural scenery [ME, fr MF, fr L *natura*, fr *natus*, pp of *nasci* to be born – more at NATION]

ˈnature reˌserve *n* an area of great botanical or zoological interest protected from exploitation by human beings

ˈnature ˌtrail *n* a walk (e g in a nature reserve) planned to indicate points of interest to the observer of nature

naturism /ˈnaychəˌriz(ə)m/ *n* nudism – **naturist** *adj or n*

naturopathy /ˌnaychəˈropəthi/ *n* treatment of disease emphasizing stimulation of the natural healing processes, including the use of herbal medicines [*nature* + *-o-* + *-pathy*] – **naturopathic** /ˌnaychərəˈpathik, nəˌtyooərə-/ *adj*

naught /nawt/ *n* **1** nothing **2** NOUGHT 2 [ME, fr OE *nāwiht*, fr *nā* no + *wiht* creature, thing – more at NO]

naughty /ˈnawti/ *adj* **1** badly behaved; wicked ⟨*you* ~ *boy!*⟩ **2** slightly improper – euph or humor [*naught* + *-y*; orig senses, inferior, bad] – **naughtily** *adv*, **naughtiness** *n*

nauplius /ˈnawpli·əs/ *n, pl* **nauplii** /ˈnawpliˌie/ a crustacean larva in the first stage after leaving the egg [NL, fr L, a shellfish, fr Gk *nauplios*]

nausea /ˈnawzi·ə/ *n* **1** a feeling of discomfort in the stomach accompanied by a distaste for food and an urge to vomit **2** extreme disgust [L, seasickness, nausea, fr Gk *nautia, nausia*, fr *nautēs* sailor] – **nauseant** *n or adj*

nauseate /ˈnawziˌayt/ *vb* to (cause to) become affected with nausea or disgust – **nauseatingly** *adv*

nauseous /ˈnawzi·əs/ *adj* causing or affected with nausea or disgust – **nauseously** *adv*, **nauseousness** *n*

nautch /nawch/ *n* an entertainment in India performed by professional dancing girls [Hindi *nāc*, fr Skt *nṛtya*, fr *nṛtyati* he dances]

nautical /ˈnawtikl/ *adj* of or associated with seamen, navigation, or ships ☞ SHIP [L *nauticus*, fr Gk *nautikos*, fr *nautēs* sailor, fr *naus* ship – more at [2]NAVE] – **nautically** *adv*

ˌnautical ˈmile *n* any of various units of distance used for sea and air navigation based on the length of a minute of arc of a great circle of the earth: e g **a** a British unit equal to 6080ft (about 1853.18m) **b** an international unit equal to 1852m (about 6076.17ft) ☞ UNIT

nautilus /ˈnawtiləs/ *n, pl* **nautiluses, nautili** /-ˌlie/ **1** any of a genus of molluscs related to the octopuses and squids that live in the Pacific and Indian oceans and have a spiral shell **2** PAPER NAUTILUS [NL, genus name, fr L, paper nautilus, fr Gk *nautilos*, lit., sailor, fr *naus* ship]

Navaho, Navajo /ˈnavəhoh/ *n, pl* **Navahos, Navajos,** *esp collectively* **Navaho, Navajo** a member of an American Indian people of N New Mexico and Arizona; *also* their language [Sp *(Apache de) Navajó*, lit., Apache of Navajó, fr *Navajó*, a pueblo]

navaid /ˈnavayd/ *n* a usu electronic device or system that assists a navigator [*na*vigation *aid*]

naval /ˈnayvl/ *adj* **1** of a navy **2** consisting of or involving warships [L *navalis*, fr *navis* ship]

naval architect *n* sby who designs ships

[1]nave /nayv/ *n* the hub of a wheel [ME, fr OE *nafu*; akin to OE *nafela* navel]

[2]nave *n* the main body of a church lying to the west of the chancel; *esp* the long central space flanked by aisles ☞ CHURCH [ML *navis*, fr L, ship; akin to OE *nōwend* sailor, Gk *naus* ship, Skt *nau*]

navel /ˈnayvl/ *n* **1** a depression in the middle of the abdomen marking the point of former attachment of the umbilical cord **2** the central point [ME, fr OE *nafela*; akin to OHG *nabalo* navel, L *umbilicus*, Gk *omphalos*]

ˈnavel ˌorange *n* a seedless orange with a pit at the top enclosing a small secondary fruit

navicular /nəˈvikyoolə/ *n or adj* (a bone, esp in the ankle) shaped like a boat [L *navicula* boat, dim. of *navis*]

navigable /ˈnavigəbl/ *adj* **1** suitable for ships to pass through or along **2** capable of being steered – **navigableness** *n*, **navigably** *adv*, **navigability** /-gəˈbiləti/ *n*

navigate /ˈnavigayt/ *vi* **1** to travel by water **2** to steer a course through a medium **3** to perform the activities (e g taking sightings and making calculations) involved in navigation ~ *vt* **1a** to sail over, on, or through **b** to make one's way over or through **2a** to steer or manage (a boat) in sailing **b** to operate or direct the course of (e g an aircraft) [L *navigatus*, pp of *navigare*, fr *navis* ship + *-igare* (fr *agere* to drive) – more at AGENT] – **navigator** *n*

navigation /ˌnaviˈgaysh(ə)n/ *n* **1** navigating **2** the science of determining position, course, and distance travelled during a journey and hence advising on the best course to be steered or taken **3** ship traffic or commerce – **navigational** *adj*, **navigationally** *adv*

navvy /ˈnavi/ *n, Br* an unskilled labourer [by shortening & alter. fr *navigator* (construction worker on canals, railways, roads)]

navy /ˈnayvi/ *n* **1** a nation's ships of war and support vessels together with the organization needed for maintenance ☞ RANK **2** *sing or pl in constr* the personnel manning a navy **3** NAVY BLUE [ME *navie*, fr MF, fr L *navigia* ships, fr *navigare*]

ˌnavy ˈblue *adj or n* deep dark blue

ˈnavy ˌyard *n, NAm* a naval dockyard

nawab /nəˈwawb, -ˈwahb/ *n* NABOB 1 ⟨*the* Nawab *of Pataudi*⟩ [Hindi & Urdu *nawwāb*]

country	adjective	language	money
Afghanistan	Afghan *sp:* Afghanistani *pl:* Afghans	Pashto Dari Persian	afghani =100 puls
Albania	Albanian	Albanian	lek =100 qindarka
Algeria	Algerian	Arabic	Algerian dinar =100 centimes
Andorra	Andorran	Catalan	French franc Spanish peseta
Angola	Angolan	Portuguese	kwanza =100 lweis
Argentina	Argentinian	Spanish	peso =100 centavos
Australia	Australian	English	Australian dollar =100 cents
Austria	Austrian	German	Schilling =100 Groschen
Bahamas	Bahamian	English	Bahamian dollar =100 cents
Bahrain	Bahraini	Arabic	Bahraini dinar =1000 fils
Bangladesh	Bangladesh *sp:* Bangladeshi	Bengali	taka =100 paise
Barbados	Barbadian	English	Barbados dollar =100 cents
Belgium	Belgian	French Dutch German	Belgian franc =100 centimes
Belize	Belizean	English	Belize dollar =100 cents
Benin (formerly Dahomey)		French	franc CFA
Bermuda	Bermudan	English	Bermuda dollar =100 cents
Bhután	Bhutani	Dzongkha	Indian rupee
Bolivia	Bolivian	Spanish	Bolivian peso =100 centavos
Botswana	Setswana *sp:* Motswana, Batswana *pl:* Batswana	English	pula =100 thebe
Brazil	Brazilian	Portuguese	cruzeiro =100 centavos
Brunei	Bruneian	Malay	Brunei dollar =100 cents
Bulgaria	Bulgarian	Bulgarian	lev =100 stotinki
Burma	Burmese	Burmese	kyat =100 pyas
Burundi	Burundian	French	Burundi franc
Cameroon	Cameroonian	French English	franc CFA
Canada	Canadian	English French	Canadian dollar =100 cents
Cape Verde	Cape Verdean	Portuguese	escudo =100 centavos
Cayman Islands	Cayman Island *sp:* Cayman Islander	English	Cayman Island dollar =100 cents
Central African Republic		French Sango	franc CFA
Chad	Chadian	French	franc CFA
Chile	Chilean	Spanish	peso =100 centavos
China	Chinese	Putonghua (Mandarin)	yuan =10 jiao or 100 fen
Colombia	Colombian	Spanish	peso =100 centavos
Comoros	Comoranian, Comoro	French	franc CFA
Congo	Congolese	French	franc CFA
Costa Rica	Costa Rican	Spanish	colon =100 céntimos
Cuba	Cuban	Spanish	peso =100 centavos
Cyprus	Cyprian. Cypriot *sp:* Cypriot	Turkish Greek	Cyprus pound =1000 mils
Czechoslovakia	Czech *p:* Czechoslovak	Czechoslovak	Koruna öre =100 haler
Denmark	Danish *sp:* Dane	Danish	krone =100 ore
Djibouti or Jibuti	Djiboutian, Jibutian	French	Djibouti franc
Dominica	Dominican	English	East Caribbean dollar =100 cents
Dominican Republic	Dominican	Spanish	peso =100 centavos
Ecuador	Ecuadorian	Spanish	sucre =100 centavos
Egypt	Egyptian	Arabic	Egyptian pound =100 piastres
El Salvador	Salvadorean	Spanish	colón =100 centavos

country	adjective	language	money
Equatorial Guinea	Equatorial Guinean *sp:* Bantu *pl:* Bantu	Spanish	ekuele
Ethiopia	Ethiopian	Amharic	Ethiopian dollar =100 cents
Falkland Islands	Falkland Island	English	Falkland Island pound=100 pence
Fiji	Fijian	English	Fiji dollar =100 cents
Finland	Finnish *sp:* Finn	Finnish	markka =100 penniä
France	French	French	franc =100 centimes
Gabon	Gabonese	French	franc CFA
The Gambia	Gambian	English	dalasi =100 bututs
Germany (Democratic Republic)	(East) German	German	Mark der Deutschen Demokratischen Republik (infml:- Ostmark) =100 Pfennig
Germany (Federal Republic)	(West) German	German	Deutsche Mark =100 Pfennig
Ghana	Ghanian	English	cedi =100 pesewa
Gibraltar	Gibraltarian	English	Gibraltar pound =100 pence
Greece	Greek	Greek	drachma =100 lepta
Grenada	Grenadian	English	East Caribbean dollar=100 cents
Guatemala	Guatemalan	Spanish	quetzal =100 centavos
Guinea	Guinean	French	syli =100 cauris
Guinea-Bissau	Guinean	Portuguese	Escudo =100 centavos
Guyana	Guyanese	English	Guyana dollar =100 cents
Haiti	Haitian	French	gourde
Honduras	Honduran	Spanish	lempira =100 centavos
Hong Kong		English	Hong Kong dollar =100 cents
Hungary	Hungarian	Hungarian (Magyar)	forint =100 fillér
Iceland	Icelandic	Icelandic	króna =100 eyrir
India	Indian	Hindi, English	rupee =100 paise
Indonesia	Indonesian	Bahasa Indonesian	rupiah =100 sen
Iran	Iranian	Farsi Persian	rial =100 dinars
Iraq	Iraqi	Arabic	Iraqi dinar =1000 fils
Irish Republic	Irish	Irish & English	Irish punt =100 pence
Israel	Israeli	Hebrew, Arabic	Israeli shekel =100 new agora
Italy	Italian	Italian	lira
Ivory Coast	Ivorian	French	franc CFA
Jamaica	Jamaican	English	Jamaican dollar =100 cents
Japan	Japanese	Japanese	yen
Jordan	Jordanian	Arabic	Jordanian dinar =1000 fils
Kampuchea	Kampuchean	Khmer	formerly riel, but money officially abolished under Pol Pot Government in 1978. Present situation unclear.
Kenya	Kenyan	English, Swahili	Kenya shilling =100 cents
Kiribati	Kiribatian	English	Australian dollar =100 cents
Korea (North)	N Korean	Korean	won =100 jeon
Korea (South)	S Korean	Korean	won =100 jeon
Kuwait	Kuwaiti	Arabic	Kuwaiti dinar =1000 fils
Laos	Laotian	Lao	kip = 100 ats
Lebanon	Lebanese	Arabic	Lebanese pound =100 piastres
Lesotho	Sesotho *sp:* Mosotho *pl:* Basotho *p:* Basotho	Sesotho, English	loti (*pl* maloti) =100 lisente
Liberia	Liberian	English	Liberian dollar =100 cents
Libya	Libyan	Arabic	Libyan dinar =1000 dirham
Liechtenstein	Liechtenstein *sp:* Liechtensteiner	German	Swiss franc

sp: single person   pl: plural   p: people

☞MAP

country	adjective	language	money
Luxemburg	Luxemburg *sp:* Luxemberger	French	Luxemburg franc =100 centimes
Macao	Macoan	Portuguese	pataca =100 avos
Madagascar	Malagasy	French	Malagasy franc
Malawi	Malawian	English	Malawi kwacha =100 tambala
Malaysia	Malaysian	Malay	ringgit (Malaysian dollar) =100 cents
Maldive Islands	Maldivian	Divehi	Maldive rupee =100 laris
Mali	Malian	French	Mali franc
Malta	Maltese	Maltese	Maltese pound =100 cents *or* 1000 mils
Mauritania	Mauritanian	Arabic, French	ouguiya =5 khoums
Mauritius	Mauritian	English	rupee =100 cents
Mexico	Mexican	Spanish	peso =100 centavos
Monaco	Monegasque	French	French franc
Mongolia	Mongolian	Khalka Mongolian	tugrik =100 mongo
Montserrat	Montserratian	English	East Caribbean dollar
Morocco	Moroccan	Arabic	dirham =100 centimes
Mozambique	Mozambiquean	Portuguese	metical =100 centavos
Namibia	Namibian	Afrikaans, English	South African rand
Nauru	Nauruan	Nauruan, English	Australian dollar
Nepal	Nepalese	Nepali	Nepalese rupee =100 paise
The Netherlands	Dutch	Dutch	florin or gulden =100 cents
The Netherlands Antilles		Dutch	Netherland Antilles florin
New Zealand	New Zealand	English	New Zealand dollar =100 cents
Nicaragua	Nicaraguan	Spanish	córdoba =100 centavos
Niger	Nigerien	French	franc CFA
Nigeria	Nigerian	English	naira =100 kobo
Norway	Norwegian	Norwegian	krone =100 öre
Oman	Omani	Arabic	rial Omani =1000 baiza
Pakistan	Pakistan	English Urdu Punjabi	Pakistan rupee =100 paisa
Panama	Panamanian	Spanish	balboa =100 cents
Papua New Guinea	Papuan	Papuan, English	kina =100 toea
Paraguay	Paraguayan	Spanish	guarani =100 céntimos
Peru	Peruvian	Spanish	sol =100 centavos
Philippines	Philippine *sp:* Filipino	Pilipino (Tagalog) English, Spanish	Philippine peso = 100 centavos
Pitcairn Islands	Pitcairn	English	New Zealand dollar
Poland	Polish	Polish	zloty =100 groszy
Portugal	Portuguese	Portuguese	escudo =100 centavos
Qatar	Qatari	Arabic	Qatar riyal =100 dirhams
Romania	Romanian	Romanian	lev =100 bani
Rwanda	Rwandan	Kinyarwanda, French	Rwanda franc
St Helena		English	St Helena pound
St Lucia		English	East Caribbean dollar
St Vincent		English	East Caribbean dollar
San Marino		Italian	Italian lira
São Tomé	St Tomean	Portuguese	dobra =100 centavos
Saudi Arabia	Saudi Arabian *sp:* Saudi or Saudi Arabian	Arabic	rial =20 qursh *or* 100 halalas
Senegal	Senegalese	French	franc CFA
Seychelles	Seychellois	English	Seychelles rupee =100 cents
Sierra Leone	Sierra Leonean	English	leone =100 cents
Singapore	Singaporean	Malay, English	Singapore dollar =100 cents
Solomon Islands	Solomon Island	English	Solomon Islands dollar =100 cents
Somalia	Somalian	Somali, English Italian, Arabic	Somali shilling =100 cents
South Africa	South African	Afrikaans, English	rand =100 cents
Spain	Spanish *sp:* Spaniard	Spanish	peseta =100 céntimos
Sri Lanka	Sinhalese	Sinhala, English, Tamil	Sri Lanka rupee =100 cents
Sudan	Sudanese	Arabic	Sudanese pound =100 piastres *or* 1000 milliemes
Suriname	Surinamese	Dutch	Surinam florin/ guilder
Swaziland	Swazi	siSwati English	lilangeni (pl emalangeni) =100 cents
Sweden	Swedish *sp:* Swede	Swedish	krona =100 öre
Switzerland	Swiss	French German Italian	Swiss franc =100 centimes *or* rappen
Syria	Syrian	Arabic	Syrian pound =100 piastres
Taiwan	Taiwanese	Mandarin	New Taiwan dollar =100 cents
Tanzania	Tanzanian	Swahili English	Tanzanian shilling =100 cents
Thailand	Thai	Thai	baht =100 stangs
Togo	Togolese	French	franc CFA
Tonga	Tongan	Tongan	pa'anga =100 seniti
Trinidad & Tobago	Trinidadian, Tobagan	English	T & T dollar =100 cents
Tunisia	Tunisian	Arabic	Tunisian dinar =1000 millimes
Turkey	Turkish *sp:* Turk	Turkish	Turkish lira =100 kurus
Tuvalu (from Ellice Islands)	Tuvalese	English, French	Tuvalu franc =100 centimes
Uganda	Ugandan	Swahili, English	Uganda shilling =100 cents
Union of Soviet Socialist Republics (USSR)	Russian *also* Soviet	Russian	rouble =100 kopecks
United Arab Emirates (UAE)		Arabic	dirham of the UAE
United Kingdom of Great Britain and Northern Ireland (UK)	British	English	pound sterling =100 pence
United States of America (USA)	American	English	dollar =100 cents
Upper Volta	Voltaic *sp:* Voltain	French	franc CFA
Uruguay	Uruguayan	Spanish	new peso =100 centésimos
Vanuaatu (formerly New Hebrides)	Vanuaatuan	English, French	Vanuaatu franc
Venezuela	Venezuelan	Spanish	bolivar =100 céntimos
Vietnam	Vietnamese	Vietnamese	dong =10 hào *or* 100 xu
Western Samoa	Samoan	English, Samoan	tala =100 sene
West Indian Associated States (Antigua & St Kitts – Nevis – Anguilla)		English	East Caribbean dollar
Yemen Arab Republic	Yemeni	Arabic	Yemeni riyal =100 fils
Peoples Democratic Republic of Yemen	Arabic		Southern Yemen dinar =1000 fils
Yugoslavia	Yugoslavian *sp:* Yugoslav	Serbo-Croat Slovene Macedonian	dinar =100 paras
Zaïre	Zaïrean	French	zaire =100 makuta (*sing* likuta) *or* 10,000 sengi
Zambia	Zambian	English	kwacha =100 ngwee
Zimbabwe	Zimbabwean	English	Zimbabwe dollar =100 cents

¹nay /nay/ *adv* **1** not merely this but also ⟨*she was happy, ~, ecstatic*⟩ **2** *N Eng or archaic* no [ME, no, fr ON *nei*, fr *ne* not + *ei* ever – more at ¹AYE]

²nay *n* **1** denial, refusal **2** a vote or voter against

Nazarene /,nazə'reen/ *n* a native or inhabitant of Nazareth [ME *Nazaren*, fr LL *Nazarenus*, fr Gk *Nazarēnos*, fr *Nazareth*, town in Palestine]

nazi /'nahtsi/ *n, often cap* a member of the German fascist party controlling Germany from 1933 to 1945 [G, by shortening & alter. fr *nationalsozialist*, fr *national* + *sozialist* socialist] – **nazi** *adj*, **nazify** /-,fie/ *vt*, **nazification** /-fi'kaysh(ə)n/ *n*

Nazism /'naht,siz(ə)m/, **Naziism** /'nahtsi,iz(ə)m/ *n* the totalitarian and racialist doctrines of the fascist National Socialist German Workers' party in the 3rd German Reich [*Nazi* + *-ism*]

NCO *n* NONCOMMISSIONED OFFICER

-nd *suffix* (→ *adj*), *chiefly Br* – used after the figure 2 to indicate the ordinal number *second* ⟨2nd⟩ ⟨72nd⟩

ne-, neo- *comb form* **1a** new; recent ⟨Neo*cene*⟩ **b** new, subsequent, or revived period or form of ⟨Neo-*platonism*⟩ ⟨neo-*Classicism*⟩ **c** in a new, subsequent, or revived form or manner ⟨Neo*lithic*⟩ ⟨neo-*Georgian*⟩ **2** New World ⟨Neo*tropical*⟩ [Gk, fr *neos* new – more at NEW]

Neanderthal /nee'andə,tahl, -th(ə)l/ *adj* being, relating to, or like Neanderthal man – **Neanderthal** *n*

Neanderthal man *n* a Middle Palaeolithic man known from skeletal remains in Europe, N Africa, and W Asia [*Neanderthal*, valley in western Germany where the remains were first discovered] – **Neanderthaloid** /-thəloyd/ *adj or n*

neap /neep/ *adj or n* (of or being) a neap tide [adj ME *neep*, fr OE *nēp* being at the stage of neap tide; n fr adj]

Neapolitan /,nee·ə'politn/ *n or adj* (a native or inhabitant) of Naples [L *neapolitanus* of Naples, fr Gk *neapolitēs* citizen of Naples, fr *Neapolis* Naples, city in Italy]

neap tide *n* a tide of minimum height occurring at the 1st and the 3rd quarters of the moon

¹near /niə/ *adv* **1** in or into a near position or manner ⟨*came ~ to tears*⟩ **2** closely approximating; nearly ⟨*a* near-*perfect performance*⟩ ⟨*isn't anywhere ~ clever enough*⟩ [ME *ner*, partly fr *ner* nearer, fr OE *nēar*, compar of *nēah* nigh; partly fr ON *nær* nearer, compar of *nā-* nigh – more at NIGH] – **near on** CLOSE ON

²near *prep* near to ⟨*went too ~ the edge*⟩ ⟨*call me* ~er *the time*⟩

³near *adj* **1** intimately connected or associated ⟨*he and I are ~ relations*⟩ **2a** not far distant in time, space, or degree ⟨*in the ~ future*⟩ **b** close, narrow ⟨*a ~ miss*⟩ ⟨*a ~ resemblance*⟩ **3a** being the closer of 2 ⟨*the ~ side*⟩ **b** being the left-hand one of a pair ⟨*the ~ wheel of a cart*⟩ – **nearness** *n*

⁴near *vb* to approach

,near'by /-'bie/ *adv or adj* close at hand ⟨*live ~*⟩ ⟨*a ~ café*⟩

Nearctic /ni'ahktik/ *adj* of or being the biogeographic subregion that includes Greenland and arctic and temperate N America

,near 'gale *n* MODERATE GALE

nearly /'niəli/ *adv* **1** in a close manner or relationship ⟨*~ related*⟩ **2** almost but not quite ⟨*very ~ identical*⟩ ⟨*~ a year later*⟩

,near'side /-'sied/ *n, Br* the left-hand side (e g of a vehicle or road) ⟨*hit a car parked on his ~*⟩ – **nearside** /'-,-/ *adj*

,near'sighted /-'sietid/ *adj* able to see near things more clearly than distant ones; myopic – **nearsightedly** *adv*, **nearsightedness** *n*

¹neat /neet/ *n, pl* **neat, neats** *archaic* the common domestic ox or cow [ME *neet*, fr OE *nēat*; akin to OHG *nōz* head of cattle, OE *nēotan* to make use of]

²neat *adj* **1a** without addition or dilution ⟨*~ gin*⟩ **b** free from irregularity; smooth **2** elegantly simple **3a** precise, well-defined ⟨*a ~ solution to the problem*⟩ **b** skilful, adroit **4** (habitually) tidy and orderly ⟨*a ~ room*⟩ ⟨*a ~ little man*⟩ **5** *chiefly NAm* fine, excellent – infml [MF *net*, fr L *nitidus* bright, neat, fr *nitēre* to shine; akin to OPer *naiba-* beautiful] – **neatly** *adv*, **neatness** *n*

³neat *adv* without addition or dilution; straight ⟨*drinks his whisky ~*⟩

neaten /'neetn/ *vt* to make neater

neath /neeth/ *prep* beneath – poetic

neat's-foot oil *n* a pale yellow oil made esp from the bones of cattle and used chiefly as a leather dressing

neb /neb/ *n, chiefly dial* **1** a nose, snout **2** a small usu pointed end; a tip [ME, fr OE; akin to ON *nef* beak]

nebula /'nebyoolə/ *n, pl* **nebulas, nebulae** /-li/ **1** a cloudy patch on the cornea **2a** any of many immense bodies of highly rarefied gas or dust in interstellar space **b** a galaxy [NL, fr L, mist, cloud; akin to OHG *nebul* fog, Gk *nephelē, nephos* cloud] – **nebular** *adj*

nebulosity /,nebyoo'losəti/ *n* **1** being nebulous **2** nebulous matter; *also* NEBULA 2

nebulous /'nebyooləs/ *adj* **1** indistinct, vague **2** of or resembling a nebula; nebular [L *nebulosus* misty, fr *nebula*] – **nebulously** *adv*, **nebulousness** *n*

necessarily /'nesəs(ə)rəli, ,nesə'serəli/ *adv* as a necessary consequence; inevitably

¹necessary /'nesəs(ə)ri, 'nesə,seri/ *n* an indispensable item; an essential

²necessary *adj* **1a** inevitable, inescapable **b(1)** logically unavoidable ⟨*a ~ conclusion*⟩ **(2)** that cannot be denied without contradiction of some other statement **c** determined by a previous state of affairs **d** acting under compulsion; not free ⟨*a ~ agent*⟩ **2** essential, indispensable [ME *necessarie*, fr L *necessarius*, fr *necesse* necessary, fr *ne-* not + *cedere* to withdraw – more at NO, CEDE]

necessitate /nə'sesitayt/ *vt* to make necessary or unavoidable – **necessitation** /-'taysh(ə)n/ *n*

necessitous /nə'sesitəs/ *adj* needy, impoverished – fml – **necessitously** *adv*, **necessitousness** *n*

necessity /nə'sesəti/ *n* **1** the quality of being necessary, indispensable, or unavoidable **2** impossibility of a contrary order or condition ⟨*physical ~*⟩ **3** poverty, want **4a** sthg necessary or indispensable ⟨*the bare* necessities *of life*⟩ **b** a pressing need or desire [ME *necessite*, fr MF *necessité*, fr L *necessitat-, necessitas*, fr *necesse*] – **of necessity** necessarily

¹neck /nek/ *n* **1a** the part of an animal that connects the head with the body; *also* a cut of beef, mutton, etc taken from this part ☞ MEAT **b** the part of a garment that covers the neck; *also* the neckline **2a** a narrow part, esp shaped like a neck ⟨*~ of a bottle*⟩

b the part of a stringed musical instrument extending from the body and supporting the fingerboard and strings **c** a narrow stretch of land **d** STRAIT 1 **e** a column of solidified magma of a volcanic pipe or laccolith **3** a narrow margin ⟨*won by a* ~⟩ [ME *nekke*, fr OE *hnecca*; akin to OHG *hnac* nape, OE *hnutu* nut – more at NUT] – **neck of the woods** area or district in which one lives; locality

²**neck** *vt* to reduce the diameter of ~ *vi* **1** to become constricted **2** to kiss and caress in sexual play – infml

ˌ**neck and** ˈ**neck** *adv* evenly matched; running level

necked /nekt/ *adj* having a (specified kind of) neck – often in combination ⟨*long*-necked⟩

neckerchief /ˈnekəˌcheef, -ˌchif/ *n, pl* **neckerchiefs** *also* **neckerchieves** /-cheevz/ a square of fabric folded and worn round the neck [ME *nekkerchef*, fr *nekke* + *kerchef* kerchief]

necklace /ˈneklis/ *n* a string of jewels, beads, etc worn round the neck as an ornament

ˈ**neckˌline** /-ˌlien/ *n* the upper edge of a garment that forms the opening for the neck and head

ˈ**neckˌtie** /-ˌtie/ *n, chiefly NAm* TIE 5

necr-, necro- *comb form* **1** corpse; corpses ⟨necr*opsy*⟩ ⟨necro*philia*⟩ **2** conversion to dead tissue ⟨necr*osis*⟩ [LL, fr Gk *nekr-, nekro-*, fr *nekros* dead body – more at NOXIOUS]

necrology /neˈkroləji/ *n* **1** a list of the recently dead **2** an obituary [NL *necrologium*, fr *necr-* + *-logium* (as in ML *eulogium* eulogy)] – **necrologist** *n*, **necrological** /ˌnekrəˈlojikl/ *adj*

necromancy /ˈnekrəˌmansi/ *n* **1** the conjuring up of the spirits of the dead in order to predict or influence the future **2** magic, sorcery [alter. of ME *nigromancie*, fr MF, fr ML *nigromantia*, by folk etymology (infl by L *nigr-, niger* black) fr LL *necromantia*, fr LGk *nekromanteia*, fr Gk *nekr-* + *-manteia* -mancy] – **necromancer** *n*, **necromantic** /-ˈmantik/ *adj*, **necromantically** *adv*

necrophagous /neˈkrofəgəs, ni-/ *adj* feeding on corpses or carrion ⟨~ *insects*⟩

necrophilia /ˌnekrəˈfili·ə/ *n* obsession with and usu erotic interest in corpses [NL] – **necrophile** /-ˌfiel/ *n*, **necrophiliac** /-ˈfiliak/ *adj or n*, **necrophilic** /-ˈfilik/ *adj*, **necrophilism** /neˈkrofiˌliz(ə)m, ni-/ *n*

necropolis /neˈkropəlis, ni-/ *n, pl* **necropolises, necropoles** /-pəleez/, **necropoleis** /-lays/, **necropoli** /-lie, -li/ a cemetery; *esp* a large elaborate cemetery of an ancient city [LL, city of the dead, fr Gk *nekropolis*, fr *nekr-* + *-polis*]

necropsy /ˈnekropsi/ *n* POSTMORTEM 1 – **necropsy** *vt*

necrosis /neˈkrohsis, ni-/ *n, pl* **necroses** /-seez/ (localized) death of living tissue [LL, fr Gk *nekrōsis*, fr *nekroun* to make dead, fr *nekros* – more at NOXIOUS] – **necrotic** /neˈkrotik, ni-/ *adj*, **necrotize** /ˈnekrəˌtiez/ *vb*

nectar /ˈnektə/ *n* **1** the drink of the gods in classical mythology; *broadly* a delicious drink **2** a sweet liquid secreted by the flowers of many plants that is the chief raw material of honey [L, fr Gk *nektar*] – **nectarous** *adj*

nectarine /ˈnektərin, -reen/ *n* (a tree that bears) a smooth-skinned peach [obs *nectarine*, adj (like nectar)]

nectary /ˈnektəri/ *n* a plant gland that secretes nectar [NL *nectarium*, irreg fr L *nectar* + *-arium* -ary]

née, nee /nay/ *adj* – used to identify a woman by her maiden name ⟨*Mrs Thomson*, ~ *Wilkinson*⟩ [F *née*, fem of *né*, lit., born, pp of *naître* to be born, fr L *nasci* – more at NATION]

¹**need** /need/ *n* **1a** a necessary duty; an obligation **b** reason or grounds for an action or condition **2a** a lack of sthg necessary, desirable, or useful ⟨*socks in* ~ *of mending*⟩ **b** a physiological or psychological requirement for the well-being of an organism **3** a condition requiring supply or relief ⟨*help in time of* ~⟩ **4** poverty, want [ME *ned*, fr OE *nīed, nēd*; akin to OHG *nōt* distress, need] – **needful** *adj*, **needfulness** *n*

²**need** *vt* **1** to be in need of; require ⟨*the soup* ~s *salt*⟩ ⟨*my socks* ~ *mending*⟩ **2** to be constrained ⟨*I'll* ~ *to work hard*⟩ ~ *va* be under necessity or obligation to ⟨~ *I go?*⟩ ⟨*he* ~ *not answer*⟩

ˈ**needful** /-f(ə)l/ *adj* necessary, requisite ⟨*do whatever is* ~⟩

¹**needle** /ˈneedl/ *n* **1a** a small slender usu steel instrument with an eye for thread at one end and a sharp point at the other, used for sewing **b** any of various similar larger instruments without an eye, used for carrying thread and making stitches (e g in crocheting or knitting) **c** the slender hollow pointed end of a hypodermic syringe for injecting or removing material **2** a slender, usu sharp-pointed, indicator on a dial; *esp* a magnetic needle **3a** a slender pointed object resembling a needle: e g **(1)** a pointed crystal **(2)** a sharp pinnacle of rock **(3)** an obelisk **b** a needle-shaped leaf, esp of a conifer **c** STYLUS b **d** a slender pointed rod controlling a fine inlet or outlet (e g in a valve) **4** a beam used to take the load of a wall while supported at each end by shores **5** *Br* a feeling of enmity or ill will – infml ⟨*a* ~ *match*⟩ [ME *nedle*, fr OE *nǣdl*; akin to OHG *nādala* needle, *nājan* to sew, L *nēre* to spin, Gk *nēn*] – **needlelike** *adj*

²**needle** *vt* **1** to sew or pierce (as if) with a needle **2** to provoke by persistent teasing or gibes – **needler** /ˈneedlə/ *n*, **needling** /ˈneed ling/ *n*

ˈ**needleˌcord** /-ˌkawd/ *n* a fine corduroy with close ribs and a flattish pile

ˈ**needleˌpoint** /-ˌpoynt/ *n* **1** lace worked over a paper or parchment pattern – compare POINT 8, PILLOW LACE **2** embroidery worked on canvas usu in a simple even stitch (e g cross- or tent stitch) – compare GROS POINT, PETIT POINT – **needlepoint** *adj*

needless /ˈneedlis/ *adj* not needed; unnecessary ⟨~ *to say*⟩ – **needlessly** *adv*, **needlessness** *n*

ˈ**needleˌwoman** /-ˌwoomən/ *n* a woman who does needlework

ˈ**needleˌwork** /-ˌwuhk/ *n* sewing; *esp* fancy work (e g embroidery)

needn't /ˈneednt/ need not – **needn't have** was under no necessity to but did ⟨*I* needn't have *worn this sweater*⟩

needs /needz/ *adv* necessarily ⟨*must* ~ *be recognized*⟩ [ME *nedes*, fr OE *nēdes*, fr gen of *nēd* need]

needy /ˈneedi/ *adj* in want, impoverished – **neediness** *n*

neep /neep/ *n, dial Scot* a turnip [ME *nepe*, fr OE *nǣp*, fr L *napus*]

ne'er /neə/ *adv* never – poetic

'ne'er-do-,well *n* an idle worthless person – **ne'er-do-well** *adj*

nefarious /ni'feəri·əs/ *adj* iniquitous, evil [L *nefarius*, fr *nefas* crime, fr *ne-* not + *fas* right, divine law; akin to L *fari* to speak] – **nefariously** *adv*, **nefariousness** *n*

negate /ni'gayt/ *vt* **1** to deny the existence or truth of **2** to make ineffective or invalid [L *negatus*, pp of *negare* to say no, deny, fr *neg-* no, not (akin to *ne-* not) – more at NO] – **negate** *n*, **negator, negater** *n*

negation /ni'gaysh(ə)n/ *n* **1a** a denial or refusal **b** a negative statement; *esp* an assertion of the falsity of a given proposition **2a** sthg that is merely the absence of sthg actual or positive ⟨*anarchy is the ~ of government*⟩ **b** sthg opposite to sthg regarded as positive [NEGATE + -ION] – **negational** *adj*

[1]**negative** /'negətiv/ *adj* **1a** marked by denial, prohibition, or refusal **b** expressing negation **2** lacking positive or agreeable features ⟨*a ~ outlook on life*⟩ **3a** less than zero and opposite in sign to a positive number that when added to the given number yields zero ⟨*–2 is a ~ number*⟩ **b** in a direction opposite to an arbitrarily chosen regular direction ⟨*~ angle*⟩ **4a** being, relating to, or charged with electricity as a result of an excess of electrons **b** having lower electric potential and constituting the part towards which the current flows from the external circuit **5a** not showing the presence or existence of the organism, condition, etc in question **b** directed or moving away from a source of stimulation ⟨*~ tropism*⟩ **6** having the light and dark parts in approximately inverse order to those of the original photographic subject – **negatively** *adv*, **negativeness** *n*, **negativity** /-'tivəti/ *n*

[2]**negative** *n* **1a** a proposition by which sthg is denied or contradicted **b** a negative reply **2** sthg that is the negation or opposite of sthg else **3** an expression (e g the word *no*) of negation or denial **4** the side that upholds the contradictory proposition in a debate **5** the plate of a voltaic or electrolytic cell that is at the lower potential **6** a negative photographic image on transparent material used for printing positive pictures

[3]**negative** *vt* **1a** to refuse to accept or approve **b** to reject, veto **2** to demonstrate the falsity of; disprove

negative income tax *n* a system of subsidy payments to families with incomes below a stipulated level, proposed as a substitute for or supplement to social-security payments

[1]**neglect** /ni'glekt/ *vt* **1** to pay insufficient attention to; disregard **2** to leave undone or unattended to [L *neglectus*, pp of *neglegere, neclegere*, fr *nec-* not (akin to *ne-* not) + *legere* to gather – more at NO, LEGEND] – **neglecter** *n*

[2]**neglect** *n* neglecting or being neglected

ne'glectful /-f(ə)l/ *adj* careless, forgetful – **neglectfully** *adv*, **neglectfulness** *n*

negligee, negligé /'neglizhay/ *n* a woman's light decorative housecoat, often designed to be worn with a matching nightdress [F *négligé*, fr pp of *négliger* to neglect, fr L *neglegere*]

negligence /'neglij(ə)ns/ *n* **1** forgetfulness; carelessness **2** failure to exercise the proper care expected of a prudent person

negligent /'neglij(ə)nt/ *adj* **1** (habitually or culpably) neglectful **2** pleasantly casual in manner [ME, fr MF & L; MF, fr L *neglegent-, neglegens*, prp of *neglegere*] – **negligently** *adv*

negligible /'neglijəbl/ *adj* trifling, insignificant [L *neglegere, negligere*] – **negligibly** *adv*, **negligibility** /-jə'biləti/ *n*

negotiable /ni'gohshyəbl/ *adj* **1** transferable to another ⟨*~ securities*⟩ **2** capable of being passed along or through ⟨*a difficult but ~ road*⟩ **3** capable of being dealt with or settled through discussion [NEGOTIATE + -ABLE] – **negotiability** /-ə'biləti/ *n*

negotiate /ni'gohshiayt/ *vi* to confer with another in order to reach an agreement or settlement ~ *vt* **1** to arrange or bring about through discussion **2a** to transfer (e g a bill of exchange) to another by delivery or endorsement **b** to convert into cash or the equivalent value ⟨*~ a cheque*⟩ **3a** to travel successfully along or over **b** to complete or deal with successfully [L *negotiatus*, pp of *negotiari* to carry on business, fr *negotium* business, fr *neg-* not + *otium* leisure – more at NEGATE] – **negotiant** /-ənt/ *n*, **negotiator** /-,aytə/ *n*, **negotiatory** /-ətri/ *adj*

negotiation /ni,gohshi'aysh(ə)n/ *n* negotiating or being negotiated; *esp* discussion of a disputed issue – often pl with sing. meaning

Negress /'neegris/ *n* a female Negro – chiefly derog and technical

Negrillo /ni'griloh/ *n, pl* **Negrillos, Negrilloes** a member of any of a group of small Negroid peoples (e g Pygmies) that inhabit Africa [Sp, dim. of *negro*]

Negrito /ni'greetoh/ *n, pl* **Negritos, Negritoes** a member of any of a group of small Negroid peoples that inhabit Oceania and SE Asia [Sp, dim. of *negro*]

negritude /'negri,tyoohd, 'nee-/ *n* conscious pride in the African heritage [F *négritude*, fr *nègre* Negro + *-i-* + *-tude*]

Negro /'neegroh/ *n, pl* **Negroes** **1** a member of the esp African branch of the black race of mankind **2** a person of Negro descent [Sp or Pg, fr *negro* black, fr L *nigr-, niger*] – **Negro** *adj, often not cap*, **Negroid** *n or adj, often not cap*

negus /'neegəs/ *n* a drink of wine, hot water, sugar, lemon juice, and nutmeg [Francis *Negus* †1732 E colonel]

Nehemiah /,nee·i'mie·ə/ *n* (a book of the Old Testament concerning) a Jewish leader of the 5th c BC who supervised the rebuilding of the city walls of Jerusalem [Heb *Nĕḥemyāh*]

neigh /nay/ *vi* to make the loud prolonged cry characteristic of a horse [ME *neyen*, fr OE *hnǣgan*; akin to MHG *nēgen* to neigh] – **neigh** *n*

[1]**neighbour,** *NAm chiefly* **neighbor** /'naybə/ *n* **1** one living or situated near another **2** a fellow human being ⟨*love thy ~*⟩ [ME *neighbor, neighebor*, fr OE *nēahgebūr*; akin to OHG *nāhgibūr* neighbour; both fr a prehistoric WGmc compound represented by OE *nēah* near & OE *gebūr* dweller – more at NIGH]

[2]**neighbour,** *NAm chiefly* **neighbor** *vt* to adjoin or lie near to

'neighbour,hood /-,hood/ *n* **1** an adjacent or surrounding region **2** an approximate amount, extent, or degree ⟨*cost in the ~ of £300*⟩ **3a** *sing or pl in constr* the neighbours **b** a district lived in by neighbours **c** (the inhabitants of) a district of a town, city etc, forming a distinct community **4** the set of all points whose distances from a given point are not greater than a given positive number [[1]NEIGHBOUR + -HOOD]

neighbouring /'nayb(ə)ring/ *adj* nearby, adjacent

'neighbourly /-li/ *adj* characteristic of congenial neighbours; *esp* friendly

[1]neither /'niedhə; *or* 'needhə/ *pron* not the one or the other ⟨~ *of us*⟩ [ME, alter. of *nauther, nother*, fr OE *nāhwæther, nōther*, fr *nā, nō* not + *hwæther* which of two, whether]

[2]neither *conj* **1** not either ⟨~ *here nor there*⟩ ⟨~ *ate, drank, nor smoked*⟩ **2** also not; nor ⟨*he didn't go and* ~ *did I*⟩

[3]neither *adj* not either ⟨~ *hand*⟩

[4]neither *adv* **1** similarly not; also not ⟨*'I can't swim.' 'Neither can I.'*⟩ **2** *chiefly dial* either

nekton /'nekton/ *n* aquatic animals (e g whales or squid) free-swimming near the surface of the water [G, fr Gk *nēkton*, neut of *nēktos* swimming, fr *nēchein* to swim; akin to L *nare* to swim – more at NOURISH] – **nektonic** /-'tonik/ *adj*

nelly /'neli/ *n* [*Nelly (Duff)*, rhyming slang for *puff* (breath, life)] – **not on your nelly** *Br* certainly not – slang

nelson /'nels(ə)n/ *n* FULL NELSON; *also* HALF NELSON [prob fr the name *Nelson*]

nemat-, nemato- *comb form* **1** thread ⟨nemato*cyst*⟩ **2** nematode ⟨nemato*logy*⟩ [NL, fr Gk *nēmat-*, fr *nēmat-, nēma*, fr *nēn* to spin – more at NEEDLE]

nematocyst /'nemətə,sist/ *n* any of the minute stinging organs of jellyfish or other coelenterates [ISV]

nematode /'nemə,tohd/ *n* any of a phylum of elongated cylindrical worms parasitic in animals or plants or free-living in soil or water [deriv of Gk *nēmat-, nēma*]

Nembutal /'nembyoo,tol, -tal/ *trademark* – used for pentobarbitone

nemertean /ni'muhti·ən/ *n* any of a phylum of often vividly coloured marine worms [deriv of Gk *Nēmertēs* Nemertes, one of the Nereids (sea nymphs)] – **nemertean** *adj*, **nemertine** /-,tien/, **nemertinean** /,nemə 'tinyən/ *adj or n*

nemesia /ni'meezh(y)ə/ *n* any of various S African plants of the figwort family cultivated for their coloured flowers [NL, genus name, fr Gk, pl of *nemesion* catchfly]

nemesis /'neməsis/ *n, pl* **nemeses** /-seez/ **1a** (an agent of) retribution or vengeance **b** a formidable enemy or opponent **2** downfall, undoing [L *Nemesis*, goddess of divine retribution, fr Gk, fr *nemesis* retribution, righteous anger, fr *nemein* to distribute – more at NIMBLE]

nene /'nay,nay/ *n* a Hawaiian goose [Hawaiian *nēnē*]

neo- – see NE-

neoclassic /,neeoh'klasik/, **neoclassical** /-kl/ *adj* of or constituting a revival or adaptation of the classical, esp in literature, music, art, or architecture – **neoclassicism** /-'klasi,siz(ə)m/ *n*, **neoclassicist** *n or adj*

,neoco'lonialism /-kə'lohnyəliz(ə)m, -ni·əl-/ *n* the economic and political policies by which a great power indirectly extends its influence over other areas – **neocolonial** *adj*, **neocolonialist** *n or adj*

,neo'dymium /-'dimi·əm/ *n* a yellow metallic element of the rare-earth group ☞ PERIODIC TABLE [NL, fr *ne-* + *-dymium* (fr *didymium*)]

Neolithic /,nee·ə'lithik/ *adj* of the last period of the Stone Age characterized by polished stone implements

neologism /ni'oləjiz(ə)m/ *n* (the use of) a new word, usage, or expression [F *néologisme*, fr *né-* ne- + *log-* + *-isme* -ism] – **neology** /-ji/ *n*, **neological** /,nee·ə'lojikl/ *adj*, **neologistic** /,nee·ələ'jistik/ *adj*

neon /'neeon/ *n* **1** a noble gaseous element used esp in electric lamps ☞ PERIODIC TABLE **2** a discharge lamp in which the gas contains a large proportion of neon [Gk, neut of *neos* new – more at NEW] – **neon** *adj*, **neoned** *adj*

neonate /'nee·ə,nayt/ *n* a newborn child (less than a month old) [NL *neonatus*, fr *ne-* + *natus*, pp of *nasci* to be born – more at NATION] – **neonatal** /-'naytl/ *adj*

neophyte /'nee·ə,fiet/ *n* **1** a new convert **2** a beginner [LL *neophytus*, fr Gk *neophytos*, fr *neophytos* newly planted, newly converted, fr *ne-* + *phyein* to bring forth – more at BE]

neoplasm /'nee·ə,plaz(ə)m/ *n* an abnormal growth of tissue; a tumour [ISV] – **neoplastic** /-'plastik/ *adj*

neoprene /'nee·ə,preen/ *n* a synthetic rubber resistant to oils [*ne-* + chloro*prene*]

neoteny /nee'ot(ə)ni/ *n* **1** attainment of sexual maturity during the larval stage (e g in the axolotl) **2** retention of some larval or immature characters in adulthood [NL *neotenia*, fr *ne-* + Gk *teinein* to stretch – more at THIN] – **neotenic** /,nee·ə'tenik/ *adj*

neoteric /,nee·ə'terik/ *adj* of recent origin; modern [LL *neotericus*, fr LGk *neōterikos*, fr Gk, youthful, fr *neōteros*, compar of *neos* new, young – more at NEW]

Neotropical /,neeoh'tropikl/ *also* **Neotropic** /-'tropik/ *adj* of or constituting the region comprising tropical America and the W Indies [ISV]

Neozoic /,nee·ə'zoh·ik/ *adj or n* Cainozoic

Nepalese /,nep(ə)l'eez/ *n or adj, pl* **Nepalese** (a) Nepali

Nepali /ni'pawli/ *n, pl* **Nepalis**, *esp collectively* **Nepali** **1** the language of Nepal ☞ LANGUAGE **2** a native or inhabitant of Nepal [Hindi *naipālī* of Nepal, fr Skt *naipālīya*, fr *Nepāla* Nepal, country in Asia] – **Nepali** *adj*

nephanalysis /,nefə'naləsis/ *n* the analysis of the clouds and related phenomena over a large area of the earth [NL, fr Gk *nephos* cloud + *analysis* – more at NEBULA]

nephew /'nefyooh/ *n* a son of one's brother or sister or of one's brother-in-law or sister-in-law [ME *nevew*, fr OF *neveu*, fr L *nepot-, nepos* grandson, nephew; akin to OE *nefa* grandson, nephew, Skt *napāt* grandson]

nephr-, nephro- *comb form* kidney; kidneys ⟨neph *rectomy*⟩ ⟨nephro*logy*⟩ [NL, fr Gk, fr *nephros*]

nephrite /'nefriet/ *n* the less valuable white to dark green or black jade that is a silicate of calcium and magnesium [G *nephrit*, fr Gk *nephros*; fr its formerly being worn as a remedy for kidney diseases]

nephritic /ni'fritik/ *adj* **1** renal **2** of or affected with nephritis

nephritis /ni'frietəs/ *n, pl* **nephritides** /ni'fritədeez/ inflammation of the kidneys [LL, fr Gk, fr *nephros* kidney; akin to ME *nere* kidney]

nephron /'nefron/ *n* a single excretory unit, esp of

the kidneys of vertebrate animals [G, fr Gk *nephros*]

ne plus ultra /,nay ploos 'ooltrə/ *n* **1** the highest point or stage **2** the greatest degree of a quality or state [NL, (go) no more beyond]

nepotism /'nepə,tiz(ə)m/ *n* favouritism shown to a relative (e g by appointment to office) [F *népotisme*, fr It *nepotismo*, fr *nepote* nephew, fr L *nepot-*, *nepos* grandson, nephew – more at NEPHEW] – **nepotist** *n*

Neptune /'neptyoohn/ *n* **1** the ocean personified **2** the planet 8th in order from the sun ☞ ASTRONOMY, SYMBOL [L *Neptunus*, Roman god of the sea] – **Neptunian** /nep'tyoohnyən, -ni·ən/ *adj*

neptunium /nep'tyoohni·əm/ *n* a radioactive metallic element chemically similar to uranium from which it is formed in nuclear reactors ☞ PERIODIC TABLE [NL, fr ISV *Neptune*]

nereis /'niəri·is/ *n, pl* **nereides** /ni'ree·ə,deez/ any of a genus of (large) marine annelid worms [NL *Nereid-*, *Nereis*, genus name, fr L, Nereid (sea nymph), fr Gk *Nēreid-*, *Nēreis*, fr *Nēreus* Nereus, god of the sea]

neritic /ne'ritik/ *adj* of or being the region of shallow water adjoining the seacoast [perh fr NL *Nerita*, genus of marine snails]

nerv-, nervi-, nervo- *comb form* neur- ⟨nervine⟩ [ME *nerv-*, fr L, fr *nervus*]

[1]**nerve** /nuhv/ *n* **1** sinew, tendon ⟨*strain every* ~⟩ **2** any of the filaments of nervous tissue that conduct nervous impulses to and from the nervous system and are made up of axons and dendrites 👁 **3a** fortitude, tenacity **b** (disrespectful) assurance or boldness **4a** a sore or sensitive subject – esp in *hit/touch a nerve* **b** *pl* acute nervousness or anxiety **5** VEIN 3 **6** the sensitive pulp of a tooth [L *nervus* sinew, nerve; akin to Gk *neuron* sinew, nerve, *nēn* to spin – more at NEEDLE]

[2]**nerve** *vt* **1** to give strength and courage to **2** to prepare (oneself) psychologically *for* – often + *up* ⟨~d *herself up for the confrontation*⟩

'nerve ,cell *n* a neuron ☞ NERVE

'nerve ,centre *n* **1** CENTRE 3 **2** a source of leadership, control, or energy

nerved *adj* having (a specified kind or number of) veins or nerves – usu in combination

'nerve ,gas *n* a deadly usu organophosphate poison gas that interferes with nerve transmission

'nerveless /-lis/ *adj* **1** lacking strength or vigour **2** not agitated or afraid; cool – **nervelessly** *adv*, **nervelessness** *n*

'nerve-,racking, 'nerve-,wracking *adj* placing a great strain on the nerves

nervosity /nuh'vosəti/ *n* the state of being nervous

nervous /'nuhvəs/ *adj* **1** of, affected by, or composed of (the) nerves or neurons **2a** easily excited or agitated **b** timid, apprehensive ⟨~ *of strangers*⟩ – **nervously** *adv*, **nervousness** *n*

,nervous 'break,down *n* (an occurrence of) a disorder in which worrying, depression, severe tiredness, etc prevent one from coping with one's responsibilities

'nervous ,system *n* the brain, spinal cord, or other nerves and nervous tissue together forming a system for interpreting stimuli from the sense organs and transmitting impulses to muscles, glands, etc ☞ NERVE

nervure /'nuhvyooə/ *n* VEIN 3 [F, fr *nerf* sinew, fr L *nervus*]

nervy /'nuhvi/ *adj* **1** suffering from nervousness or anxiety **2** brash, imprudent – infml – **nerviness** *n*

nescience /'nesi·əns, 'nesh(ə)ns/ *n* ignorance; lack of knowledge – fml [LL *nescientia*, fr L *nescient-*, *nesciens*, prp of *nescire* to not know, fr *ne-* not + *scire* to know – more at NO, SCIENCE] – **nescient** /-ənt/ *adj*

ness /nes/ *n* a cape or headland [ME *nasse*, fr OE *næss*; akin to OE *nasu* nose – more at NOSE]

-ness /-nis/ *suffix* (*adj* → *n*) **1** state or quality of ⟨*good*ness⟩; *also* instance of (a specified state or quality) ⟨*a kind*ness⟩ **2** degree or amount of ⟨*big*ness⟩ [ME *-nes*, fr OE; akin to OHG *-nissa* -ness]

[1]**nest** /nest/ *n* **1a** a bed or receptacle prepared by a bird for its eggs and young **b** a place or structure in which animals live, esp in their immature stages ⟨*an ants'* ~⟩ **2a** a place of rest, retreat, or lodging **b** a den or haunt **3a** a group of similar things **b** a hotbed **4** a series of objects made to fit close together or one inside another [ME, fr OE; akin to OHG *nest* nest, L *nidus*]

[2]**nest** *vi* **1** to build or occupy a nest **2** to fit compactly together ~ *vt* to pack or fit compactly together – **nester** *n*

'nest ,egg *n* **1** a real or artificial egg left in a nest to induce a fowl to continue to lay there **2** an amount of money saved up as a reserve

nestle /'nesl/ *vb* **nestling** /'nesling, 'nesl·ing/ *vi* **1** to settle snugly or comfortably **2** to lie in a sheltered position ~ *vt* **1** to shelter or enclose (as if) in a nest **2** to press closely and affectionately [ME *nestlen*, fr OE *nestlian*, fr *nest*]

nestling /'nes(t)ling/ *n* a young bird that has not abandoned the nest

Nestor /'nestaw/ *n, often not cap* a patriarch or mentor [L, fr Gk *Nestōr*, old wise hero in Gk mythology]

Nestorian /ne'stawri·ən/ *adj* of (a church following) the doctrine ascribed to Nestorius that divine and human persons remained separate in the incarnate Christ [ME, fr LL *Nestorianus*, fr *Nestorius* † *ab* 451 patriarch of Constantinople] – **Nestorian** *n*, **Nestorianism** *n*

[1]**net** /net/ *n* **1a** an open meshed fabric twisted, knotted, or woven together at regular intervals **b** a device for catching fish, birds, or insects **c** a net barricade which divides a tennis, badminton, etc court in half and over which a ball or shuttlecock must be hit to be in play ☞ SPORT **d** the fabric that encloses the sides and back of a soccer, hockey, etc goal **e(1)** a practice cricket pitch surrounded by nets – usu pl **(2)** a period of practice in such a net **2** an entrapping situation **3** a network of lines, fibres, etc **4** a ball hit into the net in a racket game [ME *nett*, fr OE; akin to OHG *nezzi* net, L *nodus* knot] – **netless** *adj*, **netlike** *adj*, **netty** *adj*

[2]**net** *vt* **-tt-** **1** to cover or enclose (as if) with a net **2** to catch (as if) in a net **3a** to hit (a ball) into the net for the loss of a point in a game **b** to hit or kick (a ball or puck) into the goal for a score in hockey, soccer, etc – **netter** *n*

[3]**net,** *chiefly Br* **nett** *adj* **1a** remaining after all deductions (e g for taxes, outlay, or loss) ⟨~ *earnings*⟩ – compare GROSS **b** excluding all tare ⟨~ *weight*⟩ **2** final, ultimate ⟨*the* ~ *result*⟩ [ME, clean, bright, fr MF – more at [2]NEAT]

[4]**net,** *chiefly Br* **nett** *vt* **-tt- 1** to make by way of profit **2** to get possession of

[5]**net** *n* a net amount, profit, weight, price, or score

'net,ball /-,bawl/ *n* a game, usu for women, between 2 sides of 7 players each who score goals by tossing an inflated ball through a high horizontal ring on a post at each end of a hard court

nether /'nedhə/ *adj* **1** beneath the earth's surface ⟨*the ~ regions*⟩ **2** lower, under – fml [ME, fr OE *nithera*, fr *nither* down; akin to OHG *nidar* down, Skt *ni*, Gk *en, eni* in – more at IN] – **nethermost** /-,mohst/ *adj*

'nether,world /-,wuhld/ *n* the world of the dead

netsuke /'netsooki, 'netski/ *n, pl* **netsuke, netsukes** a small and often intricately carved toggle (e g of ivory) used to fasten a pouch to a kimono sash [Jap]

netting /'neting/ *n* NETWORK 1

[1]**nettle** /'netl/ *n* **1** any of a genus of widely distributed green-flowered plants covered with stinging hairs **2** any of various plants like the nettle – used in combination ⟨*red dead* nettle⟩ [ME, fr OE *netel*; akin to OHG *nazza* nettle, Gk *adikē*]

[2]**nettle** *vt* **nettling** /'netl·ing/ **1** to strike or sting (as if) with nettles **2** to arouse to annoyance or anger

'nettle ,rash *n* urticaria

[1]**'net,work** /-,wuhk/ *n* **1** a fabric or structure of cords or wires that cross at regular intervals and are knotted or secured at the crossings **2** a system of crisscrossing lines or channels **3** an interconnected chain, group, or system **4a** a group of radio or television stations linked together so that they can broadcast the same programmes if desired **b** a radio or television company that produces programmes for broadcast over such a network

[2]**network** *vt* to present on or integrate into a radio or television network ⟨~ed *programmes*⟩

Neufchâtel /'nuh,shatel (*Fr* nœʃɑtɛl)/ *n* a soft white cheese similar to cream cheese but containing less fat [F, fr *Neufchâtel*, town in France]

neur-, neuro- *comb form* **1** nerve; nervous system ⟨neura*l*⟩ ⟨neuro*logy*⟩ ⟨neuro*surgeon*⟩ **2** neural; neural and ⟨neuro*muscular*⟩ [NL, fr Gk, nerve, sinew, fr *neuron* – more at NERVE]

neural /'nyooərəl/ *adj* **1** of or affecting a nerve or the nervous system **2** dorsal – **neurally** *adv*

neuralgia /nyoo(ə)'raljə/ *n* intense paroxysms of pain radiating along the course of a nerve without apparent cause [NL] – **neuralgic** /-jik/ *adj*

neurasthenia /,nyooərəs'theenyə/ *n* severe fatigue, depression, etc occurring as a mental disorder; NERVOUS BREAKDOWN – not now used technically [NL] – **neurasthenic** /-nik/ *adj,* **neurasthenically** *adv*

neuritis /nyooə'rietəs/ *n* inflammation or degeneration of a nerve causing pain, sensory disturbances, etc [NL] – **neuritic** /-'ritik/ *adj or n*

,neuro'chemistry /,nyooəroh-/ *n* the biochemistry of (the transmission of impulses down) nerves – **neurochemical** *adj,* **neurochemist** *n*

neuroglia /nyoo(ə)'rogli·ə, ,nyooərə'glee·ə/ *n* supporting tissue that is intermingled with the impulse-conducting cells of nervous tissue in the brain, spinal cord, and ganglia [NL, fr *neur-* + MGk *glia* glue] – **neuroglial** *adj*

neuroleptic /,nyooərə'leptik/ *n* TRANQUILLIZER [F *neuroleptique*, fr *neur-* + *-leptique* affecting, fr Gk *lēptikos* seizing, fr *lambanein* to take, seize – more at LATCH] – **neuroleptic** *adj*

neurology /nyoo(ə)'roləji/ *n* the study of (diseases of) the nervous system [NL *neurologia*, fr *neur-* + *-logia* -logy] – **neurologist** *n,* **neurologic** /-rə'lojik/, **neurological** *adj,* **neurologically** *adv*

,neuro'muscular /,nyooəroh-/ *adj* involving nervous and muscular cells, tissues, etc ⟨*a ~ junction*⟩ [ISV]

neuron /'nyooəron/ *n* any of the many specialized cells each with an axon and dendrites that form the functional impulse-transmitting units of the nervous system [NL, fr Gk, nerve, sinew – more at NERVE] – **neuronal** /'nyooərənəl, nyoo'rohnl/ *also* **neuronic** /-'ronik/ *adj*

neuropathy /nyoo(ə)'ropəthi/ *n* an abnormal (degenerative) state of the nerves or nervous system [ISV] – **neuropathic** /,nyooərə'pathik/ *adj,* **neuropathically** *adv*

neuropteran /nyoo(ə)'roptərən/ *n* any of an order of insects, usu having a fine network of veins in their wings, including the lacewings [deriv of Gk *neur-* + *pteron* wing – more at FEATHER] – **neuropteran** *adj,* **neuropterous** *adj*

neurosis /nyoo(ə)'rohsis/ *n, pl* **neuroses** /-,seez/ a nervous disorder, unaccompanied by disease of the nervous system, in which phobias, compulsions, anxiety, and obsessions make normal life difficult [NL]

neurotic /nyoo(ə)'rotik/ *n* one who is emotionally unstable or is affected with a neurosis – **neurotic** *adj,* **neurotically** *adv,* **neuroticism** /-'roti,siz(ə)m/ *n*

,neurotrans'mitter /,nyooəroh-/ *n* a substance (e g acetylcholine) that is released at a nerve ending and transmits nerve impulses across the synapse – **neurotransmission** *n*

[1]**neuter** /'nyoohtə/ *adj* **1a** of or belonging to the gender that is neither masculine nor feminine **b** intransitive **2** lacking generative organs or having nonfunctional ones ⟨*the worker bee is ~*⟩ ☞ SYMBOL [ME *neutre*, fr MF & L; MF *neutre*, fr L *neuter*, lit., neither, fr *ne-* not + *uter* which of two – more at NO, WHETHER]

[2]**neuter** *n* **1** (a word or morpheme of) the neuter gender **2a** WORKER 2 **b** a castrated animal

[3]**neuter** *vt* CASTRATE 1

[1]**neutral** /'nyoohtrəl/ *adj* **1** (of or being a country, person, etc) not engaged on either side of a war, dispute, etc ⟨*~ territory*⟩ **2a** indifferent, indefinite **b** without colour **c** NEUTER 2 **d** neither acid nor alkaline ⟨*a ~ solution*⟩ **e** not electrically charged or positive or negative; not live ⟨*the ~ wire in a mains plug is blue*⟩ **3a** produced (e g like the vowel /ə/) with the tongue in the position it has when at rest **b** produced (e g like the vowel /ah/) with the lips neither spread nor rounded [MF, fr (assumed) ML *neutralis*, fr L, of neuter gender, fr *neutr-, neuter*] – **neutrally** *adv,* **neutralism** *n,* **neutralist** *n,* **neutralistic** /-'listik/ *adj,* **neutrality** /nyooh'traləti/ *n*

[2]**neutral** *n* **1** a neutral country, person, etc **2** a neutral colour **3** a position (of a gear lever) in which gears are disengaged **4** a neutral electrical conductor

neutral·ize, -ise /'nyoohtrə,liez/ *vt* **1** to make (chemically, politically, electrically, etc) neutral **2** to nullify or counteract (the effect of) with an opposing action, force, etc ~ *vi* to become neutralized – **neutralization** /-'zaysh(ə)n/ *n*

neutrino /nyooh'treenoh/ *n, pl* **neutrinos** either of 2 forms of an uncharged elementary particle that is

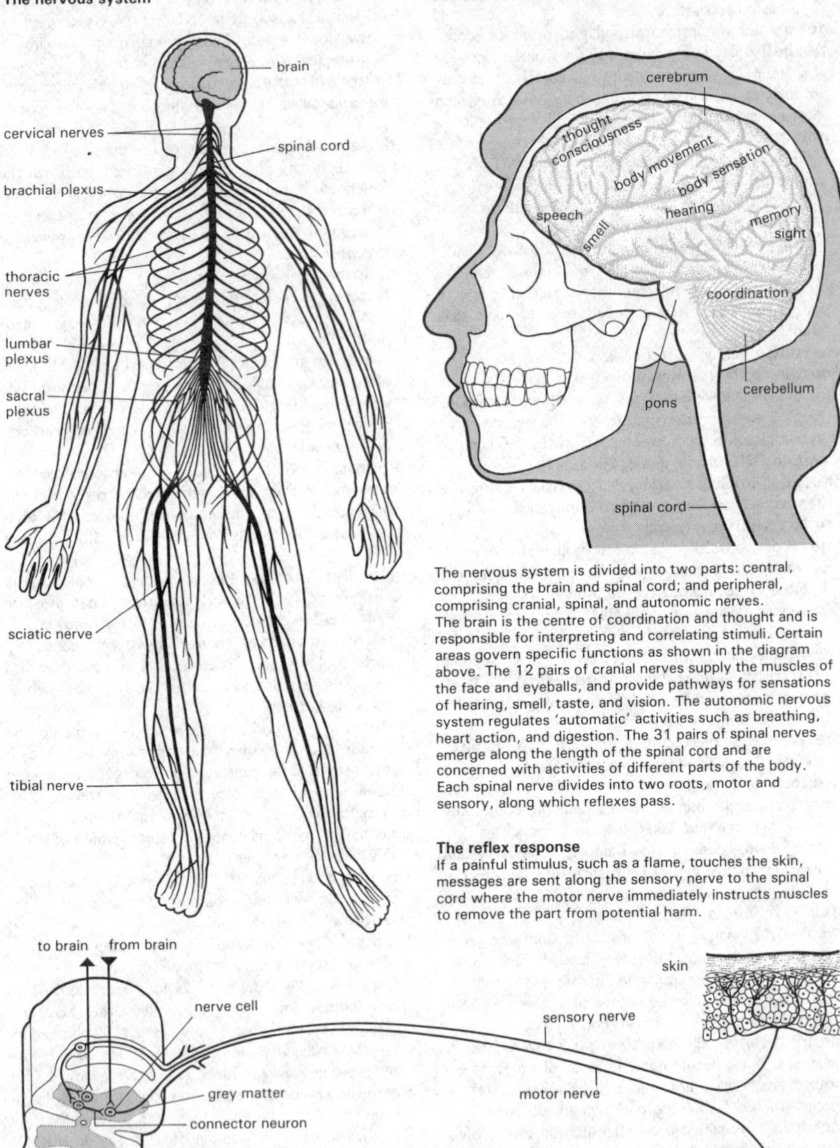

The nervous system is divided into two parts: central, comprising the brain and spinal cord; and peripheral, comprising cranial, spinal, and autonomic nerves. The brain is the centre of coordination and thought and is responsible for interpreting and correlating stimuli. Certain areas govern specific functions as shown in the diagram above. The 12 pairs of cranial nerves supply the muscles of the face and eyeballs, and provide pathways for sensations of hearing, smell, taste, and vision. The autonomic nervous system regulates 'automatic' activities such as breathing, heart action, and digestion. The 31 pairs of spinal nerves emerge along the length of the spinal cord and are concerned with activities of different parts of the body. Each spinal nerve divides into two roots, motor and sensory, along which reflexes pass.

The reflex response
If a painful stimulus, such as a flame, touches the skin, messages are sent along the sensory nerve to the spinal cord where the motor nerve immediately instructs muscles to remove the part from potential harm.

☞ ANATOMY, DIGESTION, REPRODUCTION

Skin

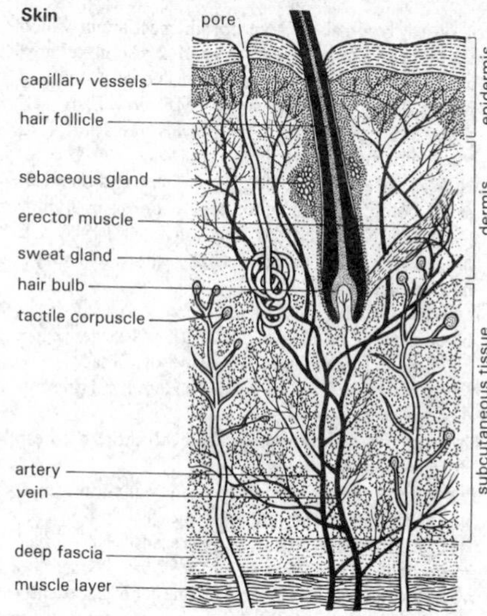

Sensory organs relay the sensations they receive to the brain where these messages are synthesized into consciousness of the world around us.

Tongue

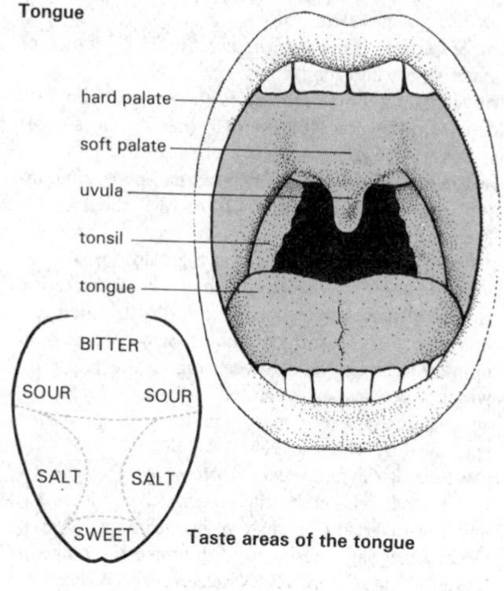

Taste areas of the tongue

Ear

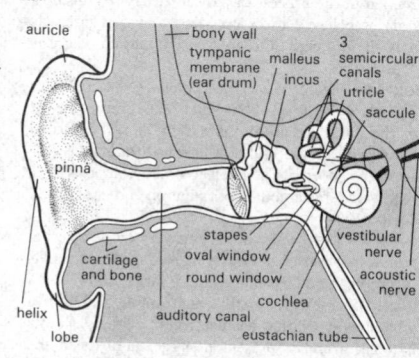

auricle
bony wall
tympanic membrane (ear drum)
malleus
incus
3 semicircular canals
utricle
saccule
pinna
stapes
oval window
round window
cochlea
vestibular nerve
acoustic nerve
cartilage and bone
helix
lobe
auditory canal
eustachian tube

Eye

sclera
choroid
retina
optic nerve
eyelid
suspensory ligaments
iris
pupil
lens
vitreous humour
cornea
blind spot
aqueous humour
ciliary body
canal of schlemm
blood vessels to retina

Nose

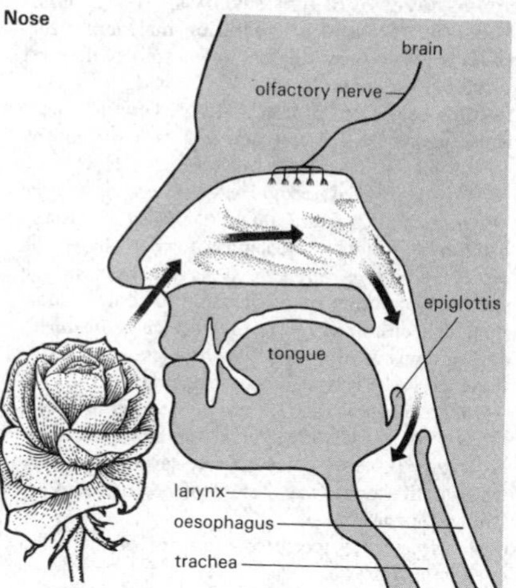

created in the process of particle decay (e g inside a star), is believed to be massless, and that interacts only slightly with other matter [It, dim. of *neutrone* neutron]

neutron /'nyooh,tron/ *n* an uncharged elementary particle with a mass about that of the proton, present in the nuclei of all atoms except those of normal hydrogen ☞ PHYSICS [prob fr *neutral*]

'neutron ,bomb *n* a nuclear bomb that produces relatively large amounts of radiation and a relatively small blast

'neutron ,star *n* any of various very dense celestial bodies that consist of closely packed neutrons resulting from the collapse of a much larger star

neutrophil /'nyoohtrə,fil/, **neutrophile** /-,fiel/ *n* a white blood cell that has neutrophilic granules in its cytoplasm and is present in large numbers in the blood ☞ ANATOMY [ISV *neutro-* neutral (fr L *neutr-, neuter* neither) + *-phil, -phile*]

neutrophilic /,nyoohtrə'filik/, **neutrophil** /'nyoohtrə,fil/ *adj* staining weakly with both acidic and basic dyes

névé /'nevay (*Fr* neve)/ *n* (a field of) partly compacted granular snow, esp forming the surface part of the upper end of a glacier [F (Swiss dial.), fr L *niv-, nix* snow – more at SNOW]

never /'nevə/ *adv* **1** not ever; at no time ⟨~ *saw him before*⟩ ⟨~ *forgotten*⟩ **2** not in any degree; not under any condition ⟨*this will* ~ *do*⟩ ⟨~ *mind*⟩ **3** surely not ⟨*you're* ~ *18!*⟩ ⟨*'I said it to his face.'* 'Never!'⟩ – chiefly infml [ME, fr OE *nǣfre*, fr *ne* not + *ǣfre* ever – more at NO] **– I never 1** – used to express amazement ⟨*well* I never⟩; chiefly infml **2** I didn't do it – nonstandard ⟨*no she* never⟩

,never'more *adv* never again

,never-'never *n, Br* HIRE PURCHASE – + *the*; infml

,never-'never ,land *n* an ideal or imaginary place

nevertheless /,nevədhə'les/ *adv* in spite of that; yet ⟨*true but* ~ *unkind*⟩

nevus /'neevəs/ *n, pl* **nevi** /-vie/ *NAm* a naevus

[1]**new** /nyooh/ *adj* **1** not old; not used previously; recent ⟨*a* ~ *book*⟩ ⟨*a* ~ *science*⟩ **2a(1)** only recently discovered, recognized, or in use; novel ⟨*the* ~ *morality*⟩ **(2)** fresh, unfamiliar ⟨*visit* ~ *places*⟩ **b** different from or replacing a former one of the same kind ⟨*a* ~ *model*⟩ **3** having been in the specified condition or relationship for only a short time; unaccustomed ⟨~ *to the job*⟩ ⟨*a* ~ *member*⟩ **4a** beginning as the repetition of a previous act or thing ⟨*a* ~ *day*⟩ **b** refreshed, regenerated ⟨*awoke, a* ~ *man*⟩ **5** *cap* MODERN 3; *esp* in use after medieval times [ME, fr OE *nīwe*; akin to OHG *niuwi* new, L *novus*, Gk *neos*] – **newish** *adj*, **newness** *n* – **new lease of life** a renewed period of healthy activity, strength, or usefulness

[2]**new** *adv* newly, recently – usu in combination ⟨new-*mown grass*⟩

,new'born /-'bawn/ *n or adj, pl* **newborn, newborns** (an individual who is) recently born

'Newcastle di,sease /'nyooh,kahsl, -,kasl/ *n* FOWL PEST [*Newcastle* upon Tyne, city in England]

'new,comer /-,kumə/ *n* **1** a recent arrival **2** a beginner, novice

New Deal *n* the programme of economic and social reform in the USA during the 1930s [fr its supposed resemblance to the situation of freshness and equality of opportunity afforded by a fresh deal in a card game]

newel /'nyooh·əl/ *n* **1** an upright post about which the steps of a spiral staircase wind **2** *also* **newel post** a principal post supporting either end of a staircase handrail ☞ ARCHITECTURE [ME *nowell*, fr MF *nouel* stone of a fruit, fr LL *nucalis* like a nut, fr L *nuc-, nux* nut – more at NUT]

,new'fangled /-'fang·gld/ *adj* modern and unnecessarily complicated or gimmicky – derog or humor [ME, fond of novelty, fr *newefangel*, fr *new* + OE *fangen*, pp of *fōn* to take, seize – more at PACT] – **newfangledness** *n*

Newfoundland /nyooh'fowndlənd/ *n* (any of) a breed of large intelligent dogs with coarse dense usu black hair [*Newfoundland*, island of Canada]

New Hebrew /'heebrooh/ *n* the Hebrew of present-day Israel

New Latin /'latin/ *n* post-medieval Latin, used esp in scientific terminology

,New 'Left *n* a radical left-wing movement originating in Britain in the late 1950s

newly /'nyoohli/ *adv* **1** lately, recently ⟨*a* ~ *married couple*⟩ **2** anew

'newly,wed /-,wed/ *n or adj* (one who is) recently married

,new 'maths *n* MODERN MATHS

,new 'moon *n* the phase of the moon when its dark side is towards the earth; *also* the thin crescent moon seen a few days after this ☞ SYMBOL

,new 'penny *n* PENNY 1a(2)

news /nyoohz/ *n pl but sing in constr* **1** (a report or series of reports of) recent (notable) events; new information about sthg ⟨*have you heard the* ~*?*⟩ ⟨*there is no* ~ *of him*⟩ **2a** news reported in a newspaper, a periodical, or a broadcast **b** material that is newsworthy **3** a radio or television broadcast of news – **newsless** *adj*

'news,agent /-,ayjənt/ *n, chiefly Br* a retailer of newspapers and magazines

'news,boy /-,boy/, *fem* **'news,girl** *n* a paperboy

'news,cast /-,kahst/ *n* NEWS 3 [*news* + broad*cast*] – **newscaster** *n*, **newscasting** *n*

'news,letter /-,letə/ *n* a printed pamphlet containing news or information of interest chiefly to a special group

'news,monger /-,mung·gə/ *n* a gossip

newspaper /'nyoohs,paypə/ *n* **1** (an organization that publishes) a paper printed and distributed usu daily or weekly and containing news, articles of opinion, features, and advertising **2** the paper on which a newspaper is printed

'news,paperman /-mən, -,man/ *n* a journalist employed by a newspaper

newspeak /'nyooh,speek/ *n, often cap* propagandistic language marked by euphemism, circumlocution, and the inversion of customary meanings [*Newspeak*, a language 'designed to diminish the range of thought," in the novel *Nineteen Eighty-Four* by George Orwell †1950 E writer]

'news,print /-,print/ *n* cheap paper made chiefly from wood pulp and used mostly for newspapers

'news,reader /-,reedə/ *n* a broadcaster who reads the news

'news,reel /-,reel/ *n* a short film dealing with current events

'news,room /-room, -,roohm/ *n* a place (e g an office) where news is prepared for publication or broadcast

'news,stand /-,stand/ *n* a stall where newspapers and periodicals are sold

'New ,Style *adj or adv* according to the Gregorian calendar

'news,vendor /-,vendə/ *n* one who sells newspapers, esp in the street at a regular place

'news,worthy /-,wuhdhi/ *adj* sufficiently interesting to warrant reporting

newsy /'nyoohzi/ *adj* full of (inconsequential) news – **newsiness** *n*

newt /nyooht/ *n* any of various small semiaquatic salamanders ☞ LIFE CYCLE [ME, alter. (by incorrect division of *an ewte*) of *ewte* – more at EFT]

,new tech'nology *n* technology that is new, esp that using microprocessors (e g in domestic appliances, cars, printing, etc)

,New 'Testament *n* the second part of the Christian Bible comprising the canonical Gospels and Epistles, the books of Acts, and the book of Revelation

newton /'nyooht(ə)n/ *n* the SI unit of force equal to the force that when acting for 1s on a free mass of 1kg will give it a velocity of 1m/s ☞ PHYSICS, UNIT [Sir Isaac *Newton* †1727 E mathematician & scientist]

Newtonian /nyooh'tohnyn, -ni·ən/ *adj* of, following, or agreeing with (the discoveries of) Isaac Newton ⟨~ *mechanics*⟩

new town *n* any of several towns in Britain planned and built as a unit since 1946

,new 'wave *n, often cap N&W* **1** a cinematic movement characterized by improvisation, abstraction, a subjective treatment of chronology and symbolism, and the frequent use of experimental photographic techniques **2** a style of rock music that developed from punk rock and is usu more complex musically while retaining an emphasis on social comment [trans of F *nouvelle vague*]

,New 'World *n* the W hemisphere; *esp* the continental landmass of N and S America

,New 'Year *n* the first day or days of a year; *esp* NEW YEAR'S DAY

,New ,Year's 'Day *n* January 1 observed as a public holiday in many countries

[1]next /nekst/ *adj* **1** immediately adjacent or following (e g in place or order) ⟨*the* ~ *house*⟩ **2** immediately after the present or a specified time ⟨~ *week*⟩ ⟨*he left the very* ~ *Monday*⟩ [ME, fr OE *nīehst*, superl of *nēah* nigh – more at NIGH]

[2]next *adv* **1** in the time, place, or order nearest or immediately succeeding ⟨~ *we drove home*⟩ ⟨*the* ~ *closest school*⟩ **2** on the first occasion to come ⟨*when* ~ *we meet*⟩

[3]next *prep* nearest or adjacent to ⟨*wear wool* ~ *the skin*⟩

[4]next *n* the next occurrence, item, or issue of a kind ⟨*to be contained in our* ~⟩

,next-'door *adj* situated or living in the next building, room, etc

next door *adv* in or to the next building, room, etc

next man *n* – **the next man** anyone else ⟨*would do it as well as* the next man⟩

,next of 'kin *n, pl* **next of kin** the person most closely related to another person

[1]'next to *prep* immediately following or adjacent to ⟨*sit* ~ *Mary*⟩ ⟨~ *gin I like sherry best*⟩

[2]next to *adv* very nearly; almost ⟨*it was* ~ *impossible to see in the fog*⟩ ⟨*the article told me* ~ *nothing*⟩

nexus /'neksəs/ *n, pl* **nexuses, nexus** **1** a connection or link **2** a connected group or series [L, fr *nexus*, pp of *nectere* to bind]

ngwee /n'gwee/ *n, pl* **ngwee** ☞ *Zambia* at NATIONALITY [native name in Zambia, lit., bright]

niacin /'nie·əsin/ *n* NICOTINIC ACID [*ni*cotinic *ac*id + *-in*]

[1]nib /nib/ *n* **1** a bill or beak **2a** the sharpened point of a quill pen **b** (each of the 2 equal divisions of) a small thin (detachable) piece of metal at the end of a pen, that tapers to a split point which is placed in contact with the paper or other surface to be marked **3** a small pointed or projecting part or article ⟨*roasted almond* ~s⟩ [prob alter. of *neb*]

[2]nib *vt* **-bb-** to make into a nib or give a nib to

[1]nibble /'nibl/ *vb* **nibbling** /'nibling/ *vt* **1a** to bite cautiously, gently, or playfully **b** to eat or chew in small bites **2** to produce by repeated small bites ~ *vi* **1** to take gentle, small, or cautious bites **2** to show cautious or qualified interest *USE* (*vi*) usu + *at* [origin unknown] – **nibbler** /'niblə/ *n*

[2]nibble *n* **1** an act of nibbling **2** a very small amount (e g of food) *USE* infml

nibs /nibz/ *n pl but sing in constr* an important or self-important person – infml; chiefly in *his nibs* or *His Nibs* [earlier *nabs*, perh alter. of *neb*]

nice /nies/ *adj* **1** showing or requiring fine discrimination or treatment ⟨*a* ~ *distinction*⟩ **2a** pleasant, agreeable **b** well done; well-executed ⟨~ *shot!*⟩ **3** inappropriate or unpleasant – usu ironic ⟨*he's a* ~ *one to talk*⟩; compare PRETTY 2 **4a** socially acceptable; well-bred **b** decent, proper [ME, foolish, wanton, fr OF, fr L *nescius* ignorant, fr *nescire* to not know – more at NESCIENCE] – **nicely** *adv*, **niceness** *n* – **nice and** to a satisfactory degree ⟨*it's* nice and *cool*⟩

Nicene Creed /'nie,seen, -'-/ *n* a Christian creed expanded from a creed issued by the first Nicene Council in AD 325, beginning 'I believe in one God" [*Nicene* (of Nicaea, ancient city in Asia Minor), fr ME, fr LL *Nicenus, Nicaenus*]

nicety /'niesəti/ *n* **1** an elegant or refined feature **2** a fine point or distinction **3** (the showing or requiring of) delicacy, discernment, or careful attention to details [ME *nicete*, fr MF *niceté* foolishness, fr *nice*, adj] – **to a nicety** to the point at which sthg is at its best ⟨*roasted* to a nicety⟩

[1]niche /neesh, nich/ *n* **1** a recess in a wall, esp for a statue **2a** a place or activity for which a person is best suited **b** the ecological role of an organism in a community, esp in regard to food consumption [F, fr MF, fr *nicher* to nest, fr (assumed) VL *nidicare*, fr L *nidus* nest – more at NEST]

[2]niche *vt* to place (as if) in a niche

Nichrome /'niekrohm/ *trademark* – used for a nickel and chromium alloy with a high electrical resistance

[1]nick /nik/ *n* **1** a small notch or groove **2** the point at which the back or side wall of a squash court meets the floor **3** EDGE 4 **4** *Br* state of health or repair – infml; esp in *in good/bad nick* ⟨*it's not in very good* ~⟩ **5** *Br* a prison or police station – slang ⟨*he's been in the* ~ *for the last 3 years*⟩ [ME *nyke*, prob alter. of *nocke* nock] – **in the nick of time** at the final critical moment; just before it would be too late

[2]nick *vt* **1a** to make a nick in **b** to cut into or wound slightly **2** *Br* **a** STEAL 1a **b** ARREST 2 ~ *vi esp of domestic animals* to complement one another genetically and produce superior offspring *USE* (*vt 2*) slang

nickel /'nik(ə)l/ *n* **1** a hard bivalent metallic transition element with magnetic properties like those of iron ☞ PERIODIC TABLE **2** (a US coin containing 1 part of nickel to 3 of copper and worth) the sum of 5 cents [prob fr Sw, fr G *kupfernickel* niccolite (a mineral largely composed of a nickel arsenide), prob fr *kupfer* copper + *nickel* goblin; fr the deceptive copper colour of niccolite]

nickelodeon /,nik(ə)l'ohdi·ən/ *n* a jukebox [prob fr *nickel* + *-odeon* (as in *melodeon* reed organ)]

nickel silver *n* a silver-white alloy of copper, zinc, and nickel

¹nicker /'nikə/ *n, pl* **nicker** *Br* the sum of £1 – slang [origin unknown]

²nicker *vi* to whinny [perh alter. of *neigh*]

nicknack /'nik,nak/ *n* a knick-knack

nickname /'nik,naym/ *n* **1** a name used in place of or in addition to a proper name **2** a familiar form of a proper name, esp of a person [ME *nekename* additional name, alter. (by incorrect division of *an ekename*) of *ekename*, fr *eke* also + *name*] – **nickname** *vt*

nicol /'nik(ə)l/, **nicol prism** two pieces of transparent calcite cemented together and used esp to obtain a ray of polarized light [William *Nicol* †1851 Sc physicist]

nicotinamide /,nikə'tinə,mied, -'tee-/ *n* a vitamin of the vitamin B complex with actions similar to those of nicotinic acid [ISV]

'nico,tinamide-,adenine ,di'nucleotide /,adəneen die'nyoohkli·ətied, ,adənin/ *n* NAD

nicotine /'nikəteen/ *n* an alkaloid that is the chief drug in tobacco and has the actions of the neurotransmitter acetylcholine on some of its receptors, esp those in skeletal muscle [F, fr NL *nicotiana*, genus name of tobacco plants, fr Jean *Nicot* †1600 F diplomat & scholar who introduced tobacco into France] – **nicotinic** /-'teenik, -'tinik/ *adj*

,nico,tinic 'acid /-'teenik, -'tinik/ *n* a vitamin of the vitamin B complex that is found widely in animals and plants and whose lack results in pellagra

nictitating membrane /'niktə,tayting/ *n* a thin membrane capable of extending across the eyeball under the eyelids of many animals (e g cats) [*nictitate* (to wink), alter. of *nictate*, fr L *nictatus*, pp of *nictare*]

nidification /,nidifi'kaysh(ə)n/ *n* the act, process, or technique of building a nest [ML *nidification-, nidificatio*, fr L *nidificatus*, pp of *nidificare* to build a nest, fr *nidus* nest]

nidus /'niedəs/ *n, pl* **nidi** /'nie,die, -di/, **niduses** **1** a nest or breeding place; *esp* a place in an animal or plant where bacteria or other organisms lodge and multiply **2** a place where sthg originates, develops, or is located [NL, fr L]

niece /nees/ *n* a daughter of one's brother or sister or of one's brother-in-law or sister-in-law [ME *nece* granddaughter, niece, fr OF *niece*, fr LL *neptia*, fr L *neptis*; akin to L *nepot-, nepos* grandson, nephew – more at NEPHEW]

niello /ni'eloh/ *n, pl* **nielli** /-,lie, -li/, **niellos** **1** a black enamel-like mixture of sulphur with silver, copper, and lead **2** (a piece of) metal decorated with incised designs filled with niello [It, fr ML *nigellum*, fr neut of L *nigellus* blackish, dim. of *niger* black] – **niello** *vt*

niff /nif/ *n, Br* an unpleasant smell – slang [E dial., perh fr *sniff*] – **niffy** *adj*

nifty /'nifti/ *adj* very good or effective; *esp* cleverly conceived or executed – infml [origin unknown] – **nifty** *adv*

niggard /'nigəd/ *n* a mean and stingy person [ME, of Scand origin; akin to ON *hnøggr* niggardly; akin to L *cinis* ashes – more at INCINERATE] – **niggard** *adj*

'niggardly /-li/ *adj* **1** grudgingly mean; miserly **2** provided in meagre amounts ⟨~ *praise*⟩ – **niggardliness** *n*, **niggardly** *adv*

nigger /'nigə/ *n* a Negro; *broadly* a member of any dark-skinned race – derog [alter. of earlier *neger*, fr MF *negre*, fr Sp or Pg *negro*, fr *negro* black, fr L *niger*]

niggle /'nigl/ *vb* **niggling** /'nigling/ *vi* **1** to waste time or effort on minor details **2** to find fault constantly in a petty way ~ *vt* to cause slight irritation to; bother [origin unknown] – **niggle** *n*, **niggler** *n*, **niggly** *adj*

niggling /'nigling/ *adj* **1** petty **2** persistently annoying ⟨~ *doubts*⟩ – **nigglingly** *adv*

nigh /nie/ *adv, adj, or prep* near (in place, time, or relation) ⟨~ *on 50 years*⟩ [ME, fr OE *nēah*; akin to OHG *nāh*, adv, nigh, & prep, nigh, after, ON *nā-* nigh]

night /niet/ *n* **1** the period of darkness from dusk to dawn caused by the earth's daily rotation **2** an evening characterized by a specified event or activity ⟨*Thursday is bingo* ~⟩ ⟨*opening* ~⟩ **3a** darkness **b** a state of affliction, ignorance, or obscurity [ME, fr OE *niht*; akin to OHG *naht* night, L *noct-, nox*, Gk *nykt-, nyx*]

night blindness *n* reduced vision in faint light (e g at night) – **night-blind** *adj*

'night,cap /-,kap/ *n* **1** a cloth cap worn in bed **2** a drink taken at bedtime

'night,club /-,klub/ *n* a place of entertainment open at night that has a floor show, provides music and space for dancing, and usu serves drinks and food

'night,dress /-,dres/ *n* a woman's or girl's nightgown

'night,fall /-,fawl/ *n* dusk

'night,gown /-,gown/ *n* a loose garment for sleeping in

'night,hawk /-,hawk/ *n* a nightjar, owl, or similar bird that flies at night

nightie, nighty /'nieti/ *n* a nightdress – infml [*nightgown* + *-ie, -y*]

nightingale /'nieting,gayl/ *n* any of several Old World thrushes noted for the sweet usu nocturnal song of the male [ME, fr OE *nihtegale*, fr *niht* + *galan* to sing – more at YELL]

'night,jar /-,jah/ *n* a Eurasian insect-eating bird that is active at night and has a characteristic churring call [fr its harsh sound]

'night,life /-,lief/ *n* late evening entertainment or social life

'night-,light *n* a dim light kept burning all night long, esp in sby's bedroom

'nightly /-li/ *adj or adv* (of, occurring, taken, or done) at or by night or every night

'night,mare /-,meə/ *n* **1** an evil spirit that causes frightening dreams **2** a frightening dream accompanied by a sense of oppression or suffocation that usu awakens the sleeper **3** an experience, situation, or object that causes acute anxiety or terror [*night*

+ *mare* (evil spirit), fr ME, fr OE] – **nightmare, nightmarish** *adj*, **nightmarishly** *adv*

'night ,owl *n* sby who tends to be most active at night – infml

nights *adv* in the night repeatedly; on any night

'night ,school *n* classes, often in subjects leading to a qualification, held in the evening

nightshade /'niet,shayd/ *n* any of various related usu poisonous plants: e g **a** bittersweet **b** DEADLY NIGHTSHADE

'night,shirt /-,shuht/ *n* a long loose shirt for sleeping in

'night ,soil *n* human excrement collected for fertilizing the soil

'night,stick /-,stik/ *n*, *NAm* a club carried by a policeman

,night 'watchman *n* **1** sby who keeps watch (e g over a building) by night **2** a relatively inexpert batsman who is sent in to bat towards the end of a day's play so that a more expert batsman need not face the bowling until the following day

nighty /'nieti/ *n* a nightie

nignog /'nig,nog/ *n*, *Br* a nigger – humor; derog [redupl of *nig*, short for *nigger*]

nigritude /'nigrityoohd/ *n* blackness – fml [L *nigritudo*, fr *nigr-*, *niger* black]

nihilism /'nie·ə,liz(ə)m, 'ni-/ *n* **1** a view that rejects all values and beliefs as meaningless or unfounded **2a** *often cap* the doctrine that social conditions are so bad as to make destruction desirable for its own sake, adhered to specif by a 19th-c Russian terrorist revolutionary party **b** terrorism [G *nihilismus*, fr L *nihil* nothing – more at NIL] – **nihilist** *n or adj*, **nihilistic** /-'listik/ *adj*

nihil obstat /,nie·il 'obstat/ *n* authoritative or official approval [L, nothing hinders]

-nik /-nik/ *suffix* (*n or adj* → *n*) one connected with or characterized by being ⟨*beat*nik⟩ ⟨*computer*nik⟩ [Yiddish, fr Russ & Pol]

nil /nil/ *n* nothing, zero ⟨*a score of 2 points to* ~⟩ [L, nothing, contr of *nihil*, fr OL *nihilum*, fr *ne-* not + *hilum* trifle – more at NO] – **nil** *adj*

nilgai /'nilgie/ *n*, *pl* **nilgais**, *esp collectively* **nilgai** a large Indian antelope [Hindi *nīlgāw* blue bull (fem *nīlgāī*), fr Skt *nīla* dark blue + *go* bull, cow]

Nilotic /nie'lotik/ *adj* of (the inhabitants or languages of) the Nile or Nile region ☞ LANGUAGE [L *Niloticus*, fr Gk *Neilōtēs*, fr *Neilos* Nile, river in E Africa]

nim /nim/ *n* any of various games in which each player in turn draws objects from 1 or more piles and attempts to take the last object or force the opponent to take it [prob fr obs *nim* (to take), fr ME *nimen*, fr OE *niman*]

nimble /'nimbl/ *adj* **1** quick, light, and easy in movement **2** quick and clever in thought and understanding [ME *nimel*, fr OE *numol* holding much, fr *niman* to take; akin to OHG *neman* to take, L *numerus* number, Gk *nemein* to distribute, manage, *nomos* pasture, *nomos* usage, custom, law] – **nimbleness** *n*, **nimbly** /'nimbli/ *adv*

nimbostratus /,nimboh'strahtəs/ *n* a low dark rainy cloud layer [NL, fr L *nimbus* + NL *stratus*]

nimbus /'nimbəs/ *n*, *pl* **nimbi** /-,bie, -bi/, **nimbuses** **1** a luminous vapour, cloud, or atmosphere surrounding a god or goddess **2** a luminous circle about the head of a representation of a god, saint, or sovereign **3** a cloud from which rain is falling ☞ WEATHER [L, rainstorm, cloud; akin to Pahlavi *namb* mist]

nimiety /ni'mie·əti/ *n* an excess, redundancy – fml [LL *nimietas*, fr L *nimius* too much, adj, fr *nimis*, adv]

niminy-piminy /,nimәni 'pimәni/ *adj* affectedly dainty or delicate [prob alter. of *namby-pamby*]

nincompoop /'ningkəm,poohp/ *n* a silly or foolish person [origin unknown]

nine /nien/ *n* **1** ☞ NUMBER **2** the ninth in a set or series **3** sthg having 9 parts or members or a denomination of 9 **4** the first or last 9 holes of an 18-hole golf course **5** *pl in constr, cap the* Common Market countries between 1973 and 1981 [ME, fr *nyne*, adj, fr OE *nigon*; akin to OHG *niun* nine, L *novem*, Gk *ennea*] – **nine** *adj or pron*, **ninefold** /-,fohld/ *adj or adv* – **to the nines** elaborately in special, formal, or party clothes ⟨*dressed up* to the nines⟩ [perh fr the use of 9 as a mystic number symbolizing perfection]

,nine ,days' 'wonder *n* sthg that creates a short-lived sensation

nineteen /nien'teen/ *n* ☞ NUMBER [ME *nynetene*, adj, fr OE *nigontēne*; akin to OE *tīen* ten] – **nineteen** *adj or pron*, **nineteenth** /-teenth/ *adj or n* – **nineteen to the dozen** very fast and volubly ⟨*talking* nineteen to the dozen⟩

,Nineteen ,Eighty-'Four *n* a (future) era envisaged as having all aspects of life controlled by an all-seeing totalitarian government [*Nineteen Eighty-Four*, futuristic novel by George Orwell †1950 E writer]

,nineteenth 'hole *n* the bar of a golf club or other gathering place – humor [fr its being resorted to after the 18 holes on a standard golf course]

ninety /'nienti/ *n* **1** ☞ NUMBER **2** *pl* (a range of temperatures, ages, or dates within a century characterized by) the numbers 90 to 99 [ME *ninety*, adj, fr OE *nigontig*, short for *hundnigontig*, fr *hundnigontig*, n, group of 90, fr *hund* hundred + *nigon* nine + *-tig* group of 10 – more at HUNDRED, EIGHTY] – **ninety** *adj or pron*, **ninetyfold** /-,fohld/ *adj or adv*, **ninetieth** /-ith/ *adj or n*

ninhydrin /nin'hiedrin/ *n* an oxidizing agent used esp for the detection of amino acids and polypeptides [fr *Ninhydrin*, a trademark]

ninny /'nini/ *n* a silly or foolish person – humor; infml [perh by shortening & alter. fr *an innocent*]

ninth /nienth/ *n* **1** ☞ NUMBER **2a** (a chord containing) a musical interval of an octave and a second **b** the note separated by this interval from a lower note – **ninth** *adj or adv*

niobium /nie'ohbi·əm/ *n* a ductile metallic element chemically resembling tantalum ☞ PERIODIC TABLE [NL, fr L *Niobe*, mythical daughter of Tantalus, fr Gk *Niobē*; fr its occurrence in tantalite]

¹nip /nip/ *vb* **-pp-** *vt* **1** to catch hold of and squeeze sharply; pinch **2a** to sever (as if) by pinching sharply – often + *off* **b** to prevent the growth or development of ⟨*her plans were* ~ped *in the bud*⟩ **3** to injure or make numb with cold ~ *vi chiefly Br* to go quickly or briefly; hurry – infml ⟨*I'll just* ~ *out to the shops*⟩ [ME *nippen*; akin to ON *hnippa* to prod, Gk *konis* ashes – more at INCINERATE]

²nip *n* **1** a sharp stinging cold ⟨*a* ~ *in the air*⟩ **2** (an instance of) nipping; a pinch **3** *chiefly NAm* a pungent flavour; a tang

³nip *n* a small measure or drink of spirits [prob short for *nipperkin* (a small liquor container)]

[4]**nip** *vb* **-pp-** to take nips of (a drink)

Nip *n* a Japanese – derog [short for *Nipponese*]

nipa /'neepə, 'nie-/ *n* (an alcoholic drink made from the juice of) an Australasian creeping palm [prob fr It, fr Malay *nipah* nipa palm]

,nip and 'tuck *adj or adv, chiefly NAm* NECK AND NECK [[2]*nip* + [2]*tuck*]

nipper /'nipə/ *n* **1** any of various devices (e g pincers) for gripping or cutting – usu pl with sing. meaning **2** *chiefly Br* a child; *esp* a small boy – infml [[1]NIP + [2]-ER]

nipple /'nipl/ *n* **1** the small protuberance of a mammary gland (e g a breast) from which milk is drawn in the female **2a** an artificial teat through which a bottle-fed infant feeds **b** a device with a hole through which the discharge of a liquid can be regulated **3** a small projection through which oil or grease is injected into machinery [earlier *neble, nible*, prob dim. of *neb, nib*]

nipplewort /'nipl,wuht/ *n* a slender composite Eurasian plant with small yellow flower heads

Nipponese /,nipə'neez/ *n or adj, pl* **Nipponese** (a) Japanese [*Nippon* (Japan), fr Jap *Dai Nippon*]

nippy /'nipi/ *adj* **1** nimble and lively; snappy **2** CHILLY 1 [[2]NIP + [1]-Y] – **nippily** *adv*, **nippiness** *n*

nirvana /niə'vahnə, nuh-/ *n, often cap* **1** a Hindu and Buddhist state of final bliss and freedom from the cycle of rebirth, attainable through the extinction of desire and individual consciousness **2** a place or state of relief from pain or anxiety [Skt *nirvāṇa*, lit., act of extinguishing, fr *nis-* out + *vāti* it blows – more at [1]WIND]

nisi /'niesie, 'neezi/ *adj* taking effect at a specified time unless previously modified or avoided ⟨*a decree* ~⟩ [L, unless, fr *ne-* not + *si* if]

'Nissen ,hut /'nis(ə)n/ *n* a prefabricated shelter with a semicircular arching roof of corrugated iron and a concrete floor [Peter *Nissen* †1930 Br mining engineer]

[1]**nit** /nit/ *n* (the egg of) a parasitic insect (e g a louse) [ME *nite*, fr OE *hnitu*; akin to OHG *hniz* nit, Gk *konid-, konis*]

[2]**nit** *n, chiefly Br* a nitwit – infml

'nit-,picking *n* petty and usu unjustified criticism [[1]*nit*] – **nitpick** *vi*

nitr-, nitro- *comb form* **1** nitrogen ⟨nitr*ate*⟩ **2** nitrate ⟨nitro*cellulose*⟩ [*nitre*]

[1]**nitrate** /'nietrayt/ *n* **1** a salt or ester of nitric acid **2** sodium or potassium nitrate used as a fertilizer [F, fr *nitrique*]

[2]**nitrate** *vt* to treat or combine with nitric acid or a nitrate – **nitrator** *n*, **nitration** /-'traysh(ə)n/ *n*

nitrazepam /nie'trazi,pam/ *n* a synthetic drug with actions similar to those of diazepam, widely used as a hypnotic in sleeping pills – compare MOGADON [*nitr-* + *-azepam* (as in *diazepam*)]

nitre, *NAm chiefly* **niter** /'nietə/ *n* POTASSIUM NITRATE – not now used technically [ME *nitre* natron, fr MF, fr L *nitrum*, fr Gk *nitron*, fr Egypt *ntry*]

nitric /'nietrik/ *adj* of or containing nitrogen (with a relatively high valency) ⟨~ *oxide*⟩ [F *nitrique*, fr *nitr-*]

,nitric 'acid *n* a corrosive inorganic liquid acid used esp as an oxidizing agent and in making fertilizers, dyes, etc

nitride /'nietried/ *n* a compound of nitrogen with 1 other element ⟨*boron* ~⟩ [ISV]

nitrification /,nietrifi'kaysh(ə)n/ *n* nitrifying; *specif* the oxidation (e g by bacteria) of ammonium salts first to nitrites and then to nitrates

nitrify /'nietrifie/ *vt* to combine or impregnate with (a compound of) nitrogen [F *nitrifier*, fr *nitr-*]

nitrile /'nietriel, -tril, -treel/ *n* an organic compound containing the cyanide group [ISV *nitr-* + *-il, -ile* (fr L *-ilis* [1]-ile)]

nitrite /'nietriet/ *n* a salt or ester of nitrous acid

nitro /'nietroh/ *adj* being the univalent group NO_2 or containing it in the molecular structure – usu in combination ⟨nitro*benzene*⟩ [*nitr-*]

nitro- – see NITR-

nitrobenzene /,nietroh'benzeen/ *n* an oily liquid with an almond smell, used esp as a solvent and in making aniline [ISV]

,nitro'cellu,lose /-'selyoo,lohs, -,lohz/ *n* CELLULOSE NITRATE [ISV]

nitrogen /'nietrəj(ə)n/ *n* a trivalent gaseous chemical element that constitutes about 78 per cent by volume of the atmosphere and is found in combined form as a constituent of all living things ☞ PERIODIC TABLE [F *nitrogène*, fr *nitr-* + *-gène* -gen] – **nitrogenous** /nie'trojənəs/ *adj*

'nitrogen ,cycle *n* the continuous circulation of nitrogen and nitrogen-containing compounds from air to soil to living organisms and back to air, involving nitrogen fixation, nitrification, decay, and denitrification

nitrogen fixation *n* (industrial or biological) assimilation of atmospheric nitrogen into chemical compounds; *specif* this process performed by soil microorganisms, esp in the root nodules of leguminous plants (e g clover) – **nitrogen-fixer** *n*, **nitrogen-fixing** *n*

nitroglycerine /,nietroh'glisəreen, -rin/ *n* an oily explosive liquid used chiefly in making dynamite and, as a weak solution in water, in medicine to dilate the blood vessels [ISV]

nitros-, nitroso- *comb form* containing the univalent group NO in the molecular structure ⟨nitros*amine*⟩ [NL *nitrosus* nitrous]

nitrosamine /nie'trohsə,meen, -min/ *n* any of various often cancer-producing compounds containing the group NNO in their molecular structure

nitrous /'nietrəs/ *adj* of or containing **a** potassium nitrate **b** nitrogen (with a relatively low valency) [NL *nitrosus*, fr L, full of natron, fr *nitrum* natron – more at NITRE]

,nitrous 'acid *n* an unstable acid containing less oxygen than nitric acid and occurring only in solution or in the form of its salts

,nitrous 'oxide *n* a gas used as a general anaesthetic, esp in obstetrics and dentistry

nitty-gritty /,niti 'griti/ *n* *the* important basic realities – infml [origin unknown] – **nitty-gritty** *adj*

nitwit /'nit,wit/ *n* a scatterbrained or stupid person – infml [prob fr G dial. *nit* not + E *wit*] – **nit-witted** *adj*

[1]**nix** /niks/, *fem* **nixie** /-si/ *n* a water sprite of Germanic folklore [G, fr OHG *nihhus*; akin to OE *nicor* water monster, Gk *nizein* to wash]

[2]**nix** *n* nothing – slang [G *nichts* nothing]

[3]**nix** *adv, NAm* no – slang

[4]**nix** *vt, NAm* to veto, forbid – slang

nizam /nie'zahm, ni-, -zam, '--/ *n* any of a line of sovereigns of Hyderabad in India, reigning from

1713 to 1950 [Hindi *nizām* order, governor, fr Ar *nizām*] – **nizamate** /-,mayt/ *n*

[1]**no** /noh/ *adv* **1** – used to negate an alternative choice ⟨*whether you like it or* ~⟩ **2** in no respect or degree – in comparisons ⟨~ *better than before*⟩ **3** – used in answers expressing negation, dissent, denial, or refusal; contrasted with *yes* ⟨~, *I'm not going*⟩ **4** – used like a question demanding assent to the preceding statement ⟨*she's pretty,* ~?⟩ **5** nay ⟨*happy,* ~, *ecstatic*⟩ **6** – used as an interjection to express incredulity ⟨*'She's 17.'* 'No!'⟩ **7** *chiefly Scot* not ⟨*it's* ~ *canny*⟩ [ME, fr OE *nā*, fr *ne* not + *ā* always; akin to ON & OHG *ne* not, L *ne-*, Gk *nē-* – more at [1]AYE]

[2]**no** *adj* **1a** not any ⟨~ *money*⟩ ⟨*there's* ~ *denying*⟩ ⟨~ *parking*⟩ **b** hardly any; very little ⟨*I'll be finished in* ~ *time*⟩ **2a** not a; quite other than a ⟨*he's* ~ *expert*⟩ **b** – used before a noun phrase to give force to an opposite meaning ⟨*in* ~ *uncertain terms*⟩; compare NOT 3

[3]**no** *n, pl* **noes, nos** a negative reply or vote

No, Noh /noh/ *n, pl* **No, Noh** a classic Japanese (form of) dance-drama [Jap *nō*, lit., talent]

[1]**nob** /nob/ *n* **1** a jack of the same suit as the card turned by the dealer in cribbage, that scores 1 point for the holder – chiefly in *his nob/nobs* ⟨*one for his* ~⟩ **2** a person's head – infml [prob alter. of *knob*]

[2]**nob** *n, chiefly Br* a wealthy or influential person – infml [perh fr [1]*nob*]

[1],**no-'ball** *interj or n* – (used as a call by an umpire to indicate) an illegal delivery of the ball in cricket which cannot take a wicket and counts 1 run to the batsman's side if the batsman does not score a run off it

[2]**no-ball** *vt , of an umpire in cricket* to declare (a bowler) to have delivered or (a delivery) to be a no-ball ~ *vi* to bowl a no-ball

nobble /'nobl/ *vt* **nobbling** /'nobling, 'nobl·ing/ *Br* **1** to incapacitate (esp a racehorse), esp by drugging **2a** to win over to one's side, esp by dishonest means **b** to get hold of, esp dishonestly **c** to swindle, cheat *USE* (*1*) infml; (*2*) slang [perh irreg freq of *nab*] – **nobbler** *n*

nobbut /'nobət/ *adv, N Eng* no more than; only ⟨*he's* ~ *a lad*⟩ [ME *no but*, fr *no* (adv) + *but*]

nobelium /noh'beeli·əm/ *n* an artificially produced radioactive metallic element ☞ PERIODIC TABLE [NL, fr Alfred *Nobel* †1896 Sw manufacturer, inventor, & philanthropist]

,**Nobel 'prize** /noh'bel/ *n* any of various annual prizes established by the will of Alfred Nobel for the encouragement of people who work for the interests of humanity (e g in the fields of peace, literature, medicine, and physics)

nobility /noh'biləti/ *n* **1** being noble **2** *sing or pl in constr* the people making up a noble class [ME *nobilite*, fr MF *nobilité*, fr L *nobilitat-*, *nobilitas*, fr *nobilis*]

[1]**noble** /'nohbl/ *adj* **1a** gracious and dignified in character or bearing **b** famous, notable ⟨*a* ~ *victory*⟩ **2** of or being high birth or exalted rank **3** of fine quality; excellent ⟨*a* ~ *vintage*⟩ **4** imposing, stately **5** having or showing a magnanimous character or high ideals ⟨*a* ~ *deed*⟩ [ME, fr OF, fr L *nobilis* knowable, well known, noble, fr *noscere* to come to know – more at KNOW] – **nobleness** *n*, **nobly** /'nohbli/ *adv*

[2]**noble** *n* **1** a person of noble rank or birth **2** a former English gold coin worth £⅓

noble gas *n* any of a group of gaseous elements that react only slightly with other elements and include helium, neon, argon, krypton, xenon, and radon

'**nobleman** /-mən/, *fem* '**noble,woman** *n* a man of noble rank

noblesse /noh'bles, no-/ *n sing or pl in constr* the members of the (French) nobility [ME, fr OF *noblesce*, fr *noble*]

noblesse oblige /,nohbles o'bleezh, no-/ *n* the obligation of honourable and responsible behaviour associated with high rank [F, lit., nobility obligates]

[1]**nobody** /'nohbədi, -,bodi/ *pron* not anybody ⟨~ *likes me*⟩

[2]**nobody** *n* a person of no influence or consequence

[1]**nock** /nok/ *n* **1** a notch cut at the end of an archer's bow to hold the string **2** (the strengthened part of an arrow carrying) a notch into which the bowstring fits [ME *nocke* notched tip on the end of a bow; akin to MD *nocke* summit, tip, L *nux* nut – more at NUT]

[2]**nock** *vt* to make a nock in (e g a bow or arrow); *also* to fit (e g a bowstring) into or by means of a nock

,**no-'claim** ,**bonus**, ,**no-'claims** ,**bonus** *n, Br* a discount allowed in (motor) insurance premiums when no claim has been made under the policy in previous years

noct-, nocti-, nocto- *comb form* night ⟨noct*ambulation*⟩ ⟨noct*urnal*⟩ [L *noct-*, *nocti-*, fr *noct-*, *nox* – more at NIGHT]

noctule /'noktyoohl/ *n* a large Eurasian reddish-brown insect-eating bat [prob fr NL *noctula*, specific epithet, fr LL, small owl, dim. of L *noctua* owl]

nocturnal /nok'tuhnl/ *adj* **1** of or occurring in the night **2** active at night ⟨*a* ~ *predator*⟩ [MF or LL; MF, fr LL *nocturnalis*, fr L *nocturnus* of night, nocturnal, fr *noct-*, *nox* night] – **nocturnally** *adv*

nocturne /'noktuhn/ *n* a work of art dealing with evening or night; *esp* a dreamy pensive composition for the piano [F, adj, nocturnal, fr L *nocturnus*]

nocuous /'nokyoo·əs/ *adj* harmful, noxious [L *nocuus*, fr *nocēre* to harm – more at NOXIOUS] – **nocuously** *adv*

[1]**nod** /nod/ *vb* **-dd-** *vi* **1** to make a short downward movement of the head (e g in assent or greeting) **2** to bend or sway gently downwards or forwards **3a** to become drowsy or sleepy ⟨~ *in front of the fire*⟩ **b** to make a slip or error in a moment of inattention ⟨*even Homer sometimes* ~s⟩ ~ *vt* **1** to incline (e g the head) in a quick downward movement **2** to express by a nod ⟨~ded *their approval*⟩ [ME *nodden*; akin to OHG *hnotōn* to shake, L *cinis* ashes – more at INCINERATE] – **nodder** *n*

[2]**nod** *n* **1** (an instance of) nodding **2** an unconsidered indication of agreement, approval, etc – infml ⟨*the motion went through on the* ~⟩

nodding /'noding/ *adj* **1** pendulous or drooping ⟨*a plant with* ~ *flowers*⟩ **2** casual, superficial ⟨*a* ~ *acquaintance with French*⟩

noddle /'nodl/ *n* a person's head – infml [ME *nodle* back of the head or neck]

noddy /'nodi/ *n* any of several stout-bodied terns of warm seas [prob short for obs *noddypoll*, alter. of *hoddypoll* (fumbling inept person)]

node /nohd/ *n* **1** a thickening or swelling (e g of a rheumatic joint) **2** either of the 2 points where the orbit of **a** a planet or comet intersects the ecliptic

☞ SYMBOL **b** an earth satellite crosses the plane of the equator **3a** a point on a stem at which 1 or more leaves are attached **b** a point at which a curve intersects itself **4** a point, line, etc of a vibrating body at which vibration is at a minimum [L *nodus* knot, node – more at [1]NET] – **nodal** *adj*, **nodally** *adv*

,node of 'Ranvier /'ranviə, 'ronhvi,ay/ *n* a constriction in the myelin sheath of a myelinated nerve fibre [Louis *Ranvier* †1922 F histologist]

nodical /'nodikl, 'noh-/ *adj* of astronomical nodes

nod off *vi* to fall asleep, esp unintentionally

nodose /'nohdohs, -'-/ *adj* having (conspicuous) protuberances [L *nodosus*, fr *nodus*] – **nodosity** /-'dosəti/ *n*

nodule /'nodyoohl/ *n* a small rounded mass: e g **a** a small rounded lump of a mineral or mineral aggregate **b** a swelling on the root of a leguminous plant (e g clover) containing symbiotic bacteria that convert atmospheric nitrogen into a form in which it can be used by the plant [L *nodulus*, dim. of *nodus*] – **nodular** *adj*, **nodulated** /'nodyoo,laytid/ *adj*, **nodulation** /-'laysh(ə)n/ *n*

nodus /'nohdəs/ *n, pl* **nodi** /-die, -di/ a difficult or complex situation [L, knot, node]

Noel, Noël /noh'el/ *n* the Christmas season [F *noël* Christmas, carol, fr L *natalis* birthday, fr *natalis* natal]

noes /nohz/ *pl of* NO

noetic /noh'etik/ *adj* of or based on the intellect [Gk *noētikos* intellectual, fr *noein* to think, fr *nous* mind]

nog /nog/ *n* (an) eggnog

noggin /'nogin/ *n* **1** a small mug or cup **2** a small measure of spirits, usu 0.142 litres (¼pt) **3** a person's head – infml [origin unknown]

no-go /,noh 'goh/ *adj* having prohibited or restricted access ⟨*a ~ military zone*⟩

Noh /noh/ *n* No

no-hoper /,noh 'hohpə/ *n, chiefly Austr* one who has no chance of success – infml

nohow /'noh,how/ *adv* in no way; not at all – chiefly dial or humor

[1]**noise** /noyz/ *n* **1** loud confused shouting or outcry **2a** a (harsh or unwanted) sound **b** unwanted signals or fluctuations in an electrical circuit **c** irrelevant or meaningless information occurring with desired information in the output of a computer **3** a usu trite remark of a specified type – usu pl ⟨*made sympathetic ~s*⟩ [ME, fr OF, strife, quarrel, noise, fr L *nausea* nausea] – **noiseless** *adj*, **noiselessly** *adv*

[2]**noise** *vt* to spread by gossip or hearsay – usu + *about* or *abroad*

noisette /nwah'zet (*Fr* nwazɛt)/ *n* a small round thick boneless slice of lamb or other meat ☞ MEAT [F, hazel nut, fr MF, fr OF, dim. of *nois, nois* nut, fr L *nuc-, nux*]

noisome /'noys(ə)m/ *adj* repellent, offensive – fml [ME *noysome*, fr *noy* annoyance, fr OF *enui, anoi* – more at ENNUI] – **noisomely** *adv*, **noisomeness** *n*

noisy /'noyzi/ *adj* **1** making noise **2** full of or characterized by noise – **noisily** *adv*, **noisiness** *n*

noli me tangere /,nohli may 'tang·gəray/ *n* a warning against touching or interference [L, do not touch me]

nolle prosequi /,noli 'prosikwie/ *n* an entry on the record of a legal action stating that the prosecutor or plaintiff will not proceed with part or all of his suit or prosecution [L, to be unwilling to pursue]

nomad /'nohmad/ *n* **1** a member of a people that wanders from place to place, usu seasonally and within a well-defined territory **2** one who wanders aimlessly from place to place [L *nomad-, nomas* member of a wandering pastoral people, fr Gk, fr *nemein* to distribute, pasture – more at NIMBLE] – **nomad** *adj*, **nomadism** *n*, **nomadic** /-'madik/ *adj*

'no-,man's-,land *n* **1a** an area of waste or unclaimed land **b** an unoccupied area between opposing armies **2** an area of anomalous, ambiguous, or indefinite character

nom de plume /,nom de 'ploohm/ *n, pl* **noms de plume** /~/ a pseudonym under which an author writes [F *nom* name + *de* of + *plume* pen]

nomen /'nohmən, -men/ *n, pl* **nomina** /'nominə/ the second of the 3 names that an ancient Roman usu had [L *nomin-, nomen* name – more at NAME]

nomenclature /no'menklәchә/ *n* **1** a name, designation **2** (an instance of) naming, esp within a particular system **3** a system of terms used in a particular science, discipline, or art [L *nomenclatura* calling by name, list of names, fr *nomen* + *calatus*, pp of *calare* to call – more at [1]LOW] – **nomenclatural** /-'klaychərəl/ *adj*

[1]**nominal** /'nominl/ *adj* **1** of or being a nominal **2** of or constituting a name **3a** being sthg in name only – compare TITULAR 1 **b** assigned as a convenient approximation (e g to an actual weight or size) **c** negligible, insignificant ⟨*a ~ rent*⟩ [ME *nominalle*, fr ML *nominalis*, fr L, of a name, fr *nomin-, nomen* name] – **nominally** *adv*

[2]**nominal** *n* a word (group) functioning as a noun

'nominal,ism /-,iz(ə)m/ *n* a theory that abstract things and general ideas are mere names and have no independent reality inside or outside the mind – **nominalist** *n*, **nominalist, nominalistic** /-'istik/ *adj*

nominate /'nominayt/ *vt* **1** to designate, specify **2a** to appoint or recommend for appointment **b** to propose for an honour, award, or candidature [L *nominatus*, pp of *nominare*, fr *nomin-, nomen* name] – **nominator** *n*, **nominee** /-'nee/ *n*, **nomination** /-'naysh(ə)n/ *n*

nominative /'nominətiv/ *adj* **1** of or being the grammatical case expressing the subject of a verb **2** nominated [fr the traditional use of the nominative form in naming a noun] – **nominative** *n*

nomogram /'nomə,gram, noh-/, **nomograph** /-,grahf, -,graf/ *n* a graphic representation that consists of several lines marked off to scale and arranged in such a way that by using a straightedge to connect known values on 2 lines an unknown value can be read at the point of intersection with another line [Gk *nomos* law + ISV *-gram* – more at NIMBLE] – **nomographic** /-'grafik/ *adj*, **nomography** /-'mogrəfi/ *n*

no more *conj* neither ⟨*he can't go and ~ can I*⟩

-nomy /-nəmi/ *comb form* (→ *n*) **1** system of laws or principles governing a (specified) field; science of ⟨*agronomy*⟩ ⟨*astronomy*⟩ **2** management ⟨*economy*⟩ **3** government, rule ⟨*autonomy*⟩ [ME *-nomie*, fr OF, fr L *-nomia*, fr Gk, fr *nemein* to distribute]

non- /non-/ *prefix* **1** not; reverse of; absence of ⟨non*conformity*⟩ ⟨non*payment*⟩ ⟨non*existence*⟩ ⟨non*alcoholic*⟩ **2** failure to be; refraining from ⟨non*smoker*⟩ ⟨non*violent*⟩ ⟨non*appearance*⟩ **3** lacking the usual characteristics of the thing specified ⟨non*event*⟩ ⟨non*appearance*⟩ **4** proof against;

designed to avoid ⟨non*stick*⟩ ⟨non-*iron*⟩ ⟨non*flammable*⟩ [ME, fr MF, fr L *non* not, fr OL *noenum*, fr *ne-* not + *oinom*, neut of *oinos* one – more at NO, ONE]

nonage /'nohnij, 'nonij/ *n* a period or state of youth or immaturity [ME, fr MF, fr *non-* + *age*]

nonagenarian /,nohnəji'neəri·ən, ,nonə-/ *n* a person between 90 and 99 years old [L *nonagenarius* containing ninety, fr *nonageni* ninety each, fr *nonaginta* ninety, fr *nona-* (akin to *novem* nine) + *-ginta* (akin to *viginti* twenty) – more at NINE, VIGESIMAL] – **nonagenarian** *adj*

nonagon /'nonəgən/ *n* a polygon of 9 angles and 9 sides ☞ MATHEMATICS [L *nonus* ninth + E *-gon* – more at NOON]

nonaligned /,nonə'liend/ *adj* not allied with other nations, esp any of the great powers – **nonalignment** *n*

nonarrestable offence *n* an offence for which a warrant is required before an arrest can be made ☞ LAW

nonce /nons/ *n* the present occasion, time, or purpose ⟨*for the* ~⟩ ⟨*a* ~ *word*⟩ [ME *nanes*, alter. (by incorrect division of *then anes* in such phrases as *to then anes* for the one purpose) of *anes* one purpose, irreg fr *an* one, fr OE *ān*]

nonchalant /'nonshələnt/ *adj* giving an impression of easy unconcern or indifference [F, fr OF, fr prp of *nonchaloir* to disregard, fr *non-* + *chaloir* to concern, fr L *calēre* to be warm – more at LEE] – **nonchalance** /-ləns/ *n*, **nonchalantly** *adv*

noncombatant /non'kombət(ə)nt, -kəm'bat(ə)nt/ *n* a civilian, army chaplain, etc who does not engage in combat – **noncombatant** *adj*

,noncom,missioned 'officer /-nonkə'mish(ə)nd/ *n* a subordinate officer (e g a sergeant) in the armed forces appointed from among the personnel who do not hold a commission

,noncom'mittal /-kə'mitl/ *adj* giving no clear indication of attitude or feeling – **noncommittally** *adv*

non compos mentis /,non ,kompəs 'mentis/ *adj* not of sound mind [L, lit., not having mastery of one's mind]

,noncon'ductor /-kən'duktə/ *n* a substance that conducts heat, electricity, etc only very slightly under normal conditions

,noncon'formist /-kən'fawmist/ *n* **1** *often cap* a person who does not conform to an established church; *specif* a member of a Protestant body separated from the Church of England **2** one who does not conform to a generally accepted pattern of thought or behaviour – **nonconformism** *n, often cap*, **nonconformist** *adj, often cap*

,noncon'formity /-kən'fawməti/ *n* **1** refusal to conform to an established creed, rule, or practice **2** absence of correspondence or agreement

,nonco,ope'ration /-koh,opə'raysh(ə)n/ *n* refusal to cooperate; *specif* CIVIL DISOBEDIENCE – **noncooperationist** *n*, **noncooperative** /-koh'op(ə)rətiv/ *adj*, **noncooperator** /-koh 'opə,raytə/ *n*

nondescript /'nondiskript/ *adj* **1** (apparently) belonging to no particular class or kind **2** lacking distinctive or interesting qualities; dull [*non-* + L *descriptus*, pp of *describere* to describe] – **nondescript** *n*

nondrying oil /,non'drie·ing/ *n* a highly saturated oil (e g olive oil) that is unable to solidify when exposed in a thin film to air

¹none /nun/ *pron, pl* **none** **1** not any; no part or thing ⟨~ *of the money is missing*⟩ ⟨~ *of the telephones are working*⟩ **2** not one person; nobody ⟨*it's* ~ *other than Tom*⟩ ⟨~ *but a fool*⟩ **3** not any such thing or person ⟨*a bad film is better than* ~ *at all*⟩ [ME, fr OE *nān*, fr *ne* not + *ān* one – more at NO, ONE]

²none *adv* **1** by no means; not at all ⟨~ *too soon to begin*⟩ **2** in no way; to no extent ⟨ ~ *the worse for wear*⟩

³none /nohn/ *n, often cap* the fifth of the canonical hours that was orig fixed for 3 pm [LL *nona*, fr L, 9th hour of the day from sunrise – more at NOON]

nonentity /no'nentiti/ *n* **1** sthg that does not exist or exists only in the imagination **2** nonexistence **3** sby or sthg of little importance or interest

nones /nohnz/ *n pl but sing or pl in constr* **1** the 9th day before the ides according to ancient Roman reckoning **2** *often cap* ³NONE [ME *nonys*, fr L *nonae*, fr fem pl of *nonus* ninth]

nonesuch *also* **nonsuch** /'nun,such/ *n* a person or thing without an equal; a paragon – **nonesuch** *adj*

nonetheless /,nundhə'les/ *adv* nevertheless

,non-eu'clidean *adj, often cap E* not assuming or in accordance with all of Euclid's postulates ⟨~ *geometry*⟩

nonevent /,noni'vent/ *n* an event that is (unexpectedly) dull or inconsequential

,non'feasance /-'feez(ə)ns/ *n* failure to act [*non-* + obs *feasance* (doing, execution), fr AF *fesance*, fr MF *faisance* act, fr OF, fr *fais-*, stem of *faire* to make, do, fr L *facere*]

,non'ferrous /-'ferəs/ *adj* of or being a metal other than or not containing iron

,non'flammable /-'flaməbl/ *adj* difficult or impossible to set alight – **nonflammability** *n*

,nonin'ductive /-in'duktiv/ *adj* not inductive; *esp* having negligible electrical inductance

,noninter'vention /-intə'vensh(ə)n/ *n* the state or policy of not intervening – **noninterventionist** *n or adj*

,noni'onic /-ie'onik/ *adj* not ionic; *esp, of a detergent* not dependent on a surface-active anion for effect

,non'joinder /-'joyndə/ *n* failure to include a necessary party in a legal action

,non'juring /-'jooəring/ *adj* being a nonjuror [*non-* + L *jurare* to swear – more at JURY]

,non'juror /-'jooərə/ *n* a person refusing to take an oath; *specif* a member of the clergy in Britain who refused to take an oath of allegiance after 1688

,non'metal /-'metl/ *n* a chemical element (e g boron or carbon) that is not a metal – **nonmetallic** /-mi'talik/

,non'nuclear /-'nyoohkli·ə/ *adj* not having or using nuclear power or weapons ⟨*a* ~ *country*⟩

no-nonsense /,noh 'nons(ə)ns/ *adj* **1** serious, businesslike **2** without trifles or frills

nonpareil /'nonpərel, ,nonpə'rayl/ *n or adj* (sby or sthg) having no equal [adj MF, fr *non-* + *pareil* equal, fr (assumed) VL *pariculus*, fr L *par* equal; n fr adj]

nonplus /,non'plus/ *vt* **-ss-** (*NAm* **-s-**, **-ss-**) to perplex or disconcert [*nonplus*, n (quandary), fr L *non plus* no more]

,non'polar /-'pohlə/ *adj* not polar; *esp* not having or requiring the presence of electrical poles

,nonpro'ductive /-prə'duktiv/ *adj* **1** failing to produce or yield **2** *of a cough* dry – **nonproductiveness** *n*

,nonpro,life'ration /-prə,lifə'raysh(ə)n/ *adj or n* (providing for) the stoppage of proliferation (e g of nuclear weapons)

,non,represen'tational /-,reprizen'taysh(ə)nl/ *adj* not representing a natural or actual object, figure, etc ⟨~ *art*⟩ – **nonrepresentationalism** *n*

,non'resident /-'rezid(ə)nt/ *adj* not residing in a particular place (e g a hotel) – **nonresident** *n*, **nonresidence, nonresidency** *n*

,nonre'sistance /-ri'zist(ə)ns/ *n* passive submission to authority; *also* the principle of not resisting violence by force

,nonre'turnable /-ri'tuhnəbl/ *adj* not returnable (to a dealer in exchange for a deposit) ⟨~ *bottles*⟩

,non'rigid /-'rijid/ *adj* maintaining form by pressure of contained gas ⟨*a ~ airship*⟩ [NON- + RIGID] – **nonrigidity** /-ri'jidəti/ *n*

,nonse'cretor /-si'kreetə/ *n* a person of blood group A, B, or AB who does not secrete the corresponding antigen in bodily fluids (e g saliva)

,nonsec'tarian /-sek'teəri·ən/ *adj* not affiliated with or restricted to a particular religious sect or denomination

nonsense /'nonsəns/ *n* **1a** meaningless words or language **b** (an instance of) foolish or absurd language, conduct, or thought **2** frivolous or insolent behaviour **3** – used interjectionally to express forceful disagreement – **nonsensical** /-'sensikl/ *adj*, **nonsensically** *adv*, **nonsensicalness** *n*

'nonsense ,verse *n* humorous or whimsically absurd verse

non sequitur /,non 'sekwitə/ *n* **1** a conclusion that does not follow from the premises **2** a statement that does not follow logically from anything previously said [L, it does not follow]

,non'skid /-'skid/ *adj, of a tyre or road* designed or equipped to prevent skidding

,non'slip /-'slip/ *adj* designed to reduce or prevent slipping

,non'standard /'standəd/ *adj* not conforming in pronunciation, grammatical construction, idiom, or word choice to accepted usage – compare SUBSTANDARD [NON- + STANDARD]

,non'starter /-'stahtə/ *n* sby or sthg that is sure to fail or prove impracticable [NON- + STARTER]

,non'stick /-'stik/ *adj* having or being a surface that prevents adherence of food during cooking [[3]*stick*]

,non'stop /-'stop/ *adj* done or made without a stop – **nonstop** *adv*

nonsuch /'nun,such/ *n* a nonesuch

,non'suit /-'sooht/ *n* a judgment against a plaintiff for failure to prosecute, or inability to establish, a case [ME, fr AF *nounsuyte*, fr *noun-* non- + OF *siute* following, pursuit – more at SUIT] – **nonsuit** *vt*

,non'trivial /-'trivi·əl/ *adj* of or being a solution to an equation in which at least 1 unknown value is not equal to zero [NON- + TRIVIAL]

non troppo /,non 'tropoh/ *adv or adj* without excess – used in music [It, lit., not too much]

,non-'U /'yooh/ *adj* not characteristic of the upper classes

,non'union /-'yoohnyən/ *adj* not belonging to or connected with a trade union ⟨~ *plumbers*⟩ ⟨*a ~ job*⟩

,non'violence /-'vie·ələns/ *n* **1** refraining from violence on moral grounds **2** passive resistance or peaceful demonstration for political ends – **nonviolent** *adj*, **nonviolently** *adv*

,non'white /-'wiet/ *n or adj* (one who is) not Caucasian

,non'zero /-'ziəroh/ *adj* not zero; either positive or negative

[1]noodle /'noohdl/ *n* a silly or foolish person – humor [perh alter. of *noddle*]

[2]noodle *n* a narrow flat ribbon of pasta made with egg [G *nudel*]

nook /nook/ *n* a small secluded or sheltered place or part [ME *noke, nok*]

noon /noohn/ *n* **1 noon, noonday** the middle of the day; midday **2** the highest or culminating point [ME, fr OE *nōn* ninth hour from sunrise, fr L *nona*, fr fem of *nonus* ninth; akin to L *novem* nine – more at NINE]

'no ,one *pron* nobody

[1]noose /noohs/ *n* a loop with a running knot that tightens as the rope is pulled [prob fr Prov *nous* knot, fr L *nodus* – more at [1]NET]

[2]noose *vt* **1** to secure by a noose **2** to make a noose in or of

Nootka /'nootkə, 'noohtkə/ *n, pl* **Nootkas**, *esp collectively* **Nootka** a member, or the language, of a people of Vancouver Island and NW Washington

nopal /'nohpl/ *n* (a plant related to) a cactus similar to the prickly pear, cultivated in Mexico as food for the cochineal insect [Sp, fr Nahuatl *nopalli*]

nope /nohp/ *adv, chiefly NAm* no – infml [by alter.]

nor /naw/ *conj* **1** – used to join 2 sentence elements of the same class or function ⟨*neither here ~ there*⟩ ⟨*not done by you ~ me ~ anyone*⟩ **2** also not; neither ⟨*it didn't seem hard, ~ was it*⟩ [ME, contr of *nother* neither, nor, fr *nother*, pron & adj, neither – more at NEITHER]

nor' /naw, nə-/ *n* north – often in combination ⟨*~-easter*⟩

noradrenalin, noradrenaline /,norə'drenəlin/ a compound from which adrenalin is formed in the body and which is the major neurotransmitter released from the nerve endings of the sympathetic nervous system [ISV *nor-* (a compound derived from another by replacing 1 or more methyl groups with hydrogen atoms; fr *normal*) + *adrenalin, adrenaline*]

[1]Nordic /'nawdik/ *adj* **1** of a tall, fair, longheaded, blue-eyed physical type characteristic of the Germanic peoples of N Europe, esp Scandinavia **2** of competitive ski events consisting of ski jumping and cross-country racing – compare ALPINE 3 [F *nordique*, fr *nord* north, fr OE *north*]

[2]Nordic *n* a person of Nordic physical type or of a supposed Nordic division of the Caucasian race; *esp* one from N Europe

norepinephrine /,norepi'nefrin, ,nori'pinəfrin/ *n, chiefly NAm* noradrenalin [*nor-* (as in *noradrenalin*) + *epinephrine*]

Norfolk jacket /'nawfək/ *n* a man's semifitted belted single-breasted jacket with box pleats ☞ GARMENT [*Norfolk*, county of England]

norm /nawm/ *n* **1** an authoritative standard; a model **2** a principle of correctness that is binding upon the members of a group, and serves to regulate action and judgment **3** the average: e g **a** a set standard of development or achievement, usu derived from the average achievement of a large group **b** a pattern typical of a social group [L *norma*, lit., carpenter's square]

¹normal /ˈnawml/ *adj* **1** PERPENDICULAR 1 **2** conforming to or constituting a norm, rule, or principle **3** occurring naturally ⟨~ *immunity*⟩ **4a** having average intelligence or development **b** free from mental disorder **5** *of a solution* having a concentration of 1 gram equivalent weight of a solute in 1l **6** of, involving, or being a normal curve or normal distribution [L *normalis*, fr *norma* carpenter's square] – **normally** /ˈnawml·i/ *adv*, **normalcy** /-si/, **normality** /-ˈmaləti/ *n*

²normal *n* **1** a line that is normal **2** sby or sthg that is normal

normal curve *n* the symmetrical bell-shaped curve of a normal distribution

normal distribution *n* a frequency distribution whose graph is a standard symmetrical bell-shaped curve ☞ STATISTICS

normal·ize, -ise /ˈnawml,iez/ *vt* to make normal – **normalizable** *adj*, **normalization** /-ˈzaysh(ə)n/ *n*

Norman /ˈnawmən/ *n* **1** a native or inhabitant of Normandy: e g **a** any of the Scandinavian conquerors of Normandy in the 10th c **b** any of the Norman-French conquerors of England in 1066 **2 Norman, Norman-French** the French language of the medieval Normans **3** a style of architecture characterized, esp in its English form, by semicircular arches and heavy pillars ☞ CHURCH [ME, fr OF *Normant*, fr ON *Northmann-, Northmathr* Norseman, fr *northr* north + *mann-, mathr* man] – **Norman** *adj*

normative /ˈnawmətiv/ *adj* serving as or prescribing a norm [F *normatif*, fr *norme* norm, fr L *norma*] – **normatively** *adv*, **normativeness** *n*

Norn /nawn/ *n* any of the 3 Norse goddesses of fate [ON]

¹Norse /naws/ *n* **1** *pl in constr* Scandinavians; *specif* Norwegians **2a** the (older forms of the) language of Norway **b** NORTH GERMANIC ☞ LANGUAGE [prob fr obs D *noorsch*, adj, Norwegian, Scandinavian, alter. of obs D *noordsch* northern, fr D *noord* north; akin to OE *north*]

²Norse *adj* Scandinavian; *esp* of ancient Scandinavia or Norway

ˈNorseman /-mən/ *n, pl* **Norsemen** /-mən/ a native or inhabitant of ancient Scandinavia

¹north /nawth/ *adj or adv* towards, at, belonging to, or coming from the north [ME, fr OE; akin to OHG *nord* north, Gk *nerteros* lower, infernal]

²north *n* **1** (the compass point corresponding to) the direction of the north terrestrial pole **2** *often cap* regions or countries lying to the north of a specified or implied point of orientation – **northward** /-,wood/ *adv, adj, or n*, **northwards** *adv*

¹,northˈeast /-ˈeest/ *adj or adv* towards, at, belonging to, or coming from the northeast

²,northˈeast *n* **1** (the general direction corresponding to) the compass point midway between north and east **2** *often cap* regions or countries lying to the northeast of a specified or implied point of orientation – **northeastward** /-wood/ *adv, adj, or n*, **northeastwards** *adv*

¹northeasterly /-ˈeestəli/ *adj or adv* northeast [²*northeast* + *-erly* (as in *easterly*)]

²northeasterly, ,northˈeaster /-ˈeestə/ *n* a wind from the northeast

,northˈeastern /-ˈeest(ə)n/ *adj* **1** *often cap* (characteristic) of a region conventionally designated Northeast **2** northeast [²*northeast* + *-ern* (as in *eastern*)] – **northeasternmost** /-,mohst/ *adj*

¹northerly /ˈnawdhəli/ *adj or adv* north [²*north* + *-erly* (as in *easterly*)]

²northerly *n* a wind from the north

northern /ˈnawdhən/ *adj* **1** *often cap* (characteristic) of a region conventionally designated North **2** north [ME *northerne*, fr OE; akin to OHG *nordrôni* northern, OE *north* north] – **northernmost** *adj*

Northerner /ˈnawdhənə/ *n* a native or inhabitant of the North

,northern ˈlights *n pl* AURORA BOREALIS **Northerner** /ˈnawdhənə/ *n* a native or inhabitant of the North

,North Gerˈmanic *n* a group of Germanic languages comprising the Scandinavian languages including Icelandic and Faroese

northing /ˈnawthing/ *n* **1** distance due north in latitude from the preceding point of measurement **2** northerly progress

ˈnorthland /-lənd, -,land/ *n, often cap* land in the north; the north of a country – poetic

ˈNorthman /-mən/ *n, pl* **Northmen** /-mən/ a Norseman

,north-,northˈeast *n* the compass point midway between north and northeast

,north-,northˈwest *n* the compass point midway between north and northwest

,north ˈpole *n* **1a** *often cap N&P* the northernmost point of the rotational axis of the earth or another celestial body **b** the northernmost point on the celestial sphere, about which the stars seem to revolve **2** the northward-pointing pole of a magnet

North Star *n* POLE STAR

¹Northumbrian /nawˈthumbri·ən/ *adj* (characteristic) of ancient or modern Northumbria or Northumberland [obs *Northumber* (inhabitant of England north of the river Humber), fr ME *Northhumbre*, fr OE *Northhymbre*, pl]

²Northumbrian *n* **1** a native or inhabitant of Northumbria or Northumberland **2** the English dialect of ancient or modern Northumbria

¹,northˈwest /-ˈwest/ *adj or adv* towards, at, belonging to, or coming from the northwest

²,northˈwest *n* **1** (the general direction corresponding to) the compass point midway between north and west **2** *often cap* regions or countries lying to the northwest of a specified or implied point of orientation – **northwestward** *adv, adj, or n*, **northwestwards** *adv*

¹,northˈwesterly /-ˈwestəli/ *adj or adv* northwest [²*northwest* + *-erly* (as in *westerly*)]

²,northˈwesterly, northwester /-ˈwestə/ *n* a wind from the northwest

,northˈwestern /-ˈwest(ə)n/ *adj* **1** *often cap* (characteristic) of a region conventionally designated Northwest **2** northwest [²*northwest* + *-ern* (as in *western*)]

Norwegian /nawˈweejən/ *n* a native or inhabitant or the language of Norway ☞ LANGUAGE [ML *Norvegia, Norwegia* Norway, country of N Europe] – **Norwegian** *adj*

nor ˈyet *conj* and also not

nos-, noso- *comb form* disease ⟨noso*logy*⟩ [Gk, fr *nosos*]

¹nose /nohz/ *n* **1a** the part of the face that bears the nostrils and covers the front part of the nasal cavity (together with the nasal cavity itself) ☞ NERVE **b**

the front part of the head above or projecting beyond the mouth; a snout, muzzle **2a** the sense or (vertebrate) organ of smell **b** aroma, bouquet **3** the projecting part or front end of sthg ☞ FLIGHT **4a** the nose as a symbol of undue curiosity or interference **b** a knack for detecting what is latent or concealed [ME, fr OE *nosu*; akin to OE *nasu* nose, OHG *nasa*, L *nasus*] – **through the nose** at an exorbitant rate ⟨*had to pay* through the nose⟩

²**nose** *vt* **1** to detect (as if) by smell; scent **2** to push (as if) with the nose **3** to touch or rub with the nose; nuzzle ~ *vi* **1** to use the nose in examining, smelling, etc; to sniff or nuzzle **2a** to pry – often + *into* **b** to search or look inquisitively – usu + *about* or *around* **3** to move ahead slowly or cautiously

ˈ**nose ˌbag** *n* a bag for feeding a horse or other animal, that covers the muzzle and is fastened on top of the head

ˈ**noseˌband** /-ˌband/ *n* the part of a bridle that passes over a horse's nose

ˈ**noseˌbleed** /-ˌbleed/ *n* an attack of bleeding from the nose

nosed /nohzd/ *adj* having a (specified kind of) nose – usu in combination ⟨*snub*-nosed⟩

ˈ**nose ˌdive** *n* **1** a downward nose-first plunge of an aircraft or other flying object **2** a sudden dramatic drop – **nose-dive** *vb*

ˈ**noseˌgay** /-ˌgay/ *n* a small bunch of flowers; a posy [¹*nose* + E dial. *gay* (ornament)]

ˈ**noseˌpiece** /-ˌpees/ *n* **1** a piece of armour for protecting the nose **2** the end piece of a microscope to which the lens nearest the specimen is attached

nosey /ˈnohzi/ *adj* nosy

¹**nosh** /nosh/ *vt* to chew, munch ~ *vi* to eat – infml [Yiddish *nashn*, fr MHG *naschen* to eat on the sly] – **nosher** *n*

²**nosh** *n* food (in sufficient quantities for a meal); a meal – infml

ˈ**nosh-ˌup** *n, Br* a large meal – infml

ˌ**no-ˈside** *n* full time in rugby

nosing /ˈnohzing/ *n* (any of various projections like) the usu rounded edge of a stair tread that projects over the riser [¹*nose* + ²*-ing*]

noso- – see NOS-

nosology /noˈsoləji/ *n* (a branch of medical science that deals with) the classification of diseases [prob fr NL *nosologia*, fr *nos-* + *-logia* -logy] – **nosological, nosologic** /ˌnosəˈlojik/ *adj*, **nosologically** *adv*

nostalgia /noˈstaljə/ *n* **1** homesickness **2** a wistful or excessively sentimental yearning for sthg past or irrecoverable [NL, fr Gk *nostos* return home + NL *-algia*; akin to OE *genesan* to survive, Skt *nasate* he approaches] – **nostalgic** *adj or n*, **nostalgically** *adv*

nostoc /ˈnostok/ *n* any of a genus of blue-green algae [NL, genus name]

nostril /ˈnostril, nostrəl/ *n* the opening of the nose to the outside (together with the adjoining nasal passage) [ME *nosethirl*, fr OE *nosthyrl*, fr *nosu* nose + *thyrel* hole; akin to OE *thurh* through]

nostrum /ˈnostrəm/ *n* **1** a medicine of secret composition recommended by its preparer usu without proof of its effectiveness **2** a facile or questionable remedy [L, neut of *noster* our, ours, fr *nos* we – more at US]

nosy, nosey /ˈnohzi/ *adj* inquisitive, prying – infml [¹*nose*] – **nosily** *adv*, **nosiness** *n*

ˌ**nosy ˈparker** /ˈpahkə/ *n, Br* a busybody – infml [prob fr the name *Parker*]

not /not/ *adv* **1** – used to negate a word or word group ⟨~ *thirsty*⟩ ⟨~ *to complain*⟩; often *n't* after auxiliary verbs ⟨*can't go*⟩ **2** – used to negate a preceding word or word group ⟨*will it rain? I hope* ~⟩ ⟨*are you ready? If* ~*, hurry up*⟩ **3** – used to give force to an opposite meaning ⟨~ *without reason*⟩ ⟨~ *a few of us*⟩ – compare ²NO 2b [ME, alter. of *nought*, fr *nought*, pron, var of *naught* – more at NAUGHT] – **not a** not even one – **not at all** – used in answer to thanks or to an apology ⟨*'Sorry to trouble you.'* 'Not at all!'⟩ – **not half 1** *chiefly Br* not nearly ⟨not half *long enough*⟩ **2** very much; totally ⟨*didn't* half *scold us*⟩ ⟨*'Are you busy?'* 'Not half!'⟩ – slang

not-, noto- *comb form* back (part) ⟨noto*chord*⟩ [NL, fr Gk *nōt-*, *nōto-*, fr *nōton*, *nōtos* back – more at NATES]

nota bene /ˌnohtə ˈbenay/ *interj* – used to call attention to sthg important [L, mark well]

notability /ˌnohtəˈbiləti/ *n* **1** a notable **2** being notable

¹**notable** /ˈnohtəbl/ *adj* **1** worthy of note; remarkable **2** distinguished, prominent – **notableness** *n*, **notably** *adv*

²**notable** *n* **1** a prominent person **2** *pl, often cap* a group of people summoned, esp in France when it was a monarchy, to act as a deliberative body

notarial /ˌnohˈteəri·əl/ *adj* of or executed by a notary – **notarially** *adv*

notar·ize, -ise /ˈnohtəˌriez/ *vt, chiefly NAm* to validate as a notary public

notary /ˈnohtəri/, **notary public** *n, pl* **notaries, notaries public, notary publics** a public officer appointed to administer oaths and draw up and authenticate documents [ME *notary* clerk, notary public, fr L *notarius* clerk, secretary, fr *notarius* of shorthand, fr *nota* note, shorthand character]

notate /nohˈtayt/ *vt* to put into notation [back-formation fr *notation*]

notation /nohˈtaysh(ə)n/ *n* **1** (a representation of sthg by) a system or set of marks, signs, symbols, figures, characters, or abbreviated expressions (e g to express technical facts or quantities) ☞ MUSIC, SYMBOL **2** *chiefly NAm* an annotation, note [L *notation-*, *notatio*, fr *notatus*, pp of *notare* to note] – **notational** *adj*

¹**notch** /noch/ *n* **1a** a V-shaped indentation **b** a slit or cut used as a record **2** a degree, step **3** *NAm* a deep narrow pass; a gap [perh alter. (by incorrect division of *an otch*) of (assumed) *otch*, fr MF *oche*] – **notched** *adj*

²**notch** *vt* **1** to make a notch in **2a** to mark or record (as if) by a notch – often + *up* **b** to score or achieve – usu + *up*

¹**note** /noht/ *vt* **1a** to take due or special notice of **b** to notice, observe **c** to record in writing **2** to make special mention of; remark [ME *noten*, fr OF *noter*, fr L *notare* to mark, note, fr *nota*] – **noter** *n*

²**note** *n* **1a(1)** a sound having a definite pitch **(2)** a call, esp of a bird **b** a written symbol used to indicate duration and pitch of a tone by its shape and position on the staff **2a** a characteristic feature of smell, flavour, etc **b** a mood or quality **3a** a memorandum **b(1)** a brief comment or explanation **(2)** a printed comment or reference set apart from the text **c** a piece of paper money **d(1)** a short informal letter **(2)** a formal diplomatic communication **e** a short essay

4a distinction, reputation **b** observation, notice [L *nota* mark, character, written note]

'note,book /-,book/ *n* a book for notes or memoranda

noted /'nohtid/ *adj* well-known, famous – **notedly** *adv*, **notedness** *n*

'note-,row /roh/ *n* a tone-row

'note,worthy /-,wuhdhi/ *adj* worthy of or attracting attention; notable – **noteworthily** *adv*, **noteworthiness** *n*

¹nothing /'nuthing/ *pron* **1** not any thing; no thing ⟨~ *greasy*⟩ ⟨~ *much to eat*⟩ ⟨*eats next to* ~⟩ **2** sthg of no consequence ⟨*it means* ~ *to me*⟩ ⟨*thinks* ~ *of walking 20 miles*⟩ ⟨*would be* ~ *without his title*⟩ **3** no truth or value ⟨*there's* ~ *in this rumour*⟩ – compare FOR NOTHING [ME, fr OE *nān thing, nāthing*, fr *nān* no + *thing* – more at NONE] – **like nothing on earth 1** severely indisposed or embarrassed **2** grotesque, outlandish

²nothing *adv* not at all; in no degree ⟨~ *like as cold*⟩

³nothing *n* **1a** sthg that does not exist **b** NOTHINGNESS 2b **2** sby or sthg of no or slight value or size ⟨*whisper sweet* ~s⟩

⁴nothing *adj* of no account; worthless

'nothingness /-nis/ *n* **1a** nonexistence **b** utter insignificance **2a** a void, emptiness **b** a metaphysical entity opposed to and devoid of being [³NOTHING + -NESS]

¹notice /'nohtis/ *n* **1a** warning of a future occurrence **b** notification of intention of terminating an agreement at a particular time **2** attention, heed **3** a written or printed announcement **4** a review (e g of a play) [ME, fr MF, acquaintance, fr L *notitia* knowledge, acquaintance, fr *notus* known, fr pp of *noscere* to come to know – more at KNOW]

²notice *vt* **1** to comment upon; refer to **2** to take notice of; mark **3** *chiefly NAm* to give a formal notice to

noticeable /'nohtisəbl/ *adj* **1** worthy of notice **2** capable of being noticed; perceptible – **noticeably** *adv*

'notice-,board *n, chiefly Br* a board on which notices may be (temporarily) displayed

notifiable /'nohti,fie·əbl/ *adj, of a disease* required by law to be reported to official health authorities [NOTIFY + -ABLE]

notification /,nohtifi'kaysh(ə)n/ *n* **1** (an instance of) notifying **2** sthg written that gives notice

notify /'nohti,fie/ *vt* **1** to give (official) notice to **2** to make known [ME *notifien*, fr MF *notifier* to make known, fr LL *notificare*, fr L *notus* known] – **notifier** *n*

notion /'nohsh(ə)n/ *n* **1a(1)** a broad general concept **(2)** a conception, impression ⟨*had no* ~ *of the poem's meaning*⟩ **b** a whim or fancy **2** *pl, chiefly NAm* small articles of merchandise (e g haberdashery) [L *notion-, notio*, fr *notus*, pp of *noscere*]

notional /'nohsh(ə)nl/ *adj* **1** theoretical, speculative **2** existing only in the mind; imaginary [NOTION + ¹-AL] – **notionally** *adv*, **notionality** /-'aləti/ *n*

noto- – see NOT-

notochord /'nohtə,kawd/ *n* a longitudinal rod that forms the supporting axis of the body in the lancelet, lamprey, etc and in the embryos of higher vertebrates [*not-* + L *chorda* cord – more at CORD] – **notochordal** /-'kawdl/ *adj*

notoriety /,nohtə'rie·əti/ *n* the quality or state of being notorious [MF or ML; MF *notorieté*, fr ML *notorietat-, notorietas*, fr *notorius*]

notorious /noh'tawri·əs/ *adj* well-known, esp for a specified (unfavourable) quality or trait [ML *notorius*, fr LL *notorium* information, indictment, fr neut of (assumed) LL *notorius* making known, fr L *notus*, pp of *noscere* to come to know – more at KNOW] – **notoriously** *adv*, **notoriousness** *n*

,no-'trump *adj* being a bid, contract, or hand in bridge suitable to play without any suit being trumps – **no-trump** *n*

¹notwithstanding /,notwidh'standing, -with-/ *prep* in spite of [ME *notwithstonding*, fr *not* + *withstonding*, prp of *withstonden* to withstand]

²notwithstanding *adv* nevertheless

³notwithstanding *conj* although

nougat /'nugət, 'nooh,gah/ *n* a sweetmeat of nuts or fruit pieces in a semisolid sugar paste [F, fr Prov, fr OProv *nogat*, fr *noga* nut, fr L *nuc-, nux* – more at NUT]

nought /nawt/ *n* **1** NAUGHT 1 **2** the arithmetical symbol 0; zero

,noughts and 'crosses *n pl but sing in constr* a game in which 2 players alternately put noughts and crosses in usu 9 square spaces arranged in a square in an attempt to get a row of 3 noughts or 3 crosses

noumenon /'noohmi,non, 'now-/ *n, pl* **noumena** /-nə/ the basis of all phenomena that according to Kant cannot be directly experienced but can be postulated by reason [G, fr Gk *nooumenon* that which is apprehended by thought, fr neut of prp passive of *noein* to think, conceive, fr *nous* mind] – **noumenal** *adj*

noun /nown/ *n* a word that is the name of a person, place, thing, substance, or state and that belongs to 1 of the major form classes in grammar [ME *nowne*, fr AF *noun* name, noun, fr OF *nom*, fr L *nomen* – more at NAME]

nourish /'nurish/ *vt* **1** to nurture, rear **2** to encourage the growth of; foster **3a** to provide or sustain with nutriment; feed **b** to cherish, entertain [ME *nurishen*, fr OF *norriss-*, stem of *norrir*, fr L *nutrire* to suckle, nourish; akin to Gk *nan* to flow, *noteros* damp, L *nare* to swim, Gk *nein*] – **nourisher** *n*, **nourishing** *adj*

'nourishment /-mənt/ *n* **1** food, nutriment **2** nourishing or being nourished

nous /nows/ *n* **1** mind, reason **2** *chiefly Br* gumption, common sense [Gk *noos, nous* mind]

nouveau riche /,noohvoh 'reesh (*Fr* nuvo riʃ)/ *n, pl* **nouveaux riches** /~/ sby who has recently become rich (and shows it) [F, lit., new rich]

nouvelle vague /,noohvel 'vahg (*Fr* nuvɛl vag)/ *n, often cap N&V* NEW WAVE 1 [F]

nova /'nohvə/ *n, pl* **novas, novae** /-vi, -vay/ a previously faint star that becomes suddenly very bright and then fades away to its former obscurity over months or years [NL, fem of L *novus* new] – **novalike** *adj*

¹novel /'novl/ *adj* **1** new and unlike anything previously known **2** original and striking, esp in conception or style [ME, fr MF, new, fr L *novellus*, fr dim. of *novus* new – more at NEW]

²novel *n* an invented prose narrative that is usu long and complex and deals esp with human experience and social behaviour [It *novella*] – **novelist** *n*, **novelistic** /-'istik/ *adj*

novelette /ˌnovl'et/ *n* a short novel or long short story, often of a sentimental nature – **novelettish** *adj*

novella /no'velə/ *n, pl* **novellas** *also* **novelle** /-li/ a short novel, usu more complex than a short story [It, fr fem of *novello* new, fr L *novellus*]

novelty /'nov(ə)lti/ *n* **1** sthg new and unusual **2** the quality or state of being novel **3** a small manufactured often cheap article for personal or household adornment [ME *novelte*, fr MF *noveleté*, fr *novel*]

November /noh'vembə/ *n* the 11th month of the Gregorian calendar [ME *Novembre*, fr OF, fr L *November* (ninth month), fr *novem* nine – more at NINE]

novena /noh'veenə/ *n* a Roman Catholic 9 days' devotion of prayers for the intercession of a particular saint for a special purpose [ML, fr L, fem of *novenus* nine each, fr *novem*]

novice /'novis/ *n* **1** a person admitted to probationary membership of a religious community **2** a beginner [ME, fr MF, fr ML *novicius*, fr L, new, inexperienced, fr *novus* – more at NEW]

novitiate /noh'vishi·ət, -ayt, nə-/ *n* **1** (the duration of) the state of being a novice **2** a house where novices are trained [F *noviciat*, fr ML *noviciatus*, fr *novicius*]

[1]**now** /now/ *adv* **1a** at the present time **b** in the immediate past **c** in the time immediately to follow; forthwith ⟨*come in* ~⟩ ⟨~ *for tea*⟩ **2** – used with the sense of present time weakened or lost **a** to introduce an important point or indicate a transition ⟨~ *if we turn to the next aspect of the problem*⟩ **b** to express command, request, or warning ⟨*oh, come* ~⟩ ⟨~, ~, *don't squabble*⟩ ⟨~ *then, what's the matter?*⟩ **3** sometimes – linking 2 or more coordinate words or phrases ⟨~ *one and* ~ *another*⟩ **4** under the changed or unchanged circumstances ⟨*he'll never believe me* ~, *after what happened*⟩ **5** at the time referred to ⟨~ *the trouble began*⟩ **6** up to the present or to the time referred to ⟨*haven't been for years* ~⟩ [ME, fr OE *nū*; akin to OHG *nū* now, L *nunc*, Gk *nyn*]

[2]**now** *conj* in view of the fact that; since ⟨~ *that we are here*⟩

[3]**now** *n* **1** the present time ⟨*been ill up to* ~⟩ ⟨*goodbye for* ~⟩ **2** the time referred to ⟨*by* ~ *the hints and rumours were fairly thick – The Economist*⟩

nowadays /'nowə,dayz/ *adv* in these modern times; today [ME *now a dayes*, fr [1]*now* + *a dayes* during the day]

ˌnow and a'gain *adv* at occasional intervals; from time to time

ˌnow and 'then *adv* NOW AND AGAIN

noway /'noh,way/, **noways** *adv* in no way whatever; not at all – fml

ˌno 'way *interj, chiefly NAm* – used to express forceful refusal; infml

[1]**nowhere** /'noh,weə/ *adv* **1** not anywhere **2** to no purpose or result ⟨*this will get us* ~⟩

[2]**nowhere** *n* a nonexistent place

ˌnowhere 'near *adv* not nearly

'no,wise /-,wiez/ *adv* noway

nowt /nowt/ *n, N Eng* nothing, naught [var of *naught*]

noxious /'nokshəs/ *adj* **1** harmful to living things ⟨~ *industrial wastes*⟩ **2** having a harmful moral influence; unwholesome [L *noxius*, fr *noxa* harm; akin to L *nocēre* to harm, *nec-*, *nex* violent death, Gk *nekros* dead body] – **noxiously** *adv*, **noxiousness** *n*

nozzle /'nozl/ *n* a projecting part with an opening that usu serves as an outlet; *esp* a short tube with a taper or constriction used on a hose, pipe, etc to speed up or direct a flow of fluid [dim. of *nose*]

-n't /-nt/ *comb form* not ⟨*isn*'t⟩

nth /enth/ *adj* **1** of or having an unspecified or indefinitely large number **2** extreme, utmost ⟨*to the* ~ *degree*⟩ [*n* + *-th*]

'n-,type *adj, of a semiconductor* having an excess of electrons – compare P-TYPE ☞ COMPUTER [*negative-type*]

nu /nyooh/ *n* the 13th letter of the Greek alphabet [Gk *ny*, of Sem origin; akin to Heb *nūn*, 14th letter of the Heb alphabet]

nuance /'nyooh,onhs (*Fr* n ɑ̃ːs)/ *n* a subtle distinction or gradation; a shade [F, fr MF, shade of colour, fr *nuer* to make shades of colour, fr *nue* cloud, fr L *nubes*; akin to Gk *nythos* dark] – **nuanced** *adj*

nub /nub/ *n* **1** a knob, lump ⟨*a* ~ *of coal*⟩ **2** *the* gist or crux [alter. of E dial. *knub*, prob fr LG *knubbe*]

nubble /'nubl/ *n* a small knob or lump [dim. of *nub*] – **nubbly** *adj*

nubile /'n(y)ooh,biel/ *adj, of a girl* of marriageable age; *esp* young and sexually attractive – often humor [F, fr L *nubilis*, fr *nubere* to marry – more at NUPTIAL] – **nubility** /-'biləti/ *n*

nuchal /'nyoohk(ə)l/ *adj* of or in (the region of) the nape of the neck [ML *nucha* nape, fr Ar *nukhā'* spinal marrow]

nucle-, nucleo- *comb form* **1** nucleus ⟨nucle*on*⟩ **2** related to nucleic acid ⟨nucleo*protein*⟩ [F *nuclé-*, *nucléo-*, fr NL *nucleus*]

nuclear /'nyoohkli·ə/ *adj* **1** of or constituting a nucleus **2** of, using, or being the atomic nucleus, atomic energy, the atom bomb, or atomic power ☞ ENERGY

ˌnuclear dis'armament *n* the reduction or giving up of a country's nuclear weapons

ˌnuclear 'family *n* a family unit that consists of husband, wife, and children – compare EXTENDED FAMILY

nuclear magnetic resonance *n* the magnetic resonance of an atomic nucleus

nuclease /'nyoohkliayz, -ays/ *n* any of various enzymes that promote the breakdown of nucleic acids

nucleate /'nyoohkli,ayt, -ət/ *vb* to form (into)a nucleus; to cluster [LL *nucleatus*, pp of *nucleare* to become stony, fr L *nucleus*] – **nucleator** *n*, **nucleation** /-'aysh(ə)n/ *n*

'nucle,ated, nucleate /-ət, -,ayt/ *adj* having a nucleus or nuclei ⟨~ *cells*⟩ [L *nucleatus*, fr *nucleus* kernel]

nu,cleic 'acid /nyooh'klayik, -'klee-/ *n* RNA, DNA, or another acid composed of a chain of nucleotide molecules linked to each other

nuclein /'nyoohkli-in/ *n* a nucleoprotein

nucleolus /nyooh'klee·ələs, ˌnyoohkli'ohləs/ *n, pl* **nucleoli** /-,lie, -li/ a spherical body in the nucleus of a cell that is prob the site of the synthesis of ribosomes [NL, fr L, dim. of *nucleus*] – **nucleolar** *adj*

nucleon /'nyoohkli,on/ *n* a proton or neutron, esp when in the atomic nucleus [ISV] – **nucleonic** /-'onik/ *adj*

nucleonics /ˌnyoohkli'oniks/ *n pl but sing or pl in*

constr the physics and technical applications of nucleons, the atomic nucleus, or nuclear energy

nucleophile /'nyoohkli·ə,fiel/ *n* a substance (e g a negative ion) with an affinity for atomic nuclei – **nucleophilic** /-'filik/ *adj*, **nucleophilicity** /-fi'lisəti/ *n*

nucleoprotein /,nyoohklioh'prohteen/ *n* a compound of a protein (e g a histone) with a nucleic acid (e g DNA), forming the major constituent of chromosomes [ISV]

nucleoside /'nyoohkli·ə,sied/ *n* any of several compounds (e g adenosine) consisting of a purine or pyrimidine base combined with deoxyribose or ribose and occurring esp as a constituent of nucleotides [ISV *nucle-* + *-ose* + *-ide*]

nucleotide /'nyoohkli·ə,tied/ *n* any of several compounds that form the structural units of RNA and DNA and consist of a nucleoside combined with a phosphate group [ISV, irreg fr *nucle-* + *-ide*]

nucleus /'nyoohkli·əs/ *n, pl* **nuclei** /-kli,ie, -kli·i/ *also* **nucleuses** **1** a small bright and dense part of a galaxy or head of a comet **2** a central point, mass, etc about which gathering, concentration, etc takes place: e g **a** a usu round membrane-surrounded cellular organelle containing the chromosomes **b** a (discrete) mass of nerve cells in the brain or spinal cord **c** the positively charged central part of an atom that accounts for nearly all of the atomic mass and consists of protons and usu neutrons [NL, fr L, kernel, dim. of *nuc-*, *nux* nut – more at NUT]

nuclide /'nyoohklied/ *n* an atom with a particular number of protons and neutrons in its nucleus [*nucl*eus + Gk *eidos* form, species – more at IDOL] – **nuclidic** /-'klidik/ *adj*

[1]nude /n(y)oohd/ *adj* **1** lacking sthg essential to legal validity ⟨*a ~ contract*⟩ **2a** without clothing; naked **b** without natural covering or adornment; bare [L *nudus* naked – more at NAKED] – **nudely** *adv*, **nudeness, nudity** *n*

[2]nude *n* **1a** a representation of a nude human figure **b** a nude person **2** the state of being nude ⟨*in the ~*⟩

nudge /nuj/ *vt* **1** to touch or push gently; *esp* to catch the attention of by a push of the elbow **2** to move (as if) by pushing gently or slowly [perh of Scand origin; akin to ON *gnaga* to gnaw; akin to OE *gnagan* to gnaw] – **nudge** *n*

nudibranch /'n(y)oohdi,brangk/ *n* any of various related shell-less marine gastropod molluscs [deriv of L *nudus* + *branchia* gill – more at BRANCHIA] – **nudibranch** *adj*, **nudibranchiate** /-'brangi·ət, -ayt/ *adj or n*

nudism /'nooh,diz(ə)m, 'nyooh-/ *n* the cult or practice of going nude as much as possible – **nudist** *adj or n*

nugatory /'nyoohgət(ə)ri/ *adj* **1** trifling, inconsequential **2** inoperative *USE* fml [L *nugatorius*, fr *nugatus*, pp of *nugari* to trifle, fr *nugae* trifles]

nugget /'nugət/ *n* a solid lump, esp of a precious metal in its natural state [perh dim. of E dial. *nug* (lump, block)]

nuisance /'nyoohs(ə)ns/ *n* **1** (legally actionable) harm or injury **2** an annoying or troublesome person or thing [ME *nusaunce*, fr AF, fr OF *nuisir* to harm, fr L *nocēre* – more at NOXIOUS]

nuke /nyoohk/ *vt or n* (to destroy with) a nuclear weapon – slang [by shortening & alter.]

[1]null /nul/ *adj* **1** having no force in law – esp in *null and void* **2** amounting to nothing; nil **3** without character or distinction **4** *of an instrument* indicating (e g by a zero reading on a scale) when current or voltage is zero **5** of or being a method of measurement that uses a null instrument [MF *nul*, lit., not any, fr L *nullus*, fr *ne-* not + *ullus* any; akin to L *unus* one – more at NO, ONE]

[2]null *n* **1** ZERO 3 **2** a minimum or zero value of an electric current or of a radio signal

nulla /'nulə/ *n* a zero, nought – used in printing [alter. of [2]*null*]

nullah /'nulə/ *n, Ind* a gully, ravine [Hindi *nālā*]

,null and 'void *adj* completely invalid

nulla-nulla /,nulə 'nulə/, **nulla** *n* a hardwood club used by Australian aborigines [native name in Australia]

null hypothesis *n* a statistical hypothesis to be tested and accepted or rejected in favour of an alternative

nullification /,nulifi'kaysh(ə)n/ *n* nullifying or being nullified

nullify /'nulifie/ *vt* **1** to make (legally) null **2** to make worthless, unimportant, or ineffective [LL *nullificare*, fr L *nullus*]

nullipara /nu'lipərə/ *n* a female that has not borne offspring [NL, fr L *nullus* none + *-para*] – **nulliparous** *adj*

nullity /'nuləti/ *n* **1** (an act or document characterized by) legal invalidity **2** sthg null [[1]NULL + -ITY]

numb /num/ *adj* **1** devoid of sensation, esp as a result of cold or anaesthesia **2** devoid of emotion [ME *nomen*, fr pp of *nimen* to take, fr OE *niman* – more at NIMBLE] – **numb** *vt*, **numbingly** /'numingli/ *adv*, **numbly** /'numli/ *adv*, **numbness** /'numnis/ *n*

[1]number /'numbə/ *n* **1a(1)** a total **(2)** *sing or pl in constr* an indefinite, usu large, total ⟨*a ~ of members were absent*⟩ **(3)** *pl* a numerous group; many; *also* an instance of numerical superiority ⟨*there is safety in ~s*⟩ **b(1)** any of an ordered set of standard names or symbols (e g 2, 5, 27th) used in counting or in assigning a position in an order; *esp* NATURAL NUMBER **(2)** an element (e g 6, -3, ⅝, √7) belonging to an arithmetical system based on or analogous to the numbers used in counting and subject to specific rules of addition, subtraction, and multiplication – compare INTEGER, RATIONAL NUMBER, COMPLEX NUMBER **c** *pl* arithmetic ⟨*teach children their ~s*⟩ **2** a distinction of word form denoting reference to singular or plural *also* a set of forms so distinguished **3a** a word, symbol, letter, or combination of symbols representing a number **b** one or more numerals or digits used to identify or designate ⟨*a car ~*⟩ ⟨*a telephone ~*⟩ **4a** a member of a sequence or collection designated by esp consecutive numbers; *also* an individual or item (e g a single act in a variety show or an issue of a periodical) singled out from a group **b** a position in a numbered sequence **5** a group of individuals ⟨*he is not of our ~*⟩ **6** *pl but sing or pl in constr* a form of US lottery in which bets are made on the appearance of a certain combination of 3 digits in sets of numbers regularly published in newspapers (e g the stock-market receipts) **7a** sthg viewed in terms of the advantage or enjoyment obtained from it ⟨*her job is a really cushy ~*⟩ ⟨*drives round in a fast little ~*⟩ **b** an article of esp women's clothing ⟨*wearing a chic little black ~*⟩ **c** a person or individual, esp an attractive girl ⟨*who's*

Cardinal numbers

NAME[1]	SYMBOL Arabic	Roman[2]
zero or nought	0	
one	1	I
two	2	II
three	3	III
four	4	IV
five	5	V
six	6	VI
seven	7	VII
eight	8	VIII
nine	9	IX
ten	10	X
eleven	11	XI
twelve	12	XII
thirteen	13	XIII
fourteen	14	XIV
fifteen	15	XV
sixteen	16	XVI
seventeen	17	XVII
eighteen	18	XVIII
nineteen	19	XIX
twenty	20	XX
twenty-one	21	XXI
twenty-two	22	XXII
twenty-three	23	XXIII
twenty-four	24	XXIV
twenty-five	25	XXV
twenty-six	26	XXVI
twenty-seven	27	XXVII
twenty-eight	28	XXVIII
twenty-nine	29	XXIX
thirty	30	XXX
thirty-one	31	XXXI
thirty-two etc	32	XXXII
forty	40	XL
forty-one etc	41	XLI
fifty	50	L
sixty	60	LX
seventy	70	LXX
eighty	80	LXXX
ninety	90	XC
one hundred	100	C
one hundred and one or one hundred one	101	CI
one hundred and two etc	102	CII
two hundred	200	CC
three hundred	300	CCC
four hundred	400	CD
five hundred	500	D
six hundred	600	DC
seven hundred	700	DCC
eight hundred	800	DCCC
nine hundred	900	CM
one thousand *or* ten hundred etc	1,000 *or* 1 000	M
two thousand etc	2,000 *or* 2 000	MM
five thousand	5,000 *or* 5 000	$\overline{V}$
ten thousand	10,000 *or* 10 000	$\overline{X}$
one hundred thousand	1000,000 *or* 100 000	$\overline{C}$
one million	1,000,000 *or* 1 000 000	$\overline{M}$

one gillion
British system 10^9 *or* one thousand million

one billion
Old British system 10^{12} *or* one million million
American system† 10^9 *or* one thousand million

one trillion
British system 10^{18} *or* one million million million
American system 10^{12} *or* one million million

one quadrillion
British system 10^{24} *or* one million million million million
American system 10^{15} *or* one thousand million million

† The American system is now replacing the British in this case.

1 Arabic numerals from 1,000 to 9,999 are often written without commas or spaces (1000, 9999). Year numbers are always written without commas (1783).

2 The Roman numerals are written either in capitals or in lower-case letters (VIII or viii).

3 The Arabic symbols for the cardinal numbers may be read as ordinals in certain contexts (January 1 = January first; 2 Samuel = Second Samuel). The Roman numerals are sometimes read as ordinals (Henry IV = Henry the Fourth); sometimes they are written with the ordinal suffixes (XIXth dynasty).

Ordinal numbers

NAME	SYMBOL[3]
first	1st
second	2d or 2nd
third	3d or 3rd
fourth	4th
fifth	5th
sixth	6th
seventh	7th
eighth	8th
ninth	9th
tenth	10th
eleventh	11th
twelfth	12th
thirteenth	13th
fourteenth	14th
fifteenth	15th
sixteenth	16th
seventeenth	17th
eighteenth	18th
nineteenth	19th
twentieth	20th
twenty-first	21st
twenty-second	22d or 22nd
twenty-third	23d or 23rd
twenty-fourth	24th
twenty-fifth	25th
twenty-six	26th
twenty-seventh	27th
twenty-eighth	28th
twenty-ninth	29th
thirtieth	30th
thirty-first	31st
thirty-second etc	32d or 32nd
fortieth	40th
forty-first	41st
forty-second etc	42d or 42nd
fiftieth	50th
sixtieth	60th
seventieth	70th
eightieth	80th
ninetieth	90th
hundredth or one hundredth	100th
hundred and first or one hundred and first	101st
hundred and second etc	102d or 102nd
two hundredth	200th
three hundredth	300th
four hundredth	400th
five hundredth	500th
six hundredth	600th
seven hundredth	700th
eight hundredth	800th
nine hundredth	900th
thousandth *or* one thousandth	1,000th *or* 1 000th
two thousandth etc	2,000th *or* 2 000th
ten thousandth	10,000th *or* 10 000th
hundred thousandth *or* one hundred thousandth	100,000th *or* 100 000th
millionth *or* one millionth	1,000,000th *or* 1 000 000th

Prime numbers (2, 3, 5, 7, 11, 13, 17, 19 . . .)
A prime number is one that only gives a whole number when divided by 1 or itself but leaves a remainder when divided by any other number.

Rational numbers (all the whole numbers and fractions such as $\frac{3}{4}$, $11\frac{27}{32}$, $\frac{1}{7}$)
A rational number is any number produced by dividing any whole number by any other whole number.

Irrational numbers ($\sqrt{2}$, $\sqrt{3}$, pi . . .)
An irrational number is a number that is not a rational number; it cannot be produced by dividing one whole number by another.

Transcendental numbers (eg pi)
A transcendental number is an irrational number that is not the answer to any equation.

Complex numbers
A complex number is a number that contains the square root of -1 (i) and has the general form $x + i \times y$ where x and y can be any sort of number except for a complex number.

Fibonacci sequence (0, 1, 1, 2, 3, 5, 8, 13, 21, 34, 55 . . .)
Each number in the sequence is produced by adding together the two previous numbers. All the numbers in the sequence are called Fibonacci numbers. There are many examples of these numbers in nature; for example the arrangement of leaves in a spiral up a stem is usually such that the number of leaves between two positions where a leaf lies exactly above another on the stem is a Fibonacci number.

the blonde ~ over there?〉 **8** insight into a person's motives or character 〈*soon had his ~*〉 *USE* (*7&8*) infml [ME *nombre*, fr OF, fr L *numerus* – more at NIMBLE] – **without number** innumerable

[2]**number** *vt* **1** to count **2** to include as part of a whole or total 〈*proud to ~ her among my friends*〉 **3** to restrict to a definite number; limit – usu pass 〈*knew his days were ~ed*〉 **4** to assign a number to 〈*~ed the team members 1 to 10*〉 〈*a ~ed road*〉 **5** to comprise in number; total 〈*the inhabitants ~ed 150,000*〉 ~ *vi* **1** to be part of a total number 〈*~s among my closest friends*〉 **2** to call *off* numbers in sequence – **numberable** *adj*

,Number '10 *n* the British government – infml [*Number 10*, Downing Street, official residence in London of the British Prime Minister]

,number '8 *n* the player positioned in the back row of scrum in rugby union ☞ SPORT

'numberless /-lis/ *adj* innumerable, countless

,number 'one *n* **1** sthg that is first in rank, order, or importance 〈*~ in her list of priorities*〉 **2** one's own interests or welfare – infml 〈*always thinking of ~*〉 **3** an act of urinating – euph; used by or to children

'number,plate /-,playt/ *n, chiefly Br* a rectangular identifying plate fastened to a vehicle and bearing the vehicle's registration number

'Numbers *n pl but sing in constr* the mainly narrative 4th book of the Old Testament

'number ,theory *n* a branch of mathematics dealing with integers and their properties

,number 'two *n* **1** a second-in-command **2** an act of defecating – euph; used by or to children

numbles /'numblz/ *n, archaic* the umbles [ME *noumbles, nombles* – more at UMBLES]

numbskull /'num,skul/ *n* a numskull

numen /'nyoohmen/ *n, pl* **numina** /-minə/ a divine force associated with a place or natural object [L, nod, divine will, numen; akin to L *nuere* to nod, Gk *neuein*]

numerable /'nyoohm(ə)rəbl/ *adj* capable of being counted – not used technically

numeracy /'nyoohm(ə)rəsi/ *n, Br* the quality or state of being numerate

[1]**numeral** /'nyoohm(ə)rəl/ *adj* of or expressing numbers [MF, fr LL *numeralis*, fr L *numerus*] – **numerally** *adv*

[2]**numeral** *n* a conventional symbol that represents a natural number or zero

numerate /'nyoohm(ə)rət/ *adj* understanding basic mathematics; able to use numbers in calculation [L *numerus* number + E *-ate* (as in *literate*)]

numeration /,nyoohmə'raysh(ə)n/ *n* **1a** counting **b** designating by a number **2** expressing in words numbers written as numerals **3** a system of numbering or counting [ME *numeracion*, fr L *numeration-, numeratio*, fr *numeratus*, pp of *numerare* to count] – **numerate** /-,rayt/ *vt*

numerator /'nyoohmə,raytə/ *n* the part of a fraction that is above the line and signifies the number of parts of the denominator that is shown by the fraction

numerical /nyooh'merikl/, **numeric** *adj* of, expressed in, or involving numbers or a number system 〈*the ~ superiority of the enemy*〉 〈*~ standing in a class*〉 〈*a ~ code*〉 [L *numerus*] – **numerically** *adv*

numerology /,nyoohmə'roləji/ *n* the study of the occult significance of numbers [L *numerus* + E *-o-* + *-logy*] – **numerologist** *n*, **numerological** /-rə'lojikl/ *adj*

numerous /'nyoohm(ə)rəs/ *adj* consisting of many units or individuals [MF *numereux*, fr L *numerosus*, fr *numerus*] – **numerously** *adv*, **numerousness** *n*

numinous /'nyoohminəs/ *adj* **1** awe-inspiring, mysterious **2** filled with a sense of the presence of divinity [L *numin-, numen* numen]

numismatics /,nyoohmiz'matiks/ *n pl but sing in constr* the study or collection of coinage, coins, paper money, medals, tokens, etc [F *numismatique*, fr *numismatique*, adj, fr L *nomismat-, nomisma* coin, fr Gk, custom, coin; akin to Gk *nomos* custom, law] – **numismatic** *adj*, **numismatically** *adv*, **numismatist** /nyooh'mizmətist/ *n*

numnah /'numnə/ *n* a piece of leather, sheepskin, etc placed under a horse's saddle to prevent chafing [Hindi *namdā*, fr Per *namad* carpet, rug]

numskull, numbskull /'num,skul/ *n* a dull or stupid person [*numb* + *skull*]

nun /nun/ *n* a female member of a religious order living in a convent under vows of chastity, poverty, etc and often engaged in educational or nursing work [ME, fr OE *nunne*, fr LL *nonna*]

Nunc Dimittis /,noongk di'mitis, nungk/ *n* a canticle based on the prayer of Simeon in Luke 2:29-32 [L, now lettest thou depart; fr the first words of the canticle]

nunciature /'nuns(h)i·əchə/ *n* the (term of) office of a papal nuncio [It *nunciatura*, fr *nuncio*]

nuncio /'nuns(h)ioh/ *n, pl* **nuncios** a papal ambassador to a civil government [It, fr L *nuntius* messenger, message]

nunnery /'nunəri/ *n* a convent of nuns

Nupe /'noohpay/ *n, pl* **Nupes**, *esp collectively* **Nupe** a member, or the Kwa language, of a Negro people of W central Nigeria

[1]**nuptial** /'nupsh(ə)l/ *adj* **1** of marriage **2** characteristic of or occurring in the breeding season 〈*a ~ flight*〉 [L *nuptialis*, fr *nuptiae*, pl, wedding, fr *nuptus*, pp of *nubere* to marry; akin to Gk *nymphē* bride, nymph]

[2]**nuptial** *n* a wedding – usu pl

nuptial plumage *n* the brilliantly coloured plumage developed in the males of many birds prior to the start of the breeding season – compare ECLIPSE PLUMAGE

[1]**nurse** /nuhs/ *n* **1a** WET NURSE **b** a woman employed to take care of a young child **2** sby skilled or trained in caring for the sick or infirm, esp under the supervision of a physician 〈*she and her brother are both ~s*〉 **3** a member of the worker caste in an ant, bee, etc society, that cares for the young [ME, fr OF *nurice*, fr LL *nutricia*, fr L, fem of *nutricius* nourishing – more at NUTRITIOUS]

[2]**nurse** *vt* **1** to suckle **2a** to rear, nurture **b** to encourage the development of; foster 〈*carefully ~d his tomatoes*〉 **3a** to attempt to cure (e g an illness or injury) by appropriate treatment **b** to care for and wait on (e g a sick person) **4** to hold in one's mind; harbour 〈*~ a grievance*〉 **5** to handle carefully in order to conserve or prolong **6** to hold (e g a baby) lovingly or caressingly ~ *vi* **1a** to suckle an offspring **b** to suck at the breast **2** to act or serve as a nurse [ME *nurshen* to nourish, contr of *nurishen*]

'nurse,maid /-,mayd/ *n* a girl or woman employed to look after children

nursery /'nuhs(ə)ri/ *n* **1** a child's bedroom or playroom **2a** a place where small children are looked after in their parents' absence **b** NURSERY SCHOOL **3** a place where young animals (e g fish) grow or are cared for **4** an area where plants, trees, etc are grown for propagation, sale, or transplanting

'nurseryman /-mən, -ˌman/ *n* one whose occupation is the cultivation of plants, usu for sale

'nursery ˌrhyme *n* a short traditional story in rhyme for children

'nursery ˌschool *n* a school for children aged usu from 2 to 5

'nursery ˌslope *n* a usu gentle ski slope for beginners

'nursing ˌhome /'nuhsing/ *n* a usu private hospital or home (where care is provided for the aged, chronically ill, etc)

'nursing ˌofficer *n* a nurse of the next rank below a senior nursing officer

nursling /'nuhsling/ *n* a child under the care of a nurse, esp in former times ['*nurse* + *-ling*]

¹nurture /'nuhchə/ *n* **1** training, upbringing **2** food, nourishment **3** all the environmental influences that affect the innate genetic potentialities of an organism [ME, fr MF *norriture*, fr LL *nutritura* act of nursing, fr L *nutritus*, pp of *nutrire* to suckle, nourish – more at NOURISH]

²nurture *vt* **1** to give care and nourishment to **2** to educate or develop

¹nut /nut/ *n* **1** (the often edible kernel of) a dry fruit or seed with a hard separable rind or shell **2** a difficult person, problem, or undertaking ⟨*a tough* ~⟩ **3** a typically hexagonal usu metal block that has a central hole with an internal screw thread cut on it, and can be screwed onto a piece, esp a bolt, with an external thread to tighten or secure sthg **4** the ridge in a stringed instrument (e g a violin) over which the strings pass on the upper end of the fingerboard **5** a small piece or lump ⟨*a* ~ *of butter*⟩ **6** *pl* nonsense – often used interjectionally **7** a person's head **8a** an insane or wildly eccentric person **b** an ardent enthusiast ***USE*** (*6, 7, & 8*) infml [ME *nute, note*, fr OE *hnutu*; akin to OHG *nuz* nut, L *nux*] – **nutlike** *adj*

²nut *vi* **-tt-** to gather or seek nuts – chiefly in *go nutting*

nutation /nyooh'taysh(ə)n/ *n* **1** (a small oscillation of the earth's axis like) the nodding oscillatory movement of the axis of a rotating body (e g a top) **2** a spontaneous (spiral) movement of a growing plant part **3** nodding the head – fml [L *nutation-, nutatio*, fr *nutatus*, pp of *nutare* to nod, rock, freq of *nuere* to nod – more at NUMEN] – **nutational** *adj*, **nutate** /ˌnyooh'tayt, '-,-/ *vi*

ˌnut-'brown *adj or n* (of) the colour of a ripe hazelnut

'nutˌcase /-ˌkays/ *n* a nut, lunatic – infml

'nutˌcracker /-ˌkrakə/ *n* an implement for cracking nuts, usu consisting of 2 hinged metal arms between which the nut is held and compressed – often pl with sing. meaning

'nutˌhatch /-ˌhach/ *n* a Eurasian tree-climbing bird with bluish grey upper parts and a black stripe through the eye region [ME *notehache*, fr *note* nut + *hache* axe, fr OF, battle-axe – more at HASH]

'nutˌhouse /-ˌhows/ *n* a madhouse – slang; humor

nutmeg /'nutmeg/ *n* (an Indonesian tree that produces) an aromatic seed used as a spice [ME *notemuge*, deriv of OProv *noz muscada*, fr *noz* nut (fr L *nuc-, nux*) + *muscada*, fem of *muscat* musky – more at MUSCAT]

nutria /'nyoohtri·ə/ *n* **1** a coypu **2** the fur of the coypu [Sp, modif of L *lutra* otter; akin to OE *oter* otter]

nutrient /'nyoohtri·ənt/ *n or adj* (sthg) that provides nourishment [L *nutrient-, nutriens*, prp of *nutrire* to nourish – more at NOURISH]

nutriment /'nyoohtrimənt/ *n* sthg that nourishes or promotes growth [L *nutrimentum*, fr *nutrire*]

nutrition /nyooh'trish(ə)n/ *n* nourishing or being nourished; *specif* all the processes by which an organism takes in and uses food [MF, fr LL *nutrition-, nutritio*, fr L *nutritus*, pp of *nutrire*] – **nutritional** *adj*, **nutritionally** *adv*, **nutritionist** *n*

nutritious /nyooh'trishəs/ *adj* nourishing [L *nutricius*, fr *nutric-, nutrix* nurse; akin to L *nutrire* to nourish] – **nutritiously** *adv*, **nutritiousness** *n*

nutritive /'nyoohtritiv/ *adj* **1** of nutrition **2** nourishing – **nutritively** *adv*

nuts /nuts/ *adj* **1** passionately keen or enthusiastic ⟨*he's* ~ *on ice-hockey*⟩ **2** crazy, mad ***USE*** infml [fr pl of ¹*nut*]

ˌnuts and 'bolts *n* **1** the working parts or elements **2** the practical workings (e g of a business or enterprise) ***USE*** infml

'nutˌshell /-ˌshel/ *n* the hard outside covering enclosing the kernel of a nut – **in a nutshell** in a brief accurate account

nutter /'nutə/ *n, chiefly Br* a nut, maniac – infml [¹*nut* + ²*-er*]

nutty /'nuti/ *adj* **1** having or producing nuts **2** having a flavour like that of nuts **3** eccentric, silly; *also* NUTS 2 – infml – **nuttiness** *n*

nux vomica /ˌnuks 'vomikə/ *n, pl* **nux vomica** (an Asian tree that bears) a poisonous seed containing strychnine and other alkaloids [NL, lit., emetic nut]

nuzzle /'nuzl/ *vb* **nuzzling** /'nuzling/ *vi* **1** to push or rub sthg with the nose **2** to lie close or snug; nestle ~ *vt* to root or rub (as if) with the nose [ME *noselen* to bring the nose towards the ground, fr *nose*]

nyala /en'yahlə/ *n, pl* **nyalas**, *esp collectively* **nyala** a S African antelope with vertical white stripes on its sides [of Bantu origin; akin to Venda *nyala* nyala, Zulu *inxala*]

nyctalopia /ˌniktə'lohpi·ə/ *n* NIGHT BLINDNESS [LL, deriv of Gk *nykt-, nyx* night + *alaos* blind + *ōps* eye]

nyctitropic /ˌnikti'tropik, -'trohpik/ *n* of or being a movement of a plant part at nightfall (e g the closing of a flower) [ISV *nyct-* (fr L, fr Gk *nykt-, nyx* night) + *-i-* + *-tropic*] – **nyctitropism** /nik'titrəˌpiz(ə)m, ˌnikti'trohpiz(ə)m/ *n*

nylon /'nielon/ *n* **1** any of numerous strong tough elastic synthetic polyamide materials fashioned into fibres, sheets, etc and used esp in textiles and plastics **2** *pl* stockings made of nylon [coined word]

nymph /nimf/ *n* **1** any of the minor female divinities of nature in classical mythology **2** any of various immature insects; *esp* a larva of a dragonfly or other insect with incomplete metamorphosis ☞ LIFE CYCLE **3** a girl – poetic [ME *nimphe*, fr MF, fr L *nympha* bride, nymph, fr Gk *nymphē* – more at NUPTIAL] – **nymphal** /'nimf(ə)l/ *adj*

nymphet /'nimfit/ *n* a sexually desirable girl in early adolescence [obs *nymphet* (young nymph), fr MF *nymphette*, dim. of *nymphe* nymph]

nympho /'nimfoh/ *n* a nymphomaniac – infml

nympholepsy /'nimfə,lepsi/ *n* a frenzy of emotion, usu inspired by sthg unattainable [*nympholept* fr Gk *nympholēptos* frenzied, lit., caught by nymphs, fr *nymphē* + *lambanein* to seize] – **nympholept** /-,lept/ *n*, **nympholeptic** /-'leptik/ *adj*

nymphomania /,nimfə'maynyə/ *n* excessive sexual desire in a female – compare SATYRIASIS [NL, fr *nymphae* inner lips of the vulva (fr L, pl of *nympha*) + LL *mania*] – **nymphomaniac** /-ni,ak/ *n or adj*, **nymphomaniacal** /,nimfohmə'nie·əkl/ *adj*

Nynorsk /n(y)ooh'nawsk/ *n* a literary form of Norwegian based on the spoken dialects of Norway – compare BOKMÅL [Norw, lit., new Norwegian]

nystagmus /ni'stagməs/ *n* a rapid involuntary oscillation of the eyeballs (e g from dizziness) [NL, fr Gk *nystagmos* drowsiness, fr *nystazein* to doze; akin to Lith *snusti* to doze] – **nystagmic** /-mik/ *adj*

O

o /oh/ *n, pl* **o's, os** *often cap* **1** (a graphic representation of or device for reproducing) the 15th letter of the English alphabet **2** sthg shaped like the letter O; *esp* zero

O /oh/ *interj or n* oh

o-, oo- *comb form* egg ⟨*oology*⟩; *specif* ovum ⟨*oogonium*⟩ [Gk *ōi-, ōio-*, fr *ōion* – more at ²EGG]

-o- – used as a connective vowel to join word elements of Greek and other origin ⟨*milometer*⟩ ⟨*elastomer*⟩ [ME, fr OF, fr L, fr Gk, thematic vowel of many nouns & adjectives in combination]

¹**-o** /-oh/ *suffix* (→ *n or adj*) (sby or sthg) that is, has the qualities of, or is associated with ⟨*cheapo*⟩ ⟨*wino*⟩ ⟨*beano*⟩ – infml [perh fr ¹*oh*]

²**-o** /-oh/ *suffix* (→ *interj*) – in interjections formed from other parts of speech ⟨*cheerio*⟩ ⟨*righto*⟩; infml [prob fr ¹*oh*]

o' *also* **o** /ə/ *prep* **1** of ⟨*one* o'*clock*⟩ **2** *chiefly dial* on [ME *o, o-*, contr of *on* & *of*]

oaf /ohf/ *n* a clumsy slow-witted person [of Scand origin; akin to ON *alfr* elf – more at ELF] – **oafish** *adj*, **oafishly** *adv*, **oafishness** *n*

oak /ohk/ *n, pl* **oaks, oak** (the tough hard durable wood of) any of various trees or shrubs of the beech family, usu having lobed leaves and producing acorns as fruits [ME *ook*, fr OE *āc*; akin to OHG *eih* oak, Gk *aigilōps*, a kind of oak] – **oaken** /'ohk(ə)n/ *adj*

'oak ,apple *n* a large round gall produced on oak stems or leaves by a gall wasp

oakum /'ohkəm/ *n* hemp or jute fibre impregnated with tar or a tar derivative and used in packing joints and stopping up gaps between the planks of a ship [ME *okum*, fr OE *ācumba* tow, fr *ā-* (separative & perfective prefix) + *-cumba* (akin to OE *camb* comb)]

¹**oar** /aw/ *n* **1** a long usu wooden shaft with a broad blade at one end used for propelling or steering a boat **2** an oarsman [ME *oor*, fr OE *ār*; akin to ON *ār* oar] – **oared** *adj*

²**oar** *vb* ¹ROW – poetic

'oar,fish /-,fish/ *n* any of several very long and thin soft-bodied sea fishes

'oar,lock /-,lok/ *n, chiefly NAm* a rowlock

oarsman /'awzmən/ *n* one who rows a boat, esp in a racing crew – **oarsmanship** *n*

oasis /oh'aysis/ *n, pl* **oases** /-seez/ **1** a fertile or green area in a dry region **2** sthg providing relaxation or relief [LL, fr Gk]

Oasis *trademark* – used for a highly water-absorbent material into which cut flowers and other plants may be stuck for display

'oast ,house /ohst/ *n* a usu circular building housing a kiln for drying hops or malting barley [*oast* fr ME *ost*, fr OE *āst*; akin to MD *eest* kiln, L *aestus* heat, *aestas* summer – more at EDIFY]

oat /oht/ *n* **1a** (any of various wild grasses related to) a widely cultivated cereal grass – usu pl **b** *pl* a crop or plot of oats **2** an oat seed [ME *ote*, fr OE *āte*] – **oaten** /-tn/ *adj*

'oat ,cake *n* a usu crisp unleavened biscuit or bread made of oatmeal

'oat ,grass *n* WILD OAT 1

oath /ohth/ *n, pl* **oaths** /ohdhz/ **1a** a solemn calling upon God or a revered person or thing to witness to the true or binding nature of one's declaration **b** sthg (e g a promise) formally confirmed by an oath ⟨*an ~ of allegiance*⟩ **c** a form of expression used in taking an oath **2** an irreverent use of a sacred name; *broadly* a swearword [ME *ooth*, fr OE *āth*; akin to OHG *eid* oath] – **on/under oath** bound by a solemn promise to tell the truth

'oat,meal /-,meel, -,miəl/ *n* **1** meal made from oats, used esp in porridge **2** a greyish beige colour

ob-, oc-, of-, op- *prefix* **1** out; forth ⟨ob*trude*⟩ ⟨of*fer*⟩; exposed ⟨ob*verse*⟩ **2** so as to involve compliance ⟨o*bey*⟩ ⟨ob*serve*⟩ **3** against; in opposition to ⟨ob*loquy*⟩ ⟨op*ponent*⟩; resisting ⟨ob*stinate*⟩ **4** in the way of; hindering ⟨ob*stacle*⟩ ⟨ob*struct*⟩ **5** hidden; concealed ⟨ob*fuscatory*⟩ ⟨oc*cult*⟩ **6** inversely ⟨ob*ovate*⟩ [ME, fr OF, fr L, in the way, against, towards, fr *ob* in the way of, on account of – more at EPI-; (6) NL, prob fr *ob*verse obversely]

Obadiah /,ohbə'die·ə/ *n* a prophetic book of the Old Testament [Heb *'Ōbhadhyāh*]

¹**obbligato** /,obli'gahtoh/ *adj* not to be omitted – used in music [It, obligatory, fr pp of *obbligare* to oblige, fr L *obligare*]

²**obbligato** *n, pl* **obbligatos** *also* **obbligati** /-ti/ an elaborate, esp melodic, accompaniment, usu played by a single instrument

obdurate /'obdyoorət, -joo-/ *adj* **1** stubbornly persistent in wrong doing **2** inflexible, unyielding [ME, fr L *obduratus*, pp of *obdurare* to harden, fr *ob-* against + *durus* hard – more at OB-, DURING] – **obdurately** *adv*, **obdurateness, obduracy** *n*

obeah /'ohbi·ə/ *n, often cap* sorcery and magic ritual as practised among Negroes, esp of the British W Indies [of African origin; akin to Twi *a¹bi²a³*, a creeper used in making charms]

'obeahman /-mən/ *n* a man who is expert in the practice of obeah

obedience /ə'beedi·əns, oh-/ *n* **1a** an act of obeying **b** the quality or state of being obedient **2** a sphere of esp ecclesiastical jurisdiction

obedient /ə'beedi·ənt, oh-/ *adj* submissive to the will or authority of a superior; willing to obey [ME, fr OF, fr L *oboedient-, oboediens*, fr prp of *oboedire* to obey – more at OBEY] – **obediently** *adv*

obeisance /oh'bay(i)səns, -'bee-/ *n* **1** a movement or gesture made as a sign of respect or submission **2** deference, homage [ME *obeisaunce* obedience, obeisance, fr MF *obeissance*, fr *obeissant*, prp of *obeir* to obey] – **obeisant** *adj*, **obeisantly** *adv*

obelisk /'obəlisk/ *n* **1** an upright 4-sided usu monolithic pillar that gradually tapers towards the top and terminates in a pyramid **2** DAGGER 2 [MF *obelisque*, fr L *obeliscus*, fr Gk *obeliskos*, fr dim. of *obelos* spit, pointed pillar]

obese /oh'bees/ *adj* excessively fat [L *obesus*, fr pp of *obedere* to eat up, fr *ob-* against + *edere* to eat – more at OB-, EAT] – **obesity** *n*

obey /ə'bay, oh'bay/ *vt* **1** to submit to the commands or guidance of ⟨~s *the teacher*⟩ ⟨~ed *a whim*⟩ **2** to comply with; execute ⟨~ed *instructions*⟩ ~ *vi* to act obediently [ME *obeien*, fr OF *obeir*, fr L *oboedire*, fr *ob-* towards + *-oedire* (akin to *audire* to hear) – more at OB-, AUDIBLE]

obfuscate /'obfus,kayt/ *vt* **1** to make obscure or difficult to understand **2** to confuse, bewilder [LL *obfuscatus*, pp of *obfuscare*, fr L *ob-* in the way + *fuscus* dark brown – more at OB-, DUSK] – **obfuscation** /-'kaysh(ə)n/ *n*, **obfuscatory** /-'kayt(ə)ri/ *adj*

[1]**obi** /'ohbi/ *n* a broad sash worn with a Japanese kimono [Jap]

[2]**obi** *n* obeah

obit /'obit, 'oh-/ *n* a memorial service held on the anniversary of the death of a founder or benefactor [ME, fr MF, fr L *obitus* death, fr *obitus*, pp of *obire* to go to meet, die, fr *ob-* in the way + *ire* to go – more at ISSUE]

obiter dictum /,obitə 'diktəm/ *n, pl* **obiter dicta** /'diktə/ **1** an incidental observation made by a judge which is not material to his judgment and therefore not binding **2** an incidental remark or observation [LL, lit., something said in passing]

obituary /ə'bityoo(ə)ri/ *n* a notice of a person's death, usu with a short biography [ML *obituarium*, fr L *obitus* death] – **obituary** *adj*

[1]**object** /'objekt/ *n* **1** sthg that is (capable of) being sensed physically or examined mentally ⟨*an* ~ *of study*⟩ **2a** sthg or sby that arouses an emotion or provokes a reaction or response ⟨*an* ~ *of derision*⟩ **b** sby or sthg that is ridiculous, outlandish, or pathetic in appearance ⟨*looked a real* ~⟩ **3** an end towards which effort, action, etc is directed; a goal ⟨*what's the* ~ *of the exercise?*⟩ **4** a noun or noun equivalent appearing in a prepositional phrase or representing the goal or the result of the action of its verb (e g *house* in *we built a house*) **5** sthg of paramount concern ⟨*if money's no* ~ *then buy it*⟩ [ME, fr ML *objectum*, fr L, neut of *obicere* to throw in the way, present, hinder, fr *ob-* in the way + *jacere* to throw – more at OB-, [2]JET] – **objectless** *adj*

[2]**object** /əb'jekt/ *vb vi* **1** to oppose sthg with words or arguments **2** to feel dislike or disapproval ⟨*I* ~ *to his condescending manner*⟩ ~ *vt* to offer in opposition or objection [ME *objecten*, fr L *objectus*, pp of *obicere* to throw in the way, object] – **objector** *n*

'**object ,ball** *n* the ball (first) struck by the cue ball in snooker, billiards, etc

objectify /əb'jekti,fie/ *vt* **1a** to cause to become an object of perception **b** to make objective **2** EXTERNALIZE 2 – **objectification** /-fi'kaysh(ə)n/ *n*

objection /əb'jeksh(ə)n/ *n* **1** a reason or argument presented in opposition **2** a feeling or statement of dislike, disapproval, or opposition [[2]OBJECT + -ION]

objectionable /əb'jeksh(ə)nəbl/ *adj* unpleasant or offensive – **objectionableness** *n*, **objectionably** *adv*

[1]**objective** /əb'jektiv/ *adj* **1a** constituting an object: e g **(1)** existing independently of the mind **(2)** belonging to the external world and observable or verifiable **(3)** *of a symptom of disease* perceptible to other people as well as the affected individual **b** concerned with or expressing the nature of external reality rather than personal feelings or beliefs **c** dealing with facts without distortion by personal feelings or prejudices **2** of or in the case that follows a preposition or a transitive verb – **objectively** *adv*, **objectiveness, objectivity** /,objek'tivəti/ *n*

[2]**objective** *n* **1** sthg towards which efforts are directed; a goal **2** sthg to be attained or achieved by a military operation **3** (a word in) the objective case **4** a lens or system of lenses that forms an image of an object

objectivism /əb'jekti,viz(ə)m/ *n* a theory stressing objective reality, esp as distinguished from subjective experience or appearance – **objectivist** *n*, **objectivistic** /-'vistik/ *adj*

'**object ,lesson** *n* **1** a lesson that takes a material object as its basis **2** sthg that serves as a concrete illustration of a principle

objet d'art /,obzhay 'dah (*Fr* ɔbʒɛ dar)/ *n, pl* **objets d'art** /~/ a usu small article of some artistic value [F, lit., art object]

objet trouvé /'troohvay, trooh'vay (*Fr* truve)/ *n, pl* **objets trouvés** /~/ a natural or man-made object displayed as having artistic value [F, lit., found object]

oblast /'oblahst/ *n, pl* **oblasts** *also* **oblasti** /-ti/ an administrative subdivision of a constituent republic of the USSR [Russ *oblast'*]

[1]**oblate** /'oblayt/ *adj* flattened or depressed at the poles ⟨*an* ~ *spheroid*⟩ – compare PROLATE [prob fr NL *oblatus*, fr *ob-* + *-latus* (as in *prolatus* prolate)] – **oblateness** *n*

[2]**oblate** *n* a (lay) member of any of several Roman Catholic communities [ML *oblatus*, lit., one offered up, fr L, pp of *offerre*]

oblation /ə'blaysh(ə)n/ *n* **1** *cap* the act of offering to God the bread and wine used at Communion **2** an offering made for religious purposes [ME *oblacioun*, fr MF *oblation*, fr LL *oblation-*, *oblatio*, fr L *oblatus*, pp of *offerre* to offer]

[1]**obligate** /'obligayt, -gət/ *adj* **1** restricted to 1 characteristic mode of life ⟨*an* ~ *parasite*⟩ **2** always happening irrespective of environmental conditions ⟨~ *parasitism*⟩ – compare FACULTATIVE – **obligately** *adv*

[2]**obligate** /'obligayt/ *vt* to constrain legally or morally [L *obligatus*, pp of *obligare*]

obligation /,obli'gaysh(ə)n/ *n* **1** sthg (e g a contract or promise) that binds one to a course of action **2** (the amount of) a financial commitment ⟨*the company was unable to meet its financial* ~s⟩ **3** sthg one is bound to do; a duty **4** (indebtedness for) a service or favour ⟨*her kindness has put me under an* ~ *to her*⟩ [[2]OBLIGATE + -ION]

obligatory /ə'bligət(ə)ri/ *adj* **1** binding in law or conscience **2** relating to or enforcing an obligation ⟨*a writ* ~⟩ **3** mandatory, compulsory **4** obligate – **obligatorily** *adv*

oblige /ə'bliej/ *vt* **1** to constrain by force or circumstance **2a** to put in one's debt by a favour or service – usu pass ⟨*we're much* ~d *to you for all your help*⟩ **b** to do a favour for ⟨~d *the assembled company with a song*⟩ ~ *vi* to do sthg as a favour; be of service ⟨*always ready to* ~⟩ [ME *obligen*, fr OF *obliger*, fr

L *obligare*, lit., to bind to, fr *ob-* towards + *ligare* to bind – more at LIGATURE]

obligee /,obli'jee/ *n* sby to whom another is obligated

obliging /ə'bliejing/ *adj* eager to help; accommodating – **obligingly** *adv*, **obligingness** *n*

obligor /,obli'gaw/ *n* one who places himself under a legal obligation

oblique /ə'bleek/ *adj* **1a** neither perpendicular nor parallel; inclined **b** having the axis not perpendicular to the base ⟨*an ~ cone*⟩ **c** having no right angle ⟨*an ~ triangle*⟩ **d** *of an angle* greater than but not a multiple of 90° **2** not straightforward or explicit; indirect ⟨*~ references to financial difficulties*⟩ **3** *of a muscle* situated obliquely with 1 end not attached to bone [ME *oblike*, fr L *obliquus*, fr *ob-* towards + *-liquus* (akin to *ulna* elbow)] – **oblique** *n*, **obliquely** *adv*, **obliqueness** *n*

oblique case *n* any grammatical case other than the nominative or vocative

obliquity /ə'blikwəti/ *n* (the amount of) deviation from being parallel or perpendicular

obliterate /ə'blitərayt/ *vt* **1** to make illegible or imperceptible **2** to destroy all trace or indication of **3** to cause (e g a blood vessel or other body part) to collapse or disappear **4** CANCEL 5 [L *oblitteratus*, pp of *oblitterare*, fr *ob* in the way of + *littera* letter] – **obliterative** /-rətiv/ *adj*, **obliterator** /-,raytə/ *n*, **obliteration** /-'raysh(ə)n/ *n*

oblivion /ə'blivi·ən/ *n* **1** the state of forgetting or being oblivious **2** the state of being forgotten **3** official disregarding of offences [ME, fr MF, fr L *oblivion-*, *oblivio*, fr *oblivisci* to forget, perh fr *ob-* in the way + *levis* smooth – more at OB-, [1]LIME]

oblivious /ə'blivi·əs/ *adj* lacking conscious knowledge; completely unaware – usu + *of* or *to* – **obliviously** *adv*, **obliviousness** *n*

oblong /'oblong/ *adj* deviating from a square by being longer; *esp* rectangular with adjacent sides unequal [ME, fr L *oblongus*, fr *ob-* towards + *longus* long] – **oblong** *n*

obloquy /'obləkwi/ *n* **1** strongly-worded condemnation **2** discredit, disgrace [LL *obloquium*, fr *obloqui* to speak against, fr *ob-* against + *loqui* to speak – more at OB-]

obnoxious /əb'nokshəs/ *adj* highly offensive or repugnant [L *obnoxius*, fr *ob* in the way of, exposed to + *noxa* harm – more at OB-, NOXIOUS] – **obnoxiously** *adv*, **obnoxiousness** *n*

oboe /'oh,boh/ *n* a double-reed woodwind instrument with a conical tube and a usual range from B flat below middle C upwards for about 2½ octaves [It, fr F *hautbois* – more at HAUTBOY] – **oboist** *n*

obol /'obol/ *n* an ancient Greek coin or weight equal to $^1/_6$ drachma [L *obolus*, fr Gk *obolos*; akin to Gk *obelos* spit]

obovate /o'bohvayt/ *adj*, *of a leaf* ovate with the narrower end nearest the stalk ☞ PLANT

obscene /əb'seen/ *adj* **1** offending standards of esp sexual propriety or decency; *specif* inciting sexual depravity ⟨*confiscated various ~ publications*⟩ **2** (morally) repugnant [MF, fr L *obscenus*, *obscaenus*] – **obscenely** *adv*

obscenity /əb'senəti/ *n* **1** the quality or state of being obscene **2** an obscene act or utterance

obscurantism /,obskyoo'rantiz(ə)m/ *n* opposition to the advance of knowledge [F *obscurantisme*, fr *obscurant* obscuring] – **obscurantist** *n or adj*

[1]**obscure** /əb'skyooə/ *adj* **1** hard to understand; abstruse **2** not well-known or widely acclaimed **3** faint, indistinct **4** constituting or representing the unstressed vowel /ə/ [ME, fr MF *obscur*, fr L *obscurus*, fr *ob-* in the way + *-scurus* (akin to Gk *keuthein* to conceal) – more at OB-, [2]HIDE] – **obscurely** *adv*, **obscureness** *n*

[2]**obscure** *vt* **1** to conceal (as if) by covering **2** to make indistinct or unintelligible – **obscuration** /,obskyoo'raysh(ə)n/ *n*

obscurity /əb'skyooərəti/ *n* **1** the quality or state of being obscure **2** an obscure person or thing

obsequious /əb'seekwi·əs/ *adj* showing a servile willingness to oblige [ME, fr L *obsequiosus* compliant, fr *obsequium* compliance, fr *obsequi* to comply, fr *ob-* towards + *sequi* to follow – more at OB-, SUE] – **obsequiously** *adv*, **obsequiousness** *n*

obsequy /'obsikwi/ *n* a funeral ceremony – usu pl with sing. meaning [ME *obsequie*, fr MF, fr ML *obsequiae* (pl), alter. of L *exsequiae* – more at EXEQUY]

observable /əb'zuhvəbl/ *adj* capable of being observed; discernible – **observable** *n*, **observably** *adv*

observance /əb'zuhv(ə)ns/ *n* **1a** a customary practice, rite, or ceremony – often pl **b** a rule governing members of a religious order **2** an act of complying with a custom, rule, or law [OBSERVE + -ANCE]

observant /əb'zuhv(ə)nt/ *adj* **1** paying close attention; watchful **2** careful to observe; mindful – + *of* **3** quick to notice; alert – **observantly** *adv*

observation /,obzə'vaysh(ə)n/ *n* **1** an act or the faculty of observing **2** the gathering of information by noting facts or occurrences ⟨*weather ~s*⟩ **3** a remark, comment **4** the condition of sby or sthg that is observed ⟨*under ~ at the hospital*⟩ [MF, fr L *observation-*, *observatio*, fr *observatus*, pp of *observare*] – **observational** *adj*

,obser'vation ,car *n*, *NAm* a railway carriage with large windows and often a partly transparent roof that affords passengers a broad view

observatory /əb'zuhvət(ə)ri/ *n* a building or institution for the observation and interpretation of natural phenomena, esp in astronomy [prob fr NL *observatorium*, fr L *observatus*]

observe /əb'zuhv/ *vt* **1a** to act in due conformity with ⟨*always ~d the law*⟩ ⟨*careful to ~ local customs*⟩ **b** to celebrate or perform (e g a ceremony or festival) according to a prescribed or traditional form ⟨*~d the fast of Ramadan*⟩ **2** to perceive or take note of, esp by concentrated attention **3** to utter as a comment ⟨*~d that things weren't what they used to be*⟩ **4** to make a scientific observation on or of [ME *observen*, fr MF *observer*, fr L *observare* to guard, watch, observe, fr *ob-* in the way, towards + *servare* to keep – more at OB-, CONSERVE]

observer /əb'zuhvə/ *n* **1** sby sent to observe but not participate officially in a gathering **2** sby who accompanies the pilot of an aircraft to make observations [OBSERVE + [2]-ER]

obsess /əb'ses/ *vt* to preoccupy intensely or abnormally [L *obsessus*, pp of *obsidēre* to besiege, beset, fr *ob-* against + *sedēre* to sit – more at OB-, SIT] – **obsessive** /-siv/ *adj or n*, **obsessively** *adv*, **obsessiveness** *n*

obsession /əb'sesh(ə)n/ *n* a persistent (disturbing) preoccupation with an often unreasonable idea; *also* an idea causing such a preoccupation – **obsessional** *adj*, **obsessionally** *adv*

obsidian /əb'sidi·ən/ *n* a usu black volcanic glass which splits to give a convex surface [NL *obsidianus*, fr L *obsidianus lapis*, false MS reading for *obsianus lapis*, lit., stone of Obsius, fr *Obsius*, a Roman traveller named by Pliny as its supposed discoverer]

obsolescent /,obsə'les(ə)nt/ *adj* going out of use; becoming obsolete [L *obsolescent-, obsolescens*, prp of *obsolescere*] – **obsolescence** *n*

obsolete /'obsəleet/ *adj* **1** no longer in use **2** outdated, outmoded [L *obsoletus*, fr pp of *obsolescere* to grow old, become disused] – **obsoleteness** /'obsəleetnis, ,--'--/ *n*

obstacle /'obstəkl/ *n* sthg that hinders or obstructs [ME, fr MF, fr L *obstaculum*, fr *obstare* to stand in the way, fr *ob-* in the way + *stare* to stand – more at OB-, STAND]

obstetric /əb'stetrik, ob-/, **obstetrical** /-kl/ *adj* of or associated with childbirth or obstetrics [prob fr (assumed) NL *obstetricus*, fr L *obstetric-, obstetrix* midwife, fr *obstare* to stand in the way, stand in front of] – **obstetrically** *adv*

ob'stetrics *n pl but sing or pl in constr* a branch of medicine dealing with the care and treatment of women before, during, and after childbirth – **obstetrician** /,obste'trish(ə)n, -stə-/ *n*

obstinate /'obstinət/ *adj* **1** clinging stubbornly to an opinion or course of action; not yielding to arguments or persuasion **2** not easily subdued, remedied, or removed ⟨*an ~ fever*⟩ [ME, fr L *obstinatus*, pp of *obstinare* to be resolved, fr *ob-* in the way + *-stinare* (akin to *stare* to stand)] – **obstinately** *adv*, **obstinacy** /-si/ *n*

obstreperous /əb'strep(ə)rəs/ *adj* **1** aggressively noisy; clamorous **2** vociferously defiant; unruly [L *obstreperus*, fr *obstrepere* to clamour against, fr *ob-* against + *strepere* to make a noise; akin to OE *thræft* discord] – **obstreperously** *adv*, **obstreperousness** *n*

obstruct /əb'strukt/ *vt* **1** to block or close up by an obstacle ⟨*the road is ~ed by a landslide*⟩ ⟨*the fence ~s the view*⟩ **2** to hinder, impede [L *obstructus*, pp of *obstruere*, fr *ob-* in the way + *struere* to build – more at OB-, STRUCTURE] – **obstructive** *adj or n*, **obstructiveness** *n*, **obstructively** *adv*, **obstructor** *n*

obstruction /əb'struksh(ə)n/ *n* **1** a condition of being clogged or blocked **2** an attempted delay of business in a deliberative body (e g Parliament) **3** sthg that obstructs [OBSTRUCT + -ION]

ob'struction,ism /-,iz(ə)m/ *n* deliberate interference with (legislative) business – **obstructionist** *n*, **obstructionistic** /-'istik/ *adj*

obtain /əb'tayn/ *vt* to acquire or attain ~ *vi* to be generally accepted or practised – fml [ME *obteinen*, fr MF & L; MF *obtenir*, fr L *obtinēre* to hold on to, possess, obtain, fr *ob-* in the way + *tenēre* to hold – more at OB-, THIN] – **obtainable** *adj*, **obtainer** *n*, **obtainment** *n*, **obtainability** /-nə'biləti/ *n*

obtest /ob'test, əb-/ *vb, archaic* to beseech, supplicate [MF *obtester*, fr L *obtestari* to call to witness, beseech, fr *ob-* towards + *testis* witness – more at OB-, TESTAMENT] – **obtestation** /,obte'staysh(ə)n/ *n*

obtrude /əb'troohd/ *vt* **1** to thrust out **2** to assert without warrant or request ~ *vi* to thrust oneself forward with unwarranted assertiveness [L *obtrudere* to thrust at, fr *ob-* in the way + *trudere* to thrust – more at OB-, THREAT] – **obtruder** *n*, **obtrusion** /-zh(ə)n/ *n*

obtrusive /əb'troohsiv, -ziv/ *adj* **1** forward in manner; pushing **2** unduly noticeable [L *obtrusus*, pp of *obtrudere*] – **obtrusively** *adv*, **obtrusiveness** *n*

obtund /ob'tund/ *vt* to reduce the edge or violence of; dull ⟨~ed *reflexes*⟩ [ME *obtunden*, fr L *obtundere*]

obturate /'obtyoo(ə),rayt/ *vt* to obstruct or close (an opening, esp the breech of a gun) [L *obturatus*, pp of *obturare*, fr *ob-* in the way + *-turare* (akin to *tumēre* to swell) – more at OB-, THUMB] – **obturator** *n*, **obturation** /-'raysh(ə)n/ *n*

obtuse /əb'tyoohs/ *adj* **1** lacking sensitivity or mental alertness **2a** being or forming an angle greater than 90° but less than 180° **b** having an obtuse angle ⟨*an ~ triangle*⟩ **c** not pointed or acute **3** *of a leaf* rounded at the end furthest from the stalk ☞ PLANT [L *obtusus* blunt, dull, fr pp of *obtundere* to beat against, blunt, fr *ob-* against + *tundere* to beat – more at OB-, STUTTER] – **obtusely** *adv*, **obtuseness** *n*

[1]**obverse** /'obvuhs/ *adj* **1** facing the observer or opponent **2** with the base narrower than the top ⟨*an ~ leaf*⟩ **3** constituting a counterpart or complement [L *obversus*, fr pp of *obvertere* to turn towards, fr *ob-* towards + *vertere* to turn – more at OB-, [1]WORTH] – **obversely** *adv*

[2]**obverse** *n* **1a** the side of a coin, medal, or currency note that bears the principal device and lettering; *broadly* a front or principal surface – compare REVERSE 4a **b** the more conspicuous of 2 possible sides or aspects **2** a counterpart to a fact or truth

obviate /'obviayt/ *vt* **1** to anticipate and dispose of in advance **2** to make unnecessary [LL *obviatus*, pp of *obviare* to meet, withstand, fr L *obviam* in the way] – **obviation** /-'aysh(ə)n/ *n*

obvious /'obvi·əs/ *adj* **1** evident to the senses or understanding **2** unsubtle ⟨*the symbolism of the novel was rather ~*⟩ [L *obvius*, fr *obviam* in the way, fr *ob* in the way of + *viam*, acc of *via* way – more at OB-, VIA] – **obviously** *adv*, **obviousness** *n*

oc- – see OB-

ocarina /,okə'reenə/ *n* a simple wind instrument with an oval body [It, fr *oca* goose, fr LL *auca*, deriv of L *avis* bird – more at AVIARY]

,**Occam's 'razor, Ockham's razor** /'okəmz/ *n* an esp philosophical principle that explanations should include as little reference as possible to unknown phenomena [William of *Occam* (or *Ockham*) †1349? E scholastic philosopher]

[1]**occasion** /ə'kayzh(ə)n/ *n* **1** a suitable opportunity or circumstance ⟨*this is hardly the ~ for laughter*⟩ **2** a state of affairs that provides a reason or grounds ⟨*you have no ~ to be annoyed*⟩ **3** the immediate or incidental cause **4** a time at which sthg occurs ⟨*on the ~ of his daughter's marriage*⟩ **5** a special event or ceremony ⟨*the wedding was a real ~*⟩ [ME, fr MF or L; MF, fr L *occasion-, occasio*, fr *occasus*, pp of *occidere* to fall, fall down, fr *ob-* towards + *cadere* to fall – more at OB-, CHANCE] – **on occasion** from time to time

[2]**occasion** *vt* to bring about; cause – fml

occasional /ə'kayzh(ə)nl/ *adj* **1** of a particular occasion **2** composed for a particular occasion ⟨*~ verse*⟩ **3** occurring at irregular or infrequent intervals **4** acting in a specified capacity from time to time

⟨*an ~ golfer*⟩ **5** designed for use as the occasion demands ⟨*an ~ table*⟩

occasionally /ə'kayzh(ə)nli, ə'kayzhnəli/ *adv* NOW AND AGAIN

Occident /'oksid(ə)nt/ *n* WEST 2a [ME, fr MF, fr L *occident-, occidens*, fr prp of *occidere* to fall, set (of the sun)]

occidental /,oksi'dentl/ *adj, often cap* of or situated in the Occident; western – **occidentalism** *n, often cap*, **occidentalize** *vt, often cap*, **occidentally** *adv, often cap*

Occidental *n* a member of any of the indigenous peoples of the Occident

occipital /ok'sipitl/ *adj* of, situated near, or being the back part of the head or skull – **occipital** *n*, **occipitally** *adv*

occiput /'oksipət/ *n, pl* **occiputs, occipita** /ok'sipitə/ the back part of the head [L *occipit-, occiput*, fr *ob-* against + *capit-, caput* head – more at OB-, HEAD]

occlude /ə'kloohd/ *vt* **1** to stop up; block **2** to obstruct, hinder **3** to sorb ~*vi* **1** *of teeth* to fit together with the cusps of the opposing teeth when the mouth is closed ⟨*his teeth do not ~ properly*⟩ **2** to become occluded [L *occludere*, fr *ob-* in the way + *claudere* to shut, close – more at OB-, [4]CLOSE] – **occludent** *adj*, **occlusive** /-siv, -ziv/ *adj*

occluded front *n* OCCLUSION 3

occlusion /ə'kloohzh(ə)n/ *n* **1** occluding or being occluded **2** the complete obstruction of the breath passage in the articulation of a speech sound **3** the meteorological front formed by a cold front overtaking a warm front and lifting the warm air above the earth's surface [prob fr (assumed) NL *occlusion-, occlusio*, fr L *occlusus*, pp of *occludere*]

[1]**occult** /'okult, -'-/ *vt* to conceal by occultation [L *occultare*, fr *occultus*, pp]

[2]**occult** *adj* **1** secret; *esp* esoteric **2** not easily understood; abstruse **3** involving (secret knowledge of) supernatural powers **4** not present, manifest, or detectable by the unaided eye ⟨*~ blood loss*⟩ [L *occultus*, fr pp of *occulere* to cover up, fr *ob-* in the way + *-culere* (akin to *celare* to conceal) – more at OB-, HELL] – **occult** *n*, **occultly** *adv*

occultation /,okul'taysh(ə)n/ *n* the eclipsing of one celestial body by another, usu much larger, one

occultism /'okul,tiz(ə)m/ *n* belief in or study of the action or influence of supernatural powers – **occultist** *n*

occupancy /'okyoopənsi/ *n* **1** the act of taking and holding possession of land, a property, etc **2** becoming or being an occupant; *also* being occupied

occupant /'okyoopənt/ *n* **1** one who acquires title by occupancy **2** a resident

occupation /,okyoo'paysh(ə)n/ *n* **1a** an activity in which one engages **b** an activity by which one earns a living **2a** the occupancy of land **b** tenure **3a** the act of taking possession or the holding and control of a place or area, esp by a foreign military force **b** *sing or pl in constr* a military force occupying a country **c** the period of time for which a place or area is occupied [ME *occupacioun*, fr MF *occupation*, fr L *occupation-, occupatio*, fr *occupatus*, pp of *occupare*]

occupational /,okyoo'paysh(ə)nl/ *adj* of or resulting from a particular occupation ⟨*~ hazards*⟩ – **occupationally** *adv*

,occu,pational 'therapy *n* creative activity used as therapy for promoting recovery or rehabilitation – **occupational therapist** *n*

occupy /'okyoopie/ *vt* **1** to engage the attention or energies of **2** to fill up (a portion of space or time) **3** to take or maintain possession of **4** to reside in or use as an owner or tenant [ME *occupien* to take possession of, occupy, modif of MF *occuper*, fr L *occupare*, fr *ob-* towards + *-cupare* (akin to *capere* to take) – more at OB-, HEAVE] – **occupier** *n*

occur /ə'kuh/ *vi* **-rr- 1** to be found; exist **2** to become the case; happen **3** to come to mind ⟨*it ~s to me that I haven't posted the letter*⟩ [L *occurrere*, fr *ob-* in the way + *currere* to run]

occurrence /ə'kurəns/ *n* **1** sthg that takes place; an event **2** the action or process of occurring

ocean /'ohsh(ə)n/ *n* **1** (any of the large expanses that together constitute) the whole body of salt water that covers nearly ¾ of the surface of the globe **2** *pl* a huge amount – infml ⟨*no need to hurry, we've got ~s of time*⟩ [ME *occean*, fr L *oceanus*, fr Gk *Ōkeanos*, a river believed to encircle the earth, ocean]

oceanarium /,ohsh(ə)n'eəri·əm/ *n, pl* **oceanariums, oceanaria** /-ri·ə/ a large marine aquarium

'ocean,going /-,goh·ing/ *adj* of or designed for travel on the ocean

oceanic /,ohshi'anik/ *adj* of, produced by, or occurring in the ocean, esp the open sea

oceanography /,ohsh(ə)n'ografi/ *n* the science dealing with oceans and their form, biology, and resources [ISV] – **oceanographer** *n*, **oceanographic** /-ə'grafik/ *also* **oceanographical** *adj*, **oceanographically** *adv*

ocellus /oh'seləs, o-/ *n, pl* **ocelli** /-lie/ a minute simple eye or eyespot of an invertebrate animal (e g an insect) ☞ ANATOMY [NL, fr L, dim. of *oculus* eye – more at EYE] – **ocellar** *adj*, **ocellate** /'osəlayt/, **ocellated** *adj*, **ocellation** /,ohse'laysh(ə)n, ,o-/ *n*

ocelot /'osə,lot/ *n* a medium-sized American wildcat with a yellow or greyish coat dotted and striped with black [F, fr Nahuatl *ocelotl* jaguar]

och /okh/ *interj, Scot & Irish* – used to express surprise, impatience, or regret [ScGael & IrGael]

oche /'oki/ *n* the line behind which a player must stand when throwing darts at a dartboard; *broadly* the place where a dart player stands when throwing [prob fr (assumed) ME *oche* groove, notch, fr MF]

ochre, *NAm chiefly* **ocher** /'ohkə/ *n* **1** the colour of esp yellow ochre **2** an earthy usu red or yellow (impure) iron ore used as a pigment [ME *oker*, fr MF *ocre*, fr L *ochra*, fr Gk *ōchra*, fr fem of *ōchros* yellow] – **ochreous** /'ohkri·əs/ *adj*

-ock /-ək/ *suffix* (→ *n*) small or young kind of ⟨*hill*ock⟩ ⟨*bull*ock⟩ [ME *-oc*, fr OE]

ocker /'okə/ *n, often cap, Austr & NZ* an Australian – infml [*Ocker*, name of a boorish character in an Australian TV series of the 1970s]

,Ockham's 'razor /'okəmz/ *n* OCCAM'S RAZOR

o'clock /ə'klok/ *adv* **1** according to the clock – used in specifying the exact hour ⟨*the time is 3 ~*⟩ **2** – used for indicating position or direction as if on a clock dial that is oriented vertically or horizontally ⟨*an aircraft approaching at 6 ~*⟩ [contr of *of the clock*]

octa- /oktə-/, **octo-** *also* **oct-** *comb form* **1** eight ⟨*oct*ane⟩ ⟨*octo*roon⟩ **2** containing 8 atoms, groups, or chemical equivalents in the molecular structure

[Gk *okta-, oktō-, okt-* (fr *oktō*) & L *octo-, oct-*, fr *octo* – more at EIGHT]

octad /'oktad/ *n* a group or series of 8 [Gk *oktad-, oktas* number 8, body of 8 men, fr *oktō*]

octagon /'oktəgon, -gən/ *n* a polygon of 8 angles and 8 sides ☞ MATHEMATICS [L *octagonum*, fr Gk *oktagōnon*, fr *okta-* + *-gōnon* -gon] – **octagonal** /ok'tagənl/ *adj*, **octagonally** *adv*

octahedral /,oktə'heedrəl/ *adj* **1** having 8 plane faces **2** of or formed in octahedrons – **octahedrally** *adv*

octahedron /-oktə'heedron, -drən/ *n, pl* **octahedrons, octahedra** /-drə/ a polyhedron of 8 faces [Gk *oktaedron*, fr *okta-* + *-edron* -hedron]

octal /'okt(ə)l/ *adj* of, being, or belonging to a number system having 8 as its base

octameter /ok'tamitə/ *n* a line of verse consisting of 8 metrical feet [LL, having 8 feet, fr LGk *oktametros*, fr *okta-* + *metron* measure – more at MEASURE]

octane /'oktayn/ *n* a liquid hydrocarbon of the alkane series that occurs esp in petroleum [ISV]

'octane ,number *n* a number that is used to measure or indicate the antiknock properties of a liquid motor fuel and that increases as the probability of knocking decreases

'octane ,rating *n* OCTANE NUMBER

octant /'oktənt/ *n* **1a** the position or aspect of a celestial body when distant from another body by 45° **b** an instrument for measuring altitudes of a celestial body from a ship or aircraft **2** any of the 8 parts into which a space is divided by 3 coordinate planes [L *octant-, octans* eighth of a circle, fr *octo*]

octave /'oktiv, 'oktayv/ *n* **1** a group of 8 lines of verse, esp the first 8 of a sonnet **2a** (the combination of 2 notes at) a musical interval of 8 diatonic degrees **b** a note separated from a lower note by this interval **c** the whole series of notes or piano, organ, etc keys within this interval that form the unit of the modern scale **3** a group of 8 [ME, fr ML *octava*, fr L, fem of *octavus* eighth, fr *octo* eight – more at EIGHT]

octavo /ok'tayvoh/ *n, pl* **octavos** (a book or page in) the size of a piece of paper cut 8 from a sheet [L, abl of *octavus* eighth]

octet /ok'tet/ *n* **1** (a musical composition for) 8 instruments, voices, or performers **2** OCTAVE 1

octo- – see OCTA-

October /ok'tohbə/ *n* the 10th month of the Gregorian calendar [ME *Octobre*, fr OF, fr L *October* (8th month of the Roman calendar), fr *octo*]

octodecimo /,oktoh'desimoh/ *n* eighteenmo [L, abl of *octodecimus* eighteenth, fr *octodecim* eighteen, fr *octo* eight + *decem* ten – more at TEN]

octogenarian /,oktəjə'neəri·ən/ *n* a person between 80 and 89 years old [L *octogenarius* containing eighty, fr *octogeni* eighty each, fr *octoginta* eighty, fr *octo* eight + *-ginta* (akin to *viginti* twenty) – more at VIGESIMAL] – **octogenarian** *adj*

octopod /'oktə,pod/ *n* an octopus or related cephalopod mollusc with 8 arms [deriv of Gk *oktōpod-, oktōpous* scorpion, fr *oktō* octa- + *pod-, pous* foot – more at FOOT] – **octopod** *adj*, **octopodan** /ok'topədən; *also* ,oktə'pohdən/ *adj or n*, **octopodous** *adj*

octopus /'oktəpəs/ *n, pl* **octopuses, octopi** /-pie/ **1** any of a genus of molluscs related to the squids and cuttlefishes with 8 muscular arms equipped with 2 rows of suckers **2** sthg having many radiating branches or far-reaching controlling influence [NL *Octopod-, Octopus*, genus name, fr Gk *oktōpous*]

octoroon /'oktə,roohn/ *n* a person of ⅛ Negro ancestry [*octa-* + *-roon* (as in *quadroon*)]

octosyllable /'oktoh,siləbl, -tə-/ *n* a word or line of 8 syllables – **octosyllabic** /-si'labik/ *adj*

ocul-, oculo- *comb form* eye (and) ⟨ocul**o**motor⟩ ⟨ocul**ist**⟩ [L *ocul-*, fr *oculus* – more at EYE]

[1]**ocular** /'okyoolə/ *adj* **1** performed or perceived with the eyes **2** of the eye ⟨~ *muscles*⟩ [LL *ocularis* of eyes, fr L *oculus* eye]

[2]**ocular** *n* an eyepiece

oculist /'okyoolist/ *n* an ophthalmologist or optician [F *oculiste*, fr L *oculus*]

od /od, ohd/ *n* a mysterious force formerly believed to pervade the universe [G (coined by Baron Karl von Reichenbach †1869 G natural philosopher)]

odalisque /'ohd(ə)l·isk/ *n* a female slave or concubine in a harem [F, fr Turk *odalk*]

odd /od/ *adj* **1a** left over when others are paired or grouped **b** not matching ⟨~ *socks*⟩ **2** not divisible by 2 without leaving a remainder ⟨*1,3,5 are ~ numbers*⟩ **3** somewhat more than the specified number – usu in combination ⟨*300*-odd *pages*⟩ **4** not regular or planned; casual, occasional ⟨~ *jobs*⟩ ⟨*at ~ moments*⟩ **5** different from the usual or conventional; strange [ME *odde*, fr ON *oddi* point of land, triangle, odd number; akin to OE *ord* point of a weapon] – **oddly** *adv*, **oddness** *n*

'odd,ball /-,bawl/ *n* an eccentric or peculiar person – infml – **oddball** *adj*

oddity /'odəti/ *n* **1** an odd person, thing, event, or trait **2** oddness, strangeness

,odd man 'out *n* sby or sthg that differs in some respect from all the others in a set or group

oddment /'odmənt/ *n* **1** sthg left over; a remnant **2** *pl* ODDS AND ENDS

odds /odz/ *n pl but sing or pl in constr* **1a** an amount by which one thing exceeds or falls short of another ⟨*won the election against considerable* ~⟩ **b** a difference in terms of advantage or disadvantage ⟨*it makes no* ~⟩ ⟨*what's the ~?*⟩ **2** the probability (expressed as a ratio) that one thing will happen rather than another ⟨*the ~ are that he will be dismissed*⟩ ⟨*the ~ are 50 to 1 against the newcomer*⟩ **3** disagreement, variance ⟨*was at ~ with management*⟩ **4** the ratio between the amount to be paid off for a winning bet and the amount of the bet ⟨*gave ~ of 3 to 1*⟩ ☞ STATISTICS

,odds and 'ends *n pl* miscellaneous items or remnants

,odds-'on *adj* **1** (viewed as) having a better than even chance to win ⟨*the ~ favourite*⟩ **2** not involving much risk ⟨*an ~ bet*⟩

odd trick *n* each trick in excess of 6 won by the declarer's side at bridge – compare BOOK 6

ode /ohd/ *n* a lyric poem, often addressed to a particular subject, marked by a usu exalted tone and varying meter and length of line [MF or LL; MF, fr LL, fr Gk *ōidē*, lit., song, fr *aeidein, aidein* to sing; akin to Gk *audē* voice, OHG *farwāzan* to deny]

-ode /-ohd/ *comb form* (→ *n*) **1** way; path ⟨*electrode*⟩ **2** electrode ⟨*diode*⟩ [Gk *-odos*, fr *hodos* road, way]

odeum /oh'dee·əm, 'ohdi·əm/ *n, pl* **odea** /-ə/ a small roofed theatre of ancient Greece and Rome [L & Gk; L, fr Gk *ōideion*, fr *ōidē* song]

odious /'ohdi·əs/ *adj* arousing hatred or revulsion

⟨*an* ~ *crime*⟩ [ME, fr MF *odieus*, fr L *odiosus*, fr *odium*] – **odiously** *adv*, **odiousness** *n*

odium /ˈohdi·əm/ *n* general condemnation or disgrace associated with a despicable act – fml [L, hatred, fr *odisse* to hate; akin to OE *atol* terrible, Gk *odyssasthai* to be angry]

odometer /ohˈdomitə/ *n* an instrument for measuring the distance travelled (e g by a vehicle) [F *odomètre*, fr Gk *hodometron*, fr *hodos* way, road + *metron* measure – more at MEASURE]

odont-, odonto- *comb form* tooth ⟨odont*itis*⟩ [F, fr Gk *odont-, odous* – more at TOOTH]

-odont /-əˌdont/ *comb form* (→ *adj*) having teeth of a (specified) nature ⟨*meso*dont⟩ [Gk *odont-, odous* tooth]

odontoglossum /ohˌdontəˈglosəm, ə-, o-/ *n* any of a genus of tropical American orchids with showy flowers [NL, genus name, fr *odont-* + Gk *glōssa* tongue – more at ²GLOSS]

oˌdontoid ˈprocess /ohˈdontoyd, ə-, o-/ *n* a toothlike projection from the front end of the second vertebra in the neck on which the first vertebra and the head rotate

odontology /ˌohdonˈtoləji, o-/ *n* the science dealing with the (structure, development, and diseases of the) teeth [F *odontologie*, fr *odont-* + *-logie* -logy] – **odontologist** *n*, **odontological** /-təˈlojikl/ *adj*

odoriferous /ˌohdəˈrif(ə)rəs/ *adj* yielding a scent or odour – **odoriferously** *adv*

odorous /ˈohd(ə)rəs/ *adj* having a scent or odour – **odorously** *adv*

odour, *NAm chiefly* **odor** /ˈohdə/ *n* **1** (the sensation resulting from) a quality of sthg that stimulates the sense of smell **2** repute, favour ⟨*in bad* ~⟩ – fml **3** a characteristic quality; a savour – chiefly derog ⟨*an* ~ *of sanctity*⟩ [ME *odour*, fr OF, fr L *odor*; akin to L *olēre* to smell, Gk *ozein* to smell, *osmē* smell, odour] – **odourless** *adj*

odyssey /ˈodəsi/ *n* a long wandering or quest [the *Odyssey*, epic poem by Homer recounting the long wanderings of Odysseus]

oecumenical /ˌekyooˈmenikl, ˌeekyoo-/ *adj* ecumenical

oedema, *NAm chiefly* **edema** /iˈdeemə/ *n* abnormal accumulation of liquid derived from serum causing abnormal swelling of the tissues [NL, fr Gk *oidēma* swelling, fr *oidein* to swell; akin to OE *ātor* pus]

Oedipus complex /ˈeedipəs, ˈedipəs/ *n* (an adult personality disorder resulting from) the sexual attraction developed by a child towards the parent of the opposite sex with accompanying jealousy of the parent of the same sex [*Oedipus*, figure in Gk mythology who unknowingly killed his father and married his mother] – **Oedipal** *adj*

oeillade /uhˈyahd (*Fr* œjad)/ *n* an (amorous or provocative) glance [F, fr MF, fr *oeil* eye, fr L *oculus* – more at EYE]

oenology, *NAm chiefly* **enology** /eeˈnoləji/ *n* the science of wine and winemaking [Gk *oinos* wine + E *-logy*] – **oenologist** *n*

oenophile, *NAm chiefly* **enophile** /ˈeenohˌfiel/ *n* a wine connoisseur

o'er /aw, ˈoh·ə/ *adv or prep* over – poetic

oersted /ˈuhstəd/ *n* the cgs unit of magnetic field strength [Hans Christian *Oersted* †1851 Dan physicist]

oesophag-, oesophago-, *NAm chiefly* **esophag-, esophago-** *comb form* **1** oesophagus ⟨oesophage*al*⟩ **2** oesophageal and ⟨oesophago*gastric*⟩

oesophagus /eeˈsofəgəs/ *n, pl* **oesophagi** /-ˌgie/ the muscular tube leading from the back of the mouth to the stomach ☞ DIGESTION [ME *ysophagus*, fr Gk *oisophagos*, fr *oisein* to be going to carry + *phagein* to eat] – **oesophageal** /eeˌsofəˈjee·əl, ˌ---ˈ--/

oestr-, oestro-, *NAm chiefly* **estr-, estro-** *comb form* (promoting) oestrus ⟨oestro*gen*⟩

oestradiol /ˌeestrəˈdieˌol, ˌestrə-/ *n* the major oestrogenic steroid sex hormone in human females, used in treating abnormal absence of menstruation and menopausal symptoms [ISV *oestra-* (fr *oestrin*, an oestrogenic hormone) + *di-* + *-ol*]

oestriol /ˈeestriˌol, ˈestriˌol/ *n* an oestrogenic steroid hormone used esp in the treatment of menopausal symptoms [*oestrin* + *tri-* + *-ol*]

oestrogen /ˈeestrəj(ə)n, ˈestrə-/ *n* a substance, esp a sex hormone, that stimulates the development of secondary sex characteristics in female vertebrates and promotes oestrus in lower mammals [NL *oestrus* + ISV *-o-* + *-gen*] – **oestrogenic** /-ˈjenik/ *adj*, **oestrogenically** *adv*

oestrone /ˈeestrohn, ˈestrohn/ *n* an oestrogenic steroid hormone that is a derivative of oestradiol and has similar actions and uses [ISV, fr *oestrin* (an oestrogenic hormone)]

oestrus /ˈeestrəs, ˈestrəs/ *n* a regularly recurrent state of sexual excitability in the female of most lower mammals when she will copulate with the male [NL, fr L *oestrus* gadfly, frenzy, fr Gk *oistros* – more at IRE] – **oestral, oestrous** *adj*

ˈoestrus ˌcycle *n* the series of changes in a female mammal occurring from one period of oestrus to the next

oeuvre /ˈuhvə (*Fr* œːvr)/ *n pl* **oeuvres** /~/ the life's work of a writer, artist, or composer [F *œuvre*, lit., work, fr L *opera* – more at OPERA]

of /əv; *strong* ov/ *prep* **1a** – used to indicate origin or derivation ⟨*a man* ~ *noble birth*⟩ ⟨*they expect it* ~ *me*⟩ **b** – used to indicate cause, motive, or reason ⟨*died* ~ *pneumonia*⟩ ⟨*did it* ~ *her own free will*⟩ **c** proceeding from; on the part of ⟨*the approval* ~ *the minister*⟩ ⟨*the buzzing* ~ *the bees*⟩ ⟨*very kind* ~ *him*⟩ **d** BY 4a(2) ⟨*the plays* ~ *Shaw*⟩ **2a(1)** composed or made from ⟨*a crown* ~ *gold*⟩ ⟨*a staff* ~ *teachers*⟩ ⟨*a family* ~ *5*⟩ **(2)** using as a material ⟨*what did he make the crown* ~*?*⟩ ⟨*made the dress* ~ *silk rather than cotton*⟩ **b** containing ⟨*cup* ~ *water*⟩ **c** – used to indicate the mass noun or class that includes the part denoted by the previous word ⟨*an inch* ~ *rain*⟩ ⟨*a blade* ~ *grass*⟩ **d** from among ⟨*most* ~ *the army*⟩ ⟨*one* ~ *his last poems*⟩ ⟨*the fattest* ~ *the girls*⟩ ⟨*members* ~ *the team*⟩ ⟨*she,* ~ *all people!*⟩ ⟨*the elder* ~ *the two*⟩ **3a** belonging to; related to ⟨*the leg* ~ *the chair*⟩ ⟨*the colour* ~ *her dress*⟩ ⟨*the relatives* ~ *those who were killed*⟩ ⟨*the wife* ~ *the managing director*⟩ ⟨*the hat* ~ *the old gentleman*⟩ **b** that is or are – used before possessive forms ⟨*a friend* ~ *John's*⟩ ⟨*that nose* ~ *his*⟩ **c** characterized by; with, having ⟨*a man* ~ *courage*⟩ ⟨*an area* ~ *hills*⟩ ⟨*a woman* ~ *no im portance*⟩ ⟨*suitcases* ~ *a suitable size*⟩ **d** connected with ⟨*the king* ~ *England*⟩ ⟨*a teacher* ~ *French*⟩ ⟨*a smell* ~ *mice*⟩ ⟨*the time* ~ *arrival*⟩ **e** existing or happening in or on ⟨*the battle* ~ *Blenheim*⟩ ⟨*my letter* ~ *the 19th*⟩ **4a** relating to (a topic); concerning ⟨*stories* ~ *his travels*⟩ ⟨*dreamed* ~ *home*⟩ ⟨*what*

~ *it?*⟩ **b** in respect to ⟨*slow ~ speech*⟩ ⟨*north ~ the lake*⟩ ⟨*have hopes ~ him*⟩ ⟨*fond ~ chocolate*⟩ ⟨*guilty ~ murder*⟩ **c** directed towards ⟨*love ~ nature*⟩ ⟨*care ~ guinea pigs*⟩ ⟨*the shooting ~ seals*⟩ ⟨*ask a question ~ him*⟩ **d** – used to show separation or removal ⟨*eased ~ pain*⟩ ⟨*cured him ~ mumps*⟩ ⟨*cheated him ~ his rights*⟩ **e** – used as a function word to indicate a whole or quantity from which a part is removed or expended ⟨*gave ~ his time*⟩ **5** – used to indicate apposition ⟨*the city ~ Rome*⟩ ⟨*the age ~ 8*⟩ ⟨*the art ~ painting*⟩ **6** *NAm* to (a specified hour) ⟨*a quarter ~ four*⟩ **7** in, during ⟨*died ~ a Monday*⟩ ⟨*go there ~ an evening*⟩ – infml [ME, off, of, fr OE, adv & prep; akin to OHG *aba* off, away, L *ab* from, away, Gk *apo*] – **of a** -like ⟨*that palace* of a *house*⟩ ⟨*that brute* of a *dog*⟩ – used after expressions of strong feeling

of- – see OB-

ofay /'oh,fay, -'-/ *n* a white person – derog [origin unknown]

[1]off /of/ *adv* **1a(1)** from a place or position ⟨*march ~*⟩ ⟨*frighten them ~*⟩; *specif* away from land ⟨*ship stood ~ to sea*⟩ **(2)** away in space or ahead in time ⟨*stood 10 paces ~*⟩ ⟨*Christmas is a week ~*⟩ **b** from a course; aside ⟨*turned ~ into a lay-by*⟩; *specif* away from the wind **c** into sleep or unconsciousness ⟨*dozed ~*⟩ **2a** so as to be not supported ⟨*rolled to the edge of the table and ~*⟩, not in close contact ⟨*took his coat ~*⟩, or not attached ⟨*handle came ~*⟩ **b** so as to be divided ⟨*surface marked ~ into squares*⟩ ⟨*a corner screened ~*⟩ **3a** to or in a state of discontinuance or suspension ⟨*shut ~ an engine*⟩ ⟨*game was rained ~*⟩ ⟨*the radio is ~*⟩ **b** so as to be completely finished or no longer existent ⟨*finish it ~*⟩ ⟨*kill them ~*⟩ ⟨*walk it ~*⟩ ⟨*sleep it ~*⟩ **c** in or into a state of putrefaction ⟨*cream's gone ~*⟩ **d** (as if) by heart ⟨*know it ~ pat*⟩ **4** away from an activity or function ⟨*the night shift went ~*⟩ ⟨*take time ~ for lunch*⟩ **5** offstage ⟨*noises ~*⟩ **6** to a sexual climax ⟨*brought him ~*⟩ – slang [ME *of*, fr OE – more at OF]

[2]off *prep* **1a** – used to indicate physical separation or distance from ⟨*take it ~ the table*⟩ ⟨*jumped ~ his bicycle*⟩ ⟨*wear it ~ the shoulder*⟩ **b** to seaward of ⟨*2 miles ~ shore*⟩ **c** lying or turning aside from; adjacent to ⟨*a shop just ~ the high street*⟩ **d** (slightly) away from – often in combination ⟨*a week ~ work*⟩ ⟨*completely ~ the point*⟩ ⟨off-*target*⟩ ⟨off-*centre*⟩ **2** – used to indicate the source from which sthg derives or is obtained ⟨*dined ~ oysters*⟩ ⟨*bought it ~ a friend*⟩ ⟨*claim it ~ tax*⟩ **3a** not occupied in ⟨*~ duty*⟩ **b** tired of; no longer interested in or using ⟨*he's ~ drugs*⟩ ⟨*I've gone ~ science fiction*⟩ **c** below the usual standard or level of ⟨*~ his game*⟩

[3]off *adj* **1a** FAR 3 **b** seaward **c** being the right-hand one of a pair ⟨*the ~ wheel of a cart*⟩ **d** situated to one side; adjoining ⟨*bedroom with dressing room ~*⟩ **2a** started on the way ⟨*~ on a spree*⟩ **b** not taking place or staying in effect; cancelled ⟨*the match is ~*⟩ **c** *of a dish on a menu* no longer being served **3a** not up to standard; unsatisfactory in terms of achievement ⟨*an ~ day*⟩ **b** slack ⟨*~ season*⟩ **4** affected (as if) with putrefaction ⟨*this fish is ~*⟩ **5** provided ⟨*well ~*⟩ ⟨*how are you ~ for socks?*⟩ **6a** in, on, through, or towards the off side of a cricket field **b** *esp of a ball bowled in cricket* moving or tending to move in the direction of the leg side ⟨*~ break*⟩ **7** *of behaviour* not what one has a right to expect; *esp* rather unkind or dishonest ⟨*it was a bit ~ to leave without a word of thanks!*⟩ – infml

[4]off *vi* to go away; leave

[5]off *n* the start or outset; *also* a starting signal ⟨*ready for the ~*⟩

offal /'ofl/ *n* **1** the by-products of milling used esp for animal feeds **2** the liver, heart, kidney, etc of a butchered animal used as food **3** refuse [ME, fr *of* off + *fall*]

,off and 'on *adv* FROM TIME TO TIME

,off'beat /-'beet/ *adj* unusual; *esp* unconventional – infml

,off 'Broadway /'brawdway/ *adj or n often cap O* (of) a part of the New York professional theatre that is located outside the theatrical Broadway area and stresses fundamental and artistic values

'off-,chance *n* a remote possibility – **on the off chance** just in case ⟨*came* on the off chance *of seeing you*⟩

,off-'colour *adj* **1** unwell ⟨*feeling a bit ~*⟩ **2** *chiefly NAm* somewhat indecent; risqué

'off,cut /-,kut/ *n* a piece (e g of paper or wood) that is left after the original piece required has been cut

offence, *NAm chiefly* **offense** /ə'fens/ *n* **1** sthg that occasions a sense of outrage **2** (an) attack, assault **3** displeasure, resentment **4a** a sin or misdeed **b** an illegal act; a crime **5** *chiefly NAm* ATTACK 6 [ME, fr MF, fr L *offensa*, fr *offensus*, pp of *offendere*] – **offenceless** *adj*

offend /ə'fend/ *vi* **1** to break a moral or divine law – often + *against* **2** to cause displeasure, difficulty, or discomfort ~ *vt* **1** to cause pain or displeasure to; hurt ⟨*colours that ~ the eye*⟩ **2** to cause to feel indignation or disgust [ME *offenden*, fr MF *offendre*, fr L *offendere* to strike against, offend, fr *ob-* against + *-fendere* to strike – more at OB-, DEFEND] – **offender** *n*

[1]offensive /ə'fensiv/ *adj* **1a** aggressive, attacking **b** of or designed for attack ⟨*~ weapons*⟩ **2** arousing physical disgust; repellent **3** causing indignation or outrage – **offensively** *adv*, **offensiveness** *n*

[2]offensive *n* **1** *the* position or attitude of an attacking party ⟨*took the ~*⟩ **2** an esp military attack on a large scale

[1]offer /'ofə/ *vt* **1** to present (e g a prayer or sacrifice) in an act of worship or devotion – often + *up* **2a** to present for acceptance, rejection, or consideration **b** to present in order to satisfy a requirement ⟨*candidates may ~ Welsh as one of their foreign languages*⟩ **3** to declare one's willingness ⟨*~ed to help me*⟩ **4** to put up ⟨*~ed stubborn resistance*⟩ **5a** to make available; afford ⟨*the hotel ~s a full range of facilities*⟩ **b** to present (goods) for sale **6** to present in performance or exhibition **7** to tender as payment; bid ~ *vi* **1** to make an offer for consideration, acceptance, etc **2** to present itself; occur [(*vt* 1) ME *offren*, fr OE *offrian*, fr LL *offerre*, fr L, to present, tender, fr *ob-* towards + *ferre* to carry; (2-7 & *vi*) ME *offren*, fr OF *offrir*, fr L *offerre* – more at OB-, [2]BEAR]

[2]offer *n* **1a** a proposal; *specif* a proposal of marriage **b** an undertaking to do or give sthg on a specific condition **2** a price named by a prospective buyer – **on offer** being offered; *specif* for sale, esp at a reduced price – **under offer** sold subject to the signing of contracts – used in connection with sales of real estate

offering /'of(ə)ring/ *n* **1** the act of one who offers **2** sthg offered; *esp* a sacrifice ceremonially offered as a part of worship **3** a contribution to the support of a church or other religious organization

offertory /'ofət(ə)ri/ *n* **1** *often cap* (a text said or sung during) the offering of the Communion bread and wine to God before consecration **2** (the collection and presentation of) the offerings of the congregation at public worship [ML *offertorium*, fr *offertus*, pp of LL *offerre*]

offhand /ˌof'hand/ *adv or adj* **1** without forethought or preparation **2** without proper attention or respect – **offhanded** *adj*, **offhandedly** *adv*, **offhandedness** *n*

office /'ofis/ *n* **1** an esp beneficial service or action carried out for another ⟨*through her good* ~s *I recovered my belongings*⟩ **2a** a position giving authority to exercise a public function ⟨*the* ~ *of Prime Minister*⟩ **b** a position with special duties or responsibilities **3** a prescribed form or service of worship; *esp, cap* DIVINE OFFICE **4a** a place, esp a large building, where the business of a particular organization is carried out **b** (a group of people sharing) a room in which the administrative, clerical, or professional work of an organization is performed **c** a place, esp a small room, where a particular service is provided ⟨*the lost property* ~⟩ **5a** *cap* a major administrative unit in some governments ⟨*the Foreign* Office⟩ **b** a subdivision of some government departments [ME, fr OF, fr L *officium* service, duty, office, fr *opus* work + *facere* to make, do – more at OPERATE, DO]

'office ˌboy, *fem* **'office ˌgirl** *n* a young person employed to run errands in an office

1officer /'ofisə/ *n* **1** a policeman **2** one who holds a position with special duties or responsibilities (e g in a government or business) **3a** one who holds a position of authority or command in the armed forces; *specif* a commissioned officer **b** a master or any of the mates of a merchant or passenger ship [ME, fr MF *officier*, fr ML *officiarius*, fr L *officium*]

2officer *vt* **1** to supply with officers **2** to command or direct as an officer

ˌofficer of 'arms *n* any of the officers of a monarch or government responsible for creating and granting heraldic arms

1official /ə'fish(ə)l/ *n* one who holds an esp public office ⟨*government* ~s⟩ – **officialdom** /-d(ə)m/ *n*, **officialese** /-'eez/ *n*

2official *adj* **1** of an office and its duties **2** holding an office **3a** authoritative, authorized **b** prescribed or recognized as authorized, esp by a pharmacopoeia **4** suitable for or characteristic of a person in office; formal – **officially** *adv*

of'ficialˌism /-ˌiz(ə)m/ *n* the lack of flexibility and excessive adherence to routine held to characterize the behaviour of esp government officials

Ofˌficial Re'ceiver *n* a public official appointed to administer a bankrupt's property

officiate /ə'fishiayt/ *vi* **1** to perform an esp religious ceremony, function, or duty ⟨~ *at a wedding*⟩ **2** to act as an official or in an official capacity – **officiant** /-ənt/ *n*, **officiation** /-'aysh(ə)n/ *n*

officinal /ˌofi'sienl/ *adj* **1** kept ready-prepared at a pharmacy ⟨~ *medicine*⟩; *also* OFFICIAL 3b **2** medicinal ⟨~ *herbs*⟩ [ML *officinalis* of a storeroom, fr *officina* storeroom, fr L, workshop, fr *opific-*, *opifex* workman, fr *opus* work + *facere* to do] – **officinal** *n*, **officinally** *adv*

officious /ə'fishəs/ *adj* **1** given to or marked by overzealousness in exercising authority or carrying out duties **2** *esp of a diplomatic agreement* informal, unofficial [L *officiosus*, fr *officium* service, office] – **officiously** *adv*, **officiousness** *n*

offing /'ofing/ *n* the part of the deep sea visible from the shore ['*off*] – **in the offing** likely to happen in the near future ⟨*thought more unemployment was in the offing*⟩

offish /'ofish/ *adj* inclined to be aloof or distant – infml ['*off*] – **offishly** *adv*, **offishness** *n*

ˌoff-'key *adj* varying in pitch from the proper tone of a melody

'off-ˌlicence *n, Br* a shop, part of a public house, etc licensed to sell alcoholic drinks to be consumed off the premises; *also* the licence permitting such sale – **off-licensee** /ˌ- --'-/ *n*

ˌoff 'limits *adv or adj, chiefly NAm & Austr* out-of-bounds

'off-ˌline *adj* not controlled directly by a computer ⟨~ *equipment*⟩ – compare ON-LINE ☞ SYMBOL – **off-line** *adv*

ˌoff-'load *vt* UNLOAD 1, 2

ˌoff-off-'Broadway *adj or n* (of) avant-garde theatrical productions in New York

ˌoff-'peak *adj* (used) at a time of less than the maximum demand or activity ⟨~ *electricity*⟩ ⟨~ *travel*⟩

'offˌprint /-ˌprint/ *n* a separately printed excerpt (e g an article from a magazine) – **offprint** *vt*

ˌoff-'putting *adj, chiefly Br* disagreeable, disconcerting – infml

'off ˌsales *n pl, Br* drinks and food sold, esp by a public house, for consumption off the premises

'offˌscouring /-ˌskowəring/ *n* refuse, dregs – often pl with sing. meaning

ˌoff'screen /-'skreen/ *adv or adj* out of sight of the film or television viewer

ˌoff-'season *n* a time of suspended or reduced activity

1'offˌset /-ˌset/ *n* **1** a short shoot or bulb growing out to the side from the base of a plant **2a** an offshoot, esp of a family or race **b** a spur in a range of hills **3** an abrupt bend in an object by which one part is turned aside out of line **4** sthg that serves to compensate for sthg else **5** a printing process in which an inked impression from a plate is first made on a rubber surface and then transferred to paper

2ˌoff'set *vt* **-tt-; offset 1a** to balance ⟨*credits* ~ *debits*⟩ **b** to compensate or make up for **2** to print (e g a book) by using the offset process

ˌoffset 'litho *n* offset printing from photolithographic plates

'offˌshoot /-ˌshooht/ *n* **1** a branch of a plant's main stem **2a** a lateral branch (e g of a mountain range) **b** a subsidiary branch, descendant, or member

ˌoff'shore /-'shaw/ *adj or adv* **1** (coming or moving) away from the shore **2** at a distance from the shore

offshore fund *n* a form of unit trust that is registered abroad, usu in countries offering tax advantages

ˌoff'side /-'sied/ *adv or adj* illegally in advance of the ball or puck in a team game

'off ,side *n* **1** the part of a cricket field on the opposite side of a line joining the middle stumps to that in which the batsman stands when playing a ball – compare LEG SIDE ☞ SPORT **2** *chiefly Br* the right side of a horse, vehicle, etc

'off,spring /-,spring/ *n, pl* **offspring** the progeny of a person, animal, or plant; young [ME *ofspring*, fr OE, fr *of* off + *springan* to spring]

,off'stage /-'stayj/ *adv or adj* **1** on a part of the stage not visible to the audience **2** behind the scenes; away from the public gaze

,off-the-'cuff *adj or adv* impromptu – infml

,off-the-'peg *adj, chiefly Br* (of or dealing in clothes) made beforehand to fit standard sizes – compare MADE-TO-MEASURE – **off-the-peg** *adv*

,off-the-'record *adj or adv* (given or made) unofficially or in confidence

,off-'white *n or adj* (a) yellowish or greyish white

oft /oft/ *adv* often – poetic [ME, fr OE; akin to OHG *ofto* often]

often /'of(t)ən/ *adv* **1** (at) many times **2** in many cases ⟨*they* ~ *die young*⟩ [ME, alter. of *oft*]

ogee /'oh,jee/ *n* **1** (a moulding in the form of) a shallow S-shaped curve **2 ogee arch, ogee** a pointed arch with shallow S-shaped sides ***USE*** ☞ ARCHITECTURE [obs *ogee* (ogive); fr the use of such mouldings in ogives]

ogham, ogam /'ogəm, 'oh·əm/ *n* a 20-character Old Irish alphabet that used notches for vowels and lines that met at or cut across a straight line (e g the edge of a stone) for consonants [IrGael *ogham*, fr MIr *ogom, ogum*] – **oghamic** /o'gamik, 'oh·əmik/ *adj*

ogival /oh'jievl/ *adj* (having the form) of an ogive or an ogee

ogive /'oh,jiev/ *n* a diagonal arch or rib across a Gothic vault [F]

ogle /'ohgl/ *vb* **ogling** /'ohgling/ to glance or stare with esp sexual interest (at) [prob fr LG *oegeln*, fr *oog* eye; akin to OHG *ouga* eye – more at EYE] – **ogle** *n*, **ogler** *n*

ogre /'ohgə/, *fem* **ogress** /'ohgris/ *n* **1** a hideous giant of folklore believed to feed on human beings **2** a dreaded person or thing – compare SPECTRE 2 [F] – **ogreish** *adj*

¹oh, O /oh/ *interj* – used to express surprise, pain, disappointment, etc [ME *o*]

²oh, O *n* nought [*o*; fr the similarity of the symbol for nought (0) to the letter *O*]

ohm /ohm/ *n* the derived SI unit of electrical resistance equal to the resistance between 2 points of a conductor when a constant potential difference of 1 volt applied to these points produces a current of 1 ampere ☞ PHYSICS [Georg Simon *Ohm* †1854 G physicist] – **ohmic** *adj*, **ohmically** *adv*

ohmmeter /'ohm,meetə/ *n* an instrument for measuring electrical resistance [ISV]

oho /oh'hoh/ *interj* – used to express amused surprise, exultation, etc [ME]

oi /oy/ *n* a style of music popular among some young white people in the early 1980s, characterized by a strong jerky rhythm and lyrics often advocating racism and violence ⟨*an* ~ *band*⟩ ⟨~ *music*⟩ [prob fr *oi, oy*, interj used to attract attention, express warning, etc]

-oic /-'oh·ik/ *suffix* (→ *adj*) containing a (derivative of a) carboxyl group ⟨*benzoic acid*⟩ [*-o-* + *-ic*]

¹-oid /-oyd/ *suffix* (→ *n*) sthg resembling (a specified object) or having (a specified quality) ⟨*globoid*⟩ ⟨*asteroid*⟩

²-oid *suffix* (→ *n, adj*) **1** resembling; having the form or appearance of ⟨*petaloid*⟩ ⟨*anthropoid*⟩ **2** bearing an imperfect resemblance to ⟨*humanoid*⟩ [MF & L; MF *-oïde*, fr L *-oïdes*, fr Gk *-oeidēs*, fr *-o-* + *eidos* appearance, form – more at ¹WISE]

oidium /oh'idi·əm/ *n, pl* **oidia** /-di·ə/ **1** any of (the small asexual spores borne in chains by) various fungi many of which are the spore-bearing stages of powdery mildews **2** a powdery mildew, esp on grapes, caused by an oidium [NL, fr *o-* + *-idium*]

¹oil /oyl/ *n* **1** any of numerous smooth greasy combustible liquids or low melting-point solids that are insoluble in water but dissolve in organic solvents **2** a substance (e g a cosmetic preparation) of oily consistency **3a** OIL PAINT ⟨*a portrait done in* ~s⟩ **b** OIL PAINTING **4** petroleum ☞ ENERGY [ME *oile*, fr OF, fr L *oleum* olive oil, fr Gk *elaion*, fr *elaia* olive] – **oil** *adj*

²oil *vt* to treat or lubricate with oil ~ *vi* to change from a solid fat into an oil by melting – **oiler** *n* – **oil the wheels** to help things run smoothly

'oil,bird /-,buhd/ *n* a nocturnal bird of S America and Trinidad valued because oil can be extracted from the fat of its young and used as a substitute for butter

'oil ,cake *n* the solid residue left after extracting the oil from seeds (e g of cotton)

'oil,can /-,kan/ *n* a vessel with a nozzle designed to release oil in a controlled flow (e g for lubricating machinery)

'oil,cloth /-,kloth/ *n* cloth treated with oil or paint and used for table and shelf coverings

'oil ,colour *n* OIL PAINT

'oil ,field *n* a region rich in petroleum deposits; *esp* one producing petroleum in commercial quantities

'oil ,gland *n* a gland that secretes oil; *esp* UROPYGIAL GLAND

'oil ,paint *n* paint consisting of ground pigment mixed with oil

'oil ,painting *n* (a product of) the art of painting with oil paints

'oil ,palm *n* an African palm with fruit that yields palm oil

'oil,seed /-,seed/ *n* a seed or crop (e g rape) grown largely for oil

'oil ,shale *n* shale from which oil can be distilled

'oil,skin /-,skin/ *n* **1** an oiled waterproof cloth used for coverings and garments **2** an oilskin or plastic raincoat **3** *pl* an oilskin or plastic suit of coat and trousers

'oil ,slick *n* a film of oil floating on water

'oil,stone /-,stohn/ *n* a sharpening stone used with a surface coating of oil

'oil ,well *n* a well drilled in the earth from which petroleum is obtained

oily /'oyli/ *adj* **1** of, resembling, containing, or covered with oil **2** unctuous, ingratiating – **oilily** *adv*, **oiliness** *n*

oink /oyngk/ *n* the grunt of a pig – humor [imit] – **oink** *vi*

ointment /'oyntmənt/ *n* a soothing or healing salve for application to the skin [ME, alter. of *oignement*, fr OF, modif of L *unguentum*, fr *unguere* to anoint; akin to OHG *ancho* butter, Skt *añjati* he salves]

Ojibwa, Ojibway /oh'jibway/ *n, pl* **Ojibwas, Ojibways**, *esp collectively* **Ojibwa, Ojibway** a member, or the Algonquian language, of an American Indian people orig of Michigan [Ojibwa *ojib-ubway*, a kind of moccasin worn by the Ojibwa]

[1]**OK, okay** /oh'kay, '-,-/ *adv, adj, or interj* ALL RIGHT [perh abbr of *oll korrect*, alter. of *all correct*]

[2]**OK, okay** /oh'kay/ *vt or n* **OK's; OK'ing; OK'd** (to give) approval or authorization (of); sanction

okapi /oh'kahpi/ *n* an African mammal closely related to the giraffe but with a shorter neck and black and cream rings on the upper parts of the legs [native name in Africa]

okeydoke /,ohki'dohk/, **okeydokey** /-'dohki/ *interj* – used to express assent [redupl of *OK*]

okra /'ohkrə, 'okrə/ *n* **1** a tall annual plant of the mallow family cultivated for its mucilaginous green pods used as a vegetable, esp in soups and stews; *also* the pods of this plant **2** GUMBO 1 [of African origin; akin to Twi ŋ'*ku'rū'mā*' okra]

-ol *suffix* (→ *n*) chemical compound containing a hydroxyl group; alcohol ⟨*glycerol*⟩ ⟨*phenol*⟩ ⟨*ethanol*⟩ [ISV, fr *alcohol*]

[1]**old** /ohld/ *adj* **1a** dating from the esp remote past ⟨~ *traditions*⟩ **b** persisting from an earlier time ⟨*an* ~ *ailment*⟩ **c** of long standing ⟨*an* ~ *friend*⟩ **2** *cap* constituting an early period in the development of a language ⟨Old *Irish*⟩ **3** having existed for a specified period of time ⟨*3 years* ~⟩ **4** advanced in years or age **5** experienced ⟨*an* ~ *hand*⟩ **6** former **7a** made long ago; *esp* worn with time or use **b** no longer in use; discarded **8a** long familiar ⟨*the same* ~ *story*⟩ **b** – used as an intensive ⟨*a high* ~ *time*⟩ ⟨*any* ~ *time*⟩ [ME, fr OE *eald*; akin to OHG *alt* old, L *alere* to nourish, *alescere* to grow, *altus* high, deep] – **oldish** *adj*, **oldness** *n*

[2]**old** *n* **1** old or earlier time ⟨*men of* ~⟩ **2** one of a specified age – usu in combination ⟨*a 3-year-old*⟩

,old 'Adam /'adəm/ *n* the sinful nature inherent in man [*Adam*, the first man & first sinner, according to the Bible (Gen 2:7-3:24)]

,old 'age *n* the final stage of the normal life span

,old age 'pension *n* a state pension paid to retired people – **old age pensioner** *n*

,old 'boy, *fem* **,old 'girl** *n, chiefly Br* **1** a former pupil of a particular, esp public, school **2** a fellow or friend – often used as an informal term of address

,old 'boy ,network *n, chiefly Br the* system of favouritism operating among people of a similar privileged background, esp among former pupils of public schools

Old Church Slavonic *n* a Slavonic language surviving as the liturgical language of the Orthodox church

,old con'temptibles *n pl, often cap O&C the* British expeditionary force in France in 1914 – infml [fr the alleged description of it by the Emperor of Germany as a 'contemptible little army']

'old ,country *n* an immigrant's country of origin

olden /'ohldn/ *adj* of a bygone era – poetic

,Old 'English *n* the English language of the 7th to 11th c ☞ LANGUAGE

Old English sheepdog *n* (any of) an English breed of medium-sized sheepdogs with a very long shaggy coat

olde-worlde /,ohld 'wuhld; *often* ,ohldi 'wuhldi/ *adj* (excessively or falsely) old-world [by alter. (pseudo-antique spelling)]

,old-'fashioned *adj* **1** (characteristic) of a past era; outdated **2** clinging to customs of a past era – **old-fashionedly** *adv*

,old-fashioned 'look *n* a knowing or disapproving look

,Old 'French *n* the French language from the 9th to approximately the late 14th c

,old 'gold *n or adj* (a) dull brownish yellow

,old 'guard *n sing or pl in constr, often cap O&G* the (original) conservative members of a group or party

,old 'hand *n* VETERAN 1

,old 'hat *adj* **1** old-fashioned **2** hackneyed, trite

,Old High 'German *n* High German before the 12th c

oldie /'ohldi/ *n* sby or sthg old; *esp* a popular song from the past

,old 'lady *n* one's wife or mother – infml

,old 'maid *n* **1** SPINSTER 2 **2** a simple card game in which each player tries to avoid holding a designated unpaired card at the end **3** a prim fussy person – infml – **old-maidish** *adj*

,old 'man *n* **1** one's husband or father **2** one in authority (e g one's employer, manager, or commander) – + *the USE* infml

,old-man's 'beard *n* TRAVELLER'S JOY

,old 'master *n* (a work by) a distinguished European painter of the 16th to early 18th c

,Old 'Nick /nik/ *n* – used as an informal or humorous name for the devil [*Nick*, nickname for *Nicholas*]

,Old North 'French *n* the northern dialects of Old French, esp of Normandy and Picardy

,old 'penny *n* PENNY 1a(1)

,Old 'Prussian *n* a Baltic language of E Prussia until the 17th c

,old 'school *n* adherents of traditional ideas and practices

,old ,school 'tie *n* **1** a tie displaying the colours of an English public school, worn by former pupils **2** the conservatism and upper-class solidarity traditionally attributed to former members of British public schools

,old 'stager /'stayjə/ *n* VETERAN 1

oldster /'ohldstə/ *n, chiefly NAm* an old or elderly person – infml

'Old ,Style *adj or adv* according to the Julian calendar

,Old 'Testament *n* a collection of writings forming the Jewish canon of Scripture and the first part of the Christian Bible

'old-,time *adj* (characteristic) of an earlier period

,old-'timer *n* **1** VETERAN 1 **2** *chiefly NAm* an old man

,old 'wives' ,tale *n* a traditional superstitious notion

,old 'woman *n* **1** one's wife or mother **2** a timid, prim, or fussy person, esp a man – derog *USE* infml

,old-'world *adj* **1** of the E hemisphere **2** reminiscent of a past age; *esp* quaintly charming

,Old 'World *n* the E Hemisphere; *specif* Europe, Asia, and Africa

ole-, oleo- *comb form* oil ⟨oleic⟩ [F *olé-, oléo-*, fr L *ole-*, fr *oleum* – more at OIL]

olé /oh'lay/ *interj* – used as a cry of approval or success, esp at bullfights [Sp *ole, olé*, fr Ar *wa-llāh*, fr *wa-* and + *allāh* God]

oleaginous /,ohli'ajinəs/ *adj* resembling, containing, or producing oil; oily [MF *oleagineux*, fr L *oleagineus* of an olive tree, fr *olea* olive tree, fr Gk *elaia*] – **oleaginously** *adv*, **oleaginousness** *n*

oleander /ˌohliˈandə/ *n* a poisonous evergreen shrub of the periwinkle family with fragrant white, pink, or red flowers [ML]

oleaster /ˌoliˈastə/ *n* any of several large shrubs or small trees having yellow flowers and planted esp to provide shelter in dry windy regions [L, fr *olea*]

olefin, olefine /ˈohliˌfin, -ˌfeen/ *n* an alkene [ISV, fr F (*gaz*) *oléfiant* ethylene, fr L *oleum*] – **olefinic** /-ˈfinik/ *adj*

oleic /ohˈlee·ik/ *adj* **1** relating to, derived from, or contained in oil **2** of oleic acid – **oleate** /ˈohliayt/ *n*

oˌleic ˈacid *n* an unsaturated fatty acid found as glycerides in natural fats and oils

oleograph /ˈohli·əˌgrahf, -ˌgraf/ *n* a chromolithograph printed on cloth to resemble an oil painting [ISV *ole-* + *-graph*] – **oleographic** /-ˈgrafik/ *adj*, **oleography** /-ˈogrəfi/ *n*

oleoresin /ˌohliohˈrezin/ *n* a solution of resin in oil occurring naturally as a plant product (e g turpentine) or made synthetically [ISV] – **oleoresinous** *adj*

oleum /ˈohli·əm/ *n* a heavy oily strongly corrosive solution of sulphur trioxide in sulphuric acid [L – more at OIL]

ˈO ˌlevel *n* ORDINARY LEVEL

olfaction /olˈfaksh(ə)n/ *n* smelling or the sense of smell [L *olfactus*, pp of *olfacere* to smell, fr *olēre* to smell + *facere* to do – more at ODOUR, DO] – **olfactive** /-tiv/, **olfactory** /-t(ə)ri/ *adj*

olig- /olig-/, **oligo-** *comb form* few ⟨oligarchy⟩ [ML, fr Gk, fr *oligos*; akin to Arm *a at* scant]

oligarch /ˈoligahk/ *n* a member of an oligarchy [Gk *oligarchēs*, fr *olig-* + *-archēs* -arch]

oligarchy /ˈoligahki/ *n* **1** government by a small group **2** a state or organization in which a small group exercises control, esp for its own interests **3** a small group exercising such control – **oligarchic** /-ˈgahkik/, **oligarchical** *adj*

Oligocene /oˈligohˌseen, ˈoligohˌseen/ *adj or n* (of or being) an epoch of the Tertiary between the Eocene and Miocene ☞ EVOLUTION [ISV]

oligochaete /ˌoligəˈkeetə, əˈligəˌkeetə, -keet, ˈoligohˌkeet(ə)/ *n or adj* (any) of a class of freshwater and ground-living annelid worms (e g the earthworm) with relatively few bristles along the body – compare POLYCHAETE [NL *Oligochaeta*, class or order name, fr Gk *olig-* + *chaitē* long hair]

oligoclase /ˈoligohˌklays, oˈligohˌklays/ *n* a common feldspar mineral of the plagioclase series found in many rocks (e g granite) [G *oligoklas*, fr *olig-* + Gk *klasis* breaking, fr *klan* to break – more at [1]HALT]

oligomer /əˈligəmə/ *n* (an intermediate in the synthesis of) a polymer containing relatively few structural units [*olig-* + *-mer* (as in *polymer*)] – **oligomeric** /-ˈmerik/ *adj*, **oligomerization** /-mərieˈzaysh(ə)n/ *n*

oligopoly /ˌoliˈgopəli/ *n* a market situation in which each of a few producers affects but does not control the market [*olig-* + mono*poly*] – **oligopolist** *n*, **oligopolistic** /-ˈlistik/ *adj*

olivaceous /ˌoliˈvayshəs/ *adj* olive

[1]**olive** /ˈoliv/ *n* **1** (an Old World evergreen tree that grows esp around the Mediterranean and bears) a small stone fruit used as a food and a source of oil **2 olive, olive green** a dull yellowish green colour resembling that of an unripe olive [ME, fr OF, fr L *oliva*, fr Gk *elaia*]

[2]**olive,** ˌ**olive ˈgreen** *adj* of the colour olive

ˈolive ˌbranch *n* an offer or gesture of conciliation or goodwill

olivine /ˈoliveen, ˌ--ˈ-/ *n* a usu greenish mineral that is a silicate of magnesium and iron [G *olivin*, fr L *oliva*] – **olivinic** /-ˈvinik/ *adj*, **olivinitic** /-viˈnitik/ *adj*

olm /ohlm, olm/ *n* a European cave-dwelling aquatic salamander with nonfunctional eyes [G, fr OHG]

ology /ˈoləji/ *n* SCIENCE 1a, c – humor [*-ology* (as in *geology, psychology*)]

oloroso /ˌohləˈrohsoh, ˌolə-/ *n, pl* **olorosos** a golden full-bodied sweet sherry [Sp, fr *oloroso* fragrant, fr *olor* odour, fr L, fr *olēre* to smell]

olympiad /əˈlimpiˌad/ *n, often cap* **1** any of the 4-year intervals between Olympian games by which time was reckoned in ancient Greece **2** OLYMPIC GAMES [MF *Olympiade*, fr L *Olympiad-, Olympias*, fr Gk, fr *Olympia*, site in Greece of ancient Olympian games]

[1]**Olympian** /əˈlimpi·ən/ *adj* of the ancient Greek region of Olympia

[2]**Olympian** *n, chiefly NAm* a participant in the Olympic Games

[3]**Olympian** *adj* **1** of Mount Olympus in Thessaly **2** lofty, detached

[4]**Olympian** *n* **1** an inhabitant of the ancient Greek region of Olympia **2** any of the ancient Greek deities dwelling on Olympus **3** a loftily detached or superior person

Oˌlympian ˈGames *n pl* a festival held every 4th year by the ancient Greek states and consisting of contests of sports, music, and literature

Olympic /əˈlimpik/ *adj* **1** [3]OLYMPIAN **2** of or executed in the Olympic Games

Oˌlympic ˈGames *n pl but sing or pl in constr, pl* **Olympic Games** an international sports meeting that is a modified revival of the Olympian games and is held once every 4 years in a different host country

Oˈlympics *n pl but sing or pl in constr, pl* **Olympics** OLYMPIC GAMES

-oma /-ˈohmə/ *suffix* (→ *n*), *pl* **-omas, -omata** /-ˈohmətə, -ˈmahtə/ tumour ⟨aden*oma*⟩ ⟨fibr*oma*⟩ [L *-omat-, -oma*, fr Gk *-ōmat-, -ōma*, fr *-ō-* (stem of causative verbs in *-oun*) + *-mat-, -ma*, suffix denoting result – more at -MENT]

omasum /ohˈmays(ə)m/ *n, pl* **omasa** /-sə/ the third stomach of a ruminant mammal, lying between the reticulum and the abomasum [NL, fr L, tripe of a bullock]

ombre /ˈombə/ *n* a 3-handed card game popular in Europe in the 17th and 18th c [F or Sp; F *hombre*, fr Sp, lit., man]

ombré /ˈombray/ *adj, esp of fabrics* graduated in colour from light to dark [F, pp of *ombrer* to shade, fr It *ombrare*, fr *ombra* shade, fr L *umbra* – more at UMBRAGE]

ombudsman /ˈomboodzmən/ *n* a government official appointed to investigate complaints made by individuals against government or public bodies [Sw, lit., representative, fr ON *umbothsmathr*, fr *umboth* commission + *mathr* man]

-ome /-ohm/ *suffix* (→ *n*) part ⟨rhiz*ome*⟩ – esp in botanical names [NL *-oma*, fr L, -oma]

omega /ˈohmigə/ *n* **1** the 24th and last letter of the

Greek alphabet **2** the last one in a series, order, etc – compare ALPHA 2 [Gk *ōmega*, lit., large o]

omelette, *NAm chiefly* **omelet** /ˈomlit/ *n* a mixture of beaten eggs cooked until set in a shallow pan and often served folded in half over a filling – compare SPANISH OMELETTE [F *omelette*, alter. of MF *alumelle*, lit., knife blade, modif of L *lamella*, dim. of *lamina* thin plate]

omen /ˈohmən/ *n* an event or phenomenon believed to be a sign of some future occurrence [L *omin-*, *omen*]

omentum /ohˈmentəm/ *n, pl* **omenta** /-tə/, **omentums** a fold of peritoneum connecting or supporting the stomach and other abdominal structures [L, fr *o-* (akin to *-uere* to put on) – more at EXUVIAE] – **omental** /-tl/ *adj*

omicron /ohˈmiekrən/ *n* the 15th letter of the Greek alphabet [Gk *o mikron*, lit., small o]

ominous /ˈominəs/ *adj* portentous; *esp* foreboding evil or disaster [L *ominosus*, fr *omin-*, *omen* omen] – **ominously** *adv*, **ominousness** *n*

omission /ohˈmish(ə)n, ə-/ *n* **1** omitting or being omitted ⟨*sins of* ~⟩ **2** sthg neglected or left undone [ME *omissioun*, fr LL *omission-*, *omissio*, fr L *omissus*, pp of *omittere*]

omit /ohˈmit, ə-/ *vt* **-tt- 1** to leave out or unmentioned **2** to fail to do or perform [ME *omitten*, fr L *omittere*, fr *ob-* towards + *mittere* to let go, send – more at OB-, SMITE] – **omissible** /ohˈmisəbl, ə-/ *adj*

ommatidium /ˌoməˈtidi·əm/ *n, pl* **ommatidia** /-di·ə/ any of the many parts of an arthropod's compound eye, each corresponding to a simple eye [NL, fr Gk *ommat-*, *omma* eye] – **ommatidial** *adj*

omni- /omni-/ *comb form* all; universally ⟨*omnidirectional*⟩ [L, fr *omnis*]

[1]omnibus /ˈomnibəs/ *n* **1** a book containing reprints of a number of works, usu by 1 author ⟨*an* ~ *edition*⟩ **2** BUS 1 – fml [F, bus, fr L, for all, dat pl of *omnis*]

[2]omnibus *adj* of, containing, or providing for many things at once

omnidirectional /ˌomnidiˈreksh(ə)nl, -die-/ *adj* present or (capable of) moving in all directions; *esp* receiving or transmitting radio waves equally well in all directions

omnipotent /omˈnipət(ə)nt/ *adj* having unlimited or very great power or influence; *specif, often cap* ALMIGHTY 1 [ME, fr MF, fr L *omnipotent-*, *omnipotens*, fr *omni-* + *potent-*, *potens* potent] – **omnipotence** *n*, **omnipotently** *adv*

Omnipotent *n* GOD 1

omnipresent /ˌomniˈprez(ə)nt/ *adj* present in all places at all times – **omnipresence** *n*

omniscient /omˈnisi·ənt, omˈnish(ə)nt/ *adj* **1** having infinite awareness or understanding **2** possessed of complete knowledge; all-knowing [NL *omniscient-*, *omnisciens*, back-formation fr ML *omniscientia* omniscience, fr L *omni-* + *scientia* science] – **omniscience** *n*, **omnisciently** *adv*

omnivorous /omˈnivərəs/ *adj* **1** feeding on both animal and vegetable substances **2** avidly taking in, and esp reading, everything [L *omnivorus*, fr *omni-* + *-vorus* -vorous] – **omnivorously** *adv*, **omnivorousness** *n*, **omnivore** /ˈomniˌvaw/ *n*

[1]on /on/ *prep* **1a(1)** in contact with or supported from below by ⟨*a fly* ~ *the ceiling*⟩ ⟨*stand* ~ *1 foot*⟩ ⟨*a book* ~ *the table*⟩ **(2)** attached or fastened to ⟨*a dog* ~ *a lead*⟩ **(3)** carried on the person of ⟨*have you a match* ~ *you?*⟩ **(4)** very near to, esp along an edge or border ⟨*towns* ~ *the frontier*⟩ ⟨*Walton-*~*-Thames*⟩ **(5)** within the limits of a usu specified area ⟨~ *the steppes*⟩ ⟨~ *page 17*⟩ **b** at the usual standard or level of ⟨~ *form*⟩ **c(1)** in the direction of ⟨~ *the right*⟩ ⟨*crept up* ~ *him*⟩ **(2)** into contact with ⟨*jumped* ~ *the horse*⟩ **(3)** with regard to; concerning ⟨*keen* ~ *sports*⟩ ⟨*unfair* ~ *me*⟩ ⟨*evidence* ~ *the matter*⟩ **(4)** with a specified person or thing as object ⟨*try it out* ~ *her*⟩ **(5)** having as a topic; about ⟨*a book* ~ *India*⟩ **(6)** staked on the success of ⟨*put £5* ~ *a horse*⟩ **(7)** doing or carrying out a specified action or activity ⟨*here* ~ *business*⟩ ⟨*went* ~ *an errand*⟩ **(8)** working for, supporting, or belonging to ⟨~ *a committee*⟩ ⟨~ *their side*⟩ **(9)** working at; in charge of ⟨*the man* ~ *the gate*⟩ **2a** having as a basis or source (e g of knowledge or comparison) ⟨*have it* ~ *good authority*⟩ ⟨*swear* ~ *the Bible*⟩ ⟨*prices are down* ~ *last year*⟩ **b** at the expense of ⟨*got it* ~ *the National Health*⟩ ⟨*drinks are* ~ *the house*⟩ **3a** in the state or process of ⟨~ *fire*⟩ ⟨~ *strike*⟩ ⟨~ *holiday*⟩ ⟨~ *offer*⟩ ⟨~ *the increase*⟩ **b** in the specified manner ⟨~ *the cheap*⟩ **c** using as a medium ⟨*played it* ~ *the clarinet*⟩; *esp* OVER 4b ⟨*talking* ~ *the telephone*⟩ **d** using by way of transport ⟨*arrived* ~ *foot*⟩ ⟨*left* ~ *the early train*⟩ **e** sustained or powered by ⟨*live* ~ *vegetables*⟩ ⟨*car runs* ~ *petrol*⟩ ⟨*people* ~ *low incomes*⟩ ⟨*dined out* ~ *the story*⟩ **f** regularly taking ⟨~ *Valium*⟩ **4** through contact with ⟨*cut himself* ~ *a piece of glass*⟩ **5a** at the time of ⟨*came* ~ *Monday*⟩ ⟨*every hour* ~ *the hour*⟩ ⟨*cash* ~ *delivery*⟩ **b** on the occasion of or immediately after and usu in consequence of ⟨*shot* ~ *sight*⟩ ⟨*fainted* ~ *hearing the news*⟩ **c** in the course of ⟨~ *a journey*⟩ ⟨~ *tour*⟩ ⟨~ *my way*⟩ **d** AFTER 2b ⟨*blow* ~ *blow*⟩ [ME *an*, *on*, prep & adv, fr OE; akin to OHG *ana* on, Gk *ana* up, on]

[2]on *adv* **1** so as to be supported from below ⟨*put the top* ~⟩, in close contact ⟨*has new shoes* ~⟩, or attached ⟨*sew the buttons* ~⟩ **2a** ahead or forwards in space or time ⟨*went* ~ *home*⟩ ⟨*do it later* ~⟩ ⟨*40 years* ~⟩ ⟨*getting* ~ *for 5*⟩ **b** with the specified part forward ⟨*cars crashed head* ~⟩ **c** without interruption ⟨*chattered* ~ *and* ~⟩ **d** in continuance or succession ⟨*and so* ~⟩ **3a** in or into (a state permitting) operation ⟨*switch the light* ~⟩ ⟨*get the potatoes* ~⟩ ⟨*put a record* ~⟩ – compare TURN ON **b** in or into an activity or function ⟨*the night shift came* ~⟩

[3]on *adj* **1a** LEG 2 ⟨~ *drive*⟩ ☞ SPORT **b** taking place ⟨*the game is* ~⟩ **c** performing or broadcasting ⟨*we're* ~ *in 10 minutes*⟩ **d** intended, planned ⟨*has nothing* ~ *for tonight*⟩ **e** worn as clothing ⟨*went out with just a cardigan* ~⟩ **2a** committed to a bet **b** in favour of a win ⟨*the odds are 2 to 1* ~⟩ **3** *chiefly Br* possible, practicable – usu neg ⟨*you can't refuse, it's just not* ~⟩ **4a** *chiefly Br* nagging ⟨*she's always* ~ *at him about his hair*⟩ **b** talking dully, excessively, or incomprehensibly ⟨*what's he* ~ *about?*⟩ *USE* (*3&4*) infml

[1]-on /-on, -ən/ *suffix* (→ *n*) chemical compound ⟨*parathion*⟩ ⟨*interferon*⟩ [ISV, alter. of *-one*]

[2]-on /-on/ *suffix* (→ *n*) **1** elementary particle ⟨*electron*⟩ ⟨*baryon*⟩ **2a** unit; quantum ⟨*photon*⟩ ⟨*magneton*⟩ **b** basic operational unit of the genetic material ⟨*cistron*⟩ ⟨*operon*⟩ [fr *-on* (in *ion*)]

[3]-on /-on/ *suffix* (→ *n*) inert gas ⟨*neon*⟩ [NL, fr *-on* (in *argon*)]

onager /ˈonəjə/ *n* **1** a small Asian wild ass with a broad stripe on its back **2** a heavy catapult-like machine used in ancient and medieval times for hurling rocks in battle [(1) ME, wild ass, fr L, fr Gk *onagros*, fr *onos* ass + *agros* field – more at ACRE; (2) LL, fr L]

ˌon and ˈoff *adv* FROM TIME TO TIME

onanism /ˈohnəˌniz(ə)m/ *n* **1** COITUS INTERRUPTUS **2** masturbation [prob fr NL *onanismus*, fr *Onan*, son of Judah (Gen 38:9)] – **onanistic** /-ˈnistik/ *adj*

[1]once /wuns/ *adv* **1** one time and no more ⟨*met only* ~⟩ ⟨*shaves* ~ *a week*⟩ **2** even 1 time; ever ⟨*if* ~ *we lose the key*⟩ **3** at some indefinite time in the past; formerly ⟨*there* ~ *lived a king*⟩ **4** by 1 degree of relationship ⟨*2nd cousin* ~ *removed*⟩ [ME *ones*, fr gen of *on* one] – **once again/more 1** now again as before ⟨*back home* once *again*⟩ **2** for 1 more time

[2]once *n* one single time ⟨~ *is enough*⟩ ⟨*just this* ~⟩ – **all at once 1** all at the same time **2** ALL OF A SUDDEN – **at once 1** at the same time; simultaneously ⟨*both spoke* at once⟩ **2** IMMEDIATELY 2 – **once and for all, once for all** for the final or only time; conclusively

[3]once *conj* from the moment when; as soon as ⟨~ *he arrives we can start*⟩ ⟨~ *over the wall we're safe*⟩

ˈonce-ˌover *n* a swift appraising glance – infml ⟨*gave him the* ~⟩

oncer /ˈwunsə/ *n, Br* a £1 note – infml [[1] *once* + [2]*-er*]

oncogenic /ˌongkohˈjenik/, **oncogenous** /-ˈjeenəs/ *adj* of or tending to cause tumour formation [Gk *onkos* mass + E *-genic* or *-genous*] – **oncogenesis** /-ˈjenəsis/ *n*, **oncogenically** *adv*, **oncogenicity** /-jəˈnisəti/ *n*

oncology /ongˈkoləji/ *n* the study and treatment of cancer and malignant tumours [Gk *onkos* mass + ISV *-logy*] – **oncologist** *n*, **oncological** /-kəˈlojikl/ *also* **oncologic** *adj*

oncoming /ˈonˌkuming/ *adj* coming nearer in time or space; advancing

on dit /on ˈdee (*Fr* ɔ̃ di)/ *n, pl* **on dits** /dee(z) (*Fr* ~)/ a piece of gossip; a rumour [F, lit., they say, it is said]

[1]one /wun/ *adj* **1a** being a single unit or thing ⟨~ *day at a time*⟩ **b** being the first – used after the noun modified ⟨*on page* ~⟩ **2** being a particular but unspecified instance ⟨*saw her early* ~ *morning*⟩ **3a(1)** the same; identical ⟨*both of* ~ *mind*⟩ ⟨*it's all* ~ *to me where we go*⟩ **(2)** constituting a unified entity ⟨*all shouted with* ~ *voice*⟩ ⟨*the combined elements form* ~ *substance*⟩ **b** being in a state of agreement; united ⟨*I am* ~ *with the rest of you in this matter*⟩ **4** being some unspecified instance – used esp of future time ⟨*will see you* ~ *day soon*⟩ ⟨*we might try it* ~ *weekend*⟩ **5a** being a particular object or person ⟨*close first* ~ *eye then the other*⟩ **b** being the only individual of an indicated or implied kind ⟨*the* ~ *and only person she wanted to marry*⟩ [ME *on*, fr OE *ān*; akin to OHG *ein* one, L *unus* (OL *oinos*), Skt *eka*] – **one and the same** the very same

[2]one *pron, pl* **ones 1** a single member or specimen of a usu specified class or group ⟨*saw* ~ *of his friends*⟩ **2** an indefinitely indicated person; anybody at all ⟨~ *has a duty to* ~*'s public*⟩ ⟨~ *never knows*⟩ **3** – used to refer to a noun or noun phrase previously mentioned or understood ⟨*2 grey shirts and 3 red* ~s⟩ ⟨*if you want a book about bees, try this* ~⟩ ⟨*the question is* ~ *of great importance*⟩ ***USE*** used as a subject or object; no pl for senses 2 and 3

[3]one *n* **1** ☞ NUMBER **2** the number denoting unity **3** the first in a set or series ⟨*takes a* ~ *in shoes*⟩ **4a** a single person or thing **b** a unified entity ⟨*is secretary and treasurer in* ~⟩ ⟨*they all rose up as* ~ *and clamoured for more pay*⟩ **c** a particular example or instance ⟨~ *of the coldest nights this year*⟩ **d** a certain specified person ⟨~ *George Hopkins*⟩ **5a** a person with a liking or interest for a specified thing; an enthusiast ⟨*he's rather a* ~ *for baroque music*⟩ **b** a bold, amusing, or remarkable character ⟨*oh! you are a* ~⟩ **6a** a blow, stroke ⟨*socked him* ~ *on the jaw*⟩ **b** a drink ⟨*just time for a quick* ~⟩ **c** a remark; *esp* a joke ⟨*have you heard this* ~*?*⟩ **7** sthg having a denomination of 1 ⟨*I'll take the money in* ~s⟩ – **at one** in harmony; in a state of agreement – **for one** even if alone; not to mention others – **one by one** singly, successively

-one /-ohn/ *suffix* (→ *n*) (compound related or analogous to a) ketone ⟨*acetone*⟩ ⟨*oestrone*⟩ [ISV, alter. of *-ene*]

ˌone and ˈall *pron pl in constr* everyone individually and collectively

ˌone aˈnother *pron* each other

ˌone-armed ˈbandit *n* FRUIT MACHINE [fr the handle pulled to make the wheels spin]

ˌone-diˈmensional *adj* lacking depth; superficial – **one- dimensionality** *n*

ˌone-ˈhorse *adj* of little importance or interest – infml ⟨*a* ~ *town*⟩

oneiric /ohˈnierik/ *adj* of or relating to dreams; dreamy [Gk *oneiros* dream; akin to Arm *anurǰ* dream]

ˌone-ˈman *adj* **1** consisting of only 1 person **2** done or produced by only 1 person

oneness /ˈwun·nis/ *n* **1** singleness **2** integrity, wholeness **3** sameness, identity **4** unity, union [[1]ONE + -NESS]

ˌone-night ˈstand *n* **1** a performance given only once in any particular locality **2** (a person with whom one has) a sexual relationship lasting only 1 night

ˌone-ˈoff *adj or n, chiefly Br* (made or intended as) a single and unrepeated item or occurrence ⟨*a* ~ *job*⟩

ˌone-ˈpiece *adj* consisting of or made in a single undivided piece ⟨*a* ~ *swimming costume*⟩

onerous /ˈohnərəs, ˈon-/ *adj* burdensome, troublesome [ME, fr MF *onereus*, fr L *onerosus*, fr *oner-*, *onus* burden; akin to Skt *anas* cart] – **onerously** *adv*, **onerousness** *n*

oneself /wunˈself/ *pron* **1** a person's self; one's own self – used reflexively ⟨*one should wash* ~⟩ or for emphasis ⟨*to do it* ~⟩ **2** one's normal self ⟨*not feeling quite* ~⟩ – compare MYSELF – **be oneself** to behave in a normal, unconstrained, or unpretentious manner – **by oneself** ON ONE'S OWN – **to oneself** for one's exclusive use or knowledge

ˌone-ˈsided *adj* **1a** having or occurring on 1 side only **b** having 1 side prominent or more developed **2** partial, biased – **one-sidedly** *adv*, **one-sidedness** *n*

ˈone-ˌstep *n* (a piece of music used for) a ballroom dance marked by quick walking steps – **one-step** *vi*

'one,time /-,tiem/ *adj* former, sometime

,one-to-'one *adj* pairing each element of a set uniquely with an element of another set

,one-'track *adj* interested or absorbed in 1 thing only ⟨*a ~ mind*⟩

,one-'two *n* **1** a combination of 2 quick blows in boxing, usu with different hands and in rapid succession **2** a pass in soccer whereby one player kicks the ball to another and runs forward immediately to receive the return

,one 'up *adj* in a position of advantage

,one-'upmanship /'upmənship/ *n* the art of gaining a psychological advantage over others by professing social or professional superiority

,one-'way *adj* **1** that moves in or allows movement in only 1 direction ⟨*~ traffic*⟩ **2** one-sided, unilateral

ongoing /'on,goh·ing/ *adj* **1** actually in progress **2** growing, developing

onion /'unyən/ *n* (the pungent edible bulb, eaten as a vegetable, of) an Asian plant of the lily family or any of various related plants [ME, fr MF *oignon*, fr L *union-*, *unio*, perh fr *unus* one]

,on-'line *adj* controlled directly by, or in direct communication with a computer ⟨*~ equipment*⟩ – compare OFF-LINE ☞ SYMBOL – **on-line** *adv*

onlooker /'on,lookə/ *n* a passive spectator – **onlooking** *adj*

[1]only /'ohnli/ *adj* **1** unquestionably the best ⟨*flying is the ~ way to travel*⟩ **2** alone in its class or kind; sole ⟨*an ~ child*⟩ ⟨*the ~ detergent that contains fabric softener*⟩ [ME, fr OE *ānlīc*, fr *ān* one – more at ONE]

[2]only *adv* **1a** nothing more than; merely ⟨*~ a little one*⟩ ⟨*if it would ~ rain!*⟩ **b** solely, exclusively ⟨*known ~ to him*⟩ **2** nothing other than ⟨*it was ~ too true*⟩ **3a** in the final outcome ⟨*will ~ make you sick*⟩ **b** with nevertheless the final result ⟨*won the battle, ~ to lose the war*⟩ **4** no earlier than ⟨*~ last week*⟩ ⟨*has ~ just left*⟩

[3]only *conj* **1** but, however ⟨*they look very nice, ~ we can't use them*⟩ **2** were it not for the fact that ⟨*I'd tell you, ~ you'll just spread it around*⟩ *USE* infml

,on-'off *adj* occurring or existing from time to time; intermittent ⟨*an ~ relationship*⟩

onomastic /,onə'mastik/ *adj* (consisting) of a name [Gk *onomastikos*, fr *onomazein* to name, fr *onoma* name – more at NAME]

onomatopoeia /,onə,matə'pee·ə/ *n* the formation or use of words intended to be a vocal imitation of the sound associated with the thing or action designated (e g in *buzz, cuckoo*) [LL, fr Gk *onomatopoiia*, fr *onomat-*, *onoma* name + *poiein* to make – more at POET] – **onomatopoeic** /-'pee·ik/ *adj*, **onomatopoeically** *adv*

onrush /'on,rush/ *n* a forceful rushing forwards

onset /'on,set/ *n* **1** an attack, assault **2** a beginning, commencement

,on'shore /-'shaw/ *adj or adv* **1** (moving) towards the shore **2** on or near the shore

,on'side /-'sied/ *adv or adj* not offside

onslaught /'on,slawt/ *n* a fierce attack [modif of D *aanslag* act of striking; akin to OE *an* on & *slēan* to strike – more at SLAY]

on 'stream *adj or adv* in or into production ⟨*more oil fields are soon due to come ~*⟩

ont- /ont-/, **onto-** *comb form* **1** being; existence ⟨*ontology*⟩ **2** organism ⟨*ontogeny*⟩ [NL, fr LGk, fr Gk *ont-*, *ōn*, prp of *einai* to be – more at IS]

-ont /-ont/ *comb form* (→ *n*) cell; organism ⟨*diplont*⟩ [Gk *ont-*, *ōn*, prp]

,on-the-'job *adj* of or being sthg learnt, gained, or done while working in a job

onto, on to /'ontə; *strong* 'ontooh/ *prep* **1** to a position on **2** in or into a state of awareness about ⟨*put the police ~ him*⟩ **3** – used as a function word to indicate a mathematical set, each element of which is the image of at least 1 element of another set ⟨*a function mapping the set* S *~ the set* T⟩ **4** *chiefly Br* in or into contact with ⟨*been ~ him about the drains*⟩; *esp* on at; nagging

ontogenesis /,ontə'jenəsis/ *n* ontogeny [NL] – **ontogenetic** /-jə'netik/ *adj*, **ontogenetically** *adv*

ontogeny /on'tojəni/ *n* the (course of) development of an individual organism [ISV]

ontological /,ontə'lojikl/ *adj* **1** of ontology **2** relating to or based on being or existence – **ontologically** *adv*

ontology /on'toləji/ *n* a branch of philosophy concerned with the nature of being [NL *ontologia*, fr *ont-* + *-logia* -logy] – **ontologist** *n*

onus /'ohnəs/ *n* **1a** duty, responsibility **b** blame **2** BURDEN OF PROOF [(1) L – more at ONEROUS; (2) NL]

onward /'onwood/ *adj* directed or moving onwards; forward

'onwards, onward *adv* towards or at a point lying ahead in space or time; forwards ⟨*from his childhood ~*⟩

-onym /-ənim/ *comb form* (→ *n*) **1** name ⟨*pseudonym*⟩ **2** word ⟨*antonym*⟩ [ME, fr L *-onymum*, fr Gk *-ōnymon*, fr *onyma* – more at NAME]

onyx /'oniks/ *n* **1** a translucent variety of quartz with layers of different colours, typically green and white or black or brown and white **2 onyx, onyx marble** a translucent or semitranslucent calcium carbonate mineral, usu calcite, with marble-like bands of colour [ME *onix*, fr OF & L; OF, fr L *onych-*, *onyx*, fr Gk, lit., claw, nail – more at NAIL]

oo- – see O-

oocyte /'oh·ə,siet/ *n* an egg before maturation or division to form female gametes [ISV]

oodles /'oohdlz/ *n pl but sing or pl in constr* a great quantity; a lot – infml [perh alter. of [2]*huddle*]

oogamete /,oh·əgə'meet, -'gameet/ *n* a relatively large immobile female gamete

oogamous /oh'ogəməs/ *adj* having or involving a small mobile male gamete and a large immobile female gamete – **oogamy** *n*

oogenesis /,oh·ə'jenəsis/ *n* the formation and maturation of eggs or ova [NL] – **oogenetic** /-jə'netik/ *adj*

ooh /ooh/ *interj* – used to express amazement or pleased surprise – **ooh** *vi*

oolite /'oh·ə,liet/ *n* a rock, esp limestone, consisting of small round grains, esp of calcium carbonate [prob fr F *oolithe*, fr *o-* + *-lithe* -lite] – **oolitic** /-'litik/ *adj*

oology /oh'oləji/ *n* the study or collecting of birds' eggs – **oological** /,oh·ə'lojikl/ *also* **oologic** *adj*, **oologically** *adv*, **oologist** /oh'oləjist/ *n*

oolong /'ooh,long/ *n* a dark china tea that is partially fermented before drying [Chin (Pek) *wu*[1] *lung*[2], lit., black dragon]

oompah /'oompah/ *n* the deep, often rhythmical,

sound of a tuba, euphonium, or similar brass band instrument [imit]

oomph /oom(p)f/ *n* vitality, enthusiasm – humor [imit]

oops /oops, oohps/ *interj* – used to express apology or surprise

oosperm /ˈoh·ə,spuhm/ *n* a zygote

oospore /ˈoh·ə,spaw/ *n* a fertilized plant spore that grows into the phase of a plant producing sexual spores – compare ZYGOSPORE [ISV]

¹ooze /oohz/ *n* **1** a soft deposit of mud, slime, debris, etc on the bottom of a body of water **2** (the muddy ground of) a marsh or bog [ME *wose*, fr OE *wāse* mire; akin to L *virus* slime – more at VIRUS] – **oozy** *adj*

²ooze *n* **1** an infusion of vegetable material (e g bark) used for tanning leather **2** sthg that oozes [ME *wose* sap, juice, fr OE *wōs*; akin to OHG *waso* damp, Gk *hearon* ewer] – **oozy** *adj*

³ooze *vi* **1a** to pass or flow slowly through small openings **b** to diminish gradually; dwindle *away* **2** to exude moisture ~ *vt* **1** to emit or give out slowly **2** to display in abundance ⟨*positively* ~d *vitality*⟩

op /op/ *n* OPERATION 3, 5 – infml

op- – see OB-

opacity /ohˈpasəti/ *n* **1** opaqueness **2** obscurity of meaning; unintelligibility **3** an opaque spot on a normally transparent structure (e g the lens of the eye) [F *opacité* shadiness, fr L *opacitat-, opacitas*, fr *opacus* shaded, dark]

opah /ˈohpə/ *n* a large brilliantly coloured marine fish with rich oily red flesh [Ibo *úbá*]

opal /ˈohp(ə)l/ *n* a transparent to translucent mineral consisting of a hydrated silica and used in its opalescent forms as a gem [L *opalus*, fr Skt *upala* stone, jewel]

opalescent /,ohplˈes(ə)nt, ,ohpəˈles(ə)nt/ *adj* reflecting a milky iridescent light – **opalescence** *n*

opaline /ˈohp(ə)l,ien/ *adj* resembling opal; opalescent

opaque /ohˈpayk/ *adj* **1** not transmitting radiant energy, esp light; not transparent **2** hard to understand; unintelligible [L *opacus*] – **opaquely** *adv*, **opaqueness** *n*

,op ˈart /op/ *n* OPTICAL ART – **op artist** *n*

¹open /ˈohp(ə)n/ *adj* **1** having no enclosing or confining barrier ⟨*the* ~ *hillside*⟩ **2** allowing passage; not shut or locked **3a** exposed to general view or knowledge; public ⟨*regarded him with* ~ *hatred*⟩ **b** vulnerable to attack or question; liable ⟨~ *to doubt*⟩ **4a** not covered or protected ⟨*an* ~ *boat*⟩ ⟨*an* ~ *wound*⟩ **b** not fastened or sealed **5** not restricted to a particular category of participants; *specif* contested by both amateurs and professionals **6** presenting no obstacle to passage or view **7** having the parts or surfaces spread out or unfolded **8** articulated with the tongue low in the mouth ⟨*an* ~ *vowel*⟩ **9a** available ⟨*the only course* ~ *to us*⟩ **b** not taken up with duties or engagements ⟨*keep an hour* ~ *on Friday*⟩ **c** not finally decided or settled ⟨*an* ~ *question*⟩ **d** available for a qualified applicant; vacant **e** remaining available for use or filling until cancelled ⟨*an* ~ *order for more items*⟩ **10a(1)** willing to consider new ideas; unprejudiced ⟨*an* ~ *mind*⟩ **(2)** willing to receive and consider ⟨*always* ~ *to suggestions*⟩ **b** candid, frank **11a** containing many small openings or spaces; *specif* porous **b** having relatively wide spacing between words or lines ⟨~ *type*⟩ **c** *of a compound word* elements separated by a space in writing or printing (e g in *ski lift*) **12a** *of a string on a musical instrument* not stopped by the finger **b** *of a note* produced on a musical instrument without fingering the strings, valves, slides, or keys **13** in operation; *esp* ready for business or use ⟨*the shop is* ~ *from 9 to 5*⟩ ⟨*the new motorway will be* ~ *next week*⟩ **14** free from checks or restraints ⟨*an* ~ *economy*⟩ **15** *of a mathematical set* containing a neighbourhood of every element ⟨*the interior of a sphere is an* ~ *set*⟩ **16** *Br, of a cheque* payable in cash to the person, organization, etc named on it; not crossed [ME, fr OE; akin to OHG *offan* open; both fr a prehistoric NGmc-WGmc word akin to OE *ūp* up] – **open** *adv*, **openness** *n*

²open *vt* **1a** to change or move from a closed position **b** to permit entry into or passage through **c** to gain access to the contents of ⟨~ *a parcel*⟩ **2a** to make available for or active in a particular use or function; *specif* to establish ⟨~ed *a new shop*⟩ **b** to declare available for use, esp ceremonially **c** to make the necessary arrangements for (e g a bank account), esp by depositing money **3a** to disclose, reveal – often + *up* **b** to make more responsive or enlightened **4a** to make 1 or more openings in **b** to loosen and make less compact ⟨~ *the soil*⟩ **5** to spread out; unfold **6** to begin, commence ⟨~ed *the meeting*⟩ **7** to begin (e g the bidding, betting, or play) in a card game **8a** to initiate (a side's innings) as one of the 2 first batsmen **b** to initiate (a side's bowling attack) by bowling one of the first 2 overs of an innings ~ *vi* **1** to become open **2** to commence, start ⟨~ed *with a prayer*⟩ **3** to give access – usu + *into* or *onto* **4** to extend, unfold – usu + *out* ⟨*the view* ~ed *out in front of us*⟩ – **openable** *adj*, **openability** /-əˈbiləti/ *n*

³open *n* **1** OUTDOORS 2 **2** *often cap* an open contest, competition, or tournament – **bring into/be in the open** to (cause to) be generally known

,open-ˈair *adj* outdoor

,open ˈair *n* OUTDOORS 2

,open-and-ˈshut *adj* easily settled ⟨*an* ~ *case*⟩

,openˈcast /-ˈkahst/ *adj*, *of a mine or mining* worked from or carried out on the earth's surface by removing material covering the mineral mined for

,open-ˈcircuit *adj* of or being television in which programmes are broadcast so that they are available to any receivers within range

,open ˈcircuit *n* an incomplete circuit of electrical components through which current cannot flow – **open-circuit, open-circuited** *adj*

,open ˈcourt *n* a court or trial to which the public are admitted

ˈopen ,day *n* a day on which an institution is open to the public

,open ˈdoor *n* a policy of equal commercial relations with all nations – **open-door** *adj*

,open-ˈended *adj* without any definite limits or restrictions (e g of time or purpose) set in advance – **open-endedness** *n*

opener /ˈohp(ə)nə/ *n* **1a** an instrument that opens sthg – usu in combination ⟨*a bottle* ~⟩ **b** one who opens; *specif* an opening batsman **2** *pl* cards of sufficient value for a player to open the betting in a poker game **3** the first item or event in a series

,openˈhanded /-ˈhandid/ *adj* generous in giving – **openhandedly** *adv*, **openhandedness** *n*

ˌopen-ˈheart *adj* of or performed on a heart surgically opened whilst its function is temporarily taken over by a heart-lung machine ⟨~ *surgery*⟩

ˌopenˈhearted /-ˈhahtid/ *adj* **1** candidly straightforward **2** kind, generous – **openheartedly** *adv*, **openheartedness** *n*

ˌopen-ˈhearth *adj* of, produced by, or used in the open-hearth steelmaking process

ˌopen-ˈhearth ˌprocess *n* a process of making steel from pig iron in a reverberatory furnace

ˌopen ˈhouse *n* ready and usu informal hospitality for all comers – esp in *keep open house*

opening /ˈohp(ə)ning/ *n* **1** an act of making or becoming open **2** a breach, aperture **3a** an often standard series of moves made at the beginning of a game of chess or draughts – compare END GAME, MIDDLE GAME **b** a first performance **4a** a favourable opportunity; a chance **b** an opportunity for employment; a vacancy

ˈopening ˌtime the time at which a business, shop, etc opens; *specif* the statutory time at which a public house may open for the sale of alcohol

ˌopen ˈletter *n* a letter, esp of protest, appeal, or explanation, usu addressed to an individual but intended for the general public, and published in a newspaper, periodical, etc

ˈopenly /-li/ *adv* in an open and frank manner

ˌopen ˈmarket a market based on free competition and an unrestricted flow of goods (e g between countries)

ˌopen-ˈminded *adj* receptive to new arguments or ideas – **open-mindedly** *adv*, **open-mindedness** *n*

ˌopenˈmouthed /-ˈmowdhd/ *adj* having the mouth open, esp in surprise

ˌopen ˈorder *n* a military formation in which the units are widely separated

open out *vi* to speak more freely and confidently

ˌopen-ˈplan *adj* having no or few internal dividing walls ⟨*an* ~ *house*⟩

ˌopen ˈprison *n* a prison that has less restrictive security than a conventional one, to which criminals considered unlikely to attempt escape may be sent

ˌopen ˈsandwich *n* a sandwich without a top slice of bread

ˈopen ˌseason *n* a period during which it is legal to kill or catch game or fish protected at other times by law

ˌopen ˈsecret *n* a supposed secret that is in fact widely known

ˌopen ˈsesame /ˈsezəmi, ˈsesəmi/ *n* a means of gaining access to sthg otherwise inaccessible [*open sesame*, the magical command used by Ali Baba to open the door of the robbers' den in the Ar folktale *Ali Baba and the Forty Thieves*]

ˌopen ˈshop *n* an establishment in which eligibility for employment is not dependent on membership of a trade union – compare CLOSED SHOP

ˌOpen Uniˈversity *n* the nonresidential British university that caters mainly for adults studying part-time, has no formal entrance requirements, and operates mainly through correspondence and broadcasting

open up *vi* **1** to commence firing **2** OPEN OUT **3** to open a door ⟨open up, *it's the police!*⟩ **4** *of a game, competition, etc* to become more interesting, esp because more closely contested ~ *vt* to make available or accessible ⟨*the deal* opened up *important now possibilities for trade*⟩

ˌopen ˈverdict *n* a verdict at an inquest that records a death but does not state its cause

ˈopenˌwork /-ˌwuhk/ *n* work (e g in fabric or metal) that is perforated or pierced – **open-worked** *adj*

¹opera /ˈop(ə)rə/ *pl of* OPUS

²opera /ˈoprə/ *n* **1** (the performance of or score for) a drama set to music and made up of vocal pieces with orchestral accompaniment and usu other orchestral music (e g an overture) **2** the branch of the arts concerned with such works **3** a company performing operas [It, work, opera, fr L, work, pains; akin to L *oper-*, *opus*] – **operatic** /op(ə)ˈratik/ *adj*, **operatically** *adv*

operable /ˈop(ə)rəbl/ *adj* suitable for surgical treatment ⟨*an* ~ *cancer*⟩ [OPERATE + -ABLE] – **operably** *adv*, **operability** /-ˈbiləti/ *n*

opéra bouffe /ˌop(ə)rə ˈboohf (*Fr* ɔpera buf)/ *n* OPERA BUFFA [F, fr It *opera buffa*]

ˌopera ˈbuffa /ˈboohfə/ *n* a farcical or satirical opera, esp of a form popular in the 18th c [It, lit., comic opera]

ˌopéra coˈmique /koˈmeek (*Fr* kɔmik)/ *n* COMIC OPERA [F]

ˈopera ˌglass *n* small binoculars suitable for use at the opera or theatre – often pl with sing. meaning

ˈopera ˌhat *n* a man's collapsible top hat ☞ GARMENT

ˈopera ˌhouse *n* a theatre designed for the performance of opera

operand /ˌopəˈrand/ *n* sthg, esp a quantity, on which an operation is performed (e g in mathematics) [L *operandum*, neut of gerundive of *operari*]

¹operant /ˈop(ə)rənt/ *adj* effective, functioning

²operant *n* behaviour (e g bar pressing by a rat to obtain food) that operates on the environment to produce rewarding effects

ˌopera ˈseria /ˈsiəri·ə/ *n* an 18th-c opera with a heroic or legendary subject [It, lit., serious opera]

operate /ˈopərayt/ *vi* **1** to exert power or influence; act ⟨*factors* operating *against our success*⟩ **2** to produce a desired effect **3a** to work, function **b** to perform surgery – usu + *on* **c** to carry on a military or naval action or mission **4** to be in action; *specif* to carry out trade or business ~ *vt* **1** to effect; BRING ABOUT **2a** to cause to function; work **b** to put or keep in operation; manage [L *operatus*, pp of *operari* to work, fr *oper-*, *opus* work; akin to OE *efnan* to perform, Skt *apas* work]

ˈoperating ˌtable /ˈopərayting/ *n* a high table on which a patient lies while undergoing surgery

ˈoperating ˌtheatre *n*, *Br* a room, usu in a hospital, where surgical operations are carried out

operation /ˌopəˈraysh(ə)n/ *n* **1a** the act, method, or process of operating **b** sthg (to be) done; an activity **2** the state of being functional or operative ⟨*the plant is now in* ~⟩ **3** a procedure carried out on a living body with special instruments, usu for the repair of damage or the restoration of health **4** any of various mathematical or logical processes (e g addition) carried out to derive one expression from others according to a rule **5** a usu military action, mission, or manoeuvre and its planning **6** a business or financial transaction **7** a single step performed by a computer in the execution of a program

operational /ˌopəˈraysh(ə)nl/ *adj* **1** of or based on operations **2a** of, involved in, or used for the execution of commercial, military, or naval operations **b** (capable of) functioning – **operationally** *adv*

operational research *n, chiefly Br* the application of scientific, esp mathematical, methods to the study and analysis of problems involving complex systems (e g business management, economic planning, and the waging of war)

operations research *n, chiefly NAm* OPERATIONAL RESEARCH

ope'rations ,room *n* a room from which esp military operations are controlled

[1]**operative** /'op(ə)rətiv/ *adj* **1a** producing an appropriate effect; efficacious **b** significant, relevant ⟨*I might come, but might is the ~ word*⟩ **2** in force or operation **3** based on, consisting of, or using an esp surgical operation – **operatively** *adv*, **operativeness** *n*

[2]**operative** *n* an operator: e g **a** a workman **b** *NAm* PRIVATE DETECTIVE

operator /'opə,raytə/ *n* **1a** one who operates a machine or device **b** one who owns or runs a business, organization, etc ⟨*a tour ~*⟩ **c** one who is in charge of a telephone switchboard **2** a mathematical or logical symbol denoting an operation to be performed **3** a shrewd and skilful manipulator – infml

operculum /o'puhkyooləm/ *n, pl* **opercula** /-lə/ *also* **operculums** **1** a lid or covering flap (e g of a moss capsule or the gills of a fish) ☞ ANATOMY **2** a hard plate at the end of the foot in many gastropod molluscs that closes the shell when the animal is retracted [NL, fr L, cover, fr *operire* to shut, cover – more at WEIR] – **opercular, operculate** /-lət, -,layt/, **operculated** /-,laytid/ *adj*

operetta /,opə'retə/ *n* a usu romantic comic opera that includes dancing [It, dim. of *opera*] – **operettist** *n*

operon /'opə,ron/ *n* a set of genes on a chromosome that function together as a unit [*oper*ator + [2]*-on*]

ophidian /o'fidi·ən/ *adj* of or resembling snakes [deriv of Gk *ophis*] – **ophidian** *n*

ophite /'ofiet/ *n* any of various usu green and often mottled rocks (e g serpentine) [L, fr Gk *ophitēs* (*lithos*), lit., serpentine (stone), fr *ophitēs* snakelike, fr *ophis* snake; akin to L *anguis* snake, *anguilla* eel, Gk *enchelys* eel, *echidna* viper, *echinos* hedgehog, OE *igil*]

ophitic /o'fitik/ *adj* having or being a texture characteristic of rocks in which lath-shaped feldspar crystals are embedded in pyroxene

ophthalm-, ophthalmo- *comb form* eye ⟨ophthal*mology*⟩; *also* eyeball ⟨ophthalm*itis*⟩ [Gk, fr *ophthalmos*]

ophthalmia /of'thalmi·ə; *also* op-/ *n* inflammation of the conjunctiva or the eyeball [ME *obtalmia*, fr LL *ophthalmia*, fr Gk, fr *ophthalmos* eye; akin to Gk *ōps* eye – more at EYE]

ophthalmic /of'thalmik; *also* op-/ *adj* of or situated near the eye

ophthalmic optician *n* an optician qualified to test eyesight and prescribe correctional lenses

ophthalmologist /,ofthal'moləjist; *also* op-/ *n* a physician who specializes in ophthalmology – compare OPTICIAN

ophthalmology /,ofthal'moləji; *also* op-/ *n* the branch of medical science dealing with the structure, functions, and diseases of the eye – **ophthalmological** /-mə'lojikl/ *also* **ophthalmologic** *adj*, **ophthalmologically** *adv*

ophthalmoscope /of'thalmə,skohp; *also* op-/ *n* an instrument used to view the retina and other structures inside the eye [ISV] – **ophthalmoscopic** /-mə'skopik/ *adj*, **ophthalmoscopy** /-'moskəpi/ *n*

-opia /-'ohpi·ə/ *comb form* (→ *n*) condition of having (a specified visual defect) ⟨*dip*lopia⟩ ⟨*my*opia⟩ [NL, fr Gk *-ōpia*, fr *ōps* eye]

[1]**opiate** /'ohpi·ət, -,ayt/ *adj* **1** containing or mixed with opium **2** inducing sleep; narcotic

[2]**opiate** *n* **1** a preparation or derivative of opium; *broadly* a narcotic **2** sthg that induces inaction or calm

opine /oh'pien/ *vt* to state as an opinion – fml [MF *opiner*, fr L *opinari* to have an opinion]

opinion /ə'pinyən/ *n* **1a** a view or judgment formed about a particular matter **b** an esp favourable estimation ⟨*I have no great ~ of his work*⟩ **2a** a belief unsupported by positive knowledge **b** a generally held view **3a** a formal expression by an expert of his/her professional judgment or advice; *esp* a barrister's written advice to a client **b** *chiefly NAm* a formal expression of the principles on which a legal decision is based [ME, fr MF, fr L *opinion-*, *opinio*; akin to L *opinari*]

opinionated /ə'pinyə,naytid/ *adj* stubbornly sticking to one's own opinions – **opinionatedly** *adv*, **opinionatedness** *n*

opium /'ohpi·əm/ *n* the dried juice of the unripe seed capsules of the opium poppy, containing morphine and other addictive narcotic alkaloids [ME, fr L, fr Gk *opion*, fr dim. of *opos* sap]

'opium ,den *n* a place where opium can be bought and smoked

'opium ,poppy *n* an annual Eurasian poppy cultivated as the source of opium or for its edible seeds or showy flowers

opossum /ə'posəm/ *n, pl* **opossums** *also esp collectively* **opossum** any of various American (tree-dwelling) marsupial mammals; *also* any of several Australian phalangers resembling this [*âpäsûm* (lit., white animal) in some Algonquian language of Virginia]

[1]**opponent** /ə'pohnənt/ *n* one who takes the opposite side in a contest, conflict, etc [L *opponent-*, *opponens*, prp of *opponere*]

[2]**opponent** *adj* OPPOSITE 2

opportune /,opə'tyoohn, '--,-/ *adj* **1** suitable or convenient for a particular occurrence ⟨*an ~ moment*⟩ **2** occurring at an appropriate time [ME, fr MF *opportun*, fr L *opportunus*, fr *ob-* towards + *portus* port, harbour – more at OB-] – **opportunely** *adv*, **opportuneness** *n*

opportunism /,opə'tyooh,niz(ə)m/ *n* the taking advantage of opportunities or circumstances, esp with little regard for principles or consequences – **opportunist** *n or adj*, **opportunistic** /-'nistik/ *adj*

opportunity /,opə'tyoohnəti/ *n* **1** a favourable set of circumstances **2** a chance for advancement or progress

opposable /ə'pohzəbl/ *adj* **1** capable of being opposed or resisted **2** *of a thumb or other digit* capable of being placed opposite and against 1 or more of the remaining digits

oppose /ə'pohz/ *vt* **1** to place opposite or against sthg so as to provide counterbalance, contrast, etc **2** to offer resistance to [F *opposer*, fr L *opponere* (perf indic *opposui*), fr *ob-* against + *ponere* to place – more at OB-, POSITION] – **opposer** *n*

op'posed *adj* set in opposition; contrary

[1]**opposite** /ˈopəzit/ *n* **1** sthg or sby opposed or contrary **2** an antonym

[2]**opposite** *adj* **1a** set over against sthg that is at the other end or side of an intervening line or space ⟨*~ ends of a diameter*⟩ **b** *of plant parts* situated in pairs at the same level on opposite sides of an axis ⟨*~ leaves*⟩ – compare ALTERNATE 2a ☞ PLANT **2a** occupying an opposing position ⟨*~ sides of the question*⟩ **b** diametrically different; contrary **3** being the other of a matching or contrasting pair ⟨*the ~ sex*⟩ [ME, fr MF, fr L *oppositus*, pp of *opponere*] – **oppositely** *adv*, **oppositeness** *n*

[3]**opposite** *adv* on or to an opposite side

[4]**opposite** *prep* **1** across from and usu facing ⟨*sat ~ each other*⟩ **2** in a role complementary to ⟨*played ~ the leading lady*⟩

ˌopposite ˈnumber *n* a counterpart

opposition /ˌopəˈzish(ə)n/ *n* **1** an opposite position of 2 celestial bodies in which their longitude differs by 180 degrees – compare CONJUNCTION 3 ☞ SYMBOL **2** the relation between 2 propositions having the same subject and predicate but differing in quantity or quality or both **3** placing opposite or being so placed **4** hostile or contrary action **5** *sing or pl in constr* **a** the body of people opposing sthg **b** *often cap* a political party opposing the party in power – **oppositional** *adj*

oppress /əˈpres/ *vt* **1** to crush by harsh or authoritarian rule **2** to weigh heavily on the mind or spirit of [ME *oppressen*, fr MF *oppresser*, fr ML *oppressare*, fr L *oppressus*, pp of *opprimere*, fr *ob-* against + *premere* to press – more at OB-, [2]PRESS] – **oppressor** *n*

oppression /əˈpresh(ə)n/ *n* **1** unjust or harsh exercise of authority or power **2** a sense of being weighed down in body or mind [OPPRESS + -ION]

oppressive /əˈpresiv/ *adj* **1** unreasonably harsh or severe **2** tyrannical **3** physically or mentally depressing or overpowering – **oppressively** *adv*, **oppressiveness** *n*

opprobrious /əˈprohbri·əs/ *adj* scurrilous and abusive ⟨*~ language*⟩ – fml – **opprobriously** *adv*

opprobrium /əˈprohbri·əm/ *n* (a cause of) public infamy or disgrace – fml [L, fr *opprobrare* to reproach, fr *ob* in the way of + *probrum* reproach, fr *prober* guilty; akin to L *pro* forwards, *ferre* to carry, bring – more at OB-, FOR, [2]BEAR]

-opsis /-ˈopsis/ *comb form, pl* **-opses** /-ˈopseez/, **-opsides** /-ˈopsideez/ (→ *n*) thing (e g a plant part) resembling ⟨*karyopsis*⟩ [NL, fr Gk, fr *opsis* appearance, vision]

opsonin /ˈopsənin/ *n* an antibody in blood serum that makes foreign cells more susceptible to the action of phagocytes [L *opsonium* relish (fr Gk *opsōnion* victuals, fr *opsōnein* to purchase victuals, fr *opson* food + *ōneisthai* to buy) + E *-in*] – **opsonic** /opˈsonik/ *adj*

-opsy /-opsi, -əpsi/ *comb form* (→ *n*) examination ⟨*necropsy*⟩ ⟨*autopsy*⟩ [Gk *-opsia*, fr *opsis*]

opt /opt/ *vi* to decide in favour of sthg *USE* – usu + *for* [F *opter*, fr L *optare* – more at OPTION]

optative /ˈoptətiv/ *adj* of or belonging to a grammatical mood (e g in Greek) expressing wish or desire – **optative** *n*

[1]**optic** /ˈoptik/ *adj* of vision or the eye [MF *optique*, fr ML *opticus*, fr Gk *optikos*, fr *opsesthai* to be going to see; akin to Gk *opsis* appearance, *ōps* eye – more at EYE]

[2]**optic** *n* **1** the eye **2** any of the lenses, prisms, or mirrors of an optical instrument

optical /ˈoptikl/ *adj* **1** of optics **2a** visual ⟨*an ~ illusion*⟩ **b** visible ⟨*an ~ galaxy*⟩ **c** designed to aid vision ⟨*an ~ instrument*⟩ **3** of or using light ⟨*~ microscopy*⟩ – **optically** *adv*

optical activity *n* the ability (of some solutions) to rotate the plane of vibration of polarized light

ˌoptical ˈart *n* abstract art that uses linear or geometric patterns to create an optical illusion

optical fibre *n* a very thin glass or plastic fibre used in fibreoptics to transmit light ☞ TELECOMMUNICATION

optical glass *n* a high-quality glass used esp for making lenses

ˌoptical ilˈlusion *n* ILLUSION 2a(1)

optic axis *n* a line in a doubly refracting medium along which double refraction does not occur

optician /opˈtish(ə)n/ *n* one who prescribes correctional lenses for eye defects or supplies (lenses for) spectacles on prescription – compare OPHTHALMOLOGIST

optics /ˈoptiks/ *n pl but sing or pl in constr* **1** the science of the nature, properties, and uses of (radiation or particles that behave like) light **2** optical properties or components

optimal /ˈoptiml/ *adj* most satisfactory; optimum – **optimally** *adv*

optimism /ˈoptiˌmiz(ə)m/ *n* **1** the doctrine that this world is the best possible world **2** a tendency to emphasize favourable aspects of situations or events or to expect the best possible outcome [F *optimisme*, fr L *optimum*, n, best, fr neut of *optimus* best; akin to L *ops* power – more at OPULENT] – **optimist** *n*, **optimistic** /-ˈmistik/ *adj*, **optimistically** *adv*

optimum /ˈoptiməm/ *n, pl* **optima** /-mə/ *also* **optimums** (the amount or degree of) sthg that is most favourable to a particular end [L] – **optimum** *adj*, **optimize** /ˈoptiˌmiez/ *vt*

[1]**option** /ˈopsh(ə)n/ *n* **1** an act of choosing **2a** the power or right to choose **b** (a contract conveying) a right to buy or sell designated securities or commodities at a specified price during a stipulated period **3a** an alternative course of action **b** an item offered in addition to or in place of standard equipment [F, fr L *option-*, *optio* free choice; akin to L *optare* to choose, Gk epi*opsesthai* to be going to choose]

[2]**option** *vt* to grant or take an option on

optional /ˈopsh(ə)nl/ *adj* not compulsory; available as a choice – **optionally** *adv*

optometry /opˈtomətri/ *n* the art or profession of examining the eye for defects and prescribing correctional lenses or exercises but not drugs or surgery [Gk *optos* (verbal of *opsesthai* to be going to see) + ISV *-metry* – more at OPTIC] – **optometrist** *n*, **optometric** /ˌoptəˈmetrik/ *adj*

opt out *vi* to choose not to participate in sthg – often + *of*

opulent /ˈopyoolənt/ *adj* **1** wealthy, rich **2** abundant, profuse [L *opulentus*, fr *ops* power, wealth, help; akin to L *opus* work, Gk *ompnē* food, prosperity, Skt *apnas* possession, property] – **opulence** *n*, **opulently** *adv*

opuntia /oˈpunsh(y)ə/ *n* PRICKLY PEAR [NL, fr L, a plant, fr fem of *opuntius* of Opus, fr *Opunt-*, *Opus* Opus, ancient city in Greece]

opus /ˈohpəs/ *n, pl* **opera** /ˈop(ə)rə/ *also* **opuses** WORK 7; *specif* a musical composition or set of compositions, usu numbered in the order of issue [L *oper-, opus* – more at OPERATE]

opuscule /o'puskyoohl/ *n* a small or minor work (e g of literature) [F, fr L *opusculum*, dim. of *opus*]

[1]**or** /ə; *strong* aw/ *conj* **1a** – used to join 2 sentence elements of the same class or function and often introduced by *either* to indicate that what immediately follows is another or a final alternative ⟨*either sink ~ swim*⟩ ⟨*red, blue, ~ green*⟩ ⟨*coffee ~ tea ~ whisky*⟩ ⟨*whether you like it ~ not*⟩ **b** – used before the second and later of several suggestions to indicate approximation or uncertainty ⟨*five ~ six days*⟩ ⟨*a place such as Venice ~ Florence ~ somewhere like that – SEU S*⟩ – compare OR SO **2** and not – used after a neg ⟨*never drinks ~ smokes*⟩ **3** that is – used to indicate equivalence or elucidate meaning ⟨*lessen ~ abate*⟩ ⟨*a heifer ~ young cow*⟩ **4** – used to indicate the result of rejecting a preceding choice ⟨*hurry ~ you'll be late*⟩ **5** – used to introduce an afterthought ⟨$e=mc^2$*– ~ am I boring you?*⟩ [ME *other, or*, fr OE *oththe*; akin to OHG *eddo* or, ON *etha*] – **or so** – used to indicate an approximation or conjecture ⟨*I've known him 20 years* or so⟩

[2]**or** /aw/ *n* a gold colour; *also* yellow – used in heraldry [MF, gold, fr L *aurum* – more at ORIOLE]

[1]**-or** /-ə/ *suffix* (→ *n*) one that performs (a specified action) ⟨*vendor*⟩ [ME, fr OF *-eur, -eor* & L *-or*; OF *-eur*, fr L *-or*; OF *-eor*, fr L *-ator* -or, fr *-atus*, pp suffix + *-or* – more at [3]-ATE]

[2]**-or** /-ə/ *suffix* (→ *n*) quality, condition, or state of ⟨*horror*⟩ ⟨*tremor*⟩; *also* instance of (a specified quality or state) ⟨*an error*⟩ [ME, fr OF *-eur*, fr L *-or*]

orache, orach /'orich/ *n* a plant of the goosefoot family cultivated and eaten like spinach; *also* any of various related plants that occur as weeds [ME *orage*, fr MF *arrache*, fr (assumed) VL *atrapic-, atrapex*, fr Gk *atraphaxys*]

oracle /'orəkl/ *n* **1a** an often cryptic answer to some question, usu regarding the future, purporting to come from a deity **b** (a shrine housing) a priest or priestess who delivers oracles **2** (a statement by) a person giving wise or authoritative decisions [ME, fr MF, fr L *oraculum*, fr *orare* to speak – more at ORATION]

Oracle *trademark* – used for a service provided by ITV which transmits information (e g the weather or sports results) on usu special channels ☞ TELEVISION

oracular /o'rakyoolə/ *adj* **1** of or being an oracle **2** resembling an oracle (e g in solemnity or obscurity of expression) [L *oraculum*] – **oracularly** *adv*

[1]**oral** /'awrəl, 'o-/ *adj* **1a** uttered in words; spoken **b** using speech **2a** of, given through, or affecting the mouth ⟨*~ contraceptive*⟩ **b** of or characterized by (passive dependency, aggressiveness, or other personality traits typical of) the first stage of sexual development in which gratification is derived from eating, sucking, and later by biting – compare ANAL, GENITAL [L *or-, os* mouth; akin to OE *ōra* border, shore, L *ora* edge, border, Skt *ās* mouth] – **orally** *adv*, **orality** /aw'raləti, o-/ *n*

[2]**oral** *n* an oral examination

[1]**orange** /'orinj/ *n* **1a** (a small evergreen tree of the rue family with hard yellow wood and fragrant white flowers that bears) a spherical fruit with a reddish yellow leathery aromatic rind and sweet juicy edible pulp **2** any of several trees or fruits resembling the orange **3** a colour whose hue resembles that of the orange and lies between red and yellow in the spectrum [ME, fr MF, fr OProv *auranja*, fr Ar *nāranj*, fr Per *nārang*, fr Skt *nāranga* orange tree, of Dravidian origin; akin to Tamil *na ru* fragrant]

[2]**orange** *adj* of the colour orange

Orange *adj* of Orangemen ⟨*an ~ lodge*⟩ – **Orangeism** *n*

'Orangeman /-mən/ *n, pl* **Orangemen** /~/ **1** a member of a Protestant loyalist society in the north of Ireland **2** a Protestant Irishman, esp of Ulster [William III of England, Prince of *Orange* (fr *Orange*, city in France) †1702 Protestant ruler who deposed the Roman Catholic James II]

'orange ,peel *n* a pitted surface (e g on porcelain) like that of an orange

orangery /'orinj(ə)ri/ *n* a protected place (e g a greenhouse) for growing oranges in cool climates

'orange-,stick *n* a thin usu orangewood stick with a pointed end used in manicuring

'orange,wood /-,wood/ *n* the wood of the orange tree used esp for turning and carving

orangish /'orinjish/ *adj* rather orange

orangutan, orangoutan /aw,rang·(y)ooh'tan/ *n* a largely plant-eating tree-dwelling anthropoid ape of Borneo and Sumatra with brown skin and hair and very long arms [Malay *orang hutan*, fr *orang* man + *hutan* forest]

orangy, orangey /'orinji/ *adj* resembling an orange, esp in taste or colour

orate /aw'rayt/ *vi* to speak in an elevated and often pompous manner [back-formation fr *oration*]

oration /aw'raysh(ə)n/ *n* a speech delivered in a formal and dignified manner [L *oration-, oratio* speech, oration, fr *oratus*, pp of *orare* to plead, speak, pray; akin to Russ *orat'* to yell, Gk *ara, arē* prayer]

orator /'orətə/ *n* **1** one who delivers an oration **2** a skilled public speaker [ME *oratour*, fr MF or L; MF *orateur*, fr L *orator*, fr *oratus*, pp]

Oratorian /,orə'tawri·ən/ *n or adj* (a member) of the Congregation of the Oratory, a Roman Catholic preaching order founded by St Philip Neri in 1564

oratorio /,orə'tawrioh/ *n, pl* **oratorios** a choral work based usu on a religious subject and composed chiefly of recitatives, arias, and choruses without action or scenery [It, fr the *Oratorio* di San Filippo Neri (Oratory of St Philip Neri) in Rome, where musical religious services were held in the 16th c]

[1]**oratory** /'orət(ə)ri/ *n* **1** a place of prayer; *esp* a private or institutional chapel **2** *cap* an Oratorian congregation, house, or church [ME *oratorie*, fr LL *oratorium*, fr L *oratus*, pp]

[2]**oratory** *n* **1** the art of public speaking **2** public speaking characterized by (excessive) eloquence [L *oratoria*, fr fem of *oratorius* oratorical, fr *oratus*, pp]

orb /awb/ *n* **1** a spherical body; *esp* a celestial sphere **2** a sphere surmounted by a cross symbolizing royal power and justice [MF *orbe*, fr L *orbis* circle, disc, orb; akin to L *orbita* track, rut]

orbicular /aw'bikyoolə/ *adj* **1** spherical **2** circular ⟨*~ leaves*⟩ ☞ PLANT [ME *orbiculer*, fr MF or LL; MF *orbiculaire*, fr LL *orbicularis*, fr L *orbiculus*, dim. of *orbis*] – **orbicularly** *adv*, **orbicularity** /-'larəti/ *n*, **orbiculate** /-lət/ *adj*

[1]**orbit** /'awbit/ *n* **1** the bony socket of the eye **2** (1 complete passage of) a path described by one body in its revolution round another (e g that of the earth round the sun) ☞ SPACE **3** a sphere of influence **4** the eye – poetic [L *orbita*] – **orbital** *adj*

[2]**orbit** *vt* **1** to revolve in an orbit round **2** to send up and make revolve in an orbit ~ *vi* to travel in circles

orbital /'awbitl/ *n* an area round an atom or molecule inside which there is a high probability of finding 1 or 2 of the electrons that orbit round the atomic nuclei

orbiter /'awbitə/ *n* a spacecraft designed to orbit a celestial body without landing on its surface [[2]ORBIT + [2]-ER]

Orcadian /aw'kaydi·ən/ *n* a native or inhabitant of the Orkney islands [L *Orcades* Orkney islands] – **Orcadian** *adj*

orchard /'awchəd/ *n* a usu enclosed area in which fruit trees are planted [ME, fr OE *ortgeard*, prob fr L *hortus* garden + OE *geard* yard – more at [2]YARD]

orchestra /'awkistrə/ *n* **1** the circular space used by the chorus in front of the stage in an ancient Greek theatre **2** the space in front of the stage in a modern theatre that is used by an orchestra **3** a group of musicians including esp string players organized to perform ensemble music [L, fr Gk *orchēstra*, fr *orcheisthai* to dance; akin to Skt *ṛghāyati* he raves]

orchestral /aw'kestrəl/ *adj* of or composed for an orchestra – **orchestrally** *adv*

orchestrate /'awki,strayt/ *vt* **1** to compose or arrange (music) for an orchestra **2** to provide with orchestration ⟨~ *a ballet*⟩ – **orchestrator** *n*

orchestration /,awki'straysh(ə)n/ *n* (the style of) the arrangement of music for performance by an orchestra

orchid /'awkid/ *n* a plant or flower of a large family of plants related to the grasses and lilies and usu having striking 3-petalled flowers with an enlarged liplike middle petal ☞ ENDANGERED [irreg fr NL *Orchis*]

orchidectomy /,awki'dektəmi/ *n* the surgical removal of 1 or both testicles [irreg fr Gk *orchis* testicle + E *-ectomy*]

orchil /'awchil, 'awkil/ *n* a violet dye obtained from certain lichens [ME *orchell*, fr OF *orcheil*, perh deriv of L *herba urceolaris* plant for polishing glass pitchers, fr *urceolus*, dim. of *urceus* pitcher]

orchis /'awkis/ *n* an orchid, esp of a genus having fleshy roots and a spurred lip [NL, genus name, fr L, orchid, fr Gk, testicle, orchid; akin to MIr *uirgge* testicle; fr the shape of the tubers]

orchitis /aw'kietəs/ *n* inflammation of the testicles [NL, fr Gk *orchis* testicle]

ordain /aw'dayn/ *vt* **1** to invest officially with priestly authority (e g by the laying on of hands) **2a** to order by appointment, decree, or law; enact **b** to destine, foreordain [ME *ordeinen*, fr OF *ordener*, fr LL *ordinare*, fr L, to put in order, appoint, fr *ordin-*, *ordo* order] – **ordainment** *n*

ordeal /aw'deel/ *n* **1** a method formerly used to determine guilt or innocence by submitting the accused to dangerous or painful tests whose outcome was believed to depend on divine or supernatural intervention ⟨~ *by fire*⟩ **2** a severe or testing experience [ME *ordal*, fr OE *ordāl*; akin to OHG *urteil* judgment; both from a prehistoric WGmc compound derived fr a compound verb represented by OHG *irteilen* to judge, distribute, fr *ir-*, perfective prefix + *teilen* to divide, render a verdict; akin to OHG *teil* part – more at DEAL]

[1]**order** /'awdə/ *n* **1a** a religious body or community living under a specific rule and often required to take vows of renunciation of earthly things **b** a military decoration **2a** any of the several grades of the Christian ministry **b** *pl* the office of a person in the Christian ministry **3a** a rank or group in a community **b** a category in the classification of living things ranking above the family and below the class **4a(1)** a rank or level **(2)** a category or kind **b** arrangement of objects or events according to sequence in space, time, value, importance, etc **c** DEGREE 7a **d** the number of times mathematical differentiation is applied successively ⟨*derivatives of higher* ~⟩ **e** the number of columns or rows in a square matrix **f** the number of elements in a finite mathematical group **5a** (a sphere of) a sociopolitical system ⟨*the present economic* ~⟩ **b** regular or harmonious arrangement **6a** customary procedure, esp in debate ⟨*point of* ~⟩ **b** a prescribed form of a religious service **7a** the rule of law or proper authority ⟨*law and* ~⟩ **b** a specific rule, regulation, or authoritative direction **8a** a style of building; *esp* any of the classical styles of building ⟨*the Doric* ~⟩ **b** a column and entablature proportioned and decorated according to one of the classical styles **9** a proper, orderly, or functioning condition ⟨*telephone is out of* ~⟩ **10a** a written direction to pay money to sby **b** a direction to purchase, sell, or supply goods or to carry out work **c** goods bought or sold **d** an assigned undertaking – chiefly in *a tall order* **11** the style of dress and equipment for a specified purpose ⟨*troops in full marching* ~⟩ [MF *ordre*, fr ML & L; ML *ordin-*, *ordo* ecclesiastical order, fr L, arrangement, group, class; akin to L *ordiri* to lay the warp, begin] – **in order that** THAT 2a(1) – **in order to** for the purpose of – **in the order of** about as much or as many as; approximately – **on order** having been ordered – **to order** according to the specifications of an order ⟨*furniture made* to order⟩

[2]**order** *vt* **1** to put in order; arrange **2a** to give an order to; command **b** to command to go or come to a specified place **c** to place an order for ⟨~ *a meal*⟩ ~ *vi* to give or place an order

,order 'arms *n* a drill position in which the rifle is held vertically beside the right leg with the butt resting on the ground [fr the command *order arms!*]

'ordered *adj* **1** well regulated or ordered **2a** having elements succeeding or arranged according to rule **b** having a specified first element ⟨*a set of* ~ *pairs*⟩

,order in 'council *n*, *often cap O&C* an order made by the British sovereign on the advice of the privy council, giving the force of law to administrative regulations ☞ LAW

[1]**orderly** /'awdəli/ *adj* **1a** arranged in order; neat, tidy **b** liking or exhibiting order; methodical **2** well behaved; peaceful – **orderliness** *n*

[2]**orderly** *n* **1** a soldier assigned to carry messages, relay orders, etc for a superior officer **2** a hospital attendant who does routine or heavy work (e g carrying supplies or moving patients)

,order of 'magnitude *n* a range of magnitude

extending from a particular value to 10 times that value

ˌorder of the ˈday *n* **1** an agenda **2** the characteristic or dominant feature or activity

ˈorder ˌpaper *n* a programme of the day's business in a legislative assembly

[1]**ordinal** /ˈawdinl/ *n* **1a** *cap* (a book containing) the forms of service for ordination **b** a book containing the Roman Catholic services proper to every day of the year **2** ORDINAL NUMBER [(1) ME, fr ML *ordinale*, fr LL, neut of *ordinalis*, adj; (2) LL *ordinalis*, fr *ordinalis*, adj]

[2]**ordinal** *adj* of a specified order or rank in a series [LL *ordinalis*, fr L *ordin-, ordo*]

ordinal number *n* a number designating the place (e g first, second, or third) occupied by an item in an ordered set – compare CARDINAL NUMBER ☞ NUMBER

ordinance /ˈawdinəns/ *n* **1** an authoritative decree; *esp* a municipal regulation **2** a prescribed usage, practice, or ceremony [ME, fr MF & ML; MF *ordenance*, lit., act of arranging, fr ML *ordinantia*, fr L *ordinant-, ordinans*, prp of *ordinare* to put in order – more at ORDAIN]

ordinand /ˈawdiˌnand/ *n* a candidate for ordination [LL *ordinandus*, gerundive of *ordinare* to ordain]

[1]**ordinary** /ˈawdn(ə)ri, ˈawd(ə)nri/ *n* **1** *often cap* the invariable parts of the Mass – compare PROPER 2 **2** the regular or customary state of affairs – chiefly in *out of the ordinary* **3** any of the simplest heraldic charges bounded by straight lines (e g a chevron) [ME *ordinarie*, fr AF & ML; AF, fr ML *ordinarius*, fr L *ordinarius*, adj]

[2]**ordinary** *adj* **1** routine, usual **2** not exceptional; commonplace [ME *ordinarie*, fr L *ordinarius*, fr *ordin-, ordo* order] – **ordinarily** /-rili, ˈawd(ə)nˌeərili, ˌ--ˈ---/ *adv*, **ordinariness** *n*

Ordinary level *n, often cap L* an examination that is the lowest of the 3 levels of the British General Certificate of Education

ˌordinary ˈseaman *n* ☞ RANK

ordinary share *n* a share which has a claim on dividends or assets only after the claims of preference shares have been met – compare PREFERENCE SHARE, DEFERRED SHARE

ordinate /ˈawdinət/ *n* the coordinate of a point in a plane Cartesian coordinate system obtained by measuring parallel to the y-axis – compare ABSCISSA [NL (*linea*) *ordinate* (*applicata*), lit., line applied in an orderly manner]

ordination /ˌawdiˈnaysh(ə)n/ *n* (an) ordaining; being ordained

ordnance /ˈawdnəns/ *n* **1** (a branch of government service dealing with) military supplies **2** cannon, artillery [ME *ordinaunce*, fr MF *ordenance*, lit., act of arranging]

ˈordnance ˌdatum *n* a standard mean sea level used by the Ordnance Survey

ˌOrdnance ˈSurvey *n* (a British or Irish government organization that produces) a survey of Great Britain or Ireland published as a series of detailed maps

ordonnance /ˈawdənəns (*Fr* ɔrdɔnɑ̃ːs)/ *n* arrangement of parts (e g of a literary composition) [F, alter. of MF *ordenance*]

Ordovician /ˌawdoˈvishyən/ *adj or n* (of or being) the period of the Palaeozoic era between the Cambrian and the Silurian ☞ EVOLUTION [L *Ordovices*, ancient people in N Wales]

ordure /ˈawdyooə/ *n* excrement [ME, fr MF, fr *ord* filthy, fr L *horridus* horrid]

ore /aw/ *n* a mineral containing a metal or other valuable constituent for which it is mined [ME *or*, fr OE *ār*; akin to OHG *ēr* bronze, L *aes* copper, bronze, Skt *ayas* metal, iron]

öre /ˈuhrə/ *n, pl* **öre** ☞ *Denmark, Norway, Sweden* at NATIONALITY [Sw *öre* & Dan & Norw *øre*, fr L *aureus*, a gold coin]

oregano /oriˈgahnoh, əˈregənoh/ *n* a bushy plant of the mint family whose leaves are used as a herb in cooking [AmerSp *orégano*, fr Sp, wild marjoram, fr L *origanum*, fr Gk *origanon*]

ˌOregon ˈpine /ˈorigən/ *n* DOUGLAS FIR [*Oregon*, state of the USA]

organ /ˈawgən/ *n* **1a** a wind instrument consisting of sets of pipes made to sound by compressed air and controlled by keyboards; *also* an electronic keyboard instrument producing a sound approximating to that of an organ **b** REED ORGAN **c** any of various similar cruder instruments **2** a differentiated structure (e g the heart or a leaf) consisting of cells and tissues and performing some specific function in an organism **3** a subordinate organization that performs specialized functions ⟨*the various* ~s *of government*⟩ **4** a periodical [ME; partly fr OE *organa*, fr L *organum*, fr Gk *organon*, lit., tool, instrument; partly fr OF *organe*, fr L *organum*; akin to Gk *ergon* work – more at [1]WORK] – **organist** *n*

organ-, organo- *comb form* **1** organ; organs ⟨organo*genesis*⟩ **2** organic ⟨organo*mercurial*⟩ [ME, fr ML, fr L *organum*]

organdie, organdy /ˈawgəndi/ *n* a very fine transparent muslin with a stiff finish [F *organdi*]

organelle /ˌawgəˈnel/ *n* a part of a cell (e g a mitochondrion) that has a specialized structure and usu a specific function [NL *organella*, fr L *organum*]

ˈorgan-ˌgrinder *n* an itinerant street musician who operates a barrel organ

organic /awˈganik/ *adj* **1a** of or arising in a bodily organ **b** affecting the structure of the organism ⟨*an* ~ *disease*⟩ – compare FUNCTIONAL 1b **2a** of or derived from living organisms **b** of or being food produced using fertilizer solely of plant or animal origin without the aid of chemical fertilizers, pesticides, etc ⟨~ *farming*⟩ **3a** forming an integral element of a whole **b** having systematic coordination of parts **c** containing carbon compounds, esp those occurring in living organisms; *also* of or being the branch of chemistry dealing with these **d** resembling or developing in the manner of an organism **4** of or constituting the law by which a government exists – **organically** *adv*

organism /ˈawgəˌniz(ə)m/ *n* **1** a complex structure of interdependent and subordinate elements **2** a living being – **organismic** /-ˈnizmik/ *adj*, **organismal** /-ˈnizml/ *adj*

organ·ization, -isation /ˌawgənieˈzaysh(ə)n/ *n* **1a** organizing or being organized **b** the condition or manner of being organized **2a** an association, society **b** an administrative and functional body – **organizational** *adj*

organ·ize, -ise /ˈawgəˌniez/ *vt* **1** to cause to develop an organic structure **2** to arrange or form into a complete or functioning whole **3a** to set up an administrative structure for **b** to persuade to associate in an organization; *esp* to unionize ⟨~d *labour*⟩ **4** to arrange by systematic planning and effort ~ *vi* **1** to arrange elements into a whole **2** to form an organization, esp a trade union – **organizer** *n*

organoleptic /,awgənoh'leptik, aw,ganə-/ *adj* **1** involving or using 1 or more of the sense organs ⟨~ *evaluation of foods*⟩ **2** being, affecting, or relating to qualities (e g taste and smell) that stimulate the sense organs [F *organoleptique*, fr *organ-* + Gk *lēptikos* disposed to take, fr *lambanein* to take – more at LATCH]

organon /'awgə,non/ *n* an instrument for acquiring or ordering knowledge [Gk, lit., tool – more at ORGAN]

organophosphate /aw,ganə'fosfayt/ *n* an organic compound, esp a war gas or pesticide, containing phosphorus – **organophosphate** *adj*

organum /'awgənəm/ *n* an organon [ML, fr L, organ]

organza /aw'ganzə/ *n* a sheer dress fabric resembling organdie, usu made of silk, rayon, or nylon [prob alter. of *Lorganza*, a trademark]

organzine /'awgən,zeen/ *n* a raw silk yarn used for warp threads in fine fabrics [F or It; F *organsin*, fr It *organzino*, prob fr *Urgench*, town in USSR, where it was first manufactured]

orgasm /'aw,gaz(ə)m/ *n* intense or paroxysmal emotional excitement; *esp* (an instance of) the climax of sexual excitement, occurring typically as the culmination of sexual intercourse [NL *orgasmus*, fr Gk *orgasmos*, fr *organ* to grow ripe, be lustful; akin to Skt *ūrjā* sap, strength] – **orgasmic** /aw'gazmik/ *adj*, **orgastic** /aw'gastik/ *adj*

orgeat /'aw,zhah; (*Fr* ɔrʒa)/ *n* a sweet syrup or drink made with almonds and usu flower water and used esp as a cocktail ingredient [F, fr MF, fr *orge* barley, fr L *hordeum*; akin to OHG *gersta* barley, Gk *kri*]

orgy /'awji/ *n* **1** the secret rites of an ancient Greek or Roman deity, often accompanied by ecstatic singing and dancing **2a** drunken revelry **b** a wild party characterized by sexual promiscuity **3** an excessive or frantic indulgence in a specified activity ⟨*an ~ of destruction*⟩ [MF *orgie*, fr L *orgia*, pl, fr Gk; akin to Gk *ergon* work – more at [1]WORK] – **orgiastic** /-'astik/ *adj*

-oria /-'awri·ə/ *pl of* -ORIUM

-orial /-'awri·əl/ *suffix* (→ *adj*) of, belonging to, or connected with ⟨*sens*orial⟩ [ME, fr L *-orius* -ory + ME *-al*]

oribi /'orəbi, 'aw-/ *n, pl* **oribis** a small graceful tan-coloured antelope of S and E Africa [Afrik]

oriel window /'awri·əl/ *n* a bay window projecting from an upper storey and supported by a corbel or bracket [ME *oriel* porch, oriel window, fr MF *oriol* porch]

[1]orient /'awri·ənt, 'o-/ *n* **1** *cap* EAST 2 **2** a pearl of great lustre [ME, fr MF, fr L *orient-*, *oriens*, fr prp of *oriri* to rise – more at RISE]

[2]orient *adj* **1** lustrous, sparkling ⟨~ *gems*⟩ **2** *archaic* ORIENTAL 1

[3]orient /'awri,ent, 'o-/ *vt* **1a** to cause to face or point towards the east; *specif* to build (a church or temple) with the longitudinal axis pointing eastwards **b** to set in a definite position, esp in relation to the points of the compass **c** to ascertain the bearings of **2a** to adjust to an environment or a situation **b** to acquaint (oneself) with the existing situation or environment [F *orienter*, fr MF, fr *orient*]

oriental /,awri'entl, ,o-/ *adj* **1** *often cap* relating to or characteristic of the Orient **2a** *of a pearl or other precious stone* of superior grade, lustre, or value **b** being corundum but simulating another specified gem in colour ⟨~ *amethyst*⟩ **3** *often cap* relating to or having the characteristics of Orientals **4** *cap* of or being the biogeographic region that includes Asia S and SE of the Himalayas and part of the Malay archipelago

Oriental *n* a member of any of the indigenous peoples of the Orient

orientalist /,awri'entl·ist, ,o-/ *n, often cap* a specialist in oriental subjects

orientate /'awri·ən,tayt, 'o-/ *vt*, *chiefly Br* to orient ~ *vi* to face east

orientation /,awri·ən'taysh(ə)n, ,o-/ *n* **1a** orienting or being oriented **b** an arrangement or alignment **2** a lasting tendency of thought, inclination, or interest **3** change of position by (a part of) an organism in response to an external stimulus – **orientational** *adj*

orienteering /,awri·ən'tiəring, ,o-/ *n* a sport in which contestants traverse a usu difficult unfamiliar course using a map and compass to navigate their way between checkpoints [modif (influenced by *-eer*) of Sw *orientering*, fr *orientera* to orient] – **orienteer** *vi*

orifice /'orifis/ *n* an opening (e g a vent or mouth) through which sthg may pass [MF, fr LL *orificium*, fr L *or-*, *os* mouth + *-ficium* (fr *-ficus* -fic) – more at ORAL] – **orificial** /-'fish(ə)l/ *adj*

origami /,ori'gahmi/ *n* the (traditional Japanese) art or process of folding paper into complex shapes [Jap]

origanum /ə'rigənəm; *also* ,ori'gahnəm/ *n* oregano; *also* marjoram [ME, fr L, wild marjoram, fr Gk *origanon*]

origin /'orijin/ *n* **1** ancestry, parentage **2** a source or starting-point **3** the more fixed, central, or large attachment or part of a muscle **4** the intersection of coordinate axes [ME *origine*, prob fr MF, fr L *origin-*, *origo*, fr *oriri* to rise – more at RISE]

[1]original /ə'rijənl/ *n* **1** that from which a copy, reproduction, or translation is made **2** an eccentric person

[2]original *adj* **1** initial, earliest **2a** not secondary, derivative, or imitative **b** being the first instance or source of a copy, reproduction, or translation **3** inventive, creative – **originally** *adv*

originality /ə,rijə'naləti/ *n* **1** freshness, novelty **2** the power of imaginative and independent thought or creation [[2]ORIGINAL + -ITY]

o,riginal 'sin *n* (the doctrine of) man's innate sinfulness resulting from Adam's fall

originate /ə'rijə,nayt/ *vb* to (cause to) begin or come into existence – **originator** *n*, **origination** /-'naysh(ə)n/ *n*

orinasal /,awri'nayzl, ,o-/ *adj* NASAL 2b [L *or-*, *os* mouth + E *nasal*]

oriole /'awri,ohl, -əl/ *n* any of a family of birds with black and either orange or yellow plumage [F *oriol*, fr L *aureolus*, dim. of *aureus* golden, fr *aurum* gold; akin to Lith *auksas* gold]

orison /'oriz(ə)n/ *n, archaic* a prayer [ME, fr OF, fr LL *oration-*, *oratio*, fr L, oration]

-orium /-'awri·əm/ *suffix pl* **-oriums, -oria** /-'awri·ə/ (→ *n*) [1]-ORY ⟨*cremat*orium⟩ [L, fr neut of *-orius* -ory]

Oriya /o'ree(y)ə/ *n* the language of Orissa in India ☞ LANGUAGE

Orlon /'awlon/ *trademark* – used for an acrylic fibre

'orlop ,deck /'awlop/ *n* the lowest deck in a ship that has 4 or more decks ☞ SHIP [ME *overlop* deck of a single-decker, fr MLG *overlōp*, lit., something that overleaps]

ormer /'awmə/ *n* an abalone [F dial., prob deriv of L *auris maris* ear of the sea]

ormolu /'awmə,looh/ *n* gilded brass or bronze used to decorate furniture, ornaments, etc [F *or moulu*, lit., ground gold]

¹ornament /'awnəmənt/ *n* **1** sthg that lends grace or beauty; (a) decoration or embellishment **2** a person who adds honour or importance to sthg **3** an embellishing note not belonging to the essential harmony or melody [ME, fr OF *ornement*, fr L *ornamentum* equipment, decoration, fr *ornare*]

²ornament /'awnə,ment/ *vt* to add ornament to; embellish

ornamental /,awnə'mentl/ *adj or n* (of or being) a decorative object, esp a plant cultivated for its beauty – **ornamentally** *adv*

ornamentation /,awnəmen'taysh(ə)n/ *n* **1** ornamenting or being ornamented **2** sthg that ornaments; an embellishment

ornate /aw'nayt/ *adj* **1** rhetorical or florid in style **2** elaborately or excessively decorated [ME *ornat*, fr L *ornatus*, pp of *ornare* to furnish, embellish; akin to L *ordinare* to order – more at ORDAIN] – **ornately** *adv*, **ornateness** *n*

ornery /'awnəri/ *adj*, *NAm* cantankerous – infml [alter. of *ordinary*] – **orneriness** *n*

ornith-, ornitho- *comb form* bird ⟨ornitho*logy*⟩ [L, fr Gk, fr *ornith-*, *ornis*]

ornithology /,awnə'tholəji/ *n* a branch of zoology dealing with birds [NL *ornithologia*, fr *ornith-* + *-logia* -logy] – **ornithologist** *n*, **ornithological** /-thə'lojikl/ *adj*

¹oro- *comb form* mountain ⟨oro*logy*⟩ ⟨oro*geny*⟩ [Gk *oros*]

²oro- *comb form* mouth ⟨oro*pharynx*⟩ [L *or-*, *os* – more at ORAL]

orography /o'rografi/ *n* a branch of physical geography that deals with mountains [ISV ¹*oro-* + geo*graphy*] – **orographic** /,oroh'grafik, ,orə-/, **orographical** *adj*

orotund /'orətund, 'oroh-/ *adj* **1** marked by fullness of sound; sonorous **2** pompous, bombastic [modif of L *ore rotundo*, lit., with round mouth] – **orotundity** /,orə'tundəti, ,oroh-/ *n*

¹orphan /'awf(ə)n/ *n* **1** a child 1 or both of whose parents are dead **2** a young animal that has lost its mother [LL *orphanus*, fr Gk *orphanos*; akin to OHG *erbi* inheritance, L *orbus* orphaned] – **orphanhood** *n*

²orphan *vt* to cause to be an orphan

orphanage /'awf(ə)n·ij/ *n* an institution for the care of orphans

orphic /'awfik/ *adj* **1** *cap* of Orpheus or the rites or doctrines ascribed to him **2** mystic, oracular [L *Orphicus*, fr Gk *Orphikos*, fr *Orpheus*, poet & musician in Gk mythology]

Orphism /'aw,fiz(ə)m/ *n* an ancient Greek mystery religion [*Orpheus*, its reputed founder]

orphrey /'awfri/ *n* an ornamental border or band, esp on an ecclesiastical vestment [ME *orfrey*, fr MF *orfreis*, fr ML *aurifrigium*, fr L *aurum* gold + *Phrygius* Phrygian – more at ORIOLE]

orpiment /'awpimənt/ *n* arsenic trisulphide occurring as an orange to lemon yellow mineral and formerly used as a pigment [ME, fr MF, fr L *auripigmentum*, fr *aurum* + *pigmentum* pigment]

orpine /'awpin/ *n* a plant with fleshy leaves and pink or purple flowers [ME *orpin*, fr MF, fr *orpiment*]

Orpington /'awpingt(ə)n/ *n* (any of) an English breed of large deep-chested domestic fowls [*Orpington*, town in Kent, England]

orrery /'orəri/ *n* a clockwork apparatus showing the relative positions and motions of bodies in the solar system [Charles Boyle †1731 4th Earl of *Orrery*, for whom one was made]

orris /'oris/ *n* (a European iris with) a fragrant rootstock used esp in perfume and perfumed sachets [prob alter. of ME *ireos*, fr ML, alter. of L *iris*]

'orris,root /-,rooht/ *n* the fragrant rootstock of orris or another iris

orth-, ortho- *comb form* **1** straight; upright; vertical ⟨ortho*rhombic*⟩ **2** correct; corrective ⟨ortho*dontics*⟩ **3** containing the highest possible number of hydroxyl groups or molecules of water ⟨ortho*phosphate*⟩ **4 ortho-** *also* **orth-** involving substitution at 2 neighbouring positions in the benzene ring ⟨ortho-*xylene*⟩ – compare META-, PARA- [ME, fr MF, straight, right, true, fr L, fr Gk, fr *orthos* – more at ARDUOUS]

orthocephalic /,awthəsi'falik/, **orthocephalous** /-'sefələs/ *adj* having a medium ratio of the height to the length or breadth of the skull [NL *orthocephalus* orthocephalic person, fr *orth-* + Gk *kephalē* head – more at CEPHALIC] – **orthocephaly** /-'sefəli/ *n*

orthochromatic /,awthəkroh'matik, -thoh-, -krə-/ *adj* **1** of or producing natural tone values of light and shade in a photograph **2** sensitive to all colours except red ⟨~ *film*⟩ [ISV]

orthoclase /'awthə,klayz, -klays/ *n* a common feldspar consisting of potassium aluminium silicate [G *orthoklas*, fr *orth-* + Gk *klasis* breaking, fr *klan* to break – more at ¹HALT]

orthodontia /,awthoh'donsh(y)ə, -thə-/ *n* orthodontics [NL]

orthodontics /,awthə'dontiks/ *n pl but sing in constr* dentistry dealing with (the correction of) irregularities of the teeth – **orthodontic** /-tik/ *adj*, **orthodontist** *n*

orthodox /'awthə,doks/ *adj* **1a** conforming to established, dominant, or official doctrine (e g in religion) **b** conventional **2a** *cap* (consisting) of the Eastern churches headed by the patriarch of Constantinople which separated from the Western church in the 9th c and have characteristic and separate doctrines, liturgy, and forms of organization **b** *cap* relating to Judaism that keeps to strict and conservative interpretation of the Torah and rabbinic tradition [MF or LL; MF *orthodoxe*, fr LL *orthodoxus*, fr LGk *orthodoxos*, fr Gk *orth-* + *doxa* opinion – more at DOXOLOGY] – **orthodoxly** *adv*

orthodoxy /'awthədoksi/ *n* **1** being orthodox **2** an orthodox belief or practice

orthoepy /'awthoh,epi/ *n* the study of (correct) pronunciation [NL *orthoepia*, fr Gk *orthoepeia*, fr *orth-* + *epos* word – more at VOICE] – **orthoepic** /-'epik/ *adj*, **orthoepist** *n*

orthogenesis /,awthoh'jenəsis/ *n* the theory that social evolution takes place through the same stages in every culture [NL] – **orthogenetic** /-jə'netik/ *adj*

orthogonal /aw'thogənl/ *adj, of lines, planes, axes, etc* perpendicular to one another [MF, fr L *orthogonius*, fr Gk *orthogōnios*, fr *orth-* + *gōnia* angle – more at -GON] – **orthogonally** *adv*

orthographic /,awthə'grafik/ *also* **orthographical** /-kl/ *adj* **1** characterized by perpendicular lines or right angles **2** of orthography – **orthographically** *adv*

orthography /aw'thogrəfi/ *n* **1** correct spelling **2** the manner of spelling ☞ ALPHABET [ME *ortografie*, fr MF, fr L *orthographia*, fr Gk, fr *orth-* + *graphein* to write – more at CARVE]

orthopaedics, *NAm chiefly* **orthopedics** /,awthə'peediks/ *n pl but sing or pl in constr* the correction or prevention of skeletal and muscular deformities, esp by surgery [F *orthopédique*, adj, fr *orthopédie* orthopaedics, fr *ortho-* + Gk *paid-, pais* child] – **orthopaedic** *adj*, **orthopaedist** *n*

orthopteran, orthopteron /aw'thoptərən/ *n, pl* **orthopterans, orthoptera** /-rə/ any of an order of large insects (e g crickets and grasshoppers) with biting mouthparts and either no wings or 2 pairs of wings [NL *Orthoptera*, group name, fr *orth-* + Gk *pteron* wing – more at FEATHER] – **orthopteran** *adj*, **orthopterous** *adj*

orthorhombic /,awthoh'rombik/ *adj* of or constituting a system of crystal structure characterized by 3 unequal axes at right angles to each other [ISV]

orthoscopic /,awthə'skopik, -thoh-/ *adj* **1** giving an image in correct and normal proportions **2** giving a flat field of view [ISV *orth-* + *-scopic* (as in *microscopic*)]

ortolan /'awtələn, 'awtl·ən/ *n* a brown and greyish-green European bunting [F or It; F, fr It *ortolano*, lit., gardener, fr L *hortulanus*, fr *hortulus*, dim. of *hortus* garden – more at ²YARD]

¹**-ory** /-(ə)ri/ *suffix* (→ *n*) **1** place of or for ⟨*observatory*⟩ ⟨*refectory*⟩ **2** sthg that serves for ⟨*directory*⟩ [ME *-orie*, fr L *-orium*, fr neut of *-orius*, adj suffix]

²**-ory** *suffix* (→ *adj*) **1** of or involving ⟨*gustatory*⟩ ⟨*compulsory*⟩ **2** serving for or producing ⟨*justificatory*⟩ [ME *-orie*, fr MF & L; MF, fr L *-orius*]

oryx /'oriks/ *n, pl* **oryxes,** *esp collectively* **oryx** any of a genus of large straight-horned African antelopes [NL, genus name, fr L, a gazelle, fr Gk, pickaxe, antelope, fr *oryssein* to dig – more at ROUGH]

Oscan /'oskən/ *n* (the language of) a member of a people of ancient Italy inhabiting Campania [L *Oscus*] – **Oscan** *adj*

¹**Oscar** /'oskə/ *n* a statuette awarded annually by a US professional organization for outstanding achievement in the cinema [*Oscar* Pierce, 20th-c US wheat and fruit grower]

²**Oscar** – a communications code word for the letter *o*

oscillate /'osi,layt/ *vi* **1a** to swing backwards and forwards like a pendulum **b** to move or travel back and forth between 2 points **2** to vary between opposing beliefs, feelings, or courses of action [L *oscillatus*, pp of *oscillare* to swing, fr *oscillum* swing] – **oscillatory** /'osilət(ə)ri/ *adj*

oscillation /,osi'laysh(ə)n/ *n* **1** oscillating **2** a variation, fluctuation **3** a flow of electricity periodically changing direction **4** a single swing (e g of sthg oscillating) from one extreme limit to the other

oscillator /'osi,laytə/ *n* **1** sby or sthg that oscillates **2** a device for producing alternating current; *esp* a radio-frequency or audio-frequency signal generator

oscillograph /ə'silə,grahf, -,graf/ *n* an instrument for recording (electrical) oscillations [F *oscillographe*, fr L *oscillare* + F *-graphe* -graph] – **oscillographic** /-'grafik/ *adj*, **oscillography** /,osi'logrəfi/ *n*

oscilloscope /ə'silə,skohp/ *n* an instrument in which electrical oscillations register as a temporary visible wave form on the fluorescent screen of a cathode-ray tube [L *oscillare* + ISV *-scope*] – **oscilloscopic** /-'skopik/ *adj*

oscine /'osien/ *adj* of or being a suborder of passerine birds with vocal cords specialized for singing [L *oscin-, oscen* bird used in divination, fr *obs-* in front of + *canere* to sing – more at OSTENSIBLE, CHANT] – **oscine** *n*

osculate /'oskyoo,layt/ *vt* to kiss – humor or fml [L *osculatus*, pp of *osculari*, fr *osculum* kiss, fr dim. of *os* mouth – more at ORAL] – **osculation** /-'laysh(ə)n/ *n*

osculum /'oskyooləm/ *n* an opening in a sponge from which a current of water flows out [NL, fr L, dim. of *os* mouth]

¹**-ose** /-ohs; *also* -ohz/ *suffix* (→ *adj*) **1** full of; possessing the quality of ⟨*verbose*⟩ ⟨*bellicose*⟩ **2** having; consisting of; resembling ⟨*frond* ose⟩ ⟨*ramose*⟩ ⟨*globose*⟩ [ME, fr L *-osus*] – **-osity** /-'osəti/ *suffix* (→ *n*)

²**-ose** /-ohz, -ohs/ *suffix* (→ *n*) **1** carbohydrate ⟨*amylose*⟩; *esp* sugar ⟨*fructose*⟩ **2** primary product of hydrolytic breakdown ⟨*pro* teose⟩ ⟨*peptose*⟩ [F, fr *glucose*]

osier /'ohzhə/ *n* **1** any of various willows whose pliable twigs are used for furniture and basketry **2** a willow rod used in basketry – compare WITHY [ME, fr MF, fr ML *auseria* osier bed]

-osis /-'ohsis/ *suffix, pl* **-oses** /-'ohseez/, **-osises** /-ohsiseez/ (→ *n*) **1a** action, process, or condition of ⟨*hypnosis*⟩ ⟨*metamorphosis*⟩ **b** abnormal or pathological condition of ⟨*thrombosis*⟩ **2** increase or formation of ⟨*leucocytosis*⟩ [ME, fr L, fr Gk *-ōsis*, fr *-ō-* (stem of causative verbs in *-oun*) + *-sis*] – **-otic** /-'otik/ *adj*, **-otically** *adv*

Osmanli /oz'manli/ *n* **1** a member of the W branch of the Turkish peoples **2** Turkish [Turk *osmanl*, fr *Osman* †1326 founder of the Ottoman Empire]

osmiridium /,ozmi'ridi·əm, os-/ *n* a hard naturally occurring alloy that consists chiefly of iridium and osmium and is used esp for pen nibs [Gk *osmē* + NL *iridium*]

osmium /'ozmi·əm/ *n* a hard grey to black polyvalent metallic element of the platinum group that is the heaviest metal known ☞ PERIODIC TABLE [NL, fr Gk *osmē* smell] – **osmic** /'ozmik/ *adj*

osmometer /oz'momitə, os-/ *n* an apparatus for measuring osmotic pressure [*osmosis* + *-meter*] – **osmometric** /-mə'metrik/ *adj*, **osmometry** /-'momitri/ *n*

osmoregulation /,ozmoh,regyoo'laysh(ə)n, ,os-/ *n* the usu automatic regulation of osmotic pressure, esp in the body of an organism [*osmosis* + *regulation*]

osmose /'ozmohs, -mohz, 'os-/ *vi* to diffuse by osmosis [back-formation fr *osmosis*]

osmosis /oz'mohsis, os-/ *n* **1** movement of a solvent through a semipermeable membrane (e g of a living cell) into a solution of higher concentration that tends to equalize the concentrations on the 2 sides of the membrane **2** a process of absorption or diffusion suggestive of osmosis [NL, short for *endosmosis*] – **osmotic** /-'motik/ *adj*

osmotic pressure /oz'motik, os-/ *n* the pressure produced by or associated with osmosis and dependent on concentration and temperature

osmunda /oz'mundə/ *n* any of a genus of large ferns [NL, genus name, fr ML, osmunda, fr OF *osmonde*]

osprey /'ospray, -pri/ *n* **1** a large fish-eating hawk with dark brown and white plumage **2** a feather trimming used for millinery [ME *ospray*, fr (assumed) MF *osfraie*, fr L *ossifraga*]

ossein /'osi·in/ *n* the collagen of bones [ISV, fr L *oss-, os*]

osseous /'osi·əs/ *adj* BONY 1 [L *osseus*, fr *oss-, os* bone; akin to Gk *osteon* bone, Skt *asthi*]

ossicle /'osikl/ *n* a small bone or bony structure (e g in the middle ear) [L *ossiculum*, dim. of *oss-, os*] – **ossicular** /o'sikyoolə/ *adj*

ossifrage /'osifrij, -,frayj/ *n* a lammergeier [L *ossifraga* sea eagle, fr fem of *ossifragus* bone-breaking, fr *oss-, os* + *frangere* to break – more at BREAK]

ossify /'osi,fie/ *vi* **1** to become bone **2** to become unfeeling, unimaginative, or rigid ~ *vt* to change (e g cartilage) into bone [prob fr (assumed) NL *ossificare*, fr L *oss-, os*] – **ossification** /-fi'kaysh(ə)n/ *n*

ossuary /'osyooəri/ *n* a container for the bones of the dead [LL *ossuarium*, fr L, neut of *ossuarius* of bones, fr OL *ossua*, pl of *oss-, os*]

oste-, osteo- *comb form* bone ⟨oste*al*⟩ ⟨osteo*myelitis*⟩ [NL, fr Gk, fr *osteon* – more at OSSEOUS]

ostensible /o'stensəbl/ *adj* being such in appearance rather than reality; professed, declared [F, fr L *ostensus*, pp of *ostendere* to show, fr *obs-* in front of (akin to *ob-* in the way) + *tendere* to stretch – more at OB-, THIN] – **ostensibly** *adv*

ostensive /o'stensiv/ *adj* of or being definition by means of displaying or pointing to the thing or quality being defined – **ostensively** *adv*

ostentation /,osten'taysh(ə)n/ *n* unnecessary display of wealth, knowledge, etc designed to impress or attract attention [ME *ostentacioun*, fr MF *ostentation*, fr L *ostentation-, ostentatio*, fr *ostentatus*, pp of *ostentare* to display ostentatiously, fr *ostentus*, pp of *ostendere*] – **ostentatious** /-shəs/ *adj*, **ostentatiously** *adv*, **ostentatiousness** *n*

osteoarthritis /,ostiohah'thrietəs/ *n* degenerative arthritis [NL] – **osteoarthritic** /-'thritik/ *adj*

osteomalacia /,ostiohmə'laysh(y)ə/ *n* softening of the bones, esp in elderly people, equivalent to rickets in young people [NL, fr *oste-* + Gk *malakia* softness, fr *malakos* soft – more at MALAC-]

osteomyelitis /,ostiohmie·ə'lietəs/ *n* an infectious inflammatory disease of bone (marrow) [NL]

osteopathy /,osti'opəthi/ *n* a system of treatment of diseases based on the theory that they can be cured by manipulation of bones [NL *osteopathia*, fr *oste-* + L *-pathia* -pathy] – **osteopath** /'osti·ə,path/ *n*, **osteopathic** /-'pathik/ *adj*

osteophyte /'osti·ə,fiet/ *n* an abnormal outgrowth from a bone [ISV] – **osteophytic** /-'fitik/ *adj*

ostinato /,osti'nahtoh/ *n, pl* **ostinatos** a musical figure repeated persistently at the same pitch throughout a composition – compare IMITATION 3, SEQUENCE 1b [It, obstinate, fr L *obstinatus*]

ostler, *chiefly NAm* **hostler** /'oslə/ *n* a groom or stableman at an inn [ME *osteler, hosteler* innkeeper, ostler, fr *hostel*]

Ostmark /'ost,mahk, 'awst-/ *n* ☞ *Germany (Democratic Republic)* at NATIONALITY [G, lit., East mark]

-ostosis /-o'stohsis/ *comb form, pl* **-ostoses** /-seez/, **-ostosises** /-səseez/ (→ *n*) conversion into bone of (a specified part) or to (a specified degree) ⟨*hyper*ostosis⟩ [NL, fr Gk *-ostōsis*, fr *osteon* bone – more at OSSEOUS]

ostracism /'ostrə,siz(ə)m/ *n* **1** temporary banishment by popular vote as practised in ancient Greece **2** exclusion by general consent from common privileges or social acceptance

ostrac·ize, -ise /'ostrə,siez/ *vt* to exile or exclude by ostracism [Gk *ostrakizein* to banish by voting with potsherds, fr *ostrakon* shell, potsherd – more at OYSTER]

ostrich /'ostrich, *also* 'ostrij/ *n* **1** a swift-footed 2-toed flightless bird that has valuable wing and tail plumes and is the largest of existing birds **2** one who refuses to face up to unpleasant realities [ME, fr OF *ostrusce*, fr (assumed) VL *avis struthio*, fr L *avis* bird + LL *struthio* ostrich, irreg fr Gk *strouthos*; (2) fr the belief that the ostrich when pursued hides its head in the sand and believes itself to be unseen]

Ostrogoth /'ostrə,goth/ *n* a member of the E branch of the Goths [LL *Ostrogothi*, pl, of Gmc origin] – **Ostrogothic** /-'gothik/ *adj*

ot-, oto- *comb form* ear ⟨ot*itis*⟩; ear and ⟨oto*laryngology*⟩ [Gk *ōt-, ōto-*, fr *ōt-, ous* – more at [1]EAR]

[1]other /'udhə/ *adj* **1a** being the 1 left of 2 or more ⟨*held on with 1 hand and waved with the ~ one*⟩ **b** being the ones distinct from that or those first mentioned ⟨*taller than the ~ boys*⟩ **c** SECOND 2 ⟨*every ~ day*⟩ **2a** not the same; different ⟨*schools ~ than her own*⟩ **b** far, opposite ⟨*lives the ~ side of town*⟩ **3** additional, further ⟨*John and 2 ~ boys*⟩ **4** recently past ⟨*the ~ evening*⟩ [ME, fr OE *ōther*; akin to OHG *andar* other, Skt *antara*]

[2]other *pron, pl* **others** *also* **other** **1** the remaining or opposite one ⟨*went from one side to the ~*⟩ ⟨*the ~s came later*⟩ **2** a different or additional one ⟨*some film or ~*⟩ ⟨*some left, but many ~s stayed*⟩ – compare ANOTHER, ONE ANOTHER

[3]other *adv* otherwise – + *than* ⟨*can't get there ~ than by swimming*⟩

,other-di'rected *adj* directed in thought and action primarily by external influences rather than by one's own values

'otherness /-nis/ *n* the state of being other or different

other rank *n, chiefly Br* a military person not holding commissioned rank

[1]'other,wise /-,wiez/ *adv* **1** in a different way **2** in different circumstances ⟨*might ~ have left*⟩ **3** in other respects ⟨*an ~ excellent dinner*⟩ **4** if not; or else ⟨*do what I say, ~ you'll be sorry*⟩ **5** not – used to express the opposite ⟨*mothers, whether married or ~*⟩ ⟨*guilty unless proved ~*⟩ **6** alias ⟨*Chee Soo, ~ Cliff Gibbs – Sportsworld*⟩ [ME, fr OE (*on*) *ōthre wīsan* in another manner]

[2]**otherwise** *adj* of a different kind ⟨*how can I be ~ than grateful*⟩

ˌ**other'worldly** *adj* concerned with spiritual or intellectual matters rather than the material world – **otherworldliness** *n*

otic /'ohtik/ *adj* of or located in the region of the ear [Gk *ōtikos*, fr *ōt-*, *ous* ear – more at [1]EAR]

-otic /-'ohtik/ *comb form* (→ *adj*) having (a specified relationship to) the ear ⟨*peri*otic⟩ [Gk *ōtikos*]

otiose /'ohshiˌohs, 'ohti-/ *adj* **1** at leisure; idle **2** futile, pointless *USE* fml [L *otiosus*, fr *otium* leisure] – **otiosely** *adv*, **otioseness** *n*

oto- – see OT-

otolith /'ohtohˌlith/ *n* any of many minute lumps of calcite and protein in the internal ear that are receptors for the sense of balance [F *otolithe*, fr *ot-* + *-lithe* -lith] – **otolithic** /-'lithik/ *adj*

Otomac /ˌohtə'mahk, -'mak/ *n* a member, or the language, of an extinct people of S Venezuela

ottava /oh'tahvə/ *adv or adj* at an octave higher or lower than written – used in music ☞ MUSIC [It, octave, fr ML *octava*]

otˌtava 'rima /'reemə/ *n, pl* **ottava rimas** a stanza of 8 lines of 10 syllables each in English or 11 in Italian with a rhyme scheme of *abababcc* [It, lit., eighth rhyme]

otter /'otə/ *n, pl* **otters,** *esp collectively* **otter** **1** (the dark brown fur or pelt of) any of several aquatic fish-eating mammals with webbed and clawed feet, related to the weasels **2a** an otterboard **b** a paravane [ME *oter*, fr OE *otor*; akin to OHG *ottar* otter, Gk *hydros* water snake, *hydōr* water – more at WATER]

'otterˌboard /-ˌbawd/ *n* either of 2 boards that keep the mouth of a trawl net open

otto /'otoh/ *n* attar [by alter.]

ottoman /'otəmən/ *n* **1** *cap* a Turk **2a** a usu heavily upholstered box or seat without a back or arms **b** a cushioned stool for the feet [(2) F *ottomane*, fr fem of *ottoman*, adj]

Ottoman *adj* TURKISH 1 [F, adj & n, prob fr It *ottomano*, fr Ar *'othmānī*, fr *'Othmān* Othman (Osman) †1326 founder of the Ottoman Empire]

ouabain /wah'bah·in, 'wahbahˌeen/ *n* a glycoside obtained from several African shrubs or trees of the periwinkle family and used medically like digitalis [ISV, fr F *ouabaïo*, an African tree, fr Somali *waba yo*]

oubliette /ˌoohbli'et/ *n* a dungeon with an opening only at the top ☞ CHURCH [F, fr MF, fr *oublier* to forget, fr L *oblitus*, pp of *oblivisci* – more at OBLIVION]

[1]**ouch** /owch/ *n, archaic* a setting for a precious stone [ME, alter. (by incorrect division of *a nouche*) of *nouche*, fr MF, of Gmc origin; akin to OHG *nusca* clasp; akin to OE *nett* net]

[2]**ouch** *interj* – used esp to express sudden sharp pain [origin unknown]

[1]**ought** /awt/ *verbal auxiliary* – used to express moral obligation ⟨*~ to pay our debts*⟩, advisability ⟨*~ to be boiled for 10 minutes*⟩, enthusiastic recommendation ⟨*you ~ to hear her sing*⟩, natural expectation ⟨*~ to have arrived by now*⟩, or logical consequence ⟨*the result ~ to be infinity*⟩; used in the negative to express moral condemnation of an action ⟨*you ~ not to treat him like that*⟩; often used with the perfect infinitive to express unfulfilled obligation ⟨*~ never to have been allowed*⟩ [ME *oughte* (1 & 3 sing. pres indic), fr *oughte*, 1 & 3 sing. past indic & subj of *owen* to own, owe – more at OWE]

[2]**ought** *n or adj* (a) zero [var of *aught*]

oughtn't /'awtnt/ ought not

ouguiya /ooh'geeə/ *n* ☞ *Mauritania* at NATIONALITY [of Ar origin]

Ouija /'weejə, -ji/ *trademark* – used for a board with the alphabet and other signs on it that is used to produce automatic writing in spiritualistic seances

[1]**ounce** /owns/ *n* **1a** ☞ UNIT **b** a small amount ⟨*an ~ of common sense*⟩ **2** FLUID OUNCE ☞ UNIT [ME, fr MF *unce*, fr L *uncia* twelfth part, ounce, fr *unus* one – more at ONE]

[2]**ounce** *n* SNOW LEOPARD [ME *unce, once*, fr OF *once*, alter. of *lonce*, fr (assumed) VL *lyncea*, fr L *lync-*, *lynx* lynx – more at LYNX]

our /'owə, ah/ *adj* of us, ourself, or ourselves, esp as possessors or possessor ⟨*~ throne*⟩, agents or agent ⟨*~ discovery*⟩, or objects or object of an action ⟨*~ being chosen*⟩; of everybody ⟨*~ Saviour*⟩ [ME *oure*, fr OE *ūre*; akin to OHG *unsēr* our, OE *ūs* us]

ˌ**Our 'Father** *n* LORD'S PRAYER [fr its opening words]

ˌ**Our 'Lady** *n* VIRGIN MARY

ours /'owəz, ahz/ *pron, pl* **ours** that which or the one who belongs to us – used without a following noun as a pronoun equivalent in meaning to the adjective *our*; compare phrases at MINE

our'self /-'self/ *pron* myself – referring to the single-person subject when *we* is used instead of *I* (e g by a sovereign)

our'selves /-'selvz/ *pron, pl in constr* **1** those identical people that are we – used reflexively ⟨*we're doing it solely for ~*⟩ or for emphasis ⟨*we ~ will never go*⟩; compare ONESELF **2** our normal selves ⟨*not feeling quite ~*⟩

-ous /-əs/ *suffix* (→ *adj*) **1** full of; characterized by; possessing the quality of ⟨*clamor*ous⟩ ⟨*envi*ous⟩ **2** having a valency relatively lower than in (specified compounds or ions named with an adjective ending in *-ic*) ⟨*ferr*ous⟩ ⟨*mercur*ous⟩ [ME; partly fr OF *-ous, -eus, -eux*, fr L *-osus*; partly fr L *-us*, nom sing. masc ending of many adjectives] – **-ously** *suffix* (→ *adv*)

ousel /'oohzl/ *n* an ouzel

oust /owst/ *vt* **1** to remove from or dispossess of property or position **2** to take the place of; supplant [AF *ouster*, fr OF *oster*, fr LL *obstare* to ward off, fr L, to stand against, fr *ob-* against + *stare* to stand – more at OB-, STAND]

ouster /'owstə/ *n* illegal dispossession [AF, to oust]

[1]**out** /owt/ *adv* **1a** away from the inside or centre ⟨*went ~ into the garden*⟩ **b** from among other things ⟨*separate ~ the bad apples*⟩ **c** away from the shore, the city, or one's homeland ⟨*~ at sea*⟩ ⟨*go ~ to Africa*⟩ ⟨*live ~ in the country*⟩ **d** away from a particular place, esp of one's home or business ⟨*~ for lunch*⟩ ⟨*~ on strike*⟩ ⟨*move ~ into lodgings*⟩ – compare OUTSIDE **e(1)** clearly in or into view ⟨*when the sun's ~*⟩ – compare COME OUT **(2)** *of a flower* in or into full bloom **2a(1)** out of the proper place ⟨*left a word ~*⟩ ⟨*put his shoulder ~*⟩ **(2)** amiss in reckoning ⟨*more than 4 lb ~ – Punch*⟩ **b** in all directions from a central point of control ⟨*lent ~ money*⟩ **c** from political power ⟨*voted them ~*⟩ **d** into shares or portions ⟨*parcelled ~ the farm*⟩ **e**

out of vogue or fashion **3a** to or in a state of extinction or exhaustion ⟨*burn* ~⟩ ⟨*before the year is* ~⟩ – compare RUN OUT **b** to the fullest extent or degree; completely ⟨*all decked* ~⟩ ⟨*hear me* ~⟩ ⟨*clean* ~ *the attic*⟩ **c** in or into a state of determined effort ⟨~ *to fight pollution*⟩ **4a** aloud ⟨*cried* ~⟩ ⟨~ *with it!*⟩ **b** in existence; ever – with a superlative; infml ⟨*the funniest thing* ~⟩ **5** so as to be put out of a game ⟨*bowled* ~⟩ **6** – used on a 2-way radio circuit to indicate that a message is complete and no reply is expected [ME, fr OE *ūt*; akin to OHG *ūz* out, Gk *hysteros* later, *hybris* arrogance, Skt *ud* up, out]

[2]**out** *vi* to become publicly known

[3]**out** *adj* **1** located outside; external **2** located at a distance; outlying ⟨*the* ~ *islands*⟩ **3** not being in operation or power ⟨*the fire's* ~⟩ **4** directed or serving to direct outwards ⟨*the* ~ *tray*⟩ **5** not allowed to continue batting **6** out of the question ⟨*your suggestion's definitely* ~⟩

[4]**out** *prep* OUT OF 1a(1)

[5]**out** *n* a way of escaping from an embarrassing or difficult situation

out- *prefix* **1** forth ⟨out*cry*⟩ ⟨out*burst*⟩ ⟨out*rush*⟩ **2** result; product ⟨out*put*⟩ ⟨out*come*⟩ **3** in a manner that goes beyond, surpasses, or excels ⟨out*manoeuvre*⟩ ⟨out*strip*⟩ [[1]*out*]

outage /'owtij/ *n* a period of nonoperation (e g of a power supply)

,out-and-'out *adj* being completely as specified at all times or from every point of view ⟨*an* ~ *liar*⟩ – **out-and-outer** *n*

'out,back /-,bak/ *n* isolated rural (Australian) country

,out'balance /-'baləns/ *vt* to outweigh in value or importance

,out'bid /-'bid/ *vt* **outbid; -dd-** to make a higher bid than

[1]**'out,board** /-,bawd/ *adj* **1** situated outboard **2** having, using, or limited to the use of an outboard motor

[2]**outboard** *adv* **1** in a lateral direction from the hull of a ship or the fuselage of an aircraft **2** in a position closer or closest to either of the wing tips of an aeroplane or of the sides of a motor vehicle

[3]**outboard** *n* **1 outboard, outboard motor** a motor, propeller, and rudder attached as a unit to the stern of a small boat **2** a boat with an outboard

'out,break /-,brayk/ *n* **1a** a sudden or violent breaking out ⟨*the* ~ *of war*⟩ **b** a sudden increase in numbers of a harmful organism or in sufferers from a disease within a particular area ⟨*an* ~ *of locusts*⟩ ⟨*an* ~ *of measles*⟩ **2** an insurrection, revolt

'out,breeding /-,breeding/ *n* interbreeding of relatively unrelated animals or plants – **outbreed** /-'-/ *vt*

'out,building /-,bilding/ *n* a smaller building (e g a stable or a woodshed) separate from but belonging to a main building

'out,burst /-,buhst/ *n* **1** a violent expression of feeling **2** a surge of activity or growth

'out,cast /-,kahst/ *n* one who is cast out by society – **outcast** *adj*

'out,caste /-,kahst/ *n* **1** a Hindu who has been ejected from his/her caste **2** one who has no caste

,out'class /-'klahs/ *vt* to excel, surpass

'out,come /-,kum/ *n* a result, consequence

[1]**'out,crop** /-,krop/ *n* **1** (the emergence of) the part of a rock formation that appears at the surface of the ground **2** an outbreak

[2]**,out'crop** *vi* **-pp-** to project as an outcrop

'out,cry /-,krie/ *n* **1** a loud cry; a clamour **2** a public expression of anger or disapproval

,out'dated /-'daytid/ *adj* outmoded

,out'distance /-'dist(ə)ns/ *vt* to go far ahead of (e g in a race)

,out'do /-'dooh/ *vt* **outdoes** /-'duz/; **outdid** /-'did/; **outdone** /-'dun/ to surpass in action or performance

'out,door /-,daw/ *also* **,out'doors** *adj* **1** of or performed outdoors **2** not enclosed; without a roof ⟨*an* ~ *restaurant*⟩ [*out* (*of*) *door, out* (*of*) *doors*]

[1]**,out'doors** *adv* outside a building; in or into the open air

[2]**,out'doors** *n pl but sing in constr* **1** *the* open air **2** *the* world remote from human habitation ⟨*the great* ~⟩

outer /'owtə/ *adj* **1** existing independently of the mind; objective **2a** situated farther out ⟨*the* ~ *limits*⟩ **b** away from a centre ⟨*the* ~ *planets*⟩ **c** situated or belonging on the outside ⟨*the* ~ *covering*⟩ [ME, fr [3]*out* + *-er*, compar suffix] – **outermost** /-,mohst/ *adj*

,outer 'ear *n* the outer visible part of the ear together with the canal through which sound waves reach the eardrum ☞ NERVE

,outer 'space *n* space outside the earth's atmosphere

,out'face /-'fays/ *vt* **1** to cause to waver or submit (as if) by staring **2** to confront unflinchingly; defy

'out,fall /-,fawl/ *n* the outlet for a river, lake, drain, sewer, etc

'out,field /-,feeld/ *n* the part of a cricket field beyond the prepared section on which wickets are laid out or of a baseball field furthest from the bases – **outfielder** *n*

[1]**'out,fit** /-,fit/ *n* **1a** a complete set of equipment needed for a particular purpose **b** a set of garments worn together, often for a specified occasion or activity **2** *sing or pl in constr* a group that works as a team – infml

[2]**outfit** *vt* **-tt-** to equip with an outfit

'out,fitter /-,fitə/ *n* one who supplies an outfit or equipment; *esp* a retailer in men's clothing

,out'flank /-'flangk/ *vt* **1** to go round or extend beyond the flank of (an opposing force) **2** to gain an advantage over by doing sthg unexpected

'out,flow /-,floh/ *n* **1** a flowing out **2** sthg that flows out – **outflow** *vi*

,out'general /-'jen(ə)rəl/ *vt* **-ll-** (*NAm* **-l-**) to surpass in generalship

'out,go /-,goh/ *n, pl* **outgoes** *NAm* expenditure

'out,going /-,goh·ing/ *adj* **1a** going away; departing **b** retiring or withdrawing from a position ⟨*the* ~ *president*⟩ **2** friendly, sociable – **outgoingness** *n*

'out,goings *n pl* expenditures; *esp* overheads

,out'grow /-'groh/ *vt* **outgrew** /-'grooh/; **outgrown** /-'grohn/ **1** to grow or increase faster than **2** to grow too large or too old for

'out,growth /-,grohth/ *n* **1** a process or product of growing out ⟨*an* ~ *of hair*⟩ **2** a consequence, by-product

,out-'Herod /'herəd/ *vt* to outdo in violence, extravagance, etc – chiefly in *out-Herod Herod* [*out-* + *Herod* Antipas, fl 4 BC ruler of Judaea, depicted in medieval mystery plays as a blustering tyrant]

'out,house /-,hows/ *n* an outbuilding; *esp, chiefly NAm* PRIVY 1

outing /'owting/ *n* a short pleasure trip

outlandish /owt'landish/ *adj* strikingly unusual; bizarre [ME, foreign, fr OE *ūtlendisc,* fr *ūtland* outlying land, foreign country] – **outlandishly** *adv*

,out'last /-'lahst/ *vt* to last longer than

1**'out,law** /-,law/ *n* **1** sby excluded from the protection of the law **2** a fugitive from the law [ME *outlawe,* fr OE *ūtlaga,* fr ON *ūtlagi,* fr *ūt* out (akin to OE *ūt* out) + *lag-, lög* law – more at OUT, LAW] – **outlaw** *adj*

2**outlaw** *vt* **1** to deprive of the protection of law **2** to make illegal – **outlawry** /-ri/ *n*

'out,lay /-,lay/ *n* expenditure, payment

outlet /'owtlit, -,let/ *n* **1a** an exit or vent **b** a means of release or satisfaction for an emotion or drive **2** an agency (e g a shop or dealer) through which a product is marketed **3** *chiefly NAm* POWER POINT ['*out* + *let,* vb]

'out,lier /-,lie·ə/ *n* sthg, esp part of a rock formation, separated or lying away from a main or related body

1**'out,line** /-,lien/ *n* **1a** a line bounding the outer limits of sthg **b** SHAPE 1, 2 **2** (a) drawing with no shading **3a** a condensed treatment of a subject **b** a summary of a written work **4** a preliminary account of a project

2**outline** /'-,-, ,-'-/ *vt* **1** to draw the outline of **2** to indicate the principal features of

,out'live /-'liv/ *vt* **1** to live longer than **2** to survive the effects of

'out,look /-,look/ *n* **1** a view from a particular place ⟨*house with a pleasant* ~⟩ **2** an attitude; POINT OF VIEW **3** a prospect for the future

,out 'loud *adv* aloud

'out,lying /-,lie·ing/ *adj* remote from a centre or main point

,outma'noeuvre, *NAm* **outmaneuver** /-mə'noohvə/ *vt* to defeat by more skilful manoeuvring

,out'match /-'mach/ *vt* to surpass, outdo

,out'moded /-'mohdid/ *adj* **1** no longer in fashion **2** no longer acceptable or usable; obsolete

,out'number /-'numbə/ *vt* to exceed in number

'out of *prep* **1a(1)** from within to the outside of ⟨*walked* ~ *the room*⟩ **(2)** – used to indicate a change in quality, state, or form ⟨*woke up* ~ *a deep sleep*⟩ **b(1)** beyond the range or limits of ⟨~ *sight*⟩ ⟨*lived a mile* ~ *the town*⟩ **(2)** – used to indicate a position or state away from a qualification or circumstance ⟨~ *practice*⟩ ⟨~ *perspective*⟩ **2a** – used to indicate origin or cause ⟨*came* ~ *fear*⟩ ⟨*did well* ~ *the war*⟩ ⟨*what do I get* ~ *it?*⟩ **b** using as a material ⟨*built* ~ *old timber*⟩ **c** having as a mother – used esp of horses ⟨*a colt* ~ *an ordinary mare*⟩; compare BY 4b(1) **3** – used to indicate exclusion from or deprivation of ⟨~ *breath*⟩ ⟨*we're right* ~ *soap*⟩ ⟨*cheated him* ~ *his savings*⟩ **4** from among; *also* IN 5 ⟨*one* ~ *4 survived*⟩ – **out of it 1** not part of a group, activity, or fashion **2** hence, away ⟨*get off* out of it⟩

,out-of-'bounds *adv or adj* outside the prescribed boundaries or limits

,out-of-'date *adj* outmoded, obsolete

,out-of-'pocket *adj* **1** requiring an outlay of cash ⟨~ *expenses*⟩ **2** having spent or lost more money than one can afford ⟨*that shopping spree has left me* ~⟩

,out-of-the-'way *adj* **1** off the beaten track; remote **2** unusual

'out,patient /-,paysh(ə)nt/ *n* a patient who is not an inmate of a hospital but visits it for diagnosis or treatment – compare INPATIENT

,out'play /-'play/ *vt* to defeat or play better than in a game ⟨~ed *his rival*⟩

,out'point /-'poynt/ *vt* to score more points than (and so defeat)

'out,post /-,pohst/ *n* **1** a post or detachment established at a distance from a main body of troops, esp to protect it from surprise attack **2a** an outlying or frontier settlement **b** an outlying branch of a main organization or body

'out,pouring /-,pawring/ *n* an effusive expression (e g of emotion) – usu pl with sing. meaning

1**output** /-,poot/ *n* **1** mineral, agricultural, or industrial production ⟨*steel* ~⟩ **2** mental or artistic production **3** the amount produced by sby in a given time **4a** sthg (e g energy, material, or data) produced by a machine or system **b** the terminal for the output on an electrical device

2**'out,put** *vt* **-tt-; output** to produce as output

1**outrage** /-,rayj/ *n* **1** an act of violence or brutality **2** an act that violates accepted standards of behaviour or taste [ME, fr OF, excess, outrage, fr *outre* beyond, in excess, fr L *ultra* – more at ULTRA-]

2**,out'rage** *vt* **1** to violate the standards or principles of **2** to rape – euph

outrageous /owt'rayjəs/ *adj* **1** not conventional or moderate; extravagant **2** going beyond all standards of propriety, decency, or taste; shocking, offensive – **outrageously** *adv,* **outrageousness** *n*

,out'rank /-'rangk/ *vt* to rank higher than

outré /'oohtray (*Fr* utre)/ *adj* violating convention or propriety; bizarre [F, fr pp of *outrer* to carry to excess]

1**,out'reach** /-'reech/ *vt* **1** to surpass in reach **2** to exceed

2**'out,reach** *n* communication with and education of other people, esp in order to convert to a particular religion ⟨*Christian* ~⟩

,out'ride /-'ried/ *vt* **outrode** /-'rohd/; **outridden** /-'rid(ə)n/ to ride out (a storm)

'out,rider /-,riedə/ *n* a mounted attendant or motorcyclist who rides ahead of or beside a carriage or car as an escort

'out,rigger /-,rigə/ *n* **1** a spar, beam, or framework run out or projecting from a ship's side (e g to help secure a mast or support a float or rowlock) **2** a member projecting from a main structure to provide additional stability or support sthg

1**,out'right** /-'riet/ *adv* **1** completely **2** instantaneously; ON THE SPOT 2

2**'out,right** *adj* being completely or exactly what is stated ⟨*an* ~ *lie*⟩

,out'run /-'run/ *vt* **outran** /-'ran/; **outrun; -nn- 1** to run faster than **2** to exceed, surpass

,out'score /-'skaw/ *vt vt* to make a larger score than

,out'sell /-'sel/ *vt* **outsold** /-'sohld/ to surpass in selling, salesmanship, or numbers sold

outset /-,set/ *n* *the* beginning, start

,out'shine /-'shien/ *vb* **outshone** /-'shon/, **outshined** *vt* **1** to shine brighter than **2** to outdo or excel (in splendour)

1**outside** /,owt'sied, '-,-/ *n* **1a** an external part; the region beyond a boundary **b** the area farthest from a point of reference: e g (1) the section of a playing area towards the sidelines; *also* a corner (2) the side of a pavement nearer the traffic **2** an outer side or surface **3** an outer manifestation; an appearance **4** the extreme limit of an estimation or guess; a maximum ⟨*the crowd numbered 10,000 at the ~*⟩

[2]**'out,side** *adj* **1a** of or being on, near, or towards the outside ⟨*an ~ lavatory*⟩ ⟨*an ~ telephone line*⟩ **b** of or being the outer side of a curve or near the middle of the road ⟨*driving on the ~ lane*⟩ **2** maximum **3a** originating elsewhere ⟨*an ~ broadcast*⟩ ⟨*~ agitators*⟩ **b** not belonging to one's regular occupation or duties ⟨*~ interests*⟩ **4** barely possible; remote ⟨*an ~ chance*⟩

[3]**,out'side** *adv* **1** on or to the outside ⟨*wait ~ in the passage*⟩ – compare OUT 1d **2** outdoors **3** *chiefly Br* not in prison – slang

[4]**outside** /'-,-, ,-'-/ *prep* **1** on or to the outside of ⟨*live a mile ~ Cambridge*⟩ **2** beyond the limits of ⟨*~ my experience*⟩ **3** except, besides ⟨*few interests ~ her children*⟩

,outside-'left *n* an attacking player on the left wing in a traditional soccer lineup ☞ SPORT

,out'side of *prep, chiefly NAm* outside

outsider /owt'siedə/ *n* **1** sby who does not belong to a particular group **2** a competitor who has only an outside chance of winning

,outside-'right *n* an attacking player on the right wing in a traditional soccer lineup ☞ SPORT

outsize /'owt,siez/ *adj or n* (of) an unusual or above standard size

'out,skirt /-,skuht/ *n* an outer area, esp of a town or city – usu pl with sing. meaning

,out'smart /-'smaht/ *vt* to get the better of; outwit

,out'spoken /-'spohkən/ *adj* direct and open in speech or expression; frank – **outspokenly** *adv*, **outspokenness** *n*

,out'standing /-'standing/ *adj* **1a** unpaid ⟨*left several bills ~*⟩ **b** continuing, unresolved **2a** standing out from a group; conspicuous **b** marked by eminence and distinction – **outstandingly** *adv*

,out'stare /-'steə/ *vt* OUTFACE 1

'out,station /-,staysh(ə)n/ *n* a remote or outlying station

,out'stay /-'stay/ *vt* **1** to overstay ⟨~ed *his welcome*⟩ **2** to surpass in staying power

,out'stretch /-'strech/ *vt* to stretch out; extend

,out'strip /-'strip/ *vt* **-pp- 1** to go faster or farther than **2** to get ahead of; leave behind [*out-* + obs *strip* (to move fast)]

'out,swing /-,swing/ *n* the swing of a bowled cricket ball from the leg to the off side – compare INSWING – **outswinger** *n*

,out'vote /-'voht/ *vt* to defeat by a majority of votes

[1]**'outward** /-wood/ *adj* **1a** situated at or directed towards the outside **b** being or going away from home ⟨*the ~ voyage*⟩ **2** of the body or external appearances ⟨*~ calm*⟩

[2]**outward** *n* external form, appearance, or reality

,outward-'bound *adj* bound in an outward direction (e g away from a home port)

'outwardly /-li/ *adv* in outward appearance; superficially

'outwards *adv* towards the outside

,out'wear /-'weə/ *vt* **outwore** /-'waw/; **outworn** /-'wawn/ to last longer than

,out'weigh /-'way/ *vt* to exceed in weight, value, or importance

,out'wit /-'wit/ *vt* **-tt-** to get the better of by superior cleverness

'out,work /-,wuhk/ *n* **1** a minor defensive position constructed outside a fortified area **2** work done for a business or organization off its premises usu by employees based at home – **outworker** *n*

,out'worn /-'wawn/ *adj* no longer useful or acceptable; outmoded

ouzel, ousel /'oohzl/ *n* **1** RING OUZEL **2** a dipper [ME *ousel*, fr OE *ōsle* blackbird]

ouzo /'oohzoh/ *n* an unsweetened Greek spirit flavoured with aniseed that is usu drunk with water [NGk *ouzon, ouzo*]

ov-, ovi-, ovo- *comb form* egg ⟨ovi*form*⟩; ovum ⟨ovi*duct*⟩ [L *ov-, ovi-*, fr *ovum* – more at [2]EGG]

ova /'ohvə/ *pl of* OVUM

[1]**oval** /'ohvl/ *adj* having the shape of an egg; *also* exactly or approximately elliptical [ML *ovalis*, fr LL, of an egg, fr L *ovum*] – **ovally** *adv*, **ovalness** *n*

[2]**oval** *n* an oval figure or object

ovariectomy /oh,veəri'ektəmi, -,vari-/ *n* the surgical removal of an ovary [NL *ovariectomia*]

ovary /'ohvəri/ *n* **1** the typically paired female reproductive organ that produces eggs and female sex hormones ☞ REPRODUCTION **2** the enlarged rounded usu basal female part of a flowering plant that bears the ovules and consists of 1 or more carpels ☞ PLANT [NL *ovarium*, fr L *ovum* egg] – **ovarian** /oh'veəri·ən, -'va-/ *adj*, **ovaritis** /,ohvə'rietəs/ *n*

ovate /'ohvayt/ *adj* (having an outline) shaped like (a longitudinal section of) an egg ⟨*an ~ leaf*⟩ ☞ PLANT

ovation /oh'vaysh(ə)n/ *n* an expression of popular acclaim [L *ovation-, ovatio*, fr *ovatus*, pp of *ovare* to exult; akin to Gk *euoi*, interjection used in bacchic revels]

oven /'uv(ə)n/ *n* a chamber used for baking, heating, or drying [ME, fr OE *ofen*; akin to OHG *ofan* oven, Gk *ipnos*, L *aulla, olla* pot]

'oven,bird /-,buhd/ *n* any of various small S American birds that build globular nests of mud [fr the shape of its nest]

'oven,ware /-,weə/ *n* heat-resistant dishes (e g casseroles) in which food can be cooked in an oven

[1]**over** /'ohvə/ *adv* **1a** across a barrier ⟨*climb ~*⟩ **b** across an intervening space ⟨*went ~ to the States*⟩; *also* ROUND 5 ⟨*ask them ~ for drinks*⟩ **c** downwards from an upright position ⟨*fell ~*⟩ ⟨*knocked him ~*⟩ **d** across the brim or brink ⟨*soup boiled ~*⟩ **e** so as to bring the underside up ⟨*turned his cards ~*⟩ ⟨*rolled ~ and ~*⟩ **f** so as to be reversed or folded ⟨*change the 2 pictures ~*⟩ ⟨*bend it ~*⟩ **g** from one person or side to another ⟨*hand it ~*⟩ ⟨*won them ~*⟩ ⟨*went ~ to the enemy*⟩ **h** ACROSS 3 ⟨*got his point ~*⟩ **2a(1)** beyond some quantity or limit ⟨*£10 or ~*⟩ ⟨*show ran a minute ~*⟩ **(2)** excessively, inordinately – often in combination ⟨over-*optimistic*⟩ ⟨over*value*⟩ **(3)** in excess; remaining ⟨*there wasn't much ~*⟩ ⟨*3 into 7 goes twice and 1 ~*⟩ **b** till a later time ⟨*stay ~ till Monday*⟩ **3** so as to cover the whole surface ⟨*windows boarded ~*⟩ **4a** at an end ⟨*the day is ~*⟩ **b** – used on a two-way radio circuit to indicate that a message is complete and a reply is expected **5a** –

used to show repetition ⟨*10 times* ~⟩ ⟨*told you ~ and ~ again*⟩ **b** *chiefly NAm* once more ⟨*do one's sums* ~⟩ [ME, adv & prep, fr OE *ofer*; akin to OHG *ubar* (prep) above, beyond, over, L *super*, Gk *hyper*]

[2]**over** *prep* **1a** higher than; above ⟨*towered ~ his mother*⟩ **b** vertically above but not touching ⟨*lamp hung ~ the table*⟩ **c** – used to indicate movement down upon ⟨*hit him ~ the head*⟩ or down across the edge of ⟨*fell ~ the cliff*⟩ **d** ACROSS 1 ⟨*climbed ~ the gate*⟩ ⟨*flew ~ the lake*⟩ **e** so as to cover ⟨*laid a blanket ~ the child*⟩ ⟨*curtains drawn ~ the windows*⟩ **f** divided by ⟨*6 ~ 2 is 3*⟩ **2a** with authority, power, or jurisdiction in relation to ⟨*respected those ~ him*⟩ **b** – used to indicate superiority, advantage, or preference ⟨*a big lead ~ the others*⟩ **3** more than ⟨*cost ~ £5*⟩ – compare OVER AND ABOVE **4a** all through or throughout ⟨*showed me all ~ the house*⟩ ⟨*went ~ his notes*⟩ **b** by means of (a medium or channel of communication) ⟨*~ the radio*⟩ ⟨*~ the phone*⟩ **5a** in the course of; during ⟨*~ the past 25 years*⟩ ⟨*wrote it ~ the weekend*⟩ **b** until the end of ⟨*stay ~ Sunday*⟩ **c** past, beyond ⟨*we're ~ the worst*⟩ **6a** – used to indicate an object of solicitude or reference ⟨*the Lord watches ~ them*⟩ ⟨*laughed ~ the incident*⟩ **b** – used to indicate an object of occupation or activity ⟨*sitting ~ their wine*⟩ ⟨*spent an hour ~ cards*⟩

[3]**over** *adj* **1** upper, higher ⟨over*lord*⟩ **2** outer, covering ⟨over*coat*⟩ **3** excessive ⟨over*imagination*⟩ ⟨over*confidence*⟩ *USE* often in combination

[4]**over** *n* any of the divisions of an innings in cricket during which 1 bowler bowls 6 or 8 balls from the same end of the pitch [fr the umpire's cry of *over* (i e change to the other end) after the 6th or 8th ball]

,overa'bundance /-ə'bund(ə)ns/ *n* an excess, surfeit – **overabundant** *adj*

,over'act /-'akt/ *vb* to perform (a part) with undue exaggeration

,over 'against *prep* as opposed to; in contrast with

[1]**overall** /,ohvə'rawl/ *adv* **1** as a whole; IN TOTO **2** from end to end, esp of a ship

[2]**overall** /'ohvə,rawl/ *n* **1** *pl* a protective garment resembling a boiler suit or dungarees **2** *chiefly Br* a usu loose-fitting protective coat worn over other clothing

[3]**overall** *adj* including everything

,over and a'bove *prep* besides – compare OVER 3

,over and 'over *adv* repeatedly

overarm /'ohvə,rahm/ *adj or adv* overhand

,over'awe /-'aw/ *vt* to fill with respect or fear

,over'balance /-'baləns/ *vt* to cause to lose balance ~ *vi chiefly Br* to lose one's balance

,over'bear /-'beə/ *vt* **overbore** /-'baw/; **overborne** *also* **overborn** /-'bawn/ **1** to bring down by superior weight or force **2a** to domineer over **b** to surpass in importance or cogency; outweigh

,over'bearing /-'beəring/ *adj* harshly masterful or domineering – **overbearingly** *adv*

,over'bid /-'bid/ *vb* **overbid; -dd-** *vi* **1** to bid in excess of value **2** to bid more than the scoring capacity of a hand at cards ~ *vt* to bid in excess of; *esp* to bid more than the value of (one's hand at cards) – **overbid** /'--,-/ *n*

[1]**,over'blown** /-'blohn/ *adj* inflated, pretentious [[1]*blow*]

[2]**overblown** *adj* past the prime of bloom ⟨*~ roses*⟩ [[3]*blow*]

'over,board /-,bawd/ *adv* **1** over the side of a ship or boat into the water **2** to extremes of enthusiasm ⟨*went ~ for the plan*⟩ **3** aside ⟨*threw the plan ~*⟩

,over'book /-'book/ *vt* to issue bookings for (e g a hotel) in excess of the space available ~ *vi* to issue bookings in excess of the space available

,over'build /-'bild/ *vb* **overbuilt** /-'bilt/ to build (houses) in excess of demand

[1]**,over'burden** /-'buhd(ə)n/ *vt* to place an excessive burden on

[2]**'over,burden** *n* soil, rock, etc overlying a useful deposit (e g of coal)

,over'call /-'kawl/ *vb* to make a higher bid than (the previous bid or player) in a card game – **overcall** /'--,-/ *n*

,over'capital·ize, -ise /-'kapitl,iez/ *vt* to put a nominal value on the capital of (a company) higher than actual cost or fair market value – **overcapitalization** /-'zaysh(ə)n/ *n*

overcast /'ohvə,kahst, ,--'-/ *adj* being, having, or characterized by a cloudy sky

'over,casting /-,kahsting/ *n* the act of stitching a raw edge of fabric to prevent unravelling; *also* the stitching so done

,over'charge /-'chahj/ *vt* **1** to charge too much or too fully **2** to fill too full **3** to exaggerate ~ *vi* to make an excessive charge – **overcharge** /'--,-/ *n*

,over'cloud /-'klowd/ *vt* to cover with clouds

'over,coat /-,koht/ *n* **1** a warm usu thick coat for wearing outdoors over other clothing **2** a protective coat (e g of paint)

,over'come /-'kum/ *vb* **overcame** /-'kaym/; **overcome** *vt* **1** to get the better of; surmount ⟨*~ difficulties*⟩ **2** to overpower, overwhelm ~ *vi* to gain superiority; win [ME *overcomen*, fr OE *ofercuman*, fr *ofer* over + *cuman* to come]

,over,compen'sation /-,kompen'saysh(ə)n, -pən-/ *n* excessive reaction to feelings of inferiority, guilt, inadequacy, etc

,over'crowd /-'krowd/ *vb* to (cause to) be too crowded

,over'do /-'dooh/ *vt* **overdoes** /-'duz/; **overdid** /-'did/; **overdone** /-'dun/ **1a** to do or use in excess **b** to exaggerate **2** to cook too much

overdose /'ohvə,dohs; *vb* '--,-, ,--'-/ *vb or n* (to give or take) too great a dose of drugs, medicine, etc

'over,draft /-,drahft/ *n* an act of overdrawing at a bank; the state of being overdrawn; *also* the sum overdrawn

,over'draw /-'draw/ *vb* **overdrew** /-'drooh/; **overdrawn** /-'drawn/ *vt* **1** to draw cheques on (a bank account) for more than the balance ⟨*his account was* overdrawn⟩ **2** to exaggerate, overstate ~ *vi* to make an overdraft

,over'drawn /-'drawn/ *adj* having an overdrawn account

[1]**,over'dress** /-'dres/ *vb* to dress (oneself) too elaborately or formally

[2]**'over,dress** *n* a dress worn over another, or over a jumper, blouse, etc

'over,drive /-,driev/ *n* a transmission gear in a motor vehicle that provides a ratio higher than the normal top gear and that drives the propeller shaft at a speed greater than the engine speed

,over'due /-'dyooh/ *adj* **1a** unpaid when due **b**

delayed beyond an appointed time **2** more than ready or ripe

,over'eat /-'eet/ *vi* **overate** /-'et, -'ayt/; **overeaten** /-'eet(ə)n/ to eat to excess

,over'estimate /-'estimayt/ *vt* **1** to estimate as being more than the actual amount or size **2** to place too high a value on; overrate – **overestimate** /-mət/ *n*, **overestimation** /-'maysh(ə)n/ *n*

,overex'tend /-ik'stend/ *vt* to extend or expand beyond a safe or reasonable point

,over'feed /-'feed/ *vb* **overfed** /-'fed/ to feed to excess

,over'fish /-'fish/ *vt* to fish excessively to the detriment of (a fishing ground) or to the depletion of (a kind of organism)

'over,flight /-,fliet/ *n* a passage over an area in an aircraft

[1]**,over'flow** /-'floh/ *vt* **1** to cover (as if) with water; inundate **2** to flow over the brim, edge, or limit of ~ *vi* to flow over or beyond a brim, edge, or limit

[2]**'over,flow** *n* **1** a flowing over; an inundation **2** sthg that flows over; *also, sing or pl in constr* the excess members of a group **3** an outlet or receptacle for surplus liquid

,over'fly /-'flie/ *vt* **overflew** /-'flooh/; **overflown** /-'flohn/ to fly over, esp in an aircraft

'over,fold /-,fohld/ *n* a geological fold that has the form of an overturned anticline ☞ GEOGRAPHY

'over,ground /-,grownd/ *adj or adv* on the surface; not underground ⟨~ *railway*⟩

,over'grow /-'groh/ *vb* **overgrew** /-'grooh/; **overgrown** /-'grohn/ *vt* **1** to grow over so as to cover with vegetation **2** to grow beyond; to outgrow ~ *vi* **1** to grow excessively **2** to become overgrown – **overgrowth** /'ohvə,grohth/ *n*

,over'grown /-'grohn/ *adj* **1** grown over or choked with vegetation **2** grown too large

'over,hand /-,hand/ *adj or adv* with the hand brought forwards and down from above shoulder level

overhand knot *n* a type of simple knot often used to prevent the end of a cord from fraying

[1]**,over'hang** /-'hang/ *vb* **overhung** /-'hung/ *vt* **1** to project over **2** to threaten ~ *vi* to project so as to be over sthg

[2]**'over,hang** *n* **1** sthg that overhangs; *also* the extent by which sthg overhangs **2** a projection of the roof or upper storey of a building beyond the wall of the lower part

,over'haul /-'hawl/ *vt* **1** to examine thoroughly and carry out necessary repairs **2** to overtake ['*over* + '*haul*; orig sense, to slacken (a rope), release (a tackle)] – **overhaul** /'--,-/ *n*

[1]**,over'head** /-'hed/ *adv* above one's head

[2]**'over,head** *adj* **1** operating, lying, or coming from above **2** of overhead expenses

[3]**'over,head** *n* **1** a business expense (e g rent, insurance, or heating) not chargeable to a particular part of the work or product – often pl with sing. meaning **2** a stroke in squash, tennis, etc made above head height; a smash

,overhead pro'jector *n* a projector that projects a magnified image of a horizontal transparency onto a screen via a mirror

,over'hear /-'hiə/ *vb* **overheard** /-'huhd/ to hear (sby or sthg) without the speaker's knowledge or intention

,over'heat /-'heet/ *vt* **1** to heat to excess **2** to stimulate or excite unduly ⟨~ing *the economy*⟩ ~ *vi* to become overheated

,over'issue /-'ish(y)ooh, -'isyooh/ *n* an issue exceeding the limit of capital, credit, or authority – **overissue** *vt*

,over'joyed /-'joyd/ *adj* extremely pleased; elated

[1]**,over'kill** /-'kil/ *vt* to obliterate (a target) with more nuclear force than required

[2]**'over,kill** *n* **1** the capability of destroying an enemy or target with a force, esp nuclear, larger than is required **2** an excess of sthg beyond what is required or suitable for a particular purpose

,over'laid /-'layd/ *adj* (having sthg) laid or lying on top

[1]**'over,land** /-,land/ *adv or adj* by, upon, or across land rather than sea or air

[2]**overland** *vb, Austr* to drive (stock) overland for long distances – **overlander** *n*

,over'lap /-'lap/ *vb* **-pp-** *vt* to extend over and cover a part of ~ *vi* to coincide partly; have sthg in common – **overlap** /'--,-/ *n*

[1]**,over'lay** /-'lay/ *vt* **overlaid** /-'layd/ to lay or spread over or across

[2]**'over,lay** *n* sthg (designed to be) laid over sthg else; *esp* a transparent sheet containing graphic matter to be superimposed on another sheet

,over'leaf /-'leef/ *adv* on the other side of the page ⟨*continued* ~⟩

,over'lie /-'lie/ *vt* **overlay** /-'lay/; **overlain** /-'layn/ to lie or be situated over

,over'load /-'lohd/ *vt* **overloaded, overladen** /-'laydn/ to load to excess – **overload** /'--,-/ *n*

'over,locking /-,loking/ *n* the act or occupation of oversewing a raw edge of fabric cut to a pattern using a small machine stitch to prevent unravelling – **overlocker** *n*

,over'long /-'long/ *adj or adv* too long

,over'look /-'look/ *vt* **1** to have or provide a view of from above **2a** to fail to notice; miss **b** to ignore **c** to excuse

'over,lord /-,lawd/ *n* **1** a lord who is superior to other lords **2** an absolute or supreme ruler – **overlordship** *n*

'overly /-li/ *adv, chiefly NAm & Scot* to an excessive degree [ME, fr '*over* + [2]*-ly*]

,over'man /-'man/ *vt* **-nn-** to have or provide too many workers for ⟨~ *a ship*⟩

'over,mantel /-,mantl/ *n* an ornamental often shelved structure above a mantelpiece

,over'master /-'mahstə/ *vt* to overpower, subdue

,over'mighty /-'mieti/ *adj* exercising or claiming undue (political) power

,over'much /-'much/ *adj or adv* too much

,over'night /-'niet/ *adv* **1** during or throughout the evening or night **2** suddenly – **overnight** /'-,-/ *adj*

'over,pass /-,pahs/ *n* a flyover; *also* the crossing of 2 roads, paths, railways, or combinations of these

,over'pay /-'pay/ *vt* to give excessively high payment to or for

,over'pitch /-'pich/ *vb* to bowl (a ball) in cricket so as to bounce nearer the batsman's wicket than intended and be easily hit

,over'play /-'play/ *vt* **1** to exaggerate (e g a dramatic role) **2** to give too much emphasis to – **overplay one's hand** to overestimate one's capacities

'over,plus /-,plus/ *n* a surplus [ME, part trans of MF *surplus*]

ˌoverˌpopuˈlation /-ˌpopyooˈlaysh(ə)n/ *n* the condition of having too dense a population, so that the quality of life is impaired – **overpopulated** /ˌ--ˈ--ˌ--/ *adj*

ˌoverˈpower /-ˈpowə/ *vt* **1** to overcome by superior force **2** to overwhelm – **overpoweringly** *adv*

ˈoverˌprint /-ˌprint/ *n* a printed marking added to a postage stamp to alter the original or to commemorate a special event – **overprint** /ˌ--ˈ-/ *vt*

ˌoverproˈduce /-prəˈdyoohs/ *vb* to produce beyond demand, need, or allocation – **overproduction** /-prəˈduksh(ə)n/ *n*

ˌoverˈproof /-ˈproohf/ *adj* containing more alcohol than proof spirit does

ˌoverˈrate /-ˈrayt/ *vt* to rate too highly

ˌoverˈreach /-ˈreech/ *vt* to defeat (oneself) by trying to do or gain too much ~ *vi, of a horse* to strike the hind foot against the forefoot

ˌoverreˈact /-riˈakt/ *vi* to show an excessive or exaggerated reaction – **overreaction** /-ˌaksh(ə)n/ *n*

[1]**ˌoverˈride** /-ˈried/ *vt* **overrode** /-ˈrohd/; **overridden** /-ˈrid(ə)n/ **1a** to prevail over; dominate ⟨*an* overriding *consideration*⟩ **b** to set aside or annul; *esp* to neutralize the action of (e g an automatic control) **2** to overlap

[2]**ˈoverˌride** *n* a device or system used to override a control

ˈover-ˌrider *n, Br* a vertical attachment to a motor vehicle bumper to prevent the locking of bumpers with other cars

ˌoverˈripe /-ˈriep/ *adj* passed beyond maturity or ripeness towards decay

ˌoverˈrule /-ˈroohl/ *vt* to rule against or set aside, esp by virtue of superior authority

ˌoverˈrun /-ˈrun/ *vt* **overran** /-ˈran/; **-nn- 1a** to defeat decisively and occupy the positions of **b** to swarm over; infest **2a** to run or go beyond or past **b** to readjust (set type) by shifting letters or words from one line into another **3** to flow over – **overrun** /ˈ--ˌ-/ *n*

[1]**ˌoverˈseas** /-ˈseez/, **oversea** /-ˈsee/ *adv* beyond or across the seas ⟨*travelled* ~⟩

[2]**ˈoverˌseas, oversea** *adj* **1** of transport across the seas **2** of, from, or in (foreign) places across the seas ⟨~ *markets*⟩ ⟨~ *students here in London*⟩

ˌoverˈsee /-ˈsee/ *vt* **oversaw** /-ˈsaw/; **overseen** /-ˈseen/ to supervise

ˈoverˌseer /-ˌsee·ə/ *n* a supervisor

ˌoverˈsell /-ˈsel/ *vt* **oversold** /-ˈsohld/ **1** to sell too much of **2** to make excessive claims for – **oversell** /ˈ--ˌ-/ *n*

ˌoverˈsensitive /-ˈsensətiv/ *adj* unduly or extremely sensitive – **oversensitiveness** *n*

ˌoverˈset /-ˈset/ *vt* **overset; -tt-** to tip over; overturn – **overset** /ˈ--ˌ-/ *n*

ˈoverˌsew /-ˌsoh/ *vt* **oversewed** /-ˌsohd/; **oversewn** /-ˌsohn/, **oversewed** to sew over (an edge or 2 edges placed together), esp with small closely worked stitches, to neaten or make a firm seam

ˌoverˈsexed /-ˈsekst/ *adj* with an abnormally strong sexual drive

ˌoverˈshadow /-ˈshadoh/ *vt* **1** to cast a shadow over **2** to exceed in importance; outweigh

ˈoverˌshoe /-ˌshooh/ *n* a usu rubber shoe worn over another as protection (e g from rain or snow)

ˌoverˈshoot /-ˈshooht/ *vt* **overshot** /-ˈshot/ to shoot or pass over or beyond, esp so as to miss – **overshoot** /ˈ--ˌ-/ *n*

ˈoverˌshot /-ˌshot/ *adj* **1** (having the upper jaw) projecting beyond the lower jaw (e g in some dogs) **2** operated by the weight of water passing over and flowing from above ⟨*an* ~ *waterwheel*⟩

ˈoverˌsight /-ˌsiet/ *n* **1** supervision **2** an inadvertent omission or error

ˌoverˈsimpliˌfy /-ˈsimpliˌfie/ *vb* to simplify (sthg) to such an extent as to cause distortion or error – **oversimplification** /-fiˈkaysh(ə)n/ *n*

oversize /ˌohvəˈsiez, ˈ--ˌ-/, **oversized** *adj* of above average or normal size

ˌoverˈsleep /-ˈsleep/ *vi* **overslept** /-ˈslept/ to sleep beyond the intended time

ˌoverˈspend /-ˈspend/ **ˌoverˈspent** /-ˈspent/ *vt* to exceed in expenditure ~ *vi* to spend beyond one's means – **overspender** *n*

ˈoverˌspill /-ˌspil/ *n, chiefly Br* people who have moved away from crowded urban areas ⟨~ *towns*⟩; *also* the movement of such people

ˌoverˈstate /-ˈstayt/ *vt* to state in too strong terms; exaggerate – **overstatement** *n*

ˌoverˈstay /-ˈstay/ *vt* to stay beyond the time or the limits of

ˈoverˌsteer /-ˌstiə/ *n* the tendency of a motor vehicle to steer into a sharper turn than the driver intends – **oversteer** /ˌ--ˈ-/ *vb*

ˌoverˈstep /-ˈstep/ *vt* **-pp-** to exceed, transgress – esp in *overstep the mark*

ˌoverˈstrung /-ˈstrung/ *adj* too highly strung; too sensitive

ˌoverˈstuff /-ˈstuf/ *vt* to cover (e g a chair) thickly with upholstery

ˌoversubˈscribe /-səbˈskrieb/ *vt* to subscribe for more of than is offered for sale – **oversubscription** /-səbˈskripsh(ə)n/ *n*

overt /ˈohvuht, ˌ-ˈ-/ *adj* public, manifest [ME, fr MF *ouvert, overt*, fr pp of *ouvrir* to open, fr (assumed) VL *operire*, alter. of L *aperire* – more at WEIR] – **overtly** *adv*

ˌoverˈtake /-ˈtayk/ *vb* **overtook** /-ˈtook/; **overtaken** /-ˈtaykən/ *vt* **1a** to catch up with **b** to catch up with and pass beyond **2** to come upon suddenly ~ *vi, chiefly Br* to catch up with and pass by another vehicle going in the same direction [ME *overtaken*, fr [1]*over* + *taken* to take]

ˌoverˈtax /-ˈtaks/ *vt* **1** to tax too heavily **2** to put too great a burden or strain on

[1]**ˌoverˈthrow** /-ˈthroh/ *vt* **overthrew** /-ˈthrooh/; **overthrown** /-ˈthrohn/ **1** to overturn, upset **2** to cause the downfall of; defeat

ˈoverˌthrow 2 *n* (a further run scored from) a return of the ball from a fielder in cricket that eludes the fielders near the wickets

ˈoverˌtime /-ˌtiem/ *n* **1** time in excess of a set limit; *esp* working time in excess of a standard working day or week **2** the wage paid for overtime – **overtime** *adv*

ˈoverˌtone /-ˌtohn/ *n* **1a** any of the higher harmonics produced simultaneously with the fundamental in a complex musical note **b** HARMONIC 2 **2** a secondary effect, quality, or meaning; a suggestion – often pl with sing. meaning

ˌoverˈtop /-ˈtop/ *vt* **-pp- 1** to rise above the top of **2** to surpass

ˌoverˈtrain /-ˈtrayn/ *vb* to train more than is desirable for maximum efficiency

ˈoverˌtrick /-ˌtrik/ *n* a card trick won in excess of the number bid

,over'trump /-'trump/ *vb* to trump with a higher trump card than the highest previously played on the same trick

overture /'ohvətyooə, -chə/ *n* **1a** an initiative towards agreement or action – often pl with sing. meaning **b** sthg introductory; a prelude **2a** the orchestral introduction to a musical dramatic work **b** an orchestral concert piece written esp as a single movement [ME, lit., opening, fr MF, fr (assumed) VL *opertura*, alter. of L *apertura* – more at APERTURE]

,over'turn /-'tuhn/ *vt* **1** to cause to turn over; upset **2** to overthrow; BRING DOWN 1 ~ *vi* TURN OVER 1 – **overturn** /'--,-/ *n*

'over,view /-,vyooh/ *n* a usu brief general survey

,over'weening /-'weening/ *adj* **1** arrogant, presumptuous **2** immoderate, exaggerated [ME *overweening*, prp of *overwenen* to be arrogant, fr *over* + *wenen* to imagine, fr OE *wēnan*]

[1]**'over,weight** /-,wayt/ *n* weight above what is normal, average, or required

[2]**,over'weight** *vt* **1** to give too much weight or consideration to **2** to weight excessively **3** to exceed in weight

[3]**,over'weight** *adj* exceeding the expected, normal, or proper (bodily) weight

,over'whelm /-'welm/ *vt* **1** to cover over completely; submerge **2** to overcome by superior force or numbers **3** to overpower with emotion [ME *overwhelmen*, fr [1]*over* + *whelmen* to turn over, cover up] – **overwhelmingly** *adv*

,over'wind /-'wiend/ *vt* **overwound** /-'wownd/ to wind more than is proper

,over'winter /-'wintə/ *vi* to survive or spend the winter

'over with *adj* finished, completed

,over'work /-'wuhk/ *vt* **1** to cause to work too hard or too long **2** to make excessive use of ~ *vi* to work too much or too long – **overwork** *n*

,over'write /-'riet/ *vb* **overwrote** /-'roht/; **overwritten** /-'ritn/ to write too much or pretentiously

,over'wrought /-'rawt/ *adj* extremely excited; agitated [pp of *overwork*]

ovi- – see OV-

oviduct /'ohvi,dukt/ *n* the tube that serves for the passage of eggs from an ovary, esp before laying [NL *oviductus*, fr *ov-* + *ductus* duct] – **oviductal** /-'duktl/ *adj*

ovine /'ohvien/ *adj* of or resembling sheep [LL *ovinus*, fr L *ovis* sheep – more at EWE] – **ovine** *n*

oviparous /oh'vipərəs/ *adj* involving or producing eggs that develop and hatch outside the mother's body ☞ LIFE CYCLE [L *oviparus*, fr *ov-* + *-parus* -parous] – **oviparously** *adv*, **oviparousness** *n*, **oviparity** /-vi'parəti/ *n*

oviposit /,ohvi'pozit/ *vi, esp of an insect* to lay eggs [prob back-formation fr *ovipositor*] – **oviposition** /-pə'zish(ə)n/ *n*

ovipositor /,ohvi'pozitə/ *n* a specialized organ, esp of an insect, for depositing eggs [NL, fr L *ov-* + *positor* sby or sthg that places, fr *positus*, pp of *ponere* to place – more at POSITION]

ovo- – see OV-

ovoid /'ohvoyd/, **ovoidal** /oh'voydl/ *adj* shaped like an egg [F *ovoïde*, fr L *ovum* egg – more at [2]EGG] – **ovoid** *n*

ovolo /'ohvə,loh/ *n, pl* **ovolos** a rounded convex moulding ☞ ARCHITECTURE [It, dim. of *uovo, ovo* egg, fr L *ovum*]

ovotestis /,ohvoh'testis/ *n* a hermaphrodite gonad (e g in some snails) [NL]

ovoviviparous /,ohvohvi'vipərəs/ *adj* producing eggs that develop and usu hatch within the mother's body ☞ LIFE CYCLE [prob fr (assumed) NL *ovoviviparus*, fr L *ov-* + *viviparus* viviparous] – **ovoviviparity** /-vivi'parəti/ *n*

ovulate /'ovyoo,layt/ *vi* to produce eggs or discharge them from an ovary – **ovulation** /-'laysh(ə)n/ *n*, **ovulatory** /-lət(ə)ri/ *adj*

ovule /'ovyoohl, 'oh-/ *n* **1** an outgrowth of the ovary of a seed plant that develops into a seed after fertilization of the egg cell it contains ☞ PLANT **2** a small egg, esp one in an early stage of growth [NL *ovulum*, dim. of L *ovum*] – **ovular** /'ovyoolə/ *adj*

ovum /'ohvəm/ *n, pl* **ova** /'ohvə/ an animal's female gamete that when fertilized can develop into a new individual ☞ REPRODUCTION [NL, fr L, egg – more at [2]EGG]

ow /ow/ *interj* – used esp to express sudden mild pain [ME]

owe /oh/ *vt* **1a** to be under obligation to pay or render **b** to be indebted to **2** to have or enjoy as a result of the action or existence of sthg or sby else ⟨~s *his fame to luck*⟩ ~ *vi* to be in debt [ME *owen* to possess, own, owe, fr OE *āgan*; akin to OHG *eigun* (1 & 3 pl pres indic) possess, Skt *īśe* he possesses]

'owing to /'oh·ing/ *prep* BECAUSE OF 1 ⟨*delayed ~ a crash*⟩

owl /owl/ *n* any of an order of chiefly nocturnal birds of prey with large head and eyes and a short hooked bill [ME *owle*, fr OE *ūle*; akin to OHG *uwila* owl, ON *ugla*]

owlet /'owlit/ *n* a small or young owl

owlish /'owlish/ *adj* having a round face or a wide-eyed stare [OWL + -ISH] – **owlishly** *adv*

[1]**own** /ohn/ *adj* belonging to, for, or relating to oneself or itself – usu after a possessive pronoun ⟨*cooked his ~ dinner*⟩ [ME *owen*, fr OE *āgen*; akin to OHG *eigan* own, ON *eiginn*, OE *āgan* to possess – more at OWE]

[2]**own** *vt* **1** to have or hold as property; possess **2** to acknowledge, admit ~ *vi* to acknowledge sthg to be true or valid – + *to* – **owner** *n*, **ownership** *n*

[3]**own** *pron, pl* **own** one belonging to oneself or itself – usu after a possessive pronoun ⟨*a country with oil of its ~*⟩ – **on one's own** **1** in solitude; alone ⟨*live* on one's own⟩ **2** without assistance or control

,own-'brand *adj* of or being goods offered for sale under the label or trade name of the retail distributor (e g a chain store)

,owner-'occupier *n* sby who owns the house he/she lives in

,own 'goal *n* a goal, esp in soccer, scored by a player against his own team

own up *vi* to confess a fault frankly

owt /owt/ *pron, N Eng* anything, aught [var of *aught*]

ox /oks/ *n, pl* **oxen** /'oks(ə)n/ *also* **ox** **1** a (domestic species of) bovine mammal **2** an adult castrated male domestic ox [ME, fr OE *oxa*; akin to OHG *ohso* ox, Gk *hygros* wet – more at HUMOUR]

ox-, oxo- *comb form* containing a carbonyl group in the molecular structure; ketone ⟨*oxoacetic acid*⟩ [F, fr *oxygène*]

oxalate /'oksə,layt/ *n* a salt or ester of oxalic acid

ox,alic 'acid /ok'salik/ *n* a poisonous strong acid that occurs in various plants and is used esp as a bleach and in making dyes [trans of F (*acide*) *oxalique*, fr L *oxalis* wood sorrel]

oxbow /'oks,boh/ *n* **1** a U-shaped collar round a draught ox's neck for supporting the yoke **2** a U-shaped river bend or lake formed from this ☞ GEOGRAPHY – **oxbow** *adj*

Oxbridge /'oks,brij/ *adj or n* (of) the universities of Oxford and Cambridge [*Ox*ford + Cam*bridge*]

oxer /'oksə/ *n* an obstacle for horses to jump consisting of a hedge, rails, and sometimes a ditch [*oxer* (hedge or fence to restrain cattle), fr *ox* + [2]*-er*]

oxeye /'oks,ei/ *n* any of several composite plants whose heads have both disc and ray flowers; *esp* OXEYE DAISY

,ox,eye 'daisy *n* a leafy-stemmed European composite plant with long white ray florets

,Oxford 'bags /'oksfəd/ *n pl in constr, pl* **Oxford bags** wide-legged trousers [*Oxford*, city in England]

'Oxford ,movement *n* a Victorian High Church movement within the Church of England

oxidant /'oksid(ə)nt/ *n* an oxidizing agent – **oxidant** *adj*

oxidative phosphorylation /'oksi,daytiv/ *n* the synthesis in mitochondria of ATP from ADP using energy obtained from the oxidation of substances formed during the Krebs cycle

oxide /'oksied/ *n* a compound of oxygen with an element or radical [F *oxide, oxyde*, fr *ox-* (fr *oxygène* oxygen) + *-ide* (fr *acide* acid)] – **oxidic** /ok'sidik/ *adj*

oxid·ize, -ise /'oksi,diez/ *vt* **1** to combine with oxygen **2** to remove hydrogen or 1 or more electrons from (e g an atom, ion, or molecule) ~ *vi* to become oxidized [*oxide* + *-ize*] – **oxidizable** *adj*, **oxidizer** *n*, **oxidation** /-'daysh(ə)n/ *n*, **oxidative** /-,daytiv/ *adj*

oxlip /'oks,lip/ *n* a Eurasian primula similar to the cowslip [(assumed) ME *oxeslippe*, fr OE *oxanslyppe*, lit., ox dung, fr *oxa* ox + *slypa, slyppe* paste – more at [5]SLIP]

oxo- – see OX-

Oxonian /ok'sohnyən, -ni·ən/ *n* a student or graduate of Oxford University [ML *Oxonia* Oxford] – **Oxonian** *adj*

oxtail /'oks,tayl/ *n* the tail of cattle (skinned and used for food, esp in soup)

'ox,tongue /-,tung/ *n* a bugloss or other plant with rough tongue-shaped leaves

oxy /'oksi/ *adj* containing or using (additional) oxygen – often in combination ⟨oxy*haemoglobin*⟩ ⟨oxy*hydrogen*⟩ [F, fr *oxygène* oxygen]

oxyacetylene /,oksi·ə'set(ə)lin, -leen/ *adj* of or using a mixture of oxygen and acetylene, esp for producing a hot flame ⟨*an ~ torch*⟩ [ISV]

oxygen /'oksij(ə)n/ *n* a bivalent gaseous chemical element that forms about 21 per cent by volume of the atmosphere, is found combined in water, most minerals, and many organic compounds, is required for most burning processes, and is essential for the life of all plants and animals ☞ PERIODIC TABLE [F *oxygène*, fr Gk *oxys*, adj, acid, lit., sharp + F *-gène* -gen; akin to L *acer* sharp – more at EDGE] – **oxygenic** /-'jenik/ *adj*

oxygenate /ok'sijənayt/ *vt* to impregnate, combine, or supply (e g blood) with oxygen – **oxygenator** *n*, **oxygenation** /-'naysh(ə)n/ *n*

'oxygen ,debt *n* a cumulative oxygen lack that develops during intense activity and must be made up when the body returns to rest

'oxygen ,mask *n* a device worn over the nose and mouth through which oxygen is supplied from a storage tank

'oxygen ,tent *n* a canopy placed over sby in bed to maintain a flow of oxygen-enriched air

oxyhaemoglobin /,oksi,heemə'glohbin/ *n* haemoglobin loosely combined with oxygen that it releases to the tissues [ISV]

oxymoron /,oksi'mawron/ *n, pl* **oxymora** /-rə/ a combination of contradictory or incongruous words (e g *cruel kindness*) [LGk *oxymōron*, fr neut of *oxymōros* pointedly foolish, fr Gk *oxys* sharp, keen + *mōros* foolish – more at MORON]

,oxy'tocin /-'tohsin/ *n* a polypeptide hormone secreted by the back lobe of the pituitary gland that stimulates the contraction of uterine muscle (e g during childbirth) and the ejection of milk [ISV, fr Gk *oxys* + *tokos* childbirth, fr *tiktein* to bear, beget] – **oxytocic** /-'tohsik/ *adj*

oy, oye /oy/ *n, Scot* a grandchild [ME (Sc) *o*, of Celt origin; akin to OIr *aue* grandson – more at UNCLE]

oyer and terminer /,oyər ənd 'tuhminə/ *n* a commission authorizing a British judge to hear and decide a criminal case [ME, part trans of AF *oyer et terminer*, lit., to hear and determine]

oyez /oh'yay, -yes/ *vb imper* – uttered by a court official or public crier to gain attention [ME, fr AF, hear ye, imper pl of *oir* to hear, fr L *audire* – more at AUDIBLE]

oyster /'oystə/ *n* **1** any of various (edible) marine bivalve molluscs with a rough irregular shell **2** a small mass of muscle on each side of the back of a fowl [ME *oistre*, fr MF, fr L *ostrea*, fr Gk *ostreon*; akin to Gk *ostrakon* shell, *osteon* bone – more at OSSEOUS]

'oyster ,bed *n* a place where oysters grow or are cultivated

'oyster,catcher /-,kachə/ *n* any of a genus of usu black-and-white stout-legged wading birds

'oyster ,farm *n* a stretch of sea bottom where oysters are bred for food

'oyster ,plant *n* salsify

ozocerite /,ohzoh'siəriet/, **ozokerite** /,ohzoh'kiəriet/ *n* a waxy mineral that is a mixture of hydrocarbons that is white when pure, is often of unpleasant smell, and is used esp in making candles, insulating, etc [G *ozokerit*, fr Gk *ozein* to smell + *kēros* wax – more at CERUMEN]

ozon-, ozono- *comb form* ozone ⟨ozonize⟩ [ISV, fr *ozone*]

ozone /'oh,zohn/ *n* **1** a form of oxygen with 3 atoms in each molecule that is a bluish irritating gas with a pungent smell and occurs naturally in the upper atmosphere where it is formed by the action of ultraviolet solar radiation on normal oxygen **2** pure and refreshing air [G *ozon*, fr Gk *ozōn*, prp of *ozein* to smell – more at ODOUR] – **ozonous** *adj*, **ozonize** *vt*, **ozonic** /oh'zohnik, -'zo-/ *adj*, **ozoniferous** /-'nifərəs/ *adj*

P

p /pee/ *n, pl* **p's, ps** *often cap* **1** (a graphic representation of or device for reproducing) the 16th letter of the English alphabet **2** a grade rating a student's work as passing [(2) *pass*]

pa /pah/ *n* father – infml [short for *papa*]

pa'anga /pah'ang(g)ə/ *n* ☞ *Tonga* at NATIONALITY [Tongan, lit., seed]

pabulum /'pabyooləm/ *n* **1** food **2** intellectual sustenance [L, food, fodder; akin to L *pascere* to feed – more at FOOD]

paca /'pakə, 'pahkə/ *n* any of a genus of large (spotted) S and Central American rodents [Pg & Sp, fr Tupi *páca*]

[1]**pace** /pays/ *n* **1a** rate of movement **b** parallel rate of growth or development ⟨*wages do not keep* ~ *with inflation*⟩ **c** rate or manner of doing sthg **2** a manner of walking **3a** STEP 2a(1) **b** the distance covered by a single step in walking, usu taken to be about 0.75m (about 30in) ☞ UNIT **4a** GAIT 2; *esp* a fast 2-beat gait of a horse in which the legs move in lateral pairs **b** *pl* an exhibition of skills or abilities ⟨*put him through his* ~s⟩ [ME *pas*, fr OF, step, fr L *passus*, fr *passus*, pp of *pandere* to spread – more at FATHOM]

[2]**pace** *vi* **1** to walk with a slow or measured tread **2** *esp of a horse* to go at a pace ~ *vt* **1a** to measure by pacing – often + *out* or *off* **b** to traverse at a walk **2** *of a horse* to cover (a course) by pacing **3** to set or regulate the pace of; *specif* to go ahead of (e g a runner) as a pacemaker – **pacer** *n*

[3]**pace** /'paysi/ *prep* with due respect to [L, abl of *pac-*, *pax* peace, permission]

pace bowler /pays/ *n* sby who bowls the ball fast and without spin in cricket

'pace ,car *n* a motor car that leads the field of competitors through a warm-up lap but does not participate in the race

'pace,maker /-,maykə/ *n* **1** sby or sthg that sets the pace for another (e g in a race) **2** (a device for applying regular electric shocks to the heart that reproduces the function of) a part of the heart that maintains rhythmic (coordinated) contractions – **pacemaking** *n*

'pace,setter /-,setə/ *n* PACEMAKER 1

pachisi /pə'cheezi, pah-/ *n* an ancient board game played with dice and counters on a cross-shaped board [Hindi *pacisi*]

pachyderm /'pakiduhm/ *n* an elephant, rhinoceros, pig, or other usu thick-skinned (hoofed) nonruminant mammal [F *pachyderme*, fr Gk *pachydermos* thick-skinned, fr *pachys* thick (akin to ON *bingr* heap, Skt *bahu* dense, much) + *derma* skin – more at DERM-] – **pachydermal** /-'duhml/ *adj*, **pachydermatous** /-'duhmətəs/ *adj*

pachytene /'pakiteen/ *n* the stage of the prophase of meiotic cell division in which the paired chromosomes become thickened and divided into chromatids [ISV *pachy-* (fr Gk *pachys*) + *-tene*]

pacific /pə'sifik/ *adj* **1** tending to bring about peace; conciliatory **2** having a mild peaceable nature **3** *cap* of (the region round) the Pacific ocean [MF *pacifique*, fr L *pacificus*, fr *pac-*, *pax* peace + *-i-* + *-ficus* -fic – more at PEACE] – **pacifically** *adv*

pacificatory /pə'sifikət(ə)ri/ *adj* PACIFIC 1

pacifism /'pasifiz(ə)m/ *n* opposition to war as a means of settling disputes; *specif* refusal to bear arms on moral or religious grounds [F *pacifisme*, fr *pacifique* pacific] – **pacifist** *n*

pacify /'pasifie/ *vt* **1** to allay the anger or agitation of **2a** to restore to a peaceful state; subdue **b** to reduce to submission [ME *pacifien*, fr L *pacificare*, fr *pac-*, *pax* peace] – **pacifiable** *adj*, **pacifier** /-,fie·ə/ *n*, **pacification** /-fi'kaysh(ə)n/ *n*

[1]**pack** /pak/ *n* **1** a bundle or bag of things carried on the shoulders or back; *specif* a knapsack **2a** a large amount or number ⟨*a* ~ *of lies*⟩ **b** a full set of playing cards **3** a method of packing ⟨*vacuum* ~⟩ **4** *sing or pl in constr* **a** a group of people with a common characteristic ⟨*a* ~ *of thieves*⟩ **b** an organized troop (e g of cub scouts) **5** *sing or pl in constr the* forwards in a rugby team, esp when acting together **6** *sing or pl in constr* **a** a group of domesticated animals trained to hunt or run together ⟨*a* ~ *of hounds*⟩ **b** a group of (predatory) animals of the same kind ⟨*a wolf* ~⟩ **7** a concentrated mass; *specif* PACK ICE **8** wet absorbent material for application to the body as treatment (e g for a bruise) **9** *chiefly NAm* a packet [ME, of LG or D origin; akin to MLG & MD *pak* pack, MFlem *pac*]

[2]**pack** *vt* **1a** to stow (as if) in a container, esp for transport or storage **b** to cover, fill, or surround with protective material **2a** to crowd together so as to fill; cram **b** to force into a smaller volume; compress **3** to bring to an end; finish – + *up* or *in* ⟨*he's* ~ing *up his job next year*⟩ **4** to gather into a pack **5** to cover or surround with a pack **6** to cause or be capable of making (an impact) ⟨*a book that* ~s *quite a punch*⟩ ~ *vi* **1** to stow goods or equipment for transporting – often + *up* **2** to crowd together **3** to become compacted in a layer or mass – **packable** *adj*, **packer** *n*, **packability** /,pakə'biləti/ *n* – **pack it in** to stop doing it; give it up – infml

[3]**pack** *vt* to influence the composition of (e g a jury) so as to bring about a desired result [obs *pack* (to make a secret agreement), perh alter. of *pact*]

[1]**package** /'pakij/ *n* **1a** a small or medium-sized pack; a parcel **b** sthg wrapped or sealed **2** a wrapper or container in which sthg is packed **3** PACKAGE DEAL [[2]PACK + -AGE]

[2]**package** *vt* to make into or enclose in a package – **packager** *n*

'package ,deal *n* an offer or agreement involving a number of related items and making acceptance of one item dependent on the acceptance of all; *also* the items so offered

packed /pakt/ *adj* **1a** that is crowded or stuffed – often in combination ⟨*an action*-packed *story*⟩ **b** compressed ⟨*hard*-packed *snow*⟩ **2** filled to capacity ⟨*played to a* ~ *house*⟩

packet /ˈpakit/ *n* **1** a small pack or parcel ⟨*a* ~ *of biscuits*⟩ **2** a passenger boat carrying mail and cargo on a regular schedule **3** *Br* a large sum of money ⟨*cost a* ~⟩ – infml [AF *pacquet*, dim. of *pack*; (2) short for *packet-boat*]

packhorse /ˈpak,haws/ *n* a horse used for carrying packs

ˈpack ˌice *n* sea ice crushed together into a large floating mass

packing /ˈpaking/ *n* **1** the action, process, or method of packing sthg **2** material used to pack

ˈpacking ˌcase *n* a usu wooden crate in which goods are packed for storage or transport

pack off *vt* to send away, esp abruptly or unceremoniously – infml ⟨pack *the kids* off *to school*⟩

ˈpack,saddle /-,sadl/ *n* a saddle designed to support a pack on an animal's back

ˈpack,thread /-,thred/ *n* strong thread or thin twine used for sewing or tying packages

pack up *vi* **1** to finish work **2** to cease to function ⟨*the engine* packed up⟩ ***USE*** infml

pact /pakt/ *n* an agreement, treaty [ME, fr MF, fr L *pactum*, fr neut of *pactus*, pp of *pacisci* to agree, contract; akin to OE *fōn* to seize, L *pangere* to fix, fasten, Gk *pēgnynai*]

¹pad /pad/ *n* **1** a thin flat mat or cushion: e g **a** padding used to shape an article of clothing **b** a padded guard worn to shield body parts, esp the legs of a batsman, against impact **c** a piece of absorbent material used as a surgical dressing or protective covering **2a** the foot of an animal **b** the cushioned thickening of the underside of the toes of cats, dogs, etc **3** a large floating leaf of a water plant **4** a number of sheets of paper (e g for writing or drawing on) fastened together at 1 edge **5a** a flat surface for a vertical takeoff or landing **b** LAUNCHING PAD **6** living quarters – infml [origin unknown]

²pad *vt* **-dd- 1** to provide with a pad or padding **2** to expand or fill out (speech or writing) with superfluous matter – often + *out*

³pad *vb* **-dd-** *vt* to go along on foot ~ *vi* to walk with a muffled step [perh fr MD *paden* to follow a path, fr *pad* path – more at PATH]

padding /ˈpading/ *n* material used to pad

¹paddle /ˈpadl/ *n* **1a** a usu wooden implement similar to but smaller than an oar, used to propel and steer a small craft (e g a canoe) **b** an implement with a short handle and broad flat blade used for stirring, mixing, hitting, etc **2** any of the broad boards at the circumference of a paddle wheel or waterwheel [ME *padell*]

²paddle *vb* **paddling** /ˈpadling/ *vi* to go on or through water (as if) by means of paddling a craft ~ *vt* to propel (as if) by a paddle – **paddler** *n*

³paddle *vi* to walk, play, or wade in shallow water [prob freq of ³*pad*] – **paddle** *n*, **paddler** *n*

ˈpaddle ˌsteamer *n* a vessel propelled by a pair of paddle wheels mounted amidships or by a single paddle wheel at the stern

ˈpaddle ˌwheel *n* a power-driven wheel with paddles, floats, or boards round its circumference used to propel a boat

paddock /ˈpadək/ *n* **1** a small usu enclosed field, esp for pasturing or exercising animals; *esp* one where racehorses are saddled and paraded before a race **2** an area at a motor-racing track where cars, motorcycles, etc are parked and worked on before a race [alter. of ME *parrok*, fr OE *pearroc*; akin to OHG *pfarrih* enclosure; both fr a prehistoric Gmc word borrowed fr (assumed) VL *parricus*]

paddy /ˈpadi/ *n* **1** (threshed unmilled) rice **2** a paddyfield [Malay *padi*]

Paddy *n* an Irishman – chiefly derog [*Paddy*, common Irish nickname for *Patrick*]

ˈpaddy,field /-,feeld/ *n* a field of wet land in which rice is grown

padlock /ˈpadlok/ *n* a portable lock with a shackle that can be passed through a staple or link and then secured [ME *padlok*, fr *pad*- (of unknown origin) + *lok* lock] – **padlock** *vt*

padre /ˈpahdri/ *n* **1** a Christian priest **2** a military chaplain [Sp or It or Pg, lit., father, fr L *pater* – more at FATHER]

paean /ˈpee·ən/ *n* a joyously exultant song or hymn of praise, tribute, thanksgiving, or triumph [L, hymn of thanksgiving esp addressed to Apollo, fr Gk *paian, paiōn*, fr *Paian, Paiōn*, epithet of Apollo in the hymn]

paed- /pe(e)d-/, **paedo-**, *NAm chiefly* **ped-**, **pedo-** *comb form* child ⟨paed*iatrics*⟩ [Gk *paid-, paido-*, fr *paid-, pais* child, boy – more at FEW]

paediatrics /,peediˈatriks/ *n pl but sing or pl in constr* medicine dealing with the development, care, and diseases of children – **paediatric** *adj*, **paediatrician** /,peedi·əˈtrish(ə)n/ *n*

paedophilia /,peedohˈfili·ə, -də-/ *n* sexual desire directed towards children [NL] – **paedophile** /-,fiel/ *n*

paella /pieˈela/ *n* a saffron-flavoured Spanish dish containing rice, meat, seafood, and vegetables [Catal, lit., pot, pan, fr MF *paelle*, fr L *patella* small pan – more at PATELLA]

paeon /ˈpee·ən/ *n* a metrical foot of 4 syllables with 1 long or stressed and 3 short or unstressed syllables [L, fr Gk *paiōn*, fr *paian, paiōn* paean]

paeony /ˈpee·əni/ *n* a peony

pagan /ˈpaygən/ *n* **1** a follower of a polytheistic religion **2** an irreligious person [ME, fr LL *paganus*, fr L, country dweller, fr *pagus* country district; akin to L *pangere* to fix – more at PACT] – **pagan** *adj*, **paganish** *adj*, **paganism** *n*, **paganize** *vt*

¹page /payj/ *n* **1a(1)** a youth being trained for the medieval rank of knight and in the personal service of a knight **(2)** a youth attending on a person of rank **b** a boy serving as an honorary attendant at a formal function (e g a wedding) **2** sby employed to deliver messages or run errands [ME, fr OF, fr It *paggio*]

²page *vt* **1** to summon by repeatedly calling out the name of (e g over a public-address system) **2** to summon by a coded signal emitted esp by a short-range radio transmitter

³page *n* **1** (a single side of) a leaf of a book, magazine, etc **2** sthg worth being recorded in writing ⟨*the brightest* ~ *of her career*⟩ **3** a sizable subdivision of computer memory used chiefly for convenience of reference in programming [MF, fr L *pagina*; akin to L *pangere* to fix, fasten]

⁴page *vt* to paginate

pageant /'paj(ə)nt/ *n* **1** an ostentatious display **2** a show, exhibition; *esp* a colourful spectacle with a series of tableaux, dramatic presentations, or a procession, expressing a common theme **3** PAGEANTRY 1 [ME *pagyn, padgeant*, lit., scene of a play, fr ML *pagina*, fr L, page]

pageantry /'paj(ə)ntri/ *n* **1** pageants and the presentation of pageants **2** colourful or splendid display; spectacle

'page ,boy *n* **1** a boy serving as a page **2** a usu shoulder-length woman's hairstyle in which the ends of the hair are turned under in a smooth roll

paginate /'pajinayt/ *vt* to number the sides of the leaves of (e g a book) in a sequence – compare FOLIATE 2 [L *pagina* page] – **pagination** /-'naysh(ə)n/ *n*

pagoda /pə'gohdə/ *n* a many-storied usu polygonal tower with upturned projecting roofs at the division of each storey and erected esp as a temple or memorial in the Far East [Pg *pagode* oriental idol, temple]

pah /pah/ *interj* – used esp to express contempt or disgust

pahlavi /'pahləvi/ *n, pl* **pahlavi, pahlavis** (a coin representing) a money unit of Iran worth 100 rials [Per *pahlawī*, fr Riza Shah *Pahlawī* †1944 Shah of Iran]

Pahlavi *n* the language of Sassanian Persia [Per *pahlawī*, fr *Pahlav* Parthia, fr OPer *Parthava-*]

paid /payd/ *past of* PAY

,paid-'up *adj* having paid the necessary fees to be a full member of a group or organization; *broadly* showing the characteristic attitudes and behaviour of a specified group to a marked degree ⟨*a* ~ *member of the awkward squad*⟩

pail /payl/ *n* (the contents of or quantity contained in) an esp wooden or metal bucket [ME *payle, paille*, prob fr OE *pægel*, a small measure of liquid; akin to MD *pegel* gauge, scale] – **pailful** *n*

paillasse /'palias, pal'yas/ *n* a palliasse

paillette /pal'yet/ *n* a small shiny object (e g a spangle) used to decorate clothing [F, fr *paille* straw – more at [1]PALLET]

[1]**pain** /payn/ *n* **1a** a basic bodily sensation induced by a noxious stimulus or physical disorder and characterized by physical discomfort (e g pricking, throbbing, or aching) **b** acute mental or emotional distress **2** *pl* the throes of childbirth **3** *pl* trouble or care taken **4** sby or sthg that annoys or is a nuisance – infml ⟨*she's a real* ~⟩ [ME, fr OF *peine*, fr L *poena*, fr Gk *poinē* payment, penalty; akin to Gk *tinein* to pay, *tinesthai* to punish, *timē* price, value, honour] – **painless** *adj*, **painlessly** *adv*, **painlessness** *n* – **on/under pain of** subject to penalty or punishment of ⟨*ordered to leave the country* on pain of *death*⟩ – **pain in the neck** a source of annoyance; a nuisance – infml

[2]**pain** *vt* to make suffer or cause distress to; hurt ~ *vi* to give or have a sensation of pain

painful /'paynf(ə)l/ *adj* **-ll-** **1a** feeling or giving pain **b** irksome, annoying **2** requiring effort or exertion ⟨*a long* ~ *trip*⟩ – **painfully** *adv*, **painfulness** *n*

'pain,killer /-,kilə/ *n* sthg, esp a drug (e g morphine or aspirin), that relieves pain – **painkilling** *adj*

painstaking /'payn,stayking/ *adj* showing diligent care and effort – **painstakingly** *adv*

[1]**paint** /paynt/ *vt* **1a** to apply colour, pigment, paint, or cosmetics to **b** to apply with a movement resembling that used in painting **2a** to represent in colours on a surface by applying pigments **b** to decorate by painting **c** to produce or evoke as if by painting ⟨*her novel* ~s *glowing pictures of rural life*⟩ **3** to depict as having specified or implied characteristics ⟨*not as black as he's* ~ed⟩ ~ *vi* to practise the art of painting [ME *painten*, fr OF *peint*, pp of *peindre*, fr L *pingere* to tattoo, embroider, paint; akin to OE *fāh* variegated, Gk *poikilos* variegated, *pikros* sharp, bitter]

[2]**paint** *n* **1a(1)** a mixture of a pigment and a suitable liquid which forms a closely adherent coating when spread on a surface **(2)** pigment, esp in compressed form **b** an applied coat of paint ⟨*wet* ~⟩ **2** (coloured) make-up – infml – **painty** *adj*

'paint,brush /-,brush/ *n* a brush for applying paint

,painted 'lady *n* a migratory butterfly with wings mottled in brown, orange, red, and white

[1]**painter** /'payntə/ *n* **1** an artist who paints **2** sby who applies paint (e g to a building), esp as an occupation [[1]PAINT + [2]-ER]

[2]**painter** *n* a line used for securing or towing a boat [ME *paynter*, prob fr MF *pendoir, pentoir* clothesline, fr *pendre* to hang – more at PENDANT]

'painterly /-li/ *adj* artistic; *also, of a painter or a painting* showing an interest in pigment and the qualities of paint as a material rather than in draughtsmanship [[1]PAINTER + [1]-LY] – **painterliness** *n*

painting /'paynting/ *n* **1** a product of painting; *esp* a painted work of art **2** the art or occupation of painting

'paint,work /-,wuhk/ *n* paint that has been applied to a surface; *also* a painted surface ⟨*damaged the* ~ *of the car*⟩

[1]**pair** /peə/ *n sing or pl in constr, pl* **pairs** *also* **pair** **1a(1)** two corresponding things usu used together ⟨*a* ~ *of shoes*⟩ **(2)** two corresponding bodily parts ⟨*a beautiful* ~ *of legs*⟩ **b** a single thing made up of 2 connected corresponding pieces ⟨*a* ~ *of trousers*⟩ **2a** two similar or associated things: e g **(1)** a couple in love, engaged, or married ⟨*were a devoted* ~⟩ **(2)** two playing cards of the same value in a hand **(3)** two horses harnessed side by side **(4)** two mated animals **b** a partnership between 2 people, esp in a contest against another partnership **c** two members from opposite sides of a deliberative body who agree not to vote on a specific issue during a time agreed on **d** a failure to score runs in either innings of a match by a batsman in cricket [ME *paire*, fr OF, fr L *paria* equal things, fr neut pl of *par* equal]

[2]**pair** *vt* **1** to arrange a voting pair between **2** to arrange in pairs ⟨*she succeeded in* ~ing *the socks*⟩

,pair of 'compasses *n* COMPASS 2b

pair off *vb* to (cause to) form pairs, esp male and female ⟨*the anxious mothers are trying to* pair off *their children*⟩ ⟨*they* paired off *for the next dance*⟩

'pair pro,duction *n* the transformation of a quantum of radiant energy into an electron and a positron

paisa /'piesə/ *n, pl* **paise** /-say/, **paisa, paisas** ☞ *Bangladesh, India, Pakistan* at NATIONALITY [Hindi *paisā*]

paisley /'payzli/ *adj, often cap* of a fabric or garment made usu of soft wool and woven or printed with colourful abstract teardrop-shaped figures [*Paisley*, town in Scotland] – **paisley** *n*

pajamas /pə'jahməz/ *n pl in constr, pl* **pajamas** *chiefly NAm* pyjamas – **pajama** *adj*

pakeha /'pahkə,hah, pah'kee·ə/ *n, pl* **pakehas,** *esp collectively* **pakeha** *NZ* one who is not a Maori; *broadly* a white person [Maori]

Paki /'paki/ *n, often not cap, Br* a Pakistani – chiefly derog

Pakistani /,paki'stahni, ,pah-/ *n* **1** a native or inhabitant of Pakistan **2** a descendant of Pakistanis [Hindustani *Pākistānī*, fr *Pākistān* Pakistan, country in S Asia] – **Pakistani** *adj*

pal /pal/ *n* **1** a close friend **2** – used as a familiar form of address, esp to a stranger *USE* infml [Romany *phral, phal* brother, friend, fr Skt *bhrātṛ* brother; akin to OE *brōthor* brother]

[1]**palace** /'palis/ *n* **1** the official residence of a ruler (e g a sovereign or bishop) **2a** a large stately house **b** a large public building **c** a large and often ornate place of public entertainment ⟨*a picture* ~⟩ [ME *palais*, fr OF, fr L *palatium*, fr *Palatium*, the Palatine Hill in Rome where the emperors' residences were built]

[2]**palace** *adj* **1** of a palace **2** of or involving the intimates of a chief executive ⟨*a* ~ *revolution*⟩ ⟨~ *politics*⟩

paladin /'palədin/ *n* a champion of a medieval prince [F, fr It *paladino*, fr ML *palatinus* courtier, fr L, palace official – more at PALATINE]

palae- /pali-/, **palaeo-,** *chiefly NAm* **pale-, paleo-** *comb form* **1** involving or dealing with ancient (e g fossil) forms or conditions ⟨palaeo*botany*⟩ **2** early; primitive; archaic ⟨Palaeo*lithic*⟩ [Gk *palai-, palaio-* ancient, fr *palaios*, fr *palai* long ago; akin to Gk *tēle* far-off, Skt *carama* last]

Palaearctic /,pali'ahktik/ *adj* of or being a biogeographic region that includes Europe and N Asia, Arabia, and Africa

,palaeo'botany /,palioh'botəni/ *n* a branch of botany dealing with fossil plants [ISV] – **palaeobotanist** *n*, **palaeobotanic** /-bə'tanik/, **palaeobotanical** *adj*, **palaeobotanically** *adv*

Palaeocene /'palioh,seen/ *adj or n* (of or being) the earliest epoch of the Tertiary period ☞ EVOLUTION

palaeoclimatology /,palioh,kliemə'toləji/ *n* a science dealing with the climate of past ages [ISV]

palaeography /,pali'ogrəfi/ *n* the study of ancient writings and inscriptions [NL *palaeographia*, fr Gk *palai-* + *-graphia* -graphy] – **palaeographer** *n*

Palaeolithic /,pali·ə'lithik/ *adj or n* (of or being) the 2nd era of the Stone Age characterized by rough or chipped stone implements [ISV]

palaeomagnetism /,palioh'magnə,tiz(ə)m/ *n* (the study of) the intensity and direction of residual magnetization in ancient rocks

palaeontology /,palion'toləji/ *n* a science dealing with the life of past geological periods as inferred from fossil remains [F *paléontologie*, fr *palé-* palae- + Gk *onta* living things (fr neut pl of *ont, ōn*, prp of *einai* to be) + F *-logie* -logy] – **palaeontologist** *n*, **palaeontological** /-,ontə'lojikl/ *adj*

,Palaeo'zoic /,pali·ə'zohik/ *adj or n* (of or being) an era of geological history that extends from the beginning of the Cambrian to the close of the Permian ☞ EVOLUTION

palais /'palay, 'pali/, **palais de dance** /~ də 'donhs/ *n* a public dance hall – chiefly infml [F *palais de danse*, lit., dance palace]

palanquin /'palənkeen/ *n* a litter formerly used in eastern Asia, esp for 1 person, and usu hung from poles borne on the bearers' shoulders [Pg *palanquim*, fr Jav *pĕlaṅki*]

palatable /'palətəbl/ *adj* **1** pleasant to the taste **2** acceptable to the mind [*palate* + *-able*] – **palatableness** *n*, **palatably** *adv*, **palatability** /-tə'biləti/ *n*

palatal /'palətl/ *adj* **1** of the palate **2** *of a speech sound (e g /y/)* formed with the front of the tongue near or touching the hard palate – **palatal** *n*, **palatalize** *vt*, **palatally** /'palətl·i/ *adv*, **palatalization** /-ie 'zaysh(ə)n/ *n*

palate /'palət/ *n* **1** the roof of the mouth, separating it from the nasal cavity ☞ NERVE **2a** the sense of taste **b** a usu intellectual taste or liking [ME, fr L *palatum*]

palatial /pə'laysh(ə)l/ *adj* **1** of or being a palace **2** suitable to a palace; magnificent [L *palatium* palace] – **palatially** *adv*, **palatialness** *n*

palatinate /pə'latinət/ *n* the territory of a palatine

[1]**palatine** /'palətien/ *n* a feudal lord (e g a count or bishop) with sovereign power [L *palatinus*, fr *palatinus*, adj, fr *palatium*]

[2]**palatine** *adj* of or lying near the palate

palaver /pə'lahvə/ *n* **1** a long parley or discussion **2** idle talk [Pg *palavra* word, speech, fr LL *parabola* parable, speech] – **palaver** *vi*

palazzo /pə'latsoh, -sə, -'ladzoh, -zə/ *n, pl* **palazzi** /-si/ a large imposing building in Italy [It, fr L *palatium* palace]

[1]**pale** /payl/ *adj* **1** deficient in (intensity of) colour **2** not bright or brilliant; dim ⟨*a* ~ *sun shining through the fog*⟩ **3** feeble, faint ⟨*a* ~ *imitation*⟩ **4** *of a colour* not intense ⟨*a* ~ *pink*⟩ [ME, fr MF, fr L *pallidus*. fr *pallēre* to be pale – more at [1]FALLOW] – **pale** *vb*, **palish** *adj*, **palely** *adv*, **paleness** *n*

[2]**pale** *n* **1** PICKET 1 **2** a territory under a particular jurisdiction [ME, fr MF *pal* stake, fr L *palus* – more at [1]POLE] – **beyond the pale** in violation of good manners, social convention etc

[3]**pale** *n* a palea

pale-, paleo- *comb form, chiefly NAm* palae-, palaeo-

palea /'paylyə/ *n, pl* **paleae** /'payli,ee/ a chaffy scale or bract, esp the upper bract of the flower of a grass [NL, fr L, chaff – more at [1]PALLET] – **paleal** /'paylyəl/ *adj*

paleface /'payl,fays/ *n* a white person, esp as distinguished from an American Indian

palette /'palit/ *n* **1** a thin board held in the hand on which an artist mixes pigments **2** a particular range, quality, or use of colour; *esp* that of an individual artist [F, fr MF, dim. of *pale* spade, shovel, fr L *pala*]

'palette ,knife *n* a knife with a flexible steel blade and no cutting edge, used esp in cooking or by artists for mixing and applying paints

palfrey /'pawlfri/ *n, archaic* a saddle horse other than a war-horse, esp for a woman [ME, fr OF *palefrei*, fr ML *palafredus*, fr LL *paraveredus* post-horse for secondary roads, fr Gk *para-* beside, subsidiary + L *veredus* post-horse, fr a Gaulish word akin to W *gorwydd* horse; akin to OIr *riadaim* I ride – more at PARA-, RIDE]

Pali /'pahli/ *n* the liturgical language of Theravada Buddhism [Skt *pāli* row, series of Buddhist sacred texts]

palimpsest /'palimpsest/ *n* writing material (e g a parchment or tablet) reused after earlier writing has been erased [L *palimpsestus*, fr Gk *palimpsēstos* scraped again, fr *palin* + *psēn* to rub, scrape – more at SAND]

palindrome /'palindrohm/ *n* a word, sentence, etc that reads the same backwards or forwards [Gk *palindromos* running back again, fr *palin* back, again (akin to Gk *polos* axis, pole) + *dramein* to run – more at [3]POLE, DROMEDARY] – **palindromic** /-'drohmik/ *adj*

paling /'payling/ *n* (a fence of) stakes or pickets [[2]*pale* + *-ing*]

palingenetic /,palinjə'netik/ *adj* of or being biological features (e g the gill slits in a human embryo) that are derivations from distant ancestral forms [*palingenesis*, n, fr Gk *palin* + L *genesis* birth]

palinode /'palinohd/ *n* a poem in which sthg is recanted or retracted [Gk *palinōidia*, fr *palin* back + *aeidein* to sing – more at ODE]

[1]**palisade** /,pali'sayd/ *n* **1** a fence of stakes, esp for defence **2** a long strong stake pointed at the top and set close with others as a defence [F *palissade*, deriv of L *palus* stake – more at [1]POLE]

[2]**palisade** *vt* to surround or fortify with palisades

palisade layer *n* a layer of cells containing many chloroplasts lying beneath the upper skin of green leaves

[1]**pall** /pawl/ *n* **1** PALLIUM 1b **2a** a square of linen used to cover the chalice containing the wine used at Communion **b** a heavy cloth draped over a coffin or tomb **3** sthg heavy or dark that covers or conceals ⟨*a ~ of thick black smoke*⟩ [ME, cloak, mantle, fr OE *pæll*, fr L *pallium*]

[2]**pall** *vi* to cease to be interesting or attractive [ME *pallen* to become weak or stale, short for *appallen* to become pale – more at APPAL]

Palladian /pə'laydi·ən/ *adj* of a neoclassic style of architecture based on the works of Andrea Palladio [Andrea *Palladio* †1580 It architect] – **Palladianism** *n*

palladium /pə'laydi·əm/ *n* a soft silver-white metallic element of the platinum group used esp in electrical contacts and as a catalyst ☞ PERIODIC TABLE [NL, fr *Pallad-*, *Pallas*, an asteroid] – **palladous** /pə'laydəs/ *adj*

pallbearer /'pawl,beərə/ *n* a person who helps to carry the coffin at a funeral or is part of its immediate escort

[1]**pallet** /'palit/ *n* **1** a straw-filled mattress **2** a small hard often makeshift bed [ME *pailet*, fr (assumed) MF *paillet*, fr *paille* straw, fr L *palea* chaff, straw; akin to Skt *palāva* chaff]

[2]**pallet** *n* **1** a flat-bladed wooden tool used esp by potters for shaping clay **2** a lever or surface in a timepiece that receives an impulse from the escapement wheel and imparts motion to a balance or pendulum **3** a portable platform intended for handling, storing, or moving materials and packages [MF *palette*, lit., small shovel – more at PALETTE]

pallet·ize, -ise /'palitiez/ *vt* to place on, transport, or store by means of pallets – **palletizer** *n*, **palletization** /-tie'zaysh(ə)n/ *n*

palliasse, paillasse /'palias, pal'yas/ *n* a thin straw mattress [*palliasse* modif of F *paillasse*, fr *paille* straw]

palliate /'paliayt/ *vt* **1** to lessen the unpleasantness of (e g a disease) without removing the cause **2** to disguise the gravity of (a fault or offence) by excuses or apologies; extenuate **3** to moderate the intensity of ⟨*trying to ~ the boredom*⟩ [LL *palliatus*, pp of *palliare* to cloak, conceal, fr *pallium* cloak] – **palliator** *n*, **palliative** /'palyətiv/ *n or adj*, **palliation** /,pali'aysh(ə)n/ *n*

pallid /'palid/ *adj* **1** lacking colour; wan **2** lacking sparkle or liveliness; dull [L *pallidus* – more at [1]PALE] – **pallidly** *adv*, **pallidness** *n*

pallium /'pali·əm/ *n, pl* **pallia** /-li·ə/, **palliums** **1a** a draped rectangular cloth worn as a cloak, esp by men of ancient Rome **b** a white woollen band in the shape of 2 Y's that meet on the shoulders, worn esp by a pope or archbishop ☞ GARMENT **2** the mantle of a mollusc, bird, etc [L] – **pallial** *adj*

pallor /'palə/ *n* deficiency of (facial) colour; paleness [L, fr *pallēre* to be pale – more at [1]FALLOW]

pally /'pali/ *adj* friendly ⟨*he was very ~ with the local vicar*⟩ – infml [*pal* + [1]*-y*]

[1]**palm** /pahm; *NAm* pah(l)m/ *n* **1** any of a family of tropical or subtropical trees, shrubs, or climbing plants related to the lilies, grasses, and orchids and usu having a simple stem and a crown of large leaves **2** a leaf of the palm as a symbol of victory, distinction, or rejoicing; *also* a branch (e g of laurel) similarly used **3** a symbol of triumph or distinction; *also* a victory, triumph [ME, fr OE; akin to OHG *palma* palm tree; both fr a prehistoric NGmc-WGmc word borrowed fr L *palma* palm of the hand, palm tree; fr the resemblance of the tree's leaves to the outstretched hand] – **palmlike** *adj*, **palmaceous** /pah'mayshəs/ *adj*

[2]**palm** *n* **1** the concave part of the human hand between the bases of the fingers and the wrist **2** a unit of measurement based on the length (e g about 200mm or 8in) or breadth (e g about 100mm or 4in) of the human hand ☞ UNIT [ME *paume*, fr MF, fr L *palma*; akin to OE *flōr* floor]

[3]**palm** *vt* **1a** to conceal in or with the hand **b** to pick up stealthily **2** to impose by fraud

palmar /'palmə, 'pahmə/ *adj* of or involving the palm of the hand

palmate /'palmayt, -mət/ *also* **palmated** /-,maytid/ *adj* (having lobes radiating from a common point) resembling a hand with the fingers spread ☞ PLANT – **palmately** *adv*, **palmation** /-'maysh(ə)n/ *n*

palm civet *n* any of various tree-dwelling African or Asian civets

palmer /'palmə, 'pahmə/ *n* a pilgrim wearing 2 crossed palm leaves as a sign of a visit to the Holy Land

palmetto /pal'metoh/ *n, pl* **palmettos, palmettoes** any of several usu low-growing fan-leaved palms [modif of Sp *palmito*, fr *palma* palm, fr L]

palmistry /'pahmistri/ *n* reading a person's character or future from the markings on his/her palms [ME *pawmestry*, prob fr *paume* palm + *maistrie* mastery] – **palmist** *n*

palmitate /'palmitayt/ *n* a salt or ester of palmitic acid

pal,mitic 'acid /pal'mitik/ *n* a waxy fatty acid occurring (as glycerides) in most fats and fatty oils [ISV, fr *palmitin* (an ester of glycerol & palmitic acid), fr F *palmitine*, prob fr *palmite* pith of the palm tree, fr Sp *palmito*]

palm off *vt* to get rid of (sthg unwanted or inferior) by deceiving sby into taking it – often + *on*

'palm ,oil *n* an edible fat obtained from the fruit of several palms and used esp in soap and candles

,Palm 'Sunday *n* the Sunday before Easter celebrated in commemoration of Christ's triumphal entry into Jerusalem [fr the palm branches strewn in Christ's path]

palmy /'pahmi, 'pahlmi/ *adj* marked by prosperity; flourishing ⟨~ *days*⟩ [[1]PALM + [1]-Y]

palmyra /pal'mie·ərə/ *n* a tall fan-leaved palm cultivated in Asia for its hard wood, fibre, and sugar-rich sap [Pg *palmeira*, fr *palma* palm, fr L]

palolo /pə'lohloh/ *n, pl* **palolos** an edible marine worm that burrows in the coral reefs of various Pacific islands and forms periodic breeding swarms [Samoan & Tongan]

palomino /,palə'meenoh/ *n, pl* **palominos** a light tan or cream usu slender-legged horse [AmerSp, fr Sp, like a dove, fr L *palumbinus*, fr *palumbes* ringdove; akin to Gk *peleia* dove, L *pallēre* to be pale – more at [1]FALLOW]

palp /palp/ *n* a segmented (touch- or taste-sensitive) feeler on the mouthparts of an insect or other arthropod ☞ ANATOMY [NL *palpus*, fr L, caress, soft palm of the hand; akin to L *palpare*] – **palpal** *adj*

palpable /'palpəbl/ *adj* **1** capable of being touched or felt; tangible **2** easily perceptible by the mind; manifest ⟨*a* ~ *falsehood*⟩ [ME, fr LL *palpabilis*, fr L *palpare* to stroke, caress – more at FEEL] – **palpably** *adv*, **palpability** /,palpə'biləti/ *n*

palpate /'palpayt/ *vt* to examine, esp medically, by touch [prob back-formation fr *palpation*, fr L *palpation-, palpatio*, fr *palpatus*, pp of *palpare*] – **palpation** /pal'paysh(ə)n/ *n*

palpebral /'palpibrəl/ *adj* of or near the eyelids [LL *palpebralis*, fr L *palpebra* eyelid; akin to L *palpare*]

palpitant /'palpit(ə)nt/ *adj* marked by trembling or throbbing

palpitate /'palpitayt/ *vi* to beat rapidly and strongly; throb ⟨*a* palpitating *heart*⟩ [L *palpitatus*, pp of *palpitare*, freq of *palpare* to stroke] – **palpitation** /-'taysh(ə)n/ *n*

palpus /'palpəs/ *n, pl* **palpi** /'palpie, -pi/ a palp

palstave /'pawl,stayv/ *n* a type of Bronze age axe designed to fit into a split wooden handle [Dan *pålstav*, fr ON *pālstafr*, a heavy missile, prob fr *pāll* spade, hoe + *stafr* staff]

[1]palsy /'pawlzi, 'polzi/ *n* paralysis or uncontrollable tremor of (a part of) the body [ME *parlesie*, fr MF *paralisie*, fr L *paralysis*]

[2]palsy *vt* to affect (as if) with palsy

palter /'pawltə, 'poltə/ *vi* **1** to act insincerely or deceitfully; equivocate **2** to haggle – + *with* [origin unknown] – **palterer** *n*

paltry /'pawltri/ *adj* **1** mean, despicable ⟨*a* ~ *trick*⟩ **2** trivial ⟨*a* ~ *sum*⟩ [obs *paltry* (trash), fr E dial. *palt, pelt*] – **paltriness** *n*

paludal /pəl'yoohdl, 'palyoodl/ *adj* of marshes or fens [L *palud-, palus* marsh; akin to Skt *palvala* pond]

palynology /,pali'noləji/ *n* a branch of botany dealing with pollen and spores [Gk *palynein* to sprinkle, fr *palē* fine meal – more at POLLEN] – **palynologist** *n*, **palynological, palynologic** /,palinə'lojik/ *adj*, **palynologically** *adv*

pampa /'pampə/ *n* an extensive (grass-covered) plain of temperate S America east of the Andes – usu pl with sing. meaning but sing. or pl in constr ☞ PLANT [AmerSp, fr Quechua & Aymara, plain]

pampas grass /'pampəs/ *n* a tall S American grass with large silky flower heads frequently cultivated as an ornamental plant [*pampas* fr AmerSp, pl of *pampa*]

pamper /'pampə/ *vt* to treat with extreme or excessive care and attention ⟨~ed *their guests*⟩ [ME *pamperen*, prob of D origin; akin to Flem *pamperen* to pamper]

pampero /pam'peəroh/ *n, pl* **pamperos** a strong cold wind from the W or SW that blows over the pampas [AmerSp, fr *pampa*]

pamphlet /'pamflit/ *n* a usu small unbound printed publication with a paper cover, often dealing with topical matters ⟨*a* ~ *on nuclear disarmament*⟩ [ME *pamflet* unbound booklet, fr *Pamphilus seu De Amore* Pamphilus or On Love, popular 12th-c Latin love poem]

pamphleteer /,pamfli'tiə/ *n* a writer of (political) pamphlets attacking sthg or urging a cause

[1]pan /pan/ *n* **1a** any of various usu broad shallow open receptacles: e g **(1)** WARMING PAN **(2)** a dustpan **(3)** a bedpan **(4)** a metal or plastic dish in a pair of scales **(5)** a round metal container or vessel usu with a long handle, used to heat or cook food – compare SAUCEPAN **b** any of various similar usu metal receptacles: e g **(1)** the hollow part of the gunlock in old guns or pistols for receiving the priming **(2)** a vessel in which gold or a similar metal is separated from waste by washing **2** a hollow or depression in land ⟨*a salt* ~⟩ **3** hardpan **4a** *chiefly Br* the bowl of a toilet **b** *chiefly NAm* TIN 2b [ME *panne*, fr OE; akin to OHG *phanna* pan; both fr a prehistoric WGmc-NGmc word borrowed fr L *patina*, fr Gk *patanē*; akin to L *patēre* to be open – more at FATHOM]

[2]pan *vb* **-nn-** *vi* **1** to wash earth, gravel, etc in a pan in search of metal (e g gold) **2** to yield precious metal in panning ~ *vt* **1a** to wash (earth, gravel, etc) in a pan **b** to separate (e g gold) by panning **2** to criticize severely – infml

[3]pan /pahn/ *n* (a substance for chewing consisting of betel nut and various spices etc wrapped in) a betel leaf [Hindi *pān*, fr Skt *parṇa* wing, leaf – more at FERN]

[4]pan /pan/ *vb* **-nn-** *vi* **1** to rotate a film or television camera horizontally so as to keep a moving object in view or obtain a panoramic effect **2** *of a camera* to undergo panning ~ *vt* to cause (a camera) to pan [*panorama*]

[5]pan /pan/ *n* the act or process of panning a camera; the movement of the camera in a panning shot

pan- /pan-/ *comb form* **1** all; completely ⟨pan*chromatic*⟩ **2a** of all of (a specified group) ⟨Pan-*American*⟩ **b** advocating or involving the union of (a specified group) ⟨Pan-*Asian*⟩ **3** whole; general ⟨pan*demic*⟩ [Gk, fr *pan*, neut of *pant-, pas* all, every; akin to Skt *śaśvat* all, every, *śvayati* he swells]

panacea /,panə'see·ə/ *n* a remedy for all ills or difficulties [L, fr Gk *panakeia*, fr *pan-* + *akeisthai* to heal, fr *akos* remedy] – **panacean** *adj*

panache /pə'nash, pa-/ *n* **1** an ornamental tuft (e g of feathers), esp on a helmet 2 dash or flamboyance in style and action; verve [MF *pennache*, fr OIt *pennacchio*, fr LL *pinnaculum* small wing – more at PINNACLE]

panada /pə'nahdə/ *n* a thick paste of flour or bread-crumbs used as a base for a sauce or as a binder for forcemeat [Sp, fr *pan* bread, fr L *panis* – more at FOOD]

panama /ˌpanə'mah/ *n, often cap* a lightweight hat of plaited straw [AmerSp *panamá*, fr *Panama*, country in Central America]

panatela, panatella /ˌpanə'tela/ *n* a long slender straight-sided cigar rounded off at the sealed mouth end [Sp, fr AmerSp, a long thin biscuit, deriv of L *panis* bread]

pancake /'panˌkayk/ *n* 1 a flat cake made from thin batter and cooked on both sides usu in a frying pan 2 make-up compressed into a flat cake or stick form

'Pancake ˌDay *n* Shrove Tuesday as marked by the eating of pancakes

pancake landing *n* a landing in which an aircraft descends in an approximately horizontal position with little forward motion

panchromatic /ˌpankroh'matik, -krə-/ *adj* sensitive to light of all colours in the visible spectrum ⟨~ *film*⟩ [ISV]

pancreas /'pangkri·əs/ *n* a large compound gland in vertebrates that secretes digestive enzymes into the intestines and the hormones insulin and glucagon into the blood ☞ DIGESTION [NL, fr Gk *pankreas*, fr *pan-* + *kreas* flesh, meat – more at RAW] – **pancreatic** /-kri'atik/ *adj*

pancreat- /'pangkri·ət-/, **pancreato-** *comb form* pancreas ⟨pancreat*ic*⟩ [NL, fr Gk *pankreat-, pankreas*]

pancreatic juice /ˌpangkri'atik/ *n* the secretion of pancreatic digestive enzymes that is poured into the duodenum

pancreatin /pang'kree·ətin, 'pangkri·əˌtin/ *n* (a preparation containing) a mixture of enzymes from the pancreatic juice

panda /'pandə/ *n* 1 a long-tailed Himalayan flesh-eating mammal resembling the American raccoon and having long chestnut fur spotted with black 2 a large black-and-white plant-eating mammal of western China resembling a bear but related to the raccoons ☞ ENDANGERED [F, fr native name in Nepal]

'panda ˌcar *n, Br* a small car used by police patrols, esp in urban areas [fr its orig having black-and-white bodywork]

pandemic /pan'demik/ *n or adj* (a disease) occurring over a wide area and affecting an exceptionally high proportion of the population [adj LL *pandemus*, fr Gk *pandēmos* of all the people, fr *pan-* + *dēmos* people – more at DEMAGOGUE; n fr adj]

pandemonium /ˌpandi'mohnyəm, -ni·əm/ *n* a wild uproar; a tumult [NL, abode of all demons, hell, fr Gk *pan-* + *daimōn* evil spirit]

¹pander /'pandə/ *n* 1 a pimp 2 sby who encourages or exploits the weaknesses or vices of others [ME *Pandare* Pandarus, mythical Gk procurer, fr L *Pandarus*, fr Gk *Pandaros*]

²pander *vi* to act as a pander; *esp* to provide gratification for others' desires – usu + *to*

pandit /'pundit/ *n* a wise or learned man in India – often used as an honorary title [Hindi *paṇḍit*, fr Skt *paṇḍita*]

Pandora's box /pan'dawrəz/ *n* a prolific source of troubles [fr the Gk myth of a box sent by the gods to Pandora, the first woman, which contained all the ills of mankind]

pane /payn/ *n* 1 a piece, section, or side of sthg; *esp* a framed sheet of glass in a window or door 2 any of the sections into which a sheet of postage stamps is cut for distribution [ME *pan, pane* strip of cloth, pane, fr MF *pan*, fr L *pannus* cloth, rag – more at VANE]

panegyric /ˌpani'jirik/ *n* a eulogistic oration or piece of writing; *also* formal or elaborate praise [L *panegyricus*, fr Gk *panēgyrikos*, fr *panēgyrikos* of or for a festival assembly, fr *panēgyris* festival assembly, fr *pan-* + *agyris* assembly; akin to Gk *ageirein* to gather – more at GREGARIOUS] – **panegyrical** *adj*, **panegyrically** *adv*, **panegyrist** /ˌpani'jirist, -'jie·ə-/ *n*

¹panel /'panl/ *n* **1a(1)** a list of people summoned for jury service **(2)** the jury so summoned **b(1)** a group of people selected to perform some service (e g investigation or arbitration) ⟨*a* ~ *of experts*⟩ **(2)** a group of people who discuss before an audience topics of usu political or social interest **(3)** a group of entertainers who appear as contestants in a quiz or guessing game on radio or television **2** a separate or distinct part of a surface: e g **a(1)** a thin usu rectangular board set in a frame (e g in a door) ☞ ARCHITECTURE **(2)** a usu sunken or raised section of a surface set off by a margin **b** a vertical section of fabric ⟨*skirt made with 8* ~s⟩ **3** a thin flat piece of wood on which a picture is painted **4a** a flat often insulated support (e g for parts of an electrical device) usu with controls on 1 face **b** a usu vertical mount for controls or dials (e g in a car or aircraft) ***USE*** (*1a(2) & 1b*) sing. or pl in constr [ME, piece of cloth, slip of parchment, jury schedule, fr MF, piece of cloth, piece, prob fr (assumed) VL *pannellus*, dim. of L *pannus* cloth]

²panel *vt* **-ll-** (*NAm* **-l-**, **-ll-**), /'panl·ing/ to furnish or decorate with panels ⟨~led *the living room*⟩

panel heating *n* space heating of rooms by means of panels containing a heat source

panellist /'panl·ist/ *n* a member of a discussion or advisory panel or of a radio or television panel

'panel ˌpin *n* a short slender nail used for woodwork

pang /pang/ *n* 1 a brief piercing spasm of pain 2 a sharp attack of mental anguish ⟨~s *of remorse*⟩ [origin unknown]

panga /'pang·gə/ *n* a large broad-bladed African knife [native name in E Africa]

pangolin /pang'gohlin/ *n* any of several Asian and African anteaters with a body covered with large overlapping horny scales [Malay *pĕngguling*]

panhandle /'panˌhandl/ *vb, NAm* to beg (from) in the street ***USE*** – infml [back-formation fr *panhandler*, prob fr *panhandle*, n; fr the extended forearm] – **panhandler** /-ˌhandlə/ *n*

¹panic /'panik/ *n* 1 a sudden overpowering fright; *esp* a sudden unreasoning terror that spreads rapidly through a group 2 a sudden widespread fright concerning financial affairs and resulting in a depression in values [F *panique*, adj, of fright caused by Pan, Gk god of woods, fr Gk *panikos*, fr *Pan*] – **panic** *adj*, **panicky** *adj*

²panic *vb* **-ck-** to (cause to) be affected with panic

ˈpanic ˌbutton *n* sthg setting off a precipitous emergency response

ˈpanic ˌgrass *n* any of various (forage or cereal) grasses [ME *panik*, fr MF or L; MF *panic* foxtail millet, fr L *panicum*, fr *panus* swelling, ear of millet]

panicle /ˈpanikl/ *n* a (pyramidal) loosely branched flower cluster or compound inflorescence ☞ PLANT [L *panicula*, fr dim. of *panus* swelling] – **panicled** *adj*, **paniculate** /pəˈnikyoolət, -ˌlayt/ *adj*

ˈpanic-ˌstricken *adj* overcome with panic

Panjabi /poonˈjahbi/ *n or adj* (a) Punjabi

panjandrum /panˈjandrəm/ *n, pl* **panjandrums** *also* **panjandra** /-drə/ a powerful personage or self-important official – humor [Grand *Panjandrum*, burlesque title of an imaginary personage in some nonsense lines by Samuel Foote †1777 E actor & dramatist]

panleucopenia /ˌpanˌloohkəˈpeenyə/ *n* an acute usu fatal epidemic virus disease of cats [NL]

panne /pan/ *n* a silk or rayon velvet with lustrous pile flattened in 1 direction [F, fr OF *penne, panne* fur used for lining, fr L *pinna* feather, wing – more at [3]PEN]

pannier, panier /ˈpanyə, ˈpani·ə/ *n* **1** a large basket; *esp* either of a pair carried on the back of an animal **2** a hoop petticoat or overskirt that gives extra width to the sides of a skirt at hip level **3** *chiefly Br* either of a pair of bags or boxes fixed on either side of the rear wheel of a bicycle or motorcycle [ME *panier*, fr MF, fr L *panarium*, fr *panis* bread – more at FOOD]

panoply /ˈpanəpli/ *n* **1a** a full suit of armour **b** ceremonial dress **2** a magnificent or impressive array ⟨*the full ~ of a military funeral*⟩ [Gk *panoplia*, fr *pan-* + *hopla* arms, armour, pl of *hoplon* tool, weapon – more at HOPLITE] – **panoplied** *adj*

panorama /ˌpanəˈrahmə/ *n* **1a** a large pictorial representation encircling the spectator **b** a picture exhibited by being unrolled before the spectator **2a** an unobstructed or complete view of a landscape or area **b** a comprehensive presentation or survey of a series of events [*pan-* + Gk *horama* sight, fr *horan* to see – more at WARY] – **panoramic** /-ˈramik/ *adj*, **panoramically** *adv*

pan out *vi* to turn out as specified; *esp* to succeed [[2]*pan*]

ˈpanˌpipe /ˈpanˌpiep, ˌ-ˈ-/ *n* a primitive wind instrument consisting of a graduated series of short vertical pipes bound together with the mouthpieces in an even row – often pl with sing. meaning [*Pan*, Gk god of woods, its alleged inventor]

pansy /ˈpanzi/ *n* **1** (a flower of) a garden plant derived from wild violets **2** an effeminate male or male homosexual – derog [MF *pensée*, fr *pensée* thought, fr fem of *pensé*, pp of *penser* to think, fr L *pensare* to ponder – more at PENSIVE]

[1]pant /pant/ *vi* **1a** to breathe quickly, spasmodically, or in a laboured manner **b** to run panting ⟨*~ing along beside the bicycle*⟩ **c** to make a puffing sound **2** to long eagerly; yearn **3** to throb, pulsate *~ vt* to utter with panting; gasp ⟨*~ed his apologies for arriving so late*⟩ [ME *panten*, fr MF *pantaisier*, fr (assumed) VL *phantasiare* to have hallucinations, fr Gk *phantasioun*, fr *phantasia* appearance, imagination – more at FANCY]

[2]pant *n* **1** a panting breath **2** a puffing sound

pant- /pant-/, **panto-** *comb form* all ⟨*pantisocracy*⟩ [MF, fr L, fr Gk, fr *pant-, pas* – more at PAN-]

pantalets, pantalettes /ˌpantəˈlets/ *n pl* a trouser-like undergarment with a ruffle at the bottom of each leg, worn esp by women and children in the early 19th c [*pantaloons*]

pantaloon /ˌpantəˈloohn/ *n* **1** a stock character in the commedia dell'arte who is usu a skinny old dotard wearing pantaloons **2** *pl* any of several kinds of men's breeches or trousers; *esp* close-fitting trousers fastened under the calf or instep and worn in the 18th and 19th c [MF & OIt; MF *Pantalon*, fr OIt *Pantaleone, Pantalone*]

pantechnicon /panˈteknikən/ *n, Br* a large van, esp for transporting household possessions, furniture, etc [short for *pantechnicon van*, fr *pantechnicon* (storage warehouse)]

pantheism /ˈpanthee·iz(ə)m/ *n* **1** a doctrine that equates God with the forces and laws of nature **2** the indiscriminate worship of all the gods of different religions and cults; *also* toleration of such worship (e g at certain periods of the Roman empire) [F *panthéisme*, fr *panthéiste* pantheist, fr E *pantheist*, fr *pan-* + *-theist*] – **pantheist** *n*, **pantheistic** /-ˈistik/, **pantheistical** *adj*, **pantheistically** *adv*

pantheon /ˈpanthi·ən, panˈthee·ən/ *n* **1** a building serving as the burial place of or containing memorials to famous dead **2** the gods of a people; *esp* the officially recognized gods [ME *Panteon*, a temple at Rome, fr L *Pantheon*, fr Gk *pantheion* temple of all the gods, fr neut of *pantheios* of all gods, fr *pan-* + *theos* god]

panther /ˈpanthə/ *n, pl* **panthers** *also esp collectively* **panther** **1** a leopard, esp of the black colour phase **2** *NAm* a puma [ME *pantere*, fr OF, fr L *panthera*, fr Gk *panthēr*]

panties /ˈpantiz/ *n pl* pants for women or children; *also* knickers

pantile /ˈpanˌtiel/ *n* a roofing tile whose transverse section is a flattened S-shape ☞ BUILDING [[1]*pan*] – **pantiled** *adj*

panto /ˈpantoh/ *n, Br* PANTOMIME 1b – infml

pantograph /ˈpantəˌgrahf, -ˌgraf/ *n* **1** an instrument for copying sthg (e g a map) on a predetermined scale consisting of 4 light rigid bars jointed in parallelogram form; *also* any of various extensible devices of similar construction **2** a collapsible and adjustable framework mounted on an electric vehicle (e g a railway locomotive) for collecting current from an overhead wire [F *pantographe*, fr *pant-* + *-graphe* -graph] – **pantographic** /-ˈgrafik/ *adj*

pantomime /ˈpantəˌmiem/ *n* **1a** any of various dramatic or dancing performances in which a story is told by bodily or facial movements **b** a British theatrical and musical entertainment of the Christmas season based on a nursery tale with stock roles and topical jokes **2** conveyance of a story by bodily or facial movements, esp in drama or dance [L *pantomimus*, fr *pant-* + *mimus* mime] – **pantomimic** /-ˈmimik/ *adj*

pantoˌthenic ˈacid /ˌpantəˈthenik/ *n* a vitamin of the vitamin B complex [Gk *pantothen* from all sides, fr *pant-, pas* all – more at PAN-]

pantry /ˈpantri/ *n* **1** a room or cupboard used for storing provisions or tableware **2** a room (e g in a hotel or hospital) for preparation of cold foods to order [ME *panetrie*, fr MF *paneterie*, fr OF, fr *panetier* servant in charge of the pantry, irreg fr *pan* bread, fr L *panis* – more at FOOD]

pants /pants/ *n pl* **1** *chiefly Br* an undergarment that covers the crotch and hips and that may extend to the waist and partly down each leg **2** *chiefly NAm* trousers [short for *pantaloons*]

'pants ,suit *n, chiefly NAm* TROUSER SUIT

'panty ,hose /'panti/ *n pl, chiefly NAm* tights

¹panzer /'panzə/ *adj* of, carried out by, or being a (WW II German) armoured unit [G *panzer-*, fr *panzer* coat of mail, armour, fr OF *pancière*, fr *pance, panche* belly – more at PAUNCH]

²panzer *n* TANK 2; *esp* a German tank of WW II

¹pap /pap/ *n, chiefly dial* a nipple, teat [ME *pappe*]

²pap *n* **1** a soft food for infants or invalids **2** sthg lacking solid value or substance [ME]

¹papa /pə'pah/ *n, chiefly Br* father – formerly used formally, esp in address [F (baby talk)]

²papa /'papə/ *n* daddy – used informally and by children

papacy /'paypəsi/ *n* **1** the (term of) office of pope **2** *cap* the system of government of the Roman Catholic church of which the pope is the supreme head [ME *papacie*, fr ML *papatia*, fr LL *papa* pope – more at POPE]

papain /pə'pay·in, pə'pie·in, 'paypə·in/ *n* an enzyme in the juice of unripe papaya, used to tenderize meat [ISV, fr *papaya*]

papal /'paypl/ *adj* of a pope or the Roman Catholic church [ME, fr MF, fr ML *papalis*, fr LL *papa*] – **papally** /'paypl·i/ *adv*

papal cross *n* a cross having a long upright shaft and 3 crossbars of successively shorter length ☞ SYMBOL

papaw /' pə'paw, *2* 'pawpaw, 'pah-/ *n* **1** papaya **2** (a N American tree that bears purple flowers and) a yellow edible fruit [prob modif of Sp *papaya*]

papaya /pə'pie·ə/ *n* (a tropical American tree that bears) a large oblong yellow edible fruit [Sp, of AmerInd origin; akin to Otomac *papai*]

¹paper /'paypə/ *n* **1a** a sheet of closely compacted vegetable fibres (e g of wood or cloth) **b** a piece of paper **2a** a piece of paper containing a written or printed statement; a document ⟨*naturalization* ~s⟩; *specif* a document carried as proof of identity or status – often pl **b** a piece of paper containing writing or print **c** a formal written composition **d** the question set or answers written in an examination in 1 subject **3** a paper container or wrapper ⟨*a sweet* ~⟩ **4** a newspaper **5** the negotiable notes or instruments of commerce **6** wallpaper [ME *papir*, fr MF *papier*, fr L *papyrus* papyrus, paper, fr Gk *papyros* papyrus] – **on paper** in theory; hypothetically

²paper *vt* **1** to cover or line with paper; *esp* to apply wallpaper to **2** to give out free tickets for ⟨~ *the theatre for the opening night*⟩ ~ *vi* to hang wallpaper – **paperer** *n*

³paper *adj* **1a** made of paper, thin cardboard, or papier-mâché **b** papery **2** of clerical work or written communication **3** existing only in theory; nominal **4** issued as paper money **5** finished with a crisp smooth surface like that of paper ⟨~ *taffeta*⟩

'paper,back /-,bak/ *n* a book with a flexible paper binding – compare HARDBACK – **paperback** *adj*

'paper,boy /-,boy/, *fem* **'paper,girl** *n* a boy who delivers or sells newspapers

paper chase *n* a game in which some of the players scatter bits of paper as a trail which others follow to find and catch them

paper clip *n* a small clip made from 2 loops of wire, used for holding sheets of paper together

'paper,hanger /-,hang·ə/ *n* sby who applies wallpaper to walls

'paper,hanging /-,hang·ing/ *n* the act of applying wallpaper

paper knife *n* a knife for slitting envelopes or uncut pages

paper money *n* bank notes

paper mulberry *n* an Asian variety of mulberry, the bark of which was formerly used in papermaking, esp in Japan

paper nautilus *n* a mollusc related to the octopuses and squids, the female of which has a delicate papery shell

paper over *vt* **1** to gloss over, explain away, or patch up (e g major differences), esp in order to maintain a semblance of unity **2** to hide, conceal

paper tiger *n* sby or sthg outwardly powerful or dangerous but inwardly weak or ineffectual ⟨*had to show that the military commitment was not a* ~⟩

'paper,weight /-,wayt/ *n* a usu small heavy object used to hold down loose papers (e g on a desk)

'paper,work /-,wuhk/ *n* routine clerical or record-keeping work, often incidental to a more important task

papery /'payp(ə)ri/ *adj* resembling paper in thinness or consistency ⟨~ *leaves*⟩ ⟨~ *silk*⟩ – **paperiness** *n*

papier-mâché /,papyay 'mashay, mə'shay, 'paypə/ *n* a light strong moulding material made of paper pulped with glue that is used for making boxes, trays, etc [F, lit., chewed paper] – **papier-mâché** *adj*

papilionaceous /pə,pilyə'nayshəs/ *adj, of a (leguminous) flower* having an irregular butterfly-shaped corolla [L *papilion-, papilio* butterfly – more at PAVILION]

papilla /pə'pilə/ *n, pl* **papillae** /-li/ a small projecting nipple-shaped body part: e g **a** a piece of connective tissue extending into and nourishing the root of a hair, feather, etc **b** any of the protuberances of the dermal layer of the skin extending into the epidermal layer **c** any of the protuberances on the upper surface of the tongue [L, nipple; akin to L *papula* pimple, Lith *papas* nipple] – **papillary** /pə'piləri/ *adj*, **papillate** /'papilayt/ *adj*, **papillose** /'papilohs/ *adj*

papilloma /,papi'lohmə/ *n, pl* **papillomas, papillomata** /-mətə/ a benign tumour (e g a wart) due to overgrowth of epithelial tissue [NL] – **papillomatous** *adj*

papillon /'papilon/ *n* (any of) a breed of small slender toy spaniels with large butterfly-shaped ears [F, lit., butterfly, fr L *papilion-, papilio*]

papist /'paypist/ *n, often cap* a Roman Catholic – chiefly derog [MF or NL; MF *papiste*, fr *pape* pope; NL *papista*, fr LL *papa* pope] – **papist** *adj*, **papistry** *n*

papoose /pə'poohs/ *n* a young N American Indian child [Narraganset *papoòs*]

pappus /'papəs/ *n, pl* **pappi** /'papie/ a (tuft of) usu hairy appendages crowning the ovary or fruit in various plants (e g the dandelion) [L, fr Gk *pappos*] – **pappose** *adj*

paprika /'paprikə, pa'preekə/ *n* (a mild to hot red condiment consisting of the finely ground dried pods of) any of various cultivated sweet peppers – compare CAYENNE PEPPER [Hung, fr Serb, fr *papar* pepper, fr Gk *peperi*]

Pap smear /pap/ *n* a method for the early detection of cancer in which cells (e g from mucous membrane) are scraped off and examined under the microscope [George N *Papanicolaou* †1962 US medical scientist]

papule /'papyoohl/ *n* a small solid usu conical projection from the skin [L *papula*] – **papular** *adj*

papyrus /pə'pie·ərəs/ *n, pl* **papyruses, papyri** /-rie/ **1** a tall sedge of the Nile valley **2** the pith of the papyrus plant, esp when made into a material for writing on **3** a usu ancient manuscript written on papyrus [ME, fr L – more at PAPER]

par /pah/ *n* **1a** the established value of the monetary unit of one country expressed in terms of the monetary unit of another country **b** the money value assigned to each share of stock in the charter of a company **2** a common level; equality – esp in *on a par with* **3a** an amount taken as an average or norm **b** an accepted standard; *specif* a usual standard of physical condition or health **4** the standard score (of a good player) for each hole of a golf course [L, one that is equal, fr *par* equal] – **par** *adj*

[1]**para** /'pahrə/ *n, pl* **paras, para** ☞ *Yugoslavia* at NATIONALITY [Turk, fr Per *pārah*, lit., piece]

[2]**para** /'parə/ *n, pl* **paras** a paratrooper

[1]**para-** /parə-/, **par-** *prefix* **1a** beside; alongside ⟨para*thyroid*⟩ ⟨par*allel*⟩ **b** beyond ⟨para*normal*⟩ ⟨para*dox*⟩ **2** involving substitution at 2 opposite positions in the benzene ring that are separated by 2 carbon atoms ⟨para*dichlorobenzene*⟩ – compare META-, ORTHO- **3a** faulty; abnormal ⟨para*esthesia*⟩ ⟨para*noia*⟩ **b** associated in a subsidiary or auxiliary capacity ⟨para*medical*⟩ **c** closely resembling or related to ⟨para*typhoid*⟩ [ME, fr MF, fr L, fr Gk, fr *para*; akin to Gk *pro* before – more at FOR]

[2]**para-** *comb form* parachute ⟨para*trooper*⟩

-para /-p(ə)rə/ *comb form* (→ *n*), *pl* **-paras, -parae** /-ri/ woman delivered of (so many) children ⟨*tri*para⟩ [L, fr *parere* to give birth to – more at PARE]

,para-a,minoben,zoic 'acid /,parə ,aminohben,-zoh·ik, ə,meenoh-/ *n* the form of aminobenzoic acid that is a growth factor of the vitamin B complex [ISV]

parabiosis /,parəbie'ohsis/ *n* anatomical and physiological union of 2 organisms [NL] – **parabiotic** /-bie'otik/ *adj*, **parabiotically** *adv*

parable /'parəbl/ *n* a usu short allegorical story illustrating a moral or religious principle [ME, fr MF, fr LL *parabola*, fr Gk *parabolē*, fr *paraballein* to compare, fr *para-* + *ballein* to throw – more at DEVIL]

parabola /pə'rabələ/ *n* a plane curve generated by a point moving so that its distance from a fixed point is equal to its distance from a fixed line; the intersection of a right circular cone with a plane parallel to a straight line in the surface of the cone – compare ELLIPSE, HYPERBOLA ☞ MATHEMATICS [NL, fr Gk *parabolē*, lit., comparison]

parabolic /,parə'bolik/ *adj* **1** expressed by or being a parable **2** of or having the form of a parabola ⟨*motion in a* ~ *curve*⟩ [(1) LL *parabola* parable; (2) NL *parabola*] – **parabolically** *adv*

paraboloid /pə'rabəloyd/ *n* a surface some plane sections of which are parabolas – compare ELLIPSOID, HYPERBOLOID – **paraboloidal** /-'loydl/ *adj*

paracetamol /,parə'seetəmol, -'setə-/ *n* a derivative of acetanilide widely used as a painkiller and as an intermediate in chemical synthesis [[1]*para-* + *acet-* + *amin-* + *-ol*]

[1]**parachute** /'parə,shooht/ *n* a folding device of light fabric used esp for ensuring a safe descent of a person or object from a great height (e g from a aeroplane) [F, fr *para-* (as in *parasol*) + *chute* fall – more at CHUTE] – **parachutist** *n*

[2]**parachute** *vi* to descend by means of a parachute

Paraclete /'parəkleet/ *n* HOLY SPIRIT [ME *Paraclit*, fr MF *Paraclet*, fr LL *Paracletus*, fr Gk *Paraklētos*, lit., advocate, intercessor, fr *parakalein* to invoke, fr *para-* + *kalein* to call – more at [1]LOW]

[1]**parade** /pə'rayd/ *n* **1** an ostentatious show; an exhibition ⟨*made a* ~ *of his superior knowledge*⟩ **2** the (ceremonial) ordered assembly of a body of troops before a superior officer **3** a public procession **4** *chiefly Br* a row of shops, esp with a service road [F, fr MF, fr *parer* to prepare – more at PARE]

[2]**parade** *vt* **1** to cause to manoeuvre or march **2** to exhibit ostentatiously ~ *vi* **1** to march in a procession **2** to promenade **3a** SHOW OFF **b** to masquerade ⟨*myths which* ~ *as modern science* – M R Cohen⟩ – **parader** *n*

paradichlorobenzene /,parədie,klawroh'benzeen/ *n* a white chlorinated benzene compound used chiefly as a fumigant against clothes moths [ISV]

paradigm /'parədiem/ *n* **1** an example or pattern **2** an example of a conjugation or declension showing a word in all its inflectional forms [LL *paradigma*, fr Gk *paradeigma*, fr *paradeiknynai* to show side by side, fr *para-* + *deiknynai* to show – more at DICTION] – **paradigmatic** /,parədig'matik/ *adj*

paradise /'parədies/ *n* **1** *often cap* **a** the garden of Eden **b** Heaven **2** a place of bliss, felicity, or delight [ME *paradis*, fr OF, fr LL *paradisus*, fr Gk *paradeisos*, lit., enclosed park, of Iranian origin; akin to Av *pairi-daēza-* enclosure; akin to Gk *peri* around, & to Gk *teichos* wall – more at PERI-, DOUGH] – **paradisaical** /,parədi'sie·əkl, -die-/ *adj*

parados /'parədos/ *n* a bank of earth behind a fortified place or trench [F, fr *para-* (as in *parasol*) + *dos* back, fr L *dorsum*]

paradox /'parə,doks/ *n* **1** a tenet contrary to received opinion **2a** a statement that is apparently contradictory or absurd and yet might be true **b** a self-contradictory statement that at first seems true **3** sthg (e g a person, condition, or act) with seemingly contradictory qualities or phases [L *paradoxum*, fr Gk *paradoxon*, fr neut of *paradoxos* contrary to expectation, fr *para-* + *dokein* to think, seem – more at DECENT]

paradoxical /,parə'doksikl/ *adj* **1** constituting a paradox **2** not being the normal or usual kind ⟨~ *pulse*⟩ – **paradoxically** *adv*, **paradoxicalness** *n*

paradoxical sleep *n* a state of sleep that is characterized esp by dreaming, rapid eye movements, and vascular congestion of the sex organs

paraesthesia, *NAm chiefly* **paresthesia** /,parees'theezyə, -zh(y)ə/ *n* a sensation of prickling or tingling on the skin with no physical cause [NL]

paraffin /'parəfin, ,--'-/ *n* **1** a usu waxy inflammable mixture of hydrocarbons obtained from distillates of wood, coal, petroleum, etc and used chiefly in candles, chemical synthesis, and cosmetics **2** an alkane **3** an inflammable liquid hydrocarbon obtained by distillation of petroleum and used esp as a fuel [G, fr L *parum* too little + *affinis* bordering on; akin to L *paucus* few – more at FEW, AFFINITY] – **paraffinic** /-'finik/ *adj*

paragon /'parəgən/ *n* a model of excellence or perfection [MF, fr OIt *paragone*, lit., touchstone, fr *paragonare* to test on a touchstone, fr Gk *parakonan* to sharpen, fr *para-* + *akonē* whetstone, fr *akē* point; akin to Gk *akmē* point – more at EDGE]

paragraph /'parə,grahf, -,graf/ *n* **1a** a usu indented division of a written composition that develops a single point or idea **b** a composition or news item that is complete in 1 paragraph **2** a sign (e g) used as a reference mark or to indicate the beginning of a paragraph ☞ SYMBOL [MF & ML; MF *paragraphe*, fr ML *paragraphus* sign marking a paragraph, fr Gk *paragraphos* line used to mark change of persons in a dialogue, fr *paragraphein* to write alongside, fr *para-* + *graphein* to write – more at CARVE] – **paragraph** *vt*, **paragraphic** /-'grafik/ *adj*

parakeet, *NAm also* **parrakeet** /,parə'keet, '--,-/ *n* any of numerous usu small slender long-tailed parrots [Sp & MF; Sp *periquito*, fr MF *perroquet* parrot]

paraldehyde /pə'raldihied/ *n* a synthetic drug used esp as a sedative and hypnotic to control convulsions

parallax /'parəlaks/ *n* the apparent displacement or the difference in apparent direction of an object as seen from 2 different points not on the same straight line [MF *parallaxe*, fr Gk *parallaxis*, fr *parallassein* to change, fr *para-* + *allassein* to change, fr *allos* other – more at ELSE] – **parallactic** /-'laktik/ *adj*

[1]**parallel** /'parəlel/ *adj* **1a** extending in the same direction, everywhere equidistant, and not meeting ⟨~ *rows of trees*⟩ ☞ SYMBOL **b** everywhere equally distant ⟨*concentric spheres are* ~⟩ ☞ SYMBOL **2** being or relating to an electrical circuit having a number of conductors in parallel **3** analogous, comparable [L *parallelus*, fr Gk *parallēlos*, fr *para* beside + *allēlōn* of one another, fr *allos* *allos* one another, fr *allos* other – more at PARA-, ELSE]

[2]**parallel** *n* **1a** a parallel line, curve, or surface ☞ MATHEMATICS, SYMBOL **b** a circle or line of latitude on (a globe or map of) the earth ☞ SYMBOL **c** a sign ‖ used as a reference mark – often pl with sing. meaning ☞ SYMBOL **2** sby or sthg equal or similar in all essential particulars; a counterpart, analogue **3** a comparison to show resemblance ⟨*drew a* ~ *between the 2 states*⟩ **4a** the state of being physically parallel **b** the arrangement of 2-terminal electrical devices in which one terminal of each device is joined to one conductor and the others are joined to another conductor – compare SERIES 7

[3]**parallel** *vt* **1** to compare **2a** to equal, match ⟨*no one has* ~ed *my success in business*⟩ **b** to correspond to

[4]**parallel** *adv* in a parallel manner

,parallel 'bars *n pl but sing or pl in constr* (a men's gymnastic event using) a pair of bars supported horizontally 1.7m (5ft 7in) above the floor usu by a common base

parallelepiped /,parə,leli'pieped, ,parəle'lepiped/ *n* a polyhedron whose faces are parallelograms [Gk *parallēlepipedon*, fr *parallēlos* + *epipedon* plane surface, fr neut of *epipedos* flat, fr *epi-* + *pedon* ground; akin to L *ped-*, *pes* foot – more at FOOT]

parallelism /'parəleliz(ə)m/ *n* **1** the quality or state of being parallel **2** a resemblance, correspondence

parallelogram /,parə'leləgram/ *n* a quadrilateral with opposite sides parallel and equal ☞ MATHEMATICS [LL or Gk; LL *parallelogrammum*, fr Gk *parallēlogrammon*, fr neut of *parallēlogrammos* bounded by parallel lines, fr *parallēlos* + *grammē* line, fr *graphein* to write – more at CARVE]

paralysis /pə'raləsis/ *n, pl* **paralyses** /-seez/ **1** (partial) loss of function, esp when involving motion or sensation in a part of the body **2** loss of the ability to move **3** a state of powerlessness or incapacity to act [L, fr Gk, fr *paralyein* to loosen, disable, fr *para-* + *lyein* to loosen – more at LOSE] – **paralyse,** *NAm* **paralyze** *vt*, **paralysation** /-'zaysh(ə)n/ *n*

[1]**paralytic** /,parə'litik/ *adj* **1** of, resembling, or affected with paralysis **2** *chiefly Br* very drunk – infml

[2]**paralytic** *n* one suffering from paralysis

paramagnetic /,parəmag'netik/ *adj* of or being a substance that in a magnetic field is (slightly) attracted towards points of higher field intensity [ISV] – **paramagnetically** *adv*, **paramagnetism** /-'magnə,tiz(ə)m/ *n*

paramecium /,parə'meesyəm/ *n, pl* **paramecia** /-s(h)yə/ *also* **parameciums** any of a genus of protozoans that have an elongated body covered with cilia and an oblique funnel-shaped groove bearing the mouth at the tip [NL, genus name, fr Gk *paramēkēs* oblong, fr *para-* + *mēkos* length; akin to Gk *makros* long – more at MEAGRE]

paramedical /,parə'medikl/ *also* **,para'medic** /-'medik/ *adj* concerned with supplementing the work of medical doctors ⟨~ *technicians*⟩

parameter /pə'ramitə/ *n* **1** an arbitrary constant whose value characterizes a member of a system (e g a family of curves) **2** a characteristic, factor ⟨*political dissent as a* ~ *of modern life*⟩ [NL, fr *para-* + Gk *metron* measure – more at MEASURE] – **parametric** /,parə'metrik/ *also* **parametrical** *adj*, **parametrically** *adv*

parameter·ize, -ise, parametr·ize, -ise /pə'ramit(ə)riez/ *vt* to express in terms of parameters – **parameterization, parametrization** /-'zaysh(ə)n/ *n*

paramilitary /,parə'milit(ə)ri/ *adj* formed on a military pattern (as a potential auxiliary military force) ⟨*a* ~ *border patrol*⟩

paramnesia /,parəm'neezi·ə, -zh(i)ə, -ram-/ *n* DÉJÀ VU 1 [NL, fr *para-* + *-mnesia* (as in *amnesia*)]

paramount /'parəmownt/ *adj* superior to all others; supreme [AF *paramont*, fr OF *par* by (fr L *per*) + *amont* above, fr *a* to (fr L *ad*) + *mont* mountain – more at FOR, [1]AT, MOUNT]

paramour /'parəmooə/ *n* an illicit lover; *esp* a mistress [ME, fr *par amour* by way of love, fr OF]

parang /'parang/ *n* a heavy Malaysian or Indonesian knife [Malay]

paranoia /,parə'noyə/ *n* **1** a mental disorder characterized by delusions of persecution or grandeur **2** a tendency towards excessive or irrational suspiciousness and distrustfulness of others [NL, fr Gk, madness, fr *paranous* demented, fr *para-* + *nous* mind] – **paranoiac** *adj or n*, **paranoid** *adj or n*

paranormal /parə'nawml/ *adj* not scientifically explainable; supernatural – **paranormally** *adv*, **paranormality** /-naw'maləti/ *n*

parapet /'parəpit, -pet/ *n* **1** a wall, rampart, or

elevation of earth or stone to protect soldiers **2** a low wall or balustrade to protect the edge of a platform, roof, or bridge ☞ ARCHITECTURE, CHURCH [It *parapetto*, fr *parare* to shield (fr L, to prepare) + *petto* chest, fr L *pectus* – more at PARE] – **parapeted** *adj*

paraph /'paraf/ *n* a flourish at the end of a signature [MF, fr L *paragraphus* paragraph]

paraphernalia /,parəfə'naylyə/ *n pl but sing or pl in constr* **1** personal belongings **2a** articles of equipment **b** accessory items [ML, personal property of a married woman, deriv of Gk *parapherna* goods a bride brings in addition to the dowry, fr *para-* + *phernē* dowry, fr *pherein* to bear – more at ²BEAR]

¹**paraphrase** /'parə,frayz/ *n* a restatement of a text, passage, or work giving the meaning in another form [MF, fr L *paraphrasis*, fr Gk, fr *paraphrazein* to paraphrase, fr *para-* + *phrazein* to point out]

²**paraphrase** *vb* to make a paraphrase (of) – **paraphrasable** *adj*, **paraphraser** *n*

paraphrastic /,parə'frastik/ *adj* explaining or translating more clearly and amply; having the nature of a paraphrase [F *paraphrastique*, fr Gk *paraphrastikos*, fr *paraphrazein*] – **paraphrastically** *adv*

paraplegia /,parə'pleejə/ *n* paralysis of the lower half of the body including the legs [NL, fr Gk *paraplēgiē* hemiplegia, fr *para-* + *-plēgia* -plegia] – **paraplegic** /-jik/ *adj or n*

,parapsy'chology /-sie'koləji/ *n* the investigation of evidence for the occurrence of psychic phenomena (e g telepathy and clairvoyance) [ISV] – **parapsychologist** *n*, **parapsychological** /-siekə'lojikl/ *adj*

paraquat /'parəkwot, -kwat/ *n* a very poisonous herbicide used esp as a weedkiller [*para-* + *quat*ernary salt of an organic compound]

paraselene /,parəse'leeni/ *n, pl* **paraselenae** /-ni, -nie/ a bright spot like a parhelion seen on lunar haloes [NL, fr *para-* + Gk *selēnē* moon – more at SELENIUM] – **paraselenic** /-'lenik/ *adj*

parashah /'parə,shah/ *n* a section of the Torah assigned for weekly reading in synagogue worship [Heb *pārāshāh*, lit., explanation]

parasite /'parəsiet/ *n* **1** an organism living in or on another organism in parasitism **2** sthg resembling a biological parasite in dependence on sthg else for existence or support without making a useful or adequate return [MF, fr L *parasitus*, fr Gk *parasitos*, fr *para-* + *sitos* grain, food] – **parasitic** /-'sitik/ *also* **parasitical** *adj*, **parasitically** *adv*, **parasitology** /-sie'toləji/ *n*, **parasitologist** *n*

parasitism /'parəsie,tiz(ə)m/ *n* an intimate association between organisms of 2 or more kinds in which a parasite benefits at the expense of a host – **parasitize** *vt*

parasol /'parəsol/ *n* a lightweight umbrella used, esp by women, as a protection from the sun [F, fr OIt *parasole*, fr *parare* to shield + *sole* sun, fr L *sol* – more at PARAPET, ¹SOLAR]

parasympathetic /,parəsimpə'thetik/ *adj* of, being, mediated by, or acting on (the nerves of) the parasympathetic nervous system [ISV]

parasympathetic nervous system *n* the part of the autonomic nervous system that contains nerve fibres in which the neurotransmitter is acetylcholine and whose activity tends to contract smooth muscle and cause the dilation of blood vessels – compare SYMPATHETIC NERVOUS SYSTEM

parasympathomimetic /,parə,simpəthohmie'metik, -mi-/ *adj* simulating parasympathetic nervous action in physiological effect [ISV]

parataxis /,parə'taksis/ *n* the placing of clauses or phrases one after another without coordinating or subordinating forms [NL, fr Gk, act of placing side by side, fr *paratassein* to place side by side, fr *para-* + *tassein* to arrange – more at TACTICS] – **paratactic** /-tik/ *adj*

parathion /,parə'thie·on/ *n* a very poisonous insecticide used esp in farming [*para-* + *thio*phosphate + *-on*]

parathyroid /,parə'thie·əroyd/, **parathyroid gland** *n* any of 4 small endocrine glands near the thyroid gland that produce a hormone ☞ DIGESTION [ISV] – **parathyroid** *adj*

paratroops /'parə,troohps/ *n pl* troops trained and equipped to parachute from an aeroplane [²*para-*] – **paratrooper** *n*

paratyphoid /,parə'tiefoyd/ *n* a disease caused by salmonella that resembles typhoid fever and is commonly contracted by eating contaminated food [ISV] – **paratyphoid** *adj*

paravane /'parəvayn/ *n* a torpedo-shaped device towed underwater by a ship to sever the moorings of mines

parboil /'pah,boyl/ *vt* to boil briefly as a preliminary or incomplete cooking procedure [ME *parboilen*, fr *parboilen* to boil thoroughly, fr MF *parboillir*, fr LL *perbullire*, fr L *per-* thoroughly (fr *per* through) + *bullire* to boil, fr *bulla* bubble]

¹**parbuckle** /'pah,bukl/ *n* a sling of rope fastened overhead that is used for hoisting or lowering a cylindrical object (e g a cask) [origin unknown]

²**parbuckle** *vt* to raise or lower by means of a parbuckle

¹**parcel** /'pahsl/ *n* **1** a plot of land **2** ¹PACK 2a **3** a wrapped bundle; a package [ME, fr MF, fr (assumed) VL *particella*, fr L *particula* small part – more at PARTICLE]

²**parcel** *vt* **-ll-** (*NAm* **-l-, -ll-**), /'pahsl·ing/ **1** to divide into parts; distribute – often + *out* **2** to make up into a parcel; wrap – often + *up* **3** to cover (e g a rope) with strips of canvas

parch /pahch/ *vt* **1** to roast (e g peas) slightly in a dry heat **2** to make dry or scorched ~ *vi* to become dry or scorched [ME *parchen*]

parchment /'pahchmənt/ *n* **1** the skin of an animal, esp of a sheep or goat, prepared for writing on **2** strong paper made to resemble parchment **3** a parchment manuscript [ME *parchemin*, fr OF, modif of L *pergamena*, fr Gk *pergamēnē*, fr fem of *Pergamēnos* of Pergamum, fr *Pergamon* Pergamum, ancient city in Asia Minor]

parclose screen /'pahklohz/ *n* a screen separating a side chapel from the main body of the church ☞ CHURCH [ME *parclose*, fr MF, enclosure, end, fr fem of *parclos*, pp of *parclore* to enclose]

pard /pahd/ *n, archaic* a leopard [ME *parde*, fr OF, fr L *pardus*, fr Gk *pardos*]

pardner /'pahdnə/ *n, chiefly NAm* a partner, chum [alter. of *partner*]

¹**pardon** /'pahdn/ *n* **1** INDULGENCE 1 **2** a release from legal penalties **3** excuse or forgiveness for a fault, offence, or discourtesy

²**pardon** *vt* **1** to absolve from the consequences of a fault or crime **2** to allow (an offence) to pass without punishment [ME *pardonen*, fr MF *pardoner*, fr LL

perdonare to grant freely, fr L *per-* thoroughly + *donare* to give – more at DONATION] – **pardonable** /'pahdnəbl/ *adj*, **pardonably** *adv*

pardoner /'pahd(ə)nə/ *n* a medieval preacher delegated to raise money by granting indulgences [[2]PARDON + [2]-ER]

pare /peə/ *vt* **1** to cut or shave off **a** (an outer surface) ⟨~ *the skin from an apple*⟩ **b** the outer surface of ⟨~ *an apple*⟩ **2** to diminish gradually (as if) by paring ⟨~ *expenses*⟩ [ME *paren*, fr MF *parer* to prepare, trim, fr L *parare* to prepare, acquire; akin to OE *fearr* bull, ox, L *parere* to give birth to, produce] – **parer** *n*

paregoric /,pari'gorik/ *n* a camphorated tincture of opium used esp to relieve pain and coughing [F *parégorique* relieving pain, fr LL *paregoricus*, fr Gk *parēgorikos*, fr *parēgorein* to talk over, soothe, fr *para-* + *agora* assembly – more at GREGARIOUS]

parenchyma /pə'rengkimə/ *n* **1** a fleshy tissue of the leaves, fruits, stems, etc of higher plants that consists of thin-walled living cells – compare COLLENCHYMA, SCLERENCHYMA **2** the essential and distinctive tissue of an organ or an abnormal growth, as distinguished from its supportive framework [NL, fr Gk, visceral flesh, fr *parenchein* to pour in beside, fr *para-* + *en-* + *chein* to pour – more at [4]FOUND] – **parenchymatous** /,parən'kiemətəs, -ki-/ *adj*

[1]**parent** /'peərənt/ *n* **1** sby who begets or brings forth offspring; a father or mother **2a** an animal or plant regarded in relation to its offspring **b** the material or source from which sthg is derived [ME, fr MF, fr L *parent-, parens*, fr prp of *parere* to give birth to] – **parent** *adj*, **parenthood** *n*, **parental** /pə'rentl/ *adj*, **parentally** *adv*

[2]**parent** *vt* to be or act as the parent of; originate, produce

parentage /'peərəntij/ *n* descent from parents or ancestors; lineage ⟨*a woman of noble* ~⟩ [[1]PARENT + -AGE]

parenteral /pa'rentərəl/ *adj* situated, occurring, or administered outside the intestines [ISV *para-* + *enteral*] – **parenterally** /-t(ə)rəli/ *adv*

parenthesis /pə'renthəsis/ *n, pl* **parentheses** /-,seez/ **1a** an amplifying or explanatory word or phrase inserted in a passage from which, in writing, it is usu set off by punctuation **b** either or both of the curved marks (or) used in writing and printing to enclose a parenthesis or to group a symbolic unit in a logical or mathematical expression **2** an interlude, interval [LL, fr Gk, lit., act of inserting, fr *parentithenai* to insert, fr *para-* + *en-* + *tithenai* to place – more at [1]DO] – **parenthetic** /,parən'thetik/, **parenthetical** *adj*, **parenthetically** *adv*

parenthes·ize, -ise /pə'renthəsiez/ *vt* to make a parenthesis of ~ *vi* to digress

parent-teacher association *n sing or pl in constr* an organization of teachers at a school and the parents of their pupils, that works for the improvement of the school

parergon /pa'ruhgon/ *n, pl* **parerga** /-gə/ supplementary or subsidiary work; work undertaken apart from one's regular employment [L, fr Gk, fr *par-* para- + *ergon* work]

paresis /pə'reesis, 'parəsis/ *n, pl* **pareses** /-,seez/ slight or partial paralysis [NL, fr Gk, fr *parienai* to let fall, fr *para-* + *hienai* to let go, send – more at [2]JET] – **paretic** /pə'retik/ *adj or n*

par excellence /pah'reks(ə)ləns (*Fr* par ɛksɛlɑ̃:s)/ *adj* being the best example of a kind; without equal – used postpositively ⟨*the dictionary* ~⟩ [F, lit., by excellence]

parfait /pah'fay/ *n* a frozen flavoured dessert that resembles custard and contains whipped cream and eggs [F, lit., sthg perfect, fr *parfait* perfect, fr L *perfectus*]

[1]**parget** /'pahjit/ *vt* to coat with plaster, esp ornamentally ☞ BUILDING [ME *pargetten*, fr MF *parjeter* to throw on top of, fr *par-* thoroughly (fr L *per-*) + *jeter* to throw – more at [2]JET]

[2]**parget** *n* plasterwork, esp in raised ornamental figures on walls ☞ BUILDING

parhelic circle /,pah'heelik/ *n* a luminous circle or halo parallel to the horizon at the altitude of the sun

parhelion /,pah'heelyən/ *n, pl* **parhelia** /-lyə/ any one of several bright spots that often appear on the parhelic circle [L *parelion*, fr Gk *parēlion*, fr *para-* + *hēlios* sun – more at [1]SOLAR] – **parhelic** /-'heelik/ *adj*

pariah /pə'rie·ə, 'pari·ə/ *n* **1** a member of a low caste of S India and Burma **2** an outcast [Tamil *paraiyan*, lit., drummer]

'**Parian** ,**ware** /'peəri·ən/ *n* a fine-grained white porcelain usu used for making unglazed classical figures, esp nudes [*Paros*, Gk island, source of marble used in classical sculpture]

parietal /pə'rie·ətl/ *adj* **1** of the walls of an anatomical part or cavity **2** of or forming the upper rear wall of the skull [MF, fr NL *pariet-, paries* wall of a cavity or hollow organ, fr L, wall]

parietal bone *n* either of a pair of bones of the top and side of the skull

pari-mutuel /,pari 'myoohtyooəl/ *n* **1** a betting pool in which those who bet on the winners of the first 3 places share the total amount bet, minus a percentage for the management **2** *NAm* a totalizator [F *pari mutuel*, lit., mutual stake]

paring /'peəring/ *n* **1** the act of cutting away an edge or surface **2** sthg pared off ⟨*apple* ~s⟩

,**Paris 'green** /'paris/ *n* a very poisonous bright green powder that is used as an insecticide and pigment [*Paris*, capital city of France]

parish /'parish/ *n* **1** the subdivision of a diocese served by a single church or clergyman **2** a unit of local government in rural England, often coinciding with an original ecclesiastical parish [ME *parisshe*, fr MF *parroche*, fr LL *parochia*, fr LGk *paroikia*, fr *paroikos* Christian, fr Gk, stranger, fr *para-* + *oikos* house – more at VICINITY]

parishioner /pə'rish(ə)nə/ *n* a member or inhabitant of a parish [ME *parisshoner*, prob modif of MF *parrochien*, fr *parroche*]

,**parish 'register** *n* a book containing records of baptisms, marriages, and burials in a parish

[1]**parity** /'parəti/ *n* **1** the quality or state of being equal or equivalent **2** equivalence of a commodity price expressed in one currency to its price expressed in another **3a** the property of an integer with respect to being odd or even ⟨*3 and 7 have the same* ~⟩ **b(1)** the state of being odd or even that is the basis of a method of detecting errors in binary-coded data **(2)** PARITY BIT **4** the property whereby a quantity (e g the charge of an elementary particle) changes from positive to negative or vice versa or remains unaltered during a particular interaction or reaction [L *paritas*, fr *par* equal]

²parity *n* the state or fact of having borne offspring; *also* the number of children previously borne [*-parous*]

'parity ,bit *n* a bit added to a group of bits (e g on magnetic tape) to correct the length of the information unit to odd or even so that a parity check can be made

'parity ,check *n* a check made on computer data by which errors are detected

¹park /pahk/ *n* **1** an enclosed area of lawns, woodland, pasture, etc attached to a country house and used as a game reserve or for recreation **2a** an area of land for recreation in or near a city or town **b** an area maintained in its natural state as a public property **3** an assigned space for military animals, vehicles, or materials **4a** *Br* a pitch where professional soccer is played **b** *NAm* an arena or stadium used for ball games [ME, fr OF *parc* enclosure, fr (assumed) VL *parricus*]

²park *vt* **1a** to leave or place (a vehicle) for a time, esp at the roadside or in a car park or garage **b** to land or leave (e g an aeroplane) **c** to establish (e g a satellite) in orbit **2** to assemble (e g equipment or stores) in a military dump or park **3** to set and leave temporarily – infml ⟨~ed *her boyfriend at the bar*⟩ ~ *vi* to park a vehicle – **parker** *n*

parka /'pahkə/ *n* **1** a hooded fur garment for wearing in the arctic **2** an anorak [Aleut, skin, outer garment, fr Russ, pelt, fr Yurak]

parkin /'pahkin/ *n* a thick heavy ginger cake made with oatmeal and treacle [origin unknown]

'parking ,lot *n, NAm* an outdoor car park

'parking ,meter *n* a coin-operated device which registers the payment and displays the time allowed for parking a motor vehicle

parkinsonism /'pahkins(ə)n,iz(ə)m/ *n* PARKINSON'S DISEASE

,Parkinson's di,sease /'pahkins(ə)nz/ *n* tremor, weakness of resting muscles, and a peculiar gait occurring in later life as a progressive nervous disease [James *Parkinson* †1824 E physician] – **parkinsonian** /-'sohnyən/ *adj*

Parkinson's Law *n* an observation in office organization: work expands so as to fill the time available for its completion [C Northcote *Parkinson b*1909 E historian]

parkland /'pahk,land/ *n* land with clumps of trees and shrubs in cultivated condition suitable for use as a park

'park,way /-,way/ *n, NAm* a broad landscaped road or highway

parky /'pahki/ *adj, Br* CHILLY 1 – infml [prob fr ¹*park* + ¹*-y*]

parlance /'pahlәns/ *n* manner of speech and esp choice of words ⟨*in legal* ~⟩ [MF, fr OF, fr *parler*]

¹parlay /'pahli/ *vt, NAm* to bet in a parlay [F *paroli*, n, parlay, fr It dial., pl of *parolo*, fr *paro* equal, fr L *par*]

²parlay *n, NAm* ACCUMULATOR 3

¹parley /'pahli/ *vi* to speak with another; confer; *specif* to discuss terms with an enemy [MF *parler* to speak, fr ML *parabolare*, fr LL *parabola* speech, parable – more at PARABLE]

²parley *n* a conference for discussion of points in dispute; *specif* a conference under truce to discuss terms with an enemy

parliament /'pahləmənt, *also* -lyə-/ *n* **1** a formal conference for the discussion of public affairs **2** *often cap* the supreme legislative body of the UK that consists of the House of Commons and the House of Lords and is called together and dissolved by the sovereign; *also* a similar body in another nation or state ☞ LAW [ME, fr OF *parlement*, fr *parler*]

parliamentarian /,pahləmən'teəri·ən, -men-, *also* -lyə-/ *n* **1** *often cap* an adherent of the parliament during the Civil War **2** an expert in parliamentary rules and practice **3** *Br* a Member of Parliament

,parlia'mentary /,pahlə'ment(ə)ri, *also* -lyə-/ *adj* **1** of, appropriate to, or enacted by a parliament **2** of or supporting the parliament during the Civil War

Parliamentary Commissioner for Administration *n* the ombudsman in the UK

¹parlour, *NAm* **parlor** /'pahlə/ *n* **1a** a room in a private house for the entertainment of guests **b** a room in an inn, hotel, or club for conversation or semiprivate uses **2** any of various business places ⟨*a funeral* ~⟩ ⟨*a beauty* ~⟩ **3** a place for milking cows [ME *parlour*, fr OF, fr *parler*]

²parlour *adj* fostered or advocated in comfortable seclusion without consequent action or application to affairs

'parlour ,game *n* an indoor word game, board game, etc

parlous /'pahləs/ *adj* full of uncertainty and danger – fml or humor [ME, alter. of *perilous*]

Parmesan /,pahmi'zan, '---/ *n* a very hard dry strongly flavoured cheese that is often used grated [F *parmesan* of Parma, fr *Parma*, city in Italy]

parochial /pə'rohki·əl/ *adj* **1** of a (church) parish **2** limited in range or scope (e g to a narrow area or region); provincial, narrow [ME *parochiall*, fr MF *parochial*, fr LL *parochialis*, fr *parochia* parish – more at PARISH] – **parochially** *adv*

parochial church council *n* a predominantly lay body administering the affairs of a Church of England parish

parochialism /pə'rohki·ə,liz(ə)m/ *n* selfish pettiness or narrowness (e g of interests, opinions, or views) [PAROCHIAL + -ISM]

¹parody /'parədi/ *n* **1** a literary or musical work in which the style of an author is imitated for comic or satirical effect **2** a feeble or ridiculous imitation [L *parodia*, fr Gk *parōidia*, fr *para-* + *aidein* to sing – more at ODE] – **parodic** /pə'rodik/ *adj*, **parodist** /'parədist/ *n*

²parody *vt* to compose a parody on ⟨~ *a poem*⟩

parol /'parəl/ *adj* given by word of mouth ⟨~ *evidence*⟩ – used in law [MF *parole*]

¹parole /pə'rohl/ *n* **1** a pledge of one's honour; *esp* the promise of a prisoner of war to fulfil stated conditions in consideration of release or the granting of privileges **2** a password given only to officers of the guard and of the day **3** a conditional release of a prisoner **4** linguistic behaviour – compare LANGUE, PERFORMANCE 6 [F, speech, parole, fr MF, fr LL *parabola* speech – more at PARABLE]

²parole *vt* to put on parole – **parolee** /pə,roh'lee/ *n*

paronomasia /,parənoh'maysyə/ *n* a play on words; a pun [L, fr Gk, fr *paronomazein* to call with a slight change of name, fr *para-* + *onoma* name – more at NAME] – **paronomastic** /-'mastik/ *adj*

paronymous /pə'ronimәs/ *adj* **1** CONJUGATE 2 **2** formed from a word in another language [Gk *parōnymos*, fr *para-* + *-ōnymos* (as in *homōnymos* homonymous)] – **paronym** /'parənim/ *n*

parotid gland /pə'rotid/ *n* either of a pair of large salivary glands below and in front of the ear [NL *parotid-, parotis*, fr L, tumour near the ear, fr Gk *parōtid-, parōtis*, fr *para-* + *ōt-, ous* ear – more at [1]EAR] – **parotid** *adj*

parotitis /,parə'tietəs/ *n* inflammation of the parotid glands; *also* mumps [NL]

-parous /-p(ə)rəs/ *comb form* (→ *adj*) giving birth to; producing (such or so many) offspring ⟨*bi*parous⟩ ⟨*vivi*parous⟩ [L *-parus*, fr *parere* to give birth to, produce]

paroxysm /'parək,siz(ə)m/ *n* **1** a fit, attack, or sudden increase or recurrence of (disease) symptoms; a convulsion ⟨*a ~ of coughing*⟩ **2** a sudden violent emotion or action ⟨*a ~ of rage*⟩ [F & ML; F *paroxysme*, fr ML *paroxysmus*, fr Gk *paroxysmos*, fr *paroxynein* to stimulate, fr *para-* + *oxynein* to provoke, fr *oxys* sharp – more at OXYGEN] – **paroxysmal** /,parək'sizməl/ *adj*

[1]**parquet** /'pahkay, -ki/ *vt* **parqueted** /'pahkayd/; **parqueting** /'pahkaying/ to furnish with a floor of parquetry

[2]**parquet** *n* parquetry [F, fr MF, small enclosure, fr *parc* park]

parquetry /'pahkitri/ *n* work in the form of usu geometrically patterned wood laid or inlaid esp for floors

parr /pah/ *n, pl* **parr** *also* **parrs** a young salmon actively feeding in fresh water [origin unknown]

parrakeet /,parə'keet, '--,-/ *n, chiefly NAm* a parakeet

parrel /'parəl/ *n* a rope loop or sliding collar by which a yard or spar is held to a mast in such a way that it may be hoisted or lowered ☞ SHIP [ME *perell*, fr alter. of *parail* apparel, short for *apparail*, fr MF *apareil*, fr *apareillier* to prepare – more at APPAREL]

parricide /'parisied/ *n* (the act of) sby who murders his/her father, mother, or a close relative [L *parricida* & *parricidium*, fr *parri-* (akin to Gk *pēos* kinsman by marriage) + *-cida* & *-cidium* – more at -CIDE] – **parricidal** /-'siedl/ *adj*

[1]**parrot** /'parət/ *n* **1** any of numerous chiefly tropical birds that have a distinctive stout hooked bill, are often crested and brightly variegated, and are excellent mimics **2** a person who parrots another's words [prob irreg fr MF *perroquet*]

[2]**parrot** *vt* to repeat or imitate (e g another's words) without understanding or thought

'parrot ,fish *n* any of numerous spiny-finned sea fishes with the teeth fused into a cutting plate like a beak

parry /'pari/ *vi* to ward off a weapon or blow ~ *vt* **1** to ward off (e g a blow) **2** to evade, esp by an adroit answer ⟨*~ an embarrassing question*⟩ [prob fr F *parez*, imper of *parer* to parry, fr OProv *parar*, fr L *parare* to prepare – more at PARE] – **parry** *n*

parse /pahz/ *vt* **1** to resolve (e g a sentence) into component parts of speech and describe them grammatically **2** to describe grammatically by stating the part of speech and the inflectional and syntactic relationships [L *pars orationis* part of speech]

parsec /'pah,sek/ *n* a unit of distance for use in astronomy equal to about 3¼ light-years ☞ PHYSICS, UNIT [*par*allax + *sec*ond]

Parsi, Parsee /,pah'see, '-,-/ *n* **1** a Zoroastrian descended from Persian refugees settled principally in Bombay **2** Pahlavi [Per *pārsī*, fr *Pārs* Persia] – **Parsiism** *n*

parsimonious /,pahsi'mohnyəs/ *adj* frugal to the point of stinginess; niggardly – **parsimoniously** *adv*

parsimony /'pahsiməni/ *n* **1** the quality of being careful with money or resources; thrift **2** the quality or state of being niggardly; stinginess [ME *parcimony*, fr L *parsimonia*, fr *parsus*, pp of *parcere* to spare]

parsley /'pahsli/ *n* an orig S European plant of the carrot family widely cultivated for its leaves used as a herb or garnish in cooking [ME *persely*, fr OE *petersilie*, fr (assumed) VL *petrosilium*, alter. of L *petroselinum*, fr Gk *petroselinon*, fr *petros* stone + *selinon* celery]

parsnip /'pahsnip/ *n* (the long edible tapering root of) a European plant of the carrot family with large leaves and yellow flowers [ME *pasnepe*, modif of MF *pasnaie*, fr L *pastinaca*, fr *pastinum* 2-pronged dibble]

parson /'pahs(ə)n/ *n* **1** the incumbent of a parish **2** a clergyman [ME *persone*, fr OF, fr ML *persona*, lit., person, fr L]

parsonage /'pahsənij/ *n* the house provided by a church for its parson

,parson's 'nose /'pahs(ə)nz/ *n* the fatty extension of the rump of a cooked fowl

[1]**part** /paht/ *n* **1a(1)** any of the often indefinite or unequal subdivisions into which sthg is (regarded as) divided and which together constitute the whole **(2)** an essential portion or integral element **b** an amount equal to another amount ⟨*mix 1 ~ of the powder with 3 ~*s *of water*⟩ **c(1)** an organ, member, or other constituent element of a plant or animal body **(2)** *pl* PRIVATE PARTS **d** a division of a literary work **e(1)** a vocal or instrumental line or melody in concerted music or in harmony **(2)** (the score for) a particular voice or instrument in concerted music **f** a constituent member of an apparatus (e g a machine); *also* SPARE PART **2** sthg falling to one in a division or apportionment; a share **3** any of the opposing sides in a conflict or dispute ⟨*took his son's ~ in the argument*⟩ **4** a portion of an unspecified territorial area ⟨*took off for unknown ~*s⟩ **5** a function or course of action performed ⟨*the government's ~ in the strike*⟩ ⟨*did you take ~ in the fighting?*⟩ **6a** an actor's lines in a play **b** ROLE 1b **7** a constituent of character or capacity; a talent ⟨*a man of many ~*s⟩ **8** *NAm* [1]PARTING 2 [ME, fr OF & OE, both fr L *part-, pars*; akin to L *parare* to prepare – more at PARE] – **for the most part** in most cases or respects; mainly – **in part** in some degree; partly – **on the part of** with regard to the one specified

[2]**part** *vi* **1a** to separate from or take leave of sby **b** to take leave of one another **2** to become separated into parts ⟨*the clouds ~*ed *and the sun appeared*⟩ **3** to become separated, detached, or broken ⟨*the strands of the rope ~*ed⟩ **4** to relinquish possession or control, esp reluctantly ⟨*hated to ~ with her money*⟩ ~ *vt* **1a** to divide into parts **b** to separate (the hair) by combing on each side of a line **2a** to remove from contact or association; separate ⟨*till death do us ~*⟩ **b** to hold (e g combatants) apart [ME *parten*, fr OF *partir*, fr L *partire* to divide, fr *part-, pars*]

[3]**part** *adv* partly ⟨*a centaur is ~ man ~ horse*⟩

[4]**part** *adj* PARTIAL 3

partake /pah'tayk/ *vi* **partook** /-'took/; **partaken** /-'taykən/ to take a part or share; participate – usu + *in* or *of*; fml [back-formation fr *partaker*, alter. of *part taker*] – **partaker** *n*

,part and 'parcel *n* an essential part or element

parterre /pah'teə/ *n* an ornamental garden with paths between the beds [F, fr MF, fr *par terre* on the ground]

,part-ex'change *n* a method of paying for sthg whereby part of the payment takes the form of goods, the balance being made up in money

,parthenogenesis /,pahthinoh'jenəsis/ *n* reproduction by development of an unfertilized gamete that occurs esp among lower plants and invertebrate animals [NL, fr Gk *parthenos* virgin + L *genesis* birth] – **parthenogenetic** /-jə'netik/ *adj*

Parthian /'pahthyən/ *adj* (characteristic) of ancient Parthia [*Parthia*, ancient country of SW Asia] – **Parthian** *n*

[1]**partial** /'pahsh(ə)l/ *adj* **1** inclined to favour one party more than the other; biased **2** markedly fond of sby or sthg – + *to* ⟨~ *to beans*⟩ **3** of a part rather than the whole; not general or total ⟨*a* ~ *solution*⟩ [ME *parcial*, fr MF *partial*, fr ML *partialis*, fr LL, of a part, fr L *part-*, *pars* part] – **partially** *adv*

[2]**partial** *n* OVERTONE 1a

partial derivative *n* the derivative of a function of several variables with respect to any one of them and with the remaining variables treated as constants

partial differentiation *n* the process of finding a partial derivative

partial fraction *n* any of the simpler fractions into which another fraction may be separated and that when summed are equivalent to that fraction

partiality /,pahshi'aləti/ *n* **1** the quality or state of being partial; a bias **2** a special taste or liking

partial pressure *n* the pressure exerted by a specified gas in a mixture of gases

partible /'pahtəbl/ *adj* capable of being divided up ⟨*bequeathed a* ~ *estate*⟩

participate /pah'tisipayt/ *vi* **1** TAKE PART **2** to have a part or share in sthg [L *participatus*, pp of *participare*, fr *particip-*, *particeps* participant, fr *part-*, *pars* part + *capere* to take – more at HEAVE] – **participator** *n*, **participant** /-pənt/ *n*, **participation** /-'paysh(ə)n/ *n*, **participatory** /pah'tisipətri/ *adj*

participle /'pahti,sipl, pah'tisipl/ *n* a verbal form (e g *singing* or *sung*) that has the function of an adjective and at the same time can be used in compound verb forms [ME, fr MF, modif of L *participium*, fr *particip-*, *particeps*] – **participial** /,pahti'sipi·əl/ *adj*

particle /'pahtikl/ *n* **1** a minute subdivision of matter (e g an electron, atom or molecule) – compare ELEMENTARY PARTICLE **2** a minute quantity or fragment **3a** a minor unit of speech including all uninflected words or all words except nouns and verbs; *esp* FUNCTION WORD **b** AFFIX 1 [ME, fr L *particula*, fr dim. of *part-*, *pars*]

parti-coloured /'pahti/ *adj* showing different colours or tints ⟨~ *threads*⟩ [*parti-* fr obs *party* (variegated), fr ME, fr MF *parti* striped, fr OF, fr *parti*, pp of *partir* to divide]

[1]**particular** /pə'tikyoolə/ *adj* **1** of or being a single person or thing; specific ⟨*the* ~ *person I had in mind*⟩ **2** detailed, exact **3** worthy of notice; special, unusual ⟨*there was nothing in the letter of* ~ *importance*⟩ **4** *of a proposition in logic* predicating a term of some but not all members of a specified class **5a** concerned over or attentive to details; meticulous **b** hard to please; exacting [ME *particuler*, fr MF, fr LL *particularis*, fr L *particula* small part] – **particularity** /pə,tikyoo'larəti/ *n*

[2]**particular** *n* an individual fact, point, circumstance, or detail ⟨*complete in every* ~⟩ – **in particular** particularly, especially

particularism /pə'tikyooləriz(ə)m/ *n* **1** exclusive or special devotion to a particular interest **2** a political theory that each political group has a right to promote its own interests without regard to those of larger groups – **particularist** *n*, **particularistic** /-'ristik/ *adj*

particular·ize, -ise /pə'tikyooləriez/ *vt* to state in detail; specify ~ *vi* to go into details – **particularization** /-rie'zaysh(ə)n/ *n*

particularly /pə'tikyooləli/ *adv* **1** in a particular manner; IN DETAIL **2** to an unusual degree

particulate /pah'tikyoolət/ *n or adj* (a substance) consisting of minute separate particles [L *particula*]

[1]**parting** /'pahting/ *n* **1** a place or point where a division or separation occurs **2 parting,** *NAm* **part** the line where the hair is parted

[2]**parting** *adj* given, taken, or performed at parting ⟨*a* ~ *kiss*⟩

parti pris /,pahti 'pree/ *n, pl* **partis pris** /~/ a preconceived opinion; a prejudice, bias [F, lit., side taken]

[1]**partisan, partizan** /'pahtizn/ *n* **1** a firm adherent to a party, faction, cause, or person; *esp* one exhibiting blind, prejudiced, and unreasoning allegiance **2** a guerrilla [MF *partisan*, fr OIt *partigiano*, fr *parte* part, party, fr L *part-*, *pars* part] – **partisan** *adj*, **partisanship** *n*

[2]**partisan, partizan** *n* a weapon of the 16th and 17th c consisting of a broad blade mounted on a long shaft [MF *partisane*, fr OIt *partigiana*, fem of *partigiano*]

partita /pah'teetə/ *n* a musical suite [It, fr *partire* to divide, fr L – more at [2]PART]

partite /'pahtiet/ *adj* **1** divided into a usu specified number of parts – usu in combination ⟨*tri*partite⟩ **2** cleft nearly to the base ⟨*a* ~ *leaf*⟩ [L *partitus*, fr pp of *partire*]

[1]**partition** /pah'tish(ə)n/ *n* **1a** division into parts **b** separation of a class or whole into constituent elements **2** sthg that divides; *esp* a light interior dividing wall **3** a part or section of a whole – **partitionist** *n*

[2]**partition** *vt* **1** to divide into parts or shares **2** to divide or separate *off* by a partition ⟨*can we* ~ *off part of the room to use as an office?*⟩

partitive /'pahtətiv/ *adj* of or denoting a part of a whole – **partitively** *adv*

partly /'pahtli/ *adv* in some measure or degree; partially

[1]**partner** /'pahtnə/ *n* **1a** either of a couple who dance together **b** sby who plays with 1 or more others in a game against an opposing side **c** a person with whom one is having a sexual relationship; a spouse, lover, etc **2** a member of a partnership [ME *partener*, alter. of *parcener*, fr AF – more at COPARCENER]

[2]**partner** *vt* **1** to act as a partner to **2** to provide with a partner

[1]**partnership** /-ship/ *n* **1** the state of being a partner; association **2** (a legal relation between) 2 or more joint principals in a business **3** an association involving close cooperation

,**part of 'speech** *n* a class of words distinguished according to the kind of idea denoted and the function performed in a sentence

partridge /'pahtrij/ *n, pl* **partridges,** *esp collectively* **partridge** any of various typically medium-sized stout-bodied Old World game birds with variegated plumage [ME *partrich,* modif of OF *perdris,* modif of L *perdic-, perdix,* fr Gk *perdik, perdix*]

'**part-,song** *n* a usu unaccompanied song consisting of 2 or more voice parts with 1 part carrying the melody

,**part-'time** *adj* involving or working less than customary or standard hours ⟨*a ~ job*⟩ ⟨*~ students*⟩ – **part-time** *adv,* **part-timer** *n*

parturient /pah'tyooəri·ənt/ *adj* **1** about to bring forth young **2** about to produce sthg (e g an idea, discovery, or literary work) – fml [L *parturient-, parturiens,* prp of *parturire* to be in labour, fr *parere* to produce – more at PARE]

parturition /,pahtyoo'rish(ə)n/ *n* the action or process of giving birth to offspring [LL *parturition-, parturitio,* fr L *parturitus,* pp of *parturire*]

partway /,paht'way/ *adv, chiefly NAm* to some extent; partially, partly

part work *n, Br* a regularly published series of magazines devoted to 1 subject that is designed to be bound together (e g in book form) ⟨*publishing a new ~ on military history*⟩

party /'pahti/ *n* **1a** a person or group taking 1 side of a question, dispute, or contest **b** *sing or pl constr* a group of people organized to carry out an activity or fulfil a function together ⟨*sent out a search ~*⟩ **2** *sing or pl in constr* a group organized for political involvement **3** one who is involved; a participant – usu + *to* ⟨*a ~ to the transaction*⟩ **4** a (festive) social gathering **5** sby who is concerned in an action or activity – chiefly fml ⟨*a third ~ was involved*⟩ ⟨*is this the guilty ~?*⟩ **6** a particular individual – infml ⟨*a shameless old ~*⟩ [ME *partie* part, party, fr OF, fr *partir* to divide – more at [2]PART]

party line *n* **1** a single telephone line connecting 2 or more subscribers with an exchange **2** the official principles of a political party

party wall *n* a wall which divides 2 adjoining properties and in which each owner has a joint interest

parvenu /'pahvənyooh/ *n* a person of low social position who has recently or suddenly acquired wealth or power; an upstart [F, fr pp of *parvenir* to arrive, fr L *pervenire,* fr *per* through + *venire* to come – more at FOR, COME] – **parvenu, parvenue** *adj*

parvis *also* **parvise** /'pahvis/ *n* an enclosed space in front of a church ☞ CHURCH [ME *parvis,* fr MF, modif of LL *paradisus* enclosed park – more at PARADISE]

pas /pah/ *n, pl* **pas** /~, pahz/ a dance step or combination of steps [F, fr L *passus* step – more at [1]PACE]

pascal /pa'skal/ *n* the SI unit of pressure equal to the pressure produced by a force of 1N applied uniformly over an area of $1m^2$ ☞ PHYSICS, UNIT [Blaise *Pascal* †1662 F mathematician & philosopher]

PASCAL /paskl/ *n* a high-level computer language suitable esp for minicomputers [Blaise *Pascal*]

Pascal's triangle /pa'skalz/ *n* a set of numbers arranged in a triangle, each of which is obtained by adding together the numbers above it, and which is used to determine the coefficients of the terms in an expansion made using the binomial theorem [Blaise *Pascal*]

Pasch /pask/ *n* the Passover [ME *pasche* Passover, Easter, fr OF, fr LL *pascha,* fr LGk, fr Gk, Passover, fr Heb *pesaḥ*]

paschal /'paskl/ *adj* **1** of the Passover **2** of or appropriate to Easter

pas de deux /,pah də 'duh/ *n, pl* **pas de deux** /~, duhz/ a dance or set of dance steps for 2 performers [F, lit., step for two]

pash /pash/ *n, chiefly Br* a hero-worshipping adolescent infatuation; a crush – infml ⟨*a silly schoolgirl hero*-pash *on him* – John Fowles⟩ [by shortening & alter. fr *passion*]

pasha /'pahshə, 'pashə/ *n* a man of high rank or office (e g in Turkey or N Africa) ⟨*Glubb* Pasha⟩ [Turk *paşa*]

Pashto /'pooshtoh/ *n* the language of the Pathan people ☞ LANGUAGE [Per *pashtu,* fr Pashto]

paso doble /,pasoh 'dohblay/ *n* (the music for) a ballroom dance in $\frac{2}{4}$ time based on a Latin American march step [Sp, lit., double step]

pasqueflower /'pask,flowə/ *n* any of several low-growing plants of the buttercup family with large, usu white or purple, early spring flowers [modif of MF *passefleur,* fr *passer* to pass + *fleur* flower, fr L *flor-, flos* – more at [3]BLOW]

pasquinade /,paskwi'nayd/ *n* a lampoon posted in a public place [MF, fr It *pasquinata,* fr *Pasquino,* name given to a statue in Rome on which lampoons were posted] – **pasquinade** *vt*

[1]**pass** /pahs/ *vi* **1** to move, proceed **2a** to go away ⟨*the panic* ~ed *very quickly*⟩ – often + *off* ⟨*his headache had* ~ed *off by lunchtime*⟩ **b** to die – often + *on* or *away*; euph **3a** to go by; move past ⟨*waved from the car window as she* ~ed⟩ **b** *of time* to elapse ⟨*4 years* ~ed *before we met again*⟩ **c** to overtake another vehicle ⟨*we can ~ once we're round this bend*⟩ **4a** to go across, over, or through ⟨*allow no one to ~*⟩ **b** to go uncensured or unchallenged ⟨*let her remark ~*⟩ **5** to go from one quality, state, or form to another ⟨~es *from a liquid to a gaseous state*⟩ **6a** to pronounce a judgment **b** to be legally pronounced **7** to go from the control or possession of one person or group to that of another ⟨*the throne* ~ed *to the king's daughter*⟩ **8** to take place as a mutual exchange or transaction ⟨*angry words* ~ed *between them*⟩ **9a** to become approved by a body (e g a legislature) ⟨*the proposal* ~ed⟩ **b** to undergo an inspection, test, or examination successfully **10a** to be accepted or regarded as adequate or fitting ⟨*it's only a quick repair but it will ~*⟩ **b** to resemble or act the part of so well as to be accepted – usu + *for* **11** to kick, throw, or hit a ball or puck to a teammate **12** to decline to bid, bet, or play in a card game ~ *vt* **1** to go beyond: e g **a** to surpass, exceed ⟨~es *all expectations*⟩ **b** to advance or develop beyond ⟨*societies that have* ~ed *the feudal stage*⟩ **c** to go by; move past **2a** to go across, over, or through ⟨*~ a barrier*⟩ **b** to spend (time) ⟨~ed *the holidays at her sister's home*⟩ **3a** to secure the approval of (e g a legislative body) **b** to succeed in satisfying the

requirements of (a test, inspection, or examination) **4a** to cause or permit to win approval or sanction ⟨~ *a law*⟩ **b** to accept (sby or sthg) after examination ⟨*I can't ~ this bad piece of work!*⟩ **5a** to put in circulation ⟨~ *bad cheques*⟩ **b** to transfer from one person to another ⟨*please ~ the salt*⟩ **c** to move or place, esp in or for a short time ⟨~ed *his hand across his brow*⟩ ⟨~ *a rope round a tree*⟩ **d** to throw, hit, or kick (a ball or puck), esp to a teammate **6a** to pronounce judicially ⟨~ *sentence*⟩ **b** to utter – esp in *pass a comment, pass a remark* **7a** to cause or permit to go past or through a barrier **b** to cause to march or go by in order ⟨~ *the troops in review*⟩ **8** to emit or discharge from a bodily part, esp the bowels or bladder **9** to hit a ball past (an opponent), esp in tennis [ME *passen*, fr OF *passer*, fr (assumed) VL *passare*, fr L *passus* step – more at [1]PACE] – **in passing** as a relevant digression; parenthetically – **pass muster** to be found adequate, esp in passing an inspection or examination – **pass the buck** to shift a responsibility to sby else – **past the time of day** to give or exchange friendly greetings – **pass water** to urinate – euph

[2]**pass** *n* a narrow passage over low ground in a mountain range [ME, fr OF *pas*, fr L *passus* step]

[3]**pass** *n* **1** a usu distressing or bad state of affairs – often in *come to a pretty pass* **2a** a written permission to move about freely in a place or to leave or enter it **b** a written leave of absence from a military post or station for a brief period **c** a permit or ticket allowing free transport or free admission **3** a movement of the hands over or along sthg **4** the passing of an examination ⟨*2 A-level* ~es⟩ **5** a single complete mechanical operation (e g in manufacturing or data processing) **6a** an act of passing in cards, soccer, rugby, etc; *also* a ball or puck passed **b** a ball hit to the side and out of reach of an opponent, esp in tennis **7** a single passage or movement of a man-made object (e g an aircraft) over a place or towards a target **8** a sexually inviting gesture or approach – usu in *make a pass at* [partly fr ME *passe*, fr MF, fr *passer* to pass; partly fr [1]*pass*]

passable /'pahsəbl/ *adj* **1** capable of being passed, crossed, or travelled on ⟨~ *roads*⟩ **2** barely good enough; tolerable – **passably** *adv*

passacaglia /,pasə'kahlyə/ *n* an instrumental musical composition in moderately slow triple time consisting of variations usu on a ground bass [modif of Sp *pasacalle*]

passage /'pasij/ *n* **1** the action or process of passing from one place or condition to another **2a** a way of exit or entrance; a road, path, channel, or course by which sthg passes **b** a corridor or lobby giving access to the different rooms or parts of a building or apartment **3a(1)** a specified act of travelling or passing, esp by sea or air ⟨*a rough* ~⟩ **(2)** a right to be conveyed as a passenger ⟨*secured a ~ to France*⟩ **b** the passing of a legislative measure **4** a right, liberty, or permission to pass **5a** a brief noteworthy portion of a written work or speech **b** a phrase or short section of a musical composition **6** passing sthg or undergoing a passing **7** incubation of a pathogen (e g a virus) in culture, a living organism, or a developing egg

'**passage,way** /-,way/ *n* a corridor

passant /'pas(ə)nt/ *adj, of a heraldic animal* walking with the farther forepaw raised – used postpositively ⟨*leopard* ~⟩ [MF, fr prp of *passer* to pass]

pass away *vi* **1** to go out of existence **2** to die – euph

'**pass,band** /-,band/ *n* a band of frequencies (e g in an electronic circuit or a light filter) that is transmitted with maximum efficiency

'**pass,book** /-,book/ *n* **1** a (building society) account-holder's book in which deposits and withdrawals are recorded **2** *SAfr* a dompass

'**pass de,gree** *n* a bachelor's degree without honours

passé /'pahsay, 'pasay/ *adj* **1** outmoded **2** behind the times [F, fr pp of *passer*]

,**passed 'pawn** *n* a chess pawn that has no enemy pawn in front of it on its own or an adjacent file

passementerie /pas'ment(ə)ri/ *n* a fancy edging or trimming made of braid, beading, metallic thread, etc [F, fr *passement* ornamental braid, fr *passer*]

passenger /'pasinjə, -s(ə)n-/ *n* **1** sby who travels in, but does not operate, a public or private conveyance **2** *chiefly Br* a member of a group who contributes little or nothing to the functioning or productivity of the group [ME *passager*, fr MF, fr *passager*, adj, passing, fr *passage* act of passing, fr OF, fr *passer*]

'**passenger ,pigeon** *n* an extinct but formerly abundant N American migratory pigeon

passe-partout /,pahs pah'tooh/ *n* **1** MASTER KEY **2** a strong paper gummed on 1 side and used esp for mounting pictures [F, fr *passe partout* pass everywhere]

passerby /,pahsə'bie/ *n, pl* **passersby** /,pahsəz-/ a person who happens by chance to pass by a particular place

passerine /'pasə,rien/ *adj* of the largest order of birds that consists chiefly of perching songbirds (e g finches, warblers, and thrushes) [L *passerinus* of sparrows, fr *passer* sparrow] – **passerine** *n*

passim /'pasim/ *adv* HERE AND THERE 1 [L, fr *passus* scattered, fr pp of *pandere* to spread – more at FATHOM]

passing /'pahsing/ *adj* **1** going by or past ⟨*a ~ pedestrian*⟩ **2** having a brief duration ⟨*a ~ whim*⟩ **3** superficial **4** of or used in or for passing ⟨*a ~ place in a road*⟩

passing note *n* a melodic but discordant note interposed between essential notes of adjacent chords

passion /'pash(ə)n/ *n* **1** *often cap* **a** the sufferings of Christ between the night of the Last Supper and his death **b** a musical setting of a gospel account of the Passion story **2a** intense, driving, or uncontrollable feeling **b** an outbreak of anger **3a** ardent affection; love **b** (the object of) a strong liking, devotion, or interest **c** strong sexual desire [ME, fr OF, fr LL *passion-*, *passio* suffering, being acted on, fr L *passus*, pp of *pati* to suffer – more at PATIENT] – **passional** *adj*

passionate /'pash(ə)nət/ *adj* **1** easily aroused to anger **2a** capable of, affected by, or expressing intense feeling, esp love, hatred, or anger **b** extremely enthusiastic; keen ⟨*a ~ interest in sport*⟩ – **passionately** *adv*, **passionateness** *n*

'**passion,flower** /-,flowə/ *n* any of a genus of chiefly tropical plants with usu showy flowers and pulpy often edible berries [fr the fancied resemblance of parts of the flower to the instruments of Christ's crucifixion]

'**passion,fruit** /-,frooht/ *n* an edible fruit from any of various passion flowers; a granadilla

'passion ,play *n, often cap 1st P* a dramatic representation of the passion and crucifixion of Christ

,Passion 'Sunday *n* the fifth Sunday in Lent

'Passion,tide /-,tied/ *n* the last 2 weeks of Lent

'Passion ,Week *n* the second week before Easter

passivate /'passivayt/ *vt* to protect or make inactive or less reactive, esp by coating ⟨~ *the surface of steel*⟩ – **passivation** /-'vaysh(ə)n/ *n*

[1]passive /'pasiv/ *adj* **1a** acted on, receptive to, or influenced by external forces or impressions **b** *of a verb form or voice* expressing an action that is done to the grammatical subject of a sentence (e g *was hit* in 'the ball was hit'') **c** *esp of an animal* placid **d** *of a person* lacking in energy, will, or initiative; meekly accepting **2a** not active or operative; inert **b** of or characterized by chemical inactivity; *esp* resistant to corrosion **c** not involving expenditure of chemical energy ⟨~ *transport across a cell membrane*⟩ **d** relating to or being an electronic component (e g a capacitor or resistor) or network of components whose characteristics cannot be controlled electronically and which show no gain **e** operating solely by means of the power of an input signal ⟨*a ~ communication satellite that reflects radio waves*⟩ **f** operating by intercepting signals emitted from a target ⟨*a ~ homing missile*⟩ **3** offering no resistance; submissive ⟨~ *surrender to fate*⟩ [ME, fr L *passivus*, fr *passus*, pp] – **passively** *adv*, **passiveness** *n*, **passivity** /pa'sivəti/ *n*

[2]passive *n* the passive voice of a verb

passive resistance *n* resistance characterized by nonviolent noncooperation

passkey /'pahs,kee/ *n* MASTER KEY

'pass ,law *n* any of several S African laws restricting the movements of nonwhites, enforcing their domicile in certain areas and requiring them to carry identification at all times – compare DOMPASS

pass off *vt* **1** to present with intent to deceive **2** to give a false identity or character to ⟨passed *herself* off *as a millionairess*⟩ ~ *vi* to take place and be completed ⟨*his stay in France* passed off *smoothly* – *TLS*⟩

pass out *vi* **1** to lose consciousness **2** *chiefly Br* to finish a period of (military) training

Passover /'pahsohvə/ *n* the Jewish celebration of the liberation of the Hebrews from slavery in Egypt [fr the exemption of the Israelites from the slaughter of the first-born in Egypt (Exod 12:23-27)]

pass over *vt* **1** to ignore in passing ⟨*I will* pass over *this aspect of the book in silence*⟩ **2** to pay no attention to the claims of; disregard ⟨*was* passed over *for the chairmanship*⟩

passport /'pahs,pawt/ *n* **1** an official document issued by a government **a** as proof of identity and nationality to one of its citizens for use when leaving or reentering the country and affording some protection when abroad **b** as a safe-conduct to a foreign citizen passing through its territory **2a** a permission or authorization to go somewhere **b** sthg that secures admission or acceptance ⟨*education as a ~ to success*⟩ [MF *passeport*, fr *passer* to pass + *port* port, fr L *portus* – more at FORD]

pass up *vt* to decline, reject

'pass,word /-,wuhd/ *n* **1** a word or phrase that must be spoken by a person before being allowed to pass a guard **2** WATCHWORD 1

[1]past /pahst/ *adj* **1a** just gone or elapsed ⟨*for the ~ few months*⟩ **b** having gone by; earlier ⟨~ *generations*⟩ ⟨*in years ~*⟩ **2** finished, ended ⟨*winter is ~*⟩ **3** of or constituting the past tense expressing elapsed time **4** preceding, former ⟨~ *president*⟩ [ME, fr pp of *passen* to pass]

[2]past *prep* **1a** beyond the age of or for ⟨*he's ~ 80*⟩ ⟨~ *playing with dolls*⟩ **b** subsequent to in time ⟨*half ~ 2*⟩ **2a** at the farther side of; beyond **b** up to and then beyond ⟨*drove ~ the house*⟩ **3** beyond the capacity, range, or sphere of ⟨~ *belief*⟩ ⟨*wouldn't put it ~ her to cheat*⟩ – **past it** no longer effective or in one's prime – infml

[3]past *n* **1a** time gone by **b** sthg that happened or was done in the past ⟨*regret the ~*⟩ **2** the past tense of a language **3** a past life, history, or course of action; *esp* one that is kept secret ⟨*she has a ~, you know*⟩

[4]past *adv* so as to pass by the speaker ⟨*children ran ~*⟩ ⟨*days crawled ~*⟩

pasta /'pastə/ *n* any of several (egg or oil enriched) flour and water doughs that are usu shaped and used fresh or dried (e g as spaghetti) [It, fr LL]

[1]paste /payst/ *n* **1a** a fat-enriched dough used esp for pastry **b** a usu sweet doughy confection ⟨*almond ~*⟩ **c** a smooth preparation of meat, fish, etc used as a spread **2** a soft plastic mixture or composition: e g **a** a preparation of flour or starch and water used as an adhesive **b** clay or a clay mixture used in making pottery or porcelain **3** a brilliant glass used in making imitation gems [ME, fr MF, fr LL *pasta* dough, paste]

[2]paste *vt* **1** to stick with paste **2** to cover with sthg pasted on

[1]'paste,board /-,bawd/ *n* board made by pasting together sheets of paper

[2]pasteboard *adj* **1** made of pasteboard **2** sham, insubstantial

[1]pastel /'pastl; *NAm* pas'tel/ *n* **1** (a crayon made of) a paste of powdered pigment mixed with gum **2** a drawing in pastel **3** any of various pale or light colours [F, fr It *pastello*, fr LL *pastellus* woad, fr dim. of *pasta*] – **pastellist** *n*

[2]pastel *adj* pale and light in colour

pastern /'pastuhn/ *n* (a part of an animal's leg corresponding to) a part of a horse's foot extending from the fetlock to the hoof ☞ ANATOMY [MF *pasturon*, fr *pasture* pasture, tether attached to a horse's foot]

'paste-,up *n* **1** a piece of copy for photographic reproduction consisting of text and artwork in the proper positions **2** DUMMY 4

pasteur·ization, -isation /,pahstyoorie'zaysh(ə)n, pa-, -stərie-/ *n* partial sterilization of a substance, esp a liquid (e g milk), by heating for a short period [Louis *Pasteur* †1895 F chemist] – **pasteurize** *vt*

pastiche /pa'steesh/ *n* **1** a literary, artistic, or musical work that imitates the style of a previous work **2** a musical, literary, or artistic composition made up of elements borrowed from various sources [F, fr It *pasticcio*, lit., pasty, fr ML *pasticius*, fr LL *pasta*]

pasties /'paystiz/ *n pl* small round coverings for a woman's nipples, worn esp by strippers [[2]*paste*]

pastille *also* **pastil** /'past(ə)l, -stil, -steel/ *n* **1** a small cone of aromatic paste, burned to fumigate or scent a room **2** an aromatic or medicated lozenge [F *pastille*, fr L *pastillus* small loaf, lozenge; akin to L *panis* bread – more at FOOD]

pastime /'pahs,tiem/ *n* sthg (e g a hobby, game, etc)

that amuses and serves to make time pass agreeably

pasting /ˈpaysting/ *n* a beating, trouncing – infml [gerund of *paste*, alter. of *baste*]

pastis /paˈstees/ *n* an alcoholic drink flavoured with aniseed [F]

ˌpast ˈmaster *n* one who is expert or experienced (in a particular activity) [alter. of *passed master*]

pastor /ˈpahstə/ *n* one having responsibility for the spiritual welfare of a group (e g a congregation) [ME *pastour*, fr OF, fr L *pastor* herdsman, fr *pastus*, pp of *pascere* to feed – more at FOOD] – **pastorate** *n*, **pastorship** *n*

[1]**pastoral** /ˈpahst(ə)rəl/ *adj* **1a(1)** (composed) of shepherds or herdsmen **(2)** used for or based on livestock rearing **b** of the countryside; not urban **c** portraying rural life, esp in an idealized and conventionalized manner ⟨~ *poetry*⟩ **d** pleasingly peaceful and innocent; idyllic **2a** of or providing spiritual care or guidance, esp of a church congregation **b** of the pastor of a church [ME, fr L *pastoralis*, fr *pastor* herdsman] – **pastoralism** *n*, **pastorally** *adv*

[2]**pastoral** *n* **1 pastoral, pastoral letter** a letter addressed by a bishop to his diocese **2a** a pastoral literary work **b** an (idealized) depiction of country life **c** a pastorale

pastorale /ˌpastəˈrahli/ *n* an instrumental composition or opera with a pastoral theme [It, fr *pastorale* of herdsmen, fr L *pastoralis*]

pastoralist /ˈpahst(ə)rəˌlist/ *n*, *Austr* a farmer who keeps grazing animals (e g cattle or sheep)

past participle *n* a participle with past, perfect, or passive meaning

past perfect *adj* of or constituting a verb tense (e g *had finished*) that expresses completion of an action at or before a past time – **past perfect** *n*

pastrami /paˈstrahmi/ *n* a highly seasoned smoked beef [Yiddish, fr Romanian *pastramă*]

pastry /ˈpaystri/ *n* **1** PASTE 1a; *esp* paste when baked (e g for piecrust) **2** (an article of) usu sweet food made with pastry [[1]*paste*]

pasturage /ˈpastyoorij, ˈpahschərij/ *n* pasture

[1]**pasture** /ˈpahschə/ *n* **1** plants (e g grass) grown for feeding (grazing) animals **2** (a plot of) land used for grazing **3** the feeding of livestock; grazing [ME, fr MF, fr LL *pastura*, fr L *pastus*, pp of *pascere* to feed – more at FOOD]

[2]**pasture** *vi* to graze on pasture ~ *vt* to feed (e g cattle) on pasture

[1]**pasty** /ˈpasti/ *n* a small filled usu savoury pie or pastry case baked without a container [ME *pastee*, fr MF *pasté*, fr *paste* dough, paste]

[2]**pasty** /ˈpaysti/ *adj* resembling paste; *esp* pallid and unhealthy in appearance – **pastiness** *n*

[1]**pat** /pat/ *n* **1** a light tap, esp with the hand or a flat instrument **2** a light tapping sound **3** a small mass of sthg (e g butter) shaped (as if) by patting [ME *patte*, prob of imit origin]

[2]**pat** *vt* **-tt- 1** to strike lightly with the open hand or some other flat surface **2** to flatten, smooth, or put into place or shape with light blows ⟨*he* ~ted *his hair into place*⟩ **3** to tap or stroke gently with the hand to soothe, caress, or show approval

[3]**pat** *adv* in a pat manner; aptly, promptly

[4]**pat** *adj* **1** prompt, immediate **2** suspiciously appropriate; contrived ⟨*a* ~ *answer*⟩ **3** learned, mastered, or memorized exactly

pataca /pəˈtahkə/ *n* ☞ *Macao* at NATIONALITY [Pg]

patagium /pəˈtayji·əm/ *n*, *pl* **patagia** /-ji·ə/ a wing membrane; *esp* the fold of skin connecting the forelimbs and hind limbs of a gliding animal (e g a flying squirrel) [NL, fr L, gold edging on a tunic]

ˈpat-ˌball *n* slow or feeble play (e g in cricket or tennis)

[1]**patch** /pach/ *n* **1** a piece of material used to mend or cover a hole or reinforce a weak spot **2** a tiny piece of black silk worn on the face, esp by women in the 17th and 18th c, to set off the complexion **3a** a cover (e g a piece of adhesive plaster) applied to a wound **b** a shield worn over the socket of an injured or missing eye **4a** a small piece; a scrap **b** a small area distinct from its surroundings ⟨*damp* ~es *on the wall*⟩ **c** a small piece of land usu used for growing vegetables ⟨*a cabbage* ~⟩ **5** a piece of cloth sewn on a garment as an ornament or insignia **6** a temporary connection in a communications system **7** a temporary correction in a faulty computer program **8** *chiefly Br* a usu specified period ⟨*poetry is going through a bad* ~ – Cyril Connolly⟩ **9** *chiefly Br* an area for which a particular individual or unit (e g of police) has responsibility [ME *pacche*, perh fr MF *pece, piece, pieche* piece] – **not a patch on** not nearly as good as

[2]**patch** *vt* **1** to mend or cover (a hole) with a patch **2** to provide with a patch ⟨*a* ~ed *pair of trousers*⟩ **3a** to make from patchwork **b** to mend or put together, esp in a hasty or shabby fashion – usu + *up* **c** to make a patch in (a computer program); *also* to make a change in (data stored on a computer) without following the standard routine for this procedure **4** to connect (e g circuits) by a patch cord

ˈpatchˌboard /-ˌbawd/ *n* a board which has sets of linked sockets for making temporary circuit connections by means of patch cords

ˈpatch ˌcord *n* a wire with a plug at each end that is used to link sockets on a patchboard

patchouli, patchouly /ˈpachooli, pəˈchoohli/ *n* **1** an E Indian shrubby plant of the mint family that yields a fragrant essential oil **2** a heavy perfume made from patchouli [Tamil *paccuḷi*]

ˈpatch ˌpocket *n* a flat pocket attached to the outside of a garment

patch up *vt* to bring (a quarrel, dispute, etc) to an end

ˈpatchˌwork /-ˌwuhk/ *n* **1** sthg composed of miscellaneous or incongruous parts **2** work consisting of pieces of cloth of various colours and shapes sewn together

patchy /ˈpachi/ *adj* **1** uneven in quality; incomplete ⟨*my knowledge of French is* ~⟩ **2** *of certain types of weather* appearing in patches ⟨~ *fog*⟩ – **patchily** *adv*, **patchiness** *n*

pate /payt/ *n* (the crown of) the head [ME] – **pated** *adj*

pâté /ˈpatay/ *n* a rich savoury paste of seasoned and spiced meat, fish, etc [F, fr OF *pasté*, fr *paste*]

patella /pəˈtelə/ *n*, *pl* **patellae** /-li/, **patellas** the kneecap ☞ ANATOMY [L, fr dim. of *patina* shallow dish] – **patellar** *adj*

paten /ˈpat(ə)n/ *n* **1** a plate holding the bread used at Communion **2** a thin circular metal disc [ME, fr OF *patene*, fr ML & L; ML *patina*, fr L, shallow dish, fr Gk *patanē*; akin to L *patēre*]

[1]**patent** /ˈpayt(ə)nt, ˈpat(ə)nt; *sense 5* ˈpayt(ə)nt/ *adj*

1a secured by or made under a patent ⟨~ *locks*⟩ **b** proprietary ⟨~ *drugs*⟩ **2a** of patents ⟨*a ~ lawyer*⟩ **b** made of patent leather ⟨~ *shoes*⟩ **3** original and ingenious as if protected by patent ⟨*a ~ way of pickling onions*⟩ **4** affording free passage; unobstructed ⟨*a ~ opening*⟩ **5** readily visible or intelligible; not hidden or obscure [ME, fr MF, fr L *patent-, patens,* fr prp of *patēre* to be open – more at FATHOM] – **patency** /'payt(ə)nsi/ *n,* **patently** /'pay-/ *adv*

[2]**patent** /'payt(ə)nt, 'pat(ə)nt/ *n* **1** LETTERS PATENT **2a** (a formal document securing to an inventor) the exclusive right to make or sell an invention **b** a patented invention **3** a privilege, licence

[3]**patent** *vt* to obtain a patent for (an invention) – **patentable** *adj*

patentee /,payt(ə)n'tee, ,pa-/ *n* sby to whom a grant is made or a privilege secured by patent

,patent 'leather /'payt(ə)nt/ *n* a leather with a hard smooth glossy surface

patent medicine /'payt(ə)nt/ *n* a medicine that is made and marketed under a patent, trademark, etc

'patent ,office /'payt(ə)nt, 'pat(ə)nt/ *n* a government office for granting patents

pater /'paytə/ *n, chiefly Br* a father – now usu humor [L]

paterfamilias /,paytəfə'mili,as/ *n, pl* **patresfamilias** /,pahtrayz-/ the male head of a household [L, fr *pater* father + *familias,* archaic gen of *familia* household – more at FATHER, FAMILY]

paternal /pə'tuhnl/ *adj* **1** fatherly ⟨~ *benevolence*⟩ **2** received or inherited from one's male parent **3** related through one's father ⟨~ *grandfather*⟩ [L *paternus,* fr *pater*] – **paternally** *adv*

pa'ternal,ism /-,iz(ə)m/ *n* a system under which a government or organization deals with its subjects or employees in an authoritarian but benevolent way, esp by supplying all their needs and regulating their conduct – **paternalist** *n or adj,* **paternalistic** /-'istik/ *adj*

paternity /pə'tuhnəti/ *n* **1** being a father **2** origin or descent from a father

pa'ternity ,test *n* the comparison of the genetic attributes (e g blood groups) of a mother, child, and man to determine whether the man could be the child's father

paternoster /,patə'nostə, ,pah-/ *n, often cap* LORD'S PRAYER [ME, fr ML, fr L *pater noster* our father]

path /pahth/ *n, pl* **paths** /pahdhz/ **1** a track formed by the frequent passage of people or animals **2** a track specially constructed for a particular use ⟨*garden ~s*⟩ – compare BRIDLE PATH **3a** a course, route ⟨*the ~ of a planet*⟩ **b** a way of life, conduct, or thought ⟨*his ~ through life was difficult*⟩ **4** the continuous series of positions or configurations that can be assumed in any motion or process of change by a moving or varying system [ME, fr OE *pæth;* akin to MD & MLG *pad* path, OHG *pfad*]

path-, patho- *comb form* pathological state; disease ⟨path*ogen*⟩ [NL, fr Gk, fr *pathos,* lit., suffering – more at PATHOS]

-path /-path/ *comb form* (→ *n*) **1** practitioner of (a specified system of medicine) ⟨*naturo*path⟩ **2** sufferer from disorder of (such a part or system) ⟨*psycho*path⟩ [(1) G, back-formation fr *-pathie* -pathy; (2) ISV, fr Gk *-pathēs* (adj) suffering, fr *pathos*]

Pathan /pə'tahn/ *n* a member of the principal ethnic group of Afghanistan [Hindi *Paṭhān*]

pathetic /pə'thetik/ *adj* **1a** PITIFUL 1 ⟨*a ~ lost child*⟩ **b** PITIFUL 2 ⟨*a ~ performance*⟩ ⟨*~ attempts to learn German*⟩ **2** marked by sorrow or melancholy; sad [MF or LL; MF *pathetique,* fr LL *patheticus,* fr Gk *pathētikos* capable of feeling, pathetic, fr *paschein* to experience, suffer – more at PATHOS] – **pathetically** *adv*

pathetic fallacy *n* the attribution of human characteristics or feelings to inanimate nature (e g in *cruel sea*)

pathfinder /'pahth,fiendə/ *n* **1** sby or sthg that explores unexplored regions to mark out a new route **2** sby who discovers new ways of doing things – **pathfinding** *n or adj*

pathless /'pahthlis/ *adj* untrod, trackless

pathogen /'pathəj(ə)n, -jen/ *n* a bacterium, virus, or other disease-causing agent [ISV] – **pathogenic** /-'jenik/ *adj,* **pathogenically** *adv,* **pathogenicity** /-jə'nisəti/ *n*

pathogenesis /,pathə'jenəsis/ *n* the origination and development of a disease [NL] – **pathogenetic** /-jə'netik/ *adj*

pathologist /pə'tholəjist/ *n* one who studies pathology; *specif* one who conducts postmortems to determine the cause of death

pathology /pə'tholəji/ *n* **1** the study of (the structure and functional changes produced by) diseases **2** sthg abnormal: **a** the anatomical and physiological abnormalities that constitute or characterize (a particular) disease **b** deviation from an assumed normal state of mentality or morality [NL *pathologia* & MF *pathologie,* fr Gk *pathologia* study of the emotions, fr *path-* + *-logia* -logy] – **pathological** /,pathə'lojikl/, **pathologic** *adj,* **pathologically** *adv*

pathos /'paythos/ *n* **1** a quality in experience or in artistic representation evoking pity or compassion **2** an emotion of sympathetic pity [Gk, suffering, experience, emotion, fr *paschein* to experience, suffer; akin to Lith *kesti* to suffer]

pathway /'pahth,way/ *n* **1** a path, course **2** the sequence of enzyme-catalysed reactions by which a substance is synthesized or an energy-yielding substance is used by living tissue ⟨*metabolic ~s*⟩

-pathy /-pəthi/ *comb form* (→ *n*) **1** feeling; being acted upon ⟨*em*pathy⟩ ⟨*tele*pathy⟩ **2** disorder of (such a part or system) ⟨*neuro*pathy⟩ **3** system of medicine based on (such a factor) ⟨*osteo*pathy⟩ [L *-pathia,* fr Gk *-patheia,* fr *-pathēs* suffering, fr *pathos*]

patience /'paysh(ə)ns/ *n* **1** the capacity, habit, or fact of being patient **2** *chiefly Br* any of various card games that can be played by 1 person and usu involve the arranging of cards into a prescribed pattern

[1]**patient** /'paysh(ə)nt/ *adj* **1** bearing pains or trials calmly or without complaint **2** manifesting forbearance under provocation or strain **3** not hasty or impetuous **4** steadfast despite opposition, difficulty, or adversity [ME *pacient,* fr MF, fr L *patient-, patiens,* fr prp of *pati* to suffer; akin to L *paene* almost, *penuria* need, Gk *pēma* suffering] – **patiently** *adv*

[2]**patient** *n* an individual awaiting or under medical care

patina /'patinə/ *n, pl* **patinas, patinae** /-ni/ **1** a (decorative) usu green film formed on copper and bronze by (simulated) weathering and valued as aesthetically pleasing **2** a surface appearance of sthg (e g polished wood) that has grown more beautiful esp with age or use [NL, fr L, shallow dish – more at PATEN]

patio /ˈpati·oh/ *n, pl* **patios** a usu paved area adjoining a dwelling [Sp]

patisserie /pəˈteesəri, -ˈti-/ *n* **1** PASTRY 2 **2** an establishment where patisserie is made and sold [F *pâtisserie*, fr MF *pastiserie* pastry, deriv of LL *pasta* dough, paste]

Patna rice /ˈpatnə/ *n* a long-grained rice suitable for use in savoury dishes [*Patna*, city in India]

patois /ˈpatwah/ *n, pl* **patois** /ˈpatwahz/ **1** a provincial dialect other than the standard or literary dialect **2** JARGON 2 [F]

patr-, patri-, patro- *comb form* father ⟨patro*nymic*⟩ [*patr-, patri-* fr L, fr *patr-, pater; patr-, patro-* fr Gk, fr *patr-, patēr* – more at FATHER]

patrial /ˈpaytri·əl/ *n* sby who has a legal right to reside in the UK because one of his/her parents or grandparents was born there [ML *patrialis* (adj) of one's fatherland, fr L *patria* fatherland – more at EXPATRIATE] – **patrial** *adj*, **patriality** /,paytriˈaləti/ *n*

patriarch /ˈpaytri,ahk, ˈpat-/ *n* **1a** any of the biblical fathers of the human race or of the Hebrew people **b** a man who is father or founder (e g of a race, science, religion, or class of people) **c(1)** the oldest member or representative of a group **(2)** a venerable old man **d** a man who is head of a patriarchy **2a** any of the bishops of the ancient or Orthodox sees of Constantinople, Alexandria, Antioch, and Jerusalem **b** the head of any of various Eastern churches [ME *patriarche*, fr OF, fr LL *patriarcha*, fr Gk *patriarchēs*, fr *patria* lineage (fr *patr-, patēr* father) + *-archēs* -arch – more at FATHER] – **patriarchal** /-ˈahkl/ *adj*

patriarchal cross *n* a cross having two horizontal crossbars, the lower crossbar being longer than the upper, and intersecting the upright at or above its middle ☞ SYMBOL

patriarchate /,paytriˈahkət, -kayt, ,patri/ *n* the (duration of) office or jurisdiction of a patriarch

patriarchy /ˈpaytri,ahki, ˈpatri-/ *n* a system or an instance of social organization marked by the supremacy of the father in the clan or family, the legal dependence of wives and children, and the reckoning of descent and inheritance in the male line

patrician /pəˈtrish(ə)n/ *n* **1** a member of any of the original citizen families of ancient Rome **2a** sby of high birth; an aristocrat **b** sby of breeding and cultivation [ME *patricion*, fr MF *patricien*, fr L *patricius*, fr *patres* senators, fr pl of *pater* father – more at FATHER] – **patrician** *adj*

patriciate /pəˈtrishi·ət, -,ayt/ *n sing or pl in constr* a patrician class

patricide /ˈpatri,sied/ *n* (the act of) sby who kills his/her father [L *patricida* & *patricidium*, fr *patr-* + *-cida* & *-cidium* – more at -CIDE] – **patricidal** /-ˈsiedl/ *adj*

patrilineal /,patriˈlini·əl/ *adj* relating to or tracing descent through the paternal line

patrimony /ˈpatriməni/ *n* **1a** property inherited from one's father or ancestor **b** sthg derived from one's father or ancestors; a heritage **2** an estate or endowment belonging to a church [ME *patrimonie*, fr MF, fr L *patrimonium*, fr *patr-, pater* father] – **patrimonial** /-ˈmohni·əl/ *adj*

patriot /ˈpaytri·ət, ˈpatri-/ *n* one who loves and zealously supports his/her country [MF *patriote*, fr LL *patriota*, fr Gk *patriōtēs*, fr *patrios* of one's father, fr *patr-, patēr* father] – **patriotism** *n*, **patriotic** /-ˈotik/ *adj*, **patriotically** *adv*

patristic /pəˈtristik/, **patristical** /-kl/ *adj* of the church fathers or their writings

[1]**patrol** /pəˈtrohl/ *n* **1a** traversing a district or beat or going the rounds of a garrison or camp for observation or the maintenance of security **b** *sing or pl in constr* a detachment of men employed for reconnaissance, security, or combat **2** *sing or pl in constr* a subdivision of a scout troop or guide company that has 6 to 8 members

[2]**patrol** *vb* **-ll-** to carry out a patrol (of) [F *patrouiller*, fr MF, to tramp round in the mud, fr *patte* paw – more at PATTEN] – **patroller** *n*

paˈtrol ,car *n* a usu high-performance car used by police to patrol esp motorways

paˈtrolman /-mən/ *n, NAm* a policeman assigned to a beat

paˈtrol ,wagon *n, NAm* an enclosed van used by police to carry prisoners

patron /ˈpaytrən; *sense 6* paˈtronh/, *fem* **patroness** /ˈpaytrənəs, -ˈnes/ *n* **1a** sby chosen, named, or honoured as a special guardian, protector, or supporter **b** a wealthy or influential supporter of an artist or writer **2** sby who uses his/her wealth or influence to help an individual, institution, or cause **3** CUSTOMER 1 **4** the holder of the right of presentation to an English ecclesiastical benefice **5** a master in ancient times who freed his slave but retained some rights over him/her **6** the proprietor of an establishment (e g an inn), esp in France [ME, fr MF, fr ML & L; ML *patronus* patron saint, patron of a benefice, pattern, fr L, defender, fr *patr-, pater*; (6) F, fr MF]

patronage /ˈpatrənij/ *n* **1** advowson **2** the support or influence of a patron **3** the granting of favours in a condescending way **4** business or activity provided by patrons **5** the power to appoint to government jobs

patron·ize, -ise /ˈpatrəniez/ *vt* **1** to act as patron of **2** to adopt an air of condescension towards **3** to be a patron of – **patronizingly** *adv*

,patron ˈsaint *n* a saint regarded as having a particular person, group, church, etc under his/her special care and protection

patronymic /,patrəˈnimik/ *n* a name derived from that of the father or a paternal ancestor, usu by the addition of an affix [LL *patronymicum*, fr neut of *patronymicus* of a patronymic, fr Gk *patronymikos*, fr *patronymia* patronymic, fr *patr-* + *onyma* name – more at NAME] – **patronymic** *adj*

patsy /ˈpatsi/ *n, NAm* one who is duped or victimized; a sucker – infml [perh fr It *pazzo* fool]

patten /ˈpatn/ *n* a sandal or overshoe set on a wooden sole or metal device to elevate the foot [ME *patin*, fr MF, fr *patte* paw, hoof, fr (assumed) VL *patta*, of imit origin]

[1]**patter** /ˈpatə/ *vb* to say or talk glibly and volubly [ME *patren*, fr *paternoster*] – **patterer** *n*

[2]**patter** *n* **1** cant **2** the sales talk of a street hawker **3** empty chattering talk **4a** the rapid-fire talk of a comedian **b** the talk with which an entertainer accompanies his/her routine

[3]**patter** *vi* **1** to strike or tap rapidly and repeatedly ⟨*rain* ~ed *against the window pane*⟩ **2** to run with quick light-sounding steps ~*vt* to cause to patter [freq of [2]*pat*] – **patter** *n*

[1]**pattern** /'pat(ə)n/ *n* **1** a form or model proposed for imitation; an example **2** a design, model, or set of instructions for making things ⟨*a dress* ~⟩ **3** a model for making a mould into which molten metal is poured to form a casting **4** a specimen, sample **5** a usu repeated decorative design (e g on fabric) **6** a natural or chance configuration ⟨*a frost* ~⟩ ⟨*the* ~ *of events*⟩ **7** the grouping on a target by bullets, bombs, etc **8** the flight path prescribed for an aircraft coming in for a landing [ME *patron*, fr MF, fr ML *patronus*]

[2]**pattern** *vt* **1** to make or model according to a pattern **2** to decorate with a design

patty /'pati/ *n* **1** a little pie or pasty **2** *NAm* a small flat cake of chopped food ⟨*a hamburger* ~⟩ [F *pâté*]

patulous /'patyooləs/ *adj* spreading widely from a centre ⟨*a tree with* ~ *branches*⟩ [L *patulus*, fr *patēre* to be open – more at FATHOM] – **patulously** *adv*, **patulousness** *n*

paucity /'pawsəti/ *n* **1** smallness of number **2** smallness of quantity; scarcity *USE* fml [ME *paucite*, fr MF or L; MF *paucité*, fr L *paucitat-, paucitas*, fr *paucus* little – more at FEW]

Pauli exclusion principle /'powli/ *n* EXCLUSION PRINCIPLE [Wolfgang *Pauli* †1958 US (Austrian-born) physicist]

Pauline /'pawlien/ *adj* of the apostle Paul, his epistles, or their doctrines or theology [ML *paulinus*, fr L *Paulus* Paul † *ab* 67 Christian apostle, fr Gk *Paulos*]

Paul Jones /,pawl 'johnz/ *n* a dance during which the couples change partners [prob fr John *Paul Jones* †1792 US naval officer]

paulownia /paw'lohni·ə/ *n* a Chinese tree of the figwort family with fragrant violet flowers [NL, genus name, fr Anna *Paulovna* †1865 Russ princess]

paunch /pawnch/ *n* **1a** the belly **b** a potbelly **2** the rumen [ME, fr MF *panche*, fr L *pantic-, pantex*]

paunchy /'pawnchi/ *adj* having a potbelly

pauper /'pawpə/ *n* a very poor person; *specif* sby supported by charity or from public funds [L, poor – more at FEW] – **pauperism** *n*

pauper·ize, -ise /'pawpə,riez/ *vt* to reduce to poverty or destitution

[1]**pause** /pawz/ *n* **1** a temporary stop **2** a caesura **3** temporary inaction, esp as caused by uncertainty; hesitation **4** the sign denoting a fermata ☞ MUSIC [ME, fr L *pausa*, fr Gk *pausis*, fr *pauein* to stop; akin to Gk *paula* rest]

[2]**pause** *vi* **1** to stop temporarily **2** to linger for a time

pavane *also* **pavan** /pə'van, pə'vahn, 'pavən/ *n* (music for or having the slow duple rhythm of) a stately court dance by couples [MF *pavane*, fr OSp *pavana*, fr OIt]

pave /payv/ *vt* **1** to lay or cover with material (e g stone or concrete) to form a firm level surface for walking or travelling on **2** to serve as a covering or pavement of ⟨*palaces* ~d *with marble*⟩ [ME *paven*, fr MF *paver*, fr L *pavire* to strike, stamp; akin to OHG *arfūrian* to castrate, L *putare* to prune, reckon, think, Gk *paiein* to strike] – **paver** *n* – **pave the way** to prepare a smooth easy way; facilitate development

pavé /'pavay/ *n or adj* (a setting in which jewels are) set closely together to conceal a metal base [n F, fr pp of *paver* to pave; adj fr n]

paved /payvd/ *adj* covered with a pavement

pavement /'payvmənt/ *n* a paved surface: e g **a** *chiefly Br* a surfaced walk for pedestrians at the side of a road **b** *NAm* the artificially covered surface of a road [ME, fr OF, fr L *pavimentum*, fr *pavire*]

'**pavement ,artist** *n* sby who draws coloured pictures on the pavement in the hope that passersby will give him/her money

[1]**pavilion** /pə'vilyən, -li·ən/ *n* **1** a large often sumptuous tent **2** a part of a building projecting from the rest **3a** a light sometimes ornamental structure in a garden, park, etc **b** a temporary structure erected at an exhibition by an individual exhibitor **4** the lower faceted part of a cut gem below the girdle **5** *chiefly Br* a permanent building on a sports ground, specif a cricket ground, containing changing rooms and often also seats for spectators [ME *pavilon*, fr OF *paveillon*, fr L *papilion-, papilio* butterfly; akin to OHG *fifaltra* butterfly, Lith *peteliške* flighty]

[2]**pavilion** *vt* to provide with or put in a pavilion

'**paving ,stone** /'payving/ *n* a thin rectangular stone or concrete block used for paving

pavior, paviour /'payvyə/ *n, Br* a person or machine that paves [ME *pavier*, fr *paven* to pave]

[1]**paw** /paw/ *n* **1** the (clawed) foot of a lion, dog, or other (quadruped) animal **2** a human hand – infml; chiefly humor [ME, fr MF *poue*]

[2]**paw** *vt* **1** to feel or touch clumsily, rudely, or indecently **2** to touch or strike at with a paw **3** to scrape or strike (as if) with a hoof ~*vi* **1** to beat or scrape sthg (as if) with a hoof **2** to touch or strike with a paw

pawky /'pawki/ *adj, chiefly Br* artfully shrewd, esp in a humorous way; canny [obs E dial. *pawk* (trick)]

pawl /pawl/ *n* a pivoted tongue or sliding bolt on one part of a machine that is adapted to fall into notches on another part (e g a ratchet wheel) so as to permit motion in only 1 direction [perh modif of D *pal* pawl]

[1]**pawn** /pawn/ *n* **1** sthg delivered to or deposited with another as a pledge or security (e g for a loan) **2** the state of being pledged – usu + *in* [ME *paun*, modif of MF *pan*]

[2]**pawn** *vt* to deposit in pledge or as security

[3]**pawn** *n* **1** any of the 8 chessmen of each colour of least value that have the power to move only forwards usu 1 square at a time and to capture only diagonally forwards, and that may be promoted to any piece except a king upon reaching the opposite side of the board **2** sby or sthg that can be used to further the purposes of another [ME *pown*, fr MF *poon*, fr ML *pedon-, pedo* foot soldier, fr LL, one with broad feet, fr L *ped-, pes* foot – more at FOOT]

'**pawn,broker** /-,brohkə/ *n* one who lends money on the security of personal property pledged in his/her keeping – **pawnbroking** *n*

'**pawn,shop** /-,shop/ *n* a pawnbroker's shop

pawpaw /'paw,paw/ *n* PAPAW 2

pax /paks/ *n* **1** a tablet decorated with a sacred figure (e g of Christ), ceremonially kissed by participants at mass 2 KISS OF PEACE 3 peace [ME, fr ML, fr L, peace – more at PEACE]

[1]**pay** /pay/ *vb* **paid,** (*7*) **paid** *also* **payed** /payd/ *vt* **1a** to make due return to for services done or property received **b** to engage for money; hire ⟨*you couldn't ~ me to do that*⟩ **2a** to give in return for goods or service ⟨*~ wages*⟩ **b** to discharge indebtedness for; settle ⟨*~ a bill*⟩ **c** to make a disposal or transfer of (money) ⟨*~ money into the bank*⟩ **3** to give or forfeit in reparation or retribution ⟨*~ the penalty*⟩ **4a** to make compensation for **b** to requite according to what is deserved ⟨*~ him back*⟩ ⟨*~ her out*⟩ **5** to give, offer, or make willingly or as fitting ⟨*~ attention*⟩ ⟨*~ heed*⟩ **6a** to be profitable to; be worth the expense or effort to ⟨*it ~*s *shopkeepers to stay open late*⟩ **b** to bring in as a return ⟨*an investment ~*ing *5 per cent*⟩ **7** to slacken (e g a rope) and allow to run out – usu + *out* ~ *vi* **1** to discharge a debt or obligation **2** to be worth the expense or effort ⟨*it ~*s *to advertise*⟩ [ME *payen,* fr OF *paier,* fr L *pacare* to pacify, fr *pac-, pax* peace] – **payer** *n,* **payee** /pay'ee/ *n*

[2]**pay** *n* **1** the status of being paid by an employer; employ ⟨*was in the ~ of the enemy*⟩ **2** sthg paid as a salary or wage

[3]**pay** *adj* **1** containing or leading to sthg valuable **2** equipped with a coin slot for receiving a fee for use ⟨*a ~ phone*⟩ **3** requiring payment

[4]**pay** *vt* **payed** *also* **paid** to coat with a waterproof composition [obs F *peier,* fr L *picare,* fr *pic-, pix* pitch]

payable /'payəbl/ *adj* that may, can, or must be paid

,pay-as-you-'earn *n* a system of deducting income tax from pay before an employee receives it

'pay,bed /-,bed/ *n* a hospital bed the use of which is paid for by the occupant rather than by the state

'pay,day /-,day/ *n* a regular day on which wages are paid

'pay,load /-,lohd/ *n* **1** the revenue-producing load that a vehicle of transport can carry **2** the explosive charge carried in the warhead of a missile **3** the load (e g instruments) carried in a spacecraft relating directly to the purpose of the flight as opposed to the load (e g fuel) necessary for operation

'pay,master /-,mahstə/ *n* an officer or agent whose duty it is to pay salaries or wages

,paymaster 'general *n, often cap P&G* a British government minister who is often made a member of the cabinet and entrusted with special functions

'payment /-mənt/ *n* **1** the act of paying **2** sthg that is paid **3** a recompense (e g a reward or punishment)

'pay,off /-,of/ *n* **1** a profit or reward, esp received by a player in a game **2** a decisive fact or factor resolving a situation or bringing about a definitive conclusion **3** the climax of an incident or chain of events; *specif, chiefly NAm* the denouement of a narrative – infml

pay off *vt* **1** to give all due wages to; *esp* to pay in full and discharge (an employee) **2** to pay (a debt or a creditor) in full ~ *vi* to yield returns ⟨*it was a risk but it* paid off⟩

payola /pay'ohlə/ *n* an undercover or indirect payment for unofficial promotion of a commercial product [prob alter. of *payoff*]

'pay-,out *n* (the act of making) a usu large payment of money – infml

'pay-,packet *n, Br* (an envelope containing) sby's wages

'pay,roll /-,rohl/ *n* **1** a list of those entitled to be paid and of the amounts due to each **2** the sum necessary to pay those on a payroll **3** *sing or pl in constr* the people on a payroll

'pay,slip /-,slip/ *n, Br* a written statement of one's gross pay, allowances, deductions, and net pay

pay up *vb* to pay in full

PCB *n* POLYCHLORINATED BIPHENYL

P-Celtic *n* the division of the Celtic languages that includes Welsh, Cornish, and Breton [fr the development in these languages of the phoneme *p* from Indo-European *qu*]

pea /pee/ *n, pl* **peas** *also* **pease** /peez; *also* pees/ **1a** (a leguminous climbing plant that bears) an edible rounded protein-rich green seed **b** *pl* the immature pods of the pea with their seeds **2** any of various leguminous plants related to or resembling the pea – usu with a qualifying term ⟨*chick*-pea⟩ ⟨*sweet ~*⟩ [back-formation fr *pease* (taken as a pl), fr ME *pese,* fr OE *pise,* fr L *pisa,* pl of *pisum,* fr Gk *pison*]

peace /pees/ *n* **1** a state of tranquillity or quiet: e g **a** freedom from civil disturbance **b** public order and security maintained by law or custom ⟨*a breach of the ~*⟩ **2** freedom from disquieting or oppressive thoughts or emotions ⟨*~ of mind*⟩ **3** harmony in personal relations **4a** mutual concord between countries **b** an agreement to end hostilities **5** – used interjectionally as a command or request for silence or calm or as a greeting or farewell [ME *pees,* fr OF *pais,* fr L *pac-, pax*; akin to L *pacisci* to agree – more at PACT] – **at peace** in a state of concord or tranquillity

peaceable /'peesəbl/ *adj* **1a** disposed to peace; not inclined to dispute or quarrel **b** quietly behaved **2** free from strife or disorder – **peaceableness** *n,* **peaceably** *adv*

'peace ,corps *n* a body of trained volunteer personnel sent by the US government to assist developing nations

'peaceful /-f(ə)l/ *adj* **1** PEACEABLE 1 **2** untroubled by conflict, agitation, or commotion; quiet, tranquil **3** of a state or time of peace – **peacefully** *adv,* **peacefulness** *n*

peaceful coexistence *n* a state in which countries with different ideologies live together in peace rather than in constant hostility

'peace ,offering *n* sthg given or done to produce peace or reconciliation

'peace ,pipe *n* a calumet

'peace ,sign *n* a sign made by holding the palm outwards and forming a V with the index and middle fingers, used to indicate the desire for peace – compare V SIGN

'peace,time /-,tiem/ *n* a time when a nation is not at war

[1]**peach** /peech/ *n* **1** (a low spreading tree of the rose family that grows in temperate areas, has stalkless usu pink spring flowers, and bears) an edible fruit with a large stone, thin downy skin, and sweet white or yellow flesh **2** light yellowish pink **3** a particularly excellent person or thing; *specif* an unusually attractive girl or young woman – infml [ME *peche,* fr MF (the fruit), fr LL *persica,* fr L *persicum,* fr neut of *persicus* Persian, fr *Persia*]

[2]**peach** *vi* to turn informer ⟨*~*ed *on his accomplices*⟩ [ME *pechen,* short for *apechen* to accuse, fr

(assumed) AF *apecher*, fr LL *impedicare* to fetter, entangle – more at IMPEACH]

peacock /'peekok/ *n* a male peafowl with very large tail feathers that are usu tipped with eyelike spots and can be erected and spread in a fan shimmering with iridescent colour; *broadly* a peafowl [ME *pecok*, fr *pe-* (fr OE *pēa* peafowl) + *cok* cock; akin to OHG *pfāwo* peacock; both fr a prehistoric WGmc-NGmc word borrowed fr L *pavon-*, *pavo* peacock]

,peacock 'blue *n* lustrous greenish blue

peacock butterfly *n* a butterfly with large eyespots on the wings

'pea,fowl /-,fowl/ *n* a very large ornamental ground-living pheasant of SE Asia and the E Indies [*pea-* (as in *peacock*) + *fowl*]

,pea 'green *n* light yellowish green

'pea,hen /-,hen/ *n* a female peafowl [ME *pehenne*, fr *pe-* + *henne* hen]

'pea ,jacket *n* a heavy woollen double-breasted jacket worn esp by sailors [by folk etymology fr D *pijjekker*, fr *pij*, a kind of cloth + *jekker* jacket]

[1]peak /peek/ *vi* to grow thin or sickly [origin unknown]

[2]peak *n* **1** a projecting part on the front of a cap or hood **2** a sharp or pointed end **3a** (the top of) a hill or mountain ending in a point ☞ GEOGRAPHY **b** sthg resembling a mountain peak **4a** the upper aftermost corner of a 4-cornered fore-and-aft sail ☞ SHIP **b** the narrow part of a ship's bow or stern **5a** the highest level or greatest degree **b** a high point in a course of development, esp as represented on a graph [perh alter. of *pike*]

[3]peak *vi* to reach a maximum

[4]peak *adj* at or reaching the maximum of capacity, value, or activity ⟨*the factory reached ~ productivity*⟩ ⟨*~ traffic hours*⟩

[1]peaked /peekt/ *adj* having a peak; pointed – **peakedness** *n*

[2]peaked *adj* peaky

peak load *n* maximum demand or density (e g of electricity or traffic)

peak time *n* the time of greatest demand for some service (e g television programmes)

peaky /'peeki/ *adj* looking pale and wan; sickly [[1]*peak* + [1]*-y*]

[1]peal /peel/ *n* **1a** a complete set of changes on a given number of bells **b** a set of bells tuned to the notes of the major scale for change ringing **2** a loud prolonged sound ⟨*~s of laughter*⟩ [ME, appeal, summons to church, short for *appel* appeal, fr *appelen* to appeal]

[2]peal *vi* to give out peals *~ vt* to utter or give forth loudly

peanut /'peenut/ *n* **1** (the pod or oily edible seed of) a low-branching widely cultivated leguminous plant with showy yellow flowers and pods containing 1 to 3 seeds that ripen in the earth **2** *pl* a trifling amount – infml

pear /peə/ *n* (a tree of the rose family that bears) a large fleshy edible fruit wider at the end furthest from the stalk [ME *pere*, fr OE *peru*, fr L *pirum*]

[1]pearl /puhl/ *n* **1a** a dense usu milky white lustrous mass of mother-of-pearl layers, formed as an abnormal growth in the shell of some molluscs, esp oysters, and used as a gem **b** mother-of-pearl **2** sby or sthg very rare or precious [ME *perle*, fr MF, fr (assumed) VL *pernula*, dim. of L *perna* haunch, sea mussel; akin to OE *fiersn* heel, Gk *pternē*]

[2]pearl *vt* **1** to set or adorn (as if) with pearls **2** to form into small round grains *~ vi* **1** to form drops or beads like pearls **2** to fish or search for pearls – **pearler** *n*

[3]pearl *adj* **1a** of or resembling pearl **b** made of or adorned with pearls **2** having medium-sized grains ⟨*~ barley*⟩

[4]pearl /puhl/ *vt or n, Br* (to) picot [alter. of *purl*]

pearl millet *n* a tall cereal grass grown in Africa, Asia, and S USA for its edible seeds and for forage

'pearl,wort /-,wuht/ *n* any of several very small plants of the pink family with usu minute white or green flowers

[1]pearly /'puhli/ *adj* resembling, containing, or decorated with pearls or mother-of-pearl

[2]pearly *n, Br* **1** a button made of mother-of-pearl **2** a member of certain cockney families who are traditionally costermongers and entitled to wear a special costume covered with pearlies

pearmain /'peə,mayn/ *n* any of various eating apples [ME *permayn*, a type of pear, fr OF *permain*, perh fr L *Parmensis* of Parma, city in Italy]

peasant /'pez(ə)nt/ *n* **1** a small landowner or farm labourer **2** a usu uneducated person of low social status [ME *paissaunt*, fr MF *paisant*, fr OF, fr *païs* country, fr LL *pagensis* inhabitant of a district, fr L *pagus* district – more at PAGAN] – **peasantry** /-tri/ *n sing or pl in constr*

pease /peez; *also* pees/ *n, chiefly Br* PEA 1a – archaic except in attributive use ⟨*~ pudding*⟩

peasecod, peascod /'peezkod/ *n* a pea pod [ME *pesecod*, fr *pese* pease + *cod* bag, husk – more at CODPIECE]

'pea,shooter /-,shoohtə/ *n* a toy blowpipe for shooting peas

,pea-'souper /'soohpə/ *also* **pea soup** *n* a heavy fog

peat /peet/ *n* (a piece of) partially carbonized vegetable tissue formed by partial decomposition in water of various plants (e g mosses), found in large bogs, and used esp as a fuel for domestic heating and as a fertilizer [ME *pete*, fr ML *peta*] – **peaty** *adj*

'peat ,moss *n* sphagnum

peavey, peavy /'peevi/ *n, NAm* CANT HOOK [prob fr the name *Peavey*]

[1]pebble /'pebl/ *n* **1** a small usu rounded stone, often worn smooth by the action of water **2** rock crystal [ME *pobble*, fr OE *papolstān*, fr *papol-* (prob imit) + *stān* stone] – **pebbly** *adj*

[2]pebble *vt* to pave or cover with (sthg resembling) pebbles

'pebble,dash /-,dash/ *n* a finish for exterior walls consisting of small pebbles embedded in a stucco base

pecan /pi'kan, 'peekan/ *n* (the smooth oblong thin-shelled edible nut of) a large hickory tree with roughish bark and hard but brittle wood [of Algonquian origin; akin to Ojibwa *pagân*, a hard-shelled nut]

peccable /'pekəbl/ *adj* prone to sin [MF, fr L *peccare*]

peccadillo /,pekə'diloh/ *n, pl* **peccadilloes, peccadillos** a slight or trifling offence [Sp *pecadillo*, dim. of *pecado* sin, fr L *peccatum*, fr neut of *peccatus*, pp of *peccare*]

peccant /ˈpekənt/ *adj* guilty, sinning [L *peccant-, peccans*, prp of *peccare* to stumble, sin] – **peccancy** *n*, **peccantly** *adv*

peccary /ˈpekəri/ *n* either of 2 largely nocturnal social American mammals resembling the related pigs [of Cariban origin; akin to Chaima *paquera* peccary]

[1]**peck** /pek/ *n* a unit of volume or capacity equal to 2gall (about 9.1l) ☞ UNIT [ME *pek*, fr OF]

[2]**peck** *vt* **1a** to strike or pierce (repeatedly) with the beak or a pointed tool **b** to make by pecking ⟨~ *a hole*⟩ **c** to kiss perfunctorily **2** to pick up with the beak ~ *vi* **1** to strike, pierce, or pick up sthg (as if) with the beak **2** to eat reluctantly and in small bites ⟨~ *at food*⟩ [ME *pecken*, alter. of *piken* to pierce – more at [1]PICK]

[3]**peck** *n* **1** an impression or hole made by pecking **2** a quick sharp stroke **3** a quick perfunctory kiss

[4]**peck** *vi, of a horse* to stumble on landing from a jump [alter. of [3]*pick* (to pitch)]

pecker /ˈpekə/ *n* **1** *chiefly Br* courage – in *keep one's pecker up*; infml **2** *NAm* a penis – vulg [[2]PECK + [2]-ER]

ˈ**pecking ˌorder** /ˈpeking/, **peck order** *n* **1** the natural hierarchy within a flock of birds, esp poultry, in which each bird pecks another lower in the scale without fear of retaliation **2** a social hierarchy

peckish /ˈpekish/ *adj, chiefly Br* agreeably hungry – infml [[2]*peck* + *-ish*]

pecten /ˈpekt(ə)n/ *n, pl* (*1*) **pectines** /-eez/, **pectens**, (*2*) **pectens** **1** a comblike body part **2** [1]SCALLOP 1 [NL *pectin-, pecten*, fr L, comb, scallop]

pectin /ˈpektin/ *n* any of various water-soluble substances that bind adjacent cell walls in plant tissues and yield a gel which acts as a setting agent in jams and fruit jellies [F *pectine*, fr *pectique* pectic, fr Gk *pēktikos* coagulating, fr *pēgnynai* to fix, coagulate – more at PACT] – **pectic** *adj*

pectinate /ˈpektinayt/, **pectinated** *adj* having narrow parallel projections or divisions suggestive of the teeth of a comb ⟨~ *antennae*⟩ [L *pectinatus*, fr *pectin-, pecten* comb; akin to Gk *kten-, kteis* comb, L *pectere* to comb – more at FEE] – **pectination** /-ˈnaysh(ə)n/ *n*

pectoral /ˈpekt(ə)rəl/ *adj* of, situated in or on, or worn on the chest [MF or L; MF, fr L *pectoralis*, fr *pector-, pectus* breast]

pectoral cross *n* a cross worn on the chest, esp by a prelate

pectoral fin *n* either of the fins of a fish that correspond to the forelimbs of a quadruped

pectoral girdle *n* the bony or cartilaginous arch that supports the forelimbs of a vertebrate

peculate /ˈpekyoolayt/ *vt* to embezzle [L *peculatus*, pp of *peculari*, fr *peculium*] – **peculator** *n*, **peculation** /-ˈlaysh(ə)n/ *n*

[1]**peculiar** /piˈkyoohli·ə, -lyə/ *adj* **1** belonging exclusively to 1 person or group **2** distinctive **3** different from the usual or normal; strange, curious [ME *peculier*, fr L *peculiaris* of private property, special, fr *peculium* private property, fr *pecu* cattle; akin to L *pecus* cattle – more at FEE] – **peculiarly** *adv*

[2]**peculiar** *n* sthg exempt from ordinary jurisdiction; *esp* a church or parish independent of the diocese in which it is situated

peculiarity /piˌkyoohliˈarəti/ *n* a distinguishing characteristic [[1]PECULIAR + -ITY]

pecuniary /piˈkyoohnyəri/ *adj* of or measured in money – fml [L *pecuniarius*, fr *pecunia* money – more at FEE] – **pecuniarily** *adv*

ped /ped/ *n* a natural soil aggregate [Gk *pedon* ground; akin to L *ped-, pes* foot – more at FOOT]

ped-, pedo- *comb form, chiefly NAm* paed-, paedo-

-ped /-ped, *also* -pəd/, **-pede** /-peed/ *comb form* (→ *n*) foot ⟨*quadru*ped⟩ ⟨*centi*pede⟩ [L *ped-, pes*]

pedagogics /ˌpedəˈgojiks, -ˈgoh-/ *n pl but sing in constr* pedagogy – **pedagogic, pedagogical** *adj*, **pedagogically** *adv*

pedagogue /ˈpedəgog/ *n* a teacher, schoolmaster – now chiefly derog [ME *pedagoge*, fr MF, fr L *paedagogus*, fr Gk *paidagōgos*, slave who escorted children to school, fr *paid-* paed- + *agōgos* leader, fr *agein* to lead – more at AGENT]

pedagogy /ˈpedəgoji, -gogi, -goh-/ *n* the science of teaching

[1]**pedal** /ˈpedl/ *n* **1** a lever pressed by the foot in playing a musical instrument **2** a foot lever or treadle by which a part is activated in a mechanism [MF *pedale*, fr It, fr L *pedalis*, adj]

[2]**pedal** *adj* of the foot [L *pedalis*, fr *ped-, pes*]

[3]**pedal** *vb* **-ll-** (*NAm* **-l-** *also* **-ll-**), /ˈpedl·ing, ˈpedling/ *vi* **1** to use or work a pedal or pedals **2** to ride a bicycle ~ *vt* to work the pedals of

pedalo /ˈpedəloh/ *n, pl* **pedalos, pedaloes** a small pleasure boat that is propelled by paddles turned by pedals

ˈ**pedal ˌpushers** *n pl* women's and girls' calf-length trousers

pedant /ˈped(ə)nt/ *n* one who is unimaginative or unnecessarily concerned with detail, esp in academic matters [MF, fr It *pedante*] – **pedantic** /piˈdantik/ *adj*, **pedantry** /ˈped(ə)ntri/ *n*

peddle /ˈpedl/ *vb* **peddling** /ˈpedling, ˈpedl·ing/ *vi* to sell goods as a pedlar ~ *vt* **1** to sell as a pedlar **2** to deal out or seek to disseminate (e g ideas or opinions) [back-formation fr *peddler, pedlar*]

peddler /ˈpedlə/ *n* **1** one who peddles dangerous or illicit drugs; a pusher **2** *NAm* a pedlar

-pede /-peed/ – see -PED

pederast, paederast /ˈpedəˌrast, ˈpee-/ *n* one who practises anal intercourse, esp with a boy [Gk *paiderastēs*, lit., lover of boys, fr *paid-* paed- + *erastēs* lover, fr *erasthai* to love – more at EROS] – **pederasty** *n*, **pederastic** /-ˈrastik/ *adj*

pedestal /ˈpedistl/ *n* **1a** a base supporting a late classic or neoclassic column ☞ ARCHITECTURE **b** the base of an upright structure (e g a statue) **2** a base, foundation **3** a position of esteem or idealized respect [MF *piedestal*, fr OIt *piedestallo*, fr *pie di stallo* foot of a stall]

[1]**pedestrian** /piˈdestri·ən/ *adj* **1** commonplace, unimaginative **2a** going or performed on foot **b** of or designed for walking ⟨*a ~ precinct*⟩ [L *pedestr-, pedester*, lit., going on foot, fr *pedes* sby going on foot, fr *ped-, pes* foot – more at FOOT] – **pedestrianism** *n*

[2]**pedestrian** *n* sby going on foot; a walker

peˌdestrian ˈcrossing *n* a usu marked stretch of road on which pedestrians crossing the road have priority over the traffic in certain circumstances

pedestrian·ize, -ise /piˈdestri·əˌniez/ *vt* to convert (an existing vehicular highway) to a usu paved area for pedestrians only – **pedestrianization** /-ˈzaysh(ə)n/ *n*

pedicel /ˈpedisel/ *n* **1** a plant stalk that supports a fruiting or spore-bearing organ **2** a narrow basal attachment of an animal organ or part [NL *pedicellus*, dim. of L *pediculus*] – **pedicellate** /-'selət/ *adj*

pedicle /'pedikl/ *n* a pedicel [L *pediculus*, fr dim. of *ped-*, *pes*] – **pedicled** *adj*

pediculosis /pi,dikyoo'lohsis/ *n* infestation with lice [NL, fr L *pediculus* louse] – **pediculous** /pi'dikyooləs/ *adj*

pedicure /'pedikyooə/ *n* **1** one who practises chiropody **2** (a) treatment for the care of the feet and toenails [F *pédicure*, fr L *ped-*, *pes* foot + *curare* to take care, fr *cura* care – more at CURE]

[1]**pedigree** /'pedigree/ *n* **1** a register recording a line of ancestors **2a** an esp distinguished ancestral line; a lineage **b** the origin and history of sthg **3** the recorded purity of breed of an individual or strain [ME *pedegru*, fr MF *pie de grue* crane's foot; fr the shape made by the lines of a genealogical chart] – **pedigreed** *adj*

[2]**pedigree** *adj* of, being, or producing pedigree animals

pediment /'pedimənt/ *n* the triangular gable of a 2-pitched roof in classic architecture [alter. of obs *periment*, prob alter. of *pyramid*] – **pedimental** /-'mentl/ *adj*

pedipalp /'pedipalp/ *n* either of the second pair of appendages of an arachnid (e g a spider) that are near the mouth and are often modified for a special (e g sensory) function [NL *pedipalpus*, fr *ped-*, *pes* foot + *palpus*]

pedlar, *NAm chiefly* **peddler** /'pedlə/ *n* **1** one who travels about offering small wares for sale **2** one who deals in or promotes sthg intangible [ME *pedlere*, alter. of *peddere*, fr *ped* wicker basket] – **pedlary** *n*

pedology /pi'doləji/ *n* SOIL SCIENCE [Gk *pedon* earth + ISV *-logy*] – **pedologist** *n*, **pedologic** /,peedə'lojik/, **pedological** *adj*

pedometer /pi'domitə/ *n* an instrument that records the distance a walker covers by responding to body motion at each step [F *pédomètre*, fr L *ped-*, *pes* foot + F *-mètre* -meter – more at FOOT]

peduncle /pi'dungkl/ *n* **1** a stalk bearing a flower, flower cluster, or fruit **2** a narrow stalklike part by which some larger part or the whole body of an organism is attached [NL *pedunculus*, dim. of L *ped-*, *pes*] – **peduncled** *adj*, **peduncular** /-kyoolə/ *adj*, **pedunculate** /-lət, -layt/, **pedunculated** *adj*

[1]**pee** /pee/ *vi* to urinate – euph [*p*iss]

[2]**pee** *n* **1** an act of urinating **2** urine *USE* euph

[3]**pee** *n*, *pl* **pee** *Br* PENNY 1a(2) – infml [*p*enny]

peek /peek/ *vi* **1** to look furtively – often + *in* or *out* **2** to take a brief look; glance [ME *piken*] – **peek** *n*

[1]**peekaboo** /'peekə,booh/ *n* a game for amusing a baby in which one repeatedly hides and comes back into view, typically exclaiming 'Peekaboo!" [*peek* + [1]*boo*]

[2]**peekaboo** *adj* trimmed with eyelet embroidery ⟨*a ~ blouse*⟩

[1]**peel** /peel/ *vt* **1** to strip off an outer layer of ⟨*~ an orange*⟩ **2** to remove by stripping ⟨*~ the label off the can*⟩ ~ *vi* **1a** to come off in sheets or scales **b** to lose an outer layer (e g of skin) ⟨*his face is ~ing*⟩ **2** to take off one's clothes – usu + *off*; infml ⟨*they ~ed off and dived into the water*⟩ [ME *pelen*, fr MF *peler*, fr L *pilare* to remove the hair from, fr *pilus* hair – more at [5]PILE] – **peeler** *n*

[2]**peel** *n* the skin or rind of a fruit

[3]**peel** *also* **pele** /peel/ *n* a small fortified tower built in the 16th c along the Scottish-English border [ME *pel* stockade, stake, fr AF, stockade & MF, stake, fr L *palus* stake – more at [1]POLE]

[4]**peel** *n* a usu long-handled (baker's) shovel for getting bread, pies, etc into or out of an oven [ME *pele*, fr MF, fr L *pala*]

peeler /'peelə/ *n*, *archaic Br* a policeman [Sir Robert *Peel* †1850 E statesman who founded the Irish constabulary]

peeling /'peeling/ *n* a strip of skin, rind, etc that has been stripped off

peel off *vi* **1** to veer away from an aircraft formation, esp when diving or landing **2** to break away from a group or formation (e g of marchers or ships in a convoy)

[1]**peen** /peen/ *vt* to draw, bend, or flatten (as if) by hammering with a peen

[2]**peen, pein** /peen/ *n* a usu hemispherical or wedge-shaped end of the head of a hammer that is opposite the face and is used esp for bending, shaping, or cutting the material struck [prob of Scand origin; akin to Norw *penn* peen]

[1]**peep** /peep/ *vi* **1** to utter a feeble shrill sound characteristic of a newly hatched bird; cheep **2** to utter a slight sound [ME *pepen*, of imit origin]

[2]**peep** *n* **1** a cheep **2** a slight sound, esp spoken – infml ⟨*don't let me hear another ~ out of you*⟩

[3]**peep** *vi* **1** to look cautiously or slyly, esp through an aperture; peek **2** to begin to emerge (as if) from concealment; show slightly [ME *pepen*, perh alter. of *piken* to peek]

[4]**peep** *n* **1** the first faint appearance ⟨*at the ~ of dawn*⟩ **2** a brief or furtive look; a glance

peeper /'peepə/ *n* **1** a voyeur **2** an eye – infml [[3]PEEP + [2]-ER]

'peep,hole /-,hohl/ *n* a hole or crevice to peep through

Peeping Tom /,peeping 'tom/ *n*, *often not cap P* a voyeur [*Peeping Tom*, legendary 11th-c figure who peeped at Lady Godiva as she rode naked through Coventry]

'peep ,show *n* an entertainment (e g a film) or object (e g a small painting) viewed through a small opening or a magnifying glass

'peep ,sight *n* a rear sight for a gun having an adjustable metal piece pierced with a small hole to peep through in aiming

[1]**peer** /piə/ *n* **1** sby who is of equal standing with another **2** a duke, marquess, earl, viscount, or baron of the British peerage [ME, fr OF *per*, fr *per*, adj, equal, fr L *par*]

[2]**peer** *adj* belonging to the same age, grade, or status group ⟨*a ~ group of adolescents*⟩

[3]**peer** *vi* to look narrowly or curiously; *esp* to look searchingly at sthg difficult to discern [perh by shortening & alter. fr *appear*]

peerage /'piərij/ *n* **1** *sing or pl in constr* the body of peers **2** the rank or dignity of a peer

peeress /'piəris/ *n* **1** the wife or widow of a peer **2** a woman having in her own right the rank of a peer

'peerless /-lis/ *adj* matchless, incomparable – **peerlessly** *adv*, **peerlessness** *n*

peeve /peev/ *vt* to make peevish or resentful; annoy – infml [back-formation fr *peevish*]

peevish /'peevish/ *adj* querulous in temperament or

mood; fretful [ME *pevish* spiteful] – **peevishly** *adv*, **peevishness** *n*

peewit, pewit /'peewit/ *n* a lapwing [imit]

[1]**peg** /peg/ *n* **1** a small usu cylindrical pointed or tapered piece of wood, metal, or plastic used to pin down or fasten things or to fit into or close holes; a pin ⟨*they secured the guy ropes with tent* ~s⟩ **2a** a projecting piece used to hold or support ⟨*he hung his hat on the* ~ *in the hall*⟩ **b** sthg (e g a fact or opinion) used as a support, pretext, or reason ⟨*the strike was simply a* ~ *for their prejudices*⟩ **3a** any of the wooden pins set in the head of a stringed instrument and turned to regulate the pitch of the strings **b** a step or degree, esp in estimation – esp in *take sby down a peg (or two)* **4** *Br* a clothes peg **5** *Br* a drink, esp of spirits ⟨*poured himself out a stiff* ~ – Dorothy Sayers⟩ [ME *pegge*, prob fr MD] – **off the peg** mass-produced; READY-MADE 1 ⟨*men over 7 feet have difficulty in finding clothes* off the peg *to fit*⟩

[2]**peg** *vt* **-gg- 1** to put a peg into **2** to pin down; restrict **3** to fix or hold (e g prices) at a predetermined level **4** *Br* to fasten (e g washing) to a clothesline with a clothes peg – often + *out*

peg away *vi, chiefly Br* to work hard and steadily – often + *at*

'peg,board /-,bawd/ *n* a material pierced at regular intervals with holes into which hooks or pegs may be inserted for the storage or display of articles

,peg 'leg *n* (one who wears) an artificial leg

pegmatite /'pegmətiet/ *n* (a formation resembling) a coarse variety of granite occurring as dykes or veins [F, fr Gk *pēgmat-*, *pēgma* sthg fastened together, fr *pēgnynai* to fasten together – more at PACT] – **pegmatitic** /-'titik/ *adj*

peg out *vi* **1** to finish a game in croquet by hitting the peg with the ball **2** *chiefly Br* DIE 1 – infml ~ *vt* to mark by pegs ⟨peg out *the boundaries of an estate*⟩

Pehlevi /'payləvi/ *n* Pahlavi

peignoir /'paynwah, ,-'-/ *n* a woman's loose negligee or dressing gown [F, lit., garment worn while combing the hair, fr MF, fr *peigner* to comb the hair, fr L *pectinare*, fr *pectin-*, *pecten* comb – more at PECTINATE]

pein /peen/ *n* a peen

pejorative /pə'jorətiv, *also* 'peej(ə)rətiv/ *adj* depreciatory, disparaging [LL *pejoratus*, pp of *pejorare* to make or become worse, fr L *pejor* worse; akin to L *pessimus* worst, Gk *pedon* ground – more at PARALLELEPIPED] – **pejorative** *n*, **pejoratively** *adv*

peke /peek/ *n, often cap* PEKINGESE 2 – infml [by shortening & alter.]

Pekingese, Pekinese /,peki'neez, ,pee-/ *n, pl* **Pekingese, Pekinese 1a** a native or inhabitant of Peking **b** Mandarin **2** (any of) a Chinese breed of small short-legged dogs with a broad flat face and a long thick soft coat [*Peking, Pekin*, city in NE China]

Peking man /pee'king/ *n* an extinct Pleistocene man known from skeletal and cultural remains at Choukoutien in China

pekoe /'peekoh/ *n* a black tea of superior quality [Chin (Amoy) *pek-ho*]

pelage /'pelij/ *n* the hairy covering of a mammal [F, fr MF, fr *poil* hair, fr L *pilus* – more at [5]PILE]

Pelagian /pe'layji·ən/ *n or adj* (one) following Pelagius in denying original sin and thus holding that man's salvation depends on his own efforts rather than divine grace [*Pelagius* † *ab* 420 Br monk & theologian] – **Pelagianism** *n*

pelagic /pe'lajik/ *adj* of, occurring, or living (at or above moderate depths) in the open sea – compare DEMERSAL [L *pelagicus*, fr Gk *pelagikos*, fr *pelagos* sea – more at [1]FLAKE]

pelargonium /,pelə'gohnyəm, -ni·əm/ *n* any of a genus of plants (e g a garden geranium) of the geranium family with showy red, pink, or white flowers [NL, genus name, irreg fr Gk *pelargos* stork]

Pelasgian /pe'lazji·ən, -gi·ən/ *n* a member of an ancient people inhabiting Greece and the E islands of the Mediterranean [Gk *pelasgios*, adj, Pelasgian, fr *Pelasgoi* Pelasgians] – **Pelasgian** *adj*, **Pelasgic** /-jik, -gik/ *adj*

pele /peel/ *n* [3]PEEL

pelerine /'peləreen/ *n* a woman's long cape usu with ends hanging down in front [obs F, neckerchief, fr F *pèlerine*, fem of *pèlerin* pilgrim, fr LL *pelegrinus* – more at PILGRIM]

pelf /pelf/ *n* money, riches [ME, fr MF *pelfre* booty]

pelican /'pelikən/ *n* any of a genus of large web-footed birds with a very large bill containing a pouch in which fish are kept [ME, fr OE *pellican*, fr LL *pelecanus*, fr Gk *pelekan*]

,pelican 'crossing *n* a crossing in the UK at which the movement of vehicles and pedestrians is controlled by pedestrian-operated traffic lights [irreg fr *pe*destrian *li*ght *con*trolled crossing]

pelisse /pe'lees/ *n* **1** a long cloak or coat made, lined, or trimmed with fur; *esp* one that is part of a hussar's uniform **2** a woman's loose cloak with wide collar and fur trimming [F, fr LL *pellicia*, fr fem of *pellicius* made of skin, fr L *pellis* skin]

pellagra /pə'laygrə, -'la-/ *n* dermatitis and nervous symptoms associated with a deficiency of nicotinic acid and protein in the diet [It, fr *pelle* skin (fr L *pellis*) + *-agra* (as in *podagra*, fr L)] – **pellagrous** *adj*

pellet /'pelit/ *n* **1** a usu small rounded or spherical body (e g of food or medicine) **2** a piece of small shot [ME *pelote*, fr MF, fr (assumed) VL *pilota*, dim. of L *pila* ball – more at [5]PILE] – **pelletal** *adj*, **pelletize** *vt*

pellicle /'pelikl/ *n* a thin skin or film [MF *pellicule*, fr ML *pellicula*, fr L, dim. of *pellis*]

[1]**pellitory** /'pelit(ə)ri/, **,pellitory-of-'Spain** *n* a composite plant resembling yarrow [ME *peletre*, fr MF *piretre*, fr L *pyrethrum*]

[2]**pellitory, ,pellitory-of-the-'wall** *n* any of a genus of plants of the nettle family with inconspicuous flowers; *specif* one that grows in cracks in walls and rocks [ME *paritorie*, fr MF *paritaire*, fr LL *parietaria*, fr fem of *parietarius* of a wall, fr L *pariet-*, *paries* wall]

pell-mell /,pel 'mel/ *adv* **1** in confusion or disorder **2** in confused haste [MF *pelemele*, fr OF *pesle mesle*, redupl of *mesle-*, stem of *mesler* to mix, mingle] – **pell-mell** *adj or n*

pellucid /pi'l(y)oohsid/ *adj* **1** transparent **2** easy to understand *USE* fml or poetic [L *pellucidus*, fr *per* through + *lucidus* lucid – more at FOR] – **pellucidly** *adv*, **pellucidity** /-'sidəti/ *n*

pelmet /'pelmit/ *n, chiefly Br* a length of board or fabric placed above a window to conceal curtain fixtures [prob modif of F *palmette* palm-leaf design, fr *palme* palm, fr L *palma*]

pelorus /pi'lawrəs/ *n* a navigational instrument having 2 sight vanes mounted on a rotatable ring by which bearings are taken [origin unknown]

pelota /pə'lotə/ *n* any of various Spanish or Latin-American court games; *specif* JAI ALAI [Sp, fr OF *pelote* little ball – more at PELLET]

[1]**pelt** /pelt/ *n* **1** a usu undressed skin with its hair, wool, or fur **2** a skin stripped of hair or wool before tanning [ME]

[2]**pelt** *vt* **1** to strike with a succession of blows or missiles ⟨~ed *him with stones*⟩ **2** to hurl, throw **3** to beat or dash repeatedly against ⟨*rain* ~ing *the windows*⟩ ~ *vi* **1** *of rain* to fall heavily and continuously **2** to move rapidly and vigorously; hurry ⟨*the children* ~ed *down the road*⟩ [ME *pelten*]

[3]**pelt** *n* – **at full pelt** as fast as possible

peltate /'peltayt/ *adj* shaped like a shield; *specif, of a leaf* having the stem or support attached to the lower surface instead of at the base or margin ☞ PLANT [prob fr (assumed) NL *peltatus*, fr L *pelta* small shield, fr Gk *peltē*]

peltry /'peltri/ *n* pelts [ME, fr AF *pelterie*]

pelvic girdle /'pelvik/ *n* the bony or cartilaginous arch that supports the hind limbs of a vertebrate

pelvis /'pelvis/ *n, pl* **pelvises, pelves** /-veez/ **1** (the cavity of) a basin-shaped structure in the skeleton of many vertebrates that is formed by the pelvic girdle and adjoining bones of the spine ☞ ANATOMY **2** the funnel-shaped cavity of the kidney into which urine is discharged [NL, fr L, basin; akin to OE & ON *full* cup, Gk *pella* wooden bowl] – **pelvic** *adj*

Pembroke table /'pembrohk, -brook/ *n* a small 4-legged table with a drawer and drop leaves [*Pembroke, Pembrokeshire*, county of Wales]

pemmican *also* **pemican** /'pemikən/ *n* a concentrated food of lean dried pounded meat mixed with melted fat traditionally made by N American Indians; *also* a similar preparation usu of beef and dried fruits used for emergency rations [Cree *pimikân*]

pemphigus /'pemfigəs, pem'fiegəs/ *n* a disease characterized by large blisters on the skin and mucous membranes often accompanied by itching [NL, fr Gk *pemphig-, pemphix* breath, pustule]

[1]**pen** /pen/ *n* **1** a small enclosure for animals **2** a small place of confinement or storage **3** a (heavily fortified) dock or slip for a submarine [ME, fr OE *penn*]

[2]**pen** *vt* **-nn-** to shut in a pen

[3]**pen** *n* **1** an implement for writing or drawing with fluid (e g ink): e g **a** a quill **b** a penholder fitted with a nib **c** FOUNTAIN PEN **d** a ballpoint **2a** a writing instrument as a means of expression ⟨*the* ~ *is mightier than the sword*⟩ **b** a writer – fml [ME *penne*, fr MF, feather, pen, fr L *penna, pinna* feather; akin to Gk *pteron* wing – more at FEATHER]

[4]**pen** *vt* **-nn-** to write – fml ⟨~ *a letter*⟩

[5]**pen** *n* a female swan [origin unknown]

penal /'peenl/ *adj* **1** of punishment **2** liable to punishment ⟨*a* ~ *offence*⟩ **3** used as a place of punishment ⟨*a* ~ *colony*⟩ [ME, fr MF, fr L *poenalis*, fr *poena* punishment – more at PAIN] – **penally** *adv*

penal·ize, -ise /'peenl·iez/ *vt* **1** to inflict a penalty on **2** to put at a serious disadvantage – **penalization** /-'zaysh(ə)n/ *n*

penalty /'pen(ə)lti/ *n* **1** a punishment legally imposed or incurred **2** a forfeiture to which a person agrees to be subject if conditions are not fulfilled **3a** disadvantage, loss, or suffering due to some action ⟨*paid the* ~ *for his heavy drinking*⟩ **b** a disadvantage imposed for violation of the rules of a sport **4** PENALTY KICK [ML *poenalitas*, fr L *poenalis*]

'**penalty ,area** *n* a rectangular area 44yd (about 40m) wide and 18yd (about 16m) deep in front of each goal on a soccer pitch ☞ SPORT

'**penalty ,box** *n* **1** PENALTY AREA **2** an area alongside an ice hockey rink to which penalized players are confined

'**penalty ,kick** *n* **1** a free kick in rugby **2** a free kick at the goal in soccer awarded for a serious offence committed in the penalty area and taken from a point 12yd (about 11m) in front of the goal with only the goalkeeper to defend it

'**penalty ,shot** *n* a shot at the goal awarded to a team for serious offences (e g in ice hockey)

'**penalty ,spot** *n* a spot 11m (12yd) in front of the goal on a soccer pitch, from which penalty kicks are taken ☞ SPORT

penance /'penəns/ *n* an act of self-abasement or devotion performed to show repentance for sin; *also* a sacramental rite of the Roman, Orthodox, and some Anglican churches involving confession and a penance directed by the confessor [ME, fr OF, fr ML *poenitentia* penitence]

penannular /pen'anyoolə/ *adj* ring-shaped with a small break in the circumference [L *paene, pene* almost + E *annular*]

Penates /pe'nahteez, -'nay-/ *n pl* the Roman gods of the household [L – more at PENETRATE]

pence /pens/ *pl of* PENNY

penchant /'penchənt, 'pon(h)shonh (*Fr* pɑ̃ʃɑ̃)/ *n* a strong leaning; a liking [F, fr prp of *pencher* to incline, fr (assumed) VL *pendicare*, fr L *pendere* to weigh]

[1]**pencil** /'pensl/ *n* **1a** an implement for writing, drawing, or marking consisting of or containing a slender cylinder or strip of a solid marking substance (e g graphite) **b** a small medicated or cosmetic roll or stick for local applications **2** a set of light rays, esp when diverging from or converging to a point **3** sthg long and thin like a pencil [ME *pensel* paintbrush, fr MF *pincel*, fr (assumed) VL *penicellus*, fr L *penicillus*, lit., little tail, fr dim. of *penis* tail, penis]

[2]**pencil** *vt* **-ll-** (*NAm* **-l-, -ll-**), /'pensl·ing/ to draw, write, or mark with a pencil – **penciller** *n*

pendant *also* **pendent** /'pend(ə)nt/ *n* **1** sthg suspended (e g an ornament allowed to hang free) **2** a companion piece or supplement **3** *chiefly Br* a pennant [ME *pendaunt*, fr MF *pendant*, fr prp of *pendre* to hang, fr (assumed) VL *pendere*, fr L *pendēre*; akin to L *pendere* to weigh, estimate, pay, *pondus* weight – more at SPAN]

pendent, pendant /'pend(ə)nt/ *adj* **1** suspended **2** jutting or leaning over; overhanging ⟨*a* ~ *cliff*⟩ **3** remaining undetermined; pending [ME *pendaunt*]

[1]**pending** /'pending/ *prep* until – fml [F *pendant*, fr prp of *pendre*]

[2]**pending** *adj* **1** not yet decided or dealt with **2** imminent, impending – **pendency** *n* /'pend(ə)nsi/

pendulous /'pendyooləs/ *adj* suspended, inclined, or hanging downwards ⟨~ *jowls*⟩ [L *pendulus*, fr *pendere* to weigh] – **pendulously** *adv*

pendulum /'pendyooləm/ *n* a body suspended from a fixed point so as to swing freely periodically under the action of gravity and commonly used to regulate movements (e g of clockwork) [NL, fr L, neut of *pendulus*]

peneplain *also* **peneplane** /'peeniplayn, ,--'-/ *n* a large almost flat land surface shaped by erosion [L *paene, pene* almost + E *plain* or *plane* – more at PATIENT]

penetralia /,peni'trayli·ə, -lyə/ *n pl* the innermost or most secret and hidden parts of a place or thing [L, neut pl of *penetralis* inner, fr *penetrare* to penetrate]

penetrate /'penitrayt/ *vt* **1a** to pass into or through **b** to enter, esp by overcoming resistance; pierce **2** to see into or through; discern **3** to diffuse through or into ~ *vi* to be absorbed by the mind; be understood ⟨*I heard what he said, but it didn't* ~⟩ [L *penetratus*, pp of *penetrare*; akin to L *penitus* inward, *Penates* household gods, Lith *peneti* to nourish] – **penetrable** /-trəbl/ *adj*, **penetrability** /-trə'biləti/ *n*, **penetrative** /-trətiv/ *adj*

penetrating /'penitrayting/ *adj* **1** having the power of entering, piercing, or pervading ⟨*a* ~ *shriek*⟩ ⟨*the cold is* ~⟩ **2** acute, discerning ⟨~ *insights into life*⟩ – **penetratingly** *adv*

penetration /,peni'traysh(ə)n/ *n* **1a** the entering of a country so that influence is established **b** the process of successfully introducing or increasing sales of a product in an existing market **2a** the depth to which sthg penetrates **b** the ability to discern deeply and acutely ⟨*a critic gifted with great powers of* ~⟩ [PENETRATE + -ION]

penetrometer /,peni'tromitə/ *n* an instrument for measuring firmness or consistency [L *penetrare* + ISV *-meter*]

'pen-,friend *n* a person, esp one in another country, with whom a friendship is made through correspondence

penguin /'peng·gwin/ *n* any of various erect short-legged flightless aquatic birds of the southern hemisphere [perh fr W *pen gwyn* white head]

'pen,holder /-,hohldə/ *n* **1** a holder or handle for a pen nib **2** a method of gripping a table-tennis bat in which the handle is held like a pen with the blade downwards

penicillate /,peni'silət, -layt/ *adj* having a tuft of fine filaments ⟨*a* ~ *stigma*⟩ [prob fr (assumed) NL *penicillatus*, fr L *penicillus* brush – more at PENCIL]

penicillin /,peni'silin/ *n* (a salt, ester, or mixture of salts and esters of) any of several antibiotics or antibacterial drugs orig obtained from moulds, that act by interfering with the synthesis of bacterial cell walls and are active against a wide range of bacteria [NL *Penicillium*, genus name of fungi, fr L *penicillus*]

penile /'peeniel/ *adj* of or affecting the penis

peninsula /pə'ninsyoolə/ *n* a piece of land jutting out into or almost surrounded by water; *esp* one connected to the mainland by an isthmus [L *paeninsula*, fr *paene* almost + *insula* island – more at PATIENT]

peninsular /pə'ninsyoolə/ *adj* of a peninsula; *specif, often cap* of Spain and Portugal

penis /'peenis/ *n, pl* **penes** /-neez/, **penises** the male organ of copulation by which semen is introduced into the female during coitus ☞ REPRODUCTION [L, penis, tail; akin to OHG *faselt* penis, Gk *peos*]

'penis ,envy *n* the unconscious desire to be a male that in psychoanalytic theory is attributed to the female

¹penitent /'penit(ə)nt/ *adj* feeling or expressing sorrow for sins or offences [ME, fr MF, fr L *paenitent-, paenitens*, fr prp of *paenitēre* to be sorry; akin to L *paene* almost – more at PATIENT] – **penitence** *n*, **penitently** *adv*

²penitent *n* **1** sby who repents of sin **2** sby under church censure but admitted to penance, esp under the direction of a confessor

penitential /,peni'tensh(ə)l/ *adj* of penitence or penance – **penitentially** *adv*

¹penitentiary /,peni'tensh(ə)ri/ *n* a prison in the USA [ME *penitenciary* officer dealing with penitents, fr ML *poenitentiarius*, fr *poenitentia*]

²penitentiary *adj, NAm* of or incurring confinement in a penitentiary

penknife /'pen,nief/ *n* a small pocketknife [fr its original use for mending quill pens]

'penman /-mən/ *n* sby with a specified quality or style of handwriting ⟨*a poor* ~⟩

'penmanship /-ship/ *n* **1** the art or practice of writing with the pen **2** quality or style of handwriting

'pen ,name *n* an author's pseudonym

pennant /'penənt/ *n* **1** any of various nautical flags used for identification or signalling **2** a flag that tapers to a point or has a swallowtail [alter. of *pendant*]

penni /'peni/ *n, pl* **pennia** /-ni·ə/, **pennis** ☞ *Finland* at NATIONALITY [Finn]

penniless /'penilis/ *adj* lacking money; poor

pennon /'penən/ *n* a long usu triangular or swallowtailed streamer typically attached to the head of a lance as a knight's personal flag [ME, fr MF *penon*, aug of *penne* feather – more at ³PEN]

,Pennsylvania 'Dutch /,pens(ə)l'vaynyə, -ni·ə/ *n* a people descended from 18th-c German immigrants to E Pennsylvania [*Pennsylvania*, state of the USA] – **Pennsylvania Dutchman** *n*

penny /'peni/ *n, pl* **pennies, pence** /pens/, (3) **pennies** **1a** (a usu bronze coin representing) (1) a former British money unit worth £$^1/_{240}$ (2) a British money unit in use since 1971 that is worth £$^1/_{100}$ **b** ☞ *Irish Republic, Gibraltar, Falkland Islands* at NATIONALITY **2** a denarius **3** *NAm* a cent [ME, fr OE *penning, penig*; akin to OHG *pfenning*, a coin] – **the penny drops** the true meaning finally dawns

-penny /-p(ə)ni; *since decimalization also* -peni/ *comb form* (→ *adj*) costing (so many) pence ⟨*ninepenny*⟩

,penny 'dreadful *n* a novel of violent adventure or crime orig costing a penny

,penny-'farthing *n, Br* an early type of bicycle having 1 small and 1 large wheel [fr the relative sizes of the old penny and farthing coins]

'penny-,pinching *adj* mean, niggardly, stingy – **penny pincher** *n*, **penny-pinching** *n*

,penny'royal /-'royəl/ *n* **1** a European mint with small aromatic leaves **2** an aromatic American plant of the mint family [prob by folk etymology fr MF *poullieul*, modif of L *pulegium*]

'penny,weight /-,wayt/ *n* a unit of troy weight equal to 24 grains (about 1.56g) ☞ UNIT

,penny-'wise *adj* prudent only in dealing with small

sums or matters – esp in *penny-wise and pound-foolish*

'penny,wort /-wuht/ *n* any of various round-leaved plants

,pennyworth /'penəth, 'peniwəth, -,wuhth/ *n, pl* **pennyworth, pennyworths 1** a penny's worth **2** value for the money spent; a bargain ⟨*got a good* ~⟩ **3** a small quantity; a modicum

penology /pee'noləji/ *n* criminology dealing with prison management and the treatment of offenders [Gk *poinē* penalty + E *-logy* – more at PAIN] – **penologist** *n*, **penological** /,peenə'lojikl/ *adj*

'pen ,pal *n* a pen-friend – infml

'pen ,pusher *n* one whose work involves usu boring or repetitive writing at a desk; *specif* CLERK 2a

pensile /'pensiel/ *adj* pendent, hanging ⟨*the* ~ *nests of some birds*⟩ [L *pensilis*, fr *pensus*, pp of *pendēre* to hang]

¹pension /'pensh(ə)n; *sense 2* 'ponhsyonh (*Fr* pɑ̃sjɔ̃)/ *n* **1** a fixed sum paid regularly to a person (e g following retirement or as compensation for a wage-earner's death) ⟨*a widow's* ~⟩ **2** (bed and board provided by) a hotel or boardinghouse, esp in continental Europe [ME, fr MF, fr L *pension-, pensio*, fr *pensus*, pp of *pendere* to pay – more at PENDANT] – **pensionless** *adj*

²pension /'pensh(ə)n/ *vt* to grant or pay a pension to

pensionable /'pensh(ə)nəbl/ *adj* (that makes sby) entitled to receive a pension ⟨~ *employment*⟩ ⟨*a* ~ *employee*⟩

pensioner /'pensh(ə)nə/ *n* one who receives or lives on an esp old-age pension

pension off *vt* **1** to dismiss or retire from service with a pension ⟨pensioned off *his faithful old servant*⟩ **2** to set aside or dispense with after long use – infml ⟨pensioned off *his old trousers*⟩

pensive /'pensiv/ *adj* sadly or dreamily thoughtful [ME *pensif*, fr MF, fr *penser* to think, fr L *pensare* to ponder, fr *pensus*, pp of *pendere* to weigh – more at PENDANT] – **pensively** *adv*, **pensiveness** *n*

penstock /'pen,stok/ *n* **1** a valve, sluice, or gate for regulating a flow (e g of water) **2** *chiefly NAm* a conduit or pipe for conducting water [¹*pen* + *stock*]

penta-, pent- *comb form* **1** five ⟨penta*hedron*⟩ ⟨penta*valent*⟩ ⟨pent*ode*⟩ **2** containing 5 atoms, groups, or chemical equivalents in the molecular structure ⟨penta*hydrate*⟩ [ME, fr Gk, fr *pente* – more at FIVE]

pentacle /'pentəkl/ *n* a pentagram [(assumed) ML *pentaculum*, fr Gk *pente*]

pentad /'pentad/ *n* a group or series of 5 [Gk *pentad-, pentas*, fr *pente*]

pentagon /'pentəgən, -,gon/ *n* a polygon of 5 angles and 5 sides ☞ MATHEMATICS [Gk *pentagōnon*, fr neut of *pentagōnos* pentagonal, fr *penta-* + *gōnia* angle – more at -GON] – **pentagonal** /pen'tagənl/ *adj*, **pentagonally** *adv*

Pentagon *n sing or pl in constr the* US military establishment [the *Pentagon* building, headquarters of the US Department of Defense in Arlington, Virginia]

pentagram /'pentə,gram/ *n* a 5-pointed star used as a magical symbol [Gk *pentagrammon*, fr *penta-* + *-grammon* (akin to *gramma* letter) – more at ²GRAM]

pentamerous /pen'tamərəs/ *adj* divided into or consisting of 5 parts; *specif, of a flower* having each whorl of petals, sepals, stamens, etc consisting of (a multiple of) 5 members [NL *pentamerus*, fr *penta-* (fr Gk) + *-merus* -merous]

pentameter /pen'tamitə/ *n* a line of verse consisting of 5 metrical feet [L, fr Gk *pentametros* having 5 metrical feet, fr *penta-* + *metron* measure – more at MEASURE]

pentane /'pentayn/ *n* a liquid hydrocarbon of the alkane series obtained from petroleum [ISV]

pentangle /'pen,tang·gl/ *n* a pentagram

pentaprism *n* a 5-sided prism, esp in a camera, which gives a constant deviation of 90° to light from any direction

Pentateuch /'pentə,tyoohk/ *n the* first 5 books of the Old Testament [LL *Pentateuchus*, fr Gk *Pentateuchos*, fr *penta-* + *teuchos* tool, vessel, book; akin to Gk *teuchein* to make – more at DOUGHTY] – **pentateuchal** /-'tyoohkl/ *adj*

pentathlete /pen'tathleet/ *n* sby who competes in the pentathlon

pentathlon /pen'tathlon/ *n* **1** a (women's) athletic contest in which all contestants compete in the 100m hurdles, shot put, high jump, long jump, and 200m sprint **2** MODERN PENTATHLON [Gk, athletic contest involving 5 events, fr *penta-* + *athlon* contest]

pentatonic /,pentə'tonik/ *adj* of, in, or being a musical scale consisting of 5 tones ⟨*a* ~ *tune*⟩

Pentecost /'pentikost/ *n* (a Christian festival on the 7th Sunday after Easter commemorating the descent of the Holy Spirit on the apostles at) the Jewish festival of Shabuoth [ME, fr OE *pentecosten*, fr LL *pentecoste*, fr Gk *pentēkostē*, lit., fiftieth day, fr *pentēkostos* fiftieth, fr *pentēkonta* fifty, fr *penta-* + *-konta* (akin to L *viginti* twenty) – more at VIGESIMAL]

,Pente'costal /-tl/ *adj* of or being (a member of) any of various fundamentalist evangelical Christian bodies laying particular emphasis on the gifts of the Holy Spirit (e g speaking in tongues and healing) – **Pentecostalism** *n*, **Pentecostalist** *n*

penthouse /'pent,hows/ *n* **1** a structure (e g a shed or roof) attached to and sloping from a wall or building **2** a structure or dwelling built on the roof of a (tall) building ⟨*a* ~ *flat*⟩ [by folk etymology fr ME *pentis*, fr MF *appentis*, prob fr ML *appenticium* appendage, fr L *appendic-, appendix* – more at APPENDIX]

pentimento /,penti'mentoh/ *n, pl* **pentimenti** /-ti/ a reappearance in a painting of underlying work which has been painted over [It, repentance, correction, fr *pentire* to repent, fr L *paenitere*]

pentobarbitone /,pentə'bahbitohn/ *n, Br* a barbiturate used, esp formerly, in sleeping pills and as an anticonvulsant [*penta-* + *-o-* + *barbitone* (barbital)]

pentose /'pentohs, -tohz/ *n* any of various monosaccharide sugars (e g ribose) that contain 5 carbon atoms in the molecule [ISV]

Pentothal /'pentə,thol/ *trademark* – used for thiopentone

pentstemon /,pent'steemən, -'stemən/ *n* any of a genus of chiefly American plants of the figwort family with showy blue, purple, red, yellow, or white flowers [NL *pentstemon*, alter. of *Penstemon*, genus name, fr Gk *penta-* + *stēmōn* thread – more at STAMEN]

,pent-'up /pent/ *adj* confined, held in check ⟨~

emotions⟩ [*pent*, pp of obs *pend* (to confine), prob alter. of [2]*pen*]

penult /pi'nult, pe-/ *n* the next to the last (syllable of a word) [L *paenultima*, fr fem of *paenultimus* almost last, fr *paene* almost + *ultimus* last]

[1]**penultimate** /pi'nultimət, pe-/ *adj* next to the last ⟨*the ~ chapter of a book*⟩ – **penultimately** *adv*

[2]**penultimate** *n* a penult

penumbra /pi'numbrə/ *n, pl* **penumbrae** /-bri/, **penumbras** **1** a region of partial darkness (e g in an eclipse) in a shadow surrounding the umbra **2** a less dark region surrounding the dark centre of a sunspot [NL, fr L *paene* almost + *umbra* shadow – more at PATIENT, UMBRAGE] – **penumbral** *adj*

penurious /pi'nyooəri·əs/ *adj* marked by or suffering from penury – fml – **penuriously** *adv*, **penuriousness** *n*

penury /'penyoori/ *n* a cramping and oppressive lack of resources, esp money; *esp* severe poverty – fml [ME, fr L *penuria* want – more at PATIENT]

peon /'pee·ən/ *n, pl* **peons, peones** /pay'ohneez/, (3) **peons** **1** an Indian or Sri Lankan infantryman, orderly, or other worker **2** an agricultural labourer in Spanish America **3** a drudge, menial [Pg *peão* & F *pion*, fr ML *pedon-*, *pedo* foot soldier – more at [3]PAWN]

peonage /'pee·ənij/ *n* **1** the condition of a peon **2** the use of labourers bound in servitude because of debt or under a convict lease system

peony, paeony /'pee·əni/ *n* any of a genus of plants with very large usu double showy red, pink, or white flowers [ME *piony*, fr MF *pioine*, fr L *paeonia*, fr Gk *paiōnia*, fr *Paiōn* Paeon, mythical physician of the gods]

[1]**people** /'peepl/ *n pl in constr*, (5) *sing or pl in constr* **1** human beings in general **2** a group of persons considered collectively ⟨*poor ~*⟩ **3** the members of a family or kinship ⟨*his ~ have been farmers for generations*⟩ **4** the mass of a community ⟨*disputes between the ~ and the nobles*⟩ **5** a body of persons that are united by a common culture and that often constitute a politically organized group ⟨*the Jewish ~*⟩ **6** the citizens of a state who are qualified to vote [ME *peple*, fr OF *peuple*, fr L *populus*] – **of all people** – used to show surprise ⟨*the Archbishop* of all people *said that?*⟩

[2]**people** *vt* **1** to supply or fill with people **2** to dwell in; inhabit [MF *peupler*, fr OF, fr *peuple*]

pep /pep/ *vt or n* **-pp-** (to liven up or instil with) brisk energy or initiative and high spirits [n short for *pepper*; vb fr n] – **peppy** *adj*, **peppiness** *n*

peplos *also* **peplus** /'pepləs/ *n* a robe or shawl worn by women of ancient Greece [L *peplus*, fr Gk *peplos*]

peplum /'pepləm/ *n* a short skirt or flounce attached to the waistline of a blouse, jacket, or dress [L, fr Gk *peplos*]

pepo /'peepoh/ *n, pl* **pepos** a fleshy many-seeded berry (e g a pumpkin, melon, or cucumber) with a hard rind [L, a melon – more at PUMPKIN]

[1]**pepper** /'pepə/ *n* **1a(1)** BLACK PEPPER **(2)** WHITE PEPPER **b** any of a genus of tropical mostly climbing shrubs with aromatic leaves; *esp* one with red berries from which black pepper and white pepper are prepared **2** any of various products similar to pepper; *esp* a pungent condiment obtained from capsicums – used with a qualifying term ⟨*cayenne ~*⟩ **3** (the usu red or green fruit of) a capsicum whose fruits are hot peppers or sweet peppers [ME *peper*, fr OE *pipor*; akin to OHG *pfeffar* pepper; both fr a prehistoric WGmc-NGmc word borrowed fr L *piper* pepper, fr Gk *peperi*] – **pepper** *adj*

[2]**pepper** *vt* **1a** to sprinkle, season, or cover (as if) with pepper **b** to shower with shot or other missiles **2** to sprinkle ⟨*~ed his report with statistics*⟩

,pepper-and-'salt *adj, of a fabric or garment* having black and white or dark and light colour intermingled in small flecks

'pepper,corn /-,kawn/ *n* a dried berry of the pepper plant

'peppercorn ,rent *n* a very small amount of money paid as a nominal rent

'pepper,mint /-,mint/ *n* **1** (an aromatic essential oil obtained from) a mint with dark green tapering leaves and whorls of small pink flowers **2** a sweet flavoured with peppermint oil – **pepperminty** *adj*

'pepper ,pot *n, Br* a small usu cylindrical container with a perforated top used for sprinkling ground pepper on food

peppery /'pep(ə)ri/ *adj* **1** hot, pungent **2** hot-tempered, touchy ⟨*a ~ old man*⟩ **3** fiery, stinging ⟨*a ~ speech*⟩ [[1]PEPPER + [1]-Y]

'pep ,pill *n* a tablet of a stimulant drug

pepsin /'pepsin/ *n* an enzyme of the stomach that breaks down most proteins in an acid environment [G, fr Gk *pepsis* digestion, fr *pessein*]

'pep ,talk *n* a usu brief, high-pressure, and emotional talk designed esp to encourage an audience (e g a sports team)

peptic /'peptik/ *adj* **1** of or promoting digestion **2** connected with or resulting from the action of digestive juices ⟨*a ~ ulcer*⟩ [L *pepticus*, fr Gk *peptikos*, fr *peptos* cooked, fr *peptein, pessein* to cook, digest – more at COOK]

peptide /'peptied/ *n* a short chain of 2 or more amino acids joined by peptide bonds [ISV, fr *peptone*] – **peptidic** /-'tidik/ *adj*

peptide bond *n* the chemical bond between the carbon of one amino acid and the nitrogen of another that links amino acids in peptides and proteins

peptone /'peptohn/ *n* any of various water-soluble products of protein breakdown [G *pepton*, fr Gk, neut of *peptos*] – **peptonize** /'peptəniez/ *vt*

per /pə; *strong* puh/ *prep* **1** by the means or agency of; through ⟨*send it ~ rail*⟩ **2** with respect to every; for each ⟨*£30 ~ head ~ week*⟩ **3** ACCORDING TO 1 ⟨*~ list price*⟩ [L, through, by means of, by – more at FOR]

per- *prefix* **1a** through; throughout ⟨per*ambulate*⟩ ⟨per*vade*⟩ **b** thoroughly; very ⟨per*fervid*⟩ ⟨per*fect*⟩ **2** to the bad; to destruction ⟨per *jure*⟩ ⟨per*dition*⟩ **3** containing an atom in a high oxidation state in its molecular structure ⟨per*chloric acid*⟩ ⟨per*chlorate*⟩ [L, through, throughout, thoroughly, to destruction, fr *per*]

peradventure /pərəd'venchə, ,puh-/ *adv, archaic* perhaps, possibly [ME *per aventure*, fr OF, by chance]

perambulate /pə'rambyoolayt/ *vt* to travel over or through on foot; traverse ~ *vi* to stroll *USE* fml [L *perambulatus*, pp of *perambulare*, fr *per-* through + *ambulare* to walk] – **perambulation** /-'laysh(ə)n/ *n*, **perambulatory** /-lət(ə)ri/ *adj*

perambulator /pə'rambyoolaytə/ *n, chiefly Br* a pram [PERAMBULATE + [1]-OR]

per 'annum /pər 'anəm/ *adv* in or for each year [ML]

percale /pə'kayl, pə'kahl, ˌpuh-/ *n* a closely woven cotton cloth variously finished for clothing, sheeting, and industrial uses [Per *pargālah*]

percaline /'puhkəlin, ˌpuhkə'leen/ *n* a lightweight cotton fabric; *esp* a glossy fabric used for bookbindings [F, fr *percale*]

per 'capita /'kapitə/ *adv or adj* per unit of population; by or for each person ⟨*the highest income ~ of any European country*⟩ [ML, by heads]

perceive /pə'seev/ *vt* **1** to understand, realize **2** to become aware of through the senses; *esp* to see, observe [ME *perceiven*, fr OF *perceivre*, fr L *percipere*, fr *per-* thoroughly + *capere* to take – more at PER-, HEAVE] – **perceivable** *adj*, **perceivably** *adv*, **perceiver** *n*

[1]**per cent** /pə 'sent/ *adv* in or for each 100 ⟨*50 ~ of our workers are married*⟩ [*per* + L *centum* hundred – more at HUNDRED]

[2]**per cent** *n, pl* **per cent** **1** one part in a 100 ⟨*gave half a ~ of her income to charity*⟩ ☞ SYMBOL **2** a percentage ⟨*a large ~ of the total*⟩

[3]**per cent** *adj* **1** reckoned on the basis of a whole divided into 100 parts ⟨*a 10 ~ increase*⟩ **2** *of bonds, securities, etc* paying interest at a specified per cent

percentage /pə'sentij/ *n* **1** a proportion (expressed as per cent of a whole) ⟨*what ~ of the population own their own houses?*⟩ ⟨*the ~ of car owners has increased to 50*⟩ **2** a share of winnings or profits ⟨*they did him out of his ~*⟩ **3** an advantage, profit – infml

percentile /pə'sentiel/ *n* a statistical measure (e g used in educational and psychological testing) that expresses a value as a percentage of all the values that are lower than or equal to it ☞ STATISTICS [prob fr *per cent* + *-ile* (as in *quartile*, n)]

per 'cents *n pl, Br* stocks that bear a specified rate of interest ⟨*took out some 10 ~*⟩

per centum /'sentəm/ *n* PER CENT

percept /'puhsept/ *n* a mental impression of a perceived object [back-formation fr *perception*]

perceptible /pə'septəbl/ *adj* capable of being perceived, esp by the senses ⟨*a ~ change in her tone*⟩ ⟨*the light became increasingly ~*⟩ – **perceptibly** *adv*, **perceptibility** /-'biləti/ *n*

perception /pə'sepsh(ə)n/ *n* **1a** a result of perceiving; an observation **b** a mental image; a concept **2** the mental interpretation of physical sensations produced by stimuli from the external world **3** intuitive discernment; insight, understanding ⟨*has little ~ of what is required*⟩ [L *perception-*, *perceptio* act of perceiving, fr *perceptus*, pp of *percipere*] – **perceptional** *adj*, **perceptual** /-chooəl/ *adj*

perceptive /pə'septiv/ *adj* **1** capable of or exhibiting (keen) perception; observant, discerning ⟨*a ~ scholar*⟩ **2** characterized by sympathetic understanding or insight – **perceptively** *adv*, **perceptiveness** *n*, **perceptivity** /-'tivəti/ *n*

[1]**perch** /puhch/ *n* **1** a roost for a bird **2** *chiefly Br* ROD 2 ☞ UNIT **3a** a resting place or vantage point; a seat **b** a prominent position ⟨*his new ~ as president*⟩ *USE* (*3*) infml [ME *perche*, fr OF, fr L *pertica* pole]

[2]**perch** *vt* to place on a perch, height, or precarious spot ~ *vi* to alight, settle, or rest, esp briefly or precariously

[3]**perch** *n, pl* **perches,** *esp collectively* **perch** a small European freshwater spiny-finned fish [ME *perche*, fr MF, fr L *perca*, fr Gk *perkē*; akin to OHG *faro* coloured, L *porcus*, a spiny fish]

perchance /pə'chahns/ *adv* perhaps, possibly – usu poetic or humor [ME *per chance*, fr MF, by chance]

Percheron /'puhshəron/ *n* any of a breed of powerful rugged draught horses that originated in the Perche region of France [F, fr *Perche*, region of N France]

percipient /pə'sipi·ənt/ *adj* perceptive, discerning – fml [L *percipient-*, *percipiens*, prp of *percipere* to perceive] – **percipience** *n*

percolate /'puhkəlayt/ *vt* **1a** to cause (esp a liquid) to pass through a permeable substance, esp for extracting a soluble constituent **b** to prepare (coffee) in a percolator **2** to be diffused through; permeate ~ *vi* **1** to ooze or filter through a permeable substance; seep **2** to become percolated **3** to become diffused ⟨*sunlight* ~d *into the room*⟩ [L *percolatus*, pp of *percolare*, fr *per-* through + *colare* to sieve – more at PER-, COLANDER] – **percolation** /-'laysh(ə)n/ *n*

percolator /'puhkəlaytə/ *n* a coffee pot in which boiling water rising through a tube is repeatedly deflected downwards through a perforated basket containing ground coffee beans [PERCOLATE + [1]-OR]

per 'contra /'kontrə/ *adv* ON THE CONTRARY [It, by the opposite side (of the ledger)]

percuss /pə'kus/ *vt* to perform percussion on (esp a body surface) [L *percussus*]

percussion /pə'kush(ə)n/ *n* **1a** the beating or striking of a musical instrument **b** the tapping of the surface of a body part (e g the chest) to learn the condition of the parts beneath (e g the lungs) by the resultant sound **2** the striking of sound on the ear **3** *sing or pl in constr* percussion instruments that form a section of a band or orchestra [L *percussion-*, *percussio*, fr *percussus*, pp of *percutere* to beat, fr *per-* thoroughly + *quatere* to shake – more at PER-, QUASH] – **percussion** *adj*, **percussive** /-siv/ *adj*

per'cussion ˌcap *n* CAP 6

per'cussion ˌinstrument *n* a musical instrument (e g a drum or xylophone) sounded by striking, shaking, or scraping

percussionist /pə'kush(ə)nist/ *n* one who plays percussion instruments

percutaneous /ˌpuhkyoo'taynyəs, -ni·əs/ *adj* done or performed through the skin – **percutaneously** *adv*

[1]**per 'diem** /'dee·em, 'die·em/ *adj or adv* (paid) by the day or for each day [ML]

[2]**per diem** *n, pl* **per diems** a daily allowance or fee

perdition /pə'dish(ə)n/ *n* eternal damnation; Hell [ME *perdicion*, fr LL *perdition-*, *perditio*, fr L *perditus*, pp of *perdere* to destroy, fr *per-* to destruction + *dare* to give – more at PER-, [2]DATE]

peregrination /ˌperigri'naysh(ə)n/ *n* a long and wandering journey, esp in a foreign country – humor [MF or L; MF, fr L *peregrination-*, *peregrinatio*, fr *peregrinatus*, pp of *peregrinari* to travel abroad, fr *peregrinus* foreigner, fr *peregrinus* foreign – more at PILGRIM] – **peregrinate** /'perigriˌnayt/ *vb*

peregrine /'perigrin/, **peregrine falcon** *n* a smallish swift widely occurring falcon formerly much used in falconry [*peregrine*, adj (wandering, widely distributed), fr ML *peregrinus*, fr L, foreign]

peremptory /pə'rempt(ə)ri/ *adj* **1** admitting no contradiction or refusal ⟨*a* ~ *conclusion*⟩ ⟨*a* ~ *command*⟩ **2** expressive of urgency or command ⟨*a* ~ *call*⟩ **3** (having an attitude or nature) characterized by imperious or arrogant self-assurance ⟨*a* ~ *disregard for safety measures*⟩ ⟨*a* ~ *tone*⟩ [LL & L; LL *peremptorius*, fr L, destructive, fr *peremptus*, pp of *perimere* to take entirely, destroy, fr *per-* to destruction + *emere* to take – more at REDEEM] – **peremptorily** *adv*, **peremptoriness** *n*

perennial /pə'renyəl, -ni·əl/ *adj* **1** present at all seasons of the year **2** *of a plant* living for several years, usu with new herbaceous growth each year **3** lasting for a long time or forever; constant ⟨*politics provide a* ~ *topic of argument*⟩ [L *perennis*, fr *per-* throughout + *annus* year – more at PER-, ANNUAL] – **perennial** *n*, **perennially** *adv*

[1]**perfect** /'puhfikt/ *adj* **1** expert, proficient ⟨*practice makes* ~⟩ **2a** entirely without fault or defect; flawless ⟨*a* ~ *gemstone*⟩ **b** satisfactory in every respect ⟨*the holiday was* ~⟩ **c** corresponding to an ideal standard or abstract concept ⟨*a* ~ *gentleman*⟩ **3a** accurate, exact ⟨~ *pitch*⟩ ⟨*a* ~ *circle*⟩ **b** lacking in no essential detail; complete **c** absolute, utter ⟨*I felt a* ~ *fool*⟩ **4** of or constituting a verb tense or form that expresses an action or state completed at the time of speaking or at a time spoken of **5a** *of the musical intervals fourth, fifth, and octave* having a character that is retained when inverted; not augmented or diminished **b** *of a cadence* passing from a dominant or subdominant to a tonic chord **6** having the stamens and carpels in the same flower [ME *parfit*, fr OF, fr L *perfectus*, fr pp of *perficere* to carry out, perfect, fr *per-* thoroughly + *facere* to make, do – more at [1]DO] – **perfectness** *n*

[2]**perfect** /pə'fekt/ *vt* **1** to make perfect; improve, refine **2** to bring to final form – **perfecter** *n*, **perfectible** *adj*, **perfectibility** /-tə'biləti/ *n*

perfection /pə'feksh(ə)n/ *n* **1a** making or being perfect **b** freedom from (moral) fault or defect **c** full development; maturity ⟨*Greek civilization slowly flowered to* ~⟩ **2** (an example of) unsurpassable accuracy or excellence ⟨*the cake was* ~⟩

perfectionism /pə'fekshə,niz(ə)m/ *n* **1** the theological doctrine that a state of freedom from sin is attainable on earth **2** a disposition to regard anything short of perfection, esp in one's own work, as unacceptable – **perfectionist** *adj or n*

perfective /pə'fektiv/ *adj, of a form of a verb* expressing action as complete – compare IMPERFECTIVE – **perfective** *n*, **perfectively** *adv*, **perfectivity** /-'tivəti/ *n*

perfectly /'puhfiktli/ *adv* to an adequate extent; quite ⟨*your dress will be* ~ *suitable for the party*⟩ [[1]PERFECT + [2]-LY]

perfect number *n* an integer (e g 6 or 28) that is equal to the sum of all its possible integral factors including 1 but excluding itself

perfecto /pə'fektoh/ *n, pl* **perfectos** a thick cigar that tapers almost to a point at each end [Sp, perfect, fr L *perfectus*]

perfect participle *n* PAST PARTICIPLE

,perfect 'pitch *n* ABSOLUTE PITCH 2

perfervid /puh'fuhvid/ *adj* excessively fervid [NL *perfervidus*, fr L *per-* thoroughly + *fervidus* fervid]

perfidy /'puhfidi/ *n* being faithless or disloyal; treachery [L *perfidia*, fr *perfidus* faithless, fr *per fidem decipere* to betray, lit., to deceive by trust] – **perfidious** /pə'fidi·əs/ *adj*, **perfidiously** *adv*, **perfidiousness** *n*

perforate /'puhfə,rayt/ *vt* **1** to make a hole through; *specif* to make a line of holes in or between (e g rows of postage stamps in a sheet) to make separation easier **2** to pass through or into (as if) by making a hole ~ *vi* to penetrate or make a hole in a surface [L *perforatus*, pp of *perforare* to bore through, fr *per-* through + *forare* to bore – more at [1]BORE] – **perforator** *n*, **perforate** /-rət/ *adj*, **perforation** /-'raysh(ə)n/ *n*

perforce /pə'faws/ *adv* by force of circumstances – fml [ME *par force*, fr MF, by force]

perform /pə'fawm/ *vt* **1** to do; CARRY OUT ⟨~ed *a small service*⟩ **2a** to do in a formal manner or according to prescribed ritual ⟨~ *a marriage ceremony*⟩ **b** to give a rendering of; present ⟨*they* ~ed *a new play*⟩ ~ *vi* **1** to carry out an action or pattern of behaviour; act, function **2** to give a performance [ME *performen*, fr AF *performer*, alter. of OF *perfournir*, fr *per-* thoroughly (fr L) + *fournir* to complete – more at FURNISH] – **performable** *adj*, **performer** *n*

performance /pə'fawməns/ *n* **1a** the execution of an action **b** sthg accomplished; a deed, feat **2** the fulfilment of a claim, promise, etc **3** a presentation to an audience of a (character in a) play, a piece of music, etc ⟨*3* ~s *a night*⟩ ⟨*gave a brilliant* ~ *in the title rôle*⟩ **4** the ability to perform or work (efficiently or well) ⟨*good engine* ~ *requires good tuning*⟩ **5** manner of reacting to stimuli; behaviour ⟨*the* ~ *of the stock market*⟩ **6** language as manifested in actual speech and writing – compare COMPETENCE 2, PAROLE 4 **7a** a lengthy or troublesome process or activity ⟨*going through the customs was such a* ~!⟩ **b** a display of bad behaviour *USE* (7) infml

performing art /pə'fawming/ *n* an art (e g music or drama) requiring public performance

[1]**perfume** /'puhfyoohm/ *n* **1** a sweet or pleasant smell; a fragrance **2** a pleasant-smelling (liquid) preparation (e g of floral essences) [MF *perfum*, prob fr OProv, fr *perfumar* to perfume, fr *per-* thoroughly (fr L) + *fumar* to smoke, fr L *fumare*]

[2]**perfume** /pə'fyoohm, 'puhfyoohm/ *vt* to fill or imbue with a sweet smell

perfumery /pə'fyoohm(ə)ri/ *n* **1** (the manufacture of) perfumes **2** a place where perfumes are made or sold – **perfumer** *n*

perfunctory /pə'fungkt(ə)ri/ *adj* characterized by routine or superficiality; mechanical, cursory ⟨*a* ~ *smile*⟩ [LL *perfunctorius*, fr L *perfunctus*, pp of *perfungi* to accomplish, get through with, fr *per-* through + *fungi* to perform – more at PER-, FUNCTION] – **perfunctorily** *adv*, **perfunctoriness** *n*

perfuse /pə'fyoohz/ *vt* **1** to suffuse **2** to force a fluid through (an organ or tissue), esp by way of the blood vessels [L *perfusus*, pp of *perfundere* to pour over, fr *per-* through + *fundere* to pour – more at [4]FOUND] – **perfusion** /-zh(ə)n/ *n*, **perfusive** /-siv, -ziv/ *adj*

pergola /'puhgələ/ *n* (an arbour made by training plants over) a support for climbing plants [It, fr L *pergula* projecting roof]

perhaps /pə'haps, p(ə)raps/ *adv* possibly but not certainly; maybe ⟨~ *I'm mistaken*⟩ ⟨~ *you would open it?*⟩ [*per* + *hap* (chance) – more at HAPPEN]

peri- /peri-/ *prefix* **1** all; round; about ⟨peri*scope*⟩ ⟨peri*patetic*⟩ **2** near ⟨peri*helion*⟩ ⟨peri*gee*⟩ **3** enclosing; surrounding ⟨peri*meter*⟩ ⟨peri*toneum*⟩ ⟨peri*style*⟩ [L, fr Gk, round, in excess, fr *peri*; akin to Gk *peran* to pass through]

perianth /'peri,anth/ *n* the external envelope of a flower, esp when not differentiated into petals and sepals [NL *perianthium*, fr *peri-* + Gk *anthos* flower – more at ANTHOLOGY]

,peri'cardium /-'kahdi·əm, -dyəm/ *n, pl* **pericardia** the membranous sac that surrounds the heart of vertebrates [NL, fr Gk *perikardion*, neut of *perikardios* round the heart, fr *peri-* + *kardia* heart – more at HEART] – **pericardial** *adj*, **pericarditis** /-kah'dietəs/ *n*

'peri,carp /-,kahp/ *n* the ripened wall of a plant ovary [NL *pericarpium*, fr Gk *perikarpion* pod, fr *peri-* + *-karpion* -carp]

,peri'chondrium /-'kondri·əm/ *n, pl* **perichondria** /-dri·ə/ the membrane of fibrous connective tissue that surrounds cartilage except at joints [NL, fr *peri-* + Gk *chondros* grain, cartilage – more at GRIND] – **perichondrial** *adj*

,peri'cranium /-'kraynyəm, -ni·əm/ *n, pl* **pericrania** /-nyə, -ni·ə/ the external membrane of the skull [NL, fr Gk *perikranion*, neut of *perikranios* round the skull, fr *peri-* + *kranion* skull] – **pericranial** *adj*

'peri,cycle /-,siekl/ *n* a thin layer of cells that surrounds the central vascular part of many stems and roots [F *péricycle*, fr Gk *perikyklos* spherical, fr *peri-* + *kyklos* circle – more at WHEEL] – **pericyclic** /-'siklik, -'sie-/ *adj*

'peri,derm /-,duhm/ *n* a thick outer protective tissue layer of woody roots and stems that consists of cork and adjacent tissues [NL *peridermis*, fr *peri-* + *-dermis*] – **peridermal** /-'duhml/, **peridermic** /-'duhmik/ *adj*

peridot /'peridot, -doh/ *n* a deep yellowish green transparent gem consisting of silicates of iron and magnesium [F *péridot*, fr OF *peritot*]

'peri,gee /-jee/ *n* the point in an orbit round the earth that is nearest the centre of the earth – compare APOGEE 1 [MF & NL; MF, fr NL *perigaeum*, *perigeum*, fr Gk *perigeion*, fr neut of *perigeios* near the earth, fr *peri-* + *gē* earth] – **perigean** /-'jee·ən/ *adj*

perigynous /pə'rijinəs/ *adj* (having floral organs) borne on a ring or cup of the receptacle surrounding an ovule – compare EPIGYNOUS, HYPOGYNOUS [NL *perigynus*, fr *peri-* + *-gynus* -gynous] – **perigyny** /-ni/ *n*

perihelion /,peri'heeli·ən, -lyən/ *n, pl* **perihelia** /-li·ə/ the point in the path of a planet, comet, etc that is nearest to the sun – compare APHELION [NL, fr *peri-* + Gk *hēlios* sun – more at [1]SOLAR] – **perihelic** /-'heelik/ *adj*

peril /'perəl, -ril/ *n* **1** exposure to the risk of being injured, destroyed, or lost; danger ⟨*fire put the city in* ~⟩ **2** sthg that imperils; a risk [ME, fr OF, fr L *periculum* – more at FEAR] – **perilous** *adj*, **perilously** *adv*, **perilousness** *n*

perilune /'peri,loohn/ *n* the point in the path of a body orbiting the moon that is nearest the centre of the moon – compare APOLUNE [*peri-* + L *luna* moon – more at LUNAR]

'peri,lymph /-,limf/ *n* the liquid inside the labyrinth of the inner ear [ISV]

perimeter /pə'rimitə/ *n* **1** (the length of) the boundary of a closed plane figure ☞ MATHEMATICS **2** a line, strip, fence, etc bounding or protecting an area ⟨*a* ~ *fence*⟩ **3** the outer edge or limits of sthg [F *périmètre*, fr L *perimetros*, fr Gk, fr *peri-* + *metron* measure – more at MEASURE]

perinatal /,peri'naytl/ *adj* (occurring) at about the time of birth

,peri'neum /-'nee·əm/ *n* the area between the anus and the back part of the genitals, esp in the female [NL, fr LL *perinaion*, fr Gk, fr *peri-* + *inein* to empty out; akin to L *ira* ire] – **perineal** *adj*

[1]**period** /'piəri·əd/ *n* **1** a well-proportioned sentence of several clauses **2a** the full pause at the end of a sentence; *also, chiefly NAm* FULL STOP **b** a stop, end **3a** a portion of time **b** the (interval of) time that elapses before a cyclic motion or phenomenon begins to repeat itself; the reciprocal of the frequency **c** (a single cyclic occurrence of) menstruation **4a** a chronological division; a stage (of history) **b** a division of geological time longer than an epoch and included in an era **5** any of the divisions of **a** the school day **b** the playing time of a game [MF *periode*, fr ML, L, & Gk; ML *periodus* period of time, punctuation mark, fr L & Gk; L, rhetorical period, fr Gk *periodos* circuit, period of time, rhetorical period, fr *peri-* + *hodos* way – more at CEDE]

[2]**period** *adj* of, representing, or typical of a particular historical period ⟨~ *furniture*⟩

periodic /,piəri'odik/ *adj* **1** recurring at regular intervals **2** consisting of or containing a series of repeated stages ⟨~ *decimals*⟩ ⟨*a* ~ *vibration*⟩ – **periodicity** /-ə'disəti/ *n*

[1]**periodical** /,piəri'odikl/ *adj* **1** PERIODIC 1 **2** *of a magazine or journal* published at fixed intervals (e g weekly or quarterly) – **periodically** *adv*

[2]**periodical** *n* a periodical publication

periodic function *n* a mathematical function (e g a sine or cosine) whose possible values all recur at regular intervals

periodic table *n* an arrangement of chemical elements in the order of their atomic numbers, that shows a periodic variation in their properties 👁

periodontal /,peri·oh'dontl/ *adj* (of or affecting tissues) surrounding a tooth – **periodontally** *adv*

,perio'dontics /-'dontiks/ *n pl but sing or pl in constr* dentistry that deals with (diseases of) the supporting structures of the teeth [NL *periodontium*, fr *peri-* + Gk *odont-*, *odous*, *odōn* tooth – more at TOOTH] – **periodontist** *n*

,periodon'tology /don'toləji/ *n* periodontics

'period ,piece *n* a piece (e g of fiction, art, furniture, or music) whose special value lies in its evocation of a historical period

periosteum /,peri'osti·əm/ *n, pl* **periostea** /-sti·ə/ the membrane of connective tissue that closely surrounds all bones except at the joints [NL, fr LL *periosteon*, fr Gk, neut of *periosteos* round the bone, fr *peri-* + *osteon* bone – more at OSSEOUS] – **periosteal** *adj*, **periostitis** /-'stietəs/ *n*

[1]**peripatetic** /,peripə'tetik/ *n* sby, esp a teacher unattached to a particular school, or sthg that travels about from place to place (on business)

[2]**peripatetic** *adj* itinerant [MF *peripatetique*, fr Gk *peripatētikos*, fr *peripatein* to walk up and down, discourse while pacing, fr *peri-* + *patein* to tread; akin to Skt *patha* path – more at FIND] – **peripatetically** *adv*

Periodic table of chemical elements

	IA	IIA	IIIA		IVA	VA	VIA	VIIA	VIII			IB	IIB	IIIB	IVB	VB	VIB	VIIB	0
1	1 **H** Hydrogen 1.008																		2 **He** Helium 4.003
2	3 **Li** Lithium 6.94	4 **Be** Beryllium 9.012												5 **B** Boron 10.81	6 **C** Carbon 12.011	7 **N** Nitrogen 14.007	8 **O** Oxygen 15.999	9 **F** Fluorine 18.998	10 **Ne** Neon 20.17
3	11 **Na** Sodium 22.990	12 **Mg** Magnesium 24.305												13 **Al** Aluminium 26.982	14 **Si** Silicon 28.08	15 **P** Phosphorus 30.974	16 **S** Sulphur 32.06	17 **Cl** Chlorine 35.453	18 **Ar** Argon 39.94
4	19 **K** Potassium 39.09	20 **Ca** Calcium 40.08	21 **Sc** Scandium 44.956		22 **Ti** Titanium 47.9	23 **V** Vanadium 50.941	24 **Cr** Chromium 51.996	25 **Mn** Manganese 54.938	26 **Fe** Iron 55.84	27 **Co** Cobalt 58.933	28 **Ni** Nickel 58.7	29 **Cu** Copper 63.54	30 **Zn** Zinc 65.38	31 **Ga** Gallium 69.72	32 **Ge** Germanium 72.5	33 **As** Arsenic 74.922	34 **Se** Selenium 78.9	35 **Br** Bromine 79.904	36 **Kr** Krypton 83.80
5	37 **Rb** Rubidium 85.467	38 **Sr** Strontium 87.62	39 **Y** Yttrium 88.906		40 **Zr** Zirconium 91.22	41 **Nb** Niobium 92.906	42 **Mo** Molyb-denum 95.9	43 **Tc** Technetium 97	44 **Ru** Ruthenium 101.0	45 **Rh** Rhodium 102.906	46 **Pd** Palladium 106.4	47 **Ag** Silver 107.868	48 **Cd** Cadmium 112.40	49 **In** Indium 114.82	50 **Sn** Tin 118.6	51 **Sb** Antimony 121.7	52 **Te** Tellurium 127.6	53 **I** Iodine 126.905	54 **Xe** Xenon 131.30
6	55 **Cs** Caesium 132.905	56 **Ba** Barium 137.34	57 **La** Lanthanum 138.905	*	72 **Hf** Hafnium 178.4	73 **Ta** Tantalum 180.947	74 **W** Tungsten 183.8	75 **Re** Rhenium 186.2	76 **Os** Osmium 190.2	77 **Ir** Iridium 192.2	78 **Pt** Platinum 195.0	79 **Au** Gold 196.967	80 **Hg** Mercury 200.5	81 **Tl** Thallium 204.3	82 **Pb** Lead 207.2	83 **Bi** Bismuth 208.980	84 **Po** Polonium 209	85 **At** Astatine 210	86 **Rn** Radon 222
7	87 **Fr** Francium 223	88 **Ra** Radium 226.025	89 **Ac** Actinium 227	†	104 **Rf** Rutherford-ium 261	105 **Hn** Hahnium 260	106 263												

Key

4 **Be** Beryllium 9.012	atomic number symbol element atomic weight

*Lanthanide Series	58 **Ce** Cerium 140.12	59 **Pr** Praseo-dymium 140.908	60 **Nd** Neodymium 144.2	61 **Pm** Promethium 147	62 **Sm** Samarium 150.4	63 **Eu** Europium 151.96	64 **Gd** Gadolinium 157.2	65 **Tb** Terbium 158.925	66 **Dy** Dysprosium 162.5	67 **Ho** Holmium 164.930	68 **Er** Erbium 167.2	69 **Tm** Thulium 168.934	70 **Yb** Ytterbium 173.0	71 **Lu** Lutetium 174.97
†Actinide Series	90 **Th** Thorium 232.038	91 **Pa** Protactin-ium 231.036	92 **U** Uranium 238.029	93 **Np** Neptunium 237.048	94 **Pu** Plutonium 244	95 **Am** Americium 243	96 **Cm** Curium 247	97 **Bk** Berkelium 247	98 **Cf** Californium 251	99 **Es** Einsteinium 254	100 **Fm** Fermium 257	101 **Md** Mendel-evium 257	102 **No** Nobelium 255	103 **Lr** Lawrencium 256

peripatus /pə'ripətəs/ *n* any of a class of primitive tropical arthropods that in some respects are intermediate between annelid worms and typical arthropods [NL, genus name, fr Gk *peripatos* act of walking about, fr *peri-* + *patein* to tread]

peripeteia /pə,ripi'tie·ə, -'tee·ə/ *n* a sudden or unexpected reversal of circumstances or situation [Gk, fr *peripiptein* to fall round, change suddenly, fr *peri-* + *piptein* to fall – more at FEATHER]

[1]**peripheral** /pə'rif(ə)rəl/ *adj* **1** of, involving, or forming a periphery ⟨~ *nerves*⟩; *also* of minor significance **2** located away from a centre or central portion; external **3** of, using, or being the outer part of the field of vision ⟨*good* ~ *vision*⟩ **4** auxiliary or supplementary ⟨~ *equipment*⟩ – **peripherally** *adv*

[2]**peripheral** *n* a device (e g a VDU) connected to a computer to provide communication (e g input and output) or auxiliary functions (e g additional storage)

periphery /pə'rif(ə)ri/ *n* **1** the perimeter of a closed curve (e g a circle or polygon) **2** the external boundary or surface of a (person's) body, esp as distinguished from its internal regions or centre [MF *peripherie*, fr LL *peripheria*, fr Gk *periphereia*, fr *peripherein* to carry round, fr *peri-* + *pherein* to carry – more at [2]BEAR]

periphrasis /pə'rifrəsis/ *n, pl* **periphrases** /-seez/ (a) circumlocution [L, fr Gk, fr *periphrazein* to express periphrastically, fr *peri-* + *phrazein* to point out]

periphrastic /,peri'frastik/ *adj* **1** of or characterized by periphrasis **2** formed by the use of function words or auxiliaries instead of by inflection (e g *more fair* as contrasted with *fairer*) – **periphrastically** *adv*

perique /pə'reek/ *n* a rich-flavoured aromatic Louisiana tobacco [LaF *périque*]

periscope /'peri,skohp/ *n* a tubular optical instrument containing lenses, mirrors, or prisms for seeing objects not in the direct line of sight [ISV]

,peri'scopic /-'skopik/ *adj* **1** providing a view all round or on all sides ⟨*a* ~ *lens*⟩ **2** of a periscope

,perise'lene /-si'leeni/ *n* the perilune [ISV *peri-* + Gk *selēnē* moon – more at SELENIUM]

perish /'perish/ *vi* **1a** to be destroyed or ruined ⟨~ *the thought!*⟩ **b** to die, esp in a terrible or sudden way – poetic or journ **2** *chiefly Br* to deteriorate, spoil ⟨*the rubber had begun to* ~⟩ ~ *vt* , *of cold or exposure* to weaken, numb ⟨*we were* ~ed *with cold*⟩ [ME *perisshen*, fr OF *periss-*, stem of *perir*, fr L *perire*, fr *per-* to destruction + *ire* to go – more at PER-, ISSUE]

perishable /'perishəbl/ *n or adj* (sthg, esp food) liable to spoil or decay ⟨*such* ~ *products as fruit, fish, butter, and eggs*⟩ – **perishability** /-'biləti/ *n*

perisher /'perishə/ *n, Br* an annoying or troublesome person or thing; *esp* a mischievous child – infml

perishing /'perishing/ *adj* **1** freezingly cold **2** damnable, confounded – **perishingly** *adv*

peristalsis /,peri'stalsis/ *n* successive waves of involuntary contraction passing along the walls of a hollow muscular structure, esp the intestine, and forcing the contents onwards [NL, fr Gk *peristaltikos* peristaltic, fr *peristellein* to wrap round, fr *peri-* + *stellein* to place – more at [1]STALL] – **peristaltic** /-tik/ *adj*, **peristaltically** *adv*

'peri,style /-,stiel/ *n* a colonnade surrounding a building or court [F *péristyle*, fr L *peristylum*, fr Gk *peristylon*, fr neut of *peristylos* surrounded by a colonnade, fr *peri-* + *stylos* pillar – more at [2]STEER]

peritoneum /,peritoh'nee·əm/ *n, pl* **peritoneums, peritonea** /-'nee·ə/ the smooth transparent membrane that lines the cavity of the mammalian abdomen [LL, fr Gk *peritonaion*, neut of *peritonaios* stretched round, fr *peri-* + *teinein* to stretch – more at THIN] – **peritoneal** *adj*, **peritoneally** *adv*

peritonitis /,peritə'nietəs/ *n* inflammation of the peritoneum [NL]

periwig /'peri,wig/ *n* a peruke [modif of MF *perruque*] – **periwigged** /-,wigd/ *adj*

[1]**periwinkle** /'peri,wingkl/ *n* any of several trailing evergreen plants with blue or white flowers [ME *perwinke*, fr OE *perwince*, fr L *pervinca*]

[2]**periwinkle** *n* any of various (related) edible marine snails [(assumed) ME, alter. of OE *pīnewincle*, fr L *pina*, a kind of mussel (fr Gk) + OE *-wincle* (akin to Dan *vincle* snail shell)]

perjure /'puhjə/ *vt* to make (oneself) guilty of perjury [MF *perjurer*, fr L *perjurare*, fr *per-* to destruction, to the bad + *jurare* to swear – more at PER-, [1]JURY] – **perjurer** *n*

perjury /'puhj(ə)ri/ *n* the voluntary violation of an oath, esp by a witness

[1]**perk** /puhk/ *n, chiefly Br* a privilege, gain, or profit incidental to regular salary or wages [by shortening & alter. fr *perquisite*]

[2]**perk** *vi, of coffee* to percolate [by shortening & alter.]

perk up *vb* to (cause to) recover one's vigour or cheerfulness, esp after a period of weakness or depression ⟨*she* perked up *when the letter arrived*⟩ ⟨*a drink will* perk *him* up⟩ [*perk* (to thrust up the head, stick up jauntily), fr ME *perken*, perh fr ONF *perquer* to perch, fr *perque* perch, fr L *pertica* pole]

perky /'puhki/ *adj* **1** briskly self-assured; cocky ⟨*a* ~ *salesman*⟩ **2** jaunty – **perkily** *adv*, **perkiness** *n*

perlite /'puhliet/ *n* volcanic glass that has a concentric structure and when expanded by heat forms a lightweight aggregate used esp in concrete and plaster [F, fr *perle* pearl] – **perlitic** /-'litik/ *adj*

[1]**perm** /puhm/ *n* a long-lasting wave set in the hair by chemicals [short for *permanent (wave)*]

[2]**perm** *vt, Br* to give a perm to

[3]**perm** *vt, Br* to permute; *specif* to pick out and combine (a specified number of teams in a football pool) in all the possible permutations ⟨~ *any 8 from 11*⟩ – **perm** *n*

permafrost /'puhmə,frost/ *n* a layer of permanently frozen ground in frigid regions ☞ PLANT [*permanent* + *frost*]

Permalloy /'puhmə,loy/ *trademark* – used for an easily magnetized and demagnetized alloy of about 80 per cent nickel and 20 per cent iron

[1]**'permanent** /'puhmənənt/ *adj* **1** continuing or enduring without fundamental or marked change; lasting, stable **2** not subject to replacement according to political circumstances ⟨~ *undersecretary at the Home Office*⟩ [ME, fr MF, fr L *permanent-*, *permanens*, prp of *permanēre* to endure, fr *per-* throughout + *manēre* to remain – more at PER-, MANSION] – **permanence, permanency** *n*, **permanently** *adv*

[2]**permanent** *n, NAm* [1]PERM

permanent magnet *n* a magnet that retains its magnetism after removal of the magnetizing force

permanent press *n* (material subjected to) a treatment for fabric in which a chemical and heat are used for setting the shape and aiding wrinkle resistance

permanent tooth *n* any of the second set of teeth of a mammal that follow the milk teeth and typically last into old age

permanent wave *n* [1]PERM

permanent way *n, Br* the rails, sleepers, and ballast that make up the track of a railway system

permanganate /pəˈmang·gənət, -ˌnayt/ *n* a usu dark purple salt containing manganese

permeability /ˌpuhmi·əˈbiləti/ *n* **1** being permeable **2** the property of a magnetizable substance that determines the effect it has on the magnetic flux in the region it occupies

permeable /ˈpuhmi·əbl/ *adj* capable of being permeated; *esp* having pores or openings that permit liquids or gases to pass through ⟨*a ~ membrane*⟩ – **permeableness** *n*, **permeably** *adv*

permeate /ˈpuhmiˌayt/ *vi* to diffuse through or penetrate sthg ~ *vt* **1** to spread or diffuse through ⟨*a room ~d with tobacco smoke*⟩ **2** to pass through the pores, gaps, cracks, etc of [L *permeatus*, pp of *permeare*, fr *per-* through + *meare* to go, pass; akin to MW *mynet* to go] – **permeance** /-mi·əns/ *n*, **permeant** *adj or n*, **permeation** /-ˈaysh(ə)n/ *n*

Permian /ˈpuhmi·ən/ *adj or n* (of or being) the last period of the Palaeozoic era ☞ EVOLUTION [*Perm*, region in E Russia]

permissible /pəˈmisəbl/ *adj* allowable [ME, fr ML *permissibilis*, fr L *permissus*, pp] – **permissibly** *adv*, **permissibility** /-ˈbiləti/ *n*

permission /pəˈmish(ə)n/ *n* formal consent; authorization [ME, fr MF, fr L *permission-*, *permissio*, fr *permissus*, pp of *permittere*]

permissive /pəˈmisiv/ *adj* **1** tolerant; *esp* accepting a relaxed social or sexual morality ⟨*the ~ age*⟩ **2** allowing (but not enforcing) ⟨*~ legislation*⟩ [F *permissif*, fr L *permissus*, pp] – **permissively** *adv*, **permissiveness** *n*

[1]**permit** /pəˈmit/ *vb* **-tt-** *vt* **1** to consent to, usu expressly or formally ⟨*~ access to records*⟩ **2** to give leave; authorize **3** to make possible ~ *vi* to give an opportunity; allow ⟨*if time ~s*⟩ ⟨*weather ~ting*⟩ [L *permittere* to let through, permit, fr *per-* through + *mittere* to let go, send – more at PER-, SMITE] – **permitter** *n*

[2]**permit** /ˈpuhmit/ *n* a written warrant allowing the holder to do or keep sthg ⟨*a gun ~*⟩

permittivity /ˌpuhmiˈtivəti/ *n* (a measure of) the ability of a dielectric material to store electrical potential energy under the influence of an electric field [[1]*permit* + *-ive* + *-ity*]

permutation /ˌpuhmyooˈtaysh(ə)n/ *n* **1** a variation or change (e g in character or condition) brought about by rearrangement of existing elements **2** (the changing from one to another of) any of the various possible ordered arrangements of a set of objects, numbers, letters, etc [ME *permutacioun* exchange, transformation, fr MF *permutation*, fr L *permutation-*, *permutatio*, fr *permutatus*, pp of *permutare*] – **permutational** *adj*

permute /pəˈmyooht/ *vt* to change the order or arrangement of; *esp* to arrange successively in all possible ways [ME *permuten*, fr MF or L; MF *permuter*, fr L *permutare*, fr *per-* + *mutare* to change – more at [1]MISS]

pernicious /pəˈnishəs, puh-/ *adj* highly injurious or destructive; deadly [MF *pernicieus*, fr L *perniciosus*, fr *pernicies* destruction, fr *per-* + *nec-*, *nex* violent death – more at NOXIOUS] – **perniciously** *adv*, **perniciousness** *n*

pernicious anaemia *n* anaemia marked by a decrease in the number of red blood cells which is caused by a reduced ability to absorb vitamin B_{12}

pernickety /pəˈnikəti/ *adj* **1** fussy about small details; fastidious ⟨*a ~ teacher*⟩ **2** requiring precision and care ⟨*a ~ job*⟩ [perh alter. of *particular*]

peroneal /ˌperəˈnee·əl/ *adj* of or near the fibula [NL *peroneus*, fr *perone* fibula, fr Gk *peronē*, lit., pin; akin to L *per* through – more at FOR]

peroration /ˌperəˈraysh(ə)n/ *n* **1** the concluding part of a discourse, in which the main points are summed up **2** a highly rhetorical speech [ME *peroracyon*, fr L *peroration-*, *peroratio*, fr *peroratus*, pp of *perorare* to speak at length, finish speaking, fr *per-* through + *orare* to speak – more at PER-, ORATION] – **perorational** *adj*, **perorate** /ˈperərayt/ *vi*

[1]**peroxide** /pəˈroksied/ *n* **1** an oxide containing a high proportion of oxygen; *esp* a compound containing the peroxy radical **2** HYDROGEN PEROXIDE [ISV] – **peroxidic** /-ˈsidik/ *adj*

[2]**peroxide** *vt* to bleach (hair) with hydrogen peroxide – **peroxidation** /-siˈdaysh(ə)n/ *n*

peroxy /pəˈroksi/ *n* the bivalent chemical radical –O–O– – usu in combination [ISV *per-* + *oxy-*]

[1]**perpendicular** /ˌpuhpənˈdikyoolə/ *adj* **1** being or standing at right angles to the plane of the horizon or a given line or plane **2** extremely steep; precipitous **3** *cap* of, being, or built in a late Gothic style of architecture prevalent in England from the 15th to the 16th c characterized by large windows, fan vaults, and an emphasis on vertical lines ☞ CHURCH [ME *perpendiculer*, fr MF, fr L *perpendicularis*, fr *perpendiculum* plumb line, fr *per-* + *pendēre* to hang – more at PENDANT] – **perpendicularly** *adv*, **perpendicularity** /-ˈlarəti/ *n*

[2]**perpendicular** *n* a line, plane, or surface at right angles to the plane of the horizon or to another line or surface

perpetrate /ˈpuhpiˌtrayt/ *vt* to be guilty of performing or doing; commit ⟨*~ a fraud*⟩ ⟨*~ a blunder*⟩ [L *perpetratus*, pp of *perpetrare*, fr *per-* through + *patrare* to accomplish] – **perpetrator** *n*, **perpetration** /-ˈtraysh(ə)n/ *n*

perpetual /pəˈpetyoo(ə)l, -choo(ə)l/ *adj* **1a** continuing or valid forever; everlasting **b** holding sthg (e g an office) for life or for an unlimited time **2** occurring continually; constant ⟨*a ~ complaint*⟩ **3** *of a plant* blooming continuously throughout the season [ME *perpetuel*, fr MF, fr L *perpetuus*, fr *per-* through + *petere* to go to – more at FEATHER] – **perpetually** *adv*

perpetual check *n* an endless succession of checks in chess which results in a draw

perpetuate /pəˈpetyooˌayt, -chooˌayt/ *vt* to make perpetual; cause to last indefinitely ⟨*~ the species*⟩ [L *perpetuatus*, pp of *perpetuare*, fr *perpetuus*] – **perpetuator** *n*, **perpetuation** /-ˈaysh(ə)n/ *n*

perpetuity /ˌpuhpiˈtyooh·əti/ *n* (the quality or state of) sthg that is perpetual; eternity ⟨*bequeathed to* *them in* ~⟩ [ME *perpetuite*, fr MF *perpetuité*, fr L *perpetuitat-, perpetuitas*, fr *perpetuus*]

perplex /pə'pleks/ *vt* **1** to puzzle, confuse ⟨*her attitude* ~es *me*⟩ ⟨*a* ~ing *problem*⟩ **2** to complicate [obs *perplex*, adj (involved, perplexed), fr L *perplexus*, fr *per-* thoroughly + *plexus* involved, fr pp of *plectere* to braid, twine – more at PER-, [1]PLY] – **perplexedly** /-sidli/ *adv*, **perplexingly** *adv*

perplexity /pə'pleksəti/ *n* (sthg that causes) the state of being perplexed or bewildered [ME *perplexite*, fr OF *perplexité*, fr LL *perplexitat-, perplexitas*, fr L *perplexus*]

perquisite /'puhkwizit/ *n* **1** sthg held or claimed as an exclusive right or possession **2** a perk – fml [ME, property acquired by other means than inheritance, fr ML *perquisitum*, fr neut of *perquisitus*, pp of *perquirere* to purchase, acquire, fr L, to search for thoroughly, fr *per-* thoroughly + *quaerere* to seek]

perry /'peri/ *n* an alcoholic drink made from fermented pear juice [ME *peirrie*, fr MF *peré*, fr (assumed) VL *piratum*, fr L *pirum* pear]

perse /puhs/ *adj or n* dark greyish blue [adj ME *pers*, fr MF, fr ML *persus*, prob fr L *Persa* Persian; n fr adj]

per se /pə 'say/ *adv* by, of, or in itself; intrinsically [L]

persecute /'puhsi,kyooht/ *vt* **1** to harass in a manner designed to injure or afflict; *specif* to cause to suffer because of race, religion, political beliefs, etc **2** to annoy with persistent or urgent approaches, attacks, pleas, etc; pester [MF *persecuter*, back-formation fr *persecuteur* persecutor, fr LL *persecutor*, fr *persecutus*, pp of *persequi* to persecute, fr L, to pursue, fr *per-* through + *sequi* to follow – more at SUE] – **persecutor** *n*, **persecution** /-'kyoohsh(ə)n/ *n*, **persecutory** /-'kyooht(ə)ri/ *adj*

perseverance /,puhsi'viərəns/ *n* **1** persevering, steadfastness **2** continuance in a state of grace

perseveration /puh,sevə'raysh(ə)n/ *n* continuation of sthg (e g repetition of a word) usu to an excessive or exceptional degree [L *perseveration-, perseveratio*, fr *perseveratus*, pp of *perseverare*] – **perseverate** /-'sevərayt/ *vi*

persevere /,puhsi'viə/ *vi* to persist in a state, enterprise, or undertaking in spite of adverse influences, opposition, or discouragement [ME *perseveren*, fr MF *perseverer*, fr L *perseverare*, fr *per-* through + *severus* severe]

Persian /'puhsh(ə)n, *also* -zh(ə)n/ *n or adj* (a native, inhabitant, or language) of ancient Persia or modern Iran [*Persia* (now Iran), country in SW Asia]

Persian cat *n* a short-nosed domestic cat with long silky fur

Persian lamb *n* (the pelt, characterized by very silky tightly curled fur, of) the young of the karakul sheep

persiflage /'puhsi,flahzh/ *n* frivolous bantering talk [F, fr *persifler* to banter, fr *per-* thoroughly + *siffler* to whistle, hiss, boo, fr L *sibilare*, of imit origin]

persimmon /puh'simən/ *n* (the orange several-seeded globular fruit of) any of a genus of American and Asian trees of the ebony family with hard fine wood [of Algonquian origin; akin to Cree *pasiminan* dried fruit]

persist /pə'sist/ *vi* **1** to go on resolutely or stubbornly in spite of opposition or warning **2** to be insistent in the repetition or pressing of an utterance (e g a question or opinion) **3** to continue to exist, esp past a usual, expected, or normal time [MF *persister*, fr L *persistere*, fr *per-* + *sistere* to take a stand, stand firm; akin to L *stare* to stand – more at STAND] – **persister** *n*

persistent /pə'sist(ə)nt/ *adj* **1** continuing to exist in spite of interference or treatment ⟨*a* ~ *cough*⟩ **2a** remaining (1) beyond the usual period ⟨*a* ~ *leaf*⟩ (2) without change in function or structure ⟨~ *gills*⟩ **b** *of a chemical substance* broken down only slowly in the environment ⟨~ *pesticides*⟩ [L *persistent-, persistens*, prp of *persistere*] – **persistence, persistency** *n*, **persistently** *adv*

persnickety /pə'snikəti/ *adj, NAm* **1** pernickety **2** snobbish [alter. of *pernickety*]

person /'puhs(ə)n/ *n* **1** a human being (considered as having a character of his/her own, or as being different from all others) ⟨*you're just the* ~ *I wanted to see*⟩ **2** any of the 3 modes of being in the Trinity as understood by Christians **3** a living human body or its outward appearance ⟨*she was small and neat of* ~⟩ ⟨*insured against damage to* ~ *and property*⟩ **4** an individual, corporation, etc with recognized legal rights and duties **5** any of 3 forms of verb or pronoun that indicate reference to the speaker, to one spoken to, or to sby or sthg spoken of [ME, fr OF *persone*, fr L *persona* actor's mask, character in a play, person, prob fr Etruscan *phersu* mask] – **in person** in one's own bodily presence ⟨*he appeared* in person *last time*⟩

persona /puh'sohnə/ *n, pl* (*1*) **personae** /-ni/, (*2*) **personas** **1** *pl* the characters in a fictional work **2** an individual's social facade that, esp in Jungian psychology, reflects the role that the individual is playing in life – compare ANIMA [L]

personable /'puhs(ə)nəbl/ *adj* pleasing in person; attractive – **personableness** *n*

personage /'puhs(ə)nij/ *n* **1** a person of rank, note, or distinction; *esp* one distinguished in presence and personal power **2** a dramatic, fictional, or historical character **3** a human individual; a person – fml

personal /'puhs(ə)nl/ *adj* **1** of or affecting a person; private ⟨*done purely for* ~ *financial gain*⟩ **2a** done in person without the intervention of another; *also* proceeding from a single person **b** carried on between individuals directly ⟨*a* ~ *interview*⟩ **3** of the person or body **4** of or referring to (the character, conduct, motives, or private affairs of) an individual, often in an offensive manner ⟨*don't make* ~ *remarks*⟩ **5** of personal property ⟨*a* ~ *estate*⟩ **6** denoting grammatical person [ME, fr MF, fr LL *personalis*, fr L *persona*]

personal equation *n* (a correction made for) variation (e g in astronomical observation) due to a person's individual peculiarities

personality /'puhs(ə)n'aləti/ *n* **1** *pl* reference, esp critical, to a particular person ⟨*let's keep* personalities *out of this debate*⟩ **2** the totality of an individual's behavioural and emotional tendencies; *broadly* a distinguishing complex of individual or group characteristics **3a** (sby having) distinction or excellence of personal and social traits **b** a person of importance, prominence, renown, or notoriety ⟨*a well-known stage* ~⟩ [ME *personalite*, fr LL *personalitat-, personalitas*, fr *personalis*]

person'ality ,cult *n* the officially encouraged slavish admiration of a leader

personal·ize, -ise /'puhs(ə)nl,iez/ *vt* **1** PERSONIFY 1 **2** to make personal or individual; *specif* to mark as the property of a particular person ⟨~d *stationery*⟩ – **personalization** /-'zaysh(ə)n/ *n*

personally /'puhs(ə)nli/ *adv* **1** IN PERSON ⟨*attend to the matter* ~⟩ **2** as a person; in personality ⟨~ *attractive but not very trustworthy*⟩ **3** for oneself; as far as oneself is concerned ⟨~, *I don't think much of it*⟩ **4** as directed against oneself in a personal way ⟨*don't take my remarks about your plan* ~⟩

personal pronoun *n* a pronoun (e g *I, you,* or *they*) that expresses a distinction of person

personal property *n* all property other than freehold estates and interests in land

personalty /'puhs(ə)nlti/ *n* PERSONAL PROPERTY [AF *personalté,* fr LL *personalitat-, personalitas* personality]

persona non grata /puh,sohnə non 'grahtə/ *adj* personally unacceptable or unwelcome [NL, person not acceptable]

personate /'puhs(ə)nayt/ *vt* **1** to impersonate, represent **2** to assume (some character or capacity) with fraudulent intent – **personator** *n,* **personative** /-ətiv/ adj, **personation** /-'aysh(ə)n/ *n*

personification /pə,sonifi'kaysh(ə)n/ *n* **1** the personifying of an abstract quality or thing **2** an embodiment, incarnation

personify /pə'sonifie/ *vt* **1** to conceive of or represent as having human qualities or form **2** to be the embodiment of in human form; incarnate ⟨*he was kindness* personified⟩ – **personifier** *n*

personnel /,puhsə'nel/ *n* **1** *sing or pl in constr* a body of people employed (e g in a factory, office, or organization) or engaged on a project **2** a division of an organization concerned with the employees and their welfare at work [F, fr G *personale, personal,* fr ML *personale,* fr LL, neut of *personalis* personal]

[1]**perspective** /pə'spektiv/ *adj* of, using, or seen in perspective ⟨*a* ~ *drawing*⟩ – **perspectively** *adv*

[2]**perspective** *n* **1a** (the technique of accurately representing on a flat or curved surface) the visual appearance of solid objects with respect to their relative distance and position **b** LINEAR PERSPECTIVE **2a** the aspect of an object of thought from a particular standpoint ⟨*try to get a different* ~ *on your problem*⟩ **b** (the capacity to discern) the true relationship or relative importance of things ⟨*get things in* ~⟩ **3** a picture or view giving a distinctive impression of distance; a vista [MF, fr ML *perspectiva,* fr fem of *perspectivus* of sight, optical, fr L *perspectus,* pp of *perspicere* to look through, see clearly, fr *per-* through + *specere* to look – more at PER-, SPY]

Perspex /'puh,speks/ *trademark* – used for a transparent acrylic plastic

perspicacious /,puhspi'kayshəs/ *adj* of acute mental vision or discernment; KEEN 3a – fml [L *perspicac-, perspicax,* fr *perspicere*] – **perspicaciously** *adv,* **perspicaciousness** *n,* **perspicacity** /-'kasəti/ *n*

perspicuous /pə'spikyoo·əs/ *adj* plain to the understanding, esp because of clarity and precision of presentation ⟨*a* ~ *argument*⟩ – fml [L *perspicuus* transparent, perspicuous, fr *perspicere*] – **perspicuously** *adv,* **perspicuousness** *n,* **perspicuity** /,puhspi'kyooh·əti/ *n*

perspiration /,puhspi'raysh(ə)n/ *n* **1** sweating **2** [2]SWEAT 1 – **perspiratory** /pə'spie·ərət(ə)ri/ *adj*

perspire /pə'spie·ə/ *vi* [1]SWEAT 1 [F *perspirer,* fr MF, fr L *per-* through + *spirare* to blow, breathe – more at PER-, SPIRIT]

persuade /pə'swayd/ *vt* **1** to move by argument, reasoning, or entreaty to a belief, position, or course of action **2** to cause to feel certain; convince ⟨*the icy roads* ~d *him of the need to drive carefully*⟩ **3** to get (sthg) with difficulty *out of* or *from* ⟨*finally* ~d *an answer out of her*⟩ [L *persuadēre,* fr *per-* thoroughly + *suadēre* to advise, urge] – **persuadable** *adj,* **persuader** *n*

persuasible /pə'swaysəbl, -zəbl/ *adj* persuadable [MF, fr L *persuasibilis* persuasive, fr *persuasus*]

persuasion /pə'swayzh(ə)n/ *n* **1a** persuading or being persuaded **b** persuasiveness ⟨*she has great powers of* ~⟩ **2a** an opinion held with complete assurance **b** (a group adhering to) a particular system of religious beliefs **3** a kind, sort ⟨*people of the same* ~⟩ [ME *persuasioun,* fr MF or L; MF *persuasion,* fr L *persuasion-, persuasio,* fr *persuasus,* pp of *persuadēre*]

persuasive /pə'swaysiv, -ziv/ *adj* tending or able to persuade – **persuasively** *adv,* **persuasiveness** *n*

pert /puht/ *adj* **1** impudent and forward; saucy **2** trim and chic; jaunty ⟨*a* ~ *little hat*⟩ [ME, open, bold, forward, modif of OF *apert,* fr L *apertus* open, fr pp of *aperire* to open] – **pertly** *adv,* **pertness** *n*

pertain /pə'tayn/ *vi* **1a** to belong *to* as a part, attribute, feature, function, or right ⟨*the destruction and havoc* ~ing *to war*⟩ **b** to be appropriate to sthg ⟨*the criteria that* ~ *elsewhere do not apply here*⟩ **2** to have reference *to* ⟨*books* ~ing *to birds*⟩ [ME *perteinen,* fr MF *partenir,* fr L *pertinēre* to reach to, belong, fr *per-* through + *tenēre* to hold]

pertinacious /,puhti'nayshəs/ *adj* clinging resolutely to an opinion, purpose, or design, often to the point of stubbornness – fml [L *pertinac-, pertinax,* fr *per-* thoroughly + *tenac-, tenax* tenacious, fr *tenēre*] – **pertinaciously** *adv,* **pertinaciousness** *n,* **pertinacity** /-'nasəti/ *n*

pertinent /'puhtinənt/ *adj* clearly relevant (to the matter in hand) ⟨~ *details*⟩ [ME, fr MF, fr L *pertinent-, pertinens,* prp of *pertinēre*] – **pertinence, pertinency** *n,* **pertinently** *adv*

perturb /pə'tuhb, puh-/ *vt* **1** to disturb greatly in mind; disquiet **2** to throw into confusion; disorder **3** to cause (a moving object, celestial body, etc) to deviate from a theoretically regular (orbital) motion [ME *perturben,* fr MF *perturber,* fr L *perturbare* to throw into confusion, fr *per-* + *turbare* to disturb – more at TURBID] – **perturbable** *adj,* **perturbation** /,puhtə'baysh(ə)n/ *n,* **perturbational** *adj*

pertussis /pə'tusis/ *n* WHOOPING COUGH [NL, fr L *per-* thoroughly + *tussis* cough]

peruke /pə'roohk/ *n* a long curly wig worn by men in the 17th and 18th c [MF *perruque,* fr OIt *parrucca, perrucca* hair, wig]

peruse /pə'roohz/ *vt* **1** to examine or consider with attention and in detail; study – fml **2** to look over the contents of (e g a book) – often humor [ME *perusen,* prob fr L *per-* thoroughly + ME *usen* to use] – **perusal** *n,* **peruser** *n*

pervade /pə'vayd, puh-/ *vt* to become diffused throughout every part of [L *pervadere* to go through, pervade, fr *per-* through + *vadere* to go – more at PER-, WADE] – **pervasion** /-zh(ə)n/ *n,* **pervasive** /-siv, -ziv/ *adj,* **pervasively** *adv,* **pervasiveness** *n*

perverse /pə'vuhs, puh-/ *adj* **1a** obstinate in opposing what is right, reasonable, or accepted; wrongheaded **b** arising from or indicative of stubbornness or obstinacy **2** unreasonably opposed to the wishes of others; uncooperative, contrary [ME, fr L *perversus*, fr pp of *pervertere*] – **perversely** *adv*, **perversity, perverseness** *n*

perversion /pə'vuhsh(ə)n, puh-/ *n* **1** perverting or being perverted **2** sthg perverted; *esp* abnormal sexual behaviour – **perversive** /-siv/ *adj*

[1]**pervert** /pə'vuht/ *vt* **1** to cause to turn aside or away from what is good, true, or morally right; corrupt **2a** to divert to a wrong end or purpose; misuse **b** to twist the meaning or sense of; misinterpret [ME *perverten*, fr MF *pervertir*, fr L *pervertere* to overturn, corrupt, pervert, fr *per-* thoroughly + *vertere* to turn – more at PER-, [1]WORTH] – **perverter** *n*

[2]**pervert** /'puhvuht/ *n* a perverted person; *specif* one given to some form of sexual perversion

perverted /pə'vuhtid, puh-/ *adj* **1** CORRUPT 1 **2** marked by perversion – **pervertedly** *adv*, **pervertedness** *n*

pervious /'puhvi·əs, -vyəs/ *adj* **1** permeable ⟨~ *soil*⟩ **2** accessible *to* ⟨~ *to reason*⟩ – fml [L *pervius*, fr *per-* through + *via* way – more at PER, VIA] – **perviousness** *n*

pesante /pe'zantay/ *adv* in a heavy manner – used as a direction in music [It, fr prp of *pesare* to weigh, fr L *pensare* to ponder – more at PENSIVE]

peseta /pə'seetə, pə'saytə/ *n* ☞ *Spain* at NATIONALITY [Sp, dim. of *peso*]

pesewa /pi'saywah/ *n, pl* **pesewas** ☞ *Ghana* at NATIONALITY [Fante]

pesky /'peski/ *adj, NAm* troublesome, vexatious – infml [prob irreg fr *pest* + *-y*]

peso /'paysoh/ *n, pl* **pesos** **1** a former silver coin of Spain and Spanish America worth 8 reals **2** (a note or coin representing) the basic money unit of certain Spanish-speaking South and Latin American countries (e g Argentina, Chile, Mexico, Uruguay) and the Philippines ☞ NATIONALITY [Sp, lit., weight, fr L *pensum* – more at [2]POISE]

pessary /'pesəri/ *n* **1** a vaginal suppository **2** a device worn in the vagina to support the uterus or prevent conception [ME *pessarie*, fr LL *pessarium*, fr *pessus, pessum*, fr Gk *pessos* oval stone for playing draughts, pessary]

pessimism /'pesi,miz(ə)m/ *n* **1** a tendency to stress the adverse aspects of a situation or event or to expect the worst possible outcome **2** the doctrine that this is the worst of all possible worlds [F *pessimisme*, fr L *pessimus* worst – more at PEJORATIVE] – **pessimist** *n*, **pessimistic** /-'mistik/ *adj*, **pessimistically** *adv*

pest /pest/ *n* **1** a pestilence **2** a plant or animal capable of causing damage or carrying disease **3** sby or sthg that pesters or annoys; a nuisance [MF *peste*, fr L *pestis*]

pester /'pestə/ *vt* to harass with petty irritations; annoy [modif of MF *empestrer* to hobble, embarrass, fr (assumed) VL *impastoriare*, fr L *in-* + (assumed) VL *pastoria* hobble, fr L *pastor* herdsman – more at PASTOR]

pesticide /'pestisied/ *n* a chemical used to destroy insects and other pests of crops, domestic animals, etc

pestiferous /pe'stif(ə)rəs/ *adj* **1** dangerous to society; pernicious **2** carrying or propagating infection [ME, fr L *pestifer* pestilential, noxious, fr *pestis* + *-fer* -ferous] – **pestiferously** *adv*

pestilence /'pestiləns/ *n* a virulent and devastating epidemic disease; *specif* BUBONIC PLAGUE

pestilent /'pestilənt/ *adj* **1** destructive of life; deadly **2** morally harmful; pernicious **3** causing displeasure or annoyance; irritating [ME, fr L *pestilent-, pestilens* pestilential, fr *pestis*] – **pestilently** *adv*

pestilential /,pesti'lensh(ə)l/ *adj* pestilent – **pestilentially** *adv*

[1]**pestle** /'pesl/ *n* **1** a usu club-shaped implement for pounding substances in a mortar **2** any of various devices for pounding, stamping, or pressing [ME *pestel*, fr MF, fr L *pistillum*; akin to MLG *vīsel* pestle, L *pilum* pestle, javelin, *pinsere* to pound, crush]

[2]**pestle** *vb* to pound or pulverize (as if) with a pestle

[1]**pet** /pet/ *n* **1** a domesticated animal kept for companionship rather than work or food **2** sby who is treated with unusual kindness or consideration; a favourite **3** *chiefly Br* DARLING 1 – used chiefly by women as an affectionate form of address [perh back-formation fr ME *pety* small – more at PETTY]

[2]**pet** *adj* **1a** kept or treated as a pet **b** for pet animals ⟨*a* ~ *shop*⟩ **2** expressing fondness or endearment ⟨*a* ~ *name*⟩ **3** favourite ⟨*his* ~ *project*⟩

[3]**pet** *vb* **-tt-** *vt* **1** to stroke in a gentle or loving manner **2** to treat with unusual kindness and consideration; pamper ~ *vi* to engage in amorous embracing, caressing, etc – **petter** *n*

[4]**pet** *n* a fit of peevishness, sulkiness, or anger [origin unknown]

peta- *comb form* thousand billion (10^{15}) ☞ PHYSICS [ISV, perh fr Gk *peta-* (in *petannynai* to spread out, *petasma* sthg spread out)]

petal /'petl/ *n* any of the modified often brightly coloured leaves of the corolla of a flower ☞ PLANT [NL *petalum*, fr Gk *petalon*; akin to Gk *petannynai* to spread out – more at FATHOM] – **petaled, petalled** *adj*, **petallike** *adj*, **petaloid** /-oyd/ *adj*

petalous /'petl·əs/ *adj* having (such or so many) petals – usu in combination ⟨*poly*petalous⟩

petard /pe'tahd, pi-/ *n* **1** a case containing an explosive for military demolitions **2** a firework that explodes with a loud report [MF, fr *peter* to break wind, fr *pet* expulsion of wind, fr L *peditum*, fr neut of *peditus*, pp of *pedere* to break wind; akin to Gk *bdein* to break wind]

peter /'peetə/ *vi* to diminish gradually and come to an end; give out – usu + *out* [origin unknown]

Peter *n* (either of 2 New Testament epistles attributed to) a fisherman of Galilee and one of the 12 apostles [LL *Petrus*, fr Gk *Petros*, fr *petra* rock]

,**Peter 'Pan** /pan/ *n* a male who seems never to age [*Peter Pan*, hero of the play *Peter Pan, or the boy who wouldn't grow up* by Sir James Barrie †1937 Sc novelist & dramatist]

Peter Pan collar *n* a usu small flat collar attached to a round neck and with rounded ends that meet in front

petersham /'peetəshəm/ *n* **1** (a coat made of) a rough nubbly woollen cloth **2** a heavy corded ribbon used for belts and put round hats [Charles Stanhope, Lord *Petersham* †1851 E colonel]

Peter's pence *n pl but sing in constr* an annual tribute of a penny formerly paid by each householder in England to the papal see [fr the tradition that St Peter founded the papal see]

pethidine /'pethideen, -din/ *n* a synthetic narcotic

drug with actions and uses similar to those of morphine but with less sedative effect [perh blend of *piperidine* and *ethyl*]

petillant /ˈpetiyohn (*Fr* petijɑ̃)/ *adj, of wine* mildly effervescent [F *pétillant*, prp of *pétiller* to effervesce with a crackling sound, fr MF *petiller* to crackle, fr *peter* to break wind – more at PETARD]

petiole /ˈpeti·ohl/ *n* the usu slender stalk by which a leaf is attached to a stem [NL *petiolus*, fr L, small foot, fruit stalk, alter. of *pediculus*, dim. of *ped-*, *pes* foot – more at FOOT] – **petiolated** *adj*, **petioled, petiolate** /-layt, -lət/ *adj*, **petiolar** /ˌpetiˈohlə/ *adj*

petit bourgeois /ˌpeti ˈbooəzh·wah (*Fr* pəti burʒwa)/ *n, pl* **petits bourgeois** /~/ a member of the petite bourgeoisie [F, lit., small bourgeois] – **petit bourgeois** *adj*

petite /pəˈteet/ *adj, esp of a woman* having a small trim figure [F, fem of *petit* small]

petite bourgeoisie /pəˌteet booəzh·wahˈzee (*Fr* pətit burʒwazi)/ *n sing or pl in constr* the lower middle class [F, lit., small bourgeoisie]

petit four /ˌpeti ˈfaw (*Fr* pəti fur)/ *n, pl* **petits fours, petit fours** /fawz (*Fr* ~)/ a small fancy cake or biscuit [F, lit., small oven]

[1]**petition** /piˈtish(ə)n/ *n* **1** an earnest request; an entreaty **2** (a document embodying) a formal written request to a superior **3** sthg asked or requested [ME, fr MF, fr L *petition-*, *petitio*, fr *petitus*, pp of *petere* to seek, request – more at FEATHER] – **petitionary** *adj*

[2]**petition** *vb* to make an esp formal written request (to or for) – **petitioner** *n*

petitio principii /piˌtishi·oh prinˈkipi·ie/ *n* a logical fallacy in which a premise is assumed to be true without justification [ML, lit., postulation of the beginning, begging the question]

petit mal /ˌpeti ˈmal/ *n* (an attack of) mild epilepsy – compare GRAND MAL [F, lit., small illness]

petit point /ˌpeti ˈpoynt (*Fr* pəti pwɛ̃)/ *n* TENT STITCH; *also* needlepoint embroidery worked on canvas across single threads in tent stitch – compare GROS POINT [F, lit., small point]

petit pois /ˌpeti ˈpwah, pəˌtee- (*Fr* pəti pwa)/ *n, pl* **petits pois** /pwɑh(z) (*Fr* ~)/ a small young slightly sweet green pea [F, small pea]

petr-, petri-, petro- *comb form* stone; rock ⟨petro*logy*⟩ [NL, fr Gk *petr-*, *petro-*, fr *petros* stone & *petra* rock]

Petrarchan sonnet /piˈtrahkən, pe-, pee-/ *n* a sonnet consisting of an octave rhyming *abba abba* and a sestet rhyming in any of various patterns (e g *cde cde* or *cdc cdc*) [*Petrarch* (Francesco *Petrarca*) †1374 It poet]

petrel /ˈpetrəl/ *n* any of numerous seabirds; *esp* any of the smaller long-winged birds (e g a storm petrel) that fly far from land [alter. of earlier *pitteral*]

petri dish /ˈpeetri/ *n* a small shallow glass or plastic dish with a loose cover used esp for cultures of microorganisms (e g bacteria) [Julius *Petri* †1921 G bacteriologist]

petrifaction /ˌpetriˈfaksh(ə)n/ *n* **1** the process of petrifying; being petrified **2** sthg petrified

petrification /ˌpetrifiˈkaysh(ə)n/ *n* petrifaction

petrify /ˈpetrifie/ *vt* **1** to convert (as if) into stone or a stony substance **2a** to make lifeless or inactive; deaden **b** to confound with fear, amazement, or awe; paralyse ⟨*is* petrified *of talking in public* – Alan Frank⟩ ~ *vi* to become stone or of stony hardness or rigidity [MF *petrifier*, fr *petr-* + *-ifier* -ify]

Petrine /ˈpeetrien/ *adj* **1** of (the doctrines associated with) the apostle Peter **2** of Peter the Great [LL *Petrus* Peter]

petrochemical /ˌpetrohˈkemikl, -trə-/ *n* a chemical obtained from petroleum or natural gas [*petro*leum + *chemical*] – **petrochemical** *adj*, **petrochemistry** /-ˈkemistri/ *n*

ˈ**petroˌdollar** /-ˌdolə/ *n* a unit of foreign exchange obtained by a petroleum-exporting country by sales abroad [*petro*leum + *dollar*]

petrography /peˈtrografi/ *n* the description and systematic classification of rocks [NL *petrographia*, fr *petr-* + L *-graphia* -graphy] – **petrographer** *n*, **petrographic** /ˌpetrəˈgrafik/, **petrographical** *adj*, **petrographically** *adv*

petrol /ˈpetrəl/ *n, chiefly Br* a volatile inflammable liquid hydrocarbon mixture refined from petroleum and used as a fuel for internal-combustion engines ☞ CAR [F *essence de pétrole*, lit., essence of petroleum]

petrolatum /ˌpetrəˈlaytəm/ *n* PETROLEUM JELLY [NL, fr ML *petroleum*]

petroleum /pəˈtrohli·əm, -lyəm/ *n* an oily inflammable usu dark liquid composed of a mixture of hydrocarbons, widely occurring in the upper strata of the earth, and refined for use as petrol, naphtha, etc ☞ ENERGY [ML, fr L *petr-* + *oleum* oil – more at OIL]

peˌtroleum ˈjelly *n* a semisolid mixture of hydrocarbons obtained from petroleum and used esp as the basis of ointments

petrology /peˈtroləji/ *n* a science that deals with the origin, structure, composition, etc of rocks [ISV] – **petrologist** *n*, **petrologic** /ˌpetrəˈlojik/, **petrological** *adj*, **petrologically** *adv*

ˈ**petrol ˌstation** *n, Br* FILLING STATION

petrous /ˈpetrəs, ˈpee-/ *adj* resembling stone, esp in hardness; *specif* of or being the hard dense part of the human temporal bone that contains the internal hearing organs [MF *petreux*, fr L *petrosus*, fr *petra* rock, fr Gk]

[1]**petticoat** /ˈpetiˌkoht/ *n* **1** an outer skirt formerly worn by women and small children **2** a skirt designed to be worn as an undergarment [ME *petycote* short tunic, petticoat, fr *pety* small + *cote* coat] – **petticoated** *adj*

[2]**petticoat** *adj* of or exercised by women; female ⟨~ *government*⟩ – chiefly humor or derog

pettifog /ˈpetiˌfog/ *vi* **-gg-** **1** to engage in legal chicanery **2** to quibble over insignificant details [back-formation fr *pettifogger*, prob fr *petty* + obs E *fogger* (perh fr *Fugger*, 15th & 16th-c G family of financiers & merchants)] **pettifogger** *n*, **pettifoggery** *n*

pettitoes /ˈpetiˌtohz/ *n pl* the feet of a pig used as food [pl of obs *pettytoe* (offal), fr MF *petite oye* small goose, goose-giblets]

petty /ˈpeti/ *adj* **1** having secondary rank or importance; *also* trivial **2** small-minded [ME *pety* small, minor, alter. of *petit*, fr MF] – **pettiness** *n*, **pettily** *adv*

petty bourgeois *n* PETIT BOURGEOIS

ˌ**petty ˈcash** *n* cash kept on hand for payment of minor items

ˌ**petty ˈlarceny** *n, NAm* larceny involving property

below a value specified by law – no longer used technically in the UK

petty officer *n* – compare NONCOMMISSIONED OFFICER ☞ RANK

petty officer first class *n* ☞ RANK

petty officer second class *n* ☞ RANK

petty officer third class *n* ☞ RANK

petulant /'petyoolənt/ *adj* characterized by temporary or capricious ill humour; peevish [L or MF; MF, fr L *petulant-, petulans*; akin to L *petere* to go to, attack, seek – more at FEATHER] – **petulance** *n*, **petulantly** *adv*

petunia /pi'tyoohnyə, -ni·ə/ *n* any of a genus of plants of the nightshade family with large brightly coloured funnel-shaped flowers [NL, genus name, fr obs F *petun* tobacco, fr Tupi *petyn*]

pew /pyooh/ *n* **1** a bench fixed in a row for the use of the congregation in a church; *also* a high compartment with such benches for the accommodation of a group (e g a family) **2** *Br* a seat ⟨*take a* ~⟩ – infml [ME *pewe*, fr MF *puie* balustrade, fr L *podia*, pl of *podium* parapet, podium, fr Gk *podion* base, dim. of *pod-, pous* foot – more at FOOT]

pewit /'pee,wit/ *n* a peewit

pewter /'pyoohtə/ *n* (utensils, vessels, etc made of) any of various tin-containing alloys; *esp* one of tin and lead [ME, fr MF *peutre*; akin to It *peltro* pewter] – **pewter** *adj*

pewterer /'pyooht(ə)rə/ *n* one who works with pewter (and makes utensils or vessels)

peyote /pay'ohti, pi-/ *n* **1** any of several American cacti; *esp* MESCAL 1 **2** MESCAL BUTTON; *also* mescaline [Mex Sp, fr Nahuatl *peyotl*]

peyotl /pay'ohtl/ *n* peyote

pfennig /'(p)fenig, -nikh (*Ger* 'pfɛniç)/ *n, pl* **pfennigs, pfennige** /-nigə (*Ger* -nigə)/ *often cap* ☞ *Germany (Federal Republic), Germany (Democratic Republic)* at NATIONALITY [G, fr OHG *pfenning* – more at PENNY]

pH /,pee 'aych/ *n* the negative logarithm of the hydrogen-ion concentration in moles per litre, used to express the acidity or alkalinity of a solution on a scale of 0 to 14 with 7 representing neutrality [G, fr *potenz* power + *H*, symbol for hydrogen]

phaeton /'fayt(ə)n/ *n* a light open 4-wheeled carriage [*Phaëthon*, character in Gk legend who attempted to drive the chariot of the sun]

phag-, phago- *comb form* eating; devouring ⟨*phagocyte*⟩ [Gk, fr *phagein* to eat – more at BAKSHEESH]

phage /fayj/ *n* a bacteriophage [by shortening]

-phagia /-'fayji·ə/ *comb form* (→ *n*) eating (a specified amount) ⟨*dys*phagia⟩; eating (a specified substance) ⟨*micro*phagia⟩ [NL, fr Gk, fr *phagein* to eat] – **-phagous** /-fəgəs/ *comb form* (→ *adj*)

phagocyte /'fagə,siet/ *n* a macrophage, white blood cell, etc that characteristically engulfs foreign material (e g bacteria) and consumes debris (e g from tissue injury) [ISV, fr Gk *phagein* + NL *-cyta* -cyte] – **phagocyte** *adj*, **phagocytic** /,fagə'sitik/ *adj*, **phagocytically** *adv*

phagocytosis /,fagəsie'tohsis/ *n, pl* **phagocytoses** /-seez/ the uptake and usu destruction of extracellular solid matter by phagocytes – compare PINOCYTOSIS [NL] – **phagocytotic** /-'totik/ *adj*, **phagocytotically** *adv*, **phagocytose** /'fagəsie,tohz/ *vt*, **phagocytize** /-,tiez/ *vt*

-phagy /-fəji/ *comb form* (→ *n*) -phagia [Gk *-phagia*, fr *phagein*]

phalanger /fə'lanjə/ *n* any of various Australian marsupial mammals ranging in size from a mouse to a large cat [NL, fr Gk *phalang-, phalanx*]

phalanstery /'falənst(ə)ri/ *n* a Fourierist cooperative community [F *phalanstère* dwelling of a Fourierist community, fr L *phalang-, phalanx* + F *-stère* (as in *monastère* monastery)]

phalanx /'falangks/ *n, pl* **phalanges** /fə'lanjeez/, **phalanxes** **1** *sing or pl in constr* a body of troops, esp those of ancient Greece, in close array **2** any of the digital bones of the hand or foot of a vertebrate ☞ ANATOMY **3** *sing or pl in constr* a massed arrangement of people, animals, or things; *esp* a body of people organized for a common purpose [L *phalang-phalanx*, fr Gk, battle line, digital bone, lit., log – more at BALK]

phalarope /'falə,rohp/ *n, pl* **phalaropes,** *esp collectively* **phalarope** any of various small wading birds that have lobed toes and are good swimmers [F, fr NL *phalaropod-, phalaropus*, fr Gk *phalaris* coot (akin to Gk *phalios* having a white spot) + *pod-, pous* foot – more at BALD, FOOT]

phallic /'falik/ *adj* of or resembling a phallus – **phallically** *adv*

phallus /'faləs/ *n, pl* **phalli** /-lie/ **phalluses** (a symbol or representation of) the penis [L, fr Gk *phallos* penis, representation of the penis – more at [1]BLOW]

phanerogam /'fanəroh,gam/ *n* a spermatophyte [F *phanérogame*, deriv of Gk *phaneros* visible (fr *phainein* to show) + *gamos* marriage – more at BIGAMY] – **phanerogamic** /,fanəroh'gamik/ *adj*, **phanerogamous** /-'rogəməs/ *adj*

phantasm /'fan,taz(ə)m/ *n* **1** an illusion **2a** a ghost, spectre **b** a figment of the imagination; a fantasy [ME *fantasme*, fr OF, fr L *phantasma*, fr Gk, fr *phantazein* to present to the mind – more at FANCY] – **phantasmal** /fan'tazm(ə)l/ *adj*, **phantasmic** /fan'tazmik/ *adj*

phantasmagoria /,fantazmə'gawri·ə/ *n* **1** an optical effect by which figures on a screen appear to dwindle into the distance or to rush towards the observer with enormous increase of size **2** a constantly shifting, confused succession of things seen or imagined (e g in a dreaming or feverish state) [F *phantasmagorie*, fr *phantasme* phantasm (fr OF *fantasme*) + *-agorie* (prob fr Gk *ageirein* to assemble, collect) – more at GREGARIOUS] – **phantasmagoric** /-mə'gorik/ *adj*

phantasy /'fantəsi/ *vb or n* (to) fantasy

[1]**phantom** /'fantəm/ *n* **1a** sthg (e g a ghost) apparent to the senses but with no substantial existence **b** sthg elusive or unreal; a will-o'-the-wisp **c** sthg existing only in the imagination ⟨*his dreams troubled by* ~s *of the past*⟩ **2** sthg existing in appearance only; a form without substance [ME *fantosme, fantome*, fr MF *fantosme*, modif of L *phantasma*] – **phantomlike** *adv or adj*

[2]**phantom** *adj* **1** of the nature of, suggesting, or being a phantom **2** fictitious, dummy ⟨~ *voters*⟩

pharaoh /'feəroh/ *n, often cap* a ruler of ancient Egypt [LL *pharaon-, pharao*, fr Gk *pharaō*, fr Heb *par'ōh*, fr Egypt *pr-‘ ’*,] – **pharaonic** /feə'ronik/ *adj, often cap*

pharaoh ant *n* a small red ant that is a household and greenhouse pest

pharisaic /,fari'say·ik/, **pharisaical** /-kl/ *adj* **1** *cap* of the Pharisees **2** marked by hypocritical self-righteousness [LL *pharisaicus*, fr LGk *pharisaikos*, fr Gk *pharisaios* Pharisee] – **pharisaism** /ˈfarisay,iz(ə)m/ *n*

pharisee /ˈfarisee/ *n* **1** *cap* a member of a Jewish party noted for strict adherence to (their own oral traditions interpreting) the Torah **2** a pharisaic person [ME *pharise*, fr OE *farise*, fr LL *pharisaeus*, fr Gk *pharisaios*, fr Aram *pĕrīshayyā*, pl of *pĕrīshā*, lit., separated]

[1]**pharmaceutical** /,fahməˈsyoohtikl/ *also* **pharmaceutic** *adj* of or engaged in pharmacy or in the manufacture of medicinal substances [LL *pharmaceuticus*, fr Gk *pharmakeutikos*, fr *pharmakeuein* to administer drugs – more at PHARMACY] – **pharmaceutically** *adv*

[2]**pharmaceutical** *n* a medicinal drug

,pharmaˈceutics /-tiks/ *n pl but sing in constr* PHARMACY 1

pharmaco- *comb form* medicine; drug ⟨pharmaco*logy*⟩ [Gk *pharmako-*, fr *pharmakon*]

pharmacology /,fahməˈkoləji/ *n* **1** the science of drugs and their effect on living things **2** the properties and effects of a usu specified drug ⟨*the ~ of morphine*⟩ – **pharmacologist** *n*, **pharmacologic** /-kəˈlojik/, **pharmacological** *adj*, **pharmacologically** *adv*

pharmacopoeia /,fahməkəˈpee·ə/ *n* **1** an (official) book describing drugs, chemicals, and medicinal preparations **2** a stock of drugs [NL, fr LGk *pharmakopoiia* preparation of drugs, fr Gk *pharmako-* + *poiein* to make – more at POET] – **pharmacopoeial** /-ˈpee·əl/ *adj*

pharmacy /ˈfahməsi/ *n* **1** the preparation, compounding, and dispensing of drugs **2a** a place where medicines are compounded or dispensed **b** CHEMIST 2 [LL *pharmacia* administration of drugs, fr Gk *pharmakeia*, fr *pharmakeuein* to administer drugs, fr *pharmakon* magic charm, poison, drug; akin to Lith *burti* to practise magic] – **pharmacist** *n*

pharyng-, pharyngo- *comb form* pharynx ⟨pharyng*itis*⟩ ⟨pharynge*al*⟩ [Gk, fr *pharyng-*, *pharynx*]

pharynx /ˈfaringks/ *n, pl* **pharynges** /faˈrinjeez/ *also* **pharynxes** the part of the vertebrate alimentary canal between the mouth cavity and the oesophagus [NL *pharyng-*, *pharynx*, fr Gk, throat, pharynx; akin to ON *barki* throat, L *forare* to bore – more at [1]BORE] – **pharyngeal** /,farinˈjee·əl/ *adj*, **pharyngitis** /,farinˈjietəs/ *n*

[1]**phase** /fayz/ *n* **1** a particular appearance or state in a regularly recurring cycle of changes ⟨~s *of the moon*⟩ **2a** a discernable part or stage in a course, development, or cycle ⟨*the early* ~s *of his career*⟩ **b** an aspect or part (e g of a problem) under consideration **3** a stage of progress in a regularly recurring motion or cyclic process (e g an alternating electric current) with respect to a starting point or standard position **4** a homogeneous and mechanically separable portion of matter present in a complex mixture [NL *phasis*, fr Gk, appearance of a star, phase of the moon, fr *phainein* to show – more at FANCY] – **phasic** /ˈfayzik/ *adj*

[2]**phase** *vt* **1** to conduct or carry out by planned phases **2** to schedule (e g operations) or contract for (e g goods or services) to be performed or supplied as required ⟨~ *a development programme*⟩

,phase-ˈcontrast *adj* of, employing, or produced by the phase-contrast microscope

phase-contrast microscope *n* a microscope that changes differences in the phase of the light transmitted through or reflected by the object into differences of intensity in the image and is used esp for examining biological specimens that have not been stained

phase in *vt* to introduce the practice, production, or use of in gradual stages ⟨phase in *a new model*⟩

phase out *vt* to discontinue the practice, production, or use of in gradual stages ⟨phase out *the old machinery*⟩ – **phaseout** *n*

-phasia /-,fayzyə, -zh(y)ə/ *comb form* (→*n*) speech disorder ⟨*dys*phasia⟩ [NL, fr Gk, speech, fr *phasis* utterance, fr *phanai* to speak, say – more at [1]BAN]

phasor /ˈfayzə/ *n* a regularly alternating quantity (e g current or voltage) that is represented graphically by a directed line segment whose length represents the magnitude and whose direction represents the phase – compare VECTOR 1a [[1]*phase* + *vector*]

phatic /ˈfatik/ *adj, of speech* expressing feelings or establishing an atmosphere of sociability rather than communicating ideas [Gk *phatos*, verbal of *phanai* to speak] – **phatically** *adv*

pheasant /ˈfez(ə)nt/ *n, pl* **pheasants**, *esp collectively* **pheasant** any of numerous large often long-tailed and brightly coloured Old World (game) birds [ME *fesaunt*, fr AF, fr OF *fesan*, fr L *phasianus*, fr Gk *phasianos*, fr *phasianos* of the Phasis river, fr *Phasis*, river in Colchis, ancient country in Asia]

phellem /ˈfeləm/ *n* an outer layer of cork cells produced in the roots or stems of woody plants by phellogen [Gk *phellos* cork + E *-em* (as in *phloem*)]

phelloderm /ˈfeloh,duhm/ *n* a layer of (parenchyma) cells produced inwardly in the roots or stems of woody plants by phellogen [Gk *phellos* + ISV *-derm*]

phellogen /ˈfeləjən/ *n* a single row of cells in the outer layer of a woody plant stem or root that divides to form phellem to the outside and phelloderm to the inside [Gk *phellos* + ISV *-gen*]

phen-, pheno- *comb form* of or derived from benzene ⟨phen*anthrene*⟩; containing phenyl ⟨pheno*barbital*⟩ ⟨phen*ol*⟩ [obs *phene* (benzene), fr F *phène*, fr Gk *phainein* to show – more at FANCY; fr its occurrence in illuminating gas]

phenacetin /fiˈnasətin/ *n* a compound related to acetanilide and formerly used as a painkiller [ISV]

phenobarbitone /,feenohˈbahbi,tohn/ *NAm chiefly* **phenobarbital** /-bit(ə)l/ *n, chiefly Br* a barbiturate used esp as a sedative and anticonvulsant in the treatment of epilepsy

phenocryst /ˈfenə,krist, ˈfee-/ *n* any of the prominent embedded crystals of a porphyry rock [F *phénocryste*, fr Gk *phainein* to show + *krystallos* crystal – more at FANCY] – **phenocrystic** /,fenəˈkristik, ,fee-/ *adj*

phenol /ˈfeenol/ *n* (any of various derivatives of benzene containing a hydroxyl group and analogous to) a caustic poisonous hydroxy benzene used in dilute solution as a disinfectant [ISV *phen-* + *-ol*] – **phenolic** /fiˈnolik/ *adj*

phenolphthalein /,feenolfˈthayli·in, -li·een/ *n* a synthetic compound used in medicine as a purgative and in chemical analysis as an indicator that is brilliant red in alkaline solutions [ISV]

phenomenal /fi'nominl/ *adj* relating to or being a phenomenon: e g **a** known through the senses rather than through thought or intuition **b** concerned with phenomena rather than with hypotheses **c** extraordinary, remarkable ⟨*a ~ success*⟩ – **phenomenally** *adv*

phe'nomenal,ism /-,iz(ə)m/ *n* a theory which holds that knowledge is limited to phenomena – **phenomenalist** *n*, **phenomenalistic** /-'istik/ *adj*, **phenomenalistically** *adv*

phenomenological /fi,nominl'ojikl/ *adj* **1** of phenomenology or phenomenalism **2** PHENOMENAL a, b – **phenomenologically** *adv*

phenomenology /fi,nomi'noləji/ *n* **1** the description of the formal structure of the objects of awareness and of awareness itself in abstraction from any causal connections with the external world **2a** the classification of a related group of phenomena ⟨*the ~ of religion*⟩ **b** an analysis produced by phenomenological investigation [G *phänomenologie*, fr *phänomenon* phenomenon + *-logie* -logy] – **phenomenologist** *n*

phenomenon /fi'nominən/ *n, pl* **phenomena** /-nə/ *also* **phenomenons** **1** an observable fact or event **2a** an object of sense perception rather than of thought or intuition **b** a fact or event that can be scientifically described and explained **3a** a rare or significant fact or event ⟨*vandalism is a social ~*⟩ **b** an exceptional, unusual, or abnormal person, thing, or event; a prodigy [LL *phaenomenon*, fr Gk *phainomenon*, fr neut of *phainomenos*, prp of *phainesthai* to appear, fr *phainein* to show – more at FANCY]

phenothiazine /,feenoh'thie·əzeen/ *n* **1** a synthetic compound used in chemical synthesis and in veterinary medicine against parasitic worms **2** any of various phenothiazine derivatives (e g chlorpromazine) used as tranquillizing agents, esp in the treatment of schizophrenia [ISV]

phenotype /'feenoh,tiep/ *n* the visible characteristics of an organism that are produced by the interaction of the organism's genes and the environment [G *phänotypus*, fr Gk *phainein* to show + *typos* type] – **phenotypic** /,feenoh'tipik/ *also* **phenotypical** *adj*, **phenotypically** *adv*

phenyl /'fenil, 'feenil, -niel, -nl/ *n* a univalent radical C_6H_5 that is derived from benzene by removal of 1 hydrogen atom – often in combination [ISV] – **phenylic** /fe'nilik, fee-/ *adj*

phenylalanine /,feni'lalәneen/ *n* an amino acid found in most proteins that is essential for human metabolism [ISV]

phenylbutazone /,fenil'byoohtə,zohn, ,fee-/ *n* a synthetic drug used esp to treat the pain and inflammation of arthritis and gout [*phenyl* + *butyric* acid + pyrazal*one* ($C_3H_4N_2O$)]

phenylketonuria /,fenil,keetə'nyooəri·ə, ,fee-/ *n* an inherited metabolic disease in human beings that results in severe mental deficiency if untreated from birth [*phenyl* + *ketone* + *-uria*] – **phenylketonuric** /-rik/ *adj or n*

phenylthiocarbamide /,fenil,thie·oh'kahbəmied, ,fee-/ *n* phenylthiourea

phenylthiourea /,fenil,thie·ohyoo'ree·ə, ,fee-/ *n* an extremely bitter compound that can be tasted only by people with a particular dominant gene

pheromone /'ferəmohn/ *n* a chemical substance that is produced by an animal and stimulates 1 or more behavioural responses in other individuals of the same species [ISV *phero-* (fr Gk *pherein* to carry) + *-mone* (as in *hormone*) – more at ²BEAR] – **pheromonal** /,ferə'mohnl/ *adj*

phew /fyooh/ *interj* – used to express shock, relief, or exhaustion

phi /fie/ *n* the 21st letter of the Greek alphabet [MGk, fr Gk *phei*]

phial /'fie·əl/ *n* a small closed or closable vessel, esp for holding liquid medicine [ME, fr L *phiala*, fr Gk *phialē*]

Phi Beta Kappa /,fie ,beetə 'kapə/ *n* (a member of) an American college fraternity whose membership is based on academic distinction [*Phi Beta Kappa* (*Society*), fr *phi* + *beta* + *kappa*, initials of the society's Gk motto *philosophia biou kybernētēs* philosophy the guide of life]

phil-, philo- *comb form* loving ⟨philo*gynist*⟩;having an affinity for ⟨philo*progenitive*⟩ [ME, fr OF, fr L, fr Gk, fr *philos* dear, friendly]

philadelphus /,filə'delfəs/ *n* any of a genus of ornamental shrubs of the hydrangea family; *esp* MOCK ORANGE [NL, genus name, fr Gk *philadelphos* brotherly, fr *phil-* + *adelphos* brother, fr *ha-, a-* (akin to *homos* same) + *delphys* womb – more at SAME, DOLPHIN]

philander /fi'landə/ *vi* **1** *of a man* to flirt **2** to have many casual love affairs [obs *philander* (lover, philanderer), prob fr *Philander*, stock name for a lover in early romances, fr Gk *philos* + *andr-, anēr* man] – **philanderer** *n*

philanthropic /,filən'thropik/ *also* **philanthropical** /-kl/ *adj* **1** of or characterized by philanthropy; humanitarian **2** dispensing or receiving aid from funds set aside for humanitarian purposes ⟨*a ~ institution*⟩ – **philanthropically** *adv*

philanthropy /fi'lanthrəpi/ *n* **1** goodwill to one's fellow men; *esp* active effort to promote the welfare of others **2** a philanthropic act or gift [LL *philanthropia*, fr Gk *philanthrōpia*, fr *philanthrōpos* loving mankind, fr *phil-* + *anthrōpos* man] – **philanthropist** *n*

philately /fi'latəli/ *n* the study and collection of (postage) stamps [F *philatélie*, fr *phil-* + Gk *ateleia* tax exemption, fr *atelēs* free from tax, fr *a-* + *telos* tax; akin to Gk *telein* to pay, *tlēnai* to bear – more at TOLERATE] – **philatelist** *n*, **philatelic** /,filə'telik/ *adj*, **philatelically** *adv*

-phile /-fiel/, **-phil** /-fil/ *comb form* (→ *n*) one having a fondness or liking for ⟨*Franco*phile⟩; *also* one having a chemical affinity for ⟨*neutro*phil⟩ [F *-phile*, fr Gk *-philos*, fr *philos*] – **-phile** *comb form* (→ *adj*)

Philemon /fie'leemon/ *n* a letter written by St Paul to a Christian living in the area of Colossae urging him to forgive his runaway slave, which is included as a book in the New Testament [Gk *Philēmōn*]

Philharmonic /,filə'monik, ,fil(h)ah-/ *n* SYMPHONY ORCHESTRA [F *philharmonique*, lit., loving harmony, fr It *filarmonico*, fr *fil-* phil- + *armonia* harmony, fr L *harmonia*]

-philia /-'fili·ə/ *comb form* (→ *n*) abnormal appetite or liking for ⟨*necro*philia⟩ [NL, fr Gk *philia* friendship, fr *philos* dear] – **-philiac** *comb form* (→ *adj*)

philibeg /'fili,beg/ *n* a filibeg

-philic /-'filik/ *comb form* (→ *adj*) having (chemical) affinity for; liking ⟨*photo*philic⟩ – compare -PHOBIC [Gk *-philos* -philous]

Philippians /fi'lipi·ənz; *also* ,fili'pee·ənz/ *n pl but sing in constr* a letter written by St Paul to the Christians of Philippi, included as a book in the New Testament

philippic /fi'lipik/ *n* a speech or declamation full of bitter invective [MF *philippique,* fr L & Gk; L *philippica, orationes philippicae,* speeches of Cicero †43 BC against Mark Antony, trans of Gk *philippikoi logoi,* speeches of Demosthenes †322 BC against Philip II of Macedon, lit., speeches relating to Philip]

philistine /'filistien/ *n* **1** *cap* a native or inhabitant of ancient Philistia **2** *often cap* a person who professes indifference or opposition to intellectual or aesthetic values [*Philistia,* ancient country in SW Palestine] – **philistine** *adj,* **philistinism** *n*

phillumenist /fi'loohmənist/ *n* one who collects books of matches or matchbox labels [*phil-* + L *lumen* light – more at LUMINARY]

philodendron /,filə'dendrən/ *n, pl* **philodendrons, philodendra** /-drə/ any of various plants of the arum family cultivated for their showy foliage [NL, fr Gk, neut of *philodendros* loving trees, fr *phil-* + *dendron* tree – more at DENDR-]

philogyny /fi'lojini/ *n* fondness for women [Gk *philogynia,* fr *phil-* + *gynē* woman – more at QUEEN]

philology /fi'loləji/ *n* (historical and comparative) linguistics [F *philologie,* fr L *philologia* love of learning and literature, fr Gk, fr *philologos* fond of learning and literature, fr *phil-* + *logos* word, speech – more at LEGEND] – **philologist** *n,* **philological** /,filə'lojikl/ *adj,* **philologically** *adv*

philosopher /fi'losəfə/ *n* **1a** a scholar, thinker **b** a specialist in philosophy **2** a person whose philosophical viewpoint enables him/her to meet trouble with equanimity [ME, modif of MF *philosophe,* fr L *philosophus,* fr Gk *philosophos,* fr *phil-* + *sophia* wisdom, fr *sophos* wise]

philosophers' stone *n* a substance believed by alchemists to have the power of transmuting base metals into gold

philosophical /,filə'sofikl/ *adj* **1** of philosophers or philosophy **2** calm in the face of trouble

philosoph·ize, -ise /fi'losəfiez/ *vi* **1** to engage in philosophical reasoning **2** to expand a trite or superficial philosophy

philosophy /fi'losəfi/ *n* **1a** the pursuit of wisdom **b** the study of the nature of knowledge and existence and the principles of moral and aesthetic value **2** the philosophical principles or teachings of a specified individual, group, or period ⟨*Kantian* ~⟩ **3a** the sum of beliefs and attitudes of a specified individual, group, or period ⟨*the vegetarian* ~⟩ **b** equanimity in the face of trouble or stress [ME *philosophie,* fr OF, fr L *philosophia,* fr Gk, fr *philosophos* philosopher]

-philous /-filəs/ *comb form* (→ *adj*) -philic ⟨*helio*philous⟩ [Gk *-philos,* fr *philos* dear, friendly]

philtre, *NAm chiefly* **philter** /'filtə/ *n* a potion or drug reputed to have the power to arouse sexual passion [MF *philtre,* fr L *philtrum,* fr Gk *philtron;* akin to Gk *philos* dear]

phizog /'fizog/ *n* FACE 1 –infml or humor [by shortening & alter. fr *physiognomy*]

phleb-, phlebo- *comb form* vein ⟨phleb*itis*⟩ [ME *fleb-,* fr MF, fr LL *phlebo-,* fr Gk *phleb-, phlebo-,* fr *phleb-, phleps;* akin to L *fluere* to flow – more at FLUID]

phlebitis /fli'bietəs/ *n* inflammation of a vein [NL]

phlebotomy /fli'botəmi/ *n* the letting or taking of blood in the treatment or diagnosis of disease [ME *fleobotomie,* fr MF *flebotomie,* fr LL *phlebotomia,* fr Gk, fr *phleb-* + *-tomia* -tomy] – **phlebotomize** *vb,* **phlebotomist** *n*

phlegm /flem/ *n* **1** that one of the 4 humours in medieval physiology that was considered to be cold and moist and to cause sluggishness **2** thick mucus secreted in abnormal quantities in the respiratory passages **3a** dull or apathetic coldness or indifference **b** intrepid coolness; composure [ME *fleume,* fr MF, fr LL *phlegmat-, phlegma,* fr Gk, flame, inflammation, phlegm, fr *phlegein* to burn – more at BLACK] – **phlegmy** *adj*

phlegmatic /fleg'matik/ *adj* **1** resembling, consisting of, or producing phlegm **2** having or showing a slow and stolid temperament – **phlegmatically** *adv*

phloem /'floh·em/ *n* a complex vascular tissue of higher plants that functions chiefly in the conduction of soluble food substances (e g sugars) – compare XYLEM [G, fr Gk *phloios, phloos* bark; akin to Gk *phallos* penis – more at [1]BLOW]

phlogistic /flo'jistik/ *adj* **1** of phlogiston **2** of inflammations and fevers [(1) NL *phlogiston;* (2) Gk *phlogistos*]

phlogiston /flo'jist(ə)n/ *n* the supposed essence of fire formerly regarded as a material substance [NL, fr Gk, neut of *phlogistos* inflammable, fr *phlogizein* to set on fire, fr *phlog-, phlox* flame, fr *phlegein*]

phlox /floks/ *n, pl* **phlox,** *esp for different types* **phloxes** any of a genus of American plants with red, purple, white, or variegated flowers [NL, genus name, fr L, a flower, fr Gk, flame, wallflower]

-phobe /-,fohb/ *comb form* (→ *n*) one afraid of or averse to ⟨*Franco*phobe⟩ [Gk *-phobos* fearing] – **-phobe** *comb form* (→*adj*)

phobia /'fohbi·ə, -byə/ *n* an exaggerated and illogical fear of sthg [NL, fr LL *-phobia,* fr Gk, fr *-phobos* fearing, fr *phobos* fear, flight; akin to Gk *phebesthai* to flee, be frightened, Lith *bėgti* to flee]

-phobia /-fohbi·ə, -byə/ *comb form* (→ *n*) abnormal fear or dislike of ⟨*claustro*phobia⟩

phobic /'fohbik/ *adj* **1** of or being a phobia **2** motivated by or based on withdrawal from an unpleasant stimulus ⟨*a* ~ *response to light*⟩

-phobic /-'fohbik/, **-phobous** *comb form* (→ *adj*) lacking (chemical) affinity for ⟨*hydro*phobic⟩; having an aversion for ⟨*Anglo*phobic⟩ – compare -PHILIC [*-phobic* fr F *-phobique,* fr LL *-phobicus,* fr Gk *-phobikos,* fr *-phobia; -phobous* fr LL *-phobus,* fr Gk *-phobos*]

Phoenician /fə'neesh(ə)n, -shyən, -'ni-/ *n* (the language of) a native or inhabitant of ancient Phoenicia ☞ ALPHABET [*Phoenicia,* ancient country in SW Asia] – **Phoenician** *adj*

phoenix /'feeniks/ *n* a mythical bird believed to live for 500 years, burn itself on a pyre, and rise alive from the ashes to live another cycle [ME *fenix,* fr OE, fr L *phoenix,* fr Gk *phoinix* purple, crimson, Phoenician, phoenix, date palm, fr *phoinos* bloodred; akin to Gk *phonos* murder, *theinein* to strike – more at DEFEND] – **phoenixlike** *adj*

phon /fon/ *n* the unit of loudness relative to a 1kHz

tone measured on a scale corresponding to the decibel scale of sound intensity [ISV, fr Gk *phōnē* voice, sound]

phon-, phono- *comb form* sound; voice; speech ⟨phon*ate*⟩ ⟨phono*graph*⟩ [L, fr Gk *phōn-, phōno-*, fr *phōnē* – more at ¹BAN]

phonate /foh'nayt/ *vi* to produce vocal, esp speech, sounds – **phonation** /foh'naysh(ə)n/ *n*

¹**phone** /fohn/ *n* **1** an earphone **2** a telephone [by shortening]

²**phone** *vb* to telephone – often + *up*

³**phone** *n* a simple speech sound [Gk *phōnē*]

-phone /-fohn/ *comb form* (→ *n*) **1** sound ⟨*homo*phone⟩ – often in names of musical instruments and sound-transmitting devices ⟨*radio*phone⟩ ⟨*xylo*phone⟩ **2** speaker of (a specified language) ⟨*Anglo*phone⟩ [Gk *-phōnos* sounding, fr *phōnē*]

'**phone ,book** *n* TELEPHONE DIRECTORY

'**phone-,in** *n* a broadcast programme in which viewers or listeners can participate by telephone

phonematic /,fohni'matik/ *adj* phonemic – **phonematically** *adv*

phoneme /'fohneem/ *n* the smallest unit of speech that can be used to differentiate the meanings of words – compare ALLOPHONE ☞ ALPHABET [F *phonème*, fr Gk *phōnēmat-, phōnēma* speech sound, utterance, fr *phōnein* to sound]

phonemic /fə'neemik/ *adj* **1** of phonemes **2** linguistically distinctive – **phonemically** *adv*

pho'nemics *n pl but sing in constr* **1** the study of phonemes **2** the phonemic system of a language

phonetic /fə'netik/, **phonetical** /-kl/ *adj* **1a** of spoken language or speech sounds **b** of the study of phonetics **2** representing speech sounds by symbols that each have 1 value only [NL *phoneticus*, fr Gk *phōnētikos*, fr *phōnein* to sound with the voice, fr *phōnē* voice] – **phonetically** *adv*

pho'netics *n pl* **1** *sing in constr* the study and classification of speech sounds **2** *sing or pl in constr* the system of speech sounds of a language ☞ ALPHABET – **phonetician** /,fohnə'tish(ə)n, ,fo-/ *n*

phoney, *NAm chiefly* **phony** /'fohni/ *adj* not genuine or real: e g **a** intended to deceive, mislead, or defraud; counterfeit **b** false, sham ⟨*a ~ name*⟩ ⟨*~ pearls*⟩ **c** *of a person* pretentious [origin unknown] – **phoney** *n*

-phonia /-'fohnyə, -ni·ə/ *comb form* (→ *n*) **1** -phony **2** -phasia ⟨*dys*phonia⟩

phonic /'fonik/ *adj* **1** of or producing sound; acoustic **2a** of speech sounds **b** of phonics – **phonically** *adv*

'**phonics** *n pl but sing in constr* a method of teaching reading and pronunciation through the phonetic value of letters, syllables, etc

phonogram /'fohnə,gram/ *n* a character used (e g in shorthand) to represent a spoken sound [ISV] – **phonogrammic, phonogramic** /,fohnə'gramik/ *adj*, **phonogrammically, phonogramically** *adv*

phonograph /'fohnə,grahf, -,graf/ *n* **1** an early device for recording or reproducing sound in which a stylus cuts or follows a groove on a cylinder **2** a gramophone – now chiefly NAm or humor

phonographic /,fohnə'grafik/ *adj* **1** of phonography **2** of a phonograph – **phonographically** *adv*

phonography /foh'nogrəfi/ *n* a spelling system, esp shorthand, based on pronunciation

phonology /fə'noləji/ *n* **1** the science of speech sounds **2** the phonetics and phonemics of a language at a particular time – **phonologist** *n*, **phonological** /,fohnə'lojikl/ *also* **phonologic** *adj*

phonon /'fohnon/ *n* a quantum of energy in the form of vibrations (e g sound) [*phon-* + ²*-on*]

phony /'fohni/ *adj, chiefly NAm* phoney

-phony /-fəni/ *also* **-phonia** /-'fohnyə, -ni·ə/ *comb form* (→ *n*) **1** sound ⟨*tele*phony⟩ ⟨*eu*phony⟩ **2** -phasia ⟨*dys*phonia⟩ [ME *-phonie*, fr OF, fr L *-phonia*, fr Gk *-phōnia*, fr *-phōnos* sounding – more at -PHONE]

phooey /'fooh·i/ *interj* – used to express scorn or incredulity; infml

-phore /-faw/ *comb form* (→*n*) bearer; carrier ⟨*gam etophore*⟩ ⟨*sema*phore⟩ [NL *-phorus*, fr Gk *-phoros*, fr *-phoros* (adj comb form) carrying, fr *pherein* to carry – more at ²BEAR] – **-phorous** *comb form* (→*adj*)

-phoresis /-fə'reesis/ *comb form* (→ *n*), *pl* **-phoreses** /-seez/ transmission ⟨*electro*phoresis⟩ [NL, fr Gk *phorēsis* act of carrying, fr *phorein* to carry, wear, freq of *pherein*]

phosgene /'fozjeen/ *n* a very poisonous colourless gas that is a severe respiratory irritant and was formerly used as a war gas [Gk *phōs* light + E *-gen, -gene*; fr its having been obtained originally by the action of sunlight upon equal volumes of chlorine & carbon monoxide]

phosph-, phospho- *comb form* **1** phosphorus ⟨phos*phide*⟩ **2** phosphate ⟨phospho*protein*⟩ ⟨phospho*lipid*⟩ [*phosphorus*]

phosphate /'fosfayt/ *n* **1** a salt or ester of a phosphoric acid **2** any of several phosphates used as fertilizers [F, fr *acide phosphorique* phosphoric acid] – **phosphatic** /fos'fatik/ *adj*

phosphene /'fosfeen/ *n* an impression of light due to excitation of the retina caused by pressure on the eyeball [Gk *phōs* light + *phainein* to show – more at FANCY]

phosphide /'fosfied/ *n* a binary compound of phosphorus with an element or radical [ISV]

phosphor *also* **phosphore** /'fosfə/ *n* a substance showing phosphorescence ☞ TELEVISION [L *phosphorus*, fr Gk *phōsphoros*, lit., light bringer, fr *phōsphoros* light-bearing, fr *phōs-* + *pherein* to carry, bring – more at ²BEAR]

phosphor-, phosphoro- *comb form* phosph- ⟨phosphoro*lysis*⟩

phosphor bronze *n* a hard elastic bronze containing a small amount of phosphorus

phosphorescence /,fosfə'res(ə)ns/ *n* **1** light emission that is caused by the absorption of radiations and continues for a noticeable time after these radiations have stopped **2** lasting emission of light without noticeable heat – **phosphorescent** *adj*, **phosphoresce** /-'res/ *vi*

phosphoric /fos'forik/ *adj* of or containing (high valency) phosphorus

phos,phoric 'acid *n* (any of several hydrated forms of) a syrupy acid used esp in preparing phosphates (e g for fertilizers), in rustproofing metals, and as a flavouring in soft drinks

phosphorite /'fosfəriet/ *n* calcium phosphate occurring as a noncrystalline apatite – **phosphoritic** /,fosfə'ritik/ *adj*

phosphorous /'fosf(ə)rəs/ *adj* of or containing (low valency) phosphorus

phosphorus /'fosf(ə)rəs/ *n* **1** a nonmetallic trivalent or pentavalent element of the nitrogen family that occurs widely, esp as phosphates, 1 form of which ignites readily in warm moist air ☞ PERIODIC TABLE **2** a phosphorescent substance or body; *esp* one that shines or glows in the dark [NL, fr Gk *phōsphoros* light-bearing – more at PHOSPHOR]

phosphorylation /fos,fori'laysh(ə)n/ *n* the combining of an organic compound with an inorganic phosphate group; *esp* the conversion of carbohydrates (e g glucose) into their phosphates in metabolic processes [*phosphoryl* (the radical PO) + *-ation*] – **phosphorylate** /-'fori,layt/ *vt*, **phosphorylative** /-'forilətiv/ *adj*

phot-, photo- *comb form* **1** light; radiant energy ⟨pho *tography*⟩ ⟨photo*philic*⟩ ⟨photo*taxis*⟩ **2** photograph; photographic ⟨photo*engraving*⟩ **3** photoelectric ⟨photo*cell*⟩ [Gk *phōt-*, *phōto-*, fr *phōt-*, *phōs* – more at FANCY]

photic /'fohtik/ *adj* **1** of or involving light, esp in its effect on living organisms **2** penetrated by (the sun's) light ⟨~ *zone of the ocean*⟩ – **photically** *adv*

[1]**photo** /'fohtoh/ *vb or n* **photos; photoing; photoed;** *pl* **photos** (to) photograph

[2]**photo** *adj* PHOTOGRAPHIC 1

'photo,call /-,kawl/ *n* a session at which a person is photographed, typically for the purpose of publicity (e g in the press)

'photo,cell /-,sel/ *n* PHOTOELECTRIC CELL [ISV]

,photo'chemistry /-'kemistri/ *n* (chemistry that deals with) the effect of radiant energy in producing chemical changes – **photochemical** /-'kemikl/ *adj*, **photochemically** *adv*, **photochemist** /-'kemist/ *n*

photochromic /,fohtə'krohmik/ *adj* (of or using a substance) capable of changing colour on exposure to radiant energy (e g light) ⟨~ *glass*⟩ [*phot-* + *chrom-* + *-ic*] – **photochromism** /'fohtə,krohmiz(ə)m/ *n*

,photo,compo'sition /-,kompə'zish(ə)n/ *n* composition of reading matter directly on film or photosensitive paper for reproduction – **photocompose** /-kəm'pohz/ *vt*, **photocomposer** *n*

,photo,conduc'tivity /-,konduk'tivəti/ *n* electrical conductivity that is affected by exposure to radiation, esp light – **photoconductive** /-kən'duktiv/ *adj*

[1]**photocopy** /'fohtə,kopi, -toh-/ *n* a photographic reproduction of graphic matter [ISV]

[2]**photocopy** *vb* to make a photocopy (of) – **photocopier** *n*

photoelectric /,fohtoh·i'lektrik/ *adj* involving, relating to, or using any of various electrical effects due to the interaction of radiation (e g light) with matter [ISV] – **photoelectrically** *adv*

photoelectric cell *n* a cell whose electrical properties are modified by the action of light

,photoe'lectron /-i'lektron/ *n* an electron released in photoemission [ISV] – **photoelectronic** /-lek'tronik/ *adj*

,photoe'mission /-i'mish(ə)n/ *n* the release of electrons from a metal by radiation, esp light – **photoemissive** /-'misiv/ *adj*

,photoen'graving /-in'grayving/ *n* (a plate made by) a process for making line and halftone blocks by photographing an image on a metal plate and then etching – **photoengrave** *vt*, **photoengraver** *n*

photo finish *n* **1** a race finish so close that the winner is only revealed (as if) by a photograph of the contestants as they cross the finishing line **2** a close contest

'photo-,fit *n, often cap* (a means of constructing) a likeness of a person's face from photographs, esp for identification – compare [1]IDENTIKIT

'photo,flood /-,flud/ *n* an electric lamp using excess voltage to give intense sustained illumination for taking photographs

photogenic /,fohtə'jenik, -'jeenik/ *adj* **1** producing or generating light; luminescent ⟨~ *bacteria*⟩ **2** suitable for being photographed – **photogenically** *adv*

photogrammetry /,fohtoh'gramitri/ *n* the use of esp aerial photographs to obtain reliable measurements [ISV *photogram* photograph (fr *phot-* + *-gram*) + *-metry*] – **photogrammetrist** *n*, **photogrammetric** /-grə'metrik/ *adj*

[1]**photograph** /'fohtə,grahf, -,graf/ *n* a picture or likeness obtained by photography

[2]**photograph** *vt* to take a photograph of ~ *vi* **1** to take a photograph **2** to undergo being photographed – **photographer** /fə'tografə/ *n*

photographic /,fohtə'grafik/ *adj* **1** relating to, obtained by, or used in photography **2** capable of retaining vivid impressions; *esp* eidetic ⟨~ *memory*⟩ – **photographically** *adv*

photography /fə'tografi/ *n* the art or process of producing images on a sensitized surface (e g a film) by the action of radiant energy, esp light ☞ CAMERA

photogravure /,fohtəgrə'vyooə/ *n* (a picture produced by) a process for making prints from an intaglio plate prepared by photographic methods [F, fr *phot-* + *gravure*]

photoheliograph /,fohtoh'heeli·ə,grahf, -,graf/ *n* a telescope adapted for photographing the sun

photolithography /,fohtohli'thografi/ *n* lithography in which photographically prepared plates are used [ISV] – **photolithographer** *n*, **photolithograph** /-'lithə,grahf, -,graf/ *n or vt*, **photolithographic** /-,lithə'grafik/ *adj*, **photolithographically** *adv*

photolysis /foh'toləsis/ *n* chemical decomposition by the action of radiant energy, esp light [NL] – **photolyse** /'fohtəliez/ *vb*, **photolytic** /fohtə'litik/ *adj*, **photolytically** *adv*

photometer /foh'tomitə/ *n* an instrument for measuring light intensity, illumination, or brightness [NL *photometrum*, fr *phot-* + *-metrum* -meter] – **photometry** *n*, **photometric** /,fohtə'metrik/ *adj*, **photometrically** *adv*

photomicrograph /,fohtə'miekrə,grahf, -,graf/ *n* a photograph of an object magnified under a microscope [*phot-* + *micr-* + *-graph*] – **photomicrograph** *vt*, **photomicrography** /-mie'krografi/ *n*, **photomicrographic** /-,miekrə'grafik/ *also* **photomicrographical** *adj*

,photo'multiplier /-'multi,plie·ə/ *n* a device that increases the brightness of an electronic image (e g a television picture) by multiplying the number of electrons released by photoelectric emission

photon /'fohton/ *n* a quantum of electromagnetic radiation [*phot-* + [2]*-on*] – **photonic** /,foh'tonik/ *adj*

,photo-'offset /'ofset/ *n* offset printing from photolithographic plates

,photo'period /-'piəri·əd/ *n* the relative lengths of alternating periods of lightness and darkness as they affect the growth and maturity of an organism – **photoperiodism** *n*, **photoperiodic** /-piəri'odik/ *adj*, **photoperiodically** *adv*

,photo'phobia /-'fohbi·ə, -byə/ *n* painful sensitiveness to strong light [NL] – **photophobic** /-'fohbik/ *adj*

ˈphoto,phore /-ˌfaw/ *n* a light-emitting organ; *esp* any of the luminous spots on various marine mostly deep-sea fishes [ISV]

photophosphorylation /ˌfohtohfosˌforiˈlaysh(ə)n/ *n* the synthesis of ATP from ADP and phosphate that occurs in a plant using radiant energy absorbed during photosynthesis [*phot-* + *phosphorylation*]

photopic /ˌfohˈtopik, -ˈtohpik/ *adj* of or being vision in bright light with light-adapted eyes – compare SCOTOPIC [NL *photopia*, fr *phot-* + *-opia*] – **photopia** /-ˈtohpi·ə/ *n*

ˌphotoˈpolymer /-ˈpolimə/ *n* a photosensitive plastic used for making printing plates

ˌphotoreˈceptor /-riˈseptə/ *n* a receptor for light stimuli – **photoreception** /-ˈsepsh(ə)n/ *n*, **photoreceptive** /-ˈseptiv/ *adj*

ˌphotoˈsensitive /-ˈsensətiv/ *adj* sensitive or sensitized to radiant energy, esp light – **photosensitivity** /-ˌsensəˈtivəti/ *n*

ˌphotoˈsensit·ize, -ise /-ˈsensitiez/ *vt* to make (abnormally) sensitive to the influence of radiant energy, esp light – **photosensitive** *adj*, **photosensitization** /-ˌsensəˈtiezaysh(ə)n/ *n*

ˈphoto,setting /-ˌseting/ *n* photocomposition – **photosetter** *n*

photosphere /ˈfohtəˌsfiə/ *n* the luminous surface layer of the sun or other star – **photospheric** /ˌfohtəˈsferik/ *adj*

photostat /ˈfohtəˌstat/ *vt* to copy on a Photostat device; *broadly* to photocopy – **photostat** *n*, **photostatic** /ˌfohtəˈstatik/ *adj*

Photostat *trademark* – used for a device for making a photographic copy of graphic matter

photosynthesis /ˌfohtohˈsinthəsis/ *n* the synthesis of organic chemical compounds from carbon dioxide using radiant energy, esp light; *esp* the formation of carbohydrates in the chlorophyll-containing tissues of plants exposed to light ☞ ENERGY, FOOD [NL] – **photosynthesize** /-siez/ *vi*, **photosynthetic** /-sinˈthetik/ *adj*, **photosynthetically** *adv*

phototropism /fohˈtotrəˌpiz(ə)m/ *n* a tropism in which light is the orienting factor [ISV] – **phototropic** /ˌfohtəˈtropik, -ˈtrohpik/ *adj*, **phototropically** *adv*

ˌphototyˈpography /-tieˈpogrəfi/ *n* photocomposition [ISV] – **phototypographic** /-ˌtiepəˈgrafik/ *adj*

ˌphotovolˈtaic /-volˈtayik/ *adj* of or using the generation of an electromotive force when radiant energy falls on the boundary between dissimilar substances [ISV]

phrasal /ˈfrayzl/ *adj* (consisting) of a phrase – **phrasally** *adv*

¹phrase /frayz/ *n* **1** a mode or form of speech; diction **2** a brief usu idiomatic or pithy expression; *esp* a catchphrase ⟨*good at turning a* ~⟩ **3** a group of musical notes forming a natural unit of melody that is usu 3 or 4 bars in length **4** a group of 2 or more grammatically related words that do not form a clause; *esp* a preposition with the words it governs [L *phrasis*, fr Gk, fr *phrazein* to point out, explain, tell]

²phrase *vt* **1** to express in words or in appropriate or telling terms ⟨*a politely* ~d *rejection*⟩ **2** to divide into melodic phrases

ˈphrase ˌbook *n* a book containing words and idiomatic expressions of a foreign language and their translation

phraseogram /ˈfrayzi·əˌgram/ *n* a symbol for a phrase in some shorthand systems [*phraseo-* (as in *phraseology*) + *-gram*]

ˈphraseo,graph /-ˌgrahf, -ˌgraf/ *n* a phrase for which a phraseogram is used

phraseology /ˌfrayziˈoləji/ *n* **1** a mode of organization of words and phrases into longer elements; a style **2** choice of words [NL *phraseologia*, fr Gk *phrase-*, *phrasis* + *-logia* -logy] – **phraseological** /-zi·əˈlojikl/ *adj*, **phraseologically** *adv*

phrasing /ˈfrayzing/ *n* **1** a style of expression; phraseology **2** the art, act, method, or result of grouping notes into musical phrases

phratry /ˈfraytri/ *n* a tribal subdivision [Gk *phratria*, fr *phratēr* member of the same clan, member of a phratry – more at BROTHER]

phreatic /friˈatik/ *adj* of or being water in the earth [Gk *phreat-*, *phrear* well]

phren- /frin-, fren-/, **phreno-** *comb form* **1** mind ⟨phreno*logy*⟩ **2** diaphragm ⟨phren*ic*⟩ [Gk, fr *phren-*, *phrēn* diaphragm, mind]

phrenetic /friˈnetik/ *adj* frenetic

phrenic /ˈfrenik/ *adj* of the diaphragm [NL *phrenicus*, fr *phren-*]

phrenology /friˈnoləji/ *n* the study of the conformation of the skull as a supposed indicator of mental faculties and character – **phrenologist** *n*, **phrenological** /ˌfrenəˈlojikl, ˌfree-/ *adj*, **phrenologically** *adv*

Phrygian /ˈfriji·ən/ *n* a native or inhabitant of ancient Phrygia [*Phrygia*, ancient country of Asia Minor] – **Phrygian** *adj*

ˌphthalic ˈacid /ˈ(f)thalik/ *n* an acid obtained by oxidation of various benzene derivatives [ISV, short for obs *naphthalic acid*, fr *naphthalene*]

phthisis /ˈthiesis/ *n*, *pl* **phthises** /-ˌseez/ a progressive wasting condition; *esp* lung tuberculosis [L, fr Gk, fr *phthinein* to waste away; akin to Skt *kṣiṇoti* he destroys]

¹phut /fut/ *n* a dull sound as of sthg bursting [imit]

²phut, fut *adv*, *chiefly Br* WRONG 4 – chiefly in *go phut*; infml ⟨*steam iron went* ~⟩

phyl- /fil-/, **phylo-** *comb form* tribe; race; phylum ⟨phylogeny⟩ [L, fr Gk, fr *phylē*, *phylon*; akin to Gk *phyein* to bring forth – more at BE]

phylactery /fiˈlakt(ə)ri/ *n* either of 2 small square leather boxes containing passages from scripture, traditionally worn on the left arm and forehead by Jewish men during morning weekday prayers [ME *philaterie*, fr ML *philaterium*, alter. of LL *phylacterium*, fr Gk *phylaktērion* amulet, phylactery, fr *phylassein* to guard, fr *phylak-*, *phylax* guard]

phyll- /fil-/, **phyllo-** *comb form* leaf ⟨phyll*oid*⟩ ⟨phyllo*phagous*⟩ [NL, fr Gk, fr *phyllon* – more at BLADE]

phyllode /ˈfilohd/ *n* a flat expanded leaf stalk that resembles the blade of a foliage leaf and fulfils the same functions [NL *phyllodium*, fr Gk *phyllōdēs* like a leaf, fr *phyllon* leaf]

phyllopod /ˈfilohˌpod/ *n* any of a group of crustaceans that typically have leaflike swimming appendages that also serve as gills [deriv of Gk *phyllon* leaf + *pod-*, *pous* foot – more at FOOT] – **phyllopod** *adj*, **phyllopodan** /fiˈlopəd(ə)n/ *adj or n*, **phyllopodous** /fiˈlopədəs/ *adj*

phyllotaxy /ˈfilohˌtaksi/ *also* **phyllotaxis** /ˌfilohˈtaksis/ *n* (the study of) the arrangement of leaves on a stem [NL *phyllotaxis*, fr *phyll-* + *-taxis*] – **phyllotactic** /ˌfiloh'taktik/ *adj*

phylloxera /ˌfilok'siərə/ *n* any of various plant lice that are destructive to many plants (e g grapevines) [NL, genus name, fr *phyll-* + Gk *xēros* dry – more at SERENE] – **phylloxeran** *adj or n*

phylogenesis /ˌfieloh'jenəsis/ *n* phylogeny [NL, fr *phyl-* + L *genesis*] – **phylogenetic** /-ji'netik/ *adj*, **phylogenetically** *adv*

phylogeny /fi'lojəni/ *n* (the history of) the evolution of a genetically related group of organisms (e g a race or species) [ISV] – **phylogenic** /ˌfiloh'jenik/ *adj*

phylum /'filəm/ *n, pl* **phyla** /-lə/ a major group of related species in the classification of plants and animals [NL, fr Gk *phylon* tribe, race – more at PHYL-]

-phyre /-fie·ə/ *comb form* (→ *n*) porphyritic rock ⟨*grano*phyre⟩ [F, fr *porphyre* porphyry, fr ML *porphyrium* – more at PORPHYRY]

physi-, physio- *comb form* **1** nature ⟨physio*graphy*⟩ **2** physical ⟨physio*therapy*⟩ [L, fr Gk, fr *physis* – more at PHYSICS]

[1]**physic** /'fizik/ *n* a medicinal preparation (e g a drug); *esp* a purgative [ME *physik, phisic* natural science, art of medicine, fr OF *fisique*, fr L *physica* (sing.) natural science, fr Gk *physikē*, fr fem of *physikos* – more at PHYSICS]

[2]**physic** *vt* **-ck-** *archaic* to administer medicine to; *esp* to purge [ME *phisiken*, fr *phisik*]

physical /'fizikl/ *adj* **1a** having material existence; perceptible, esp through the senses, and subject to the laws of nature **b** of material things **2a** of natural science **b** of or involving physics ⟨~ *chemistry*⟩ **3a** of the body ⟨~ *education*⟩ **b** concerned or preoccupied with the body and its needs, as opposed to spiritual matters [ME, fr ML *physicalis*, fr L *physica* physics] – **physically** *adv*

ˌphysical ge'ography *n* geography that deals with the exterior physical features and changes of the earth

physicality /ˌfizi'kaləti/ *n* intensely physical orientation; predominance of the physical, usu at the expense of the mental, spiritual, or social

ˌphysical 'jerks *n* bodily exercises – infml

ˌphysical 'science *n* the natural sciences (e g physics, astronomy, etc) that deal primarily with nonliving materials – **physical scientist** *n*

physician /fi'zish(ə)n/ *n* a person skilled in the art of healing; *specif* a doctor of medicine [ME *fisicien*, fr OF, fr *fisique* medicine]

physico- /fizikoh-/ *comb form* **1** physical ⟨phys*icogeographical*⟩ **2** physical and ⟨physico*chemical*⟩ [NL, fr L *physicus*, fr Gk *physikos*]

physics /'fiziks/ *n pl but sing or pl in constr* **1** a science that deals with (the properties and interactions of) matter and energy in such fields as mechanics, heat, electricity, magnetism, atomic structure, etc **2** the physical properties and phenomena of a particular system [L *physica*, pl, natural science, fr Gk *physika*, fr neut pl of *physikos* of nature, fr *physis* growth, nature, fr *phyein* to bring forth – more at BE] – **physicist** /'fizisist/ *n*

Physiocrat /'fizioh,krat/ *n* a member of a school of political economists of 18th-c France, who believed in allowing the operation of natural economic laws [F *physiocrate*, fr *physi-* + *-crate* -crat] – **physiocratic** /ˌfizi·ə'kratik/ *adj, often cap*

physiognomy /ˌfizi'onəmi/ *n* **1** the art of judging character from outward appearance **2** the facial features, esp when revealing qualities of mind or character **3** an external aspect; *also* inner character or quality revealed outwardly ⟨*the* ~ *of a political party*⟩ [ME *phisonomie*, fr MF, fr LL *physiognomonia, physiognomia*, fr Gk *physiognōmonia*, fr *physiognōmōn* judging character by the features, fr *physis* nature, physique, appearance + *gnōmōn* interpreter – more at GNOMON] – **physiognomic** /ˌfizi·ə'nomik/, **physiognomical** *adj*, **physiognomically** *adv*

physiography /ˌfizi'ografi/ *n* **1** a description of nature or natural phenomena **2** physical geography [prob fr (assumed) NL *physiographia*, fr NL *physi-* + L *-graphia* -graphy] – **physiographer** *n*, **physiographic** /-zi·ə'grafik/ *also* **physiographical** *adj*

physiological /ˌfizi·ə'lojikl/, **physiologic** *adj* **1** of physiology **2** characteristic of or appropriate to an organism's healthy or normal functioning ⟨*the* ~ *level of a substance in the blood*⟩ – **physiologically** *adv*

physiological saline *n* a solution of a salt or salts that is similar in concentration to tissue fluids or blood

physiology /ˌfizi'oləji/ *n* **1** biology that deals with the functions and activities of life or of living matter (e g organs, tissues, or cells) and the physical and chemical phenomena involved – compare ANATOMY **2** the physiological activities of (part of) an organism or a particular bodily function ⟨*the* ~ *of sex*⟩ [L *physiologia* natural science, fr Gk, fr *physi-* + *-logia* -logy] – **physiologist** *n*

physiotherapy /ˌfizi·oh'therəpi/ *n* the treatment of disease by physical and mechanical means (e g massage and regulated exercise) [NL *physiotherapia*, fr *physi-* + *therapia* therapy] – **physiotherapist** *n*

physique /fi'zeek/ *n* the form or structure of a person's body [F, fr *physique* physical, bodily, fr L *physicus* of nature, fr Gk *physikos*]

phyt- /fiet-/, **phyto-** *comb form* plant ⟨phyto *chemistry*⟩ ⟨phyto*pathology*⟩ [NL, fr Gk, fr *phyton*, fr *phyein* to bring forth – more at BE]

-phyte /-ˌfiet/ *comb form* (→ *n*) **1** plant having (a specified characteristic or habitat) ⟨*sapro*phyte⟩ **2** pathological growth ⟨*osteo*phyte⟩ [ISV, fr Gk *phyton* plant] – **-phytic** /-'fitik/ *comb form* (→ *adj*)

phytography /fie'tografi/ *n* descriptive botany, sometimes including plant taxonomy [NL *phytographia*, fr *phyt-* + L *-graphia* -graphy]

phytophagous /fie'tofəgəs/ *adj, esp of an insect* feeding on plants – **phytophagy** *n*

phytoplankton /ˌfietoh'plangktən/ *n* planktonic plant life – compare ZOOPLANKTON [ISV] – **phytoplanktonic** /-plangk'tonik/ *adj*

ˌphyto'toxic /-'toksik/ *adj* poisonous to plants – **phytotoxicity** /-tok'sisəti/ *n*

[1]**pi** /pie/ *n, pl* **pis** /piez/ **1** the 16th letter of the Greek alphabet **2** (the symbol π denoting) the ratio of the circumference of a circle to its diameter with a value, to 8 decimal places, of 3.14159265 ☞ SYMBOL [MGk, fr Gk *pei*, of Sem origin; akin to Heb *pē*, 17th letter of the Heb alphabet]

[2]**pi** *vt* **pies; piing, pieing; pied** *chiefly NAm* [3]PIE

[3]**pi** *adj, Br* pious – derog [by shortening]

piaffe /pi'af/ *vi, of a horse* to move at a slow trot [F *piaffer*, lit., to strut]

piaffer /pi'afə/ *n* the action or an instance of piaffing

Base SI units

unit	*symbol*	*concept*
ampere	A	electric current
candela	cd	luminous intensity
kelvin	K	thermodynamic temperature
kilogram	kg	mass
metre	m	length
mole	mol	amount of substance
second	s	time

Derived SI units with names

coulomb	C	electric charge
farad	F	capacitance
henry	H	inductance
hertz	Hz	frequency
joule	J	work or energy
lumen	lm	luminous flux
lux	lx	illumination
newton	N	force
ohm	Ω	electric resistance
pascal	Pa	pressure
tesla	T	magnetic flux density
volt	V	electric potential (difference)
watt	W	power
weber	Wb	magnetic flux

Supplementary SI units

radian	rad	plane angle
steradian	sr	solid angle

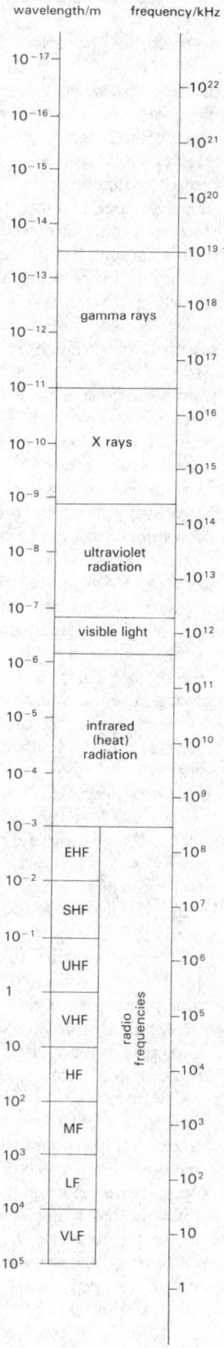

Fundamental constants

constant	*symbol*	*value*
velocity of light in a vacuum	c	2.998×10^{8} m s^{-1}
charge on electron	e	1.602×10^{-19} C
rest mass of an electron	m_e	9.110×10^{-31} kg
rest mass of a proton	m_p	1.673×10^{-27} kg
rest mass of a neutron	m_n	1.675×10^{-27} kg
Avogadro's constant	L, N_A	6.022×10^{23} mol^{-1}
standard atmospheric pressure		1.013 Pa
acceleration due to gravity	g	9.807 m s^{-2}
velocity of sound at sea level at 0°C		331.46 m s^{-1}
magnetic constant (permeability of free space)	μ_0 .	$4\pi \times 10^{-7}$ H m^{-1}
electric constant (permittivity of free space)	$\epsilon_0 = \mu_0^{-1}c^{-2}$	8.854×10^{-12} F m^{-1}
Planck's constant	h	6.626×10^{-34} J s
Boltzmann's constant	$k = \frac{R}{L}$	1.381×10^{-23} J K^{-1}
universal gas constant	$R = Lk$	8.314 J K^{-1} mol^{-1}
Faraday constant	$F = Ne$	9.649×10^{4} C mol^{-1}
gravitational constant	G	6.673×10^{-11} N m^{2} kg^{-2}

Other units used with SI (in specialized fields)

unit	*symbol*	*value*	*concept*
ångstrom	Å	10^{-10} m	length
astronomical unit	AU	149,600,000 km	length
degree celsius	C	1 K	temperature
electron volt	eV	1.60219×10^{-19} J	energy
parsec	pc	30857×10^{12} m	length

Metric prefixes

exa	E	10^{18}	1 000 000 000 000 000 000
peta	P	10^{15}	1 000 000 000 000 000
tera	T	10^{12}	1 000 000 000 000
giga	G	10^{9}	1 000 000 000
mega	M	10^{6}	1 000 000
kilo	k	10^{3}	1000
hecto	h	10^{2}	100
deca	da	10^{1}	10
deci	d	10^{-1}	0.1
centi	c	10^{-2}	0.01
milli	m	10^{-3}	0.001
micro	μ	10^{-6}	0.000 001
nano	n	10^{-9}	0.000 000 001
pico	p	10^{-12}	0.000 000 000 001
femto	f	10^{-15}	0.000 000 000 000 001
atto	a	10^{-18}	0.000 000 000 000 000 001

Spectrum of electromagnetic radiation

wavelength/m: 10^{-17}, 10^{-16}, 10^{-15}, 10^{-14}, 10^{-13}, 10^{-12}, 10^{-11}, 10^{-10}, 10^{-9}, 10^{-8}, 10^{-7}, 10^{-6}, 10^{-5}, 10^{-4}, 10^{-3}, 10^{-2}, 10^{-1}, 1, 10, 10^{2}, 10^{3}, 10^{4}, 10^{5}

frequency/kHz: 10^{22}, 10^{21}, 10^{20}, 10^{19}, 10^{18}, 10^{17}, 10^{16}, 10^{15}, 10^{14}, 10^{13}, 10^{12}, 10^{11}, 10^{10}, 10^{9}, 10^{8}, 10^{7}, 10^{6}, 10^{5}, 10^{4}, 10^{3}, 10^{2}, 10, 1

gamma rays

X rays

ultraviolet radiation

visible light

infrared (heat) radiation

radio frequencies: EHF, SHF, UHF, VHF, HF, MF, LF, VLF

pia mater /ˌpie·ə 'mahtə, 'maytə/ *n* the thin membrane that envelops the brain and spinal cord and is internal to the dura mater [ME, fr ML, fr L, tender mother]

pianissimo /ˌpee·ə'nisimoh/ *adv or adj* very soft – used in music [It, superl of *piano* softly]

pianist /'pee·ənist/ *n* a performer on the piano

pianistic /ˌpee·ə'nistik/ *adj* **1** of or characteristic of the piano **2** skilled in or well adapted to piano playing – **pianistically** *adv*

[1]**piano** /pi'ahnoh, 'pyah-/ *adv or adj* in a soft or quiet manner – used in music [It, fr LL *planus* smooth, fr L, level – more at FLOOR]

[2]**piano** /pi'anoh/ *n, pl* **pianos** a stringed instrument having steel wire strings that sound when struck by felt-covered hammers operated from a keyboard [It, short for *pianoforte*, fr *piano e forte* soft and loud]

pianoforte /ˌpyanoh'fawti, piˌah-, piˌa-/ *n* a piano [It]

piano hinge *n* a hinge that extends along the full length of the parts to be joined

Pianola /ˌpee·ə'nohlə/ *trademark* – used for a mechanical piano operated by the pressure of air through perforations in a paper roll

piassava /piə'sahvə/ *n* any of several stiff coarse fibres obtained from palms and used esp in making ropes or brushes [Pg *piassaba*, fr Tupi *piaçaba*]

piastre, *NAm* **piaster** /pi'astə/ *n* (a note or coin representing) a unit worth $^1/_{100}$ of the basic money unit of certain Middle Eastern countries (e g Egypt, Syria) ☞ NATIONALITY [F *piastre*, fr It *piastra* thin metal plate, coin]

piazza /pi'atsə, pi'adzə/ *n, pl* **piazzas, piazze** /-si/ **1** an open square, esp in an Italian town **2** *NAm* a veranda [It, fr L *platea* broad street – more at PLACE]

pibroch /'peebrok(h)/ *n* a set of martial or mournful variations for the Scottish Highland bagpipe [ScGael *piobaireachd* pipe-music]

pic /pik/ *n, pl* **pics, pix** /piks/ a photograph – infml [short for *picture*]

[1]**pica** /'piekə/ *n* **1** a unit of 4.23 mm (about $^1/_6$ in) used in measuring typographical material **2** a typewriter type providing 10 characters to the linear inch [prob fr ML, collection of church rules]

[2]**pica** *n* the pathological craving for and eating of inappropriate substances (e g chalk or ashes) [NL, fr L, magpie – more at [1]PIE]

picador /'pikəˌdaw/ *n, pl* **picadors, picadores** /-dawˌrayz/ a horseman who in a bullfight prods the bull with a lance to weaken its neck and shoulder muscles [Sp, fr *picar* to prick, fr (assumed) VL *piccare* – more at [3]PIKE]

picaresque /ˌpikə'resk/ *adj* of or being fiction narrating in loosely linked episodes the adventures of a rogue [Sp *picaresco*, fr *pícaro* rogue]

picayune / ˌpikə'yoohn/ *adj, NAm* of little value; paltry; *also* petty, small-minded [F *picaillon* halfpenny, fr Prov *picaioun*, fr *picaio* money, fr *pica* to prick, jingle, fr (assumed) VL *piccare*] – **picayune** *n*, **picayunish** *adj*

piccalilli /ˌpikə'lili/ *n* a hot relish of chopped vegetables, mustard, and spices [prob alter. of *pickle*]

piccaninny, *chiefly NAm* **picaninny, pickaninny** /'pikəˌnini, ˌ--'--/ *n* a small Negro child – chiefly derog [prob modif of Pg *pequenino* very little, fr *pequeno* small]

piccolo /'pikəˌloh/ *n, pl* **piccolos** a small shrill flute whose range is an octave higher than that of an ordinary flute [It, short for *piccolo flauto* small flute] – **piccoloist** *n*

pice /pies/ *n, pl* **pice** a paisa [Hindi *paisā*]

piceous /'pisi·əs, 'pie-/ *adj* of or resembling pitch, esp in colour [L *piceus*, fr *pic-, pix* pitch – more at [1]PITCH]

[1]**pick** /pik/ *vt* **1** to pierce, penetrate, or break up with a pointed instrument ⟨~ed *the hard clay*⟩ **2a** to remove bit by bit ⟨~ *meat from bones*⟩ **b** to remove covering or clinging matter from ⟨~ed *the bones clean*⟩ **3a** to gather by plucking ⟨~ed *flowers*⟩ **b** to choose, select ⟨*tried to* ~ *the shortest route*⟩ ⟨*she* ~ed *out the most expensive dress*⟩ **4** to pilfer from; rob ⟨~ *pockets*⟩ **5** to provoke ⟨~ *a quarrel*⟩ **6a** to dig into, esp in order to remove unwanted matter; probe ⟨~ *his teeth*⟩ ⟨~ *his nose*⟩ **b** to pluck with a plectrum or with the fingers ⟨~ *a guitar*⟩ **c** to loosen or pull apart with a sharp point ⟨~ *wool*⟩ **7** to unlock with a device (e g a wire) other than the key ⟨~ *a lock*⟩ **8** to make (one's way) carefully on foot ~ *vi* to gather or harvest sthg by plucking [ME *piken*, partly fr (assumed) OE *pīcian* (akin to MD *picken* to prick); partly fr MF *piquer* to prick – more at [3]PIKE] – **pick and choose** to select with care and deliberation – **pick at 1** to find fault with, esp in a petty way **2** to eat sparingly and with little interest; toy with – **pick on 1** to single out for unpleasant treatment or an unpleasant task **2** to single out for a particular purpose or for special attention – **pick someone's brains** to obtain ideas or information from sby – **pick someone/something to pieces** to subject to systematic adverse criticism

[2]**pick** *n* **1** the act or privilege of choosing or selecting; a choice ⟨*take your* ~⟩ **2** *sing or pl in constr* the best or choicest ⟨*the* ~ *of the herd*⟩ **3** the portion of a crop gathered at 1 time ⟨*the first* ~ *of grapes*⟩

[3]**pick** *vt* to throw (a shuttle) across the loom [ME *pykken*, alter. of *picchen* to pitch]

[4]**pick** *n* **1** a throw of the shuttle across a loom **2** one weft thread taken as a unit of fineness of fabric – compare [2]COUNT 5

[5]**pick** *n* **1** a heavy wooden-handled iron or steel tool with a head that is pointed at one or both ends – compare MATTOCK **2** a toothpick **3** a plectrum [ME *pik*]

pickaback /'pikəˌbak/ *n, adv, or adj* (a) piggyback

pickaninny /'pikəˌnini, ˌ--'--/ *n, chiefly NAm* a piccaninny

pickaxe /'pikˌaks/ *n* [5] PICK 1 [alter. of ME *pikois, pikeis*, fr OF *picois*, fr *pic* pick, fr L *picus* woodpecker – more at [1]PIE]

picked *adj* choice, prime

picker /'pikə/ *n* **1** a person or machine that picks sthg, esp crops **2** a person or the part of the loom that threads the shuttle

pickerel /'pik(ə)rəl/ *n, pl* **pickerels**, *esp collectively* **pickerel** *dial chiefly Br* a young or small pike [ME *pikerel*, dim. of *pike*]

[1]**picket** /'pikit/ *n* **1** a pointed or sharpened stake or post **2** *sing or pl in constr* **a** a small body of troops detached to guard an army from surprise attack **b** a detachment kept ready in camp for such duty **3** a person posted by a trade union at a place of work affected by a strike; *also* a person posted for a demonstration or protest [F *piquet*, fr MF, fr *piquer* to prick – more at [3]PIKE]

²picket *vt* **1** to enclose, fence, or fortify with pickets **2** to tether **3** to guard with or post as a picket **4a** to post pickets at **b** to walk or stand in front of as a picket ~*vi* to serve as a picket – **picketer** *n*

'picket ˌline *n* a line of people picketing a business, organization, etc

pickings /'pikingz/ *n pl* sthg picked (up): e g **a** gleanable or eatable fragments; scraps **b** yield or return for effort expended; *esp* rewards obtained by dishonest or dubious means

¹pickle /'pikl/ *n* **1** a solution or bath for preserving or cleaning: e g **a** a brine or vinegar solution in which meat, fish, vegetables, etc are preserved **b** an acidic solution for cleaning metal **2** (an article of) food preserved in a pickle; *also* chutney – often pl **3** a difficult situation – infml ⟨*I could see no way out of the* ~ *I was in* – R L Stevenson⟩ **4** *Br* a mischievous or troublesome child – infml [ME *pekille*, prob fr MD *pekel, peekel*]

²pickle *vt* **pickling** /'pikling/ to treat, preserve, or clean in or with a pickle

³pickle *n, Scot* a small quantity [perh fr Sc *pickle* (to trifle, pilfer), fr ME *pikelen*, fr *piken* to pick]

'pickled *adj* DRUNK 1 – infml

'pick-me-ˌup *n* sthg that stimulates or restores; a tonic

pick off *vt* to shoot or bring down one by one ⟨*the sniper* picked off *the enemy troops*⟩

pick out *vt* **1** to make clearly visible, esp as distinguished from a background ⟨*the fences were* picked out *in red*⟩ **2** to play the notes of by ear or one by one ⟨*learned to* pick out *tunes on the piano*⟩

pick over *vt* to examine in order to select the best or discard the unwanted ⟨picked over *the berries*⟩

'pickˌpocket /-ˌpokit/ *n* one who steals from pockets or bags

pickup /-ˌup/ *n* **1** the act or process of picking up **2** sby or sthg picked up: e g **a** a hitchhiker who is given a lift **b** a temporary casual acquaintance; *esp* one made with the intention of having sex **3** a device (e g on a record player) that converts mechanical movements into electrical signals **4** a device (e g a microphone or a television camera) for converting sound or an image into electrical signals **5** interference (e g to reception) from an adjacent electrical circuit or system **6** a light motor truck having an open body with low sides and tailboard

pick up *vt* **1a** to take hold of and lift up ⟨picked up *the pencil*⟩ **b** to gather together; collect ⟨picked up *all the pieces*⟩ **2** to take (passengers or freight) into a vehicle **3a** to acquire casually or by chance ⟨picked up *a valuable antique at a jumble sale*⟩ ⟨picked up *some money doing odd jobs*⟩ **b** to acquire by study or experience; learn ⟨picking up *a great deal of information in the process*⟩ **c** to collect ⟨picked up *his clothes at the cleaners*⟩ **d** to accept for the purpose of paying ⟨*the government should* pick up *the bill for the damaged ship*⟩ **4** to enter informally into conversation or companionship with (a previously unknown person), usu with the intention of having sex **5a** to take into custody **b** to discover and follow ⟨picked up *the outlaw's trail*⟩ **c** to bring within range of sight, hearing, or a sensor ⟨picked up *the planes on the radar*⟩ **6** to revive **7** to resume after a break; continue **8** *chiefly NAm* to clean up; tidy ~*vi* **1** to recover speed, vigour, or activity; improve ⟨*after the strike, business* picked up⟩ **2** to put things in order; tidy

Pickwickian /pik'wiki·ən, -kyən/ *adj, of a word or expression* intended or taken in a sense other than the obvious or literal one [Samuel *Pickwick*, character in the novel *Pickwick Papers* by Charles Dickens †1870 E novelist]

picky /'piki/ *adj, chiefly NAm* fussy, choosy ⟨*a* ~ *eater*⟩

¹picnic /'piknik/ *n* **1** (the food eaten at) an outing that includes an informal meal, usu lunch, eaten in the open **2** a pleasant or amusingly carefree experience ⟨*don't expect marriage to be a* ~⟩; *also* an easily accomplished task or feat – infml [G or F; G *picknick*, fr F *pique-nique*] – **picnicky** *adj*

²picnic *vi* **-ck-** to go on a picnic – **picnicker** *n*

pico- /peekoh-, peekə-/ *comb form* one million millionth (10^{-12}) part of (a specified unit) ⟨picogram⟩ ☞ PHYSICS [ISV, perh fr It *piccolo* small]

picot /'peekoh/ *vt or n* (to finish with an edging of) any of a series of small ornamental loops on ribbon or lace [n F, lit., small point, fr MF, fr *pic* prick, fr *piquer* to prick – more at ³PIKE; vb fr n]

picotee /ˌpikə'tee/ *n* a flower (e g some carnations or tulips) having 1 basic colour with a margin of another colour [F *picoté* pointed, fr *picoter* to mark with points, fr *picot*]

picr-, picro- *comb form* bitter ⟨picric *acid*⟩ ⟨picrotoxin⟩ [F, fr Gk *pikr-, pikro-*, fr *pikros* – more at PAINT]

ˌpicric 'acid /'pikrik/ *n* an explosive yellow strong acid used esp in powerful explosives and as an antiseptic [ISV]

Pict /pikt/ *n* a member of a possibly non-Celtic people who once occupied Britain and later became amalgamated with the Scots [ME *Pictes*, pl, Picts, fr LL *Picti*, perh fr L *picti* painted people, fr *pictus*, pp of *pingere* to paint] – **Pictish** *adj*

Pictish *n* the language of the Picts

pictograph /'piktəˌgrahf, -ˌgraf/, **pictogram** /-ˌgram/ *n* **1** an ancient or prehistoric drawing or painting on a rock wall **2** any of the symbols used in a system of picture writing – compare IDEOGRAM, LOGOGRAM **3** a diagram representing statistical data by pictorial forms [L *pictus* + E *-o-* + *-graph*] – **pictography** /-'togrəfi/ *n*, **pictographic** /ˌpiktə'grafik/ *adj*

pictorial /pik'tawri·əl/ *adj* **1** of (a) painting or drawing ⟨~ *perspective*⟩ **2** consisting of or illustrated by pictures ⟨~ *records*⟩ **3** suggesting or conveying visual images [LL *pictorius*, fr L *pictor* painter, fr *pictus*, pp] – **pictorially** *adv*, **pictorialness** *n*

¹picture /'pikchə/ *n* **1** a design or representation made by painting, drawing, etc **2a** a description so vivid or graphic as to suggest a mental image or give an accurate idea of sthg ⟨*painted a vivid* ~ *of life in Victorian England*⟩ **b** a presentation of the relevant or characteristic facts concerning a problem or situation ⟨*drew an alarming* ~ *of the economic future*⟩ **3a** an image, copy ⟨*he was the* ~ *of his father*⟩ **b** the perfect example ⟨*he looked the* ~ *of health*⟩ **c** a striking or picturesque sight ⟨*his face was a* ~ *when he heard the news*⟩ **4a** a transitory visible image or reproduction ⟨*adjusted the television for a brighter* ~⟩ **b** FILM 3a, b **c** *pl, chiefly Br* CINEMA 1b, 2 – infml ⟨*what's on at the* ~*s?*⟩ **5** a situation ⟨*a look at the overall political* ~⟩ [ME, fr L *pictura*, fr *pictus*, pp of *pingere* to paint – more at PAINT] – **in the picture** fully informed and up to date

[2]**picture** *vt* **1** to paint or draw a representation, image, or visual conception of; depict **2** to describe graphically in words **3** to form a mental image of; imagine

picture hat *n* a woman's usu decorated hat with a broad brim ☞ GARMENT

,**picture-'postcard** *adj* picturesque ⟨~ *villages*⟩

picturesque /,pikchə'resk/ *adj* **1** quaint, charming **2** evoking striking mental images; vivid ⟨~ *language*⟩ [F & It; F *pittoresque*, fr It *pittoresco*, fr *pittore* painter, fr L *pictor*, fr *pictus*, pp] – **picturesquely** *adv*, **picturesqueness** *n*

picture window *n* a large esp single-paned window usu facing an attractive view

[1]**piddle** /'pidl/ *vi* **piddling** /'pidling/ **1** to act or work in an idle or trifling manner **2** to urinate *USE* infml [origin unknown]

[2]**piddle** *n* **1** urine **2** an act of urinating *USE* infml

piddling /'pidling/ *adj* trivial, paltry – infml

piddock /'pidək/ *n* a bivalve mollusc that bores holes in wood, clay, and rocks [origin unknown]

pidgin /'pijin/ *n* a language based on 2 or more languages and used esp for trade between people with different native languages – compare CREOLE 4 [*Pidgin English*, oriental modif of *business English*] – **pidginize** *vt*

[1]**pie** /pie/ *n* **1** MAGPIE 1 **2** a variegated animal [ME, fr OF, fr L *pica*; akin to L *picus* woodpecker, OHG *speh*]

[2]**pie** *n* a dish consisting of a sweet or savoury filling covered or encased by pastry and baked in a container [ME]

[3]**pie,** *chiefly NAm* **pi** *vt* to spill or throw (type or typeset matter) into disorder [origin unknown] – **pie** *n*

[1]**piebald** /'pie,bawld/ *adj* **1** *esp of a horse* of different colours; *specif* spotted or blotched with different colours, esp black and white **2** composed of incongruous parts; heterogeneous [[1]*pie* + *bald* (streaked with white)]

[2]**piebald** *n* a piebald horse or other animal

[1]**piece** /pees/ *n* **1a** a part of a whole; *esp* a part detached, cut, or broken from a whole ⟨~ *of string*⟩ **b** a portion marked off ⟨*bought a* ~ *of land*⟩ **2** an object or individual regarded as a unit of a kind or class; an example ⟨*fine teak tables copied from antique* ~s⟩ **3** a standard quantity (e g of length, weight, or size) in which sthg is made or sold **4a** a literary, artistic, dramatic, or musical work **b** a passage to be recited **5** a coin, esp of a specified value ⟨*a 5-pence* ~⟩ **6** a man used in playing a board game; *esp* a chessman of rank superior to a pawn **7** a gun used for a specified purpose ⟨*an artillery* ~⟩ **8** a person; *esp* a woman – slang [ME, fr OF, fr (assumed) VL *pettia*, of Gaulish origin; akin to Bret *pez* piece] – **piece of one's mind** a severe scolding – **of a piece** alike, consistent – **to pieces 1** into fragments **2** out of control ⟨*went* to pieces *from shock*⟩

[2]**piece** *vt* **1** to repair, renew, or complete by adding pieces; patch – often + *up* **2** to join into a whole – often + *together* ⟨*he* ~d *the story together from the accounts of witnesses*⟩ – **piecer** *n*

,**piece by 'piece** *adv* by degrees; piecemeal

pièce de résistance /,pyes də rəzis'tahn(h)s (*Fr* pjɛs də rezistɑ̃:s)/ *n, pl* **pièces de résistance** /~/ **1** the chief dish of a meal **2** an outstanding item; a showpiece [F, lit., piece of resistance]

'**piece-,dye** *vt* to dye after weaving or knitting

'**piece ,goods** *n pl* **1** fabrics made and sold in standard lengths **2** *chiefly NAm* fabrics sold from the bolt by the retailer in lengths specified by the customer

[1]'**piece,meal** /-meel/ *adv* **1** one piece at a time; gradually **2** in pieces or fragments; apart

[2]**piecemeal** *adj* done, made, or accomplished piece by piece or in a fragmentary way

,**piece of 'cake** *n* sthg easily accomplished – infml

,**piece of 'eight** *n* a peso

'**piece ,rate** *n* a system whereby wages are calculated according to a set rate per unit produced

'**piece,work** /-,wuhk/ *n* work that is paid for at a set rate per unit – **pieceworker** *n*

piecrust /'pie,krust/ *n* the baked pastry covering of a pie

pied /pied/ *adj* having patches of 2 or more colours

pied-à-terre /,pyay ɑh 'teə (*Fr* pje a tɛ:r/ *n, pl* **pieds-à-terre** /~/ a temporary or second lodging (e g a flat in a city kept by sby who lives in the country) [F, lit., foot to the ground]

,**pied 'piper** /pied/ *n, often cap both Ps* one who offers strong but delusive enticement [*The Pied Piper of Hamelin*, title & hero of a poem by Robert Browning †1889 E poet]

,**pie-'eyed** *adj* DRUNK 1 – infml [prob fr [3]*pie*]

,**pie in the 'sky** *n* a prospect or promise of deferred and often illusory happiness or prosperity – infml

pier /piə/ *n* **1** an intermediate support for the adjacent ends of 2 bridge spans **2** a structure extending into navigable water for use as a landing place, promenade, etc **3** a vertical structural support (e g for a wall) ☞ CHURCH [ME *per*, fr OE, fr ML *pera*]

pierce /piəs/ *vt* **1** to enter or thrust into sharply or painfully; stab ⟨*the thorn* ~d *his finger*⟩ **2** to make a hole in or through; perforate **3** to force or make a way into or through ⟨*a light* ~d *the darkness*⟩ **4** to penetrate with the eye or mind; discern **5** to move or affect the emotions of, esp sharply or painfully ⟨*grief* ~d *his heart when he heard of his son's death*⟩ **6** to sound sharply through ⟨*a shriek* ~d *the stillness of the evening*⟩ **7** *of cold* to penetrate ⟨*the cold* ~d *them to the bone*⟩ ~ *vi* to force a way into or through sthg [ME *percen*, fr OF *percer*, perh fr (assumed) VL *pertusiare*, fr L *pertusus*, pp of *pertundere* to pierce, fr *per* through + *tundere* to beat, pound]

pierced *adj* having holes; *esp* decorated with perforations

piercing /'piəsing/ *adj* penetrating: e g **a** loud, shrill ⟨~ *cries*⟩ **b** perceptive ⟨~ *eyes*⟩ **c** penetratingly cold; biting ⟨*a* ~ *winter wind*⟩ **d** cutting, incisive ⟨~ *sarcasm*⟩ – **piercingly** *adv*

'**pier ,glass** *n* a tall mirror; *esp* one designed to occupy the wall space between 2 windows

Pierrot /'piə,roh/ *n* a stock comic character of old French pantomime usu having a whitened face [F, dim. of *Pierre* Peter]

pietà /,pee·ay'tah, ,pyay-/ *n, often cap* a representation of the Virgin Mary mourning over the dead body of Christ [It, lit., pity, fr L *pietat-*, *pietas*]

pietism /'pie·ə,tiz(ə)m/ *n* **1** *cap* a religious movement originating in 17th-c Germany stressing Bible study and personal religious experience **2a** emphasis on personal devotional experience rather than theology **b** exaggerated religious sentiment – **pietist** *n, often cap*, **pietistic** /ˌpie·əˈtistik/, **pietistical** *adj*, **pietistically** *adv*

piety /ˈpie·əti/ *n* **1** the quality or state of being pious; devoutness **2** dutifulness, esp to parents ⟨*inspired by filial* ~⟩ **3** an act inspired by piety [F *pieté* piety, pity, fr L *pietat-, pietas*, fr *pius* dutiful – more at PIOUS]

piezo- *comb form* pressure ⟨piezo*meter*⟩ ⟨piezo*electric*⟩ [Gk *piezein* to press; akin to Skt *pīḍayati* he squeezes]

piezoelectricity /pieˌeezohiˌlekˈtrisəti, -ˌeelek-/ *n* electricity or electric polarity due to pressure, esp in a crystalline substance (e g quartz) [ISV] – **piezoelectric** /-iˈlektrik/ *adj*

piezometer /ˌpie·iˈzomitə/ *n* an instrument for measuring pressure or compressibility – **piezometry** *n*, **piezometric** /pieˌeezəˈmetrik/ *adj*

piffle /ˈpifl/ *n* trivial nonsense – infml [prob imit]

piffling /ˈpifling/ *adj* trivial, derisory – infml

[1]**pig** /pig/ *n* **1a** *chiefly Br* any of various (domesticated) stout-bodied short-legged omnivorous mammals with a thick bristly skin and a long mobile snout **b** *NAm* a young pig **2** pork **3** sby like or suggestive of a pig in habits or behaviour (e g in dirtiness, greed, or selfishness) ⟨*a male chauvinist* ~⟩ ⟨*made a* ~ *of himself by eating all the cake*⟩ **4** an animal related to or resembling the pig – usu in combination ⟨*guinea* ~⟩ **5** a shaped mass of cast crude metal, esp iron **6** a policeman – slang; derog [ME *pigge*] – **piglet** /-lit/ *n*

[2]**pig** *vb* **-gg-** *vi* **1** to farrow **2** to live like a pig – + *it* ~ *vt* **1** to farrow (piglets) **2a** to eat (food) greedily ⟨~ged *all the cream cakes*⟩ **b** to overindulge (oneself) ⟨~ged *himself on cream cakes*⟩ *USE* (*vt 2*) infml

pigeon /ˈpij(ə)n/ *n* **1** any of a family of birds with a stout body and smooth and compact plumage, many of which are domesticated or live in urban areas ☞ ANATOMY **2** a matter of special concern; business – infml ⟨*that's not my* ~; *someone else can deal with it*⟩ [ME, fr MF *pijon*, fr LL *pipion-, pipio* young bird, fr L *pipire* to chirp; (2) alter. of *pidgin*]

[1]ˈ**pigeonˌhole** /-ˌhohl/ *n* **1** a small open compartment (e g in a desk or cabinet) for letters or documents **2** a neat category which usu fails to reflect actual complexities ⟨*a psychological* ~ *for every misfit*⟩

[2]**pigeonhole** *vt* **1a** to place (as if) in the pigeonhole of a desk **b** to lay aside; shelve **2** to assign to a category; classify

ˌ**pigeon-ˈtoed** *adj* having the toes turned in

piggery /ˈpig(ə)ri/ *n* **1** a place where pigs are kept **2** dirty or nasty behaviour ⟨*male chauvinist* ~⟩

piggish /ˈpigish/, **piggy** /ˈpigi/ *adj* of or resembling a pig, esp in being dirty, greedy, or ill mannered ⟨*embarrassed by his* ~ *eating habits*⟩ – **piggishly** *adv*, **piggishness** *n*

piggy /ˈpigi/ *n* a pig; *esp* a little pig – used esp by or to children

[1]ˈ**piggyˌback** /-ˌbak/ *adv* up on the back and shoulders ⟨*carried the child* ~ *up the stairs*⟩ [alter. of earlier *a pick back, a pick pack*, of unknown origin]

[2]**piggyback** *n* a ride on the back and shoulders of another ⟨*gave his injured friend a* ~⟩

[3]**piggyback** *adj* **1** being up on the shoulders and back ⟨*children love* ~ *rides*⟩ **2** being or relating to sthg carried as an extra load on the back of a vehicle (e g an aircraft)

ˈ**piggy ˌbank** *n* a coin bank often in the shape of a pig

pigheaded /pigˈhedid/ *adj* obstinate, stubborn – **pigheadedness** *n*

ˌ**pig in a ˈpoke** *n* sthg offered in such a way as to obscure its real nature or worth [E dial. *poke* (sack, bag), fr ME, fr ONF – more at POCKET]

ˈ**pig ˌiron** *n* crude iron from the blast furnace before refining

ˈ**pig ˌlead** *n* lead cast in pigs

[1]**pigment** /ˈpigmənt/ *n* **1** a substance that colours other materials; *esp* a powdered substance that is mixed with a liquid in which it is relatively insoluble and is used to colour paints, inks, plastics, etc **2** (a colourless substance related to) any of various colouring matters in animals and plants [L *pigmentum*, fr *pingere* to paint – more at PAINT] – **pigmentary** /-t(ə)ri/ *adj*

[2]**pigment** /pigˈment/ *vt* to colour (as if) with pigment

pigmentation /ˌpigmenˈtaysh(ə)n/ *n* (excessive) coloration with, or deposition of, (bodily) pigment

pigmy /ˈpigmi/ *n* a pygmy

pignut /ˈpigˌnut/ *n* a common plant of the carrot family

ˈ**pigˌpen** /-ˌpen/ *n, NAm* a pigsty

ˈ**pigˌskin** /-ˌskin/ *n* (leather made from) the skin of a pig

ˈ**pigˌsticking** /-ˌstiking/ *n* the hunting of wild boar on horseback with a spear

ˈ**pigˌsty** /-ˌstie/ *n* **1** an enclosure with a covered shed for pigs **2** a dirty, untidy, or neglected place

ˈ**pigˌtail** /-ˌtayl/ *n* **1** a tight plait of hair, esp when worn singly at the back of the head **2** either of 2 bunches of hair worn loose or plaited at either side of the head by young girls – **pigtailed** *adj*

pika /ˈpeekə, ˈpiekə/ *n* any of various short-eared small Asian and N American mammals related to the rabbits [Tungusic *piika*]

[1]**pike** /piek/ *n, Br* a mountain or hill, esp in the Lake District, with a peaked summit [ME, perh of Scand origin; akin to Norw dial. *pīk* pointed mountain]

[2]**pike** *n, pl* **pike**, *esp for different types* **pikes** (any of various fishes related to or resembling) a large long-snouted fish-eating bony fish widely distributed in cooler parts of the N hemisphere [ME, fr *pike* pikestaff, spike; fr the shape of its head]

[3]**pike** *n* a weapon consisting of a long wooden shaft with a pointed steel head that was used by foot soldiers until superseded by the bayonet [MF *pique*, fr *piquer* to prick, fr (assumed) VL *piccare*, fr *piccus* woodpecker, fr L *picus* – more at [1]PIE] – **pike** *vt*

[4]**pike** *n* a body position (e g in diving) in which the hands touch the toes or clasp the legs at the knees, the hips are bent forwards, and the knees are straight [prob fr [2]*pike*]

pikelet /ˈpieklit/ *n, dial Br* a crumpet [by shortening & alter. fr earlier *bara-picklet*, fr W *bara pyglyd* pitchy bread]

pikestaff /-ˌstahf/ *n* **1** a spiked staff for use on slippery ground **2** the staff of a foot soldier's pike

pil- /piel-/, **pili-**, **pilo-** *comb form* hair ⟨pil*eous*⟩ ⟨pil*iferous*⟩ [L *pilus* – more at [5]PILE]

pilaf, pilaff /'pee,laf, 'pi-/ *n* a dish of seasoned rice and often meat [Per & Turk *pilāu*]

pilaster /pi'lastə/ *n* an upright rectangular column that is usu embedded in a wall [MF *pilastre*, fr It *pilastro*]

pilau /'pilow, 'pee,low/ *n* (a) pilaf

pilchard /'pilchəd/ *n* (any of several sardines related to) a fish of the herring family that occurs in great schools along the coasts of Europe [origin unknown]

[1]**pile** /piel/ *n* a beam of timber, steel, reinforced concrete, etc driven into the ground to carry a vertical load [ME, dart, stake, fr OE *pīl*; akin to OHG *pfīl* dart; both fr a prehistoric WGmc word borrowed fr L *pilum* javelin – more at PESTLE]

[2]**pile** *vt* to drive piles into

[3]**pile** *n* **1a** a quantity of things heaped together **b** a heap of wood for burning a corpse or a sacrifice **c** a large quantity, number, or amount ⟨*a ~ of stuff still to be read*⟩ ⟨~s *of friends*⟩ **2** a large building or group of buildings **3** a great amount of money; a fortune ⟨*now that he has made his ~, he can live in luxury*⟩ **4** a vertical series of alternate discs of 2 dissimilar metals (e g copper and zinc) separated by discs of cloth or paper moistened with an electrolyte for producing an electric current **5** REACTOR 2 [ME, fr MF, fr L *pila* pillar]

[4]**pile** *vt* **1** to lay or place in a pile; stack – often + *up* **2** to heap in abundance; load ⟨~d *potatoes on his plate*⟩ ~ *vi* to move or press forwards (as if) in a mass; crowd ⟨~d *into the car*⟩ – **pile it on** to exaggerate

[5]**pile** *n* **1** soft hair, down, fur, or wool **2** a soft raised surface on a fabric or carpet consisting of cut threads or loops [ME, fr L *pilus* hair; akin to L *pila* ball, *pilleus, pileus* felt cap, Gk *pilos*] – **piled** *adj*

[6]**pile** *n* a haemorrhoid – usu pl [ME, fr L *pila* ball]

'pile ,driver *n* a machine for driving piles into the ground

'pile,up /-,up/ *n* a collision involving usu several motor vehicles and causing damage or injury

pile up *vi* **1** to accumulate ⟨*his work* piled up *over the holidays*⟩ **2** to become involved in a pileup of vehicles

pileus /'pieli·əs/ *n, pl* **pilei** /-li,ie/ the (umbrella-shaped) fruiting body of many fungi (e g mushrooms) [NL, fr L] – **pileate** /-li·ət, -ayt/ *adj*

pilfer /'pilfə/ *vb* to steal stealthily in small amounts or to small value [MF *pelfrer*, fr *pelfre* booty] – **pilferage** *n*, **pilferer** *n*

pilgrim /'pilgrim/ *n* a person making a pilgrimage [ME, fr OF *peligrin*, fr LL *pelegrinus*, alter. of L *peregrinus* foreigner, fr *peregrinus* foreign, fr *pereger* being abroad, fr *per* through + *agr-, ager* land – more at FOR, ACRE]

pilgrimage /'pilgrimij/ *n* **1** a journey to a shrine or sacred place as an act of devotion, in order to acquire spiritual merit, or as a penance **2** the course of life on earth

,Pilgrim 'Fathers *n pl* the English colonists who settled at Plymouth, Massachusetts, in 1620

pili- – see PIL-

Pilipino /,pilə'peenoh, ,pee-/ *n* the Tagalog-based official language of the Philippines [Pilipino, fr Sp *Filipino* Philippine]

pill /pil/ *n* **1a** a small rounded solid mass of medicine to be swallowed whole **b** an oral contraceptive in the form of an (oestrogen- and progestogen-containing) pill taken daily by a woman over a monthly cycle – + *the* **2** sthg repugnant or unpleasant that must be accepted or endured ⟨*the loss of salary was a bitter ~ to swallow*⟩ **3** sthg resembling a pill in size or shape **4** a disagreeable or tiresome person – infml [L *pilula*, fr dim. of *pila* ball]

[1]**pillage** /'pilij/ *n* **1** the act of looting or plundering, esp in war **2** sthg taken as booty [ME, fr MF, fr *piller* to plunder, fr *peille* rag, fr L *pilleum, pilleus* felt cap]

[2]**pillage** *vb* to plunder ruthlessly; loot – **pillager** *n*

[1]**pillar** /'pilə/ *n* **1a** a firm upright support for a superstructure **b** a usu ornamental column or shaft **2** a chief supporter; a prop ⟨*a ~ of the Establishment*⟩ **3** a solid mass of coal, ore, etc left standing to support a mine roof [ME *piler*, fr OF, fr ML *pilare*, fr L *pila*] – **from pillar to post** from one place or one situation to another

[2]**pillar** *vt* to support or decorate (as if) with pillars

'pillar ,box *n* a red pillar-shaped public letter box

,pillar-box 'red *adj or n* vivid scarlet

pillbox /'pil,boks/ *n* **1** a box for pills; *esp* a shallow round box made of pasteboard **2** a small low concrete weapon emplacement **3** a small round brimless hat with a flat crown and straight sides, worn esp by women ☞ GARMENT

[1]**pillion** /'pilyən/ *n* a saddle or seat for a passenger on a motorcycle or motor scooter ⟨*a ~ passenger*⟩ [ScGael *pillean* or IrGael *pillīn*, dim. of *peall* covering, couch; orig sense in E, light saddle]

[2]**pillion** *adv* (as if) on a pillion ⟨*ride ~*⟩

[1]**pillory** /'piləri/ *n* **1** a device for publicly punishing offenders consisting of a wooden frame with holes for the head and hands **2** a means for exposing one to public scorn or ridicule [ME, fr OF *pilori*]

[2]**pillory** *vt* **1** to put in a pillory **2** to expose to public contempt, ridicule, or scorn

[1]**pillow** /'piloh/ *n* **1** a usu rectangular cloth bag (e g of cotton) filled with soft material (e g down) and used to support the head of a reclining person **2** sthg resembling a pillow, esp in form [ME *pilwe*, fr OE *pyle*; akin to OHG *pfuliwi* pillow; both fr a prehistoric WGmc word borrowed fr L *pulvinus* pillow]

[2]**pillow** *vt* **1** to rest or lay (as if) on a pillow **2** to serve as a pillow for

'pillow,case /-,kays/ *n* a removable washable cover, esp of cotton or nylon, for a pillow

'pillow ,lace *n* lace worked with bobbins over a padded support – compare NEEDLEPOINT 1, POINT 8

'pillow ,lava *n* lava solidified in rounded masses

'pillow ,slip *n* a pillowcase

pilo- – see PIL-

pilose /'pie,lohs/ *adj* covered with (soft) hair [L *pilosus*, fr *pilus* hair – more at [5]PILE] – **pilosity** /pie'losəti/ *n*

[1]**pilot** /'pielət/ *n* **1** sby qualified and usu licensed to conduct a ship into and out of a port or in specified waters **2** a guide, leader **3** sby who handles or is qualified to handle the controls of an aircraft or spacecraft **4** a piece that guides a tool or machine part [MF *pilote*, fr It *pilota*, alter. of *pedota*, fr (assumed) MGk *pēdōtēs*, fr Gk *pēda* steering oars, pl of *pēdon* oar; akin to Gk *pod-, pous* foot – more at FOOT] – **pilotage** *n*, **pilotless** *adj*

[2]**pilot** *vt* **1** to act as a guide to; lead or conduct over

a usu difficult course **2a** to direct the course of ⟨~ *a ship*⟩ **b** to act as pilot of ⟨~ *a plane*⟩

[3]**pilot** *adj* serving as a guide, activator, or trial ⟨~ *holes*⟩ ⟨~ *lamps*⟩ ⟨*a* ~ *scheme*⟩

'pilot-,cloth *n* a thick blue woollen cloth used esp for seamen's coats

pilot engine *n* a locomotive going in advance of a train to make sure that the way is clear

'pilot ,fish *n* an oceanic fish that often swims in company with a shark

'pilot ,lamp *n* PILOT LIGHT 1

'pilot ,light *n* **1** an indicator light showing whether power is on or where a switch or circuit breaker is located **2** a small permanent flame used to ignite gas at a burner

pilot officer *n* ☞ RANK

pilsner /'pilznə/ *n* a light beer with a strong flavour of hops [G, lit., of Pilsen (now Plzen), city in Czechoslovakia]

,Piltdown 'man /'pilt,down/ *n* a supposedly very early primitive modern man based on skull fragments uncovered in a gravel pit at Piltdown [*Piltdown*, site in East Sussex, England]

pilule /'pilyoohl/ *n* a little pill [MF, fr L *pilula* pill, dim. of *pila* ball] – **pilular** /'pilyoolə/ *adj*

pilus /'pieləs/ *n, pl* **pili** /-lie, -li/ (a structure resembling) a hair [L – more at [5]PILE]

pimento /pi'mentoh/ *n, pl* **pimentos, pimento** **1** a pimiento **2** allspice [Sp *pimienta* allspice, pepper, fr LL *pigmenta*, pl of *pigmentum* plant juice, fr L, pigment – more at PIGMENT]

pimiento /pi'myentoh/ *n, pl* **pimientos** any of various sweet peppers with a mild sweet flavour that are used esp as a garnish and as a stuffing for olives [Sp, fr *pimienta*]

pimp /pimp/ *n* a man who solicits clients for a prostitute or brothel [origin unknown] – **pimp** *vi*

pimpernel /'pimpə,nel/ *n* any of several plants of the primrose family: e g **a** SCARLET PIMPERNEL **b** YELLOW PIMPERNEL [ME *pimpernele*, fr MF *pimprenelle*, fr LL *pimpinella*, a medicinal herb, perh deriv of L *piper* pepper]

pimple /'pimpl/ *n* (a swelling or protuberance like) a small solid inflamed (pus-containing) elevation of the skin [ME *pinple*] – **pimpled** *adj*, **pimply** *adj*

[1]**pin** /pin/ *n* **1a** a piece of solid material (e g wood or metal) used esp for fastening separate articles together or as a support **b** sthg resembling a pin, esp in slender elongated form **2a** a small thin pointed piece of metal with a head used esp for fastening cloth, paper, etc **b** sthg of small value; a trifle ⟨*doesn't care a* ~ *for anyone*⟩ **c** an ornament or badge fastened to clothing with a pin **d** SAFETY PIN **3a** any of the wooden pieces constituting the target in various games (e g skittles and tenpin bowling) **b** the peg at which a quoit is pitched **c** the staff of the flag marking a hole on a golf course **4** a projecting metal bar on a plug which is inserted into a socket **5** PEG 3a **6** a leg – infml; usu pl ⟨*wobbly on his* ~s⟩ [ME, fr OE *pinn*; akin to OHG *pfinn* peg] – **pinned** *adj*

[2]**pin** *vt* **-nn-** **1a** to fasten, join, or secure with a pin **b** to hold fast or immobile ⟨~ned *him against the wall*⟩ **2a** to attach, hang ⟨~ned *his hopes on a miracle*⟩ **b** to assign the blame or responsibility for ⟨~ *the robbery on a night watchman*⟩ **3** to make (a chess opponent's piece) unable to move without exposing the king to check or a valuable piece to capture

pinafore /'pinə,faw/ *n* **1** an apron, usu with a bib **2** *also* **pinafore dress** a sleeveless usu low-necked dress designed to be worn over another garment (e g a blouse) ☞ GARMENT [[2]*pin* + *afore*]

pinball /'pin,bawl/ *n* a game in which a ball is propelled across a sloping surface at pins and targets that score points if hit

'pinball ma,chine *n* an amusement device for playing pinball and automatically recording the score

pince-nez /'pans ,nay, 'pins- (*Fr* pɛ̃s ne)/ *n, pl* **pince-nez** /~/ glasses clipped to the nose by a spring [F, fr *pincer* to pinch + *nez* nose, fr L *nasus* – more at NOSE]

pincer /'pinsə/ *n* **1a** *pl* an instrument having 2 short handles and 2 grasping jaws working on a pivot and used for gripping things **b** a claw (e g of a lobster) resembling a pair of pincers **2** either part of a double military envelopment of an enemy position [ME *pinceour*, prob deriv of MF *pincier* to pinch] – **pincerlike** *adj*

[1]**pinch** /pinch/ *vt* **1a** to squeeze or compress painfully (e g between the finger and thumb or between the jaws of an instrument) **b** to prune the tip of (a plant or shoot), usu to induce branching – + *out* or *back* **c** to cause to appear thin or shrunken ⟨*faces* ~ed *with hunger and fatigue*⟩ **2** to subject to strict economy or want; straiten **3** to sail (a ship) too close to the wind **4a** STEAL 1 – slang **b** ARREST 2 – slang ~ *vi* **1** to compress, squeeze **2** to press painfully ⟨*my new shoes* ~⟩ **3** *of a ship* to sail too close to the wind [ME *pinchen*, fr (assumed) ONF *pinchier*] – **pincher** *n*

[2]**pinch** *n* **1a** a critical juncture; an emergency ⟨*when it comes to the* ~, *he'll let you down*⟩ **b(1)** pressure, stress ⟨*when the* ~ *of foreign competition came at last* – G M Trevelyan⟩ **(2)** hardship, privation ⟨*after a year of sanctions, they began to feel the* ~⟩ **2a** an act of pinching; a squeeze **b** as much as may be taken between the finger and thumb ⟨*a* ~ *of snuff*⟩ – **at a pinch** in an emergency – **with a pinch of salt** with reservations as to the validity of sthg

pinchbeck /'pinch,bek/ *n* an alloy of copper and zinc used esp to imitate gold in jewellery [Christopher *Pinchbeck* †1732 E watchmaker] – **pinchbeck** *adj*

pincushion /'pin,koosh(ə)n/ *n* a small cushion in which pins are stuck ready for use, esp in sewing

Pindaric /pin'darik/ *adj* of or written in a style characteristic of the poet Pindar [L *pindaricus*, fr Gk *pindarikos*, fr *Pindaros* Pindar †443 BC Gk lyric poet]

Pindarics *n pl* Pindaric verse

pin down *vt* **1** to force (sby) to state his/her position or make a decision **2** to define precisely ⟨*a vague feeling of unease that she couldn't quite* pin down⟩ **3** to fasten down; prevent from moving

[1]**pine** /pien/ *vi* **1** to lose vigour or health (e g through grief); languish – often + *away* **2** to yearn intensely and persistently, esp for sthg unattainable; long ⟨*pining for her lost youth*⟩ [ME *pinen*, fr OE *pīnian*, fr (assumed) OE *pīn* punishment, fr L *poena* – more at PAIN]

[2]**pine** *n* **1** (any of various trees related to) any of a genus of coniferous evergreen trees which have slender elongated needles **2** the straight-grained white or yellow usu durable and resinous wood of a pine

[ME, fr OE *pīn*, fr L *pinus*; akin to Gk *pitys* pine, L *opimus* fat – more at FAT] – **piny, piney** *adj*

pineal body /ˈpini·əl/ *n* PINEAL GLAND

pineal gland *n* a small appendage of the brain of most vertebrates that has the structure of an eye in a few reptiles, and that secretes melatonin and other hormones [*pineal* fr F *pinéal*, fr MF, fr L *pinea* pinecone, fr fem of *pineus* of pine, fr *pinus*] – **pineal** *adj*

pineapple /ˈpienapl/ *n* **1** (the large oval edible succulent yellow-fleshed fruit of) a tropical plant related to the grasses, lilies, and orchids, with rigid spiny leaves and a dense head of small flowers **2** a hand grenade – slang [ME *pinappel* pinecone, fr *pin, pine* pine + *appel* apple, fruit]

ˈpineapple ˌweed *n* a composite plant with a small rounded head of yellow flowers that smell of pineapple when crushed

ˈpine,cone /ˈpien,kohn/ *n* a cone of a pine tree

ˈpine ˌmarten *n* a slender Eurasian marten with a yellow patch on the chest and throat

ˈpine ˌnut *n* the edible seed of any of several chiefly western N American pines

ˈpine ˌtar *n* tar obtained by destructive distillation of the wood of the pine tree and used esp in roofing and soaps, and in the treatment of skin diseases

pinetum /pieˈneetəm/ *n, pl* **pineta** /-tə/ a plantation of pine trees; *also* a scientific collection of living coniferous trees [L, fr *pinus*]

pinfall /ˈpin,fawl/ *n* FALL 8a

ˈpin,fold /-,fohld/ *n* ⁴POUND 1 [ME, fr OE *pundfald*, fr *pund-* enclosure + *fald* fold] – **pinfold** *vt*

ping /ping/ *vi or n* (to make) a sharp ringing sound [imit]

Ping-Pong /ˈping ˌpong/ *trademark* – used for table tennis

pinhead /ˈpin,hed/ *n* **1** sthg very small or insignificant **2** a very dull or stupid person; a fool – infml

ˌpinˈheaded /-ˈhedid/ *adj* lacking intelligence or understanding; dull, stupid – infml – **pinheadedness** *n*

pinhole camera /ˈpin,hohl/ *n* a photographic camera having a minute aperture and no lens

¹pinion /ˈpinyən/ *n* **1** (the end section of) a bird's wing **2** a bird's feather; a quill [ME, fr MF *pignon*] – **pinioned** *adj*

²pinion *vt* **1** to restrain (a bird) from flight, esp by cutting off the pinion of a wing **2a** to disable or restrain by binding the arms **b** to bind fast; shackle

³pinion *n* a gear with a small number of teeth designed to mesh with a larger gear wheel or rack [F *pignon*, fr MF *peignon*, fr *peigne* comb, fr L *pecten* – more at PECTINATE]

¹pink /pingk/ *vt* **1** to pierce slightly; stab **2a** to perforate in an ornamental pattern **b** to cut a zigzag or saw-toothed edge on [ME *pinken*]

²pink *n* a sailing vessel with a narrow overhanging stern [ME, fr MD *pinke*]

³pink *n* any of a genus of plants related to the carnation and widely grown for their white, pink, red, or variegated flowers [origin unknown] – **in the pink** in the best of health – infml

⁴pink *adj* **1** of the colour pink **2** holding moderately radical political views – **pinkish** *adj*, **pinkness** *n*

⁵pink *n* **1** any of various shades of pale red **2** (the scarlet colour of) a fox hunter's coat

⁶pink *adv* to a high degree; enormously – in *tickled pink*; infml

⁷pink *vi, Br, of an internal-combustion engine* to make a series of sharp popping noises because of faulty combustion of the fuel-air mixture [imit]

ˌpink ˈelephants *n pl* any of various hallucinations arising esp from heavy drinking or use of drugs – infml

ˈpink,eye /-,ie/ *n* a highly contagious conjunctivitis of human beings and various domestic animals

ˌpink ˈgin *n* a drink consisting of gin flavoured with angostura bitters

pinkie, pinky /ˈpingki/ *n, NAm & dial Br* LITTLE FINGER [prob fr D *pinkje*, dim. of *pink* little finger]

ˈpinking ˌshears /ˈpingking/ *n pl* shears with a saw-toothed inner edge on the blades, used in sewing for making a zigzag cut in cloth to prevent fraying [¹*pink*]

pinko /ˈpingkoh/ *n, pl* **pinkos, pinkoes** sby who holds moderately radical political views – chiefly derog [⁴*pink* 2 + ¹*-o*]

ˈpin ˌmoney *n* **1a** extra money earned by sby, esp a married woman (e g in a part-time job) **b** money set aside for the purchase of incidentals **2** a trivial amount of money

pinna /ˈpinə/ *n, pl* **pinnae** /-ni/, **pinnas** **1** a leaflet or primary division of a pinnate leaf or frond **2** the largely cartilaginous projecting portion of the outer ear [NL, fr L, feather, wing – more at ³PEN] – **pinnal** *adj*

pinnace /ˈpinəs/ *n* any of various ship's boats [MF *pinace*, prob fr OSp *pinaza*, fr *pino* pine, fr L *pinus*]

¹pinnacle /ˈpinəkl/ *n* **1** an architectural ornament resembling a small spire and used esp to crown a buttress ☞ CHURCH **2** a structure or formation suggesting a pinnacle; *specif* a lofty mountain **3** the highest point of development or achievement [ME *pinacle*, fr MF, fr LL *pinnaculum* gable, fr dim. of L *pinna* wing, battlement]

²pinnacle *vt* to raise (as if) on a pinnacle

pinnate /ˈpinayt, -nət/ *adj* resembling a feather, esp in having similar parts arranged on opposite sides of an axis like the barbs on the shaft of a feather ⟨*a* ~ *leaf*⟩ ☞ PLANT [NL *pinnatus*, fr L, feathered, fr *pinna*] – **pinnately** *adv*, **pinnation** /piˈnaysh(ə)n/ *n*

pinnule /ˈpinyoohl/ *n* **1** any of the secondary branches of a pinnate leaf or organ **2** a small fish fin separated from a major fin [NL *pinnula*] – **pinnulate** /-lət, -,layt/, **pinnulated** /-,laytid/ *adj*

pinny /ˈpini/ *n* PINAFORE 1 – infml [by shortening & alter.]

pinochle /ˈpee,nukl/ *n* (the combination of the queen of spades and jack of diamonds in) a card game similar to bezique played with a 48-card pack containing 2 each of the ace, king, queen, jack, ten, and nine in each suit [prob modif of G dial. *binokel*, a game resembling bezique, fr F dial. *binocle*]

pinocytosis /ˌpienohsieˈtohsis, ˌpin-/ *n, pl* **pinocytoses** /-,seez/ the uptake of extracellular fluid by a cell by invagination of the cell membrane and formation of a fluid-filled sac inside the cell – compare PHAGOCYTOSIS, EXOCYTOSIS [NL, fr Gk *pinein* to drink + NL *cyt-* + *-osis* – more at POTABLE] – **pinocytic** /-ˈsietik, -ˈsitik/ *adj*, **pinocytically** *adv*, **pinocytotic** /-ˈtotik/ *adj*, **pinocytotically** *adv*, **pinocytose** /-ˈsietohz/ *vb*

pinole /pi'nohli/ *n* (any of various flours resembling) a finely ground flour made from parched corn and used (sweetened) esp in Mexico and SW USA [AmerSp, fr Nahuatl *pinolli*]

piñon /'pinyohn, 'pinyən, pin'yohn/ *n* (the edible nut-like seed of) any of various low-growing pines [AmerSp *piñón*, fr Sp, pine nut, fr *piña* pinecone, fr L *pinea*]

[1]**pinpoint** /'pin,poynt/ *vt* **1** to fix, determine, or identify with precision **2** to cause to stand out conspicuously; highlight

[2]**pinpoint** *adj* **1** extremely small, fine, or precise ⟨*a ~ target*⟩ **2** located, fixed, or directed with extreme precision

[3]**pinpoint** *n* a very small point or area ⟨*saw a ~ of light at the end of the tube*⟩

'pin,prick /-,prik/ *n* **1** a small puncture made (as if) by a pin **2** a petty irritation or annoyance

,pins and 'needles *n pl* a pricking tingling sensation in a limb recovering from numbness

'pin,stripe /-,striep/ *n* **1** a very thin stripe, esp on a fabric **2** a suit or trousers with pinstripes – often pl with sing. meaning – **pin-striped** *adj*

pint /pient/ *n* **1** either of 2 units of liquid capacity equal to ⅛gal: ☞ UNIT **a** a British unit of about 0.568l ☞ UNIT **b** a US unit of about 0.473l ☞ UNIT **2** a pint of liquid, esp milk or beer [ME *pinte*, fr MF, fr ML *pincta*, fr (assumed) VL, fem of *pinctus*, pp of L *pingere* to paint – more at PAINT]

'pin,table /-,taybl/ *n* PINBALL MACHINE

'pin,tail /-,tayl/ *n, pl* **pintails**, *esp collectively* **pintail** a bird with elongated central tail feathers: e g **a** a slender grey and white dabbling duck **b** any of several grouse

pintle /'pintl/ *n* a usu upright pivot on which another part turns [ME *pintel*, lit., penis, fr OE; akin to MLG *pint* penis, OE *pinn* pin]

pinto /'pintoh/ *n, pl* **pintos** *also* **pintoes** *NAm* a spotted or blotched horse or pony [AmerSp, fr *pinto* spotted, fr obs Sp, fr (assumed) VL *pinctus*]

'pint-,size, 'pint-,sized *adj* small – chiefly derog

'pin ,tuck *n* a very narrow usu ornamental tuck in a garment

pinup /'pin,up/ *n* (a person whose glamorous qualities make him/her a suitable subject of) a photograph pinned up on an admirer's wall – **pinup** *adj*

'pin,wheel /-,weel/ *n* **1** CATHERINE WHEEL **2** *NAm* WINDMILL 2

'pin,worm /-,wuhm/ *n* a threadworm

piolet /piə'lay (*Fr* pjɔlɛ)/ *n* an ice axe [F]

pion /'pie·on/ *n* any of several positive, negative, or neutral unstable elementary particles of the meson family responsible for the force between nucleons [contr of *pi-meson*] – **pionic** /pie'onik/ *adj*

[1]**pioneer** /,pie·ə'niə/ *n* **1** a member of a military unit (e g engineers) engaging in light construction and defensive works **2a** a person or group that originates or helps open up a new line of thought or activity or a new method or technical development **b** any of the first people to settle in a territory [MF *pionier*, fr OF *peonier* foot soldier, fr *peon* foot soldier, fr ML *pedon-*, *pedo* – more at [3]PAWN]

[2]**pioneer** *adj* **1** original, earliest **2** (characteristic) of early settlers or their time

[3]**pioneer** *vi* to act as a pioneer ~ *vt* **1** to open or prepare for others to follow; *esp* to settle **2** to originate or take part in the development of

pious /'pie·əs/ *adj* **1** devout **2** sacred or devotional as distinct from the profane or secular **3** dutiful **4** marked by sham or hypocritical virtue; sanctimonious [L *pius*; akin to L *piare* to appease] – **piously** *adv*, **piousness** *n*

[1]**pip** /pip/ *n* **1** (a disorder marked by formation of) a scale or crust on a bird's tongue **2** a fit of irritation, low spirits, or disgust – chiefly infml; esp in *to give one the pip* [ME *pippe*, fr MD; akin to OHG *pfiffiz* pip; both fr a prehistoric WGmc word borrowed fr (assumed) VL *pipita*, alter. of L *pituita* phlegm, pip]

[2]**pip** *n* **1a** any of the dots on dice and dominoes that indicate numerical value **b** SPOT 2c **2** a star worn, esp on the shoulder, to indicate an army officer's rank [origin unknown]

[3]**pip** *vt* **-pp-** to beat by a narrow margin – infml – **pip at the post** to beat at the very last minute (e g in a race or competition)

[4]**pip** *n* a small fruit seed of an apple, orange, etc [short for *pippin*]

[5]**pip** *vt* **-pp-** to remove the pips from (a fruit)

[6]**pip** *n* a short high-pitched tone, esp broadcast in a series as a time signal [imit]

pipal /'peepl/ *n* a large long-lived Indian fig tree [Hindi *pīpal*, fr Skt *pippala*]

[1]**pipe** /piep/ *n* **1a** a tubular wind instrument; *specif* a small fipple flute held in and played with one hand, esp while a tabor is played with the other **b(1)** FLUE PIPE **(2)** REED PIPE **c** a bagpipe – usu pl with sing. meaning **2** a long tube or hollow body for conducting a liquid, gas, etc **3a** a tubular or cylindrical object, part, or passage **b** a roughly cylindrical body of ore **4** a large cask used esp for wine (e g port) and oil **5** (tobacco or other plant material held by the bowl of) a wood, clay, etc tube with a mouthpiece at one end, and at the other a small bowl in which plant material, esp tobacco, is burned for smoking ⟨*he lit his ~*⟩ [ME, fr OE *pīpa*; akin to OHG *pfīfa* pipe; both fr a prehistoric WGmc word borrowed fr (assumed) VL *pipa* pipe, fr L *pipare* to cheep, of imit origin]

[2]**pipe** *vi* **1a** to play on a pipe **b** to convey orders or direct by signals on a boatswain's pipe **2a** to speak in a high or shrill voice **b** to make a shrill sound ~ *vt* **1a** to play (a tune) on a pipe **b** to utter in the shrill tone of a pipe **2** to lead, accompany, or announce ceremonially **3a** to trim with piping **b** to force (e g cream or icing) through a piping tube or nozzle in order to achieve a decorative effect **4** to supply or equip with pipes **5** to convey (as if) by pipes; *specif* to transmit by wire or coaxial cable

'pipe-,clay *vt* to whiten or clean with pipe clay

'pipe ,clay *n* a fine white clay used esp for making tobacco pipes and for whitening leather

'pipe ,cleaner *n* a piece of flexible wire covered with tufted fabric which is used to clean the stem of a tobacco pipe

,piped 'music /piept/ *n* recorded background music in public places

pipe down *vi* to stop talking or making noise – infml [[2]*pipe*]

'pipe ,dream *n* an illusory or fantastic plan, hope, or story [fr the fantasies brought about by the smoking of opium]

'pipe,fish /-,fish/ *n* any of various long slender fishes that are related to the sea horses and have a tube-shaped snout

'pipe,line /-,lien/ *n* **1** a line of pipe with pumps, valves, and control devices for conveying liquids, gases, etc **2a** the processes through which supplies pass from source to user **b** sthg considered as a continuous set of processes which the individual must go through or be subjected to ⟨*children in the educational* ~⟩ ⟨*the housing* ~⟩ **3** *NAm* a direct channel for information

,pipe 'major *n* the principal player in a band of bagpipes

,pipe of 'peace *n* a calumet

'pipe ,organ *n* ORGAN 1a

piper /'piepə/ *n* **1** one who or that which plays on a pipe **2** a maker, layer, or repairer of pipes

piperidine /pi'perə,deen, -din/ *n* a liquid heterocyclic organic compound with a peppery smell like that of ammonia [ISV, blend of *piperine* (an alkaloid; fr L *piper* pepper) and *-ide*]

pipette, *NAm* **pipet** /pi'pet/ *n* a narrow tube into which fluid is drawn (e g for dispensing or measuring) by suction and retained by closing the upper end [F *pipette*, dim. of *pipe* pipe, cask, fr (assumed) VL *pipa, pippa* pipe]

pipe up *vi* to begin to play or to sing or speak, esp unexpectedly

piping /'pieping/ *n* **1a** the music of a pipe **b** a sound, note, or call like that of a pipe **2** a quantity or system of pipes **3a** a narrow trimming consisting of a folded strip of cloth often enclosing a cord, used to decorate upholstery, garments, etc **b** a thin cordlike line of icing piped onto a cake

'piping ,bag *n* a conical usu polythene bag with a hole at the narrow end to which nozzles are fitted, that is used in cookery to pipe esp icing

,piping 'hot *adj* so hot as to sizzle or hiss; *broadly* very hot

pipistrelle /,pipi'strel/ *n* any of a genus of insect-eating bats [F, fr It *pipistrello*, alter. of *vispistrello*, fr L *vespertilio* bat]

pipit /'pipit/ *n* any of various small birds resembling larks [imit]

pippin /'pipin/ *n* any of numerous apples with usu yellow skins strongly flushed with red [ME *pepin*, fr OF]

,pip-'pip *interj, Br* goodbye – now chiefly humor [origin unknown]

'pip-,squeak *n* a small or insignificant person – infml

piquant /'peekənt/ *adj* **1** agreeably stimulating to the palate; savoury **2** pleasantly stimulating to the mind [MF, fr prp of *piquer*] – **piquancy** *n*, **piquantly** *adv*, **piquantness** *n*

[1]**pique** /peek/ *n* (a fit of) resentment resulting from wounded vanity

[2]**pique** *vt* **1** to arouse anger or resentment in; *specif* to offend by slighting **2a** to excite or arouse by a provocation, challenge, or rebuff **b** to pride or congratulate (oneself), esp in respect of a particular accomplishment ⟨*he* ~s *himself on his skill as a cook*⟩ [F *piquer*, lit., to prick – more at [3]PIKE]

piqué, pique /'peekay/ *n* a durable ribbed fabric of cotton, rayon, or silk [F *piqué*, fr pp of *piquer* to prick, quilt]

piquet /pi'ket/ *n* **1** a 2-handed card game played with a 32-card pack with no cards below the 7 **2** PICKET 2 [F]

piracy /'pie·ərəsi/ *n* **1** robbery or illegal violence on the high seas; *also* a similar act (e g hijacking) against an aircraft in flight **2** the infringement of a copyright, patent, etc **3** an act (as if) of piracy [ML *piratia*, fr LGk *peirateia*, fr Gk *peiratēs* pirate]

piranha /pi'rahn(y)ə/ *n* a small S American fish capable of attacking and (fatally) wounding human beings and large animals [Pg, fr Tupi]

[1]**pirate** /'pie·ərət/ *n* **1** (a ship used by) sby who commits piracy **2** an unauthorized radio station; *esp* one located on a ship in international waters ⟨*a* ~ *radio station*⟩ [ME, fr MF or L; MF, fr L *pirata*, fr Gk *peiratēs*, fr *peiran* to attempt – more at FEAR] – **piratical** /pie'ratikl/ *adj*, **piratically** *adv*

[2]**pirate** *vt* **1** to commit piracy on **2** to take or appropriate by piracy **3** to reproduce without authorization ~ *vi* to commit or practise piracy

pirouette /,piroo'et/ *n* a rapid whirling about of the body; *specif* a full turn on the toe or ball of one foot in ballet [F, lit., teetotum] – **pirouette** *vi*

pis /piez/ *pl of* PI

pis aller /,peez a'lay/ *n, pl* **pis allers** /-'lay(z)/ a last resource or device; an expedient [F, lit., to go worst]

pisc-, pisci- *comb form* fish ⟨*pisci*culture⟩ ⟨*pisci*vorous⟩ [L *pisci-*, fr *piscis* fish]

piscary /'pisk(ə)ri/ *n* **1** the right of fishing in waters belonging to another **2** FISHERY 2 [(1) ME *piscarie*, fr ML *piscaria*, fr L, neut pl of *piscarius* of fish, fr *piscis*; (2) ML *piscaria*, fr L, fem of *piscarius*]

piscatory /'piskət(ə)ri/, **piscatorial** /,piskə'tawri·əl/ *adj* of or dependent on fishermen or fishing [L *piscatorius*, fr *piscatus*, pp of *piscari* to fish, fr *piscis*]

Pisces /'pieseez/ *n pl but sing in constr* (sby born under) the 12th sign of the zodiac in astrology, which is pictured as 2 fishes ☞ SYMBOL [ME, fr L, fr pl of *piscis* fish – more at [1]FISH] – **Piscean** /'piesi·ən/ *adj or n*

piscina /pi'seenə/ *n* a basin with a drain for disposing of water from liturgical ablutions ☞ CHURCH [ML, fr L, fishpond, fr *piscis*]

piscine /'pisien/ *adj* (characteristic) of fish [L *piscinus*, fr *piscis*]

pish /pish/ *interj* – used to express disdain or contempt [origin unknown]

pisiform /'pisi,fawm/ *adj* pea-shaped [L *pisum* pea + E *-iform* – more at PEA]

pisiform bone *n* a bone of the wrist or carpus on the side of the little finger or ulna in most mammals

pismire /'pis,mie·ə/ *n, dial* an ant [ME *pissemire*, fr *pisse* urine + *mire* ant, of Scand origin; akin to ON *maurr* ant; akin to L *formica* ant, Gk *myrmēx*]

[1]**piss** /pis/ *vi* **1** to urinate **2** to rain heavily – often with *down* ~ *vt* **1** to urinate in or on ⟨~ *the bed*⟩ **2** to discharge (as if) as urine ⟨*to* ~ *blood*⟩ *USE* vulg [ME *pissen*, fr OF *pissier*, fr (assumed) VL *pissiare*, of imit origin]

[2]**piss** *n* **1** urine **2** an act of urinating *USE* vulg

pissed *adj, Br* drunk – slang

piss off *vb, Br vi* to go away ~ *vt* to cause to be annoyed or fed up *USE* vulg

pissoir /,pi'swah, '-,-/ *n* a public urinal in the street in some European countries [F, fr MF, fr *pisser* to urinate, fr OF *pissier*]

'piss-,up *n, chiefly Br* a heavy drinking session – vulg

pistachio /pi'stahshi·oh/ *n, pl* **pistachios** **1** (the green edible nut of) a small tree of the sumach family **2** the vivid green colour of the pistachio nut [It *pistacchio,* fr L *pistacium* pistachio nut, fr Gk *pistakion,* fr *pistakē* pistachio tree, fr Per *pistah*]

piste /peest/ **1** a prepared slope for skiing **2** a rectangular area 14m (about 46ft) by 2m (about 6ft 7in) on which a fencing bout takes place [F, lit., trail, track, fr MF, fr OIt *pista,* fr *pistare* to trample down, pound – more at PISTON]

pistil /ˈpistil/ *n* a carpel [NL *pistillum,* fr L, pestle – more at PESTLE]

pistillate /ˈpistilət, -,layt/ *adj* having pistils but no stamens

pistol /ˈpistl/ *n* a short firearm intended to be aimed and fired with 1 hand [MF *pistole,* fr G, fr MHG dial. *pischulle,* fr Czech *píšťal,* lit., pipe; akin to Russ *pischal* arquebus]

pistole /piˈstohl/ *n* any of several former European, esp Spanish, gold coins [ME]

pistoleer /,pistəˈliə/ *n* a person armed with a pistol

ˈpistol ,grip *n* a grip on a shotgun, rifle, tool, etc shaped like a pistol stock

ˈpistol-,whip *vt* to beat with a pistol; *broadly* to assail violently and intemperately

piston /ˈpist(ə)n/ *n* **1** a sliding disc or short cylinder fitting within a cylindrical vessel along which it moves back and forth by or against fluid pressure ☞ CAR **2a** a sliding valve in a cylinder in a brass instrument that is used to lower its pitch **b** a button on an organ console for bringing in a preselected registration [F, fr It *pistone,* fr *pistare* to pound, fr ML, fr L *pistus,* pp of *pinsere* to crush – more at PESTLE]

ˈpiston ,ring *n* a springy split metal ring for sealing the gap between a piston and a cylinder wall

ˈpiston ,rod *n* a rod by which a piston is moved or communicates motion

[1]**pit** /pit/ *n* **1a(1)** a hole, shaft, or cavity in the ground **(2)** a mine **b(1)** an area often sunken or depressed below the adjacent floor area **(2)** ORCHESTRA 2 **2** Hell – + *the* **3** a hollow or indentation, esp in the surface of a living plant or animal: e g **a** a natural hollow in the surface of the body **b** any of the indented scars left in the skin by a pustular disease (e g smallpox) **4** any of the areas alongside a motor-racing track used for refuelling and repairing the vehicles during a race – usu pl with sing. meaning; + *the* **5** *chiefly Br* the floor of a theatre auditorium; *esp* the area between the stalls and the stage [ME, fr OE *pytt;* akin to OHG *pfuzzi* well]

[2]**pit** *vb* **-tt-** *vt* **1** to make pits in; *esp* to scar or mark with pits **2a** to set (e g fighting cocks) to fight (as if) in a cockpit – often + *against* **b** to set into opposition or rivalry; oppose ~ *vi* to become marked with pits; *esp* to preserve for a time an indentation made by pressure

[3]**pit** *n, NAm* STONE 2 [D, fr MD – more at PITH]

[4]**pit** *vt* **-tt-** *chiefly NAm* to remove the pit from (a fruit)

,pit-a-ˈpat *n* pitter-patter [imit] – **pit-a-pat** *adv or adj*

[1]**pitch** /pich/ *n* **1** (any of various bituminous substances similar to) a black or dark viscous substance obtained as a residue in the distillation of organic materials, esp tars **2** resin obtained from various conifers [ME *pich,* fr OE *pic,* fr L *pic-, pix;* akin to L *opimus* fat]

[2]**pitch** *vt* to cover, smear, or treat (as if) with pitch

[3]**pitch** *vt* **1** to erect and fix firmly in place ⟨~ *a tent*⟩ **2** to throw, fling ⟨~ *hay onto a wagon*⟩ ⟨~ed *a couple of drunks out of the party*⟩: e g **a** to throw (a baseball) to a batter **b** to toss (e g coins) so as to fall at or near a mark **3a(1)** to cause to be at a particular level or of a particular quality **(2)** to set in a particular musical pitch or key **b** to cause to be set at a particular angle; slope ⟨*a* ~ed *roof*⟩ ☞ ARCHITECTURE **4** to hit (a golf ball) in a high arc with backspin **5** to bowl (a ball) in cricket to a specified place or in a specified manner ~ *vi* **1a** to fall precipitately or headlong **b(1)** *of a ship* to move so that the bow is alternately rising and falling **(2)** *of an aircraft* to turn about a lateral axis so that the nose rises or falls in relation to the tail **c** BUCK 1 **2** to encamp **3** to incline downwards; slope **4** to pitch a baseball or golf ball **5** *of a ball, esp a bowled cricket ball* to bounce [ME *pichen*]

[4]**pitch** *n* **1** pitching; *esp* an up-and-down movement – compare YAW **2a** a slope; *also* the degree of slope **b(1)** distance between one point on a gear tooth and the corresponding point on the next tooth **(2)** distance from any point on the thread of a screw to the corresponding point on an adjacent thread measured parallel to the axis **c** the distance advanced by a propeller in 1 revolution **d** the number of teeth on a gear or of threads on a screw per unit distance **e** the degree to which a blade of a propeller is slanted in relation to the axis of rotation **3a** the relative level, intensity, or extent of some quality or state ⟨*were at a high* ~ *of excitement*⟩ **b(1)** the property of a sound, esp a musical note, that is determined by the frequency of the waves producing it; highness or lowness of sound **(2)** a standard frequency for tuning instruments **4** an often high-pressure sales talk or advertisement **5** WICKET 4b **6** *chiefly Br* **a** a usu specially marked area used for playing soccer, rugby, hockey, etc **b** an area or place, esp in a street, to which a person lays unofficial claim for carrying out business or activities – **pitched** *adj*

,pitch-ˈblack *adj* intensely dark or black

pitchblende /ˈpich,blend/ *n* a radium-containing uranium oxide occurring as a brown to black lustrous mineral [part trans of G *pechblende,* fr *pech* pitch + *blende*]

,pitched ˈbattle *n* an intense battle; *specif* one fought on previously chosen ground

[1]**pitcher** /ˈpichə/ *n* **1** a large deep usu earthenware vessel with a wide lip and a handle or 2 ear-shaped handles, for holding and pouring liquids; *broadly* a large jug **2** a modified leaf of a pitcher plant in which the hollowed stalk and base of the blade form an elongated receptacle [ME *picher,* fr OF *pichier,* fr ML *bicarius* goblet, fr Gk *bikos* earthen jug]

[2]**pitcher** *n* the player who pitches in a baseball game [[3]PITCH + [2]-ER]

ˈpitcher ,plant *n* a plant with leaves modified into pitchers containing liquids in which insects are trapped and digested

[1]**pitchfork** /ˈpich,fawk/ *n* a long-handled fork with 2 or 3 long curved prongs used esp for pitching hay [ME *pikfork,* fr *pik* pick + *fork*]

[2]**pitchfork** *vt* **1** to lift and toss (as if) with a pitchfork ⟨~ed *the hay into the wagon*⟩ **2** to thrust (sby) into a position, office, etc suddenly or without preparation

pitch in *vi* **1** to begin to work **2** to contribute to a common endeavour

ˈpitch ,pipe *n* a small instrument of 1 or more reed

or fine pipes blown to establish the pitch in singing or in tuning an instrument

piteous /ˈpiti·əs/ *adj* causing or deserving pity or compassion – **piteously** *adv*, **piteousness** *n*

pitfall /ˈpit,fawl/ *n* **1** a trap or snare; *specif* a camouflaged pit used to capture animals **2** a hidden or not easily recognized danger or difficulty

[1]**pith** /pith/ *n* **1a** a (continuous) central area of spongy tissue in the stems of most vascular plants **b** the white tissue surrounding the flesh and directly below the skin of a citrus fruit **2a** the essential part; the core ⟨*individuality, which was the very ~ of liberty* – H J Laski⟩ **b** substantial quality (e g of meaning) ⟨*made a speech that lacked ~*⟩ [ME, fr OE *pitha*; akin to MD & MLG *pit* pith, pit]

[2]**pith** *vt* **1** to destroy the spinal cord or central nervous system of (e g cattle or a frog) **2** to remove the pith from (a plant part)

pithead /ˈpit,hed; *in mining communities usu* ,pitˈhed/ *n* (the ground and buildings adjacent to) the top of a mining pit

pithecanthropus /,pithikanˈthrohpəs, ,pithiˈkanthrəpəs/ *n, pl* **pithecanthropi** /-,pie/ any of the primitive extinct men known from skeletal remains from Javanese Pliocene gravels – compare JAVA MAN [NL, fr Gk *pithēkos* ape + *anthrōpos* human being] – **pithecanthropoid** /-ˈkanthrə,poyd/ *adj*

pithy /ˈpithi/ *adj* **1** consisting of or having much pith **2** tersely cogent – **pithily** *adv*, **pithiness** *n*

pitiable /ˈpiti·əbl/ *adj* deserving or exciting pity or contempt, esp because of inadequacy ⟨*a ~ excuse*⟩ – **pitiableness** *n*, **pitiably** *adv*

pitiful /ˈpitif(ə)l/ *adj* **1** deserving or arousing pity or commiseration **2** exciting pitying contempt (e g by meanness or inadequacy) – **pitifully** *adv*, **pitifulness** *n*

pitiless /ˈpitilis/ *adj* devoid of pity; merciless – **pitilessly** *adv*, **pitilessness** *n*

ˈ**pitman** /-mən/ *n, pl* (*1*) **pitmen** /-mən/, (*2*) **pitmans** **1** a male mine worker **2** *NAm* CONNECTING ROD

piton /piˈton(h) (*Fr* pitɔ̃)/ *n* a spike or peg that is driven into a rock or ice surface as a support, esp for a rope, in mountaineering [F]

ˈ**Pitot ,tube** /ˈpeetoh/ *n* a tube with a short right-angled bend that is used with a manometer to measure the velocity of fluid flow [F (*tube de*) *Pitot*, fr Henri *Pitot* †1771 F physicist]

ˈ**pit ,saw** *n* a handsaw worked by 2 men, one of whom stands on or above the log being sawn and the other below it, usu in a pit

pitta bread /ˈpitə/ *n* slightly leavened bread, typically flat and oval in shape, with a hollow in the centre [MGk *pitta* cake, pie, fr Gk, pitch]

pittance /ˈpit(ə)ns/ *n* a small amount or allowance; *specif* a meagre wage or remuneration [ME *pitance*, fr OF, piety, pity, fr ML *pietantia*, fr *pietant-*, *pietans*, prp of *pietari* to be charitable, fr L *pietas*]

ˈ**pitter-,patter** /ˈpitə/ *n* a rapid succession of light sounds [imit] – **pitter-patter** *adv or adj*, **pitter-patter** *vi*

pituitary /piˈtyooh·it(ə)ri/ *adj or n* (of) the pituitary gland [L *pituita* phlegm; fr the former belief that the pituitary gland secreted phlegm]

piˈtuitary ,gland *n* a small endocrine organ attached to the brain that consists of a front lobe and a rear lobe that secrete many important hormones controlling growth, metabolism, etc ☞ DIGESTION

ˈ**pit ,viper** *n* any of various mostly New World venomous snakes with a sensory pit on each side of the head and hollow perforated fangs

[1]**pity** /ˈpiti/ *n* **1a** (the capacity to feel) sympathetic sorrow for one suffering, distressed, or unhappy **b** a contemptuous feeling of regret aroused by the inferiority or inadequacy of another **2** sthg to be regretted ⟨*it's a ~ you can't go*⟩ [ME *pite*, fr OF *pité*, fr L *pietat-*, *pietas* piety, pity, fr *pius* pious]

[2]**pity** *vb* to feel pity (for) – **pitier** *n*, **pityingly** *adv*

pityriasis /,pitəˈrie·əsis/ *n* dry scaly or scurfy patches of skin in human beings or domesticated animals [NL, fr Gk, fr *pityron* scurf]

piupiu /ˈpeeooh,peeooh/ *n, pl* **piupius** *NZ* a traditional Maori skirt made of rolled strips of flax and worn by men and women [Maori]

[1]**pivot** /ˈpivət/ *n* **1** a shaft or pin on which sthg turns **2a** a person, thing, or factor having a major or central role, function, or effect ⟨*as if the ~ and pole of his life was his Mother* – D H Lawrence⟩ **b** a key player or position; *specif* [6]POST 2b [F]

[2]**pivot** *vi* to turn (as if) on a pivot ~ *vt* **1** to provide with, mount on, or attach by a pivot **2** to cause to pivot – **pivotable** *adj*

[3]**pivot** *adj* **1** turning (as if) on a pivot **2** pivotal

ˈ**pivotal** /-tl/ *adj* **1** of or constituting a pivot **2** vitally important; crucial – **pivotally** *adv*

pix /piks/ *pl of* PIC

pixie, pixy /ˈpiksi/ *n* a (mischievous) fairy [origin unknown] – **pixieish** *adj*

pixilated /ˈpiksi,laytid/ *adj, chiefly NAm* **1** somewhat unbalanced mentally; *also* bemused **2** drunk [irreg fr *pixie*] – **pixilation** /,piksiˈlaysh(ə)n/ *n*

pizza /ˈpeetsə/ *n* a round thin cake of baked bread dough spread with a mixture of tomatoes, cheese, herbs, etc [It, fr (assumed) VL *picea*, fr L, fem of *piceus* of pitch, fr *pic-*, *pix* pitch]

pizzeria /,peetsəˈriə/ *n* an establishment where pizzas are made or sold [It, fr *pizza*]

pizzicato /,pitsiˈkahtoh/ *n, adv, or adj, pl* **pizzicati** /-ti/ (a note or passage played) by means of plucking instead of bowing – used in music [It, pp of *pizzicare* to pinch, pluck]

[1]**placard** /ˈplakahd/ *n* a notice for display or advertising purposes, usu printed on or fixed to a stiff backing material [ME *placquart*, a formal document, fr MF, fr *plaquier* to plate – more at PLAQUE]

[2]**placard** *vt* **1** to cover (as if) with placards **2** to give public notice of by means of placards

placate /pləˈkayt/ *vt* to soothe or mollify, esp by concessions; appease [L *placatus*, pp of *placare* – more at PLEASE] – **placation** /pləˈkaysh(ə)n/ *n*, **placative** /pləˈkaytiv, ˈplakətiv/ *adj*, **placatory** /pləˈkayt(ə)ri, ˈplakət(ə)ri/ *adj*

[1]**place** /plays/ *n* **1a** physical environment; a space **b** physical surroundings; atmosphere **2a** an indefinite region or expanse; an area **b** a building or locality used for a usu specified purpose ⟨*a ~ of amusement*⟩ ⟨*a ~ of worship*⟩ **3a** a particular region or centre of population **b** a house, dwelling ⟨*invited them to his ~ for the evening*⟩ **4** a particular part of a surface or body; a spot **5** relative position in a scale or series: e g **a** a particular part in a piece of writing; *esp* the point at which a reader has temporarily stopped **b** an important or valued position ⟨*there was never much of a ~ in his life for women*⟩ **c** degree of prestige ⟨*put her in her ~*⟩ **d** a (numbered) point in an argument, explanation, etc ⟨*in the first ~, you're*

wrong⟩ **6** a leading place, esp second or third, in a competition **7a** a proper or designated niche ⟨*thought that a woman's ~ was in the home*⟩ ⟨*put it back in its ~*⟩ **b** an appropriate moment or point ⟨*this is not the ~ to discuss legal liability*⟩ **8a** an available seat or accommodation **b** PLACE SETTING ⟨*lay another ~ for our guest*⟩ **9** the position of a figure in relation to others of a row or series; *esp* the position of a digit within a numeral ⟨*in 316 the figure 1 is in the tens ~*⟩ **10a** remunerative employment; a job; *esp* public office **b** prestige accorded to one of high rank; status ⟨*an endless quest for preferment and ~ – Time*⟩ **c** a duty accompanying a position of responsibility ⟨*it was not his ~ to sack the employee*⟩ **11** a public square **12** *chiefly Br* an available vacancy ⟨*got a university ~*⟩ [ME, fr MF, open space, fr L *platea* broad street, fr Gk *plateia (hodos)*, fr fem of *platys* broad, flat; akin to Skt *pṛthu* broad, L *planta* sole of the foot] – **in place of** so as to replace

[2]**place** *vt* **1** to distribute in an orderly manner; arrange ⟨*~ these documents in their correct order*⟩ **2a** to put in, direct to, or assign to a particular place ⟨*~d her on the right of the host*⟩ ⟨*could always ~ the dart exactly where he wanted to*⟩ **b** to put in a particular state ⟨*~ a performer under contract*⟩ **3** to appoint to a position ⟨*~d him in charge of the class*⟩ **4** to find employment or a home for **5a** to assign to a position in a series or category **b** to estimate ⟨*~d the value of the estate too high*⟩ **c** to identify by connecting with an associated context ⟨*couldn't quite ~ her face*⟩ **d** to put, lay ⟨*the teacher ~s a great deal of stress on correct spelling*⟩ **6a** to give (an order) to a supplier **b** to give an order for ⟨*~ a bet*⟩ – **placeable** *adj*, **placement** *n*

placebo /plə'seeboh/ *n, pl* **placebos 1** the Roman Catholic vespers for the dead **2a(1)** a medication that has no physiological effect and is prescribed more for the mental relief of the patient **(2)** an inert substance against which an active substance (e g a drug) is tested in a controlled trial **b** sthg tending to soothe or gratify [(1) ME, fr L, I shall please, fr *placēre* to please; (2) L]

pla'cebo ef,fect *n* improvement in the condition of a sick person that occurs in response to treatment but is prob more connected with mental factors than with the specific treatment

'place ,card *n* a card indicating the place a guest is to occupy at table during a formal dinner

placed *adj, chiefly Br* in a leading place, esp second or third, at the end of a competition, horse race, etc

'place,kick /-,kik/ *vt or n* (to kick or score by means of) a kick at a ball (e g in rugby) placed or held in a stationary position on the ground – **placekicker** *n*

'placeman /-mən/ *n* a political appointee to a public office, esp in 18th-c Britain

'place-,name *n* the name of a geographical locality 👁

placenta /plə'sentə/ *n, pl* **placentas, placentae** /-ti/ **1** the organ in all higher mammals that unites the foetus to the maternal uterus and provides for the nourishment of the foetus and the elimination of waste ☞ REPRODUCTION **2** the part of a flowering plant to which the ovules are attached ☞ PLANT [NL, fr L, flat cake, fr Gk *plakount-, plakous*, fr *plak-, plax* flat surface – more at PLEASE] – **placental** *adj or n*

placentation /,plasen'taysh(ə)n/ *n* **1** the development of the placenta and attachment of the foetus to the uterus during pregnancy **2** the particular type of form and structure of a mammalian or plant placenta

placer /'plasə/ *n* an alluvial or glacial deposit containing particles of valuable minerals, esp gold [Sp, fr Catal, submarine plain, fr *plaza* place, fr L *platea* broad street – more at PLACE]

'place ,setting *n* a table service for 1 person

placid /'plasid/ *adj* serenely free of interruption or disturbance ⟨*~ summer skies*⟩ ⟨*a ~ disposition*⟩ [L *placidus*, fr *placēre* to please – more at PLEASE] – **placidly** *adv*, **placidness, placidity** /pla'sidəti/ *n*

placket /'plakit/ *n* a slit in a garment, esp a skirt, for a fastening or pocket [origin unknown]

placoid /'plakoyd/ *adj* of or being a scale with an enamel-tipped spine characteristic of cartilaginous fishes [Gk *plak-, plax* flat surface]

plagal /'playgl/ *adj* **1** *of a church mode* having the keynote on the 4th scale step **2** *of a cadence* passing from a subdominant to a tonic chord [ML *plagalis*, deriv of Gk *plagios* oblique, sideways, fr *plagos* side; akin to L *plaga* net, region, Gk *pelagos* sea – more at [1]FLAKE]

plage /plahzh/ *n* a bright region on the sun caused by light from gas clouds and often associated with a sunspot [F, beach, luminous surface, fr It *piaggia* beach, fr LL *plagia*, fr Gk *plagios* oblique]

plagiarism /'playj(y)ə,riz(ə)m/ *n* **1** plagiarizing **2** sthg plagiarized – **plagiarist** *n*, **plagiaristic** /,playj(y)ə'ristik/ *adj*

plagiar·ize, -ise /'playj(y)ə,riez/ *vt* to appropriate and pass off (the ideas or words of another) as one's own *~ vi* to present as new and original an idea or product derived from an existing source [*plagiary* (one who plagiarizes, plagiarism), fr L *plagiarius*, lit., plunderer, fr *plagium* hunting net, fr *plaga* net] – **plagiarizer** *n*

plagioclase /'playji·ə,klays, -,klayz/ *n* a triclinic feldspar; *esp* one containing calcium or sodium [Gk *plagios* + *klasis* breaking, fr *klan* to break – more at [1]HALT]

[1]**plague** /playg/ *n* **1a** a disastrous evil or affliction; a calamity **b** a large destructive influx ⟨*a ~ of locusts*⟩ **2** any of several epidemic virulent diseases that cause many deaths; *esp* a fever caused by a bacterium that occurs in several forms **3a** a cause of irritation; a nuisance **b** a sudden unwelcome outbreak ⟨*a ~ of burglaries*⟩ [ME *plage*, fr MF, fr LL *plaga*, fr L, blow; akin to L *plangere* to strike – more at PLAINT]

[2]**plague** *vt* **1** to infest or afflict (as if) with disease, calamity, etc **2a** to cause worry or distress to **b** to disturb or annoy persistently – **plaguer** *n*

plaguey, plaguy /'playgi/ *adj* causing irritation or annoyance; troublesome – infml

plaice /plays/ *n, pl* **plaice** any of various flatfishes; *esp* a large European flounder [ME, fr OF *plaïs*, fr LL *platensis*, prob fr Gk *platys* broad, flat]

plaid /plad/ *n* **1** a rectangular length of tartan worn over the left shoulder as part of Highland dress **2** a usu twilled woollen fabric with a tartan pattern **3** a tartan [ScGael *plaide*] – **plaid** *adj*, **plaided** *adj*

[1]**plain** /playn/ *n* **1a** an extensive area of level or rolling treeless country **b** a broad unbroken expanse **2** [2]KNIT [ME, fr OF, fr L *planum*, fr neut of *planus* flat, plain – more at FLOOR]

Place-name elements in Britain and Ireland

The etymology of place names is often complex or uncertain, and this list should be taken only as a brief guide.

G = Gaelic OE = Old English W = Welsh L = Latin ON = Old Norse

modern forms	explanation	source
Aber-	confluence; place at the mouth of a river	W *aber*
Ach-, Auch-(Scotland) Agh-, Augh-, -agha-, -agh (Ireland)	field	G *achadh*
Ard-, -ard	high	G *ard*
Ath-, Agh-, Augh-, -agh, -ah	ford	G *ath*
Auchter-	upper part, summit; high field	G *uachdar*
Bal-, Ball-, Bally-	village; farmhouse	G *baile*
Beath, -beath, -beith	birch tree	G *beath, beith*
Blair	a plain	G *blàr*
-borough, -burgh, -bury	fortified place	OE *burgh*
Brock-, Brough-, -broke, -brook	brook, stream	OE *broc*
Burn-, -borne, -bourne, -burn	stream, spring	OE *burna*
-by	farmstead, village	ON *by*
Caer-, Car-	fort, castle	W *caer*
Carrick-	rock	G *carraic, carraig craig, creag*
Chester, -caster, -cester, -chester	Roman town, ancient fort	OE *ceaster*
Clon-, Cloon-	meadow	G *cluain*
Comb-, Comp-, -combe, -coombe	valley	OE *cumb*
-cot, -cote	cottage, shelter	OE *cot*
Craig-, -craig	rock, crag	G *carraic, carraig craig, creag*
Dal-	field	G *dail*
Den-, -dean, -den	valley	OE *denu*
-den	(chiefly in Kent & Sussex) pasture	OE *denn*
Derri-, -derry	an oak wood	G *doire, daire*
Drum-, Drom-, -drum	back; ridge	G *druim*
Dun-, Don-, Doon-, Doon	castle, fort; hill	G *dùn*
-ea, -ey, -y	land between streams; island	OE *eg, ieg*
Ennis-, Inis-, Inish-, Inch-, Inch	island; flat part of a meadow by a river	G *inis*
Ford-, -ford, -forth	ford	OE *ford*
-gill	ravine; deep valley	ON *gil*
Glen-, -glen	glen	G *gleann*
-hall, -ale, -all	remote valley; water meadow	OE *halh, healh*
Ham-, -ham	village; homestead; manor	OE *ham*
Hampstead, -hampstead, -hamstead	homestead	OE *hamstede*
Hampton, -hampton	home farm	OE *hamtun*
Head-, -head	headland, bluff	OE *heafod*
Holt, -holt	wood	OE *holt*
Hop-, -hope	small valley	OE *hop*
Hull, Hil-, Hill-, -hill, -hull	hill	OE *hyll*
-hurst, -hirst	wood; hillock	OE *hyrst*
-ington	-used to denote association of a settlement with a particular individual	OE *ing + tun*
Inver-, Inner-	mouth of a river; confluence	G *inbhir*
Kil- (Scotland) Kil-, Kill-, Cal-, Kilty-, Keel, -keel, -kyle (Ireland)	1 hermit's cell, church 2 wood	G *cill, ceall* G *coille*
Kin- (Scotland) Kin-, Ken-, Can- (Ireland)	head, promontory	G *ceann, cinn*
Kir-, Kirk-, -kirk	church	ON *kirkja*
Leigh-, -leigh, -ley	glade, clearing; wood, forest	OE *leah*
Lis-	fort	G *lios*
Llan-	church	W *llan*
-low	hill, mound	OE *hlaw*
Maghera, Maghera-, Machery	a plain	G *machaire*
-mer, -mere	lake, mere	OE *mere*
-minster	monastery, church	OE *mynster*
Mor-, More-, -moor	moor, waste, fen	OE *mor*
-mouth	mouth	OE *muþ*
-ness, -nes, Nas-,	headland, cape	OE *naess, ness*
Nass-, Naz-	projecting ridge	ON *nes*
Pen-, Pem-	head	W *penn*
Pont-	bridge	W *pont* from L *pons*
Poole, Pool-, -pole, -pool	pool, tidal stream	OE *pol*
Port-, -port	harbour; market town	OE *port* from L *portus*
Pwll-	pool	W *pwll*
Rhos-	moor	W *rhos*
Ros-	cape, headland (Scotland and N. Ireland) wood (S. Ireland)	G *ros*
Roth-	fort	G *rath*
-shot	strip of land	OE *sceat*
Stan-, Stone-, -ston, -stone	stone (eg a boundary stone)	OE *ston*
-stead, -sted	place, site	OE *stede, styde*
Stoke, Stock-, Stoke-, -stock, -stoke	place; outlying farm or hamlet; monastery	OE *stoc*
Stow, Stowe, -stoe, -stow, -stowe	place – esp a religious site	OE *stow*
Strat-, Streat-, Stret-, -street	Roman road	OE *straet, stret*
Stra-, Strath-	valley	G *srath*
Thorpe, -thorpe	outlying farm or hamlet	Old Danish *þorp*
-thwaite	meadow, clearing	ON *þveit*
-toft	site of a house	Old Danish *toft*
Ton-, -ton, -tone	homestead, village	OE *tun*
Tra-, -tray	strand	G *traigh, tracht*
Tre-	homestead, village, town	W *tre, tref*
-trey, -try	tree	OE *treow*
-wald, -wold	high forest-land	OE *wald, weald*
-wark	fortification	OE *weorc*
-wich, -wick	dwelling-place; dairy farm	OE *wic*
-worth, -worthy	homestead	OE *worþ, worþig*

The places marked on this map illustrate some of the commonest place-name elements in Britain and Ireland. These are printed in bold type and are listed, with their meanings, in alphabetical order on the page opposite.

[2]**plain** *adj* **1** lacking ornament; undecorated **2** free of added substances; pure **3** free of impediments to view; unobstructed **4a** evident to the mind or senses; obvious ⟨*it's perfectly* ~ *that they will resist*⟩ **b** clear ⟨*made his intentions* ~⟩ **5** free from deceitfulness or subtlety; candid **6** lacking special distinction or affectation; ordinary **7a** characterized by simplicity; not complicated ⟨~ *home cooking*⟩ **b** not rich or elaborately prepared or decorated **8** unremarkable either for physical beauty or for ugliness **9** *of flour* not containing a raising agent – **plainly** *adv*, **plainness** *n*

[3]**plain** *adv* in a plain manner; clearly, simply; *also* totally, utterly ⟨*it's just* ~ *daft*⟩

'plain,chant /-,chahnt/ *n* plainsong [F *plain-chant*, lit., plain song]

,plain 'clothes *n* ordinary civilian dress as opposed to (police) uniform – often attrib in *plain-clothes man*

,plain 'dealing *n* straightforward honesty ⟨*a businessman noted for his* ~⟩

,plain 'sailing *n* easy progress along an unobstructed course (e g of action)

'plain,song /-,song/ *n* **1** the nonmetrical monophonic music of the medieval church; *esp* GREGORIAN CHANT **2** a liturgical chant of any of various Christian rites

,plain'spoken /-'spohkən/ *adj* candid, frank – **plainspokenness** *n*

'plain ,stitch *n* [2]KNIT

plaint /playnt/ *n* a protest [ME, lamentation, protest, fr MF, fr L *planctus*, fr *planctus*, pp of *plangere* to strike, beat one's breast, lament; akin to OHG *fluokhōn* to curse, Gk *plēssein* to strike]

'plain,text /-,tekst/ *n* the intelligible form (e g the original form) of an encoded text

plaintiff /'playntif/ *n* sby who commences a civil legal action – compare DEFENDANT [ME *plaintif*, fr MF, fr *plaintif*, adj]

plaintive /'playntiv/ *adj* expressive of suffering or woe; melancholy, mournful [ME *plaintif*, fr MF, fr *plaint*] – **plaintively** *adv*, **plaintiveness** *n*

plain weave *n* a simple weave in which the weft yarns pass alternatively over and under the warp yarns – **plain-weave** *adj*, **plain-woven** *adj*

[1]**plait** *also* **plat** /plat/ *n* **1** a pleat **2** a length of plaited material, esp hair [ME *pleit*, fr MF, fr (assumed) VL *plictus*, fr *plictus*, pp of L *plicare* to fold – more at [1]PLY]

[2]**plait,** *also* **plat** *vt* **1** to pleat **2a** to interweave the strands of **b** to make by plaiting – **plaiter** *n*

[1]**plan** /plan/ *n* **1** a drawing or diagram drawn on a plane: e g **a** a top or horizontal view of an object ☞ BUILDING **b** a large-scale map of a small area **2a** a method for achieving an end **b** an often customary method of doing sthg; a procedure ⟨*the usual* ~ *is to both arrive and leave early*⟩ **c** a detailed formulation of a programme of action **d** a goal, aim ⟨*his* ~ *was to get a degree in engineering*⟩ [F, plane, foundation, ground plan; partly fr L *planum* level ground, fr neut of *planus* level; partly fr F *planter* to plant, fix in place, fr LL *plantare* – more at FLOOR, [1]PLANT] – **planless** *adj*, **planlessly** *adv*

[2]**plan** *vb* **-nn-** *vt* **1** to design **2** to arrange in advance **3** to have in mind; intend ~ *vi* to make plans – **planner** *n*

plan-, plano- *comb form* **1** flat ⟨plano*sol*⟩; flat and ⟨plano-*concave*⟩ **2** flatly ⟨plano*spiral*⟩ [L *planus*]

planar /'playnə, -nah/ *adj* of, being, or lying in a plane – **planarity** /play'narəti/ *n*

planarian /plə'neəri·ən/ *n* any of several related small cilia-bearing and mostly aquatic flatworms [NL *Planaria*, type genus of the family]

planchet /'plahnchit/ *n* a plain metal disc before stamping as a coin [dim. of *planch* (flat plate)]

[1]**plane** /playn/ *vt* **1** to make flat or even with a plane ⟨~d *the sides of the door*⟩ **2** to remove by planing – often + *away* or *down* [ME *planen*, fr MF *planer*, fr LL *planare*, fr L *planus* level – more at FLOOR] – **planer** *n*

[2]**plane, 'plane ,tree** *n* any of a genus of trees with large deeply cut lobed leaves and flowers in spherical heads [ME, fr MF, fr L *platanus*, fr Gk *platanos*; akin to Gk *platys* broad – more at PLACE]

[3]**plane** *n* a tool with a sharp blade protruding from the base of a flat metal or wooden stock for smoothing or shaping a wood surface [ME, fr MF, fr LL *plana*, fr *planare*]

[4]**plane** *n* **1a** a surface such that any 2 included points can be joined by a straight line lying wholly within the surface **b** a flat or level physical surface **2** a level of existence, consciousness, or development ⟨*on the intellectual* ~⟩ **3a** any of the main supporting surfaces of an aeroplane **b** an aeroplane [L *planum*, fr neut of *planus* level; (3B) by shortening]

[5]**plane** *adj* **1** having no elevations or depressions; flat **2a** of or dealing with geometric planes **b** lying in a plane ⟨*a* ~ *curve*⟩ [L *planus*]

[6]**plane** *vi* **1** to fly keeping the wings motionless **2** to skim across the surface of the water [F *planer*, fr *plan* plane; fr the plane formed by the wings of a soaring bird]

planet /'planit/ *n* **1** any of the bodies, except a comet, meteor, or satellite, that revolve round a star, esp the sun in our solar system; *specif* Mercury, Venus, Earth, Mars, Jupiter, Saturn, Uranus, Neptune, or Pluto ☞ ASTRONOMY **2** STAR 2a(1) [ME *planete*, fr OF, fr LL *planeta*, modif of Gk *planēt-*, *planēs*, lit., wanderer, fr *planasthai* to wander; akin to ON *flana* to rush around]

plane table *n* a field surveying instrument that consists essentially of a drawing board on a tripod together with an alidade

planetarium /,plani'teəri·əm/ *n, pl* **planetariums, planetaria** /-ri·ə/ **1** a model of the solar system **2** (a building or room housing) an optical projector for projecting images of celestial bodies and effects as seen in the night sky

planetary /'planit(ə)ri/ *adj* **1a** of or being a planet **b** having a motion like that of a planet ⟨~ *electrons*⟩ **2** of or belonging to the earth; terrestrial **3** erratic, wandering – poetic

planetesimal /,plani'tesim(ə)l/ *n* any of numerous small solid celestial bodies that may have aggregated to form the planets of the solar system [*planet* + *-esimal* (as in *infinitesimal*)]

planetoid /'planitoyd/ *n* an asteroid – **planetoidal** /,plani'toydl/ *adj*

planform /'plan,fawm/ *n* a view of an object (e g an aircraft) from above

plangent /'planj(ə)nt/ *adj* **1** loudly reverberating **2** having an expressive, esp plaintive, quality [L *plangent-*, *plangens*, prp of *plangere* to strike, lament] – **plangency** /-si/ *n*, **plangently** *adv*

planimeter /pla'nimitə/ *n* an instrument for measuring the area of a plane figure by tracing its boundary line [F *planimètre*, fr L *planum* plane + F *-mètre* -meter] – **planimetric** /ˌplaniˈmetrik/ *adj*

planish /ˈplanish/ *vt* to toughen and finish (metal) by hammering [MF *planiss-*, stem of *planir* to make smooth, fr *plan* level, fr L *planus*] – **planisher** *adj*

planisphere /ˈplaniˌsfiə/ *n* a polar projection of the celestial sphere and the stars on a plane to show celestial phenomena at any given time [ML *planisphaerium*, fr L *planum* plane + *sphaera* sphere] – **planispheric** /ˌplaniˈsferik/ *adj*

[1]**plank** /plangk/ *n* **1a** a long thick piece of wood; *specif* one 2 to 4in (about 50 to 100mm) thick and at least 8in (about 200mm) wide **2a** an article in a political platform **b** a (principal) item of a policy or programme [ME, fr ONF *planke*, fr L *planca*]

[2]**plank** *vt* to cover or floor with planks

plankton /ˈplangktən/ *n* the floating or weakly swimming minute animal and plant organisms of a body of water [G, fr Gk, neut of *planktos* drifting, fr *plazesthai* to wander, drift, passive of *plazein* to drive astray; akin to L *plangere* to strike – more at PLAINT] – **planktonic** /plangkˈtonik/ *adj*

planning /ˈplaning/ *n* the establishment of goals, policies, and procedures for a social or economic unit ⟨*town* ~⟩

ˌ**plano-conˈcave** /ˌplaynoh/ *adj* flat on one side and concave on the other

ˌ**plano-conˈvex** *adj* flat on one side and convex on the other

planography /pləˈnogrəfi/ *n* a process (e g lithography) for printing from a plane surface – **planographic** /ˌplaynəˈgrafik/ *adj*

[1]**plant** /plahnt/ *vt* **1a** to put in the ground, soil, etc for growth ⟨~ *seeds*⟩ **b** to set or sow (land) with seeds or plants **c** to implant **2a** to establish, institute **b** to place (animals) in a new locality **c** to stock with animals **3** to place firmly or forcibly ⟨~ed *a hard blow on his chin*⟩ **4** to position secretly; *specif* to conceal in order to observe or deceive ⟨*the spy* ~ed *a microphone in the hotel room*⟩ ~ *vi* to plant sthg [ME *planten*, fr OE *plantian*, fr LL *plantare* to plant, fix in place, fr L, to plant, fr *planta* plant] – **plantable** *adj*

[2]**plant** *n* **1a** a tree, vine, etc that is or can be planted; *esp* a small herbaceous plant **b** any of a kingdom of living things (e g a green alga, moss, fern, conifer, or flowering plant) typically lacking locomotive movement or obvious nervous or sensory organs **2a** the buildings, machinery, etc employed in carrying on a trade or an industrial business **b** a factory or workshop for the manufacture of a particular product **3** an act of planting **4** sthg or sby planted ⟨*left muddy footprints as a* ~ *to confuse the police*⟩ [ME *plante*, fr OE, fr L *planta*] – **plantlike** *adj*

Plantagenet /planˈtaj(ə)nit/ *adj* of the English royal house that ruled from 1154 to 1399 [*Plantagenet*, nickname of the family adopted as surname] – **Plantagenet** *n*

[1]**plantain** /ˈplantayn, -tin/ *n* any of a genus of short-stemmed plants bearing dense spikes of minute greenish or brownish flowers ☞ PLANT [ME, fr OF, fr L *plantagin-*, *plantago*, fr *planta* sole of the foot – more at PLACE; fr its broad leaves]

[2]**plantain** *n* (the angular greenish starchy fruit of) a type of banana plant [Sp *plántano* plane tree, banana tree, fr ML *plantanus* plane tree, alter. of L *platanus* – more at [2]PLANE]

plantar /ˈplantə/ *adj* of the sole of the foot [L *plantaris*, fr *planta* sole – more at PLACE]

plantation /plahnˈtaysh(ə)n, plan-/ *n* **1** (a place with) a usu large group of plants, esp trees, under cultivation **2** a settlement in a new country or region; a colony **3** an agricultural estate, usu worked by resident labour

planter /ˈplahntə/ *n* **1** one who owns or operates a plantation ⟨*a tea* ~⟩ **2** one who settles or founds a new colony **3** a container in which ornamental plants are grown **4** a planting machine [[1]PLANT + [2]-ER]

plantigrade /ˈplantiˌgrayd/ *adj* (designed for) walking on the sole with the heel touching the ground ⟨*human beings are* ~ *animals*⟩ – compare DIGITIGRADE [F, fr L *planta* sole + F *-grade*] – **plantigrade** *n*

ˈ**plant ˌkingdom** *n* the one of the 3 basic groups of natural objects that includes all living and extinct plants – compare ANIMAL KINGDOM, MINERAL KINGDOM

ˈ**plant ˌlouse** *n* an aphid or other small insect parasitic on plants

plantocracy /plahnˈtokrəsi/ *n* a controlling class of plantation owners [*plant*er + *-o-* + *-cracy*]

plant out *vb* to transplant (e g seedlings or a house plant) from a pot, seed tray, etc to open ground

plaque /plak, plahk/ *n* **1a** an ornamental brooch; *esp* the badge of an honorary order **b** a commemorative or decorative inscribed tablet of ceramic, wood, metal, etc **2a** a localized abnormal patch on a body part or surface **b** a film of mucus on a tooth that harbours bacteria – compare [1]TARTAR 2 [F, fr MF, metal sheet, fr *plaquier* to plate, fr MD *placken* to piece, patch; akin to MD *placke* piece, MHG *placke* patch]

[1]**plash** /plash/ *n* a shallow or muddy pool [ME *plasche*, fr OE *plæsc*; akin to MD *plasch*, *plas* pool]

[2]**plash** *vt* to interweave (branches and twigs) to form a hedge; *also* to form (a hedge) thus [ME *plashen*, fr MF *plaissier*, fr OF, fr *plais* hedge]

[3]**plash** *vt* to break the surface of (water); splash ~ *vi* to cause a splashing or spattering effect [perh fr D *plassen*, fr MD, of imit origin] – **plash** *n*

[1]**plashy** /ˈplashi/ *adj* marshy, boggy [[1]*plash*]

[2]**plashy** *adj* splashy, plashing [[3]*plash*]

-plasia /-playzyə, -zh(y)ə/, **-plasy** /-playzi/ *comb form* (→ *n*) development; formation ⟨*hyper*plasia⟩ [NL *-plasia*, fr Gk *plasis* moulding, fr *plassein*] – **-plastic** /-plastik/ *comb form* (→ *adj*)

plasm /ˈplaz(ə)m/ *n* plasma [LL *plasma* something moulded]

plasm-, **plasmo-** *comb form* plasma; cytoplasm ⟨plas *modium*⟩ ⟨plasmo*lysis*⟩ [F, fr NL *plasma*]

-plasm /-ˌplaz(ə)m/ *comb form* (→ *n*) structural material of a living organism (e g a cell or tissue) ⟨*endo*plasm⟩ [G *-plasma*, fr NL *plasma*]

plasma /ˈplazmə/ *n* **1** the fluid part of blood, lymph, or milk as distinguished from suspended material **2** protoplasm **3** a highly ionized gas (e g in the atmospheres of stars) containing approximately equal numbers of positive ions and electrons [G, fr LL, something moulded, fr Gk, fr *plassein* to mould – more at PLASTER] – **plasmatic** /plazˈmatik/ *adj*

plasmalemma /ˌplazməˈlemə/ *n* PLASMA MEMBRANE 1 [NL, fr *plasma* + Gk *lemma* husk, fr *lepein* to peel]

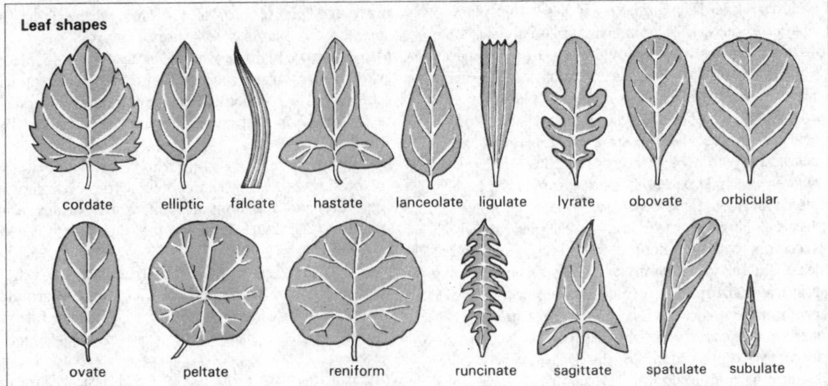
Leaf shapes
cordate
elliptic
falcate
hastate
lanceolate
ligulate
lyrate
obovate
orbicular
ovate
peltate
reniform
runcinate
sagittate
spatulate
subulate

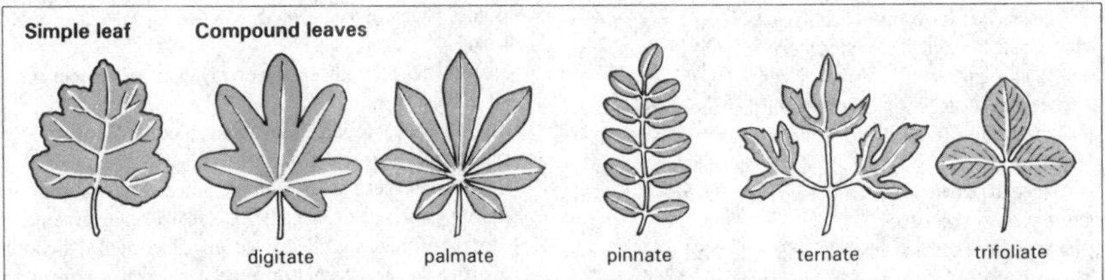
Simple leaf
Compound leaves
digitate
palmate
pinnate
ternate
trifoliate

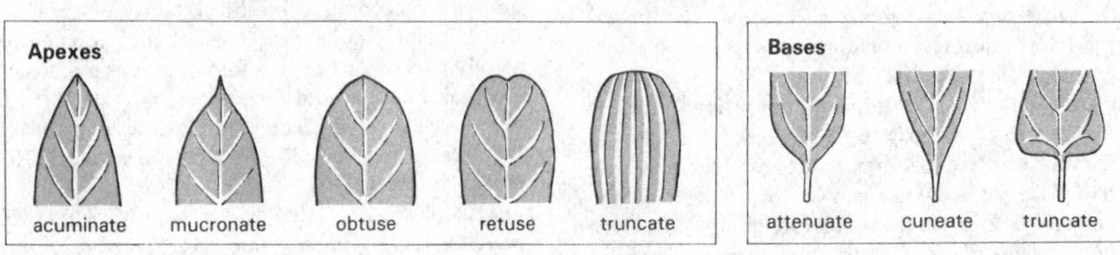
Apexes
acuminate
mucronate
obtuse
retuse
truncate
Bases
attenuate
cuneate
truncate

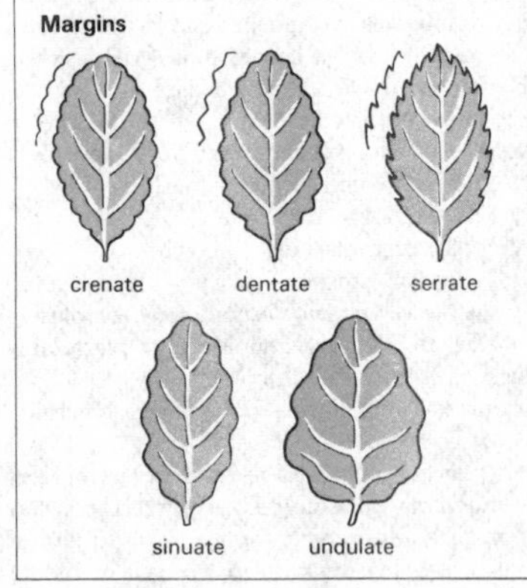
Margins
crenate
dentate
serrate
sinuate
undulate

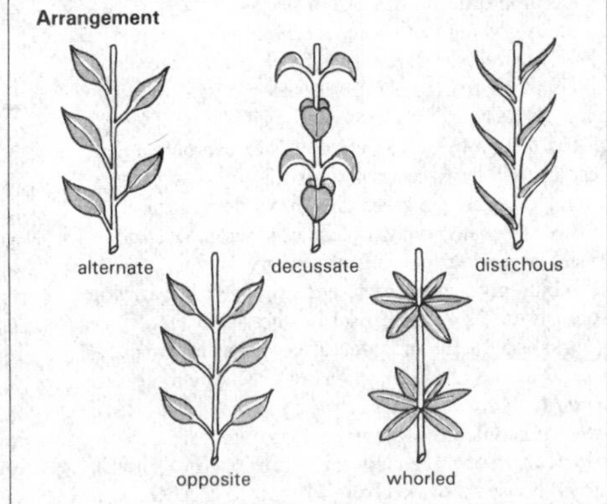
Arrangement
alternate
decussate
distichous
opposite
whorled

Structure and function of a typical flower

A flower is a specialized reproductive shoot producing seeds which give rise to the next generation. The flower parts are attached to the receptacle in rings, or whorls. The innermost whorl of one or more carpels is encircled by a whorl of stamens. In most flowers, these reproductive organs are surrounded by a whorl of petals. Coloured, scented petals with a nectary at the base attract insects which, as they collect nectar, bring about cross-pollination by transferring pollen from the anthers of one flower to the stigma of another. An outer whorl of leaflike sepals encloses and protects the other flower parts as they develop at the bud stage.

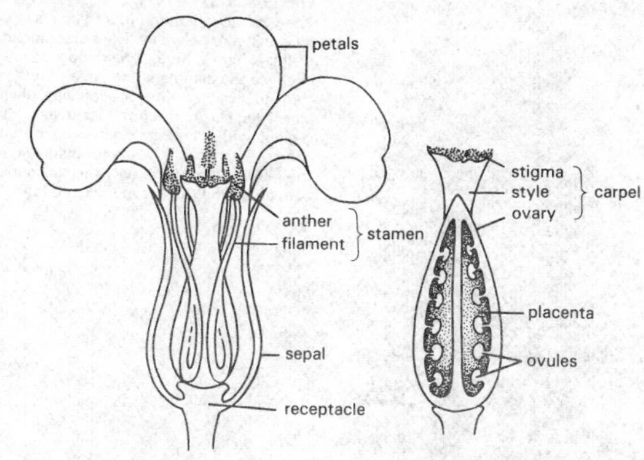

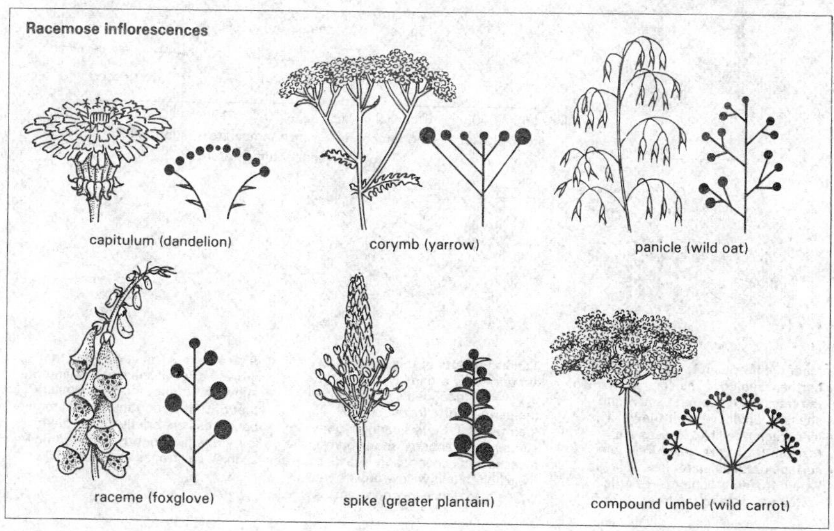

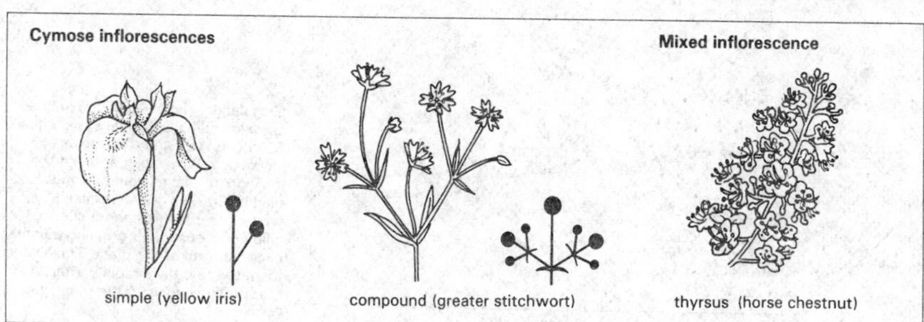

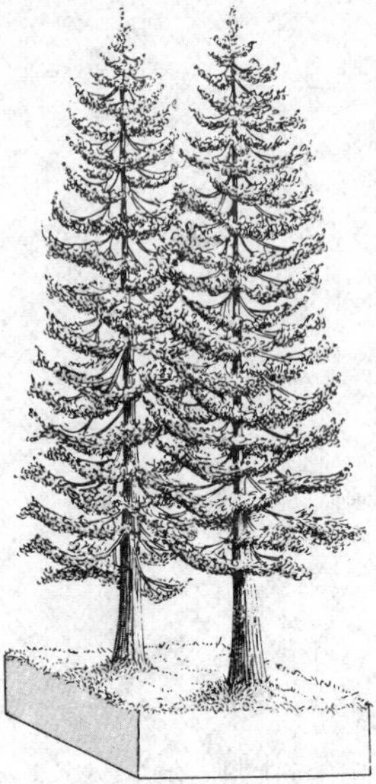

Plant habitats
The natural vegetation of a region is largely determined by climate. The boreal forest or taiga of the N hemisphere, for example, is coniferous because the climate is too severe for deciduous trees to survive. A major ecological division or biome (eg scrub or tundra) includes all those regions with a broadly similar vegetation and climate – the scrub biome for instance, includes the Mediterranean maquis, the N American chaparral, and the European heathland.

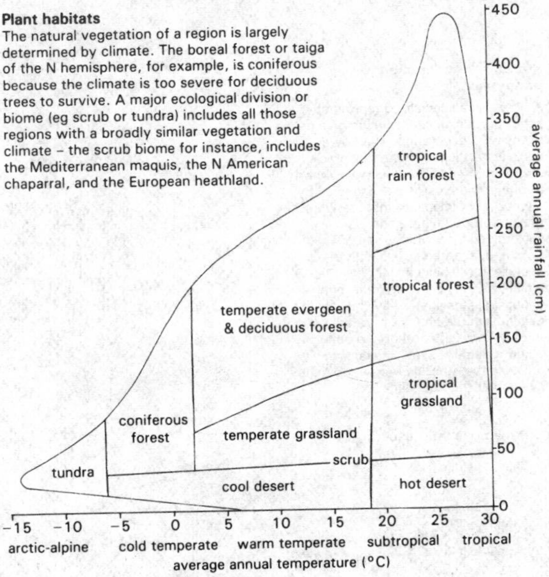

tropical rain forest
tropical forest
temperate evergeen & deciduous forest
tropical grassland
coniferous forest
temperate grassland
scrub
tundra
cool desert
hot desert
450 400 350 300 250 200 150 100 50 0
average annual rainfall (cm)
−15 −10 −5 0 5 10 15 20 25 30
arctic-alpine cold temperate warm temperate subtropical tropical
average annual temperature (°C)

Most **coniferous forests** are in cold northern regions. The conical shape of the trees both supports snow and sheds it rapidly when it thaws. The evergreen needlelike leaves are resistant to freezing and their waxy surface reduces water loss in areas where frozen ground makes little water available to the tree.

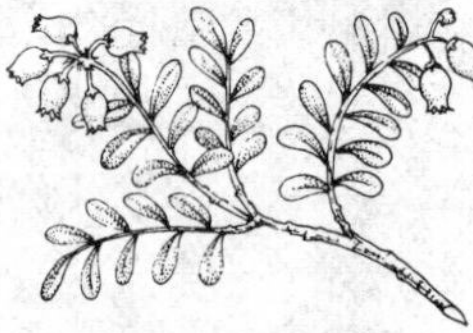

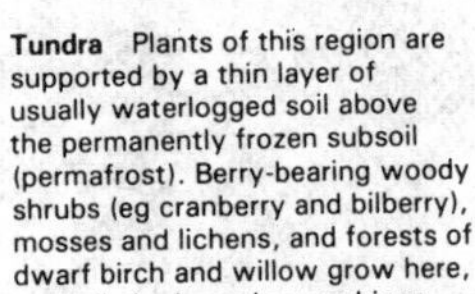

Tundra Plants of this region are supported by a thin layer of usually waterlogged soil above the permanently frozen subsoil (permafrost). Berry-bearing woody shrubs (eg cranberry and bilberry), mosses and lichens, and forests of dwarf birch and willow grow here, typically in dense low cushions.

Alpine zone The vegetation that grows between the tree line and the snow line of mountains is similar to that of the Arctic tundra. In summer, both areas are briefly covered with low-growing, brightly coloured flowers such as saxifrages and cranesbills.

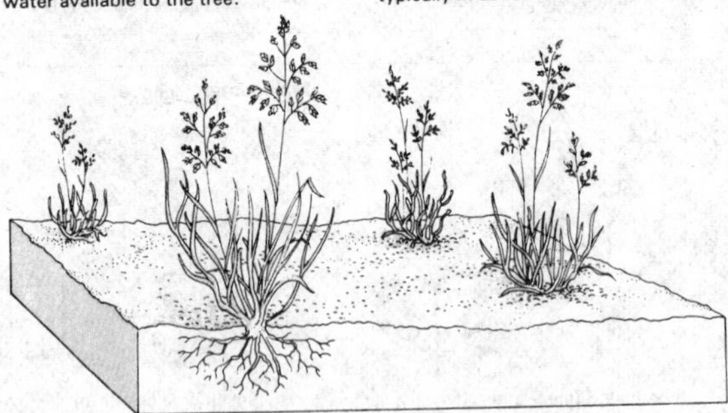

Grassland The N American prairie, Eurasian steppe, S American pampa, S African veld, and the tropical savanna are the major areas of the 45 million km² (18 million mi²) grassland biome. Grasses grow successfully where other plants cannot survive, chiefly because their growing point is near the base of the plant. This allows them to grow back rapidly after grazing by animals, cutting, or fire.

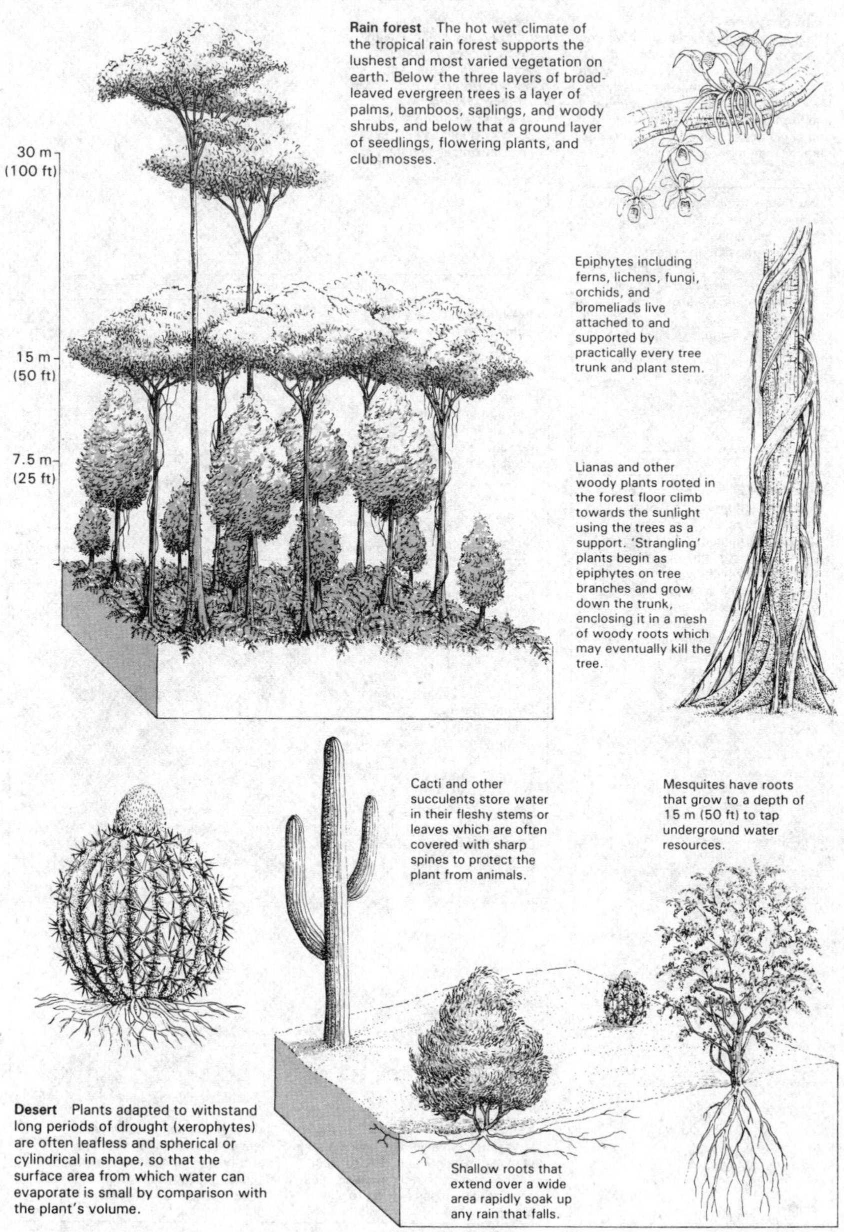

Rain forest The hot wet climate of the tropical rain forest supports the lushest and most varied vegetation on earth. Below the three layers of broad-leaved evergreen trees is a layer of palms, bamboos, saplings, and woody shrubs, and below that a ground layer of seedlings, flowering plants, and club mosses.

Epiphytes including ferns, lichens, fungi, orchids, and bromeliads live attached to and supported by practically every tree trunk and plant stem.

Lianas and other woody plants rooted in the forest floor climb towards the sunlight using the trees as a support. 'Strangling' plants begin as epiphytes on tree branches and grow down the trunk, enclosing it in a mesh of woody roots which may eventually kill the tree.

Cacti and other succulents store water in their fleshy stems or leaves which are often covered with sharp spines to protect the plant from animals.

Mesquites have roots that grow to a depth of 15 m (50 ft) to tap underground water resources.

Desert Plants adapted to withstand long periods of drought (xerophytes) are often leafless and spherical or cylindrical in shape, so that the surface area from which water can evaporate is small by comparison with the plant's volume.

Shallow roots that extend over a wide area rapidly soak up any rain that falls.

Plant divisions

The plant kingdom can be divided into higher or seed-bearing plants and lower (non-seed-bearing) plants. More detailed classification, particularly of the lower plants, varies considerably and in many systems bacteria, fungi, and algae are excluded from both the plant and animal kingdoms.

Bacteria and blue-green algae live in most environments. Although blue-green algae can photosynthesize and most bacteria cannot, they are classed together because of the similarity of their simple cell structure which, unlike that of practically every other living organism, has no nucleus.

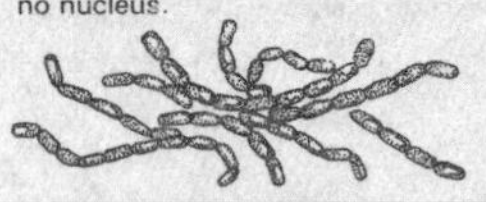

Thallophytes have a plant body not differentiated into leaves, stems, and roots. This diverse group of organisms includes the yeasts, moulds, mushrooms, and toadstools which live as parasites or saprophytes wherever organic matter is available, and algae ranging from minute single-celled varieties to giant seaweeds up to 100 m (328 ft) long.

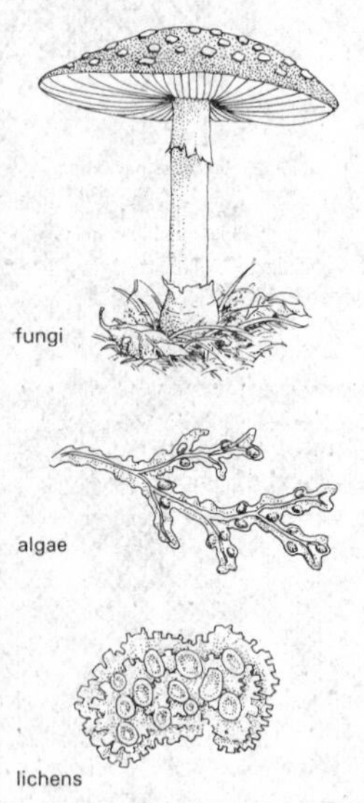

Bryophytes are small primitive land plants with no true roots or water-conducting tissue. They absorb water through their surface and are most abundant in damp areas such as bogs, river banks, and in tropical climates.

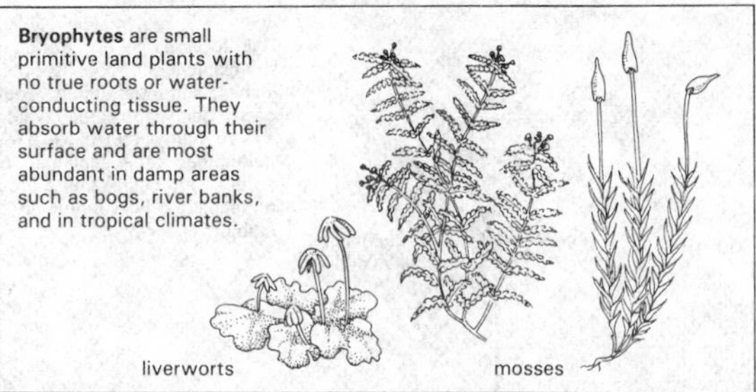

Pteridophytes were the dominant plants in the vast forests of the Carboniferous period, 300 million years ago. Like the higher plants they have vascular tissue for food and water conduction but they reproduce by means of spores rather than seeds.

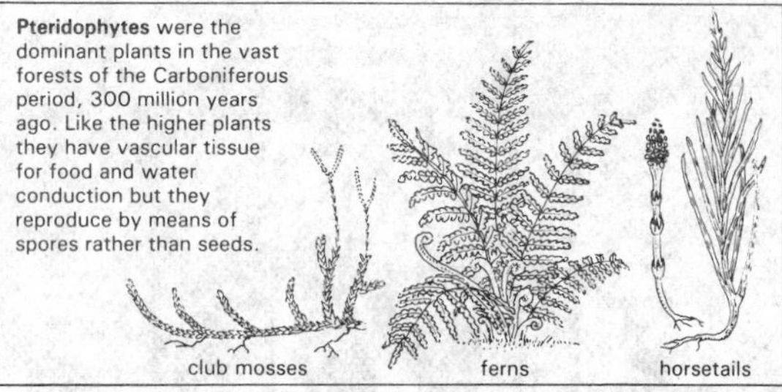

Spermatophytes are seed-bearing plants and include the Gymnosperms and Angiosperms.

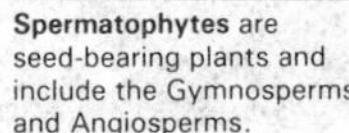

Gymnosperms are the oldest group of seed-bearing plants. Included in this group of woody, mostly evergreen trees and shrubs are the yews, the tropical palmlike cycads, the ginkgo or maidenhair tree – now practically extinct, and the conifers which bear the seeds on scales arranged in cones.

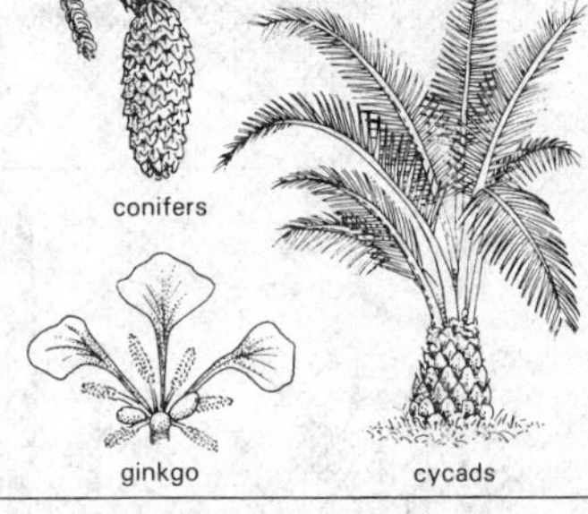

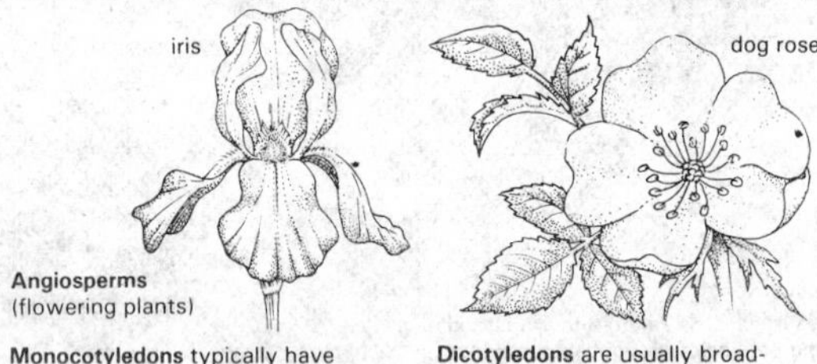

Angiosperms
(flowering plants)

Monocotyledons typically have long narrow leaves with parallel veins. All the grasses, the rushes, palms, and the highly evolved lilies, orchids, and irises belong to this group.

Dicotyledons are usually broad-leaved plants. Most garden plants and flowering trees are included in this category which contains over threequarters of all flowering plants.

plasma membrane *n* **1** the semipermeable surface bounding a cell **2** the tonoplast

plasma torch *n* a device that heats a gas by electrical means to form a plasma for high-temperature operations (e g melting metal)

plasmid /'plazmid/ *n* a piece of DNA or RNA in some cells, esp bacteria, that exists and reproduces independently of the cell's chromosomes [*plasma* + [2]*-id*]

plasmin /'plazmin/ *n* an enzyme that breaks down the fibrin of blood clots

plasminogen /plaz'minəjən/ *n* the substance found in blood plasma and serum from which plasmin is formed

plasmodesma /,plazmə'dezmə/ *also* **plasmodesm** /'plazmə,dez(ə)m/ *n, pl* **plasmodesmata** /-'dezmətə, -dez'mahtə/, **plasmodesmas** any of the strands of cytoplasm that provide living bridges between some plant cells [NL *plasmodesma*, fr *plasma* + Gk *desmat-, desma* bond, fr *dein* to bind – more at DIADEM]

plasmodium /plaz'mohdi·əm/ *n, pl* **plasmodia** /-di·ə/ **1** (an organism consisting of) a (mobile) mass of living matter containing many nuclei and resulting from fusion of amoeba-like cells **2** an individual malaria parasite [NL, fr *plasm-* + *-odium* thing resembling, fr Gk *-ōdēs* like]

plasmolysis /plaz'moləsis/ *n* shrinking of the cytoplasm away from the wall of a living (plant) cell due to water loss by exosmosis [NL] – **plasmolyse** /'plazmə,liez/ *vb*, **plasmolytic** /,plazmə'litik/ *adj*, **plasmolytically** *adv*

-plast /-plast, -plahst/ *comb form* (→ *n*) organized particle or subcellular granule; cell ⟨*proto*plast⟩ [MF *-plaste* thing moulded, fr LL *-plastus*, fr Gk *-plastos*, fr *plastos* moulded, fr *plassein*]

[1]**plaster** /'plahstə/ *n* **1** a medicated or protective dressing consisting of a film of cloth, plastic, etc often spread with a medicated substance; STICKING PLASTER **2** a pastelike mixture (e g of lime, water, and sand) that hardens on drying and is used esp for coating walls, ceilings, and partitions ☞ BUILDING **3 plaster, plaster cast** a rigid dressing of gauze impregnated with plaster of paris for immobilizing a diseased or broken body part [ME, fr OE, fr L *emplastrum*, fr Gk *emplastron*, fr *emplassein* to plaster on, fr *en-* + *plassein* to mould, plaster; akin to L *planus* level, flat] – **plastery** *adj*

[2]**plaster** *vt* **1** to overlay or cover with plaster **2** to apply a plaster to **3a** to cover over or conceal as if with a coat of plaster **b** to smear (sthg) thickly (on); coat ⟨*he* ~ed *butter on his bread*⟩ ⟨*she* ~ed *her face with make-up*⟩ **c** to cause to lie flat or stick to another surface ⟨~ed *his hair down*⟩ ⟨*the rain* ~ed *his shirt to his body*⟩ **4** to fasten (sthg) (to) or place (sthg) (on), esp conspicuously or in quantity ⟨*walls* ~ed *with posters*⟩ ⟨~ed *posters all over the walls*⟩ **5** to inflict heavy damage, injury, or casualties on, esp by a concentrated or unremitting attack – infml ~ *vi* to apply plaster – **plasterer** *n*

'**plaster,board** /-,bawd/ *n* a board with a plaster core used esp as a substitute for plaster on walls

'**plastered** *adj* drunk – infml

plastering /'plahst(ə)ring/ *n* **1** a coating (as if) of plaster **2** a decisive defeat – infml

,**plaster of 'paris** /'paris/ *n, often cap 2nd P* a white powdery plaster made from gypsum that when mixed with water forms a quicksetting paste used chiefly for casts and moulds [*Paris*, capital city of France]

'**plaster,work** /-,wuhk/ *n* plastering applied as a finish on architectural constructions ☞ BUILDING

[1]**plastic** /'plastik; *also* 'plahstik/ *adj* **1** formative, creative ⟨~ *forces in nature*⟩ **2a** capable of being moulded or modelled ⟨~ *clay*⟩ **b** supple, pliant **3** sculptural **4** made or consisting of a plastic **5** capable of being bent or stretched continuously and permanently in any direction without breaking **6** of, involving, or being plastic surgery **7** formed by or adapted to an artificial or conventional standard; synthetic – chiefly derog ⟨*takes a positive effort of will to avoid* ~ *food,* ~ *living, and* ~ *entertainment* – L E Sissman⟩ [L *plasticus* of moulding, fr Gk *plastikos*, fr *plassein* to mould, form] – **plastically** *adv*, **plasticize** /-ti,siez/ *vt*, **plasticization** /,plastisie'zaysh(ə)n/ *n*

[2]**plastic** *n* any of numerous (synthetic) organic polymers that can be moulded, cast, extruded, etc into objects, films, or filaments

-plastic /-plastik/ *comb form* (→ *adj*) of sthg designated by a term ending in *-plasm, -plast, -plasty*, or *-plasy* ⟨*homo*plastic⟩ ⟨*neo*plastic⟩ [Gk *-plastikos*, fr *plassein*]

plastic art *n* art concerned with modelling or representing three-dimensional things; *specif* any of the visual arts (e g painting, sculpture, or film)

Plasticine /'plasti,seen; *also* 'plahs-/ *trademark* – used for a modelling substance that remains plastic for a long period

plasticity /plas'tisəti, plahs-/ *n* **1** being plastic; *esp* capacity for being moulded or altered **2** the ability to retain a shape produced by pressure deformation

plastic·izer, -iser /'plasti,siezə, 'plahs-/ *n* a chemical added to rubbers and plastics, esp to give flexibility [PLASTICIZE + [2]-ER]

,**plastic 'surgery** *n* surgery concerned with the repair, restoration, or cosmetic improvement of parts of the body chiefly by the grafting of tissue – **plastic surgeon** *n*

plastid /'plastid/ *n* any of various organelles of plant cells that function as centres of photosynthesis, store starch, oil, etc, or contain pigment [G, fr Gk *plastos* moulded] – **plastidial** /plas'tidi·əl/ *adj*

plastron /'plastrən/ *n* **1a** a metal breastplate **b** a quilted pad worn in fencing to protect the chest, waist, and sides **2** the lower part of the shell of a tortoise or turtle [MF, fr OIt *piastrone*, aug of *piastra* thin metal plate] – **plastral** *adj*

-plasty /-,plahsti/ *comb form* (→ *n*) replacement or formation of (sthg specified) by means of plastic surgery ⟨*osteo*plasty⟩ ⟨*rhino*plasty⟩ [F *-plastie*, fr LGk *-plastia* moulding, fr Gk *-plastēs* moulder, fr *plassein*]

plat /plat/ *vt or n* **-tt-** (to) plait

platan /'plat(ə)n/ *n* a plane tree [ME, fr L *platanus*]

plat du jour /,plah doo 'zhooə (*Fr* pla dy ʒuːr)/ *n, pl* **plats du jour** /~/ a dish featured by a restaurant on a particular day [F, lit., plate of the day]

[1]**plate** /playt/ *n* **1a** a smooth flat thin usu rigid piece of material **b** a very thin layer of metal deposited on a surface of a base metal by plating **c** (armour of) broad metal plates **d** an (external) scale or rigid layer of bone, horn, etc forming part of an animal body **e**

any of the huge movable segments into which the earth's crust is divided ☞ GEOGRAPHY **2a** domestic utensils and tableware made of or plated with gold, silver, or base metals **b** a shallow usu circular vessel, made esp of china, from which food is eaten or served **c** a plateful **3a** a prepared surface from which printing is done **b** a sheet of material (e g glass) coated with a light-sensitive photographic emulsion **c** an electrode in an accumulator **4** a flat piece or surface bearing letters or a design **5** a horizontal structural member (e g a timber) that provides bearing and anchorage, esp for rafters or joists **6** the part of a denture that fits to the mouth; *broadly* a denture **7** a full-page book illustration, often on different paper from the text pages **8** *NAm* **a** a complete main course served on a plate **b** food and service supplied to 1 person ⟨*a dinner at £5 a* ~⟩ **9** *NAm* the anode of an electron tube [ME, fr OF, fr *plate*, fem of *plat* flat, fr (assumed) VL *plattus*, prob fr Gk *platys* broad, flat – more at PLACE] – **platelike** *adj* – **on a plate** so as not to require effort – infml

²**plate** *vt* **1** to cover or equip with plate: e g **a** to arm with armour plate **b** to cover permanently with an adherent layer, esp of metal; *also* to deposit (e g a layer) on a surface **2** to fix or secure with a plate – **plater** *n*

plateau /'platoh/ *n, pl* **plateaus, plateaux** /-tohz/ **1** a usu extensive relatively flat land area raised sharply above adjacent land on at least 1 side **2** a relatively stable level, period, or condition ⟨*a price* ~ *interrupting an inflationary spiral*⟩ [F, fr MF, platter, fr *plat* flat]

'plateful /-f(ə)l/ *n* as much or as many as a plate will hold

,plate 'glass *n* rolled, ground, and polished sheet glass

'plate,layer /-,layə/ *n, Br* a person who lays and maintains railway track

'platelet /-lit/ *n* BLOOD PLATELET ☞ ANATOMY

'plate-,mark *n* a hallmark

platen /'plat(ə)n/ *n* **1** a flat plate that exerts pressure, esp in a printing press **2** the roller of a typewriter [MF *plateine*, fr *plate*]

plateresque /,platə'resk/ *adj, often cap* of or being a 16th-c Spanish architectural style suggestive of silverplate [Sp *plateresco*, fr *platero* silversmith, fr *plata* silver]

plate tectonics *n pl but sing in constr* the study of the formation of the major structures of the earth's surface by the movement and interaction of the plates of the earth's crust – **platetectonic** /,--'--/ *adj*, **platetectonically** /,--'---/ *adv*

platform /'platfawm/ *n* **1** a declaration of (political) principles and policies **2a** a horizontal flat surface, usu higher than the adjoining area; *esp, Br* a raised surface at a railway station to facilitate access to trains **b** a raised flooring (e g for speakers) **c** a raised metal structure secured to the sea bed by posts and serving as a base for the extraction of oil ☞ ENERGY **3** a place or opportunity for public discussion **4** (a shoe with) a thick sole ☞ GARMENT **5** *chiefly Br* the area next to the entrance or exit of a bus [MF *plate-forme* diagram, map, lit., flat form]

platin-, platino- *comb form* platinum ⟨platin*iridium*⟩ [NL *platinum*]

plating /'playting/ *n* **1** a coating of metal plates **2** a thin coating of metal

platinic /plə'tinik/ *adj* of or containing (tetravalent) platinum

platin·ize, -ise /'platiniez/ *vt* to cover, treat, or combine with (a compound of) platinum

platinous /'platinəs/ *adj* of or containing (bivalent) platinum

platinum /'platinəm/ *n* a heavy precious greyish white noncorroding metallic element used esp as a catalyst and for jewellery ☞ PERIODIC TABLE [NL, fr Sp *platina*, fr dim. of *plata* silver, fr (assumed) VL *plattus* flat – more at PLATE]

,platinum 'black *n* a soft dull black powder of platinum used as a catalyst

,platinum 'blonde *n* (sby having hair of) a pale silvery blond colour usu produced in human hair by bleach and bluish rinse

platitude /'platityoohd/ *n* a banal, trite, or stale remark, esp when presented as if it were original and significant [F, fr *plat* flat, dull]

platitudin·ize, -ise /,plati'tyoohdi,niez/ *vi* to utter platitudes [*platitudinous*]

,plati'tudinous /-nəs/ *adj* having the characteristics of a platitude; full of platitudes ⟨~ *remarks*⟩ [*platitude* + *-inous* (as in *multitudinous*)] – **platitudinously** *adv*

platonic /plə'tonik/ *adj* **1** *cap* (characteristic) of Plato or Platonism **2a** of or being a close relationship between 2 people in which sexual desire is absent or has been repressed or sublimated **b** nominal, theoretical [L *platonicus*, fr Gk *platōnikos*, fr *Platōn* Plato †349 BC Gk philosopher] – **platonically** *adv*

Platonism /'playtə,niz(ə)m/ *n* the philosophy of Plato stressing that actual things and ideas (e g of truth or beauty) are copies of transcendent ideas which are the objects of true knowledge – **Platonist** *n*, **Platonistic** /,playtə'nistik/ *adj*

platoon /plə'toohn/ *n sing or pl in constr* **1** a subdivision of a military company normally consisting of 2 or more sections or squads **2** a group of people sharing a common characteristic or activity ⟨*a* ~ *of waiters*⟩ [F *peloton* small detachment, lit., ball, fr *pelote* little ball – more at PELLET]

Plattdeutsch /'plat,doych, ,plaht-/ *n* a colloquial language of N Germany [G, fr D *Platduitsch*, lit., Low German, fr *plat* flat, low + *duitsch* German]

platteland /'plutə,lunt/ *n, SAfr* the backveld [Afrik, fr D, lit., flatland]

platter /'platə/ *n* **1** a large often oval plate used esp for serving meat **2** *NAm* a gramophone record [ME *plater*, fr AF, fr MF *plat* plate] – **platterful** *n*

platyhelminth /,plati'helminth/ *n* any of a phylum of soft-bodied flattened worms (e g the planarians, flukes, and tapeworms) [deriv of Gk *platys* broad, flat + *helminth-*, *helmis* helminth] – **platyhelminthic** /-hel'minthik/ *adj*

platypus /'platipəs/ *n, pl* **platypuses** *also* **platypi** /-pie/ a small aquatic Australian and Tasmanian primitive mammal that lays eggs and has a fleshy bill resembling that of a duck, webbed feet, and a broad flattened tail [NL, fr Gk *platypous* flat-footed, fr *platys* broad, flat + *pous* foot – more at PLACE, FOOT]

plaudit /'plawdit/ *n* enthusiastic approval – usu pl with sing. meaning ⟨*received the* ~s *of the critics*⟩ [L *plaudite* applaud, pl imper of *plaudere* to applaud]

plausible /'plawzəbl/ *adj* **1** apparently fair, reasonable, or valid but often specious ⟨*a ~ pretext*⟩ **2** *of a person* persuasive but deceptive [L *plausibilis* worthy of applause, fr *plausus*, pp of *plaudere*] – **plausibleness** *n*, **plausibly** *adv*, **plausibility** /,plawzə'biləti/ *n*

[1]**play** /play/ *n* **1** the conduct, course, or (a particular) action in or of a game **2a** (children's spontaneous) recreational activity **b** the absence of serious or harmful intent; jest ⟨*said it in ~*⟩ **c** a playing on words or speech sounds **d** gaming, gambling **3a** operation, activity ⟨*bringing other forces into ~*⟩ **b** light, quick, transitory, or fitful movement ⟨*the ~ of sunlight and shadows through the trees*⟩ **c** free or unimpeded motion (e g of a part of a machine) **d** scope or opportunity for action **4a** the dramatized representation of an action or story on stage **b** a dramatic composition (for presentation in a theatre) **5** *chiefly NAm* **a** an act or manoeuvre, esp in a game **b** a move or series of moves calculated to arouse friendly feelings – usu + *make* ⟨*made a big ~ for the blonde*⟩ [ME, fr OE *plega*; akin to OE *plegan* to play, MD *pleyen*] – **in/into play** **1** in/into condition or position to be legitimately played **2** in/into operation or consideration – **out of play** not in play

[2]**play** *vi* **1a** to engage in sport or recreation **b(1)** to behave aimlessly; toy, trifle ⟨*don't ~ with your food*⟩ **(2)** to deal or behave frivolously, mockingly, or playfully – often + *around* or *about* **(3)** to deal in a light speculative manner ⟨*liked to ~ with ideas*⟩ **(4)** to make use of double meaning or of the similarity of sound of 2 words for stylistic or humorous effect – usu in *play on words* **2a** to take advantage ⟨*~ing on fears*⟩ **b** to move or operate in a lively, irregular, or intermittent manner ⟨*watch the light ~ing on the water*⟩ ⟨*a faint smile ~s on her lips*⟩ **c** to move or function freely within prescribed limits ⟨*a piston rod ~s within cylinders*⟩ **d** to discharge repeatedly or in a stream ⟨*hoses ~ing on a fire*⟩ **3a(1)** to perform music **(2)** to sound in performance ⟨*the organ is ~ing*⟩ **(3)** to reproduce or emit sounds ⟨*his radio is ~ing*⟩ **b(1)** to act in a dramatic production **(2)** to be presented at a place of entertainment (e g a theatre) **c** to act with special consideration so as to gain favour, approval, or sympathy – usu + *up to* **4a** to engage, take part, or make a move in a game **b** to perform (e g in a sport) in a specified position or manner ⟨*the fullbacks are ~ing deep*⟩ **c** to gamble **d(1)** to behave (or conduct oneself) in a specified way ⟨*~ safe*⟩ ⟨*the pitch will ~ well*⟩ **(2)** to feign a specified state or quality ⟨*~ dead*⟩ **(3)** to take part in or assent to some activity; cooperate ⟨*~ along with his scheme*⟩ **5** to have (promiscuous or illicit) sexual relations – euph; usu in *play around* ~ *vt* **1a(1)** to engage in or occupy oneself with ⟨*~ football*⟩ **(2)** to deal with, handle, or manage ⟨*decided to ~ the dispute another way*⟩ – often + *it* ⟨*trying to ~ it cool*⟩ **(3)** to exploit, manipulate ⟨*~ the stock market*⟩ **b** to pretend to engage in ⟨*children ~ing cops and robbers*⟩ **c(1)** to perform or execute for amusement or to deceive or mock ⟨*~ a trick*⟩ **(2)** to wreak ⟨*~ havoc*⟩ **2a(1)** to put on a performance of (a play) **(2)** to act in the character or part of **(3)** to act or perform in ⟨*~ed leading theatres*⟩ **b** to perform or act the part of ⟨*~ the fool*⟩ **3a(1)** to contend against in a game **(2)** to use as a contestant in a game ⟨*the selectors did not ~ him*⟩ **(3)** to perform the duties associated with (a certain position) ⟨*~ed fullback*⟩ **b(1)** to make bets on ⟨*~ the horses*⟩ **(2)** to operate on the basis of ⟨*~ a hunch*⟩ **c** to put into action in a game ⟨*~ the ace*⟩ ⟨*~ the knight*⟩ **d** to direct the course of (e g a ball); hit **4a** to perform (music) on an instrument ⟨*~ a waltz*⟩ **b** to perform music on ⟨*~ the violin*⟩ **c** to perform music of (a specified composer) **d** to reproduce sounds, esp music, on (an apparatus) ⟨*~s her radio all day long*⟩ ⟨*~ us your favourite record*⟩ **5a** to aim and fire or set off with continuous effect ⟨*~ed the hose on the burning building*⟩ **b** to cause to move or operate lightly and irregularly or intermittently ⟨*~ed his torch along the fence*⟩ **c** to allow (a hooked fish) to become exhausted by pulling against a line – **playable** *adj*, **player** *n*, **playability** /,playə'biləti/ *n* – **play ball** to cooperate – **play by ear** to deal with from moment to moment rather than making plans in advance – **play fast and loose** to act in a reckless, irresponsible, or craftily deceitful way – **play into the hands of** to act so as to prove advantageous to (an opponent) – **play second fiddle** to take a subordinate position – **play the field** to have a number of boyfriends or girl friends rather than committing oneself exclusively to one person – **play the game** to act according to a code or set of standards – **play with oneself** to masturbate – **to play with** at one's disposal ⟨*a lot of funds* to play with⟩

playa /'plah·yə/ *n* the flat bottom of an undrained desert basin that becomes at times a shallow lake [Sp, lit., beach]

playact /'play,akt/ *vi* **1** to make believe **2** to behave in a misleading or insincere manner ~ *vt* ACT OUT 1a [back-formation fr *playacting*]

'play,back /-,bak/ *n* (a device that provides for) the reproduction of recorded sound or pictures

play back *vt* to listen to or look at material on (a usu recently recorded disc or tape)

'play,boy /-,boy/ *n* a man who lives a life devoted chiefly to the pursuit of pleasure

'play ,down *n* to cause to seem less important; minimize

,played 'out *adj* worn or tired out

player piano /'playə/ *n* a piano containing a mechanical device that operates the keys automatically

'play,fellow /-,feloh/ *n* a playmate

'playful /-f(ə)l/ *adj* **1** full of fun; frolicsome ⟨*a ~ kitten*⟩ **2** humorous, lighthearted ⟨*the ~ tone of her voice*⟩ – **playfully** *adv*, **playfulness** *n*

'play,ground /-,grownd/ *n* **1** a piece of land for children to play on **2** an area favoured for recreation or amusement ⟨*that town was a gambler's ~*⟩

'play,group /-,groohp/ *n*, *chiefly Br* a supervised group of children below school age who play together regularly

'play,house /-,hows/ *n* **1** a theatre **2** *chiefly NAm* WENDY HOUSE

'playing ,card /'playing/ *n* any of a set of usu 52 thin rectangular pieces, usu of cardboard, marked on one side to show one of 13 ranks in one of 4 suits and used in playing any of numerous games

'playing ,field *n* a field used for playing organized games and often divided into several separate pitches – often pl with sing. meaning

'play,mate /-,mayt/ *n* a companion in play

'play-,off *n* a final contest to determine a winner

play off *vt* **1** to decide the winner of (a competition) or break (a tie) by a play-off **2** to set in opposition for one's own gain ⟨*survived by* playing *his enemies* off *against each other*⟩

ˌplay on ˈwords *n* a pun

play out *vt* **1** to finish; USE UP **2** to unreel, unfold

ˈplayˌpen /-ˌpen/ *n* a portable usu collapsible enclosure in which a baby or young child may play

ˈplayˌsuit /-ˌs(y)ooht/ *n* a garment, esp dungarees, for children to play in

ˈplayˌthing /-ˌthing/ *n* a toy

play up *vt* **1** to give special emphasis or prominence to ⟨*the press* played up *the divorce story*⟩ **2** *Br* to cause pain or distress to ⟨*my corns have been* playing *me* up *again*⟩ ~ *vi* to behave in a disobedient or annoying manner; ACT UP

ˈplayˌwright /-ˌriet/ *n* one who writes plays [[1]*play* + obs *wright* (maker), fr ME, fr OE *wryhta* – more at WRIGHT]

plaza /ˈplahzə/ *n* a public square in a city or town [Sp, fr L *platea* broad street – more at PLACE]

plea /plee/ *n* **1** an allegation made by a party in support of his/her case **2** an accused person's answer to an indictment ⟨*a* ~ *of guilty*⟩ **3** sthg offered by way of excuse or justification **4** an earnest entreaty; an appeal [ME *plaid, plai,* fr OF *plait, plaid,* fr ML *placitum,* fr L, decision, decree, fr neut of *placitus,* pp of *placēre* to please, be decided – more at PLEASE]

plea bargaining *n* pleading guilty to a lesser charge in order to avoid standing trial for a more serious one

pleach /pleech/ *vt* to interlace, plash [ME *plechen,* fr ONF *plechier,* fr L *plexus,* pp of *plectere* to braid – more at [1]PLY]

plead /pleed/ *vb* **pleaded, pled** /pled/ *vi* **1** to argue a case as an advocate in a court **2** to make or answer an allegation in a legal proceeding **3** to make a specified plea ⟨~ *not guilty*⟩ **4a** to urge reasons for or against sthg **b** to entreat or appeal earnestly; implore ~ *vt* **1** to maintain (e g a case) in a court **2** to offer as a (legal) plea ⟨*to* ~ *ignorance*⟩ [ME *plaiden* to institute a lawsuit, fr OF *plaidier,* fr *plaid* plea] – **pleadable** *adj,* **pleader** *n,* **pleadingly** *adv*

pleading /ˈpleeding/ *n* **1** advocacy of a case in a court **2** any of the formal usu written allegations made alternately by the parties in a legal action

pleasant /ˈplez(ə)nt/ *adj* **1** having qualities that tend to give pleasure; agreeable ⟨*a* ~ *day*⟩ **2** *of a person* likable, friendly [ME *plesaunt,* fr MF *plaisant,* fr prp of *plaisir*] – **pleasantly** *adv,* **pleasantness** *n*

pleasantry /ˈplez(ə)ntri/ *n* **1** an agreeable remark (made in order to be polite) **2** a humorous act or remark; a joke

please /pleez/ *vi* **1** to afford or give pleasure or satisfaction **2** to like, wish ⟨*do as you* ~⟩ **3** to be willing – usu used in the imperative (1) to express a polite request ⟨*coffee,* ~⟩ ⟨~ *come in*⟩ (2) to make polite a request for attention ⟨~, *Sir, I don't understand*⟩ (3) to express polite acceptance ⟨*Coffee?* Please*!*⟩ (4) to turn an apparent question into a request ⟨*can you shut it,* ~*?*⟩ ~ *vt* **1** to give pleasure to; gratify **2** to be the will or pleasure of ⟨*may it* ~ *your Majesty*⟩ – fml [ME *plesen,* fr MF *plaisir,* fr L *placēre*; akin to L *placare* to placate, OE *flōh* flat stone, Gk *plak-, plax* flat surface] – **pleasing** *adj,* **pleasingly** *adv*

pleasurable /ˈplezh(ə)rəbl/ *adj* pleasant, enjoyable – **pleasurableness** *n,* **pleasurably** *adv,* **pleasurability** /ˌplezh(ə)rəˈbiləti/ *n*

[1]pleasure /ˈplezh·ə/ *n* **1** a state of gratification **2a** sensual gratification ⟨*he abandoned the monastery for a life of* ~⟩ **b** enjoyment, recreation ⟨*are you here on business or for* ~*?*⟩ **3** a source of delight or joy ⟨*it's always a* ~ *to talk to her*⟩ **4** a wish, desire – fml [ME *plesure,* alter. of *plesir,* fr MF *plaisir,* fr *plaisir* to please]

[2]pleasure *vt, archaic* to give (sexual) pleasure to

[1]pleat /pleet/ *vt* to fold; *esp* to arrange in pleats ⟨~ *a skirt*⟩ [ME *pleten,* fr *pleit, plete* plait] – **pleater** *n*

[2]pleat *n* a fold in cloth made by doubling material over on itself; *also* sthg resembling such a fold [ME *plete*] – **pleated** *adj,* **pleatless** *adj*

pleb /pleb/ *n* a plebeian – chiefly derog

plebby /ˈplebi/ *adj, chiefly Br* plebeian – derog

[1]plebeian /pliˈbee·ən/ *n* a member of the (Roman) common people [L *plebeius* of the common people, fr *plebs* common people; akin to Gk *plēthos* throng, *plēthein* to be full] – **plebeianism** *n*

[2]plebeian *adj* **1** of plebeians **2** crude or coarse in manner or style; common – **plebeianly** *adv*

plebiscite /ˈplebiˌsiet/ *n* a vote by the people of an entire country or district for or against a proposal, esp on a choice of government or ruler [L *plebis scitum* law voted by the comitia, lit., decree of the common people] – **plebiscitary** /pləˈbisit(ə)ri/ *adj*

plectrum /ˈplektrəm/ *n, pl* **plectra** /-trə/, **plectrums** a small thin piece of plastic, metal, etc used to pluck the strings of a stringed instrument [L, fr Gk *plēktron,* fr *plēssein* to strike – more at PLAINT]

pled /pled/ *past of* PLEAD

[1]pledge /plej/ *n* **1** a chattel delivered as security for an obligation (e g a debt) or for the performance of an act **2** the state of being held as a security ⟨*his watch is in* ~⟩ **3** a token, sign, or earnest of sthg else **4** TOAST 3 **5** a binding promise to do or forbear [ME, security, fr MF *plege,* fr LL *plebium,* fr (assumed) LL *plebere* to pledge]

[2]pledge *vt* **1** to make a pledge of; *specif* to deposit as security for fulfilment of a contract or obligation **2** to drink the health of **3** to bind by a pledge **4** to give a promise of ⟨~ *allegiance to the flag*⟩ – **pledger, pledgor** /pleˈjaw/ *n*

pledgee /pleˈjee/ *n* one to whom a pledge is given

pledget /ˈplejit/ *n* a compress or pad used to apply medication or absorb discharges (e g from a wound) [origin unknown]

-plegia /-ˈpleeji·ə/ *comb form* (→ *n*) paralysis ⟨*hemiplegia*⟩ [NL, fr Gk *-plēgia,* fr *plēssein* to strike – more at PLAINT]

Pleiades /ˈplie·əˌdeez/ *n pl* a conspicuous cluster of stars in the constellation Taurus [L, fr Gk]

plein air /ˌplayn ˈeə/ *adj* of (impressionist) painting done out of doors which attempts to capture the atmospheric effects of outdoor daylight [F, open air] – **pleinairist** *n*

pleio-, pleo-, plio- *comb form* more ⟨pleo*nasm*⟩ [Gk *pleiōn, pleōn* – more at PLUS]

Pleistocene /ˈpliestəˌseen, -stoh-/ *adj or n* (of or being) the earlier epoch of the Quaternary ☞ EVOLUTION, GEOGRAPHY [Gk *pleistos* most + ISV *-cene*; akin to Gk *pleiōn* more]

plenary /ˈpleenəri/ *adj* **1** absolute, unqualified ⟨~ *power*⟩ **2** attended by all entitled to be present ⟨*a* ~

session⟩ [LL *plenarius*, fr L *plenus* full – more at [1]FULL]

plenipotentiary /ˌplenipəˈtensh(ə)ri/ *n or adj* (sby, esp a diplomatic agent) invested with full power to transact business [ML *plenipotentiarius*, adj & n, deriv of LL *plenipotent-, plenipotens*, adj, fr L *plenus* + *potent-, potens* powerful]

plenitude /ˈplenityoohd/ *n* **1** fullness, completeness **2** abundance *USE* fml [ME *plenitude*, fr MF or L; MF, fr L *plenitudo*, fr *plenus* full]

plenteous /ˈplentyəs/ *adj* plentiful – fml or poetic [ME *plentevous, plenteous*, fr OF *plentiveus*, fr *plentif* abundant, fr *plenté* plenty] – **plenteously** *adv*, **plenteousness** *n*

plentiful /ˈplentif(ə)l/ *adj* **1** containing or yielding plenty ⟨*a ~ land*⟩ **2** characterized by, constituting, or existing in plenty – **plentifully** *adv*, **plentifulness** *n*

[1]**plenty** /ˈplenti/ *n* **1a** *sing or pl in constr* a full or more than adequate amount or supply ⟨*had ~ of time to finish the job*⟩ ⟨*there's ~ more*⟩ **b** a large number or amount ⟨*he's in ~ of trouble*⟩ **2** copiousness, plentifulness ⟨*years of ~*⟩ [ME *plente*, fr OF *plenté*, fr LL *plenitat-, plenitas*, fr L, fullness, fr *plenus* full]

[2]**plenty** *adj, chiefly NAm* ample ⟨*~ work to be done – Time*⟩

[3]**plenty** *adv* **1** quite, abundantly ⟨*~ warm enough*⟩ **2** *chiefly NAm* to a considerable or extreme degree; very ⟨*~ hungry*⟩ *USE* infml

pleochroism /pleeˈokroh,iz(ə)m/ *n* the property of a crystal of showing different colours when viewed by light from different angles [ISV *pleochroic* (fr *pleio-* + Gk *chrōs* skin, colour) + *-ism* – more at GRIT] – **pleochroic** /ˌplee·əˈkrohik/ *adj*

pleomorphism /ˌplee·ohˈmaw,fiz(ə)m/ *n* the having, assumption, or occurrence of more than 1 distinct form [ISV] – **pleomorphic** /-fik/ *adj*

pleonasm /ˈplee·ə,naz(ə)m/ *n* the use of more words than are necessary to convey the intended sense [LL *pleonasmus*, fr Gk *pleonasmos*, fr *pleonazein* to be excessive, fr *pleiōn, pleōn* more – more at PLUS] – **pleonastic** /ˌplee·əˈnastik/ *adj*, **pleonastically** *adv*

plesiosaur /ˈpleesi·ə,saw/ *n* a Mesozoic marine reptile with a flattened body and limbs modified into paddles [deriv of Gk *plēsios* close (fr *pelas* near) + *sauros* lizard]

plethora /ˈplethərə/ *n* **1** an abnormal excess of blood in the body – not now used technically **2** a superfluity, excess ⟨*a ~ of regulations*⟩ [ML, fr Gk *plēthōra*, lit., fullness, fr *plēthein* to be full – more at [1]FULL] – **plethoric** /pleˈthorik/ *adj*

pleur- /plooər-/, **pleuro-** *comb form* **1a** pleura ⟨pleuro*pneumonia*⟩; pleura and ⟨pleuro*peritoneum*⟩ **b** pleural and ⟨pleuro*cerebral*⟩ **2** side; lateral ⟨pleu*ron*⟩ [(1) NL, fr *pleura*; (2) Gk, fr *pleura*]

pleura /ˈplooərə/ *n, pl* **pleurae** /-ri/, **pleuras** the delicate membrane that lines each half of the thorax of mammals and surrounds the lung of the same side [Gk, rib, side] – **pleural** *adj*

pleurisy /ˈplooərəsi/ *n* inflammation of the pleura, usu with fever, painful breathing, and oozing of liquid into the pleural cavity [ME *pluresie*, fr MF *pleuresie*, fr LL *pleurisis*, alter. of L *pleuritis*, fr Gk, fr *pleura* side] – **pleuritic** /plooəˈritik/ *adj*

pleuron /ˈplooəron/ *n* a side part of the middle segment of an insect [NL, fr Gk, rib, side]

pleuropneumonia /ˌplooərohnyoohˈmohnyə, -ni·ə/ *n* combined inflammation of the pleura and lungs, esp in cattle [NL]

pleuston /ˈploohston, -stən/ *n* floating living organisms forming a layer on or near the surface of a body of fresh water [(assumed) Gk *pleustos* (verbal of *plein* to sail, float) + ISV *-on* (as in *plankton*)] – **pleustonic** /ploohˈstonik/ *adj*

Plexiglas /ˈpleksi,glahs/ *trademark* – used for acrylic plastic sheets and moulding powders

plexus /ˈpleksəs/ *n* **1** a network of interlacing blood vessels or nerves **2** a network of parts or elements in a structure or system [NL, fr L, braid, network, fr *plexus*, pp of *plectere* to braid – more at [1]PLY] – **plexiform** /ˈpleksi,fawm/ *adj*

pliable /ˈplie·əbl/ *adj* **1** easily bent without breaking; flexible **2** yielding readily to others; compliant [ME, fr MF, fr *plier* to bend, fold – more at [1]PLY] – **pliableness** *n*, **pliably** *adv*, **pliability** /ˌplie·əˈbiləti/ *n*

pliant /ˈplie·ənt/ *adj* PLIABLE 1 – **pliantly** *adv*, **pliantness, pliancy** /-si/ *n*

plicate /ˈpliekayt/ *also* **plicated** /ˈpliekaytid/ *adj* folded lengthways like a fan; pleated, ridged ⟨*a ~ leaf*⟩ [L *plicatus*, pp of *plicare* to fold] – **plicately** *adv*, **plicateness** *n*

plication /pliˈkaysh(ə)n, plie-/ *n* **1** folding **2** a fold or being folded

plié /ˈplee·ay/ *n* the action in ballet of bending the knees outwards while holding the back straight [F, fr pp of *plier* to bend]

pliers /ˈplie·əz/ *n pl, pl* **pliers** a pair of pincers with long jaws for holding small objects or for bending and cutting wire [[1]*ply* + [2]*-er* + [1]*-s*]

[1]**plight** /pliet/ *vt* to put or give in pledge; engage ⟨*~ one's troth*⟩ [ME *plighten*, fr OE *plihtan* to endanger, fr *pliht* danger; akin to OHG *pflegan* to take care of]

[2]**plight** *n* an (unpleasant or difficult) state; a predicament [ME *plit*, fr AF, fr (assumed) VL *plictus* fold – more at PLAIT]

plimsoll /ˈplims(ə)l, -sol, -sohl/ *n, Br* a shoe with a rubber sole and canvas top worn esp for sports [prob fr the supposed resemblance of the upper edge of the rubber to the Plimsoll line on a ship]

Plimsoll line *n* a set of markings indicating the draught levels to which a vessel may legally be loaded in various seasons and waters [Samuel *Plimsoll* †1898 E leader of shipping reform]

Plimsoll mark *n* PLIMSOLL LINE

plinth /plinth/ *n* **1** a usu square block serving as a base (e g of a pedestal) **2** a part of a structure forming a continuous foundation or base *USE* ☞ ARCHITECTURE [L *plinthus*, fr Gk *plinthos*]

plio- *comb form* pleio-

Pliocene /ˈplie·oh,seen/ *adj or n* (of or being) the latest epoch of the Tertiary ☞ EVOLUTION

plissé, plisse /ˈpleesay/ *n* (a fabric with) a permanently puckered finish [F *plissé*, fr pp of *plisser* to pleat, fr MF, fr *pli* fold, fr *plier* to fold – more at [1]PLY]

plod /plod/ *vb* **-dd-** *vi* **1a** to walk heavily or slowly; trudge **b** to proceed slowly or tediously ⟨*the film just ~s along*⟩ **2** to work laboriously and monotonously ⟨*~ding through stacks of unanswered letters*⟩ *~ vt* to tread slowly or heavily along or over ⟨*~ded the streets all day, looking for work*⟩ [imit] – **plod** *n*, **plodder** *n*, **ploddingly** *adv*

-ploid /-ployd/ *comb form* (→ *adj*) having a chromosome number that bears (such) a relationship to or is (so many) times the haploid number ⟨*poly*ploid⟩ – compare -SOMIC [ISV, fr *diploid* & *haploid*] – **-ploid** *comb form* (→ *n*)

ploidy /'ploydi/ *n* degree of repetition of the haploid number of chromosomes [fr such words as *diploidy, hexaploidy*]

[1]plonk /plongk/ *vt* PLUNK 2

[2]plonk *n, chiefly Br* cheap or inferior wine – infml [short for earlier *plink-plonk*, perh modif of F *vin blanc* white wine]

plop /plop/ *vb* **-pp-** *vi* **1** to drop or move suddenly with a sound suggestive of sthg dropping into water **2** to allow the body to drop heavily ⟨~ped *into a chair*⟩ ~ *vt* to set, drop, or throw heavily [imit] – **plop** *n*

plosion /'plohzh(ə)n/ *n* the release of obstructed breath that occurs in the articulation of stop consonants [fr *explosion, implosion*] – **plosive** /'plohsiv, -ziv/ *adj or n*

[1]plot /plot/ *n* **1** a small piece of land, esp one used or designated for a specific purpose ⟨*a vegetable* ~⟩ **2** the plan or main story of a literary work **3** a secret plan for accomplishing a usu evil or unlawful end; an intrigue **4** a chart or other graphic representation **5** *NAm* GROUND PLAN [ME, fr OE] – **plotless** *adj*, **plotlessness** *n*

[2]plot *vb* **-tt-** *vt* **1a** to make a plot, map, or plan of **b** to mark or note (as if) on a map or chart **2** to lay out in plots **3a** to assign a position to (a point) by means of coordinates **b** to draw (a curve) by means of plotted points **c** to represent (an equation) by means of a curve so constructed **4** to plan or contrive, esp secretly ⟨~ted *his revenge*⟩ **5** to invent or devise the plot of (a literary work) ~ *vi* to form a plot; scheme – **plotter** *n*

[1]plough, *NAm* **plow** /plow/ *n* **1** (any of various devices operating like) an implement used to cut, lift, and turn over soil, esp in preparing ground for sowing **2** ploughed land **3** *cap* URSA MAJOR – + *the* [ME, fr OE *plōh* hide of land; akin to OHG *pfluog* plough]

[2]plough, *NAm* **plow** *vi* **1a** to use a plough **b** to bear or undergo ploughing **2** to force a way, esp violently ⟨*the car* ~ed *into a group of spectators*⟩ **3** to proceed steadily and laboriously; plod ⟨*had to* ~ *through a summer reading list*⟩ ~ *vt* **1a** to turn, break up, or work (as if) with a plough **b** to make (e g a furrow) with a plough **2** to cut into, open, or make furrows or ridges in (as if) with a plough – often + *up* – **ploughable** *adj*, **plougher** *n*

plough back *vt* to reinvest (profits) in an industry

'ploughman /-mən/ *n* one who guides a plough; *broadly* a farm labourer

,ploughman's 'lunch /-mənz/ *n* a cold lunch of bread, cheese, and usu pickled onions often served in a public house

'plough,share /-,sheə/ *n* the part of a mouldboard plough that cuts the furrow [ME, fr *plough* + *schare* ploughshare – more at [3]SHARE]

plover /'pluvə/ *n, pl* **plovers,** *esp collectively* **plover** any of numerous wading birds with a short beak and usu a stout compact build [ME, fr MF, fr (assumed) VL *pluviarius*, fr L *pluvia* rain – more at PLUVIAL]

ploy /ploy/ *n* sthg devised or contrived, esp to embarrass or frustrate an opponent [prob fr *employ*]

[1]pluck /pluk/ *vt* **1** to pull or pick off or out ⟨*she* ~ed *out a grey hair*⟩ **2** to remove sthg from (as if) by plucking; *esp* to remove the feathers from (e g a chicken) **3** to pick, pull, or grasp at; *also* to play (an instrument) in this manner ~ *vi* to tug *at* ⟨~ed *at the folds of her skirt*⟩ [ME *plucken*, fr OE *pluccian*; akin to MHG *pflücken* to pluck] – **plucker** *n*

[2]pluck *n* **1** an act or instance of plucking or pulling **2** the heart, liver, and lungs of a slaughtered animal, esp as food **3** courage and determination

plucky /'pluki/ *adj* marked by courage; spirited – **pluckily** *adv*, **pluckiness** *n*

[1]plug /plug/ *n* **1a** a piece used to fill a hole; a stopper **b** an obtruding or obstructing mass of material resembling a stopper ⟨*a volcanic* ~⟩ **2** a flat compressed cake of (chewing) tobacco; *also* a piece cut from this for chewing **3** a small core or segment removed from a larger object **4** a fire hydrant **5a** any of various devices resembling or functioning like an electrical plug **b** a device having usu 3 pins projecting from an insulated case for making electrical connection with a suitable socket; *also* the electrical socket **6** a piece of favourable publicity (e g for a commercial product) usu incorporated in general matter – infml [D, fr MD *plugge*; akin to MHG *pfloc* plug]

[2]plug *vb* **-gg-** *vt* **1** to block, close, or secure (as if) by inserting a plug **2** to hit with a bullet; SHOOT 2a **3** to advertise or publicize insistently ~ *vi* to work doggedly and persistently ⟨~ged *away at his homework*⟩ – **plugger** *n*

plug in *vi* to establish an electric circuit by inserting a plug ~ *vt* to attach or connect to a power point

plum /plum/ *n* **1** (any of numerous trees and shrubs of the rose family, that bear) an edible globular to oval smooth-skinned fruit with an oblong seed **2** a raisin when used in a pudding, cake, etc ⟨~ *cake*⟩ **3** sthg excellent or superior; *esp* an opportunity or position offering exceptional advantages ⟨*a* ~ *job*⟩ **4** a dark reddish purple [ME, fr OE *plūme*; akin to OHG *pflūmo* plum tree; both fr a prehistoric WGmc word borrowed fr L *prunum* plum, fr Gk *proumnon*] – **plum** *adj*, **plumlike** *adj*

plumage /'ploohmij/ *n* the entire covering of feathers of a bird [ME, fr MF, fr OF, fr *plume* feather – more at PLUME] – **plumaged** *adj*

[1]plumb /plum/ *n* **1** a lead weight attached to a cord and used to indicate a vertical line **2** any of various weights (e g a sinker for a fishing line or a lead for sounding) [ME, fr (assumed) OF *plomb*, fr OF *plon* lead, fr L *plumbum*]

[2]plumb *adv* **1** straight down or up; vertically **2** exactly, precisely ⟨*his house is* ~ *in the middle of the island*⟩ **3** *chiefly dial NAm* completely, absolutely USE (2&3) chiefly infml

[3]plumb *vt* **1** to measure the depth of with a plumb **2** to examine minutely and critically, esp so as to achieve complete understanding ⟨~ing *the book's complexities*⟩ **3** to adjust or test by a plumb line **4** to supply with or install as plumbing – often + *in* [(4) back-formation fr *plumber*]

[4]plumb *adj* **1** exactly vertical or true **2** *of a cricket wicket* flat and allowing little or no horizontal or vertical deviation of the bowled ball **3** downright, complete – infml

plumb-, plumbo- *comb form* lead ⟨plumb*ism*⟩ [L *plumb-*, fr *plumbum*]

plumbaginous /plum'bajinəs/ *adj* resembling, consisting of, or containing graphite

plumbago /plum'baygoh/ *n, pl* **plumbagos** **1** graphite **2** any of a genus of plants of the thrift family with spikes of showy flowers [L *plumbagin-, plumbago* galena, leadwort, fr *plumbum*]

plumb bob *n* the metal bob of a plumb line

plumbeous /'plumbi·əs/ *adj* consisting of or resembling lead [L *plumbeus*, fr *plumbum*]

plumber /'plumə/ *n* **1** sby who installs, repairs, and maintains water piping and fittings **2** *obs* a dealer or worker in lead [ME, dealer or worker in lead, fr MF *plombier*, fr L *plumbarius*, fr *plumbarius*, adj, of or relating to lead, fr *plumbum*]

plumbic /'plumbik/ *adj* of or containing (tetravalent) lead

plumbing /'pluming/ *n* **1** a plumber's occupation or trade **2** the apparatus (e g pipes and fixtures) concerned in the distribution and use of water in a building

plumbism /'plumbiz(ə)m/ *n* (chronic) lead poisoning

'**plumb** ,**line** *n* a line that has a weight at one end and is used esp to determine verticality ☞ BUILDING

plumbous /'plumbəs/ *adj* of or containing (bivalent) lead

[1]**plume** /ploohm/ *n* **1a** a (large showy) bird's feather **b** a cluster of distinctive feathers **2** a usu large feather or cluster of feathers worn esp as an ornament **3** sthg resembling a feather (e g in shape, appearance, or lightness): e g **a** a feathery or feather-like animal or plant part; *esp* a full bushy tail **b** a trail of smoke, blowing snow, etc [ME, fr MF, fr L *pluma* small soft feather] – **plumed** *adj*

[2]**plume** *vt* **1** to provide or deck with plumes **2** to pride or congratulate (oneself) *on* or *upon* **3a** *of a bird* to preen and arrange the feathers of (itself) **b** to preen and arrange (feathers)

[1]**plummet** /'plumit/ *n* a plumb (line) [ME *plomet*, fr MF *plombet* ball of lead, fr *plomb* lead, fr (assumed) OF – more at [1]PLUMB]

[2]**plummet** *vi* to fall sharply and abruptly ⟨*prices* ~ed⟩

plummy /'plumi/ *adj* **1** *of the voice* rich and mellow, often to the point of affectation **2** choice, desirable ⟨*got a* ~ *role in the film*⟩ – infml [PLUM + [1]-Y]

plumose /'ploohmohs/ *adj* **1** having feathers or plumes **2** feathery **3** having a main shaft bearing small filaments ⟨*the* ~ *antennae of an insect*⟩ – **plumosely** *adv*

[1]**plump** /plump/ *vi* to drop or sink suddenly or heavily ⟨~ed *down in the chair*⟩ ~ *vt* to drop, cast, or place suddenly or heavily [ME *plumpen*, of imit origin] – **plump for** to decide on out of several choices or courses of action ⟨plumped for *beer rather than wine*⟩

[2]**plump** *adv* **1** with a sudden or heavy drop **2** without qualification; directly

[3]**plump** *n* (the sound of) a sudden plunge, fall, or blow

[4]**plump** *adj* having a full rounded form; slightly fat [MD, dull, blunt] – **plumpish** *adj*, **plumply** *adv*, **plumpness** *n*

[5]**plump** *vb* to make or become plump – often + *up* or *out*

,**plum** '**pudding** *n* a rich boiled or steamed pudding containing dried fruits (e g raisins) and spices

plump up *vt* to cause to fill or swell out ⟨plumped up *the pillows when she made the bed*⟩

plumule /'ploohmyoohl/ *n* the primary bud of a plant embryo [NL *plumula*, fr L, dim. of *pluma*] – **plumulose** /'ploohmyoolohs/ *adj*

[1]**plunder** /'plundə/ *vt* **1** to pillage, sack **2** to take, esp by force (e g in war); steal ~ *vi* to commit robbery or looting [G *plündern*, fr MHG *plundern*, fr *plunder* household goods, clothes] – **plunderer** *n*

[2]**plunder** *n* **1** an act of plundering; pillaging **2** sthg taken by force, theft, or fraud; loot

[1]**plunge** /plunj/ *vt* **1a** to cause to penetrate quickly and forcibly **b** to sink (a potted plant) in the ground **2** to cause to enter a thing, state, or course of action, usu suddenly, unexpectedly, or violently ~ *vi* **1** to thrust or cast oneself (as if) into water **2a** to be thrown headlong or violently forwards and downwards ⟨*the car stopped abruptly and he* ~d *through the windscreen*⟩; *also* to move oneself in such a manner **b** to act with reckless haste; enter suddenly or unexpectedly ⟨*the firm* ~d *into debt*⟩ **3** to descend or dip suddenly **4** to bet or gamble heavily and recklessly – infml [ME *plungen*, fr MF *plonger*, fr (assumed) VL *plumbicare*, fr L *plumbum* lead]

[2]**plunge** *n* a dive; *also* a swim

plunger /'plunjə/ *n* **1a** a device (e g a piston in a pump) that acts with a plunging or thrusting motion **b** a rubber suction cup on a handle used to free plumbing from blockages **2** a reckless gambler or speculator – chiefly infml [[1]PLUNGE + [2]-ER]

plunging fire /'plunjing/ *n* direct fire from a superior elevation resulting in the projectiles striking the target at a steep angle

plunk /plungk/ *vt* **1** to pluck so as to produce a hollow, metallic, or harsh sound **2** to set down suddenly; plump – chiefly infml [imit] – **plunk** *n*, **plunker** *n*

plunk down *vi* to drop abruptly; settle into position ~ *vt* **1** to put down usu firmly or abruptly ⟨plunked *his money* down *on the counter*⟩ **2** to settle (oneself) into position ⟨plunked *himself* down *on the bench*⟩ *USE* chiefly infml

pluperfect /plooh'puhfikt/ *adj* PAST PERFECT [modif of LL *plusquamperfectus*, lit., more than perfect] – **pluperfect** *n*

plural /'plooərəl/ *adj* **1** of or being a word form (e g *we, houses, cattle*) denoting more than 1, or in some languages more than 2 or 3, persons, things, or instances **2** consisting of or containing more than 1 (kind or class) ⟨*a* ~ *society*⟩ [ME, fr MF & L; MF *plurel*, fr L *pluralis*, fr *plur-, plus* more – more at PLUS] – **plural** *n*, **plurally** *adv*, **pluralize** *vt*

pluralism /'plooərə,liz(ə)m/ *n* **1** the holding of 2 or more offices or positions (e g benefices) at the same time **2** a state of society in which members of diverse social groups develop their traditional cultures or special interests within a common civilization [PLURAL + -ISM] – **pluralist** *adj or n*, **pluralistic** /-'listik/ *adj*, **pluralistically** *adv*

plurality /plooə'ralәti/ *n* **1a** the state of being plural or numerous **b** a large number or quantity **2** (a benefice held by) pluralism

pluri- /plooəri-/ *comb form* having or being more than 1; several; multi- ⟨pluri*axial*⟩ [L, fr *plur-, plus*]

[1]**plus** /plus/ *prep* **1** increased by; with the addition of ⟨*4* ~ *5*⟩ ⟨*the debt* ~ *interest*⟩ ☞ SYMBOL **2** and also ⟨*the job needs experience* ~ *patience*⟩ [L, adv,

more, fr neut of *plur-, plus,* adj, more; akin to Gk *pleiōn* more, L *plenus* full – more at [1]FULL]

[2]**plus** *n, pl* **-s-** *also* **-ss-** **1** an added quantity **2** a positive factor, quantity, or quality **3** a surplus

[3]**plus** *adj* **1** algebraically or electrically positive **2** additional and welcome ⟨*a ~ factor is its nearness to the shops*⟩ **3** greater than that specified ⟨*had a B ~ for his essay*⟩

[4]**plus** *conj* and moreover ⟨*~ he has to watch what he says – Punch*⟩

,plus 'fours *n pl* loose wide trousers gathered on a band and finishing just below the knee [fr the extra 4 inches of length allowed for looseness]

[1]**plush** /plush/ *n* a fabric with an even pile longer and less dense than that of velvet [MF *peluche*]

[2]**plush** *adj* **1** (made) of or resembling plush **2** PLUSHY 2 – **plushly** *adv,* **plushness** *n*

plushy /'plushi/ *adj* **1** having the texture of or covered with plush **2** luxurious, showy – **plushiness** *n*

'plus ,sign *n* a sign + denoting addition or a positive quantity ☞ SYMBOL

Pluto /'ploohtoh/ *n* the planet furthest from the sun ☞ ASTRONOMY, SYMBOL [NL, fr L *Pluton-, Pluto,* god of the underworld, fr Gk *Ploutōn*]

plutocracy /plooh'tokrəsi/ *n* (government by) a controlling class of wealthy people [Gk *ploutokratia,* fr *ploutos* wealth] – **plutocrat** /'ploohtə,krat/ *n,* **plutocratic** /,ploohtə'kratik/ *adj,* **plutocratically** *adv*

pluton /'ploohton/ *n* a typically large (exposed) body of plutonic rock [prob back-formation fr *plutonic*]

plutonian /plooh'tohnyən, -ni·ən/ *adj, often cap* infernal [L *plutonius,* fr Gk *ploutōnios,* fr *Ploutōn*]

plutonic /plooh'tonik/ *adj, of igneous rock* formed by solidification of a molten magma deep within the earth [L *Pluton-, Pluto*]

plutonium /plooh'tonyəm, -ni·əm/ *n* a radioactive metallic element similar to uranium that is formed in atomic reactors and is used in weapons and as a fuel for atomic reactors ☞ ENERGY, PERIODIC TABLE [NL, fr *Pluton-, Pluto,* the planet Pluto]

[1]**pluvial** /'ploohvi·əl/ *adj* **1** of or caused by rain **2** characterized by abundant rainfall [L *pluvialis,* fr *pluvia* rain, fr fem of *pluvius* rainy, fr *pluere* to rain – more at FLOW]

[2]**pluvial** *n* a prolonged geological period of wet climate

[1]**ply** /plie/ *vt* to twist together ⟨*~ 2 single yarns*⟩ [ME *plien* to fold, fr MF *plier,* fr L *plicare;* akin to OHG *flehtan* to braid, L *plectere,* Gk *plekein*]

[2]**ply** *n* **1a** a strand in a yarn, wool, etc **b** any of several layers (e g of cloth) usu sewn or laminated together **2a** (any of the veneer sheets forming) plywood **b** a layer of paper or paperboard

[3]**ply** *vt* **1a** to use or wield diligently ⟨*busily ~ing his axe*⟩ **b** to practise or perform diligently ⟨*~ing his trade*⟩ **2** to keep furnishing or supplying sthg to ⟨plied *them with drinks*⟩ **3** to go or travel over or on regularly *~ vi* **1** to apply oneself steadily **2** *of a boatman, taxi driver, etc* to wait regularly in a particular place for custom – esp in *ply for hire* **3** to go or travel regularly ⟨*a steamer ~ing between opposite shores of the lake*⟩ [ME *plien,* short for *applien* to apply]

,Plymouth 'Brethren /'plimǝth/ *n pl* a strongly puritanical Christian religious body founded about 1830 in Plymouth

,Plymouth 'Rock *n* any of an American breed of medium-sized domestic fowls [*Plymouth Rock* in Massachusetts, USA, on which the Pilgrim Fathers are supposed to have landed in 1620]

plywood /'plie,wood/ *n* a light structural material of thin sheets of wood glued or cemented together with the grains of adjacent layers arranged crosswise usu at right angles

-pnea /-pnee·ə/ *comb form* (→ *n*), *chiefly NAm* -PNOEA

pneum- /nyoohm-/, **pneumo-** *comb form* **1** air; gas ⟨pneumo*thorax*⟩ **2a** lung ⟨pneum*ectomy*⟩ **b** pulmonary and ⟨pneumo*gastric*⟩ **3** respiration ⟨pneumo*graph*⟩ **4** pneumonia ⟨pneumo*coccus*⟩ [NL; partly fr Gk *pneum-* (fr *pneuma*), partly fr Gk *pneumōn* lung]

pneumat- /nyoohmat-, nyoohmət-/, **pneumato-** *comb form* **1** spirit ⟨pneumato*logy*⟩ **2** air; vapour; gas ⟨pneumat*ics*⟩ **3** respiration ⟨pneumato*meter*⟩ [Gk, fr *pneumat-, pneuma*]

pneumatic /nyooh'matik/ *adj* of or using gas (e g air or wind): **a** moved or worked by air pressure **b** adapted for holding or inflated with compressed air **c** having air-filled cavities [L *pneumaticus,* fr Gk *pneumatikos,* fr *pneumat-, pneuma* air, breath, spirit, fr *pnein* to breathe – more at SNEEZE] – **pneumatically** *adv*

pneu,matic 'drill *n* a machine in which air causes a tool (e g a chisel for breaking up road surfaces) to strike repeatedly

pneumaticity /,nyoohmə'tisəti/ *n* a condition marked by the presence of air cavities ⟨*~ of bird bones*⟩

pneu'matics *n pl but sing in constr* a science that deals with the mechanical properties of gases

pneumatophore /'nyoohmətoh,faw, nyoo'matoh-faw, -tə-/ *n* a muscular gas-containing sac that serves as a float on a hydrozoan colony [ISV] – **pneumatophoric** /,nyoohmətoh'forik, ,nyoohmatə'forik, nyoo,matə'forik/ *adj*

pneumococcus /,nyoohmoh'kokəs/ *n, pl* **pneumococci** /-'kok(s)ie/ a bacterium that causes acute pneumonia [NL] – **pneumococcal** /-kl/ *also* **pneumococcic** /-kok(s)ik/ *adj*

,pneumo,coni'osis /-,koni'ohsis/ *n, pl* **pneumoconioses** /-seez/ a crippling disease of the lungs, esp of miners, caused by the habitual inhalation of irritant mineral or metallic particles – compare SILICOSIS [NL, fr *pneum-* + Gk *konis* dust – more at INCINERATE]

,pneumo'gastric /-'gastrik/ *adj* **1** of the lungs and stomach **2** vagal

,pneumo'nectomy /-'nektəmi/ *n* excision of (1 or more lobes of) a lung [Gk *pneumōn* + ISV *-ectomy*]

pneumonia /nyooh'mohnyə, -ni·ə/ *n* localized or widespread inflammation of the lungs with change from an air-filled to a solid consistency, caused by infection or irritants [NL, fr Gk, fr *pneumōn* lung, alter. of *pleumōn* – more at PULMONARY]

pneumonic /nyooh'monik/ *adj* **1** of the lungs **2** of or affected with pneumonia [NL *pneumonicus,* fr Gk *pneumonikos,* fr *pneumōn*]

pneumothorax /,nyoohmoh'thawraks/ *n* the presence of gas, esp air, in the pleural cavity occurring esp as a result of disease or injury [NL]

-pnoea, *NAm chiefly* **-pnea** /-pneeə/ *comb form* breath; breathing ⟨apnoea⟩ [NL, fr Gk *-pnoia*, fr *pnoia*, fr *pnein* to breathe]

po /poh/ *n, pl* **pos** *Br* CHAMBER POT – infml [F *pot (de chambre)*]

[1]**poach** /pohch/ *vt* to cook (e g fish or an egg) in simmering liquid [ME *pochen*, fr MF *pocher*, fr OF *pochier*, lit., to put into a bag, fr *poche* bag, pocket, of Gmc origin; akin to OE *pocca* bag]

[2]**poach** *vt* **1** to trample or cut up (e g turf) (as if) with hoofs **2a** to trespass on ⟨*a field* ~ed *too frequently by the amateur – TLS*⟩ **b** to take (game or fish) illegally **c** to take or acquire by unfair or underhand means ~ *vi* **1** *of land* to become soft or muddy when trampled on **2a** to (trespass while attempting to) take game or fish illegally **b** to trespass *on* or *upon* ⟨*what happens to a poet when he* ~es *upon a novelist's preserves* – Virginia Woolf⟩ [MF *pocher*, of Gmc origin; akin to ME *poken* to poke] – **poacher** *n*

pochard /'pohchəd/ *n* any of numerous rather heavy-bodied diving ducks; *esp* a common Old World duck the male of which has a chestnut head and grey upper parts [origin unknown]

pock /pok/ *n* (a spot resembling) a pustule in an eruptive disease (e g smallpox) [ME *pokke*, fr OE *pocc*; akin to MLG & MD *pocke* pock, L *bucca* cheek, mouth] – **pock** *vt*, **pocky** *adj*

[1]**pocket** /'pokit/ *n* **1** a small bag that is sewn or inserted in a garment so that it is open at the top or side **2** a supply of money; means ⟨*has houses to suit all* ~s⟩ **3a** a receptacle, container **b** any of several openings at the corners or sides of a billiard table into which balls are propelled **4a** a small isolated area or group ⟨~s *of unemployment*⟩ **b** a cavity (e g in the earth) containing a deposit (e g of gold or water) **c** AIR POCKET **5** *chiefly SAfr* (the amount contained in) a bag [ME *poket*, fr ONF *pokete*, dim. of *poke* bag, of Gmc origin; akin to OE *pocca* bag] – **pocketful** *n* – **in pocket** in the position of having made a profit – **out of pocket** having suffered a financial loss

[2]**pocket** *vt* **1a** to put or enclose (as if) in one's pocket ⟨~ed *his change*⟩ **b** to appropriate to one's own use; steal ⟨~ed *the money she had collected for charity*⟩ **2** to accept; PUT UP WITH ⟨~ *an insult*⟩ **3** to set aside, suppress ⟨~ed *his pride*⟩ **4** to drive (a ball) into a pocket of a billiard table

[3]**pocket** *adj* **1** small enough to be carried in the pocket ⟨*a* ~ *camera*⟩ **2** small, miniature ⟨*a* ~ *submarine*⟩

pocket battleship *n* a small battleship built so as to come within treaty limitations of tonnage and armament

'pocket,book /-,book/ *n* **1** a pocket-size container for (paper) money and personal papers **2** *NAm* **a** a small, esp paperback, book that can be carried in the pocket **b** a purse **c** a strapless handbag

pocket borough *n* an English constituency controlled before parliamentary reform by 1 person or family

'pocket e,dition *n* a miniature form of sthg

,pocket-'handkerchief *n* a handkerchief

'pocket,knife /-,nief/ *n* a knife that has 1 or more blades that fold into the handle so that it can be carried in the pocket

'pocket ,money *n* money for small personal expenses, esp as given to a child

'pocket-,size, 'pocket-,sized *adj* [3]POCKET 1

pockmark /'pok,mahk/ *n* a mark or pit (like that) caused by smallpox – **pockmarked** *adj*

poco /'pohkoh/ *adv* slightly, somewhat – used in music ⟨~ *allegro*⟩ [It, little, fr L *paucus* – more at FEW]

,poco a 'poco /ah/ *adv* gradually – used in music [It]

[1]**pod** /pod/ *n* **1** a long seed vessel or fruit, esp of the pea, bean, or other leguminous plant **2** an egg case of a locust or similar insect **3** a streamlined compartment under the wings or fuselage of an aircraft used as a container (e g for fuel) **4** a detachable compartment on a spacecraft or aircraft [prob alter. of *cod* bag – more at CODPIECE]

[2]**pod** *vb* **-dd-** *vi* to produce pods ~ *vt* to remove (e g peas) from the pod

[3]**pod** *n* a small group of animals (e g seals) close together [origin unknown]

-pod /-pod/ *comb form* (→ *n*) foot; part resembling a foot ⟨*pleo*pod⟩ [Gk *-podos*, fr *pod-*, *pous* foot – more at FOOT]

podagra /pə'dagrə/ *n* GOUT 1 [ME, fr L, fr Gk, fr *pod-*, *pous* + *agra* hunt, catch; akin to L *agere* to drive – more at AGENT] – **podagral** *adj*

podge /poj/ *n, chiefly Br* a fatty – infml [prob alter. of *pudge*, of unknown origin]

podgy /'poji/ *adj* short and plump; chubby

podiatry /po'dieətri/ *n, NAm* chiropody [Gk *pod-*, *pous* + E *-iatry*] – **podiatrist** *n*, **podiatric** /,podie'atrik/ *adj*

podium /'pohdiəm/ *n, pl* **podiums, podia** /-diə/ **1** a low wall serving as a foundation or terrace wall: e g **a** one round the arena of an ancient amphitheatre **b** the stone base supporting the columns of a classical structure **2** a small raised platform (for an orchestral conductor) [L – more at PEW]

-podium /-pohdium/ *comb form* (→ *n*), *pl* **-podia** /-diə/ -pod ⟨*pseudo*podium⟩ [NL, fr Gk *podion*, dim. of *pod-*, *pous* foot]

podophyllin /,podoh'filin, ,pohdə'fielin, -doh-/ *n* a bitter resin from the underground stem of the mayapple, used esp as a purgative [ISV, fr NL *Podophyllum*, genus of herbs including the mayapple]

podsol /podsol/ *n* podzol

podzol /'podzol/ *n* any of a group of soils that have a grey upper layer from which humus and iron and aluminium compounds have leached to enrich the layer below [Russ] – **podzolize** /'podzo,liez/ *vb*, **podzolic** /pod'zolik/ *adj*, **podzolization** /,podzolie'zaysh(ə)n/ *n*

poem /'pohim/ *n* **1** an individual work of poetry **2** a creation, experience, or object suggesting a poem ⟨*the interior was a* ~ *of chinoiserie*⟩ [MF *poeme*, fr L *poema*, fr Gk *poiēma*, fr *poiein*]

poesy /'pohizi, -si/ *n* **1** a poem or body of poems **2** the art or composition of poetry [ME *poesie*, fr MF, fr L *poesis*, fr Gk *poiēsis*, lit., creation, fr *poiein*]

poet /'pohit/, *fem* **poetess** /'pohites, ,pohi'tes/ *n* **1** one who writes poetry **2** a creative artist with special sensitivity to his/her medium ⟨*a* ~ *of the piano*⟩ [ME, fr OF *poete*, fr L *poeta*, fr Gk *poiētēs* maker, poet, fr *poiein* to make, create; akin to Skt *cinoti* he heaps up]

poetaster /,pohi'tastə/ *n* an inferior poet [NL, fr L *poeta* + *-aster* -aster]

poetic /poh'etik/, **poetical** /-kl/ *adj* **1a** (characteristic) of poets or poetry **b** having the qualities associated with poetry **2** written in verse – **poetically** *adv*, **poeticism** /poh'eti,siz(ə)m/ *n*

poetic·ize, -ise /poh'etisiez/ *vt* to give a poetic quality to

poetic justice *n* an outcome in which vice is punished and virtue rewarded in an (ironically) appropriate manner

poetics /poh'etiks/ *n, pl* **poetics** **1** a treatise on poetry or aesthetics **2** *sing or pl in constr* poetic theory or practice

poet·ize, -ise /'poh·itiez/ *vi* to compose poetry ~ *vt* to poeticize – **poetizer** *n*

,poet 'laureate *n, pl* **poets laureate, poet laureates** **1** a distinguished poet honoured for achievement in his/her art **2** a poet appointed for life by the sovereign as a member of the British royal household and expected to compose poems for state occasions

poetry /'poh·itri/ *n* **1a** metrical writing; verse **b** a poet's compositions; poems **2** writing that is arranged to formulate a concentrated imaginative awareness of experience through meaning, sound, and rhythm **3** a quality of beauty, grace, and great feeling ⟨~ *in motion*⟩

,po-'faced /poh/ *adj, Br* having a foolishly solemn or humourless expression – chiefly infml [*po* + *-faced*]

pogey /'pohgi/ *n, Can* DOLE 2 – infml [origin unknown]

'pogo ,stick /'pohgoh/ *n* a pole with a spring at the bottom and 2 footrests on which sby stands and can move along with a series of jumps [fr *Pogo*, a trademark]

pogrom /'pogrəm/ *n* an organized massacre, esp of Jews [Yiddish, fr Russ, lit., devastation]

pohutukawa /pə'hoohtə,kah·wə/ *n* an evergreen New Zealand tree of the myrtle family with brilliant red flowers [Maori]

-poiesis /-poy'eesis/ *comb form* (→ *n*), *pl* **-poieses** /-seez/ production; formation ⟨*erythro*poiesis⟩ ⟨*mytho*poiesis⟩ [NL, fr Gk *poiēsis* creation – more at POESY] – **-poietic** *comb form* (→ *adj*)

poignant /'poynyənt/ *adj* **1a** painfully affecting the feelings; distressing **b** deeply affecting; touching **2** designed to make an impression; cutting ⟨~ *satire*⟩ [ME *poinaunt*, fr MF *poignant*, prp of *poindre* to prick, sting, fr L *pungere* – more at PUNGENT] – **poignancy** *n*, **poignantly** *adv*

poikilotherm /,poy'kiləthuhm/ *n* a living organism (e g a frog) with a variable body temperature usu slightly higher than the temperature of its environment; a cold-blooded organism [Gk *poikilos* variegated + ISV *-therm*; akin to L *pingere* to paint – more at PAINT] – **poikilothermic** /-kiloh'thuhmik/ *adj*, **poikilothermism** /-'thuhmiz(ə)m/ *n*

poilu /'pwahlooh/ *n* a French private soldier (in the front line during WW I) [F, fr *poilu* hairy, fr MF, fr *poil* hair, fr L *pilus* – more at ^{5}PILE]

poinciana /,poynsi'ahnə/ *n* any of a genus of ornamental tropical leguminous trees or shrubs with bright orange or red flowers [NL, genus name, fr De *Poinci*, 17th-c governor of part of the French W Indies]

poinsettia /poyn'seti·ə/ *n* any of various spurges bearing flower clusters opposite brightly coloured bracts [NL, fr Joel R *Poinsett* †1851 US diplomat]

^{1}**point** /poynt/ *n* **1a(1)** an individual detail; an item **(2)** a distinguishing detail ⟨*tact is one of her strong* ~s⟩ **b** the most important essential in a discussion or matter ⟨*missed the whole* ~ *of the joke*⟩ **2** an end or object to be achieved; a purpose ⟨*did not see what* ~ *there was in continuing the discussion*⟩ **3a(1)** a geometric element that has a position but no extent or magnitude **(2)** a geometric element determined by an ordered set of coordinates **b** (a narrowly localized place having) a precisely indicated position ⟨*walked to a* ~ *50 yards north of the building*⟩ **c(1)** an exact moment ⟨*at this* ~ *he was interrupted*⟩ **(2)** a time interval immediately before sthg indicated; *the* verge ⟨*at the* ~ *of death*⟩ **d(1)** a particular step, stage, or degree in development ⟨*had reached the* ~ *where nothing seemed to matter any more*⟩ **(2)** a definite position in a scale ⟨*boiling* ~⟩ **4a** the sharp or narrowly rounded end of sthg; a tip **b** the tip of the toes – used in ballet; usu pl **c** *pl* a contact breaker **5a** a projecting usu tapering piece of land **b(1)** the tip of a projecting body part **(2)** TINE 2 **(3)** *pl* (the markings of) the extremities of an animal, esp when of a different colour from the rest of the body **6a** a very small mark **b(1)** PUNCTUATION MARK; *esp* FULL STOP **(2)** DECIMAL POINT **7** any of the 32 evenly spaced compass directions; *also* the 11° 15′ interval between 2 successive points **8a** lace worked with a needle; NEEDLEPOINT 1 **b** lace imitating needlepoint worked with bobbins; PILLOW LACE **9a** a unit of counting in the scoring of a game or contest **b** a unit used in evaluating the strength of a bridge hand **c** a unit used in quoting prices (e g of shares, bonds, and commodities) **d** a unit of 0.351mm (about $^{1}/_{72}$in) used to measure the body size of printing type **10a** the action of pointing **b** the rigidly intent attitude of a gundog when marking game for a hunter **11** (the position of) a defensive player in lacrosse **12** a fielding position in cricket near to the batsman and on a direct line with the popping crease on the off side ☞ SPORT **13** *pl, Br* a device made of usu 2 movable rails and necessary connections and designed to turn a locomotive or train from one track to another [ME; partly fr OF, puncture, small spot, point in time or space, fr L *punctum*, fr neut of *punctus*, pp of *pungere* to prick; partly fr OF *pointe* sharp end, fr (assumed) VL *puncta*, fr L, fem of *punctus*, pp – more at PUNGENT] – **beside the point** irrelevant – **to the point** relevant, pertinent ⟨*a suggestion that was* to the point⟩

^{2}**point** *vt* **1a** to provide with a point; sharpen ⟨~*ing a pencil with a knife*⟩ **b** to give added force, emphasis, or piquancy to ⟨~ *up a remark*⟩ **2** to scratch out the old mortar from the joints of (e g a brick wall) and fill in with new material **3a** to punctuate **b** to mark signs or points in (e g psalms or Hebrew words) **4** *of a gundog* to indicate the presence and place of (game) for a hunter by a point **5** to cause to be turned in a particular direction ⟨~ *a gun*⟩ ⟨~ed *the boat upstream*⟩ ~ *vi* **1a** to indicate the fact or probability of sthg specified ⟨*everything* ~s *to a bright future*⟩ **b** to indicate the position or direction of sthg, esp by extending a finger ⟨~ *at the map*⟩ **c** to point game ⟨*a dog that* ~s *well*⟩ **2** to lie extended, aimed, or turned in a particular direction ⟨*the signpost* ~ed *north*⟩

,point-'blank *adj* **1** so close to a target that a missile fired will travel in a straight line to the mark **2** direct, blunt ⟨*a* ~ *refusal*⟩ – **point-blank** *adv*

point d'appui /,pwahn da'pwee (*Fr* pwẽ dap i)/ *n*,

pl **points d'appui** /~/ a base, esp for a military operation [F, lit., point of support]

'point-,duty *n* traffic regulation carried out usu by a policeman stationed at a particular point

pointe /pwant (*Fr* pwɛ̃ːt)/ *n* a ballet position in which the body is balanced on the extreme tip of the toe [F, lit., point]

pointed /'poyntid/ *adj* **1** having a point **2a** pertinent; TO THE POINT **b** aimed at a particular person or group **3** conspicuous, marked ⟨~ *indifference*⟩ – **pointedly** *adv*, **pointedness** *n*

pointer /'poyntə/ *n* **1** a rod used to direct attention **2** a large strong slender smooth-haired gundog that hunts by scent and indicates the presence of game by pointing **3** a useful suggestion or hint; a tip [[2]POINT + [2]-ER]

Pointers *n pl* the 2 stars in Ursa Major which are in line with and are therefore used to locate the Pole Star

pointillism /'pwanti,liz(ə)m, 'poyn-, -ti,yiz(ə)m/ *n* the technique in art of applying small strokes or dots of pure colour to a surface so that from a distance they blend together [F *pointillisme*, fr *pointiller* to stipple, fr *point* spot – more at POINT] – **pointillist** *also* **pointilliste** /-list, -'yeest/ *n or adj*

point lace *n* POINT 8; *esp* NEEDLEPOINT 1

'pointless /-lis/ *adj* devoid of meaning, relevance, or purpose; senseless ⟨*a* ~ *remark*⟩ – **pointlessly** *adv*, **pointlessness** *n*

,point of 'honour *n* a matter which one considers to have a serious effect on one's honour or reputation

point of no return *n* **1** the point in a long-distance journey after which return to the starting point is impossible **2** a critical point (e g in a course of action) at which turning back or reversal is not possible

,point of 'order *n* a question relating to procedure in an official meeting

,point-of-'sale *adj* of or being advertising or promotional material accompanying a product at its place of distribution, esp in a retail shop

,point of 'view *n* a position from which sthg is considered or evaluated

point out *vt* to direct sby's attention to ⟨point out *a mistake*⟩

pointsman /'poyntsmən/ *n* **1** a policeman on point-duty **2** *Br* a person in charge of railway points

point source *n* a source of radiation (e g light) that is concentrated at a point and considered to have no spatial extension

,point-to-'point *n* a usu cross-country steeplechase for amateur riders – **point-to-pointer** *n*

[1]poise /poyz/ *vt* **1a** to balance; *esp* to hold or carry in equilibrium ⟨*walked along gracefully with a water jar* ~d *on her head*⟩ **b** to hold supported or suspended without motion in a steady position **2** to hold or carry in a particular way **3** to put into readiness; brace ~ *vi* to hang (as if) suspended; hover [ME *poisen* to weigh, ponder, fr MF *pois-*, stem of *peser*, fr L *pensare* – more at PENSIVE]

[2]poise *n* **1** a stably balanced state ⟨*a* ~ *between widely divergent impulses* – F R Leavis⟩ **2a** easy self-possessed assurance of manner **b** a particular way of carrying oneself [ME *poyse* weight, heaviness, fr MF *pois*, fr L *pensum*, fr neut of *pensus*, pp of *pendere* to weigh – more at PENDANT]

[3]poise /pwahz/ *n* a cgs unit of dynamic viscosity [F, fr Jean Louis Marie *Poiseuille* †1869 F physician & anatomist]

poised /poyzd/ *adj* **1** marked by balance or equilibrium or by easy composure of manner **2** in readiness ⟨~ *for flight*⟩ ⟨~ *for action*⟩

[1]poison /'poyz(ə)n/ *n* **1a** a substance that through its chemical action kills, injures, or impairs an organism ☞ SYMBOL **b** sthg destructive or harmful **2** a substance that inhibits the activity of another substance or the course of a reaction or process ⟨*a catalyst* ~⟩ [ME, fr OF, drink, poisonous drink, poison, fr L *potion-*, *potio* drink – more at POTION] – **poison** *adj*

[2]poison *vt* **1a** to injure or kill with poison **b** to treat, taint, or impregnate with poison **2** to exert a harmful influence on; corrupt ⟨~ed *their minds*⟩ **3** to inhibit the activity, course, or occurrence of – **poisoner** *n*

poison gas *n* a poisonous gas or a liquid or solid giving off poisonous vapours designed to kill, injure, or disable by inhalation or contact

,poison 'ivy *n* (any of several plants related to) a N American climbing plant of the sumach family that has greenish flowers and white berries and produces an oil that causes an intensely itching skin rash

poisonous /'poyz(ə)nəs/ *adj* having the properties or effects of poison – **poisonously** *adv*

,poison-'pen *adj* written with malice and spite and usu anonymously ⟨~ *letter*⟩

[1]poke /pohk/ *n, chiefly dial NAm* a bag, sack [ME, fr ONF – more at POCKET]

[2]poke *vt* **1a(1)** to prod, jab ⟨~d *him in the ribs and grinned broadly*⟩ **(2)** to stir the coals or logs of (a fire) so as to promote burning **b** to produce by piercing, stabbing, or jabbing ⟨~ *a hole*⟩ **2** to cause to project ⟨~d *her head out of the window*⟩ **3** to hit, punch ⟨~d *him in the nose*⟩ – infml **4** *of a man* to have sexual intercourse with –vulg ~ *vi* **1** to make a prodding, jabbing, or thrusting movement, esp repeatedly **2a** to look about or through sthg without system; rummage ⟨*found it while* poking *around in the attic*⟩ **b** to meddle **3** to move or act slowly or aimlessly; potter ⟨*just* ~d *about at home and didn't accomplish much*⟩ **4** to become stuck out or forwards; protrude **5** *of a man* to have sexual intercourse – vulg [ME *poken*; akin to MD *poken* to poke] – **poke fun at** to mock – **poke one's nose into** to meddle in or interfere with (esp sthg that does not concern one)

[3]poke *n* **1** a quick thrust; a jab **2** a punch – infml **3** an act of sexual intercourse – vulg

'poke ,bonnet *n* a woman's bonnet with a projecting brim at the front ☞ GARMENT

[1]poker /'pohkə/ *n* a metal rod for poking a fire [[2]POKE + [2]-ER]

[2]poker *n* any of several card games in which a player bets that the value of his/her hand is greater than that of the hands held by others and in which each subsequent player must either equal or raise the last bet or drop out [prob modif of F *poque*, a card game similar to poker]

'poker ,dice *n* (any of) a set of usu 5 dice, each carrying the representation of the 6 highest playing cards

'poker ,face *n* an inscrutable face that reveals no hint of a person's thoughts or feelings [[2]*poker*; fr the need of the poker player to conceal the true quality of his/her hand] – **poker-faced** /,-- '-/ *adj*

'poker,work /-,wuhk/ *n* (the art of doing) decorative work burnt into a material by a heated instrument

pokeweed /'pohk,weed/ *n* a coarse American plant with white flowers, dark purple juicy berries, and a poisonous root [*poke* (pokeweed), modif of *puccoon*, a plant used in dyeing, of Algonquian origin]

pokey /'pohki/ *n, NAm* a jail – slang [origin unknown]

poky *also* **pokey** /'pohki/ *adj* small and cramped – infml [[2]*poke*] – **pokily** *adv*, **pokiness** *n*

Polack /'pohlak/ *n, archaic or NAm* a Pole – now derog [Pol *Polak*]

polar /'pohlə/ *adj* **1a** of, coming from, or characteristic of (the region round) a geographical pole **b** *esp of an orbit* passing over a planet's N and S poles **2** of 1 or more poles (e g of a magnet) **3** diametrically opposite **4** exhibiting polarity; *esp* having (molecules with) groups with opposing properties at opposite ends ⟨*a ~ molecule*⟩ ⟨*a ~ solvent*⟩ **5** resembling a pole or axis round which all else revolves; pivotal **6** of or expressed in polar coordinates ⟨*~ equations*⟩; *also* of a polar coordinate system [NL *polaris*, fr L *polus* pole]

,polar 'bear *n* a large creamy-white bear that inhabits arctic regions

,polar 'circle *n* either the Arctic or Antarctic circle

,polar co'ordinate *n* either of 2 numbers that locate a point in a plane by its distance along a line from a fixed point and the angle this line makes with a fixed line

polarimeter /,pohlə'rimitə/ *n* **1** an instrument for determining the amount of polarization of light **2** an instrument for measuring the amount of optical rotation (e g of a sugar solution) [ISV, fr *polarization*] – **polarimetry** *n*, **polarimetric** /-ri'metrik/ *adj*

Polaris /pə'lahris, poh-/ *n* POLE STAR [NL, fr *polaris* polar]

polariscope /poh'lari,skohp/ *n* **1** an instrument for studying the properties of or examining substances in polarized light **2** POLARIMETER 2 [ISV, fr *polarization*] – **polariscopic** /-,lari'skopik/ *adj*

polarity /pə'larəti, poh-/ *n* **1** the quality or condition of a body that has opposite or contrasted properties or powers in opposite directions **2** attraction towards a particular object or in a specific direction **3** the particular electrical state of being either positive or negative **4** (an instance of) diametric opposition

polar·ize, -ise /'pohləriez/ *vt* **1a** to affect (radiation, esp light) so that the vibrations of the wave assume a definite form (e g restriction to vibration in 1 plane) **b** to give electrical or magnetic polarity to **2** to divide into opposing factions or groupings *~ vi* to become polarized [F *polariser*, fr NL *polaris* polar] – **polarizable** *adj*, **polarizability** /,pohləriezə'biləti/ *n*, **polarization** /,pohlərie'zaysh(ə)n/ *n*

Polaroid /'pohləroyd/ *trademark* – used esp for a light-polarizing material used esp in glasses to prevent glare and in various optical devices

polder /'poldə, pohl-/ *n* an area of low land reclaimed from a body of water, esp in the Netherlands [D]

[1]pole /pohl/ *n* **1a** a long slender usu cylindrical object (e g a length of wood) **b** a shaft which extends from the front axle of a wagon between the draught animals **2** ROD 2 ☞ UNIT **3** the most favourable front-row position on the starting line of a (motor) race [ME, fr OE *pāl* stake, pole, fr L *palus* stake; akin to L *pangere* to fix – more at PACT]

[2]pole *vb* to push or propel (oneself or sthg) with poles

[3]pole *n* **1** either extremity of an axis of (a body, esp the earth, resembling) a sphere **2a** either of 2 related opposites **b** a point of guidance or attraction **3a** either of the 2 terminals of an electric cell, battery, or dynamo **b** any of 2 or more regions in a magnetized body at which the magnetic flux density is concentrated **4** either of the anatomically or physiologically differentiated areas at opposite ends of an axis in an organism or cell [ME *pool*, fr L *polus*, fr Gk *polos* pivot, pole; akin to Gk *kyklos* wheel – more at WHEEL]

Pole *n* a native or inhabitant of Poland [G, of Slav origin; akin to Pol *Polak* Pole]

[1]poleaxe /'pohl,aks/ *n* **1** a battle-axe with a short handle and often a hook or spike opposite the blade **2** an axe used, esp formerly, in slaughtering cattle [ME *polax, pollax*, fr *pol, polle* poll + *ax* axe]

[2]poleaxe *vt* to attack, strike, or fell (as if) with a poleaxe

polecat /'pohl,kat/ *n, pl* **polecats,** *esp collectively* **polecat** **1** a European flesh-eating mammal of which the ferret is considered a domesticated variety **2** *NAm* SKUNK 1 [ME *polcat*, prob fr MF *poul, pol* cock + ME *cat*; prob fr its preying on poultry – more at PULLET]

polemic /pə'lemik, po-, poh-, -'lee-/ *n* **1** an aggressive attack on or refutation of the opinions or principles of another **2** the art or practice of disputation or controversy – usu pl with sing. meaning but sing. or pl in constr [F *polémique*, fr MF, fr *polemique* controversial, fr Gk *polemikos* warlike, hostile, fr *polemos* war; akin to OE eal*felo* baleful, Gk *pallein* to brandish] – **polemic, polemical** *adj*, **polemicist** /-misist/ *n*

polemic·ize, -ise /-mi,siez/ *vi* to polemize

polem·ize, -ise /'polimiez/ *vi* to engage in controversy; dispute aggressively – **polemist** *n*

polenta /po'lentə, poh-, pə-/ *n* a porridge made with maize meal or semolina [It]

polestar /'pohl,stah/ *n* **1** a directing principle; a guide **2** a centre of attraction

Pole Star *n* the star in the constellation Ursa Minor that lies very close to the N celestial pole

'pole ,vault *n* (an athletic field event consisting of) a jump for height over a crossbar with the aid of a pole – **pole-vault** *vi*, **pole-vaulter** *n*

[1]police /pə'lees/ *n* **1** the department of government concerned with maintenance of public order and enforcement of laws **2a** *sing or pl in constr* POLICE FORCE **b** *pl in constr* policemen **3** *sing or pl in constr* an organized body having similar functions to a police force within a more restricted sphere ⟨*railway ~*⟩ [MF, government, fr LL *politia*, fr Gk *politeia*, fr *politeuein* to be a citizen, engage in political activity, fr *politēs* citizen, fr *polis* city, state; akin to Skt *pur* city]

[2]police *vt* **1** to control by use of police **2** to put in order **3** to supervise the operation of

po'lice ,dog *n* a dog trained to assist the police (e g in tracking criminals or detecting drugs)

po'lice ,force *n sing or pl in constr* a body of trained people entrusted by a government with maintenance of public order and enforcement of laws

po'liceman /-mən/, *fem* **po'lice,woman** *n* a member of a police force

police state *n* a political unit characterized by repressive governmental control of political, economic, and social life, usu enforced by (secret) police

po'lice ,station *n* the headquarters of a local police force

[1]**policy** /'polisi/ *n* **1** procedure based primarily on material interest; wisdom ⟨*it's bad ~ to smoke*⟩ **2a** a definite course of action selected from among alternatives to guide and determine present and future decisions **b** an overall plan embracing general goals and procedures, esp of a governmental body [ME *policie* government, policy, fr MF, government, regulation, fr LL *politia*]

[2]**policy** *n* (a document embodying) a contract of insurance [alter. of earlier *police*, fr MF, certificate, fr OIt *polizza*, modif of ML *apodixa* receipt, fr MGk *apodeixis*, fr Gk, proof, fr *apodeiknynai* to demonstrate – more at APODICTIC]

po'licy,holder /-,hohldə/ *n* a person granted an insurance policy

polio /'pohli·oh/ *n* poliomyelitis

poliomyelitis /,pohli·oh,mie·ə'lietis/ *n* an infectious virus disease, esp of children, characterized by inflammation of the nerve cells of the spinal cord, paralysis of the motor nerves, and atrophy of skeletal muscles often with permanent disability and deformity [NL, fr Gk *polios* grey + *myelos* marrow – more at [1]FALLOW, MYEL-] – **poliomyelitic** /-'litik/ *adj*

-polis /-pəlis/ *comb form* (→ *n*) city ⟨*megalo*polis⟩ [LL, fr Gk, fr *polis*]

[1]**polish** /'polish/ *vt* **1** to make smooth and glossy, usu by friction **2** to refine in manners or condition **3** to bring to a highly developed, finished, or refined state; perfect – often + *up* ~ *vi* to become smooth or glossy (as if) by friction [ME *polisshen*, fr OF *poliss-*, stem of *polir*, fr L *polire*] – **polisher** *n*

[2]**polish** *n* **1a** a smooth glossy surface **b** freedom from rudeness or coarseness **2** the action or process of polishing ⟨*give the table a ~*⟩ **3** a preparation used to produce a gloss and often a colour for the protection and decoration of a surface ⟨*furniture ~*⟩ ⟨*nail ~*⟩

[1]**Polish** /'pohlish/ *adj* (characteristic) of Poland [*Pole*]

[2]**Polish** *n* the language of the Poles ☞ LANGUAGE

polish off *vt* to dispose of rapidly or completely

politburo /'polit,byooəroh, -'-,--/ *n* the principal committee of a Communist party [Russ *politbyuro*, fr *politicheskoye byuro* political bureau]

polite /pə'liet/ *adj* **1** showing or characterized by correct social usage; refined **2** marked by an appearance of consideration and deference; courteous [L *politus*, fr pp of *polire*] – **politely** *adv*, **politeness** *n*

politic /'politik/ *adj* **1** *of a person* shrewd and sagacious in managing, contriving, or dealing **2** *of a policy* expedient [ME *politik*, fr MF *politique*, fr L *politicus*, fr Gk *politikos*, fr *politēs* citizen – more at POLICE]

political /pə'litikl/ *adj* **1** of government **2a** of (party) politics **b** sensitive to politics ⟨*highly ~ students*⟩ **3** involving or charged with acts against a government ⟨*~ criminals*⟩ [L *politicus*] – **politically** *adv*

political economy *n* a social science dealing with the interrelationship of political and economic processes – **political economist** *n*

political levy *n* a levy that trade-union members may pay and that is used for political purposes, esp affiliation to the Labour party

political science *n* a social science concerned chiefly with political institutions and processes – **political scientist** *n*

politician /,poli'tish(ə)n/ *n* a person experienced or engaged in politics

politic·ize, -ise /pə'litisiez/ *vi* to discuss politics ~ *vt* to give a political tone to – **politicization** /pə,litisie'zaysh(ə)n/ *n*

politico /pə'litikoh/ *n, pl* **politicos** *also* **politicoes** a politician – infml [It *politico* or Sp *político*, derivs of L *politicus* political]

politico- *comb form* political and ⟨*politico-diplomatic*⟩ [L *politicus*]

politics /'politiks/ *n pl but sing or pl in constr* **1a** the art or science of government **b** POLITICAL SCIENCE **2a** political affairs; *specif* competition between interest groups in a government **b** political life as a profession **3** sby's political sympathies **4** the total complex of relations between human beings in society [Gk *politika*, fr neut pl of *politikos* political]

polity /'poləti/ *n* (the form of) a politically organized unit [LL *politia* – more at POLICE]

polka /'polkə/ *n* (music for or in the rhythm of) a vivacious dance of Bohemian origin in duple time [F & G, fr Czech *půlka* half-step, fr *půl* half] – **polka** *vi*

'polka ,dot *n* any of many regularly distributed dots in a textile design – **polka-dot, polka-dotted** *adj*

[1]**poll** /pohl/ *n* **1** (the hairy top or back of) the head **2** the broad or flat end of the head of a striking tool (e g a hammer) **3a** the casting of votes **b** the place where votes are cast – usu pl with sing. meaning ⟨*at the ~s*⟩ **c** the number of votes recorded ⟨*a heavy ~*⟩ **4** a survey conducted by the questioning of people selected at random or by quota – compare GALLUP POLL [ME *pol, polle*, fr MLG; (3, 4) fr the idea of counting heads and hence votes]

[2]**poll** *vt* **1** to cut off or cut short **a** the hair or wool of **b** the horns of (a cow) **c** (e g wool) **2** to remove the top of (e g a tree); *specif* to pollard **3** to receive and record the votes of **4** to receive (votes) **5** to question in a poll ~ *vi* to cast one's vote – **pollee** /,poh'lee/ *n*, **poller** *n*

[3]**poll** *n* a polled animal [prob fr obs *poll*, adj, naturally hornless, short for *polled*]

pollack /'polək/ *n, pl* **pollack** a N Atlantic food fish related to and resembling the cods but darker; *also* a coley [Sc *podlok*, of unknown origin]

[1]**pollard** /'poləd/ *n* **1** a hornless animal of a usu horned kind **2** a tree cut back to the main stem to promote the growth of a dense head of foliage [[2]*poll*]

[2]**pollard** *vt* to make a pollard of (a tree)

polled /pohld/ *adj* hornless

pollen /'polən/ *n* (a fine dust of) the minute granular spores discharged from the anther of the flower of a flowering plant that serve to fertilize the ovules [NL *pollin-, pollen*, fr L, fine flour; akin to L *pulvis* dust, Gk *palē* fine meal] – **pollinic** /pə'linik/ *adj*

'pollen ,basket *n* a smooth area on each hind leg of a bee that serves to collect and transport pollen

'pollen ,count *n* a figure representing the amount of

pollen in the air, available as a warning to people allergic to pollen

'pollen ,tube *n* a tube formed by a pollen grain in contact with the stigma of a flowering plant that conveys the sperm to the ovary

pollex /'poleks/ *n, pl* **pollices** /-li,seez/ the first digit of the forelimb; the thumb [NL *pollic-, pollex*, fr L, thumb, big toe] – **pollical** /-likl/ *adj*

pollin- /polən-/, **pollini-** *comb form* pollen ⟨*pollinate*⟩ [NL *pollin-, pollen*]

pollinate /'polə,nayt/ *vt* to place pollen on the stigma of and so fertilize – **pollinator** *n*, **pollination** /,polə'naysh(ə)n/ *n*

polliniferous /,polə'nif(ə)rəs/ *adj* producing or (adapted for) bearing pollen

pollinium /pə'lini·əm/ *n, pl* **pollinia** /-ni·ə/ a coherent mass of pollen grains, often with a stalk bearing an adhesive disc that clings to insects [NL, fr *pollin-*]

pollinosis, pollenosis /,polə'nohsis/ *n* hay fever caused by allergic sensitivity to specific pollens [NL *pollinosis*, fr *pollin-*]

polliwog, pollywog /'poliwog/ *n, NAm & dial Br* a tadpole [alter. of ME *polwygle*, prob fr *pol* poll + *wiglen* to wiggle]

pollock /'polək/ *n, pl* **pollock** a pollack

pollster /'pohlstə/ *n* one who conducts a poll or compiles data obtained by a poll

'poll ,tax *n* a tax of a fixed amount per person levied on adults

pollute /pə'looht/ *vt* **1** to make morally impure; defile **2** to make physically impure or unclean; *esp* to contaminate (an environment), esp with man-made waste [ME *polluten*, fr L *pollutus*, pp of *polluere*, fr *por-* (akin to L *per* through) + *-luere* (akin to L *lutum* mud, Gk *lyma* dirt, defilement)] – **pollutant** *n*, **polluter** *n*, **pollutive** *adj*

pollution /pə'loohsh(ə)n/ *n* **1** polluting or being polluted **2** material that pollutes

Pollyanna /,poli'anə/ *n* an irrepressible optimist [*Pollyanna*, heroine of the novel *Pollyanna* by Eleanor Porter †1920 US fiction-writer] – **Pollyannaish, Pollyannish** /-'anish/ *adj*

polo /'pohloh/ *n* a game of oriental origin played by teams of usu 4 players on ponies or canoes, bicycles, etc using mallets with long flexible handles to drive a wooden ball into the opponent's goal [Balti, ball]

polonaise /,polə'nayz/ *n* **1** a short-sleeved elaborate dress with a fitted waist and panniers at the sides and back drawn up on cords **2** (music in moderate $\frac{3}{4}$ time for) a stately Polish processional dance [F, fr fem of *polonais* Polish, fr *Pologne* Poland, fr ML *Polonia*]

polo neck *n, chiefly Br* (a jumper with) a very high closely fitting collar worn folded over ☞ GARMENT

polonium /pə'lohnyəm, -ni·əm/ *n* a radioactive metallic element that occurs esp in pitchblende ☞ PERIODIC TABLE [NL, fr ML *Polonia* Poland]

polony /pə'lohni/ *n* a dry sausage of partly cooked meat, esp pork; *also* a cooked sausage made from soya and meat and eaten cold [alter. of *bologna (sausage)*]

poltergeist /'poltə,giest/ *n* a noisy mischievous ghost believed to be responsible for unexplained noises and physical damage [G, fr *poltern* to knock + *geist* spirit, fr OHG – more at GHOST]

poltroon /pol'troohn/ *n* a spiritless coward [MF *poultron*, fr OIt *poltrone*, fr aug of *poltro* colt, deriv of L *pullus* young of an animal – more at FOAL]

poly /'poli/ *n, pl* **polys** *Br* a polytechnic – infml

poly- *comb form* **1a** many; several; much; multi- ⟨poly *phonic*⟩ ⟨poly*gyny*⟩ **b** excessive; abnormally great; hyper- ⟨poly*phagia*⟩ **2a** containing 2 or more (specified ions or radicals) in the molecular structure ⟨poly*sulphide*⟩ **b** polymeric; polymer of (a specified monomer) ⟨poly*ethylene*⟩ ⟨poly*nucleotide*⟩ [ME, fr L, fr Gk, fr *polys*; akin to OE *full* full]

polyamide /,poli'amied, -mid/ *n* a (polymeric) compound characterized by more than 1 amide group [ISV]

,poly'androus /-'andrəs/ *adj* **1** having many usu free stamens **2** of or practising polyandry [(1) *poly-* + *-androus* (2) *polyandry* + *-ous*]

polyandry /'poli,andri/ *n* **1** having more than 1 husband at a time – compare POLYGAMY, POLYGYNY **2** the state of being polyandrous [Gk *polyandria* having many men, populousness, fr *polyandros*, adj, having many men or many husbands, fr *poly-* + *andr-, anēr* man, husband – more at ANDR-]

,poly'anthus /-'anthəs/ *n, pl* **polyanthuses, polyanthi** /-thie/ any of various cultivated hybrid primroses [NL, fr Gk *polyanthos* blooming, fr *poly-* + *anthos* flower – more at ANTHOLOGY]

'poly,chaete /-,keet/ *n or adj* (any) of a class of chiefly sea-living annelid worms with many bristles, usu arranged in pairs, along the body – compare OLIGOCHAETE [deriv of Gk *polychaitēs* having much hair, fr *poly-* + *chaitē long hair*] – **polychaetous** /-'keetəs/ *adj*

polychlorinated biphenyl /,poli'klawri,naytid/ *n* any of several compounds (e g dieldrin) that are hydrocarbons with some hydrogen atoms replaced by chlorine and are poisonous environmental pollutants which tend to accumulate in animal tissues

,polychro'matic /-kroh'matik/ *adj* **1** showing a variety or a change of colours; multicoloured **2** of or being radiation composed of more than 1 wavelength [Gk *polychrōmatos*, fr *poly-* + *chrōmat-, chrōma* colour – more at CHROMATIC]

'poly,chrome /-,krohm/ *adj* relating to, made with, or decorated in several colours ⟨~ *pottery*⟩ [Gk *polychrōmos*, fr *poly-* + *chrōma*] – **polychromy** *n*

,polycrystall,ine /-'kristl,ien/ *adj* composed of several (variously oriented) crystals – **polycrystal** /'--,--/ *n*

,polycy'thaemia /-sie'theemi·ə/ *n* a condition marked by an abnormal increase in the number of circulating red blood cells [NL, fr *poly-* + *cyt-* + *-haemia*] – **polycythaemic** /-'theemik/ *adj*

,poly'dactyl /-'daktil/, **polydactylous** /-ləs/ *adj* having more digits than normal [Gk *polydaktylos*, fr *poly-* + *daktylos* digit] – **polydactyly** *n*

polyene /'poli·een/ *n* an organic compound containing many double bonds, esp in a long aliphatic chain [ISV] – **polyenic** /-'eenik/ *adj*

,poly'ester /-'estə/ *n* a polymer containing ester groups used esp in making fibres, resins, or plastics [ISV] – **polyesterification** /poli,estrifi'kaysh(ə)n/ *n*

,poly'ethylene /-'ethi,leen/ *n* polythene

polygamous /pə'ligəməs/, **polygamic** /,poli'gamik/ *adj* **1a** of or practising polygamy **b** having more than 1 mate at a time ⟨*baboons are* ~⟩ **2** bearing both hermaphrodite and unisexual flowers on the same plant [Gk *polygamos*, fr *poly-* + *-gamos* -gamous] – **polygamously** *adv*

polygamy /pə'ligəmi/ *n* **1** being married to more than 1 person at a time; *esp* marriage to more than 1 wife – compare POLYANDRY, POLYGYNY **2** the state of being polygamous [MF *polygamie*, fr LL *polygamia*, fr Gk, fr *poly-* + *-gamia* -gamy] – **polygamist** *n*, **polygamize** *vi*

,poly'genesis /-'jenəsis/ *n* origin from more than 1 ancestral line or stock [NL] – **polygenesist** *n*, **polygenetic** /-jə'netik/ *adj*, **polygenetically** *adv*

¹'poly,glot /-,glot/ *n* **1** one who is polyglot **2** *cap* a book, esp a bible, containing versions of the same text in several languages **3** a mixture or confusion of languages [Gk *polyglōttos*, adj, polyglot, fr *poly-* + *glōtta* language – more at ²GLOSS] – **polyglottal** /,--'--/ *adj*

²polyglot *adj* **1** MULTILINGUAL 2 **2** containing matter in several languages ⟨*a* ~ *sign*⟩

polygon /'poligən, -gon/ *n* a closed plane figure bounded by straight lines ☞ MATHEMATICS [LL *polygonum*, fr Gk *polygōnon*, fr neut of *polygōnos* polygonal, fr *poly-* + *gōnia* angle – more at -GON] – **polygonal** /pə'lig(ə)nl/ *adj*, **polygonally** *adv*

'poly,graph /-,grahf, -,graf/ *n* an instrument for recording variations of the pulse, blood pressure, etc simultaneously; *broadly* LIE DETECTOR – **polygraphic** /-'grafik/ *adj*

polygynous /pə'lijinəs/ *adj* **1** of or practising polygyny **2** *of a plant* having many ovaries

polygyny /pə'lijini/ *n* having more than 1 wife at a time – compare POLYANDRY, POLYGAMY

polyhedron /,poli'heedrən/ *n, pl* **polyhedrons, polyhedra** /-drə/ a solid formed by plane faces ☞ MATHEMATICS [NL] – **polyhedral** *adj*

,Poly'hymnia /-'himni·ə/ *n* the Greek Muse of sacred song [L, fr Gk *Polyymnia*]

'poly,math /-,math/ *n* one who has a wide range of learning or accomplishments [Gk *polymathēs* very learned, fr *poly-* + *manthanein* to learn – more at MATHEMATICAL] – **polymath** *adj*, **polymathic** /,poli'mathik/ *adj*, **polymathy** /pə'limathi/ *n*

polymer /'polimə/ *n* a chemical compound or mixture of compounds containing repeating structural units and formed by chemical combination of many small molecules [ISV, back-formation fr *polymeric*, fr Gk *polymerēs* having many parts, fr *poly-* + *meros* part – more at MERIT] – **polymerize** /'polimәriez, pə'limәriez/ *vb*, **polymerization** *n*, **polymeric** /,poli'merik/ *adj*, **polymerically** *adv*

,poly'morphic /-'mawfik/, **polymorphous** /-fəs/ *adj* having, assuming, or occurring in various forms, characters, or styles [Gk *polymorphos*, fr *poly-* + *-morphos* -morphous] – **polymorphically, polymorphously** *adv*, **polymorphism** *n*

polymorphonuclear leucocyte /,poli,mawfoh'nyoohkli·ə/ *n* a granulocyte

Polynesian /,poli'neez(h)yən, -s(h)yən/ *n* **1** a native or inhabitant of Polynesia **2** a group of languages spoken in Polynesia [*Polynesia*, island group in central and south Pacific, fr *poly-* + Gk *nēsos* island] – **Polynesian** *adj*

,polyneu'ritis /-nyooə'rietəs/ *n* inflammation or degeneration of several nerves at the same time caused by poisons, vitamin deficiency, etc [NL]

¹,poly'nomial /-'nohmyəl/ *n* an algebraic expression of 2 or more terms ⟨$a + bx + cx^2$ *is a* ~⟩ [*poly-* + *-nomial* (as in *binomial*)]

²polynomial *adj* (composed) of or expressed as 1 or more polynomials ⟨~ *functions*⟩

,poly'nucleotide /-'nyoohkli·ətied/ *n* a polymeric nucleotide chain (e g a nucleic acid) [ISV]

polyp /'polip/ *n* **1** a coelenterate with a hollow cylindrical body attached at one end and having a central mouth surrounded by tentacles at the other **2** a projecting mass of tissue (e g a tumour) [MF *polype* octopus, nasal tumour, fr L *polypus*, fr Gk *polypous*, fr *poly-* + *pous* foot – more at FOOT] – **polypoid** *adj*, **polypous** *adj*

polypary /'polip(ə)ri/ *n* the common structure or tissue in which the polyps of compound coelenterates (e g corals) are embedded

,poly'peptide /-'peptied/ *n* a long chain of amino acids joined by peptide bonds [ISV] – **polypeptidic** /-pep'tidik/ *adj*

,poly'phagia /-fayjyə/ *n* pathologically excessive appetite or eating [Gk fr *polyphagos*]

polyphagous /pə'lifəgəs/ *adj* feeding on many kinds of food [Gk *polyphagos* eating too much, fr *poly-* + *-phagos* -phagous] – **polyphagy** *n*

polyphase /'poli,fayz/, **polyphasic** /,poli'fayzik/ *adj* having, using, or producing 2 or more phases of alternating current ⟨*a* ~ *machine*⟩ [ISV]

,poly'phonic /-'fonik/, **polyphonous** /pə'lifənəs/ *adj* of or marked by polyphony – compare HOMOPHONIC – **polyphonically** *adv*, **polyphonously** *adv*

polyphony /pə'lifəni/ *n* a style of musical composition in which 2 or more independent but organically related voice parts sound against one another [Gk *polyphōnia* variety of tones, fr *polyphōnos* having many tones or voices, fr *poly-* + *phōnē* voice – more at ¹BAN]

polyphyletic /,polifi'letik/ *adj* derived from more than 1 ancestral line or more than 1 stock [ISV, fr Gk *polyphylos* of many tribes, fr *poly-* + *phylē* tribe – more at PHYL-] – **polyphyletically** *adv*, **polyphyleticism** /-'letisiz(ə)m/ *n*

'poly,ploid /-ployd/ *adj* having or being a chromosome number that is a multiple greater than 2 of the haploid number – compare HAPLOID, DIPLOID [ISV] – **polyploid** *n*, **polyploidy** *n*

polypody /pə'lipədi/ *n* a widely distributed fern that has creeping rootstocks [ME *polypodie*, fr L *polypodium*, fr Gk *polypodion*, fr *poly-* + *pod-*, *pous* foot – more at FOOT]

polypropylene /,poli'prohpileen/ *n* any of various plastics or fibres that are polymers of propylene

'poly,rhythm /-,ridh(ə)m/ *n* the simultaneous combination of contrasting rhythms in a musical composition – **polyrhythmic** /,poli'ridhmik/ *adj*, **polyrhythmically** *adv*

,poly'saccharide /-'sakəried/ *n* a carbohydrate (e g cellulose or starch) consisting of chains of monosaccharide molecules [ISV]

polysemous /,poli'seeməs, pə'lisiməs/ *adj* having many meanings [LL *polysemus*, fr Gk *polysēmos*, fr *poly-* + *sēma* sign] – **polysemy** /-'seemi, -'lisəmi/ *n*

,poly'styrene /-'stie·əreen/ *n* a rigid transparent polymer of styrene used esp in moulded products, foams, and sheet materials

,polysyl'labic /-si'labik/, **polysyllabical** /-kl/ *adj* **1** having more than 3 syllables **2** characterized by polysyllables [ML *polysyllabus*, fr Gk *polysyllabos*, fr *poly-* + *syllabē* syllable] – **polysyllabically** *adv*

'poly,syllable /-,siləbl/ *n* a polysyllabic word [modif of ML *polysyllaba*, fr fem of *polysyllabus*]

[1]**,poly'technic** /-'teknik/ *adj* relating to or devoted to instruction in many technical arts or applied sciences [F *polytechnique*, fr Gk *polytechnos* skilled in many arts, fr *poly-* + *technē* art – more at TECHNICAL]

[2]**polytechnic** *n* a polytechnic school; *specif* any of a number of British institutions offering full-time, sandwich, and part-time courses in various subjects but with a bias towards the vocational

,polytetra,fluoro'ethylene /-tetrə,flooəroh'ethileen/ *n* a tough translucent fluorine-containing plastic used esp for moulding articles and for nonstick coatings (e g in cooking utensils)

'polythe,ism /-thi,iz(ə)m/ *n* belief in or worship of 2 or more gods [F *polythéisme*, fr LGk *polytheos* polytheistic, fr Gk, of many gods, fr *poly-* + *theos* god] – **polytheist** *adj or n*, **polytheistic** /-'istik/ *adj*

'polythene /-theen/ *n* any of various lightweight ethylene polymers used esp for packaging and bowls, buckets, etc [contr of *polyethylene*]

,polyto'nality /-toh'naləti/ *n* the simultaneous use of 2 or more musical keys – **polytonal** /-'tohnl/ *adj*, **polytonally** *adv*

,polyun'saturated /-un'sachooraytid/ *adj, of a fat or oil* rich in unsaturated chemical bonds

,poly'urethane /-'yooəri,thayn/ *n* any of various polymers used esp in foams and paints [ISV]

,poly'valent /-'vaylənt/ *adj* **1** having a valency greater usu than 2 **2** having more than 1 valency [ISV] – **polyvalence** *n*

,polyvinyl 'chloride /-'vienl/ *n* a plastic used esp as a rubber substitute (e g for raincoats and insulation for wires) [ISV *polyvinyl* + E *chloride*]

,poly'zoan /-'zoh·ən/ *n* a bryozoan [NL *Polyzoa*, phylum name, fr *poly-* + *-zoa*] – **polyzoan** *adj*

pom /pom/ *n, often cap* **1** a Pomeranian **2** a Pommy *USE* infml

pomace /'pumis/ *n* sthg (e g apples) crushed to a pulpy mass (e g to extract juice for cider-making) [prob fr ML *pomacium* cider, fr LL *pomum* apple, fr L, fruit]

pomade /pə'mahd, po-/ *n* a perfumed ointment for the hair or scalp [MF *pommade* ointment formerly made from apples, fr It *pomata*, fr *pomo* apple, fr LL *pomum*] – **pomade** *vt*

pomander /po'mandə, pə-/ *n* a mixture of aromatic substances enclosed in a perforated bag or box and used to scent clothes or linen or formerly carried as a guard against infection [ME, modif of MF *pome d'ambre*, lit., apple or ball of amber]

pome /pohm/ *n* a fruit (e g an apple) with an outer thickened fleshy layer and a central core with the seeds enclosed in a capsule [ME, fr MF *pome, pomme* apple, pome, ball, fr LL *pomum*]

pomegranate /'pomi,granət/ *n* (an Old World tree that bears) a thick-skinned reddish fruit about the size of an orange that contains many seeds each surrounded by a tart edible crimson pulp [ME *poumgarnet*, fr MF *pomme grenate*, lit., seedy apple]

Pomeranian /,pomə'raynyən, -ni·ən/ *n* (any of) a breed of very small compact long-haired dogs [*Pomeranian*, adj, fr *Pomerania*, region of N Europe]

'Pomfret ,cake /'pumfrit, 'pom-/ *n* PONTEFRACT CAKE [*Pomfret*, earlier form of *Pontefract*]

pomiferous /po'mif(ə)rəs/ *adj* bearing pomes [L *pomifer* fruitbearing, fr *pomum* + *-fer* -ferous]

[1]**pommel** /'puməl, 'po-/ *n* **1** the knob on the hilt of a sword **2** the protuberance at the front and top of a saddle **3** either of the pair of removable handles on the top of a pommel horse [ME *pomel*, fr MF, fr (assumed) VL *pomellum* ball, knob, fr dim. of LL *pomum* apple]

[2]**pommel** /'puməl/ *vt* **-ll-** (*NAm* **-l-, -ll-**), /'puml·ing/ to pummel [[1]*pommel*]

'pommel ,horse *n* (a men's gymnastic event using) a leather-covered horizontal rectangular or cylindrical form with 2 handles on the top that is supported above the ground and is used for swinging and balancing feats

Pommy, Pommie /'pomi/ *n, often not cap, Austr & NZ* a British person; *esp* a British immigrant [prob short for *pomegranate*, prob alter. (fr the redness of the fruit and British complexions) of rhyming slang *Jimmy Grant* immigrant] – **Pommy, Pommie** *adj*

pomology /po'moləji, poh-/ *n* fruit growing [NL *pomologia*, fr L *pomum* fruit + *-logia* -logy] – **pomological** /,pomə'lojikl/ *adj*, **pomologically** *adv*, **pomologist** /po'moləjist/ *n*

pomp /pomp/ *n* **1** a show of magnificence; splendour **2** ostentatious or specious display [ME, fr MF *pompe*, fr L *pompa* procession, pomp, fr Gk *pompē* act of sending, escort, procession, pomp]

pompadour /'pompə,dooə, -,daw/ *n* a woman's hairstyle in which the hair is turned back into a loose full roll round the face [Marquise de *Pompadour* †1764 mistress of Louis XV of France]

[1]**pom-pom** /'pom ,pom/ *n* an automatic gun mounted on ships in pairs, fours, or eights [imit]

[2]**pom-pom** *n* an ornamental ball or tuft used esp on clothing, hats, etc [alter. of *pompon*]

pompon /'pompon(h)/ *n* a chrysanthemum or dahlia with small rounded flower heads [F, fr MF *pompe* tuft of ribbons]

pomposity /pom'posəti/ *n* **1** pompous demeanour, speech, or behaviour **2** a pompous gesture, habit, or act

pompous /'pompəs/ *adj* **1** self-important, pretentious ⟨*a ~ politician*⟩ **2** excessively elevated or ornate ⟨*~ rhetoric*⟩ [POMP + -OUS] – **pompously** *adv*, **pompousness** *n*

[1]**ponce** /pons/ *n, Br* **1** a pimp **2** a man who behaves in an effeminate manner – infml [perh fr *pounce* (talon of bird of prey, act of pouncing)]

[2]**ponce** *vi, Br* **1** to pimp **2** to act in a frivolous, showy, or effeminate manner – usu + *around* or *about*; infml

poncho /'ponchoh/ *n, pl* **ponchos** a cloak resembling a blanket with a slit in the middle for the head ☞ GARMENT [AmerSp, fr Araucanian *pontho* woollen fabric]

poncy, poncey /'ponsi/ *adj, Br* (characteristic) of a ponce – infml

pond /pond/ *n* a body of (fresh) water usu smaller than a lake [ME *ponde* artificially confined body of water, alter. of *pounde* enclosure – more at [4]POUND]

ponder /'pondə/ *vt* **1** to weigh in the mind; assess **2** to review mentally; think over ⟨*~ed the events of the day*⟩ *~ vi* to think or consider, esp quietly, soberly, and deeply [ME *ponderen*, fr MF *ponderer*, fr L *ponderare* to weigh, ponder, fr *ponder-, pondus* weight – more at PENDANT] – **ponderer** *n*

ponderosa pine /ˌpondə'rohsə/ *n* (the strong reddish wood of) a tall N American pine with long needles [NL *ponderosa*, specific epithet of *Pinus ponderosa*, species name, fr L, fem of *ponderosus* ponderous]

ponderous /'pond(ə)rəs/ *adj* **1** unwieldy or clumsy because of weight and size **2** oppressively or unpleasantly dull; pedestrian ⟨~ *prose*⟩ [ME, fr MF *ponderetux*, fr L *ponderosus*, fr *ponder-*, *pondus*] – **ponderously** *adv*, **ponderousness** *n*

pond skater *n* any of various long-legged insects that move about on the surface of the water

'pondˌweed /-ˌweed/ *n* any of a genus of aquatic plants with jointed stems, floating or submerged leaves, and spikes of greenish flowers

pong /pong/ *vi or n, Br* (to emit) an unpleasant smell; stink – infml [origin unknown]

pongee /pon'jee/ *n* a thin silk beige or tan fabric of Chinese origin; *also* an imitation of this fabric in cotton or rayon [Chin (Pek) *pen*[3] *chi*[1], fr *pen*[3] own + *chi*[1] loom]

poniard /'ponyəd/ *n* a small dagger [MF *poignard*, fr *poing* fist, fr L *pugnus* – more at PUNGENT]

pons /ponz/ *n, pl* **pontes** /'ponteez/ a broad mass of nerve fibres on the lower front surface of the brain ☞ NERVE [NL, short for *pons Varolii*]

pons Varolii /və'rohli·ie/ *n* the pons [NL, lit., bridge of Varoli, fr Costanzo *Varoli* †1575 It surgeon & anatomist]

Pontefract cake /'pontifrakt/ *n* a small flat circular liquorice sweet [*Pontefract*, town in Yorkshire, England, place of its manufacture]

pontifex /'pontifeks/ *n, pl* **pontifices** /pon'tifiˌseez/ a member of the council of priests in ancient Rome [L *pontific-*, *pontifex*, prob fr *pont-*, *pons* bridge + *facere* to make – more at FIND, [1]DO]

pontifex maximus /'maksiməs/ *n* the pope [L, greatest pontiff]

pontiff /'pontif/ *n* a bishop; *specif* the pope [F *pontife*, fr L *pontific-*, *pontifex*]

[1]**pontifical** /pon'tifikl/ *adj* **1** of a pontiff or pontifex **2** pretentiously dogmatic [L *pontificalis*, fr *pontific-*, *pontifex*] – **pontifically** *adv*

[2]**pontifical** *n* **1** episcopal dress; *specif* the full vestments of bishophood worn by a prelate when celebrating a pontifical mass – usu pl with sing. meaning **2** a book containing the forms for sacraments and rites performed by a bishop

pontifical mass *n* the solemn celebration of the mass by a bishop

[1]**pontificate** /pon'tifikət/ *n* the state, office, or term of office of the pope [L *pontificatus*, fr *pontific-*, *pontifex*]

[2]**pontificate** /pon'tifikayt/ *vi* **1** to officiate as a pontiff **2** to deliver oracular utterances or dogmatic opinions [ML *pontificatus*, pp of *pontificare*, fr L *pontific-*, *pontifex*] – **pontificator** *n*, **pontification** /-'kaysh(ə)n/ *n*

pontine /'pontien/ *adj* of the pons [ISV *pont-* (fr NL *pont-*, *pons*) + *-ine*]

[1]**pontoon** /pon'toohn/ *n* a flat-bottomed boat or portable float (used in building a floating temporary bridge) [F *ponton* floating bridge, punt, fr L *ponton-*, *ponto*, fr *pont-*, *pons* bridge]

[2]**pontoon** *n* a gambling card game in which the object is to be dealt cards scoring more than those of the dealer up to but not exceeding 21 [prob alter. of *vingt-et-un*]

pony /'pohni/ *n* **1** a small horse; *esp* a member of any of several breeds of very small stocky horses under 14.2 hands in height **2** a racehorse – usu pl; slang **3** *Br* the sum of £25 – slang [prob fr obs F *poulenet*, dim. of F *poulain* colt, fr ML *pullanus*, fr L *pullus* young of an animal, foal – more at FOAL]

'ponyˌtail /-ˌtayl/ *n* a hairstyle in which the hair is drawn back tightly and tied high at the back of the head

'pony ˌtrekking *n* the pastime of riding ponies long distances across country in a group

pooch /poohch/ *n* DOG 1a – slang [origin unknown]

poodle /'poohdl/ *n* (any of) a breed of active intelligent dogs with a thick curly coat which is of 1 colour only [G *pudel*, short for *pudelhund*, fr *pudeln* to splash (fr *pudel* puddle, fr LG) + *hund* dog (fr OHG *hunt*) – more at PUDDLE, HOUND]

poof, pouf /poohf, poof/ *n, Br* an effeminate man or male homosexual – chiefly derog [perh fr *poof* (interj used to express contempt)]

poofter /'pooftə/ *n, Br* a poof – chiefly derog [irreg fr *poof*]

pooh /pooh/ *interj* – used to express contempt, disapproval, or distaste at an unpleasant smell [imit]

'pooh-ˌbah /bah/ *n, often cap P&B* a person holding many public or private offices [*Pooh-Bah*, character bearing the title Lord- High-Everything-Else in the comic opera *The Mikado* by W S Gilbert †1911 E librettist & poet]

ˌpooh-'pooh *vb* to express contempt (for) [*pooh*]

[1]**pool** /poohl/ *n* **1a** a small and relatively deep body of usu fresh water (e g a still place in a stream or river) **b** sthg resembling a pool (e g in depth or shape) ⟨~s *of light*⟩ **2** a small body of standing liquid; a puddle ⟨*lay in a* ~ *of blood*⟩ **3** SWIMMING POOL [ME, fr OE *pōl*; akin to OHG *pfuol* pool]

[2]**pool** *n* **1** an aggregate stake to which each player of a game has contributed **2** any of various games played on a billiard table with 6 pockets and often 15 numbered balls **3** a combination of the interests or property of different parties that subjects each party to the same controls and a common liability **4** a readily available supply; *esp* the whole quantity of a particular material present in the body and available for metabolism **5** a facility, service, or group of people providing a service for a number of people (e g the members of a business organization) ⟨*a typing* ~⟩ **6** *pl* FOOTBALL POOLS [F *poule*, lit., hen, fr OF, fem of *poul* cock – more at PULLET; perh fr a hen being set as the target and prize in a game]

[3]**pool** *vt* to contribute to a common stock (e g of resources or effort)

[1]**poop** /poohp/ *n* an enclosed superstructure at the stern of a ship above the main deck ☞ SHIP [MF *poupe*, fr L *puppis*]

[2]**poop** *vt* **1** to break over the stern of **2** to receive (a sea or wave) over the stern

[3]**poop** *vb, chiefly NAm vt* to put out of breath; *also* to tire out ~ *vi* to become exhausted *USE* (*vt & vi*) usu + *out*; infml [origin unknown]

poor /pooə, paw/ *adj* **1a** lacking material possessions **b** of or characterized by poverty **2** less than adequate; meagre ⟨*a* ~ *harvest*⟩ **3** exciting pity ⟨~ *old soul!*⟩ **4** inferior in quality, value, or workmanship ⟨*in* ~ *health*⟩ ⟨*a* ~ *essay*⟩ **5** humble, unpretentious ⟨*in my* ~ *opinion*⟩ **6** *of land* barren, unproductive [ME *poure*, fr OF *povre*, fr L *pauper*; akin to L *paucus* little and to L *parere* to produce, *parare* to acquire – more at FEW, PARE] – **poorish** *adj*, **poorly** *adv*, **poorness** *n*

'poor ,box *n* a box (e g in a church) into which money for the poor can be put

,Poor 'Clare /kleə/ *n* a member of an austere order of nuns founded by St Clare in 1212

'poor,house /-,hows/ *n* WORKHOUSE 1

'poor ,law *n* a law that in former times provided for the relief of the poor

poorly /'pooəli/ *adj* somewhat ill

,poor-'spirited *adj* lacking zest, confidence, or courage – **poor-spiritedly** *adv*, **poor-spiritedness** *n*

poor white *n* a member of an inferior or underprivileged white social group – chiefly derog

poove /poohv/ *n, Br* a poof – chiefly derog [by alter.]

[1]**pop** /pop/ *vb* **-pp-** *vt* **1** to strike or knock sharply; hit ⟨~ped *him one on the jaw*⟩ **2** to push, put, or thrust suddenly ⟨~ped *a sweet into his mouth*⟩ **3** to cause to explode or burst open **4** to shoot at **5** to take (drugs) orally or by injection ⟨*he* ~ped *pills*⟩ **6** *Br* to pawn ~ *vi* **1a** to go, come, or enter suddenly or quickly ⟨*just* ~ped *out to do some shopping*⟩ **b** to escape or break away from sthg (e g a point of attachment) usu suddenly or unexpectedly **2** to make or burst with a sharp explosive sound **3** to protrude from the sockets ⟨*eyes* ~ping *in amazement*⟩ *USE* (*vt & vi*) infml [ME *poppen*, of imit origin] – **pop the question** to propose marriage – infml

[2]**pop** *n* **1** a popping sound **2** a flavoured carbonated beverage **3** *Br* PAWN 2 *USE* (*1 & 3*) infml ['*pop*; (2) fr the sound made by pulling a cork from a bottle]

[3]**pop** *adv* like or with a pop; suddenly – infml

[4]**pop** *n, chiefly NAm* a father – infml [short for *poppa*]

[5]**pop** *adj* popular: e g **a** of pop music ⟨~ *singer*⟩ **b** of or constituting a mass culture widely disseminated through the mass media ⟨~ *society*⟩

[6]**pop** *n* POP MUSIC

pop art *n, often cap P&A* art that incorporates everyday objects from popular culture and the mass media (e g comic strips) – **pop artist** *n*

'pop,corn /-,kawn/ *n* (the popped kernels of) a maize whose kernels burst open when heated to form a white starchy mass

pope /pohp/ *n* **1** *often cap* the prelate who as bishop of Rome is the head of the Roman Catholic church **2** a priest of an Eastern church **3** [1]RUFF [ME, fr OE *pāpa*, fr LL *papa*, fr Gk *pappas, papas*, title of bishops, lit., papa; (2) Russ *pop*, fr OSlav *popŭ*, fr (assumed) WGmc *papo*, fr Gk *pappas, papas*]

popery /'pohp(ə)ri/ *n* ROMAN CATHOLICISM – chiefly derog

'pop-,eyed *adj* having staring or bulging eyes (e g as a result of surprise or excitement)

'pop,gun /-,gun/ *n* a toy gun that shoots a cork or pellet and produces a popping sound; *also* an inadequate or inefficient firearm

popinjay /'popin,jay/ *n* a strutting supercilious person [ME *papejay* parrot, fr MF *papegai, papejai*, fr Ar *babghā'*]

popish /'pohpish/ *adj* of popery – chiefly derog [*pope*] – **popishly** *adv*

poplar /'poplə/ *n* **1** (the wood of) any of a genus of slender quick-growing trees (e g an aspen) of the willow family **2** TULIP TREE [ME *poplere*, fr MF *pouplier*, fr *pouple* poplar, fr L *populus*]

poplin /'poplin/ *n* a strong usu cotton fabric in plain weave with crosswise ribs [F *papeline*]

popliteal /pop'liti·əl, ,popli'tee·əl/ *adj* of the back part of the leg behind the knee joint [NL *popliteus*, fr L *poplit-, poples* ham of the knee]

pop music *n* modern commercially promoted popular music that is usu short and simple and has a strong beat

pop off *vi* **1** to leave suddenly **2** to die unexpectedly *USE* infml

poppa /'popə/ *n, NAm* a father – infml [alter. of *papa*]

poppadom /'popədom/ *n* a crisp wafer-thin pancake of deep-fried dough eaten chiefly with Indian food [Tamil-Malayalam *pappaṭam*]

popper /'popə/ *n, chiefly Br* PRESS-STUD ['POP + [2]-ER]

poppet /'popit/ *n* **1** a valve that rises up and down from its seat **2** *chiefly Br* a lovable or enchanting person or animal – infml [ME *popet* doll, puppet – more at PUPPET]

poppie /'popi/ *n, SAfr* GIRLFRIEND – infml [Afrik, fr *pop* doll + *-ie*, dim. suffix]

'popping ,crease /'poping/ *n* either of the lines drawn perpendicularly across a cricket pitch 4ft (about 1.22m) in front of each wicket and behind which the batsman must have a foot or his/her bat on the ground to avoid being run out or stumped – compare BOWLING CREASE ☞ SPORT

poppy /'popi/ *n* any of several genera of plants with showy flowers and capsular fruits including the opium poppy and several other plants cultivated for their ornamental value [ME *popi*, fr OE *popæg, popig*, modif of L *papaver*]

'poppy,cock /-,kok/ *n* empty talk; nonsense – infml [D dial. *pappekak*, lit., soft dung, fr D *pap* pap + *kak* dung]

popsy /'popsi/ *n, Br* GIRLFRIEND – infml; often derog [*pop* (short for *poppet*) + *-s* + [4]*-y*]

populace /'popyooləs/ *n sing or pl in constr* the (common) people; the masses [MF, fr It *popolaccio* rabble, pejorative of *popolo* the people, fr L *populus*]

popular /'popyoolə/ *adj* **1** of the general public **2** suited to the needs, means, tastes, or understanding of the general public ⟨*a* ~ *history of the war*⟩ **3** having general currency **4** commonly liked or approved ⟨*a very* ~ *girl*⟩ [L *popularis* of the people, fr *populus* the people, a people] – **popularly** *adv*, **popularity** /,popyoo'larəti/ *n*

,popular 'front *n, often cap P&F* a coalition of left-wing political parties against a common opponent

popular·ize, -ise /'popyoolə,riez/ *vt* **1** to cause to be liked or esteemed **2** to present in a generally understandable or interesting form – **popularizer** *n*, **popularization** /-rie'zaysh(ə)n/ *n*

populate /'popyoolayt/ *vt* **1** to have a place in; occupy, inhabit **2** to supply or provide with inhabitants; people [ML *populatus*, pp of *populare* to people, fr L *populus* people]

population /,popyoo'laysh(ə)n/ *n* **1** *sing or pl in constr* the whole number of people or inhabitants in a country or region **2** *sing or pl in constr* a body of people or individuals having a quality or characteristic in common ⟨*a floating* ~ *of drifters*⟩ **3** all the particles in a particular energy level – used esp with reference to atoms in a laser **4** the group of organisms inhabiting a particular area **5** a set (e g of individual people or items) from which samples are taken for statistical measurement [LL *population-, populatio,* fr L *populus*]

population explosion *n* a vast usu rapid increase in the size of a living population

populist /'popyoolist/ *n* **1** a member of a political party claiming to represent the common people **2** a believer in the rights, wisdom, or virtues of the common people [L *populus* the people] – **populism** *n,* **populist** *also* **populistic** /-'listik/ *adj*

populous /'popyooləs/ *adj* densely populated [L *populosus,* fr *populus* people] – **populously** *adv,* **populousness** *n*

[1]**'pop-,up** *adj* of or having a device that causes its contents to spring up or stand out in relief ⟨*a* ~ *toaster*⟩ ⟨*a* ~ *book*⟩

pop up *vi* to arise suddenly or unexpectedly; CROP UP – infml

porbeagle /'paw,beegl/ *n* a small shark of the N Atlantic and Pacific oceans with a pointed nose and crescent-shaped tail [Corn *porgh-bugel*]

porcelain /'paws(ə)lin/ *n* **1a** a type of hard nonporous translucent white ceramic ware made from a mixture of kaolin, quartz, and feldspar fired at a high temperature **b** a type of translucent ceramic ware made from a mixture of refined clay and ground glass fired at a low temperature **2** porcelain ware [MF *porcelaine* cowrie shell, porcelain (fr the resemblance of its finish to the surface of the shell), fr It *porcellana,* fr *porcello* vulva, lit., little pig, fr L *porcellus,* dim. of *porcus* pig, vulva; fr the shape of the shell] – **porcelaneous, porcellaneous** /,pawsə'laynyəs, -ni·əs/ *adj*

porch /pawch/ *n* **1** a covered usu projecting entrance to a building ☞ CHURCH **2** *NAm* a veranda [ME *porche,* fr OF, fr L *porticus* portico, fr *porta* gate – more at [2]PORT]

porcine /'pawsien/ *adj* of or like pigs; *esp* obese [L *porcinus,* fr *porcus* pig – more at FARROW]

porcupine /'pawkyoopien/ *n* any of various ground-living or tree-dwelling relatively large rodents with stiff sharp erectile bristles mingled with the hair [ME *porkepin,* fr MF *porc espin,* fr OIt *porcospino,* fr L *porcus* pig + *spina* spine, prickle]

[1]**pore** /paw/ *vi* **1** to study closely or attentively **2** to reflect or meditate steadily ***USE*** usu + *on, over,* or *upon* [ME *pouren*]

[2]**pore** *n* a minute opening; *esp* one (e g in a membrane, esp the skin, or between soil particles) through which fluids pass or are absorbed ☞ NERVE [ME, fr MF, fr L *porus,* fr Gk *poros* passage, pore – more at [1]FARE] – **pored** *adj*

porgy /'pawgi/ *n, pl* **porgies,** *esp collectively* **porgy** (any of various fishes related to) a blue-spotted crimson spiny-finned food fish of the coasts of Europe and America [partly fr earlier *pargo* (porgy); partly fr earlier *scuppaug* (porgy)]

poriferan /paw'rif(ə)rən/ *n* SPONGE 1b [deriv of L *porus* pore + *-fer* -ferous] – **poriferan, poriferal** *adj*

pork /pawk/ *n* the flesh of a pig used as food ☞ MEAT [ME, fr OF, pig, fr L *porcus*]

porker /'pawkə/ *n* PIG 1a; *esp* a young pig fattened for food

,porkpie 'hat /,pawk'pie/ a man's hat with a low crown, flat top, and usu a turned-up brim [fr its shape]

porky /'pawki/ *adj* fat, fleshy ⟨*a* ~ *young man*⟩ – infml [PORK + [1]-Y]

porn /pawn/ *n* pornography – infml

pornographer /paw'nogrəfə/ *n* one who produces or deals in pornography

pornography /paw'nogrəfi/ *n* (books, photographs, films, etc containing) the depiction of erotic behaviour intended to cause sexual excitement [Gk *pornographos,* adj, writing of prostitutes, fr *pornē* prostitute + *graphein* to write; akin to Gk *pernanai* to sell, *poros* journey – more at [1]FARE, CARVE] – **pornographic** /,pawnə'grafik/ *adj,* **pornographically** *adv*

porous /'pawrəs/ *adj* **1** having or full of pores or spaces **2** permeable to liquids – **porously** *adv,* **porousness** *n,* **porosity** /paw'rosəti/ *n*

porphyria /paw'firi·ə/ *n* any of various usu hereditary abnormalities of porphyrin metabolism characterized esp by discoloured, usu red, urine, extreme sensitivity to light, and phases of mental derangement [NL, fr ISV *porphyrin*]

porphyrin /'pawfirin/ *n* any of various compounds from which others, esp of chlorophyll or haemoglobin, are formed [ISV, fr Gk *porphyra* purple]

porphyry /'pawfiri/ *n* an igneous rock consisting of crystals (e g of feldspar) embedded in a compact mass of surrounding rock [ME *porfurie,* fr ML *porphyrium,* alter. of L *porphyrites,* fr Gk *porphyritēs* (*lithos*), lit., stone like Tyrian purple, fr *porphyra* purple] – **porphyritic** /,pawfi'ritik/ *adj*

porpoise /'pawpəs/ *n* (any of several small gregarious toothed whales related to) a blunt-snouted usu largely black whale about 2m (6ft) long [ME *porpoys,* fr MF *porpois,* fr ML *porcopiscis,* fr L *porcus* pig + *piscis* fish – more at FARROW, [1]FISH]

porrect /pə'rekt/ *adj* extended forwards ⟨*an insect with* ~ *antennae*⟩ [L *porrectus,* pp of *porrigere* to stretch out, fr *por-* forwards + *regere* to direct – more at PORTEND, [1]RIGHT]

porridge /'porij/ *n* **1** (sthg with the consistency of) a soft food made by boiling a cereal product, esp oatmeal, in milk or water until thick **2** *Br* time spent in prison – slang [alter. of *pottage*]

porringer /'porinjə/ *n* a small bowl from which esp soft or liquid foods (e g porridge) are eaten [alter. of ME *poteger, potinger,* fr AF *potageer,* fr MF *potager* of pottage, fr *potage* pottage]

[1]**port** /pawt/ *n* **1** a town or city with a harbour where ships, hovercraft, etc may take on or discharge cargo or passengers **2** a place where goods and people may be permitted to pass into or out of a country [ME, fr OE & OF, fr L *portus* – more at FORD]

[2]**port** *n* **1** an opening (e g in machinery) for intake or exhaust of a fluid **2** an opening in a ship's side to admit light or air or to load cargo **3** a hole in an armoured vehicle or fortification through which guns may be fired [ME *porte,* fr MF, gate, door, fr L *porta* passage, gate; akin to L *portus* port]

[3]**port** *n* the position in which a military weapon is carried at the command *port arms* [ME, deportment, bearing, fr MF, fr *porter* to carry, fr L *portare*]

[4]**port** *adj or n* (of or at) the left side of a ship or aircraft looking forwards – compare STARBOARD ☞ SHIP [prob fr [1]*port* or [2]*port*]

5port *vt* to turn or put (a helm) to the left – used chiefly as a command

6port *n* a fortified sweet wine of rich taste and aroma made in Portugal [*Oporto*, seaport in Portugal]

portable /'portəbl/ *n or adj* (sthg) capable of being carried or moved about ⟨*a* ~ *typewriter*⟩ ⟨*a* ~ *sawmill*⟩ [adj ME, fr MF, fr LL *portabilis*, fr L *portare* to carry – more at 1FARE; n fr adj] – **portably** *adv*, **portability** /,portə'biləti/ *n*

1portage /'pawtij/ *n* **1** the carrying of boats or goods overland from one body of water to another **2** the route followed in portage; *also* a place where such a transfer is necessary [ME, fr MF, fr *porter* to carry]

2portage *vt* to carry over a portage ~ *vi* to move gear over a portage

1portal /'pawtl/ *n* **1** a (grand or imposing) door or entrance **2** the point at which sthg (e g a disease-causing agent) enters the body [ME, fr MF, fr ML *portale* city gate, porch, fr neut of *portalis* of a gate, fr L *porta* gate – more at 2PORT]

2portal *adj* **1** of the transverse fissure on the underside of the liver where most of the vessels enter **2** of or being a portal vein [NL *porta* transverse fissure of the liver, fr L, gate]

portal vein *n* a vein that transfers blood from one part of the body to another without passing through the heart; *esp* the vein carrying blood from the digestive organs and spleen to the liver

portamento /,pawtə'mentoh/ *n, pl* **portamenti** /-ti/ a continuous gliding movement from one note to another by the voice, a trombone, or a bowed stringed instrument [It, lit., act of carrying, fr *portare* to carry, fr L]

portcullis /pawt'kulis/ *n* a usu iron or wood grating that can prevent entry through the gateway of a fortified place by sliding down between grooves [ME *port colice*, fr MF *porte coleïce*, lit., sliding door]

port de bras /,paw də 'brah/ *n* the technique and practice of arm movement in ballet [F, lit., carriage of the arm]

Porte /pawt/ *n* the government of the Ottoman empire [F, short for *Sublime Porte*, lit., sublime gate; fr the gate of the sultan's palace where justice was administered]

portend /paw'tend/ *vt* **1** to give an omen or anticipatory sign of; bode **2** to indicate, signify [ME *portenden*, fr L *portendere*, fr *por-* forwards (akin to *per* through) + *tendere* to stretch – more at FOR, THIN]

portent /'pawt(ə)nt, -tent/ *n* **1** sthg foreshadowing a coming event; an omen **2** prophetic indication or significance [L *portentum*, fr neut of *portentus*, pp of *portendere*]

portentous /paw'tentəs/ *adj* **1** eliciting amazement or wonder; prodigious **2** self-consciously weighty; pompous – **portentously** *adv*, **portentousness** *n*

1porter /'pawtə/, *fem* **portress** /-tris/ *n, chiefly Br* a gatekeeper or doorkeeper, esp of a large building, who usu regulates entry and answers enquiries [ME, fr OF *portier*, fr LL *portarius*, fr L *porta* gate – more at 2PORT]

2porter *n* **1** sby who carries burdens; *specif* sby employed to carry luggage (e g in a hotel or railway station) **2** a heavy dark brown beer **3** *NAm* a sleeping car attendant [ME *portour*, fr MF *porteour*, fr LL *portator*, fr L *portatus*, pp of *portare* to carry – more at 1FARE; (2) short for *porter's beer*]

porterage /'pawt(ə)rij/ *n* (the charge made for) the work performed by a porter

'porter,house /-,hows/ *n* a large steak cut from the back end of the sirloin above the ribs and containing part of the fillet ☞ MEAT [arch *porterhouse* (house where porter and other liquors were sold, and where such steaks were served)]

portfolio /pawt'fohli·oh/ *n, pl* **portfolios** **1** a hinged cover or flexible case for carrying loose papers, pictures, etc **2** the office of a government minister or member of a cabinet ⟨*the defence* ~⟩ **3** the securities held by an investor [It *portafoglio*, fr *portare* to carry (fr L) + *foglio* leaf, sheet, fr L *folium* – more at BLADE; (2) fr the use of such a case to carry documents of state]

porthole /'pawt,hohl/ *n* **1** a usu glazed opening, esp in the side of a ship or aircraft **2** 2PORT 2 [2*port*]

portico /'pawtikoh/ *n, pl* **porticoes, porticos** a colonnade or covered veranda, usu at the entrance of a building and characteristic of classical architecture [It, fr L *porticus* – more at PORCH]

portiere /,pawti'eə/ *n* a curtain hanging across a doorway [F *portière*, fr OF, fem of *portier* porter, doorkeeper]

1portion /'pawsh(ə)n/ *n* **1** a part or share of sthg: e g **a** a helping of food **b** *archaic* a dowry **2** an individual's lot or fate [ME, fr OF, fr L *portion-, portio*; akin to L *part-, pars* part]

2portion *vt* to divide into portions; distribute – often + *out*

'portionless /-lis/ *adj* having no portion; *esp* having no dowry or inheritance

portland cement /'pawtlənd/ *n* a hydraulic cement made from lime and clay [fr its resemblance to portland stone]

portland stone *n* a limestone much used in building [Isle of *Portland*, peninsula in Dorset, England, where the limestone is found]

portly /'pawtli/ *adj* rotund, stout [3*port* (deportment, bearing) + 1*-ly*; orig sense, of dignified bearing] – **portliness** *n*

1portmanteau /pawt'mantoh/ *n, pl* **portmanteaus, portmanteaux** /-tohz/ a trunk for a traveller's belongings that opens into 2 equal parts [MF *portemanteau*, fr *porter* to carry (fr L *portare*) + *manteau* mantle, fr L *mantellum*]

2portmanteau *adj* combining more than 1 use or quality

portmanteau word *n* BLEND 2

,port of 'call *n* **1** a port where ships customarily stop during a voyage **2** a stop included in an itinerary

portrait /'pawtrit, -trayt/ *n* **1** a pictorial likeness of a person **2** a verbal portrayal or representation [MF, fr pp of *portraire*] – **portraitist** *n*

portraiture /'pawtrichə/ *n* the art of making portraits

portray /paw'tray/ *vt* **1** to make a picture of; depict **2a** to describe in words **b** to play the role of [ME *portraien*, fr MF *portraire*, fr L *protrahere* to draw forth, reveal, expose, fr *pro-* forth + *trahere* to draw – more at 1PRO-, DRAW] – **portrayer** *n*

portrayal /paw'tray(ə)l/ *n* **1** the act or process of portraying; representation **2** a portrait

portress /'pawtris/ *n* a female porter

Port Salut /,paw sa'looh (*Fr* pɔr saly)/ *n* a pale yellow mild-flavoured cheese [F *port-du-salut, port-salut*, fr *Port du Salut*, Trappist abbey in NW France]

Portuguese /ˌpawchoo'geez, ˌpawtyoo'geez/ *n, pl* **Portuguese** **1** a native or inhabitant of Portugal **2** the language of esp Portugal and Brazil ☞ LANGUAGE [Pg *português,* adj & n, fr *Portugal,* country in SW Europe, fr L *Portus Cale* Oporto, seaport in NW Portugal] – **Portuguese** *adj*

Portuguese man-of-war *n* any of several large floating jellyfishes with very long stinging tentacles

[1]**pose** /pohz/ *vt* **1** to place (e g a model) in a studied attitude **2** to put or set forth; offer ⟨*this attitude* ~s *a threat to our hopes for peace*⟩ **3** to present for attention or consideration ⟨*let me* ~ *a question*⟩ ~*vi* **1** to assume a posture or attitude, usu for artistic purposes **2** to affect an attitude or character; posture ⟨~d *as an honest man*⟩ [ME *posen,* fr MF *poser,* fr (assumed) VL *pausare* (influenced in meaning by L *pos-,* perfect stem of *ponere* to put, place), fr LL, to stop, rest, pause, fr L *pausa* pause]

[2]**pose** *n* **1** a sustained posture; *esp* one assumed for artistic purposes **2** an assumed attitude of mind or mode of behaviour

[1]**poser** /'pohzə/ *n* a puzzling or baffling question [*pose* (to puzzle, baffle), short for earlier *appose,* fr ME *apposen,* alter. of *opposen* to oppose, fr MF *opposer* – more at OPPOSE]

[2]**poser** *n* a poseur [[1]POSE + [2]-ER]

poseur /poh'zuh/ *n* an affected or insincere person [F, lit., poser, fr *poser* to pose]

[1]**posh** /posh/ *adj* **1** very fine; splendid ⟨*a* ~ *new car*⟩ **2** socially exclusive or fashionable; *broadly* upper-class ⟨*a* ~ *Knightsbridge address*⟩ – often derog ***USE*** infml [perh fr earlier *posh,* n (money, dandy)]

[2]**posh** *adv* in a posh accent – infml ⟨*talk* ~⟩

posit /'pozit/ *vt* to assume or affirm the existence of; postulate [L *positus,* pp]

[1]**position** /pə'zish(ə)n/ *n* **1** the statement of a proposition or thesis **2** an opinion; POINT OF VIEW ⟨*made her* ~ *on the issue clear*⟩ **3** a market commitment in securities or commodities; *also* the inventory of a market trader **4a** the place occupied by sby or sthg ⟨*house in an attractive* ~ *overlooking the sea*⟩; *also* the proper place ⟨*the cars are now in the starting* ~⟩ **b** a disposition or attitude of (a part of) the body ⟨*rose to a standing* ~⟩ **5a** a condition, situation ⟨*is now in a* ~ *to make important decisions on his own*⟩ **b** social or official rank or status **c** a situation that confers advantage or preference ⟨*jockeying for* ~⟩ **6** the disposition of the notes of a chord **7** a post, job – fml [MF, fr L *position-, positio,* fr *positus,* pp of *ponere* to lay down, put, place, fr (assumed) OL *posinere,* fr *po-* away (akin to Gk *apo-*) + L *sinere* to lay, leave – more at SITE]

[2]**position** *vt* to put in a proper or specified position

positional /pə'zish(ə)nl/ *adj* of or fixed by position ⟨~ *astronomy*⟩

[1]**positive** /'pozətiv/ *adj* **1a** expressed clearly or peremptorily ⟨*her answer was a* ~ no⟩ **b** fully assured; confident ⟨~ *that he is right*⟩ **2** of or constituting the simple form of an adjective or adverb that expresses no degree of comparison **3** incontestable ⟨~ *proof*⟩ **4** utter ⟨*a* ~ *disgrace*⟩ **5** real, active ⟨*a* ~ *influence for good in the community*⟩ **6a** capable of being constructively applied; helpful ⟨~ *advice*⟩ **b** concentrating on what is good or beneficial; optimistic ⟨*has a* ~ *attitude towards his illness*⟩ **7a** having or expressing actual existence or quality as distinguished from deficiency **b** not speculative; empirical **8** having the light and dark parts similar in tone to those of the original photographic subject **9a** in a direction arbitrarily or customarily taken as that of increase or progression ⟨~ *angles*⟩ **b** directed or moving towards a source of stimulation ⟨*a* ~ *response to light*⟩ **10** numerically greater than zero ⟨*+2 is a* ~ *integer*⟩ **11a** of being, or charged with electricity as a result of a deficiency of electrons **b** having higher electric potential and constituting the part from which the current flows to the external circuit **12a** marked by or indicating acceptance, approval, or affirmation **b** showing the presence of sthg sought or suspected to be present ⟨*a* ~ *test for blood*⟩ **13** *of a lens* converging light rays and forming a real inverted image [ME, formally laid down, fr OF *positif,* fr L *positivus,* fr *positus*] – **positively** *adv,* **positiveness** *n*

[2]**positive** *n* sthg positive: e g **a** the positive degree or form of an adjective or adverb **b** sthg about which an affirmation can be made; reality **c** a positive photograph or a print from a negative

positivism /'pozitiviz(ə)m/ *n* **1** a theory rejecting theology and metaphysics in favour of knowledge based on the scientific observation of natural phenomena **2** LOGICAL POSITIVISM [F *positivisme,* fr *positif* positive + *-isme* -ism] – **positivist** *adj or n,* **positivistic** /-'vistik/ *adj*

positron /'pozitron/ *n* a positively charged elementary particle that has the same mass and magnitude of charge as the electron and is the antiparticle of the electron [*posi*tive + *-tron* (as in *electron*)]

positronium /ˌpozi'trohnyəm, -ni·əm/ *n* a short-lived system that consists of a positron and an electron bound together [*positron* + *-ium*]

posse /'posi/ *n sing or pl in constr* **1** a body of people summoned by a sheriff, esp in N America, to assist in preserving the public peace, usu in an emergency **2** a large group, often with a common interest [ML *posse comitatus,* lit., power or authority of the county]

possess /pə'zes/ *vt* **1a** to make the owner or holder – + *of* or *with* **b** to have possession of **2a** to have and hold as property; own **b** to have as an attribute, knowledge, or skill **3a** to take into one's possession **b** to influence so strongly as to direct the actions ⟨*whatever* ~ed *her to act like that?*⟩; *also, of a demon, evil spirit, etc* to enter into and control [ME *possessen,* fr MF *possesser* to have possession of, take possession of, fr L *possessus,* pp of *possidēre,* fr *potis* able, in power + *sedēre* to sit – more at POTENT, SIT] – **possessor** *n*

pos'sessed *adj* **1** influenced or controlled by sthg (e g an evil spirit or a passion) **2** mad, crazed – **possessedly** /-sidli/ *adv,* **possessedness** /-sidnis/ *n*

possession /pə'zesh(ə)n/ *n* **1a** the act of having or taking into control **b** ownership; *also* control or occupancy (e g of property) without regard to ownership **2a** sthg owned, occupied, or controlled **b** *pl* wealth, property **3** domination by sthg (e g an evil spirit or passion) – **possessional** *adj*

[1]**possessive** /pə'zesiv/ *adj* **1** manifesting possession or the desire to own or dominate ⟨*a* ~ *mother*⟩ **2** of or being the grammatical possessive – **possessively** *adv,* **possessiveness** *n*

[2]**possessive** *n* (a form in) a grammatical case expressing ownership or a similar relation – compare GENITIVE

possessory /pə'zes(ə)ri/ *adj* of or having possession ⟨*a ~ interest*⟩

posset /'posit/ *n* a comforting hot beverage of sweetened and spiced milk curdled with ale or wine; *also* a dessert made with cream, eggs, sugar and usu lemon [ME *poshet, possot*]

possibility /,posə'biləti/ *n* **1** the condition or fact of being possible **2** sthg possible **3** potential or prospective value – usu pl with sing. meaning ⟨*the house had great* possibilities⟩

[1]**possible** /'posəbl/ *adj* **1** within the limits of ability, capacity, or realization **2** capable of being done or occurring according to nature, custom, or manners **3** that may or may not occur ⟨*it is ~ but not probable that he will win*⟩ **4** having a specified potential use, quality, etc ⟨*a ~ housing site*⟩ [ME, fr MF, fr L *possibilis*, fr *posse* to be able, fr *potis, pote* able + *esse* to be – more at POTENT, IS]

[2]**possible** *n* **1** sthg possible ⟨*politics is the art of the ~*⟩ **2** sby or sthg that may be selected for a specified role, task, etc ⟨*a ~ for the post of Chancellor*⟩

possibly /'posəbli/ *adv* **1** it is possible that; maybe ⟨*~ there is life on Mars*⟩ ⟨*he may ~ have caught a later train*⟩ **2** – used as an intensifier with *can* or *could* ⟨*you can't ~ eat all that cake*⟩ ⟨*I'll do all I ~ can to have it ready on time*⟩

possum /'pos(ə)m/ *n* an opossum – not used technically

[1]**post** /pohst/ *n* **1** a piece of timber, metal, etc fixed firmly in an upright position, esp as a stay or support **2** a pole marking the starting or finishing point of a horse race **3** a goalpost [ME, fr OE; akin to OHG *pfosto* post; both fr a prehistoric WGmc word borrowed fr L *postis*; akin to Gk *pro* before & to Gk *histasthai* to stand – more at FOR, STAND]

[2]**post** *vt* **1** to fasten to a wall, board, etc in order to make public – often + *up* **2** to publish, announce, or advertise (as if) by use of a placard

[3]**post** *n* **1** (a single despatch or delivery of) the mail handled by a postal system **2** *chiefly Br* a postal system or means of posting **3** *archaic* (the distance between) any of a series of stations for keeping horses for relays [MF *poste* relay station, courier, fr OIt *posta* relay station, fr fem of *posto*, pp of *porre* to place, fr L *ponere* – more at POSITION]

[4]**post** *vt* **1** to send by post ⟨*~ a letter*⟩ **2a** to transfer or carry from a book of original entry to a ledger **b** to make transfer entries in **3** to provide with the latest news; inform ⟨*kept her ~*ed *on the latest gossip*⟩

[5]**post** *adv* with post-horses; express

[6]**post** *n* **1a** the place at which a soldier is stationed **b** a station or task to which one is assigned **c** the place at which a body of troops is stationed **2a** an office or position to which a person is appointed **b** (the position of) a player in basketball who provides the focal point of the attack **3** a trading post, settlement **4** *Br* either of 2 bugle calls giving notice of the hour for retiring at night [MF *poste*, fr OIt *posto*, fr pp of *porre* to place]

[7]**post** *vt* **1** to station ⟨*guards were ~*ed *at the doors*⟩ **2** *chiefly Br* to assign to a unit or location

post- *prefix* **1a** after; subsequent; later ⟨post*date*⟩ **b** posterior; following after ⟨post*script*⟩ ⟨post*consonantal*⟩ **2a** subsequent to; later than ⟨post*operative*⟩ ⟨post-*Pleistocene*⟩ **b** situated behind ⟨post*orbital*⟩ [ME, fr L, fr *post*, adv & prep; akin to Skt *paśca* behind, after, Gk *apo* away from – more at OF]

postage /'pohstij/ *n* (markings or stamps representing) the fee for a postal service

'**postage ,meter** *n, NAm* a franking machine

'**postage ,stamp** *n* an adhesive or imprinted stamp used as evidence of prepayment of postage

postal /'pohstl/ *adj* **1** of or being a system for the conveyance of written material, parcels, etc between a large number of users **2** conducted by post ⟨*~ chess*⟩ – **postally** *adv*

'**postal ,order** *n, Br* an order issued by a post office for payment of a specified sum of money usu at another post office

'**post,bag** /-,bag/ *n, Br* **1** a mailbag **2** a single batch of mail usu delivered to 1 address

'**post,box** /-,boks/ *n* a secure receptacle for the posting of outgoing mail

'**post,boy** /-,boy/ *n* **1** a postilion **2** *chiefly Br* a boy or man who deals with post

'**post,card** /-,kahd/ *n* a card that can be posted without an enclosing envelope

,**post 'chaise** /shayz/ *n* a usu closed 4-wheeled carriage seating 2 to 4 people [[3]*post*]

,**post'classical** /-'klasikl/, **postclassic** *adj* of or being a period (e g in art, literature, or civilization) following a classical one

'**post,code** /-,kohd/ *n* a combination of letters and numbers that is used in the postal address of a place in the UK to assist sorting – compare ZIP CODE

,**post'date** /-'dayt/ *vt* **1a** to date with a date later than that of execution ⟨*~ a cheque*⟩ **b** to assign (an event) to a date subsequent to that of actual occurrence – compare BACKDATE **2** to follow in time

poster /'pohstə/ *n* a (decorative) bill or placard for display often in a public place [[2]*post*]

poste restante /,pohst 'restont/ *n, chiefly Br* mail that is intended for collection from a post office [F, lit., waiting mail] – **poste restante** *adv*

[1]**posterior** /po'stiəri·ə/ *adj* **1** later in time; subsequent **2** situated behind or towards the back: e g **a** *of an animal part* near the tail; caudal **b** *of the human body or its parts* dorsal **3** *of a plant part* (on the side) facing towards the stem or axis; *also* SUPERIOR 5a ***USE*** compare ANTERIOR [L, compar of *posterus* coming after, fr *post* after – more at POST-] – **posteriorly** *adv*, **posteriority** /po,stiəri'orəti/ *n*

[2]**posterior** *n* the buttocks

posterity /po'sterəti/ *n* **1** *sing or pl in constr* all the descendants of 1 ancestor **2** all future generations [ME *posterite*, fr MF *posterité*, fr L *posteritat-, posteritas*, fr *posterus* coming after]

postern /'postuhn, 'poh-/ *n* a back door or gate [ME *posterne*, fr OF, alter. of *posterle*, fr LL *posterula*, dim. of *postera* back door, fr L, fem of *posterus*] – **postern** *adj*

'**poster ,paint** *n* an opaque watercolour paint containing gum

,**post-'free** *adv, chiefly Br* postpaid

,**post'graduate** /-'gradyoo·ət/ *n* a student continuing higher education after completing a first degree – **postgraduate** *adj*

,**post'haste** /-'hayst/ *adv* with all possible speed [[3]*post* (courier) + *haste*]

'**post ,horn** *n* a simple wind instrument with cupped mouthpiece used esp by postilions in the 18th and 19th c

'post-,horse *n* a horse formerly kept for use by couriers or mail carriers

posthumous /'postyooməs/ *adj* **1** born after the death of the father **2** published after the death of the author or composer **3** following or occurring after death ⟨~ *fame*⟩ [L *posthumus*, alter. (influenced by *humus* ground) of *postumus* late-born, posthumous, fr superl of *posterus* coming after – more at POSTERIOR] – **posthumously** *adv*, **posthumousness** *n*

posthypnotic suggestion /,pohst·hip'notik/ *n* the giving of instructions or suggestions to a hypnotized person which he/she will act on when no longer in a trance

postiche /po'steesh/ *n* a wig; *esp* a toupee [F, fr Sp *postizo*]

postie /'pohsti/ *n* a postal worker – infml [[3]*post* (courier, postman) + *-ie*]

postilion, postillion /po'stilyən/ *n* sby who rides as a guide on the near horse of one of the pairs attached to a coach or post chaise, esp without a coachman [MF *postillon* mail carrier using post-horses, fr It *postiglione*, fr *posta* post]

Postimpressionism /,pohstim'preshəniz(ə)m/ *n* a theory or practice in art that reacted against impressionism by stressing the formal or subjective elements in a painting [F *postimpressionisme*, fr *post-* + *impressionisme* impressionism] – **Postimpressionist** *adj or n*, **Postimpressionistic** /-,preshə'nistik/ *adj*

[1]**posting** /'pohsting/ *n* the act of transferring an entry to the proper account in a ledger; *also* the resultant entry [[4]*post*]

[2]**posting** *n* an appointment to a post or a command [[7]*post*]

'postman /-mən/, *fem* **'post,woman** *n* sby who delivers the post

,postman's 'knock *n* a children's game in which a kiss is the reward for the pretended delivery of a letter

'post,mark /-,mahk/ *vt or n* (to mark with) a cancellation mark showing the post office and date of posting of a piece of mail

'post,master /-,mahstə/, *fem* **'post,mistress** *n* sby who has charge of a post office – **postmastership** *n*

,postmaster 'general *n, pl* **postmasters general** an official in charge of a national post office

,post me'ridiem /mə'ridi·əm/ *adj* being after noon – abbr **pm** [L]

,postmil'lennial /-mi'leni·əl/ *adj* coming after or relating to the period after the millennium

[1]**,post'mortem** /-'mawtəm/ *adj* **1** occurring after death **2** following the event ⟨*a ~ appraisal of the game*⟩ [L *post mortem* after death]

[2]**postmortem** *n* **1** *also* **postmortem examination** an examination of a body after death for determining the cause of death or the character and extent of changes produced by disease **2** an examination of a plan or event that failed, in order to discover the cause of failure

,post'natal /-'naytl/ *adj* subsequent to birth; *also* of or relating to a newborn child [ISV] – **postnatally** *adv*

,post'nuptial /-'nupsh(ə)l/ *adj* made or occurring after marriage or mating – **postnuptially** *adv*

,post-'obit /-'obit, -'ohbit/ *adj* occurring or taking effect after death [L *post obitum* after death]

'post ,office *n* **1** a national usu governmental organization that runs a postal system; *specif, cap P&O* the corporation that fulfils this function in the UK **2** a local branch of a national post office **3** *NAm* POSTMAN'S KNOCK

,post'operative /-'op(ə)rətiv/ *adj* following a surgical operation [ISV] – **postoperatively** *adv*

,post'paid /-'payd/ *adv* with the postage paid by the sender and not chargeable to the receiver

postpartum /-'pahtəm/ *adj* following birth ⟨~ *period*⟩ [NL *post partum* after birth] – **postpartum** *adv*

postpone /pə'spohn, ,pohs(t)'pohn/ *vt* to hold back to a later time; defer [L *postponere* to place after, postpone, fr *post-* + *ponere* to place – more at POSITION] – **postponable** *adj*, **postponement** *n*, **postponer** *n*

,post'positive /-'pozətiv/ *adj* placed after or at the end of another word [LL *postpositivus*, fr L *postpositus*, pp of *postponere*] – **postpositively** *adv*

,post'prandial /-'prandi·əl/ *adj* following a meal – fml or humor

postscript /'pohs(t),skript/ *n* **1** a note or series of notes appended to a completed article, a book, or esp a letter **2** a subordinate or supplementary part [NL *postscriptum*, fr L, neut of *postscriptus*, pp of *postscribere* to write after, fr *post-* + *scribere* to write – more at [1]SCRIBE]

,post-'structuralism /'strukch(ə)rəlizəm, -izm/ *n* a critical approach that is a reaction against structuralism, that draws on Freudian psychoanalytic theories, and that regards a text (e g in literature or history) as being autonomous and as yielding an indeterminate number of possible interpretations – **post-structuralist** *n or adj*

,postsy'naptic /-si'naptik/ *adj* situated or occurring just after a nerve synapse – **postsynaptically** *adv*

postulant /'postyoolənt/ *n* a person seeking admission to a religious order [F, petitioner, candidate, postulant, fr MF, fr prp of *postuler* to demand, solicit, fr L *postulare*] – **postulancy** *n*

[1]**postulate** /'postyoo,layt/ *vt* **1** to assume or claim as true **2** to assume as a postulate or axiom [L *postulatus*, pp of *postulare*, fr (assumed) *postus*, pp of L *poscere* to ask; akin to OHG *forsca* question, Skt *pṛcchati* he asks] – **postulation** /-'laysh(ə)n/ *n*, **postulational** *adj*

[2]**postulate** /'postyoolət/ *n* **1** a hypothesis advanced as a premise in a train of reasoning **2** AXIOM 2a [ML *postulatum*, fr neut of *postulatus*, pp of *postulare* to assume, fr L, to demand]

[1]**posture** /'poschə/ *n* **1** the position or bearing of (relative parts of) the body **2** a state or condition, esp in relation to other people or things ⟨*put the country in a ~ of defence*⟩ **3** a frame of mind; an attitude ⟨*his ~ of moral superiority*⟩ [F, fr It *postura*, fr L *positura*, fr *positus*, pp of *ponere* to place – more at POSITION] – **postural** *adj*

[2]**posture** *vi* **1** to assume a posture; *esp* to strike a pose for effect **2** to assume an artificial or insincere attitude; attitudinize – **posturer** *n*

postwar /,pohst'waw/ *adj* of or being the period after a war, esp WW I or II

posy /'pohzi/ *n* a small bouquet of flowers; a nosegay [alter. of *poesy*]

[1]**pot** /pot/ *n* **1a** any of various usu rounded vessels (e g of metal or earthenware) used for holding liquids or solids, esp in cooking **b** a potful ⟨*a ~ of coffee*⟩ **2** an enclosed framework for catching fish or lobsters

3 a drinking vessel (e g of pewter) used esp for beer 4 the total of the bets at stake at 1 time 5 *Br* a shot in billiards or snooker in which an object ball is pocketed 6 *NAm* the common fund of a group 7 a large amount (of money) – usu pl with sing. meaning; infml 8 a potbelly – infml 9 cannabis; *specif* marijuana – slang [ME, fr OE *pott*; akin to MLG *pot* pot]

²**pot** *vb* **-tt-** *vt* **1a** to place in a pot **b** to preserve in a sealed pot, jar, or can ⟨~ted *chicken*⟩ 2 to shoot (e g an animal) for food 3 to make or shape (earthenware) as a potter 4 to embed (e g electronic components) in a container with an insulating or protective material (e g plastic) 5 to sit (a young child) on a potty ~*vi* to take a potshot

potable /'pohtəbl/ *adj* suitable for drinking [LL *potabilis*, fr L *potare* to drink; akin to L *bibere* to drink, Gk *pinein*] – **potableness** *n*, **potability** /ˌpohtə'biləti/ *n*

potage /po'tahzh/ *n* a thick soup – compare POTTAGE [MF, fr OF, pottage]

potash /'potash/ *n* **1a** potassium carbonate, esp from wood ashes **b** potassium hydroxide **2** potassium or a potassium compound, esp as used in agriculture or industry [earlier *pot ashes*, trans of obs D *potaschen*; fr its being orig obtained by leaching wood ashes & evaporating the lye in iron pots]

potassium /pə'tasyəm, -si·əm/ *n* a soft light univalent metallic element of the alkali metal group that occurs abundantly in nature, esp combined in minerals ☞ PERIODIC TABLE [NL, fr *potassa* potash, fr E *potash*] – **potassic** *adj*

poˌtassium 'chlorate *n* a salt that is used as an oxidizing agent in matches, fireworks, and explosives

poˌtassium 'cyanide *n* a very poisonous salt used esp in electroplating

poˌtassium 'nitrate *n* a salt that occurs as a product of nitrification in arable soils, is a strong oxidizer, and is used esp in making gunpowder and in preserving meat

poˌtassium per'manganate *n* a dark purple salt used as an oxidizer and disinfectant

potassium sodium tartrate *n* ROCHELLE SALT

potation /poh'taysh(ə)n/ *n* an act or instance of drinking; *also* a usu alcoholic drink – fml or humor [ME *potacioun*, fr MF *potation*, fr L *potation-*, *potatio* act of drinking, fr *potatus*, pp of *potare*]

potato /pə'taytoh/ *n, pl* **potatoes** 1 SWEET POTATO 2 a plant of the nightshade family widely cultivated in temperate regions for its edible starchy tubers; *also* a potato tuber eaten as a vegetable [Sp *batata*, fr Taino]

potato chip *n* 1 *chiefly Br* CHIP 6a 2 *NAm* a crisp

potato crisp *n, chiefly Br* a crisp

ˌpot'belly /-'beli/ *n* an enlarged, swollen, or protruding abdomen – **potbellied** *adj*

'potˌboiler /-ˌboylə/ *n* a usu inferior work (e g of art or literature) produced chiefly to make money

'pot-ˌbound *adj, of a potted plant* having roots so densely matted as to allow little or no space for further growth

'potˌboy /-ˌboy/ *n* a boy who serves drinks in a tavern

poteen, potheen /po'cheen, po'teen/ *n* Irish whiskey illicitly distilled; *broadly* any distilled alcoholic drink made at home [IrGael *poitin*, dim. of *pota* pot, fr E *pot*]

potent /'poht(ə)nt/ *adj* 1 having or wielding force, authority, or influence; powerful ⟨~ *arguments*⟩ 2 achieving or bringing about a particular result; effective 3 chemically or medicinally effective ⟨*a* ~ *vaccine*⟩ 4 producing an esp unexpectedly powerful reaction; strong ⟨*this whisky is* ~ *stuff*⟩ 5 *esp of a male* able to have sexual intercourse [ME (Sc), fr L *potent-*, *potens*, fr prp of (assumed) L *potēre* to be powerful, fr L *potis*, *pote* able; akin to Goth *brūthfaths* bridegroom, Gk *posis* husband, Skt *pati* master] – **potently** *adv*, **potence** /-t(ə)ns/ *n*, **potency** *n*

potentate /'poht(ə)nˌtayt/ *n* one who wields controlling power

¹**potential** /pə'tensh(ə)l/ *adj* 1 existing in possibility; capable of being made real ⟨~ *benefits*⟩ 2 of or constituting a verb phrase expressing possibility [ME, fr LL *potentialis*, fr *potentia* potentiality, fr L, power, fr *potent-*, *potens*] – **potentially** *adv*

²**potential** *n* 1 sthg that can develop or become actual; possible capacity or value ⟨*a* ~ *for violence*⟩ 2 **potential, potential difference** the difference between the voltages at 2 points (e g in an electrical circuit or in an electrical field) ☞ PHYSICS

potential energy *n* the energy that sthg has because of its position or because of the arrangement of parts

potentiality /pəˌtenshi'aləti/ *n* POTENTIAL 1

potentiate /pə'tenshiˌayt/ *vt* to make effective or more effective; *specif* to act on (a drug or its effects) so as to produce a greater overall effect – **potentiator** *n*, **potentiation** /-'aysh(ə)n/ *n*

potentilla /ˌpoht(ə)n'tilə/ *n* any of a large genus of herbaceous plants and shrubs (e g a cinquefoil) of the rose family [NL, genus name, fr ML, garden heliotrope, fr L *potent-*, *potens*]

potentiometer /pəˌtenshi'omitə/ *n* 1 an instrument for measuring electromotive force 2 a resistor that can be tapped at any point to provide a range of potential differences from a single power source [ISV *potential* + *-o-* + *-meter*] – **potentiometric** /-shi·ə'metrik/ *adj*, **potentiometrically** *adv*

'potful /-f(ə)l/ *n* as much or as many as a pot will hold

potheen /po'cheen, po'teen/ *n* poteen

¹**pother** /'podhə/ *n* 1 a noisy disturbance; a commotion 2 needless agitation over a trivial matter; fuss [origin unknown]

²**pother** *vb* to put into or be in a pother

potherb /'potˌhuhb/ *n* a herb whose leaves or stems are cooked for use as greens; *also* one (e g parsley) used to season food

¹**'potˌhole** /-ˌhohl/ *n* 1 a circular hole worn in the rocky bed of a river by stones or gravel whirled round by the water 2 a natural vertically descending hole in the ground or in the floor of a cave; *also* a system of these usu linked by caves 3 an unwanted hole in a road surface – **potholed** *adj*

²**pothole** *vi* to explore pothole systems – **potholer** *n*

'potˌhook /-ˌhook/ *n* 1 a curved, esp S-shaped, hook for hanging or lifting pots and kettles 2 a written character resembling a pothook

'potˌhunter /-ˌhuntə/ *n* sby who shoots animals indiscriminately rather than as a sport – **pothunting** *n*

potion /'pohsh(ə)n/ *n* a mixed drink, esp of medicine, often intended to produce a specified effect ⟨*a love* ~⟩ [ME *pocioun*, fr MF *potion*, fr L *potion-*, *potio* drink, potion, fr *potus*, pp of *potare* to drink – more at POTABLE]

potlatch /'pot,lach/ *n* a ceremonial feast of N American Indians marked by the giving and receiving of lavish gifts [Chinook Jargon, fr Nootka *patshatl* giving] – **potlatch** *vb*

,pot'luck /-'luk/ *n* **1** food that is available without special preparations being made **2** whatever luck or chance brings – esp in *take potluck*

potoroo /,pohtə'rooh/ *n, pl* **potoroos** RAT KANGAROO [native name in New South Wales, Australia]

[1]**'pot,plant** *n* a plant grown in a pot, usu for ornament (e g in a house)

potpourri /,pohpə'ree, poh'pooəri/ *n* **1** a mixture of dried flowers, herbs, and spices, usu kept in a jar for its fragrance **2** a miscellaneous collection; a medley [F *pot pourri*, lit., rotten pot]

'pot,roast *n* a joint of meat cooked by braising, usu on the top of a cooker – **pot-roast** *vt*

'pot,sherd /-,shuhd/ *n* a pottery fragment [ME *pot-sherd*, fr *pot* + *sherd* shard]

'pot,shot /-,shot/ *n* **1** a shot taken in a casual manner or at an easy target **2** a critical remark made in a careless manner [fr the notion that such a shot is unsportsmanlike and worthy only of sby wishing to fill a cooking pot]

pottage /'potij/ *n* a thick soup of vegetables (and meat) – compare POTAGE [ME *potage*, fr OF, fr *pot* pot, of Gmc origin; akin to OE *pott* pot]

potted /'potid/ *adj* **1** planted or grown in a pot **2** *chiefly Br* abridged or summarized, usu in a simplified or popular form ⟨~ *biographies*⟩

[1]**potter** /'potə/ *n* one who makes pottery [ME *pottere*, fr OE, fr *pott* pot]

[2]**potter** *vi* **1** to spend time in aimless or unproductive activity – often + *around* or *about* ⟨*loves to* ~ *around at home*⟩ **2** to move or travel in a leisurely or random fashion ⟨*avoided the motorways and* ~ed *along country lanes*⟩ [prob freq of E dial. *pote* (to poke), fr ME *poten*, fr OE *potian*]

potter's field *n* a public burial place for paupers, unknown people, and criminals [fr the mention in Mt 27:7 of the purchase of a potter's field for use as a graveyard]

potter's wheel *n* a horizontal disc revolving on a vertical spindle, on which clay is shaped by a potter

pottery /'pot(ə)ri/ *n* **1** a place where ceramic ware is made and fired **2a** the art or craft of the potter **b** the manufacture of pottery **3** articles of fired clay; *esp* coarse or hand-made ceramic ware

potto /'potoh/ *n, pl* **pottos** any of several African primates; *esp* a W African primate that has a vestigial index finger and tail [of Niger-Congo origin; akin to Wolof *pata*, a tailless monkey]

[1]**potty** /'poti/ *adj, chiefly Br* **1** slightly crazy ⟨*that noise is driving me* ~⟩ **2** foolish, silly ⟨*a* ~ *idea*⟩ **3** having a great interest or liking ⟨~ *about her new boyfriend*⟩ *USE* infml [prob fr [1]*pot*] – **pottiness** *n*

[2]**potty** *n* a chamber pot, esp for a small child [[1]*pot* + [4]*-y*]

[1]**pouch** /powch/ *n* **1** a small drawstring bag carried on the person **2** a bag of small or moderate size for storing or transporting goods; *specif* a lockable bag for mail or diplomatic dispatches **3** an anatomical structure resembling a pouch: e g **a** a pocket of skin in the abdomen of marsupials for carrying their young **b** a pocket of skin in the cheeks of some rodents used for storing food **c** a loose fold of skin under the eyes **4** an arrangement of cloth (e g a pocket) resembling a pouch [ME *pouche*, fr MF, of Gmc origin; akin to OE *pocca* bag] – **pouched** *adj*

[2]**pouch** *vt* **1** to put (as if) into a pouch **2** to form (as if) into a pouch ⟨*his face was* ~ed *and lined from fatigue*⟩ ~ *vi* to form a pouch

pouf /poof, poohf/ *n* a poof

pouffe, pouf /poohf/ *n* a large stuffed cushion that serves as a low seat or footrest [F *pouf* sthg inflated, of imit origin]

Poujadism /pooh'zhah,diz(ə)m/ *n* advocacy of the political rights and interests of the petite bourgeoisie [Pierre *Poujade b* 1920 F politician] – **Poujadist** *adj or n*

[1]**poult** /pohlt/ *n* a young turkey or other fowl [ME *polet, pulte* young fowl – more at PULLET]

[2]**poult** *n* a plain-weave silk fabric with slight crosswise ribs [short for *poult-de-soie*, fr F *pou-de-soie, poult-de-soie*]

poulterer /'pohlt(ə)rə/ *n* one who deals in poultry, poultry products, or game [alter. of ME *pulter*, fr MF *pouletier*]

[1]**poultice** /'pohltis/ *n* a soft usu heated and sometimes medicated mass spread on cloth and applied to inflamed or injured parts (e g sores) [ML *pultes* pap, fr L, pl of *pult-, puls* porridge – more at [1]PULSE]

[2]**poultice** *vt* to apply a poultice to

poultry /'pohltri/ *n* domesticated birds (e g chickens) kept for eggs or meat [ME *pultrie*, fr MF *pouleterie*, fr OF, fr *pouletier* poulterer, fr *polet* – more at PULLET]

[1]**pounce** /powns/ *vi* **1** to swoop on and seize sthg (as if) with talons **2** to make a sudden assault or approach [ME *pounce* talon, sting, prob by shortening & alter. fr *punson* pointed tool, dagger, fr MF *poinçon* – more at [1]PUNCH]

[2]**pounce** *n* the act of pouncing

[3]**pounce** *n* **1** a fine powder formerly used to prevent ink from blotting **2** a fine powder for making stencilled patterns [F *ponce* pumice, fr LL *pomic-, pomex*, alter. of L *pumic-, pumex* – more at FOAM]

[1]**pound** /pownd/ *n, pl* **pounds** *also* **pound** **1** a unit of mass and weight equal to 16oz avoirdupois (about 0.453kg) ☞ UNIT **2** the basic money unit of the UK and many other countries ☞ NATIONALITY [ME, fr OE *pund*; akin to ON *pund* pound; both fr a prehistoric Gmc word borrowed fr L *pondo* pound; akin to L *pondus* weight – more at PENDANT; (2) fr its being orig a pound weight of silver]

[2]**pound** *vt* **1** to reduce to powder or pulp by beating or crushing ⟨~ *the meat to a paste*⟩ **2** to strike heavily or repeatedly ⟨~ed *the door with his fists*⟩ **3** to move or run along with heavy steps ⟨*the policeman* ~s *his beat*⟩ ~ *vi* **1** to strike heavy repeated blows ⟨~ing *angrily on the table*⟩ **2** to move with or make a dull repetitive sound ⟨*his heart was* ~ing *with fear*⟩ [alter. of ME *pounen*, fr OE *pūnian*]

[3]**pound** *n* an act or sound of pounding

[4]**pound** *n* **1** an enclosure for animals; *esp* a public enclosure for stray or unlicensed animals **2** a place for holding personal property until redeemed by the owner ⟨*a car* ~⟩ [ME, enclosure, fr OE *pund-*]

[1]**poundage** /'powndij/ *n* **1** a charge per pound of weight **2** weight in pounds

[2]**poundage** *n* impounding or being impounded

poundal /'powndl/ *n* a unit of force that gives to a mass of one pound an acceleration of one foot per second per second ☞ UNIT [*pound* + *-al* (as in *quintal*)]

pounder /'powndə/ *n* **1** one having a usu specified weight or value in pounds – usu in combination ⟨*caught a 9-*pounder *with his new fly rod*⟩ **2** a gun firing a projectile of a specified weight – in combination ⟨*the artillery were using 25-*pounders⟩

pound out *vt* to produce (as if) by striking repeated heavy blows ⟨pounded out *a story on the typewriter*⟩

,**pound 'sterling** *n* the pound used as the money unit of the UK

[1]**pour** /paw/ *vt* **1** to cause to flow in a stream ⟨~ *the dirty water down the sink*⟩ **2** to dispense (a drink) into a container ⟨~ *me a whisky*⟩ **3** to supply or produce freely or copiously ⟨*she* ~ed *money into the firm*⟩ ~ *vi* **1** to move or issue with a continuous flow and in large quantities; stream ⟨*people* ~ed *out of the offices at the end of the day*⟩ **2** to rain hard – often + *down* [ME *pouren*] – **pourable** *adj*, **pourer** *n*, **pouringly** *adv* – **pour cold water on** to be critical or unenthusiastic about ⟨*he* poured cold water on *all their proposals*⟩ – **pour oil on troubled waters** to calm or defuse a heated situation

[2]**pour** *n* sthg that is poured ⟨*a* ~ *of concrete*⟩

pour out *vt* to speak or express volubly or at length ⟨poured out *his woes*⟩

pourparler /pooə'pahlay/ *n* an informal discussion preliminary to negotiations [F]

poussin /pooh'sanh (*Fr* pusɛ̃)/ *n* a young chicken that has been reared esp for food [F, fr LL *pullicenus* young table fowl, dim. of L *pullus* young bird, young of an animal – more at FOAL]

[1]**pout** /powt/ *n, pl* **pout,** *esp for different types* **pouts** any of several large-headed fishes (e g a bullhead or eelpout) [prob fr (assumed) ME *poute*, a fish with a large head, fr OE *-pūte*; akin to ME *pouten* to pout, Skt *budbuda* bubble]

[2]**pout** *vi* **1a** to show displeasure by thrusting out the lips or wearing a sullen expression **b** to sulk **2** *of lips* to protrude ~ *vt* to cause to protrude, usu in displeasure ⟨~ed *her lips*⟩ [ME *pouten*]

[3]**pout** *n* **1** an act of pouting **2** *pl* a fit of pique – usu + *the*

pouter /'powtə/ *n* a domestic pigeon of a breed characterized by erect carriage and a distensible crop [[2]POUT + [2]-ER]

poverty /'povəti/ *n* **1a** the lack of sufficient money or material possessions **b** the renunciation of individual property by a person entering a religious order **2a** a scarcity, dearth ⟨*a* ~ *of ideas and images*⟩ **b** the condition of lacking desirable elements; deficiency ⟨*the* ~ *of our critical vocabulary*⟩ *USE* (*2*) fml [ME *poverte*, fr OF *poverté*, fr L *paupertat-, paupertas*, fr *pauper* poor – more at POOR]

'**poverty-,stricken** *adj* very poor; destitute

'**poverty ,trap** *n* a situation in which the total income of a poor family is reduced due to the loss of social security and other benefits when its earned income increases above a certain level

[1]**powder** /'powdə[r]/ *n* **1** matter reduced to a state of dry loose particles (e g by crushing or grinding) **2a** a preparation in the form of fine particles, esp for medicinal or cosmetic use **b** fine dry light snow **3** any of various solid explosives used chiefly in gunnery and blasting [ME *poudre*, fr OF, fr L *pulver-, pulvis* dust – more at POLLEN] – **powdery** *adj*

[2]**powder** *vt* **1** to sprinkle or cover (as if) with powder **2** to reduce or convert to powder ~ *vi* to become powder – **powderer** *n*

,**powder 'blue** *adj or n* pale blue [fr its being orig composed of powdered smalt]

'**powder ,horn** *n* a flask (made from horn) for carrying gunpowder

'**powder ,keg** *n* an explosive place or situation ⟨*the problem of race is a potential* ~⟩

powder metallurgy *n* the production of (metallic objects from) powdered metals

'**powder ,monkey** *n* sby who carries or has charge of explosives (e g in blasting operations) [perh fr the small size and agility of the boys known as powder monkeys employed to carry gunpowder to the guns on warships]

'**powder ,puff** *n* a small (fluffy) pad for applying powder to the skin

'**powder ,room** *n* a public toilet for women in a hotel, department store, etc

[1]**power** /'pow·ə/ *n* **1a** possession of control, authority, or influence over others **b** a sovereign state **c** a controlling group – often in *the powers that be* **2a** ability to act or produce or undergo an effect **b** legal or official authority or capacity ⟨*the police had no* ~ *to intervene*⟩ **3a** physical might **b** mental or moral efficacy; vigour ⟨*the* ~ *and insight of his analysis*⟩ **c** political control or influence ⟨*the balance of* ~⟩ **4a** the number of times, as indicated by an exponent, that a number has to be multiplied by itself ⟨*2 to the* ~ *3 is* 2^3 = *2x2x2*⟩ **b** EXPONENT 1 **5a** a source or means of supplying energy; *specif* electricity **b** the rate at which work is done or energy emitted or transferred **6** MAGNIFICATION 2 **7** a large amount *of* – infml ⟨*the walk did him a* ~ *of good*⟩ *USE* (*5*) ☞ PHYSICS [ME, fr OF *poeir*, fr *poeir* to be able, fr (assumed) L *potēre* to be powerful – more at POTENT]

[2]**power** *vt* **1** to supply with esp motive power **2** to make (one's way) in a powerful and vigorous manner ⟨~ed *her way to the top*⟩ ~ *vi* to move in a powerful and rigorous manner ⟨~ing *down the back straight*⟩

[3]**power** *adj* driven by a motor ⟨*a* ~ *saw*⟩ ⟨*a* ~ *mower*⟩

'**power ,cut** *n* a failure in or reduction of the supply of electric power to an area

'**power ,dive** *n* a dive of an aircraft accelerated by the power of the engine – **power-dive** *vi*

'**powerful** /-f(ə)l/ *adj* having great power, prestige, or influence – **powerfully** *adv*

'**power,house** /-,hows/ *n* **1** POWER STATION **2** a dynamic individual of great physical or mental force

'**powerless** /-lis/ *adj* **1** devoid of strength or resources; helpless **2** lacking the authority or capacity to act ⟨*the police were* ~ *to intervene*⟩ – **powerlessly** *adv*, **powerlessness** *n*

power of attorney *n* a legal document authorizing one to act as the agent of the grantor

'**power ,pack** *n* a unit for converting a power supply (e g mains electricity) to a voltage suitable for an electronic circuit

'**power ,plant** *n* **1** POWER STATION **2** an engine and related parts supplying the motive power of a self-propelled object

'power ,point *n, Br* a set of terminals that are connected to the electric mains and to which an electrical device may be connected

power politics *n pl but sing or pl in constr* international politics characterized by attempts to advance national interests by force

power series *n* an infinite series whose terms are successive integral powers of a variable multiplied by constants

'power ,station *n* an electricity generating station ☞ ENERGY

power take-off *n* a supplementary mechanism enabling the engine power to be used to operate a separate apparatus

[1]**powwow** /'pow,wow/ *n* **1** a N American Indian medicine man **2** a N American Indian ceremony **3** a meeting for discussion – infml [of Algonquian origin; akin to Natick *pauwau* conjurer]

[2]**powwow** *vi* to hold a powwow

pox /poks/ *n, pl* **pox, poxes** **1** a virus disease (e g chicken pox) characterized by eruptive spots **2** syphilis – infml **3** *archaic* smallpox **4** *archaic* a disastrous evil; a plague ⟨*a ~ on him*⟩ [alter. of *pocks*, pl of *pock*]

poxy /'poksi/ *adj* awful, disgusting – slang [POX + [1]-Y]

pozzolana /,potsə'lahnə/ *n* volcanic ash used in making hydraulic cement [It *pozz(u)olana*, fr *pozz(u)olana*, fem of *pozz(u)olano* of Pozzuoli, fr *Pozzuoli*, town near Naples in Italy] – **pozzolanic** /-'lanik/ *adj*

pozzuolana /,potswə'lahnə/ *n* pozzolana

praam /pram, prahm/ *n* [1]PRAM

practicable /'praktikəbl/ *adj* **1** capable of being carried out; feasible **2** usable ⟨*the road was ~ despite the weather conditions*⟩ [modif of F *praticable*, fr MF, fr *pratiquer* to practise, put into practice] – **practicableness** *n*, **practicably** *adv*, **practicability** /,praktikə'biləti/ *n*

[1]**practical** /'praktikl/ *adj* **1a** of or manifested in practice or action ⟨*for all ~ purposes*⟩ **b** being such in practice or effect; virtual ⟨*a ~ failure*⟩ **2** capable of being put to use or account; useful ⟨*he had a ~ knowledge of French*⟩ **3** suitable for use ⟨*a table of ~ design*⟩ **4a** disposed to or capable of positive action as opposed to speculation; *also* prosaic **b** qualified by practice or practical training ⟨*a good ~ mechanic*⟩ [LL *practicus*, fr Gk *praktikos*, fr *prassein* to pass over, fare, do; akin to Gk *peran* to pass through – more at [1]FARE] – **practicalness** *n*, **practicality** /,prakti'kaləti/ *n*

[2]**practical** *n* a practical examination or lesson

,practical 'joke *n* a trick or prank played on sby to derive amusement from his/her discomfiture – **practical joker** *n*

practically /'praktikli/ *adv* almost, nearly ⟨~ *everyone went to the party*⟩ [[1] PRACTICAL + [2]-LY]

practice, *NAm also* **practise** /'praktis/ *n* **1a** actual performance or application ⟨*ready to carry out in ~ what she advocated in principle*⟩ **b** a repeated or customary action; a habit ⟨*he made a ~ of going to bed early*⟩ **c** the usual way of doing sthg ⟨*it's wise to conform to local ~*s⟩ **d** the established method of conducting legal proceedings **e** dealings, conduct – esp in *sharp practice* **2** (an instance of) regular or repeated exercise in order to acquire proficiency; *also* proficiency or experience gained in this way ⟨*must get back into ~*⟩ **3a** the continuous exercise of a profession, esp law or medicine **b** a professional business [fr *practise*, vb (by analogy to *advice* : *advise*)]

practise, *NAm chiefly* **practice** /'praktis/ *vt* **1** to perform or work at repeatedly so as to become proficient ⟨~d *the drums every day*⟩ **2a** to apply; CARRY OUT 1 ⟨~ *what he preaches*⟩ **b** to make a habit or practice of **c** to be professionally engaged in ⟨~ *medicine*⟩ ~ *vi* **1** to exercise repeatedly so as to achieve proficiency **2** to pursue a profession actively ⟨~s *as a lawyer*⟩ [ME *practisen*, fr MF *practiser*, fr *practique, pratique* practice, fr LL *practice*, fr Gk *praktikē*, fr fem of *praktikos*] – **practiser** *n*

[1]**practised,** *NAm chiefly* **practiced** *adj* **1** experienced, skilled **2** learned by practice – often derog ⟨*a ~ smile*⟩

practitioner /prak'tish(ə)nə/ *n* **1** one who practises a profession, esp law or medicine ⟨*a legal ~*⟩ **2** one who practises a skill or art – sometimes derog ⟨*a ~ of fiction*⟩ [alter. of earlier *practician*, fr ME (Sc) *pratician*, fr MF *practicien*, fr *pratique*]

praedial, predial /'preedi·əl/ *adj* of land or its products – fml [ML *praedialis*, fr L *praedium* landed property, fr *praed-, praes* bondsman]

praemunire /,preemyoo'nie·əri/ *n* an offence against the Crown orig committed by asserting papal supremacy in England [ME *praemunire facias*, fr ML, that you cause to warn; fr prominent words in the writ]

praesidium /pri'sidi·əm, -'zidi-/ *n* a presidium

praetor, *chiefly NAm* **pretor** /'preetə/ *n* an ancient Roman magistrate ranking below a consul [ME *pretor*, fr L *praetor*] – **praetorship** *n*, **praetorial** /pree'tawri·əl/ *adj*

praetorian /pree'tawri·ən/ *adj, often cap* of the Roman imperial bodyguard – **praetorian** *n, often cap*

pragmatic /prag'matik/ *adj* concerned with practicalities or expediency rather than theory or dogma; realistic [L *pragmaticus* skilled in law or business, fr Gk *pragmatikos*, fr *pragmat-, pragma* deed, fr *prassein* to do – more at PRACTICAL] – **pragmatically** *adv*

pragmatic sanction *n* a solemn decree of a sovereign on a matter of primary importance (e g the regulation of the succession) that has the force of fundamental law

pragmatism /'pragmə,tiz(ə)m/ *n* **1** a practical approach to problems and affairs ⟨*tried to strike a balance between principles and ~*⟩ **2** an American philosophical movement asserting that the meaning or truth of a concept depends on its practical consequences – **pragmatist** *adj or n*, **pragmatistic** /,pragmə'tistik/ *adj*

prairie /'preəri/ *n* an extensive area of level or rolling (practically) treeless grassland, esp in N America ☞ PLANT [F, fr (assumed) VL *prataria*, fr L *pratum* meadow; akin to L *pravus* crooked, MIr *rāth* earthworks]

prairie oyster *n* a raw egg (yolk) beaten with seasonings and swallowed whole, esp as a remedy for an alcoholic hangover

[1]**praise** /prayz/ *vt* **1** to express a favourable judgment of; commend **2** to glorify or extol (e g God or a god) [ME *praisen*, fr MF *preisier* to prize, praise, fr LL *pretiare* to prize, fr L *pretium* price – more at PRICE] – **praiser** *n*

[2]**praise** *n* **1** expression of approval; commendation ⟨*won high* ~ *for her efforts*⟩ **2** worship

'praise,worthy /-,wuhdhi/ *adj* laudable, commendable – **praiseworthily** *adv*, **praiseworthiness** *n*

Prakrit /'prahkrit/ *n* any of the ancient or modern Indic languages or dialects other than Sanskrit [Skt *prākṛta*, fr *prākṛta* natural]

praline /'prahleen/ *n* (sthg, esp a powder or paste, made from) a confection of nuts, esp almonds, caramelized in boiling sugar [F, fr Count Plessis-*Praslin* †1675 F soldier, whose cook invented it]

[1]**pram, praam** /pram, prahm/ *n* a small lightweight nearly flat-bottomed boat with a broad transom and usu squared-off bow [D *praam*; akin to MLG *prām* pram]

[2]**pram** /pram/ *n, chiefly Br* a usu 4-wheeled carriage for 1 or 2 babies that is pushed by a person on foot [by shortening & alter. fr *perambulator*]

[1]**prance** /prahns/ *vi* **1** *esp of a horse* to spring from the hind legs or move by so doing **2** to walk or move in a gay, lively, or haughty manner [ME *prauncen*] – **prancer** *n*, **prancingly** *adv*

[2]**prance** *n* a prancing movement

prandial /'prandyəl/ *adj* of a meal [L *prandium* late breakfast, luncheon]

prang /prang/ *vt* to crash or damage a vehicle or aircraft – slang; no longer in vogue [imit] – **prang** *n*

prank /prangk/ *n* a mildly mischievous act; a trick [obs *prank* (to play tricks)]

prankster /'prangkstə/ *n* one who plays pranks

prase /prayz/ *n* a translucent leek-green gem-quartz [F, fr L *prasius*, fr Gk *prasios*, fr *prasios*, adj, leek green, fr *prason* leek; akin to L *porrum* leek]

praseodymium /,prayzi·oh'dimi·əm/ *n* a trivalent metallic element of the rare-earth group ☞ PERIODIC TABLE [NL, alter. of *pra seodidymium*, irreg fr Gk *prasios*, adj + NL *didymium*]

prat /prat/ *n, Br* a foolish or contemptible person – slang [prob fr *prat* (buttocks)]

prate /prayt/ *vi* to talk foolishly and excessively *about*; chatter ⟨*he* ~d *on about his new car*⟩ [ME *praten*, fr MD; akin to MLG *pratten* to pout] – **prater** *n*, **pratingly** *adv*

pratie /'prayti/ *n, chiefly Irish* a potato [by alter.]

pratincole /'prating,kohl/ *n* any of a genus of Old World wading birds [deriv of L *pratum* meadow + *incola* inhabitant, fr *in-* + *colere* to cultivate – more at PRAIRIE, WHEEL]

pratique /'prateek/ *n* clearance given to an incoming ship by the health authority of a port [F, lit., practice – more at PRACTISE]

[1]**prattle** /'pratl/ *vi* **prattling** /'pratling/ to chatter in an artless or childish manner [LG *pratelen*; akin to MD *praten* to prate] – **prattler** *n*, **prattlingly** *adv*

[2]**prattle** *n* idle or childish talk

prau /prow/ *n* a proa

prawn /prawn/ *n* any of numerous widely distributed edible 10-legged crustaceans that resemble large shrimps [ME *prane*]

praxis /'praksis/ *n, pl* **praxes** /-seez/ **1** exercise or practice of an art, science, or skill, as opposed to theory **2** customary practice or conduct – fml [ML, fr Gk, doing, action, fr *prassein* to pass through, practise – more at PRACTICAL]

pray /pray/ *vt* to entreat, implore – often used to introduce a question, request, or plea; fml ⟨~ *tell me*⟩ ~ *vi* **1** to request earnestly or humbly **2** to address prayers to God or a god [ME *prayen*, fr OF *preier*, fr L *precari*, fr *prec-*, *prex* request, prayer; akin to OHG *frāgēn* to ask, Skt *pṛcchati* he asks] – **prayer** /'prayə/ *n*

prayer /preə/ *n* **1a(1)** an address to God or a god in word or thought, with a petition, confession, thanksgiving, etc **(2)** a set order of words used in praying **b** an earnest request **2** the act or practice of praying **3** a religious service consisting chiefly of prayers – often pl with sing. meaning **4** sthg prayed for **5** a slight chance ⟨*tried hard but didn't have a* ~⟩ – infml [ME, fr OF *preiere*, fr ML *precaria*, fr L, fem of *precarius* obtained by entreaty, fr *prec-*, *prex*] – **prayerful** *adj*

prayer book *n* a book containing directions for worship; *specif, often cap P&B* the official service book of the Anglican church

prayer mat *n* a small Oriental rug used by Muslims to kneel on when praying

prayer shawl *n* a tallith

prayer wheel *n* a revolving cylinder to which written prayers may be attached, used by Tibetan Buddhists

,praying 'mantis /'praying/ *n* a (large green) mantis [fr its posture, with forelimbs extended as if in prayer]

pre- /,pree-, pri-/ *prefix* **1a(1)** earlier than; prior to ⟨*Pre cambrian*⟩ ⟨*prehistoric*⟩; *specif* immediately preceding ⟨*preadolescence*⟩ **(2)** preparatory or prerequisite to ⟨*premedical*⟩ **b** in advance; beforehand ⟨*precancel*⟩ ⟨*prefabricate*⟩ **2** situated in front of; anterior to ⟨*preaxial*⟩ ⟨*premolar*⟩ [ME, fr OF & L; OF, fr L *prae-*, fr *prae* in front of, before – more at FOR]

preach /preech/ *vi* **1** to deliver a sermon **2** to urge acceptance or abandonment of an idea or course of action, esp in an officious manner ~ *vt* **1** to set forth in a sermon **2** to advocate earnestly ⟨~ed *revolution*⟩ **3** to deliver (e g a sermon) publicly [ME *prechen*, fr OF *prechier*, fr LL *praedicare*, fr L, to proclaim publicly, fr *prae-* pre- + *dicare* to proclaim – more at DICTION] – **preacher** *n*, **preachingly** *adv*

preamble /'pree,ambl/ *n* **1** an introductory statement; *specif* that of a constitution or statute **2** an introductory or preliminary fact or circumstance [ME, fr MF *preambule*, fr ML *preambulum*, fr LL, neut of *praeambulus* walking in front of, fr L *prae-* + *ambulare* to walk]

,pre'amplifier /-'amplifie·ə/ *n* an amplifier used to amplify and often to equalize a relatively weak signal (e g from a microphone or gramophone pick-up) before feeding it to the main amplifier

,prear'range /-ə'raynj/ *vt* to arrange beforehand ⟨*at a* ~d *signal*⟩ – **prearrangement** *n*

,prea'tomic /-ə'tomik/ *adj* of a time before the use of the atom bomb and atomic energy

prebend /'prebənd/ *n* (a clergyman receiving) a stipend furnished by a cathedral or collegiate church to a member of its chapter [ME *prebende*, fr MF, fr ML *praebenda*, fr LL, subsistence allowance granted by the state, fr L, fem of *praebendus*, gerundive of *praebēre* to offer, fr *prae-* + *habēre* to hold – more at GIVE] – **prebendal** /pri'bendl/ *adj*

prebendary /'prebənd(ə)ri/ *n* a canon in a cathedral chapter, often in receipt of a prebend

prebiological /,preebie·ə'lojikl/ *adj* of or being

chemical or environmental precursors of the origin of life ⟨~ *molecules*⟩

,prebi'otic /-bie'otik/ *adj* prebiological

,Pre'cambrian /-'kambri·ən/ *adj or n* (of or being) the earliest era of geological history equivalent to the Archaeozoic and Proterozoic eras ☞ EVOLUTION

precarious /pri'keəri·əs/ *adj* **1** dependent on chance or uncertain circumstances; doubtful **2** characterized by a lack of security or stability; dangerous [L *precarius* obtained by entreaty, uncertain – more at PRAYER] – **precariously** *adv*, **precariousness** *n*

precast /,pree'kahst/ *adj* being concrete that is cast in the form of a panel, beam, etc before being placed in final position

precative /'prekətiv/ *adj* of or being a verb form expressing a wish [LL *precativus* precatory, beseeching, fr L *precatus*, pp of *precari* to pray – more at PRAY]

precatory /'prekət(ə)ri/ *adj* expressing a wish – fml [LL *precatorius*, fr *precatus*, pp]

precaution /pri'kawsh(ə)n/ *n* **1** care taken in advance; foresight ⟨*warned of the need for* ~⟩ **2** a measure taken beforehand to avoid possible harmful or undesirable consequences; a safeguard [F *précaution*, fr LL *praecaution-*, *praecautio*, fr L *praecautus*, pp of *praecavēre* to guard against, fr *prae-* + *cavēre* to be on one's guard – more at HEAR] – **precautionary** *adj*

precede /pri'seed/ *vt* **1** to surpass in rank, dignity, or importance **2** to be, go, or come ahead or in front of **3** to be earlier than **4** to cause to be preceded; preface ⟨*he* ~d *his address with a welcome to the visitors*⟩ ~ *vi* to go or come before [ME *preceden*, fr MF *preceder*, fr L *praecedere*, fr *prae-* pre- + *cedere* to go – more at CEDE] – **preceding** *adj*

precedence /'presid(ə)ns/ *also* **precedency** /-d(ə)nsi/ *n* **1** the fact of preceding in time **2** the right to superior honour on a ceremonial or formal occasion **3** priority of importance; preference

[1]**precedent** /pri'seed(ə)nt, 'presid(ə)nt/ *adj* prior in time, order, arrangement, or significance [ME, fr MF, fr L *praecedent-*, *praecedens*, prp of *praecedere*]

[2]**precedent** /'presid(ə)nt/ *n* **1** an earlier occurrence of sthg similar **2** sthg done or said that may serve as an example or rule to justify a similar subsequent act or statement; *specif* a judicial decision that serves as a rule for subsequent similar cases

precentor /pri'sentə/ *n* **1** a leader of the singing of a choir or congregation **2** the officer of a church, esp a cathedral, who directs choral services [LL *praecentor*, fr L *praecentus*, pp of *praecinere* to sing before, fr *prae-* + *canere* to sing – more at CHANT] – **precentorship** *n*, **precentorial** /,preesen'tawri·əl/ *adj*

precept /'preesept/ *n* a command or principle intended as a general rule of conduct [ME, fr L *praeceptum*, fr neut of *praeceptus*, pp of *praecipere* to take beforehand, instruct, fr *prae-* + *capere* to take – more at HEAVE] – **preceptive** /pri'septiv/ *adj*

preceptor /pri'septə/, *fem* **preceptress** /-tris/ *n* a teacher, tutor – **preceptorial** /,preesep'tawri·əl/ *adj*

precess /pri'ses/ *vb* to (cause to) progress with a movement of precession [back-formation fr *precession*]

precession /pri'sesh(ə)n/ *n* a slow movement of the axis of rotation of a spinning body about another line intersecting it caused by the application of a turning force tending to change the direction of the axis of rotation [NL *praecession-*, *praecessio*, fr ML, act of preceding, fr L *praecessus*, pp of *praecedere* to precede] – **precessional** *adj*

precession of the equinoxes *n* the slow westward motion of the equinoctial points along the ecliptic causing the earlier occurrence of the equinoxes in each successive sidereal year

,pre-'Christian *adj* before the beginning of the Christian era

precinct /'preesingkt/ *n* **1a** an enclosure bounded by the walls of a building – often pl with sing. meaning **b** *pl* the region immediately surrounding a place; environs **c** the boundary – often pl with sing. meaning ⟨*a ruined tower within the* ~s *of the squire's grounds* – T L Peacock⟩ **2** an area of a town or city containing a shopping centre and not allowing access to traffic ⟨*a shopping* ~⟩ **3** *NAm* an administrative district for election purposes or police control [ME, fr ML *praecinctum*, fr L, neut of *praecinctus*, pp of *praecingere* to gird about, fr *prae-* pre- + *cingere* to gird – more at CINCTURE]

preciosity /,pres(h)i'osəti/ *n* (an instance of) fastidious or excessive refinement (e g in language)

[1]**precious** /'preshəs/ *adj* **1** of great value or high price ⟨~ *stone*⟩ **2** highly esteemed or cherished; dear ⟨*his friendship was* ~ *to her*⟩ **3** excessively refined; affected **4** highly valued but worthless – used as an intensive ⟨*you can keep your* ~ *Costa Brava: I prefer Blackpool!*⟩ [ME, fr OF *precios*, fr L *pretiosus*, fr *pretium* price – more at PRICE] – **preciously** *adv*, **preciousness** *n*

[2]**precious** *adv* very, extremely ⟨*has* ~ *little to say*⟩

[3]**precious** *n* a dear one; darling ⟨*my* ~⟩

precipice /'presipis/ *n* **1** a very steep, perpendicular, or overhanging surface (e g of a rock or mountain) **2** the brink of disaster [MF, fr L *praecipitium*, fr *praecipit-*, *praeceps* headlong, fr *prae-* + *caput* head – more at HEAD]

precipitant /pri'sipit(ə)nt/ *adj* unduly hasty or sudden; precipitate [F *précipitant*, fr L *praecipitant-*, *praecipitans*, prp of *praecipitare*] – **precipitance** *n*, **precipitancy** *n*, **precipitantly** *adv*, **precipitantness** *n*

[1]**precipitate** /pri'sipitayt/ *vt* **1** to throw violently; hurl **2** to bring about suddenly, unexpectedly, or too soon ⟨*the failure of government policy* ~d *a general election*⟩ **3a** to cause to separate from solution or suspension **b** to cause (vapour) to condense and fall as rain, snow, etc ~ *vi* **1** to separate from solution or suspension **2** to fall as rain, snow, etc [L *praecipitatus*, pp of *praecipitare*, fr *praecipit-*, *praeceps*] – **precipitable** *adj*, **precipitator** *n*, **precipitative** /-tətiv/ *adj*

[2]**precipitate** /pri'sipitət/ *n* a substance separated from a solution or suspension by chemical or physical change, usu as an insoluble amorphous or crystalline solid [NL *praecipitatum*, fr L, neut of *praecipitatus*]

[3]**precipitate** /pri'sipitət/ *adj* **1** exhibiting violent or undue haste ⟨*a* ~ *departure*⟩ **2** lacking due care or consideration; rash – **precipitately** *adv*, **precipitateness** *n*

precipitation /pri,sipi'taysh(ə)n/ *n* **1** a precipitating or the forming of a precipitate **2** (the amount of) a deposit of rain, snow, hail, etc on the earth **3** a precipitate

precipitous /pri'sipitəs/ *adj* **1** PRECIPITATE 1 **2** resembling a precipice, esp in being dangerously steep or perpendicular [F *précipiteux*, fr MF, fr L *precipitium* precipice] – **precipitously** *adv*, **precipitousness** *n*

1**précis** /'praysee/ *n, pl* **précis** a concise summary of essential points, facts, etc [F, fr *précis* precise]

2**précis** *vt* **précising** /'praysi·ing/; **précised** /'praysid/ to make a précis of; summarize

precise /pri'sies/ *adj* **1** exactly or sharply defined or stated ⟨~ *images*⟩ **2** highly exact ⟨~ *timing*⟩ **3** strictly conforming to a rule, convention, etc; punctilious **4** distinguished from every other; very ⟨*at that ~ moment*⟩ [MF *precis*, fr L *praecisus*, pp of *praecidere* to cut off, fr *prae-* + *caedere* to cut – more at CONCISE] – **precisely** *adv*, **preciseness** *n*

1**precision** /pri'sizh(ə)n/ *n* **1** being precise; exactness **2** the degree of refinement with which an operation is performed or a measurement stated – **precisionist** *n*

2**precision** *adj* **1** adapted for extremely accurate measurement or operation ⟨~ *instruments*⟩ **2** marked by precision of execution ⟨~ *bombing*⟩

preclinical /,pree'klinikl/ *adj* **1** of a period before symptoms appear **2** of or being a medical student's period of theoretical study before patients are encountered – **preclinical** *n*

preclude /pri'kloohd/ *vt* **1** to make ineffectual or impracticable; exclude **2** to make impossible; prevent [L *praecludere*, fr *prae-* + *claudere* to close – more at 4CLOSE] – **preclusion** /-'kloohzh(ə)n/ *n*, **preclusive** /'kloohsiv/ *adj*, **preclusively** *adv*

precocial /pri'kohsh(ə)l/ *adj, of a bird* (having young) capable of a high degree of independent activity from birth ⟨*ducklings are ~*⟩ – compare ALTRICIAL [NL *praecoces* precocial birds, fr L, pl of *praecoc-, praecox*]

precocious /pri'kohshəs/ *adj* **1** exceptionally early in development or occurrence **2** exhibiting mature qualities at an unusually early age [L *praecoc-, praecox* early ripening, precocious, fr *prae-* + *coquere* to cook – more at COOK] – **precociously** *adv*, **precociousness** *n*, **precocity** /pri'kosəti/ *n*

precognition /,preekog'nish(ə)n/ *n* clairvoyance relating to a future event [LL *praecognition-, praecognitio*, fr L *praecognitus*, pp of *praecognoscere* to know beforehand, fr *prae-* + *cognoscere* to know – more at COGNITION] – **precognitive** /-'kognitiv/ *adj*

,pre'conceive /-kən'seev/ *vt* to form (e g an opinion) prior to actual knowledge or experience

,precon'ception /-kən'sepsh(ə)n/ *n* **1** a preconceived idea **2** a prejudice

,precon'cert /-kən'suht/ *vt* to organize beforehand; prearrange ⟨*her little plans and* ~ed *speeches had all left her* – George Eliot⟩

,precon'dition /-kən'dish(ə)n/ *n* a prerequisite

,pre'conscious /-'konshəs/ *adj* not present in consciousness but capable of being readily recalled – **preconsciously** *adv*

precursor /pri'kuhsə/ *n* **1a** sby or sthg that precedes and signals the approach of sby or sthg else; a forerunner **b** a predecessor **2** a substance from which another substance is formed [L *praecursor*, fr *praecursus*, pp of *praecurrere* to run before, fr *prae-* pre- + *currere* to run – more at CAR]

precursory /pri'kuhs(ə)ri/ *adj* having the character of a precursor; preliminary

predacious, predaceous /pri'dayshəs/ *adj* living by preying on other animals; predatory [L *praedari* to prey upon (fr *praeda* prey) + E *-aceous* or *-acious* (as in *rapacious*)]

predate /,pree'dayt/ *vt* to antedate

predation /pri'daysh(ə)n/ *n* **1** the act of preying or plundering; depredation **2** a mode of life of certain animals in which food is primarily obtained by the killing and consuming of other animals ☞ FOOD [L *praedation-, praedatio*, fr *praedatus*, pp of *praedari*] – **predator** /'predətə/ *n*

predatory /'predət(ə)ri/ *adj* **1a** of or carrying out plunder or robbery **b** showing a disposition to injure or exploit others for one's own gain **2** living by predation; predacious; *also* adapted to predation – **predatorily** *adv*

predecease /,preedi'sees/ *vt* to die before (another person) – **predecease** *n*

predecessor /'preedi,sesə/ *n* **1** the previous occupant of a position or office to which another has succeeded **2** an ancestor [ME *predecessour*, fr MF *predecesseur*, fr LL *praedecessor*, fr L *prae-* pre- + *decessor* retiring governor, fr *decessus*, pp of *decedere* to depart, retire from office – more at DECEASE]

,predesti'narian /-desti'neəri·ən/ *n* a person who believes in predestination [*predestination* + *-arian*] – **predestinarian** *adj*, **predestinarianism** *n*

1**,pre'destinate** /-'destinət/ *adj* destined or determined beforehand [ME, fr L *praedestinatus*, pp of *praedestinare*]

2**,pre'destinate** /-'destinayt/ *vt* to predestine [ME *predestinaten*, fr L *praedestinatus*, pp] – **predestinator** *n*

,predesti'nation /-desti'naysh(ə)n/ *n* the doctrine of God's foreknowledge of all events; *esp* the doctrine that salvation or damnation is foreordained

,pre'destine /-'destin/ *vt* to destine or determine (e g damnation or salvation) beforehand [ME *predestinen*, fr MF or L; MF *predestiner*, fr L *praedestinare*, fr *prae-* + *destinare* to determine – more at DESTINE]

,prede'termine /-di'tuhmin/ *vt* **1** to determine or arrange beforehand ⟨*at a* ~d *signal*⟩ **2** to impose a direction or tendency on beforehand [LL *praedeterminare*, fr L *prae-* + *determinare* to determine] – **predetermination** /-di,tuhmi'naysh(ə)n/ *n*

,prede'terminer /-di'tuhminə/ *n* a limiting noun modifier (e g *both* or *twice*) occurring before the determiner in a noun phrase

predial /'preedyəl/ *adj* praedial

predicable /'predikəbl/ *adj* capable of being asserted [ML *praedicabilis*, fr LL *praedicare* to predicate]

predicament /pri'dikəmənt/ *n* a (difficult, perplexing, or trying) situation [ME, category of predication, fr LL *praedicamentum*, fr *praedicare*]

1**predicate** /'predikət/ *n* **1** sthg that is stated or denied of the subject in a logical proposition **2** the part of a sentence or clause that expresses what is said of the subject [LL *praedicatum*, fr neut of *praedicatus*]

2**predicate** /'predikayt/ *vt* **1** to affirm, declare **2** to assert to be a quality or property ⟨~s *intelligence of man*⟩ **3** to imply **4** *chiefly NAm* BASE 2 – usu + *on* or *upon* ⟨*his theory is* ~d *on recent findings*⟩ *USE* chiefly fml [LL *praedicatus*, pp of *praedicare* to assert, predicate logically, preach, fr L, to proclaim publicly, assert – more at PREACH]

predication /ˌpredi'kaysh(ə)n/ *n* **1** the expression of action, state, or quality by a grammatical predicate **2** the affirmation of a predicate in logic [[2]PREDICATE + -ION]

predicative /pri'dikətiv/ *adj* **1** of a predicate **2** joined to a modified noun by a copula (e g *red* in *the dress is red*) – compare ATTRIBUTIVE – **predicatively** *adv*

predict /pri'dikt/ *vt* to declare in advance; *esp* to foretell (sthg) on the basis of observation, experience, or scientific reason [L *praedictus*, pp of *praedicere*, fr *prae-* pre- + *dicere* to say – more at DICTION] – **predictable** *adj*, **predictably** *adv*, **predictor** *n*, **predictability** /-tə'biləti/ *n*

prediction /pri'diksh(ə)n/ *n* sthg that is predicted; a forecast [PREDICT + -ION] – **predictive** /-tiv/ *adj*, **predictively** *adv*

predigest /ˌpreedi'jest, -die-/ *vt* to prepare (e g food or a book) in an easier form (for consumption) – **predigestion** /-chən/ *n*

predilection /preedi'leksh(ə)n, pre-/ *n* a liking, preference ⟨*has a ~ for classical music*⟩ [F *prédilection*, fr ML *praedilectus*, pp of *praediligere* to love more, prefer, fr L *prae-* + *diligere* to love – more at DILIGENT]

ˌprediˈspose /-di'spohz/ *vt* **1** to incline, esp in advance ⟨*a good teacher ~s children to learn*⟩ **2** to make susceptible *to* – **predisposition** /-dispə'zish(ə)n/ *n*

prednisolone /pred'nisəˌlohn/ *n* a synthetic steroid drug that is a glucocorticoid and is used to reduce inflammation and inhibit the action of the immune system, esp in the treatment of rheumatoid arthritis [blend of *prednisone* and *-ol*]

prednisone /pred'nisohn/ *n* a synthetic drug that has similar uses to prednisolone [prob fr *pre*gnane (a saturated steroid hydrocarbon) + *d*ie*ne* (compound containing 2 double bonds) + cort*isone*]

predominant /pri'dominənt/ *adj* having superior strength, influence, or authority; prevailing [MF, fr ML *praedominant-*, *praedominans*, prp of *praedominari* to predominate, fr L *prae-* + *dominari* to rule, govern – more at DOMINATE] – **predominance** *n*, **predominantly** *adv*

predominate /pri'dominayt/ *vi* **1** to exert controlling power or influence; prevail **2** to hold advantage in numbers or quantity [ML *praedominatus*, pp of *praedominari*] – **predomination** /-'naysh(ə)n/ *n*

ˌpre-eˈclampsia /e'klampsi·ə/ *n* a serious abnormal condition that develops in late pregnancy and is characterized by a sudden rise in blood pressure and generalized oedema

preeminent /pri'eminənt/ *adj* excelling all others; paramount [LL *praeeminent-*, *praeeminens*, fr L, prp of *praeeminēre* to be outstanding, fr *prae-* + *eminēre* to stand out – more at EMINENT] – **preeminence** *n*, **preeminently** *adj*

preempt /pri'empt/ *vt* **1** to acquire by preemption **2** to seize on to the exclusion of others; appropriate ⟨*the movement was then ~ed by a lunatic fringe*⟩ **3** to take the place of; replace **4** to invalidate or render useless by taking action or appearing in advance ⟨*the government decision to build an airport ~ed the council's plans*⟩ *~vi* to make a preemptive bid in bridge [back-formation fr *preemption*] – **preemptor** *n*

preemption /pri'empsh(ə)n/ *n* **1a** the right of purchasing before others **b** a purchase under this right **2** a prior seizure or appropriation [ML *praeemptus*, pp of *praeemere* to buy before, fr L *prae-* pre- + *emere* to buy – more at REDEEM]

preemptive /pri'emptiv/ *adj* **1** (capable) of preemption **2** of or being a bid in bridge high enough to shut out bids by the opponents **3** carried out in order to forestall intended action by others ⟨*a ~ attack that disabled the enemy*⟩ – **preemptively** *adv*

preen /preen/ *vt* **1** to trim or dress (as if) with a beak **2** to dress or smarten (oneself) up **3** to pride or congratulate (oneself) *on* *~vi* **1** to smarten oneself, esp in a vain way ⟨*~ing in front of the mirror*⟩ **2** to appear to be congratulating oneself; gloat ⟨*couldn't help ~ing after his campaign victory*⟩ **3** *of a bird* to trim and arrange the feathers [ME *preinen*] – **preener** *n*

preexistence /ˌpree·ig'zist(ə)ns/ *n* existence in a former state or previous to sthg else; *esp* existence of the soul before incarnation – **preexist** *vi*, **preexistent** *adj*

prefab /'preefab/ *n* a prefabricated structure or building – **prefab** *adj*

prefabricate /pri'fabrikayt/ *vt* **1** to fabricate the parts of (e g a building) at a factory ready for assembly elsewhere **2** to produce artificially – **prefabricator** *n*, **prefabrication** /-'kaysh(ə)n/ *n*

[1]preface /'prefəs/ *n* **1** an introduction to a book, speech, etc **2** sthg that precedes or heralds; a preliminary [ME, fr MF, fr ML *prephatia*, alter. of L *praefation-*, *praefatio* foreword, fr *praefatus*, pp of *praefari* to say beforehand, fr *prae-* pre- + *fari* to say – more at [1]BAN]

[2]preface *vt* **1** to introduce *by* or provide *with* a preface **2** to be a preliminary or preface to – **prefacer** *n*

prefatory /'prefət(ə)ri/ *adj* of or constituting a preface; introductory [L *praefatus*, pp] – **prefatorily** /-t(ə)rəli/ *adv*

prefect /'preefekt/ *n* **1** any of various high officials or magistrates in ancient Rome **2** a chief officer or chief magistrate (e g in France or Italy) **3** a monitor in a secondary school, usu with some authority over other pupils [ME, fr MF, fr L *praefectus*, fr pp of *praeficere* to place at the head of, fr *prae-* + *facere* to make – more at [1]DO]

prefecture /'preefekchə/ *n* the office or official residence of a prefect – **prefectural** /-'fekchoo(ə)rəl/ *adj*

prefer /pri'fuh/ *vt* **-rr-** **1** to choose or esteem above another; like better ⟨*~s sports to reading*⟩ **2** to give (a creditor) priority **3** to bring against sby ⟨*won't ~ charges*⟩ **4** to bring forward or submit for consideration [ME *preferren*, fr MF *preferer*, fr L *praeferre* to put before, prefer, fr *prae-* + *ferre* to carry – more at [2]BEAR] – **preferrer** *n*, **preferable** /'pref(ə)rəbəl/ *adj*, **preferably** *adv*

preference /'pref(ə)rəns/ *n* **1** the power or opportunity of choosing ⟨*gave him first ~*⟩ **2** sby or sthg preferred; a choice ⟨*which is your ~?*⟩ **3** special favour or consideration ⟨*give ~ to those with qualifications*⟩ **4** priority in the settlement of an obligation [F *préférence*, fr ML *praeferentia*, fr L *praeferent-*, *praeferens*, prp of *praeferre*] – **preferential** /ˌprefə'rensh(ə)l/ *adj*, **preferentially** *adv* – **for preference** as being the more desirable; preferably ⟨*use red wine* for preference⟩

ˈpreference ˌshare *n* a share guaranteed priority over ordinary shares in the payment of dividends and usu in the distribution of assets – compare DEFERRED SHARE, ORDINARY SHARE

preferment /pri'fuhmənt/ *n* (an esp ecclesiastical appointment affording) advancement or promotion in rank, station, etc [PREFER + -MENT]

prefigure /,pree'figə/ *vt* **1** to represent or suggest in advance; foreshadow **2** to picture or imagine beforehand; foresee [ME *prefiguren*, fr LL *praefigurare*, fr L *prae-* pre- + *figurare* to shape, picture, fr *figura* figure] – **prefigurement** *n*, **prefigurative** /-'figrətiv/ *adj*, **prefiguration** /-figə'raysh(ə)n/ *n*

[1]**prefix** /'preefiks/ *vt* **1** to attach as a prefix **2** to add to the beginning ⟨~ed *a brief introduction to the article*⟩ [partly fr ME *prefixen* to fix or appoint beforehand, fr MF *prefixer*, fr *pre-* + *fixer* to fix, fr *fix* fixed, fr L *fixus* – more at FIX; partly [2]*prefix*]

[2]**prefix** *n* **1** an affix (e g *un* in *unhappy*) placed at the beginning of a word or before a root – compare INFIX, SUFFIX **2** a title used before a person's name [NL *praefixum*, fr L, neut of *praefixus*, pp of *praefigere* to fasten before, fr *prae-* + *figere* to fasten] – **prefixal** /'pree,fiksl/ *adj*, **prefixally** *adv*

preform /,pree'fawm/ *vt* to form or shape beforehand [L *praeformare*, fr *prae-* + *formare* to form, fr *forma* form] – **preform** *n*, **preformation** /,preefaw'maysh(ə)n/ *n*

preggers /'pregəz/ *adj*, *Br* PREGNANT 3 – infml [by alter.]

pregnancy /'pregnənsi/ *n* **1** the condition or quality of being pregnant ☞ REPRODUCTION **2** fertility of mind; inventiveness

pregnant /'pregnənt/ *adj* **1** full of ideas or resourcefulness; inventive **2** rich in significance or implication; meaningful ⟨*a* ~ *pause*⟩ **3** containing unborn young within the body **4** showing signs of the future; portentous ⟨*the* ~ *years of the prewar era*⟩ **5** full, teeming – usu + *with* ⟨*nature* ~ *with life*⟩ [ME, fr L *praegnant-*, *praegnans*, alter. of *praegnas*, fr *prae-* pre- + *-gnas* (akin to *gignere* to produce) – more at KIN] – **pregnantly** *adv*

prehensile /pri'hensiel, ,pree-/ *adj* adapted for seizing or grasping, esp by wrapping round ⟨*a* ~ *tail*⟩ [F *préhensile*, fr L *prehensus*, pp of *prehendere* to grasp, fr *prae-* + *-hendere* (akin to ON *geta* to get) – more at GET] – **prehensility** /,preehen'siləti/ *n*

prehension /pri'hensh(ə)n/ *n* the act of taking hold, seizing, or grasping

prehistoric /,preehi'storik/, **prehistorical** /-kl/ *adj* of or existing in times antedating written history – **prehistorically** *adv*

,pre'history /-'histəri/ *n* (the study of) the prehistoric period of human beings' evolution – **prehistorian** /-hi'stawri·ən/ *n*

,preig'nition /-ig'nish(ə)n/ *n* the premature detonation of the explosive charge in the cylinder of an internal-combustion engine

,pre'judge /-'juj/ *vt* to pass judgment on prematurely or before a full and proper examination [MF *prejuger*, fr L *praejudicare*, fr *prae-* + *judicare* to judge – more at JUDGE] – **prejudger** *n*, **prejudgment** *n*

[1]**prejudice** /'prejoodis, -jə-/ *n* **1** disadvantage resulting from disregard of one's (legal) rights **2a** (an instance of) a preconceived judgment or opinion; *esp* a biased and unfavourable one formed without sufficient reason or knowledge **b** an irrational attitude of hostility directed against an individual, group, or race [ME, fr OF, fr L *praejudicium* previous judgment, damage, fr *prae-* + *judicium* judgment – more at JUDICIAL]

[2]**prejudice** *vt* **1** to injure by some judgment or action **2** to cause (sby) to have an unreasonable bias

'**prejudiced** *adj* having a prejudice or bias in favour of or esp against

prejudicial /prejə'dish(ə)l/, **prejudicious** /-'dishəs/ *adj* **1** detrimental **2** leading to prejudiced judgments – **prejudicially** *adv*, **prejudicialness** *n*, **prejudiciously** *adv*

prelacy /'preləsi/ *n* **1** the office of a prelate **2** episcopal church government

prelate /'prelət/ *n* an ecclesiastic (e g a bishop or abbot) of high rank [ME *prelat*, fr OF, fr ML *praelatus*, lit., one receiving preferment, fr L (pp of *praeferre* to prefer), fr *prae-* + *latus*, pp of *ferre* to carry – more at TOLERATE, [2]BEAR]

prelibation /,preelie'baysh(ə)n/ *n* a foretaste – fml [L *praelibation-*, *praelibatio*, fr *praelibatus*, pp of *praelibare* to taste beforehand, fr *prae-* + *libare* to pour as an offering, taste – more at LIBATION]

prelim /'preelim/ *n* a preliminary

[1]**preliminary** /pri'limin(ə)ri/ *n* sthg that precedes or is introductory or preparatory: e g **a** a preliminary scholastic examination **b** *pl*, *Br* matter (e g a list of contents) preceding the main text of a book [F *préliminaires*, pl, fr ML *praeliminaris*, adj, preliminary, fr L *prae-* pre- + *limin-*, *limen* threshold – more at [1]LIMB]

[2]**preliminary** *adj* preceding and preparing for what is to follow; introductory – **preliminarily** *adv*

preliterate /,pree'litərət/ *adj* not yet employing writing – **preliterate** *n*

[1]**prelude** /'prelyoohd/ *n* **1** an introductory or preliminary performance, action, or event; an introduction **2a** a musical section or movement introducing the theme or chief subject or serving as an introduction (e g to an opera) **b** a short separate concert piece, usu for piano or orchestra [MF, fr ML *praeludium*, fr *praeludere* to play beforehand, fr *prae-* + *ludere* to play – more at LUDICROUS] – **preludial** /,pree'l(y)oohdi·əl, pri-/ *adj*

[2]**prelude** *vt* to serve as prelude to; foreshadow – **preluder** /'prelyoohdə/ *n*

prelusive /pri'l(y)oohsiv/, **prelusory** /pri'l(y)oohzəri/ *adj* constituting or having the form of a prelude; introductory – fml [L *praelusus*, pp of *praeludere*] – **prelusively** *adv*

preman /,pree'man, '-,-/ *n* a primate (e g Peking man) that is a direct ancestor of man

premature /'preməchə, ,premə'tyooə, 'premə,tyooə/ *adj* happening, arriving, existing, or performed before the proper or usual time; *esp, of a human* born after a gestation period of less than 37 weeks [L *praematurus* too early, fr *prae-* + *maturus* ripe, mature] – **prematureness** *n*, **prematurely** *adv*, **prematurity** /-'tyoo(ə)rəti/ *n*

premeditate /pri'meditayt, ,pree-/ *vt* to think over and plan beforehand ⟨~d *murder*⟩ [L *praemeditatus*, pp of *praemeditari*, fr *prae-* + *meditari* to meditate] – **premeditator** *n*, **premeditative** /-tətiv/ *adj*

premeditation /pri,medi'taysh(ə)n/ *n* planning of an act beforehand, as evidence of intent to commit that act [PREMEDITATE + -ION]

premenstrual /,pree'menstrooəl/ *adj* of or occurring in the period just before menstruation ⟨~ *tension*⟩ – **premenstrually** *adv*

[1]**premier** /'premyə, 'premi·ə/ *adj* **1** first in position,

rank, or importance; principal **2** first in time; earliest [ME *primier*, fr MF *premier* first, chief, fr L *primarius* of the first rank – more at PRIMARY]

[2]**premier** *n* PRIME MINISTER [F, fr *premier*, adj] – **premiership** *n*

premiere /'premi,eə, 'premi·ə/ *n* a first public performance or showing ⟨*the ~ of a play*⟩ [F *première*, fr fem of *premier* first] – **premiere** *vt*

premillennial /,preemi'leni·əl/ *adj* coming before a millennium [*pre-* + *millennium*] – **premillennially** *adv*

[1]**premise** /'premis/ *n* **1** *Br also* **premiss** a proposition taken as a basis of argument or inference; *specif* either of the first 2 propositions of a syllogism **2** *pl, Br also* **premiss** matters previously stated; *specif* the preliminary and explanatory part of a deed **3** *pl* **a** a piece of land with the buildings on it **b** (part of) a building [(1) ME *premisse*, fr MF, fr ML *praemissa*, fr L, fem of *praemissus*, pp of *praemittere* to place ahead, fr *prae-* pre- + *mittere* to send – more at SMITE; (2, 3) ME *premisses*, fr ML *praemissa*, fr L, neut pl of *praemissus*; (3) fr its being identified in the premises of the deed]

[2]**premise** *vt* **1** to state as a premise or introduction **2** to presuppose, postulate

[1]**premium** /'preemyəm, -mi·əm/ *n* **1a** a reward or recompense for a particular act **b** a sum above a fixed price or remuneration, paid chiefly as an incentive; a bonus ⟨*willing to pay a ~ for immediate delivery*⟩ **c** a sum in advance of or in addition to the nominal value of sthg **2** the sum paid for a contract of insurance **3** a high value or a value in excess of that normally expected ⟨*put a ~ on accuracy*⟩ [L *praemium* booty, profit, reward, fr *prae-* + *emere* to take, buy – more at REDEEM] – **at a premium** valuable because rare or difficult to obtain ⟨*flats in London are* at a premium⟩

[2]**premium** *adj, chiefly NAm* of exceptional quality or amount ⟨*wine made from ~ grapes*⟩

premium bond *n* a government bond that is issued in units of £1 and which instead of earning interest is entered into a monthly draw for money prizes

premolar /,pree'mohlə/ *n or adj* (a tooth) situated in front of the true molar teeth ☞ DIGESTION

premonition /,premə'nish(ə)n, ,pree-/ *n* **1** a previous notice or warning; a forewarning ⟨*a ~ of the troubles that lay in store*⟩ **2** an anticipation of an event without conscious reason; a presentiment ⟨*felt a ~ of danger*⟩ [MF, fr LL *praemonition-, praemonitio*, fr L *praemonitus*, pp of *praemonēre* to warn in advance, fr *prae-* + *monēre* to warn – more at MIND] – **premonitory** /pri'monit(ə)ri/ *adj*

Premonstratensian /,pree,monstrə'tensh(ə)n/ *n* a member of a religious order founded by St Norbert at Prémontré in France in 1120 [ML *praemonstratensis*, fr *praemonstratensis* of Prémontré, fr *Praemonstratus* Prémontré, abbey in N France]

premorse /pri'maws/ *adj* having an abrupt and ragged end as if bitten off ⟨*a ~ root*⟩ [L *praemorsus*, fr pp of *praemordēre* to bite off in front, fr *prae-* + *mordēre* to bite – more at SMART]

prenatal /,pree'naytl/ *adj* occurring or being in a stage before birth – **prenatally** *adv*

,pre'notion /-'nohsh(ə)n/ *n* a preconception [L *praenotion-, praenotio* preconception, fr *prae-* + *notio* idea, conception – more at NOTION]

preoccupation /pri,okyoo'paysh(ə)n, ,pree-/ *n* (sthg that causes) complete mental absorption [L *praeoccupation-, praeoccupatio* act of seizing beforehand, fr *praeoccupatus*, pp of *praeoccupare* to seize beforehand, fr *prae-* + *occupare* to seize, occupy]

,pre'occupied /-'okyoopied/ *adj* lost in thought; engrossed

,pre'occupy /-'okyoopie/ *vt* **1** to engage or engross the attention of to the exclusion of other things **2** to take possession of or occupy in advance or before another [*pre-* + *occupy*]

,pre'operative /-'op(ə)rətiv/ *adj* occurring in the period preceding a surgical operation – **preoperatively** *adv*

,preor'dain /-aw'dayn/ *vt* to decree or determine in advance – **preordainment** *n*, **preordination** /-awdinaysh(ə)n/ *n*

prep /prep/ *n, Br* homework done at or away from school [short for *preparation*]

prepackage /,pree'pakij/ *vt* to package (e g food) before offering for sale to the consumer

preparation /,prepə'raysh(ə)n/ *n* **1** preparing **2** a state of being prepared; readiness **3** a preparatory act or measure – usu pl ⟨*made his ~s for the journey*⟩ **4** sthg prepared; *esp* a medicine ⟨*a ~ for colds*⟩ [ME *preparacion*, fr MF *preparation*, fr L *praeparation-, praeparatio*, fr *praeparatus*, pp of *praeparare*]

preparative /pri'parətiv/ *n* sthg that prepares the way for or serves as a preliminary to sthg else

[1]**preparatory** /pri'parət(ə)ri/, **preparative** /-tiv/ *adj* preparing or serving to prepare for sthg; introductory – **preparatorily** *adv*

[2]**preparatory** *adv* by way of preparation; in a preparatory manner – usu + *to* ⟨*took a deep breath ~ to drinking*⟩

pre'paratory ,school *n* a private school preparing pupils **a** *Br* for public schools **b** *NAm* for college

prepare /pri'peə/ *vt* **1a** to make ready beforehand for some purpose, use, or activity ⟨*~ food for dinner*⟩ **b** to put into a suitable frame of mind for sthg ⟨*~d her gradually for the shocking news*⟩ **2** to work out the details of; plan in advance ⟨preparing *his strategy for the coming campaign*⟩ **3a** to put together ⟨*~ a prescription*⟩ **b** to draw up in written form ⟨*~ a report*⟩ ~ *vi* to get ready; make preparations ⟨preparing *for a career in teaching*⟩ [ME *preparen*, fr MF *preparer*, fr L *praeparare*, fr *prae-* pre- + *parare* to procure, prepare – more at PARE] – **preparer** *n*

pre'pared *adj* subjected to a special process or treatment

preparedness /pri'peə(ri)dnis/ *n* adequate preparation (in case of war) [PREPARED + -NESS]

prepay /,pree'pay/ *vt* **prepaid** to pay or pay the charge on in advance ⟨*carriage* prepaid⟩ – **prepayment** *n*

preponderant /pri'pond(ə)rənt/ *also* **preponderate** /-rət/ *adj* **1** having superior weight, force, or influence; predominant **2** occurring in greater number or quantity – **preponderance** *n*, **preponderantly** *adv*

preponderate /pri'pondərayt/ *vi* **1** to predominate in influence, power, or importance **2** to predominate in number or frequency [L *praeponderatus*, pp of *praeponderare*, fr *prae-* + *ponder-, pondus* weight – more at PENDANT] – **preponderation** /-'raysh(ə)n/ *n*

preposition /,prepə'zish(ə)n/ *n* a linguistic form (e g *by, of, for*) that combines with a noun, pronoun, or noun equivalent to form a phrase with a relation to some other word [ME *preposicioun*, fr L *praepo-*

sition-, praepositio, fr *praepositus*, pp of *praeponere* to put in front, fr *prae-* pre- + *ponere* to put – more at POSITION] – **prepositional** *adj*, **prepositionally** *adv*

prepositive /pri'pozətiv/ *adj* prefixed [LL *praepositivus* put before, fr L *praepositus*] – **prepositively** *adv*

prepossess /,preepə'zes/ *vt* to prejudice, esp in favour of sby or sthg

,prepos'sessing /-pə'zesing/ *adj* tending to create a favourable impression; attractive – **prepossessingly** *adv*, **prepossessingness** *n*

,prepos'session /-pə'zesh(ə)n/ *n* **1** an opinion or impression formed beforehand; a prejudice **2** an exclusive concern with 1 idea or object; a preoccupation

preposterous /pri'post(ə)rəs/ *adj* contrary to nature or reason; absurd; *also* ridiculous ⟨*look at that ~ outfit*⟩ [L *praeposterus*, lit., with the hindside in front, fr *prae-* + *posterus* hinder, following – more at POSTERIOR] – **preposterously** *adv*, **preposterousness** *n*

prepotent /,pree'poht(ə)nt/ *adj* having great or the most power, authority, or influence; preeminent – fml [ME, fr L *praepotent-, praepotens*, fr *prae-* + *potens* powerful – more at POTENT] – **prepotency** *n*, **prepotently** *adv*

,pre'prandial /-'prandyəl/ *adj* of or suitable for the time just before a meal ⟨*a ~ drink*⟩

,pre'print /-'print/ *n* a printing of a speech or paper before its formal publication or delivery

'prep ,school /prep/ *n* PREPARATORY SCHOOL

prepuce /'pree,pyoohs/ *n* the foreskin; *also* a similar fold surrounding the clitoris [ME, fr MF, fr L *praeputium*, fr *prae-* + *-putium* (akin to Belorussian *potka* penis)] – **preputial** /-'pyoohsh(ə)l/ *adj*

Pre-Raphaelite /,pree 'rafəliet, -fyə-/ *adj or n* (of or relating to) a member of the Pre-Raphaelite Brotherhood – **Pre-Raphaelitism** /-'raf(ə)lətiz(ə)m, -fyə-/ *n*

Pre-Raphaelite Brotherhood *n* a group of English artists formed in 1848 which aimed to restore the artistic principles and practices of the early Renaissance and whose work is characterized by richness of colour and detail and religious and legendary subjects painted from nature [*Raphael* (Raffaello Santi) †1520 It painter]

prerecord /,preeri'kawd/ *vt* to record (e g a radio or television programme) in advance of presentation or use

[1],pre-re'lease /ri'lees/ *vt* to release (e g a film or record) before the official date – **pre-release** *adj*

[2]pre-release *n* sthg pre-released; *also* a public showing of a film before its official date of release

prerequisite /pri'rekwizit/ *n* a requirement that must be satisfied in advance – **prerequisite** *adj*

prerogative /pri'rogətiv/ *n* **1** an exclusive or special right or privilege belonging esp to a person or group of people by virtue of rank or status **2** the discretionary power inhering in the Crown [ME, fr MF & L; MF, fr L *praerogativa*, Roman century voting first in one of the public assemblies, privilege, fr fem of *praerogativus* voting first, fr *praerogatus*, pp of *praerogare* to ask for an opinion before another, fr *prae-* + *rogare* to ask – more at [1]RIGHT] – **prerogatived** *adj*

[1]presage /'presij/ *n* **1** sthg that foreshadows or portends a future event; an omen **2** an intuition of what is going to happen in the future; a presentiment [ME, fr L *praesagium*, fr *praesagire* to forebode, fr *prae-* + *sagire* to perceive keenly – more at SEEK] – **presageful** *adj*

[2]presage /'presij, pri'sayj/ *vt* **1** to give an omen or warning of; portend **2** to forecast, predict **3** to have a presentiment of ~ *vi* to make or utter a prediction

presby- /prezbi-/, **presbyo-** *comb form* old age ⟨presby*opia*⟩ [NL, fr Gk *presby-* elder, fr *presbys* old man]

presbyopia /,prezbi'ohpyə/ *n* a visual condition of old age in which loss of elasticity of the lens of the eye causes defective accommodation and inability to focus sharply for near vision [NL] – **presbyopic** /-bi'opik/ *adj or n*

presbyter /'prezbitə/ *n* **1** a member of the governing body of an early Christian church **2** [1]ELDER 3 [LL, elder, priest – more at PRIEST] – **presbyterate** /-'bitərət/ *n*

presbyterial /prezbi'tiəri·əl/ *adj* of presbyters or a presbytery

[1]Presbyterian /,prezbi'tiəri·ən/ *adj* of or constituting a Christian church governed by elected representative bodies and traditionally Calvinistic in doctrine – **Presbyterianism** *n*

[2]Presbyterian *n* a member of a Presbyterian church

presbytery /'prezbit(ə)ri/ *n* **1** the part of a church (e g the E end of the chancel) reserved for the officiating clergy **2** a local ruling body in Presbyterian churches **3** the house of a Roman Catholic parish priest [ME & LL; ME *presbytory* part of church reserved for clergy, fr LL *presbyterium* group of presbyters, part of church reserved for clergy, fr Gk *presbyterion* group of presbyters, fr *presbyteros* elder, priest – more at PRIEST]

preschool /,pree'skoohl/ *adj* of the period from infancy to first attendance at primary school

prescience /'presi·əns, -sh(ə)ns, -shi·əns/ *n* foreknowledge of events; *also* foresight [ME, fr LL *praescientia*, fr L *praescient-, praesciens*, prp of *praescire* to know beforehand, fr *prae-* + *scire* to know – more at SCIENCE] – **prescient** *adj*, **presciently** *adv*

prescind /pri'sind/ *vt* to separate in the mind; abstract ~ *vi* to withdraw one's attention ***USE*** usu + *from*; fml [L *praescindere* to cut off in front, fr *prae-* + *scindere* to cut – more at [1]SHED]

prescribe /pri'skrieb/ *vi* **1** to claim a title to sthg by right of prescription **2** to lay down a rule; dictate **3** to write or give medical prescriptions ~ *vt* **1a** to ordain; LAY DOWN 2b **b** to specify with authority **2** to designate or order the use of as a remedy [L *praescribere* to write at the beginning, dictate, order, fr *prae-* + *scribere* to write – more at [1]SCRIBE; (*vi* 1) ME *prescriben*, fr ML *praescribere*, fr L, to write at the beginning] – **prescriber** *n*

prescript /pri'skript, 'pree,skript/ *n or adj* (sthg) prescribed as a rule [ME, fr L *praescriptus*, pp]

prescription /pri'skripsh(ə)n/ *n* **1** the establishment of a claim to sthg by use and enjoyment of it over a long period **2** the action of laying down authoritative rules or directions **3** a written direction or order for the preparation and use of a medicine; *also* the medicine prescribed **4** (a claim founded on) ancient or long-standing custom [partly fr ME *prescripcion* establishment of a claim, fr MF *prescrip-*

tion, fr LL *praescription-*, *praescriptio*, fr L, act of writing at the beginning, order, limitation of subject matter, fr *praescriptus*, pp of *praescribere*; partly fr L *praescription-*, *praescriptio* order]

prescriptive /pri'skriptiv/ *adj* **1** serving to prescribe **2** established by, founded on, or arising from prescription or long-standing custom **3** authoritarian as regards language use – **prescriptively** *adv*

preselector /,preesi'lektə/ *n* a system of gears (e g of a motor vehicle transmission) that can be selected in advance of use

presence /'prez(ə)ns/ *n* **1** the fact or condition of being present ⟨*requested his* ~ *at the meeting*⟩ **2a** the immediate vicinity of a specified person ⟨*never looked at ease in my* ~⟩ **b** the vicinity of one of superior, esp royal, rank ⟨*bowed before withdrawing from the* ~⟩ **3a** sby or sthg present; *also* a spirit felt to be present **b** a body of people from a specified place (e g a country), present and playing an influential role in another organization or nation ⟨*the withdrawal of the American* ~ *in Vietnam*⟩ **4a** a personal magnetism that attracts and holds the attention of others **b** a usu dignified or stately bearing or appearance **5** a quality of poise or distinction that enables a person, esp a performer, to impress, or have a strong effect on, others ⟨*she had great stage* ~⟩

presence chamber *n* the room where a great personage receives those entitled to come into his/her presence

presence of mind *n* the ability to retain one's self-possession and act calmly in emergencies or difficult situations

[1]**present** /'prez(ə)nt/ *n* sthg presented; a gift [ME, fr OF, fr *presenter*]

[2]**present** /pri'zent/ *vt* **1a** to introduce (sby) esp to another of higher rank **b** to bring (e g a play) before the public **2** to make a gift to **3** to give or bestow formally **4** to lay (e g a charge) before a court **5** to nominate (a clergyman) to a benefice **6a** to offer for show; exhibit ⟨~ *a bedraggled appearance*⟩ **b** to offer for approval or consideration ⟨~ *this report again next week in greater detail*⟩ **7** to act as a presenter of (e g a television or radio programme) **8** to act the part of **9** to level or aim (e g a weapon) ~ *vi* to come to notice or into view ⟨*the patient* ~ed *with abdominal pain*⟩ [ME *presenten*, fr OF *presenter*, fr L *praesentare*, fr *praesent-*, *praesens*, adj]

[3]**present** / pri'zent/ *n* PRESENT ARMS ⟨*his gun held at the* ~⟩

[4]**present** /'prez(ə)nt/ *adj* **1** now existing or in progress ⟨*under the* ~ *system of government*⟩ **2a** in or at a usu specified place ⟨*he wasn't* ~ *at the meeting*⟩ **b** existing in sthg mentioned or understood ⟨*methane and air had to be* ~ *in the right quantities for combustion to take place*⟩ **c** vividly felt, remembered, or imagined – usu + *to* or *in* ⟨*the events of a decade ago are still* ~ *to our minds*⟩ **3** being discussed, dealt with, or considered ⟨*as far as the* ~ *writer is concerned*⟩ **4** of or being a verb tense that expresses present time or the time of speaking [ME, fr OF, fr L *praesent-*, *praesens*, fr prp of *praeesse* to be before one, fr *prae-* pre- + *esse* to be – more at IS] – **presentness** *n*

[5]**present** /'prez(ə)nt/ *n* **1** (a verb form in) the present tense of a language **2** the present time **3** *pl* the present words or statements – fml

presentable /pri'zentəbl/ *adj* **1** fit to be seen or inspected **2** fit (e g in dress or manners) to appear in company ⟨*must make myself* ~ *for dinner*⟩ [[2]PRESENT + -ABLE] – **presentableness** *n*, **presentably** *adv*, **presentability** /tə'biləti/ *n*

present arms /pri'zent/ *n* a saluting position in which the firearm is held vertically in front of the body [fr the command *present arms!*]

presentation /,prezən'taysh(ə)n/ *n* **1a** sthg offered or given; a gift **b** sthg put forward for consideration or notice **c** a descriptive or persuasive account (e g by a salesman of a product) **2a** the manner in which sthg is set forth, laid out, or presented ⟨*his* ~ *of the argument was masterly*⟩ ⟨*the* ~ *of the final dish is important in cookery*⟩ **b** the position in which the foetus lies in the uterus in labour with respect to the mouth of the uterus **3** an immediate object of perception, cognition, or memory [[2]PRESENT + -ATION] – **presentational** *adj*

,presen'tation,ism /-,iz(ə)m/ *n* the theory that the mind is directly aware of items in the external world – compare REPRESENTATIONALISM

presentative /pri'zentətiv/ *adj* known or capable of being known directly rather than through cogitation

,present-'day /'prez(ə)nt/ *adj* now existing or occurring

presenter /pri'zentə/ *n* one who presents; *specif* a broadcaster who introduces and provides comments on broadcast material during a programme

presentient /pri'sensh(ə)nt, -ti·ənt, -zen-/ *adj* having a presentiment – fml [L *praesentient-*, *praesentiens*, prp of *praesentire*]

presentiment /pri'zentimənt/ *n* a feeling that sthg will or is about to happen; a premonition [F *pressentiment*, fr MF, fr *pressentir* to have a presentiment, fr L *praesentire* to feel beforehand, fr *prae-* + *sentire* to feel – more at SENSE] – **presentimental** /-'mentl/ *adj*

presently /'prez(ə)ntli/ *adv* **1** before long; soon **2** *chiefly NAm & Scot* at the present time; now

presentment /pri'zentmənt/ *n* **1** the act of presenting a formal statement to an authority; *specif* a statement made on oath by a jury of a matter of fact within their own knowledge **2** an act of offering a document that calls for acceptance or payment

present participle /'prez(ə)nt/ *n* a participle (e g *dancing, being*) with present or active meaning

present perfect *adj or n* (of or being) a verb tense (e g *have finished*) that expresses completion of an action at or before the time of speaking

preservationist /,prezə'vaysh(ə)nist/ *n* a conservationist

preservative /pri'zuhvətiv/ *n or adj* (sthg) that preserves or has the power to preserve; *specif* (sthg) used to protect against decay, discoloration, or spoilage

[1]**preserve** /pri'zuhv/ *vt* **1** to keep safe from harm or destruction; protect **2a** to keep alive, intact, or free from decay **b** to maintain ⟨~s *her habitual calm at all times*⟩ **3a** to keep or save from decomposition **b** to can, pickle, or similarly prepare (a perishable food) for future use **c** to make a preserve of (fruit) **4** to keep and protect (e g land or game) for private, esp sporting, use ~ *vi* **1** to make preserves **2** to withstand preserving (e g by canning) ⟨*some fruits do not* ~ *well*⟩ [ME *preserven*, fr MF *preserver*, fr ML *praeservare*, fr LL, to observe beforehand, fr L *prae-* + *servare* to keep, guard, observe – more at

CONSERVE] – **preservable** *adj*, **preserver** *n*, **preservation** /prezə'vaysh(ə)n/ *n*

[2]**preserve** *n* **1** a preparation (e g a jam or jelly) consisting of fruit preserved by cooking whole or in pieces with sugar **2** an area restricted for the preservation of natural resources (e g animals or trees); *esp* one used for regulated hunting or fishing **3** sthg (e g a sphere of activity) reserved for certain people

preset /,pree'set/ *vt* **-tt-; preset** to set beforehand – **preset** *adj*, **presettable** *adj*

,pre'shrunk /-'shrungk/ *adj* of or being material subjected to a process during manufacture designed to reduce later shrinking

preside /pri'zied/ *vi* **1** to occupy the place of authority **2** to exercise guidance, authority, or control *over* **3** to perform as featured or chief instrumentalist – usu + *at* ⟨~d *at the organ*⟩ **4** to be prominent ⟨*the* presiding *genius of the company*⟩ [L *praesidēre* to guard, preside over, lit., to sit in front of, sit at the head of, fr *prae-* + *sedēre* to sit – more at SIT] – **presider** *n*

presidency /'prezid(ə)nsi/ *n* **1** the office of president **2** the term during which a president holds office **3** the action or function of one who presides; superintendence

president /'prezid(ə)nt/ *n* **1** an official chosen to preside over a meeting or assembly **2** an elected head of state in a republic **3** *chiefly NAm* the chief officer of an organization (e g a business corporation or university) [ME, fr MF, fr L *praesident-*, *praesidens*, fr prp of *praesidēre*] – **presidential** /-'densh(ə)l/ *adj*, **presidentially** *adv*

presidium /pri'sidi·əm, -'zi-/ *n, pl* **presidia** /-di·ə/, **presidiums** a permanent executive committee in a Communist country [Russ *prezidium*, fr L *praesidium* garrison]

,pre-So'cratic /,pree-/ *adj* of or being Greek philosophers before Socrates – **pre-Socratic** *n*

[1]**press** /pres/ *n* **1** a crowd of people; a throng; *also* crowding **2** an apparatus or machine by which pressure is applied (e g for shaping material, extracting liquid, or compressing sthg) **3** a cupboard; *esp* one for books or clothes **4** an action of pressing or pushing; pressure **5a** PRINTING PRESS **b** the act or process of printing **c** (a building containing) a publishing house or printing firm **6a** *sing or pl in constr, often cap* **(1)** *the* newspapers and magazines collectively **(2)** *the* journalists collectively **b** comment or notice in newspapers and magazines [ME *presse*, fr OF, fr *presser* to press]

[2]**press** *vt* **1** to push firmly and steadily against **2** to assail, harass – esp in *hard-pressed* **3a** to squeeze out the juice or contents of (e g citrus fruits) **b** to squeeze with apparatus or instruments to a desired density, smoothness, or shape ⟨~ed *flowers*⟩ **c** IRON 1 ⟨~ed *his trousers*⟩ **4a** to exert influence on; constrain **b** to try hard to persuade; entreat **5** to move by means of pressure ⟨~ *this button*⟩ **6** to lay emphasis or insist on ⟨*continued to* ~ *his point*⟩ **7** to follow through (a course of action) ⟨~ed *his claim*⟩ **8** to clasp in affection or courtesy ⟨~ed *his hand*⟩ **9** to make (a gramophone record) from a matrix ~ *vi* **1** to crowd closely; mass **2** to force or push one's way ⟨~ing *through the crowd*⟩ **3** to seek urgently; contend ⟨~ing *for salary increases*⟩ **4** to require haste or speed in action ⟨*time is* ~ing⟩ **5** to exert pressure **6** to come to a desired condition, esp of smoothness, by being pressed [ME *pressen*, fr MF *presser*, fr L *pressare*, fr *pressus*, pp of *premere* to press; akin to L *prelum* press, & perh to Russ *peret'* to press] – **presser** *n*

[3]**press** *vt* **1** to force into military service, esp in an army or navy **2a** to take by authority, esp for public use; commandeer **b** to take and force into any, usu temporary, service [alter. of obs *prest* (to enlist by giving pay in advance), fr *prest* (loan of money, advance on wages), fr ME, fr MF, deriv of L *praed-*, *praes* surety, bondsman]

[4]**press** *n* impressment into service, esp in a navy

'press ,agent *n* an agent employed to establish and maintain good public relations through publicity [[1]*press*]

'press ,button *n* PUSH BUTTON

'press ,conference *n* an interview given by a public figure to journalists by appointment

'press ,cutting *n, Br* a paragraph or article cut from a newspaper or magazine

'press-,gang *n sing or pl in constr* a detachment empowered to press men into military or naval service [[4]*press*]

press gang *vt* to force into service (as if) by a press-gang ⟨*was* press ganged *into playing cricket in a charity match*⟩

[1]**pressing** /'presing/ *adj* **1** very important; critical **2** earnest, insistent ⟨*a* ~ *invitation*⟩ – **pressingly** *adv*

[2]**pressing** *n* one or more gramophone records produced from a single matrix

'pressman /-mən; *sense 2 or* -,man/, *fem* **'press,woman** *n* **1** the operator of a printing press **2** *Br* a newspaper reporter

'press,mark /-,mahk/ *n, chiefly Br* a combination of characters assigned to a book to indicate its place in a library [[1]*press* 3]

press on *vi* **1** to continue on one's way ⟨press on *along the Blackpool road*⟩ **2** to proceed in an urgent or resolute manner ⟨*the firm is* pressing on *with its plans for expansion*⟩

'press-,stud *n, Br* a metal fastener consisting of 2 parts joined by pressing

'press-,up *n* an exercise performed in a prone position by raising and lowering the body with the arms while supporting it only on the hands and toes

[1]**pressure** /'preshə/ *n* **1a** the burden of physical or mental distress ⟨*the* ~ *of family anxieties*⟩ **b** trouble or difficulty resulting from social or economic constraints ⟨*under severe financial* ~⟩ **2** the application of force to sthg by sthg else in direct contact with it; compression **3a** the action of a force against an opposing force **b** the force or thrust exerted over a surface divided by its area **4** the stress of urgent matters ⟨*people who work well under* ~⟩ **5a** influence or compulsion directed towards achieving a particular end ⟨*the unions put* ~ *on the government to increase wages*⟩ **b** repeated persistent attack; harassment ⟨*the English batsmen were under* ~ *from the Australian bowlers*⟩ **6** the atmospheric pressure *USE* (*2&3*) ☞ PHYSICS [L *pressura* action of pressing, pressure, fr *pressus*, pp of *premere* to press; (1) ME, fr LL *pressura*, fr L]

[2]**pressure** *vt* **1** to apply pressure to **2** *chiefly NAm* to pressurize

'pressure ,cooker *n* a metal vessel with an airtight lid in which superheated steam under pressure produces a very high temperature, used for cooking food quickly – **pressure-cook** *vb*

'**pressure ,gauge** *n* a gauge for indicating the pressure of a fluid

'**pressure ,group** *n* an interest group organized to influence public, esp governmental, policy

'**pressure ,point** *n* a point where a blood vessel may be compressed against a bone (e g to check bleeding)

'**pressure ,suit** *n* an inflatable suit to protect the body from low pressure

pressur·ize, -ise /'preshəriez/ *vt* **1** to maintain near-normal atmospheric pressure in (e g an aircraft cabin) **2** to apply pressure to ⟨*the team* ~d *the opponents' goal and eventually scored*⟩; *specif* to coerce ⟨*the prisoner's hunger strike* ~d *the authorities into action*⟩ **3** to design to withstand pressure – **pressurizer** *n*, **pressurization** *n* /-'zaysh(ə)n/

Prestel /pre'stel/ *trademark* – used for a service provided by British Telecom which transmits information (e g the weather or sports results) on a television screen to subscribers who call it up by means of a special push-button telephone ☞ TELECOMMUNICATION, TELEVISION

prestidigitation /,presti,diji'taysh(ə)n/ *n* conjuring; SLEIGHT OF HAND [F, fr *prestidigitateur* prestidigitator, fr *preste* nimble, quick (fr It *presto*) + L *digitus* finger – more at TOE] – **prestidigitator** /-'diji,taytə/ *n*

prestige /pre'steezh, -'steej/ *n* **1** high standing or esteem in the eyes of others **2** superiority or desirability in the eyes of society resulting from associations of social rank or material success ⟨*a* ~ *executive suite*⟩ [F, fr MF, conjuror's trick, illusion, fr LL *praestigium*, fr L *praestigiae*, pl, conjuror's tricks, irreg fr *praestringere* to tie up, blindfold, fr *prae-* + *stringere* to bind tight – more at [2]STRAIN]

pre'stigeful /-f(ə)l/ *adj* prestigious

prestigious /pre'stijəs/ *adj* having or conferring prestige [L *praestigiosus* full of tricks, deceitful, fr *praestigiae*] – **prestigiously** *adv*, **prestigiousness** *n*

[1]**presto** /'prestoh/ *n, adv, or adj, pl* **prestos** (a musical passage or movement played) at a rapid tempo – used in music [It, quick, quickly, fr L *praestus* ready, fr *praesto*, adv, on hand; akin to L *prae* before – more at FOR]

[2]**presto** *interj* HEY PRESTO

prestress /,pree'stres/ *vt* to introduce internal stresses into (e g a structural beam) to counteract stresses that will result from an applied load – **prestress** *n*

presume /pri'zyoohm/ *vt* **1** to undertake without leave or justification; dare ⟨*I wouldn't* ~ *to tell you how to do your job*⟩ **2** to suppose or assume, esp with some degree of certainty **3** to take for granted; imply ~ *vi* **1** to act or proceed on a presumption; take sthg for granted **2** to take liberties **3** to take advantage, esp in an unscrupulous manner – usu + *on* or *upon* ⟨*don't* ~ *on his kindness*⟩ [ME *presumen*, fr LL & MF; LL *praesumere* to dare, fr L, to anticipate, assume, fr *prae-* + *sumere* to take; MF *presumer* to assume, fr L *praesumere* – more at CONSUME] – **presumable** *adj*, **presumably** *adv*, **presumer** *n*

presuming /pri'zyoohming/ *adj* presumptuous – **presumingly** *adv*

presumption /pri'zumpsh(ə)n, pri'zumsh(ə)n/ *n* **1** presumptuous attitude or conduct; effrontery **2a** an attitude or belief based on reasonable evidence or grounds; an assumption **b** a ground or reason for presuming sthg **3** a legal inference as to the existence or truth of a fact [ME *presumpcioun*, fr OF *presumption*, fr LL & L; LL *praesumption-, praesumptio* presumptuous attitude, fr L, assumption, fr *praesumptus*, pp of *praesumere*]

presumptive /pri'zum(p)tiv/ *adj* **1** giving grounds for reasonable opinion or belief ⟨~ *evidence*⟩ **2** based on probability or presumption ⟨*heir* ~⟩ – **presumptively** *adv*

presumptuous /pri'zum(p)choo·əs, -tyoo·əs/ *adj* overstepping due bounds; forward [ME, fr MF *presumptueux*, fr LL *praesumptuosus*, irreg fr *praesumptio*] – **presumptuously** *adv*, **presumptuousness** *n*

presuppose /,preesə'pohz/ *vt* **1** to suppose beforehand **2** to require as an antecedent in logic or fact [ME *presupposen*, fr MF *presupposer*, fr ML *praesupponere* (perf indic *praesupposui*), fr L *prae-* + ML *supponere* to suppose – more at SUPPOSE] – **presupposition** /-,supə'zish(ə)n/ *n*

,presy'naptic /-si'naptik/ *adj* situated or occurring just before a nerve synapse – **presynaptically** *adv*

pret-a-porter /,pret ah 'pawtay/ *adj, of a garment* off-the-peg [F *prêt à porter* ready to wear]

pretax /,pree'taks/ *adj* existing before provision for taxes

pretence, *NAm chiefly* **pretense** /pri'tens/ *n* **1** a claim made or implied; *esp* one not supported by fact ⟨*made no* ~ *to learning*⟩ **2a** mere ostentation; pretentiousness ⟨*a man entirely free of pomp and* ~⟩ **b** a false or feigning act or assertion **3** an outward and often insincere or inadequate show; a semblance ⟨*struggling to maintain some* ~ *of order in the meeting*⟩ **4** a professed rather than a real intention or purpose; a pretext – esp in *false pretences* [ME, fr MF *pretensse*, fr (assumed) ML *praetensa*, fr LL, fem of *praetensus*, pp of L *praetendere*]

[1]**pretend** /pri'tend/ *vt* **1** to give a false appearance of; feign ⟨*he* ~ed *deafness*⟩ **2** to claim or assert falsely; profess ⟨~ing *an emotion he could not really feel*⟩ ⟨~ed *affection*⟩ ~ *vi* **1** to feign an action, part, or role (as if) in play **2** to lay claim ⟨*did not* ~ *to high office*⟩ [ME *pretenden*, fr L *praetendere* to allege as an excuse, lit., to stretch in front of like a curtain, fr *prae-* pre- + *tendere* to stretch – more at THIN] – **pretended** *adj*, **pretendedly** *adv*

[2]**pretend** *adj* make-believe – used esp by children

pretender /pri'tendə/ *n* **1** sby who lays claim to sthg; *specif* a (false) claimant to a throne **2** sby who makes a false or hypocritical show ⟨*a* ~ *to spirituality*⟩ [[1]PRETEND + [2]-ER]

pretension /pri'tensh(ə)n/ *n* **1** (an effort to establish) an esp unjustified claim ⟨*have no* ~ *to be a great writer*⟩ **2** vanity, pretentiousness [ML *praetension-, praetensio*, fr LL *praetensus*, pp] – **pretensionless** *adj*

pretentious /pri'tenshəs/ *adj* making usu unjustified or excessive claims (e g of value or standing) [F *prétentieux*, fr *prétention* pretension, fr ML *praetention-, praetentio*, fr L *praetentus*, pp of *praetendere*] – **pretentiously** *adv*, **pretentiousness** *n*

preterite, *chiefly NAm* **preterit** /'pretərit/ *adj* of or constituting a verb tense that expresses action in the past without reference to duration, continuance, or repetition [ME *preterit*, fr MF, fr L *praeteritus*, fr pp of *praeterire* to go by, pass, fr *praeter* beyond, past, by (fr compar of *prae* before) + *ire* to go – more at FOR, ISSUE] – **preterite** *n*

preternatural /ˌpreetəˈnacharəl/ *adj* **1** exceeding what is natural or regular; extraordinary **2** lying beyond or outside normal experience *USE* fml [ML *praeternaturalis,* fr L *praeter naturam* beyond nature] – **preternaturally** *adv,* **preternaturalness** *n*

pretext /ˈpreetekst/ *n* a false reason given to disguise the real one; an excuse [L *praetextus,* fr *praetextus,* pp of *praetexere* to assign as a pretext, lit., to weave in front, fr *prae-* + *texere* to weave – more at TECHNICAL]

pretor /ˈpreetə/ *n, chiefly NAm* a praetor – **pretorian** /priˈtawri·ən/ *adj*

prettify /ˈpritifie/ *vt* to make pretty or depict prettily, esp in an inappropriate way; *also* to palliate ⟨*attempts to* ~ *criminal violence*⟩ – **prettification** /-fiˈkaysh(ə)n/ *n*

[1]**pretty** /ˈpriti/ *adj* **1a** attractive or aesthetically pleasing, esp because of delicacy or grace, but less than beautiful ⟨*a* ~ *girl*⟩ **b** outwardly pleasant but lacking strength, purpose, or intensity ⟨~ *words that make no sense* – Elizabeth Barrett Browning⟩ **2** miserable, terrible ⟨*a* ~ *mess you've got us into*⟩ **3** moderately large; considerable ⟨*a very* ~ *profit*⟩ **4** *of a man* having delicate features; *specif* effeminate – derog [ME *praty, prety* artful, dainty, fr OE *prættig* tricky, fr *prætt* trick; akin to ON *prettr* trick] – **prettily** *adv,* **prettiness** *n,* **prettyish** *adj*

[2]**pretty** *adv* **1a** in some degree; moderately ⟨~ *comfortable*⟩; *esp* somewhat excessively ⟨*felt* ~ *sick*⟩ **b** very – used to emphasize *much* or *nearly* ⟨~ *nearly ready*⟩ **2** in a pretty manner; prettily – infml

[3]**pretty** *n, archaic* a dear or pretty child or young woman – in *my pretty*

ˌpretty ˈpenny *n* a considerable amount of money ⟨*could be worth a* ~ *one of these days*⟩ – infml

ˌpretty-ˈpretty *adj* excessively pretty, esp in an insipid or inappropriate way [redupl of [1]*pretty*]

pretty up *vt* to make pretty – infml ⟨*curtains to* pretty up *the room*⟩

ˌpretty ˈwell *adv* very nearly; almost

pretzel /ˈpretsl/ *n* a brittle glazed and salted biscuit typically having the form of a loose knot [G *brezel,* deriv of L *brachiatus* having branches like arms, fr *brachium, bracchium* arm – more at BRACE]

prevail /priˈvayl/ *vi* **1** to gain ascendancy through strength or superiority; triumph – often + *against* or *over* **2** to persuade successfully – + *on, upon,* or *with* ⟨~ed *on him to sing*⟩ **3** to be frequent; predominate ⟨*the west winds that* ~ *in the mountains*⟩ **4** to be or continue in use or fashion; persist ⟨*a custom that still* ~s⟩ [ME *prevailen,* fr L *praevalēre,* fr *prae-* pre- + *valēre* to be strong – more at WIELD] – **prevailing** *adj,* **prevailingly** *adj*

prevalence /ˈprevələns/ *n* **1** being prevalent **2** the degree to which sthg is prevalent

prevalent /ˈprevələnt/ *adj* generally or widely occurring or existing; widespread [L *praevalent-, praevalens* very powerful, fr prp of *praevalēre*] – **prevalently** *adv*

prevaricate /priˈvarikayt/ *vi* to speak or act evasively so as to hide the truth; equivocate [L *praevaricatus,* pp of *praevaricari* to walk crookedly, fr *prae-* + *varicare* to straddle, fr *varicus* having the feet spread apart, fr *varus* bent, knock-kneed; prob akin to OE *wōh* crooked, L *vacillare* to sway, *vagus* wandering] – **prevaricator** *n,* **prevarication** /-ˈkaysh(ə)n/ *n*

prevenient /priˈveenyənt, -ni·ənt/ *adj* antecedent, anticipatory – fml [L *praevenient-, praeveniens,* prp of *praevenire*] – **preveniently** *adv*

prevent /priˈvent/ *vt* **1** to keep from happening or existing ⟨*steps to* ~ *war*⟩ *vt* **2** to hold or keep back; stop – often + *from* [ME *preventen* to anticipate, fr L *praeventus,* pp of *praevenire* to come before, anticipate, forestall, fr *prae-* + *venire* to come – more at COME] – **preventable** *also* **preventible** *adj,* **preventer** *n,* **prevention** /-sh(ə)n/ *n,* **preventability** /-təˈbiləti/ *n*

[1]**preventive** /priˈventiv/, **preventative** /-tətiv/ *n* sthg that prevents (disease)

[2]**preventive, preventative** *adj* **1** intended or serving to prevent; precautionary **2** undertaken to forestall anticipated hostile action ⟨~ *war*⟩ – **preventively** *adv,* **preventiveness** *n*

preventive detention *n, Br* a term of imprisonment for habitual criminals over 30

[1]**preview** /ˈpree,vyooh/ *vt* to see beforehand; *specif* to view or show in advance of public presentation

[2]**preview** *n* **1** an advance showing or performance (e g of a film or play) **2** a brief view or foretaste of sthg that is to come **3** *also* **prevue** *chiefly NAm* a film or television trailer

previous /ˈpreevyəs, -vi·əs/ *adj* **1** going before in time or order **2** acting too soon; premature ⟨*she was a bit* ~ *when she said she'd got the job*⟩ – infml [L *praevius* leading the way, fr *prae-* pre- + *via* way – more at VIA] – **previously** *adv,* **previousness** *n*

previous question *n* a parliamentary motion that the pending question be put to an immediate vote, which if defeated has the effect of closing the debate

ˈprevious to *prep* before; PRIOR TO

prevision /ˌpreeˈvizh(ə)n/ *n* **1** foreknowledge, prescience **2** a forecast, prognostication [LL *praevision-, praevisio,* fr L *praevisus,* pp of *praevidēre* to foresee, fr *prae-* + *vidēre* to see – more at WIT] – **previsional** *adj,* **previsionary** *adj*

ˌpreˈwar /-ˈwaw/ *adj* of or being the period preceding a war, esp WW I or II

[1]**prey** /pray/ *n* **1a** an animal taken by a predator as food **b** sby or sthg helpless or unable to resist attack; a victim **2** the act or habit of preying [ME *preie* booty, prey, fr OF, fr L *praeda;* akin to L *prehendere* to grasp, seize – more at PREHENSILE]

[2]**prey** *vi* **1** to make raids for booty ⟨*pirates* ~ed *on the coast*⟩ **2a** to seize and devour prey – often + *on* or *upon* ⟨*kestrels* ~ *upon mice*⟩ **b** to live by extortion, deceit, or exerting undue influence ⟨*confidence tricksters* ~ing *on elderly women*⟩ **3** to have continuously oppressive or distressing effect ⟨*problems that* ~ *on one's mind*⟩ [ME *preyen,* fr OF *preier,* fr L *praedari,* fr *praeda*] – **preyer** /ˈprayə/ *n*

priapic /prieˈaypik, -ˈapik/ *adj* phallic [L *priapus* lecher, fr *Priapus,* god of male generative power, fr Gk *Priapos*]

[1]**price** /pries/ *n* **1** the money, or amount of goods or services, that is exchanged or demanded in barter or sale **2** the terms for the sake of which sthg is done or undertaken: e g **a** an amount sufficient to bribe sby ⟨*believed every man had his* ~⟩ **b** a reward for the catching or killing of sby ⟨*a man with a* ~ *on his head*⟩ **3** the cost at which sthg is done or obtained ⟨*the* ~ *of his carelessness was a broken window*⟩ **4** *archaic* value, worth ⟨*her* ~ *is far above rubies* – Prov 31:10(AV)⟩ [ME *pris,* fr OF, fr L *pretium*

price, money; akin to Skt *prati-* against, in return – more at PROS-]

[2]**price** *vt* **1** to set a price on **2** to find out the price of – **pricer** *n*

-priced /-priest/ *comb form* (→ *adj*) set at (such) a price ⟨*low-*priced *merchandise*⟩

'**priceless** /-lis/ *adj* **1** having a worth beyond any price; invaluable **2** particularly amusing or absurd ⟨*told me this* ~ *story*⟩ – infml

'**price-,ring** *n* a group of traders acting in agreement to maintain prices

'**price ,tag** *n* **1** a label on merchandise showing the price at which it is offered for sale **2** price, cost ⟨*the council was asked to put a* ~ *on the new nursery school*⟩

'**price ,war** *n* a period of commercial competition characterized by the repeated cutting of prices below those of competitors

pricey *also* **pricy** /'priesi/ *adj, chiefly Br* expensive – infml

[1]**prick** /prik/ *n* **1** a mark or shallow hole made by a pointed instrument **2** a pointed instrument, weapon, etc **3** an instance of pricking or the sensation of being pricked: e g **a** a nagging or sharp feeling of sorrow or remorse **b** a sharp localized pain ⟨*the* ~ *of a needle*⟩ **4** the penis – vulg **5** a disagreeable person – chiefly vulg [ME *prikke*, fr OE *prica*; akin to MD *pric* prick]

[2]**prick** *vt* **1** to pierce slightly with a sharp point **2** to affect with sorrow or remorse ⟨*his conscience began to* ~ *him*⟩ **3** to mark, distinguish, or note by means of a small mark **4** to trace or outline with punctures **5** to cause to be or stand erect ⟨*a dog* ~ing *his ears*⟩ – often + *up* ~ *vi* **1** to prick sthg or cause a pricking sensation **2** to feel discomfort as if from being pricked – **pricker** *n* – **prick up one's ears** to start to listen intently

pricket /'prikit/ *n* **1** (a candlestick with) a spike on which a candle is stuck **2** a buck, esp a male fallow deer, 2 years old – compare BROCKET [ME *priket*, fr *prikke*; (2) prob fr the straightness of its horns]

[1]**prickle** /'prikl/ *n* **1** a sharp pointed spike arising from the skin or bark of a plant **2** a prickling sensation [ME *prikle*, fr OE *pricle*; akin to OE *prica* prick]

[2]**prickle** *vb* **prickling** /'prikling, 'prikl·ing/ *vt* to prick slightly ~ *vi* to cause or feel a prickling or stinging sensation; tingle

prickly /'prik(ə)li/ *adj* **1** full of or covered with prickles **2** marked by prickling; stinging ⟨*a* ~ *sensation*⟩ **3a** troublesome, vexatious ⟨~ *issues*⟩ **b** easily irritated ⟨*had a* ~ *disposition*⟩ – **prickliness** *n*

,**prickly 'heat** *n* a skin eruption of red spots with intense itching and tingling caused by inflammation round the sweat ducts

prickly pear *n* (the pulpy pearshaped edible fruit of) any of a genus of cacti having yellow flowers and bearing spines or prickly hairs

prickly poppy *n* any of a genus of plants of the poppy family with prickly leaves and white or yellow flowers

prick out *vt* to transplant (seedlings) from the place of germination to a more permanent position (e g in a flower bed)

pricy /'priesi/ *adj* pricey

[1]**pride** /pried/ *n* **1a** inordinate self-esteem; conceit **b** a reasonable or justifiable self-respect **c** delight or satisfaction arising from some act, possession, or relationship ⟨*parental* ~⟩ **2** a source of pride; *esp, sing or pl in constr* the best in a group or class ⟨*this pup is the* ~ *of the litter*⟩ **3** *sing or pl in constr* a group of lions [ME, fr OE *prȳde*, fr *prūd* proud – more at PROUD]

[2]**pride** *vt* to be proud of (oneself) – + *on* or *upon* ⟨*he* ~d *himself on his generosity*⟩

,**pride of 'place** *n* the highest or first position ⟨*gave* ~ *on the mantelpiece to a photograph of his granddaughter*⟩

prie-dieu /'pree ,dyuh/ *n, pl* **prie-dieux** /~/ **1** a kneeling bench with a raised shelf, designed for use by a person at prayer **2** a low armless upholstered chair with a high straight back [F, lit., pray God]

prier /'prie·ə/ *n* an inquisitive person [[1]PRY + [2]-ER]

priest /preest/ *n* a person authorized to perform the sacred rites of a religion; *specif* a clergyman ranking below a bishop and above a deacon (e g in the Anglican and Roman Catholic churches) [ME *preist*, fr OE *prēost*, modif of LL *presbyter*, fr Gk *presbyteros* elder, priest, compar of *presbys* old man] – **priestly** *adj*, **priestliness** *n*, **priesthood** /-,hood/ *n*

priestess /pree'stes, 'preestis/ *n* a female priest of a non-Christian religion

prig /prig/ *n* one who is excessively self-righteous or affectedly precise about the observance of proprieties (e g of speech or manners) [prob fr *prig* (thief), fr *prig* (to steal)] – **priggish** *adj*, **priggishly** *adv*, **priggishness** *n*, **priggery** /-gəri/ *n*

prim /prim/ *adj* **-mm-** **1** stiffly formal and proper; decorous **2** prudish [perh deriv of OF *prin, prime* excellent, fr L *primus* first] – **primly** *adv*, **primness** *n*

prima ballerina /'preemə/ *n* the principal female dancer in a ballet company [It, leading ballerina]

primacy /'priemәsi/ *n* **1** the office or rank of an ecclesiastical primate **2** the state of being first (e g in importance, order, or rank); preeminence – fml

prima donna /,preemә 'donə/ *n, pl* **prima donnas** **1** a principal female singer (e g in an opera company) **2** an extremely sensitive or temperamental person [It, lit., first lady]

primaeval /prie'meevl/ *adj, chiefly Br* primeval

[1]**prima facie** /,priemə 'fayshi/ *adv* at first view; on the first appearance ⟨*his arguments appear* ~ *true*⟩ [L]

[2]**prima facie** *adj* true, valid, or sufficient at first impression; apparent ⟨*the theory offers a* ~ *solution*⟩

primal /'priem(ə)l/ *adj* **1** original, primitive ⟨*village life continues in its* ~ *innocence* – Van Wyck Brookes⟩ **2** first in importance; fundamental ⟨*our* ~ *concern*⟩ [ML *primalis*, fr L *primus* first – more at [2]PRIME] – **primality** /-'maləti/ *n*

primarily /'priem(ə)rəli, *also* prie'merəli/ *adv* **1** for the most part, chiefly **2** in the first place; originally

[1]**primary** /'priem(ə)ri/ *adj* **1a** first in order of time or development; primitive **b** of or being formations of the Palaeozoic and earlier periods **2a** of first rank, importance, or value; principal **b** basic, fundamental **c** *of Latin, Greek, or Sanskrit tense* expressing present or future time **d** of or constituting the strongest degree of stress in speech **3a** direct, firsthand ⟨~ *sources of information*⟩ **b** not derivable from other colours, odours, or tastes **c** preparatory to sthg else in a continuing process; elementary ⟨~

instruction⟩ **d** of or at a primary school ⟨~ *education*⟩ **e** belonging to the first group or order in successive divisions, combinations, or ramifications ⟨~ *nerves*⟩ **f** of or being the inducing current or its circuit in an induction coil or transformer **g** of or being the amino acid sequence in proteins ⟨~ *protein structure*⟩ **4** of, involving, or derived directly from plant-forming tissue, specif meristem, at a growing point ⟨~ *tissue*⟩ ⟨~ *growth*⟩ **5** of or being an industry that produces raw materials ⟨*mining is a ~ industry*⟩ – compare SECONDARY, TERTIARY [LL *primarius* basic, primary, fr L, principal, fr *primus*]

[2]**primary** *n* **1** sthg that stands first in rank, importance, or value; a fundamental – usu pl **2** any of the usu 9 or 10 strong feathers on the joint of a bird's wing furthest from the body ☞ ANATOMY **3** PRIMARY COLOUR **4** a caucus **5** PRIMARY SCHOOL

primary cell *n* a cell that converts chemical energy into electrical energy by irreversible chemical reactions

primary colour *n* **1** any of the 3 spectral bands red, green, and bluish violet from which all other colours can be obtained by suitable combinations **2** any of the 3 coloured pigments red, yellow, and blue that cannot be matched by mixing other pigments

primary consumer *n* a herbivore – compare SECONDARY CONSUMER, TERTIARY CONSUMER ☞ FOOD

'primary ,school *n* a school usu for pupils from 5 to 11, but sometimes also including nursery school

primary syphilis *n* the first stage of syphilis which is marked by the development of a deep ulcer and the spread of the causative bacterium in the tissues of the body

primate /'priemayt *or* (*esp in sense* [1]) -mət/ *n* **1** *often cap* a bishop having precedence (e g in a nation) **2** any of an order of mammals including human beings, the apes, monkeys, and related forms (e g lemurs and tarsiers) [ME *primat*, fr OF, fr ML *primat-*, *primas* archbishop, fr L, leader, fr *primus*] – **primateship** *n*, **primatial** /-'maysh(ə)l/ *adj*, **primatology** /-mə'toləji/ *n*, **primatologist** *n*, **primatological** /-mətə'lojikl/ *adj*

[1]**prime** /priem/ *n* **1** *often cap* the second of the canonical hours, orig fixed for 6 am **2** the most active, thriving, or successful stage or period ⟨*in the ~ of his life*⟩ **3** the chief or best individual or part; the pick ⟨~ *of the flock, and choicest of the stall* – Alexander Pope⟩ **4 prime, prime number** a positive integer that has no factor except itself and 1 ☞ NUMBER **5** the symbol ′ used in mathematics as a distinguishing mark (e g in denoting derivatives of a function) [ME, fr OE *prīm*, fr L *prima hora* first hour]

[2]**prime** *adj* **1** first in time; original **2** having no factor except itself and 1 ⟨*3 is a ~ number*⟩ **3a** first in rank, authority, or significance; principal **b** *of meat, esp beef* of the highest grade or best quality regularly marketed **4** not deriving from sthg else; primary [ME, fr MF, fem of *prin* first, fr L *primus*; akin to L *prior*] – **primely** *adv*, **primeness** *n*

[3]**prime** *vt* **1** to fill, load; *esp* to fill or ply (a person) *with* liquor **2** to prepare (a firearm or charge) for firing by supplying with priming or a primer **3** to apply a first coat (e g of paint or oil) to (a surface), esp in preparation for painting **4** to put into working order by filling or charging with sthg, esp a liquid ⟨~ *a pump with water*⟩ **5** to instruct beforehand; prepare ⟨~d *the witness*⟩ [prob fr [1]*prime*]

prime meridian *n* *the* meridian (at Greenwich) of 0° longitude from which other longitudes E and W are reckoned

,prime 'minister *n* **1** the chief minister of a ruler or state **2** the chief executive of a parliamentary government – **prime ministership** *n*, **prime ministry** *n*

prime mover *n* **1** God as the creator of (motion in) the physical universe **2a** an initial source of motive power (e g a windmill, water wheel, turbine, or internal-combustion engine) **b** a powerful tractor or lorry **3** the original or most influential force in a development or undertaking ⟨*he was a ~ of the constitutional reform*⟩ [trans of ML *primus motor*]

[1]**primer** /'priemə/ *n* a small book for teaching children to read [ME, fr ML *primarium*, fr LL, neut of *primarius* primary]

[2]**primer** *n* **1** a device (e g a percussion cap) used for igniting a charge **2** material used in priming a surface [[3]PRIME + [2]-ER]

prime rate, prime interest rate *n* an interest rate at which preferred customers can borrow from banks and which is the lowest commercial interest rate available at a particular time and place

prime time *n* the peak television viewing time, for which the highest rates are charged to advertisers

primeval, *Br also* **primaeval** /prie'meevl/ *adj* **1** of the earliest age or ages **2** existing in or persisting from the beginning (e g of a universe) [L *primaevus*, fr *primus* first + *aevum* age – more at [1]AYE] – **primevally** *adv*

priming /'prieming/ *n* the explosive used for igniting a charge [[3]PRIME + [2]-ING]

primipara /prie'mipərə/ *n, pl* **primiparas, primiparae** /-ri/ **1** a woman bearing a first child **2** a woman who has borne only 1 child [L, fr *primus* first + *-para*] – **primiparity** /-'mip(ə)rəti/ *n*, **primiparous** *adj*

[1]**primitive** /'primətiv/ *adj* **1** original, primary **2a** of the earliest age or period; primeval **b** belonging to or characteristic of an early stage of development or evolution ⟨~ *technology*⟩ **3a** elemental, natural **b** of or produced by a relatively simple people or culture ⟨~ *art*⟩ **c** lacking in sophistication or subtlety; crude; *also* uncivilized **d(1)** self-taught, untutored **(2)** produced by a self-taught artist [ME *primitif*, fr L *primitivus*, fr *primitus* originally, fr *primus* first – more at [2]PRIME] – **primitively** *adv*, **primitiveness** *n*, **primitivism** *n*, **primitivist** *n*, **primitivistic** /-'vistik/ *adj*, **primitivity** /-'tivəti/ *n*

[2]**primitive** *n* **1a** a primitive concept, term, or proposition **b** a root word **2a(1)** an artist of an early, esp pre-Renaissance, period **(2)** a later imitator of such an artist **b** an artist, esp self-taught, whose work is marked by directness and naiveté **c** a primitive work of art **3a** a member of a primitive people **b** an unsophisticated person

primo /'preemoh/ *n, pl* **primos** /-mohz/ the first or leading part (e g in a duet or trio) [It, fr *primo* first, fr L *primus*]

primogenitor /,priemoh'jenətə/ *n* an ancestor, forefather [LL, fr L *primus* + *genitor* begetter, fr *genitus*, pp of *gignere* to beget – more at KIN]

,primo'geniture /-'jenichə/ *n* **1** the state or fact of being the firstborn of the children of the same parents **2** the principle by which right of inheritance belongs to the eldest son [LL *primogenitura*, fr L *primus* + *genitura* birth, fr *genitus*, pp]

primordial /prie'mawdyəl/ *adj* **1a** existing from or at the beginning; primeval **b** earliest formed in the development of an individual or structure **2** fundamental, primary [ME, fr LL *primordialis*, fr L *primordium* origin, fr neut of *primordius* original, fr *primus* first + *ordiri* to begin – more at [2]PRIME, ORDER] – **primordially** *adv*

primordium /prie'mawdyəm/ *n, pl* **primordia** /-di·ə/ the earliest stage in the development of a part or organ [NL, fr L]

primp /primp/ *vt* to dress, adorn, or arrange in a careful or fastidious manner ~ *vi* to dress or groom oneself carefully [perh alter. of [1]*prim*]

primrose /'primrohz/ *n* **1** any of a genus of perennial plants with showy, esp yellow, flowers ☞ ENDANGERED **2** pale yellow [ME *primerose*, fr MF, fr ML *prima rosa*, lit., first (early) rose]

primrose path *n* a path of ease or pleasure; *esp* one leading to disaster

primula /'primyoolə/ *n* PRIMROSE 1 [ML, fr *primula veris*, lit., firstling of spring]

primum mobile /,priemoom 'mohbili/ *n, pl* **primum mobiles** /-leez/ the outermost concentric sphere conceived in medieval astronomy as carrying the spheres of the fixed stars and the planets in its daily revolution [ME, fr ML, lit., first moving thing]

Primus /'priemәs/ *trademark* – used for a portable oil-burning stove used chiefly for cooking (e g when camping)

primus inter pares /,priemәs intә 'peәreez/ *n* first among equals [L]

prince /prins/ *n* **1** a sovereign ruler, esp of a principality **2** a foreign nobleman of varying rank and status **3** a person of high rank or standing in his class or profession ⟨*a* ~ *among poets*⟩ [ME, fr OF, fr L *princip-, princeps*, lit., one who takes the first part, fr *primus* first + *capere* to take – more at HEAVE] – **princedom** *n*, **princeship** *n*

,prince 'charming *n* an ideal suitor [*Prince Charming*, hero of the fairy tale *Cinderella*, trans by Robert Samber *fl* 1729 E writer of *Cendrillon* by Charles Perrault †1703 F writer]

,prince 'consort *n, pl* **princes consort** the husband of a reigning female sovereign – used only after the title has been specif conferred by the sovereign

'princeling /-ling/ *n* a petty or insignificant prince

'princely /-li/ *adj* **1** of a prince **2** befitting a prince; noble ⟨~ *manners*⟩ **3** magnificent, lavish ⟨*a* ~ *sum*⟩ – **princely** *adv*, **princeliness** *n*

,Prince of 'Wales /waylz/ *n* the male heir apparent to the British throne – used only after the title has been specif conferred by the sovereign

,prince's-'feather *n* a showy annual plant of the amaranth family often cultivated for its dense usu red flower spikes

[1]princess /,prin'ses *as an ordinary word, usu* 'prinses *or* 'prinsәs *before a name*/ *n* **1** a female member of a royal family; *esp* a daughter of a sovereign **2** the wife or widow of a prince **3** a woman having in her own right the rank of a prince **4** a woman, or sthg personified as female, that is outstanding in a specified respect

[2]princess, princesse /prin'ses, 'prinses/ *adj* closely fitting at the top, flared from the hips to the hemline, and having gores or panels ⟨*dress with* ~ *line*⟩ [F *princesse* princess, fr *prince*]

[1]principal /'prinsipl/ *adj* most important, consequential, or influential; chief [ME, fr OF, fr L *principalis*, fr *princip-, princeps*] – **principally** *adv*

[2]principal *n* **1** a person who has controlling authority or is in a leading position: e g **a** the head of an educational institution **b** one who employs another to act for him/her **c** the chief or an actual participant in a crime – no longer used technically **d** the person ultimately liable on a legal obligation **e** a leading performer **2** a matter or thing of primary importance: e g **a** a capital sum placed at interest, due as a debt, or used as a fund **b** a main rafter of a roof – **principalship** *n*

principal boy *n* the role of the hero in British pantomime traditionally played by a girl

principality /,prinsi'paləti/ *n* the office or territory of a prince

,principal 'parts *n pl* that series of verb forms from which all the other forms of a verb can be derived

principle /'prinsipl/ *n* **1a** a universal and fundamental law, doctrine, or assumption **b(1)** a rule or code of conduct **(2)** habitual devotion to right principles ⟨*a man of* ~⟩ **(3)** a fundamental implication ⟨*he objects to the* ~ *of the thing, not the method*⟩ **c** the laws or facts of nature underlying the working of an artificial device **2** a primary source; a fundamental element ⟨*the ancients emphasized the opposing* ~s *of heat and cold*⟩ **3** an underlying faculty or endowment ⟨*such* ~s *of human nature as greed and curiosity*⟩ **4** an ingredient (e g a chemical) that exhibits or imparts a characteristic quality [ME, modif of MF *principe*, fr L *principium* beginning, fr *princip-, princeps* one taking the first part – more at PRINCE] – **in principle** with respect to fundamentals ⟨*prepared to accept the proposition* in principle⟩

'principled *adj* exhibiting, based on, or characterized by principle – often used in combination ⟨*high*-principled⟩

prink /pringk/ *vb* to primp [prob alter. of [2]*prank* (to dress or adorn showily), prob fr D *pronken* to strut] – **prinker** *n*

[1]print /print/ *n* **1a** a mark made by pressure; an impression **b** sthg impressed with a print or formed in a mould **2** printed state or form **3** printed matter or letters – compare SMALL PRINT **4a(1)** a copy made by printing (e g from a photographic negative) **(2)** a reproduction of an original work of art (e g a painting) **(3)** an original work of art (e g a woodcut or lithograph) intended for graphic reproduction **b** (an article made from) cloth with a pattern applied by printing **c** a photographic copy, esp from a negative [ME *preinte*, fr OF, fr *preint*, pp of *preindre* to press, fr L *premere* – more at [2]PRESS] – **in print** obtainable from the publisher – **out of print** not obtainable from the publisher

[2]print *vt* **1** to stamp (e g a mark or design) in or on sthg **2a** to make a copy of by impressing paper against an inked printing surface **b** to impress with a design or pattern **c** to publish in print **3** to write each letter of separately, not joined together **4** to make (a positive picture) on sensitized photographic surface from a negative or a positive ~ *vi* **1** to form a printed image **2a** to work as a printer **b** to produce printed matter **3** to produce sthg by printing **4** to use unjoined letters like those of roman type

printable /'printəbl/ *adj* **1** capable of being printed or of being printed from or on 2 considered fit to publish – **printability** /-'biləti/ *n*

,printed 'circuit *n* a circuit for electronic apparatus consisting of conductive material in thin continuous paths from terminal to terminal on an insulating surface

printer /'printə/ *n* 1 a person engaged in printing 2 a machine for printing from photographic negatives 3 a device (e g a line printer) that produces printout [[2]PRINT + [2]-ER]

printing /'printing/ *n* 1 reproduction in printed form 2 the art, practice, or business of a printer 3 IMPRESSION 4c

'printing ,press *n* a machine that produces printed copies

'print,out /-,owt/ *n* a printed record produced automatically (e g by a computer) ☞ COMPUTER – **print out** *vt*

[1]**prior** /'prie·ə/ *n* 1 the deputy head of a monastery ranking next below the abbot 2 the head (of a house) of any of various religious communities [ME, fr OE & MF, fr ML, fr LL, administrator, fr L, former, superior] – **priorate** /-rət/ *n*, **priorship** *n*

[2]**prior** *adj* 1 earlier in time or order 2 taking precedence (e g in importance) [L, former, superior, compar of OL *pri* before; akin to L *priscus* ancient, *prae* before – more at FOR] – **priorly** *adv*

prioress /'prie·əris, -res/ *n* a nun corresponding in rank to a prior

priority /prie'orəti/ *n* 1a being prior b(1) superiority in rank (2) legal precedence in exercise of rights 2 sthg meriting prior attention

'prior to *prep* before in time; in advance of – fml

priory /'prie·əri/ *n* (the church of) a religious house under a prior or prioress

prise /priez/ *vt, chiefly Br* [5]PRIZE

prism /'priz(ə)m/ *n* 1 a polyhedron whose ends are similar, equal, and parallel polygons and whose faces are parallelograms 2 a transparent body that is bounded in part by 2 nonparallel plane faces and is used to deviate or disperse a beam of light [LL *prismat-, prisma*, fr Gk, lit., anything sawn, fr *priein* to saw]

prismatic /priz'matik/ *adj* 1 of, like, or being a prism 2 formed, dispersed, or refracted (as if) by a prism ⟨~ *effects*⟩ ⟨~ *colours*⟩ – **prismatically** *adv*

prison /'priz(ə)n/ *n* 1 a state of confinement or captivity 2 a place of enforced confinement; *specif* a building in which people are confined for safe custody while on trial or for punishment after conviction [ME, fr OF, fr L *prehension-, prehensio* act of seizing, fr *prehensus*, pp of *prehendere* to seize – more at PREHENSILE] – **prison** *vt*

prisoner /'priz(ə)nə/ *n* sby kept under involuntary confinement; *esp* sby on trial or in prison

,prisoner of 'war *n* a person captured in war

prisoner's base *n* a game in which players on each of 2 teams try to tag and imprison players of the other team who have ventured out of their home territory

prissy /'prisi/ *adj* prim and over-precise; finicky [prob blend of *prim* and *sissy*] – **prissily** *adv*, **prissiness** *n*

pristine /'pristeen, -tien/ *adj* 1 belonging to the earliest period or state 2 free from impurity or decay; fresh and clean as if new [L *pristinus*; akin to L *prior*] – **pristinely** *adv*

prithee /'pridhee/ *interj, archaic* – used to express a wish or request [alter. of (*I*) *pray thee*]

privacy /'prievəsi, pri-/ *n* 1 being apart from the company or observation of others; seclusion 2 freedom from undesirable intrusions and esp publicity [ME *privacie*, fr *privat* private]

[1]**private** /'prievit/ *adj* 1a intended for or restricted to the use of a particular person, group, etc ⟨*a* ~ *park*⟩ b belonging to or concerning an individual person, company, or interest ⟨*a* ~ *house*⟩ c(1) restricted to the individual or arising independently of others ⟨*my* ~ *opinion is that the whole scheme's ridiculous*⟩ (2) independent of the usual institutions ⟨~ *study*⟩ d not general in effect ⟨*a* ~ *statute*⟩ e of or receiving medical treatment in Britain for which fees are charged and in which the patient has more privileges than a patient being treated under the National Health Service f of or administered by a private individual or organization as opposed to a governmental institution or agency ⟨*a* ~ *pension scheme*⟩ 2a(1) not holding public office or employment ⟨*a* ~ *citizen*⟩ (2) not related to one's official position; personal ⟨~ *correspondence*⟩ b having the rank of a private ⟨*a* ~ *soldier*⟩ 3a(1) withdrawn from company or observation; sequestered (2) not seeking or having the companionship of others ⟨*she was a very* ~ *person*⟩ b not (intended to be) known publicly; secret [ME *privat*, fr L *privatus*, fr pp of *privare* to deprive, release, fr *privus* private, set apart; akin to L *pro* for – more at FOR] – **privately** *adv*, **privateness** *n*

[2]**private** *n* ☞ RANK – **in private** not openly or in public

private company *n* a company that has a limited number of shareholders and whose shares are not offered to the general public – compare PUBLIC COMPANY

,private de'tective *n* a person concerned with the maintenance of legal conduct or the investigation of crime either as a regular employee of a private interest (e g a hotel) or as a contractor for fees

private enterprise *n* FREE ENTERPRISE

privateer /,prievə'tiə/ *n* 1 an armed private ship commissioned to cruise against the commerce or warships of an enemy 2 the commander or any of the crew of a privateer – **privateer** *vi*

,private 'eye *n* PRIVATE DETECTIVE

private first class *n* ☞ RANK

private law *n* a branch of law concerned with private people and property

private member's bill *n* a bill that is not part of the government's legislative programme

private parts *n pl* the external genital and excretory organs

private practice *n* the practice of a doctor or dentist outside the National Health Service

private school *n* an independent school that is not a British public school

private sector *n* the part of the economy that is not owned or directly controlled by the state – compare PUBLIC SECTOR

private treaty *n* a sale of property on terms determined by negotiation between the seller and buyer – compare AUCTION

privation /prie'vaysh(ə)n/ *n* 1 an act or instance of depriving; deprivation 2 being deprived; *esp* lack of the usual necessities of life [ME *privacion*, fr MF *privation*, fr L *privation-, privatio*, fr *privatus*, pp of *privare* to deprive – more at PRIVATE]

privative /ˈprivətiv/ *adj* constituting or predicating lack or absence of a quality ⟨*a-, un-, and non- are ~ prefixes*⟩ – **privative** *n*

privat·ization, -isation /ˌprievətieˈzaysh(ə)n/ **1** the avoiding of involvement in anything beyond one's immediate interests **2** the restoration of a nationalized body to private ownership – **privatize** /ˈprievəˌtiez/ *vt*

privet /ˈprivit/ *n* an ornamental shrub with half-evergreen leaves widely planted for hedges [origin unknown]

[1]**privilege** /ˈpriv(i)lij/ *n* a right, immunity, or advantage granted exclusively to a particular person, class, or group; a prerogative; *esp* such an advantage attached to a position or office [ME, fr OF, fr L *privilegium* law for or against a private person, fr *privus* private + *leg-, lex* law]

[2]**privilege** *vt* to grant a privilege to

ˈ**privileged** *adj* **1** having or enjoying 1 or more privileges ⟨*~ classes*⟩ **2** not subject to disclosure in court ⟨*a ~ communication*⟩

privity /ˈprivəti/ *n* **1** joint, usu secret, knowledge of a private matter **2** the relation between people who have a legal interest in the same transaction [ME *privite*, fr OF, fr ML *privitat-, privitas*, fr L *privus* private – more at PRIVATE]

[1]**privy** /ˈprivi/ *adj* **1** sharing in a secret – + *to* ⟨*~ to the conspiracy*⟩ **2** *archaic* secret, private [ME *prive*, fr OF *privé*, fr L *privatus* private] – **privily** *adv*

[2]**privy** *n* **1** a small building containing a bench with a hole in it used as a toilet **2** *NAm* TOILET 2b

Privy Council *n* an advisory council nominally chosen by the British monarch and usu functioning through its committees – **Privy Councillor** *n*

privy purse *n, often cap both Ps* an allowance for the monarch's private expenses

[1]**prize** /priez/ *n* **1** sthg offered or striven for in competition or in a contest of chance **2** sthg exceptionally desirable or precious [ME *pris* prize, price – more at PRICE]

[2]**prize** *adj* **1a** awarded or worthy of a prize ⟨*a ~ pupil*⟩ **b** awarded as a prize ⟨*a ~ medal*⟩ **2** outstanding of a kind ⟨*a ~ idiot*⟩

[3]**prize** *vt* **1** to estimate the value of; rate **2** to value highly; esteem [ME *prisen*, fr MF *prisier*, fr LL *pretiare*, fr L *pretium* price, value – more at PRICE]

[4]**prize** *n* property or shipping lawfully captured at sea in time of war [ME *prise* booty, fr OF, act of taking, fr *prendre* to take, fr L *prehendere* – more at PREHENSILE]

[5]**prize,** *Br also* **prise** /priez/ *vt* **1** to press, force, or move with a lever **2** to open, obtain, or remove with difficulty ⟨*tried to ~ information out of him*⟩ [[4]*prize* (lever)]

ˈ**prize,fighting** /-ˌfieting/ *n* boxing – **prizefight** *n*, **prizefighter** *n*

ˈ**prize ,money** *n* **1** a part of the proceeds of a captured ship formerly divided among the officers and men taking the prize **2** money offered as a prize

ˈ**prize,winning** /-ˌwining/ *adj* having won or of a quality to win a prize ⟨*a ~ design*⟩

[1]**pro** /proh/ *n, pl* **pros** **1** an argument or piece of evidence in favour of a particular proposition or view ⟨*an appraisal of the ~s and cons*⟩ **2** one who favours or supports a particular proposition or view [ME, fr L, prep, for – more at FOR]

[2]**pro** *adv* in favour or affirmation ⟨*much has been written ~ and con*⟩ [*pro-*]

[3]**pro** *prep* for; IN FAVOUR OF 1 [L]

[4]**pro** *n or adj, pl* **pros** (a) professional – infml

[5]**pro** *n, pl* **pros** a prostitute – slang

[1]**pro-** *prefix* **1a** earlier than; prior to; before ⟨pro*logue*⟩ **b** rudimentary; prot- ⟨pro*nucleus*⟩ **2** projecting ⟨prog*nathous*⟩ [ME, fr OF, fr L, fr Gk, before, forwards, forth, for, fr *pro* – more at FOR]

[2]**pro-** /proh-/ *prefix* **1** taking the place of; substituting for ⟨pro*cathedral*⟩ ⟨pro*proctor*⟩ **2** favouring; supporting; championing ⟨pro-*American*⟩ **3** onwards; forwards ⟨pro*gress*⟩ ⟨pro*pel*⟩ [L *pro* in front of, before, for – more at FOR]

proa /ˈproh·ə/ *n* a fast Malay boat shaped like a canoe and equipped with oars, a large triangular sail, and an outrigger [Malay *pĕrahu*]

pro-am /ˌproh ˈam/ *n* an esp golf competition in which amateurs play professionals [*pro*fessional + *am*ateur]

probabilistic /ˌprobəbəˈlistik/ *adj* of or based on probability

probability /ˌprobəˈbiləti/ *n* **1** being probable **2** sthg (e g an occurrence or circumstance) probable **3** a measure of the likelihood that a given event will occur, usu expressed as the ratio of the number of times it occurs in a test series to the total number of trials in the series ☞ STATISTICS

probability function *n* a function of a discrete random variable that gives the probability that a specified value will occur

[1]**probable** /ˈprobəbl/ *adj* **1** supported by evidence strong enough to establish likelihood but not proof **2** likely to be or become true or real ⟨*~ events*⟩ [ME, fr MF, fr L *probabilis*, fr *probare* to test, approve, prove – more at PROVE] – **probably** *adv*

[2]**probable** *n* sby or sthg probable; *esp* sby who will probably be selected ⟨*she's a ~ for the new post*⟩

proband /ˈproh,band/ *n* SUBJECT 3b(1) [L *probandus*, gerundive of *probare*]

probang /ˈproh,bang/ *n* a slender flexible rod with a sponge on one end used esp for removing obstructions from the oesophagus [alter. (prob influenced by [1]*probe*) of earlier *provang* (so named by the inventor), of unknown origin]

[1]**probate** /ˈprohbayt, -bət/ *n* the judicial determination of the validity of a will; *also* an official copy of a will certified as valid [ME *probat*, fr L *probatum*, neut of *probatus*, pp of *probare*]

[2]**probate** *vt, NAm* to establish (a will) by probate

probation /prəˈbaysh(ə)n, proh-/ *n* **1a** subjection of an individual to a period of testing to ascertain fitness **b** a method of dealing with (young) offenders by which sentence is suspended subject to regular supervision by a probation officer **2** the state or a period of being subject to probation – **probational** *adj*, **probationally** *adv*, **probationary** *adj*

probationer /prəˈbaysh(ə)nə/ *n* **1** one (e g a newly admitted student nurse) whose fitness for a post is being tested during a trial period **2** an offender on probation

proˈbation ,officer *n* an officer appointed to supervise the conduct of offenders on probation

probative /ˈprohbətiv/ *adj* serving to prove; substantiating – fml

[1]**probe** /prohb/ *n* **1** a slender surgical instrument for

examining a cavity **2a** a slender pointed metal conductor (e g of electricity or sound) that is temporarily connected to or inserted in the monitored device or quantity **b** a device used to investigate or send back information, esp from interplanetary space ☞ SPACE **3a** the action of probing **b** a tentative exploratory survey **c** a penetrating or critical investigation; an inquiry – journ [ML *proba* examination, fr L *probare*]

[2]**probe** *vt* **1** to examine (as if) with a probe **2** to investigate thoroughly – journ ~*vi* to make an exploratory investigation – **prober** *n*

probit /'prohbit/ *n* a unit of measurement of probability based on deviations from the mean of a normal distribution [*prob*ability un*it*]

probity /'prohbəti/ *n* adherence to the highest principles and ideals; uprightness – fml [MF *probité*, fr L *probitat-, probitas*, fr *probus* honest – more at PROVE]

[1]**problem** /'probləm/ *n* **1a** a question raised for inquiry, consideration, or solution **b** a proposition in mathematics or physics stating sthg to be done **2a** a situation or question that is difficult to understand or resolve **b** sby who is difficult to deal with or understand [ME *probleme*, fr MF, fr L *problema*, fr Gk *problēma*, lit., something thrown forwards, fr *proballein* to throw forwards, fr *pro-* forwards + *ballein* to throw – more at [1]PRO-, DEVIL]

[2]**problem** *adj* **1** dealing with a social or human problem ⟨*a ~ play*⟩ **2** difficult to deal with; presenting a problem ⟨*a ~ child*⟩

problematic /,problə'matik/, **problematical** /-kl/ *adj* **1** difficult to solve or decide; puzzling **2** open to question or debate; questionable **3** *of a proposition in logic* asserted as possible – **problematically** *adv*

proboscidean, proboscidian /,prohbə'sidi·ən/ *n* any of an order of large mammals comprising the elephants and extinct related forms [deriv of L *proboscid-, proboscis*] – **proboscidean** *adj*

proboscis /prə'bosis/ *n, pl* **proboscises** *also* **proboscides** /-,deez/ **1** a long flexible snout (e g the trunk of an elephant) **2** any of various elongated or extendable tubular parts (e g the sucking organ of a mosquito) of an invertebrate ☞ ANATOMY **3** the human nose – infml; humor [L, fr Gk *proboskis*, fr *pro-* + *boskein* to feed; akin to Lith *gauja* herd]

proboscis monkey *n* a large monkey of Borneo with a long fleshy nose

procaryote /,proh'kari·oht/ *n* a prokaryote – **procaryotic** /-'otik/ *adj*

procedural /prə'seej(ə)rəl, -dyoorəl, -dyə-/ *adj* of procedure – **procedurally** *adv*

procedure /prə'seejə, proh-/ *n* **1** a particular way of acting or accomplishing sthg **2** a series of ordered steps ⟨*legal ~*⟩ **3** an established method of doing things ⟨*a stickler for ~*⟩ [F *procédure*, fr MF, fr *proceder*]

proceed /prə'seed, proh-/ *vi* **1** to arise from a source; originate ⟨*this trouble ~ed from a misunderstanding*⟩ **2** to continue after a pause or interruption **3** to begin and carry on an action, process, or movement **4** to move along a course; advance [ME *proceden*, fr MF *proceder*, fr L *procedere*, fr *pro-* forwards + *cedere* to go – more at [1]PRO-, CEDE]

proceeding /prə'seeding, proh-/ *n* **1** a procedure **2** *pl* events, goings-on **3** *pl* legal action ⟨*divorce ~s*⟩ **4** *pl* an official record of things said or done **5** (an) affair, transaction – fml in sing.; usu pl with sing. meaning

proceeds /'prohseedz/ *n pl* **1** the total amount brought in ⟨*the ~ of a sale*⟩ **2** the net amount received [pl of obs *proceed* (proceeds)]

[1]**process** /'prohses/ *n* **1a** a moving forwards, esp as part of a progression or development ⟨*the historical ~*⟩ **b** sthg going on; a proceeding **2a** a natural phenomenon marked by gradual changes that lead towards a particular result ⟨*the ~ of growth*⟩ **b** a series of actions or operations designed to achieve an end; *esp* a continuous operation or treatment (e g in manufacture) **3a** a whole course of legal proceedings **b** a summons, writ **4** a prominent or projecting part of a living organism or an anatomical structure ⟨*a bone ~*⟩ [ME *proces*, fr MF, fr L *processus*, fr *processus*, pp of *procedere*]

[2]**process** *vt* **1** to subject to a special process or treatment (e g in the course of manufacture) **2** to take appropriate action on ⟨*~ an insurance claim*⟩ – **processible, processable** *adj*

[3]**process** *vi, chiefly Br* to move in a procession [back-formation fr *procession*]

procession /prə'sesh(ə)n/ *n* **1** a group of individuals moving along in an orderly way, esp as part of a ceremony or demonstration **2** a succession, sequence

[1]**processional** /prə'sesh(ə)nl/ *n* a musical composition (e g a hymn) designed for a procession

[2]**processional** *adj* of or moving in a procession – **processionally** *adv*

processor /'prohsesə/ *n* **1a** a computer **b** the part of a computer system that operates on data **2** a computer program that puts data into a form acceptable to the computer ***USE*** ☞ COMPUTER [[2]PROCESS + [1]-OR]

procès-verbal /proh,say vuh'bal (*Fr* prɔsɛ vɛrbal)/ *n, pl* **procès-verbaux** /vuhboh (*Fr* vɛrbo)/ a written statement in support of a charge in French law [F, lit., verbal trial]

proclaim /prə'klaym, proh-/ *vt* **1** to declare publicly and usu officially; announce **2** to give outward indication of; show [ME *proclamen*, fr MF or L; MF *proclamer*, fr L *proclamare*, fr *pro-* before + *clamare* to cry out – more at PRO-, CLAIM] – **proclaimer** *n*

proclamation /,proklə'maysh(ə)n/ *n* **1** proclaiming or being proclaimed **2** an official public announcement [ME *proclamacion*, fr MF *proclamation*, fr L *proclamation-, proclamatio*, fr *proclamatus*, pp of *proclamare*]

proclitic /proh'klitik/ *adj, of a word* (*e g* at *in* at *home*) being without independent accent and pronounced with the following word as a phonetic unit [NL *procliticus*, fr Gk *pro-* + LL *-cliticus* (as in *encliticus* enclitic)] – **proclitic** *n*

proclivity /prə'klivəti, proh-/ *n* an inclination or predisposition towards sthg, esp sthg reprehensible – often pl with sing. meaning [L *proclivitas*, fr *proclivis* sloping, prone, fr *pro-* forwards + *clivus* hill – more at PRO-, DECLIVITY]

proconsul /,proh'konsl/ *n* **1** a governor or military commander of an ancient Roman province **2** an administrator in a modern dependency or occupied area [ME, fr L, fr *pro consule* for a consul] – **proconsulship** *n*, **proconsular** /-'konsyoolə/ *adj*, **proconsulate** /-syoolət/ *n*

procrastinate /proh'krastinayt, prə-/ *vi* to delay intentionally and reprehensibly in doing sthg necessary – fml [L *procrastinatus*, pp of *procrastinare*, fr *pro-* forwards + *crastinus* of tomorrow, fr *cras* tomorrow] – **procrastinator** *n*, **procrastination** /-ˈnaysh(ə)n/ *n*

procreate /ˌprohkriˈayt/ *vb* to beget or bring forth (young) [L *procreatus*, pp of *procreare*, fr *pro-* forth + *creare* to create] – **procreative** *adj*, **procreator** *n*, **procreation** /-ˈaysh(ə)n/ *n*

procrustean /prohˈkrustyən, -ti·ən/ *adj, often cap* seeking to enforce or establish conformity (e g to a policy or doctrine) by arbitrary and often violent means [*Procrustes*, mythical robber of ancient Greece who forced his victims to fit a certain bed by stretching them or lopping off their legs, fr L, fr Gk *Prokroustēs*, lit., stretcher]

proctology /prokˈtoləji/ *n* a branch of medicine dealing with the structure and diseases of the anus, rectum, and lower part of the large intestine [Gk *prōktos* anus + E *-logy*] – **proctologist** *n*, **proctologic** /-təˈlojik/, **proctological** *adj*

proctor /ˈproktə/ *n* a supervisor, monitor; *specif* one appointed to maintain student discipline at Oxford or Cambridge [ME *procutour* procurator, proctor, alter. of *procuratour*] – **proctorship** *n*, **proctorial** /-ˈtawri·əl/ *adj*

procumbent /prohˈkumbənt/ *adj* being or having stems that trail along the ground without rooting [L *procumbent-*, *procumbens*, prp of *procumbere* to fall or lean forwards, fr *pro-* forwards + *-cumbere* to lie down – more at RECUMBENT]

procuration /ˌprokyooˈraysh(ə)n/ *n* **1** the authority vested in an attorney **2** the action of obtaining sthg (e g supplies); procurement – fml [ME *procuratioun*, fr MF *procuration*, fr L *procuration-*, *procuratio*, fr *procuratus*, pp of *procurare*]

procurator /ˈprokyooˌraytə/ *n* **1** an agent **2** an administrator of the Roman empire entrusted with the financial management of a province – **procuratorial** /-rəˈtawri·əl/ *adj*

ˌprocurator-ˈfiscal *n, often cap P&F* a local public prosecutor in Scotland

procure /prəˈkyooə/ *vt* **1** to get and provide (esp women) to act as prostitutes **2** to obtain, esp by particular care and effort **3** to achieve; BRING ABOUT ~ *vi* to procure women ***USE*** (*vt 2&3*) fml [ME *procuren* to contrive, obtain, fr LL *procurare*, fr L, to take care of, fr *pro-* for + *cura* care] – **procurable** *adj*, **procurance** *n*, **procurement** *n*

procurer /prəˈkyooərə/, *fem* **procuress** /-ris/ *n* sby who procures women for prostitution [PROCURE + [2]-ER]

[1]**prod** /prod/ *vb* **-dd-** *vt* **1** to poke or jab (as if) with a pointed instrument **2** to incite to action; stir ~ *vi* to make a prodding or jabbing movement, esp repeatedly [perh alter. of E dial. *brod* (to goad); fr or akin to ON *broddr* spike] – **prodder** *n*

[2]**prod** *n* **1** a pointed instrument **2** a prodding action; a jab **3** an incitement to act

[1]**prodigal** /ˈprodigl/ *adj* **1** recklessly extravagant or wasteful **2** yielding abundantly; lavish ⟨~ *of new ideas*⟩ – fml [L *prodigus*, fr *prodigere* to drive away, squander, fr *pro-*, *prod-* forth + *agere* to drive – more at PRO-, AGENT] – **prodigally** *adv*, **prodigality** /-ˈgaləti/ *n*

[2]**prodigal** *n* **1** a repentant sinner or reformed wastrel **2** one who spends or gives lavishly and foolishly

prodigious /prəˈdijəs/ *adj* **1** exciting amazement or wonder **2** extraordinary in bulk, quantity, or degree; enormous – **prodigiously** *adv*, **prodigiousness** *n*

prodigy /ˈprodiji/ *n* **1a** sthg extraordinary, inexplicable, or marvellous **b** an exceptional and wonderful example ⟨*a* ~ *of patience*⟩ **2** a person, esp a child, with extraordinary talents [L *prodigium* omen, monster, fr *pro-*, *prod-* + *-igium* (akin to *aio* I say) – more at ADAGE]

[1]**produce** /prəˈdyoohs/ *vt* **1** to offer to view or notice; exhibit **2** to give birth or rise to **3** to extend in length, area, or volume ⟨~ *a side of a triangle*⟩ **4** to act as a producer of **5** to give being, form, or shape to; make; *esp* to manufacture **6** to (cause to) accumulate ~ *vi* to bear, make, or yield sthg [ME (Sc) *producen*, fr L *producere*, fr *pro-* forwards + *ducere* to lead – more at [1]TOW] – **producible** *adj*

[2]**produce** /ˈprodyoohs/ *n* agricultural products; *esp* fresh fruits and vegetables as distinguished from grain and other staple crops

producer /prəˈdyoohsə/ *n* **1** an individual or entity that grows agricultural products or manufactures articles **2a** sby who has responsibility for the administrative aspects of the production of a film (e g casting, schedules, and esp finance) **b** *Br* DIRECTOR 3 **3** an organism, usu a photosynthetic green plant, that can synthesize organic matter from inorganic materials and that often serves as food for other organisms – compare CONSUMER ☞ FOOD [[1]PRODUCE + [2]-ER]

producer gas *n* a manufactured fuel gas consisting chiefly of carbon monoxide, hydrogen, and nitrogen

product /ˈprodəkt, -dukt/ *n* **1** the result of the multiplying together of 2 or more numbers or expressions **2** sthg produced by a natural or artificial process; *specif* a result of a combination of incidental causes or conditions ⟨*a typical* ~ *of an arts education*⟩ **3** a salable or marketable commodity ⟨*tourism should be regarded as a* ~⟩ [(1) ME, fr ML *productum*, fr L, sthg produced, fr neut of *productus*, pp of *producere*; (2, 3) L *productum*]

production /prəˈduksh(ə)n/ *n* **1a** sthg produced; a product **b(1)** a literary or artistic work **(2)** a work presented on the stage or screen or over the air **2a** the act or process of producing **b** the creation of utility; *esp* the making of goods available for human wants **3** total output, esp of a commodity or an industry – **productional** *adj*

production line *n* LINE 5h

productive /prəˈduktiv/ *adj* **1** having the quality or power of producing, esp in abundance ⟨~ *fishing waters*⟩ **2** effective in bringing about; being the cause *of* **3a** yielding or furnishing results or benefits ⟨*a* ~ *programme of education*⟩ **b** yielding or devoted to the satisfaction of wants or the creation of utilities – **productively** *adv*, **productiveness** *n*, **productivity** /ˌprodukˈtivəti/ *n*

proem /ˈproh·em/ *n* **1** a preface or introduction, esp to a book or speech **2** a prelude [ME *proheme*, fr MF, fr L *prooemium*, fr Gk *prooimion*, fr *pro-* + *oimē* song] – **proemial** /-ˈeemi·əl/ *adj*

proenzyme /ˌproh·ˈenziem/ *n* a zymogen [ISV]

prof /prof/ *n* a professor – slang

profanation /ˌprofəˈnaysh(ə)n/ *n* (a) profaning

[1]**profane** /prəˈfayn/ *vt* **1** to treat (sthg sacred) with abuse, irreverence, or contempt; desecrate **2** to debase by an unworthy or improper use – **profaner** *n*

[2]**profane** *adj* **1** not concerned with religion or religious purposes **2** debasing or defiling what is holy; irreverent **3a** not among the initiated **b** not possessing esoteric or expert knowledge [ME *prophane*, fr MF, fr L *profanus*, fr *pro-* before + *fanum* temple – more at PRO-, FEAST] – **profanely** *adv*, **profaneness** *n*

profanity /prə'fanəti/ *n* **1a** being profane **b** (the use of) profane language **2** a profane utterance

profess /prə'fes/ *vt* **1** to receive formally into a religious community **2a** to declare or admit openly or freely; affirm **b** to declare falsely; pretend **3** to confess one's faith in or allegiance to **4** to be a professor of (an academic discipline) ~ *vi* to make a profession or avowal [(1) ME *professen*, fr *profes*, adj, having professed one's vows, fr OF, fr LL *professus*, fr L, pp of *profitēri* to profess, confess, fr *pro-* before + *fatēri* to acknowledge; (2–4 & vi) L *professus*, pp – more at CONFESS]

pro'fessed *adj* **1** openly and freely admitted or declared ⟨*a* ~ *atheist*⟩ **2** professing to be qualified ⟨*a* ~ *solicitor*⟩ **3** pretended, feigned ⟨~ *misery*⟩ – **professedly** /-sidli/ *adv*

profession /prə'fesh(ə)n/ *n* **1** the act of taking the vows of a religious community **2** an act of openly declaring or claiming a faith, opinion, etc; a protestation **3** an avowed religious faith **4a** a calling requiring specialized knowledge and often long and intensive academic preparation **b** a principal calling, vocation, or employment **c** *sing or pl in constr* the whole body of people engaged in a particular calling

[1]**professional** /prə'fesh(ə)nl/ *adj* **1a** (characteristic) of a profession **b** engaged in 1 of the learned professions **c(1)** characterized by or conforming to the technical or ethical standards of a profession ⟨~ *conduct*⟩ **(2)** characterized by conscientious workmanship ⟨*a sound* ~ *novel*⟩ ⟨*did a really* ~ *job on the garden*⟩ **2a** engaging for gain or livelihood in an activity or field of endeavour often engaged in by amateurs **b** engaged in by professionals ⟨~ *football*⟩ **3** following a line of conduct as though it were a profession ⟨*a* ~ *agitator*⟩ – derog **4** *of a breaking of rules, esp in sport* intentional – euph – **professionalize** *vt*, **professionally** *adv*

[2]**professional** *n* **1** one who engages in a pursuit or activity professionally **2** one with sufficient experience or skill in an occupation or activity to resemble a professional ⟨*a real* ~ *when it comes to mending cars*⟩ – infml

pro'fessionalism /-iz(ə)m/ *n* **1** the esp high and consistent conduct, aims, or qualities that characterize a profession or a professional person **2** the following for gain or livelihood of an activity often engaged in by amateurs

professor /prə'fesə/ *n* **1** sby who professes or declares sthg (e g a faith or opinion) **2a** a staff member of the highest academic rank at a university; *esp* the head of a university department **b** sby who teaches or professes special knowledge of an art, sport, or occupation requiring skill **c** *NAm* a teacher at a university, college, or sometimes secondary school – **professorship** *n*, **professorate** /-rət/ *n*, **professorial** /,profə'sawri·əl/ *adj*

professoriate, professoriat /,profə'sawri·ət/ *n* **1** the body of professors **2** a professorship [modif of F *professorat*, fr *professeur* professor, fr L *professor*, fr *professus*]

proffer /'profə/ *vt* to present for acceptance; tender [ME *profren*, fr AF *profrer*, fr OF *poroffrir*, fr *porforth* (fr L *pro-*) + *offrir* to offer – more at PRO-]

proficient /prə'fish(ə)nt/ *adj* well advanced or expert in an art, skill, branch of knowledge, etc [L *proficient-*, *proficiens*, prp of *proficere* to go forwards, accomplish, fr *pro-* forwards + *facere* to make – more at PRO-, [1]DO] – **proficiency** *n*, **proficient** *n*, **proficiently** *adv*

[1]**profile** /'prohfiel/ *n* **1** a side view, esp of the human face **2** an outline seen or represented in sharp relief; a contour **3** a side or sectional elevation: e g **a** a drawing showing a vertical section of the ground **b** a vertical section of a soil from the ground surface to the underlying material **4** a concise written or spoken biographical sketch [It *profilo*, fr *profilare* to draw in outline, fr *pro-* forwards (fr L) + *filare* to spin, fr LL – more at [5]FILE]

[2]**profile** *vt* **1** to represent in profile or by a profile; produce a profile of (e g by drawing or writing) **2** to shape the outline of by passing a cutter round – **profiler** *n*

[1]**profit** /'profit/ *n* **1** a valuable return; a gain **2** the excess of returns over expenditure **3** compensation for the assumption of risk in business enterprise, as distinguished from wages or rent [ME, fr MF, fr L *profectus* advance, profit, fr *profectus*, pp of *proficere*] – **profitless** *adj*

[2]**profit** *vi* to derive benefit; gain – usu + *from* or *by* ⟨~ed *greatly from these lessons*⟩ ~ *vt* to be of service to; benefit ⟨*it will not* ~ *you to start an argument*⟩

profitable /'profitəbl/ *adj* affording financial or other gains or profits – **profitableness** *n*, **profitably** *adv*, **profitability** /-tə'biləti/ *n*

profiteer /,profi'tiə/ *n* one who makes an unreasonable profit, esp on the sale of scarce and essential goods – **profiteer** *vi*

profiterole /'profitə,rohl, ,---'-, prə'fitə,rohl/ *n* a small hollow ball of cooked choux pastry that is filled with a sweet or savoury preparation; *esp* one filled with whipped cream and covered with a chocolate sauce [F, fr *profiter* to profit]

profit sharing *n* a system or process under which employees receive a part of the profits of an industrial or commercial enterprise

[1]**profligate** /'profligət/ *adj* **1** utterly dissolute; immoral **2** wildly extravagant; prodigal [L *profligatus*, fr pp of *profligare* to strike down, fr *pro-* forwards, down + *-fligare* (akin to *fligere* to strike); akin to Gk *thlibein* to squeeze] – **profligacy** *n*, **profligately** *adv*

[2]**profligate** *n* a person given to wildly extravagant and usu grossly self-indulgent expenditure

pro forma /,proh 'fawmə/ *adj* **1** made or carried out in a perfunctory manner or as a formality **2** provided in advance to prescribe form or describe items ⟨~ *invoice*⟩ [L]

profound /prə'fownd/ *adj* **1a** having intellectual depth and insight **b** difficult to fathom or understand **2a** extending far below the surface **b** coming from, reaching to, or situated at a depth; deep-seated ⟨*a* ~ *sigh*⟩ **3a** characterized by intensity of feeling or quality **b** all encompassing; complete ⟨~ *sleep*⟩ [ME, fr MF *profond* deep, fr L *profundus*, fr *pro-* before + *fundus* bottom – more at PRO-, BOTTOM] – **profoundly** *adv*, **profoundness** *n*

profundity /prə'fundəti/ *n* **1a** intellectual depth **b**

sthg profound or abstruse **2** being profound or deep [ME *profundite*, fr MF *profundité*, fr L *profunditat-, profunditas* depth, fr *profundus*]

profuse /prə'fyoohs/ *adj* **1** liberal, extravagant ⟨~ *in their thanks*⟩ **2** greatly abundant; bountiful ⟨*a ~ harvest*⟩ [ME, fr L *profusus*, pp of *profundere* to pour forth, fr *pro-* forth + *fundere* to pour – more at [4]FOUND] – **profusely** *adv*, **profuseness** *n*

profusion /prə'fyoohzh(ə)n/ *n* **1** being profuse **2** a large or lavish amount

progenitor /,proh'jenitə/ *n* **1a** a direct ancestor; a forefather **b** a biologically ancestral form **2** a precursor, originator [ME, fr MF *progeniteur*, fr L *progenitor*, fr *progenitus*, pp of *progignere* to beget, fr *pro-* forth + *gignere* to beget – more at KIN]

progeny /'projini/ *n* **1** *sing or pl in constr* **a** descendants, children **b** offspring of animals or plants **2** an outcome, product – fml [ME *progenie*, fr OF, fr L *progenies*, fr *progignere*]

progestational /,prohje'staysh(ə)nl/ *adj* preceding pregnancy or gestation; *esp* associated with ovulation

progesterone /proh'jestə,rohn/ *n* a steroid progestational hormone [*progestin* + *sterol* + *-one*]

progestin /proh'jestin/ *n* a progestational hormone; *esp* progesterone [*pro-* + *gestation* + *-in*]

progestogen /proh'jestəjin/ *n* any of several progestational steroids (e g progesterone) [*progestational* + *-ogen* (as in *oestrogen*)]

proglottid /proh'glotid/ *n* a segment of a tapeworm containing both male and female reproductive organs [NL *proglottid-, proglottis*, fr Gk *proglōttis* tip of the tongue, fr *pro-* + *glōtta* tongue – more at [2]GLOSS; fr its shape] – **proglottidean** /-,gloti'dee·ən, -glo'tidi·ən/ *adj*

,pro'glottis /-'glotis/ *n, pl* **proglottides** /-ti,deez/ a proglottid

prognathic /prog'nathik/ *adj* prognathous

prognathous /prog'naythəs/ *adj* having the jaws projecting beyond the upper part of the face

prognosis /prog'nohsis/ *n, pl* **prognoses** /-seez/ **1** the prospect of recovery as anticipated from the usual course of disease or peculiarities of a particular case **2** a forecast, prognostication – fml [LL, fr Gk *prognōsis*, lit., foreknowledge, fr *progignōskein* to know before, fr *pro-* + *gignōskein* to know – more at KNOW]

prognostic /prog'nostik/ *n* **1** sthg that foretells; a portent **2** prognostication, prophecy *USE* fml [ME *pronostique*, fr MF, fr L *prognosticum*, fr Gk *prognōstikon*, fr neut of *prognōstikos* foretelling, fr *progignōskein*] – **prognostic** *adj*

prognosticate /prog'nosti,kayt/ *vt* **1** to foretell from signs or symptoms; predict **2** to indicate in advance; presage *USE* fml – **prognosticator** *n*, **prognosticative** /-kətiv/ *adj*, **prognostication** /-'kaysh(ə)n/ *n*

prograde /,proh'grayd/ *adj, of orbital or rotational movement* in the same direction as neighbouring celestial bodies – compare RETROGRADE [L *pro-* forwards + *gradi* to go – more at PRO-, GRADE]

[1]**program** /'prohgram/ *n* **1a** a plan for the programming of a mechanism (e g a computer) ☞ COMPUTER **b** a sequence of coded instructions that can be inserted into a mechanism (e g a computer) or that is part of an organism **2** *chiefly NAm* a programme

[2]**program** *vt* **-mm-** (*NAm* **-mm-, -m-**) **1** to work out a sequence of operations to be performed by (a computer or similar mechanism); provide with a program **2** *chiefly NAm* to programme – **programmable** *adj*, **programmability** /-mə'biləti/ *n*

programmatic /,prohgrə'matik/ *adj* **1** of programme music **2** of, resembling, or having a programme – **programmatically** *adv*

[1]**programme,** *NAm chiefly* **program** /'prohgram/ *n* **1a** a brief usu printed (pamphlet containing a) list of the features to be presented, the people participating, etc (e g in a public performance or entertainment) **b** the performance of a programme **c** a radio or television broadcast characterized by some feature (e g a presenter, a purpose, or a theme) giving it coherence and continuity ☞ TELEVISION **2** a systematic plan of action ⟨*a rehousing ~*⟩ **3** a curriculum **4** a prospectus, syllabus **5** matter for programmed instruction [F *programme* agenda, public notice, fr Gk *programma*, fr *prographein* to write before, fr *pro-* before + *graphein* to write]

[2]**programme,** *NAm chiefly* **program** *vt* **1a** to arrange or provide a programme of or for **b** to enter in a programme **2** to cause to conform to a pattern (e g of thought or behaviour); condition ⟨*our visions of marriage have been ~*d *by Hollywood*⟩ – **programmable** *adj*, **programming** *n*, **programmability** /-mə'biləti/ *n*

'programmed, *NAm also* **programed** *adj* (in the form) of programmed instruction

programmed instruction *n* instruction given in small steps with each requiring a correct response by the learner before going on to the next step

programme music *n* music intended to suggest a sequence of images or incidents

programmer, *NAm also* **programer** /'prohgramə/ *n* **1** a person or device that prepares and tests programs for mechanisms **2** a person or device that programs a mechanism (e g a computer) **3** one who prepares educational programmes [[2]PROGRAM, [2]PROGRAMME + [2]-ER]

[1]**progress** /'prohgres/ *n* **1a** a ceremonial journey; *esp* a monarch's tour of his/her dominions **b** an expedition, journey, or march **2** a forward or onward movement (e g to an objective or goal); an advance **3** gradual improvement; *esp* the progressive development of mankind [ME, fr L *progressus* advance, fr *progressus*, pp of *progredi* to go forth, fr *pro-* forwards + *gradi* to go – more at PRO-, GRADE] – **in progress** occurring; going on

[2]**progress** /prə'gres/ *vi* **1** to move forwards; proceed **2** to develop to a higher, better, or more advanced stage ~ *vt* **1** to oversee and ensure the satisfactory progress or running of (e g a project) ⟨*the editor must ~ articles from conception to publication*⟩ **2** to ascertain and attempt to bring forward the delivery or completion date of ⟨*~ these orders*⟩

progression /prə'gresh(ə)n/ *n* **1** a sequence of numbers in which each term is related to its predecessor by a uniform law **2a** progressing, advance **b** a continuous and connected series; a sequence **3** succession of musical notes or chords – **progressional** *adj*

[1]**progressive** /prə'gresiv/ *adj* **1a** of or characterized by progress or progression **b** making use of or interested in new ideas, findings, or opportunities **c** of or being an educational theory marked by emphasis on the individual, informality, and self-expression **2** moving forwards continuously or in stages; advanc-

ing **3** increasing in extent or severity ⟨*a* ~ *disease*⟩ **4** of or constituting a verb form (e g *am working*) that expresses action in progress **5** increasing in rate as the base increases ⟨*a* ~ *tax*⟩ – **progressively** *adv*, **progressiveness** *n*, **progressivism** *n*, **progressivist** *n or adj*, **progressivistic** /-'vistik/ *adj*

²**progressive** *n* **1** sby or sthg progressive **2** sby believing in moderate political change, esp social improvement; *esp, cap* a member of a political party that advocates these beliefs

prohibit /prə'hibit, proh-/ *vt* **1** to forbid by authority **2a** to prevent from doing sthg **b** to preclude [ME *prohibiten*, fr L *prohibitus*, pp of *prohibēre* to hold away, fr *pro-* forwards + *habēre* to hold]

prohibition /,proh·hi'bish(ə)n/ *n* **1** the act of prohibiting by authority **2** an order to restrain or stop **3** *often cap* the forbidding by law of the manufacture and sale of alcohol **4** a judicial writ prohibiting a lower court from proceeding in a case beyond its jurisdiction – **prohibitionist** *n*

prohibitive /prə'hibətiv, proh-/, **prohibitory** /-t(ə)ri/ *adj* **1** tending to prohibit or restrain **2** tending to preclude the use or acquisition of sthg ⟨*the running expenses seemed* ~⟩ – **prohibitively** *adv*, **prohibitiveness** *n*

¹**project** /'projekt; *also* proh-/ *n* **1** a specific plan or design; a scheme **2** a planned undertaking: e g **a** a definitely formulated piece of research **b** a large undertaking, esp a public works scheme **c** a task or problem engaged in usu by a group of pupils, esp to supplement and apply classroom studies [ME *proiecte*, modif of MF *pourjet*, fr *pourjeter* to throw out, spy, plan, fr *pour-* (fr L *porro* forwards) + *jeter* to throw; akin to Gk *pro* forwards – more at FOR, ²JET]

²**project** /prə'jekt/ *vt* **1a** to devise in the mind; design **b** to plan, figure, or estimate for the future **2** to throw forwards or upwards, esp by mechanical means **3** to present or transport in imagination ⟨*a book that tries to* ~ *how the world will look in 2100*⟩ **4** to cause to protrude **5** to cause (light or an image) to fall into space or on a surface **6** to reproduce (e g a point, line, or area) on a surface by motion in a prescribed direction **7a** to cause (one's voice) to be heard at a distance **b** to communicate vividly, esp to an audience **c** to present or express (oneself) in a manner that wins approval ⟨*must learn to* ~ *yourself better if you want the job*⟩ **8** to attribute (sthg in one's own mind) to a person, group, or object ⟨*a nation is an entity on which one can* ~ *many of the worst of one's instincts – TLS*⟩ ~ *vi* **1** to jut out; protrude **2** to attribute sthg in one's own mind to a person, group, or object [partly modif of MF *pourjeter*; partly fr L *projectus*, pp of *proicere* to throw forwards, fr *pro-* + *jacere* to throw – more at ²JET] – **projectable** *adj*

¹**projectile** /prə'jektiel/ *n* **1** a body projected by external force and continuing in motion by its own inertia; *esp* a missile (e g a bullet, shell, or grenade) fired from a weapon **2** a self-propelling weapon (e g a rocket)

²**projectile** *adj* **1** projecting or impelling **2** capable of being thrust forwards

projection /prə'jeksh(ə)n/ *n* **1a** a systematic representation on a flat surface of latitude and longitude from the curved surface of the earth, celestial sphere, etc **b** (a graphic reproduction formed by) the process of reproducing a spatial object on a surface by projecting its points **2** the act of throwing or shooting forward; ejection **3a** a jutting out **b** a part that juts out **4** the act of perceiving a subjective mental image as objective **5** the attribution of one's own ideas, feelings, or attitudes to other people or to objects, esp as a defence against feelings of guilt or inadequacy **6** the display of films or slides by projecting an image from them onto a screen **7** an estimate of future possibilities based on a current trend – **projectional** *adj*

projectionist /prə'jekch(ə)nist/ *n* the operator of a film projector or television equipment

projective /prə'jektiv/ *adj* of, produced by, or involving projection – **projectively** *adv*

projector /prə'jektə/ *n* an apparatus for projecting films or pictures onto a surface ☞ TELEVISION [²PROJECT + ¹-OR]

prokaryote, procaryote /proh'kari,oht/ *n* an organism (e g a bacterium or a blue-green alga) that does not have a distinct nucleus – compare EUKARYOTE [*pro-* + *kary-* + *-ote* (as in *zygote*)] – **prokaryotic** /-'otik/ *adj*

prolactin /proh'laktin/ *n* a pituitary hormone that causes milk production in some mammals [²*pro-* + *lact-* + *-in*]

prolapse /'proh,laps/ *n* the falling down or slipping of a body part (e g the uterus) from its usual position or relations [NL *prolapsus*, fr LL, fall, fr L *prolapsus*, pp of *prolabi* to fall or slide forwards, fr *pro-* forwards + *labi* to slide – more at PRO-, SLEEP] – **prolapse** *vi*

prolate /'proh,layt/ *adj* elongated in the direction of a line joining the poles ⟨*a* ~ *spheroid*⟩ – compare OBLATE [L *prolatus* (pp of *proferre* to bring forwards, extend), fr *pro-* forwards + *latus*, pp of *ferre* to carry]

prole /prohl/ *n or adj* (a) proletarian – derog

proleg /'proh,leg/ *n* a fleshy leg on an abdominal segment of some insect larvae ☞ ANATOMY

prolegomenon /,prohle'gominən, ,pro-/ *n, pl* **prolegomena** /-minə/ an introductory section, esp to a learned work [Gk, neut prp passive of *prolegein* to say beforehand, fr *pro-* before + *legein* to say] – **prolegomenous** *adj*

prolepsis /proh'lepsis/ *n, pl* **prolepses** /-,seez/ anticipation; *esp* the representation of a future act or development as already existing or accomplished – fml [Gk *prolēpsis*, fr *prolambanein* to take beforehand, fr *pro-* before + *lambanein* to take – more at LATCH] – **proleptic** /-'leptik/ *adj*

proletarian /,prohli'teəri·ən/ *n or adj* (a member) of the proletariat [n L *proletarius*, member of the lowest social class who served the state by producing offspring, fr *proles* progeny, fr *pro-* forth + *-olescere* (fr *alescere* to grow) – more at OLD; adj fr n] – **proletarianize** *vt*, **proletarianization** /-'zaysh(ə)n/ *n*

proletariat /,prohli'teəri·ət/ *n sing or pl in constr* **1** the lowest class of a community **2** WORKING CLASS; *esp* those workers who lack their own means of production and hence sell their labour to live [F *prolétariat*, fr L *proletarius*]

¹**proliferate** /prə'lifərayt/ *vi* to grow or increase (as if) by rapid production of new parts, cells, buds, etc [back-formation fr *proliferation*, fr F *prolifération*, fr *proliférer* to proliferate, fr *prolifère* proliferous, fr L

proles + *-fer* -ferous] – **proliferative** /-'lif(ə)rətiv/ *adj*, **proliferatively** *adv*, **proliferation** /-'raysh(ə)n/ *n*

²**proliferate** /prə'lif(ə)rət/ *adj* increased in number or quantity [back-formation fr *proliferation*]

proliferous /prə'lif(ə)rəs/ *adj* undergoing proliferation; *specif, of a plant* reproducing by putting out runners, side shoots, etc – **proliferously** *adv*

prolific /prə'lifik/ *adj* **1** producing young or fruit (freely) **2** marked by abundant inventiveness or productivity ⟨*a* ~ *writer*⟩ [F *prolifique*, fr L *proles* progeny] – **prolificacy** /-kəsi/ *n*, **prolifically** *adv*, **prolificness** *n*, **prolificity** /-li'fisəti/ *n*

prolix /'proh,liks/ *adj* **1** unduly prolonged or repetitious ⟨*a* ~ *speech*⟩ **2** given to verbosity in speaking or writing; long-winded [ME, fr MF & L; MF *prolixe*, fr L *prolixus* extended, fr *pro-* forwards + *liquēre* to be fluid – more at LIQUID] – **prolixity** /-'liksəti/ *n*, **prolixly** *adv*

prologue, *NAm also* **prolog** /'prohlog/ *n* **1** the preface or introduction to a literary work **2** (the actor delivering) a speech, often in verse, addressed to the audience at the beginning of a play **3** an introductory or preceding event or development [ME *prolog*, fr OF *prologue*, fr L *prologus* preface to a play, fr Gk *prologos* part of a Greek play preceding the entry of the chorus, fr *pro-* before + *legein* to speak – more at PRO-, LEGEND]

prolong /prə'long/ *vt* **1** to lengthen in time; continue **2** to lengthen in space ⟨*to* ~ *a line*⟩ [ME *prolongen*, fr MF *prolonguer*, fr LL *prolongare*, fr L *pro-* forwards + *longus* long] – **prolonger** /-'long·ə, -'long·gə, proh-/ *n*, **prolongation** /,proh,long'gaysh(ə)n, ,pro-/ *n*

prom /prom/ *n* **1** PROMENADE CONCERT **2** *Br* PROMENADE 2

¹**promenade** /'promə,nahd, ,--'-/ *n* **1** a leisurely stroll or ride taken for pleasure, usu in a public place and often as a social custom **2** a place for strolling; *esp, Br* a paved walk along the seafront at a resort [F, fr *promener* to take for a walk, fr L *prominare* to drive forwards, fr *pro-* forwards + *minare* to drive – more at AMENABLE]

²**promenade** *vi* to take or go on a promenade ~ *vt* **1** to walk about in or on **2** to display (as if) by promenading around ⟨~d *his new bicycle in front of his friends*⟩

promenade concert *n* a concert at which some of the audience stand or can walk about

promenade deck *n* an upper deck or an area on a deck of a passenger ship where passengers may stroll

promenader /promə'nahdə/ *n* sby attending a promenade concert [²PROMENADE + ²-ER]

Promethean /prə'meethyən/ *adj* daringly original or creative [*Prometheus*, demigod of Greek myth who stole fire from Zeus & gave it to man, fr L, fr Gk *Promētheus*]

promethium /prə'meethyəm/ *n* a metallic element of the rare-earth group obtained as a fission product of uranium ☞ PERIODIC TABLE [NL, fr L *Prometheus*]

prominence /'prominəns/ *n* **1** being prominent or conspicuous **2** sthg prominent; a projection ⟨*a rocky* ~⟩ **3** a large mass of gas arising from the lower solar atmosphere

prominent /'prominənt/ *adj* **1** projecting beyond a surface or line; protuberant **2a** readily noticeable; conspicuous **b** widely and popularly known; leading [L *prominent-*, *prominens*, fr prp of *prominēre* to jut forwards, fr *pro-* forwards + *-minēre* (akin to *mont-*, *mons* mountain) – more at ¹MOUNT] – **prominently** *adv*

promiscuity /,promi'skyooh·əti/ *n* **1** a miscellaneous mixture or mingling of people or things **2** promiscuous sexual behaviour

promiscuous /prə'miskyoo·əs/ *adj* **1** composed of a mixture of people or things **2** not restricted to 1 class or person; indiscriminate; *esp* not restricted to 1 sexual partner **3** casual, irregular ⟨~ *eating habits*⟩ [L *promiscuus*, fr *pro-* forth + *miscēre* to mix – more at PRO-, MIX] – **promiscuously** *adv*, **promiscuousness** *n*

¹**promise** /'promis/ *n* **1a** a declaration that one will do or refrain from doing sthg specified **b** a legally binding declaration **2** grounds for expectation usu of success, improvement, or excellence ⟨*show* ~⟩ **3** sthg promised [ME *promis*, fr L *promissum*, fr neut of *promissus*, pp of *promittere* to send forth, promise, fr *pro-* forth + *mittere* to send – more at PRO-, SMITE]

²**promise** *vt* **1** to pledge oneself to do, bring about, or provide (sthg for) ⟨~ *aid*⟩ ⟨*but you* ~d *me*⟩ **2** to assure ⟨*it can be done, I* ~ *you*⟩ **3** to betroth **4** to suggest beforehand; indicate ⟨*dark clouds* ~ *rain*⟩ ~ *vi* **1** to make a promise **2** to give grounds for expectation, esp of sthg good

promised land *n* a place or condition believed to promise final satisfaction or realization of hopes [fr God's promise to Abram (Abraham) in Gen 12:7]

promisee /,promi'see/ *n* sby to whom a promise is made

promising /'promising/ *adj* full of promise; likely to succeed or to yield good results – **promisingly** *adv*

promisor /,promi'saw, 'promisə/ *n* one who makes a (legally binding) promise

promissory /'promis(ə)ri/ *adj* containing or conveying a promise [ML *promissorius*, fr L *promissus*, pp]

promissory note *n* a written promise to pay, either on demand or at a fixed or determinable future time, a sum of money to a specified individual or to the bearer

promo /'promoh/ *n*, *pl* **promos** *chiefly Austr* an advertising promotion – infml [short for *promotion*]

promontory /'promənt(ə)ri/ *n* **1** HEADLAND 2 **2** a bodily prominence [L *promunturium*, *promonturium*; prob akin to *prominēre* to jut forth – more at PROMINENT]

promote /prə'moht/ *vt* **1a** to advance in station, rank, or honour; raise **b** to change (a pawn) into a more valuable piece in chess by moving to the 8th rank **c** to assign to a higher division of a sporting competition (e g a football league) – compare RELEGATE **2a** to contribute to the growth or prosperity of; further ⟨~ *international understanding*⟩ **b** to help bring (e g an enterprise) into being; launch **c** to present (e g merchandise) for public acceptance through advertising and publicity [L *promotus*, pp of *promovēre*, lit., to move forwards, fr *pro-* forwards + *movēre* to move] – **promoter** *n*, **promotive** *adj*

promotion /prə'mohsh(ə)n/ *n* **1** the act or fact of being raised in position or rank; preferment **2a** the act of furthering the growth or development of sthg, esp sales or public awareness **b** sthg (e g a price reduction or free sample) intended to promote esp sales of merchandise – **promotional** *adj*

[1]**prompt** /'prompt/ *vt* **1** to move to action; incite ⟨*curiosity* ~ed *him to ask the question*⟩ **2** to assist (sby acting or reciting) by saying the next words of sthg forgotten or imperfectly learnt **3** to serve as the inciting cause of; urge ⟨~s *serious anxiety about unemployment*⟩ [ME *prompten*, fr ML *promptare*, fr L *promptus* prompt] – **prompter** *n*

[2]**prompt** *adj* of or for prompting actors

[3]**prompt** *adj* **1a** ready and quick to act as occasion demands **b** PUNCTUAL 2 **2** performed readily or immediately ⟨~ *assistance*⟩ [ME, fr MF or L; MF, fr L *promptus* ready, prompt, fr pp of *promere* to bring forth, fr *pro-* forth + *emere* to take – more at REDEEM] – **promptly** *adv*, **promptness** *n*

[4]**prompt** *n* **1** the act or an instance of prompting; a reminder **2** (the contract fixing) a limit of time given for payment of an account for goods purchased

promptitude /'prompti,tyoohd/ *n* the quality or habit of being prompt; promptness – fml [ME, fr MF or LL; MF, fr LL *promptitudo*, fr L *promptus*]

promulgate /'prom(ə)l,gayt/ *vt* to make known by open declaration; proclaim – fml [L *promulgatus*, pp of *promulgare* to proclaim] – **promulgator** *n*, **promulgation** /-'gaysh(ə)n/ *n*

pronate /proh'nayt/ *vt* to rotate (the hand or forearm) so that the palm faces downwards or backwards [LL *pronatus*, pp of *pronare* to bend forwards, fr L *pronus*] – **pronation** /-'naysh(ə)n/ *n*

prone /prohn/ *adj* **1** having a tendency or inclination; disposed *to* **2** having the front or ventral surface downwards; prostrate – compare SUPINE 1a [ME, fr L *pronus* bent forwards, tending; akin to L *pro* forwards – more at FOR] – **prone** *adv*, **pronely** *adv*, **proneness** *n*

[1]**prong** /prong/ *n* **1** any of the slender sharp-pointed parts of a fork **2** a subdivision of an argument, attacking force, etc [ME *pronge, prange* fork; perh akin to MHG *pfrengen* to press, Lith *branktas* whiffletree]

[2]**prong** *vt* to stab, pierce, or break up (as if) with a prong

pronged *adj* having or divided into prongs; *esp* having more than 1 attacking force, each coming from a different direction – usu in combination ⟨*a 3-*pronged *attack*⟩

'**prong,horn** /-,hawn/ *n, pl* **pronghorns,** *esp collectively* **pronghorn** a ruminant mammal of treeless parts of western N America that resembles an antelope

pronominal /,proh'nominl, prə-/ *adj* of, resembling, or constituting a pronoun [LL *pronominalis*, fr L *pronomin-, pronomen*] – **pronominally** *adv*

pronoun /'prohnoun/ *n* a word used as a substitute for a noun or noun equivalent and referring to a previously named or understood person or thing [ME *pronom*, fr L *pronomin-, pronomen*, fr *pro-* for + *nomin-, nomen* name – more at PRO-, NAME]

pronounce /prə'nowns/ *vt* **1** to declare officially or ceremoniously ⟨*the priest* ~d *them man and wife*⟩ **2** to declare authoritatively or as an opinion ⟨*doctors* ~d *him fit to resume duties*⟩ **3** to utter the sounds of; *esp* to say correctly ~ *vi* **1** to pass judgment; declare one's opinion definitely or authoritatively – often + *on* or *upon* **2** to produce speech sounds ⟨*she* ~s *abominably*⟩ [ME *pronouncen*, fr MF *prononcier*, fr L *pronuntiare*, fr *pro-* forth + *nuntiare* to report, fr *nuntius* messenger – more at PRO-] – **pronounceable** *adj*, **pronouncer** *n*

pro'nounced *adj* strongly marked; decided – **pronouncedly** /-sidli/ *adv*

pro'nouncement /-mənt/ *n* **1** a usu formal declaration of opinion **2** an authoritative announcement

pronto /'prontoh/ *adv* without delay; quickly – infml [Sp, fr L *promptus* prompt]

pronunciamento /prə,nunsi·ə'mentoh/ *n, pl* **pronunciamentos, pronunciamentoes** a declaration; *esp* one made by the leaders of a revolt announcing a change of government [Sp *pronunciamiento*, fr *pronunciar* to pronounce, fr L *pronuntiare*]

pronunciation /prə,nunsi'aysh(ə)n/ *n* the act or manner of pronouncing sthg ☞ ALPHABET [ME *pronunciacion*, fr MF *prononciation*, fr L *pronuntiation-, pronuntiatio*, fr *pronuntiatus*, pp of *pronuntiare*] – **pronunciational** *adj*

pro-oestrus /,proh 'eestrəs/ *n* a period immediately preceding oestrus characterized by preparatory physiological changes [NL]

[1]**proof** /proohf/ *n* **1** the cogency of evidence that compels acceptance of a truth or a fact **2** an act, effort, or operation designed to establish or discover a fact or the truth; a test **3** legal evidence **4a** an impression (e g from type) taken for examination or correction **b** a proof impression of an engraving, lithograph, etc **c** a test photographic print **5** a test of the quality of an article or substance **6** the alcoholic content of a beverage compared with the standard for proof spirit [ME, alter. of *preove*, fr OF *preuve*, fr LL *proba*, fr L *probare* to prove – more at PROVE]

[2]**proof** *adj* **1** designed for or successful in resisting or repelling; impervious – often in combination ⟨*water*proof⟩ ⟨*sound*proof⟩ **2** used in proving or testing or as a standard of comparison **3** of standard strength or quality or alcoholic content

[3]**proof** *vt* **1** to make or take a proof of **2** to give a resistant quality to; make (sthg) proof *against* – **proofer** *n*

'**proof,read** /-,reed/ *vt* to read and mark corrections on (a proof) [back-formation fr *proofreader*] – **proofreader** *n*

proof spirit *n* a mixture of alcohol and water containing a standard amount of alcohol, in Britain 57.1% by volume

[1]**prop** /prop/ *n* **1** a rigid usu auxiliary vertical support (e g a pole) ⟨*pit* ~⟩ **2** a source of strength or support ⟨*his son was his chief* ~ *in his old age*⟩ **3** PROP FORWARD [ME *proppe*, fr MD, stopper; akin to MLG *proppe* stopper]

[2]**prop** *vt* **-pp- 1** to support by placing sthg under or against **2** to support by placing against sthg *USE* often + *up*; compare PROP UP

[3]**prop** /prop/ *n* any article or object used in a play or film other than painted scenery or costumes [short for *property*]

[4]**prop** /prop/ *n* a propeller

propaganda /,propə'gandə/ *n* **1** *cap* a division of the Roman curia having jurisdiction over missionary territories and related institutions **2** (the usu organized spreading of) ideas, information, or rumour designed to promote or damage an institution, movement, person, etc [NL, fr *Congregatio de propaganda fide* Congregation for propagating the faith, organization established by Pope Gregory XV †1623]

propagand·ize, -ise /ˌpropəˈgandiez/ *vb* to subject to or carry on propaganda – **propagandism** *n*, **propagandist** *n or adj*, **propagandistic** /-ˈdistik/ *adj*, **propagandistically** *adv*

propagate /ˈpropəˌgayt/ *vt* **1** to reproduce or increase by sexual or asexual reproduction **2** to pass down (e g a characteristic) to offspring **3a** to cause to spread out and affect a greater number or area; disseminate **b** to publicize ⟨~ *the Gospel*⟩ **c** to transmit ~ *vi* **1** to multiply sexually or asexually **2** to increase, extend [L *propagatus*, pp of *propagare* to set slips, propagate, fr *propages* slip, offspring, fr *pro-* before + *pangere* to fasten – more at PRO-, PACT] – **propagator** *n*, **propagable** /ˈpropəgəbl/ *adj*, **propagative** /-gətiv/ *adj*

propagation /ˌpropəˈgaysh(ə)n/ *n* **1** an increase (e g of a type of organism) in numbers **2** the spreading of sthg (e g a belief) abroad or into new regions **3** an enlargement or extension (e g of a crack) in a solid body [PROPAGATE + -ION] – **propagational** *adj*

propane /ˈprohpayn/ *n* a hydrocarbon of the alkane series used as a fuel [ISV, fr *propionic (acid)* + *-ane*]

propel /prəˈpel/ *vt* **-ll-** **1** to drive forwards by means of a force that imparts motion **2** to urge on; motivate [ME *propellen*, fr L *propellere*, fr *pro-* before + *pellere* to drive – more at FELT]

propellant *also* **propellent** /prəˈpelənt/ *n* sthg that propels: e g **a** a fuel for propelling projectiles **b** fuel plus oxidizer used by a rocket engine **c** a gas in a pressurized container for expelling the contents when the pressure is released

propellent, propellant /prəˈpelənt/ *adj* capable of propelling

proˈpeller *also* **propellor** /prəˈpelə/ *n* SCREW PROPELLER [PROPEL + ²-ER, ¹-OR]

propeller shaft *n* a shaft that transmits mechanical power, esp from an engine ☞ CAR

propelling pencil /prəˈpeling/ *n*, *Br* a usu metal or plastic pencil whose lead can be extended by a screw device

propensity /prəˈpensəti/ *n* a natural inclination or tendency – fml [arch *propense* (leaning towards, disposed), fr L *propensus*, pp of *propendēre* to lean or incline towards, fr *pro-* before + *pendēre* to hang – more at PENDANT]

¹proper /ˈpropə/ *adj* **1** suitable, appropriate **2** appointed for the liturgy of a particular day **3** belonging to one; own **4** represented heraldically in natural colour **5** belonging characteristically *to* a species or individual; peculiar **6** being strictly so-called ⟨*the borough is not part of the city* ~⟩ **7a** strictly accurate; correct **b** strictly decorous; genteel ⟨*a very prim and* ~ *gentleman*⟩ **8** *chiefly Br* thorough, complete ⟨*I felt a* ~ *Charlie!*⟩ [ME *propre* proper, own, fr OF, fr L *proprius* own, special] – **properness** *n*

²proper *n* the parts of the mass that vary according to the liturgical calendar

³proper *adv*, *chiefly dial* in a thorough manner; completely

proper fraction *n* a fraction in which the numerator is less or of lower degree than the denominator

ˈproperly /-li/ *adv* **1** in a fit manner; suitably **2** strictly in accordance with fact; correctly ⟨~ *speaking*⟩ **3** *chiefly Br* to the full extent; completely

proper name *n* PROPER NOUN

proper noun *n* a noun that designates a particular being or thing and is usu capitalized (e g *Janet*, *London*)

propertied /ˈpropətid/ *adj* possessing property, esp land

property /ˈpropəti/ *n* **1a** a quality, attribute, or power inherent in sthg **b** an attribute common to all members of a class **2a** sthg owned or possessed; *specif* a piece of real estate **b** ownership **c** sthg to which a person has a legal title **3** ³PROP [ME *proprete*, fr MF *propreté*, *propriété*, fr L *proprietat-*, *proprietas*, fr *proprius* own, characteristic] – **propertyless** *adj*

prop forward *n* (the position of) either of the 2 players in rugby on either side of the hooker in the front row of the scrum ☞ SPORT [¹*prop*]

prophase /ˈprohfayz/ *n* **1** the initial phase of mitosis in which chromosomes are condensed from the resting form and split into paired chromatids **2** the initial stage of meiosis in which the chromosomes become visible as paired chromatids and the nuclear membrane disappears [ISV] – **prophasic** /-ˈfayzik/ *adj*

prophecy /ˈprofisi/ *n* **1** the function or vocation of a prophet; (the capacity to utter) an inspired declaration of divine will and purpose **2** a prediction of an event [ME *prophecie*, fr OF, fr LL *prophetia*, fr Gk *prophēteia*, fr *prophētēs* prophet]

prophesy /ˈprofisie/ *vt* **1** to utter (as if) by divine inspiration **2** to predict with assurance or on the basis of mystic knowledge ~ *vi* **1** to speak as if divinely inspired **2** to make a prediction [ME *prophesien*, fr MF *prophesier*, fr OF, fr *prophecie*] – **prophesier** /-ˌsie·ə/ *n*

prophet /ˈprofit/, *fem* **prophetess** /-tes, -ˈtes/ *n* **1** a person who utters divinely inspired revelations; *specif*, *often cap* the writer of any of the prophetic books of the Old Testament **2** one gifted with more than ordinary spiritual and moral insight **3** one who foretells future events; a predictor **4** a spokesman for a doctrine, movement, etc ⟨*a* ~ *of socialism*⟩ [ME *prophete*, fr OF, fr L *propheta*, fr Gk *prophētēs*, fr *pro* for + *phanai* to speak – more at FOR, ¹BAN]

prophetic /prəˈfetik/, **prophetical** /-kl/ *adj* **1** (characteristic) of a prophet or prophecy **2** foretelling events; predictive – **prophetically** *adv*

Prophets /ˈprofits/ *n pl* the second part of the Jewish scriptures

prophylactic /ˌprofiˈlaktik/ *adj* **1** guarding or protecting from or preventing disease **2** tending to prevent or ward off; preventive – fml [Gk *prophylaktikos*, fr *prophylassein* to keep guard before, fr *pro-* before + *phylassein* to guard, fr *phylak-*, *phylax* guard] – **prophylactic** *n*, **prophylactically** *adv*

prophylaxis /ˌprofiˈlaksis/ *n*, *pl* **prophylaxes** /-ˈlakˌseez/ measures designed to preserve health and prevent the spread of disease [NL, fr Gk *prophylaktikos*]

propinquity /prəˈpingkwəti/ *n* **1** nearness of blood; kinship **2** nearness in place or time; proximity *USE* fml [ME *propinquite*, fr L *propinquitat-*, *propinquitas* kinship, proximity, fr *propinquus* near, akin, fr *prope* near – more at APPROACH]

propionate /ˈprohpi·ənayt/ *n* a salt or ester of propionic acid [ISV]

propiˌonic ˈacid /ˌprohpiˈonik/ *n* a rancid-smelling fatty acid found in milk and distillates of wood, coal, and petroleum and used esp in making flavourings and perfumes [ISV [1]*pro-* + Gk *piōn* fat; akin to L *opimus* fat – more at FAT]

propitiate /prə'pishi,ayt/ *vt* to gain or regain the favour or goodwill of; appease [L *propitiatus*, pp of *propitiare*, fr *propitius* propitious] – **propitiator** *n*, **propitiable** *adj*, **propitiatory** /-ət(ə)ri/ *adj*, **propitiation** /-'aysh(ə)n/ *n*

propitious /prə'pishəs/ *adj* **1** favourably disposed; benevolent **2** boding well; auspicious **3** tending to favour; opportune ⟨*a ~ moment for the revolt to break out*⟩ [ME *propicious*, fr L *propitius*, fr *pro-* for + *petere* to seek – more at PRO-, FEATHER] – **propitiously** *adv*, **propitiousness** *n*

propjet /'prop,jet/ *n* a turboprop [[4]*prop* + *jet*]

propolis /'propəlis/ *n* a brownish resinous material of waxy consistency collected by bees from the buds of trees and used as a cement [L, fr Gk, suburb, bee-glue, fr *pro-* for + *polis* city – more at PRO-, POLICE]

proponent /prə'pohnənt/ *n* one who argues in favour of sthg; an advocate [L *proponent-, proponens*, prp of *proponere* to propound]

[1]**proportion** /prə'pawsh(ə)n/ *n* **1** the relation of one part to another or to the whole with respect to magnitude, quantity, or degree **2** harmonious relation of parts to each other or to the whole; balance **3** a statement of equality of 2 ratios (e g in $4/2=10/5$) **4a** proper or equal share ⟨*each did his ~ of the work*⟩ **b** a quota, percentage **5** *pl* size, dimension [ME *proporcion*, fr MF *proportion*, fr L *proportion-, proportio*, fr *pro* for + *portion-, portio* portion – more at FOR]

[2]**proportion** *vt* **1** to adjust (a part or thing) in proportion to other parts or things **2** to make the parts of harmonious or symmetrical

[1]**proportional** /prə'pawsh(ə)nl/ *adj* **1a** proportionate – usu + *to* ⟨a *is ~ to* b⟩ **b** having the same or a constant ratio **2** regulated or determined in proportionate amount or degree ***USE*** (*1*) ☞ SYMBOL – **proportionally** *adv*, **proportionality** /-'aləti/ *n*

[2]**proportional** *n* a number or quantity in a proportion

proportional representation *n* an electoral system designed to represent in a legislative body each political group in proportion to its voting strength in the electorate

[1]**proportionate** /prə'pawsh(ə)nət/ *adj* being in due proportion – **proportionately** *adv*

[2]**proportionate** /prə'pawsh(ə),nayt/ *vt* to make proportionate; proportion

proposal /prə'pohzl/ *n* **1** an act of putting forward or stating sthg for consideration **2a** a proposed idea or plan of action; a suggestion **b** an offer of marriage **3** an application for insurance

propose /prə'pohz/ *vi* **1** to form or put forward a plan or intention ⟨*man ~s, but God disposes*⟩ **2** to make an offer of marriage ~ *vt* **1a** to present for consideration or adoption ⟨~d *terms for peace*⟩ **b** to establish as an aim; intend ⟨~d *to spend the summer in study*⟩ **2a** to recommend to fill a place or vacancy; nominate **b** to nominate (oneself) for an insurance policy **c** to offer as a toast ⟨~ *the health of the bridesmaids*⟩ [ME *proposen*, fr MF *proposer*, fr L *proponere* (perf indic *proposui*) – more at PROPOUND] – **proposer** *n*

[1]**proposition** /,propə'zish(ə)n/ *n* **1a** sthg offered for consideration or acceptance; *specif* a proposal of sexual intercourse **b** a formal mathematical statement to be proved **2** an expression, in language or signs, of sthg that can be either true or false **3** a project, situation, or individual requiring to be dealt with ⟨*the firm is not a paying ~*⟩ – **propositional** *adj*

[2]**proposition** *vt* to make a proposal to; *specif* to propose sexual intercourse to

propound /prə'pownd/ *vt* to offer for discussion or consideration – fml [alter. of earlier *propone*, fr ME (Sc) *proponen*, fr L *proponere* to display, propound, fr *pro-* before + *ponere* to put, place – more at PRO-, POSITION] – **propounder** *n*

propranolol /proh'pranəlol/ *n* a synthetic drug that blocks the action of adrenalin on beta-receptors and is used esp in the treatment of abnormal heart rhythms and to lower high blood pressure [prob alter. of earlier *propanolol*, fr *propanol* (propyl alcohol) + *-ol*]

[1]**proprietary** /prə'prie·ət(ə)ri/ *n* a body of proprietors [ME *proprietarie* owner, fr LL *proprietarius*, fr *proprietarius*, adj]

[2]**proprietary** *adj* **1** (characteristic) of a proprietor ⟨~ *rights*⟩ **2** made and marketed under a patent, trademark, etc ⟨*a ~ process*⟩ **3** privately owned and managed ⟨*a ~ clinic*⟩ [LL *proprietarius*, fr L *proprietas* property – more at PROPERTY]

proprietary colony *n* a colony granted to a proprietor with full prerogatives of government

proprietor /prə'prie·ətə/, *fem* **proprietress** /-tris/ *n* **1** an owner **2** sby having an interest less than absolute right [alter. of [1]*proprietary*] – **proprietorship** *n*, **proprietorial** /-'tawri·əl/ *adj*

propriety /prə'prie·əti/ *n* **1** the quality or state of being proper; fitness **2** the standard of what is socially or morally acceptable in conduct or speech, esp between the sexes; decorum **3** *pl* the conventions and manners of polite society ***USE*** fml [ME *propriete*, fr MF *proprieté* property, quality of a person or thing – more at PROPERTY]

proprioception /,prohpri·ə'sepsh(ə)n/ *n* the reception of stimuli produced within the organism [L *proprius* own + E *-ception* (as in *reception*)] – **proprioceptive** /-'septiv/ *adj*

proprioceptor /,prohpri·ə'septə/ *n* a sensory receptor excited by proprioceptive stimuli

proptosis /prop'tohsis/ *n* forward projection or displacement, esp of the eyeball [NL, fr LL, falling forwards, fr Gk *proptōsis*, fr *propiptein* to fall forwards, fr *pro-* + *piptein* to fall – more at PRO-, FEATHER]

propulsion /prə'pulsh(ə)n/ *n* **1** the action or process of propelling **2** sthg that propels [L *propulsus*, pp of *propellere* to propel]

propulsive /prə'pulsiv/ *adj* having power to or tending to propel [L *propulsus*]

prop up *vt* to give nonmaterial (e g moral or financial) support to ⟨*government* propping up *ailing industries*⟩

propyl /'prohpil, -piel/ *n* a univalent hydrocarbon radical C_3H_7 derived from propane [ISV, fr *propionic (acid)* + *-yl*] – **propylic** /-'pilik/ *adj*

propylene /'propileen/ *n* a hydrocarbon of the alkene series used chiefly in organic synthesis

pro rata /,proh 'rahtə/ *adv* proportionately according to an exactly calculable factor [L] – **pro rata** *adj*

prorate /,proh'rayt, '-,-/ *vt* to divide, distribute, or assess proportionately ~ *vi* to make a pro rata distribution [*pro rata*] – **proration** /-'raysh(ə)n/ *n*

prorogue /prə'rohg, ,proh-/ *vt* to terminate a session of (e g a parliament) by royal prerogative ~ *vi* to suspend a legislative session [ME *prorogen*, fr MF *proroguer*, fr L *prorogare*, fr *pro-* before + *rogare* to ask – more at PRO-, [1]RIGHT] – **prorogation** /,prorə'gaysh(ə)n/ *n*

pros /prohz/ *pl of* PRO

pros- /pros/ *prefix* **1** near; towards ⟨pros*elyte*⟩ **2** replacement; substitute ⟨pros*thesis*⟩ [LL, fr Gk, fr *proti, pros* face to face with, towards, in addition to, near; akin to Skt *prati-* near, towards, against, in return, Gk *pro* before – more at FOR]

prosaic /proh'zayik, prə-/ *adj* **1a** characteristic of prose as distinguished from poetry **b** dull, unimaginative **2** belonging to the everyday world; commonplace [LL *prosaicus*, fr L *prosa* prose] – **prosaically** *adv*

prosaism /'prohzay,iz(ə)m, 'prohzi-/ *n* **1** a prosaic manner, style, or quality **2** a prosaic expression – usu pl *USE* fml

prosaist /proh'zayist/ *n* a prosaic person – fml [L *prosa* prose]

proscenium /proh'seenyəm, prə-, -ni·əm/ *n* the stage of an ancient Greek or Roman theatre [L, fr Gk *proskēnion*, fr *pro-* + *skēnē* building forming the background for a dramatic performance – more at SCENE]

proscenium arch *n* the arch in a conventional theatre through which the spectator sees the stage

prosciutto /prə'shootoh/ *n, pl* **prosciutti** /-ti/, **prosciuttos** /-tohz/ smoked spiced Italian ham [It, alter. of obs *presciutto*, fr *pre-* pre- + *-sciutto*, fr L *exsuctus* dried up, sucked out, pp of *exsugere* to suck out]

proscribe /proh'skrieb/ *vt* **1a** to put outside the protection of the law **b** to outlaw, exile; *specif, in ancient Rome* to outlaw by publishing the name of (a person) **2** to condemn or forbid as harmful; prohibit [L *proscribere* to publish, proscribe, fr *pro-* before + *scribere* to write – more at [1]SCRIBE] – **proscriber** *n*

proscription /prə'skripsh(ə)n, proh-/ *n* **1** proscribing or being proscribed **2** an imposed restraint or restriction; a prohibition [ME *proscripcion*, fr L *proscription-, proscriptio*, fr *proscriptus*, pp of *proscribere*] – **proscriptive** /-tiv/ *adj*, **proscriptively** *adv*

prose /prohz/ *n* **1a** ordinary nonmetrical language **b** a literary medium distinguished from poetry esp by its closer correspondence to the patterns of everyday speech **2** a commonplace quality or character; ordinariness [ME, fr MF, fr L *prosa*, fr fem of *prorsus, prosus* straightforward, being in prose, contr of *proversus*, pp of *provertere* to turn forwards, fr *pro-* forwards + *vertere* to turn – more at PRO-, [1]WORTH] – **prose** *adj*

prosecute /'prosikyooht/ *vt* **1a** to institute and pursue criminal proceedings against **b** to institute legal proceedings with reference to ⟨~ *a claim*⟩ **2** to follow through, pursue ⟨*determined to* ~ *the investigation*⟩ **3** CARRY OUT 1 ~ *vi* to institute and carry on a prosecution *USE* (*2&3*) fml [ME *prosecuten*, fr L *prosecutus*, pp of *prosequi* to pursue – more at PURSUE]

prosecution /prosi'kyoohsh(ə)n/ *n* **1** prosecuting; *specif* the formal institution of a criminal charge **2** *sing or pl in constr* the party by whom criminal proceedings are instituted or conducted

prosecutor /'prosikyoohtə/ *n* sby who institutes or conducts an official prosecution

[1]**proselyte** /'prosiliet/ *n* a new convert, esp to Judaism [ME *proselite*, fr LL *proselytus* proselyte, alien resident, fr Gk *prosēlytos*, fr *pros* near + *-ēlytos* (akin to *elthein* to go); akin to Gk *elaunein* to drive – more at PROS-, ELASTIC]

[2]**proselyte** *vb, chiefly NAm* to proselytize

proselytism /'prosili,tiz(ə)m/ *n* religious conversion

proselyt·ize, -ise /'prosili,tiez/ *vt* to convert (sby), esp to a new religion ~ *vi* to (try to) make converts, esp to a new religion – **proselytizer** *n*, **proselytization** /-'zaysh(ə)n/ *n*

'**prose ,poem** *n* a work in prose that has some of the qualities of a poem – **prose poet** *n*

prosit /'prohzit/, **prost** /prohst/ *interj* – used to wish sby good health, esp before drinking [G, fr L *prosit* may it be beneficial, fr *prodesse* to be useful – more at PROUD]

prosody /'prosədi/ *n* the study of versification and esp of metrical structure [ME, fr L *prosodia* accent of a syllable, fr Gk *prosōidia* song sung to instrumental music, accent, fr *pros* in addition to + *ōidē* song – more at PROS-, ODE] – **prosodist** *n*, **prosodic** /prə'sodik/ *adj*

prosopopoeia /,prosəpə'pee·ə/ *n* a figure of speech in which an imaginary or absent person is represented as speaking or acting; *esp* PERSONIFICATION 1 [L, fr Gk *prosōpopoiia*, fr *prosōpon* mask, person (fr *pros-* + *ōps* face) + *poiein* to make – more at EYE, POET]

[1]**prospect** /'prospekt/ *n* **1** an extensive view; a scene **2a** a mental picture of sthg to come ⟨*doesn't like the* ~ *of more examinations*⟩ **b** expectation, possibility ⟨*has a fine career in* ~⟩ **c** *pl* **(1)** financial and social expectations **(2)** chances, esp of success **3a** a place showing signs of containing a mineral deposit **b** a partly developed mine **c** the mineral yield of a tested sample of ore or gravel **4** a potential client, candidate, etc [ME, fr L *prospectus* view, prospect, fr *prospectus*, pp of *prospicere* to look forwards, exercise foresight, fr *pro-* forwards + *specere* to look – more at PRO-, SPY]

[2]**prospect** /prə'spekt/ *vb* to explore (an area), esp for mineral deposits – **prospector** *n*

prospective /prə'spektiv/ *adj* **1** likely to come about; expected **2** likely to be or become ⟨*a* ~ *mother*⟩ – **prospectively** *adv*

prospectus /prə'spektəs/ *n* a printed statement, brochure, etc describing an organization or enterprise and distributed to prospective buyers, investors, or participants [L, prospect]

prosper /prospə/ *vi* to succeed, thrive; *specif* to achieve economic success ~ *vt* to cause to succeed or thrive ⟨*may the gods* ~ *our city*⟩ [ME *prosperen*, fr MF *prosperer*, fr L *prosperare* to cause to succeed, fr *prosperus* favourable]

prosperity /pro'sperəti, prə-/ *n* the condition of being successful or thriving; *esp* economic well-being

prosperous /'prosp(ə)rəs/ *adj* marked by esp financial success [ME, fr MF *prospereux*, fr *prosperer* to prosper + *-eux* -ous] – **prosperously** *adv*

prostaglandin /,prostə'glandin/ *n* any of various cyclic fatty acids that are important locally acting hormones in humans and animals and of which one is widely used to induce abortions [*prostate gland* + *-in*; fr its occurrence in the sexual glands of animals]

[1]**prostate** /'prostayt/, **prostate gland** *n* a partly muscular, partly glandular body situated around the base of the male mammalian urethra that secretes a major constituent of the ejaculatory fluid ☞ REPRODUCTION [NL *prostata*, fr Gk *prostatēs*, fr *proïstanai* to put in front, fr *pro-* before + *histanai* to cause to stand – more at PRO-, STAND]

[2]**prostate** *also* **prostatic** /pro'statik, prə-/ *adj* of or being the prostate gland

prosthesis /'prosthəsis; *sense* ' *or* -'thee-/ *n, pl* **prostheses** /-,seez/ **1** an artificial device to replace a missing part of the body **2** prothesis [NL, fr Gk, addition, fr *prostithenai* to add to, fr *pros-* in addition to + *tithenai* to put – more at PROS-, [1]DO]

prosthetic /pros'thetik/ *adj* of a prosthesis or prosthetics – **prosthetically** *adv*

pros'thetics *n pl but sing or pl in constr* the surgical and dental specialities concerned with the artificial replacement of missing parts

[1]**prostitute** /'prosti,tyooht/ *vt* **1** to make a prostitute of **2** to devote to corrupt or unworthy purposes; debase ⟨~ *one's talents*⟩ [L *prostitutus*, pp of *prostituere*, fr *pro-* before + *statuere* to station – more at PRO-, STATUTE] – **prostitution** /-'tyoohsh(ə)n/ *n*

[2]**prostitute** *n* a person, esp a woman, who engages in sexual practices for money

prostomium /proh'stohmyəm, -mi·əm/ *n, pl* **prostomia** /-myə, -mi·ə/ the portion of the head of various worms and molluscs that is situated in front of the mouth [NL, fr Gk *pro-* + *stoma* mouth – more at STOMACH] – **prostomial** *adj*

[1]**prostrate** /'prostrayt/ *adj* **1** lying full-length face downwards, esp in adoration or submission **2a** physically and emotionally weak; overcome ⟨~ *with grief*⟩ **b** physically exhausted **3** *of a plant* trailing on the ground [ME *prostrat*, fr L *prostratus*, pp of *prosternere*, fr *pro-* before + *sternere* to spread out, throw down – more at STREW]

[2]**prostrate** /pro'strayt/ *vt* **1** to throw or put into a prostrate position **2** to put (oneself) in a humble and submissive posture or state **3** to reduce to submission, helplessness, or exhaustion; overcome – **prostration** /pro'straysh(ə)n/ *n*

prosy /'prohzi/ *adj* dull, commonplace; *esp* tedious in speech or manner [[1]*prose* + [1]*-y*] – **prosily** *adv*

prot-, proto- *comb form* **1** first in time; earliest; original ⟨proto*lithic*⟩ ⟨proto*type*⟩ **2** first-formed; primary ⟨proto*xylem*⟩ **3** *cap* of or constituting the recorded or assumed language that is ancestral to (a specified language or group of related languages or dialects) ⟨Proto-*Indo-European*⟩ [ME *protho-*, fr MF, fr LL *proto-*, fr Gk *prōt-*, *prōto-*, fr *prōtos*; akin to Gk *pro* before – more at FOR]

protactinium /,prohtak'tini·əm/ *n* an artificially produced metallic radioactive element of relatively short life ☞ PERIODIC TABLE [NL]

protagonist /proh'tagənist, prə-/ *n* **1** one who takes the leading part in a drama, novel, or story **2** a leader or notable supporter of a cause [Gk *prōtagōnistēs*, fr *prōt-* prot- + *agōnistēs* competitor at games, actor, fr *agōnizesthai* to compete, fr *agōn* contest, competition at games – more at AGONY]

protamine /'prohtəmeen, -min/ *n* any of various simple proteins that are strong chemical bases, are associated with nucleic acids, and typically contain much arginine [ISV *prot-* + *amine*]

protasis /'prohtəsis/ *n, pl* **protases** /-,seez/ the subordinate clause of a conditional sentence – compare APODOSIS [LL, fr Gk, premise of a syllogism, conditional clause, fr *proteinein* to stretch out before, put forwards, fr *pro-* + *teinein* to stretch – more at THIN] – **protatic** /proh'tatik, prə-/ *adj*

prote-, proteo- *comb form* protein ⟨proteo*lysis*⟩ [ISV, fr F *protéine*]

protea /'prohti·ə/ *n* any of a genus of evergreen shrubs of the S hemisphere grown for their dense flower heads [NL, genus name, fr L *Proteus* Proteus]

protean /proh'tee·ən/ *adj* **1** readily assuming different shapes or roles **2** displaying great diversity or variety [*Proteus*, mythological sea god with the power of assuming different shapes, fr L, fr Gk *Prōteus*]

protect /prə'tekt/ *vt* **1** to cover or shield *from* injury or destruction; guard *against* **2** to shield or foster (a home industry) by a protective tariff [L *protectus*, pp of *protegere*, fr *pro-* in front + *tegere* to cover – more at PRO-, THATCH] – **protectant** *n*, **protective** /-tiv/ *adj*, **protectively** *adv*, **protectiveness** *n*

protection /prə'teksh(ə)n/ *n* **1** protecting or being protected **2** sthg that protects **3** the shielding of the producers of a country from foreign competition by import tariffs **4a** immunity from threatened violence, often purchased under duress **b** money extorted by racketeers posing as a protective association **5** COVERAGE 3a

pro'tectionist /-ist/ *n* an advocate of government economic protection – **protectionism** *n*, **protectionist** *adj*

pro,tective 'custody *n* detention of sby (allegedly) for his/her own safety

pro'tector /prə'tektə/, *fem* **protectress** /-tris/ *n* **1a** a guardian **b** a device used to prevent injury; a guard **2** *often cap* the executive head of the Commonwealth from 1653 to 1659 [PROTECT + [1]-OR] – **protectorship** *n*

protectorate /prə'tekt(ə)rət/ *n* **1a** government by a protector **b** *often cap* the government of the Commonwealth from 1653 to 1659 **c** the rank or (period of) rule of a protector **2a** the relationship of one state over another dependent state which it partly controls but has not annexed **b** the dependent political unit in such a relationship

protectory /prə'tekt(ə)ri/ *n* an institution for the care usu of homeless or delinquent children

protégé, *fem* **protégée** /'protə,zhay, 'proh-, -tay- (*Fr* prɔteʒe)/ *n* a person under the protection, guidance, or patronage of sby influential [F, fr pp of *protéger* to protect, fr L *protegere*]

protein /'prohteen/ *n* any of numerous genetically specified naturally occurring extremely complex combinations of amino acids linked by peptide bonds that are essential constituents of all living cells and are an essential part of the diet of animals and humans [F *protéine*, fr LGk *prōteios* primary, fr Gk *prōtos* first – more at PROT-] – **proteinaceous** /,prohti'nayshəs/ *adj*

proteinase /'prohti,nayz, -,nays/ *n* an enzyme that breaks down proteins, esp into peptides [ISV]

pro tem /,proh 'tem/ *adv* for the time being [short for *pro tempore*, fr L]

proteo- – see PROTE-

proteolysis /,prohti'oləsis/ *n* the breakdown of proteins or peptides resulting in the formation of simpler (soluble) products [NL] – **proteolytic** /-ə'litik/ *adj*

Proterozoic /,prohtərə'zoh·ik/ *adj or n* (of or being) an era of geological history between the Archaeozoic and the Palaeozoic ☞ EVOLUTION [Gk *proteros* former, earlier (fr *pro* before) + ISV *-zoic* – more at FOR]

[1]**protest** /'prohtest/ *n* **1a** a sworn declaration that a note or bill has been duly presented and that payment has been refused **b** a formal declaration of dissent from an act of esp a legislature **c** a formal declaration of disapproval ⟨*reprieved in response to international* ~s⟩ **2** protesting; *esp* an organized public demonstration of disapproval **3** an objection or display of unwillingness ⟨*went to the dentist under* ~⟩

[2]**protest** /prə'test/ *vt* **1** to make formal or solemn declaration or affirmation of **2** to execute or have executed a formal protest against (e g a bill or note) **3** *NAm* to make a formal protest against **4** *NAm* to remonstrate against ⟨*unwilling to* ~ *the cost of her ticket*⟩ ~ *vi* **1** to make a protestation **2** to enter a protest [ME *protesten*, fr MF *protester*, fr L *protestari*, fr *pro-* forth + *testari* to call to witness – more at PRO-, TESTAMENT] – **protester, protestor** *n*

protestant /'protistənt/ *n* **1** *cap* **a** any of a group who protested against an edict of the Diet of Spires in 1529 intended to suppress the Lutheran movement **b** a Christian who denies the universal authority of the pope and affirms the principles of the Reformation **2** one who makes or enters a protest [MF, fr L *protestant-, protestans*, prp of *protestari*] – **Protestantism** *n*

Protestant *adj*, of Protestants, their churches, or their religion

protestation /,prote'staysh(ə)n, proh-, -ti-/ *n* **1** an act of protesting **2** a solemn declaration or avowal

prothalamion /,prohthə'laymi·ən/, **prothalamium** /-mi·əm/ *n, pl* **prothalamia** /-mi·ə/ a song or poem in celebration of a forthcoming marriage [NL, fr Gk *pro-* + *-thalamion* (as in *epithalamion* epithalamium)]

prothallium /proh'thalyəm, -li·əm/ *n, pl* **prothallia** /-lyə/ (a tiny structure of a flowering plant corresponding to) the gamete-producing form of a fern or related plant [NL, fr *pro-* + *thallus*] – **prothallial** *adj*

prothallus /proh'thaləs/ *n* the prothallium [NL, fr *pro-* + *thallus*]

prothesis /'prothəsis/ *n, pl* **protheses** /-,seez/ the addition of a sound to the beginning of a word [LL, alter. of *prosthesis*, fr Gk, lit., addition – more at PROSTHESIS] – **prothetic** /,pro'thetik, prə-/ *adj*

prothorax /,proh'thawraks/ *n* the front segment of the thorax of an insect [NL *prothorac-, prothorax*, fr [1]*pro-* + *thorax*] – **prothoracic** /-'rasik, ,pro-/ *adj*

prothrombin /proh'thrombin/ *n* a plasma protein produced in the liver in the presence of vitamin K and converted into thrombin in the clotting of blood [ISV]

protist /'prohtist/ *n* any of a major group of usu single-celled organisms including bacteria, protozoans, and various algae and fungi [deriv of Gk *prōtistos* very first, primal, fr superl of *prōtos* first – more at PROT-] – **protistan** *adj or n*

protium /'prohtyəm/ *n* the ordinary light hydrogen isotope of atomic mass 1 – compare DEUTERIUM, TRITIUM [NL, fr Gk *prōtos* first]

proto- – see PROT-

protochordate /,prohtoh'kawdayt/ *n* any of a major division of chordate animals that do not have a vertebral column and include the hemichordates, lancelets, and tunicates [NL *Protochordata*, division name]

protocol /'prohtəkol/ *n* **1** an original draft or record of a document or transaction **2** a preliminary memorandum often formulated and signed by diplomatic negotiators as a basis for a final treaty **3** a code of correct etiquette and precedence **4** *NAm* the plan of a scientific experiment or treatment [MF *prothocole*, fr ML *protocollum*, fr LGk *prōtokollon* first sheet of a papyrus roll bearing date of manufacture, fr Gk *prōt-* prot- + *kollan* to glue together, fr *kolla* glue; akin to MD *helen* to glue]

proton /'prohton/ *n* an elementary particle that is identical with the nucleus of the hydrogen atom, that along with neutrons is a constituent of all other atomic nuclei, that carries a positive charge numerically equal to the charge of an electron, that has a mass of 1.672×10^{-27}kg, and that is classified as a baryon ☞ PHYSICS [Gk *prōton*, neut of *prōtos* first – more at PROT-] – **protonic** /prə'tonik, proh-/ *adj*

protonotary /,prohtə'noht(ə)ri, proh'tonət(ə)ri/, **prothonotary** /-t(h)ə-, -'t(h)o-/ *n* a chief clerk of any of various courts of law [ME *prothonotarie*, fr LL *protonotarius*, fr *prot-* + L *notarius* notary]

protoplasm /'prohtə,plaz(ə)m/ *n* **1** the organized complex of organic and inorganic substances (e g proteins and salts in solution) that constitutes the living nucleus, cytoplasm, plastids, and mitochondria of the cell **2** cytoplasm [G *protoplasma*, fr *prot-* + NL *plasma*] – **protoplasmic** /-'plazmik/ *adj*

protoplast /'prohtə,plast/ *n* the nucleus, cytoplasm, and plasma membrane of a cell as distinguished from nonliving walls and inclusions (e g vacuoles) [MF *protoplaste*, fr LL *protoplastus* first man, fr Gk *prōtoplastos* first formed, fr *prōt-* prot- + *plastos* formed, fr *plassein* to mould – more at PLASTER] – **protoplastic** /-'plastik/ *adj*

prototrophic /,prohtə'trofik/ *adj* deriving nutriment from inorganic sources [ISV] – **prototroph** /'prohtə,trohf/ *n*, **prototrophy** /prə'totrəfi/ *n*

prototype /'prohtə,tiep, -toh-/ *n* **1** an original model on which sthg is based; an archetype **2** sby or sthg that has the essential features of a later type ⟨*the battle chariot is the* ~ *of the modern tank*⟩ **3** sby or sthg that exemplifies the essential or typical features of a type ⟨*mathematics is the* ~ *of logical thinking*⟩ **4** a first full-scale and usu operational form of a new type or design of a construction (e g an aeroplane) [F, fr Gk *prōtotypon*, fr neut of *prōtotypos* archetypal, fr *prōt-* + *typos* type] – **prototypal** /-'tiepl/ *adj*

protozoan /,prohtə'zoh·ən/ *n* any of a phylum or subkingdom of minute single-celled animals which have varied structure and physiology and often complex life cycles [NL *Protozoa*, phylum name, fr *prot-* + *-zoa*] – **protozoal** *adj*, **protozoan** *adj*, **protozoic** /-ik/ *adj*

protozoology /,prohtohzooh'oləji, -zoh-, -tə-/ *n* a branch of zoology dealing with protozoans [NL *Protozoa* + ISV *-logy*] – **protozoologist** *n*, **protozoological** /-ə'lojikl/ *adj*

protozoon /,prohtə'zoh·on/ *n, pl* **protozoa** /-'zoh·ə/ a protozoan [NL, fr sing. of *Protozoa*]

protract /prə'trakt/ *vt* **1** to prolong in time or space **2** to lay down the lines and angles of with scale and protractor **3** to extend forwards or outwards [L *protractus*, pp of *protrahere*, lit., to draw forwards, fr *pro-* forwards + *trahere* to draw – more at PRO-, DRAW] – **protraction** /-'traksh(ə)n/ *n*, **protractive** /-tiv/ *adj*

protractile /prə'traktiel/ *adj* capable of being thrust out ⟨~ *jaws*⟩ [L *protractus*]

protractor /prə'traktə/ *n* **1** a muscle that extends a body part – compare RETRACTOR **2** an instrument that is used for marking out or measuring angles in drawing [PROTRACT + [1]-OR]

protrude /prə'troohd/ *vb* to (cause to) jut out from the surrounding surface or place [L *protrudere*, fr *pro-* + *trudere* to thrust – more at THREAT] – **protrusion** /-zh(ə)n/ *n*, **protrusive** /-siv/ *adj*

protuberant /prə'tyoohb(ə)rənt/ *adj* thrusting or projecting out from a surrounding or adjacent surface [LL *protuberant-*, *protuberans*, prp of *protuberare* to bulge out, fr L *pro-* forwards + *tuber* hump, swelling] – **protuberance** *n*

proud /prowd/ *adj* **1a** having or displaying excessive self-esteem **b** much pleased; exultant **c** having proper self-respect **2a** stately, magnificent **b** giving reason for pride; glorious ⟨*the* ~est *moment of her life*⟩ **3** projecting slightly from a surrounding surface [ME, fr OE *prūd*, prob fr OF *prod, prud, prou* capable, good, valiant, fr LL *prode* advantage, advantageous, back-formation fr L *prodesse* to be advantageous, fr *pro-*, *prod-* for, in favour + *esse* to be – more at PRO-, IS] – **proudly** *adv*

prove /proohv/ *vb* **proved, proven** /'proohv(ə)n/ *vt* **1a** to test the quality of; try out ⟨*the exception* ~s *the rule*⟩ **b** to subject to a testing process **2a** to establish the truth or validity of by evidence or demonstration **b** to check the correctness of (e g an arithmetical operation) **3a** to verify the genuineness of; *specif* to obtain probate of **b** PROOF 1 **4** to allow (bread dough) to rise and become light before baking ~ *vi* **1** to turn out, esp after trial ⟨*the new drug* ~d *to be effective*⟩ **2** *of bread dough* to rise and become aerated through the action of yeast [ME *proven*, fr OF *prover*, fr L *probare* to test, approve, prove, fr *probus* good, honest, fr *pro-* for, in favour + *-bus* (akin to OE *bēon* to be)]

provenance /'provənəns/ *n* an origin, source – used esp with reference to works of art or literature [F, fr *provenir* to come forth, originate, fr L *provenire*, fr *pro-* forth + *venire* to come – more at PRO-, COME]

Provençal /,provonh'sahl (*Fr* prɔvɑ̃sal)/ *n* **1** a native or inhabitant of Provence **2** a Romance language of SE France [MF, fr *provençal* of Provence, fr *Provence*, region of SE France] – **Provençal** *adj*

provender /'provində/ *n* **1** dry food for domestic animals **2** food, provisions – humor [ME, fr MF *provende, provendre*, fr ML *provenda*, alter. of *praebenda* prebend]

proventriculus /,prohven'trikyooləs/ *n, pl* **proventriculi** /-lie, -li/ a pouch of the digestive tract (e g of an insect); *esp* the glandular stomach of a bird situated between the crop and gizzard [NL]

proverb /'provuhb/ *n* a brief popular epigram or maxim; an adage [ME *proverbe*, fr MF, fr L *proverbium*, fr *pro-* + *verbum* word – more at WORD]

proverbial /prə'vuhbyəl, -bi·əl/ *adj* **1** of or like a proverb **2** that has become a proverb or byword; commonly spoken of – **proverbially** *adv*

Proverbs /'provuhbz/ *n pl but sing in constr* a collection of moral sayings forming a book of the Old Testament

provide /prə'vied/ *vi* **1** to take precautionary measures ⟨~d *against future loss*⟩ **2** to make a proviso or stipulation ⟨*the regulations* ~ *for 2 directors*⟩ **3** to supply what is needed for sustenance or support ⟨~s *for a large family*⟩ ~ *vt* **1a** to furnish, equip *with* ⟨~ *the children with new shoes*⟩ **b** to supply, afford ⟨*curtains* ~ *privacy*⟩ **2** to stipulate [ME *providen*, fr L *providēre*, lit., to see ahead, fr *pro-* forwards + *vidēre* to see – more at PRO-, WIT]

pro'vided *conj* providing [pp of *provide*]

providence /'provid(ə)ns/ *n* **1** *cap* God conceived as the power sustaining and guiding human destiny **2** being provident [ME, fr MF, fr L *providentia*, fr *provident-*, *providens*]

provident /'provid(ə)nt/ *adj* making provision for the future, esp by saving [L *provident-*, *providens*, fr prp of *providēre*] – **providently** *adv*

providential /,provi'densh(ə)l/ *adj* of or determined (as if) by Providence; lucky – **providentially** *adv*

'provident so,ciety *n* FRIENDLY SOCIETY

provider /prə'viedə/ *n* one who provides for his/her family [PROVIDE + [2]-ER]

providing /prə'vieding/ *conj* on condition; if and only if ⟨*may come* ~ *that you pay for yourself*⟩ [prp of *provide*]

province /'provins/ *n* **1a** an administrative district of a country **b** *pl* all of a country except the metropolis – usu + *the* **2** a territorial unit of religious administration **3a** proper or appropriate function or scope; sphere **b** a field of knowledge or activity [F, fr L *provincia*]

[1]**provincial** /prə'vinsh(ə)l/ *n* **1** the head of a province of a Roman Catholic religious order **2** one living in or coming from a province **3a** a person with a narrow outlook **b** a person lacking polish or refinement

[2]**provincial** *adj* **1** of or coming from a province **2a** limited in outlook; narrow **b** lacking polish; unsophisticated – **provincialism** /-,iz(ə)m/ *n*, **provincialize** /-,iez/ *vt*

'proving ,ground /'proohving/ *n* **1** a place designed for or used in scientific experimentation or testing; *esp* a place for testing vehicles **2** a place where sthg new is tried out

[1]**provision** /prə'vizh(ə)n/ *n* **1a** providing **b** a measure taken beforehand; a preparation ⟨*no* ~ *made for replacements*⟩ **2** *pl* a stock of food or other necessary goods **3** a proviso, stipulation [ME, fr MF, fr LL & L; LL *provision-*, *provisio* act of providing, fr L, foresight, fr *provisus*, pp of *providēre* to see ahead]

[2]**provision** *vt* to supply with provisions

provisional /prə'vizh(ə)nl/ *adj* serving for the time being; temporary; *specif* requiring later confirmation ⟨*gave her* ~ *consent*⟩ – **provisionally** *adv*

Provisional *adj* of or being the secret terrorist wing of the IRA – **Provisional** *n*

proviso /prə'viezoh/ *n, pl* **provisos, provisoes** **1** a clause that introduces a condition **2** a conditional stipulation [ME, fr ML *proviso quod* provided that]

provisory /prə'viez(ə)ri/ *adj* **1** conditional **2** provisional

provitamin /proh'vitəmin, -'vie-/ *n* a substance convertible in the body into a specific vitamin

[1]**Provo** /'prohvoh/ *n* a member of a militant Dutch antiestablishment group [D, short for *provocateur,* fr F, fr *provoquer*]

[2]**Provo** /'provoh/ *n* a member of the Provisional wing of the IRA – infml [by shortening & alter. fr *provisional*]

provocation /,provə'kaysh(ə)n/ *n* **1** an act of provoking; incitement **2** sthg that provokes or arouses [ME *provocacioun,* fr MF *provocation,* fr L *provocation-, provocatio,* fr *provocatus,* pp of *provocare*]

provocative /prə'vokətiv/ *adj* serving or tending to provoke or arouse to indignation, sexual desire, etc – **provocatively** *adv,* **provocativeness** *n*

provoke /prə'vohk/ *vt* **1** to incite to anger; incense **2a** to call forth; evoke **b** to stir up on purpose; induce ⟨*always trying to* ~ *an argument*⟩ [ME *provoken,* fr MF *provoquer,* fr L *provocare,* fr *pro-* forth + *vocare* to call – more at PRO-, VOICE]

provoking /prə'vohking/ *adj* causing mild anger; annoying – **provokingly** *adv*

provost /'provəst/ *n* **1** the head of a collegiate or cathedral chapter; *specif* one who is also the incumbent of a parish of which the cathedral is the church **2** the chief magistrate of a Scottish burgh **3** the head of certain colleges at Oxford, Cambridge, etc [ME, fr OE *profost* & OF *provost,* fr ML *propositus,* alter. of *praepositus,* fr L, one in charge, director, fr pp of *praeponere* to place at the head – more at PREPOSITION]

pro,vost 'marshal /prə'voh/ *n* an officer who supervises the military police of a command

prow /prow/ *n* **1** the bow of a ship **2** a pointed projecting front part [MF *proue,* prob fr OIt dial. *prua,* fr L *prora,* fr Gk *prōira*]

prowess /'prowis/ *n* **1** outstanding (military) valour and skill **2** outstanding ability [ME *prouesse,* fr OF *proesse,* fr *prou* valiant – more at PROUD]

[1]**prowl** /prowl/ *vb* to move about (in) or roam (over) in a stealthy or predatory manner [ME *prollen*] – **prowler** *n*

[2]**prowl** *n* an act or instance of prowling

proximal /'proksim(ə)l/ *adj, esp of an anatomical part* next to or nearest the point of attachment or origin – compare DISTAL [L *proximus*] – **proximally** *adv*

proximate /'proksimət/ *adj* **1a** very near; close **b** forthcoming; imminent **2** next preceding or following; *specif* next in a chain of cause and effect ***USE*** fml [L *proximatus,* pp of *proximare* to approach, fr *proximus* nearest, next, superl of *prope* near – more at APPROACH] – **proximately** *adv,* **proximateness** *n*

proximity /prok'siməti/ *n* being close in space, time, or association; *esp* nearness – fml [MF *proximité,* fr L *proximitat-, proximitas,* fr *proximus*]

prox'imity ,fuse *n* a fuse that detonates a projectile within effective range of the target

proximo /'proksimoh/ *adj* of or occurring in the next month after the present – compare ULTIMO [L *proximo mense* in the next month]

proxy /'proksi/ *n* **1** (the agency, function, or office of) a deputy authorized to act as a substitute for another ⟨*marriage by* ~⟩ **2** (a document giving) authority to act or vote for another [ME *procucie,* contr of *procuracie,* fr AF, fr ML *procuratia,* alter. of L *procuratio* procuration] – **proxy** *adj*

prude /proohd/ *n* one who shows or affects extreme modesty or propriety, esp in sexual matters [F, good woman, prudish woman, short for *prudefemme* good woman, fr OF *prode femme*]

prudence /'proohd(ə)ns/ *n* **1** discretion or shrewdness in the management of affairs **2** skill and good judgment in the use of resources; frugality **3** caution or circumspection with regard to danger or risk ⟨*conservative from* ~ – T S Eliot⟩

prudent /'proohd(ə)nt/ *adj* characterized by, arising from, or showing prudence [ME, fr MF, fr L *prudent-, prudens,* contr of *provident-, providens* – more at PROVIDENT] – **prudently** *adv*

prudential /prooh'densh(ə)l/ *adj* **1** of or proceeding from prudence **2** exercising prudence, esp in business matters – **prudentially** *adv*

prudery /'proohd(ə)ri/ *n* **1** the quality of being a prude **2** a prudish act or remark

prudish /'proohdish/ *adj* marked by prudery; priggish – **prudishly** *adv,* **prudishness** *n*

pruinose /'prooh·inohs/ *adj* covered with whitish dust or bloom ⟨~ *stems*⟩ [L *pruinosus* covered with hoarfrost, fr *pruina* hoarfrost]

[1]**prune** /proohn/ *n* a plum dried or capable of drying without fermentation [ME, fr MF, plum, fr L *prunum* – more at PLUM]

[2]**prune** *vt* **1** to cut off the dead or unwanted parts of (a usu woody plant or shrub) **2a** to reduce by eliminating superfluous matter ⟨~d *the text*⟩ **b** to remove as superfluous ⟨~ *away all ornamentation*⟩ ~ *vi* to cut away what is unwanted [ME *prouynen,* fr MF *proignier,* prob alter. of *provigner* to layer, fr *provain* layer, fr L *propagin-, propago,* fr *pro-* forwards + *pangere* to fix – more at PRO-, PACT]

prurient /'prooəri·ənt/ *adj* inclined to, having, or arousing an excessive or unhealthy interest in sexual matters [L *prurient-, pruriens,* prp of *prurire* to itch, crave, be wanton; akin to L *pruna* glowing coal, Skt *ploṣati* he singes] – **prurience** *n*

prurigo /proo(ə)'riegoh/ *n* a chronic inflammatory skin disease marked by raised itching spots [NL, fr L, itch, fr *prurire*] – **pruriginous** /-'rijənəs/ *adj*

pruritic /proo(ə)'ritik/ *adj* of or marked by itching

pruritus /proo(ə)'rietəs/ *n* ITCH 1 [L, fr *pruritus,* pp of *prurire*]

,Prussian 'blue /'prush(ə)n/ *n* **1** any of numerous blue iron pigments **2** a dark blue hydrated salt of iron and cyanide used as a test for ferric iron **3** a strong greenish blue colour [*Prussia,* former kingdom & state of N Germany]

'prussian·ize, -ise /-iez/ *vt, often cap* to make Prussian in character (e g by imposing authoritarian control or rigid discipline) – **prussianization** /-'zaysh(ə)n/ *n, often cap*

,prussic 'acid /'prusik/ *n* HYDROCYANIC ACID [part trans of F *acide prussique,* fr *acide* acid + *prussique* of Prussian blue]

prutah, pruta /prooh'tah/ *n, pl* **prutoth, prutot** /-toht(h), -tohs/ (a coin representing) a former money unit of Israel equivalent to $^{1}/_{1000}$ pound [NHeb *pĕrūṭāh,* fr LHeb, a small coin]

[1]**pry** /prie/ *vi* **1** to inquire in an overinquisitive or impertinent manner *into* **2** to look closely or inquisitively at sby's possessions, actions, etc ⟨~ing *neighbours*⟩ [ME *prien*]

[2]**pry** *vt, chiefly NAm* [5]PRIZE [by alter.]

Przewalski's horse /ˌpuhzhəˈvalskiz/ *n* a primitive wild horse of Central Asia that is prob the ancestor of the domesticated horse and has a dun-coloured coat with a brown upright mane [Nikolai *Przhevalski* †1888 Russ soldier & explorer]

psalm /sahm/ *n, often cap* any of the sacred songs attributed to King David and collected in the Book of Psalms [ME, fr OE *psealm*, fr LL *psalmus*, fr Gk *psalmos*, lit., twanging of a harp, fr *psallein* to pluck, play a stringed instrument]

psalmody /ˈsahmədi, ˈsalmədi/ *n* **1** (the practice or art of) singing psalms in worship **2** a collection of psalms [ME *psalmodie*, fr LL *psalmodia*, fr LGk *psalmōidia*, lit., singing to the harp, fr *psalmos* + *aidein* to sing – more at ODE]

Psalms /sahmz/ *n pl but sing in constr* a collection of 150 sacred poems forming a book of the Old Testament

Psalter /ˈsawltə/ *n* a book containing a collection of Psalms for liturgical or devotional use [ME, fr OE *psalter* & OF *psaltier*, fr LL *psalterium*, fr LGk *psaltērion*, fr Gk, psaltery]

psaltery *also* **psaltry** /ˈsawlt(ə)ri/ *n* an ancient stringed musical instrument similar to the dulcimer but plucked [ME *psalterie*, fr MF, fr L *psalterium*, fr Gk *psaltērion*, fr *psallein* to play on a stringed instrument]

p's and q's /ˌpeez ən(d) ˈkyoohz/ *n pl* sthg, esp manners or language, that one should be mindful of ⟨*mind your* ~ *in front of your great-aunt*⟩ – infml [fr the phrase *mind one's p's and q's*, prob alluding to the difficulty a child learning to write may have in distinguishing between *p* and *q*]

psephology /seˈfoləji/ *n* the scientific study of elections [Gk *psēphos* pebble, ballot, vote; fr the use of pebbles by the ancient Greeks in voting] – **psephologist** *n*, **psephological** /-fəˈlojikl/ *adj*

pseud /s(y)oohd/ *n, chiefly Br* an intellectually or socially pretentious person – infml [*pseudo-*] – **pseud** *adj*, **pseudy** *adj*

pseudo /ˈs(y)oohdoh/ *adj* apparent rather than actual; spurious ⟨*distinction between true and* ~ *freedom*⟩ [ME, fr *pseudo-*]

pseudo-, pseud- *comb form* false; sham; spurious ⟨pseu doscience⟩ ⟨pseud*axis*⟩ ⟨pseudo-*intellectual*⟩ [ME, fr LL, fr Gk, fr *pseudēs*]

pseudocyesis /ˌs(y)oohdohsieˈeesis/ *n* FALSE PREGNANCY [NL, fr *pseud-* + *cyesis* pregnancy, fr Gk *kyēsis*, fr *kyein* to be pregnant – more at [1]CAVE]

pseudomorph /ˈs(y)oohdəˌmawf, -doh-/ *n* a mineral having the outward form of another mineral type [prob fr F *pseudomorphe*, fr *pseud-* + *-morphe* -morph] – **pseudomorphic** /-ˈmawfik/ *adj*, **pseudomorphism** /-ˌfiz(ə)m/ *n*, **pseudomorphous** /-fəs/ *adj*

pseudonym /ˈs(y)oohdəˌnim/ *n* a fictitious name; *esp* one used by an author [F *pseudonyme*, fr Gk *pseudōnymos* bearing a false name]

pseudonymous /s(y)oohˈdoniməs/ *adj* bearing, using, or being a pseudonym [Gk *pseudōnymos*, fr *pseud-* + *onoma, onyma* name] – **pseudonymously** *adv*

pseudopod /ˈs(y)oohdəˌpod/ *n* a pseudopodium [NL *pseudopodium*]

pseudopodium /ˌs(y)oohdəˈpohdi·əm/ *n, pl* **pseudopodia** /-di·ə/ a temporary protrusion of a cell (e g an amoeba) that serves to take in food, move the cell, etc [NL]

pseudopregnancy /ˌs(y)oohdohˈpregnənsi/ *n* **1** FALSE PREGNANCY **2** a state resembling pregnancy that occurs in various mammals usu after an infertile copulation and during which oestrus does not occur – **pseudopregnant** *adj*

pshaw /(p)shaw/ *interj* – used to express irritation, disapproval, or disbelief

psi /(p)sie/ *n* the 23rd letter of the Greek alphabet [LGk, fr Gk *psei*]

psilocybin /ˌsieləˈsiebin/ *n* a hallucinogenic organic compound obtained from a mushroom [NL *Psilocybe*, genus name + *-in*]

psittacine /ˈ(p)sitəˌsien, -ˌseen, -sin/ *adj* of the parrots [L *psittacinus*, fr *psittacus* parrot, fr Gk *psittakos*] – **psittacine** *n*

psittacosis /ˌ(p)sitəˈkohsis/ *n* a severe infectious disease of birds caused by a rickettsia that causes a serious pneumonia when transmitted to human beings [NL, fr L *psittacus*] – **psittacotic** /-ˈkotik/ *adj*

psoriasis /(p)soˈrie·əsis, (p)sə-/ *n* a chronic skin condition characterized by distinct red patches covered by white scales [NL, fr Gk *psōriasis*, fr *psōrian* to have the itch, fr *psōra* itch; akin to Gk *psēn* to rub] – **psoriatic** /ˌ(p)soriˈatik/ *adj or n*

psych, psyche /siek/ *vt* **1** *NAm* to psychoanalyse **2** *chiefly NAm* **a** to anticipate correctly the intentions or actions of; outguess **b** to analyse or work out (e g a problem or course of action) ⟨*I* ~ed *it all out by myself*⟩ **3** *chiefly NAm* **a** to make psychologically uneasy; intimidate – often + *out* **b** to make (oneself) psychologically ready for some action, test, etc – usu + *up* ⟨~ed *herself up for the race*⟩ *USE* infml [by shortening]

psych- /siek-/, **psycho-** *comb form* **1** psyche ⟨psycho*gnosis*⟩ **2a** mind; mental processes ⟨psycho*active*⟩ ⟨psycho*logy*⟩ **b** using psychoanalytical methods ⟨psycho*therapy*⟩ **c** brain ⟨psycho*surgery*⟩ **d** mental and ⟨psycho*somatic*⟩ [Gk, fr *psychē* breath, principle of life, life, soul; akin to Gk *psychein* to breathe, blow, cool, Skt *babhasti* he blows]

psyche /ˈsieki/ *n* **1** the soul, self **2** the mind [Gk *psychē*]

psychedelic /ˌsiekəˈdelik/ *adj* **1a** *of drugs* capable of producing altered states of consciousness that involve changed mental and sensory awareness, hallucinations, etc **b** produced by or associated with the use of psychedelic drugs **2a** imitating or reproducing effects (e g distorted or bizarre images or sounds) resembling those produced by psychedelic drugs ⟨*a* ~ *light show*⟩ **b** *of colours* fluorescent [Gk *psychē* soul + *dēloun* to show]

psychiatry /sieˈkie·ətri/ *n* a branch of medicine that deals with mental, emotional, or behavioural disorders [prob fr (assumed) NL *psychiatria*, fr *psych-* + *-iatria* -iatry] – **psychiatrist** *n*, **psychiatric** /-kiˈatrik/ *adj*, **psychiatrically** *adv*

[1]**psychic** /ˈsiekik/ *also* **psychical** /-kl/ *adj* **1** of or originating in the psyche **2** lying outside the sphere of physical science or knowledge **3** *of a person* sensitive to nonphysical or supernatural forces and influences [Gk *psychikos* of the soul, fr *psychē*] – **psychically** *adv*

[2]**psychic** *n* **1** a psychic person **2** MEDIUM 2e

psycho /ˈsiekoh/ *n, pl* **psychos** a psychopath, psychotic – infml – **psycho** *adj*

,psycho'active /-ˈaktiv/ *adj* affecting the mind or behaviour ⟨~ *drugs*⟩

,psycho'analyse /-ˈanəliez/ *vt* to treat by means of psychoanalysis

,psychoa'nalysis /-əˈnaləsis/ *n* a method of analysing unconscious mental processes and treating mental disorders, esp by allowing the patient to talk freely about early childhood experiences, dreams, etc [ISV] – **psychoanalyst** /-ˈanəlist/ *n*, **psychoanalytic** /-anəˈlitik/, **psychoanalytical** *adj*

,psychody'namics /-dieˈnamiks/ *n* the psychology of mental or emotional forces or processes and their effects on behaviour and mental states; *also* explanation or interpretation (e g of behaviour) in terms of these forces – **psychodynamic** *adj*

psychogenic /,siekohˈjenik, -kə-/ *adj* originating in the mind or in mental or emotional conflict

psychokinesis /,siekohkiˈneesis/ *n* apparent movement in physical objects produced by the power of the mind without physical contact [NL, fr *psych-* + Gk *kinēsis* motion, fr *kinein* to move] – **psychokinetic** /-ˈnetik/ *adj*

,psycholin'guistics /-lingˈgwistiks/ *n pl but sing in constr* the study of the interrelation between linguistic behaviour and the minds of speaker and hearer (e g the production and comprehension of speech) – **psycholinguistic** *adj*, **psycholinguist** /-ˈling,gwist/ *n*

psychological /,siekəˈlojikl/ *adj* **1a** of psychology **b** mental **2** directed towards or intended to affect the will or mind ⟨~ *warfare*⟩ – **psychologically** *adv*

psycho,logical 'moment *n* the occasion when conditions are most conducive to achieving a particular effect

psycholog·ize, -ise /sieˈkoləjiez/ *vb* to explain or interpret (sthg) in psychological terms

psychology /sieˈkoləji/ *n* **1** the science or study of mind and behaviour **2** the mental or behavioural characteristics of an individual or group [NL *psychologia*, fr *psych-* + *-logia* -logy] – **psychologist** *n*

psychometrics /,siekohˈmetriks/ *n pl but sing in constr* psychometry

psychometry /sieˈkomətri/ *n* **1** divination of facts concerning an object or its owner through physical contact or proximity **2** the psychological theory and technique of the measurement of mental capacities and attributes – **psychometrist** *n*, **psychometric** /,siekohˈmetrik/ *adj*

psychomotor /,siekohˈmohtə/ *adj* relating to motor action directly proceeding from mental activity ⟨*a ~ seizure*⟩ [ISV]

,psychoneu'rosis /-nyoo(ə)ˈrohsis/ *n* a neurosis (based on emotional conflict) [NL] – **psychoneurotic** /-ˈrotik/ *adj or n*

psychopath /ˈsiekəpath/ *n* a person suffering from a severe emotional and behavioural disorder characterized by antisocial tendencies and usu the pursuit of immediate gratification through often violent acts; *broadly* a dangerously violent mentally ill person [ISV] – **psychopathic** /-ˈpathik/ *adj*, **psychopathy** /sieˈkopəthi/ *n*

psychopathology /,siekohpəˈtholəji/ *n* (the study of) psychological and behavioural aberrations occurring in mental disorder [ISV *psych-* + *pathology*] – **psychopathologist** *n*, **psychopathological** /-pathəˈlojikl/ *adj*

,psychopharma'cology /-fahməˈkoləji/ *n* the study of the effect of drugs on the mind and behaviour – **psychopharmacologist** *n*, **psychopharmacological** /-kəˈlojikl/ *adj*

,psycho'physics /-ˈfiziks/ *n pl but sing in constr* a branch of psychology that deals with the relationship between the physical attributes of a stimulus and the characteristics of the resulting sensation or perception [ISV] – **psychophysical** /-ˈfisikl/ *adj*

,psycho'sexual /-ˈseksy(oo)əl, -sh(ə)l/ *adj* of the emotional, mental, or behavioural aspects of sex – **psychosexuality** /-ˈaləti/ *n*

psychosis /sieˈkohsis/ *n, pl* **psychoses** /-,seez/ severe mental derangement (e g schizophrenia) that results in the impairment or loss of contact with reality [NL] – **psychotic** /-ˈkotik/ *adj or n*, **psychotically** *adv*

,psycho'social /-ˈsohsh(ə)l/ *adj* relating social conditions to mental health ⟨~ *medicine*⟩

,psychoso'matic /-səˈmatik/ *adj* of or resulting from the interaction of psychological and somatic factors, esp the production of physical symptoms by mental processes ⟨~ *medicine*⟩ [ISV]

,psycho'surgery /-ˈsuhjəri/ *n* brain surgery used to treat mental disorder – **psychosurgical** /-jikl/ *adj*

,psycho'therapy /-ˈtherəpi/ *n* treatment by psychological methods for mental, emotional, or psychosomatic disorders [ISV] – **psychotherapist** *n*

psychotropic /siekəˈtrohpik/ *adj* psychoactive

psychro- *comb form* cold ⟨psychro*meter*⟩ [Gk, fr *psychros*, fr *psychein* to cool – more at PSYCH-]

psychrometer /sieˈkromitə/ *n* a hygrometer consisting of 2 similar thermometers with the bulb of 1 being kept wet so that the resulting cooling provides a measure of the dryness of the atmosphere [ISV] – **psychrometric** /-krohˈmetrik/ *adj*, **psychrometry** /-ˈkromətri/ *n*

ptarmigan /ˈtahmigən/ *n, pl* **ptarmigans,** *esp collectively* **ptarmigan** any of various grouse of northern regions whose plumage turns white in winter ☞ DEFENCE [modif of ScGael *tārmachan*]

,P 'T ,boat *n, NAm* MOTOR TORPEDO BOAT [*p*atrol *t*orpedo]

PTC *n* phenylthiocarbamide [*p*henyl*t*hio*c*arbamide]

pter-, ptero- *comb form* wing ⟨ptero*dactyl*⟩ [NL, fr Gk, fr *pteron* wing, feather – more at FEATHER]

pterid-, pterido- *comb form* fern ⟨pterid*oid*⟩ ⟨pterido*logy*⟩ [Gk *pterid-, pteris*; akin to Gk *pteron* wing, feather]

pteridology /,teriˈdoləji/ *n* the study of ferns – **pteridologist** *n*, **pteridological** /-dəˈlojik(ə)l/ *adj*

pteridophyte /ˈteridoh,fiet, -də-/ *n* any of a group of ferns or other vascular plants that have roots, stems, and leaves but no flowers or seeds ☞ PLANT [deriv of Gk *pterid-, pteris* + *phyton* plant – more at PHYT-] – **pteridophytic** /-ˈfitik/, **pteridophytous** /-ˈdofitəs/ *adj*

pterodactyl /,terəˈdaktil/ *n* any of an order of extinct flying reptiles without feathers [NL *Pterodactylus*, genus of reptiles, fr Gk *pteron* + *daktylos* finger]

pteropod /ˈterə,pod/ *n* SEA BUTTERFLY [NL *Pteropoda*, group name, fr Gk *pteron* + NL *-poda*] – **pteropod** *adj*, **pteropodan** /-ˈpohdn/ *adj or n*

pterosaur /ˈterə,saw/ *n* a pterodactyl [deriv of Gk *pteron* + *sauros* lizard]

pterygoid /ˈterigoyd/ *adj* of or lying in the region of the lower part of the wedge-shaped bone at the base of the vertebrate skull [NL *pterygoides*, fr Gk *pterygoeidēs*, lit., shaped like a wing, fr *pteryg-*, *pteryx* wing; akin to Gk *pteron* wing]

PTFE *n* polytetrafluoroethylene [*p*oly*t*etra*f*luoro*e*thylene]

Ptolemaic system /,tolə'mayik/ *n* the system of planetary motions according to which the sun, moon, and planets revolve round a stationary earth [*Ptolemy* (Claudius *Ptolemaeus*) † *ab* 168 Egyptian astronomer & geographer] – **Ptolemaist** *n*

ptomaine /'tohmayn/ *n* any of various often very poisonous organic compounds formed by the action of putrefactive bacteria on nitrogen-containing matter [It *ptomaina*, fr Gk *ptōma* fall, fallen body, corpse, fr *piptein* to fall – more at FEATHER]

ptomaine poisoning *n* food poisoning caused by (substances formed by) bacteria

ptosis /'tohsis/ *n, pl* **ptoses** /-seez/ a drooping of the upper eyelid [NL, fr Gk *ptōsis* act of falling, fr *piptein*]

ptyalin /'tie·ə,lin/ *n* an enzyme found in the saliva of many animals that breaks down starch into sugar [Gk *ptyalon* saliva, fr *ptyein* to spit – more at SPEW]

'p-,type *adj, of a semiconductor* having an excess of positvely charged current carriers – compare N-TYPE COMPUTER [*p*ositive-*type*]

pub /pub/ *n* an establishment where alcoholic beverages are sold and consumed; *esp, chiefly Br* PUBLIC HOUSE [short for *public (house)*]

pubby /'pubi/ *adj* having the (informal and friendly) atmosphere of a pub

'pub ,crawl *n, chiefly Br* a visit to a series of pubs, usu involving at least 1 drink at each – infml

puberty /'pyoohbəti/ *n* **1** the condition of being or the period of becoming capable of reproducing sexually **2** the age at which puberty occurs [ME *puberte*, fr L *pubertas*, fr *puber* pubescent] – **pubertal** *adj*

pubes /'pyoohbeez/ *n, pl* **pubes** the pubic region or hair [NL, fr L, manhood, body hair, pubic region; akin to L *puber* pubescent]

pubescence /pyooh'bes(ə)ns/ *n* **1** being pubescent **2** a pubescent covering or surface

pubescent /pyooh'bes(ə)nt/ *adj* **1** arriving at or having reached puberty **2** covered with fine soft short hairs – compare HISPID [L *pubescent-*, *pubescens*, prp of *pubescere* to reach puberty, become covered as with hair, fr *pubes*]

pubic /'pyoohbik/ *adj* of or situated in or near the region of the pubis or the pubic hair

,pubic 'hair *n* the hair that appears at puberty round the genitals

pubis /'pyoohbis/ *n, pl* **pubes** /-beez/ the bottom front of the 3 principal bones that form either half of the pelvis [NL *os pubis*, lit., bone of the pubic region]

[1]**public** /'publik/ *adj* **1a** of or affecting all the people or the whole area of a nation or state ⟨~ *law*⟩ **b** of or being in the service of the community ⟨~ *affairs*⟩ **2** general, popular ⟨*increasing* ~ *awareness*⟩ **3** of national or community concerns as opposed to private affairs; social **4a** accessible to or shared by all members of the community ⟨*a* ~ *park*⟩ **b** capitalized in shares that can be freely traded on the open market ⟨*the company has gone* ~⟩ **5a** exposed to general view; open ⟨*a* ~ *quarrel*⟩ **b** well-known, prominent ⟨~ *figures*⟩ [ME *publique*, fr MF, fr L *publicus*, prob alter. of *poplicus*, fr *populus* the people]

[2]**public** *n* **1** *the* people as a whole; *the* populace **2** a group or section of people having common interests or characteristics ⟨*the motoring* ~⟩ – **in public** in the presence, sight, or hearing of strangers

,public-ad'dress ,system *n* an apparatus including a microphone and loudspeakers used to address a large audience

publican /'publikən/ *n* **1** a Jewish tax collector for the ancient Romans **2** *chiefly Br* the licensee of a public house [ME, fr MF, fr L *publicanus* tax farmer, fr *publicum* public revenue, fr neut of *publicus*]

publication /,publi'kaysh(ə)n/ *n* **1** the act or process of publishing **2** a published work [ME *publicacioun*, fr MF *publication*, fr LL *publication-*, *publicatio*, fr L *publicatus*, pp of *publicare* to make public, publish]

,public 'bar *n, Br* a plainly furnished and often relatively cheap bar in a public house – compare SALOON BAR

,public 'company *n* a company whose shares are offered to the general public – compare PRIVATE COMPANY

,public con'venience *n, Br* public toilet facilities provided by local government

,public corpo'ration *n* a corporation responsible for running a nationalized service or industry

,public do'main *n* the status in law of property rights that are unprotected by copyright or patent and are subject to appropriation by anyone

,public 'enemy *n* sby, esp a notorious wanted criminal, who is a danger to the public

,public 'health *n* (the theory and practice of) the protection and improvement of community health, esp sanitation, by government regulation and community effort

,public 'house *n, chiefly Br* an establishment where alcoholic beverages are sold to be drunk on the premises

publicist /'publisist/ *n* an expert or commentator on public affairs

publicity /pu'blisəti/ *n* **1a** information with news value issued as a means of gaining public attention or support **b** paid advertising **c** the dissemination of information or promotional material **2** public attention or acclaim **3** being public ⟨*the* ~ *of an open court*⟩ – fml

public·ize, -ise /'publisiez/ *vt* to give publicity to

,public 'law *n* a branch of law regulating the relations of individuals with the government and the organization and conduct of the government itself

,public 'lending ,right *n, often cap P, L, & R* the right of authors to a royalty on issues of their books from public libraries

publicly /'publikli/ *adv* **1** in a manner observable by or in a place accessible to the public; openly **2a** by the people generally; communally **b** by a government ⟨~ *provided medical care*⟩

,public 'prosecutor *n* an official who conducts criminal prosecutions on behalf of the state

,public re'lations *n pl but usu sing in constr* the business of inducing the public to have understanding for and goodwill towards a person, organization, or institution; *also* the degree of understanding and goodwill achieved

ˌpublic ˈsale *n* AUCTION 1

ˌpublic ˈschool *n* **1** an endowed independent usu single-sex school in Britain, typically a large boarding school preparing pupils for higher education **2** *NAm & Scot* STATE SCHOOL

public sector *n* the part of the economy owned or controlled by the state – compare PRIVATE SECTOR

ˌpublic ˈservant *n* a government employee

ˌpublic ˈservice *n* **1** the business of supplying electricity, transport, etc to a community **2** a service rendered in the public interest **3** government employment

ˌpublic ˈspeaking *n* **1** making speeches in public **2** the art or science of effective oral communication with an audience ⟨*took a course in* ~⟩

ˌpublic-ˈspirited *adj* motivated by concern for the general welfare

ˌpublic ˈworks *n pl* schools, roads, etc constructed for public use, esp by the government

publish /ˈpublish/ *vt* **1a** to make generally known **b** to announce publicly **2a** to produce or release for publication; *specif* to print **b** to issue the work of (an author) ~ *vi* to put out an edition (e g of a newspaper) [ME *publishen*, modif of MF *publier*, fr L *publicare*, fr *publicus* public] – **publishing** *n*

publisher /ˈpublishə/ *n* a person or company whose business is publishing [PUBLISH + ²-ER]

puce /pyoohs/ *adj or n* brownish purple [n F, lit., flea, fr L *pulic-*, *pulex*; adj fr n]

¹puck /puk/ *n* a mischievous sprite [ME *puke*, fr OE *pūca*; akin to ON *pūki* devil]

²puck *n* a vulcanized rubber disc used in ice hockey [E dial. *puck* (to poke, hit), alter. of E ²*poke*]

¹pucker /ˈpukə/ *vb* to (cause to) become wrinkled or irregularly creased [prob irreg fr ¹*poke*]

²pucker *n* a crease or wrinkle in a normally even surface

puckish /ˈpukish/ *adj* impish, whimsical [¹*puck*]

pud /pood/ *n*, *Br* a pudding – infml

pudding /ˈpooding/ *n* **1** BLACK PUDDING **2** WHITE PUDDING **3a** any of various sweet or savoury dishes of a soft to spongy or fairly firm consistency that are made from rice, tapioca, flour, etc and are cooked by boiling, steaming, or baking ⟨*sponge* ~⟩ ⟨*steak and kidney* ~⟩ **b** dessert **4** a small podgy person – infml [ME]

ˈpudding ˌstone *n* (a) conglomerate rock

¹puddle /ˈpudl/ *n* **1** a small pool of liquid; *esp* one of usu muddy rainwater **2** a mixture (e g of clay, sand, and gravel) used as a waterproof covering [ME *podel*; akin to LG *pudel* puddle, OE *pudd* ditch]

²puddle *vt* **puddling** /ˈpudling, ˈpudl·ing/ **1** to work (a wet mixture of earth or concrete) into a dense impervious mass **2** to subject (iron) to puddling – **puddler** *n*

puddling /ˈpudling, ˈpudl·ing/ *n* the conversion of pig iron into wrought iron by heating and stirring with oxidizing substances

pudendum /pyoohˈdendəm/ *n*, *pl* **pudenda** /-də/ the external genital organs of a (female) human being – usu pl with sing. meaning [NL, sing. of L *pudenda*, fr neut pl of *pudendus*, gerundive of *pudēre* to be ashamed] – **pudendal** *adj*

pudgy /ˈpuji/ *adj* podgy [origin unknown] – **pudginess** *n*

pueblo /ˈpwebloh, pooˈebloh/ *n*, *pl* **pueblos** the communal dwelling of an American Indian village of Arizona or New Mexico, consisting of adjoining flat-roofed stone or adobe houses [Sp, village, lit., people, fr L *populus*]

puerile /ˈpyooəriel/ *adj* **1** juvenile **2** not befitting an adult; childish ⟨~ *remarks*⟩ [F or L; F *puéril*, fr L *puerilis*, fr *puer* boy, child; akin to Gk *pais* boy, child – more at FEW] – **puerilism** /-riˌliz(ə)m/ *n*, **puerility** /-ˈriləti/ *n*

puerperal /pyoohˈuhp(ə)rəl/ *adj* of or occurring during (the period immediately following) childbirth [L *puerpera* woman in childbirth, fr *puer* child + *parere* to give birth to – more at PARE]

puerperal fever *n* an often serious condition caused by infection of the placental site following childbirth or abortion

¹puff /puf/ *vi* **1a(1)** to blow in short gusts **(2)** to exhale or blow forcibly ⟨~ed *into a blowpipe to shape the molten glass*⟩ **b** to breathe hard and quickly; pant **c** to emit small whiffs or clouds (e g of smoke or steam) **2** to become distended; swell – usu + *up* ~ *vt* **1a** to emit, propel, or blow (as if) by puffs; waft **b** to draw on (a pipe, cigarette, etc) with intermittent exhalations of smoke **2a** to distend (as if) with air or gas; inflate **b** to make proud or conceited ⟨*extravagant praise* ~ed *up his ego*⟩ **c** to praise extravagantly and usu exaggeratedly; *also* to advertise by this means **3** to make (one's way) emitting puffs of breath or smoke ⟨~ed *her way up the hill*⟩ *USE (2a&b)* usu + *up* [ME *puffen*, fr OE *pyffan*, of imit origin]

²puff *n* **1a** an act or instance of puffing **b** a slight explosive sound accompanying a puff **c** a small cloud (e g of smoke) emitted in a puff **d** DRAW 1a **2** a light round hollow pastry made of puff paste **3** a highly favourable notice or review, esp one that publicizes sthg or sby **4** *chiefly Br* BREATH 2a ⟨*sat down until she got her* ~ *back*⟩ – infml **5** *NAm* a quilted bed cover; an eiderdown **6** a poof – slang – **puffy** *adj*, **puffiness** *n*

ˈpuff ˌadder *n* a large venomous African viper that inflates its body and hisses loudly when disturbed ☞ LIFE CYCLE

ˈpuffˌball /-ˌbawl/ *n* any of various spherical and often edible fungi

puffed /puft/ *adj*, *chiefly Br* out of breath – infml

puffer /ˈpufə/ *n* a globefish [¹PUFF + ²-ER]

puffin /ˈpufin/ *n* any of several seabirds that have a short neck and a deep grooved multicoloured bill [ME *pophyn*]

puff out *vt* **1** to extinguish by blowing **2** to cause to enlarge, esp by filling or inflating with air ~ *vi* to be enlarged with air

puff pastry *n* a light flaky pastry made with a rich dough containing a large quantity of butter

puff sleeve *n* a short full sleeve gathered at the upper and lower edges

¹pug /pug/ *n* a small sturdy compact dog with a tightly curled tail and broad wrinkled face [obs *pug* (hobgoblin, monkey), perh alter. of ¹*puck*]

²pug *vt* **-gg-** to work and mix (e g clay) when wet [perh alter. of ²*poke*]

³pug *n* a footprint, esp of a wild mammal [Hindi *pag* foot]

puggaree, pugaree, puggree /ˈpug(ə)ri/ *n* a light turban or scarf wrapped round a sun helmet [Hindi *pagṛī* turban]

pugilism /ˈpyoohjiˌliz(ə)m/ *n* boxing – fml [L *pugil* boxer; akin to L *pugnus* fist – more at PUNGENT] – **pugilist** *n*, **pugilistic** /-ˈlistik/ *adj*

pugnacious /pug'nayshəs/ *adj* inclined to fight or quarrel; belligerent [L *pugnac-, pugnax*, fr *pugnare* to fight – more at PUNGENT] – **pugnaciousness** *n*, **pugnacity** /-'nasəti/ *n*

pug nose *n* a nose having a slightly concave bridge and flattened nostrils [[1]*pug*] – **pug-nosed** *adj*

puisne /'pyoohni/ *adj, esp of a judge* lower in rank [MF *puisné* younger – more at PUNY] – **puisne** *n*

puissance /'pyooh·is(ə)ns, 'pwis(ə)ns, pyoo(h)'is(ə)ns; *in showjumping* 'pweesahnhs (*Fr* pɥisɑ̃:s)/ *n* **1** a showjumping competition which tests the horse's power to jump high obstacles **2** strength, power – fml or poetic [ME, power, fr MF, fr OF, fr *puissant* powerful, fr *poeir* to be able, be powerful – more at POWER] – **puissant** *adj*

puke /pyoohk/ *vb* to vomit – slang [perh imit] – **puke** *n*

pukka /'pukə/ *adj* **1** genuine, authentic; *also* first-class **2** *chiefly Br* stiffly formal or proper [Hindi *pakkā* cooked, ripe, solid, fr Skt *pakva*; akin to Gk *pessein* to cook – more at COOK]

puku /'poohkooh/ *n, NZ* the stomach [Maori]

pul /poohl/ *n, pl* **puls, puli** /-li, -lee/ ☞ *Afghanistan* at NATIONALITY [Per *pūl*]

pula /'poolə/ *n* ☞ *Botswana* at NATIONALITY [of Bantu origin]

pulchritude /'pulkri,tyoohd/ *n* physical beauty – fml [ME, fr L *pulchritudin-, pulchritudo*, fr *pulchr-, pulcher* beautiful] – **pulchritudinous** /-'tyoohdinəs/ *adj*

pule /pyoohl/ *vi* to whine, whimper [prob imit]

[1]**pull** /pool/ *vt* **1a** to draw out from the skin ⟨~ *feathers from a cock's tail*⟩ **b** to pick from a plant or pluck by the roots ⟨~ *flowers*⟩ ⟨~ *turnips*⟩ **c** to extract ⟨~ *a tooth*⟩ **2a** to exert force upon so as to (tend to) cause motion towards the force; tug at **b** STRAIN 2b ⟨~ed *a tendon*⟩ **c** to hold back (a horse) from winning a race **d** to work (an oar) **3** to hit (e g a ball in cricket or golf) towards the left from a right-handed swing or towards the right from a left-handed swing **4** to draw apart; tear **5** to print (e g a proof) by impression **6** to bring out (a weapon) ready for use ⟨~ed *a knife on him*⟩ **7** to draw from the barrel, esp by pulling a pump handle ⟨~ *a pint*⟩ **8a** to carry out, esp with daring and imagination ⟨~ *a robbery*⟩ ⟨~ed *another financial coup*⟩ **b** to do, perform, or say with a deceptive intent ⟨*been* ~ing *these tricks for years*⟩ **9** to (attempt to) seduce or attract ⟨*spends his weekends* ~ing *the birds*⟩ ⟨~ *votes*⟩ ~ *vi* **1a** to use force in drawing, dragging, or tugging **b** to move, esp through the exercise of mechanical energy ⟨*the car* ~ed *out of the driveway*⟩ **c** to draw or inhale hard in smoking **d** *of a horse* to strain against the bit **2** to be capable of being pulled ***USE*** (*vt 8a, 8b, & 9*) infml [ME *pullen*, fr OE *pullian*] – **pull a fast one** to perpetrate a trick or fraud – infml – **pull oneself together** to regain one's self-possession or self-control – **pull one's punches** to refrain from using all the force at one's disposal – **pull one's weight** to do one's full share of the work – **pull out all the stops** to do everything possible to achieve an effect or action – **pull rank on somebody** to assert one's authority in order to get sthg pleasant – **pull someone's leg** to deceive sby playfully; hoax – **pull strings** to exert (secret) personal influence – **pull the wool over someone's eyes** to blind sby to the true situation; hoodwink sby – **pull together** to work in harmony towards a common goal; cooperate

[2]**pull** *n* **1a** the act or an instance of pulling **b(1)** a draught of liquid **(2)** an inhalation of smoke (e g from a cigarette) **c** the effort expended in moving ⟨*a long* ~ *uphill*⟩ **d** an attacking stroke in cricket made by hitting the ball to the leg side with a horizontal bat **e** force required to overcome resistance to pulling **2** (special influence exerted to obtain) an advantage **3** PROOF 4a **4** a force that attracts, compels, or influences

pull away *vi* **1** to draw oneself back or away; withdraw **2** to move off or ahead ⟨pulled away *from the leaders on the last lap*⟩

pull down *vt* to demolish, destroy

pullet /'poolit/ *n* a young female domestic fowl less than a year old [ME *polet* young fowl, fr MF *poulet*, fr OF, dim. of *poul* cock, fr LL *pullus*, fr L, young of an animal, chicken, sprout – more at FOAL]

pulley /'pooli/ *n* **1** a wheel with a grooved rim that is used with a rope or chain to change the direction and point of application of a pulling force; *also* such a wheel together with a block in which it runs **2** a wheel used to transmit power or motion by means of a belt, rope, or chain passing over its rim [ME *pouley*, fr MF *poulie*, prob deriv of Gk *polos* axis, pole]

'pull-,in *n, chiefly Br* a place where vehicles may pull in and stop; *also* a roadside café

pull in *vt* **1** to arrest **2** to acquire as payment or profit ⟨pulls in *£10,000 a year*⟩ – infml ~ *vi* **1** *esp of a train or road vehicle* to arrive at a destination or stopping place **2** *of a vehicle or driver* to move to the side of or off the road in order to stop

Pullman /'poolmən/ *n* a railway passenger carriage with extra-comfortable furnishings, esp for night travel [George M *Pullman* †1897 US inventor]

pull off *vt* to carry out or accomplish despite difficulties

'pull-,on *n* a garment (e g a hat) that has no fastenings and is pulled onto the head or body – **pull-on** *adj*

'pull,out /-,owt/ *n* **1** a larger leaf in a book or magazine that when folded is the same size as the ordinary pages **2** a removable section of a magazine, newspaper, or book ⟨*see this week's handy TV guide* ~⟩

pull out *vi* **1** *esp of a train or road vehicle* to leave, depart **2a** to withdraw from a military position **b** to withdraw from a joint enterprise or agreement **3** *of an aircraft* to resume horizontal flight after a dive ⟨pulled out *at 400 feet*⟩ **4** *of a motor vehicle* **a** to move into a stream of traffic **b** to move out from behind a vehicle (e g when preparing to overtake)

'pull,over /-,ohvə/ *n* a garment for the upper body, esp a jumper, put on by being pulled over the head

pull over *vi, of a driver or vehicle* to move towards the side of the road, esp in order to stop

pull round *vb* to return to good health or spirits

'pull,through /-,throoh/ *n* a weighted cord with a piece of cloth attached that is passed through a tube (e g the barrel of a rifle or a woodwind instrument) to clean it

pull through *vb* to (cause to) survive a dangerous or difficult situation (e g illness)

pullulate /'pulyoo,layt/ *vi* **1a** to germinate, sprout **b** to breed or produce rapidly and abundantly **2** to swarm, teem – fml [L *pullulatus*, pp of *pullulare*, fr *pullulus*, dim. of *pullus* chicken, sprout] – **pullulation** /-'laysh(ə)n/ *n*

ˈpull-ˌup *n* **1** an exercise performed by drawing oneself up while hanging by the hands until the chin is level with the support **2** *chiefly Br* a pull-in

pull up *vt* **1** to bring to a stop; halt **2** to reprimand, rebuke ⟨*her manager* pulled *her* up *for her carelessness*⟩ – infml ~ *vi* **1** to come to a halt; stop **2** to draw even with or gain on others (e g in a race) – **pull one's socks up** *or* **pull up one's socks** to make an effort to show greater application or improve one's performance

pulmonary /ˈpoolmən(ə)ri, ˈpul-/, **pulmonic** /-ˈmonik/ *adj* of, associated with, or carried on by the lungs [L *pulmonarius*, fr *pulmon-*, *pulmo* lung; akin to Gk *pleumōn* lung]

ˌpulmonary ˈartery *n* an artery that conveys deoxygenated blood from the heart to the lungs ☞ ANATOMY

ˌpulmonary ˈvalve *n* the heart valve between the right ventricle and the pulmonary artery that stops blood flowing back into the right ventricle

ˌpulmonary ˈvein *n* a valveless vein that returns oxygenated blood from the lungs to the heart ☞ ANATOMY

pulmonate /ˈpulmənət/ *adj* **1** having (organs resembling) lungs **2** of a large order of gastropod molluscs that includes most land snails and slugs and many freshwater snails [L *pulmon-*, *pulmo* lung]

¹pulp /pulp/ *n* **1a** the soft juicy or fleshy part of a fruit or vegetable **b** a soft mass of vegetable matter from which most of the water has been pressed **c** the soft sensitive tissue that fills the central cavity of a tooth ☞ DIGESTION **d** a material prepared by chemical or mechanical means from rags, wood, etc that is used in making paper **2** pulverized ore mixed with water **3** a soft shapeless mass, esp produced by crushing or beating ⟨*smashed his face to a* ~⟩ **4** a magazine or book cheaply produced on rough paper and containing sensational material [MF *poulpe*, fr L *pulpa* flesh, pulp] – **pulpiness** *n*, **pulpy** *adj*

²pulp *vt* **1** to reduce to pulp **2** to remove the pulp from **3** to produce or reproduce (written matter) in pulp form ~ *vi* to become pulp or pulpy

pulpit /ˈpoolˌpit/ *n* **1** a raised platform or high reading desk in church from which a sermon is preached ☞ CHURCH **2** *the* clergy as a profession [ME, fr LL *pulpitum*, fr L, staging, platform]

ˈpulpˌwood /-ˌwood/ *n* a wood (e g hemlock, pine, or spruce) used in making pulp for paper

pulsar /ˈpulˌsah/ *n* a celestial source, prob a rotating neutron star, of uniformly pulsating radio waves [*pulse* + *-ar* (as in *quasar*)]

pulsate /pulˈsayt/ *vi* **1** to beat with a pulse **2** to throb or move rhythmically; vibrate [L *pulsatus*, pp of *pulsare*, fr *pulsus*, pp of *pellere*] – **pulsatory** /ˈpulsət(ə)ri, pulˈsaytəri/ *adj*

pulsation /pulˈsaysh(ə)n/ *n* rhythmic throbbing or vibrating (e g of an artery); *also* a single beat or throb – **pulsatile** /ˈpulsəˌtiel/ *adj*

pulsator /pulˈsaytə/ *n* a device that works with a throbbing movement

¹pulse /puls/ *n* the edible seeds of any of various leguminous crops (e g peas, beans, or lentils); *also* the plant yielding these [ME *puls*, fr OF *pouls* porridge, fr L *pult-*, *puls*; akin to L *pollen* fine flour – more at POLLEN]

²pulse /puls/ *n* **1a** a regular throbbing caused in the arteries by the contractions of the heart; *also* a single movement of such throbbing **b** the number of beats of a pulse in a specific period of time **2a** (an indication of) underlying sentiment or opinion ⟨*felt the political* ~ *of the nation at Westminster*⟩ **b** a feeling of liveliness; vitality **3a** rhythmical vibrating or sounding **b** a single beat or throb **4a** a short-lived variation of electrical current, voltage, etc whose value is normally constant **b** an electromagnetic wave or sound wave of brief duration [ME *puls*, fr MF *pouls*, fr L *pulsus*, lit., beating, fr *pulsus*, pp of *pellere* to drive, push, beat – more at FELT]

³pulse *vi* to pulsate, throb ~ *vt* **1** to drive (as if) by a pulsation **2** to cause to pulsate **3** to produce or modulate (e g electromagnetic waves) in the form of pulses ⟨~d *waves*⟩ – **pulser** *n*

pulsimeter /pulˈsimitə/ *n* an instrument for measuring esp the force and rate of the pulse

pulver·ize, -ise /ˈpulvəriez/ *vt* **1** to reduce (e g by crushing or grinding) to very small particles **2** to annihilate, demolish ~ *vi* to become pulverized [MF *pulveriser*, fr LL *pulverizare*, fr L *pulver-*, *pulvis* dust, powder – more at POLLEN] – **pulverizable** *adj*, **pulverizer** *n*, **pulverization** /-ˈzaysh(ə)n/ *n*

pulverulent /pulˈver(y)oolənt/ *adj* **1** consisting of or reducible to fine powder **2** being or looking dusty – fml [L *pulverulentus* dusty, fr *pulver-*, *pulvis*]

puma /ˈpyoohmə/ *n, pl* **pumas,** *esp collectively* **puma** a powerful tawny big cat formerly widespread in the Americas but now extinct in many areas [Sp, fr Quechua]

¹pumice /ˈpumis/ *n* a light porous volcanic rock used esp as an abrasive and for polishing [ME *pomis*, fr MF, fr L *pumic-*, *pumex* – more at FOAM] – **pumiceous** /pyooˈmishəs/ *adj*

²pumice *vt* to dress or polish with pumice

pummel /ˈpuml/ *vb* **-ll-** (*NAm* **-l-**, **-ll-**), /ˈpuml·ing/ to pound or strike repeatedly, esp with the fists [alter. of *pommel*]

¹pump /pump/ *n* **1a** a device that raises, transfers, or compresses fluids or that reduces the density of gases, esp by suction or pressure or both **b** a mechanism (e g the sodium pump) for pumping atoms, ions, or molecules **2** the heart **3** an act or the process of pumping [ME *pumpe, pompe*, fr MLG *pumpe* or MD *pompe*, prob fr Sp *bomba*, of imit origin]

²pump *vt* **1a** to raise (e g water) with a pump **b** to draw fluid from with a pump – often + *out* **2** to pour out or inject (as if) with a pump ⟨~ed *money into the economy*⟩ **3** to question persistently ⟨~ed *her for information*⟩ **4** to move (sthg) rapidly up and down as if working a pump handle ⟨~ed *her hand warmly*⟩ **5a** to inflate by means of a pump or bellows – usu + *up* **b** to supply with air by means of a pump or bellows ⟨~ *an organ*⟩ ~ *vi* **1** to work a pump; raise or move a fluid with a pump **2** to move in a manner resembling the action of a pump handle **3** to spurt out intermittently

³pump *n* **1** a low shoe without fastenings that grips the foot chiefly at the toe and heel **2** *Br* a plimsoll [origin unknown]

pumpernickel /ˈpumpəˌnikl, ˈpoom-/ *n* a dark coarse slightly sour-tasting bread made from wholemeal rye [G]

pumpkin /ˈpum(p)kin/ *n* (a usu hairy prickly plant that bears) a very large usu round fruit with a deep yellow to orange rind and edible flesh [alter. of earlier *pumpion*, modif of F *popon, pompon* melon, pumpkin, fr L *pepon-*, *pepo*, fr Gk *pepōn*, fr *pepōn* ripened; akin to Gk *pessein* to cook, ripen – more at COOK]

'pump ,room *n* a room at a spa in which the water is distributed and drunk

[1]pun /pun/ *vt* to consolidate (e g earth, concrete, or hardcore) by repeated ramming or pounding [ME *pounen* to pound]

[2]pun *n* a humorous use of a word with more than 1 meaning or of words with (nearly) the same sound but different meanings [prob short for obs *punnet, pundigrion,* perh alter. of It *puntiglio* fine point, quibble – more at PUNCTILIO]

[3]pun *vi* **-nn-** to make puns

puna /'poohnə/ *n* a windswept tableland in the higher Andes [AmerSp, fr Quechua]

[1]punch /punch/ *vt* **1** to strike, esp with a hard and quick thrust of the fist **2** to drive or push forcibly (as if) by a punch **3** to hit (a ball) with less than a full swing of a bat, racket, etc **4** to emboss, cut, or make (as if) with a punch ~ *vi* to punch sthg [ME *punchen,* fr MF *poinçonner* to prick, stamp, fr *poinçon* puncheon (pointed tool), fr (assumed) VL *punction-, punctio,* fr *punctiare* to prick, fr L *punctus,* pp of *pungere* to prick – more at PUNGENT] – **puncher** *n*

[2]punch *n* **1** a blow (as if) with the fist **2** effective energy or forcefulness ⟨*an opening paragraph that packs a lot of* ~⟩

[3]punch *n* **1** a tool, usu in the form of a short steel rod, used esp for perforating, embossing, cutting, or driving the heads of nails below a surface **2** a device for cutting holes or notches in paper or cardboard [prob short for *puncheon* (pointed tool)]

[4]punch *n* a hot or cold drink usu made from wine or spirits mixed with fruit, spices, water, and occas tea – compare CUP 6 [perh fr Hindi *p ac* five, fr Skt *pañca*; akin to Gk *pente* five; fr the number of ingredients]

'punch-,bag *n* **1** an inflated or stuffed bag punched with the fists as a form of exercise or training **2** sby who serves as a stooge or butt

'punch ,ball *n, Br* a punch-bag

'punch ,bowl *n* a large bowl in which a beverage, esp punch, is mixed and served

'punch-,drunk *adj* **1** suffering brain damage as a result of repeated punches or blows to the head **2** behaving as if punch-drunk; dazed

,punched 'card, 'punch ,card *n* a card used in data processing in which a pattern of holes or notches has been cut to represent information or instructions ☞ SYMBOL

punched tape *n* a strip of paper having rows of typically 8 holes punched across it which represent information or instructions used in computers and other machines ☞ SYMBOL

puncheon /'punch(ə)n/ *n* a large cask of varying capacity [ME *poncion,* fr MF *ponchon, poinçon,* of unknown origin]

Punchinello /,punchi'neloh/ *n* a short fat humpbacked clown or buffoon in Italian puppet shows [modif of It dial. *polecenella*]

'punching ,bag /'punching/ *n, NAm* a punch-bag

'punch ,line *n* a sentence or phrase, esp a joke, that forms the climax to a speech or dialogue

'punch-,up *n, chiefly Br* a usu spontaneous fight, esp with the bare fists – infml

punchy /'punchi/ *adj* having punch; forceful

punctate /'pung(k)tayt/ *adj* marked with minute spots or depressions ⟨*a* ~ *leaf*⟩ [NL *punctatus,* fr L *punctum* point – more at POINT] – **punctation** /-'taysh(ə)n/ *n*

punctilio /pung(k)'tilioh/ *n, pl* **punctilios** **1** a minute detail of ceremony or observance **2** careful observance of forms (e g in social conduct) [It & Sp; It *puntiglio* point of honour, scruple, fr Sp *puntillo,* fr dim. of *punto* point, fr L *punctum*]

punctilious /pung(k)'tili·əs/ *adj* strict or precise in observing codes of conduct or conventions – **punctiliously** *adv,* **punctiliousness** *n*

punctual /'pung(k)chooəl, -tyoo-/ *adj* **1** relating to or having the nature of a point **2** (habitually) arriving, happening, performing, etc at the exact or agreed time [ML *punctualis,* fr L *punctus* pricking, point, fr *punctus,* pp of *pungere* to prick – more at PUNGENT] – **punctually** *adv,* **punctuality** /-'aləti/ *n*

punctuate /'pung(k)choo,ayt, -tyoo-/ *vt* **1** to mark or divide with punctuation marks **2** to break into or interrupt at intervals ~ *vi* to use punctuation marks [ML *punctuatus,* pp of *punctuare* to point, provide with punctuation marks, fr L *punctus* point] – **punctuator** *n*

punctuation /,pung(k)choo'aysh(ə)n, -tyoo-/ *n* the dividing of writing with marks to clarify meaning; *also* a system of punctuation [PUNCTUATE + -ION]

punctu'ation ,mark *n* a standardized mark or sign used in punctuation

[1]puncture /'pung(k)chə/ *n* a perforation (e g a hole or narrow wound) made by puncturing; *esp* a small hole made accidentally in a pneumatic tyre [L *punctura,* fr *punctus,* pp of *pungere*]

[2]puncture *vt* **1** to pierce with a pointed instrument or object **2** to cause a puncture in **3** to make useless or deflate as if by a puncture ⟨*failures* ~d *her confidence*⟩ ~ *vi* to become punctured

pundit /'pundit/ *n* **1** a learned man or teacher; *specif* a pandit **2** one who gives opinions in an authoritative manner; an authority [Hindi *paṇḍit,* fr Skt *paṇḍita,* fr *paṇḍita* learned] – **punditry** /-tri/ *n*

pungent /'punj(ə)nt/ *adj* **1** having a stiff and sharp point ⟨~ *leaves*⟩ **2a** marked by a sharp incisive quality; caustic **b** to the point; highly expressive ⟨~ *prose*⟩ **3** having a strong sharp smell or taste; *esp* acrid [L *pungent-, pungens,* prp of *pungere* to prick, sting; akin to L *pugnus* fist, *pugnare* to fight, Gk *pygmē* fist] – **pungency** /-si/ *n*

Punic /'pyoohnik/ *n or adj* (the dialect) of Carthage or the Carthaginians [adj L *punicus,* fr *Poenus* inhabitant of Carthage, modif of Gk *Phoinix* Phoenician; n fr adj]

punish /'punish/ *vt* **1** to impose a penalty on (an offender) or for (an offence) **2** to treat roughly or damagingly ⟨~ *an engine*⟩ – infml ~ *vi* to inflict punishment [ME *punisshen,* fr MF *puniss-,* stem of *punir,* fr L *punire,* fr *poena* penalty – more at PAIN] – **punishable** *adj,* **punisher** *n*

'punishment /-mənt/ *n* **1a** punishing or being punished **b** a judicial penalty **2** rough or damaging treatment – infml ⟨*the contender took plenty of* ~ *in the last round*⟩

punitive /'pyoohnətiv/ *adj* inflicting or intended to inflict punishment ⟨*a* ~ *blow*⟩ ⟨*a* ~ *schedule*⟩ [F *punitif,* fr ML *punitivus,* fr L *punitus,* pp of *punire*]

,punitive 'damages *n pl* damages awarded in excess of normal compensation to the plaintiff to punish a defendant

Punjabi /pun'jahbi, poon-/ *n* (the language spoken

by) a native or inhabitant of the Punjab of NW India and Pakistan ☞ LANGUAGE [Hindi *pañjābī*, fr *pañjābī* of Punjab, fr Per, fr *Pañjāb* Punjab] – **Punjabi** *adj*

[1]**punk** /pungk/ *n* **1** sby following punk styles in music, dress, etc **2** *chiefly NAm* sby considered worthless or inferior; *esp* a petty criminal [origin unknown]

[2]**punk** *adj* **1** of or being a movement among young people of the 1970s and 1980s in Britain characterized by a violent rejection of established society and expressed through punk rock and the wearing of aggressively outlandish clothes and hairstyles **2** *chiefly NAm* of very poor quality; inferior – slang

[3]**punk** *n* a dry spongy substance prepared from fungi and used to ignite fuses [perh alter. of *spunk*]

punkah /'pungkə/ *n* a fan used esp formerly in India consisting of a cloth-covered frame suspended from the ceiling and swung to and fro by means of a cord [Hindi *pãkhā*]

,punk 'rock *n* a style of rock music characterized by a driving tempo, crude or obscene lyrics, and an aggressive delivery

punnet /'punit/ *n, chiefly Br* a small basket of wood, plastic, etc, esp for soft fruit or vegetables [origin unknown]

punster /'punstə/ *n* one who is given to punning

[1]**punt** /punt/ *n* a long narrow flat-bottomed boat with square ends, usu propelled with a pole [(assumed) ME, fr OE, fr L *ponton-, ponto* – more at [1]PONTOON]

[2]**punt** *vt* to propel (e g a punt) with a pole; *also* to transport by punt ~*vi* to propel a punt; go punting

[3]**punt** *vi* **1** to play against the banker at a gambling game **2** *Br* to gamble [F *ponter*, fr *ponte* point in some games, play against the banker, fr Sp *punto* point, fr L *punctum* – more at POINT]

[4]**punt** *vb* to kick (a football) by means of a punt [origin unknown]

[5]**punt** *n* the act of kicking a football with the top or tip of the foot after it is dropped from the hands and before it hits the ground

[6]**punt** /poont/ *n* ☞ *Irish Republic* at NATIONALITY [IrGael, pound]

punter /'puntə/ *n* **1** a con-man's (potential) victim **2** a prostitute's client; *broadly* a client, customer **3** *chiefly Br* sby who gambles and esp bets with a bookmaker ***USE*** (*1&2*) slang [[2] [3] [4]PUNT + [2]-ER]

puny /'pyoohni/ *adj* slight or inferior in power, size, or importance; weak [MF *puisné* younger, lit., born afterwards, fr *puis* afterwards + *né* born] – **puniness** *n*

[1]**pup** /pup/ *n* a young dog; *also* a young seal, rat, etc [short for *puppy*]

[2]**pup** *vi* **-pp-** to give birth to pups

pupa /'pyoohpə/ *n, pl* **pupae** /-pi/, **pupas** the intermediate usu inactive form of an insect that undergoes metamorphism (e g a bee, moth, or beetle) that occurs between the larva and the imago stages ☞ LIFE CYCLE [NL, fr L *pupa* girl, doll] – **pupal** *adj*

pupate /pyooh'payt/ *vi* to become a pupa – **pupation** /-'paysh(ə)n/ *n*

[1]**pupil** /'pyoohpl/ *n* **1** a child or young person at school or receiving tuition **2** one who has been taught or influenced by a distinguished person [ME *pupille* minor ward, fr MF, fr L *pupillus* male ward (fr dim. of *pupus* boy) & *pupilla* female ward, fr dim. of *pupa* girl, doll, puppet]

[2]**pupil** *n* the contractile usu round dark opening in the iris of the eye ☞ NERVE [MF *pupille*, fr L *pupilla*, fr dim. of *pupa* doll; fr the tiny image of oneself seen reflected in another's eye] – **pupilar** /-pilə/ *adj*, **pupillary** /-piləri/ *adj*

pupillage, pupilage /'pyoohpilij/ *n* the state or period of being a pupil, specif to a barrister

,pupil 'teacher *n* a young person who in former times taught in an elementary school while concurrently receiving education

pupiparous /pyooh'pip(ə)rəs/ *adj* producing mature larvae that are ready to pupate at birth [NL *pupa* + E *-i-* + *-parous*]

puppet /'pupit/ *n* **1a** a small-scale toy figure (e g of a person or animal) usu with a cloth body and hollow head that fits over and is moved by the hand **b** a marionette **2** one whose acts are controlled by an outside force or influence ⟨*a ~ government*⟩ [ME *popet*, fr MF *poupette*, dim. of (assumed) *poupe* doll, fr L *pupa*] – **puppetry** *n*, **puppeteer** /-'tiə/ *n*

puppy /'pupi/ *n* **1** a young dog (less than a year old) **2** a conceited or ill-mannered young man [ME *popi*, fr MF *poupée* doll, toy, fr (assumed) *poupe* doll]

'puppy ,fat *n* temporary plumpness in children and adolescents

'puppy ,love *n* short-lived romantic affection felt by an adolescent for sby of the opposite sex

'pup ,tent *n* a small shelter tent

Purbeck stone /'puhbek/ *n* a hard limestone used esp for building [Isle of *Purbeck*, district in Dorset, England]

purblind /'puh,bliend/ *adj* **1** partly blind **2** lacking in vision or insight; obtuse – fml [ME *pur blind*, fr *pur* purely, wholly, fr *pur* pure] – **purblindness** *n*

[1]**purchase** /'puhchəs/ *vt* **1a** to acquire (real estate) by means other than inheritance **b** to obtain by paying money or its equivalent; buy **c** to obtain by labour, danger, or sacrifice ⟨~d *life at the expense of honour*⟩ **2** to move or raise by a device (e g a lever or pulley) **3** to constitute the means for buying ⟨*a pound seems to ~ less each year*⟩ [ME *purchacen*, fr OF *purchacier* to seek to obtain, fr *por-, pur-* for, forwards (modif of L *pro-*) + *chacier* to pursue, chase – more at PRO-] – **purchasable** *adj*, **purchaser** *n*

[2]**purchase** *n* **1** sthg obtained by payment of money or its equivalent **2a** a mechanical hold or advantage (e g that applied through a pulley or lever); *broadly* an advantage used in applying power or influence **b** a means, esp a mechanical device, by which one gains such an advantage

'purchase ,tax *n* a tax levied on the sale of goods and services that is usu calculated as a percentage of the purchase price – compare VALUE-ADDED TAX

purdah /'puhdah, -də/ *n* the seclusion of women from public view among Muslims and some Hindus, esp in India; *also* a screen used for this purpose [Hindi *parda*, lit., screen, veil]

pure /pyooə/ *adj* **1a(1)** unmixed with any other matter ⟨*~ gold*⟩ **(2)** free from contamination ⟨*~ food*⟩ **(3)** spotless; *specif* free from moral fault **b** *of a musical sound* being in tune and free from harshness **c** *of a vowel* monophthongal **2a** sheer, unmitigated ⟨*~ folly*⟩ **b** abstract, theoretical ⟨*~ science*⟩ **3a** free from anything that vitiates or weakens ⟨*the ~ religion of our fathers*⟩ **b** containing nothing that does not properly belong ⟨*the ~ text*⟩ **c** of unmixed ancestry **4a** chaste **b** ritually clean [ME *pur*, fr OF, fr L *purus*; akin to Skt *punāti* he cleanses, MIr *ūr* fresh, green] – **pureness** *n*

ˈpure,blood /-ˌblud/, **pure-blooded** /-ˈbludid/ *adj* PURE 3c – **pureblood** *n*

ˈpure,bred /-ˌbred/ *adj* bred over many generations from members of a recognized breed, strain, or kind without mixture of other blood – **purebred** *n*

¹puree, purée /ˈpyooəray/ *n* a thick pulp (e g of fruit or vegetable) usu produced by rubbing cooked food through a sieve or blending in a liquidizer; *also* a thick soup made from pureed vegetables [F, fr MF, fr fem of *puré*, pp of *purer* to purify, strain, fr L *purare* to purify, fr *purus*]

²puree, purée *vt* to reduce to a puree

purely /ˈpyooəli/ *adv* **1** without addition, esp of anything harmful **2** simply, merely ⟨*read ~ for relaxation*⟩ **3** in a chaste or innocent manner **4** wholly, completely ⟨*a selection based ~ on merit*⟩

purfle /ˈpuhfl/ *vt* to ornament the border or edges of [ME *purfilen*, fr MF *porfiler*] – **purfle** *n*

purgation /puhˈgaysh(ə)n/ *n* the act or result of purging

purgative /ˈpuhgətiv/ *n or adj* (a medicine) causing evacuation of the bowels

purgatory /ˈpuhgət(ə)ri/ *n* **1** a place or state of punishment in which, according to Roman Catholic doctrine, the souls of those who die in God's grace may make amends for past sins and so become fit for heaven **2** a place or state of temporary suffering or misery – infml ⟨*the return trip was absolute ~*⟩ [ME, fr AF or ML; AF *purgatorie*, fr ML *purgatorium*, fr LL, neut of *purgatorius* purging, fr L *purgatus*, pp of *purgare*] – **purgatorial** /-ˈtawri·əl/ *adj*

¹purge /puhj/ *vt* **1a** to clear of guilt **b** to free from moral or physical impurity **2a** to cause evacuation from (e g the bowels) **b(1)** to rid (e g a nation or party) of unwanted or undesirable members, often summarily or by force **(2)** to get rid of (e g undesirable people) by means of a purge [ME *purgen*, fr OF *purgier*, fr L *purigare*, *purgare* to purify, purge, fr *purus* pure + *-igare* (akin to *agere* to drive, do) – more at AGENT]

²purge *n* **1** an (esp political) act of purging **2** a purgative

purificatory /ˌpyoo(ə)rifiˈkaytəri, -tri/ *adj* serving, tending, or intended to purify

purify /ˈpyooərifie/ *vt* **1** to free of physical or moral impurity or imperfection **2** to free from undesirable elements ~ *vi* to grow or become pure or clean [ME *purifien*, fr MF *purifier*, fr L *purificare*, fr L *purus* + *-ificare* -ify] – **purifier** *n*, **purificator** /-fiˌkaytə/ *n*, **purification** /-fiˈkaysh(ə)n/ *n*

purine /ˈpyooəreen, -rin/ *n* (either of the bases adenine or guanine that are constituents of DNA and RNA and are derivatives of) a compound from which uric acid and related compounds are made in the body [G *purin*, fr L *purus* pure + NL *uricus* uric, fr E *uric*]

purist /ˈpyooərist/ *n* one who keeps strictly and often excessively to established or traditional usage, esp in language – **purism** *n*

puritan /ˈpyooərit(ə)n/ *n* **1** *cap* a member of a 16th- and 17th-c mainly calvinist Protestant group in England and New England which wished to purify the Church of England of all very ceremonial worship **2** one who practises or preaches a rigorous or severe moral code [prob fr LL *puritas* purity] – **puritan** *adj, often cap*

puritanical /ˌpyooəriˈtanikl/ *adj* **1** puritan **2** of or characterized by a rigid morality; strict

puritanism /ˈpyooəritəˌniz(ə)m/ *n* **1** *cap* the beliefs and practices of the Puritans **2** strictness and austerity, esp in matters of religion or conduct

purity /ˈpyooərəti/ *n* **1** pureness **2** SATURATION 1 [ME *purete*, fr OF *pureté*, fr LL *puritat-*, *puritas*, fr L *purus* pure]

¹purl /puhl/ *n* **1** a thread of twisted gold or silver wire used for embroidering or edging **2 purl, purl stitch** a basic knitting stitch made by inserting the needle into the back of a stitch that produces a raised pattern on the back of the work – compare KNIT STITCH **3** *Br* an ornamental edging of small loops or picots on lace, ribbon, or braid [obs *pirl* (to twist), of unknown origin]

²purl *vt* **1a** to decorate, edge, or border with gold or silver thread **b** to edge with loops; picot **2** to knit in purl stitch ~ *vi* to do knitting in purl stitch

³purl *n* a gentle murmur or movement (e g of water) [perh of Scand origin; akin to Norw *purla* to ripple]

⁴purl *vi, of a stream, brook, etc* to flow in eddies with a soft murmuring sound

purler /ˈpuhlə/ *n, chiefly Br* a heavy headlong fall – infml [*purl* (to whirl, capsize, upset), alter. of obs *pirl* (to twist)]

purlieus /ˈpuhlyoohz/ *n pl* **1** environs, neighbourhood **2** confines, bounds – fml [ME *purlewe* land severed from an English royal forest by perambulation, fr AF *puralé* perambulation, fr OF *puraler* to go through, fr *pur-* for, through + *aler* to go – more at PURCHASE, ¹ALLEY]

purlin /ˈpuhlin/ *n* a horizontal beam in a roof supporting the rafters ☞ ARCHITECTURE [origin unknown]

purloin /puhˈloyn, pə-/ *vt* to take dishonestly; steal – fml [ME *purloinen* to put away, render ineffectual, fr AF *purloigner*, fr OF *porloigner* to put off, delay, fr *por-* forwards + *loing* at a distance, fr L *longe*, fr *longus* long]

¹purple /ˈpuhpl/ *adj* **1** of the colour purple **2** highly rhetorical; ornate ⟨~ *prose*⟩ [ME *purpel*, alter. of *purper*, fr OE *purpuran*, gen of *purpure* purple colour, fr L *purpura*, fr Gk *porphyra*]

²purple *n* **1a** a colour falling about midway between red and blue in hue **b** cloth dyed purple; *also* a purple robe worn as an emblem of rank or authority **c(1)** a mollusc yielding a purple dye, esp the Tyrian purple of ancient times **(2)** a pigment or dye that colours purple **2** imperial, regal, or very high rank ⟨*born to the* ~⟩

³purple *vb* to make or become purple

ˌpurple ˈheart *n* a light blue tablet containing the drug phenobarbitone and formerly prescribed as a hypnotic or sedative

ˌpurple ˈpassage *n* a piece of obtrusively ornate writing [trans of L *pannus purpureus* purple patch; fr the traditional splendour of purple cloth in contrast with more shabby materials]

purplish /ˈpuhplish/ *adj* rather purple

¹purport /ˈpuhpawt, -pət/ *n* professed or implied meaning; import; *also* substance – fml [ME, fr AF, content, tenor, fr *purporter* to contain, fr OF *por-*

porter to convey, fr *por-* forwards + *porter* to carry – more at PURCHASE, [3]PORT]

[2]**purport** /pə'pawt, puh'pawt, 'puhpət/ *vt* to (be intended to) seem; profess ⟨*a book that* ~s *to be an objective analysis*⟩

[1]**purpose** /'puhpəs/ *n* **1** the object for which sthg exists or is done; the intention **2** resolution, determination [ME *purpos*, fr OF, fr *purposer* to purpose, fr L *proponere* (perf indic *proposui*) to propose – more at PROPOSE] – **purposeless** *adj* – **on purpose** with intent; intentionally

[2]**purpose** *vt* to have as one's intention – fml

,**purpose-'built** *n, chiefly Br* designed to meet a specific need ⟨*a* ~ *conference centre*⟩

'**purposeful** /-f(ə)l/ *adj* **1** full of determination **2** having a purpose or aim ⟨~ *activities*⟩ – **purposefully** *adv*, **purposefulness** *n*

'**purposely** /-li/ *adv* with a deliberate or express purpose

purposive /'puhpəsiv/ *adj* **1** serving or effecting a useful function though not necessarily as a result of deliberate intention **2** having or tending to fulfil a conscious purpose; purposeful *USE* fml – **purposively** *adv*, **purposiveness** *n*

purpura /'puhpyoorə/ *n* any of several states characterized by patches of purplish discoloration on the skin and mucous membranes and caused by abnormalities in the blood [NL, fr L, purple colour] – **purpuric** /-'pyooərik/ *adj*

purpure /'puhpyooə/ *n* purple – used in heraldry [ME, fr OE, purple]

purr /puh/ *vi* **1** to make the low vibratory murmur of a contented cat **2** to make a sound resembling a purr [imit] – **purr** *n*

[1]**purse** /puhs/ *n* **1** a small flattish bag for money; *esp* a wallet with a compartment for holding change **2a** resources, funds **b** a sum of money offered as a prize or present; *also* the total amount of money offered in prizes for a given event **3** *NAm* a handbag [ME *purs*, fr OE, modif of ML *bursa*, fr LL, oxhide, fr Gk *byrsa*]

[2]**purse** *vt* to pucker, knit

purser /'puhsə/ *n* an officer on a ship responsible for documents and accounts and on a passenger ship also for the comfort and welfare of passengers [ME, fr [1]*purse* + [2]*-er*]

'**purse** ,**strings** *n pl* control over expenditure ⟨*she holds the* ~⟩

purslane /'puhslin/ *n* a fleshy-leaved trailing plant with tiny yellow flowers [ME, fr MF *porcelaine*, fr LL *porcillagin-*, *porcillago*, alter. of L *porcillaca*, alter. of *portulaca*]

pursuance /pə'syooh·əns/ *n* a carrying out or into effect (e g of a plan or order); prosecution ⟨*in* ~ *of her duties*⟩ – fml [PURSUE + -ANCE]

pursue /pə'syooh/ *vt* **1** to follow in order to overtake, capture, kill, or defeat **2** to find or employ measures to obtain or accomplish ⟨~ *a goal*⟩ **3** to proceed along ⟨~s *a northern course*⟩ **4a** to engage in ⟨~ *a hobby*⟩ **b** to follow up ⟨~ *an argument*⟩ **5** to continue to afflict; haunt ⟨*was* ~d *by horrible memories*⟩ ~ *vi* to go in pursuit [ME *pursuen*, fr AF *pursuer*, fr OF *poursuir*, fr L *prosequi*, fr *pro-* forwards + *sequi* to follow – more at PRO-, SUE]

pursuer /pə'syooh·ə/ *n, Scot* **1** a plaintiff **2** a prosecutor [PURSUE + [2]-ER]

pursuit /pə'syooht/ *n* **1** an act of pursuing **2** an activity that one regularly engages in (e g as a pastime or profession) [ME, fr OF *poursuite*, fr *poursuir*]

pursuivant /'puhsiv(ə)nt; *also* -swi-/ *n* an officer of arms ranking below a herald [ME *pursevant* attendant of a herald, fr MF *poursuivant*, lit., follower, fr prp of *poursuir, poursuivre* to pursue]

pursy /'puhsi/ *adj* (short-winded, esp because) corpulent [ME *pursy*, fr AF *pursif*, alter. of MF *polsif*, fr *poulser, polser* to beat, push, pant – more at PUSH] – **pursiness** *n*

purulent /'pyooərələnt/ *adj* **1** containing, consisting of, or being pus ⟨*a* ~ *discharge*⟩ **2** accompanied by suppuration [L *purulentus*, fr *pur-*, *pus* pus] – **purulence** *n*

purvey /pə'vay, puh-/ *vt* to supply (e g provisions), esp in the course of business [ME *purveien*, fr MF *porveeir*, fr L *providēre* to provide] – **purveyance** *n*

purveyor /pə'vayə, puh-/ *n* a victualler or caterer [PURVEY + [1]-OR]

purview /'puh,vyooh/ *n* **1** the body or enacting part of a statute **2** the range or limit of authority, responsibility, or concern **3** the range of vision or understanding *USE* (*2&3*) fml [ME *purveu*, fr AF *purveu est* it is provided (opening phrase of a statute)]

pus /pus/ *n* thick opaque usu yellowish white fluid matter formed by suppuration (e g in an abscess) [L *pur-*, *pus* – more at FOUL]

[1]**push** /poosh/ *vt* **1a** to apply a force to (sthg) in order to cause movement away from the person or thing applying the force **b** to move (sthg) away or forwards by applying such a force ⟨*to* ~ *a car uphill*⟩ **2** to cause (sthg) to change in quantity or extent as if under pressure ⟨*scarcity of labour* ~ed *up wages*⟩ **3a** to develop (e g an idea or argument), esp to an extreme degree **b** to urge or press the advancement, adoption, or practice of; *specif* to make aggressive efforts to sell ⟨*a drive to* ~ *tinned foods*⟩ **c** to press or urge (sby) to sthg; pressurize ⟨*keeps* ~ing *me to give her a rise*⟩ **4** to force towards or beyond the limits of capacity or endurance ⟨*poverty* ~ed *them to breaking point*⟩ **5** to hit (a ball) towards the right from a right-handed swing or towards the left from a left-handed swing **6** to approach in age or number ⟨*the old man was* ~ing *75*⟩ – infml **7** to engage in the illicit sale of (drugs) – slang ~ *vi* **1** to press against sthg with steady force (as if) in order to move it away **2** to press forwards energetically against obstacles or opposition ⟨*explorers* ~ed *out into the Antarctic*⟩ **3** to exert oneself continuously or vigorously to achieve an end ⟨*unions* ~ing *for higher wages*⟩ [ME *pusshen*, fr OF *poulser* to beat, push, fr L *pulsare*, fr *pulsus*, pp of *pellere* to drive, strike – more at FELT] – **push one's luck** to take an increasing risk

[2]**push** *n* **1a** a vigorous effort to attain an end; a drive **b** a military assault or offensive **c** an advance that overcomes obstacles **2a** an act or action of pushing **b** a nonphysical pressure; an urge ⟨*the* ~ *and pull of conflicting emotions*⟩ **c** vigorous enterprise or energy ⟨*she'll need a lot of* ~ *to get to the top*⟩ **3a** an exertion of influence to promote another's interests ⟨*his father's* ~ *took him to the top*⟩ **b** stimulation to activity; an impetus **4** a time for action; an emergency ⟨*when it came to the* ~ *I forgot my lines*⟩ **5** *Br* dismissal – esp in *get/give the push* ⟨*he'll get the* ~ *if he's late again*⟩ *USE* (*4&5*) infml – **at a push**

chiefly Br if really necessary; if forced by special conditions

push around *vt* to order about; bully

'push-,bike *n, Br* a pedal bicycle

'push-,button *adj* **1** operated by means of a push button **2** characterized by the use of long-range weapons rather than physical combat ⟨~ *warfare*⟩

'push ,button *n* a small button or knob that when pushed operates or triggers sthg, esp by closing an electric circuit

'push,chair /-,cheə/ *n, Br* a light folding chair on wheels in which young children may be pushed

pushed /poosht/ *adj* having difficulty in finding enough time, money, etc ⟨*you'll be ~ to finish that by tonight*⟩ – infml

pusher /'pooshə/ *n* **1** a utensil used by a child for pushing food onto a spoon or fork **2** one who sells drugs illegally – slang [[1]PUSH + [2]-ER]

push in *vi* to join a queue at a point in front of others already waiting, esp by pushing or jostling

pushing /'pooshing/ *adj* aggressively ambitious and self-assertive

push off *vi* to go away, esp hastily or abruptly – infml

push on *vi* to continue on one's way, esp despite obstacles or difficulties

'push,over /-,ohvə/ *n* **1** an opponent who is easy to defeat or a victim who is incapable of effective resistance **2** sby unable to resist a usu specified attraction; a sucker ⟨*he's a ~ for blondes*⟩ **3** sthg accomplished without difficulty; a cinch *USE* infml

,push-'pull *adj* of or being an arrangement of 2 thermionic valves or transistors in which an alternating input causes alternate valves or transistors to drive the load – **push-pull** *n*

'push,rod /-,rod/ *n* a rod put into action by a cam to open or close a valve in an internal-combustion engine

Pushtu /'pushtooh/ *n* Pashto

pushy /'pooshi/ *adj* self-assertive often to an objectionable degree; forward – infml – **pushily** *adv*, **pushiness** *n*

pusillanimous /,pyoohsi'lanimәs/ *adj* lacking courage and resolution; contemptibly timid – fml [LL *pusillanimis*, fr L *pusillus* very small (dim. of *pusus* small child) + *animus* spirit; akin to L *puer* child – more at PUERILE, ANIMATE] – **pusillanimity** /-lə'nimәti/ *n*

puss /poos/ *n* **1** a cat – used chiefly as a pet name or calling name **2** a girl ⟨*a saucy little ~*⟩ *USE* infml [origin unknown]

'puss ,moth *n* a large grey and white moth

[1]**pussy** /'poosi/ *n* **1** a catkin of the pussy willow **2** a cat – infml; used chiefly as a pet name

[2]**pussy** *n* the vulva – vulg [earlier *puss* (perh of LG or Scand origin) + *-y*; akin to ON *pūss* pocket, pouch, LG *pūse* vulva, OE *pusa* bag, Gk *byein* to stuff, plug]

'pussy,cat /-,kat/ *n* a cat – used chiefly by or to children

'pussy,foot /-,foot/ *vi* **1** to tread or move warily or stealthily **2** to avoid committing oneself (e g to a course of action)

,pussy 'willow *n* any of various willows having grey silky catkins

pustulant /'pustyoolәnt/ *n or adj* (sthg, esp a chemical, for) inducing the formation of pustules

pustular /'pustyoolə/ *adj* of, resembling, or covered with pustules

pustulation /,pustyoo'laysh(ә)n/ *n* **1** the producing of pustules; being covered with pustules **2** a pustule

pustule /'pustyoohl/ *n* **1** a small raised spot on the skin having an inflamed base and containing pus **2** a small raised area like a blister or pimple [ME, fr L *pustula* – more at [2]FOG]

[1]**put** /poot/ *vb* **put; -tt-** *vt* **1a** to place in or move into a specified position or relationship ⟨~ *the book on the table*⟩ ⟨~ *a child to bed*⟩ **b** to thrust (e g a weapon) into or through sthg **c** to throw (a shot, weight, etc) with a put, esp in the shot put **d** to bring into a specified condition ⟨~ *a rule into effect*⟩ ⟨~ *the matter right*⟩ **2a** to cause to endure or undergo; subject ⟨~ *me to a lot of expense*⟩ **b** to impose, establish ⟨~ *a tax on luxuries*⟩ **3a** to formulate for judgment or decision ⟨~ *the question*⟩ ⟨~ *the motion*⟩ **b** to express, state ⟨~ting *it mildly*⟩ **4a** to turn into language or literary form ⟨~ *her feelings into words*⟩ **b** to adapt, set ⟨*lyrics ~ to music*⟩ **5a** to devote, apply ⟨~ *his mind to the problem*⟩ **b** to cause to perform an action; urge ⟨~ *the horse at the fence*⟩ **c** to impel, incite ⟨~ *them into a frenzy*⟩ **6a** to repose, rest ⟨~s *his faith in reason*⟩ **b** to invest ⟨~ *his money into steel*⟩ **7** to give as an estimate ⟨~ *her age at about 40*⟩; *also* to imagine as being ⟨~ *yourself in my place*⟩ **8** to write, inscribe ⟨~ *their names to what they wrote* – Virginia Woolf⟩ **9** to bet, wager ⟨~ *£5 on the favourite*⟩ ~ *vi*, *of a ship* to take a specified course ⟨~ *back to port*⟩ [ME *putten*; akin to OE *put*ung instigation, MD *poten* to plant] – **put a foot wrong** to make the slightest mistake – **put a good/bold face on** to represent (a matter) or confront (an ordeal) as if all were well – **put a sock in it** *Br* to stop talking; SHUT UP – slang – **put a spoke in someone's wheel** to thwart sby's plans – **put forth 1a** to assert, propose **b** to make public; issue **2** to bring into action; exert **3** to produce or send out by growth ⟨put forth *leaves*⟩ – **put in mind** to remind – often + of – **put it across someone** *Br* to deceive sby into believing or doing sthg – compare PUT ACROSS – **put it past someone** to think sby at all incapable or unlikely ⟨*wouldn't* put it past him *to cheat*⟩ – **put it there** – used as an invitation to shake hands – **put one's best foot forward** to make every effort – **put one's finger on** to identify ⟨put his finger on *the cause of the trouble*⟩ – **put one's foot down** to take a firm stand – **put one's foot in it** to make an embarrassing blunder – **put one's shirt on** to risk all one's money on – **put one's shoulder to the wheel** to make an effort, esp a cooperative effort – **put on the map** to cause to be considered important – **put paid to** *Br* to ruin; FINISH 1a ⟨*St George* putting paid to *the dragon – Scottish Field*⟩ – **put someone's nose out of joint** to supplant sby distressingly – **put the lid on** *chiefly Br* to be the culminating misfortune of (a series) – **put the wind up** *Br* to scare, frighten – infml – **put to bed** to make the final preparations for printing (e g a newspaper) – **put together** to create as a united whole; construct – **put to it** to give difficulty to; press hard ⟨*had been* put to it *to keep up*⟩ – **put to shame** to disgrace by comparison ⟨*their garden* puts *ours* to shame⟩ – **put two and two together** to draw the proper conclusion

from given premises – **put wise** to inform, enlighten – infml

[2]**put** *n* a throw made with an overhand pushing motion; *specif* the act or an instance of putting the shot

[3]**put** *adj* in the same position, condition, or situation – in *stay put*

put about *vi*, *of a ship* to change direction ~ *vt* to cause (a ship) to put about

put across *vt* to convey (the meaning or significance of sthg) effectively

putative /ˈpyoohtətiv/ *adj* **1** commonly accepted or supposed **2** assumed to exist or to have existed *USE* fml [ME, fr LL *putativus*, fr L *putatus*, pp of *putare* to think – more at PAVE] – **putatively** *adv*

put away *vt* **1** to discard, renounce **2a** to place for storage when not in use ⟨put *the knives* away *in the drawer*⟩ **b** to save (money) for future use **3a** to confine, esp in an asylum **b** to kill; *esp* PUT DOWN 2 **4** to eat or drink up; consume ⟨*used to* put away *a bottle without blinking*⟩ – infml

put by *vt* PUT AWAY 2

ˈ**put-ˌdown** *n* a humiliating remark; a snub – infml

put down *vt* **1** to bring to an end; suppress ⟨put down *a riot*⟩ **2** to kill (e g a sick or injured animal) painlessly **3a** to put in writing ⟨put *it* down *on paper*⟩ **b** to enter in a list (e g of subscribers) ⟨put *me* down *for £5*⟩ **4** to pay as a deposit **5a** to place in a category ⟨*I* put *him* down *as an eccentric*⟩ **b** to attribute ⟨put *it* down *to inexperience*⟩ **6** to store or set aside (e g bottles of wine) for future use **7a** to disparage, belittle **b** to humiliate, snub ~ *vi*, *of an aircraft or pilot* to land *USE* (7) infml

put forward *vt* **1** to propose (e g a theory) **2** to bring into prominence ⟨*have no wish to* put *myself* forward⟩

put in *vt* **1** to make a formal offer or declaration of ⟨put in *a plea of guilty*⟩ **2** to come in with; interpose ⟨put in *a word for her brother*⟩ **3** to spend (time) at an occupation or job ⟨put in *6 hours at the office*⟩ ~ *vi* **1** to call at or enter a place, harbour, etc **2** to make an application, request, or offer *for* ⟨*decided to* put in *for a pension*⟩

putlog /ˈputˌlog/ *n* a piece of timber between a wall and the uprights of a scaffold that supports scaffolding planks [prob alter. of earlier *putlock*, perh fr [3]*put* + *lock*]

put off *vt* **1** to disconcert, distract **2a** to postpone ⟨*decided to* put off *their departure*⟩ **b** to get rid of or persuade to wait, esp by means of excuses or evasions ⟨put *his creditors* off *for another few days*⟩ **3a** to repel, discourage **b** to dissuade ⟨*so keen it was impossible to* put *her* off⟩ **4** to take off; rid oneself of

[1]ˈ**put-ˌon** *adj* pretended, assumed

[2]**put-on** *n* an instance of deliberately misleading sby; *also, chiefly NAm* a parody, spoof

put on *vt* **1a** to dress oneself in; don **b** to make part of one's appearance or behaviour **c** to feign, assume ⟨put on *a saintly manner*⟩ **2** to cause to act or operate; apply ⟨put on *more speed*⟩ **3** to come to have an increased amount of ⟨put on *weight*⟩ **4** to stage, produce (e g a play) **5** to bet (a sum of money) **6** to bring to or cause to speak on the telephone ⟨*is your father there?* Put *him* on, *then*⟩ **7** to mislead deliberately, esp for amusement – infml

Putonghua /ˌpoohtongˈhwah/ *n* a modern language of China based on Mandarin as spoken in Peking – used in place of Mandarin as the name for the official language of China [Chin *p'u-t'ung-hua* common language]

put out *vt* **1** to extinguish ⟨put *the fire* out⟩ **2** to publish, issue **3** to produce for sale **4a** to disconcert, confuse **b** to annoy, irritate **c** to inconvenience ⟨*don't* put *yourself* out *for us*⟩ **5** to cause to be out (in baseball, cricket, etc) **6** to give or offer (a job of work) to be done by another outside the premises ~ *vi* **1** to set out from shore **2** to make an effort

put over *vt* PUT ACROSS

putrefaction /ˌpyoohtriˈfaksh(ə)n/ *n* **1** the decomposition of organic matter; *esp* the breakdown of proteins by bacteria and fungi, typically in the absence of oxygen, with the formation of foul-smelling incompletely oxidized products **2** being putrefied; corruption [ME *putrefaccion*, fr LL *putrefaction-*, *putrefactio*, fr L *putrefactus*, pp of *putrefacere*] – **putrefactive** /-tiv/ *adj*

putrefy /ˈpyoohtrifie/ *vb* to make or become putrid [ME *putrefien*, fr MF & L; MF *putrefier*, fr L *putrefacere*, fr *putrēre* to be rotten + *facere* to make – more at [1]DO]

putrescent /ˌpyoohˈtres(ə)nt/ *adj* of or undergoing putrefaction [L *putrescent-*, *putrescens*, prp of *putrescere* to grow rotten, fr *putrēre*] – **putrescence** *n*

putrid /ˈpyoohtrid/ *adj* **1a** in a state of putrefaction **b** (characteristic) of putrefaction; *esp* foul-smelling **2** very unpleasant – slang [L *putridus*, fr *putrēre* to be rotten, fr *puter, putris* rotten; akin to L *putēre* to stink] – **putridness** *n*, **putridity** /-ˈtridəti/ *n*

putsch /pooch/ *n* a secretly plotted and suddenly executed attempt to overthrow a government [G]

putt /put/ *n* a gentle golf stroke made to roll the ball towards or into the hole on a putting green [alter. of [2]*put*] – **putt** *vb*

puttee /ˈputi, puˈtee/ *n* **1** a long cloth strip wrapped spirally round the leg from ankle to knee, esp as part of an army uniform **2** *NAm* a usu leather legging secured by a strap or catch or by laces [Hindi *paṭṭī* strip of cloth, fr Skt *paṭṭikā*]

[1]**putter** /ˈputə/ *n* a golf club used for putting [PUTT + [2]-ER]

[2]**putter** /ˈputə/ *vi, NAm* to potter [by alter.]

put through *vt* **1** to carry into effect or to a successful conclusion **2a** to make a telephone connection for **b** to obtain a connection for (a telephone call)

ˈ**putting ˌgreen** /ˈputing/ *n* a smooth grassy area at the end of a golf fairway containing the hole into which the ball must be played

putto /ˈpootoh/ *n, pl* **putti** /-ti/ a figure of a Cupid-like boy, esp in Renaissance painting [It, lit., boy, fr L *putus*; akin to Skt *putra* son – more at FEW]

[1]**putty** /ˈputi/ *n* **1** a pasty substance consisting of hydrated lime and water **2** a dough-like cement, usu made of whiting and boiled linseed oil, used esp in fixing glass in sashes and stopping crevices in woodwork [F *potée*, lit., potful, fr OF, fr *pot* – more at POTTAGE]

[2]**putty** *vt* to use putty on or apply putty to

ˈ**put-ˌup** *adj* contrived secretly beforehand ⟨*the vote was obviously a* ~ *job*⟩ – infml

put up *vt* **1** to sheathe (a sword) **2** to flush (game) from cover **3** to nominate for election **4** to offer up (e g a prayer) **5** to offer for public sale ⟨put *her possessions* up *for auction*⟩ **6** to give food and shelter to; accommodate **7** to build, erect **8a** to make a display of; show ⟨*desperate as she was, she* put up *a brave front*⟩ **b** CARRY ON 2 ⟨put up *a struggle against considerable odds*⟩ **9a** to contribute, pay **b** to offer as a prize or stake **10** to increase the amount of; raise ~*vi* **1** to shelter, lodge ⟨*we'll* put up *here for the night*⟩ **2** to present oneself as a candidate in an election – usu + *for* – **put someone's back up** to annoy or irritate sby – **put up to** to urge on, instigate ⟨*they* put *him* up to *playing the prank*⟩ – **put up with** to endure or tolerate without complaint or protest

'put-u,pon *adj* imposed upon; taken advantage of

puy /pwee/ *n* a hill of volcanic origin, esp in the Auvergne in France [F, fr L *podium* balcony – more at PEW]

[1]puzzle /'puzl/ **puzzling** /'puzling, 'puzl·ing/ *vt* to offer or represent a problem difficult to solve or a situation difficult to resolve; perplex; *also* to exert (e g oneself) over such a problem or situation ⟨*they* ~d *their brains to find a solution*⟩ ~ *vi* to be uncertain as to action, choice, or meaning – usu + *over* or *about* [origin unknown] – **puzzlement** *n*, **puzzler** *n*

[2]puzzle *n* **1** being puzzled; perplexity **2a** sthg that puzzles **b** a problem, contrivance, etc designed for testing one's ingenuity

puzzle out *vt* to find (a solution or meaning) by means of mental effort

PVC *n* POLYVINYL CHLORIDE [*p*oly*v*inyl *c*hloride]

py- /pie-/, **pyo-** *comb form* pus ⟨py*aemia*⟩ ⟨py*orrhoea*⟩ [Gk, fr *pyon* pus – more at FOUL]

pya /pyah, pi'ah/ *n* ☞ *Burma* at NATIONALITY [Burmese]

pyaemia /pie'eemyə, -mi·ə/ *n* blood poisoning accompanied by multiple abscesses [NL]

'pye-,dog /pie/ *n* a half-wild dog common in and around Asian villages [prob by shortening & alter. fr *pariah dog*]

pyel-, pyelo- *comb form* renal pelvis ⟨pyelo*graphy*⟩ [NL, pelvis, fr Gk *pyelos* trough; akin to Gk *plein* to sail – more at FLOW]

pyelitis /,pie·ə'lietis/ *n* inflammation of the lining of the renal pelvis [NL]

pygidium /pie'jidi·əm, -'gidi-/ *n, pl* **pygidia** /-di·ə/ the end structure (e g a tail) or end part of the body of various invertebrates [NL, fr Gk *pygidion*, dim. of *pygē* rump; akin to L *pustula* pustule] – **pygidial** *adj*

pygmy /'pigmi/ *n* **1** *cap* a member of a people of equatorial Africa under 1.5m (about 5ft) in height **2** a very short person; a dwarf **3** one who is insignificant or inferior in a specified sphere or manner ⟨*a political* ~⟩ [ME *pigmei*, fr L *pygmaeus* of a pygmy, dwarfish, fr Gk *pygmaios*, fr *pygmē* fist, measure of length – more at PUNGENT] – **pygmoid** /-,moyd/ *adj*

pyjamas, *NAm chiefly* **pajamas** /pə'jahməz/ *n pl, chiefly Br* **1** loose lightweight trousers traditionally worn in the East **2** a suit of loose lightweight jacket and trousers for sleeping in [Hindi *pājāma*, fr Per *pā* leg + *jāma* garment] – **pyjama** *adj*

pyknic /'piknik/ *adj* characterized by short stature and stocky build [ISV, fr Gk *pyknos* dense, stocky] – **pyknic** *n*

pylon /'pielon, -lən/ *n* **1** either of 2 towers with sloping sides flanking the entrance to an ancient Egyptian temple **2** a tower for supporting either end of a wire, esp electricity power cables, over a long span **3** a rigid structure on the outside of an aircraft for supporting sthg [Gk *pylōn*, fr *pylē* gate]

pylorus /pie'lawrəs/ *n, pl* **pylori** /-rie, -ri/ the opening from the vertebrate stomach into the intestine [LL, fr Gk *pylōros*, lit., gatekeeper, fr *pylē*] – **pyloric** *adj*

pyo- – see PY-

pyogenic /,pie·ə'jenik/ *adj* producing pus [ISV]

pyorrhoea /,pie·ə'riə/ *n* an inflammation of the sockets of the teeth leading usu to loosening of the teeth [NL]

pyr-, pyro- *comb form* **1** fire; heat ⟨pyro*meter*⟩ ⟨pyro*mania*⟩ **2** produced (as if) by the action of heat ⟨pyro*electricity*⟩ [ME, fr MF, fr LL, fr Gk, fr *pyr* – more at FIRE]

pyracantha /,pierə'kanthə/ *n* any of a genus of Eurasian thorny shrubs of the rose family with white flowers and red or orange berries [NL, genus name, fr Gk *pyrakantha*, a tree, fr *pyr-* + *akantha* thorn]

pyramid /'pirəmid/ *n* **1a** an ancient massive structure having typically a square ground plan and tapering smooth or stepped walls that meet at the top **b** a structure or object of similar form **2** a polyhedron having for its base a polygon and for faces triangles with a common vertex **3** a nonphysical structure or system (e g a social or organizational hierarchy) having a broad supporting base and narrowing gradually to an apex [L *pyramid-*, *pyramis*, fr Gk] – **pyramidal** /pi'ramidl/ *adj*

'pyramid ,selling *n* a fraudulent financial system whereby agents for the sale of a product are induced to recruit further agents on ever-dwindling commissions

pyre /'pie·ə/ *n* a heap of combustible material for burning a dead body as part of a funeral rite; *broadly* a pile of material to be burned [L *pyra*, fr Gk, fr *pyr* fire – more at FIRE]

pyrenoid /pie'reenoyd, 'pierinoyd/ *n* any of the protein bodies that act as centres for starch deposition in some algae and other lower organisms [ISV, fr NL *pyrena* stone of a fruit, fr Gk *pyrēn*]

pyrethrin /pie'reethrin/ *n* either of 2 oily liquid insecticides that occur esp in pyrethrum flowers [ISV, fr L *pyrethrum*]

pyrethrum /pie'reethrəm/ *n* **1** any of several chrysanthemums with finely divided often aromatic leaves **2** an insecticide consisting of the dried heads of any of several Old World chrysanthemums [L, pellitory, fr Gk *pyrethron*, fr *pyr* fire]

pyretic /pie'retik/ *adj* of fever [NL *pyreticus*, fr Gk *pyretikos*, fr *pyretos* fever, fr *pyr*]

Pyrex /'piereks/ *trademark* – used for glass and glassware that is resistant to heat, chemicals, and electricity

pyrexia /pie'reksi·ə/ *n* abnormal elevation of body temperature [NL, fr Gk *pyressein* to be feverish, fr *pyretos*] – **pyrexial** *adj*, **pyrexic** /-sik/ *adj*

pyrheliometer /pə,heeli'omitə/ *n* an instrument for measuring the radiant energy from the sun that is received at the earth [ISV] – **pyrheliometric** /pə,heeli·ə'metrik/ *adj*

pyridine /'pierideen, -din/ *n* a pungent liquid that is an organic chemical base, is obtained from coal, and is used as a solvent and in the manufacture of medicines and waterproofing substances [*pyr-* + *-id* + *-ine*]

pyridoxine *also* **pyridoxin** /,pieri'dokseen, -sin/ *n* a vitamin B_6 found esp in cereal foods and convertible in the body into phosphate compounds that are important coenzymes [*pyridine* + *ox-* + *-ine*]

pyrimidine /pie'rimideen, -din/ *n* any of the bases cytosine, thymine, or uracil that are constituents of DNA and RNA [ISV, alter. of *pyridine*]

pyrite /'pie·əriet/ *n* IRON PYRITES [L *pyrites*]

pyrites /pie'rieteez, pi-/ *n, pl* **pyrites** any of various metallic-looking sulphide minerals; *esp* IRON PYRITES [L, flint, fr Gk *pyritēs* of or in fire, fr *pyr* fire] – **pyritic** /-'ritik/ *adj*

pyro- – see PYR-

pyrocatechol /,pieroh'katəkol, -rə-/ *n* a phenol, usu made synthetically, used esp as a photographic developer and in organic synthesis [ISV *pyr-* + *catechol*, fr *catechu* + *-ol*]

pyroclastic /,pieroh'klastik, -rə-/ *adj* formed from fragments resulting from volcanic action

pyrogallol /,pieroh'galol/ *n* a phenol with weak acid properties that is used esp in photographic developers and in dye manufacture [ISV *pyrogallic* (acid) + *-ol*]

pyrogen /'pieroh,jen, -rə-/ *n* a fever-producing substance [ISV]

pyrogenic /,pieroh'jenik/ *adj* **1** producing or produced by heat or fever **2** IGNEOUS 2 [ISV] – **pyrogenicity** /-jə'nisəti/ *n*

pyroligneous /,pieroh'ligni·əs/ *adj* obtained by destructive distillation of wood [F *pyroligneux*, fr *pyr-* + *ligneux* woody, fr L *lignosus*, fr *lignum* wood – more at LIGN-]

pyrolyse, *NAm chiefly* **pyrolyze** /'pierəliez/ *vt* to subject to pyrolysis

pyrolysis /pie'roləsis/ *n* chemical change brought about by the action of heat [NL] – **pyrolytic** /,pierə'litik/ *adj*

pyromania /,pierə'maynyə, -ni·ə/ *n* a compulsive urge to start fires [NL] – **pyromaniac** /-'mayniak/ *n*, **pyromaniacal** /-mə'nie·əkl/ *adj*

pyrometer /pie'romitə/ *n* an instrument for measuring temperatures, esp when beyond the range of mercury thermometers [ISV] – **pyrometry** /-mətri/ *n*, **pyrometric** /-rə'metrik/ *adj*

pyrope /'pie,rohp/ *n* a deep red magnesium-aluminium garnet commonly used as a gem [ME *pirope*, a red gem, fr MF, fr L *pyropus*, a red bronze, fr Gk *pyrōpos*, lit., fiery-eyed, fr *pyr-* + *ōp-*, *ōps* eye – more at EYE]

pyrophoric /,pierə'forik/ *adj* **1** igniting spontaneously **2** *of an alloy* emitting sparks when scratched or struck, esp with steel [NL *pyrophorus*, fr Gk *pyrophoros* fire-bearing, fr *pyr-* + *-phoros* -phorous]

pyrotechnic /,pierə'teknik/ *n* **1** a firework **2** *pl* a brilliant or spectacular display (e g of oratory or extreme virtuosity) ⟨*his verbal* ~s *are entertaining* – *TLS*⟩ [*pyrotechnic*, adj, fr F *pyrotechnique*, fr Gk *pyr* fire + *technē* art] – **pyrotechnic** *adj*, **pyrotechnist** *n*

pyroxene /'pierok,seen, -'--/ *n* any of a group of silicate minerals that commonly contain calcium, magnesium, or iron and are chief constituents of many igneous rocks [F *pyroxène*, fr Gk *pyr-* + *xenos* stranger] – **pyroxenoid** /pie'roksi,noyd/ *adj or n*

pyroxenite /pie'roksiniet/ *n* a coarse-grained igneous rock composed mainly of pyroxene – **pyroxenitic** /-'nitik/ *adj*

pyroxylin /pie'roksilin/ *n* an inflammable mixture of cellulose nitrates that is used esp in making plastics and coatings [ISV *pyr-* + Gk *xylon* wood]

pyrrhic /'pirik/ *n* a metrical foot consisting of 2 short or unaccented syllables [L *pyrrhichius*, fr Gk (*pous*) *pyrrhichios*, fr *pyrrhichē*, a kind of dance] – **pyrrhic** *adj*

,Pyrrhic 'victory *n* a victory won at excessive cost [*Pyrrhus* †272 BC King of Epirus who sustained heavy losses in defeating the Romans]

pyruvate /pie'roohvayt/ *n* a salt or ester of pyruvic acid

py,ruvic 'acid /pie'roohvik/ *n* a liquid organic acid that smells like acetic acid and is an important intermediate compound in metabolism and fermentation [ISV *pyr-* + L *uva* grape; fr its importance in fermentation – more at UVULA]

Pythagoras' theorem /pie'thagərəs(iz)/ *n, chiefly Br* a theorem in geometry: the square of the length of the hypotenuse of a right-angled triangle equals the sum of the squares of the lengths of the other 2 sides [*Pythagoras* † *ab* 500 BC Gk philosopher & mathematician]

Pythagorean /,piethagə'ree·ən, pi-/ *adj* of or associated with the philosophy of Pythagoras and his followers asserting the mystical significance of numbers and the transmigration of souls

Pythian /'pithi·ən/ *adj* of Delphi or its oracle [L *pythius* of Delphi, fr Gk *pythios*, fr *Pythō* Pytho, former name of Delphi, town in Greece]

python /'pieth(ə)n/ *n* a large boa or other constrictor; *esp* any of a genus that includes the largest living snakes [L, monstrous serpent killed by Apollo, fr Gk *Pythōn*] – **pythonine** /-,nien, -,neen/ *adj*

pythoness /'piethənes, -is, -'es/ *n* an oracular priestess of Apollo [ME *Phitonesse*, fr MF *pithonisse*, fr LL *pythonissa*, fr Gk *Pythōn*, spirit of divination, fr *Pythō*, seat of the Delphic oracle] – **pythonic** /-'thonik/ *adj*

pyuria /,pie'yooəri·ə/ *n* (a condition characterized by) pus in the urine [NL]

pyx /piks/ *n* **1** a container in which the bread used at Communion is kept; *esp* one used for carrying the Eucharist to the sick **2** a box in a mint for deposit of sample coins reserved for testing [ME, fr ML *pyxis*, fr L, box, fr Gk – more at [2]BOX]

pyxidium /pik'sidi·əm/ *n, pl* **pyxidia** /-di·ə/ a capsular fruit that opens at maturity with the upper part falling off like a cap [NL, fr Gk *pyxidion*, dim. of *pyxis*]

pyxis /'piksis/ *n, pl* **pyxides** /'piksi,deez/ a pyxidium [NL, fr L, box]

Q

q /kyooh/ *n, pl* **q's, qs** *often cap* (a graphic representation of or device for reproducing) the 17th letter of the English alphabet

Q *n* a source posited by biblical critics for the material common to the gospels of Matthew and Luke that is not derived from that of Mark [fr initial letter of G *quelle* source]

qadi, cadi, kadi /'kahdi, 'kaydi/ *n* a Muslim judge who administers the religious law [Ar *qāḍī*, fr *qaḍā* to judge]

'Q ,fever *n* a mild disease characterized by high fever, chills, and muscular pains that is caused by a rickettsia and is transmitted by raw milk, by contact, or by ticks [*q*uery; fr its cause being orig unknown]

qindar /kin'dah/, **qintar** /'kintah, kin'tah/ *n, pl* **qindarka** /kin'dahkə/ ☞ *Albania* at NATIONALITY [Alb]

'Q-,ship *n* an armed ship disguised as a merchant or fishing vessel and used chiefly in WW I to decoy enemy submarines into gun range [*q*uery]

QSO *n* a quasar [*q*uasi-*s*tellar *o*bject]

qua /kway, kwah/ *prep* in the capacity or character of; as [L, which way, as, fr abl sing. fem of *qui* who – more at WHO]

¹quack /kwak/ *vi or n* (to make) the characteristic cry of a duck [imit]

²quack *n* **1** one who has or pretends to have medical skill **2** CHARLATAN 2 *USE* infml [short for *quacksalver* (charlatan), fr obs D (now *kwakzalver*)] – **quackery** *n*, **quackish** *adj*

³quack *adj* (characteristic) of a quack ⟨~ *medicines*⟩

¹quad /kwod/ *n* a quadrangle

²quad *n* a type-metal space that is 1 or more ems in width [short for *quadrat*]

³quad *n* a quadruplet

⁴quad *adj* quadraphonic

quadr- – see QUADRI-

Quadragesima /,kwodrə'jesimə/ *n* the first Sunday in Lent [LL, fr L, fem of *quadragesimus* fortieth, fr *quadraginta* forty, fr *quadra-* (akin to L *quattuor* four) + *-ginta* – more at QUINQUAGESIMA]

quadrangle /'kwodrang·gl/ *n* **1** a quadrilateral **2** a 4-sided enclosure surrounded by buildings [ME, fr MF, fr LL *quadriangulum*, fr L, neut of *quadriangulus* quadrangular, fr *quadri-* + *angulus* angle] – **quadrangular** /kwo'drang·gyoolə/ *adj*

quadrant /'kwodrənt/ *n* **1a** an instrument for measuring angles, consisting commonly of a graduated arc of 90° **b** a device or mechanical part shaped like or suggestive of the quadrant of a circle **2** (the area of 1 quarter of a circle that is bounded by) an arc of a circle containing an angle of 90° **3** any of the 4 quarters into which sthg is divided by 2 real or imaginary lines that intersect each other at right angles [ME, fr L *quadrant-, quadrans* fourth part; akin to L *quattuor* four – more at FOUR] – **quadrantal** /kwo'drantl/ *adj*

quadraphonic /,kwodrə'fonik/ *adj* of or being an audio system that uses 4 signal channels by which the signal is conveyed from its source to its final point of use [irreg fr *quadri-* + *phonic*] – **quadraphonics** *n*, **quadraphony** /kwo'draf(ə)ni/ *n*

quadrat /'kwodrət, 'kwodrat/ *n* ²QUAD [alter. of ²*quadrate*]

¹quadrate /'kwodrət, 'kwodrayt/ *adj* **1** (approximately) square **2** of or being a bony or cartilaginous part on each side of the skull to which the lower jaw is hinged in most lower vertebrates [ME, fr L *quadratus*, pp of *quadrare* to make square, fit; akin to L *quattuor*]

²quadrate *n* **1** an approximately square or cubical area, space, or body **2** a quadrate bone

quadratic /kwo'dratik/ *n or adj* (an equation or expression) of or involving (terms of) the second power or order – **quadratically** *adv*

quadrature /'kwodrəchə/ *n* **1** the process of finding a square equal in area to a given area **2** a configuration in which 2 celestial bodies have a separation of 90° ☞ SYMBOL **3** a phase difference of 1 quarter cycle (e g between the currents in a 2-phase power distribution system) [L *quadratura* square, act of squaring, fr *quadrare*]

quadrennial /kwo'dreni·əl/ *adj* **1** consisting of or lasting for 4 years **2** occurring every 4 years – **quadrennial** *n*, **quadrennially** *adv*

quadrennium /kwo'dreni·əm/ *n, pl* **quadrenniums, quadrennia** /-ni·ə/ a period of 4 years [L *quadriennium*, fr *quadri-* + *annus* year – more at ANNUAL]

quadri-, quadr-, quadru- *comb form* **1** four ⟨quad*rilateral*⟩ ⟨quadri*valent*⟩ **2** square ⟨quad*ric*⟩ **3** fourth ⟨quadri*centennial*⟩ ⟨quad*roon*⟩ [ME, fr L; akin to L *quattuor* four]

quadric /'kwodrik/ *adj* quadratic ⟨*a* ~ *surface*⟩ – used where there are more than 2 variables [ISV] – **quadric** *n*

quadricentennial /,kwodrisen'teni·əl/ *adj or n* (of) a quatercentenary

quadriceps /'kwodri,seps/ *n* the large muscle at the front of the thigh that acts to straighten the leg at the knee joint [NL *quadricipit-, quadriceps*, fr *quadri-* + *-cipit-, -ceps* (as in *bicipit-, biceps* biceps)]

quadrilateral /,kwodri'lat(ə)rəl/ *n or adj* (a polygon) having 4 sides [prob fr (assumed) NL *quadrilateralis*, fr L *quadrilaterus*, fr *quadri-* + *later-, latus* side]

quadrille /kwə'dril/ *n* **1** a 4-handed variant of ombre played with a pack of 40 cards and popular esp in the 18th c **2** (the music for) a square dance for 4 couples made up of 5 or 6 figures [F, group of knights engaged in a carousel, variant of ombre, fr Sp *cuadrilla* troop, fr It *quadriglia* band, troop, company, fr *cuadra, quadra* square]

quadrillion /kwo'drilyən/ *n* **1** *Br* a million million million millions (10^{24}) **2** *chiefly NAm* a thousand million millions (10^{15}) *USE* ☞ NUMBER [F, fr MF, fr *quadri-* + *-illion* (as in *million*)] – **quadrillion** *adj*, **quadrillionth** *adj or n*

quadripartite /,kwodri'pahtiet/ *adj* **1** consisting of or divided into 4 parts **2** shared or participated in by 4 parties or people ⟨*a* ~ *agreement*⟩ [ME, fr L *quadripartitus*, fr *quadri-* + *partitus*, pp of *partire* to divide, fr *part-*, *pars* part]

quadriplegic /,kwodri'pleejik/ *n* affected with paralysis of both arms and both legs [*quadriplegia*, fr NL] – **quadriplegia** /-j(y)ə/ *n*

quadrivium /kwo'drivi·əm/ *n* arithmetic, music, geometry, and astronomy, forming the division of the 7 liberal arts studied after the trivium in medieval universities – compare TRIVIUM [LL, fr L, crossroads, fr *quadri-* + *via* way – more at VIA]

quadroon /kwo'droohn/ *n* sby of one-quarter Negro ancestry [modif of Sp *cuarterón*, fr *cuarto* fourth, fr L *quartus*; akin to L *quattuor* four]

quadru- – see QUADRI-

quadrumana /kwo'droohmənə/ *n pl* primates, excluding human beings, considered as a group distinguished by hand-shaped feet [NL, fr *quadri-* + L *manus* hand – more at MANUAL] – **quadrumanal, quadrumanous** /-mənəs/ *adj*, **quadrumane** /'kwodrooh,mayn/ *adj or n*

quadruped /'kwodroo,ped/ *n* an animal having 4 feet [L *quadruped-*, *quadrupes*, fr *quadruped-*, *quadrupes*, adj, having 4 feet, fr *quadri-* + *ped-*, *pes* foot – more at FOOT] – **quadruped, quadrupedal** /kwo'droopidl, ,kwodroo'peedl/ *adj*

[1]**quadruple** /'kwodroopl, kwo'droohpl/ *vb* to make or become 4 times as great or as many

[2]**quadruple** *n* a sum 4 times as great as another

[3]**quadruple** *adj* **1** having 4 units or members **2** being 4 times as great or as many **3** marked by 4 beats per bar ⟨~ *time*⟩ [MF or L; MF, fr L *quadruplus*, fr *quadri-* + *-plus* multiplied by – more at DOUBLE] – **quadruply** /-pli/ *adv*

quadruplet /'kwodrooplit, kwo'droohplit/ *n* **1** any of 4 offspring born at 1 birth **2** a combination of 4 of a kind **3** a group of 4 musical notes performed in the time of 3 notes of the same value [fr [3]*quadruple*, by analogy to *double : doublet*]

[1]**quadruplicate** /kwo'droohplikət/ *adj* **1** consisting of or existing in 4 corresponding or identical parts or examples ⟨~ *invoices*⟩ **2** being the fourth of 4 things exactly alike [L *quadruplicatus*, pp of *quadruplicare* to quadruple, fr *quadruplic-*, *quadruplex* fourfold, fr *quadri-* + *-plic-*, *-plex* fold – more at [1]SIMPLE]

[2]**quadruplicate** /kwo'droohplikayt/ *vt* **1** to make quadruple or fourfold **2** to prepare in quadruplicate – **quadruplication** /-'kaysh(ə)n/ *n*

[3]**quadruplicate** /kwo'droohplikət/ *n* **1** any of 4 identical copies **2** 4 copies all alike – + *in* ⟨*typed in* ~⟩

quadruplicity /,kwodroo'plisəti/ *n* the state of being quadruple or quadruplicate

quadrupole /'kwodroo,pohl/ *n* a system composed of 2 electric, magnetic, etc dipoles of equal but oppositely directed moment [ISV *quadri-* + *pole*] – **quadrupolar** /-'pohlə/ *adj*

quaestor /'kweestə/ *n* any of numerous ancient Roman officials concerned chiefly with financial administration [ME *questor*, fr L *quaestor*, fr *quaestus*, pp of *quaerere* to seek, ask]

quaff /kwof, kwahf/ *vb* to drink (a beverage) deeply in long draughts ⟨~ed *his ale*⟩ [origin unknown] – **quaffer** *n*

quag /kwag, kwog/ *n* a marsh, bog [origin unknown] – **quaggy** *adj*

quagga /'kwagə/ *n* a recently extinct wild zebra of southern Africa [obs Afrik (now *kwagga*), prob of Bantu origin]

quagmire /'kwag,mie·ə, 'kwog-/ *n* **1** soft miry land that shakes or yields under the foot **2** a predicament from which it is difficult to extricate oneself

quaich, quaigh /kwayk, kwaykh/ *n, chiefly Scot* a small shallow drinking cup with 2 handles [ScGael *cuach*]

[1]**quail** /kwayl/ *n, pl* **quails,** *esp collectively* **quail** **1** a migratory Old World game bird **2** any of various small American game birds [ME *quaille*, fr MF, fr ML *quaccula*, of imit origin]

[2]**quail** *vi* to shrink back in fear; cower ⟨*the strongest* ~ *before financial ruin* – Samuel Butler †1902⟩ [ME *quailen* to curdle, fr MF *quailler*, fr L *coagulare* – more at COAGULATE]

quaint /kwaynt/ *adj* **1** unusual or different in character or appearance; odd **2** pleasingly or strikingly old-fashioned or unfamiliar [ME *cointe* skilled, elegant, fastidious, strange, fr OF, fr L *cognitus*, pp of *cognoscere* to know – more at COGNITION] – **quaintly** *adv*, **quaintness** *n*

[1]**quake** /kwayk/ *vi* **1** to shake or vibrate, usu from shock or instability **2** to tremble or shudder, esp inwardly from fear [ME *quaken*, fr OE *cwacian*; akin to OE *cweccan* to shake, vibrate]

[2]**quake** *n* **1** a quaking **2** an earthquake – infml

Quaker /'kwaykə/ *n* a member of a pacifist Christian sect that stresses Inner Light and rejects sacraments and an ordained ministry [[1]QUAKE + [2]-ER] – **Quakerish** *adj*, **Quakerism** *n*, **Quakerly** *adj*

qualifiable /'kwoli,fie·əbl/ *adj* capable of being qualified or modified

qualification /,kwolifi'kaysh(ə)n/ *n* **1** a restriction in meaning or application; a limiting modification **2a** a quality or skill that fits a person (e g for a particular task or appointment) ⟨*the applicant with the best* ~s⟩ **b** a condition that must be complied with (e g for the attainment of a privilege) ⟨*a* ~ *for membership*⟩ [ML *qualification-*, *qualificatio*, fr *qualificatus*, pp of *qualificare*]

qualified /'kwolified/ *adj* **1a** fitted (e g by training or experience) for a usu specified purpose; competent **b** complying with the specific requirements or conditions (e g for appointment to an office); eligible **2** limited or modified in some way ⟨~ *approval*⟩

qualifier /'kwoli,fie·ə/ *n* one who or that which qualifies: e g **a** a sby or sthg that satisfies requirements or meets a specified standard **b** a grammatical modifier **c** a preliminary heat or contest

qualify /'kwolifie/ *vt* **1a** to reduce from a general to a particular or restricted form; modify **b** to make less harsh or strict; moderate **c** MODIFY 2 **2** to characterize or describe *as* ⟨*cannot* ~ *it as either glad or sad*⟩ **3a** to fit by training, skill, or ability for a special purpose **b** to render legally capable or entitled ~ *vi* **1** to be fit (e g for an office) ⟨qualifies *for the job by virtue of his greater experience*⟩ **2** to reach an accredited level of competence ⟨*has just* qualified *as a lawyer*⟩ **3** to exhibit a required degree of ability or achievement in a preliminary contest [MF *qualifier*, fr ML *qualificare*, fr L *qualis* of what kind]

qualitative /'kwolitətiv/ *adj* of or involving quality or kind – **qualitatively** *adv*

,qualitative a'nalysis *n* chemical analysis designed to identify the components of a substance or mixture

[1]**quality** /'kwoləti/ *n* **1a** peculiar and essential character; nature **b** an inherent feature; a property **2a** degree of excellence; grade ⟨*a decline in the* ~ *of applicants*⟩ **b** superiority in kind ⟨*proclaimed the* ~ *of his wife* – Compton Mackenzie⟩ **3** high social position ⟨*a man of* ~⟩ **4** a distinguishing attribute; a characteristic ⟨*listed all her good* qualities⟩ **5** the identifying character of a vowel sound **6** *archaic* a capacity, role ⟨*in the* ~ *of reader and companion* – Joseph Conrad⟩ [ME *qualite*, fr OF *qualité*, fr L *qualitat-*, *qualitas*, fr *qualis* of what kind; akin to L *qui* who – more at WHO]

[2]**quality** *adj* **1** concerned with or displaying excellence ⟨~ *control*⟩ ⟨~ *goods*⟩ **2** *of a newspaper* aiming to appeal to an educated readership ⟨*the* ~ *Sundays*⟩

qualm /kwahm, kwawm/ *n* **1** a sudden and brief attack of illness, faintness, or nausea **2** a sudden feeling of anxiety or apprehension **3** a scruple or feeling of uneasiness, esp about a point of conscience or honour [origin unknown] – **qualmish** *adj*

quandary /'kwond(ə)ri/ *n* a state of perplexity or doubt [origin unknown]

quango /'kwang·goh/ *n, pl* **quangos** *Br* an autonomous body (e g the Race Relations Board) set up by the British government and having statutory powers in a specific field [*qu*asi-*a*utonomous *n*on-*g*overnmental *o*rganization]

quantify /'kwontifie/ *vt* **1** to specify the logical quantity of **2** to determine, express, or measure the quantity of [ML *quantificare*, fr L *quantus* how much] – **quantifier** *n*, **quantifiable** *adj*, **quantification** /-fi'kaysh(ə)n/ *n*

quantitative /'kwontitətiv/ *adj* **1** (expressible in terms) of quantity **2** of or involving the measurement of quantity or amount **3** *of classical verse* based on the relative duration of sequences of sounds – compare ACCENTUAL – **quantitatively** *adv*, **quantitativeness** *n*

,quantitative a'nalysis *n* chemical analysis designed to determine the amounts or proportions of the components of a substance

quantity /'kwontəti/ *n* **1a** an indefinite amount or number **b** a known, measured or estimated amount ⟨*precise* quantities *of 4 ingredients*⟩ **c** the total amount or number **d** a considerable amount or number – often pl with sing. meaning ⟨*wept like anything to see such* quantities *of sand* – Lewis Carroll⟩ **2a** the aspect in which a thing is measurable in terms of degree of magnitude **b** the number, value, etc subjected to a mathematical operation **c** sby or sthg to take into account or be reckoned with ⟨*an unknown* ~ *as military leader*⟩ **3** the relative duration of a speech sound or sound sequence, specif a prosodic syllable **4** the character of a logical proposition as universal, particular, or singular [ME *quantite*, fr OF *quantité*, fr L *quantitat-*, *quantitas*, fr *quantus* how much, how large; akin to L *quam* how, as, *quando* when, *qui* who – more at WHO]

quantity surveyor *n* sby who estimates or measures quantities (e g for builders) – **quantity surveying** *n*

quant·ize, -ise /'kwontiez/ *vt* **1** to subdivide (e g energy) into quanta **2** to calculate or express in terms of quantum mechanics [*quant*um + *-ize*] – **quantizer** *n*, **quantization** /-tie'zaysh(ə)n, -ti-/ *n*

quantum /'kwontəm/ *n, pl* **quanta** /-tə/ **1a** a quantity, amount **b** a portion, part **2** any of the very small parcels or parts into which many forms of energy are subdivided and which cannot be further subdivided *USE* (*1*) fml [L, neut of *quantus* how much]

quantum mechanics *n pl but sing or pl in constr* the mathematical description of the interactions of matter and radiation in terms of the quantum theory – **quantum mechanical** *adj*, **quantum mechanically** *adv*

'quantum ,number *n* any of a set of integers or odd half integers that indicate the magnitude of various discrete quantities (e g electric charge) of a particle or system and that serve to define its state

'quantum ,theory *n* a theory in physics based on the acceptance of the idea that all energy can be divided into quanta

[1]**quarantine** /'kworən,teen/ *n* **1** (the period of) a restraint on the activities or communication of people or the transport of goods or animals, designed to prevent the spread of disease or pests **2** a place in which people, animals, vehicles, etc under quarantine are kept **3** a state of enforced isolation [It *quarantina* period of forty days, fr MF *quarantaine*, fr OF, fr *quarante* forty, fr L *quadraginta*, fr *quadra-* (akin to *quattuor* four) + *-ginta* (akin to *viginti* twenty) – more at FOUR, VIGESIMAL]

[2]**quarantine** *vt* **1** to detain in or exclude by quarantine **2** to isolate from normal relations or communication

quark /kwahk/ *n* a hypothetical particle that carries a fractional electric charge and is held to be a constituent of known elementary particles [coined by Murray Gell-Mann *b* 1929 US physicist]

[1]**quarrel** /'kworəl/ *n* a short heavy square-headed arrow or bolt, esp for a crossbow [ME, fr MF & OF; MF, square of glass, fr OF, square-headed arrow, building stone, fr (assumed) VL *quadrellum*, dim. of L *quadrum* square; akin to L *quattuor* four – more at FOUR]

[2]**quarrel** *n* **1** a reason for dispute or complaint ⟨*have no* ~ *with his reasoning*⟩ **2** a usu verbal conflict between antagonists; a dispute [ME *querele*, fr MF, complaint, fr L *querela*, fr *queri* to complain – more at WHEEZE]

[3]**quarrel** *vi* **-ll-** (*NAm* **-l-**, **-ll-**) **1** to find fault *with* ⟨*the teacher invariably found something to* ~ *with in her essays*⟩ **2** to contend or dispute actively; argue – **quarreller** *n*

'quarrelsome /-səm/ *adj* inclined or quick to quarrel, esp in a petty manner – **quarrelsomely** *adv*, **quarrelsomeness** *n*

[1]**quarry** /'kwori/ *n* the prey or game of a predator, esp a hawk, or of a hunter [ME *querre* entrails of game given to the hounds, fr MF *cuiree*, fr OF, prob alter. (influenced by *cuir* leather & *curer* to disembowel) of *coree* entrails, fr LL *corata* (pl), fr L *cor* heart]

[2]**quarry** *n* **1** an open excavation from which building materials (e g stone, slate, and sand) are obtained **2** a source from which useful material, esp information, may be extracted [ME *quarey*, alter. of *quarrere*, fr MF *quarriere*, fr (assumed) OF *quarre* squared stone, fr L *quadrum* square]

[3]**quarry** *vt* **1** to obtain (as if) from a quarry **2** to make

a quarry in ~ *vi* to dig (as if) in a quarry – **quarrier** *n*

'quarry ,tile *n* an unglazed floor tile

quart /kwawt/ *n* either of 2 units of liquid capacity equal to 2pt: **a** a British unit equal to about 1.136l **b** a US unit equal to about 0.946l *USE* ☞ UNIT [ME, one quarter of a gallon, fr MF *quarte*, fr OF, fr fem of *quart*, adj, fourth, fr L *quartus*; akin to L *quattuor* four – more at FOUR]

quartan /'kwawtn/ *n* an intermittent fever, esp malaria, that recurs at approximately 72-hour intervals [ME *quarteyne*, fr OF *(fievre) quartaine*, fr L *(febris) quartana*, fr *quartanus* of the fourth, fr *quartus*] – **quartan** *adj*

¹quarter /'kwawtə/ *n* **1** any of 4 equal parts into which sthg is divisible **2** any of various units equal to or derived from a fourth of some larger unit; *specif* a quarter of either an American or British hundredweight ☞ UNIT **3** a fourth of a measure of time: e g **a** any of 4 3-month divisions of a year **b** a quarter of an hour – used in designation of time ⟨~ *past four*⟩ **4** (a coin worth) a quarter of a (US) dollar **5** a limb of a 4-limbed animal or carcass together with the adjacent parts; *esp* a hindquarter **6a** (the direction of or region round) a (cardinal) compass point **b** a person, group, direction, or place not specifically identified ⟨*had financial help from many* ~s⟩ ⟨*did little trade in that* ~⟩ **7** a division or district of a town or city ⟨*the Chinese* ~⟩ **8a** an assigned station or post – usu pl ⟨*battle* ~s⟩ **b** *pl* living accommodation; lodgings; *esp* accommodation for military personnel or their families **9** merciful consideration of an opponent; *specif* the clemency of not killing a defeated enemy ⟨*gave him no* ~⟩ **10** a fourth part of the moon's periodic cycle **11** any of the 4 or more parts of a heraldic shield that are marked off by horizontal and vertical lines **12** the part of a ship's side towards the stern; *also* any direction to the rear of abeam and from a specified side ⟨*light on the port* ~⟩ **13** any of the 4 equal periods into which the playing time of some games is divided [ME, fr OF *quartier*, fr L *quartarius*, fr *quartus* fourth]

²quarter *vt* **1** to divide into 4 (almost) equal parts; *broadly* to divide into parts **2** to provide with lodgings or shelter; *esp* to assign (a member of the armed forces) to accommodation ⟨~ed *his men on the villagers*⟩ **3** *esp of a gun dog* to crisscross (an area) in many directions in search of game, or in order to pick up an animal's scent **4a** to arrange or bear (e g different coats of arms) in heraldic quarters on 1 shield **b** to add (a coat of arms) to others on 1 heraldic shield **c** to divide (a heraldic shield) into 4 or more sections **5** *archaic* to divide (esp a traitor's body) into 4 parts, usu after hanging ~ *vi* **1** to lodge, dwell **2** to strike on a ship's quarter ⟨*the wind was* ~ing⟩

³quarter *adj* consisting of or equal to a quarter

quarterage /'kwawt(ə)rij/ *n* a quarterly payment, tax, wage, or allowance

,quarter-'bound *adj, of a book* bound in 2 materials with the better material on the spine only – **quarter binding** *n*

'quarter ,day *n* a day which begins a quarter of the year and on which a quarterly payment often falls due

'quarter,deck /-,dek/ *n* **1** the stern area of a ship's upper deck ☞ SHIP **2** *sing or pl in constr, chiefly Br* the officers of a ship or navy – compare LOWER DECK

'quarter,final /-,fienl/ *n* a match whose winner goes through to the semifinals of a knockout tournament; *also, pl* a round made up of such matches – **quarterfinal** *adj*, **quarterfinalist** *n*

'quarter ,horse *n, NAm* a muscular horse capable of high speed for short distances [fr its high speed over distances up to a quarter of a mile]

quartering /'kwawt(ə)ring/ *n* the division of a heraldic shield into 4 or more heraldic quarters; *also* any of the heraldic quarters so formed or the coat of arms it bears

'quarter ,light *n, Br* a small usu triangular panel in a motor vehicle side window that can usu be opened for ventilation

¹quarterly /'kwawtəli/ *n* a periodical published at 3-monthly intervals

²quarterly *adj* **1** computed for or payable at 3-monthly intervals ⟨*a* ~ *premium*⟩ **2** recurring, issued, or spaced at 3-monthly intervals – **quarterly** *adv*

'quarter,master /-,mahstə/ *n* **1** a petty officer or seaman who attends to a ship's compass, tiller or wheel, and signals **2** an army officer who provides clothing, subsistence, and quarters for a body of troops

quartern /'kwawtən/ *n* a quarter, esp of a pint [ME *quarteron*, fr OF, quarter of a pound, quarter of a hundred, fr *quartier* quarter]

'quarter ,note *n, NAm* a crotchet

'quarter ,sessions *n pl, often cap Q&S* a former English local court with limited criminal and civil jurisdiction, held quarterly

'quarter,staff /-,stahf/ *n, pl* **quarterstaves** /-,stayvz, -,stahvz/ a long stout staff formerly used as a weapon

'quarter ,tone *n* a musical interval of ½ a semitone

quartet *also* **quartette** /kwaw'tet/ *n* **1** (a musical composition for) a group of 4 instruments, voices, or performers **2** *sing or pl in constr* a group or set of 4 [It *quartetto*, fr *quarto* fourth, fr L *quartus* – more at QUART]

quartic /'kwawtik/ *n or adj* (an equation or expression) of or involving (terms of) the fourth power or order [L *quartus* fourth]

quartile /'kwawtiel/ *n* any of 3 numbers that divide a frequency distribution into 4 equal intervals ☞ STATISTICS [ISV, fr L *quartus*]

quarto /'kwawtoh/ *n, pl* **quartos** **1** (a book or page of) the size of a piece of paper cut 4 from a sheet **2** *Br* a size of paper usu 10 × 8in (about 25 × 20cm) – not used technically [L, abl of *quartus* fourth]

¹quartz /kwawts/ *n* a mineral consisting of a silicon dioxide occurring in colourless and transparent or coloured hexagonal crystals or in crystalline masses [G *quarz*, fr MHG] – **quartzose** /-ohs, -ohz/ *adj*

²quartz *adj* controlled by the oscillations of a quartz crystal ⟨*a* ~ *watch*⟩

'quartz ,glass *n* a glass made of high purity silica prepared from quartz and noted for its transparency to ultraviolet radiation

quartzite /'kwawtsiet/ *n* a compact granular quartz rock derived from sandstone [ISV] – **quartzitic** /-'sitik/ *adj*

quasar /'kwaysah/ *n* any of various unusually bright very distant star-like celestial objects that have spectra with large red shifts ☞ ASTRONOMY [*quasi-stellar* radio source]

quash /kwosh/ *vt* **1a** to nullify (by judicial action) **b** to reject (a legal document) as invalid **2** to suppress or extinguish summarily and completely; subdue [ME *quassen*, fr MF *casser, quasser* to annul, fr LL *cassare*, fr L *cassus* void, without effect; akin to L *carēre* to be without – more at CASTE; (2) partly fr ME *quashen* to smash, fr MF *quasser, casser*, fr L *quassare*, to shake violently, shatter, fr *quassus*, pp of *quatere* to shake; akin to OE *hūdenian* to shake]

quasi /ˈkwahzi, ˈkwayzie, -sie/ *adj* having some resemblance to ⟨*a ~ corporation*⟩

quasi- *comb form* to some degree; partly; seemingly ⟨quasi-*officially*⟩ ⟨quasi-*stellar object*⟩ [L *quasi* as if, as it were, approximately, fr *quam* as + *si* if – more at QUANTITY, SO]

quasi-stellar object *n* a quasar

quassia /ˈkwoshə/ *n* a drug obtained from the heartwood of various tropical trees, used esp as a bitter tonic and remedy for roundworms in children, and as an insecticide [NL, genus name, fr *Quassi*, 18th-c Surinam Negro slave who discovered its medicinal value]

quatercentenary /ˌkwatəsenˈteenəri, -ˈtenəri/ *n* (the celebration of) a 400th anniversary [L *quater* four times + E *centenary*]

[1]**quaternary** /kwəˈtuhnəri/ *adj* **1** of or consisting of four (parts) **2** *cap* of or being the geological period from the end of the Tertiary to the present time ☞ EVOLUTION **3** characterized by or resulting from the substitution of 4 atoms or groups in a molecule; *esp* being or containing an atom united by 4 bonds to carbon atoms [L *quaternarius*, fr *quaterni* four each]

[2]**quaternary** *n* **1** a member of a group of 4 things **2** *cap* the Quaternary period or system of rocks

quaternion /kwəˈtuhnyən, -ni·ən/ *n* **1** a set of 4 parts, things, or people **2** a generalized complex number that depends on 1 real and 3 imaginary units [ME *quaternyoun*, fr LL *quaternion-, quaternio*, fr L *quaterni* four each, fr *quater* four times; akin to L *quattuor* four – more at FOUR]

quaternity /kwəˈtuhnəti/ *n* a group or set of 4 [LL *quaternitas*, fr L *quaterni* four each]

quatrain /ˈkwotrayn/ *n* a stanza of 4 lines [F, fr MF, fr *quatre* four, fr L *quattuor*]

quatrefoil /ˈkatrəˌfoyl/ *n* **1** a stylized figure or ornament in the form of a 4-lobed leaf or flower ☞ ARCHITECTURE **2** a design enclosed by 4 joined foils [ME *quaterfoil* set of four leaves, fr MF *quatre* + ME *-foil* (as in *trefoil*)]

quattrocento /ˌkwatrohˈchentoh/ *n, often cap* the 15th c in Italy, esp with reference to its literature and art [It, lit., four hundred, fr *quattro* four (fr L *quattuor*) + *cento* hundred, fr L *centum* – more at HUNDRED]

[1]**quaver** /ˈkwayvə/ *vi* **1** *esp of the voice* to tremble, shake **2** to speak or sing in a trembling voice ~ *vt* to utter in a quavering voice [ME *quaveren*, freq of *quaven* to tremble] – **quaveringly** *adv*, **quavery** *adj*

[2]**quaver** *n* **1** a musical note with the time value of ½ that of a crotchet ☞ MUSIC **2** a tremulous sound

quay /kee/ *n* an artificial landing place beside navigable water for loading and unloading ships [alter. of earlier *key*, fr ME, fr MF *cai*, fr OF *kay*, of Celt origin; akin to Corn *kē* hedge, fence; akin to OE *hecg* hedge] – **quayage** /ˈkee·ij/ *n*

ˈquayˌside /-ˌsied/ *n* land forming or bordering a quay

quean /kween/ *n, chiefly Scot* a woman; *esp* one who is young or unmarried [ME *quene*, fr OE *cwene*; akin to OE *cwēn* woman, queen]

queasy *also* **queazy** /ˈkweezi/ *adj* **1** causing or suffering from nausea **2** causing or feeling anxiety or uneasiness [ME *coysy, qwesye*] – **queasily** *adv*, **queasiness** *n*

Quebec /kwiˈbek/ – a communications code word for the letter *q* [*Quebec*, city in Canada]

Quebecois, Québecois /ˌkwibeˈkwah, ˌki-/ *n, pl* **Quebecois, Québecois** a (French-speaking) native or inhabitant of Quebec [F *Québecois*, fr *Québec* Quebec]

quebracho /kayˈbrahchoh/ *n* (the wood of) a S American tree of the periwinkle family whose dried bark was formerly used in the treatment of asthma [AmerSp, alter. of *quiebracha*, fr Sp *quiebra* it breaks + *hacha* axe]

Quechua /ˈkechwə/ *n, pl* **Quechuas,** *esp collectively* **Quechua** **1** a member of an American Indian people of central Peru **2** the language of the Quechua people; *also* the language family to which this belongs ☞ LANGUAGE [Sp, fr Quechua *kkechúwa* plunderer, robber] – **Quechuan** *adj or n*

[1]**queen** /kween/ *n* **1** the wife or widow of a king **2** a female monarch **3** (sthg personified as) a woman who is preeminent in a specified respect ⟨*a beauty ~*⟩ ⟨*Paris, ~ of cities*⟩ **4** the most powerful piece of each colour in a set of chessmen, which has the power to move any number of squares in any direction **5** a playing card marked with a stylized figure of a queen and ranking usu below the king **6** the fertile fully developed female in a colony of bees, ants, or termites **7** a mature female cat **8** an aging male homosexual – used esp by male homosexuals [ME *quene*, fr OE *cwēn* woman, wife, queen; akin to Goth *qens* wife, Gk *gynē* woman, wife, Skt *jani*]

[2]**queen** *vi*, *of a pawn* to become a queen in chess ~ *vt* to promote (a pawn) to a queen in chess – **queen it** to put on airs

ˌQueen ˈAnne /an/ *adj* (having the characteristics) of **a** a style of furniture prevalent in Britain esp during Queen Anne's reign (the first half of the 18th c), marked by extensive use of upholstery, marquetry, and Oriental fabrics **b** a style of English building of the early 18th c characterized by restrained classic detail and the use of red brickwork [*Queen Anne* of Britain †1714]

ˌqueen ˈconsort *n, pl* **queens consort** the wife of a reigning king

ˌqueen ˈmother *n* a woman who is the widow of a king and the mother of the reigning sovereign

ˈqueen ˌpost *n* either of 2 vertical posts connecting the principal rafters of a timber roof truss with the tie beam – compare KING POST ☞ ARCHITECTURE

ˌQueen's ˈBench, Queen's Bench Division *n* a division of the High Court hearing both civil and criminal cases – used when the British monarch is a queen ☞ LAW

ˌQueen's ˈCounsel *n* a barrister who has been appointed by the Crown to a senior rank with special privileges – used when the British monarch is a queen

ˌQueen's ˈEnglish *n* – used instead of *King's English* when the British monarch is a queen

ˈqueen ˌsubstance *n* a pheromone secreted by queen bees that is consumed by worker bees and inhibits the development of their ovaries

queen truss *n* a truss in a timber roof that is framed with queen posts

[1]queer /kwiə/ *adj* **1a** eccentric, unconventional **b** mildly insane **2** questionable, suspicious ⟨~ *goings-on*⟩ **3** not quite well; queasy – infml **4** homosexual – derog [perh fr G *quer* athwart, oblique, perverse] – **queerish** *adj*, **queerly** *adv*, **queerness** *n*

[2]queer *vt* to spoil the effect or success of ⟨~ *one's plans*⟩ – **queer someone's pitch** to prejudice or ruin sby's chances in advance

[3]queer *n* a usu male homosexual – derog

ˈqueer ˌstreet *n, often cap Q&S* a condition of financial embarrassment

quell /kwel/ *vt* **1** to overwhelm thoroughly and reduce to submission or passivity **2** to quiet, pacify ⟨~ *fears*⟩ [ME *quellen* to kill, quell, fr OE *cwellan* to kill; akin to OHG *quellen* to torture, kill, *quāla* torment, Gk *belonē* needle] – **queller** *n*

quench /kwench/ *vt* **1a** to put out (the light or fire of) ⟨~ed *the fire by throwing on sand*⟩ ⟨~ed *the glowing coals*⟩ **b** to cool (e g hot metal) suddenly by immersion in oil, water, etc; *broadly* to cause to lose heat or warmth **2a** to bring (sthg immaterial) to an end, esp by satisfying, damping, or decreasing ⟨*the praise that* ~es *all desire to read the book* – T S Eliot⟩ **b** to terminate (as if) by destroying; eliminate ⟨~ *a rebellion*⟩ **c** to relieve or satisfy with liquid ⟨~ed *his thirst at a wayside spring*⟩ [ME *quenchen*, fr OE *-cwencan*; akin to OE *-cwincan* to vanish, OFris *quinka*] – **quenchable** *adj*, **quencher** *n*, **quenchless** *adj*

quenelle /kəˈnel/ *n* a small ball of a seasoned meat or fish mixture (e g of pike) [F, fr G *knödel* dumpling, fr MHG, dim. of *knode* knot, fr OHG *knodo, knoto* – more at [1]KNOT]

quern /kwuhn/ *n* a primitive hand mill for grinding grain [ME, fr OE *cweorn*; akin to OHG *quirn* mill, OSlav *žrŭny*]

querulous /ˈkwer(y)ooləs/ *adj* habitually complaining; fretful, peevish [L *querulus*, fr *queri* to complain] – **querulously** *adv*, **querulousness** *n*

[1]query /ˈkwiəri/ *n* **1** a question, esp expressing doubt or uncertainty **2** QUESTION MARK; *esp* one used to question the accuracy of a text [alter. of earlier *quere*, fr L *quaere*, imper of *quaerere* to ask]

[2]query *vt* **1** to put as a question ⟨*"what's wrong?" she* queried⟩ **2** to question the accuracy of (e g a statement) **3** to mark with a query **4** *chiefly NAm* to ask questions of – **querier** *n*

[1]quest /kwest/ *n* **1** (the object of) a pursuit or search ⟨*went in* ~ *of gold*⟩ **2** an adventurous journey undertaken by a knight in medieval romance [ME, search, pursuit, investigation, inquest, fr MF *queste* search, pursuit, fr (assumed) VL *quaesta*, fr L, fem of *quaestus*]

[2]quest *vi* **1** *of a dog* to search for a trail or game **2** to go on a quest ⟨~ing *after gold*⟩ ~ *vt* to search for – chiefly poetic

[1]question /ˈkwesch(ə)n/ *n* **1a** a command or an interrogative expression used to elicit information or test knowledge ⟨*unable to answer the exam* ~⟩ **b** an interrogative sentence or clause **2** an act or instance of asking; an inquiry **3a** a subject or concern that is uncertain or in dispute; an issue ⟨*the abortion* ~⟩; *broadly* a problem, matter ⟨*it's only a* ~ *of time*⟩ **b** a subject or point of debate or a proposition to be voted on in a meeting ⟨*the* ~ *before the House*⟩ **c** the specific point at issue **4a** (room for) doubt or objection ⟨*her integrity is beyond* ~⟩ ⟨*called into* ~ *the veracity of his statement*⟩ **b** chance, possibility ⟨*no* ~ *of escape*⟩ [ME, fr MF, fr L *quaestion-, quaestio*, fr *quaesitus, quaestus*, pp of *quaerere* to seek, ask] – **in question** under discussion – **out of the question** preposterous, impossible

[2]question *vt* **1a** to ask a question of **b** to interrogate ⟨~ed *her as to her whereabouts*⟩ **2** to doubt, dispute ⟨~ed *the wisdom of his decision*⟩ **3** to subject (facts or phenomena) to analysis; examine ~ *vi* to ask questions; inquire – **questioner** *n*

questionable /ˈkweschənəbl/ *adj* **1** open to doubt or challenge; not certain or exact **2** of doubtful morality or propriety; shady – **questionableness** *n*, **questionably** *adv*

ˈquestion ˌmark *n* a punctuation mark ? used in writing and printing at the end of a sentence to indicate a direct question

ˈquestion-ˌmaster *n* one who puts questions during a quiz

questionnaire /ˌkweschəˈneə; *also* ˌkes-/ *n* (a form having) a set of questions to be asked of a number of people to obtain statistically useful information [F, fr *questionner* to question, fr MF, fr *question*, n]

ˈquestion ˌtime *n* a period during which members of a parliamentary body may put questions to a minister

quetzal /ˈketsl/ *n, pl* **quetzals, quetzales** /ketˈsahlays/ **1** a Central American bird that has brilliant plumage and the male of which has very long upper tail feathers **2** ☞ *Guatemala* at NATIONALITY [AmerSp, fr Nahuatl *quetzaltototl*, fr *quetzalli* brilliant tail feather + *tototl* bird]

Quetzalcoatl /ˌketslkohˈatl, ˌketslˈkwahtl/ *n* a chief Toltec and Aztec god identified with the wind and air and represented by means of a plumed serpent [Nahuatl]

[1]queue /kyooh/ *n* **1** a pigtail **2a** a waiting line, esp of people or vehicles **b** WAITING LIST ⟨*a housing* ~⟩ [F, lit., tail, fr L *cauda, coda*]

[2]queue *vi* **queuing, queueing** to line up or wait in a queue – **queuer** *n*

ˈqueue-ˌjump *vi* to join a queue at a point in front of (some of) those already waiting; PUSH IN – **queue-jumper** *n*

[1]quibble /ˈkwibl/ *n* a minor objection or criticism, esp used as an equivocation [prob dim. of obs *quib* (quibble), prob fr L *quibus*, dat & abl pl of *qui* who, which]

[2]quibble *vi* **quibbling** /ˈkwibl·ing, ˈkwibling/ **1** to equivocate **2** to bicker – **quibbler** *n*

quiche /keesh/ *n* a pastry shell filled with a rich savoury egg and cream custard and various other ingredients (e g ham, cheese, or vegetables) – compare FLAN [F, fr G dial. (Lorraine) *küche*, dim. of *kuchen* cake, fr OHG *kuocho* – more at CAKE]

[1]quick /kwik/ *adj* **1a** fast in understanding, thinking, or learning; mentally agile ⟨*a* ~ *mind*⟩ ⟨~ *thinking*⟩ **b** reacting with speed and keen sensitivity **2a** fast in development or occurrence ⟨*a* ~ *succession of events*⟩ **b** done or taking place with rapidity ⟨*gave them a* ~ *look*⟩ **c** marked by speed, readiness, or promptness of physical movement ⟨*walked with* ~

steps⟩ **d** inclined to hastiness (e g in action or response) ⟨~ *to find fault*⟩ **e** capable of being easily and speedily prepared ⟨*a* ~ *and tasty dinner*⟩ **3** *archaic* alive [ME *quik*, fr OE *cwic* alive; akin to ON *kvikr* living, L *vivus* living, *vivere* to live, Gk *bios, zōē* life] – **quickly** *adv*, **quickness** *n*

[2]**quick** *adv* in a quick manner

[3]**quick** *n* **1** painfully sensitive flesh, esp under a fingernail, toenail, etc **2** the inmost sensibilities ⟨*cut to the* ~ *by the remark*⟩ [prob of Scand origin; akin to ON *kvika* sensitive flesh, fr *kvikr* living]

quicken /'kwikən/ *vt* **1** to enliven, stimulate **2** to make more rapid; accelerate ⟨~ed *her steps*⟩ ~ *vi* **1** to come to life **2** to reach the stage of gestation at which foetal motion is felt **3** to become more rapid ⟨*her pulse* ~ed *at the sight*⟩ – **quickener** *n*

'quick,fire /-,fie·ə/ *adj* coming or operating quickly; *esp* coming in quick succession ⟨*the* ~ *patter of the auctioneer*⟩

,quick-'freeze *vt* **quick-froze; quick-frozen** to freeze (food) for preservation so rapidly that the natural juices and flavour are preserved intact

quickie /'kwiki/ *n* sthg done or made in a hurry – infml

'quick,lime /-,liem/ *n* LIME 2a

'quick,sand /-,sand/ *n* (a deep mass of) loose sand, esp mixed with water, into which heavy objects readily sink

'quick,set /-,set/ *n, chiefly Br* plant cuttings, esp hawthorn, set in the ground to grow into a hedgerow; *also* a hedge formed in this way

'quick,silver /-,silvə/ *n* MERCURY 1 – **quicksilver** *adj*

'quick,step /-,step/ *n* (a piece of music composed for) a fast fox-trot characterized by a combination of short rapid steps

,quick-'tempered *adj* easily angered; irascible

'quick,thorn /-,thawn/ *n* the hawthorn

'quick ,time *n* a rate of marching of about 120 steps in a minute

,quick-'witted *adj* quick in understanding; mentally alert – **quick-wittedly** *adv*, **quick-wittedness** *n*

[1]**quid** /kwid/ *n, pl* **quid** *also* **quids** *Br* the sum of £1 – infml [perh fr L *quid* what, anything, something] – **quids in** in the state of having made a usu large profit – infml ⟨*if we sell them at £5 each, we'll be* quids in⟩

[2]**quid** *n* a wad of sthg, esp tobacco, for chewing [E dial., cud, fr ME *quide*, fr OE *cwidu, cwudu* – more at CUD]

quiddity /'kwidəti/ *n* that which makes sthg what it is; essence – fml [ML *quidditas* essence, lit., whatness, fr L *quid* what, neut of *quis* who – more at WHO]

quid pro quo /,kwid proh 'kwoh/ *n* sthg given or received in exchange for sthg else [L, something for something]

quiescent /kwi'es(ə)nt/ *adj* **1** causing no trouble **2** at rest; inactive – fml [L *quiescent-, quiescens*, prp of *quiescere* to become quiet, rest, fr *quies*] – **quiescence** *n*, **quiescently** *adv*

[1]**quiet** /'kwie·ət/ *n* being quiet; tranquillity [ME, fr L *quiet-, quies* rest, quiet – more at WHILE] – **on the quiet** without telling anyone; discreetly, secretly

[2]**quiet** *adj* **1a** marked by little or no motion or activity; calm ⟨*a* ~ *day at the office*⟩ ⟨*business had been very* ~ *recently*⟩ **b** free from noise or uproar; still ⟨*a* ~ *little village in the Cotswolds*⟩ **c** secluded ⟨*a* ~ *nook*⟩ **d** enjoyed in peace and relaxation; undisturbed ⟨*a* ~ *cup of tea*⟩ **e** informal and usu involving small numbers of people ⟨*a* ~ *wedding*⟩ **2a** gentle, reserved ⟨*a* ~ *temperament*⟩ **b** unobtrusive, conservative ⟨~ *clothes*⟩ **3** private, discreet ⟨*can I have a* ~ *word with you?*⟩ [ME, fr MF, fr L *quietus*, fr pp of *quiescere*] – **quietly** *adv*, **quietness** *n*

[3]**quiet** *adv* in a quiet manner

[4]**quiet** *vt* to calm, soothe ⟨*did nothing to* ~ *her fears*⟩ ~ *vi* , *chiefly NAm* to become quiet – usu + *down* – **quieter** *n*

quieten /'kwie·ətn/ *vb, chiefly Br* to make or become quiet – often + *down*

quietism /'kwie·ə,tiz(ə)m/ *n* (a system of religious mysticism teaching) a passive withdrawn attitude or policy towards the world or worldly affairs – **quietist** *adj or n*

quietude /'kwie·ətyoohd/ *n* being quiet; repose – fml [MF, fr LL *quietudo*, fr L *quietus*]

quietus /kwie'eetəs, -'aytəs/ *n* removal from activity; *esp* death [ME *quietus est*, fr ML, he is quit, formula of discharge from obligation]

quiff /kwif/ *n, Br* a lock of hair brushed so as to stand up over the forehead [origin unknown]

[1]**quill** /kwil/ *n* **1a** a bobbin, spool, or spindle on which yarn is wound **b** a hollow shaft often surrounding another shaft and used in various mechanical devices **c** a roll of dried bark ⟨*cinnamon* ~s⟩ **2a** the hollow horny barrel of a feather ☞ ANATOMY **b** any of the large stiff feathers of a bird's wing or tail **c** any of the hollow sharp spines of a porcupine, hedgehog, etc **3** sthg made from or resembling the quill of a feather; *esp* a pen for writing **4** a float for a fishing line [ME *quil* hollow reed, bobbin; akin to MHG *kil* large feather]

[2]**quill** *vt* to wind (thread or yarn) on a quill

[1]**quilt** /kwilt/ *n* **1** a thick warm top cover for a bed consisting of padding held in place between 2 layers of cloth by lines of stitching – compare EIDERDOWN, DUVET **2** a usu thinnish cover for a bed; a bedspread [ME *quilte* mattress, quilt, fr OF *cuilte*, fr L *culcita* mattress]

[2]**quilt** *vt* **1a** to fill, pad, or line like a quilt ⟨*a* ~ed *jacket*⟩ **b** to fasten between 2 pieces of material **2** to stitch or sew together in layers with padding in between ~ *vi* to make quilts or quilted work – **quilter** *n*, **quilting** *n*

quim /kwim/ *n* the female genitals – vulg [origin unknown]

quin /kwin/ *n, Br* a quintuplet

quin- /kwin-/, **quino-** *comb form* cinchona (bark) ⟨quin*ine*⟩ [Sp *quina* – more at QUININE]

quince /kwins/ *n* (a central Asian tree of the rose family that bears) a fruit resembling a hard-fleshed yellow apple, used for marmalade, jelly, and preserves [ME *quynce* quinces, pl of *coyn, quyn* quince, fr MF *coin*, fr L *cotoneum, cydoneum (malum)* Cydonian (apple), fr Gk *kydōnion*, fr *kydōnia* Cydonia, ancient city in Crete]

quincentenary /,kwinsen'teenəri, -'tenəri/ *n* (the celebration of) a 500th anniversary [L *quin*que five + E *centenary*]

quincunx /'kwin,kungks/ *n* an arrangement of 5 things (e g marks on a playing card) with 1 at each corner and 1 in the middle of a square or rectangle [L *quincunc-, quincunx*, lit., five-twelfths, fr *quinque* five + *uncia* twelfth part – more at FIVE, OUNCE] – **quincuncial** /-'kungksh(ə)l/ *adj*

quinine /'kwineen, -'-/ *n* an alkaloid with a bitter taste that is obtained from cinchona bark, is used as a tonic, and was formerly the major drug in the treatment of malaria [Sp *quina* cinchona, short for *quinaquina*, fr Quechua]

quinone /kwi'nohn, '--/ *n* **1** a chemical compound that is a derivative of benzene and is used as an oxidizing agent in photography **2** any of various related compounds including several that are biologically important as coenzymes, hydrogen acceptors, or vitamins [ISV *quin*ine + *-one*]

Quinquagesima /,kwingkwə'jesimə/ *n* the Sunday before Lent [ML, fr L, fem of *quinquagesimus* fiftieth, fr *quinquaginta* fifty, fr *quinque* + *-ginta* (akin to *viginti* twenty – more at VIGESIMAL)]

quinque-, **quinqu-** *comb form* five ⟨quinquennium⟩ [L, fr *quinque* – more at FIVE]

quinquennial /kwing'kweni·əl, kwin-/ *adj* **1** consisting of or lasting for 5 years **2** occurring or being done every 5 years – **quinquennial** *n*, **quinquennially** *adv*

quinquennium /kwing'kweni·əm, kwin-/ *n, pl* **quinquenniums, quinquennia** /-ni·ə/ a period of 5 years [L, fr *quinque* + *annus* year – more at ANNUAL]

quinsy /'kwinzi/ *n* a severe inflammation of the throat or adjacent parts with swelling and fever [ME *quinesie*, fr MF *quinancie*, fr LL *cynanche*, fr Gk *kynanchē*, fr *kyn-*, *kyōn* dog + *anchein* to strangle – more at HOUND, ANGER]

quint /kwint/ *n, NAm* a quintuplet

quintain /'kwintin/ *n* (the exercise of tilting at) a post having a revolving crosspiece with a target at one end and a sandbag at the other end providing jousting practice, esp in medieval times [ME *quintaine*, fr MF, fr L *quintana* street in a Roman camp separating the fifth maniple from the sixth where military exercises were performed, fr fem of *quintanus* fifth in rank, fr *quintus* fifth]

quintal /'kwintl/ *n* **1** a hundredweight **2** a metric unit of weight equal to 100kg (about 220.5lb) [ME, fr MF, fr ML *quintale*, fr Ar *quinṭār*, fr LGk *kentēnarion*, fr LL *centenarium*, fr L, neut of *centenarius* consisting of a hundred – more at CENTENARY]

quintessence /kwin'tes(ə)ns/ *n* **1** the pure and concentrated essence of sthg; the most significant or typical element in a whole **2** the most typical example or representative (e g of a quality or class) ⟨*the ~ of pride*⟩ [ME, fr MF *quinte essence*, fr ML *quinta essentia*, lit., fifth essence] – **quintessential** /,kwinti'sensh(ə)l/ *adj*, **quintessentially** *adv*

quintet *also* **quintette** /kwin'tet/ *n* **1** (a musical composition for) a group of 5 instruments, voices, or performers **2** *sing or pl in constr* a group or set of 5 [*quintet* fr It *quintetto*, fr *quinto* fifth, fr L *quintus; quintette* fr F, fr It *quintetto*]

[1]**quintuple** /'kwintyoopl, kwin'tyoohpl/ *adj* **1** having 5 units or members **2** being 5 times as great or as many [MF, fr LL *quintuplex*, fr L *quintus* fifth + *-plex* -fold; akin to L *quinque* five – more at FIVE, [1]SIMPLE] – **quintuple** *n*

[2]**quintuple** *vb* to make or become 5 times as great or as many

quintuplet /'kwintyooplit, kwin'tyoohplit/ *n* **1** a combination of 5 of a kind **2** any of 5 offspring born at 1 birth **3** a group of 5 equal musical notes performed in the time given to 3, 4, etc of the same value [fr [1]*quintuple*, by analogy to *double* : *doublet*]

[1]**quintuplicate** /kwin'tyoohplikət/ *adj* **1** consisting of or existing in 5 corresponding or identical parts or examples ⟨*~ invoices*⟩ **2** being the fifth of 5 things exactly alike [L *quintuplicatus*, pp of *quintuplicare* to quintuple, fr *quintuplic-*, *quintuplex* quintuple]

[2]**quintuplicate** *n* **1** any of 5 identical copies **2** 5 copies all alike – + *in* ⟨*typed in ~*⟩

[3]**quintuplicate** /-,kayt/ *vt* **1** to make quintuple or fivefold **2** to prepare in quintuplicate

quip /kwip/ *vi or n* (to make) a clever, witty, or sarcastic observation or response [n earlier *quippy*, perh fr L *quippe* indeed, to be sure (often ironical), fr *quid* what, neut of *quis* who; vb fr n] – **quipster** /-stə/ *n*

[1]**quire** /kwie·ə/ *n* **1** twenty-four sheets of paper of the same size and quality **2** a set of folded sheets (e g of a book) fitting one within another [ME *quair* 4 sheets of paper folded once, collection of sheets, fr MF *quaer*, fr (assumed) VL *quadernum*, alter. of L *quaterni* 4 each, set of 4 – more at QUATERNION]

[2]**quire** *n, archaic* a choir ☞ CHURCH

quirk /kwuhk/ *n* **1** an odd or peculiar trait; an idiosyncrasy **2** an accident, vagary ⟨*by some ~ of fate*⟩ **3** a groove separating a bead or other moulding from adjoining members [origin unknown] – **quirky** *adj*

quirt /kwuht/ *vt or n* (to strike or drive with) a riding whip with a short handle and a leather lash [n MexSp *cuarta*; vb fr n]

quisling /'kwizling/ *n* a traitor who collaborates with invaders [Vidkun *Quisling* †1945 Norw politician who collaborated with the Germans in WW II]

[1]**quit** /kwit/ *adj* released from obligation, charge, or penalty – + *of* [ME *quite, quit*, fr OF *quite*]

[2]**quit** *vb* **-tt-; quitted** (*NAm chiefly* **quit**) *vt* **1** to leave, depart from (a person or place) ⟨*~ted her without a backward glance*⟩ ⟨*ready to ~ the building at a moment's notice*⟩ **2** to relinquish (e g a way of thinking or acting); stop ⟨*~ moaning!*⟩ **3** to give up (e g an activity or employment) ⟨*he ~ his job*⟩ **4** *archaic* to conduct (oneself) in a usu specified way ⟨*~ themselves with great courage*⟩ *~ vi* **1** to cease doing sthg; *specif* to give up one's job **2** *of a tenant* to vacate occupied premises ⟨*the landlord gave them notice to ~*⟩ **3** to admit defeat; GIVE UP – infml [ME *quiten, quitten*, fr MF *quiter, quitter*, fr OF, fr *quite* free of, released, lit., at rest, fr L *quietus* quiet, at rest]

quitch /kwich/, **quitch grass** /'-,-/ *n* COUCH GRASS [(assumed) ME *quicche*, fr OE *cwice*; akin to OHG *quecca* couch grass, OE *cwic* living – more at [1]QUICK]

quitclaim /'kwit,klaym/ *n* a legal instrument by which one person renounces his/her right in favour of another [ME *quite-claim*, fr MF *quiteclame*, fr *quiteclamer*, lit., to declare free, fr OF, fr *quite* [1]quit + *clamer* to declare, claim – more at CLAIM]

quite /kwiet/ *adv or adj* **1a** wholly, completely ⟨*not ~ all*⟩ ⟨*~ sure*⟩ **b** positively, certainly ⟨*~ the best I've seen*⟩ **2** more than usually; rather ⟨*took ~ a while*⟩ ⟨*that was ~ some party!*⟩ **3** *chiefly Br* to only a moderate degree ⟨*~ good but not perfect*⟩ [ME, fr *quite*, adj, quit] – **quite so** JUST SO 2

quitrent /'kwit,rent/ *n* a fixed rent payable to a

feudal superior in place of the performing of services [ME *quiterent*, fr *quite, quit* [1]quit + *rent*]

quits /kwits/ *adj* on even terms as a result of repaying a debt or retaliating for an injury [ME, quit, prob fr ML *quittus*, alter. of L *quietus* at rest]

quittance /ˈkwit(ə)ns/ *n* (a document giving proof of) discharge from a debt

quitter /ˈkwitə/ *n* one who gives up too easily; a defeatist [[2]QUIT + [2]-ER]

[1]quiver /ˈkwivə/ *n* a case for carrying or holding arrows [ME, fr OF *quivre*, of Gmc origin; akin to OE *cocer* quiver, OHG *kohhari*]

[2]quiver *vi* to shake or move with a slight trembling motion [ME *quiveren*, prob fr *quiver* agile, quick, fr (assumed) OE *cwifer*] – **quiver** *n*

qui vive /ˌkee ˈveev/ *n* the alert, lookout – in *on the qui vive* [F *qui-vive*, fr *qui vive?* long live who?, challenge of a French sentry]

quixotic /kwikˈsotik/, **quixotical** /-kl/ *adj* idealistic or chivalrous in a rash or impractical way [Don *Quixote*, hero of the novel *Don Quixote de la Mancha* by Miguel de Cervantes Saavedra †1616 Sp novelist] – **quixotically** *adv*

[1]quiz /kwiz/ *n* **-zz-** **1** a public test of (general) knowledge, esp as a television or radio entertainment ⟨*a ~ programme*⟩ **2** *NAm* an informal test given by a teacher to a student or class [origin unknown]

[2]quiz *vt* **-zz-** **1** to question closely – journ **2** *NAm* to test (a student or class) informally – **quizzer** *n*

quizzical /ˈkwizikl/ *adj* **1** gently mocking; teasing **2** indicating a state of puzzlement; questioning ⟨*a ~ glance*⟩ – **quizzically** *adv*, **quizzicality** /-ˈkaləti/ *n*

[1]quoin /koyn; *also* kwoyn/ *n* (any of the distinguishing blocks forming) a solid exterior angle of a building [alter. of [1]*coin*]

[2]quoin *vt* to provide with quoins ⟨*~ed walls*⟩

quoit /koyt; *also* kwoyt/ *n* **1** a ring (e g of rubber or iron) used in a throwing game **2** *pl but sing in constr* a game in which quoits are thrown at an upright pin in an attempt to ring the pin or come as near to it as possible [ME *coite*]

quondam /ˈkwondam, -dəm/ *adj* former, sometime ⟨*a ~ friend*⟩ – fml [L, at one time, formerly, fr *quom, cum* when; akin to L *qui* who – more at WHO]

Quonset /ˈkwonsit/ *trademark, NAm* – used for a prefabricated shelter similar to a Nissen hut

quorate /ˈkwawrət, -rayt/ *adj* having a quorum ⟨*is this meeting ~?*⟩

quorum /ˈkwawrəm/ *n* the number of members of a body that when duly assembled is constitutionally competent to transact business [ME, quorum of justices of the peace, fr L, of whom, gen pl of *qui* who; fr the wording of the commission formerly issued to justices of the peace]

quota /ˈkwohtə/ *n* **1** a proportional part or share; *esp* the share or proportion to be either contributed or received by an individual or body ⟨*most factories fulfilled their production ~*⟩ **2** the number or amount constituting a proportional share **3** a numerical limit set on some class of people or things ⟨*an immigration ~*⟩ [ML, fr L *quota pars* how great a part]

quotable /ˈkwohtəbl/ *adj* **1** fit for or worth quoting **2** made with permission for publication (e g in a newspaper) ⟨*were the Minister's remarks ~ or off the record?*⟩

quotation /kwohˈtaysh(ə)n/ *n* **1** sthg quoted; *esp* a passage or phrase quoted from printed literature **2** quoting **3a** (the naming or publishing of) current bids and offers for or prices of shares, securities, commodities, etc **b** ESTIMATE 4

quoˈtation ˌmark *n* either of a pair of punctuation marks ' " or ' ' used to indicate the beginning and end of a direct quotation

[1]quote /kwoht/ *vt* **1a** to repeat (a passage or phrase previously said or written, esp by another) in writing or speech, usu with an acknowledgment **b** to repeat a passage or phrase from, esp in substantiation or illustration ⟨*to ~ the Scriptures*⟩ **2** to cite in illustration ⟨*~ cases*⟩ **3a** to name (the current or recent buying or selling price) of a commodity, stock, share, etc **b** to make an estimate of or give exact information on (e g the price of a commodity or service) **4** to set off by quotation marks *~ vi* **1** to repeat sthg previously said or written ⟨*the Prime Minister said, and I ~, 'We have beaten inflation'*⟩ **2** to name one's price [ML *quotare* to mark the number of, number references, fr L *quotus* of what number or quantity, fr *quot* how many, (as) many as; akin to L *qui* who – more at WHO]

[2]quote *n* **1** a quotation **2** QUOTATION MARK – often used orally to indicate the beginning of a direct quotation

quoth /kwohth/ *vb past, archaic* said – chiefly in the 1st and 3rd persons with a subject following ⟨*~ he*⟩ [ME, past of *quethen* to say, fr OE *cwethan*; akin to OHG *quedan* to say]

quotidian /kwoˈtidi·ən/ *adj* **1** occurring or recurring every day ⟨*~ fever*⟩ **2** commonplace, ordinary – fml [ME *cotidian*, fr MF, fr L *quotidianus, cotidianus*, fr *quotidie* every day, fr *quot* (as) many as + *dies* day – more at DEITY]

quotient /ˈkwohsh(ə)nt/ *n* **1** the result of the division of one number or expression by another **2** the ratio, usu multiplied by 100, between a test score and a measurement on which that score might be expected largely to depend – compare INTELLIGENCE QUOTIENT **3** a quota, share – nonstandard [ME *quocient*, modif of L *quotiens* how many times, fr *quot* how many]

Quran, Qur'an /kooˈrahn, -ˈran/ *n* the Koran

qursh /kooəsh/ *n, pl* **qursh** ☞ *Saudi Arabia* at NATIONALITY [Ar *qirsh*]

R

r /ah/ *n, pl* **r's, rs** *often cap* (a graphic representation of or device for reproducing) the 18th letter of the English alphabet

[1]**-r** *suffix* – used to form the comparative degree of adjectives and adverbs of 1 syllable, and of some adjectives and adverbs of 2 or more syllables, that end in *e* ⟨*truer*⟩ ⟨*freer*⟩; compare [1]-ER

[2]**-r** *suffix* [2]-ER – used with nouns that end in *e* ⟨*old- timer*⟩ ⟨*teenager*⟩ ⟨*diner*⟩

[1]**rabbet** /'rabit/ *n* a channel, groove, or recess cut out of an edge or surface; *specif* one intended to receive another piece (e g a panel) [ME *rabet*, fr MF *rabat* act of beating down, fr OF *rabattre* to beat down, reduce – more at [1]REBATE]

[2]**rabbet** *vt* **1** to cut a rabbet in **2** to unite the rabbeted edges of

rabbi /'rabie/ *n* **1** a Jew qualified to expound and apply Jewish law **2** a Jew trained and ordained for professional religious leadership; *specif* the official leader of a Jewish congregation [LL, fr Gk *rhabbi*, fr Heb *rabbī* my master, fr *rabh* master + *-ī* my]

rabbinate /'rabinət/ *n* **1** the office or tenure of a rabbi **2** the whole body of rabbis [*rabbin* (rabbi), fr F]

rabbinic /rə'binik/, **rabbinical** /-kl/ *adj* **1** of rabbis or their writings **2** of or preparing for the rabbinate – **rabbinically** *adv*

[1]**rabbit** /'rabit/ *n, pl* **rabbits,** (*1*) *esp collectively* **rabbit 1** (the fur of) a small long-eared mammal that is related to the hares but differs from them in producing naked young and in its burrowing habits ☞ LIFE CYCLE **2** *Br* an unskilful player (e g in golf, cricket, or tennis) [ME *rabet*, prob fr Walloon *robett, robete*, fr MD *robbe*] – **rabbity** *adj*

[2]**rabbit** *vi* **1** to hunt rabbits **2** *Br* to talk aimlessly or inconsequentially – infml; often + *on* [(2) rhyming slang *rabbit (and pork)* talk] – **rabbiter** *n*

'rabbit ,punch *n* a short chopping blow delivered to the back of the neck [fr the manner in which a rabbit is stunned before being killed]

rabble /'rabl/ *n* **1** a disorganized or disorderly crowd of people; a mob **2** *the* common people; *the* lowest class of society – derog [ME *rabel* pack of animals]

'rabble-,rouser *n* one who stirs up the common people (e g to hatred or violence); a demagogue

Rabelaisian /,rabi'layzyən, -zh(y)ən/ *adj* marked by the robust humour, extravagant caricature, or bold naturalism characteristic of Rabelais or his works [François *Rabelais* †1553 F humorist & satirist]

rabid /'rabid; *sense 2 also* 'raybid/ *adj* **1** unreasoning or fanatical in an opinion or feeling ⟨*a ~ racialist*⟩ **2** affected with rabies [L *rabidus* mad, fr *rabere*] – **rabidly** *adv*, **rabidness, rabidity** /rə'bidəti/ *n*

rabies /'raybeez, -biz/ *n, pl* **rabies** a fatal short-lasting virus disease of the nervous system of warm-blooded animals, transmitted esp through the bite of an affected animal, and characterized by extreme fear of water and convulsions [NL, fr L, madness, fr *rabere* to rave – more at RAGE]

raccoon, racoon /rə'koohn/ *n, pl* **raccoons,** *esp collectively* **raccoon** (the fur of) a small flesh-eating mammal of N America that has a bushy ringed tail and lives chiefly in trees [*äräkhun* (in some Algonquian language of Virginia, USA)]

[1]**race** /rays/ *n* **1a** a strong or rapid current of water in the sea, a river, etc **b** (the current flowing in) a watercourse used industrially (e g to turn the wheel of a mill) **2a** a contest of speed (e g in running or riding) **b** *pl* a meeting in which several races (e g for horses) are run **c** a contest or rivalry for an ultimate prize or position ⟨*the ~ for the league championship*⟩ **3** a track or channel in which sthg rolls or slides; *specif* a groove for the balls in a ball bearing **4** *archaic* the course of life [ME *ras*, fr ON *rās*; akin to OE *rǣs* rush, L *rorarii* skirmishers, Gk *erōē* rush]

[2]**race** *vi* **1** to compete in a race **2** to go or move at top speed or out of control ⟨*his pulse was* racing⟩ **3** *of a motor, engine, etc* to revolve too fast under a diminished load ~ *vt* **1** to have a race with ⟨~d *her brother to the garden gate*⟩ **2a** to enter in a race ⟨*always* ~s *his horses at Chepstow*⟩ **b** to drive at high speed **c** to transport or propel at maximum speed **3** to accelerate (e g an engine) without a working load or with the transmission disengaged – **racer** *n*

[3]**race** *n* **1** a family, tribe, people, or nation belonging to the same stock **2** an actually or potentially interbreeding group within a species; *also* a category (e g a subspecies) in classification representing such a group **3a** a division of mankind having traits that are transmissible by descent and sufficient to characterize it as a distinct human type **b** human beings collectively ⟨*the human ~*⟩ **4** the division of mankind into races ⟨*the brotherhood of man independent of colour, creed, or ~*⟩ [MF, generation, fr OIt *razza*]

'race,course /-,kaws/ *n* a place where or the track on which races, esp horse races, are held

racemate /ray'seemayt, rə-, 'rasi-/ *n* a racemic compound or mixture

raceme /ray'seem, rə-/ *n* a simple stalk of flowers (e g that of the lily of the valley) in which the flowers are borne on short side-stalks of about equal length along an elongated main stem ☞ PLANT [L *racemus* bunch of grapes]

racemic /rə'seemik, -'se-/ *adj* of or being a compound or mixture that is composed of equal amounts of dextrorotatory and laevorotatory forms of the same compound, and is optically inactive [F *racémique*, fr L *racemus*]

racem·ization, -isation /,rasimie'zaysh(ə)n/ *n* the action or process of changing from an optically active compound into a racemic compound or mixture – **racemize** /'--,-/ *vb*

racemose /'rasimohs/ *adj* having or growing in the form of a raceme ☞ PLANT [L *racemosus* full of clusters, fr *racemus*]

'racemose ,gland *n* a compound gland of freely branching ducts

'race ,riot *n* a riot caused by racial dissensions

rachi-, rachio- *comb form* spine ⟨rachi*tic*⟩ [Gk *rhachi-*, fr *rhachis*; akin to Gk *rhachos* thorn, Lith *ražas* stubble]

rachis /'raykis/ *n, pl* **rachises** *also* **rachides** /'rakideez, 'ray-/ **1** SPINAL COLUMN **2** an axial structure: e g **a(1)** the main stem of a plant's inflorescence **(2)** an extension of the stalk of a compound leaf that bears the leaflets **b** the part of the shaft of a feather that bears the barbs [NL *rachid-, rachis*, modif of Gk *rhachis*]

rachitis /ra'kietəs/ *n* rickets [NL, fr Gk *rhachitis* disease of the spine, fr *rhachis*] – **rachitic** /ra'kitik/ *adj*

Rachmanism /'rakmə,niz(ə)m/ *n, Br* the unscrupulous exploitation of poor tenants by corrupt landlords [Peter *Rachman fl* 1960 E landlord]

racial /'raysh(ə)l/ *adj* **1** of or based on a race **2** existing or occurring between (human) races ⟨*strove for ~ harmony*⟩; *also* directed towards a particular race ⟨*~ discrimination*⟩ – **racially** *adv*

racialism /'rayshə,liz(ə)m/ *n* **1** racial prejudice or discrimination **2** RACISM 1 – **racialist** *n or adj*, **racialistic** /-'listik/ *adj*

racism /'raysiz(ə)m/ *n* **1** a belief that racial differences produce an inherent superiority of a particular race **2** RACIALISM 1 – **racist** *n or adj*

[1]rack /rak/ *n* a wind-driven mass of high often broken clouds [ME *rak*, prob of Scand origin; akin to Sw dial. *rak* wreck; akin to OE *wrecan* to drive – more at WREAK]

[2]rack *vi, of clouds* to fly or scud in high wind

[3]rack *n* **1** a framework for holding fodder for livestock **2** an instrument of torture on which the victim's body is stretched – usu + *the* **3** a framework, stand, or grating on or in which articles are placed ⟨*a luggage ~*⟩ **4** a bar with teeth on 1 face for meshing with a pinion or worm gear ⟨*~ and pinion*⟩ [ME, prob fr MD *rec* framework; akin to OE *reccan* to stretch, Gk *oregein* – more at [1]RIGHT] – **on the rack** under great mental or emotional stress

[4]rack *vt* **1** to torture on the rack **2** to cause to suffer torture, pain, or anguish ⟨*~ed by headaches*⟩ **3a** to stretch or strain considerably ⟨*~ed his brains*⟩ **b** to raise (rents) oppressively **4** to place in a rack

[5]rack *vt* to draw off (e g wine) from the lees [ME *rakken*, fr OProv *arraca*, fr *raca* stems and husks of grapes after pressing]

[6]rack *n* the front rib section of lamb used for chops or as a roast [perh fr [3]*rack*]

[7]rack *n* destruction – chiefly in *rack and ruin* [var of *wrack*]

[1]racket *also* **racquet** /'rakit/ *n* **1** a lightweight implement that consists of a netting stretched in an open frame with a handle attached and that is used for striking the ball or shuttle in any of various games (e g tennis, squash, or badminton) **2** *pl but sing in constr* a game for 2 or 4 players played with a ball and rackets on a 4-walled court [MF *raquette*, fr It *racchetta*, fr Ar *rāḥah* palm of the hand]

[2]racket *n* **1** a loud and confused noise; a din **2a** a fraudulent enterprise made workable esp by bribery or intimidation **b** an easy and lucrative means of livelihood – infml **c** a usu specified occupation or business – slang ⟨*he's in the publicity ~*⟩ [prob imit]

[3]racket *vi* **1** to engage in an active, esp a dissipated, social life – usu + *about* or *round* **2** to move with or make a racket

racketeer /,raki'tiə/ *n* one who extorts money or advantages by threats, blackmail, etc – **racketeer** *vi*

rack railway *n* a railway having between its running rails a rack that meshes with a gear wheel or pinion on a locomotive

'rack ,rent *vt or n* (to subject to) an excessive or unreasonably high rent [[4]*rack*]

'rack-,renter *n* sby who pays or exacts rack rent

raconteur /,rakon'tuh/ *n* one who excels in telling anecdotes [F, fr MF, fr *raconter* to tell, fr OF, fr *re-* + *aconter, acompter* to tell, count – more at ACCOUNT]

racoon /rə'koohn/ *n* a raccoon

racy /'raysi/ *adj* **1** full of zest or vigour **2** having a strongly marked quality; piquant ⟨*a ~ flavour*⟩ **3** risqué, suggestive [[2]*race* (characteristic flavour or quality)] – **racily** *adv*, **raciness** *n*

rad /rad/ *n* a unit of absorbed dose of ionizing radiation (e g X-rays) [short for *radiation*]

radar /'raydah/ *n* an electronic device that generates high-frequency radio waves and locates objects in the vicinity by analysis of the radio waves reflected back from them [*ra*dio *d*etection *a*nd *r*anging]

raddle /'radl/ *n* red ochre [prob alter. of *ruddle*, fr arch *rud* (red colour), fr ME *rude*, fr OE *rudu*]

raddled /'radld/ *adj* broken down; dilapidated; *esp* haggard with age or dissipation [origin unknown]

radi- – see RADIO-

[1]radial /'raydyəl/ *adj* **1** (having parts) arranged like rays or radii from a central point or axis **2a** relating to, placed like, or moving along a radius **b** characterized by divergence from a centre **3** of or situated near a radius bone (e g in the human forearm) [ML *radialis*, fr L *radius* ray] – **radially** *adv*

[2]radial *n* **1** any line in a system of radial lines **2** a radial body part (e g an artery) **3 radial, radial tyre** a pneumatic tyre in which the ply cords are laid at a right angle to the centre line of the tread ☞ CAR

,radial 'engine *n* a usu internal-combustion engine with cylinders arranged radially round the crankshaft

,radial 'symmetry *n* the condition of having similar parts symmetrically arranged around a central axis – **radially symmetrical** *adj*

radian /'raydyən/ *n* a unit of angular measurement that is equal to the angle at the centre of a circle subtended by a part of the circumference equal in length to the radius ☞ PHYSICS [*radius* + *-an*]

[1]radiant /'raydyənt/ *adj* **1a** radiating rays or reflecting beams of light **b** vividly bright and shining; glowing **2** marked by or expressive of love, confidence, or happiness ⟨*a ~ smile*⟩ **3a** emitted or transmitted by radiation ⟨*~ energy*⟩ **b** of or emitting radiant heat [ME, fr L *radiant-, radians*, prp of *radiare*] – **radiance, radiancy** *n*, **radiantly** *adv*

[2]radiant *n* **1** the apparent point of origin of a meteor shower **2** a point or object from which light or heat emanates; *specif* the part of a gas or electric heater that becomes incandescent [[1]RADIATE + [1]-ANT]

,radiant 'energy *n* energy in the form of electromagnetic waves (e g heat, light, or radio waves)

,radiant 'flux *n* the rate of emission or transmission of radiant energy

,radiant 'heat *n* heat transmitted by radiation rather than by conduction or convection

[1]radiate /'raydi,ayt/ *vi* **1** to send out rays of light, heat, or any other form of radiation **2** to issue in rays **3** to proceed in a direct line from or towards a centre ~ *vt* **1a** to send out in rays **b** to show or display clearly ⟨~s *health and vitality*⟩ **2** to disseminate (as if) from a centre [L *radiatus*, pp of *radiare*, fr *radius* ray]

[2]radiate /-ət/ *adj* having rays or radial parts; *specif* having radial symmetry – **radiately** *adv*

radiation /,raydi'aysh(ə)n/ *n* **1** the action or process of radiating; *esp* the process of emitting radiant energy in the form of waves or particles **2** energy radiated in the form of waves or particles; *esp* electromagnetic radiation (e g light) or emission from radioactive sources (e g alpha rays) **3** a radial arrangement – **radiational** *adj*

radi'ation ,sickness *n* sickness that results from overexposure to ionizing radiation (e g X-rays), commonly marked by fatigue, nausea, vomiting, loss of teeth and hair, and, in more severe cases, leukaemia

radiator /'raydi,aytə/ *n* **1** a room heater (with a large surface area for radiating heat); *specif* one through which hot water or steam circulates as part of a central-heating system **2** a device with a large surface area used for cooling an internal-combustion engine by means of water circulating through it [[1]RADIATE + [1]-OR]

[1]radical /'radikl/ *adj* **1a** of or growing from the root or the base of a stem – compare CAULINE **b** of or constituting a linguistic root **c** of or involving a mathematical root **d** designed to remove the root of a disease or all diseased tissue ⟨~ *surgery*⟩ **2** essential, fundamental **3a** departing from the usual or traditional; extreme **b** affecting or involving the basic composition or nature of sthg; thoroughgoing ⟨~ *changes*⟩ **c** tending or disposed to make extreme changes in existing views, conditions, institutions, etc **d** of or constituting a political group advocating extreme measures ⟨*the* ~ *right*⟩ [ME, fr LL *radicalis*, fr L *radic-*, *radix* root – more at [1]ROOT] – **radicalism** *n*, **radicalize** *vt*, **radically** *adv*, **radicalness** *n*, **radicalization** /-ie'zaysh(ə)n/ *n*

[2]radical *n* **1** ROOT 6 **2** sby who is a member of a radical party or who holds radical views **3** a group of atoms that is replaceable in a molecule by a single atom and is capable of remaining unchanged during a series of reactions **4a radical, radical expression** a mathematical expression involving radical signs **b** RADICAL SIGN

,radical 'chic *n, often cap R&C* fashionable and usu superficial left-wing radicalism – derog

'radical ,sign *n* the sign $\sqrt{}$ placed before an expression to denote that the square root, or some other root corresponding to an index number placed over the sign, is to be calculated

radices /'raydi,seez/ *pl of* RADIX

radicle /'radikl/ *n* **1** the lower part of the axis of a plant embryo or seedling, including the embryonic root **2** the rootlike beginning of an anatomical vessel or part **3** a radical [L *radicula*, dim. of *radic-*, *radix*] – **radicular** /ra'dikyoolə/ *adj*

radii /'raydi,ie/ *pl of* RADIUS

[1]radio /'raydi,oh/ *n, pl* **radios** **1** (the use of) the system of wireless transmission and reception of signals by means of electromagnetic waves **2** a radio receiver **3a** a radio transmitter (e g in an aircraft) **b** a radio broadcasting organization or station ⟨Radio *London*⟩ **c** the radio broadcasting industry **d** the medium of radio communication [short for *radiotelegraphy*]

[2]radio *adj* **1** of electric currents or phenomena of frequencies between about 15,000 and 10^{11}Hz **2a** of, used in, or transmitted or received by a radio **b** making or participating in radio broadcasts **c** controlled or directed by or using radio

[3]radio *vb* **radios; radioing; radioed** *vt* **1** to send or communicate by radio **2** to send a radio message to ~ *vi* to send or communicate sthg by radio

radio-, radi- *comb form* **1** radial ⟨radio*symmetrical*⟩ **2a** radiant energy; radiation ⟨radio*dermatitis*⟩ **b** radioactive ⟨radio*element*⟩ ⟨radio*nuclide*⟩ **c** using ionizing radiation ⟨radio*therapy*⟩ **d** radioactive isotopes of (a specified element) ⟨radio*carbon*⟩ **e** radio ⟨radio*telegraphy*⟩ [F, fr L *radius* ray]

,radioac'tivity /,raydioh·ak'tivəti/ *n* the property possessed by some elements (e g uranium) of spontaneously emitting alpha or beta rays and sometimes also gamma rays by the disintegration of the nuclei of atoms ☞ ENERGY, SYMBOL [ISV] – **radioactive** *adj*, **radioactively** *adv*

,radio a'stronomy *n* astronomy using radio telescopes

,radio'carbon /-'kahbən/ *n* radioactive carbon; *esp* CARBON 14 [ISV]

,radio'chemistry /-'kemistri/ *n* a branch of chemistry dealing with radioactive substances and phenomena, and including the use of radioactive tracers – **radiochemical** *adj*, **radiochemically** *adv*, **radiochemist** *n*

,radio'element /-'eləmənt/ *n* a radioactive element [ISV]

'radio ,frequency *n* a frequency (e g of electromagnetic waves) intermediate between audio frequencies and infrared frequencies and used esp in radio and television transmission ☞ PHYSICS

,radio'genic /-'jenik/ *adj* produced by radioactivity

radiogram /'raydi·ə,gram, -dioh-/ *n* **1** a radiograph **2** *Br* a combined radio receiver and record player

radiograph /'raydi·ə,grahf, -,graf, -dioh-/ *n* a picture produced on a sensitive surface by a form of radiation other than light; *specif* an X-ray or gamma-ray photograph – **radiograph** *vt*, **radiographic** /-'grafik/ *adj*, **radiographically** *adv*, **radiographer** /,raydi'ografə/ *n*

radioisotope /,raydioh'iesətohp/ *n* a radioactive isotope [ISV] – **radioisotopic** /-,iesə'topik, -'toh-/ *adj*, **radioisotopically** *adv*

radiolarian /,raydioh'leəri·ən/ *n* any of a large order of marine protozoans with a skeleton made of silica and radiating threadlike pseudopodia [NL *Radiolaria*, order name, fr LL *radiolus* small sunbeam, fr dim. of L *radius* ray]

radiology /,raydi'oləji/ *n* the study and use of radioactive substances and high-energy radiations; *esp* the use of radiant energy (e g X rays and gamma rays) in the diagnosis and treatment of disease – **radiologist** *n*, **radiological** /ˌraydi·əˈlojikl/ *adj*

radiometer /ˌraydiˈomitə/ *n* an instrument for measuring the intensity of radiant or sound energy – **radiometry** /-mətri/ *n*

radiomimetic /ˌraydiohmiˈmetik, -mie-/ *adj, esp of chemical compounds* producing effects on living tissue similar to those of ionizing radiation (e g X rays) [ISV]

radiopaque /ˌraydiohˈpayk/ *adj* (almost) opaque to various forms of radiation (e g X rays)

radiophonic /ˌraydi·əˈfonik, -dioh-/ *adj* of, being, or creating sounds that are electronically produced ⟨*the BBC* Radiophonic *Workshop*⟩ – **radiophonically** *adv*

radioscopy /ˌraydiˈoskəpi/ *n* observation of objects opaque to light, esp by means of X rays [ISV] – **radioscopic** /ˌraydi·əˈskopik/ *adj*

radiosonde /ˈraydiohˌsond/ *n* a miniature radio transmitter carried (e g by an unmanned balloon) into the atmosphere together with instruments for broadcasting back details of humidity, temperature, air pressure, etc [ISV]

radiotelegraphy /ˌraydiohtəˈlegrəfi/ *n* telegraphy carried out by means of radio waves [ISV] – **radiotelegraphic** /-ˌteliˈgrafik/ *adj*

ˌradioˈtelephone /-ˈtelifohn/ *n* an apparatus for enabling telephone messages to be sent by radio (e g from a moving vehicle) [ISV] – **radiotelephony** /-təˈlefəni/ *n*

ˌradio ˈtelescope *n* a radio receiver connected to a large often dish-shaped aerial for recording and measuring radio waves from celestial bodies

ˌradioˈtherapy /-ˈtherəpi/ *n* the treatment of disease (e g cancer) by means of X rays or radiation from radioactive substances [ISV] – **radiotherapist** *n*

ˌradio-ˈulna *n* a bone in the forelimb of an amphibian (e g a frog) that represents the fused radius and ulna of less primitive vertebrate animals (e g mammals) [NL]

ˈradio ˌwave *n* an electromagnetic wave of radio frequency

radish /ˈradish/ *n* (a plant of the mustard family with) a pungent fleshy typically dark red root, eaten raw as a salad vegetable [ME, alter. of OE *rædic*, fr L *radic-*, *radix* root, radish – more at [1]ROOT]

radium /ˈraydyəm/ *n* an intensely radioactive metallic element that occurs in minute quantities in pitchblende and some other minerals and is used chiefly in luminous materials and in the treatment of cancer ☞ PERIODIC TABLE [NL, fr L *radius* ray]

ˈradium ˌtherapy *n* radiotherapy using radium

[1]**radius** /ˈraydi·əs/ *n, pl* **radii** /-diˌie/ *also* **radiuses** **1** the bone on the thumb side of the human forearm; *also* a corresponding part in forms of vertebrate animals higher than fishes ☞ ANATOMY **2** (the length of) a straight line extending from the centre of a circle or sphere to the circumference or surface ☞ MATHEMATICS **3a** the circular area defined by a stated radius **b** a bounded or circumscribed area ⟨*alerted all police cars within a 2 mile* ~⟩ **4** a radial part (e g a spoke of a wheel) [L, ray, radius]

[2]**radius** *vt* to give a rounded edge to (e g a machine part)

ˈradius ˌvector *n* **1** the length of a line segment from a fixed point (e g the origin in a polar coordinate system) to a variable point **2** an imaginary straight line joining the centre of an attracting body with a body in orbit round it

radix /ˈraydiks/ *n, pl* **radices** /-ˌseez/, **radixes** **1** BASE 4d(1) **2** a root or rootlike part [L, root]

radome /ˈrayˌdohm/ *n* a housing sheltering a radar antenna, esp on an aircraft [*radar dome*]

radon /ˈraydon/ *n* a radioactive noble gaseous element formed by disintegration of radium ☞ PERIODIC TABLE [ISV, fr *radium*]

radula /ˈradyoolə/ *n, pl* **radulae** /-li/ *also* **radulas** a horny band covered with minute teeth found in some molluscs (e g snails) and used to tear up food and draw it into the mouth [NL, fr L, scraper, fr *radere* to scrape – more at RAT] – **radular** *adj*

raffia, raphia /ˈrafi·ə/ *n* the fibre of the raffia palm used esp for making baskets, hats, and table mats [Malagasy *rafia*]

ˈraffia ˌpalm *n* a palm of Madagascar with enormous fan-shaped leaves

raffish /ˈrafish/ *adj* marked by careless unconventionality; rakish [*raff* (jumble, rubbish, disreputable person), fr ME *raf*, perh fr MF *raffe, rafle* act of snatching, sweeping] – **raffishly** *adv*, **raffishness** *n*

raffle /ˈrafl/ *vt or n* **raffling** /ˈrafling, ˈrafl·ing/ (to dispose of by means of) a lottery in which the prizes are usually goods ⟨~ *a turkey*⟩ [n ME, kind of game with dice, fr MF; vb fr n]

[1]**raft** /rahft/ *n* **1a** a collection of logs or timber fastened together for transport by water **b** a flat usu wooden structure designed to float on water and used as a platform or vessel **2** a foundation slab for a building, usu made of reinforced concrete [ME *rafte* rafter, raft, fr ON *raptr* rafter]

[2]**raft** *vt* **1a** to transport in the form of or by means of a raft **b** to cross (e g a lake or river) by raft **2** to make into a raft ~ *vi* to travel by raft

[3]**raft** *n, chiefly NAm* a large collection or quantity ⟨*assembled a* ~ *of facts and figures – New Yorker*⟩ [alter. (influenced by [1]*raft*) of *raff* (jumble)]

[1]**rafter** /ˈrahftə/ *n* any of the parallel beams that form the framework of a roof ☞ ARCHITECTURE [ME, fr OE *ræfter*; akin to ON *raptr*]

[2]**rafter** *n* one who manoeuvres logs into position and binds them into rafts [[2]*raft*]

[1]**rag** /rag/ *n* **1a** (a waste piece of) worn cloth **b** *pl* clothes, esp when in poor or ragged condition **2** a scrap or unevenly shaped fragment of sthg ⟨*a* ~ *of cloud*⟩ **3** a usu sensational or poorly written newspaper [ME *ragge*, fr (assumed) OE *ragg*, fr ON *rögg* tuft, shagginess – more at RUG]

[2]**rag** *n* any of various hard rocks used in building [origin unknown]

[3]**rag** *vb* **-gg-** *vt* to torment, tease ~ *vi* to engage in horseplay [origin unknown]

[4]**rag** *n, chiefly Br* **1** an outburst of boisterous fun; a prank **2** a series of processions and stunts organized by students to raise money for charity ⟨~ *week*⟩

[5]**rag** *n* (a composition or dance in) ragtime [short for *ragtime*]

raga /ˈrahgə/ *n* (an improvisation based on) any of the ancient traditional melodic patterns or modes in Indian music [Skt *rāga*, lit., colour, tone]

ragamuffin /ˈragəˌmufin/ *n* a ragged often disreputable person, esp a child [*Ragamoffyn*, a demon in the poem *Piers Plowman* by William Langland †1400 E poet]

ˌrag-and-ˈbone ˌman *n, chiefly Br* a usu itinerant dealer in old clothes, furniture, etc

ragbag /'rag,bag/ *n* **1** a dishevelled or slovenly person **2** a miscellaneous collection ⟨*a* ~ *of prejudices*⟩ *USE* infml

'rag ,bolt *n* a bolt that has barbs on its shank to grip the material in which it is set [[1]*rag* (jagged projection on cast metal)]

,rag 'doll *n* a stuffed cloth doll

[1]**rage** /rayj/ *n* **1** (a fit or bout of) violent and uncontrolled anger **2** violent action (e g of the wind or sea) **3** an intense feeling; passion **4** (an object of) fashionable and temporary enthusiasm ⟨*enormous hats were all the* ~⟩ – infml [ME, fr MF, fr LL *rabia*, fr L *rabies* rage, madness, fr *rabere* to be mad; akin to Skt *rabhas* violence]

[2]**rage** *vi* **1** to be in a rage **2** to be violently stirred up or in tumult ⟨*the wind* ~d *outside*⟩ **3** to be unchecked in violence or effect ⟨*the controversy still* ~s⟩

ragged /'ragid/ *adj* **1** having an irregular edge or outline **2** torn or worn to tatters **3** wearing tattered clothes **4a** straggly **b** showing irregularities; uneven – **raggedly** *adv*, **raggedness** *n*

,ragged 'robin *n* a perennial Eurasian plant of the pink family with ragged pink flowers

raggle-taggle /'ragl ,tagl/ *adj* motley, unkempt [irreg fr *ragtag* (ragged, unkempt), fr [1]*rag* + [1]*tag*]

ragi, raggee /'rahgee, 'ra-/ *n* (the seeds of) an E Indian cereal grass forming a staple food crop in the Orient [Hindi *rāgī*]

raglan /'raglən/ *n* a loose overcoat with raglan sleeves [F J H Somerset, Baron *Raglan* †1855 E field-marshal]

raglan sleeve *n* a sleeve that extends to the neckline with slanted seams from the underarm to the neck

ragout /'ragooh, -'-/ *n* a well-seasoned stew, esp of meat and vegetables, cooked in a thick sauce [F *ragoût*, fr *ragoûter* to revive the taste, fr *re-* + *a-* ad- (fr L *ad-*) + *goût* taste, fr L *gustus*; akin to L *gustare* to taste – more at CHOOSE]

ragtime /'rag,tiem/ *n* (music having) rhythm characterized by strong syncopation in the melody with a regularly accented accompaniment [prob fr *ragged* + *time*]

'rag ,trade *n* *the* clothing trade – infml

ragweed /'rag,weed/ *n* any of various chiefly N American composite plants whose pollen is a major cause of hay fever

ragworm /'rag,wuhm/ *n* any of various marine annelid worms used esp as bait

ragwort /'rag,wuht/ *n* any of several yellow-flowered composite plants that have deeply cut leaves and are common weeds

rah *also* **ra** /rah/ *interj, chiefly NAm* hurrah

[1]**raid** /rayd/ *n* **1a** a usu hostile incursion made in order to seize sby or sthg ⟨*a cattle* ~⟩ **b** a surprise attack by a small force **2** a sudden invasion by the police (e g in search of criminals or stolen goods) **3** an attempt to depress share prices by concerted selling **4** an act of robbery [Sc dial., fr OE *rād* ride, raid – more at ROAD]

[2]**raid** *vt* to make a raid on ~ *vi* to take part in a raid – **raider** *n*

[1]**rail** /rayl/ *n* **1a** an esp horizontal bar, usu supported by posts, which may serve as a barrier (e g across a balcony) or as a support on or from which sthg (e g a curtain) may be hung **b** a horizontal structural support (e g in a door) ☞ ARCHITECTURE **2a** RAILING 1 **b** either of the fences on each side of a horse-racing track – usu pl with sing. meaning **3a** either of a pair of lengths of rolled steel forming a guide and running surface (e g a railway) for wheeled vehicles **b** the railway ⟨*always travels by* ~⟩ [ME *raile*, fr MF *reille* ruler, bar, fr L *regula* ruler, fr *regere* to keep straight, direct, rule – more at [1]RIGHT] – **off the rails** **1** away from the proper or normal course; awry **2** mad, crazy

[2]**rail** *vt* to enclose or separate with a rail or rails – often + *off*

[3]**rail** *n, pl* **rails,** *esp collectively* **rail** any of numerous wading birds of small or medium size, usu having very long toes which enable them to run on soft wet ground [ME *raile*, fr MF *raale*]

[4]**rail** *vi* to utter angry complaints or abuse – often + *against* or *at* [ME *railen*, fr MF *railler* to mock, fr OProv *ralhar* to babble, joke, fr (assumed) VL *ragulare* to bray, fr LL *ragere* to neigh] – **railer** *n*

railcar /'rayl,kah/ *n* a self-propelled railway carriage

railhead /'rayl,hed/ *n* the farthest point reached by a railway; *also* the point at which goods are transferred to or from road transport

railing /'rayling/ *n* **1** a usu vertical rail in a fence or similar barrier **2** (material for making) rails

raillery /'rayl(ə)ri/ *n* (a piece of) good-humoured teasing [F *raillerie*, fr MF, fr *railler* to mock]

[1]**railroad** /'rayl,rohd/ *n, NAm* a railway

[2]**railroad** *vt* **1a** to push through hastily or without due consideration **b** to hustle into taking action or making a decision **2** *NAm* to transport by rail **3** *NAm* to convict with undue haste or by unjust means – **railroader** *n*

railway /'rayl,way/ *n, chiefly Br* **1** a line of track usu having 2 parallel lines or rails fixed to sleepers on which vehicles run to transport goods and passengers; *also* such a track and its assets (e g rolling stock and buildings) constituting a single property **2** an organization which runs a railway network ⟨*works as a clerk on the* ~⟩

railwayman /'raylwaymən/ *n, pl* **railwaymen** /~/ *Br* a railway worker

raiment /'raymənt/ *n* garments, clothing – poetic ⟨*the heroine garbed in flowing* ~ *– New York Times*⟩ [ME *rayment*, short for *arrayment*, fr *arrayen* to array]

[1]**rain** /rayn/ *n* **1a** (a descent of) water falling in drops condensed from vapour in the atmosphere ☞ WEATHER **b** rainwater **2** *pl* the rainy season **3** rainy weather **4** a dense flow or fall of sthg ⟨*a steady* ~ *of fire from the helicopters*⟩ ⟨*greeted him with a* ~ *of abuse*⟩ [ME *reyn*, fr OE *regn, rēn*; akin to OHG *regan* rain]

[2]**rain** *vi* **1** *of rain* to fall in drops from the clouds **2** to fall in profusion ~ *vt* **1** to cause to fall; pour or send down **2** to bestow abundantly – **rain cats and dogs** to rain heavily

rainbow /'raynboh/ *n* **1** an arch in the sky consisting of a series of concentric arcs of the colours red, orange, yellow, green, blue, indigo, and violet, formed esp opposite the sun by the refraction, reflection, and interference of light rays in raindrops, spray, etc **2** an array of bright colours

'rainbow-,coloured *adj* of many colours

,rainbow 'trout *n* a large stout-bodied trout of Europe and western N America

'rain,coat /-,koht/ *n* a coat made from waterproof or water-resistant material

'rain,fall /-,fawl/ *n* **1** a fall of rain; a shower **2** the amount of rain that has fallen in a given area during a given time, usu measured by depth

'rain ,forest *n* a dense tropical woodland with an annual rainfall of at least 2500mm (about 100in) and containing lofty broad-leaved evergreen trees forming a continuous canopy ☞ PLANT

'rain ,gauge *n* an instrument for measuring rainfall

rain off *vt, chiefly Br* to interrupt or prevent (e g a sporting fixture) by rain – usu pass

'rain,proof /-,proohf/ *vt or adj* (to make) impervious to rain

'rain ,shadow *n* an area of relatively light rainfall in the lee of a mountain range

'rain,water /-,wawtə/ *n* water that has fallen as rain and is therefore usu soft

rainy /'rayni/ *adj* **1** having or characterized by heavy rainfall **2** wet with rain ⟨~ *streets*⟩

,rainy 'day *n* a future period of usu financial want or need ⟨*keep it for a* ~⟩

[1]**raise** /rayz/ *vt* **1** to cause or help to rise to an upright or standing position **2a** to awaken, arouse **b** to stir up; incite **c** to recall (as if) from death **d** to establish radio communication with **3a** to build, erect **b** to lift up **c** to place higher in rank or dignity **d** to invigorate ⟨~ *the spirits*⟩ **e** to end the operation of ⟨~ *a siege*⟩ **4a** to levy, obtain ⟨~ *funds*⟩ **b** to assemble, collect ⟨~ *an army*⟩ **5a** to grow, cultivate **b** to rear (e g a child) **6a** to give rise to; provoke ⟨~ *a laugh*⟩ **b** to give voice or expression to ⟨~ *a cheer*⟩ **7** to bring up for consideration or debate ⟨~ *an issue*⟩ **8a** to increase the strength, intensity, degree, or pitch of ⟨~ *the temperature*⟩ **b** to cause to rise in level or amount ⟨~ *the rent*⟩ **c(1)** to increase the amount of (a poker bet) **(2)** to bet more than (a previous better) **9** to make light and porous, esp by adding yeast ⟨~ *dough*⟩ **10** to multiply (a quantity) by the same quantity a number of times so as to produce a specified power ⟨*2* ~d *to the power 3 equals 8*⟩ **11** to bring in sight on the horizon by approaching ⟨~ *land*⟩ **12a** to bring up the nap of (cloth), esp by brushing **b** to bring (e g a design) into relief **c** to cause (e g a blister) to form on the skin **13** to pronounce (a vowel sound) with the tongue unusually near the roof of the mouth **14** *chiefly NAm* to increase the nominal value of fraudulently ⟨~ *a cheque*⟩ [ME *raisen*, fr ON *reisa* – more at REAR] – **raiser** *n* – **raise Cain/hell/the roof** to create a usu angry and noisy disturbance; *esp* to complain vehemently – infml – **raise an eyebrow/eyebrows** to cause surprise, doubt, or disapproval ⟨*his ideas would* raise eyebrows *in political circles*⟩

[2]**raise** *n* **1** an act of raising or lifting **2a** an increase of a bet or bid **b** *chiefly NAm* RISE 4b

raisin /'rayz(ə)n/ *n* a dried grape [ME, fr MF, grape, fr L *racemus* cluster of grapes or berries]

'raising ,agent /'rayzing/ *n* LEAVEN 1

raison d'être /,rayzon(h) 'detrə, (*Fr* rezɔ̃ dɛtr)/ *n* a reason or justification for existence [F]

raj /rahj/ *n* RULE 3; *specif, cap* British rule in India [Hindi *rāj*, fr Skt *rājya*; akin to Skt *rājan* king]

rajah, raja /'rahjə/ *n* **1** an Indian or Malay prince or chief **2** a person bearing a Hindu title of nobility [Hindi *rājā*, fr Skt *rājan* king – more at ROYAL]

Rajput, Rajpoot /'rahjpoot/ *n* a member of a landowning military Indo-Aryan caste of N India [Hindi *rājpūt*, fr Skt *rājaputra* king's son, fr *rājan* king + *putra* son – more at FEW]

[1]**rake** /rayk/ *n* **1** a long-handled implement with a head on which a row of projecting prongs is fixed for gathering hay, grass, etc or for loosening or levelling the surface of the ground; *also* any of several implements similar in shape or use (e g a tool used to draw together the money or chips on a gaming table) **2** a mechanical implement, usu with rotating pronged wheels, used for gathering hay [ME, fr OE *racu*; akin to OHG *rehho* rake]

[2]**rake** *vt* **1** to gather, loosen, or level (as if) with a rake **2** to search through, esp in a haphazard manner – often + *through* or *among* **3** to sweep the length of, esp with gunfire – **raker** *n*

[3]**rake** *vb* to (cause to) incline from the perpendicular [origin unknown]

[4]**rake** *n* **1** inclination from the perpendicular; *esp* the overhang of a ship's bow or stern **2** the angle of inclination or slope, esp of a stage in a theatre

[5]**rake** *n* a dissolute man, esp in fashionable society [short for arch *rakehell* (dissolute person), fr [2]*rake* + *hell*]

rake in *vt* to earn or gain (money) rapidly or in abundance – infml

'rake-,off *n* a share of usu dishonestly gained profits – infml [[2]*rake* + *off*; fr the use of a rake by a croupier to collect the operator's profits in a gambling casino]

rake up *vt* **1** to uncover, revive ⟨raked up *an old grievance*⟩ **2** to find or collect, esp with difficulty ⟨*managed to* rake up *enough money for the rent*⟩

[1]**rakish** /'raykish/ *adj* dissolute, licentious [[5]RAKE + -ISH]

[2]**rakish** *adj* **1** *of a ship, boat, etc* having a smart stylish appearance suggestive of speed **2** dashing, jaunty ⟨*with her hat at a* ~ *angle*⟩ [prob fr [3]*rake*; fr the raking masts of pirate ships] – **rakishly** *adv*, **rakishness** *n*

rale /rahl/ *n* an abnormal wheezing sound that accompanies breathing, due esp to liquid in the lungs [F *râle*, fr *râler* to rattle]

rallentando /,ralən'tandoh/ *n, adj, or adv, pl* **rallentandos, rallentandi** /-di/ (a passage performed) with a gradual decrease in tempo – used in music [It, lit., slowing down, fr *rallentare* to slow down again, fr *re-* + *allentare* to slow down, fr LL, fr L *al-* ad- + *lentus* slow, pliant]

[1]**rally** /'rali/ *vt* **1** to bring together for a common cause **2a** to arouse for or recall to order or action ⟨rallied *his wits to face the problem*⟩ **b** to rouse from depression or weakness ⟨rallied *his strength*⟩ ~ *vi* **1** to join in a common cause ⟨*thousands will* ~ *to the new party*⟩ **2** to come together again to renew an effort ⟨*the troops* rallied *and drove back the enemy*⟩ **3** to recover, revive ⟨*began to* ~ *after his long illness*⟩ [F *rallier*, fr OF *ralier*, fr *re-* + *alier* to unite – more at ALLY]

[2]**rally** *n* **1a** a mustering of scattered forces to renew an effort **b** a recovery of strength or courage after weakness or dejection **c** an increase in price after a decline **2** a mass meeting of people sharing a common interest or supporting a common, usu political, cause **3** a series of strokes interchanged between players (e g in tennis) before a point is won **4** *also* **rallye** a motor race, usu over public roads, designed to test both speed and navigational skills [(4) F *rallye*, fr E [1]*rally*]

rallycross /'rali,kros/ *n* a motor sport in which specially adapted saloon cars race round a 1-mile circuit [[2]*rally* + *-cross* (as in *cyclocross*)]

[1]**ram** /ram/ *n* **1** an uncastrated male sheep **2a** BATTERING RAM **b** a heavy beak on the prow of a warship for piercing enemy vessels; *also* a warship equipped with a ram **3a** the plunger of a hydrostatic press or force pump **b** the weight that strikes the blow in a pile driver [ME, fr OE *ramm*; akin to OHG *ram*]

[2]**ram** *vb* **-mm-** *vi* to strike with violence ⟨*her car* ~med *into a tree*⟩ ~*vt* **1** to force down or in by driving, pressing, or pushing ⟨~med *his hat down over his ears*⟩ **2** to force passage or acceptance of ⟨~ *home an idea*⟩ **3** to strike against violently and usu head-on – **rammer** *n* – **ram something down someone's throat** to force sby to accept or listen to sthg, esp by constant repetition

Ramadan, Ramadhan /'ramədan, -dahn, ,--'-/ *n* the 9th month of the Muslim year, during which fasting is practised daily from dawn to sunset [Ar *Ramadān*]

[1]**ramble** /'rambl/ *vi* **rambling** /'rambling, 'rambl·ing/ **1** to walk for pleasure, esp without a planned route **2** to talk or write in a disconnected long-winded fashion **3** to grow or extend irregularly ⟨*a* rambling *old house*⟩ [perh fr ME *romblen*, freq of *romen* to roam] – **ramblingly** *adv*

[2]**ramble** *n* a leisurely walk taken for pleasure and often without a planned route

rambler /'ramblə/ *n* any of various climbing roses with small, often double, flowers in large clusters [[1]RAMBLE + [2]-ER]

rambunctious /ram'bungkshəs/ *adj, NAm* rumbustious, unruly – infml [prob alter. of *rumbustious*] – **rambunctiously** *adv*, **rambunctiousness** *n*

rambutan /ram'boohtn/ *n* (a tree that bears) a bright red spiny Malayan fruit closely related to the litchi [Malay, fr *rambut* hair]

ramekin, ramequin /'ram(i)kin/ *n* **1** a preparation of cheese with breadcrumbs, puff pastry, or eggs baked in an individual mould **2** an individual baking and serving dish [F *ramequin*, fr LG *ramken*, dim. of *ram* cream, fr MLG *rōm*]

ramification /,ramifi'kaysh(ə)n/ *n* **1a** the act or process of branching out **b** the arrangement of branches (e g on a plant) **2a** a branch, subdivision **b** a branched structure **3** a usu extended or complicated consequence ⟨*the* ~s *of a problem*⟩

ramiform /'rami,fawm, 'ray-/ *adj* resembling or constituting branches [L *ramus* + E *-iform*]

ramify /'ramifie/ *vb* to (cause to) separate or split up into branches, divisions, or constituent parts [MF *ramifier*, fr ML *ramificare*, fr L *ramus* branch; akin to L *radix* root – more at ROOT]

ramjet /'ram,jet/ *n* a jet engine that uses the flow of compressed air produced by the forward movement of the aeroplane, rocket, etc to burn the fuel [[2]*ram* + *jet*]

ramose /'raymohs/ *adj* consisting of or having branches [L *ramosus*, fr *ramus* branch] – **ramosely** *adv*

ramp /ramp/ *n* **1** a sloping floor, walk, or roadway leading from one level to another **2** a stairway for entering or leaving an aircraft [F *rampe*, fr *ramper* to crawl, rear, of Gmc origin; akin to MLG *ramp* cramp, OHG *rimpfan* to wrinkle]

[1]**rampage** /ram'payj/ *vi* to rush about wildly or violently [Sc, perh irreg fr *ramp* (to rear, rage, climb), fr ME *rampen*, fr OF *ramper*]

[2]**rampage** /ram'payj, '--/ *n* – **on the rampage** engaged in violent or uncontrolled behaviour

rampant /'rampənt/ *adj* **1** *of a heraldic animal* rearing upon the hind legs with forelegs extended – used postpositively **2a** characterized by wildness or absence of restraint (e g of opinion or action) ⟨*a* ~ *militarist*⟩ **b** spreading or growing unchecked ⟨*a* ~ *crime wave*⟩ [ME, fr MF, prp of *ramper*] – **rampancy** *n*, **rampantly** *adv*

rampart /'rampaht/ *n* **1** a broad embankment raised as a fortification (e g around a fort or city) and usu surmounted by a parapet ☞ CHURCH **2** a protective barrier; a bulwark [MF *rampart, rempart*, fr *ramparer, remparer* to fortify, strengthen, fr *re-* + *emparer* to defend, protect, deriv of L *ante* before + *parare* to prepare]

rampion /'rampyən/ *n* a European plant that is related to the harebell and whose tuberous root is sometimes eaten in salads [prob modif of MF *raiponce*, fr OIt *raponzo*, prob fr *rapa, rapo* turnip, fr L *rapa, rapum* rape, turnip]

ramrod /'ram,rod/ *n* **1** a rod for ramming home the charge in a muzzle-loading firearm **2** a rod for cleaning the barrels of rifles and other small arms

ramshackle /'ramshakl/ *adj* badly constructed or needing repair; rickety [alter. of earlier *ransackled*, fr pp of obs *ransackle*, freq of *ransack*]

ramsons /'ramsənz, -zənz/ *n pl but sing in constr* (the root, eaten as a relish, of) a broad-leaved garlic [ME *ramsyn*, fr OE *hramsan*, pl of *hramsa* wild garlic]

ran /ran/ *past of* RUN

[1]**ranch** /rahnch/ *n* **1** a large farm for raising livestock esp in N America and Australia **2** *chiefly NAm* a farm or area devoted to raising a particular crop or animal ⟨*a poultry* ~⟩ [MexSp *rancho* small ranch, fr Sp, camp, hut & Sp dial., small farm, fr OSp *ranchear (se)* to take up quarters, fr MF *(se) ranger* to take up a position, fr *ranger* to set in a row – more at [2]RANGE]

[2]**ranch** *vi* to own, work, or live on a ranch – **rancher** *n*

rancid /'ransid/ *adj* (smelling or tasting) rank [L *rancidus*, fr *rancēre* to be rancid] – **rancidness, rancidity** /ran'sidəti/ *n*

rancour, *NAm* **rancor** /'rangkə/ *n* bitter and deep-seated ill will or hatred [ME *rancour*, fr MF *ranceur*, fr LL *rancor* rancidity, rancour, fr L *rancēre*] – **rancorous** *adj*

rand /rand/ *n, pl* **rand** ☞ *South Africa* at NATIONALITY [the *Rand*, gold-mining district of S Africa]

[1]**random** /'randəm/ *n* [ME, impetuosity, fr MF *randon*, fr OF, fr *randir* to run, of Gmc origin; akin to OHG *rinnan* to run – more at RUN] – **at random** without definite aim, direction, rule, or method

[2]**random** *adj* **1** lacking a definite plan, purpose, or pattern **2** (of, consisting of, or being events, parts, etc) having or relating to a probability of occurring equal to that of all similar parts, events, etc – **randomly** *adv*, **randomness** *n*

,random-'access *adj* permitting access to stored data in any order the user desires ⟨*a* ~ *computer memory*⟩ ☞ COMPUTER

random·ize, -ise /'randəmiez/ *vt* to arrange (e g samples) so as to simulate a chance distribution and yield unbiased statistical data – **randomizer** *n*

,random 'walk *n* a process (e g the random movement of molecules or genetic drift) consisting of a sequence of steps, each of whose characteristics (e g magnitude and direction) are determined by chance

randy /'randi/ *adj* sexually aroused; lustful – infml [prob fr obs *rand* (to rant), fr obs D *randen, ranten*]

rang /rang/ *past of* RING

[1]range /raynj/ *n* **1a** a series of mountains **b** a number of objects or products forming a distinct class or series **c** a variety, cross-section ⟨*a good ~ of people here*⟩ **2** a usu solid-fuel fired cooking stove with 1 or more ovens, a flat metal top, and 1 or more areas for heating pans **3a** an open region over which livestock may roam and feed, esp in N America **b** the region throughout which a kind of living organism or ecological community naturally lives or occurs **4a(1)** the distance to which a projectile can be propelled (2) the distance between a weapon and the target **b** the maximum distance a vehicle can travel without refuelling **c** a place where shooting (e g with guns or missiles) is practised **5a** the space or extent included, covered, or used **b** the extent of pitch within a melody or within the capacity of a voice or instrument **6a** a sequence, series, or scale between limits ⟨*a wide ~ of patterns*⟩ **b** (the difference between) the least and greatest values of an attribute or series ☞ STATISTICS **7** the set of values a function may take; *esp* the values that a dependent variable may have **8** LINE 9 [ME, row of persons, fr OF *renge*, fr *rengier* to range]

[2]range *vt* **1a** to set in a row or in the proper order ⟨*troops were ~d on either side*⟩ **b** to place among others in a specified position or situation ⟨*~d himself with the radicals in the party*⟩ **2** to roam over or through **3** to determine or give the elevation necessary for (a gun) to propel a projectile to a given distance ~ *vi* **1** to roam at large or freely ⟨*the talk ~d over current topics*⟩ **2** *esp of printing type* to align **3** to extend in a usu specified direction **4** *of a gun or projectile* to have a usu specified range **5** to change or differ within limits ⟨*their ages ~d from 5 to 65*⟩ **6** to live, occur in, or be native to, a specified region [ME *rangen*, fr MF *ranger*, fr OF *rengier*, fr *renc, reng* line, place, row – more at [2]RANK]

'range,finder *n* a device for indicating or measuring the distance between a gun and a target or a camera and an object

ranger /'raynjə/ *n* **1a** the keeper of a British royal park or forest **b** an officer who patrols a N American national park or forest **2a** a member of any of several bodies of armed men in N America who range over a usu specified region, esp to enforce the law **b** a soldier in the US army specially trained in close-range fighting and raiding tactics **3** *often cap* a private in an Irish line regiment **4** *cap* a senior member of the British Guide movement aged from 14 to 19 [[2]RANGE + [2]-ER]

'ranging ,rod /'raynjing/ *n* a rod, usu painted with alternate red and white stripes, used in surveying to mark a straight line

rangy /'raynji/ *adj* **1** *of an animal* long-limbed and long-bodied **2** *of a person* tall and slender [[1, 2]*range* + [1]*-y*] – **ranginess** *n*

rani, ranee /rah'nee, '--/ *n* a Hindu queen or princess; *esp* the wife of a rajah [Hindi *rānī*, fr Skt *rājñī*, fem of *rājan* king – more at ROYAL]

[1]rank /rangk/ *adj* **1** (covered with vegetation which is) excessively vigorous and often coarse in growth **2** offensively gross or coarse **3a** shockingly conspicuous; flagrant ⟨*lecture him on his ~ disloyalty*⟩ **b** complete – used as an intensive ⟨*a ~ outsider*⟩ **4** offensive in odour or flavour [ME, fr OE *ranc* overbearing, strong; akin to OE *riht* right – more at RIGHT] – **rankly** *adv*, **rankness** *n*

[2]rank *n* **1a** a row, line, or series of people or things **b(1)** *sing or pl in constr* a line of soldiers ranged side by side in close order (2) *pl* RANK AND FILE **c** any of the 8 rows of squares that extend across a chessboard perpendicular to the files **2** an esp military formation – often pl with sing. meaning ⟨*to break ~s*⟩ **3a** a degree or position in a hierarchy or order; *specif* an official position in the armed forces **b** (high) social position ⟨*the privileges of ~*⟩ **4** the number of rows in a mathematical matrix **5** *Br* a place where taxis wait to pick up passengers [MF *renc, reng*, of Gmc origin; akin to OHG *hring* ring – more at [1]RING]

[3]rank *vt* **1** to arrange in lines or in a regular formation **2** to determine the relative position of; rate **3** *NAm* to outrank ~ *vi* to take or have a position in relation to others

,rank and 'file *n sing or pl in constr* **1** the body of members of an armed force as distinguished from the officers **2** the individuals constituting the body of an organization, society, or nation as distinguished from the leading or principal members ⟨*~ members of the orchestra*⟩ – **rank and filer** *n*

ranker /'rangkə/ *n* one who serves or has served in the ranks; *esp* a commissioned officer promoted from the ranks

ranking /'rangking/ *adj, chiefly NAm* having a high or the highest position

rankle /'rangkl/ *vi* **rankling** /'rangkling, 'rangkl·ing/ to cause continuing anger, irritation, or bitterness [ME *ranclen* to fester, fr MF *rancler*, fr OF *draoncler, raoncler*, fr *draoncle, raoncle* festering sore, fr (assumed) VL *dracunculus*, fr L, dim. of *draco* serpent – more at DRAGON]

ransack /'ransak/ *vt* **1** to search in a disordered but thorough manner **2** to rob, plunder [ME *ransaken*, fr ON *rannsaka*, fr *rann* house + *-saka* (akin to OE *sēcan* to seek)] – **ransacker** *n*

[1]ransom /'ransəm/ *n* **1** a price paid or demanded for the release of a captured or kidnapped person **2** the act of ransoming [ME *ransoun*, fr OF *rançon*, fr L *redemption-, redemptio* – more at REDEMPTION]

[2]ransom *vt* **1** to deliver or redeem, esp from sin or its consequences **2** to free from captivity or punishment by paying a ransom – **ransomer** *n*

[1]rant /rant/ *vi* to talk in a noisy, excited, or declamatory manner ~ *vt* to declaim bombastically [obs D *ranten, randen*] – **ranter** *n*, **rantingly** *adv*

[2]rant *n* (a) bombastic extravagant speech

ranunculus /rə'nungkyooləs/ *n, pl* **ranunculuses, ranunculi** /-lie/ any of a large widely distributed genus of plants of the buttercup family including the buttercups and crowfoots [NL, genus name, fr L, tadpole, crowfoot, dim. of *rana* frog]

[1]rap /rap/ *n* **1** (the sound made by) a sharp blow or knock **2** blame, punishment – infml ⟨*I ended up taking the ~*⟩ [ME *rappe*, prob of imit origin]

[2]rap *vb* **-pp-** *vt* **1** to strike with a sharp blow **2** to utter (e g a command) abruptly and forcibly – usu + *out* **3** to express or communicate (e g a message) by

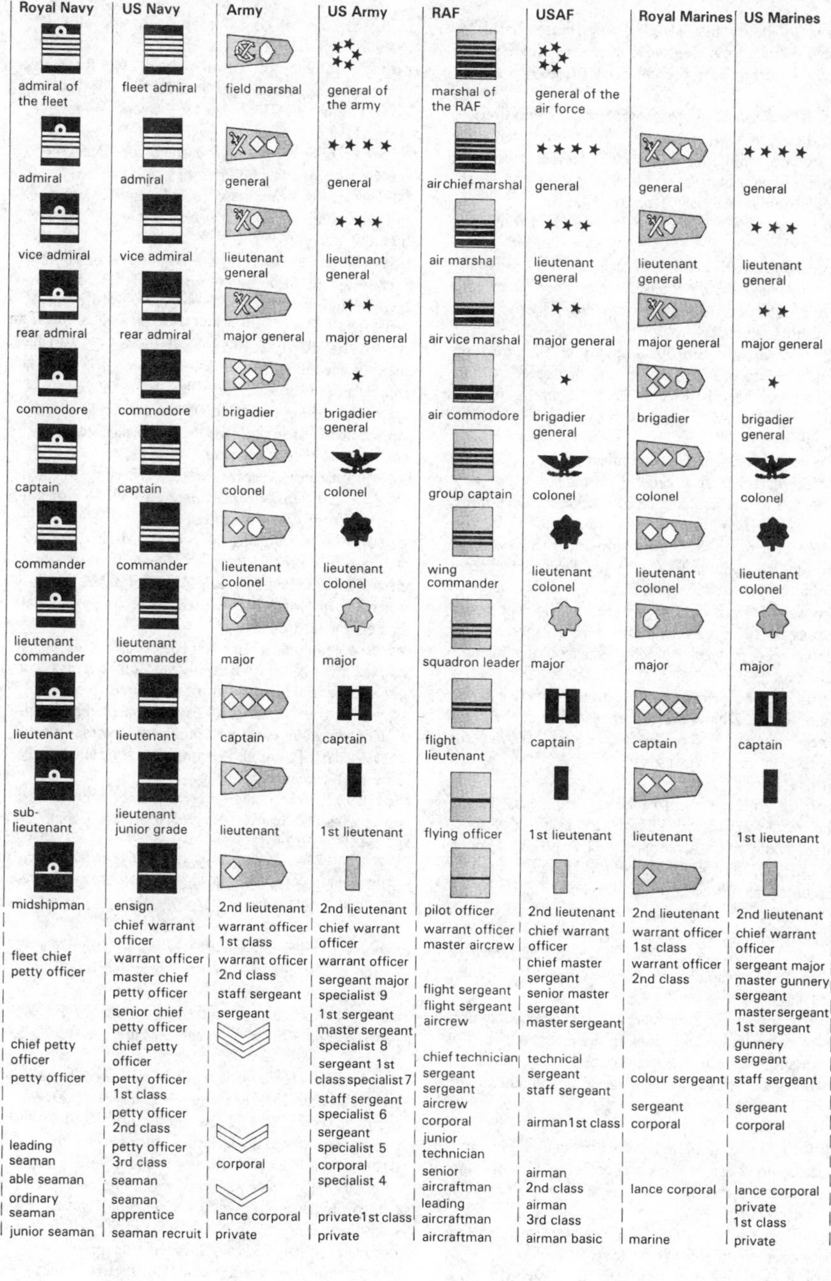
Royal Navy
admiral of the fleet
admiral
vice admiral
rear admiral
commodore
captain
commander
lieutenant commander
lieutenant
sub-lieutenant
midshipman
fleet chief petty officer
chief petty officer
petty officer
leading seaman
able seaman
ordinary seaman
junior seaman
US Navy
fleet admiral
admiral
vice admiral
rear admiral
commodore
captain
commander
lieutenant commander
lieutenant
lieutenant junior grade
ensign
chief warrant officer
warrant officer
master chief petty officer
senior chief petty officer
chief petty officer
petty officer 1st class
petty officer 2nd class
petty officer 3rd class
seaman
seaman apprentice
seaman recruit
Army
field marshal
general
lieutenant general
major general
brigadier
colonel
lieutenant colonel
major
captain
lieutenant
2nd lieutenant
warrant officer 1st class
warrant officer 2nd class
staff sergeant
sergeant
corporal
lance corporal
private
US Army
general of the army
general
lieutenant general
major general
brigadier general
colonel
lieutenant colonel
major
captain
1st lieutenant
2nd lieutenant
chief warrant officer
warrant officer
sergeant major specialist 9
1st sergeant master sergeant specialist 8
sergeant 1st class specialist 7
staff sergeant specialist 6
sergeant specialist 5
corporal specialist 4
private 1st class
private
RAF
marshal of the RAF
air chief marshal
air marshal
air vice marshal
air commodore
group captain
wing commander
squadron leader
flight lieutenant
flying officer
pilot officer
warrant officer master aircrew
flight sergeant flight sergeant aircrew
chief technician
sergeant
sergeant aircrew
corporal
junior technician
senior aircraftman
leading aircraftman
aircraftman
USAF
general of the air force
general
lieutenant general
major general
brigadier general
colonel
lieutenant colonel
major
captain
1st lieutenant
2nd lieutenant
chief warrant officer
chief master sergeant
senior master sergeant
master sergeant
technical sergeant
staff sergeant
airman 1st class
airman 2nd class
airman 3rd class
airman basic
Royal Marines
general
lieutenant general
major general
brigadier
colonel
lieutenant colonel
major
captain
lieutenant
2nd lieutenant
warrant officer 1st class
warrant officer 2nd class
colour sergeant
sergeant
corporal
lance corporal
marine
US Marines
general
lieutenant general
major general
brigadier general
colonel
lieutenant colonel
major
captain
1st lieutenant
2nd lieutenant
chief warrant officer
sergeant major
master gunnery sergeant
master sergeant
1st sergeant
gunnery sergeant
staff sergeant
sergeant
corporal
lance corporal
private 1st class
private

means of raps – usu + *out* **4** to criticize sharply – journ ⟨*judge* ~s *police*⟩ ~ *vi* to strike a quick sharp blow **– (a) rap over the knuckles** (to give) a scolding

[3]**rap** *n* the least bit (e g of care or consideration) – infml ⟨*doesn't care a* ~⟩ [arch *rap* (counterfeit coin in Ireland, smallest coin), prob fr IrGael *ropaire*]

[4]**rap** *n, chiefly NAm* talk, conversation – slang [perh by shortening & alter. fr *repartee*]

[5]**rap** *vi* **-pp-** *chiefly NAm* to talk freely and frankly – slang

rapacious /rə'payshəs/ *adj* **1** excessively grasping or covetous **2** *of an animal* living on prey [L *rapac-, rapax*, fr *rapere* to seize] – **rapaciously** *adv*, **rapaciousness, rapacity** /rə'pasəti/ *n*

[1]**rape** /rayp/ *n* a European plant of the mustard family grown as a forage crop and for its seeds which yield rapeseed oil [ME, fr L *rapa, rapum* turnip, rape; akin to OHG *rāba* turnip, rape, Gk *rhapys* turnip]

[2]**rape** *vt* **1** to despoil **2** to commit rape on [ME *rapen* to take by force, fr L *rapere*] – **rapist** *n*

[3]**rape** *n* **1** an act or instance of robbing or despoiling ⟨*the* ~ *of the countryside*⟩ **2** (an instance of) the crime of forcing sby, esp a woman, to have sexual intercourse against his/her will **3** an outrageous violation ⟨*a* ~ *of Justice*⟩

rapeseed /'rayp,seed/ *n* the seed of the rape plant

rapeseed oil *n* an oil obtained from rapeseed and turnip seed and used chiefly as a cooking oil and lubricant

raphe, rhaphe /'ray,fee/ *n* a seam or ridge (e g at the union of the 2 halves of a part or organ of the body or on a seed) [NL, fr Gk *rhaphē* seam, fr *rhaptein* to sew – more at RHAPSODY]

raphia /'rafi·ə/ *n* raffia

raphide /'rafied/ *n, pl* **raphides** /'rafi,deez/ any of the needle-shaped crystals, usu of calcium oxalate, that develop in some plant cells [F & NL; F *raphide*, fr NL *raphides*, pl, modif of Gk *rhaphides*, pl of *rhaphid-, rhaphis* needle, fr *rhaptein*]

[1]**rapid** /'rapid/ *adj* moving, acting, or occurring with speed; swift [L *rapidus* seizing, sweeping, rapid, fr *rapere* to seize, sweep away; akin to OE *refsan* to blame] – **rapidly** *adv*, **rapidness, rapidity** /rə'pidəti/ *n*

[2]**rapid** *n* a part of a river where the water flows swiftly over a steep usu rocky slope in the river bed – usu pl with sing. meaning ☞ GEOGRAPHY

,rapid 'eye ,movement *n* rapid movement of the eyes that occurs during the phases of sleep when dreaming is taking place

,rapid-'fire *adj* **1** (adapted for) firing shots in rapid succession **2** *esp of speech* proceeding with or characterized by rapidity, liveliness, or sharpness ⟨~ *interrogation*⟩

,rapid 'transit *n, NAm* fast passenger transport (e g by underground) in urban areas

rapier /'raypi·ə/ *n* a straight 2-edged sword with a narrow pointed blade [MF (*espee*) *rapiere*]

rapine /'rapien/ *n* pillage, plunder [ME *rapyne*, fr L *rapina*, fr *rapere* to seize, rob]

rapparee /,rapə'ree/ *n* a 17th-c Irish irregular soldier or bandit [IrGael *rāpaire*]

rappee /ra'pee/ *n* a pungent snuff [F (*tabac*) *râpé*, lit., grated tobacco, fr *tabac* tobacco + *râpé*, pp of *râper* to grate]

rappel /ra'pel/ *vi* to abseil [F, lit., recall, fr OF *rapel*, fr *rapeler* to recall, fr *re-* + *apeler* to appeal, call – more at APPEAL] – **rappel** *n*

rappen /'rahpən, 'ra-/ *n, pl* **rappen** /~/ the Swiss centime ☞ *Switzerland* at NATIONALITY [G, lit., raven; akin to OHG *hraban* raven – more at [1]RAVEN]

rapport /ra'paw/ *n* a sympathetic or harmonious relationship [F, fr *rapporter* to bring back, refer, fr OF *raporter* to bring back, fr *re-* + *aporter* to bring, fr L *apportare*, fr *ad-* + *portare* to carry – more at [1]FARE]

rapporteur /,rapaw'tuh/ *n* a person responsible for preparing and presenting reports (e g from a committee to a higher body) [F, fr *rapporter* to bring back, report]

rapprochement /ra'proshmonh/ *n* the reestablishment of cordial relations, esp between nations [F, fr *rapprocher* to bring together, fr MF, fr *re-* + *approcher* to approach, fr OF *aprochier*]

rapscallion /rap'skalyən/ *n* a rascal [alter. of earlier *rascallion*, fr [1]*rascal*]

rapt /rapt/ *adj* **1** enraptured **2** wholly absorbed [ME, fr L *raptus*, pp of *rapere* to seize – more at RAPID] – **raptly** *adv*, **raptness** *n*

raptor /'raptə/ *n* a bird of prey [deriv of L *raptor* plunderer, fr *raptus*]

raptorial /rap'tawri·əl/ *adj* **1** *esp of a bird* PREDATORY 2 **2** *of birds' feet* adapted for seizing prey **3** of or being a bird of prey

rapture /'rapchə/ *n* **1a** a state or experience of being carried away by overwhelming emotion **b** a mystical experience in which the spirit is exalted to a knowledge of divine things **2** an expression or manifestation of ecstasy or extreme delight ⟨*went into* ~s *over the new car*⟩ [L *raptus*] – **rapturous** *adj*, **rapturously** *adv*, **rapturousness** *n*

rara avis /,rahrə 'ayvis, ,reərə/ *n, pl* **rara avises, rarae aves** /,rahri 'ayveez, ,reəri/ a rare person or thing [L, rare bird]

[1]**rare** /reə/ *adj, of meat* cooked so that the inside is still red [alter. of earlier *rere*, fr ME, fr OE *hrēre* boiled lightly; akin to OE *hrēran* to stir, OHG *hruoren*]

[2]**rare** *adj* **1** lacking in density; thin ⟨*a* ~ *atmosphere*⟩ **2** marked by unusual quality, merit, or appeal ⟨*to show* ~ *tact*⟩ **3** seldom occurring or found ⟨*a* ~ *moth*⟩ **4** superlative or extreme – infml ⟨*gave her a* ~ *fright*⟩ [ME, fr L *rarus*] – **rarely** *adv*, **rareness** *n*

,rare 'earth *n* (an oxide of) any of a series of metallic elements that includes the elements with atomic numbers from 58 to 71, usu lanthanum, and sometimes yttrium and scandium – **rare-earth** *adj*

rarefaction /,reəri'faksh(ə)n/ *n* **1** rarefying or being rarefied **2** a state or region of minimum pressure in a medium through which longitudinal waves (e g sound waves) pass [F or ML; F *raréfaction*, fr ML *rarefaction-, rarefactio*, fr L *rarefactus*, pp of *rarefacere* to rarefy] – **rarefactional, rarefactive** /-'faktiv/ *adj*

rarefied *also* **rarified** /'reərified/ *adj* **1** esoteric, abstruse **2** very high or exalted (e g in rank) ⟨*moved in* ~ *political circles*⟩

rarefy *also* **rarify** /'reərifie/ *vt* **1** to make rare, porous, or less dense **2** to make more spiritual, refined, or abstruse ~ *vi* to become less dense [ME *rarefien, rarifien*, fr MF *rarefier*, modif of L *rarefacere*, fr *rarus* rare + *facere* to make – more at DO]

raring /ˈreəring/ *adj* full of enthusiasm or eagerness ⟨~ *to go*⟩ [fr prp of E dial. *rare* (to rear), alter. of E *rear*]

rarity /ˈreərəti/ *n* **1** the quality, state, or fact of being rare **2** sby or sthg rare

rascal /ˈrahsk(ə)l/ *n* **1** an unprincipled or dishonest person **2** a mischievous person or animal – usu humor or affectionate [ME *rascaile* rabble, one of the rabble, prob fr ONF *rasque* mud] – **rascally** *adj or adv*

raschel /rahˈshel/ *n* a type of warp-knitted fabric usu with openwork patterns – compare TRICOT [*Raschel (machine)*, a kind of loom, fr G *Raschelmaschine*, fr *Rachel* (Elisa Félix) †1858 F actress]

rase /rayz/ *vt* to raze

[1]rash /rash/ *adj* acting with, characterized by, or proceeding from undue haste or impetuosity [ME (northern) *rasch* quick; akin to OHG *rasc* fast] – **rashly** *adv*, **rashness** *n*

[2]rash *n* **1** an outbreak of spots on the body **2** a large number of instances of a specified thing during a short period ⟨*a* ~ *of arrests*⟩ [obs F *rache* scurf, fr OF *rasche*, fr (assumed) VL *rasica*, fr *rasicare* to scratch, fr L *rasus*, pp of *radere* to scrape]

rasher /ˈrashə/ *n* a thin slice of bacon or ham ☞ MEAT [perh fr obs *rash* (to cut), fr ME *rashen*]

[1]rasp /rahsp/ *vt* **1** to rub with sthg rough; *specif* to abrade with a rasp **2** to grate upon; irritate **3** to utter in a grating tone ~ *vi* to produce a grating sound [ME *raspen*, fr (assumed) MF *rasper*, of Gmc origin; akin to OHG *raspōn* to scrape together] – **rasper** *n*, **raspingly** *adv*

[2]rasp *n* a coarse file with rows of cutting teeth

raspberry /ˈrahzb(ə)ri/ *n* **1** (a widely grown shrub that bears) any of various usu red edible berries **2** a rude sound made by sticking the tongue out and blowing noisily – slang [E dial. *rasp* (raspberry) + E *berry*; (2) rhyming slang *raspberry (tart)* fart]

Rasta /ˈrastə/ *n or adj* (a) Rastafarian

Rastafarian /ˌrastəˈfeəri·ən/ *n or adj* (an adherent) of a puritanical religious and political movement among black W Indians which believes the former Emperor of Ethiopia, Haile Selassie, to be God, and looks for the redemption of the black race and the establishment of a homeland in Ethiopia [*Ras Tafari*, Haile Selassie †1974 Emperor of Ethiopia] – **Rastafarianism** *n*

Rastaman /ˈrastəˌman/ *n* a Rastafarian

raster /ˈrastə/ *n* a pattern of parallel lines whose intensity is controlled to form an image on a television screen [G, fr L *raster, rastrum* rake, fr *radere* to scrape]

[1]rat /rat/ *n* **1** any of numerous rodents that are considerably larger than the related mice **2a** a contemptible or wretched person; *specif* one who betrays or deserts his party, friends, or associates **b** a blackleg ***USE*** (*2*) infml [ME, fr OE *ræt*; akin to OHG *ratta* rat, L *rodere* to gnaw, *radere* to scrape, shave] – **ratlike** *adj*

[2]rat *vi* **-tt-** **1** to betray, desert, or inform on one's associates – usu + *on* **2** to catch or hunt rats **3** to work as a blackleg

rata /ˈrahtə/ *n* either of 2 New Zealand trees of the myrtle family that bear bright red flowers and yield a hard dark red wood [Maori]

ratable /ˈraytəbl/ *adj* rateable – **ratably** *adv*

ratafia /ˌratəˈfiə/ *n* a small sweet almond-flavoured biscuit or cake – compare MACAROON [F, liqueur flavoured with almonds]

ratal /ˈraytl/ *n* the amount on which rates are assessed

rataplan /ˌratəˈplan, ˈ--,-/ *n* the sound of drumming [F, of imit origin]

rat-a-tat /ˌrat ə ˈtat/, **rat-a-tat-tat** /ˌrat ə tat ˈtat/ *n* a sharp repeated knocking or tapping sound [imit]

ratatouille /ˌratəˈtooh·i (*Fr* ratatuːj)/ *n* a dish containing vegetables (e g tomatoes, aubergines, etc) stewed slowly in a vegetable stock until most of the liquid has evaporated [F, fr *touiller* to stir, fr L *tudiculare*, fr *tudes* hammer]

ratbag /ˈratˌbag/ *n* an unpleasant or disagreeable person – slang

ratchet /ˈrachit/ *n* **1** a mechanism that consists of a bar or wheel having inclined teeth into which a pawl drops so that motion is allowed in 1 direction only **2** *also* **ratchet wheel** a toothed wheel held in position or turned by a pawl [alter. of earlier *rochet*, fr F, alter. of MF *rocquet* lance head, of Gmc origin; akin to OHG *rocko* distaff, ON *rokkr* distaff, OHG *roc* coat]

[1]rate /rayt/ *vt, archaic* to scold angrily [ME *raten*]

[2]rate *n* **1** valuation ⟨*appraised him at a low* ~⟩ **2a** a fixed ratio between 2 things **b** a charge, payment, or price fixed according to a ratio, scale, or standard ⟨~ *of exchange*⟩ ⟨~ *of interest*⟩ **c** *Br* a tax levied by a local authority – usu pl with sing. meaning **3** a quantity, amount, or degree of sthg measured per unit of sthg else [ME, fr MF, fr ML *rata*, fr L (*pro*) *rata (parte)* according to a fixed proportion] – **at any rate** in any case; anyway

[3]rate *vt* **1** to consider to be; value as ⟨*was* ~d *an excellent pianist*⟩ **2** to determine or assign the relative rank or class of **3** to assign a rate to **4** to be worthy of; deserve ⟨*now* ~s *his own show*⟩ **5** to think highly of; consider to be good – infml ⟨*doesn't* ~ *Spurs' chances of avoiding relegation*⟩ ~ *vi* to be estimated at a specified level ⟨~s *as the best show ever staged in London*⟩

-rate /-rayt/ *comb form* of the specified level of quality ⟨*fifth*-rate⟩

rateable, ratable /ˈraytəbl/ *adj* capable of or susceptible to being rated, estimated, or apportioned

rateable value *n* the estimated value of a property on which annual rate payments are calculated

rate-capping *n, Br* restriction by central government legislation of the level of rates which a local authority can levy

ratel /ˈraytl, -tel/ *n* an African or Asiatic nocturnal flesh-eating mammal resembling the badger [Afrik, lit., rattle, fr MD – more at RATTLE]

ratepayer /ˈraytˌpayə/ *n* a taxpayer; *also, Br* a person liable to pay rates

rath /rahth/ *n* a usu circular earthwork serving as the stronghold or residence of an ancient Irish chieftain [IrGael *rāth*]

rather /ˈrahdhə/ *adv or adj* **1** more readily or willingly; sooner ⟨*left* ~ *than cause trouble*⟩ ⟨*I'd* ~ *not go*⟩ – often used interjectionally, esp by British speakers, to express enthusiastic affirmation ⟨*"will you come?"* "Rather!"⟩ **2** more properly, reasonably, or truly ⟨*my father, or* ~ *my stepfather*⟩ **3** to some degree; somewhat ⟨*it's* ~ *warm*⟩ ⟨~ *too big*⟩ ⟨*I* ~ *thought so*⟩; esp somewhat excessively ⟨*it's* ~ *far for* me⟩ **4** on the contrary ⟨*was nothing bettered, but ~ grew worse* – Mk 5:26 (AV)⟩ [ME, fr OE *hrathor*, compar of *hrathe* quickly; akin to OHG *rado* quickly, OE *hræd* quick]

ratify /'ratifie/ *vt* to approve or confirm formally [ME *ratifien*, fr MF *ratifier*, fr ML *ratificare*, fr L *ratus* determined, fr pp of *reri* to think, calculate – more at REASON] – **ratification** /-fi'kaysh(ə)n/ *n*

rating /'rayting/ *n* **1** a classification according to grade **2** relative estimate or evaluation **3** *pl* any of various indexes which list television programmes, new records, etc in order of popularity – usu + *the* **4** *chiefly Br* ORDINARY SEAMAN ☞ RANK

ratio /'rayshioh/ *n, pl* **ratios** **1** the indicated division of one mathematical expression by another **2** the relationship in quantity, number, or degree between things or between one thing and another thing [L, computation, reason – more at REASON]

ratiocinate /,rati'osinayt/ *vi* to reason logically or formally – fml [L *ratiocinatus*, pp of *ratiocinari* to reckon, fr *ratio*] – **ratiocinator** *n*, **ratiocinative** /-nətiv/ *adj*, **ratiocination** /-'naysh(ə)n/ *n*

[1]**ration** /'rash(ə)n/ *n* a share or amount (e g of food) which one permits oneself or which one is permitted ⟨*the petrol ~*⟩ [F, fr L *ration-, ratio* computation, reason]

[2]**ration** *vt* **1** to distribute or divide (e g commodities in short supply) in fixed quantities – often + *out* **2a** to limit (a person or commodity) to a fixed ration ⟨*sugar was strictly ~ed*⟩ **b** to use sparingly

[1]**rational** /'rash(ə)nl/ *adj* **1** having, based on, or compatible with reason; reasonable ⟨*~ behaviour*⟩ **2** of, involving, or being (a mathematical expression containing) 1 or more rational numbers [ME *racional*, fr L *rationalis*, fr *ration-, ratio*] – **rationally** *adv*, **rationalness, rationality** /,rashə'naləti/ *n*

[2]**rational** *n* sthg rational; *specif* RATIONAL NUMBER

rationale /,rashə'nahl/ *n* **1** an explanation of controlling principles of opinion, belief, practice, or phenomena **2** an underlying reason; basis [L, neut of *rationalis*]

rationalism /'rash(ə)nə,liz(ə)m/ *n* **1** reliance on reason for the establishment of religious truth **2** a theory that reason is a source of knowledge superior to and independent of sense perception – **rationalist** *n*, **rationalist, rationalistic** /-'listik/ *adj*, **rationalistically** *adv*

rational·ize, -ise /'rash(ə)nəliez/ *vt* **1** to free (a mathematical expression) from irrational parts ⟨*~ a denominator*⟩ **2** to bring into accord with reason or cause to seem reasonable; *specif* to attribute (e g one's actions) to rational and creditable motives without analysis of true, esp unconscious, motives in order to provide plausible but untrue reasons for conduct **3** to increase the efficiency of (e g an industry) by more effective organization *~ vi* to provide plausible but untrue reasons for one's actions, opinions, etc – **rationalizer** *n*, **rationalization** /-'zay sh(ə)n/ *n*

,rational 'number *n* a number (e g 2, $^{5}/_{2}$, - ½) that can be expressed as the result of dividing one integer by another – compare [2]IRRATIONAL, SURD ☞ NUMBER

ratite /'ratiet/ *n or adj* (a bird, esp an ostrich, emu, moa, or kiwi) having a flat breastbone [adj deriv of L *ratitus* marked with the figure of a raft, fr *ratis* raft; n fr adj]

rat kangaroo *n* any of various small ratlike kangaroos

ratline /'ratlin/ *n* any of the short transverse ropes attached to the shrouds of a ship to form rungs ☞ SHIP [origin unknown]

[1]**ratoon** /ra'toohn/ *n* a new shoot that develops from the root of the sugarcane or other perennial plant after cropping [Sp *retoño*, fr *retoñar* to sprout, fr *re-* (fr L) + *otoñar* to grow in autumn, fr *otoño* autumn, fr L *autumnus*]

[2]**ratoon** *vi* to sprout from the root

'rat ,race *n* a fiercely competitive and wearisome activity; *specif* the struggle to maintain one's position in a career or survive the pressures of modern urban life

ratsbane /'rats,bayn/ *n, archaic* sthg poisonous to rats

rattan /rə'tan/ *n* **1** a climbing palm with very long tough stems **2** a part of the stem of a rattan used esp for walking sticks and wickerwork [Malay *rotan*]

[1]**rattle** /'ratl/ *vb* **rattling** /'ratling, 'ratl·ing/ *vi* **1** to make a rapid succession of short sharp sounds **2** to chatter incessantly and aimlessly – often + *on* **3** to move with a clatter or rattle *~ vt* **1** to say or perform in a brisk lively fashion – often + *off* ⟨*~d off a long list of examples*⟩ **2** to cause to make a rattling sound **3** to upset to the point of loss of poise and composure ⟨*he looked severely ~d*⟩ – infml [ME *ratelen*; akin to MD *ratel* rattle, OE *hratian* to rush – more at CARDINAL]

[2]**rattle** *n* **1** a rattling sound **2a** a child's toy consisting of loose pellets in a hollow container that rattles when shaken **b** a device that consists of a springy tongue in contact with a revolving ratchet wheel which is rotated or shaken to produce a loud noise **3** the sound-producing organ on a rattlesnake's tail **4** a throat noise caused by air passing through mucus and heard esp at the approach of death

rattler /'ratlə/ *n, chiefly NAm* a rattlesnake [[1]RATTLE + [2]-ER]

'rattle,snake /-,snayk/ *n* any of various American poisonous snakes with horny interlocking joints at the end of the tail that rattle when shaken

[1]**rattling** /'ratling/ *adj* lively, brisk ⟨*moved at a ~ pace*⟩ – not now in vogue – **rattlingly** *adv*

[2]**rattling** *adv* to an extreme degree; very – chiefly in *rattling good*; infml

ratty /'rati/ *adj* irritable – infml [[1]RAT + [1]-Y]

raucous /'rawkəs/ *adj* disagreeably harsh or strident; noisy [L *raucus* hoarse; akin to OE *rēon* to lament – more at RUMOUR] – **raucously** *adv*, **raucousness** *n*

raunchy /'rawnchi/ *adj* earthy, gutsy ⟨*a group with a confident ~ sound*⟩ – infml [origin unknown] – **raunchily** *adv*, **raunchiness** *n*

[1]**ravage** /'ravij/ *n* damage resulting from ravaging – usu pl with sing. meaning ⟨*the ~s of time*⟩ [F, fr MF, fr *ravir* to ravish – more at RAVISH]

[2]**ravage** *vb* to wreak havoc (on); cause (violent) destruction (to) – **ravagement** *n*, **ravager** *n*

[1]**rave** /rayv/ *vi* **1** to talk irrationally (as if) in delirium; *broadly* to rage, storm **2** to talk with extreme or passionate enthusiasm ⟨*~d about her beauty*⟩ [ME *raven*]

[2]**rave** *n* **1** a raving **2** an extravagantly favourable review ⟨*the play opened to ~ notices*⟩ **3** a wild exciting period, experience, or event – slang ⟨*the party was a real ~*⟩

[1]**ravel** /'ravl/ *vb* **-ll-** (*NAm* **-l-, -ll-**), /'ravling, 'ravl-·ing/ *vt* **1** to unravel, disentangle – usu + *out* **2** to entangle, confuse ~ *vi* to fray [D *rafelen*, fr *rafel* loose thread; akin to OE *ræfter* rafter]

[2]**ravel** *n* **1** a tangle or tangled mass **2** a loose thread

ravelin /'rav(ə)lin/ *n* a (detached) triangular temporary fortification, usu situated between 2 bastions [MF, fr OIt *ravellino*, alter. of *rivellino*, dim. of *riva* bank, fr L *ripa*]

[1]**raven** /'rayv(ə)n/ *n* a very large glossy black bird of the crow family [ME, fr OE *hræfn*; akin to OHG *hraban* raven, L *corvus*, Gk *korax*, L *crepare* to rattle, crack]

[2]**raven** *adj* glossy black ⟨~ *hair*⟩

[3]**raven** /'rav(ə)n/ *vt* **1** to devour greedily **2** to despoil ⟨*men* ~ *the earth, destroying its resources – New Yorker*⟩ ~ *vi* **1** to (seek after) prey **2** to plunder [MF *raviner* to rush, take by force, fr *ravine* rapine] – **ravener** /'rav(ə)nə/ *n*

ravenous /'rav(ə)nəs/ *adj* **1** urgently seeking satisfaction, gratification, etc; grasping, insatiable **2** fiercely eager for food; famished – **ravenously** *adv*, **ravenousness** *n*

raver /'rayvə/ *n, chiefly Br* an energetic and uninhibited person who enjoys a hectic social life; *also* a sexually uninhibited or promiscuous person – slang [[1]RAVE + [2]-ER]

'**rave-,up** *n, chiefly Br* a wild party – slang

ravine /rə'veen/ *n* a narrow steep-sided valley smaller than a canyon and usu worn by running water [F, fr MF, rapine, rush, fr L *rapina* rapine]

[1]**raving** /'rayving/ *n* irrational, incoherent, wild, or extravagant utterance or declamation – usu pl with sing. meaning

[2]**raving** *adj* extreme, marked ⟨*a* ~ *beauty*⟩ – infml

ravioli /,ravi'ohli/ *n* little cases of pasta containing meat, cheese, etc [It, fr It dial., pl of *raviolo*, lit., little turnip, dim. of *rava* turnip, fr L *rapa* – more at [1]RAPE]

ravish /'ravish/ *vt* **1** to overcome with joy, delight, etc ⟨~ed *by the beauty of the scene*⟩ **2** to rape, violate [ME *ravisshen*, fr MF *raviss-*, stem of *ravir*, fr (assumed) VL *rapire*, alter. of L *rapere* to seize – more at RAPID] – **ravisher** *n*, **ravishment** *n*

ravishing /'ravishing/ *adj* unusually attractive or pleasing – **ravishingly** *adv*

[1]**raw** /raw/ *adj* **1** not cooked **2a(1)** not processed or purified; in the natural state ⟨~ *fibres*⟩ ⟨~ *sewage*⟩ **(2)** not diluted or blended ⟨~ *spirits*⟩ **b** not in a polished, finished, or processed form ⟨~ *data*⟩ ⟨*hem this* ~ *edge to stop it fraying*⟩ **3** having the surface abraded or chafed ⟨~ *skin*⟩ **4** lacking experience, training, etc; new ⟨*a* ~ *recruit*⟩ **5** disagreeably damp or cold [ME, fr OE *hrēaw*; akin to OHG *hrō* raw, L *crudus* raw, *cruor* blood, Gk *kreas* flesh] – **rawly** *adv*, **rawness** *n*

[2]**raw** *n* a sensitive place or state ⟨*touched her on the* ~⟩ – **in the raw** **1** in the natural or crude state ⟨*life* in the raw⟩ **2** naked ⟨*slept* in the raw⟩

,**raw'boned** /-'bohnd/ *adj* having a heavy or clumsy frame that seems inadequately covered with flesh

,**raw 'deal** *n* an instance of unfair treatment

'**raw,hide** /-,hied/ *n* (a whip of) untanned hide

,**raw ma'terial** *n* material that can be converted by manufacture, treatment, etc into a new and useful product

,**raw 'umber** *n* (the dark yellowish brown colour of) umber that has not been calcined – compare BURNT UMBER

[1]**ray** /ray/ *n* any of numerous fishes having the eyes on the upper surface of a flattened body and a long narrow tail [ME *raye*, fr MF *raie*, fr L *raia*]

[2]**ray** *n* **1a** any of the lines of light that appear to radiate from a bright object **b** a narrow beam of radiant energy (e g light or X rays) **c** a stream of (radioactive) particles travelling in the same line – compare ALPHA RAY, BETA RAY, COSMIC RAY **2a** a thin line suggesting a ray **b** any of a group of lines diverging from a common centre **3a** any of the bony rods that support the fin of a fish **b** any of the radiating parts of the body of a radially symmetrical animal (e g a starfish) **4** RAY FLOWER **5** a slight manifestation or trace (e g of intelligence or hope) [ME, fr MF *rai*, fr L *radius* rod, ray] – **rayed** *adj*, **rayless** *adj*

[3]**ray** *vi* **1** to shine (as if) in rays **2** to radiate from a centre ~ *vt* to emit in rays; radiate

'**ray ,flower** *n* any of the strap-shaped florets forming **a** the outer ring of the head of a composite plant (e g an aster or daisy) having central disc florets **b** the entire flower head of a composite plant (e g a dandelion) lacking disc florets

rayon /'rayon, -ən/ *n* (a fabric made from) a yarn or fibre produced by forcing and drawing cellulose through minute holes [irreg fr [2]*ray*]

raze, rase /rayz/ *vt* to destroy or erase completely; *specif* to lay (e g a town or building) level with the ground [ME *rasen*, fr MF *raser*, fr (assumed) VL *rasare*, fr L *rasus*, pp of *radere* to scrape, shave]

razor /'rayzə/ *n* a sharp-edged cutting implement for shaving or cutting (facial) hair [ME *rasour*, fr OF *raseor*, fr *raser*] – **razor** *vt*

,**razor-'backed, 'razor,back** *adj* having a sharp narrow back ⟨*a* ~ *whale*⟩

'**razor,bill** /-,bil/ *n* a N Atlantic auk with a flattened sharp-edged bill

'**razor-,shell** *n* any of numerous marine bivalve molluscs having a long narrow curved thin shell

razz /raz/ *vt, NAm* to heckle, deride ⟨*the fans* ~ed *the visiting players*⟩ – infml [short for *razzberry* (sound of contempt), alter. of *raspberry*]

razzle /'razl/ *n, chiefly Br* a spree, binge – usu in *on the razzle*; slang [short for *razzle-dazzle*]

razzle-dazzle /,--'--, '--,--/ *n* razzmatazz – infml [irreg redupl of *dazzle*]

razzmatazz /'razmə,taz, ,--'-/ *n* noisy, colourful, and often gaudily showy atmosphere or activity ⟨*the* ~ *of professional sport*⟩ – infml [prob alter. of *razzle-dazzle*]

[1]**re** /ray, ree/ *n* the 2nd note of the diatonic scale in solmization [ML – more at GAMUT]

[2]**re** /ree/ *prep* WITH REGARD TO; concerning [L, abl of *res* thing – more at [1]REAL]

re- *prefix* **1a** again; anew ⟨*re*born⟩ ⟨*re*print⟩ **b(1)** again in a new, altered, or improved way ⟨*re*hash⟩ ⟨*re*write⟩ ⟨*re*house⟩ **(2)** repeated, new, or improved version of ⟨*re*tread⟩ ⟨*re*broadcast⟩ ⟨*re*make⟩ **2** back; backwards ⟨*re*call⟩ ⟨*re*tract⟩ [ME, fr OF, fr L *re-*, *red-* back, again, against]

'**re** /ə/ *vb* are ⟨*you*'re *right*⟩

[1]**reach** /reech/ *vt* **1** to stretch out ⟨~ *out your hand to her*⟩ **2a** to touch or grasp by extending a part of the body (e g a hand) or an object ⟨*couldn't* ~ *the apple*⟩ **b** to pick up and draw towards one; pass ⟨~ *me my hat, will you?*⟩ **c(1)** to extend to ⟨*the shadow*

~ed *the wall*⟩ **(2)** to get up to or as far as; arrive at ⟨*took 2 days to ~ the mountains*⟩ ⟨*they hoped to ~ an agreement*⟩ **d** to contact or communicate with ⟨~ed *her by phone at the office*⟩ ~*vi* **1a** to make a stretch (as if) with one's hand ⟨~ed *towards the book on the top shelf*⟩ **b** to strain after sthg ⟨~ing *for the unattainable*⟩ **2a** to project, extend ⟨*her land* ~es *to the river*⟩ **b** to arrive at or come to sthg ⟨*as far as the eye could* ~⟩ **3** to sail on a reach [ME *rechen*, fr OE *rǣcan*; akin to OHG *reichen* to reach, Lith *raižytis* to stretch oneself repeatedly] – **reachable** *adj*

[2]**reach** *n* **1a** the action or an act of reaching **b** the distance or extent of reaching or of ability to reach **c** a range; *specif* comprehension ⟨*an idea well beyond his* ~⟩ **2** a continuous stretch or expanse; *esp* a straight uninterrupted portion of a river or canal **3** the tack sailed by a vessel with the wind blowing more or less from the side **4** *pl* groups or levels in a usu specified activity or occupation; echelons ⟨*the higher* ~es *of academic life*⟩

'reach-me-,down *n or adj, chiefly Br* (sthg) passed on from another ⟨~ *clothes*⟩ – infml

react /ri'akt/ *vi* **1** to exert a reciprocal or counteracting force or influence – often + *on* or *upon* **2** to respond to a stimulus **3** to act in opposition to a force or influence – usu + *against* **4** to undergo chemical reaction ~*vt* to cause to react chemically [NL *reactus*, pp of *reagere*, fr L *re-* + *agere* to act – more at AGENT]

reactance /ri'akt(ə)ns/ *n* the part of the impedance of an alternating-current circuit that is due to capacitance and/or inductance and that is expressed in ohms

reactant /ri'akt(ə)nt/ *n* a substance that reacts chemically with another

reaction /ri'aksh(ə)n/ *n* **1a** a reacting **b** tendency towards a former and usu outmoded (political or social) order or policy **2** bodily response to or activity aroused by a stimulus: e g **a** the response of tissues to a foreign substance (e g an antigen or infective agent) **b** a mental or emotional response to circumstances **3** the force that sthg subjected to the action of a force exerts equally in the opposite direction **4a** a chemical transformation or change; an action between atoms, molecules, etc to form 1 or more new substances **b** a process involving change in atomic nuclei resulting from interaction with a particle or another nucleus

reactionary /ri'akshən(ə)ri/ *also* **reactionist** *n or adj* (a person) opposing radical social change or favouring a return to a former (political) order

re'action ,engine *n* an engine (e g a jet engine) that develops thrust by expelling a jet of fluid or a stream of particles

reactivate /ri'aktivayt/ *vb* to make or become active again – **reactivation** /-'vaysh(ə)n/ *n*

reactive /ri'aktiv/ *adj* **1** of or marked by reaction or reactance **2** tending to or liable to react ⟨*highly ~ chemicals*⟩ – **reactively** *adv*, **reactiveness, reactivity** /-'tivəti/ *n*

reactor /ri'aktə/ *n* **1** a vat for an industrial chemical reaction **2** an apparatus in which a chain reaction of fissile material (e g uranium or plutonium) is started and controlled, esp for the production of nuclear power or elementary particles ☞ ENERGY [REACT + [1]-OR]

[1]**read** /reed/ *vb* **read** /red/ *vt* **1a(1)** to look at or otherwise sense (e g letters, symbols, or words) with mental assimilation of the communication represented ⟨*can't ~ his handwriting*⟩ ⟨*to ~ a book*⟩ ⟨*~ music*⟩ ⟨*~ braille*⟩ **(2)** to look at, interpret, and understand (signs, communicative movements, etc) ⟨*~ lips*⟩ ⟨*~ semaphore*⟩ **(3)** to utter aloud (interpretatively) the printed or written words of ⟨*~ them a story*⟩ – often + *out* **b** to learn or get to know by reading ⟨*~ that he had died*⟩ **c(1)** to study (a subject), esp for a degree ⟨*~ law*⟩ **(2)** to read (the) works of (an author or type of literature) ⟨~s *science fiction mainly*⟩ **d** to receive and understand (a message) by radio **2a** to understand, comprehend ⟨*can ~ you like a book*⟩ ⟨*~ his thoughts*⟩ **b** to interpret the meaning or significance of ⟨~s *dreams*⟩ ⟨*can ~ the situation in 2 ways*⟩ **c** to interpret the action of or in so as to anticipate what will happen or what needs doing ⟨*in football the sweeper must be able to ~ the game*⟩ **d** to attribute (a meaning) to sthg read or considered ⟨*~ a nonexistent meaning into her words*⟩ **3** to use as a substitute for or in preference to another written or printed word, character, etc ⟨~ hurry *for* harry⟩ **4** to indicate ⟨*the thermometer* ~s *zero*⟩ **5a** to sense the meaning of (information stored or recorded on punched cards, in a computer memory, etc) **b** *esp of a computer* to take (information) from storage ~*vi* **1a** to perform the act of reading; read sthg **b(1)** to learn about sthg by reading – usu + *up* ⟨~ing *up on astronomy*⟩ **(2)** to study a subject in order to qualify *for* ⟨*to ~ for the Bar*⟩ **2** to yield a (particular) meaning or impression when read ⟨*Hebrew* ~s *from right to left*⟩ ⟨*the poem* ~s *rather badly*⟩ [ME *reden* to advise, interpret, read, fr OE *rǣdan*; akin to OHG *rātan* to advise, Gk *arariskein* to fit – more at [1]ARM]

[2]**read** /reed/ *n* **1** sthg to read with reference to the interest, enjoyment, etc it provides ⟨*the book is a terrific* ~⟩ **2** *chiefly Br* a period of reading ⟨*had a ~ and went to bed early*⟩

[3]**read** /red/ *adj* instructed by or informed through reading ⟨*well*-read⟩ ⟨*widely ~ in contemporary literature*⟩

readable /'reedəbl/ *adj* **1** legible **2** pleasurable or interesting to read – **readably** *adv*, **readability** /-'biləti/, **readableness** *n*

reader /'reedə/ *n* **1a** one appointed to read to others; *esp* LAY READER **b(1)** one who reads and corrects proofs **(2)** one who evaluates manuscripts **2** a member of a British university staff between the ranks of lecturer and professor **3** a device that reads or displays coded information on a tape, microfilm, punched cards, etc **4** a usu instructive (introductory) book or anthology [[1]READ + [2]-ER]

readership /'reedə,ship/ *n* **1** the office, duties, or position of a (university) reader **2** *sing or pl in constr* a collective body of readers; *esp* the readers of a particular publication or author [READER + -SHIP]

readily /'redəli/ *adv* **1** without hesitating ⟨*he ~ accepted advice*⟩ **2** without much difficulty ⟨*for reasons that anyone could ~ understand*⟩ [[1]READY + [2]-LY]

reading /'reeding/ *n* **1a** material read or for reading ⟨*his biography makes fine* ~⟩ **b** the extent to which a person has read ⟨*a man of wide* ~⟩ **c** an event at which a play, poetry, etc is read to an audience **d** an act of formally reading a bill that constitutes any of 3 successive stages of approval by a legislature, specif Parliament ☞ LAW **2a** a form or version of a particular (passage in a) text ⟨*the generally accepted* ~⟩ **b** the value indicated or data produced by an instrument ⟨*examined the thermometer* ~⟩ **3a** a particular interpretation ⟨*what is your* ~ *of the situation?*⟩ **b** a particular performance of sthg (e g a musical work)

'reading ,desk *n* a desk designed to support a book in a convenient position for a (standing) reader

'reading ,room *n* a room in a library, club, etc with facilities for reading or study

'read,out /-,owt/ *n* (a device used for) the removal of information from storage (e g in a computer memory or on magnetic tape) for display in an understandable form (e g as a printout); *also* the information displayed

¹ready /'redi/ *adj* **1a** prepared mentally or physically for some experience or action **b** prepared or available for immediate use ⟨*dinner is* ~⟩ ⟨*had little* ~ *cash*⟩ **2a(1)** willingly disposed ⟨~ *to agree to his proposal*⟩ **(2)** likely or about to do the specified thing ⟨~ *to cry with vexation*⟩ **b** spontaneously prompt ⟨*always has a* ~ *answer*⟩ ⟨*a* ~ *wit*⟩ **c** (presumptuously) eager ⟨*he is very* ~ *with his criticism*⟩ ⟨~ *acceptance*⟩ [ME *redy*; akin to OHG *reiti* ready, Goth *garaiths* arrayed, Gk *arariskein* to fit – more at ¹ARM] – **readiness** *n*

²ready *vt* to make ready

³ready *n* (ready) money – sometimes pl with sing. meaning; infml – **at/to the ready 1** *of a gun* prepared and in the position for immediate aiming and firing **2** ¹READY 1b

⁴ready *adv* in advance ⟨*food that is bought* ~ *cooked*⟩

,ready-'made *adj* **1** made beforehand, esp for general sale or use rather than to individual specifications ⟨~ *suits*⟩ **2** lacking originality or individuality ⟨~ *opinions*⟩ **3** readily available ⟨*her illness provided a* ~ *excuse*⟩

,ready 'reckoner *n, Br* an arithmetical table (e g a list of numbers multiplied by a fixed per cent) or set of tables for aid in calculating

,ready-to-'wear *adj, of a garment* off-the-peg

reafforest /,ree·ə'forəst/ *vt, chiefly Br* to renew the forest cover of by seeding or planting – **reafforestation** /-'staysh(ə)n/ *n*

reagent /ri'ayj(ə)nt/ *n* a substance that takes part in or brings about a particular chemical reaction, used esp to detect sthg [NL *reagent-*, *reagens*, prp of *reagere* to react – more at REACT]

¹real /reel, riəl/ *adj* **1** of or being fixed or immovable property (e g land or buildings) **2a** not artificial, fraudulent, illusory, fictional, etc; *also* being precisely what the name implies; genuine **b** of practical or everyday concerns or activities ⟨*left university to live in the* ~ *world*⟩ **c** belonging to or concerned with the set of real numbers ⟨*the* ~ *roots of an equation*⟩ **d** formed by light rays converging at a point ⟨*a* ~ *image*⟩ – compare VIRTUAL 2 **e** measured by purchasing power rather than the paper value of money ⟨~ *income*⟩ **f** complete, great – used chiefly for emphasis ⟨*a* ~ *surprise*⟩ [ME, real, relating to things (in law), fr MF, fr ML & LL; ML *realis* relating to things (in law), fr LL, real, fr L *res* thing, fact; akin to Skt *rai* property] – **realness** *n*

²real *n* – **for real** in earnest; seriously ⟨*they were fighting* for real⟩

³real *adv, chiefly NAm & Scot* very

⁴real /ray'ahl/ *n, pl* **reals, reales** /-lays/ (a coin representing) a former money unit of Spain and Spanish colonies [Sp, fr *real* royal, fr L *regalis* – more at ROYAL]

'real e,state *n* property in buildings and land

realgar /ri'algə/ *n* an orange-red mineral consisting of arsenic sulphide [ME, fr ML, fr Catal, fr Ar *rahj al-ghār* powder of the mine]

realign /,ree·ə'lien/ *vt* to reorganize or make new groupings of [RE- + ALIGN] – **realignment** *n*

realism /'ree,liz(ə)m, 'riə-/ *n* **1** concern for fact or reality and rejection of the impractical and visionary **2** the belief that objects of sense perception have real existence independent of the mind **3** fidelity in art, literature, etc to nature and to accurate representation without idealization – **realist** *adj or n*, **realistic** /-'listik/ *adj*, **realistically** *adv*

reality /ri'aləti/ *n* **1** being real **2a** a real event, entity, or state of affairs ⟨*his dream became a* ~⟩ **b** the totality of real things and events ⟨*trying to escape from* ~⟩ – **in reality** AS A MATTER OF FACT

real·ize, -ise /'reeliez, 'riə-/ *vt* **1a** to convert into actual fact; accomplish ⟨*finally* ~d *his goal*⟩ **b** to cause to seem real ⟨*a book in which the characters are carefully* ~d⟩ **2a** to convert into actual money ⟨~ *his assets*⟩ **b** to bring or get by sale, investment, or effort ⟨*the painting will* ~ *several thousand pounds*⟩ **3** to be fully aware of ⟨*she did not* ~ *the risk he was taking*⟩ **4** to play or write (music) in full (e g from a figured bass) [F *réaliser*, fr MF *realiser*, fr *real* real] – **realizable** *adj*, **realization** /-'zaysh(ə)n/ *n*

really /'reeli, 'riəli/ *adv* **1a** in reality, actually ⟨*did he* ~ *say that?*⟩ ⟨*not very difficult* ~⟩ **b** without question; thoroughly ⟨~ *cold weather*⟩ ⟨~ *hates him*⟩ **2** more correctly – used to give force to an injunction ⟨*you should* ~ *have asked me first*⟩ **3** – expressing surprise or indignation ⟨*'she wants to marry him.'* 'Really?'⟩ ⟨~, *you're being ridiculous*⟩

realm /relm/ *n* **1** a kingdom **2** a sphere, domain – often pl with sing. meaning ⟨*within the* ~s *of possibility*⟩ [ME *realme*, fr OF, modif of L *regimen* rule – more at REGIMEN]

,real 'number *n* a number (e g a square root of a positive number, an integer, or pi) that does not include a part that is a multiple of the square root of minus one – compare COMPLEX NUMBER

realpolitik /ray'ahlpoliteek, ray'al-/ *n* politics based on practical factors rather than on moral objectives [G, fr *real* practical + *politik* politics]

,real 'presence *n, often cap R&P* the doctrine that Christ's body and blood are actually present in the Eucharist – compare TRANSUBSTANTIATION

,real 'tennis *n* a game played with a racket and ball in an irregularly-shaped indoor court divided by a net

,real-'time *adj* being or involving the almost instantaneous processing, presentation, or use of data by a computer

realtor /'reeltə, -taw, 'riəl-/ *n, NAm* a real estate agent, esp a member of the National Association of Real Estate Boards

realty /'reelti, 'riəl-/ *n* REAL ESTATE [*real* + *-ty* (as in *property*)]

¹ream /reem/ *n* **1** a quantity of paper equal to 20 quires or variously 480, 500, or 516 sheets **2** a great amount (e g of sthg written or printed) – usu pl with sing. meaning ⟨*composed* ~s *of poetry*⟩ [ME *reme*, fr MF *raime*, fr Ar *rizmah*, lit., bundle]

[2]**ream** *vt* **1** to enlarge or widen (a hole) with a reamer **2** *NAm* to press the juice from (a citrus fruit) [perh fr (assumed) ME dial. *remen* to open up, fr OE dial. *rēman*; akin to OE *rȳman* to open up, *rūm* room – more at ROOM]

reamer /'reemə/ *n* **1** a rotating finishing tool with cutting edges used to enlarge or shape a hole **2** *NAm* LEMON SQUEEZER [[2]REAM + [2]-ER]

reap /reep/ *vt* **1a** to cut (a crop) with a sickle, scythe, or reaping machine; *also* to harvest thus **b** to clear (e g a field) of a crop by reaping **2** to obtain or win, esp as the reward for effort ⟨*to* ~ *lasting benefits from study*⟩ ~ *vi* to reap sthg [ME *repen*, fr OE *reopan*; akin to OE *rāw*, *rǣw* row – more at [3]ROW] – **reaper** *n*

[1]**rear** /riə/ *vt* **1** to build or construct **2** to raise upright **3a** to breed and tend (an animal) or grow (e g a crop) for use or sale **b** BRING UP 1 ~ *vi* **1** to rise to a height **2** *of a horse* to rise up on the hind legs [ME *reren*, fr OE *rǣran*; akin to ON *reisa* to raise, OE *rīsan* to rise] – **rearer** *n*

[2]**rear** *n* **1** the back part of sthg: e g **a** the part (e g of an army) away from the enemy **b** the part of sthg located opposite its front ⟨*the* ~ *of a house*⟩ **c** the buttocks **2** the space or position at the back ⟨*moved to the* ~⟩ [prob fr *rear-* (in such terms as *rear guard*)]

[3]**rear** *adj* at the back ⟨*a* ~ *window*⟩ – **rearmost** *adj*

,rear 'admiral *n* ☞ RANK

'rear,guard /-,gahd/ *adj* of vigorous resistance in the face of defeat ⟨*a* ~ *action*⟩

'rear ,guard *n* a military detachment for guarding the rear of a main body or force, esp during a retreat [ME *reregarde*, fr MF, fr OF, fr *rere* backward, behind (fr L *retro*) + *garde* guard – more at RETRO-]

rearm /,ree'ahm/ *vt* to arm (e g a nation or military force) again, esp with new or better weapons ~ *vi* to become armed again – **rearmament** /-məmənt/ *n*

,rearview 'mirror /-vyooh/ *n* a mirror (e g in a motor car) that gives a view of the area behind a vehicle

[1]**'rear,ward** /-,wood/ *n* the rear; *esp* the rear division (e g of an army) ⟨*to* ~ *of the main column*⟩ [ME *rerewarde*, fr AF; akin to OF *reregarde* rear guard]

[2]**'rearward** /-wood/ *adj* located at or directed towards the rear [[2]*rear* + *-ward*]

'rearwards /-woodz/ *also* **rearward** *adv* at or towards the rear; backwards

[1]**reason** /'reez(ə)n/ *n* **1a** (a statement offered as) an explanation or justification **b** a rational ground or motive ⟨*a good* ~ *to act soon*⟩ **c** that which makes some phenomenon intelligible; cause ⟨*wanted to know the* ~ *for earthquakes*⟩ **2a(1)** the power of comprehending, inferring, or thinking, esp in orderly rational ways; intelligence **(2)** proper exercise of the mind **b** sanity ⟨*lost his* ~⟩ [ME *resoun*, fr OF *raison*, fr L *ration-*, *ratio* reason, computation; akin to Goth *garathjan* to count, L *reri* to calculate, think, Gk *arariskein* to fit – more at [1]ARM] – **within reason** within reasonable limits – **with reason** with good cause

[2]**reason** *vi* **1** to use the faculty of reason so as to arrive at conclusions **2** to talk or argue *with* another so as to influence his/her actions or opinions ⟨*can't* ~ *with them*⟩ ~ *vt* **1** to persuade or influence by the use of reason ⟨~ed *myself out of such fears*⟩ **2** to formulate, assume, analyse, or conclude by the use of reason – often + *out* ⟨*to* ~ *out a plan*⟩ – **reasoner** *n*

reasonable /'reez(ə)nəbl/ *adj* **1a** in accord with reason ⟨*a* ~ *theory*⟩ **b** not extreme or excessive ⟨~ *requests*⟩ **c** moderate, fair ⟨*a* ~ *boss*⟩ ⟨~ *weather*⟩ **d** inexpensive **2a** having the faculty of reason; rational **b** sensible – **reasonableness** *n*, **reasonably** *adv*

reasoning /'reez(ə)ning/ *n* the drawing of inferences or conclusions through the use of reason

reassure /,ree·ə'shooə, -'shaw/ *vt* **1** to assure anew ⟨~d *him that the work was satisfactory*⟩ **2** to restore confidence to ⟨*I was* ~d *by his promise*⟩ – **reassurance** *n*, **reassuringly** *adv*

rebarbative /ri'bahbətiv/ *adj* repellent, unattractive – fml [F *rébarbatif*, fr MF, fr *rebarber* to be repellent, fr *re-* + *barbe* beard, fr L *barba* – more at BEARD]

[1]**rebate** /'reebayt/ *n* **1** a return of part of a payment ⟨*tax* ~⟩ **2** a deduction from a sum before payment; a discount ⟨*10%* ~⟩ [F *rabat*, fr MF *rabattre* to beat down again, reduce, fr OF, fr *re-* + *abattre* to beat down, fr *a-* (fr L *ad-*) + *battre* to beat, fr L *battuere* – more at BATTLE]

[2]**rebate** /'rabit, 'reebayt/ *vt or n* (to) rabbet [by alter.]

rebec, rebeck /'reebek/ *n* a medieval pear-shaped usu 3-stringed musical instrument played with a bow [MF *rebec*, alter. of OF *rebebe*, fr OProv *rebeb*, fr Ar *rebāb*]

[1]**rebel** /'rebl/ *adj* **1** in rebellion **2** of rebels ⟨*the* ~ *camp*⟩ [ME, fr OF *rebelle*, fr L *rebellis*, fr *re-* + *bellum* war, fr OL *duellum* – more at DUEL]

[2]**rebel** *n* one who rebels against a government, authority, convention, etc

[3]**rebel** /ri'bel/ *vi* **-ll- 1a** to oppose or disobey (one in) authority or control **b** to resist by force the authority of one's government **2a** to act in or show opposition ⟨~led *against the conventions of polite society*⟩ **b** to feel or exhibit anger or revulsion ⟨~led *at the injustice of life*⟩

rebellion /ri'belyən/ *n* **1** opposition to (one in) authority or dominance **2** (an instance of) open armed resistance to an established government

rebellious /ri'belyəs/ *adj* **1a** in rebellion ⟨~ *troops*⟩ **b** (characteristic) of or inclined towards rebellion ⟨*a* ~ *speech*⟩ ⟨*a* ~ *people*⟩ **2** REFRACTORY 1 – **rebelliously** *adv*, **rebelliousness** *n*

rebirth /,ree'buhth/ *n* **1a** a new or second birth **b** spiritual regeneration **2** a renaissance, revival ⟨*a* ~ *of nationalism*⟩

rebore /,ree'baw/ *vt* to enlarge and renew the bore of a cylinder in (an internal-combustion engine) – **rebore** /'-,-/ *n*

reborn /,ree'bawn/ *adj* born again; regenerated; *specif* spiritually renewed

[1]**rebound** /ri'bownd/ *vi* **1** to spring back (as if) on collision or impact with another body **2** to return with an adverse effect to a source or starting point ⟨*their hatred* ~ed *on themselves*⟩ [ME *rebounden*, fr MF *rebondir*, fr OF, fr *re-* + *bondir* to bound – more at [5]BOUND]

[2]**rebound** /'ree,bownd; *also* ri'bownd/ *n* **1a** a rebounding, recoil **b** a recovery ⟨*a sharp* ~ *in*

prices⟩ **2** a shot (e g in basketball or soccer) that rebounds **– on the rebound** (whilst) in an unsettled or emotional state resulting from setback, frustration, or crisis ⟨on the rebound *from an unhappy love affair*⟩

rebuff /ri'buf/ *vt or n* (to) snub [vb MF *rebuffer*, fr OIt *ribuffare* to reprimand; n fr vb]

rebuke /ri'byoohk/ *vt or n* (to) reprimand [vb ME *rebuken*, fr ONF *rebuker*; n fr vb]

rebus /'reebəs/ *n* (a riddle using) a representation of words or syllables by pictures that suggest the same sound [L, by things, abl pl of *res* thing – more at [1]REAL]

rebut /ri'but/ *vt* **-tt- 1** to drive back; repel **2** to disprove or expose the falsity of; refute [ME *rebuten*, fr OF *reboter*, fr *re-* + *boter* to butt – more at [1]BUTT] – **rebuttable** *adj*, **rebuttal** *n*

[1]**rebutter** /ri'butə/ *n* a defendant's answer to a plaintiff's surrejoinder [AF *rebuter*, fr OF *reboter* to rebut]

[2]**rebutter** *n* a refutation [REBUT + [2]-ER]

recalcitrant /ri'kalsitrənt/ *adj* **1** obstinately defiant of authority or restraint **2** difficult to handle or control [LL *recalcitrant-*, *recalcitrans*, prp of *recalcitrare* to be stubbornly disobedient, fr L, to kick back, fr *re-* + *calcitrare* to kick, fr *calc-*, *calx* heel] – **recalcitrance** *n*, **recalcitrant** *n*

[1]**recall** /ri'kawl/ *vt* **1a** to call or summon back ⟨~ed *their ambassador*⟩ **b** to bring back to mind ⟨~s *his early years*⟩ **2** to cancel, revoke – **recallable** *adj*

[2]**recall** /ri'kawl, 'ree,kawl/ *n* **1** a call or summons to return ⟨*a ~ of workers after a layoff*⟩ **2** remembrance of what has been learned or experienced ⟨*had almost perfect visual ~*⟩ **3** the act of revoking or the possibility of being revoked **4** the ability (e g of an information retrieval system) to retrieve stored material

recant /ri'kant/ *vt* to withdraw or repudiate (a statement or belief) formally and publicly; renounce ~ *vi* to make an open confession of error; *esp* to disavow a religious or political opinion or belief [L *recantare*, fr *re-* + *cantare* to sing – more at CHANT] – **recantation** /-'taysh(ə)n/ *n*

[1]**recap** /'ree,kap/ *vt* **-pp-** *NAm* to partially retread (a worn pneumatic tyre) [*re-* + [2]*cap*] – **recappable** /-'kapəbl/ *adj*

[2]**recap** /'ree,kap, ri'kap/ *vb* **-pp-** to recapitulate [by shortening] – **recap** /'-,-/ *n*

recapitulate /,reekə'pityoolayt/ *vb* to repeat the principal points or stages of (e g an argument or discourse) in summing up [LL *recapitulatus*, pp of *recapitulare* to restate by heads, sum up, fr L *re-* + *capitulum* division of a book]

recapitulation /,reekəpityoo'laysh(ə)n/ *n* **1** recapping; a concise summary **2** the supposed occurrence in the development of an embryo of successive stages resembling the series of ancestral types from which the organism has evolved **3** a modified repetition of the main themes forming the third section of a musical movement written in sonata form

recapture /,ree'kapchə/ *vt* **1a** to capture again **b** to experience again ⟨*to ~ the atmosphere of the past*⟩ **2** *NAm* to take (excess earnings or profits) by law – **recapture** *n*

recast /,ree'kahst/ *vt* **recast** to cast again ⟨*~ a gun*⟩ ⟨*~ a play*⟩; *also* to remodel, refashion ⟨~s *his political image to fit the times*⟩ – **recast** /'-,-/ *n*

[1]**recce** /'reki/ *n* a reconnaissance – infml [by shortening & alter.]

[2]**recce** *vb* **recceing; recced, recceed** to reconnoitre – infml [by shortening & alter.]

[1]**recede** /ri'seed/ *vi* **1a** to move back or away; withdraw **b** to slant backwards ⟨*a* receding *chin*⟩ **2** to grow less, smaller, or more distant; diminish ⟨*fears that demand will ~*⟩ ⟨*hope* ~d⟩ [L *recedere* to go back, fr *re-* + *cedere* to go – more at CEDE]

[2]**recede** /,ree'seed/ *vt* to cede (e g land) back to a former possessor [*re-* + *cede*]

[1]**receipt** /ri'seet/ *n* **1** the act or process of receiving ⟨*please acknowledge ~ of the goods*⟩ **2** sthg (e g goods or money) received – usu pl with sing. meaning ⟨*took the days's ~*s *to the bank*⟩ **3** a written acknowledgment of having received goods or money [ME *receite*, fr ONF, fr ML *recepta*, prob fr L, neut pl of *receptus*, pp of *recipere* to receive]

[2]**receipt** *vt* to give a receipt for or acknowledge, esp in writing, the receiving of

receive /ri'seev/ *vt* **1a** to (willingly) come into possession of or be provided with **b** to accept for consideration; give attention to ⟨*had to ~ their unwanted attentions*⟩ ⟨*~ a petition*⟩ **2a** to act as a receptacle or container for; *also* to take (an impression, mark, etc) **b** to assimilate through the mind or senses ⟨*~ new ideas*⟩ **3a** to permit to enter; admit ⟨~d *into the priesthood*⟩ **b** to welcome, greet; *also* to entertain **c** to act in response to ⟨*how did she ~ the offer?*⟩ ⟨*well* ~d *on his tour*⟩ **4** to accept as authoritative or true ⟨~d *wisdom*⟩ **5a** to take the force or pressure of ⟨*these pillars ~ the weight of the roof*⟩ **b** to suffer the hurt or injury of ⟨*~ a broken nose*⟩ **6** to be the player who returns (the service of his/her opponent) in tennis, squash, etc **7** to convert (an incoming signal, esp radio waves) into a form suitable for human perception ~ *vi* to be a recipient: e g **a** to be at home to visitors **b** to accept stolen goods [ME *receiven*, fr ONF *receivre*, fr L *recipere*, fr *re-* + *capere* to take – more at HEAVE] – **receivable** *adj*

Re,ceived Pronunci'ation *n* a form of nonlocal British English pronunciation used by many educated British people, esp those who have attended public schools, and usu by the BBC

Re,ceived 'Standard *n, chiefly NAm* RECEIVED PRONUNCIATION

re'ceiver /ri'seevə/ *n* **1** a person appointed to hold in trust and administer property of a bankrupt or insane person or property under litigation – compare OFFICIAL RECEIVER **2** one who receives stolen goods **3a** a radio, television, or other part of a communications system that receives the signal ☞ TELEVISION **b** the part of a telephone that contains the mouthpiece and earpiece [RECEIVE + [2]-ER] – **receivership** *n*

recension /ri'sensh(ə)n/ *n* **1** a critical revision of a text **2** a revised text [L *recension-*, *recensio* enumeration, fr *recensēre* to review, fr *re-* + *censēre* to assess, tax]

recent /'rees(ə)nt/ *adj* **1a** of a time not long past ⟨*the ~ election*⟩ **b** having lately come into existence ⟨*the ~ snow*⟩ **2** *cap* of or being the present or post-Pleistocene geological epoch ☞ EVOLUTION [MF or L; MF, fr L *recent-*, *recens*; akin to Gk *kainos* new] – **recency** /-si/, **recentness** *n*, **recently** *adv*

receptacle /ri'septəkl/ *n* **1** an object that receives and contains sthg 2 the end of the flower stalk of a flowering plant upon which the floral organs are borne ☞ PLANT [L *receptaculum*, fr *receptare* to receive, fr *receptus*, pp of *recipere* to receive]

reception /ri'sepsh(ə)n/ *n* 1 receiving or being received: e g a an admission ⟨*his ~ into the church*⟩ b a response, reaction ⟨*the play met with a mixed ~*⟩ c the receiving of a radio or television broadcast 2 a formal social gathering during which guests are received 3 *Br* an office or desk where visitors or clients (e g to an office, factory, or hotel) are received on arrival [ME *recepcion*, fr MF or L; MF *reception*, fr L *reception-*, *receptio*, fr *receptus*, pp of *recipere*]

receptionist /ri'sepshənist/ *n* one employed to greet and assist callers or clients

re'ception ,room *n* 1 a waiting room for dental or medical patients 2 a room used primarily for the reception of guests or visitors

receptive /ri'septiv/ *adj* 1 open and responsive to ideas, impressions, or suggestions 2 able to receive and transmit stimuli; sensory – **receptively** *adv*, **receptiveness** *n*, **receptivity** /,reesep'tivəti/ *n*

receptor /ri'septə/ *n* 1 a cell or group of cells that receives stimuli; SENSE ORGAN 2 a molecule or group of molecules, esp on the surface of a cell, that have an affinity for a particular chemical (e g a neurotransmitter)

[1]**recess** /ri'ses, 'reeses/ *n* 1 a hidden, secret, or secluded place – usu pl ⟨*illuminating the ~es of American politics – TLS*⟩ 2a an indentation or cleft (e g in an anatomical or geological structure) b an alcove ⟨*a pleasant ~ lined with books*⟩ 3 a suspension of business or activity, usu for a period of rest or relaxation ⟨*Parliament is in ~*⟩; *specif, NAm* a break between school classes [L *recessus*, fr *recessus*, pp of *recedere* to recede]

[2]**recess** /ri'ses/ *vt* 1 to put in a recess ⟨*~ed lighting*⟩ 2 to make a recess in 3 *chiefly NAm* to interrupt for a recess ~ *vi*, *chiefly NAm* to take a recess

recession /ri'sesh(ə)n/ *n* 1 a withdrawal 2 the withdrawal of clergy and choir at the end of a church service 3 a period of reduced economic activity – **recessional, recessionary** *adj*

recessional /ri'sesh(ə)nl/ *n* a hymn or musical piece at the conclusion of a church service

recessive /ri'sesiv/ *adj* 1 receding or tending to recede 2 being the one of a pair of (genes determining) contrasting inherited characteristics that is suppressed if a dominant gene is present – compare DOMINANT 4 – **recessively** *adv*

recharge /,ree'chahj/ *vi* to charge again; *esp* to renew the active materials in (a storage battery) – **recharge** /'--/ *n*, **rechargeable** *adj*

réchauffé /ray'shohfay (*Fr* reʃofe)/ *n* 1 a warmed-up dish of food 2 a rehash [F]

recherché /rə'sheəshay (*Fr* rəʃɛrʃe)/ *adj* 1 exotic, rare ⟨*discusses all manner of words – common, ~, and slang – New Yorker*⟩ 2 precious, affected ⟨*his ~ highbrow talk*⟩ [F]

recidivist /ri'sidivist/ *n* one who relapses, specif into criminal behaviour [F *récidiviste*, fr *récidiver* to relapse, fr ML *recidivare*, fr L *recidivus* recurring, fr *recidere* to fall back, fr *re-* + *cadere* to fall – more at CHANCE] – **recidivism** *n*, **recidivist, recidivistic** /-'vistik/ *adj*

recipe /'resipi/ *n* 1 PRESCRIPTION 3 2 a list of ingredients and instructions for making sthg, specif a food dish 3 a procedure for doing or attaining sthg ⟨*a ~ for success*⟩ [L, take, imper of *recipere* to take, receive – more at RECEIVE]

recipient /ri'sipi·ənt/ *n* sby who or sthg that receives [L *recipient-*, *recipiens*, prp of *recipere*] – **recipient** *adj*

[1]**reciprocal** /ri'siprəkl/ *adj* 1 *esp of mathematical functions* inversely related 2 shared, felt, or shown by both sides ⟨*~ love*⟩ 3 consisting of or functioning as a return in kind ⟨*did not expect ~ benefit*⟩ 4 mutually corresponding; equivalent ⟨*~ trade agreements*⟩ [L *reciprocus* returning the same way, alternating, irreg fr *re-* + *pro-*] – **reciprocally** *adv*

[2]**reciprocal** *n* 1 either of a pair of numbers (e g ⅔, ³⁄₂) that when multiplied together equal 1 ⟨*the ~ of 2 is 0.5*⟩ 2 the inverse of a number under multiplication

re,ciprocal 'pronoun *n* a pronoun (e g *each other*) used to denote mutual action or relationship

reciprocate /ri'siprə,kayt/ *vt* 1 to give and take mutually 2 to return in kind or degree ⟨*~ a compliment gracefully*⟩ ~ *vi* 1 to make a return for sthg ⟨*we hope to ~ for your kindness*⟩ 2 to move forwards and backwards alternately ⟨*a* reciprocating *valve*⟩ – **reciprocator** *n*, **reciprocative** /-kətiv/ *adj*, **reciprocation** /-'kaysh(ə)n/ *adj*

re,ciprocating 'engine /ri'siprə,kayting/ *n* an engine in which the to-and-fro motion of a piston is transformed into circular motion of the crankshaft

reciprocity /,resi'prosəti/ *n* 1 mutual dependence, action, or influence 2 a mutual exchange of privileges, specif between countries or institutions [[1]RECIPROCAL + -ITY]

recital /ri'sietl/ *n* 1a a reciting b a detailed account ⟨*a ~ of her troubles*⟩ c a discourse, narration 2 a concert or public performance given by a musician, small group of musicians, or dancer – **recitalist** *n*

recitative /,resitə'teev/ *n* (a passage delivered in) a rhythmically free declamatory style for singing a narrative text [It *recitativo*, fr *recitare* to recite, fr L] – **recitative** /ri'sietətiv/ *adj*

recite /ri'siet/ *vt* 1 to repeat from memory or read aloud, esp before an audience 2 to relate in detail; enumerate ⟨*~d a catalogue of offences*⟩ ~ *vi* to repeat or read aloud sthg memorized or prepared [ME *reciten* to state formally, fr MF or L; MF *reciter* to recite, fr L *recitare*, fr *re-* + *citare* to summon – more at CITE] – **reciter** *n*, **recitation** /,resi'taysh(ə)n/ *n*

reck /rek/ *vt* 1 to take account of ⟨*he little ~ed what the outcome might be*⟩ 2 to matter to; concern ⟨*what ~s it me that I shall die tomorrow?*⟩ *USE* archaic or poetic [ME *recken* to take heed, fr OE *reccan*; akin to OHG *ruohhen* to take heed]

reckless /'reklis/ *adj* marked by lack of proper caution; careless of consequences ⟨*~ driving*⟩ ⟨*~ courage*⟩ – **recklessly** *adv*, **recklessness** *n*

reckon /'rekən/ *vt* 1a to count – usu + *up* b to estimate, compute ⟨*~ the height of a building*⟩ c to determine by reference to a fixed basis ⟨*the Gregorian calendar is ~ed from the birth of Christ*⟩ 2 to consider or think of in a specified way ⟨*she is ~ed the leading expert*⟩ 3 to suppose, think ⟨*I ~ they're not coming*⟩ 4 to esteem highly ⟨*the boys ~ him because he's one of the lads*⟩ – infml ~ *vi* 1 to settle accounts 2 to make a calculation 3 to place reliance ⟨*I'm ~ing on your support*⟩ [ME *rekenen*, fr OE *-recenian* (as in *gerecenian* to narrate); akin to OE *reccan*] – **reckon with** to take into account, esp because formidable – **reckon without** to fail to consider; ignore

reckoning /'rekəning/ *n* **1a** a calculation or counting **b** an account, bill **2** a settling of accounts ⟨*day of* ~⟩ **3** an appraisal

reclaim /ri'klaym/ *vt* **1** to rescue or convert from an undesirable state; reform **2** to make available for human use by changing natural conditions ⟨~ed *marshland*⟩ **3** to obtain from a waste product [ME *reclamen*, fr OF *reclamer* to call back, fr L *reclamare* to cry out against, fr *re-* + *clamare* to cry out – more at CLAIM] – **reclaimable** *adj*, **reclamation** /,reklə'maysh(ə)n/ *n*, **reclamator** /'rekləmaytə, ri'klamətə/ *n*

réclame /,ray'klahm (*Fr* reklaːm)/ *n* public acclaim [F, advertising, fr *réclamer* to appeal, fr OF *reclamer*]

recline /ri'klien/ *vb* **1** (to cause or permit) to incline backwards ⟨~d *the seat a little*⟩ **2** to place or be in a recumbent position; lean, repose ⟨~s *her head on the pillow*⟩ [ME *reclinen*, fr MF or L; MF *recliner*, fr L *reclinare*, fr *re-* + *clinare* to bend – more at [1]LEAN]

recluse /ri'kloohs/ *n or adj* (sby) leading a secluded or solitary life [adj ME, fr OF *reclus*, lit., shut up, fr LL *reclusus*, pp of *recludere* to shut up, fr L *re-* + *claudere* to close – more at [4]CLOSE; n fr adj] – **reclusive** *adj*, **reclusion** /-zh(ə)n/ *n*

recognition /,rekəg'nish(ə)n/ *n* **1** recognizing or being recognized: e g **a** (formal) acknowledgment (e g of a government or claim) **b** perception of sthg as identical with sthg already known in fact or by description ⟨~ *of a former friend*⟩ ⟨~ *of a fine claret*⟩ **2** special notice or attention ⟨*a writer who has received much* ~⟩ **3** the sensing and coding of printed or written data by a machine ⟨*optical character* ~⟩ ⟨*machine* ~ *of handwritten characters*⟩ [L *recognition-, recognitio*, fr *recognitus*, pp of *recognoscere*]

recognizance /ri'kogniz(ə)ns/ *n* (the sum pledged as a guarantee for) a bond entered into before a court or magistrate that requires a person to do sthg (e g pay a debt or appear in court at a later date) [alter. of ME *reconissaunce*, fr MF *reconoissance* recognition, fr *reconoistre* to recognize]

recogn·ize, -ise /'rekəgniez/ *vt* **1a** to perceive to be sthg or sby previously known or encountered ⟨~d *the word*⟩ **b** to perceive clearly ⟨~d *his own inadequacy*⟩ **2a** to show appreciation of (e g by praise or reward) **b** to acknowledge acquaintance with ⟨~ *an old crony with a nod*⟩ **c** to admit the fact of ⟨~s *his obligation*⟩ **3a** to admit as being of a particular status or having validity ⟨~d *her as legitimate representative*⟩ **b** to allow to speak in a meeting [modif of MF *reconoiss-*, stem of *reconoistre*, fr L *recognoscere*, fr *re-* + *cognoscere* to know – more at COGNITION] – **recognizable** *adj*, **recognizably** *adv*, **recognizability** /-zə'biləti/ *n*

[1]**recoil** /ri'koyl/ *vi* **1** to shrink back physically or emotionally (e g in horror, fear, or disgust) **2** to spring back; rebound: e g **a** to fly back into an uncompressed position ⟨*the spring* ~ed⟩ **b** *esp of a firearm* to move backwards sharply when fired **3** REBOUND 2 [ME *reculen*, fr OF *reculer*, fr *re-* + *cul* backside, fr L *culus*]

[2]**recoil** /'ree,koyl, ri'koyl/ *n* recoiling; *esp* the backwards movement of a gun on firing

recollect /,rekə'lekt/ *vt* **1** to bring back to the level of conscious awareness; remember, recall **2** to bring (oneself) back to a state of composure or concentration ~ *vi* to call sthg to mind [ML *recollectus*, pp of *recolligere*, fr L, to gather again] – **recollection** /-'leksh(ə)n/ *n*, **recollective** /-tiv/ *adj*

recombinant /,ree'kombinənt/ *adj* **1** exhibiting genetic recombination ⟨~ *progeny*⟩ **2** of or being DNA prepared in the laboratory by combining pieces of DNA from several different species of organisms – **recombinant** *n*

recombination /,reekombi'naysh(ə)n/ *n* the formation of new combinations of genes in progeny that did not occur in the parents – **recombinational** *adj*

recommend /,rekə'mend/ *vt* **1a** to declare to be worthy of acceptance or trial ⟨~ed *the restaurant*⟩ **b** to endorse as fit, worthy, or competent ⟨~s *her for the position*⟩ **2** to make acceptable ⟨*has other points to* ~ *it*⟩ **3** to advise ⟨~ *that the matter be dropped*⟩ **4** *archaic* to entrust, commit ⟨~ed *his soul to God*⟩ [ME *recommenden* to praise, fr ML *recommendare*, fr L *re-* + *commendare* to commend] – **recommendable** *adj*, **recommendation** /-'daysh(ə)n/ *n*, **recommendatory** /-'mendət(ə)ri/ *adj*

[1]**recompense** /'rekəmpens/ *vt* **1** to give sthg to by way of compensation ⟨~d *him for his losses*⟩ **2** to make or amount to an equivalent or compensation for ⟨*a pleasure that* ~s *our trouble*⟩ [ME *recompensen*, fr MF *recompenser*, fr LL *recompensare*, fr L *re-* + *compensare* to compensate]

[2]**recompense** *n* an equivalent or a return for sthg done, suffered, or given ⟨*offered in* ~ *for injuries*⟩

reconcile /'rekənsiel/ *vt* **1a** to restore to friendship or harmony **b** to settle, resolve ⟨~ *differences*⟩ **2** to make consistent or congruous ⟨~ *an ideal with reality*⟩ **3** to cause to submit to or accept ⟨*was* ~d *to hardship*⟩ [ME *reconcilen*, fr MF or L; MF *reconcilier*, fr L *reconciliare*, fr *re-* + *conciliare* to conciliate] – **reconcilable** *adj*, **reconciler, reconcilement** *n*, **reconciliation** /-,sili'aysh(ə)n/ *n*, **reconciliatory** /-'sili·ət(ə)ri/ *adj*

recondite /ri'kondiet, 'rekən-/ *adj* (of or dealing with sthg) little known, abstruse, or obscure ⟨*the* ~ *literature of the Middle Ages*⟩ ⟨*a* ~ *subject*⟩ [L *reconditus*, pp of *recondere* to conceal, fr *re-* + *condere* to store up, fr *com-* + *-dere* to put – more at DO] – **reconditely** *adv*, **reconditeness** *n*

recondition /,reekən'dish(ə)n/ *vt* to restore to good (working) condition (e g by replacing parts)

reconnaissance /ri'konəs(ə)ns/ *n* a preliminary survey to gain information; *esp* an exploratory military survey of enemy territory or positions [F, lit., recognition, fr MF *reconoissance*]

reconnoitre, *NAm* **reconnoiter** /,rekə'noytə/ *vb* to make a reconnaissance (of) [obs F *reconnoître*, lit., to recognize, fr MF *reconoistre* – more at RECOGNIZE]

reconsider /,reekən'sidə/ *vb* to consider (sthg) again with a view to change, revision, or revocation – **reconsideration** /-'raysh(ə)n/ *n*

reconstitute /ree'konstityooht, -chooht/ *vt* to constitute again or anew; *esp* to restore to a former condition by adding water ⟨~ *powdered milk*⟩ – **reconstitution** /-'tyoohsh(ə)n/ *n*

reconstruct /,reekən'strukt/ *vt* **1a** to restore to a previous condition **b** RECREATE a ⟨~ing *a dinosaur* *from its bones*⟩ **2** to reorganize, reestablish ⟨~ing *society during the postwar period*⟩ **3** to build up a mental image or physical representation of (e g a crime or a battle) from the available evidence – **reconstructible** *adj*, **reconstruction** /-'struksh(ə)n/

[1]**record** /ri'kawd/ *vt* **1a** to commit to writing so as to supply written evidence **b** to state or indicate (as if) for a record ⟨*said he wanted to* ~ *certain reservations*⟩ **c(1)** to register permanently by mechanical or other means ⟨*earthquake shocks* ~ed *by a seismograph*⟩ **(2)** to indicate, read **2** to give evidence of; show **3** to convert (e g sound) into a permanent form fit for reproduction ~ *vi* to record sthg [ME *recorden*, lit., to recall, fr OF *recorder*, fr L *recordari*, fr *re-* + *cord-, cor* heart – more at HEART] – **recordable** *adj*

[2]**record** /'rekawd, 'rekəd/ *n* **1** the state or fact of being recorded **2a** sthg recorded or on which information, evidence, etc has been registered **b** sthg that recalls, relates, or commemorates past events or feats **c** an authentic official document **d** the official copy of the papers used in a law case **3a(1)** a body of known or recorded facts regarding sthg or sby **(2)** a list of previous criminal convictions **b** a performance, occurrence, or condition that goes beyond or is extraordinary among others of its kind; *specif* the best recorded performance in a competitive sport **4** (the sound recorded on) a flat usu plastic disc with a spiral groove whose undulations represent recorded sound for reproduction on a gramophone – **off the record** not for publication ⟨*remarks that were* off the record⟩ – **on record** in or into the status of being known, published, or documented ⟨*he is* on record *as saying this*⟩

'record ,deck *n* the apparatus including a turntable and stylus on which a gramophone record is played

re,corded de'livery *adv or n* (by) a postal service available in the UK in which the delivery of a posted item is recorded

recorder /ri'kawdə/ *n* **1** *often cap* a magistrate formerly presiding over the court of quarter sessions **2** any of a group of wind instruments consisting of a slightly tapering tube with usu 8 finger holes and a mouthpiece like a whistle [[1]RECORD + [2]-ER; (2) arch *record* (to practise a tune)]

recording /ri'kawding/ *n* sthg (e g sound or a television programme) that has been recorded electronically

recordist /ri'kawdist/ *n* one who records sound (e g on magnetic tape)

'record ,player /'rekawd, -kəd/ *n* an electronically-operated system for playing records; a gramophone

[1]**recount** /ri'kownt/ *vt* to relate in detail [ME *recounten*, fr MF *reconter*, fr *re-* + *conter, compter* to count, relate – more at [1]COUNT]

[2]**recount** /,ree'kownt/ *vt* to count again [*re-* + *count*]

[3]**recount** /'ree,kownt/ *n* a recounting, esp of votes

recoup /ri'koohp/ *vt* **1** to rightfully withhold part of (a sum due) **2a** to get an equivalent for (e g losses) **b** to pay (a person, organization, etc) back; compensate **3** to regain ⟨*an attempt to* ~ *his fortune*⟩ ~ *vi* to make up for sthg lost [F *recouper* to cut back, fr OF, fr *re-* + *couper* to cut – more at [3]COPE] – **recoupable** *adj*

recourse /ri'kaws/ *n* **1** (a turning or resorting to) a source of help, strength, or protection ⟨*to have* ~ *to the law*⟩ **2** the right to demand payment [ME *recours*, fr MF, fr LL *recursus*, fr L, act of running back, fr *recursus*, pp of *recurrere* to run back – more at RECUR]

recover /ri'kuvə/ *vt* **1** to get back: e g **a** to regain possession or use of ⟨*quickly* ~ed *his senses*⟩ **b** RECLAIM 2 **2** to bring back to a normal position or condition ⟨*stumbled, then* ~ed *himself*⟩ **3a** to make up for ⟨~ *one's costs*⟩ **b** to obtain by legal action ⟨~ *damages*⟩ **4** to obtain from an ore, waste product, or by-product ~ *vi* to regain a normal or stable position or condition (e g of health) ⟨~ing *from a cold*⟩ [ME *recoveren*, fr MF *recoverer*, fr L *recuperare*; akin to L *recipere* to receive – more at RECEIVE] – **recoverable** *adj*, **recoverability** /-rə'biləti/ *n*

recovery /ri'kuv(ə)ri/ *n* a recovering: e g **a** a return to normal health **b** a regaining of balance or control (e g after a stumble or mistake) **c** an economic upturn (e g after a depression)

recreant /'rekri·ənt/ *adj* **1** cowardly **2** unfaithful to duty or allegiance ***USE*** fml or poetic [ME, fr MF, fr prp of *recroire* to renounce one's cause in a trial by battle, fr *re-* + *croire* to believe, fr L *credere* – more at CREED] – **recreant** *n*

recreate /,reekri'ayt/ *vt* to create again: e g **a** to reproduce so as to resemble exactly ⟨~d *an old frontier town for the film*⟩ **b** to visualize or create again in the imagination – **recreatable** *adj*, **recreation** /-'aysh(ə)n/ *n*

recreation /,rekri'aysh(ə)n/ *n* (a means of) pleasurable activity, diversion, etc ⟨*his favourite* ~ *was spying on his neighbours*⟩ [ME *recreacion*, fr MF *recreation*, fr L *recreation-, recreatio* restoration to health, fr *recreatus*, pp of *recreare* to create anew, restore, refresh, fr *re-* + *creare* to create] – **recreational** *adj*

recriminate /ri'krimi,nayt/ *vi* to indulge in bitter mutual accusations [ML *recriminatus*, pp of *recriminare*, fr L *re-* + *criminari* to accuse – more at CRIMINATE] – **recriminative** /-nətiv/, **recriminatory** /-nət(ə)ri/ *adj*, **recrimination** /-'naysh(ə)n/ *n*

recrudesce /,reekrooh'des/ *vi, of sthg undesirable, esp a disease* to break out or become active again – fml [L *recrudescere* to become raw again, fr *re-* + *crudescere* to become raw, fr *crudus* raw – more at RAW] – **recrudescence** *n*, **recrudescent** *adj*

[1]**recruit** /ri'krooht/ *n* a newcomer to a field or activity; *specif* a newly enlisted member of the armed forces [F *recrute, recrue* fresh growth, new levy of soldiers, fr MF, fr *recroistre* to grow up again, fr L *recrescere*, fr *re-* + *crescere* to grow – more at CRESCENT]

[2]**recruit** *vt* **1a(1)** to enlist recruits for (e g an army, regiment, or society) **(2)** to enlist (a person) as a recruit **b** to secure the services of; hire **2** to replenish, renew ~ *vi* to enlist new members – **recruiter** *n*, **recruitment** *n*

rect-, recto- *comb form* rectum ⟨*rectal*⟩ [NL *rectum*]

rectal /'rekt(ə)l/ *adj* of, affecting, or near the rectum – **rectally** *adv*

rectangle /'rektang·gl/ *n* a parallelogram all of whose angles are right angles; *esp* one that is not a square ☞ MATHEMATICS [ML *rectangulus* having a right angle, fr L *rectus* right + *angulus* angle – more at RIGHT, [1]ANGLE]

rectangular /rek'tang·gyoolə/ *adj* **1** shaped like a rectangle ⟨*a* ~ *area*⟩ **2a** crossing, lying, or meeting at a right angle ⟨~ *axes*⟩ **b** having faces or surfaces shaped like rectangles ⟨*volume of a* ~ *solid*⟩ ⟨~ *blocks*⟩ – **rectangularly** *adv*, **rectangularity** /-'larəti/ *n*

rec,tangular co'ordinate *n* a coordinate in a Cartesian system having axes perpendicular to each other

rectifier /'rekti,fie·ə/ *n* a device for converting alternating current into direct current [RECTIFY + ²-ER]

rectify /'rekti,fie/ *vt* **1** to set right; remedy ⟨*to* ~ *mistakes*⟩ **2** to purify (e g alcohol), esp by repeated or fractional distillation **3** to correct by removing errors ⟨~ *the calendar*⟩ **4** to convert (alternating current) to direct current [ME *rectifien*, fr MF *rectifier*, fr ML *rectificare*, fr L *rectus* right] – **rectifiable** *adj*, **rectification** /-fi'kaysh(ə)n/ *n*

rectilinear /,rekti'lini·ə/ *adj* **1** (moving) in or forming a straight line ⟨~ *motion*⟩ **2** characterized by straight lines [LL *rectilineus*, fr L *rectus* + *linea* line] – **rectilinearly** *adv*

rectitude /'rekti,tyoohd/ *n* **1** moral integrity **2** correctness in judgment or procedure [ME, fr MF, fr LL *rectitudo*, fr L *rectus* straight, right]

recto /'rektoh/ *n*, *pl* **rectos** a right-hand page – compare VERSO [NL *recto* (*folio*) the page being straight]

recto- – see RECT-

rector /'rektə/ *n* **1a** a clergyman in charge of a parish; *specif* one in a Church of England parish where the tithes were formerly paid to the incumbent **b** a Roman Catholic priest directing a church with no pastor or one whose pastor has other duties **2** the head of a university or college [L, director, fr *rectus*, pp of *regere* to direct – more at ¹RIGHT] – **rectorship** *n*, **rectorate** /'rekt(ə)rət/, **rectorial** /rek'tawri·əl/ *adj*

rectory /'rekt(ə)ri/ *n* a rector's residence or benefice

rectrix /'rektriks/ *n*, *pl* **rectrices** /-seez/ any of a bird's tail feathers that are important in controlling flight direction [NL, fr L, fem of *rector* director]

rectum /'rektəm/ *n*, *pl* **rectums, recta** /-tə/ the last part of the intestine of a vertebrate, ending at the anus ☞ DIGESTION [NL, fr *rectum intestinum*, lit., straight intestine]

rectus /'rektəs/ *n*, *pl* **recti** /-tie/ any of several straight abdominal muscles [NL, fr *rectus musculus* straight muscle]

recumbent /ri'kumbənt/ *adj* **1** in an attitude suggestive of repose ⟨*comfortably* ~ *against a tree*⟩ **2** lying down [L *recumbent-*, *recumbens*, prp of *recumbere* to lie down, fr *re-* + *-cumbere* to lie down (akin to L *cubare* to lie, recline) – more at ²HIP] – **recumbency** /-si/ *n*, **recumbently** *adv*

recuperate /ri'k(y)oohpə,rayt/ *vt* to regain ⟨~ *financial losses*⟩ ~ *vi* to regain a former (healthy) state or condition [L *recuperatus*, pp of *recuperare* – more at RECOVER] – **recuperation** /-'raysh(ə)n/ *n*, **recuperative** /-p(ə)rətiv/ *adj*

recur /ri'kuh/ *vi* **-rr-** to occur again, esp repeatedly or after an interval: e g **a** to come up again for consideration ⟨*knew the difficulties would only* ~⟩ **b** to come again to mind ⟨~ring *thoughts*⟩ [ME *recurren* to return, fr L *recurrere*, lit., to run back, fr *re-* + *currere* to run – more at CAR] – **recurrence** /ri'kurəns/ *n*

recurrent /ri'kurənt/ *adj* **1** *esp of nerves and anatomical vessels* running or turning back in a direction opposite to a former course **2** returning or happening repeatedly or periodically ⟨~ *complaints*⟩ [L *recurrent-*, *recurrens*, prp of *recurrere*] – **recurrently** *adv*

re,curring 'decimal /ri'kuhring/ *n* a decimal in which a particular digit or sequence of digits repeats itself indefinitely at some stage after the decimal point

recursion /ri'kuhsh(ə)n/ *n* **1** a return **2** the repeated application of a particular mathematical procedure to the previous result to determine either a sequence of numbers or a more accurate approximation to a square root, fraction, etc [LL *recursion-*, *recursio*, fr *recursus*, pp of *recurrere* to run back] – **recursive** /-siv/ *adj*, **recursively** *adv*

recurved /ri'kuhvd/ *adj* curved backwards or inwards

recusancy /'rekyooz(ə)nsi/, **recusance** *n* refusal to accept or obey established authority; *specif* the refusal of Roman Catholics to attend services of the Church of England, a statutory offence from about 1570 until 1791 [*recusant*, n, fr L *recusant-*, *recusans*, prp of *recusare* to refuse, fr *re-* + *causari* to give a reason, fr *causa* cause, reason] – **recusant** *n or adj*

recycle /,ree'siekl/ *vt* to pass through a series of changes or treatments so as to return to a previous stage in a cyclic process; *specif* to process (sewage, waste paper, glass, etc) for conversion back into a useful product ~ *vi esp of an electronic device* to return to an original condition so that operation can begin again – **recyclable** *adj*, **recycler** *n*

¹red /red/ *adj* **-dd-** **1** of the colour red **2a** flushed, esp with anger or embarrassment **b** bloodshot ⟨*eyes* ~ *from crying*⟩ **c** *of hair or the coat of an animal* in the colour range between a medium orange and russet or bay **d** tinged with or rather red ⟨*a* ~ *sky*⟩ **3** *cap* of a communist country, esp the Soviet Union **4** failing to show a profit ⟨*a* ~ *financial statement*⟩ – compare BLACK 8 **5a** inciting or endorsing radical social or political change, esp by force **b** *often cap* communist ***USE*** (*5*) infml or derog [ME, fr OE *rēad*; akin to OHG *rōt* red, L *ruber* & *rufus*, Gk *erythros*] – **reddish** *adj*, **reddishness** *n*, **redly** *adv*, **redness** *n*

²red *n* **1** a colour whose hue resembles that of blood or of the ruby or is that of the long-wave extreme of the visible spectrum **2** sthg that is of or gives a red or reddish colour **3** the condition of being financially in debt or of showing a loss – usu in *in/out of the red*; compare BLACK 7 **4** a red traffic light meaning 'stop" **5a** a revolutionary radical **b** *cap* a communist ***USE*** (*5*) chiefly derog

redact /ri'dakt/ *vt* to prepare for publication; edit [back-formation fr *redaction*, fr F *rédaction*, fr LL *redaction-*, *redactio* act of reducing, compressing, fr L *redactus*, pp of *redigere* to bring back, reduce, fr *re-*, *red-* re- + *agere* to lead – more at AGENT] – **redaction** /ri'daksh(ə)n/ *n*, **redactor** *n*

,red 'admiral *n* a common N American and European butterfly that has broad orange-red bands on the fore wings and feeds on nettles in the larval stage

,red 'alga *n* any of many algae that are seaweeds with a predominantly red colour

,red 'blood ,cell, red cell *n* any of the haemoglobin-containing cells that carry oxygen to the tissues and are responsible for the red colour of vertebrate blood – compare WHITE BLOOD CELL

,red 'blood ,corpuscle, red corpuscle *n* RED BLOOD CELL

,red-'blooded *adj* full of vigour; virile

'red,breast /-,brest/ *n* a robin

'red,brick /-,brik/ *n or adj* (an English university) founded between 1800 and WW II [fr the common use of red brick in the buildings of recently-founded universities]

,red 'campion *n* a red-flowered Eurasian plant of the pink family

'red,cap /-,kap/ *n* **1** *Br* a military policeman **2** *NAm* a (railway) porter

,red 'carpet *n* a greeting or reception marked by ceremonial courtesy – usu in *roll out the red carpet* – **red-carpet** *adj*

,red 'cedar *n* (the wood of) an American juniper

,red 'cent *n, chiefly NAm* a trivial amount; a whit ⟨*not worth a* ~⟩

'red,coat /-,koht/ *n* a British soldier, esp formerly when scarlet jackets were worn

,red'currant /-'kurənt/ *n* (the small red edible fruit of) a widely cultivated European currant bush

redd /red/ *vt* **redded, redd** *chiefly NAm & Scot* to set in order; make tidy [ME *redden* to clear, prob alter. of *ridden* – more at RID]

redden /'red(ə)n/ *vt* to make red or reddish ~ *vi* to become red; *esp* to blush

redeem /ri'deem/ *vt* **1a** to repurchase (e g sthg pledged or lodged as security against a sum of money) ⟨*to ~ a pawned ring*⟩ **b** to get or win back ⟨~ed *his losses of the previous night's gambling*⟩ **2** to free from what distresses or harms: e g **a** to free from captivity by payment of ransom **b** to release from blame or debt ⟨*hoped to ~ himself by these heroics*⟩ **c** to free from the consequences of sin **3a** to eliminate another's right to (sthg) by payment of a debt **b(1)** to remove the obligation of (e g a bond) by making a stipulated payment ⟨*the government ~ savings bonds on demand*⟩; *specif* to convert (paper money) into money in coin **(2)** to convert (trading stamps, tokens, etc) into money or goods **c** to make good; fulfil ⟨~ed *his promise*⟩ **4a** to atone for ⟨*to ~ an error*⟩ **b(1)** to offset the bad effect of ⟨*flashes of wit* ~ed *a dreary speech*⟩ **(2)** to make worthwhile; retrieve ⟨*no efforts of hers could ~ such a hopeless undertaking*⟩ [ME *redemen*, modif of MF *redimer*, fr L *redimere*, fr *re-, red-* re- + *emere* to take, buy; akin to Lith *imti* to take] – **redeemable** *adj*

Redeemer /ri'deemə/ *n* Jesus [REDEEM + ²-ER]

redemption /ri'dempsh(ə)n, -'demsh(ə)n/ *n* redeeming or being redeemed; *also* sthg that redeems [ME *redempcioun*, fr MF *redemption*, fr L *redemption-, redemptio*, fr *redemptus*, pp of *redimere* to redeem] – **redemptive** /-tiv/ *adj*

redeploy /,reedi'ploy/ *vb* to transfer (e g troops or workers) from one area or activity to another – **redeployment** *n*

redevelop /,reedi'veləp/ *vt* to design, develop, or build again; *specif* to renovate a deteriorating or depressed (urban) area – **redeveloper** *n*, **redevelopment** *n*

,red 'giant *n* a star that has a low surface temperature and a large diameter relative to the sun

,Red 'Guard *n* a member of a militant youth organization in China formed to preserve popular enthusiasm for the communist regime

,red 'gum *n* (the hard reddish wood of or the reddish brown gum yielded by) any of several Australian eucalyptus trees

,red-'handed *adv or adj* in the act of committing a crime or misdeed ⟨*caught* ~⟩

'red,head /-,hed/ *n* a person with red hair – **red-headed** *adj*

,red 'heat *n* being red-hot; *also* the temperature at which a substance is red-hot

,red 'herring *n* **1** a herring cured by salting and slow smoking to a dark brown colour **2** sthg irrelevant that distracts attention from the real issue [(2) fr the practice of drawing a red herring across a trail to confuse hunting dogs]

,red-'hot *adj* **1** glowing with heat; extremely hot **2a** ardent, passionate ⟨~ *anger*⟩ **b** sensational; *specif* salacious ⟨*this ~ story of a Regency love affair*⟩ **c** full of energy, vigour, or enterprise ⟨*a ~ band*⟩ **d** arousing enthusiasm; currently extolled ⟨*a ~ favourite for the National*⟩ **3** new, topical ⟨~ *news*⟩

,red-hot 'poker *n* any of various S African plants of the lily family with tall erect spikes of yellow flowers changing to bright red towards the top

redia /'reedi·ə/ *n, pl* **rediae** /-di,ee/ *also* **redias** a larva of any of various parasitic trematode worms that either produces another generation of rediae or develops into a cercaria [NL, fr Francesco *Redi* †1697 It naturalist]

,Red 'Indian *n* a N American Indian

redingote /'reding,goht/ *n* **1** an overcoat with a large collar worn, esp by men, in the 18th and 19th c **2** a woman's lightweight coat with a cut-away front below the waist [F, modif of E *riding coat*]

redirect /,reedi'rekt, -die'rekt/ *vt* to change the course or direction of – **redirection** /-'reksh(ə)n/ *n*

,red 'lead /led/ *n* an orange-red to brick-red lead oxide used in storage battery plates, in glass and ceramics, and as a paint pigment

,red-'letter *adj* of special (happy) significance [fr the practice of marking holy days in red letters in church calendars]

,red 'light *n* **1** a red warning light, esp on a road or railway commanding traffic to stop **2** a cautionary sign ⟨*saw her warning as a ~ to potential troublemakers*⟩

,red-'light ,district *n* a district having many brothels

'red ,man *n* a N American Indian – chiefly derog

,red 'meat *n* dark-coloured meat (e g beef or lamb) – compare WHITE MEAT

,red 'mullet *n* MULLET b

redo /,ree'dooh/ *vt* **redoes; redoing; redid; redone 1** to do over again **2** to decorate (a room or interior of a building) anew

,red 'ochre *n* a red earthy haematite used as a pigment

redolent /'redələnt/ *adj* **1** full of a specified fragrance ⟨*air ~ of seaweed*⟩ **2** evocative, suggestive ⟨*a city ~ of antiquity*⟩ [ME, fr MF, fr L *redolent-, redolens*, prp of *redolēre* to emit a scent, fr *re-, red-* + *olēre* to smell – more at ODOUR] – **redolence** *n*, **redolently** *adv*

redouble /ri'dubl; *sense 2* ,ree-/ *vb* **redoubling** /-'dubl·ing, -'dubling/ **1** to make or become greater, more numerous, or more intense ⟨*to* ~ *our efforts*⟩ **2** to double (an opponent's double) in bridge – **redouble** *n*

redoubt /ri'dowt/ *n* **1** a small usu temporary enclosed defensive fortified structure **2** a secure place; a stronghold [F *redoute*, fr It *ridotto*, fr ML *reductus* secret place, fr L, withdrawn, fr pp of *reducere* to lead back – more at REDUCE]

redoubtable /ri'dowtəbl/ *adj* **1** formidable ⟨*a* ~ *adversary*⟩ **2** inspiring or worthy of awe or reverence [ME *redoutable*, fr MF, fr *redouter* to dread, fr *re-* + *douter* to doubt] – **redoubtably** *adv*

redound /ri'downd/ *vi* **1** to have a direct effect; lead or contribute *to* ⟨*can only* ~ *to our advantage*⟩ **2** to rebound *on* or *upon* ⟨*the President's behaviour* ~s *on his Party*⟩ *USE* fml [ME *redounden* to overflow, fr MF *redonder*, fr L *redundare*, fr *re-*, *red-* re- + *unda* wave – more at WATER]

redox /'ree,doks/ *adj* of or involving both oxidation and reduction ⟨*a* ~ *reaction*⟩ [*red*uction + *ox*idation]

,red 'pepper *n* CAYENNE PEPPER

'red,poll /-,pol/ *n* any of several small finches that resemble and are closely related to the linnet [[1]*poll*]

'red ,poll *n, often cap R&P* any of a British breed of large red hornless dairy and beef cattle [[3]*poll*]

[1]redress /ri'dres/ *vt* **1a** to set right ⟨*to* ~ *social wrongs*⟩ **b** to make or exact reparation for **2** to adjust evenly; make stable or equal again ⟨*to* ~ *the balance of power*⟩ [ME *redressen*, fr MF *redresser*, fr OF *redrecier*, fr *re-* + *drecier* to make straight – more at DRESS]

[2]redress *n* **1** compensation for wrong or loss **2** the (means or possibility of) putting right what is wrong

,red 'salmon *n* a sockeye

'red,shank /-,shangk/ *n* a common Old World wading bird with pale red legs and feet

'red ,shift *n* a displacement of the spectrum of a celestial body towards longer wavelengths, that is a consequence of the Doppler effect or the gravitational field of the source

'red,skin /-,skin/ *n* a N American Indian – chiefly derog

,red 'snow *n* snow coloured red by airborne dusts or by a growth of red-coloured algae

,red 'spider *n* any of several small mites that attack crop plants

,red 'squirrel *n* a reddish brown Eurasian squirrel native to British woodlands that is gradually being replaced by the grey squirrel

'red,start /-,staht/ *n* a small Old World bird with chestnut tail and underparts [*red* + obs *start* (handle, tail), fr ME *stert*, fr OE *steort*]

,red 'tape *n* excessively complex bureaucratic routine that results in delay [fr the red tape formerly used to bind legal documents in Britain]

,red 'tide *n* sea water discoloured and made toxic by the presence of large numbers of red-coloured protozoans

reduce /ri'dyoohs/ *vt* **1** to diminish in size, amount, extent, or number; make less ⟨~ *taxes*⟩ ⟨~ *the likelihood of war*⟩ **2** to bring or force to a specified state or condition ⟨*was* ~d *to tears of frustration*⟩ **3** to force to capitulate ⟨~d *Alexandria after a lengthy siege*⟩ **4** to bring to a systematic form or character ⟨~ *natural events to laws*⟩ **5** to correct (e g a fracture) by bringing displaced or broken parts back into normal position **6** to lower in grade, rank, status, or condition ⟨~d *to the ranks*⟩ ⟨*living in* ~d *circumstances*⟩ **7a** to diminish in strength, density, or value **b** to lower the price of ⟨*shoes* ~d *in the sale*⟩ **8** to change the denominations or form of without changing the value ⟨~ *fractions to a common denominator*⟩ **9** to break down by crushing, grinding, etc **10a** to convert (e g an ore) to a metal by removing nonmetallic elements **b** to combine with or subject to the action of hydrogen **c** to change (an atom, molecule, ion, etc) from a higher to a lower oxidation state, esp by adding electrons ~ *vi* **1** to become diminished or lessened; *esp* to lose weight by dieting **2** to become reduced ⟨*ferric iron* ~s *to ferrous iron*⟩ [ME *reducen* to lead back, fr L *reducere*, fr *re-* + *ducere* to lead – more at [1]TOW] – **reducer** *n*, **reducible** *adj*, **reducibility** /-sə'biləti/ *n*

re'ducing ,agent /ri'dyoohsing/ *n* a substance that reduces a chemical compound, usu by donating electrons

reductant /ri'duktənt/ *n* REDUCING AGENT

reductio ad absurdum /ri,dukti·oh ad ab'suhdəm/ *n* proof of the falsity of a proposition by revealing the absurdity of its logical consequences [LL, lit., reduction to the absurd]

reduction /ri'duksh(ə)n/ *n* **1** a reducing or being reduced **2a** sthg made by reducing; *esp* a reproduction (e g of a picture) in a smaller size **b** the amount by which sthg is reduced [ME *reduccion* restoration, fr MF *reduction*, fr LL & L; LL *reduction-*, *reductio* reduction (in a syllogism), fr L, restoration, fr *reductus*, pp of *reducere*] – **reductive** /-tiv/ *adj*

re'duction di,vision *n* (the first division of) meiosis of cells

reductionism /ri'dukshə,niz(ə)m/ *n* a procedure or theory that reduces complex data or phenomena to simple terms; *esp* oversimplification – **reductionist** *n or adj*, **reductionistic** /-'nistik/ *adj*

redundancy /ri'dundənsi/ *n* **1** being redundant **2** the part of a message that can be eliminated without loss of essential information **3** *chiefly Br* dismissal from a job

redundant /ri'dundənt/ *adj* **1a** superfluous **b** characterized by or containing an excess; *specif* excessively verbose ⟨*a* ~ *literary style*⟩ **2** serving as a backup so as to prevent failure of an entire system (e g a spacecraft) in the event of failure of a single component **3** *chiefly Br* unnecessary, unfit, or no longer required for a job [L *redundant-*, *redundans*, prp of *redundare* to overflow – more at REDOUND] – **redundantly** *adv*

reduplication /,ree,doohpli'kaysh(ə)n, -,dyooh-/ *n* **1** a doubling or reiterating **2** the doubling of (part of) a word with or without partial modification (e g in *hocus pocus* or *dilly-dally*) – **reduplicate** /-kayt/ *vt or* /-kət/ *adj*, **reduplicative** /-kətiv/ *adj*

,red 'wine *n* a wine with a predominantly red colour derived during fermentation from the natural pigment in the skins of dark-coloured grapes

'red,wing /-,wing/ *n* a Eurasian thrush with red patches beneath its wings

'red,wood /-,wood/ *n* (the wood of) a commercially important Californian timber tree of the pine family that often reaches a height of 100m (about 300ft)

reecho /,ree'ekoh/ *vb* **reechoes; reechoing; reechoed** *vi* to repeat or return an echo ~ *vt* to echo back; repeat

reed /reed/ *n* **1a** (the slender, often prominently jointed, stem of) any of various tall grasses that grow esp in wet areas **b** a person or thing too weak to rely on **2** a growth or mass of reeds; *specif* reeds for thatching **3a** a thin elastic tongue or flattened tube (e g of cane or plastic) fastened over an air opening in a musical instrument (e g an organ or clarinet) and set in vibration by an air current **b** a woodwind instrument having a reed ⟨*the* ~s *of an orchestra*⟩ **4** a device on a loom resembling a comb, used to space warp yarns evenly **5** a semicircular convex moulding that is usu 1 of several set parallel [ME *rede*, fr OE *hrēod*; akin to OHG *hriot* reed, Lith *krutėti* to stir]

'reed ,bunting *n* a common Eurasian bunting that frequents marshy places

'reed,mace /-,mays/ *n* any of a genus of tall reedy marsh plants with brown furry fruiting spikes

'reed ,organ *n* a keyboard wind instrument in which the wind acts on a set of reeds

'reed ,pipe *n* an organ pipe producing its tone by vibration of a beating reed in an air current

reeducate /,ree'edyookayt, -'ejoo-/ *vt* to rehabilitate through education – **reeducative** /-kətiv/ *adj*, **reeducation** /-'kaysh(ə)n/ *n*

'reed ,warbler *n* any of several Eurasian warblers that frequent marshy places

reedy /'reedi/ *adj* **1** full of, covered with, or made of reeds **2** slender, frail **3** having the tonal quality of a reed instrument; *esp* thin and high

[1]reef /reef/ *n* a part of a sail taken in or let out to regulate the area exposed to the wind ☞ SHIP [ME *riff*, fr ON *rif*]

[2]reef *vt* to reduce the area of (a sail) exposed to the wind by rolling up or taking in a portion

[3]reef *n* **1** a ridge of rocks or sand at or near the surface of water **2** a lode [D *rif*, prob of Scand origin; akin to ON *rif* reef of a sail] – **reefy** *adj*

[1]reefer /'reefə/, **'reefer ,jacket** *n* a close-fitting usu double-breasted jacket of thick cloth [[2]REEF + [2]-ER]

[2]reefer *n* JOINT 4 [prob fr [1]*reef* (sthg rolled up) + [2]*-er*]

'reef ,knot *n* a symmetrical knot made of 2 half-knots tied in opposite directions and commonly used for joining 2 pieces of material

[1]reek /reek/ *n* **1** a strong or disagreeable smell **2** *chiefly Scot & N Eng* smoke, vapour [ME *rek* smoke, fr OE *rēc*; akin to OHG *rouh* smoke] – **reeky** *adj*

[2]reek *vi* **1** to emit smoke or vapour **2a** to give off or become permeated with a strong or offensive smell **b** to give a strong impression (of some usu undesirable quality or feature) – + *of* or *with* ⟨*an area that* ~s *of poverty*⟩ ⟨*man who* ~s *of charm*⟩

[1]reel /reel, riəl/ *n* a revolvable device on which sthg flexible is wound: e g **a** a small wheel at the butt of a fishing rod for winding the line **b** a flanged spool for photographic film, magnetic tape, etc **c** *chiefly Br* a small spool for sewing thread [ME, fr OE *hrēol*; akin to ON *hræll* weaver's reed, Gk *krekein* to weave]

[2]reel *vt* **1** to wind (as if) on a reel **2** to draw by reeling a line ⟨~ *a fish in*⟩

[3]reel *vi* **1** to be giddy; be in a whirl ⟨*his mind was* ~ing⟩ **2** to waver or fall back (e g from a blow) ⟨~ed *back in horror*⟩ **3** to walk or (appear to) move unsteadily (e g from dizziness or intoxication) [ME *relen*, prob fr *reel*, n] .

[4]reel *n* a reeling motion

[5]reel *n* (the music for) a lively esp Scottish-Highland or Irish dance in which 2 or more couples perform a series of circular figures and winding movements [prob fr [4]*reel*]

reel off *vt* **1** to tell or repeat readily and without pause ⟨reeled off *all the facts and figures*⟩ **2** to chalk up, usu as a series ⟨*to* reel off *6 wins in succession*⟩

,reel-to-'reel *adj* of or utilizing magnetic tape passing between 2 reels that are unconnected and not in a cassette or cartridge ⟨*a* ~ *tape recorder*⟩ ☞ COMPUTER

reentrant /,ree'entrənt/ *n or adj* (an angle, point, etc) directed or pointing inwards

reentry /,ree'entri/ *n* **1** the retaking of possession **2** a second or new entry ⟨*a* ~ *visa*⟩; *esp* the return to and entry of the earth's atmosphere by a space vehicle – **reenter** /-'entə/ *vb*

[1]reeve /reev/ *n* a medieval English manor officer [ME *reve*, fr OE *gerēfa*, fr *ge-* (associative prefix) + *-rēfa* (akin to OE *-rōf* number, OHG *ruova*)]

[2]reeve *vt* **rove** /rohv/, **reeved** **1** to pass (e g a rope) through a hole or opening **2** to fasten by passing through a hole or round sthg **3** to pass a rope through (e g a block) [origin unknown]

[3]reeve *n* the female of the ruff [prob alter. of *ruff*]

ref /ref/ *n* REFEREE 2 – infml

refection /ri'feksh(ə)n/ *n* (the taking of) a light meal – fml [ME *refeccioun*, fr MF *refection*, fr L *refection-*, *refectio*, fr *refectus*, pp of *reficere* to restore, fr *re-* + *facere* to make – more at DO]

refectory /ri'fekt(ə)ri/ *n* a dining hall in an institution (e g a monastery or college) [LL *refectorium*, fr L *refectus*]

refectory table *n* a long narrow dining table with heavy legs

refer /ri'fuh/ *vb* **-rr-** *vt* **1a** to explain in terms of a general cause ⟨~s *their depression to the weather*⟩ **b** to allot to a specified place, stage, period, or category ⟨*to* ~ *the fall of Rome to 410* AD⟩ **c** to experience (e g pain) as coming from or located in a different area from its source ⟨*the pain in appendicitis may be* ~red *to any area of the abdomen*⟩ **2** to send or direct for treatment, aid, information, testimony, or decision ⟨*to* ~ *a patient to a specialist*⟩ ⟨~s *students to her other works*⟩ ~ *vi* **1a** to relate *to* sthg **b** to direct attention (by clear and specific mention); allude ⟨*the numbers* ~ *to footnotes*⟩ ⟨*no one* ~red *to yesterday's quarrel*⟩ **2** to have recourse; glance briefly for information ⟨~red *frequently to his notes while speaking*⟩ [ME *referren*, fr L *referre* to bring back, report, refer, fr *re-* + *ferre* to carry – more at [2]BEAR] – **referable** *adj*, **referral** *n*

[1]referee /,refə'ree/ *n* **1** a person to whom sthg is referred: e g **a** one to whom a legal matter is referred for investigation or settlement **b** one who reviews a (technical) paper before publication **c** REFERENCE 4a **2** an official who supervises the play and enforces the laws in any of several sports (e g football and boxing)

[2]referee *vb* to act as a referee (in or for)

[1]reference /'ref(ə)rəns/ *n* **1** referring or consulting ⟨*a manual designed for ready* ~⟩ **2** (a) bearing on or connection with a matter – often in *in/with reference to* **3** sthg that refers: e g **a** an allusion, mention **b** sthg that refers a reader or consulter to another source of information (e g a book or passage) **4** one referred to or consulted: e g **a** a person to whom inquiries as to character or ability can be made **b** a statement of the qualifications of a person seeking employment or appointment given by sby familiar with him/her **c** a source of information (e g a book or passage) to which a reader or inquirer is referred **d** a standard for measuring, evaluating, etc [REFER + -ENCE] – **referential** /ˌrefəˈrensh(ə)l/ *adj*

²**reference** *vt* to provide (e g a book) with references to authorities and sources of information

ˈ**reference** ˌ**book** *n* a book (e g a dictionary, encyclopedia, or atlas) intended primarily for consultation rather than for consecutive reading

ˈ**reference** ˌ**group** *n* a group to which sby aspires or belongs that influences his/her attitudes and behaviour by providing a source of comparison

ˈ**reference** ˌ**mark** *n* a conventional sign (e g * or †) to direct the reader's attention, esp to a footnote

referendum /ˌrefəˈrendəm/ *n, pl* **referendums** *also* **referenda** /-də/ the submitting to popular vote of a measure proposed by a legislative body or by popular initiative; *also* a vote on a measure so submitted [NL, fr L, neut of *referendus,* gerundive of *referre* to refer]

referent /ˈref(ə)rənt/ *n* the thing that a symbol (e g a word or sign) stands for [L *referent-, referens,* prp of *referre*]

refill /ˈreeˌfil/ *n* a fresh or replacement supply (for a device) ⟨*a* ~ *for a ballpoint pen*⟩ – **refill** /ˌreeˈfil/ *vb,* **refillable** /-ˈfiləbl/ *adj*

refine /riˈfien/ *vt* **1** to free from impurities ⟨~ *sugar*⟩ **2** to improve or perfect by pruning or polishing ⟨~ *a poetic style*⟩ **3** to free from imperfection, esp from what is coarse, vulgar, or uncouth ~ *vi* **1** to become pure or perfected **2** to make improvement by introducing subtleties or distinctions – **refiner** *n*

reˈfined *adj* **1** fastidious, cultivated **2** *esp of food* processed to the extent that desirable ingredients may be lost in addition to impurities or imperfections

reˈfinement /-mənt/ *n* **1** refining or being refined **2a** a (highly) refined feature, method, or distinction ⟨*pursued the delicate art of suggestion to its furthest* ~*s* – Maurice Bowra⟩ **b** a contrivance or device intended to improve or perfect ⟨*a new model of car with many* ~*s*⟩

refinery /riˈfien(ə)ri/ *n* a plant where raw materials (e g metals, oil or sugar) are refined or purified

refit /ˌreeˈfit/ *vt* **-tt-** to fit out or supply again; *esp* to renovate and modernize (e g a ship) – **refit** /ˈ-ˌ-/ *n*

reflation /ˌreeˈflaysh(ə)n/ *n* an expansion in the volume of available money and credit or in the economy, esp as a result of government policy [*re-* + *-flation* (as in *deflation*)] – **reflationary** /-shən(ə)ri/ *adj,* **reflate** /-ˈflayt/ *vb*

reflect /riˈflekt/ *vt* **1** to send or throw (light, sound, etc) back or at an angle ⟨*a mirror* ~*s light*⟩ **2** to show as an image or likeness; mirror ⟨*the clouds were* ~*ed in the water*⟩ **3** to make manifest or apparent; give an idea of ⟨*the pulse* ~*s the condition of the heart*⟩ **4** to consider ~ *vi* **1** to throw back light or sound **2** to think quietly and calmly **3a** to tend to bring reproach or discredit – usu + *on* or *upon* ⟨*an investigation that* ~*s on all the members of the department*⟩ **b** to tend to bring about a specified appearance or impression – usu + *on* ⟨*an act which* ~*s favourably on her*⟩ [ME *reflecten,* fr L *reflectere* to bend back, fr *re-* + *flectere* to bend]

reflecting telescope /riˈflekting/ *n* REFLECTOR 2

reflection, *Br also* **reflexion** /riˈfleksh(ə)n/ *n* **1** a reflecting of light, sound, etc **2** sthg produced by reflecting: e g **a** an image given back (as if) by a reflecting surface **b** an effect produced by or related to a specified influence or cause ⟨*a high crime rate is a* ~ *of an unstable society*⟩ **3** an often obscure or indirect criticism **4** (a thought, opinion, etc formed by) consideration of some subject matter, idea, or purpose ⟨*on* ~ *it didn't seem such a good plan*⟩ **5** a transformation of a figure with respect to a reference line producing a mirror image of the figure [ME, alter. of *reflexion,* fr LL *reflexion-, reflexio* act of bending back, fr L *reflexus,* pp of *reflectere*] – **reflectional** *adj*

reflective /riˈflektiv/ *adj* **1** capable of reflecting light, images, or sound waves **2** thoughtful, deliberative **3** of or caused by reflection ⟨*the* ~ *glare of the snow*⟩ – **reflectively** *adv,* **reflectiveness, reflectivity** /-ˈtivəti/ *n*

reflector /riˈflektə/ *n* **1** a polished surface for reflecting radiation, esp light **2** a telescope in which the principal focussing element is a mirror [REFLECT + ¹-OR]

¹**reflex** /ˈreefleks/ *n* **1a** reflected heat, light, or colour **b** a mirrored image **c** a reproduction or reflection that corresponds to some usu specified original; *specif* a word (element) in a form determined by development from an earlier stage of the language **2a** an automatic response to a stimulus that does not reach the level of consciousness ☞ NERVE **b** *pl* the power of acting or responding with adequate speed **c** an (automatic) way of behaving or responding ⟨*lying became a natural* ~ *for him*⟩ [L *reflexus,* pp of *reflectere* to reflect]

²**reflex** *adj* **1** bent, turned, or directed back ⟨*a stem with* ~ *leaves*⟩ **2** directed back upon the mind or its operations; introspective **3** occurring as an (automatic) response **4** *of an angle* greater than 180° but less than 360° **5** of, being, or produced by a reflex without intervention of consciousness [L *reflexus*] – **reflexly** *adv*

ˌ**reflex** ˈ**arc** *n* the complete nervous path involved in a reflex

ˌ**reflex** ˈ**camera** *n* a camera in which the image formed by the lens is reflected onto a ground-glass screen or is seen through the viewfinder for focussing and composition

reflexed /ˈreeflekst, riˈflekst/ *adj* bent or curved backwards or downwards ⟨~ *petals*⟩ [L *reflexus* + E *-ed*]

¹**reflexive** /riˈfleksiv/ *adj* **1** directed or turned back on itself **2** of, denoting, or being an action (e g in *he perjured himself*) directed back upon the agent or the grammatical subject [ML *reflexivus,* fr L *reflexus*] – **reflexively** *adv*

²**reflexive** *n* a reflexive verb or pronoun

reflux /riˈfluks, ˈreeˌfluks/ *vb* to (cause to) flow back or return; *esp* (to heat so as) to form vapours that condense and return to be heated again – **reflux** /ˈreeˌfluks/ *n*

¹**reform** /riˈfawm/ *vt* **1** to amend or alter for the better **2** to put an end to (an evil) by enforcing or introducing a better method or course of action **3** to

induce or cause to abandon evil ways ⟨~ *a drunkard*⟩ ~*vi* to become changed for the better [ME *reformen*, fr MF *reformer*, fr L *reformare*, fr *re-* + *formare* to form] – **reformable** *adj*, **reformative** /-mətiv/, **reformatory** /-mət(ə)ri/ *adj*

[2]**reform** *n* **1** amendment of what is defective or corrupt ⟨*educational* ~⟩ **2** (a measure intended to effect) a removal or correction of an abuse, a wrong, or errors

reformation /ˌrefə'maysh(ə)n/ *n* **1** reforming or being reformed **2** *cap the* 16th-c religious movement marked ultimately by the rejection of papal authority and some Roman Catholic doctrines and practices, and the establishment of the Protestant churches – **reformational** *adj*

reformatory /ri'fawmət(ə)ri/ *n, chiefly NAm* a penal institution to which young or first offenders or women are sent for reform – no longer used technically in Br

Reformed /ri'fawmd/ *adj* Protestant; *specif* of the Calvinist Protestant churches

reformer /ri'fawmə/ *n* **1** one who works for or urges reform **2** *cap* a leader of the Protestant Reformation

reformism /ri'fawmiz(ə)m/ *n* a doctrine, policy, or movement of reform – **reformist** *n*

Re,form 'Judaism /ri'fawm/ *n* a liberalizing and modernizing branch of Judaism

re'form ,school *n, chiefly NAm* a reformatory for young offenders – no longer used technically in Br

refract /ri'frakt/ *vt* **1** to deflect (light or another wave motion) from one straight path to another when passing from one medium (e g glass) to another (e g air) in which the velocity is different **2** to determine the refracting power of [L *refractus*, pp of *refringere* to break open, break up, refract, fr *re-* + *frangere* to break – more at BREAK] – **refraction** /-ri'fraksh(ə)n/ *n*, **refractive** /-tiv/ *adj*, **refractivity** /-'tivəti/ *n*

refracting telescope /ri'frakting/ *n* a refractor

refractive index /ri'fraktiv/ *n* the ratio of the velocity of a radiation (e g light) in 2 adjacent mediums

refractometer /ˌreefrak'tomitə/ *n* an instrument for measuring refractive indexes [ISV] – **refractometric** /ˌrifraktə'metrik/ *adj*, **refractometry** /ˌreefrak'tomətri/ *n*

refractor /ri'fraktə/ *n* a telescope whose principal focussing element is usu an achromatic lens

[1]**refractory** /ri'frakt(ə)ri/ *adj* **1** resisting control or authority; stubborn, unmanageable **2a** resistant to treatment or cure ⟨*a* ~ *cough*⟩ **b** immune ⟨*after recovery they were* ~ *to infection*⟩ **3** difficult to fuse, corrode, or draw out; *esp* capable of enduring high temperatures [alter. of *refractary*, fr L *refractarius*, irreg fr *refragari* to oppose, fr *re-* + *-fragari* (as in *suffragari* to support with one's vote)] – **refractorily** *adv*, **refractoriness** *n*

[2]**refractory** *n* a heat-resisting ceramic material

[1]**refrain** /ri'frayn/ *vi* to keep oneself from doing, feeling, or indulging in sthg, esp from following a passing impulse – usu + *from* [ME *refreynen*, fr MF *refraindre*, fr L *refringere* to break up, destroy, check – more at REFRACT]

[2]**refrain** *n* (the musical setting of) a regularly recurring phrase or verse, esp at the end of each stanza or division of a poem or song; a chorus [ME *refreyn*, fr MF *refrain*, fr *refraindre* to resound, fr L *refringere* to break up, refract]

refrangible /ri'franjəbl/ *adj* capable of being refracted [irreg fr L *refringere* to refract] – **refrangibility** /-'biləti/ *n*

refresh /ri'fresh/ *vt* **1** to restore strength or vigour to; revive (e g by food or rest) **2** to restore or maintain by renewing supply; replenish ⟨*the waiter* ~ed *our glasses*⟩ **3** to arouse, stimulate (e g the memory) [ME *refresshen*, fr MF *refreschir*, fr OF, fr *re-* + *freis* fresh – more at FRESH]

refresher /ri'freshə/ *n* **1** sthg (e g a drink) that refreshes **2 refresher, refresher course** a course of instruction designed to keep one abreast of developments in one's professional field

refreshing /ri'freshing/ *adj* agreeably stimulating because of freshness or newness – **refreshingly** *adv*

re'freshment /-mənt/ *n* **1** refreshing or being refreshed **2a** sthg (e g food or drink) that refreshes **b** assorted foods, esp for a light meal – usu pl with sing. meaning

refrigerate /ri'frijərayt/ *vb* to make or keep cold or cool; *specif* to freeze or chill (e g food) or remain frozen for preservation [L *refrigeratus*, pp of *refrigerare*, fr *re-* + *frigerare* to cool, fr *frigor-*, *frigus* cold – more at FRIGID] – **refrigerant** *n or adj*, **refrigeration** /-'raysh(ə)n/ *n*

refrigerator /ri'frijəraytə/ *n* an insulated cabinet or room for keeping food, drink, etc cool [REFRIGERATE + [1]-OR]

refringent /ri'frinj(ə)nt/ *adj* refractive, refracting [L *refringent-*, *refringens*, prp of *refringere* to refract] – **refringence, refrigency** *n*

refuel /ˌree'fyooh·əl/ *vb* **-ll-** (*NAm* **-l-**, **-ll-**) to provide with or take on additional fuel

refuge /'refyoohj/ *n* **1** (a place that provides) shelter or protection from danger or distress ⟨*to seek* ~ *in flight*⟩ ⟨*a mountain* ~⟩ **2** a person, thing, or course of action that offers protection or is resorted to in difficulties ⟨*patriotism is the last* ~ *of a scoundrel* – Samuel Johnson⟩ [ME, fr MF, fr L *refugium*, fr *refugere* to escape, fr *re-* + *fugere* to flee – more at FUGITIVE]

refugee /ˌrefyoo'jee/ *n* one who flees for safety, esp to a foreign country to escape danger or avoid political, religious, or racial persecution [F *réfugié*, pp of (*se*) *réfugier* to take refuge, fr L *refugium*]

refulgence /ri'fulj(ə)ns/ *n* radiance, brilliance – fml [L *refulgentia*, fr *refulgent-*, *refulgens*, prp of *refulgēre* to shine brightly, fr *re-* + *fulgēre* to shine – more at FULGENT] – **refulgent** *adj*, **refulgently** *adv*

[1]**refund** /ri'fund/ *vt* **1** to return (money) in restitution, repayment, or balancing of accounts **2** to pay (sby) back [ME *refunden*, fr MF & L; MF *refonder*, fr L *refundere*, lit., to pour back, fr *re-* + *fundere* to pour – more at [4]FOUND] – **refundable** *adj*

[2]**refund** /'ree,fund/ *n* **1** a refunding **2** a sum refunded

[3]**refund** /ˌree'fund/ *vt* to fund (a debt) again [*re-* + *fund*]

refurbish /ˌree'fuhbish/ *vt* to renovate – **refurbishment** *n*

refusal /ri'fyoohzl/ *n* **1** a refusing, denying, or being refused **2** the right or option of refusing or accepting sthg before others

[1]**refuse** /ri'fyoohz/ *vt* **1** to express oneself as unwilling to accept **2a** to show or express unwillingness to

do or comply with ⟨*the engine* ~d *to start*⟩ **b** to deny ⟨*they were* ~d *admittance to the game*⟩ **3** to decline to jump over – used esp of a horse ⟨~d *the water jump*⟩ ~ *vi* **1** to withhold acceptance, compliance, or permission **2** *of a horse* to decline to jump a fence, wall, etc ⟨~d *at the third fence*⟩ [ME *refusen*, fr MF *refuser*, fr (assumed) VL *refusare*, fr L *refusus*, pp of *refundere* to pour back] – **refusable** *adj*, **refuser** *n*

[2]**refuse** /'refyoohs/ *n* worthless or useless stuff; rubbish, garbage [ME, fr MF *refus* rejection, fr OF, fr *refuser*]

refute /ri'fyooht/ *vt* **1** to prove wrong by argument or evidence **2** to deny the truth or accuracy of [L *refutare*, fr *re-* + *-futare* to beat – more at [1]BEAT] – **refutable** /'refyootəbl, ri'fyooh-/ *adj*, **refutably** *adv*, **refutation** /,refyoo'taysh(ə)n/ *n*

regain /ri'gayn, ,ree-/ *vt* to gain or reach again; recover

regal /'reegl/ *adj* **1** of or suitable for a king or queen **2** stately, splendid [ME, fr MF or L; MF, fr L *regalis* – more at ROYAL] – **regally** *adv*, **regality** /ree'galəti/ *n*

regale /ri'gayl/ *vt* **1** to entertain sumptuously **2** to give pleasure or amusement to ⟨~d *us with stories of her exploits*⟩ [F *régaler*, fr MF, fr *regale* feast, fr *re-* + *gale* pleasure merrymaking – more at GALLANT]

regalia /ri'gaylyə/ *n pl but sing or pl in constr* **1** (the) ceremonial emblems or symbols indicative of royalty **2** special dress; *esp* official finery [ML, fr L, neut pl of *regalis*]

[1]**regard** /ri'gahd/ *n* **1** a gaze, look **2a** attention, consideration ⟨*due* ~ *should be given to all facets of the question*⟩ **b** a protective interest ⟨*ought to have more* ~ *for his health*⟩ **3a** a feeling of respect and affection ⟨*her hard work won her the* ~ *of her colleagues*⟩ **b** *pl* friendly greetings ⟨*give him my* ~s⟩ **4** an aspect to be taken into consideration ⟨*is a small school, and is fortunate in this* ~⟩ [ME, fr MF, fr OF, fr *regarder*] – **regardful** *adj* – **in/with regard to** with reference to; on the subject of

[2]**regard** *vt* **1** to pay attention to; take into consideration or account **2** to look steadily at **3** to relate to; concern **4** to consider and appraise in a specified way or from a specified point of view ⟨*he is highly* ~ed *as a mechanic*⟩ [ME *regarden*, fr MF *regarder* to look back at, regard, fr OF, fr *re-* + *garder* to guard, look at] – **as regards** WITH REGARD TO

regarding /ri'gahding/ *prep* WITH REGARD TO

[1]**re'gardless** /-lis/ *adj* heedless, careless – **regardlessly** *adv*, **regardlessness** *n*

[2]**regardless** *adv* despite everything ⟨*went ahead with their plans* ~⟩

re'gardless of *prep* IN SPITE OF ⟨regardless of *our mistakes*⟩

regatta /ri'gatə/ *n* a series of rowing, speedboat, or sailing races [It]

regelation /,reeji'laysh(ə)n/ *n* the freezing again of water, derived from ice that has melted under high pressure, when the pressure is relieved – **regelate** /'reeji,layt/ *vi*

regency /'reej(ə)nsi/ *n* **1** the office, period of rule, or government of a regent or regents **2** *sing or pl in constr* a body of regents

Regency *adj* of or resembling the styles (e g of furniture or dress) prevalent during the time of the Prince Regent [fr the regency (1811-20) of George, Prince of Wales (afterwards George IV) †1830]

[1]**regenerate** /ri'jenərət/ *adj* **1** formed or created again **2** spiritually reborn or converted **3** restored to a better, higher, or more worthy state [ME *regenerat*, fr L *regeneratus*, pp of *regenerare* to regenerate, fr *re-* + *generare* to beget – more at GENERATE] – **regenerate** *n*, **regeneracy** /-si/ *n*

[2]**regenerate** /ri'jenərayt/ *vi* **1** to become regenerate or regenerated **2** *of a body or body part* to undergo renewal or regrowth (e g after injury) ~ *vt* **1a** to subject to spiritual or moral renewal or revival **b** to change radically and for the better **2a** to generate or produce anew; *esp* to replace (a body part) by a new growth of tissue **b** to produce from a derivative or modified form, esp by chemical treatment ⟨~d *cellulose*⟩ **3** to restore to original strength or properties – **regenerator** *n*, **regenerable** /-rəbl/ *adj*, **regenerative** /-tiv/ *adj*, **regeneration** /-'raysh(ə)n/ *n*

regent /'reej(ə)nt/ *n* one who governs a kingdom in the minority, absence, or disability of the sovereign [ME, fr MF or ML; MF, fr ML *regent-*, *regens*, fr L, prp of *regere* to rule – more at [1]RIGHT] – **regent** *adj*

reggae /'regay/ *n* popular music of West Indian origin that is characterized by a strongly accented subsidiary beat [Jamaican E, fr *rege* rag]

regicide /'reji,sied/ *n* (the act of) one who kills a king [prob fr (assumed) NL *regicida* & *regicidium*, fr L *reg-*, *rex* king + *-cida* & *-cidium* – more at ROYAL, -CIDE] – **regicidal** /-'siedl/ *adj*

regime *also* **régime** /ray'zheem/ *n* **1a** a regimen **b** a regular pattern of occurrence or action (e g of seasonal rainfall) **2a** a form of management or government ⟨*a socialist* ~⟩ **b** a government in power [F *régime*, fr L *regimin-*, *regimen*]

regimen /'rejimən/ *n* a systematic plan (e g of diet, exercise, or medical treatment) adopted esp to achieve some end [ME, fr L *regimin-*, *regimen* rule, fr *regere*]

[1]**regiment** /'rejimənt/ *n sing or pl in constr* **1** a permanent military unit consisting usu of a number of companies, troops, batteries, or sometimes battalions **2** a large number or group [ME, government, area governed, fr MF, fr LL *regimentum*, fr L *regere*] – **regimental** /'-mentl/ *adj*, **regimentally** *adv*

[2]**regiment** /'reji,ment/ *vt* **1** to form into a regiment **2** to subject to strict and stultifying organization or control ⟨~ *an entire country*⟩ – **regimentation** /-'taysh(ə)n/ *n*

regimentals /,reji'mentlz/ *n pl* **1** the uniform of a regiment **2** military dress

Regina /ri'jienə/ *n* CROWN 5a – used when a queen is ruling [L, queen, fem of *reg-*, *rex* king]

region /'reej(ə)n/ *n* **1** an administrative area **2a** an indefinite area of the world or universe **b** a broadly uniform geographical or ecological area ⟨*desert* ~s⟩ **3** an indefinite area surrounding a specified body part ⟨*the abdominal* ~⟩ **4** a sphere of activity or interest ⟨*the abstract* ~ *of higher mathematics*⟩ **5** any of the zones into which the atmosphere is divided according to height or the sea according to depth [ME, fr MF, fr L *region-*, *regio*, fr *regere* to rule] – **in the region of** approximating to; MORE OR LESS

regional /'reejənl/ *adj* **1** (characteristic) of a region **2** affecting a particular region; localized – **regionally** *adv*

regionalism /'reejənl,iz(ə)m/ *n* **1** loyalty to a region **2** development of an administrative system based on areas – **regionalist** *n or adj*

regional·ize, -ise /'reejənl,iez/ *vt* to arrange in (administrative) regions – **regionalization** /-'zaysh(ə)n/ *n*

regisseur, régisseur /,rayzhi'suh (*Fr* reʒisœːr)/ *n* a director responsible for staging a theatrical work (e g a ballet) [F *régisseur*, fr *régir* to direct, rule, fr L *regere*]

¹register /'rejistə/ *n* **1** a written record containing (official) entries of items, names, transactions, etc **2a** a roster of qualified or available individuals ⟨*the electoral* ~⟩ **b** a school attendance record **3a** an organ stop **b** (a part of) the range of a human voice or a musical instrument **4** the language style and vocabulary appropriate to a particular subject matter **5** a device regulating admission of air, esp to solid fuel **6** REGISTRATION 1 **7** an automatic device registering a number or a quantity **8** a condition of correct alignment or proper relative position (e g of the plates used in colour printing) – often in *in/out of register* **9** a device (e g in a computer) for storing and working on small amounts of data [ME *registre*, fr MF, fr ML *registrum*, alter. of LL *regesta*, pl, register, fr L, neut pl of *regestus*, pp of *regerere* to bring back, fr *re-* + *gerere* to bear – more at CAST]

²register *vt* **1a** to make or secure official entry of in a register ⟨~ed *the birth of their daughter*⟩ **b** to enrol formally **c** to record automatically; indicate ⟨*this dial* ~s *speed*⟩ **d** to make a (mental) record of; note **2** to secure special protection for (a piece of mail) by prepayment of a fee **3** to convey an impression of ⟨~ed *surprise at the telegram*⟩ **4** to achieve, win ⟨~ed *an impressive victory*⟩ ~ *vi* **1a** to put one's name in a register ⟨~ed *at the hotel*⟩ **b** to enrol formally (as a student) **2** to make or convey an impression ⟨*the name didn't* ~⟩ – **registrable** /'rejistrəbl/ *adj*

'registered *adj* qualified formally or officially

'register ,office *n* REGISTRY OFFICE

'register ,ton *n* a unit of internal capacity for ships equal to 100ft³ (about 2.83m³)

registrar /,reji'strah, '--,-/ *n* **1** an official recorder or keeper of records: e g **a** a senior administrative officer of a university **b** a court official who deals with administrative and interlocutory matters and acts as a subordinate judge ☞ LAW **2** (the post, senior to that of a senior house officer, of) a British hospital doctor in training [alter. of ME *registrer*, fr MF *registreur*, fr *registrer* to register, fr ML *registrare*, fr *registrum*]

registration /,reji'straysh(ə)n/ *n* **1** registering or being registered **2** an entry in a register

,regi'stration ,document *n, chiefly Br* a document kept with a motor vehicle that gives the registration number, make, engine size, etc and details of the current ownership

,regi'stration ,mark *n, Br* an identifying combination of letters and numbers assigned to a motor vehicle

registry /'rejistri/ *n* **1** REGISTRATION 1 **2** a place of registration; *specif* a registry office

'registry ,office *n, Br* a place where births, marriages, and deaths are recorded and civil marriages conducted

,regius pro'fessor /'reejəs/ *n* a holder of a professorship founded by royal subsidy at a British university [NL, royal professor]

regnal /'regnəl/ *adj* of a reign; *specif* calculated from a monarch's accession ⟨*in his 8th* ~ *year*⟩ [ML *regnalis*, fr L *regnum* reign – more at REIGN]

regnant /'regnənt/ *adj* reigning ⟨*a queen* ~⟩ [L *regnant-, regnans*, prp of *regnare* to reign, fr *regnum*]

¹regress /'ree,gres/ *n* **1** REGRESSION 2a **2** an act of going or coming back – fml [ME, fr L *regressus*, fr *regressus*, pp of *regredi* to go back, fr *re-* + *gradi* to go – more at GRADE]

²regress /ri'gres/ *vi* **1** to undergo or exhibit backwards movement, esp to an earlier state **2** to tend to approach or revert to a mean ~ *vt* to induce, esp by hypnosis, a state of psychological regression in

regression /ri'gresh(ə)n/ *n* **1** the act or an instance of regressing; *esp* (a) retrograde movement **2a** a trend or shift towards a lower, less perfect, or earlier state or condition **b** reversion to an earlier mental or behavioural level **3** the statistical analysis of the association between 2 or more variables, esp so that predictions (e g of sales over a future period of time) can be made – **regressive** /-siv/ *adj*, **regressively** *adv*

¹regret /ri'gret/ *vt* **-tt-** **1** to mourn the loss or death of **2** to be very sorry about ⟨~s *his mistakes*⟩ [ME *regretten*, fr MF *regreter*, fr OF, fr *re-* + *-greter* (of Scand origin; akin to ON *grāta* to weep) – more at ²GREET] – **regrettable** *adj*

²regret *n* **1** (an expression of) the emotion arising from a wish that some matter or situation could be other than what it is; *esp* grief or sorrow tinged esp with disappointment, longing, or remorse **2** *pl* a conventional expression of disappointment, esp on declining an invitation ⟨*couldn't come to tea, and sent her* ~s⟩ – **regretful** *adj*, **regretfully** *adv*, **regretfulness** *n*

regrettably /ri'gretəbli/ *adv* **1** in a regrettable manner; to a regrettable extent ⟨*a* ~ *steep decline in wages*⟩ **2** it is regrettable that ⟨~, *we had failed to consider alternatives*⟩

¹regular /'regyoolə/ *adj* **1** belonging to a religious order – compare SECULAR 2 **2a** formed, built, arranged, or ordered according to some rule, principle, or type ⟨*a* ~ *curve*⟩ **b(1)** both equilateral and equiangular ⟨*a* ~ *polygon*⟩ **(2)** having faces that are identical regular polygons with identical angles between them ⟨*a* ~ *polyhedron*⟩ ⟨*a* ~ *solid*⟩ **c** perfectly (radially) symmetrical or even **3a** steady or uniform in course, practice, or occurrence; habitual, usual, or constant ⟨~ *habits*⟩ **b** recurring or functioning at fixed or uniform intervals ⟨*a* ~ *income*⟩ **c** defecating or having menstrual periods at normal intervals **4a** constituted, conducted, or done in conformity with established or prescribed usages, rules, or discipline **b** real, absolute ⟨*the office seemed like a* ~ *madhouse*⟩ **c** inflecting normally; *specif* WEAK 7 **5** of or being a permanent standing army **6** *chiefly NAm* thinking or behaving in an acceptable manner ⟨*wanted to prove he was a* ~ *guy*⟩ – infml *USE* (2b) ☞ MATHEMATICS [ME *reguler*, fr MF, fr LL *regularis* regular, fr L, of a bar, fr *regula* rule – more at RULE] – **regularly** *adv*, **regularize** /-,riez/ *vt*, **regularization** /-'zaysh(ə)n/ *n*, **regularity** /-'larəti/ *n*

²regular *n* **1a** a member of the regular clergy **b** a soldier in a regular army **2** one who is usu present or participating; *esp* one who habitually visits a particular place

regulate /ˈregyoo͵layt/ *vt* **1** to govern or direct according to rule **2** to bring order, method, or uniformity to ⟨~ *one's habits*⟩ **3** to fix or adjust the time, amount, degree, or rate of ⟨~ *the pressure of a tyre*⟩ [LL *regulatus*, pp of *regulare*, fr L *regula*] – **regulative** /-͵lətiv/, **regulatory** /-t(ə)ri, -ˈlay-/ *adj*, **regulator** /-ˈlaytə/ *n*

¹**regulation** /͵regyooˈlaysh(ə)n/ *n* **1** regulating or being regulated **2a** an authoritative rule dealing with details or procedure ⟨*safety* ~s *in a factory*⟩ **b** a rule or order having the force of law ⟨*EEC* ~s⟩

²**regulation** *adj* conforming to regulations; official ⟨~ *uniform*⟩

regulo /ˈregyooloh/ *n, chiefly Br* the temperature in a gas oven expressed as a specified number ⟨*meat cooked on* ~ *4*⟩ [fr *Regulo*, a trademark]

regulus /ˈregyooləs/ *n, pl* **reguluses, reguli** /-lie/ the impure metallic mass formed in smelting ores [ML, metallic antimony, fr L, petty king, fr *reg-*, *rex* king – more at ROYAL]

regurgitate /riˈguhji͵tayt/ *vb* to vomit or pour back or out (as if) from a cavity [ML *regurgitatus*, pp of *regurgitare*, fr L *re-* + LL *gurgitare* to engulf, fr L *gurgit-*, *gurges* whirlpool – more at VORACIOUS] – **regurgitation** /-ˈtaysh(ə)n/ *n*

rehabilitate /͵ree(h)əˈbilitayt/ *vt* **1** to reestablish the good name of **2a** to restore to a former capacity or state (e g of efficiency, sound condition, or solvency) ⟨~ *slum areas*⟩ **b** to restore to a condition of health or useful and constructive activity (e g after illness or imprisonment) [ML *rehabilitatus*, pp of *rehabilitare*, fr L *re-* + LL *habilitare* to qualify, fr L *habilitas* ability – more at ABILITY] – **rehabilitative** /-tətiv/ *adj*, **rehabilitation** /-ˈtaysh(ə)n/ *n*

¹**rehash** /͵reeˈhash/ *vt* to present or use again in another form without substantial change or improvement

²**rehash** /ˈree͵hash, ͵-ˈ-/ *n* sthg presented in a new form without change of substance

͵**reˈhear** /-ˈhiə/ *vt* **reheard** /-ˈhuhd/ to hear (a trial or lawsuit) over again – **rehearing** *n*

rehearsal /riˈhuhsl/ *n* **1** a rehearsing **2** a practice session, esp of a play, concert, etc preparatory to a public appearance

rehearse /riˈhuhs/ *vt* **1** to present an account of (again) ⟨~ *a familiar story*⟩ **2** to recount in order ⟨*had* ~d *their grievances in a letter to the governor*⟩ **3a** to give a rehearsal of; practice **b** to train or make proficient by rehearsal ~ *vi* to engage in a rehearsal of a play, concert, etc [ME *rehersen*, fr MF *rehercier*, lit., to harrow again, fr *re-* + *hercier* to harrow, fr *herce* harrow – more at HEARSE] – **rehearser** *n*

reheat /͵reeˈheet/ *n* the injection of fuel into the tailpipe of a turbojet engine to obtain extra thrust by combustion with uncombined air in the exhaust gases

rehouse /͵reeˈhowz, -ˈhows/ *vt* to establish in new or better-quality housing

rehydrate /͵reeˈhiedrayt, ˈ---/ *vt* to restore fluid lost in dehydration to – **rehydration** /-ˈdraysh(ə)n/ *n*

reify /ˈree·ifie/ *vt* to regard (sthg abstract) as a material thing [L *res* thing – more at ¹REAL] – **reification** /-fiˈkaysh(ə)n/ *n*

¹**reign** /rayn/ *n* **1a** royal authority; sovereignty **b** the dominion, sway, or influence of one resembling or likened to a monarch ⟨*the* ~ *of the military dictators*⟩ **2** the time during which sby or sthg reigns [ME *regne*, fr OF, fr L *regnum*, fr *reg-*, *rex* king – more at ROYAL]

²**reign** *vi* **1a** RULE 1a **b** to hold office as head of state although possessing little governing power ⟨*the queen* ~s *but does not rule*⟩ **2** to be predominant or prevalent ⟨*chaos* ~ed *in the classroom*⟩

͵**reign of ˈterror** *n* a period of ruthless violence committed by those in power [*Reign of Terror*, a period of the French Revolution that was conspicuous for mass executions of political suspects]

reimburse /͵ree·imˈbuhs/ *vt* **1** to pay back to sby ⟨~ *travel expenses*⟩ **2** to make restoration or payment to ⟨~ *you*⟩ [*re-* + obs *imburse* (to put in the pocket, pay)] – **reimbursable** *adj*, **reimbursement** *n*

¹**rein** /rayn/ *n* **1** a long line fastened usu to both sides of a bit, by which a rider or driver controls an animal **2a** a restraining influence **b** controlling or guiding power ⟨*the* ~s *of government*⟩ **c** opportunity for unhampered activity or use ⟨*gave free* ~ *to his emotions*⟩ *USE* (*1 & 2b*) usu pl with sing. meaning [ME *reine*, fr MF *rene*, fr (assumed) VL *retina*, fr L *retinēre* to restrain – more at RETAIN]

²**rein** *vt* to check or stop (as if) by pulling on reins – often + *in* ⟨~ed *in his horse*⟩ ⟨*couldn't* ~ *his impatience*⟩

reincarnate /͵reeˈinkahnayt, ͵--ˈ--/ *vt* **1** to incarnate again; give a new form or fresh embodiment to **2** to cause (a person or his/her soul) to be reborn in another (human) body after death – usu in pass; compare TRANSMIGRATE – **reincarnate** /-ˈkahnət/ *adj*, **reincarnation** /-ˈnaysh(ə)n/ *n*, **reincarnationist** *n*

reindeer /ˈrayn͵diə/ *n* any of several deer that inhabit N Europe, Asia, and America, have antlers in both sexes, and are often domesticated [ME *reindere*, fr ON *hreinn* reindeer + ME *deer*]

reindeer moss *n* a grey lichen that constitutes a large part of the food of reindeer

reinforce /͵ree·inˈfaws/ *vt* **1** to strengthen by additional assistance, material, or support; make stronger or more pronounced **2** to strengthen or increase (e g an army) by fresh additions **3** to stimulate (an experimental subject) with a reward following a correct or desired performance; *also* to encourage (a response) with a reward [*re-* + *inforce*, alter. of *enforce*] – **reinforceable** *adj*, **reinforcement** *n*, **reinforcer** *n*

͵**reinforced ˈconcrete** /͵ree·inˈfawst, ˈ--͵-/ *n* concrete in which metal is embedded for strengthening

reinstate /͵ree·inˈstayt/ *vt* **1** to place again (e g in possession or in a former position) **2** to restore to a previous effective state or condition – **reinstatement** *n*

reinsurance /͵ree·inˈshooərəns, -ˈshaw-/ *n* insurance by another insurer of all or a part of a risk previously assumed by an insurance company

reinsure /͵ree·inˈshooə, -ˈshaw-/ *vt* to insure (a risk or person) by reinsurance – **reinsurer** *n*

reinvent /͵ree·inˈvent/ *vt* to remake or redo completely (and unnecessarily) – **reinvention** /-ˈvensh(ə)n/ *n*

reinvest /͵ree·inˈvest/ *vt* to invest (e g earnings or investment income) rather than take or distribute the surplus as dividends or profits – **reinvestment** *n*

reissue /͵reeˈish(y)ooh, -ˈisyooh/ *vt* to issue again; *esp* to cause to become available again – **reissue** *n*

reiterate /͵reeˈitərayt/ *vt* to say or do over again or repeatedly, sometimes with wearying effect [L *reiteratus*, pp of *reiterare* to repeat, fr *re-* + *iterare* to iterate] – **reiteration** /-'raysh(ə)n/ *n*, **reiterative** /-rətiv/ *adj*, **reiteratively** *adv*

Reiter's syndrome /'rietəz/ *n* a disease of uncertain cause that is characterized by arthritis, conjunctivitis, and urethritis [Hans *Reiter* *b* 1881 G physician]

[1]reject /ri'jekt/ *vt* **1a** to refuse to accept, consider, submit to, or use **b** to refuse to accept or admit ⟨*the underprivileged feel* ~ed *by society*⟩ **2** to eject; *esp* VOMIT 1 **3** to fail to accept (e g a skin graft or transplanted organ) as part of the organism because of immunological differences [ME *rejecten*, fr L *rejectus*, pp of *reicere*, fr *re-* + *jacere* to throw – more at [2]JET] – **rejecter, rejector** *n*, **rejection** /-sh(ə)n/ *n*

[2]reject /'reejekt/ *n* a rejected person or thing; *esp* a substandard article of merchandise

rejig /,ree'jig/ *vt* **-gg-** to rearrange or reequip (e g a factory) so as to perform different work; *broadly* to adjust, reorganize ⟨*recommended* ~ging *the timetable – TES*⟩

rejoice /ri'joys/ *vt* to give joy to; gladden ~ *vi* to feel or express joy or great delight [ME *rejoicen*, fr MF *rejoiss-*, stem of *rejoir*, fr *re-* + *joir* to rejoice, fr L *gaudēre* – more at JOY] – **rejoicer** *n*, **rejoicingly** *adv*

rejoin /ri'joyn/ *vt* to say (sharply or critically) in response [ME *rejoinen* to answer to a legal charge, fr MF *rejoin-*, stem of *rejoindre*, fr *re-* + *joindre* to join – more at JOIN]

rejoinder /ri'joyndə/ *n* (an answer to) a reply [ME *rejoiner*, fr MF *rejoindre* to rejoin]

rejuvenate /,ree'joohvə,nayt, ri-/ *vt* **1** to make young or youthful again **2** to restore to an original or new state ⟨~ *old cars*⟩ ~ *vi* to cause or undergo rejuvenation [*re-* + L *juvenis* young – more at YOUNG] – **rejuvenator** *n*, **rejuvenation** /-'naysh(ə)n/ *n*

rejuvenescence /ri,joohvə'nes(ə)ns/ *n* a renewal of youthfulness or vigour; rejuvenation [ML *rejuvenescere* to become young again, fr L *re-* + *juvenescere* to become young, fr *juvenis*] – **rejuvenescent** *adj*, **rejuvenesce** *vb*

[1]relapse /ri'laps, 'ree,laps/ *n* a relapsing or backsliding; *esp* a recurrence of symptoms of a disease after a period of improvement [L *relapsus*, pp of *relabi* to slide back, fr *re-* + *labi* to slide – more at SLEEP]

[2]relapse /ri'laps/ *vi* **1** to slip or fall back into a former worse state **2** to sink, subside ⟨~ *into deep thought*⟩

re,lapsing 'fever /ri'lapsing/ *n* a bacterial disease transmitted by lice and ticks that is marked by recurring high fever

relate /ri'layt/ *vt* **1** to give an account of; tell **2** to show or establish logical or causal connection between ~ *vi* **1** to have relationship or connection **2** to respond, esp favourably ⟨*can't* ~ *to that kind of music*⟩ *USE* (*vi*) often + *to* [L *relatus* (pp of *referre* to carry back), fr *re-* + *latus*, pp of *ferre* to carry – more at TOLERATE, [2]BEAR] – **relatable** *adj*, **relater** *n*

re'lated *adj* **1** connected by reason of an established or discoverable relation **2** connected by common ancestry or sometimes by marriage – **relatedness** *n*

relation /ri'laysh(ə)n/ *n* **1** the act of telling or recounting **2** an aspect or quality (e g resemblance) that connects 2 or more things as belonging or working together or as being of the same kind **3a** RELATIVE 3a **b** kinship **4** reference, respect, or connection ⟨*in* ~ *to*⟩ **5** the interaction between 2 or more people or groups – usu pl with sing. meaning ⟨*race* ~s⟩ **6** *pl* **a** dealings, affairs ⟨*foreign* ~s⟩ **b** communication, contact ⟨*broke off all* ~ *with her family*⟩ **c** sexual intercourse – euph – **relational** *adj*

re'lationship /-ship/ *n* **1** the state or character of being related or interrelated ⟨*show the* ~ *between 2 things*⟩ **2** (a specific instance or type of) kinship **3** a state of affairs existing between those having relations or dealings ⟨*had a good* ~ *with his family*⟩

[1]relative /'relətiv/ *n* **1** a word referring grammatically to an antecedent **2** sthg having or a term expressing a relation to, connection with, or necessary dependence on another thing **3a** a person connected with another by blood relationship or marriage **b** an animal or plant related to another by common descent

[2]relative *adj* **1** introducing a subordinate clause qualifying an expressed or implied antecedent ⟨*a* ~ *pronoun*⟩; *also* introduced by such a connective ⟨*a* ~ *clause*⟩ **2** relevant, pertinent ⟨*matters* ~ *to world peace*⟩ **3a** not absolute or independent; comparative ⟨*the* ~ *isolation of life in the country*⟩ **b** expressing, having, or existing in connection with or reference to sthg else (e g a standard) ⟨~ *density*⟩ ⟨*supply is* ~ *to demand*⟩ **4** *of major and minor keys and scales* having the same key signature – **relatively** *adv*, **relativeness** *n*

,relative hu'midity *n* the ratio of the actual water vapour pressure in the air to that when the air is saturated with water vapour at the same temperature

'relative to *prep* WITH REGARD TO

relativism /'relәti,viz(ə)m/ *n* a theory that knowledge and moral principles are relative and have no objective standard – **relativist** *n*

relativistic /,relәti'vistik/ *adj* **1** of or characterized by relativity or relativism **2** moving at or being a velocity that causes a significant change in properties (e g mass) in accordance with the theory of relativity ⟨*a* ~ *electron*⟩ – **relativistically** *adv*

relativity /,relә'tivәti/ *n* **1** being relative **2a** *also* **special theory of relativity** a theory (based on the 2 postulates (1) that the speed of light in a vacuum is constant and independent of the source or observer and (2) that all motion is relative) that leads to the assertion that mass and energy are equivalent and that mass, dimension, and time will change with increased velocity **b** *also* **general theory of relativity** an extension of this theory to include gravitation and related acceleration phenomena

relator /ri'laytə/ *n* one on whose suggestion or information a legal action is commenced [RELATE + [1]-OR]

relax /ri'laks/ *vt* **1** to make less tense or rigid ⟨~ed *her muscles*⟩ **2** to make less severe or stringent ⟨~ *immigration laws*⟩ **3** to lessen the force, intensity, or strength of ⟨~ing *his concentration*⟩ **4** to relieve from nervous tension ~ *vi* **1** to become lax, weak, or loose **2** to become less intense or severe **3** to cast off inhibition, nervous tension, or anxiety ⟨*couldn't* ~ *in crowds*⟩ **4** to seek rest or recreation [ME *relaxen* to make less compact, fr L *relaxare*, fr *re-* + *laxare* to loosen, fr *laxus* loose – more at [1]SLACK] – **relaxant** *adj or n*, **relaxer** *n*

relaxation /ˌreelakˈsaysh(ə)n/ *n* **1** relaxing or being relaxed **2** a relaxing or recreational state, activity, or pastime **3** the attainment of an equilibrium state following the abrupt removal of some influence (e g light, high temperature, or stress)

reˈlaxed *adj* easy of manner; informal – **relaxedly** /-sidli/ *adv*

relaxin /riˈlaksin/ *n* a hormone produced by the corpus luteum in the ovary of a pregnant mammal that makes birth easier by causing relaxation of the pelvic ligaments

[1]**relay** /ˈreeˌlay/ *n* **1a** a fresh supply (e g of horses) arranged beforehand for successive use **b** a number of people who relieve others in some work ⟨*worked in* ~s *around the clock*⟩ **2** a race between teams in which each team member successively covers a specified portion of the course **3** a device set in operation by variation in an electric circuit and operating other devices in turn **4** the act of passing sthg along by stages; *also* such a stage **5** sthg, esp a message, relayed

[2]**relay** /ˈreeˌlay, riˈlay/ *vt* **1** to provide with relays **2** to pass along by relays ⟨*news was* ~ed *to distant points*⟩ [ME *relayen*, fr MF *relaier*, fr OF, fr *re-* + *laier* to leave – more at DELAY]

[1]**release** /riˈlees/ *vt* **1** to set free from restraint, confinement, or servitude **2** to relieve from sthg that confines, burdens, or oppresses ⟨*was* ~d *from her promise*⟩ **3** to relinquish (e g a claim or right) in favour of another **4** to give permission for publication, performance, exhibition, or sale of, on but not before a specified date; *also* to publish, issue ⟨*the commission* ~d *its findings*⟩ [ME *relesen*, fr OF *relessier*, fr L *relaxare* to relax]

[2]**release** *n* **1** relief or deliverance from sorrow, suffering, or trouble **2a** discharge from obligation or responsibility **b** (a document effecting) relinquishment or conveyance of a (legal) right or claim **3** freeing or being freed; liberation (e g from jail) **4** a device adapted to release a mechanism as required **5a** (the act of permitting) performance or publication **b** the matter released: e g **(1)** a statement prepared for the press **(2)** a (newly issued) gramophone record – **releaser** *n*

relegate /ˈreləˌgayt/ *vt* **1** to assign to a place of insignificance or oblivion; put out of sight or mind; *specif* to demote to a lower division of a sporting competition (e g a football league) – compare PROMOTE 1c **2a** to assign to an appropriate place or situation on the basis of classification or appraisal **b** to submit or refer to sby or sthg for appropriate action [L *relegatus*, pp of *relegare*, fr *re-* + *legare* to send with a commission – more at LEGATE] – **relegation** /-ˈgaysh(ə)n/ *n*

relent /riˈlent/ *vi* **1** to become less severe, harsh, or strict, usu from reasons of humanity **2** to slacken; LET UP [ME *relenten* to melt, dissolve, fr (assumed) ML *relentare* to soften, fr L *re-* + *lentare* to bend, fr *lentus* flexible, slow]

reˈlentless /-lis/ *adj* persistent, unrelenting – **relentlessly** *adv*, **relentlessness** *n*

relevant /ˈreliv(ə)nt/ *adj* **1** having significant and demonstrable bearing on the matter at hand **2** having practical application, esp to the real world [ML *relevant-*, *relevans*, fr L, prp of *relevare* to raise up – more at RELIEVE] – **relevance, relevancy** *n*, **relevantly** *adv*

reliable /riˈlie·əbl/ *adj* suitable or fit to be relied on; dependable – **reliableness** *n*, **reliably** /-bli/ *adv*, **reliability** /-ˈbiləti/ *n*

reliance /riˈlie·əns/ *n* **1** the act of relying; the condition or attitude of one who relies ⟨~ *on military power to achieve political ends*⟩ **2** sthg or sby relied on – **reliant** *adj*, **reliantly** *adv*

relic /ˈrelik/ *n* **1** a part of the body of or some object associated with a saint or martyr, that is preserved as an object of reverence **2** sthg left behind after decay, disintegration, or disappearance ⟨~s *of ancient cities*⟩ **3** a trace of sthg past, esp an outmoded custom, belief, or practice **4** *pl, archaic* remains, corpse [ME *relik*, fr OF *relique*, fr ML *reliquia*, fr LL *reliquiae*, pl, remains of a martyr, fr L, remains, fr *relinquere* to leave behind – more at RELINQUISH]

relict /ˈrelikt/ *n* **1** a (type of) plant or animal that is a remnant of an otherwise extinct flora, fauna, or kind of organism **2** a geological or geographical feature (e g a lake or mountain) or a rock remaining after other parts have disappeared or substantially altered **3** *archaic* a widow [(1, 2) *relict*, adj (residual), fr L *relictus*, pp of *relinquere*; (3) LL *relicta*, fr L, fem of *relictus*]

relief /riˈleef/ *n* **1a** removal or lightening of sthg oppressive, painful, or distressing ⟨*sought* ~ *from asthma by moving to the coast*⟩ **b** aid in the form of money or necessities, esp for the poor ⟨*a* ~ *organization*⟩ **c** military assistance to an endangered or surrounded post or force **d** a means of breaking or avoiding monotony or boredom ⟨*studied medieval theology for light* ~⟩ **2** (release from a post or duty by) one who takes over the post or duty of another ⟨*a* ~ *teacher*⟩ **3** legal compensation or amends **4** (a method of) sculpture in which the design stands out from the surrounding surface – compare BAS-RELIEF, HIGH RELIEF **5** sharpness of outline due to contrast ⟨*a roof in bold* ~ *against the sky*⟩ **6** the differences in elevation of a land surface [ME, fr MF, fr OF, fr *relever*; (4) F]

relief map *n* a map representing topographical relief **a** graphically by shading, hachures, etc **b** by means of a three-dimensional scale model

relief printing *n* LETTERPRESS 1

relieve /riˈleev/ *vt* **1a** to free from a burden; give aid or help to **b** to set free from an obligation, condition, or restriction – often + *of* **2** to bring about the removal or alleviation of **3** to release from a post, station, or duty **4** to remove or lessen the monotony of **5** to raise in relief **6** to give relief to (oneself) by urinating or defecating ~ *vi* to bring or give relief [ME *releven*, fr MF *relever* to raise, relieve, fr L *relevare*, fr *re-* + *levare* to raise – more at LEVER] – **relievable** *adj*

reˈlieved *adj* experiencing or showing relief, esp from anxiety or pent-up emotions – **relievedly** /-vidli/ *adv*

religio- *comb form* religion ⟨religio*centric*⟩; religion and ⟨religio*philosophical*⟩

religion /riˈlij(ə)n/ *n* **1a(1)** the (organized) service and worship of a god, gods, or the supernatural **(2)** personal commitment or devotion to religious faith or observance **b** the state of a member of a religious order **2** a cause, principle, or system of beliefs held to with ardour and faith; sthg considered to be of supreme importance [ME *religioun*, fr L *religion-*, *religio* reverence, religion, prob fr *religare* to tie back – more at RELY]

religionist /ri'lijənist/ *n* a person adhering (zealously) to a religion – **religionism** *n*

religiose /ri'liji,ohs/ *adj* excessively, obtrusively, or sentimentally religious – **religiosity** /-'osəti/ *n*

[1]religious /ri'lijəs/ *adj* **1** of or manifesting faithful devotion to an acknowledged ultimate reality or deity ⟨*a ~ man*⟩ **2** of, being, or devoted to the beliefs or observances of a religion **3** scrupulously and conscientiously faithful ⟨*~ in his observance of rules of health*⟩ [ME, fr OF *religieus*, fr L *religiosus*, fr *religio*] – **religiously** *adv*, **religiousness** *n*

[2]religious *n, pl* **religious** a member of a religious order under monastic vows [ME, fr OF *religieus*, fr *religieus*, adj]

relinquish /ri'lingkwish/ *vt* **1** to renounce or abandon; GIVE UP 3b **2a** to stop holding physically ⟨*~ed his grip*⟩ **b** to give over possession or control of ⟨*few leaders willingly ~ power*⟩ [ME *relinquisshen*, fr MF *relinquiss-*, stem of *relinquir*, fr L *relinquere* to leave behind, fr *re-* + *linquere* to leave – more at LOAN] – **relinquishment** *n*

reliquary /'relikwəri/ *n* a container or shrine in which sacred relics are kept [F *reliquaire*, fr ML *reliquiarium*, fr *reliquia* relic – more at RELIC]

reliquiae /ri'likwi,ee/ *n pl* remains of the dead; *esp* relics [L – more at RELIC]

[1]relish /'relish/ *n* **1** characteristic, pleasing, or piquant flavour or quality **2** enjoyment of or delight in sthg (that satisfies one's tastes, inclinations, or desires) ⟨*eat with ~*⟩ ⟨*little ~ for sports*⟩ **3** sthg that adds an appetizing or savoury flavour; *esp* a highly seasoned sauce (e g of pickles or mustard) eaten with plainer food [alter. of ME *reles* taste, fr OF, something left behind, release, fr *relessier* to release]

[2]relish *vt* **1** to add relish to **2** to enjoy; have pleasure from – **relishable** *adj*

relive /,ree'liv/ *vt* to live over again; *esp* to experience again in the imagination

reluctance /ri'luktəns/ *n* **1** being reluctant **2** the opposition offered by a magnetic substance to magnetic flux; *specif* the ratio of the magnetic potential difference to the corresponding flux

reluctant /ri'luktənt/ *adj* holding back; unwilling ⟨*~ to condemn him*⟩ [L *reluctant-*, *reluctans*, prp of *reluctari* to struggle against, fr *re-* + *luctari* to struggle – more at [1]LOCK] – **reluctantly** *adv*

rely /ri'lie/ *vi* **1** to have confidence based on experience ⟨*her husband was a man she could ~ on*⟩ **2** to be dependent ⟨*they ~ on a spring for their water*⟩ *USE* + *on* or *upon* [ME *relien* to rally, fr MF *relier* to connect, rally, fr L *religare* to tie back, fr *re-* + *ligare* to tie – more at LIGATURE]

rem /rem/ *n* a unit of ionizing radiation equal to the dosage that will cause the same biological effect as one röntgen of X-ray or gamma-ray radiation [*r*öntgen *e*quivalent *m*an]

REM *n* RAPID EYE MOVEMENT

remain /ri'mayn/ *vi* **1a** to be sthg or a part not destroyed, taken, or used up ⟨*only a few ruins ~*⟩ **b** to be sthg yet to be shown, done, or treated ⟨*it ~s to be seen*⟩ **2** to stay in the same place or with the same person or group; *specif* to stay behind **3** to continue to be ⟨*~ faithful*⟩ [ME *remainen*, fr MF *remaindre*, fr L *remanēre*, fr *re-* + *manēre* to remain – more at MANSION]

[1]remainder /ri'mayndə/ *n* **1** a future interest in property that is dependent upon the termination of a previous interest created at the same time **2a** a remaining group, part, or trace **b(1)** the number left after a subtraction **(2)** the final undivided part after division, that is less than the divisor **3** a book sold at a reduced price by the publisher after sales have fallen off [ME, fr AF, fr MF *remaindre*]

[2]remainder *vt* to dispose of (copies of a book) as remainders

remains /ri'maynz/ *n* **1** a remaining part or trace ⟨*threw away the ~ of the meal*⟩ **2** writings left unpublished at a writer's death ⟨*literary ~*⟩ **3** a dead body

[1]remake /,ree'mayk/ *vt* **remade** to make anew or in a different form

[2]'re,make *n* a new version of a film

remand /ri'mahnd/ *vt* **1** to adjourn (a case) for further enquiries **2** to return to custody [ME *remaunden*, fr MF *remander*, fr LL *remandare* to send back word, fr L *re-* + *mandare* to order – more at MANDATE] – **remand** *n*

re'mand ,home *n, Br* a temporary centre for (juvenile) offenders – not now in technical use; compare COMMUNITY HOME

remanence /'remənəns/ *n* the magnetic induction remaining in a magnetized substance when the magnetizing force has become zero

remanent /'remənənt/ *adj* **1** of, being, or characterized by remanence **2** residual, remaining – fml [ME, fr L *remanent-*, *remanens*, prp of *remanēre* to remain]

[1]remark /ri'mahk/ *vt* **1** to express as an observation or comment **2** to take notice of; observe – chiefly fml ~ *vi* to notice sthg and make a comment or observation *on* or *upon* [F *remarquer*, fr MF, fr *re-* + *marquer* to mark – more at MARQUE]

[2]remark *n* **1** mention or notice of that which deserves attention ⟨*would merit ~ in any political history*⟩ **2** a casual expression of an opinion or judgment ⟨*heartily sick of his snide ~*s⟩

remarkable /ri'mahkəbl/ *adj* worthy of being or likely to be noticed, esp as being uncommon or extraordinary – **remarkableness** *n*, **remarkably** *adv*

remedial /ri'meedi·əl, -dyəl/ *adj* **1** intended as a remedy ⟨*~ treatment*⟩ **2** concerned with the correction of faulty study habits ⟨*~ reading courses*⟩ – **remedially** *adv*

[1]remedy /'remədi/ *n* **1** a medicine, application, or treatment that relieves or cures a disease **2** sthg that corrects or counteracts an evil or deficiency ⟨*the firing squad made a simple ~ for discontent*⟩ **3** (legal) compensation or amends [ME *remedie*, fr AF, fr L *remedium*, fr *re-* + *mederi* to heal – more at MEDICAL]

[2]remedy *vt* to provide or serve as a remedy for – **remediable** /ri'meedi·əbl, -dyəbl/ *adj*

remember /ri'membə/ *vt* **1** to bring to mind or think of again (for attention or consideration) ⟨*~s the old days*⟩ ⟨*~ me in your prayers*⟩ **2** to give or leave (sby) a present, tip, etc ⟨*was ~ed in the will*⟩ **3** to retain in the memory ⟨*~ the facts until the test is over*⟩ **4** to convey greetings from ⟨*~ me to your mother*⟩ **5** to commemorate ~ *vi* **1** to exercise or have the power of memory **2** to have a recollection or remembrance [ME *remembren*, fr MF *remembrer*, fr LL *rememorari*, fr L *re-* + LL *memorari* to be mindful of, fr L *memor* mindful – more at MEMORY]

remembrance /ri'membrəns/ *n* **1** the state of bearing in mind **2** the period over which one's memory extends **3** an act of recalling to mind ⟨~ *of the offence angered him all over again*⟩ **4** a memory of a person, thing, or event ⟨*had only a dim* ~ *of that night*⟩ **5a** sthg that serves to keep in or bring to mind **b** a commemoration, memorial **c** a greeting or gift recalling or expressing friendship or affection

remembrancer /ri'membrənsə/ *n* one who or that which reminds; *esp, cap* any of several English officials having orig the duty of bringing a matter to the attention of the proper authority

Re,membrance 'Sunday *n* the Sunday closest to November 11, set aside in commemoration of fallen Allied servicemen and of the end of hostilities in 1918 and 1945 – compare VETERANS DAY

remind /ri'miend/ *vt* to put in mind of sthg; cause to remember – **reminder** *n*

reminisce /,remi'nis/ *vi* to indulge in reminiscence [back-formation fr *reminiscence*]

reminiscence /,remi'nis(ə)ns/ *n* **1** the process or practice of thinking or telling about past experiences **2a** a remembered experience **b** an account of a memorable experience – often pl ⟨*published the* ~s *of the old settler*⟩ **3** sthg that recalls or is suggestive of sthg else [LL *reminiscentia*, fr L *reminiscent-, reminiscens*, prp of *reminisci* to remember, fr *re-* + *-minisci* (akin to L *ment-, mens* mind) – more at MIND]

reminiscent /,remi'nis(ə)nt/ *adj* **1** of (the character of) reminiscence **2** marked by or given to reminiscence **3** tending to remind one (e g of sthg seen or known before) ⟨*a technology* ~ *of the Stone Age*⟩

remiss /ri'mis/ *adj* **1** negligent in the performance of work or duty **2** showing neglect or inattention ⟨*service was* ~ *in most of the hotels*⟩ [ME, fr L *remissus*, fr pp of *remittere* to send back, relax] – **remissly** *adv*, **remissness** *n*

remission /ri'mish(ə)n/ *n* **1** the act or process of remitting **2** a state or period during which sthg (e g the symptoms of a disease) is remitted **3** reduction of a prison sentence

[1]**remit** /ri'mit/ *vb* **-tt-** *vt* **1a** to release sby from the guilt or penalty of (sin) **b** to refrain from inflicting or exacting ⟨~ *a tax*⟩ ⟨~ *the penalty of loss of pay*⟩ **c** to give relief from (suffering) **2a** to desist from (an activity) **b** to let (e g attention or diligence) slacken **3** to refer for consideration; *specif* to return (a case) to a lower court **4** to put back **5** to postpone, defer **6** to send (money) to a person or place ~ *vi* **1a** to moderate **b** *of a disease or abnormality* to become less severe for a period **2** to send money (e g in payment) [ME *remitten*, fr L *remittere* to send back, fr *re-* + *mittere* to send – more at SMITE] – **remitment** *n*, **remittable** *adj*, **remitter** *n*

[2]**remit** *n* **1** an act of remitting **2** sthg remitted to another person or authority for consideration or judgment

remittal /ri'mitl/ *n* a remission

remittance /ri'mit(ə)ns/ *n* **1a** a sum of money remitted **b** a document by which money is remitted **2** transmittal of money

remittent /ri'mit(ə)nt/ *adj, of a disease* marked by alternating periods of abatement and increase of symptoms [L *remittent-, remittens*, prp of *remittere*] – **remittently** *adv*

remnant /'remnənt/ *n* **1a** a usu small part or trace remaining **b** a small surviving group – often pl **2** an unsold or unused end of fabric [ME, contr of *remenant*, fr MF, fr prp of *remenoir* to remain, fr L *remanēre* – more at REMAIN]

remodel /,ree'modl/ *vt* to reconstruct

remonet·ize, -ise /,ree'muni,tiez/ *vt* to restore to use as legal tender [*re-* + *monetize* (to coin money, establish as legal tender), fr L *moneta* mint, money] – **remonetization** /-'zaysh(ə)n/ *n*

remonstrance /ri'monstrəns/ *n* an act or instance of remonstrating

remonstrate /'remən,strayt, ri'mon-/ *vt* to say or plead in protest, reproof, or opposition ~ *vi* to present and urge reasons in opposition – often + *with* [ML *remonstratus*, pp of *remonstrare* to demonstrate, fr L *re-* + *monstrare* to show – more at MUSTER] – **remonstration** /,remən'straysh(ə)n/ *n*, **remonstrative** /ri'monstrətiv/ *adj*, **remonstratively** *adv*, **remonstrator** /'remən,straytə/ *n*

remora /'remərə/ *n* any of several fishes that have a sucking disc on the head by means of which they cling to other fishes and to ships [L, lit., delay, fr *remorari* to delay, fr *re-* + *morari* to delay – more at MORATORIUM; fr a former belief that it held ships back]

remorse /ri'maws/ *n* a deep and bitter distress arising from a sense of guilt for past wrongs [ME, fr MF *remors*, fr ML *remorsus*, fr LL, act of biting again, fr L *remorsus*, pp of *remordēre* to bite again, fr *re-* + *mordēre* to bite – more at SMART] – **remorseful** *adj*, **remorsefully** *adv*

re'morseless /-lis/ *adj* **1** merciless ⟨~ *cruelty*⟩ **2** persistent, indefatigable – **remorselessly** *adv*, **remorselessness** *n*

remote /ri'moht/ *adj* **1** far removed in space, time, or relation ⟨*the* ~ *past*⟩ ⟨*comments* ~ *from the truth*⟩ **2** out-of-the-way, secluded **3** acting on or controlling indirectly or from a distance ⟨~ *computer operation*⟩ **4** small in degree ⟨*a* ~ *possibility*⟩ **5** distant in manner [L *remotus*, fr pp of *removēre* to remove] – **remotely** *adv*, **remoteness** *n*

re,mote con'trol *n* control over an operation (e g of a machine or weapon) exercised from a distance usu by means of an electrical circuit or radio waves ☞ TELEVISION

[1]**remould** /,ree'mohld/ *vt* to refashion the tread of (a worn tyre)

[2]**remould** /'ree,mohld/ *n* a remoulded tyre

[1]**remount** /,ree'mownt/ *vt* **1** to mount again ⟨~ *a picture*⟩ **2** to provide (e g a unit of cavalry) with remounts ~ *vi* to mount again [ME *remounten*; partly fr *re-* + *mounten* to mount; partly fr MF *remonter*, fr *re-* + *monter* to mount]

[2]**remount** /'ree,mownt, ,-'-/ *n* a fresh riding horse; *esp* one used as a replacement for one which is exhausted

removable /ri'moohvəbl/ *adj* capable of being removed – **removableness** *n*, **removably** *adv*, **removability** /-'biləti/ *n*

removal /ri'moohvl/ *n* **1** *Br* the moving of household goods from one residence to another **2** removing or being removed; *specif* MOVE 2c – fml ⟨*our* ~ *to Hampton Wick*⟩

[1]**remove** /ri'moohv/ *vt* **1** to change the location, position, station, or residence of ⟨~ *soldiers to the front*⟩ **2** to move by lifting, pushing aside, or taking away or off ⟨~s *his hat in church*⟩ **3** to get rid of ⟨~ *a tumour surgically*⟩ ~ *vi* to change location,

station, or residence – fml ⟨removing *from the city to the suburbs*⟩ [ME *removen*, fr OF *removoir*, fr L *removēre*, fr *re-* + *movēre* to move] – **remover** *n*

[2]**remove** *n* **1a** a distance or interval separating one person or thing from another ⟨*poems that work best at a slight ~ from the personal*⟩ **b** a degree or stage of separation ⟨*a repetition, at many ~s, of the theme of her first book*⟩ **2** a form intermediate between 2 others in some British schools

re'moved *adj* **1a** distant in degree of relationship **b** of a younger or older generation ⟨*a second cousin's child is a second cousin once ~*⟩ **2** separate or remote in space, time, or character

remunerate /ri'myoohnə,rayt/ *vt* **1** to pay an equivalent for **2** to recompense [L *remuneratus*, pp of *remunerare* to recompense, fr *re-* + *munerare* to give, fr *muner-*, *munus* gift – more at [1]MEAN] – **remunerator** *n*, **remuneration** /-'raysh(ə)n/ *n*, **remunerative** /-rətiv/ *adj*

renaissance /ri'nays(ə)ns, ri'nesonhs/ *n* **1** *cap the* (period of the) humanistic revival of classical influence in Europe from the 14th c to the 17th c, expressed in a flowering of the arts and literature and by the beginnings of modern science **2** *often cap* a movement or period of vigorous artistic and intellectual activity **3** a rebirth, revival [F, fr MF, rebirth, fr *renaistre* to be born again, fr L *renasci*, fr *re-* + *nasci* to be born – more at NATION]

Renaissance man *n* a person of wide interests and expertise; *specif* a person equally at home in the arts and sciences

renal /'reenl/ *adj* relating to, involving, or located in the region of the kidneys [F or LL; F *rénal*, fr LL *renalis*, fr L *renes* kidneys]

renascence /ri'nays(ə)ns/ *n* a renaissance

re'nascent /ri'nays(ə)nt/ *adj* rising again into being or vigour – fml [L *renascent-*, *renascens*, prp of *renasci*]

rend /rend/ *vb* **rent** /rent/ *vt* **1** to wrest, split, or tear apart or in pieces (as if) by violence **2** to tear (the hair or clothing) as a sign of anger, grief, or despair **3a** to lacerate mentally or emotionally **b** to pierce with sound ~ *vi* to become torn or split [ME *renden*, fr OE *rendan*; akin to OFris *renda* to tear, Skt *randhra* hole]

render /'rendə/ *vt* **1a** to melt down; extract by melting ⟨~ *lard*⟩ **b** to treat so as to convert into industrial fats and oils or fertilizer **2a** to yield; GIVE UP 1 **b** to deliver for consideration, approval, or information **3a** to give in return or retribution **b** to restore; GIVE BACK **c** to give in acknowledgment of dependence or obligation **d** to do (a service) for another **4a** to cause to be or become ⟨*enough rain to ~ irrigation unnecessary*⟩ **b(1)** to reproduce or represent by artistic or verbal means **(2)** to give a performance of **c** to translate **5** to direct the execution of; administer ⟨~ *justice*⟩ **6** to apply a coat of plaster or cement directly to [ME *rendren*, fr MF *rendre* to give back, yield, fr (assumed) VL *rendere*, alter. of L *reddere*, partly fr *re-* + *dare* to give & partly fr *re-* + *-dere* to put – more at [2]DATE, DO]

rendering /'rend(ə)ring/ *n* a covering material, usu of cement, sand, and a small percentage of lime, applied to exterior walls

rendezvous /'rondi,vooh, -day-, 'ronh-/ *n, pl* **rendezvous** **1** a place (appointed) for assembling or meeting **2** a meeting at an appointed place and time [MF, fr *rendez vous* present yourselves] – **rendezvous** *vi*

rendition /ren'dish(ə)n/ *n* the act or result of rendering: e g **a** a translation **b** a performance, interpretation [obs F, fr MF, alter. of *reddition*, fr LL *reddition-*, *redditio*, fr L *redditus*, pp of *reddere*]

renegade /'reni,gayd/ *n* **1** a deserter from one faith, cause, or allegiance to another **2** an individual who rejects lawful or conventional behaviour [Sp *renegado*, fr ML *renegatus*, fr pp of *renegare* to deny, fr L *re-* + *negare* to deny – more at NEGATE] – **renegade** *adj*

renege /ri'neeg, ri'nayg/ *vi* to go back on a promise or commitment ⟨~d *on her contract*⟩ [ML *renegare*] – **reneger** *n*

renew /ri'nyooh/ *vt* **1** to restore to freshness, vigour, or perfection ⟨*as we ~ our strength in sleep*⟩ **2** to make new spiritually; regenerate **3a** to revive **b** to make changes in; rebuild **4** to make or do again **5** to begin again; resume **6** to replace, replenish ⟨~ *water in a tank*⟩ **7a** to grant or obtain an extension of or on (e g a subscription, lease, or licence) **b** to grant or obtain a further loan of ⟨~ *a library book*⟩ ~ *vi* to make a renewal (e g of a lease) – **renewable** *adj*, **renewably** *adv*, **renewal** *n*, **renewer** *n*, **renewability** /-ə'biləti/ *n*

reni-, reno- *comb form* kidney ⟨reni*form*⟩ [L *renes* kidneys]

reniform /'reni,fawm, 'ree-/ *adj* kidney-shaped ☞ PLANT [NL *reniformis*, fr *reni-* + *-formis* -form]

renin /'reenin, 'renin/ *n* an enzyme of the kidney that plays a major role in the release of angiotensin [ISV, fr L *renes*]

rennet /'renit/ *n* **1a** the contents of the stomach of an unweaned animal, esp a calf **b** (a preparation from) the lining membrane of a stomach (e g the fourth of a ruminant) used for curdling milk **2** (a substitute for) rennin [ME, fr (assumed) ME *rennen* to cause to coagulate, fr OE *gerennan*, fr *ge-* together + (assumed) OE *rennan* to cause to run; akin to OHG *rennen* to cause to run, OE *rinnan* to run]

rennin /'renin/ *n* any of several enzymes that coagulate milk and are used in making cheese and junkets; *esp* one from the mucous membrane of the stomach of a calf [*rennet* + [1]*-in*]

renounce /ri'nowns/ *vt* **1** to give up, refuse, or resign, usu by formal declaration ⟨~ *his errors*⟩ **2** to refuse to follow, obey, or recognize any further **3** to fail to follow with a card from (the suit led) in a card game [ME *renouncen*, fr MF *renoncer*, fr L *renuntiare*, fr *re-* + *nuntiare* to report, fr *nuntius* messenger] – **renouncement** *n*, **renouncer** *n*

renovate /'renə,vayt/ *vt* **1** to restore to life, vigour, or activity **2** to restore to a former or improved state (e g by cleaning, repairing, or rebuilding) [L *renovatus*, pp of *renovare*, fr *re-* + *novare* to make new, fr *novus* new – more at NEW] – **renovator** *n*, **renovation** /-'vaysh(ə)n/ *n*

renown /ri'nown/ *n* a state of being widely acclaimed; fame [ME, fr MF *renon*, fr OF, fr *renomer* to celebrate, fr *re-* + *nomer* to name, fr L *nominare*, fr *nomin-*, *nomen* name – more at NAME]

re'nowned *adj* celebrated, famous

[1]**rent** /rent/ *n* **1a** a usu fixed periodical return made by a tenant or occupant of property or user of goods to the owner for the possession and use thereof **b** an

amount paid or collected as rent 2 the portion of the income of an economy (e g of a nation) attributable to land as a factor of production in addition to capital and labour [ME *rente*, fr OF, income from a property, fr (assumed) VL *rendita*, fr fem of *renditus*, pp of *rendere* to yield – more at RENDER]

[2]rent *vt* **1** to take and hold under an agreement to pay rent **2** to grant the possession and use of for rent ~ *vi* **1** to obtain the possession and use of a place or article for rent **2** to allow the possession and use of property for rent – **rentable** *adj*, **rentability** /-tə'biləti/ *n*

[3]rent *past of* REND

[4]rent *n* **1** an opening or split made (as if) by rending **2** an act or instance of rending [E dial. *rent* (to rend), var of *rend*]

[1]rental /'rentl/ *n* **1** an amount paid or collected as rent **2** an act of renting **3** *NAm* sthg (e g a house) that is rented

[2]rental *adj* of or relating to rent or renting

renter /'rentə/ *n* the lessee or tenant of property [[2]RENT + [2]-ER]

rentier /'ronti,ay, 'ronh- (*Fr* rɑ̃tje)/ *n* one who receives a fixed income (e g from land or shares) [F, fr OF, fr *rente*]

'rent ,strike *n* a refusal by a group of tenants to pay rent

renumber /,ree'numbə/ *vt* to number again or differently

renunciation /ri,nunsi'aysh(ə)n/ *n* the act or practice of renouncing; *specif* self-denial practised for religious reasons [ME, fr L *renuntiation-, renuntiatio*, fr *renuntiatus*, pp of *renuntiare*] – **renunciative** /ri'nunsi·ətiv, -syə-/ *adj*, **renunciatory** /-si·ət(ə)ri, -syə-/ *adj*

reoffer /,ree'ofə/ *vt* to offer (a security issue) for public sale

reopen /,ree'ohp(ə)n/ *vt* **1** to open again **2** to resume (discussion or consideration of) ⟨~ *a contract*⟩ **3** to begin again ~ *vi* to open again ⟨*school* ~s *in September*⟩

reorder /,ree'awdə/ *vt* to arrange in a different way

[1]rep, repp /rep/ *n* a plain-weave fabric with raised crosswise ribs [F *reps*, modif of E *ribs*, pl of *rib*]

[2]rep *n* a representative; *specif, chiefly Br* SALES REPRESENTATIVE – infml

[3]rep *n* REPERTORY 2b, c – infml

[1]repair /ri'peə/ *vi* to betake oneself; go ⟨~ed *to his home*⟩ – fml [ME *repairen*, fr MF *repairier* to go back to one's country, fr LL *repatriare*, fr L *re-* + *patria* native country – more at EXPATRIATE]

[2]repair *vt* **1** to restore by replacing a part or putting together what is torn or broken **2** to restore to a sound or healthy state **3** to remedy [ME *repairen*, fr MF *reparer*, fr L *reparare*, fr *re-* + *parare* to prepare – more at PARE] – **repairer** *n*, **repairable** *adj*, **repairability** /-rə'biləti/ *n*

[3]repair *n* **1** an instance or the act or process of repairing **2** relative condition with respect to soundness or need of repairing ⟨*the car is in reasonably good* ~⟩

reparable /'rep(ə)rəbl/ *adj* capable of being repaired

reparation /,repə'raysh(ə)n/ *n* **1a** the act of making amends, offering expiation, or giving satisfaction for a wrong or injury **b** sthg done or given as amends or satisfaction **2** damages; *specif* compensation payable by a defeated nation for war damages – usu pl with sing. meaning [ME, fr MF, fr LL *reparation-, reparatio*, fr L *reparatus*, pp of *reparare*] – **reparative** /ri'parətiv/ *adj*

repartee /,repah'tee/ *n* **1** a quick and witty reply **2** (skill in) amusing and usu light sparring with words [F *repartie*, fr *repartir* to retort, fr MF, fr *re-* + *partir* to divide – more at [2]PART]

repass /,ree'pahs/ *vi* to pass again, esp in the opposite direction ~ *vt* to pass through, over, or by again ⟨~ *the house*⟩ [ME *repassen*, fr MF *repasser*, fr OF, fr *re-* + *passer* to pass] – **repassage** /,ree'pasij/ *n*

repast /ri'pahst/ *n* [1]MEAL – fml [ME, fr MF, fr OF, fr *repaistre* to feed, fr *re-* + *paistre* to feed, fr L *pascere* – more at FOOD]

repatriate /,ree'patri,ayt, ri-, -'pay-/ *vt* to restore to the country of origin [LL *repatriatus*, pp of *repatriare* to go back to one's country – more at [1]REPAIR] – **repatriate** /-tri·ət/ *n*, **repatriation** /-'aysh(ə)n/ *n*

repay /ri'pay, ,ree-/ *vt* **repaid** /-'payd/ **1a** to pay back ⟨~ *a loan*⟩ **b** to give or inflict in return or requital ⟨~ *evil for evil*⟩ **2** to compensate, requite **3** to recompense ⟨*a company which* ~s *hard work*⟩ – **repayable** *adj*, **repayment** *n*

repeal /ri'peel/ *vt* to revoke (a law) [ME *repelen*, fr MF *repeler*, fr OF, fr *re-* + *apeler* to appeal, call] – **repeal** *n*, **repealable** *adj*

[1]repeat /ri'peet/ *vt* **1a** to say or state again **b** to say through from memory **c** to say after another ⟨~ *these words after me*⟩ **2a** to make, do, perform, present, or broadcast again ⟨~ *an experiment*⟩ **b** to experience again **3** to express or present (oneself or itself) again in the same words, terms, or form ~ *vi* **1** to say, do, or accomplish sthg again **2** *of food* to continue to be tasted intermittently after being swallowed – often + *on* [ME *repeten*, fr MF *repeter*, fr L *repetere*, fr *re-* + *petere* to go to, seek – more at FEATHER] – **repeatable** *adj*, **repeatability** /-tə'biləti/ *n*

[2]repeat *n* **1** the act of repeating **2a** sthg repeated; *specif* a television or radio programme that has previously been broadcast at least once **b** (a sign placed before or after) a musical passage to be repeated in performance ☞ MUSIC

re'peated *adj* **1** renewed or recurring again and again ⟨~ *changes of plan*⟩ **2** said, done, or presented again

repeatedly /ri'peetidli/ *adv* again and again

repeater /ri'peetə/ *n* **1** a watch that strikes the time when a catch is pressed **2** a firearm that fires several times without having to be reloaded [[1]REPEAT + [2]-ER]

repeating decimal /ri'peeting/ *n* RECURRING DECIMAL

repechage /,repi'shahzh, '--,-/ *n* a heat (e g in rowing) in which losers from earlier heats are given another chance to qualify for the finals [F *repêchage* second chance, reexamination for a candidate who has failed, fr *repêcher* to fish out, rescue, fr *re-* + *pêcher* to fish, fr L *piscari* – more at PISCATORY]

repel /ri'pel/ *vt* **-ll-** **1** to drive back; repulse **2a** to drive away **b** to be incapable of sticking to, mixing with, taking up, or holding ⟨*a fabric that* ~s *moisture*⟩ **c** to (tend to) force away or apart by mutual action at a distance ⟨*2 like electric charges* ~ *one another*⟩ **3** to cause aversion in; disgust [ME *repellen*, fr L *repellere*, fr *re-* + *pellere* to drive]

[1]repellent *also* **repellant** /ri'pelənt/ *adj* **1** serving or tending to drive away or ward off **2** repulsive [L *repellent-, repellens,* prp of *repellere*] – **repellently** *adv*

[2]**repellent** *also* **repellant** *n* sthg that repels; *esp* a substance used to prevent insect attacks

[1]**repent** /ri'pent/ *vi* **1** to turn from sin and amend one's life **2** to feel regret or contrition ~ *vt* to feel sorrow, regret, or contrition for [ME *repenten,* fr OF *repentir,* fr *re-* + *pentir* to be sorry, fr L *paenitēre* – more at PENITENT] – **repentance** *n,* **repentant** *adj,* **repenter** *n*

[2]**repent** /'reepənt/ *adj, of a plant part* creeping, prostrate [L *repent-, repens,* prp of *repere* to creep – more at REPTILE]

repercussion /,reepə'kush(ə)n/ *n* **1** an echo, reverberation **2a** an action or effect given or exerted in return **b** a widespread, indirect, or unforeseen effect of an act, action, or event [L *repercussion-, repercussio,* fr *repercussus,* pp of *repercutere* to drive back, fr *re-* + *percutere* to beat – more at PERCUSSION] – **repercussive** /-siv/ *adj*

repertoire /'repə,twah/ *n* **1a** a list or supply of dramas, operas, pieces, or parts that a company or person is prepared to perform **b** a range of skills, techniques, or expedients **2a** the complete list or range of skills, techniques, or ingredients used in a particular field, occupation, or practice **b** a list or stock of capabilities ⟨*the instruction* ~ *of a computer*⟩ [F *répertoire,* fr LL *repertorium*]

repertory /'repət(ə)ri/ *n* **1** a repository **2a** a repertoire **b** (a theatre housing) a company that presents several different plays in the course of a season at one theatre **c** the production and presentation of plays by a repertory company ⟨*acting in* ~⟩ [LL *repertorium* list, fr L *repertus,* pp of *reperire* to find, fr *re-* + *parere* to produce – more at PARE]

répétiteur /ri,peti'tuh/ *n* sby who coaches opera singers [F, fr L *repetitus,* pp]

repetition /,repi'tish(ə)n/ *n* **1** repeating or being repeated **2** a reproduction, copy [L *repetition-, repetitio,* fr *repetitus,* pp of *repetere* to repeat] – **repetitional** *adj*

repetitious /,repi'tishəs/ *adj* characterized or marked by repetition; *esp* tediously repeating – **repetitiously** *adv,* **repetitiousness** *n*

repetitive /ri'petətiv/ *adj* repetitious – **repetitively** *adv,* **repetitiveness** *n*

repine /ri'pien/ *vi* to feel or express dejection or discontent –fml – **repiner** *n*

replace /ri'plays/ *vt* **1** to restore to a former place or position ⟨~ *cards in a file*⟩ **2** to take the place of, esp as a substitute or successor **3** to put sthg new in the place of ⟨~ *a worn carpet*⟩ – **replaceable** *adj,* **replacer** *n*

re'placement /-mənt/ *n* **1** replacing or being replaced **2** sthg or sby that replaces another

replant /,ree'plahnt/ *vt* **1** to plant again or anew **2** to provide with new plants

[1]**replay** /,ree'play/ *vt* to play again

[2]**replay** /'reeplay/ *n* **1a** an act or instance of replaying **b** the playing of a tape (e g a videotape) **2** a repetition, reenactment ⟨*don't want a* ~ *of our old mistakes*⟩ **3** a match played to resolve a tie in an earlier match

replenish /ri'plenish/ *vt* to stock or fill up again ⟨~ed *his glass*⟩ [ME *replenisshen,* fr MF *repleniss-,* stem of *replenir* to fill, fr OF, fr *re-* + *plein* full, fr L *plenus* – more at [1]FULL] – **replenishment** *n*

replete /ri'pleet/ *adj* **1** fully or abundantly provided or filled **2** abundantly fed; sated [ME, fr MF & L; MF *replet,* fr L *repletus,* pp of *replēre* to fill up, fr *re-* + *plēre* to fill] – **repleteness** *n,* **repletion** /ri'pleesh(ə)n/ *n*

replevin /ri'plevin/ *n* the recovery of goods detained, upon security being given to try the matter in court [ME, fr AF *replevine,* fr *replevir* to give security, fr OF, fr *re-* + *plevir* to pledge, fr (assumed) LL *plebere*]

replevy /ri'plevi/ *vt* to get back by replevin [AF *replevir*]

replica /'replikə/ *n* **1** a close reproduction or facsimile, esp by the maker of the original **2** a copy, duplicate [It, repetition, fr *replicare* to repeat, fr LL, fr L, to fold back]

replicate /'repli,kayt/ *vt* **1** to duplicate, repeat ⟨~ *a statistical experiment*⟩ **2** to fold or bend back ~ *vi* to produce a replica of itself ⟨replicating *virus particles*⟩ [LL *replicatus,* pp of *replicare;* (2) L *replicatus*] – **replicable** /'replikəbl/ *adj,* **replicative** /-kətiv, -,kaytiv/ *adj,* **replicability** /-kə'biləti/ *n*

replication /,repli'kaysh(ə)n/ *n* **1a** an answer (to a reply); a rejoinder **b** a plaintiff's reply to a defendant **2** the action or process of reproducing

[1]**reply** /ri'plie/ *vi* **1a** to respond in words or writing **b** to make a legal replication **2** to do sthg in response ~ *vt* to give as an answer [ME *replien,* fr MF *replier* to fold again, fr L *replicare* to fold back, fr *re-* + *plicare* to fold – more at [1]PLY]

[2]**reply** *n* sthg said, written, or done in answer or response

[1]**report** /ri'pawt/ *n* **1a** (an account spread by) common talk **b** character or reputation ⟨*a man of good* ~⟩ **2a** a usu detailed account or statement ⟨*a news* ~⟩ **b** an account of a judicial opinion or decision **c** a usu formal record of the proceedings of a meeting or inquiry **d** a statement of a pupil's performance at school usu issued every term to the pupil's parents or guardian **3** a loud explosive noise [ME, fr MF, fr OF, fr *reporter* to report, fr L *reportare,* fr *re-* + *portare* to carry – more at [1]FARE]

[2]**report** *vt* **1** to give information about; relate **2a** to convey news of **b** to relate the words or sense of (sthg said) **c** to make a written record or summary of **d** to present the newsworthy aspects or developments of in writing or for broadcasting **3a** to announce or relate (as the result of examination or investigation) ⟨~ed *no sign of disease*⟩ **b** to make known to the relevant authorities ⟨~ *a fire*⟩ **c** to make a charge of misconduct against ~ *vi* **1a** to give an account **b** to present oneself ⟨~ *at the main entrance*⟩ **c** to account for oneself as specified ⟨~ed *sick on Friday*⟩ **2** to make, issue, or submit a report **3** to act in the capacity of a news reporter – **reportable** *adj*

reportage /,repaw'tahzh, ri'pawtij/ *n* **1** the act or process of reporting news **2** writing intended to give a usu factual account of events [F, fr *reporter* to report]

reportedly /ri'pawtidli/ *adv* reputedly

re,ported 'speech /ri'pawtid/ *n* the report of one utterance grammatically adapted for inclusion in another

reporter /ri'pawtə/ *n* sby who or sthg that reports: e g **a** one who makes a shorthand record of a proceeding **b** a journalist who writes news stories **c** one who gathers and broadcasts news

re'port ,stage *n* the stage in the British legislative process before the third reading of a bill ☞ LAW

¹repose /ri'pohz/ *vt* to lay at rest ⟨~ *her head on the cushion*⟩ ~ *vi* **1a** to lie resting **b** to lie dead ⟨reposing *in state*⟩ **2** to take rest **3** to rest for support – chiefly fml ⟨*a bowl* reposing *on the table*⟩ [ME *reposen*, fr MF *reposer*, fr OF, fr LL *repausare*, fr L *re-* + LL *pausare* to stop, fr L *pausa* pause – more at PAUSE]

²repose *n* **1** a place or state of rest or resting; *esp* rest in sleep **2a** calm, tranquillity **b** a restful effect (e g of a painting or colour scheme) **3** cessation or absence of activity, movement, or animation ⟨*the appearance of his face in* ~⟩ **4** composure of manner – **reposeful** *adj*

repository /ri'pozət(ə)ri/ *n* **1** a place, room, or container where sthg is deposited or stored **2** sby who or sthg that holds or stores sthg nonmaterial (e g knowledge) **3** sby to whom sthg is confided or entrusted [L *repositorium*, fr *repositus*, pp of *reponere* to replace, fr *re-* + *ponere* to place – more at POSITION]

repossess /,reepə'zes/ *vt* **1** to regain possession of **2** to resume possession of in default of the payment of instalments due – **repossession** /-'zesh(ə)n/ *n*

repoussé /rə'poohsay/ *n or adj* (metalwork) decorated with patterns in relief made by hammering on the reverse side [adj F, pp of *repousser* to press back, fr MF, fr *re-* + *pousser* to push, thrust, fr OF *poulser* – more at PUSH; n fr adj]

repp /rep/ *n* ¹REP

reprehend /,repri'hend/ *vt* to voice disapproval of; censure [ME *reprehenden*, fr L *reprehendere*, lit., to hold back, fr *re-* + *prehendere* to grasp – more at PREHENSILE]

reprehensible /,repri'hensəbl/ *adj* deserving censure; culpable [ME, fr LL *reprehensibilis*, fr *reprehensus*, pp of *reprehendere*] – **reprehensibleness** *n*, **reprehensibly** *adv*, **reprehensibility** /-'biləti/ *n*

represent /,repri'zent/ *vt* **1** to convey a mental impression of ⟨*a book which* ~s *the character of Tudor England*⟩ **2** to serve as a sign or symbol of ⟨*the snake* ~s *Satan*⟩ **3** to portray or exhibit in art; depict **4a(1)** to take the place of in some respect; stand in for **(2)** to act in the place of **b** to serve, esp in a legislative body, by delegated authority **5** to attribute a specified character or identity to ⟨~s *himself as a friend of the workingman*⟩ **6** to serve as a specimen, exemplar, or instance of **7** to form a mental impression of [ME *representen*, fr MF *representer*, fr L *repraesentare*, fr *re-* + *praesentare* to present] – **representable** *adj*, **representer** *n*

representation /,reprizen'taysh(ə)n/ *n* **1** sby who or sthg that represents: e g **a** an artistic likeness or image **b** a statement made to influence opinion – usu pl with sing. meaning **c** a usu formal protest ⟨*a* ~ *in parliament*⟩ **2** representing or being represented: e g **a** the action or fact of one person standing in place of another so as to have the rights and obligations of the person represented **b** representing or being represented on or in some formal, esp legislative, body **3** the people representing a constituency – **representational** *adj*

representational /,reprizen'taysh(ə)nl/ *adj* **1** of representation **2** of realistic depiction of esp physical objects or appearances in the graphic or plastic arts

representationalism /,reprizen'tayshn·liz(ə)m/ *n* the theory that the perceived object is an idea in the mind that represents an item in the external world – compare PRESENTATIONISM – **representationalist** *n*

¹representative /,repri'zentətiv/ *adj* **1** serving to represent ⟨*a painting* ~ *of strife*⟩ **2a** standing or acting for another, esp through delegated authority **b** of or based on representation of the people in government by election **3** serving as a typical or characteristic example ⟨*a* ~ *area*⟩ **4** of representation – **representatively** *adv*, **representativeness** *n*

²representative *n* **1** a typical example of a group, class, or quality **2** one who represents another or others: e g **a(1)** one who represents a constituency **(2)** a member of a House of Representatives or of a US state legislature **b** a deputy, delegate **c** one who represents a business organization; *esp* SALES REPRESENTATIVE **d** one who represents another as successor or heir

repress /ri'pres/ *vt* **1a** to curb ⟨*injustice was* ~ed⟩ **b** to put down by force ⟨~ *an insurrection*⟩ **2a** to hold in or prevent the expression of, by self-control ⟨~ed *a laugh*⟩ **b** to exclude (e g a feeling) from consciousness by psychological repression – compare SUPPRESS 3a [ME *repressen*, fr L *repressus*, pp of *reprimere* to check, fr *re-* + *premere* to press – more at ²PRESS] – **repressible** *adj*, **repressive** /-siv/ *adj*, **repressor** *n*

repression /ri'presh(ə)n/ *n* **1a** repressing or being repressed ⟨~ *of unpopular opinions*⟩ **b** an instance of repressing ⟨*racial* ~s⟩ **2** a psychological process by which unacceptable desires or impulses are excluded from conscious awareness

¹reprieve /ri'preev/ *vt* **1** to delay or remit the punishment of (e g a condemned prisoner) **2** to give temporary relief or rest to [perh fr MF *repris*, pp of *reprendre* to take back]

²reprieve *n* **1a** reprieving or being reprieved **b** (a warrant for) a suspension or remission of a (death) sentence **2** a temporary remission (e g from pain or trouble)

¹reprimand /'repri,mahnd/ *n* a severe (and formal) reproof [F *réprimande*, fr L *reprimenda*, fem of *reprimendus*, gerundive of *reprimere* to check]

²reprimand /'--,-, ,--'-/ *vt* to criticize sharply or formally censure, usu from a position of authority

reprint /'ree,print/ *n* **1** a subsequent impression of a book previously published in the same form **2** matter (e g an article) that has appeared in print before – **reprint** /,ree'print/ *vt*

reprisal /ri'priezl/ *n* **1** (a) retaliation by force short of war **2** the usu forcible retaking of sthg (e g territory) **3** a retaliatory act [ME *reprisail*, fr MF *reprisaille*, fr OIt *ripresaglia*, fr *ripreso*, pp of *riprendere* to take back, fr *ri-* re- (fr L *re-*) + *prendere* to take, fr L *prehendere* – more at PREHENSILE]

reprise /ri'preez; *sense* ¹ *also* ri'priez/ *n* **1** a deduction or charge made yearly out of a manor or estate – usu pl **2** a repetition of a musical passage, theme, or performance [ME, fr MF, lit., action of taking back, fr OF, fr *reprendre* to take back, fr *re-* + *prendre* to take, fr L *prehendere*]

¹reproach /ri'prohch/ *n* **1** (a cause or occasion of) discredit or disgrace ⟨*the poverty of millions is a constant* ~⟩ **2** the act or action of reproaching or disapproving ⟨*was beyond* ~⟩ **3** an expression of rebuke or disapproval [ME *reproche*, fr MF, fr OF, fr *reprochier* to reproach, fr (assumed) VL *repropiare*, fr L *re-* + *prope* near – more at

APPROACH] – **reproachful** *adj*, **reproachfully** *adv*, **reproachfulness** *n*

[2]**reproach** *vt* to express disappointment and displeasure with (a person) for conduct that is blameworthy or in need of amendment – **reproachable** *adj*, **reproacher** *n*, **reproachingly** *adv*

[1]**reprobate** /'reprə,bayt/ *vt* **1** to condemn strongly as unworthy, unacceptable, or evil **2** to predestine to damnation [ME *reprobaten*, fr LL *reprobatus*, pp of *reprobare* – more at REPROVE] – **reprobation** /-'baysh(ə)n/ *n*, **reprobative** /'reprəbətiv/ *adj*, **reprobatory** /-t(ə)ri/ *adj*

[2]**reprobate** /'reprəbayt/ *adj* **1** predestined to damnation **2** morally dissolute; unprincipled – **reprobate** *n*

reproduce /,reeprə'dyoohs/ *vt* **1** to produce (new living things of the same kind) by a sexual or asexual process **2** to cause to exist again or anew **3** to imitate closely ⟨*sound-effects that ~ the sound of thunder*⟩ **4** to make an image or copy of **5** to translate (a recording) into sound or an image ~ *vi* **1** to undergo reproduction in a usu specified manner ⟨*the picture ~s well*⟩ **2** to produce offspring [RE- + [1]PRODUCE] – **reproducer** *n*, **reproducible** *adj*, **reproducibility** /-sə'biləti/ *n*

reproduction /,reeprə'duksh(ə)n/ *n* **1** the act or process of reproducing; *specif* the sexual or asexual process by which plants and animals give rise to offspring **2** sthg (e g a painting) that is reproduced – **reproductive** /-'duktiv/ *adj*

reprography /ri'prografi/ *n* the science or practice of reproducing graphic matter (e g by photocopying) [*reproduction* + *-graphy*] – **reprographic** /,reprə'grafik/ *adj*

reproof /ri'proohf/ *n* criticism for a fault [ME *reprof*, fr MF *reprove*, fr OF, fr *reprover*]

reprove /ri'proohv/ *vt* **1** to call attention to the remissness of ⟨*~ a child's bad manners*⟩ *vt* **2** to express disapproval of; censure ⟨*~ a child for her bad manners*⟩ [ME *reproven*, fr MF *reprover*, fr LL *reprobare* to disapprove, condemn, fr L *re-* + *probare* to test, approve – more at PROVE] – **reprover** *n*, **reprovingly** *adv*

reptile /'reptiel/ *n* **1** any of a class of air-breathing vertebrates that include the alligators and crocodiles, lizards, snakes, turtles, and extinct related forms (e g the dinosaurs) and have a bony skeleton and a body usu covered with scales or bony plates EVOLUTION **2** a grovelling or despicable person [ME *reptil*, fr MF or LL; MF *reptile* (fem), fr LL *reptile* (neut), fr neut of *reptilis* creeping, fr L *reptus*, pp of *repere* to creep; akin to OHG *reba* tendril]

[1]**reptilian** /rep'tilyən/ *adj* **1** resembling or having the characteristics of a reptile **2** of the reptiles

[2]**reptilian** *n* REPTILE 1

republic /ri'publik/ *n* **1a** a state whose head is not a monarch **b** a state in which supreme power resides in the people and is exercised by their elected representatives governing according to law **c** a (specified) republican government ⟨*the French Fourth* Republic⟩ **2** a body of people freely and equally engaged in a common activity ⟨*the ~ of letters*⟩ **3** a constituent political and territorial unit of the USSR or Yugoslavia [F *république*, fr MF *republique*, fr L *respublica*, fr *res* thing, wealth + *publica*, fem of *publicus* public – more at [1]REAL, PUBLIC]

[1]**republican** /ri'publikən/ *adj* **1a** of or like a republic **b** advocating a republic **2** *cap* of or constituting a political party of the USA that is usu primarily associated with business, financial, and some agricultural interests and is held to favour a restricted governmental role in social and economic life – **republicanism** *n*

[2]**republican** *n* **1** one who favours republican government **2** *cap* a member of the US Republican party

repudiate /ri'pyoohdi,ayt/ *vt* **1** to refuse to have anything to do with; disown **2a** to refuse to accept; *esp* to reject as unauthorized or as having no binding force **b** to reject as untrue or unjust ⟨*~ a charge*⟩ **3** to refuse to acknowledge or pay ⟨*~ a debt*⟩ [L *repudiatus*, pp of *repudiare*, fr *repudium* divorce] – **repudiation** /-'aysh(ə)n/ *n*

repugnance /ri'pugnəns/ *n* **1** the quality or fact or an instance of being contradictory or incompatible **2** strong dislike, aversion, or antipathy

repugnant /ri'pugnənt/ *adj* **1** incompatible, inconsistent **2** arousing strong dislike or aversion [ME, opposed, contradictory, incompatible, fr MF, fr L *repugnant-*, *repugnans*, prp of *repugnare* to fight against, fr *re-* + *pugnare* to fight – more at PUNGENT] – **repugnantly** *adv*

[1]**repulse** /ri'puls/ *vt* **1** to drive or beat back ⟨*~ the invading army*⟩ **2** to repel by discourtesy, coldness, or denial **3** to cause repulsion in [L *repulsus*, pp of *repellere* to repel]

[2]**repulse** *n* **1** a rebuff, rejection **2** repelling an assailant or being repelled

repulsion /ri'pulsh(ə)n/ *n* **1** repulsing or being repulsed **2** a force (e g between like electric charges or like magnetic poles) tending to produce separation **3** a feeling of strong aversion

repulsive /ri'pulsiv/ *adj* **1** tending to repel or reject; forbidding **2** serving or able to repulse **3** arousing strong aversion or disgust – **repulsively** *adv*, **repulsiveness** *n*

reputable /'repyootəbl/ *adj* held in good repute; well regarded – **reputably** *adv*, **reputability** /,repyootə'biləti/ *n*

reputation /,repyoo'taysh(ə)n/ *n* **1a** overall quality or character as seen or judged by others **b** recognition by other people of some characteristic or ability ⟨*has the ~ of being clever*⟩ **2** a place in public esteem or regard; good name

[1]**repute** /ri'pyooht/ *vt* to believe, consider ⟨~d *to be the oldest specimen*⟩ ⟨~d *honest*⟩ [ME *reputen*, fr MF *reputer*, fr L *reputare* to reckon up, think over, fr *re-* + *putare* to reckon – more at PAVE]

[2]**repute** *n* **1** the character, quality, or status commonly ascribed **2** the state of being favourably known or spoken of

re'puted *adj* being such according to general or popular belief ⟨*the ~ father of the child*⟩ – **reputedly** *adv*

[1]**request** /ri'kwest/ *n* **1** the act or an instance of asking for sthg **2** sthg asked for **3** the condition or fact of being requested ⟨*available on ~*⟩ **4** the state of being sought after ⟨*a book in great ~*⟩ [ME *requeste*, fr MF, fr (assumed) VL *requaesta*, fr fem of *requaestus*, pp of *requaerere* to require]

[2]**request** *vt* **1** to make a request to or of ⟨~ed *her to write a paper*⟩ **2** to ask as a favour or privilege ⟨*he ~s to be excused*⟩ **3** to ask for ⟨~ed *a brief delay*⟩

requiem /'rekwi·əm, -,em/ *n* **1** a mass for the dead **2** sthg that resembles a solemn funeral chant in tone or function ⟨'Requiem *for a Nun*" – William Faulkner⟩ **3** *often cap* **a** a musical setting of the mass for the dead **b** a musical composition in honour of the dead [ME, fr L (first word of the introit of the requiem mass), acc of *requies* rest, fr *re-* + *quies* quiet, rest – more at WHILE]

require /ri'kwie·ə/ *vt* **1** to claim or demand by right and authority **2a** to call for as suitable or appropriate ⟨*the occasion* ~s *formal dress*⟩ **b** to call for as necessary or essential; have a compelling need for ⟨*all living beings* ~ *food*⟩ **3** to impose an obligation or command on; compel [ME *requeren*, fr MF *requerre*, fr (assumed) VL *requaerere* to seek for, need, require, alter. of L *requirere*, fr *re-* + *quaerere* to seek, ask] – **requirement** *n*

requisite /'rekwizit/ *adj* necessary, required ⟨*make the* ~ *payment*⟩ [ME, fr L *requisitus*, pp of *requirere*] – **requisite** *n*, **requisiteness** *n*

requisition /,rekwi'zish(ə)n/ *n* **1** the act of formally requesting sby to perform an action **2a** the act of requiring sthg to be supplied **b** a formal and authoritative (written) demand or application ⟨~ *for army supplies*⟩ [MF or ML; MF, fr ML *requisition-*, *requisitio*, fr L, act of searching, fr *requisitus*] – **requisition** *vt*

requite /ri'kwiet/ *vt* **1** to make retaliation for **2a** to make suitable return to (for a benefit or service) **b** to compensate sufficiently for (an injury) [*re-* + obs *quite* (to quit, pay), fr ME *quiten* – more at [2]QUIT] – **requital** /ri'kwitl/ *n*

reredos /'riə,dos, 'riəri,dos, 'reərə-/ *n* a usu ornamental wood or stone screen or partition wall behind an altar [ME, fr AF *areredos*, fr MF *arrere* behind + *dos* back, fr L *dorsum* – more at ARREAR]

rerun /'ree,run/ *n* a presentation of a film or television programme after its first run – **rerun** /,ree'run/ *vt*

rescind /ri'sind/ *vt* **1** to annul; TAKE BACK ⟨*refused to* ~ *her harsh order*⟩ **2** to repeal, revoke (e g a law, custom, etc) [L *rescindere*, fr *re-* + *scindere* to cut – more at [1]SHED] – **rescinder** *n*, **rescindment** *n*, **rescission** /ri'sizh(ə)n/ *n*

rescript /'ree,skript/ *n* **1** a written answer (e g of a pope) to a legal inquiry or petition **2** an act or instance of rewriting [L *rescriptum*, fr neut of *rescriptus*, pp of *rescribere* to write in reply, fr *re-* + *scribere* to write – more at [1]SCRIBE]

rescue /'reskyooh/ *vt* to free from confinement, danger, or evil [ME *rescuen*, fr MF *rescourre*, fr OF, fr *re-* + *escourre* to shake out, fr L *excutere*, fr *ex-* + *quatere* to shake – more at QUASH] – **rescue** *n*, **rescuer** *n*

[1]**research** /ri'suhch, 'reesuhch/ *n* **1** careful or diligent search **2** scientific or scholarly inquiry; *esp* study or experiment aimed at the discovery, interpretation, reinterpretation, or application of (new) facts, theories, or laws [MF *recerche*, fr *recerchier* to investigate thoroughly, fr OF, fr *re-* + *cerchier* to search – more at SEARCH]

[2]**research** *vt vt* **1** to search or investigate thoroughly ⟨~ *a problem*⟩ **2** to engage in research on or for ⟨~ *a book*⟩ ⟨~ *the life of Chaucer*⟩ ~ *vi* to perform research – **researchable** /ri'suhchəbl/ *adj*, **researcher** /ri'suhchə, 'ree-/ *n*

resect /ri'sekt/ *vt* to remove surgically a part of (an organ or structure) [L *resectus*, pp of *resecare* to cut off, fr *re-* + *secare* to cut – more at [2]SAW] – **resectable** *adj*, **resectability** /-tə'biləti/ *n*, **resection** /ri'seksh(ə)n/ *n*

reseda /'residə/ *n* any of a genus of Old World plants (e g mignonette) [NL, genus name, fr L, a plant used to reduce tumours]

resemble /ri'zembl/ *vt* **resembling** /ri'zembling, -'zembl·ing/ to be like or similar to [ME *resemblen*, fr MF *resembler*, fr OF, fr *re-* + *sembler* to be like, seem, fr L *similare* to copy, fr *similis* like – more at SAME] – **resemblance** /ri'zembləns/ *n*

resent /ri'zent/ *vt* to harbour or express ill will or bitterness at [F *ressentir* to feel strongly about, fr OF, fr *re-* + *sentir* to feel, fr L *sentire* – more at SENSE] – **resentful** *adj*, **resentfully** *adv*, **resentfulness** *n*, **resentment** *n*

reserpine /'resəpin/ *n* an alkaloid extracted esp from the root of a tropical shrub of the periwinkle family and sometimes used in the treatment of mildly raised blood pressure [G *reserpin*, prob irreg fr NL *Rauwolfia serpentina*, a shrub of the genus Rauwolfia]

reservation /,rezə'vaysh(ə)n/ *n* **1** an act of reserving sthg; *esp* (a promise, guarantee, or record of) an arrangement to have sthg (e g a hotel room) held for one's use **2** a tract of land set aside; *specif* one designated for the use of American Indians by treaty **3a** (the specifying of) a limiting condition ⟨*agreed, but with* ~s⟩ **b** a specific doubt or objection ⟨*had* ~s *about the results*⟩ **4** a strip of land separating carriageways **5** *chiefly NAm* an area in which hunting is not permitted; *esp* one set aside as a secure breeding place [[1]RESERVE + -ATION]

[1]**reserve** /ri'zuhv/ *vt* **1** to hold in reserve; keep back ⟨~ *grain for seed*⟩ **2** to set aside (part of the consecrated elements) at the Eucharist for future use **3** to defer ⟨~ *one's judgment on a plan*⟩ [ME *reserven*, fr MF *reserver*, fr L *reservare*, lit., to keep back, fr *re-* + *servare* to keep – more at CONSERVE]

[2]**reserve** *n* **1** sthg retained for future use or need **2** sthg reserved or set aside for a particular use or reason: e g **a(1)** a military force withheld from action for later use – usu pl with sing. meaning **(2)** the military forces of a country not part of the regular services; *also* a reservist **b** *chiefly Br* a tract (e g of public land) set apart for the conservation of natural resources or (rare) flora and fauna ⟨*a nature* ~⟩; *also* one used for regulated hunting or fishing ⟨*a game* ~⟩ **3** an act of reserving ⟨*accepted without* ~⟩ **4** restraint, closeness, or caution in one's words and actions **5** money, gold, foreign exchange, etc kept in hand or set apart usu to meet liabilities – often pl with sing. meaning **6** a player or participant who has been selected to substitute for another if the need should arise – **in reserve** held back ready for use if needed

re'served *adj* **1** restrained in speech and behaviour **2** kept or set apart or aside for future or special use – **reservedly** /-vidli/ *adv*, **reservedness** /-vidnis/ *n*

re'serve ,price *n* a price announced at an auction as the lowest that will be considered

reservist /ri'zuhvist/ *n* a member of a military reserve

reservoir /'rezə,vwah/ *n* **1** a place where sthg is kept in store: e g **a** an artificial lake where water is collected and kept in quantity for use **b** a part of an apparatus in which a liquid is held **2** an available but unused extra source or supply ⟨*an untapped* ~ *of ideas*⟩ [F *réservoir*, fr MF, fr *reserver*]

reset /,ree'set/ *vt* **-tt-; reset 1** to set again or anew

The reproductive system

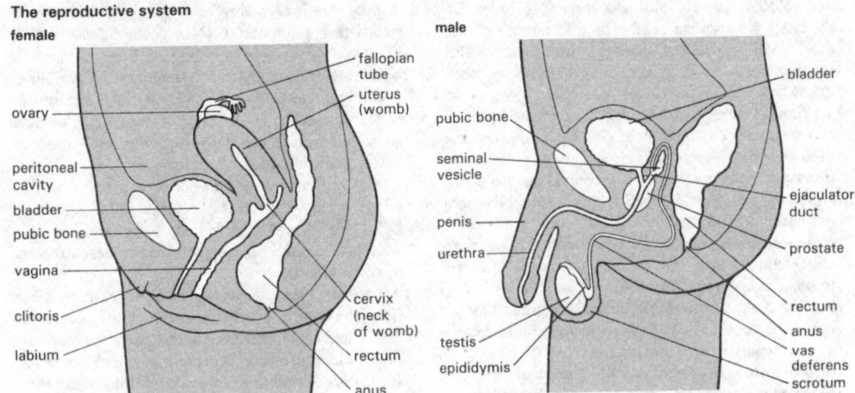

female

fallopian tube
uterus (womb)
ovary
peritoneal cavity
bladder
pubic bone
vagina
clitoris
labium
cervix (neck of womb)
rectum
anus

male

bladder
pubic bone
seminal vesicle
ejaculatory duct
penis
prostate
urethra
rectum
anus
testis
vas deferens
epididymis
scrotum

fallopian tube
uterus (womb)
ovum fertilized
ovum about to be released
ovary
cervical canal
implanted ovum
cervix (neck of womb)
vagina

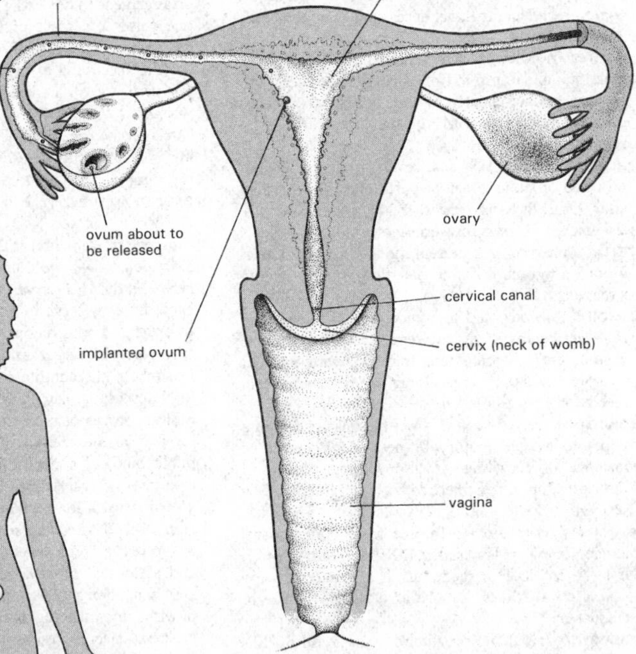

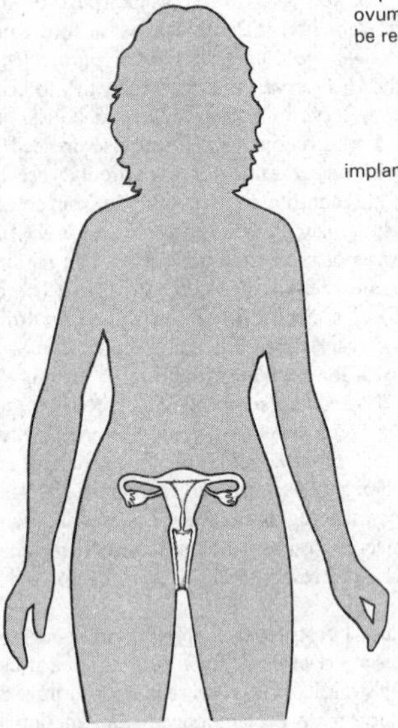

The female figure on the left shows the relative position and size of the internal organs. The above diagram shows the structures in more detail and illustrates the passage of the ovum from the ovary to the uterus, a journey which takes several days.

☞ ANATOMY, DIGESTION, NERVE

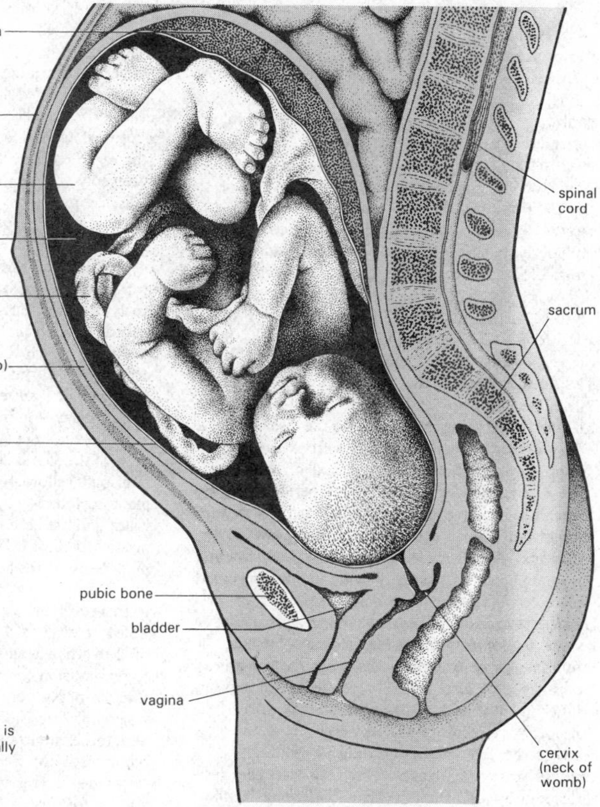

placenta
abdominal wall
foetus or embryo
amniotic fluid
umbilical cord
uterus (womb)
amnion
pubic bone
bladder
vagina
spinal cord
sacrum
cervix (neck of womb)

Pregnancy

The diagram on the right shows a foetus at full term – that is, when it is ready to be born. Pregnancy is usually 40 weeks long, the estimated birth date being calculated from the first day of the last menstrual period.

Menstrual cycle

The menstrual cycle is, on average, 28 days long though it is frequently shorter or longer than this. The day on which menstruation begins is counted as the first day of the cycle, and at the same time an ovum begins to develop in a follicle in the ovary. This ovum is released on or about the fourteenth day. It then passes down the fallopian tube to the uterus where, if the ovum has been fertilized, it embeds itself in the lining and starts to develop. If the ovum has not been fertilized it passes out of the uterus with the menstrual flow.

release of ovum (ovulation)
most likely time for conception
development of ovum in follicle
1
4
14
17
28 days
menstruation (menstrual period)
lining of uterus building up to receive ovum

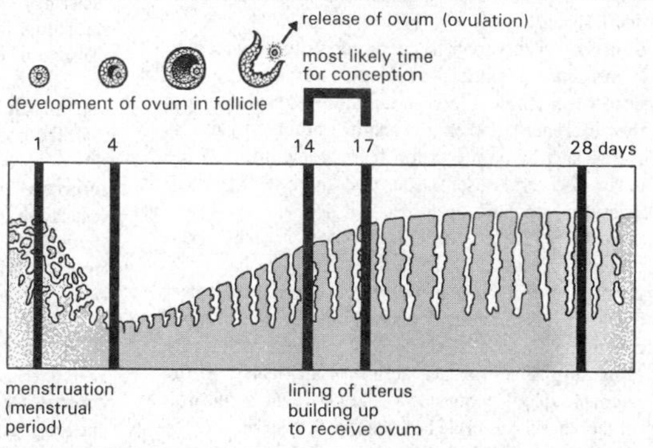

⟨~ *type*⟩ **2** to change the reading of ⟨~ *a meter*⟩ – **resettable** *adj*

res gestae /,reez 'jestee/ *n pl* facts relevant to legal proceedings and admissible as evidence [L, things done]

reshape /,ree'shayp/ *vt* to give a new form or orientation to – **reshaper** *n*

reshuffle /,ree'shufl/ *vt* to reorganize by the redistribution of (existing) elements ⟨*the cabinet was* ~d *by the Prime Minister*⟩ – **reshuffle** *n*

reside /ri'zied/ *vi* **1a** to dwell permanently or continuously; occupy a place as one's legal domicile **b** to make one's home for a time ⟨*the King* ~d *at Lincoln*⟩ **2a** to be present as an element or quality **b** to be vested as a right [ME *residen,* fr MF or L; MF *resider,* fr L *residēre* to sit back, remain, abide, fr *re-* + *sedēre* to sit – more at SIT]

residence /'rezid(ə)ns/ *n* **1a** the act or fact of dwelling in a place **b** the act or fact of living in or regularly attending some place for the discharge of a duty or the enjoyment of a benefit **2** a (large or impressive) dwelling **3a** the period of abode in a place ⟨*after a* ~ *of 30 years*⟩ **b** a period of study, teaching, etc at a college or university **4** *chiefly NAm* housing or a unit of housing provided for students – **residency** *n* – **in residence 1** serving in a regular capacity **2** actually living in a usu specified place ⟨*the Queen is* in residence *at Windsor*⟩

[1]**resident** /'rezid(ə)nt/ *adj* **1a** living in a place, esp for some length of time **b** serving in a regular or full-time capacity ⟨*the* ~ *engineer for a highway department*⟩; *also* being in residence **2** present, inherent **3** *of an animal* not migratory [ME, fr L *resident-, residens,* prp of *residēre*]

[2]**resident** *n* one who resides in a place

residential /,rezi'densh(ə)l/ *adj* **1a** used as a residence or by residents ⟨~ *accommodation*⟩ **b** entailing residence ⟨*a* ~ *course*⟩ **2** given over to private housing as distinct from industry or commerce ⟨*a* ~ *neighbourhood*⟩ **3** of residence or residences – **residentially** *adv*

[1]**residual** /ri'zidyooəl/ *adj* of or constituting a residue [L *residuum* residue] – **residually** *adv*

[2]**residual** *n* sthg left over; a remainder, residue: e g **a** the difference between **(1)** results obtained by observation and by computation from a formula **(2)** the mean of several observations and any one of them **b** a residual product or substance

re,siduary lega'tee /ri'zidyooəri/ *n* sby who inherits a residue

residue /'rezidyooh/ *n* sthg that remains after a part is taken, separated, or designated; a remnant, remainder: e g **a** that part of a testator's estate remaining after the satisfaction of all debts and the payment of all bequests **b** a constituent structural unit of a usu complex molecule (e g a protein or nucleic acid) [ME, fr MF *residu,* fr L *residuum,* fr neut of *residuus* left over, fr *residēre* to remain]

residuum /ri'zidyooəm/ *n, pl* **residua** /-dyooə/ sthg residual: e g **a** RESIDUE a **b** a residual product (e g left after the distillation of petroleum) [L]

resign /ri'zien/ *vt* **1** to renounce voluntarily; *esp* to relinquish (e g a right or position) by a formal act **2** to reconcile, consign; *esp* to give (oneself) over without resistance ⟨~ed *herself to her fate*⟩ ~ *vi* to give up one's office or position [ME *resignen,* fr MF *resigner,* fr L *resignare,* lit., to unseal, cancel, fr *re-* + *signare* to sign, seal – more at [2]SIGN] – **resigner** *n*

resignation /,rezig'naysh(ə)n/ *n* **1a** an act or instance of resigning sthg **b** a formal notification of resigning ⟨*handed in her* ~⟩ **2** the quality or state of being resigned

re'signed *adj* marked by or expressing submission to sthg regarded as inevitable ⟨*a* ~ *look on his face*⟩ – **resignedly** /ri'zienidli/ *adv,* **resignedness** /-nidnis/ *n*

resilience /ri'zilyəns/, **resiliency** /-si/ *n* **1** the ability of a body to recover its original form after deformation (e g due to stretching or applying pressure) **2** an ability to recover quickly from or adjust easily to misfortune, change, or disturbance

resilient /ri'zilyənt/ *adj* characterized or marked by resilience; *esp* capable of withstanding shock without permanent deformation or rupture [L *resilient-, resiliens,* prp of *resilire* to jump back, recoil, fr *re-* + *salire* to leap – more at SALLY] – **resiliently** *adv*

[1]**resin** /'rezin/ *n* (a synthetic polymer or plastic with some of the characteristics of) any of various solid or semisolid yellowish to brown inflammable natural plant secretions (e g amber) that are insoluble in water and are used esp in varnishes, sizes, inks, and plastics [ME, fr MF *resine,* fr L *resina,* fr Gk *rhētinē* pine resin] – **resinoid** /-noyd/ *adj or n,* **resinous** *adj*

[2]**resin** *vt* to treat with resin

[1]**resist** /ri'zist/ *vt* **1** to withstand the force or effect of **2** to strive against ⟨~ed *the enemy valiantly*⟩ **3** to refrain from ⟨*could never* ~ *a joke*⟩ ~ *vi* to exert force in opposition [ME *resisten,* fr MF or L; MF *resister,* fr L *resistere,* fr *re-* + *sistere* to take a stand; akin to L *stare* to stand – more at STAND] – **resistible** *adj,* **resistibility** /-tə'biləti/ *n*

[2]**resist** *n* sthg (e g a protective coating) applied to a surface to cause it to resist or prevent the action of a particular agent (e g an acid or dye)

resistance /ri'zist(ə)ns/ *n* **1** an act or instance of resisting **2** the ability to resist **3** an opposing or retarding force **4a** the opposition offered to the passage of a steady electric current through a substance, usu measured in ohms **b** a resistor **5** *often cap* an underground organization of a conquered country engaging in sabotage ***USE*** *(4)* ☞ PHYSICS

resistant /ri'zist(ə)nt/ *adj* capable of or offering resistance – often in combination ⟨*heat-*resistant *paint*⟩

resister /ri'zistə/ *n, chiefly NAm* one who actively opposes the policies of a government [[1]RESIST + [2]-ER]

resistive /ri'zistiv/ *adj* resistant – **resistively** *adv,* **resistiveness** *n*

resistivity /,rezis'tivəti/ *n* **1** (electrical) resistance **2** the longitudinal electrical resistance of a uniform rod of a specified substance of unit length and unit cross-sectional area

resistless /ri'zistlis/ *adj* **1** irresistible **2** unable to resist – **resistlessly** *adv,* **resistlessness** *n*

resistor /ri'zistə/ *n* a component included in an electrical circuit to provide resistance

resolute /'rezəl(y)ooht/ *adj* **1** firmly resolved; determined **2** bold, unwavering [L *resolutus,* pp of *resolvere*] – **resolutely** *adv,* **resoluteness** *n*

resolution /,rezə'loohsh(ə)n, -'lyoohsh(ə)n/ *n* **1** the act or process of reducing to simpler form: e g **a** the act of making a firm decision **b** the act of finding out sthg (e g the answer to a problem); solving **c** the passing of a voice part from a dissonant to a consonant note or the progression of a chord from dissonance to consonance **d** the separating of a chemical compound or mixture into its constituents **e** the analysis of a vector into 2 or more vectors of which it is the sum **f** the process or capability (e g of a microscope) of making individual parts or closely adjacent images distinguishable **2** the subsidence of inflammation, esp in a lung **3a** sthg that is resolved **b** firmness of resolve **4** a formal expression of opinion, will, or intent voted by a body or group

[1]**resolve** /ri'zolv/ *vt* **1a** to break up or separate into constituent parts **b** to reduce by analysis ⟨~ *the problem into simple elements*⟩ **2** to cause or produce the resolution of **3a** to deal with successfully ⟨~ *doubts*⟩ ⟨~ *a dispute*⟩ **b** to find an answer to **c** to find a mathematical solution of **d** to express (e g a vector) as the sum of 2 or more components **4** to reach a firm decision about ⟨~ *disputed points in a text*⟩ **5** to declare or decide by a formal resolution and vote **6** to make (e g voice parts) progress from dissonance to consonance ~ *vi* **1** to become separated into constituent parts; *also* to become reduced by dissolving or analysis **2** to form a resolution; determine ⟨*he* ~d *against overeating at Christmas*⟩ **3** to progress from dissonance to consonance [L *resolvere* to unloose, dissolve, fr *re-* + *solvere* to loosen, release – more at SOLVE] – **resolvable** *adj*, **resolver** *n*

[2]**resolve** *n* **1** sthg that is resolved **2** fixity of purpose **3** a legal or official decision; *esp* a formal resolution

resolvent /ri'zolv(ə)nt/ *n or adj* (sthg, esp a drug) capable of reducing inflammation [adj L *resolvent-*, *resolvens*, prp of *resolvere*; n fr adj]

re'solving ,power /ri'zolving/ *n* the ability of an (optical) system to form distinct images of objects separated by small distances

resonance /'rezənəns/ *n* **1a** the quality or state of being resonant **b** (the state of adjustment that produces) strong vibration in a mechanical or electrical system caused by the stimulus of a relatively small vibration of (nearly) the same frequency as that of the natural vibration of the system **2a** the intensification and enrichment of a musical tone by supplementary vibration **b** a quality imparted to voiced sounds by a buildup esp of vibrations in the vocal tract **3** the possession by a molecule, radical, etc of 2 or more possible structures differing only in the distribution of electrons

resonant /'rezənənt/ *adj* **1** continuing to sound **2a** capable of inducing resonance **b** relating to or exhibiting resonance **3** intensified and enriched by resonance – **resonant** *n*, **resonantly** *adv*

resonate /'rezə,nayt/ *vi* to produce or exhibit resonance ~ *vt* to make resonant [L *resonatus*, pp of *resonare* to resound – more at RESOUND]

resonator /'rezənaytə/ *n* sthg that resounds or resonates: e g **a** a device that responds to and can be used to detect a particular frequency **b** a device for increasing the resonance or amplifying the sound of a musical instrument

resorb /ri'sawb/ *vt* to swallow, suck in, or absorb again ~ *vi* to undergo resorption [L *resorbēre*, fr *re-* + *sorbēre* to suck up – more at ABSORB]

resorcin /ri'zawsin/, **resorcinol** /-nol/ *n* a synthetic phenol used in making dyes, medicines, and resins [ISV *res-* (fr L *resina* resin) + *orcin* (a natural or synthetic phenol)]

resorption /ri'sawpsh(ə)n/ *n* resorbing, esp of distinct tissues in the body, or being resorbed [L *resorptus*, pp of *resorbēre*] – **resorptive** /-tiv/ *adj*

[1]**resort** /ri'zawt/ *n* **1a** sby who or sthg that is looked to for help; a refuge ⟨*saw her as a last* ~⟩ **b** recourse ⟨*have* ~ *to force*⟩ **2a** frequent, habitual, or general visiting ⟨*a place of popular* ~⟩ **b** a frequently visited place (e g a village or town), esp providing accommodation and recreation for holidaymakers [ME, fr MF, resource, recourse, fr *resortir* to rebound, resort, fr OF, fr *re-* + *sortir* to escape, sally]

[2]**resort** *vi* **1** to go, esp frequently or in large numbers **2** to have recourse ⟨~ *to force*⟩

resound /ri'zownd/ *vi* **1** to become filled with sound **2** to produce a sonorous or echoing sound **3** to become renowned ~ *vt* to extol loudly or widely [ME *resounen*, fr MF *resoner*, fr L *resonare*, fr *re-* + *sonare* to sound; akin to L *sonus* sound – more at [3]SOUND]

resounding /ri'zownding/ *adj* **1a** resonating **b** impressively sonorous **2** vigorously emphatic; unequivocal ⟨*a* ~ *success*⟩ – **resoundingly** *adv*

resource /ri'zaws, ri'saws/ *n* **1a** an available means of support or provision **b** a natural source of wealth or revenue ☞ ENERGY **c** computable wealth **d** a source of information or expertise **2** a means of occupying one's spare time **3** the ability to deal with a difficult situation; resourcefulness ***USE*** (*1a, b, c*) usu pl [F *ressource*, fr OF *ressourse* relief, resource, fr *resourdre* to relieve, lit., to rise again, fr L *resurgere* – more at RESURRECTION]

re'sourceful /-f(ə)l/ *adj* skilful in handling situations; capable of devising expedients – **resourcefully** *adv*, **resourcefulness** *n*

[1]**respect** /ri'spekt/ *n* **1** a relation to or concern with sthg usu specified; reference – in *with/in respect to* ⟨*with* ~ *to your last letter*⟩ **2a** high or special regard; esteem **b** the quality or state of being esteemed ⟨*achieving* ~ *among connoisseurs*⟩ **c** *pl* expressions of respect or deference ⟨*paid his* ~s⟩ **3** an aspect; detail ⟨*a good plan in some* ~s⟩ [ME, fr L *respectus*, lit., act of looking back, fr *respectus*, pp of *respicere* to look back, regard, fr *re-* + *specere* to look – more at SPY] – **in respect of 1** from the point of view of **2** in payment of

[2]**respect** *vt* **1a** to consider worthy of high regard **b** to refrain from interfering with ⟨~ *the sovereignty of a state*⟩ **c** to show consideration for ⟨~ *a person's privacy*⟩ **2** to have reference to – **respecter** *n*

respectability /ri,spektə'biləti/ *n* the quality or state of being socially respectable

respectable /ri'spektəbl/ *adj* **1** worthy of respect **2** decent or conventional in character or conduct **3a** acceptable in size or quantity ⟨~ *amount*⟩ **b** fairly good; tolerable **4** presentable ⟨~ *clothes*⟩ – **respectability** *n*, **respectably** *adv*

re'spectful /-f(ə)l/ *adj* marked by or showing respect or deference – **respectfully** *adv*, **respectfulness** *n*

respecting /ri'spekting/ *prep* with regard to; concerning

respective /ri'spektiv/ *adj* of or relating to each; particular, separate ⟨*their* ~ *homes*⟩ – **respectiveness** *n*

re'spectively /-li/ *adv* **1** in particular; separately **2**

in the order given ⟨*Mary and Anne were 12 and 16 years old* ~⟩

respell /,ree'spel/ *vt* to spell again or in another way and esp according to a phonetic system

respirable /'respirəbl, ri'spie·ərəbl/ *adj* fit for breathing; *also* capable of being taken in by breathing ⟨~ *particles of ash*⟩

respiration /,respi'raysh(ə)n/ *n* **1a** the process by which air or dissolved gases are brought into intimate contact with the circulating medium of a multicellular organism (e g by breathing) **b** (a single complete act of) breathing **2** the processes by which an organism supplies its cells with the oxygen needed for metabolism and removes the carbon dioxide formed in energy-producing reactions **3** any of various energy-yielding reactions involving oxidation that occur in living cells – **respirational** *adj*, **respiratory** /'respirət(ə)ri, ri'spirət(ə)ri, ri'spie·ə-/ *adj*

respirator /'respi,raytə/ *n* **1** a device worn over the mouth or nose to prevent the breathing of poisonous gases, harmful dusts, etc **2** a device for maintaining artificial respiration

respiratory pigment /'respirət(ə)ri, ri'spirət(ə)ri, ri'spie·ərət(ə)ri/ *n* any of various proteins that function in the transfer of oxygen in cellular respiration

respire /ri'spie·ə/ *vi* **1** to breathe **2** *of a cell or tissue* to take up oxygen and produce carbon dioxide during respiration ~ *vt* to breathe [ME *respiren*, fr L *respirare*, fr *re-* + *spirare* to blow, breathe – more at SPIRIT]

respite /'respiet, 'respit/ *n* **1** a period of temporary delay; *esp* REPRIEVE 1B **2** an interval of rest or relief [ME *respit*, fr OF, fr ML *respectus*, fr L, act of looking back – more at RESPECT]

resplendent /ri'splend(ə)nt/ *adj* characterized by splendour ⟨*the Queen sat* ~ *on her throne*⟩ [L *resplendent-*, *resplendens*, prp of *resplendēre* to shine back, fr *re-* + *splendēre* to shine – more at SPLENDID] – **resplendently** *adv*, **resplendence** *n*

1**respond** /ri'spond/ *vi* **1** to write or speak in reply; make an answer ⟨~ *to the appeal for aid*⟩ **2a** to react in response ⟨~ *to a stimulus*⟩ **b** to show favourable reaction ⟨~ *to surgery*⟩ ~ *vt* to reply [MF *respondre*, fr L *respondēre* to promise in return, answer, fr *re-* + *spondēre* to promise – more at SPOUSE] – **responder** *n*

2**respond** *n* an engaged pillar or pier supporting an arch or terminating a colonnade or arcade

1**respondent** /ri'spond(ə)nt/ *n* one who responds: e g **a** a defendant, esp in an appeal or divorce case **b** a person who replies to a poll [L *respondent-*, *respondens*, prp of *respondēre*]

2**respondent** *adj* making response

response /ri'spons/ *n* **1** an act of responding **2** sthg constituting a reply or reaction: e g **a** sthg (e g a verse) sung or said by the people or choir after or in reply to the officiant in a liturgical service ☞ SYMBOL **b** a change in the behaviour of an organism resulting from stimulation **c** the output of a transducer or detecting device that results from a given input and is often considered as a function of some variable (e g frequency) [ME & L; ME *respounse*, fr MF *respons*, fr L *responsum* reply, fr neut of *responsus*, pp of *respondēre*]

responsibility /ri,sponsə'biləti/ *n* **1** the quality or state of being responsible: e g **a** moral or legal obligation **b** reliability, trustworthiness **2** sthg or sby that one is responsible for

responsible /ri'sponsəbl/ *adj* **1a** liable to be required to justify **b(1)** liable to be called to account as the agent or primary cause ⟨*the woman* ~ *for the job*⟩ **(2)** being the reason or cause ⟨*mechanical defects were* ~ *for the accident*⟩ **2a** able to answer for one's own conduct **b** able to discriminate between right and wrong **3** marked by or involving responsibility or liability ⟨~ *financial policies*⟩ ⟨*a* ~ *job*⟩ **4** *esp of the British cabinet* required to submit to the electorate if defeated by the legislature – **responsibleness** *n*, **responsibly** *adv*

responsive /ri'sponsiv/ *adj* **1** giving response; constituting a response ⟨*a* ~ *glance*⟩ ⟨~ *aggression*⟩ **2** quick to respond or react appropriately or sympathetically – **responsively** *adv*, **responsiveness** *n*

responsory /ri'spons(ə)ri/ *n* a set of phrases and responses sung or said after a reading in church

responsum /ri'sponsəm/ *n*, *pl* **responsa** /-sə/ a written decision from a rabbinic authority in response to a submitted question or problem [NL, fr L, reply, formal opinion of a jurist]

1**rest** /rest/ *n* **1** repose, sleep **2a** freedom or a break from activity or labour **b** a state of motionlessness or inactivity **c** the repose of death **3** a place for resting, lodging, or taking refreshment ⟨*sailor's* ~⟩ **4** peace of mind or spirit **5a** (a character representing) a silence in music of a specified duration ☞ MUSIC **b** a brief pause in reading **6** sthg (e g an armrest) used for support [ME, fr OE; akin to OHG *rasta* rest, *ruowa* calm, Gk *erōē* respite] – **at rest** resting or reposing, esp in sleep or death

2**rest** *vi* **1a** to relax by lying down; *esp* to sleep **b** to lie dead ⟨~ *in peace*⟩ **2** to cease from action or motion; desist from labour or exertion **3** to be free from anxiety or disturbance **4** to be set or lie fixed or supported ⟨*a column* ~s *on its pedestal*⟩ **5** to be based or founded ⟨*the verdict* ~ed *on several sound precedents*⟩ **6** to depend for action or accomplishment ⟨*the answer* ~s *with him*⟩ **7** *of farmland* to remain idle or uncropped **8** to stop introducing evidence in a law case ~ *vt* **1** to give rest to **2** to set at rest **3** to place on or against a support **4a** to cause to be firmly based or founded ⟨~ed *all hope in his son*⟩ **b** to stop presenting evidence pertinent to (a case at law) – **rester** *n*

3**rest** *n* a collection or quantity that remains over ⟨*ate the* ~ *of the chocolate*⟩ [ME, fr MF *reste*, fr *rester* to remain, fr L *restare*, lit., to stand back, fr *re-* + *stare* to stand – more at STAND]

restate /,ree'stayt/ *vt* to state again or in a different way (e g more emphatically) – **restatement** *n*

restaurant /'rest(ə)ronh, -ront, -rənt/ *n* a place where refreshments, esp meals, are sold usu to be eaten on the premises [F, fr prp of *restaurer* to restore, fr L *restaurare*]

'restaurant ,car *n* DINING CAR

restauranteur /,rest(ə)ron'tuh/ *n* a restaurateur [modif of F *restaurateur*]

restaurateur /,rest(ə)rə'tuh, ,resto-/ *n* the manager or proprietor of a restaurant [F, fr LL *restaurator* restorer, fr L *restauratus*, pp of *restaurare*]

restful /'restf(ə)l/ *adj* **1** marked by, affording, or suggesting rest and repose ⟨*a* ~ *colour scheme*⟩ **2** quiet, tranquil – **restfully** *adv*, **restfulness** *n*

restitution /,resti'tyoohsh(ə)n/ *n* **1** restoration: e g **a** the returning of sthg (e g property) to its rightful owner **b** the making good of or giving a compensation for an injury **2** a legal action serving to cause restoration of a previous state [ME, fr OF, fr L *restitution-, restitutio,* fr *restitutus,* pp of *restituere* to restore, fr *re-* + *statuere* to set up – more at STATUTE]

restive /'restiv/ *adj* **1** stubbornly resisting control **2** restless, uneasy [ME *restif* (of animals) refusing to move, fr MF, fr *rester* to stop behind, remain] – **restively** *adv,* **restiveness** *n*

'restless /-lis/ *adj* **1** affording no rest ⟨*a ~ night*⟩ **2** continuously agitated ⟨*the ~ ocean*⟩ **3** characterized by or manifesting unrest, esp of mind ⟨*~ pacing*⟩; *also* changeful, discontented – **restlessly** *adv,* **restlessness** *n*

'rest ,mass *n* the mass of a body when it is at rest

restoration /,restə'raysh(ə)n/ *n* **1** restoring or being restored: e g **a** a reinstatement **b** a handing back of sthg **2** a representation or reconstruction of the original form (e g of a fossil or building) **3** *cap* the reestablishment of the monarchy in England in 1660 under Charles II; *also* the reign of Charles II ⟨Restoration *drama*⟩

restorative /ri'stawrətiv, -'sto-/ *n or adj* (sthg capable of) restoring esp health or vigour – **restoratively** *adv*

restore /ri'staw/ *vt* **1** to give back ⟨*~ the book to its owner*⟩ **2** to bring back into existence or use **3** to bring back to or put back into a former or original (unimpaired) state ⟨*to ~ a painting*⟩ **4** to put again in possession of sthg ⟨*newly ~*d *to health*⟩ [ME *restoren,* fr OF *restorer,* fr L *restaurare* to renew, rebuild, alter. of *instaurare* to renew – more at STORE] – **restorable** *adj,* **restorer** *n*

restrain /ri'strayn/ *vt* **1a** to prevent *from* doing sthg ⟨*~*ed *the boy from jumping*⟩ **b** to limit, repress, or keep under control ⟨*she found it hard to ~ her anger*⟩ **2** to deprive of liberty; *esp* to place under arrest [ME *restraynen,* fr MF *restraindre,* fr L *restringere* to restrain, restrict, fr *re-* + *stringere* to bind tight – more at [2]STRAIN] – **restrainable** *adj,* **restrainer** *n*

re'strained *adj* characterized by restraint; being without excess or extravagance – **restrainedly** /-nidli/ *adv*

restraint /ri'straynt/ *n* **1a** restraining or being restrained **b** a means of restraining; a restraining force or influence **2** moderation of one's behaviour; self-restraint [ME, fr MF *restrainte,* fr *restraindre*]

restrict /ri'strikt/ *vt* **1** to confine within bounds **2** to regulate or limit as to use or distribution [L *restrictus,* pp of *restringere*]

re'stricted *adj* **1a** not general; limited **b** available only to particular groups or for a particular purpose **c** subject to control, esp by law **d** not intended for general circulation ⟨*a ~ document*⟩ **2** narrow, confined – **restrictedly** *adv*

restriction /ri'striksh(ə)n/ *n* **1** a regulation that restricts or restrains ⟨*~*s *for motorists*⟩ **2** restricting or being restricted

restrictive /ri'striktiv/ *adj* **1** restricting or tending to restrict ⟨*~ regulations*⟩ **2** identifying rather than describing a modified word or phrase ⟨*a ~ clause*⟩ – **restrictively** *adv,* **restrictiveness** *n*

re,strictive 'practice *n* **1** a practice by the members of a trade union that limits the flexibility of management **2** an antisocial trading agreement (e g as to conditions of sale or quantities to be manufactured)

'rest ,room *n, NAm* public toilet facilities in a public building (e g a restaurant)

restructure /,ree'strukchə/ *vt* to change the make-up, organization, or pattern of ⟨*~ local government*⟩

[1]result /ri'zult/ *vi* **1** to proceed or arise as a consequence, effect, or conclusion, usu from sthg specified ⟨*injuries ~*ing *from skiing*⟩ **2** to have a usu specified outcome or end ⟨*errors that ~ in tragedy*⟩ [ME *resulten,* fr ML *resultare,* fr L, to rebound, fr *re-* + *saltare* to leap – more at SALTIRE]

[2]result *n* **1** sthg that results as a (hoped for or required) consequence, outcome, or conclusion **2** sthg obtained by calculation or investigation ⟨*showed us the ~ of the calculations*⟩ **3a** a win or tie as the conclusion of a cricket match **b** a win (e g in soccer)

[1]resultant /ri'zult(ə)nt/ *adj* derived or resulting from sthg else, esp as the total effect of many causes – **resultantly** *adv*

[2]resultant *n* the single vector that is the sum of a given set of vectors

resume /ri'zyoohm/ *vt* **1** to take or assume again ⟨*~*d *his seat by the fire* – Thomas Hardy⟩ **2** to return to or begin again after interruption *~ vi* to begin again after an interruption ⟨*the meeting will ~ after lunch*⟩ [ME *resumen,* fr MF or L; MF *resumer,* fr L *resumere,* fr *re-* + *sumere* to take up, take – more at CONSUME] – **resumption** /ri'zumpsh(ə)n/ *n*

résumé, resumé *also* **resume** /'rezyoo,may/ *n* a summary: e g **a** a summing up of sthg (e g a speech or narrative) **b** *NAm* CURRICULUM VITAE [F *résumé,* fr pp of *résumer* to resume, summarize]

resupinate /ri'syoohpinət/ *adj* (appearing to be) upside down [L *resupinatus,* pp of *resupinare* to bend back to a supine position, fr *re-* + *supinus* supine] – **resupination** /-'naysh(ə)n/ *n*

resurgence /ri'suhj(ə)ns/ *n* a rising again into life, activity, or influence [*resurgent* fr L *resurgent-, resurgens,* prp of *resurgere* to rise again] – **resurge** *vi,* **resurgent** *adj*

resurrect /,rezə'rekt/ *vt* **1** to bring back to life from the dead **2** to bring back into use or view [back-formation fr *resurrection*]

resurrection /,rezə'reksh(ə)n/ *n* **1a** *cap* the rising of Christ from the dead **b** *often cap* the rising again to life of all the human dead before the last judgment **2** a resurgence, revival, or restoration [ME, fr LL *resurrection-, resurrectio* act of rising from the dead, fr *resurrectus,* pp of *resurgere* to rise from the dead, fr L, to rise again, fr *re-* + *surgere* to rise – more at SURGE] – **resurrectional** *adj*

resurrectionist /,rezə'reksh(ə)nist/ *n* BODY SNATCHER

resuscitate /ri'susə,tayt/ *vt* to revive from apparent death or from unconsciousness; *also* to revitalize *~ vi* to revive; COME TO [L *resuscitatus,* pp of *resuscitare,* lit., to stir up again, fr *re-* + *suscitare* to stir up, fr *sub-, sus-* up + *citare* to put in motion, stir – more at SUB-, CITE] – **resuscitation** /-'taysh(ə)n/ *n,* **resuscitative** /-tətiv/ *adj,* **resuscitator** /-,taytə/ *n*

ret /ret/ *vt* **-tt-** to soak (e g flax) so that the fibres are loosened from the woody tissue [ME *reten,* fr MD]

[1]retail /'ree,tayl; *sense 2 often* ri'tayl/ *vt* **1** to sell (goods) in carrying on a retail business **2** [1]RECOUNT ~ *vi* to be sold at retail ⟨*tomatoes* ~ *at a higher price*⟩ [ME *retailen*, fr MF *retaillier* to cut back, divide into pieces, fr OF, fr *re-* + *taillier* to cut – more at TAILOR] – **retailer** /'ree,taylə/ *n*

[2]retail /'reetayl/ *adj, adv, or n* (of, being, or concerned with) the sale of commodities or goods in small quantities to final consumers who will not resell them – compare WHOLESALE

,retail 'price ,index *n* a price index showing the cost of living in Britain that is revised every month

retain /ri'tayn/ *vt* **1a** to keep in possession or use **b** to engage by paying a retainer ⟨~ *a lawyer*⟩ **c** to keep in mind or memory **2** to hold secure or intact; contain in place ⟨*lead* ~s *heat*⟩ [ME *reteinen, retainen*, fr MF *retenir*, fr L *retinēre* to hold back, keep, restrain, fr *re-* + *tenēre* to hold – more at THIN] – **retainable** *adj*

[1]retainer /ri'taynə/ *n* a fee paid to a lawyer or professional adviser for services [ME *reteiner* act of withholding, fr *reteinen* + AF *-er* (as in *weyver* waiver)]

[2]retainer *n* an old and trusted domestic servant [RETAIN + [2]-ER]

re'taining ,wall /ri'tayning/ *n* a wall built to withstand a mass of earth, water, etc

[1]retake /,ree'tayk/ *vt* **retook** /,ree'took/; **retaken** /,ree'tayk(ə)n/ **1** to recapture **2** to photograph again

[2]retake /'reetayk/ *n* a second photographing or photograph

retaliate /ri'tali,ayt/ *vi* to return like for like; *esp* to get revenge [LL *retaliatus*, pp of *retaliare*, fr *re-* + *talio* legal retaliation] – **retaliation** /-'aysh(ə)n/ *n*, **retaliative** /ri'talyətiv/, **retaliatory** /-t(ə)ri/ *adj*

retard /ri'tahd/ *vt* to slow down or delay, esp by preventing or hindering advance or accomplishment [L *retardare*, fr *re-* + *tardus* slow] – **retardant** *adj or n*, **retardation** /,reetah'daysh(ə)n/ *n*

retarded /ri'tahdid/ *adj* slow in intellectual or emotional development or academic progress

retch /rech/ *vb* to (make an effort to) vomit [(assumed) ME *rechen* to spit, retch, fr OE *hrǣcan* to spit, hawk; akin to L *crepare* to rattle – more at [1]RAVEN] – **retch** *n*

retention /ri'tensh(ə)n/ *n* **1a** retaining or being retained **b** abnormal retaining of a fluid (e g urine) in a body cavity **2** retentiveness [ME *retencioun*, fr L *retention-, retentio*, fr *retentus*, pp of *retinēre* to retain – more at RETAIN]

retentive /ri'tentiv/ *adj* able or tending to retain; *esp* retaining knowledge easily ⟨*a* ~ *mind*⟩ – **retentively** *adv*, **retentiveness** *n*

rethink /,ree'thingk/ *vb* **rethought** /,ree'thawt/ to think (about) again; *esp* to reconsider (a plan, attitude, etc) with a view to changing – **rethinker** *n*, **rethink** /'-,-/ *n*

reticent /'retis(ə)nt/ *adj* **1** inclined to be silent or reluctant to speak **2** restrained in expression, presentation, or appearance [L *reticent-, reticens*, prp of *reticēre* to keep silent, fr *re-* + *tacēre* to be silent – more at TACIT] – **reticence** *n*, **reticently** *adv*

reticle /'retikl/ *n* a graticule visible in the eyepiece of an optical instrument [L *reticulum* network]

[1]reticulate /ri'tikyoolət/, **reticular** /-lə/ *also* **reticulose** /-lohs, -lohz/ *adj* resembling a net; *esp* having veins, fibres, or lines crossing [L *reticulatus*, fr *reticulum*] – **reticulately** *adv*

[2]reticulate /ri'tikyoo,layt/ *vb* to divide, mark, or arrange (sthg) so as to form a network [back-formation fr *reticulated*, adj (reticulate)] – **reticulation** /-'laysh(ə)n/ *n*

reticule /'retikyoohl/ *n* **1** a reticle **2** a decorative drawstring bag used as a handbag by women in the 18th and 19th c [F *réticule*, fr L *reticulum* network, network bag, fr dim. of *rete* net]

reticulocyte /ri'tikyooloh,siet, -lə-/ *n* a young non-nucleated red blood cell [NL *reticulum* + ISV *-cyte*] – **reticulocytic** /-'sitik/ *adj*

reticulum /ri'tikyooləm/ *n* **1** the second stomach of a ruminant mammal in which folds of the lining form hexagonal cells **2** a reticulate formation; a network [NL, fr L, network]

retiform /'reetifawm, 're-/ *adj* reticulate [NL *retiformis*, fr L *rete* + *-iformis* -iform]

retin- /retin-/, **retino-** *comb form* retina ⟨retin*itis*⟩ ⟨retino*pathy*⟩ [*retina*]

retina /'retinə/ *n, pl* **retinas, retinae** /-ni/ the sensory membrane at the back of the eye that receives the image formed by the lens and is connected with the brain by the optic nerve ☞ NERVE [ME *rethina*, fr ML *retina*, prob fr L *rete* net; akin to Gk *erēmos* lonely, solitary, Lith *rėtis* sieve] – **retinal** *adj*

retinal /,reti'nal/ *n* a derivative of vitamin A that in combination with proteins forms the visual pigments of the retinal rods and cones [*retin-* + [3]*-al*]

retinol /'retinol/ *n* the chief and typical vitamin A [*retin-* + [1]*-ol*; fr its being the source of retinal]

retinue /'reti,nyooh/ *n* a group of retainers or attendants accompanying an important personage (e g a head of state) [ME *retenue*, fr MF, fr fem of *retenu*, pp of *retenir* to retain]

retire /ri'tie·ə/ *vi* **1** to withdraw **a** from action or danger ⟨~ *from the scene of the crime*⟩ **b** for rest or seclusion; go to bed **2** to recede; FALL BACK **3** to give up one's position or occupation; conclude one's working or professional career ⟨*has* ~d *from the civil service*⟩ ~ *vt* **1a** to order (a military force) to withdraw **b** to withdraw (e g currency or shares) from circulation **2** to cause to retire from a position or occupation [MF *retirer*, fr *re-* + *tirer* to draw, fr OF – more at TIRADE] – **retirement** *n*

re'tired *adj* **1** remote from the world; secluded **2** having concluded one's career **3** received or due in retirement ⟨~ *pay*⟩

retiring /ri'tie·əring/ *adj* reserved, shy – **retiringly** *adv*

retool /,ree'toohl/ *vt* to equip (esp a factory) with new tools

[1]retort /ri'tawt/ *vt* **1** to fling back or return aggressively **2** to say or exclaim in reply or as a counter argument **3** to answer (e g an argument) by a counter argument ~ *vi* to answer back sharply or tersely; retaliate [L *retortus*, pp of *retorquēre*, lit., to twist back, hurl back, fr *re-* + *torquēre* to twist – more at TORTURE]

[2]retort *n* a terse, witty, or cutting reply; *esp* one that turns the first speaker's words against him/her

[3]retort *vt or n* (to treat by heating in) a vessel in which substances are distilled or decomposed by heat [n MF *retorte*, fr ML *retorta*, fr L, fem of *retortus*, pp; fr its bent shape; vb fr n]

retouch /,ree'tuch/ *vt* **1** TOUCH UP 1 **2** to alter (e g a photographic negative) to produce a more acceptable appearance ~ *vi* to retouch sthg [F *retoucher*, fr MF, fr *re-* + *toucher* to touch] – **retouch** /'-,-/ *n*, **retoucher** *n*

retrace /,ree'trays/ *vt* to trace again or back ⟨~d *her footsteps*⟩ [F *retracer*, fr MF *retracier*, fr *re-* + *tracier* to trace]

retract /ri'trakt/ *vt* **1** to draw back or in ⟨*cats can ~ their claws*⟩ **2a** to withdraw; TAKE BACK ⟨~ *a confession*⟩ **b** to refuse to admit or abide by ~ *vi* **1** to draw back **2** to recant or disavow sthg [ME *retracten*, fr L *retractus*, pp of *retrahere*] – **retractable** *adj*

retractile /ri'traktiel/ *adj* capable of being retracted – **retractility** /,reetrak'tiləti/ *n*

retraction /ri'traksh(ə)n/ *n* an act of recanting; *specif* a statement made by one retracting [RETRACT + -ION]

retractor /ri'traktə/ *n* **1** a surgical instrument for holding open the edges of a wound **2** a muscle that draws in a body part – compare PROTRACTOR [RETRACT + [1]-OR]

retranslate /,reetrans'layt, -trahns-, -tranz-, -trahnz-/ *vt* to translate (a translation) into another language, esp the original one – **retranslation** /-'laysh(ə)n/ *n*

[1]**retread** /,ree'tred/ *vt* to replace and vulcanize the tread of (a worn tyre)

[2]**retread** /'ree,tred/ *n* (a tyre with) a new tread

[1]**retreat** /ri'treet/ *n* **1a** an act or process of withdrawing, esp from what is difficult, dangerous, or disagreeable; *specif* (a signal for) the forced withdrawal of troops from an enemy or position **b** the process of receding from a position or state attained ⟨*the ~ of a glacier*⟩ **c** a bugle call sounded at about sunset **2** a place of privacy or safety; a refuge **3** a period of usu group withdrawal for prayer, meditation, and study [ME *retret*, fr MF *retrait*, fr pp of *retraire* to withdraw, fr L *retrahere*, lit., to draw back, fr *re-* + *trahere* to draw – more at DRAW]

[2]**retreat** *vi* **1** to make a retreat; withdraw **2** RECEDE 1b ~ *vt* to draw or lead back; *specif* to move (a piece) back in chess – **retreater** *n*

retrench /ri'trench/ *vt* **1** to reduce ⟨~ *company expenditure*⟩ **2a** to cut out; excise ⟨~ *offending paragraphs from an article*⟩ **b** *Austr & WI* to make (a worker) redundant ~ *vi* to make reductions, esp in expenses; economize [obs F *retrencher* (now *retrancher*), fr MF *retrenchier*, fr *re-* + *trenchier* to cut] – **retrenchment** *n*

retribution /,retri'byoohsh(ə)n/ *n* **1** requital for an insult or injury **2** (the dispensing or receiving of reward or) punishment – used esp with reference to divine judgment [ME *retribucioun*, fr MF *retribution*, fr LL *retribution-*, *retributio*, fr L *retributus*, pp of *retribuere* to pay back, fr *re-* + *tribuere* to pay – more at TRIBUTE] – **retributively** *adv*, **retributive** /ri'tribyootiv/, **retributory** /ri'tribyoot(ə)ri/ *adj*

retrieval /ri'treevl/ *n* a retrieving

retrieve /ri'treev/ *vt* **1** to discover and bring in (killed or wounded game) **2** to call to mind again **3a** to get back again; recover (and bring back) ⟨~d *the keys he left on the bus*⟩ **b** to rescue, save ⟨~ *him from moral ruin*⟩ **4** to return (e g a ball that is difficult to reach) successfully **5** to remedy the ill effects of ⟨~ *the situation*⟩ **6** to recover (e g information) from storage, esp in a computer memory ~ *vi*, *esp of a dog* to retrieve game; *also* to bring back an object thrown by a person [ME *retreven*, modif of MF *retrouver* to find again, fr *re-* + *trouver* to find, prob fr (assumed) VL *tropare* to compose, fr L *tropus* trope] – **retrievable** *adj*, **retrievability** /-və'biləti/ *n*, **retrievably** *adv*

retriever /ri'treevə/ *n* a medium-sized dog with water-resistant coat used esp for retrieving game [RETRIEVE + [2]-ER]

retro- *prefix* **1a** back towards the past ⟨retro*spect*⟩ ⟨retro*grade*⟩ **b** backwards ⟨retro*cede*⟩ ⟨retro*flex*⟩ **2** situated behind ⟨ret ro*choir*⟩ ⟨retro*sternal*⟩ [ME, fr L, fr *retro*, fr *re-* + *-tro* (as in *intro* within) – more at INTRO-]

retroaction /,retroh'aksh(ə)n/ *n* a reciprocal action; a reaction

,retro'active /-'aktiv/ *adj* extending in scope or effect to a prior time ⟨*a ~ tax*⟩ [F *retroactif*, fr L *retroactus*, pp of *retroagere* to drive back, reverse, fr *retro-* + *agere* to drive – more at AGENT] – **retroactively** *adv*, **retroactivity** /-'tivəti/ *n*

,retro'fit /-'fit/ *vt* **-tt-** to provide with new parts or equipment not available at the time of manufacture – **retrofit** /'retroh,fit/ *n*

retroflex /'retrəfleks/, **retroflexed** *adj* articulated with the tongue tip turned up or curled back just under the hard palate ⟨*a ~ vowel*⟩ [ISV, fr NL *retroflexus*, fr L *retro-* + *flexus*, pp of *flectere* to bend] – **retroflexion, retroflection** /-'fleksh(ə)n/ *n*

[1]**retrograde** /'retrəgrayd/ *adj* **1a** *of orbital or rotational movement* in a direction contrary to neighbouring celestial bodies – compare PROGRADE **b** moving or directed backwards **c** ordered in a manner that is opposite to normal ⟨*a ~ alphabet*⟩ **2** tending towards or resulting in a worse or less advanced or specialized state [ME, fr L *retrogradus*, fr *retro-* + *gradi* to go] – **retrogradely** *adv*

[2]**retrograde** *vi* **1** to move back; recede ⟨*a glacier* ~s⟩ **2** to undergo retrogression [L *retrogradi*, fr *retro-* + *gradi* to go – more at GRADE] – **retrogradation** /-grə'daysh(ə)n, -gray-/ *n*

retrogress /,retrə'gres/ *vi* to revert, regress, or decline from a better to a worse state [L *retrogressus*, pp of *retrogradi*] – **retrogressive** *adj*, **retrogressively** *adv*

retrogression /,retrə'gresh(ə)n/ *n* **1** REGRESSION 3 **2** a reversal in development or condition; *esp* a return to a less advanced or specialized state during the development of an organism

'retro,rocket /'retroh/ *n* a rocket on an aircraft, spacecraft, etc that produces thrust in a direction opposite to or at an angle to its motion for slowing it down or changing its direction

retrorse /ri'traws/ *adj* bent backwards or downwards [L *retrorsus*, contr of *retroversus*] – **retrorsely** *adv*

retrospect /'retrəspekt/ *n* a survey or consideration of past events [*retro-* + *-spect* (as in *prospect*)] – **in retrospect** in considering the past or a past event

retrospection /,retrə'speksh(ə)n/ *n* the act or process or an instance of surveying the past [L *retrospectus*, pp of *retrospicere* to look back at, fr *retro-* + *specere* to look – more at SPY]

[1]**retrospective** /,retrə'spektiv/ *adj* **1a** of, being, or given to retrospection **b** based on memory ⟨*a ~ report*⟩ **2** relating to or affecting things past; retroactive – **retrospectively** *adv*

[2]**retrospective** *n* an exhibition showing the evolution of an artist's work over a period of years

retroussé /rə'troohsay/ *adj, esp of a nose* turned up (at the end) [F, fr pp of *retrousser* to tuck up, fr MF, fr *re-* + *trousser* to truss, tuck up]

retroversion /,retroh'vuhsh(ə)n/ *n* the act or process of turning back or regressing [L *retroversus* turned backwards, fr *retro-* + *versus*, pp of *vertere* to turn – more at [1]WORTH]

retsina /ret'seenə/ *n* a white resin-flavoured Greek wine [NGk, perh fr It *resina* resin, fr L]

[1]**return** /ri'tuhn/ *vi* **1a** to go back or come back again ⟨~ed *home*⟩ **b** to go back *to* in thought, conversation, or practice ⟨*soon* ~ed *to her old habits*⟩ **2** to pass back to an earlier possessor ⟨*the estate* ~ed *to a distant branch of the family*⟩ **3** to reply, retort – fml ~*vt* **1a** to state officially, esp in answer to a formal demand ⟨~ed *details of her income*⟩ **b** to elect (a candidate) **c** to bring in (a verdict) **2** to restore to a former or proper place, position, or state ⟨~ *the book to the shelf*⟩ **3** to retort ⟨*she* ~ed *a pretty sharp answer*⟩ **4** to bring in (e g a profit) **5a** to repay ⟨*I cannot* ~ *the compliment*⟩ **b** to give or send back, esp to an owner **6** to lead (a card) or a card of (a suit) in response to one's partner's earlier action, esp in bridge **7** to play (a ball or shuttlecock) hit, esp served, by an opponent [ME *retournen*, fr MF *retourner*, fr OF, fr *re-* + *tourner* to turn – more at TURN] – **returnable** *adj*, **returner** *n*

[2]**return** *n* **1** the act or process of coming back to or from a place or condition **2a** a (financial) account or formal report **b** a report or declaration of the results of an election – usu pl with sing. meaning **3a** the continuation, usu at a right angle, of the facade of a building or of a moulding **b** a means for conveying sthg (e g water) back to its starting point **4** the profit from labour, investment, or business – often pl with sing. meaning **5a** the act of returning sthg, esp to a former place, condition, or owner **b** sthg returned; *esp, pl* unsold newspapers, magazines, etc returned to the publisher for a refund **6** the returning of a ball (e g in tennis) or shuttlecock **7** *Br* a ticket bought for a trip to a place and back again – compare SINGLE 5 – **by return (of post)** by the next returning post – **in return** in compensation or repayment

[3]**return** *adj* **1** doubled back on itself ⟨*a* ~ *flue*⟩ **2** played, delivered, or given in return; taking place for the second time ⟨*a* ~ *match*⟩ **3** used or followed on returning ⟨*the* ~ *road*⟩ **4** permitting return ⟨*a* ~ *valve*⟩ **5** of or causing a return to a place or condition

re'turn ,crease *n* any of the 4 lines on a cricket pitch at right angles to the bowling and popping creases from inside which the ball must be bowled ☞ SPORT

returning officer /ri'tuhning/ *n, Br* an official who presides over an election count and declares the result

retuse /ri'tyoohs/ *adj, of a leaf* having a rounded and notched end ☞ PLANT [L *retusus* blunted, fr pp of *retundere* to pound back, blunt, fr *re-* + *tundere* to beat, pound – more at [1]STINT]

reunion /ree'yoohnyən/ *n* **1** reuniting or being reunited **2** a gathering of people (e g relatives or associates) after a period of separation

reunite /,reeyoo'niet/ *vb* to come or bring together again ⟨*the child was* ~d *with its parents*⟩ [ML *reunitus*, pp of *reunire*, fr L *re-* + LL *unire* to unite – more at UNITE]

reuse /,ree'yoohz/ *vt* to use again, esp after reclaiming or reprocessing ⟨*the need to* ~ *scarce resources*⟩ – **reusable** *adj*, **reuser** *n*

[1]**rev** /rev/ *n* a revolution of a motor [short for *revolution*]

[2]**rev** *vb* **-vv-** *vt* to increase the number of revolutions per minute of (esp an engine) – often + *up* ~*vi* to operate at an increased speed of revolution – usu + *up*

revalue /,ree'valyooh/ *vt* **1** to change, specif to increase, the exchange rate of (a currency) **2** to reappraise

revamp /,ree'vamp/ *vt* **1** to renovate, reconstruct **2** to revise without fundamental alteration – **revamp** *n*

revanche /ri'vahnsh/ *n* a policy designed to recover lost territory or status [F, fr MF, alter. of *revenche* – more at [2]REVENGE] – **revanchism** *n*, **revanchist** *n or adj*

[1]**reveal** /ri'veel/ *vt* **1** to make known through divine inspiration **2** to make known (sthg secret or hidden) ⟨~ *a secret*⟩ **3** to open up to view ⟨*the uncurtained window* ~ed *a gloomy room*⟩ [ME *revelen*, fr MF *reveler*, fr L *revelare* to uncover, reveal, fr *re-* + *velare* to cover, veil, fr *velum* veil] – **revealable** *adj*, **revealer** *n*, **revealment** *n*

[2]**reveal** *n* the side of an opening (e g for a window) between a frame and the outer surface of a wall; *also* a jamb ☞ ARCHITECTURE [alter. of earlier *revale*, fr ME *revalen* to lower, fr MF *revaler*, fr *re-* + *val* valley – more at VALE]

revealing /ri'veeling/ *adj* exposing sthg usu intended to be concealed ⟨*a* ~ *dress*⟩ ⟨*the answer was* ~⟩

reveille /ri'vali, -'ve-/ *n* a call or signal to get up in the morning; *specif* a military bugle call [modif of F *réveillez*, imper pl of *réveiller* to awaken, fr *re-* + *eveiller* to awaken, fr (assumed) VL *exvigilare*, fr L *ex-* + *vigilare* to keep watch, stay awake, fr *vigil* awake]

[1]**revel** /'revl/ *vi* **-ll-** (*NAm* **-l-, -ll-**), **revelling** /'revl·ing/ **1** to take part in a revel **2** to take intense satisfaction *in* ⟨~led *in his discomfiture*⟩ [ME *revelen*, fr MF *reveler*, lit., to rebel, fr L *rebellare*] – **reveller** *n*

[2]**revel** *n* a usu riotous party or celebration – often pl with sing. meaning

revelation /,revə'laysh(ə)n/ *n* **1** (the communicating of) a divine truth revealed by God to man **2** *cap* a prophetic book of the New Testament – often pl with sing. meaning but sing. in constr **3** a revealing or sthg revealed; *esp* a sudden and illuminating disclosure [ME, fr MF, fr LL *revelation-*, *revelatio*, fr L *revelatus*, pp of *revelare* to reveal]

revelatory /'revələt(ə)ri, ,revə'layt(ə)ri/ *adj* serving to reveal sthg

revelry /'revlri/ *n* exuberant festivity or merrymaking

revenant /'revinənt/ *n* one who returns from the dead or after a long absence [F, fr prp of *revenir* to return] – **revenant** *adj*

[1]**revenge** /ri'venj/ *vt* **1** to inflict injury in return for (an insult, slight, etc) **2** to avenge (e g oneself) usu by retaliating in kind or degree [ME *revengen*, fr MF *revengier*, fr OF, fr *re-* + *vengier* to avenge – more at VENGEANCE] – **revenger** *n*

[2]**revenge** *n* **1** (a desire for) retaliating in order to get even ⟨*exacted* ~ *for the insult*⟩ ⟨*saw* ~ *in her eyes*⟩ **2** an opportunity for getting satisfaction or requital

[MF *revenge, revenche*, fr *revengier, revenchier* to revenge]

revenue /'revənyooh/ *n* **1** the total yield of income; *esp* the income of a national treasury **2** a government department concerned with the collection of revenue [ME, fr MF, fr *revenir* to return, fr L *revenire*, fr *re-* + *venire* to come]

reverb /ri'vuhb, 'ree,vuhb/ *n* (a usu electronic device for producing) an artificial echo effect in recorded music [short for *reverberation*]

reverberate /ri'vuhbə,rayt/ *vi* **1a** to be reflected **b** to continue (as if) in a series of echoes **2** to produce a continuing strong effect ⟨*the scandal* ~d *round Whitehall*⟩ ~ *vt* to reflect or return (light, heat, sound, etc) [L *reverberatus*, pp of *reverberare* to strike back, fr *re-* + *verberare* to lash, fr *verber* rod – more at VERVAIN] – **reverberator** *n*, **reverberant, reverberative** /-rətiv/, **reverberatory** /-b(ə)rətri/ *adj*, **reverberation** /-'raysh(ə)n/ *n*

reverberatory /ri'vuhb(ə)rətri/, **reverberatory furnace** *n* a furnace or kiln in which heat is reflected from the curved roof onto the material treated

revere /ri'viə/ *vt* to regard with deep and devoted or esp religious respect [L *revereri*, fr *re-* + *vereri* to fear, respect – more at WARY]

[1]**reverence** /'rev(ə)rəns/ *n* **1** honour or respect felt or shown; *esp* profound respect accorded to sthg sacred **2** a gesture (e g a bow) denoting respect **3** being revered ⟨*we hold her in* ~⟩ **4** – used as a title for a clergyman – **reverential** /,revə'rensh(ə)l/ *adj*, **reverentially** *adv*

[2]**reverence** *vt* to regard or treat with reverence – **reverencer** *n*

[1]**reverend** /'rev(ə)rənd/ *adj* **1** revered **2** *cap* being a member of the clergy – used as a title, usu preceded by *the* ⟨*the* Reverend *David Brown*⟩ ⟨*the* Reverend *Mr Brown*⟩ [ME, fr MF, fr L *reverendus*, gerundive of *revereri*]

[2]**reverend** *n* a member of the clergy – infml

,Reverend 'Mother *n* the Mother Superior of a convent – used esp as a term of address

reverent /'rev(ə)rənt/ *adj* expressing or characterized by reverence [ME, fr L *reverent-, reverens*, prp of *revereri*] – **reverently** *adv*

reverie, revery /'revəri/ *n* **1** a daydream **2** the condition of being lost in thought or dreamlike fantasy [F *rêverie*, fr MF, delirium, fr *resver, rever* to wander, be delirious]

revers /ri'viə/ *n, pl* **revers** /ri'viəz/ a wide turned-back or applied facing along each of the front edges of a garment; *specif* a lapel, esp on a woman's garment [F, lit., reverse, fr MF, fr *revers*, adj]

reversal /ri'vuhsl/ *n* **1** reversing **2** a conversion of a photographic positive into a negative or vice versa **3** a change for the worse ⟨*his condition suffered a* ~⟩

[1]**reverse** /ri'vuhs/ *adj* **1a** (acting, operating, or arranged in a manner) opposite or contrary to a previous, normal, or usual condition ⟨*put them in* ~ *order*⟩ **b** having the front turned away from an observer or opponent **2** effecting reverse movement ⟨*the* ~ *gear*⟩ [ME *revers*, fr MF, fr L *reversus*, pp of *revertere* to turn back – more at REVERT] – **reversely** *adv*

[2]**reverse** *vt* **1a** to turn or change completely about in position or direction ⟨~ *the order of the words*⟩ **b** to turn upside down **2a** to overthrow (a legal decision) **b** to change (e g a policy) to the contrary **3** to cause (e g a motor car) to go backwards or in the opposite direction ~ *vi* **1** to turn or move in the opposite direction **2** to go or drive in reverse – **reverser** *n* – **reverse the charges** *Br* to arrange for the recipient of a telephone call to pay for it

[3]**reverse** *n* **1** the opposite of sthg **2** reversing or being reversed **3** a misfortune; REVERSAL 3 **4a** the side of a coin, medal, or currency note that does not bear the principal device – compare OBVERSE 1a **b** the back part of sthg; *esp* the back cover of a book **5** a gear that reverses sthg – **in reverse** backwards

[1]**reversible** /ri'vuhsəbl/ *adj* **1** capable of going through a sequence (e g of changes) either backwards or forwards ⟨*a* ~ *chemical reaction*⟩ **2a** having 2 finished sides ⟨~ *fabric*⟩ **b** *of clothing* designed to be worn with either side outwards [[2]REVERSE + -IBLE] – **reversibly** *adv*, **reversibility** /-sə'biləti/ *n*

[2]**reversible** *n* a reversible cloth or article of clothing

reversion /ri'vuhsh(ə)n/ *n* **1** (an owner's future interest in) property temporarily granted to another **2** the right of future possession or enjoyment **3a** the process of reverting **b** (an organism showing) a return to an ancestral type or reappearance of an ancestral character [ME, fr MF, fr L *reversion-, reversio* act of returning, fr *reversus*, pp] – **reversionary** /-n(ə)ri/ *adj*

reversioner /ri'vuhsh(ə)nə/ *n* the beneficiary of a reversion

revert /ri'vuht/ *vi* **1a** to return, esp to a lower, worse, or more primitive condition or to an ancestral type **b** to go back in thought or conversation ⟨~ed *to the subject of finance*⟩ **2** *esp of property* to return to (the heirs of) the original owner after an interest granted away has expired [ME *reverten*, fr MF *revertir*, fr L *revertere*, vt, to turn back & *reverti*, vi, to return, come back, fr *re-* + *vertere, verti* to turn – more at [1]WORTH] – **reverter** *n*, **revertible** *adj*

revet /ri'vet/ *vt* **-tt-** to face (an embankment, wall, etc) esp with masonry [F *revêtir*, lit., to clothe again, dress up, fr L *revestire*, fr *re-* + *vestire* to clothe – more at [1]VEST]

re'vetment /-mənt/ *n* **1** a facing of stone, concrete, etc to retain an embankment **2** RETAINING WALL

[1]**review** /ri'vyooh/ *n* **1** REVISION 1 ⟨*prices are subject to* ~⟩ **2** a formal military or naval inspection **3a** a general survey (e g of current affairs) **b** a retrospective view or survey (e g of one's life) **4** an act of inspecting or examining **5** judicial reexamination of a case **6a** a critical evaluation of a book, play, etc **b** (a part of) a magazine or newspaper devoted chiefly to reviews and essays [MF *revue*, fr *revoir* to look over, fr OF, fr *re-* + *voir* to see – more at VIEW]

[2]**review** *vt* **1** to take a retrospective view of ⟨~ *the past year*⟩ **2a** to go over (again) or examine critically or thoughtfully ⟨~ed *the results of the study*⟩ **b** to give a review of (a book, play, etc) **3** to hold a review of (troops, ships, etc)

reviewer /ri'vyooh·ə/ *n* a writer of critical reviews [[2]REVIEW + [2]-ER]

revile /ri'viel/ *vt* to subject to harsh verbal abuse [ME *revilen*, fr MF *reviler* to despise, fr *re-* + *vil* vile] – **revilement** *n*, **reviler** *n*

revise /ri'viez/ *vt* **1** to look over again in order to correct or improve **2** to make an amended, improved, or up-to-date version of ⟨~ *a dictionary*⟩ **3** *Br* to refresh knowledge of (e g a subject), esp before an exam ⟨*busy* revising *her physics*⟩ ~ *vi*, *Br* to refresh one's knowledge of a subject, esp in preparation for an exam [F *reviser*, fr L *revisere* to look at again, fr *revisus*, pp of *revidēre* to see again, fr *re-* + *vidēre* to see – more at WIT] – **revisable** *adj*, **reviser, revisor** *n*

Re,vised ,Standard 'Version *n* a revised English translation of the Bible derived from the Revised Version and published in the USA in 1946 and 1952

Re,vised 'Version *n* a British revision of the Authorized Version of the Bible published in 1881 and 1885

revision /ri'vizh(ə)n/ *n* **1** the action or an act of revising ⟨~ *of a manuscript*⟩ ⟨~ *for an examination*⟩ **2** a revised version – **revisionary** /-n(ə)ri/ *adj*

revisionism /ri'vizhə,niz(ə)m/ *n* **1** advocacy of revision (e g of a doctrine) **2** a movement in Marxist socialism favouring an evolutionary rather than a revolutionary transition to socialism – chiefly derog – **revisionist** *adj or n*

revital·ize, -ise /,ree'vietl,iez/ *vt* to impart new life or vigour to ⟨~ *urban development*⟩ – **revitalization** /-ie'zaysh(ə)n/ *n*

revival /ri'vievl/ *n* reviving or being revived: e g **a** renewed attention to or interest in sthg **b** a new presentation or production (e g of a play) **c** a period of renewed religious fervour **d** an often emotional evangelistic meeting or series of meetings **e** restoration of an earlier fashion, style, or practice

re'vival,ism /-,iz(ə)m/ *n* the spirit or evangelistic methods characteristic of religious revivals – **revivalist** *n or adj*, **revivalistic** /-'istik/ *adj*

revive /ri'viev/ *vb* to return to consciousness, life, health, (vigorous) activity, or current use, esp from a depressed, inactive, or unused state ⟨*she soon* ~d *in the fresh air*⟩ ⟨~d *an old musical*⟩ ⟨~d *memories of the war*⟩ [ME *reviven*, fr MF *revivre*, fr L *revivere* to live again, fr *re-* + *vivere* to live – more at [1]QUICK] – **revivable** *adj*, **reviver** *n*

revivify /,ree'vivifie/ *vt* to revive [F *révivifier*, fr LL *revivificare*, fr L *re-* + LL *vivificare* to vivify] – **revivification** /-fi'kaysh(ə)n/ *n*

[1]**revoke** /ri'vohk/ *vt* to annul, rescind, or withdraw ⟨~ *a will*⟩ ~ *vi* to fail to follow suit when able in a card game, in violation of the rules [ME *revoken*, fr MF *revoquer*, fr L *revocare*, fr *re-* + *vocare* to call – more at VOICE] – **revoker** *n*, **revocable** /'revəkəbl/ *also* **revokable** /ri'vohkəbl/ *adj*, **revocation** /,revə'kaysh(ə)n/ *n*

[2]**revoke** *n* an act or instance of revoking in a card game

[1]**revolt** /ri'vohlt/ *vi* **1** to renounce allegiance or subjection to a government, employer, etc; rebel **2** to experience or recoil from disgust or abhorrence ⟨~ *at their behaviour*⟩ ~ *vt* to cause to recoil with disgust or loathing; nauseate [MF *revolter*, fr OIt *rivoltare* to overthrow, fr (assumed) VL *revolvitare*, freq of L *revolvere* to revolve, roll back] – **revolter** *n*

[2]**revolt** *n* **1** a (determined armed) rebellion **2** a movement or expression of vigorous opposition

revolting /ri'vohlting/ *adj* extremely offensive; nauseating

[1]**revolute** /'revəl(y)ooht/ *adj* rolled backwards or downwards ⟨*a leaf with* ~ *margins*⟩ [L *revolutus*, pp]

[2]**revolute** *vi* to undertake social or political revolution – slang [back-formation fr *revolution*]

revolution /,revə'loohsh(ə)n/ *n* **1a** the action of or time taken by a celestial body in going round in an orbit **b** (a single recurrence of) a cyclic process or succession of related events **c** the motion of a figure or object about a centre or axis; ROTATION 1a, b ⟨*33⅓* ~s *per minute*⟩ **2a** a sudden or far-reaching change **b** a fundamental (political) change; *esp* (activity supporting) the overthrow of one government and the substitution of another by the governed [ME *revolucioun*, fr MF *revolution*, fr LL *revolution-, revolutio*, fr L *revolutus*, pp of *revolvere*] – **of revolution** *of a solid shape* formed by the rotation of a plane figure or curve about an axis ⟨*a cone* of revolution⟩

[1]**revolutionary** /,revə'loohshən(ə)ri/ *adj* **1a** of or being a revolution ⟨~ *war*⟩ **b** promoting or engaging in revolution ⟨*a* ~ *speech*⟩; *also* extremist ⟨*a* ~ *outlook*⟩ **2** completely new and different – **revolutionarily** *adv*, **revolutionariness** *n*

[2]**revolutionary** *n* sby who advocates or is engaged in a revolution

Revo,lutionary 'calendar *n* the calendar of the first French republic adopted in 1793, dated from September 22, 1792, and divided into 12 months of 30 days with 5 extra days in a regular year

,revo'lutionist /-ist/ *n, NAm* a revolutionary

,revo'lution·ize, -ise /-iez/ *vt* to cause a revolution in; change fundamentally or completely ⟨*an idea that has* ~d *the steel industry*⟩

[1]**revolve** /ri'volv/ *vt* **1** to ponder ⟨~d *a scheme in his mind*⟩ **2** to cause to turn round (as if) on an axis ~ *vi* **1** to recur ⟨*the seasons* ~d⟩ **2** to be considered in turn ⟨*all sorts of ideas* ~d *in her head*⟩ **3** to move in a curved path round (and round) a centre or axis; turn round (as if) on an axis **4** to be centred on a specified theme or main point ⟨*the dispute* ~d *around wages*⟩ [ME *revolven*, fr L *revolvere* to roll back, cause to return, fr *re-* + *volvere* to roll – more at VOLUBLE] – **revolvable** *adj*

[2]**revolve** *n, Br* a device used on a stage to allow a piece of scenery to be rotated

revolver /ri'volvə/ *n* a handgun with a revolving cylinder of several chambers each holding 1 cartridge and allowing several shots to be fired without reloading [[1]REVOLVE + [2]-ER]

revue /ri'vyooh/ *n* a theatrical production consisting typically of brief loosely connected often satirical sketches, songs, and dances [F, fr MF, review – more at REVIEW]

revulsion /ri'vulsh(ə)n/ *n* **1** a sudden or violent reaction or change **2** a feeling of utter distaste or repugnance [L *revulsion-, revulsio* act of tearing away, fr *revulsus*, pp of *revellere* to pluck away, fr *re-* + *vellere* to pluck – more at VULNERABLE] – **revulsive** *adj*

[1]**reward** /ri'wawd/ *vt* **1** to give a reward to or for **2** to recompense [ME *rewarden*, fr ONF *rewarder* to regard, reward, fr *re-* + *warder* to watch, guard, of Gmc origin; akin to OHG *wartēn* to watch – more at WARD OFF] – **rewardable** *adj*, **rewarder** *n*, **rewardless** *adj*

[2]**reward** *n* sthg that is given in return for good or evil done or received; *esp* sthg offered or given for some service, effort, or achievement

rewarding /ri'wawding/ *adj* yielding a reward; personally satisfying ⟨*a very* ~ *experience*⟩

rewind /ˌree'wiend/ *vt* **rewound** /ˌree'wownd/ to wind (film, tape, etc) back onto a spool – **rewind** /'-ˌ-/ *n*

rewire /ˌree'wie·ə/ *vt* to provide (e g a house) with new electric wiring

reword /ˌree'wuhd/ *vt* to alter the wording of; *also* to restate in different words

rework /ˌree'wuhk/ *vt* to treat again or anew: e g **a** to revise ⟨~ *a musical composition*⟩ **b** to reprocess (e g used material) for further use

[1]**rewrite** /ˌree'riet/ *vb* **rewrote** /ˌree'roht/; **rewritten** /ˌree'ritn/ to revise (sthg previously written) – **rewriter** /'reeˌrietə, ˌ-'--/ *n*

[2]**rewrite** /'reeˌriet/ *n* (the result, esp a rewritten news story, of) rewriting

reynard /'renəd, 'ray-, -nahd/ *n, often cap* a fox – used esp in stories as a name for the fox [ME *Renard*, name of the fox who is hero of the 13th-c F poem *Roman de Renart*, fr MF *Renart, Renard*]

rhadamanthine /ˌradə'manthien/ *adj, often cap* rigorously just or uncompromising [*Rhadamanthus*, mythical judge of souls in the underworld, fr L, fr Gk *Rhadamanthos*]

Rhaeto-Romanic /ˌreetoh roh'manik/ *n* any of a group of Romance languages of E Switzerland and the Tyrol, including Romansh [L *Rhaetus* of Rhaetia, ancient Roman province + E *Romanic*]

rhaphe /'rayˌfee/ *n* a raphe

rhapsod·ize, -ise /'rapsədiez/ *vi* to speak or write rhapsodically or emotionally – **rhapsodist** *n*

rhapsody /'rapsədi/ *n* **1** a part of an epic poem suitable for recitation **2a** a highly rapturous or emotional utterance or literary composition **b** rapture, ecstasy **3** a musical composition of irregular form suggesting improvisation [L *rhapsodia*, fr Gk *rhapsōidia* recitation of selections from epic poetry, rhapsody, fr *rhaptein* to sew, stitch together (akin to OHG *worf* scythe handle, Gk *rhepein* to bend, incline) + *aidein* to sing – more at ODE] – **rhapsodic** /rap'sodik/, **rhapsodical** *adj*, **rhapsodically** *adv*

rhea /'riə/ *n* any of several large tall flightless S American birds like but smaller than the ostrich [NL, genus of birds, prob fr L *Rhea*, mother of Zeus in mythology, fr Gk]

rhenium /'reenyəm, 'reeni·əm/ *n* a hard metallic element similar to manganese and used esp in catalysts and thermocouples ☞ PERIODIC TABLE [NL, fr L *Rhenus* Rhine river]

rheo- *comb form* flow; current ⟨rheo*stat*⟩ [Gk *rhein* to flow – more at STREAM]

rheology /ri'oləji/ *n* a science dealing with the deformation and flow of matter [ISV] – **rheologist** *n*, **rheological** /ˌree·ə'lojikl/ *adj*, **rheologically** *adv*

rheostat /'riəstat/ *n* an adjustable resistor for regulating an electric current – **rheostatic** /-'statik/ *adj*

'**rhesus ˌfactor** /'reesəs/ *n* any of several antigens in red blood cells that can induce intense allergic reactions [fr its being first detected in rhesus monkeys]

rhesus monkey *n* a pale brown E Indian monkey [NL *Rhesus*, genus of monkeys, fr L, a mythical king of Thrace, fr Gk *Rhēsos*]

ˌ**rhesus 'negative** *adj* lacking rhesus factor in the red blood cells

ˌ**rhesus 'positive** *adj* containing rhesus factor in the red blood cells

rhetoric /'retərik/ *n* **1** the art of speaking or writing effectively; *specif* (the study of) the principles and rules of composition **2a** skill in the effective use of speech **b** insincere or exaggerated language (that is calculated to produce an effect) [ME *rethorik*, fr MF *rethorique*, fr L *rhetorica*, fr Gk *rhētorikē*, lit., art of oratory, fr fem of *rhētorikos* of an orator, fr *rhētōr* orator, rhetorician, fr *eirein* to say, speak – more at WORD]

rhetorical /ri'torikl/ *adj* **1** employed (merely) for rhetorical effect **2** given to rhetoric; grandiloquent – **rhetorically** *adv*

rheˌtorical 'question *n* a question asked merely for effect with no answer expected

rhetorician /ˌretə'rish(ə)n/ *n* **1 rhetorician, rhetor a** a master or teacher of rhetoric **b** an orator **2** an eloquent or grandiloquent writer or speaker

rheum /roohm/ *n* a watery discharge from the mucous membranes of the eyes, nose, etc [ME *reume*, fr MF, fr L *rheuma*, fr Gk, lit., flow, flux, fr *rhein* to flow] – **rheumy** *adj*

[1]**rheumatic** /rooh'matik, roo-/ *adj* of, being, characteristic of, or suffering from rheumatism [ME *rewmatik* subject to rheum, fr L *rheumaticus*, fr Gk *rheumatikos*, fr *rheumat-, rheuma*] – **rheumatically** *adv*

[2]**rheumatic** *n* sby suffering from rheumatism

rheuˌmatic 'fever *n* inflammation and pain in the joints, pericardium, and heart valves, occurring together with fever as a short-lasting disease, esp in children

rheumaticky /rooh'matiki, roo-/ *adj* rheumatic – not used technically

rheumatics *n pl* rheumatism – not used technically

rheumatism /'roohməˌtiz(ə)m/ *n* **1** any of various conditions characterized by inflammation and pain in muscles, joints, or fibrous tissue **2** RHEUMATOID ARTHRITIS [L *rheumatismus* flux, rheum, fr Gk *rheumatismos*, fr *rheumatizesthai* to suffer from a flux, fr *rheumat-, rheuma* flux]

rheumatoid /'roohməˌtoyd/ *adj* characteristic of or affected with rheumatism or rheumatoid arthritis [ISV, fr *rheumatism*]

ˌ**rheumatoid arth'ritis** *n* painful inflammation and swelling of joint structures occurring as a progressively worsening disease of unknown cause

rheumatology /ˌroohmə'toləji/ *n* a branch of medicine dealing with rheumatic diseases – **rheumatologist** /-'toləjist/ *n*

rhin-, rhino- *comb form* nose ⟨rhino*ceros*⟩ ⟨rhin*al*⟩; nose and ⟨rhino*laryngology*⟩ [NL, fr Gk, fr *rhin-, rhis*]

rhinal /'rienl/ *adj* nasal

rhine /rien/ *n, dial Br* a wide drainage ditch or watercourse [earlier *royne*, prob alter. of ME *rune* watercourse, fr OE *ryne* flow, watercourse; akin to OFris *rene* flow]

'**rhineˌstone** /-ˌstohn/ *n* a lustrous imitation gem made of glass, paste, quartz, etc [*Rhine*, river in W Europe]

rhinitis /rie'nietis/ *n* inflammation of the mucous membrane of the nose [NL]

rhino /'rienoh/ *n, pl* **rhinos**, *esp collectively* **rhino** a rhinoceros – infml

rhinoceros /rie'nos(ə)rəs/ *n, pl* **rhinoceroses** /-siz/, *esp collectively* **rhinoceros** any of various large plant-eating very thick-skinned hoofed African or Asian mammals with 1 or 2 horns on the snout [ME *rinoceros*, fr L *rhinocerot-, rhinoceros*, fr Gk *rhinokerōt-, rhinokerōs*, fr *rhin-* + *keras* horn – more at HORN]

rhiz- /riez-/, **rhizo-** *comb form* root ⟨rhizo*carpous*⟩ ⟨rhizo*genic*⟩ [NL, fr Gk, fr *rhiza* – more at ROOT]

-rhiza, -rrhiza /-riezə/ *comb form* (→ *n*), *pl* **-rhizae** /-si/, **-rhizas** (part resembling or connected with a) root ⟨*myco*rrhiza⟩ [NL, fr Gk *rhiza*]

rhizocarp /ˌriezoh'kahpik/ *n* a plant with perennial underground parts but annual stems and foliage [ISV] – **rhizocarpic, rhizocarpous** *adj*

rhizome /'riezohm/ *n* an elongated (thickened and horizontal) underground plant stem distinguished from a true root in having buds and usu scalelike leaves [NL *rhizomat-, rhizoma*, fr Gk *rhizōmat-, rhizōma* mass of roots, fr *rhizoun* to cause to take root, fr *rhiza* root – more at ROOT] – **rhizomic** /-'zohmik, -'zomik/, **rhizomatous** /ˌriezoh'mahtəs, -'zohmətəs/ *adj*

rhizopod /'riezohpod/ *n* any of various related protozoans (e g an amoeba) with lobed rootlike pseudopodia [deriv of Gk *rhiza* + *pod-, pous* foot – more at FOOT] – **rhizopodal** /rie'zopədl, riezə'pohdl/, **rhizopodous** /riez'opədəs, riezə'pohdəs/, **rhizopodan** /ˌriez'opədən, ˌriezə'pohdən/ *adj*

rho /roh/ *n* the 17th letter of the Greek alphabet [Gk *rhō*, of Sem origin; akin to Heb *rēsh*, 20th letter of the Heb alphabet]

rhod-, rhodo- *comb form* rose; rose-red ⟨rhod*ium*⟩ ⟨rhodo*lite*⟩ [NL, fr L, fr Gk, fr *rhodon* rose]

rhodamine /'rohdəmeen, -min/ *n* any of a group of (brilliant) yellowish red to blue fluorescent dyes [ISV]

Rhode Island Red *n* (any of) an American breed of brownish red domestic fowls [*Rhode Island*, state of the USA]

'Rhodes ˌscholar *n* the holder of any of numerous scholarships founded by Cecil Rhodes that can be used at Oxford university by candidates from the Commonwealth and the USA [Cecil *Rhodes* †1902 E statesman & financier in S Africa]

rhodium /'rohdyəm/ *n* a white hard usu trivalent metallic element similar to and used in alloys with platinum ☞ PERIODIC TABLE [NL, fr Gk *rhodon* rose]

rhododendron /ˌrohdə'dendrən/ *n* any of a genus of showy-flowered shrubs and trees of the heath family; *esp* one with leathery evergreen leaves [NL, genus name, fr L, rosebay, fr Gk, fr *rhod-* + *dendron* tree – more at DENDR-]

rhodolite /'rohdəliet/ *n* a pink or purple garnet used as a gem

rhodonite /'rohdəniet/ *n* a pale red ornamental mineral consisting mainly of manganese silicate [G *rhodonit*, fr Gk *rhodon* rose]

rhodopsin /roh'dopsin/ *n* a light-sensitive pigment in the retinal rods of marine fishes and most higher vertebrates whose presence determines the sensitivity of the rods to differing intensities of illumination – compare IODOPSIN [ISV *rhod-* + Gk *ops*is sight, vision + ISV *-in* – more at OPTIC]

rhomb /rom/ *n* **1** a rhombus **2** a rhombohedron [MF *rhombe*, fr L *rhombus*]

rhomb-, rhombo- *comb form* rhombus ⟨rhombo*hedron*⟩ [MF, fr L, fr Gk, fr *rhombos*]

rhombic /'rombik/ *adj* **1** shaped like a rhombus **2** orthorhombic

rhombohedron /ˌromboh'heedrən/ *n, pl* **rhombohedrons, rhombohedra** /-drə/ a 6-sided solid whose faces are rhombuses [NL] – **rhombohedral** *adj*

¹rhomboid /'romboyd/ *n* a parallelogram that is neither a rhombus nor a square [MF *rhomboïde*, fr L *rhomboides*, fr Gk *rhomboeidēs* resembling a rhombus, fr *rhombos*]

²rhomboid, rhomboidal /rom'boydl/ *adj* shaped like a rhombus or rhomboid

rhombus /'rombəs/ *n, pl* **rhombuses, rhombi** /-bie/ a parallelogram with equal sides but unequal angles; a diamond-shaped figure ☞ MATHEMATICS [L, fr Gk *rhombos*]

rhubarb /'roohbahb/ *n* **1** (the thick succulent stems, edible when cooked, of) any of several plants of the dock family **2** *chiefly Br* – used by actors to suggest the sound of (many) people talking in the background **3** *chiefly Br* nonsense, rubbish – slang or humor **4** *chiefly NAm* a heated or noisy dispute – slang [ME *rubarbe*, fr MF *reubarbe*, fr ML *reubarbarum*, alter. of *rha barbarum*, lit., foreign rhubarb]

rhumb /rum/ *n* any of the 32 points of the mariner's compass [Sp *rumbo* rhumb, rhumb line]

rhumba /'rumbə/ *n* a rumba

'rhumb ˌline *n* a line that makes equal oblique angles with all meridians and that is the course sailed by a ship following a single compass direction

¹rhyme /riem/ *n* **1a** correspondence in the sound of (the last syllable of) words, esp those at the end of lines of verse **b** a word that provides a rhyme for another **2** (a) rhyming verse [alter. of ME *rime*, fr OF, prob deriv of L *rhythmus* rhythm] – **rhymeless** *adj*

²rhyme *vi* **1** to make rhymes; *also* to compose rhyming verse **2a** *of a word or (line of) verse* to end in syllables that rhyme **b** to constitute a rhyme ⟨date ~s *with* fate⟩ ~ *vt* **1** to put into rhyme **2** to cause to rhyme; use as (a) rhyme – **rhymer** *n*

ˌrhyme or 'reason *n* good sense; reasonableness – esp in *without rhyme or reason*

'rhyme ˌscheme *n* the pattern of rhymes in a stanza or poem

rhymester /'riemstə/ *n* a poetaster

rhyming slang *n* slang in which the word actually meant is replaced by a rhyming phrase of which only the first element is usu pronounced (e g 'head' becomes 'loaf of bread'' and then 'loaf ')

rhyolite /'rie·əliet/ *n* a fine-grained acid volcanic rock similar to granite but formed from lava [G *rhyolith*, fr Gk *rhyax* stream, stream of lava (fr *rhein*) + G *-lith* -lite] – **rhyolitic** /-'litik/ *adj*

rhythm /'ridh(ə)m/ *n* **1a** the pattern of recurrent alternation of strong and weak elements in the flow of sound and silence in speech **b** ²METRE 1 **2a** (the aspect of music concerning) the regular recurrence of a pattern of stress and length of notes **b** a characteristic rhythmic pattern ⟨*music in rumba* ~⟩; *also* ²METRE 2 **c rhythm, rhythm section** *sing or pl in constr* the group of instruments in a band (e g the drums, piano, and bass) supplying the rhythm **3** movement or fluctuation marked by a regular recurrence of elements (e g pauses or emphases) **4** a regularly recurrent change in a biological process or state (e g with night and day) **5** the effect created by the interaction of the elements in a play, film, or novel that relate to the development of the action **6** **rhythm, rhythm method** birth control by abstinence from sexual intercourse during the period when ovulation is most likely to occur [MF & L; MF *rhythme*, fr L *rhythmus*, fr Gk *rhythmos*, fr *rhein* to flow – more at STREAM]

,rhythm and 'blues *n* popular music with elements of blues and Negro folk music

rhythmic /'ridhmik/, **rhythmical** /-kl/ *adj* **1** of or involving rhythm **2** moving or progressing with a pronounced or flowing rhythm **3** regularly recurring – **rhythmically** *adv*, **rhythmicity** /ridh'misəti/ *n*

ria /riə/ *n* a narrow inlet caused by the submergence of (part of) a river valley [Sp *ría*, fr *río* river, fr L *rivus*]

¹rial /ri'ahl, 'rie·əl/ *n* ☞ *Iran, Oman* at NATIONALITY [Per, fr Ar *riyāl* riyal]

²rial /ree'awl, -'ahl/ *n* a riyal

¹rib /rib/ *n* **1a** any of the paired curved rods of bone or cartilage that stiffen the body walls of most vertebrates and protect the heart, lungs, etc ☞ ANATOMY **b** a cut of meat including a rib ☞ MEAT **2** sthg resembling a rib in shape or function: e g **a** a transverse member of the frame of a ship that runs from keel to deck **b** any of the stiff strips supporting an umbrella's fabric **c** an arched support or ornamental band in Romanesque and Gothic vaulting ☞ CHURCH **3** an elongated ridge: e g **a** a vein of a leaf or insect's wing **b** any of the ridges in a knitted or woven fabric; *also* ribbing [ME, fr OE; akin to OHG *rippi* rib, Gk *erephein* to roof over]

²rib *vt* **-bb-** **1** to provide or enclose with ribs ⟨~ *bed vaulting*⟩ **2** to form a pattern of vertical ridges in by alternating knit stitches and purl stitches

³rib *vt* **-bb-** to tease – infml [prob fr ¹*rib*; fr the tickling of the ribs to cause laughter]

ribald /'rib(ə)ld, 'rie,bawld/ *adj* **1** crude, offensive ⟨~ *language*⟩ **2** characterized by coarse or indecent humour ⟨*a* ~ *youth*⟩ [ME, menial retainer, rascal, fr OF *ribaut, ribauld* wanton, rascal, fr *riber* to be wanton, of Gmc origin; akin to OHG *rīban* to be wanton, lit., to twist; akin to Gk *rhiptein* to throw] – **ribaldry** /'ribəldri/ *n*

riband /'ribənd/ *n* a ribbon used esp as a decoration [ME, alter. of *riban*]

ribbing /'ribing/ *n* an arrangement of ribs; *esp* a knitted pattern of ribs

ribbon /'ribən/ *n* **1a** a (length of a) narrow band of decorative fabric used for ornamentation (e g of hair), fastening, tying parcels, etc **b** a piece of usu multicoloured ribbon worn as a military decoration or in place of a medal **2** a long narrow ribbonlike strip; *esp* a strip of inked fabric or plastic used in a typewriter **3** *pl* tatters, shreds ⟨*her coat was in* ~s⟩ [ME *riban*, fr MF *riban, ruban*] – **ribbonlike** *adj*

,ribbon de'velopment *n* haphazard development of buildings and settlements along main roads

'ribbon,fish /-,fish/ *n* any of various long thin fishes

'ribbon ,worm *n* a nemertean

'rib ,cage *n* the enclosing wall of the chest consisting chiefly of the ribs and their connections

ribgrass /'rib,grahs/ *n, chiefly NAm* ribwort

riboflavin, riboflavine /,rieboh'flayvin/ *n* a yellow vitamin of the vitamin B complex occurring esp in milk and liver [ISV *ribose* + L *flavus* yellow – more at ¹BLUE]

,ribonu,cleic 'acid /,riebohnyooh'klee·ik, -'klayik/ *n* RNA [*ribose* + *nucleic acid*]

ribonucleotide /,rieboh'nyoohkli·ətied/ *n* a nucleotide containing ribose rather than deoxyribose and occurring esp as a constituent of RNA [*ribose* + *nucleotide*]

ribose /'riebohs, -bohz/ *n* a pentose sugar occurring esp in ribonucleotides [ISV, deriv of *arabinose* (a sugar obtained from gums), fr (*gum*) *arabic*]

ribosome /'riebəsohm/ *n* any of the minute granules containing RNA and protein that occur in cells and are the sites where proteins are synthesized [*ribo-*nucleic (acid) + *-some*] – **ribosomal** /-'sohml/ *adj*

ribwort /'rib,wuht/ *n* an Old World plantain with long narrow ribbed leaves

rice /ries/ *n* (the seed, important as a food, of) a cereal grass widely cultivated in warm climates [ME *rys*, fr OF *ris*, fr OIt *riso*, fr Gk *oryza, oryzon*]

'rice ,paper *n* a very thin edible paper made from the pith of an oriental tree [fr its resemblance to paper made of rice straw]

'rice ,polishings *n pl* the inner bran layer of rice when rubbed off in milling

rich /rich/ *adj* **1** having abundant possessions, esp material and financial wealth **2a** having high worth, value, or quality ⟨*a* ~ *crop*⟩ **b** well supplied or endowed – often + *in* ⟨~ *in natural talent*⟩ **3** sumptuous **4a** vivid and deep in colour ⟨*a* ~ *red*⟩ **b** full and mellow in tone and quality ⟨*a* ~ *voice*⟩ **c** pungent ⟨~ *odours*⟩ **5** highly productive or remunerative; giving a high yield ⟨~ *farmland*⟩ **6a** *of soil* having abundant plant nutrients **b** (of food that is) highly seasoned, fatty, oily, or sweet ⟨*a* ~ *diet*⟩ **c** *esp of mixtures of fuel with air* high in the combustible component; containing more petrol than normal **7a** highly amusing; *also* laughable – infml **b** full of import ⟨~ *allusions*⟩ [ME *riche*, fr OE *rīce*; akin to OHG *rīhhi* rich, OE *rīce* kingdom, OHG *rīhhi*; all fr prehistoric Gmc words borrowed fr Celt words akin to OIr *rī* (gen *rīg*) king – more at ROYAL] – **richen** *vt*, **richness** *n*

riches /'richiz/ *n pl* (great) wealth [ME, sing. or pl, fr *richesse*, lit., richness, fr OF, fr *riche* rich, of Gmc origin; akin to OE *rīce* rich]

richly /'richli/ *adv* in full measure; amply ⟨*praise* ~ *deserved*⟩ [RICH + ²-LY]

'Richter ,scale /'riktə, 'rikhtə/ *n* a logarithmic scale for expressing the magnitude of a seismic disturbance (e g an earthquake) [Charles *Richter* *b* 1900 US seismologist]

¹rick /rik/ *n* a stack (e g of hay) in the open air [ME *reek*, fr OE *hrēac*; akin to ON *hraukr* rick]

²rick *vt* to pile (e g hay) in ricks

³rick *vt, chiefly Br* to wrench or sprain (e g one's neck) [perh fr ME *wrikken* to move unsteadily]

rickets /'rikits/ *n pl but sing in constr* soft and deformed bones in children caused by failure to assimilate and use calcium and phosphorus, normally due to a lack of sunlight or vitamin D [origin unknown]

rickettsia /ri'ketsi·ə/ *n, pl* **rickettsias, rickettsiae** /-si,ee/ any of a family of microorganisms similar to bacteria that are intracellular parasites and cause various diseases (e g typhus) [NL, genus of microorganisms, fr Howard T *Ricketts* †1910 US pathologist] – **rickettsial** *adj*

rickety /'rikiti/ *adj* **1** suffering from rickets **2a** feeble in the joints ⟨*a* ~ *old man*⟩ **b** shaky, unsound ⟨~ *stairs*⟩

rickrack, ricrac /'rik,rak/ *n* a flat braid woven to

form zigzags and used esp as trimming on clothing [redupl of [4]*rack*]

rickshaw, ricksha /'rik,shaw/ *n* a small covered 2-wheeled vehicle pulled by 1 or more people [modif of Jap *jinrikisha*, fr *jin* man + *riki* strength + *sha* vehicle]

[1]**ricochet** /'rikəshay; *also* -shet/ *n* the glancing rebound of a projectile (e g a bullet) off a hard or flat surface [F]

[2]**ricochet** *vi* **ricocheting** /-'shaying/, **ricocheted** /-,shayd/; **ricochetting** /-,sheting/, **ricochetted** /-,shetid/ to proceed (as if) with glancing rebounds

ricotta /ri'kotə/ *n* a soft white bland Italian cheese made from the whey of sheep's milk [It, fr fem of pp of *ricuocere* to cook again, fr L *recoquere*, fr *re-* + *coquere* to cook – more at COOK]

rictus /'riktəs/ *n* **1** the (gape of a bird's) mouth **2** an unnatural gaping grin or grimace [NL, fr L, open mouth, fr *rictus*, pp of *ringi* to open the mouth; akin to OSlav *ręgnoti* to gape] – **rictal** *adj*

rid /rid/ *vt* **-dd-; rid** *also* **ridded** to relieve, disencumber ⟨~ *himself of his troubles*⟩ [ME *ridden* to clear, fr ON *rythja*; akin to L *ruere* to dig up – more at RUG]

riddance /'rid(ə)ns/ *n* deliverance, relief – often in *good riddance* [RID + -ANCE]

-ridden /,rid(ə)n/ *comb form* (→ *adj*) **1** afflicted or excessively concerned with ⟨*conscience*-ridden⟩ **2** excessively full of or supplied with ⟨*slum*-ridden⟩ [fr pp of [1]*ride*]

[1]**riddle** /'ridl/ *n* **1** a short and esp humorous verbal puzzle **2** a mystifying problem or fact ⟨*the* ~ *of her disappearance*⟩ **3** sthg or sby difficult to understand [ME *redels, ridel*, fr OE *rǣdelse* opinion, conjecture, riddle; akin to OE *rǣdan* to interpret – more at READ]

[2]**riddle** *vi* **riddling** /'ridl·ing/ to speak in or propound riddles – **riddler** *n*

[3]**riddle** *n* a coarse sieve (e g for sifting grain or gravel) [ME *riddil*, fr OE *hriddel*; akin to L *cribrum* sieve, *cernere* to sift – more at CERTAIN]

[4]**riddle** *vt* **1** to separate (e g grain from chaff) with a riddle; sift **2** to cover with holes ⟨~d *with bullets*⟩ **3** to spread through, esp as an affliction ⟨*the state* – *was* ~d *with poverty* – Thomas Wood⟩

[1]**ride** /ried/ *vb* **rode** /rohd/; **ridden** /'rid(ə)n/ *vi* **1a** to sit and travel mounted on and usu controlling an animal **b** to travel on or in a vehicle **2** to be sustained ⟨rode *on a wave of popularity*⟩ **3a** to lie moored or anchored **b** to appear to float ⟨*the moon* rode *in the sky*⟩ **4** to become supported on a point or surface **5** to continue without interference ⟨*let it* ~⟩ **6** to be contingent; depend ⟨*everything* ~s *on her initial success*⟩ **7** to work up the body ⟨*shorts that* ~ *up*⟩ **8** to be bet ⟨*his money is* riding *on the favourite*⟩ **9** to move from a correct or usual position ⟨*the screwdriver tends to* ~ *out of the slot*⟩ **10** *of a racetrack* to be in a usu specified condition for horse riding ~ *vt* **1a** to travel mounted on and in control of ⟨~ *a bike*⟩ **b** to move with or float on ⟨~ *the waves*⟩ **2a** to traverse by car, horse, etc **b** to ride a horse in ⟨~ *a race*⟩ **3** to survive without great damage or loss; last *out* ⟨*rode out the gale*⟩ **4** *esp of a male animal* to mount in copulation **5** to obsess, oppress ⟨ridden *by anxiety*⟩ **6** to give with (a punch) to soften the impact **7** *NAm* to harass persistently [ME *riden*, fr OE *rīdan*; akin to OHG *rītan* to ride, OIr *rīadaim* I ride, travel] – **ride high** to experience success – **ride roughshod over** to disregard in a high-handed or arrogant way

[2]**ride** *n* **1** a trip on horseback or by vehicle **2** a usu straight road or path in a wood, forest, etc used for riding, access, or as a firebreak **3** any of various mechanical devices (e g at a funfair) for riding on **4** the quality of travel comfort in a vehicle ⟨*gives a rough* ~⟩ **5** *chiefly NAm* a trip on which gangsters take a victim to murder him/her – euph

rider /'riedə/ *n* **1** sby who rides; *specif* sby who rides a horse **2** sthg added by way of qualification or amendment **3** sthg used to overlie another or to move along on another piece

ridge /rij/ *n* **1a** a range of hills or mountains **b** an elongated elevation of land ☞ GEOGRAPHY **2** the line along which 2 upward-sloping surfaces meet; *specif* the top of a roof at the intersection of 2 opposite slopes ☞ ARCHITECTURE **3** an elongated part that is raised above a surrounding surface (e g the raised part between furrows on ploughed ground) [ME *rigge*, fr OE *hrycg*; akin to OHG *hrukki* ridge, back, L *cruc-, crux* cross, *curvus* curved – more at [1]CROWN] – **ridge** *vt*, **ridged** *adj*, **ridger** *n*

'ridge,piece /-,pees/ *n* a horizontal beam in a roof that supports the upper ends of the rafters

'ridge,pole /-,pohl/ *n* the horizontal pole at the top of a tent

'ridge,way /-,way/ *n, Br* a path or road along the ridge of a hill

[1]**ridicule** /'ridikyoohl/ *n* exposure to laughter [F or L; F, fr L *ridiculum* jest]

[2]**ridicule** *vt* to mock; MAKE FUN OF

ridiculous /ri'dikyooləs/ *adj* arousing or deserving ridicule [L *ridiculosus* (fr *ridiculum* jest, fr neut of *ridiculus*) or *ridiculus*, lit., laughable, fr *ridēre* to laugh; akin to Skt *vrīḍate* he is ashamed] – **ridiculously** *adv*, **ridiculousness** *n*

riding /'rieding/ *n* **1** any of the 3 former administrative jurisdictions of Yorkshire **2** an administrative or electoral district of a Commonwealth dominion [ME, alter. of (assumed) OE *thriding*, fr ON *thrithjungr* third part, fr *thrithi* third; akin to OE *thridda* third – more at THIRD]

riem /reem/ *n, SAfr* a soft pliable thong [Afrik, lit., strap, belt, fr MD *rieme*]

riempie /'reempi/ *n, SAfr* a narrow riem used esp in furniture construction [Afrik *riempje*, dim. of *riem*]

Riesling /'reezling/ *n* a typically medium-dry white table wine; *also* the grape variety from which this is made [G]

rife /rief/ *adj* **1** prevalent, esp to a rapidly increasing degree ⟨*fear was* ~ *in the city*⟩ **2** abundant, common **3** abundantly supplied – usu + *with* ⟨~ *with rumours*⟩ [ME *ryfe*, fr OE *rȳfe*; akin to ON *rīfr* abundant]

riff /rif/ *n* (a piece based on) a constantly repeated phrase in jazz or rock music, typically played as a background to a solo improvisation [prob by shortening & alter. fr *refrain*] – **riff** *vi*

[1]**riffle** /'rifl/ *n* **1** (the sound made while) shuffling sthg (e g cards) **2** *NAm* a shallow stretch of rough water in a stream **3** *NAm* RIPPLE 1 [perh alter. of *ruffle*]

[2]**riffle** *vb* **riffling** /'rifling/ *vi* to leaf cursorily ⟨~ *through files*⟩ ~ *vt* **1** to ruffle slightly ⟨*the wind* ~d *the waters*⟩ **2a** to leaf through rapidly; *specif* to leaf

through (e g a pile of papers) by running a thumb along the edge of the leaves **b** to shuffle (playing cards) by separating the deck into 2 parts and riffling with the thumbs so the cards become mixed together

[3]**riffle** *n* **1** any of a series of blocks, rails, etc laid on the bottom of a sluice to make grooves to catch and retain a mineral (e g gold) **2** a groove so formed [prob fr [1]*riffle*]

riffraff /ˈrif,raf/ *n sing or pl in constr* **1** disreputable people **2** rabble [ME *riffe raffe*, fr *rif and raf* every single one, fr MF *rif et raf* completely, fr *rifler* to plunder + *raffe* act of sweeping]

[1]**rifle** /ˈriefl/ *vt* **rifling** /ˈriefling, ˈriefl·ing/ to search through, esp in order to steal and carry away sthg [ME *riflen*, fr MF *rifler* to scratch, file, plunder, of Gmc origin; akin to obs D *rijffelen* to scrape] – **rifler** *n*

[2]**rifle** *vt* to cut spiral grooves into the bore of (a rifle, cannon, etc) [F *rifler* to scratch, file]

[3]**rifle** *n* **1** a shoulder weapon with a rifled bore **2** *pl* a body of soldiers armed with rifles – **rifleman** /-mən/ *n*

[4]**rifle** *vt* to propel (e g a ball) with great force or speed [[3]*rifle*]

[1]**rift** /rift/ *n* **1** a fissure or crack, esp in the earth **2** an opening made by tearing or splitting apart **3** an estrangement [ME, of Scand origin; akin to Dan & Norw *rift* fissure, ON *rīfa* to rive – more at RIVE]

[2]**rift** *vt* to tear apart; split

rift valley *n* a valley formed by the subsidence of the earth's crust between at least 2 faults ☞ GEOGRAPHY

[1]**rig** /rig/ *vt* **-gg-** **1** to fit out (e g a ship) with rigging **2** to clothe, dress up – usu + *out* **3** to supply with special gear **4** to put together, esp for temporary use – usu + *up* [ME *riggen*]

[2]**rig** *n* **1** the distinctive shape, number, and arrangement of sails and masts of a ship **2** an outfit of clothing worn for an often specified occasion or activity ⟨*in ceremonial* ~⟩ **3** tackle, equipment, or machinery fitted for a specified purpose

[3]**rig** *vt* **-gg-** to manipulate, influence, or control for dishonest purposes ⟨~ *the election*⟩ [*rig*, n (ridicule, trick, swindle), of unknown origin]

rigatoni /,rigəˈtohni/ *n* pasta in the form of short, ridged, and sometimes curved tubes [It, pl, fr *rigato* furrowed, fluted, fr pp of *rigare* to furrow, flute, fr *riga* line, of Gmc origin; akin to OHG *rīga* line – more at [3]ROW]

rigger /ˈrigə/ *n* a ship of a specified rig ⟨*square*-rigger⟩ [[1]RIG + [2]-ER]

rigging /ˈriging/ *n* **1** lines and chains used aboard a ship, esp for controlling sails and supporting masts and spars ☞ SHIP **2** a network similar to a ship's rigging used (e g in theatrical scenery) for support and manipulation

[1]**right** /riet/ *adj* **1** in accordance with what is morally good, just, or proper **2** conforming to facts or truth **3** suitable, appropriate ⟨*the* ~ *woman for the job*⟩ **4** straight ⟨*a* ~ *line*⟩ **5a** of, situated on, or being the side of the body that is away from the heart **b** located nearer to the right hand than to the left; *esp* located on the right hand when facing in the same direction as an observer ⟨*stage* ~⟩ **c** located on the right when facing downstream ⟨*the* ~ *bank of a river*⟩ **d** being the side of a fabric that should show or be seen when made up **6** having its axis perpendicular to the base ⟨~ *cone*⟩ **7** of or being the principal or more prominent side of an object **8** acting or judging in accordance with truth or fact; not mistaken **9** in a correct, proper, or healthy state ⟨*not in his* ~ *mind*⟩ **10** conforming to or influencing what is socially favoured or acceptable **11** *often cap* of the Right, esp in politics **12** *chiefly Br* real, utter – infml [ME, fr OE *riht*; akin to OHG *reht* right, L *rectus* straight, right, *regere* to lead straight, direct, rule, *rogare* to ask, Gk *oregein* to stretch out] – **rightness** *n*

[2]**right** *n* **1** qualities (e g adherence to duty) that together constitute the ideal of moral conduct or merit moral approval **2a** a power, privilege, interest, etc to which one has a just claim **b** a property interest in sthg – often pl with sing. meaning ⟨*mineral* ~s⟩ **3** sthg one may legitimately claim as due **4** the cause of truth or justice ⟨*trust that* ~ *may prevail*⟩ **5a** (a blow struck with) the right hand **b** the location or direction of the right side **c** the part on the right side **6** the quality or state of being factually or morally correct **7** *sing or pl in constr, often cap* the members of a European legislative body occupying the right of a legislative chamber as a result of holding more conservative political views than other members **8a** *sing or pl in constr, cap* those professing conservative political views **b** *often cap* a conservative position [ME, fr OE *riht*, fr *riht*, adj] – **by rights** with reason or justice; properly – **in one's own right** by virtue of one's own qualifications or properties – **to rights** into proper order

[3]**right** *adv* **1** in a right, proper, or correct manner ⟨*guessed* ~⟩ ⟨*knew he wasn't doing it* ~⟩ **2** in the exact location or position ⟨~ *in the middle of the floor*⟩ **3** in a direct line or course; straight ⟨*go* ~ *home*⟩ **4** all the way; completely ⟨*blew* ~ *out of the window*⟩ **5a** without delay; straight ⟨~ *after lunch*⟩ **b** immediately ⟨~ *now*⟩ **6** to the full ⟨*entertained* ~ *royally*⟩ – often in British titles **7** on or to the right ⟨*looked left and* ~⟩

[4]**right** *vt* **1** to avenge **2a** to adjust or restore to the proper state or condition; correct **b** to bring or restore (e g a boat) to an upright position – **righter** *n*

ˈ**right ,angle** *n* the angle bounded by 2 lines perpendicular to each other; an angle of 90° ☞ MATHEMATICS, SYMBOL – **right-angled, right-angle** *adj*

right atrioventricular valve /,aytriohvenˈtrikyoolə/ *n* TRICUSPID VALVE

,**right aˈway** *adv* without delay or hesitation

ˈ**right-,back** *n* a fullback playing on the right side of the pitch in a traditional soccer lineup ☞ SPORT

righteous /ˈriechəs/ *adj* **1** acting in accord with divine or moral law; free from guilt or sin **2a** morally right or justified **b** arising from an outraged sense of justice [alter. of earlier *rightuous*, alter. of ME *rightwise, rightwos*, fr OE *rihtwīs*, fr *riht*, n, right + *wīs* wise] – **righteously** *adv*, **righteousness** *n*

rightful /ˈrietf(ə)l/ *adj* **1** just, equitable **2a** having a just claim ⟨*the* ~ *owner*⟩ **b** held by right ⟨~ *authority*⟩ – **rightfully** *adv*, **rightfulness** *n*

,**right-ˈhalf** *n* a halfback playing on the right side of the pitch in a traditional soccer lineup ☞ SPORT

,**right-ˈhand** *adj* **1** situated on the right **2** right-handed **3** chiefly or constantly relied on

,**right ˈhand** *n* **1a** the hand on the right-hand side of the body **b** a reliable or indispensable person **2a** the right side **b** a place of honour

,**right-ˈhanded** *adj* **1** using the right hand habitually or more easily than the left; *also* swinging from right to left ⟨*a ~ batsman*⟩ **2** relating to, designed for, or done with the right hand **3** clockwise – used of a twist, rotary motion, or spiral curve as viewed from a given direction with respect to the axis of rotation – **right-handed** *adv*, **right-handedly** *adv*, **right-handedness** *n*

ˌright-ˈhander /ˈhandə/ *n* **1** a blow struck with the right hand **2** a right-handed person

ˌright ˈhonourable *adj* entitled to great honour – used as a title for privy councillors

rightism /ˈrieˌtiz(ə)m/ *n, often cap* (advocacy of) the doctrines of the Right – **rightist** *n or adj, often cap*

rightly /ˈrietli/ *adv* **1** in accordance with right conduct; fairly **2** in the right manner; properly **3** according to truth or fact **4** with certainty ⟨*I can't ~ say*⟩

ˌright-ˈminded *adj* thinking and acting by just or honest principles – **right-mindedness** *n*

righto /ˈrietˌoh/ *interj, chiefly Br* – used to express agreement

ˌright ˈoff *adv* RIGHT AWAY, AT ONCE – infml

ˌright of ˈsearch *n* the right to stop and search a merchant vessel on the high seas to ascertain whether it is liable to seizure

ˌright of ˈway *n, pl* **rights of way** **1** a legal right of passage over another person's property **2a** the course along which a right of way exists **b** the strip of land over which a public road is built **c** the land occupied by a railway for its tracks **3** a precedence in passing accorded to one vehicle over another by custom, decision, or statute

ˌright ˈon *interj* – used to express agreement or approval; slang

ˌRight ˈReverend *adj* – used as a title for high ecclesiastical officials

ˈrights ˌissue *n* an issue of new shares available to existing shareholders only

rightward /ˈrietwood/ *adj* being towards or on the right

ˈrightwards /-woodz/, *chiefly NAm* **rightward** *adv* towards or on the right

ˈright ˌwhale *n* any of several large whalebone whales with no dorsal fin, very long whalebone, and a large head [fr its being formerly considered the right whale to hunt]

ˌright ˈwing *n sing or pl in constr, often cap R&W* the more conservative division of a group or party – **right-wing** *adv*, **rightwinger** *n*

rigid /ˈrijid/ *adj* **1a** deficient in or devoid of flexibility **b** fixed in appearance ⟨*her face ~ with pain*⟩ **2a** inflexibly set in opinions or habits **b** strictly maintained ⟨*a ~ schedule*⟩ **3** firmly inflexible rather than lax or indulgent **4** precise and accurate in procedure **5a** having the gas containers enclosed within compartments of a fixed fabric-covered framework ⟨*a ~ airship*⟩ **b** having the outer shape maintained by a fixed framework [MF or L; MF *rigide*, fr L *rigidus*, fr *rigēre* to be stiff] – **rigidly** *adv*, **rigidness** *n*, **rigidify** /riˈjidifie/ *vb*, **rigidity** /riˈjidəti/ *n*

rigmarole /ˈrigməˌrohl/ *n* **1** confused or nonsensical talk **2** an absurd and complex procedure [alter. of obs *ragman roll* (long list, catalogue)]

rigor /ˈrigə/ *n* **1** a tremor caused by a chill **2** rigidness or insensitivity of organs or tissue **3** *NAm* rigour [(1, 2) NL, fr L]

ˌrigor ˈmortis /ˈmawtis/ *n* the temporary rigidity of muscles that occurs after death [NL, stiffness of death]

rigorous /ˈrigərəs/ *adj* **1** manifesting, exercising, or favouring rigour; very strict ⟨*~ standards of hygiene*⟩ **2** harsh, severe **3** scrupulously accurate – **rigorously** *adv*

rigour /ˈrigə/ *n* **1a(1)** harsh inflexibility in opinion, temper, or judgment **(2)** the quality of being unyielding or inflexible **(3)** severity of life; austerity **b** an act or instance of strictness or severity – often pl **2** a condition that makes life difficult, challenging, or painful; *esp* extremity of cold – often pl **3** strict precision ⟨*logical ~*⟩ [ME, fr MF *rigueur*, fr L *rigor*, lit., stiffness, fr *rigēre*]

rigout /ˈrigowt/ *n* a complete outfit of clothing – infml

rile /riel/ *vt* **1** to make angry or resentful **2** *NAm* ROIL 1 [alter. of *roil*]

¹rill /ril/ *n* a small brook – chiefly poetic [D *ril* or LG *rille*; akin to OE *rīth* rivulet]

²rill, rille /ril/ *n* any of several long narrow valleys on the moon's surface [G *rille*, lit., channel made by a small stream, fr LG, rill]

¹rim /rim/ *n* **1** an outer usu curved edge or border **2** the outer ring of a wheel not including the tyre ☞ CAR [ME, fr OE *rima*; akin to ON *rimi* strip of land, Gk *ērema* gently, Lith *remti* to support]

²rim *vt* **-mm-** to serve as a rim for; border

¹rime /riem/ *n* **1** FROST 1b **2** an accumulation of granular ice tufts on the windward sides of exposed objects at low temperatures [ME *rim*, fr OE *hrīm*; akin to ON *hrīm* frost, Latvian *kreims* cream] – **rimy** *adj*

²rime *vt* to cover (as if) with rime

rimmed /rimd/ *adj* having a rim – usu in combination ⟨*dark*-rimmed *glasses*⟩

rimu /ˈreeˌmooh/ *n* (the wood of) a large coniferous New Zealand tree [Maori]

¹rind /riend/ *n* **1** the bark of a tree **2** a usu hard or tough outer layer of fruit, cheese, bacon, etc [ME, fr OE; akin to OHG *rinda* bark, OE *rendan* to rend]

²rind *vt* to remove the rind or bark from

rinderpest /ˈrindəˌpest/ *n* an infectious fever, esp of cattle [G, fr *rinder*, pl, cattle + *pest* pestilence]

¹ring /ring/ *n* **1** a circular band for holding, connecting, hanging, moving, fastening, etc or for identification **2** a circlet usu of precious metal, worn on the finger **3a** a circular line, figure, or object **b** an encircling arrangement **c** a circular or spiral course **4a** an often circular space, esp for exhibitions or competitions; *esp* such a space at a circus **b** a square enclosure in which boxers or wrestlers contest **5** any of the concentric bands that revolve round some planets (e g Saturn or Uranus) **6** ANNUAL RING **7** *sing or pl in constr* an exclusive association of people for a selfish and often corrupt purpose ⟨*a drug ~*⟩ **8** a closed chain of atoms in a molecule **9** a set of elements closed under 2 binary operations (e g addition and multiplication) which is a commutative group under the first operation and in which the second operation is associative and is distributive relative to the first **10** boxing as a profession ⟨*retired after 9 years in the ~*⟩ **11** an electric element or gas burner in the shape of a circle, set into the top of a cooker, stove, etc, which provides a source of heat for cooking – compare GAS RING [ME, fr OE *hring*; akin to OHG *hring* ring, L *curvus* curved – more at ¹CROWN] – **ringlike** *adj*

[2]ring *vt* **ringed** **1** to place or form a ring round; encircle **2** to attach a ring to ⟨~ *migrating geese*⟩ **3** GIRDLE 3 **4** to throw a ring over (the peg) in a game (e g quoits)

[3]ring *vb* **rang** /rang/; **rung** /rung/ *vi* **1** to sound resonantly ⟨*the doorbell* rang⟩ ⟨*cheers* rang *out*⟩ **2a** to be filled with resonant sound; resound **b** to have the sensation of a continuous humming sound **3** to sound a bell as a summons **4a** to be filled with talk or report **b** to sound repeatedly ⟨*praise* rang *in her ears*⟩ **5** *chiefly Br* to telephone – often + *up* ~ *vt* **1** to cause to ring, esp by striking **2** to sound (as if) by ringing a bell **3** to announce (as if) by ringing – often + *in* or *out* **4** *chiefly Br* to telephone – usu + *up* [ME *ringen*, fr OE *hringan*; akin to MD *ringen* to ring, Lith *krankti* to croak] – **ring a bell** to sound familiar – **ring the changes** to run through the range of possible variations – **ring true** to appear to be true or authentic

[4]ring *n* **1** a set of bells **2** a clear resonant sound made by vibrating metal; *also* a similar sound **3** resonant tone **4** a loud sound continued, repeated, or reverberated **5** a sound or character suggestive of a particular quality or feeling **6a** an act or instance of ringing **b** a telephone call – usu in *give somebody a ring*

ringbark /'ring,bahk/ *vt* GIRDLE 1d

ring binder *n* a loose-leaf binder in which split metal rings attached to a metal back hold perforated sheets of paper in place

'ring,bolt /-,bohlt/ *n* an eyebolt with a ring through its loop

'ring,bone /-,bohn/ *n* a bony outgrowth on a horse's pastern bones, usu causing lameness – **ringboned** *adj*

'ring,dove /-,duv/ *n* a woodpigeon [fr the white patch on each side of its neck]

ringed /ringd/ *adj* encircled or marked (as if) with rings

ringer /'ring·ə/ *n* **1** sby who rings bells **2** *NAm* sby or sthg that strongly resembles another – often + *dead* ⟨*she's a dead* ~ *for the senator*⟩ **3** a horse entered in a race under false representations; *broadly* an impostor – infml [[3]RING + [2]-ER]

'ring ,finger *n* the third finger, esp of the left hand, counting the index finger as the first

ringgit /'ring·git/ *n* ☞ *Malaysia* at NATIONALITY [Malay]

ringhals /'ring,hals/ *n* a poisonous African snake that spits its venom at the eyes of its victim [Afrik *rinkals* (formerly *ringhals*), fr *ring* ring + *hals* neck]

ringing /'ring·ing/ *adj* **1** resounding **2** vigorously unequivocal ⟨*a* ~ *condemnation*⟩ – **ringingly** *adv*

'ring,leader /-,leedə/ *n* a leader of a group that engages in objectionable activities

ringlet /'ringlit/ *n* **1** a small ring or circle **2** a long lock of hair curled in a spiral

'ring ,main *n, Br* a domestic wiring circuit in which a number of power points are connected to supply cables which form a closed loop

'ring,master /-,mahstə/ *n* one in charge of performances in a ring (e g of a circus)

'ring,neck /-,nek/ *adj* ring-necked – **ringneck** *n*

,ring-'necked *adj* having a ring of colour about the neck

ring off *vi, chiefly Br* to terminate a telephone conversation

'ring ,ouzel /'oohz(ə)l/ *n* an Old World thrush, the male of which is black with a broad white bar across the breast

'ring-,pull *n* a built-in device for opening a tin consisting of a ring that, when pulled, removes a hermetically sealed tab or lid

'ring ,road *n, Br* a road round a town or town centre designed to relieve traffic congestion

[1]'ring,side /-,sied/ *n* **1** the area surrounding a ring, esp providing a close view of a contest **2** a place that gives a close view

[2]ringside *adj or adv* at the ringside

'ring-,tailed *adj* having a tail marked with rings of differing colours

ring up *vt* **1** to record by means of a cash register **2** to record, achieve [fr the bell that rings when a sum is recorded by a cash register]

ringworm /'ring,wuhm/ *n* any of several contagious fungous diseases of the skin, hair, or nails in which ring-shaped discoloured blister-covered patches form on the skin

rink /ringk/ *n* **1a** (a building containing) a surface of ice for ice-skating **b** an enclosure for roller-skating **2** part of a bowling green being used for a match [ME (Sc) *rinc* area in which a contest takes place, fr MF *renc* place, row – more at [2]RANK]

[1]rinse /rins/ *vt* **1** to cleanse (e g from soap) with liquid (e g clean water) – often + *out* **2** to remove (dirt or impurities) by washing lightly [ME *rincen*, fr MF *rincer*, fr OF *recincier*, perh fr (assumed) VL *recentiare*, fr L *recent-*, *recens* fresh, recent] – **rinser** *n*

[2]rinse *n* **1** (a) rinsing **2a** liquid used for rinsing **b** a solution that temporarily tints the hair

riot /'rie·ət/ *n* **1** unrestrained revelry **2** (a) violent public disorder; *specif* a disturbance of the peace by 3 or more people **3** a profuse and random display ⟨*the woods were a* ~ *of colour*⟩ **4** sby or sthg wildly funny [ME, fr OF, dispute] – **riot** *vi*, **rioter** *n*

'riot ,gun *n* a small firearm used to disperse rioters rather than to inflict serious injury

riotous /'rie·ətəs/ *adj* **1** participating in a riot **2a** wild and disorderly **b** exciting, exuberant ⟨*the party was a* ~ *success*⟩ – **riotously** *adv*, **riotousness** *n*

[1]rip /rip/ *vb* **-pp-** *vi* **1** to become ripped; rend **2** to rush along ⟨~ped *past the finishing post*⟩ **3** to start or proceed without restraint ⟨*let it* ~⟩ ~ *vt* **1a** to tear or split apart, esp in a violent manner **b** to saw or split (wood) along the grain **2** to slit roughly (as if) with a sharp blade **3** to remove by force – + *out* or *off* [prob fr Flem *rippen* to strip off roughly] – **ripper** *n*

[2]rip *n* a rough or violent tear

[3]rip *n* a body of rough water formed **a** by the meeting of opposing currents, winds, etc **b** by passing over ridges [perh fr [2]*rip*]

[4]rip *n* **1** a worn-out worthless horse **2** a mischievous usu young person [perh by shortening & alter. fr *reprobate*]

riparian /rie'peəri·ən/ *adj* of or occurring on the bank of a body of water, esp a river [L *riparius* – more at RIVER]

'rip ,cord *n* a cord or wire for releasing a parachute from its pack

'rip ,current *n* a riptide

ripe /riep/ *adj* **1** fully grown and developed; mature **2** mature in knowledge, understanding, or judgment **3** of advanced years **4a** fully arrived; propitious ⟨*the* *time seemed ~ for the experiment*⟩ **b** fully prepared; ready *for* **5** brought by aging to full flavour or the best state; mellow ⟨*~ cheese*⟩ **6** ruddy, plump, or full like ripened fruit **7** smutty, indecent – euph [ME, fr OE *rīpe*; akin to OE *rīpan, reopan* to reap – more at REAP] – **ripely** *adv,* **ripen** *vb,* **ripener** *n,* **ripeness** *n*

ripieno /ri'pyenoh/ *n, pl* **ripieni** /-ni/, **ripienos** a supplementary or accompanying group of instruments or musical parts; *esp* all the instruments or musical parts except the soloist [It, lit., filled up]

'rip-,off *n* **1** an act or instance of stealing **2** an instance of financial exploitation; *esp* the charging of an exorbitant price *USE* infml

rip off *vt* **1** to rob; *also* to steal **2** to defraud *USE* infml

riposte /ri'pohst, -post/ *n* **1** a fencer's quick return thrust following a parry **2** a piece of retaliatory banter **3** a usu rapid retaliatory manoeuvre or measure [F, modif of It *risposta,* lit., answer, fr *rispondere* to respond, fr L *respondēre*] – **riposte** *vi*

¹ripple /'ripl/ *vb* **rippling** /'ripling, 'ripl·ing/ *vi* **1a** to become covered with small waves **b** to flow in small waves or undulations **2** to flow with a light rise and fall of sound or inflection **3** to proceed with an undulating motion (so as to cause ripples) **4** to spread irregularly outwards, esp from a central point ~ *vt* **1** to stir up small waves on **2** to impart a wavy motion or appearance to ⟨rippling *his muscles*⟩ [perh freq of ¹*rip*] – **rippler** *n*

²ripple *n* **1** a small wave or succession of small waves **2a** RIPPLE MARK **b** a sound like that of rippling water ⟨*a ~ of laughter*⟩ **3** *NAm* RIFFLE 1

'ripple ,mark *n* any of a series of small ridges produced, esp on sand, by wind or water

riprap /'rip,rap/ *n, NAm* (stone used for) a foundation or sustaining wall of loose stones [obs *riprap* (sound of rapping), redupl of ¹*rap*] – **riprap** *vt*

'rip-,roaring *adj* noisily excited or exciting; exuberant

ripsaw /'rip,saw/ *n* a coarse-toothed saw having teeth only slightly bent to alternate sides that is designed to cut wood in the direction of the grain – compare CROSSCUT SAW

riptide /'rip,tied/ *n* a strong surface current flowing outwards from a shore

Ripuarian /,ripyoo'eəri·ən/ *adj* of or constituting a group of Franks who settled in the 4th c on the Rhine near Cologne [ML *Ripuarius*]

¹rise /riez/ *vi* **rose** /rohz/; **risen** /'riz(ə)n/ **1a** to assume an upright position, esp from lying, kneeling, or sitting **b** to get up from sleep or from one's bed **2** to return from death **3** to take up arms **4a** to respond warmly or readily; applaud – usu + *to* **b** to respond to nasty words or behaviour, esp by annoyance or anger ⟨*despite the innuendos, he didn't ~*⟩ **5** to end a session; adjourn **6** to appear above the horizon **7a** to move upwards; ascend **b** to increase in height or volume **8** to extend above other objects or people **9a** to become cheered or encouraged **b** to increase in fervour or intensity **10a** to attain a higher office or rank **b** to increase in amount or number **11a** to occur; TAKE PLACE **b** to come into being; originate **12** to show oneself equal to a challenge [ME *risen,* fr OE *rīsan*; akin to OHG *rīsan* to rise, L *oriri* to rise, *rivus* stream, Gk *ornynai* to rouse]

²rise *n* **1** rising or being risen: e g **a** a movement upwards **b** emergence (e g of the sun) above the horizon **c** the upward movement of a fish to seize food or bait **2** origin ⟨*behaviour that gave ~ to much speculation*⟩ **3** the vertical height of sthg; *specif* the vertical height of a step **4a** an increase, esp in amount, number, or intensity **b** an increase in price, value, rate, or sum; *specif, chiefly Br* an increase in pay **5a** an upward slope or gradient **b** a spot higher than surrounding ground **6** a rising-pitch intonation in speech **– get/take a rise out of** to provoke to annoyance by teasing

riser /'riezə/ *n* the upright part between 2 consecutive stair treads ☞ ARCHITECTURE [¹RISE + ²-ER]

risible /'rizəbl/ *adj* **1** inclined or susceptible to laughter **2** arousing or provoking laughter **3** associated with or used in laughter [LL *risibilis,* fr L *risus,* pp of *ridēre* to laugh – more at RIDICULOUS] – **risibility** /-'biləti/ *n*

¹rising /'riezing/ *n* an insurrection, uprising

²rising *adv* approaching a specified age

¹risk /risk/ *n* **1** possibility of loss, injury, or damage **2** a dangerous element or factor; hazard **3a** the chance of loss or the dangers to that which is insured in an insurance contract **b** sby who or sthg that is a specified hazard to an insurer ⟨*a poor ~ for insurance*⟩ **c** an insurance hazard from a specified cause ⟨*war ~*⟩ [F *risque,* fr It *risco*] – **risky** *adj,* **riskily** *adv,* **riskiness** *n* **– at risk** in danger (e g of infection or of behaving in ways which are considered antisocial) **– on risk** *of an insurer* having assumed and accepting liability for a risk

²risk *vt* **1** to expose to hazard or danger **2** to incur the risk or danger of

risorgimento /ri,sawji'mentoh/ *n, pl* **risorgimentos** a time of renewal or revival; *specif, often cap* the 19th-c movement for Italian political unity [It, fr *risorgere* to rise again, fr L *resurgere* – more at RESURRECTION]

risotto /ri'zotoh, -'so-/ *n, pl* **risottos** an Italian dish of rice cooked in meat stock with onion, green pepper, etc [It, fr *riso* rice]

risqué /'reeskay, 'ri-/ *adj* verging on impropriety or indecency [F, fr pp of *risquer* to risk, fr *risque*]

rissole /'risohl/ *n* a small fried cake or ball of cooked minced food, esp meat [F, fr MF *roissole,* fr (assumed) VL *russeola,* fr L *russeus* reddish, fr *russus* red]

ritardando /,ritah'dandoh/ *adv, adj, or n, pl* **ritardandos** (with) a gradual slackening in musical tempo [It, fr L *retardandum,* gerund of *retardare* to retard]

rite /riet/ *n* **1** (a prescribed form of words or actions for) a ceremonial act or action **2** the characteristic liturgy of a church or group of churches [ME, fr L *ritus*; akin to OE *rīm* number, Gk *arithmos* number – more at ARITHMETIC]

ritenuto /,reete'n(y)oohtoh, ,ritə'nyoohtoh/ *adv, adj, or n, pl* **ritenutos** (with) an immediate slackening of musical tempo [It, pp of *ritenere* to hold back, retain, fr L *retinēre*]

,rite of 'passage *n* a ritual associated with a change of status (e g assuming adult status and responsibilities) in the life of an individual [trans of F *rite de passage*]

ritornello /,ritaw'neloh/ *n, pl* **ritornelli** /-li/, **ritornellos** **1** a short recurrent instrumental passage in a vocal composition **2** a tutti passage in a concerto or rondo refrain [It, dim. of *ritorno* return, fr *ritornare* to return]

[1]**ritual** /ˈrichooəl, -tyoo-/ *adj* **1** of rites or a ritual; ceremonial ⟨*a ~ dance*⟩ **2** according to religious law or social custom – **ritually** *adv*

[2]**ritual** *n* **1** the form or order of words prescribed for a religious ceremony **2** (a) ritual observance; *broadly* any formal and customary act or series of acts

ritualism /ˈrichooə,liz(ə)m, -tyoo-/ *n* (excessive devotion to) the use of ritual – **ritualist** *n*, **ritualistic** /-ˈlistik/ *adj*

ritual·ize, -ise /ˈrichooə,liez, -tyoo-/ *vi* to practise ritualism ~ *vt* to convert into a ritual – **ritualization** /-ˈzaysh(ə)n/ *n*

ritzy /ˈritsi/ *adj* ostentatiously smart – infml [*Ritz* hotels, noted for their opulence] – **ritziness** *n*

[1]**rival** /ˈrievl/ *n* **1a** any of 2 or more competing for a single goal **b** sby who tries to compete with and be superior to another **2** sby who or sthg that equals another in desirable qualities [MF or L; MF, fr L *rivalis* one using the same stream as another, rival in love, fr *rivalis* of a stream, fr *rivus* stream – more at RISE] – **rivalry** /-ri/ *n*

[2]**rival** *adj* having comparable pretensions or claims

[3]**rival** *vt* **-ll-** (*NAm* **-l, -ll-**), /ˈrievl·ing/ **1** to be in competition with; contend with **2** to strive to equal or excel **3** to possess qualities that approach or equal (those of another)

rive /riev/ *vb* **rived; riven** /ˈriv(ə)n/ *also* **rived** *vt* **1a** to wrench open or tear apart or to pieces **b** to split with force or violence; cleave **2** to rend with distress or dispute ~ *vi* to become split [ME *riven*, fr ON *rīfa*; akin to L *ripa* shore, Gk *ereipein* to tear down, OE *rāw* row]

river /ˈrivə/ *n* **1** a natural stream of water of considerable volume ☞ GEOGRAPHY **2a** a flow that matches a river in volume ⟨*a ~ of lava*⟩ **b** *pl* a copious or overwhelming quality [ME *rivere*, fr OF, fr (assumed) VL *riparia*, fr L, fem of *riparius* riparian, fr *ripa*]

riverine /ˈrivərien/ *adj* **1** of, formed by, or resembling a river **2** living or situated on the banks of a river

[1]**rivet** /ˈrivit/ *n* a headed metal pin used to unite 2 or more pieces by passing the shank through a hole in each piece and then beating or pressing down the plain end so as to make a second head [ME *rivette*, fr MF *river* to be attached]

[2]**rivet** *vt* **1** to fasten (as if) with rivets **2** to hammer or flatten the end or point of (e g a metal pin, rod, or bolt) so as to form a head **3** to fix firmly **4** to attract and hold (e g the attention) completely – **riveter** *n*

riviera /,riviˈeərə/ *n, often cap* a coastal region, usu with a mild climate, frequented as a resort [the *Riviera*, region in SE France and NW Italy]

rivulet /ˈrivyoolit/ *n* a small stream [It *rivoletto*, dim. of *rivolo*, fr L *rivulus*, dim. of *rivus* stream – more at RISE]

[1]**riyal** /riˈyahl/ *n* ☞ *Qatar, Saudi Arabia, Yemen Arab Republic* at NATIONALITY [Ar *riyāl*, fr Sp *real* real]

[2]**riyal** *n* a rial

RNA *n* any of various nucleic acids similar to DNA that contain ribose and uracil as structural components instead of deoxyribose and thymine, and are associated with the control of cellular chemical activities [*ribonucleic acid*]

[1]**roach** /rohch/ *n, pl* **roach** *also* **roaches** a silver-white European freshwater fish of the carp family [ME *roche*, fr MF]

[2]**roach** *n* a concave or convex curvature in the edge of a sail [origin unknown]

[3]**roach** *n, NAm* **1** a cockroach **2** the butt of a marijuana cigarette – slang

road /rohd/ *n* **1** a relatively sheltered stretch of water near the shore where ships may ride at anchor – often pl with sing. meaning **2a** an open usu paved way for the passage of vehicles, people, and animals **b** the part of a paved surface used by vehicles **3** a route or path [ME *rode*, fr OE *rād* ride, journey, raid; akin to OE *rīdan* to ride] – **roadless** *adj* – **off the road** *of a vehicle* not roadworthy – **on the road** travelling or touring on business

ˈroad,bed /-,bed/ *n* **1** the bed on which the sleepers, rails, and ballast of a railway rest **2a** the earth foundation of a road prepared for surfacing **b** *NAm* ROAD 2b

ˈroad,block /-,blok/ *n* **1** a road barricade set up by an army, the police, etc **2** an obstruction in a road **3** *chiefly NAm* an obstacle to progress or success

ˈroad ,hog *n* a driver of a motor vehicle who obstructs or intimidates others

ˈroad,holding /-,hohlding/ *n, chiefly Br* the ability of a moving vehicle to remain stable

ˈroad,house /-,hows/ *n* an inn situated usu on a main road in a country area

roadie /ˈrohdi/ *n* sby who looks after the transport, setting up, etc, of the equipment of entertainers, esp a rock group

roadman /ˈrohdmən, -,man/ *n* one who mends or builds roads

ˈroad ,metal *n* broken stone used in making and repairing roads or ballasting railways

ˈroad,runner /-,runə/ *n* a largely ground-living fast-running American bird of the cuckoo family

ˈroad ,show *n* a theatrical performance given by a troupe on tour

ˈroad,side /-,sied/ *n* the strip of land beside a road; the side of a road

roadster /ˈrohdstə/ *n* **1** a horse for riding or driving on roads **2a** an open sports car that seats usu 2 people **b** *Br* a sturdy bicycle for ordinary use on common roads

ˈroad ,test *n* a test of a vehicle taken under practical operating conditions on the road – **road test** *vt*

ˈroad,way /-,way/ *n* a road

ˈroad,work /-,wuhk/ *n* **1** conditioning for an athletic contest (e g a boxing match) consisting mainly of long runs **2** *pl, Br* (the site of) the repair or construction of roads

ˈroad,worthy /-,wuhdhi/ *adj, of a vehicle* in a fit condition to be used on the roads; in proper working order – **roadworthiness** *n*

roam /rohm/ *vi* **1** to go aimlessly from place to place; wander **2** to travel unhindered through a wide area ~ *vt* to range or wander over [ME *romen*] – **roam** *n*, **roamer** *n*

[1]**roan** /rohn/ *adj, esp of horses and cattle* having a coat of a usu reddish brown base colour that is muted and lightened by some white hairs [MF, fr OSp *roano*]

[2]**roan** *n* (the colour of) an animal (e g a horse) with a roan, specif a bay roan, coat

[1]**roar** /ˈraw/ *vi* **1a** to give a roar **b** to sing or shout with full force **2a** to make or emit loud reverber-

ations **b** to laugh loudly and deeply **3** to be boisterous or disorderly – usu + *about* **4** *of a horse suffering from roaring* to make a loud noise in breathing ~ *vt* to utter with a roar [ME *roren*, fr OE *rārian*; akin to OHG *rērēn* to bleat, Skt *rāyati* he barks]

[2]**roar** *n* **1** the deep prolonged cry characteristic of a wild animal **2** a loud cry, call, etc (e g of pain, anger, or laughter) **3** a loud continuous confused sound ⟨*the ~ of the waves*⟩

[1]**roaring** /ˈrawring/ *n* noisy breathing in a horse occurring during exertion and caused by muscular paralysis

[2]**roaring** *adj* **1** making or characterized by a sound resembling a roar **2** marked by energetic or successful activity ⟨*did a ~ trade*⟩

[3]**roaring** *adv* extremely, thoroughly – infml ⟨*went and got ~ drunk*⟩

ˌroaring ˈforties *n pl* either of 2 areas of stormy westerly winds between latitudes 40° and 50° N and S

[1]**roast** /rohst/ *vt* **1a** to cook by exposing to dry heat (e g in an oven) or by surrounding with hot embers **b** to dry and brown slightly by exposure to heat ⟨*~ coffee*⟩ ⟨*~ chestnuts*⟩ **2** to heat (ore or other inorganic material) with air to cause the removal of volatile material, oxidation, etc **3** to heat to excess **4** *chiefly NAm* to criticize severely ~ *vi* **1** to cook food by roasting **2** to be subject to roasting [ME *rosten*, fr OF *rostir*, of Gmc origin; akin to OHG *rōsten* to roast]

[2]**roast** *n* **1** a piece of meat roasted or suitable for roasting **2** *NAm* a party at which food is roasted, esp in the open air

[3]**roast** *adj* roasted ⟨*~ beef*⟩

roaster /ˈrohstə/ *n* **1** a device for roasting **2** a pig, fowl, vegetable, etc suitable for roasting [[1]ROAST + [2]-ER]

rob /rob/ *vb* **-bb-** *vt* **1** to steal sthg from (a person or place), esp by violence or threat **2** to deprive of sthg due, expected, or desired ~ *vi* to commit robbery [ME *robben*, fr OF *rober*, of Gmc origin; akin to OHG *roubōn* to rob – more at BEREAVE] – **robber** *n*

robbery /ˈrobəri/ *n* the act of robbing; *specif* theft accompanied by violence or threat

[1]**robe** /rohb/ *n* **1** a long flowing outer garment; *esp* one used for ceremonial occasions or as a symbol of office or profession – sometimes pl with sing. meaning **2** *NAm* a woman's dressing gown [ME, fr OF, robe, booty, of Gmc origin; akin to OHG *roubōn* to rob]

[2]**robe** *vt* to clothe or cover (as if) with a robe ~ *vi* to put on a robe; *broadly* DRESS 1a

robin /ˈrobin/, **robin ˈredˌbreast** /ˈred,brest/ *n* **1** a small brownish European thrush resembling a warbler and having an orange red throat and breast **2** a large N American thrush with a dull reddish breast and underparts [ME *robin redbrest*, fr *Robin*, nickname for *Robert*]

robot /ˈrohbot/ *n* **1a** a (fictional) humanoid machine that walks and talks **b** sby efficient or clever who lacks human warmth or sensitivity **2** an automatic apparatus or device that performs functions ordinarily ascribed to human beings or operates with what appears to be almost human intelligence **3** sthg guided by automatic controls [Czech, fr *robota* work; akin to OHG *arabeit* trouble, L *orbus* orphaned]

robotics /rohˈbotiks, rə-/ *n pl but sing in constr* a field of interest concerned with the construction, maintenance, and behaviour of robots ⟨*~ is a major science-fiction theme*⟩

robust /rohˈbust, ˈ--/ *adj* **1a** having or exhibiting vigorous health or stamina **b** firm in purpose or outlook **c** strongly formed or constructed **2** earthy, rude **3** requiring strenuous exertion **4** full-bodied ⟨*a ~ red wine*⟩ [L *robustus* oaken, strong, fr *robor-*, *robur* oak, strength] – **robustly** *adv*, **robustness** *n*

roc /rok/ *n* a mythical bird of great size and strength [Ar *rukhkh*]

rocambole /ˈrokəmbohl/ *n* a European leek used for flavouring [F, fr G *rockenbolle*, fr *rocken, roggen* rye + *bolle* bulb]

Rochelle salt /roˈshel/ *n* sodium potassium tartrate, used esp in baking powders and in piezoelectric crystals [La *Rochelle*, city in W France]

roche moutonnée /ˌrosh moohtoˈnay/ *n, pl* **roches moutonnées** /~/ a long ice-sculptured rock mound [F, lit., fleecy rock]

rochet /ˈrochit/ *n* a white ceremonial vestment resembling a surplice, worn esp by bishops [ME, fr MF, fr OF, fr (assumed) OF *roc* coat, of Gmc origin; akin to OHG *roc* coat]

[1]**rock** /rok/ *vt* **1** to move gently back and forth (as if) in a cradle **2a** to cause to sway back and forth **b(1)** to daze or stun **(2)** to disturb, upset ~ *vi* **1** to become moved rapidly or violently backwards and forwards (e g under impact) **2** to move rhythmically back and forth [ME *rokken*, fr OE *roccian*; akin to OHG *rucken* to cause to move] – **rock the boat** to disturb the equilibrium of a situation ⟨*even though you're right you can't afford to* rock the boat⟩

[2]**rock, rock and roll, rock 'n' roll** /ˌrok (ə)n ˈrohl/ *n* popular music, usu played on electronically amplified instruments and characterized by a persistent heavily accented beat, much repetition of simple phrases, and often country, folk, and blues elements

[3]**rock** *n* **1** a large mass of stone forming a cliff, promontory, or peak **2** a large concreted mass of stony material **3** consolidated or unconsolidated solid mineral matter **4a** sthg like a rock in firmness; a firm or solid foundation or support **b** sthg that threatens or causes disaster – often pl with sing. meaning **5** a coloured and flavoured sweet produced in the form of a usu cylindrical stick **6** ROCK SALMON – used esp by fishmongers **7** *NAm* a small stone **8** a gem; *esp* a diamond – slang [ME *rokke*, fr ONF *roque*, fr (assumed) VL *rocca*] – **rock** *adj*, **rocklike** *adj* – **on the rocks** **1** in or into a state of destruction or wreckage ⟨*their marriage was* on the rocks⟩ **2** on ice cubes ⟨*Scotch* on the rocks⟩

ˌrock-ˈbottom *adj* being the lowest possible

ˌrock ˈbottom *n* the lowest or most fundamental part or level

ˈrockˌbound /-ˌbownd/ *adj* surrounded or strewn with rocks; rocky

rock crystal *n* transparent colourless quartz

ˈrock ˌdove *n* a bluish grey Old World wild pigeon that is the ancestor of the domestic pigeons

rocker /ˈrokə/ *n* **1a** either of the 2 curved pieces of wood or metal on which an object (e g a cradle) rocks **b** sthg mounted on rockers; *specif* ROCKING CHAIR **c** any object (with parts) resembling a rocker (e g a skate with a curved blade) **2** a device that works with a rocking motion **3** a member of a group of aggressive leather-jacketed young British motorcyclists in the 1960s who waged war on the mods – compare HELL'S ANGEL [[1]ROCK + [2]-ER] – **off one's rocker** crazy, mad – infml

rockery /'rokəri/ *n* a bank of rocks and earth where rock plants are grown

[1]**rocket** /'rokit/ *n* any of numerous plants of the mustard family [MF *roquette*, fr OIt *rochetta*, dim. of *ruca* garden rocket, fr L *eruca*]

[2]**rocket** *n* **1a** a firework consisting of a long case filled with a combustible material fastened to a guiding stick and projected through the air by the rearward discharge of gases released in combustion **b** such a device used as an incendiary weapon or as a propelling unit (e g for a lifesaving line or whaling harpoon) **2** a jet engine that carries with it everything necessary for its operation and is thus independent of the oxygen in the air **3** a rocket-propelled bomb, missile, or projectile ☞ SPACE **4** *chiefly Br* a sharp reprimand – infml [It *rocchetta*, lit., small distaff, fr dim. of *rocca* distaff, of Gmc origin; akin to OHG *rocko* distaff] – **rocketeer** /-'tiə/ *n*

[3]**rocket** *vi* **1** to rise or increase rapidly or spectacularly **2** to travel with the speed of a rocket

rocketry /'rockitri/ *n* the study of, experimentation with, or use of rockets

rockfish /'rok,fish/ *n* any of various fishes that live among rocks or on rocky bottoms

'rock ,garden *n* a garden containing 1 or more rockeries; *also* a rockery

'rocking ,chair /'roking/ *n* a chair mounted on rockers

'rocking ,horse *n* a toy horse mounted on rockers

rockling /'rokling/ *n* any of several rather small elongated marine fishes of the cod family

,rock 'lobster *n* SPINY LOBSTER

rock 'n' roll /,rok (ə)n 'rohl/ *n* [2]ROCK

'rock ,oil *n* petroleum

'rock ,plant *n* a small esp alpine plant that grows among rocks or in rockeries

'rock,rose /-,rohz/ *n* any of various showy-flowered woody plants or shrubs

,rock 'salmon *n* a dogfish – not now used technically

'rock ,salt *n* common salt occurring as a solid mineral

'rock,shaft /-,shahft/ *n* a shaft (e g in a steam engine) that rocks on its bearings instead of revolving

'rock ,wool *n* mineral wool made from limestone or siliceous rock

[1]**rocky** /'roki/ *adj* **1** full of or consisting of rocks **2** filled with obstacles; difficult [[1]*rock*] – **rockiness** *n*

[2]**rocky** *adj* unsteady, tottering [[1]*rock*] – **rockiness** *n*

[1]**rococo** /ro'kohkoh, rə-/ *adj* **1a** (typical) of a style of architecture and decoration in 18th-c Europe characterized by elaborate curved forms and shell motifs **b** of an 18th-c musical style marked by light gay ornamentation **2** excessively ornate or florid [F, irreg fr *rocaille* rock-work, fr *roc* rock, alter. of MF *roche*, fr (assumed) VL *rocca*]

[2]**rococo** *n* rococo work or style

rod /rod/ *n* **1a(1)** a straight slender stick **(2)** (a stick or bundle of twigs used for) punishment **(3)** a pole with a line for fishing **b(1)** a slender bar (e g of wood or metal) **(2)** a wand or staff carried as a sign of office, power, or authority **2** a unit of length equal to 5½yd (about 5m) ☞ UNIT **3** any of the relatively long rod-shaped light receptors in the retina that are sensitive to faint light – compare CONE 3a **4** an angler [ME, fr OE *rodd*; akin to ON *rudda* club] – **rodless** *adj*, **rodlike** *adj*

rode /rohd/ *past of* RIDE

rodent /'rohd(ə)nt/ *n* any of an order of relatively small gnawing mammals including the mice, rats, squirrels, and beavers [deriv of L *rodent-*, *rodens*, prp of *rodere* to gnaw – more at RAT] – **rodent** *adj*, **rodenticide** /roh'denti,sied/ *n*

rodent ulcer *n* a skin cancer that appears as an ulcer of exposed skin, esp on the face, and spreads slowly outwards destroying other tissue [L *rodent-*, *rodens* gnawing]

rodeo /roh'dayoh, 'rohdi,oh/ *n, pl* **rodeos** **1** a roundup **2** a public performance featuring the riding skills of cowboys [Sp, fr *rodear* to surround, fr *rueda* wheel, fr L *rota* – more at ROLL]

rodomontade /,rohdəmon'tayd, -'tahd/ *n* **1** a bragging speech **2** vain boasting or bluster; bombast [MF, fr It *Rodomonte*, character in *Orlando Innamorato* by Matteo Boiardo †1494 It poet] – **rodomontade** *adj*

roe /roh/ *n* **1** the eggs of a female fish, esp when still enclosed in a membrane, or the corresponding part of a male fish **2** the eggs or ovaries of an invertebrate (e g a lobster) [ME *roof*; akin to OHG *rogo* roe, Lith *kurkulai* frog's eggs]

roebuck /'roh,buk/ *n, pl* **roebuck, roebucks** a (male) roe deer

'roe ,deer *n* a small Eurasian deer with erect cylindrical antlers that is noted for its nimbleness and grace [*roe* (roe deer), fr ME *ro*, fr OE *rā*; akin to OHG *rēh* roe deer, OIr *riabach* dappled]

roentgen /'rontgən, 'rentgən, -jən (əer rœntgən)/ *n* a röntgen

roentgenogram /ront'genə,gram, rent-, -'je-/ *n* a röntgenogram

roent'geno,graph /-,grahf, -,graf/ *n* a röntgenograph

Ro'gation ,Day /roh'gaysh(ə)n/ *n* any of the days of prayer, esp for the harvest, observed on the 3 days before Ascension Day and by Roman Catholics also on April 25 [ME *rogacioun* litany, supplication, fr L *rogation-*, *rogatio*, fr *rogatus*, pp of *rogare* to ask, beg – more at [1]RIGHT]

[1]**roger** /'rojə/ *vt* to have sexual intercourse with – slang [obs *roger* (penis), fr the name *Roger*]

roger 2 *interj* – used esp in radio and signalling to indicate that a message has been received and understood [*Roger*, former communications codeword for the letter *r*]

[1]**rogue** /rohg/ *n* **1** a wilfully dishonest or corrupt person **2** a mischievous person; a scamp **3** sby or sthg that displays a chance variation making it inferior to others [perh fr obs *roger* (beggar), perh fr L *rogare* to ask] – **roguish** *adj*, **roguishly** *adv*, **roguishness** *n*

[2]**rogue** *vb* **roguing, rogueing** to weed out inferior, diseased, etc plants (from)

[3]**rogue** *adj*, *of an animal* (roaming alone and) vicious and destructive ⟨*a ~ elephant*⟩

roguery /'rohg(ə)ri/ *n* an act characteristic of a rogue

,rogues' 'gallery *n* a collection of pictures of people arrested as criminals

roil /royl/ *vt* **1a** to make muddy or opaque by

stirring up the sediment of **b** to stir up **2** to annoy, rile [origin unknown]

roister /'roystə/ *vi* to engage in noisy revelry [arch *roister* (roisterer), fr MF *rustre* boor, ruffian, fr *ruste* rude, rough, fr L *rusticus* rustic] – **roisterer** *n*

role, rôle /rohl/ *n* **1a(1)** a character assigned or assumed **(2)** a socially expected behaviour pattern, usu determined by an individual's status in a particular society **b** a part played by an actor or singer **2** a function [F *rôle*, lit., roll, fr OF *rolle*]

'role ,playing *n* behaving in a way typical of another or of a stereotype, often for therapeutic or educational purposes

1roll /rohl/ *n* **1a** a written document that may be rolled up; *specif* one bearing an official or formal record **b** a list of names or related items; a catalogue **c** an official list of people (e g members of a school or of a legislative body) **2** sthg rolled up to resemble a cylinder or ball; e g **a** a quantity (e g of fabric or paper) rolled up to form a single package **b** any of various food preparations rolled up for cooking or serving; *esp* a small piece of baked yeast dough **3** ROLLER 1a(1) **4** *NAm* paper money folded or rolled into a wad [ME *rolle*, fr OF, fr L *rotula*, dim. of *rota* wheel; akin to OHG *rad* wheel, Skt *ratha* wagon]

2roll *vt* **1a** to propel forwards by causing to turn over and over on a surface **b** to cause (sthg fixed) to revolve (as if) on an axis **c** to cause to move in a circular manner **d** to form into a mass by revolving and compressing **e** to carry forwards with an easy continuous motion ⟨*the river* ~s *its waters to the sea*⟩ **2a** to put a wrapping round **b** to wrap round on itself; shape into a ball or roll – often + *up* **3a** to press, spread, or level with a roller; make thin, even, or compact **b** to spread out ⟨~ *out the red carpet*⟩ **4** to move as specified on rollers or wheels **5a** to sound with a full reverberating tone **b** to make a continuous beating sound on ⟨~ed *their drums*⟩ **c** to utter with a trill **6** *NAm* to rob (sby sleeping or unconscious) – infml ⟨~ *a drunk*⟩ ~ *vi* **1a** to travel along a surface with a rotary motion **b(1)** to turn over and over **(2)** to luxuriate *in* an abundant supply; wallow **2a** to move onwards in a regular cycle or succession **b** to shift the gaze continually and erratically ⟨*eyes* ~ing *in terror*⟩ **c** to revolve on an axis **3a** to flow with an undulating motion **b** to flow in an abundant stream; pour **c** to extend in broad undulations ⟨~ing *hills*⟩ **4a** to become carried on a stream **b** to move on wheels **5** to make a deep reverberating sound ⟨*the thunder* ~s⟩ **6a** to rock from side to side **b** to walk with a swinging gait **c** to move so as to reduce the impact of a blow – + *with* ⟨~ed *with the punch*⟩ **7** to take the form of a cylinder or ball – often + *up* **8a** to begin to move or operate ⟨*let the cameras* ~⟩ **b** to move forwards; develop and maintain impetus

3roll *n* **1a** a sound produced by rapid strokes on a drum **b** a rhythmic sonorous flow (of speech) **c** a reverberating sound **2** (an action or process involving) a rolling movement: e g **a** a swaying movement of the body (e g in walking or dancing) **b** a side-to-side movement (e g of a ship) **c** a flight manoeuvre in which a complete revolution about the longitudinal axis of an aircraft is made with the horizontal direction of flight being approximately maintained

roll back *vt* to cause to retreat or withdraw; push back

'roll ,call *n* the calling out of a list of names (e g for checking attendance)

1roller /'rohlə/ *n* **1a(1)** a revolving cylinder over or on which sthg is moved or which is used to press, shape, or apply sthg **(2)** a hair curler **b** a cylinder or rod on which sthg (e g a blind) is rolled up **2** a long heavy wave [2ROLL + 2-ER]

2roller *n* **1** any of a group of mostly brightly coloured Old World birds noted for performing aerial rolls in their nuptial display **2** a canary that has a song in which the notes are soft and run together [G, fr *rollen* to roll, reverberate, fr MF *roller*, fr (assumed) VL *rotulare*, fr L *rotula*]

roller bearing *n* a bearing in which the rotating part turns on rollers held in a cylindrical housing

'roller ,coaster *n* an elevated railway (e g in a funfair) constructed with curves and inclines on which the cars roll

'roller ,skate *n* (a shoe fitted with) a metal frame holding usu 4 small wheels that allows the wearer to glide over hard surfaces – **roller-skate** *vi*, **roller-skater** *n*

'roller ,towel *n* a continuous towel hung from a roller

1rollicking /'roliking/ *adj* boisterously carefree [*rollick* (to romp), perh blend of *romp* and *frolic*]

2rollicking *n, Br* a severe scolding – infml [prob alter. of *bollocking*]

roll in *vi* to come or arrive in large quantities

'rolling ,mill /'rohling/ *n* an establishment or machine in which metal is rolled into plates and bars

'rolling ,pin *n* a long usu wooden cylinder for rolling out dough

'rolling ,stock *n* **1** the vehicles owned and used by a railway **2** *NAm* the road vehicles owned and used by a company

,rolling 'stone *n* one who leads a wandering or unsettled life

rollmop /'rohl,mop/ *n* a herring fillet rolled up and pickled by being marinated in spiced vinegar or brine [back-formation fr *rollmops*, pl of *rollmops* (rolled herring fillet), fr G, fr *rollen* to roll + *mops* simpleton, pugnosed dog, fr LG]

roll neck *n* a loose high collar, esp on a jumper, worn rolled over

'roll-,on *n* **1** a woman's elasticated girdle without fastenings **2** a liquid preparation (e g deodorant) applied to the skin by means of a rolling ball in the neck of the container

,roll 'on *interj, Br* – used to urge on a desired event ⟨~ *summer!*⟩

roll-,on roll-'off *adj* allowing vehicles to drive on or off ⟨*a* ~ *ship*⟩

rollout /'rohl,owt/ *n* the public introduction or unveiling of a new aircraft

,rolltop 'desk /'rohl,top/ *n* a writing desk with a sliding cover often of parallel slats fastened to a flexible backing

'roll-,up *n, Br* a hand-rolled cigarette – infml

roll up *vi* **1** to arrive in a vehicle **2** to turn up at a destination, esp unhurriedly

1roly-poly /,rohli 'pohli/ *n* a dish, esp a pudding, consisting of pastry spread with a filling (e g jam), rolled, and baked or steamed [redupl of *roly*, fr 2*roll* + 3*-y*]

2,roly-'poly *adj* short and plump – infml

Romaic /roh'mayik/ *n* the modern Greek vernacular [NGk *Rhōmaiikos*, fr Gk *Rhōmaïkos* Roman, fr *Rhōmē* Rome, capital city of Italy] – **Romaic** *adj*

[1]Roman /'rohmən/ *n* **1** a native or inhabitant of (ancient) Rome **2** ROMAN CATHOLIC **3** *not cap* roman letters or type [partly fr ME, fr OE, fr L *Romanus*, adj & n, fr *Roma* Rome; partly fr ME *Romain*, fr OF, fr L *Romanus*]

[2]Roman *adj* **1** (characteristic) of Rome or the (ancient) Romans **2** *not cap, of numbers and letters* not slanted; perpendicular ☞ ALPHABET **3** of the see of Rome or the Roman Catholic church

roman à clef /roh,monh a 'klay (*Fr* rɔmɑ̃ a kle)/ *n, pl* **romans à clef** /~/ a novel in which real people or actual events are fictionally disguised [F, lit., novel with a key]

,Roman 'candle *n* a cylindrical firework that discharges balls or stars of fire at intervals

[1],Roman 'Catholic *n* a member of the Roman Catholic church

[2]Roman Catholic *adj* of the body of Christians headed by the pope, with a hierarchy of priests and bishops under the pope, a liturgy centred on the Mass, and a body of dogma formulated by the church as the infallible interpreter of revealed truth; *specif* of the Western rite of this church marked by a formerly Latin liturgy – **Roman Catholicism** *n*

[1]romance /roh'mans, rə-/ *n* **1a(1)** a medieval usu verse tale dealing with chivalric love and adventure **(2)** a prose narrative dealing with imaginary characters involved in usu heroic, adventurous, or mysterious events that are remote in time or place **(3)** a love story **b** such literature as a class **2** sthg lacking any basis in fact **3** an emotional aura attaching to an enthralling era, adventure, or pursuit **4** LOVE AFFAIR [ME *romauns*, fr OF *romans* French, something written in French, fr L *romanice* in the Roman manner, fr *romanicus* Roman, fr *Romanus*]

[2]romance *vi* **1** to exaggerate or invent detail or incident **2** to entertain romantic thoughts or ideas

[3]romance *n* a short instrumental piece of music in ballad style [F, fr Sp, fr OSp, Spanish, something written in Spanish, fr L *romanice*]

Romance *adj* of or constituting the languages developed from Latin

romancer /rə'mansə, roh-/ *n* **1** a writer of romance **2** sby prone to romancing

,Roman 'collar *n* CLERICAL COLLAR; *specif* one worn by Roman Catholic clergy

Romanesque /,rohmə'nesk/ *adj* of a style of architecture developed in Italy and western Europe and characterized after 1000 AD by the use of the round arch and vault, decorative arcading, and elaborate mouldings – compare NORMAN – **Romanesque** *n*

roman-fleuve /roh,monh 'fluhv (*Fr* rɔmɑ̃ flœːv)/ *n, pl* **romans-fleuves** /~/ a novel in the form of a long and leisurely chronicle of a family or community [F, lit., river novel]

,Roman 'holiday *n* an entertainment at the expense of others' suffering [fr the bloody combats staged as entertainment in ancient Rome]

Romanian, Rumanian *also* **Roumanian** /roo'maynyən, roh-, rə-, -ni·ən/ *n* **1** a native or inhabitant of Romania **2** the Romance language of the Romanians ☞ LANGUAGE [*Romania* (Rumania, Roumania), country in E Europe] – **Romanian** *adj*

Romanic /roh'manik/ *adj* **1** Romance **2** descended or derived from the Romans – **Romanic** *n*

Romanism /'rohmə,niz(ə)m/ *n* ROMAN CATHOLICISM

Romanist /'rohmənist/ *n* **1** ROMAN CATHOLIC **2** a specialist in the language, culture, or law of ancient Rome – **Romanist, Romanistic** /-'nistik/ *adj*

roman·ize, -ise /'rohməniez/ *vt* **1** *often cap* to make Roman; Latinize **2** to write or print (e g a language) in the roman alphabet – **romanization** /-'zaysh(ə)n/ *n, often cap*

,roman 'law *n, often cap R* the legal system of the ancient Romans which forms the basis of many modern legal codes

,Roman 'nose *n* a nose with a prominent slightly aquiline bridge

,Roman 'numeral *n* a numeral in a system of notation based on the ancient Roman system using the symblos i, v, x, l, c, d, m ☞ NUMBER

Romans /'rohmənz/ *n pl but sing in constr* a letter on doctrine written by St Paul to the Christians at Rome and included as a book in the New Testament

Romansh, Romansch /roh'mahnsh/ *n* the Rhaeto-Romanic dialects spoken in parts of Switzerland and Italy ☞ LANGUAGE [Romansh *romonsch*]

[1]romantic /rə'mantik, roh-/ *adj* **1** consisting of or like a romance **2** having no basis in real life **3** impractical or fantastic in conception or plan **4a** marked by the imaginative appeal of the heroic, remote, or mysterious **b** *often cap* (having the characteristics) of romanticism **c** of or being (a composer of) 19th-c music characterized by an emphasis on subjective emotional qualities and freedom of form **5a** having an inclination for romance **b** marked by or constituting strong feeling, esp love [F *romantique*, fr obs F *romant* romance, fr OF *romans*] – **romantically** *adv*

[2]romantic *n* **1** a romantic person **2** *cap* a romantic writer, artist, or composer

romanticism /roh'manti,siz(ə)m, rə-/ *n, often cap* (adherence to) a chiefly late 18th- and early 19th-c literary, artistic, and philosophical movement that reacted against neoclassicism by emphasizing individual aspirations, nature, the emotions, and the remote and exotic – **romanticist** *n, often cap*

romantic·ize, -ise /roh'manti,siez, rə-/ *vt* to give a romantic character to ~ *vi* **1** to hold romantic ideas **2** to present incidents or people in a (misleadingly) romantic way – **romanticization** /-'zaysh(ə)n/ *n*

Romany /'rohməni/ *n* **1** GIPSY 1 **2** the Indic language of the Gipsies [Romany *romani*, adj, gypsy, fr *rom* gypsy man, fr Skt *ḍomba* man of a low caste of musicians] – **Romany** *adj*

[1]Romeo /'rohmi·oh, -myoh/ *n, pl* **Romeos** a romantic male lover [*Romeo*, hero of the play *Romeo and Juliet* by William Shakespeare †1616 E poet & dramatist]

[2]Romeo – a communications code word for the letter *r*

Romish /'rohmish/ *adj* ROMAN CATHOLIC – chiefly derog

[1]romp /romp/ *n* **1** boisterous or bawdy entertainment or play **2** an effortless winning pace [partly alter. of [2]*ramp* (act of rearing or raging); partly alter. of *ramp* (bold woman), fr ME *rampe*, perh fr *rampen* to ramp, rage]

[2]romp *vi* **1** to play in a boisterous manner **2** to win easily [alter. of *ramp* (to rear, rage, climb) – more at RAMPAGE]

romper /ˈrompə/, **ˈromper ˌsuit** *n* a 1-piece child's garment combining a top or bib and short trousers – usu pl with sing. meaning [[2]ROMP + [2]-ER]

rondavel /ˈrondəˌvel, ˌronˈdahvl/ *n, SAfr* a circular 1-roomed hut in the grounds of a house, used as a guest room or for storage [Afrik *rondawel*]

rondeau /ˈrondoh/ *n, pl* **rondeaux** /ˈrondoh(z)/ (a poem in) a form of verse using only 2 rhymes, in which the opening words of the first line are used as a refrain [MF *rondel, rondeau*]

rondel /ˈrondl/ *n* **1** (a poem in) a particular form of rondeau **2** RONDELLE 1 [ME *rondel, rondelle*, fr OF, lit., small circle – more at ROUNDEL]

rondelle /ronˈdel/ *n* **1** a circular object **2** RONDEL 1

rondo /ˈrondoh/ *n, pl* **rondos** an instrumental composition, esp a movement in a concerto or sonata, typically having a refrain or recurring theme [It *rondò*, fr MF *rondeau*]

Roneo /ˈrohnioh/ *trademark* – used for a duplicating machine that uses stencils

röntgen, roentgen, rontgen /ˈrontgən, ˈrentgən, -jən (əer rœntgən)/ *n* a unit of ionizing radiation equal to the amount that produces ions of 1 sign carrying a charge of 2.58×10^{-4} coulomb in 1kg of air [ISV, fr Wilhelm Conrad *Röntgen* †1923 G chemist]

röntgenogram, roentgenogram, rontgenogram /rontˈgenəgram, rent-, -ˈje-/ *n* an X-ray photograph [ISV]

röntˈgenoˌgraph, roentgenograph, rontgenograph /-ˌgrahf, -ˌgraf/ *n* a röntgenogram – **röntgenographic** /-ˈgrafik/ *adj*, **röntgenographically** *adv*, **röntgenography** /-ˈnogrəfi/ *n*

röntgenology, roentgenology, rontgenology /ˌrontgəˈnoləji, rent-, -jə-/ *n* radiology dealing with the use of X rays for diagnosis or treatment of disease [ISV] – **röntgenologic** /-nəˈlojik/, **röntgenological** *adj*, **röntgenologically** *adv*, **röntgenologist** /-ˈnoləjist/ *n*

roo /rooh/ *n, pl* **roos,** *esp collectively* **roo** *Austr* a kangaroo – infml

rood /roohd/ *n* **1** a cross, crucifix; *specif* a large crucifix on a beam or screen at the entrance to the chancel of a medieval church ☞ CHURCH **2** a British unit of land area equal to ¼ acre (about 1011m²) ☞ UNIT [ME, fr OE *rōd* rod, rood; akin to OHG *ruota* rod, OSlav *ratište* shaft of a lance]

[1]**roof** /roohf/ *n, pl* **roofs** *also* **rooves** /roohvz/ **1a** the upper usu rigid cover of a building ☞ ARCHITECTURE **b** a dwelling, home ⟨*why not share the same* ~ – Virginia Woolf⟩ **2a** the highest point or level **b** sthg resembling a roof in form or function **3** the vaulted or covering part of the mouth, skull, etc [ME, fr OE *hrōf*; akin to ON *hrōf* roof of a boathouse, OSlav *stropŭ* roof] – **roofed** *adj*, **roofless** *adj*, **rooflike** *adj*, **roofing** *n*

[2]**roof** *vt* **1** to cover (as if) with a roof **2** to serve as a roof over

ˈroofˌtop /-ˌtop/ *n* the outer surface of a usu flat roof

ˈroofˌtree /-ˌtree/ *n* a ridgepiece

[1]**rook** /rook/ *n* a common Old World social bird similar to the related carrion crow but having a bare grey face [ME, fr OE *hrōc*; akin to OE *hræfn* raven – more at [1]RAVEN]

[2]**rook** *vt* to defraud by cheating (e g at cards) – infml [*rook*, n (cheat, swindler), fr [1]*rook*]

[3]**rook** *n* either of 2 pieces of each colour in a set of chessmen having the power to move along the ranks or files across any number of consecutive unoccupied squares [ME *rok*, fr MF *roc*, fr Ar *rukhkh*, fr Per]

rookery /ˈrookəri/ *n* **1a** (the nests, usu built in the upper branches of trees, of) a colony of rooks **b** (a breeding ground or haunt of) a colony of penguins, seals, etc **2** a crowded dilapidated tenement or maze of dwellings

rookie /ˈrooki/ *n* a recruit; *also, chiefly NAm* a novice [alter. of *recruit*]

[1]**room** /roohm, room/ *n* **1** an extent of space occupied by, or sufficient or available for, sthg **2a** a partitioned part of the inside of a building **b** such a part used as a separate lodging – often pl **3** suitable or fit occasion; opportunity + *for* ⟨~ *for improvement*⟩ [ME, fr OE *rūm*; akin to OHG *rūm* room, L *rur-, rus* open land]

[2]**room** /roohm/ *vt* to accommodate with lodgings ~ *vi* , *NAm* to occupy a room; lodge

roomed /roohmd, roomd/ *adj* containing rooms – usu in combination ⟨*a 6-*roomed *house*⟩

roomer /ˈroohmə/ *n, NAm* a lodger

roommate /ˈroohmˌmayt, ˈroom-/ *n* any of 2 or more people sharing the same room (e g in a university hall)

ˈroom ˌservice *n* the facility by which a hotel guest can have food, drinks, etc brought to his/her room

roomy /ˈroohmi/ *adj* spacious – **roominess** *n*

[1]**roost** /roohst/ *n* **1** a support or place where birds roost **2** a group of birds roosting together [ME, fr OE *hrōst*; akin to MD *roest* roost, OSlav *krada* pile of wood]

[2]**roost** *vi, esp of a bird* to settle down for rest or sleep; perch

rooster /ˈroohstə/ *n, chiefly NAm* COCK 1a

[1]**root** /rooht/ *n* **1a** the (underground) part of a flowering plant that usu anchors and supports it and absorbs and stores food **b** a (fleshy and edible) root, bulb, tuber, or other underground plant part **2a** the end of a nerve nearest the brain and spinal cord **b** the part of a tooth, hair, the tongue, etc by which it is attached to the body **3a** sthg that is an underlying cause or basis (e g of a condition or quality) **b** one or more progenitors of a group of descendants **c** the essential core, the heart **d** *pl* a feeling of belonging established through close familiarity or family ties with a particular place ⟨*the need for* ~s⟩ ⟨~s *in Scotland*⟩ **4a** a number which produces a given number when taken an indicated number of times as a factor ⟨*2 is a fourth* ~ *of 16*⟩ ☞ SYMBOL **b** a number that reduces an equation to an identity when it is substituted for 1 variable **5a** the lower part; the base **b** the part by which an object is attached to or embedded in sthg else **6** the basis from which a word is derived **7** the tone from whose overtones a chord is composed; the lowest note of a chord in normal position [ME, fr OE *rōt*, fr ON; akin to OE *wyrt* root, L *radix*, Gk *rhiza*] – **rooted** *adj*, **rootedness** *n*, **rootless** *adj*, **rootlet** *n*, **rootlike** *adj*, **rooty** *adj*

[2]**root** *vt* **1** to give or enable to develop roots **2** to fix or implant (as if) by roots ~ *vi* **1** to grow roots or take root **2** to have an origin or base

[3]**root** *vi* **1** *esp of a pig* to dig with the snout **2** to poke

or dig about *in*; search (unsystematically) for sthg [ME *wroten*, fr OE *wrōtan*; akin to OHG *ruozzan* to root]

⁴**root** *vi, chiefly NAm* to lend vociferous or enthusiastic support to sby or sthg – + *for* [perh alter. of *rout* (to bellow), fr ME *rowten*, fr ON *rauta*] – **rooter** *n*

rootage /'roohtij/ *n* a developed system of roots

,root and 'branch *adv* so as to leave no remnant; completely – **root-and-branch** *adj*

'root ,cap *n* a protective cap of cells that covers the growing point at the end of most root tips

'root ,crop *n* a crop (e g turnips or sugar beet) grown for its enlarged roots

rootle /'roohtl/ *vi* **rootling** /'roohtling, 'roohtl·ing/ *Br* ³ROOT [freq of ³*root*]

,root-,mean-'square *n* the square root of the arithmetic mean of the squares of a set of numbers

root out *vt* **1** to discover or cause to emerge by rooting **2** to get rid of or destroy completely

'root,stock /-,stok/ *n* **1** an underground plant part formed from several stems **2** a stock for grafting consisting of (a piece of) root; *broadly* STOCK 2b, 4

¹**rope** /rohp/ *n* **1a** a strong thick cord composed of strands of fibres or wire twisted or braided together **b** a long slender strip of material (used) like rope **c** a hangman's noose **2** a row or string consisting of things united (as if) by braiding, twining, or threading **3** *pl* special methods or procedures [ME, fr OE *rāp*; akin to OHG *reif* hoop]

²**rope** *vt* **1a** to bind, fasten, or tie with a rope **b** to enclose, separate, or divide by a rope **c** to connect (a party of climbers) with a rope **2** to enlist (sby reluctant) *in* a group or activity **3** *NAm* to lasso ~ *vi* to put on a rope for climbing; *also* to climb *down* or *up* – **roper** *n*

'rope,dancer /-,dahnsə/ *n* one who dances, walks, or performs acrobatic feats on a rope high in the air – **ropedancing** *n*

rope ladder *n* a ladder having rope sides and rope, wood, or metal rungs

'rope,walk /-,wawk/ *n* a long covered area where ropes are made

'rope,walker /-,wawkə/ *n* an acrobat who walks along a rope high in the air

'rope,way /-,way/ *n* an endless aerial cable moved by a stationary engine and used to transport goods (e g logs and ore)

ropy, ropey /'rohpi/ *adj* **1a** capable of being drawn out into a thread **b** gelatinous or slimy from bacterial or fungal contamination ⟨~ *milk*⟩ ⟨~ *flour*⟩ **2** like rope in texture or appearance **3** *Br* **a** of poor quality; shoddy **b** somewhat unwell *USE* (*3*) infml – **ropiness** *n*

Roquefort /'rok(ə),faw, (*Fr* rɔkfɔ:r)/ *trademark* – used for a strong-flavoured crumbly French cheese with bluish green veins, made from the curds of ewes' milk

¹**roquet** /'rohki/ *vt, of a croquet ball or the player who strikes it* to hit (another ball) [prob alter. of *croquet*]

²**roquet** *n* an act or instance of roqueting

rorqual /'rawkwəl/ *n* any of a genus of large whalebone whales (e g a fin whale) having the skin of the throat marked with deep longitudinal furrows [F, fr Norw *rørhval*, fr ON *reytharhvalr*, fr *reythr* rorqual + *hvalr* whale]

Rorschach /'raw,shahk/ *adj* of, used in connection with, or resulting from the Rorschach test

'Rorschach ,test *n* a personality test based on the interpretation of sby's reactions to a set of standard inkblot designs [Hermann *Rorschach* †1922 Swiss psychiatrist]

rosaceous /roh'zayshəs/ *adj* of or belonging to the rose family [deriv of L *rosa*]

rosaniline /roh'zanilien, -lin, -leen/ *n* **1** an organic chemical compound from which many dyes are derived **2** fuchsine [L *rosa* rose + ISV *aniline*]

rosary /'rohz(ə)ri/ *n* a string of beads used in counting prayers [ML *rosarium*, fr L, rose garden, fr neut of *rosarius* of roses, fr *rosa* rose]

rosary pea *n* **1** an E Indian climbing plant of the pea family that produces jequirity beans and has a root that is used as a substitute for liquorice **2** the seed of the rosary pea, often used for beads

¹**rose** /rohz/ *past of* RISE

²**rose** *n* **1** (the showy often double flower of) any of a genus of widely cultivated usu prickly shrubs **2a** COMPASS CARD **b** (the form of) a gem, esp a diamond, with a flat base and triangular facets rising to a point **c** a perforated outlet for water (e g from a shower or watering can) **d** an electrical fitting that anchors the flex of a suspended light bulb to a ceiling **3** a pale to dark pinkish colour [ME, fr OE, fr L *rosa*] – **roselike** *adj*

³**rose** *adj* **1a** of, containing, or used for roses **b** flavoured, sweetly scented, or coloured with or like roses **2** of the colour rose

rosé /roh'zay, '--/ *n* a light pink table wine made from red grapes by removing the skins after fermentation has begun [F, fr *rosé* pink, fr OF, fr *rose* rose, fr L *rosa*]

roseate /'rohzi·ət/ *adj* **1** resembling a rose, esp in colour **2** marked by unrealistic optimism [L *roseus* rosy, fr *rosa*] – **roseately** *adv*

,roseate 'tern *n* a graceful tern with a deeply forked tail

rosebay willowherb /,rohzbay 'wiloh,huhb/ *n* a tall Eurasian and N American perennial plant of the evening primrose family with long spikes of pinkish purple flowers

rosebud /'rohz,bud/ *n* the bud of a rose

'rose,bush /-,boosh/ *n* a shrubby rose plant

'rose ,chafer /'chayfə/ *n* a metallic green European beetle that feeds on (rose) leaves and flowers as an adult

'rose-,coloured *adj* representing a person, situation, etc in an overoptimistic light

rosella /roh'zelə/ *n* **1** any of several brightly coloured parakeets **2** *Austr* a sheep that has shed most of its wool [irreg fr *Rosehill*, district of SE Australia]

rose mallow *n* **1** any of several hibiscuses with large rose-coloured flowers **2** a hollyhock

rosemary /'rohzməri/ *n* a fragrant shrubby Eurasian plant used as a cooking herb [ME *rosmarine*, fr L *rosmarinus*, fr *ror-*, *ros* dew + *marinus* of the sea – more at MARINE]

roseola /roh'zee·ələ/ *n* (German measles or a similar virus disease, esp of children, accompanied by) a rash of pink spots [NL, fr L *roseus* rosy, fr *rosa* rose] – **roseolar** *adj*

rosette /roh'zet, rə-/ *n* **1** an ornament usu made of material gathered so as to resemble a rose and worn as a badge, trophy, or trimming **2** a stylized carved or moulded rose used as a decorative motif in architecture **3** a rosette-shaped structure or marking on an animal **4** a cluster of leaves in crowded circles or spirals (e g in the dandelion) [F, lit., small rose, fr OF, fr *rose*, fr L *rosa*]

rose window *n* a circular window filled with tracery radiating from its centre ☞ ARCHITECTURE

'rose,wood /-,wood/ *n* (any of various esp leguminous tropical trees yielding) a valuable dark red or purplish wood, streaked and variegated with black

Rosh Hashanah /,rosh hə'shahnə, -'sha-/ *n* the Jewish New Year [LHeb *rōsh hashshānāh*, lit., beginning of the year]

Rosicrucian /,rohzi'kroohsh(y)ən/ *n* an adherent or member of an organization held to derive from a 17th- and 18th-c movement devoted to occult or esoteric wisdom [Christian *Rosenkreutz* (NL *Rosa Crucis*) reputed 15th-c founder of the movement] – **Rosicrucianism** *n*

[1]**rosin** /'rozin/ *n* a translucent resin that is the residue from the distillation of turpentine and is used esp in making varnish and soldering flux and for rubbing on violin bows [ME, modif of MF *resine* resin]

[2]**rosin** *vt* to rub or treat (e g the bow of a violin) with rosin

rostellum /ro'steləm/ *n* a small beaklike body part; a small rostrum [NL, fr L, dim. of *rostrum* beak] – **rostellar** *adj*

roster /'rostə/ *n* **1** a list or register giving the order in which personnel are to perform a duty, go on leave, etc **2** an itemized list [D *rooster*, lit., gridiron; fr the parallel lines]

rostrum /'rostrəm/ *n, pl* **rostrums, rostra** /'rostrə/ **1a** a stage for public speaking **b** a raised platform (on a stage) **2** a body part (e g an insect's snout or beak) shaped like a bird's bill [L, beak, ship's beak, fr *rodere* to gnaw – more at RAT; (1) L *Rostra* (pl), a stage in Rome ornamented with prows of captured ships] – **rostral** *adj*

rosy /'rohzi/ *adj* **1a** ROSE 2 **b** having a rosy complexion – often in combination ⟨rosy-*cheeked youngsters*⟩ **2** characterized by or encouraging optimism – **rosily** *adv*, **rosiness** *n*

[1]**rot** /rot/ *vb* **-tt-** *vi* **1a** to undergo decomposition, esp from the action of bacteria or fungi – often + *down* **b** to become unsound or weak (e g from chemical or water action) **2a** to go to ruin **b** to become morally corrupt ~ *vt* to cause to decompose or deteriorate [ME *roten*, fr OE *rotian*; akin to OHG *rōzzēn* to rot, L *rudus* rubble – more at RUDE]

[2]**rot** *n* **1** (sthg) rotting or being rotten; decay **2** any of several plant or animal diseases, esp of sheep, with breakdown and death of tissues **3** nonsense, rubbish – often used interjectionally

rota /'rohtə/ *n, chiefly Br* **1** a list specifying a fixed order of rotation (e g of people or duties) **2** an ordered succession [L, wheel – more at ROLL]

Rotarian /roh'teəri·ən/ *n* a member of a Rotary Club

[1]**rotary** /'roht(ə)ri/ *adj* **1a** turning on an axis like a wheel **b** proceeding about an axis ⟨~ *motion*⟩ **2** having a principal part that turns on an axis **3** characterized by rotation **4** of or being a printing press using a rotating curved printing surface [ML *rotarius*, fr L *rota* wheel]

[2]**rotary** *n* **1** a rotary machine **2** *NAm* a roundabout

'Rotary ,Club *n* an organization of business and professional men devoted to serving the community and advancing world peace

,rotary 'cultivator *n* a machine with rapidly revolving blades or claws for tilling or breaking up the soil

[1]**rotate** /'rohtayt/ *adj, of a flower* with petals or sepals radiating like the spokes of a wheel [L *rota*]

[2]**rotate** /roh'tayt/ *vi* **1** to turn about an axis or a centre; revolve **2a** to take turns at performing an act or operation **b** to perform an ordered series of actions or functions ~ *vt* **1** to cause to turn about an axis or centre **2** to order in a recurring sequence [L *rotatus*, pp of *rotare*, fr *rota* wheel – more at ROLL] – **rotatable** *adj*, **rotative** /'rohtətiv/ *adj*, **rotatory** /'rohtət(ə)ri, roh'tayt(ə)ri/ *adj*

rotation /roh'taysh(ə)n/ *n* **1a(1)** a rotating or being rotated (as if) on an axis or centre **(2)** the act or an instance of rotating sthg **b** one complete turn; the angular displacement required to return a rotating body or figure to its original orientation **2a** recurrence in a regular series **b** the growing of different crops in succession in 1 field, usu in a regular sequence **3** the turning of a limb about its long axis – **rotational** *adj*

rote /roht/ *n* the mechanical use of the memory [ME]

rotgut /'rot,gut/ *n* spirits of low quality – infml

roti /'rohti/ *n, pl* **roti** a flat cake of unleavened bread [Hindi]

rotifer /'rohtifə/ *n* any of a class or phylum of minute aquatic invertebrate animals with circles of cilia at the front that look like rapidly revolving wheels [deriv of L *rota* + *-fer*]

rotisserie /roh'tisəri, -'tee-/ *n* **1** a restaurant specializing in roast and barbecued meats **2** an appliance fitted with a spit on which food is cooked [F *rôtisserie*, fr MF *rostisserie*, fr *rostir* to roast – more at ROAST]

rotor /'rohtə/ *n* **1** a part that revolves in a machine; *esp* the rotating member of an electrical machine **2** a complete system of more or less horizontal blades that supplies (nearly) all the force supporting an aircraft (e g a helicopter) in flight [contr of *rotator*, fr [2]*rotate* + [1]*-or*]

rotovator /'rohtə,vaytə/ *n* ROTARY CULTIVATOR [alter. of *rotavator*, fr *rot*ary culti*vator*] – **rotovate** /-,vayt/ *vb*

rotten /'rot(ə)n/ *adj* **1** having rotted; putrid **2** morally or politically corrupt **3** extremely unpleasant or inferior **4** marked by illness, discomfort, or unsoundness *USE* (*3, 4*) infml [ME *roten*, fr ON *rotinn*; akin to OE *rotian* to rot] – **rottenly** *adv*, **rottenness** *n*

rotten borough *n* an election district with very few voters – used esp of certain English constituencies before 1832

'rotten,stone /-,stohn/ *n* a much weathered limestone rich in silica, used for polishing

rotter /'rotə/ *n* a thoroughly objectionable person – often humor

rotund /roh'tund/ *adj* **1** rounded **2** high-flown or sonorous **3** markedly plump [L *rotundus* – more at ROUND] – **rotundity** /-dəti/ *n*, **rotundly** *adv*, **rotundness** *n*

rotunda /roh'tundə/ *n* a round building; *esp* one covered by a dome [It *rotonda*, fr L *rotunda*, fem of *rotundus*]

roturier /roh'tyooəri,ay/ *n* a member of the common people [MF]

rouble, ruble /'roohbl/ *n* ☞ *Union of Soviet Socialist Republics* at NATIONALITY [Russ *rubl'*]

roué /'rooh·ay/ *n* a debauched man; *esp* one past his prime [F, lit., broken on the wheel, fr pp of *rouer* to break on the wheel, fr ML *rotare*, fr L, to rotate; fr an implication that such a person deserves this punishment]

[1]**rouge** /roohzh/ *n* **1** a red cosmetic, esp for the cheeks **2** ferric oxide as a red powder, used as a pigment and in polishing glass, metal, or gems [F, fr MF, fr *rouge* red, fr L *rubeus* reddish – more at RUBY]

[2]**rouge** *vt* to apply rouge to

[1]**rough** /ruf/ *adj* **1** having an irregular or uneven surface: e g **a** not smooth **b** covered with or made up of coarse hair **c** covered with boulders, bushes, etc **2a** turbulent, stormy **b(1)** harsh, violent **(2)** requiring strenuous effort ⟨*had a ~ day*⟩ **(3)** unfortunate and hard to bear – often + *on* ⟨*it's rather ~ on his wife*⟩ **3** coarse or rugged in character or appearance: e g **a** harsh to the ear **b** crude in style or expression **c** ill-mannered, uncouth **4a** crude, unfinished **b** executed hastily or approximately ⟨*a ~ draft*⟩ **5** *Br* poorly or exhausted, esp through lack of sleep or heavy drinking – infml [ME, fr OE *rūh*; akin to L *ruga* wrinkle, Gk *oryssein* to dig, ON *rögg* tuft – more at RUG] – **roughish** *adj*, **roughness** *n*

[2]**rough** *n* **1** uneven ground covered with high grass, brush, and stones; *specif* such ground bordering a golf fairway **2** the rugged or disagreeable side or aspect **3a** sthg, esp written or illustrated, in a crude or preliminary state **b** broad outline **c** a quick preliminary drawing or layout **4** a hooligan, ruffian

[3]**rough** *adv, chiefly Br* in want of material comforts; without proper lodging – esp in *live/sleep rough*

[4]**rough** *vt* to roughen – **rough it** to live in uncomfortable or primitive conditions

roughage /'rufij/ *n* coarse bulky food (e g bran) that is relatively high in fibre and low in digestible nutrients and that by its bulk stimulates intestinal peristalsis

,rough-and-'ready *adj* crudely or hastily constructed or conceived; makeshift

,rough-and-'tumble *n* disorderly unrestrained fighting or struggling – **rough-and-tumble** *adj*

[1]**roughcast** /'ruf,kahst/ *n* a plaster of lime mixed with shells or pebbles used for covering buildings

[2]**roughcast** *vt* **roughcast** to plaster with roughcast

,rough 'diamond *n* sby without social graces but of an upright or amiable nature

,rough-'dry *vt* to dry (laundry) without ironing or pressing – **rough-dry** *adj*

roughen /'ruf(ə)n/ *vb* to make or become (more) rough

,rough-'hew *vt* **rough-hewn** **1** to hew (e g timber) coarsely without smoothing or finishing **2** to form crudely

,rough-'hewn *adj* **1** in a rough or unfinished state **2** lacking refinement

roughhouse /'ruf,hows/ *n* an instance of brawling or excessively boisterous play – infml – **roughhouse** *vi*

roughly /'rufli/ *adv* **1a** with insolence or violence **b** in primitive fashion; crudely **2** without claim to completeness or exactness [[1]ROUGH + [2]-LY]

roughneck /'ruf,nek/ *n* **1** a worker who handles the heavy drilling equipment of an oil rig **2** *NAm* a ruffian, tough

rough out *vt* **1** to shape or plan in a preliminary way **2** to outline

roughshod /'ruf,shod, ,-'-/ *adv* forcefully and without justice or consideration

rough shooting *n* the sport of shooting game (e g pigeons or rabbits) on unprepared ground with no beaters

'rough ,stuff *n* violent behaviour; violence – infml

rough up *vt* to beat up – infml

roulade /,rooh'lahd/ *n* an elaborate vocal embellishment sung to 1 syllable [F, lit., act of rolling]

[1]**rouleau** /'rooh,loh/ *n, pl* **rouleaux** /'rooh,loh(z)/ **1** a little roll; *esp* a roll of coins in paper **2** a decorative piping or rolled strip used esp as a trimming [F]

[2]**rouleau** *adj* made from or provided with a rouleau

roulette /rooh'let, roo-/ *n* **1** a gambling game in which players bet on which compartment of a revolving wheel a small ball will come to rest in **2** any of various toothed wheels or discs (e g for producing rows of dots on engraved plates or for perforating paper) [F, lit., small wheel, fr OF *roelete*, dim. of *roele* small wheel, fr LL *rotella*, dim. of L *rota* wheel – more at ROLL]

Roumanian /roo'maynyən, roh-, rə-, -ni·ən/ *n or adj* (a) Romanian

[1]**round** /rownd/ *adj* **1a(1)** having every part of the surface or circumference equidistant from the centre **(2)** cylindrical ⟨*a ~ peg*⟩ **b** approximately round ⟨*a ~ face*⟩ **2** well filled out; plump ⟨*~ cheeks*⟩ **3a** complete, full ⟨*a ~ dozen*⟩ **b** approximately correct; *esp* exact only to a specific decimal **c** substantial in amount ⟨*a good ~ sum*⟩ **4** direct in expression ⟨*a ~ oath*⟩ **5a** moving in or forming a ring or circle **b** following a roughly circular route ⟨*a ~ tour of the Cotswolds*⟩ **6** presented with lifelike fullness **7a** having full resonance or tone **b** pronounced with rounded lips; labialized **8** *of handwriting* not angular; curved [ME, fr OF *roont*, fr L *rotundus*; akin to L *rota* wheel – more at ROLL] – **roundness** *n*

[2]**round** *adv* **1a** in a circular or curved path **b** with revolving or rotating motion ⟨*wheels go ~*⟩ **c** in circumference ⟨*a tree 5 feet ~*⟩ **d** in, along, or through a circuitous or indirect route ⟨*the road goes ~ by the lake*⟩ **e** in an encircling position ⟨*a field with a fence all ~*⟩ **2a** in close from all sides so as to surround ⟨*the children crowded ~*⟩ **b** near, about **c** here and there in various places **3a** in rotation or recurrence ⟨*your birthday will soon be ~ again*⟩ **b** from beginning to end; through ⟨*all the year ~*⟩ **c(1)** in or to the other or a specified direction ⟨*turn ~*⟩ ⟨*talk her ~*⟩ **(2)** TO 4 **(3)** in the specified order or relationship ⟨*got the story the wrong way ~*⟩ **4** about, approximately ⟨*~ 1900*⟩ **5** to a particular person or place ⟨*invite them ~ for drinks*⟩ – **round about** **1** approximately; MORE OR LESS **2** in a ring round; on all sides of

[3]**round** *prep* **1a** so as to revolve or progress about (a centre) **b** so as to encircle or enclose ⟨*seated ~ the table*⟩ **c** so as to avoid or get past; beyond the obstacle of ⟨*got ~ his objections*⟩ ⟨*lives just ~ the corner*⟩ **d** near to; about **2a** in all directions outwards from ⟨*looked ~ her*⟩ **b** here and there in or throughout ⟨*travel ~ Europe*⟩ **3** so as to have a

centre or basis in ⟨*a movement organized ~ the idea of service*⟩ **4** continuously during; throughout

[4]**round** *n* **1a** sthg round (e g a circle, curve, or ring) **b** a circle of people or things **2** a musical canon sung in unison in which each part is continuously repeated **3** a rung of a ladder or chair **4a** a circling or circuitous path or course **b** motion in a circle or a curving path **5a** a route or assigned territory habitually traversed (e g by a milkman or policeman) **b** a series of visits made by **(1)** a general practitioner to patients in their homes **(2)** a hospital doctor to the patients under his/her care **c** a series of customary social calls ⟨*doing the* ~s *of her friends*⟩ **6** a set of usu alcoholic drinks served at 1 time to each person in a group **7** a recurring sequence of actions or events ⟨*a ~ of talks*⟩ **8** a period of time that recurs in fixed succession ⟨*the daily ~*⟩ **9** a unit of ammunition consisting of the parts necessary to fire 1 shot **10a** any of a series of units of action in a game or sport (e g covering a prescribed time) **b** a division of a tournament in which each contestant plays 1 other **11** a prolonged burst (e g of applause) **12a** a cut of beef between the rump and the lower leg ☞ MEAT **b** a single slice of bread or toast; *also* a sandwich made with 2 whole slices of bread **13** a rounded or curved part *USE* (*5b, c*) usu pl with sing. meaning – **in the round 1** in full sculptured form unattached to a background **2** with a centre stage surrounded by an audience ⟨*theatre* in the round⟩

[5]**round** *vt* **1a** to make round or rounded **b(1)** to make (the lips) round and protruded **(2)** to produce (e g the vowel /ooh/) with rounded lips; labialize **2** to go round (e g a bend, corner) ⟨*the ship* ~ed *the headland*⟩ **3** to encircle, encompass **4** to bring to completion or perfection – often + *off* or *out* **5** to express as a round number – often + *off, up,* or *down* ⟨*11.3572 ~ed off to 3 decimal places becomes 11.357*⟩ ~ *vi* **1a** to become round, plump, or smooth in outline **b** to reach fullness or completion – usu + *off* or *out* **2** to follow a winding or circular course ⟨~ing *into the home stretch*⟩ – **round on** to turn against and attack; *esp* to suddenly scold

[1]**roundabout** /'rowndə,bowt/ *n, Br* **1** a merry-go-round; *also* a rotatable platform that is an amusement in a children's playground **2** a road junction formed round a central island about which traffic moves in 1 direction only; *also* a paved or planted circle in the middle of this

[2]**roundabout** *adj* circuitous, indirect – **roundaboutness** *n*

round bracket *n, chiefly Br* PARENTHESIS 1b

'**round,dance** *n* **1** a folk dance in which participants form a ring **2** a ballroom dance in which couples progress round the room

rounded /'rowndid/ *adj* **1** made round; smoothly curved **2** fully developed; mature – **roundedness** *n*

roundel /'rowndl/ *n* **1** a round figure or object: e g **a** a circular panel, window, etc **b** a circular mark identifying the nationality of an aircraft, esp a warplane **2** (an English modification of) the rondeau [ME, fr OF *rondel,* fr *roont* round – more at ROUND]

roundelay /'rowndi,lay/ *n* **1** a simple song with a refrain **2** a poem with a refrain recurring frequently or at fixed intervals [modif of MF *rondelet,* dim. of *rondel*]

rounder /'rowndə/ *n* **1** *pl but sing in constr* a game with bat and ball that resembles baseball **2** a boxing or wrestling match lasting a specified number of rounds ⟨*a 10*-rounder⟩ [[4] [5]ROUND + [2]-ER]

Roundhead /'rownd,hed/ *n* an adherent of Parliament in its contest with Charles I [fr the short-cropped hair of some of the Parliamentarians]

roundheaded /,rownd'hedid/ *adj* brachycephalic

roundhouse /'rownd,hows/ *n* **1** a cabin or apartment on the after part of a quarterdeck **2** *chiefly NAm* a circular building for housing and repairing locomotives

roundly /'rowndli/ *adv* **1** in a round or circular form or manner **2** in a blunt or severe manner ⟨~ *rebuked him*⟩

,**round 'robin** *n* **1** a written petition or protest; *esp* one on which the signatures are arranged in a circle so that no name heads the list **2** a tournament in which every contestant plays every other contestant in turn [prob fr the name *Robin*]

,**round-'shouldered** *adj* having stooping or rounded shoulders

roundsman /'rowndzmən/ *n* sby (e g a milkman) who takes, orders, sells, or delivers goods on an assigned route

,**round 'table** *n* a meeting or conference of several people on equal terms – **round-table** *adj*

,**round-the-'clock** *adj* lasting or continuing 24 hours a day; constant

,**round 'trip** *n* a trip to a place and back, usu over the same route

'**round,up** /-,up/ *n* **1a** the collecting in of cattle by riding round them and driving them **b** a gathering in of scattered people or things **2** a summary of information (e g from news bulletins)

round up *vt* **1** to collect (cattle) by a roundup **2** to gather in or bring together from various quarters

'**round,worm** /-,wuhm/ *n* a nematode

roup /roohp/ *n* a virus disease of poultry in which soft whitish lesions form on the mouth, throat, and eyes [origin unknown]

rouse /rowz/ *vi* **1** to become aroused **2** to become stirred ~ *vt* **1** to stir up; provoke **2** to arouse from sleep or apathy [ME *rousen*]

rousing /'rowzing/ *adj* giving rise to enthusiasm; stirring

roustabout /'rowstə,bowt/ *n, Br* **1** a deck hand or docker **2** an unskilled or semiskilled labourer, esp in an oil field or refinery [*roust* (to rouse roughly), alter. of *rouse*]

[1]**rout** /rowt/ *n* **1** a disorderly crowd of people; a mob **2** *archaic* a fashionable social gathering [ME *route,* fr MF, troop, defeat, fr (assumed) VL *rupta,* fr L, fem of *ruptus,* pp of *rumpere* to break – more at BEREAVE]

[2]**rout** *vi* [3]ROOT 1 ~ *vt* to gouge out or make a furrow in [alter. of [3]*root*]

[3]**rout** *n* **1** a state of wild confusion; *specif* a confused retreat; headlong flight **2** a disastrous defeat [MF *route* troop, defeat]

[4]**rout** *vt* **1** to disorganize completely; wreak havoc among **2** to put to headlong flight **3** to defeat decisively or disastrously

[1]**route** /rooht/ *n* **1a** a regularly travelled way ⟨*the trunk ~ north*⟩ **b** a means of access **2** a line of travel **3** an itinerary [ME, fr OF, fr (assumed) VL *rupta* (*via*), lit., broken way, fr L *rupta,* fem of *ruptus,* pp]

2route *vt* **1** to send by a selected route; direct **2** to divert in a specified direction

'route,man /-,man/ *n, NAm* a roundsman

'route ,march *n* a usu long and tiring march, esp as military training

1routine /rooh'teen/ *n* **1a** a regular course of procedure **b** habitual or mechanical performance of an established procedure **2** a fixed piece of entertainment often repeated ⟨*a dance* ~⟩ **3** a particular sequence of computer instructions for carrying out a given task [F, fr MF, fr *route* travelled way]

2routine *adj* **1** commonplace or repetitious in character **2** of or in accordance with established procedure – **routinely** *adv*

rout out /rowt/ *vt* ROOT OUT

roux /rooh/ *n, pl* **roux** /rooh(z)/ a cooked mixture of fat and flour used as a thickening agent in a sauce [F, fr (*beurre*) *roux* browned (butter)]

1rove /rohv/ *vb* to wander aimlessly or idly (through or over) [ME *roven* to shoot at rovers (random targets in archery)]

2rove *past of* REEVE

3rove *vt* to join (textile fibres) with a slight twist and draw out into roving [origin unknown]

4rove *n* roving

'rove ,beetle *n* any of numerous often predatory long-bodied beetles [perh fr 1*rove*]

1rover /'rohvə/ *n* a pirate [ME, fr MD, fr *roven* to rob; akin to OE *rēafian* to plunder]

2rover *n* a wanderer [ME, random target in archery, wanderer, fr *roven* to shoot at random, wander]

1roving /'rohving/ *adj* **1** not restricted as to location or area of concern **2** inclined to ramble or stray ⟨*a* ~ *fancy*⟩ [1*rove*]

2roving *n* a slightly twisted roll or strand of textile fibres [3*rove*]

,roving 'eye *n* promiscuous sexual interests [1*roving*]

1row /roh/ *vi* **1** to propel a boat by means of oars **2** to move (as if) by the propulsion of oars ~ *vt* **1a** to propel (as if) with oars **b** to compete against in rowing **2** to transport in a boat propelled by oars **3** to occupy a specified position in a rowing crew [ME *rowen*, fr OE *rōwan*; akin to MHG *rüejen* to row, L *remus* oar] – **rower** *n*

2row /roh/ *n* an act of rowing a boat

3row /roh/ *n* **1** a number of objects arranged in a (straight) line; *also* the line along which such objects are arranged **2** a way, street [ME *rawe*; akin to OE *rǣw* row, OHG *riga* line, L *rima* slit] – **in a row** one after another; successively

4row /row/ *n* **1** a noisy quarrel or stormy dispute **2** excessive or unpleasant noise [origin unknown]

5row /row/ *vi* to engage in quarrelling

rowan /'roh·ən/ *n* (the red berry of) a small Eurasian tree of the rose family that bears flat clusters of white flowers [of Scand origin; akin to ON *reynir* rowan; akin to OE *rēad* red – more at RED]

rowboat /'roh,boht/ *n* ROWING BOAT

rowdy /'rowdi/ *n or adj* (sby) coarse or boisterous [perh irreg fr 4*row*] – **rowdily** *adv*, **rowdiness** *n*, **rowdyism** *n*

rowel /'rowəl/ *n* a revolving disc with sharp marginal points at the end of a spur [ME *rowelle*, fr MF *rouelle* small wheel, fr OF *roele* – more at ROULETTE]

'rowing ,boat /'roh·ing/ *n, Br* a small boat designed to be rowed

rowlock /'rolək; *also (not tech)* 'roh,lok/ *n, chiefly Br* a device for holding an oar in place and providing a fulcrum for its action [prob alter. of *oarlock*]

1royal /'roy(ə)l/ *adj* **1a** of monarchical ancestry ⟨*the* ~ *family*⟩ **b** of the crown ⟨*the* ~ *estates*⟩ **c** in the crown's service ⟨Royal *Air Force*⟩ **2** suitable for royalty; regal, magnificent **3** of superior size, magnitude, or quality **4** of or being a part of the rigging of a sailing ship next above the topgallant [ME *roial*, fr MF, fr L *regalis*, fr *reg-, rex* king; akin to OIr *rī* (gen *rīg*) king, Skt *rājan*, L *regere* to rule – more at 1RIGHT] – **royally** *adv*

2royal *n* **1** a stag of 8 years or more having antlers with at least 12 points **2** a royal sail or mast **3** a size of paper usu 25 x 20in (635 × 508mm) **4** sby of royal blood – infml

,Royal As'sent *n* *the* formal ratification of a parliamentary bill by a British sovereign ☞ LAW

,royal 'blue *adj or n* rich purplish blue

,Royal Com'mission *n* a committee of inquiry appointed by the Crown

,royal 'flush *n* a straight flush having an ace as the highest card

royalist /'royəlist/ *n, often cap* a supporter of a king or of monarchical government (e g a Cavalier) – **royalism** *n*, **royalist** *adj*

,royal 'jelly *n* a highly nutritious secretion of the honeybee that is fed to the very young larvae and to all larvae that will develop into queens

,royal pre'rogative *n* the constitutional rights of the monarch

royal road *n* the most direct way *to* a condition or object of study

royalty /'royəlti/ *n* **1a** royal sovereignty **b** a monetary benefit received by a sovereign (e g a percentage of minerals) **2** regal character or bearing **3a** people of royal blood **b** a privileged class of a specified type **4** a right of jurisdiction granted by a sovereign **5a** a share of the product or profit reserved by one who grants esp an oil or mining lease **b** a payment made to an author, composer, or inventor for each copy or example of his/her work sold [ME *roialte*, fr MF *roialté*, fr OF, fr *roial*]

rozzer /'rozə/ *n, Br* a policeman – slang [origin unknown]

-rrhagia /-'rayj(y)ə/ *comb form* (→ *n*) abnormal or excessive discharge or flow ⟨*menor*rhagia⟩ [NL, fr Gk, fr *rhēgnynai* to break, burst; akin to OSlav *rězati* to cut]

-rrhiza /-'riezə/ – see -RHIZA

-rrhoea, *chiefly NAm* **-rrhea** /-'riə/ *comb form* (→ *n*) flow; discharge ⟨*leucor*rhoea⟩ [ME *-ria*, fr LL *-rrhoea*, fr Gk *-rrhoia*, fr *rhoia*, fr *rhein* to flow – more at STREAM]

1rub /rub/ *vb* **-bb-** *vi* to move along a surface with pressure and friction ~ *vt* **1** to subject to pressure and friction, esp with a back-and-forth motion **2a** to cause (a body) to move with pressure and friction along a surface **b** to treat in any of various ways by rubbing **3** to bring into reciprocal back-and-forth or rotary contact [ME *rubben*; akin to Icel *rubba* to scrape] – **rub shoulders** to associate closely; mingle socially – **rub the wrong way** to arouse the antagonism or displeasure of; irritate

2rub *n* **1a** an obstacle, difficulty – usu + *the* **b** sthg grating to the feelings (e g a gibe or harsh criticism) **2** the application of friction and pressure

rub along *vi* **1** to continue coping in a trying situation **2** to remain on friendly terms

rubato /rooh'bahtoh/ *n, pl* **rubatos** expressive fluctuation of speed within a musical phrase [It, pp of *rubare* to rob, of Gmc origin]

¹rubber /'rubə/ *n* **1a** an instrument or object used in rubbing, polishing, or cleaning **b** *Br* a small piece of rubber or plastic used for rubbing out esp pencil marks on paper, card, etc **2** (any of various synthetic substances like) an elastic substance obtained by coagulating the milky juice of the rubber tree or other plant that is essentially a polymer of isoprene and is used, esp when toughened by chemical treatment, in car tyres, waterproof materials, etc **3** sthg like or made of rubber: e g **a** *NAm* a galosh **b** *NAm* a condom [¹RUB + ²-ER; (2) fr its use in erasers] – **rubber** *adj*, **rubbery** *adj*

²rubber *n* a contest consisting of an odd number of games won by the side that takes a majority [origin unknown]

,rubber 'band *n* a continuous band of rubber used for holding small objects together

rubber·ize, -ise /'rubəriez/ *vt* to coat or impregnate with (a solution of) rubber

¹rubberneck /'rubə,nek/ *also* **rubbernecker** /-,nekə/ *n, NAm* **1** an overinquisitive person **2** a tourist, sightseer; *esp* one on a guided tour ***USE*** derog

²rubberneck *vi, NAm* **1** to show exaggerated curiosity – infml **2** to engage in sightseeing – derog

'rubber ,plant *n* a tall Asian tree of the fig family frequently dwarfed and grown as an ornamental plant

,rubber-'stamp *vt* **1** to imprint with a rubber stamp **2** to approve, endorse, or dispose of as a matter of routine or at the dictate of another

,rubber 'stamp *n* **1** a stamp of rubber for making imprints **2** sby who unthinkingly assents to the actions or policies of others **3** a routine endorsement or approval

'rubber ,tree *n* a S American tree of the spurge family that is cultivated in plantations and is the chief source of rubber

rubbing /'rubing/ *n* an image of a raised surface obtained by placing paper over it and rubbing the paper with charcoal, chalk, etc ⟨*a brass* ~⟩

¹rubbish /'rubish/ *n* **1** worthless or rejected articles; trash **2** sthg worthless; NONSENSE 1a, b – often used interjectionally [ME *robys*] – **rubbishy** *adj*

²rubbish *vt* **1** to condemn as rubbish **2** to litter with rubbish

rubble /'rubl/ *n* **1** broken fragments of building material (e g brick, stone, etc) **2** rough broken stones or bricks used in coarse masonry or in filling courses of walls **3** rough stone from the quarry [ME *robyl*]

rubdown /'rub,down/ *n* a brisk rubbing of the body

rubefacient /,roohbi'faysh(y)ənt/ *n* a substance for external application that produces redness of the skin [L *rubefacient-, rubefaciens*, prp of *rubefacere* to make red, fr *rubeus* reddish + *facere* to make – more at RUBY, DO] – **rubefacient** *adj*

rubella /rooh'belə/ *n* GERMAN MEASLES [NL, fr L, fem of *rubellus* reddish, fr *ruber* red – more at RED]

rubellite /'roohbə,liet/ *n* a pink-red tourmaline used as a gem [L *rubellus*]

rubeola /rooh'bee·ələ/ *n* measles [NL, fr neut pl of (assumed) NL *rubeolus* reddish, fr L *rubeus* – more at RUBY]

Rubicon /'roohbikən/ *n* a bounding or limiting line; *esp* one that when crossed commits sby irrevocably [L *Rubicon-, Rubico*, river of N Italy, forming part of the boundary between Cisalpine Gaul and Italy, whose crossing by Julius Caesar in 49 BC began a civil war]

rubicund /'roohbikənd/ *adj* ruddy [L *rubicundus*, fr *rubēre* to be red; akin to L *rubeus*] – **rubicundity** /-'kundəti/ *n*

rubidium /rooh'bidi·əm/ *n* a soft metallic element of the alkali metal group ☞ PERIODIC TABLE [NL, fr L *rubidus* red, fr *rubēre*]

rubiginous /rooh'bijinəs/ *adj* rust-coloured [L *robiginosus, rubiginosus* rusty, fr *robigin-, robigo* rust; akin to L *rubēre*]

Rubik's cube, Rubik cube /'roohbik/ *n* a puzzle consisting of a usu plastic cube having each face divided into nine small coloured or distinctively marked square segments and rotatable about a central square, that must be restored to an initial condition in which each face shows nine identical squares [Ernö *Rubik b* 1944 Hung designer]

rub in *vt* to harp on (e g sthg unpleasant or embarrassing)

ruble /'roohbl/ *n* a rouble

rub off *vi* **1** to disappear as the result of rubbing **2** to exert an influence through contact or example

rub out *vt* **1** to remove (e g pencil marks) with a rubber; *broadly* to obliterate **2** *chiefly NAm* to kill, murder – slang

rubric /'roohbrik/ *n* **1** a heading (e g in a book or manuscript) written or printed in a distinctive colour (e g red) or style **2a** a heading under which sthg is classed **b** an authoritative rule; *esp* a rule for the conduct of church ceremonial **c** an explanatory or introductory commentary [ME *rubrike* red ochre, heading in red letters of part of a book, fr MF *rubrique*, fr L *rubrica*, fr *rubr-, ruber* red] – **rubric, rubrical** *adj*

rubricate /'roohbri,kayt/ *vt* to write or print as a rubric – **rubricator** *n*, **rubrication** /-'kaysh(ə)n/ *n*

rub up *vt* to revive or refresh knowledge of; revise

¹ruby /'roohbi/ *n* **1** a red corundum used as a gem **2a** the dark red colour of the ruby **b** sthg like a ruby in colour [ME, fr MF *rubis, rubi*, irreg fr L *rubeus* reddish; akin to L *ruber* red – more at RED]

²ruby *adj* of or marking a 40th anniversary ⟨~ *wedding*⟩

ruche /roohsh/, **ruching** /'roohshing/ *n* a pleated or gathered strip of fabric used for trimming [F *ruche*, fr ML *rusca* bark of a tree, of Celt origin] – **ruched** *adj*

¹ruck /ruk/ *n* **1a** an indistinguishable mass **b** *the* usual run of people or things **2** a situation in Rugby Union in which 1 or more players from each team close round the ball when it is on the ground and try to kick the ball out to their own team – compare MAUL 1 [ME *ruke* pile of combustible material, of Scand origin; akin to ON *hraukr* rick – more at ¹RICK]

²ruck *vb* to wrinkle, crease – often + *up* [*ruck*, n (wrinkle), of Scand origin; akin to ON *hrukka* wrinkle]

rucksack /'ruk,sak/ *n* a lightweight bag carried on the back and fastened by straps over the shoulders, used esp by walkers and climbers [G, fr *rucken* (alter. of *rücken* back) + *sack* bag]

ruckus /'rukəs/ *n, chiefly NAm* a row or disturbance – infml [prob blend of *ruction* and *rumpus*]

ruction /'ruksh(ə)n/ *n* **1** a violent dispute **2** a disturbance, uproar *USE* infml [perh by shortening & alter. fr *insurrection*]

rudbeckia /rud'beki·ə/ *n* any of a genus of N American composite plants with showy yellow flower heads [NL, genus name, fr Olof *Rudbeck* †1702 Sw scientist]

rudd /rud/ *n* a freshwater European fish of the carp family resembling the roach [prob fr *rud* (redness, red ochre), fr ME *rude*, fr OE *rudu* – more at RUDDY]

rudder /'rudə/ *n* **1** a flat piece or structure of wood or metal hinged vertically to a ship's stern for changing course with **2** a movable auxiliary aerofoil, usu attached to the fin, that serves to control direction of flight of an aircraft in the horizontal plane ☞ FLIGHT [ME *rother*, fr OE *rōther* paddle; akin to OE *rōwan* to row] – **rudderless** *adj*

ruddock /'rudək/ *n* ROBIN 1 [ME *ruddok*, fr OE *rudduc*; akin to OE *rudu*]

ruddy /'rudi/ *adj* **1** having a healthy reddish colour **2** red, reddish **3** *Br* BLOODY 4 – euph [ME *rudi*, fr OE *rudig*, fr *rudu* redness; akin to OE *rēad* red – more at RED] – **ruddily** /'rudəli/ *adv*, **ruddiness** *n*

rude /roohd/ *adj* **1a** in a rough or unfinished state **b** primitive, undeveloped **c** simple, elemental **2** lacking refinement or propriety: e g **a** discourteous **b** vulgar, indecent **c** uncivilized **d** ignorant, unlearned **3** showing or suggesting lack of training or skill **4** robust, vigorous – esp in *rude health* **5** sudden and unpleasant; abrupt ⟨*a ~ awakening*⟩ [ME, fr MF, fr L *rudis*; akin to L *rudus* rubble, *ruere* to fall – more at RUG] – **rudely** *adv*, **rudeness** *n*, **rudery** /'roohd(ə)ri/ *n*

rudiment /'roohdimənt/ *n* **1** a basic principle or element or a fundamental skill **2a** sthg as yet unformed or undeveloped **b(1)** a deficiently developed body part or organ; VESTIGE 2 **(2)** a primordium *USE* usu pl with sing. meaning [L *rudimentum* beginning, fr *rudis* raw, rude] – **rudimental** /-'mentl/ *adj*

rudimentary /,roohdi'ment(ə)ri/ *adj* **1** basic, fundamental **2** of a primitive kind; crude **3** very poorly developed or represented only by a vestige ⟨*the ~ tail of a hyrax*⟩ – **rudimentarily** *adv*

[1]**rue** /rooh/ *vt* to feel penitence or bitter regret for [ME *ruen*, fr OE *hrēowan*; akin to OHG *hriuwan* to regret]

[2]**rue** *n* a strong-scented woody plant with bitter leaves formerly used in medicine [ME, fr MF, fr L *ruta*, fr Gk *rhytē*]

rueful /'roohf(ə)l/ *adj* **1** arousing pity or compassion **2** mournful, regretful; *also* feigning sorrow – **ruefully** *adv*, **ruefulness** *n*

rufescent /rooh'fes(ə)nt/ *adj* reddish [L *rufescent-*, *rufescens*, prp of *rufescere* to become reddish, fr *rufus* red – more at RED]

[1]**ruff, ruffe** /ruf/ *n* a small freshwater European perch [ME *ruf*]

[2]**ruff** *n* **1** a broad starched collar of fluted linen or muslin worn in the late 16th and early 17th c ☞ GARMENT **2** a fringe or frill of long hairs or feathers growing round the neck **3** *fem* **reeve** a Eurasian sandpiper the male of which has a large ruff of erectable feathers during the breeding season [prob back-formation fr *ruffle*] – **ruffed** *adj*

[3]**ruff** *vt* TRUMP 1 [*ruff*, n (former card-game, kind of trump), fr MF *roffle, ronfle*] – **ruff** *n*

ruffian /'rufi·ən/ *n* a brutal and lawless person [MF *rufian*] – **ruffianism** *n*, **ruffianly** *adj*

[1]**ruffle** /'rufl/ *vb* **ruffling** /'rufling, 'rufl·ing/ *vt* **1a** to disturb the smoothness of **b** to trouble, vex ⟨*~d his composure*⟩ **2** to erect (e g feathers) (as if) in a ruff **3** to make into a ruffle ~ *vi* to become ruffled [ME *ruffelen*; akin to LG *ruffelen* to crumple]

[2]**ruffle** *n* **1** a disturbance of surface evenness (e g a ripple or crumple) **2a** a strip of fabric gathered or pleated on 1 edge **b** [2]RUFF 2

rufous /'roohfəs/ *adj, esp of an animal* reddish brown [L *rufus* red – more at RED]

rug /rug/ *n* **1** a heavy mat, usu smaller than a carpet and with a thick pile, which is used as a floor covering **2a** a woollen blanket, often with fringes on 2 opposite edges, used as a wrap esp when travelling **b** a blanket for an animal (e g a horse) [(assumed) ME, rag, tuft, of Scand origin; akin to ON *rögg* tuft; akin to L *ruere* to rush, fall, dig up, Skt *ravate* he breaks up]

rugby /'rugbi/ *n, often cap* a football game that is played with an oval football, that features kicking, lateral hand-to-hand passing, and tackling, and in which forward passing is prohibited ☞ SPORT [*Rugby* School, in Warwickshire, England]

,Rugby 'League *n* the 1 of the 2 forms of rugby that is played by teams of 13 players each, features a 6-man scrum, and permits professionals to play

,Rugby 'Union *n* the 1 of the 2 forms of rugby that is played by teams of 15 players each, features an 8-man scrum, and is restricted to amateurs

rugged /'rugid/ *adj* **1** having a rough uneven surface or outline ⟨*~ mountains*⟩ **2** seamed with wrinkles and furrows ⟨*a ~ face*⟩ **3** austere, stern; *also* uncompromising ⟨*~ individualism*⟩ **4a** strongly built or constituted; sturdy **b** presenting a severe test of ability or stamina [ME, fr (assumed) ME *rug*] – **ruggedly** *adv*, **ruggedness** *n*

rugger /'rugə/ *n, Br* rugby – infml [by alter.]

rugose /'rooh,gohs/ *adj* wrinkled, ridged ⟨*~ leaves*⟩ [L *rugosus*, fr *ruga* wrinkle – more at ROUGH] – **rugosely** *adv*, **rugosity** /rooh'gosəti/ *n*

[1]**ruin** /'rooh·in/ *n* **1** physical, moral, economic, or social collapse **2a** the state of being wrecked or decayed ⟨*the city lay in ~s*⟩ **b** the remains of sthg destroyed – usu pl with sing. meaning **3** (a cause of) destruction or downfall ⟨*whisky was his ~*⟩ ⟨*the ~ of modern drama* – T S Eliot⟩ **4** a ruined person or structure [ME *ruine*, fr MF, fr L *ruina*; akin to L *ruere* to fall – more at RUG] – **ruination** /-'naysh(ə)n/ *n*

[2]**ruin** *vt* **1** to reduce to ruins **2a** to damage irreparably; spoil **b** to reduce to financial ruin – **ruiner** *n*

ruinous /'rooh·inəs/ *adj* **1** dilapidated, ruined **2** causing (the likelihood of) ruin ⟨*~ sales performance*⟩ – **ruinously** *adv*, **ruinousness** *n*

[1]**rule** /roohl/ *n* **1a** a prescriptive specification of conduct or action **b** the laws or regulations prescribed by the founder of a religious order for observance by its members **c** an established procedure, custom, or habit **d** a legal precept or doctrine **2a(1)** a usu valid generalization **(2)** a generally prevailing quality, state, or form **b** a standard of judgment **c**

a regulating principle, esp of a system ⟨*the* ~s *of grammar*⟩ **3** the exercise or a period of dominion **4** a strip or set of jointed strips of material marked off in units and used for measuring or marking off lengths [ME *reule*, fr OF, fr L *regula* straightedge, rule, fr *regere* to lead straight – more at [1]RIGHT] – **as a rule** generally; FOR THE MOST PART

[2]**rule** *vt* **1a** to exert control, direction, or influence on **b** to exercise control over, esp by restraining ⟨~d *her appetites firmly*⟩ **2a** to exercise power or firm authority over **b** to be preeminent in; dominate ⟨*an actor who* ~s *the stage*⟩ **3** to lay down authoritatively, esp judicially **4a** to mark with lines drawn (as if) along the straight edge of a ruler **b** to mark (a line) on sthg with a ruler ~ *vi* **1** to exercise supreme authority **2** to make a judicial decision

,rule of 'thumb *n* a rough practical or common-sense method rather than a precise or technical one

rule out *vt* **1a** to exclude, eliminate **b** to deny the possibility of ⟨rule out *further discussion*⟩ **2** to make impossible; prevent

ruler /'roohlə/ *n* **1** sby, specif a sovereign, who rules **2** a smooth-edged strip of material that is usu marked off in units (e g centimetres) and is used for guiding a pen or pencil in drawing lines, for measuring, or for marking off lengths – **rulership** *n*

[1]**ruling** /'roohling/ *n* an official or authoritative decision

[2]**ruling** *adj* **1** exerting power or authority **2** chief, predominant

[1]**rum** /rum/ *adj* **-mm-** *chiefly Br* queer, strange ⟨*she's a* ~ *customer*⟩ – infml [earlier *rome*, perh fr Romany *rom* gypsy man]

[2]**rum** *n* a spirit distilled from a fermented cane product (e g molasses) [prob short for obs *rumbullion* (rum), of unknown origin]

Rumanian /rooh'maynyən, roo-, rə-, -ni·ən/ *n or adj* (a) Romanian

rumba, rhumba /'rumbə/ *n* (the music for) a ballroom dance of Cuban Negro origin marked by steps with a delayed transfer of weight and pronounced hip movements [AmerSp *rumba*]

[1]**rumble** /'rumbl/ *vb* **rumbling** /'rumbling, 'rumbl·-ing/ *vi* **1** to make a low heavy rolling sound **2** *NAm* to engage in a street fight – infml ~ *vt* **1** to utter or emit with a low rolling sound **2** to reveal or discover the true character of – infml [ME *rumblen*; akin to MHG *rummeln* to rumble] – **rumbler** *n*

[2]**rumble** *n* **1a** a rumbling sound **b** low-frequency noise from a record deck caused by the vibrations of the turntable **2** *NAm* a street fight, esp between gangs – infml

rumbustious /rum'buschəs/ *adj, chiefly Br* irrepressibly or coarsely exuberant [alter. of *robustious*, fr *robust*] – **rumbustiousness** *n*

rumen /'roohmen/ *n, pl* **rumina** /-minə/, **rumens** the large first compartment of the stomach of a ruminant mammal in which cellulose is broken down, esp by the action of symbiotic bacteria [NL *rumin-, rumen*, fr L, gullet]

[1]**ruminant** /'roohminənt/ *n* a ruminant mammal

[2]**ruminant** *adj* **1a** that chews the cud **b** of or being (a member of) a group of hoofed mammals including the cattle, sheep, giraffes, and camels that chew the cud and have a complex 3- or 4-chambered stomach **2** meditative

ruminate /'roohmi,nayt/ *vb* **1** to chew again (what has been chewed slightly and swallowed) **2** to engage in contemplation (of) [L *ruminatus*, pp of *ruminari* to chew the cud, muse upon, fr *rumin-, rumen* gullet; akin to Skt *romantha* ruminant] – **ruminator** *n*, **ruminative** /-nətiv/ *adj*, **ruminatively** *adv*, **rumination** /-'naysh(ə)n/ *n*

[1]**rummage** /'rumij/ *n* **1** a thorough search, esp among a jumbled assortment of objects **2a** *chiefly NAm* JUMBLE 2 **b** *NAm* a miscellaneous or confused accumulation [obs *rummage* (act of packing cargo), modif of MF *arrimage*]

[2]**rummage** *vt* **1** to make a thorough search of (an untidy or congested place) **2** to uncover by searching – usu + *out* ~ *vi* to engage in a haphazard search – **rummager** *n*

'rummage ,sale *n, chiefly NAm* JUMBLE SALE

rummer /'rumə/ *n* a tall often elaborately engraved drinking glass, used esp for wine [G or D; G *römer*, fr D *roemer*]

rummy /'rumi/ *n* any of several card games for 2 or more players in which each player tries to assemble combinations of 3 or more related cards and to be the first to turn all his/her cards into such combinations [perh fr *rummy* (queer, strange), fr [1]*rum* + [1]*-y*]

[1]**rumour,** *NAm chiefly* **rumor** /'roohmə/ *n* **1** a statement or report circulated without confirmation of its truth **2** talk or opinion widely disseminated but with no identifiable source [ME *rumour*, fr MF, fr L *rumor*; akin to OE *rēon* to lament, Gk *ōryesthai* to howl]

[2]**rumour,** *NAm chiefly* **rumor** *vt* to tell or spread by rumour

rump /rump/ *n* **1** the rear part of a quadruped mammal, bird, etc; the buttocks **2** a cut of beef between the loin and round ☞ MEAT **3** a small or inferior remnant of a larger group (e g a parliament) [ME, of Scand origin; akin to Icel *rumpr* rump; akin to MHG *rumph* torso]

[1]**rumple** /'rumpl/ *n* a fold, wrinkle

[2]**rumple** *vb* **rumpling** /'rumpl·ing/ *vt* **1** to wrinkle, crumple **2** to make unkempt; tousle ~ *vi* to become rumpled [D *rompelen*; akin to OHG *rimpfan* to wrinkle, L *curvus* curved]

rumpus /'rumpəs/ *n* a usu noisy commotion [perh alter. of *rumble*]

[1]**run** /run/ *vb* **-nn-; ran** /ran/; **run** *vi* **1a** to go faster than a walk; *specif* to go steadily by springing steps so that both feet leave the ground for an instant in each step **b** *of a horse* to move at a fast gallop **c** to flee, escape ⟨*dropped his gun and* ran⟩ **2a** to go without restraint ⟨*let his chickens* ~ *loose*⟩ ⟨~ *about barefoot*⟩ **b** to sail before the wind as distinct from reaching or sailing close-hauled – compare REACH 3, BEAT 4 **3a** to hasten with a specified often distressing purpose ⟨~ *and fetch the doctor*⟩ **b** to make a quick, easy, or casual trip or visit ⟨~ *up to town for the day*⟩ **4** to contend in a race; *also* to finish a race in the specified place ⟨ran *third*⟩ **5a** to move (as if) on wheels ⟨*a chair that* ~s *on castors*⟩ **b** to pass or slide freely or cursorily ⟨*a thought* ran *through my mind*⟩ **6** to sing or play quickly ⟨~ *up the scale*⟩ **7a** to go back and forth; ply ⟨*made the trains* ~ *on time*⟩ **b** *of fish* to migrate or move in schools; *esp* to ascend a river to spawn **8** to function, operate ⟨*don't touch the engine while it's* ~ning⟩ ⟨*the engine* ~s *on petrol*⟩ ⟨*everything's* ~ning *smoothly at the office*⟩ **9a** to continue in force ⟨*the lease has 2 more years to* ~⟩ **b** to continue to

accumulate or become payable ⟨*interest on the loan* ~s *from July 1st*⟩ **10** to pass, esp by negligence or indulgence, into a specified state ⟨~ *to waste*⟩ ⟨*money* ran *low*⟩ **11a(1)** to flow, course ⟨~ning *water*⟩ **(2)** to become by flowing ⟨*the water* ran *cold*⟩ **(3)** to discharge liquid ⟨*made my nose* ~⟩ ⟨*left the tap* ~ning⟩ **(4)** to reach a specified state by discharging liquid ⟨*the well* ran *dry*⟩ **b** MELT 1 ⟨*butter started to* ~⟩ **c** to spread, dissolve ⟨*colours guaranteed not to* ~⟩ **d** to discharge pus or serum ⟨*a* ~ning *sore*⟩ **12a** to develop rapidly in some specific direction; *esp* to throw out an elongated shoot **b** to have a tendency; be prone ⟨*they* ~ *to big noses in that family*⟩ **13a** to lie or extend in a specified position, direction, or relation to sthg ⟨*the road* ~s *through a tunnel*⟩ **b** to extend in a continuous range ⟨*shades* ~ *from white to dark grey*⟩ **c** to be in a certain form or expression ⟨*the letter* ~s *as follows*⟩ **14a** to occur persistently ⟨*a note of despair* ~s *through the narrative*⟩ **b** to continue to be as specified ⟨*profits were* ~ning *high*⟩ **c** to play or be featured continuously (e g in a theatre or newspaper) ⟨*the musical* ran *for 6 months*⟩ **15** to spread quickly from point to point ⟨*chills* ran *up his spine*⟩ **16** to ladder **17** *chiefly NAm* STAND 10 ⟨~ *for President*⟩ ~ *vt* **1a** to bring to a specified condition (as if) by running ⟨ran *himself to death*⟩ **b** to go in pursuit of; hunt ⟨*dogs that* ~ *deer*⟩ ⟨ran *the rumour to its source*⟩ **c** to drive, chase ⟨~ *him out of town*⟩ **d** to enter, register, or enrol as a contestant in a race **e** to put forward as a candidate for office **2a** to drive (livestock), esp to a grazing place **b** to provide pasturage for (livestock) **3a** to cover, accomplish, or perform (as if) by running ⟨ran *10 miles*⟩ ⟨~ *errands for his mother*⟩ ⟨ran *the whole gamut of emotions*⟩ **b** to slip through or past ⟨~ *a blockade*⟩ **4a** to cause or allow to penetrate or enter ⟨ran *a splinter into his toe*⟩ **b** to stitch **c** to cause to lie or extend in a specified position or direction ⟨~ *a wire in from the aerial*⟩ **d** to cause to collide ⟨ran *his head into a post*⟩ **e** to smuggle ⟨~ *guns*⟩ **5** to cause to pass lightly, freely, or cursorily ⟨ran *a comb through her hair*⟩ **6a(1)** to cause or allow (a vehicle or vessel) to go ⟨~ *his car off the road*⟩ ⟨~ *the ship aground*⟩ **(2)** to cause to ply or travel along a regular route ⟨~ *an extra train on Saturdays*⟩ **(3)** to own and drive ⟨*she* ~s *an old banger*⟩ **(4)** to convey in a vehicle ⟨*can I* ~ *you home?*⟩ **b** to operate ⟨~ *a lathe*⟩ ⟨~ *your razor off the mains*⟩ **c** to carry on, manage, or control ⟨~ *a factory*⟩ **7** to be full of; flow with ⟨*streets* ran *blood*⟩ **8a** to cause to move or flow in a specified way or into a specified position **b(1)** to cause to pour out liquid ⟨~ *the hot tap*⟩ **(2)** to fill from a tap ⟨~ *a hot bath*⟩ **9a** to melt and cast in a mould **b** to subject to a treatment or process ⟨~ *a problem through a computer*⟩ **10** to make oneself liable to ⟨~ *risks*⟩ **11** to permit (e g charges) to accumulate before settling ⟨~ *an account at the grocer's*⟩ **12a** RUN OFF 1b ⟨*a book to be* ~ *on lightweight paper*⟩ **b** to carry in a printed medium; print [ME *ronnen*, alter. of *rinnen*, vi (fr OE *iernan, rinnan* & ON *rinna*) & of *rennen*, vt, fr ON *renna*; akin to OHG *rinnan*, vi, to run, OE *rīsan* to rise] – **run across** to meet with or discover by chance – **run after** to pursue, chase; *esp* to seek the company of – **run a temperature** to be feverish – **run foul of 1** to collide with ⟨run foul of *a hidden reef*⟩ **2** to come into conflict with ⟨run foul of *the law*⟩ – **run into 1a** to merge with **b** to mount up to ⟨*income often* runs into *five figures*⟩ **2a** to collide with **b** to encounter, meet ⟨ran into *an old friend the other day*⟩ – **run into the ground** to tire out or use up with heavy work – **run it fine** to leave only the irreducible margin – **run on** to be concerned with; dwell on ⟨*her mind keeps* running on *the past*⟩ – **run rings round** to show marked superiority over; defeat decisively – **run riot 1** to act or function wildly or without restraint ⟨*let one's imagination* run riot⟩ **2** to grow or occur in profusion – **run short 1** to become insufficient **2** to come near the end of available supplies ⟨*we* ran short *of tea*⟩ – **run somebody off his/her feet 1** to tire sby out with running **2** to keep sby very busy – **run through 1** to squander **2a** RUN THROUGH *vt* 2 ⟨ran through *it quickly*⟩ **b** to deal with rapidly and usu perfunctorily – **run to 1** to extend to ⟨*the book* runs to *500 pages*⟩ **2a** to afford **b** *of money* to be enough for ⟨*his salary won't* run to *a car*⟩ – **run to earth/ground** to find after protracted search

²**run** *n* **1a** an act or the activity of running; continued rapid movement **b** a quickened gallop; *broadly* the gait of a runner **c** (a school of fish) migrating or ascending a river to spawn **d** a running race ⟨*a mile* ~⟩ **2a** the direction in which sthg (e g a vein of ore or the grain of wood) lies **b** general tendency or direction ⟨*watching the* ~ *of the stock market*⟩ **3** a continuous series or unbroken course, esp of identical or similar things ⟨*a* ~ *of bad luck*⟩: e g **a** a rapid passage up or down a musical scale **b** a number of rapid small dance steps executed in even tempo **c** an unbroken course of performances or showings **d** a set of consecutive measurements, readings, or observations **e** a persistent and heavy commercial or financial demand ⟨*a* ~ *on gilt-edged securities*⟩ **f** three or more playing cards usu of the same suit in consecutive order of rank **4** the quantity of work turned out in a continuous operation **5** the average or prevailing kind or class ⟨*the general* ~ *of students*⟩ **6a** the distance covered in a period of continuous journeying **b(1)** a regularly travelled course or route ⟨*ships on the Far East* ~⟩ **(2)** a short excursion in a car ⟨*went for a Sunday* ~⟩ **c** the distance a golf ball travels after touching the ground **d** freedom of movement in or access to a place ⟨*has the* ~ *of the house*⟩ **7a** a way, track, etc frequented by animals **b** an enclosure for domestic animals where they may feed or exercise **c** an inclined passageway **8a** an inclined course (e g for skiing) **b** a support or channel (e g a track, pipe, or trough) along which sthg runs **9** a unit of scoring in cricket made typically by each batsman running the full length of the wicket **10** LADDER 2b – **runless** *adj* – **on the run 1** in haste; without pausing **2** in hiding or running away, esp from lawful authority – **run for one's money** the profit or enjoyment to which one is legitimately entitled

runabout /ˈrunə,bowt/ *n* a light motor car, aeroplane, or motorboat

run along *vi* to go away; depart – often used as an order or request

runaround /ˈrunə,rownd/ *n, chiefly NAm* delaying action, esp in response to a request

¹**runaway** /ˈrunə,way/ *n* **1** a fugitive **2** sthg (e g a horse) that is running out of control

²**runaway** *adj* **1** fugitive **2** accomplished as a result of running away ⟨*a* ~ *marriage*⟩ **3** won by a long

lead; decisive ⟨*a ~ victory*⟩ **4** out of control ⟨*~ inflation*⟩

run away *vi* **1a** to take to flight **b** to flee from home; *esp* to elope **2** to run out of control; stampede, bolt – **run away with** **1** to take away in haste or secretly; *esp* to steal **2** to believe too easily ⟨*don't* run away with *the idea that you needn't go*⟩ **3** to carry beyond reasonable limits ⟨*his imagination* ran away with *him*⟩

,runcible 'spoon /'runsəbl/ *n* a sharp-edged fork with 3 broad curved prongs [coined with indefinite meaning by Edward Lear †1888 E writer & painter]

runcinate /'runsinət, -,nayt/ *adj, of a leaf* having large downward-pointing teeth ⟨*the ~ leaves of the dandelion*⟩ ☞ PLANT [L *runcinatus*, pp of *runcinare* to plane off, fr *runcina* plane]

rundown /'run,down/ *n* **1** the running down of sthg ⟨*the ~ of the steel industry*⟩ **2** an item-by-item report; a résumé

,run-'down *adj* **1** in a state of disrepair **2** in poor health **3** *NAm* completely unwound ⟨*a ~ clock*⟩

run down *vt* **1a** to knock down, esp with a motor vehicle **b** to run against and cause to sink **2a** to chase to exhaustion or until captured **b** to find by searching ⟨run down *a book in the library*⟩ **3** to disparage ⟨*don't* run *him* down*; he's an honest fellow*⟩ **4** to allow the gradual decline or closure of ⟨*the lead mines are being gradually* run down⟩ ~ *vi* **1** to cease to operate because of the exhaustion of motive power ⟨*that battery* ran down *weeks ago*⟩ **2** to decline in physical condition

rune /roohn/ *n* **1** any of the characters of an alphabet prob derived from Latin and Greek and used in medieval times, esp in carved inscriptions, by the Germanic peoples **2** a magical or cryptic utterance or inscription [ON & OE *rūn* mystery, runic character, writing; akin to OHG *rūna* secret discussion] – **runic** /'roohnik/ *adj*

[1]**rung** /rung/ *past part of* RING

[2]**rung** *n* **1a** a rounded part placed as a crosspiece between the legs of a chair **b** any of the crosspieces of a ladder **2** a level or stage in sthg that can be ascended ⟨*the bottom ~ of the social scale*⟩ [ME, fr OE *hrung*; akin to OE *hring* ring – more at [1]RING]

'run-,in *n* **1** the final part of a race(track) **2** *NAm* a quarrel

run in *vt* **1** to make (typeset matter) continuous without a paragraph or other break **2** to use (e g a motor car) cautiously for an initial period **3** to arrest, esp for a minor offence – infml

runnel /'runl/ *n* a small stream; a brook [alter. of ME *rinel*, fr OE *rynel*; akin to OE *rinnan* to run – more at RUN]

runner /'runə/ *n* **1** an entrant for a race who actually competes in it **2a** a bank or stockbroker's messenger **b** sby who smuggles or distributes illicit or contraband goods – usu in combination ⟨*a dope*-runner⟩ **3** a straight piece on which sthg slides: e g **a** a longitudinal piece on which a sledge or ice skate slides **b** a groove or bar along which sthg (e g a drawer or sliding door) slides **4** a stolon **5a** a long narrow carpet (e g for a hall or staircase) **b** a narrow decorative cloth for a table or dresser top **6** RUNNER BEAN **7** a player who runs in place of an injured batsman in cricket [[1]RUN + [2]-ER]

,runner 'bean *n, chiefly Br* (the long green edible pod of) a widely cultivated orig tropical American high-climbing bean with large usu bright red flowers

,runner-'up *n, pl* **runners-up** *also* **runner-ups** a competitor other than the outright winner whose attainment still merits a prize

[1]**running** /'runing/ *n* **1** the state of competing, esp with a good chance of winning – in *in/out of the running* **2** management, operation ⟨*the ~ of a small business*⟩ ⟨*the ~ of a company car*⟩

[2]**running** *adj* **1** runny **2a** having stages that follow in rapid succession ⟨*a ~ battle*⟩ **b** made during the course of a process or activity ⟨*a ~ commentary*⟩ ⟨*~ repairs*⟩ **3** being part of a continuous length ⟨*cost of timber per ~ metre*⟩ **4** cursive, flowing **5** designed or used for races on foot ⟨*a ~ track*⟩

[3]**running** *adv* in succession ⟨*for 3 days ~*⟩

'running ,board *n* a footboard, esp at the side of a motor car

'running ,gear *n* the working parts of a machine (e g a locomotive)

,running 'head *n* a headline repeated on consecutive pages

running knot *n* a knot that slips along the rope or line round which it is tied

'running ,light *n* any of the lights carried by a moving ship, aeroplane, car, etc esp at night, that indicate size, position, and direction of movement

'running ,mate *n* a candidate standing for a subordinate place in a US election

'running ,shed *n, Br* a building for housing and repairing railway rolling stock

'running ,stitch *n* a small even sewing stitch run in and out of cloth (e g for gathering)

runny /'runi/ *adj* tending to run ⟨*a ~ nose*⟩

runoff /'run,of/ *n* a final decisive race, contest, or election

run off *vt* **1a** to compose rapidly or glibly **b** to produce with a printing press or copier ⟨run off *a few copies*⟩ **c** to decide (e g a race) by a runoff **2** to drain off (a liquid) **3** *NAm* to steal (e g cattle) by driving away ~ *vi* RUN AWAY 1 – **run off with** RUN AWAY WITH 1

,run-of-the-'mill *adj* average, commonplace

'run-,on *n* sthg (e g a dictionary entry) run on

run on *vi* **1** to keep going without interruption ⟨*the opera* ran on *for 4 hours*⟩ **2** to talk or narrate at length ~ *vt* **1** to continue (written material) without a break or a new paragraph **2** to place or add (e g an entry in a dictionary) at the end of a paragraphed item

run out *vi* **1a** to come to an end ⟨*time* ran out⟩ **b** to become exhausted or used up ⟨*the petrol* ran out⟩ **2** to finish a course or contest in the specified position ⟨ran out *the winner*⟩ **3** *of a horse* to evade a fence by turning aside ~ *vt* **1** to dismiss (a batsman who is outside his crease and attempting a run) by breaking the wicket with the ball **2** *chiefly NAm* to compel to leave ⟨run *him* out *of town*⟩ – **run out of** to use up the available supply of – **run out on** [3]DESERT

runover /'run,ohvə/ *n* typeset matter that exceeds the allotted space

run over *vi* **1** to overflow **2** to exceed a limit ⟨*meetings that* run over *into the next day*⟩ ~ *vt* **1** to glance over, repeat, or rehearse quickly **2** to injure or kill with a motor vehicle ⟨ran *the dog* over⟩

runt /runt/ *n* **1** an animal unusually small of its

kind; *esp* the smallest of a litter of pigs **2** a puny person [origin unknown] – **runty** *adj*

'run-,through *n* **1** a cursory reading, summary, or rehearsal **2** a sequence of actions performed for practice

run through *vt* **1** to pierce with a weapon (e g a sword) **2** to perform, esp for practice or instruction

'run-,up *n* **1** (the track or area provided for) an approach run to provide momentum (e g for a jump or throw) **2** *Br* a period that immediately precedes an action or event ⟨*the ~ to the last election*⟩

run up *vt* **1** to make (esp a garment) quickly **2a** to erect hastily **b** to hoist (a flag) **3** to accumulate or incur (debts) – **run up against** to encounter (e g a difficulty)

runway /'run,way/ *n* **1** a (beaten) path made by or for animals **2** an artificially surfaced strip of ground on an airfield for the landing and takeoff of aeroplanes

rupee /rooh'pee/ *n* (a note or coin representing) the basic money unit of various countries of the Indian subcontinent and the Indian Ocean (e g India, Pakistan, Seychelles, and Sri Lanka) ☞ NATIONALITY [Hindi *rūpaiyā*, fr Skt *rūpya* coined silver]

rupiah /rooh'pee·ə, rooh'pie·ə/ *n, pl* **rupiah, rupiahs** ☞ *Indonesia* at NATIONALITY [Hindi *rūpaiyā*]

¹rupture /'rupchə/ *n* **1** breach of peace or concord; *specif* open hostility between nations **2a** the tearing apart of a tissue, esp muscle **b** a hernia **3a** a breaking apart or bursting **b** the state of being broken apart or burst [ME *ruptur*, fr MF or L; MF *rupture*, fr L *ruptura* fracture, fr *ruptus*, pp of *rumpere* to break – more at BEREAVE]

²rupture *vt* **1a** to part by violence; break, burst **b** to create a breach of **2** to produce a rupture in ~ *vi* to have or undergo a rupture

rural /'rooərəl/ *adj* of the country, country people or life, or agriculture [ME, fr MF, fr L *ruralis*, fr *rur-*, *rus* open land – more at ROOM] – **rurally** *adv*

,rural 'dean *n* a priest supervising 1 district of a diocese

Ruritanian /,rooəri'taynyən, -ni·ən/ *adj* (characteristic) of an imaginary Central European country used as a setting for contemporary cloak-and-dagger court intrigues [*Ruritania*, fictional kingdom in the novel *The Prisoner of Zenda* by Anthony Hope (Sir Anthony Hope Hawkins) †1933 E writer]

ruse /roohz/ *n* a wily subterfuge [F, fr MF, fr *ruser* to dodge, deceive]

¹rush /rush/ *n* any of various often tufted marsh plants with cylindrical (hollow) leaves, used for the seats of chairs and for plaiting mats [ME, fr OE *risc*; akin to MHG *rusch* rush, L *restis* rope] – **rushy** *adj*

²rush *vi* to move forwards, progress, or act quickly or eagerly or without preparation ~ *vt* **1** to push or impel forwards with speed or violence **2** to perform or finish in a short time or at high speed ⟨~ed *his breakfast*⟩ **3** to urge to an excessive speed **4** to run against in attack, often with an element of surprise; charge [ME *russhen*, fr MF *ruser* to put to flight, repel, deceive, fr L *recusare* to refuse – more at RECUSANCY] – **rusher** *n*

³rush *n* **1a** a rapid and violent forward motion **b** a sudden onset of emotion ⟨*a quick ~ of sympathy*⟩ **2a** a surge of activity; *also* busy or hurried activity ⟨*the bank holiday ~*⟩ **b** a burst of productivity or speed **3** a great movement of people, esp in search of wealth **4** the unedited print of a film scene processed directly after shooting – usu pl **5** ²FLASH 9

⁴rush *adj* requiring or marked by special speed or urgency

rush candle *n* a rushlight

'rush ,hour *n* a period of the day when traffic is at a peak

rushlight /'rush,liet/ *n* a candle that consists of the pith of a rush dipped in grease

rusk /rusk/ *n* (a light dry biscuit similar to) a piece of sliced bread baked again until dry and crisp [modif of Sp & Pg *rosca* coil, twisted roll]

russet /'rusit/ *n* **1** a reddish to yellowish brown **2** any of various russet-coloured winter eating apples [ME, fr OF *rousset*, fr *rousset*, adj, russet, fr *rous* russet, fr L *russus* red; akin to L *ruber* red – more at RED] – **russet** *adj*

Russian /'rush(ə)n/ *n* **1** a native or inhabitant of Russia; *broadly* a native or inhabitant of the USSR **2** a Slavonic language of the Russians ☞ ALPHABET, LANGUAGE – **Russian** *adj*

,Russian rou'lette *n* an act of bravado consisting of spinning the cylinder of a revolver loaded with 1 cartridge, pointing the muzzle at one's own head, and pulling the trigger

,Russian 'salad *n* a salad of cold diced cooked vegetables (e g carrot and potato) in mayonnaise

Russki *also* **Russky** /'ruski/ *n or adj* (a) Russian – derog [Russ *Russkiĭ*, adj & n, fr *Rus'*, old name for Russia]

Russo- /rusoh-/ *comb form* **1** Russian nation, people, or culture ⟨Russo*phobia*⟩ **2** Russian; Russian and ⟨Russo-*Japanese*⟩ [*Russia* & *Russian*]

¹rust /rust/ *n* **1a** brittle reddish hydrated ferric oxide that forms as a coating on iron, esp iron chemically attacked by moist air **b** a comparable coating produced on another metal **c** sthg like rust **2** corrosive or injurious influence or effect **3** (a fungus causing) any of numerous destructive diseases of plants in which reddish brown pustular lesions form **4** a reddish brown to orange colour [ME, fr OE *rūst*; akin to OE *rēad* red – more at RED]

²rust *vi* **1** to form rust; become oxidized ⟨*iron* ~s⟩ **2** to degenerate, esp through lack of use or advancing age **3** to become reddish brown as if with rust **4** to be affected with a rust fungus ~ *vt* to cause (a metal) to form rust

¹rustic /'rustik/ *adj* **1** of or suitable for the country **2a** made of the rough limbs of trees ⟨*~ furniture*⟩ **b** finished by rusticating ⟨*a ~ joint in masonry*⟩ **3** characteristic of country people [ME *rustik*, fr MF *rustique*, fr L *rusticus*, fr *rus* open land – more at ROOM] – **rustically** *adv*, **rusticity** /ru'stisəti/ *n*

²rustic *n* an unsophisticated rural person

rusticate /'rusti,kayt/ *vt* **1** to suspend (a student) from college or university **2** to bevel or cut a groove, channel etc in (e g the edges of stone blocks) to make the joints conspicuous ⟨*a* ~d *stone wall*⟩ ☞ ARCHITECTURE **3** to impart a rustic character to – **rusticator** *n*, **rustication** /-'kaysh(ə)n/ *n*

¹rustle /'rusl/ *vb* **rustling** /'rusling, 'rusl·ing/ *vi* **1a** to make or cause a rustle **b** to move with a rustling sound **2** *chiefly NAm* to steal cattle or horses ~ *vt*, *chiefly NAm* to steal (e g cattle) [ME *rustelen*, of imit origin] – rustler /'ruslə/ *n*

[2]rustle *n* a quick succession or confusion of faint sounds

rustproof /'rust,proof/ *adj* able to resist rust

rusty /'rusti/ *adj* **1** affected (as if) by rust; *esp* stiff (as if) with rust ⟨*the creaking of ~ hinges*⟩ **2** inept and slow through lack of practice or advanced age **3a** of the colour rust **b** dulled in colour by age and use; shabby ⟨*a ~ old suit of clothes*⟩ – **rustily** *adv*, **rustiness** *n*

[1]rut /rut/ *n* **1** an annually recurrent state of readiness to copulate, in the male deer or other mammal; *also* oestrus, heat **2** the period during which rut normally occurs – often + *the* [ME *rutte*, fr MF *rut* roar, fr LL *rugitus*, fr L *rugitus*, pp of *rugire* to roar; akin to OE *rēoc* wild, MIr *rucht* roar]

[2]rut *n* **1** a track worn by habitual passage, esp of wheels on soft or uneven ground **2** an established practice; *esp* a tedious routine ⟨*get into a ~*⟩ [perh modif of MF *route* way, route]

[3]rut *vt* **-tt-** to make a rut in

rutabaga /,roohtə'baygə, ,roo-, -'begə/ *n, NAm* SWEDE 2 [Sw dial. *rotabagge*, fr *rot* root + *bagge* bag]

Ruth /roohth/ *n* (a short narrative book of the Old Testament telling of) a Moabite woman who left her own country to return with her mother-in-law, Naomi, to Bethlehem, where she married Boaz and became the ancestress of David [Heb *Rūth*]

ruthenium /rooh'theenyəm, -ni·əm/ *n* a polyvalent rare metallic element of the platinum group used in hardening platinum alloys ☞ PERIODIC TABLE [NL, fr ML *Ruthenia* Russia] - **ruthenic** /-nik/ *adj*, **ruthenious** *adj*

ruthless /'roohthlis/ *adj* showing no pity or compassion [*ruth* (compassion), fr ME *ruthe*, fr *ruen* to rue] – **ruthlessly** *adv*, **ruthlessness** *n*

rutile /'roohtil, -,tiel/ *n* a usu reddish brown lustrous mineral consisting of titanium dioxide [G *rutil*, fr L *rutilus* reddish; akin to L *ruber* red – more at RED]

ruttish /'rutish/ *adj* lustful ['*rut* + *-ish*] – **ruttishly** *adv*, **ruttishness** *n*

-ry /-ri/ – see -ERY ⟨*citizenry*⟩ ⟨*wizardry*⟩ [ME *-rie*, fr OF, short for *-erie* -ery]

rye /rie/ *n* (the seeds, from which a wholemeal flour is made, of) a hardy grass widely grown for grain [ME, fr OE *ryge*; akin to OHG *rocko* rye, Lith *rugys*]

ryegrass /'rie,grahs/ *n* any of several grasses used esp for pasture [alter. of obs *raygrass*, fr obs *ray* (darnel)]

,rye 'whisky *n* a whisky distilled from rye or from rye and malt

S

s /es/ *n, pl* **s's, ss** /'esiz/ *often cap* (a graphic representation of or device for reproducing) the 19th letter of the English alphabet

[1]**-s** /-s *after voiceless consonant sounds other than* s, sh, ch; z *after vowel sounds & voiced consonant sounds other than* z, zh, j; iz *after* s, sh, ch, z, zh, j/ *suffix* (→ *n pl*) **1a** – used to form the plural of most nouns that do not end in *s, z, sh, ch,* or postconsonantal *y* ⟨*cat*s⟩ ⟨*head*s⟩ ⟨*book*s⟩ ⟨*boy*s⟩ ⟨*belief*s⟩; compare [1]-ES 1 **b** – used with or without a preceding apostrophe to form the plural of abbreviations, numbers, letters, and symbols used as nouns ⟨*MC*s⟩ ⟨*4*s⟩ ⟨*the 1940*'s⟩ ⟨*£*s⟩ ⟨*B*'s⟩; compare [1]-ES 1 **2** *chiefly NAm* – used to form adverbs denoting usual or repeated action or state ⟨*always at home Sunday*s⟩ ⟨*morning*s *he stops by the newsstand*⟩ [(1) ME *-es, -s,* fr OE *-as,* nom & acc pl ending of some masc nouns; akin to OS *-os*; (2) ME *-es, -s,* pl ending of nouns, fr *-es,* gen sing. ending of nouns (functioning adverbially), fr OE *-es*]

[2]**-s** *suffix* (→ *vb*) – used to form the third person singular present of most verbs that do not end in *s, z, sh, ch,* or postconsonantal *y* ⟨*fall*s⟩ ⟨*take*s⟩ ⟨*play*s⟩; compare [2]-ES [ME (Northern & N Midland) *-es,* fr OE (Northumbrian) *-es, -as,* prob fr OE *-es, -as,* 2 sing. pres indic ending]

[1]**'s** /*like* - oXs/ *vb* **1** is ⟨*she*'s *here*⟩ **2** has ⟨*he*'s *seen them*⟩ **3** does – in questions ⟨*what*'s *he want?*⟩

[2]**'s** *pron* us – + *let* ⟨*let*'s⟩

-'s *suffix* (→ *n* or *pron*) – used to form the possessive of singular nouns ⟨*boy*'s⟩, of plural nouns not ending in *s* ⟨*children*'s⟩, of some pronouns ⟨*anyone*'s⟩, and of word groups functioning as nouns ⟨*the man in the corner*'s *hat*⟩ or pronouns ⟨*someone else*'s⟩ [ME *-es, -s,* gen sing. ending, fr OE *-es*; akin to OHG *-es,* gen sing. ending, Gk *-oio, -ou,* Skt *-asya*]

sabadilla /,sabə'dilə/ *n* (the seeds, used as a source of the drug veratrine, of) a Mexican plant of the lily family [Sp *cebadilla*]

Sabaoth /sa'bayoth/ *n pl* armed hosts – used in the biblical title *Lord of Sabaoth* for God [LL, fr Gk *Sabaōth,* fr Heb *ṣĕbāōth,* pl of *ṣābā* army]

sabbat /'sabət, -bat/ *n, often cap* a midnight assembly of witches held to renew allegiance to the devil [F, lit., sabbath, fr L *sabbatum*]

Sabbatarian /sabə'teəri·ən/ *n* **1** a person who observes the Sabbath on Saturday in strict conformity with the 4th commandment **2** an adherent of Sabbatarianism [L *sabbatarius,* fr *sabbatum* sabbath] – **Sabbatarian** *adj*

Sabbatarianism /sabə'teəri·ə,niz(ə)m/ *n* the avoidance of work and suppression of enjoyment on the Sabbath

sabbath /'sabəth/ *n* **1** *often cap* the 7th day of the week observed from Friday evening to Saturday evening as a day of rest and worship by Jews **2** *often cap* Sunday observed among Christians as a day of rest and worship **3** a sabbat [ME *sabat,* fr OF & OE, fr L *sabbatum,* fr Gk *sabbaton,* fr Heb *shabbāth,* lit., rest]

[1]**sabbatical** /sə'batikl/, **sabbatic** *adj* **1** of the sabbath ⟨~ *laws*⟩ **2** of or being a sabbatical [LL *sabbaticus,* fr Gk *sabbatikos,* fr *sabbaton*]

[2]**sabbatical** *n* a leave, often with pay, granted usu every 7th year (e g to a university teacher)

sabbatical year *n, often cap S* a year of rest for the land observed every 7th year in ancient Judaea

Sabine /'sabien/ *n* a member of an ancient people of the Apennines NE of Latium [ME *Sabin,* fr L *Sabinus*] – **Sabine** *adj*

[1]**sable** /'saybl/ *n, pl* **sables,** (*1*) **sables,** *esp collectively* **sable 1** (the valuable dark brown fur of) a N Asian and European flesh-eating mammal related to the martens **2** BLACK 2 – poetic or used technically in heraldry [ME, sable or its fur, the heraldic colour black, black, fr MF, sable or its fur, the heraldic colour black, fr MLG *sabel* sable or its fur, fr MHG *zobel,* of Slav origin; akin to Russ *sobol'* sable or its fur]

[2]**sable** *adj* of the colour sable

sabot /'saboh/ *n* **1** a wooden shoe worn in various European countries **2** a thrust-transmitting carrier that positions a smaller projectile in a larger gun barrel or launching tube and that prevents the escape of gas ahead of the missile so as to increase the muzzle velocity of the projectile [F]

[1]**sabotage** /'sabə,tahzh/ *n* **1** destructive or obstructive action carried on by a civilian or enemy agent, intended to hinder military activity **2** deliberate subversion (e g of a plan or project) [F, fr *saboter* to clatter with sabots, botch, sabotage, fr *sabot*]

[2]**sabotage** *vt* to practise sabotage on

saboteur /,sabə'tuh/ *n* one who commits sabotage [F, fr *saboter*]

sabra /'sabrə/ *n, often cap* a native-born Israeli [NHeb *ṣabrāh*]

[1]**sabre,** *NAm chiefly* **saber** /'saybə/ *n* **1** a cavalry sword with a curved blade, thick back, and guard **2** a light fencing or duelling sword having an arched guard that covers the back of the hand and a tapering flexible blade with a full cutting edge along one side – compare ÉPÉE, FOIL [F *sabre,* modif of G dial. *sabel,* fr MHG, of Slav origin; akin to Russ *sablya* sabre]

[2]**sabre,** *NAm chiefly* **saber** *vt* to strike or kill with a sabre

'**sabre ,rattling** *n* blustering display of military power

sabretache /'sabə,tash, 'say-/ *n* a flat leather case worn suspended on the left from a waist belt by men of some cavalry regiments [F, fr G *säbeltasche,* fr *säbel* sabre + *tasche* pocket]

,**sabre-toothed 'tiger** *n* an extinct big cat with long curved upper canines

sabreur /sa'bruh/ *n* one who carries or fences with a sabre [F, fr *sabrer* to strike with a sabre, fr *sabre*]

sac /sak/ *n* a (fluid-filled) pouch within an animal or plant [F, lit., bag, fr L *saccus* – more at [1]SACK] – **saclike** *adj*

saccade /sa'kahd/ *n* a small rapid jerky movement of the eye, esp as it jumps from fixation on one point to another (e g in reading) [F, twitch, jerk, fr MF, fr *saquer* to pull, draw] – **saccadic** /sa'kahdik/ *adj*

saccate /'sakayt, -kət/ *adj* having the form of a sac or pouch ⟨*a ~ corolla*⟩ [NL *saccatus*, fr L *saccus*]

sacchar-, sacchari-, saccharo- *comb form* sugar ⟨sacchar*ide*⟩ [L *saccharum*, fr Gk *sakcharon*, fr Pali *sakkharā*, fr Skt *śarkarā* gravel, sugar]

saccharide /'sakəried/ *n* SUGAR 1b

saccharin /'sak(ə)rin/ *n* a compound containing no calories that is several hundred times sweeter than cane sugar and is used as a sugar substitute (e g in low-calorie diets) [ISV]

saccharine /'sak(ə)rin, -reen/ *adj* **1** of, like, or containing sugar ⟨*~ taste*⟩ **2** excessively sweet; mawkish ⟨*~ sentiment*⟩ [L *saccharum*] – **saccharinity** /-'rinəti/ *n*

saccharometer /,sakə'romitə/ *n* a device for measuring the amount of sugar in a solution

saccharose /'sakərohs, -rohz/ *n* sucrose

saccular /'sakyoolə/ *adj* resembling a sac

sacculate /'sakyoolət, -,layt/, **sacculated** /-,laytid/ *adj* having or formed of a series of saclike expansions – **sacculation** /-'laysh(ə)n/ *n*

saccule /'sakyoohl/ *n* a little sac; *specif* the smaller chamber of the membranous labyrinth of the ear ☞ NERVE [NL *sacculus*, fr L, dim. of *saccus* bag – more at [1]SACK]

sacculus /'sakyooləs/ *n, pl* **sacculi** /-li, -lie/ a saccule [NL]

sacerdotal /,sasə'dohtl/ *adj* of priests or a priesthood [ME, fr MF, fr L *sacerdotalis*, fr *sacerdot-*, *sacerdos* priest, fr *sacer* sacred + *-dot-*, *-dos* (akin to *facere* to make) – more at SACRED, DO] – **sacerdotally** *adv*

,sacer'dotal,ism /-,iz(ə)m/ *n* religious belief emphasizing the role of priests as essential mediators between God and human beings – **sacerdotalist** *n*

sachem /'saych(ə)m, 'sach(ə)m/ *n* a N American Indian chief [Narraganset & Pequot *sachima*] – **sachemic** /sa'chemik/ *adj*

sachet /'sashay/ *n* **1** a small usu plastic bag or packet; *esp* one holding just enough of sthg (e g shampoo or sugar) for use at 1 time **2** a small bag containing a perfumed powder used to scent clothes and linens [F, fr OF, dim. of *sac* bag – more at SAC] – **sacheted** /'sashayd/ *adj*

[1]**sack** /sak/ *n* **1** a usu rectangular large bag (e g of paper or canvas) **2** the amount contained in a sack **3** a garment without shaping: e g **a** a loosely fitting dress **b** a loose coat or jacket; *esp* one worn by men in the 19th c **4** dismissal from employment – usu + *get* or *give* + *the*; infml [ME *sak* bag, sackcloth, fr OE *sacc*; akin to OHG *sac* bag; both fr a prehistoric Gmc word borrowed fr L *saccus* bag & LL *saccus* sackcloth, both fr Gk *sakkos* bag, sackcloth, of Sem origin; akin to Heb *śaq* bag, sackcloth] – **sackful** *n*

[2]**sack** *vt* **1** to place in a sack **2** to dismiss from a job – infml – **sacker** *n*

[3]**sack** *n* any of various dry white wines formerly imported to England from S Europe [modif of MF *sec* dry, fr L *siccus*; akin to OHG *sīhan* to filter, Gk *hikmas* moisture]

[4]**sack** *n* the plundering of a place captured in war [MF *sac*, fr OIt *sacco*, lit., bag, fr L *saccus*]

[5]**sack** *vt* **1** to plunder (e g a town) after capture **2** to strip (a place) of valuables – **sacker** *n*

sackbut /'sak,but/ *n* the renaissance trombone [MF *saqueboute*, lit., hooked lance, fr OF, fr *saquer* to pull + *bouter, boter* to push – more at BUTT]

sackcloth /'sak,kloth/ *n* **1** sacking **2** a garment of sackcloth worn as a sign of mourning or penitence [[1]*sack*]

sacking /'saking/ *n* material for sacks; *esp* a coarse fabric (e g hessian)

'sack ,race *n* a jumping race in which each contestant has his/her legs enclosed in a sack

[1]**sacr-, sacro-** *comb form* sacred; holy ⟨sacro*sanct*⟩ [ME *sacr-*, fr MF & L; MF, fr L, fr *sacr-*, *sacer* – more at SACRED]

[2]**sacr-, sacro-** *comb form* **1** sacrum ⟨sacr*al*⟩ **2** sacral and ⟨sacro*iliac*⟩ [NL, fr *sacrum*, fr L, neut of *sacr-*, *sacer* sacred]

[1]**sacral** /'saykrəl/ *adj* of or lying near the sacrum

[2]**sacral** *adj* holy, sacred [L *sacr-*, *sacer*]

sacrament /'sakrəmənt/ *n* **1** a formal religious act (e g baptism) functioning as a sign or symbol of a spiritual reality **2** *cap* the bread and wine used at Communion; *specif* the consecrated Host [ME *sacrement, sacrament*, fr OF & LL; OF, fr LL *sacramentum*, fr L, oath of allegiance, obligation, fr *sacrare* to consecrate]

sacramental /,sakrə'mentl/ *adj* (having the character) of a sacrament – **sacramentally** *adv*

,sacra'mental,ism /-,iz(ə)m/ *n* belief in or use of sacramental rites, acts, or objects; *specif* belief that the sacraments are inherently efficacious and necessary for salvation

sacred /'saykrid/ *adj* **1a** dedicated or set apart for the service or worship of a god or gods **b** dedicated as a memorial ⟨*~ to his memory*⟩ **2a** worthy of religious veneration **b** commanding reverence and respect **3** of religion; not secular or profane [ME, fr pp of *sacren* to consecrate, fr OF *sacrer*, fr L *sacrare*, fr *sacr-*, *sacer* holy, cursed; akin to L *sancire* to make sacred, Hitt *saklais* rite] – **sacredly** *adv*, **sacredness** *n*

,sacred ba'boon *n* HAMADRYAD 2b [fr its veneration by the ancient Egyptians]

,sacred 'cow *n* sby or sthg granted unreasonable immunity from criticism [fr the veneration of the cow by the Hindus]

[1]**sacrifice** /'sakrifies/ *n* **1** an act of offering to a deity; *esp* the killing of a victim on an altar **2** sthg offered in sacrifice **3a** destruction or surrender of one thing for the sake of another of greater worth or importance **b** sthg given up or lost ⟨*the ~s made by parents*⟩ [ME, fr OF, fr L *sacrificium*, fr *sacr-*, *sacer* + *facere* to make – more at DO]

[2]**sacrifice** *vt* **1** to offer as a sacrifice **2** to give up or lose for the sake of an ideal or end *~ vi* to offer up or perform rites of a sacrifice – **sacrificer** *n*

sacrificial /,sakri'fish(ə)l/ *adj* of or involving sacrifice – **sacrificially** *adv*

sacrilege /'sakrilij/ *n* **1** a technical violation of what is sacred **2** gross irreverence toward sby or sthg sacred [ME, fr OF, fr L *sacrilegium*, fr *sacrilegus* one who steals sacred things, fr *sacr-*, *sacer* + *legere* to gather, steal – more at LEGEND] – **sacrilegious** /-ˈlijəs/ *adj*, **sacrilegiously** *adv*, **sacrilegiousness** *n*

sacristan /ˈsakristən/ *n* a person in charge of the sacristy and ceremonial equipment; *also* a sexton [ME, fr ML *sacristanus*, fr *sacrista*]

sacristy /ˈsakristi/ *n* a room in a church where sacred vessels and vestments are kept and where the clergy put on their vestments [ML *sacristia*, fr *sacrista* sacristan, fr L *sacr-*, *sacer*]

sacro- – see SACR-

sacrosanct /ˈsakrəsangkt/ *adj* accorded the highest reverence and respect; *also* regarded with unwarranted reverence [L *sacrosanctus*, prob fr *sacro sanctus* hallowed by a sacred rite] – **sacrosanctity** /-ˈsangktəti/ *n*

sacrum /ˈsaykrəm/ *n*, *pl* **sacra** /ˈsaykrə/ the part of the vertebral column that is directly connected with or forms part of the pelvis and in humans consists of 5 united vertebrae ☞ ANATOMY [NL, fr LL *os sacrum* last bone of the spine, lit., holy bone]

sad /sad/ *adj* **-dd-** **1a** affected with or expressing unhappiness **b(1)** causing or associated with unhappiness **(2)** deplorable, regrettable ⟨*a ~ decline in standards*⟩ **2** of a dull sombre colour **3** *of baked goods* [1]HEAVY 9b [ME, fr OE *sæd* sated; akin to OHG *sat* sated, L *satis* enough] – **sadly** *adv*, **sadness** *n*

sadden /ˈsadn/ *vb* to make or become sad

saddhu /ˈsah,dooh/ *n* a sadhu

[1]**saddle** /ˈsadl/ *n* **1a(1)** a usu padded and leather-covered seat secured to the back of a horse, donkey, etc for the rider to sit on **(2)** a part of a harness for a draught animal (e g a horse pulling a carriage) comparable to a saddle that is used to keep in place the strap that passes under the animal's tail **b** a seat in certain types of vehicles (e g a bicycle or agricultural tractor) **2** sthg like a saddle in shape, position, or function **3** a ridge connecting 2 peaks **4a** a large cut of meat from a sheep, hare, rabbit, deer, etc consisting of both sides of the unsplit back including both loins ☞ MEAT **b** the rear part of a male fowl's back extending to the tail **5** a saddle-shaped marking on the back of an animal [ME *sadel*, fr OE *sadol*; akin to OHG *satul* saddle] – **saddleless** *adj* – **in the saddle** in control

[2]**saddle** *vt* **saddling** /ˈsadl·ing/ **1** to put a saddle on **2** to encumber ⟨*got ~d with the paperwork*⟩

ˈ**saddle,back** /-,bak/ *n* any of several animals with saddle-shaped markings on the back; *esp* a medium-sized black pig with a white band crossing the back

ˈ**saddle,bag** /-,bag/ *n* a pouch or bag on the back of a horse behind the saddle, or either of a pair laid across behind the saddle or hanging over the rear wheel of a bicycle or motorcycle

ˈ**saddle ,blanket** *n* a saddlecloth

ˈ**saddle,bow** /-,boh/ *n* the arch in or the pieces forming the front of a saddle

ˈ**saddle,cloth** /-,kloth/ *n* a piece of cloth, leather, etc placed under a horse's saddle to prevent rubbing

ˈ**saddle ,horse** /-,haws/ *n* a horse suited or trained for riding

saddler /ˈsadlə/ *n* one who makes, repairs, or sells furnishings (e g saddles) for horses

saddlery /ˈsadləri/ *n* **1** the trade, articles of trade, or shop of a saddler **2** a set of the equipment used for sitting on and controlling a riding horse

ˈ**saddle ,soap** *n* a mild oily soap used for cleansing and conditioning leather

ˈ**saddle-,stitched** *adj* fastened by staples through the fold ⟨*a ~ magazine*⟩

ˈ**saddle,tree** /-,tree/ *n* the frame of a saddle

sadhu, saddhu /ˈsah,dooh/ *n* an Indian ascetic usu mendicant holy man [Skt *sādhu*]

sadiron /ˈsad,ie·ən/ *n* a flatiron that is pointed at both ends [*sad* (compact, heavy) + *iron*]

sadism /ˈsaydiz(ə)m/ *n* **1** a sexual perversion in which pleasure is obtained by inflicting physical or mental pain on others – compare MASOCHISM **2** delight in inflicting pain [ISV, fr Marquis (really Count) de *Sade* †1814 F writer] – **sadist** *adj or n*, **sadistic** /səˈdistik/ *adj*, **sadistically** *adv*

sadomasochism /,saydohˈmasəkiz(ə)m/ *n* sadism and masochism occurring together in the same person [ISV *sadism* + *-o-* + *masochism*] – **sadomasochist** *n*, **sadomasochistic** /-,masəˈkistik/ *adj*

sad sack *n*, *NAm* an inept person – infml

sae /,es,ayˈee/ *n* a stamped addressed envelope

[1]**safari** /səˈfahri/ *n* (the caravan and equipment of) a hunting or scientific expedition, esp in E Africa [Ar *safarīy* of a trip] – **safari** *vi*

[2]**safari** *adj* made of lightweight material, esp cotton, and typically having 2 breast pockets and a belt ☞ GARMENT

saˈ**fari ,park** *n* a park stocked with usu big game animals (e g lions) so that visitors can observe them in natural-appearing surroundings

[1]**safe** /sayf/ *adj* **1** freed from harm or risk **2** secure from threat of danger, harm, or loss **3** affording safety from danger **4a** not threatening or entailing danger ⟨*is your dog ~?*⟩ **b** unlikely to cause controversy ⟨*keeping to ~ subjects*⟩ **5a** not liable to take risks **b** trustworthy, reliable **6** being a constituency where the MP was elected with a large majority – compare MARGINAL [ME *sauf*, fr OF, fr L *salvus* safe, healthy; akin to L *salus* health, safety, *salubris* healthful, *solidus* solid, Gk *holos* whole, safe] – **safe** *adv*, **safely** *adv*, **safeness** *n*

[2]**safe** *n* **1** a room or receptacle for the safe storage of valuables **2** a receptacle, esp a cupboard, for the temporary storage of fresh and cooked foods that typically has at least 1 side of wire mesh to allow ventilation while preventing flies from entering

ˈ**safe,blower** /-,bloh·ə/ *n* a safecracker who uses explosives – **safeblowing** *n*

ˈ**safe,breaker** /-,braykə/ *n* a safecracker – **safebreaking** *n*

,**safe-ˈconduct** *n* (a document authorizing) protection given to a person passing through a military zone or occupied area [ME *sauf conduit*, fr OF, safe conduct]

ˈ**safe,cracker** /-,krakə/ *n* one who breaks open safes to steal – **safecracking** *n*

[1]ˈ**safe,guard** /-,gahd/ *n* **1** a pass, safe-conduct **2** a precautionary measure or stipulation [ME *saufgarde*, fr MF *saufegarde*, fr OF, fr *sauve* safe + *garde* guard]

[2]**safeguard** *vt* **1** to provide a safeguard for **2** to make safe; protect

,**safeˈkeeping** /-ˈkeeping/ *n* keeping safe or being kept safe

ˈ**safe,light** /-,liet/ *n* a darkroom lamp with a filter to screen out rays that are harmful to photographic film or paper

'safe ˌperiod *n* the time during or near the menstrual period when conception is least likely to occur

safety /'sayfti/ *n* **1** the condition of being safe from causing or suffering hurt, injury, or loss **2** SAFETY CATCH **3** a billiard shot made with no attempt to score or so as to leave the balls in an unfavourable position for the opponent [ME *saufte*, fr MF *sauveté*, fr OF, fr *sauve*, fem of *sauf* safe]

'safety ˌbelt *n* a belt fastening a person to an object to prevent falling or injury

'safety ˌcatch *n* a device (e g on a gun or machine) designed to prevent accidental use

'safety ˌcurtain *n* a fireproof curtain which can isolate the stage from the auditorium in case of fire

'safety ˌglass *n* glass strengthened by tempering so that when broken, it shatters into relatively safe rounded granules

'safety ˌlamp *n* a miner's lamp constructed to avoid ignition of inflammable gas, usu by enclosing the flame in wire gauze

'safety ˌmatch *n* a match capable of being ignited only on a specially prepared surface

'safety ˌpin *n* a pin in the form of a clasp with a guard covering its point when fastened

'safety ˌrazor *n* a razor with a guard for the blade

'safety ˌvalve *n* **1** an automatic escape or relief valve (e g for a steam boiler) **2** an outlet for pent-up energy or emotion ⟨*a* ~ *for life's frustrations*⟩

safflower /'saˌflowə/ *n* (a red dye prepared from the large orange or red flower heads of) an Old World composite plant [MF *saffleur*, fr OIt *saffiore*, fr Ar *aṣfar* a yellow plant]

saffron /'safron, 'safrən/ *n* **1** (the deep orange aromatic pungent dried stigmas, used to colour and flavour foods, of) a purple-flowered crocus **2** orange-yellow [ME, fr OF *safran*, fr ML *safranum*, fr Ar *za'farān*]

safranine /'safrənin, -neen/, **safranin** /-nin/ *n* **1** a usu red synthetic dye **2** any of various mixtures of safranine salts used in dyeing and for staining specimens for microscopy [ISV, fr F or G *safran* saffron]

[1]**sag** /sag/ *vi* **-gg- 1** to droop, sink, or settle (as if) from weight, pressure, or loss of tautness **2** to lose firmness or vigour ⟨*spirits* ~ging *from overwork*⟩ **3** to fail to stimulate or retain interest ⟨~ged *a bit in the last act*⟩ [ME *saggen*, prob of Scand origin; akin to Sw *sacka* to sag]

[2]**sag** *n* **1** a sagging part ⟨*the* ~ *in a rope*⟩ **2** an instance or amount of sagging ⟨~ *is inevitable in a heavy unsupported span*⟩

saga /'sahgə/ *n* **1** (a modern heroic narrative resembling) a medieval Icelandic narrative dealing with historic or legendary figures and events **2** a long detailed account **3** a roman-fleuve [ON – more at [4]SAW]

sagacious /sə'gayshəs/ *adj* **1** of keen and farsighted judgment ⟨~ *judge of character*⟩ **2** prompted by or indicating acute discernment ⟨~ *purchase of stock*⟩ [L *sagac-*, *sagax*; akin to L *sagire* to perceive keenly – more at SEEK] – **sagaciously** *adv*, **sagaciousness, sagacity** /sə'gasəti/ *n*

[1]**sage** /sayj/ *adj* **1** wise on account of reflection and experience **2** proceeding from or indicating wisdom and sound judgment ⟨~ *counsel*⟩ [ME, fr OF, fr (assumed) VL *sapius*, fr L *sapere* to taste, have good taste, be wise; akin to OE *sefa* mind, Oscan *sipus* knowing] – **sagely** *adv*, **sageness** *n*

[2]**sage** *n* **1** sby (e g a great philosopher) renowned for wise teachings **2** a venerable man of sound judgment

[3]**sage** *n* **1** a plant of the mint family whose greyish green aromatic leaves are used esp in flavouring meat **2** sagebrush [ME, fr MF *sauge*, fr L *salvia*, fr *salvus* healthy – more at SAFE; fr its use as a medicinal herb]

'sageˌbrush /-ˌbrush/ *n* any of several composite undershrubs that cover large areas of plains in the W USA

sage cheese *n* a cheese (e g Derby) flecked with green and flavoured with sage

ˌsage 'green *adj or n* greyish green

saggar /'sagə/ *n* a box made of fireclay in which delicate ceramic pieces are fired [prob alter. of *safeguard*]

sagittal /'sajitl/ *adj* **1** of the join between the parietal bones that stretches from the front to the back of the top of the skull **2** of, situated in, or being (a plane parallel to) the middle plane or midline of the body [L *sagitta* arrow] – **sagittally** *adv*

Sagittarius /ˌsaji'teəri·əs/ *n* (sby born under) the 9th sign of the zodiac in astrology, pictured as a centaur shooting an arrow SYMBOL [L, lit., archer, fr *sagitta*] – **Sagittarian** /-ri·ən/ *adj or n*

sagittate /'sajiˌtayt/ *adj*, *of a plant or animal part, esp a leaf* shaped like an arrowhead PLANT [L *sagitta*]

sago /'saygoh/ *n*, *pl* **sagos** a dry powdered starch prepared from the pith of a sago palm and used esp as a food (e g in a milk pudding) [Malay *sagu* sago palm]

'sago ˌpalm *n* any of various tall Indian and Malaysian palms that yield sago

saguaro /sə'gwahroh/ *n*, *pl* **saguaros** a treelike cactus of N American and Mexican deserts with a tall (sparsely branched) trunk, white flowers, and an edible fruit [MexSp]

sahib /'sah·(h)ib/ *n* sir, master – used, esp among Hindus and Muslims in colonial India, when addressing or speaking of a European of some social or official status [Hindi *sāhib*, fr Ar]

said /sed/ *adj* aforementioned [pp of *say*]

saiga /'seigə/ *n* an antelope of the Asian plains that has a swollen snout [Russ *saĭga*]

[1]**sail** /sayl/ *n*, *pl* **sails,** (*1b*) **sail** *also* **sails 1a** an expanse of fabric which is spread to catch or deflect the wind as a means of propelling a ship, sand yacht, etc **b** (a ship equipped with) sails **2** sthg like a sail in function or form ⟨*the* ~s *of a windmill*⟩ **3** a voyage by ship ⟨*a 5-day* ~ *from the nearest port*⟩ [ME, fr OE *segl*; akin to OHG *segal* sail, L *secare* to cut – more at [2]SAW] – **sailed** *adj* – **under sail** in motion with sails set

[2]**sail** *vi* **1a** to travel in a boat or ship **b** to make journeys in or manage a sailing boat for pleasure **2a** to travel on water, esp by the action of wind on sails **b** to move without visible effort or in a stately manner ⟨~ed *gracefully into the room* – L C Douglas⟩ **3** to begin a journey by water ⟨~ *with the tide*⟩ ~ *vt* **1** to travel over (a body of water) in a ship ⟨~ *the 7 seas*⟩ **2** to direct or manage the operation of (a ship or boat) – **sailable** *adj* – **sail into** to attack vigorously or sharply ⟨sailed into *his dinner*⟩ ⟨sailed into *me for being late*⟩ – **sail close to the wind 1** to sail as

nearly as possible against the main force of the wind 2 to be near to dishonesty or improper behaviour

'sail,board /-,bawd/ *n* a flat buoyant board that is equipped with a sail, centreboard, and rudder and is used in the sport of wind-surfing

'sail,boat /-,boht/ *n, chiefly NAm* SAILING BOAT

'sail,cloth /-,kloth/ *n* a heavy canvas used for sails, tents, or upholstery; *also* a lightweight canvas used for clothing

'sail,fish /-,fish/ any of a genus of large marine fishes related to the swordfish but having a very large dorsal fin

'sailing ,boat /'sayling/ *n* a boat fitted with sails for propulsion

'sailing ,ship *n* a ship fitted with sails for propulsion

sailor /'saylə/ *n* **1a** a seaman, mariner **b** a member of a ship's crew other than an officer **2** a traveller by water; *esp* one considered with reference to any tendency to seasickness ⟨*a bad* ~⟩ [alter. of *sailer*, fr [2]*sail* + [2]*-er*]

'sailor ,collar *n* a broad collar that has a square flap across the back and tapers to a V in the front

sailplane /'sayl,playn/ *n* a glider designed to rise in an upward air current – **sailplane** *vi*, **sailplaner** *n*

sainfoin /'san,foyn/ *n* a Eurasian red or pink-flowered leguminous plant widely grown for forage [F, fr MF, fr *sain* healthy (fr L *sanus*) + *foin* hay, fr L *fenum*]

saint /saynt; *before a name usu* s(ə)nt/ *n* **1** a person officially recognized through canonization as being outstandingly holy and so worthy of veneration **2a** any of the spirits of the departed in heaven **b** ANGEL 1 ⟨Saint *Michael the Archangel*⟩ **3** any (of various Christian groups regarding themselves as) of God's chosen people **4** a person of outstanding piety or virtue [ME, fr MF, fr LL *sanctus*, fr L, sacred, fr pp of *sancire* to make sacred – more at SACRED] – **sainthood** /-,hood/ *n*, **saintlike** *adj*, **saintly** *adj*, **saintliness** *n*

Saint ,Agnes' 'Eve /s(ə)nt 'agnis(iz)/ *n* the night of January 20, when a girl is traditionally held to see her future husband in a dream [*St Agnes* †304 virgin martyr]

Saint ,Andrew's 'cross /'androohz/ *n* a cross consisting of 2 intersecting diagonal bars ☞ SYMBOL [*St Andrew* † *ab* AD 60, 1 of the 12 apostles]

Saint 'Andrew's ,Day *n* November 30 observed in honour of St Andrew, the patron saint of Scotland

Saint ,Anthony's 'fire /'antəniz; *also* 'anth-/ *n* any of several inflammations or gangrenous conditions (e g erysipelas or ergotism) of the skin [*St Anthony* †356 Egyptian monk]

Saint Bernard /'buhnəd/ *n* (any of) a Swiss alpine breed of tall powerful working dogs used, esp formerly, in aiding lost travellers [the hospice of Grand *St Bernard*, Switzerland, where such dogs were first bred]

Saint 'David's ,Day /'dayvidz/ *n* March 1 observed in honour of St David, the patron saint of Wales [*St David* †601 W bishop]

Saint ,Elmo's 'fire /'elmohz/ *n* a flame-like electrical discharge sometimes seen in stormy weather at prominent points (e g on an aeroplane, ship, or building) [*St Elmo* (*Erasmus*) †303 It bishop & patron saint of sailors]

Saint 'George's ,Day /'jawjiz/ *n* April 23 observed in honour of St George, the patron saint of England [*St George* † *ab* 303 Christian martyr]

Saint-,John's-'wort /jonz/ *n* any of a genus of plants and shrubs with often showy yellow flowers [*St John* the Baptist *fl ab* 27 prophet]

Saint 'Patrick's ,Day /'patriks/ *n* March 17 observed in honour of St Patrick, the patron saint of Ireland [*St Patrick* † *ab* 461 Christian missionary]

'saint's ,day /'saynts/ *n* a day in a church calendar on which a saint is commemorated

Saint 'Swithin's ,Day /'swidh(ə)nz/ July 15 that traditionally indicates 40 days of rain if rainy or 40 dry days if dry [*St Swithin* †862 E bishop]

Saint 'Valentine's ,Day /'valəntienz/ *n* February 14 observed in honour of St Valentine and as a time for sending valentines [*St Valentine* † *ab* 270 It priest]

Saint ,Vitus's 'dance /'vietəs(iz)/ *n* chorea [*St Vitus*, 3rd-c Christian child martyr]

saith /seth, sayth/ *archaic pres 3 sing of* SAY

saithe /sayth/ *n, pl* **saithe** a coley [of Scand origin; akin to ON *seithr* coalfish]

[1]**sake** /sayk/ *n* [ME, dispute, guilt, purpose, fr OE *sacu* guilt, action at law; akin to OHG *sahha* action at law, cause, OE *sēcan* to seek – more at SEEK] – **for the sake of, for someone's/something's sake 1** for the purpose of ⟨for the sake of *argument*⟩ **2** so as to get, keep, or improve ⟨for *conscience* sake⟩ ⟨*study Latin* for *its own* sake⟩ **3** so as to help, please, or honour ⟨*to go to the sea* for the sake of *the children*⟩ ⟨for *old times'* sake⟩ – **for God's/goodness/Heaven's/pity's sake** – used in protest or supplication

[2]**sake, saki** /'sahki/ *n* a Japanese alcoholic drink of fermented rice [Jap *sake*]

saker /'saykə/ *n* a large Old World falcon used in falconry [ME *sagre*, fr MF *sacre*, fr Ar *saqr*]

saki /'sahki/ *n* any of several S American long-tailed monkeys [F, fr Tupi *sagui*]

Sakti /'s(h)ahkti/ *n* Shakti – **Saktism** /-,tiz(ə)m/ *n*

sal /sal/ *n* (the wood of) an E Indian timber tree [Hindi *sāl*, fr Skt *śāla*]

[1]**salaam** /sə'lahm/ *n* **1** a ceremonial greeting in E countries **2** an obeisance made by bowing low and placing the right palm on the forehead [Ar *salām*, lit., peace]

[2]**salaam** *vb* to perform a salaam (to)

salable, saleable /'sayləbl/ *adj* capable of being or fit to be sold – **salability** /-'biləti/ *n*

salacious /sə'layshəs/ *adj* **1** arousing or appealing to sexual desire **2** lecherous, lustful [L *salac-*, *salax* fond of leaping, lustful, fr *salire* to leap – more at SALLY] – **salaciously** *adv*, **salaciousness** *n*

salad /'saləd/ *n* **1a** (mixed) raw vegetables (e g lettuce, watercress, or tomato) often served with a dressing **b** a dish of raw or (cold) cooked foods often cut into small pieces and combined with a dressing ⟨*fruit* ~⟩ **2** a vegetable or herb eaten raw (in salad); *esp* lettuce [ME *salade*, fr MF, fr OProv *salada*, fr *salar* to salt, fr *sal* salt, fr L – more at SALT]

'salad ,days *n pl* time of youthful inexperience or indiscretion ⟨*my* ~ *when I was green in judgment* – Shak⟩

'salad ,oil *n* an edible vegetable oil (e g olive oil) used in salad dressings

salamander /'salə,mandə, ,--'--/ *n* **1** a mythical animal with the power to endure fire without harm

2 any of numerous scaleless amphibians superficially resembling lizards ☞ DEFENCE [ME *salamandre*, fr MF, fr L *salamandra*, fr Gk] – **salamandrine** /-drin/ *adj*

salami /sə'lahmi/ *n, pl* **salamis** a highly seasoned, esp pork, sausage often containing garlic [It, pl of *salame* salami, fr *salare* to salt, fr *sale* salt, fr L *sal* – more at SALT]

salary /'saləri/ *n* a fixed usu monthly payment for regular services, esp of a nonmanual kind – compare WAGE [ME *salarie*, fr L *salarium* salt money, pension, salary, fr neut of *salarius* of salt, fr *sal* salt – more at SALT] – **salaried** *adj*

salbutamol /sal'byoohtə,mol/ *n* a synthetic drug used in the treatment of asthma to relax the muscles of the bronchioles of the lungs and make breathing easier [*sal* (salt, fr L) + *butyl* + *amin-* + *-ol*]

salchow /'salkow/ *n* a jump in ice-skating with a turn in the air [Ulrich *Salchow* 20th-c Sw skating champion]

sale /sayl/ *n* **1** the act or an instance of selling; *specif* the transfer of ownership of and title to property or goods from one person to another for a price **2a** opportunity of selling or being sold ⟨*counting on a large ~ for the new product*⟩ **b** quantity sold – often pl with sing. meaning ⟨*total ~*s *rose last year*⟩ **3** an event at which goods are offered for sale ⟨*an antiques ~*⟩ **4** public disposal to the highest bidder **5** a selling of goods at bargain prices **6a** *pl* operations and activities involved in promoting and selling goods or services ⟨*manager in charge of ~*s⟩ **b** gross receipts obtained from selling [ME, fr OE *sala*, fr ON – more at SELL] – **on/for sale** available for purchase

saleable /'sayləbl/ *adj* salable

salep /'saləp/ *n* the starchy dried tubers of various Old World orchids used for food [F or Sp, fr Ar dial. *saḥlab*, alter. of Ar (*khuṣy ath-*) *tha'lab*, lit., testicles of the fox]

saleratus /,salə'raytəs/ *n, NAm* a raising agent consisting of potassium or sodium bicarbonate [NL *sal aeratus* aerated salt]

saleroom /'saylroohm, -room/ *n, chiefly Br* a place where goods are displayed for sale, esp by auction

sales /saylz/ *adj* of, engaged in, or used in selling

'sales,clerk /-,klahk; *NAm* -,kluhk/ *n* SHOP ASSISTANT

'sales,girl /-,guhl/ *n* a female shop assistant

'sales,lady /-,laydi/ *n* a female shop assistant

'salesman /-mən/, *fem* **'sales,woman** *n, pl* **salesmen** /~/, *fem* **'sales ,women** a salesperson – **salesmanship** *n*

'sales,person /-,puhs(ə)n/ *n* sby employed to sell goods or a service (e g in a shop or within an assigned territory)

'sales repre,sentative *n* a person who travels, usu in an assigned territory, to win orders for his/her firm's goods

sali- *comb form* salt ⟨sali*ferous*⟩ [L, fr *sal* – more at SALT]

Salic /'saylik, 'salik/ *adj* of or being a Frankish people that settled on the Ijssel river early in the 4th c [MF or ML; MF *salique*, fr ML *Salicus*, fr LL *Salii* Salic Franks]

salicin /'salisin/ *n* a bitter glucoside obtained from the bark and leaves of any of several willows and used in medicine like salicylic acid [F *salicine*, fr L *salic-*, *salix* willow – more at [1]SALLOW]

,Salic 'law /'salik/ *n* the legal code of the Salic Franks; *also* a rule held to derive from this code excluding females from succession to a throne

salicylate /sə'lisilayt/ *n* a salt or ester of salicylic acid

sali,cylic 'acid /,sali'silik/ *n* an acid whose derivatives (e g aspirin) are used to relieve pain and fever [ISV, fr the radical *salicyl*]

[1]**salient** /'saylyənt, -li·ənt/ *adj* **1** pointing upwards or outwards ⟨*a ~ angle*⟩ **2a** projecting beyond a line or level **b** standing out conspicuously ⟨*~ characteristics*⟩ [L *salient-*, *saliens*, prp of *salire* to leap – more at SALLY] – **saliently** *adv*, **salience** /-əns/, **saliency** *n*

[2]**salient** *n* an outwardly projecting part of a fortification, trench system, or line of defence

salientian /,sayli'ensh(ə)n/ *n* any of an order of amphibians including the frogs and toads, that lack a tail as adults and have long hind limbs suited to leaping and swimming [deriv of L *salient-*, *saliens*] – **salientian** *adj*, **salient** /'saylyənt, -li·ənt/ *adj*

salina /sə'lienə/ *n* a salt marsh, lake, spring, etc [Sp, fr L *salinae* saltworks, fr fem pl of *salinus*]

[1]**saline** /'say,lien/ *adj* **1** (consisting) of, containing, or resembling salt ⟨*a ~ solution*⟩ **2** *esp of a purgative* containing salts of potassium, sodium, or magnesium [ME, fr L *salinus*, fr *sal* salt – more at SALT] – **salinity** /sə'linəti/ *n*

[2]**saline** *n* **1** a purgative salt of potassium, sodium, or magnesium **2** a saline solution (similar in concentration to body fluids)

Salish /'saylish/ *n* a language stock of the Mosan phylum ☞ LANGUAGE – **Salishan** *adj*

saliva /sə'lievə/ *n* a slightly alkaline mixture of water, protein, salts, and often enzymes that is secreted into the mouth by glands, and that lubricates ingested food and often begins the breakdown of starches [L – more at [2]SALLOW] – **salivary** /'saliv(ə)ri/ *adj*

salivate /'salivayt/ *vi* to have an (excessive) flow of saliva – **salivation** /-'vaysh(ə)n/ *n*

Salk vaccine /sawlk/ *n* a vaccine against polio [Jonas *Salk b* 1914 US physician]

sallet /'salit/ *n* a light 15th-c helmet with a projection over the neck [ME, fr MF *sallade*]

salley, sally /'sali/ *n, chiefly dial* a sallow [by alter.]

[1]**sallow** /'saloh/ *n* any of various Old World broad-leaved willows some of which are important sources of charcoal [ME, fr OE *sealh*; akin to OHG *salha* sallow, L *salix* willow]

[2]**sallow** *adj* of a sickly yellowish colour [ME *salowe*, fr OE *salu*; akin to OHG *salo* murky, L *saliva* spittle] – **sallowish** *adj*, **sallowness** *n*

[1]**sally** *n* **1** a rushing forth; *esp* a sortie of troops from a besieged position **2a** a brief outbreak ⟨*a ~ of rage*⟩ **b** a witty or penetrating remark **3** a short excursion; a jaunt [MF *saillie*, fr OF, fr *saillir* to rush forwards, fr L *salire* to leap; akin to Gk *hallesthai* to leap]

[2]**sally** *vi* **1** to rush out or issue forth suddenly **2** to set out (e g on a journey) – usu + *forth*

salmagundi /,salmə'gundi/ *n* **1** a dish of chopped meats, anchovies, eggs, and vegetables often arranged in rows for contrast **2** a mixture composed of many usu unrelated elements [F *salmigondis*]

salmi /'salmi/ *n* a ragout of partly roasted game stewed in a rich wine sauce [F *salmis*, short for *salmigondis*]

salmon /ˈsamən/ *n, pl* **salmon,** *esp for different types* **salmons** **1** (any of various fishes related to) a large soft-finned game and food fish of the N Atlantic that is highly valued for its pink flesh **2** orangy-pink [ME *samon,* fr MF, fr L *salmon-, salmo*] – **salmonoid** /ˈsalmə,noyd/ *adj*

salmonella /,salməˈnelə/ *n, pl* **salmonellae** /-li/, **salmonellas, salmonella** any of a genus of bacteria that cause diseases, esp food poisoning, in warm-blooded animals [NL, genus name, fr Daniel E *Salmon* †1914 US veterinarian] – **salmonellosis** /,salməneˈlohsis/ *n*

salmon trout *n* SEA TROUT

salon /ˈsalonh/ *n* **1** an elegant reception room or living room **2** a gathering of literary figures, statesmen, etc held at the home of a prominent person and common in the 17th and 18th c **3** *cap* an exhibition, esp in France, of works of art by living artists **4** a stylish business establishment or shop ⟨*a beauty* ~⟩ [F]

saloon /səˈloohn/ *n* **1** a public apartment or hall (e g a ballroom, exhibition room, or shipboard social area) **2** a railway carriage with no compartments **3** *Br* an enclosed motor car having no partition between the driver and passengers **4a** *Br* SALOON BAR **b** *NAm* a room or establishment in which alcoholic beverages are sold and consumed [F *salon,* fr It *salone,* aug of *sala* hall, of Gmc origin; akin to OHG *sal* hall; akin to Lith *sala* village]

saˈloon ,bar *n, Br* a comfortable, well-furnished, and often relatively expensive bar in a public house – compare PUBLIC BAR

Salopian /səˈlohpi·ən/ *n or adj* (a native or inhabitant) of Shropshire [*Salop,* alternative name of Shropshire]

salping-, salpingo- *comb form* salpinx ⟨salping*itis*⟩ ⟨salping*ectomy*⟩ [NL, fr *salping-, salpinx*]

salpinx /ˈsalpingks/ *n, pl* **salpinges** /salˈpinjeez/ **1** EUSTACHIAN TUBE **2** FALLOPIAN TUBE [NL *salping-, salpinx,* fr Gk, trumpet]

salsify /ˈsalsifie, -fi/ *n* (the long tapering edible root of) a European composite plant [F *salsifis,* modif of It *sassefrica,* fr LL *saxifrica,* any of various herbs, fr L *saxum* rock + *fricare* to rub – more at SAXIFRAGE, FRICTION]

¹salt /sawlt, solt/ *n* **1a** sodium chloride, occurring naturally esp as a mineral deposit and dissolved in sea water, and used esp for seasoning or preserving **b** any of numerous compounds resulting from replacement of (part of) the hydrogen ion of an acid by a (radical acting like a) metal **c** *pl* **(1)** a mixture of the salts of alkali metals or magnesium (e g Epsom salts) used as a purgative **(2)** SMELLING SALTS **2a** an ingredient that imparts savour, piquancy, or zest **b** sharpness of wit **3** an experienced sailor ⟨*a tale worthy of an old* ~⟩ **4** a saltcellar [ME, fr OE *sealt;* akin to OHG *salz* salt, L *sal,* Gk *hals* salt, sea] – **saltlike** *adj* – **above/below the salt** placed, esp seated, in a socially advantageous/disadvantageous position – **worth one's salt** worthy of respect; competent, effective

²salt *vt* **1** to treat, provide, season, or preserve with common salt or brine **2** to give flavour or piquancy to (e g a story) **3** to enrich (e g a mine) fraudulently by adding valuable matter, esp mineral ores **4** to sprinkle (as if) with a salt ⟨~ing *clouds with silver iodide*⟩ – **salter** *n*

³salt *adj* **1a** saline, salty **b** being or inducing a taste similar to that of common salt that is one of the 4 basic taste sensations – compare BITTER, SOUR, SWEET **2** cured or seasoned with salt; salted ⟨~ *pork*⟩ **3** containing, overflowed by, or growing in salt water ⟨*a* ~ *marsh*⟩ **4** sharp, pungent ⟨*a* ~ *wit* – John Buchan⟩ – **saltness** *n*

saltarello /,saltəˈreloh/ *n, pl* **salterellos** an Italian dance with a lively hop step beginning each measure [It, fr *saltare* to leap, fr L]

salt away *vt* to put by in reserve; save ⟨salted *his money* away⟩

ˈsalt,bush /-,boosh/ *n* an orache; *esp* one that is an important grazing plant in dry regions

ˈsalt,cellar /-,selə/ *n* a cruet for salt [ME *salt saler,* fr *salt* + *saler* salt cellar, fr MF, fr L *salarius* of salt – more at SALARY]

ˈsalt ,dome *n* a dome-shaped arch in sedimentary rock that has a mass of rock salt as its core

saltern /ˈsawltən, ˈsoltən/ *n* a place where salt is made (e g by boiling sea water) [OE *sealtern,* fr *sealt* salt + *ærn* house; akin to ON *rann* house]

salting /ˈsawlting, ˈsolting/ *n, chiefly Br* a marshy area flooded regularly by tides – usu pl with sing. meaning [fr gerund of ²*salt*]

saltire /ˈsaltie·ə/ *n* a diagonal heraldic cross [ME *sautire,* fr MF *saultoir* X-shaped animal barricade that can be jumped over by people, saltire, fr *saulter* to jump, fr L *saltare,* fr *saltus,* pp of *salire* to leap, jump]

ˈsalt ,lick *n* LICK 3

salt marsh *n* flat land frequently flooded by seawater

,salt of the ˈearth *n* an individual or group exhibiting essential human qualities (e g honesty or humour) [fr reference in Matt 5:13]

salt out *vb* to precipitate or separate (a dissolved substance) from a solution by the addition of salt

ˈsalt,pan /-,pan/ *n* a depression (e g made in rock) or vessel for evaporating brine

,saltˈpetre, *NAm* **saltpeter** /-ˈpeetə/ *n* POTASSIUM NITRATE [alter. of earlier *salpeter,* fr ME, fr MF *salpetre,* fr ML *sal petrae,* lit., salt of the rock]

,saltˈwater /-ˈwawtə/ *adj* of, living in, or being salt water

ˈsalt,wort /-,wuht/ *n* any of a genus of plants of the goosefoot family that grow esp in salty habitats

salty /ˈsawlti, ˈsolti/ *adj* **1** of, seasoned with, or containing salt **2** having a taste of (too much) salt **3a** piquant, witty **b** earthy, coarse – **saltily** *adv,* **saltiness** *n*

salubrious /səˈl(y)oohbri·əs/ *adj* **1** favourable to health or well-being ⟨*a* ~ *climate*⟩ **2** RESPECTABLE 2 ⟨*not a very* ~ *district*⟩ [L *salubris* – more at SAFE] – **salubriously** *adv,* **salubriousness, salubrity** /səˈloohbrəti/ *n*

saluki /səˈloohki/ *n* (any of) a N African and Asian breed of tall slender keen-eyed silky-coated hunting dogs [Ar *salūqīy* of Saluq, fr *Salūq* Saluq, ancient city in Arabia]

salutary /ˈsalyoot(ə)ri/ *adj* having a beneficial or edifying effect [MF *salutaire,* fr L *salutaris,* fr *salut-, salus* health] – **salutariness** *n,* **salutarily** /-trəli/ *adv*

salutation /,salyooˈtaysh(ə)n/ *n* **1a** an expression of greeting or courtesy by word or gesture **b** *pl* regards **2** the word or phrase of greeting (e g *Dear Sir*) that conventionally comes immediately before the body of a letter or speech [[1]SALUTE + -ATION] – **salutational, salutatory** /sə'l(y)oohtət(ə)ri/ *adj*

[1]**salute** /sə'l(y)ooht/ *vt* **1** to address with expressions of greeting, goodwill, or respect **2a** to honour by a conventional military or naval ceremony **b** to show respect and recognition to (a military superior) by assuming a prescribed position **c** to praise ⟨~d *her courage*⟩ **3** *archaic* to become apparent to (one of the senses) ~ *vi* to make a salute [ME *saluten*, fr L *salutare*, fr *salut-*, *salus* health, safety, greeting – more at SAFE] – **saluter** *n*

[2]**salute** *n* **1** a greeting, salutation **2a** a sign or ceremony expressing goodwill or respect ⟨*the festival was a ~ to the arts*⟩ **b** an act of saluting a military superior; *also* the position (e g of the hand or weapon) or the entire attitude of a person saluting a superior

[1]**salvage** /'salvij/ *n* **1a** compensation paid to those who save property from loss or damage; *esp* compensation paid for saving a ship from wreckage or capture **b** the act of saving or rescuing a ship or its cargo **c** the act of saving or rescuing property in danger (e g from fire) **2a** property saved from a calamity (e g a wreck or fire) **b** sthg of use or value extracted from waste material [F, fr MF, fr *salver* to save – more at [1]SAVE]

[2]**salvage** *vt* to rescue or save (e g from wreckage or ruin) – **salvager** *n*, **salvageable** *adj*, **salvageability** /-'biləti/ *n*

salvation /sal'vaysh(ə)n/ *n* **1** (an agent or means which effects) deliverance from the power and effects of sin **2** deliverance from danger, difficulty, or destruction [ME, fr OF, fr LL *salvation-*, *salvatio*, fr *salvatus*, pp of *salvare* to save – more at [1]SAVE] – **salvational** *adj*

Sal,vation 'Army *n* an international Christian group organized on military lines and founded in 1865 by William Booth for evangelizing and performing social work among the poor

salvationism /sal'vayshə,niz(ə)m/ *n* religious teaching emphasizing the saving of the soul

Salvationist /sal'vayshənist/ *n* a member of the Salvation Army – **salvationist** *adj, often cap*

[1]**salve** /salv, sahv/ *n* **1** an ointment for application to wounds or sores **2** a soothing influence or agency ⟨*a ~ to their hurt feelings*⟩ [ME, fr OE *sealf*; akin to OHG *salba* salve, Gk *olpē* oil flask]

[2]**salve** *vt* **1** to remedy (as if) with a salve **2** to ease ⟨~ *a troubled conscience*⟩

salver /'salvə/ *n* a tray; *esp* an ornamental tray (e g of silver) on which food or beverages are served or letters and visiting cards are presented [modif of F *salve*, fr Sp *salva* sampling of food to detect poison, tray, fr *salvar* to save, sample food to detect poison, fr LL *salvare* to save – more at [1]SAVE]

salvia /'salvi·ə/ *n* any of a genus of herbs or shrubs of the mint family; *esp* one grown for its scarlet or purple flowers [NL, genus name, fr L, sage – more at [3]SAGE]

salvo /'salvoh/ *n, pl* **salvos, salvoes** **1a** a simultaneous discharge of 2 or more guns or missiles in military or naval action or as a salute **b** the release at one moment of several bombs or missiles from an aircraft **2** a sudden or emphatic burst (e g of cheering or approbation) [It *salva*, fr F *salve*, fr L, hail!, imper of *salvēre* to be healthy, fr *salvus* healthy – more at SAFE]

sal volatile /,sal və'latili/ *n* an aromatic solution of ammonium carbonate in alcohol or ammonia water used as smelling salts [NL, lit., volatile salt]

salvor /'salvə/ *n* a person or ship making a salvage at sea [*salvage* + *-or*]

samara /'samərə/ *n* KEY 9 [NL, fr L, seed of the elm]

Samaritan /sə'marit(ə)n/ *n* **1** a native or inhabitant of ancient Samaria **2a** *often not cap* one who selflessly gives aid to those in distress **b** a member of an organization that offers help to those in despair [ME, fr LL *samaritanus*, n & adj, fr Gk *samaritēs* inhabitant of Samaria, fr *Samaria*, district & city of ancient Palestine; (2) fr the parable of the good Samaritan, Lk 10:30–37] – **samaritan** *adj, often cap*

samarium /sə'meəri·əm/ *n* a metallic transition element used esp in alloys that form permanent magnets ☞ PERIODIC TABLE [NL, fr F *samarskite* a mineral, fr Colonel von *Samarski* 19th-c Russ mine official]

samba /'sambə/ *n* (the music for) a Brazilian dance of African origin characterized by a dip and spring upwards at each beat of the music [Pg] – **samba** *vi*

sambar, sambur /'sahmbə, 'sam-/ *n* a large Asian deer with 3-pointed antlers and long coarse hair on the throat [Hindi *s abar*, fr Skt *śambara*]

sambo /'samboh/ *n, often cap* **1** sby of ¾ Negro ancestry **2** a Negro – derog [AmerSp *zambo* Negro, mulatto]

[1]**same** /saym/ *adj* **1** being 1 single thing, person, or group; identical ⟨*wear the ~ shoes for a week*⟩ – often as an intensive ⟨*born in this very ~ house*⟩ **2** being the specified one or ones – + *as* or *that* ⟨*made the ~ mistake as last time*⟩ **3** corresponding so closely as to be indistinguishable ⟨*2 brothers have the ~ nose*⟩ [ME, fr ON *samr*; akin to OHG *sama* same, L *similis* like, *simul* together, at the same time, *sem-* one, Gk *homos* same, *hama* together, *hen-*, *heis* one] – **at the same time** for all that; nevertheless

[2]**same** *pron, pl* **same** **1** *the* same thing, person, or group ⟨*do the ~ for you*⟩ ⟨*happy Christmas!* Same *to you!*⟩ **2** sthg previously mentioned ⟨*ordered a drink and refused to pay for ~*⟩

[3]**same** *adv* in the same manner – + *the* ⟨*2 words spelt the ~*⟩

sameness /'saymnis/ *n* **1** identity, similarity **2** monotony, uniformity [[1]SAME + -NESS]

samisen /'sami,sen/ *n* a 3-stringed Japanese musical instrument resembling a banjo [Jap]

samizdat /'samizdat/ *n* a system in the USSR by which literature suppressed by the government is clandestinely printed and distributed; *also* such literature [Russ, lit., self-publishing]

samlet /'samlit/ *n* a parr [irreg fr *salmon* + *-let*]

Samoan /sə'moh·ən/ *n* **1** a native or inhabitant of Samoa **2** the Polynesian language of the Samoans ☞ LANGUAGE [*Samoa*, group of islands in the Pacific Ocean] – **Samoan** *adj*

samovar /'samәvah, ,--'-/ *n* a metal urn with a tap at its base and an interior heating tube, that is used, esp in Russia, to boil water for tea [Russ, fr *samo-* self + *varit'* to boil]

Samoyed *also* **Samoyede** /,samoy'ed, ,samə'yed; *sense 2* sə'moy,ed/ *n* **1** a member of a people of the coastal regions of the N USSR and NW Siberia **2** (any of) a Siberian breed of deep-chested thick coated white or cream sledge dogs [Russ *samoed*] –

Samoyed *adj*, **Samoyedic** /ˌsamoyˈedik, ˌsaməˈyedik/ *adj*

samp /samp/ *n*, *NAm* (a boiled porridge made from) coarsely ground maize [Narranganset *nasaump* corn mush]

sampan /ˈsamˌpan/ *n* a small flat-bottomed boat used in rivers and harbours in the Far East [Chin (Pek) *san*[1] *pan*[3], fr *san*[1] three + *pan*[3] board, plank]

samphire /ˈsamˌfie·ə/ *n* **1** a European seacoast rock plant of the carrot family whose fleshy leaves are sometimes eaten boiled and pickled **2** glasswort [alter. of earlier *sampiere*, fr MF (*herbe de*) *Saint Pierre*, lit., St Peter's herb]

[1]**sample** /ˈsahmpl/ *n* **1** an item serving to show the character or quality of a larger whole or group **2** a part of a statistical population whose properties are studied to gain information about the whole [ME, fr MF *essample*, fr L *exemplum* – more at EXAMPLE]

[2]**sample** *vt* **sampling** /ˈsahmpl·ing, ˈsahmpling/ to take a sample of or from; *esp* to test the quality of by a sample ⟨~d *his output for defects*⟩

[3]**sample** *adj* intended as an example

[1]**sampler** /ˈsahmplə/ *n* a decorative piece of needlework typically having letters or verses embroidered on it in various stitches as an example of skill

[2]**sampler** *n* **1** sby or sthg that collects, prepares, or examines samples **2** *NAm* a collection of representative specimens ⟨*a* ~ *of 18 poets*⟩

sampling /ˈsahmpling/ *n* **1** a small (statistical) sample **2** the act, process, or technique of selecting a suitable sample

samsara /samˈsahrə/ *n* the Hindu cycle of indefinitely repeated reincarnation [Skt *saṁsāra*, lit., passing through]

samsoe /ˈsamzoh/ *n* a Danish cheese with a firm texture, mild slightly sweet flavour, and a few medium-sized holes [*Samsø*, island in Denmark]

Samuel /ˈsamyəl, ˈsamyooəl/ *n* (either of 2 narrative and historical books of the Old Testament telling of) the early Hebrew judge who anointed first Saul, then David as king [LL, fr Gk *Samouel*, fr Heb *Shĕmūʼēl*]

samurai /ˈsam(y)ooˌrie/ *n*, *pl* **samurai** **1** a military retainer of a Japanese feudal baron **2** the warrior aristocracy of Japan [Jap]

sanative /ˈsanətiv/ *adj* having the power to heal – fml [ME *sanatif*, fr MF, fr LL *sanativus*, fr L *sanatus*, pp of *sanare* to cure, fr *sanus* healthy]

sanatorium /ˌsanəˈtawri·əm/ *n*, *pl* **sanatoriums, sanatoria** /-ri·ə/ an establishment that provides therapy, rest, or recuperation for convalescents, the chronically ill, etc [NL, fr LL, neut of *sanatorius* curative, fr *sanatus*]

sanctify /ˈsangktiˌfie/ *vt* **1** to set apart for a sacred purpose or for religious use **2** to free from sin **3** to give moral or social sanction to **4** to make productive of holiness or piety ⟨*keep the sabbath day to* ~ *it* – Deut 5:12 (AV)⟩ [ME *sanctifien*, fr MF *sanctifier*, fr LL *sanctificare*, fr L *sanctus* sacred – more at SAINT] – **sanctification** /-fiˈkaysh(ə)n/ *n*

sanctimonious /ˌsangktiˈmohnyəs, -ni·əs/ *adj* self-righteous [L *sanctimonia* devoutness, fr *sanctus*] – **sanctimoniously** *adv*, **sanctimoniousness** *n*

[1]**sanction** /ˈsangksh(ə)n/ *n* **1** a formal ecclesiastical decree **2** sthg that makes an oath or moral precept binding **3** a penalty annexed to an offence **4a** a consideration that determines moral action or judgment **b** a mechanism of social control (e g shame) for enforcing a society's standards **c** official permission or authoritative ratification **5** an economic or military coercive measure adopted to force a nation to conform to international law [MF or L; MF, fr L *sanction-*, *sanctio*, fr *sanctus*, pp of *sancire* to make holy – more at SACRED]

[2]**sanction** *vt* **1** to make valid; ratify **2** to give authoritative consent to

sanctity /ˈsangktəti/ *n* **1** holiness of life and character **2** the quality or state of being holy or sacred [ME *saunctite*, fr MF *saincteté*, fr L *sanctitat-*, *sanctitas*, fr *sanctus* sacred]

sanctuary /ˈsangktyoo(ə)ri, -chəri/ *n* **1** a consecrated place: e g **a** the ancient temple at Jerusalem or its holy of holies **b** the most sacred part of a religious building; *esp* the part of a Christian church in which the altar is placed **c** a place (e g a church or a temple) for worship **2a(1)** a place of refuge and protection **(2)** a refuge for (endangered) wildlife where predators are controlled and hunting is illegal ⟨*a bird* ~⟩ **b** the immunity from law attached to a sanctuary [ME *sanctuarie*, fr MF *sainctuarie*, fr LL *sanctuarium*, fr L *sanctus*]

sanctum /ˈsangktəm/ *n*, *pl* **sanctums** *also* **sancta** /-tə/ a place of total privacy and security (e g a study) [LL, fr L, neut of *sanctus* sacred]

ˌsanctum sancˈtorum /sangkˈtawrəm/ *n* **1** HOLY OF HOLIES **2** a sanctum – humor [LL]

Sanctus /ˈsangktəs/ *n* a hymn of adoration sung or said before the prayer of consecration in the celebration of the Eucharist [ME, fr LL *Sanctus, sanctus, sanctus* Holy, holy, holy, opening of a hymn sung by the angels in Isa 6:3]

ˈSanctus ˌbell *n* a bell rung by the server at important points during the Mass

[1]**sand** /sand/ *n* **1** loose granular particles smaller than gravel and coarser than silt that result from the disintegration of (silica-rich) rocks **2** an area of sand; a beach – usu pl with sing. meaning **3** moments of time measured (as if) with an hourglass – usu pl with sing. meaning ⟨*the* ~s *of this government run out very rapidly* – H J Laski⟩ **4** yellowish grey [ME, fr OE; akin to OHG *sant* sand, L *sabulum*, Gk *psammos* & *ammos* sand, *psēn* to rub]

[2]**sand** *vt* **1** to sprinkle (as if) with sand **2** to cover or choke with sand – usu + *up* **3** to smooth or dress by grinding or rubbing with an abrasive (e g sandpaper) – often + *down* – **sander** *n*

sandal /ˈsandl/ *n* a shoe consisting of a sole held on to the foot by straps or thongs [ME *sandalie*, fr L *sandalium*, fr Gk *sandalion*, dim. of *sandalon* sandal]

ˈsandalˌwood /-ˌwood/ *n* **1** (the compact close-grained fragrant yellowish heartwood, used in ornamental carving and cabinetwork, of) an Indo-Malayan tree **2** (any of various trees yielding) fragrant wood similar to true sandalwood [*sandal* (sandalwood) (fr ME, fr MF, fr ML *sandalum*, fr LGk *santalon*, deriv of Skt *candana*, of Dravidian origin; akin to Tamil *cāntu* sandalwood tree) + *wood*]

ˈsandalwood ˌoil *n* any of several essential oils obtained from sandalwoods and used esp in perfumes and soaps

sandarac /ˈsandəˌrak/ *n* a resin obtained esp from an African tree of the pine family and used chiefly in making varnish and as incense [L *sandaraca* red colouring, fr Gk *sandarakē* realgar, red pigment from realgar]

[1]**sandbag** /'sand,bag/ *n* a bag filled with sand and used in usu temporary fortifications or constructions, as ballast, or as a weapon

[2]**sandbag** *vt* **-gg-** to barricade, stop up, or weight with sandbags

'sand,bank /-,bangk/ *n* a large deposit of sand, esp in a river or coastal waters

'sand,bar /-,bah/ *n* a sandbank

'sand,blast /-,blahst/ *vt or n* (to treat with) a high-speed jet of sand propelled by air or steam (e g for cutting or cleaning glass or stone) – **sandblaster** *n*

'sand-,blind *adj, archaic* having poor eyesight; purblind [ME, prob fr (assumed) ME *samblind*, fr OE *sam-* half + *blind*; akin to OHG *sāmi-* half – more at SEMI-]

'sand,boy /-,boy/ *n* sby who is cheerfully absorbed or engrossed – chiefly in *happy as a sandboy* [*sandboy* (pedlar of sand)]

'sand,castle /-,kahsl/ *n* a model of a castle made in damp sand, esp at the seaside

'sand ,crack *n* a fissure in the wall of a horse's hoof often causing lameness

'sand ,dollar *n* any of numerous flat circular sea urchins that live chiefly in shallow water on sandy bottoms

'sand ,eel *n* any of various silvery eel-like sea fishes

sanderling /'sandəling/ *n* a small sandpiper with largely grey-and-white plumage [perh irreg fr *sand* + *-ling*]

'sand ,flea *n* a sandhopper

'sand ,fly *n* any of various small biting two-winged flies

sandhi /'sandi/ *n* modification of a speech sound according to context (e g the pronunciation of *-ed* as /d/ in *glazed* and as /t/ in *paced*) [Skt *saṁdhi*, lit., placing together]

sandhopper /'sand,hopə/ *n* any of numerous crustaceans that live on beaches and leap like fleas

'sand ,martin *n* a small martin of the N hemisphere that usu nests in colonies in holes in banks of sand

[1]**'sand,paper** /-,paypə/ *n* paper to which a thin layer of sand has been glued for use as an abrasive; *broadly* any abrasive paper (e g glasspaper) – **sandpapery** *adj*

[2]**sandpaper** *vt* to rub (as if) with sandpaper

'sand,piper /-,piepə/ *n* any of numerous small wading birds with longer bills than the plovers

'sand,pit /-,pit/ *n* an enclosure containing sand for children to play in

'sand,shoe /-,shooh/ *n, chiefly Br* a plimsoll

'sand,stone /-,stohn/ *n* a sedimentary rock consisting of cemented (quartz) sand

'sand,storm /-,stawm/ *n* a storm driving clouds of sand, esp in a desert

[1]**sandwich** /'san(d)wij, -wich/ *n* **1a** two slices of usu buttered bread containing a layer of any of various sweet or savoury foods (e g meat, cheese, or jam); *also* a bread roll stuffed with a filling **b** a sponge cake containing a filling **2** sthg like a sandwich in having a layered or banded arrangement [John Montagu, 4th Earl of *Sandwich* †1792 E diplomat]

[2]**sandwich** *vt* **1** to insert *between* 2 things of a different quality or character **2** to create room or time for – often + *in* or *between*

[3]**sandwich** *adj* **1** of or used for sandwiches ⟨~ *bread*⟩ **2** *Br* of a sandwich course

'sandwich ,board *n* either of 2 boards hung at the front of and behind the body by straps from the shoulders and used esp for advertising

'sandwich ,course *n* a British vocational course consisting of alternate periods of some months' duration in college and in employment

'sandwich ,man *n* sby who advertises a business by wearing sandwich boards

sandwort /'sand,wuht/ *n* any of several usu short tufted plants of the pink family that grow usu in dry sandy regions

sandy /'sandi/ *adj* **1** consisting of, containing, or sprinkled with sand **2** resembling sand in colour or texture – **sandiness** *n*

'sand ,yacht *n* a light wheeled vehicle that is propelled by sails and is used for recreation and racing on sand

sane /sayn/ *adj* (produced by a mind that is) mentally sound; able to anticipate and appraise the effect of one's actions [L *sanus* healthy, sane] – **sanely** *adv*, **saneness** *n*

sang /sang/ *past of* SING

sangfroid /,song'frwah/ *n* imperturbability, esp under strain [F *sang-froid*, lit., cold blood]

sangría /sang'gree·ə/, **sangria** /'sang·gri·ə, ~/ *n* a usu cold punch made of red wine, fruit juice, and soda water [Sp]

sanguinary /'sang·gwin(ə)ri/ *adj* **1** bloodthirsty, murderous **2** accompanied by bloodshed **3** readily punishing with death *USE* fml [L *sanguinarius*, fr *sanguin-, sanguis* blood] – **sanguinarily** /-gwinrəli/ *adv*

sanguine /'sang·gwin/ *adj* **1** (having the bodily conformation and temperament marked by sturdiness, high colour, and cheerfulness held to be characteristic of sby) having blood as the predominating bodily humour – used in medieval physiology **2** confident, optimistic **3a** SANGUINARY 1 **b** ruddy *USE* (*3*) fml [ME *sanguin*, fr MF, fr L *sanguineus*, fr *sanguin-, sanguis*] – **sanguinity** /-'gwinəti/ *n*

sanguineous /sang'gwini·əs/ *adj* of or containing blood [L *sanguineus*]

Sanhedrin /'sanidrin, san'heedrin, -'hedrin/ *n* the supreme council and tribunal of the Jews before 70 AD headed by the High Priest and having religious, civil, and criminal jurisdiction [LHeb *sanhedhrin gĕdhōlāh* great council]

sanicle /'sanikl/ *n* any of several plants of the carrot family whose roots were formerly used in medicine [ME, fr MF, fr ML *sanicula*]

sanitary /'sanit(ə)ri/ *adj* **1** of or promoting health ⟨~ *measures*⟩ **2** free from danger to health [F *sanitaire*, fr L *sanitas*]

'sanitary ,belt *n* a narrow belt which is worn to hold a sanitary towel in place

'sanitary ,towel *n* a disposable absorbent pad worn after childbirth or during menstruation to absorb the flow from the womb

'sanitary ,ware *n* ceramic plumbing fixtures (e g sinks or toilet bowls)

sanitation /,sani'taysh(ə)n/ *n* (the promotion of hygiene and prevention of disease by) maintenance or improvement of sanitary conditions – **sanitate** /'sani,tayt/ *vt*

sanit·ize, -ise /'sani,tiez/ *vt* **1** to make sanitary by cleaning, sterilizing, etc **2** to make more acceptable by removing objectionable features [L *sanitas*] – **sanitization** /-'zaysh(ə)n/ *n*

sanity /'sanəti/ *n* being sane; *esp* soundness or health of mind [ME *sanite*, fr L *sanitat-*, *sanitas* health, sanity, fr *sanus* healthy, sane]

sank /sangk/ *past of* SINK

sans /sanz/ *prep*, *archaic* without ⟨*my love to thee is sound,* ~ *crack or flaw* – Shak⟩ [ME *saun*, *sans*, fr MF *san*, *sans*, modif of L *sine* without – more at SUNDER]

sansculotte /,sanzkyoo'lot (*Fr* sɑ̃kylɔt)/ *n* **1** an extreme radical republican of Revolutionary France **2** a violent political extremist [F *sans-culotte*, lit., without breeches] – **sansculottic** /-'lotik/ *adj*, **sansculottish** *adj*, **sansculottism** *n*

Sanskrit /'sanskrit/ *n* an ancient sacred Indic language of India and of Hinduism ☞ ALPHABET [Skt *saṁskṛta*, lit., perfected, fr *sam* together + *karoti* he makes] – **Sanskrit** *adj*

sans serif, sanserif /,san 'serif/ *n* a letter or typeface with no serifs [prob fr *sans* + *serif*]

Santa Claus /'santə ,klawz, ,-- '-/ *n* FATHER CHRISTMAS [modif of D *Sinterklaas*, alter. of *Sint Nikolaas* Saint Nicholas *fl* 4th c, bishop of Myra in Asia Minor and patron saint of children]

santolina /,santə'leenə/ *n* any of a genus of aromatic Mediterranean composite undershrubs [NL, genus name, alter. of L *santonica*]

[1]sap /sap/ *n* **1a** a watery solution that circulates through a plant's vascular system **b** (a fluid essential to life or) bodily health and vigour **2** a foolish gullible person – infml [ME, fr OE *sæp*; akin to OHG *saf* sap]

[2]sap *vt* **-pp-** to drain or deprive of sap

[3]sap *n* the extension of a trench from within the trench itself to a point near an enemy's fortifications [MF & OIt; MF *sappe* hoe, fr OIt *zappa*]

[4]sap *vb* **-pp-** *vi* to proceed by or dig a sap ~ *vt* **1** to destroy (as if) by undermining ⟨~ped *the morale of their troops*⟩ **2** to weaken or exhaust gradually **3** to operate against or pierce by a sap

sapajou /'sapəjooh/ *n* CAPUCHIN 3 [F, fr Tupi]

sapele /sə'peeli/ *n* (the lightweight pinkish to deep reddish brown cedar-scented mahogany obtained from) any of several African trees [native name in W Africa]

sapid /'sapid/ having (a strong agreeable) flavour [L *sapidus* tasty, fr *sapere* to taste – more at [1]SAGE] – **sapidity** /sə'pidəti/ *n*

sapient /'saypyənt/ *adj* possessing or expressing great wisdom or discernment – fml [ME, fr MF, fr L *sapient-*, *sapiens*, fr prp of *sapere* to taste, be wise] – **sapience** *n*, **sapiently** *adv*

sapless /'saplis/ *adj* feeble, lacking vigour [[1]SAP + -LESS] – **saplessness** *n*

sapling /'sapling/ *n* **1** a young tree **2** YOUTH 2a [ME, fr [1]*sap* + *-ling*]

sapodilla /,sapə'dilə/ *n* (the rough-skinned brownish edible fruit of) a tropical evergreen tree with hard reddish wood and latex that yields chicle [Sp *zapotillo*, dim. of *zapote* sapodilla, fr Nahuatl *tzapotl*]

saponaceous /,sapə'nayshəs/ *adj* like or containing soap [NL *saponaceus*, fr L *sapon-*, *sapo* soap, of Gmc origin; akin to OE *sāpe* soap]

saponify /sə'ponifie/ *vt* to convert (e g fat) into soap and glycerol by decomposition with alkali; *broadly* to decompose (an ester) into an acid and alcohol ~ *vi* to undergo saponifying [F *saponifier*, fr L *sapon-*, *sapo*] – **saponifier** *n*, **saponifiable** /-'fie·əbl/ *adj*, **saponification** /-fi 'kaysh(ə)n/ *n*

saponin /'sapənin/ *n* any of various compounds obtained from plants, that produce a soapy lather and are used esp in detergents and foaming agents [F *saponine*, fr L *sapon-*, *sapo*]

sapor /'saypaw, -pə/ *n* savour or flavour [ME, fr L – more at SAVOUR] – **saporous** /'saypərəs/ *adj*

sappanwood /'sapən,wood/ *n* (an E Indian tree related to the laburnum that has) a red wood from which a dye can be obtained [Malay *sapang* heartwood of sappanwood + E *wood*]

sapper /'sapə/ *n* a (private) soldier of the Royal Engineers [[4]SAP + [2]-ER]

[1]sapphic /'safik/ *adj* **1** (consisting) of a 4-line stanza made up of chiefly trochaic and dactylic feet **2** lesbian [*Sappho fl ab* 600 BC Gk poetess & reputed homosexual]

[2]sapphic *n* a verse in sapphic stanzas

sapphire /'safie·ə/ *n* **1** a semitransparent corundum of a colour other than red, used as a gem; *esp* a transparent rich blue sapphire **2** deep purplish blue [ME *safir*, fr OF, fr L *sapphirus*, fr Gk *sappheiros*, fr Heb *sappīr*, fr Skt *śanipriya*, lit., dear to the planet Saturn, fr *Śani* Saturn + *priya* dear] – **sapphire** *adj*

sapphirine /'safirien/ *adj* **1** made of sapphire **2** resembling a sapphire, esp in colour

sapphism /'safiz(ə)m/ *n* lesbianism [*Sappho* + *-ism*] – **sapphist** *n*

sappy /'sapi/ *adj* **1** resembling or consisting largely of sapwood **2** *NAm* SOPPY 2 – **sappiness** *n*

sapr-, sapro- *comb form* dead or decaying organic matter ⟨sapro*phyte*⟩ [Gk, fr *sapros* rotten]

saprogenic /,saproh'jenik, ,saprə-/ *adj* of, causing, or resulting from putrefaction – **saprogenicity** /,saprohjə'nisəti/ *n*

saprophagous /sa'profəgəs, sə-/ *adj* feeding on decaying matter [NL *saprophagus*, fr *sapr-* + *-phagus* -phagous]

saprophytic /,saproh'fitik, ,saprə-/ *adj*, *esp of a plant* obtaining food by absorbing the products of organic breakdown and decay or other dissolved organic material ☞ FOOD [ISV] – **saprophytically** *adv*, **saprophyte** /'saprə,fiet/ *n*

sapwood /'sap,wood/ *n* the younger softer usu lighter-coloured living outer part of wood that lies between the bark and the heartwood

saraband, sarabande /'sarəband, ,--'-/ *n* **1** a stately court dance resembling the minuet **2** a musical composition or movement in slow triple time with the accent on the second beat [F *sarabande*, fr Sp *zarabanda*]

Saracen /'sarəs(ə)n/ *n* a member of a nomadic people of the desert area between Syria and Arabia; *broadly* a Muslim at the time of the Crusades [ME, fr LL *Saracenus*, fr LGk *Sarakēnos*] – **Saracen** *adj*, **Saracenic** /-'senik/ *adj*

Saran /sə'ran/ *trademark* – used for a tough flexible thermoplastic that can be formed into fibres, moulded articles, protective coatings, etc

sarc-, sarco- *comb form* **1** flesh ⟨sarco*phagous*⟩ **2** striated muscle ⟨sarco*plasmic*⟩ [Gk *sark-*, *sarko-*, fr *sark-*, *sarx*]

sarcasm /'sahkaz(ə)m/ *n* (the use of) caustic and often ironic language to express contempt or bitterness, esp towards an individual [F *sarcasme*, fr LL *sarcasmos*, fr Gk *sarkasmos*, fr *sarkazein* to tear flesh, bite the lips in rage, sneer, fr *sark-*, *sarx* flesh; akin to Av *thwarəs* to cut] – **sarcastic** /-'kastik/ *adj*, **sarcastically** *adv*

sarcoma /sah'kohmə/ *n, pl* **sarcomas, sarcomata** /sah'kohmətə/ a cancer arising in connective tissue, bone, or muscle [NL, fr Gk *sarkōmat-*, *sarkōma* fleshy growth, fr *sarkoun* to grow flesh, fr *sark-*, *sarx*] – **sarcomatous** /-kohmətəs/ *adj*

sarcophagus /sah'kofəgəs/ *n, pl* **sarcophagi** /-gie/ *also* **sarcophaguses** a stone coffin [L *sarcophagus* (*lapis*) limestone used for coffins, fr Gk (*lithos*) *sarkophagos*, lit., flesh-eating stone, fr *sark-* sarc- + *phagein* to eat]

sarcoplasm /'sahkoh,plaz(ə)m, 'sahkə-/ *n* the cytoplasm of a striated muscle fibre [NL *sarcoplasma*] – **sarcoplasmic** /-'plazmik/ *adj*

sard /sahd/ *n* a deep orange-red variety of quartz used as a gemstone [F *sarde*, fr L *sarda*]

sardine /sah'deen/ *n, pl* **sardines** *also* **sardine** the young of the European pilchard, or another small or immature fish, when of a size suitable for preserving for food [ME *sardeine*, fr MF *sardine*, fr L *sardina*]

Sardinian /sah'dinyən, -ni·ən/ *n* **1** a native or inhabitant of Sardinia **2** the Romance language of Sardinia [*Sardinia*, island in the Mediterranean] – **Sardinian** *adj*

sardonic /sah'donik/ *adj* disdainfully or cynically humorous; derisively mocking [F *sardonique*, fr Gk *sardonios*] – **sardonically** *adv*

sardonyx /'sahdəniks/ *n* a quartz mineral consisting of parallel layers of orange-red sard and milky-white chalcedony and used as a gemstone [ME *sardonix*, fr L *sardonyx*, fr Gk]

sargasso /sah'gasoh/ *n, pl* **sargassos** a large mass of floating vegetation, esp sargassums, in the sea [Pg *sargaço*]

sargassum /sah'gasəm/ *n* any of a genus of floating seaweeds that have air bladders [NL, genus name, fr ISV *sargasso*]

sarge /sahj/ *n* a sergeant – infml [by shortening & alter.]

sari *also* **saree** /'sahri/ *n* a garment worn by Hindu women that consists of a length of lightweight cloth draped so that one end forms a skirt and the other a head or shoulder covering ☞ GARMENT [Hindi *sāṛī*, fr Skt *śāṭī*]

sarking /'sahking/ *n, Br* boards or felt fixed between rafters and roofing material [ME (Sc), fr *serken* to clothe in a shirt, sheathe, fr *serk* shirt, fr OE *serc*]

sarky /'sahki/ *adj, Br* sarcastic – infml [by shortening & alter.]

sarod /sə'rohd/ *n* a lute of N India [Hindi, fr Per] – **sarodist** *n*

sarong /sə'rong, 'sahrong/ *n* **1** a loose skirt made of a long strip of cloth wrapped round the body and traditionally worn by men and women in Malaysia and the Pacific islands **2** cloth for sarongs [Malay *kain sarong* cloth sheath]

saros /'sayros/ *n* a cycle of about 6,585 days during which a particular sequence of eclipses occurs and after which the centres of the sun and moon return to the same relative positions [Gk, fr Assyr-Bab *shāru*]

sarrusophone /sə'roohzəfohn, -'ru-/ *n* a double-reed woodwind instrument that is made of metal [*Sarrus*, 19th-c F bandmaster + *-o-* + *-phone*]

sarsaparilla /,sahs(ə)pə'rilə/ *n* **1** (the dried roots, used esp as a flavouring, of) any of various tropical American trailing plants of the lily family **2** *chiefly NAm* a sweetened fizzy drink flavoured with birch oil and sassafras [Sp *zarzaparilla*, fr *zarza* bush + *parrilla*, dim. of *parra* vine]

sarsen /'sahs(ə)n/ *n* a large mass of stone left after the erosion of a continuous bed or layer [short for *sarsen stone*, prob alter. of *Saracen stone*, i e a pagan stone or monument]

sartorial /sah'tawri·əl/ *adj* with regard to clothing ⟨~ *elegance*⟩ – fml; humor; used esp with reference to men [L *sartor* tailor] – **sartorially** *adv*

sartorius /sah'tawri·əs/ *n, pl* **sartorii** /-ri,ie/ a long muscle that crosses the front of the thigh obliquely [NL, fr L *sartor* tailor, fr *sartus*, pp of *sarcire* to mend – more at EXORCISE]

[1]**sash** /sash/ *n* a band of cloth worn round the waist or over 1 shoulder as a dress accessory or as the emblem of an honorary or military order [Ar *shāsh* muslin] – **sashed** *adj*

[2]**sash** *n, pl* **sash** *also* **sashes** the framework in which panes of glass are set in a window or door; *also* such a framework together with its panes forming a usu sliding part of a window ☞ ARCHITECTURE [prob modif of F *châssis* chassis (taken as pl)]

sashay /sa'shay/ *vi, NAm* **1a** to saunter **b** to strut ostentatiously **2** to proceed in a zigzag manner ***USE*** infml [alter. of *chassé*]

'sash ,cord *n* a cord used to connect a sash weight to a window sash

'sash ,weight *n* either of 2 counterweights for balancing a window sash in a desired position

,sash 'window *n* a window having 2 sashes that slide vertically in a frame ☞ ARCHITECTURE

Sasquatch /'saskwach/ *n* a hairy manlike animal reported as existing in W Canada [native name]

sassafras /'sasəfras/ *n* (the dried root bark, used esp as a flavouring, of) a tall N American tree of the laurel family with mucilage-containing twigs and leaves [Sp *sasafrás*]

Sassanian, Sasanian /sə'saynyən, -ni·ən/ *n* a Sassanid

Sassanid /'sasənid/ *n or adj* (a member) of a dynasty of Persian kings of the 3rd to the 7th c AD [NL *Sassanidae* Sassanids, fr *Sassan*, founder of the dynasty]

Sassenach /'sasənakh/ *n, Scot & Irish* an English person – chiefly derog [IrGael *Sasanach*, of Gmc origin; akin to OE *Seaxan* Saxons]

sat /sat/ *past of* SIT

Satan /'sayt(ə)n/ *n* the adversary of God and lord of evil in Judaism and Christianity [ME, fr OE, fr LL, fr Gk, fr Heb *śāṭān* adversary, plotter]

satanic /sə'tanik/ *adj* **1** (characteristic) of Satan or satanism ⟨~ *pride*⟩ ⟨~ *rites*⟩ **2** extremely cruel or malevolent – **satanically** *adv*

satanism /'sayt(ə)niz(ə)m/ *n, often cap* **1** diabolism **2** obsession with or affinity to evil; *specif* the worship of Satan marked by the travesty of Christian rites – **satanist** *n, often cap*

satchel /'sachəl/ *n* a usu stiff bag often with a shoulder strap; *esp* one carried by schoolchildren [ME *sachel*, fr MF, fr L *sacellus*, dim. of *saccus* bag – more at [1]SACK] – **satchelful** *n*

sate /sayt/ *vt* **1** to surfeit with sthg **2** to satisfy (e g a thirst) by indulging to the full [prob by shortening & alter. fr *satiate*]

sateen /sa'teen/ *n* a smooth durable lustrous fabric in which the weft predominates on the face [alter. of *satin*]

satellite /'satl·iet/ *n* **1** an obsequious follower **2a** a celestial body orbiting another of larger size ☞ ASTRONOMY **b** a man-made object or vehicle intended to orbit a celestial body ☞ SPACE, TELECOMMUNICATION, TELEVISION, WEATHER **3** sby or sthg attendant or dependent; *esp* a country subject to another more powerful country **4** an urban community that is physically separate from an adjacent city but dependent on it [MF, fr L *satellit-, satelles* attendant] – **satellite** *adj*

satiable /'saysh(y)əbl/ *adj* capable of being satisfied – fml

satiate /'sayshi,ayt/ *vt* to satisfy (e g a need or desire) to the point of excess [L *satiatus*, pp of *satiare*, fr *satis* enough – more at SAD] – **satiation** /-'aysh(ə)n/ *n*

satiety /sə'tie·əti, 'sayshyəti/ *n* **1** being fed or gratified to or beyond capacity **2** the aversion caused by overindulgence [MF *satieté*, fr L *satietat-, satietas*, fr *satis*]

[1]**satin** /'satin/ *n* a fabric (e g of silk) in satin weave with lustrous face and dull back [ME, fr MF, prob fr Ar *zaytūnī*, fr *Zaytūn* (now Tseutung), seaport in China]

[2]**satin** *adj* **1** made of satin **2** like satin, esp in lustrous appearance or smoothness – **satiny** *adj*

satinet /,sati'net/ *n* **1** a thin silk satin or imitation satin **2** a variation of satin weave used in making satinet

'satin ,stitch *n* a long embroidery stitch nearly alike on both sides and worked in straight parallel lines so closely as to resemble satin

'satin ,weave *n* a weave in which warp threads predominate on the surface to produce a smooth-faced fabric

satinwood /'satin,wood/ *n* (the lustrous yellowish brown wood of) an E Indian tree of the mahogany family or any of various trees with similar wood

satire /'satie·ə/ *n* **1** a literary work holding up human vices and follies to ridicule or scorn; *also* the genre of such literature **2** biting wit, irony, or sarcasm intended to expose foolishness or vice [MF, fr L *satura, satira*, fr (*lanx*) *satura* full plate, medley, fr fem of *satur* sated; akin to L *satis* enough – more at SAD] – **satirical** /sə'tirikl/ *adj*

satirist /'satirist/ *n* one who satirizes; *esp* a writer of satires

satir·ize, -ise /'sati,riez/ *vi* to utter or write satire ~ *vt* to censure or ridicule by means of satire

satisfaction /,satis'faksh(ə)n/ *n* **1a** the payment through penance of the temporal punishment incurred by a sin **b** reparation for sin and fulfilment of the demands of divine justice, achieved for mankind by the death of Christ **2a** fulfilment of a need or want **b** being satisfied **c** a source of pleasure or fulfilment **3a** compensation for a loss, insult, or injury **b** the discharge of a legal claim **c** vindication of one's honour, esp through a duel **4** full assurance or certainty [ME, fr MF, fr LL *satisfaction-, satisfactio*, fr L, reparation, amends, fr *satisfactus*, pp of *satisfacere* to satisfy]

satisfactory /,satis'fakt(ə)ri/ *adj* satisfying needs or requirements; adequate – **satisfactorily** *adv*, **satisfactoriness** *n*

satisfy /'satis,fie/ *vt* **1a** to discharge; CARRY OUT **b** to meet a financial obligation to **2a** to make content **b** to gratify to the full **c** to meet the requirements of ⟨~ *the examiners*⟩ **3a** to convince **b** to put an end to ⟨~ *every objection*⟩ **4a** to conform to (e g criteria) **b** to make valid by fulfilling a condition ~ *vi* to be adequate; suffice; *also* to please ⟨*a taste that* satisfies⟩ [ME *satisfien*, fr MF *satisfier*, modif of L *satisfacere*, fr *satis* enough + *facere* to do, make – more at SAD, [1]DO] – **satisfyingly** *adv*, **satisfiable** /-'fie,əbl/ *adj*

satori /sə'tawri/ *n* a state of intuitive illumination sought in Zen Buddhism [Jap]

satsuma /sat'soohmə/ *n* a sweet seedless type of mandarin orange [*Satsuma*, former province of Japan]

saturate /'sachoorayt/ *vt* **1** to treat or provide with sthg to the point where no more can be absorbed, dissolved, or retained ⟨*water* ~d *with salt*⟩ **2a** to fill completely with sthg that permeates or pervades ⟨*moonglow* ~s *an empty sky* – Henry Miller⟩ **b** to fill to capacity **3** to cause to combine chemically until there is no further tendency to combine [L *saturatus*, pp of *saturare*, fr *satur* sated – more at SATIRE] – **saturant** *adj or n*, **saturator** *n*

'satu,rated *adj* **1** full of moisture; thoroughly soaked **2a** *of a solution* of the highest possible concentration **b** *of an organic compound, esp a fat* containing no double or triple bonds

saturation /,satchoo'raysh(ə)n/ *n* **1** the chromatic purity of a colour; freedom from dilution with white **2** the point at which a market is supplied with all the goods it will absorb **3** an overwhelming concentration of military forces or firepower [SATURATE + -ION]

Saturday /'satəday, -di/ *n* the day of the week following Friday ☞ SYMBOL [ME *saterday*, fr OE *sæterndæg*; akin to OFris *sāterdei*; both fr a prehistoric WGmc compound whose first component was borrowed fr L *Saturnus* Saturn and whose second is represented by OE *dæg* day] – **Saturdays** *adv*

Saturn /'satən, 'sa,tuhn/ *n* the planet 6th in order from the sun and conspicuous for its rings ☞ ASTRONOMY, SYMBOL [L *Saturnus*, fr *Saturnus* Saturn, god of agriculture]

saturnalia /,satə'naylyə/ *n, pl* **saturnalias** *also* **saturnalia** **1** *pl but sing or pl in constr* the festival of Saturn in ancient Rome beginning on December 17, observed as a time of general and unrestrained merrymaking **2** an unrestrained (licentious) celebration [L, fr neut pl of *saturnalis* of Saturn, fr *Saturnus*] – **saturnalian** *adj*

Saturnian /sə'tuhnyən/ *adj* of or influenced by the planet Saturn

saturniid /sə'tuhni·id/ *n* any of a large family of moths with stout bodies and strong, usu brightly coloured, wings [deriv of NL *Saturnia*, genus of moths, fr L, daughter of the god Saturn] – **saturniid** *adj*

saturnine /'satə,nien/ *adj* **1** gloomy **2** sullen **3** of or being lead poisoning [(1,2) ME, lit., born under or influenced by the planet Saturn, fr MF *saturnin*, fr (assumed) ML *saturninus*, fr L *Saturnus*; (3) arch *saturn* (lead), fr ME *saturne*, fr ML *saturnus*, fr L *Saturnus*] – **saturninely** *adv*

satyagraha /'sutyə,grah·hə, su'tyahgrə·hə/ *n*

friendly passive resistance as practised by Mahatma Gandhi [Skt *satyāgraha*, lit., insistence on truth]

satyr /'satə/ *n* **1** *often cap* a Greek minor woodland deity having certain characteristics of a horse or goat and associated with Dionysian revelry **2** a lecherous man (having satyriasis) [ME, fr L *satyrus*, fr Gk *satyros*] – **satyric** /sə'tirik/ *adj*

satyriasis /,satə'rie·əsis/ *n* excessive sexual desire in a male – compare NYMPHOMANIA [LL, fr Gk, fr *satyros*]

satyrid /sə'tie·ərid/ *n* any of a family of usu brownish butterflies [NL *Satyridae*, group name, deriv of Gk *satyros*] – **satyrid** *adj*

[1]**sauce** /saws/ *n* **1a** a liquid or soft preparation used as a relish, dressing, or accompaniment to food ⟨*tomato* ~⟩ **b** *NAm* stewed or tinned fruit eaten as a dessert **2** sthg adding zest or piquancy **3** CHEEK 3 – infml [ME, fr MF, fr L *salsa*, fem of *salsus* salted, fr pp of *sallere* to salt, fr *sal* salt – more at SALT]

[2]**sauce** *vt* **1** to dress or prepare with a sauce or seasoning **2** to be impudent to – infml

'**sauce,box** /-,boks/ *n* a saucy impudent person – infml

saucepan /'sawspən/ *n* a deep usu cylindrical cooking pan typically having a long handle and a lid

saucer /'sawsə/ *n* **1** a small usu circular shallow dish with a central depression in which a cup is set **2** sthg like a saucer; *esp* FLYING SAUCER [ME, plate containing sauce, fr MF *saussier*, fr *sausse, sauce*] – **saucerlike** *adj*

saucy /'sawsi/ *adj* **1a** disrespectfully bold and impudent **b** engagingly forward and flippant **2** smart, trim ⟨*a* ~ *ship*⟩ – **saucily** *adv*, **sauciness** *n*

sauerkraut /'sowə,krowt/ *n* finely cut cabbage fermented in a brine made from its juice – compare COLESLAW [G, fr *sauer* sour + *kraut* cabbage]

sauna /'sawnə/ *n* (a room or building for) a Finnish steam bath in which water is thrown on hot stones [Finn]

saunter /'sawntə/ *vi* to walk about in a casual manner [prob fr ME *santren* to muse] – **saunter** *n*, **saunterer** *n*

saurian /'sawri·ən/ *n* any of a group of reptiles including the lizards and formerly the crocodiles and dinosaurs [deriv of Gk *sauros* horse mackerel, lizard; akin to Gk *psauein* to touch, graze] – **saurian** *adj*

saury /'sawri/ *n* a slender long-beaked Atlantic fish [NL *saurus* lizard, fr Gk *sauros*]

sausage /'sosij; *NAm* 'saw-/ *n* (sthg shaped like) a fresh, precooked, or dried cylindrical mass of seasoned minced pork or other meat often mixed with a filler (e g bread) and enclosed in a casing usu of prepared animal intestine [ME *sausige*, fr ONF *saussiche*, fr LL *salsicia*, fr L *salsus* salted – more at SAUCE]

,**sausage 'roll** *n* a small pastry-encased roll or oblong of sausage meat

sauté /'sawtay, 'soh-/ *vt* **sautéing; sautéed, sautéd** /-tayd/ to fry in a small amount of fat [F, pp of *sauter* to jump, fr L *saltare*] – **sauté** *n or adj*

Sauternes, *NAm* **Sauterne** /soh'tuhn, '--/ *n* a usu sweet golden-coloured Bordeaux made in the commune of Sauternes in France

[1]**savage** /'savij/ *adj* **1a** not domesticated or under human control; untamed **b** lacking in social or moral restraints **2** rugged, rough **3** boorish, rude **4** lacking a developed culture – now usu taken to be offensive [ME *sauvage*, fr MF, fr ML *salvaticus*, alter. of L *silvaticus* of the woods, wild, fr *silva* wood, forest] – **savagely** *adv*, **savageness, savagery** /-j(ə)ri/ *n*

[2]**savage** *n* **1** a member of a primitive society **2** a brutal, rude, or unmannerly person

[3]**savage** *vt* to attack or treat brutally; *esp* to maul

savanna, savannah /sə'vanə/ *n* a tropical or subtropical grassland with scattered trees ☞ FOOD, PLANT [Sp *zavana*, fr Taino *zabana*]

savant /'sav(ə)nt/ *n* one who has exceptional knowledge of a particular field (e g science or literature) [F, fr prp of *savoir* to know, fr L *sapere* to be wise – more at [1]SAGE]

savarin /'sav(ə)rin/ *n* a rich yeast-leavened cake baked in a ring mould and soaked with a liqueur-flavoured syrup; *also* the mould for a savarin [F, fr Anthelme Brillat-*Savarin* †1826 F politician & gourmet]

savate /sə'vat/ *n* a form of boxing in which blows are delivered with either hands or feet [F, lit., old shoe]

[1]**save** /sayv/ *vt* **1a** to deliver from sin **b** to rescue from danger or harm **c** to preserve from injury, destruction, or loss **2a** to put aside as a store **b** to put aside for a particular use **c** to keep from being spent, wasted, or lost ⟨~d *time by taking a short cut*⟩ **d** to economize in the use of; conserve **3a** to make unnecessary ⟨~s *me going into town*⟩ **b** to prevent an opponent from scoring, winning, or scoring with ⟨~d *the goal*⟩ ⟨~d *the shot*⟩ **4** to maintain ⟨~ *appearances*⟩ ~ *vi* **1** to rescue sby (e g from danger) **2a** to put aside money – often + *up* **b** to be economical in use or expenditure **3** to make a save [ME *saven*, fr OF *salver*, fr LL *salvare*, fr L *salvus* safe – more at SAFE] – **savable, saveable** *adj*, **saver** *n*

[2]**save** *n* an action (e g by a goalkeeper) that prevents an opponent from scoring

[3]**save** *prep* BUT 1a – chiefly fml [ME *sauf*, fr OF, fr *sauf*, adj, safe – more at SAFE]

[4]**save** *conj* were it not; only ⟨*would have protested* ~ *that he was a friend*⟩ – chiefly fml

,**save-as-you-'earn** *n* a savings scheme whereby a person undertakes to contribute a particular amount from his/her pay each week or month

saveloy /'saviloy/ *n* a precooked highly seasoned dry sausage [modif of F *cervelas*, deriv of L *cerebellum*, dim. of *cerebrum* brain]

savin /'savin/ *n* **1** a Eurasian juniper with dark foliage and small yellowish green berries **2** RED CEDAR [ME, fr MF *savine*, fr L *sabina*]

[1]**saving** /'sayving/ *n* **1** preservation from danger or destruction **2** sthg saved ⟨*a* ~ *of 40 per cent*⟩ **3a** *pl* money put by over a period of time **b** the excess of income over expenditures – often pl [gerund of *save*]

[2]**saving** *prep* **1** except, save **2** without disrespect to [prp of *save*]

,**saving 'grace** *n* a redeeming quality or feature

'**savings ,stamp** *n* a stamp which is bought and saved and which may be cashed when required or used in payment of a bill

saviour, *NAm chiefly* **savior** /'sayvyə/ *n* **1** one who brings salvation; *specif, cap* Jesus **2** one who saves sby or sthg from danger or destruction [ME *saveour*, fr MF, fr LL *salvator*, fr *salvatus*, pp of *salvare* to save]

savoir faire /,savwah 'feə/ *n* polished self-assurance

in social behaviour [F *savoir-faire*, lit., knowing how to do]

savory /'sayv(ə)ri/ *n* any of several aromatic plants of the mint family used as herbs in cooking [ME *saverey*]

[1]**savour,** *NAm chiefly* **savor** /'sayvə/ *n* **1** the characteristic taste or smell of sthg **2** a particular flavour or smell **3** a (pleasantly stimulating) distinctive quality ⟨*felt that argument added ~ to conversation*⟩ [ME, fr OF, fr L *sapor*; akin to L *sapere* to taste – more at [1]SAGE]

[2]**savour,** *NAm chiefly* **savor** *vi* to have a specified smell or quality; smack ⟨*arguments that ~ of cynicism*⟩ ~ *vt* **1** to taste or smell with pleasure; relish **2a** to have (pleasurable) experience of, esp at length **b** to delight in; enjoy

[1]**savoury,** *NAm chiefly* **savory** /'sayv(ə)ri/ *adj* **1** piquantly pleasant to the mind **2** morally wholesome **3a** pleasing to the palate **b** salty, spicy, meaty, etc, rather than sweet [SAVOUR + [1]-Y]

[2]**savoury,** *NAm chiefly* **savory** *n* a dish of piquant or stimulating flavour served usu at the end of a main meal but sometimes as an appetizer

savoy, savoy cabbage /sə'voy; *often* 'savoy *when attrib/ n* a hardy cabbage with compact heads of wrinkled and curled leaves [trans of F (*chou de*) *Savoie* (cabbage of) Savoy, fr *Savoy*, region of SE France]

[1]**savvy** /'savi/ *vb* to know, understand – slang [modif of Sp *sabe* he knows, fr *saber* to know, fr L *sapere* to be wise – more at [1]SAGE]

[2]**savvy** *n* practical know-how; shrewd judgment – slang – **savvy** *adj*

[1]**saw** /saw/ *past of* SEE

[2]**saw** *n* a hand or power tool with a toothed part (e g a blade or disc) used to cut wood, metal, bone, etc [ME *sawe*, fr OE *sagu*; akin to OHG *sega* saw, L *secare* to cut, *secula* sickle] – **sawlike** *adj*

[3]**saw** *vb* **sawed, sawn** /sawn/ *vt* **1** to cut with a saw **2** to shape by cutting with a saw **3** to cut through as though with a saw ~ *vi* **1a** to use a saw **b** to cut (as if) with a saw **2** to make motions as though using a saw – **sawer** *n*

[4]**saw** *n* a maxim, proverb [ME *sawe*, fr OE *sagu* discourse; akin to OHG & ON *saga* tale, OE *secgan* to say – more at [1]SAY]

sawbill /'saw,bil/ *n* a merganser or related fish-eating duck with a serrated slender beak

'saw,bones /-,bohnz/ *n* a doctor; *specif* a surgeon – humor

'saw,dust /-,dust/ *n* fine particles of wood produced in sawing

,saw-'edged *adj* having a toothed or jagged edge

,sawed-'off *adj, chiefly NAm* sawn-off

'saw,fish /-,fish/ *n* any of a family of large elongated rays with a long flattened serrated snout

'saw,fly /-,flie/ *n* any of numerous insects whose female usu has a pair of serrated blades in her egg-laying organ and whose larva resembles a plant-feeding caterpillar

'saw,horse /-,haws/ *n* a rack on which wood is laid for sawing

'saw,mill /-,mil/ *n* a factory or machine that cuts wood

sawney /'sawni/ *n* a simpleton – infml [prob alter. of *zany*] – **sawney** *adj*

,sawn-'off *adj* having the end removed by sawing; *specif, of a shotgun* having the end of the barrel sawn off

'saw-,off *n, Can* a trade-off

'saw-,pit *n* the pit in which the lower sawyer stands while timber is being cut with a pit saw

'saw ,set *n* an instrument used to set the teeth of saws

'saw,tooth, ,saw-'toothed *adj* (having parts) arranged like the teeth of a saw ⟨*a ~ roof*⟩

sawyer /'sawyə/ *n* sby employed to saw timber

sax /saks/ *n* a saxophone

'sax,horn /-,hawn/ *n* any of a group of valved brass instruments with a conical tube, oval shape, and cup-shaped mouthpiece [(Antoine Joseph) Adolphe *Sax* †1894 Belgian maker of musical instruments + E *horn*]

saxicolous /,sak'sikələs/, **saxicoline** /-,lien/ *adj* inhabiting or growing among rocks ⟨*~ lichens*⟩ [L *saxum* rock + *-cola* inhabitant; akin to L *colere* to inhabit – more at WHEEL]

saxifrage /'saksifrij, -,frayj/ *n* any of a genus of usu showy-flowered plants often with tufted leaves, many of which are grown in rock gardens [ME, fr MF, fr LL *saxifraga*, fr L, fem of *saxifragus* breaking rocks, fr *saxum* rock (akin to OE *sæx* knife, *sagu* saw) + *frangere* to break – more at [2]SAW, BREAK]

Saxon /'saks(ə)n/ *n* **1a(1)** a member of a Germanic people that invaded England along with the Angles and Jutes in the 5th c AD and merged with them to form the Anglo-Saxon people **(2)** an Englishman or Lowlander as distinguished from a Welshman, Irishman, or Highlander **b** a native or inhabitant of Saxony **2** the Germanic language or dialect of any of the Saxon peoples [ME, fr LL *Saxones* Saxons, of Gmc origin; akin to OE *Seaxan* Saxons] – **Saxon** *adj*

saxony /'saksəni/ *n, often cap* **1** a fine soft woollen fabric **2** a fine closely twisted knitting yarn [*Saxony*, region of Germany]

saxophone /'saksə,fohn/ *n* any of a group of single-reed woodwind instruments having a conical metal tube and finger keys and used esp in jazz and popular music [F, fr Adolphe *Sax* + F *-phone*] – **saxophonist** /,sak'sofənist/ *n*

[1]**say** /say/ *vb* **says** /sez/; **said** /sed/ *vt* **1a** to state in spoken words **b** to form an opinion as to ⟨*can't ~ when I met him*⟩ **2a** to utter, pronounce ⟨*can't ~ her 'h' 's*⟩ **b** to recite, repeat ⟨said *his prayers*⟩ **3a** to indicate, show ⟨*the clock ~*s *12*⟩ **b** to give expression to; communicate ⟨I said *to myself 'That's funny'*⟩ ⟨*it ~*s *press button A*⟩ **4a** to suppose, assume **b** to allege – usu pass ⟨*the house is* said *to be 300 years old*⟩; compare SAID ~ *vi* **1** to speak, declare ⟨*I'd rather not ~*⟩ **2** *NAm* I SAY – used interjectionally [ME *sayen*, fr OE *secgan*; akin to OHG *sagen* to say, Gk en*nepein* to speak, tell] – **sayer** *n* – **I say** *chiefly Br* – used as a weak expression of surprise or to attract attention – **not to say** and indeed; or perhaps even ⟨*impolite,* not to say *rude*⟩ – **say boo to a goose** to brave even trivial dangers – usu neg – **say fairer** *Br* to express oneself any more generously ⟨*you can't* say fairer *than that*⟩ – **say when** to tell sby when to stop, esp when pouring a drink – **that is to say 1** in other words; IN EFFECT **2** or at least ⟨*he's coming,* that is to say *he promised to*⟩ – **to say nothing of** without even considering; not to mention

[2]**say** *n* **1** an expression of opinion – esp in *have one's*

say 2 a right or power to influence action or decisions; *esp* the authority to make final decisions

[3]**say** *adv* **1** at a rough estimate ⟨*the picture is worth,* ~, *£200*⟩ **2** FOR EXAMPLE ⟨*we could leave next week,* ~ *on Monday*⟩ [fr imper of [1]*say*]

saying *n* a maxim, proverb

'**say-,so** *n* **1** one's unsupported assertion **2** the right of final decision

sayyid /'sie·id/ *n* sir, master – used as a courtesy title for a Muslim of rank or lineage [Ar]

[1]**scab** /skab/ *n* **1** scabies of domestic animals **2** a crust of hardened blood and serum over a wound **3a** a contemptible person **b** BLACKLEG 3 **4** any of various plant diseases characterized by crusted spots; *also* any of these spots [ME, of Scand origin; akin to OSw *skabbr* scab; akin to OE *sceabb* scab, L *scabies* mange, *scabere* to scratch, shave – more at SHAVE] – **scabby** *adj*

[2]**scab** *vi* **-bb-** **1** to become covered with a scab **2** to act as a scab

scabbard /'skabəd/ *n* a sheath for a sword, dagger, or bayonet [ME *scaubert*, fr AF *escaubers*]

scabies /'skaybiz/ *n, pl* **scabies** a skin disease, esp contagious itch or mange, caused by a parasitic mite and usu characterized by oozing scabs [L] – **scabietic** /,skaybi'etik/ *adj*

[1]**scabious** /'skaybi·əs/ *n* any of a genus of plants with flowers in dense heads at the end of usu long stalks [ME *scabiose*, fr ML *scabiosa*, fr L, fem of *scabiosus*, adj]

[2]**scabious** *adj* **1** scabby **2** of or resembling scabies [L *scabiosus*, fr *scabies*]

scabrous /'skaybrəs/ *adj* **1** rough to the touch with scales, scabs, raised patches, etc **2** dealing with indecent or offensive themes **3** intractable, knotty *USE* (*2 & 3*) fml [L *scabr-*, *scaber* rough, scurfy; akin to L *scabies* mange – more at SCAB] – **scabrously** *adv*, **scabrousness** *n*

scaffold /'skafohld, -f(ə)ld/ *n* **1a** a temporary platform for workmen to stand or sit on when working at a height above the floor or ground **b** a platform on which a criminal is executed **c** a platform above ground or floor level **2** a supporting framework [ME, fr ONF *escafaut*, modif of (assumed) VL *catafalicum* – more at CATAFALQUE]

scaffolding /'skafəlding/ *n* **1** material used in scaffolds **2** SCAFFOLD 1a, 2

scagliola /skal'yohlə/ *n* imitation marble consisting of finely ground gypsum mixed with glue [It, lit., little chip]

[1]**scalar** /'skaylə/ *adj* **1** having a continuous series of steps ⟨~ *chain of authority*⟩ **2a** capable of being represented by a point on a scale ⟨*a* ~ *quantity*⟩ **b** of a scalar or scalar product ⟨~ *multiplication*⟩ [L *scalaris*, fr *scalae* stairs, ladder – more at [5]SCALE]

[2]**scalar** *n* **1** a real number rather than a vector **2** a quantity (e g mass or time) that has a magnitude describable by a real number, and no direction – compare VECTOR

,**scalar 'product** *n* a real number obtained by multiplying together the lengths of 2 vectors and the cosine of their included angle

scalawag /'skaləwag/ *n, NAm* a scallywag

[1]**scald** /skawld/ *vt* **1** to burn (as if) with hot liquid or steam **2a** to subject to boiling water or steam **b** to heat to just short of boiling ⟨~ *milk*⟩ [ME *scalden*, fr ONF *escalder*, fr LL *excaldare* to wash in warm water, fr L *ex-* + *calida, calda* warm water, fr fem of *calidus* warm – more at CAULDRON]

[2]**scald** *n* an injury to the body caused by scalding

scalding /'skawlding/ *adj* **1** boiling hot **2** biting, scathing

[1]**scale** /skayl/ *n* **1a** either pan of a balance **b** a beam that is supported freely in the centre and has 2 pans of equal weight suspended from its ends **2** an instrument or machine for weighing *USE* (*1b, 2*) usu pl with sing. meaning [ME, bowl, scale of a balance, fr ON *skāl*; akin to ON *skel* shell – more at SHELL]

[2]**scale** *vi* to have a specified weight on scales

[3]**scale** *n* **1** (a small thin plate resembling) a small flattened rigid plate forming part of the external body covering of a fish, reptile, etc ☞ ANATOMY **2** a small thin dry flake shed from the skin **3** a thin coating, layer, or incrustation: **a** a (black scaly) coating of oxide forming on the surface of metals, esp iron when heated **b** a hard incrustation usu of calcium sulphate or carbonate that is deposited on the inside of a kettle, boiler, etc by the evaporation or constant passage of hard water **4** a usu thin, membranous, chaffy, or woody modified leaf **5** infestation with or disease caused by scale insects [ME, fr MF *escale*, of Gmc origin; akin to OE *scealu* shell, husk – more at SHELL] – **scaled** *adj*, **scaleless** *adj*

[4]**scale** *vt* **1** to remove scale or scales from (e g by scraping) **2** to remove in thin layers or scales ⟨~ *paint from a wall*⟩ **3** to cover with scale ⟨*hard water* ~*s a boiler*⟩ ~ *vi* **1** to shed or separate or come off in scales; flake **2** to become encrusted with scale – **scaler** *n*

[5]**scale** *n* **1** a graduated series of musical notes ascending or descending in order of pitch according to a specified scheme of their intervals **2** sthg graduated, esp when used as a measure or rule: e g **a** a linear region divided by lines into a series of spaces and used to register or record sthg (e g the height of mercury in a barometer) **b** a graduated line on a map or chart indicating the length used to represent a larger unit of measure **c** an instrument having a scale for measuring or marking off distances or dimensions **3** a graduated system ⟨*a* ~ *of taxation*⟩ **4** a proportion between 2 sets of dimensions (e g between those of a drawing and its original) **5** a graded series of tests [ME, fr LL *scala* ladder, staircase, fr L *scalae*, pl, stairs, rungs, ladder; akin to L *scandere* to climb – more at SCAN] – **scale** *adj* – **to scale** according to the proportions of an established scale of measurement ⟨*floor plans drawn* to scale⟩

[6]**scale** *vt* **1** to climb up or reach (as if) by means of a ladder **2a** to change the scale of **b** to pattern, make, regulate, set, or estimate according to some rate or standard ⟨*a production schedule* ~d *to actual need*⟩ ⟨~ *down imports*⟩ *USE* (*2*) often + *up* or *down* – **scaler** *n*

scale armour *n* armour of small metallic scales fastened on leather or cloth

scale insect *n* any of numerous small insects with scale-like females attached to the host plant and young that suck plant juices

scale leaf *n* a modified usu small and scaly leaf (e g of a cypress)

scalene /'skayleen/ *adj, of a triangle* having the 3 sides of unequal length [LL *scalenus*, fr Gk *skalēnos*, lit., uneven; akin to Gk *skolios* crooked – more at CYLINDER]

'**scale,pan** /-,pan/ *n* a pan of a scale for weighing

scall /skawl/ *n* scurf or a scabby disorder (e g of the scalp) [ME, fr ON *skalli* bald head]

scallion /ˈskalyən/ *n* **1** a leek **2** an onion forming a thick basal part without a bulb; *also* SPRING ONION **3** *chiefly NAm* a shallot [ME *scaloun*, fr AF *scalun*, fr (assumed) VL *escalonia*, fr L *ascalonia* (*caepa*) onion of Ascalon, fr fem of *ascalonius* of Ascalon, fr *Ascalon-, Ascalo* Ascalon, seaport in southern Palestine]

[1]**scallop** /ˈskoləp/ *n* **1** (a large muscle, used as food, of) any of various marine bivalve molluscs that have a shell consisting of 2 wavy-edged halves each with a fan-shaped pattern of ridges and that swim by opening and closing the halves of the shell **2** a scallop shell or a similarly shaped dish used for baking esp seafood **3** any of a continuous series of circle segments or angular projections forming a border [ME *scalop*, fr MF *escalope* shell, of Gmc origin; akin to MD *schelpe* shell]

[2]**scallop** *vt* **1** to bake in a scallop shell or shallow baking dish, usu with a sauce covered with breadcrumbs **2a** to shape, cut, or finish (e g an edge or border) in scallops **b** to form scallops in

scallywag /ˈskali,wag/, *NAm chiefly* **scalawag** /ˈskaləwag/ *n* a troublemaking or dishonest person; a rascal [origin unknown]

[1]**scalp** /skalp/ *n* **1** (the part of a lower mammal corresponding to) the skin of the human head, usu covered with hair in both sexes **2a** a part of the human scalp with attached hair cut or torn from an enemy as a trophy, esp formerly by N American Indian warriors **b** a trophy of victory **3** *chiefly Scot* a projecting rocky mound [ME, of Scand origin; akin to ON *skālpr* sheath; akin to MD *schelpe* shell]

[2]**scalp** *vt* **1** to remove the scalp of **2** *NAm* **a** to buy and sell to make small quick profits **b** to obtain speculatively and resell at greatly increased prices ⟨~ *theatre tickets*⟩ **USE** (*2*) infml – **scalper** *n*

scalpel /ˈskalpl/ *n* a small very sharp straight thin-bladed knife used esp in surgery [L *scalpellus, scalpellum*, dim. of *scalper, scalprum* chisel, knife, fr *scalpere* to carve – more at SHELF]

scalp lock *n* a long tuft of hair left on the crown of the shaved head of a N American Indian warrior

scaly /ˈskayli/ *adj* **1** covered with or composed of scale or scales **2** flaky – **scaliness** *n*

scaly anteater *n* a pangolin

scammony /ˈskaməni/ *n* (the large thick root, formerly used as a purgative, of) an Asian convolvulus [ME *scamonie*, fr L *scammonia*, fr Gk *skammōnia*]

[1]**scamp** /skamp/ *n* an impish or playful young person [obs *scamp* (to roam about idly)] – **scampish** *adj*

[2]**scamp** *vt* to perform in a hasty, careless, or haphazard manner [perh of Scand origin; akin to ON *skammr* short – more at SCANT]

[1]**scamper** /ˈskampə/ *vi* to run about nimbly and playfully [prob fr obs D *schampen* to flee, fr MF *escamper*, fr It *scampare*, fr (assumed) VL *excampare* to decamp, fr L *ex-* + *campus* field – more at [1]CAMP]

[2]**scamper** *n* a playful scurry

scampi /ˈskampi/ *n, pl* **scampi** a (large) prawn (often prepared with a batter coating) [It, pl of *scampo*, a European lobster]

[1]**scan** /skan/ *vb* **-nn-** *vt* **1** to read or mark (a piece of text) so as to show metrical structure **2a** to subject to critical examination **b** to examine all parts of in a systematic order **c** to check or read hastily or casually ⟨~*ned the small ads*⟩ **3a** to traverse (a region) with a controlled beam: e g **(1)** to observe (a region) using a radar scanner **(2)** to translate (an image) into an electrical signal by moving an electron beam across it according to a predetermined pattern (e g for television transmission); *also* to reproduce (an image) from such a signal **(3)** to make a detailed examination of (e g the human body) using any of a variety of sensing devices (e g ones using ultrasonics, thermal radiation, X rays, or radiation from radioactive materials) **b** to examine (a computer data source; e g a punched card) for the presence of recorded data ~ *vi, of verse* to conform to a metrical pattern [ME *scannen*, fr LL *scandere*, fr L, to climb; akin to Gk *skandalon* trap, stumbling block, offence, Skt *skandati* he leaps]

[2]**scan** *n* **1** a scanning **2** a radar or television trace

scandal /ˈskandl/ *n* **1** loss of reputation caused by (alleged) breach of moral or social propriety **2** a circumstance or action that causes general offence or indignation or that disgraces those associated with it **3** malicious or defamatory gossip **4** indignation, chagrin, or bewilderment brought about by a flagrant violation of propriety or religious opinion [LL *scandalum* stumbling block, offence, fr Gk *skandalon*]

scandal·ize, -ise /ˈskandl,iez/ *vt* to offend the moral sense of – **scandalizer** *n*, **scandalization** /-ˈzaysh(ə)n/ *n*

ˈ**scandal,monger** /-,mung·gə/ *n* sby who circulates scandal

scandalous /ˈskandl·əs/ *adj* **1** libellous, defamatory **2** offensive to propriety – **scandalously** *adv*, **scandalousness** *n*

Scandinavian /,skandiˈnayvyən, -vi·ən/ *n* **1** a native or inhabitant of Scandinavia **2** NORTH GERMANIC – **Scandinavian** *adj*

scandium /ˈskandi·əm/ *n* a trivalent metallic transition element ☞ PERIODIC TABLE [NL, fr L *Scandia*, ancient name of southern Scandinavian peninsula]

scanner /ˈskanə/ *n* **1** a device that automatically monitors a system or process **2** a device for sensing recorded data **3** the rotating aerial of a radar set [[1]SCAN + [2]-ER]

scansion /ˈskansh(ə)n/ *n* (the analysis of) the way in which a piece of verse scans [LL *scansion-, scansio*, fr L, act of climbing, fr (assumed) L *scansus*, pp of L *scandere*]

[1]**scant** /skant/ *adj* **1a** barely sufficient; inadequate **b** lacking in quantity **2** having a small or insufficient supply [ME, fr ON *skamt*, neut of *skammr* short; akin to Gk *koptein* to cut] – **scantly** *adv*, **scantness** *n*

[2]**scant** *vt* to restrict or withhold the supply of

scantling /ˈskantling/ *n* **1a** the dimensions of timber and stone used in building **b** the dimensions of a frame or strake used in shipbuilding **2** a small piece of timber (e g an upright piece in house framing) [alter. of ME *scantilon*, lit., mason's or carpenter's gauge, fr ONF *escantillon*]

scanty /ˈskanti/ *adj* scant; *esp* deficient in coverage [E dial. *scant* (scanty supply), fr ME, fr ON *skant*, fr neut of *skammr* short] – **scantily** *adv*, **scantiness** *n*

scape /skayp/ *n* **1** a leafless flower stalk arising directly from the root of a plant (e g in the dandelion)

2 the shaft of an animal part (e g an antenna or feather) [L *scapus* shaft, stalk – more at SHAFT]

-scape /-,skayp/ *comb form* (→ *n*) view of (a specified type of scene); *also* pictorial representation of (such a scene) ⟨*seascape*⟩ [*landscape*]

'scape,goat /-,goht/ *n* **1** a goat on whose head are symbolically placed the sins of the people after which he is sent into the wilderness in the biblical ceremony for Yom Kippur **2** sby or sthg made to bear the blame for others' faults [*scape* (short for *escape*); intended as trans of Heb *'azāzēl* (prob name of a demon), as if *'ēz 'ōzēl* goat that departs, Lev 16:8] – **scapegoat** *vt*

'scape,grace /-,grays/ *n* an incorrigible rascal [*scape* (short for *escape*)]

¹scaphoid /'skafoyd/ *adj* navicular [NL *scaphoides*, fr Gk *skaphoeidēs*, fr *skaphos* boat]

²scaphoid *n* the navicular of the carpus or tarsus

scaphopod /'skafə,pod/ *n* TOOTH SHELL [deriv of Gk *skaphos* boat + *pod-*, *pous* foot]

scapula /'skapyoolə/ *n, pl* **scapulae** /-li/, **scapulas** a large flat triangular bone at the upper part of each side of the back forming most of each half of the shoulder girdle; SHOULDER BLADE ☞ ANATOMY [NL, fr L, shoulder blade, shoulder]

¹scapular /'skapyoolə/ *n* **1a** a long wide band of cloth with an opening for the head worn front and back over the shoulders as part of a monastic habit **b** a pair of small cloth squares joined by shoulder tapes and worn under the clothing on the chest and back as a sacramental and often also as a badge of a third order or confraternity **2** any of the feathers covering the base of a bird's wing [ME *scapulare*, fr LL, fr L *scapula* shoulder]

²scapular *adj* of the shoulder, the shoulder blade, or scapular feathers [NL *scapularis*, fr *scapula*]

¹scar /skah/ *n* a steep rocky place on a mountainside [ME *skere*, fr ON *sker* skerry; akin to ON *skera* to cut – more at SHEAR]

²scar *n* **1** a mark left (e g on the skin) by the healing of injured tissue **2** CICATRIX 2 **3** a mark of damage or wear **4** a lasting moral or emotional injury [ME *escare*, *scar*, fr MF *escare* scab, fr LL *eschara*, fr Gk, hearth, scab] – **scarless** *adj*

³scar *vb* **-rr-** *vt* **1** to mark with a scar **2** to do lasting injury to ~ *vi* **1** to form a scar **2** to become scarred

scarab /'skarəb/ *n* **1** a scarabaeus or other scarabaeid beetle **2** a representation of a beetle, usu made of stone or glazed earthenware, used in ancient Egypt esp as a talisman [MF *scarabee*, fr L *scarabaeus*]

scarabaeid /,skarə'bee·id/ *n* any of a family of stout-bodied beetles including the dung beetles and the Goliath and Hercules beetles [deriv of L *scarabaeus*] – **scarabaeid** *adj*

scarabaeus /,skarə'bee·əs/ *n* **1** a large (nearly) black dung beetle **2** SCARAB 2 [L]

Scaramouch, Scaramouche /'skarə,moohsh, -,mowch/ *n* a stock character in the commedia dell'arte characterized by boastfulness and cowardice [F *Scaramouche*, fr It *Scaramuccia*]

¹scarce /skeəs/ *adj* **1** not plentiful or abundant **2** few in number; rare [ME *scars*, fr ONF *escars*, fr (assumed) VL *excarpsus*, lit., plucked out, pp of L *excerpere* to pluck out – more at EXCERPT] – **scarceness** *n*, **scarcity** *n*

²scarce *adv, archaic* scarcely, hardly

'scarcely /-li/ *adv* **1a** by a narrow margin; only just ⟨*had ~ finished eating*⟩ **b** almost not ⟨*~ ever went to parties*⟩ ⟨*could ~ have been better qualified*⟩ **2** not without unpleasantness or discourtesy ⟨*could ~ interfere in a private dispute*⟩

¹scare /skeə/ *vt* **1** to frighten suddenly **2** to drive off by frightening ~ *vi* to become scared [ME *skerren*, fr ON *skirra*, fr *skjarr* shy, timid] – **scarer** *n*

²scare *n* **1** a sudden or unwarranted fright **2** a widespread state of alarm or panic ⟨*a bomb ~*⟩ – **scare** *adj*

'scare,crow /-,kroh/ *n* **1** an object usu suggesting a human figure, set up to frighten birds away from crops **2** a skinny or ragged person – infml

'scare,monger /-,mung·gə/ *n* sby who (needlessly) encourages panic – **scaremongering** *n*

scarey /'skeəri/ *adj* scary

¹scarf /skahf/ *n, pl* **scarves** /skahvz/, **scarfs** a strip or square of cloth worn round the shoulders or neck or over the head for decoration or warmth [ONF *escarpe* sash, sling]

²scarf *n, pl* **scarfs** **1** either of the chamfered or cut away ends that fit together to form a scarf joint **2** **scarf, scarf joint** a joint made by chamfering, halving, or notching 2 pieces to correspond and lapping and bolting them [ME *skarf*, prob of Scand origin; akin to ON *skarfr* scarf; akin to Gk *skorpios* scorpion]

³scarf, scarph /skahf/ *vt* **1** to unite by a scarf joint **2** to form a scarf on

'scarf,skin /-,skin/ *n* the epidermis; *esp* that forming the cuticle of a nail [¹*scarf*]

scarify /'skeərifie, 'skari-/ *vt* **1** to make scratches or small cuts in (e g the skin) **2** to wound the feelings of (e g by harsh criticism) **3** to break up and loosen the surface of (e g a field or road) [MF *scarifier*, fr LL *scarificare*, alter. of L *scarifare*, fr Gk *skariphasthai* to scratch an outline, sketch – more at ¹SCRIBE] – **scarifier** *n*, **scarification** /-fikaysh(ə)n/ *n*

scarious /'skeəri·əs/ *adj* dry and membranous in texture ⟨*a ~ bract*⟩ [NL *scariosus*]

scarlatina /,skahlə'teenə/ *n* SCARLET FEVER [NL, fr ML *scarlata* scarlet] – **scarlatinal** *adj*

scarlet /'skahlət/ *adj or n* (of) a vivid red colour tinged with orange [ME *scarlat*, *scarlet*, fr OF or ML; OF *escarlate*, fr ML *scarlata*, fr Per *saqalāt*, a kind of rich cloth]

scarlet fever *n* an infectious fever caused by a streptococcus in which there is a red rash and inflammation of the nose, throat, and mouth

scarlet pimpernel *n* a common pimpernel with usu red flowers that close in cloudy weather

scarlet runner *n* RUNNER BEAN

scarlet woman *n* a prostitute – euph [fr description of 'the great whore' in Rev 17:1-6]

¹scarp /skahp/ *n* **1** the inner side of a ditch below the parapet of a fortification **2** a steep slope, esp a cliff face, produced by faulting or erosion [It *scarpa*]

²scarp *vt* to cut down to form a vertical or steep slope

scarper /'skahpə/ *vi, Br* to run away (e g from creditors) – infml [perh fr It *scappare*, fr (assumed) VL *excappare* – more at ESCAPE]

scarph /skahf/ *vt* to scarf

scary, scarey /'skeəri/ *adj* **1** causing fright; alarming **2** easily scared; timid *USE* infml

¹scat /skat/ *vi* **-tt-** to depart rapidly – infml [*scat* (interj used to drive away a cat), perh short for *scatter*]

[2]**scat** *n* jazz singing with nonsense syllables [perh imit] – **scat** *vi*

[1]**scathe** /skaydh/ *n, archaic* harm, injury [ME *skathe*, fr ON *skathi*; akin to OE *sceatha* injury, Gk *askēthēs* unharmed] – **scatheless** *adj*

[2]**scathe** *vt* to do harm to; *specif* to scorch or sear – poetic

scathing /'skaydhing/ *adj* bitterly severe ⟨*a* ~ *condemnation*⟩ – **scathingly** *adv*

scatology /ska'toləji/ *n* **1** the biologically oriented study of excrement (e g for the determination of diet) **2** (literature characterized by) interest in or treatment of obscene matters [*scat* (excrement), fr Gk *skat-, skōr*] – **scatological** /ˌskatə'lojikl/ *adj*

[1]**scatter** /'skatə/ *vt* **1** to cause (a group or collection) to separate widely **2a** to distribute at irregular intervals **b** to distribute recklessly and at random **3** to sow (seed) by casting in all directions **4** to reflect or disperse (e g a beam of radiation or particles) irregularly and diffusely ~ *vi* to separate and go in various directions [ME *scateren*] – **scatterer** *n*, **scatteringly** *adv*

[2]**scatter** *n* **1** the act of scattering **2** a small supply or number irregularly distributed **3** the state or extent of being scattered

'**scatter,brain** /-ˌbrayn/ *n* sby incapable of concentration – **scatterbrained** *adj*

'**scatter-,gun** *n, chiefly NAm* a shotgun

scattering /'skat(ə)ring/ *n* **1** an act or process in which sthg scatters or is scattered **2** a small number or quantity interspersed here and there ⟨*a* ~ *of visitors*⟩

scatter rug *n* a small rug used, esp with others, in a room (e g to fill a vacant area of floor)

scatty /'skati/ *adj, Br* scatterbrained – infml [prob fr *scatter*brain + *-y*]

scaup /skawp/ *n, pl* **scaups,** *esp collectively* **scaup** any of several diving ducks [perh alter. of *scalp* (bed of shellfish); fr its fondness for shellfish]

scavenge /'skavinj/ *vt* **1** to salvage from discarded or refuse material; *also* to salvage usable material from **2** to feed on (carrion or refuse) **3a** to remove (burnt gases) from the cylinder of an internal-combustion engine after a working stroke **b** to remove (e g an undesirable constituent) by chemical or physical means **c** to clean and purify (molten metal) by making foreign elements from chemical compounds ~ *vi* **1** to search for reusable material **2** to obtain food by scavenging ⟨*dogs* scavenging *on kitchen waste*⟩ [back-formation fr *scavenger*]

scavenger /'skavinjə/ *n* **1** a refuse collector **2** a chemical used to remove or make innocuous an undesirable substance **3** an organism that feeds on refuse or carrion ☞ FOOD [alter. of earlier *scavager*, fr ME *skawager* collector of a toll on goods sold by nonresident merchants, fr *skawage* toll on goods sold by nonresident merchants, fr ONF *escauwage* inspection]

scenario /si'nahri·oh, -'neə-/ *n, pl* **scenarios** **1** an outline or synopsis of a dramatic work **2a** a screenplay **b** a shooting script **3** an account or synopsis of a projected course of action [It, fr L *scaenarium*, fr *scaena* stage]

[1]**scend** /send/ *vi* to rise upwards on a wave [alter. of *send*]

[2]**scend** *n* the lifting motion of a wave

scene /seen/ *n* **1** any of the smaller subdivisions of a dramatic work: e g **a** a division of an act presenting continuous action in 1 place **b** an episode, sequence, or unit of dialogue in a play, film, or television programme **2** a vista suggesting a stage setting **3** the place of an occurrence or action ⟨~ *of the crime*⟩ **4** an exhibition of unrestrained feeling ⟨*make a* ~⟩ **5** a sphere of activity or interest – slang ⟨*the drug* ~⟩ ⟨*philosophy is not my* ~⟩ [MF, stage, fr L *scena, scaena* stage, scene, fr Gk *skēnē* temporary shelter, tent, building forming the background for a dramatic performance, stage; akin to Gk *skia* shadow – more at SHINE] – **behind the scenes** out of the public view; IN SECRET

scene dock *n* a space near the stage in a theatre where scenery is stored

scenery /'seen(ə)ri/ *n* **1** the painted scenes or hangings and accessories used on a theatre stage **2** landscape, esp when considered attractive

'**scene,shifter** /-ˌshiftə/ *n* a worker who moves the scenery in a theatre

scenic /'seenik/ *also* **scenical** /-kl/ *adj* **1** of the stage, a stage setting, or stage representation **2** of or displaying (fine) natural scenery **3** representing graphically an action or event – **scenically** *adv*

[1]**scent** /sent/ *vt* **1a** to perceive by the sense of smell **b** to get or have an inkling of **2** to fill with a usu pleasant smell ~ *vi* to use the nose in seeking or tracking prey [ME *senten*, fr MF *sentir* to feel, smell, fr L *sentire* to perceive, feel – more at SENSE]

[2]**scent** *n* **1** odour: e g **a** a smell left by an animal on a surface it passes over ⟨*hounds followed the* ~ *of the fox*⟩ **b** a characteristic or particular, esp agreeable, smell **c** PERFUME 2 **2a** power of smelling; the sense of smell ⟨*a keen* ~⟩ **b** power of detection; a nose ⟨*a* ~ *for heresy*⟩ **3** a course of pursuit or discovery ⟨*threw him off the* ~⟩ **4** a hint, suggestion ⟨*a* ~ *of trouble*⟩ – **scentless** *adj*

'**scented** *adj* having scent; *esp* having a perfumed smell

scepsis /'skepsis/ *n* philosophical doubt or scepticism [NL, fr Gk *skepsis* examination, doubt, sceptical philosophy, fr *skeptesthai*]

sceptic /'skeptik/ *n* a person disposed to scepticism, esp regarding religion or religious principles [L or Gk; L *scepticus*, fr Gk *skeptikos*, fr *skeptikos* thoughtful, fr *skeptesthai* to look, consider – more at SPY]

sceptical /'skeptikl/ *adj* relating to, characteristic of, or marked by scepticism

scepticism /'skeptiˌsiz(ə)m/ *n* **1** doubt concerning basic religious principles (e g immortality, providence, or revelation) **2** the doctrine that certain knowledge is unattainable either generally or in a particular sphere **3** an attitude of doubt, esp associated with implied criticism

sceptre, *NAm chiefly* **scepter** /'septə/ *n* **1** a staff borne by a ruler as an emblem of sovereignty **2** royal or imperial authority [ME *sceptre*, fr OF *ceptre*, fr L *sceptrum*, fr Gk *skēptron* staff, sceptre – more at SHAFT]

schadenfreude /'shahdnˌfroydə/ *n* enjoyment obtained from contemplation of others' misfortunes [G, fr *schaden* damage + *freude* joy]

[1]**schedule** /'shedyool, -jəl; *also, esp NAm* 'skedyool, -jəl/ *n* **1** a statement of supplementary details appended to a document **2** a list, catalogue, or inventory **3** (the times fixed in) a timetable **4** a programme, proposal **5** a body of items to be dealt with [ME *cedule*, fr MF, slip of paper, note, fr LL

schedula slip of paper, dim. of L *scheda, scida* sheet of papyrus, fr (assumed) Gk *schidē*; akin to Gk *schizein* to split – more at [1]SHED]

[2]**schedule** *vt* **1a** to place on a schedule **b** to make a schedule of **2** to appoint or designate for a fixed time **3** *Br* to place on a list of buildings or historical remains protected by state legislation – **scheduler** *n*

scheelite /'sheeliet/ *n* calcium tungstate occurring as a mineral [G *scheelit*, fr Karl *Scheele* †1786 Sw chemist]

schema /'skeemə/ *n, pl* **schemata** /-mətə/ a diagrammatic representation; a plan [Gk *schēmat-, schēma*]

schematic /ski'matik/ *adj* of a scheme or schema; diagrammatic [NL *schematicus*, fr Gk *schēmat-, schēma*] – **schematically** *adv*

schemat·ize, -ise /'skeemə,tiez/ *vt* **1** to form into a systematic arrangement **2** to express or depict schematically [Gk *schēmatizein*, fr *schēmat-, schēma*] – **schematization** /-'zaysh(ə)n/ *n*

[1]**scheme** /skeem/ *n* **1** a concise statement or table **2** a plan or programme of action; a project ⟨*a hydro-electric* ~⟩ **3** a crafty or secret strategy **4** a systematic arrangement of parts or elements [L *schemat-, schema* arrangement, figure, fr Gk *schēmat-, schēma*, fr *echein* to have, hold, be in (such) a condition; akin to OE *sige* victory, Skt *sahate* he prevails]

[2]**scheme** *vt* to form a scheme for ~ *vi* to make plans; *also* to plot, intrigue – **schemer** *n*

scheming /'skeeming/ *adj* shrewdly devious and intriguing

schemozzle /shi'mozl/ *n* a shemozzle

scherzando /skeət'sandoh/ *n, adv, or adj, pl* **scherzandos** (a passage or movement played) in a sprightly or playful manner – used in music [It, fr verbal of *scherzare* to joke, of Gmc origin; akin to MHG *scherzen* to leap for joy, joke; akin to Gk *skairein* to gambol – more at CARDINAL]

scherzo /'skeətsoh/ *n, pl* **scherzos, scherzi** /-tsi/ a lively instrumental musical composition or movement in quick usu triple time [It, lit., joke, fr *scherzare*]

schilling /'shiling/ *n* ☞ *Austria* at NATIONALITY [G, fr OHG *skilling*, a gold coin – more at SHILLING]

schipperke /'shipəki/ *n* (any of) a breed of small tailless usu black dogs with erect triangular ears [Flem, dim. of *schipper* skipper; fr its use as a watchdog on boats]

schism /'siz(ə)m, 'skiz(ə)m/ *n* **1** separation into opposed factions **2a** formal division in or separation from a religious body **b** the offence of promoting schism [ME *scisme*, fr MF *cisme*, fr LL *schismat-, schisma*, fr Gk, cleft, division, fr *schizein* to split]

[1]**schismatic** /siz'matik, skiz-/ *n* a person who creates or takes part in schism

[2]**schismatic** *also* **schismatical** /-kl/ *adj* **1** (having the character) of schism **2** guilty of schism – **schismatically** *adv*

schismat·ize, -ise /'sizmətiez, 'skiz-/ *vi* to take part in schism; *esp* to make a breach of union (e g in the church)

schist /shist/ *n* a metamorphic crystalline rock composed of thin layers of minerals and splitting along approx parallel planes [F *schiste*, fr L *schistos* (*lapis*), lit., fissile stone, fr Gk *schistos* that may be split, fr *schizein*] – **schistose** /'shistohs/ *adj*

schistosome /'shistə,sohm/ *n* any of a family of elongated worms that parasitize the blood vessels of birds and mammals [NL *Schistosoma*, genus name, fr Gk *schistos* + *sōma* body – more at [2]SOMA] – **schistosome** *adj*, **schistosomal** /-'sohml/ *adj*

schistosomiasis /,shistəsoh'mie·əsis/ *n, pl* **schistosomiases** /-,seez/ a severe endemic disease of human beings in much of Asia, Africa, and S America marked esp by blood loss and tissue damage [NL, fr *Schistosoma*]

schiz- /skits-/, **schizo-** *comb form* **1** split; cleft ⟨schizo*carp*⟩ **2** characterized by or involving cleavage ⟨schizo*genesis*⟩ [NL, fr Gk *schizo-*, fr *schizein* to split]

schizo /'skitsoh/ *n, pl* **schizos** a schizophrenic person – infml – **schizo** *adj*

schizocarp /'skitsoh,kahp/ *n* a dry compound fruit that splits into several indehiscent single-seeded parts [ISV]

schizoid /'skitsoyd/ *adj* characterized by, resulting from, tending towards, or suggestive of schizophrenia [ISV] – **schizoid** *n*

schizomycete /,skitsoh'mieseet, -mie'seet/ *n* a bacterium [deriv of Gk *schizo-* schiz- + *mykēt-, mykēs* fungus – more at MYC-] – **schizomycetous** /-mie'seetəs/ *adj*

schizophrenia /,skitsə'freenyə/ *n* a mental disorder characterized by loss of contact with reality and disintegration of personality, usu with hallucinations and disorder of feeling, behaviour, etc [NL] – **schizophrenic** /-'frenik/ *adj or n*, **schizophrenically** *adv*

schizothymia /,skitsoh'thiemyə/ *n* a tendency towards an introverted temperament that while remaining within the bounds of normality somewhat resembles schizophrenia [NL] – **schizothymic** /-mik/ *n or adj*

schlep, schlepp /shlep/ *vt, chiefly NAm* to drag, haul [Yiddish *shleppen*, fr MHG *sleppen*, fr MLG *slēpen*]

schlieren /'shliərən/ *n pl* regions of varying refractive index in a transparent medium caused by differences in pressure, concentration, etc and detected esp by photographing the passage of a beam of light [G] – **schlieric** /-rik/ *adj*

schlock /shlok/ *adj, chiefly NAm* of low quality or value ⟨*churn out* ~ *TV series* – Clive James⟩ [Yiddish *shlak*, fr *shlak* curse, cheap merchandise, lit., blow, fr MHG *slag, slac*, fr OHG *slag*, fr *slahan* to strike – more at SLAY] – **schlock** *n*

schmaltz, schmalz /shmalts/ *n* excessive sentimentalism, esp in music or art [Yiddish *shmalts*, lit., rendered fat, fr MHG *smalz*; akin to OHG *smelzan* to melt – more at [2]SMELT] – **schmaltzy** *adj*

schnapps /shnaps/ *n, pl* **schnapps** strong gin as orig made in the Netherlands [G *schnaps*, lit., dram of liquor, fr LG, fr *snappen* to snap]

schnauzer /'shnowzə, 'shnowtsə/ *n* (any of) an orig German breed of dog with a long head and a wiry coat [G, fr *schnauze* snout – more at SNOUT]

schnitzel /'shnits(ə)l/ *n* a veal escalope [G, lit., shaving, chip, fr MHG, dim. of *sniz* slice; akin to OHG *snīdan* to cut, OE *snithan*, Czech *snět* bough]

schnorkel /'s(h)nawkl/ *vi or n* (to) snorkel

scholar /'skolə/ *n* **1** one who attends a school or

studies under a teacher 2 one who has done advanced study 3 the holder of a scholarship [ME *scoler*, fr OE *scolere* & OF *escoler*, fr ML *scholaris*, fr LL, of a school, fr L *schola* school]

'scholarly /-li/ *adj* learned, academic

'scholarship /-ship/ *n* **1** a grant of money to a student **2** the character, methods, or attainments of a scholar; learning **3** a fund of knowledge and learning

Scholarship level *n, often cap L* an examination that is the highest of the 3 levels of the British General Certificate of Education and is a partial qualification for university entrance

scholastic /skə'lastik/ *adj* **1a** *often cap* of Scholasticism **b** suggestive or characteristic of a scholar or pedant, esp in specious subtlety or dryness **2** of schools or scholars [ML & L; ML *scholasticus* of the schoolmen, fr L, of a school, fr Gk *scholastikos*, fr *scholazein* to keep a school, fr *scholē* school] – **scholastically** *adv*

scholasticism /skə'lasti,siz(ə)m/ *n* **1** *cap* a chiefly late medieval philosophical movement that applied Aristotelian concepts and principles to the interpretation of religious dogma **2** pedantic adherence to the traditional teachings or methods of a school

scholiast /'skohli,ast/ *n* a maker of scholia; an annotator [MGk *scholiastēs*, fr *scholiazein* to write scholia on, fr Gk *scholion*] – **scholiastic** /-'astik/ *adj*

scholium /'skolyəm/ *n, pl* **scholia** /-yə/, **scholiums** a marginal annotation or comment, esp made by an early grammarian [NL, fr Gk *scholion* comment, scholium, fr dim. of *scholē* lecture]

¹school /skoohl/ *n* **1a** an institution for the teaching of children **b(1)** any of the 4 faculties of a medieval university **(2)** a part of a university ⟨*the ~ of engineering*⟩ **c** an establishment offering specialized instruction ⟨*driving ~s*⟩ **d** *pl, cap* the final honours examination for the Oxford BA **e** *NAm* a college, university **2a(1)** the process of teaching or learning, esp at a school **(2)** a session of a school **b** a school building **3a** people with a common doctrine or teacher (e g in philosophy or theology) ⟨*the Frankfurt ~*⟩ **b** a group of artists under a common stylistic influence **4** a body of people with similar opinions ⟨*a ~ of thought*⟩ [ME *scole*, fr OE *scōl*, fr L *schola*, fr Gk *scholē* leisure, discussion, lecture, school; akin to Gk *echein* to hold – more at SCHEME]

²school *vt* **1** to educate in an institution of learning **2a** to teach or drill in a specific knowledge or skill ⟨*~ a horse*⟩ **b** to discipline or habituate to sthg

³school *n* a large number of fish or aquatic animals of 1 kind swimming together [ME *scole*, fr MD *schole*; akin to OE *scolu* multitude, *scylian* to separate – more at SKILL]

⁴school *vi* to swim or feed in a school

school age *n* the age at which children are legally required to start attending school; *also* the period of life during which such attendance is required

'school,boy /-,boy/, *fem* **'school,girl** *n* a schoolchild

'school,child /-,chield/ *n* a child attending school

'school,fellow /-,feloh/ *n* a schoolmate

'school,house /-,hows/ *n* a building used as a school; *esp* a country primary school

schooling /'skoohling/ *n* **1a** instruction in school **b** training or guidance from practical experience **2** the cost of instruction and maintenance at school **3** the training of a horse to service; *esp* the teaching and exercising of horse and rider in the formal techniques of horse riding

'school,kid /-,kid/ *n* a schoolchild – infml

,school-'leaver *n, Br* a pupil who is about to leave or has recently left school

'school,marm, schoolma'am /-,mahm/ *n* **1** a prim censorious woman **2** *chiefly NAm* a female schoolteacher; *esp* a rural or small-town schoolmistress [*school* + *marm*, alter. of *ma'am*]

'school,master /-,mahstə/, *fem* **'school,mistress** *n* a schoolteacher

'school,mate /-,mayt/ *n* a companion at school

'school,room /-,roohm/ *n* a room where children are taught

Schools Council *n* the official British body that conducts inquiries into school curricula

'school,teacher /-,teechə/ *n* a person who teaches in a school

'school,work /-,wuhk/ *n* lessons

schooner /'skoohnə/ *n* **1** a fore-and-aft rigged sailing vessel having 2 or more masts **2a** *Br* **(1)** a relatively tall narrow glass used esp for a large measure of sherry or port **(2)** the capacity of a schooner used as a measure (e g for sherry) **b** *chiefly NAm & Austr* a large tall drinking glass, esp for beer [origin unknown]

schorl /shawl/ *n* (black) tourmaline [G *schörl*] – **schorlaceous** /shaw'layshəs/ *adj*

schottische /sho'teesh/ *n* (music for) a round dance in duple time resembling a slow polka [G, fr *schottisch* Scottish, fr *Schotte* Scot; akin to OE *Scottas* Scots]

schuss /shoos/ *vi or n* (to ski down) a straight high-speed ski run [n G, lit., shot, fr OHG *scuz* – more at SHOT; vb fr n]

schwa /shwah/ *n* (the symbol /ə/ used for) an unstressed vowel that is the usual sound of the first and last vowels of *banana* [G, fr Heb *shĕwā*]

Schwann cell /shvan/ *n* a cell whose plasma membrane forms the myelin sheath of a nerve fibre [Theodor *Schwann* †1882 G naturalist]

sciagram /'sie·ə,gram/ *n* a figure formed by shading in the outline of a shadow [ISV *scia-* (fr Gk *skia* shadow) + *-gram* – more at SHINE]

sciatic /sie'atik/ *adj* **1** of or situated near the hip **2** of or caused by sciatica ⟨*~ pains*⟩ [MF *sciatique*, fr LL *sciaticus*, alter. of L *ischiadicus* of sciatica, fr Gk *ischiadikos*, fr *ischiad-*, *ischias* sciatica, fr *ischion* ischium]

sciatica /sie'atikə/ *n* pain in the back of the thigh, buttocks, and lower back caused esp by pressure on the sciatic nerve [ME, fr ML, fr LL, fem of *sciaticus*]

sciatic nerve *n* either of the 2 largest nerves in the body that pass out of the pelvis and down the back of the thigh, one on each side of the body, and supply the pelvic region and leg

science /'sie·əns/ *n* **1a** a department of systematized knowledge ⟨*the ~ of theology*⟩ **b** sthg (e g a skill) that may be learned systematically ⟨*the ~ of boxing*⟩ **c** any of the natural sciences **2a** coordinated knowledge of the operation of general laws, esp as obtained and tested through scientific method **b** such knowledge of the physical world and its phenomena; NATURAL SCIENCE **3** a system or method (purporting to be) based on scientific principles

[ME, fr MF, fr L *scientia*, fr *scient-, sciens* having knowledge, fr prp of *scire* to know; akin to L *scindere* to cut – more at [1]SHED]

ˌ**science 'fiction** *n* fiction of a type orig set in the future and dealing principally with the impact of science on society or individuals, but now including also works of literary fantasy

scientific /ˌsie·ən'tifik/ *adj* of or exhibiting the methods of science [ML *scientificus* producing knowledge, fr L *scient-, sciens* + *-i-* + *-ficus* -fic] – **scientifically** *adv*

scientific notation *n* a system in which numbers are expressed as products consisting of a number between 1 and 10 multiplied by a power of 10

scientism /'sie·ən,tiz(ə)m/ *n* **1** methods and attitudes (held to be) typical of the natural scientist **2** an exaggerated trust in the efficacy of scientific methods for explaining social or psychological phenomena or problems

scientist /'sie·əntist/ *n* an expert in a science, esp natural science; a scientific investigator [L *scientia*]

Scientology /ˌsie·ən'toləji/ *trademark* – used for a religious and psychotherapeutic movement begun in 1952 by L Ron Hubbard

sci-fi /'sie ˌfie/ *adj or n* (of or being) science fiction

scilicet /'sieli,set/ *adv* namely; TO WIT – used to introduce a word (e g in clarification or reiteration) [ME, fr L, surely, to wit, fr *scire* to know + *licet* it is permitted, fr *licēre* to be permitted – more at LICENCE]

scilla /'silə/ *n* any of a genus of Old World bulb-forming plants of the lily family with clusters of pink, blue, or white flowers [NL, genus name, fr L, squill – more at SQUILL]

scimitar /'simitə, -tah/ *n* a chiefly Middle Eastern sword having a curved blade which narrows towards the hilt and is sharpened on the convex side [It *scimitarra*, perh fr Per *shimshīr*]

scintigraphy /sin'tigrəfi/ *n* the production of a two-dimensional picture of a body part by detection of the emitted radiation after administration of a radioisotope [*scinti*llation + *-graphy*; fr the scintillation counter used to record radiation on the picture] – **scintigraphic** /ˌsinti'grafik/ *adj*

scintilla /sin'tilə/ *n* an iota, trace [L]

scintillate /'sinti,layt/ *vi* **1** to emit sparks **2** to emit flashes as if throwing off sparks; *also* to sparkle, twinkle **3** to be brilliant or animated ⟨scintillating *wit*⟩ [L *scintillatus*, pp of *scintillare* to sparkle, fr *scintilla* spark] – **scintillant** *adj*

scintillation /ˌsinti'laysh(ə)n/ *n* **1** the twinkling of a celestial body **2a** a spark or flash emitted in scintillating **b** a flash of light produced when a substance capable of phosphorescence is hit by a single electron, alpha particle, photon, etc **3** a dazzling outburst (e g of wit) [SCINTILLATE + -ION]

scintillation counter *n* a device for measuring the amount of radioactivity in a sample by detecting and counting the flashes of light in a crystal or phosphor that result from the emission of radioactive particles from the sample

scion /'sie·ən/ *n* **1** a detached living part of a plant joined to a stock in grafting and usu supplying parts above ground of the resulting graft **2** a (male) descendant or offspring [ME, fr MF *cion*, of Gmc origin; akin to OHG *chīnan* to sprout, split open, OE *cīnan* to gape]

scirocco /shi'rokoh, si-/ *n* a sirocco

scirrhus /'sirəs/ *n, pl* **scirrhi** /'sirie/ a hard slow-growing malignant tumour, esp in the breast, consisting mostly of fibrous tissue [NL, fr Gk *skiros, skirrhos*, fr *skiros* hard] – **scirrhous** /'sirəs/ *adj*

scissile /'sisiel/ *adj* capable of being cut smoothly or split easily [F, fr L *scissilis*, fr *scissus*, pp of *scindere* to split – more at [1]SHED]

scission /'sizh(ə)n/ *n* cutting, splitting, etc or a cut, split, etc [F, fr LL *scission-, scissio*, fr L *scissus*, pp]

scissor /'sizə/ *vt* to cut (out) (as if) with scissors

scissors /'sizəz/ *n pl* **1** a cutting instrument with 2 blades pivoted so that their cutting edges slide past each other **2** *sing or pl in constr* a gymnastic feat in which the leg movements suggest the opening and closing of scissors [ME *sisoure*, fr MF *cisoire*, fr LL *cisorium* cutting instrument, irreg fr L *caesus*, pp of *caedere* to cut – more at CONCISE] – **scissor** *adj*

scissors kick *n* a swimming kick in which the legs move from the hip and come together like scissor blades

scler- /skliə-/, **sclero-** *comb form* hard ⟨sclera⟩ ⟨sclero*derma*⟩ [NL, fr Gk *sklēr-, sklēro-*, fr *sklēros* – more at SKELETON]

sclera /'skliərə/ *n* the opaque white outer coat enclosing the eyeball except for the part covered by the cornea ☞ NERVE [NL, fr Gk *sklēros* hard] – **scleral** /'skliərəl, 'sklerəl/ *adj*

sclerenchyma /skliə'rengkimə/ *n* a supporting tissue in higher plants composed of cells with thickened and woody walls – compare COLLENCHYMA, PARENCHYMA [NL] – **sclerenchymatous** /ˌskliəreng'kimətəs/ *adj*

sclerosis /sklə'rohsis/ *n* **1** (a disease characterized by) abnormal hardening of tissue, esp from overgrowth of fibrous tissue **2** the natural hardening of plant cell walls usu by the formation of lignin [ME *sclirosis*, fr ML, fr Gk *sklērōsis* hardening, fr *sklēroun* to harden, fr *sklēros*] – **sclerose** /'sklerohs, -rohz/ *vb*

[1]**sclerotic** /sklə'rotik/ *adj* **1** being or relating to the sclera **2** of or affected with sclerosis

[2]**sclerotic** *n* the sclera [ML *sclerotica*, fr (assumed) Gk *sklērōtos*, verbal of Gk *sklēroun* to harden]

sclerotium /sklə'rohshyəm/ *n, pl* **sclerotia** /-tyə/ a compact mass of hardened fungal mycelium that becomes detached and remains dormant until a favourable opportunity for growth occurs [NL, fr (assumed) Gk *sklērōtos*] – **sclerotial** /-sh(ə)l/ *adj*

[1]**scoff** /skof/ *n* an expression of scorn, derision, or contempt [ME *scof*, prob of Scand origin; akin to obs Dan *skof* jest; akin to OFris *skof* mockery]

[2]**scoff** *vi* to show contempt by derisive acts or language – often + *at* ⟨~ *at conventional wisdom*⟩ – **scoffer** *n*

[3]**scoff** *vt, chiefly Br* to eat, esp greedily, rapidly, or in an ill-mannered way – infml [prob alter. of earlier *scaff*, of unknown origin]

[1]**scold** /skohld/ *n* a woman who habitually nags or quarrels [ME *scald, scold*, prob of Scand origin; akin to ON *skāld* poet, skald, Icel *skālda* to make scurrilous verse]

[2]**scold** *vi* to find fault noisily and at length ~*vt* to reprove sharply – **scolder** *n*

scolex /'skohleks/ *n, pl* **scolices** /sko'lee,seez/ the head of a tapeworm [NL *scolic-, scolex*, fr Gk *skōlēk-, skōlēx* worm; akin to Gk *skelos* leg – more at CYLINDER]

scoliosis /ˌskoli'ohsis/ *n, pl* **scolioses** /-ˌseez/ a sideways curvature of the spine – compare KYPHOSIS, LORDOSIS [NL, fr Gk *skoliōsis* crookedness of a bodily part, fr *skolios* crooked – more at CYLINDER] – **scoliotic** /-tik/ *adj*

scollop /'skoləp/ *n* a scallop [by alter.]

scombroid /'skombroyd/ *n* any of a suborder of spiny-finned sea fishes (e g the mackerel) used for food [deriv of Gk *skombros* mackerel] – **scombroid** *adj*

[1]**sconce** /skons/ *n* a bracket candlestick or group of candlesticks; *also* an electric light fixture patterned on a candle sconce [ME, fr MF *esconse* screened lantern, fr OF, fr fem of *escons*, pp of *escondre* to hide, fr L *abscondere* – more at ABSCOND]

[2]**sconce** *n* a detached defensive work (e g a fort or mound) [D *schans*, fr G *schanze*]

[3]**sconce** *n, Br* (the mug used for) a forfeit formerly common at Oxford and Cambridge universities that involves drinking or supplying drink (e g beer) [perh fr archaic *sconce* (head)] – **sconce** *vt*

scone /skohn; *or* skon/ *n* any of several small light cakes made from a dough or batter containing a raising agent and baked in a hot oven or on a griddle [perh fr D *schoonbrood* fine white bread, fr *schoon* pure, clean + *brood* bread]

[1]**scoop** /skoohp/ *n* **1a** a large ladle for taking up or skimming liquids **b** a deep shovel for lifting and moving granular material (e g corn or sand) **c** a handled utensil of shovel shape or with a hemispherical bowl for spooning out soft food (e g ice cream) **d** a small spoon-shaped utensil for cutting or gouging (e g in surgical operations) **2a** an act or the action of scooping **b** the amount held by a scoop ⟨*a ~ of sugar*⟩ **3** a cavity **4** material for publication or broadcast, esp when obtained ahead or to the exclusion of competitors [ME *scope*, fr MD *schope*; akin to OHG *skepfen* to shape – more at SHAPE] – **scoopful** *n*

[2]**scoop** *vt* **1** to take out or up (as if) with a scoop **2** to empty by scooping **3** to make hollow; dig out **4** to obtain a news story in advance or to the exclusion of (a competitor) **5** to obtain by swift action or sudden good fortune – chiefly infml ⟨*~ the lion's share of an aid programme*⟩

scoot /skooht/ *vi* to go suddenly and swiftly – infml [prob of Scand origin; akin to ON *skjōta* to shoot – more at [1]SHOOT] – **scoot** *n*

scooter /'skoohtə/ *n* **1** a child's foot-operated vehicle consisting of a narrow board with usu 1 wheel at each end and an upright steering handle **2** MOTOR SCOOTER

[1]**scope** /skohp/ *n* **1** space or opportunity for unhampered action, thought, or development **2a** extent of treatment, activity, or influence **b** extent of understanding or perception [It *scopo* purpose, goal, fr Gk *skopos*; akin to Gk *skeptesthai* to watch, look at – more at SPY]

[2]**scope** *n* a periscope, telescope, or other optical instrument – infml [*-scope*]

-scope /-skohp/ *comb form* (→ *n*) instrument for viewing or observing ⟨*micro*scope⟩ [NL *-scopium*, fr Gk *-skopion*; akin to Gk *skeptesthai*]

scopolamine /skoh'poləmeen, -min/ *n* hyoscine [G *scopolamin*, fr NL *Scopolia*, genus of plants + G *amin* amine]

-scopy /-skəpi/ *comb form* (→ *n*) viewing; observation ⟨*radio*scopy⟩ [Gk *-skopia*, fr *skeptesthai*]

scorbutic /skaw'byoohtik/ *adj* of, resembling, or diseased with scurvy [NL *scorbuticus*, fr *scorbutus* scurvy, prob of Gmc origin; akin to OE *scurf*] – **scorbutically** *adv*

[1]**scorch** /skawch/ *vt* **1** to burn so as to produce a change in colour and texture **2a** to parch (as if) with intense heat **b** to criticize or deride bitterly **3** to devastate completely, esp before abandoning – used in *scorched earth*, of property of possible use to an enemy *~ vi* **1** to become scorched **2** to travel at (excessive) speed [ME *scorcnen, scorchen*, prob of Scand origin; akin to ON *skorpna* to shrivel up – more at SHRIMP] – **scorchingly** *adv*

[2]**scorch** *n* a mark resulting from scorching

scorcher /'skawchə/ *n* a very hot day – infml [[1]SCORCH + [2]-ER]

[1]**score** /skaw/ *n, pl* **scores**, (*1a, b*) **scores, score** **1a** twenty **b** a group of 20 things – used in combination with a cardinal number ⟨*five*score⟩ **c** *pl* an indefinite large number **2a** a line (e g a scratch or incision) made (as if) with a sharp instrument **b** a notch used for keeping a tally **3a** an account or reckoning kept by making incisions **b** an account of debts **c** an amount due **4** a grudge ⟨*settle an old ~*⟩ **5a** a reason, ground ⟨*complain on the ~ of maltreatment*⟩ **b** a subject, topic ⟨*have no doubts on that ~*⟩ **6a** the copy of a musical composition in written or printed notation **b** the music for a film or theatrical production **c** a complete description of a dance composition in choreographic notation **7a** a number that expresses accomplishment (e g in a game or test) **b** an act (e g a goal, run, or try) in any of various games or contests that increases such a number **8** the inescapable facts of a situation ⟨*knows the ~*⟩ [ME *scor*, fr ON *skor* notch, tally, twenty; akin to OE *scieran* to cut – more at SHEAR]

[2]**score** *vt* **1a** to record (as if) by notches on a tally **b** to enter (a debt) in an account – usu + *to* or *against* **c** to cancel or strike out (e g record of a debt) with a line or notch – often + *out* **2** to mark with grooves, scratches, or notches **3a(1)** to gain (e g points) in a game or contest ⟨*~d 8 runs*⟩ **(2)** to have as a value in a game or contest ⟨*a try ~s 4 points*⟩ **b** to gain, win ⟨*~d a success with his latest novel*⟩ **4a** to write or arrange (music) for specific voice or instrumental parts **b** to orchestrate **c** to compose a score for (e g a film) *~ vi* **1** to record the scores or make a score in a game or contest **2** to obtain a rating or grade ⟨*~ high in intelligence tests*⟩ **3a** to gain or have an advantage or a success **b** to obtain illicit drugs – slang **c** to achieve a sexual success – slang – **scorer** *n* – **score off someone** *Br* to get the better of sby in debate or argument

'score,board /-ˌbawd/ *n* a usu large board for displaying the state of play (e g the score) in a game or match

scoria /'skawri·ə/ *n, pl* **scoriae** /-riˌee/ **1** the refuse from smelting ores or melting metals **2** rough cindery lava [ME, fr L, fr Gk *skōria*, fr *skōr* excrement; akin to OE *scearn* dung, L *muscerda* mouse dropping] – **scoriaceous** /ˌskawri'ayshəs/ *adj*

[1]**scorn** /skawn/ *n* **1** vigorous contempt; disdain **2** an expression of extreme contempt **3** an object of extreme disdain or derision [ME, fr OF *escarn*, of

Gmc origin; akin to OHG *scern* jest; akin to Gk *skairein* to gambol] – **scornful** *adj*

[2]**scorn** *vt* to reject with outspoken contempt – **scorner** *n*

Scorpio /ˈskawpioh/ *n* (sby born under) the 8th sign of the zodiac in astrology, which is pictured as a scorpion ☞ SYMBOL [L, fr Gk *Skorpios*, lit., scorpion] – **Scorpian** *adj or n*

scorpioid /ˈskawpi,oyd/ *adj* curved at the end like a scorpion's tail ⟨*a ~ inflorescence*⟩ [Gk *skorpioeidēs* resembling a scorpion, fr *skorpios*]

scorpion /ˈskawpyən/ *n* **1** any of an order of arachnids having an elongated body and a narrow tail bearing a venomous sting at the tip **2** a whip studded with metal spikes [ME, fr OF, fr L *scorpion-*, *scorpio*, fr Gk *skorpios*; akin to OE *scieran* to cut – more at SHEAR]

ˈ**scorpion ,fish** *n* any of several spiny-finned sea fishes; *esp* one with a venomous spine on the dorsal fin

ˈ**scorpion ,fly** *n* any of a family of flesh-eating insects that have cylindrical bodies and the male genitalia enlarged into a swollen bulb

scorzonera /,skawzəˈniərə/ *n* (a European composite plant with) a black edible root similar to that of salsify [NL, genus name, fr It]

Scot /skot/ *n* **1** a member of a Gaelic people orig of N Ireland that settled in Scotland about AD 500 **2** a native or inhabitant of Scotland [ME *Scottes* Scots, fr OE *Scottas* Irishmen, Scots, fr LL *Scotus* Irishman]

[1]**scotch** /skoch/ *vt* **1a** to stamp out; crush **b** to hinder, thwart ⟨*~ schemes for sponsorship*⟩ **2** to repudiate by exhibiting as false ⟨*~ rumours*⟩ [ME *scocchen* to gash]

[2]**scotch** *n* a slight cut

[1]**Scotch** *adj* Scottish [contr of *Scottish*]

[2]**Scotch** *n* **1** Scots **2** *pl in constr the* Scots **3** *often not cap* SCOTCH WHISKY; *broadly* (a) whisky

,**Scotch ˈbroth** *n* soup made from beef or mutton, vegetables, and barley

,**Scotch ˈegg** *n* a hard-boiled egg covered with sausage meat, coated with breadcrumbs, and deep-fried

,**Scotch ˈpine** *n* SCOTS PINE

Scotch tape *trademark* – used for any of numerous adhesive tapes

,**Scotch ˈterrier** *n* SCOTTISH TERRIER

,**Scotch ˈwhisky** *n* whisky distilled in Scotland, esp from malted barley

,**Scotch ˈwoodcock** *n* buttered toast spread with anchovy paste and scrambled egg

scoter /ˈskohtə/ *n, pl* **scoters,** *esp collectively* **scoter** any of several mostly black sea ducks [origin unknown]

,**scot-ˈfree** *adj* without any penalty, payment, or injury [*scot* (payment, tax), fr ME, fr ON *skot* shot, contribution – more at SHOT]

scotia /ˈskohshə/ *n* a deep concave moulding, esp on the base of a column ☞ ARCHITECTURE [L, fr Gk *skotia*, fr fem of *skotios* dark, shadowy, fr *skotos* darkness – more at SHADE]

,**Scotland ˈYard** /ˈskotlənd/ *n sing or pl in constr* the criminal investigation department of the London metropolitan police force [*Scotland Yard*, street in London formerly the headquarters of the metropolitan police]

scotoma /skəˈtohmə/ *n, pl* **scotomas, scotomata** /-mətə/ a blind or dark spot in the visual field [NL *scotomat-, scotoma*, fr ML, dimness of vision, fr Gk *skotōmat-, skotōma*, fr *skotoun* to darken, fr *skotos*] – **scotomatous** /-ˈtomətəs/ *adj*

scotopic /skəˈtopik, -ˈtoh-/ *adj* relating to or being vision in dim light with eyes adapted to the dark – compare PHOTOPIC [NL *scotopia* scotopic vision, fr Gk *skotos* darkness + NL *-opia*] – **scotopia** /-pi·ə/ *n*

[1]**Scots** /skots/ *adj* Scottish –used esp of the people and language or in legal context [ME *Scottis*, alter. of *Scottish*] – **Scotsman** *n*

[2]**Scots** *n* the English language of Scotland

,**Scots ˈpine** *n* a N European and Asian pine with spreading branches, short twisted needles, and hard yellow wood that provides valuable timber

Scotticism /ˈskoti,siz(ə)m/ *n* a characteristic feature of Scottish English, esp as contrasted with standard English [LL *scotticus* of the ancient Scots, fr *Scotus* Scot]

scottie /ˈskoti/ *n* **1** *cap* a (male) Scot – used esp as a nickname **2** SCOTTISH TERRIER [*Scot* + *-ie*]

[1]**Scottish** /ˈskotish/ *adj* (characteristic) of Scotland [ME, fr *Scottes* Scots] – **Scottishness** *n*

[2]**Scottish** *n* Scots

,**Scottish ˈterrier** *n* (any of) a Scottish breed of terrier with short legs and a very wiry coat of usu black hair

scoundrel /ˈskowndrəl/ *n* a wicked or dishonest fellow [origin unknown] – **scoundrelly** *adj*

[1]**scour** /ˈskowə/ *vt* **1** to move through or range over usu swiftly **2** to make a rapid but thorough search of [ME *scuren*, prob of Scand origin; akin to Sw *skura* to rush]

[2]**scour** *vt* **1a** to rub vigorously in order to cleanse **b** to remove by rubbing, esp with rough or abrasive material **2** to clean out by purging **3** to free from impurities (as if) by washing **4** to clear, excavate, or remove (as if) by a powerful current of water ~ *vi* **1** to undertake scouring **2** *esp of cattle* to suffer from diarrhoea or dysentery **3** to become clean and bright by being rubbed [ME *scouren*] – **scourer** /ˈskow(ə)rə/ *n*

[3]**scour** *n* **1** scouring action (e g of a glacier) **2** diarrhoea or dysentery, esp in cattle – usu pl with sing. meaning but sing. or pl in constr

[1]**scourge** /skuhj/ *n* **1** a whip used to inflict punishment **2a** a means of vengeance or criticism **b** a cause of affliction [ME, fr AF *escorge*, fr (assumed) OF *escorgier* to whip, fr OF *es-* ex- + L *corrigia* whip]

[2]**scourge** *vt* **1** to flog **2a** to punish severely **b** to subject to affliction; devastate **c** to subject to scathing criticism – **scourger** *n*

scouring /ˈskow(ə)ring/ *n* material removed by scouring or cleaning

scouring rush *n* a plant with stems containing hard granules of silica formerly used for scouring; *specif* a horsetail

Scouse /skows/ *n or adj* (a native or inhabitant or the dialect) of Merseyside – chiefly infml [short for *lobscouse*; fr the popularity of lobscouse in Merseyside]

[1]**scout** /skowt/ *vi* to make an advance survey (e g to obtain military information) ~ *vt* **1** to observe or explore in order to obtain information **2** to find by making a search – often + *out* or *up* [ME *scouten*,

fr MF *escouter* to listen, fr L *auscultare* – more at AUSCULTATION]

[2]**scout** *n* **1** the act or an instance of scouting **2a** sby or sthg sent to obtain (military) information **b** TALENT SCOUT **3** an Oxford university college servant – compare BEDDER, GYP **4** *often cap* a member of a worldwide movement of boys and young men that was founded with the aim of developing leadership and comradeship and that lays stress on outdoor activities; *specif* a British boy member aged from 11 to 15

ˈ**scout ˌcar** *n* a fast armoured military reconnaissance vehicle

Scouter /ˈskowtə/ *n* an adult leader in the Scout movement

Scouting /ˈskowting/ *n* the activities of the Scout movement

ˈ**scoutˌmaster** /-ˌmahstə/ *n* the adult leader of a troop of scouts – no longer used technically

scow /skow/ *n* a large flat-bottomed usu unpowered boat used chiefly for transporting ore, sand, refuse, etc [D *schouw*; akin to OHG *scalta* punt pole]

[1]**scowl** /skowl/ *vi* **1** to frown or wrinkle the brows in expression of displeasure **2** to exhibit a gloomy or threatening aspect [ME *skoulen*, prob of Scand origin; akin to Dan *skule* to scowl] – **scowler** *n*

[2]**scowl** *n* an angry frown

[1]**scrabble** /ˈskrabl/ *vi* **scrabbling** /ˈskrabling/ **1** to scratch or scrape about **2a** to scramble, clamber **b** to struggle frantically ⟨*urchins* scrabbling *for leftovers*⟩ *USE* infml [D *schrabbelen* to scratch] – **scrabbler** *n*

[2]**scrabble** *n* **1** a persistent scratching or clawing **2** a scramble *USE* infml

Scrabble *trademark* – used for a board game of word-building from individual letters ☞ WORD

[1]**scrag** /skrag/ *n* **1** a scraggy person or animal **2** (the bony end nearest the head of) a neck of mutton or veal ☞ MEAT [perh alter. of Sc & E dial. *crag* neck, fr ME, fr MD *crāghe*]

[2]**scrag** *vt* **-gg- 1** to kill or execute by hanging, garrotting, or wringing the neck of **2** to attack in anger – infml

scraggly /ˈskragli/ *adj, NAm* irregular; *also* ragged, unkempt – infml

scraggy /ˈskragi/ *adj* lean and lanky in growth or build

scram /skram/ *vi* **-mm-** to go away at once – infml [short for *scramble*]

[1]**scramble** /ˈskrambl/ *vb* **scrambling** /ˈskrambling/ *vi* **1a** to move or climb using hands and feet, esp hastily **b** to move with urgency or panic **2** to struggle eagerly or chaotically for possession of sthg **3a** to spread or grow irregularly **b** *of a plant* to climb over a support **4** *esp of an aircraft or its crew* to take off quickly in response to an alert ~ *vt* **1** to collect by scrambling – + *up* or *together* ⟨~d *up a hasty supper*⟩ **2a** to toss or mix together **b** to prepare (eggs) in a pan by stirring during cooking **3** to cause or order (an aircraft) to scramble **4** to encode (the elements of a telecommunications transmission) in order to make unintelligible on unmodified receivers [perh alter. of [1]*scrabble*]

[2]**scramble** *n* **1** a scrambling movement or struggle **2** a disordered mess; a jumble **3** a rapid emergency takeoff of aircraft **4** a motorcycle race over very rough ground

scrambling /ˈskrambling/ *n* moto-cross

[1]**scrap** /skrap/ *n* **1** *pl* fragments of discarded or leftover food **2a** a small detached fragment **b** an excerpt from sthg written or printed **c** the smallest piece **3** *pl* the remains of animal fat after rendering; cracklings **4a** the residue from a manufacturing process **b** manufactured articles or parts, esp of metal, rejected or discarded and useful only for reprocessing [ME, fr ON *skrap* scraps; akin to ON *skrapa* to scrape]

[2]**scrap** *vt* **-pp- 1** to convert into scrap ⟨~ *a battleship*⟩ **2** to abandon or get rid of, as without further use ⟨~ *outworn methods*⟩

[3]**scrap** *vi or n* **-pp-** (to engage in) a minor fight or dispute – infml [origin unknown]

ˈ**scrapˌbook** /-ˌbook/ *n* a blank book in which miscellaneous items (e g newspaper cuttings or postcards) may be pasted

[1]**scrape** /skrayp/ *vt* **1a** to remove (clinging matter) from a surface by usu repeated strokes of an edged instrument **b** to make (a surface) smooth or clean with strokes of an edged or rough instrument **2a** to grate harshly over or against **b** to damage or injure by contact with a rough surface **c** to draw roughly or noisily over a surface **3** to collect or procure (as if) by scraping – often + *up* or *together* ⟨~ *up the price of a pint*⟩ ~ *vi* **1** to move in sliding contact with a rough or abrasive surface **2** to accumulate money by small but difficult economies ⟨scraping *and saving to educate their children*⟩ **3** to draw back the foot along the ground in making a bow – chiefly in *bow and scrape* **4** to get by with difficulty or succeed by a narrow margin – often + *in, through,* or *by* ⟨*the candidate* ~d *through with a majority of 6*⟩ [ME *scrapen*, fr ON *skrapa*; akin to OE *scrapian* to scrape, L *scrobis* ditch, Gk *keirein* to cut – more at SHEAR] – **scraper** *n*

[2]**scrape** *n* **1a** an act, process, or result of scraping **b** the sound of scraping **2** a disagreeable predicament, esp as a result of foolish behaviour – infml

scraperboard /ˈskraypəˌbawd/ *n* prepared cardboard on which a design may be produced by scraping away parts of a black surface

ˈ**scrap ˌheap** *n* **1** a pile of discarded materials, esp metal **2** the place to which useless things are consigned

scrapie /ˈskraypi/ *n* a usu fatal virus disease of sheep characterized by twitching, intense itching, emaciation, and finally paralysis [[1]*scrape*]

scrappy /ˈskrapi/ *adj* consisting of scraps ⟨*a* ~ *education*⟩

ˈ**scrapˌyard** /-ˌyahd/ *n, chiefly Br* a yard where scrap (metal) is collected or processed

[1]**scratch** /skrach/ *vt* **1** to scrape or dig with the claws or nails **2** to tear, mark, or cut the surface of with sthg sharp or jagged **3** to scrape or rub lightly (e g to relieve itching) **4** to scrape together ⟨~ *a precarious living – Punch*⟩ **5** to write or draw on a surface ⟨~ed *his initials on the desk*⟩ **6a** to cancel or erase (as if) by drawing a line through **b** to withdraw (an entry) from competition ~ *vi* **1** to use the claws or nails in digging, tearing, or wounding **2** to scrape or rub oneself (e g to relieve itching) **3** to acquire money by hard work and saving **4** to make a thin grating sound ⟨*this pen* ~es⟩ [blend of E dial. *scrat* (to scratch) and obs E *cratch* (to scratch)] – **scratcher** *n*

[2]**scratch** *n* **1** a mark, injury, or slight wound (produced by scratching) **2** the sound of scratching **3** the

most rudimentary beginning – in *from scratch* **4** standard or satisfactory condition or performance ⟨*not up to* ~⟩

[3]scratch *adj* **1** made or done by chance and not as intended ⟨*a* ~ *shot*⟩ **2** arranged or put together haphazardly or hastily ⟨*a* ~ *team*⟩ **3** without handicap or allowance ⟨*a* ~ *golfer*⟩

scratchy /ˈskrachi/ *adj* **1** tending to scratch or irritate ⟨~ *wool*⟩ **2** making a scratching noise ⟨*a* ~ *pen*⟩ **3** made (as if) with scratches ⟨~ *drawing*⟩ **4** uneven in quality **5** irritable, fractious – **scratchiness** *n*

scrawl /skrawl/ *vb* to write or draw awkwardly, hastily, or carelessly [origin unknown] – **scrawl** *n*, **scrawler** *n*, **scrawly** *adj*

scrawny /ˈskrawni/ *adj* exceptionally thin and slight ⟨~ *cattle*⟩ [origin unknown] – **scrawniness** *n*

[1]scream /skreem/ *vi* **1a(1)** to voice a sudden piercing cry, esp in alarm or pain **(2)** to produce harsh high tones **b** to move with or make a shrill noise like a scream **2** to speak or write violently or hysterically ⟨*a* ~ing *headline*⟩ **3** to produce a vivid or startling effect ⟨*a* ~ing *red*⟩ ~ *vt* **1** to utter (as if) with a scream or screams **2** to bring to a specified state by screaming ⟨~ *oneself hoarse*⟩ [ME *scremen*; akin to OHG *scrīan* to scream] – **screamer** *n*

[2]scream *n* **1** a shrill penetrating cry or noise **2** sby or sthg that provokes screams of laughter ⟨*he's a* ~ *after a drink or 2*⟩ – infml

screamingly /ˈskreemingli/ *adv* extremely ⟨~ *funny*⟩

scree /skree/ *n* (a mountain slope covered with) loose stones or rocky debris ☞ GEOGRAPHY [of Scand origin; akin to ON *skritha* landslide, fr *skrītha* to creep; akin to OHG *scrītan* to go, Lith *skrytis* rim of a wheel]

[1]screech /skreech/ *vi* **1** to utter a shrill piercing cry; cry out, esp in terror or pain **2** to make a sound like a screech ⟨*the car* ~ed *to a halt*⟩ [alter. of earlier *scritch*, fr ME *scrichen*; akin to ON *skrækja* to screech] – **screecher** *n*

[2]screech *n* a shrill sound or cry

ˈscreech ˌowl *n* a barn owl or other owl with a harsh shrill cry

screed /skreed/ *n* **1** an overlong usu dull piece of writing **2** a strip (e g of plaster) serving as a guide to the thickness of a subsequent coat **3** a levelling device drawn over freshly poured concrete [ME *screde* fragment, fr OE *scrēade* – more at SHRED]

[1]screen /skreen/ *n* **1a** a usu movable piece of furniture that gives protection from heat or draughts or is used as an ornament ⟨*fire* ~⟩ **b** an ornamental partition **2a** sthg that shelters, protects, or conceals ⟨*a* ~ *of light infantry*⟩ **b** a shield for secret usu illicit practices **3a** a sieve or perforated material set in a frame used to separate coarser from finer parts **b** a device that shields from interference (e g by electrical or magnetic fields) **c** a frame holding a netting used esp in a window or door to exclude mosquitoes and other pests **4a** a surface on which images are projected or reflected **b** the surface on which the image appears in a television or radar receiver ☞ TELEVISION **c** a ruled glass plate through which an image is photographed in making a halftone **5a** *the* film industry; films ⟨*a star of stage and* ~⟩ **b** *the* medium of television [ME *screne*, fr MF *escren*, fr MD *scherm*; akin to OHG *skirm* screen, L *corium* skin – more at CUIRASS]

[2]screen *vt* **1** to guard from injury, danger, or punishment **2a** to separate (as if) with a screen **b** to provide with a screen to keep out pests (e g insects) **3a** to pass (e g coal, gravel, or ashes) through a screen to separate the fine part from the coarse; *also* to remove (as if) by a screen **b(1)** to examine systematically so as to separate into different groups ⟨~ *visa applications*⟩ **(2)** to test or check by a screening process **4a** to show or broadcast (a film or television programme) **b** to present in a film or on television – **screenable** *adj*, **screener** *n*

screening /ˈskreening/ *n* **1** *pl but sing or pl in constr* material (e g waste or fine coal) separated out by a screen **2** metal or plastic mesh (e g for window screens) **3** a showing of a film or television programme

ˈscreenˌplay /-ˌplay/ *n* the script of a film including description of characters, details of scenes and settings, dialogue, and stage directions

screen printing *n* SILK SCREEN – **screen-printed** *adj*

ˈscreenˌwriter /-ˌrietə/ *n* a writer of screenplays

[1]screw /skrooh/ *n* **1** a simple machine of the inclined plane type in which the applied force acts along a spiral path about a cylinder while the resisting force acts along the axis of the cylinder **2a** a usu pointed tapering metal rod having a raised thread along all or part of its length and a usu slotted head which may be driven into a body by rotating (e g with a screwdriver) **b** a screw-bolt that can be turned by a screwdriver **3a** sthg like a screw in form or function; a spiral **b** a turn of a screw; *also* a twist resembling such a turn **4** SCREW PROPELLER **5** a thumbscrew **6** backspin, esp when given to a cue ball in billiards, snooker, etc **7** *chiefly Br* a small twisted paper packet (e g of tobacco) **8** sby who drives a hard bargain – slang **9** a prison guard – slang **10** an act of sexual intercourse – vulg [ME, fr MF *escroe* female screw, nut, fr ML *scrofa*, fr L, sow] – **screwlike** *adj*

[2]screw *vt* **1a(1)** to attach, close, operate, adjust, etc by means of a screw **(2)** to unite or separate by means of a screw or a twisting motion ⟨~ *the 2 pieces together*⟩ **b** to cause to rotate spirally about an axis **2a(1)** to contort (the face) or narrow (the eyes) (e g with effort or an emotion) – often + *up* **(2)** to crush into irregular folds **b** to make a spiral groove or ridge in **3** to increase the intensity, quantity, or effectiveness of ⟨~ *up one's courage*⟩ **4** to give backwards spin to (a ball) **5a** to make oppressive demands on ⟨~ed *him for every penny he'd got*⟩ **b** to extract by pressure or threat – usu + *from* or *out of* **6** to copulate with ~ *vi* **1a** to rotate like or as a screw **b** to become secured (as if) by screwing – usu + *on* or *up* ⟨*panels that* ~ *on*⟩ **2** to turn or move with a twisting motion **3** to copulate *USE* (*vt 2a(2), 3*) usu + *up*; (*vt 5*) slang; (*vt 6; vi 3*) vulg – **screwer** *n*

ˈscrewˌball /-ˌbawl/ *n or adj, chiefly NAm* (sby) crazily eccentric or whimsical – infml

ˈscrew-ˌbolt *n* a blunt-tipped metal rod or pin for fastening objects together that has a head at one end and a screw thread at the other for screwing into a threaded hole (e g on a nut)

ˈscrewˌdriver /-ˌdrievə/ *n* a tool for turning screws

screwed *adj* drunk – infml [fr pp of [2]*screw*]

screw eye *n* a device with a pointed threaded shaft and a head in the form of a loop

screw pine *n* any of a genus of tropical plants with slender palmlike stems and crowns of swordlike leaves

screw propeller *n* a device that consists of a central hub with radiating blades and is used to propel a vehicle (e g a ship or aeroplane)

screw thread *n* the projecting spiral rib of a screw

screw top *n* (an opening designed to take) a cover secured by twisting

screw up *vt* **1** to fasten or lock (as if) by a screw **2** to bungle, botch **3** to cause to become anxious or neurotic *USE* (*2, 3*) slang

screwy /ˈskrooh·i/ *adj* crazily absurd, eccentric, or unusual; *also* mad – infml – **screwiness** *n*

scribble /ˈskribl/ *vb* **scribbling** /ˈskribling/ to write or draw without regard for legibility or coherence [ME *scriblen*, fr ML *scribillare*, fr L *scribere* to write] – **scribble** *n*

scribbler /ˈskriblə/ *n* a minor or worthless author [SCRIBBLE + [2]-ER]

[1]**scribe** /skrieb/ *n* **1** a member of a learned class of lay jurists in ancient Israel up to New Testament times **2** a copier of manuscripts **3** an author; *specif* a journalist – chiefly humor [ME, fr L *scriba* official writer, fr *scribere* to write; akin to Gk *skariphasthai* to scratch an outline, *keirein* to cut – more at SHEAR] – **scribal** *adj*

[2]**scribe** *vt* **1** to mark a line on by scoring with a pointed instrument **2** to make (e g a line) by scratching or gouging [prob short for *describe*]

scriber /ˈskriebə/ *n* a sharp-pointed tool for making marks, esp on material (e g metal) to be cut

scrimmage /ˈskrimij/ *vi or n* (to take part in) **a** a confused fight or minor battle; a mêlée **b** the interplay between 2 American football teams that begins with the passing back of the ball from the ground and continues until the ball is dead [alter. of [1]*skirmish*]

scrimp /skrimp/ *vi* to be frugal or niggardly – esp in *scrimp and save* ~ *vt* to be niggardly in providing (for) ⟨~ *provisions*⟩ ⟨~s *his family*⟩ [perh of Scand origin; akin to Sw *skrympa* to shrink, ON *skorpna* to shrivel up – more at SHRIMP] – **scrimpy** *adj*

scrimshank /ˈskrim,shangk/ *vi, Br* to avoid duties or obligations – infml [origin unknown] – **scrimshanker** *n*

scrimshaw /ˈskrim,shaw/ *n* carved or coloured work made esp by sailors from ivory or whalebone [origin unknown] – **scrimshaw** *vb*

scrip /skrip/ *n* any of various documents used as evidence that the holder or bearer is entitled to receive sthg [short for *script*]

[1]**script** /skript/ *n* **1a** sthg written; text ⟨*handed him several pages of* ~⟩ **b** an original document **c** the written text of a stage play, film, or broadcast (used in production or performance) **d** an examination candidate's written answers ⟨*a pile of* ~s *to mark*⟩ **2a** (printed lettering resembling) handwriting **b** the characters used in the alphabet of a particular language ⟨*unable to decipher Cyrillic* ~⟩ ☞ ALPHABET [L *scriptum* thing written, fr neut of *scriptus*, pp of *scribere* to write – more at [1]SCRIBE]

[2]**script** *vt* to prepare a script for or from

scriptural /ˈskripchərəl/ *adj* of, contained in, or according to a sacred writing; *esp* biblical – **scripturally** *adv*

scripture /ˈskripchə/ *n* **1a** *often cap* the sacred writings of a religion; *esp* the Bible – often pl with sing. meaning **b** a passage from the Bible **2** an authoritative body of writings [ME, fr LL *scriptura*, fr L, act or product of writing, fr *scriptus*]

scriptwriter /ˈskript,rietə/ *n* one who writes screenplays or radio or television programmes

scrivener /ˈskrivn·ə/ *n* a notary [ME *scriveiner*, alter. of *scrivein*, fr MF *escrivein*, fr (assumed) VL *scriban-*, *scriba*, alter. of L *scriba* scribe]

scrod /skrod/ *n, NAm* a young cod, haddock, or other fish [perh fr obs D *schrood* shred; akin to OE *scrēade* shred – more at SHRED]

scrofula /ˈskrofyoolə/ *n* tuberculosis of lymph glands, esp in the neck [ML, fr LL *scrofulae*, pl, swellings of the lymph glands of the neck, fr pl of *scrofula*, dim. of L *scrofa* breeding sow]

scrofulous /ˈskrofyooləs/ *adj* of or affected (as if) with scrofula or a similar disease

scroll /skrohl/ *n* **1** a written document in the form of a roll **2** a stylized ornamental design imitating the spiral curves of a scroll [ME *scrowle*, alter. of *scrowe*, fr MF *escroue* scrap, scroll, of Gmc origin; akin to OE *scrēade* shred] – **scrolled** *adj*

ˈscroll ˌsaw *n* a thin handsaw for cutting curves or irregular designs

scrooge /skroohj/ *n, often cap* a miserly person – infml [Ebenezer *Scrooge*, character in *A Christmas Carol*, story by Charles Dickens †1870 E writer]

scrotum /ˈskrohtəm/ *n, pl* **scrota** /-tə/, **scrotums** the external pouch of most male mammals that contains the testes ☞ REPRODUCTION [L; akin to L *scrupus* sharp stone – more at SHRED] – **scrotal** *adj*

[1]**scrounge** /skrownj/ *vt* to beg, wheedle ⟨*can I* ~ *a cigarette off you?*⟩ ~ *vi* **1** to hunt *around* **2** to wheedle [alter. of E dial. *scrunge* (to wander about idly)] – **scrounger** *n*

[2]**scrounge** *n* – **on the scrounge** attempting to obtain sthg by wheedling or cajoling

[1]**scrub** /skrub/ *n* **1** (an area covered with) vegetation consisting chiefly of stunted trees or shrubs ⟨~ *land*⟩ ⟨~ *vegetation*⟩ ☞ PLANT **2a** a usu inferior type of domestic animal of mixed or unknown parentage; a mongrel **b** a small or insignificant person; a runt **3** *NAm* a player not in the first team; *also* a team composed of such players [ME, alter. of *schrobbe* shrub – more at SHRUB]

[2]**scrub** *vb* **-bb-** *vt* **1a** to clean by rubbing, esp with a stiff brush **b** to remove by scrubbing **2** WASH 6b **3** to abolish; DO AWAY WITH ⟨*let's* ~ *that idea*⟩ – infml ~ *vi* to use hard rubbing in cleaning [of LG or Scand origin; akin to MLG & MD *schrubben* to scrub, Sw *skrubba*]

scrubber /ˈskrubə/ *n* **1** an apparatus for removing impurities, esp from gases **2** *Br* a girl who is readily available for casual sex; *also* a prostitute **3** *Br* a coarse or unattractive person *USE* (*2, 3*) slang [[2]SCRUB + [2]-ER]

ˈscrubbing ˌbrush /ˈskrubing/, *NAm* **scrub brush** *n* a brush with hard bristles used for heavy cleaning, esp washing floors

scrubby /ˈskrubi/ *adj* **1** inferior in size or quality; stunted ⟨~ *cattle*⟩ **2** covered with or consisting of scrub 3 lacking distinction; trashy – infml [[1]*scrub*]

'scrub ,pine *n* a small or inferior pine tree

scrub up *vi, of a surgeon, nurse, etc* to clean the hands and arms thoroughly by scrubbing before an operation

[1]**scruff** /skruf/ *n* the back of the neck; the nape [alter. of earlier *scuff*, of unknown origin]

[2]**scruff** *n* an untidily dressed or grubby person – infml [E dial. *scruff* (dandruff, sthg worthless), alter. of *scurf*]

scruffy /'skrufi/ *adj* 1 seedy, disreputable ⟨*a ~ neighbourhood*⟩ 2 slovenly and untidy, esp in appearance – **scruffiness** *n*

scrum /skrum/ *n* 1 a set piece in rugby in which the forwards of each side crouch in a tight formation with the 2 front rows of each team meeting shoulder to shoulder so that the ball can be put in play between them ☞ SPORT 2 a disorderly struggle – chiefly humor ⟨*the morning ~ to board the bus*⟩ [short for *scrummage*]

scrum down *vi* to form a scrum

,scrum-'half *n* the player in rugby who puts the ball into the scrum ☞ SPORT

scrummage /'skrumij/ *vi or n* (to take part in) a scrum [alter. of *scrimmage*]

scrump /skrump/ *vt, Br* to pilfer (e g apples) from an orchard – infml [perh alter. of *scrimp*]

scrumptious /'skrum(p)shəs/ *adj, esp of food* delicious – infml [prob alter. of *sumptuous*] – **scrumptiously** *adv*, **scrumptiousness** *n*

scrumpy /'skrumpi/ *n, Br* dry rough cider [E dial. *scrump* (sthg shrivelled, shrivelled apple)]

scrunch /skrunch/ *vt* 1 to crunch, crush 2 to crumple – often + *up* ⟨*~ up a sheet of cardboard*⟩ ~ *vi* 1 to move making a crunching sound ⟨*her boots ~ed in the snow*⟩ 2 *NAm* to hunch up [alter. of [1]*crunch*] – **scrunch** *n*

[1]**scruple** /'skroohpl/ *n* 1 ☞ UNIT 2 *archaic* a minute part or quantity [ME *scriple*, fr L *scrupulus* a unit of weight, fr *scrupulus* small sharp stone]

[2]**scruple** *n* a moral consideration that inhibits action [MF *scrupule*, fr L *scrupulus* small sharp stone, cause of mental discomfort, scruple, dim. of *scrupus* sharp stone – more at SHRED]

[3]**scruple** *vi* to be reluctant on grounds of conscience

scrupulous /'skroohpyooləs/ *adj* 1 inclined to have moral scruples 2 painstakingly exact ⟨*working with ~ care*⟩ [ME, fr L *scrupulosus*, fr *scrupulus*] – **scrupulously** *adv*, **scrupulousness** *n*, **scrupulosity** /-'losəti/ *n*

scrutineer /,skroohti'niə/ *n, Br* sby who examines or observes sthg, esp the counting of votes at an election

scrutin·ize, -ise /'skroohti,niez/ *vt* to examine painstakingly – **scrutinizer** *n*

scrutiny /'skroohtini/ *n* 1 a searching study, inquiry, or inspection 2 a searching or critical look 3 close watch ⟨*keep prisoners under ~*⟩ [L *scrutinium*, fr *scrutari* to search, examine, fr *scruta* rubbish]

scry /skrie/ *vi* to divine by crystal gazing [short for *descry*]

scuba /'sk(y)oohbə/ *n* an aqualung ⟨*~ diving*⟩ [*s*elf-*c*ontained *u*nderwater *b*reathing *a*pparatus]

[1]**scud** /skud/ *vi* **-dd-** 1 to move or run swiftly, esp as if swept along ⟨*clouds ~ding along*⟩ 2 *of a ship* to run before a gale [prob of Scand origin; akin to Norw *skudda* to push; akin to L *quatere* to shake]

[2]**scud** *n* 1a a sudden slight shower b ocean spray or loose vaporizing clouds driven swiftly by the wind 2 a gust of wind

[1]**scuff** /skuf/ *vi* 1 to slouch along without lifting the feet 2 to become scratched or roughened by wear ⟨*patent leather soon ~s*⟩ ~ *vt* 1 to shuffle (the feet) along while walking or back and forth while standing 2 to scratch, chip, or abrade the surface of [prob of Scand origin; akin to Sw *skuffa* to push]

[2]**scuff** *n* 1 (a blemish or injury caused by) scuffing 2 *NAm* a noise (as if) of scuffing

[1]**scuffle** /'skufl/ *vi* **scuffling** /'skufling/ 1 to struggle confusedly and at close quarters 2 to move (hurriedly) about with a shuffling gait [prob of Scand origin; akin to Sw *skuffa* to push]

[2]**scuffle** *n* a confused impromptu usu brief fight

[1]**scull** /skul/ *n* 1 an oar worked to and fro over the stern of a boat as a means of propulsion 2 either of a pair of light oars used by a single rower [ME *sculle*]

[2]**scull** *vt* to propel (a boat) by sculls or by a large oar worked to and fro over the stern ~ *vi* to scull a boat – **sculler** *n*

scullery /'skul(ə)ri/ *n* a room for menial kitchen work (e g washing dishes and preparing vegetables) [ME, department of household in charge of dishes, fr MF *escuelerie*, fr *escuelle* bowl, fr L *scutella* drinking bowl – more at [1]SCUTTLE]

scullion /'skulyən/ *n, archaic* a kitchen servant [ME *sculion*, fr MF *escouillon* dishcloth, alter. of *escouvillon*, fr *escouve* broom, fr L *scopa*, lit., twig; akin to L *scapus* stalk – more at SHAFT]

sculpin /'skulpin/ *n, pl* **sculpins** *also* **sculpin** any of a family of spiny large-headed broad-mouthed usu scaleless fishes [origin unknown]

sculpt /skulpt/ *vt* to sculpture [F *sculpter*, alter. of obs *sculper*, fr L *sculpere*]

sculptor /'skulptə/, *fem* **sculptress** /-tris/ *n* an artist who sculptures [L, fr *sculptus*, pp of *sculpere*]

[1]**sculpture** /'skulpchə/ *n* 1a the art of creating three-dimensional works of art out of mouldable or hard materials by carving, modelling, casting, etc b (a piece of) work produced by sculpture 2 (a pattern of) impressed or raised marks, esp on a plant or animal part [ME, fr L *sculptura*, fr *sculptus*, pp of *sculpere* to carve, alter. of *scalpere* – more at SHELF] – **sculptural** *adj*, **sculpturally** *adv*, **sculpturesque** /-'resk/ *adj*

[2]**sculpture** *vt* 1a to represent in sculpture b to form (e g wood or stone) into a sculpture 2 to shape by erosion or other natural processes 3 to shape (as if) by carving or moulding

[1]**scum** /skum/ *n* 1 pollutants or impurities risen to or collected on the surface of a liquid 2 *pl in constr* the lowest class; the dregs ⟨*the ~ of the earth*⟩ [ME, fr MD *schum*; akin to OHG *scūm* foam] – **scummy** *adj*

[2]**scum** *vi* **-mm-** to become covered (as if) with scum

[1]**scumble** /'skumbl/ *vt* **scumbling** /'skumbling, 'skumbl·ing/ to soften the lines or colours of a (a drawing) by rubbing lightly b (a painting) by covering with a thin opaque coat of colour [freq of [2]*scum*]

[2]**scumble** *n* 1 the effect of scumbling 2 a material used for scumbling

scungy /'skunji/ *adj, Austr* grotty [perh fr Sc *scunge* a sly or vicious person]

scunner /'skunə/ *n, Scot* (the object of) an unreasonable dislike or prejudice ⟨*took a ~ at him*⟩ [ME (Sc) *skunniren* to be annoyed]

'scunnered *adj, Scot* extremely fed up or exasperated

[1]**scupper** /'skupə/ *n* an opening in a ship's side for draining water from the deck [ME *skopper*]

[2]**scupper** *vt, Br* to wreck; PUT PAID TO ⟨~ed *our plans for a reunion*⟩ – infml [origin unknown]

scurf /skuhf/ *n* thin dry scales detached from the skin; *specif* dandruff [ME, of Scand origin; akin to Icel *skurfa* scurf; akin to OHG *scorf* scurf, L *carpere* to pluck – more at HARVEST] – **scurfy** *adj*

scurrilous /'skuriləs/ *adj* **1a** using or given to coarse language **b** wicked and unscrupulous in behaviour ⟨*~ impostors who rob poor people*⟩ **2** containing obscenities or coarse abuse [L *scurrilis* jeering, fr *scurra* buffoon, jester] – **scurrilously** *adv*, **scurrilousness** *n*, **scurrility** /sku'riləti/ *n*

scurry /'skuri/ *vi* to move briskly, esp with short hurried steps, and often in some agitation or confusion; scamper [short for *hurry-scurry*, redupl of *hurry*] – **scurry** *n*

[1]**scurvy** /'skuhvi/ *adj* disgustingly mean or contemptible ⟨*a ~ trick*⟩ [*scurf*] – **scurvily** *adv*, **scurviness** *n*

[2]**scurvy** *n* a deficiency disease caused by a lack of vitamin C and marked by spongy gums, loosening of the teeth, and bleeding under the skin

'scurvy ,grass *n* any of several small plants of the mustard family whose leaves were formerly eaten to prevent scurvy

scut /skut/ *n* a short erect tail (e g of a hare) [origin unknown]

scutage /'skyoohtij/ *n* a tax levied on a tenant of a knight's estate in place of military service [ME, fr ML *scutagium*, fr L *scutum* shield – more at ESQUIRE]

scutch /skuch/ *vt* to separate the woody fibre from (flax or hemp) by beating [(assumed) F *escoucher* to beat, fr (assumed) VL *excuticare* to beat out, fr L *executere*, fr *ex-* + *quatere* to shake, strike]

scute /skyooht/ *n* an external hard plate or large scale (e g on the belly of a snake) [NL *scutum*, fr L, shield – more at ESQUIRE]

scutellum /skyooh'teləm/ *n, pl* **scutella** /-lə/ any of several small usu hard (shield-shaped) plates or scales on a plant or animal (e g on the feet of a bird) [NL, dim. of L *scutum* shield] – **scutellar** *adj*, **scutellate** /'skyoohti,layt, -lit/, **scutellated** *adj*

scutter /'skutə/ *vi, chiefly Br* [4]SCUTTLE [by alter.]

[1]**scuttle** /'skutl/ *n* a vessel that resembles a bucket and is used for storing, carrying, and dispensing coal indoors [ME *scutel*, fr L *scutella* drinking bowl, tray, dim. of *scutra* platter]

[2]**scuttle** *n* **1** a small opening or hatchway with a movable lid in the deck of a ship **2** *Br* the top part of a motor-car body forward of the 2 front doors, to which the windscreen and instrument panel are attached [ME *skottell*]

[3]**scuttle** *vt* **scuttling** /'skutling/ **1** to sink (a ship) by making holes in the hull or opening the sea-cocks **2** to destroy, wreck ⟨*~ attempts to reach agreement*⟩

[4]**scuttle** *vi* to scurry, scamper [prob blend of *scud* and *shuttle*]

[5]**scuttle** *n* **1** a quick shuffling pace **2** a short swift dash; *esp* a swift departure

'scuttle,butt /-,but/ *n* **1** a cask on a ship's deck containing fresh water **2** *NAm* GOSSIP 2a – infml [[2]*scuttle*]

scutum /'skyoohtəm/ *n, pl* **scuta** /-tə/ a scute [NL, fr L, shield – more at ESQUIRE]

[1]**scythe** /siedh/ *n* a long curving blade fastened at an angle to a long handle for cutting standing plants, esp grass [ME *sithe*, fr OE *sīthe*; akin to OE *sagu* saw – more at [2]SAW]

[2]**scythe** *vt* to cut (as if) with a scythe

Scythian /'sidhi·ən/ *n* **1** a member of an ancient nomadic people inhabiting Scythia **2** the Iranian language of the Scythians [L *Scytha*, fr Gk *Skythēs*] – **Scythian** *adj*

sea /see/ *n* **1a** OCEAN 1; *broadly* the waters of the earth as distinguished from the land and air – often pl with sing. meaning **b** a large (partially) landlocked or inland body of salt water **c** a freshwater lake ⟨*the* Sea *of Galilee*⟩ **2** (the direction of) surface motion caused by the wind on a large body of water; *also* a heavy swell or wave **3** sthg vast or overwhelming likened to the sea ⟨*a ~ of faces*⟩ **4** the seafaring life ⟨*to run away to ~*⟩ **5** [2]MARE [ME *see*, fr OE *sǣ*; akin to OS & OHG *sē* sea] – **at sea 1** on the sea; *specif* on a sea voyage **2** unable to understand; bewildered ⟨*he was all* at sea, *having never done such work before*⟩

'sea ,anchor *n* a device, typically of canvas, thrown overboard to slow the drifting of a ship or seaplane and to keep its head to the wind

'sea a,nemone *n* any of numerous usu solitary and brightly coloured polyps with a cluster of tentacles superficially resembling a flower ☞ DEFENCE

'sea ,bass /bas/ *n* any of numerous marine fishes related to the groupers

'sea,bird /-,buhd/ *n* a bird (e g a gull or albatross) frequenting the open sea

'sea,board /-,bawd/ *n, chiefly NAm* (the land near) a seashore – **seaboard** *adj*

'sea,borne /-,bawn/ *adj* conveyed on or over the sea ⟨*~ trade*⟩

'sea ,bream *n* any of numerous marine spiny-finned food fishes

sea breeze *n* a cool breeze blowing usu during the day inland from the sea

,sea 'butterfly *n* any of a group of small marine gastropod molluscs with the foot expanded into broad winglike swimming organs

'sea ,captain *n* the master of a (merchant) vessel

'sea ,change *n* a complete transformation

'sea ,chest *n* a sailor's personal storage chest

'sea ,coal *n, archaic* mineral coal as opposed to charcoal

'sea-,cock *n* a valve in the hull of a vessel through which water may be admitted

'sea ,cow *n* **1** a dugong **2** a manatee

,sea 'cucumber *n* a holothurian; *esp* one whose body is cucumber-shaped

'sea,dog /-,dog/ *n* a fogbow

'sea ,dog *n* a veteran sailor

'sea-,ear *n* an abalone

,sea 'elephant *n* ELEPHANT SEAL

'sea ,fan *n* a polyp with a fan-shaped skeleton

'sea,farer /-,feərə/ *n* a sailor [*sea* + [1]*fare* + [2]*-er*]

'sea,faring /-,feəring/ *n* travel by sea; *esp* the occupation of a sailor – **seafaring** *adj*

'sea,food /-,foohd/ *n* edible marine fish, shellfish, crustaceans, etc

'sea,front /-,frunt/ *n* the waterfront of a seaside town

'sea,girt /-,guht/ *adj* surrounded by the sea – poetic ⟨*this* ~ *isle*⟩

'sea,going /-,goh·ing/ *adj* of or designed for travel on the sea

,sea 'gooseberry *n* a ctenophore

,sea 'green *adj or n* bluish or yellowish green

'sea ,gull *n* [1]GULL

'sea ,hare *n* any of various large shell-less molluscs with tentacles that project like ears

'sea ,holly *n* a European coastal plant of the carrot family with bluish spiny leaves and pale blue flowers

'sea ,horse *n* 1 a mythical creature half horse and half fish 2 any of numerous small fishes whose head and body are shaped like the head and neck of a horse

'sea,kale /-,kayl/ *n* 1 a fleshy European plant of the mustard family used as a herb in cooking 2 *also* **seakale beet** chard

[1]**seal** /seel/ *n, pl* **seals,** *esp collectively* **seal** 1 any of numerous marine flesh-eating mammals chiefly of cold regions with limbs modified into webbed flippers for swimming 2 sealskin [ME *sele,* fr OE *seolh;* akin to OHG *selah* seal]

[2]**seal** *vi* to hunt seal

[3]**seal** *n* **1a** sthg that confirms, ratifies, or makes secure **b(1)** an emblem or word impressed or stamped on a document as a mark of authenticity (2) an article used to impress such a word or emblem (e g on wax); *also* a disc, esp of wax, bearing such an impression **2a** a closure (e g a wax seal on a document or a strip of paper over the cork of a bottle) that must be broken in order to give access, and so guarantees that the item so closed has not been tampered with **b** a tight and effective closure (e g against gas or liquid) [ME *seel,* fr OF, fr L *sigillum* seal, fr dim. of *signum* sign, seal] – **under seal** with an authenticating seal attached

[4]**seal** *vt* 1 to confirm or make secure (as if) by a seal ⟨~ed *the agreement with a handshake*⟩ **2a** to attach an authenticating seal to; *also* to authenticate, ratify **b** to mark with a stamp or seal (e g as evidence of size, accuracy, or quality) **3a** to fasten (as if) with a seal, esp to prevent or disclose interference **b** to close or make secure against access, leakage, or passage by a fastening or coating; *esp* to make airtight **c** to fix in position or close breaks in with a filling (e g of plaster) 4 to determine irrevocably ⟨*that answer* ~ed *our fate*⟩

'sea-,lane *n* an established sea route

sealant /'seelənt/ *n* a sealing agent ⟨*radiator* ~⟩

sea lavender *n* any of a genus of mostly coastal plants with bluish-purple flowers

,sealed-'beam /seeld/ *adj* of or being an electric light in which a reflector is an integral part of the bulb

'sea ,legs *n pl* bodily adjustment to the motion of a ship, indicated esp by ability to walk steadily and by freedom from seasickness

'sea ,leopard *n* a spotted antarctic seal

[1]**sealer** /'seelə/ *n* 1 a coat (e g of size) applied to prevent subsequent coats of paint or varnish from being too readily absorbed 2 *chiefly NAm* an official who certifies conformity to a standard of correctness [[3]*seal*]

[2]**sealer** *n* a person or ship engaged in hunting seals [[1]*seal*]

'sea ,level *n* the mean level of the surface of the sea midway between high and low tide

'sea ,lily *n* a (stalked) crinoid

'sealing ,wax /'seeling/ *n* a resinous composition that becomes soft when heated and is used for sealing letters, parcels, etc

'sea ,lion *n* any of several large Pacific seals

'sea ,loch *n* a loch connecting with the sea

seal off *vt* to close securely, esp in order to prevent passage ⟨*troops* sealed off *the airport*⟩

'sea-,lord *n, often cap* either of 2 members of the Admiralty Board of the Ministry of Defence who are also serving naval officers

'seal,skin /,skin/ *n* 1 (leather made from) the skin of a seal 2 a garment of sealskin – **sealskin** *adj*

,Sealyham 'terrier /'seeli·əm/ *n* (any of) a breed of short-legged wirehaired chiefly white Welsh terriers [*Sealyham,* estate in Pembrokeshire, Wales]

[1]**seam** /seem/ *n* 1 a line of stitching joining 2 separate pieces of fabric, esp along their edges 2 the space between adjacent planks or strakes of a ship **3a** a line, groove, or ridge formed at the meeting of 2 edges **b** a layer or stratum of coal, rock, etc **c** a line left by a cut or wound; *also* a wrinkle [ME *seem,* fr OE *sēam;* akin to OE *sīwian* to sew – more at SEW] – **seamless** *adj*

[2]**seam** *vt* 1 to join (as if) by sewing 2 to mark with a seam, furrow, or scar

seaman /'seemən/ *n* 1 a sailor, mariner 2 ☞ RANK – **seamanlike** *adj,* **seamanly** *adj,* **seamanship** *n*

seaman apprentice *n* ☞ RANK

seaman recruit *n* ☞ RANK

'sea,mark /-,mahk/ *n* a conspicuous object serving as a guide for navigators

seam bowling *n* usu faster bowling in cricket in which the ball is made to bounce on its seam and thereby deviate from a straight line

seamer /'seemə/ *n* (a delivery bowled by) a bowler of seam bowling [[2]SEAM + [2]-ER]

'sea ,mew *n* [1]GULL

sea mile *n* NAUTICAL MILE

'sea,mount /-,mownt/ *n* an underwater mountain

'sea ,mouse *n* a large broad marine worm covered with hairlike bristles

seamstress /'seemstris/ *n* a woman whose occupation is sewing [fem of *seamster* one who sews, fr ME *semester, semster,* fr OE *sēamestre* seamstress, tailor, fr *sēam* seam]

seamy /'seemi/ *adj* unpleasant, sordid ⟨*the* ~ *side of the building trade*⟩ [*seam* + *-y;* orig sense, having the rough side of the seam showing] – **seaminess** *n*

séance /'say·on(h)s/ *n* a meeting at which spiritualists attempt to communicate with the dead [F, fr *seoir* to sit, fr L *sedēre* – more at SIT]

'sea ,otter *n* a rare large marine otter of N Pacific coasts that feeds largely on shellfish ☞ ENDANGERED

'sea ,pen *n* any of numerous sea invertebrates related to the corals and living in large social groups that have a feathery form

,sea-'pink *n* a thrift with dense pink or white flower heads that grows esp on the seashore

'sea,plane /-,playn/ *n* an aeroplane designed to take off from and land on the water

'sea,port /-,pawt/ *n* a port, harbour, or town accessible to seagoing ships

'sea ,power *n* (a nation that commands) naval strength

'sea ,purse *n* the horny egg case of skates and some sharks

'sea,quake /-,kwayk/ *n* an underwater earthquake [*sea* + *-quake* (as in *earthquake*)]

¹sear /siə/ *adj* sere

²sear *vt* **1** to make withered and dried up **2** to burn, scorch, or injure (as if) with a sudden application of intense heat **3** to mark (as if) with a branding iron ⟨*a sight which was* ~ed *on my memory*⟩ [ME *seren*, fr OE *sēarian* to become sere, fr *sēar* sere] – **searingly** *adv*

³sear *n* a mark or scar left by searing

⁴sear *n* the catch that holds the hammer of a gunlock at cock or half cock [prob fr MF *serre* grasp, fr *serrer* to press, grasp, fr LL *serare* to bolt, latch, fr L *sera* bar for fastening a door]

¹search /suhch/ *vt* **1a** to look through or over carefully or thoroughly in order to find or discover sthg ⟨~ed *the horizon*⟩ ⟨~ed *the house for clues*⟩ **b** to examine (a person) for concealed articles (e g weapons or drugs) **c** to scrutinize, esp in order to discover intention or nature ⟨~ed *her heart*⟩ **2** to uncover or ascertain by investigation – usu + *out* ⟨~ *out the relevant facts*⟩ **3** to cover (an area) with gunfire ~ *vi* **1** to look or inquire carefully or thoroughly ⟨~ed *for the papers*⟩ **2** to make painstaking investigation or examination ⟨~ed *into the matter very thoroughly*⟩ [ME *cerchen*, fr MF *cerchier* to go about, survey, search, fr LL *circare* to go about, fr L *circum* round about] – **searchable** *adj*, **searcher** *n* – **search me** – used to express ignorance of an answer

²search *n* **1** an act or process of searching; *esp* an organized act of searching ⟨*the* ~ *for the escaped convicts is still in progress*⟩ ⟨*a* ~ *party*⟩ **2** an exercise of the right of search

searching /'suhching/ *adj* piercing, penetrating ⟨*a* ~ *gaze*⟩ – **searchingly** *adv*

'search,light /-,liet/ *n* (an apparatus for projecting) a movable beam of light

'search ,warrant *n* a warrant authorizing a search of premises for unlawful possessions

'sea ,room *n* room for a ship to manoeuvre at sea

'sea ,rover *n, archaic* a pirate

'sea,scape /-,skayp/ *n* (a picture representing) a view of the sea

'sea ,scout *n, often cap* a member of a Scout troop that specializes in sea and water activities

'sea ,serpent *n* a large monster resembling a serpent often reported to have been seen but never proved to exist

'sea,shell /-,shel/ *n* the shell of a sea animal, esp a mollusc

,sea'shore /-'shaw/ *n* land (between high and low water marks) next to the sea

'sea,sick /-,sik/ *adj* suffering from the motion sickness associated with travelling by boat or hovercraft – **seasickness** *n*

'sea,side /-,sied/ *n* (a holiday resort or beach on) land bordering the sea

'sea ,slug *n* a shell-less marine gastropod mollusc

'sea ,snail *n* **1** a creeping spiral-shelled marine gastropod mollusc (e g a whelk) **2** any of numerous small slimy fishes usu with the pelvic fins modified to form a sucker

'sea ,snake *n* **1** SEA SERPENT **2** any of various highly poisonous aquatic snakes of the Pacific regions with a tail shaped like an oar

¹season /'seez(ə)n/ *n* **1a** any of the 4 quarters into which the year is commonly divided **b** a period characterized by a particular kind of weather ⟨*the dry* ~⟩ **c** a period of the year characterized by or associated with a particular activity or phenomenon ⟨*the holiday* ~⟩ ⟨*the hunting* ~⟩ ⟨*an animal's mating* ~⟩ **d** the time of year when a place is most frequented ⟨*difficult to find accommodation there at the height of the* ~⟩ **e** the time of a major holiday; *specif* the Christmas season ⟨*send the* ~*'s greetings*⟩ **2** *archaic* an indefinite length of time [ME, fr OF *saison*, fr L *sation-, satio* action of sowing, fr *satus*, pp of *serere* to sow – more at ²sow] – **in season 1** *of food* readily available and in the best condition for eating **2** *of game* legally available to be hunted or caught **3** *of an animal* on heat ⟨*the bitch is* in season⟩ **4** *esp of advice* given when most needed or most welcome ⟨*a word* in season⟩ – **out of season** not in season

²season *vt* **1a** to give (food) more flavour by adding seasoning or savoury ingredients **b** to make less harsh or unpleasant; relieve **c** to enliven ⟨*conversation* ~ed *with wit*⟩ **2a** to treat or expose (e g timber) over a period so as to prepare for use **b** to make fit or expert by experience ⟨*a* ~ed *veteran*⟩ [ME *sesounen*, fr MF *assaisoner* to ripen, season, fr OF, fr *a-* (fr L *ad-*) + *saison* season] – **seasoner** *n*

seasonable /'seez(ə)nnəbl/ *adj* **1** occurring in good or proper time; opportune **2** suitable to the season or circumstances – **seasonableness** *n*, **seasonably** *adv*

seasonal /'seez(ə)nl/ *adj* **1** of, occurring, or produced at a particular season ⟨~ *rainfall*⟩ **2** determined by seasonal need or availability ⟨~ *employment*⟩ ⟨~ *industries*⟩ – **seasonally** *adv*

seasoning /'seez(ə)ning/ *n* a condiment, spice, herb, etc added to food primarily for the savour that it imparts

'season ,ticket *n, Br* a ticket sold, usu at a reduced price, for an unlimited number of trips over the same route during a limited period

'sea ,squirt *n* any of various tunicate sea animals that are permanently attached to a surface for all their adult lives

¹seat /seet/ *n* **1a** a piece of furniture (e g a chair, stool, or bench) for sitting in or on **b** the part of sthg on which one rests when sitting ⟨*the* ~ *of a chair*⟩ ⟨*trouser* ~⟩; *also* the buttocks **c** a place for sitting ⟨*took his* ~ *next to her*⟩ **d** a unit of seating accommodation ⟨*a* ~ *for the game*⟩ **2a** a special chair (e g a throne) of sby in authority; *also* the status symbolized by it **b** a right of sitting ⟨*lost her* ~ *in the Commons*⟩ **c** a large country mansion **3a** a place where sthg is established or practised ⟨*an ancient* ~ *of learning*⟩ **b** a place from which authority is exercised ⟨*the* ~ *of government*⟩ **4** a bodily part in which a particular function, disease, etc is centred **5** posture in or a way of sitting on horseback **6a** a part at or forming the base of sthg **b** a part or surface on or in which another part or surface rests ⟨*a valve* ~⟩ [ME *sete*, fr ON *sæti*; akin to OE *sittan* to sit]

²seat *vt* **1a** to cause to sit or assist in finding a seat ⟨~ed *her next to the door*⟩ **b** to provide seats for ⟨*a*

theatre ~ing *1000 people*⟩ **c** to put (e g oneself) in a sitting position **2** to fit correctly on a seat **3** to fit to or with a seat ⟨~ *a valve*⟩ ~ *vi*, *of a garment* to become baggy in the area covering the buttocks ⟨*your woollen dress has* ~ed *badly*⟩ – **seater** *n*

'seat ,belt *n* an arrangement of straps designed to secure a person in a seat in an aeroplane, vehicle, etc

seating /'seeting/ *n* **1a** the act of providing with seats **b** the arrangement of seats (e g in a theatre) **2a** material for upholstering seats **b** a base on or in which sthg rests ⟨*a valve* ~⟩

'sea ,trout *n* a European and N African fish related to the salmon that migrates into fresh water to spawn

'sea ,urchin *n* any of a class of echinoderms usu with a thin shell covered with movable spines

,sea'wall /-'wawl/ *n* a wall or embankment to protect the shore from erosion or to act as a breakwater

'sea,way /-,way/ *n* **1** a ship's headway **2** the sea as a route for travel **3** a deep inland waterway that admits ocean shipping

'sea,weed /-,weed/ *n* (an abundant growth of) a plant, specif an alga, growing in the sea, typically having thick slimy fronds

'sea,worthy /-,wuhdhi/ *adj* fit or safe for a sea voyage ⟨*a* ~ *ship*⟩ – **seaworthiness** *n*

seax /saks/ *n* a heraldic sword resembling the scimitar but having a semicircular notch on the concave edge [ME *sexe* knife, short sword, fr OE *seax, sæx*; akin to ON *sax* knife, sword]

sebaceous /si'bayshəs/ *adj* of, secreting, or being sebum or other fatty material ☞ NERVE [L *sebaceus* made of tallow, fr *sebum* tallow – more at SOAP]

seborrhoea /,sebə'riə/ *n* excessive discharge of sebum (e g on the scalp) [NL, fr L *sebum* + NL *-rrhoea*]

sebum /'seebəm/ *n* fatty lubricant matter secreted by sebaceous glands of the skin [L, tallow, grease]

¹sec /sek/ *n, Br* a second, moment – infml ⟨*hang on a* ~*!*⟩

²sec *adj, of wine* not sweet; dry [F, lit., dry – more at ³SACK]

secant /'seekənt/ *n* **1** a straight line cutting a curve at 2 or more points – compare ²CHORD 2 **2** the trigonometric function that is the reciprocal of the cosine [NL *secant-, secans,* fr L, prp of *secare* to cut – more at ²SAW]

secateur /'sekə,tuh, ,--'-/ *n, chiefly Br* a pair of pruning shears – usu pl with sing. meaning [F *sécateur*, fr L *secare* to cut]

secco /'sekoh/ *n* FRESCO SECCO [It, fr *secco* dry, fr L *siccus* – more at ³SACK]

secede /si'seed/ *vi* to withdraw from an organization (e g a church or federation) [L *secedere*, fr *sed-, se-* apart (*fr sed, se* without) + *cedere* to go – more at IDIOT, CEDE] – **seceder** *n*

secession /si'sesh(ə)n/ *n* an act of seceding [L *secession-, secessio,* fr *secessus,* pp of *secedere*] – **secessionism** *n*, **secessionist** *n*

seclude /si'kloohd/ *vt* to remove or separate from contact with others [ME *secluden* to keep away, fr L *secludere* to separate, seclude, fr *se-* apart + *claudere* to close – more at SECEDE, ⁴CLOSE]

se'cluded *adj* **1** screened or hidden from view **2** living in seclusion – **secludedly** *adv*, **secludedness** *n*

seclusion /si'kloohzh(ə)n/ *n* **1** secluding or being secluded **2** a secluded or isolated place [ML *seclusion-, seclusio,* fr L *seclusus,* pp of *secludere*] – **seclusive** *adj*, **seclusively** *adv*, **seclusiveness** *n*

¹second /'sekənd/ *adj* **1a** next to the first in place or time ⟨*was* ~ *in line*⟩ **b(1)** next to the first in value, quality, or degree **(2)** inferior, subordinate ⟨*was* ~ *to none*⟩ **c** standing next below the top in authority or importance ⟨~ *mate*⟩ **2** alternate, other ⟨*elects a mayor every* ~ *year*⟩ **3** resembling or suggesting a prototype ⟨*a* ~ *Napoleon*⟩ **4** being the forward gear or speed 1 higher than first in a motor vehicle **5** relating to or having a part typically subordinate to or lower in pitch than the first part in concerted or ensemble music [ME, fr OF, fr L *secundus* second, following, favourable, fr *sequi* to follow – more at SUE] – **second, secondly** *adv* – **at second hand** from or through an intermediary ⟨*heard the news* at second hand⟩

²second *n* **1a** ☞ NUMBER **b** sthg that is next after the first in rank, position, authority, or precedence ⟨*the* ~ *in line*⟩ **2** sby who aids, supports, or stands in for another; *esp* the assistant of a duellist or boxer **3a** (the combination of 2 notes at) a musical interval of 2 diatonic degrees **b** the supertonic **4** a slightly flawed or inferior article (e g of merchandise) **5a** a place next below the first in a contest **b** *also* **second class** *often cap* the second level of British honours degree **6** the second forward gear or speed of a motor vehicle **7** *pl* a second helping of food – infml

³second *n* **1a** a 60th part of a minute of time or of a minute of angular measure **b** the SI unit of time equal to the duration of a certain number of periods of vibration of a specific radiation of a particular caesium isotope ☞ PHYSICS **2** a moment ⟨*wait a* ~ *will you*⟩ [ME *secunde,* fr ML *secunda,* fr L, fem of *secundus* second; fr its being the second sexagesimal division of a unit, as a minute is the first]

⁴second *vt* **1** to give support or encouragement to **2** to endorse (a motion or nomination) [L *secundare,* fr *secundus* second, favourable] – **seconder** *n*

⁵second /si'kond/ *vt, chiefly Br* to release (e g a teacher, businessman, or military officer) from a regularly assigned position for temporary duty with another organization [F *second,* n, second position (in the phrase *en second* in second place, subordinate), fr *second,* adj] – **secondment** *n*

¹secondary /'sekənd(ə)ri/ *adj* **1a** of second rank or importance ⟨~ *streams*⟩ **b** of or constituting the second strongest degree of stress in speech **2a** immediately derived from sthg primary or basic; derivative ⟨~ *sources*⟩ **b** of or being the induced current or its circuit in an induction coil or transformer ⟨*a* ~ *coil*⟩ ⟨~ *voltage*⟩ **3a** not first in order of occurrence or development **b** of the second order or stage in a series or sequence **c** produced away from a growing point by the activity of plant formative tissue, esp cambium ⟨~ *growth*⟩ ⟨~ *phloem*⟩ ⟨~ *thickening*⟩ **d** of or being the (feathers growing on the) second segment of the wing of a bird **e** of a secondary school **4** of or being a manufacturing industry – compare PRIMARY, TERTIARY – **secondarily** *adv*, **secondariness** *n*

²secondary *n* **1** a secondary electrical circuit or coil **2** a secondary feather ☞ ANATOMY **3** SECONDARY SCHOOL

secondary cell *n* an electric cell that converts chemical energy into electrical energy by reversible chemical reactions and that may be recharged by the passing of an appropriate current – compare ACCUMULATOR

secondary colour *n* a colour formed by mixing primary colours in equal or equivalent quantities

secondary consumer *n* a carnivore that eats herbivores – compare PRIMARY CONSUMER, TERTIARY CONSUMER ☞ FOOD

secondary modern, secondary modern school *n* a secondary school formerly providing a practical rather than academic type of education

secondary school *n* a school intermediate between primary school and higher education

secondary sex characteristic *n* a physical or mental attribute characteristic of a particular sex (e g the breasts of a female mammal) that appears at puberty or in the breeding season, and is not directly concerned with reproduction

secondary syphilis *n* the second stage of syphilis, from 2 to 6 months after infection, in which a long-lasting skin rash appears

,second-'best *adj* next after the best

second best *n* sby or sthg that comes after the best in quality or worth

,second 'childhood *n* dotage

¹,second-'class *adj* **1** of a second class ⟨*a ~ honours degree*⟩ **2** inferior, mediocre; *also* socially, politically, or economically deprived ⟨*~ citizens*⟩

²second-class *adv* **1** in accommodation next below the best ⟨*travel ~*⟩ **2** by second-class mail ⟨*send the letters ~*⟩

second class *n* the second and usu next to highest group in a classification

Second Coming *n* the return of Christ to judge the world on the last day

second-degree burn *n* a burn characterized by blistering and surface destruction of the skin – compare FIRST-DEGREE BURN, THIRD-DEGREE BURN

Second Empire *adj* (characteristic) of a style (e g of furniture) popular in mid-19th-c France and marked by heavy ornate modification of Empire styles

¹,second'hand /-'hand/ *adj* **1a** received from or through an intermediary ⟨*~ information*⟩ **b** not original; derivative **2a** acquired after being owned by another ⟨*a ~ car*⟩ **b** dealing in secondhand goods ⟨*a ~ bookshop*⟩

²secondhand *adv* indirectly; AT SECOND HAND

,second-in-com'mand *n* one who is immediately subordinate to a commander; a deputy commander

second lieutenant *n* ☞ RANK

second man *n, Br* a train driver's assistant

,second 'nature *n* an action or ability that practice has made instinctive

secondo /se'kondoh/ *n, pl* **secondi** /-di/ the second, usu lower, part in a concerted piece or duet [It, fr *secondo,* adj, second, fr L *secundus*]

second person *n* (any of) a set of linguistic forms referring to the person or thing addressed (e g 'you'')

,second-'rate *adj* of inferior quality or value – **second-rateness** *n,* **second-rater** *n*

second reading *n* **1** the stage in the British legislative process providing for debate on the principal features of a bill ☞ LAW **2** the stage in the US legislative process that occurs when a bill has been reported back from committee and that provides an opportunity for full debate and amendment

,second 'sight *n* clairvoyance, precognition

second-story man *n, NAm* CAT BURGLAR

,second-'string *adj, chiefly NAm* being a substitute as distinguished from a regular player (e g in a football team); *broadly* substitute [fr the reserve bowstring carried by an archer in case the first breaks]

,second 'thoughts *n pl* a reconsideration of a previous decision ⟨*began to have ~*⟩

,second 'wind /wind/ *n* renewed energy or endurance after a period of severe exertion – esp in *get one's second wind*

secrecy /'seekrəsi/ *n* **1** the habit or practice of keeping secrets or maintaining privacy or concealment **2** the condition of being hidden or concealed ⟨*complete ~ surrounded the conference*⟩ [alter. of earlier *secretie,* fr ME *secretee,* fr *secre* secret, fr MF *secré,* fr L *secretus*]

¹secret /'seekrit/ *adj* **1a** kept or hidden from knowledge or view ⟨*determined to keep his mission ~*⟩ **b** marked by the practice of discretion; secretive **c** conducted in secret ⟨*~ negotiations*⟩ **2** retired, secluded **3** revealed only to the initiated; esoteric ⟨*~ rites*⟩ **4** containing information whose unauthorized disclosure could endanger national security – compare RESTRICTED, TOP SECRET [ME, fr MF, fr L *secretus,* fr pp of *secernere* to separate, distinguish, fr *se-* apart + *cernere* to sift – more at SECEDE, CERTAIN] – **secretly** *adv*

²secret *n* **1a** sthg kept hidden or unexplained **b** a fact concealed from others or shared confidentially with a few ⟨*a trade ~*⟩ **2** sthg taken to be the means of attaining a desired end ⟨*the ~ of longevity*⟩ – **in secret** in a private place or manner; in secrecy

secret agent *n* a spy

secretaire /,sekrə'teə/ *n* a writing desk with a top section for books [F *secrétaire* escritoire, secretary (person), fr MF *secretaire* secretary (person), fr ML *secretarius*]

secretariat /,sekrə'teəri·ət/ *n* **1** the office of secretary **2** the clerical staff of an organization **3** a government administrative department [F *secrétariat,* fr ML *secretariatus,* fr *secretarius*]

secretary /'sekrətri, -,teri/ *n* **1** sby employed to handle correspondence and manage routine work for a superior **2a** COMPANY SECRETARY **b** an officer of an organization or society responsible for its records and correspondence **3** an officer of state who superintends a government administrative department [ME *secretarie,* fr ML *secretarius* confidential employee, secretary, fr L *secretum* secret, fr neut of *secretus,* pp] – **secretaryship** *n,* **secretarial** /,sekri'teəri·əl/ *adj*

'secretary ,bird *n* a large long-legged African bird of prey that feeds largely on reptiles [prob fr the resemblance of its crest to a bunch of quill pens stuck behind the ear]

,secretary-'general *n, pl* **secretaries-general** a principal administrative officer (e g of the United Nations)

secret ballot *n* an official ballot that is marked in secret

¹secrete /si'kreet/ *vt* to form and give off (a secretion) [back-formation fr *secretion*] – **secretory** /-təri/ *adj*

[2]**secrete** *vt* to deposit in a hidden place ⟨~ *opium about his person*⟩ [alter. of obs *secret*, fr [1]*secret*]

secretion /si'kreesh(ə)n/ *n* **1** (a product formed by) the bodily process of making and releasing some material either functionally specialized (e g a hormone, saliva, latex, or resin) or isolated for excretion (e g urine) **2** the act of hiding sthg [(1) F *sécrétion*, fr L *secretion-*, *secretio* separation, fr *secretus*, pp of *secernere* to separate – more at SECRET; (2) [2]*secrete*] – **secretionary** *adj*

secretive /'seekrətiv/ *adj* inclined to secrecy; not open or outgoing in speech or behaviour [back-formation fr *secretiveness*, part trans of F *secrétivité*] – **secretively** *adv*, **secretiveness** *n*

,secret po'lice *n* a police organization operating largely in secrecy, esp for political purposes

secret service *n* a (secret) governmental agency concerned with national security; *esp, cap both Ss* a British government intelligence department

,secret so'ciety *n* a society whose members keep their activities secret from others

sect /sekt/ *n* **1** a (heretical) dissenting or schismatic religious body **2a** a group maintaining strict allegiance to a doctrine or leader **b** a party; *esp* a faction **3** a denomination – chiefly derog [ME *secte*, fr MF & LL & L; MF, group, sect, fr LL *secta* organized ecclesiastical body, fr L, way of life, class of persons, fr *sequi* to follow]

-sect /-sekt/ *comb form* (→ *vb*) cut; divide ⟨*bi*sect⟩ [L *sectus*, pp of *secare* to cut – more at [2]SAW]

[1]**sectarian** /sek'teəri·ən/ *n* **1** a (fanatical) adherent of a sect **2** a bigoted person

[2]**sectarian** *adj* **1** (characteristic) of a sect or sectarian **2** limited in character or scope; parochial – **sectarianism** *n*, **sectarianize** *vb*

[1]**section** /'seksh(ə)n/ *n* **1a** the action or an instance of (separating by) cutting; *esp* the action of dividing sthg (e g tissues) surgically ⟨*caesarean* ~⟩ **b** a part separated (as if) by cutting **2** a distinct part or portion of sthg written; *esp* a subdivision of a chapter **3** the profile of sthg as it would appear if cut through by an intersecting plane ☞ BUILDING **4** a sign used in printing as a mark for the beginning of a section **5** a distinct part of an area, community, or group **6** a part when considered in isolation ⟨*the northern* ~ *of the route*⟩ **7** *sing or pl in constr* a subdivision of a platoon, troop, or battery that is the smallest tactical military unit **8** a very thin slice (e g of tissue) suitable for microscopic examination **9** any of several component parts that may be separated and reassembled ⟨*a bookcase in* ~s⟩ **10** a division of an orchestra composed of 1 class of instruments **11** a printed sheet that is folded to form part (e g 8 leaves) of a book [L *section-*, *sectio*, fr *sectus*]

[2]**section** *vt* **1** to cut or separate into sections **2** to represent in sections (e g by a drawing)

sectional /'seksh(ə)nl/ *adj* **1** restricted to a particular group or locality ⟨~ *interests*⟩ **2** composed of or divided into sections ⟨~ *furniture*⟩ – **sectionalize** *vt*, **sectionally** *adv*

sectionalism /'seksh(ə)nl,iz(ə)m/ *n* an excessive concern for the interests of a region or group

sector /'sektə/ *n* **1** a part of a circle consisting of 2 radii and the portion of the circumference between them – compare SEGMENT 2a ☞ MATHEMATICS **2a** a portion of a military area of operation **b** a part of a field of activity, esp of business, trade, etc ⟨*employment in the public and private* ~s⟩ [LL, fr L, cutter, fr *sectus*]

sectorial /sek'tawri·əl/ *adj* (having the shape) of a sector of a circle

[1]**secular** /'sekyoolə/ *adj* **1a** of this world rather than the heavenly or spiritual **b** not overtly or specifically religious **2** not bound by monastic vows or rules; *specif* of or being clergy not belonging to a particular religious order **3a** taking place once in an age or a century **b** surviving or recurring through ages or centuries [ME, fr OF *seculer*, fr LL *saecularis*, fr L, coming once in an age, fr *saeculum* breed, generation; akin to L *serere* to sow – more at [2]SOW] – **secularly** *adv*, **secularity** /,sekyoo'larəti/ *n*

[2]**secular** *n*, *pl* **seculars**, **secular** a layman

secularism /'sekyoolə,riz(ə)m/ *n* disregard for or rejection of religious beliefs and practices – **secularist** *n or adj*, **secularistic** /-'ristik/ *adj*

secular·ize, -ise /'sekyoolə,riez/ *vt* **1** to transfer (e g property) from ecclesiastical to civil use **2** to release from monastic vows **3** to convert to or imbue with secularism – **secularizer** *n*, **secularization** /-'zaysh(ə)n/ *n*

[1]**secure** /si'kyooə/ *adj* **1a** calm in mind **b** confident in opinion or hope **2a** free from danger **b** free from risk of loss ⟨~ *employment*⟩ **c** affording safety ⟨*a* ~ *hideaway*⟩ **d** firm, dependable; *esp* firmly fastened ⟨~ *foundation*⟩ **3** assured, certain ⟨*when the reinforcements arrived, victory was* ~⟩ **4** *archaic* overconfident [L *securus* safe, secure, fr *se* without + *cura* care – more at IDIOT, CURE] – **securely** *adv*, **secureness** *n*

[2]**secure** *vt* **1a** to make safe from risk or danger ⟨~d *the lid with a padlock*⟩ **b** to guarantee against loss or denial ⟨*a bill to* ~ *the rights of strikers*⟩ **c** to give pledge of payment to (a creditor) or of (an obligation) ⟨~ *a note by a pledge of collateral*⟩ **2** to make fast; shut tightly ⟨~ *a door*⟩ **3** to obtain or bring about, esp as the result of effort ⟨~d *a cabin for the voyage home*⟩ ⟨*spared no effort to* ~ *his ends*⟩ – **securement** *n*, **securer** *n*

security /si'kyooərəti/ *n* **1** being secure: e g **a** freedom from danger, fear, or anxiety **b** stability, dependability **2a** sthg pledged to guarantee the fulfilment of an obligation **b** a surety **3** an evidence of debt or of ownership (e g a stock certificate) **4a** protection **b(1)** measures taken to protect against esp espionage or sabotage **(2)** *sing or pl in constr* an organization whose task is to maintain security

Security Council *n* a permanent council of the United Nations responsible for the maintenance of peace and security

sedan /si'dan/ *n*, *NAm & Austr* SALOON 3

sedan chair *n* a portable often enclosed chair, esp of the 17th and 18th c, designed to seat 1 person and be carried on poles by 2 people [*sedan* perh deriv of L *sella* saddle]

[1]**sedate** /si'dayt/ *adj* calm and even in temper or pace [L *sedatus*, fr pp of *sedare* to calm; akin to *sedēre* to sit – more at SIT] – **sedately** *adv*, **sedateness** *n*

[2]**sedate** *vt* to give a sedative to [back-formation fr *sedative*]

sedation /si'daysh(ə)n/ *n* (the induction, esp with a sedative, of) a relaxed easy state

sedative /'sedətiv/ *n or adj* (sthg, esp a drug) tending to calm or to tranquillize nervousness or excitement

sedentary /'sed(ə)ntri/ *adj* **1** *esp of birds* not migratory **2** doing or involving much sitting ⟨*a ~ occupation*⟩ **3** permanently attached ⟨*~ barnacles*⟩ [MF *sedentaire*, fr L *sedentarius*, fr *sedent-, sedens*, prp of *sedēre* to sit]

seder /'saydə/ *n, often cap* a Jewish domestic ceremonial dinner held on the first evening of the Passover in commemoration of the exodus from Egypt [Heb *sēdher* order]

sedge /sej/ *n* any of a family of usu tufted marsh plants differing from the related grasses esp in having solid stems [ME *segge*, fr OE *secg*; akin to MHG *segge* sedge, OE *sagu* saw – more at [2]SAW] – **sedgy** *adj*

sedge warbler *n* a small Old World warbler that breeds in marshy places

sedilia /sə'dili·ə/ *n* seats of masonry on the south side of the chancel for the celebrant, deacon, and subdeacon ☞ CHURCH [L, pl of *sedile* seat, fr *sedēre*]

sediment /'sedimənt/ *n* **1** the matter that settles to the bottom of a liquid **2** material deposited by water, wind, or glaciers [MF, fr L *sedimentum* settling, fr *sedēre* to sit, sink down] – **sediment** /-,ment/ *vb*

sedimentary /,sedi'ment(ə)ri/ *adj* **1** of or containing sediment ⟨*~ deposits*⟩ **2** formed by or from deposits of sediment ⟨*~ rock*⟩

sedimentation /,sedimen'taysh(ə)n/ *n* the forming or depositing of sediment

sedition /si'dish(ə)n/ *n* incitement to defy or rise up against lawful authority [ME, fr MF, fr L *sedition-, seditio*, lit., separation, fr *se-* apart + *ition-, itio* act of going, fr *itus*, pp of *ire* to go – more at SECEDE, ISSUE] – **seditionary** *adj*

seditious /si'dishəs/ *adj* **1** tending to arouse or take part in sedition; guilty of sedition **2** of or constituting sedition – **seditiously** *adv*, **seditiousness** *n*

seduce /si'dyoohs/ *vt* **1** to incite to disobedience or disloyalty **2** to lead astray, esp by false promises **3** to effect the physical seduction of [LL *seducere*, fr L, to lead away, fr *se-* apart + *ducere* to lead – more at [1]TOW] – **seducer** *n*

seduction /si'duksh(ə)n/ *n* **1** the act of seducing to wrong; *specif* enticement to sexual intercourse **2** a thing or quality that attracts by its charm ⟨*the ~ of riches*⟩ ⟨*the ~s of articles in shop windows*⟩ [MF, fr LL *seduction-, seductio*, fr L, act of leading aside, fr *seductus*, pp of *seducere*]

seductive /si'duktiv/ *adj* tending to seduce; alluring ⟨*a ~ woman*⟩ – **seductively** *adv*, **seductiveness** *n*

seductress /si'duktris/ *n* a female seducer [obs *seductor* (male seducer), fr LL, fr *seductus*, pp of *seducere* to seduce]

sedulous /'sedyooləs/ *adj* **1** involving or accomplished with steady perseverance ⟨*~ craftsmanship*⟩ **2** diligent in application or pursuit ⟨*a ~ student*⟩ *USE* fml [L *sedulus*, fr *sedulo* sincerely, diligently, fr *se* without + *dolus* guile – more at TALE] – **sedulously** *adv*, **sedulousness** *n*

sedum /'seedəm/ *n* a stonecrop or related fleshy plant [NL, genus name, fr L, houseleek]

[1]**see** /see/ *vb* **saw** /saw/; **seen** /seen/ *vt* **1a** to perceive by the eye ⟨*looked for her but couldn't ~ her in the crowd*⟩ ⟨saw *that she was in difficulties*⟩ **b** to look at; inspect ⟨*can I ~ your ticket please?*⟩ **2a** to have experience of; undergo ⟨*~ army service*⟩ ⟨*shoes that ~ a lot of wear*⟩ ⟨*a coat that has ~n better days*⟩ **b** to (try to) find out or determine ⟨*~ if you can mend it*⟩ **3a** to form a mental picture of; imagine, envisage ⟨*can't ~ him objecting*⟩ **b** to regard ⟨*couldn't ~ him as a crook*⟩ **4** to perceive the meaning or importance of; understand ⟨*I ~ what you mean*⟩ ⟨*failed to ~ that it was important*⟩ ⟨*couldn't ~ the point of it*⟩ **5a** to observe, watch ⟨*want to ~ how he handles the problem*⟩ **b** to be a witness of ⟨*can't ~ her neglected*⟩ **c(1)** to read ⟨*~ page 17*⟩ **(2)** to read of ⟨saw *it in the paper*⟩ **d** to attend as a spectator ⟨*~ a play*⟩ **6** to ensure; MAKE CERTAIN 2 ⟨*~ that order is kept*⟩ **7a** to prefer to have ⟨*I'll ~ him hanged first*⟩ **b** to find acceptable or attractive ⟨*can't understand what he ~s in her*⟩ **8** *of a period of time* to be marked by ⟨*the 5th century* saw *the collapse of the Western Roman Empire*⟩ **9a** to call on; visit ⟨*~ the dentist*⟩ **b(1)** to keep company with ⟨*they've been ~ing each other regularly for some time*⟩ **(2)** to meet to a specified extent ⟨*haven't ~n much of her lately*⟩ **c** to grant an interview to ⟨*the president will ~ you*⟩ **d** to accompany, escort ⟨*~ the girls home*⟩ **10** to meet (a bet) in poker or equal the bet of (a player) ~ *vi* **1a** to have the power of sight **b** to apprehend objects by sight ⟨*too dark to ~*⟩ **2a** to give or pay attention ⟨*~ here!*⟩ **b** to look about ⟨*come to the window and ~*⟩ **3** to have knowledge ⟨*~ into the future*⟩ **4** to make investigation or inquiry; consider, deliberate ⟨*let me ~*⟩ [ME *seen*, fr OE *sēon*; akin to OHG *sehan* to see, OE *secgan* to say – more at [1]SAY] – **see about 1** to deal with **2** to consider further ⟨*we'll* see about *that*⟩ – **see eye to eye** to have a common viewpoint; agree – **see fit** to consider proper or advisable ⟨saw fit *to warn him of his impending dismissal*⟩ – **see one's way to** to feel capable of – **see red** to become suddenly enraged – **see someone right** to protect and reward (a protégé) – **see someone through** to provide for, support, or help sby until the end of (a time of difficulty) ⟨*enough supplies to* see *us* through *the winter*⟩ ⟨saw *him* through *his divorce*⟩ – **see the light 1a** to be born **b** to be published **2** to undergo conversion – **see the wood for the trees** to grasp the total picture without being confused by detail – **see through** to grasp the true nature of; penetrate ⟨saw through *his deceptions*⟩ – **see to** to attend to; care for

[2]**see** *n* a bishopric [ME *se*, fr OF, fr L *sedes* seat; akin to L *sedēre* to sit – more at SIT]

[1]**seed** /seed/ *n, pl* **seeds**, *esp collectively* **seed 1a(1)** the grains or ripened ovules of plants used for sowing **(2)** the fertilized ripened ovule of a (flowering) plant that contains an embryo and is capable of germination to produce a new plant **b** semen or milt **c** SPAT 2 **d** the condition or stage of bearing seed ⟨*in ~*⟩ **2** a source of development or growth ⟨*sowed the ~s of discord*⟩ **3** sthg (e g a tiny particle) that resembles a seed in shape or size **4** a competitor who has been seeded in a tournament **5** *archaic* progeny [ME, fr OE *sǣd*; akin to OHG *sāt* seed, OE *sāwan* to sow – more at [2]SOW] – **seed** *adj*, **seeded** *adj*, **seedless** *adj*, **seedlike** *adj* – **go/run to seed 1** to develop seed **2** to decay; *also* to become unattractive by being shabby or careless about appearance

[2]**seed** *vi* **1** to sow seed **2** *of a plant* to produce or shed seeds ~ *vt* **1a** to plant seeds in; sow 1 ⟨*~ land to grass*⟩ **b** PLANT 1a **2** to treat with solid particles to stimulate crystallization, condensation, etc; *esp* to treat (a cloud) in this way to produce rain, snow, etc **3** to extract the seeds from (e g raisins) **4** to schedule

(tournament players or teams) so that superior ones will not meet in early rounds

'seed,bed /-,bed/ *n* a place where sthg specified develops ⟨*the* ~ *of revolution*⟩

'seed,cake /-,kayk/ *n* a sweet cake containing aromatic seeds (e g caraway seeds)

'seed,eater /-,eetə/ *n* a bird (e g a finch) whose diet consists basically of seeds

seeder /'seedə/ *n* sby who or sthg that seeds clouds to produce precipitation [[2]SEED + [2]-ER]

'seed ,leaf *n* COTYLEDON 2

seedling /'seedling/ *n* **1** a plant grown from seed rather than from a cutting **2** a young plant; *esp* a nursery plant before permanent transplantation – **seedling** *adj*

seed oyster *n* a young oyster, esp of a size suitable for transferring to another bed to start a new colony

seed pearl *n* a very small often imperfect pearl

seedsman /'seedzmən/ *n* sby who sows or deals in seeds

'seed,time /-,tiem/ *n* the sowing season

seed vessel *n* a pericarp

seedy /'seedi/ *adj* **1** containing or full of seeds ⟨*a* ~ *fruit*⟩ **2a** shabby, grubby ⟨~ *clothes*⟩ **b** somewhat disreputable; run-down ⟨*a* ~ *district*⟩ **c** slightly unwell – infml ⟨*felt* ~ *and went home early*⟩ – **seedily** *adv*, **seediness** *n*

seeing /'see·ing/ *conj* in view of the fact; since – often + *that* or, in nonstandard use, *as how* [fr prp of *see*]

seeing eye *n* GUIDE DOG

seek /seek/ *vb* **sought** /sawt/ *vt* **1** to resort to; go to ⟨~ *the shade on a hot day*⟩ **2a** to go in search of – often + *out* **b** to try to discover ⟨~ *a solution to the problem*⟩ **3** to ask for ⟨~s *advice*⟩ **4** to try to acquire or gain ⟨~ *fame*⟩ **5** to make an effort; aim – + infinitive ⟨~ *to cater for every taste*⟩ ~ *vi* to make a search or inquiry [ME *seken*, fr OE *sēcan*; akin to OHG *suohhen* to seek, L *sagire* to perceive keenly, Gk *hēgeisthai* to lead] – **seeker** *n*

seem /seem/ *vi* **1** to give the impression of being ⟨*he* ~s *unhappy*⟩ ⟨*she* ~s *a bore*⟩ **2** to appear to the observation or understanding ⟨*I* ~ *to have caught a cold*⟩ ⟨*it* ~s *he lost his passport*⟩ **3** to give evidence of existing ⟨*there* ~s *no reason*⟩ [ME *semen*, of Scand origin; akin to ON *sōma* to beseem, befit, *samr* same – more at SAME] – **not seem** somehow not ⟨*I don't* seem *to feel hungry*⟩ ⟨*he can't* seem *to lift it*⟩ – **would seem** to seem to one ⟨*it* would seem *to be raining*⟩

seeming /'seeming/ *adj* apparent rather than real [fr prp of *seem*]

'seemingly /-li/ *adv* **1** so far as can be seen or judged **2** to outward appearance only

seemly /'seemli/ *adj* in accord with good taste or propriety [ME *semely*, fr ON *sœmiligr*, fr *sœmr* becoming; akin to ON *sōma* to beseem] – **seemliness** *n*

see off *vt* **1** to be present at the departure of ⟨saw *his parents* off *on holiday*⟩ **2** to avert, repel

see out *vt* **1** to escort to the outside (e g of a room, office, or house) **2** to last until the end of ⟨*enough fuel to* see *the winter* out⟩

seep /seep/ *vi* to pass slowly (as if) through fine pores or small openings ⟨*water* ~ed *in through a crack*⟩ [alter. of earlier *sipe*, fr ME *sipen*, fr OE *sipian*; akin to MLG *sipen* to seep] – **seepage** *n*

seer /siə/ *n* **1a** sby who predicts future events **b** sby credited with exceptional moral and spiritual insight **2** sby who practises divination [[1]SEE + [2]-ER]

seersucker /'siə,sukə/ *n* a light slightly puckered fabric of linen, cotton, or rayon [Hindi *śīrśakar*, fr Per *shīr-o-shakar*, lit., milk and sugar]

[1]seesaw /'see,saw/ *n* **1** an alternating up-and-down or backwards-and-forwards movement; *also* anything (e g a process or movement) that alternates ⟨*a* ~ *of shame and defiance*⟩ **2** (a game in which 2 or more children ride on opposite ends of) a plank balanced in the middle so that one end goes up as the other goes down [prob redupl of [3]*saw*] – **seesaw** *adj or adv*

[2]seesaw *vi* **1a** to move backwards and forwards or up and down **b** to play at seesaw **2a** to alternate **b** to vacillate ~ *vt* to cause to move with a seesaw motion

seethe /seedh/ *vi* **1a** to be in a state of agitated usu confused movement **b** to churn or foam as if boiling **2** to feel or express violent emotion ⟨*he* ~d *with rage*⟩ [ME *sethen*, fr OE *sēothan*; akin to OHG *siodan* to seethe, Lith *siausti* to rage]

seething /'seedhing/ *adj* **1** intensely hot ⟨*a* ~ *inferno*⟩ **2** constantly moving or active

'see-,through *adj* transparent

see through *vt* to undergo or endure to the end ⟨*bravely* saw *the fight* through⟩

[1]segment /'segmənt/ *n* **1a** a separated piece of sthg ⟨*chop the stalks into short* ~s⟩ **b** any of the constituent parts into which a body, entity, or quantity is divided or marked off ⟨*all* ~s *of the population agree*⟩ **2** a portion cut off from a geometrical figure by 1 or more points, lines, or planes: e g **a** a part of a circular area bounded by a chord of that circle and the arc subtended by it – compare SECTOR 1 **b** a part of a sphere cut off by a plane or included between 2 parallel planes **c** the part of a line between 2 points in the line ***USE*** *(2)* ☞ MATHEMATICS [L *segmentum*, fr *secare* to cut – more at [2]SAW] – **segmentary** /-mənt(ə)ri/ *adj*, **segmental** /-'mentl/ *adj*

[2]segment /seg'ment/ *vt* to separate into segments

segmentation /,segmən'taysh(ə)n, -men-/ *n* the formation of many cells from a single cell (e g in a developing egg) [[2]SEGMENT + -ATION]

segno /'senyoh/ *n, pl* **segnos** the sign that marks the beginning or end of a musical repeat ☞ MUSIC [It, sign, fr L *signum*]

segregate /'segri,gayt/ *vt* **1** to separate or set apart **2** to cause or force separation of (e g criminals from society) or in (e g a community) ~ *vi* **1** to withdraw **2** to undergo (genetic) segregation [L *segregatus*, pp of *segregare*, fr *se-* apart + *greg-*, *grex* herd – more at SECEDE, GREGARIOUS] – **segregative** /-,gaytiv/ *adj*

'segre,gated *adj* **1** set apart from others of the same kind **2** administered separately for different groups or races ⟨~ *education*⟩

segregation /,segri'gaysh(ə)n/ *n* **1a** the separation or isolation of a race, class, or ethnic group **b** the separation for special treatment or observation of individuals or items from a larger group ⟨*the* ~ *of political prisoners from common criminals*⟩ **2** the separation of pairs of genes controlling the same hereditary characteristic, that occurs during meiotic cell division [SEGREGATE + -ION] – **segregationist** *n*

seguidilla /,segi'dilyə, -'deel-/ *n* a Spanish dance in triple time [Sp, dim. of *seguida* sequence, fr *seguir* to follow, fr L *sequi*]

seiche /saysh/ *n* an oscillation of the surface of a lake or landlocked sea [F]

ˈSeidlitz ˌpowder /ˈsedlits/ *n* a mild purgative consisting of one powder of sodium bicarbonate and sodium potassium tartrate and another of tartaric acid that are mixed in water and drunk while effervescing [*Seidlitz* (Sedlčany), village in Bohemia, Czechoslovakia; fr the similarity of its effect to that of the water of the village]

seigneur /sayˈnyuh/ *n* a feudal lord [MF, fr ML *senior*, fr L, adj, elder – more at SENIOR]

seigneury /ˈsaynyəri/ *n* the territory or authority of a feudal lord

seigniorage, seignorage /ˈsaynyərij/ *n* a government revenue from the manufacture of coins calculated as being the difference between the face value and the metal value of the coins [ME *seigneurage*, fr MF, right of the lord (esp to coin money), fr *seigneur*]

seine /sayn/ *vb or n* (to catch with, fish in with, or use) a large net with weights on one edge and floats on the other that hangs vertically in the water and is used to enclose fish when its ends are pulled together or drawn ashore [n ME, fr OE *segne*; akin to OHG *segīna* seine; both fr a prehistoric WGmc word borrowed fr L *sagena* seine, fr Gk *sagēnē*; vb fr n]

seism-, seismo- *comb form* earthquake; vibration ⟨seismo*meter*⟩ [Gk, fr *seismos*]

seismic /ˈsiezmik/, **seismal** /-ml/ *adj* **1** of or caused by an earth vibration, specif an earthquake **2** of a vibration on the moon or other celestial body comparable to a seismic event on earth [Gk *seismos* shock, earthquake, fr *seiein* to shake; akin to Skt *tvesati* he is violently moved] – **seismicity** /-ˈmisəti/ *n*

seismogram /ˈsiezməˌgram/ *n* a record made by a seismograph [ISV]

ˈseismoˌgraph /-ˌgrahf, -ˌgraf/ *n* an apparatus to measure and record earth tremors [ISV] – **seismographer** /-ˈmogrəfə/ *n*, **seismography** /-ˈmogrəfi/ *n*, **seismographic** /-məˈgrafik/ *adj*

seismology /seizˈmoləji/ *n* a science that deals with earth vibrations, esp earthquakes [ISV] – **seismologist** *n*, **seismological** /-məˈlojikl/ *adj*

seismometry /seizˈmomitri/ *n* the scientific study and measurement of earthquakes [ISV]

ˈsei ˌwhale /say/ *n* a common and widely distributed small white-spotted rorqual [part trans of Norw *seihval*, fr *sei* coalfish + *hval* whale; fr its habit of following the coalfish in search of food]

seize /seez/ *vt* **1** *also* **seise** /~/ to put in possession of **2** to confiscate, esp by legal authority **3a** to take possession of by force **b** to take prisoner **4** to take hold of abruptly or eagerly ⟨~d *his arm and pulled him clear of the fire*⟩ **5a** to attack or afflict physically ⟨~d *with an attack of arthritis*⟩ **b** to possess (the mind) completely or overwhelmingly **6** to bind or fasten together with a lashing of cord or twine ~ *vi* **1** to lay hold of sthg suddenly, forcibly, or eagerly – usu + *on* or *upon* ⟨~d *on her idea for a new TV series*⟩ **2a** *of brakes, pistons, etc* to become jammed through excessive pressure, temperature, or friction – often + *up* **b** *of an engine* to fail to operate owing to the seizing of a part [ME *saisen*, fr OF *saisir* to put in possession of, fr ML *sacire*, of Gmc origin; akin to OHG *sezzen* to set – more at [1]SET]

seizure /ˈseezhə/ *n* **1** the taking possession of sby or sthg by legal process **2** a sudden attack (e g of disease) [SEIZE + -URE]

selachian /siˈlayki·ən/ *n* any of a group of cartilaginous fishes usu considered to include the sharks and dogfishes and sometimes the rays [deriv of Gk *selachos* cartilaginous phosphorescent fish; akin to Gk *selas* brightness – more at SELENIUM] – **selachian** *adj*

[1]seldom /ˈseldəm/ *adv* in few instances; rarely, infrequently [ME, fr OE *seldan*; akin to OHG *seltan* seldom, L *sed, se* without – more at IDIOT]

[2]seldom *adj* rare, infrequent

[1]select /siˈlekt/ *adj* **1** picked out in preference to others **2a** of special value or quality **b** exclusively or fastidiously chosen, esp on the basis of social characteristics ⟨*a* ~ *membership*⟩ **3** judicious in choice ⟨~ *appreciation*⟩ [L *selectus*, pp of *seligere* to select, fr *se-* apart (fr *sed, se* without) + *legere* to gather, select – more at LEGEND] – **selectness** *n*

[2]select *vt* to take according to preference from among a number; pick out ~ *vi* to make a selection or choice

select committee *n* a temporary committee of a legislative body, established to examine 1 particular matter

selectee /siˌlekˈtee/ *n, NAm* a conscript

selection /siˈleksh(ə)n/ *n* **1** sby or sthg selected; *also* a collection of selected items **2** a range of things from which to choose **3** a natural or artificially imposed process that results in the survival and propagation only of organisms with desired or suitable attributes so that their heritable characteristics only are perpetuated in succeeding generations – compare NATURAL SELECTION [[2]SELECT + -ION]

selective /siˈlektiv/ *adj* of or characterized by selection; selecting or tending to select – **selectively** *adv*, **selectiveness** *n*, **selectivity** /-ˈtivəti/ *n*

seˌlective ˈservice *n, NAm* a system under which people are called up for military service

selector /siˈlektə/ *n, Br* sby who chooses the members of a sports team [[2]SELECT + [1]-OR]

[1]selen-, seleno- *comb form* moon ⟨seleno*graphy*⟩ [L *selen-*, fr Gk *selēn-*, fr *selēnē* – more at SELENIUM]

[2]selen-, seleni-, seleno- *comb form* selenium ⟨selen*ide*⟩ ⟨selen*ic*⟩ [Sw, fr NL *selenium*]

selenite /ˈseliniet/ *n* calcium sulphate occurring in transparent crystals or crystalline masses [L *selenites*, fr Gk *selēnitēs* (*lithos*), lit., stone of the moon, fr *selēnē*; fr the belief that it waxed and waned with the moon]

selenium /siˈleeni·əm/ *n* a nonmetallic solid element resembling sulphur and tellurium chemically, 1 form of which varies in electrical conductivity under the influence of light and is used in electronic devices (e g solar cells) ☞ PERIODIC TABLE [NL, fr Gk *selēnē* moon; akin to Gk *selas* brightness, L *sol* sun – more at [1]SOLAR] – **selenic** /-nik/ *adj*

selenium cell *n* a strip of selenium used as a light-sensitive element in a photoelectric cell

selenocentric /siˌleenohˈsentrik/ *adj* of or seen from the centre of the moon [ISV]

selenography /ˌseliˈnogrəfi/ *n* (the study of) the physical features of the moon – **selenographer** *n*, **selenographic** /-nohˈgrafik/ *adj*

selenology /ˌseliˈnoləji/ *n* a branch of astronomy dealing with the moon – **selenologist** *n*, **selenological** /-nohˈlojikl/ *adj*

Seleucid /si'loohsid/ *n or adj* (a member) of a 3rd-c BC Syrian and W Asian dynasty under which Greek language and culture were introduced into Syria [n NL *seleucides*, fr *Seleucus I* †280 BC Macedonian general & founder of Seleucid dynasty + L *-ides*, masc patronymic suffix; adj fr n]

^{1}**self** /self/ *pron* myself, himself, herself [ME (intensive pron), fr OE; akin to OHG *selb*, intensive pron, L *sui* (reflexive pron) of oneself – more at SUICIDE]

^{2}**self** *adj* identical throughout, esp in colour

^{3}**self** *n, pl* **selves** /selvz/ **1** the entire being of an individual **2** a (part or aspect of a) person's individual character ⟨*his true ~ was revealed*⟩ **3** the body, emotions, thoughts, sensations, etc that constitute the individuality and identity of a person **4** personal interest, advantage, or welfare ⟨*took no thought of ~*⟩

self- *comb form* **1a** oneself; itself ⟨self-*supporting*⟩ **b** of oneself or itself ⟨self-*abasement*⟩ **c** by oneself or itself ⟨self- *propelled*⟩ ⟨self-*made*⟩ ⟨self-*starting*⟩ **2a** to, with, for, or in oneself or itself ⟨self-*confident*⟩ ⟨self-*addressed*⟩ ⟨self-*love*⟩ **b** of or in oneself or itself inherently ⟨self-*evident*⟩ ⟨self-*explanatory*⟩ [ME, fr OE, fr *self*]

ˌself-aˈbandonment *n* **1** a surrender of selfish interests or desires **2** a lack of self-restraint

ˌself-aˈbasement *n* humiliation of oneself, esp in response to a sense of guilt

ˌself-ˈabnegating *adj* self-denying – **self-abnegation** *n*

ˌself-abˈsorbed *adj* preoccupied with one's own thoughts, activities, or welfare – **self-absorption** *n*

ˌself-aˈbuse *n* masturbation

ˌself-adˈdressed *adj* addressed for return to the sender ⟨*a ~ envelope*⟩

ˌself-adˈjusting *adj* adjusting by itself

ˌself-agˈgrandizing *adj* acting or seeking to enhance one's power or status – **self-aggrandizement** *n*

ˌself-annihiˈlation *n* annihilation of self-awareness (e g in mystical contemplation of God)

ˌself-approˈbation *n* (excessive) satisfaction with one's own actions and achievements

ˌself-asˈsertion *n* the act of asserting oneself or one's own rights, claims, or opinions, esp aggressively or conceitedly – **self-assertive** *adj*

ˌself-asˈsurance *n* self-confidence

ˌself-ˈbinder *n* a harvesting machine that cuts grain and binds it into bundles

ˌself-ˈcatering *adj* provided with lodging and kitchen facilities but not meals ⟨*a ~ holiday*⟩ ⟨*~ chalets*⟩

ˌself-ˈcentred *adj* concerned excessively with one's own desires or needs

ˌself-ˈcocking *adj* cocked by the operation of some part of the mechanism ⟨*~ on closing the bolt*⟩

ˌself-ˈcolˈlected *adj* self-possessed

ˌself-ˈcoloured *adj* of a single colour ⟨*a ~ flower*⟩

ˌself-comˈmand *n* self-control

ˌself-comˈposed *adj* having or showing mental or spiritual composure

ˌself-ˈconcept *n* a self-image

ˌself-conˈfessed *adj* openly acknowledged ⟨*a ~ debauchee*⟩

ˌself-ˈconfidence *n* confidence in oneself and one's powers and abilities – **self-confident** *adj*

ˌself-congratuˈlation *n* a complacent acknowledgment of one's own superiority or good fortune – **self-congratulatory** *adj*

ˌself-ˈconscious *adj* **1a** conscious of oneself as a possessor of mental states and originator of actions **b** intensely aware of oneself **2** uncomfortably conscious of oneself as an object of notice; ill at ease – **self-consciously** *adv*, **self-consciousness** *n*

ˌself-conˈsistent *adj* having each element logically consistent with the rest; internally consistent ⟨*a ~ set of proofs*⟩ – **self-consistency** *n*

ˌself-conˈtained *adj* **1** complete in itself ⟨*a ~ flat*⟩ **2a** showing self-possession **b** formal and reserved in manner – **self-containedly** /-nidli/ *adv*

ˌself-conˈtent *n* a feeling or expression of self-satisfaction – **self-contentment** *n*

ˌself-contraˈdiction *n* **1** contradiction of oneself **2** a statement that contains 2 contradictory elements or ideas – **self-contradictory** *adj*

ˌself-conˈtrol *n* restraint of one's own impulses or emotions – **self-controlled** *adj*

ˌself-ˈcritical *adj* **1** unduly critical of oneself **2** able to judge one's own motives or actions impartially

ˌself-ˈcriticism *n* the act of or capacity for criticizing one's own faults or shortcomings

ˌself-deˈception *n* the act of deceiving oneself; the state of being deceived by oneself (e g about one's character or motives)

ˌself-deˈfeating *adj* having the effect of preventing its own success

ˌself-deˈfence *n* **1** the act of defending or justifying oneself **2** the legal right to defend oneself with reasonable force – **self-defensive** *adj*

ˌself-deˈlusion *n* self-deception

ˌself-deˈnial *n* the restraint or limitation of one's desires or their gratification

ˌself-deˈnying *adj* showing self-denial

ˌself-ˈdeprecating *adj* given to self-depreciation

ˌself-depreciˈation *n* disparagement or understatement of oneself

ˌself-deˈstruct *vi, chiefly NAm* to destroy itself

ˌself-deˈstruction *n* destruction of oneself or itself; *esp* suicide – **self-destructive** *adj*

ˌself-determiˈnation *n* **1** free choice of one's own actions or states without outside influence **2** determination by a territorial unit of its own political status – **self-determined** *adj*, **self-determining** *adj*

ˌself-ˈdiscipline *n* the act of disciplining or power to discipline one's thoughts and actions, usu for the sake of improvement – **self-disciplined** *adj*

ˌself-ˈdoubt *n* a lack of confidence in oneself; diffidence – **self-doubting** *adj*

self-drive *adj, chiefly Br, of a hired vehicle* intended to be driven by the hirer

ˌself-efˈfacement *n* the act of making oneself inconspicuous, esp because of modesty; humility – **self-effacing** *adj*, **self-effacingly** *adv*

ˌself-emˈployed *adj* earning income directly from one's own business, trade, or profession rather than as salary or wages from an employer – **self-employment** *n*

ˌself-enˈrichment *n* the act or process of increasing one's intellectual or spiritual resources

ˌself-eˈsteem *n* **1** confidence and satisfaction in oneself; self-respect **2** vanity

ˌself-ˈevident *adj* requiring no proof; obvious – **self-evidence** *n*, **self-evidently** *adv*

ˌself-examiˈnation *n* the analysis of one's conduct, motives, etc

ˌself-ˈexecuting *adj* taking effect immediately without prior legislative procedures ⟨*a* ~ *treaty*⟩

ˌself-eˈxistent *adj* existing independently of any cause or agency – **self-existence** *n*

ˌself-exˈplanatory *adj* capable of being understood without explanation

ˌself-exˈpression *n* **1** the expression of one's individual characteristics (e g through painting or poetry) **2** the assertion of one's own character through uninhibited behaviour – **self-expressive** *adj*

ˌself-ˈfeeder *n* a device for feeding animals that automatically provides the food required

ˌself-fertiliˈzation *n* fertilization by the union of ova with pollen or sperm from the same individual – compare CROSS-FERTILIZATION – **self-fertile** *adj*, **self-fertility** *n*, **self-fertilized** *adj*, **self-fertilizing** *adj*

ˌself-fulˈfilling *adj* **1** marked by or achieving self-fulfilment **2** attaining fulfilment by virtue of having been asserted or assumed beforehand ⟨*a* ~ *prophecy*⟩

ˌself-fulˈfilment *n* fulfilment of oneself or itself

ˌself-ˈgenerated *adj* generated or originated from within oneself ⟨~ *humour*⟩

ˌself-ˈgiving *adj* self-sacrificing, unselfish

ˌself-ˈgoverned *adj* not influenced or controlled by others

ˌself-ˈgoverning *adj* having control over oneself; *specif* having self-government

ˌself-ˈgovernment *n* control of one's own (political) affairs – compare HOME RULE

ˌself-ˈhate *n* self-hatred

ˌself-ˈhatred *n* hatred of oneself; *specif* hatred redirected towards oneself in frustration or despair – **self-hating** *adj*

ˈself-ˌheal *n* a small violet-flowered plant of the mint family or other plant held to possess healing properties

ˌself-ˈhelp *n* the bettering or helping of oneself without dependence on others

ˈselfhood /-hood/ *n* **1a** the state of existing as a unique individual **b** personality **2** selfishness

ˌself-ˈimage *n* one's conception of oneself or of one's role

ˌself-imˈportance *n* **1** an exaggerated sense of one's own importance **2** arrogant or pompous behaviour – **self-important** *adj*

ˌself-inˈduced *adj* induced by oneself or itself

ˌself-inˈductance *n* inductance due to self-induction

ˌself-inˈduction *n* induction of an electromotive force in a circuit by a varying current in the same circuit

ˌself-inˈdulgence *n* excessive or unrestrained gratification of one's own appetites, desires, or whims – **self-indulgent** *adj*

ˌself-ˈinterest *n* (a concern for) one's own advantage and well-being ⟨*acted out of* ~ *and fear*⟩ – **self-interested** *adj*

selfish /ˈselfish/ *adj* concerned with or directed towards one's own advantage, pleasure, or well-being without regard for others [[3]*self* + *-ish*] – **selfishly** *adv*, **selfishness** *n*

ˌself-justifiˈcation *n* the making of excuses for oneself – **self-justificatory** *adj*

ˌself-ˈjustifying *adj* automatically justifying its existence or occurrence ⟨~ *extravagance*⟩

ˌself-ˈknowledge *n* knowledge or understanding of one's own capabilities, character, feelings, or motives

ˈselfless /-lis/ *adj* having no concern for self; unselfish – **selflessly** *adv*, **selflessness** *n*

ˌself-ˈloading *adj, of a firearm* semiautomatic

ˌself-ˈlove *n* **1** conceit, narcissism **2** an esp selfish concern for one's own happiness or advantage – **self-loving** *adj*

ˌself-ˈmade *adj* raised from poverty or obscurity by one's own efforts ⟨*a* ~ *man*⟩

ˌself-ˈmastery *n* self-control

ˌself-oˈpinionated *adj* **1** conceited **2** stubbornly holding to one's own opinion; opinionated

ˌself-perˈception *n* an appraisal of oneself; *esp* a self-image

ˌself-perˈpetuating *adj* capable of continuing or renewing oneself or itself indefinitely ⟨~ *board of trustees*⟩

ˌself-ˈpity *n* a self-indulgent dwelling on one's own sorrows or misfortunes – **self-pitying** *adj*

ˌself-polliˈnation *n* the transfer of pollen from the anther of a flower to the stigma of the same or a genetically identical flower – compare CROSS-POLLINATION

ˌself-ˈportrait *n* **1** a portrait of an artist done by him-/herself **2** a description of one's character or personality given by oneself

ˌself-posˈsessed *adj* having or showing self-possession; composed in mind or manner; calm – **self-possessedly** /-sidli/ *adv*

ˌself-posˈsession *n* control of one's emotions or behaviour, esp when under stress; composure

ˌself-preserˈvation *n* an instinctive tendency to act so as to safeguard one's own existence

ˌself-proˈclaimed *adj* self-styled

ˌself-proˈpelled *adj* **1** propelled by one's or its own power; *specif* containing within itself the means for its own propulsion ⟨*a* ~ *vehicle*⟩ **2** mounted on a vehicle rather than towed ⟨*a* ~ *artillery piece*⟩

ˌself-ˈquestioning *n* examination of one's own actions and motives

ˌself-ˈraising ˌflour *n* a commercially prepared mixture of flour containing a raising agent

ˌself-realiˈzation *n* fulfilment by oneself of the possibilities inherent in one's nature

ˌself-ˈrecording *adj, of an instrument* making an automatic record

ˌself-reˈgard *n* **1** concern or consideration for oneself or one's own interests **2** self-respect – **self-regarding** *adj*

ˌself-ˈregistering *adj* registering automatically ⟨*a* ~ *barometer*⟩

ˌself-ˈregulating *adj* regulating itself; *esp* automatic ⟨*a* ~ *mechanism*⟩

ˌself-reˈliance *n* reliance on one's own efforts and abilities; independence – **self-reliant** *adj*

ˌself-renunciˈation *n* renunciation of one's own desires or ambitions, esp for the sake of others

ˌself-reˈproach *n* the act of blaming or censuring oneself – **self-reproachful** *adj*, **self-reproaching** *adj*

ˌself-reˈspect *n* a proper respect for one's human dignity

ˌself-reˈspecting *adj* having or characterized by self-respect or integrity

ˌself-reˈstraint *n* restraint imposed on oneself, esp on the expression of one's feeling

ˌself-ˈrighteous *adj* assured of one's own righteousness, esp in contrast with the actions and beliefs of others; narrow-mindedly moralistic – **self-righteously** *adv*, **self-righteousness** *n*

,self-'righting *adj* capable of righting itself when capsized ⟨*a* ~ *boat*⟩

,self-'sacrifice *n* sacrifice of oneself or one's well-being for the sake of an ideal or for the benefit of others – **self-sacrificing** *adj*

'self,same *adj* precisely the same; identical ⟨*he left the* ~ *day*⟩

,self-satis'faction *n* a smug satisfaction with oneself or one's position or achievements

,self-'satisfied *adj* feeling or showing self-satisfaction ⟨*a* ~ *smile*⟩

,self-'sealing *adj* capable of sealing itself (e g after puncture) ⟨*a* ~ *fuel tank*⟩

,self-'seeker *n* sby self-seeking

,self-'seeking *adj* seeking only to safeguard or further one's own interests; selfish – **self-seeking** *n*

,self-'service *n* the serving of oneself (e g in a cafeteria or supermarket) with things to be paid for at a cashier's desk, usu upon leaving – **self-service** *adj*

,self-'serving *adj* serving one's own interests, esp at the expense of honesty or the welfare of others

,self-'sow /soh/ *vi* **self-sown** /sohn/, **self-sowed** /sohd/ *of a plant* to grow from seeds spread naturally (e g by wind or water)

,self-'starter *n* an electric motor used to start an internal-combustion engine

,self-'starting *adj* capable of starting by oneself or itself

,self-'sterile *adj* not self-fertile – **self-sterility** *n*

,self-'styled *adj* called by oneself, esp without justification ⟨~ *experts*⟩

,self-suf'ficient *adj* **1** able to maintain oneself or itself without outside aid; capable of providing for one's own needs ⟨*a community* ~ *in dairy products*⟩ **2** having unwarranted assurance of one's own ability or worth – **self-sufficiency** *n*

,self-suf'ficing *adj* self-sufficient – **self-sufficingly** *adv*

,self-sup'porting *adj* **1** meeting one's needs by one's own labour or income **2** supporting itself or its own weight ⟨*a* ~ *wall*⟩

,self-su'stained *adj* self-sustaining

,self-su'staining *adj* **1** maintaining or able to maintain oneself by independent effort **2** maintaining or able to maintain itself once started ⟨*a* ~ *nuclear reaction*⟩

,self-'will *n* stubborn or wilful adherence to one's own desires or ideas; obstinacy – **self-willed** *adj*

,self-'winding /'wiending/ *adj* not needing to be wound by hand ⟨*a* ~ *watch*⟩

[1]sell /sel/ *vb* **sold** /sohld/ *vt* **1** to deliver or give up in violation of duty, trust, or loyalty; betray – often + *out* **2a(1)** to give up (property) in exchange, esp for money **(2)** to offer for sale ⟨~s *insurance*⟩ **b** to give up or dispose of foolishly or dishonourably (in return for sthg else) ⟨*juries who* sold *the verdicts*⟩ **3** to cause or promote the sale of ⟨*advertising* ~s *newspapers*⟩ **4** to achieve a sale of ⟨*a book which* sold *a million copies*⟩ **5a** to make acceptable, believable, or desirable by persuasion ⟨~ *an idea*⟩ **b** to persuade to accept or enjoy sthg – usu + *on*; infml ⟨~ *children on reading*⟩ **6** to deceive, cheat – usu pass; infml ⟨*we've been* sold!⟩ ~ *vi* **1** to transfer sthg to another's ownership by sale **2** to achieve a sale; *also* to achieve satisfactory sales ⟨*hoped that the new line would* ~⟩ **3** to have a specified price – + *at* or *for* [ME *sellen*, fr OE *sellan*; akin to OHG *sellen* to sell, ON *sala* sale, Gk *helein* to take] – **sellable** *adj* – **sell down the river** to betray the faith of

[2]sell *n* **1** the act or an instance of selling **2** a deliberate deception; a hoax – infml

seller /'selə/ *n* a product offered for sale and selling well, to a specified extent, or in a specified manner ⟨*a million-copy* ~⟩ ⟨*a poor* ~⟩ [[1]SELL + [2]-ER]

seller's market *n* a market in which demand exceeds supply – compare BUYER'S MARKET

'selling ,plate /'seling/ *n* a race in which the winning horse is auctioned [*plate* (a race for which the prize is a gold or silver cup or similar trophy), fr [1]*plate*]

'selling-,plater /,playtə/ *n* **1** a horse that runs chiefly in selling plates **2** an inferior racehorse

sell off *vt* to dispose of completely by selling, esp at a reduced price

sellotape /'selə,tayp/ *vt* to fix (as if) with Sellotape

Sellotape *trademark* – used for a usu transparent adhesive tape

'sell-,out *n* **1** a performance, exhibition, or contest for which all tickets or seats are sold **2** a betrayal – infml

sell out *vt* **1** to dispose of entirely by sale **2** to betray or be unfaithful to (e g one's cause or associates), esp for the sake of money ~ *vi* **1** SELL UP **2** to betray one's cause or associates – usu + *on*

sell up *vb, chiefly Br* to sell (e g one's house or business) in a conclusive or forced transaction ⟨sold up *and emigrated to Australia*⟩

seltzer /'seltsə/ *n* a natural or artificially prepared mineral water containing carbon dioxide [modif of G *Selterser* (*wasser*) water of Selters, fr Nieder*selters*, village in Hesse, Germany]

selvage, selvedge /'selvij/ *n* **1a** the edge on either side of a (woven) fabric, so finished as to prevent unravelling; *specif* a narrow border often of different or heavier threads than the fabric and sometimes in a different weave **b** an edge (e g of wallpaper) meant to be cut off and discarded **2** a border, edge [ME *selvage*, prob fr MFlem *selvegge, selvage*, fr *selv* self + *egge* edge; akin to OE *self* and to OE *ecg* edge – more at EDGE]

selves /selvz/ *pl of* SELF

semantic /si'mantik/ *adj* of meaning in language [Gk *sēmantikos* significant, fr *sēmainein* to signify, mean, fr *sēma* sign, token; akin to Skt *dhyāyati* he thinks] – **semantically** *adv*

se'mantics *n pl but sing or pl in constr* **1** the branch of linguistics concerned with meaning **2** a branch of semiotics dealing with the relation between signs and the objects they refer to – **semanticist** /-sist/ *n*

[1]semaphore /'semə,faw/ *n* **1** an apparatus for conveying information by visual signals (e g by the position of 1 or more pivoted arms) **2** a system of visual signalling by 2 flags held 1 in each hand [Gk *sēma* sign, signal + ISV *-phore*]

[2]semaphore *vt* to convey (information) (as if) by semaphore ~ *vi* to send signals (as if) by semaphore

sematic /si'matik/ *adj, of a poisonous or unpleasant animal's (bright) colours* warning of danger ⟨*the* ~ *coloration of the skunk*⟩ [Gk *sēmat-, sēma* sign]

semblance /'sembləns/ *n* outward and often deceptive appearance; a show ⟨*wrapped in a* ~ *of* *euphoria*⟩ [ME, fr MF, fr OF *sembler* to be like, seem – more at RESEMBLE]

semeiology /ˌsemi'oləji, ˌsee-/ *n* semiology

semen /'seemən/ *n* a suspension of spermatozoa produced by the male reproductive glands that is conveyed to the female reproductive tract during coitus [NL, fr L, seed; akin to OHG *sāmo* seed, L *serere* to sow – more at [2]SOW]

semester /si'mestə/ *n* an academic term lasting half a year, esp in America and Germany [G, fr L *semestris* half-yearly, fr *sex* six + *mensis* month – more at SIX, MOON]

semi /'semi/ *n, Br* a semidetached house – infml

semi- /semi-/ *prefix* **1a** precisely half of **b** forming a bisection of ⟨semi*ellipse*⟩ ⟨semi*oval*⟩ **c** occurring halfway through (a specified period of time) ⟨semi*annual*⟩ ⟨semi*centenary*⟩ – compare BI- **2** to some extent; partly; incompletely ⟨semi*civilized*⟩ ⟨semi-*independent*⟩ ⟨semi*dry*⟩ ⟨semi*acid*⟩ – compare DEMI-, HEMI- **3a** partial; incomplete ⟨semi*consciousness*⟩ ⟨semi*darkness*⟩ **b** having some of the characteristics of ⟨semi*porcelain*⟩ ⟨semi*metal*⟩ **c** quasi ⟨semi*judicial*⟩ ⟨semi*governmental*⟩ ⟨semi*monastic*⟩ [ME, fr L; akin to OHG *sāmi-* half, Gk *hēmi-*]

ˌsemi'annual /-'anyoo(ə)l/ *adj* occurring every 6 months or twice a year – compare BIANNUAL – **semiannually** *adv*

ˌsemiauto'matic /-awtə'matik/ *adj* not fully automatic – **semiautomatic** *n*, **semiautomatically** *adv*

'semiˌbreve /-ˌbreev/ *n* a musical note with the time value of 2 minims or 4 crotchets ☞ MUSIC

ˌsemicen'tenary /-sen'teenəri, -'tenəri/ *n* (the celebration of) a 50th anniversary – **semicentenary** *adj*

ˌsemicen'tennial /-sen'teni·əl/ *n* a semicentenary – **semicentennial** *adj*

'semiˌcircle /-ˌsuhkl/ *n* (an object or arrangement in the form of) a half circle [L *semicirculus*, fr *semi-* + *circulus* circle] – **semicircular** *adj*

ˌsemiˌcircular ca'nal /ˌsemi'suhkyoolə/ *n* any of the 3 loop-shaped tubular parts of the inner ear that together constitute a sensory organ associated with the maintenance of bodily equilibrium ☞ NERVE

ˌsemi'classical /-'klasikl/ *adj* having some of the characteristics of the classical

ˌsemi'colon /-'kohlon/ *n* a punctuation mark ; used chiefly to coordinate major sentence elements where there is no conjunction

ˌsemicon'ducting /-kən'dukting/ *adj* (having the characteristics) of a semiconductor

ˌsemicon'ductor /-kən'duktə/ *n* a substance (e g silicon) whose electrical conductivity at room temperature is between that of a conductor and that of an insulator

ˌsemi'conscious /-'konshəs/ *adj* not fully aware or responsive – **semiconsciously** *adv*, **semiconsciousness** *n*

ˌsemicy'lindrical /-si'lindrikl/ *adj* having the shape of a longitudinal half of a cylinder

ˌsemi'darkness /-'dahknis/ *n* partial darkness; shade

ˌsemide'tached /-di'tacht/ *adj* forming 1 of a pair of residences joined into 1 building by a common wall – **semidetached** *n*

ˌsemidi'ameter /-die'amitə/ *n* a radius; *specif* the apparent radius of a generally spherical celestial body

ˌsemidi'urnal /-die'uhnl/ *adj* **1** relating to, lasting, or accomplished in half a day **2** occurring twice a day

ˌsemidocu'mentary /-dokyoo'ment(ə)ri/ *n* a film or television programme that incorporates factual material in presenting a fictional story – **semidocumentary** *adj*

'semiˌdome /-ˌdohm/ *n* a half dome covering a semicircular structure or recess – **semidomed** *adj*

ˌsemi'drying /-'drie·ing/ *adj* that dries imperfectly or slowly ⟨*cottonseed oil is a* ~ *oil*⟩

[1]ˌsemi'final /-'fienl/ *adj* **1** next to the last in a knockout competition **2** of or participating in a semifinal

[2]semifinal /ˌ--'--, '--ˌ--/ *n* a semifinal match or round – often pl with sing. meaning – **semifinalist** /ˌ--'---/ *n*

ˌsemi'fitted /-'fitid/ *adj* conforming roughly to the lines of the body

ˌsemi'fluid /-'flooh·id/ *adj* having qualities intermediate between those of a liquid and a solid; viscous – **semifluid** *n*

ˌsemi'formal /-'fawml/ *adj* being or suitable for an occasion of moderate formality ⟨*a* ~ *dinner*⟩ ⟨~ *gowns*⟩

ˌsemi'liquid /-'likwid/ *adj* semifluid – **semiliquid** *n*

ˌsemi'lunar /-'loohnə/ *adj* crescent-shaped [NL *semilunaris*, fr L *semi-* + *lunaris* lunar]

ˌsemilunar 'valve *n* (any of the crescent-shaped cusps that occur in) the aortic valve or the pulmonary valve

ˌsemi'metal /-'metl/ *n* an element (e g arsenic) with some metallic properties – **semimetallic** /-mi'talik/ *adj*

ˌsemi'monthly /-'munthli/ *adv* twice a month

seminal /'seminl/ *adj* **1** (consisting) of, storing, or conveying seed or semen ⟨~ *duct*⟩ ⟨~ *vesicle*⟩ ☞ REPRODUCTION **2** containing or contributing the seeds of future development; original and influential ⟨*a* ~ *book*⟩ ⟨*one of the most* ~ *of the great poets*⟩ [ME, fr MF, fr L *seminalis*, fr *semin-*, *semen* seed – more at SEMEN] – **seminally** *adv*

seminar /'semiˌnah/ *n* **1** an advanced or graduate class often featuring informality and discussion **2** a meeting for exchanging and discussing information [G, fr L *seminarium* seminary]

seminarian /ˌsemi'neəri·ən/ *n* a student in a seminary, esp of the Roman Catholic church

seminarist /'seminərist/ *n* a seminarian

seminary /'semin(ə)ri/ *n* **1** an institution of education **2** an institution for the training of candidates for the (Roman Catholic) priesthood [ME, seedbed, nursery, seminary, fr L *seminarium*, fr *semin-*, *semen* seed]

seminiferous /ˌsemi'nif(ə)rəs, ˌsee-/ *adj* producing or bearing seed or semen [L *semin-*, *semen* seed + E *-iferous*]

ˌsemiof'ficial /-ə'fish(ə)l/ *adj* having some official authority or standing ⟨*a* ~ *statement*⟩ – **semiofficially** *adv*

semiology, semeiology /ˌsemi'oləji, ˌsee-/ *n* the study of signs; *esp* semiotics [Gk *sēmeion* sign] – **semiological** /-ə'lojikl/ *adj*

semiotics /ˌsemi'otiks, ˌsee-/ *n pl but sing or pl in constr* a general philosophical theory of signs and symbols that includes syntactics and semantics [Gk *sēmeiōtikos* observant of signs, fr *sēmeiousthai* to interpret signs, fr *sēmeion* sign; akin to Gk *sēma* sign – more at SEMANTIC] – **semiotic** *adj*

ˌsemiˈpermanent /-ˈpuhmənənt/ *adj* **1** lasting or intended to last for a long time but not permanent **2** having the characteristics of sthg permanent but subject to change or review ⟨*a* ~ *agreement*⟩ – **semipermanently** *adv*

ˌsemiˈpermeable /ˈpuhmi·əbl/ *adj, esp of a membrane* permeable to small molecules but not to larger ones – **semipermeability** /-əˈbiləti/ *n*

ˌsemiˈplastic /-ˈplastik; *also* ˈplah-/ *adj* not fully plastic

ˌsemiˈprecious /-ˈpreshəs/ *adj, of a gemstone* of less commercial value than a precious stone

ˌsemiˈpro /-ˈproh/ *n or adj* (a) semiprofessional – infml

[1]**ˌsemiproˈfessional** /-prəˈfesh(ə)nl/ *adj* **1** engaging in an activity for pay or gain but not as a full-time occupation ⟨*a* ~ *dance band*⟩ **2** engaged in by semiprofessional players – **semiprofessionally** *adv*

[2]**semiprofessional** *n* one who engages in an activity (e g a sport) semiprofessionally

ˈsemiˌquaver /-ˌkwayvə/ *n* a musical note with time value of $\frac{1}{2}$ of a quaver ☞ MUSIC

ˌsemiˈrigid /-ˈrijid/ *adj* having a flexible cylindrical gas container with an attached stiffening keel that carries the load ⟨*a* ~ *airship*⟩

ˌsemiˈskilled /-ˈskild/ *adj* of, being, or requiring workers who have less training than skilled workers and more than unskilled workers

ˌsemiˈsoft /-ˈsoft/ *adj* firm but easily cut ⟨~ *cheese*⟩

ˌsemiˈsolid /-ˈsolid/ *adj* having the qualities of both a solid and a liquid; highly viscous – **semisolid** *n*

ˌsemisynˈthetic /-sinˈthetik/ *adj* produced by chemical alteration of a natural starting material ⟨~ *penicillins*⟩

Semite /ˈseemiet/ *n* a member of any of a group of peoples of SW Asia chiefly represented now by the Jews and Arabs [F *sémite*, fr *Sem* Shem, eldest son of Noah, fr LL, fr Gk *Sēm*, fr Heb *Shēm*]

[1]**Semitic** /siˈmitik/ *adj* **1** of or characteristic of the Semites; *specif* Jewish **2** of a branch of the Afro-Asiatic language family that includes Hebrew, Aramaic, Arabic, and Ethiopic ☞ ALPHABET

[2]**Semitic** *n* (any of) the Semitic languages

Semitism /ˈsemiˌtiz(ə)m/ *n* a policy favourable to Jews; predisposition in favour of Jews

ˈsemiˌtone /-ˌtohn/ *n* the musical interval (e g E–F or F–F♯) equal to the interval between 2 adjacent keys on a keyboard instrument – **semitonic** /-ˈtonik/ *adj*

ˈsemiˌtrailer /-ˌtraylə/ *n* a trailer having rear wheels but supported by a towing tractor at the front

ˌsemiˈtropical /-ˈtropikl/ *adj* subtropical

ˈsemiˌvowel /-ˌvowl/ *n* (a letter representing) a speech sound (e g /y/ or /w/) intermediate between vowel and consonant

ˌsemiˈweekly /-ˈweekli/ *adj or adv* appearing or taking place twice a week ⟨*a* ~ *news bulletin*⟩

semolina /ˌseməˈleenə/ *n* the purified hard parts left after milling of (hard) wheat used for pasta and in milk puddings [It *semolino*, dim. of *semola* bran, fr L *simila* finest wheat flour]

sempiternal /ˌsempiˈtuhnl/ *adj* everlasting, eternal – chiefly poetic [ME, fr LL *sempiternalis*, fr L *sempiternus*, fr *semper* ever, always, fr *sem-* one, same (akin to ON *samr* same) + *per* through – more at SAME, FOR] – **sempiternally** *adv*

sempre /ˈsempri; *also* ˈsempray/ *adv* always – used in music ⟨~ *legato*⟩ [It, fr L *semper*]

sempstress /ˈsem(p)stris/ *n* a seamstress [fem of *sempster*, var of *seamster* – more at SEAMSTRESS]

sen /sen/ *n, pl* **sen** ☞ *Indonesia, Malaysia* at NATIONALITY [Indonesian *sén*, prob fr E *cent*; Malaysian prob fr Indonesian]

senary /ˈseen(ə)ri/ *adj* of, based on, or characterized by 6; compounded of 6 things or parts ⟨~ *scale*⟩ ⟨~ *division*⟩ [L *senarius* consisting of six]

senate /ˈsenit/ *n sing or pl in constr* **1a** the supreme council of the ancient Roman republic and empire **b** the 2nd chamber in some legislatures that consist of 2 houses **2** the governing body of some universities [ME *senat*, fr OF, fr L *senatus*, lit., council of elders, fr *sen-*, *senex* old, old man – more at SENIOR]

senator /ˈsenətə/ *n* a member of a senate [ME *senatour*, fr OF *senateur*, fr L *senator*, fr *senatus*] – **senatorial** /-ˈtawri·əl/ *adj*, **senatorship** *n*

[1]**send** /send/ *vb* **sent** /sent/ *vt* **1** to direct or cause to go in a specified direction, esp violently ⟨sent *a blow to his chin*⟩ ⟨*the crash* sent *them scuttling out of their houses*⟩ **2** *of God, fate, etc* to cause to be; grant; BRING ABOUT ⟨~ *her victorious*⟩ **3** to dispatch by a means of communication ⟨~ *a telegram*⟩ **4a** to cause, direct, order, or request to go ⟨sent *her to buy some milk*⟩ **b** to dismiss ⟨*was* sent *home*⟩ **5** to cause to assume a specified state ⟨sent *him into a rage*⟩ **6** to cause to issue: e g **a** to pour out; discharge ⟨*clouds* ~ing *forth rain*⟩ **b** to utter ⟨~ *forth a cry*⟩ **c** to emit ⟨sent *out waves of perfume*⟩ **d** to grow out (parts) in the course of development ⟨*a plant* ~ing *forth shoots*⟩ **7** to consign to a destination (e g death or a place of imprisonment) **8** to delight, thrill – infml ⟨*that music really* ~s *me*⟩ ~ *vi* **1a** to dispatch sby to convey a message or do an errand ⟨~ *out for coffee*⟩ **b** to dispatch a request or order ⟨*have to* ~ *to Germany for spares*⟩ **2** to scend **3** to transmit [ME *senden*, fr OE *sendan*; akin to OHG *sendan* to send, OE *sīth* road, journey, OIr *sét*] – **sender** *n* – **send for** to request by message to come; summon – **send packing** to dismiss roughly or in disgrace

[2]**send** *n* a scend

send down *vt, Br* **1** to suspend or expel from a university **2** to send to jail – infml

send in *vt* **1** to cause to be delivered to an authority, group, or organization ⟨send in *a letter of complaint*⟩ **2** to assign with a view to tackling a crisis or difficulty ⟨send *a receiver* in *to deal with the bankruptcy*⟩

ˈsend-ˌoff *n* a usu enthusiastic demonstration of goodwill at the beginning of a venture (e g a trip)

send off *vt* **1** to dispatch **2** to attend to the departure of – compare SEE OFF

send on *vt* **1** to dispatch (e g luggage) in advance **2** to forward (readdressed mail)

send out *vt* **1** to issue for circulation ⟨*had* sent *the invitations* out⟩ **2** to dispatch (e g an order) from a shop or place of storage

send round *vt* to circulate ⟨*a notice is being* sent round⟩

ˈsend-ˌup *n, Br* a satirical imitation, esp on stage or television; a parody

send up *vt* **1** *chiefly Br* to make an object of mockery or laughter; ridicule **2** *chiefly NAm* SEND DOWN 2

sene /ˈsaynay/ *n* ☞ *Western Samoa* at NATIONALITY [Samoan, fr E *cent*]

senectitude /siˈnekti,tyoohd/ *n* old age – fml [ML *senectitudo*, alter. of L *senectus* old age, fr *sen-*, *senic-*, *senex* old, old man – more at SENIOR]

senescence /siˈnes(ə)ns/ *n* being or becoming old or withered [*senescent* fr L *senescent-*, *senescens*, prp of *senescere* to grow old, fr *sen-*, *senex* old] – **senesce** *vi*, **senescent** *adj*

seneschal /ˈsenish(ə)l/ *n* the agent or bailiff of a feudal lord's estate [ME, fr MF, of Gmc origin; akin to Goth *sineigs* old, OHG *scalc* servant – more at ²SENIOR]

sengi /ˈseng·gi/ *n, pl* **sengi** ☞ *Zaire* at NATIONALITY [native name in Zaire]

senhor /seˈnyaw/ *n, pl* **senhors, senhores** /-rees, -reez/ a Portuguese or Brazilian gentleman – used as a title equivalent to *Mr* or as a generalized term of direct address [Pg, fr ML *senior* superior, lord, fr L, adj, elder]

senhora /seˈnyawrə/ *n* a married Portuguese or Brazilian woman – used as a title equivalent to *Mrs* or as a generalized term of direct address [Pg, fem of *senhor*]

senhorita /,senyəˈreetə/ *n* an unmarried Portuguese or Brazilian girl or woman – used as a title equivalent to *Miss* [Pg, fr dim. of *senhora*]

senile /ˈseeniel/ *adj* of, exhibiting, or characteristic of (the mental or physical weakness associated with) old age [L *senilis*, fr *sen-*, *senex* old, old man] – **senility** /siˈniləti/ *n*

¹**senior** /ˈseenyə, ˈseeni·ə/ *n* **1** sby who is older than another ⟨*5 years his* ~⟩ **2a** sby of higher standing or rank **b** *NAm* a student in the final year before graduation from school, university, etc [ME, fr L, fr *senior*, adj]

²**senior** *adj* **1** elder – used, chiefly in the USA, to distinguish a father with the same name as his son **2** higher in standing or rank ⟨~ *officers*⟩ [ME, fr L, older, elder, compar of *sen-*, *senex* old; akin to Goth *sineigs* old, Gk *henos*]

,**senior ˈaircraftman** *n* ☞ RANK

senior chief petty officer *n* ☞ RANK

,**senior ˈcitizen** *n* sby beyond the usual age of retirement – euph

Senior Common Room *n* a staff sitting room in a college

senior house officer *n* (a doctor holding) the training grade of British hospital doctor senior to houseman

seniority /,seeniˈorəti/ *n* a privileged status attained by length of continuous service (e g in a company) [²SENIOR + -ITY]

senior master sergeant *n* ☞ RANK

senior nursing officer *n* sby who is in charge of the nursing staff in a British hospital

senior registrar *n* (one holding) the grade of British hospital doctor senior to registrar

senior wrangler *n* the winner of the highest mark in the first class of the old Cambridge mathematical tripos

seniti /ˈseniti/ *n, pl* **seniti** ☞ *Tonga* at NATIONALITY [Tongan, modif of E *cent*]

senna /ˈsenə/ *n* (the dried leaflets or pods, used as a purgative, of) any of a genus of leguminous plants, shrubs, and trees of warm regions [NL, fr Ar *sanā*]

sennet /ˈsenit/ *n* a signal call on a trumpet or cornet for entrance or exit on the stage [prob alter. of obs *signet* (signal)]

sennit /ˈsenit/ *n* a braided cord or fabric (e g of plaited rope yarns) [perh fr F *coussinet*, dim. of *coussin* cushion; fr its use to protect cables from fraying]

senor, señor /seˈnyaw/ *n, pl* **senors, señores** /-rays/ a Spanish-speaking man – used as a title equivalent to *Mr* or as a generalized term of direct address [Sp *señor*, fr ML *senior* superior, lord, fr L, adj, elder]

senora, señora /seˈnyawrə/ *n* a married Spanish-speaking woman – used as a title equivalent to *Mrs* or as a generalized term of direct address [Sp *señora*, fem of *señor*]

senorita, señorita /,senyəˈreetə/ *n* an unmarried Spanish-speaking girl or woman – used as a title equivalent to *Miss* [Sp *señorita*, fr dim. of *señora*]

¹**sensate** /ˈsensayt/ *adj* endowed with bodily senses ⟨*a* ~ *being*⟩ – fml [LL *sensatus*, fr L *sensus* sense]

²**sensate** *adj* relating to or apprehended through the senses [ML *sensatus*, fr LL, endowed with sense, fr L *sensus* sense] – **sensately** *adv*

sensation /senˈsaysh(ə)n/ *n* **1a** a mental process (e g seeing or hearing) resulting from stimulation of a sense organ **b** a state of awareness of a usu specified type resulting from internal bodily conditions or external factors; a feeling or sense ⟨~s *of fatigue*⟩ **2a** a surge of intense interest or excitement ⟨*their elopement caused a* ~⟩ **b** a cause of such excitement; *esp* sby or sthg in some respect remarkable or outstanding [ML *sensation-*, *sensatio*, fr LL *sensatus* endowed with sense]

sensational /senˈsaysh(ə)nl/ *adj* **1** arousing an immediate, intense, and usu superficial interest or emotional reaction **2** exceptionally or unexpectedly excellent or impressive – infml [SENSATION + ¹-AL] – **sensationalize** *vt*, **sensationally** *adv*

senˈsational,ism /-,iz(ə)m/ *n* the use of sensational subject matter or style – **sensationalist** *n*

¹**sense** /sens/ *n* **1** a meaning conveyed or intended; *esp* any of a range of meanings a word or phrase may bear, esp as isolated in a dictionary entry **2** (the faculty of perceiving the external world or internal bodily conditions by means of) any of the senses of feeling, hearing, sight, smell, taste, etc **3** soundness of mind or judgment – usu pl with sing. meaning ⟨*when he came to his* ~s *he was shocked to hear what he had done*⟩ **4a** an ability to use the senses for a specified purpose ⟨*a good* ~ *of balance*⟩ **b** a definite but often vague awareness or impression ⟨*felt a* ~ *of insecurity*⟩ **c** an awareness that motivates action or judgment ⟨*done out of a* ~ *of justice*⟩ **d** a capacity for discernment and appreciation ⟨*her* ~ *of humour*⟩ ⟨*a highly-developed critical* ~⟩ **5** the prevailing view; a consensus ⟨*the* ~ *of the meeting*⟩ **6** an ability to put the mind to effective use; practical intelligence **7** either of 2 opposite directions (of motion) [MF or L; MF *sens* sensation, feeling, mechanism of perception, meaning, fr L *sensus*, fr *sensus*, pp of *sentire* to perceive, feel; akin to OHG *sin* mind, sense, OE *sith* journey – more at SEND]

²**sense** *vt* **1a** to perceive by the senses **b** to be or become conscious of ⟨~ *danger*⟩ **2** to grasp, comprehend ⟨~ *the import of a remark*⟩ **3** to detect (e g a symbol or radiation) automatically

ˈ**senseless** /-lis/ *adj* deprived of, deficient in, or contrary to sense: e g **a** unconscious ⟨*knocked* ~⟩

b foolish, stupid ⟨*it was some ~ practical joke* – A Conan Doyle⟩ **c** meaningless, purposeless ⟨*a ~ murder*⟩ – **senselessly** *adv*, **senselessness** *n*

'sense ,organ *n* a bodily structure that responds to a stimulus (e g heat or sound waves) by initiating impulses in nerves that convey them to the central nervous system where they are interpreted as sensations

sensibility /,sensə'biləti/ *n* **1** ability to have sensations ⟨*tactile ~*⟩ **2** heightened susceptibility to feelings of pleasure or pain (e g in response to praise or blame) – often pl with sing. meaning ⟨*a man of strong* sensibilities⟩ **3** the ability to discern and respond freely to sthg (e g emotion in another) **4** (exaggerated) sensitiveness in feelings and tastes

sensible /'sensəbl/ *adj* **1** capable of sensing ⟨*~ to pain*⟩ **2** having, containing, or indicative of good sense or sound reason ⟨*~ men*⟩ ⟨*made a ~ answer*⟩ **3a** perceptible to the senses or to understanding ⟨*his distress was ~ from his manner*⟩ **b** large enough to be observed or noticed; considerable ⟨*a ~ decrease*⟩ **4** aware, conscious *of USE* (*3 & 4*) fml [ME, fr MF, fr L *sensibilis*, fr *sensus*, pp] – **sensibleness** *n*, **sensibly** *adv*

sensitive /'sensətiv/ *adj* **1** capable of being stimulated or excited by external agents (e g light, gravity, or contact) ⟨*a photographic emulsion ~ to red light*⟩ **2** highly responsive or susceptible: e g **a(1)** easily provoked or hurt emotionally **(2)** finely aware of the attitudes and feelings of others or of the subtleties of a work of art **b** hypersensitive ⟨*~ to egg protein*⟩ **c** capable of registering minute differences; delicate ⟨*~ scales*⟩ **d** readily affected or changed by external agents (e g light or chemical stimulation) **e** *of a radio receiving set* highly responsive to incoming waves **3** concerned with highly classified information ⟨*a ~ document*⟩ [ME, fr MF *sensitif*, fr ML *sensitivus*, irreg fr L *sensus*] – **sensitively** *adv*, **sensitiveness** *n*, **sensitivity** /-'tivəti/ *n*

sensitive plant *n* any of several mimosas or other plants with leaves that fold or droop when touched

sensit·ize, -ise /'sensətiez/ *vb* to make or become sensitive or hypersensitive [*sensit*ive + *-ize, -ise*] – **sensitizer** *n*, **sensitization** /-'zaysh(ə)n/ *n*

sensor /'sensə, -saw/ *n* a device that responds to heat, light, sound, pressure, magnetism, etc and transmits a resulting impulse (e g for measurement or operating a control) [L *sensus*, pp of *sentire* to perceive – more at SENSE]

sensorial /sen'sawri·əl/ *adj* sensory

sensorium /sen'sawri·əm/ *n, pl* **sensoriums, sensoria** /-ri·ə/ (the parts of the brain or the mind concerned with the reception and interpretation of stimuli from) all the sensory apparatus [LL, sense organ, fr L *sensus* sense]

sensory /'sens(ə)ri/ *adj* of sensation or the senses ☞ NERVE

sensual /'sensyoo·əl, -shoo-/ *adj* **1** sensory **2** relating to or consisting in the gratification of the senses or the indulgence of appetites **3a** devoted to or preoccupied with the senses or appetites, rather than the intellect or spirit **b** voluptuous [ME, fr LL *sensualis*, fr L *sensus* sense + *-alis* -al] – **sensualism** *n*, **sensualist** *n*, **sensualize** *vt*, **sensually** *adv*, **sensuality** /-'aləti/ *n*

sensuous /'sensyoo·əs, -shoo·əs/ *adj* **1a** of (objects perceived by) the senses **b** providing or characterized by gratification of the senses; appealing strongly to the senses ⟨*~ pleasure*⟩ **2** suggesting or producing rich imagery or sense impressions ⟨*~ verse*⟩ **3** readily influenced by sense perception [L *sensus* sense + E *-ous*] – **sensuously** *adv*, **sensuousness** *n*, **sensuosity** /-'osəti/ *n*

Sensurround /'sens(y)ə,rownd/ *trademark* – used for a sound- reproducing system developed for use in films that employs low frequencies to heighten the spectators' sense of physical involvement with the action depicted on the screen

sent /sent/ *past of* SEND

[1]sentence /'sentəns/ *n* **1a** a judgment formally pronounced by a court and specifying a punishment **b** the punishment so imposed ⟨*serve a ~*⟩ **2** a grammatically self-contained speech unit that expresses an assertion, a question, a command, a wish, or an exclamation and is usu shown in writing with a capital letter at the beginning and with appropriate punctuation at the end [ME, fr OF, fr L *sententia*, lit., feeling, opinion, fr (assumed) *sentent-, sentens*, irreg prp of *sentire* to feel – more at SENSE] – **sentential** /-'tensh(ə)l/ *adj*

[2]sentence *vt* **1** to impose a judicial sentence on **2** to consign to a usu unpleasant fate ⟨*development that ~s rural industries to extinction*⟩

sententia /sen'tenshə/ *n, pl* **sententiae** /-shi,ee/ an aphorism – usu pl; fml [L, lit., feeling, opinion – more at SENTENCE]

sententious /sen'tenshəs/ *adj* **1** terse, pithy **2** given to or full of **a** terse or pithy sayings **b** pompous, moralizing [ME, fr L *sententiosus*, fr *sententia* sentence, maxim] – **sententiously** *adv*, **sententiousness** *n*

sentience /'sensh(ə)ns/ *n* **1** a sentient quality or state **2** rudimentary feeling and perception as distinguished from thought and the higher emotions *USE* chiefly fml

sentient /'sensh(ə)nt/ *adj* **1** capable of perceiving through the senses; conscious **2** keenly sensitive in perception or feeling *USE* chiefly fml [L *sentient-, sentiens*, prp of *sentire* to perceive, feel] – **sentiently** *adv*

sentiment /'sentimənt/ *n* **1a** (an attitude, thought, or judgment prompted or coloured by) feeling or emotion **b** a specific view or attitude; an opinion – usu pl with sing. meaning ⟨*held similar ~s on the matter*⟩ **2a** sensitive feeling; refined sensibility, esp as expressed in a work of art **b** indulgently romantic or nostalgic feeling **3** the emotional significance of a communication as distinguished from its overt meaning ⟨*the ~ is admirable, though it is clumsily expressed*⟩ [F or ML; F, fr ML *sentimentum*, fr L *sentire*]

sentimental /,senti'mentl/ *adj* **1** resulting from feeling rather than reason ⟨*kept the gift for its ~ value*⟩ **2** having an excess of superficial sentiment – **sentimentalism** *n*, **sentimentalist** *n*, **sentimentalize** *vb*, **sentimentally** *adv*, **sentimentality** /-'taləti/ *n*

[1]sentinel /'sentinl/ *n* sby who or sthg that keeps guard [MF *sentinelle*, fr OIt *sentinella*, fr *sentina* vigilance, fr *sentire* to perceive, fr L]

[2]sentinel *vt* **-ll-** (*NAm* **-l-, -ll-**) **1** to watch over as a sentinel **2** to post as a sentinel

sentry /'sentri/ *n* a guard, watch; *esp* a soldier standing guard at a gate, door, etc [perh fr obs *sentry* (sanctuary, watch tower), alter. of ME *seintuarie* sanctuary]

'sentry ,box *n* a shelter for a standing sentry

'sentry-,go *n* duty as a sentry [fr the phrase *Sentry, go!*]

senza /'sentsah/ *prep* without – used in music directions ⟨~ *sordini*⟩ [It]

sepal /'sepl/ *n* any of the modified leaves comprising the calyx of a flower ☞ PLANT [NL *sepalum*, fr *sepa-* (fr Gk *skepē* covering) + *-lum* (as in *petalum* petal); akin to Lith *kepurė* head covering] – **sepaloid** /'seepl,oyd/ *adj*

-sepalous /-'sepələs/ *comb form* (→ *adj*) having (such or so many) sepals ⟨*gamo*sepalous⟩ [*sepal*]

separable /,sep(ə)rəbl/ *adj* capable of being separated or dissociated [ME, fr L *separabilis*, fr *separare* to separate] – **separableness** *n*, **separably** *adv*, **separability** /-'biləti/ *n*

[1]separate /'sepərayt/ *vt* **1a** to set or keep apart; detach, divide **b** to make a distinction between; distinguish ⟨~ *religion from magic*⟩ **c** to disperse in space or time; scatter ⟨*widely* ~d *hamlets*⟩ **2** to part (a married couple) by separation **3** to isolate, segregate **4a** to isolate from a mixture or compound ⟨~ *cream from milk*⟩ **b** to divide into constituent parts or types **5** *NAm* to discharge ⟨*was* ~d *from the army*⟩ ~ *vi* **1** to become divided or detached; draw or come apart **2a** to sever an association; withdraw ⟨~ *from a federation*⟩ **b** to cease to live together as man and wife, esp by formal arrangement **3** to go in different directions **4** to become isolated from a mixture ***USE*** (*vt 4*; *vi 4*) often + *out* [ME *separaten*, fr L *separatus*, pp of *separare*, fr *se-* apart + *parare* to prepare, procure – more at SECEDE, PARE] – **separative** /'sep(ə)rətiv/ *adj*

[2]separate /'sep(ə)rət/ *adj* **1** set or kept apart; detached, separated **2** not shared with another; individual ⟨~ *rooms*⟩ **3a** existing independently; autonomous **b** different in kind; distinct ⟨*6* ~ *ways of cooking an egg*⟩ – **separately** *adv*, **separateness** *n*

separates /'sep(ə)rəts/ *n pl* garments (e g skirts, shirts, and trousers) that are designed to be worn together to form an interchangeable outfit

separation /,sepə'raysh(ə)n/ *n* **1a** a point, line, or means of division **b** an intervening space; a gap, break **2** cessation of cohabitation between husband and wife by mutual agreement or judicial decree [[1]SEPARATE + -ION]

separatism /'sep(ə)rə,tiz(ə)m/ *n* a belief or movement advocating separation (e g schism, secession, or segregation)

'separatist /-tist/ *n* one who favours separatism: e g **a** *cap* any of a group of 16th- and 17th-c English Protestants preferring to separate from the Church of England rather than reform it **b** an advocate of racial or cultural separation – **separatist** *adj, often cap*

separator /'sepə,raytə/ *n* a device for separating liquids of different specific gravities (e g cream from milk) or liquids from solids [[1]SEPARATE + [1]-OR]

Sephardi /si'fahdi/ *n, pl* **Sephardim** /-dim/ a member or descendant of the non-Yiddish-speaking branch of European Jews that settled in Spain and Portugal – compare ASHKENAZI [LHeb *sěphāradhī*, fr *sěphāradh* Spain, fr Heb, region where Jews were once exiled (Obad 1: 20)] – **Sephardic** /-dik/ *adj*

[1]sepia /'seepyə/ *n* **1** (a brown melanin-containing pigment from) the inky secretion of cuttlefishes **2** rich dark brown [NL, genus comprising cuttlefish, fr L, cuttlefish, fr Gk *sēpia*; akin to Gk *sēpein* to make putrid, *sapros* rotten]

[2]sepia *adj* **1** of the colour sepia **2** made of or done in sepia ⟨*a* ~ *print*⟩

sepoy /'seepoy/ *n* an Indian soldier employed by a European power, esp Britain [Pg *sipai*, fr Hindi *sipāhī*, fr Per, cavalryman]

sepsis /'sepsis/ *n, pl* **sepses** /-seez/ the spread of bacteria from a focus of infection; *esp* septicaemia [NL, fr Gk *sēpsis* decay, fr *sēpein* to make putrid]

septate /'septayt/ *adj* divided by or having a septum

September /sep'tembə, səp-/ *n* the 9th month of the Gregorian calendar [ME *Septembre*, fr OF, fr L *September* (seventh month of ancient Roman calendar), fr *septem* seven – more at SEVEN]

septennial /sep'tenyəl/ *adj* **1** consisting of or lasting for 7 years **2** occurring or performed every 7 years [LL *septennium* period of seven years, fr L *septem* + *-ennium* (as in *biennium*)] – **septennially** *adv*

septet /sep'tet/ *n* **1** a musical composition for 7 instruments, voices, or performers **2** *sing or pl in constr* a group or set of 7; *esp* the performers of a septet [G, fr L *septem*]

septic /'septik/ *adj* **1** putrefactive **2** relating to, involving, or characteristic of sepsis [L *septicus*, fr Gk *sēptikos*, fr *sēpein* to make putrid – more at SEPIA]

septicaemia /,septi'seemyə, -mi·ə/ *n* invasion of the bloodstream by microorganisms from a focus of infection with chills, fever, etc [NL, fr L *septicus* + NL *-aemia*]

,septic 'tank *n* a tank in which the solid matter of continuously flowing sewage is disintegrated by bacteria

septuagenarian /,sepchooəji'neəri·ən, ,septwə-/ *n* sby between 70 and 79 years old [LL *septuagenarius* 70 years old, fr L, of or containing 70, fr *septuageni* 70 each, fr *septuaginta*] – **septuagenarian** *adj*

Septuagesima /,sepchooə'jesimə, ,septwə-/ *n* the third Sunday before Lent [ME, fr LL, fr L, fem of *septuagesimus* 70th, fr *septuaginta* seventy; fr its being the 70th day before Easter]

Septuagint /'sepchooə,jint, 'septwə-/ *n* a pre-Christian Greek version of the Jewish Scriptures arranged and edited by Jewish scholars about 300 BC [LL *Septuaginta*, fr L, seventy, irreg fr *septem* seven + *-ginta* (akin to L *viginti* twenty); fr the approximate number of its translators – more at SEVEN, VIGESIMAL]

septum /'septəm/ *n, pl* **septa** /-tə/ a dividing wall or membrane, esp between bodily spaces or masses of soft tissue [NL, fr L *saeptum* enclosure, fence, wall, fr *saepire* to fence in, fr *saepes* fence, hedge; akin to Gk *haimasia* stone wall] – **septal** *adj*

sepulchral /si'pulkrəl/ *adj* **1** of the burial of the dead **2** suited to or suggestive of a tomb; funereal ⟨*a* ~ *whisper*⟩ – **sepulchrally** *adv*

sepulchre, *NAm chiefly* **sepulcher** /'sep(ə)lkə/ *n* **1** a place of burial; a tomb **2** a receptacle (in an altar) for religious relics [ME *sepulcre*, fr OF, fr L *sepulcrum, sepulchrum*, fr *sepelire* to bury; akin to Gk *hepein* to care for, Skt *saparyati* he pays homage, *sapati* he serves]

sepulture /'sep(ə)lchə/ *n* burial, interment – fml [ME, fr OF, fr L *sepultura*, fr *sepultus*, pp of *sepelire*]

sequel /'seekwəl/ *n* **1** a consequence, result **2a** subsequent development or course of events **b** a play, film, or literary work continuing the course of a narrative begun in a preceding one [ME, fr MF *sequelle*, fr L *sequela*, fr *sequi* to follow – more at SUE]

sequela /si'kweelə/ *n, pl* **sequelae** /-lee/ an aftereffect of disease or injury [NL, fr L, sequel]

[1]**sequence** /'seekwəns/ *n* **1** a continuous or connected series: e g **a** an extended series of poems united by theme ⟨*a sonnet* ~⟩ **b** RUN 3f **c** a succession of repetitions of a melodic phrase or harmonic pattern each in a new position – compare IMITATION 3, OSTINATO **d** a set of elements following the same order as the natural numbers **e** an episode, esp in a film **2a** order of succession **b** the order of amino acids in a protein, nucleotide bases in DNA or RNA, etc **3** a subsequent but not resultant occurrence or course **4** a continuous progression [ME, fr ML *sequentia*, fr LL, sequel, lit., act of following, fr L *sequent-, sequens*, prp of *sequi*]

[2]**sequence** *vt* **1** to place in ordered sequence **2** to determine the amino acid sequence of (a protein), nucleotide sequence of (a nucleic acid), etc – **sequencer** *n*

sequent /'seekwənt/ *adj* **1** consecutive, succeeding **2** consequent, resultant *USE* fml [L *sequent-, sequens*, prp]

sequential /si'kwensh(ə)l/ *adj* **1** of or arranged in a sequence; serial ⟨~ *file systems*⟩ **2** following in sequence – **sequentially** *adv*

sequester /si'kwestə/ *vt* **1a** to set apart; segregate **b** to seclude, withdraw ⟨~ *oneself from urban life*⟩ ⟨*a quiet* ~ed *spot*⟩ **2** to seize (e g a debtor's property) judicially **3** to chelate [ME *sequestren*, fr MF *sequestrer*, fr LL *sequestrare* to surrender for safekeeping, set apart, fr L *sequester* agent, depositary, bailee; akin to L *sequi* to follow]

sequestrate /si'kwestrayt/ *vt* SEQUESTER 2 [LL *sequestratus*, pp of *sequestrare*] – **sequestration** /,seekwe'straysh(ə)n/ *n*

sequin /'seekwin/ *n* **1** a former gold coin of Italy and Turkey **2** a very small disc of shining metal or plastic used for ornamentation, esp on clothing [F, fr It *zecchino*, fr *zecca* mint, fr Ar *sikkah* die, coin]

sequoia /si'kwoyə/ *n* either of 2 huge coniferous Californian trees: **a** BIG TREE **b** a redwood [NL, genus name, fr *Sequoya* (George Guess) †1843 AmerInd scholar]

sera /'siərə/ *pl of* SERUM

serac /'seerak/ *n* a pinnacle, sharp ridge, or block of ice among the crevasses of a glacier [F *sérac*, lit., a kind of white cheese, fr ML *seracium* whey, fr L *serum* whey – more at SERUM]

seraglio /se'rahli·oh, -lyoh/ *n, pl* **seraglios** HAREM 1a [It *serraglio* enclosure, seraglio; partly fr ML *serraculum* bar of a door, bolt, fr LL *serare* to bolt; partly fr Turk *saray* palace – more at [4]SEAR]

serai /se'rie/ *n* a caravanserai [Turk & Per; Turk *saray* mansion, palace, fr Per *sarāī* mansion, inn]

serang /sə'rang/ *n* a boatswain [Per *sarhang* commander, boatswain, fr *sar* chief + *hang* authority]

seraph /'serəf/ *n, pl* **seraphim** /-fim/, **seraphs** any of the 6-winged angels standing in the presence of God [LL *seraphim*, pl, seraphs, fr Heb *śĕrāphīm*] – **seraphic** /si'rafik/ *adj*

Serb /suhb/, **Serbian** /'suhbi·ən/ *n* **1** a native or inhabitant of Serbia **2** the Serbo-Croatian language as spoken in Serbia – compare CROATIAN ☞ LANGUAGE [*Serb*, fr Serb *Srb*; *Serbian*, fr *Serbia*, former Balkan kingdom, now a republic of Yugoslavia, fr Serb *Srbija*] – **Serb, Serbian** *adj*

Serbo-Croatian /,suhboh kroh'aysh(ə)n/ *n* **1** the Slavonic language of the Serbs and Croats **2** one whose native language is Serbo-Croatian – **Serbo-Croatian** *adj*

[1]**sere, sear** /siə/ *adj* shrivelled, withered – chiefly poetic [ME, fr OE *sēar* dry; akin to OHG *sōrēn* to wither, Gk *hauos* dry]

[2]**sere** *n* a series of successive ecological communities established in 1 area [L *series* series] – **seral** /'siərəl/ *adj*

[1]**serenade** /,serə'nayd/ *n* **1** a complimentary vocal or instrumental performance (given outdoors at night for a woman) **2** an instrumental composition in several movements written for a small ensemble [F *sérénade*, fr It *serenata*, fr *sereno* clear, calm (of weather), fr L *serenus*]

[2]**serenade** *vb* to perform a serenade (in honour of) – **serenader** *n*

serendipity /,serən'dipəti/ *n* the faculty of discovering pleasing or valuable things by chance [fr its possession by the heroes of the Per fairy tale *The Three Princes of Serendip; Serendip*, ancient name for Sri Lanka, fr Ar *Sarandīb* Sri Lanka, deriv of Skt *Siṃhalānāṃ Dvipaḥ*, lit., island of the Sinhalese] – **serendipitous** /-'dipitəs/ *adj*

serene /sə'reen/ *adj* **1** free of storms or adverse changes; clear, fine ⟨~ *skies*⟩ ⟨~ *weather*⟩ **2** having or showing tranquillity and peace of mind ⟨*a* ~ *smile*⟩ [L *serenus*; akin to OHG *serawēn* to become dry, Gk *xēros* dry] – **serenely** *adv*, **sereneness** *n*, **serenity** /sə'renəti/ *n*

serf /suhf/ *n* a member of a class of agricultural labourers in a feudal society, bound in service to a lord, and esp transferred with the land they worked if its ownership changed hands [F, fr L *servus* slave, servant, serf – more at SERVE] – **serfage** *n*, **serfdom** *n*

serge /suhj/ *n* a durable twilled fabric having a smooth clear face and a pronounced diagonal rib on the front and the back [ME *sarge*, fr MF, fr (assumed) VL *sarica*, fr L *serica*, fem of *sericus* silken – more at SERICEOUS]

sergeant /'sahj(ə)nt/ *n* **1** a police officer ranking in Britain between constable and inspector **2** ☞ RANK [ME, servant, attendant, sergeant, fr OF *sergent, serjant*, fr L *servient-, serviens*, prp of *servire* to serve]

sergeant aircrew *n* ☞ RANK

,sergeant-at-'arms *n, pl* **sergeants-at-arms** *often cap S&A* an officer attending the British Speaker or Lord Chancellor; *also* a similar officer in other legislatures

sergeant first class *n* ☞ RANK

,sergeant 'major *n, pl* **sergeant majors, sergeants major** **1** ☞ RANK **2** a warrant officer in the British army or Royal Marines

[1]**serial** /'siəri·əl/ *adj* **1** of or constituting a series, rank, or row ⟨~ *order*⟩ **2** appearing in successive instalments ⟨*a* ~ *story*⟩ **3** of or being music based on a series of notes in an arbitrary but fixed order without regard for traditional tonality ⟨~ *technique*⟩ – **serially** *adv*

[2]**serial** *n* **1** a work appearing (e g in a magazine or on

television) in parts at usu regular intervals **2** a publication issued as 1 of a consecutively numbered continuing series – **serialist** *n*

serialism /'siəri-ə,liz(ə)m/ *n* (the theory or practice of composing) serial music

'serial·ize, -ise /-liez/ *vt* to arrange or publish in serial form – **serialization** /-'zaysh(ə)n/ *n*

'serial ,number *n* a number used as a means of identification that indicates position in a series

seriate /'siəri,ayt/ *vt or adj* (to cause to be) arranged in a series – fml [adj fr (assumed) NL *seriatus*, fr L *series*; vb fr adj]

seriatim /,siəri'atim/ *adv or adj* in regular order [adv ML, fr L *series*; adj fr adv]

sericeous /si'rishəs/ *adj* finely hairy ⟨*a* ~ *leaf*⟩ [LL *sericeus* silken, fr L *sericum* silk garment, silk, fr neut of *sericus* silken, fr Gk *sērikos*, fr *Sēres*, an eastern Asiatic people producing silk in ancient times]

sericulture /'seri,kulchə/ *n* the production of raw silk by breeding silkworms [L *sericum* silk + E *culture*] – **sericultural** /-'kulchərəl/ *adj*, **sericulturist** *n*

series /'siəriz, -reez/ *n, pl* **series** **1** a number of things or events of the same kind following one another in spatial or temporal succession ⟨*a concert* ~⟩ ⟨*the hall opened into a* ~ *of small rooms*⟩; *broadly* any group of systematically related items **2** a usu infinite mathematical sequence whose terms are to be added together **3** the coins or currency of a particular country and period **4** a succession of issues of volumes published with continuous numbering or usu related subjects or authors and format **5** a division of rock formations that is smaller than a system and comprises rocks deposited during an epoch **6** a group of chemical compounds or elements related in structure and properties **7** an arrangement of devices in an electrical circuit in which the whole current passes through each device – compare PARALLEL 4b **8** a number of games (e g of cricket) played between 2 teams ⟨*a 5-match* ~ *between England and Australia*⟩ [L, fr *serere* to join, link together; akin to Gk *eirein* to string together, *hormos* chain, necklace]

serif /'serif/ *n* a short line stemming from the stroke of a letter ☞ ALPHABET [prob fr D *schreef* stroke, line, fr MD, fr *schriven* to write, fr L *scribere* – more at [1]SCRIBE] – **seriffed** *adj*

serigraph /'seri,grahf, -,graf/ *n* a print made by a silk-screen process [L *sericum* silk + Gk *graphein* to write, draw – more at CARVE] – **serigrapher** /sə'rigrəfə/ *n*, **serigraphy** /-fi/ *n*

serin /'serin/ *n* a small European finch related to the canary [F]

serine /'sereen, 'siə-, -rin/ *n* an amino acid that occurs in most proteins [ISV *sericin* a gelatinous protein that cements the 2 fibroin filaments in a silk fibre (fr L *sericum* silk) + *-ine*]

seriocomic /,siərioh'komik/ *adj* having a mixture of the serious and the comic [*serious* + *-o-* + *comic*] – **seriocomically** *adv*

serious /'siəri·əs/ *adj* **1** grave or thoughtful in appearance or manner; sober **2a** requiring careful attention and concentration ⟨~ *study*⟩ **b** of or relating to a weighty or important matter ⟨*a* ~ *play*⟩ **3a** not jesting or deceiving; in earnest **b** deeply interested or committed ⟨~ *fishermen*⟩ **4** having important or dangerous consequences; critical ⟨*a* ~ *injury*⟩ [ME *seryows*, fr MF or LL; MF *serieux*, fr LL *seriosus*, alter. of L *serius*] – **seriousness** *n*

'seriously /-li/ *adv* **1a** in a sincere manner; earnestly **b** to speak in a serious way ⟨~, *you should be more careful*⟩ **2** to a serious extent; severely ⟨~ *injured*⟩

,serious-'minded *adj* having a serious outlook on life – **serious-mindedly** *adv*

serjeant /'sahj(ə)nt/ *n* a sergeant

sermon /'suhmən/ *n* **1** a religious discourse delivered in public, usu by a clergyman as a part of a religious service **2** a speech on conduct or duty; *esp* one that is unduly long or tedious [ME, fr OF, fr ML *sermon-*, *sermo*, fr L, speech, conversation, fr *serere* to link together – more at SERIES]

sermon·ize, -ise /'suhmə,niez/ *vi* to give moral advice in an officious or dogmatic manner – **sermonizer** *n*

sero- *comb form* serum ⟨sero*logy*⟩ [L *serum*]

serology /si'roləji/ *n* the medical study of the reactions and properties of (blood) serum [ISV] – **serologist** *n*, **serological** /,siərə'lojikl/ *adj*

serosa /si'rohsə, -zə/ *n* SEROUS MEMBRANE [NL, fr fem of *serosus* serous, fr L *serum*] – **serosal** *adj*

serotonin /,serə'tohnin/ *n* an amine that causes constriction of small blood vessels and occurs esp in blood platelets and as a neurotransmitter in the brain [*sero-* + *tonic* + *-in*]

serous membrane /'siərəs/ *n* a thin membrane (e g the peritoneum) with cells that secrete a watery liquid [*serous* fr MF *sereux*, fr *serum*, fr L]

serpent /'suhpənt/ *n* **1** a (large) snake **2** *the* Devil **3** a wily treacherous person **4** an old-fashioned bass woodwind instrument of serpentine form [ME, fr MF, fr L *serpent-*, *serpens*, fr prp of *serpere* to creep; akin to Gk *herpein* to creep, Skt *sarpati* he creeps]

[1]serpentine /'suhpən,tien/ *adj* **1** of or like a serpent (e g in form or movement) **2** subtly tempting; wily, artful **3** winding or turning one way and another [ME, fr MF *serpentin*, fr LL *serpentinus*, fr L *serpent-*, *serpens*]

[2]serpentine *n* sthg wavy or winding; *specif* a serpentine movement in dressage

[3]serpentine *n* a usu dull green mottled mineral consisting mainly of hydrated magnesium silicate [ME, fr ML *serpentina*, *serpentinum*, fr LL, fem & neut of *serpentinus* resembling a serpent]

serpiginous /suh'pijinəs/ *adj, of an ulcer, ringworm, etc* creeping, spreading [ML *serpigin-*, *serpigo* creeping skin disease, fr L *serpere* to creep]

serranid /'serənid/ *n* any of a large family of flesh-eating spiny-finned marine fishes with toothed scales [deriv of L *serra* saw] – **serranid** *adj*, **serranoid** /-noyd/ *adj or n*

[1]serrate /se'rayt, sə-/ *vt* to mark or provide with serrations [LL *serratus*, pp of *serrare* to saw, fr L *serra*]

[2]serrate /'serət, -rayt/ *adj* notched or having (forwards-pointing) teeth on the edge ⟨*a* ~ *leaf*⟩ ☞ PLANT [L *serratus*, fr *serra* saw]

serration /se'raysh(ə)n, sə-/ *n* **1** a formation resembling the teeth of a saw **2** any of the teeth of a serrated edge [[2]SERRATE + -ION]

serried /'serid/ *adj* crowded or pressed together; compact ⟨*the crowd collected in a* ~ *mass* – W S Maugham⟩ [fr pp of arch *serry* (to press close), fr MF *serré*, pp of *serrer* to press, crowd, fr LL *serare* to bolt, latch, fr L *sera* lock, bolt]

serum /'siərəm/ *n, pl* **serums, sera** /'siərə/ the watery part of an animal liquid (remaining after coagulation): **a** blood serum, esp when containing specific antibodies **b** whey [L, whey, serum; akin to Gk *oros* whey, serum, *hormē* onset, assault, Skt *sarati* it flows] – **serous** *adj*

serum hepatitis *n* an often fatal inflammation of the liver caused by a virus that is contracted esp by contact with an infected person's blood

serval /'suhv(ə)l/ *n* a long-legged long-eared African wildcat with a tawny black-spotted coat [F, fr Pg *lobo cerval* lynx, fr ML *lupus cervalis*, lit., cervine wolf]

servant /'suhv(ə)nt/ *n* sby who or sthg that serves others; *specif* sby employed to perform personal or domestic duties for another [ME, fr OF, fr prp of *servir*]

[1]**serve** /suhv/ *vi* **1a** to act as a servant **b** to do military or naval service **2** to act as server at Mass **3a** to be of use; fulfil a specified purpose – often + *as* **b** to be favourable, opportune, or convenient ⟨*told the story whenever occasion* ~d⟩ **c** to prove reliable or trustworthy ⟨*it was last year, if memory* ~s⟩ **d** to hold a post or office; discharge a duty ⟨~ *on a jury*⟩ **4** to prove adequate or satisfactory; suffice ⟨*dress that* ~s *for all occasions*⟩ **5** to distribute drinks or helpings of food **6** to attend to customers in a shop **7** to put the ball or shuttle in play in any of various games (e g tennis or volleyball) ~ *vt* **1a** to act as a servant to **b** to give military or naval service to ⟨~d *France in the last war*⟩ **c** to perform the duties of ⟨~d *his presidency*⟩ **2** to act as server at (Mass) **3a** to work through or perform (a term of service) ⟨~d *his time as a mate*⟩ **b** to undergo (a term of imprisonment) **4** to supply (food or drink) to (guests or diners) **5a(1)** to provide with sthg needed or desired ⟨*3 schools* ~ *the area*⟩ **(2)** to attend to (a customer) in a shop **b** to supply (sthg needed or desired) ⟨*garages refused to* ~ *petrol*⟩ **6** to prove adequate for; suffice ⟨*a smile would* ~ *him for encouragement*⟩ ⟨*this sharp stone will* ~ *my purposes*⟩ **7** to treat or act towards in a specified way ⟨*he* ~d *me ill*⟩ **8** to make legal service of (e g a writ or summons) or upon (a person there named) **9** *of a male animal* to copulate with **10** to wind yarn or wire tightly round (a rope or stay) for protection **11** to act so as to help or benefit ⟨*the citizen's duty to* ~ *society*⟩ **12** to put (the ball or shuttle) in play [ME *serven*, fr OF *servir*, fr L *servire* to be a slave, serve, fr *servus* slave, servant, perh of Etruscan origin] – **serve someone right** to be a deserved punishment for sby

[2]**serve** *n* the act of putting the ball or shuttle in play in any of various games (e g volleyball, badminton, or tennis); *also* a turn to serve

server /'suhvə/ *n* **1** sby who serves food or drink **2** the player who serves (e g in tennis) **3** sthg (e g tongs) used in serving food or drink **4** an assistant to the celebrant of a low mass

servery /'suhv(ə)ri/ *n* a room, counter, or hatch (e g in a public house) from which food is served

serve up *vt* to provide or supply (sthg required or expected) – chiefly infml

[1]**service** /'suhvis/ *n* **1a** work or duty performed for sby ⟨*on active* ~⟩ **b** employment as a servant ⟨*entered* ~ *when she was 14*⟩ **2a** the function performed by sby who or sthg that serves ⟨*these shoes have given me good* ~⟩ **b** help, use, benefit ⟨*be of* ~ *to them*⟩ **c** disposal for use or assistance ⟨*I'm always at your* ~⟩ **3a** a form followed in a religious ceremony **b** a meeting for worship **4** the act of serving: e g **a** a helpful act; a favour ⟨*did him a* ~⟩ **b** a piece of useful work that does not produce a tangible commodity – usu pl with sing. meaning ⟨*charge for professional* ~s⟩ **c** a serve **5** a set of articles for a particular use; *specif* a set of matching tableware ⟨*a 24-piece dinner* ~⟩ **6a** an administrative division ⟨*the consular* ~⟩ **b** any of a nation's military forces (e g the army or navy) **7a(1)** a facility supplying some public demand ⟨*telephone* ~⟩ ⟨*bus* ~⟩ **(2)** *pl* utilities (e g gas, water sewage, or electricity) available or connected to a building **b(1)** a facility providing maintenance and repair ⟨*television* ~⟩ **(2)** the usu routine repair and maintenance of a machine or motor vehicle ⟨*the car is due for its 6000 mile* ~⟩ **c** a facility providing broadcast programmes ⟨*East European* Service⟩ **8** the bringing of a legal writ, process, or summons to notice as prescribed **9** the act of copulating with a female animal [ME, fr OF, fr L *servitium* condition of a slave, body of slaves, fr *servus* slave]

[2]**service** *adj* **1** of the armed services **2** used in serving or delivering ⟨*tradesmen use the* ~ *entrance*⟩ **3** providing services ⟨*the* ~ *industries*⟩

[3]**service** *vt* to perform services for: e g **a** to repair or provide maintenance for **b** to meet interest and sinking fund payments on (e g government debt) **c** to perform any of the business functions auxiliary to production or distribution of **d** *of a male animal* SERVE 9 – **servicer** *n*

[4]**service, 'service ,tree** *n* an Old World tree of the rose family resembling the related mountain ashes but with larger flowers and larger edible fruits [ME *serves*, pl of *serve* serviceberry, service tree, fr OE *syrfe*, fr (assumed) VL *sorbea*, fr L *sorbus* service tree]

serviceable /'suhvisəbl/ *adj* **1** fit to use; suited for a purpose **2** wearing well in use; durable – **serviceableness** *n*, **serviceably** *adv*, **serviceability** /-'biləti/ *n*

'serviceberry /-b(ə)ri/ *n* any of various N American trees and shrubs of the rose family with showy white flowers and edible purple or red fruits [[4]*service* + *berry*]

'service ,box *n* a rectangular area 1.6m (5ft 3in) square on each side of a squash court, inside which a player must stand to serve ☞ SPORT

'service ,cap *n* a flat-topped visor cap worn as part of a military uniform – compare GARRISON CAP

'service ,car *n, NZ* a coach, bus

'service ,charge *n* a proportion of a bill added onto the total bill to pay for service, usu instead of tips

'service ,flat *n, Br* a flat of which the rent includes a charge for certain services (e g cleaning)

'service ,line *n* a line marked on a court in various games (e g tennis) to mark a boundary which must not be overstepped in serving ☞ SPORT

'serviceman /-mən/, *fem* **'service,woman** *n* **1** a member of the armed forces **2** *chiefly NAm* sby employed to repair or maintain equipment

'service ,mark *n* a mark or device used in the USA to identify a commercial service

'service ,road *n* a road that provides access for local traffic only

'service ,station *n* a retail station for servicing motor vehicles, esp with oil and petrol

'service ,tree *n* [4]SERVICE

serviette /,suhvi'et/ *n, chiefly Br* a table napkin [F, fr MF, fr *servir* to serve]

servile /'suhviel/ *adj* **1** of or befitting a slave or a menial position ⟨*a ~ task*⟩ **2** slavishly or unctuously submissive; abject, obsequious [ME, fr L *servilis*, fr *servus* slave – more at SERVE] – **servilely** *adv*, **servility** /-'viləti/ *n*

serving /'suhving/ *n* a single portion of food or drink; a helping

servitude /'suhvityoohd/ *n* **1** lack of liberty; bondage ⟨*penal ~*⟩ **2** a right by which sthg owned by one person is subject to a specified use or enjoyment by another [ME, fr MF, fr L *servitudo* slavery, fr *servus* slave]

servo /'suhvoh/ *n, pl* **servos** a servomotor or servomechanism

servomechanism /'suhvoh,mekəniz(ə)m/ *n* an automatic device for controlling large amounts of power by means of very small amounts of power and automatically correcting performance of a mechanism [*servo-* (as in *servomotor*) + *mechanism*]

servomotor /'suhvoh,mohtə/ *n* a power-driven mechanism that supplements a primary control operated by a comparatively feeble force (e g in a servomechanism) [F *servo-moteur*, fr L *servus* slave, servant + F *-o-* + *moteur* motor, fr L *motor* mover – more at MOTOR]

-ses /-seez/ *pl of* -SIS

sesame /'sesəmi/ *n* (an E Indian plant with) small flattish seeds used as a source of oil and as a flavouring agent [alter. of earlier *sesam, sesama*, fr L *sesamum, sesama*, fr Gk *sēsamon, sēsamē*, of Sem origin; akin to Assyr *šamaššamu* sesame, Ar *simsim*]

sesamoid /'sesəmoyd/ *adj or n* (of or being) a small round mass of bone or cartilage in a tendon, esp at a joint or bony prominence [Gk *sēsamoeidēs*, lit., resembling sesame seed, fr *sēsamon*]

sesqui- /seskwi-/ *comb form* **1** one and a half times ⟨sesqui*centennial*⟩ **2** containing 3 atoms or equivalents of a specified element or radical, esp combined with 2 of another ⟨sesqui*oxide*⟩ [L, one and a half, half again, lit., and a half, fr *semis* half (fr *semi-*) + *-que* (enclitic) and; akin to Gk *te* and, Skt *ca*, Goth *-h, -uh*]

sesquicentenary /,seskwisen'teenəri, -'tenəri/ *n* a sesquicentennial

,sesquicen'tennial /-sen'teni·əl/ *n* (the celebration of) a 150th anniversary – **sesquicentennial** *adj*

,sesquipe'dalian /-pə'daylyən/ *adj* many-syllabled [L *sesquipedalis*, lit., a foot and a half long, fr *sesqui-* + *ped-, pes* foot – more at FOOT]

sessile /'sesiel/ *adj* **1** attached directly by the base without a stalk ⟨*a ~ leaf*⟩ **2** permanently attached or established and not free to move about ⟨*~ polyps*⟩ [L *sessilis* of or fit for sitting, low, dwarf (of plants), fr *sessus*, pp] – **sessility** /se'siləti/ *n*

,sessile 'oak *n* a durmast

session /'sesh(ə)n/ *n* **1** a meeting or series of meetings of a body (e g a court or council) for the transaction of business; a sitting **2** the period between the meeting of a legislative or judicial body and the final adjournment of that meeting **3** the period in which a school conducts classes **4** a period devoted to a particular activity, esp by a group of people ⟨*a recording ~*⟩ [ME, fr MF, fr L *session-*, *sessio*, lit., act of sitting, fr *sessus*, pp of *sedēre* to sit – more at SIT] – **sessional** *adj*

sesterce /'sestuhs/ *n* an ancient Roman coin worth ¼ denarius [L *sestertius*, fr *sestertius* two and a half times as great (fr its being equal originally to two and a half asses), fr *semis* half (fr *semi-*) + *tertius* third – more at THIRD]

sestertium /ses'tuhti·əm/ *n, pl* **sestertia** /-ti·ə/ a money unit in ancient Rome worth 1000 sesterces [L, fr gen pl of *sestertius* (in the phrase *milia sestertium* thousands of sesterces)]

ses'tertius /-ti·əs/ *n, pl* **sestertii** /-ti,ie/ a sesterce

sestet /ses'tet/ *n* a poem or stanza of 6 lines; *specif* the last 6 lines of an Italian sonnet [It *sestetto*, fr *sesto* sixth, fr L *sextus* – more at SEXT]

sestina /se'steenə/ *n* a lyrical poem form consisting of 6 6-line stanzas and a 3-line envoy with an elaborate scheme of repeated words [It, fr *sesto* sixth]

[1]set /set/ *vb* **-tt-; set,** (*vt 10*) **setted** *vt* **1** to cause to sit; place in or on a seat **2a** to place with care or deliberate purpose and with relative stability ⟨*~ a ladder against the wall*⟩ **b** TRANSPLANT 1 ⟨*~ seedlings*⟩ **c** to make (e g a trap) ready to catch prey **3** to cause to assume a specified condition ⟨*~ the room to rights*⟩ ⟨*she ~ my mind at rest*⟩ **4a** to appoint or assign to an office or duty ⟨*~ him over them as foreman*⟩ **b** to post, station ⟨*~ sentries*⟩ **5a** to place in a specified relation or position ⟨*a dish to ~ before a king*⟩ **b** to place in a specified setting ⟨*the story is ~ in 17th-c Spain*⟩ **6a** to fasten **b** to apply ⟨*~ pen to paper*⟩ ⟨*~ a match to the fire*⟩ **7** to fix or decide on as a time, limit, or regulation; prescribe ⟨*~ a wedding day*⟩ **8a** to establish as the most extreme, esp the highest, level ⟨*~ a new record*⟩ **b** to provide as a pattern or model ⟨*~ an example*⟩ ⟨*~ a fashion*⟩ **c** to allot as or compose for a task ⟨*~ the children some homework*⟩ **9a** to adjust (a device, esp a measuring device) to a desired position ⟨*~ the alarm for 7:00*⟩ **b** to restore to normal position or connection after dislocation or fracturing ⟨*~ a broken bone*⟩; *also* REDUCE 5 ⟨*~ a fracture*⟩ **c** to spread to the wind ⟨*~ the sails*⟩ **10a** to divide (an age-group of pupils) into sets **b** to teach (a school subject) by dividing the pupils into sets ⟨*maths and science are ~*ted⟩ **11a** to make ready for use ⟨*~ the stage*⟩ ⟨*~ another place for dinner*⟩ **b** to provide music or instrumentation for (a text) **c(1)** to arrange (type) for printing **(2)** to put into type or its equivalent (e g on film) **12a** to put a fine edge on by grinding or honing ⟨*~ a razor*⟩ **b** to bend slightly the alternate teeth of (a saw) in opposite directions **c** to sink (the head of a nail) below the surface **13** to fix in a desired position **14** to fix (the hair) in a desired style by waving, curling, or arranging, usu while wet **15a** to adorn or surround with sthg attached or embedded; stud, dot ⟨*river all ~ about with fever trees* – Rudyard Kipling⟩ **b** to fix (e g a gem) in a metal setting **16a** to fix at a specified amount ⟨*~ bail at £500*⟩ **b** to value, rate ⟨*his promises were ~ at naught*⟩ **c** to place as an estimate of worth ⟨*~ a high value on life*⟩ **17** to place in relation for comparison ⟨*~ her beside Michelangelo*⟩; *also* to offset ⟨*~ our gains against our losses*⟩ **18a** to direct to action ⟨*~ her to write a report*⟩ **b** to put into activity or motion ⟨*~ the clock going*⟩ ⟨*it ~ me wondering*⟩ **c** to incite to attack or antagonism ⟨*war ~s brother against brother*⟩ **19** *of a gundog* to point out the position of (game) by holding a fixed attitude

20 to defeat (an opponent or his/her contract) in bridge **21** to fix firmly; give rigid form to ⟨~ *his jaw in determination*⟩ **22** to cause to become firm or solid ⟨~ *jelly by adding gelatin*⟩ **23** to cause (e g fruit) to develop ~ *vi* **1** – used as an interjection to command runners to put themselves into the starting position before a race **2** *of a plant part* to undergo development, usu as a result of pollination **3** to pass below the horizon; go down ⟨*the sun* ~s⟩ **4** to make an attack – + *on* or *upon* **5** to have a specified direction in motion; flow, tend ⟨*the wind was* ~ting *south*⟩ **6** to apply oneself to some activity ⟨~ *to work*⟩ **7** *of a gundog* to indicate the position of game by crouching or pointing **8** to dance face to face with another in a square dance ⟨~ *to your partner*⟩ **9a** to become solid or thickened by chemical or physical attention ⟨*the cement* ~s *rapidly*⟩ **b** *of a broken bone* to become whole by knitting together **c** *of metal* to acquire a permanent twist or bend from strain **10** *chiefly dial* to sit [ME *setten*, fr OE *settan*; akin to OHG *sezzen* to set, OE *sittan* to sit] – **set about 1** to begin to do ⟨*how to* set about *losing weight*⟩ **2** to attack ⟨set about *the intruder with a rolling pin*⟩ – **set foot** to pass over the threshold; enter – + *in, on,* or *inside* – **set in motion** to get (sthg) started; initiate ⟨set *an inquiry* in motion⟩ – **set on** to cause to attack or pursue ⟨set *the dog* on *the trespassers*⟩ – **set one's face against** to oppose staunchly – **set one's hand to** to become engaged in – **set one's heart** to resolve; *also* to want (sthg) very much – + *on* or *upon* ⟨*she* set her heart *on succeeding*⟩ – **set one's house in order** to introduce necessary reforms – **set one's sights** to focus one's concentration or intentions; aim – **set one's teeth on edge** to give one an unpleasant sensation (e g that caused by an acid flavour or squeaky noise) – **set sail** to begin a voyage ⟨set sail *for America*⟩ – **set store by** to consider valuable, trustworthy, or worthwhile, esp to the specified degree ⟨*don't* set *much* store by *his advice*⟩ – **set the scene** to provide necessary background information – **set to work** to apply oneself; begin ⟨*he* set to work *to undermine their confidence*⟩

[2]**set** *adj* **1** intent, determined ⟨~ *on going*⟩ **2** fixed by authority or binding decision; prescribed, specified ⟨*there are 3* ~ *books for the examination*⟩ **3** *of a meal* consisting of a specified combination of dishes available at a fixed price **4** reluctant to change; fixed by habit ⟨~ *in his ways*⟩ **5** immovable, rigid ⟨*a* ~ *frown*⟩ **6** ready, prepared ⟨*all* ~ *for an early morning start*⟩ **7** conventional, stereotyped ⟨*her speech was full of* ~ *phrases*⟩ [ME *sett*, fr pp of *setten* to set]

[3]**set** *n* **1** setting or being set **2a** a mental inclination, tendency, or habit **b** predisposition to act in a certain way in response to an anticipated stimulus or situation **3** a number of things, usu of the same kind, that belong or are used together or that form a unit ⟨*a chess* ~⟩ ⟨*a* ~ *of Dickens*⟩ ⟨*a good* ~ *of teeth*⟩ **4** direction of flow ⟨*the* ~ *of the wind*⟩ **5** the form or carriage of the body or of its parts ⟨*the graceful* ~ *of his head*⟩ **6** the amount of deviation from a straight line; *specif* the degree to which the teeth of a saw have been set **7** permanent change of form due to repeated or excessive stress **8** the arrangement of the hair by curling or waving **9a** a young plant or rooted cutting ready for transplanting **b** a small bulb, corm, or (piece of) tuber used for propagation ⟨*onion* ~s⟩ **10** an artificial setting for a scene of a theatrical or film production **11** a division of a tennis match won by the side that wins at least 6 games beating the opponent by 2 games or that wins a tie breaker **12** the basic formation in a country dance or square dance **13** (the music played at) a session of music (e g jazz or rock music), usu followed by an intermission **14** *sing or pl in constr* a group of people associated by common interests ⟨*the smart* ~⟩ **15** a collection of mathematical elements (e g numbers or points) **16** an apparatus of electronic components assembled so as to function as a unit ⟨*a radio* ~⟩ **17** *sing or pl in constr* a group of pupils of roughly equal ability in a particular subject who are taught together – compare STREAM **18** a sett

seta /ˈseetə/ *n, pl* **setae** /-ti/ a slender bristle or similar part of an animal or plant [NL, fr L *saeta, seta* bristle – more at SINEW] – **setaceous** /siˈtayshəs/ *adj,* **setaceously** *adv,* **setal** /ˈseetl/ *adj*

set apart *vt* **1** SET ASIDE 2 **2** to make noticeable or outstanding ⟨*his height* sets *him* apart⟩

set aside *vt* **1** to put to one side; discard **2** to reserve for a particular purpose; save **3** to reject from consideration **4** to annul or overrule (a sentence, verdict, etc)

ˈ**set,back** /-ˌbak/ *n* **1** an arresting of or hindrance in progress **2** a defeat, reverse

set back *vt* **1** to prevent or hinder the progress of; impede, delay **2** to cost ⟨*a new suit* set *him* back *a full week's wages*⟩ – infml [[1]*set* + [2]*back*]

set by *vt* to put aside for future use; reserve

set down *vt* **1** to place at rest on a surface or on the ground; deposit **2** to cause or allow (a passenger) to alight from a vehicle **3** to land (an aircraft) on the ground or water **4** to put in writing **5a** to regard, consider ⟨set *him* down *as a liar*⟩ **b** to attribute, ascribe ⟨set *her success* down *to sheer perseverance*⟩

ˈ**set-,in** *adj* cut separately and stitched in ⟨~ *sleeves*⟩

set in *vt* to insert; *esp* to stitch (a small part) into a larger article ⟨set in *a sleeve of a dress*⟩ ~ *vi* **1** to become established ⟨*the rot has* set in⟩ **2** to blow or flow towards the shore ⟨*the wind was beginning to* set in⟩

ˈ**set,line** /-ˌlien/ *n, NAm* a long heavy fishing line to which several hooks are attached in series

ˈ**set-,off** *n* **1** sthg set off against another thing: **a** a decoration, adornment **b** a counterbalance, compensation **2** the discharge of a debt by setting against it a sum owed by the creditor to the debtor

set off *vt* **1a** to put in relief; show up by contrast **b** to adorn, embellish **c** to make distinct or outstanding; enhance **2** to treat as a compensating item ⟨set off *the 3 totals against one another*⟩ **3a** to set in motion; cause to begin **b** to cause to explode; detonate **4** *chiefly NAm* to compensate for; offset ~ *vi* to start out on a course or journey ⟨set off *for home*⟩

set out *vt* **1** to state or describe at length; expound ⟨*a pamphlet* setting out *his ideas in full*⟩ **2a** to arrange and present graphically or systematically **b** to mark out (e g a design) **c** to create or construct according to a plan or design ⟨set *gardens* out *on waste ground*⟩ **3** to begin with a definite purpose or goal; intend, undertake ⟨*you* set out *deliberately to annoy me*⟩ ~ *vi* to start out on a course, journey, or career

set piece *n* **1** (a part of) a work of art, literature, etc with a formal pattern or style **2** an arrangement of fireworks that forms a pattern while burning **3** any of various moves in soccer or rugby (e g a corner kick or free kick) by which the ball is put back into play after a stoppage

set point *n* a situation (e g in tennis) in which one player will win the set by winning the next point

'set,screw /-,skrooh/ *n* **1** a screw that is tightened to prevent relative movement between parts (e g of a machine) and keep them in a set position **2** a screw that serves to adjust a machine

set square *n, chiefly Br* a flat triangular instrument with 1 right angle and 2 other precisely known angles, used to mark out or test angles

sett, set /set/ *n* **1** the burrow of a badger **2** a usu rectangular block of stone or wood formerly used for paving streets [alter. of [3]*set*]

settee /se'tee/ *n* a long often upholstered seat with a back and usu arms for seating more than 1 person; *broadly* a sofa [alter. of [1]*settle*]

setter /'setə/ *n* a large gundog trained to point on finding game; *specif* IRISH SETTER [[1]SET + [2]-ER]

set theory *n* a branch of mathematics or of symbolic logic that deals with the nature and relations of sets

setting /'seting/ *n* **1** the manner, position, or direction in which sthg (e g a dial) is set **2** the (style of) frame in which a gem is mounted **3a** the background, surroundings **b** the time and place of the action of a literary, dramatic, or cinematic work **c** the scenery used in a theatrical or film production **4** the music composed for a text (e g a poem) **5** PLACE SETTING

[1]settle /'setl/ *n* a wooden bench with arms, a high solid back, and an enclosed base which can be used as a chest [ME, place for sitting, seat, chair, fr OE *setl*; akin to OHG *sezzal* seat, L *sella* seat, chair, saddle, OE *sittan* to sit]

[2]settle *vb* **settling** /'setling/ *vt* **1** to place firmly or comfortably ⟨~d *herself in an armchair*⟩ **2a** to establish in residence ⟨~ *refugees on farmland*⟩ **b** to supply with inhabitants; colonize **3a** to cause to sink and become compacted ⟨*rain* ~d *the dust*⟩ **b** to clarify by causing the sediment to sink ⟨*put eggshells in the coffee to* ~ *it*⟩ **4a** to free from pain, discomfort, disorder, or disturbance ⟨*took a drink to* ~ *his nerves*⟩ **b** to make subdued or well-behaved ⟨*one word from the referee* ~d *him*⟩ **5** to fix or resolve conclusively ⟨~ *the question*⟩ **6a** to bestow legally for life – usu + *on* ⟨~d *her estate on her son*⟩ **b** to arrange for or make a final disposition of ⟨~d *her affairs*⟩ **7** to pay (a bill or money claimed) ~ *vi* **1** to come to rest ⟨*a sparrow* ~d *on the windowsill*⟩ **2a** to sink gradually to the bottom; subside ⟨*let the dust* ~ *before applying paint*⟩ **b** to become clearer by the deposit of sediment or scum **c** *of a building, the ground, etc* to sink slowly to a lower level; subside **3a** to become fixed or permanent ⟨*his mood* ~d *into apathy*⟩ **b** to establish a residence or colony ⟨~d *in Canada for a few years*⟩ **4a** to become calm or orderly – often + *down* **b** to adopt an ordered or stable life-style – usu + *down* ⟨*marry and* ~ *down*⟩ **5a** to adjust differences or accounts – often + *with* or *up* **b** to end a legal dispute by the agreement of both parties, without court action ⟨~d *out of court*⟩ [ME *settlen* to seat, bring to rest, come to rest, fr OE *setlan*, fr *setl* seat] – **settle for** to be content with; accept

settle in *vi* to become comfortably established ⟨*children quickly* settle in *at a new school*⟩ ~ *vt* to assist in becoming comfortably established

'settlement /-mənt/ *n* **1** settling **2a** an act of bestowing possession under legal sanction **b** an estate, income, etc legally bestowed on sby **3a** a newly settled place or region **b** a small, esp isolated, village **4** an organization providing various community services in an underprivileged area **5** an agreement resolving differences ⟨*reached a* ~ *on the strike*⟩

settler /'setlə/ *n* one who settles sthg (e g a new region)

settling /'setling/ *n* sediment, dregs – usu pl with sing. meaning

settlor /'setlə/ *n* one who makes a legal settlement

'set-,to *n, pl* **set-tos** a usu brief and vigorous conflict – chiefly infml

set to *vi* **1** to make an eager or determined start on a job or activity **2** to begin fighting

'set-,up *n* **1** an arrangement; *also* an organization **2** *chiefly NAm* carriage of the body; bearing **3** *chiefly NAm* a task or contest with a prearranged or artificially easy course – chiefly infml

set up *vt* **1a** to raise into position; erect ⟨set up *a statue*⟩ ⟨set up *road blocks*⟩ **b** to put forward (e g a theory) for acceptance; propound **2a** to assemble and prepare for use or operation ⟨set up *a printing press*⟩ **b** to put (a machine) in readiness or adjustment for operation **3a** to give voice to, esp loudly; raise ⟨set up *a din*⟩ **b** to create; BRING ABOUT ⟨*issues that* set up *personal tensions*⟩ **4** to place in a high office or powerful position ⟨set up *the general as dictator*⟩ **5** to claim (oneself) to be a specified thing ⟨sets *herself* up *as an authority*⟩ **6a** to found, institute ⟨set up *a fund for orphans*⟩ **b** to install oneself in ⟨set up *house together*⟩ **7a** to provide with an independent livelihood ⟨set *her* up *in business*⟩ **b** to provide with what is necessary or useful – usu + *with* or *for* ⟨*we're well* set up *with logs for the winter*⟩ **8** to bring or restore to health or success ⟨*a drink will* set *you* up⟩ **9** to prepare detailed plans for ⟨set up *a bank robbery*⟩ ~ *vi* to start business ⟨set up *as a house agent*⟩ – **set up shop** to establish one's business

seven /'sev(ə)n/ *n* **1** ☞ NUMBER **2** the seventh in a set or series ⟨*the* ~ *of diamonds*⟩ **3** sthg having 7 parts or members or a denomination of 7 **4** *pl but sing or pl in constr* a rugby game played with teams of 7 players each [ME, fr *seven*, adj, fr OE *seofon*; akin to OHG *sibun* seven, L *septem*, Gk *hepta*] – **seven** *adj or pron*, **sevenfold** *adj or adv*

,seven 'seas *n pl* all the oceans of the world

seventeen /,sev(ə)n'teen/ *n* ☞ NUMBER [*seventeen*, adj, fr ME *seventene*, fr OE *seofontēne*; akin to OE *tien* ten] – **seventeen** *adj or pron*, **seventeenth** *adj or n*

seventh /'sev(ə)nth/ *n* **1** ☞ NUMBER **2a** (the combination of 2 notes at) a musical interval of 7 diatonic degrees **b** LEADING NOTE – **seventh** *adj or adv*

,Seventh-Day 'Adventist *n* a member of a group of Adventist Christians who advocate or observe Saturday as the Christian Sabbath

,seventh 'heaven *n* a state of supreme rapture or

bliss ⟨*she was in the ~ with her new train set*⟩ [fr the seventh being the highest of the 7 heavens of Muslim and cabalist doctrine]

seventy /ˈsev(ə)nti/ *n* **1** ☞ NUMBER **2** *pl* the numbers 70 to 79; *specif* a range of temperatures, ages, or dates within a century characterized by those numbers [*seventy*, adj, fr ME, fr OE *seofontig*, short for *hundseofontig*, fr *hundseofontig*, n, group of seventy, fr *hund* hundred + *seofon* seven + *-tig* group of ten – more at HUNDRED, [1]-TY] – **seventieth** *adj or n*, **seventy** *adj or pron*

ˌseventy-ˈeight *n* **1** ☞ NUMBER **2** a gramophone record that plays at 78 revolutions per minute – usu written 78 – **seventy-eight** *adj or pron*

ˌseven-year ˈitch *n* marital discontent allegedly leading to infidelity after about 7 years of marriage

sever /ˈsevə/ *vt* **1** to put or keep apart; separate; *esp* to remove (a major part or portion) (as if) by cutting **2** to break off; terminate ⟨~ *economic links*⟩ ~ *vi* to become separated [ME *severen*, fr MF *severer*, fr L *separare* – more at SEPARATE] – **severable** *adj*, **severance** *n*

[1]**several** /ˈsev(ə)rəl/ *adj* **1** more than 2 but fewer than many ⟨~ *hundred times*⟩ **2** separate or distinct from one another; respective ⟨*specialists in their ~ fields*⟩ – chiefly fml [ME, separate, different, fr AF, fr ML *separalis*, fr L *separ* separate, back-formation fr *separare* to separate]

[2]**several** *pron, pl in constr* an indefinite number more than 2 and fewer than many ⟨~ *of the guests*⟩ – **severalfold** *adj or adv*

severally /ˈsev(ə)rəli/ *adv* each by itself or him-/herself; separately – chiefly fml

ˈ**severalty** /-ti/ *n* **1** possession by a single person only ⟨*tenants in* ~⟩ **2** the quality or state of being several or distinct – fml [MF *severalte*, fr AF *severalté*, fr *several*]

ˈ**severance ˌpay** *n* an amount payable to an employee on termination of employment

severe /siˈviə/ *adj* **1** having a stern expression or character; austere **2** rigorous in judgment, requirements, or punishment; stringent ⟨~ *penalties*⟩ ⟨~ *legislation*⟩ **3** strongly critical or condemnatory; censorious ⟨*a ~ critic*⟩ **4** sober or restrained in decoration or manner; plain **5** marked by harsh or extreme conditions ⟨~ *winters*⟩ **6** requiring much effort; arduous ⟨*a ~ test*⟩ **7** serious, grave ⟨~ *depression*⟩ ⟨*a ~ illness*⟩ [MF or L; MF, fr L *severus*] – **severely** *adv*, **severity** /siˈverəti/ *n*

Seville orange /seˈvil, ˈsevl/ *n* (an orange tree that bears) a reddish-orange fruit with bitter rind and sour flesh, used esp for making marmalade [*Seville*, province & city in SW Spain]

Sèvres /ˈseəvrə/ *n* an elaborately decorated fine porcelain [*Sèvres*, town in France]

sew /soh/ *vb* **sewed** /sohd/; **sewn** /sohn/, **sewed** *vt* **1** to unite, fasten, or attach by stitches made with a needle and thread **2** to close or enclose by sewing ⟨~ *the money in a bag*⟩ **3** to make or mend by sewing ~ *vi* to practise or engage in sewing [ME *sewen*, fr OE *sīwian*; akin to OHG *siuwen* to sew, L *suere*] – **sewer** *n*

sewage /ˈs(y)ooh·ij, ˈs(y)oo·ij/ *n* waste matter carried off by sewers [*sewer*]

sewer /ˈs(y)ooə/ *n* an artificial usu underground conduit used to carry off waste matter, esp excrement, from houses, schools, towns, etc and surface water from roads and paved areas [ME, fr MF *esseweur, seweur*, fr *essewer* to drain, fr (assumed) VL *exaquare*, fr L *ex-* + *aqua* water – more at ISLAND]

sewerage /ˈs(y)ooərij/ *n* **1** sewage **2** the removal and disposal of surface water by sewers **3** a system of sewers

sewing /ˈsoh·ing/ *n* **1** the act, action, or work of one who sews **2** work that has been or is to be sewn

sew up *vt* **1** to mend, close (e g a hole), or enclose by sewing **2** to bring to a successful or satisfactory conclusion ⟨sew up *pay negotiations*⟩ – chiefly infml

[1]**sex** /seks/ *n* **1** either of 2 divisions of organisms distinguished as male or female **2** the structural, functional, and behavioural characteristics that are involved in reproduction and that distinguish males and females **3** SEXUAL INTERCOURSE [ME, fr L *sexus*]

[2]**sex** *vt* to identify the sex of ⟨~ *chicks*⟩

sex-, sexi- *comb form* six ⟨sexi*valent*⟩ ⟨sex*partite*⟩ [L *sex* – more at SIX]

sexagenarian /ˌseksəjiˈneəri·ən/ *n* a person between 60 and 69 years old [L *sexagenarius* of or containing 60, 60 years old, fr *sexageni* 60 each, fr *sexaginta* sixty, irreg fr *sex* six + *-ginta* (akin to L *viginti* twenty) – more at SIX, VIGESIMAL] – **sexagenarian** *adj*

Sexagesima /ˌseksəˈjesimə/ *n* the second Sunday before Lent [LL, fr L, fem of *sexagesimus* sixtieth; fr its being approximately 60 days before Easter]

sexagesimal /-ˈjesiməl/ *adj* of or based on the number 60 [L *sexagesimus* sixtieth, fr *sexaginta* sixty]

ˈ**sex apˌpeal** *n* physical attractiveness for members of the opposite sex

sex chromosome *n* a chromosome concerned directly with the inheritance of male or female sex

sexed /sekst/ *adj* having sex, sex appeal, or sexual instincts, esp to a specified degree ⟨*highly* ~⟩ ⟨*under* ~⟩

sexism /ˈsekˌsiz(ə)m/ *n* **1** a belief that sex determines intrinsic capacities and role in society and that sexual differences produce an inherent superiority of one sex, usu the male **2** discrimination on the basis of sex; *esp* prejudice against women on the part of men [[1]*sex* + *-ism* (as in *racism*)] – **sexist** *adj or n*

ˈ**sex ˌkitten** *n* a woman who makes a display of her sex appeal – infml

ˈ**sexless** /-lis/ *adj* **1** lacking sexuality or sexual intercourse ⟨~ *marriage*⟩ **2** lacking sex appeal

ˈ**sex-ˌlinked** *adj* (determined by a gene) located in a sex chromosome ⟨*a ~ gene*⟩ ⟨*a ~ characteristic*⟩ – **sex-linkage** *n*

sexology /sekˈsoləji/ *n* the study of (human) sexual behaviour

sexploitation /ˌseksployˈtaysh(ə)n/ *n* the employment of sex for commercial gain, esp in films and publications [blend of *sex* and *exploitation*]

ˈ**sexˌpot** /-ˌpot/ *n* SEX KITTEN – humor

sext /sekst/ *n, often cap* the fourth of the canonical hours, orig fixed for 12 noon [ME *sexte*, fr LL *sexta*, fr L, sixth hour of the day, fr fem of *sextus* sixth, fr *sex* six]

sextant /ˈsekstənt/ *n* an instrument for measuring angles that is used, esp in navigation, to observe the altitudes of celestial bodies and so determine the observer's position on the earth's surface [NL *sex-*

tant-, sextans sixth part of a circle, fr L, sixth part, fr *sextus* sixth]

sextet /sek'stet/ *n* **1** (a musical composition for) a group of 6 instruments, voices, or performers **2** *sing or pl in constr* a group or set of 6 [alter. of *sestet*]

sexton /'sekstən/ *n* a church officer who takes care of the church property and is often also the gravedigger [ME *secresteyn, sexteyn,* fr MF *secrestain,* fr ML *sacristanus* – more at SACRISTAN]

¹sextuple /'sekstyoopl/ *adj* **1** having 6 units or members **2** being 6 times as great or as many [prob fr ML *sextuplus,* fr L *sextus* sixth + *-plus* multiplied by – more at DOUBLE] – **sextuple** *n*

²sextuple *vb* to make or become 6 times as much or as many

sextuplet /'sekstyooplit/ *n* **1** a combination of 6 of a kind **2** any of 6 offspring born at 1 birth **3** a group of 6 equal musical notes performed in the time ordinarily given to 4 of the same value

sexual /'seksyoo(ə)l, -sh(ə)l/ *adj* **1** of or associated with sex or the sexes ⟨~ *conflict*⟩ **2** having or involving sex ⟨~ *reproduction*⟩ [LL *sexualis,* fr L *sexus* sex] – **sexually** *adv,* **sexuality** /-'aləti/ *n*

sexual intercourse *n* intercourse with genital contact **a** involving penetration of the vagina by the penis; coitus **b** other than penetration of the vagina by the penis

sexual·ize, -ise /'seksyoo(ə)liez, -shəliez/ *vt* to make sexual; endow with a sexual character or significance

sexy /'seksi/ *adj* sexually suggestive or stimulating; erotic – **sexily** *adv,* **sexiness** *n*

Seyfert galaxy /'seefət, 'siefət/ *n* any of a class of spiral galaxies that have small compact bright nuclei that send out radio waves [Carl K *Seyfert* †1960 US astronomer]

sforzando /sfawt'sandoh/ *n, adj, or adv, pl* **sforzandos, sforzandi** /-di/ (a note or chord played) with prominent stress or accent – used in music [It, gerund & prp of *sforzare* to force]

sgraffito /sgra'feetoh/ *n, pl* **sgraffiti** /-ti/ decoration in which parts of a surface layer (e g of plaster) are cut or scratched away to expose a different coloured background [It, fr pp of *sgraffire* to scratch, produce sgraffito]

sh /sh/ *interj* – used often in prolonged or reduplicated form to urge or command silence [alter. of *hush*]

Shabbat /sha'baht, 'shahbəs/ *n, pl* **Shabbatim** /shə'bahtim, -'bawsəm/ the Jewish Sabbath [Heb *shabbāth*]

shabby /'shabi/ *adj* **1a** threadbare or faded from wear ⟨*a* ~ *sofa*⟩ **b** dilapidated, run-down ⟨*a* ~ *district*⟩ **2** dressed in worn or grubby clothes; seedy ⟨*a* ~ *tramp*⟩ **3** shameful, despicable ⟨*what a* ~ *trick, driving off and leaving me to walk home!*⟩ [obs *shab* (scab, a low fellow), fr ME] – **shabbily** *adv,* **shabbiness** *n*

shabraque, shabrack /'shabrak/ *n* a type of saddlecloth used esp by historical European light cavalry regiments [F *schabraque,* fr G *schabracke,* fr Hung *csáprág,* fr Turk *çaprak*]

Shabuoth /shah'vooh·oth, -əs/ *n* a Jewish holiday observed in commemoration of the revelation of the Ten Commandments at Mt Sinai [Heb *shābhū'ōth,* lit., weeks]

shack /shak/ *n* a small crudely built dwelling or shelter [perh back-formation fr E dial. *shackly* (rickety)]

¹shackle /'shakl/ *n* **1** (a metal ring like) a manacle or handcuff **2** sthg that restricts or prevents free action or expression – usu pl with sing. meaning **3** a U-shaped piece of metal with a pin or bolt to close the opening [ME *schakel,* fr OE *sceacul;* akin to ON *skökull* pole of a cart]

²shackle *vt* **1a** to bind with shackles; fetter **b** to make fast with shackles **2** to deprive of freedom of thought or action by means of restrictions or handicaps; impede

shack up *vi* to live with and have a sexual relationship with sby; *also* to spend the night as a partner in sexual intercourse – usu + *together* or *with;* infml

shad /shad/ *n, pl* **shad** any of several fishes of the herring family that have a relatively deep body and are important food fishes of Europe and N America [(assumed) ME, fr OE *sceadd;* akin to L *scatēre* to bubble]

shaddock /'shadək/ *n* (a tree that bears) a very large usu pear-shaped citrus fruit closely related to the grapefruit but often with coarse dry pulp [Captain *Shaddock,* 17th-c E ship commander]

¹shade /shayd/ *n* **1a** partial darkness caused by the interception of rays of light **b** relative obscurity or insignificance **2** a place sheltered (e g by foliage) from the direct heat and glare of the sun **3** a transitory or illusory appearance **4** *pl* the shadows that gather as night falls **5** GHOST 2 **6** sthg that intercepts or diffuses light or heat: e g **a** a lampshade **b** *chiefly NAm* **(1)** *pl* sunglasses – infml **(2)** a window blind **7** the reproduction of shade in a picture **8a** a colour produced by a pigment mixed with some black **b** a particular level of depth or brightness of a colour ⟨*a* ~ *of pink*⟩ **9** a minute difference or amount ⟨*the* ~s *of meaning in a poem*⟩ [ME, fr OE *sceadu;* akin to OHG *scato* shadow, Gk *skotos* darkness] – **a shade** a tiny bit; somewhat ⟨a shade *too much salt*⟩ – **shades of** – used interjectionally to indicate that one is reminded of or struck by a resemblance to a specified person or thing

²shade *vt* **1a** to shelter or screen by intercepting radiated light or heat **b** to cover with a shade **2** to darken or obscure (as if) with a shadow **3a** to represent the effect of shade on **b** to mark with shading or gradations of colour **4** to change by gradual transition ~ *vi* to pass by slight changes or imperceptible degrees – usu + *into* or *off into*

'shade ˌtree *n* a tree grown primarily to produce shade

shading /'shayding/ *n* an area of filled-in outlines to suggest three-dimensionality, shadow, or degrees of light and dark in a picture

¹shadow /'shadoh/ *n* **1a** partial darkness caused by an opaque body interposed so as to cut off rays from a light source ⟨*the thieves lurked in the* ~ *of the house*⟩ **b** a dark area resembling shadow ⟨~s *under his eyes from fatigue*⟩ **2a** a faint representation or suggestion ⟨~s *of future difficulties*⟩ **b** a mere semblance or imitation of sthg ⟨*she wore herself to a* ~ *by studying too hard*⟩ **3** a dark figure cast on a surface by a body intercepting light rays ⟨*the trees cast their* ~s *on the wall*⟩ **4** a phantom **5** *pl* darkness **6** a shaded or darker portion of a picture **7** an attenuated form; a vestige ⟨*after his illness he was only a* ~ *of his former self*⟩ **8a** an inseparable companion or follower **b** one (e g a spy or detective) who shadows **9** a small degree or portion; a trace ⟨*without a ~ of doubt*⟩ **10** a source of gloom or disquiet ⟨*her death cast a ~ on the festivities*⟩ **11** a pervasive and often disabling influence ⟨*governed under the ~ of his predecessor*⟩ [ME *shadwe*, fr OE *sceaduw-, sceadu* shade, shadow]

[2]**shadow** *vt* **1** to cast a shadow over **2** to follow (a person) secretly; keep under surveillance **3** to shade

[3]**shadow** *adj* **1** identical with another in form but without the other's power or status ⟨*a ~ government in exile*⟩; *specif* of or constituting the probable cabinet when the opposition party is returned to power ⟨*the ~ spokesman on employment*⟩ **2a** having an indistinct pattern ⟨*~ plaid*⟩ **b** having darker sections of design ⟨*~ lace*⟩ **3** shown by throwing the shadows of performers or puppets on a screen ⟨*a ~ dance*⟩

'shadow-,box *vi* to box with an imaginary opponent, esp as a form of training [back-formation fr *shadow-boxing*] – **shadow-boxing** *n*

shadowy /'shadoh·i/ *adj* **1a** of the nature of or resembling a shadow; insubstantial **b** scarcely perceptible; indistinct **2** lying in or obscured by shadow ⟨*deep ~ interiors*⟩ – **shadowiness** *n*

shady /'shaydi/ *adj* **1** producing or affording shade ⟨*a ~ tree*⟩ **2** sheltered from the direct heat or light of the sun ⟨*a ~ spot*⟩ **3a** of questionable merit; uncertain, unreliable ⟨*a ~ deal*⟩ **b** of doubtful integrity; disreputable ⟨*she's a ~ character*⟩ – chiefly infml – **shadily** *adv*, **shadiness** *n*

[1]**shaft** /shahft/ *n* **1a** (the long handle of) a spear, lance, or similar weapon **b** a pole; *specif* either of 2 poles between which a horse is hitched to a vehicle **c** an arrow, esp for a longbow **2** a sharply delineated beam of light shining from an opening **3** sthg resembling the shaft of a spear, lance, etc, esp in having a long slender cylindrical form: e g **a** the trunk of a tree **b** the cylindrical pillar between the capital and the base of a column ☞ ARCHITECTURE, **c** the handle of a tool or implement (e g a hammer or golf club) **d** a usu cylindrical bar used to support rotating pieces or to transmit power or motion by rotation **e** a man-made vertical or inclined opening leading underground to a mine, well, etc **f** a vertical opening or passage through the floors of a building ⟨*a lift ~*⟩ **g** the central stem of a feather ☞ ANATOMY **4** a scornful, satirical, or pithily critical remark; a barb [ME, fr OE *sceaft*; akin to OHG *scaft* shaft, L *scapus* shaft, stalk, Gk *skēptron* staff]

[2]**shaft** *vt, NAm* to treat unfairly or harshly – slang

shafting /'shahfting/ *n* (material for) shafts

[1]**shag** /shag/ *n* **1a** an unkempt or uneven tangled mass or covering (e g of hair) **b** long coarse or matted fibre or nap **2** a strong coarse tobacco cut into fine shreds **3** a European bird smaller than the closely related cormorant [(assumed) ME *shagge*, fr OE *sceacga*; akin to ON *skegg* beard, OSlav *skokŭ* leap] – **shaggy** *adj*, **shaggily** *adv*

[2]**shag** *vt* **-gg- 1** to fuck, screw – vulg **2** *Br* to make utterly exhausted – usu + *out*; slang [origin unknown]

[3]**shag** *n* an act of sexual intercourse – vulg

shagbark /'shag,bahk/ *n* (the wood of) a N American hickory with a grey shaggy outer bark that peels off in long strips

shaggy-dog story /'shagi/ *n* a protracted and inconsequential funny story whose humour lies in the pointlessness or irrelevance of the conclusion

shagreen /sha'green/ *n* **1** an untanned leather covered with small round granulations and usu dyed green **2** the rough skin of various sharks and rays [by folk etymology fr F *chagrin*, fr Turk *sağr*] – **shagreen** *adj*

shah /shah/ *n, often cap* a sovereign of Iran [Per *shāh* king – more at CHECK] – **shahdom** /-d(ə)m/ *n*

[1]**shake** /shayk/ *vb* **shook** /shook/; **shaken** /'shaykən/ *vi* **1** to move to and fro with rapid usu irregular motion **2** to vibrate, esp from the impact of a blow or shock **3** to tremble as a result of physical or emotional disturbance **4** to shake hands ⟨*if you've agreed then ~ on it*⟩ ~ *vt* **1** to brandish, wave, or flourish, esp in a threatening manner **2** to cause to move with a rapidly alternating motion **3** to cause to quake, quiver, or tremble **4** to cause to waver; weaken ⟨*~ one's faith*⟩ **5** to put in a specified state by repeated quick jerky movements ⟨shook *himself free from the woman's grasp*⟩ **6** to dislodge or eject by quick jerky movements of the support or container ⟨shook *the dust from the cloth*⟩ **7** to clasp (hands) in greeting or farewell or to convey goodwill or agreement **8** to agitate the feelings of; upset ⟨*the news* shook *him*⟩ [ME *shaken*, fr OE *sceacan*; akin to ON *skaka* to shake, Skt *khajati* he agitates] – **shakable, shakeable** *adj* – **shake a leg** to hurry up; hasten – infml – **shake one's head** to move one's head from side to side to indicate disagreement, denial, disapproval, etc

[2]**shake** *n* **1** an act of shaking ⟨*indicated her disapproval with a ~ of the head*⟩ **2** *pl* a condition of trembling (e g from chill or fever); *specif* DELIRIUM TREMENS **3** a wavering, vibrating, or alternating motion caused by a blow or shock **4** TRILL 1 ☞ MUSIC **5** *chiefly NAm* MILK SHAKE **6** *chiefly NAm* an earthquake **7** a moment ⟨*I'll be round in 2 ~*s⟩ *USE* (*6&7*) infml

[1]**'shake,down** /-,down/ *n* **1** a makeshift bed (e g one made up on the floor) **2** *NAm* an act or instance of shaking sby down; *esp* extortion **3** *NAm* a thorough search *USE* (*2&3*) infml

[2]**shakedown** *adj* designed to test a new ship, aircraft, etc and allow the crew to become familiar with it ⟨*a ~ cruise*⟩ [[1]*shakedown* (period or process of adjustment)]

shake down *vi* **1** to stay the night or sleep, esp in a makeshift bed **2** to become comfortably established, esp in a new place or occupation ~ *vt* **1** to settle (as if) by shaking **2** to give a shakedown test to **3** *NAm* to obtain money from in a dishonest or illegal manner **4** *NAm* to make a thorough search of (a person); frisk *USE* (*3&4*) infml

shake off *vt* to free oneself from ⟨shook off *a heavy cold*⟩

shaker /'shaykə/ *n* **1** a container or utensil used to sprinkle or mix a substance by shaking ⟨*a flour ~*⟩ ⟨*a cocktail ~*⟩ **2** *cap* a member of an American sect practising celibacy and a self-denying communal life, and looking forward to the millennium [[1]SHAKE + [2]-ER; (2) fr a dance with shaking movements performed as part of worship] – **Shaker** *adj*, **Shakerism** *n*

Shakespearean, Shakespearian *also* **Shaksperean, Shaksperian** /shayk'spiəri·ən/ *n or adj* (an authority on or devotee) of Shakespeare [William *Shakespeare*

†1616 E dramatist & poet] – **Shakespeareana, Shakespeariana** /-ri'ahnə/ *n pl*

Shakespearean sonnet *n* a sonnet consisting of 3 quatrains and a couplet with a rhyme scheme of *abab cdcd efef gg*

'shake-,up *n* an act or instance of shaking up; *specif* an extensive and often drastic reorganization (e g of a company) – infml

shake up *vt* **1** to jar (as if) by a physical shock ⟨*the collision* shook up *both drivers*⟩ **2** to reorganize by extensive and often drastic measures – infml

shako /'shahkoh, 'shakoh/ *n, pl* **shakos, shakoes** a stiff military hat with a high crown and plume [F, fr Hung *csákó*]

Shakta /'shuktə/ *n or adj* (an adherent) of Shaktism [Skt *śākta*, fr *Śakti*]

Shakti /'shukti/ *n* the dynamic energy of a Hindu god personified as his female consort; *broadly* cosmic energy as conceived in Hindu thought [Skt *Śakti*]

Shaktism /'shuk,tiz(ə)m/ *n* a Hindu cult of devotion to the female principle, often celebrated with magical rites and orgies

shaky /'shayki/ *adj* **1a** lacking stability; precarious ⟨*a ~ coalition*⟩ **b** lacking in firmness (e g of beliefs or principles) **2a** unsound in health; poorly **b** characterized by or affected with shaking **3** likely to give way or break down; rickety ⟨*a ~ chair*⟩ – **shakily** *adv*, **shakiness** *n*

shale /shayl/ *n* a finely stratified or laminated rock formed by the consolidation of clay, mud, or silt [ME, shell, scale, fr OE *scealu* – more at SHELL]

shale oil *n* a crude dark oil obtained from oil shale by heating

shall /shəl; *strong* shal/ *verbal auxiliary, pres sing & pl* **shall;** *past* **should** /shəd; *strong* shood/ **1** – used to urge or command ⟨*you ~ go*⟩ or denote what is legally mandatory ⟨*it ~ be unlawful to carry firearms*⟩ **2a** – used to express what is inevitable or seems likely to happen in the future ⟨*we ~ have to be ready*⟩ ⟨*we ~ see*⟩ **b** – used in the question form to express simple futurity ⟨*when ~ we expect you?*⟩ or with the force of an offer or suggestion ⟨*~ I open the window?*⟩ **3** – used to express determination ⟨*they ~ not pass*⟩ [ME *shal* (1 & 3 sing. pres indic), fr OE *sceal*; akin to OHG *scal* (1 & 3 sing. pres indic) ought to, must, Lith *skola* debt]

shallot /shə'lot/ *n* (any of the small clusters of bulbs, used esp for pickling and in seasoning, produced by) a perennial plant that resembles the related onion [modif of F *échalote*, deriv of (assumed) VL *escalonia* – more at SCALLION]

¹shallow /'shaloh/ *adj* **1** having little depth ⟨*~ water*⟩ **2** superficial in knowledge, thought, or feeling **3** not marked or accentuated ⟨*the plane went into a ~ dive*⟩ ⟨*a ~ curve*⟩ [ME *schalowe*] – **shallowly** *adv*, **shallowness** *n*

²shallow *vi* to become shallow

³shallow *n* a shallow place in a body of water – usu pl with sing. meaning but sing. or pl in constr

shalom /shə'lohm, shə'lom/ *interj* – used as a Jewish greeting and farewell [Heb *shālōm* peace]

sha,lom a'leichem /ə'layk(h)əm/ *interj* – used as a traditional Jewish greeting [Heb *shālōm 'alēkhem* peace unto you]

shalt /shalt/ *archaic pres 2 sing of* SHALL

¹sham /sham/ *n* **1** cheap falseness; hypocrisy ⟨*the ~ ... of the empty pageant* – Oscar Wilde⟩ **2** an imitation or counterfeit purporting to be genuine **3** a person who shams [perh fr E dial. *sham* (shame), alter. of E *shame*] – **sham** *adj*

²sham *vb* **-mm-** *vt* to act so as to counterfeit ⟨*I ~ med a headache to get away*⟩ ~ *vi* to create a deliberately false impression

shaman /'shahmən, 'shay-/ *n* a priest believed to exercise magic power (e g for healing and divination), esp through ecstatic trances [Russ or Tungus; Russ, fr Tungus *šaman*] – **shamanism** *n*, **shamanist** *n*

shamateur /'shamətə, ,shamə'tuh/ *n* a sports player who is officially classed as amateur but who takes payment – derog [blend of *sham* and *amateur*] – **shamateurism** /-'tuhriz(ə)m/ *n*

¹shamble /'shambl/ *vi* **shambling** /'shambling/ to walk awkwardly with dragging feet; shuffle [*shamble* (bowed, malformed)]

²shamble *n* a shambling gait

shambles /'shamblz/ *n, pl* **shambles** **1** a slaughterhouse **2a** a place of carnage **b** a scene or a state of great destruction, chaos, or confusion; a mess ⟨*the place was left a ~ by hooligans*⟩ [*shamble* (meat market) & obs *shamble* (table for exhibition of meat for sale), fr ME *shamel*, fr OE *scamul, sceamul* stool, table]

shambolic /sham'bolik/ *adj, Br* utterly chaotic or confused – infml [irreg fr *shambles*]

¹shame /shaym/ *n* **1a** a painful emotion caused by consciousness of guilt, shortcomings, impropriety, or disgrace **b** susceptibility to such emotion ⟨*was not upset because she had no ~*⟩ **2** humiliating disgrace or disrepute; ignominy **3** sthg bringing regret or disgrace ⟨*it's a ~ you weren't there*⟩ [ME, fr OE *scamu*; akin to OHG *scama* shame]

²shame *vt* **1** to bring shame to; disgrace **2** to put to shame by outdoing **3** to fill with a sense of shame **4** to compel by causing to feel guilty ⟨~d *into confessing*⟩

,shame'faced /-'fayst/ *adj* **1** showing modesty; bashful **2** showing shame; ashamed [alter. of arch *shamefast* (bound by shame), fr ME, fr OE *scamfæst*, fr *scamu* + *fæst* fixed, fast] – **shamefacedly** /-'faysidli/ *adv*, **shamefacedness** /-'faysidnis/ *n*

'shameful /-f(ə)l/ *adj* **1** bringing disrepute or ignominy; disgraceful **2** arousing the feeling of shame – **shamefully** *adv*, **shamefulness** *n*

'shameless /-lis/ *adj* **1** insensible to disgrace **2** showing lack of shame; disgraceful – **shamelessly** *adv*

shammy /'shami/ *n* CHAMOIS 2 [by alter.]

¹shampoo /sham'pooh/ *vt* **shampoos; shampooing; shampooed** **1** to clean (esp the hair or a carpet) with shampoo **2** to wash the hair of [Hindi *c apo*, imper of *c apnā* to press, shampoo] – **shampooist** *n*

²shampoo *n, pl* **shampoos** **1** a washing of the hair esp by a hairdresser **2** a soap, detergent, etc used for shampooing

shamrock /'sham,rok/ *n* any of several plants (e g a wood sorrel or some clovers) whose leaves have 3 leaflets and are used as a floral emblem by the Irish [IrGael *seamrōg*]

shandy /'shandi/ *n* a drink consisting of beer mixed with lemonade or ginger beer [short for *shandygaff*, of unknown origin]

shanghai /,shang'hie/ *vt* **shanghais; shanghaiing; shanghaied** /-hied/ **1** to compel to join a ship's crew, esp by the help of drink or drugs – compare PRESS-GANG **2** to put into an awkward or unpleasant position by trickery [*Shanghai*, seaport in E China; fr the formerly widespread use of this method to procure sailors for voyages to the Orient]

Shangri-la /,shang·gri 'lah/ *n* a remote imaginary place where life approaches perfection [*Shangri-La*, imaginary land depicted in the novel *Lost Horizon* by James Hilton †1954 E novelist]

shank /shangk/ *n* **1a** a leg; *specif* the part of the leg between the knee and the ankle in human beings or the corresponding part in various other vertebrates **b** a cut of beef, veal, mutton, or lamb from the upper or the lower part of the leg **2** a straight narrow usu vital part of an object: e g **a** the straight part of a nail or pin **b** the stem or stalk of a plant **c** the part of an anchor between the ring and the crown **d** the part of a fishhook between the eye and the bend **e** the part of a key between the handle and the bit **f** the narrow part of the sole of a shoe beneath the instep **3** a part of an object by which it can be attached to sthg else: e g **a(1)** a projection on the back of a solid button **(2)** a short stem of thread that holds a sewn button away from the cloth **b** the end (e g of a drill bit) that is gripped in a chuck [ME *shanke*, fr OE *scanca*; akin to ON *skakkr* crooked, Gk *skazein* to limp]

,shanks's 'mare /'shangksiz/ *n, chiefly NAm* SHANKS'S PONY

,shanks's 'pony *n* one's own feet or legs considered as a means of transport ⟨*went home by* ~⟩ – humor [*shanks*, pl of *shank*]

shanny /'shani/ *n* a small European blenny [origin unknown]

shan't /shahnt/ shall not

shantung /,shan'tung/ *n* a silk fabric in plain weave with a slightly irregular surface [*Shantung*, province in NE China]

[1]shanty /'shanti/ *n* a small crudely built or dilapidated dwelling or shelter; a shack [CanF *chantier*, fr F, gantry, fr L *cantherius* trellis]

[2]shanty *n* a song sung by sailors in rhythm with their work [modif of F *chanter* to sing – more at CHANT]

'shanty,town /-,town/ *n* (part of) a town consisting mainly of shanties

[1]shape /shayp/ *vt* **1** to form, create; *esp* to give a particular form or shape to ⟨~d *the clay into a cube*⟩ **2** to adapt in shape so as to fit neatly and closely ⟨*a dress* ~d *to fit*⟩ **3** to guide or mould into a particular state or condition ⟨shaping *her plans for the future*⟩ **4a** to determine or direct the course of (e g a person's life) **b** to cause to take a particular form or course ⟨~ *the course of history*⟩ [ME *shapen*, alter. of OE *scieppan*; akin to OHG *skepfen* to shape] – **shapable, shapeable** *adj*, **shaper** *n*

[2]shape *n* **1a** the visible or tactile form of a particular (kind of) item **b(1)** spatial form ⟨*all solids have* ~⟩ **(2)** a circle, square, or other standard geometrical form **2** the contour of the body, esp of the trunk; the figure **3a** a phantom, apparition **b** an assumed appearance; a guise ⟨*the devil in the* ~ *of a serpent*⟩ **4** definite form (e g in thought or words) ⟨*the plan slowly took* ~⟩ **5** a general structure or plan ⟨*the final* ~ *of society*⟩ **6** sthg made in a particular form ⟨*a* ~ *for moulding jellies*⟩ **7a** the condition of a person or thing, esp at a particular time ⟨*in excellent* ~ *for his age*⟩ **b** a fit or ordered condition ⟨*got the car into* ~⟩ – **shaped** *adj*

'shapeless /-lis/ *adj* **1** having no definite shape **2** deprived of usual or proper shape; misshapen ⟨*a* ~ *old hat*⟩ – **shapelessly** *adv*, **shapelessness** *n*

'shapely /-li/ *adj* having a pleasing shape; well-proportioned – **shapeliness** *n*

shape up *vi* to (begin to) behave or perform satisfactorily

shard /shahd/ *n* **1** a piece or fragment of sthg brittle (e g earthenware) **2** SHERD 2 [ME, fr OE *sceard*; akin to OE *scieran* to cut – more at SHEAR]

[1]share /sheə/ *n* **1a** a portion belonging to, due to, or contributed by an individual **b** a full or fair portion ⟨*she's had her* ~ *of fun*⟩ **2a** the part allotted or belonging to any of a number owning property or interest together **b** any of the equal portions into which property or invested capital is divided **c** *pl, chiefly Br* the proprietorship element in a company, usu represented by transferable certificates [ME, fr OE *scearu* cutting, tonsure; akin to OE *scieran* to cut – more at SHEAR]

[2]share *vt* **1** to divide and distribute in shares; apportion – usu + *out* **2** to partake of, use, experience, or enjoy with others ~ *vi* to have a share or part – often + *in* – **shareable, sharable** *adj*, **sharer** *n*

[3]share *n* a ploughshare [ME *schare*, fr OE *scear*, akin to OHG *scaro* ploughshare, OE *scieran* to cut]

'share,cropper /-,kropə/ *n, NAm* a tenant farmer, esp in the southern USA, who lives on credit provided by the landlord and receives an agreed share of the value of the crop – **sharecrop** *vb*

'share,holder /-,hohldə/ *n* the holder or owner of a share in property

'share,milking /-,milking/ *n, NZ* the system of helping an owner of dairy cattle with milking in exchange for a share in the profits – **sharemilker** *n*

'share-,pusher *n, Br* a dealer who sells shares other than through the usual channels and often fraudulently

sharif /sha'reef/ *n* a descendant of the prophet Muhammad through his daughter Fatima; *broadly* one of noble ancestry or political preeminence in a predominantly Islamic country [Ar *sharīf*, lit., illustrious] – **sharifian** /shə'reefi·ən/ *adj*

[1]shark /shahk/ *n* any of numerous mostly large typically grey marine fishes that are mostly active, voracious, and predators and have gill slits at the sides and a mouth on the under part of the body [origin unknown]

[2]shark *n* **1** a greedy unscrupulous person who exploits others by usury, extortion, or trickery **2** *NAm* one who excels greatly, esp in a specified field – infml [prob modif (influenced in form & meaning by [1]*shark*) of G *schurke* scoundrel]

'shark,skin /-,skin/ *n* **1** (leather from) the hide of a shark **2** a smooth stiff durable fabric in twill or basket weave with small woven designs

[1]sharp /shahp/ *adj* **1** (adapted to) cutting or piercing: e g **a** having a thin keen edge or fine point **b** bitingly cold; icy ⟨*a* ~ *wind*⟩ **2a** keen in intellect, perception, attention, etc ⟨~ *sight*⟩ ⟨*keep a* ~ *lookout*⟩ **b** paying shrewd usu selfish attention to personal gain ⟨*a* ~ *trader*⟩ **3a** brisk, vigorous ⟨*a* ~ *trot*⟩ **b** capable of acting or reacting strongly; *esp* caustic ⟨*a* ~ *soap*⟩ **4** severe, harsh: e g **a** marked by irritability or anger; fiery ⟨*a* ~ *temper*⟩ **b** causing intense usu sudden anguish ⟨*a* ~ *pain*⟩ **c** cutting in language or implication ⟨*a* ~ *rebuke*⟩ **5** affecting the senses or sense organs intensely: e g **a(1)** pungent, tart, or acid, esp in flavour (2) acrid **b** shrill, piercing **c** issuing in a brilliant burst of light ⟨*a* ~ *flash*⟩ **6a** characterized by hard lines and angles ⟨~ *features*⟩ **b** involving an abrupt change in direction ⟨*a* ~ *turn*⟩ **c** clear in outline or detail; distinct ⟨*a* ~ *image*⟩ **d** conspicuously clear ⟨~ *contrast*⟩ **7** *of a musical note* raised a semitone in pitch **8** stylish, dressy – infml [ME, fr OE *scearp*; akin to OE *scieran* to cut – more at SHEAR] – **sharply** *adv*, **sharpness** *n*

[2]**sharp** *adv* **1** in an abrupt manner ⟨*the car pulled up* ~⟩ ⟨*turn* ~ *right*⟩ **2** exactly, precisely ⟨*4 o'clock* ~⟩ **3** above the proper musical pitch ⟨*they're playing* ~⟩

[3]**sharp** *n* **1a** a musical note 1 semitone higher than another indicated or previously specified note **b** a character on the musical staff indicating a raising in pitch of a semitone ☞ MUSIC **2** a relatively long needle with a sharp point and a small rounded eye for use in general sewing **3** *chiefly NAm* a swindler, sharper

sharpen /'shahpən/ *vb* to make or become sharp or sharper – **sharpener** *n*

'**sharpening ,stone** *n* WHETSTONE 1

sharper /'shahpə/ *n* a cheat, swindler; *esp* a gambler who habitually cheats ['*sharp* + [2]*-er*]

sharpish /'shahpish/ *adv, Br* with haste; somewhat quickly – infml ⟨*we'd better move* ~ *to get some tea*⟩

,**sharp 'practice** *n* dealing in which advantage is taken or sought unscrupulously

'**sharp,shooter** /-,shoohtə/ *n* a good marksman – **sharpshooting** *n*

,**sharp-'tongued** *adj* cutting or sarcastic in speech; quick to rebuke

shat /shat/ *past of* SHIT

shatter /'shatə/ *vt* **1a** to break into pieces (e g by a sudden blow) **b** to cause to break down; impair, disable ⟨*his nerves were* ~ed⟩ **2** to have a forceful or violent effect on the feelings of ⟨*she was absolutely* ~ed *by the news*⟩ **3** to cause to be utterly exhausted ⟨*felt* ~ed *by the long train journey*⟩ ~ *vi* to break suddenly apart; disintegrate *USE* (*vt 2&3*) infml [ME *schateren*] – **shatteringly** *adv*

[1]**shave** /shayv/ *vb* **shaved, shaven** /'shayv(ə)n/ *vt* **1a** to remove in thin layers or shreds – often + *off* ⟨~ *off a thin slice of cheese*⟩ **b** to cut off thin layers or slices from **c** to cut or trim closely ⟨*a closely* ~d *lawn*⟩ **2a** to remove the hair from by cutting close to the roots **b** to cut off (hair or beard) close to the skin **3** to come very close to or brush against in passing ~ *vi* to cut off hair or beard close to the skin [ME *shaven*, fr OE *scafan*; akin to L *scabere* to shave, *capo* capon]

[2]**shave** *n* **1** a tool or machine for shaving **2** an act or process of shaving

'**shave,hook** /-,hook/ *n* a tool for scraping that has a usu triangular blade set at right angles to a shaft

shaver /'shayvə/ *n* **1** an electric-powered razor **2** a boy, youngster – infml ['SHAVE + [2]-ER]

'**shave,tail** /-,tayl/ *n, NAm* a (newly broken in) pack mule [fr the practice of shaving the tails of newly broken mules to distinguish them from untrained ones]

Shavian /'shayvyən/ *n or adj* (an admirer or devotee) of G B Shaw, his writings, or his social and political theories [NL *Shavius*, latinized form of George Bernard *Shaw* †1950 Br (Ir-born) author & socialist]

shaving /'shayving/ *n* sthg shaved off – usu pl ⟨*wood* ~s⟩

shaw /shaw/ *n, chiefly Br* the stalks and leaves of a cultivated crop (e g potatoes or turnips) [prob alter. of *show*]

shawl /shawl/ *n* a usu decorative square, oblong, or triangular piece of fabric that is worn to cover the head or shoulders [Per *shāl*]

shawl collar *n* a collar that is rolled back and follows a continuous line round the neck and down the front edges of a garment ☞ GARMENT

shawm /shawm/ *n* an early double-reed woodwind instrument [ME *schalme*, fr MF *chalemie*, modif of LL *calamellus*, dim. of L *calamus* reed, fr Gk *kalamos* – more at HAULM]

Shawnee /shaw'nee/ *n, pl* **Shawnees,** *esp collectively* **Shawnee** (the Algonquian language of) a member of a N American Indian people orig of the central Ohio valley [back-formation fr obs E *Shawnese*, fr Shawnee *Shaawanwaaki*, lit., those in the south]

[1]**she** /shi; *strong* shee/ *pron* **1** that female person or creature who is neither speaker nor hearer ⟨~ *is my mother*⟩ **2** – used to refer to sthg regarded as feminine (e g by personification) ⟨~ *was a fine ship*⟩ [ME, prob alter. of *hye*, alter. of OE *hēo* she – more at HE]

[2]**she** /shee/ *n* a female person or creature ⟨*is the baby a he or a* ~⟩ – often in combination ⟨she-*cat*⟩

shea butter /shiə/ *n* a pale solid fat from the seeds of the shea tree used in food, soap, and candles

sheaf /sheef/ *n, pl* **sheaves** /sheevz/ **1** a quantity of plant material, esp the stalks and ears of a cereal grass, bound together **2** a collection of items laid or tied together ⟨*a* ~ *of papers*⟩ [ME *sheef*, fr OE *scēaf*; akin to OHG *scoub* sheaf, Russ *chub* forelock]

[1]**shear** /shiə/ *vb* **sheared, shorn** /shawn/ *vt* **1a** to cut off the hair from ⟨*with* shorn *scalp*⟩ **b** to cut or clip (hair, wool, a fleece, etc) from sby or sthg; *also* to cut sthg from ⟨~ *a lawn*⟩ **c** to cut (as if) with shears ⟨~ *a metal sheet in 2*⟩ **2** to cut with sthg sharp **3** to deprive of sthg as if by cutting off – usu passive + *of* ⟨*has been* shorn *of her authority*⟩ **4** to subject to a shear force ~ *vi* **1** to become divided or separated under the action of a shear force ⟨*the bolt may* ~ *off*⟩ **2** *chiefly Scot* to reap crops with a sickle [ME *sheren*, fr OE *scieran*; akin to ON *skera* to cut, L *curtus* shortened, Gk *keirein* to cut, shear] – **shearer** *n*, **shearing** *n*

[2]**shear** *n* **1a** a cutting implement similar to a pair of scissors but typically larger **b** any of various cutting tools or machines operating by the action of opposed cutting edges of metal **c** *also* **sheer** a sheerlegs – usu pl with sing. meaning but sing. or pl in constr **2** an action or force that causes or tends to cause 2 parts of a body to slide on each other in a direction parallel to their plane of contact *USE* (*1a, b*) usu pl with sing. meaning

'**shearling** /-ling/ *n, chiefly Br* a sheep after its first shearing

'**shear,water** /-,wawtə/ *n* any of numerous seabirds that usu skim close to the waves in flight

sheatfish /'sheet,fish/ *n* a wels [alter. of *sheathfish*, fr *sheath* + *fish*]

sheath /sheeth/ *n, pl* **sheaths** /sheedhz/ **1** a case or cover for a blade (e g of a knife or sword) **2** a cover or case of a (part of a) plant or animal body ⟨*the leaves of grasses form a* ~ *round the main stalk*⟩ **3**

a cover or support (applied) like the sheath of a blade **4** a condom [ME *shethe,* fr OE *scēath*; akin to OHG *sceida* sheath, L *scindere* to cut – more at [1]SHED]

sheathe /sheedh/ *vt* **1** to put into or provide with a sheath ⟨~d *her dagger*⟩ **2** to withdraw (a claw) into a sheath **3** to encase or cover with sthg protective (e g thin boards or sheets of metal) [ME *shethen,* fr *shethe* sheath]

sheath knife *n* a knife that has a fixed blade and is carried in a sheath

shea tree /shiə/ *n* a tropical African tree of the sapodilla family with fatty nuts that yield shea butter [Bambara *si*]

[1]**sheave** /sheev/ *n* a grooved wheel (e g in a pulley block) [ME *sheve*; akin to OE *scēath* sheath]

[2]**sheave** *vt* to gather and bind into a sheaf [*sheaf*]

shebang /shi'bang/ *n, chiefly NAm* an affair, business ⟨*she's head of the whole* ~⟩ – infml [perh alter. of *shebeen*]

shebeen /shi'been/ *n, chiefly Irish* an unlicensed or illegally operated drinking establishment [IrGael *sībin* little mug, bad ale]

[1]**shed** /shed/ *vb* **-dd-; shed** *vt* **1** to be incapable of holding or absorbing; repel ⟨*a duck's plumage* ~s *water*⟩ **2a** to cause (blood) to flow by wounding or killing **b** to pour forth; let flow ⟨~ *tears*⟩ **c** to give off or out; cast ⟨*the book* ~s *some light on this subject*⟩ **3** to cast off or let fall (a natural covering) ~ *vi* to cast off hairs, threads etc; moult ⟨*the dog is* ~*ding*⟩ [ME *sheden* to divide, separate, fr OE *scēadan*; akin to OHG *skeidan* to separate, L *scindere* to cut, split, Gk *schizein* to split]

[2]**shed** *n* WATERSHED 1

[3]**shed** *n* a usu single-storied building for shelter, storage, etc, esp with 1 or more sides open [alter. of earlier *shadde,* prob fr ME *shade* shade]

she'd /shid; *strong* sheed/ she had; she would

sheen /sheen/ *n* **1** a bright or shining quality or condition; brightness, lustre **2** a subdued shininess or glitter of a surface **3** a lustrous surface imparted to textiles through finishing processes or use of shiny yarns [ME *shene* beautiful, bright, fr OE *sciene*; akin to OE *scēawian* to look – more at SHOW] – **sheeny** *adj*

sheeny /'sheeni/ *n* a Jew – derog [origin unknown]

sheep /sheep/ *n, pl* **sheep** **1** any of numerous ruminant mammals related to the goats but stockier and lacking a beard in the male; *specif* one domesticated, esp for its flesh and wool **2** an inane or docile person; *esp* one easily influenced or led [ME, fr OE *scēap*; akin to OHG *scāf* sheep]

'sheep,cote /-,kot, -,koht/ *n, chiefly Br* a sheepfold

'sheep-,dip *n* a liquid preparation into which sheep are plunged, esp to destroy parasites

'sheep,dog /-,dog/ *n* a dog used to tend, drive, or guard sheep; *esp* BORDER COLLIE

'sheep,fold /-,fohld/ *n* a pen or shelter for sheep

'sheep,herder /-,huhdə/ *n, NAm* a shepherd

sheepish /'sheepish/ *adj* embarrassed by consciousness of a fault ⟨*a* ~ *look*⟩ [SHEEP + -ISH] – **sheepishly** *adv,* **sheepishness** *n*

sheep ked /ked/ *n* a wingless bloodsucking fly that feeds chiefly on sheep [*sheep* + *ked* (sheep ked), of unknown origin]

sheep's eyes *n pl* wistful amorous glances ⟨*making* ~ *at her*⟩

sheep's fescue /'feskyooh/ *n* a hardy European grass with very thin leaves

'sheep,shank /-,shangk/ *n* a knot for shortening a rope

'sheep,shearing /-,shiəring/ *n* (the time for or a festival at) the shearing of sheep – **sheepshearer** *n*

'sheep,skin /-,skin/ *n* **1** (leather from) the skin of a sheep **2** the skin of a sheep dressed with the wool on ⟨*a* ~ *coat*⟩

sheep tick *n* a bloodsucking tick whose young cling to bushes and readily attach themselves to passing animals

sheep walk *n, chiefly Br* a tract of land on which sheep are pastured

[1]**sheer** /shiə/ *adj* **1** transparently fine; diaphanous ⟨~ *tights*⟩ **2a** unqualified, utter ⟨~ *ignorance*⟩ **b** not mixed or mingled with anything else; pure, unadulterated **3** marked by great and unbroken steepness; precipitous ⟨*a* ~ *cliff*⟩ [ME *schere* freed from guilt, prob alter. of *skere,* fr ON *skærr* pure; akin to OE *scīnan* to shine]

[2]**sheer** *adv* **1** altogether, completely ⟨*his name went* ~ *out of my head*⟩ **2** straight up or down without a break ⟨*rugged cliffs rose* ~ *out of the sea*⟩

[3]**sheer** *vb* to (cause to) deviate from a course [perh alter. of [1]*shear*]

[4]**sheer** *n* a turn, deviation, or change in a course (e g of a ship)

[5]**sheer** *n* the curvature from front to rear of a ship's deck as observed when looking from the side [perh alter. of [2]*shear*]

[6]**sheer** *n* SHEAR 1c – usu pl with sing. meaning but sing. or pl in constr

'sheer,legs /-,legz/ *n sing or pl in constr, pl* **sheerlegs** a hoisting apparatus consisting of 2 or more upright beams fastened together at their upper ends and having tackle for lifting heavy loads (e g masts or guns)

sheer off *vi, chiefly Br* to depart or turn away abruptly, esp in order to evade

[1]**sheet** /sheet/ *n* **1** a broad piece of cloth; *specif* a rectangle of cloth (e g of linen or cotton) used as an article of bed linen **2a** a usu rectangular piece of paper **b** a printed section for a book, esp before it has been folded, cut, or bound – usu pl **c** the unseparated postage stamps printed by 1 impression of a plate on a single piece of paper **3** a broad usu flat expanse ⟨*a* ~ *of ice*⟩ **4** a suspended or moving expanse ⟨*a* ~ *of flame*⟩ ⟨~s *of rain*⟩ **5a** a piece of sthg that is thin in comparison to its length and breadth **b** a flat metal baking utensil [ME *shete,* fr OE *scȳte*; akin to OE *scēotan* to shoot – more at [1]SHOOT]

[2]**sheet** *vt* to form into, provide with, or cover with a sheet or sheets ~ *vi* to come down in sheets ⟨*the rain* ~*ed against the windows*⟩

[3]**sheet** *adj* rolled into or spread out in a sheet ⟨~ *steel*⟩

[4]**sheet** *n* **1** a rope that regulates the angle at which a sail is set in relation to the wind ☞ SHIP **2** *pl* the spaces at either end of an open boat [ME *shete,* fr OE *scēata* lower corner of a sail; akin to OE *scȳte* sheet]

sheet anchor *n* **1** an emergency anchor formerly carried in the broadest part of a ship **2** a principal support or dependence, esp in danger; a mainstay [alter. (prob influenced by [4]*sheet*) of earlier *shoot anchor,* fr ME *shute anker*]

sheet bend *n* a knot or hitch used for temporarily fastening one rope to a loop in another

,sheet 'glass *n* glass made in large sheets directly from the furnace

sheeting /'sheeting/ *n* (material suitable for making into) sheets

sheet lightning *n* lightning in diffused or sheet form due to reflection and diffusion by clouds

,sheet 'metal *n* metal in the form of a thin sheet

sheet music *n* music printed on large unbound sheets of paper

sheikh, sheik /shayk, sheek/ *n* **1** an Arab chief **2** **sheik, sheikh** a romantically attractive or dashing man [Ar *shaykh*] – **sheikhdom** /-d(ə)m/ *n*

sheila, sheilah /'sheelə/ *n, Austr, NZ, & SAfr* a young woman; a girl – infml [alter. (influenced by girl's name *Sheila*) of E dial. *shaler*]

shekel /'shekl/ *n* **1** an ancient Hebrew gold or silver coin **2** ☞ *Israel* at NATIONALITY **3** *pl* money – infml [Heb *sheqel*]

sheldrake /'sheldrayk/ *n* a shelduck [ME, fr *sheld-* (akin to MD *schillede* parti-coloured) + *drake*]

shelduck /'shelduk/ *n* any of various Old World ducks; *esp* a common mostly black and white duck slightly larger than the mallard [*shel-* (as in *sheldrake*) + *duck*]

shelf /shelf/ *n, pl* **shelves** /shelvz/ **1** a thin flat usu long and narrow piece of material (e g wood) fastened horizontally (e g on a wall or in a cupboard, bookcase, etc) at a distance from the floor to hold objects **2** sthg resembling a shelf in form or position: e g **a** a (partially submerged) sandbank or ledge of rocks **b** a flat projecting layer of rock **c** CONTINENTAL SHELF [ME, prob fr OE *scylfe*; akin to L *scalpere, sculpere* to carve, OE *sciell* shell] – **off the shelf 1** available from stock **2** OFF THE PEG – **on the shelf 1** in a state of inactivity or uselessness **2** *of a single woman* considered as unlikely to marry, esp because too old

'shelf-,life *n* the length of time for which a product (e g a tinned or packaged food) may be stored or displayed without serious deterioration

[1]shell /shel/ *n* **1a** a hard rigid often largely calcium-containing covering of an animal (e g a turtle, oyster, or beetle) **b** a seashell **c** the hard or tough outer covering of an egg, esp a bird's egg **2** the covering or outside part of a fruit or seed, esp when hard or fibrous **3** shell material or shells ⟨*an ornament made of* ~⟩ **4** sthg like a shell: e g **a** a framework or exterior structure; *esp* the outer frame of a building that is unfinished or has been destroyed (e g by fire) **b** a hollow form devoid of substance ⟨*mere effigies and* ~s *of men* – Thomas Carlyle⟩ **c** an edible case for holding a filling ⟨*a pastry* ~⟩ **5** a cold and reserved attitude that conceals the presence or absence of feeling ⟨*wish she'd come out of her* ~⟩ **6** a narrow light racing rowing boat propelled by 1 or more rowers **7** any of various spherical regions surrounding the nucleus of an atom at various distances from it and each occupied by a group of electrons of approximately equal energy **8a** a projectile for a cannon containing an explosive bursting charge **b** a metal or paper case which holds the charge in cartridges, fireworks, etc [ME, fr OE *sciell*; akin to OE *scealu* shell, ON *skel*, L *silex* pebble, flint, Gk *skallein* to hoe] – **shelly** *adj*

[2]shell *vt* **1** to take out of a natural enclosing cover (e g a shell, husk, pod, or capsule) ⟨~ *peanuts*⟩ **2** to fire shells at, on, or into ~ *vi* **1** to fall or scale off in thin pieces **2** to fall out of the pod or husk ⟨*nuts which* ~ *on falling from the tree*⟩

she'll /shil; *strong* sheel/ she will; she shall

[1]shellac /'shelak/ *n* the purified form of a resin produced by various insects, usu obtained as yellow or orange flakes; *also* a solution of this in alcohol used esp in making varnish ['*shell* + *lac*; trans of F *laque en écailles* lac in thin flakes]

[2]shellac *vt* **-ck-** to treat, esp by coating, with shellac

shelled *adj* **1** having a shell, esp of a specified kind – often in combination ⟨*pink*-shelled⟩ ⟨*thick*-shelled⟩ **2a** having the shell removed ⟨~ *oysters*⟩ ⟨~ *nuts*⟩ **b** removed from the pod or cob ⟨~ *peas*⟩

'shell,fish /-,fish/ *n* an aquatic invertebrate animal with a shell; *esp* an edible mollusc or crustacean

'shell ,jacket *n* a short tight military jacket worn buttoned up the front

shell out *vb* to pay (money) – infml

,shell 'pink *n or adj* (a) light yellowish pink

'shell,proof /-,proohf/ *adj* constructed so as to resist attack by shells or bombs

'shell ,shock *n* a mental disorder characterized by neurotic and often hysterical symptoms that occurs under conditions (e g wartime combat) that cause intense stress – **shell-shock** *vt*

Shelta /'sheltə/ *n* a secret jargon of Irish vagrants [origin unknown]

[1]shelter /'sheltə/ *n* **1** sthg, esp a structure, affording cover or protection ⟨*an air-raid* ~⟩ **2** the state of being covered and protected; refuge ⟨*took* ~⟩ [perh fr obs *sheltron* (phalanx), fr OE *scieldtruma*, fr *scield* shield + *truma* troop]

[2]shelter *vt* **1** to serve as a shelter for; protect ⟨*a thick hedge* ~ed *the orchard*⟩ **2** to keep concealed or protected ⟨~ed *her family in a mountain cave*⟩ ~ *vi* to take shelter

shelty, sheltie /'shelti/ *n* a Shetland pony or sheepdog [prob of Scand origin; akin to ON *Hjalti* Shetlander]

shelve /shelv/ *vt* **1** to provide with shelves **2** to place on a shelf **3a** to remove from active service; dismiss **b** to put off or aside ⟨~ *a project*⟩ ~ *vi* to slope gently [*shelf*]

shelving /'shelving/ *n* (material for constructing) shelves

Shema /shə'mah/ *n* the Jewish confession of faith beginning 'Hear, O Israel...' [Heb *shĕma'* hear, first word of Deut 6:4]

shemozzle /shi'mozl/ *n* a source or scene of confusion or dispute; a to-do, mix-up – infml [modif of Yiddish *shlimazel* bad luck, difficulty, misfortune, fr *shlim* bad, ill + *mazel* luck]

shenanigan /shi'nanigən/ *n* **1** deliberate deception; trickery **2** boisterous mischief; high jinks – usu pl with sing. meaning *USE* infml [origin unknown]

Sheol /'shee,ohl, ,-'-/ *n* the abode of the dead in early Hebrew thought [Heb *Shĕ'ōl*]

[1]shepherd /'shepəd/ *n* **1** *fem* **shepherdess** /-des/ one who tends sheep **2** a pastor [ME *sheepherde*, fr OE *scēaphyrde*, fr *scēap* sheep + *hierde* herdsman; akin to OE *heord* herd]

[2]shepherd *vt* **1** to tend as a shepherd **2** to guide, marshal, or conduct (people) like sheep ⟨~ed *the children onto the train*⟩

'shepherd ,dog *n* a sheepdog

ˌshepherd's ˈpie *n* a hot dish of minced meat, esp lamb, with a mashed potato topping – compare COTTAGE PIE

ˌshepherd's ˈpurse *n* a white-flowered annual plant of the mustard family that has small flat heart-shaped seed pods and is a common weed

sherard·ize, -ise /ˈsherədiez/ *vt* to coat (e g iron or steel) with zinc by heating with zinc dust [*Sherard* Cowper-Coles †1936 E inventor]

Sheraton /ˈsherət(ə)n/ *adj* of or being a style of furniture that originated in England around 1800 and is characterized by straight lines and graceful proportions [Thomas *Sheraton* †1806 E furniture designer]

sherbet /ˈshuhbət/ *n* **1** (a drink made with) a sweet powder that effervesces in liquid and is eaten dry or used to make fizzy drinks **2** a water ice with egg white, gelatin, or sometimes milk added [Turk & Per; Turk *şerbet*, fr Per *sharbat*, fr Ar *sharbah* drink]

sherd /shuhd, shahd/ *n* **1** SHARD 1 **2** fragments of pottery vessels

sheriff /ˈsherif/ *n* **1** the honorary chief executive officer of the Crown in each English county who has mainly judicial and ceremonial duties **2** the chief judge of a Scottish county or district **3** a county law enforcement officer in the USA [ME *shirreve*, fr OE *scīrgerēfa*, fr *scīr* shire + *gerēfa* reeve – more at ¹REEVE] – **sheriffdom** /-d(ə)m/ *n*

Sheriff court *n* the main inferior court in Scotland, dealing with both civil and criminal cases, and having appeal to the High Court of Justiciary ☞ LAW

Sherpa /ˈshuhpə/ *n* a member of a Tibetan people living on the high southern slopes of the Himalayas

sherry /ˈsheri/ *n* a blended fortified wine from S Spain that varies in colour from very light to dark brown [alter. of earlier *sherris* (taken as pl), fr *Xeres* (now *Jerez*), city in Spain]

she's /shiz; *strong* sheez/ she is; she has

Shetland /ˈshetlənd/ *n* **1** a Shetland pony or sheepdog **2** *often not cap* (a garment made from) a lightweight loosely twisted yarn of Shetland wool used for knitting and weaving [*Shetland* Islands off N Scotland]

ˌShetland ˈpony *n* (any of) a breed of small stocky shaggy hardy ponies that originated in the Shetland islands

ˌShetland ˈsheepdog *n* any of a breed of small dogs that resemble miniature collies

Shetland wool *n* (yarn spun from) fine wool from sheep raised in the Shetland islands

Shevuoth /sheˈvooh·oth/ *n* Shabuoth

shew /show/ *vb, archaic Br* to show

shewbread, showbread /ˈshoh,bred/ *n* consecrated unleavened bread ritually placed by the Jewish priests of ancient Israel on a table in the sanctuary of the Tabernacle on the Sabbath [trans of G *schaubrot*]

Shia /ˈshee·ə/ *n pl in constr* the members of the major branch of Islam deriving authority from Muhammad's cousin and son-in-law Ali and his appointed successors, the Imams – compare SUNNI 1 [Ar *shī'ah* sect]

shibboleth /ˈshibə,leth/ *n* **1a** a catchword, slogan **b** a use of language that distinguishes a group of people **c** a commonplace belief or saying ⟨*the ~ that crime does not pay*⟩ **2** a custom that characterizes members of a particular group [Heb *shibbōleth* stream; fr the use of this word as a test to distinguish Gileadites from Ephraimites, who pronounced it *sibbōleth*]

shickered /ˈshikəd/ *adj, Austr & NZ* drunk – infml [Yiddish *shiker*, fr Heb *shikkōr*, fr *shikhar* to be drunk]

¹shield /sheeld/ *n* **1** a piece of armour (e g of wood, metal, or leather) carried on the arm or in the hand and used esp for warding off blows **2** sby or sthg that protects or defends; a defence **3** a piece of material or a pad attached inside a garment (e g a dress) at the armpit to protect the garment from perspiration **4** sthg designed to protect people from injury from moving parts of machinery, live electrical conductors, etc **5** a defined area, the surface of which constitutes a heraldic field, on which heraldic arms are displayed; *esp* one that is wide at the top and rounds to a point at the bottom **6** an armoured screen protecting an otherwise exposed gun **7** a protective structure (e g a carapace, scale, or plate) of some animals **8** the Precambrian central rock mass of a continent **9** sthg resembling a shield: e g **a** a trophy awarded in recognition of achievement (e g in a sporting event) **b** a decorative or identifying emblem [ME *sheld*, fr OE *scield*; akin to OE *sciell* shell]

²shield *vt* **1** to protect (as if) with a shield; provide with a protective cover or shelter **2** to cut off from observation; hide ⟨*accomplices who ~ a thief*⟩

ˈshield,bug /-,bug/ *n* any of various true bugs that emit a disagreeable odour [fr the shield-like shape of its scutellum]

shieling /ˈsheeling, -lən/ *n, dial Br* **1** a mountain hut used as a shelter by shepherds **2** a summer pasture in the mountains [Sc *shiel* (shed, hut), fr ME (northern) *schele, shale*]

¹shift /shift/ *vt* **1** to exchange for or replace by another; change ⟨*the traitor ~ed his allegiance*⟩ **2** to change the place, position, or direction of; move ⟨*I can't ~ the grand piano*⟩ **3** to get rid of; dispose of – infml *~vi* **1** to change place, position, or direction ⟨*~ing uneasily in his chair*⟩ ⟨*the wind ~ed*⟩ **2a** to assume responsibility ⟨*had to ~ for herself*⟩ **b** to resort to expedients; GET BY **3** *NAm* to change gear in a motor vehicle [ME *shiften*, fr OE *sciftan* to divide, arrange; akin to OE *scēadan* to divide – more at ¹SHED]

²shift *n* **1a** a deceitful or underhand scheme or method; a subterfuge, dodge **b** an expedient tried in difficult circumstances – usu pl **2** a loose unfitted slip or dress **3a** a change in direction ⟨*a ~ in the wind*⟩ **b** a change in emphasis, judgment, or attitude **4a** *sing or pl in constr* a group who work (e g in a factory) in alternation with other groups **b** a scheduled period of work or duty ⟨*on the night ~*⟩ **5** a change in place or position: e g **a** the relative displacement of rock masses on opposite sides of a fault **b** a change in position of a line or band in a spectrum – compare DOPPLER EFFECT **6** systematic sound change as a language evolves **7** *NAm* the gear change in a motor vehicle

ˈshift ˌkey *n* a key on a keyboard (e g of a typewriter) that when held down permits a different set of characters, esp the capitals, to be printed

ˈshiftless /-lis/ *adj* **1** lacking resourcefulness; inefficient **2** lacking ambition or motivation; lazy [*shift* (resourcefulness)] – **shiftlessly** *adv*, **shiftlessness** *n*

shifty /-ti/ *adj* **1** given to deception, evasion, or fraud; slippery **2** indicative of a fickle or devious nature ⟨~ *eyes*⟩ – **shiftily** *adv*, **shiftiness** *n*

shigella /shi'gelə/ *n, pl* **shigellae** /-li/ *also* **shigellas** any of a genus of bacteria that cause dysentery in animals, esp human beings [NL, genus name, fr Kiyoshi *Shiga* †1957 Jap bacteriologist]

Shiite /'shee·iet/ *n or adj* (an adherent) of Islam as taught by the Shia – **Shiism** *n*

shillelagh /shi'layli/ *n* an Irish cudgel [*Shillelagh*, town in County Wicklow, Eire, famed for its oak trees]

shilling /'shiling/ *n* **1a** (a coin representing) a former money unit of the UK worth 12 old pence or £1/20 **b** a money unit equal to £1/20 of any of various other countries (formerly) in the Commonwealth **2** (a coin or note representing) the basic money unit of certain E African countries ☞ *Kenya, Somalia, Tanzania, Uganda* at NATIONALITY [ME, fr OE *scilling*; akin to OHG *skilling*, a gold coin; both fr a prehistoric Gmc compound represented by OE *scield* shield and by OE *-ling*]

shilly-shally /'shili ,shali/ *vi* to show hesitation or lack of decisiveness [*shilly-shally*, adv, irreg redupl of *shall I*] – **shilly-shally** *n*

[1]**shim** /shim/ *n* a thin piece of wood, metal, etc used to fill in the space between things (e g for support or adjustment of fit) [origin unknown]

[2]**shim** *vt* **-mm-** to fill out or level up by the use of 1 or more shims

[1]**shimmer** /'shimə/ *vi vi* **1** to shine with a softly tremulous or wavering light; glimmer **2** to (cause sthg to) appear in a fluctuating wavy form ⟨*the* ~ing *heat from the pavement*⟩ [ME *schimeren*, fr OE *scimerian*; akin to OE *scīnan* to shine – more at SHINE]

[2]**shimmer** *n* **1** a shimmering light **2** a wavering and distortion of the visual image of a far object usu resulting from heat-induced changes in atmospheric refraction – **shimmery** *adj*

[1]**shimmy** /'shimi/ *n* **1** a chemise **2** a jazz dance characterized by a shaking of the body from the shoulders downwards [(1) by alter.; (2) short for *shimmy-shake* & *shimmy-shiver*]

[2]**shimmy** *vi* to shake, quiver, or tremble (as if) in dancing a shimmy

[1]**shin** /shin/ *n* the front part of the leg of a vertebrate animal below the knee; *also* a cut of meat from this part, esp from the front leg of a quadruped ⟨*a* ~ *of beef*⟩ ☞ MEAT [ME *shine*, fr OE *scinu*; akin to OHG *scina* shin, OE *scēadan* to divide – more at [1]SHED]

[2]**shin** *vb* **-nn-** *vi* to climb by gripping with the hands or arms and the legs and hauling oneself up or lowering oneself down ⟨~ned *up the tree*⟩ ~ *vt* **1** to kick on the shins **2** to climb by shinning

'shin,bone /-,bohn/ *n* TIBIA 1 ☞ ANATOMY

shindig /'shindig/ *n* a usu boisterous social gathering – infml [prob alter. of *shindy*]

shindy /'shindi/ *n, pl* **shindys, shindies** a quarrel, brawl – infml [prob alter. of *shinny* – more at SHINTY]

[1]**shine** /shien/ *vb* **shone** /shon/, (*vt 2*) **shined** *vi* **1** to emit light **2** to be bright with reflected light **3** to be outstanding or distinguished ⟨*she always* ~s *in mathematics*⟩ **4** to have a radiant or lively appearance ⟨*his face* shone *with enthusiasm*⟩ ~ *vt* **1a** to cause to emit light **b** to direct the light of ⟨shone *her torch into the corner*⟩ **2** to make bright by polishing ⟨~d *his shoes*⟩ [ME *shinen*, fr OE *scīnan*; akin to OHG *skīnan* to shine, Gk *skia* shadow]

[2]**shine** *n* **1** brightness caused by the emission or reflection of light **2** brilliance, splendour ⟨*pageantry that has kept its* ~ *over the centuries*⟩ **3** fine weather; sunshine ⟨*come rain, come* ~⟩ **4** an act of polishing shoes **5** *chiefly NAm* a fancy, crush – esp in *take a shine to*; infml

shiner /'shienə/ *n* BLACK EYE – slang [[1]SHINE + [2]-ER]

[1]**shingle** /'shing·gl/ *n* **1** a small thin piece of building material for laying in overlapping rows as a covering for the roof or sides of a building **2** a woman's short haircut in which the hair is shaped into the nape of the neck [ME *schingel*]

[2]**shingle** *vt* **1** to cover (as if) with shingles **2** to cut (hair) in a shingle

[3]**shingle** *n* (a place, esp a seashore, strewn with) small rounded pebbles [prob of Scand origin; akin to Norw *singel* coarse gravel] – **shingly** /'shing·g(ə)li/ *adj*

shingles /'shing·glz/ *n pl but sing in constr* severe short-lasting inflammation of certain ganglia of the nerves that leave the brain and spinal cord, caused by a virus and associated with a rash of blisters and often intense neuralgic pain [ME *schingles*, by folk etymology fr ML *cingulus*, fr L *cingulum* girdle, fr *cingere* to gird– more at CINCTURE]

shining /'shiening/ *adj* **1** emitting or reflecting light; bright **2** possessing a distinguished quality; outstanding ⟨*a* ~ *example of bravery*⟩

Shinto /'shintoh/ *n* the indigenous animistic religion of Japan, including the veneration of the Emperor as a descendant of the sun-goddess [Jap *shintō*] – **Shinto** *adj*, **Shintoism** *n*, **Shintoist** *n or adj*, **Shintoistic** /-'istik/ *adj*

shinty /'shinti/ *n* a variation of hurling played in Scotland [alter. of *shinny* (kind of hockey), perh fr [1]*shin* + [1]*-y*]

shiny /'shieni/ *adj* **1** bright or glossy in appearance; lustrous, polished ⟨~ *new shoes*⟩ **2** *of material, clothes, etc* rubbed or worn to a smooth surface that reflects light – **shininess** *n*

[1]**ship** /ship/ *n* **1a** a large seagoing vessel **b** a square-rigged sailing vessel having a bowsprit and usu 3 masts **2** a boat (propelled by power or sail) **3** *sing or pl in constr* a ship's crew **4** an airship, aircraft, or spacecraft [ME, fr OE *scip*; akin to OHG *skif* ship, OE *scēadan* to divide – more at [1]SHED] – **when one's ship comes in** when one becomes rich

[2]**ship** *vb* **-pp-** *vt* **1** to place or receive on board a ship for transportation **2** to put in place for use ⟨~ *the tiller*⟩ **3** to take into a ship or boat ⟨~ *the gangplank*⟩ **4** to engage for service on a ship **5** to cause to be transported or sent away ⟨~ped *him off to boarding school*⟩ – infml ~ *vi* **1** to embark on a ship **2** to go or travel by ship **3** to engage to serve on shipboard – **shippable** *adj*

-ship /-ship/ *suffix* (*n* → *n*) **1** state, condition, or quality of ⟨*friend*ship⟩ **2a** office, status, or profession of ⟨*professor*ship⟩ **b** period during which (a specified office or position) is held ⟨*during his dictator*ship⟩ **3** art or skill of ⟨*horseman*ship⟩ ⟨*scholar*ship⟩ **4** *sing or pl in constr* whole group or body sharing (a specified clan or state) ⟨*reader*ship⟩ ⟨*member*ship⟩ **5** one entitled to (a specified rank, title, or appellation) ⟨*his Lord*ship⟩ [ME, fr OE

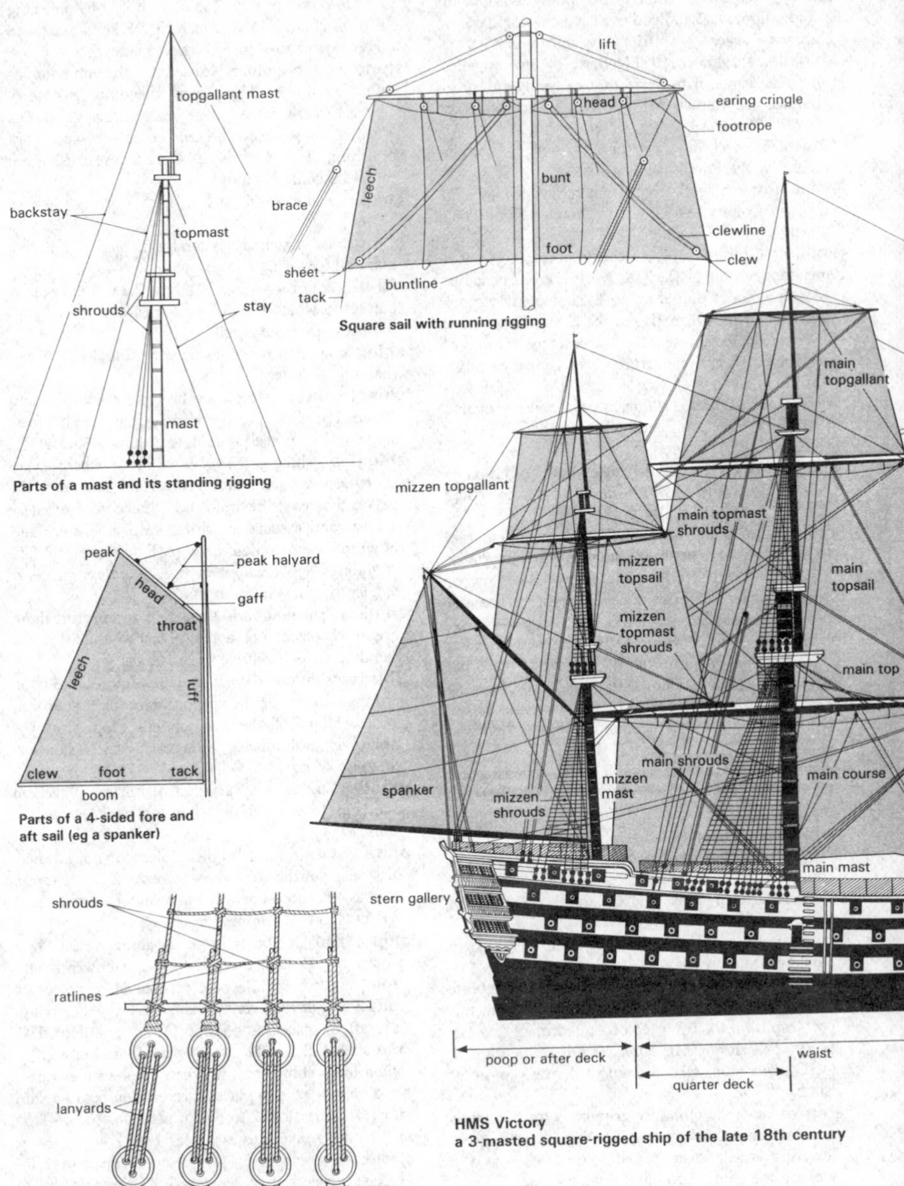

Parts of a mast and its standing rigging

Square sail with running rigging

Parts of a 4-sided fore and aft sail (eg a spanker)

Shrouds

HMS Victory
a 3-masted square-rigged ship of the late 18th century

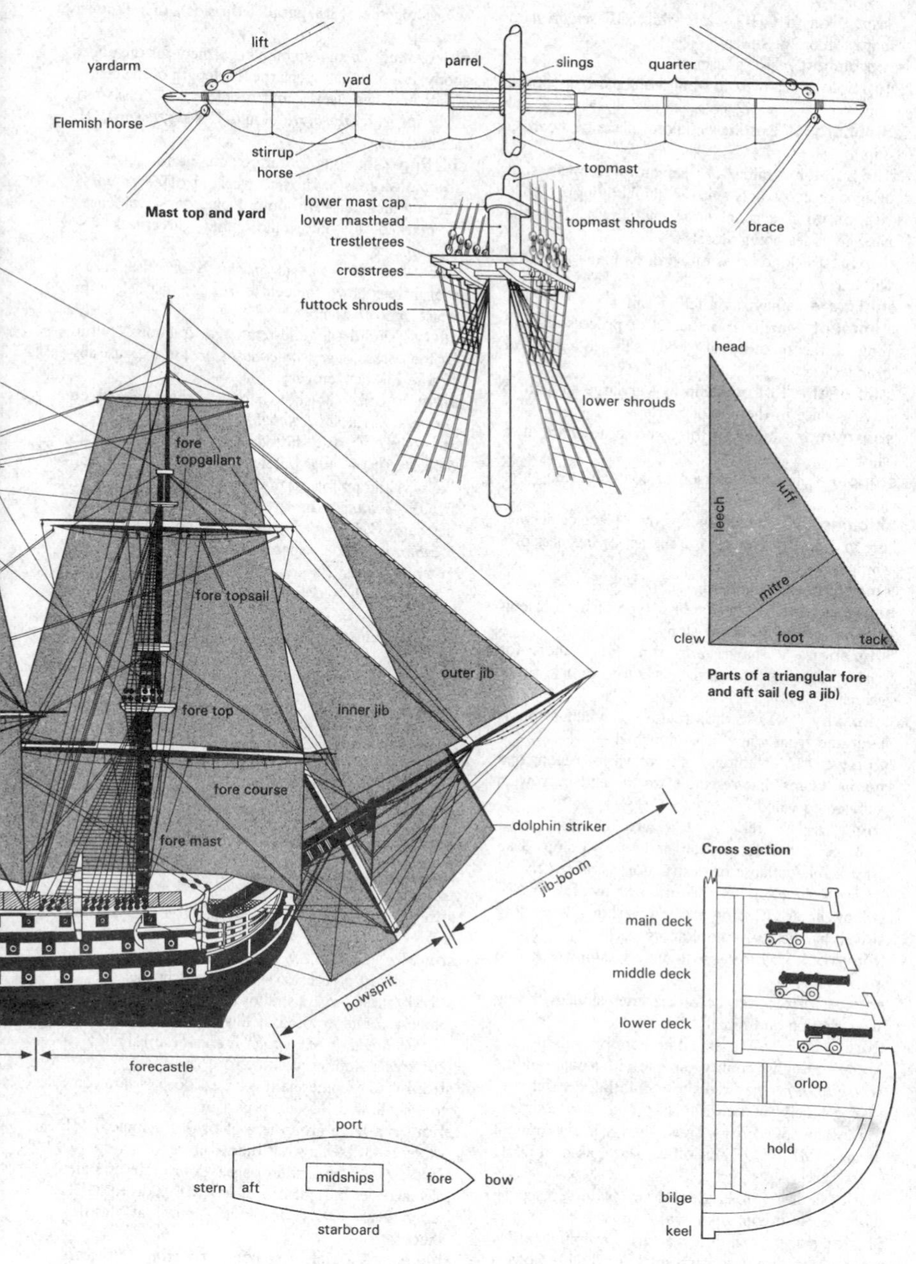
lift
yardarm
yard
parrel
slings
quarter
Flemish horse
stirrup
horse
topmast
Mast top and yard
lower mast cap
lower masthead
trestletrees
crosstrees
futtock shrouds
topmast shrouds
brace
lower shrouds
head
leech
luff
mitre
clew
foot
tack
fore topgallant
fore topsail
fore top
inner jib
outer jib
fore course
fore mast
dolphin striker
jib-boom
bowsprit
forecastle
Cross section
main deck
middle deck
lower deck
orlop
hold
bilge
keel
port
stern
aft
midships
fore
bow
starboard
Parts of a triangular fore and aft sail (eg a jib)

-*scipe*; akin to OHG -*scaft* -ship, OE *scieppan* to shape – more at SHAPE]

ship biscuit *n* SHIP'S BISCUIT

¹'ship,board /-,bawd/ *n* – **on shipboard** on board ship

²shipboard *adj* existing or taking place on board a ship

'ship,builder /-,bildə/ *n* a person or company that designs or constructs ships – **shipbuilding** *n*

ship canal *n* a canal large enough to allow the passage of sea-going vessels

'ship,load /-,lohd/ *n* as much or as many as a ship will carry

'ship,mate /-,mayt/ *n* a fellow sailor

'shipment /-mənt/ *n* **1** the act or process of shipping **2** the quantity of goods shipped ⟨*a ~ of oranges*⟩

,ship of the 'line *n* a ship of war large enough to have a place in the line of battle

'ship,owner /-,ohnə/ *n* the owner of (a share in) a ship

shipper /'shipə/ *n* a person or company that ships goods

shipping /'shiping/ *n* **1** ships (in 1 place or belonging to 1 port or country) **2** the act or business of a shipper

,ship-'rigged /-'rigd/ *adj* square-rigged

ship's biscuit *n, chiefly Br* a type of hard biscuit orig for eating on board ship

'ship,shape /-,shayp/ *adj* trim, tidy [short for earlier *shipshapen*, fr *ship* + *shapen*, archaic pp of *shape*]

'ship,way /-,way/ *n* the structure on which a ship is built and from which it is launched

'ship,worm /-,wuhm/ *n* any of various elongated marine clams that resemble worms and burrow in submerged wood

¹'ship,wreck /-,rek/ *n* **1** a wrecked ship or its remains **2** the destruction or loss of a ship **3** an irrevocable collapse or destruction ⟨*suffered the ~ of his fortune*⟩ [alter. of earlier *shipwrack*, fr ME *schipwrak*, fr OE *scipwræc*, fr *scip* ship + *wræc* sthg driven by the sea – more at WRACK]

²shipwreck *vt* **1** to cause to undergo shipwreck **2** to ruin

'ship,wright /-,riet/ *n* a carpenter skilled in ship construction and repair

shire /shie·ə/ *n* **1a** an administrative subdivision; *specif* an English county, esp one with a name ending in -*shire* **b** *pl the* English fox-hunting district consisting chiefly of Leicestershire and Northamptonshire **2** any of a British breed of large heavy draught horses [ME, fr OE *scīr* office, shire; akin to OHG *scīra* care]

shirk /shuhk/ *vt* to evade or dodge (a duty, responsibility, etc) [origin unknown] – **shirker** *n*

Shirley poppy /'shuhli/ *n* a variable annual garden poppy with bright solitary single or double flowers [*Shirley* vicarage, near Croydon, Surrey, where first developed]

shirr /shuh/ *vt, chiefly NAm* to bake (eggs removed from the shell) in a small dish until set [origin unknown]

shirring /'shuhring/ *n* a decorative gathering, esp in cloth, made by drawing up the material along 2 or more parallel lines of stitching or by stitching in rows of elastic thread or an elastic webbing [*shirr* (to draw cloth together with parallel threads), of unknown origin]

shirt /shuht/ *n* an (esp man's) garment for the upper body; *esp* one that opens the full length of the centre front and has sleeves and a collar ☞ GARMENT [ME *shirte*, fr OE *scyrte*; akin to ON *skyrta* shirt, OE *scort* short]

shirting /'shuhting/ *n* fabric suitable for shirts

'shirt-,sleeve *also* **shirt-sleeves, shirt-sleeved** *adj* **1** (having members) without a jacket ⟨*a ~ audience*⟩ **2** marked by informality and directness ⟨*~ diplomacy*⟩

'shirt,waister /-,waystə/ *n, chiefly Br* a fitted dress that fastens down the centre front to just below the waist or to the hem

shirty /'shuhti/ *adj* bad-tempered, fractious – infml [fr the phrase *to get someone's shirt out* to cause sby to lose his/her temper]

shish kebab /,shish ki'bab/ *n* kebab cooked on skewers [Arm *shish kabab*]

¹shit /shit/ *vb* **-tt-; shitted, shit, shat** /shat/ *vb* to defecate (in) – vulg [alter. (influenced by ²*shit* and the past and pp forms) of earlier *shite*, fr ME *shiten*, fr OE -*scītan*; akin to MLG & MD *schiten* to defecate, OHG *scīzan*, ON *skīta* to defecate, OE *scēadan* to divide, separate – more at ¹SHED]

²shit *n* **1** faeces **2** an act of defecation **3a** nonsense, foolishness **b** a despicable person ***USE*** vulg [fr (assumed) ME, fr OE *scite* (attested only in place names); akin to MD *schit, schitte* excrement, OE *scītan* to defecate]

shite /shiet/ *vb or n, Br* (to) shit – vulg [ME *shiten*]

shitty /'shiti/ *adj* nasty, unpleasant – vulg

Shiva /'sheevə/ *n* Siva

¹shiver /'shivə/ *n* any of the small pieces that result from the shattering of sthg brittle [ME; akin to OE *scēadan* to divide – more at ¹SHED]

²shiver *vb* to break into many small fragments; shatter

³shiver *vi vi* to tremble, esp with cold or fever [ME *shiveren*, alter. of *chiveren*]

⁴shiver *n* an instance of shivering; a tremor – **shivery** *adj*

shivoo /shie'vooh/ *n, Austr* a party, spree – infml [perh modif of F *chez vous* at your house]

¹shoal /shohl/ *n* **1** a shallow **2** an underwater sandbank; *esp* one exposed at low tide [alter. of earlier *shold, shoald*, fr ME *shold*, fr *shold* (adj) shallow, fr OE *sceald* – more at SKELETON]

²shoal *vi* to become shallow or less deep ~ *vt* to come to a shallow or less deep part of

³shoal *n* a large group (e g of fish) [(assumed) ME *shole*, fr OE *scolu* multitude – more at ³SCHOOL]

¹shock /shok/ *n* a pile of sheaves of grain or stalks of maize set upright in a field [ME; akin to MHG *schoc* heap, OE *hēah* high – more at HIGH] – **shock** *vt*

²shock *n* **1** a violent shaking or jarring ⟨*an earthquake ~*⟩ **2a(1)** a disturbance in the equilibrium or permanence of sthg (e g a system) **(2)** a sudden or violent disturbance of thoughts or emotions **b** sthg causing such disturbance ⟨*the news came as a terrible ~*⟩ **3** a state of serious depression of most bodily functions associated with reduced blood volume and pressure and caused usu by severe injuries, bleeding, or burns **4** sudden stimulation of the nerves and convulsive contraction of the muscles caused by the passage of electricity through the body [MF *choc*, fr *choquer* to strike against, fr OF *choquier*, prob of Gmc origin; akin to MD *schocken* to jolt]

[3]**shock** *vt* **1a** to cause to feel sudden surprise, terror, horror, or offence **b** to cause to undergo a physical or nervous shock **2** to cause (e g an animal) to experience an electric shock **3** to impel (as if) by a shock ⟨~ed *her into realizing her selfishness*⟩

[4]**shock** *n* a thick bushy mass, usu of hair [perh fr [1]*shock*]

'**shock ab,sorber** *n* any of various devices for absorbing the energy of sudden impulses or shocks in machinery, vehicles, etc

shocker /'shokə/ *n* **1** sthg horrifying or offensive (e g a sensational work of fiction or drama) **2** an incorrigible or naughty person (e g a child) – infml [[3]SHOCK + [2]-ER]

,**shock-'headed** *adj* having a thick bushy mass of hair

shocking /'shoking/ *adj* **1** giving cause for indignation or offence **2** very bad ⟨*had a ~ cold*⟩ – infml – **shockingly** *adv*

,**shocking 'pink** *adj or n* striking, vivid, bright, or intense pink

'**shock,proof** /-,proohf/ *adj* resistant to shock; constructed so as to absorb shock without damage ⟨*a ~ watch*⟩

'**shock ,therapy** *n* a treatment for some serious mental disorders that involves artificially inducing a coma or convulsions

'**shock ,treatment** *n* SHOCK THERAPY

'**shock ,troops** *n pl* troops trained and selected for assault

'**shock ,wave** *n* **1** BLAST 5 **2** a compressional wave formed whenever the speed of a body (e g an aircraft) relative to a medium (e g the air) exceeds that at which the medium can transmit sound **3** a violent disturbance or reaction ☞ GEOGRAPHY

shod /shod/ *adj* **1a** wearing shoes, boots, etc **b** equipped with (a specified type of) tyres **2** furnished or equipped with a shoe – often in combination [ME, fr pp of *shoen* to shoe, fr OE *scōgan*, fr *scōh* shoe]

[1]**shoddy** /'shodi/ *n* **1** a wool of better quality and longer fibre length than mungo, reclaimed from materials that are not felted **2** a fabric often of inferior quality manufactured wholly or partly from reclaimed wool [origin unknown]

[2]**shoddy** *adj* **1** made wholly or partly of shoddy **2a** cheaply imitative; vulgarly pretentious **b** hastily or poorly done; inferior **c** shabby – **shoddily** *adv*, **shoddiness** *n*

[1]**shoe** /shooh/ *n* **1a** an outer covering for the human foot that does not extend above the ankle and has a thick or stiff sole and often an attached heel ☞ GARMENT **b** a metal plate or rim for the hoof of an animal **2** sthg resembling a shoe in shape or function **3** *pl* a situation, position; *also* a predicament ⟨*I wouldn't be in the president's* ~s *for anything*⟩ **4** the part of a vehicle braking system that presses on the brake drum [ME *shoo*, fr OE *scōh*; akin to OHG *scuoh* shoe, OE *hȳd* hide]

[2]**shoe** *vt* **shoeing; shod** /shod/ *also* **shoed** /shoohd/ **1** to fit (e g a horse) with a shoe **2** to protect or reinforce with a usu metal shoe

[1]'**shoe,horn** /-,hawn/ *n* a curved piece of metal, plastic, etc used to ease the heel into the back of a shoe

[2]'**shoe-,horn** *vt* to force into a limited space ⟨*soon be* ~ing *passengers into the trains – The Guardian*⟩

'**shoe,lace** /-,lays/ *n* a lace or string for fastening a shoe

'**shoe,maker** /-,maykə/ *n* sby whose occupation is making or repairing footwear

[1]'**shoe,string** /-,string/ *n* **1** a shoelace **2** an amount of money inadequate or barely adequate to meet one's needs ⟨*run a business on a* ~⟩ [(2)fr shoestrings being a typical item sold by pedlars]

[2]**shoestring** *adj* operating on, accomplished with, or consisting of a small amount of money ⟨*a ~ budget*⟩

shofar /'shohfah, -fə/ *n, pl* **shofroth** /-'froht(h), -'frohs/ a ram's-horn trumpet used in synagogues before and during Rosh Hashanah and at the conclusion of Yom Kippur [Heb *shōphār*]

shogun /'shohgən/ *n* any of a line of Japanese military governors ruling before the revolution of 1867–68 [Jap *shōgun* general] – **shogunate** /-nət, -nayt/ *n*

shone /shon/ *past of* SHINE

[1]**shoo** /shooh/ *interj* – used in frightening away an (esp domestic) animal [ME *schowe*]

[2]**shoo** *vt* to drive away (as if) by crying 'Shoo!"

'**shoo-,in** *n, NAm* one (e g a contestant) who is a certain and easy winner – infml

[1]**shook** /shook/ *past & chiefly dial past part of* SHAKE

[2]**shook** *n* **1** [1]SHOCK **2** *NAm* a set of wooden staves and end pieces for making a hogshead, cask, or barrel [origin unknown]

,**shook-'up** *adj, chiefly NAm* upset, shaken ⟨*I'm all ~ B*⟩ – *infml* [[1]*shook*]

shoon /shoohn, shohn/ *chiefly dial pl of* SHOE

[1]**shoot** /shooht/ *vb* **shot** /shot/ *vt* **1a** to eject or impel or cause to be ejected or impelled by a sudden release of tension (e g of a bowstring or by a flick of a finger) ⟨~ *an arrow*⟩ ⟨~ *a marble*⟩ **b** to drive forth or cause to be driven forth **(1)** by an explosion (e g of a powder charge in a firearm or of ignited fuel in a rocket) **(2)** by a sudden release of gas or air ⟨~ *darts from a blowpipe*⟩ **c** to drive (e g a ball) forth or away by striking or pushing with the arm, hand, or foot or with an implement **d(1)** to utter (e g words or sounds) rapidly, suddenly, or violently ⟨~ *out a stream of invective*⟩ **(2)** to emit (e g light or flame) suddenly and rapidly **(3)** to send forth with suddenness or intensity ⟨shot *a look of anger at her*⟩ **e** to discharge or empty (e g rubbish) from a container **2a** to strike and esp wound or kill with a bullet, arrow, shell, etc shot from a gun, bow, etc **b** to remove or destroy by use of firearms; *also* to wreck, explode **3a** to push or slide (a bolt) in order to fasten or unfasten a door **b** to pass (a shuttle) through the warp threads in weaving **c** to push or thrust forwards; stick out – usu + *out* ⟨*toads* ~ing *out their tongues*⟩ **d** to put forth in growing – usu + *out* **4a** to engage in (a sport, game, or part of a game that involves shooting); play ⟨~ *pool*⟩ **b** to score by shooting ⟨~ *a basket*⟩ **5** to hunt over with a firearm or bow ⟨~ *a tract of woodland*⟩ **6a** to cause to move suddenly or swiftly forwards ⟨shot *the car onto the highway*⟩ **b** to send or carry quickly; dispatch **7** to pass swiftly by, over, or along ⟨~ing *rapids*⟩ **8** to plane (e g the edge of a board) straight or true **9** to take a picture or series

of pictures or television images of; film; *also* to make (a film, videotape, etc) **10** to pass through (a road junction or traffic lights) without slowing down or stopping – infml **11** to take (a drug) by hypodermic needle – slang ~ *vi* **1a** to go or pass rapidly or violently ⟨*sparks* ~ing *up*⟩ **b** to move ahead by superior speed, force, momentum, etc **c** to stream out suddenly; spurt ⟨*blood* shot *from the wound*⟩ **d** to dart (as if) in rays from a source of light **e** to dart with a piercing sensation ⟨*pain* shot *up his arm*⟩ **2a** to cause a weapon or other device to discharge a missile **b** to use a firearm or bow, esp for sport **3** to propel a missile ⟨*guns that* ~ *many miles*⟩ **4** to protrude, project – often + *out* ⟨*a mountain-range* ~ing *out into the sea*⟩ **5** to grow or sprout (as if) by putting forth shoots **6a** to propel an object (e g a ball) in a particular way **b** to drive the ball or puck in football, hockey, etc towards a goal **7** to slide into or out of a fastening ⟨*a bolt that* ~s *in either direction*⟩ **8a** to record a series of visual images (e g on cinefilm or videotape); make a film or videotape **b** to operate a camera or set cameras in operation [ME *sheten, shuten*, fr OE *scēotan*; akin to ON *skjōta* to shoot, Lith *skudrus* quick] – **shoot a line** to invent romantic or boastful detail – infml – **shoot one's bolt** to exhaust one's capabilities and resources – **shoot one's mouth off** to talk foolishly or indiscreetly

[2]**shoot** *n* **1a** a stem or branch with its leaves, buds, etc, esp when not yet mature **b** an offshoot **2a** a shooting trip or party **b** (land over which is held) the right to shoot game **c** a shooting match **3** a sudden or rapid advance **4** (a rush of water down) a descent in a stream **5** *chiefly NAm* a momentary darting sensation; a twinge [(4) prob by folk etymology fr F *chute* – more at CHUTE]

shoot down *vt* to assert or show the invalidity of; *also* to veto – infml

shooter /'shoohtə/ *n* a repeating pistol – usu in combination ⟨*six*-shooter⟩ ['SHOOT + [2]-ER]

shooting /'shoohting/ *n, chiefly Br* SHOOT 2

'shooting ,brake *n, Br* ESTATE CAR

'shooting ,gallery *n* a usu covered range equipped with targets for practice in shooting with firearms

'shooting ,iron *n, NAm* a firearm – slang

'shooting ,match *n* an affair, matter – chiefly in *the whole shooting match*; infml

,shooting 'star *n* a meteor appearing as a temporary streak of light in the night sky

'shooting ,stick *n* a spiked stick with a handle that opens out into a seat

'shoot-,out *n* a usu decisive battle fought with handguns or rifles

shoot through *vi, Austr & NZ* to leave; *specif* to make a hasty departure ⟨*a well-known absconder,* shooting through *at the slightest opportunity – The Age (Melbourne)*⟩

shoot up *vi* **1** to grow or increase rapidly ⟨*house prices have* shot up *in recent months*⟩ **2** to inject a narcotic drug into a vein – slang

[1]**shop** /shop/ *n* **1** a building or room for the retail sale of merchandise or for the sale of services **2** a place or part of a factory where a particular manufacturing or repair process takes place **3** the jargon or subject matter peculiar to an occupation or sphere of interest – chiefly in *talk shop* [ME *shoppe*, fr OE *sceoppa* booth; akin to OHG *scopf* shed]

[2]**shop** *vb* **-pp-** *vi* **1** to visit a shop with intent to purchase goods **2** to make a search; hunt ⟨~ *for winning designs*⟩ ~ *vt* to inform on; betray ⟨*the robber who changed sides and* ~ped *his mates – Daily Mirror*⟩ – slang – **shopper** *n*

shop around *vi* to investigate a market or situation in search of the best buy or alternative

'shop ,assistant *n, Br* one employed to sell goods in a retail shop

,shop'floor /-'flaw/ *n* the area in which machinery or workbenches are located in a factory or mill, esp considered as a place of work; *also, sing or pl in constr* the workers in an establishment as distinct from the management

'shop,front /-,frunt/ *n* the front side of a shop (building) facing the street

'shop,keeper /-,keepə/ *n* one who runs a retail shop

'shop,lift /-,lift/ *vb* to steal from a shop [back-formation fr *shoplifter*] – **shoplifter** *n*, **shoplifting** *n*

shopping /'shoping/ *n* goods purchased on a shopping trip

'shopping ,centre *n* a group of retail shops and service establishments of different types, often designed to serve a community or neighbourhood

'shop,soiled /-,soyld/ *adj, chiefly Br* **1** deteriorated (e g soiled or faded) through excessive handling or display in a shop **2** no longer fresh or effective; clichéd ⟨*the* ~ *slogans of fascism*⟩

,shop 'steward *n* a union member elected to represent usu manual workers

'shop,walker /-,wawkə/ *n, Br* sby employed in a large shop to oversee the shop assistants and aid customers

,shop'window /-'windoh/ *n* **1** a usu large window in which a shop displays merchandise **2** SHOWCASE 2

'shop,worn /-,wawn/ *adj, chiefly NAm* shopsoiled

shoran /'shaw,ran/ *n* a system of short-range aircraft navigation in which radar signals are sent out and returned by 2 ground stations of known position [*short-range navigation*]

[1]**shore** /shaw/ *n* **1** the land bordering the sea or another (large) body of water **2** land as distinguished from the sea [ME, fr (assumed) OE *scor*; akin to OE *scieran* to cut – more at SHEAR]

[2]**shore** *vt* **1** to support with shores; prop **2** to give support to; brace, sustain – usu + *up* ⟨~ *up farm prices*⟩ [ME *shoren*; akin to ON *skortha* to prop]

[3]**shore** *n* a prop for preventing sinking or sagging

'shore ,leave *n* time granted to members of a ship's crew to go ashore

'shorewards /-woodz/ *adv* towards the shore

shoring /'shawring/ *n* **1** the act of supporting (as if) with shores **2** a system or quantity of shores

shorn /shawn/ *past part of* SHEAR

[1]**short** /shawt/ *adj* **1** having little or insufficient length or height **2a** not extended in time; brief ⟨*a* ~ *vacation*⟩ **b** *of the memory* not retentive **c** quick, expeditious ⟨*made* ~ *work of the problem*⟩ **d** seeming to pass quickly ⟨*made great progress in just a few* ~ *years*⟩ **3a** *of a speech sound* having a relatively short duration **b** *of a syllable in prosody* **(1)** of relatively brief duration **(2)** unstressed **4** limited in distance ⟨*a* ~ *walk*⟩ **5a** not coming up to a measure or requirement ⟨*in* ~ *supply*⟩ ⟨*the throw was* ~ *by 5 metres*⟩ **b** insufficiently supplied ⟨~ *of cash*⟩ **6a** abrupt, curt **b** quickly provoked ⟨*a* ~ *temper*⟩ **7** SHORT-TERM 2 **8a** *of pastry, biscuits, etc* crisp and

easily broken owing to the presence of fat **b** *of metal* brittle **9** made briefer; abbreviated ⟨*Sue is ~ for Susan*⟩ **10** being or relating to a sale of securities or commodities that the seller does not possess at the time of the sale ⟨*~ sale*⟩ **11a** of or occupying a fielding position in cricket near the batsman ☞ SPORT **b** *of a bowled ball* bouncing relatively far from the batsman [ME, fr OE *scort*] – **shortness** *n* – **by the short hairs, by the short and curlies** totally at one's mercy ⟨*if he signs, we've got him* by the short hairs⟩ – **in the short run** for the immediate future – compare IN THE LONG RUN

[2]**short** *adv* **1** curtly ⟨*tends to talk ~ with people when he's busy*⟩ **2** for or during a brief time ⟨short-*lasting*⟩ **3** in an abrupt manner; suddenly ⟨*the car stopped ~*⟩ **4** at a point or degree before a specified or intended goal or limit ⟨*the shells fell ~*⟩ ⟨*stopped ~ of murder*⟩ – **be taken/caught short** *Br* to feel a sudden embarrassing need to defecate or urinate

[3]**short** *n* **1** a short sound or signal **2** *pl* a by-product of wheat milling that includes the germ, bran, and some flour **3** *pl* knee-length or less than knee-length trousers **4** *pl* short-term bonds **5** SHORT CIRCUIT **6** a brief often documentary or educational film **7** *Br* a drink of spirits – **for short** as an abbreviation – **in short** by way of summary; briefly

[4]**short** *vt* to short-circuit

shortage /'shawtij/ *n* a lack, deficit

short back and sides *n* a man's hairstyle in which the hair round the ears and at the neck is cut very short

'short,bread /-,bred/ *n* a thick biscuit made from flour, sugar, and fat

'short,cake /-,kayk/ *n* **1** shortbread **2** a thick short cake resembling biscuit that is usu sandwiched with a layer of fruit and cream and eaten as a dessert

,short'change /-'chaynj/ *vt* **1** to give less than the correct amount of change to **2** to cheat – infml

,short-'circuit *vt* **1** to apply a short circuit to or cause a short circuit in (so as to render inoperative) **2** to bypass, circumvent

,short 'circuit *n* the accidental or deliberate joining by a conductor of 2 parts of an electric circuit

'short,coming /-,kuming/ *n* a deficiency, defect ⟨*felt his ~s made him unsuited to management*⟩

shortcrust pastry /-,krust/ *n* a basic pastry used for pies, flans, and tarts and made with half as much fat as flour

'short,cut /-,kut/ *n* a route or procedure quicker and more direct than one customarily followed

shorten /'shawt(ə)n/ *vt* **1** to make short or shorter **2** to add fat to (e g pastry dough) **3** to reduce the area or amount of (sail that is set)

shortening /'shawt(ə)n·ing/ *n* an edible fat (e g butter or lard) used to shorten pastry, biscuits, etc [SHORTEN + [2]-ING]

'short,fall /-,fawl/ *n* (the degree or amount of) a deficit

'short,hand /-,hand/ *n* **1** a method of rapid writing that substitutes symbols and abbreviations for letters, words, or phrases ☞ ALPHABET **2** a system or instance of rapid or abbreviated communication ⟨*verbal ~*⟩ – **shorthand** *adj*

,short'handed /-'handid/ *adj* short of the usual or requisite number of staff; undermanned

,shorthand 'typist *n* sby who takes shorthand notes, esp from dictation, then transcribes them using a typewriter

'short,horn /-,hawn/ *n, often cap* any of a breed of beef cattle originating in the N of England and including good milk-producing strains

shortie /'shawti/ *n or adj* (a) shorty – infml

short line *n* a line from side to side of the floor of a squash court, halfway between the front and back walls, behind which the player must stand when serving ☞ SPORT

'short-,list *vt, Br* to place on a short list

'short ,list *n, Br* a list of selected candidates (e g for a job) from whom a final choice must be made

,short-'lived *adj* not living or lasting long

'shortly /-li/ *adv* **1a** in a few words; briefly **b** in an abrupt manner **2a** in a short time ⟨*we will be there ~*⟩ **b** at a short interval ⟨*~ after sunset*⟩

short order *n, NAm* an order for food that can be quickly cooked – **in short order** quickly

,short-'range *adj* **1** SHORT-TERM 1 **2** relating to, suitable for, or capable of travelling (only) short distances ⟨*a ~ missile*⟩

short shrift *n* **1** a brief respite for confession before execution **2** summary or inconsiderate treatment [*shrift* (confession), fr ME, fr OE *scrift*, fr *scrīfan* to shrive – more at SHRIVE]

,short 'sight *n* myopia

,short'sighted /-'sietid/ *adj* **1** able to see near objects more clearly than distant objects; myopic **2** lacking foresight – **shortsightedly** *adv*, **shortsightedness** *n*

,short 'story *n* a piece of prose fiction usu dealing with a few characters and often concentrating on mood rather than plot

,short-'tempered *adj* having a quick temper

,short-'term *adj* **1** involving a relatively short period of time ⟨*~ plans*⟩ **2** of or constituting a financial operation or obligation based on a brief term, esp one of less than a year

short time *n* reduced working hours because of a lack of work

short ton /tun/ *n* a US unit of weight that is equal to 2000lb (about 746.48kg)

,short-'waisted *adj* unusually short from the shoulders to the waist

'short,wave /-,wayv/ *n* a band of radio waves having wavelengths between about 120m and 20m and typically used for amateur transmissions or long-range broadcasting – often pl with sing. meaning

,short-'winded *adj* **1** affected with or characterized by shortness of breath **2** brief or concise in speaking or writing

shorty, shortie /'shawti/ *n or adj* (sby or sthg) short – infml

[1]**shot** /shot/ *n* **1a** an action of shooting **b** a directed propelling of a missile; *specif* a directed discharge of a firearm **c** a stroke or throw in a game (e g tennis, cricket, or basketball); *also* an attempt to kick the ball into the goal in soccer **d** a hypodermic injection **2a(1)** small lead or steel pellets (for a shotgun) **(2)** a single (nonexplosive) projectile for a gun or cannon **b(1)** a metal sphere that is thrown for distance as an athletic field event **(2)** this event **3** the distance that a missile is or can be projected **4** one who shoots; *esp* a marksman **5a** an attempt, try ⟨*had a ~ at mending the puncture*⟩ **b** a guess, conjecture **6a** a single photographic exposure **b** an image or series of

images in a film or a television programme shot by 1 camera from 1 angle without interruption **7** a charge of explosives **8** a small amount applied at one time; a dose ⟨*a dramatist could inject a* ~ *of colloquialism into a tragic aria* – Kenneth Tynan⟩ – infml [ME, fr OE *scot*; akin to ON *skot* shot, OHG *scuz,* OE *scēotan* to shoot – more at [1]SHOOT] – **like a shot** very rapidly – **shot in the arm** a stimulus, boost – **shot in the dark** a wild guess

[2]**shot** *adj* **1a** *of a fabric* having contrasting and changeable colour effects; iridescent ⟨~ *silk*⟩ **b** suffused or streaked with (a different) colour ⟨*hair* ~ *with grey*⟩ **c** infused or permeated *with* a quality or element ⟨~ *through with wit*⟩ **2** utterly exhausted or ruined ⟨*her nerves are* ~⟩ – infml – **be/get shot of** *chiefly Br* GET RID OF – infml

[1]'**shot,gun** /-,gun/ *n* an often double-barrelled smoothbore shoulder weapon for firing quantities of metal shot at short ranges

[2]**shotgun** *adj* enforced ⟨*a* ~ *merger*⟩ ⟨*a* ~ *wedding*⟩

'**shot ,put** /poot/ *n* SHOT 2b – **shot-putter** *n,* **shot-putting** *n*

shotten /'shot(ə)n/ *adj, of a fish* having ejected the spawn and so of inferior food value [ME *shotyn,* fr pp of *shuten* to shoot]

should /shəd; *strong* shood/ *past of* SHALL **1** – used (e g in the main clause of a conditional sentence) to introduce a contingent fact, possibility, or presumption ⟨*I* ~ *be surprised if he wrote*⟩ ⟨*it's odd that you* ~ *mention that*⟩ **2** ought to ⟨*you* ~ *brush your teeth after every meal*⟩ **3** – used in reported speech to represent *shall* or *will* ⟨*she banged on the door and said we* ~ *be late* – *Punch*⟩ **4** will probably ⟨*with an early start, they* ~ *be here by noon*⟩ **5** – used to soften direct statement ⟨*I* ~ *have thought it was colder than that*⟩ ⟨*who* ~ *open the door but Fred*⟩ [ME *sholde,* fr OE *sceolde* owed, was obliged to; akin to OHG *scolta* owed, was obliged to]

[1]**shoulder** /'shohldə/ *n* **1a** the part of the human body formed of bones, joints, and muscles that connects the arm to the trunk **b** a corresponding part of a lower vertebrate **2** *pl* **a** the 2 shoulders and the upper part of the back ⟨*shrugged his* ~s⟩ **b** capacity for bearing a burden (e g of blame or responsibility) ⟨*placed the guilt squarely on his* ~s⟩ **3** a cut of meat including the upper joint of the foreleg and adjacent parts ☞ MEAT **4** an area adjacent to a higher, more prominent, or more important part: e g **a(1)** the slope of a mountain near the top **(2)** a lateral protrusion of a mountain **b** that part of a road to the side of the surface on which vehicles travel **5** a rounded or sloping part (e g of a stringed instrument or a bottle) where the neck joins the body [ME *sholder,* fr OE *sculdor*; akin to OHG *scultra* shoulder, OE *sciell* shell – more at SHELL] – **shouldered** *adj*

[2]**shoulder** *vt* **1** to push or thrust (as if) with the shoulder ⟨~ed *his way through the crowd*⟩ **2a** to place or carry on the shoulder ⟨~ed *his rucksack*⟩ **b** to assume the burden or responsibility of ⟨~ *the costs*⟩ ~ *vi* to push aggressively with the shoulders; jostle

'**shoulder ,bag** *n* a bag that has a strap attached at each side of sufficient length for the bag to be hung over the shoulder

'**shoulder ,blade** *n* the scapula ☞ ANATOMY

'**shoulder ,strap** *n* a strap that passes across the shoulder and holds up a garment

shouldest /shoodist/, **shouldst** /shoodst/ *archaic past 2 sing of* SHALL

shouldn't /'shoodnt/ should not

[1]**shout** /showt/ *vi* **1** to utter a sudden loud cry **2** *Austr & NZ* to buy a round of drinks ~ *vt* **1** to utter in a loud voice **2** *Austr & NZ* **a** to buy sthg, esp a drink, for (another person) **b** to buy (sthg, esp a drink) for sby ⟨*dropped in to see if you'd* ~ *an old friend a drink* – *The Sun (Melbourne)*⟩ *USE* (*vi 2, vt 2*) infml [ME *shouten*] – **shouter** *n*

[2]**shout** *n* **1** a loud cry or call **2** [4]ROUND 6 – infml

shout down *vt* to drown the words of (a speaker) by shouting

shove /shuv/ *vt* **1** to push along with steady force **2** to push in a rough, careless, or hasty manner; thrust ⟨~d *the book into his coat pocket*⟩ ~ *vi* **1** to force a way forwards ⟨*bargain hunters* shoving *up to the counter*⟩ **2** to move sthg by pushing ⟨*you pull and I'll* ~⟩ [ME *shoven,* fr OE *scūfan* to thrust away; akin to OHG *scioban* to push, OSlav *skubati* to tear] – **shove** *n,* **shover** /'shuvə/ *n*

,**shove-'halfpenny** *n* a game played on a special flat board on which players shove discs (e g coins) into marked scoring areas

[1]**shovel** /'shuvl/ *n* **1a(1)** an implement consisting of a broad scoop or a dished blade with a handle, used to lift and throw loose material **(2)** (a similar part on) a digging or earth-moving machine **b** sthg like a shovel **2** a shovelful [ME, fr OE *scofl*; akin to OHG *scūfla* shovel, OE *scūfan* to thrust away]

[2]**shovel** *vb* **-ll-** (*NAm* **-l-, -ll-**), /'shuvl·ing, 'shuvling/ *vt* **1** to dig, clear, or shift with a shovel **2** to convey clumsily or in a mass as if with a shovel ⟨~led *his food into his mouth*⟩ ~ *vi* to use a shovel

'**shovelful** /-f(ə)l/ *n, pl* **shovelfuls** *also* **shovelsful** as much as a shovel will hold

shoveller /'shuvl·ə, 'shuvlə/ *n* any of several dabbling ducks that have a large and very broad beak [[2]SHOVEL + [2]-ER]

shove off *vi* to go away; leave – infml

[1]**show** /shoh/ *vb* **shown** /shohn/, **showed** *vt* **1** to cause or permit to be seen; exhibit **2** to present as a public spectacle **3** to reveal by one's condition, nature, or behaviour ⟨*was reluctant to* ~ *his feelings*⟩ **4** to demonstrate by one's achievements ⟨~ed *herself to be a fine pianist*⟩ **5a** to point out to sby ⟨~ed *him where she lived*⟩ **b** to conduct, usher ⟨~ed *me to an aisle seat*⟩ **6** to accord, grant ⟨~ *respect to one's elders*⟩ **7a** to make evident; indicate ⟨*a letter that* ~ed *his true feelings*⟩ **b** to have as an attribute; manifest ⟨*trade figures* ~ed *a large deficit*⟩ ⟨*the patient is* ~ing *some improvement*⟩ **8a** to establish or make clear by argument or reasoning ⟨~ *a plan to be faulty*⟩ **b** to inform, instruct ⟨~ed *me how to solve the problem*⟩ **9** to present (an animal) for judging in a show ~ *vi* **1** to be or come in view; be noticeable ⟨*he has a tear in his coat but it doesn't* ~⟩ **2** to appear in a specified way ⟨~ *to good advantage*⟩ **3** to be staged or presented **4** *chiefly NAm* SHOW UP 2 ⟨*failed to* ~ *for the award*⟩ [ME *shewen, showen,* fr OE *scēawian* to look, look at, see; akin to OHG *scouwōn* to look, look at, L *cavēre* to be on one's guard] – **shower** /'shoh·ə/ *n* – **show one's hand** to declare one's intentions or reveal one's resources – **show one's true colours** to show one's real nature or opinions – **show over** *chiefly Br*

to take on a tour or inspection of ⟨*prospective buyers were* shown over *the new house*⟩ – **show someone the door** to tell sby to get out

²show *n* **1** a display ⟨*a* ~ *of hands*⟩ – often + *on* ⟨*all antiques on* ~ *are genuine*⟩ **2a** a false semblance; a pretence ⟨*he made a* ~ *of friendship*⟩ **b** a more or less true appearance of sthg; a sign ⟨*a* ~ *of reason*⟩ **c** an impressive display ⟨*a* ~ *of strength*⟩ **d** ostentation **3** sthg exhibited, esp for wonder or ridicule; a spectacle **4a** a large display or exhibition arranged to arouse interest or stimulate sales **b** a competitive exhibition of animals, plants, etc to demonstrate quality in breeding, growing, etc **5** a public presentation: e g **a** a theatrical presentation **b** a radio or television programme **6** an enterprise, affair ⟨*he ran the whole* ~⟩ **7** *chiefly NAm* a chance – esp in *give someone a show* *USE* (*6&7*) infml

'show ,biz /biz/ *n* SHOW BUSINESS – infml [by shortening & alter.]

'show,bread /-,bred/ *n* shewbread

'show ,business *n* the arts, occupations, and businesses (e g theatre, films, and television) that comprise the entertainment industry

'show,case /-,kays/ *n* **1** a case, box, or cabinet with a transparent usu glass front or top used for displaying and protecting articles in a shop or museum **2** a setting or surround for exhibiting sthg to best advantage

'show,down /-,down/ *n* the final settlement of a contested issue or the confrontation by which it is settled

¹shower /'showə/ *n* **1** a fall of rain, snow, etc of short duration ☞ WEATHER **2** sthg like a rain shower ⟨*a* ~ *of tears*⟩ ⟨~s *of sparks from a bonfire*⟩ **3** an apparatus that provides a stream of water for spraying on the body; *also* an act of washing oneself using such an apparatus **4** *sing or pl in constr, Br* a motley or inferior collection of people – infml [ME *shour*, fr OE *scūr*; akin to OHG *scūr* shower, L *caurus* northwest wind] – **showery** *adj*

²shower *vi* **1** to descend (as if) in a shower ⟨*letters* ~ed *on him in praise and protest*⟩ **2** to take a shower ~ *vt* **1a** to wet copiously (e g with water) in a spray, fine stream, or drops **b** to cause to fall in a shower ⟨*factory chimneys* ~ed *soot on the neighbourhood*⟩; *also* to cover (as if) with a shower **2** to bestow or present in abundance ⟨~ed *him with honours*⟩

'shower,proof /-,proohf/ *adj, of a fabric or garment* treated so as to give protection from a slight wetting

showgirl /'shoh,guhl/ *n* a young woman who dances or sings in the chorus of a theatrical production; *broadly* a female stage performer whose presence is purely decorative

showing /'shoh·ing/ *n* **1** an act of putting sthg on view; a display, exhibition **2** performance in competition ⟨*made a good* ~ *in the finals*⟩ **3** a statement or presentation of a case; evidence

'show,jumping /-,jumping/ *n* the competitive riding of horses 1 at a time over a set course of obstacles in which the winner is judged according to ability and speed – **showjumper** *n*

'showman /-mən/ *n* **1** one who presents a theatrical show; *also* the manager of a circus or fairground **2** a person with a flair for dramatically effective presentation – **showmanship** *n*

'show-,off *n* one who shows off; an exhibitionist

show off *vt* to exhibit proudly ⟨*wanted to* show *his new car* off⟩ ~ *vi* to seek attention or admiration by conspicuous behaviour ⟨*boys* showing off *on their bicycles*⟩

'show,piece /-,pees/ *n* a prime or outstanding example used for exhibition

'show,place /-,plays/ *n* a place (e g an estate or building) regarded as an example of beauty or excellence

'show,room /-,roohm/ *n* a room where (samples of) goods for sale are displayed

show up *vt* **1** to expose (e g a defect, deception, or impostor) **2** to embarrass ~ *vi* **1a** to be plainly evident; STAND OUT **b** to appear in a specified light or manner ⟨showed up *badly in the semifinals*⟩ **2** to arrive ⟨showed up *late for his own wedding*⟩ *USE* (*vt 2; vi 2*) infml

showy /'shoh·i/ *adj* **1** making an attractive show; striking ⟨~ *blossoms*⟩ **2** given to or marked by pretentious display; gaudy – **showily** *adv*, **showiness** *n*

shrank /shrangk/ *past of* SHRINK

shrapnel /'shrapnəl/ *n, pl* **shrapnel** **1** a hollow projectile that contains bullets or pieces of metal and that is exploded by a bursting charge to produce a shower of fragments **2** bomb, mine, or shell fragments thrown out during explosion [Henry *Shrapnel* †1842 E artillery officer]

¹shred /shred/ *n* a narrow strip cut or torn off; *also* a fragment, scrap [ME *shrede*, fr OE *scrēade*; akin to OHG *scrōt* piece cut off, L *scrupus* sharp stone, OE *scieran* to cut – more at SHEAR]

²shred *vb* **-dd-** *vt* to cut or tear into shreds ~ *vi* to come apart in or be reduced to shreds – **shredder** *n*

shrew /shrooh/ *n* **1** any of numerous small chiefly nocturnal mammals having a long pointed snout, very small eyes, and velvety fur **2** an ill-tempered nagging woman; a scold [ME *shrewe* evil or scolding person, fr OE *scrēawa* shrewmouse]

shrewd /shroohd/ *adj* **1** marked by keen discernment and hardheaded practicality ⟨~ *common sense*⟩ **2** wily, artful ⟨*a* ~ *operator*⟩ [ME *shrewed* wicked, mischievous, fr *shrewe* + *-ed*] – **shrewdly** *adv*, **shrewdness** *n*

shrewish /'shrooh·ish/ *adj* ill-tempered, intractable – **shrewishly** *adv*, **shrewishness** *n*

'shrew,mouse /-,mows/ *n* SHREW 1

¹shriek /shreek/ *vi* to utter or make a shrill piercing cry; screech ⟨~ *with laughter*⟩ ~ *vt* to utter with a shriek or sharply and shrilly – often + *out* [prob irreg fr ME *shriken* to shriek; akin to ME *scremen* to scream]

²shriek *n* (a sound similar to) a shrill usu wild cry

shrieval /'shreevl/ *adj* of a sheriff [obs *shrieve* (sheriff), fr ME *shirreve* – more at SHERIFF]

shrievalty /'shreev(ə)lti/ *n, chiefly Br* the (term of) office or jurisdiction of a sheriff

shrike /shriek/ *n* any of numerous usu largely grey or brownish birds that often impale their (insect) prey on thorns [perh fr (assumed) ME *shrik*, fr OE *scrīc* thrush; akin to ME *shriken* to shriek]

¹shrill /shril/ *vi* to utter or emit a high-pitched piercing sound ⟨*alarm bells* ~ed *as the robbers raced away*⟩ ~ *vt* to scream [ME *shrillen*]

²shrill *adj* having, making, or being a sharp high-pitched sound – **shrillness** *n*, **shrilly** *adv*

¹shrimp /shrimp/ *n, pl* **shrimps**, (*1*) **shrimps**, *esp* *collectively* **shrimp** **1** any of numerous mostly small marine 10-legged crustacean animals with a long slender body, compressed abdomen, and long legs **2** a very small or puny person – infml; humor [ME *shrimpe*; akin to ON *skorpna* to shrivel up, L *curvus* curved – more at [1]CROWN] – **shrimpy** *adj*

[2]**shrimp** *vi* to fish for or catch shrimps – usu in *go shrimping*

shrine /shrien/ *n* **1a** a receptacle for sacred relics **b** a place in which devotion is paid to a saint or deity **2** a receptacle (e g a tomb) for the dead **3** a place or object hallowed by its history or associations ⟨*Oxford is a ~ of learning*⟩ [ME, fr OE *scrīn*, fr L *scrinium* case, chest] – **shrine** *vt*

[1]**shrink** /shringk/ *vb* **shrank** /shrangk/ *also* **shrunk** /shrungk/; **shrunk, shrunken** /ˈshrungkən/ *vi* **1** to draw back or cower away (e g from sthg painful or horrible) **2** to contract to a smaller volume or extent (e g as a result of heat or moisture) **3** to show reluctance (e g before a difficult or unpleasant duty); recoil ~ *vt* to cause to contract; *specif* to compact (cloth) by a treatment (e g with water or steam) that results in contraction [ME *shrinken*, fr OE *scrincan*; akin to MD *schrinken* to draw back, L *curvus* curved – more at [1]CROWN] – **shrinkable** *adj*, **shrinkage** *n*, **shrinker** *n*

[2]**shrink** *n* **1** shrinkage **2** a psychoanalyst or psychiatrist – humor [(2) short for *headshrinker*]

ˈ**shrink-ˌwrap** *vt* **-pp-** to wrap (e g a book or meat) in tough clear plastic film that is then shrunk (e g by heating) to form a tightly fitting package

shrive /shriev/ *vt* **shrived, shrove** /shrohv/; **shriven** /ˈshriv(ə)n/, **shrived** *archaic* to hear the confession of and absolve [ME *shriven*, fr OE *scrīfan* to shrive, prescribe; akin to OHG *scrīban* to write; both fr a prehistoric WGmc word borrowed fr L *scribere* to write – more at [1]SCRIBE]

shrivel /ˈshrivl/ *vb* **-ll-** (*NAm* **-l-, -ll-**), /ˈshrivl·ing/ to (cause to) contract into wrinkles, esp through loss of moisture [perh of Scand origin; prob akin to Sw dial. *skryvla* to wrinkle]

[1]**shroud** /shrowd/ *n* **1** a burial garment (e g a winding-sheet) **2** sthg that covers, conceals, or guards **3** any of the ropes or wires giving support, usu in pairs, to a ship's mast ☞ SHIP [ME, fr OE *scrūd*; akin to OE *scrēade* shred – more at SHRED]

[2]**shroud** *vt* **1a** to envelop and conceal ⟨*trees* ~ed *by a thick mist*⟩ **b** to obscure, disguise **2** to dress for burial

ˈ**shroud-ˌlaid** *adj*, *of a rope* having 4 strands and a core

Shrovetide /ˈshrovh,tied/ *n* the period immediately before Ash Wednesday [ME *schroftide*, fr *schrof-* (fr *shriven* to shrive) + *tide*]

ˌ**Shrove** ˈ**Tuesday** *n* the Tuesday before Ash Wednesday; PANCAKE DAY [ME *schroftewesday*, fr *schrof-* (as in *schroftide*) + *tewesday* Tuesday]

shrub /shrub/ *n* a low-growing usu several-stemmed woody plant [ME *schrobbe*, fr OE *scrybb* brushwood; akin to Norw *skrubbe*bær a cornel of a dwarf species] – **shrubby** *adj*

shrubbery /ˈshrub(ə)ri/ *n* a planting or growth of shrubs

shrug /shrug/ *vb* **-gg-** to lift and contract (the shoulders), esp to express aloofness, aversion, or doubt [ME *schruggen*] – **shrug** *n*

shrug off *vt* to brush aside; disregard, belittle ⟨shrugs *the problem* off⟩

shrunk /shrungk/ *past & past part of* SHRINK

shrunken /ˈshrungkən/ *past part of* SHRINK

shtetl *also* **shtetel** /ˈshtetl/ *n, pl* **shtetlach** /-lahkh/ a small Jewish town or village formerly found in E Europe [Yiddish, fr MHG *stetel*, dim. of *stat* place, town, city, fr OHG, place – more at STEAD]

[1]**shuck** /shuk/ *n* **1** a pod, husk **2** *NAm* sthg of no value – usu pl with sing. meaning ⟨*not worth* ~s⟩ **3** *pl* – used interjectionally to express mild annoyance or disappointment; infml [origin unknown]

[2]**shuck** *vt, NAm* **1** to strip of shucks **2** to remove or dispose of like a shuck – often + *off* ⟨~ *off clothing*⟩ ⟨~ *off bad habits*⟩ – **shucker** *n*

shudder /ˈshudə/ *vi* **1** to tremble with a sudden brief convulsive movement **2** to quiver, vibrate [ME *shoddren*; akin to OHG *skutten* to shake, Lith *kuteti* to shake up] – **shudder** *n*

[1]**shuffle** /ˈshufl/ *vb* **shuffling** /ˈshufling, ˈshufl·ing/ *vt* **1** to mix together in a confused mass; jumble **2** to rearrange (e g playing cards or dominoes) to produce a random order **3** to move (the feet) by sliding clumsily along or back and forth without lifting ~ *vi* **1** to act or speak in a shifty or evasive manner **2a** to move or walk by sliding or dragging the feet **b** to dance in a lazy nonchalant manner with scraping and tapping motions of the feet **3** to mix playing cards by shuffling [perh irreg fr *shove*] – **shuffler** *n*

[2]**shuffle** *n* **1a** shuffling (e g of cards) **b** a right or turn to shuffle ⟨*it's your* ~⟩ **2** (a dance characterized by) a dragging sliding movement

ˈ**shuffleˌboard** /-ˌbawd/ *n* a game in which players use long-handled cues to shove wooden discs into scoring areas of a diagram marked on a smooth surface [alter. of obs *shove-board*]

shufti /ˈshufti/ *n, Br* a look, glance ⟨*have a* ~ *at the radar screen*⟩ – infml [perh of Ar origin; akin to Ar dial. *shaufa* sight, view]

shul /shool/ *n* a synagogue [Yiddish, fr MHG *schuol*, lit., school]

shun /shun/ *vt* **-nn-** to avoid deliberately, esp habitually ⟨*actors who* ~ *publicity*⟩ [ME *shunnen*, fr OE *scunian*] – **shunner** *n*

[1]**shunt** /shunt/ *vt* **1a** to move (e g a train) from one track to another **b** *Br* to move (railway vehicles) to different positions on the same track within terminal areas **2** to provide with or divert by means of an electrical shunt **3** to divert (blood) by means of a surgical shunt ~ *vi* **1** to move into a side track **2** to travel back and forth ⟨~ed *between the 2 towns*⟩ [ME *shunten* to flinch] – **shunter** *n*

[2]**shunt** *n* **1** a means or mechanism for turning or thrusting aside: e g **a** a conductor joining 2 points in an electrical circuit so as to form a parallel path through which a portion of the current may pass **b** a surgical passage created between 2 blood vessels to divert blood from one part to another **c** *chiefly Br* a siding **2** a usu minor collision of motor vehicles – infml

[1]**shush** /sh, shush/ *n* **1** – used interjectionally to demand silence **2** peace and quiet; silence – infml ⟨*quiet, please, children! Let's have a bit of* ~*!*⟩ [imit]

[2]**shush** *vt* to tell to be quiet, esp by saying 'Shush!' – infml

shut /shut/ *vb* **-tt-; shut** *vt* **1** to place in position to close an opening ⟨~ *the lid*⟩ ⟨~ *the door*⟩ **2** to confine (as if) by enclosure ⟨~ *him in the cupboard*⟩ **3** to fasten with a lock or bolt **4** to close by bringing enclosing or covering parts together ⟨~ *the eyes*⟩ **5** to cause to cease or suspend operation ⟨~ *up shop*⟩ ~ *vi* **1** to become closed ⟨*flowers that* ~ *at night*⟩ **2** to cease or suspend operation *USE* (*vt 5; vi 2*) often + *up* or *down* [ME *shutten,* fr OE *scyttan;* akin to OE *scēotan* to shoot – more at [1]SHOOT]

shut away *vt* to remove or isolate from others ⟨*governments that* shut *dissidents* away⟩

'shut,down /-,down/ *n* the cessation or suspension of an activity (e g work in a mine or factory)

'shut-,eye *n* sleep – infml

'shut,off /-,of/ *n, chiefly NAm* a stoppage, interruption

shut off *vt* **1a** to cut off, stop ⟨shut *the water* off⟩ **b** to stop the operation of (e g a machine) ⟨shut *the motor* off⟩ **2** to isolate, separate – usu + *from* ⟨*a village* shut off *from the rest of the world*⟩ ~ *vi* to cease operating; stop ⟨*the heater* shuts off *automatically*⟩

shut out *vt* **1** to exclude **2** *chiefly NAm* to prevent (an opponent) from scoring in a game or contest

[1]**shutter** /'shutə/ *n* **1a** a usu hinged outside cover for a window, often fitted as one of a pair **b** a usu movable cover or screen (e g over a door or as part of stage scenery) **2** a device that opens and closes the lens aperture of a camera ☞ CAMERA **3** the movable slots in the box enclosing the swell organ part of a pipe organ, which are opened to increase the volume of the sound [SHUT + [2]-ER] – **shutterless** *adj*

[2]**shutter** *vt* to provide or close with shutters

shuttering /'shut(ə)ring/ *n* a temporary mould placed to support concrete while setting

[1]**shuttle** /'shutl/ *n* **1a** a usu spindle-shaped device that holds a bobbin and is used in weaving for passing the thread of the weft between the threads of the warp **b** a spindle-shaped device holding the thread in tatting, knotting, or netting **c** a sliding thread holder that carries the lower thread in a sewing machine through a loop of the upper thread to make a stitch **2** a lightweight conical object with a rounded nose that is hit as the object of play in badminton and consists of (a moulded plastic imitation of) a cork with feathers stuck in it **3a** (a route or vehicle for) a regular going back and forth over a usu short route **b** a reusable space vehicle for use esp between earth and outer space [ME *shittle,* prob fr OE *scytel* bar, bolt; akin to ON *skutill* bolt, OE *scēotan* to shoot – more at [1]SHOOT]

[2]**shuttle** *vb* **shuttling** /'shutl·ing, 'shutling/ **1** to (cause to) move to and fro rapidly **2** to transport or be transported (as if) in or by a shuttle – **shuttler** *n*

'shuttle,cock /-,kok/ *n* SHUTTLE 2 [[1]*shuttle* + *cock* (bird)]

shuttle diplomacy *n* diplomacy carried out by an intermediary who travels frequently between the countries concerned

shut up *vt* to cause (sby) to be silent; *esp* to force (a speaker) to stop talking ~ *vi* to become silent; *esp* to stop talking *USE* infml

[1]**shy** /shie/ *adj* **shier, shyer; shiest, shyest 1** easily alarmed; timid, distrustful – often in combination ⟨*camera-shy*⟩ **2** wary *of* ⟨~ *of disclosing his age*⟩ **3** sensitively reserved or retiring; bashful; *also* expressive of such a state or nature ⟨*spoke in a* ~ *voice*⟩ **4** *chiefly NAm* lacking, short ⟨*we're 3 points* ~ *of what we need to win*⟩ – infml [ME *schey,* fr OE *scēoh;* akin to OHG *sciuhen* to frighten off, OSlav *šćuti* to chase] – **shyly** *adv,* **shyness** *n*

[2]**shy** *vi* **1** to start suddenly aside in fright or alarm; recoil **2** to move or dodge to evade a person or thing – usu + *away* or *from* ⟨*they* shied *away from buying the flat when they learnt the full price*⟩ – **shy** *n*

[3]**shy** *vt* to throw (e g a stone) with a jerking movement; fling ~ *vi* to make a sudden throw *USE* infml [perh fr [1]*shy*]

[4]**shy** *n* **1** a toss, throw **2** a verbal sally ⟨*took a few* shies *at the integrity of his opponent*⟩ **3** a stall (e g at a fairground) in which people throw balls at targets (e g coconuts) in order to knock them down **4** an attempt *USE* (*1, 2, & 4*) infml

shylock /'shielok/ *n* an extortionate moneylender [*Shylock,* evil moneylender in *The Merchant of Venice,* play by William Shakespeare †1616 E dramatist & poet]

shyster /'shiestə/ *n, chiefly NAm* sby (esp a lawyer) who is professionally unscrupulous [prob fr *Scheuster fl* 1840 US attorney frequently rebuked in a New York court for pettifoggery]

si /see/ *n* ti [It]

SI *n* a system of units whose basic units are the metre, kilogram, second, ampere, kelvin, candela, and mole and which uses prefixes (e g micro-, kilo-, and mega-) to indicate multiples or fractions of 10 – compare METRIC [F *Système International d'Unités* international system of units]

sial /'sie·əl/ *n* the outer layers of the earth, composed chiefly of relatively light rock rich in silica and alumina [ISV, fr *si*lica + *al*umina] – **sialic** /sie'alik/ *adj*

sialagogue /sie'aləgog/ *n* a drug that promotes the flow of saliva [NL *sialagogus* promoting the expulsion of saliva, fr Gk *sialon* saliva + LL *-agogus* -agogue]

[1]**Siamese** /,sie·ə'meez/ *adj* Thai [*Siam* (now Thailand), country in SE Asia]

[2]**Siamese** *n, pl* **Siamese 1** Thai **2** *also* **Siamese cat** any of a breed of slender blue-eyed short-haired domestic cats of oriental origin with pale fawn or grey body and darker ears, paws, tail, and face

Siamese fighting fish *n* a brightly coloured highly aggressive long-finned freshwater fish

,Siamese 'twin *n* either of a pair of congenitally joined twins [fr Chang †1874 and Eng †1874 congenitally joined twins born in Siam]

[1]**sib** /sib/ *adj* related by blood [ME, fr OE *sibb,* fr *sibb* kinship; akin to OHG *sippa* kinship, family, L *suus* one's own – more at SUICIDE]

[2]**sib** *n* **1** a blood relation **2** a brother or sister considered irrespective of sex; *broadly* any plant or animal of a group sharing a degree of genetic relationship corresponding to that of human sibs

[1]**sibilant** /'sibilənt/ *adj* having, containing, or producing a hissing sound (e g /sh, zh, s, z/) [L *sibilant-, sibilans,* prp of *sibilare* to hiss, whistle, of imit origin] – **sibilance, sibilancy** *n,* **sibilantly** *adv*

[2]**sibilant** *n* a sibilant speech sound

sibling /'sibling/ *n* SIB 2; *also* any of 2 or more individuals having 1 parent in common

sibyl /'sibil/ *n, often cap* any of several female prophets credited to widely separate parts of the ancient world; *broadly* any female prophet [ME *sibile, sybylle,* fr MF & L; MF *sibile,* fr L *sibylla,* fr Gk] – **sibylline** /-lien, -leen/, **sibylic, sibyllic** /si'bilik/ *adj*

sic /sik/ *adv* intentionally so written – used after a printed word or passage to indicate that it is intended exactly as printed or that it exactly reproduces an original ⟨*said he seed* [~] *it all*⟩ [L, so, thus – more at so]

siccative /'sikətiv/ *n* DRIER 1 [LL *siccativus* making dry, fr L *siccatus*, pp of *siccare* to dry, fr *siccus* dry – more at ³SACK]

¹sick /sik/ *adj* **1a(1)** ill, ailing ⟨*a ~ child*⟩ **(2)** of or intended for use in illness ⟨*~ pay*⟩ ⟨*a ~ ward*⟩ **b** queasy, nauseated; likely to vomit ⟨*felt ~ in the car*⟩ – often in combination ⟨*car*sick⟩ ⟨*air*sick⟩ **2a** sickened by intense emotion (e g shame or fear) ⟨*~ with fear*⟩ ⟨*worried ~*⟩ **b** disgusted or weary, esp because of surfeit ⟨*gossip that makes one ~*⟩ ⟨*~ of flattery*⟩ **c** distressed and longing for sthg that one has lost or been parted from **3a** mentally or emotionally disturbed; morbid **b** macabre, sadistic ⟨*~ jokes*⟩ **4a** lacking vigour; sickly **b** badly outclassed ⟨*looked ~ in the contest*⟩ – infml [ME *sek, sik*, fr OE *sēoc*; akin to OHG *sioh* sick, MIr *socht* depression] – **sickish** *adj*, **sickly** *adv* – **be sick** *chiefly Br* to vomit ⟨was sick *on the rug*⟩

²sick *n, Br* vomit

,sick and 'tired *adj* thoroughly bored or sated; FED UP ⟨*I'm ~ of you nattering*⟩

'sick ,bay *n* a compartment or room (e g in a ship) used as a dispensary and hospital

'sick,bed /-,bed/ *n* the bed on which one lies sick

'sick ,call *n* a usu daily (army) parade at which individuals report as sick to the medical officer

sicken /'sikən/ *vt* **1** to cause to feel ill or nauseous **2** to drive to the point of despair or loathing *~ vi* to become ill; show signs of illness ⟨*looked as if she was ~*ing *for a cold*⟩

sickening /'sikəning/ *adj* **1** causing sickness ⟨*a ~ smell*⟩ **2** very horrible or repugnant ⟨*fell to the floor with a ~ thud*⟩ – **sickeningly** *adv*

sick headache *n, chiefly NAm* migraine

sickie /'siki/ *n, chiefly Austr* a day's absence from work claimed as sick leave – slang

¹sickle /'sikl/ *n* **1** an agricultural implement for cutting plants or hedges, consisting of a curved metal blade with a short handle **2** a cutting mechanism (e g of a combine harvester) consisting of a bar with a series of cutting parts [ME *sikel*, fr OE *sicol*; akin to OHG *sichila* sickle; both fr a prehistoric WGmc word borrowed fr L *secula* sickle – more at ²SAW]

²sickle *adj* having a curve resembling that of a sickle blade ⟨*the ~ moon*⟩

³sickle *vt* **1** to mow, reap, or cut with a sickle **2** to form (a red blood cell) into a crescent shape *~ vi* to become crescent-shaped ⟨*the ability of red blood cells to ~*⟩

'sick ,leave *n* absence from work because of illness

'sickle ,cell *n* an abnormal red blood cell of crescent shape that occurs in the blood of people affected with sickle-cell anaemia

sickle-cell anaemia *n* a hereditary anaemia occurring primarily in Negroes, in which the sickling of most of the red blood cells causes recurrent short periods of fever and pain

sickly /'sikli/ *adj* **1** somewhat unwell; *also* habitually ailing **2** associated with sickness ⟨*a ~ complexion*⟩ **3** producing or tending to produce disease ⟨*a ~ climate*⟩ **4** suggesting sickness: **a** strained, uneasy ⟨*a ~ smile*⟩ **b** feeble, weak ⟨*a ~ plant*⟩ **5a** tending to produce nausea ⟨*a ~ taste*⟩ **b** mawkish, saccharine ⟨*~ sentiment*⟩ – **sickliness** *n*

'sickness /-nis/ *n* **1** ill health **2** a specific disease **3** nausea, queasiness

'sick ,pay *n* salary or wages paid to an employee while on sick leave

'sick,room /-,roohm, -,room/ *n* a room set aside for or occupied by sick people

sick up *vt, Br* to vomit – infml

siddur /'sidə, 'sidooə/ *n, pl* **siddurim** /si'dooərəm/ a prayer book of the Jewish daily liturgy [MHeb *siddūr*, lit., order, arrangement]

¹side /sied/ *n* **1a** the right or left part of the wall or trunk of the body ⟨*a pain in the ~*⟩ **b** the right or left half of the animal body or of a meat carcass **2** a location, region, or direction considered in relation to a centre or line of division ⟨*the south ~ of the city*⟩ ⟨*surrounded on all ~*s⟩ **3** a surface forming a border or face of an object **4** a slope of a hill, ridge, etc **5a** a bounding line of a geometrical figure ⟨*each ~ of a square*⟩ ☞ MATHEMATICS **b** FACE 5a(5) **c** either surface of a thin object ⟨*one ~ of a record*⟩ ⟨*the right ~ of the cloth*⟩ **6** company ⟨*he never left her ~*⟩ **7a** *sing or pl in constr* a person or group in competition or dispute with another **b** the attitude or activity of such a person or group; a part ⟨*took my ~ of the argument*⟩ **8** a line of descent traced through a parent ⟨*the grandfather on his mother's ~*⟩ **9** an aspect or part of sthg viewed in contrast with some other aspect or part ⟨*the better ~ of his nature*⟩ **10** a position viewed as opposite to or contrasted with another ⟨*2 ~*s *to every question*⟩ **11** *the* direction of a specified tendency – + *on* ⟨*she was somewhat on the short ~*⟩ **12** *Br* a television channel **13** *Br* sideways spin imparted to a billiard ball [ME, fr OE *sīde*; akin to OHG *sīta* side, OE *sīd* ample, wide, *sāwan* to sow – more at ²sow] – **on the side 1** in addition to a principal occupation; *specif* as a dishonest or illegal secondary activity **2** *NAm* in addition to the main portion

²side *adj* **1** at, from, towards, etc the side **2a** incidental, subordinate ⟨*a ~ issue*⟩ **b** made on the side, esp in secret ⟨*a ~ payment*⟩ **c** additional to the main part or portion ⟨*a ~ order for more rolls*⟩

³side *vi* to take sides; join or form sides ⟨*~*d *with the rebels*⟩

'side ,arm *n* a weapon (e g a sword, revolver, or bayonet) worn at the side or in the belt

'side,band /-,band/ *n* a band of frequencies resulting from modulation (e g of radio waves) close to but either greater than or less than the carrier frequency

'side,board /-,bawd/ *n* **1** a usu flat-topped piece of dining-room furniture having compartments and shelves for holding articles of table service **2** *pl, Br* whiskers on the side of the face that extend from the hairline to below the ears

'side,burns /-,buhnz/ *n pl* SIDEBOARDS 2 [alter. of earlier *burnsides*, fr Ambrose *Burnside* †1881 US general]

,side by 'side *adv* beside one another ⟨*walked ~ down the aisle*⟩ – **side-by-side** *adj*

'side,car /-,kah/ *n* a car attached to the side of a motorcycle or motor scooter for 1 or more passengers

sided /'siedid/ *adj* having sides, usu of a specified number or kind ⟨*one*-sided⟩ ⟨*glass*-sided⟩ – **sidedness** *n*

ˈside ˌdish *n* any of the foods accompanying and subordinate to the main dish of a course

ˈside ˌdrum *n* SNARE DRUM

ˈside efˌfect *n* a secondary and usu adverse effect (e g of a drug) ⟨*forced to stop taking the drug by the* ~s⟩

ˈsideˌkick /-ˌkik/ *n, chiefly NAm* sby closely associated with another, esp as a subordinate – infml

ˈsideˌlight /-ˌliet/ *n* **1** incidental or additional information **2a** the red port light or the green starboard light carried by ships travelling at night **b** a light at the side of a (motor) vehicle

ˈsideˌline /-ˌlien/ *n* **1** a line at right angles to a goal line or end line and marking a side of a court or field of play ☞ SPORT **2a** a line of goods manufactured or esp sold in addition to one's principal line **b** a business or activity pursued in addition to a full-time occupation **3** *pl* the standpoint of people not immediately participating – chiefly in *on the sidelines*

¹ˈsideˌlong /-ˌlong/ *adv* towards the side; obliquely [alter. of *sideling* (sideways), fr ME *sidling*, fr ¹*side* + *-ling*]

²sidelong *adj* **1** inclining or directed to one side ⟨~ *glances*⟩ **2** indirect rather than straightforward

ˈsideˌman /-ˌman/ *n* a member of a band or orchestra, esp a jazz or swing orchestra, other than the leader or featured performer

ˌside-ˈon *adv* with 1 side facing in a given direction; *also* in profile

sider-, sidero- *comb form* iron ⟨sidero*lite*⟩ ⟨sider*osis*⟩ [MF, fr L, fr Gk *sidēr-, sidēro-*, fr *sidēros*]

sidereal /sieˈdiəri·əl/ *adj* of or expressed in relation to stars or constellations [L *sidereus*, fr *sider-, sidus* star, constellation; akin to Lith *svidus* shining]

sidereal day *n* the interval between 2 successive transits of the March equinox over the upper meridian of a particular place; 23h, 56min, 4.09s of solar time

sidereal time *n* time based on the sidereal day

sidereal year *n* the time in which the earth completes 1 revolution in its orbit round the sun measured with respect to the fixed stars; 365 days, 6h, 9min, and 9.54s of solar time

¹siderite /ˈsiedəriet/ *n* ferrous carbonate occurring as a mineral [G *siderit*, fr Gk *sidēros* iron] – **sideritic** /-ˈritik/ *adj*

²siderite *n* a nickel-iron meteorite [*sider-* + *-ite*]

sidesaddle /ˈsiedˌsadl/ *n* a saddle for women in which the rider sits with both legs on the same side of the horse – **sidesaddle** *adv*

ˈsideˌshow /-ˌshoh/ *n* **1a** a minor show offered in addition to a main exhibition (e g of a circus) **b** a fairground booth or counter offering a game of luck or skill **2** an incidental diversion

ˈsideˌslip /-ˌslip/ *vi* **-pp-** to move sideways through the air in a downward direction – **sideslip** *n*

sidesman /ˈsiedzmən/ *n* any of a group of people in an Anglican church who assist the churchwardens, esp in taking the collection in services

ˈsideˌspin /-ˌspin/ *n* rotary motion of a moving ball about a vertical axis

ˈsideˌsplitting /-ˌspliting/ *adj* causing raucous laughter

ˈsideˌstep /-ˌstep/ *vb* **-pp-** *vi* **1** to step sideways or to one side **2** to evade an issue or decision ~ *vt* **1** to move quickly out of the way of ⟨~ *a blow*⟩ **2** to bypass, evade ⟨*adept at* ~ping *awkward questions*⟩

ˈside ˌstep *n* **1** a step aside (e g in boxing to avoid a punch) **2** a step taken sideways (e g when climbing on skis)

ˈside ˌstreet *n* a minor street branching off a main thoroughfare

ˈsideˌstroke /-ˌstrohk/ *n* a swimming stroke executed while lying on one's side

sideswipe /-ˌswiep/ *n* an incidental deprecatory remark, allusion, or reference – infml

ˈside ˌtable *n* a table designed to be placed against a wall or away from a main table

¹ˈsideˌtrack /-ˌtrak/ *n* **1** an unimportant line of thinking that is followed instead of a more important one **2** *NAm* a siding

²sidetrack *vt* to divert from a course or purpose; distract

ˈsideˌwalk /-ˌwawk/ *n, NAm* a pavement

ˈsidewards /-woodz/, *NAm chiefly* **sideward** *adv* towards one side

ˈsideˌways /-ˌwayz/, *NAm also* **sideway** /-ˌway/ *adv or adj* **1** to or from the side ⟨*a* ~ *movement*⟩; *also* askance **2** with 1 side forward ⟨*turn it* ~⟩ **3** to a position of equivalent rank ⟨*he was promoted* ~⟩

ˈside-ˌwhiskers *n pl* (long) facial sideboards

ˈsideˌwinder /-ˌwiendə/ *n, chiefly NAm* a heavy swinging blow from the side – infml

ˈsideˌwise /-ˌwiez/ *adv or adj* sideways

siding /ˈsieding/ *n* a short railway track connected with the main track

sidle /ˈsiedl/ *vi* **sidling** /ˈsiedling/ **1** to move obliquely **2** to walk timidly or hesitantly; edge along – usu + *up* [prob back-formation fr *sideling* (sideways) – more at SIDELONG] – **sidle** *n*

siege /seej/ *n* a military blockade of a city or fortified place to compel it to surrender; *also* the duration of or operations carried out in a siege [ME *sege*, fr OF, seat, blockade, fr (assumed) VL *sedicum*, fr *sedicare* to settle, fr L *sedēre* to sit – more at SIT] – **lay siege to 1** to besiege militarily ⟨laid siege to *the town*⟩ **2** to pursue diligently or persistently

siemens /ˈseemənz/ *n, pl* **siemens** the SI unit of conductance ☞ PHYSICS [Werner von *Siemens* †1892 G electrical engineer]

sienna /siˈenə/ *n* an earthy substance containing oxides of iron and usu of manganese that is brownish yellow when raw and orange red or reddish brown when burnt and is used as a pigment [It *terra di Siena*, lit., Siena earth, fr *Siena, Sienna*, town in Italy]

sierra /siˈeərə/ *n* a range of mountains, esp with a serrated or irregular outline [Sp, lit., saw, fr L *serra*]

Sierra – a communication code word for the letter *s*

siesta /siˈestə/ *n* an afternoon nap or rest [Sp, fr L *sexta* (*hora*) noon, lit., sixth hour – more at SEXT]

ˈsieva ˌbean /ˈseevə/ *n* any of several small-seeded beans closely related to and sometimes classed as lima beans; *also* the seed of a lima bean [origin unknown]

¹sieve /siv/ *n* a device with a meshed or perforated bottom that will allow the passage of liquids or fine solids while retaining coarser material or solids [ME *sive*, fr OE *sife*; akin to OHG *sib* sieve, Serb *sípiti* to drizzle]

²sieve *vt* to sift

sieve cell *n* an elongated tapering cell that is present in the phloem of conifers and lower vascular plants and is important in the conduction of nutrients through the plant

sieve tube *n* a tube consisting of an end-to-end series of thin-walled living cells that is present in plant phloem and is held to function chiefly in the conduction of nutrient solutions of organic compounds (e g sugars)

siffleur /si'fluh, 'siflə/ *n* one who whistles, esp as a musical performer [F, fr *siffler* to whistle]

sift /sift/ *vt* **1a** to put through a sieve ⟨~ *flour*⟩ **b** to separate (out) (as if) by passing through a sieve **2** to scatter (as if) with a sieve ⟨~ *sugar on a cake*⟩ [ME *siften*, fr OE *siftan*; akin to OE *sife* sieve] – **sift through** to make a close examination of (things in a mass or group)

sifter /'siftə/ *n* [2]CASTOR 2 [SIFT + [2]-ER]

[1]**sigh** /sie/ *vi* **1** to take a long deep audible breath (e g in weariness or grief) **2** *esp of the wind* to make a sound like sighing **3** to grieve, yearn – usu + *for* ⟨~ing *for the days of his youth*⟩ ~ *vt* to express by or with sighs [ME *sihen*, alter. of *sichen*, fr OE *sīcan*; akin to MD ver*siken* to sigh] – **sigher** *n*

[2]**sigh** *n* **1** an act of sighing, esp when expressing an emotion or feeling (e g weariness or relief) **2** a sound of or resembling sighing ⟨~s *of the summer breeze*⟩

[1]**sight** /siet/ *n* **1** sthg seen; *esp* a spectacle ⟨*the familiar* ~ *of the postman coming along the street*⟩ **2a** a thing (e g an impressive or historic building) regarded as worth seeing – often pl ⟨*see the* ~s *of Paris*⟩ **b** sthg ridiculous or displeasing in appearance ⟨*you must get some sleep, you look a* ~⟩ **3a** the process, power, or function of seeing; *specif* the one of the 5 basic physical senses by which light received by the eye is interpreted by the brain as a representation of the forms, brightness, and colour of the objects of the real world **b** a manner of regarding; an opinion **4a** the act of looking at or beholding sthg ⟨*fainted at the* ~ *of blood*⟩ **b** a view, glimpse ⟨*got a* ~ *of the Queen*⟩ **c** an observation (e g by a navigator) to determine direction or position **5a** a perception of an object by the eye **b** the range of vision **6a** a device for guiding the eye (e g in aiming a firearm or bomb) **b** a device with a small aperture through which objects are to be seen and by which their direction is ascertained **7** a great deal; a lot ⟨*earned a* ~ *more as a freelance*⟩ – infml [ME, fr OE *gesiht* faculty or act of sight, thing seen; akin to OHG *gisiht* sight, OE *sēon* to see] – **sightless** *adj*, **sightlessness** *n* – **at first sight** when viewed without proper investigation ⟨at first sight *the place seems very dull*⟩ – **at/on sight** as soon as presented to view – **out of sight** **1** beyond all expectation or reason ⟨*wages have risen* out of sight *during the past year*⟩ **2** *chiefly NAm* marvellous, wonderful – infml; no longer in vogue – **sight for sore eyes** sby or sthg whose appearance or arrival is an occasion for joy or relief

[2]**sight** *vt* **1** to get or catch sight of ⟨*several whales were* ~ed⟩ **2** to aim (e g a weapon) by means of sights **3a** to equip (e g a gun) with sights **b** to adjust the sights of ~ *vi* to take aim (e g in shooting) – **sighting** *n*

'**sighted** *adj* having sight, esp of a specified kind – often in combination ⟨*clear*-sighted⟩

'**sightly** /-li/ *adj* **1** pleasing to the eye; attractive **2** *chiefly NAm* affording a fine view ⟨*homes in a* ~ *location*⟩ – **sightliness** *n*

'**sight-,read** /reed/ *vb* **sight-read** /red/ *vt* to read (e g a foreign language) or perform (music) without previous preparation or study ~ *vi* to read at sight; *esp* to perform music at sight [back-formation fr *sight reader*] – **sight reader** *n*

sight screen *n* a screen placed on the boundary of a cricket field behind the bowler to improve the batsman's view of the ball

'**sight,seeing** /-,see·ing/ *n* the act or pastime of touring interesting or attractive sights – often in *go sightseeing* ⟨*went on holiday* ~ *in Scotland*⟩ ⟨*a* ~ *trip*⟩ – **sightseer** /-,see·ə/ *n*

siglum /'sigləm/ *n, pl* **sigla** /-lə/ an abbreviation (e g a special character) used in a manuscript, coin, or seal [LL, perh fr L *sigillum* little figure, dim. of *signum*]

sigma /'sigmə/ *n* **1** the 18th letter of the Greek alphabet **2** *also* **sigma particle** an unstable elementary particle of the baryon family about 2000 times heavier than an electron and existing in positive, negative, and neutral charge states [Gk, of Sem origin; akin to Heb *sāmekh*, 15th letter of the Heb alphabet]

sigmoid /'sigmoyd/ *also* **sigmoidal** /-'moydl/ *adj* curved like the letter C or S [Gk *sigmoeidēs*, fr *sigma*; fr a common form of sigma shaped like the Roman letter C] – **sigmoidally** *adv*

[1]**sign** /sien/ *n* **1a** a motion or gesture by which a thought, command, or wish is made known **b** SIGNAL 1 **2** a mark with a conventional meaning, used to replace or supplement words ☞ SYMBOL **3** any of the 12 divisions of the zodiac **4a(1)** a character (e g a flat or sharp) used in musical notation **(2)** a segno **b** a character (e g ÷) indicating a mathematical operation; *also* either of 2 characters + and – that form part of the symbol of a number and characterize it as positive or negative **5** a board or notice bearing information or advertising matter or giving warning, command, or identification **6a** sthg material or external that stands for or signifies sthg spiritual **b** sthg serving to indicate the presence or existence of sby or sthg ⟨*saw no* ~ *of him anywhere*⟩ **c** a presage, portent ⟨~s *of an early spring*⟩ **d** objective evidence of plant or animal disease **7** a remarkable event indicating the will of a deity [ME *signe*, fr OF, fr L *signum* mark, token, sign, image, seal; prob akin to L *secare* to cut – more at [2]SAW]

[2]**sign** *vt* **1a** to place a sign on **b** to indicate, represent, or express by a sign **2a** to put a signature to **b** to assign formally ⟨~ed *over his property*⟩ **c(1)** to write down (one's name) **(2)** to write as the name of (oneself) ⟨~ed *herself 'R E Swan'*⟩ **3** to warn, order, or request by a sign ⟨~ed *him to enter*⟩ **4** to engage by securing the signature of on a contract of employment ⟨~ed *a new striker from Arsenal*⟩ – often + *on* or *up* ~ *vi* **1** to write one's signature, esp in token of assent, responsibility, or obligation **2** to make a sign or signal [ME *signen*, fr MF *signer*, fr L *signare* to mark, sign, seal, fr *signum*] – **signer** *n*

[1]**signal** /'signəl/ *n* **1** an act, event, or watchword agreed on as the occasion of concerted action ⟨*waited for the* ~ *to begin the attack*⟩ **2** sthg that occasions action ⟨*his scolding was a* ~ *for the little girl to start crying*⟩ **3** a conventional sign (e g a siren or flashing light) made to give warning or command

⟨*a ~ that warns of an air raid*⟩ **4a** an object used to transmit or convey information beyond the range of human voice **b** the sound or image conveyed in telegraphy, telephony, radio, radar, or television **c** the variations of a physical quantity (e g pressure or voltage) by which information may be transmitted: e g **(1)** the wave that is used to modulate a carrier ⟨*the video ~*⟩ **(2)** the wave produced by the modulation of a carrier by a signal ⟨*a radio ~*⟩ [ME, fr MF, fr ML *signale*, fr LL, neut of *signalis* of a sign, fr L *signum*]

[2]**signal** *vb* **-ll-** (*NAm* **-l-**, **-ll-**) *vt* **1** to warn, order, or request by a signal ⟨~led *the fleet to turn back*⟩ **2** to communicate by signals ⟨~led *their refusal*⟩ **3** to be a sign of; mark ⟨*his resignation* ~led *the end of a long career*⟩ ~ *vi* to make or send a signal – **signaller,** *NAm chiefly* **signaler** *n*

[3]**signal** *adj* **1** used in signalling ⟨*a ~ beacon*⟩ **2** distinguished from the ordinary; conspicuous ⟨*a ~ achievement*⟩ – chiefly fml [modif of F *signalé*, pp of *signaler* to distinguish, fr OIt *segnalare* to signal, distinguish, fr *segnale* signal, fr ML *signale*]

'signal,box /-,boks/ *n, Br* a raised building above a railway line from which signals and points are worked

signal·ize, -ise /'signəliez/ *vt* **1** *chiefly NAm* to point out carefully or distinctly; draw attention to **2** to make noteworthy; distinguish ⟨*a performance* ~d *by consummate artistry*⟩ – fml [[3]*signal*] – **signalization** /-'zaysh(ə)n/ *n*

signally /'signəli/ *adv* in a signal manner; remarkably ⟨*a ~ tactless decision*⟩ – chiefly fml

'signalman /-mən/ *n, pl* **signalmen** /-mən/ sby employed to operate signals (e g for a railway)

signatory /'signət(ə)ri/ *n* a signer with another or others; *esp* a government bound with others by a signed convention [L *signatorius* of sealing, fr *signatus*, pp] – **signatory** *adj*

signature /'signəchə/ *n* **1a** the name of a person written with his/her own hand **b** the act of signing one's name **2** a letter or figure placed usu at the bottom of the first page on each sheet of printed pages (e g of a book) as a direction to the binder in gathering the sheets; *also* the sheet itself [MF or ML; MF, fr ML *signatura*, fr L *signatus*, pp of *signare* to sign, seal]

'signature ,tune *n* a melody, passage, or song used to identify a programme, entertainer, etc

signboard /'sien,bawd/ *n* SIGN 5

signet /'signit/ *n* **1** a personal seal used officially in lieu of signature **2** the impression made (as if) by a signet **3** a small intaglio seal (e g in a finger ring) [ME, fr MF, dim. of *signe* sign, seal]

signet ring *n* a finger ring engraved with a signet, seal, or monogram

significance /sig'nifikəns/ *n* **1a** sthg conveyed as a meaning, often latently or indirectly **b** the quality of conveying or implying **2a** the quality of being important; consequence **b** the quality of being statistically significant ☞ STATISTICS

significant /sig'nifikənt/ *adj* **1** having meaning; *esp* expressive ⟨*the painter's task to pick out the ~ details* – Herbert Read⟩ **2** suggesting or containing a veiled or special meaning ⟨*perhaps her glance was ~*⟩ **3a** having or likely to have influence or effect; important ⟨*the budget brought no ~ changes*⟩ **b** probably caused by sthg other than chance ⟨*statistically ~ correlation between vitamin deficiency and disease*⟩ **c** being any of the figures that comes before or after the decimal point of a number and is not zero or is the first figure after the decimal point that is an exact zero [L *significant-, significans*, prp of *significare* to signify] – **significantly** *adv*

signification /,signifi'kaysh(ə)n/ *n* **1** signifying by symbolic means (e g signs) **2** the meaning that a term, symbol, or character normally conveys or is intended to convey

significative /sig'nifikətiv/ *adj* **1** indicative **2** significant, suggestive – **significatively** *adv*, **significativeness** *n*

signify /'signifie/ *vt* **1** to mean, denote **2** to show, esp by a conventional token (e g a word, signal, or gesture) ~ *vi* to have significance; matter [ME *signifien*, fr OF *signifier*, fr L *significare* to indicate, signify, fr *signum* sign] – **signifiable** /-,fie·əbl/ *adj*, **signifier** /-,fie·ə/ *n*

sign in *vi* to record one's arrival by signing a register or punching a card ~ *vt* to record the arrival of (a person) or receipt of (an article) by signing ⟨*all deliveries must be* signed in *at the main gate*⟩

'sign ,language *n* **1** a system of hand gestures used for communication (e g by the deaf) **2** unsystematic communication chiefly by gesture between people speaking different languages

,sign 'manual *n, pl* **signs manual** a signature; *specif* the sovereign's signature on a grant or charter [[1]*sign* + *manual*, adj]

sign off *vi* **1** to announce the end of a message, programme, or broadcast and finish broadcasting **2** to end a letter (e g with a signature) – **sign-off** *n*

sign of the cross *n* a gesture of the hand forming a cross, esp on forehead, shoulders, and chest, to profess Christian faith or invoke divine protection or blessing

sign on *vi* **1** to commit oneself to a job by signature or agreement ⟨sign on *as a member of the crew*⟩ **2** *Br* to register as unemployed, esp at an employment exchange

signor /'seen,yaw, ,-'-/ *n, pl* **signors, signori** /-ri/ an Italian man – used as a title equivalent to *Mr* [It *signore, signor*, fr ML *senior* superior, lord – more at SENOR]

signora /seen'yawrə/ *n, pl* **signoras, signore** /-ray/ an Italian married woman – used as a title equivalent to *Mrs* or as a generalized term of direct address [It, fem of *signore, signor*]

signore /seen'yawray/ *n, pl* **signori** /-ri/ – used as a generalized term of direct address when speaking to an Italian man [It]

signorina /,seenyaw'reenə/ *n, pl* **signorinas, signorine** /-nay/ an unmarried Italian girl or woman – used as a title equivalent to *Miss* [It, fr dim. of *signora*]

sign out *vi* to indicate one's departure by signing in a register ⟨signed out *of the hospital*⟩ ~ *vt* to record or approve the release or withdrawal of ⟨sign *books* out *of a library*⟩

[1]**'sign,post** /-,pohst/ *n* a post (e g at a road junction) with signs on it to direct travellers

[2]**signpost** *vt* **1** to provide with signposts or guides **2** to indicate, mark

sign up *vi* to join an organization or accept an obligation by signing a contract; *esp* to enlist in the armed services ~ *vt* to cause to sign a contract

sika deer /'seekə/ *n* a small deer introduced into

Britain from Japan and now living wild in many areas [Jap *shika*]

Sikh /seek/ *n or adj* (an adherent) of a monotheistic religion of India marked by rejection of idolatry and caste [Hindi, lit., disciple] – **Sikhism** *n*

silage /'sielij/ *n* fodder converted, esp in a silo, into succulent feed for livestock [short for *ensilage*]

silane /'silayn, 'sie-/ *n* any of various compounds of silicon and hydrogen that are analogous to hydrocarbons of the methane series [ISV *sil*icon + meth*ane*]

sild /sild/ *n, pl* **silds,** *esp collectively* **sild** a young herring other than a brisling that is canned as a sardine, esp in Norway [Norw]

¹**silence** /'sielǝns/ *n* **1** forbearance from speech or noise; muteness – often interjectional **2** absence of sound or noise; stillness **3** failure to mention a particular thing ⟨*can't understand the government's ~ on such an important topic*⟩ **4a** oblivion, obscurity ⟨*promising writers who vanish into ~*⟩ **b** secrecy [ME, fr OF, fr L *silentium,* fr *silent-, silens*]

²**silence** *vt* **1** to put or reduce to silence; still **2** to restrain from expression; suppress **3** to cause (a gun, mortar, etc) to cease firing by return fire, bombing, etc

silencer /'sielǝnsǝ/ *n* **1** a silencing device for a small firearm **2** *chiefly Br* a device for deadening the noise of the exhaust gas release of an internal-combustion engine [²SILENCE + ²-ER]

silent /'sielǝnt/ *adj* **1a** making no utterance; mute, speechless **b** disinclined to speak; not talkative **2** free from sound or noise; still **3a** endured without utterance ⟨*~ grief*⟩ **b** conveyed by refraining from reaction or comment; tacit ⟨*~ assent*⟩ **4** making no mention; uninformative ⟨*history is ~ about this man*⟩ **5** MUTE 3 ⟨*~* b *in* doubt⟩ **6** lacking spoken dialogue ⟨*a ~ film*⟩ [L *silent-, silens,* fr prp of *silēre* to be silent; akin to Goth ana*silan* to subside, L *sinere* to let go, lay – more at SITE] – **silently** *adv,* **silentness** *n*

,silent ma'jority *n sing or pl in constr* a majority who do not assert their (moderate) views

silent partner *n, chiefly NAm* SLEEPING PARTNER

¹**silhouette** /,silooh'et/ *n* **1** a portrait in profile cut from dark material and mounted on a light background **2** the shape of a body as it appears against a lighter background [F, fr Étienne de *Silhouette* †1767 F controller-general of finances; prob fr his petty economies]

²**silhouette** *vt* to represent by a silhouette; *also* to project on a background like a silhouette

silic-, silico- *comb form* silicon ⟨silicone⟩ [*silicon*]

silica /'silikǝ/ *n* silicon dioxide occurring in many rocks and minerals (e g quartz, opal, and sand) [NL, fr L *silic-, silex* flint, quartz]

silica gel *n* silica resembling coarse white sand in appearance but possessing many fine pores and therefore extremely adsorbent

silicate /'silikǝt, -kayt/ *n* any of numerous insoluble often complex compounds that contain silicon and oxygen, constitute the largest class of minerals, and are used in building materials (e g cement, bricks, and glass) [*silicic (acid)*]

siliceous, silicious /si'lishǝs/ *adj* of or containing silica or a silicate [L *siliceus* of flint, fr *silic-, silex*]

silici- *comb form* silica ⟨siliciferous⟩ [NL *silica*]

silicic /si'lisik/ *adj* of or derived from silica or silicon [NL *silica* & NL *silicium* silicon (fr *silica*)]

silicify /si'lisifie/ *vt* to convert into or impregnate with silica ~ *vi* to become silicified – **silicification** /-fi'kaysh(ǝ)n/ *n*

silicon /'silikǝn/ *n* a tetravalent nonmetallic element that occurs, in combination with other elements, as the most abundant element next to oxygen in the earth's crust and is used esp in alloys ☞ PERIODIC TABLE [NL *silica* + E *-on* (as in *carbon*)]

silicon chip *n* CHIP 4 ☞ COMPUTER

silicone /'silikohn/ *n* any of various polymeric organic silicon compounds obtained as oils, greases, or plastics and used esp for water-resistant and heat-resistant lubricants, varnishes, and electrical insulators

silicosis /sili'kohsis/ *n* a disease of the lungs marked by hardening of the tissue and shortness of breath and caused by prolonged inhalation of silica dusts [NL] – **silicotic** /-'kotik/ *adj or n*

siliqua /'silikwǝ, -lee-/ *n* a long narrow seed capsule that is characteristic of plants of the mustard family [NL, fr L, pod, husk; akin to L *silic-, silex* flint]

silique /si'leek/ *n* a siliqua [F, fr NL *siliqua*]

silk /silk/ *n* **1** a fine continuous protein fibre produced by various insect larvae, usu for cocoons; *esp* a lustrous tough elastic fibre produced by silkworms and used for textiles **2** thread, yarn, or fabric made from silk filaments **3** a King's or Queen's Counsel **4** *pl* the cap and shirt of a jockey made in the registered racing colour of his/her stable **5** a silky material or filament (e g that produced by a spider) [ME, fr OE *seolc,* prob of Baltic or Slav origin; akin to OPruss *silkas* silk, OSlav *shelkŭ*; (3) fr the silk gown worn by a King's or Queen's Counsel]

'silk ,cotton *n* kapok or another silky or cottony seed covering

silken /'silkǝn/ *adj* **1** made of silk **2** resembling silk, esp in softness or lustre

'silk ,gland *n* a gland (e g in an insect larva or spider) that produces a sticky fluid that is extruded in filaments and hardens into silk on exposure to air

,silk 'hat *n* a hat with a tall cylindrical crown and a silk-plush finish worn by men as a dress hat

'silk ,moth *n* a silkworm

silk screen, silk-screen printing *n* a stencil process in which paint or ink is forced onto the material to be printed, through the meshes of a prepared silk or organdie screen – **silk-screen** *vt*

'silk,worm /-,wuhm/ *n* a moth whose larva spins a large amount of strong silk in constructing its cocoon

silky /'silki/ *adj* **1** silken **2** having or covered with fine soft hairs, plumes, or scales – **silkily** *adv,* **silkiness** *n*

sill /sil/ *n* **1** a horizontal piece (e g a timber) that forms the lowest member or one of the lowest members of a framework or supporting structure (e g a window frame or door frame) ☞ ARCHITECTURE **2** a horizontal sheet of intrusive igneous rock running between strata of other rocks ☞ GEOGRAPHY [ME *sille,* fr OE *syll*; akin to OHG *swelli* beam, threshold, Gk *selis* crossbeam]

sillabub /'silǝ,bub/ *n* (a) syllabub

sillimanite /'silimǝniet/ *n* a brown, greyish, or pale green mineral consisting of an aluminium silicate [Benjamin *Silliman* †1864 US geologist]

silly /'sili/ *adj* **1a** showing a lack of common sense or sound judgment ⟨*a very ~ mistake*⟩ **b** trifling, frivolous ⟨*a ~ remark*⟩ ⟨*he's just being ~*⟩ **2** stunned, dazed ⟨*scared ~*⟩ ⟨*knocked me ~*⟩ **3** of or occupying a fielding position in cricket in front of and dangerously near the batsman ⟨*~ mid-off*⟩ ☞ SPORT [ME *sely, silly* happy, innocent, pitiable, feeble, fr (assumed) OE *sǣlig*, fr OE *sǣl* happiness; akin to OHG *sālig* happy, L *solari* to console, Gk *hilaros* cheerful] – **sillily** *adv*, **silliness** *n*, **silly** *n or adv*

silly-billy /,-- '--, '-- ,--/ *n* sby absurd or silly – used esp by or to children [*silly* + *Billy*, nickname for *William*; prob fr William IV †1837 King of England]

silo /'sieloh/ *n, pl* **silos** **1** a trench, pit, or esp a tall cylinder (e g of wood or concrete) usu sealed to exclude air and used for making and storing silage **2** an underground structure for housing a guided missile [Sp, perh of Celt origin; akin to OIr *sīl* seed, OE *sāwan* to sow – more at [2]sow]

[1]**silt** /silt/ *n* a deposit of sediment (e g at the bottom of a river) [ME *cylte*, prob of Scand origin; akin to Dan *sylt* salt marsh; akin to OHG *sulza* salt marsh, OE *sealt* salt] – **silty** *adj*

[2]**silt** *vb* to make or become choked or obstructed with silt – often + *up* – **siltation** /-'taysh(ə)n/ *n*

'**silt,stone** /-,stohn/ *n* a rock composed chiefly of hardened silt

Silures /'silyooreez/ *n pl* a people of ancient Britain chiefly inhabiting S Wales [L]

Silurian /sie'l(y)ooəri·ən/ *adj* **1** of the Silures or their dwelling-place **2** of or being the period of the Palaeozoic era between the Ordovician and Devonian ☞ EVOLUTION [L *Silures*] – **Silurian** *n*

silvan /'silvən/ *adj* sylvan

[1]**silver** /'silvə/ *n* **1** a white ductile and malleable metallic element that takes a very high degree of polish, is chiefly univalent in compounds, and has the highest thermal and electrical conductivity of any substance ☞ PERIODIC TABLE **2** silver as a commodity **3** coins made of silver or cupro-nickel **4** articles, esp tableware, made of or plated with silver; *also* cutlery made of other metals **5** a whitish grey colour **6** SILVER MEDAL [ME, fr OE *seolfor*; akin to OHG *silbar* silver]

[2]**silver** *adj* **1** made of silver **2a** resembling silver, esp in having a white lustrous sheen **b** giving a soft, clear, ringing sound **c** eloquently persuasive ⟨*a ~ tongue*⟩ **3** consisting of or yielding silver ⟨*~ ore*⟩ **4** relating to or characteristic of silver **5** of or marking a 25th anniversary ⟨*~ wedding*⟩

[3]**silver** *vt* **1** to cover with (a substance resembling) silver **2** to impart a silvery lustre or whiteness to – **silverer** *n*

,**silver 'birch** *n* a common Eurasian birch with a silvery-white trunk

,**silver 'fir** *n* any of various firs with leaves that have a white or silvery white undersurface

'**silver,fish** /-,fish/ *n* **1** any of various silvery fishes **2** any of various small wingless insects; *esp* one found in houses and sometimes injurious to sized paper (e g wallpaper) or starched fabrics

,**silver 'foil** *n* **1** SILVER PAPER **2** tinfoil

,**silver 'fox** *n* a genetically determined colour phase of the common red fox in which the pelt is black tipped with white

,**silver 'grey** *adj or n* light lustrous grey

,**silver 'lining** *n* a consoling or hopeful prospect [fr metaphorical use of the phrase *every cloud has a silver lining* (i e a white edge)]

,**silver 'medal** *n* a medal of silver awarded to one who comes second in a competition – **silver medallist** *n*

,**silver 'paper** *n* paper with a coating or lamination resembling silver

,**silver 'plate** *n* **1** a plating of silver **2** tableware and cutlery of silver or a silver-plated metal

,**silver 'screen** *n* *the* film industry

'**silver,side** /-,sied/ *n, Br* a cut of beef from the outer part of the top of the leg below the aitchbone, that is boned and often salted ☞ MEAT [fr its being considered the best cut]

'**silver,smith** /-,smith/ *n* sby who works in silver

'**silver,ware** /-,weə/ *n* SILVER PLATE 2

'**silver,weed** /-,weed/ *n* any of various somewhat silvery plants; *esp* a cinquefoil with leaves covered in a dense mat of silvery hairs on the underside

silvery /'silv(ə)ri/ *adj* **1** having a soft clear musical tone **2** having the lustre or whiteness of silver **3** containing or consisting of silver – **silveriness** *n*

silviculture /'silvi,kulchə/ *n* a branch of forestry dealing with the development and care of forests [F, fr L *silva, sylva* forest + *cultura* culture] – **silvicultural** /-'kulch(ə)rəl/ *adj*, **silviculturist** *n*

simian /'simi·ən/ *adj or n* (of or resembling) a monkey or ape [L *simia* ape, perh fr *simus* snub-nosed, fr Gk *simos*]

similar /'similə/ *adj* **1** marked by correspondence or resemblance, esp of a general kind ⟨*~ but not identical*⟩ **2** alike in 1 or more essential aspects ⟨*no 2 signatures are exactly ~*⟩ **3** differing in size but not in shape ⟨*~ triangles*⟩ – compare CONGRUENT 2 [F *similaire*, fr L *similis* like, similar – more at SAME] – **similarly** *adv*, **similarity** /-'larəti/ *n*

simile /'simili/ *n* a figure of speech explicitly comparing 2 unlike things (e g in *cheeks like roses*) – compare METAPHOR [L, comparison, fr neut of *similis*]

similitude /si'milityoohd/ *n* (an instance of) correspondence in kind, quality, or appearance – fml [ME, fr MF, resemblance, likeness, fr L *similitudo*, fr *similis*]

simmer /'simə/ *vi* **1a** *of a liquid* to bubble gently below or just at the boiling point **b** *of food* to cook in a simmering liquid **2a** to develop, ferment ⟨*ideas ~ing in the back of his mind*⟩ **b** to be agitated by suppressed emotion ⟨*~ with anger*⟩ ~ *vt* to cook (food) in a simmering liquid [alter. of E dial. *simper*, fr ME *simperen*, of imit origin]

simmer down *vi* to become calm or less excited

'**simnel ,cake** /'simnəl/ *n, Br* a rich fruit cake traditionally filled with a layer of almond paste and baked esp for mid-Lent and Easter [ME *simenel*, fr OF, fr L *simila* fine wheat flour]

simony /'simәni, 'sie-/ *n* the buying or selling of a church office or ecclesiastical promotion [LL *simonia*, fr *Simon* Magus 1st c AD Samaritan sorcerer (Acts 8:9–24)] – **simoniac** /si'mohniak/ *adj or n*, **simoniacal** /,siemə'nie·əkl/ *adj*

simoom /si'moohm/ *n* a hot dry violent dust-laden wind blowing from an Asian or African desert [Ar *samūm*]

simoon /si'moohn/ *n* a simoom

simp /simp/ *n, chiefly NAm* a simpleton – infml

[1]**simper** /'simpə/ *vi* to smile in a foolish self-conscious manner ~ *vt* to say with a simper ⟨*~ed her apolo-*

gies⟩ [perh of Scand origin; akin to Dan dial. *simper* affected, coy] – **simperer** *n*

²**simper** *n* a foolish self-conscious smile

¹**simple** /'simpl/ *adj* **1a** free from guile or vanity; unassuming **b** free from elaboration or showiness; unpretentious ⟨*wrote in a ~ style*⟩ **2** of humble birth or lowly position ⟨*a ~ farmer*⟩ **3a** lacking intelligence; *esp* mentally retarded **b** lacking sophistication; naive **4a** sheer, unqualified ⟨*the ~ truth of the matter*⟩ **b** free of secondary complications ⟨*a ~ fracture*⟩ **c** *of a sentence* consisting of only 1 main clause and no subordinate clauses **d** composed essentially of 1 substance **e** not made up of many like units ⟨*a ~ eye*⟩ **5a** not subdivided into branches or leaflets ☞ PLANT **b** consisting of a single carpel **c** *of a fruit* developing from a single ovary **6** not limited; unconditional ⟨*a ~ obligation*⟩ **7** readily understood or performed; straightforward ⟨*a ~ task*⟩ ⟨*the adjustment was ~ to make*⟩ [ME, fr OF, plain, uncomplicated, artless, fr L *simplus* (fr *sem-, sim-* one + *-plus* multiplied by) & *simplic-, simplex* (fr *sem-, sim-* + *-plic-, -plex* -fold), lit., single; akin to Gk di*plak-*, di*plax* double – more at SAME, DOUBLE] – **simpleness** *n*

²**simple** *n, archaic* a medicinal plant [*simple* (uncompounded substance, medicine with only 1 ingredient), fr ¹*simple*]

simple fraction *n* a fraction having whole numbers for the numerator and denominator – compare COMPLEX FRACTION

simple harmonic motion *n* a vibratory motion (e g the swing of a pendulum) in which the acceleration is proportional and opposite to the displacement of the body from an equilibrium position

ˌ**simple-'hearted** *adj* having a sincere and unassuming nature; artless

simple interest *n* interest paid or calculated on only the original capital sum of a loan

simple machine *n* any of various elementary mechanisms formerly considered as the elements of which all machines are composed and including the lever, the wheel and axle, the pulley, the inclined plane, the wedge, and the screw

ˌ**simple'minded** /-'miendid/ *adj* devoid of subtlety; unsophisticated; *also* mentally retarded – **simplemindedly** *adv*, **simplemindedness** *n*

simpleton /'simplt(ə)n/ *n* sby lacking common sense or intelligence [¹*simple* + *-ton* (as in surnames such as *Washington*)]

simple vow *n* a vow taken by a member of a Roman Catholic order under which retention of individual property is permitted and marriage, though illicit, is valid under canon law – compare SOLEMN VOW

simplex /'simpleks/ *adj* **1** simple, single **2** allowing telecommunication in only 1 direction at a time [L *simplic-, simplex* – more at ¹SIMPLE]

simplicity /sim'plisəti/ *n* **1** the state or quality of being simple **2** lack of subtlety or penetration; naivety **3** freedom from affectation or guile; sincerity, straightforwardness **4a** directness of expression; clarity **b** restraint in ornamentation; austerity, plainness [ME *simplicite*, fr MF *simplicité*, fr L *simplicitat-, simplicitas*, fr *simplic-, simplex*]

simplify /'simplifie/ *vt* to make simple or simpler: e g **a** to reduce to basic essentials **b** to diminish in scope or complexity; streamline ⟨*~ a manufacturing process*⟩ **c** to make more intelligible; clarify ~ *vi* to become simple or simpler [F *simplifier*, fr ML *simplificare*, fr L *simplus* simple] – **simplifier** *n*, **simplification** /-fi'kaysh(ə)n/ *n*

simplistic /sim'plistik/ *adj* deliberately or affectedly uncomplicated – **simplistically** *adv*

simply /'simpli/ *adv* **1a** without ambiguity; clearly ⟨*a ~ worded reply*⟩ **b** without ornamentation or show ⟨*~ furnished*⟩ **c** without affectation or subterfuge; candidly **2a** solely, merely ⟨*eats ~ to keep alive*⟩ **b** without any question ⟨*the concert was ~ marvellous*⟩

simulacrum /ˌsimyoo'laykrəm/ *n, pl* **simulacra** /-krə/ *also* **simulacrums** an often superficial or misleading likeness of sthg; a semblance – fml [L, fr *simulare*]

simulate /'simyooˌlayt/ *vt* **1** to assume the outward qualities or appearance of, usu with the intent to deceive **2** to make a functioning model of (a system, device, or process) (e g by using a computer) [L *simulatus*, pp of *simulare* to copy, represent, feign, fr *similis* like – more at SAME] – **simulator** *n*, **simulation** /-'laysh(ə)n/ *n*

simultaneous /ˌsiməl'taynyəs, -ni·əs/ *adj* **1** existing, occurring, or functioning at the same time **2** satisfied by the same values of the variables ⟨*~ equations*⟩ [(assumed) ML *simultaneus*, fr L *simul* at the same time – more at SAME] – **simultaneously** *adv*, **simultaneousness, simultaneity** /-tə'nayəti, -'nee-/ *n*

¹**sin** /sin/ *n* **1a** an offence against moral or religious law or divine commandments **b** an action considered highly reprehensible ⟨*it's a ~ to waste food*⟩ **2** a state of estrangement from God [ME *sinne*, fr OE *synn*; akin to OHG *sunta* sin] – **sinless** *adj*, **sinlessly** *adv*, **sinlessness** *n*

²**sin** *vi* **-nn- 1** to commit a sin **2** to commit an offence – often + *against* ⟨*writers who ~ against good taste*⟩ – **sinner** *n*

Sinanthropus /si'nanthrəpəs/ *n* PEKING MAN [NL, fr LL *Sinae*, pl, Chinese + Gk *anthrōpos* man – more at SINOLOGUE]

'sin ˌbin *n* **1** a brothel – euph **2** an enclosure occupied by a player (e g in ice hockey) who has been temporarily sent off – infml

¹**since** /sins/ *adv* **1** continuously from then until now ⟨*has stayed there ever ~*⟩ **2** before now; ago ⟨*should have done it long ~*⟩ **3** between then and now; subsequently ⟨*has ~ become rich*⟩ *USE* + tenses formed with *to have* [ME *sins*, contr of *sithens*, fr *sithen*, fr OE *siththan*, fr *sith tham* since that, fr *sith* since + *tham*, dat of *thæt* that; akin to OHG *sid* since, L *serus* late, OE *sāwan* to sow]

²**since** *prep* in the period between (a specified past time) and now ⟨*haven't met ~ 1973*⟩; from (a specified past time) until now ⟨*it's a long time ~ breakfast*⟩ – + present tenses and tenses formed with *to have*

³**since** *conj* **1** between now and the past time when ⟨*has held 2 jobs ~ he left school*⟩; continuously from the past time when ⟨*ever ~ he was a child*⟩ **2** in view of the fact that; because ⟨*more interesting, ~ rarer*⟩

sincere /sin'siə/ *adj* free from deceit or hypocrisy; honest, genuine ⟨*~ interest*⟩ [MF, fr L *sincerus*] – **sincerely** *adv*, **sincereness, sincerity** /sin'serəti/ *n*

sinciput /'sinsiput/ *n, pl* **sinciputs, sincipita** /sin'sipitə/ **1** the forehead **2** the upper half of the skull [L *sincipit-, sinciput*, fr *semi-* + *caput* head – more at HEAD]

sine /sien/ *n* the trigonometric function that for an acute angle in a right-angled triangle is the ratio between the side opposite the angle and the hypotenuse ☞ MATHEMATICS [ML *sinus*, fr L, curve]

sinecure /ˈsinikyooə, ˈsie-/ *n* an office or position that provides an income while requiring little or no work [ML *(beneficium) sine cura* (benefice) without cure of souls]

sine die /ˌsieni ˈdee·ay, ˈdie·ee, ˌsini/ *adv* without any future date being designated (e g for resumption) ⟨*the meeting adjourned* ~⟩ [L, without day]

sine qua non /ˌsini kway ˈnon, kway ˈnohn, ˌsieni/ *n* an absolutely indispensable or essential thing [LL, without which not]

sinew /ˈsinyooh/ *n* **1** a tendon; *also* one prepared for use as a cord or thread **2a** solid resilient strength; vigour ⟨*intellectual and moral* ~ – G K Chalmers⟩ **b** the chief means of support; mainstay – usu pl ⟨*the* ~*s of political stability*⟩ [ME *sinewe*, fr OE *seono*; akin to OHG *senawa* sinew, L *saeta* bristle] – **sinewy** *adj*

ˈ**sine** ˌ**wave** /sien/ *n* a wave form that represents periodic oscillations in which the amount of vertical displacement at each point is proportional to the sine of the horizontal distance from a reference point

sinfonia /ˌsinfəˈnee·ə/ *n, pl* **sinfonie** /-ˈnee,ay/, **sinfonias** SYMPHONY 1 [It, fr L *symphonia* symphony]

sinfonietta /sin,fohniˈetə/ *n* **1** a short or lightly-orchestrated symphony **2** a small symphony orchestra; *also* a small orchestra of strings only [It, dim. of *sinfonia*]

sinful /ˈsinf(ə)l/ *adj* tainted with, marked by, or full of sin; wicked – **sinfully** *adv*, **sinfulness** *n*

sing /sing/ *vb* **sang** /sang/, **sung** /sung/; **sung** *vi* **1a** to produce musical sounds by means of the voice **b** to utter words in musical notes and with musical inflections and modulations (as a trained or professional singer) **2** to make a shrill whining or whistling sound **3** to produce musical or melodious sounds **4** to buzz, ring ⟨*a punch that made his ears* ~⟩ **5** to make a loud clear utterance **6** to give information or evidence – slang ~ *vt* **1** to utter with musical inflections; *esp* to interpret in musical notes produced by the voice **2a** to relate or celebrate in verse **b** to express vividly or enthusiastically ⟨~ *his praises*⟩ **3** to chant, intone ⟨~ *a requiem mass*⟩ **4** to bring to a specified state by singing ⟨~*s the child to sleep*⟩ [ME *singen*, fr OE *singan*; akin to OHG *singan* to sing, Gk *omphē* voice] – **singable** *adj*, **singer** *n*

singe /sinj/ *vt* **singeing; singed** to burn superficially or slightly; scorch; *esp* to remove the hair, down, or nap from, usu by brief exposure to a flame [ME *sengen*, fr OE *sengan*; akin to OHG bi*sengan* to singe] – **singe** *n*

Singhalese /ˌsing·gəˈleez/ *n or adj, pl* **Singhalese** (a) Sinhalese

[1]**single** /ˈsing·gl/ *adj* **1a** not married **b** of the unmarried state **2** not accompanied by others; sole ⟨*the* ~ *survivor of the disaster*⟩ **3a** consisting of or having only 1 part or feature ⟨*use double, not* ~ *thread*⟩ **b** *of a plant or flower* having the normal number of petals or ray flowers – compare DOUBLE **4** consisting of a separate unique whole; individual ⟨*food is our most important* ~ *need*⟩ **5** *of combat* involving only 2 people **6** of, suitable for, or involving only 1 person ⟨*a* ~ *portion of food*⟩ [ME, fr MF, fr L *singulus* one only; akin to L *sem-* one – more at SAME] – **singleness** *n*, **singly** /ˈsing·gli/ *adv*

[2]**single** *n* **1a** a single thing or amount; *esp* a single measure of spirits **b** a (young) unmarried adult ⟨*a* ~*s club*⟩ **2** a flower having the number of petals or ray flowers typical of the species **3** a single run scored in cricket **4** a gramophone record, esp of popular music, with a single short track on each side **5** *Br* a ticket bought for a trip to a place but not back again – compare RETURN 7

[3]**single** *vt* to select or distinguish from a number or group – usu + *out*

ˌ**single-ˈaction** *adj, of a firearm* that requires the hammer to be cocked before firing

single bed *n* a bed designed for 1 person to sleep in – **single-bedded** *adj*

ˌ**single-ˈblind** *adj* of or being an experimental procedure which is designed to eliminate false results, in which the experimenters, but not the subjects, know the make-up of the test and control groups during the actual course of the experiments – compare DOUBLE-BLIND

ˌ**single-ˈbreasted** *adj* having a centre fastening with 1 row of buttons ⟨*a* ~ *coat*⟩ – compare DOUBLE-BREASTED

single cream *n* cream that is thinner and lighter than double cream, contains 18 per cent butterfat, and is suitable for pouring – compare DOUBLE CREAM

ˌ**single ˈfile** *n* a line (e g of people) moving one behind the other

ˌ**single-ˈhanded** *adj* **1** performed or achieved by 1 person or with 1 on a side **2** working or managing alone or unassisted by others – **single-handed, single-handedly** *adv*, **single-handedness** *n*

ˌ**single-ˈminded** *adj* having a single overriding purpose – **single-mindedly** *adv*, **single-mindedness** *n*

ˌ**single-ˈphase** *adj* of or being an electrical circuit energized by a single alternating electromotive force

single reed *n* a thin flat cane reed attached to the mouthpiece of woodwind instruments of the clarinet family

ˈ**singles** *n, pl* **singles** a game (e g of tennis) with 1 player on each side

ˌ**single-ˈspace** *vt* to type (copy) leaving no blank lines between lines of text

ˈ**single,stick** /-ˌstik/ *n* one-handed fighting or fencing with a wooden stick; *also* the stick used

singlet /ˈsing·glit/ *n, chiefly Br* VEST 1; *also* a similar garment worn by athletes [fr its having only 1 thickness of cloth]

singleton /ˈsing·glt(ə)n/ *n* **1** a card that is the only one of its suit in a dealt hand **2** an individual as opposed to a pair or group; *specif* an offspring born singly [[1]*single* + *-ton* (as in *simpleton*)]

singsong /ˈsing,song/ *n* **1** a voice delivery characterized by a monotonous cadence or rhythm or rising and falling inflection **2** *Br* a session of group singing

[1]**singular** /ˈsing·gyoolə/ *adj* **1a** of a separate person or thing; individual **b** of or being a word form denoting 1 person, thing, or instance **2** distinguished by superiority; exceptional ⟨*a man of* ~ *attainments*⟩ **3** not general ⟨*a* ~ *proposition in logic*⟩ **4** very unusual or strange; peculiar ⟨*the* ~ *events leading up to the murder*⟩ **5** *of a mathematical matrix* having a determinant equal to zero [ME

singuler, fr MF, fr L *singularis*, fr *singulus* only one – more at SINGLE] – **singularize** *vt*, **singularly** *adv*

²**singular** *n* the singular number, the inflectional form denoting it, or a word in that form

singularity /ˌsing·gyooˈlarəti/ *n* **1** sthg singular: e g **a** a separate unit **b** an unusual or distinctive trait; a peculiarity **2** BLACK HOLE [¹SINGULAR + -ITY]

Sinhalese /ˌsinhəˈleez/ *n, pl* **Sinhalese** **1** a member of the predominant people that inhabit Sri Lanka **2** the Indic language of the Sinhalese ☞ LANGUAGE [Skt *Simhala* Sri Lanka (Ceylon), island in the Indian Ocean] – **Sinhalese** *adj*

sinister /ˈsinistə/ *adj* **1** (darkly or insidiously) evil or productive of vice **2** threatening evil or ill fortune; ominous **3** of or situated on the left side or to the left of sthg, esp in heraldry [ME *sinistre*, fr L *sinistr-, sinister* on the left side, unlucky, inauspicious] – **sinisterly** *adv*, **sinisterness** *n*

sinistral /ˈsinistrəl/ *adj* of or inclined to the left: e g **a** left-handed **b** *of the shell of a gastropod mollusc* having whorls that turn in a clockwise direction from the top to the bottom as viewed with the top towards the observer – compare DEXTRAL – **sinistrally** *adv*

sinistrorse /ˈsiniˌstraws, ˌ--ˈ-/ *adj* **1** *of a plant* twining spirally upwards round an axis from right to left – compare DEXTRORSE **2** SINISTRAL b [NL *sinistrorsus*, fr L, towards the left side, fr *sinistr-, sinister* + *versus*, pp of *vertere* to turn – more at ¹WORTH]

¹**sink** /sink/ *vb* **sank** /sangk/, **sunk** /sungk/; **sunk** *vi* **1a** to go down below a surface (e g of water or a soft substance) **2a** to fall or drop to a lower place or level ⟨sank *to his knees*⟩ **b** to disappear from view ⟨*a red sun* ~ing *slowly in the west*⟩ **c** to take on a hollow appearance ⟨*my cakes always* ~ *in the middle*⟩ **3** to become deeply absorbed ⟨sank *into a reverie*⟩ **4** to go downwards in quality, state, condition, amount, or worth ⟨sank *into apathy*⟩ ⟨~ing *spirits*⟩ **5** to deteriorate physically ⟨*the patient was* ~ing *fast and hadn't long to live*⟩ ~ *vt* **1a** to cause to sink ⟨~ *a battleship*⟩ **b** to force down, esp into the ground **c** to cause (sthg) to penetrate ⟨sank *the dagger into his chest*⟩ **2** to engage (oneself) completely *in* ⟨sank *himself in his work*⟩ **3** to dig or bore (a well or shaft) in the earth **4** to overwhelm, defeat ⟨*if we don't reach the frontier by midnight we're* sunk⟩ **5** to pay no heed to; ignore, suppress ⟨sank *their differences*⟩ **6** to invest **7** *Br* to drink down ⟨sank *a couple of pints*⟩ – infml [ME *sinken*, fr OE *sincan*; akin to OHG *sinkan* to sink, Arm *ankanim* I fall] – **sinkable** *adj*

²**sink** *n* **1a** a cesspool **b** a sewer **c** a basin, esp in a kitchen, connected to a drain and usu a water supply for washing up **2** a place of vice or corruption **3a** a depression in which water (e g from a river) collects and becomes absorbed or evaporated **b** SINKHOLE 2 **4** a body or process that stores or dissipates sthg (e g energy); *specif* HEAT SINK

sinkage /ˈsingkij/ *n* **1** the degree of sinking **2** a sunken area; a depression

sinker /ˈsingkə/ *n* a weight for sinking a fishing line, seine, or sounding line [¹SINK + ²-ER]

ˈ**sink** ˌ**hole** /-ˌhohl/ *n* **1** SINK 3a **2** a hollow, esp in a limestone region, that communicates with an underground cavern or passage

sink in *vi* **1** to enter a solid through the surface ⟨*don't leave the ink to* sink in⟩ **2** to become understood

ˈ**sinking** ˌ**fund** /ˈsingking/ *n* a fund set up and added to for paying off the original capital sum of a debt when it falls due

ˈ**sink-**ˌ**tidy** *n* **1** a small usu triangular container with a perforated base allowing wet kitchen waste to drain into the sink while retaining the solid waste for separate disposal **2** a container for washing-up implements, soap, etc kept near the sink

Sino- /sienoh-/ *comb form* **1** Chinese nation, people, or culture ⟨Sino*phile*⟩ **2** Chinese and ⟨Sino-*Tibetan*⟩ [F, fr LL *Sinae*]

sinologue /ˈsienəlog, ˈsinə-/ *n* a sinologist [F, fr LL *Sinae*, pl, Chinese (fr Gk *Sinai*, fr Ar *Sīn* China) + F *-logue*]

sinology /sieˈnoləji, si-/ *n* the study of the Chinese and esp of their language, literature, history, and culture [prob fr F *sinologie*, fr *sino-* + *-logie* -logy] – **sinologist** *n*, **sinological** /-nəˈlojikl/ *adj*

Sino-Tibetan /ˌsienoh tiˈbet(ə)n/ *adj or n* (of or being) a language family comprising Tibeto-Burman and Chinese

¹**sinter** /ˈsintə/ *n* a silica- or calcium-containing deposit formed by the evaporation of (hot) spring water [G, fr OHG *sintar* slag – more at CINDER]

²**sinter** *vb* to make into or become a coherent mass by heating without melting – **sinterability** /-rəˈbiləti/ *n*

sinuate /ˈsinyooˌayt/ *adj, esp of a leaf* having a wavy edge with strong indentations ☞ PLANT [L *sinuatus*, pp of *sinuare* to bend, fr *sinus* curve] – **sinuately** *adv*

sinuous /ˈsinyoo·əs/ *adj* **1a** of or having a serpentine or wavy form; winding **b** lithe, supple ⟨*dancers with a* ~ *grace*⟩ **2** intricate, tortuous ⟨~ *argumentation*⟩ [L *sinuosus*, fr *sinus*] – **sinuously** *adv*, **sinuousness**, **sinuosity** /-ˈosəti/ *n*

sinus /ˈsienəs/ *n* a cavity, hollow: e g **a** a narrow passage by which pus is discharged from a deep abscess or boil **b(1)** any of several cavities in the skull that usu communicate with the nostrils and contain air **(2)** a channel for blood from the veins **(3)** a wider part in a body duct or tube (e g a blood vessel) **c** a cleft or indentation between adjoining lobes (e g of a leaf) [NL, fr L, curve, fold, hollow]

sinusitis /ˌsienəˈsietis/ *n* inflammation of a nasal sinus [NL]

ˌ**sinus veˈnosus** /viˈnohsəs/ *n* an enlarged pouch that adjoins the heart and is the passage through which blood from the veins enters the heart in lower vertebrates and in the embryos of higher vertebrates [NL, venous sinus]

Sion /ˈsie·ən/ *n* Zion

Siouan /ˈsooh·ən/ *n* **1** a language stock of central and eastern N America ☞ LANGUAGE **2** a Sioux – **Siouan** *adj*

Sioux /sooh/ *n, pl* **Sioux** /sooh(z)/ a member of any of the peoples speaking Siouan languages [F, short for *Nadowessioux*, fr Ojibwa *Nadoweisiw*]

¹**sip** /sip/ *vb* **-pp-** to drink (sthg) delicately or a little at a time [ME *sippen*; akin to LG *sippen* to sip] – **sipper** *n*

²**sip** *n* (a small quantity imbibed by) sipping

¹**siphon, syphon** /ˈsiefən/ *n* **1a** a tube by which a liquid can be transferred up over the wall of a container to a lower level by using atmospheric pressure **b** a bottle for holding carbonated water that is driven out through a tube by the pressure of the carbon dioxide in the bottle, when a valve in the tube is opened **2** any of various tubular organs in animals,

esp molluscs or arthropods [F *siphon*, fr L *siphon-*, *sipho* tube, pipe, siphon, fr Gk *siphōn*]

[2]**siphon, syphon** *vt* to convey, draw off, or empty (as if) by a siphon ~ *vi* to pass or become conveyed (as if) by a siphon

siphonophore /sie'fonəfaw, 'siefə-/ *n* any of an order of transparent free-swimming or floating marine invertebrate animals that live as colonies [deriv of Gk *siphōn* + *pherein* to carry – more at [2]BEAR]

sippet /'sipit/ *n, chiefly Br* a small usu triangular piece of dry toast or fried bread used esp as garnish [alter. of *sop*]

sir /sə; *strong* suh/ *n* **1a** a man of rank or position **b** a man entitled to be addressed as *sir* – used as a title before the Christian name of a knight or baronet **2a** – used as a usu respectful form of address to a male **b** *cap* – used as a conventional form of address at the beginning of a letter [ME, fr *sire*]

sirdar /'suh,dah, ,-'-/ *n* **1** sby of high rank (e g a hereditary noble or military chief), esp in India **2** sby holding a position of authority in India [Hindi *sardār*, fr Per]

[1]**sire** /sie·ə/ *n* **1** the male parent of a (domestic) animal **2** *archaic* **a** a father **b** a male ancestor **3** a man of rank or authority; *esp* a lord – used formerly as a title and form of address [ME, father, master, fr OF, fr L *senior* older – more at SENIOR]

[2]**sire** *vt* **1** to beget – esp with reference to a male domestic animal **2** to bring into being; originate

siren /'sierən/ *n* **1** *often cap* any of a group of mythological partly human female creatures that lured mariners to destruction by their singing **2** a dangerously alluring or seductive woman; a temptress **3a** an apparatus producing musical tones by the rapid interruption of a current of air, steam, etc by a perforated rotating disc **b** a usu electrically operated device for producing a penetrating warning sound ⟨*an ambulance* ~⟩ ⟨*air-raid* ~s⟩ [ME, fr MF & L; MF *sereine*, fr LL *sirena*, fr L *siren*, fr Gk *seirēn*]

sirenian /sie'reenyən, -ni·ən/ *n* any of an order of aquatic plant-eating mammals including the manatee and dugong [NL *Sirenia*, order name, fr L *siren*]

'siren ,suit *n* a one-piece garment like a boiler suit with usu a zip in the front from the crotch to the neck edge [fr its being easy to put on when an air-raid siren sounded]

sirloin /'suh,loyn/ *n* a cut of beef from the upper part of the hind loin just in front of the rump ☞ MEAT [alter. of earlier *surloin*, modif of MF *surlonge*, fr *sur* over (fr L *super*) + *loigne, longe* loin – more at [1]OVER]

sirocco /si'rokoh/ *n, pl* **siroccos** **1** a hot dust-laden wind from the Libyan deserts that blows onto the N Mediterranean coast **2** a warm moist oppressive southeasterly wind in the same regions [It *scirocco, sirocco*, fr Ar *sharq* east]

sirrah *also* **sirra** /'sirə/ *n, obs* – used as a form of address implying inferiority in the person addressed [alter. of *sir*]

sirree *also* **siree** /sə'ree/ *n, NAm* sir – used for emphasis, usu after *yes* or *no* [by alter.]

sirup /'sirəp/ *n, NAm* (a) syrup – **sirupy** *adj*

sis /sis/ *n, chiefly NAm* SISTER 1, 5 – infml; used esp in direct address

-sis /-sis/ *suffix* (→ *n*), *pl* **-ses** /-seez/ process or action of ⟨*peristalsis*⟩ ⟨*analysis*⟩ [L, fr Gk, fem suffix of action]

sisal /'siesl/ *n* (a widely cultivated W Indian agave plant whose leaves yield) a strong white fibre used esp for ropes and twine [MexSp, fr *Sisal*, port in Yucatán, Mexico]

siskin /'siskin/ *n* a small Old World chiefly greenish and yellowish finch related to the goldfinch [G dial. *sisschen*, dim. of MHG *zīse* siskin, of Slav origin; akin to Czech *čížek* siskin]

sissy /'sissi/ *n or adj* (a) cissy – **sissy** *adj*

[1]**sister** /'sistə/ *n* **1a** a female having the same parents as another person ⟨*Mary and I are* ~s⟩ **b** HALF SISTER **2** *often cap* **a** a member of a women's religious order; *specif* (the title given to) a Roman Catholic nun **b** a female fellow member of a Christian church **3** a woman related to another person by a common tie or interest (e g adherence to feminist principles) **4** *chiefly Br* a female nurse; *esp* one who is next in rank below a nursing officer and is in charge of a ward or a small department **5** a girl, woman – used esp in direct address; infml [ME *suster, sister*, partly fr OE *sweostor* and partly of Scand origin; akin to ON *systir* sister; akin to L *soror* sister] – **sisterly** *adj*

[2]**sister** *adj* related (as if) by sisterhood; essentially similar ⟨~ *ships*⟩

'sisterhood /-hood/ *n* **1** the relationship between sisters **2** a society of women bound by religious vows

'sister-in-,law *n, pl* **sisters-in-law** **1** the sister of one's spouse **2** the wife of one's brother

,sister of 'mercy *n* a nun engaged in educational or charitable work

sistrum /'sistrəm/ *n, pl* **sistrums, sistra** /'sistrə/ an ancient percussion instrument, used esp in Egypt, with metal rods or loops that jingle when shaken [ME, fr L, fr Gk *seistron*, fr *seiein* to shake – more at SEISMIC]

Sisyphean, Sisyphian /,sisi'fee·ən/ *adj* both endless and fruitless ⟨*a* ~ *task*⟩ [*Sisyphus*, mythical king condemned in Hades to roll uphill a heavy stone that constantly rolled down again, fr L, fr Gk *Sisyphos*]

[1]**sit** /sit/ *vb* **-tt-; sat** /sat/ *vi* **1a** to rest on the buttocks or haunches ⟨~ *in a chair*⟩ **b** to perch, roost **2** to occupy a place as a member of an official body ⟨~ *on the parish council*⟩ **3** to be in session for official business ⟨*visited London when Parliament was* ~ting⟩ **4** to cover eggs for hatching **5a** to take up a position for being photographed or painted **b** to act as a model **6** to lie or hang relative to a wearer ⟨*the collar* ~s *awkwardly*⟩ **7** to lie, rest ⟨*a kettle* ~ting *on the stove*⟩ **8** to be situated ⟨*the house* ~s *well back from the road*⟩ **9** to remain inactive or unused ⟨*the car just* ~s *in the garage all day*⟩ **10** to take an examination **11** to baby-sit ~ *vt* **1** to cause to be seated; place on or in a seat **2** to sit on (eggs) **3** to keep one's seat on ⟨~ *a horse*⟩ **4** *Br* to take part in (an examination) as a candidate [ME *sitten*, fr OE *sittan*; akin to OHG *sizzen* to sit, L *sedēre*, Gk *hezesthai* to sit, *hedra* seat] – **sit on** **1** to repress, squash **2** to delay action or decision concerning – **sit on one's hands** to fail to take action – **sit on the fence** to adopt a position of neutrality or indecision

[2]**sit** *n* an act or period of sitting ⟨*had a long* ~ *at the station between trains*⟩

sitar /si'tah/ *n* an Indian lute with a long neck and a varying number of strings [Hindi *sitār*] – **sitarist** *n*

sit back *vi* to relinquish one's efforts or responsibility ⟨*magistrates who* sit back *and accept police objections – Yorkshire Post*⟩

sitcom /'sit,kom/ *n* SITUATION COMEDY [*sit*uation *com*edy]

[1]site /siet/ *n* **1a** an area of ground that was, is, or will be occupied by a structure or set of structures (e g a building, town, or monument) ⟨*an archaeological* ~⟩ **b** an area of ground or scene of some specified activity ⟨*caravan* ~⟩ ⟨*battle* ~⟩ ⟨*building* ~⟩ **2** the place, scene, or point of sthg ⟨*the* ~ *of the wound*⟩ [ME, place, position, fr MF or L; MF, fr L *situs*, fr *situs*, pp of *sinere* to leave, place, lay; akin to L *serere* to sow – more at [2]SOW]

[2]site *vt* to place on a site or in position; locate

'sit-,in *n* a continuous occupation of a building by a body of people as a protest and means towards forcing compliance with demands

sit in *vi* **1** to participate as a visitor or observer – usu + *on* ⟨sit in *on a group discussion*⟩ **2** to stage a sit-in

Sitka spruce /'sitkə/ *n* a tall spruce native to N America [*Sitka*, town in Alaska]

sit out *vt* **1** to remain until the end of or the departure of ⟨sit *the film* out⟩ **2** to refrain from participating in

sitter /'sitə/ *n* **1** sby who sits (e g as an artist's model) **2** a baby-sitter

[1]sitting /'siting/ *n* **1** a single occasion of continuous sitting (e g for a portrait or meal) **2** a batch of eggs for incubation **3** a session [[1]SIT + [2]-ING]

[2]sitting *adj* **1** that is sitting ⟨*a* ~ *hen*⟩ **2** in office or actual possession ⟨*the* ~ *member for Leeds East*⟩ – **sitting pretty** in a highly favourable or satisfying position

,sitting 'duck *n* an easy or defenceless target for attack, criticism, or exploitation

'sitting ,room *n* a room, esp in a private house, used for recreation and relaxation

,sitting 'target SITTING DUCK

,sitting 'tenant *n, Br* a tenant who is at the present time in occupation (e g of a house or flat)

[1]situate /'sityoo,ayt, 'sichoo-, -ət/ *adj* having a site; located – fml [ML *situatus*, pp of *situare* to place, fr L *situs*]

[2]situate /'sityoo,ayt, 'sichoo-/ *vt* to place in a site, situation, or category; locate

situated /'sityoo,aytid, 'sichoo-/ *adj* **1** located **2** supplied to the specified extent with money or possessions ⟨*comfortably* ~⟩ **3** being in the specified situation ⟨*rather awkwardly* ~⟩

,situ'ation /,sityoo'aysh(ə)n, ,sichoo-/ *n* **1a** the way in which sthg is placed in relation to its surroundings **b** a locality ⟨*a house in a windswept* ~⟩ **2** position with respect to conditions and circumstances ⟨*the military* ~ *remains obscure*⟩ **3a** the circumstances at a particular moment; *esp* a critical or problematic state of affairs ⟨*the* ~ *called for swift action*⟩ **b** a particular (complicated) state of affairs at a stage in the action of a narrative or drama **4** a position of employment; a post – chiefly fml ⟨*found a* ~ *as a gardener*⟩ – **situational** *adj*

situation comedy *n* a radio or television comedy series that involves the same basic cast of characters in a succession of connected or unconnected episodes

sit up *vi* **1a** to rise from a reclining to a sitting position **b** to sit with the back straight **2** to show interest, alertness, or surprise ⟨*news that made him* sit up⟩ **3** to stay up after the usual time for going to bed ⟨sat up *to watch the late film*⟩

situs /'sietəs/ *n* the place where sthg exists or originates; *specif* the place where sthg (e g a right) is held to be located in law [L – more at SITE]

Siva, Shiva /'s(h)ivə, 's(h)eevə/ *n* the god of destruction and regeneration in the Hindu sacred triad – compare BRAHMA, VISHNU [Skt *Śiva*]

six /siks/ *n* **1** ☞ NUMBER **2** the sixth in a set or series ⟨*the* ~ *of spades*⟩ **3** sthg having 6 parts or members or a denomination of 6: e g **a** a shot in cricket that crosses the boundary before it bounces and so scores 6 runs **b** the smallest unit in a cub-scout or brownie- guide pack **c** *pl in constr, cap the* Common Market countries before 1973 [ME, fr *six*, adj, fr OE *siex*; akin to OHG *sehs* six, L *sex*, Gk *hex*] – **six** *adj or pron*, **sixfold** *adj or adv* – **at sixes and sevens** in disorder, confused, or in a muddle – **for six** so as to be totally wrecked or defeated ⟨*trade balance went* for six – *The Economist*⟩

sixer /'siksə/ *n* the leader of a cub-scout or brownie-guide six

'six-,gun *n* a 6-chambered revolver

,six of the 'best *n, Br* a severe beating

'six-,pack *n* (a container for) 6 bottles or cans bought together

'six-,shooter *n* a six-gun

sixteen /,sik'steen/ *n* **1** ☞ NUMBER **2** *pl but sing in constr* a book format in which a folded sheet forms 16 leaves [ME *sixtene*, fr OE *sixtȳne*, adj; akin to OE *tīen* ten] – **sixteen** *adj or pron*, **sixteenth** *adj or n*

sixteenth note /siks'teenth/ *n, NAm* a semiquaver

sixth /siksth/ *n* **1** ☞ NUMBER **2a** (the combination of 2 notes at) a musical interval of 6 diatonic degrees **b** the submediant – **sixth** *adj or adv*, **sixthly** *adv*

'sixth ,form *n* the highest section of a British secondary school – **sixth-former** *n*

,sixth 'sense *n* a keen intuitive power viewed as analogous to the 5 physical senses

sixty /'siksti/ *n* **1** ☞ NUMBER **2** *pl* the numbers 60-69; *specif* a range of temperatures, ages, or dates in a century characterized by those numbers [ME, fr *sixty*, adj, fr OE *siextig*, n, group of sixty, fr *siex* six + *-tig* group of ten – more at [1]-TY] – **sixtieth** /-ith/ *adj or n*, **sixty** *adj or pron*, **sixtyfold** /-,fohld/ *adj or adv*

,sixty-'nine *n* **1** ☞ NUMBER **2** soixante-neuf

sizable, sizeable /'siezəbl/ *adj* fairly large; considerable – **sizableness** *n*, **sizably** *adv*

sizar /'siezə/ *n* a poor student (e g at Cambridge) who paid lower fees and orig acted as a servant to other students in return [*sizar* alter. of *sizer*, fr [1]*size* (in obs sense of fixed portion of food and drink allowed esp to a university student)]

[1]size /siez/ *n* **1a** physical magnitude, extent, or bulk; relative or proportionate dimensions **b** relative amount or number **c** bigness ⟨*you should have seen the* ~ *of him*⟩ **2** any of a series of graduated measures, esp of manufactured articles (e g of clothing), conventionally identified by numbers or letters

⟨*a ~ 7 hat*⟩ **3** *the* actual state of affairs – infml ⟨*that's about the ~ of it*⟩ [ME *sise* assize, fr MF, fr OF, short for *assise* – more at ASSIZE]

[2]**size** *vt* **1** to make in a particular size ⟨*systems ~d to fit anyone's living room*⟩ **2** to arrange or grade according to size or bulk

[3]**size** *n* any of various thick and sticky materials (e g preparations of glue, flour, varnish, or resins) used for filling the pores in surfaces (e g of paper, textiles, leather, or plaster) or for applying colour or metal leaf (e g to book edges or covers) [ME *sise*, prob fr MF, setting, fixing, fr OF, settlement, assize]

[4]**size** *vt* to cover, stiffen, or glaze (as if) with size

[5]**size** *adj* SIZED 1 – usu in combination ⟨*a bite-*size *biscuit*⟩

sized /siezd/ *adj* **1** having a specified size or bulk – usu in combination ⟨*a small-*sized *house*⟩ **2** arranged or graded according to size

size up *vt* to form a judgment of

sizing /ˈsiezing/ *n* [3]SIZE

sizzle /ˈsizl/ *vi* **sizzling** /ˈsizling, ˈsizl·ing/ to make a hissing sound (as if) in frying [perh freq of *siss* (to hiss), fr ME *sissen*, of imit origin] – **sizzle** *n*, **sizzler** *n*

sizzling /ˈsizling, ˈsizl·ing/ *adj* full of zest or pungency; racy

sjambok /ˈshambok/ *n* a whip of rhinoceros hide used esp in S Africa [Afrik, *sambok, sjambok*, fr Malay *cambok* large whip, fr Hindi *cābuk*]

ska /skah/ *n* popular music of W Indian origin that is the forerunner of and similar to reggae [Jamaican E, of imit origin]

skald /skawld, skold/ *n* a poet of ancient Scandinavia; *broadly* a bard [ON *skāld* – more at SCOLD] – **skaldic** *adj*

[1]**skate** /skayt/ *n, pl* **skate,** *esp for different types* **skates** any of numerous rays that have greatly developed pectoral fins and many of which are important food fishes [ME *scate*, fr ON *skata*]

[2]**skate** *n* **1a** ROLLER SKATE **b** ICE SKATE **2** a period of skating [modif of D *schaats* stilt, skate, fr (assumed) ONF *escache* stilt; akin to OF *eschace* stilt]

[3]**skate** *vi* **1** to glide along on skates propelled by the alternate action of the legs **2** to glide or slide as if on skates **3** to proceed in a superficial manner ~ *vt* to go along or through (a place) or perform (an action) by skating – **skater** *n*

ˈ**skate,board** /-ˌbawd/ *n* a narrow board about 60cm (2ft) long mounted on roller-skate wheels – **skateboarder** *n*, **skateboarding** *n*

skedaddle /skiˈdadl/ *vi* **skedaddling** /skiˈdadling, -ˈdadl·ing/ to run away; *specif* to disperse rapidly – often imper; infml [origin unknown]

skeet /skeet/ *n* trapshooting in which clay targets are hurled across the shooting range from traps on either side [modif of ON *skjōta* to shoot – more at [1]SHOOT]

skein /skayn/ *n* **1** a loosely coiled length of yarn or thread; HANK 1 **2** sthg suggesting the twists or coils of a skein; a tangle ⟨*unravel the ~ of evidence*⟩ **3** a flock of wildfowl (e g geese) in flight [ME *skeyne*, fr MF *escaigne*]

skeletal /ˈskelitl/ *adj* of, forming, attached to, or resembling a skeleton – **skeletally** /-tli/ *adv*

skeleton /ˈskelitn/ *n* **1** a supportive or protective usu rigid structure or framework of an organism; *esp* the bony or more or less cartilaginous framework supporting the soft tissues and protecting the internal organs of a vertebrate (e g a fish or mammal) ☞ ANATOMY **2** sthg reduced to its bare essentials **3** an emaciated person or animal **4** a basic structural framework **5** a secret cause of shame, esp in a family – often in *skeleton in the cupboard* [NL, fr Gk, neut of *skeletos* dried up; akin to Gk *skellein* to dry up, *sklēros* hard, OE *sceald* shallow] – **skeleton** *adj*, **skeletonize** *vt*, **skeletonic** /ˌskeliˈtonik/ *adj*

skeleton key *n* a key, esp one with most or all of the serrations absent, that is able to open many simple locks

skelp /skelp/ *n, chiefly Scot* a slap, spank – chiefly infml [ME, fr *skelpen* to strike, slap, prob of imit origin] – **skelp** *vt*

skep /skep/ *n* **1** a farm basket used esp in mucking out stables **2** a beehive (of twisted straw) [ME *skeppe* basket, basketful, fr OE *sceppe*, fr ON *skeppa* bushel; akin to OE *scieppan* to form, create – more at SHAPE]

skepsis /ˈskepsis/ *n, chiefly NAm* scepsis

skeptic /ˈskeptik/ *n, chiefly NAm* a sceptic – **skeptical** *adj*, **skeptically** *adv*, **skepticism** /-ˌsiz(ə)m/ *n*

skerry /ˈskeri/ *n* a rocky island; a reef [of Scand origin; akin to ON *sker* skerry & to ON *ey* island; akin to L *aqua* water – more at [1]SCAR, ISLAND]

[1]**sketch** /skech/ *n* **1** a preliminary study or draft; *esp* a rough often preliminary drawing representing the chief features of an object or scene **2** a brief description or outline ⟨*gave a ~ of his personality*⟩ **3a** a short discursive literary composition **b** a short musical composition, usu for piano **c** a short theatrical piece having a single scene; *esp* a comic variety act [D *schets*, fr It *schizzo*, fr *schizzare* to splash]

[2]**sketch** *vt* to make a sketch, rough draft, or outline of ~ *vi* to draw or paint a sketch – **sketcher** *n*

ˈ**sketch,block** /-ˌblok/ *n* a sketchbook

ˈ**sketch,book** /-ˌbook/ *n* a book of usu detachable leaves of paper used for sketching

sketchy /ˈskechi/ *adj* lacking completeness, clarity, or substance; superficial, scanty [[1]SKETCH + [1]-Y] – **sketchily** *adv*, **sketchiness** *n*

[1]**skew** /skyooh/ *vi* to take an oblique course; twist ~ *vt* **1** to cause to skew **2** to distort from a true value or symmetrical curve ⟨~ed *statistical data*⟩ [ME *skewen* to escape, skew, fr ONF *escuer* to shun, of Gmc origin; akin to OHG *sciuhen* to frighten off – more at [1]SHY]

[2]**skew** *adj* **1** set, placed, or running obliquely **2** more developed on one side or in one direction than another; not symmetrical – **skewness** *n*

[3]**skew** *n* a deviation from a straight line or symmetrical curve

ˈ**skew,bald** /-ˌbawld/ *n or adj* (an animal) marked with spots and patches of white and another colour, esp not black [*skewed* (skewbald) + *bald*]

[1]**skewer** /ˈskyooh·ə/ *n* **1** a long pin of wood or metal used chiefly to fasten a piece of meat together while roasting or to hold small pieces of food for grilling (e g for a kebab) **2** sthg like a meat skewer in form or function [alter. of E dial. *skiver*, of unknown origin]

[2]**skewer** *vt* to fasten or pierce (as if) with a skewer

ˌ**skew-ˈwhiff** /ˈwif/ *adj, Br* askew – infml [[1]*skew* + *whiff*, vb]

[1]**ski** /skee/ *n, pl* **skis** **1a** a long narrow strip usu of wood, metal, or plastic that curves upwards in front and is typically one of a pair used esp for gliding over snow **b** WATER SKI **2** a runner on a vehicle [Norw,

fr ON *skīth* stick of wood, ski; akin to OHG *skīt* stick of wood, OE *scēadan* to divide – more at [1]SHED]

[2]**ski** *vb* **skiing; skied** to glide (over) on skis as a way of travelling or as a recreation or sport – **skiable** *adj*, **skier** *n*

skibob /'skee,bob/ *n* a bicycle-like vehicle with short skis in place of wheels that is used for gliding downhill over snow by a rider wearing miniature skis for balance [[1]*ski* + *bob* (as in *bobsleigh*)] – **skibobber** *n*, **skibobbing** *n*

[1]**skid** /skid/ *n* **1** a plank or log used to support or elevate a structure or object **2** a ship's fender **3** a device placed under a wheel to prevent its turning or used as a drag **4** the act of skidding; a slide **5** a runner used as part of the undercarriage of an aircraft **6** *pl* a road to defeat or downfall – in *hit the skids, on the skids*; infml [perh of Scand origin; akin to ON *skīth* stick of wood] – **skiddy** *adj*

[2]**skid** *vb* **-dd-** *vt* **1** to apply a brake or skid to **2** to haul along, slide, hoist, or store on skids ~ *vi of a vehicle, wheel, driver, etc* to slip or slide, esp out of control – **skidder** *n*

skiddoo /ski'dooh/ *vi* **skiddoos; skiddooing; skiddooed** *chiefly NAm* to go away; leave – often imper; infml [prob alter. of *skedaddle*]

'skid-,lid *n, Br* a motorcyclist's crash helmet – infml

'skid,pan /-,pan/ *n, chiefly Br* a slippery surface on which vehicle drivers may practise the control of skids

,skid 'row /roh/ *n, chiefly NAm* a district frequented by down-and-outs and alcoholics [alter. of *skid road* (road along which logs are skidded, part of town frequented by lumberjacks)]

skiey /'skie·i/ *adj* skyey

skiff /skif/ *n* a light rowing or sailing boat [MF or OIt; MF *esquif*, fr OIt *schifo*, of Gmc origin; akin to OE *scip* ship]

skiffle /'skifl/ *n* jazz or folk music played by a group and using nonstandard instruments or noisemakers (e g washboards or Jew's harps) [perh imit]

skilful, *NAm chiefly* **skillful** /'skilf(ə)l/ *adj* possessing or displaying skill; expert – **skilfully** *adv*

'ski ,lift *n* a power-driven conveyer consisting usu of a series of bars or seats suspended from an endless overhead moving cable and used for transporting skiers or sightseers up and down a long slope or mountainside

skill /skil/ *n* **1** the ability to utilize one's knowledge effectively and readily **2** a developed aptitude or ability in a particular field ⟨*knitted with remarkable* ~⟩ [ME *skil*, fr ON, distinction, knowledge; akin to OE *scylian* to separate, *sciell* shell – more at SHELL] – **skill-less** *adj*

skilled *adj* **1** having mastery of or proficiency in sthg (e g a technique or trade) **2** of, being, or requiring workers with skill and training in a particular occupation or craft – compare UNSKILLED, SEMISKILLED

skillet /'skilit/ *n* **1** *chiefly Br* a small saucepan usu having 3 or 4 legs and used for cooking on the hearth **2** *chiefly NAm* FRYING PAN [ME *skelet*, perh fr MF *escuelete* small platter, dim. of *escuele* platter, deriv of L *scutella*]

skillion /'skilyən/ *n, Austr* a roof (e g of a lean-to) that slopes in only 1 direction [alter. of E dial. *skeeling, skilling* (outbuilding attached like a lean-to to another), fr ME *skelyng*]

[1]**skim** /skim/ *vb* **-mm-** *vt* **1a** to clear (a liquid) of floating matter ⟨~ *boiling syrup*⟩ **b** to remove (e g film or scum) from the surface of a liquid **c** to remove cream from by skimming **d(1)** to remove the best or most accessible contents from **(2)** to remove (the choicest part or members) from sthg; cream **2** to read, study, or examine cursorily and rapidly; *specif* to glance through (e g a book) for the chief ideas or the plot **3** to throw so as to ricochet along the surface of water **4** to pass swiftly or lightly over ~ *vi* **1** to glide lightly or smoothly along or just above a surface **2** to give a cursory glance or consideration *USE* (*vt 1b & 1d(2)*) often + *off* [ME *skimmen*, prob alter. of *scumen* to remove scum from, fr *scum*]

[2]**skim** *n* **1** a thin layer, coating, or film **2** the act of skimming

[3]**skim** *adj* having the cream removed by skimming ⟨~ *milk*⟩

skimmer /'skimə/ *n* **1** a flat perforated scoop or spoon used for skimming **2** any of several long-winged sea birds that feed by flying with the elongated lower part of the beak immersed in the sea [[1]SKIM + [2]-ER]

skimming /'skiming/ *n* that which is skimmed from a liquid – usu pl with sing. meaning

skimp /skimp/ *vt* to give insufficient or barely sufficient attention or effort to or money for ~ *vi* to save (as if) by skimping sthg [*skimp* (barely sufficient), perh alter. of *scrimp* (scanty)]

skimpy /'skimpi/ *adj* inadequate in quality, size, etc; scanty ⟨*a* ~ *meal*⟩ – **skimpily** *adv*, **skimpiness** *n*

[1]**skin** /skin/ *n* **1a** the external covering of an animal (e g a fur-bearing mammal or a bird) separated from the body, usu with its hair or feathers; pelt **b(1)** the pelt of an animal prepared for use as a trimming or in a garment ⟨*it took 40* ~s *to make the coat*⟩ – compare [4]HIDE **(2)** a container (e g for wine or water) made of animal skin **2a** the external limiting layer of an animal body, esp when forming a tough but flexible cover ☞ NERVE **b** any of various outer or surface layers (e g a rind, husk, or film) ⟨*a sausage* ~⟩ **3** the life or welfare of a person – esp in *save one's skin* **4** a sheathing or casing forming the outside surface of a ship, aircraft, etc [ME, fr ON *skinn*; akin to OE *scinn* skin, MHG *schint* fruit peel, W *ysgythru* to cut] – **skinless** *adj* – **by the skin of one's teeth** by a very narrow margin – **under the skin** beneath apparent or surface differences; fundamentally

[2]**skin** *vb* **-nn-** *vt* **1a** to cover (as if) with skin **b** to heal over with skin **2a** to strip, scrape, or rub away an outer covering (e g the skin or rind) of **b** to strip or peel off like skin ⟨~ *the insulation from the wire*⟩ **c** to cut, graze, or damage the surface of ⟨*fell and* ~ned *his knee*⟩ **3** to strip of money or property; fleece – infml ~ *vi* to become covered (as if) with skin – usu + *over* ⟨*the wound had* ~ned *over within a week*⟩

,skin-'deep *adj* **1** as deep as the skin **2** superficial ⟨*beauty is only* ~⟩

'skin ,diving *n* swimming under water with a face mask and flippers and sometimes with an aqualung – **skin diver** *n*

'skin ef,fect *n* an effect characteristic of the distribution of an electrical current in a conductor at high frequencies by virtue of which most of the current passes through the surface of the conductor rather than in its interior

ˈskin ˌflick *n* a film characterized by nudity and explicit sexual situations – infml

ˈskinˌflint /-ˌflint/ *n* a miser, niggard [[2]*skin* + *flint*]

ˈskinˌful /-f(ə)l/ *n* an ample or satisfying quantity, esp of alcoholic drink – infml

ˈskin ˌgame *n, NAm* a swindling game or trick [[2]*skin*]

ˈskin ˌgraft *n* a piece of skin that is taken from one area to replace skin in a defective or damaged area – **skin grafting** *n*

ˈskinˌhead /-ˌhed/ *n* **1** a person whose hair is cut very short **2** any of a group of young British people with very short hair and a distinctive way of dressing

skink /skingk/ *n* any of a family of mostly small lizards that have small scales [L *scincus*, fr Gk *skinkos*]

skinned /skind/ *adj* having skin, esp of a specified kind – usu in combination ⟨*dark*-skinned⟩

skinner /ˈskinə/ *n* one who deals in skins, pelts, or hides

skinny /ˈskini/ *adj* very thin; lean, emaciated – infml [[1]SKIN + [1]-Y] – **skinniness** *n*

skint /skint/ *adj, Br* penniless – infml [alter. of *skinned*, pp of [2]*skin*]

ˌskinˈtight /-ˈtiet/ *adj* extremely closely fitted to the body ⟨~ *jeans*⟩

[1]skip /skip/ *vb* **-pp-** *vi* **1a(1)** to move or proceed with light leaps and bounds; gambol **(2)** to swing a rope round the body from head to toe, making a small jump each time it passes beneath the feet **b** to rebound from one point or thing after another; ricochet **2** to leave hurriedly or secretly; abscond ⟨~ped *out without paying his bill*⟩ **3** to pass over or omit an interval, section, or step ⟨*the story* ~s *to the present day*⟩ ~ *vt* **1** to leave out (a step in a progression or series); omit **2** to cause to ricochet across a surface; skim ⟨~ *a stone over a pond*⟩ **3** to fail to attend ⟨*decided to* ~ *church that Sunday*⟩ **4** *chiefly NAm* to depart from quickly and secretly ⟨~ped *town*⟩ – infml [ME *skippen*, perh of Scand origin; akin to Sw dial. *skopa* to hop]

[2]skip *n* **1** a light bounding step or gait **2** an act of omission (e g in reading)

[3]skip *n* the captain of a side in some games (e g curling or bowls) [short for [2]*skipper*]

[4]skip *n* **1** SKEP 1 **2** a bucket or cage for carrying men and materials (e g in mining or quarrying) **3** a large open container for waste or rubble [alter. of *skep*]

ˈskipˌjack /-jak/ *n, pl* **skipjacks** CLICK BEETLE [[1]*skip* + [1]*jack*; fr its habit of suddenly springing into the air]

[1]skipper /ˈskipə/ *n* any of numerous small butterflies that differ from the typical butterflies in the arrangement of the veins in the wings and the form of the antennae [[1]SKIP + [2]-ER]

[2]skipper *n* **1** the master of a fishing, small trading, or pleasure boat **2** the captain or first pilot of an aircraft **3** *Br* the captain of a sports team *USE* (*2&3*) infml [ME, fr MD *schipper*, fr *schip* ship; akin to OE *scip* ship – more at SHIP]

[3]skipper *vt* to act as skipper of (e g a boat)

ˈskipping-ˌrope /ˈskiping/ *n* a length of rope that is rotated over the head and jumped over as it passes under the feet as an exercise or game

skirl /skuhl/ *vi or n* (to emit) the high shrill sound of a bagpipe [vb ME (Sc) *skrillen, skirlen*, of Scand origin; akin to OSw *skrælla* to rattle; akin to OE *scrallettan* to sound loudly; n fr vb]

[1]skirmish /ˈskuhmish/ *n* **1** a minor or irregular fight in war, usu between small outlying detachments **2** a brief preliminary conflict; *broadly* any minor or petty dispute [ME *skyrmissh*, alter. of *skarmish*, fr MF *escarmouche*, fr OIt *scaramuccia*, of Gmc origin; akin to OHG *skirmen* to defend]

[2]skirmish *vi* to engage in a skirmish – **skirmisher** *n*

skirr /skuh/ *vi* to move rapidly, esp with a whirring or grating sound ⟨*birds* ~ed *off from the bushes* – D H Lawrence⟩ [perh alter. of [1]*scour*]

[1]skirt /skuht/ *n* **1a(1)** a free-hanging part of a garment (e g a coat) extending from the waist down **(2)** a garment or undergarment worn by women and girls that hangs from and fits closely round the waist ☞ GARMENT **b** either of 2 usu leather flaps on a saddle covering the bars on which the stirrups are hung **c** a flexible wall containing the air cushion of a hovercraft **2** the borders or outer edge of an area or group – often pl with sing. meaning **3** a part or attachment serving as a rim, border, or edging **4** *Br* any of various usu membranous and gristly cuts of beef from the flank **5** a girl, woman – slang [ME, fr ON *skyrta* shirt, kirtle – more at SHIRT] – **skirted** *adj*

[2]skirt *vt* **1** to extend along or form the border or edge of; border **2** to provide a skirt for **3** to go or pass round; *specif* to avoid through fear of difficulty, danger, or dispute ⟨~ed *the minefield*⟩ ⟨~ed *the crucial issues*⟩ ~ *vi* to be, lie, or move along an edge, border, or margin ⟨~ *round the coast*⟩ – **skirter** *n*

skirting /ˈskuhting/ *n* fabric suitable for skirts [[2]SKIRT + [2]-ING]

ˈskirting ˌboard *n, Br* a board, esp with decorative moulding, that is fixed to the base of a wall and that covers the joint of the wall and floor

ˈski ˌrun /skee/ *n* a slope or trail for skiing

skit /skit/ *n* a satirical or humorous story or sketch ⟨*did a* ~ *on Queen Victoria*⟩ [origin unknown]

skite /skiet/ *vi, Austr & NZ* to brag, boast – infml [perh fr E dial. *skite* (to defecate), fr ME *skyten*, fr ON *skīta*]

skitter /ˈskitə/ *vi* **1a** to glide or skip lightly or swiftly **b** to skim along a surface **2** to twitch a fishing lure or baited hook through or along the surface of water ~ *vt* to cause to skitter [prob freq of E dial. *skite* (to move quickly), prob of Scand origin] – **skitter** *n*

skittish /ˈskitish/ *adj* **1a** lively or frisky in behaviour; capricious **b** variable, fickle **2** easily frightened; restive ⟨*a* ~ *horse*⟩ [ME] – **skittishly** *adv*, **skittishness** *n*

skittle /ˈskitl/ *n* **1** *pl but sing in constr* any of various bowling games played with 9 pins and wooden balls or discs **2** a pin used in skittles [perh of Scand origin; akin to ON *skutill* bolt – more at SHUTTLE]

skittle out *vt* to dismiss (a batting side in cricket) for a low score

skive /skiev/ *vt* to cut off (e g leather or rubber) in thin layers or pieces; pare ~ *vi*, *Br* to evade one's work or duty, esp out of laziness; shirk – often + *off*; infml [of Scand origin; akin to ON *skifa* to slice; akin to OE *scēadan* to divide – more at [1]SHED]

skiver /'skievə/ *n* **1** a thin soft leather made from a split sheepskin **2** *Br* sby who skives off – infml

[1]**skivvy** /'skivi/ *n, Br* a female domestic servant [origin unknown]

[2]**skivvy** *vi, Br* to perform menial domestic tasks; act as a skivvy

skoal /skohl/ *n* cheers, health – usu used interjectionally as a toast [Dan *skaal*, lit., cup; akin to ON *skāl* bowl – more at [1]SCALE]

skolly /'skoli/ *n, chiefly SAfr* a young non-white thug [Afrik, prob fr D *schoelje* rogue, rascal]

skua /'skyooh·ə/ *n* any of several large dark-coloured seabirds of northern and southern seas that tend to harass weaker birds until they drop or disgorge the fish they have caught [NL, fr Faeroese *skūgvur*, akin to ON *skūfr* tassel, skua, OE *scēaf* sheaf – more at SHEAF]

skulduggery, skullduggery /skul'dugəri/ *n* devious trickery; *esp* underhand or unscrupulous behaviour [alter. of earlier *sculduddery* (gross or lewd conduct), of unknown origin]

skulk /skulk/ *vi* **1** to move in a stealthy or furtive manner; slink **2** to hide or conceal oneself, esp out of cowardice or fear or for a sinister purpose; lurk [ME *skulken*, of Scand origin; akin to Dan *skulke* to shirk, play truant] – **skulker** *n*

skull /skul/ *n* **1** the skeleton of the head of a vertebrate animal forming a bony or cartilaginous case that encloses and protects the brain and chief sense organs and supports the jaws ☞ ANATOMY **2** the seat of understanding or intelligence; the brain – usu derog ⟨*get that fact into your thick* ~*!*⟩ [ME *skulle*, of Scand origin; akin to Sw *skulle* skull] – **skulled** *adj*

,skull and 'crossbones /'kros,bohnz/ *n, pl* **skulls and crossbones** a representation of a human skull over crossbones, usu used as a warning of danger to life

'skull,cap /-,kap/ *n* **1** a closely fitting cap; *esp* a light brimless cap for indoor wear **2** any of various plants having a helmet-shaped calyx

skunk /skungk/ *n, pl* **skunks,** *esp collectively* **skunk** **1a** any of various common black-and-white New World mammals that have a pair of anal glands from which a foul-smelling secretion is ejected ☞ DEFENCE **b** the fur of a skunk **2** a thoroughly obnoxious person – infml [of Algonquian origin; akin to Abnaki *segākw* skunk]

[1]**sky** /skie/ *n* **1** the upper atmosphere when seen as an apparent great vault over the earth; the firmament, heavens **2** HEAVEN 2 **3a** weather as manifested by the condition of the sky ⟨*a clear* ~⟩ **b** climate [ME, cloud, sky, fr ON *sk*ȳ cloud; akin to OE *scēo* cloud, L *cutis* skin – more at [4]HIDE]

[2]**sky** *vt* **skied, skyed** *chiefly Br* to throw, toss, or hit (e g a ball) high in the air

,sky 'blue *adj or n* (of) the light blue colour of the sky on a clear day

'sky,diving /-,dieving/ *n* jumping from an aeroplane and executing body manoeuvres while in free-fall before pulling the rip cord of a parachute – **sky diver** *n*

,Skye 'terrier /skie/ *n* (any of) a Scottish breed of short-legged terriers [*Skye*, island of Inner Hebrides, Scotland]

skyey, skiey /'skie·i/ *adj* of the sky; ethereal

,sky-'high *adv or adj* **1a** very high **b** to a high level or degree ⟨*prices rose* ~⟩ **2** to bits; apart – in *blow sthg sky-high*

'sky,jack /-jak/ *vt* to hijack (an aircraft) [*sky* + *-jack* (as in *hijack*)] – **skyjacker** *n*

[1]**'sky,lark** /-,lahk/ *n* a common largely brown Old World lark noted for its song, esp as uttered in vertical flight or while hovering

[2]**skylark** *vi* to act in a high-spirited or mischievous manner; frolic – **skylarker** *n*

'sky,light /-,liet/ *n* **1** the diffused and reflected light of the sky **2** a window or group of windows in a roof or ceiling

'sky,line /-,lien/ *n* **1** the apparent juncture of earth and sky; the horizon **2** an outline (e g of buildings or a mountain range) against the background of the sky

[1]**'sky,rocket** /-,rokit/ *n* [2]ROCKET 1a

[2]**skyrocket** *vi* to shoot up abruptly ⟨*shares in copper are* ~ing⟩

skysail /'skie,sayl, -sl/ *n* a sail set above the royal sail on a mast

'sky,scape /-,skayp/ *n* an expanse of sky, esp as depicted by an artist

'sky,scraper /-,skraypə/ *n* a many-storeyed building; *esp* one containing offices

'skywards /-woodz/ *adv* towards the sky; *also* upwards

'sky,way /-,way/ *n* a route used by aircraft

'sky,writing /-,rieting/ *n* (the formation of) writing in the sky by means of a visible substance (e g smoke) emitted from an aircraft

slab /slab/ *n* a thick flat usu large plate or slice (e g of stone, wood, or bread) [ME *slabbe*]

[1]**slack** /slak/ *adj* **1** insufficiently prompt, diligent, or careful; negligent **2a** characterized by slowness, indolence, or languor ⟨*a* ~ *pace*⟩ **b** *of tide* flowing slowly; sluggish **3a** not taut; relaxed ⟨*a* ~ *rope*⟩ **b** lacking in usual or normal firmness and steadiness; lax ⟨~ *muscles*⟩ ⟨~ *supervision*⟩ **4** wanting in activity ⟨*a* ~ *market*⟩ [ME *slak*, fr OE *sleac*; akin to OHG *slah* slack, L *laxus* slack, loose, *languēre* to languish, Gk *lēgein* to stop] – **slackly** *adv*, **slackness** *n*

[2]**slack** *vt* **1a** to be sluggish or negligent in performing or doing **b** to lessen, moderate ⟨~ed *his pace as the sun grew hot*⟩ **2** to release tension in; loosen **3a** to cause to abate or moderate **b** SLAKE 2 ~ *vi* **1** to be or become slack ⟨*our enthusiasm* ~ed *off*⟩ **2** to shirk or evade work or duty – **slacker** *n*

[3]**slack** *n* **1** cessation in movement or flow; *specif* SLACK WATER **2** a part of sthg (e g a sail or a rope) that hangs loose without strain **3** *pl* trousers, esp for casual wear **4** a lull or decrease in activity; a dull season or period

[4]**slack** *n* the finest particles of coal produced at a mine [ME *sleck*]

slacken /'slakən/ *vb* **1** to make or become less active, rapid, or intense – often + *off* **2** to make or become slack

slack water *n* the period at the turn of the tide when there is no apparent tidal motion

slag /slag/ *n* **1** waste matter from the smelting of metal ores; dross **2** the rough cindery lava from a volcano **3** *Br* a dirty slovenly (immoral) woman – slang [MLG *slagge*]

slain /slayn/ *past part of* SLAY

slake /slayk/ *vt* **1** to satisfy, quench ⟨~ *your thirst*⟩ **2** to cause (e g lime) to heat and crumble by treatment with water [ME *slaken* to abate, allay, loosen, fr OE *slacian* to slacken, fr *sleac* slack]

slalom /'slahləm/ *n* a skiing or canoeing race against time on a zigzag or wavy course between obstacles [Norw, lit., sloping track]

[1]**slam** /slam/ *n* GRAND SLAM [origin unknown]

[2]**slam** *n* a banging noise; *esp* one made by a door [prob of Scand origin; akin to Icel *slæma* to slam]

[3]**slam** *vb* **-mm-** *vt* **1** to strike or beat vigorously; knock ⟨~med *him about the head with a book*⟩ **2** to shut forcibly and noisily; bang **3a** to put or throw down noisily and violently ⟨~med *his books on the table and stomped out*⟩ **b** to force into sudden and violent action ⟨~ *on the brakes*⟩ **4** to criticize harshly – infml ~*vi* **1** to make a banging noise ⟨*the door* ~med *to behind him*⟩ **2** to move violently or angrily ⟨*he* ~med *out of his office*⟩ – infml

[1]**slander** /'slahndə/ *n* **1** the utterance of false charges which do damage to another's reputation **2** a false defamatory oral statement – compare LIBEL [ME *sclaundre, slaundre*, fr OF *esclandre*, fr LL *scandalum* stumbling block, offence – more at SCANDAL] – **slanderous** /'slahnd(ə)rəs/ *adj*, **slanderously** *adv*, **slanderousness** *n*

[2]**slander** *vt* to utter slander against – **slanderer** *n*

[1]**slang** /slang/ *n* **1** language peculiar to a particular group: e g **a** argot **b** JARGON 2 **2** informal usu spoken vocabulary that is composed typically of coinages, novel senses of words, and picturesque figures of speech [origin unknown] – **slang** *adj*, **slangy** *adj*

[2]**slang** *vt* to abuse with harsh or coarse language ⟨*the two drivers are* ~ing *each other* – *Punch*⟩ ~*vi* to use harsh or vulgar abuse

'**slanging ,match** /'slang·ing/ *n, chiefly Br* a usu futile bout of abuse between 2 or more opposed parties – infml

[1]**slant** /slahnt/ *vi* **1** to turn or incline from a horizontal or vertical line or a level **2** to take a diagonal course, direction, or path ~*vt* **1** to give an oblique or sloping direction to **2** to interpret or present in accord with a particular interest; bias ⟨*stories* ~ed *towards youth*⟩ [ME *slenten* to fall obliquely, of Scand origin; akin to Sw *slinta* to slide; akin to OE *slīdan* to slide] – **slantingly** *adv*

[2]**slant** *n* **1** a slanting direction, line, or plane; a slope ⟨*placed the mirror at a* ~⟩ **2** SOLIDUS 2 **3a** a particular or personal point of view, attitude, or opinion **b** an unfair bias or distortion (e g in a piece of writing) – **slant** *adj*, **slantways** /-wayz/ *adv*, **slantwise** /-wiez/ *adv or adj*

'**slant ,height** *n* the length of a line from the perimeter of the base to the vertex of a cone

[1]**slap** /slap/ *n* a quick sharp blow, esp with the open hand [LG *slapp*, of imit origin] – **slap in the face** a rebuff, insult

[2]**slap** *vt* **-pp-** **1** to strike sharply (as if) with the open hand **2** to put, place, or throw with careless haste or force ⟨~ *paint on a wall*⟩

[3]**slap** *adv* directly, smack ⟨*landed* ~ *on top of a holly bush*⟩ [prob fr LG *slapp*, fr *slapp*, n]

,**slap and 'tickle** *n* playful lovemaking – infml; humor

,**slap-'bang** *adv* **1** in a highly abrupt or forceful manner **2** precisely ⟨~ *in the middle*⟩ *USE* infml

'**slap,dash** /-,dash/ *adj* haphazard, slipshod

slap down *vt* to restrain or quash the initiative of rudely or forcefully

'**slap,happy** /-,hapi/ *adj* **1** punch-drunk **2** irresponsibly casual ⟨*the* ~ *state of our democracies* – Alistair Cooke⟩ **3** buoyantly carefree; happy-go-lucky

'**slap,stick** /-,stik/ *n* **1** a wooden device that makes a loud noise when used by an actor to strike sby **2** comedy stressing farce and horseplay; knockabout comedy – **slapstick** *adj*

'**slap-,up** *adj, chiefly Br* marked by lavish consumption or luxury – infml ⟨*a* ~ *Christmas nosh* – *Sunday Mirror*⟩

[1]**slash** /slash/ *vt* **1a** to cut with violent usu random sweeping strokes **b** to make (one's way) (as if) by cutting down obstacles **2** LASH 1 ⟨~ *him with bridle reins* – Sir Walter Scott⟩ **3** to cut slits in (e g a garment) so as to reveal an underlying fabric or colour **4** to criticize cuttingly **5** to reduce drastically; cut ~*vi* **1** to cut or hit recklessly or savagely **2** *esp of rain* to fall hard and slantingly [ME *slaschen*, prob fr MF *eslachier* to break] – **slasher** *n*

[2]**slash** *n* **1** the act of slashing; *also* a long cut or stroke made (as if) by slashing **2** an ornamental slit in a garment **3** *chiefly Br* an act of urinating – vulg

slashing /'slashing/ *adj* **1** incisively satirical or critical **2** driving, pelting ⟨*journeyed through* ~ *rain*⟩ – **slashingly** *adv*

[1]**slat** /slat/ *n* **1** a thin narrow flat strip, esp of wood or metal (e g a lath, louvre, or stave) **2** [1]SLOT 1a [ME, slate, fr MF *esclat* splinter, fr OF, fr *esclater* to burst, splinter] – **slat** *adj*

[2]**slat** *vt* **-tt-** to make or equip with slats

[1]**slate** /slayt/ *n* **1** a piece of slate rock used as roofing material **2** a fine-grained metamorphic rock consisting of compressed clay, shale, etc and easily split into (thin) layers **3** a tablet of material, esp slate, used for writing on **4** dark bluish or greenish grey **5** *NAm* a list of candidates for nomination or election [ME, fr MF *esclat* splinter] – **slate** *adj*, **slatelike** *adj*, **slaty** *adj*

[2]**slate** *vt* **1** to cover with slate ⟨~ *a roof*⟩ **2** *NAm* to designate for action or appointment

[3]**slate** *vt, chiefly Br* to criticize or censure severely – infml [prob alter. of *slat* (to hurl or throw smartly), prob of Scand origin; akin to ON *sletta* to slap, throw]

slater /'slaytə/ *n* **1** a woodlouse **2** any of various marine crustaceans [[1]*slate*; fr its colour]

slather /'sladhə/ *n, chiefly NAm* a great quantity – usu pl with sing. meaning; infml [origin unknown]

slattern /'slatən/ *n* an untidy slovenly woman; a slut [prob fr G *schlottern* to hang loosely, slouch; akin to D *slodderen* to hang loosely, *slodder* slut]

'**slatternly** /-li/ *adj* **1** untidy and dirty through persistent neglect; *also* careless, disorderly **2** (characteristic) of a slut – **slatternliness** *n*

[1]**slaughter** /'slawtə/ *n* **1** the act of killing; *specif* the butchering of livestock for market **2** killing of many people (e g in battle); carnage [ME, of Scand origin; akin to ON *slātra* to slaughter; akin to OE *sleaht* slaughter, *slēan* to slay – more at SLAY]

[2]**slaughter** *vt* **1** to kill (animals) for food **2** to kill violently or in large numbers – **slaughterer** *n*

'**slaughter,house** /-,hows/ *n* an establishment where animals are killed for food

Slav /slahv/ *n* one who speaks a Slavonic language as his/her native tongue [ME *Sclav*, fr ML *Sclavus*, fr LGk *Sklabos*, fr *Sklabēnoi* Slavs, of Slav origin; akin to OSlav *Slověne*, a Slavonic people in N Greece]

[1]**slave** /slayv/ *n* **1** sby held in servitude as the property of another **2** sby who is dominated by a specified thing or person ⟨*a* ~ *to drink*⟩ **3** a device whose actions are controlled by and often mimic those of another **4** a drudge ⟨*women who are merely kitchen* ~s⟩ [ME *sclave*, fr OF or ML; OF *esclave*, fr ML *sclavus*, fr *Sclavus* Slav; fr the reduction to slavery of many Slavonic peoples of central Europe] – **slave** *adj*

[2]**slave** *vi* **1** to work like a slave; toil **2** to traffic in slaves

'**slave ,driver** *n* **1** an overseer of slaves **2** a harsh taskmaster

[1]**slaver** /'slavə/ *vi* to drool, slobber [ME *slaveren*, of Scand origin; akin to ON *slafra* to slaver; akin to MD *slabben* to slaver, L *labi* to slip – more at SLEEP]

[2]**slaver** /'slayvə/ *n* **1** sby engaged in the slave trade **2** a ship used in the slave trade

slavery /'slayv(ə)ri/ *n* **1** drudgery, toil **2a** the state of being a slave **b** the practice of owning slaves

'**slave ,state** *n* a state of the USA in which Negro slavery was legal until the American Civil War

'**slave ,trade** *n* traffic in slaves; *esp* the transportation of Negroes to America for profit

Slavic /'slahvik, 'slavik/ *adj or n* Slavonic – **Slavicist** /-visist/ *n*, **Slavist** *n*

slavish /'slayvish/ *adj* **1** (characteristic) of a slave; *esp* abjectly servile **2** obsequiously imitative; devoid of originality **3** *archaic* despicable, base – **slavishly** *adv*, **slavishness** *n*

[1]**Slavonian** /slə'vohnyən, -ni·ən/ *n* SLOVENE 1b [*Slavonia*, region of SE Europe, fr ML *Sclavonia, Slavonia* land of the Slavs, fr *Sclavus* Slav]

[2]**Slavonian** *adj* Slovene

[1]**Slavonic** /slə'vonik/ *adj* (characteristic) of the Slavs [NL *slavonicus*, fr ML *Sclavonia, Slavonia*]

[2]**Slavonic** *n* a branch of the Indo-European language family containing Byelorussian, Bulgarian, Czech, Polish, Serbo-Croatian, Slovene, Russian, and Ukrainian

slavophil /'slahvəfil, 'slavə-/, **slavophile** /-fiel/ *n*, *often cap* a foreign admirer of the Slavs

slay /slay/ *vt* **slew** /slooh/; **slain** /slayn/ **1** to kill violently or with great bloodshed; slaughter **2** to affect overpoweringly (e g with awe or delight); overwhelm – infml [ME *slen*, fr OE *slēan* to strike, slay; akin to OHG *slahan* to strike, MIr *slacain* I beat] – **slayer** *n*

sleazy /'sleezi/ *adj* squalid and disreputable [origin unknown] – **sleaziness** *n*

[1]**sled** /sled/ *n*, *chiefly NAm* [2]SLEDGE [ME *sledde*, fr MD; akin to OE *slīdan* to slide]

[2]**sled** *vb* **-dd-** *chiefly NAm* to sledge – **sledder** *n*

[1]**sledge** /slej/ *n* a sledgehammer [ME *slegge*, fr OE *slecg*; akin to ON *sleggja* sledgehammer, OE *slēan* to strike – more at SLAY]

[2]**sledge** *n* **1** a vehicle with runners that is pulled by reindeer, horses, dogs, etc and is used esp over snow or ice **2** *Br* a toboggan [D dial. *sleedse*; akin to MD *sledde* sled]

[3]**sledge** *vb*, *chiefly Br vi* to ride or be conveyed in a sledge ~ *vt* to transport on a sledge

'**sledge,hammer** /-,hamə/ *n* a large heavy hammer that is wielded with both hands [[1]*sledge*]

'**sledge-,hammer** *adj* clumsy, heavy-handed ⟨*a* ~ *package of spending cuts*⟩

[1]**sleek** /sleek/ *vt* to slick [ME *sleken*, alter. of *sliken*]

[2]**sleek** *adj* **1a** smooth and glossy as if polished ⟨~ *dark hair*⟩ **b** having a smooth well-groomed look ⟨*a* ~ *cat*⟩ **c** having a well fed or flourishing appearance **2** excessively or artfully suave; ingratiating **3** elegant, stylish [alter. of [2]*slick*] – **sleeken** *vt*, **sleekly** *adv*, **sleekness** *n*

sleekit /'sleekit/ *adj*, *chiefly Scot* crafty, sly [Sc, fr pp of [1]*sleek*]

[1]**sleep** /sleep/ *n* **1** the natural periodic suspension of consciousness that is essential for the physical and mental well-being of higher animals **2** a sleeplike state: e g **a** torpor **b** a state marked by a diminution of feeling followed by tingling ⟨*his foot went to* ~⟩ **c** the state of an animal during hibernation **d** death – euph ⟨*put a cat to* ~⟩ **3** a period spent sleeping ⟨*need a good long* ~⟩ [ME *slepe*, fr OE *slæp*; akin to OHG *slāf* sleep, L *labi* to slip, slide] – **sleeplike** *adj*

[2]**sleep** *vb* **slept** /slept/ *vi* **1** to rest in a state of sleep **2** to be in a state (e g of quiescence or death) resembling sleep **3** to have sexual relations – + *with* or *together*; infml ~ *vt* **1** to get rid of or spend in sleep ⟨~ *away the hours*⟩ ⟨~ *off a headache*⟩ **2** to provide sleeping accommodation for ⟨*the boat* ~s *6*⟩ **3** to be slumbering in ⟨slept *the sleep of the dead*⟩ – poetic – **sleep on** to consider (sthg) fully before discussing again the next day – **sleep rough** SLEEP OUT 1

sleep around *vi* to be sexually promiscuous – infml

sleeper /'sleepə/ *n* **1** a timber, concrete, or steel transverse support to which railway rails are fixed **2** SLEEPING CAR **3** a ring or stud worn in a pierced ear to keep the hole open **4** *chiefly NAm* sby or sthg unpromising or unnoticed that suddenly attains prominence or value – infml [[1]SLEEP + [2]-ER]

sleep in *vi* **1** LIVE IN **2** to sleep late, either intentionally or accidentally

'**sleeping ,bag** /'sleeping/ *n* a large thick envelope or bag of warm material for sleeping in esp when camping

'**sleeping ,car** *n* a railway carriage divided into compartments having berths for sleeping

,**sleeping 'partner** *n* a partner who takes no active part or an unknown part in the running of a firm's business

'**sleeping ,pill** *n* a drug in the form of a tablet or capsule that is taken to induce sleep

'**sleeping ,sickness** *n* a serious disease that is prevalent in much of tropical Africa, is marked by fever and protracted lethargy, and is caused by either of 2 trypanosomes and transmitted by tsetse flies

'**sleepless** /-lis/ *adj* **1** not able to sleep **2** unceasingly active – **sleeplessly** *adv*, **sleeplessness** *n*

sleep out *vi* **1** to sleep out of doors **2** LIVE OUT

'**sleep,walker** /-,wawkə/ *n* a somnambulist – **sleepwalk** *vi*

sleepy /'sleepi/ *adj* **1a** ready to fall asleep **b** (characteristic) of sleep **2** lacking alertness; sluggish, lethargic **3** sleep-inducing – **sleepily** *adv*, **sleepiness** *n*

'**sleepy,head** /-,hed/ *n* a sleepy person – humor

[1]**sleet** /sleet/ *n* precipitation in the form of partly

frozen rain, or snow and rain falling together [ME *slete*; akin to MHG *slōz* hailstone, ME *sloor* mud – more at [3]SLUR] – **sleety** *adj*

[2]sleet *vi* to send down sleet

sleeve /sleev/ *n* **1** a part of a garment covering the arm **2** a tubular machine part designed to fit over another part **3** a paper or often highly distinctive cardboard covering that protects a gramophone record when not in use [ME *sleve*, fr OE *sliefe*; akin to OE *slēfan* to slip (clothes) on, *slūpan* to slip, OHG *sliofan*, L *lubricus* slippery] – **sleeved** *adj*, **sleeveless** *adj* – **up one's sleeve** held secretly in reserve

sleeving /ˈsleeving/ *n* the covering of an insulated electric cable

[1]sleigh /slay/ *n* [2]SLEDGE 1 [D *slee*, alter. of *slede*; akin to MD *sledde* sled]

[2]sleigh *vi* to drive or travel in a sleigh

ˈsleigh ˌbell *n* any of various bells attached to (the harness of a horse drawing) a sleigh

sleight /sliet/ *n*, *archaic* deceitful craftiness; *also* a stratagem [ME, fr ON *slœgth*, fr *slœgr* sly – more at SLY]

ˌsleight of ˈhand *n* **1** manual skill and dexterity in conjuring or juggling **2** adroitness in deception

slender /ˈslendə/ *adj* **1a** gracefully slim **b** small or narrow in circumference or width in proportion to length or height **2a** flimsy, tenuous ⟨*a* ~ *hope*⟩ **b** limited or inadequate in amount; meagre ⟨*a man of* ~ *means*⟩ [ME *sclendre, slendre*] – **slenderly** *adv*, **slenderness** *n*

sleuth /sloohth/ *vi or n* (to act as) a detective – infml [n short for *sleuthhound*; vb fr n]

ˈsleuthˌhound /-ˌhownd/ *n* **1** a bloodhound **2** a detective [ME, fr *sleuth* track of an animal or person (fr ON *slōth*) + *hound*]

ˈS ˌlevel /es/ *n* SCHOLARSHIP LEVEL

[1]slew /slooh/ *past of* SLAY

[2]slew *vt* to turn or twist (sthg) about a fixed point that is usu the axis ~ *vi* **1** to turn, twist, or swing about **2** to skid [origin unknown] – **slew** *n*

[3]slew *n*, *NAm* a large number or quantity – infml [IrGael *sluagh*]

[1]slice /slies/ *n* **1a** a thin broad flat piece cut from a usu larger whole ⟨*a* ~ *of ham*⟩ **b** a wedge-shaped piece (e g of pie or cake) **2** an implement with a broad blade used for lifting, turning, or serving food ⟨*a fish* ~⟩ **3** (a flight of) a ball that deviates from a straight course in the direction of the dominant hand of the player propelling it – compare HOOK **4a** a portion, share ⟨*a* ~ *of the profits*⟩ **b** a part or section detached from a larger whole ⟨*a sizable* ~ *of the public – Punch*⟩ [ME, fr MF *esclice* splinter, fr OF, fr *esclicier* to splinter, of Gmc origin; akin to OHG *slīzan* to tear apart – more at SLIT]

[2]slice *vt* **1** to cut through (as if) with a knife ⟨~ *a melon in 2*⟩ **2** to cut into slices ⟨~d *bread*⟩ **3** to hit (a ball) so that a slice results ~ *vi* to slice sthg – **sliceable** *adj*, **slicer** *n*

[1]slick /slik/ *vt* to make sleek or smooth [ME *sliken*; akin to OHG *slīhhan* to glide, Gk *leios* smooth]

[2]slick *adj* **1** superficially plausible; glib **2a** characterized by suave or wily cleverness **b** deft, skilful ⟨~ *goal-keeping*⟩ **3** *of a tyre* having no tread **4** *chiefly NAm* smooth, slippery – **slickly** *adv*, **slickness** *n*

[3]slick *n* (a patch of water covered with) a smooth film of crude oil

slickenside /ˈslikənsied/ *n* a smooth often scratched or grooved surface on rock, produced by movement of one surface over another – usu pl with sing. meaning [E dial. *slicken* smooth (alter. of E [2]*slick*) + E *side*]

slicker /ˈslikə/ *n*, *NAm* an artful crook; a swindler – infml [*slick* (to defraud cleverly), fr [2]*slick*]

[1]slide /slied/ *vb* **slid** /slid/ *vi* **1a** to move in continuous contact with a smooth surface **b** to glide over snow or ice (e g on a toboggan) **2** to slip or fall by loss of grip or footing **3** to pass quietly and unobtrusively; steal **4** to take an undirected course; drift ⟨*let his affairs* ~⟩ **5** to pass by smooth or imperceptible gradations ⟨*the economy* slid *from recession to depression*⟩ ~ *vt* **1** to cause to glide or slip **2** to place or introduce unobtrusively or stealthily ⟨slid *the bill into his hand*⟩ [ME *sliden*, fr OE *slīdan*; akin to MHG *slīten* to slide, Gk *leios* smooth – more at [1]LIME] – **slider** *n*

[2]slide *n* **1a** an act or instance of sliding **b** a portamento **2** a sliding part or mechanism: e g **a** a U-shaped section of tube in the trombone that is pushed out and in to produce notes of different pitch **b** a moving piece of a mechanism that is guided by a part along which it slides **3** a landslide, avalanche **4a(1)** a track or slope suitable for sliding or tobogganing **(2)** a chute with a slippery surface down which children slide in play **b** a channel or track down or along which sthg is slid **5a** a flat piece of glass on which an object is mounted for examination using a light microscope **b** a photographic transparency on a small plate or film suitably mounted for projection ☞ TELEVISION **6** *Br* a hair-slide

ˈslide ˌrule *n* an instrument consisting in its simple form of a ruler with a central slide both of which are graduated in such a way that the addition of lengths corresponds to the multiplication of numbers

ˈslide ˌvalve *n* a valve that opens and closes a passageway by sliding over a hole

sliding scale /ˈslieding/ *n* a flexible scale (e g of fees or subsidies) adjusted to the needs or income of individuals

[1]slight /sliet/ *adj* **1a** having a slim or frail build **b** lacking strength or bulk; flimsy **c** trivial **d** not serious or involving risk; minor ⟨*caught a* ~ *chill*⟩ **2** small of its kind or in amount; scanty, meagre [ME, smooth, slight, prob fr MD *slicht*; akin to OHG *slīhhan* to glide – more at SLICK] – **slightly** *adv*, **slightness** *n*

[2]slight *vt* **1** to treat as slight or unimportant ⟨~ed *my efforts at reform*⟩ **2** to treat with disdain or pointed indifference; snub **3** *NAm* to perform or attend to carelessly or inadequately

[3]slight *n* **1** an act of slighting **2** a humiliating affront

slighting /ˈslieting/ *adj* characterized by disregard or disrespect; disparaging ⟨*a* ~ *remark*⟩ – **slightingly** *adv*

slily /ˈslieli/ *adv* slyly

[1]slim /slim/ *adj* **-mm- 1** of small or narrow circumference or width, esp in proportion to length or height **2** slender in build **3** scanty, slight ⟨*a* ~ *chance of success*⟩ [D, bad, inferior, fr MD *slimp* crooked, bad; akin to MHG *slimp* awry] – **slimly** *adv*, **slimness** *n*

[2]slim *vb* **-mm-** *vt* to cause to be or appear slender ⟨*a style that* ~s *the waist*⟩ ~ *vi* to become thinner (e g by dieting)

[1]slime /sliem/ *n* **1** soft moist soil or clay; *esp* viscous mud **2** a viscous or glutinous substance; *esp* mucus or a mucus-like substance secreted by slugs, catfish, etc [ME, fr OE *slīm*; akin to OHG *slīmen* to smooth, L *lima* file – more at [1]LIME]

[2]**slime** *vt* to smear or cover with slime

slime mould *n* any of a group of living organisms usu held to be lower fungi that consist of a mobile mass of fused cells and reproduce by spores

slimmer /ˈslimə/ *n* a person who slims (e g by dieting and exercise)

slimy /ˈsliemi/ *adj* **1** of or resembling slime; viscous; *also* covered with or yielding slime **2** characterized by obsequious flattery; offensively ingratiating **3** *chiefly NAm* vile, offensive *USE* (*2&3*) infml – **slimily** *adv*, **sliminess** *n*

[1]**sling** /sling/ *vt* **slung** /slung/ **1** to cast with a careless and usu sweeping or swirling motion; fling ⟨slung *the coat over her shoulder*⟩ **2** to throw (e g a stone) with a sling **3** *Br* to cast forcibly and usu abruptly ⟨*was* slung *out of the team for misconduct*⟩ – infml [ME *slingen*, prob fr ON *slyngva* to hurl; akin to OE & OHG *slingan* to worm, twist, Lith *slinkti*] – **slinger** *n*

[2]**sling** *n* an act of slinging or hurling a stone or other missile

[3]**sling** *n* **1** a device that gives extra force to a stone or other missile thrown by hand and usu consists of a short strap that is looped round the missile, whirled round, and then released at 1 end **2a** a usu looped line used to hoist, lower, or carry sthg (e g a rifle); *esp* a bandage suspended from the neck to support an arm or hand **b** a rope attached to a mast which supports a yard ☞ SHIP **c** a device (e g a rope net) for enclosing material to be hoisted by a tackle or crane

[4]**sling** *vt* **slung** /slung/ to place in a sling for hoisting or lowering

[5]**sling** *n* a drink made of whisky, brandy, or esp gin with water and sugar [origin unknown]

ˈ**sling,back** /-ˌbak/ *n* a backless shoe that is held on at the heel by a strap passing round the back of the ankle ☞ GARMENT

ˈ**sling,shot** /-ˌshot/ *n*, *NAm* a catapult

[1]**slink** /slingk/ *vb* **slunk** /slungk/ *also* **slinked** *vi* **1** to go or move stealthily or furtively (e g in fear or shame); steal **2** to move in a graceful provocative manner ~ *vt* to give premature birth to – used with reference to an animal [ME *slinken*, fr OE *slincan* to creep; akin to OE *slingan* to worm, twist]

[2]**slink** *n* (the flesh or skin of) the prematurely born young (e g a calf) of an animal

slinky /ˈslingki/ *adj* **1** characterized by slinking; stealthily quiet ⟨~ *movements*⟩ **2** sleek and flowing in movement or outline; *esp* following the lines of the body in a flowing and sensual manner ⟨*a* ~ *catsuit*⟩ – **slinkily** *adv*, **slinkiness** *n*

[1]**slip** /slip/ *vb* **-pp-** *vi* **1a** to move with a smooth sliding motion **b** to move quietly and cautiously; steal **2** *of time* to elapse, pass **3a** to slide out of place or away from a support or one's grasp ⟨*I didn't break the vase, it just* ~ped*!*⟩ **b** to slide on or down a slippery surface ⟨~ *on the stairs*⟩ **4** to get speedily *into* or *out of* clothing ⟨~ *into his coat*⟩ **5** to fall off from a standard or accustomed level by degrees; decline ~ *vt* **1** to cause to move easily and smoothly; slide **2a** to free oneself from ⟨*the dog* ~ped *his collar*⟩ **b** to escape from (one's memory or notice) **3** to put (a garment) on hurriedly **4a** to let loose from a restraining leash or grasp **b** to cause to slip open; release, undo ⟨~ *a knot*⟩ **c** to let go of **d** to detach (an anchor) instead of bringing it on board **5a** to insert, place, or pass quietly or secretly **b** to give or pay on the sly ⟨~ped *him a fiver*⟩ **6** to give birth to prematurely; abort – used with reference to an animal **7** to dislocate ⟨~ped *his shoulder*⟩ **8** to transfer (a stitch) from one needle to another in knitting without working a stitch **9** to keep in partial engagement by resting a foot continuously on the pedal ⟨~ *the clutch*⟩ [ME *slippen*, fr MD or MLG; akin to Gk *olibros* slippery, *leios* smooth – more at [1]LIME] – **slippage** *n*

[2]**slip** *n* **1** a sloping ramp extending out into the water to serve as a place for landing, repairing, or building ships **2** *the* act or an instance of eluding or evading ⟨*gave his pursuer the* ~⟩ **3a** a mistake in judgment, policy, or procedure; a blunder **b** an inadvertent and trivial fault or error ⟨*a* ~ *of the tongue*⟩ **4** a leash so made that it can be quickly unfastened **5a** the act or an instance of slipping ⟨*a* ~ *on the ice*⟩ **b** (a movement producing) a small geological fault **c** a fall from some level or standard **6a** a women's sleeveless undergarment with shoulder straps that resembles a light dress **b** a case into which sthg is slipped; *specif* a pillowcase **7** a disposition or tendency to slip easily **8** any of several fielding positions in cricket that are close to the batsman and just to the (off) side of the wicketkeeper ☞ SPORT

[3]**slip** *n* **1** a small shoot or twig cut for planting or grafting; a scion **2a** a long narrow strip of material (e g paper or wood) **b** a small piece of paper; *specif* a printed form **3** a young and slim person ⟨*a mere* ~ *of a girl*⟩ [ME *slippe*, prob fr MD or MLG, split, slit, flap]

[4]**slip** *vt* **-pp-** to take cuttings from (a plant); divide into slips

[5]**slip** *n* a semifluid mixture of clay and water used by potters (e g for coating or decorating ware) [ME *slyp* slime, fr OE *slypa* slime, paste; akin to OE *slūpan* to slip – more at SLEEVE]

slip carriage *n* a railway carriage that can be detached without stopping the train

ˈ**slip,case** /-ˌkays/ *n* a protective container with 1 open end, for 1 or more books

slip coach *n* SLIP CARRIAGE

ˈ**slip,knot** /-ˌnot/ *n* **1** RUNNING KNOT **2** a knot that can be untied by pulling

[1]ˈ**slip-,on** *n* a slip-on shoe

[2]**slip-on** *adj*, *esp of a garment* easily slipped on or off

ˌ**slipped** ˈ**disc** /slipt/ *n* a protrusion of 1 of the cartilage discs that normally separate the spinal vertebrae, producing pressure on spinal nerves and usu resulting in intense pain, esp in the region of the lower back

slipper /ˈslipə/ *n* a light shoe that is easily slipped on the foot; *esp* a flat-heeled shoe that is worn while resting at home [ME, fr *slippen* to slip]

slippery /ˈslip(ə)ri/ *adj* **1a** causing or tending to cause sthg to slide or fall ⟨~ *roads*⟩ **b** tending to slip from the grasp **2** not to be trusted; shifty [alter. of ME *slipper*, fr OE *slipor*; akin to MLG *slipper* slippery, *slippen* to slip] – **slipperiness** *n*

slippy /ˈslipi/ *adj* slippery – **be/look slippy** *chiefly Br* to be quick; hurry up – infml

slipshod /ˈslip,shod/ *adj* careless, slovenly ⟨~ *reasoning*⟩ [[1]*slip* + *shod*; orig sense, wearing loose shoes]

ˈslip ˌstitch *n* **1** a concealed stitch for sewing folded edges (e g hems) made by alternately running the needle inside the fold and picking up a thread or 2 from the body of the article **2** an unworked stitch; *specif* a knitting stitch that is transferred from one needle to another without working it – **slip-stitch** *vt*

¹ˈslipˌstream /-ˌstreem/ *n* **1** a stream of fluid (e g air or water) driven backwards by a propeller **2** an area of reduced air pressure and forward suction immediately behind a rapidly moving vehicle **3** sthg that sweeps one along in its course

²slipstream *vi* to drive or ride in a slipstream and so gain the advantage of reduced air resistance (e g in a bicycle race)

ˈslip-ˌup *n* a mistake, oversight

slip up *vi* to make a mistake; blunder

ˈslipˌway /-ˌway/ *n* a slip (on which ships are built)

¹slit /slit/ *vt* **-tt-; slit 1** to make a slit in **2** to cut or tear into long narrow strips [ME *slitten*; akin to MHG *slitzen* to slit, OHG *slīzan* to tear apart, OE *sciell* shell – more at SHELL] – **slitter** *n*

²slit *n* a long narrow cut or opening – **slit** *adj*, **slitless** *adj*

slither /ˈslidhə/ *vi* **1** to slide unsteadily, esp (as if) on a slippery surface **2** to slip or slide like a snake ~ *vt* to cause to slide [ME *slideren*, fr OE *slidrian*, freq of *slīdan* to slide] – **slithery** *adj*

slit trench *n* a narrow trench, esp for shelter in battle

¹sliver /ˈslivə/ *n* a small slender piece cut, torn, or broken; a splinter [ME *slivere*, fr *sliven* to slice off, fr OE *-slīfan*; akin to OE *-slǣfan* to cut]

²sliver *vt* to cut or break into slivers ~ *vi* to become split into slivers; splinter

slivovitz /ˈslivəvits, ˈslee-, -vich/ *n* a dry usu colourless plum brandy [Serbo-Croatian *šljivovica*, fr *šljiva, sliva* plum; akin to Russ *sliva* plum – more at LIVID]

slob /slob/ *n* a slovenly or uncouth person – infml [Ir *slab* mud] – **slobbish** *adj*

¹slobber /ˈslobə/ *vi* **1** to let saliva dribble from the mouth; drool **2** to express emotion effusively and esp oversentimentally – often + *over* ~ *vt* to smear (as if) with food or saliva dribbling from the mouth ⟨*the baby* ~ed *his bib*⟩ [ME *sloberen*; akin to LG *slubberen* to sip, Lith *lūpa* lip] – **slobberer** *n*

²slobber *n* **1** saliva drooled from the mouth **2** oversentimental language or conduct – **slobbery** *adj*

sloe /sloh/ *n* (the small dark spherical astringent fruit of) the blackthorn [ME *slo*, fr OE *slāh* – more at LIVID]

ˌsloe-ˈeyed *adj* **1** having soft dark bluish or purplish black eyes **2** having slanted eyes

sloe gin *n* a liqueur consisting of gin in which sloes have been steeped

¹slog /slog/ *vb* **-gg-** *vt* **1** to hit (e g a cricket ball or an opponent in boxing) hard and often wildly **2** to plod (one's way) with determination, esp in the face of difficulty ~ *vi* **1** to walk, move, or travel slowly and laboriously ⟨~ged *through the snow*⟩ **2** to work laboriously; toil [origin unknown] – **slogger** *n*

²slog *n* **1** a hard and often wild blow **2** persistent hard work **3** an arduous march or tramp

slogan /ˈslohgən/ *n* **1** a phrase used to express and esp make public a particular view, position, or aim **2** a brief catchy phrase used in advertising or promotion [alter. of earlier *slogorn*, fr ScGael *sluagh-ghairm* army cry]

sloop /sloohp/ *n* a fore-and-aft rigged sailing vessel with 1 mast and a single foresail [D *sloep*]

ˌsloop of ˈwar *n* a small warship carrying guns on 1 deck only

sloot /slooht/ *n, SAfr* a small watercourse or irrigation channel [Afrik, fr D, ditch, fr MD]

¹slop /slop/ *n* **1** thin tasteless drink or liquid food **2** liquid spilt or splashed **3a** waste food or a thin gruel fed to animals **b** liquid household refuse (e g dirty water or urine) **4** mawkish sentiment in speech or writing; gush *USE* (*1&3*) usu pl with sing. meaning [ME *sloppe* slush, mud, prob fr OE *sloppe* dung; akin to OE *slyppe, slypa* slime, paste – more at ³SLIP]

²slop *vb* **-pp-** *vt* **1a** to cause (a liquid) to spill over the side of a container **b** to splash or spill liquid on **2** to serve messily ⟨~ *soup into a bowl*⟩ **3** to feed slops to ⟨~ *the pigs*⟩ ~ *vi* **1** to tramp through mud or slush **2** to become spilled or splashed **3** to show mawkish sentiment; gush **4** to slouch, flop ⟨*spends his whole day* ~ping *around the house*⟩

ˈslop ˌbasin *n, Br* a bowl for receiving the dregs left in tea or coffee cups at table

ˈslop ˌbowl *n, Br* SLOP BASIN

¹slope /slohp/ *vi* **1** to take an oblique course **2** to lie at a slant; incline ~ *vt* to cause to incline or slant [ME *slope* obliquely]

²slope *n* **1** a piece of inclined ground **2** upward or downward inclination or (degree of) slant **3** GRADIENT 1

slope off *vi* to go away, esp furtively; sneak off – infml

slop out *vi, of a prisoner* to empty slops from a chamber pot

ˈslop ˌpail *n* a pail for household slops

sloppy /ˈslopi/ *adj* **1a** wet so as to splash; slushy ⟨*a* ~ *racetrack*⟩ **b** wet or smeared (as if) with sthg slopped over **2** slovenly, careless ⟨*she's a* ~ *dresser*⟩ **3** disagreeably effusive ⟨~ *sentimentalism*⟩ – **sloppily** *adv*, **sloppiness** *n*

slops /slops/ *n pl* articles (e g clothing) sold to sailors [ME *sloppe* loose smock or overall, prob fr MD *slop*; akin to OE *oferslop* surplice, overall]

¹slosh /slosh/ *n* **1** slush **2** the slap or splash of liquid **3** *chiefly Br* a heavy blow; a bash – infml [prob blend of *slop* and *slush*]

²slosh *vi* **1** to flounder or splash through water, mud, etc **2** to flow with a splashing motion ⟨*water* ~ed *all round him*⟩ ~ *vt* **1** to splash (sthg) about in liquid **2** to splash (a liquid) about, on, or into sthg **3** to make wet by splashing **4** *chiefly Br* to hit, beat ⟨~ed *him on the head with a bucket*⟩ – infml

sloshed /slosht/ *adj* drunk – infml

¹slot /slot/ *n* **1a** a narrow opening, groove, or passage; a slit **b** a passage through an aerofoil directing air rearwards from the lower to the upper surface so as to increase lift and delay stalling **2** a place or position in an organization or sequence; a niche [ME, the hollow of the breastbone, fr MF *esclot*, of unknown origin]

²slot *vb* **-tt-** *vt* **1** to cut a slot in **2** to place in or assign to a slot – often + *in* or *into* ⟨~ted *some reading in as he waited*⟩ ~ *vi* to be fitted (as if) by means of a slot or slots ⟨*a do-it-yourself bookcase that* ~s *together in seconds*⟩

³slot *n, pl* **slot** the track of an animal (e g a deer) [MF *esclot* hoofprint, track, prob of Scand origin; akin to ON *slōth* track]

sloth /slohth/ *n* **1** disinclination to action or work; indolence **2** any of several slow-moving tree-dwelling mammals that inhabit tropical forests of S and Central America, hang face upwards from the branches, and feed on leaves, shoots, and fruits [ME *slouthe*, fr *slow*] – **slothful** *adj*, **slothfully** *adv*, **slothfulness** *n*

'sloth ,bear *n* a common bear of India and Sri Lanka with a long snout

'slot ma,chine *n* **1** a machine (e g for selling cigarettes, chocolate, etc or for gambling) whose operation is begun by dropping a coin or disc into a slot – compare VENDING MACHINE **2** *chiefly NAm* FRUIT MACHINE

[1]slouch /slowch/ *n* **1** a lazy, incompetent, or awkward person **2** a gait or posture characterized by stooping or excessive relaxation of body muscles [origin unknown] – **slouchy** *adj*

[2]slouch *vi* **1** to sit, stand, or walk with a slouch ⟨~ed *behind the wheel*⟩ **2** to hang down limply; droop ~ *vt* to cause to droop ⟨~ed *his shoulders*⟩; *specif* to turn down one side of (a hat brim) – **sloucher** *n*

slouch hat *n* a soft usu felt hat with a wide flexible brim

[1]slough /slow/ *n* **1a** a place of deep mud or mire **b** a swamp **2** a state of dejection ⟨*a ~ of self-pity*⟩ [ME *slogh*, fr OE *slōh*; akin to MHG *slouche* ditch]

[2]slough *also* **sluff** /sluf/ *n* **1** the cast-off skin of a snake **2** a mass of dead tissue separating from an ulcer **3** sthg that may be shed or cast off ⟨*when shall this ~ of sense be cast* – A E Housman⟩ [ME *slughe*; akin to MHG *slūch* snakeskin, Lith *šliaužti* to crawl]

[3]slough *also* **sluff** /sluf/ *vi* **1** to become shed or cast off **2** to cast off a skin **3** to separate in the form of dead tissue from living tissue ~ *vt* **1** to cast off (e g a skin or shell) **2a** to get rid of or discard as irksome or objectionable – usu + *off* **b** to dispose of (a losing card in bridge) by discarding

,slough of de'spond /slow/ *n* a state of extreme despondency [fr the *Slough of Despond*, deep bog into which the protagonist Christian falls in the allegory *Pilgrim's Progress* by John Bunyan †1688 E preacher & writer]

Slovak /'slohvak/ *n* **1** a member of a Slavonic people of E Czechoslovakia **2** the Slavonic language of the Slovaks ☞ LANGUAGE [Slovak *Slovák*, lit., Slav] – **Slovak** *adj*, **Slovakian** /sloh'vaki·ən/ *adj or n*

sloven /'sluvn/ *n* one habitually negligent of neatness or cleanliness, esp in personal appearance [ME *sloveyn* rascal, perh fr Flem *sloovin* woman of low character]

Slovene /'slohveen/ *n* **1a** a member of a S Slavonic people inhabiting Yugoslavia **b** a native or inhabitant of Slovenia **2** the Slavonic language of the Slovenes ☞ LANGUAGE [G, fr Slovene *Sloven*] – **Slovene** *adj*, **Slovenian** /-'veenyən, -'veeni·ən/ *adj or n*

slovenly /'sluvnli, 'slo-/ *adj* **1** untidy, esp in personal appearance or habits **2** lazily slipshod; careless – **slovenliness** *n*

[1]slow /sloh/ *adj* **1a** lacking in intelligence; dull **b** naturally inert or sluggish ⟨*a ~ imagination*⟩ **2a** lacking in readiness, promptness, or willingness ⟨*a shop with ~ service*⟩ **b** not quickly aroused or excited ⟨*was ~ to anger*⟩ **3a** flowing or proceeding with little or less than usual speed ⟨*traffic was ~*⟩ **b** exhibiting or marked by retarded speed ⟨*he moved with ~ deliberation*⟩ **c** low, feeble ⟨*~ fire*⟩ **4** requiring a long time; gradual ⟨*a ~ convalescence*⟩ **5a** having qualities that hinder or prevent rapid movement ⟨*a ~ putting green*⟩ **b** (designed) for slow movement ⟨*learner drivers should keep to the ~ lane*⟩ **6** registering a time earlier than the correct one ⟨*his clock is ~*⟩ **7** lacking in liveliness or variety; boring [ME, fr OE *slāw*; akin to OHG *slēo* dull, Skt *srēvayati* he causes to fail] – **slowish** *adj*, **slowly** *adv*, **slowness** *n*

[2]slow *adv* in a slow manner; slowly

[3]slow *vb* to make or become slow or slower ⟨*~ a car*⟩ ⟨*production of new cars ~*ed⟩ – often + *down* or *up*

slowcoach /'sloh,kohch/ *n* one who thinks or acts slowly

slow match *n* a slow-burning match or fuse used esp for firing blasting charges

,slow 'motion *n* a technique in filming which allows an action to be shown as if it is taking place unnaturally slowly, which usu involves increasing the number of frames exposed in a given time and then projecting the film at the standard speed – **slow-motion** *adj*

slow neutron *n* a neutron with low kinetic energy

'slow,poke /-,pohk/ *n*, *chiefly NAm* a slowcoach

,slow-'witted *adj* slow in perception and understanding; mentally dull

'slow,worm /-,wuhm/ *n* a legless European lizard popularly believed to be blind [ME *sloworm*, fr OE *slāwyrm*, fr *slā-* (akin to Sw *slå* earthworm) + *wyrm* worm]

slub /slub/ *n* a small thickened section in a yarn or thread [origin unknown] – **slub** *adj*

sludge /sluj/ *n* **1** (a deposit of) mud or ooze **2** a slimy or slushy mass, deposit, or sediment: e g **a** precipitated solid matter produced by water and sewage treatment processes **b** muddy sediment in a steam boiler **c** a precipitate from a mineral oil (e g in an internal combustion engine) [prob alter. of *slush*] – **sludgy** *adj*

[1]slue /slooh/ *vb*, *chiefly NAm* [2]SLEW

[2]slue *n*, *chiefly NAm* a slew

[1]slug /slug/ *n* any of numerous slimy elongated chiefly ground-living gastropod molluscs that are found in most damp parts of the world and have no shell or only a rudimentary one [ME *slugge* sluggard, of Scand origin; akin to Norw dial. *slugga* to walk sluggishly; akin to ME *sloor* mud – more at [3]SLUR]

[2]slug *n* **1** a lump, disc, or cylinder of material (e g plastic or metal): e g **a** a bullet – slang **b** *NAm* a disc for insertion in a slot machine; *esp* one used illegally instead of a coin **2a** a strip of metal thicker than a printer's lead **b** a line of type cast as 1 piece **3** a unit of mass being equal to 32.174lb (about 14.59kg) ☞ UNIT **4** *chiefly NAm* a quantity of spirits that can be swallowed at a single gulp – slang [prob fr [1]*slug*]

[3]slug *n* a heavy blow, esp with the fist – infml [prob var of [2]*slog*]

[4]slug *vt* **-gg-** to hit hard (as if) with the fist or a bat – infml – **slugger** *n*

sluggard /ˈslugəd/ *n* a lazy person or animal [ME *sluggart*] – **sluggard** *adj*, **sluggardly** *adj*

sluggish /ˈslugish/ *adj* **1** averse to activity or exertion; indolent; *also* torpid **2** slow to respond (e g to stimulation or treatment) ⟨*a ~ engine*⟩ **3** markedly slow in movement, flow, or growth – **sluggishly** *adv*, **sluggishness** *n*

¹sluice /sloohs/ *n* **1a** an artificial passage for water (e g in a millstream) fitted with a valve or gate for stopping or regulating flow **b** a body of water pent up behind a floodgate **2** a dock gate **3** a stream flowing through a floodgate **4** a long inclined trough (e g for washing ores or gold-bearing earth) [alter. of ME *scluse*, fr MF *escluse*, fr LL *exclusa*, fr L, fem of *exclusus*, pp of *excludere* to exclude]

²sluice *vt* **1** to draw off by or through a sluice **2a** to wash with or in water running through or from a sluice **b** to drench with a sudden vigorous flow; flush ~ *vi* to pour (as if) from a sluice

ˈsluice ˌgate *n* a small gate for emptying the chamber of a canal lock or regulating the amount of water passing through a channel

ˈsluiceˌway /-ˌway/ *n* an artificial channel into which water is let by a sluice

¹slum /slum/ *n* **1** a poor overcrowded run-down area, esp in a city – often pl with sing. meaning **2** a squalid disagreeable place to live [origin unknown] – **slummy** *adj*

²slum *vi* **-mm- 1** to live in squalor or on very slender means – often + *it* **2** to amuse oneself by visiting a place on a much lower social level; *also* to affect the characteristics of a lower social class – **slummer** *n*

¹slumber /ˈslumbə/ *vi* **1** to sleep **2** to lie dormant or latent ⟨*a ~ing volcano*⟩ [ME *slumberen*, freq of *slumen* to doze, prob fr *slume* slumber, fr OE *slūma*; akin to Lith *slugti* to diminish – more at ³SLUR] – **slumberer** *n*

²slumber *n* sleep – often pl with sing. meaning

slumbrous, slumberous /ˈslumbrəs/ *adj* **1** heavy with sleep; sleepy ⟨*~ eyelids*⟩ **2** inducing sleep; soporific **3** marked by or suggestive of a state of sleep or lethargy; drowsy

¹slump /slump/ *vi* **1a** to fall or sink abruptly ⟨*morale ~ed with news of the defeat*⟩ **b** to drop down suddenly and heavily; collapse ⟨*~ed to the floor*⟩ **2** to assume a drooping posture or carriage; slouch **3** to go into a slump ⟨*sales ~ed*⟩ [prob of Scand origin; akin to Norw *slumpa* to fall; akin to L *labi* to slide – more at SLEEP]

²slump *n* a marked or sustained decline, esp in economic activity or prices

slung /slung/ *past of* SLING

slunk /slungk/ *past of* SLINK

¹slur /sluh/ *vb* **-rr-** *vi* to pass *over* without due mention, consideration, or emphasis ⟨*~red over certain facts*⟩ ~ *vt* **1** to perform (successive notes of different pitch) in a smooth or connected manner **2** to run together, omit, or pronounce unclearly (words, sounds, etc) [prob fr LG *slurrn* to shuffle; akin to ME *sloor* mud]

²slur *n* **1** (a curved line connecting) notes to be sung to the same syllable or performed without a break ☞ MUSIC **2** a slurring manner of speech

³slur *vb* **-rr-** *vt* **1** to cast aspersions on; disparage **2** to make indistinct; obscure ~ *vi of a sheet being printed* to slip so as to cause a slur [obs E dial. *slur* (thin mud), fr ME *sloor*; akin to MHG *slier* mud, Lith *slugti* to diminish]

⁴slur *n* **1a** an insulting or disparaging remark; a slight **b** a shaming or degrading effect; a stigma **2** a blurred spot in printed matter

slurp /sluhp/ *vb* to eat or drink noisily or with a sucking sound [D *slurpen*; akin to MLG *slorpen* to slurp] – **slurp** *n*

slurry /ˈsluri/ *n* a watery mixture of insoluble matter (e g mud, manure, or lime) [ME *slory*]

slush /slush/ *n* **1** partly melted or watery snow **2** liquid mud; mire **3** worthless and usu oversentimental material (e g literature) [perh of Scand origin; akin to Norw *slusk* slush] – **slushy** *adj*

ˈslush ˌfund *n, chiefly NAm* a fund for bribing (public) officials or carrying on corrupting propaganda

slut /slut/ *n* **1** a dirty slovenly woman **2** an immoral woman; *esp* a prostitute [ME *slutte*] – **sluttish** *adj*, **sluttishly** *adv*, **sluttishness** *n*

sly /slie/ *adj* **slier** *also* **slyer; sliest** *also* **slyest 1a** clever in concealing one's ends or intentions; furtive **b** lacking in integrity and candour; crafty **2** humorously mischievous; roguish ⟨*gave me a ~ glance*⟩ [ME *sli*, fr ON *slœgr*; akin to OE *slēan* to strike – more at SLAY] – **slyly** *adv*, **slyness** *n* –**on the sly** in a manner intended to avoid notice; secretly

¹smack /smak/ *n* (a slight hint of) a characteristic taste, flavour, or aura [ME, fr OE *smæc*; akin to OHG *smac* taste, Lith *smaguriauti* to nibble]

²smack *vi* – **smack of** to have a trace or suggestion of ⟨*a proposal that* smacks of *treason*⟩

³smack *vt* **1** to slap smartly, esp in punishment **2** to strike or put down with the sound of a smack **3** to open (the lips) with a sudden sharp sound, esp in anticipation of food or drink ~ *vi* to make or give a smack [akin to MD *smacken* to strike]

⁴smack *n* **1** a sharp blow, esp from sthg flat; a slap **2** a noisy parting of the lips **3** a loud kiss **4** *chiefly NAm* heroin – slang

⁵smack *adv* squarely and with force; directly – infml ⟨*drove ~ into the car parked opposite*⟩

⁶smack *n* a small inshore fishing vessel [D *smak* or LG *smack*]

smacker /ˈsmakə/ *n, Br* **1** ¹POUND 2 **2** ⁴SMACK 3 *USE* infml [³SMACK + ²-ER]

smacking /ˈsmaking/ *adj* brisk, lively

¹small /smawl/ *adj* **1a** having relatively little size or dimensions **b** immature, young ⟨*~ children*⟩ **2a** little in quantity, value, amount, etc **b** made up of few individuals or units ⟨*a ~ audience*⟩ **3a** lower-case **b** implying a general application rather than a specific reference, esp to a political party ⟨*my philosophy is a liberal one, with a ~ 'l'* – Reg Prentice⟩ **4** lacking in strength ⟨*a ~ voice*⟩ **5a** operating on a limited scale ⟨*a ~ farmer*⟩ **b** minor in power, influence, etc ⟨*only has a ~ say in the matter*⟩ **c** limited in degree ⟨*paid ~ heed to his warning*⟩ **d** humble, modest ⟨*a ~ beginning*⟩ **6** of little consequence; trivial ⟨*a ~ matter*⟩ **7a** mean, petty **b** reduced to a humiliating position [ME *smal*, fr OE *smæl*; akin to OHG *smal* small, L *malus* bad] – **smallish** *adj*, **smallness** *n*

²small *adv* **1** in or into small pieces **2** in a small manner or size ⟨*write ~*⟩

³small *n* **1** a part smaller and esp narrower than the remainder; *specif* the narrowest part of the back **2** *pl, Br* small articles of underwear – infml; used with reference to laundry

ˈsmall ˌad /ad/ *n, Br* a classified advertisement

ˈsmall ˌarm *n* a firearm fired while held in the hands – usu pl

ˌsmall ˈbeer *n* people or matters of small importance – infml

ˌsmall-ˈbore *adj* of a relatively small calibre, esp 5.6mm (0.22in)

ˌsmall ˈcalorie *n* CALORIE 1a

ˌsmall ˈcapital *n* a letter having the form of but smaller than a capital letter (e g in THESE WORDS)

ˌsmall ˈchange *n* coins of low denomination

ˈsmall ˌfry *n pl in constr* young or insignificant people or things; *specif* children – **small-fry** *adj*

ˈsmallˌgoods /-ˌgoodz/ *n, Austr* meat (e g bacon or sausages) sold in a form (partially) prepared for eating

ˈsmallˌholding /-ˌhohlding/ *n, chiefly Br* a small agricultural farm – **smallholder** *n*

small hours *n pl* the hours immediately following midnight

ˌsmall inˈtestine *n* the part of the intestine that lies between the stomach and colon, consists of duodenum, jejunum, and ileum, secretes digestive enzymes, and is the chief site of the absorption of digested nutrients ☞ DIGESTION

ˌsmall-ˈminded *adj* **1** having narrow interests or outlook; narrow-minded ⟨*a ~ man*⟩ **2** characterized by petty meanness – **small-mindedly** *adv*, **small-mindedness** *n*

small potatoes *n pl but sing or pl in constr* matters of trivial importance – infml

smallpox /ˈsmawlˌpoks/ *n* an acute infectious feverish virus disease characterized by skin eruption with pustules, sloughing, and scar formation

small print *n* sthg made deliberately obscure; *specif* a part of a document (e g a contract) specifying restrictions and conditions that is often confusingly worded or in small type

ˌsmall-ˈscale *adj* small in scope or extent; *esp* small in operation ⟨*a ~ undertaking*⟩

small screen *n* TELEVISION 3b – + *the*

ˈsmallˌsword /-sawd/ *n* a light tapering sword for thrusting

ˈsmall ˌtalk *n* light or casual conversation; chitchat

ˌsmall-ˈtime *adj* insignificant in operation and status; petty ⟨*~ hoodlums*⟩ – **small-timer** *n*

smalt /smawlt, smolt/ *n* a deep blue pigment used esp as a colouring for glass and ceramics [MF, fr OIt *smalto*, of Gmc origin; akin to OHG *smelzan* to melt – more at ²SMELT]

smarm /smahm/ *vt* **1** to plaster, smear ⟨*~ on a thick layer of make-up*⟩ **2** to make (one's way) by obsequiousness or fawning *USE* infml [origin unknown]

smarmy /ˈsmahmi/ *adj* marked by flattery or smugness; unctuous – infml

¹smart /smaht/ *vi* **1** to be (the cause or seat of) a sharp pain; *also* to feel or have such a pain **2** to feel or endure mental distress ⟨*~ing from a rebuke*⟩ **3** to pay a heavy penalty ⟨*would have to ~ for this foolishness*⟩ [ME *smerten*, fr OE *smeortan*; akin to OHG *smerzan* to pain, L *mordēre* to bite, Gk *marainein* to waste away]

²smart *adj* **1** making one smart; causing a sharp stinging ⟨*gave him a ~ blow with the ruler*⟩ **2** forceful, vigorous **3** brisk, spirited ⟨*walking at a ~ pace*⟩ **4a** mentally alert; bright **b** clever, shrewd ⟨*a ~ investment*⟩ **5** witty, persuasive ⟨*a ~ talker*⟩ **6a** neat or stylish in dress or appearance ⟨*a ~ new coat of paint*⟩ **b** characteristic of or frequented by fashionable society ⟨*a ~ restaurant*⟩ – **smartly** *adv*, **smartness** *n*

³smart *adv* in a smart manner; smartly

⁴smart *n* **1** a smarting pain; *esp* a stinging local pain **2** poignant grief or remorse ⟨*was not the sort to get over ~s – Sir Winston Churchill*⟩

ˈsmart ˌalec, smart aleck /ˈalik/ *n* an arrogant person with pretensions to knowledge or cleverness – derog [*Alec*, nickname for *Alexander*] – **smart-alecky, smart-alec** *adj*

smart bomb *n* a bomb that can be guided (e g by a laser beam) to its target

smarten /ˈsmaht(ə)n/ *vt* to make smart or smarter; *esp* to spruce *~ vi* to smarten oneself *USE* usu + *up*

smartish /ˈsmahtish/ *adv, Br* in a rapid manner; quickly ⟨*better get dressed ~*⟩ – infml

smart money *n* (money ventured by) those having inside information or much experience ⟨*the ~ is talking of an economic recovery*⟩ [²*smart*]

ˈsmart ˌset *n* fashionable society – + *the*

smarty-pants /ˈsmahti ˌpants/ *n, pl* **smarty-pants** SMART ALEC – infml

¹smash /smash/ *vt* **1** to break in pieces by violence; shatter **2a** to drive, throw, or hit violently, esp causing breaking or shattering; crash **b** to hit (e g a ball) with a forceful stroke, specif a smash **3** to destroy utterly; wreck – often + *up* *~ vi* **1** to crash *into*; collide ⟨*~ed into a tree*⟩ **2** to become wrecked **3** to go to pieces suddenly under collision or pressure **4** to execute a smash (e g in tennis) [perh blend of *smack* and *mash*]

²smash *n* **1a(1)** a smashing blow, attack, or collision ⟨*a 5-car ~*⟩ **(2)** the result of smashing; *esp* a wreck due to collision **b** a forceful overhand stroke (e g in tennis or badminton) **2** the condition of being smashed or shattered **3a** the action or sound of smashing **b** utter collapse; ruin; *esp* bankruptcy **4** SMASH HIT – infml

³smash *adv* with a resounding crash

ˌsmash-and-ˈgrab *n or adj, chiefly Br* (a robbery) committed by smashing a shop window and snatching the goods on display

smashed *adj* extremely drunk – infml

smasher /ˈsmashə/ *n, chiefly Br* sby or sthg very fine or attractive – infml [¹SMASH + ²-ER]

ˌsmash ˈhit *n* an outstanding success ⟨*his latest play is a ~*⟩

smashing /ˈsmashing/ *adj* extremely good; excellent ⟨*a ~ film*⟩ – infml – **smashingly** *adv*

ˈsmash-ˌup *n* a serious accident; a crash ⟨*a 10-car ~ on the M1*⟩

smattering /ˈsmat(ə)ring/ *n* a piecemeal or superficial knowledge *of* [fr gerund of *smatter* (to spatter, speak with superficial knowledge, dabble in), fr ME *smateren*]

smaze /smayz/ *n, NAm* a combination of haze and smoke similar to but drier than smog [*sm*oke + h*aze*]

¹smear /smiə/ *n* **1** a mark or blemish made (as if) by smearing a substance **2** material smeared on a surface; *also* material taken or prepared for microscopic examination by smearing on a slide ⟨*a vaginal ~*⟩ **3** a usu unsubstantiated accusation ⟨*took the article as a personal ~*⟩ [ME *smere*, fr OE *smeoru* grease, ointment; akin to OHG *smero* grease, Gk *smyris* emery, *myron* unguent]

[2]**smear** *vt* **1a** to spread with sthg sticky, greasy, or viscous; daub **b** to spread esp thickly over a surface **2a** to stain or dirty (as if) by smearing **b** to sully, besmirch; *specif* to blacken the reputation of **3** to obscure or blur (as if) by smearing ~ *vi* to become smeared ⟨*don't touch the paint or it will* ~⟩ – **smearer** *n*, **smeary** *adj*

smegma /ˈsmegmə/ *n* the secretion of a sebaceous gland; *specif* the cheesy sebaceous matter that collects between the glans penis and the foreskin or round the clitoris and labia minora [NL, fr L, detergent, soap, fr Gk *smēgma*, fr *smēchein* to wash off, clean]

[1]**smell** /smel/ *vb* **smelled, smelt** /smelt/ *vt* **1** to perceive the odour of (as if) by use of the sense of smell **2** to detect or become aware of by instinct ⟨*I could* ~ *trouble*⟩ ~ *vi* **1** to exercise the sense of smell **2a(1)** to have a usu specified smell ⟨*these clothes* ~ *damp*⟩ **(2)** to have a characteristic aura; be suggestive *of* ⟨*reports of survivors seemed to* ~ *of truth*⟩ **b** to have an offensive smell; stink [ME *smellen*; akin to MD *smölen* to scorch, Russ *smalit'*] – **smeller** *n* – **smell a rat** to have a suspicion of sthg wrong

[2]**smell** *n* **1a** the process, function, or power of smelling **b** the one of the 5 basic physical senses by which the qualities of gaseous or volatile substances in contact with certain sensitive areas in the nose are interpreted by the brain as characteristic odours **2** an odour **3** a pervading quality; an aura **4** an act or instance of smelling

ˈsmelling ˌsalts /ˈsmeling/ *n pl but sing or pl in constr* a usu scented preparation of ammonium carbonate and ammonia water sniffed as a stimulant to relieve faintness

smell out *vt* **1** to detect or discover (as if) by smelling ⟨*the dog* smelt out *the criminal*⟩ **2** to fill with an esp offensive smell ⟨*the cigarettes* smelt out *the room*⟩

smelly /ˈsmeli/ *adj* having an esp unpleasant smell

[1]**smelt** /smelt/ *n, pl* **smelts,** *esp collectively* **smelt** any of various small fishes that closely resemble the trouts in general structure and have delicate oily flesh with a distinctive smell and taste [ME, fr OE; akin to Norw *smelte* whiting]

[2]**smelt** *vt* **1** to melt (ore) to separate the metal **2** to separate (metal) by smelting [D or LG *smelten*; akin to OHG *smelzan* to melt, OE *meltan*] – **smelter** *n*, **smeltery** *n*

smew /smyooh/ *n* a sawbill duck of northern Europe and Asia, the male of which is mostly white [akin to MHG *smiehe* smew]

smidgin, smidgeon, smidgen /ˈsmijin/ *n, chiefly NAm* a small amount; a bit [prob alter. of E dial. *smitch* (soiling mark)]

smilax /ˈsmielaks/ *n* **1** SARSAPARILLA 1 **2** a tender twining plant that is often grown for ornament [L, bindweed, yew, fr Gk]

[1]**smile** /smiel/ *vi* **1** to have or assume a smile **2a** to look with amusement or scorn ⟨~d *at his own weakness*⟩ **b** to bestow approval ⟨*Heaven seemed to* ~ *on her labours*⟩ **c** to appear pleasant or agreeable ⟨*a green and* smiling *landscape*⟩ ~ *vt* **1** to affect with or change by smiling ⟨~d *away his embarrassment*⟩ **2** to utter or express with a smile ⟨~d *her thanks*⟩ [ME *smilen*; akin to OE *smerian* to laugh, L *mirari* to wonder, Skt *smayate* he smiles] – **smiler** *n*, **smilingly** *adv*

[2]**smile** *n* **1** a change of facial expression in which the corners of the mouth curve slightly upwards and which expresses esp amusement, pleasure, approval, or sometimes scorn **2** a pleasant or encouraging appearance – **smiley** *adj*

smirch /smuhch/ *vt* **1** to make dirty or stained, esp by smearing **2** to bring discredit or disgrace on ⟨~ed *his reputation*⟩ [ME *smorchen*] – **smirch** *n*

smirk /smuhk/ *vi* to smile in a fatuous or scornful manner [ME *smirken*, fr OE *smearcian* to smile; akin to OE *smerian* to laugh] – **smirk** *n*, **smirkingly** *adv*

smite /smiet/ *vb* **smote** /smoht/; **smitten** /ˈsmit(ə)n/, **smote** *vt* **1** to strike sharply or heavily, esp with (an implement held in) the hand **2** to kill, injure, or damage by smiting **3a** to attack or afflict suddenly and injuriously ⟨smitten *by disease*⟩ **b** to have a sudden powerful effect on; afflict ⟨smitten *with grief*⟩; *specif* to attract strongly ⟨smitten *by her beauty*⟩ **4** to cause to strike ⟨smote *his hand against his side*⟩ ~ *vi* to beat down or come forcibly *on* or *upon* [ME *smiten*, fr OE *smītan*; akin to OHG *bismīzan* to defile, & perh to L *mittere* to let go, send] – **smiter** *n*

smith /smith/ *n* **1** a worker in metals; *specif* a blacksmith **2** a maker – often in combination ⟨*gun*smith⟩ ⟨*song*smith⟩ [ME, fr OE; akin to OHG *smid* smith, Gk *smilē* wood-carving knife]

smithereens /ˌsmidhəˈreenz, ˈ--ˌ-/ *n pl* fragments, bits ⟨*the house was blown to* ~ *by the explosion*⟩ [IrGael *smidirīn*, dim. of *smiodar* fragment]

smithery /ˈsmith(ə)ri/ *n* the work, art, or trade of a smith

smithy /ˈsmidhi/ *n* the workshop of a smith

[1]**smock** /smok/ *n* a light loose garment resembling a smock frock, esp in being gathered into a yoke; *also* SMOCK FROCK [ME *smok*, fr OE *smoc*; akin to OHG *smocco* adornment]

[2]**smock** *vt* to ornament (e g a garment) with smocking

smock frock *n* an outer garment worn chiefly by farm labourers, esp in the 18th and 19th c, and resembling a long loose shirt gathered into a yoke ☞ GARMENT

smocking /ˈsmoking/ *n* a decorative embroidery or shirring made by gathering cloth in regularly spaced round or diamond-shaped tucks held in place with ornamental stitching

smog /smog/ *n* a fog made heavier and darker by smoke and chemical fumes [blend of *smoke* and *fog*] – **smoggy** *adj*, **smogless** *adj*

[1]**smoke** /smohk/ *n* **1a** the gaseous products of burning carbon-containing materials made visible by the presence of small particles of carbon **b** a suspension of particles in a gas **2** fumes or vapour resembling smoke **3** sthg of little substance, permanence, or value **4** sthg that obscures **5a** sthg (e g a cigarette) that is smoked **b** an act or spell of smoking esp tobacco [ME, fr OE *smoca*; akin to MHG *smouch* smoke, Gk *smychein* to smoulder] – **smokelike** *adj*

[2]**smoke** *vi* **1** to emit smoke **2** to (habitually) inhale and exhale the fumes of burning plant material, esp tobacco ~ *vt* **1a** to fumigate **b** to drive out or away by smoke ⟨~ *a fox from its den*⟩ **2** to colour or darken (as if) with smoke ⟨~d *glasses*⟩ **3** to cure (e g meat or fish) by exposure to smoke, traditionally

from green wood or peat **4** to inhale and exhale the smoke of (e g cigarettes)

smokejack /'smohk,jak/ *n* a device for turning a spit that is driven by rising gases in a chimney

'smokeless /-lis/ *adj* **1** producing little or no smoke ⟨~ *fuel*⟩ **2** in which no smoke is allowed ⟨*a* ~ *zone*⟩

smoke out *vt* **1** SMOKE 1b **2** to bring to public view or knowledge

smoker /'smohkə/ *n* **1** sby who regularly or habitually smokes tobacco **2** a carriage or compartment in which smoking is allowed [[2]SMOKE + [2]-ER]

'smoke ,screen *n* **1** a screen of smoke to hinder observation **2** sthg designed to conceal, confuse, or deceive

'smoke,stack /-,stak/ *n* a chimney or funnel through which smoke and gases are discharged, esp from a locomotive or steamship

'smoking ,jacket /'smohking/ *n* a loosely fitting jacket formerly worn by men while smoking

'smoking ,room *n* a room (e g in a club or hotel) set aside for smokers

smoko, smoke-oh /'smohkoh/ *n, Austr & NZ* a short rest period – infml [[1]*smoke* 5b + *o, oh,* interj]

smoky *also* **smokey** /'smohki/ *adj* **1** emitting smoke, esp in large quantities ⟨*a* ~ *fire*⟩ **2a** having the characteristics or appearance of smoke **b** suggestive of smoke, esp in flavour, smell, or colour **3a** filled with smoke **b** made black or grimy by smoke – **smokily** *adv*, **smokiness** *n*

smolder /'smohldə/ *vi, NAm* to smoulder

smolt /smohlt/ *n* a young salmon or sea trout that is about 2 years old and is assuming the silvery colour of the adult [ME (Sc)]

smooch /smoohch/ *vi* to kiss, caress ⟨~ing *on the dimly lit dance floor*⟩ – infml [alter. of *smouch* (to kiss loudly), of imit origin] – **smoocher** *n*, **smoochy** *adj*

[1]**smooth** /smoohdh/ *adj* **1a** having a continuous even surface **b** free from hair or hairlike projections **c** *of liquid* of an even consistency; free from lumps **d** giving no resistance to sliding; frictionless **2** free from difficulties or obstructions **3** even and uninterrupted in movement or flow **4a** equable, composed ⟨*a* ~ *disposition*⟩ **b** urbane, courteous **c** excessively and often artfully suave; ingratiating ⟨*a* ~ *salesman*⟩ **5** not sharp or acid ⟨*a* ~ *sherry*⟩ [ME *smothe*, fr OE *smōth*; akin to OS *smōthi* smooth] – **smooth** *adv*, **smoothly** *adv*, **smoothness** *n*

[2]**smooth** *vt* **1** to make smooth **2** to free from what is harsh or disagreeable **3** to dispel or alleviate (e g enmity or perplexity) – often + *away* or *over* **4** to free from obstruction or difficulty **5** to press flat – often + *out* **6** to cause to lie evenly and in order – often + *down* ⟨~ed *down his hair*⟩ **7** to free (e g a graph or data) from irregularities by ignoring random variations ~ *vi* to become smooth – **smoother** *n*

[3]**smooth** *n* a smooth or agreeable side or aspect ⟨*take the rough with the* ~⟩

,smooth'bore /-'baw/ *adj, of a firearm* not rifled – **smoothbore** *n*

smoothen /'smoohdh(ə)n/ *vb* to make or become smooth

smoothie, smoothy /'smoohdhi/ *n* a person, esp a man, who behaves with suave and often excessive self-assurance – infml

smooth muscle *n* muscle that consists of fibres usu bound in thin sheets, is present in the walls of the gut, bladder, blood vessels, etc, and is not under voluntary control – compare STRIATED MUSCLE

,smooth-'tongued *adj* ingratiating and persuasive in speech

smorgasbord /'smawgəs,bawd, 'smuh-/ *n* a luncheon or supper buffet offering a variety of foods and dishes (e g hors d'oeuvres, hot and cold meats, smoked and pickled fish, cheeses, salads, and relishes) [Sw *smörgåsbord*, fr *smörgås* open sandwich + *bord* table]

smote /smoht/ *past of* SMITE

[1]**smother** /'smudhə/ *n* **1** a dense cloud of gas, smoke, dust, etc **2** a confused mass of things; a welter [ME, alter. of *smorther*, fr *smoren* to smother, fr OE *smorian* to suffocate; akin to MD *smoren* to suffocate] – **smothery** *adj*

[2]**smother** *vt* **1** to overcome or kill with smoke or fumes **2a** to kill by depriving of air **b** to overcome or discomfort (as if) through lack of air **c** to suppress (a fire) by excluding oxygen **3a** to suppress expression or knowledge of; conceal ⟨~ *a yawn*⟩ **b** to prevent the growth or development of; suppress **4a** to cover thickly; blanket ⟨*snow* ~ed *the trees and hedgerows*⟩ **b** to overwhelm ⟨*aunts who always* ~ed *him with kisses*⟩ ~ *vi* to become smothered

[1]**smoulder,** *NAm chiefly* **smolder** /'smohldə/ *n* a smouldering fire [ME *smolder*; akin to ME *smellen* to smell]

[2]**smoulder,** *NAm chiefly* **smolder** *vi* **1** to burn feebly with little flame and often much smoke **2** to exist in a state of suppressed ferment ⟨*resentment* ~ed *in her*⟩ **3** to show suppressed anger, hate, jealousy, etc ⟨*eyes* ~ing *with hate*⟩

[1]**smudge** /smuj/ *vt* **1** to soil (as if) with a smudge **2a** to smear, daub **b** to make indistinct; blur ⟨*couldn't read the* ~d *address*⟩ **3** *NAm* to disinfect or protect by means of smoke ~ *vi* **1** to make a smudge **2** to become smudged [ME *smogen*]

[2]**smudge** *n* **1** a blurry spot or streak **2** an indistinct mass; a blur – **smudgily** *adv*, **smudginess** *n*, **smudgy** *adj*

smug /smug/ *adj* **-gg-** highly self-satisfied and complacent ⟨~ *self-righteous moralists*⟩ [prob modif of LG *smuck* neat, fr MLG, fr *smucken* to dress; akin to OE *smoc* smock] – **smugly** *adv*, **smugness** *n*

smuggle /'smugl/ *vb* **smuggling** /'smugling/ *vt* **1** to import or export secretly contrary to the law, esp without paying duties **2** to convey or introduce surreptitiously ⟨~d *his notes into the examination*⟩ ~ *vi* to import or export sthg in violation of customs laws [LG *smuggeln* & D *smokkelen*; akin to OE *smoc* smock] – **smuggler** *n*

[1]**smut** /smut/ *vb* **-tt-** *vt* **1** to stain or taint with smut **2** to affect (a crop or plant) with smut ~ *vi* to become affected by smut [prob alter. of earlier *smot* (to stain), fr ME *smotten*; akin to MHG *smutzen* to stain]

[2]**smut** *n* **1** matter, esp a particle of soot, that soils or blackens; *also* a mark made by this **2** any of various destructive fungous diseases, esp of cereal grasses, marked by transformation of plant organs into dark masses of spores **3** obscene language or matter – **smuttily** *adv*, **smuttiness** *n*, **smutty** *adj*

[1]**snack** /snak/ *vi, chiefly NAm* to eat a snack [ME *snaken* to bite, prob fr MD *snacken* to snap at, bite]

[2]**snack** *n* a light meal; food eaten between regular meals – **snack** *adj*

[1]**snaffle** /'snafl/ *n* a simple usu jointed bit for a bridle [origin unknown]

[2]**snaffle** *vt* **snaffling** /'snafling/ to appropriate, esp by devious means; pinch – infml [origin unknown]

[1]**snafu** /sna'fooh/ *adj, chiefly NAm* snarled up; awry – infml [*s*ituation *n*ormal *a*ll *f*ucked *u*p]

[2]**snafu** *vt or n, chiefly NAm* (to bring into a state of) total confusion – infml

[1]**snag** /snag/ *n* **1a** a stub or stump remaining after a branch has been lopped **b** a tree or branch embedded in a lake or stream bed and constituting a hazard to navigation **2a** a sharp or jagged projecting part **b** any of the secondary branches of an antler **3** a concealed or unexpected difficulty or obstacle ⟨*the ~ is, there's no train on Sundays*⟩ **4** an irregular tear or flaw made (as if) by catching on a snag ⟨*a ~ in her stocking*⟩ [of Scand origin; akin to ON *snagi* clothes peg] – **snaggy** *adj*

[2]**snag** *vb* **-gg-** *vt* **1** to catch (as if) on a snag **2** to clear (e g a river) of snags **3** *chiefly NAm* to halt or impede as if by catching on a snag **4** *chiefly NAm* to catch or obtain by quick action ⟨*~ged a taxi*⟩ *~ vi* to become snagged

snail /snayl/ *n* **1** a gastropod mollusc; *esp* one that has an external enclosing spiral shell **2** a slow-moving or sluggish person or thing [ME, fr OE *snægl*; akin to OHG *snecko* snail, *snahhan* to creep, Lith *snāke* snail] – **snaillike** *adj*

,snail-'paced /payst/ *adj* moving very slowly

[1]**snake** /snayk/ *n* **1** any of numerous limbless scaly reptiles with a long tapering body and with salivary glands often modified to produce venom which is injected through grooved or tubular fangs **2** a sly treacherous person **3** sthg long, slender, and flexible; *specif* a flexible rod for freeing clogged pipes **4** *often cap* a system in which the values of the currencies of countries in the European Economic Community are allowed to vary against each other within narrow limits [ME, fr OE *snaca*; akin to OE *snægl* snail] – **snakelike** *adj*

[2]**snake** *vt* to wind (e g one's way) in the manner of a snake *~ vi* to crawl, move, or extend silently, secretly, or windingly

'snake ,charmer *n* an entertainer who exhibits the power to control venomous snakes supposedly by magic

,snake in the 'grass *n* a secretly treacherous friend or associate

'snake,root /-,rooht/ *n* any of numerous plants which have roots sometimes believed to cure snakebites

'snake's-,head *n* a European fritillary plant

'snake,skin /-,skin/ *n* (leather made from) the skin of a snake

'snake,weed /-,weed/ *n* any of several plants associated with snakes (e g in appearance, habitat, or use in treatment of snakebite)

snaky /'snayki/ *adj* **1** (formed) of or entwined with snakes **2** serpentine, snakelike ⟨*the ~ arms of an octopus*⟩ **3** slyly venomous or treacherous **4** full of snakes – **snakily** *adv*

[1]**snap** /snap/ *vb* **-pp-** *vi* **1a** to make a sudden closing of the jaws; seize sthg sharply with the mouth ⟨*fish ~ping at the bait*⟩ **b** to grasp or snatch at sthg eagerly ⟨*~ at any chance*⟩ **2** to utter sharp biting words; give an irritable retort ⟨*~ped at his pupil when she apologized for being late*⟩ **3a** to make a sharp or cracking sound **b** to break suddenly, esp with a sharp cracking sound ⟨*the twig ~ped*⟩ **c** to close or fit in place with an abrupt movement or sharp sound ⟨*the catch ~ped shut*⟩ *~ vt* **1** to seize (as if) with a snap of the jaws ⟨*~ped the food right out of his hand*⟩ **2** to take possession or advantage of suddenly or eagerly – usu + *up* ⟨*shoppers ~ping up bargains*⟩ **3** to utter curtly or abruptly ⟨*~ped out an answer*⟩ **4a** to cause to make a snapping sound ⟨*~ped her fingers*⟩ **b** to cause to break suddenly, esp with a sharp cracking sound ⟨*~ped the end off the twig*⟩ **c** to put into or remove from a particular position with a sudden movement or sharp sound ⟨*~ the lid shut*⟩ **5a** to take photographically ⟨*~ a picture*⟩ **b** to photograph [D or LG *snappen*; akin to MHG *snappen* to snap] – **snap out of it** to free oneself from sthg (e g a mood) by an effort of will – infml

[2]**snap** *n* **1** an abrupt closing (e g of the mouth in biting or of scissors in cutting) **2** an act or instance of seizing abruptly; a sudden snatch or bite **3** a brief usu curt retort **4a** a sound made by snapping **b** a sudden sharp breaking of sthg thin or brittle **5** a sudden spell of harsh weather ⟨*a cold ~*⟩ **6** a thin brittle biscuit ⟨*ginger ~*⟩ **7** a snapshot **8** vigour, energy **9** a card game in which each player tries to be the first to shout '*snap*'' when 2 cards of identical value are laid successively **10** *dial NEng* **a** a small meal or snack; *esp* elevenses **b** food; *esp* the food taken by a workman to eat at work **11** *NAm* sthg that is easy and presents no problems; a cinch – infml

[3]**snap** *interj, Br* – used to draw attention to an identity or similarity ⟨*~! You're reading the same book as me*⟩

[4]**snap** *adv* with (the sound of) a snap

[5]**snap** *adj* **1** performed suddenly, unexpectedly, or without deliberation ⟨*a ~ judgment*⟩ **2** *NAm* very easy or simple ⟨*a ~ course*⟩

snapdragon /'snap,drag(ə)n/ *n* any of several garden plants of the figwort family having showy white, red, or yellow 2-lipped flowers [fr the fancied resemblance of the flowers to the face of a dragon]

snap fastener *n, NAm* a press-stud

'snap-,on *adj* designed to snap into position and fit tightly ⟨*~ cuffs*⟩

snapper /'snapə/ *n, pl* **snappers,** (*3*) **snappers,** *esp collectively* **snapper 1** SNAPPING TURTLE **2** CLICK BEETLE **3** any of numerous flesh-eating fishes of warm seas important as food and often as sport fishes [[1]SNAP + [2]-ER]

snapping turtle /'snaping/ *n* a large American turtle that has powerful jaws

snappish /'snapish/ *adj* **1a** given to curt irritable speech **b** bad-tempered, testy ⟨*a ~ reply*⟩ **2** inclined to snap or bite ⟨*a ~ dog*⟩ – **snappishly** *adv,* **snappishness** *n*

snappy /'snapi/ *adj* **1** SNAPPISH 1 **2a** brisk, quick ⟨*make it ~*⟩ **b** lively, animated ⟨*~ repartee*⟩ **c** stylish, smart ⟨*a ~ dresser*⟩ – **snappily** *adv,* **snappiness** *n*

snapshot /'snap,shot/ *n* a casual photograph made typically by an amateur with a small hand-held camera and without regard to technique

[1]**snare** /sneə/ *n* **1a** a trap often consisting of a noose for catching animals **b** sthg by which one is trapped or deceived **2** any of the catgut strings or metal spirals of a snare drum which produce a rattling

sound **3** a surgical instrument consisting usu of a wire loop used for removing tissue masses (e g tonsils) [ME, fr OE *sneare*, fr ON *snara*; akin to Gk *narkē* numbness, OHG *snuor* cord – more at NARROW]

[2]**snare** *vt* **1a** to capture (as if) by use of a snare **b** to procure by artful or skilful actions ⟨~ *a top job*⟩ **2** to entangle or hold as if in a snare – **snarer** *n*

'**snare ,drum** *n* a small double-headed drum with 1 or more snares stretched across its lower head

[1]**snarl** /snahl/ *n* **1** a tangle, esp of hair or thread; a knot **2** a confused or complicated situation; *also, chiefly NAm* a snarl-up [ME *snarle*, prob dim. of *snare*] – **snarly** *adj*

[2]**snarl** *vt* **1** to cause to become knotted and intertwined; tangle **2** to make excessively confused or complicated ~ *vi* to become snarled *USE* (*vt2; vi*) often + *up* – **snarler** *n*

[3]**snarl** *vi* **1** to growl with bared teeth **2** to speak in a vicious or bad-tempered manner ~ *vt* to utter or express viciously or in a snarling manner [freq of obs E *snar* (to growl)] – **snarl** *n*, **snarler** *n*

'**snarl-,up** *n* an instance of confusion, disorder, or obstruction; *specif* a traffic jam

[1]**snatch** /snach/ *vi* to attempt to seize sthg suddenly – often + *at* ⟨~ *at a rope*⟩ ~ *vt* **1** to take or grasp abruptly or hastily ⟨~ *a quick glance*⟩ **2** to seize or grab suddenly and usu forcibly, wrongfully, or with difficulty [ME *snacchen* to give a sudden snap, seize; akin to MD *snacken* to snap at] – **snatcher** *n*

[2]**snatch** *n* **1** a snatching at or of sthg **2a** a brief period of time or activity ⟨*sleep came in* ~es⟩ **b** sthg fragmentary or hurried ⟨*caught a brief* ~ *of their conversation*⟩ **3** a robbery – infml

'**snatch ,block** *n* a block that can be opened on one side to receive a rope

snatchy /'snachi/ *adj* marked by breaks in continuity; spasmodic

snazzy /'snazi/ *adj* stylishly or flashily attractive – infml [perh blend of *snappy* and *jazzy*]

[1]**sneak** /sneek/ *vb* **sneaked,** *NAm also* **snuck** /snuk/ *vi* **1** to go or leave stealthily or furtively; slink ⟨*boys* ~ing *over the orchard wall*⟩ **2** to behave in a furtive or servile manner **3** *Br* to tell tales ⟨*pupils never* ~ *on their classmates*⟩ – infml ~ *vt* to put, bring, or take in a furtive or artful manner ⟨~ed *a glance at the report*⟩ [akin to OE *snīcan* to sneak along, OHG *snahhan* to creep – more at SNAIL] – **sneak up on** to approach or act on stealthily

[2]**sneak** *n* **1** a person who acts in a stealthy or furtive manner **2** the act or an instance of sneaking **3** *Br* a person, esp a schoolchild, who tells tales against others – infml – **sneaky** *adj*

sneaker /'sneekə/ *n, chiefly NAm* a plimsoll – usu pl [[1]SNEAK + [2]-ER]

sneaking /'sneeking/ *adj* **1** furtive, underhand **2** mean, contemptible **3a** not openly expressed; secret ⟨*a* ~ *desire for publicity*⟩ **b** instinctively felt but unverified ⟨*a* ~ *suspicion*⟩ – **sneakingly** *adv*

'**sneak ,thief** *n* a thief who steals without using violence or breaking into buildings

sneck /snek/ *n, dial Br* a latch [ME *snekke*]

[1]**sneer** /sniə/ *vi* **1** to smile or laugh with a curl of the lips to express scorn or contempt **2** to speak or write in a scornfully jeering manner ~ *vt* to utter with a sneer [prob akin to MHG *snerren* to chatter, gossip – more at SNORE] – **sneerer** *n*

[2]**sneer** *n* a sneering expression or remark

sneeze /sneez/ *vi or n* (to make) a sudden violent involuntary audible expiration of breath [ME *snesen*, alter. of *fnesen*, fr OE *fnēosan*; akin to MHG *pfnūsen* to snort, sneeze, Gk *pnein* to breathe] – **sneezer** *n*, **sneezy** *adj* – **sneeze at** to make light of

'**sneeze,wort** /-,wuht/ *n* a strong-scented Eurasian composite perennial plant

snell /snel/ *adj, chiefly Scot* keen, piercing ⟨*a* ~ *wind smote us – Scotsman*⟩ [ME, fr OE; akin to OHG *snel* bold, agile]

[1]**snick** /snik/ *vt* **1** to cut slightly; nick **2** EDGE 4 [prob fr obs *snick or snee* to engage in cut-and-thrust fighting – more at SNICKERSNEE]

[2]**snick** *n* EDGE 4

snicker /'snikə/ *vi or n* (to) snigger [imit] – **snickerer** *n*, **snickery** *adj*

snickersnee /,snikə'snee, '--,-/ *n* a large knife [obs *snick or snee* (to engage in cut-and-thrust fighting), alter. of earlier *steake or snye*, fr D *steken of snijden* to thrust or cut]

snicket /'snikit/ *n, N Eng* a narrow pathway bordered by bushes or hedges [E dial. *snicket* (something small or insignificant)]

snide /snied/ *adj* **1** slyly disparaging; insinuating ⟨~ *remarks*⟩ **2** *chiefly NAm* mean, low ⟨*a* ~ *trick*⟩ [origin unknown] – **snidely** *adv*, **snideness** *n*

[1]**sniff** /snif/ *vi* **1** to draw air audibly up the nose, esp for smelling ⟨~ed *at the flowers*⟩ **2** to show or express disdain or scorn *at* ⟨*not to be* ~ed *at*⟩ ~ *vt* **1** to smell or take by inhalation through the nose **2** to utter in a haughty manner **3** to detect or become aware of (as if) by smelling [ME *sniffen*, of imit origin]

[2]**sniff** *n* **1** an act or sound of sniffing **2** a quantity that is sniffed ⟨*a good* ~ *of sea air*⟩

sniffer /'snifə/ *n* a person who illicitly takes drugs by sniffing ⟨*a glue* ~⟩ [[1]SNIFF + [2]-ER]

[1]**sniffle** /'snifl/ *vi* **sniffling** /'snifling, 'snifl·ing/ to sniff repeatedly [freq of *sniff*] – **sniffler** *n*

[2]**sniffle** *n* **1** an act or sound of sniffling **2** *often pl* a head cold marked by nasal discharge ⟨*he's got the* ~s⟩

sniffy /'snifi/ *adj* having or expressing a haughty attitude; supercilious – infml – **sniffily** *adv*, **sniffiness** *n*

snifter /'sniftə/ *n* a small drink of spirits – infml [E dial., sniff, snort, fr ME *snifteren* to sniff, snort]

snig /snig/ *vt* **-gg-** *Austr & NZ* to drag (logs) without using a sledge [origin unknown]

snigger /'snigə/ *vi* to laugh in a partly suppressed often derisive manner [alter. of *snicker*] – **snigger** *n*, **sniggerer** *n*

[1]**snip** /snip/ *n* **1a** a small piece snipped off; *also* a fragment, bit **b** a cut or notch made by snipping **c** an act or sound of snipping **2** *pl but sing or pl in constr* shears used esp for cutting sheet metal by hand **3** *Br* a bargain **4** *Br* CINCH 2a – infml [fr or akin to D & LG *snip*]

[2]**snip** *vb* **-pp-** *vt* to cut (as if) with shears or scissors, esp with short rapid strokes ~ *vi* to make a short rapid cut (as if) with shears or scissors – **snipper** *n*

[1]**snipe** /sniep/ *n, pl* **snipes,** *esp collectively* **snipe** any of various birds that usu have long slender straight bills; *esp* any of several game birds that occur esp in marshy areas and resemble the related woodcocks [ME, of Scand origin; akin to ON *snīpa* snipe; akin to OHG *snepfa* snipe]

[2]**snipe** *vi* **1** to shoot *at* exposed individuals usu from in hiding at long range **2** to aim a snide or obliquely critical attack *at* [*snipe* (to shoot or hunt snipe)] – **sniper** *n*

snippet /ˈsnipit/ *n* a small part, piece, or item; *esp* a fragment of writing or conversation [[1]*snip* + *-et*] – **snippety** *adj*

snit /snit/ *n, NAm, Austr, & NZ* a bad or sulky mood – chiefly in *in a snit*; infml [origin unknown]

[1]**snitch** /snich/ *vi* to turn informer; squeal on sby – infml ~ *vt* to pilfer, pinch – infml [prob fr *snitch, snitchel* (fillip on the nose, nose); vt prob influenced by [1]*snatch*] – **snitcher** *n*

[2]**snitch** *n* an esp petty theft – infml

snivel /ˈsnivl/ *vi* **-ll-** (*NAm* **-l-, -ll-**), /ˈsnivl·ing/ **1** to run at the nose **2** to sniff mucus up the nose audibly **3** to whine, snuffle **4** to speak or act in a whining, tearful, cringing, or weakly emotional manner [ME *snivelen*, fr (assumed) OE *snyflan*; akin to D *snuffelen* to snuffle, *snuffen* to sniff, Gk *nan* to flow – more at NOURISH] – **snivel** *n*, **sniveller** *n*

snob /snob/ *n* **1** one who blatantly attempts to cultivate or imitate those he/she admires as social superiors **2a** one who tends to patronize or avoid those he/she regards as inferior **b** one who has an air of smug superiority in matters of knowledge or taste ⟨*a cultural* ~⟩ [obs *snob* (member of the lower classes, vulgar or ostentatious person), fr E dial., shoemaker] – **snobbish, snobby** *adj*, **snobbishly** *adv*, **snobbishness** *n*, **snobbism** *n*

snobbery /ˈsnob(ə)ri/ *n* (an instance of) snobbishness

Sno-Cat /ˈsnoh ˌkat/ *trademark* – used for a track-laying vehicle designed for travel on snow

snog /snog/ *vi* **-gg-** *Br* to kiss and cuddle – slang [perh alter. of [2]*snug*] – **snog** *n*

snood /snoohd/ *n* **1** a net or fabric bag, formerly worn at the back of the head by women, to hold the hair **2** *Scot* a ribbon or band for a woman's hair [(assumed) ME, fr OE *snōd*; akin to OIr *snáth* thread, OE *nǣdl* needle] – **snood** *vt*

snook /snoohk/ *n* a gesture of derision made by putting the thumb to the nose and spreading the fingers out – compare COCK A SNOOK [origin unknown]

[1]**snooker** /ˈsnoohkə/ *n* **1** a variation of pool played with 15 red balls and 6 variously coloured balls **2** a position of the balls in snooker in which a direct shot would lose points [prob fr earlier slang *snooker* (new military cadet); fr the game's origin among military officers in India in the 1870s]

[2]**snooker** *vt* **1** to prevent (an opponent) from making a direct shot in snooker by playing the cue ball so that another ball rests between it and the object ball **2** to present an obstacle to; thwart – infml – **snookered** *adj*

snoop /snoohp/ *vi* to look or pry in a sneaking or interfering manner [D *snoepen* to buy or eat on the sly; akin to D *snappen* to snap] – **snoop** *n*, **snooper** *n*

snooty /ˈsnoohti/ *adj* **1** haughty, disdainful **2** characterized by snobbish attitudes ⟨*a* ~ *neighbourhood*⟩ *USE* infml [obs *snoot* (nose), fr ME *snute*] – **snootily** *adv*, **snootiness** *n*

snooze /snoohz/ *vi or n* (to take) a nap – infml [origin unknown] – **snoozer** *n*

snore /snaw/ *vi or n* (to breathe with) a rough hoarse noise due to vibration of the soft palate during sleep [vb ME *snoren*; akin to MLG *snorren* to drone, MHG *snerren* to chatter; n fr vb] – **snorer** *n*

[1]**snorkel** /ˈsnawkl/ *n* **1** a tube housing an air intake and exhaust pipes that can be extended above the surface of the water from a submerged submarine **2** a J-shaped tube allowing a skin diver to breathe while face down in the water [G *schnorchel*]

[2]**snorkel** *vi* **snorkeled; snorkeling** /ˈsnawkl·ing/ to operate or swim submerged using a snorkel – **snorkeler** /ˈsnawklə/ *n*

[1]**snort** /snawt/ *vb vi* **1** to force air violently through the nose with a rough harsh sound **2** to express scorn, anger, or surprise by a snort ~ *vt* **1** to utter with or express by a snort ⟨~ed *his contempt*⟩ **2** to take in (a drug) by inhalation ⟨~ *coke*⟩ – infml [ME *snorten*]

[2]**snort** *n* **1** an act or sound of snorting **2** a snifter – infml

snorter /ˈsnawtə/ *n* sthg extremely powerful, difficult, or impressive – infml [[1]SNORT + [2]-ER]

snot /snot/ *n* **1** nasal mucus **2** a snotty person – slang [ME, fr OE *gesnot*; akin to OHG *snuzza* nasal mucus, Gk *nan* to flow – more at NOURISH]

snotty /ˈsnoti/ *adj* **1** soiled with nasal mucus – infml **2** arrogantly or snobbishly unpleasant **3** contemptible, despicable *USE* (*2&3*) slang

snout /snowt/ *n* **1a(1)** a long projecting nose (e g of a pig) **(2)** a forward prolongation of the head of various animals **b** the human nose, esp when large or grotesque **2** tobacco – slang [ME *snute*; akin to G *schnauze* snout] – **snouted** *adj*, **snoutish** *adj*, **snouty** *adj*

[1]**snow** /snoh/ *n* **1a** (a descent of) water falling in the form of white flakes consisting of small ice crystals formed directly from vapour in the atmosphere **b** fallen snow **2a** any of various congealed or crystallized substances resembling snow in appearance **b** cocaine – slang [ME, fr OE *snāw*; akin to OHG *snēo* snow, L *niv-, nix*, Gk *nipha* (acc)] – **snowless** *adj*

[2]**snow** *vi* to fall in or as snow ~ *vt* **1** to cause to fall like or as snow **2** to cover, shut in, or block (as if) with snow – usu + *in* or *up* ⟨*found themselves* ~ed *in after the blizzard*⟩ **3** *chiefly NAm* to deceive, persuade, or charm glibly

[1]**ˈsnowˌball** /-ˌbawl/ *n* a round mass of snow pressed or rolled together for throwing

[2]**snowball** *vt* to throw snowballs at ~ *vi* **1** to throw snowballs **2** to increase or expand at a rapidly accelerating rate

ˈsnowberry /-b(ə)ri/ *n* any of several white-berried (garden) shrubs

ˈsnow ˌblindness *n* inflammation and painful sensitiveness to light caused by exposure of the eyes to ultraviolet rays reflected from snow or ice – **snow-blind, snow-blinded** *adj*

ˈsnowˌblink /-ˌblingk/ *n* a white glare in the sky over an expanse of snow

ˈsnowˌbound /-ˌbownd/ *adj* confined or surrounded by snow

ˈsnow-ˌbroth /-ˌbroth/ *n* newly melted snow

snow bunting /ˈbunting/ *n* a Eurasian and N American bunting that is a winter visitor to Europe

ˈsnowˌcap /-ˌkap/ *n* a covering cap of snow (e g on a mountain top) – **snowcapped** *adj*

ˈsnowˌdrift /-ˌdrift/ *n* a bank of drifted snow

ˈsnowˌdrop /-ˌdrop/ *n* a bulbous European plant of

the daffodil family bearing nodding white flowers in spring

'**snow,fall** /-,fawl/ *n* the amount of snow falling at one time or in a given period

'**snow,flake** /-,flayk/ *n* a flake or crystal of snow

snow goose *n* a large white goose with black-tipped wings

snow job *n, chiefly NAm* an attempt to persuade or deceive by overwhelming with information or flattery [[2]*snow* 3]

snow leopard *n* a big cat of upland central Asia with long heavy fur that is irregularly blotched with brownish black in summer and almost pure white in winter

snow line *n* the lower margin of a permanent expanse of snow

'**snow,man** /-,man/ *n* a pile of snow shaped to resemble a human figure

snowmobile /'snohmə,beel/ *n* any of various automotive vehicles for travel on snow [[1]*snow* + *automobile*]

[1]'**snow,plough** /-,plow/ *n* **1** any of various vehicles or devices used for clearing snow **2** a turn in skiing with the skis in the snowploughing position

[2]**snowplough** *vi* to force the heels of one's ski's outwards, keeping the tips together, in order to descend slowly or to stop

'**snow,shoe** /-,shooh/ *n* a light oval wooden frame that is strung with thongs and attached to the foot to enable a person to walk on soft snow without sinking

'**snow,storm** /-,stawm/ *n* a storm of or with snow

snow under *vt* **1** to overwhelm, esp in excess of capacity to handle or absorb sthg ⟨snowed under *with applications for the job*⟩ **2** *NAm* to defeat by a large margin

,**snow-'white** *adj* spotlessly white

snowy /'snoh·i/ *adj* **1a** composed of (melted) snow **b** characterized by or covered with snow **2a** whitened (as if) by snow ⟨*ground ~ with fallen blossom*⟩ **b** snow-white – **snowily** *adv*, **snowiness** *n*

,**snowy 'owl** *n* a very large white round-headed arctic owl that is a winter visitor to Europe and N America

[1]**snub** /snub/ *vt* **-bb-** **1** to check or interrupt with a cutting retort; rebuke **2** to restrain (e g a rope) suddenly while running out, esp by wrapping round a fixed object; *also* to halt the motion of by snubbing a line **3** to treat with contempt, esp by deliberately ignoring [ME *snubben*, of Scand origin; akin to ON *snubba* to scold; akin to Icel *sneypa* to scold]

[2]**snub** *n* an act or an instance of snubbing; *esp* a slight

[3]**snub** *adj* short and stubby ⟨*a ~ nose*⟩ [[1]*snub* (to shorten, cut off)] – **snubness** *n*

,**snub-'nosed** /nohzd/ *adj* **1** having a short and slightly turned-up nose **2** having a very short barrel ⟨*a ~ revolver*⟩

snuck /snuk/ *NAm past of* SNEAK

[1]**snuff** /snuf/ *n* the charred part of a candle wick [ME *snoffe*]

[2]**snuff** *vt* **1** to trim the snuff of (a candle) by pinching or by the use of snuffers **2a** to extinguish (a flame) by the use of snuffers **b** to make extinct; put an end to – usu + *out* ⟨*an accident that ~ed out a life*⟩ – **snuff it** to die – infml

[3]**snuff** *vb or n* (to) sniff [akin to D *snuffen* to sniff, snuff – more at SNIVEL]

[4]**snuff** *n* a preparation of pulverized often scented tobacco inhaled usu through the nostrils [D *snuf*, short for *snuftabak*, fr *snuffen* to snuff + *tabak* tobacco]

'**snuff,box** /-,boks/ *n* a small box for holding snuff, usu carried about the person

snuffer /'snufə/ *n* **1** an instrument resembling a pair of scissors for trimming the wick of a candle – usu pl but sing. or pl in constr **2** an instrument consisting of a small hollow cone attached to a handle, used to extinguish candles

snuffle /'snufl/ *vb* **snuffling** /'snufling, 'snufl·ing/ *vi* **1a** to sniff, usu audibly and repeatedly **b** to draw air through an obstructed nose with a sniffing sound **2** to speak (as if) through the nose ~ *vt* to utter with much snuffling [akin to D *snuffelen* to snuffle – more at SNIVEL] – **snuffle** *n*, **snuffler** *n*

[1]**snuffy** /'snufi/ *adj* **1** quick to become annoyed; huffy **2** supercilious, disdainful [[3]*snuff*]

[2]**snuffy** *adj* **1** resembling snuff **2** addicted to the use of snuff **3** soiled with snuff [[5]*snuff*]

[1]**snug** /snug/ *adj* **-gg-** **1** fitting closely and comfortably ⟨*a ~ coat*⟩ **2a** enjoying or affording warm secure comfortable shelter **b** marked by relaxation and cordiality ⟨*a ~ evening among friends*⟩ **3** affording a degree of comfort and ease ⟨*a ~ income*⟩ [perh of Scand origin; akin to Sw *snygg* tidy; akin to ON *snöggr* shorn, bald, L *novacula* razor] – **snug** *adv*, **snugly** *adv*, **snugness** *n*

[2]**snug** *vi* **-gg-** to snuggle

[3]**snug** *n, Br* a small private room or compartment in a pub; *also* a snuggery [short for *snuggery*]

snuggery /'snug(ə)ri/ *n, chiefly Br* a snug cosy place; *esp* a small room

snuggle /'snugl/ *vb* **snuggling** /'snugling/ *vi* to curl up comfortably or cosily; nestle – infml ~ *vt* to draw close, esp for comfort or in affection ⟨*the dog ~d his muzzle under his master's arm*⟩ – infml [freq of [2]*snug*]

[1]**so** /soh; *also (occasional weak form)* sə/ *adv* **1a(1)** in this way; thus ⟨*since he was ~ high*⟩ – often used as a substitute for a preceding word or word group ⟨*do you really think ~?*⟩ ⟨*are you ready? if ~, let's go*⟩ **(2)** most certainly; indeed ⟨*I hope to win and ~ I shall*⟩ **b(1)** in the same way; also ⟨*worked hard and ~ did she*⟩ – used after *as* to introduce a parallel ⟨*as the French drink wine, ~ the British like their beer*⟩ **(2)** as an accompaniment – after *as* ⟨*as the wind increased, ~ the sea grew rougher*⟩ **c** in such a way – used esp before *as* or *that*, to introduce a result ⟨*the book is ~ written that a child could understand it*⟩ or to introduce the idea of purpose ⟨*hid ~ as not to get caught*⟩ **2a** to such an extreme degree ⟨*had never been ~ happy*⟩ – used before *as* to introduce a comparison, esp in the negative ⟨*not ~ fast as mine*⟩, or, esp before *as* or *that*, to introduce a result ⟨*was ~ tired I went to bed*⟩ **b** very ⟨*I'm ~ glad you could come*⟩ **c** to a definite but unspecified extent or degree ⟨*can only do ~ much in a day*⟩ **3** therefore, consequently ⟨*the witness is biased and ~ unreliable*⟩ **4** then, subsequently ⟨*and ~ home and to bed*⟩ **5** *chiefly dial & NAm* – used, esp by children, to counter a negative charge ⟨*you did ~!*⟩ [ME, fr OE *swā*; akin to OHG *sō* so, L *sic* so, thus, *si* if, Gk *hōs* so, thus, L *suus* one's own – more at SUICIDE]

[2]**so** /soh/ *conj* **1** with the result that ⟨*her diction is*

good, ~ *every word is clear*⟩ **2** in order that; THAT 2(1) ⟨*be quiet* ~ *he can sleep*⟩ **3a** for that reason; therefore ⟨*don't want to go,* ~ *I won't*⟩ **b(1)** – used as an introductory particle ⟨~ *here we are*⟩ often to belittle a point under discussion ⟨~ *what?*⟩ **(2)** – used interjectionally to indicate awareness of a discovery ⟨~, *that's who did it*⟩ or surprised dissent

[3]**so** /soh/ *adj* **1** conforming with actual facts; true ⟨*said things that were not* ~⟩ **2** disposed in a definite order ⟨*his books are always exactly* ~⟩

[4]**so** /soh/ *pron* such as has been specified or suggested; the same ⟨*became chairman and remained* ~⟩ **– or so** – used to indicate an approximation or conjecture ⟨*I've known him 20 years* or so⟩

[5]**so, soh** /soh/ *n* [1]SOL

[1]**soak** /sohk/ *vi* **1** to lie immersed in liquid (e g water), esp so as to become saturated or softened ⟨*put the clothes to* ~⟩ **2a** to enter or pass through sthg (as if) by pores or small openings; permeate **b** to become fully felt or appreciated – usu + *in* or *into* ~ *vt* **1** to permeate so as to wet, soften, or fill thoroughly **2** to place in a surrounding element, esp liquid, to wet or permeate thoroughly **3** to extract (as if) by steeping ⟨~ *the dirt out*⟩ **4a** to draw in (as if) by absorption ⟨~ed *up the sunshine*⟩ **b** to intoxicate (oneself) with alcohol – infml **5** to charge an excessive amount of money – infml ⟨~ed *the taxpayers*⟩ [ME *soken,* fr OE *socian;* akin to OE *sūcan* to suck] – **soakage** *n,* **soaker** *n*

[2]**soak** *n* **1a** soaking or being soaked **b** that (e g liquid) in which sthg is soaked **2** a drunkard – infml

ˈsoakaˌway /-əˌway/ *n, Br* a depression dug in permeable ground into which surface water flows and naturally drains away

ˈso-and-ˌso *n, pl* **so-and-sos, so-and-so's** **1** an unnamed or unspecified person or thing ⟨*Miss* So-and-so⟩ **2** a disliked or unpleasant person – euph ⟨*the cheeky* ~*!*⟩

[1]**soap** /sohp/ *n* **1** a cleansing and emulsifying agent that lathers when rubbed in water and consists essentially of sodium or potassium salts of fatty acids **2** a salt of a fatty acid [ME *sope,* fr OE *sāpe;* akin to OHG *seifa* soap, L *sebum* tallow]

[2]**soap** *vt* **1** to rub soap over or into **2** to flatter – often + *up;* infml

ˈsoapberry /-b(ə)ri, -ˌberi/ *n* any of a genus of chiefly tropical woody plants with fruits that are typically rich in saponin

ˈsoapˌbox /-ˌboks/ *n* an improvised platform used by an informal orator – **soapbox** *adj*

ˈsoap ˌopera *n* a radio or television drama characterized by stock domestic situations and melodramatic or sentimental treatment [fr its frequently being sponsored in the USA by soap manufacturers]

ˈsoapˌstone /-ˌstohn/ *n* a soft greyish green or brown stone having a soapy feel and composed mainly of magnesium silicate

ˈsoapˌwort /-ˌwuht/ *n* a European perennial plant of the pink family whose leaves yield a detergent when bruised

soapy /ˈsohpi/ *adj* **1** containing or combined with soap or saponin **2a** smooth and slippery **b** suave, ingratiating – **soapily** *adv,* **soapiness** *n*

[1]**soar** /saw/ *vi* **1a** to fly high in the air **b(1)** to sail or hover in the air, often at a great height **(2)** *of a glider* to fly without engine power and without loss of altitude **2** to rise rapidly or to a very high level ⟨*temperatures* ~ed *into the upper 30s*⟩ **3** to rise upwards in position or status ⟨*a* ~ing *reputation*⟩ **4** to be of imposing height or stature; tower ⟨*mountains* ~ed *above us*⟩ [ME *soren,* fr MF *essorer* to air, soar, fr (assumed) VL *exaurare* to air, fr L *ex-* + *aura* air – more at AURA] – **soarer** *n*

[2]**soar** *n* (the range, distance, or height attained in) soaring

soaring /ˈsawring/ *n* the act or sport of flying a heavier-than-air craft without power by using ascending air currents

[1]**sob** /sob/ *vb* **-bb-** *vi* **1** to weep with convulsive catching of the breath **2** to make a sound like that of a sob or sobbing ~ *vt* **1** to bring (e g oneself) to a specified state by sobbing ⟨~bed *himself to sleep*⟩ **2** to express or utter with sobs ⟨~bed *out her grief*⟩ [ME *sobben*]

[2]**sob** *n* an act or sound of sobbing; *also* a similar sound

[1]**sober** /ˈsohbə/ *adj* **1** not drunk or addicted to drink **2** gravely or earnestly thoughtful **3** calmly self-controlled; sedate **4a** well balanced; realistic ⟨*a* ~ *estimate*⟩ **b** sane, rational **5** subdued in tone or colour [ME *sobre,* fr MF, fr L *sobrius;* akin to L *ebrius* drunk] – **soberly** *adv,* **soberness** *n*

[2]**sober** *vb* to make or become sober – usu + *up*

ˌsoberˈsided /-ˈsiedid/ *adj* excessively earnest or serious-minded – infml

ˈsoberˌsides /-ˌsiedz/ *n, pl* **sobersides** a sobersided person – infml

sobriety /səˈbrie-əti/ *n* being sober – fml [ME *sobrietie,* fr MF *sobrieté,* fr L *sobrietat-, sobrietas,* fr *sobrius*]

sobriquet /ˈsohbriˌkay/ *n* a nickname [F, fr MF *soubriquet* tap under the chin, nickname]

ˈsob ˌstory *n* a sentimental story or account intended chiefly to elicit sympathy – infml

ˈsob ˌstuff *n* material designed to have a sentimental or strongly emotional appeal – infml

socage, soccage /ˈsokij/ *n* a feudal tenure of land by nonmilitary service or by payment of rent [ME, fr *soc* soke] – **socager** *n*

ˌso-ˈcalled *adj* **1** commonly named; popularly so termed ⟨*involved in* ~ *campus politics*⟩ **2** falsely or improperly so named ⟨*deceived by his* ~ *friend*⟩

soccer /ˈsokə/ *n* a football game that is played with a round ball between teams of 11 players each, that features the kicking and heading of the ball, and in which use of the hands and arms is prohibited except to the goalkeepers ☞ SPORT [by shortening & alter. fr *association (football)*]

sociable /ˈsohsh(i)əbl/ *adj* **1** inclined to seek or enjoy companionship; companionable **2** conducive to friendliness or cordial social relations ⟨*spent a* ~ *evening at the club*⟩ [MF or L; MF, fr L *sociabilis,* fr *sociare* to join, associate, fr *socius*] – **sociableness** *n,* **sociably** *adv,* **sociability** /-əˈbiləti/ *n*

[1]**social** /ˈsohsh(ə)l/ *adj* **1** involving allies or confederates ⟨*the* Social *War between the Athenians and their allies*⟩ **2a** sociable **b** of or promoting companionship or friendly relations ⟨*a* ~ *club*⟩ **3a** tending to form cooperative relationships; gregarious ⟨*man is a* ~ *being*⟩ **b** living and breeding in more or less organized communities ⟨~ *insects*⟩ **c** *of a plant* tending to grow in patches or clumps so as to form a pure stand **4** of human society ⟨~ *institutions*⟩ **5a** of or based on status in a particular society ⟨*his* ~ *set*⟩ **b** (characteristic) of the upper classes ⟨*writes a column of* ~ *gossip*⟩ [L *socialis,* fr *socius* compan-

ion, ally, associate; akin to L *sequi* to follow – more at SUE] – **socially** *adv*

[2]**social** *n* a social gathering, usu connected with a church or club

,social 'climber *n* one who strives to gain a higher social position or acceptance in fashionable society – derog – **social climbing** *n*

,social 'contract *n* **1** an actual or supposed agreement among individuals forming an organized society or between (part of) the community and the governing power ruler that defines and limits the rights and duties of each **2** an unwritten agreement whereby trade unions regulate wage demands in return for governmental concessions [trans of F *contrat social*]

,social de'mocracy *n* a political movement advocating a gradual and democratic transition to socialism – **social democrat** *n*, **social democratic** *adj*

social disease *n* VENEREAL DISEASE

socialism /'sohsh(ə)l,iz(ə)m/ *n* **1** an economic and political theory advocating, or a system based on, collective or state ownership and administration of the means of production and distribution of goods **2** a transitional stage of society in Marxist theory distinguished by unequal distribution of goods according to work done

[1]**'socialist** /-ist/ *n* **1** one who advocates or practises socialism **2** *cap* a member of a socialist party or group

[2]**socialist** *adj* **1** of socialism **2** *cap* of or constituting a party advocating socialism

,social'istic /-'istik/ *adj* of or tending towards socialism – **socialistically** *adv*

socialist realism *n* a Marxist aesthetic theory calling for the instructive and educational use of the arts to develop social consciousness – **social realist** *n*

socialite /'sohsh(ə)liet/ *n* a socially active or prominent person

sociality /,sohshi'aləti/ *n* the tendency to associate in or form social groups

social·ize, -ise /'sohsh(ə)l,iez/ *vt* **1** to make social; *esp* to fit or train for life in society **2** to adapt to social needs or uses ⟨~ *science*⟩ **3** to constitute on a socialist basis ⟨~ *industry*⟩ ~ *vi* to act in a sociable manner ⟨*likes to* ~ *with his students*⟩ – **socializer** *n*, **socialization** /-ie'zaysh(ə)n/ *n*

socialized medicine *n*, *NAm* medical services administered by an organized group (e g a state agency) and paid for by assessments, philanthropy, or taxation

,social 'science *n* **1** the scientific study of human society and the relationships between its members **2** a science (e g economics or politics) dealing with a particular aspect of human society – **social scientist** *n*

,social se'curity *n* **1** provision by the state through pensions, unemployment benefit, sickness benefit, etc for its citizens' economic security and social welfare **2** SUPPLEMENTARY BENEFIT

,social 'service *n* activity designed to promote social welfare; *esp* an organized service (e g education or housing) provided by the state

'social ,work *n* any of various professional activities concerned with the aid of the economically underprivileged and socially maladjusted – **social worker** *n*

societal /sə'sie·ətl/ *adj* of society ⟨~ *forces*⟩ – **societally** *adv*

[1]**society** /sə'sie·əti/ *n* **1** companionship or association with others; company **2** *often cap* **a** the human race considered in terms of its structure of social institutions ⟨~ *cannot tolerate lawlessness*⟩ **b(1)** a community having common traditions, institutions, and collective interests ⟨*the* Society *of Friends*⟩ **(2)** an organized group working together or periodically meeting because of common interests, beliefs, or profession ⟨*the Royal* Society⟩ **3a** a clearly identifiable social circle ⟨*literary* ~⟩ **b** a fashionable leisure class ⟨*not seen in the best* ~⟩ **4** a natural group of plants, usu of a single species or habit [MF *societé*, fr L *societat-*, *societas*, fr *socius* companion – more at SOCIAL]

[2]**society** *adj* (characteristic) of fashionable society ⟨*a* ~ *wedding*⟩

socio- /,sohs(h)ioh-/ *comb form* **1** society ⟨socio*graphy*⟩ **2** social (and) ⟨socio*political*⟩ [F, fr L *socius* companion]

sociobiology /,sohs(h)iohbie'oləji/ *n* the scientific study of animal behaviour from the point of view that all behaviour has evolved by natural selection – **sociobiological** *adj*, **sociobiologically** *adv*, **socibiologist** *n*

,socio'cultural /-'kulchərəl/ *adj* combining social and cultural factors – **socioculturally** *adv*

,socio,eco'nomic /-,ekə'nomik, -,eekə-/ *adj* of or involving a combination of social and economic factors

,sociolin'guistics /-ling'gwistiks/ *n pl but sing in constr* the study of linguistic behaviour as determined by social and cultural factors – **sociolinguist** *n*, **sociolinguistically** *adv*, **sociolinguistic** *adj*

sociology /,sohs(h)i'oləji/ *n* the science of social institutions and relationships; *specif* the study of the behaviour of organized human groups [F *sociologie*, fr *socio-* + *-logie* -logy] – **sociologist** *n*, **sociological** /-ə'lojikl/ *adj*

sociometry /,sohs(h)i'omətri/ *n* the study and measurement of social relations (e g friendships in a small group of people) [ISV] – **sociometric** /-i·ə'metrik/ *adj*

[1]**sock** /sok/ *n*, *pl* **socks**, *NAm also* **sox** a knitted or woven covering for the foot usu extending above the ankle and sometimes to the knee [ME *socke*, fr OE *socc* light shoe, fr L *soccus*]

[2]**sock** *vt* to hit or apply forcefully – infml [prob of Scand origin; akin to ON *sökkva* to cause to sink; akin to OE *sincan* to sink] – **sock it to** to subject to vigorous or powerful attack – infml

[3]**sock** *n* a vigorous or forceful blow; a punch ⟨*gave him a* ~ *on the chin*⟩ – infml

[1]**socket** /'sokit/ *n* an opening or hollow that forms a holder for sthg ⟨*the eye* ~⟩ ⟨*put the plug in the* ~⟩; *also* an electrical plug [ME *soket*, fr AF, dim. of OF *soc* ploughshare, of Celt origin; akin to MIr *soc* ploughshare, lit., snout of a hog; akin to OE *sugu* sow – more at [1]sow]

[2]**socket** *vt* to provide with or place in a socket

sockeye /'sok,ie/ *n* a small commercially important Pacific salmon that ascends rivers chiefly from Columbia northwards to spawn in spring [by folk etymology fr Salish dial. *suk-kegh*]

socking /'soking/ *adv*, *chiefly Br* extremely – infml; usu + *great* ⟨*a* ~ *great pile of bricks*⟩

Socratic /so'kratik/ *adj* of Socrates, his followers, or his philosophical method of systematic doubt and questioning [*Socrates* †399 BC Gk philosopher] – **Socratically** *adv*

Socratic irony *n* a pretence of ignorance in order to elicit the false conceptions of another through adroit questioning

¹sod /sod/ *n* **1** TURF 1; *also* the grass-covered surface of the ground **2** one's native land – infml [ME, fr MD or MLG *sode*; akin to OFris *sātha* sod]

²sod *n, Br* **1** an objectionable person, esp male **2** a fellow ⟨*he's not a bad little* ~ – Noel Coward⟩ *USE* slang [short for *sodomite*]

³sod *vt* **-dd-** *Br* to damn – usu used as an oath ⟨~ *you!*⟩ or in the present participle as a meaningless intensive; slang

soda /ˈsohdə/ *n* (*2b*) *pl* **sodas** **1a** SODIUM CARBONATE **b** SODIUM BICARBONATE **c** SODIUM HYDROXIDE **2a** SODA WATER **b** *chiefly NAm* a sweet drink consisting of soda water, flavouring, and often ice cream [It, barilla plant, soda, fr (assumed) ML, barilla plant]

ˈsoda ˌfountain *n* **1** *chiefly NAm* an apparatus with a delivery tube and taps for drawing soda water **2** *NAm* a counter where sodas, sundaes, and ice cream are prepared and served

sodalist /ˈsohdl·ist/ *n* a member of a sodality

sodality /sohˈdaləti/ *n* **1** a brotherhood, community **2** a devotional or charitable association of Roman Catholic laity [L *sodalitat-, sodalitas* comradeship, club, fr *sodalis* comrade]

ˈsoda ˌwater *n* a beverage consisting of water highly charged with carbonic acid gas

sodden /ˈsod(ə)n/ *adj* **1** full of moisture or water; saturated ⟨*the* ~ *ground*⟩ **2** heavy, damp, or doughy because of imperfect cooking ⟨~ *bread*⟩ **3** dull or expressionless, esp from habitual drunkenness ⟨*his* ~ *features*⟩ [ME *soden*, fr pp of *sethen* to seethe] – **soddenly** *adv*, **soddenness** *n*

sodium /ˈsohdi·əm, ˈsohdyəm/ *n* a silver white soft ductile element of the alkali metal group that occurs abundantly in nature in combined form and is very active chemically ☞ PERIODIC TABLE [NL, fr E *soda*]

ˌsodium biˈcarbonate *n* a white weakly alkaline salt used esp in baking powders, fire extinguishers, and medicine as an antacid

ˌsodium ˈcarbonate *n* a sodium salt of carbonic acid used esp in making soaps and chemicals, in water softening, in cleaning and bleaching, and in photography; *also* WASHING SODA

ˌsodium ˈchloride *n* SALT 1a

ˌsodium ˌcromoˈglycate /ˌkrohmohˈgliekayt/ *n* a synthetic drug used to prevent and treat allergic reactions, esp asthma and inflammation of the mucous membrane of the nose – compare INTAL [*cromoglycate* fr *cromoglycic acid*, fr *chrom-* + *glyc-* + *-ic*]

ˌsodium hyˈdroxide *n* a white brittle solid that is a strong caustic alkali used esp in making soap, rayon, and paper

ˈsodium ˌpump *n* the process by which sodium ions are actively transported across a cell membrane

ˌsodium ˌthioˈsulphate /ˌthie·ohˈsulfayt/ *n* a salt used esp as a photographic fixing agent and a bleaching agent

ˌsodium-ˈvapour ˌlamp, ˈsodium ˌlamp *n* an electric lamp in which the discharge takes place through sodium vapour causing a characteristic yellow-orange light and which is used esp for street lighting

ˌsod ˈoff /sod/ *vi, Br* to go away – slang

sodomite /ˈsodəmiet/ *n* one who practises sodomy

sodomy /ˈsodəmi/ *n* a sexual act, resembling copulation, other than normal coitus: e g **a** the penetration of the penis into the mouth or esp the anus of another, esp another male **b** sexual relations between a human being and an animal [ME, fr OF *sodomie*, fr LL *Sodoma* Sodom, city of ancient Palestine; fr the homosexual leanings of the men of that city (Gen 19:1–11)]

soe'er /sohˈeə/ *adv* soever – poetic

soever /sohˈevə/ *adv* to any possible or known extent – used after an adjective preceded by *how* ⟨*how fair* ~ *she may be*⟩; poetic [*-soever* (as in *howsoever*)]

sofa /ˈsohfə/ *n* a long upholstered seat with a back and 2 arms or raised ends that typically seats 2 to 4 people [Ar *ṣuffah* long bench]

sofa bed *n* a bedsettee

so ˈfar as *conj* INSOFAR AS

soffit /ˈsofit/ *n* the underside of an overhang, staircase, arch, etc ☞ ARCHITECTURE [F *soffite*, fr It *soffitto*, fr (assumed) VL *suffictus*, pp of L *suffigere* to fasten underneath – more at SUFFIX]

¹soft /soft/ *adj* **1a** yielding to physical pressure ⟨*a* ~ *mattress*⟩ ⟨~ *ground*⟩ **b** of a consistency that may be shaped, moulded, spread, or easily cut ⟨~ *dough*⟩ ⟨~ *cheese*⟩ **c** relatively lacking in hardness ⟨~ *wood*⟩ **d** easily magnetized and demagnetized **e** deficient in or free from salts (e g of calcium or magnesium) that prevent lathering of soap ⟨~ *water*⟩ **f** having relatively low energy ⟨~ *X rays*⟩ **g** intended to avoid or prevent damage on impact ⟨~ *landing of a spacecraft on the moon*⟩ **2a** pleasing or agreeable to the senses; bringing ease or quiet **b** having a bland or mellow taste **c** not bright or glaring; subdued ⟨*a* ~ *glow*⟩ **d(1)** quiet in pitch or volume; not harsh **(2)** *of c and g* pronounced /s/ and /j/ respectively (e g in *acid* and *age*) – not used technically **(3)** *of a consonant sound* articulated with or followed by /y/ (e g in Russian) **e(1)** *of the eyes* having a liquid or gentle appearance **(2)** having a gently curved outline ⟨~ *hills against the horizon*⟩ **f** smooth or delicate in texture ⟨~ *cashmere*⟩ **g(1)** balmy or mild in weather or temperature **(2)** falling or blowing with slight force or impact ⟨~ *breezes*⟩ **3** marked by a kindness, lenience, or moderation: e g **a(1)** not being or involving harsh or onerous terms ⟨~ *option*⟩ **(2)** demanding little effort; easy ⟨*a* ~ *job*⟩ **(3)** based on negotiation and conciliation rather than on a show of power or on threats ⟨*took a* ~ *line towards the enemy*⟩ **b(1)** mild, low-key; *specif* not of the most extreme or harmful kind ⟨~ *porn*⟩ **(2)** *of a drug* considered less detrimental than a hard drug; not (strongly) addictive **4a** lacking resilience or strength, esp as a result of having led a life of ease **b** not protected against enemy attack; vulnerable ⟨*a* ~ *aboveground landing site*⟩ **c** mentally deficient; feebleminded ⟨~ *in the head*⟩ **5a** impressionable **b** readily influenced or imposed upon; compliant **c(1)** lacking firmness or strength of character; feeble **(2)** marked by a gradually declining trend; not firm ⟨*wool prices are increasingly* ~⟩ **d** amorously attracted, esp covertly – + *on* ⟨*has been* ~ *on her for years*⟩ **6** dealing with ideas, opinions, etc, rather than facts and figures ⟨*the ~ sciences*⟩ [ME, fr OE *sōfte*, alter. of *sēfte*; akin to OHG *semfti* soft] – **softish** *adj*, **softly** *adv*, **softness** *n*

[2]soft *n* a soft object, material, or part ⟨*the ~ of the thumb*⟩

[3]soft *adv* in a soft or gentle manner; softly

'soft,ball /-,bawl/ *n* a game similar to baseball played on a smaller field with a ball larger than a baseball

,soft-'boil *vt* to boil (an egg in its shell) to the point at which the white solidifies but the yolk remains unset [back-formation fr *soft-boiled*]

soft coal *n* bituminous coal

'soft-,core *adj* SOFT 3b(1)

,soft-'cover *adj* bound in flexible, not hard, covers; *specif* paperback

,soft 'drink *n* a drink typically based on soda water and often served chilled

soften /'sof(ə)n/ *vt* **1** to make soft or softer **2a** to weaken the military resistance or the morale of **b** to impair the strength or resistance of ⟨*~ him up with compliments*⟩ ~ *vi* to become soft or softer *USE* (2) often + *up* – **softener** *n*

soft fruit *n, chiefly Br* edible fruit (e g strawberries, raspberries, and blackcurrants) that is small, stoneless, and grows on low bushes

,soft 'furnishing *n, chiefly Br* (the practice of furnishing with) a cloth article (e g a curtain or chair cover) that increases the comfort, utility, or decorativeness of a room or piece of furniture – usu pl

soft goods *n pl* textiles and textile products (e g clothing)

,soft'headed /-'hedid/ *adj* foolish, stupid – **softheadedly** *adv*, **softheadedness** *n*

,soft'hearted /-'hahtid/ *adj* kind, compassionate – **softheartedly** *adv*, **softheartedness** *n*

softie /'softi/ *n* a softy

,soft-'land *vb* to (cause to) make a soft landing on a celestial body (e g the moon) [back-formation fr *soft landing*] – **soft-lander** *n*

soft palate *n* the fold at the back of the hard palate that partially separates the mouth and pharynx

soft-paste porcelain *n* PORCELAIN 1b

,soft-'pedal *vb* **-ll-** (*NAm* **-l-**, **-ll-**) to attempt to minimize the importance of (sthg), esp by talking cleverly or evasively ⟨*~ the issue of arms sales*⟩

soft pedal *n* a foot pedal on a piano that reduces the volume of sound

soft sell *n* the use of suggestion or gentle persuasion in selling rather than aggressive pressure – compare HARD SELL

,soft-'shell, ,soft-'shelled *adj* having a soft or fragile shell, esp as a result of recent shedding

,soft-'shoe *adj* of or being tap dancing done in soft-soled shoes without metal taps

,soft-'soap *vt* to persuade or mollify with flattery or smooth talk – infml – **soft-soaper** *n*

soft soap *n* **1** a semifluid soap **2** flattery – infml

,soft-'spoken *adj* having a mild or gentle voice; *also* suave

soft spot *n* a sentimental weakness ⟨*has a ~ for him*⟩

soft touch *n* sby easily imposed on or taken advantage of – infml

'soft,ware /-,weə/ *n* **1** the entire set of programs, procedures, and related documentation associated with a system, esp a computer system; *specif* computer programs **2** sthg contrasted with hardware; *esp* materials for use with audiovisual equipment

'soft,wood /-,wood/ *n* the wood of a coniferous tree – **softwood** *adj*

softy, softie /'softi/ *n* **1** an excessively sentimental or susceptible person **2** a feeble, effeminate, or foolish person *USE* infml

soggy /'sogi/ *adj* **1a** waterlogged, soaked ⟨*a ~ lawn*⟩ **b** SODDEN 2 **2** heavily dull ⟨*~ prose*⟩ [E dial. *sog* (to soak)] – **soggily** *adv*, **sogginess** *n*

soh /soh/ *n* [1]SOL [by alter.]

soi-disant /,swah 'deezonh (*Fr* swa dizɑ̃)/ *adj* self-styled, so-called ⟨*a ~ artist*⟩ [F]

soigné /'swahnyay, -'-/, *fem* **soignée** /~/ *adj* well-groomed; *also* elegant [F, fr pp of *soigner* to take care of, fr ML *soniare*]

[1]soil /soyl/ *vt* **1** to stain or make unclean, esp superficially; dirty **2** to defile morally; corrupt **3** to blacken or tarnish (e g a person's reputation) ~ *vi* to become soiled or dirty [ME *soilen*, fr OF *soiller* to wallow, soil, fr *soil* pigsty, prob fr L *suile*, fr *sus* pig – more at [1]SOW]

[2]soil *n* **1** stain, defilement **2** sthg (e g refuse or sewage) that spoils or pollutes

[3]soil *n* **1** firm land; earth **2a** the upper layer of earth that may be dug or ploughed and in which plants grow **b** the superficial unconsolidated and usu weathered part of the mantle of a planet, esp the earth **3** country, land ⟨*his native ~*⟩ **4** a medium in which sthg takes hold and develops [ME, fr AF, fr L *solium* seat; prob akin to L *sedēre* to sit – more at SIT] – **soily** *adj*

'soilless /-lis/ *adj* carried on without soil ⟨*~ agriculture*⟩

soil pipe *n* a pipe for carrying off wastes from toilets

soil science *n* the scientific study of soils

soiree, soirée /'swahray/ *n* a party or reception held in the evening [F *soirée* evening period, evening party, fr MF, fr *soir* evening, fr L *sero* at a late hour, fr *serus* late – more at SINCE]

soixante-neuf /,swasont 'nuhf/ *n* mutual cunnilingus and fellatio; mutual fellatio; mutual cunnilingus [F, lit., 69]

sojourn /'sojən, 'su-/ *vi or n* (to make) a temporary stay – fml [vb ME *sojornen*, fr OF *sojorner*, fr (assumed) VL *subdiurnare*, fr L *sub* under, during + LL *diurnum* day – more at SUB-, JOURNEY; n ME *sojorn*, fr OF, fr *sojorner*] – **sojourner** *n*

soke /sohk/ *n* **1** the right in Anglo-Saxon and early English law to hold a local court of justice and receive certain fees and fines **2** the district included in a soke jurisdiction [ME *soc, soke*, fr ML *soca*, fr OE *sōcn* inquiry, jurisdiction; akin to OE *sēcan* to seek]

[1]sol /sol/ *n* the 5th note of the diatonic scale in solmization [ML – more at GAMUT]

[2]sol /sohl/ *n, pl* **soles** /-lays/ ☞ *Peru* at NATIONALITY [AmerSp, fr Sp, sun, fr L]

[3]sol /sol/ *n* a fluid colloidal system; *esp* one in which the continuous phase is a liquid [*-sol* (as in *hydrosol*), fr *solution*]

[1]solace /'soləs/ *n* (a source of) consolation or comfort in grief or anxiety [ME *solas*, fr OF, fr L *solacium*, fr *solari* to console – more at SILLY]

[2]solace *vt* **1** to give solace to; console **2** to alleviate, relieve ⟨*~ grief*⟩ – **solacement** *n*, **solacer** *n*

solan goose /'sohlən/ *n* a gannet [ME *soland*, fr

ON *sūla* pillar, gannet + *önd* duck; akin to OE *sȳl* pillar & to OHG *anut* duck, L *anas*]

solanine /ˈsolənin, -neen/, **solanin** /-nin/ *n* a bitter poisonous alkaloid found in several plants of the nightshade family, esp tomatoes and green potatoes [F *solanine*, fr L *solanum* nightshade]

[1]solar /ˈsohlə/ *adj* **1** of or derived from the sun, esp as affecting the earth **2** (of or reckoned by time) measured by the earth's course in relation to the sun **3** produced or operated by the action of the sun's light or heat; *also* using the sun's rays ☞ ENERGY, FOOD [ME, fr L *solaris*, fr *sol* sun; akin to OE & ON *sōl* sun, Gk *hēlios*]

[2]solar *n* an upper room in a medieval house [ME, fr OE; akin to MD *solre* loft, flat roof, OHG *solāri* loft; all fr a prehistoric WGmc word borrowed fr L *solarium* part of a house exposed to the sun]

solar cell *n* a photovoltaic cell or thermopile that is able to convert the energy of sunlight into electrical energy and is used as a power source ☞ ENERGY, SPACE

solar constant *n* the quantity of radiant solar heat received by a given area of the earth's surface in a given time

solar day *n* the interval between transits of the apparent or mean sun across the meridian

solarium /səˈleəri·əm/ *n, pl* **solaria** /-ri·ə/ *also* **solariums** a room exposed to the sun (e g for relaxation or treatment of illness) [L, fr *sol*]

solar·ize, -ise /ˈsohləriez/ *vt* **1** to expose to sunlight; *specif* to affect by the action of the sun's rays **2** to subject (photographic materials) to intense or continued exposure so as to change the relative tonal values of parts of the picture – **solarization** /-ˈzaysh(ə)n/ *n*

solar panel *n* a large number of solar cells grouped together (e g on a spacecraft) ☞ ENERGY

ˌsolar ˈplexus /ˈpleksəs/ *n* **1** an interlacing network of nerves in the abdomen behind the stomach **2** the pit of the stomach [fr the radiating nerve fibres]

ˈsolar ˌsystem *n* the sun together with the group of celestial bodies that are held by its attraction and revolve round it ☞ ASTRONOMY

ˌsolar ˈwind /wind/ *n* the continuous flow of charged particles from the sun's surface into space

solatium /səˈlaysh(i)əm/ *n, pl* **solatia** /-sh(i)ə/ a compensation (e g money) given as solace for suffering, loss, hurt feelings, etc [LL *solacium, solatium*, fr L, solace]

sold /sohld/ *past of* SELL

[1]solder /ˈsohldə, ˈsoldə/ *n* an alloy, esp of tin and lead, used when melted to join metallic surfaces [ME *soudure*, fr MF, fr *souder* to solder, fr L *solidare* to make solid, fr *solidus* solid]

[2]solder *vt* **1** to unite or make whole (as if) by solder **2** to hold or join together; unite ⟨*a friendship* ~*ed by common interests*⟩ ~ *vi* to become united or repaired (as if) by solder – **solderer** *n*, **solderability** /-rəˈbiləti/ *n*

ˈsoldering ˌiron /ˈsohld(ə)ring, ˈsol-/ *n* a usu electrically heated device that is used for melting and applying solder

[1]soldier /ˈsohljə/ *n* **1a** sby engaged in military service, esp in the army **b** an enlisted man or woman **c** a person of usu specified military skill ⟨*a good* ~⟩ **2** any of a caste of ants or wingless termites having a large head and jaws [ME *soudier*, fr OF, fr *soulde* pay, fr LL *solidus* solidus] – **soldierly** *adj or adv*, **soldiership** *n*

[2]soldier *vi* **1** to serve as a soldier **2** to press doggedly forward – usu + *on* ⟨~*ed on without a windscreen*⟩

soldier beetle *n* any of various brightly coloured soft-bodied beetles

soldier of fortune *n* sby who seeks an adventurous, esp military, life wherever chance allows

soldiery /ˈsohljəri/ *n sing or pl in constr* **1** a body of soldiers **2** a set of soldiers of a specified sort ⟨*a drunken* ~⟩

ˌsold-ˈout *adj* **1** having all available tickets or places sold, esp in advance **2** having sold the entire stock of a specified product ⟨*wanted petrol but the garage was* ~⟩

[1]sole /sohl/ *n* **1a** the undersurface of a foot **b** the part of a garment or article of footwear on which the sole rests **2** the usu flat bottom or lower part of sthg or the base on which sthg rests [ME, fr MF, fr L *solea* sandal; akin to L *solum* base, ground, soil] – **soled** *adj*

[2]sole *vt* to provide with a sole ⟨~ *a shoe*⟩

[3]sole *n* any of several flatfish including some valued as superior food fishes [ME, fr MF, fr L *solea* sandal, a flatfish]

[4]sole *adj* **1** being the only one; only ⟨*she was her mother's* ~ *confidante*⟩ **2** belonging or relating exclusively to 1 individual or group ⟨~ *rights of publication*⟩ **3** *esp of a woman* not married – used in law [ME, alone, fr MF *seul*, fr L *solus*] – **soleness** *n*

solecism /ˈsoliˌsiz(ə)m/ *n* **1** a minor blunder in speech or writing **2** a deviation from what is proper or normal; *esp* a breach of etiquette or decorum [L *soloecismus*, fr Gk *soloikismos*, fr *soloikos* speaking incorrectly, lit., inhabitant of Soloi, fr *Soloi*, city in ancient Cilicia where a substandard form of Attic was spoken] – **solecistic** /-ˈsistik/ *adj*

solely /ˈsohl(l)i/ *adv* **1** without another; singly ⟨*was* ~ *responsible*⟩ **2** to the exclusion of all else ⟨*done* ~ *for money*⟩

solemn /ˈsoləm/ *adj* **1** performed so as to be legally binding ⟨*a* ~ *oath*⟩ **2** marked by the observance of established form or ceremony; *specif* celebrated with full liturgical ceremony **3a** conveying a deep sense of reverence or exaltation; sublime ⟨*was stirred by the* ~ *music*⟩ **b** marked by seriousness and sobriety **c** sombre, gloomy [ME *solemne*, fr MF, fr L *sollemnis* regularly appointed, solemn] – **solemnly** *adv*, **solemnness** *n*, **solemnify** /səˈlemnifie/ *vt*

solemnity /səˈlemnəti/ *n* **1** formal or ceremonious observance of an occasion or event **2** a solemn event or occasion **3** solemn character or state ⟨*the* ~ *of his words*⟩

solemn·ize, -ise /ˈsoləmniez/ *vt* **1** to observe or honour with solemnity **2** to perform with pomp or ceremony; *esp* to celebrate (a marriage) with religious rites **3** to make solemn or serious; dignify – **solemnization** /-ˈzaysh(ə)n/ *n*

solemn mass *n* HIGH MASS

solemn vow *n* an absolute and irrevocable vow taken by a member of a Roman Catholic order, under which ownership of property is prohibited and marriage is invalid under canon law – compare SIMPLE VOW

solenoid /ˈsolənoyd/, ˈsoh-/ *n* a coil of wire commonly in the form of a long cylinder that when carrying a current produces a magnetic field and draws in a movable usu ferrous core [F *solénoïde*, fr Gk *sōlēnoeidēs* pipe- shaped, fr *sōlēn* pipe – more at SYRINGE] – **solenoidal** /-'noydl/ *adj*

soleplate /'sohl,playt/ *n* the undersurface of an iron used for pressing cloth or clothing

solera /soh'leərə/ *n* (the system of sherry and Madeira production using) a group of barrels for the gradual blending of young and mature wines [Sp, traverse beam, stone base, lees of wine, fr *suelo* ground, lees, fr L *solum* ground, base]

sol-fa /'sol ,fah/ *n* **1** *also* **sol-fa syllables** the syllables *do, re, mi,* etc used in singing the notes of the scale **2** solmization **3** TONIC SOL-FA

solfatara /,solfə'tahrə/ *n* a volcanic outlet that yields only hot (sulphurous) vapours and gases [It, sulphur mine, fr *solfo* sulphur, fr L *sulfur*]

solfège /sol'fezh/ *n* (a singing exercise or practice in sight-reading vocal music using) the application of the sol-fa syllables to a musical scale or a melody [F, fr It *solfeggio*]

solfeggio /sol'feji·oh/ *n* solfège [It, fr *sol-fa*]

solicit /sə'lisit/ *vt* **1** to make a formal or earnest appeal or request to; entreat **2a** to attempt to lure or entice, esp into evil **b** *of a prostitute* to proposition publicly **3** to try to obtain by usu urgent requests or pleas ⟨~ *military aid*⟩ **4** to require; CALL FOR ⟨*the situation* ~s *the closest attention*⟩ – fml ~*vi* **1** to ask earnestly *for*; importune **2** *of a prostitute* to proposition sby publicly [ME *soliciten* to disturb, take charge of, fr MF *solliciter*, fr L *sollicitare* to disturb, fr *sollicitus* anxious, fr *sollus* whole (fr Oscan; akin to Gk *holos* whole) + *citus*, pp of *ciēre* to move] – **solicitant** *n*, **solicitation** /-'taysh(ə)n/ *n*

solicitor /sə'lisitə/ *n* **1** a qualified lawyer who advises clients, represents them in the lower courts, and prepares cases for barristers to try in higher courts **2** the chief law officer of a US municipality, county, etc [SOLICIT + [1]-OR] – **solicitorship** *n*

so,licitor 'general *n, pl* **solicitors general** **1** *often cap S&G* a Crown law officer ranking after the attorney general in England **2** a federally appointed assistant to the US attorney general

solicitous /sə'lisitəs/ *adj* **1** showing consideration or anxiety; concerned ⟨~ *about the future*⟩ **2** desirous *of*; eager *to* – fml [L *sollicitus*] – **solicitously** *adv*, **solicitousness** *n*

solicitude /sə'lisityoohd/ *n* **1** being solicitous; concern; *also* excessive care or attention **2** a cause of care or concern – usu pl with sing. meaning

[1]**solid** /'solid/ *adj* **1a** without an internal cavity ⟨*a* ~ *ball of rubber*⟩ **b** having no opening or division ⟨*a* ~ *wall*⟩ **c(1)** set in type or printed with minimum spacing (e g without leads) between lines **(2)** joined without a hyphen ⟨*a* ~ *compound*⟩ **2** of uniformly close and coherent texture; compact **3** of good substantial quality or kind ⟨~ *comfort*⟩: e g **a** well constructed from durable materials ⟨~ *furniture*⟩ **b** sound, cogent ⟨~ *reasons*⟩ **4a** having, involving, or dealing with 3 dimensions or with solids **b** neither gaseous nor liquid **5a** without interruption; full ⟨*waited 3* ~ *hours*⟩ **b** unanimous ⟨*had the* ~ *support of his party*⟩ **6** of a single substance or character ⟨~ *rock*⟩: e g **a** (almost) entirely of 1 metal ⟨~ *gold*⟩ **b** of uniform colour or tone **7a** reliable, reputable, or acceptable ⟨*are his opinions* ~*?*⟩ **b** serious in character or intent ⟨*sent the President a* ~ *memorandum – The Economist*⟩ **8** *chiefly NAm* in staunch or intimate association ⟨~ *with his boss*⟩ – infml [ME *solide*, fr MF, fr L *solidus*; akin to Gk *holos* whole – more at SAFE] – **solidly** *adv*, **solidness** *n*, **solidify** /sə'lidifie/ *vb*, **solidifier** *n*, **solidity** /sə'lidəti/ *n*, **solidification** /sə,lidifi'kaysh(ə)n/ *n*

[2]**solid** *adv* in a solid manner ⟨*the grease had set* ~⟩; *also* unanimously

[3]**solid** *n* **1** a substance that does not flow perceptibly under moderate stress **2** the part of a solution or suspension that when freed from solvent or suspending medium has the qualities of a solid – usu pl with sing. meaning ⟨*milk* ~s⟩ **3** a geometrical figure (e g a cube or sphere) having 3 dimensions **4** sthg solid; *esp* a solid colour

solid angle *n* a 3-dimensional spread of directions from a point that is measured by the area in which lines having these directions intercept the surface of a sphere of unit radius having that point as a centre

solidarity /,soli'darəti/ *n* unity based on shared interests and standards [F *solidarité*, fr *solidaire* characterized by solidarity, fr L *solidum* whole sum, fr neut of *solidus* solid]

solid geometry *n* a branch of geometry that deals with figures of 3-dimensional space

,solid-'state *adj* **1** relating to the properties, structure, or reactivity of solid material; *esp* relating to the arrangement or behaviour of ions, molecules, nucleons, electrons, and holes in the crystals of a substance (e g a semiconductor) or to the effect of crystal imperfections on the properties of a solid substance ⟨~ *physics*⟩ **2** using the electric, magnetic, or photic properties of solid materials; not using thermionic valves ⟨*a* ~ *stereo system*⟩ *USE* ☞ COMPUTER

solidus /'solidəs/ *n, pl* **solidi** /-die, -di/ **1** an ancient Roman gold coin introduced by Constantine and used until the fall of the Byzantine Empire **2** a punctuation mark / used esp to denote 'per' (e g in *feet/second*), 'or' (e g in *straggler/deserter*), or 'cum' (e g in *restaurant/bar*) or to separate shillings and pence (e g in *2/6* and *7/-*), the terms of a fraction, or esp numbers in a list ☞ SYMBOL **3** a curve, usu on a temperature and composition graph for a mixture, below which only the solid phase can exist – compare LIQUIDUS [(1) ME, fr LL, fr L, solid; (2) ML, shilling, fr LL; fr its use as a symbol for shillings; (3) L, solid]

solifluction /,soli'fluksh(ə)n/ *n* the slow creeping, esp of saturated soil, down a slope that usu occurs in regions of perennial frost [L *solum* soil + *-i-* + *fluction-*, *fluctio* act of flowing, fr *fluctus*, pp of *fluere* to flow – more at FLUID]

soliloquy /sə'liləkwi/ *n* **1** the act of talking to oneself **2** a dramatic monologue that gives the illusion of being a series of unspoken reflections [LL *soliloquium*, fr L *solus* alone + *loqui* to speak] – **soliloquist** *n*, **soliloquize** *vi*

solipsism /'solip,siz(ə)m/ *n* a theory holding that only the self exists and that the external world is merely an idea generated by the self [L *solus* alone + *ipse* self] – **solipsist** *n*, **solipsistic** /-'sistik/ *adj*

solitaire /'soli,teə, ,--'-/ *n* **1** a gem, esp a diamond, set by itself **2** a game played by 1 person in which a number of pieces are removed from a cross-shaped pattern according to certain rules **3** *chiefly NAm* PATIENCE 2 [F, fr *solitaire*, adj, solitary, fr L *solitarius*]

¹solitary /'solit(ə)ri/ *adj* **1a** (fond of) being or living alone or without companions ⟨*a ~ disposition*⟩ **b** dispirited by isolation; lonely ⟨*left ~ by his wife's death*⟩ **2** taken, spent, or performed without companions ⟨*a ~ weekend*⟩ **3** growing or living alone; not gregarious, colonial, social, or compound **4** being the only one; sole ⟨*the ~ example*⟩ **5** unfrequented, remote ⟨*lived in a ~ place*⟩ [ME, fr L *solitarius*, fr *solitas* aloneness, fr *solus* alone] – **solitariness** *n*, **solitarily** /-t(ə)rəli, -'terəli/ *adv*

²solitary *n* one who habitually seeks solitude

solitude /'solityoohd/ *n* **1** being alone or remote from society; seclusion **2** a lonely place; a fastness [ME, fr MF, fr L *solitudin-*, *solitudo*, fr *solus*]

solmization /,solmie'zaysh(ə)n/ *n* the act, practice, or system of using syllables to denote musical notes or the degrees of a musical scale [F *solmisation*, fr *solmiser* to sol-fa, fr *sol* (fr ML) + *mi* (fr ML) + *-iser* -ize]

¹solo /'sohloh/ *n, pl* **solos** **1** a (musical composition for) performance by a single voice or instrument with or without accompaniment **2** a flight by 1 person alone in an aircraft; *esp* a person's first solo flight [It, fr *solo* alone, fr L *solus*] – **solo** *adj*, **soloist** *n*

²solo *adv* without a companion; alone ⟨*fly ~*⟩

Solomon's seal /'soləmənz/ *n* any of a genus of perennial plants of the lily family with drooping usu greenish-white flowers [prob fr the fancied resemblance of scars on the rhizome to *Solomon's seal*, an occult symbol of two interlinked triangles forming a 6-pointed star, fr *Solomon* † *ab* 933 BC King of Israel]

,so 'long *interj* – used to express farewell; infml [prob by folk etymology fr Gael *slán*, lit., health, security, fr OIr *slān*; prob akin to L *salvus* safe – more at SAFE]

so 'long as *conj* **1** during and up to the end of the time that; while **2** provided that

solo whist *n* a game of whist in which a player attempts to win by a previously declared margin against the other players

solstice /'solstis/ *n* (the time when the sun passes) either of the 2 points on the ecliptic at which the distance from the celestial equator is greatest and which is reached by the sun each year about June 22nd and December 22nd [ME, fr OF, fr L *solstitium*, fr *sol* sun + *status*, pp of *sistere* to come to a stop, cause to stand; akin to L *stare* to stand – more at ¹SOLAR, STAND]

solstitial /sol'stish(ə)l/ *adj* (characteristic) of or happening at a solstice [L *solstitialis*, fr *solstitium*]

soluble /'solyoobl/ *adj* **1a** capable of being dissolved (as if) in a liquid **b** capable of being emulsified **2** capable of being solved or explained ⟨*~ questions*⟩ [ME, fr MF, capable of being loosened or dissolved, fr LL *solubilis*, fr L *solvere* to loosen, dissolve – more at SOLVE] – **solubilize** *vt*, **solubleness** *n*, **solubly** *adv*, **solubility** /-'biləti/ *n*

soluble glass *n* WATER GLASS 2

solute /so'lyooht/ *n* a dissolved substance [L *solutus*, pp]

solution /sə'loohsh(ə)n/ *n* **1a** an act or the process by which a solid, liquid, or gaseous substance is uniformly mixed with a liquid or sometimes a gas or solid **b** a typically liquid uniform mixture formed by this process **c** a liquid containing a dissolved substance **d** the condition of being dissolved **2a** an action or process of solving a problem **b** an answer to a problem [ME, fr MF, fr L *solution-*, *solutio*, fr *solutus*, pp of *solvere* to loosen, solve]

Solutrean, **Solutrian** /,solyoo'tree·ən, sə'lyoohtri·ən/ *adj* of an Upper Palaeolithic culture characterized by finely flaked stone implements [*Solutré*, village in France]

solvable /'solvəbl/ *adj* SOLUBLE 2 – **solvability** /-və'biləti/ *n*

solvate /'solvayt/ *vb or n* (to make or become) a combination of a solute with a solvent or of a dispersed phase with a dispersion medium [*solv*ent + *-ate*] – **solvation** /-'vaysh(ə)n/ *n*

solve /solv/ *vt* to find a solution for ⟨*~ a problem*⟩ ~ *vi* to solve sthg ⟨*substitute the known values of the constants and ~ for* x⟩ [ME *solven* to loosen, fr L *solvere* to loosen, solve, dissolve, fr *sed-*, *se-* apart + *luere* to release – more at SECEDE, LOSE] – **solver** *n*

¹solvent /'solvənt/ *adj* **1** able to pay all legal debts; *also* in credit **2** that dissolves or can dissolve ⟨*~ fluids*⟩ ⟨*~ action of water*⟩ [L *solvent-*, *solvens*, prp of *solvere* to dissolve, pay] – **solvency** *n*, **solvently** *adv*

²solvent *n* a usu liquid substance capable of dissolving or dispersing 1 or more other substances

solvolysis /sol'voləsis/ *n* a chemical reaction (e g hydrolysis) of a solvent and solute that results in the formation of new compounds [NL, fr E *solv*ent + *-o-* + NL *-lysis*] – **solvolytic** /,solvə'litik/ *adj*

¹soma /'sohmə/ *n* an intoxicating plant juice used in ancient India as an offering and a drink of immortality in Vedic ritual, and itself worshipped as a deity [Skt; akin to Av *haoma*, a Zoroastrian ritual drink, Gk *hyein* to rain – more at SUCK]

²soma *n* all of an organism except the germ cells [NL *somat-*, *soma*, fr Gk *sōmat-*, *sōma* body; akin to L *tumēre* to swell – more at THUMB]

Somali /sə'mahli, soh-/ *n, pl* **Somalis**, *esp collectively* **Somali** a member, or the language, of a people of Somaliland ☞ LANGUAGE

so many *adj* **1** a certain number of ⟨*read ~ chapters each night*⟩ **2** – used as an intensive before plurals ⟨*behaved like ~ animals*⟩

somatic /soh'matik, sə-/ *adj* **1** of or affecting the body, esp as distinguished from the germ cells or the mind **2** of the wall of the body; parietal [Gk *sōmatikos*, fr *sōmat-*, *sōma*] – **somatically** *adv*

somatic cell *n* any of the cells of the body that compose its tissues, organs, and other parts other than the germ cells

somatoplasm /soh'matə,plaz(ə)m/ *n* somatic cells as distinguished from germ cells – **somatoplastic** /-'plastik/ *adj*

somatotrophic hormone /soh,matə'trohfik/ *n* GROWTH HORMONE 1 [*somat-* + *-trophic*]

somatotropin /soh,matə'trohpin/ *n* GROWTH HORMONE 1 [*somatotropic* (fr *somat-* + *-tropic*) + *-in*]

somatotype /soh'matə,tiep/ *n* body type; physique – **somatotypic** /-'tipik/ *adj*, **somatotypically** *adv*

sombre, *NAm chiefly* **somber** /'sombə/ *adj* **1** dark, gloomy **2** of a dull, dark, or heavy shade or colour **3a** serious, grave **b** depressing, melancholy ⟨*~ thoughts*⟩ [F *sombre*] – **sombrely** *adv*

sombrero /som'breəroh/ *n, pl* **sombreros** a high-crowned hat of felt or straw with a very wide brim, worn esp in Mexico [Sp, fr *sombra* shade]

¹some /sum; *senses* ¹c *and* ¹d səm; *strong* sum/ *adj* **1a** being an unknown, undetermined, or unspecified unit or thing ⟨~ *film or other*⟩ **b** being an unspecified member of a group or part of a class ⟨~ *gems are hard*⟩ **c** being an appreciable number, part, or amount of ⟨*have ~ consideration for others*⟩ **d** being of an unspecified amount or number ⟨*give me ~ water*⟩ – used as an indefinite pl of A ⟨*have ~ apples*⟩ **2a** important, striking, or excellent ⟨*that was ~ party*⟩ – chiefly infml **b** no kind of ⟨~ *friend you are!*⟩ – chiefly infml [ME *som*, adj & pron, fr OE *sum*; akin to OHG *sum* some, Gk *hamē* somehow, *homos* same – more at SAME]

[2]**some** /sum/ *pron* **1** *sing or pl in constr* some part, quantity, or number but not all ⟨~ *of my friends*⟩ **2** *chiefly NAm* an indefinite additional amount ⟨*ran a mile and then ~*⟩

[3]**some** /sum/ *adv* **1** ABOUT 3 ⟨~ *80 houses*⟩ **2** somewhat – used in Br English in *some more* and more widely in NAm – **some little** a fair amount of – **some few** quite a number of

[1]**-some** /-s(ə)m/ *suffix* (→ *adj*) characterized by a (specified) thing, quality, state, or action ⟨*awe*some⟩ ⟨*burden*some⟩ ⟨*cuddle*some⟩ [ME *-som*, fr OE *-sum*; akin to OHG *-sam* -some, OE *sum* some]

[2]**-some** *suffix* (→ *n*) group of (so many) members, esp people ⟨*four*some⟩ [ME (northern) *-sum*, fr ME *sum*, pron, one, some]

[3]**-some** /-,sohm/ *comb form* (→ *n*) **1** intracellular particle ⟨*lyso*some⟩ **2** chromosome ⟨*mono*some⟩ [NL *-somat-*, *-soma*, fr Gk *sōmat-*, *sōma* – more at [2]SOMA]

[1]**somebody** /'sumbədi/ *pron* some indefinite or unspecified person

[2]**somebody** *n* a person of position or importance

somehow /'sum,how/ *adv* **1a** by some means not known or designated **b** no matter how ⟨*got to get across ~*⟩ **2** for some mysterious reason

someone /'sumwən, -,wun/ *pron* somebody

someplace /'sum,plays/ *adv, chiefly NAm* somewhere

somersault /'sumə,sawlt/ *n* a leaping or rolling movement in which a person turns forwards or backwards in a complete revolution bringing the feet over the head and finally landing on the feet [MF *sombresaut* leap, deriv of L *super* over + *saltus* leap, fr *saltus*, pp of *salire* to leap – more at [1]OVER, SALLY] – **somersault** *vi*

[1]**something** /'sumthing/ *pron* **1a** some indeterminate or unspecified thing ⟨*look for ~ cheaper*⟩ – used to replace forgotten matter or to express vagueness ⟨*he's ~ or other in the Foreign Office*⟩ **b** some part; a certain amount ⟨*seen ~ of her work*⟩ **2a** a person or thing of consequence ⟨*make ~ of one's life*⟩ ⟨*their daughter is quite ~*⟩ **b** some truth or value ⟨*there's ~ in what you say*⟩ – **something of a** a fairly notable ⟨*is* something of a *raconteur*⟩

[2]**something** *adv* **1** in some degree; somewhat ⟨~ *over £5*⟩ ⟨*shaped ~ like a funnel*⟩ – also used to suggest approximation ⟨*there were ~ like 1,000 people there*⟩ **2** to an extreme degree ⟨*swears ~ awful*⟩ – infml

,something 'else *pron* sthg or sby that makes others pall in comparison – infml ⟨*her apple strudels were ~*⟩

[1]**sometime** /'sum,tiem/ *adv* **1** at some unspecified future time ⟨*I'll do it ~*⟩ **2** at some point of time in a specified period ⟨~ *last night*⟩ ⟨~ *next week*⟩

[2]**sometime** *adj* having been formerly; LATE 2b ⟨*the ~ chairman*⟩

[1]**'some,times** *adv* at intervals; occasionally; NOW AND AGAIN

[2]**sometimes** *adj, archaic* sometime, former

somewhat /'sumwot/ *adv* to some degree; slightly

[1]**somewhere** /'sum,weə/ *adv* **1** in, at, or to some unknown or unspecified place **2** to a place or state symbolizing positive accomplishment or progress ⟨*at last we're getting ~*⟩ **3** in the vicinity of; approximately ⟨~ *about 9 o'clock*⟩

[2]**somewhere** *n* an undetermined or unnamed place

-somic /-sohmik/ *comb form* (→ *adj*) having (so many) times the haploid number of one of the chromosomes ⟨*tri*somic⟩ – compare -PLOID [ISV [3]*-some* + *-ic*] – **-somy** *comb form* (→ *n*)

somite /'sohmiet/ *n* any of the longitudinal series of body segments of a higher invertebrate or embryonic vertebrate [ISV, fr Gk *sōma* body – more at [2]SOMA] – **somitic** /-'mitik/ *adj*

sommelier /,suməl'yay/ *n* a waiter in a restaurant who has charge of wines and their service [F, fr MF, court official charged with transportation of supplies, pack-animal driver, fr OProv *saumalier* pack-animal driver, fr *sauma* pack animal, load of a pack animal, fr LL *sagma* packsaddle, fr Gk]

somnambulist /som'nambyoolist/ *n* sby who walks in his/her sleep [NL *somnambulus*, fr L *somnus* sleep + *ambulare* to walk] – **somnambulant** *adj*, **somnambulism** *n*, **somnambulate** /-layt/ *vi*, **somnambulistic** /-'listik/ *adj*, **somnambulistically** *adv*

somniferous /som'nifərəs/ *adj* soporific [L *somnifer*, fr *somnus* + *-fer* -ferous] – **somniferously** *adv*

somnolent /'somnələnt/ *adj* **1** inclined to or heavy with sleep **2** tending to induce sleep ⟨*a ~ sermon*⟩ [ME *sompnolent*, fr MF, fr L *somnolentus*, fr *somnus* sleep; akin to OE *swefn* sleep, Gk *hypnos*] – **somnolence** *n*, **somnolently** *adv*

[1]**'so much** *adv* to the degree indicated or suggested ⟨*if they lose their way, ~ the better for us*⟩ – compare MUCH 1a(1)

[2]**so much** *adj* **1** a certain amount of ⟨*can spend only ~ time on it*⟩ – compare MUCH 1 **2** – used as an intensive before mass nouns ⟨*sounded like ~ nonsense*⟩

[3]**so much** *pron* **1** sthg (e g an amount or price) unspecified or undetermined ⟨*charge ~ a mile*⟩ **2** all that can or need be said or done ⟨~ *for the history of the case*⟩ – compare MUCH 1

so 'much as *adv* even ⟨*can't ~ remember his name now*⟩

son /sun/ *n* **1a** a male offspring, esp of human beings **b** a male adopted child **c** a male descendant – often pl **2** *cap* the second person of the Trinity; Christ **3** a person closely associated with or deriving from a specified background, place, etc ⟨*a ~ of the welfare state*⟩ [ME *sone*, fr OE *sunu*; akin to OHG *sun* son, Gk *hyios*] – **sonless** *adj*, **sonship** *n*

sonant /'sohnənt/ *adj* **1** *of a speech sound* voiced **2** *of a consonant sound* syllabic [L *sonant-*, *sonans*, prp of *sonare* to sound – more at [3]SOUND] – **sonant** *n*

sonar /'sohnə/ *n* an apparatus that detects the presence and location of a submerged object (by reflected sound waves) [*so*und *na*vigation *r*anging]

sonata /sə'nahtə/ *n* an instrumental musical composition typically for 1 or 2 players and of 3 or 4 movements in contrasting forms and keys [It, fr *sonare* to sound, fr L]

sonata form *n* a musical form that consists basically of an exposition, a development, and a recapitulation and that is used esp for the first movement of a sonata or symphony

sonatina /ˌsonəˈteenə/ *n* a short usu simplified sonata [It, dim. of *sonata*]

sonde /sond/ *n* any of various devices for testing physical conditions (e g at high altitudes); *esp* a radiosonde [F, lit., sounding line – more at [6]SOUND]

son et lumière /ˌson ay loohˈmyeə/ *n* an entertainment held at night at a historical site (e g a cathedral or stately home) that uses lighting and recorded sound to present the place's history [F, lit., sound and light]

song /song/ *n* **1** the act, art, or product of singing **2** poetry ⟨*famous in ~ and story*⟩ **3** (the melody of) a short musical composition usu with words **4** a very small sum ⟨*sold for a ~*⟩ [ME, fr OE *sang*; akin to OE *singan* to sing]

ˌsong and ˈdance *n, chiefly Br* a fuss, commotion ⟨*it's nothing to make a ~ about*⟩ – infml

ˈsongˌbird /-ˌbuhd/ *n* **1** a bird that utters a succession of musical tones **2** a passerine bird

Song of Solomon /ˈsoləmən/ *n* a collection of love poems forming a book in canonical Jewish and Christian Scripture [fr the opening verse: 'The song of songs, which is Solomon's"]

Song of Songs *n* SONG OF SOLOMON [trans of Heb *shīr hashshīrīm*]

songster /ˈsongstə/, *fem* **songstress** /-stris/ *n* a skilled singer

ˈsong ˌthrush *n* a common Old World thrush that is largely brown above and white below

ˈsongˌwriter /-ˌrietə/ *n* a person who composes words or music for (popular) songs – **songwriting** *n*

sonic /ˈsonik/ *adj* **1** *of waves and vibrations* having a frequency within the audibility range of the human ear **2** using, produced by, or relating to sound waves ⟨*~ altimeter*⟩ **3** of or being the speed of sound in air at sea level (about 340 m/s or 741 mph) [L *sonus* sound – more at [3]SOUND] – **sonically** *adv*

ˌsonic ˈboom *n* a sound resembling an explosion produced when a shock wave formed at the nose of an aircraft travelling at supersonic speed reaches the ground

ˈson-in-ˌlaw *n, pl* **sons-in-law** the husband of one's daughter

sonnet /ˈsonit/ *n* (a poem in) a fixed verse form with any of various rhyming schemes, consisting typically of 14 lines of 10 syllables each [It *sonetto*, fr OProv *sonet* little song, fr *son* sound, song, fr L *sonus* sound]

sonneteer /ˌsoniˈtiə/ *n* a composer of sonnets, esp without high standards

sonny /ˈsuni/ *n* a young boy – usu used in address; infml [*son* + [4]*-y*]

sonobuoy /ˈsohnohˌboy/ *n* a buoy equipped for detecting underwater sounds and transmitting them by radio [L *sonus* sound + E *-o-* + *buoy* – more at [3]SOUND]

son of a bitch *n, pl* **sons of bitches** BASTARD 3 – slang

son of God *n* **1** *cap S* MESSIAH 1 **2** a person established in the love of God by divine promise

son of man /man/ *n, pl* **sons of men** **1** a human being – usu pl **2** *often cap S&M* God's messiah destined to preside over the final judgment of mankind

sonorous /ˈsonərəs, ˈsoh-/ *adj* **1** giving out sound (e g when struck) **2** pleasantly loud **3** impressive in effect or style ⟨*made a ~ speech to the assembly*⟩ [L *sonorus*; akin to L *sonus* sound] – **sonorously** *adv*, **sonorousness** *n*, **sonority** /səˈnorəti/ *n*

sonsy, sonsie /ˈsunzi/ *adj, chiefly Scot* buxom, comely [Sc *sons* health, fr or akin to IrGael *sonas* good fortune]

sool /soohl, sool/ *vt, Austr & NZ* to incite, urge *on* [E dial. *sool* (to pull by the ears), of unknown origin]

[1]**soon** /soohn/ *adv* **1** before long; without undue time lapse ⟨*~ after sunrise*⟩ **2** in a prompt manner; speedily ⟨*as ~ as possible*⟩ ⟨*the ~er the better*⟩ **3** in agreement with one's preference; willingly – in comparisons ⟨*I'd ~er walk than drive*⟩ ⟨*I'd just as ~ not*⟩ [ME *soone*, fr OE *sōna*; akin to OHG *sān* immediately] – **no sooner ... than** at the very moment that ⟨no sooner *built* than *knocked down again*⟩

[2]**soon** *adj* advanced in time; early ⟨*the ~est date that can be arranged – The Times*⟩

ˌsooner or ˈlater /ˈsoohnə/ *adv* at some uncertain future time; eventually

[1]**soot** /soot/ *n* a fine black powder that consists chiefly of carbon and is formed by combustion, or separated from fuel during combustion [ME, fr OE *sōt*; akin to OIr *sūide* soot, OE *sittan* to sit]

[2]**soot** *vt* to coat or cover with soot

soothe /soohdh/ *vt* **1** to calm (as if) by showing attention or concern; placate **2** to relieve, alleviate **3** to bring comfort or reassurance to ~ *vi* to bring peace or ease [ME *sothen* to prove the truth, fr OE *sōthian*, fr *sōth* true; akin to OHG *sand* true, Gk *etos*, L *esse* to be] – **soother** *n*, **soothingly** *adv*

soothsay /ˈsoohthˌsay/ *vi* to predict the future; prophesy [back- formation fr *soothsayer*, fr ME *sothseyer*, fr *soth, sooth* truth + *seyer, sayer* sayer] – **soothsayer** *n*

sooty /ˈsooti/ *adj* **1a** producing soot ⟨*~ fires*⟩ **b** dirtied with soot **2** of the colour of soot – **sootily** *adv*, **sootiness** *n*

[1]**sop** /sop/ *n* **1** a piece of food, esp bread, dipped, steeped, or for dipping in a liquid (e g soup) **2** sthg offered as a concession, appeasement, or bribe [ME *soppe*, fr OE *sopp*; akin to OE *sūpan* to swallow – more at SUP]

[2]**sop** *vt* **-pp-** to soak or dip (as if) in liquid ⟨*~ bread in gravy*⟩ – compare SOP UP

sophism /ˈsofiz(ə)m/ *n* **1** an argument apparently correct but actually fallacious; *esp* such an argument used to deceive **2** use of sophisms; sophistry – **sophistic** /-ˈfistik/, **sophistical** *adj*, **sophistically** *adv*

sophist /ˈsofist/ *n* a faultfinding or fallacious reasoner [L *sophista*, fr Gk *sophistēs*, lit., expert, wise man, fr *sophizesthai* to become wise, deceive, fr *sophos* clever, wise]

sophisticate /səˈfistikət/ *n* a sophisticated person

sophisticated /səˈfistiˌkaytid/ *adj* **1a** highly complicated or developed; complex ⟨*~ electronic devices*⟩ **b** worldly-wise, knowing ⟨*a ~ adolescent*⟩ **2** intellectually subtle or refined ⟨*a ~ novel*⟩ **3** not in a natural, pure, or original state; adulterated ⟨*a ~*

oil⟩ [ML *sophisticatus*, pp of *sophisticare* to adulterate, corrupt, complicate, fr L *sophisticus* sophistic, fr Gk *sophistikos*, fr *sophistēs* sophist] – **sophisticatedly** *adv*, **sophistication** /-'kaysh(ə)n/ *n*

sophistry /'sofistri/ *n* speciously subtle reasoning or argument

sophomore /'sofə,maw/ *n, NAm* a student in his/her second year at college or secondary school [prob fr Gk *sophos* wise + *mōros* foolish – more at MORON] – **sophomoric** /-'morik/ *adj*

-sophy /-səfi/ *comb form* (→ *n*) knowledge; wisdom; science ⟨*theo*sophy⟩ [ME *-sophie*, fr OF, fr L *-sophia*, fr Gk, fr *sophia* wisdom, fr *sophos*]

[1]**soporific** /,sopə'rifik/ *adj* **1** causing or tending to cause sleep **2** of or marked by sleepiness or lethargy [prob fr F *soporifique*, fr L *sopor* deep sleep; akin to L *somnus* sleep – more at SOMNOLENT]

[2]**soporific** *n* a soporific agent; *specif* HYPNOTIC 1

[1]**sopping** /'soping/ *adj* wet through; soaking [fr prp of [2]*sop*]

[2]**sopping** *adv* to an extreme degree of wetness ⟨~ *wet*⟩

soppy /'sopi/ *adj* **1** weakly sentimental; mawkish ⟨*you get so* ~ *about couples* – Iris Murdoch⟩ **2** *chiefly Br* silly, inane ***USE*** infml [[1]*sop* + [1]*-y*] – **soppily** *adv*, **soppiness** *n*

sopranino /,soprə'neenoh/ *n, pl* **sopraninos** a musical instrument (e g a recorder or saxophone) higher in pitch than the soprano [It, dim. of *soprano*]

soprano /sə'prahnoh/ *n, pl* **sopranos 1** the highest part in 4-part harmony **2** (a person with) the highest singing voice of women, boys, or castrati **3** a member of a family of instruments having the highest range [It, adj & n, fr *sopra* above, fr L *supra* – more at SUPRA-] – **soprano** *adj*

sop up /sop/ *vt* to mop up (e g water) so as to leave a dry surface

[1]**sorb** /sawb/ *n* [4]SERVICE [F *sorbe* fruit of the service tree, fr L *sorbum*]

[2]**sorb** *vt* to take up and hold by either adsorption or absorption [back-formation fr *absorb* & *adsorb*] – **sorbable** *adj*, **sorbent** *n*, **sorbability** /-bə'biləti/ *n*, **sorption** /'sawpsh(ə)n/ *n*

Sorb *n* Wendish [G *Sorbe*, fr Sorbian *Serb*] – **Sorbian** *adj or n*

sorbet /'sawbit/ *n* WATER ICE; *also* SHERBET 2 [MF, a fruit drink, fr OIt *sorbetto*, fr Turk *şerbet* – more at SHERBET]

sorcerer /'saws(ə)rə/, *fem* **sorceress** /-ris/ *n* a person who uses magical power, esp with the aid of evil spirits; a wizard

sorcery /'saws(ə)ri/ *n* the arts and practices of a sorcerer [ME *sorcerie*, fr OF, fr *sorcier* sorcerer, fr (assumed) VL *sortiarius*, fr L *sort-, sors* chance, lot]

sordid /'sawdid/ *adj* **1a** dirty, filthy **b** wretched, squalid **2** base, vile ⟨~ *motives*⟩ **3** meanly avaricious; niggardly **4** of a dull or muddy colour [L *sordidus*, fr *sordes* dirt – more at SWARTHY] – **sordidly** *adv*, **sordidness** *n*

sordino /saw'deenoh/ *n, pl* **sordini** /-ni/ MUTE 3 ⟨*con* sordini⟩ [It, fr *sordo* silent, fr L *surdus* – more at SURD]

[1]**sore** /saw/ *adj* **1a** causing pain or distress **b** painfully sensitive ⟨~ *muscles*⟩ **c** hurt or inflamed so as to be or seem painful ⟨~ *runny eyes*⟩ **2a** causing irritation or offence ⟨*overtime is a* ~ *point with him*⟩ **b** causing great difficulty or anxiety; desperate ⟨*in* ~ *straits*⟩ **3** *chiefly NAm* angry, vexed [ME *sor*, fr OE *sār*; akin to OHG *sēr* sore, L *saevus* fierce] – **soreness** *n*

[2]**sore** *n* **1** a localized sore spot on the body; *esp* one (e g an ulcer) with the tissues ruptured or abraded and usu infected **2** a source of pain or vexation; an affliction

[3]**sore** *adv, archaic* sorely

'sore,head /-,hed/ *n, NAm* a person easily angered or disgruntled – infml – **sorehead, soreheaded** /-'hedid/ *adj*

sorely /'sawli/ *adv* **1** painfully, grievously **2** much, extremely ⟨~ *needed changes*⟩

sorghum /'sawgəm/ *n* any of an economically important genus of Old World tropical grasses similar to maize in habit but with the spikelets in pairs on a hairy stalk [NL, genus name, fr It *sorgo*]

sorority /sə'rorəti/ *n* a club of women students usu living in the same house in some American universities – compare FRATERNITY [ML *sororitas* sisterhood, fr L *soror* sister – more at SISTER]

[1]**sorrel** /'sorəl/ *n* **1** brownish orange to light brown **2** a sorrel-coloured animal; *esp* a sorrel-coloured horse [ME *sorelle*, fr MF *sorel*, n & adj, fr *sor* reddish brown]

[2]**sorrel** *n* **1** [1]DOCK **2** WOOD SORREL [ME *sorel*, fr MF *surele*, fr OF, fr *sur* sour, of Gmc origin; akin to OHG *sūr* sour – more at SOUR]

[1]**sorrow** /'soroh/ *n* **1** deep distress and regret (e g over the loss of sthg precious) **2** a cause or display of grief or sadness [ME *sorow*, fr OE *sorg*; akin to OHG *sorga* sorrow, OSlav *sraga* sickness]

[2]**sorrow** *vi* to feel or express sorrow – **sorrower** *n*

'sorrowful /-f(ə)l/ *adj* expressive of or inducing sorrow ⟨*a* ~ *tale*⟩ – **sorrowfully** *adv*, **sorrowfulness** *n*

sorry /'sori/ *adj* **1** feeling regret, penitence, or pity ⟨*felt* ~ *for the poor wretch*⟩ **2** inspiring sorrow, pity, or scorn ⟨*looked a* ~ *sight in his torn clothes*⟩ [ME *sory*, fr OE *sārig*, fr *sār* sore] – **sorriness** *n*

[1]**sort** /sawt/ *n* **1a** a group constituted on the basis of any common characteristic; a class, kind **b** an instance of a kind ⟨*a* ~ *of herbal medicine*⟩ **2** nature, disposition ⟨*people of an evil* ~⟩ **3** a letter or piece of type in a fount **4** a person, individual – infml ⟨*he's not a bad* ~⟩ [ME, fr MF *sorte*, prob fr ML *sort-, sors*, fr L, chance, lot] – **of sorts/of a sort** of an inconsequential or mediocre quality – **out of sorts 1** somewhat ill **2** grouchy, irritable

[2]**sort** *vt* **1** to put in a rank or particular place according to kind, class, or quality ⟨~ *the good apples from the bad*⟩ – often + *through* **2** *chiefly Scot* to put in working order; mend ⟨~ *a vacuum cleaner*⟩ – **sortable** *adj*, **sorter** *n* – **sort with** to correspond to; agree with – fml

sortie /'sawti/ *n* **1** a sudden issuing of troops from a defensive position **2** a single mission or attack by 1 aircraft **3** a brief trip to a hostile or unfamiliar place [F, fr MF, fr *sortir* to go out, escape] – **sortie** *vi*

'sort of *adv* **1** to a moderate degree; rather **2** KIND OF ⟨~ *7 to half past – SEU S*⟩ ***USE*** infml

'sort-,out *n, chiefly Br* an act of putting things in order ⟨*my study needs a good* ~⟩

sort out *vt* **1** to clarify or resolve, esp by thoughtful consideration ⟨sorting out *his problems*⟩ **2a** to separate from a mass or group ⟨sort out *the important papers and throw the rest away*⟩ **b** to clear up; tidy

⟨*will take ages to* sort out *this mess*⟩ **3** to make (e g a person) less confused or unsettled ⟨*hoped the doctor would* sort *him out*⟩ **4** *chiefly Br* to punish, esp by violent means – infml

sorus /'sawrəs/ *n, pl* **sori** /-rie/ a cluster of plant reproductive bodies of a lower plant; *esp* any of the dots on the underside of a fertile fern frond consisting of a cluster of spores [NL, fr Gk *sōros* heap; akin to L *tumēre* to swell – more at THUMB]

SOS /,es oh 'es/ *n* **1** an internationally recognized signal of distress which is rendered in Morse code as · · · – – – · · · **2** a call or request for help or rescue [letters chosen purely for being simple to transmit & recognize in Morse code]

[1]**so-so** /'soh ,soh/ *adv* moderately well; tolerably

[2]**so-so** *adj* neither very good nor very bad; middling

sostenuto /,sostə'nyoohtoh/ *adj or adv* sustained to or beyond the note's full value – used in music [It, fr pp of *sostenere* to sustain, fr L *sustinēre*]

sot /sot/ *n* a habitual drunkard [ME, fool, fr OE *sott*] – **sottish** *adj*

soteriology /soh,tiəri'oləji/ *n* theology dealing with salvation, esp as effected by Jesus [Gk *sōtērion* salvation, fr *sōtēr* saviour, fr *sōzein* to save; akin to Gk *sōma* body – more at [2]SOMA] – **soteriological** /-ri-ə'lojikl/ *adj*

'**so that** *conj* THAT 2(1)

sotto voce /,sotoh 'vohchi/ *adv or adj* **1** under the breath; in an undertone; *also* in a private manner **2** at a very low volume – used in music [It *sottovoce*, lit., under the voice]

sou /sooh/ *n, pl* **sous** /sooh(z)/ **1** any of various former French coins of low value **2** the smallest amount of money ⟨*hadn't a* ~ *to his name*⟩ [F, fr OF *sol*, fr LL *solidus* solidus]

soubrette /sooh'bret/ *n* (an actress who plays) a coquettish maid or frivolous young woman in comedies [F, fr Prov *soubreto*, fem of *soubret* coy, fr *soubra* to surmount, exceed, fr L *superare* – more at INSUPERABLE]

soubriquet /'soohbri,kay/ *n* a sobriquet

souchong /sooh'chong, -'shong/ *n* a large-leaved black tea, esp from China [Chin (Pek) *hsiao*[3] *chung*[3], lit., small sort]

[1]**soufflé** /'soohflay/ *n* a light fluffy baked or chilled dish made with a thick sauce into which egg yolks, stiffly beaten egg whites, and sometimes gelatin are incorporated [F, fr *soufflé*, pp of *souffler* to blow, puff up, fr L *sufflare*, fr *sub-* + *flare* to blow – more at [1]BLOW]

[2]**soufflé, souffléed** /'soohflayd/ *adj* puffed or made light by or in cooking

sough /sow/ *vi* to make a sound like that of wind in the trees [ME *swoughen*, fr OE *swōgan*; akin to Goth *gaswogjan* to groan, Lith *svagėti* to sound] – **sough** *n*

sought /sawt/ *past of* SEEK

'**sought-,after** *adj* greatly desired or courted ⟨*the world's most* ~ *concert entertainers – Saturday Review*⟩

souk /soohk/ *n* an often covered market in a Muslim country [Ar *sūq* market]

[1]**soul** /sohl/ *n* **1** the immaterial essence or animating principle of an individual life **2** the spiritual principle embodied in human beings, all rational and spiritual beings, or the universe **3** all that constitutes a person's self **4a** an active or essential part ⟨*minorities are the very* ~ *of democracy*⟩ **b** a moving spirit; a leader ⟨*the* ~ *of the rebellion*⟩ **5** spiritual vitality; fervour **6** a person ⟨*she's a kind old* ~⟩ **7** exemplification, personification ⟨*he's the* ~ *of integrity*⟩ **8a** a strong positive feeling esp of intense sensitivity and emotional fervour conveyed esp by American Negro performers **b** negritude **c** music that originated in American Negro gospel singing, is closely related to rhythm and blues, and is characterized by intensity of feeling and earthiness [ME *soule*, fr OE *sāwol*; akin to OHG *sēula* soul] – **souled** *adj*

[2]**soul** *adj* (characteristic) of American Negroes or their culture

'**soul ,brother** *n* a male Negro – used esp by other Negroes

'**soul-de,stroying** *adj* giving no chance for the mind to work; very uninteresting

'**soul ,food** *n* food (e g chitterlings and ham hocks) traditionally eaten by southern US Negroes

'**soulful** /-f(ə)l/ *adj* full of or expressing esp intense or excessive feeling ⟨*a* ~ *song*⟩ – **soulfully** *adv*, **soulfulness** *n*

'**soulless** /-lis/ *adj* **1** having no soul or no warmth of feeling **2** bleak, uninviting ⟨*a* ~ *room*⟩ – **soullessly** *adv*, **soullessness** *n*

'**soul ,mate** *n* either of 2 people, esp of opposite sex, having a very close affinity with one another; a lover

'**soul-,searching** *n* scrutiny of one's mind and conscience, esp with regard to aims and motives

[1]**sound** /sownd/ *adj* **1a** healthy **b** free from defect or decay ⟨~ *timber*⟩ **2** solid, firm; *also* stable **3a** free from error, fallacy, or misapprehension ⟨~ *reasoning*⟩ **b** exhibiting or grounded in thorough knowledge and experience ⟨~ *scholarship*⟩ **c** conforming to accepted views; orthodox **4a** deep and undisturbed ⟨*a* ~ *sleep*⟩ **b** thorough, severe ⟨*a* ~ *whipping*⟩ **5** showing integrity and good judgment [ME, fr OE *gesund*; akin to OHG *gisunt* healthy] – **soundly** *adv*, **soundness** *n*

[2]**sound** *adv* fully, thoroughly ⟨~ *asleep*⟩

[3]**sound** *n* **1a** the sensation perceived by the sense of hearing **b** a particular auditory impression or quality ⟨*the* ~ *of children playing*⟩ **c** mechanical radiant energy that is transmitted by longitudinal pressure waves in a material medium (e g air) and is the objective cause of hearing **2** a speech sound ⟨-cher *of 'teacher" and* -ture *of 'creature" have the same* ~⟩ ☞ ALPHABET **3** the impression conveyed by sthg ⟨*he's having a rough time by the* ~ *of it*⟩ **4** hearing distance; earshot **5** a characteristic musical style ⟨*the Liverpool* ~ *of the 1960s*⟩ **6** radio broadcasting as opposed to television [ME *soun*, fr OF *son*, fr L *sonus*; akin to OE *swinn* melody, L *sonare* to sound, Skt *svanati* it sounds] – **soundless** *adj*, **soundlessly** *adv*

[4]**sound** *vi* **1a** to make a sound **b** to resound **c** to give a summons by sound ⟨*the bugle* ~s *to battle*⟩ **2** to have a specified import when heard; seem ⟨*his story* ~s *incredible*⟩ ~ *vt* **1a** to cause to emit sound ⟨~ *a trumpet*⟩ **b** to give out (a sound) ⟨~ *an A*⟩ **2** to put into words; voice **3a** to make known; proclaim ⟨~ *his praises far and wide*⟩ **b** to order, signal, or indicate by a sound ⟨~ *the alarm*⟩ **4** to examine by causing to emit sounds – **soundable** *adj*

[5]**sound** *n* **1a** a long broad sea inlet **b** a long passage of water connecting 2 larger bodies or separating a mainland and an island **2** the air bladder of a fish

[ME, fr OE *sund* swimming, sea & ON *sund* swimming, strait; akin to OE *swimman* to swim]

[6]**sound** *vt* **1** to measure the depth of ⟨~ *a well*⟩ **2** to explore or examine (a body cavity) with sound ~ *vi* **1** to determine the depth of water, esp with a sounding line **2** *of a fish or whale* to dive down suddenly [ME *sounden*, fr MF *sonder*, fr *sonde* sounding line, prob of Gmc origin; akin to OE *sundline* sounding line, *sund* sea]

[7]**sound** *n* a probe for exploring or sounding body cavities [F *sonde*, fr MF, lit., sounding line]

ˈsound ˌbarrier *n* a sudden large increase in aerodynamic drag that occurs as an aircraft nears the speed of sound

ˈsoundˌboard /-ˌbawd/ *n* **1** a thin resonant board so placed in a musical instrument as to reinforce its sound by sympathetic vibration **2** SOUNDING BOARD 1a(1)

ˈsound ˌbow /boh/ *n* the thick part of a bell against which the clapper strikes

ˈsound ˌbox *n* the hollow resonating chamber in the body of a musical instrument (e g a violin)

ˈsound efˌfect *n* an effect that corresponds to and esp imitates a sound required for a dramatic production (e g a play or radio programme) – usu pl

sounder /ˈsowndə/ *n* a device for making soundings [[6]SOUND + [2]-ER]

ˈsound ˌhole *n* an opening in the soundboard of a musical instrument for increasing resonance

[1]**sounding** /ˈsownding/ *n* **1a** measurement by sounding **b** the depth so determined **2** the measurement of atmospheric conditions **3** a probe, test, or sampling of opinion or intention – often pl [[6]*sound*]

[2]**sounding** *adj* **1** sonorous, resounding **2** making a usu specified sound or impression – usu in combination ⟨*odd* ~⟩ [[4]*sound*] – **soundingly** *adv*

ˈsounding ˌboard *n* **1a(1)** a structure behind or over a pulpit, rostrum, or platform to direct sound forwards **(2)** SOUNDBOARD 1 **b** a device or agency that helps disseminate opinions or ideas **2** sby or sthg used to test reaction to new ideas, plans, etc

ˈsounding ˌline *n* a line or wire weighted at one end for sounding

sound off *vi* **1** to voice opinions freely and vigorously **2** *chiefly NAm* to speak loudly *USE* infml

sound out *vt* to attempt to find out the views or intentions of ⟨sound *him* out *about the new proposals*⟩

[1]**ˈsoundˌproof** /-ˌproohf/ *adj* impervious to sound ⟨~ *glass*⟩

[2]**soundproof** *vt* to insulate so as to obstruct the passage of sound

ˈsound ˌshift *n* SHIFT 6

ˈsound ˌtrack *n* the area on a film that carries the sound recording; *also* the recorded music accompanying a film

soup /soohp/ *n* **1** a liquid food typically having a meat, fish, or vegetable stock as a base and often thickened and containing pieces of solid food **2** an awkward or embarrassing predicament – infml ⟨*he's really in the* ~ *over that business last night*⟩ **3** nitroglycerine – slang [F *soupe* sop, soup, of Gmc origin; akin to ON *soppa* soup, OE *sopp* sop] – **soupy** *adj*

soupçon /ˈsooh(p)son, -sonh/ *n* a little bit; a dash [F, lit., suspicion, fr (assumed) VL *suspection-, suspectio*, fr L *suspectus*, pp of *suspicere* to suspect – more at [3]SUSPECT]

ˈsoup ˌkitchen *n* an establishment dispensing minimum food (e g soup and bread) to the needy

soup up *vt* **1** to increase the power of (an engine or car) **2** to make more attractive, interesting, etc *USE* infml [prob fr E slang *soup* (drug injected into a racehorse to stimulate it)]

[1]**sour** /sowə/ *adj* **1** being or inducing the one of the 4 basic taste sensations that is produced chiefly by acids ⟨~ *pickles*⟩ – compare BITTER, SALT, SWEET **2a(1)** having the acid taste or smell (as if) of fermentation ⟨~ *cream*⟩ **(2)** of or relating to fermentation **b** smelling or tasting of decay; rotten ⟨~ *breath*⟩ **c** wrong, awry ⟨*a project gone* ~⟩ **3a** unpleasant, distasteful **b** morose, bitter **4** *esp of soil* acid in reaction **5** *esp of petroleum products* containing foul-smelling sulphur compounds [ME, fr OE *sūr*; akin to OHG *sūr* sour, Lith *suras* salty] – **sourish** *adj*, **sourly** *adv*, **sourness** *n*

[2]**sour** *n* **1** the primary taste sensation produced by sthg sour **2** *chiefly NAm* a cocktail made with a usu specified spirit, lemon or lime juice, sugar, and sometimes soda water ⟨*a whisky* ~⟩

[3]**sour** *vb* to make or become sour

source /saws/ *n* **1** the point of origin of a stream of water **2a(1)** a generative force; a cause **(2)** a means of supply ⟨*a secret* ~ *of wealth*⟩ **b(1)** a place of origin; a beginning **(2)** sby or sthg that initiates **(3)** a person, publication, etc that supplies information, esp at firsthand **3** *archaic* a spring, fountain [ME *sours*, fr MF *sors, sourse*, fr OF, fr pp of *sourdre* to rise, spring forth, fr L *surgere* – more at SURGE] – **sourceless** *adj*

sourdough /ˈsowəˌdoh/ *n, NAm* an old-timer, esp a prospector, of Alaska or NW Canada [fr the use of fermenting yeast for making bread in prospectors' camps]

ˌsour ˈgrapes *n pl* disparagement of sthg achieved or owned by another because unable to attain it oneself [fr the fable ascribed to Aesop of the fox who, finding himself unable to reach some grapes, disparaged them as sour]

ˈsourˌpuss /-ˌpoos/ *n* a habitually gloomy or bitter person – infml [*sour* + *puss* (face), fr IrGael *pus* mouth, fr MIr *bus*]

sousaphone /ˈsoohzəˌfohn/ *n* a large tuba that has a flared adjustable bell and is designed to encircle the player and rest on the left shoulder [John Philip *Sousa* †1932 US bandmaster & composer]

[1]**souse** /sows/ *vt* **1** to pickle ⟨~d *herring*⟩ **2a** to plunge in liquid; immerse **b** to drench, saturate **3** to make drunk; inebriate – infml ~ *vi* to become immersed or drenched [ME *sousen*, fr MF *souz, souce* pickling solution, of Gmc origin; akin to OHG *sulza* brine, OE *sealt* salt]

[2]**souse** *n* **1** an act of sousing; a wetting **2** *chiefly NAm* sthg pickled; *esp* seasoned and chopped pork trimmings, fish, or shellfish

soutane /soohˈtan/ *n* a cassock [F, fr It *sottana*, lit., undergarment, fr fem of *sottano* being underneath, fr ML *subtanus*, fr L *subtus* underneath; akin to L *sub* under – more at UP]

souter /ˈsoohtə/ *n, chiefly Scot & NEng* a shoemaker [ME, fr OE *sūtere*, fr L *sutor*, fr *sutus*, pp of *suere* to sew – more at SEW]

[1]**south** /sowth; *also* sowdh *(in names) before words beginning with a vowel*/ *adj or adv* towards, at, belonging to, or coming from the south [ME, fr OE *sūth*; akin to OHG *sund-* south, OE *sunne* sun]

[2]south *n* **1** (the compass point corresponding to) the direction of the south terrestrial pole **2** *often cap* regions or countries lying to the south of a specified or implied point of orientation – **southward** *adv, adj, or n,* **southwards** *adv*

,South 'African *n* a native or inhabitant of the Republic of South Africa – **South African** *adj*

Southdown /'sowth,down/ *n* any of an English breed of small hornless meat-producing sheep with medium-length wool [*South Downs,* hills in SE England]

[1],south'east /-'eest/ *adj or adv* towards, at, belonging to, or coming from the southeast

[2]southeast *n* **1** (the general direction corresponding to) the compass point midway between south and east **2** *often cap* regions or countries lying to the southeast of a specified or implied point of orientation – **southeastward** *adv, adj, or n,* **southeastwards** *adv*

[1],south'easterly /-'eestəli/ *adj or adv* southeast [[2]*southeast* + *-erly* (as in *easterly*)]

[2]southeasterly, southeaster *n* a wind from the SE

,south'eastern /-'eestən/ *adj* **1** *often cap* (characteristic) of a region conventionally designated Southeast **2** southeast [[2]*southeast* + *-ern* (as in *eastern*)] – **southeasternmost** /-'eestən,mohst/ *adj*

[1]southerly /'sudhəli/ *adj or adv* south [[2]*south* + *-erly* (as in *easterly*)]

[2]southerly *n* a wind from the S

southern /'sudhən/ *adj* **1** *often cap* (characteristic) of a region conventionally designated South **2** south [ME *southern, southren,* fr OE *sūtherne*; akin to OHG *sundrōni* southern, OE *sūth* south] – **southernmost** *adj*

Southerner /'sudhənə/ *n* a native or inhabitant of the South

,southern 'lights *n pl* AURORA AUSTRALIS

'southern,wood /-,wood/ *n* a shrubby fragrant European wormwood with bitter foliage

southing /'sowdhing, -thing/ *n* **1** distance due south in latitude from the preceding point of measurement **2** southerly progress

'south,paw /-,paw/ *n* a left-hander; *specif* a boxer who leads with the right hand and guards with the left – **southpaw** *adj*

,south 'pole *n* **1a** *often cap S&P* the southernmost point of the rotational axis of the earth or another celestial body **b** the southernmost point on the celestial sphere, about which the stars seem to revolve **2** the southward-pointing pole of a magnet

south-southeast /,- -'-; *esp tech* ,sow sow'eest/ *n* a compass point midway between south and southeast

south-southwest /,- -'-; *esp tech* ,sow sow'est/ *n* a compass point midway between south and southwest

[1]southwest /,sowth'west; *esp tech* ,sow'west/ *adj or adv* towards, at, belonging to, or coming from the southwest

[2]southwest *n* **1** (the general direction corresponding to) the compass point midway between south and west **2** *often cap* regions or countries lying to the southwest of a specified or implied point of orientation – **southwestward** *adv, adj, or n,* **southwestwards** *adv*

southwester /,sowth'westə; *esp tech* ,sow'westə/ *n* a southwesterly

[1],south'westerly /-li/ *adj or adv* southwest

[2]southwesterly, southwester *n* a wind from the SW [[2]*southwest* + *-erly* (as in *westerly*)]

,south'western /-'westən/ *adj* **1** *often cap* (characteristic) of a region conventionally designated Southwest **2** southwest [[2]*southwest* + *-ern* (as in *western*)] – **southwesternmost** *adj*

[1]souvenir /,soohvə'niə/ *n* sthg that serves as a reminder (e g of a place or past event); a memento [F, lit., act of remembering, fr MF, fr (*se*) *souvenir* to remember, fr L *subvenire* to come up, come to mind – more at SUBVENTION] – **souvenir** *adj*

[2]souvenir *vt, Austr* to steal, pilfer – infml

sou'wester /,sow'westə/ *n* **1** a southwesterly **2a** a long usu oilskin waterproof coat worn esp at sea during stormy weather **b** a waterproof hat with a wide slanting brim longer at the back than in front ☞ GARMENT

[1]sovereign /'sovrin/ *n* **1a** one possessing sovereignty **b** an acknowledged leader ⟨*the rose,* ~ *among flowers*⟩ **2** a former British gold coin worth 1 pound [ME *soverain,* fr OF, fr *soverain,* adj]

[2]sovereign *adj* **1a** possessing supreme (political) power ⟨~ *ruler*⟩ **b** unlimited in extent; absolute ⟨~ *power*⟩ **c** enjoying political autonomy ⟨*a* ~ *state*⟩ **2a** of outstanding excellence or importance ⟨*their* ~ *sense of humour* – Sir Winston Churchill⟩ **b** of an unqualified nature; utmost ⟨~ *contempt*⟩ **3** (characteristic) of or befitting a sovereign [ME *soverain,* fr MF, fr OF, fr (assumed) VL *superanus,* fr L *super* over, above – more at [1]OVER] – **sovereignly** *adv,* **sovereignty** *n*

soviet /'sohvyət, 'so-/ *n* **1** an elected council in a Communist country **2** *pl, cap* the people, esp the leaders, of the USSR [Russ *sovet*] – **soviet** *adj, often cap,* **sovietism** *n, often cap*

sovran /'sovrən/ *n or adj* (a) sovereign – poetic [by alter. (influenced by It *sovrano,* adj)]

[1]sow /sow/ *n* **1** an adult female pig; *also* the adult female of various other animals (e g the grizzly bear) **2** (a mass of metal solidified in) a channel that conducts molten metal, esp iron, to moulds [ME *sowe,* fr OE *sugu*; akin to OE & OHG *sū* sow, L *sus* pig, swine, hog, Gk *hys*]

[2]sow /soh/ *vb* **sowed; sown** /sohn/, **sowed** *vi* to plant seed for growth, esp by scattering ~ *vt* **1a** to scatter (e g seed) on the earth for growth; *broadly* PLANT 1a **b** to strew (as if) with seed **c** to introduce into a selected environment **2** to implant, initiate ⟨~ *suspicion*⟩ **3** to disperse, disseminate [ME *sowen,* fr OE *sāwan*; akin to OHG *sāwen* to sow, L *serere*] – **sower** *n* – **sow one's wild oats** to indulge in youthful wildness and dissipation, usu before settling down to a steady way of life

'sow ,thistle /sow/ *n* any of a genus of spiny Old World composite plants widely naturalized as weeds

soy /soy/ *n* **1** an oriental brown liquid sauce made by subjecting soya beans to long fermentation and to digestion in brine **2** SOYA BEAN [Jap *shōyu,* fr Chin (Cant) *shî-yaū,* lit., soya-bean oil]

soya /'soyə/ *n* soy [D *soja,* fr Jap *shōyu*]

soya bean *n* (the edible oil-rich and protein-rich seeds of) an annual Asiatic leguminous plant widely grown for its seed and soil improvement

soya-bean oil *n* a pale yellow oil that is obtained from soya beans and is used chiefly as a cooking oil, in paints, varnishes, linoleum, printing ink, and soap, and as a source of phospholipids, fatty acids, and sterols

'soy,bean /-,been/ *n* SOYA BEAN

sozzled /'soz(ə)ld/ *adj, chiefly Br* drunk – slang; often humor [*sozzle* (to splash, souse, intoxicate)]

spa /spah/ *n* **1** a usu fashionable resort with mineral springs **2** a spring of mineral water [*Spa*, watering place in Belgium]

¹space /spays/ *n* **1** (the duration of) a period of time **2a** a limited extent in 1, 2, or 3 dimensions; distance, area, or volume **b** an amount of room set apart or available ⟨*parking* ~⟩ **3** any of the degrees between or above or below the lines of a musical staff **4a** a boundless 3-dimensional extent in which objects and events occur and have relative position and direction **b** physical space independent of what occupies it **5** the region beyond the earth's atmosphere ☞ ASTRONOMY **6** (a piece of type giving) a blank area separating words or lines (e g on a page) **7** a set of mathematical points, each defined by a set of coordinates **8** a brief interval during which a telegraph key is not causing electrical contact to be made [ME, fr OF *espace*, fr L *spatium* area, room, interval of space or time – more at SPEED] – **spaceless** *adj*

²space *vt* to place at intervals or arrange with space between – **spacer** *n*

'space,craft /-,krahft/ *n* a device designed to travel beyond the earth's atmosphere ☞ SPACE

,spaced-'out *adj* dazed or stupefied (as if) by a narcotic substance – slang

'space,flight /-,fliet/ *n* flight beyond the earth's atmosphere

space heating *n* the heating of spaces (e g by electricity, solar radiation, or fossil fuels), esp for human comfort, with the heater either within the space or external to it – **space heater** *n*

'space,man /-,man/, *fem* **'space,woman** *n* **1** one who travels outside the earth's atmosphere **2** a visitor to earth from outer space

'space ,mark *n* the mark

space platform *n* SPACE STATION

'space,ship /-,ship/ *n* a manned spacecraft

'space ,shuttle *n* a vehicle that has usu 2 stages and is designed to serve as a reusable transport between the earth and an orbiting space station ☞ SPACE

'space ,station *n* a manned artificial satellite designed for a fixed orbit about the earth and to serve as a base ☞ SPACE

'space ,suit *n* a suit equipped with life supporting provisions to make life in space possible for its wearer

,space-'time *n* **1** a system of 1 temporal and 3 spatial coordinates by which any physical object or event can be located **2** (the properties characteristic of) the whole or a portion of physical reality determinable by a four-dimensional coordinate system

'space ,walk *n* a trip outside a spacecraft made by an astronaut in space – **space walk** *vi*, **spacewalker** *n*, **spacewalking** *n*

spacey /'spaysi/ *adj* of or in a spaced-out state – slang ⟨*music with a* ~ *effect*⟩

spacing /'spaysing/ *n* **1a** the act of providing with spaces or placing at intervals **b** an arrangement in space ⟨*alter the* ~ *of the chairs*⟩ **2** the distance between any 2 objects in a usu regularly arranged series

spacious /'spayshəs/ *adj* **1** containing ample space; roomy **2a** broad or vast in area ⟨*a country of* ~ *plains*⟩ **b** large in scale or space; expansive [ME, fr MF *spacieux*, fr L *spatiosus*, fr *spatium* space, room] – **spaciously** *adv*, **spaciousness** *n*

¹spade /spayd/ *n* a digging implement that can be pushed into the ground with the foot [ME, fr OE *spadu*; akin to Gk *spathē* blade of a sword or oar, OHG *spān* chip of wood – more at ¹SPOON] – **spadeful** *n*

²spade *vt* to dig up, shape, or work (as if) with a spade

³spade *n* **1a** a playing card marked with 1 or more black figures shaped like a spearhead **b** *pl but sing or pl in constr* the suit comprising cards identified by these figures **2** a Negro – derog [It *spada* or Sp *espada* broad sword (used as a mark on playing cards); both fr L *spatha*, fr Gk *spathē* blade] – **in spades** in the extreme [fr spades being the highest suit in some card games]

'spade,work /-,wuhk/ *n* the routine preparatory work for an undertaking

spadix /'spaydiks/ *n, pl* **spadices** /-di,seez/ a spike of crowded flowers (e g in an arum) with a fleshy or succulent axis usu enclosed in a spathe [NL *spadic-*, *spadix*, fr L, frond torn from a palm tree, fr Gk *spadik-*, *spadix*, fr *span* to draw, pull – more at SPAN]

spaghetti /spə'geti/ *n* pasta in the form of thin often solid strings of varying widths smaller in diameter than macaroni [It, fr pl of *spaghetto*, dim. of *spago* cord, string]

spahi /'spah,(h)ee/ *n* **1** any of a former corps of irregular Turkish cavalry **2** any of a former corps of Algerian native cavalry in the French Army [MF, fr Turk *sipahi*, fr Per *sipāhī* cavalryman]

spake /spayk/ *archaic past of* SPEAK

¹spall /spawl/ *n* a small splinter or chip, esp of stone [ME *spalle*]

²spall *vt* to break up (stone, ore, etc) into fragments ~ *vi* **1** to break off fragments; chip **2** to undergo spallation – **spallable** *adj*

spallation /spə'laysh(ə)n/ *n* a nuclear reaction resulting in several particles being ejected as the result of a collision [²*spall*]

Spam /spam/ *trademark* – used for a tinned pork luncheon meat

¹span /span/ *archaic past of* SPIN

²span *n* **1** the distance from the end of the thumb to the end of the little finger of a spread hand; *also* a former English unit of length equal to 9in (about 0.23m) ☞ UNIT **2** an extent, distance, or spread between 2 limits: e g **a** a limited stretch (e g of time); *esp* an individual's lifetime **b** the full reach or extent ⟨*the remarkable* ~ *of his memory*⟩ **c** the distance or extent between abutments or supports (e g of a bridge); *also* a part of a bridge between supports **d** a wingspan [ME, fr OE *spann*; akin to OHG *spanna* span, MD *spannen* to stretch, hitch up, L *pendere* to weigh, Gk *span* to draw, pull]

³span *vt* **-nn-** **1** to measure (as if) by the hand with fingers and thumb extended **2a** to extend across ⟨*his career* ~ned *4 decades*⟩ **b** to form an arch over ⟨*a small bridge* ~ned *the pond*⟩ **c** to place or construct a span over

spandrel, spandril /'spandrəl/ *n* the space between the right or left exterior curve of an arch and an enclosing right angle [ME *spandrell*, fr AF *spaundre*, fr OF *espandre* to spread out – more at SPAWN]

[1]**spangle** /ˈspang·gl/ *n* **1** a sequin **2** a small glittering object or particle ⟨*gold* ~s *of dew* – Edith Sitwell⟩ [ME *spangel*, dim. of *spang* shiny ornament, prob of Scand origin; akin to ON *spöng* spangle; akin to OE *spang* buckle, MD *spannen* to stretch]

[2]**spangle** *vb* **spangling** /ˈspang·gling/ *vt* to set or sprinkle (as if) with spangles ~ *vi* to glitter as if covered with spangles; sparkle

Spaniard /ˈspanyəd/ *n* a native or inhabitant of Spain [ME *Spaignard*, fr MF *Espaignart*, fr *Espaigne* Spain, country in SW Europe, fr L *Hispania*]

spaniel /ˈspanyəl/ *n* **1** any of several breeds of small or medium-sized mostly short-legged dogs usu having long wavy hair, feathered legs and tail, and large drooping ears **2** a fawning servile person [ME *spaniell*, fr MF *espaignol*, lit., Spaniard, fr (assumed) VL *Hispaniolus*, fr L *Hispania* Spain]

Spanish /ˈspanish/ *n* **1** the official Romance language of Spain and of the countries colonized by Spaniards ☞ LANGUAGE **2** *pl in constr* the people of Spain [*Spanish*, adj, fr ME *Spainish*, fr *Spain*] – **Spanish** *adj*

,Spanish 'American *n* a native or inhabitant of any of the Spanish-speaking countries of America; *also* a citizen of the USA of Spanish descent – **Spanish-American** *adj*

Spanish chestnut *n* a large widely cultivated edible chestnut

Spanish fly *n* **1** a green blister beetle of S Europe **2** a preparation of Spanish flies used esp as an aphrodisiac

,Spanish 'omelette *n* an omelette containing cooked chopped vegetables and usu not folded in half

,Spanish 'onion *n* a large mild-flavoured onion

[1]**spank** /spangk/ *vt* to strike, esp on the buttocks, (as if) with the open hand [imit] – **spank** *n*

[2]**spank** *vi* to move quickly or spiritedly ⟨~ing *along in his new car*⟩ [back-formation fr *spanking*]

spanker /ˈspangkə/ *n* a fore-and-aft sail set on the aftermost mast of a square-rigged ship ☞ SHIP [origin unknown]

[1]**spanking** /ˈspangking/ *adj* **1** remarkable of its kind; striking **2** vigorous, brisk ⟨*rode off at a* ~ *pace*⟩ [origin unknown] – **spankingly** *adv*

[2]**spanking** *adv* completely and impressively ⟨*a* ~ *new car*⟩

spanner /ˈspanə/ *n*, *chiefly Br* a tool with 1 or 2 ends shaped for holding or turning nuts or bolts with nut-shaped heads [G, instrument for winding springs, fr *spannen* to stretch; akin to MD *spannen* to stretch – more at SPAN] – **(put) a spanner in the works** (to cause) obstruction or hindrance (e g to a plan or operation) – infml

[1]**spar** /spah/ *n* **1** a stout pole **2a** a mast, boom, gaff, yard, etc used to support or control a sail ☞ SHIP **b** any of the main longitudinal members of the wing or fuselage of an aircraft [ME *sparre*; akin to OE *spere* spear]

[2]**spar** *vi* **-rr- 1a** [5]BOX; *esp* to gesture without landing a blow to draw one's opponent or create an opening **b** to engage in a practice bout of boxing **2** to skirmish, wrangle **3** FENCE 1b(2) [prob alter. of [2]*spur*; orig sense, to strike with feet or spurs like a gamecock]

[3]**spar** *n* any of various nonmetallic minerals which usu split easily [LG; akin to OE *spærstān* gypsum, *spæren* of plaster]

[1]**spare** /speə/ *vt* **1** to refrain from destroying, punishing, or harming **2** to refrain from using ⟨~ *the rod, and spoil the child*⟩ **3** to relieve of the necessity of doing, undergoing, or learning sthg ⟨~ *yourself the trouble*⟩ **4** to refrain from; avoid ⟨~d *no expense*⟩ **5** to use or dispense frugally – chiefly neg ⟨*don't* ~ *the butter*⟩ **6a** to give up as surplus to requirements ⟨*do you have any cash to* ~*?*⟩ **b** to have left over, unused, or unoccupied ⟨*time to* ~⟩ ~ *vi* to be frugal ⟨*some will spend and some will* ~ – Robert Burns⟩ [ME *sparen*, fr OE *sparian*; akin to OHG *sparōn* to spare, OE *spær*, adj, spare] – **spareable** *adj*

[2]**spare** *adj* **1** not in use; *esp* reserved for use in emergency ⟨*a* ~ *tyre*⟩ **2a** in excess of what is required; surplus **b** not taken up with work or duties; free ⟨~ *time*⟩ **3** sparing, concise ⟨*a* ~ *prose style*⟩ **4** healthily lean; wiry **5** not abundant; meagre – infml **6** *Br* extremely angry or distraught – infml ⟨*nearly went* ~ *with worry*⟩ [ME, fr OE *spær*; akin to OSlav *sporŭ* abundant, OE *spēd* prosperity – more at SPEED] – **sparely** *adv*, **spareness** *n*

[3]**spare** *n* **1** a spare or duplicate item or part; *specif* a spare part for a motor vehicle **2** the knocking down of all 10 pins with the first 2 balls in a frame in tenpin bowling

,spare 'part *n* a replacement for a component that may cease or has ceased to function ⟨*went to the garage for* spare parts⟩ ⟨spare-part *surgery*⟩

,spare'rib /-ˈrib/ *n* a pork rib with most of the surrounding meat removed for use as bacon ☞ MEAT [by folk etymology fr LG *ribbesper* pickled pork ribs roasted on a spit, fr MLG, fr *ribbe* rib + *sper* spear, spit]

,spare 'tyre *n* a roll of fat at the waist – infml

sparing /ˈspeəring/ *adj* **1** not wasteful; frugal ⟨*we must be* ~ *with the butter*⟩ **2** meagre, scant – **sparingly** *adv*

[1]**spark** /spahk/ *n* **1a** a small particle of a burning substance thrown out by a body in combustion or remaining when combustion is nearly completed **b** a hot glowing particle struck from a larger mass ⟨~s *flying from under a hammer*⟩ **2** a luminous disruptive electrical discharge of very short duration between 2 conductors of opposite high potential separated by a gas (e g air) **3** a sparkle, flash **4** sthg that sets off or stimulates an event, development, etc **5** a trace, esp one which may develop; a germ ⟨*still retains a* ~ *of decency*⟩ **6** *pl but sing in constr* a radio operator on a ship – infml [ME *sparke*, fr OE *spearca*; akin to MD *sparke* spark, L *spargere* to scatter, Gk *spargan* to swell]

[2]**spark** *vi* to produce or give off sparks ~ *vt* **1** to cause to be suddenly active; precipitate – usu + *off* ⟨*the question* ~ed *off a lively discussion*⟩ **2** to stir to activity; incite ⟨*a player can* ~ *his team to victory*⟩ [ME *sparken*, fr *sparke*] – **sparker** *n*

[3]**spark** *n* a lively and usu witty person – esp in *bright spark* [perh of Scand origin; akin to ON *sparkr* sprightly] – **sparkish** *adj*

[4]**spark** *vb*, *chiefly NAm* to woo, court [[3]*spark* (attractive person, lover)] – **sparker** *n*

'spark ,chamber *n* a device that is usu used to detect the path of a high-energy particle by observable electric discharges

'spark ,coil *n* an induction coil for producing the spark for an internal-combustion engine

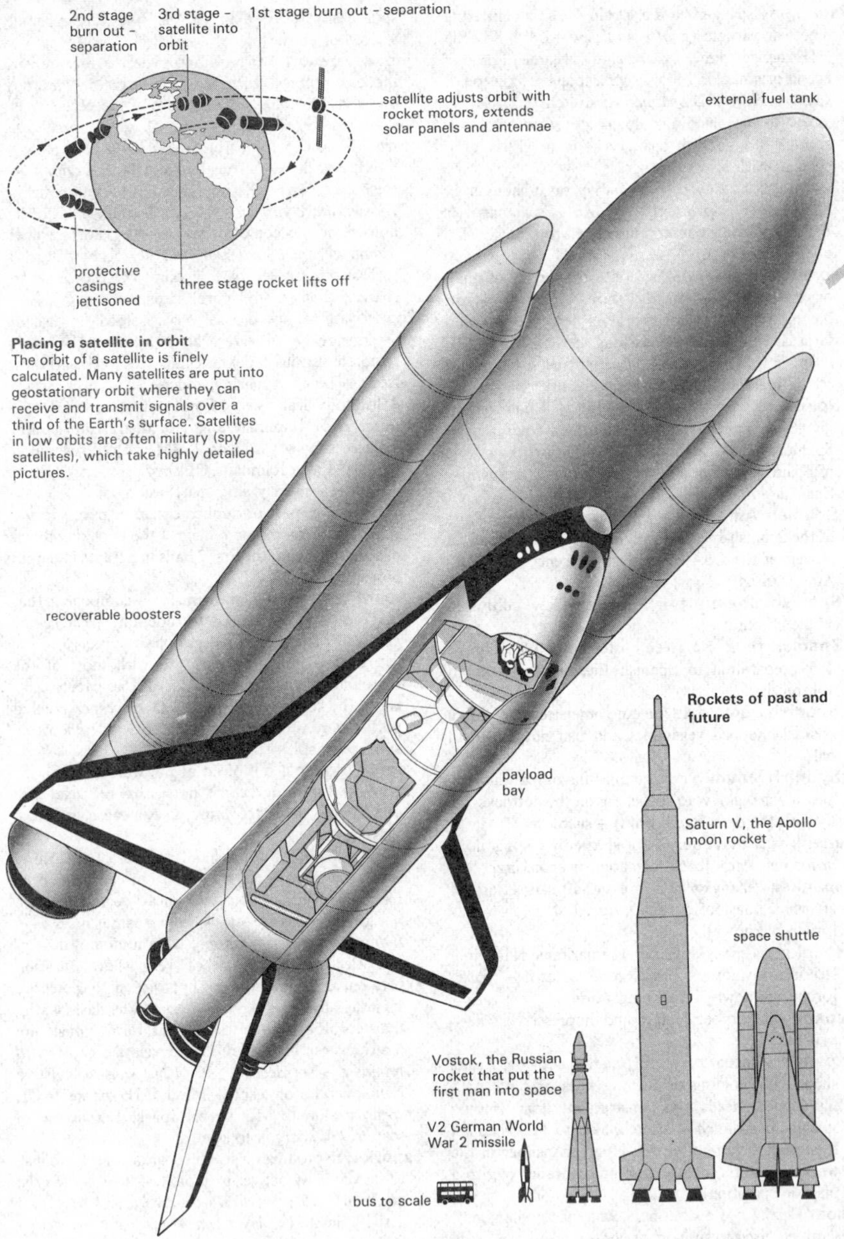

Placing a satellite in orbit
The orbit of a satellite is finely calculated. Many satellites are put into geostationary orbit where they can receive and transmit signals over a third of the Earth's surface. Satellites in low orbits are often military (spy satellites), which take highly detailed pictures.

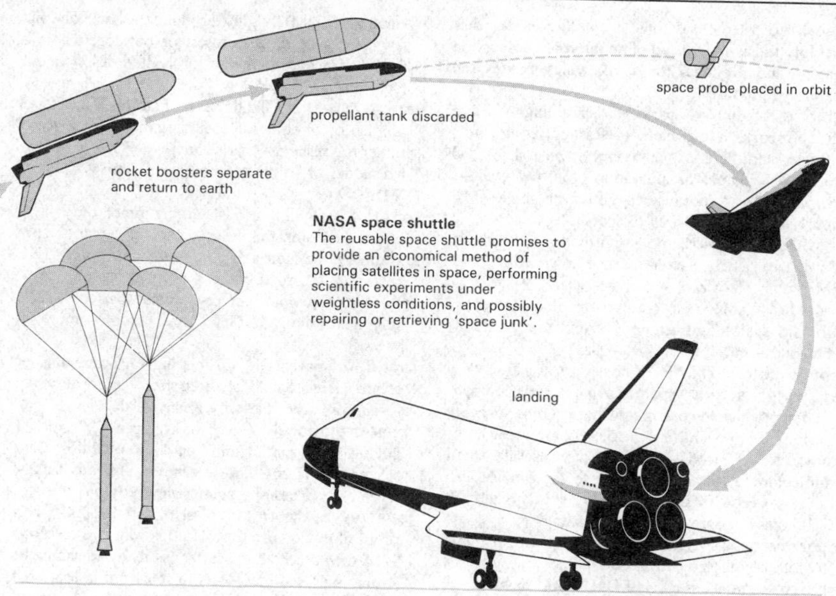

NASA space shuttle
The reusable space shuttle promises to provide an economical method of placing satellites in space, performing scientific experiments under weightless conditions, and possibly repairing or retrieving 'space junk'.

Salyut-6
Russian space station
Salyut-6 was the scene of the 185 days endurance in space record, and many pairs of cosmonauts have worked there for weeks at a time since the station was launched in 1977. Two Soyuz space craft are able to dock with Salyut, and unmanned Progress supply ships bring food and equipment from Earth.

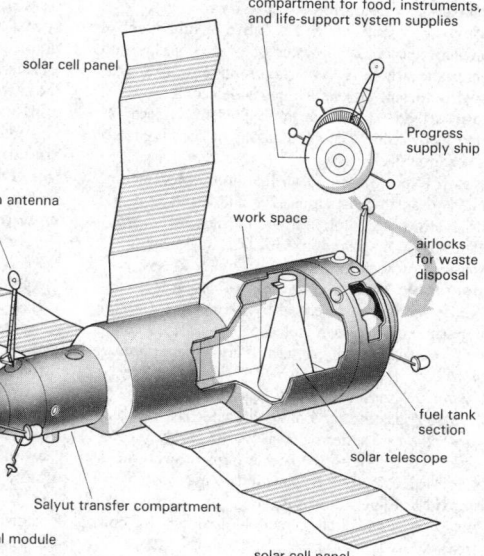

compartment for food, instruments, and life-support system supplies
solar cell panel
Progress supply ship
navigation antenna
work space
solar cell panel
airlocks for waste disposal
command capsule
fuel tank section
solar telescope
Salyut transfer compartment
Soyuz orbital module
solar cell panel

'sparking ,plug /'spahking/ *n, chiefly Br* a part that fits into the cylinder head of an internal-combustion engine and produces the spark which ignites the explosive mixture

[1]**sparkle** /'spahkl/ *vb* **sparkling** /'spahkling/ *vi* **1a** to give off sparks **b** to give off or reflect glittering points of light; scintillate **2** to effervesce ⟨*wine that* ~s⟩ **3** to show brilliance or animation ⟨*the dialogue* ~s *with wit*⟩ ~ *vt* to cause to glitter or shine [ME *sparklen*, freq of *sparken* to spark]

[2]**sparkle** *n* **1** a little spark; a scintillation **2** sparkling **3a** vivacity, gaiety **b** effervescence ⟨*a wine full of* ~⟩ [ME, dim. of *sparke*]

sparkler /'spahklə/ *n* **1** a firework that throws off brilliant sparks on burning **2** a (cut and polished) diamond – infml [[1]SPARKLE + [2]-ER]

'spark ,plug *n, chiefly NAm* SPARKING PLUG

'sparring ,partner /'spahring/ *n* a boxer's companion for practice in sparring during training; *broadly* a habitual opponent (e g in friendly argument)

sparrow /'sparoh/ *n* any of several small dull-coloured songbirds related to the finches; *esp* HOUSE SPARROW [ME *sparow*, fr OE *spearwa*; akin to OHG *sparo* sparrow, Gk *psar* starling]

'sparrow,grass /-,grahs/ *n, chiefly dial* asparagus [by folk etymology fr *asparagus*]

'sparrow ,hawk *n* a small Old World hawk

sparse /spahs/ *adj* of few and scattered elements; *esp* not thickly grown or settled [L *sparsus* spread out, fr pp of *spargere* to scatter – more at [1]SPARK] – **sparsely** *adv*, **sparseness** *n*, **sparsity** *n*

[1]**Spartan** /'spaht(ə)n/ *n* **1** a native or inhabitant of ancient Sparta **2** a person of great courage and endurance [ME, fr L *Spartanus*, adj & n, fr *Sparta*, city in ancient Greece] – **Spartanism** *n*

[2]**Spartan** *adj* **1** of Sparta in ancient Greece **2a** rigorously strict; austere **b** having or showing courage and endurance

spasm /'spaz(ə)m/ *n* **1** an involuntary and abnormal muscular contraction **2** a sudden violent and brief effort or emotion ⟨~s *of helpless mirth* – *Punch*⟩ [ME *spasme*, fr MF, fr L *spasmus*, fr Gk *spasmos*, fr *span* to draw, pull – more at SPAN]

spasmodic /spaz'modik/ *adj* **1a** relating to, being, or affected or characterized by spasm **b** resembling a spasm, esp in sudden violence ⟨*a* ~ *jerk*⟩ **2** acting or proceeding fitfully; intermittent ⟨~ *attempts at studying*⟩ [NL *spasmodicus*, fr Gk *spasmōdēs*, fr *spasmos*] – **spasmodical** *adj*, **spasmodically** *adv*

[1]**spastic** /'spastik/ *adj* **1** of or characterized by spasm ⟨*a* ~ *colon*⟩ **2** suffering from spastic paralysis ⟨*a* ~ *child*⟩ [L *spasticus*, fr Gk *spastikos* drawing in, fr *span*] – **spastically** *adv*, **spasticity** /spa'stisəti/ *n*

[2]**spastic** *n* **1** one who is suffering from spastic paralysis **2** an ineffectual person – used esp by children

spastic paralysis *n* paralysis with involuntary contraction or uncontrolled movements of the affected muscles – compare CEREBRAL PALSY

[1]**spat** /spat/ *past of* SPIT

[2]**spat** *n, pl* **spats,** *esp collectively* **spat** a young oyster or other bivalve mollusc [origin unknown]

[3]**spat** *n* a cloth or leather gaiter covering the instep and ankle ☞ GARMENT [short for *spatterdash* (legging)]

[4]**spat** *n* **1** *NAm* a light splash ⟨*a* ~ *of rain*⟩ **2** a petty argument – infml [prob imit]

spatchcock /'spach,kok/ *vt* **1** to cook (a fowl or small game bird) by splitting along the backbone and frying or grilling **2** to insert or put together in a forced or incongruous way [prob alter. of *spitchcock* (split and grilled eel)]

spate /spayt/ *n* **1** flood ⟨*a river in full* ~⟩ **2a** a large number or amount, esp occurring in a short space of time ⟨*the recent* ~ *of fire bombs* – *The Guardian*⟩ **b** a sudden or strong outburst; a rush ⟨*a* ~ *of anger*⟩ [ME]

spathe /spaydh/ *n* a sheathing bract or pair of bracts enclosing the inflorescence of a plant, esp a spadix on the same axis ⟨*the* ~ *of cuckoopint*⟩ [NL *spatha*, fr L, broad sword – more at [3]SPADE]

spathic /'spathik/ *adj* resembling spar [G *spath*, *spat* spar; akin to OHG *spān* chip – more at [1]SPOON]

spatial /'spaysh(ə)l/ *adj* relating to, occupying, or occurring in space [L *spatium* space – more at SPEED] – **spatially** *adv*, **spatiality** /,spayshi'aləti/ *n*

spatiotemporal /,spayshioh'temp(ə)rəl/ *adj* **1** having both spatial and temporal qualities **2** of space-time [L *spatium* + *tempor-*, *tempus* time – more at TEMPORAL] – **spatiotemporally** *adv*

[1]**spatter** /'spatə/ *vt* **1** to splash or sprinkle (as if) with drops of liquid; *also* to soil in this way ⟨*his coat was* ~ed *with mud*⟩ **2** to scatter (as if) by splashing or sprinkling ⟨~ *water*⟩ ~ *vi* to spurt out in scattered drops ⟨*blood* ~ing *everywhere*⟩ [akin to Flem *spetteren* to spatter]

[2]**spatter** *n* **1** (the sound of) spattering **2** a drop spattered on sthg or a stain due to spattering

spatula /'spatyoolə, -chələ/ *n* a flat thin usu metal implement used esp for spreading, mixing, etc soft substances or powders [LL, spoon, spatula – more at EPAULETTE]

spatulate /'spatyoolət, -chə-/ *adj* shaped like a spatula ⟨~ *spines of a caterpillar*⟩ ☞ PLANT

spavin /'spavin/ *n* a bony enlargement or soft swelling of the hock of a horse associated with strain [ME *spavayne*, fr MF *espavain*] – **spavined** /-vind/ *adj*

[1]**spawn** /spawn/ *vt* **1** *of an aquatic animal* to produce or deposit (eggs) **2** to bring forth, esp abundantly ~ *vi* **1** to deposit spawn **2** to produce young, esp in large numbers [ME *spawnen*, fr AF *espaundre*, fr OF *espandre* to spread out, expand, fr L *expandere*] – **spawner** *n*

[2]**spawn** *n* **1** the large number of eggs of frogs, oysters, fish, etc **2** *sing or pl in constr* (numerous) offspring **3** mycelium, esp for propagating mushrooms

spay /spay/ *vt* to remove the ovaries of [ME *spayen*, fr MF *espeer* to cut with a sword, fr OF, fr *espee* sword, fr L *spatha* sword – more at SPADE]

speak /speek/ *vb* **spoke** /spohk/; **spoken** /'spohkən/ *vi* **1a** to utter words or articulate sounds with the ordinary voice; talk **b(1)** to give voice to thoughts or feelings ⟨*why don't you* ~ *for yourself?* – H W Longfellow⟩ **(2)** to be on speaking terms ⟨*still were not* ~ing *after the dispute*⟩ **c** to address a group ⟨*the professor* spoke *on his latest discoveries*⟩ **2a** to express thoughts or feelings in writing ⟨*diaries that* ~ *of his ambition*⟩ **b** to act as spokesman *for* **3** to communicate by other than verbal means ⟨*actions* ~ *louder than words*⟩ **4** to make a claim *for*, reserve ⟨*5 of the 10 new houses are already* spoken *for*⟩ **5** to make a characteristic or natural sound ⟨*the thunder* spoke⟩ **6** to be indicative or suggestive ⟨*his battered shoes* spoke *of a long journey*⟩ ~ *vt* **1a** to utter with the speaking voice; pronounce **b** to express orally; declare ⟨*free to ~ their minds*⟩ **2** to make known in writing **3** to (be able to) use in oral communication ⟨~s *Spanish*⟩ [ME *speken*, fr OE *sprecan, specan*; akin to OHG *sprehhan* to speak, Gk *spharageisthai* to crackle] – **speakable** *adj* – **so to speak** – used as an apologetic qualification for an imprecise, unusual, ambiguous, or unclear phrase ⟨*this bus service has gone downhill,* so to speak⟩ – **to speak of** worth mentioning – usu neg

speakeasy /ˈspeek,eezi/ *n* a place where alcoholic drinks were illegally sold during Prohibition in the USA in the 1920's and 30's [fr the need to *speak easy* (softly) in ordering illicit goods]

speaker /ˈspeekə/ *n* **1a** one who speaks, esp at public functions **b** one who speaks a specified language ⟨*an Italian*-speaker⟩ **2** the presiding officer of a deliberative or legislative assembly **3** a loudspeaker – **speakership** *n*

speaking /ˈspeeking/ *adj* **1a** capable of speech **b** containing chiefly native speakers of a specified language – usu in combination ⟨*English*-speaking *countries*⟩ **2** highly significant or expressive; eloquent **3** able to speak a specified language ⟨*French*-speaking⟩

ˈspeaking ˌtube *n* a pipe through which conversation may be conducted (e g between different parts of a building)

speak out *vi* **1** to speak loudly enough to be heard **2** to speak boldly; express an opinion frankly ⟨spoke out *on the issues*⟩

speak up *vi* **1** to speak more loudly – often imper **2** to express an opinion boldly ⟨speak up *for justice*⟩

[1]spear /spiə/ *n* **1** a thrusting or throwing weapon with long shaft and sharp head or blade used esp by hunters or foot soldiers **2** a sharp-pointed instrument with barbs used in spearing fish **3** a spearman [ME *spere*, fr OE; akin to OHG *sper* spear, L *sparus*, Gk *sparos*, a marine fish]

[2]spear *vt* to pierce, strike, or take hold of (as if) with a spear ⟨~ed *a sausage from the dish*⟩

[3]spear *n* a usu young blade, shoot, or sprout (e g of asparagus or grass) [alter. of [1]*spire*]

ˈspear,fish /-ˌfish/ *n* any of several large powerful oceanic fishes related to the marlins and sail fishes

[1]ˈspear,head /-ˌhed/ *n* **1** the sharp-pointed head of a spear **2** a leading element or force in a development, course of action, etc

[2]spearhead *vt* to serve as leader or leading force of

ˈspear,man /-ˌman/ *n* one armed with a spear

ˈspear,mint /-ˌmint/ *n* a common mint grown esp for its aromatic oil

ˈspear ˌside *n* the male branch of a family – compare DISTAFF

spec /spek/ *n* a speculation – infml ⟨*one company worth trying as a ~ – The Economist*⟩ – **on spec** *Br* as a risk or speculation ⟨*houses built* on spec⟩; *also* as a risk in the hope of finding or obtaining sthg desired ⟨*the play may be sold out, but it would be worth going to the theatre* on spec⟩ – infml

[1]special /ˈspesh(ə)l/ *adj* **1** distinguished from others of the same category, esp because in some way superior **2** held in particular esteem ⟨*a ~ friend*⟩ **3** SPECIFIC 4 **4** other than or in addition to the usual ⟨*a ~ day of thanksgiving*⟩ **5** designed, undertaken, or used for a particular purpose or need ⟨*devised a ~ method of restoring paintings*⟩ **6** established or designed for the use or education of the handicapped ⟨*a ~ school*⟩ [ME, fr OF or L; OF *especial*, fr L *specialis* individual, particular, fr *species* species] – **specially** *adv*, **specialness** *n*

[2]special *n* **1** sthg that is not part of a series **2** sby or sthg reserved or produced for a particular use or occasion ⟨*caught the commuter ~ to work*⟩ **3** *Br* SPECIAL CONSTABLE; *esp* B SPECIAL

special constable *n*, *Br* sby employed as an extra policeman (e g in times of emergency)

ˌspecial efˈfect *n* an unusual visual or acoustic effect; *esp* one introduced into a film or prerecorded television production by special processing – usu pl

specialism /ˈspesh(ə)l,iz(ə)m/ *n* **1** specialization in an occupation or branch of knowledge **2** a field of specialization; a speciality

specialist /ˈspesh(ə)list/ *n* **1a** one who devotes him-/herself to a special occupation or branch of knowledge **b** a medical practitioner limiting his/her practice to a specific group of complaints ⟨*a child ~*⟩ ⟨*an ear, nose, and throat ~*⟩ **2** a rank in the US Army enabling an enlisted man/woman to draw extra pay because of technical qualifications ☞ RANK – **specialist, specialistic** /-ˈistik/ *adj*

speciality /ˌspeshiˈaləti/ *n* **1** (the state of having) a distinctive mark or quality **2** a product or object of particular quality ⟨*bread pudding was mother's ~*⟩ **3a** a special aptitude or skill **b** a particular occupation or branch of knowledge

special·ize, -ise /ˈspesh(ə)liez/ *vt* to apply or direct to a specific end or use ~ *vi* **1** to concentrate one's efforts in a special or limited activity or field **2** to undergo structural adaptation of a body part to a particular function or of an organism for life in a particular environment – **specialization** /-ˈzaysh(ə)n/ *n*

special licence *n* a British form of marriage license permitting marriage without the publication of banns or at a time and place other than those prescribed by law

special pleading *n* **1** the allegation of special or new matter in a legal action, as distinguished from a direct denial of the matter pleaded by the opposite side **2** an argument that ignores the damaging or unfavourable aspects of a case

special school *n* a school for handicapped children

special theory of relativity *n* RELATIVITY 2a

specialty /ˈspesh(ə)lti/ *n* **1** a legal agreement embodied in a sealed document **2** *chiefly NAm* a speciality [ME *specialte*, fr MF *especialté*, fr LL *specialitat-, specialitas*, fr L *specialis* special]

special verdict *n* a verdict that sets out the facts as proved and leaves the court to decide legal guilt or innocence

specie /ˈspeeshi/ *n* money in coin [fr *in specie*, fr L, in kind] – **in specie** in the same or similar form or kind ⟨*ready to return insult* in specie⟩

species /ˈspeeshiz/ *n, pl* **species** **1a** a class of individuals having common attributes and designated by a common name **b(1)** a category in the biological classification of living things that ranks immediately below a genus, comprises related organisms or populations potentially capable of interbreeding, and is designated by a name (e g *Homo sapiens*) that consists of the name of a genus followed by a Latin or latinized uncapitalized noun or adjective **(2)** an individual or kind belonging to a biological species **c** a particular kind of atomic nucleus, atom, molecule, or ion **2** the consecrated bread and wine of the Roman Catholic or Eastern Orthodox eucharist **3** a kind, sort – chiefly derog ⟨*a dangerous ~ of criminal*⟩ [L, appearance, kind, species – more at SPY]

[1]**specific** /spə'sifik/ *adj* **1a** constituting or falling into a specifiable category **b** being or relating to those properties of sthg that allow it to be assigned to a particular category ⟨*the ~ qualities of a drug*⟩ **2a** confined to a particular individual, group, or circumstance ⟨*a disease ~ to horses*⟩ **b** having a specific rather than a general influence (e g on a body part or a disease) ⟨*antibodies ~ for the smallpox virus*⟩ **3** free from ambiguity; explicit ⟨*~ instructions*⟩ **4** of or constituting a (biological) species **5a** being any of various arbitrary physical constants, esp one relating a quantitative attribute to unit mass, volume, or area **b** imposed at a fixed rate per unit (e g of weight or amount) ⟨*~ import duties*⟩ – compare AD VALOREM [LL *specificus*, fr L *species*] – **specifically** *adv*, **specificity** /,spesi'fisəti/ *n*

[2]**specific** *n* **1** a drug or remedy having a specific effect on a disease **2a** a characteristic quality or trait **b** *pl, chiefly NAm* particulars ⟨*haggling over the legal and financial ~s – Time*⟩

specification /,spesifi'kaysh(ə)n/ *n* **1** specifying **2a** a detailed description of sthg (e g a building or car), esp in the form of a plan – usu pl with sing. meaning **b** a written description of an invention for which a patent is sought

spe,cific 'gravity *n* the ratio of the density of a substance to the density of a substance (e g pure water or hydrogen) taken as a standard when both densities are obtained by weighing in air

spe,cific 'heat *n* heat required to raise the temperature of a unit mass of a substance by unit temperature – usu measured in joules per kilogram per kelvin

spe,cific per'formance *n* performance of a legal contract according to its terms, ordered where damages would be inadequate

specify /'spesifie/ *vt* **1** to name or state explicitly or in detail **2** to include as an item in a specification ⟨*~ oak flooring*⟩ [ME *specifien*, fr OF *specifier*, fr LL *specificare*, fr *specificus*] – **specifiable** *adj*, **specifier** *n*

specimen /'spesimin/ *n* **1** an item, part, or individual typical of a group or category; an example **2** a person, individual – chiefly derog [L, fr *specere* to look at, look]

speciosity /,spees(h)i'osəti/ *n* being specious; speciousness – fml

specious /'speesh(y)əs/ *adj* **1** having deceptive attraction or fascination **2** superficially sound or genuine but fallacious ⟨*~ reasoning*⟩ [ME, fr L *speciosus* beautiful, plausible, fr *species*] – **speciously** *adv*, **speciousness** *n*

[1]**speck** /spek/ *n* **1** a small spot or blemish, esp from stain or decay **2** a small particle ⟨*a ~ of sawdust*⟩ [ME *specke*, fr OE *specca*]

[2]**speck** *vt* to mark with specks

[1]**speckle** /'spekl/ *n* a little speck (e g of colour) [ME; akin to OE *specca*]

[2]**speckle** *vt* **speckling** /'spekling, 'spekl·ing/ to mark (as if) with speckles ⟨*the ~d eggs of a thrush*⟩

specs /speks/ *n pl* **1** specifications **2** GLASSES 2b(2) – infml [(1) by contr; (2) contr of *spectacles*]

spectacle /'spektəkl/ *n* **1a** sthg exhibited as unusual, noteworthy, or entertaining; *esp* a striking or dramatic public display or show **b** an object of scorn or ridicule, esp due to odd appearance or behaviour ⟨*made a ~ of himself*⟩ **2** *pl* GLASSES 2b(2) [ME, fr MF, fr L *spectaculum*, fr *spectare* to watch, fr *spectus*, pp of *specere* to look, look at – more at SPY]

'spectacled *adj* having (markings suggesting) a pair of spectacles ⟨*the ~ salamander*⟩

[1]**spectacular** /spek'takyoolə/ *adj* of or being a spectacle; sensational ⟨*a ~ display of fireworks*⟩ [L *spectaculum*] – **spectacularly** *adv*

[2]**spectacular** *n* sthg (e g a stage show) that is spectacular

spectate /spek'tayt, '-,-/ *vi* to be present as a spectator (e g at a sports event) [back-formation fr *spectator*]

spectator /spek'taytə/ *n* **1** one who attends an event or activity in order to watch **2** one who looks on without participating; an onlooker ⟨*rescuers were hampered by ~s*⟩ [L, fr *spectatus*, pp of *spectare* to watch] – **spectator** *adj*

spectral /'spektrəl/ *adj* **1** of or suggesting a spectre **2** of or made by a spectrum – **spectrally** *adv*, **spectralness** *n*, **spectrality** /-'traləti/ *n*

spectre, *NAm chiefly* **specter** /'spektə/ *n* **1** a visible ghost **2** sthg that haunts or perturbs the mind; a phantasm ⟨*the ~ of hunger*⟩ – compare OGRE 2 [F *spectre*, fr L *spectrum* appearance, spectre, fr *specere* to look, look at – more at SPY]

spectro- *comb form* spectrum ⟨spectro*scope*⟩ [NL *spectrum*]

spectrogram /'spektrə,gram/ *n* a photograph or diagram of a spectrum [ISV]

'spectro,graph /-,grahf, -,graf/ *n* an instrument for dispersing light, sound waves, etc into a spectrum (and recording or mapping it) [ISV] – **spectrographic** /-'grafik/ *adj*, **spectrographically** *adv*, **spectrography** /spek'trogrəfi/ *n*

spectroheliogram /,spektroh'heelyə,gram/ *n* a photograph of the sun at one wavelength showing its bright regions and prominences

,spectro'heliograph /-'heelyə,grahf, -,graf/ *n* an apparatus for making spectroheliograms [ISV] – **spectroheliography** /-,heeli'ogrəfi/ *n*

,spectro'helioscope /-'heelyə,skohp/ *n* **1** a spectroheliograph **2** an instrument similar to a spectroheliograph used for visual as distinguished from photographic observations [ISV]

spectrometer /spek'tromitə/ *n* a spectroscope fitted for measurements of the spectra observed with it [ISV] – **spectrometry** /-mətri/ *n*, **spectrometric** /,spektrə'metrik/ *adj*

spectrophotometer /,spektrohfoh'tomitə/ *n* an instrument for measuring the intensity of (a substance's absorption of) light at various wavelengths [ISV] – **spectrophotometric** /,-fohtə'metrik/, **spectrophotometrical** *adj*, **spectrophotometrically** *adv*, **spectrophotometry** /-foh'tomətri/ *n*

spectroscope /'spektrə,skohp/ *n* an instrument for forming and examining optical spectra [ISV] – **spectroscopic** /-'skopik/, **spectroscopical** *adj*, **spectroscopically** *adv*, **spectroscopist** /spek'troskəpist/ *n*, **spectroscopy** *n*

spectrum /'spektrəm/ *n, pl* **spectra** /-trə/, **spectrums** **1** an array of the components of an emission or wave separated and arranged in the order of some varying characteristic (e g wavelength, mass, or energy): e g **a** a series of images formed when a beam of radiant energy is subjected to dispersion and brought to focus so that the component waves are arranged in the order of their wavelengths (e g when a beam of sunlight that is refracted and dispersed by a prism forms a display of colours) **b** ELECTROMAGNETIC SPECTRUM **c** the range of frequencies of sound waves **2** a sequence, range ⟨*a wide* ~ *of interests*⟩ [NL, fr L, appearance – more at SPECTRE]

specular /ˈspekyoolə/ *adj* **1** (having the qualities) of a mirror **2** conducted with the aid of a medical speculum [L *specularis* of a mirror, fr *speculum*] – **specularly** *adv*, **specularity** /-ˈlarəti/ *n*

speculate /ˈspekyoolayt/ *vi* **1** to meditate *on* or ponder *about* sthg; reflect **2** to assume a business risk in the hope of gain; *esp* to buy or sell in expectation of profiting from market fluctuations [L *speculatus*, pp of *speculari* to spy out, examine, fr *specula* watchtower, fr *specere* to look, look at] – **speculator** *n*, **speculation** /-ˈlaysh(ə)n/ *n*

speculative /ˈspekyoolətiv/ *adj* **1** involving, based on, or constituting speculation; *also* theoretical rather than demonstrable **2** questioning, inquiring ⟨*a* ~ *glance*⟩ – **speculatively** *adv*

speculum /ˈspekyooləm/ *n, pl* **specula** /-lə/ *also* **speculums** **1** an instrument inserted into a body passage for medical inspection or treatment **2** a reflector in an optical instrument **3** a patch of colour on the secondary feathers of many birds, esp ducks [L, mirror, fr *specere*]

speech /speech/ *n* **1a** the communication or expression of thoughts in spoken words **b** conversation **2** a public discourse; an address **3a** a language, dialect **b** an individual manner of speaking **4** the power of expressing or communicating thoughts by speaking [ME *speche*, fr OE *spræc, spæc*; akin to OE *sprecan* to speak – more at SPEAK]

ˈspeech ˌday *n* an annual ceremonial day at a British school when prizes are presented

speechify /ˈspeechifie/ *vi* to speak or make a speech in a pompous manner

ˈspeechless /-lis/ *adj* **1a** unable to speak; dumb **b** deprived of speech (e g through horror or rage) **2** refraining from speech; silent **3** incapable of being expressed in words ⟨*a shape of* ~ *beauty* – P B Shelley⟩ – **speechlessly** *adv*, **speechlessness** *n*

[1]**speed** /speed/ *n* **1a** moving swiftly; swiftness **b** rate of motion; *specif* the magnitude of a velocity irrespective of direction **2** rate of performance or execution ⟨*tried to increase his reading* ~⟩ **3a** the sensitivity of a photographic film, plate, or paper expressed numerically **b** the light-gathering power of a lens or optical system **c** the duration of a photographic exposure **4** *chiefly NAm* a transmission gear in motor vehicles **5** (a drug related to) methamphetamine – slang [ME *spede* success, prosperity, swiftness, fr OE *spēd*; akin to OHG *spuot* prosperity, swiftness, L *spes* hope, *spatium* space] – **at speed** at a fast speed; while travelling rapidly

[2]**speed** *vb* **sped** /sped/, **speeded** *vi* **1** to move or go quickly ⟨sped *to her bedside*⟩ **2** to travel at excessive or illegal speed ⟨*drivers who are fined for* ~ing⟩ ~ *vt* **1** to promote the success or development of **2** to cause to move quickly; hasten – **speeder** *n*, **speedster** *n*

ˈspeedˌball /-ˌbawl/ *n* cocaine mixed with heroin or morphine or an amphetamine and usu taken by injection – slang

ˈspeed ˌlimit *n* the maximum speed permitted by law in a given area or under specified circumstances

speedometer /speeˈdomitə, spi-/ *n* **1** an instrument for indicating speed; a tachometer **2** an instrument for indicating distance travelled as well as speed; *also* an odometer

ˈspeed ˌtrap *n* a stretch of road along which police officers, radar devices, etc are stationed so as to catch vehicles exceeding the speed limit

ˈspeed-ˌup *n* an acceleration

speed up *vb* to (cause to) move, work, or take place faster; accelerate

ˈspeedˌway /-ˌway/ *n* **1** a usu oval racecourse for motorcycles **2** the sport of racing motorcycles usu belonging to professional teams on closed cinder or dirt tracks

ˈspeedˌwell /-ˌwel/ *n* any of a genus of plants of the figwort family that mostly have slender stems and small blue or whitish flowers

speedy /ˈspeedi/ *adj* swift, quick – **speedily** *adv*, **speediness** *n*

speiss /spies/ *n* a mixture of metallic arsenic compounds produced when smelting certain ores [G *speise*, lit., food, fr (assumed) VL *spesa*, fr LL *expensa* expense]

speleology /ˌspeeliˈoləji/ *n* the scientific study of caves [L *speleum* cave (fr Gk *spēlaion*) + ISV *-o-* + *-logy*] – **speleologist** *n*, **speleological** /-li·əˈlojikl/ *adj*

[1]**spell** /spel/ *n* **1a** a spoken word or form of words held to have magic power **b** a state of enchantment **2** a compelling influence or attraction [ME, talk, tale, fr OE; akin to OHG *spel* talk, tale, Gk *apeilē* boast]

[2]**spell** *vb* **spelt** /spelt/, *NAm chiefly* **spelled** *vt* **1** to name or write the letters of (e g a word) in order; *also, of letters* to form (e g a word) ⟨*c-a-t* ~s *cat*⟩ **2** to amount to; mean ⟨*crop failure would* ~ *famine for the whole region*⟩ – chiefly journ ~ *vi* to form words using the correct combination of letters ⟨*graduates who still can't* ~⟩ [ME *spellen*, fr OF *espeller*, of Gmc origin; akin to OE *spell* talk]

[3]**spell** *vb* **spelled** *vt* **1** to give a brief rest to **2** *chiefly NAm* to relieve for a time; stand in for ⟨*the 2 guards* ~ed *each other*⟩ ~ *vi* , *chiefly Austr* to rest from work or activity for a time [ME *spelen*, fr OE *spelian*; akin to OE *spala* substitute]

[4]**spell** *n* **1** a period spent in a job or occupation ⟨*did a* ~ *in catering*⟩ **2** a short or indefinite period or phase ⟨*there will be cold* ~s *throughout April*⟩ **3** [2]FIT 1b **4** *chiefly Austr* a period of rest from work, activity, or use

ˈspellˌbinder /-ˌbiendə/ *n* sby or sthg that holds one spellbound; *esp* a speaker of compelling eloquence [back-formation fr *spellbound*] – **spellbinding** *adj*

ˈspellˌbound /-ˌbownd/ *adj* held (as if) by a spell ⟨*a* ~ *audience*⟩

speller /ˈspelə/ *n* a book for teaching spelling [[2]SPELL + [2]-ER]

spelling /ˈspeling/ *n* **1** the forming of or ability to form words from letters **2** the sequence of letters that make up a particular word

ˈspelling ˌbee *n* a spelling competition

spell out *vt* **1** to read slowly and haltingly **2** to come to understand; discern ⟨*tried in vain to* spell out *his meaning*⟩ **3** to explain clearly and in detail

¹spelt /spelt/ *n* a primitive wheat whose ears contain 2 light red kernels [ME, fr OE, fr LL *spelta*, of Gmc origin; akin to MHG *spelte* split piece of wood, OHG *spaltan* to split – more at SPILL]

²spelt *chiefly Br past of* ²SPELL

spelter /'speltə/ *n* zinc, esp cast in slabs for commercial use [prob modif of MD *speauter*]

spelunker /spi'lungkə/ *n, NAm* one who makes a hobby of exploring and studying caves [L *spelunca* cave, fr Gk *spēlynx*; akin to Gk *spēlaion* cave] – **spelunking** *n*

spend /spend/ *vb* **spent** /spent/ *vt* **1** to use up or pay out; expend ⟨spent *£90 on a new suit*⟩ **2** to wear out, exhaust ⟨*the storm gradually* spent *itself*⟩ **3** to cause or permit to elapse; pass ⟨spent *the summer at the beach*⟩ ~ *vi* to pay out resources, esp money [ME *spenden*, fr OE & OF; OE *spendan*, fr L *expendere* to expend; OF *despendre*, fr L *dispendere* to weigh out – more at DISPENSE] – **spendable** *adj*, **spender** *n* – **spend a penny** *Br* to urinate – euph

'spending ,money *n* POCKET MONEY

'spend,thrift /-,thrift/ *n* one who spends carelessly or wastefully – **spendthrift** *adj*

spent /spent/ *adj* **1a** used up; consumed **b** exhausted of useful components or qualities ⟨~ *grain*⟩ ⟨~ *matches*⟩ **2** drained of energy; exhausted ⟨~ *after his nightlong vigil*⟩ **3** exhausted of spawn or sperm ⟨*a* ~ *salmon*⟩ [ME, fr pp of *spenden* to spend]

sperm /spuhm/ *n, pl* **sperms,** *esp collectively* **sperm** **1a** the male fertilizing fluid; semen **b** a male gamete **2** spermaceti, oil, etc from the sperm whale [ME, fr MF *esperme*, fr LL *spermat-, sperma*, fr Gk, lit., seed; akin to Gk *speirein* to sow – more at SPROUT]

sperm- /spuhm-/, **spermo-, sperma-, spermi-** *comb form* seed; germ; sperm ⟨*sperma*theca⟩ ⟨*spermi*cidal⟩ [Gk *sperm-, spermo-*, fr *sperma*]

spermaceti /,spuhmə'seeti, -'seti/ *n* a waxy solid obtained from the oil of whales, esp sperm whales, and used in ointments, cosmetics, and candles [ME *sperma cete*, fr ML *sperma ceti* whale sperm]

spermary /'spuhməri/ *n* an organ in which male gametes are developed [NL *spermarium*, fr Gk *sperma*]

spermat- /spuhmət-/, **spermato-** *comb form* sperm- ⟨*sper matid*⟩ ⟨*spermato*cyte⟩ [MF, fr LL, fr Gk, fr *spermat-, sperma*]

spermatheca /,spuhmə'theekə/ *n* a sac for sperm storage in the female reproductive tract of many lower animals [NL] – **spermathecal** *adj*

spermatic /spuh'matik/ *adj* relating to, resembling, carrying, or full of sperm

spermatic cord *n* a cord that suspends the testis within the scrotum

spermatid /'spuhmətid/ *n* any of the cells that form spermatozoa

spermatium /spuh'mayti·əm, -shi·əm/ *n, pl* **spermatia** /-ti·ə, -shi·ə/ a nonmotile cell functioning or held to function as a male gamete in some lower plants [NL, fr Gk *spermation*, dim. of *spermat-, sperma*] – **spermatial** /-tyəl, -sh(y)əl/ *adj*

spermatocyte /spuh'matəsiet/ *n* a cell giving rise to sperm cells; *esp* a cell of the (next to) last generation preceding the spermatozoon

spermatogenesis /spuh,matə'jenəsis/ *n* the process of male gamete formation including meiotic cell division and transformation of the 4 resulting spermatids into spermatozoa [NL] – **spermatogenic** /-'jenik/ *adj*, **spermatogenetic** /-jə'netik/ *adj*

spermatogonium /,spuhmatə'gohnyəm, -ni·əm/ *n, pl* **spermatogonia** /-nyə, -ni·ə/ a primitive male germ cell [NL] – **spermatogonial** *adj*

spermatophore /spuh'matə,faw/ *n* a capsule, packet, or mass enclosing spermatozoa produced by the male and conveyed to the female in the insemination of various invertebrates (e g the spider) [ISV]

sper'mato,phyte /-,fiet/ *n* any of a group of higher plants constituting those that produce seeds ☞ PLANT [deriv of NL *spermat-* + Gk *phyton* plant – more at PHYT-] – **spermatophytic** /-'fitik/ *adj*

spermatozoid /,spuhmətə'zoh·id/ *n* a motile male gamete of a plant, usu produced in an antheridium [ISV, fr NL *spermatozoa*]

,spermato'zoon /-'zoh·ən/ *n, pl* **spermatozoa** /-'zoh·ə/ **1** a motile male gamete of an animal, usu with rounded or elongated head and a long tail-like flagellum **2** a spermatozoid [NL] – **spermatozoal** *adj*

'sperm ,cell *n* a male gamete or germ cell

spermi- /spuhmi-/ – see SPERM-

spermicide /'spuhmisied/ *n* sthg that kills sperm – **spermicidal** /-'siedl/ *adj*

spermiogenesis /,spuhmi·oh'jenəsis/ *n* **1** transformation of a spermatid into a spermatozoon **2** spermatogenesis [NL, fr *spermium* spermatozoon + *-o-* + L *genesis*]

spermo- – see SPERM-

'sperm ,oil *n* a pale yellow oil obtained from the sperm whale

'sperm ,whale *n* a large toothed whale that has a vast blunt head in the front part of which is a cavity containing a fluid mixture of spermaceti and oil [short for *spermaceti whale*]

¹spew /spyooh/ *vi* **1** to vomit **2** to come forth in a flood or gush ~ *vt* to propel or eject with violence or in great quantity ⟨*a volcano* ~ing *ash and lava*⟩ [ME *spewen*, fr OE *spīwan*; akin to OHG *spīwan* to spit, L *spuere*, Gk *ptyein*] – **spewer** *n*

²spew *n* **1** vomit **2** material that gushes or is ejected from a source

sphagnum /'sfagnəm, 'spagnəm/ *n* any of a large genus of atypical mosses that grow only in wet acid areas (e g bogs) where their remains become compacted with other plant debris to form peat [NL, genus name, fr L *sphagnos*, a moss, fr Gk]

sphalerite /'sfaləriet/ *n* zinc sulphide occurring as a mineral [G *sphalerit*, fr Gk *sphaleros* deceitful, fr *sphallein* to cause to fall – more at SPILL; fr its often being mistaken for galena]

sphenodon /'sfeenədon, 'sfenə-/ *n* the tuatara [NL, deriv of Gk *sphēn* wedge + *odōn* tooth – more at TOOTH] – **sphenodont** /-dont/ *adj*

sphenoid /'sfenoyd/ *n or adj* (a bone at the base of the skull) shaped like a wedge [adj NL *sphenoides*, fr Gk *sphēnoeidēs* wedge-shaped, fr *sphēn* wedge; n fr adj] – **sphenoidal** *adj*

spher- /sfiər-, sfer-/, **sphero-** *also* **sphaer-, sphaero-** *comb form* sphere ⟨*spher*ule⟩ ⟨*sphero*meter⟩ [L *sphaer-*, fr Gk *sphair-, sphairo-*, fr *sphaira* sphere]

¹sphere /sfiə/ *n* **1a** (a globe depicting) the apparent surface of the heavens of which half forms the dome of the visible sky **b** any of the revolving spherical transparent shells in which, according to ancient astronomy, the celestial bodies are set **2a** a globular body; a ball **b** a planet, star **c** (a space or solid enclosed by) a surface, all points of which are equidistant from the centre **3** natural or proper place; *esp* social position or class **4** a field of action, existence, or influence [ME *spere* globe, celestial sphere, fr MF *espere*, fr L *sphaera*, fr Gk *sphaira*, lit., ball] – **spheral** *adj*, **spheric** /'sferik/ *adj*, **sphericity** /sfi'risəti/ *n*

[2]**sphere** *vt* **1** to place or enclose in a sphere **2** to form into a sphere

spherical /'sferikl/ *adj* **1** having the form of (a segment of) a sphere **2** relating to or dealing with (the properties of) a sphere – **spherically** *adv*

spherical aberration *n* aberration that is caused by the spherical form of a lens or mirror and that gives different foci for central and marginal rays

spherical angle *n* the angle between 2 intersecting arcs of great circles of a sphere

spherical coordinate *n* any of 3 coordinates that are used to locate a point in space and that comprise 1 length and 2 angles

spheroid /'sfiəroyd/ *n* a figure resembling a sphere – **spheroidal** /-'roydl/ *adj*, **spheroidally** *adv*

spherometer /ˌsfiə'romitə/ *n* an instrument for measuring the curvature of a surface [ISV]

spherule /'sfiər(y)oohl, 'sfe-/ *n* a little sphere or spherical body [LL *sphaerula*, dim. of L *sphaera*]

spherulite /'sfiər(y)ooˌliet, 'sfe-/ *n* a spherical body of radiating crystal fibres found in some volcanic rocks – **spherulitic** /-'litik/ *adj*

sphincter /'sfingktə/ *n* a muscular ring, surrounding and able to contract or close a bodily opening ☞ DIGESTION [LL, fr Gk *sphinktēr*, lit., band, fr *sphingein* to bind tight] – **sphincteral** *adj*

sphingid /'sfinjid/ *n* a hawkmoth [deriv of Gk *sphing-*, *sphinx* sphinx]

sphinx /sfinks/ *n, pl* **sphinxes, sphinges** /-jeez/ **1a** *cap* a female monster in Greek mythology, with a lion's body and a human head, that killed those who failed to answer a riddle she asked **b** an enigmatic or mysterious person **2** an ancient Egyptian image in the form of a recumbent lion, usu with a human head **3** a hawkmoth [L, fr Gk; akin to Gk *sphinktēr* sphincter]

sphygmomanometer /ˌsfigməmə'nomitə/ *n* an instrument for measuring (arterial) blood pressure [Gk *sphygmos* pulse + ISV *manometer*; akin to Gk *asphyxia* stopping of the pulse – more at ASPHYXIA] – **sphygmomanometry** /-mə'nomətri/ *n*, **sphygmomanometric** /-ˌmanə 'metrik/ *adj*, **sphygmomanometrically** *adv*

spic, spick /spik/ *n, NAm* a spik

spica /'spiekə/ *n, pl* **spicae** /-ˌsee/, **spicas** a bandage applied in successive crossing loops to immobilize a limb, esp at a joint [L, spike of grain – more at [3]SPIKE]

spicate /'spiekayt/ *adj* pointed, spiked ⟨*a ~ inflorescence*⟩ [L *spicatus*, pp of *spicare* to arrange in the shape of heads of grain, fr *spica*]

spiccato /spi'kahtoh/ *n or adj, pl* **spiccatos** (a technique, performance, or passage) played using the bow so that it rebounds from the string – used in music [It, pp of *spiccare* to detach, pick off]

[1]**spice** /spies/ *n* **1a** any of various aromatic vegetable products (e g pepper, ginger, or nutmeg) used to season or flavour foods **b** such products collectively **2** sthg that adds zest or relish ⟨*variety's the very ~ of life* – William Cowper⟩ **3** a pungent or aromatic smell [ME, fr OF *espice*, fr LL *species* spices, fr L, species]

[2]**spice** *vt* **1** to season with spice **2** to add zest or relish to ⟨*cynicism ~d with wit*⟩

'**spiceˌbush** /-ˌboosh/ *n* an aromatic N American shrub of the laurel family

spicery /'spies(ə)ri/ *n* spices

spick-and-span, spic-and-span /ˌspik ənd 'span/ *adj* spotlessly clean and tidy; spruce [short for *spick-and-span-new*, fr obs E *spick* (spike) + E *and* + *span-new* (brand-new; fr ME, part trans of ON *spānnȳr*, fr *spānn* chip of wood + *nȳr* new)]

spicule /'spikyoohl, 'spie-/ *n* **1** a minute slender pointed usu hard body; *esp* any of the minute bodies composed of calcium carbonate or silica that together support the tissue of various invertebrates (e g a sponge) **2** a jet of relatively cool gas rising through the lower atmosphere of the sun [NL & L; NL *spicula*, fr ML, arrowhead, alter. of L *spiculum*, dim. of *spica* spike of grain] – **spiculate** /-lət, -layt/ *adj*, **spiculiferous** /-'lifərəs/ *adj*

spicy /'spiesi/ *adj* **1** lively, spirited ⟨*a ~ temper*⟩ **2** piquant, zestful **3** somewhat scandalous; risqué ⟨*~ gossip*⟩ ['SPICE + [1]-Y] – **spicily** *adv*, **spiciness** *n*

spider /'spiedə/ *n* any of an order of arachnids having a body with 2 main divisions, 4 pairs of walking legs, and 2 or more pairs of abdominal spinnerets for spinning threads of silk used for cocoons, nests, or webs [ME, alter. of *spithre*; akin to OE *spinnan* to spin]

spider crab *n* any of numerous crabs with extremely long legs and nearly triangular bodies

spider mite *n* RED SPIDER

spider monkey *n* any of a genus of New World monkeys with long slender limbs, a rudimentary or absent thumb, and a very long prehensile tail

spider's web *n* the (geometrically patterned) silken web spun by most spiders and used as a resting place and a trap for small prey

'**spiderˌweb** /-ˌweb/ *n, NAm* SPIDER'S WEB

'**spiderˌwort** /-ˌwuht/ *n* tradescantia

spidery /'spied(ə)ri/ *adj* **1a** resembling a spider in form or manner; *specif* long, thin, and sharply angular like the legs of a spider **b** resembling a spider's web; *esp* composed of fine threads or lines in a weblike arrangement ⟨*~ handwriting*⟩ **2** infested with spiders

spiegeleisen /'shpeegəˌliez(ə)n, 'spee-/ *n* pig iron containing 15 to 30 per cent manganese [G, fr *spiegel* mirror + *eisen* iron]

[1]**spiel** /s(h)peel/ *vb, chiefly NAm vi* to talk volubly or extravagantly ~ *vt* to utter or express volubly or extravagantly – usu + *off* *USE* infml [G *spielen* to play, fr OHG *spilōn*; akin to OE *spilian* to revel] – **spieler** *n*

[2]**spiel** *n, chiefly NAm* a voluble talk designed to influence or persuade; patter – infml

spiffing /'spifing/ *adj, Br* extremely good; excellent ⟨*auntie is a ~ cook*⟩ – not now in vogue [E dial. *spiff* (dandified)]

spifflicate /'spiflikayt/ *vt, Br* to defeat or destroy utterly; flatten – humor [origin unknown]

spigot /'spigət/ *n* **1** a small plug used to stop up the vent of a cask **2** the part of a tap, esp on a barrel, which controls the flow **3** a plain end of a piece of piping or guttering that fits into an adjoining piece [ME, prob deriv of L *spica* spike of grain]

spik, spic /spik/ *n, NAm* a Spanish-speaking (Latin)

American – derog [alter. of *spig*, short for *spigotty*, prob fr the broken E utterance *no speaka de English* ('I don't speak English"), supposed to be much used by Spanish Americans]

[1]**spike** /spiek/ *n* **1** a very large nail **2a** any of a row of pointed iron pieces (e g on the top of a wall or fence) **b(1)** any of several metal projections set in the sole and heel of a shoe to improve traction **(2)** *pl* a pair of (athletics) shoes having spikes attached **3** the act or an instance of spiking in volleyball **4a** a pointed element in a graph or tracing **b** an unusually high and sharply defined maximum (e g of amplitude in a wave train) [ME, prob fr MD; akin to L *spina* thorn – more at SPINE]

[2]**spike** *vt* **1** to fasten or provide with spikes ⟨~ *the soles of climbing boots*⟩ **2** to disable (a muzzle-loading cannon) by driving a spike into the vent **3** to pierce with or impale on a spike; *specif* to reject (newspaper copy), orig by impaling on a spike **4** to add spirits to (a nonalcoholic drink) **5** to drive (a volleyball) sharply downwards into an opponent's court **6** *chiefly NAm* to suppress or thwart completely ⟨~d *the rumour*⟩ – **spiker** *n* – **spike someone's guns** to frustrate sby's opposition; foil an opponent

[3]**spike** *n* **1** an ear of grain **2** an elongated plant inflorescence with the flowers stalkless on a single main axis ☞ PLANT [ME *spik* head of grain, fr L *spica*; akin to L *spina* thorn]

spiked *adj* **1** having an inflorescence that is a spike **2** having a sharp projecting point

spikelet /'spieklit/ *n* a small or secondary spike; *specif* any of the small spikes that make up the compound inflorescence of a grass or sedge

spikenard /'spieknahd/ *n* (an E Indian aromatic plant of the valerian family believed to have given rise to) a fragrant ointment of the ancients [ME, fr MF or ML; MF *spicanarde*, fr ML *spica nardi*, lit., spike of nard]

spiky /'spieki/ *adj* **1** having a sharp projecting point or points **2** caustic, aggressive ⟨*a* ~ *retort*⟩

[1]**spile** /spiel/ *n* **1** SPIGOT 1 **2** *NAm* a spout inserted in a tree to draw off sap [prob fr D *spijl* stake; akin to L *spina* thorn – more at SPINE]

[2]**spile** *vt* to supply with a spile

[1]**spill** /spil/ *vb* **spilt** /spilt/, *NAm chiefly* **spilled** *vt* **1** to cause (blood) to be shed **2a** to cause or allow to fall or flow out so as to be lost or wasted, esp accidentally **b** to empty, discharge ⟨*train* spilt *its occupants onto the platform*⟩ **3** to empty (a sail) of wind **4** to throw off or out ⟨*his horse* spilt *him*⟩ **5** to let out; divulge ⟨~ *a secret*⟩ – infml ~ *vi* **1a** to fall or flow out or over and become wasted, scattered, or lost **b** to cause or allow sthg to spill **2** to spread profusely or beyond limits ⟨*crowds* spilt *into the streets*⟩ [ME *spillen*, fr OE *spillan* to kill, destroy, squander; akin to OHG *spaltan* to split, L *spolia* spoils, Gk *sphallein* to cause to fall] – **spillable** *adj*, **spiller** *n* – **spill the beans** to divulge information indiscreetly – infml

[2]**spill** *n* **1** a fall from a horse or vehicle **2** a quantity spilt

[3]**spill** *n* a thin twist of paper or sliver of wood used esp for lighting a fire [ME *spille*]

spillikin /'spilikin/ *n* **1** any of the pieces used in spillikins **2** *pl but sing in constr* a game in which a set of thin rods or straws is allowed to fall in a heap with each player in turn trying to remove them 1 at a time without disturbing the rest [prob alter. of obs D *spelleken* small peg]

spillway /'spil,way/ *n* a passage for surplus water from a dam

[1]**spin** /spin/ *vb* **-nn-; spun** /spun/ *vi* **1** to draw out and twist fibre into yarn or thread **2** *esp of a spider or insect* to form a thread by forcing out a sticky rapidly hardening fluid **3a** to revolve rapidly; whirl **b** to have the sensation of spinning; reel ⟨*my head is* ~ning⟩ **4** to move swiftly, esp on wheels or in a vehicle **5** to fish with a spinning lure **6** *of an aircraft* to fall in a spin ~ *vt* **1a** to draw out and twist into yarns or threads **b** to produce (yarn or thread) by drawing out and twisting a fibrous material **2** to form (e g a web or cocoon) by spinning **3** to compose and tell (a usu involved or fictitious story) ⟨*is always* ~ning *yarns*⟩ **4** to cause to revolve rapidly ⟨~ *a top*⟩; *also* to cause (a cricket ball) to revolve in the manner characteristic of spin bowling **5** to shape into threadlike form in manufacture; *also* to manufacture by a whirling process [ME *spinnen*, fr OE *spinnan*; akin to OHG *spinnan* to spin, L *sponte* voluntarily, Gk *span* to draw – more at SPAN]

[2]**spin** *n* **1a** the act or an instance of spinning sthg **b** the whirling motion imparted (e g to a cricket ball) by spinning **c** a short excursion, esp in or on a motor vehicle **2** an aerial manoeuvre or flight condition consisting of a combination of roll and yaw with the longitudinal axis of the aircraft inclined steeply downwards and its wings in a state of (partial) stall **3** the property of an elementary particle that corresponds to intrinsic angular momentum, that can be thought of as rotation of the particle about its axis, and that is mainly responsible for magnetic properties **4** a state of mental confusion; a panic ⟨*in a* ~⟩ – infml – **spinless** *adj*

spina bifida /,spienə 'bifidə/ *n* a congenital condition in which there is a defect in the formation of the spine allowing the meninges to protrude and usu associated with disorder of the nerves supplying the lower part of the body [NL, bifid spinal column]

spinach /'spinij, -nich/ *n* (the leaves, eaten as food, of) a plant of the goosefoot family cultivated for its edible leaves [MF *espinache, espinage*, fr OSp *espinaca*, fr Ar *isfānākh*, fr Per]

spinach beet *n* a beet that lacks a fleshy root and is grown solely for its leaves that resemble spinach in flavour; *also* the leaves of spinach beet eaten as a vegetable

spinal /'spienəl/ *adj* **1** of or situated near the backbone **2** of or affecting the spinal cord ⟨~ *reflexes*⟩ **3** of or resembling a spine – **spinally** *adv*

spinal canal *n* a canal that contains the spinal cord

spinal column *n* the skeleton running the length of the trunk and tail of a vertebrate that consists of a jointed series of vertebrae and protects the spinal cord

spinal cord *n* the cord of nervous tissue that extends from the brain lengthways along the back in the spinal canal, carries impulses to and from the brain, and serves as a centre for initiating and coordinating many reflex actions ☞ NERVE

spinal nerve *n* any of the paired nerves that arise from the spinal cord, supply muscles of the trunk and limbs, and normally form 31 pairs in human beings

spin bowling *n* usu slower bowling in cricket in

which the ball is made to spin by the bowler and so deviate from a straight line as it bounces

[1]**spindle** /'spindl/ *n* **1a** a round stick with tapered ends used to form and twist the yarn in hand spinning **b** the long slender pin by which the thread is twisted in a spinning wheel **c** any of various rods or pins holding a bobbin in a textile machine (e g a spinning frame) **d** the pin in a loom shuttle **e** the bar or shaft, usu of square section, that carries the knobs and actuates the latch or bolt of a lock **2** a spindle-shaped figure seen in microscopic sections of dividing cells along which the chromosomes are distributed **3a** a turned often decorative piece (e g in a baluster) **b** a newel **c** a pin or axis about which sthg turns [ME *spindel*, fr OE *spinel*; akin to OE *spinnan* to spin]

[2]**spindle** *vi* **spindling** /'spindling/ to grow into or have a long slender stalk – **spindler** *n*

'spindle ,tree *n* any of a genus of often evergreen shrubs, small trees, or climbing plants typically having red fruits and a hard wood formerly used for spindle making

spindly /'spindli/ *adj* having an unnaturally tall or slender appearance, esp suggestive of physical weakness ⟨~ *legs*⟩

spindrift /'spindrift/ *n* sea spray [alter. of Sc *speendrift*, fr *speen* to drive before a strong wind + E *drift*]

,spin-'dry *vt* to remove water from (wet laundry) by placing in a rapidly rotating drum – **spin-drier** *n*

spine /spien/ *n* **1a** SPINAL COLUMN ☞ ANATOMY **b** sthg like a spinal column or constituting a central axis or chief support **c** the back of a book, usu lettered with the title and author's name **2** a stiff pointed plant part; *esp* one that is a modified leaf or leaf part **3** a sharp rigid part of an animal or fish; *also* a pointed prominence on a bone [ME, thorn, spinal column, fr L *spina*; akin to Latvian *spina* twig] – **spined** *adj*

'spine-,chilling *adj* causing fear or terror – **spine-chiller** *n*

spinel /spi'nel/ *n* any of a group of hard minerals that have a similar crystal structure and are oxides of 2 metals; *esp* a colourless to ruby-red or black oxide of magnesium and aluminium used as a gem [It *spinella*, dim. of *spina* thorn, fr L]

spineless /'spienlis/ *adj* **1** free from spines, thorns, or prickles **2a** having no spinal column; invertebrate **b** lacking strength of character – **spinelessly** *adv*, **spinelessness** *n*

spinet /'spinit, spi'net/ *n* a small harpsichord having the strings at an angle to the keyboard [It *spinetta*, prob fr Giovanni *Spinetti fl* 1503, its reputed inventor]

spinifex /'spienifeks/ *n* any of several Australian grasses with spiny seeds or stiff sharp leaves [NL, genus name, fr L *spina* + *facere* to make – more at [1]DO]

spinnaker /'spinəkə/ *n* a large triangular sail set forward of a yacht's mast on a long light pole and used when running before the wind [origin unknown]

spinner /'spinə/ *n* **1** a fisherman's lure consisting of a spoon, blade, or set of wings that revolves when drawn through the water **2** a conical fairing attached to an aircraft propeller hub and revolving with it **3** (a delivery bowled by) a bowler of spin bowling [[1]SPIN + [2]-ER]

spinneret /,spinə'ret/ *n* **1** an organ, esp of a spider or caterpillar, for producing threads of silk from the secretion of silk glands **2** *also* **spinnerette** a small metal plate, thimble, or cap with fine holes through which a chemical solution (e g of cellulose) is forced in the spinning of man-made filaments

spinney /'spini/ *n*, *Br* a small wood with undergrowth [MF *espinaye* thorny thicket, fr *espine* thorn, fr L *spina*]

'spinning ,frame /'spining/ *n* a machine that draws, twists, and winds yarn

,spinning 'jenny /'jeni/ *n* an early multiple-spindle machine for spinning wool or cotton [*Jenny*, nickname for *Jane*]

'spinning ,wheel *n* a small domestic machine for spinning yarn or thread by means of a spindle driven by a hand- or foot-operated wheel

'spin-,off *n* a by-product ⟨*household products that are* ~s *of space research*⟩; *also* sthg which is a further development of some idea or product ⟨*a* ~ *from a successful TV series*⟩

spinose /'spienohs, -nohz/ *adj* SPINY 1 ⟨*a fly with black* ~ *legs*⟩ – **spinosely** *adv*, **spinosity** /-'nosəti/ *n*

spinous /'spienəs/ *adj* **1** difficult or unpleasant to handle or meet **2** SPINY 1, 3 ⟨~ *appendages*⟩ ⟨*a* ~ *larva*⟩

spin out *vt* **1** to cause to last longer, esp by thrift ⟨spinning out *their meagre rations*⟩ **2** to extend, prolong ⟨spin out *a repair job*⟩ **3** to dismiss (a batsman in cricket) by spin bowling

spinster /'spinstə/ *n* **1** an unmarried woman **2** a woman who is past the usual age for marrying or who seems unlikely to marry [ME *spinnestere* woman engaged in spinning, fr *spinnen* to spin + *-estere* -ster] – **spinsterhood** *n*, **spinsterish** *adj*

spinthariscope /spin'thariskohp/ *n* an instrument that consists of a fluorescent screen and a magnifying lens system for visual detection of alpha particles [Gk *spintharis* spark + E *-scope*]

spinule /'spienyoohl/ *n* a minute spine [L *spinula*, dim. of *spina* thorn – more at SPINE] – **spinulose** /-yoolohs/ *adj*

spiny /'spieni/ *adj* **1** covered or armed with spines; *broadly* bearing spines, prickles, or thorns **2** full of difficulties or annoyances; thorny ⟨~ *problems*⟩ **3** slender and pointed like a spine – **spininess** *n*

spiny anteater *n* the echidna

spiny lobster *n* any of several edible crustaceans distinguished from the true lobster by the simple unenlarged first pair of legs and the spiny carapace

spir-, spiri-, spiro- *comb form* coil; twist ⟨spir*ula*⟩ ⟨spiro*chaete*⟩ [LL *spir-*, fr L *spira* – more at [3]SPIRE]

spiracle /'spierəkl, 'spirəkl/ *n* a breathing orifice (e g the blowhole of a whale or a tracheal opening in an insect) ☞ ANATOMY [L *spiraculum*, fr *spirare* to breathe – more at SPIRIT] – **spiracular** /-'rakyoolə/ *adj*

spiraea /spie'riə/ *n* any of a genus of herbaceous plants or shrubs of the rose family that have small white or pink flowers in dense clusters and are commonly grown in gardens [NL, genus name, fr L, a plant, fr Gk *speiraia*, prob fr *speira* [3]spire]

[1]**spiral** /'spie·ərəl/ *adj* **1a** winding round a centre or pole and gradually approaching or receding from it ⟨*the* ~ *curve of a watch spring*⟩ **b** helical **2** of the

advancement to higher levels through a series of cyclical movements ⟨*a ~ theory of social development*⟩ [ML *spiralis*, fr L *spira* coil] – **spirally** *adv*

[2]**spiral** *n* **1a** the path of a point in a plane moving round a central point while continuously receding from or approaching it **b** a 3-dimensional curve (e g a helix) with 1 or more turns about an axis **2** a single turn or coil in a spiral object **3a** sthg with a spiral form **b** a spiral flight **4** a continuously expanding and accelerating increase or decrease ⟨*wage ~s*⟩

[3]**spiral** *vb* **-ll-** (*NAm* **-l-**, **-ll-**) *vi* to go, esp to rise, in a spiral course ⟨*prices ~led*⟩ ~ *vt* to cause to take a spiral form or course

spiral binding *n* a book or notebook binding in which a continuous spiral wire or plastic strip is passed through holes along 1 edge – **spiral-bound** *adj*

spiral galaxy *n* a galaxy with a nucleus from which extend usu 2 spiral arms

spiral nebula *n* SPIRAL GALAXY

spirant /'spie·ərənt/ *n* a fricative [ISV, fr L *spirant-*, *spirans*, prp of *spirare* to breathe – more at SPIRIT] – **spirant** *adj*

[1]**spire** /spie·ə/ *n* **1** a slender tapering blade or stalk (e g of grass) **2** the upper tapering part of sthg (e g a tree or antler) **3** a tall tapering roof or other construction on top of a tower – compare STEEPLE [ME, fr OE *spīr*; akin to MD *spier* blade of grass, L *spina* thorn – more at SPINE] – **spired** *adj*, **spiry** *adj*

[2]**spire** *vi* to taper up to a point like a spire

[3]**spire** *n* **1** a spiral, coil **2** the inner or upper part of a spiral gastropod shell [L *spira* coil, fr Gk *speira*; akin to Gk *sparton* rope, esparto, Lith *springti* to choke in swallowing] – **spired** *adj*

[4]**spire** *vi* to spiral

spiri- – see SPIR-

spirillum /spi'riləm/ *n*, *pl* **spirilla** /-lə/ any of a genus of long curved bacteria; *broadly* a spirochaete or other spiral filamentous bacterium [NL, genus name, fr dim. of L *spira* coil]

[1]**spirit** /'spirit/ *n* **1** an animating or vital principle of living organisms **2** a supernatural being or essence: e g **a** *cap* HOLY SPIRIT **b** SOUL 2 **c** a being that has no body but can become visible; *specif* GHOST 2 **d** a malevolent being that enters and possesses a human being **3** temper or state of mind – often pl with sing. meaning ⟨*in high ~s*⟩ **4** the immaterial intelligent or conscious part of a person **5** the attitude or intention characterizing or influencing sthg ⟨*undertaken in a ~ of fun*⟩ **6** liveliness, energy; *also* courage **7** devotion, loyalty ⟨*team ~*⟩ **8** a person of a specified kind or character ⟨*she's such a kind ~*⟩ **9a** distilled liquor of high alcoholic content – usu pl with sing. meaning ⟨*a glass of ~s*⟩ **b** any of various volatile liquids obtained by distillation or cracking (e g of petroleum, shale, or wood) – often pl with sing. meaning **c** ALCOHOL 1 **10a** prevailing characteristic ⟨*~ of the age*⟩ **b** the true meaning of sthg (e g a rule or instruction) in contrast to its verbal expression **11** an alcoholic solution of a volatile substance ⟨*~ of camphor*⟩ [ME, fr OF or L; OF, fr L *spiritus*, lit., breath; akin to L *spirare* to blow, breathe, ON *fisa* to break wind] – **spiritless** *adj* – **in spirits** in a cheerful or lively frame of mind – **out of spirits** in a gloomy or depressed frame of mind

[2]**spirit** *vt* to carry off, esp secretly or mysteriously – usu + *away* or *off* ⟨*was ~ed away to a mountain hideout*⟩

'**spirited** *adj* **1** full of energy, animation, or courage ⟨*a ~ discussion*⟩ **2** having a specified frame of mind – often in combination ⟨*low-*spirited⟩ – **spiritedly** *adv*, **spiritedness** *n*

spiritism /'spiri,tiz(ə)m/ *n* SPIRITUALISM 2 – **spiritist** *n*, **spiritistic** /-'tistik/ *adj*

'**spirit ,level** *n* a level that uses the position of a bubble in a curved transparent tube of liquid to indicate whether a surface is level ☞ BUILDING

,**spirit of 'hartshorn** /'hahts,hawn/, **spirits of hartshorn** *n* a solution of ammonia in water

spiritous /'spiritəs/ *adj* spirituous

spirit rapping *n* communication by raps (e g on a table) held to be made by the spirits of the dead

[1]**spiritual** /'spirichooəl/ *adj* **1** (consisting) of spirit; incorporeal ⟨*man's ~ needs*⟩ **2a** of sacred matters **b** ecclesiastical rather than lay or temporal **3** concerned with religious values **4** based on or related through sympathy of thought or feeling **5** of supernatural beings or phenomena [ME, fr MF & LL; MF *spirituel*, fr LL *spiritualis*, fr L, of breathing, of wind, fr *spiritus*] – **spiritualize** *vt*, **spiritually** *adv*, **spiritualness** *n*

[2]**spiritual** *n* a usu emotional religious song of a kind developed esp among Negroes in the southern USA

spiritualism /'spirichooə,liz(ə)m/ *n* **1** the doctrine that spirit is the ultimate reality **2** a belief that spirits of the dead communicate with the living, esp through a medium or at a séance – **spiritualist** *n, often cap*, **spiritualistic** /-'listik/ *adj*

spirituality /,spirichoo'aləti/ *n* **1** sensitivity or attachment to religious values **2** a practice of personal devotion and prayer [ME *spiritualte*, fr MF *spiritualté*, fr ML *spiritualitat-*, *spiritualitas*, fr LL *spiritualis* spiritual]

spirituel /'spirichoo,el/ *adj* having or marked by a refined and esp witty nature [F, lit., spiritual]

spirituous /'spirichooəs/ *adj* containing or impregnated with alcohol obtained by distillation ⟨*~ liquors*⟩ [prob fr F *spiritueux*, fr L *spiritus* spirit]

spiro- – see SPIR-

spirochaete, *NAm chiefly* **spirochete** /'spie·ərohkeet/ *n* any of an order of slender spirally undulating bacteria including those causing syphilis and relapsing fever [NL *Spirochaeta*, genus of bacteria, fr L *spira* coil + Gk *chaitē* long hair – more at [3]SPIRE] – **spirochaetal** *adj*

spirograph /'spie·ərə,grahf, -,graf/ *n* an instrument for recording respiratory movements [ISV] – **spirographic** /-'grafik/ *adj*, **spirography** /spie·ə'rogrəfi/ *n*

spirogyra /,spie·ərə'jie·ərə/ *n* any of a genus of freshwater green algae whose cells contain spiral chlorophyll bands [NL, genus name, fr Gk *speira* coil + *gyros* ring, circle – more at [3]SPIRE, COWER]

spirometer /spie·ə'romitə/ *n* an instrument for measuring the air entering and leaving the lungs [ISV] – **spirometry** *n*, **spirometric** /-rə'metrik/ *adj*

spirt /spuht/ *vb or n* [2] [3]SPURT

[1]**spit** /spit/ *n* **1** a slender pointed rod for holding meat over a source of heat (e g an open fire) **2** a small point of land, esp of sand or gravel, running into a river mouth, bay, etc ☞ GEOGRAPHY [ME, fr OE *spitu*; akin to L *spina* thorn, spine]

[2]**spit** *vt* **-tt-** to fix (as if) on a spit; impale

[3]**spit** *vb* **-tt-; spat** /spat/, **spit** *vt* **1** to eject (e g saliva) from the mouth **2a** to express (hostile or malicious feelings) (as if) by spitting ⟨spat *his contempt*⟩ **b** to utter vehemently or with a spitting sound ⟨spat *out his words*⟩ **3** to emit as if by spitting ⟨*the guns* spat *fire*⟩ ~ *vi* **1a** to eject saliva from the mouth (as an expression of aversion or contempt) **b** to exhibit contempt **2** to rain or snow slightly or in flurries **3** to sputter [ME *spitten*, fr *OE spittan*, of imit origin] – **spit it out** to utter promptly what is in the mind

[4]**spit** *n* **1a(1)** spittle, saliva **(2)** the act or an instance of spitting **b** a frothy secretion exuded by some insects **2** perfect likeness – often in *spit and image* ⟨*he's the very* ~ *and image of his father*⟩

,spit and 'polish *n* extreme attention to cleanliness, orderliness, and ceremonial [fr the practice of cleaning objects such as shoes by spitting on them before polishing them]

[1]**spite** /spiet/ *n* petty ill will or malice [ME, short for *despite*] – **spiteful** *adj*, **spitefully** *adv* – **in spite of** in defiance or contempt of ⟨*sorry* in spite of *himself*⟩

[2]**spite** *vt* to treat vindictively or annoy out of spite

spitfire /'spit,fie·ə/ *n* a quick-tempered or volatile person

spitting cobra /'spiting/ *n* either of 2 venomous African snakes that eject their venom towards the victim without striking

spitting image *n* [4]SPIT 2 [alter. of *spit and image*]

spittle /'spitl/ *n* **1** saliva (ejected from the mouth) **2** [4]SPIT 1b [ME *spetil*, fr OE *spætl*; akin to OE *spittan*]

'spittle,bug /-,bug/ *n* a froghopper

spittoon /spi'toohn/ *n* a receptacle for spit [[4]*spit* + *-oon* (as in *balloon*)]

spiv /spiv/ *n, Br* a slick individual who lives by sharp practice or petty fraud; *specif* a black marketeer operating esp after WW II [alter. of E dial. *spiff* (flashy dresser), fr *spiff* (dandified)] – **spivvery** *n*

splanchnic /'splangknik/ *adj* of the viscera [NL *splanchnicus*, fr Gk *splanchnikos*, fr *splanchna*, pl, viscera; akin to Gk *splēn* spleen]

[1]**splash** /splash/ *vi* **1a** to strike and move about a liquid ⟨~ed *about in the bath*⟩ **b** to move through or into a liquid and cause it to spatter ⟨~ *through a puddle*⟩ **2a(1)** to become spattered about **(2)** to spread or scatter in the manner of splashed liquid ⟨*sunlight* ~ed *over the lawn*⟩ **b** to flow, fall, or strike with a splashing sound ⟨*a brook* ~ing *over rocks*⟩ **3** *chiefly Br* to spend money liberally; splurge – usu + *out* ⟨~ed *out on a bottle of champagne*⟩ ~ *vt* **1a** to dash a liquid or semiliquid substance on or against **b** to soil or stain with splashed liquid; spatter **c** to display very conspicuously ⟨*the affair was* ~ed *all over the local papers – Woman's Journal*⟩ **2a** to cause (a liquid or semiliquid substance) to spatter about, esp with force **b** to spread or scatter in the manner of a splashed liquid ⟨*sunset* ~ed *its colours across the sky*⟩ [alter. of *plash*] – **splasher** *n*

[2]**splash** *n* **1a** a spot or daub (as if) from splashed liquid ⟨*a mud* ~ *on the wing*⟩ **b** a usu vivid patch of colour or of sthg coloured ⟨~es *of yellow tulips*⟩ **2a** (the sound of) splashing **b** a short plunge **3** (a vivid impression created esp by) an ostentatious display **4** a small amount, esp of a mixer added to an alcoholic drink; a dash – **splashy** *n*

'splash,back /-,bak/ *n* a panel or screen (e g behind a sink or cooker) to protect the wall from splashes

'splash,down /-,down/ *n* the landing of a spacecraft in the ocean – **splash down** *vi*

splat /splat/ *n* a single flat often ornamental piece of wood forming the centre of a chair back [obs *splat* (to spread flat), fr ME *splatten*]

splatter /'splatə/ *vt* to spatter ~ *vi* to scatter or fall (as if) in heavy drops ⟨*rain* ~ed *against the windscreen*⟩ [prob blend of *splash* and *spatter*] – **splatter** *n*

[1]**splay** /splay/ *vt* **1** to spread out **2** to make (e g the edges of an opening) slanting ~ *vi* **1** to become splayed **2** to slope, slant [ME *splayen*, short for *displayen* – more at DISPLAY]

[2]**splay** *adj* turned outwards ⟨~ *knees*⟩

'splay,foot /-,foot/ *n* a foot abnormally flattened and spread out – **splayfoot, splayfooted** /-'footid/ *adj*

spleen /spleen/ *n* **1** a highly vascular ductless organ near the stomach or intestine of most vertebrates that is concerned with final destruction of blood cells, storage of blood, and production of lymphocytes **2** bad temper; spite **3** *archaic* melancholy [ME *splen*, fr MF or L; MF *esplen*, fr L *splen*, fr Gk *splēn*; akin to L *lien* spleen] – **spleeny** *adj*, **spleenful** *adj*

'spleen,wort /-,wuht/ *n* any of a genus of ferns having spore clusters borne obliquely on the upper side of a leaf vein [fr the belief in its power to cure disorders of the spleen]

splen-, spleno- *comb form* spleen ⟨splen*ectomy*⟩ ⟨spleno*megaly*⟩ [L, fr Gk *splēn-*, *splēno-*, fr *splēn*]

splendent /'splendənt/ *adj* shining, glossy [ME, fr LL *splendent-*, *splendens*, fr L, prp of *splendēre*]

splendid /'splendid/ *adj* **1a** shining, brilliant **b** magnificent, sumptuous **2** illustrious, distinguished **3** of the best or most enjoyable kind; excellent ⟨*a* ~ *picnic*⟩ [L *splendidus*, fr *splendēre* to shine; akin to Gk *splēdos* ashes, Skt *sphuliṅga* spark] – **splendidly** *adv*, **splendidness** *n*

splendiferous /splen'dif(ə)rəs/ *adj* splendid – infml ⟨*his* ~ *eruption of eloquence – TLS*⟩ [*splendour* + *-i-* + *-ferous*] – **splendiferously** *adv*, **splendiferousness** *n*

splendour, *NAm chiefly* **splendor** /'splendə/ *n* **1a** great brightness or lustre; brilliance **b** grandeur, pomp **2** sthg splendid [ME *splendure*, fr AF *splendur*, fr L *splendor*, fr *splendēre*] – **splendorous, splendrous** *adj*

splenectomy /spli'nektəmi/ *n* surgical removal of the spleen [ISV] – **splenectomized** /-miezd/ *adj*

splenetic /spli'netik/ *adj* **1** bad tempered, spiteful **2** *archaic* given to melancholy [LL *spleneticus*, fr L *splen* spleen] – **splenetic** *n*, **splenetically** *adv*

splenic /'spleenik, 'splenik/ *adj* of or located in the spleen ⟨~ *blood flow*⟩ [L *splenicus*, fr Gk *splēnikos*, fr *splēn* spleen]

splenius /'spleenyəs/ *n, pl* **splenii** /-ni,ie/ a flat oblique muscle of each side of the back of the neck [NL, fr L *splenium* plaster, compress, fr Gk *splēnion*, fr *splēn*]

splenomegaly /,spleenoh'megəli/ *n* enlargement of the spleen [ISV *splen-* + Gk *megal-*, *megas* large – more at MUCH]

[1]**splice** /splies/ *vt* **1a** to join (e g ropes) by interweaving the strands **b** to unite (e g film, magnetic tape, or timber) by overlapping the ends or binding with

adhesive tape **2** *Br* to unite in marriage; marry – infml [obs D *splissen*; akin to MD *splitten* to split] – **splicer** *n*

[2]**splice** *n* a joining or joint made by splicing

spline /splien/ *n* a key, ridge, or groove that prevents a shaft from turning freely in a surrounding sleeve [origin unknown] – **splined** *adj*

[1]**splint** /splint/ *n* **1** a thin strip of wood suitable for interweaving (e g into baskets) **2** material or a device used to protect and immobilize a body part (e g a broken arm) **3** a bony enlargement on the upper part of the cannon bone of a horse, usu on the inside of the leg [ME, fr MLG *splinte, splente*; akin to OHG *spaltan* to split – more at SPILL]

[2]**splint** *vt* to support and immobilize (as if) with a splint

splint bone *n* either of the 2 slender rudimentary bones on either side of the cannon bone in the limbs of horses and related animals

[1]**splinter** /ˈsplintə/ *n* **1** a sharp thin piece, esp of wood or glass, split or broken off lengthways **2** a small group or faction broken away from a parent body [ME, fr MD; akin to MLG *splinte* splint] – **splinter** *adj*, **splintery** *adj*

[2]**splinter** *vt* **1** to split or rend into long thin pieces; shatter **2** to split into fragments, parts, or factions ~ *vi* to become splintered

[1]**split** /split/ *vb* **-tt-; split** *vt* **1** to divide, esp lengthways **2a(1)** to tear or rend apart; burst **(2)** to subject (an atom or atomic nucleus) to artificial disintegration, esp by fission **b** to affect as if by shattering or tearing apart ⟨*a roar that* ~ *the air*⟩ **3** to divide into parts or portions: e g **a** to divide between people; share ⟨~ *a bottle of wine at dinner*⟩ **b** to divide into opposing factions, parties, etc ⟨*the bill* ~ *the opposition*⟩ **c** to break down (a chemical compound) into constituents ⟨~ *a fat into glycerol and fatty acids*⟩; *also* to remove by such separation **d** *NAm* to mark (a ballot) or cast (a vote) so as to vote for opposed candidates **4** to separate (constituent parts) by interposing sthg ⟨~ *an infinitive*⟩ ~ *vi* **1a** to become split lengthways or into layers **b** to break apart; burst **2a** to become divided up or separated off ⟨~ *into factions*⟩ **b** to sever relations or connections – often + *up* ⟨~ *up after 6 months' marriage*⟩ **3** to share sthg (e g loot or profits) with others – often + *with*; infml **4** to let out a secret; act as an informer – often + *on*; slang ⟨*on the point of* ~ting *on the gang* – Dorothy Sayers⟩ **5** to leave, esp hurriedly; depart – slang [D *splitten*, fr MD; akin to OHG *spaltan* to split – more at [1]SPILL] – **splitter** *n* – **split hairs** to make oversubtle or trivial distinctions – **split one's sides** to laugh heartily – **split the difference** to compromise by taking the average of 2 amounts

[2]**split** *n* **1** a narrow break made (as if) by splitting **2** a piece broken off by splitting **3** a division into divergent groups or elements; a breach ⟨*a* ~ *in party ranks*⟩ **4a** splitting **b** *pl but sing in constr* the act of lowering oneself to the floor or leaping into the air with legs extended at right angles to the trunk **5** a wine bottle holding a quarter of the usual amount; *also* a small bottle of mineral water, tonic water, etc **6** a sweet dish composed of sliced fruit, esp a banana, ice cream, syrup, and often nuts and whipped cream

[3]**split** *adj* **1** divided, fractured **2** prepared for use by splitting ⟨~ *bamboo*⟩ ⟨~ *hides*⟩

split infinitive *n* an infinitive with a modifier between *to* and the verb

ˌ**split-ˈlevel** *adj* divided so that the floor level in one part is less than a full storey higher than an adjoining part ⟨*a* ~ *house*⟩ – **split-level** *n*

split pea *n* a dried pea in which the cotyledons are usu split apart

split personality *n* a personality composed of 2 or more internally consistent groups of behaviour tendencies and attitudes each acting more or less independently of the other

split pin *n* a strip of metal folded double that can be used as a fastener by inserting it through a hole and then bending back the ends

split ring *n* a metal ring of 2 flat turns on which keys may be kept

ˌ**split ˈsecond** *n* a fractional part of a second; a flash – **split-second** *adj*

split shift *n* a shift of working hours divided into 2 or more widely-separated working periods

splitting /ˈspliting/ *adj* causing a piercing sensation ⟨*a* ~ *headache*⟩

splodge /sploj/ *vt or n, Br* (to) splotch – infml [by alter.] – **splodgy** *adj*

splosh /splosh/ *vb or n* (to) splash – infml [by alter.]

[1]**splotch** /sploch/ *n* a large irregular spot or smear; a blotch [perh blend of *spot* and *blotch*] – **splotchy** *adj*

[2]**splotch** *vt* to mark with a splotch or splotches

[1]**splurge** /spluhj/ *n* **1** an ostentatious display or enterprise **2** an extravagant spending spree *USE* infml [perh blend of *splash* and *surge*]

[2]**splurge** *vi* **1** to make a splurge **2** to spend money extravagantly – often + *on* ⟨~ *on a slap-up meal*⟩ ~ *vt* to spend extravagantly or ostentatiously *USE* infml

splutter /ˈsplutə/ *vi* **1** to make a noise as if spitting **2** SPUTTER 2 ~ *vt* to utter hastily and confusedly [prob alter. of *sputter*] – **splutter** *n*, **splutterer** *n*, **spluttery** *adj*

Spode /spohd/ *n* fine ceramic ware (e g bone china) made at the works established by Josiah Spode at Stoke [Josiah *Spode* †1827 E potter]

spodumene /ˈspodyoomeen/ *n* a mineral that is a lithium aluminium silicate occurring as (very large) variously coloured crystals [prob fr F *spodumène*, fr G *spodumen*, fr Gk *spodoumenos*, prp of *spodousthai* to be burnt to ashes, fr *spodos* ashes]

[1]**spoil** /spoyl/ *n* **1a** plunder taken from an enemy in war or a victim in robbery; loot – often pl with sing. meaning **b** sthg gained by special effort or skill – usu pl with sing. meaning **2** earth and rock excavated or dredged [ME *spoile*, fr MF *espoille*, fr L *spolia*, pl of *spolium* – more at SPILL]

[2]**spoil** *vb* **spoilt** /spoylt/, **spoiled** *vt* **1a** to damage seriously; ruin ⟨*heavy rain* ~t *the crops*⟩ **b** to impair the enjoyment of; mar ⟨*a quarrel* ~t *the celebration*⟩ **2a** to impair the character of by overindulgence or excessive praise ⟨~ *an only child*⟩ **b** to treat indulgently; pamper **c** to cause to be unsatisfied with sthg inferior – usu + *for* ⟨*the good meals at this hotel will* ~ *us for canteen food*⟩ ~ *vi* **1** to lose good or useful qualities, usu as a result of decay ⟨*fruit soon* ~s *in warm weather*⟩ **2** to have an eager desire *for* – esp in *spoiling for a fight* [ME *spoilen*, fr MF *espoillier*, fr L *spoliare*, fr *spolium*] – **spoilable** *adj*

spoilage /'spoylij/ *n* **1** sthg spoiled or wasted **2** loss by being spoiled

spoiler /'spoylə/ *n* **1** a long narrow plate along the upper surface of an aircraft wing that may be raised for reducing lift and increasing drag ☞ FLIGHT **2** an air deflector at the front or rear of a motor vehicle to reduce the tendency to lift off the road at high speeds [[2]SPOIL + [2]-ER]

'spoil,sport /-,spawt/ *n* one who spoils the fun of others – infml

[1]spoke /spohk/ *past & archaic past part of* SPEAK

[2]spoke *n* **1** any of the small radiating bars inserted in the hub of a wheel to support the rim **2** a rung of a ladder [ME, fr OE *spāca*; akin to MD *spike* spike]

[3]spoke *vt* to provide (as if) with spokes

spoken /'spohkən/ *adj* **1a** delivered by word of mouth; oral ⟨*a ~ request*⟩ **b** used in speaking or conversation; uttered ⟨*the ~ word*⟩ **2** characterized by speaking in a specified manner – in combination ⟨*soft*-spoken⟩ ⟨*plain*spoken⟩ [pp of *speak*]

'spoke,shave /-,shayv/ *n* a plane having a blade set between 2 handles and used for shaping curved surfaces [[2]*spoke*]

spokesman /'spohksmən/, *fem* **'spokes,woman** *n* one who speaks on behalf of another or others [prob irreg fr *spoke*, obs pp of *speak*]

'spokes,person /-,puhs(ə)n/ *n* a spokesman or spokeswoman

spoliate /'spohli·ayt/ *vt* to despoil [L *spoliatus*, pp]

spoliation /,spohli'aysh(ə)n/ *n* **1a** the act of plundering **b** the state of being plundered, esp in war **2** the act of damaging or injuring, esp irreparably [ME, fr L *spoliation-, spoliatio*, fr *spoliatus*, pp of *spoliare* to plunder – more at [2]SPOIL] – **spoliator** *n*

spondee /'spondee/ *n* a metrical foot consisting of 2 long or stressed syllables [ME *sponde*, fr MF or L; MF *spondee*, fr L *spondeum*, fr Gk *spondeios*, fr *spondeios* of a libation, fr *spondē* libation; fr its use in music accompanying libations] – **spondaic** /-'dayik/ *adj or n*

spondulicks /spon'dyoohliks/ *n pl* funds, money – slang; chiefly humor [perh fr Gk *spondylikos*, adj, fr *spondylos* species of shell sometimes used as currency]

spondylitis /,spondi'lietəs/ *n* inflammation of the spinal vertebrae [NL, fr Gk *sphondylos, spondylos* vertebra, lit., whorl; akin to Gk *sphadazein* to jerk, *sphendonē* sling]

[1]sponge /spunj, spunzh/ *n* **1a(1)** an elastic porous mass of interlacing horny fibres that forms the internal skeleton of various marine animals and is able when wetted to absorb water **(2)** a piece of sponge (e g for cleaning) **(3)** a porous rubber or cellulose product used similarly to a sponge **b** any of a phylum of aquatic lower invertebrate animals that are essentially double-walled cell colonies and permanently attached as adults **2** a sponger **3a** raised dough (e g for yeast bread) **b** a sponge cake or sweet steamed pudding made from a sponge-cake mixture **c** a metal (e g platinum) in the form of a porous solid composed of fine particles [ME, fr OE, fr L *spongia*, fr Gk]

[2]sponge *vt* **1** to cleanse, wipe, or moisten (as if) with a sponge **2** to remove or erase by rubbing (as if) with a sponge **3** to obtain by sponging on another ⟨*~ the price of a pint*⟩ **4** to soak up (as if) with or in the manner of a sponge *~ vi* to obtain esp financial assistance by exploiting natural generosity or organized welfare facilities – usu + *on*

'sponge ,bag *n, Br* a small waterproof usu plastic bag for holding toilet articles

'sponge ,cake *n* a light sweet cake made with (approximately) equal quantities of sugar, flour, and eggs but no shortening

sponger /'spunjə/ *n* one who lives off others, esp by exploiting natural generosity [[2]SPONGE + [2]-ER]

,sponge 'rubber *n* cellular rubber resembling a natural sponge in structure

spongy /'spunji/ *adj* **1** resembling a sponge, esp in being soft, porous, absorbent, or moist **2** *of a metal* in the form of a sponge – **sponginess** *n*

sponson /'spuns(ə)n/ *n* **1** a projection from the side of a ship or tank enabling a gun to fire forwards **2** a light air-filled structure protruding from the hull of a seaplane to steady it on water [prob by shortening & alter. fr *expansion*]

[1]sponsor /'sponsə/ *n* **1** sby who presents a candidate for baptism or confirmation and undertakes responsibility for his/her religious education or spiritual welfare **2** sby who assumes responsibility for some other person or thing **3** sby who or sthg that pays for a project or activity [LL, fr L, guarantor, surety, fr *sponsus*, pp of *spondēre* to promise – more at SPOUSE] – **sponsorship** *n*, **sponsorial** /-'sawri·əl/ *adj*

[2]sponsor *vt* to be or stand as sponsor for

spontaneous /spon'taynyəs, -ni·əs/ *adj* **1** proceeding from natural feeling or innate tendency without external constraint ⟨*a ~ expression of gratitude*⟩ **2** springing from a sudden impulse ⟨*a ~ offer of help*⟩ **3** controlled and directed internally **4** developing without apparent external influence, force, cause, or treatment ⟨*~ recovery from a severe illness*⟩ **5** not contrived or manipulated; natural [LL *spontaneus*, fr L *sponte* of one's free will, voluntarily – more at SPIN] – **spontaneously** *adv*, **spontaneousness** *n*, **spontaneity** /,spontə'nayəti/ *n*

spontaneous combustion *n* self-ignition of combustible material through chemical action (e g oxidation) of its constituents

spontaneous generation *n* abiogenesis

spontoon /spon'toohn/ *n* a short pike formerly borne by subordinate officers of infantry [F *sponton*, fr It *spuntone*, fr *punta* sharp point, fr (assumed) VL *puncta* – more at POINT]

[1]spoof /spoohf/ *vt* **1** to deceive, hoax **2** to make good-natured fun of; lampoon *USE* infml [*Spoof*, a hoaxing game invented by Arthur Roberts †1933 E comedian]

[2]spoof *n* **1** a hoax, deception **2** a light, humorous, but usu telling parody *USE* infml – **spoof** *adj*

[1]spook /spoohk/ *n* a ghost, spectre – chiefly infml [D; akin to MLG *spōk* ghost] – **spookish** *adj*

[2]spook *vb, chiefly NAm vt* to make frightened or frantic; *esp* to startle into violent activity (e g stampeding) ⟨*~ed the herd of horses*⟩ *~ vi* to become frightened

spooky /'spoohki/ *adj* causing irrational fear, esp because suggestive of supernatural presences; eerie – chiefly infml [[1]SPOOK + [1]-Y]

[1]spool /spoohl/ *n* **1** a cylindrical device on which wire, yarn, film, etc is wound **2** (the amount of) material wound on a spool **3** *chiefly NAm* [1]REEL c [ME *spole*, fr MF or MD; MF *espole*, fr MD *spoele*; akin to OHG *spuola* spool]

[2]**spool** *vt* to wind on a spool

[1]**spoon** /spoohn/ *n* **1a** an eating, cooking, or serving implement consisting of a small shallow round or oval bowl with a handle **b** a spoonful **2** sthg curved like the bowl of a spoon (e g a usu metal or shell fishing lure) [ME, fr OE *spōn* splinter, chip; akin to OHG *spān* splinter, chip, Gk *sphēn* wedge]

[2]**spoon** *vt* **1** to take up and usu transfer (as if) in a spoon ⟨~ed *soup into his mouth*⟩ **2** to propel (a ball) weakly upwards *vi* to indulge in caressing and amorous talk – not now in vogue [vi fr *spoon*, n (simpleton, doting lover, sweetheart), fr [1]*spoon*]

'**spoon,bill** /-,bil/ *n* any of several wading birds, that have the bill greatly expanded and flattened at the tip

spoonerism /'spoohnə,riz(ə)m/ *n* a transposition of usu initial sounds of 2 or more words (e g in *tons of soil* for *sons of toil*) [William *Spooner* †1930 E clergyman & scholar]

'**spoon-,feed** *vt* **1** to feed by means of a spoon **2a** to present (e g information or entertainment) in an easily assimilable form that precludes independent thought or critical judgment ⟨~ *political theory to students*⟩ **b** to present information to in this manner

'**spoonful** /-f(ə)l/ *n, pl* **spoonfuls** *also* **spoonsful** as much as a spoon will hold

[1]**spoor** /spooə, spaw/ *n* a track, a trail, or droppings, esp of a wild animal [Afrik, fr MD; akin to OE *spor* footprint, spoor, *spurnan* to kick – more at SPURN]

[2]**spoor** *vb* to track (sthg) by a spoor

spor-, spori-, sporo- *comb form* seed; spore ⟨spor*angium*⟩ ⟨spori*cidal*⟩ [NL *spora*]

sporadic /spə'radik, spaw-/ *adj* occurring occasionally or in scattered instances [ML *sporadicus*, fr Gk *sporadikos*, fr *sporadēn* here and there, fr *sporad-*, *sporas* scattered; akin to Gk *speirein* to sow] – **sporadically** *adv*

sporangiophore /spə'ranji·ə,faw/ *n* a stalk or receptacle bearing sporangia

sporangium /spə'ranji·əm/ *n, pl* **sporangia** /-ji·ə/ a case or cell within which usu asexual spores are produced [NL, fr *spor-* + Gk *angeion* vessel – more at ANGI-] – **sporangial** *adj*

spore /spaw/ *n* a primitive usu single-celled hardy reproductive body produced by plants, protozoans, bacteria, etc and capable of development into a new individual either on its own or after fusion with another spore [NL *spora* seed, spore, fr Gk, act of sowing, seed, fr *speirein* to sow – more at SPROUT] – **spored** *adj*, **sporiferous** /spaw'rifərəs, spə-/ *adj*

sporocyst /'spawrohsist, -rə-/ *n* a resting cell (e g in slime moulds and algae) that may give rise to asexual spores [ISV] – **sporocystic** /-'sistik/ *adj*

,**sporo'genesis** /-'jenəsis/ *n* reproduction by or formation of spores [NL]

sporogenous /spə'rojinəs/ *adj* of, involving, or reproducing by sporogenesis

sporophyte /'spawrə,fiet/ *n* (a member of) the generation of a plant exhibiting alternation of generations that bears asexual spores [ISV] – **sporophytic** /-'fitik/ *adj*

-sporous /-sp(ə)rəs/ *comb form* (→ *adj*) having (such or so many) spores ⟨*homo*sporous⟩ [NL *spora* spore] – **-spory** *comb form* (→ *n*)

sporozoan /,spawrə'zoh·ən/ *n* any of a large class of strictly parasitic protozoans that have a complicated life cycle usu involving both asexual and sexual generations often in different hosts and include important pathogens (e g malaria parasites and coccidia) [NL *Sporozoa*, class name, fr *spor-* + *-zoa*] – **sporozoan** *adj*

sporozoite /,spawrə'zoh·iet/ *n* an infectious form of some sporozoans that is a product of sporogony and initiates an asexual cycle in the new host [NL *Sporozoa* + ISV *-ite*]

sporran /'sporən/ *n* a pouch of animal skin with the hair or fur on that is worn in front of the kilt with traditional Highland dress ☞ GARMENT [ScGael *sporan* purse]

[1]**sport** /spawt/ *vt* **1** to exhibit for all to see; show off ⟨~ *a new hat*⟩ **2** to put forth as a sport or bud variation ~ *vi* **1** to play about happily; frolic ⟨*lambs* ~ing *in the meadow*⟩ **2** to speak or act in jest; trifle **3** to deviate or vary abruptly from type [ME *sporten* to divert, disport, short for *disporten*; (vt 2 & vi 3) [2]*sport* 5]

[2]**sport** *n* **1a** a source of diversion or recreation; a pastime **b(1)** physical activity engaged in for recreation **(2)** a particular activity (e g hunting or athletics) so engaged in 👁 **2a** pleasantry, jest ⟨*only made the remark in* ~⟩ **b** mockery, derision **3** sby or sthg manipulated by outside forces ⟨*was made the* ~ *of fate*⟩ **4** sby who is fair, generous, and esp a good loser **5** an individual exhibiting a sudden deviation from type beyond the normal limits of individual variation **6** *chiefly NAm* a playboy **7** *Austr* – used in informal address, chiefly to men

sporting /'spawting/ *adj* **1a** concerned with, used for, or suitable for sport **b** marked by or calling for sportsmanship **c** involving such risk as a sports competitor might take or encounter ⟨*a* ~ *chance*⟩ **d** fond of or taking part in sports ⟨~ *nations*⟩ **2** *chiefly NAm* of or for sports that involve betting or gambling – **sportingly** *adv*

sportive /'spawtiv/ *adj* frolicsome, playful – **sportively** *adv*, **sportiveness** *n*

sports /spawts/, *NAm chiefly* **sport** *adj* of or suitable for sports ⟨~ *equipment*⟩; *esp* styled in a manner suitable for casual or informal wear ⟨~ *coats*⟩

'**sports ,car** *n* a low fast usu 2-passenger motor car

'**sportsman** /-mən/, *fem* '**sports,woman** *n* **1** sby who engages in sports, esp blood sports **2** sby who is fair, a good loser, and a gracious winner – **sportsmanlike** *adj*

'**sportsmanship** /-ship/ *n* conduct becoming to a sportsman

sporty /'spawti/ *adj* **1** fond of sport **2a** notably loose or dissipated; fast ⟨*ran around with a very* ~ *crowd*⟩ **b** flashy, showy ⟨~ *clothes*⟩ **3** suggestive of or capable of giving good sport ⟨*the car had a very* ~ *feel*⟩ *USE* infml – **sportily** *adv*, **sportiness** *n*

sporulation /,spor(y)oo'laysh(ə)n/ *n* the formation of spores; *esp* division into many small spores [ISV, fr NL *sporula*, dim. of *spora* spore] – **sporulate** /-layt/ *vi*, **sporulative** /-lətiv/ *adj*

[1]**spot** /spot/ *n* **1** a blemish on character or reputation; a stain **2a** a small usu round area different (e g in colour or texture) from the surrounding surface **b(1)** an area marred or marked (e g by dirt) **(2)** a small surface patch of diseased or decayed tissue ⟨*the* ~s *that appear in measles*⟩ ⟨*rust* ~s *on a leaf*⟩; *also* a pimple **c** a conventionalized design used on playing cards to distinguish suits and indicate values **3** a

small amount; a bit ⟨*had a ~ of bother with the car*⟩ **4** a particular place or area ⟨*a nice ~ for a picnic*⟩ **5a** a particular position (e g in an organization or hierarchy) ⟨*a good ~ as the director's secretary*⟩ **b** a place on an entertainment programme **6** SPOTLIGHT 1a **7** a usu difficult or embarrassing position; FIX 1 **8** *chiefly NAm* an object having a specified number of spots or a specified numeral on its surface [ME; akin to MD *spotte* stain, speck, ON *spotti* small piece] – **on the spot 1** in one place; without travelling away ⟨*running* on the spot⟩ **2** at the place of action; available at the appropriate place and time **3** in an awkward or embarrassing position ⟨*his subordinate's mistake put him* on the spot⟩

[2]spot *vb* **-tt-** *vt* **1** to sully the character or reputation of; disgrace **2** to mark or mar (as if) with spots **3a** to single out; identify **b** to detect, notice ⟨*~ a mistake*⟩ **c** to watch for and record the sighting of ⟨*~ a rare species of duck*⟩ **4** to locate accurately ⟨*~ an enemy position*⟩ **5a** to lie at intervals in or on **b** to fix in or as if in the beam of a spotlight ~ *vi* **1** to become stained or discoloured in spots **2** to cause a spot; leave a stain **3** to act as a spotter; *esp* to locate targets **4** *chiefly Br* to fall lightly in scattered drops ⟨*it's ~ting with rain again*⟩ – **spottable** *adj*

[3]spot *adj* **1a** being, originating, or done on the spot or in or for a particular spot **b** available for immediate delivery after sale ⟨*~ commodities*⟩ **c(1)** paid out immediately ⟨*~ cash*⟩ **(2)** involving immediate cash payment ⟨*a ~ sale*⟩ **d** broadcast between scheduled programmes ⟨*~ announcements*⟩ **2** given on the spot or restricted to a few random places or instances ⟨*a ~ check*⟩ ⟨*~ prizes*⟩; *also* selected at random or as a sample

,spot-'check *vb* to make a quick or random sampling or investigation (of)

'spotless /-lis/ *adj* **1** free from dirt or stains; immaculate ⟨*~ kitchens*⟩ **2** pure, unblemished ⟨*~ reputation*⟩ – **spotlessly** *adv*, **spotlessness** *n*

[1]'spot,light /-,liet/ *n* **1a** a projected spot of light used for brilliant illumination of a person or object on a stage **b** full public attention ⟨*held the political ~*⟩ **2a** a light designed to direct a narrow intense beam on a small area **b** sthg that illuminates brightly or elucidates

[2]spotlight *vt* to illuminate (as if) with a spotlight

,spot-'on *adj, Br* **1** absolutely correct or accurate **2** exactly right ⟨*a shirt that looks ~ with jeans*⟩ *USE* infml – **spot-on** *adv*

spotted /'spotid/ *adj* **1** marked with spots **2** sullied, tarnished ⟨*inherited a ~ name*⟩

,spotted 'dick /dik/ *n, Br* a steamed or boiled sweet suet pudding containing currants [*Dick*, nickname for *Richard*]

spotter /'spotə/ *n* **1** sby or sthg that makes or applies a spot (e g for identification) **2** sby or sthg that keeps watch or observes; *esp* a person who watches for and notes down vehicles (e g aircraft or trains)

spotty /'spoti/ *adj* **1a** marked with spots **b** having spots, esp on the face ⟨*a ~ youth*⟩ **2** lacking evenness or regularity, esp in quality ⟨*~ attendance*⟩ – **spottily** *adv*, **spottiness** *n*

spouse /spows, spowz/ *n* a married person; a husband or wife [ME, fr OF *espous* (masc) & *espouse* (fem), fr L *sponsus* betrothed man, groom & *sponsa* betrothed woman, bride, fr *sponsus*, pp of *spondēre* to promise, betroth; akin to Gk *spendein* to make a libation, promise, *spondē* libation (pl, treaty)]

[1]spout /spowt/ *vt* **1** to eject (e g liquid) in a copious stream ⟨*wells ~ing oil*⟩ **2** to speak or utter in a strident, pompous, or hackneyed manner; declaim ⟨*~ party slogans*⟩ – infml ~ *vi* **1** to issue with force or in a jet; spurt **2** to eject material, esp liquid, in a jet **3** to declaim – infml [ME *spouten*; akin to MD *spoiten* to spout, OE *spīwan* to spew] – **spouter** *n*

[2]spout *n* **1** a projecting tube or lip through which liquid issues from a teapot, roof, kettle, etc **2** a discharge or jet of liquid (as if) from a pipe – **spouted** *adj* – **up the spout 1** beyond hope of improvement; ruined – infml **2** pregnant – slang

[1]sprain /sprayn/ *n* **1** a sudden or violent twist or wrench of a joint with stretching or tearing of ligaments **2** a sprained condition [origin unknown]

[2]sprain *vt* to subject to sprain

sprang /sprang/ *past of* SPRING

sprat /sprat/ *n* a small or young herring; *also* the young of a similar fish [alter. of ME *sprot*, fr OE *sprott*]

[1]sprawl /sprawl/ *vi* **1** to lie or sit with arms and legs spread out carelessly or awkwardly **2** to spread or develop irregularly ⟨*a town that ~s across the countryside*⟩ ~ *vt* to cause (e g one's limbs) to spread out [ME *sprawlen*, fr OE *sprēawlian*]

[2]sprawl *n* **1** a sprawling position **2** an irregular spreading mass or group ⟨*a ~ of buildings*⟩

[1]spray /spray/ *n* **1** a usu flowering branch or shoot **2** a decorative arrangement of flowers and foliage (e g on a dress) **3** sthg (e g a jewelled pin) resembling a spray [ME]

[2]spray *n* **1** fine droplets of water blown or falling through the air ⟨*the ~ from the waterfall*⟩ **2a** a jet of vapour or finely divided liquid **b** a device (e g an atomizer or sprayer) by which a spray is dispersed or applied **c(1)** an application of a spray ⟨*give the roses a ~*⟩ **(2)** a substance (e g paint or insecticide) so applied **3** sthg (e g a number of small flying objects) resembling a spray [obs *spray* (to sprinkle), fr MD *sprayen*; akin to Gk *speirein* to scatter – more at SPROUT]

[3]spray *vt* **1** to discharge, disperse, or apply as a spray **2** to direct a spray on – **sprayer** *n*

'spray ,gun *n* an apparatus resembling a gun for applying a substance (e g paint or insecticide) in the form of a spray

[1]spread /spred/ *vb* **spread** *vt* **1a** to open or extend over a larger area – often + *out* ⟨*~ out the map*⟩ **b** to stretch out; extend ⟨*~ its wings for flight*⟩ **c** to form (the lips) into a long narrow slit (e g when pronouncing the vowel /ee/) **2a** to distribute over an area ⟨*~ manure*⟩ **b** to distribute over a period or among a group ⟨*~ the work over a few weeks*⟩ **c(1)** to apply as a layer or covering **(2)** to cover or overlay with sthg ⟨*~ bread with butter*⟩ **d** to prepare for dining; set ⟨*~ the table*⟩ **3a** to make widely known ⟨*~ the news*⟩ **b** to extend the range or incidence of ⟨*~ a disease*⟩ **c** to diffuse, emit ⟨*flowers ~ing their fragrance*⟩ **4** to force apart ~ *vi* **1a** to become dispersed, distributed, or scattered ⟨*a race that ~ across the globe*⟩ **b** to become known or disseminated ⟨*panic ~ rapidly*⟩ **2** to cover a greater area; expand **3** to be forced apart (e g from pressure or weight) [ME *spreden*, fr OE *sprǣdan*; akin to OHG *spreiten* to spread, OE *-sprūtan* to sprout – more at

Rugby Union

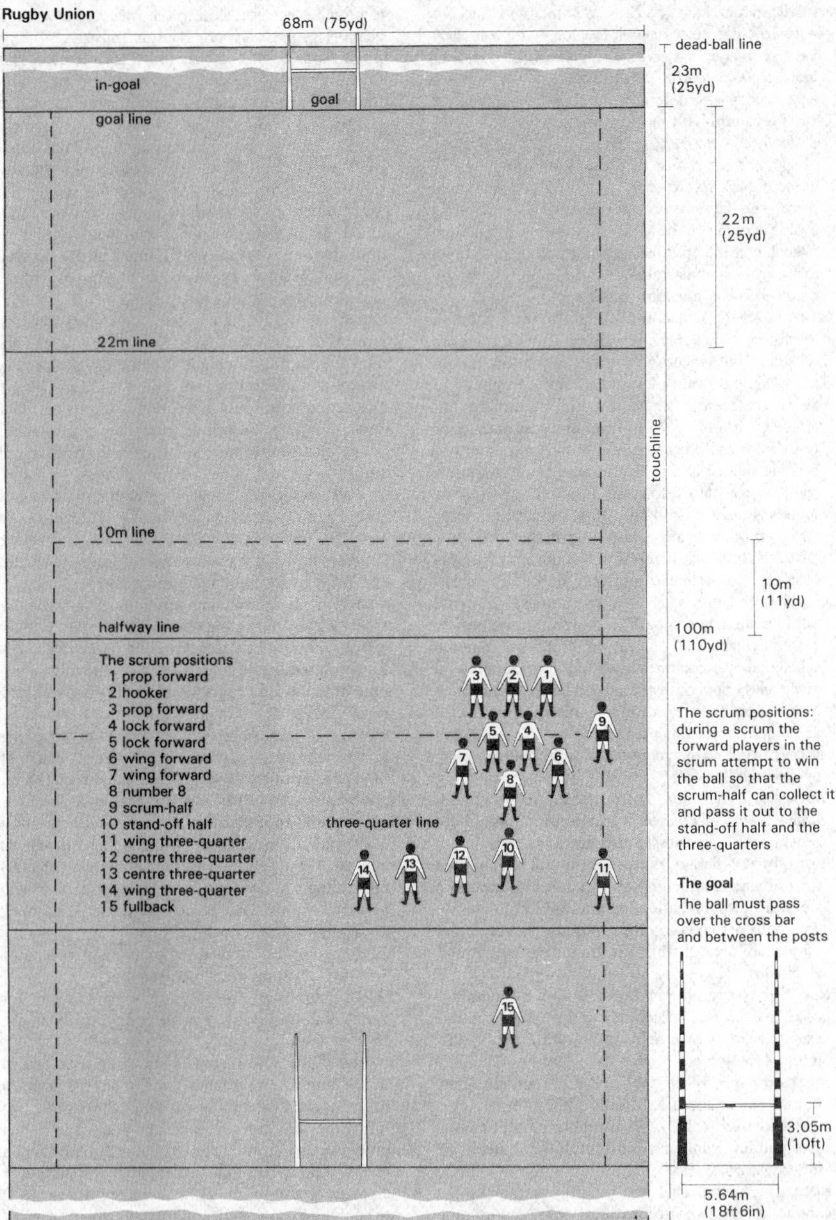

The scrum positions: during a scrum the forward players in the scrum attempt to win the ball so that the scrum-half can collect it and pass it out to the stand-off half and the three-quarters

The goal

The ball must pass over the cross bar and between the posts

Soccer

The terminology of the modern lineup is not so settled as that of the traditional lineup, but the commonest names for the positions are shown here.

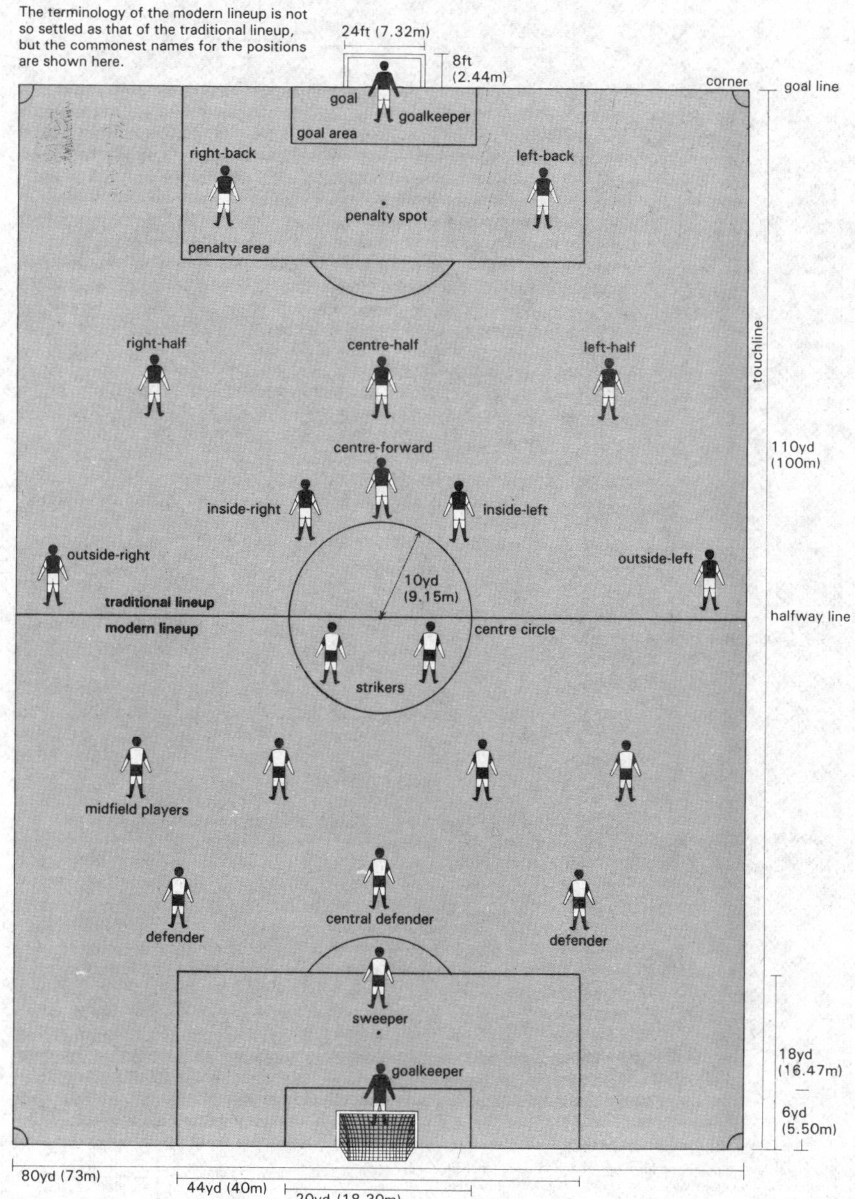

Cricket

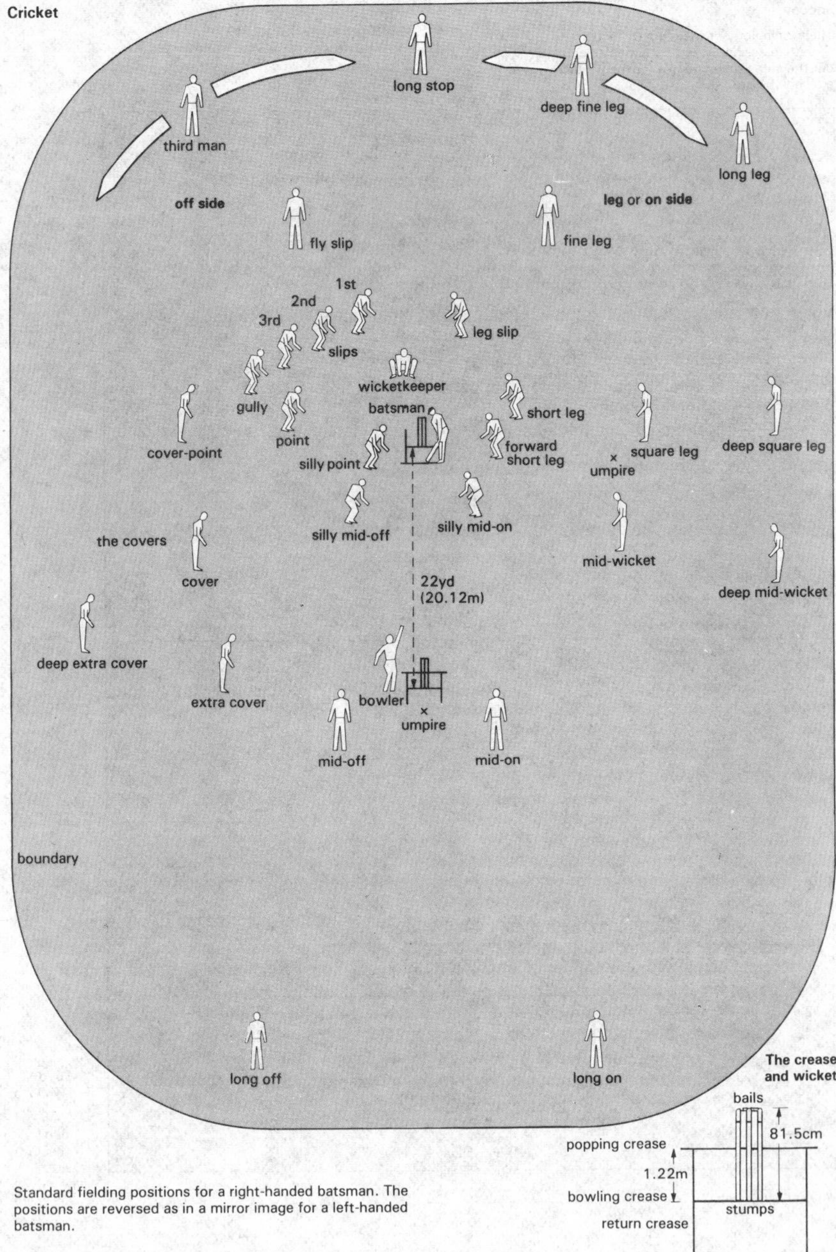

Standard fielding positions for a right-handed batsman. The positions are reversed as in a mirror image for a left-handed batsman.

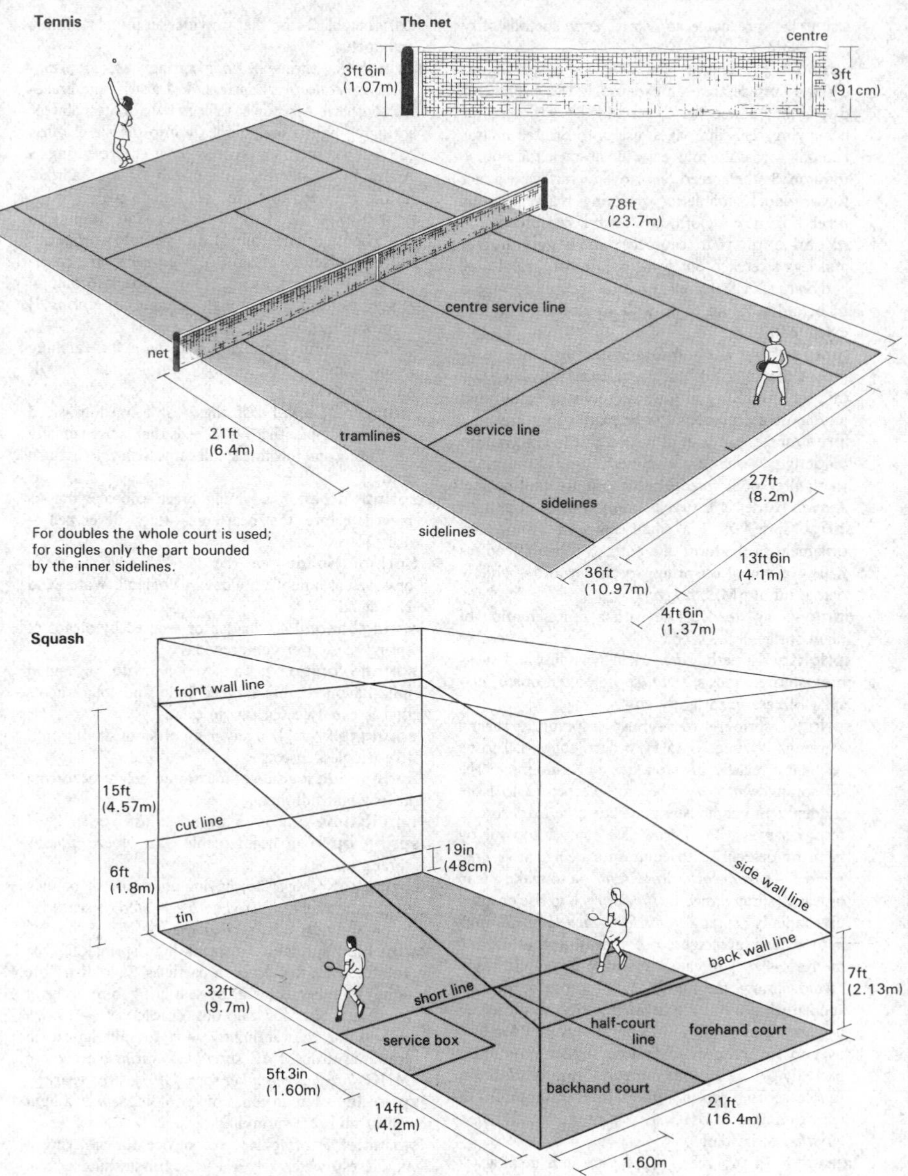

The court is bounded by the front, side, and back wall lines; any ball that hits the wall above them is out of play. Players serve from the service boxes, and the served ball must hit the front wall between the front wall line and the cut line.

SPROUT] – **spreadable** *adj*, **spreader** *n*, **spreadability** /-dəˈbiləti/ *n*

[2]**spread** *n* **1** (extent of) spreading **2** sthg spread out: e g **a** a surface area; an expanse **b(1)** a prominent display in a newspaper or periodical **(2)** (the matter occupying) 2 facing pages, usu with printed matter running across the fold **c** a wide obstacle for a horse to jump **3** sthg spread on or over a surface: e g **a** a food product suitable for spreading **b** a sumptuous meal; a feast **c** a cloth cover; *esp* a bedspread

ˈ**spread-ˌeagle** *vb* to (cause to) stand or lie with arms and legs stretched out wide; (cause to) sprawl ⟨*lay* ~d *on the lawn*⟩ [*spread eagle* (a representation, esp in heraldry, of an eagle with wings raised & legs extended)]

ˈ**spreadˌsheet** *n* a software system in which large groups of numerical data can be displayed on a VDU in a set format (e g in rows and columns) and rapid automatic calculations can be made

spree /spree/ *n* a bout of unrestrained indulgence in an activity ⟨*went on a shopping* ~⟩; *esp* a binge [perh alter. of Sc *spreath* cattle raid, foray, fr ScGael *sprēidh* cattle, fr L *praeda* booty – more at PREY]

[1]**sprig** /sprig/ *n* **1** a small shoot or twig **2** an ornament in the form of a sprig **3** a small headless nail **4** a young offspring; *specif* a youth – chiefly derog; infml [ME *sprigge*]

[2]**sprig** *vt* **-gg-** to decorate with a representation of plant sprigs

sprightly /ˈsprietli/ *adj* marked by vitality and liveliness; spirited [obs *spright* (sprite), alter. of *sprite*] – **sprightliness** *n*, **sprightly** *adv*

[1]**spring** /spring/ *vb* **sprang** /sprang/, **sprung** /sprung/; **sprung** *vi* **1a(1)** to dart, shoot **(2)** to be resilient or elastic; *also* to move by elastic force ⟨*the lid* sprang *shut*⟩ **b** to become warped **2** to issue suddenly and copiously; pour out ⟨*the tears* sprang *from her eyes*⟩ **3a** to grow as a plant **b** to issue by birth or descent **c** to come into being; arise ⟨*the project* ~s *from earlier research*⟩ **4a** to make a leap or leaps ⟨sprang *towards the door*⟩ **b** to rise or jump up suddenly ⟨sprang *to his feet when the bell rang*⟩ **5** to extend in height; rise ⟨*the tower* ~s *to 90 metres*⟩ ~ *vt* **1** to cause to spring **2** to split, crack ⟨*wind* sprang *the mast*⟩ **3a** to cause to operate suddenly ⟨~ *a trap*⟩ **b** to bring into a specified state by pressing or bending ⟨~ *a bar into place*⟩ **4** to leap over **5** to produce or disclose suddenly or unexpectedly ⟨~ *a surprise on them*⟩ ⟨sprang *a leak*⟩ **6** to release from prison – infml [ME *springen*, fr OE *springan*; akin to OHG *springan* to jump, Gk *sperchesthai* to hasten]

[2]**spring** *n* **1a** a source of supply; *esp* an issue of water from the ground **b** an ultimate source, esp of thought or action ⟨*the inner* ~s *of being*⟩ **2** a time or season of growth or development; *specif* the season between winter and summer comprising, in the northern hemisphere, the months of March, April, and May **3** a mechanical part that recovers its original shape when released after deformation ☞ CAR **4a** the act or an instance of leaping up or forward; a bound **b(1)** capacity for springing; resilience **(2)** bounce, energy ⟨*a man with* ~ *in his step*⟩

spring balance *n* a device using a spiral spring for measuring weight or force

ˈ**springˌboard** /-ˌbawd/ *n* **1** a flexible board secured at one end that a diver or gymnast jumps off to gain extra height **2** sthg that provides an initial stimulus or impetus

springbok /ˈspringbok/ *n, pl* **springboks**, (*1*) **springboks**, *esp collectively* **springbok** **1** a swift and graceful southern African gazelle noted for its habit of springing lightly and suddenly into the air **2** *often cap* a sportsman or sportswoman representing S Africa in an international match or tour abroad [Afrik, fr *spring* to jump + *bok* male goat]

ˌ**spring-ˈclean** *vt* **1** to give a thorough cleaning to (e g a house or furnishings) **2** to put into a proper or more satisfactory order ⟨~ *a government department*⟩ ~ *vi* to spring-clean a house [back-formation fr *spring-cleaning* (thorough cleaning), fr [2]*spring* 2] – **spring-clean** *n*

springe /sprinj, sprinzh/ *n* a snare for catching small animals [ME *sprenge, springe*; akin to OE *springan* to spring]

springer spaniel /ˈspring·ə/ *n* a medium-sized sporting dog of either of 2 breeds that is used chiefly for finding and flushing small game [[1]*spring* (to flush game)]

ˌ**spring ˈgreen** *n* a young green cabbage that is picked before the heart has fully developed – usu pl

ˌ**Spring ˈHoliday** *n* the last Monday in May observed as a public holiday in England, Wales, and N Ireland

ˌ**spring-ˈloaded** *adj* loaded or secured by means of spring tension or compression

ˌ**spring ˈonion** *n* an onion with a small mild-flavoured thin-skinned bulb and long shoots that is chiefly eaten raw in salads

ˈ**springˌtail** /-ˌtayl/ *n* any of an order of small primitive wingless insects

ˌ**spring ˈtide** *n* a tide of maximum height occurring at new and full moon

ˈ**springˌtime** /-ˌtiem/ *n* SPRING 2; *also* YOUTH 1

spring up *vi* to begin to blow ⟨*a breeze quickly* sprang up⟩

springy /ˈspring·i/ *adj* having an elastic or bouncy quality; resilient ⟨*walked with a* ~ *step*⟩ [[2]SPRING + [1]-Y] – **springily** *adv*, **springiness** *n*

[1]**sprinkle** /ˈspringkl/ *vb* **sprinkling** /ˈspringkling/ *vt* **1** to scatter in fine drops or particles **2a** to distribute (sthg) at intervals (as if) by scattering **b** to occur at (random) intervals on; dot ⟨*meadows* ~d *with flowers*⟩ **c** to wet lightly ~ *vi* to rain lightly in scattered drops [ME *sprenklen, sprinclen*; akin to MHG *spreckel, sprenkel* spot, OE *spearca* spark]

[2]**sprinkle** *n* **1** an instance of sprinkling; *specif* a light fall of rain **2** a sprinkling

sprinkler /ˈspringklə/ *n* a device for spraying a liquid, esp water: e g **a** a fire extinguishing system that works automatically on detection of smoke or a high temperature **b** an apparatus for watering a lawn – **sprinklered** *adj*

sprinkling /ˈspringkling/ *n* a small quantity or number, esp falling in scattered drops or particles or distributed randomly

[1]**sprint** /sprint/ *vi* to run or ride a bicycle at top speed, esp for a short distance [of Scand origin; akin to Sw dial. *sprinta* to jump, hop; akin to OHG *sprinzan* to jump up, Gk *spyrthizein*] – **sprinter** *n*

[2]**sprint** *n* **1** (an instance of) sprinting **2a** a short fast running, swimming, or bicycle race **b** a burst of speed

sprit /sprit/ *n* a spar that crosses a 4-cornered

fore-and-aft sail diagonally to support the peak [ME *spret, sprit,* fr OE *sprēot* pole, spear; akin to OE *-sprūtan* to sprout]

sprite /spriet/ *n* a (playful graceful) fairy [ME *sprit,* fr OF *esprit,* fr L *spiritus* spirit]

spritsail /'sprits(ə)l, -,sayl/ *n* a sail extended by a sprit

sprocket /'sprokit/ *n* **1** a tooth or projection on the rim of a wheel, shaped so as to engage the links of a chain **2** *also* **sprocket wheel** a wheel or cylinder having sprockets (e g to engage a bicycle chain) [origin unknown]

[1]**sprout** /sprowt/ *vi* **1** to grow, spring up, or come forth as (if) a shoot **2** to send out shoots or new growth ~ *vt* to send forth or up; cause to develop or grow [ME *sprouten,* fr OE *-sprūtan;* akin to OHG *spriozan* to sprout, Gk *speirein* to scatter, sow]

[2]**sprout** *n* **1** a (young) shoot (e g from a seed or root) **2** BRUSSELS SPROUT

[1]**spruce** /sproohs/ *n* any of a genus of evergreen coniferous trees with a conical head of dense foliage and soft light wood [obs *Spruce* (Prussia), fr ME, alter. of *Pruce,* fr OF]

[2]**spruce** *adj* neat or smart in dress or appearance; trim ⟨*his ~ black coat and his bowler hat* – W S Maugham⟩ [perh fr obs *Spruce leather* (leather imported from Prussia)] – **sprucely** *adv,* **spruceness** *n*

[3]**spruce** *vt* to make spruce ~ *vi* to make oneself spruce *USE* usu + *up*

[1]**sprue** /sprooh/ *n* a tropical long-lasting disease marked esp by diarrhoea and symptoms of food and vitamin deficiency [D *spruw;* akin to MLG *sprūwe,* a kind of tumour]

[2]**sprue** *n* (a waste piece moulded in) the hole through which molten metal or plastic enters a mould [origin unknown]

spruit /sprayt/ *n, SAfr* a small watercourse that is usu dry except in the rainy season [Afrik, sprout, small stream, fr MD *sprute,* fr *spruten* to sprout]

sprung /sprung/ *adj,* **1** *past of* SPRING **2** equipped with springs ⟨*a ~ mattress*⟩

sprung rhythm *n* a poetic rhythm designed to approximate the natural rhythm of speech

spry /sprie/ *adj* **sprier, spryer; spriest, spryest** vigorously active; nimble [perh of Scand origin; akin to Sw dial. *sprygg* spry] – **spryly** *adv,* **spryness** *n*

[1]**spud** /spud/ *n* **1** a small narrow spade **2** a potato – infml [ME *spudde* dagger]

[2]**spud** *vb* **-dd-** *vt* **1** to dig up or remove with a spud **2** to begin to drill (an oil well) ~ *vi* to begin to drill an oil well

'spud-,bashing *n* the peeling of potatoes, esp when done as a punishment in a military camp – infml

spume /spyoohm/ *vi or n* (to) froth, foam [n ME, fr MF, fr L *spuma* – more at FOAM; vb fr n] – **spumous, spumy** *adj*

spun /spun/ *past of* SPIN

,spun 'glass *n* fibreglass

spunk /spungk/ *n* **1** any of various fungi used to make tinder **2** spirit, pluck **3** *Br* semen – vulg [ScGael *spong* sponge, tinder, fr L *spongia* sponge] – **spunky** *adj*

,spun 'silk *n* a yarn or fabric made from silk waste that has been boiled to remove the natural gum

,spun 'sugar *n* sugar boiled until it forms long threads on cooling, then shaped and used to decorate cold desserts or heaped on a stick as a sweet – compare CANDY FLOSS

,spun 'yarn *n* **1** a textile yarn spun from staple fibres **2** a small rope or cord formed of 2 or more rope yarns loosely twisted together

[1]**spur** /spuh/ *n* **1a** a pointed device secured to a rider's heel and used to urge on a horse **b** *pl* recognition and reward for achievement ⟨*won his academic ~s*⟩ **2** a goad to action; a stimulus **3** sthg projecting like or suggesting a spur: e g **a(1)** a stiff sharp spine (e g on the wings or legs of a bird or insect); *esp* one on a cock's leg **(2)** a metal spike fitted to a fighting cock's leg **b** a hollow projection from a plant's petals or sepals (e g in larkspur or columbine) **4** a lateral projection (e g a ridge) of a mountain (range) ☞ GEOGRAPHY **5** a short piece of road or railway connecting with a major route (e g a motorway) [ME *spure,* fr OE *spura;* akin to OE *spurnan* to kick – more at SPURN; (1b) fr the acquisition of spurs by a man gaining knighthood] – **spurred** *adj* – **on the spur of the moment** on impulse; suddenly

[2]**spur** *vb* **-rr-** *vt* **1** to urge (a horse) on with spurs **2** to incite to usu faster action or greater effort; stimulate – usu + *on* ~ *vi* to spur a horse on; ride hard

spurge /spuhj/ *n* any of various mostly shrubby plants with a bitter milky juice [ME, fr MF, purge, spurge, fr *espurgier* to purge, fr L *expurgare* – more at EXPURGATE]

spur gear *n* a gear wheel with teeth projecting away from its axis

spurge laurel *n* a low-growing Eurasian shrub with oblong evergreen leaves and yellowish flowers

spurious /'spyooəri·əs/ *adj* **1** of illegitimate birth **2** having a superficial usu deceptive resemblance or correspondence; false **3a** of deliberately falsified or mistakenly attributed origin; forged **b** based on mistaken ideas ⟨*it would be ~ to claim special privileges*⟩ [LL & L; LL *spurius* false, fr L, of illegitimate birth, fr *spurius,* n, bastard] – **spuriously** *adv,* **spuriousness** *n*

spurn /spuhn/ *vt* to reject with disdain or contempt; scorn [ME *spurnen,* fr OE *spurnan;* akin to OHG *spurnan* to kick, L *spernere* to spurn, Gk *spairein* to quiver] – **spurn** *n*

spurrey, spurry /'spuri/ *n* any of several small usu white-flowered plants of the pink family [D *spurrie,* fr MD *sporie,* fr ML *spergula*]

spurrier /'spuhri·ə/ *n* one who makes spurs

[1]**spurt** /spuht/ *vi or n* (to make) a sudden brief burst of increased effort, activity, or speed [origin unknown]

[2]**spurt** *vb* to (cause to) gush out in a jet [perh akin to MHG *spürzen* to spit, OE *-sprūtan* to sprout – more at SPROUT]

[3]**spurt** *n* a sudden forceful gush; a jet

spurtle /'spuhtl/ *n, chiefly Scot* a wooden stick for stirring porridge [origin unknown]

'spur ,wheel *n* SPUR GEAR

sputnik /'sputnik, 'spootnik/ *n* SATELLITE 2b – used esp with reference to Soviet satellites [Russ, lit., travelling companion, fr *s, so* with + *put'* path; akin to Gk *hama* together & to Skt *patha* way – more at SAME, FIND]

[1]**sputter** /'sputə/ *vt* **1** to utter hastily or explosively in confusion, anger, or excitement; splutter **2** to dislodge (atoms) from the surface of a material by collision with high energy particles (e g electrons); *also* to deposit (a metallic film) by such a process

~ *vi* **1** to eject particles of food or saliva noisily from the mouth **2** to speak in an explosive or incoherent manner **3** to make explosive popping sounds [akin to D *sputteren* to sputter, OE *-sprūtan* to sprout] – **sputterer** *n*

[2]**sputter** *n* **1** confused and excited speech **2** (the sound of) sputtering

sputum /'spyoohtəm/ *n, pl* **sputa** /-tə/ matter, made up of discharges from the respiratory passages and saliva, that is coughed up [L, fr neut of *sputus*, pp of *spuere* to spit – more at SPEW]

[1]**spy** /spie/ *vt* **1** to keep under secret surveillance, usu for hostile purposes ⟨~ *out the land*⟩ **2** to catch sight of; see ⟨spied *him lurking in the bushes*⟩ **3** to search or look for intently ⟨~ *out a means of escape*⟩ ~ *vi* **1** to observe or search for sthg; look **2** to watch secretly; act as a spy – often + *on USE* (*vt 1&3*) usu + *out* [ME *spien*, fr OF *espier*, of Gmc origin; akin to OHG *spehōn* to spy; akin to L *specere* to look, look at, *species* appearance, species, Gk *skeptesthai* & *skopein* to watch, look at, consider]

[2]**spy** *n* **1** one who keeps secret watch on sby or sthg **2** one who attempts to gain information secretly from a country, company, etc and communicate it to another

'**spy,glass** /-,glahs/ *n* a small telescope

squab /skwob/ *n, pl* **squabs**, (*1*) **squabs**, *esp collectively* **squab** **1** a fledgling bird, esp a pigeon **2** a thick cushion for a chair, car seat, etc [prob of Scand origin; akin to Sw dial. *skvabb* anything soft and thick]

squabble /'skwobl/ *vi or n* **squabbling** /'skwobling/ (to engage in) a noisy or heated quarrel, esp over trifles [prob of Scand origin; akin to Sw dial. *skvabbel* dispute] – **squabbler** *n*

squad /skwod/ *n sing or pl in constr* **1** a small group of military personnel assembled for a purpose ⟨*a drill* ~⟩ **2** a small group working as a team ⟨*a special police* ~⟩ [MF *esquade*, fr OSp & OIt; OSp *escuadra* & OIt *squadra*, derivs of (assumed) VL *exquadrare* to make square – more at SQUARE]

'**squad ,car** *n, chiefly NAm* a police car having radio communication with headquarters

squaddy /'skwodi/ *n, Br* a person of lowest rank in the armed forces; *esp* a private – infml [alter. (influenced by *squad*) of *swaddy*, fr *swad* (soldier), prob fr *swad* (bumpkin, lout)]

squadron /'skwodrən/ *n sing or pl in constr* a unit of military organization: **a** a unit of cavalry or of an armoured regiment, usu consisting of 3 or more troops **b** a variable naval unit consisting of a number of warships on a particular operation **c** a unit of an air force consisting usu of between 10 and 18 aircraft [It *squadrone*, aug of *squadra* squad]

squadron leader *n* ☞ RANK

squalid /'skwolid/ *adj* **1** filthy and degraded from neglect or poverty ⟨~ *ramshackle tenements*⟩ **2** SORDID 2 [L *squalidus* – more at SQUALOR] – **squalidly** *adv*, **squalidness** *n*

[1]**squall** /skwawl/ *vb* to cry out raucously; scream [of Scand origin; akin to ON *skval* useless chatter] – **squall** *n*, **squaller** *n*

[2]**squall** *n* **1** a sudden violent wind, often with rain or snow **2** a short-lived commotion ⟨*a minor domestic* ~⟩ [prob of Scand origin; akin to Sw *skval* rushing water] – **squally** *adj*

squalor /'skwolə/ *n* the quality or state of being squalid [L; akin to L *squalidus* squalid, *squama* scale]

squam-, squamo- *comb form* scale; squama ⟨squam*ous*⟩ [NL, fr L *squama*]

squama /'skwaymə, 'skwahmə/ *n, pl* **squamae** /-mi/ (a structure resembling) a scale [L] – **squamate** /-mayt/ *adj*

'**squamous** /'skwayməs, 'skwahməs/ *also* **squamose** /-mohs/ *adj* **1** covered with or consisting of scales **2** of or being a surface tissue consisting of a single layer of flat scalelike cells [L *squamosus*, fr *squama*]

squander /'skwondə/ *vt* to spend extravagantly, foolishly, or wastefully; dissipate ⟨~ed *his earnings on drink*⟩ [origin unknown] – **squanderer** *n*

[1]**square** /skweə/ *n* **1** an instrument (e g a set square or T square) with at least 1 right angle and 2 straight edges, used to draw or test right angles or parallel lines **2** a rectangle with all 4 sides equal ☞ MATHEMATICS **3** sthg shaped like a square: e g **a** a square scarf **b** an area of ground for a particular purpose (e g military drill) **c** an arrangement of letters, numbers, etc in a square – compare MAGIC SQUARE **4** any of the rectangular, square, etc spaces marked out on a board used for playing games **5** the product of a number multiplied by itself **6** an open space in a town, city, etc formed at the meeting of 2 or more streets, and often laid out with grass and trees **7** a solid object or piece approximating to a cube or having a square as its principal face **8** one who is excessively conventional or conservative in tastes or outlook – infml; no longer in vogue [ME, fr MF *esquarre*, fr (assumed) VL *exquadra*, fr *exquadrare* to square, fr L *ex-* + *quadrare* to square – more at QUADRATE] – **out of square** not at an exact right angle

[2]**square** *adj* **1a** having 4 equal sides and 4 right angles **b** forming a right angle ⟨*a* ~ *corner*⟩ **2a** approximating to a cube ⟨*a* ~ *cabinet*⟩ **b** of a shape or build suggesting strength and solidity; broad in relation to length or height ⟨~ *shoulders*⟩ **c** square in cross section ⟨*a* ~ *tower*⟩ **3a** *of a unit of length* denoting the area equal to that of a square whose edges are of the specified length ⟨*a* ~ *yard*⟩ **b** being of a specified length in each of 2 equal dimensions meeting at a right angle ⟨*10 metres* ~⟩ **4a** exactly adjusted, arranged, or aligned; neat and orderly **b** fair, honest, or straightforward ⟨~ *in all his dealings*⟩ **c** leaving no balance; settled ⟨*the accounts are all* ~⟩ **d** even, tied **5** of, occupying, or passing through a fielding position near or on a line perpendicular to the line between the wickets and level with the batsman's wicket ⟨~ *leg*⟩ ☞ SPORT **6** excessively conservative; dully conventional – infml; no longer in vogue – **squarely** *adv*, **squareness** *n*, **squarish** *adj*

[3]**square** *vt* **1a** to make square or rectangular ⟨~ *a building stone*⟩ **b** to test for deviation from a right angle, straight line, or plane surface **2** to set approximately at right angles or so as to present a rectangular outline ⟨~d *his shoulders*⟩ **3a** to multiply (a number) by the same number; to raise to the second power **b** to find a square equal in area to ⟨~ *the circle*⟩ **4a** to balance, settle ⟨~ *an account*⟩ **b** to even the score of (a contest) **5** to mark *off* into squares or rectangles **6a** to bring into agreement; reconcile ⟨~ *theory with practice*⟩ **b** to bribe – infml ~ *vi* **1** to match or agree precisely – usu + *with* **2** to settle matters; *esp* to pay the bill – often + *up*

– square up to **1** to prepare oneself to meet (a challenge) ⟨squared up to *the situation*⟩ **2** to take a fighting stance towards (an opponent)

[4]**square** *adv* **1** in a straightforward or honest manner ⟨*told him* ~⟩ **2a** so as to face or be face to face ⟨*the house stood* ~ *to the road*⟩ **b** at right angles **3** DIRECTLY 1 ⟨*hit the nail* ~ *on the head*⟩

square away *vt, NAm* to put in order or readiness – infml

'square-,bashing *n, chiefly Br* military drill, esp marching, on a barrack square

,square 'bracket *n* either of 2 written or printed marks [ ] used to enclose a mathematical expression or other written or printed matter

'square ,dance *n* a dance for 4 couples who form a hollow square – **square dancer** *n*, **square dancing** *n*

,square 'deal *n* an honest and fair arrangement or transaction ⟨*got a* ~ *on that trade-in*⟩

'square,head /-,hed/ *n, NAm* a German, Dutch, or Scandinavian (immigrant) – derog

,square 'meal *n* a nutritionally balanced and satisfying meal

,square 'one *n* the starting point ⟨*our plan failed so we were back to* ~⟩

square rig *n* a sailing ship rig in which the principal sails are square sails ☞ SHIP – **square-rigged** *adj*, **square-rigger** *n*

,square 'root *n* a (positive) number whose square is a usu specified number ⟨*the* ~ *of 9 is* ±*3*⟩ ☞ SYMBOL

square sail *n* a 4-sided sail held open by a rod that is suspended at its centre from a mast

,square-'shouldered *adj* having shoulders that present a rectangular outline – compare ROUND-SHOULDERED

square wave *n* the rectangular wave form of a quantity that varies periodically and abruptly from one to the other of 2 constant values

[1]**squash** /skwosh/ *vt* **1a** to press or beat into a pulp or a flat mass; crush **b** to apply pressure to by pushing or squeezing ⟨*got* ~ed *on the crowded platform*⟩ **2** to reduce to silence or inactivity; PUT DOWN ⟨~ed *her with a cutting remark*⟩ ⟨~ *a revolt*⟩ ~ *vi* **1** to flatten out under pressure or impact **2** to squeeze, press ⟨*we* ~ed *into the front row of spectators*⟩ [MF *esquasser*, fr (assumed) VL *exquassare*, fr L *ex-* + *quassare* to shake – more at QUASH] – **squashy** *adj*, **squashily** *adv*, **squashiness** *n*

[2]**squash** *n* **1** the act or soft dull sound of squashing **2** a crushed mass; *esp* a mass of people crowded into a restricted space **3** *also* **squash rackets** a game played in a 4-walled court with long-handled rackets and a rubber ball that can be played off any number of walls ☞ SPORT **4** *Br* a beverage made from sweetened and often concentrated citrus fruit juice, usu drunk diluted

[3]**squash** *n, pl* **squashes, squash** any of various (plants of the cucumber family bearing) fruits widely cultivated as vegetables and for livestock feed [by shortening & alter. fr earlier *isquoutersquash*, fr Natick & Narraganset *askútasquash*]

[1]**squat** /skwot/ *vi* **-tt-** **1** to crouch close to the ground as if to escape detection ⟨*a* ~ting *hare*⟩ **2** to assume or maintain a position in which the body is supported on the feet and the knees are bent, so that the haunches rest on or near the heels **3** to occupy property as a squatter [ME *squatten*, fr MF *esquatir*, fr *es-* ex- (fr L *ex-*) + *quatir* to press, fr (assumed) VL *coactire* to press together, fr L *coactus*, pp of *cogere* to drive together – more at COGENT]

[2]**squat** *n* **1a** squatting **b** the posture of sby or sthg that squats **2** an empty building occupied by or available to squatters – infml

[3]**squat** *adj* **-tt-** **1** with the heels drawn up under the haunches **2** disproportionately short or low and broad – **squatly** *adv*, **squatness** *n*

squatter /'skwotə/ *n* **1** one who occupies usu otherwise empty property without rights of ownership or payment of rent **2** *Austr* one who owns large tracks of grazing land [[1]SQUAT + [2]-ER]

squaw /skwaw/ *n* a N American Indian (married) woman [of Algonquian origin; akin to Natick *squáas* woman]

squawk /skwawk/ *vi or n* **1** (to utter) a harsh abrupt scream **2** (to make) a loud or vehement protest [prob blend of *squall* and *squeak*] – **squawker** *n*

'squaw ,man *n* a white man married to a N American Indian

[1]**squeak** /skweek/ *vi* **1** to utter or make a squeak **2** SQUEAL 2a – infml ~ *vt* to utter in a squeak [ME *squeken*] – **squeaker** *n*

[2]**squeak** *n* **1** a short shrill cry or noise **2** an escape – usu in *a narrow squeak*; infml – **squeaky** *adj*

[1]**squeal** /skweel/ *vi* **1** to utter or make a squeal **2a** to turn informer ⟨*bribed to* ~ *on his boss*⟩ **b** to complain, protest ~ *vt* to utter with a squeal *USE* (*vi 2*) infml [ME *squelen*] – **squealer** *n*

[2]**squeal** *n* a shrill sharp cry or noise

squeamish /'skweemish/ *adj* **1** easily nauseated **2a** excessively fastidious in manners, scruples, or convictions **b** easily shocked or offended [ME *squaymisch*, modif of AF *escoymous*] – **squeamishly** *adv*, **squeamishness** *n*

[1]**squeegee** /'skweejee/ *n* a usu rubber bladed tool used for spreading liquid on or removing it from a surface (e g a window); *also* a roller or other device used similarly in lithography or photography [prob imit]

[2]**squeegee** *vt* to smooth, wipe, or treat with a squeegee

[1]**squeeze** /skweez/ *vt* **1a** to apply physical pressure to; compress the (opposite) sides of **b** to extract or discharge under pressure ⟨~ *juice from a lemon*⟩ **c** to force, thrust, or cram (as if) by compression ⟨~ *clothes into a suitcase*⟩ ⟨~d *his way across the room*⟩ **2a** to obtain by force or extortion ⟨*dictators who* ~ *money from the poor*⟩ **b** to reduce by extortion, oppressive measures, etc ⟨squeezing *the profits*⟩ **c** to cause (economic) hardship to **3** to fit into a limited time span or schedule – usu + *in* or *into* **4** to force (another player) to discard a card to his/her disadvantage, esp in bridge ~ *vi* **1** to force one's way ⟨~ *through a door*⟩ **2** to pass, win, or get by narrowly ⟨*managed to* ~ *through the month on sick pay*⟩ [alter. of obs *quease*, fr ME *queysen*, fr OE *cwȳsan*; akin to Icel *kveisa* stomach cramps] – **squeezable** *adj*, **squeezer** *n*

[2]**squeeze** *n* **1a** a squeezing or compressing **b** a handshake; *also* an embrace **2a** a quantity squeezed out from sthg ⟨*a* ~ *of lemon*⟩ **b** a condition of being crowded together; a crush ⟨*it was a tight* ~ *with 6 in the car*⟩ **3a** a financial pressure caused by narrowing margins or by shortages **b** pressure brought to bear on sby – chiefly in *put the squeeze on*; infml

'squeeze-,box *n* an accordion – infml

squelch /skwelch/ *vt* **1** to fall or stamp on so as to crush **2** to suppress completely; quell, squash ~ *vi* **1** to emit a sucking sound like that of an object being withdrawn from mud **2** to walk or move, esp through slush, mud, etc, making a squelching noise [imit] – **squelch** *n,* **squelchy** *adj*

squib /skwib/ *n* **1** a small firework that burns with a fizz and finishes with a small explosion **2** a short witty or satirical speech or piece of writing [origin unknown]

squid /skwid/ *n, pl* **squids,** *esp collectively* **squid** any of numerous 10-armed cephalopod molluscs, related to the octopus and cuttlefish, that have a long tapered body and a tail fin on each side [origin unknown]

squidgy /'skwiji/ *adj, chiefly Br* soft and squashy – infml [*squidge* (squelch), of imit origin]

squiffy /'skwifi/ *adj* slightly drunk, tipsy – infml [origin unknown]

squiggle /'skwigl/ *vi or n* (to draw) a short wavy twist or line, esp in handwriting or drawing [blend of *squirm* and *wriggle*] – **squiggly** /'skwigli/ *adj*

squill /skwil/ *n* **1** a Mediterranean plant of the lily family that reproduces by bulbs **2** a scilla **3** a squilla [ME, fr L *squilla, scilla* sea onion, fr Gk *skilla*]

squilla /'skwilə/ *n, pl* **squillas, squillae** /-li/ any of various crustaceans that burrow in mud or beneath stones in shallow water along the seashore [NL, genus name, fr L, squill, prawn]

squinch /skwinch/ *n* an arch, lintel, etc placed across the interior corner of a square to support a dome [alter. of earlier *scunch* (back part of the side of an opening), deriv of MF *coing, coin* wedge, corner]

[1]**squint** /skwint/ *adj* having a squint; squinting [short for *asquint,* adv, fr ME]

[2]**squint** *vi* **1** to have or look with a squint **2** to look or peer with eyes partly closed – **squinter** *n,* **squintingly** *adv*

[3]**squint** *n* **1** (a visual disorder marked by) inability to direct both eyes to the same object because of imbalance of the muscles of the eyeball **2** a hagioscope **3** a glance, look – esp in *have/take a squint at*; infml – **squinty** *adj*

[1]**squire** /skwie·ə/ *n* **1** a shield-bearer or armour-bearer of a knight **2** an owner of a country estate; *esp* the principal local landowner **3** *Br* PAL 2 – infml [ME *squier,* fr OF *esquier* – more at ESQUIRE]

[2]**squire** *vt* to attend on or escort (a woman)

squirearchy, squirarchy /'skwie·ə,rahki/ *n sing or pl in constr* the gentry or landed-proprietor class – **squirearchical** /-'rahkikl/ *adj*

squirm /skwuhm/ *vi* **1** to twist about like a worm; wriggle **2** to feel or show acute discomfort at sthg embarrassing, shameful, or unpleasant [perh imit] – **squirm** *n,* **squirmer** *n*

squirrel /'skwirəl/ *n* (the usu grey or red fur of) any of various New or Old World small to medium-sized tree-dwelling rodents that have a long bushy tail and strong hind legs [ME *squirel,* fr MF *esquireul,* fr (assumed) VL *scuriolus,* dim. of *scurius,* alter. of L *sciurus,* fr Gk *skiouros,* prob fr *skia* shadow + *oura* tail; akin to OHG *ars* buttocks, OIr *err* tail – more at SHINE]

'squirrel ,cage *n* (a type of induction motor having) a rotor with cylindrically arranged metal bars [fr its resemblance to the toy treadmill often provided in the cage of a squirrel or other small animal]

squirrel monkey *n* a small soft-haired S American monkey with a long prehensile tail

[1]**squirt** /skwuht/ *vi* to issue in a sudden forceful stream from a narrow opening ~ *vt* **1** to cause to squirt **2** to direct a jet or stream of liquid at ⟨~ed *his sister with a water pistol*⟩ [ME *squirten*; akin to LG *swirtjen* to squirt]

[2]**squirt** *n* **1** a small rapid stream of liquid; a jet **2** a small or insignificant (impudent) person – infml

squish /skwish/ *vi or n* (to make or move with) a slight squelching or sucking sound [alter. of *squash*]

squishy /'skwishi/ *adj* soft and moist – **squishiness** *n*

SS /,es 'es/ *n sing or pl in constr* Hitler's bodyguard and special police force [G, abbr for *Schutzstaffel* elite guard]

[1]**-st** *suffix* (*adj or adv* → *adj or adv*) – used to form the superlative degree of adjectives and adverbs of 1 syllable, and of some adjectives and adverbs of 2 or more syllables, that end in *e* ⟨*sure*st⟩ ⟨*complete*st⟩; compare [1]-EST

[2]**-st** – see [2]-EST

[1]**stab** /stab/ *n* **1** a wound produced by a pointed weapon **2a** a thrust (as if) with a pointed weapon **b(1)** a sharp spasm of pain **(2)** a pang of intense emotion ⟨*felt a* ~ *of remorse*⟩ **3** an attempt, try – infml [ME *stabbe*]

[2]**stab** *vb* **-bb-** *vt* **1** to pierce or wound (as if) with a pointed weapon **2** to thrust, jab ⟨~bed *his finger at the page*⟩ ~ *vi* to thrust *at* sby or sthg (as if) with a pointed weapon – **stabber** *n*

stabile /'staybiel/ *n* an abstract sculpture or construction similar to a mobile but stationary [prob fr F, fr L *stabilis* stable]

stabil·izer, -iser /'staybl,iezə/ *n* **1** a chemical substance added to another substance or to a system to prevent or retard an unwanted alteration of physical state **2** a device to keep ships steady in a rough sea **3** *chiefly NAm* the horizontal tailplane of an aircraft [STABILIZE + [2]-ER]

[1]**stable** /'staybl/ *n* **1** a building in which domestic animals, esp horses, are sheltered and fed – often pl with sing. meaning **2** *sing or pl in constr* **a** the racehorses or racing cars owned by one person or organization **b** a group of athletes (e g boxers) or performers under one management **c** a group, collection ⟨*a tycoon who owns a* ~ *of newspapers*⟩ [ME, fr OF *estable,* fr L *stabulum,* fr *stare* to stand – more at STAND]

[2]**stable** *vt* to put or keep in a stable ~ *vi* to dwell (as if) in a stable

[3]**stable** *adj* **1a** securely established; fixed ⟨*a* ~ *community*⟩ **b** not subject to change or fluctuation; unvarying ⟨*a* ~ *population*⟩ ⟨*a* ~ *currency*⟩ **c** permanent, enduring **2** not subject to feelings of mental or emotional insecurity **3a(1)** placed or constructed so as to resist forces tending to cause (change of) motion **(2)** that develops forces that restore the original condition of equilibrium when disturbed **b(1)** able to resist alteration in chemical, physical, or biological properties **(2)** not spontaneously radioactive ⟨*a* ~ *isotope*⟩ [ME, fr OF *estable,* fr L *stabilis,* fr *stare* to stand] – **stably** *adv,* **stabilize** *vb,* **stableness, stabilization** /-ie'zaysh(ə)n/ *n,* **stability** /stə'biləti/ *n*

'stable ˌlad *n* a groom in a racing stable

stabling /'staybling/ *n* indoor accommodation for animals

staccato /stə'kahtoh/ *n, adv, or adj, pl* **staccatos** (a manner of speaking or performing, or a piece of music performed) in a sharp, disconnected, or abrupt way ☞ MUSIC [adj It, fr pp of *staccare* to detach, deriv of OF *destachier* – more at DETACH; n & adv fr adj]

staccato mark *n* a pointed vertical stroke or a dot placed over or under a musical note to be produced staccato

¹stack /stak/ *n* **1** a large usu circular or square pile of hay, straw, etc **2** an (orderly) pile or heap **3a** CHIMNEY STACK **b** a smokestack **4** a pyramid of 3 interlocked rifles **5** a structure of shelves for compact storage of books – usu pl with sing. meaning **6** a stacked group of aircraft **7** a group of loudspeakers for a public address sound system **8** a high pillar of rock rising out of the sea, that was detached from the mainland by the erosive action of waves ☞ GEOGRAPHY **9** a large quantity or number – often pl with sing. meaning ⟨~s *of money*⟩; infml [ME *stak*, fr ON *stakkr*; akin to OE *staca* stake]

²stack *vt* **1** to arrange in a stack; pile **2** to arrange secretly for cheating ⟨*the cards were* ~ed⟩ **3** to assign (an aircraft) to a particular altitude and position within a group of aircraft circling before landing – **stackable** *adj*

stacked /stakt/ *adj, of a woman* shapely and having large breasts – slang

staddle /'stadl/ *n* a base or framework for a stack of hay or straw [ME *stathel* base, support, fr OE *stathol*; akin to OE *stede* place – more at STEAD]

stadium /'staydi·əm/ *n, pl* **stadiums** *also* **stadia** /-di·ə/ **1** any of various ancient Greek units of length, usu of about 185m **2** a sports ground surrounded by a large usu unroofed building with tiers of seats for spectators **3** a stage in a life history; *esp* one between successive moults in the development of an insect [ME, fr L, fr Gk *stadion*, alter. of *spadion*, fr *span* to pull – more at SPAN]

¹staff /stahf/ *n, pl* **staffs, staves** /stayvz/, (*5*) **staffs** **1a** a long stick carried in the hand for use in walking or as a weapon **b** a supporting rod; *esp* a flagstaff **c** sthg which gives strength or sustains ⟨*bread is the* ~ *of life*⟩ **2a** a crosier **b** a rod carried as a symbol of office or authority **3** a set of usu 5 parallel horizontal lines on which music is written ☞ MUSIC **4** any of various graduated sticks or rules used for measuring **5** *sing or pl in constr* **a** the body of people in charge of the internal operations of an institution, business, etc **b** a group of officers appointed to assist a military commander **c** the teachers at a school or university **d** the personnel who assist a superior [ME *staf*, fr OE *stæf*; akin to OHG *stab* staff, *stampfōn* to stamp – more at STAMP]

²staff *vt* **1** to supply with a staff or with workers **2** to serve as a staff member of

staffer /'stahfə/ *n, chiefly NAm* a member of a staff (e g of a newspaper)

'staff ˌnurse *n, Br* a qualified nurse in the staff of a hospital who is next in rank below a sister

'staff ˌofficer *n* a commissioned officer assigned to a military commander's staff

staff sergeant *n* ☞ RANK

¹stag /stag/ *n, pl* **stags,** (*1*) **stags,** *esp collectively* **stag** **1** an adult male red deer; *broadly* the male of any of various deer **2** *Br* a person who buys newly issued shares in the hope of selling them to make a quick profit [ME *stagge*, fr OE *stagga*; akin to ON *andarsteggi* drake, OE *stingan* to sting]

²stag *adj* of or intended for men only ⟨*a* ~ *night*⟩ ⟨*a* ~ *party*⟩

'stag ˌbeetle *n* any of numerous mostly large beetles having males with long and often branched mandibles suggesting the antlers of a stag

¹stage /stayj/ *n* **1** any of a series of positions or stations one above the other **2a(1)** a raised platform **(2)** the area of a theatre where the acting takes place, including the wings and storage space **(3)** *the* acting profession; *also* *the* theatre as an occupation or activity **b** a centre of attention or scene of action **3a** a scaffold for workmen **b** the small platform of a microscope on which an object is placed for examination **4a** a place of rest formerly provided for those travelling by stagecoach **b** the distance between 2 stopping places on a road **c** a stagecoach **5a** a period or step in a progress, activity, or development **b** any of the distinguishable periods of growth and development of a plant or animal ⟨*the larval* ~ *of an insect*⟩ **c** any of the divisions (e g 1 day's riding or driving between predetermined points) of a race or rally that is spread over several days **6** a connected group of components in an electrical circuit that performs some well-defined function (e g amplification) and that forms part of a larger electrical circuit **7** a propulsion unit of a rocket with its own fuel and container ☞ SPACE **8** *chiefly Br* a bus stop from or to which fares are calculated; a fare stage [ME, fr OF *estage*, fr (assumed) VL *staticum*, fr L *stare* to stand – more at STAND]

²stage *vt* **1** to produce (e g a play) on a stage **2** to produce and organize, esp for public view ⟨~d *the event to get maximum publicity*⟩

'stageˌcoach /-ˌkohch/ *n* a horse-drawn passenger and mail coach that in former times ran on a regular schedule between established stops

'stageˌcraft /-ˌkrahft/ *n* the effective management of theatrical devices or techniques

'stage diˌrection *n* a description (e g of a character or setting) or direction (e g to indicate sound effects or the movement or positioning of actors) provided in the text of a play

ˌstage 'door *n* the entrance to a theatre that is used by those who work there

'stage ˌfright *n* nervousness felt at appearing before an audience

'stageˌhand /-ˌhand/ *n* a theatre worker who handles scenery, props, or lights

ˌstage 'left *adv* on or to an actor's left when he/she is facing the audience

'stage-ˌmanage *vt* to arrange or direct, esp from behind the scenes, so as to achieve a desired result [back-formation fr *stage manager*]

ˌstage 'manager *n* one who is in charge of the stage during a performance and supervises related matters beforehand

stager /'stayjə/ *n* an experienced person; a veteran – chiefly in *old stager*

ˌstage 'right *adv* on or to an actor's right when he/she is facing the audience

'stageˌstruck /-'struk/ *adj* fascinated by the stage; *esp* having an ardent desire to become an actor or actress

stage whisper *n* **1** a loud whisper by an actor,

audible to the audience, but supposedly inaudible to others on stage 2 a whisper that is deliberately made audible

stagflation /stag'flaysh(ə)n/ *n* a state of affairs in which inflation in the economy is accompanied by zero growth in industrial production [blend of *stagnation* and *inflation*]

[1]stagger /'stagə/ *vi* to reel from side to side (while moving); totter ~ *vt* 1 to dumbfound, astonish 2 to arrange in any of various alternating or overlapping positions or times ⟨~ *work shifts*⟩ [alter. of earlier *stacker*, fr ME *stakeren*, fr ON *stakra*, freq of *staka* to push; akin to OE *staca* stake] – **staggerer** *n*

[2]stagger *n* 1 *pl but sing or pl in constr* an abnormal condition of domestic mammals and birds associated with damage to the brain and spinal cord and marked by lack of muscle coordination and a reeling unsteady gait 2 a reeling or unsteady walk or stance

staggering /'stag(ə)ring/ *adj* astonishing, overwhelming – **staggeringly** *adv*

staging /'stayjing/ *n* 1 a scaffolding or other temporary platform 2 the business of running stagecoaches

stagnant /'stagnənt/ *adj* 1a not flowing in a current or stream; motionless ⟨~ *water*⟩ b stale ⟨*long disuse had made the air ~ and foul* – Bram Stoker⟩ 2 dull, inactive – **stagnancy** /-si/ *n*, **stagnantly** *adv*

stagnate /stag'nayt/ *vi* to become or remain stagnant [L *stagnatus*, pp of *stagnare*, fr *stagnum* body of standing water; akin to Gk *stazein* to drip] – **stagnation** /-'naysh(ə)n/ *n*

stagy, stagey /'stayji/ *adj* marked by showy pretence or artificiality; theatrical [[1]STAGE + [1]-Y] – **stagily** *adv*, **staginess** *n*

staid /stayd/ *adj* sedate and often primly self-restrained; sober [fr pp of [3]*stay*] – **staidly** *adv*, **staidness** *n*

[1]stain /stayn/ *vt* 1 to discolour, soil 2 to suffuse with colour 3 to taint with guilt, vice, corruption, etc; bring dishonour to 4 to colour (e g wood or a biological specimen) by using (chemical) processes or dyes affecting the material itself ~ *vi* 1 to become stained 2 to cause staining [ME *steynen*, partly fr MF *desteindre* to discolour (fr OF, fr *des*- dis- + *teindre* to dye, fr L *tingere* to wet, dye) & partly of Scand origin; akin to ON *steina* to paint] – **stainable** *adj*, **stainer** *n*

[2]stain *n* 1 a soiled or discoloured spot 2 a moral taint or blemish 3a a preparation (e g of dye or pigment) used in staining; *esp* one capable of penetrating the pores of wood b a dye or mixture of dyes used in microscopy to make minute and transparent structures visible, to differentiate tissue elements, or to produce specific chemical reactions

,stained 'glass /staynd/ *n* glass coloured or stained for use in windows

'stainless /-lis/ *adj* 1 free from stain or stigma 2 (made from materials) resistant to stain, specif rust – **stainlessly** *adv*

,stainless 'steel *n* steel containing chromium and highly resistant to rusting and corrosion

stair /steə/ *n* 1 a series of (flights of) steps for passing from one level to another – usu pl with sing. meaning ☞ ARCHITECTURE 2 any step of a stairway [ME *steir*, fr OE *stǣger*; akin to OE & OHG *stīgan* to rise, Gk *steichein* to walk]

'stair,case /-,kays/ *n* 1 the structure or part of a building containing a stairway 2 a flight of stairs with the supporting framework, casing, and balusters

'stair,way /-,way/ *n* one or more flights of stairs, usu with intermediate landings

'stair,well /-,wel/ *n* a vertical shaft in which stairs are located

staithe /staydh/ *n*, *Br* a wharf from which coal may be loaded on a vessel [ME *stathe*, of Scand origin; akin to ON *stöth* landing place, staithe; akin to OE *stæth* bank, shore, OHG *stad*, *stado*]

[1]stake /stayk/ *n* 1 a pointed piece of material (e g wood) for driving into the ground as a marker or support 2a a post to which sby was bound for execution by burning b execution by burning at a stake – + *the* 3a sthg, esp money, staked for gain or loss b the prize in a contest, esp a horse race – often pl with sing. meaning c an interest or share in an undertaking (e g a commercial venture) 4 *pl but sing or pl in constr, often cap* a horse race in which all the horses are evenly matched (e g in age and amount of weight carried) – chiefly in names of races [ME, fr OE *staca*; akin to MLG *stake* stake, L *tignum* beam] – **at stake** in jeopardy; AT ISSUE

[2]stake *vt* 1 to mark the limits of (as if) by stakes – often + *off* or *out* 2 to tether to a stake 3 to bet, hazard 4 to fasten up or support (e g plants) with stakes 5 *chiefly NAm* to back financially – **stake a/one's claim** to state that sthg is one's by right

stake out *vt*, *NAm* to conduct a surveillance of (a suspected area, person, etc) – **stakeout** *n*

Stakhanovite /sta'kanə,viet/ *n* a Soviet industrial worker awarded recognition and privileges for outstanding productivity [Alexei G *Stakhanov* b 1905 Russ miner] – **Stakhanovism** /-nə,viz(ə)m/ *n*

stalactite /'staləktiet/ *n* an icicle-like deposit of calcium carbonate hanging from the roof or sides of a cavern [NL *stalactites*, fr Gk *stalaktos* dripping, fr *stalassein* to let drip] – **stalactitic** /-'titik/ *adj*

stalag /'stahlag/ *n* a German prison camp for non-commissioned officers and lower ranks [G, short for *stammlager* base camp, fr *stamm* base + *lager* camp]

stalagmite /'staləgmiet/ *n* a deposit of calcium carbonate like an inverted stalactite formed on the floor of a cavern [NL *stalagmites*, fr Gk *stalagma* drop or *stalagmos* dripping; akin to Gk *stalassein* to let drip] – **stalagmitic** /-'mitik/ *adj*

[1]stale /stayl/ *adj* 1a tasteless or unpalatable from age b *of air* musty, foul 2 tedious from familiarity ⟨~ *jokes*⟩ 3 impaired in legal force through lack of timely action ⟨*a* ~ *debt*⟩ 4 impaired in vigour or effectiveness, esp from overexertion [ME, aged (of ale); akin to MD *stel* stale] – **stalely** *adv*, **staleness** *n*

[2]stale *vb* to make or become stale

[3]stale *vi*, *esp of horses and cattle* to urinate [ME *stalen*; akin to MLG *stallen* to urinate]

stalemate /'stayl,mayt/ *vt or n* (to bring into) a a drawing position in chess in which only the king can move and although not in check can move only into check b a deadlock [n obs *stale* (stalemate; fr ME, fr AF *estale*, lit., fixed position, fr OF *estal* place, position) + E *mate*; vb fr n]

Stalinism /'stahli,niz(ə)m, 'sta-/ *n* the theory and practice of communism developed by Stalin from Marxism-Leninism and characterized esp by rigid authoritarianism [Joseph *Stalin* †1953 Russ political leader] – **Stalinist** *n or adj*

[1]**stalk** /stawk/ *vi* **1** to pursue or approach quarry or prey stealthily **2** to walk stiffly or haughtily ~ *vt* **1** to pursue by stalking ⟨~ *deer*⟩ **2** to go through (an area) in search of prey or quarry ⟨~ *the woods for deer*⟩ [ME *stalken*, fr OE *bestealcian*; akin to OE *stealc* lofty, *stelan* to steal – more at STEAL] – **stalker** *n*

[2]**stalk** *n* **1** the stalking of quarry or prey **2** a stiff or haughty walk

[3]**stalk** *n* **1a** the main stem of a herbaceous plant, often with its attached parts **b** STEM 1b **2** a slender upright supporting or connecting (animal) structure [ME *stalke*; akin to OE *stealc* lofty] – **stalked** *adj*, **stalkless** *adj*, **stalky** *adj*

ˌ**stalk-'eyed** *adj, esp of crustaceans* having the eyes raised on stalks

'**stalking-ˌhorse** /'stawking/ *n* sthg used to mask a purpose

[1]**stall** /stawl/ *n* **1** any of usu several compartments for domestic animals in a stable or barn **2a** a wholly or partly enclosed seat in the chancel of a church **b** a church pew **3a** a booth, stand, or counter at which articles are displayed or offered for sale **b** SIDESHOW 1b **4** a protective sheath for a finger or toe **5** a small compartment ⟨*a shower* ~⟩ **6** *Br* a seat on the main floor of an auditorium (e g in a theatre) [ME, fr OE *steall*; akin to OHG *stal* place, stall, L *locus* (OL *stlocus*) place, Gk *stellein* to set up, place, send]

[2]**stall** *vt* **1** to put or keep in a stall **2a** to bring to a standstill; block **b** to cause (e g a car engine) to stop, usu inadvertently **c** to cause (an aircraft or aerofoil) to go into a stall ~ *vi* **1** to come to a standstill; *esp, of an engine* to stop suddenly from failure **2** to experience a stall in flying

[3]**stall** *n* the condition of an aerofoil or aircraft when the airflow is so obstructed (e g from moving forwards too slowly) that lift is lost ☞ FLIGHT

[4]**stall** *vi* to play for time; delay ~ *vt* to divert or delay, esp by evasion or deception [obs *stall*, n (lure, decoy), alter. of earlier *stale*, fr ME, fr AF] – **stall** *n*

'**stallˌholder** /-ˌhohldə/ *n* one who runs a (market) stall

stallion /'stalyən/ *n* an uncastrated male horse; *esp* one kept for breeding [ME *stalion*, fr MF *estalon*, of Gmc origin; akin to OHG *stal* stall]

[1]**stalwart** /'stawlwət/ *adj* **1** strong in body, mind, or spirit **2** dependable, staunch [ME, alter. of *stalworth*, fr OE *stǣlwierthe* serviceable] – **stalwartly** *adv*, **stalwartness** *n*

[2]**stalwart** *n* a stalwart person; *specif* a staunch supporter

stamen /'staymən/ *n* the organ of a flower that produces the male gamete in the form of pollen, and consists of an anther and a filament ☞ PLANT [L, warp, thread; akin to Gk *stēmōn* thread, *histanai* to cause to stand – more at STAND]

stamin- /stamin-/, **stamini-** *comb form* stamen ⟨*staminal*⟩ ⟨stamini*ferous*⟩ [L *stamin-*, *stamen*]

stamina /'staminə/ *n* (capacity for) endurance [L, pl of *stamen* warp, thread of life spun by the Fates]

staminate /'staminət, -nayt/ *adj* **1** having or producing stamens **2** MALE 1a(2)

stammer /'stamə/ *vb* to speak or utter with involuntary stops and repetitions – compare STUTTER [ME *stameren*, fr OE *stamerian*; akin to OHG *stamalōn* to stammer, Lith *stumti* to push] – **stammer** *n*, **stammerer** *n*

[1]**stamp** /stamp/ *vt* **1** to pound or crush (e g ore) with a pestle or heavy instrument **2a** to strike or beat forcibly with the bottom of the foot **b** to bring down (the foot) forcibly **3a** to impress, imprint ⟨~ *'paid" on the bill*⟩ ⟨*an image* ~ed *on his memory*⟩ **b(1)** to attach a (postage) stamp to **(2)** to mark with an (official) impression, device, etc **4** to cut out, bend, or form with a stamp or die **5a** to provide with a distinctive character ⟨~ed *with an air of worldly wisdom*⟩ **b** CHARACTERIZE 2 ~ *vi* **1** POUND 2 **2** to strike or thrust the foot forcibly or noisily downwards [ME *stampen*; akin to OHG *stampfōn* to stamp, L *temnere* to despise, Gk *stembein* to shake up] – **stamper** *n*

[2]**stamp** *n* **1** a device or instrument for stamping **2** the impression or mark made by stamping or imprinting **3a** a distinctive feature, indication, or mark ⟨*the* ~ *of genius*⟩ **b** a lasting imprint ⟨*the* ~ *of time*⟩ **4** the act of stamping **5** a printed or stamped piece of paper that for some restricted purpose is used as a token of credit or occasionally of debit: e g **a** POSTAGE STAMP **b** a stamp used as evidence that tax has been paid **c** TRADING STAMP

'**stamp ˌduty** *n* a tax on certain legal documents

[1]**stampede** /stam'peed/ *n* **1** a wild headlong rush or flight of frightened animals **2** a sudden mass movement of people [AmerSp *estampida*, fr Sp, crash, fr *estampar* to stamp, of Gmc origin; akin to OHG *stampfōn* to stamp]

[2]**stampede** *vb* to (cause to) run away or rush in panic or on impulse

'**stamping ˌground** /'stamping/ *n* a favourite or habitual haunt

'**stamping ˌmill** *n* STAMP MILL

'**stamp ˌmill** *n* a mill in which ore is crushed

stamp out *vt* to eradicate, destroy ⟨stamp out *crime*⟩

stance /stahns, stans/ *n* **1a** a way of standing or being placed **b** intellectual or emotional attitude ⟨*took an anti-union* ~⟩ **2** the position of body or feet from which a sportsman (e g a batsman or golfer) plays [MF *estance* position, posture, stay, fr (assumed) VL *stantia*, fr L *stant-*, *stans*, prp of *stare* to stand]

stanch, staunch /stawnch, stahnch/ *vt* to check or stop the flow of ⟨~ed *her tears*⟩; *also* to stop the flow of blood from (a wound) [ME *staunchen*, fr MF *estancher*, fr (assumed) VL *stanticare*, fr L *stant-*, *stans*, prp]

stanchion /'stahnsh(ə)n/ *vt or n* (to provide with) an upright bar, post, or support (e g for a roof) [n ME *stanchon*, fr MF *estanchon*, fr OF, aug of *estance* stay, prop; vb fr n]

[1]**stand** /stand/ *vb* **stood** /stood/ *vi* **1a** to support oneself on the feet in an erect position **b** to be a specified height when fully erect ⟨~s *6ft 2*⟩ **c** to rise to or maintain an erect or upright position ⟨*his hair* stood *on end*⟩ **2a** to take up or maintain a specified position or posture ⟨~ *aside*⟩ **b** to maintain one's position ⟨~ *firm*⟩ **3** to be in a specified state or situation ⟨~s *accused*⟩ **4** to sail in a specified direction ⟨~ing *into harbour*⟩ **5a** to have or maintain a relative position (as if) in a graded scale ⟨~s *first in his class*⟩ **b** to be in a position to gain or lose because of an action taken or a commitment made

⟨~s *to make quite a profit*⟩ **6** to occupy a place or location ⟨*the house* ~s *on a hill*⟩ **7** to remain stationary or inactive ⟨*the car* stood *in the garage for a week*⟩ **8** to agree, accord – chiefly in *it stands to reason* **9a** to exist in a definite (written or printed) form ⟨*copy a passage exactly as it* ~s⟩ ⟨*that is how the situation* ~s *at present*⟩ **b** to remain valid or effective ⟨*the order given last week still* ~s⟩ **10** *chiefly Br* to be a candidate in an election ~ *vt* **1a** to endure or undergo ⟨~ *trial*⟩ ⟨*this book will* ~ *the test of time*⟩ **b** to tolerate, bear; PUT UP WITH ⟨*can't* ~ *his boss*⟩ **c** to benefit from; do with ⟨*looks as if he could* ~ *a good sleep*⟩ **2** to remain firm in the face of ⟨~ *a siege*⟩ **3** to perform the duty of ⟨~ *guard*⟩ **4** to cause to stand; set upright **5** to pay the cost of; pay for ⟨*I'll* ~ *you a dinner*⟩ – infml [ME *standen*, fr OE *standan*; akin to OHG *stantan, stān* to stand, L *stare*, Gk *histanai* to cause to stand, set, *histasthai* to stand, be standing] – **stand a chance** to have a chance – **stand by** to remain loyal or faithful to ⟨stand by *the agreement*⟩ – **stand for** **1** to be a symbol for; represent **2** to permit; PUT UP WITH – **stand on** to insist on ⟨*never* stands on *ceremony*⟩ – **stand one in good stead** to be of advantage or service to one – **stand one's ground** to remain firm and unyielding in the face of opposition – **stand on one's own feet** to think or act independently

[2]**stand** *n* **1** an act, position, or place of standing ⟨*took up a* ~ *near the exit*⟩ **2a** a standstill; *also* a halt for defence or resistance **b** a usu defensive effort of some length or success ⟨*a united* ~ *against the plans for the new motorway*⟩ ⟨*a last-wicket* ~ *of 53 runs*⟩ **c** a stop made by a touring theatrical company, rock group, etc to give a performance **3** a strongly or aggressively held position, esp on a debatable issue **4a** a structure of tiered seats for spectators – often pl with sing. meaning **b** a raised platform serving as a point of vantage or display (e g for a speaker or exhibit) **5** a small usu temporary and open-air stall where goods are sold or displayed ⟨*a hot dog* ~⟩ **6** a place where a passenger vehicle awaits hire ⟨*a taxi* ~⟩ **7** a frame on or in which sthg may be placed for support ⟨*an umbrella* ~⟩ **8** a group of plants or trees growing in a continuous area **9** *NAm the* witness-box

[1]**standard** /'standəd/ *n* **1** a conspicuous flag, object, etc used to mark a rallying point, esp in battle, or to serve as an emblem **2a** a (long narrow tapering) flag **b** the personal flag of a member of a royal family or of the head of a state **3a** sthg established by authority, custom, or general consent as a model or example; a criterion **b** a (prescribed) degree of quality or worth **c** *pl* moral integrity; principles **4** sthg set up and established by authority as a rule for the measure of quantity, weight, value, or quality **5a** the fineness and legally fixed weight of the metal used in coins **b** the basis of value in a money system **6** an upright support **7a** a shrub or herbaceous plant grown with an erect main stem so that it forms or resembles a tree **b** a fruit tree grafted on a stock that does not induce dwarfing **8** sthg standard: e g **a** a model of car supplied without optional extras **b** a musical composition, specif a popular song, that has become a part of the established repertoire [ME, fr MF *estandard* rallying point, standard, of Gmc origin; akin to OE *standan* to stand & to OE *ord* point – more at ODD]

[2]**standard** *adj* **1a** being or conforming to a standard, esp as established by law or custom ⟨~ *weight*⟩ **b** sound and usable but not of top quality **2a** regularly and widely used, available, or supplied ⟨*a* ~ *socket*⟩ **b** well established and familiar ⟨*the* ~ *weekend television programmes*⟩ **3** having recognized and permanent value ⟨*a* ~ *reference work*⟩ – **standardize** *vt*, **standardization** /-die'zaysh(ə)n/ *n*

'**standard-,bearer** *n* **1** one who carries a standard or banner **2** the leader of an organization, movement, or party

,**standard devi'ation** *n* a measure of the extent to which values of a variable are scattered about a mean value in a frequency distribution ⟨*the larger the* ~, *the more widely dispersed are the values*⟩ ☞ STATISTICS, SYMBOL

,**standard 'error** *n* the standard deviation of the distribution of values of a statistic (e g the mean) obtained from a large number of samples

'**standard ,lamp** *n* a lamp with a tall support that stands on the floor

,**standard of 'living** *n* a level of welfare or subsistence maintained by an individual, group, or community and shown esp by the level of consumption of necessities, comforts, and luxuries

'**standard ,time** *n* the officially established time, with reference to Greenwich Mean Time, of a region or country

[1]**standby** /'stand,bie/ *n, pl* **standbys** /-,biez/ one who or that which is held in reserve and can be relied on, made, or used in case of necessity

[2]**standby** *adj* **1** held near at hand and ready for use ⟨~ *equipment*⟩ **2** relating to the act or condition of standing by ⟨~ *duty*⟩

stand by *vi* **1** to be present but remain aloof or inactive ⟨*calmly* stood by *and watched those trying to help*⟩ **2** to wait in a state of readiness ⟨stand by *for action*⟩

stand down *vi* **1** to leave the witness-box **2** *chiefly Br* to relinquish (candidature for) an office or position **3** *chiefly Br, of a soldier* to go off duty ~*vt chiefly Br* to send (soldiers) off duty; *broadly* to dismiss (workers); LAY OFF

'**stand-,in** *n* **1** one who is employed to occupy an actor's place while lights and camera are made ready **2** a substitute – **stand in** *vi*

[1]**standing** /'standing/ *adj* **1** used or designed for standing in ⟨~ *places*⟩ **2** not yet cut or harvested ⟨~ *timber*⟩ ⟨~ *grain*⟩ **3** not flowing; stagnant ⟨~ *water*⟩ **4** continuing in existence or use indefinitely ⟨*a* ~ *offer*⟩ **5** established by law or custom ⟨*a* ~ *joke*⟩ **6** done from a standing position ⟨*a* ~ *jump*⟩ ⟨*a* ~ *ovation*⟩

[2]**standing** *n* **1a** length of service or experience, esp as determining rank, pay, or privilege **b** position, status, or condition, esp in relation to a group or other individuals in a similar field; *esp* good reputation ⟨*his* ~ *in the Labour party*⟩ **2** maintenance of position or condition; duration ⟨*a custom of long* ~⟩

standing army *n* a permanent army of paid soldiers

,**standing 'order** *n* **1** a rule governing the procedure of an organization, which remains in force until specifically changed **2** an instruction (e g to a banker or newsagent) in force until specifically changed

'**standing ,room** *n* space for standing; *esp* accommodation available for spectators or passengers after all seats are filled

standing stone *n* a menhir

standing wave *n* a vibration of a body or physical system in which the amplitude varies from point to point but is constant at any particular point

'stand,off /-,of/ *n, NAm* a tie, deadlock

'stand-,off, stand-off half *n* the player in rugby positioned between the scrum-half and the three-quarter backs ☞ SPORT

stand off *vi, of a horse* to take off early for a jump

standoffish /,stand'ofish/ *adj* reserved, aloof – **standoffishly** *adv*

stand out *vi* **1a** to appear (as if) in relief; project **b** to be prominent or conspicuous **2** to be stubborn in resolution or resistance

'stand,over /-,ohvə/ *adj or n, Austr* (of or being) a violent criminal ⟨*a ~ gang*⟩

'stand,pipe /-,piep/ *n* a pipe fitted with a tap and used for outdoor water supply

'stand,point /-,poynt/ *n* a position from which objects or principles are viewed and according to which they are compared and judged

'stand,still /-,stil/ *n* a state in which motion or progress is absent; a stop

stand to *vi* to take up a position of readiness (e g for action or inspection) ⟨*ordered the men to* stand to⟩

'stand-,up *adj* **1** stiffened to stay upright without folding over ⟨*a ~ collar*⟩ **2** performed in or requiring a standing position ⟨*a ~ meal*⟩ **3** (having an act) consisting of jokes usu performed solo standing before an audience ⟨*a ~ comedian*⟩

stand up *vi* **1** to rise to or maintain a standing or upright position **2** to remain sound and intact under stress, attack, or close scrutiny ~ *vt* to fail to keep an appointment with – **stand up for** to defend against attack or criticism – **stand up to 1** to withstand efficiently or unimpaired ⟨*a car which can* stand up *to rough handling*⟩ **2** to face boldly

Stanford-Binet test /,stanfəd bi'nay/ *n* an intelligence test prepared at Stanford University as a revision of the Binet-Simon scale [*Stanford* University, California, USA]

stang /stang/ *n* ☞ *Thailand* at NATIONALITY [Thai]

stank /stangk/ *past of* STINK

stannary /'stanəri/ *n* a region containing tinworks – usu pl with sing. meaning [ML *stannaria* tin mine, fr LL *stannum* tin]

stannic /'stanik/ *adj* of or containing (tetravalent) tin [prob fr F *stannique,* fr LL *stannum* tin, fr L, an alloy of silver and lead, prob of Celt origin; akin to Corn *stēn* tin]

stannous /'stanəs/ *adj* of or containing (bivalent) tin [ISV, fr LL *stannum*]

stanza /'stanzə/ *n* a division of a poem consisting of a series of lines arranged together in a usu recurring pattern of metre and rhyme [It, stay, abode, room, stanza, fr (assumed) VL *stantia* stay – more at STANCE] – **stanzaic** /-'zayik/ *adj*

stapes /'staypeez/ *n, pl* **stapes, stapedes** /'staypi,deez/ the innermost of the chain of 3 small bones in the ear of a mammal; the stirrup ☞ NERVE [NL *staped-, stapes,* fr ML, stirrup, alter. of LL *stapia*]

staph /staf/ *n* a staphylococcus – **staph** *adj*

staphylococcus /,stafiloh'kokəs/ *n, pl* **staphylococci** /-'kok(s)ie, -si/ any of various spherical bacteria that include parasites of skin and mucous membranes and cause boils, septic infections of wounds, etc [NL, genus name, fr Gk *staphylē* bunch of grapes (akin to OE *stæf* staff) + NL *-coccus*] – **staphylococcal** /-'kokl/ *also* **staphylococcic** /-'kok(s)ik/ *adj*

[1]**staple** /'staypl/ *vt or n* (to provide with or secure by) **a** a U-shaped metal loop both ends of which can be driven into a surface (e g to secure sthg) **b** a small piece of wire with ends bent at right angles which can be driven through thin sheets of material, esp paper, and clinched to secure the items [n ME *stapel* post, staple, fr OE *stapol* post; akin to MD *stapel* step, heap, emporium, OE *steppan* to step; vb fr n]

[2]**staple** *n* **1** a chief commodity or production of a place **2a** a commodity for which the demand is constant **b** sthg having widespread and constant use or appeal **c** the sustaining or principal element; substance **3** RAW MATERIAL **4a** a textile fibre (e g wool or rayon) of relatively short length that when spun and twisted forms a yarn rather than a filament **b** the length of a piece of such textile fibre as a distinguishing characteristic of the raw material [ME, trading centre, fr MD *stapel* emporium]

[3]**staple** *adj* **1** used, needed, or enjoyed constantly, usu by many individuals **2** produced regularly or in large quantities ⟨*~ crops such as wheat and rice*⟩ **3** principal, chief

stapler /'stayplə/ *n* a small usu hand-operated device for inserting wire staples [[1]STAPLE + [2]-ER]

[1]**star** /stah/ *n* **1** any natural luminous body visible in the sky, esp at night; *specif* any of many celestial bodies of great mass that give out light and are fuelled by nuclear fusion reactions ☞ ASTRONOMY **2a(1)** a planet or a configuration of the planets that is held in astrology to influence a person's destiny – often pl **(2)** *pl* an astrological forecast; a horoscope **b** a waxing or waning fortune or fame ⟨*her ~ was rising*⟩ **3a** a figure with 5 or more points that represents a star; *esp* an asterisk ☞ SYMBOL **b** an often star-shaped ornament or medal worn as a badge of honour, authority, or rank or as the insignia of an order **c** any of a group of stylized stars used to place sthg in a scale of value or quality – often in combination ⟨*a 4-*star *hotel*⟩ **4a** a (highly publicized) performer in the cinema or theatre who plays leading roles **b** an outstandingly talented performer ⟨*a ~ of the running track*⟩ [ME *sterre,* fr OE *steorra*; akin to OHG *sterno* star, L *stella,* Gk *astēr, astron*] – **starless** *adj,* **starlike** *adj*

[2]**star** *vb* **-rr-** *vt* **1** to sprinkle or adorn (as if) with stars **2** to mark with a star or an asterisk **3** to advertise or display prominently; feature ⟨*the film ~*s *a famous stage personality*⟩ ~ *vi* to play the most prominent or important role ⟨*now ~*ring *in a West-End musical*⟩

[3]**star** *adj* of, being, or appropriate to a star ⟨*received ~ treatment*⟩

'star ,apple *n* (the apple-shaped edible fruit of) a tropical American tree of the sapodilla family grown for ornament or fruit

[1]**starboard** /'stahbəd/ *adj or n* (of or at) the right side of a ship or aircraft looking forwards – compare PORT ☞ SHIP [ME *sterbord,* fr OE *stēorbord,* fr *stēor-* steering oar + *bord* ship's side – more at [2]STEER, BOARD]

[2]**starboard** *vt* to turn or put (a helm or rudder) to the right

[1]**starch** /stahch/ *vt* to stiffen (as if) with starch [ME

sterchen, prob fr (assumed) OE *stercan* to stiffen; akin to OE *stearc* stiff – more at STARK]

[2]**starch** *n* **1** an odourless tasteless complex carbohydrate that is the chief storage form of carbohydrate in plants, is an important foodstuff, and is used also in adhesives and sizes, in laundering, and in pharmacy and medicine **2** a stiff formal manner; formality

Star Chamber *n* a court in England that was abolished in 1641, had both civil and criminal jurisdiction, and was noted for its arbitrary and oppressive procedures; *broadly, often not cap* any oppressive tribunal

starchy /ˈstahchi/ *adj* **1** of or containing (much) starch ⟨~ *foods*⟩ **2** marked by formality or stiffness – **starchily** *adv*, **starchiness** *n*

ˈstar-ˌcrossed *adj* not favoured by the stars; ill-fated ⟨*a pair of* ~ *lovers take their life* – Shak⟩

ˈstardom /-d(ə)m/ *n* the status or position of a celebrity or star ⟨*the actress quickly reached* ~⟩

ˈstarˌdust /-ˌdust/ *n* a feeling or impression of romance or magic

[1]**stare** /steə/ *vi* **1** to look fixedly, often with wide-open eyes **2** to stand out conspicuously ⟨*the error* ~d *from the page*⟩ **3** *esp of an animal's coat* to appear rough and lustreless ~ *vt* to bring to a specified state by staring ⟨~d *his opponent into submission*⟩ [ME *staren*, fr OE *starian*; akin to OHG *starēn* to stare, L *strenuus* strenuous, Gk *stereos* solid, Lith *starinti* to stiffen]

[2]**stare** *n* a staring look

starfish /ˈstahˌfish/ *n* any of a class of sea animals that are echinoderms, have a body consisting of a central disc surrounded by 5 equally spaced arms, and feed largely on molluscs (e g oysters)

ˈstarˌgaze /-ˌgayz/ *vi* **1** to gaze at stars **2** to gaze raptly, contemplatively, or absentmindedly; *esp* to daydream [back-formation fr *stargazer*]

ˈstarˌgazer /-ˌgayzə/ *n* **1** an astrologer **2** an astronomer *USE* chiefly humor

[1]**stark** /stahk/ *adj* **1** sheer, utter ⟨~ *nonsense*⟩ **2a(1)** barren, desolate **(2)** having few or no ornaments; bare ⟨*a* ~ *white room*⟩ **b** harsh, blunt ⟨*the* ~ *reality of death*⟩ **3** sharply delineated ⟨*a* ~ *outline*⟩ [ME, stiff, strong, fr OE *stearc*; akin to OHG *starc* strong, Lith *starinti* to stiffen – more at STARE] – **starkly** *adv*, **starkness** *n*

[2]**stark** *adv* to an absolute or complete degree; wholly ⟨~ *raving mad*⟩

starkers /ˈstahkəz/ *adj, Br* completely naked – used predicatively; slang [*stark* + *-er* (as in *soccer*) + *-s*]

starlet /ˈstahlit/ *n* a young film actress being coached and publicized for starring roles

starling /ˈstahling/ *n* any of a family of usu dark social birds; *esp* a dark brown (or in summer, glossy greenish black) European bird that lives in large social groups [ME, fr OE *stærlinc*, fr *stær* starling + *-ling, -linc* -ling; akin to OHG *stara* starling, L *sturnus*]

ˌstar-of-ˈBethlehem /ˈbethlihem/ *n* any of a genus of plants of the lily family with leaves resembling those of grass and white star-shaped flowers [fr the star above the town of Bethlehem at the time of Christ's birth (Matt 2:9)]

Star of David /ˈdayvid/ *n* a 6-pointed star made from 2 superimposed equilateral triangles that is a symbol of Judaism and the State of Israel ☞ SYMBOL [*David*, King of Judah in biblical accounts]

starry /ˈstahri/ *adj* **1a** adorned or studded with stars **b** shining like stars; sparkling **2** (seemingly) as high as the stars ⟨~ *speculations*⟩

ˌstarry-ˈeyed *adj* given to thinking in a dreamy, impractical, or overoptimistic manner

Stars and Stripes *n pl but sing in constr* the flag of the USA, having 13 alternately red and white horizontal stripes and a blue rectangle in the top left-hand corner with white stars representing the states

star sapphire *n* a sapphire that reflects light in the form of a star-shaped figure, esp when cut with a convex surface

star shell *n* a shell that on bursting releases a brilliant light for illumination and signalling

ˈstar-ˌspangled *adj* studded with stars

ˈstar-ˌstudded *adj* full of or covered with stars ⟨*a* ~ *cast*⟩ ⟨*a* ~ *uniform*⟩

[1]**start** /staht/ *vi* **1a** to move suddenly and violently; spring ⟨~ed *angrily to his feet*⟩ **b** to react with a sudden brief involuntary movement ⟨~ed *when a shot rang out*⟩ **2a** to issue with sudden force ⟨*blood* ~ing *from the wound*⟩ **b** to come into being, activity, or operation ⟨*when does the film* ~?⟩ **3** to (seem to) protrude ⟨*his eyes* ~ing *from their sockets*⟩ **4a** to begin a course or journey ⟨~ed *out at dawn*⟩ **b** to range from a specified initial point ⟨*holiday prices* ~ *from around £80*⟩ **5** to begin an activity or undertaking; *esp* to begin work **6** to be a participant at the start of a sporting contest ~ *vt* **1** to cause to leave a place of concealment; flush ⟨~ *a rabbit*⟩ **2** to bring into being ⟨~ *a rumour*⟩ **3** to begin the use or employment of ⟨~ *a fresh loaf of bread*⟩ **4a** to cause to move, act, operate, or do sthg specified ⟨*the noise* ~ed *the baby crying*⟩ ⟨~ *the motor*⟩ **b** to act as starter of (e g a race) **c** to cause to enter or begin a game, contest, or business activity ⟨*only had £500 to* ~ *him*⟩; *broadly* to put in a starting position **5** to perform or undergo the first stages or actions of; begin ⟨~ed *studying music at the age of 5*⟩ [ME *sterten*; akin to MHG *sterzen* to stand up stiffly, move quickly, Lith *starinti* to stiffen – more at STARE] – **start something** to cause trouble – **to start with 1** at the beginning; initially **2** taking the first point to be considered

[2]**start** *n* **1** a sudden involuntary bodily movement or reaction (e g from surprise or alarm) **2** a beginning of movement, activity, or development **3a** a lead conceded at the start of a race or competition **b** an advantage, lead; HEAD START ⟨*gained a 3 days'* ~ *on the police*⟩ ⟨*his background gave him a good* ~ *in politics*⟩ **4** a place of beginning

starter /ˈstahtə/ *n* **1** one who initiates or sets going; *esp* one who gives the signal to start a race **2a** one who is in the starting lineup of a race or competition **b** one who begins to engage in an activity or process **3** sby who or sthg that causes sthg to begin operating: e g **a** a self-starter **b** material containing microorganisms used to induce a desired fermentation **c** a compound used to start a chemical reaction **4a** sthg that is the beginning of a process, activity, or series **b** *chiefly Br* the first course of a meal – often pl with sing. meaning

ˈstarting ˌhandle /ˈstahting/ *n, Br* a crank used to start an internal-combustion engine

startle /ˈstahtl/ *vb* **startling** /ˈstahtling/ to (cause to) be suddenly frightened or surprised and usu to (cause to) make a sudden brief movement [ME *stertlen*, freq of *sterten* to start] – **startling** *adj*, **startlingly** *adv*

starve /stahv/ *vi* **1a** to die from lack of food **b** to suffer or feel extreme hunger **2** to suffer or perish from deprivation ⟨~d *for affection*⟩ **3** *archaic or dial* to suffer or perish from cold ~*vt* to cause to starve [ME *sterven* to die, fr OE *steorfan*; akin to OHG *sterban* to die, Lith *starinti* to stiffen – more at STARE] – **starvation** /-'vaysh(ə)n/ *n*

starveling /'stahvling/ *n* a person or animal that is thin (as if) from lack of food

[1]**stash** /stash/ *vt* to store in a usu secret place for future use – often + *away* [origin unknown]

[2]**stash** *n, chiefly NAm* **1** a hiding place; a cache **2** sthg stored or hidden away

stasis /'staysis/ *n, pl* **stases** /-seez/ **1** a slowing or stoppage of the normal flow of body fluids **2** a state of static balance; stagnation [NL, fr Gk, act or condition of standing, stopping, fr *histasthai* to stand – more at STAND]

-stasis /-'staysis/ *comb form* (→ *n*), *pl* **-stases** /-stayseez/ **1** stoppage; slowing down; inhibition ⟨*haemo*stasis⟩ ⟨*bacterio*stasis⟩ **2** stable state ⟨*homoeo*stasis⟩ [NL, fr Gk *stasis* standing, stopping]

-stat /-stat/ *comb form* (→ *n*) agent or device for regulating ⟨*thermo*stat⟩ ⟨*rheo*stat⟩ [NL *-stata*, fr Gk *-statēs* one who or that which stops or steadies, fr *histanai* to cause to stand – more at STAND]

[1]**state** /stayt/ *n* **1a** a mode or condition of being (with regard to circumstances, health, temperament, etc) ⟨*a ~ of readiness*⟩ ⟨*a highly nervous ~*⟩ **b** a condition of abnormal tension or excitement ⟨*don't get in a ~ about it*⟩ **2a** a condition or stage in the physical being of sthg ⟨*the gaseous ~ of water*⟩ **b** any of various conditions characterized by definite quantities (e g of energy, angular momentum, or magnetic moment) in which an atomic system may exist **3a** social position; *esp* high rank **b(1)** luxurious style of living **(2)** formal dignity; pomp – usu + *in* **4** ESTATE 1 **5** a politically organized (sovereign) body, usu occupying a definite territory; *also* its political organization **6** the operations of the government ⟨*matters of ~*⟩ **7** *often cap* a constituent unit of a nation having a federal government [ME *stat*, fr OF & L; OF *estat*, fr L *status*, fr *status*, pp of *stare* to stand – more at STAND] – **statehood** *n*

[2]**state** *vt* **1** to set, esp by regulation or authority; specify **2** to express the particulars of, esp in words; *broadly* to express in words – **statable, stateable** *adj*, **stated** *adj*, **statedly** *adv*

state capitalism *n* an economic system in which capitalism is modified by some state control

'state,craft /-,krahft/ *n* the art of conducting state affairs

State Enrolled Nurse *n* a nurse who has successfully followed a 2-year course in practical nursing in Britain

'state,house /-,hows/ *n* the building in which a US state legislature sits

'stateless /-lis/ *adj* having no nationality ⟨*a ~ person*⟩ – **statelessness** *n*

'stately /-li/ *adj* **1** imposing, dignified ⟨*~ language*⟩ **2** impressive in size or proportions – **stateliness** *n*, **stately** *adv*

,stately 'home *n, Br* a large country residence, usu of historical or architectural interest and open to the public

statement /'staytmənt/ *n* **1** stating orally or on paper **2** sthg stated: e g **a** a report of facts or opinions **b** a single declaration or remark; an assertion **3** PROPOSITION 2 **4** the presentation of a theme in a musical composition **5** a summary of a financial account **6** an outward expression of thought, feeling, etc made without words ⟨*painted the room bright blue to make a definite ~*⟩

,state-of-the-'art *adj* using (the most advanced) technology available at the present time ⟨*a ~ aircraft design*⟩

stater /'staytə/ *n* any of various ancient gold or silver coins of the Greek city-states [ME, fr LL, fr Gk *statēr*, lit., a unit of weight, fr *histanai* to cause to stand, weigh – more at STAND]

State Registered Nurse *n* a fully qualified nurse in Britain

'stateroom /-,roohm, -room/ *n* **1** a large room in a palace or similar building for use on ceremonial occasions **2** a (large and comfortable) private cabin in a ship

States /stayts/ *n pl but sing or pl in constr* **the** USA

state school *n* a British school that is publicly financed and provides compulsory free education

,state's 'evidence *n, often cap S* (one who gives) evidence for the prosecution in US criminal proceedings

States General *n pl* **1** the assembly of the 3 French estates before the Revolution **2** the legislature of the Netherlands from the 15th c to 1796

'state,side /-,sied/ *adj or adv* of, in, or to the USA

'statesman /-mən/, *fem* **'states,woman** *n, pl* **statesmen** /-mən/, *fem* **stateswomen** **1** one versed in or esp engaged in the business of a government **2** one who exercises political leadership wisely and without narrow partisanship – **statesmanlike, statesmanly** *adj*, **statesmanship** *n*

state socialism *n* an economic system with limited socialist characteristics introduced gradually by political action

states' rights *n pl, often cap S&R* all rights not vested by the US Constitution in the federal government nor forbidden by it to the separate states

state trial *n* a trial for offences against the state

[1]**static** /'statik/ *also* **statical** /-kl/ *adj* **1** exerting force by reason of weight alone without motion ⟨*~ load*⟩ ⟨*~ pressure*⟩ **2** of or concerned with bodies at rest or forces in equilibrium **3** characterized by a lack of movement, animation, progression, or change ⟨*a ~ population*⟩ **4** of, producing, or being stationary charges of electricity **5** of or caused by radio static [NL *staticus*, fr Gk *statikos* causing to stand, skilled in weighing, fr *histanai* to cause to stand, weigh – more at STAND] – **statically** *adv*

[2]**static** *n* (the electrical disturbances causing) unwanted signals in a radio or television system; atmospherics [*static electricity*]

-static *comb form* (→ *adj*) **1** causing slowing of; inhibiting ⟨*bacterio*static⟩ **2** regulating; maintaining in a steady state ⟨*ther mo*static⟩ ⟨*homoeo*static⟩

statice /'statisi/ *n* SEA LAVENDER [NL, genus of herbs, fr L, an astringent plant, fr Gk *statikē*, fr fem of *statikos* causing to stand, astringent]

statics /'statiks/ *n pl but sing or pl in constr* a

branch of mechanics dealing with the relations of forces that produce equilibrium among solid bodies

[1]**station** /'staysh(ə)n/ *n* **1** the place or position in which sthg or sby stands or is assigned to stand or remain **2** a stopping place; *esp* (the buildings at) a regular or major stopping place for trains, buses, etc **3a** a post or sphere of duty or occupation **b** a post or area to which a military or naval force is assigned; *also, sing or pl in constr* the officers or society at a station **c** a stock farm or ranch in Australia or New Zealand **4** standing, rank ⟨*a woman of high* ~⟩ **5** a place for specialized observation and study of scientific phenomena ⟨*a marine biology* ~⟩ **6** a place established to provide a public service; *esp* POLICE STATION **7a** (the equipment in) an establishment equipped for radio or television transmission or reception **b** CHANNEL 1F(2) [ME *stacioun*, fr MF *station*, fr L *station-, statio*, fr *status*, pp of *stare* to stand – more at STAND]

[2]**station** *vt* to assign to or set in a station or position; post

stationary /'stayshən(ə)ri/ *adj* **1a** having a fixed position; immobile **b** geostationary **2** unchanging in condition

stationary wave *n* STANDING WAVE

stationer /'stayshənə/ *n* one who deals in stationery [ME *staciouner*, fr ML *stationarius*, fr *station-, statio* shop, fr L, station]

stationery /'stayshən(ə)ri/ *n* materials (e g paper) for writing or typing; *specif* paper and envelopes for letter writing [*stationer*]

'**station,master** /-,mahstə/ *n* an official in charge of a railway station

stations of the cross *n pl, often cap S&C* (a devotion involving meditation before) a series of images or pictures, esp in a church, that represent the 14 stages of Christ's sufferings and death

'**station ,wagon** *n, chiefly NAm* ESTATE CAR

statism /'stay,tiz(ə)m/ *n* concentration of economic controls and planning in the hands of the state – **statist** *n or adj*

statistic /stə'tistik/ *n* a single term or quantity in or computed from a collection of statistics; *specif* (a function used to obtain) a numerical value (e g the standard deviation or mean) used in describing and analysing statistics [back-formation fr *statistics*]

statistical mechanics /stə'tistikl/ *n pl but sing in constr* a branch of mechanics dealing with the application of the principles of statistics to the mechanics of a system consisting of a large number of parts having motions that differ by small steps over a large range

statistics /stə'tistiks/ *n pl but sing or pl in constr* **1** a branch of mathematics dealing with the collection, analysis, interpretation, and presentation of masses of numerical data 👁 **2** a collection of quantitative data [G *statistik* study of political facts and figures, fr NL *statisticus* of politics, fr L *status* state] – **statistical** *adj*, **statistically** *adv*, **statistician** /,stati'stish(ə)n/ *n*

stator /'staytə/ *n* a stationary part in a machine in or about which a rotor revolves [NL, fr L, one who or that which stands, fr *status*, pp of *stare* to stand – more at STAND]

[1]**statuary** /'statyooəri/ *n* statues collectively

[2]**statuary** *adj* of or suitable for statues ⟨~ *marble*⟩

statue /'statyooh, -chooh/ *n* a likeness (e g of a person or animal) sculptured, cast, or modelled in a solid material (e g bronze or stone) [ME, fr MF, fr L *statua*, fr *statuere* to set up – more at STATUTE] – **statuette** /-'et/ *n*

,**statu'esque** /-'esk/ *adj* resembling a statue, esp in dignity, shapeliness, or formal beauty – **statuesquely** *adv*, **statuesqueness** *n*

stature /'stachə/ *n* **1** natural height (e g of a person) in an upright position **2** quality or status gained by growth, development, or achievement [ME, fr OF, fr L *statura*, fr *status*, pp of *stare* to stand – more at STAND]

status /'staytəs/ *n* **1** the condition of sby or sthg (in the eyes of the law) **2** (high) position or rank in relation to others or in a hierarchy [L – more at STATE]

,**status 'quo** /kwoh/ *n* the existing state of affairs ⟨*seeks to preserve the* ~⟩ [L, state in which]

'**status ,symbol** *n* a possession serving to indicate high social status or wealth

statute /'statyooht/ *n* **1** a law passed by a legislative body and recorded ☞ LAW **2** a rule made by a corporation or its founder, intended as permanent [ME, fr OF *statut*, fr LL *statutum* law, regulation, fr L, neut of *statutus*, pp of *statuere* to set up, station, fr *status* position, condition, state]

statute book *n* the whole body of legislation of a given jurisdiction

statute law *n* enacted written law

statute mile *n* MILE 1a

statute of limitations *n* a statute stipulating a time after which rights cannot be enforced or offences punished

statutory /'statyoot(ə)ri/, **statutable** /-təbl/ *adj* established, regulated, or imposed by or in conformity to statute ⟨*a* ~ *age limit*⟩ – **statutorily** /-t(ə)rəli/, **statutably** *adv*

statutory instrument *n* an official document recording any law which has been made by a minister exercising his or her delegated legislative powers and which has not gone through parliament ☞ LAW

[1]**staunch** /stawnch/ *vt* to stanch

[2]**staunch** *adj* steadfast in loyalty or principle [ME, fr MF *estanche*, fem of *estanc*, fr OF, fr *estancher* to stanch] – **staunchly** *adv*, **staunchness** *n*

[1]**stave** /stayv/ *n* **1** STAFF 1a, 2 **2** any of the narrow strips of wood or iron placed edge to edge to form the sides, covering, or lining of a vessel (e g a barrel) or structure **3** a supporting bar; *esp* RUNG 1b **4** a stanza **5** STAFF 3 [back-formation fr *staves*, pl of *staff*]

[2]**stave** *vt* **staved, stove** /stohv/ **1** to crush or break inwards – usu + *in* **2** to provide with staves

stave off *vt* to ward or fend off, esp temporarily

staves *pl of* STAFF

[1]**stay** /stay/ *n* a strong rope, now usu of wire, used to support a ship's mast or similar tall structure (e g a flagstaff) ☞ SHIP [ME, fr OE *stæg*; akin to ON *stag* stay, OE *stēle* steel]

[2]**stay** *vt* to support (e g a chimney) (as if) with stays

[3]**stay** *vi* **1** to continue in a place or condition; remain ⟨~ *here*⟩ ⟨~ed *awake*⟩ **2** to take up temporary residence; lodge **3a** to keep even in a contest or rivalry ⟨~ *with the leaders*⟩ **b** *of a racehorse* to run well over long distances **4** *archaic* to stop going forwards; pause **5** *archaic* to stop doing sthg; cease ~ *vt* **1** to last out (e g a race) **2** to stop or delay the

proceeding, advance, or course of; halt ⟨~ *an execution*⟩ [ME *stayen*, fr MF *ester* to stand, stay, fr L *stare* – more at STAND] – **stay put** to be firmly fixed, attached, or established

[4]stay *n* **1a** stopping or being stopped **b** a suspension of judicial procedure ⟨*a* ~ *of execution*⟩ **2** a residence or sojourn in a place

[5]stay *n* **1** sby who or sthg that serves as a prop; a support **2** a corset stiffened with bones – usu pl with sing. meaning [MF *estaie*, of Gmc origin; akin to OHG *stān* to stand – more at STAND]

[6]stay *vt* to provide physical or moral support for; sustain

'stay-at-,home *n or adj* (one) preferring to remain in his/her own home, locality, or country

stayer /'stayə/ *n* a racehorse that habitually stays the course [[3]STAY + [2]-ER]

'staying ,power /'staying/ *n* stamina

staysail /'stay,sayl; *tech* -səl/ *n* a fore-and-aft sail hoisted on a stay

'stay ,stitch *n* a line of stitches sewn round an edge (e g a neckline) before making up a garment in order to prevent the cloth from stretching

stead /sted/ *n* the office, place, or function ordinarily occupied or carried out by sby or sthg else ⟨*acted in his brother's* ~⟩ [ME *stede* place, site, advantage, fr OE, place; akin to OHG *stat* place, *stān* to stand]

steadfast /'sted,fahst, -fəst/ *adj* **1a** firmly fixed in place or position ⟨*a* ~ *gaze*⟩ **b** not subject to change **2** firm in belief, determination, or adherence; loyal – **steadfastly** *adv*, **steadfastness** *n*

steading /'steding/ *n* a small farm [ME *steding*, fr *stede* place, farm]

[1]steady /'stedi/ *adj* **1a** firm in position; not shaking, rocking, etc **b** direct or sure; unfaltering ⟨*a* ~ *hand*⟩ **2** showing or continuing with little variation or fluctuation; stable, uniform ⟨~ *prices*⟩ ⟨*a* ~ *pace*⟩ **3a** not easily moved or upset; calm ⟨~ *nerves*⟩ **b** dependable, constant **c** not given to dissipation; sober [*stead* + [1]-*y*] – **steadily** *adv*, **steadiness** *n*

[2]steady *vb* to make, keep, or become steady – **steadier** *n*

[3]steady *adv* **1** in a steady manner; steadily **2** on the course set – used as a direction to the helmsman of a ship

[4]steady *n* a boyfriend or girlfriend with whom one is going steady – infml

,steady 'state *n* a dynamically balanced state or condition of a system or process that tends to remain when once achieved

steady state theory *n* a theory in cosmology: the universe has always existed and has always been expanding with matter being created continuously – compare BIG BANG THEORY

steak /stayk/ *n* **1a** a slice of meat cut from a fleshy part (e g the rump) of a (beef) carcass and suitable for grilling or frying ☞ MEAT **b** a poorer-quality less tender beef cut, usu from the neck and shoulder, suitable for braising or stewing **2** a cross-sectional slice from between the centre and tail of a large fish – compare CUTLET 2 [ME *steke*, fr ON *steik*; akin to ON *steikja* to roast on a stake, *stik* stick, stake – more at [1]STICK]

steal /steel/ *vb* **stole** /stohl/; **stolen** /'stohlən/ *vi* **1** to take the property of another **2** to come or go secretly or unobtrusively ~ *vt* **1a** to take without leave, esp secretly or by force and with intent to keep **b** to appropriate entirely to oneself or beyond one's proper share ⟨~ *the show*⟩ **2** to accomplish, obtain, or convey in a secretive, unobserved, or furtive manner ⟨~ *a visit*⟩ ⟨stole *a glance at him*⟩ **3** to seize or gain by trickery or skill ⟨*a footballer adept at* ~ing *the ball*⟩ [ME *stelen*, fr OE *stelan*; akin to OHG *stelan* to steal] – **stealer** *n* – **steal a march** to gain an advantage unobserved – usu + *on* – **steal someone's thunder** to appropriate or adapt sthg devised by another in order to take the credit due to him/her

stealth /stelth/ *n* **1** the act or action of proceeding furtively or unobtrusively **2** the state of being furtive or unobtrusive [ME *stelthe*; akin to OE *stelan* to steal]

stealthy /'stelthi/ *adj* **1** slow, deliberate, and secret in action or character **2** intended to escape observation; furtive – **stealthily** *adv*, **stealthiness** *n*

[1]steam /steem/ *n* **1** a vapour given off by a heated substance **2a** the vapour into which water is converted when heated to its boiling point **b** the mist formed by the condensation of water vapour when cooled **3a** energy or power generated (as if) by steam under pressure **b** driving force; power ⟨*got there under his own* ~⟩ – infml [ME *stem*, fr OE *stēam*; akin to D *stoom* steam] – **let/blow off steam** to release pent-up emotions

[2]steam *vi* **1** to rise or pass off as vapour **2** to give off steam or vapour **3a** to move or travel (as if) by steam power (e g in a steamship) **b** to proceed quickly **4** to become cooked by steam **5** to be angry; boil ⟨~ing *over the insult he had received*⟩ **6** to become covered *up* or *over* with steam or condensation ⟨*his glasses* ~ed *up*⟩ ~ *vt* **1** to give out as fumes; exhale **2** to apply steam to; *esp* to expose to the action of steam (e g for softening or cooking)

'steam,boat /-,boht/ *n* a boat propelled by steam power

'steam ,chest *n* the chamber from which steam is distributed to a cylinder of a steam engine

'steam ,engine *n* a stationary or locomotive engine driven or worked by steam

steamer /'steemə/ *n* **1** a device in which articles are steamed; *esp* a vessel in which food is cooked by steam **2a** a ship propelled by steam **b** an engine, machine, or vehicle operated or propelled by steam [[2]STEAM + [2]-ER]

'steam ,iron *n* an electric iron with a compartment holding water that is converted to steam by the iron's heat and emitted through the soleplate onto the fabric being pressed

steam radio *n*, *Br* radio considered as antiquated in comparison with television – humor

[1]'steam,roller /-,rohlə/ *n* **1** a machine equipped with wide heavy rollers for compacting the surfaces of roads, pavements, etc **2** a crushing force, esp when ruthlessly applied to overcome opposition

[2]steamroller *also* **steamroll** *vt* **1** to crush (as if) with a steamroller ⟨~ *the opposition*⟩ **2** to force to a specified state or condition by the use of overwhelming pressure ⟨~ed *the bill through Parliament*⟩ ~ *vi* to move or proceed with irresistible force

'steam,ship /-,ship/ *n* STEAMER 2a

steam turbine *n* a turbine driven by the pressure of steam against the turbine blades

steam up *vt* to make angry or excited; arouse

steamy /'steemi/ *adj* **1** consisting of, characterized

Statistics is the compilation, presentation and analysis of many related items of data, which as individual items are unreliable or insignificant. The word originally meant 'state arithmetic', as the first statistics were compiled for census or tax purposes. It now means (a) an assembly of related facts or (b) the mathematical technique of drawing probable conclusions from them. Thus a compilation of totals of smokers and non-smokers, showing the numbers of each who died from lung cancer over a certain period of time, is statistics in the first sense. The deduction from the figures that lung cancer is significantly correlated with smoking requires statistics in the second sense.

Statistical data can be presented in tabular form, or in many forms of graphic display. Thus this table shows the percentage of the major elements in the earth's crust:

Element	%
Oxygen	46
Silicon	27
Aluminium	8
Iron	5
Calcium	4
Sodium	3
Others	7
Total	100

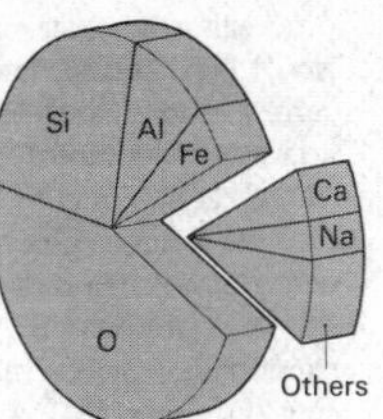

A graphical presentation – a 'pie chart' in this case – can give the data much more effectively.

Histograms and statistical distributions. The diagram shows the scatter of shots from a gun aimed at a distant target. The shots are divided into specific error-bands, and the height of each block in the histogram represents the number of shots falling within that band. The tallest block represents the most 'popular' single error-band, the *mode* of the distribution. The *median* of the distribution is the value which divides the shots evenly into two, half falling nearer than the median value, and half falling further away. Similarly, the median and the *upper* and *lower quartiles* divide the shots into four equal groups. The conventional average or *mean*, obtained by adding all the errors and dividing by the total number of shots, need not coincide with either mode or median. Here it is greater than either, being heavily influenced by the long 'tail' of very wide shots. Divided into sufficiently narrow blocks, the histogram would shade into the *limiting distribution curve* shown, which could be mathematically analysed.

Correlation. The diagram shows the (hypothetical) sales of eggs and of bacon over a year. It is clear that they tend to fluctuate together, ie are correlated to some degree, though the results for any one month (eg May) would not reveal it very convincingly. A statistical analysis would show the degree of correlation, as well as a measure of the likelihood that it had happened by chance.

☞ SYMBOL

The normal distribution is one of the most fundamental of statistical distributions. The heights of European males, the number of 'heads' in a set of penny-tossings, and the production errors in many processes are all phenomena which are 'normally distributed'. The mean, median, and mode of the distribution all coincide at its peak, *P*, and its spread is defined by a single number – the *standard deviation* σ (sigma). 68% of a normally distributed set of values will be found within 1σ of the mean value. And while the distribution theoretically 'tails' to infinity in both directions, only 0.26% of values are further than 3σ from the mean.

Probability: the educated guess

In a population of 300 people
150 have brown hair
96 have fair hair
54 have black hair
the probability of a person chosen at random having brown hair will be

Pr (brown hair) $\dfrac{\text{no. with brown hair}}{\text{total}}$

$= \dfrac{150}{300} = ½$ ie 1 in 2

the 'probability' is the estimated relative frequency of something happening or being true. All probabilities are greater than or equal to 0 and less than or equal to 1:

$0 \leqslant P \leqslant 1$

Probabilities can be presented on a scale:

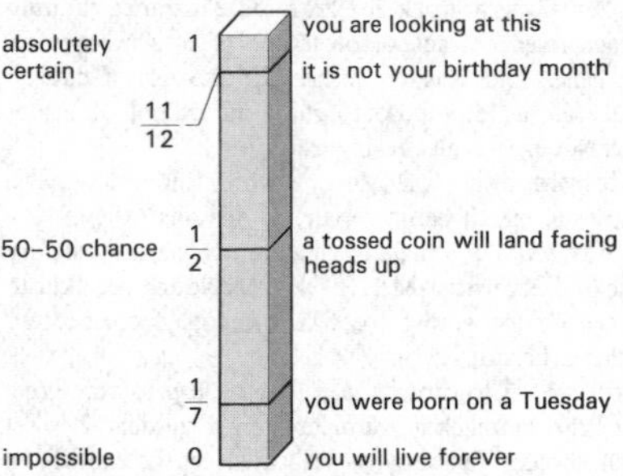

There are two laws of probability.

The *multiplication law* – for events which are completely independent. If a coin is tossed, and at the same moment a die is thrown, the probability of obtaining 'heads' and a six is given by:

Pr (heads, six) $\dfrac{1}{2} \times \dfrac{1}{6} = \dfrac{1}{12}$

ie a 1 in 12 chance.

The *addition law* – for different outcomes of the same event. If a coin is tossed and a die thrown what is the probability of getting heads + six OR tails + five?

Pr (heads, six) $= \dfrac{1}{12}$

Pr (tails, five) $= \dfrac{1}{12}$

Pr (heads, six; or tails, five)

$= \dfrac{1}{12} + \dfrac{1}{12} = \dfrac{1}{6}$

The laws of probability govern all forms of gambling.

Horse racing has a 'probability language' all of its own. The odds offered by bookies are trading figures, rather than actual probabilities: odds of A:B *on* mean that A + B are the total chances presented, of which A are favourable (horse wins) but B are unfavourable (horse loses). If these odds represented the true probability then the chances of the horse winning would be $\dfrac{A}{A+B}$.

So odds of 2:1 on implies 2 chances of winning for every 1 of losing. The bookie, offered £2 on such terms, would undertake to return £3 if the horse won. But its real chance of winning must be less than ⅔, otherwise the bookie could not make any profit.

Similarly, odds of 6:1 *against* means 6 chances of losing to 1 of winning: the bookie would accept a £1 bet and return £7 if the horse won.

On the racecourse itself the odds and the number of the horse are signalled to the bookies by their tic tac men, using a code of signals that varies in detail depending on the country in which the race is taking place.

Fruit machine theory

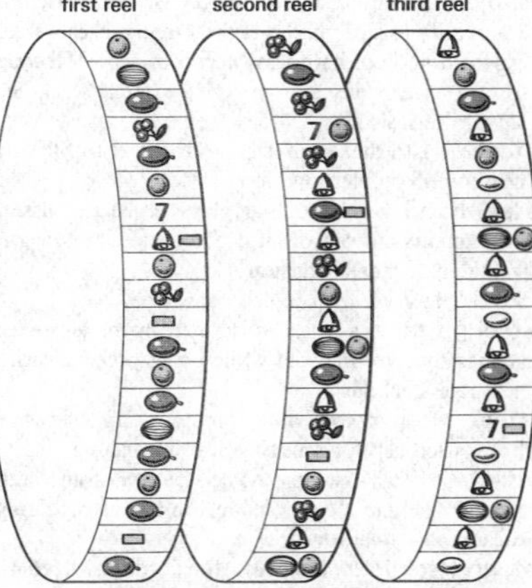

Each reel of this slot machine contains 7 different symbols, which means there are 343 (7 × 7 × 7) possible combinations. Only twelve of these pay back any money, but some of the twelve can be made several ways on the top line. The combination of one cherry plus any two other symbols can be made with either of 2 cherries on the first reel and anything not a cherry on the second and third reel. But a line of 3 sevens, for example, can only be made one way, thus reducing the chances of a large winning.

by, or full of steam **2** erotic ⟨*a ~ love scene*⟩ – **steamily** *adv*, **steaminess** *n*

stearate /'stiərayt/ *n* a salt or ester of stearic acid

stearic acid /'stiərik, sti'arik/ *n* a fatty acid that is obtained from hard fat (e g tallow) and whose salts are used in soap manufacture [*stearic* fr F *stéarique*, fr Gk *stear* fat]

stearin /'stiərin/ *n* **1** an ester of glycerol and stearic acid **2** the solid portion of a fat [F *stéarine*, fr Gk *stear*]

steat- /stee·ət-/, **steato-** *comb form* fat ⟨steato*lysis*⟩ [Gk, fr *steat-*, *stear* – more at STONE]

steatite /'stee·ətiet/ *n* soapstone [L *steatitis*, a precious stone, fr Gk, fr *steat-*] – **steatitic** /-'titik/ *adj*

steatopygia /,stee·ətoh'piji·ə/ *n* the development of excess fat on the buttocks, esp among Hottentot females [NL, fr *steat-* + Gk *pygē* rump, buttocks; akin to Latvian *pauga* cushion, Gk *physan* to blow – more at [2]FOG] – **steatopygic, steatopygous** /-'pigəs/ *adj*

steed /steed/ *n* a horse; *esp* a spirited horse for state or war – chiefly poetic [ME *stede*, fr OE *stēda* stallion; akin to OE *stōd* stud – more at [1]STUD]

[1]**steel** /steel/ *n* **1** commercial iron distinguished from cast iron by its malleability and lower carbon content **2** an instrument or implement (characteristically) of steel: e g **a** a fluted round steel rod with a handle for sharpening knives **b** a piece of steel for striking sparks from flint **c** a strip of steel used for stiffening **3** a quality (e g of mind or spirit) that suggests steel, esp in strength or hardness ⟨*nerves of ~*⟩ [ME *stele*, fr OE *stȳle*, *stēle*; akin to OHG *stahal* steel, Skt *stakati* he resists]

[2]**steel** *vt* **1** to make unfeeling; harden **2** to fill with resolution or determination

steel band *n* a band that plays tuned percussion instruments cut out of oil drums, developed orig in Trinidad – **steelbandsman** *n*

,**steel 'grey** *adj or n* bluish dark grey

steel guitar *n* a usu electric instrument with steel strings that are plucked while being pressed with a movable steel bar

,**steel 'wool** *n* long fine loosely compacted steel fibres used esp for scouring and burnishing

'**steel,works** /-,wuhks/ *n, pl* **steelworks** an establishment where steel is made – often pl with sing. meaning – **steelworker** *n*

steely /'steeli/ *adj* of or like (the hardness, strength, or colour of) steel – **steeliness** *n*

'**steel,yard** /-,yahd/ *n* a balance in which an object to be weighed is suspended from the shorter arm of a lever and the weight determined by moving a counterbalance along a graduated scale on the longer arm until equilibrium is attained [prob fr *steel*, adj + *yard* (rod)]

steenbok /'steen,bok/, **steinbok** /~, 'stienbok/ *n* any of a genus of small antelopes of the plains of S and E Africa [Afrik *steenbok*; akin to OE *stānbucca* ibex; both fr a prehistoric WGmc compound whose elements are represented respectively by OE *stān* stone & OE *bucca* buck]

[1]**steep** /steep/ *adj* **1** making a large angle with the plane of the horizon; almost vertical **2** being or characterized by a rapid and severe decline or increase **3** difficult to accept, comply with, or carry out; excessive – infml [ME *stepe*, fr OE *stēap* high, steep, deep; akin to MHG *stief* steep, ON *staup* lump, knoll, cup] – **steepen** *vb*, **steepish** *adj*, **steeply** *adv*, **steepness** *n*

[2]**steep** *vt* **1** to soak in a liquid at a temperature below its boiling point (e g for softening or bleaching) **2** to cover with or plunge into a liquid (e g in bathing, rinsing, or soaking) **3** to imbue with or subject thoroughly to – usu + *in* ⟨*~ed in history*⟩ ~ *vi* to undergo soaking in a liquid [ME *stepen*; akin to Sw *stöpa* to steep, & prob to ON *staup* cup]

[3]**steep** *n* **1** being steeped **2** a liquid in which sthg is steeped

steeple /'steepl/ *n* (a tower with) a tall spire on a church [ME *stepel*, fr OE *stēpel* tower; akin to OE *stēap* steep]

'**steeple,chase** /-,chays/ *n* **1a** a horse race across country **b** a horse race over jumps; *specif* one over a course longer than 2mi (about 3.2km) containing fences higher than 4ft 6in (about 1.4m) – compare FLAT RACE, HURDLE 2b **2** a middle-distance running race over obstacles; *specif* one of 3000m over 28 hurdles and 7 water jumps [fr the use of church steeples as landmarks to guide the riders] – **steeplechaser** *n*, **steeplechasing** *n*

'**steeple,jack** /-jak/ *n* one who climbs chimneys, towers, etc to paint, repair, or demolish them

[1]**steer** /stiə/ *n* a male bovine animal castrated before sexual maturity [ME, fr OE *stēor* young ox; akin to OHG *stior* young ox, Skt *sthavira*, *sthūra* stout, thick, broad]

[2]**steer** *vt* **1** to direct the course of; *esp* to guide (e g a ship) by mechanical means (e g a rudder) **2** to set and hold to (a course) ~ *vi* **1** to direct the course (e g of a ship or motor vehicle) **2** to pursue a course of action **3** to be subject to guidance or direction ⟨*a car that ~s well*⟩ [ME *steren*, fr OE *stīeran*; akin to OE *stēor-* steering oar, Gk *stauros* stake, cross, *stylos* pillar, Skt *sthavira*, *sthūra* stout, thick, L *stare* to stand – more at STAND] – **steerable** *adj*, **steerer** *n* – **steer clear** to keep entirely away – often + *of*

steerage /'stiərij/ *n* **1** the act or practice of steering; *broadly* direction **2** a large section in a passenger ship for passengers paying the lowest fares [(2) fr its orig being located near the rudder]

'**steerage-,way** *n* a rate of motion sufficient to make a ship or boat respond to movements of the rudder

'**steering ,column** /'stiəring/ *n* the column that encloses the links between the steering wheel and the steering gear of a vehicle

'**steering com,mittee** *n* a committee that determines the order in which business will be taken up (e g in Parliament)

'**steering ,wheel** *n* a handwheel by means of which one steers a motor vehicle, ship, etc

steersman /'stiəzmən/ *n* a helmsman

stegosaur /'stegə,saw/ *n* any of a large group of dinosaurs with strongly developed bony plates along the back [NL *Stegosauria*, group name, fr *Stegosaurus*, genus name]

stegosaurus /,stegə'sawrəs/ *n* any of a genus of large armoured dinosaurs of the Upper Jurassic rocks of Colorado and Wyoming ☞ EVOLUTION [NL, genus name, fr Gk *stegos* roof + *sauros* lizard – more at THATCH, SAURIAN]

stein /s(h)tien/ *n* a usu earthenware beer mug often with a hinged lid [prob fr G *steingut* stoneware, fr *stein* stone + *gut* goods]

steinbok /'steenbok, 'stienbok/ *n* a steenbok

stele /'steeli, steel/ *n* **1** a usu carved or inscribed stone slab or pillar used esp as a gravestone **2** the (cylindrical) central vascular portion of the stem of a vascular plant [Gk *stēlē* pillar; akin to Gk *stellein* to set up – more at [1]STALL] – **stelar** /'steelə, -lah/ *adj*

stellar /'stelə/ *adj* of or composed of (the) stars [LL *stellaris*, fr L *stella* star – more at STAR]

stellate /'stelət, -layt/ *also* **stellated** /-,laytid/ *adj* resembling a star, esp in shape [L *stella*]

stelliform /'steli,fawm/ *adj* star-shaped [NL *stelliformis*, fr L *stella* + *-iformis* -iform]

stellular /'stelyoolə/ *adj* **1** star-shaped **2** marked with stars

[1]**stem** /stem/ *n* **1a** the main trunk of a plant; *specif* a primary plant axis that develops buds and shoots instead of roots **b** a branch, petiole, or other plant part that supports a leaf, fruit, etc **2** the bow or prow of a vessel; *specif* the principal frame member at the bow to which the sides are fixed – compare STERN ☞ SHIP **3** a line of ancestry; *esp* a fundamental line from which others have arisen **4** that part of a word which has unchanged spelling when the word is inflected **5** sthg that resembles a plant stem: e g **a** a main (vertical) stroke of a letter or musical note **b** the tubular part of a tobacco pipe from the bowl outwards, through which smoke is drawn **c** the often slender and cylindrical upright support between the base and bowl of a wineglass **d** a shaft of a watch used for winding [ME, fr OE *stefn, stemn* stem of a plant or ship; OE *stefn* akin to OE *stæf* staff; OE *stemn* akin to OE *standan* to stand] – **stemless** *adj*, **stemmed** *adj*

[2]**stem** *vt* **-mm-** **1** to make headway against (e g an adverse tide, current, or wind) **2** to check or go counter to (sthg adverse) [[1]*stem* 2]

[3]**stem** *vb* **-mm-** *vi* to originate – usu + *from* ~ *vt* to remove the stem from [[1]*stem* 1]

[4]**stem** *vt* **-mm-** to stop or check (as if) by damming ⟨~ *a flow of blood*⟩ [ME *stemmen* to dam up, fr ON *stemma*; akin to OE *stamerian* to stammer]

stem cell *n* an unspecialized cell (e g in bone marrow) that gives rise to differentiated cells (e g blood cells)

stem christie, stem christy /'kristi/ *n* a turn in skiing in which the back end of one ski is forced outwards from the line of progress and the other ski is then brought parallel to it [*stem* (an act of slowing oneself on skis; fr [4]*stem*) + *christie, christy* (a skiing turn), by shortening & alter. fr *christiania*]

stemma /'stemə/ *n, pl* **stemmata** /-mətə/ **1** a simple eye present in some insects **2** a genealogical list [L, wreath, pedigree (fr the wreaths placed on ancestral images), fr Gk, wreath, fr *stephein* to crown, enwreathe]

Sten /sten/, **Sten gun** *n* a lightweight British submachine gun [Major *S*heppard, 20th-c E army officer + Mr *T*urpin, 20th-c E civil servant + *En*gland]

sten- /sten-/, **steno-** *comb form* narrow; little ⟨steno*grapher*⟩ ⟨steno*sis*⟩ [Gk, fr *stenos* narrow, close, scanty]

stench /stench/ *n* a stink [ME, fr OE *stenc*; akin to OE *stincan* to emit a smell – more at STINK]

[1]**stencil** /'stens(ə)l/ *n* **1** (a printing process using, or a design, pattern, etc produced by means of) an impervious material (e g a sheet of paper or metal) perforated with a design or lettering through which a substance (e g ink or paint) is forced onto the surface below **2** a sheet of strong tissue paper impregnated or coated (e g with paraffin or wax) for use esp in typing a stencil [ME *stanselen* to ornament with sparkling colours, fr MF *estanceler*, fr *estancele* spark, fr (assumed) VL *stincilla*, fr L *scintilla*]

[2]**stencil** *vt* **-ll-** (*NAm* **-l-**, **-ll-**); **stencilling**, /'stens(ə)l·ing/ **1** to produce by means of a stencil **2** to mark or paint with a stencil – **stenciller** *n*

stenography /ste'nogrəfi/ *n* the writing and transcription of shorthand – **stenographer** *n*, **stenographic** /,stenə'grafik/ *adj*, **stenographically** *adv*

stenosis /sti'nohsis/ *n, pl* **stenoses** /-seez/ a narrowing or constriction of the diameter of a bodily passage or orifice [NL, fr Gk *stenōsis* act of narrowing, fr *stenoun* to narrow, fr *stenos*] – **stenosed** /-nohzd, -nohst/ *adj*, **stenotic** /ste'notik/ *adj*

stenotype /'stenətiep/ *trademark* – used for a small machine rather like a typewriter, used to record speech by means of phonograms (e g shorthand characters) – **stenotype** *vt*, **stenotypist** /-,tiepist/ *n*, **stenotypy** /'stenə,tiepi, ste'notipi/ *n*

stentorian /sten'tawri·ən/ *adj* extremely loud [*Stentor*, mythical Gk herald noted for his loud voice, fr L, fr Gk *Stentōr*]

[1]**step** /step/ *n* **1** a rest for the foot in ascending or descending: e g **a** a single tread and riser on a stairway; a stair **b** a ladder rung **2a(1)** (the distance or space passed over in) an advance or movement made by raising the foot and bringing it down at another point **(2)** a combination of foot (and body) movements constituting a unit or a repeated pattern ⟨*a dance* ~⟩ **(3)** manner of walking; stride **b** FOOTPRINT 1 **c** the sound of a footstep ⟨*heard his* ~s *in the hall*⟩ **3** a short distance ⟨*just a* ~ *from the beach*⟩ **4** *pl* a course, way ⟨*directed his* ~s *towards the river*⟩ **5a** a degree, grade, or rank in a scale **b** a stage in a process ⟨*was guided through every* ~ *of her career*⟩ **6** a block supporting the base of a mast **7** an action, proceeding, or measure often occurring as 1 in a series – often pl with sing. meaning ⟨*is taking* ~s *to improve the situation*⟩ **8** a steplike offset or part, usu occurring in a series **9** *pl* a stepladder [ME, fr OE *stæpe*; akin to OHG *stapfo* step, *stampfōn* to stamp] – **steplike** *adj*, **stepped** *adj* – **in step** **1** with each foot moving to the same time as the corresponding foot of others or in time to music **2** in harmony or agreement – **out of step** not in step

[2]**step** *vb* **-pp-** *vi* **1a** to move by raising the foot and bringing it down at another point or by moving each foot in succession **b** to dance **2a** to go on foot; walk **b** to be on one's way; leave – often + *along* **3** to press down *on* sthg with the foot ⟨~ *on the brake*⟩ ~ *vt* **1** to take by moving the feet in succession ⟨~ *3 paces*⟩ **2** to go through the steps of; perform ⟨~ *a minuet*⟩ **3** to make (e g a mast) erect by fixing the lower end in a step **4** to measure by steps ⟨~ *50 yards*⟩ – usu + *off* or *out* **5** to construct or arrange (as if) in steps ⟨*craggy peaks with terraces* ~ped *up the sides – Time*⟩ – **step into** to attain or adopt (sthg) with ease ⟨stepped into *a fortune*⟩ – **step on it/the gas** to increase one's speed; hurry up – infml

step- *comb form* related by remarriage and not by blood ⟨step*parent*⟩ ⟨step*sister*⟩ [ME, fr OE *stēop-*; akin to OHG *stiof-* step-]

'step,brother /-,brudhə/ *n* a son of one's stepparent by a former marriage

,step-by-'step *adj* marked by successive degrees, usu of limited extent; gradual

'step,child /-,chield/ *n, pl* **stepchildren** /-,childrən/ a child of one's wife or husband by a former marriage

'step ,dance *n* a dance in which steps are emphasized rather than gesture or posture

'step,daughter /-,dawtə/ *n* a daughter of one's wife or husband by a former marriage

step down *vt* to lower (the voltage at which an alternating current is operating) by means of a transformer ~ *vi* to retire, resign ⟨step down *as chairman*⟩ – **step-down** *adj*

'step,father /-,fahdhə/ *n* the husband of one's mother by a subsequent marriage

stephanotis /,stefə'nohtis/ *n* any of a genus of Old World tropical woody climbing plants with fragrant white flowers [NL, genus name, fr Gk *stephanōtis* fit for a crown, fr *stephanos* crown, fr *stephein* to crown]

'step-,in *adj, of clothes* put on by being stepped into

step in *vi* **1** to make a brief informal visit **2** to intervene in an affair or dispute

'step,ladder /-,ladə/ *n* a portable set of steps with a hinged frame

'step,mother /-,mudhə/ *n* the wife of one's father by a subsequent marriage

step out *vi* **1** to leave or go outside, usu for a short time ⟨stepped out *for a smoke*⟩ **2** to go or march at a vigorous or increased pace

'step,parent /-,peərənt/ *n* the husband or wife of one's parent by a subsequent marriage

steppe /step/ *n* a vast usu level and treeless plain, esp in SE Europe or Asia ☞ PLANT [Russ *step'*]

'stepping-,stone *n* **1** a stone on which to step (e g in crossing a stream) **2** a means of progress or advancement

'step,sister /-,sistə/ *n* a daughter of one's stepparent by a former marriage

'step,son /-,sun/ *n* a son of one's husband or wife by a former marriage

step up *vt* **1** to increase (the voltage at which an alternating current is operating) by means of a transformer **2** to increase, augment, or advance by 1 or more steps ⟨step up *production*⟩ ~ *vi* **1** to come forward ⟨step up *to the front*⟩ **2** to undergo an increase – **step-up** *adj*

'step,wise /-wiez/ *adj* marked by or proceeding in steps

-ster /-stə/ *comb form* (→ *n*) **1** sby who or sthg that does, handles, or operates ⟨*tap*ster⟩ ⟨*team*ster⟩ **2** sby who or sthg that makes or uses ⟨*song*ster⟩ ⟨*pun*ster⟩ **3** sby who or sthg that is associated with or participates in ⟨*game*ster⟩ ⟨*gang*ster⟩ **4** sby who or sthg that is ⟨*young*ster⟩ [ME, fr OE *-estre* female agent; akin to MD *-ster*]

steradian /stə'raydyən/ *n* a unit of solid angular measurement that is equal to the solid angle at the centre of a sphere subtended by an area on the surface of the sphere equal to the square of the radius of the sphere ☞ PHYSICS [*stere-* + *radian*]

stere /stiə/ *n* a metric unit of volume equal to one cubic metre (about 1.3 cubic yd) [F *stère*, fr Gk *stereos*]

stere- /steri-, stiəri-/, **stereo-** *comb form* **1** solid (body) ⟨stereo*taxis*⟩ ⟨stereo*metry*⟩ **2a** stereoscope ⟨stereo*psis*⟩ ⟨stereo*graphy*⟩ **b** having, involving, or dealing with 3 dimensions of space ⟨stereo*chemistry*⟩ [NL, fr Gk, fr *stereos* solid – more at STARE]

¹stereo /'sterioh, 'stiərioh/ *n, pl* **stereos** **1** a stereoscopic method, system, or effect **2a** stereophonic reproduction **b** a stereophonic sound system [(1) short for *stereoscopy*; (2) short for *stereophonic*]

²stereo *adj* **1** stereoscopic **2** stereophonic

'stereo,bate /-,bayt/ *n* a solid structure of masonry used as a foundation [F or L; F *stéréobate*, fr L *stereobata* foundation, fr Gk *stereobatēs*, fr *stere-* + *bainein* to step, go – more at COME]

,stereo'chemistry /-'kemistri/ *n* (a branch of chemistry that deals with) the spatial arrangement of atoms and groups in molecules [ISV] – **stereochemical** /-'kemikl/ *adj*, **stereochemically** *adv*

stereography /,steri'ografi, ,stiəri-/ *n* the art, process, or technique of drawing solid bodies on a plane surface – **stereographic** /-ri·ə'grafik/ *adj*, **stereographically** *adv*

stereoisomer /sterioh'iesəmə, stiəri-/ *n* any of a group of related isomers of a molecule in which atoms are linked in the same order but differ in their spatial arrangement [ISV] – **stereoisomeric** /-,iesoh'merik/ *adj*, **stereoisomerism** /-ie'somə,riz(ə)m/ *n*

stereophonic /,steri·ə'fonik, ,stiəri-, -rioh-/ *adj* of or being (a system for) sound reproduction in which the sound is split into and reproduced by 2 different channels to give spatial effect [ISV] – **stereophonically** *adv*, **stereophony** /-ri'ofəni/ *n*

stereoscope /'steri·ə,skohp, 'stiəri·ə-/ *n* an optical instrument with 2 eyepieces through which the observer views 2 pictures taken from points of view a little way apart to get the effect of a single three-dimensional picture

stereoscopy /,steri'oskəpi, ,stiəri-/ *n* the seeing of objects in 3 dimensions [ISV] – **stereoscopic** /-ri·ə'skopik/ *adj*, **stereoscopically** *adv*

¹stereo,type /'steri·ə,tiep, 'stiəri-/ *n* **1** a plate made by making a cast, usu in type metal, from a mould of a printing surface **2** sby who or sthg that conforms to a fixed or general pattern; *esp* a standardized, usu oversimplified, mental picture or attitude held in common by members of a group [F *stéréotype*, fr *stéré-* stere- + *type*] – **stereotypical** /-'tipikl/ *also* **stereotypic** *adj*

²stereotype *vt* **1** to make a stereotype from **2a** to repeat without variation; make hackneyed **b** to develop a mental stereotype about – **stereotyper** *n*

'stereo,typed *adj* lacking originality or individuality

steric /'stiərik, 'sterik/ *adj* of or involving the arrangement of atoms in space [ISV *stere-* + *-ic*] – **sterically** *adv*

sterile /'steriel/ *adj* **1** failing or not able to produce or bear fruit, crops, or offspring **2a** deficient in ideas or originality **b** free from living organisms, esp microorganisms **3** bringing no rewards or results; not productive ⟨*the* ~ *search for jobs*⟩ [L *sterilis*; akin to Goth *stairo* sterile, Gk *steira*] – **sterilely** *adv*, **sterilize** /'steriliez/ *vt*, **sterilizable** *adj*, **sterilizer** *n*, **sterilant** *n*, **sterilization** /-'zaysh(ə)n/ *n*, **sterility** /stə'riləti/ *n*

¹sterling /'stuhling/ *n* **1** British money **2** (articles of) sterling silver [ME, silver penny]

²sterling *adj* **1** of or calculated in terms of British sterling **2a** *of silver* having a fixed standard of purity; *specif* 92.5 per cent pure **b** made of sterling silver **3** conforming to the highest standard ⟨~ *character*⟩

sterling area *n* a group of countries whose currencies are tied to British sterling

¹stern /stuhn/ *adj* **1a** hard or severe in nature or manner; austere **b** expressive of severe displeasure; harsh **2** forbidding or gloomy in appearance **3** inexorable, relentless ⟨~ *necessity*⟩ **4** sturdy, firm ⟨*a* ~ *resolve*⟩ [ME *sterne*, fr OE *styrne*; akin to OE *starian* to stare] – **sternly** *adv*, **sternness** *n*

²stern *n* **1** the rear end of a ship or boat – compare STEM ☞ SHIP **2** a back or rear part; the last or latter part [ME, rudder, prob of Scand origin; akin to ON *stjórn* act of steering; akin to OE *stīeran* to steer – more at ²STEER] – **sternmost** *adj*, **sternwards** /-woodz/ *adv*

'stern,post /-,pohst/ *n* the principal supporting structure at the stern of a ship extending from keel to deck

sternum /'stuhnəm/ *n, pl* **sternums, sterna** /-nə/ a bone or cartilage at the front of the body that connects the ribs, both sides of the shoulder girdle, or both; the breastbone ☞ ANATOMY [NL, fr Gk *sternon* chest, breastbone; akin to OHG *stirna* forehead, L *sternere* to spread out – more at STREW] – **sternal** *adj*

sternutation /,stuhnyoo'taysh(ə)n/ *n* sneezing – used technically [L *sternutation-, sternutatio*, fr *sternutatus*, pp of *sternutare* to sneeze, fr *sternutus*, pp of *sternuere* to sneeze; akin to Gk *ptarnysthai* to sneeze] – **sternutatory** /stuh'nyoohtət(ə)ri/ *adj*

sternutator /'stuhnyoo,taytə/ *n* sthg (e g an irritant gas) that induces sneezing and often tears and vomiting

sternway /'stuhn,way/ *n* backwards movement of a ship

,stern-'wheeler *n* a steamer having a paddle wheel at the stern

steroid /'steroyd, 'stiə-/ *n* any of numerous compounds of similar chemical structure, including the sterols and various hormones (e g testosterone) and glycosides (e g digitalis) [ISV *sterol* + *-oid*] – **steroidal** /stə'roydl/ *adj*

sterol /'sterol/ *n* any of various solid alcohols (e g cholesterol) widely distributed in animal and plant fats [ISV, fr *-sterol* (as in *cholesterol*)]

stertorous /'stuhtərəs/ *adj* characterized by a harsh snoring or gasping sound [NL *stertor* act of snoring, fr L *stertere* to snore; akin to L *sternuere* to sneeze] – **stertorously** *adv*

stet /stet/ *vt* **-tt-** to direct retention of (a word or passage previously ordered to be deleted or omitted) by annotating, usu with the word *stet* [L, let it stand, fr *stare* to stand – more at STAND]

stethoscope /'stethə,skohp/ *n* an instrument used to detect and study sounds produced in the body [F *stéthoscope*, fr Gk *stēthos* chest + F *-scope*] – **stethoscopic** /-'skopik/ *adj*, **stethoscopically** *adv*, **stethoscopy** /ste'thoskəpi/ *n*

stetson /'stets(ə)n/ *n* a broad-brimmed high-crowned felt hat [fr *Stetson*, a trademark]

¹stevedore /'steevədaw/ *n* a docker [Sp *estibador*, fr *estibar* to pack, fr L *stipare* to press together – more at STIFF]

²stevedore *vb* to handle (cargo) as a stevedore; *also* to load or unload the cargo of (a ship) in port

¹stew /styooh/ *n* **1a** a savoury dish, usu of meat and vegetables stewed and served in the same liquid **b** a mixture composed of many usu unrelated parts **2** a state of excitement, worry, or confusion – infml [ME *stu* cauldron, heated room, brothel, fr MF *estuve*, fr (assumed) VL *extufa*, fr *extufare* to stew]

²stew *vt* to cook (e g meat or fruit) slowly by boiling gently or simmering in liquid ~ *vi* **1** to become cooked by stewing **2** to swelter, esp from confinement in a hot atmosphere **3** to become agitated or worried; fret *USE* (*vi 2&3*) infml

¹steward /'styooh·əd/ *n* **1** one employed to look after a large household or estate **2** SHOP STEWARD **3a** one who manages the provisioning of food and attends to the needs of passengers (e g on an airliner, ship, or train) **b** one who supervises the provision and distribution of food and drink in a club, college, etc **4** an official who actively directs affairs (e g at a race meeting) [ME, fr OE *stīweard*, fr *stī* hall, sty + *weard* ward] – **stewardship** *n*

²steward *vb* to act as a steward (for)

stewardess /'styooh·ədis, ,styooh·ə'des/ *n* a woman who performs the duties of a steward; *esp* HOSTESS 2a

stewed /styoohd/ *adj* **1** *of tea* bitter-tasting because allowed to infuse for too long **2** DRUNK 1 – infml

stibnite /'stibniet/ *n* a sulphide of antimony occurring as a lead-grey mineral [alter. of obs *stibine*, fr F, fr L *stibium* antimony, fr Gk *stibi*, fr Egypt *sṭm*]

¹stick /stik/ *n* **1a** a (dry and dead) cut or broken branch or twig **b** a cut or broken branch or piece of wood gathered esp for fuel or construction material **2a** a long slender piece of wood: e g **(1)** a club or staff used as a weapon **(2)** a walking stick **b** an implement used for striking an object in a game (e g hockey) **c** sthg used to force compliance **d** a baton symbolizing an office or dignity; a rod **3** any of various implements resembling a stick in shape, origin, or use: e g **a** COMPOSING STICK **b** a joystick **4** sthg prepared (e g by cutting, moulding, or rolling) in a relatively long and slender often cylindrical form ⟨*a* ~ *of toffee*⟩ **5** a person of a specified type ⟨*a decent old* ~ – Robert Graves⟩ **6** a stick-shaped plant stalk (e g of rhubarb or celery) **7** several bombs, parachutists, etc released from an aircraft in quick succession **8** *pl the* wooded or rural and usu backward districts **9** a piece of furniture **10** *Br* hostile comment or activity ⟨*gave the Local Authority plenty of* ~⟩ *USE* (*8, 9, &10*) infml [ME *stik*, fr OE *sticca*; akin to ON *stik* stick, OE *stician* to stick]

²stick *vt* to provide a stick as a support for (e g a plant)

³stick *vb* **stuck** /stuk/ *vt* **1a** to pierce with sthg pointed; stab **b** to kill by piercing ⟨~ *a pig*⟩ **2a** to push or thrust so as or as if to pierce **b** to fasten in position (as if) by piercing ⟨stuck *a pistol in his belt*⟩ **3** to push, thrust ⟨stuck *his head out of the window*⟩ **4** to cover or adorn (as if) by sticking things on ⟨*a crown* stuck *with rubies*⟩ **5** to attach (as if) by causing to adhere to a surface **6a** to halt the movement or action of **b** to baffle, stump ⟨*got* stuck *doing his maths homework*⟩ **7** to put or set in a specified place or position ⟨~ *your coat over there*⟩ **8** to refrain from granting, giving, or allowing (sthg indignantly rejected by the speaker); stuff ⟨*you can* ~ *the job for all I care!*⟩ **9** to saddle with sthg disadvantageous or disagreeable ⟨*why do I always get* stuck *with the gardening?*⟩ **10** *chiefly Br* to bear, stand ⟨*can't ~ his voice*⟩ ~ *vi* **1a** to become fixed in place by means of a pointed end **b** to become fast (as if) by adhesion ⟨stuck *in the mud*⟩ **2a** to remain in a place, situation, or environment ⟨*don't want to ~ in this job for the rest of my life*⟩ **b** to hold fast or adhere resolutely; cling ⟨*~ to the truth*⟩ **c** to remain effective ⟨*the charge will not ~*⟩ **d** to keep close in a chase or competition ⟨~ing *with the leaders*⟩ **3** to become blocked, wedged, or jammed **4a** to hesitate, stop ⟨*would ~ at nothing to get what they wanted*⟩ **b** to be unable to proceed **5** to project, protrude – often + *out* or *up* *USE* (*vt 7, 8, 9, & 10*) infml [ME *stikken*, fr OE *stician*; akin to OHG *sticken* to prick, L *instigare* to urge on, goad, Gk *stizein* to tattoo] – **stick by** to continue to support – **stick one's neck out** to take a risk (e g by saying sthg unpopular) and make oneself vulnerable – infml – **stuck on** infatuated with ⟨*he's really* stuck on *her*⟩ – infml

[4]**stick** *n* adhesive quality or substance

stick around *vi* to stay or wait about; linger – infml

sticker /ˈstikə/ *n* **1** sby who or sthg that pierces with a point **2a** sby who or sthg that sticks or causes sticking **b** a slip of paper with gummed back that, when moistened, sticks to a surface

stick figure *n* a stylized drawing of a human being showing the body or limbs as straight lines

sticking plaster *n* an adhesive plaster, esp for covering superficial wounds

sticking point *n* an item resulting or likely to result in an impasse

ˈstick ˌinsect *n* any of various usu wingless insects with a long thin body resembling a stick ☞ DEFENCE

ˈstick-in-the-ˌmud *n* one who dislikes and avoids change

stickleback /ˈstikl,bak/ *n* any of numerous small scaleless fishes that have 2 or more spines in front of the dorsal fin [ME *stykylbak*, fr OE *sticel* goad (akin to OE *stician* to stick) + ME *bak* back]

stickler /ˈstiklə/ *n* one who insists on exactness or completeness in the observance of sthg ⟨*a ~ for obedience*⟩ [*stickle* (to act as umpire, contend, scruple), fr ME *stightlen* to arrange, strive, freq of *stighten* to arrange, fr OE *stihtan*; akin to OE *stǣger* stair – more at STAIR]

stick out *vi* **1** to be prominent or conspicuous – often in *stick out a mile, stick out like a sore thumb* **2** to be persistent (e g in a demand or an opinion) – usu + *for* ~ *vt* to endure to the end – often + *it*

stick up *vt* to rob at gunpoint – infml – **stickup** *n* – **stick up for** to speak or act in defence of; support

sticky /ˈstiki/ *adj* **1a** adhesive ⟨*~ tape*⟩ **b(1)** viscous, gluey **(2)** coated with a sticky substance ⟨*~ hands*⟩ **2** humid, muggy; *also* clammy **3a** disagreeable, unpleasant ⟨*came to a ~ end*⟩ **b** awkward, stiff ⟨*after a ~ beginning became good friends*⟩ **c** difficult, problematic ⟨*a rather ~ question*⟩ – **stickily** *adv*, **stickiness** *n*

ˌsticky ˈwicket *n* **1** a cricket pitch drying after rain and therefore difficult to bat on **2** a difficult situation – infml; often in *on a sticky wicket*

[1]**stiff** /stif/ *adj* **1a** not easily bent; rigid **b** lacking in suppleness and often painful ⟨*~ muscles*⟩ **c** *of a mechanism* impeded in movement **d** incapable of normal alert response ⟨*scared ~*⟩ **2a** firm, unyielding **b(1)** marked by reserve or decorum; formal **(2)** lacking in ease or grace; stilted **3** hard fought ⟨*a ~ match*⟩ **4a** exerting great force; forceful ⟨*a ~ wind*⟩ **b** potent ⟨*a ~ drink*⟩ **5** of a dense or glutinous consistency; thick **6a** harsh, severe ⟨*a ~ penalty*⟩ **b** arduous ⟨*a ~ climb*⟩ **7** expensive, steep ⟨*paid a ~ price*⟩ [ME *stif*, fr OE *stīf*; akin to MD *stijf* stiff, L *stipare* to press together, Gk *steibein* to tread on] – **stiffen** *vb*, **stiffener** *n*, **stiffening** *n*, **stiffish** *adj*, **stiffly** *adv*, **stiffness** *n*

[2]**stiff** *adv* in a stiff manner; stiffly

[3]**stiff** *n* a corpse – slang

ˌstiff-ˈnecked *adj* haughty, stubborn

stiff upper lip *n* the facing of misfortune impassively or without appearing perturbed

[1]**stifle** /ˈstiefl/ *n* the joint next above the hock in the hind leg of a quadruped (e g a horse) corresponding to the knee in human beings [ME]

[2]**stifle** *vb* **stifling** /ˈstiefling/ *vt* **1a** to overcome or kill by depriving of oxygen; suffocate, smother **b** to muffle ⟨*~ noises*⟩ **2a** to cut off (e g the voice or breath) **b** to prevent the development or expression of; check, suppress ⟨~d *his anger*⟩ ⟨*~ a revolt*⟩ ~ *vi* to become suffocated (as if) by lack of oxygen [alter. of ME *stuflen*] – **stiflingly** *adv*

stigma /ˈstigmə/ *n, pl* **stigmata** /stigˈmahtə, ˈstigmətə/, **stigmas,** (*2*) **stigmata** **1a** a mark of shame or discredit **b** an identifying mark or characteristic; *specif* a specific diagnostic sign of a disease **2** *pl* marks resembling the wounds of the crucified Christ, believed to be impressed on the bodies of holy or saintly people **3a** a small spot, scar, or opening on a plant or animal **b** the portion of the female part of a flower which receives the pollen grains and on which they germinate ☞ PLANT [L *stigmat-*, *stigma* mark, brand, fr Gk, fr *stizein* to tattoo – more at [3]STICK] – **stigmatic** /-ˈmatik/ *adj*, **stigmatically** *adv*

stigmatic /stigˈmatik/, **stigmatist** /ˈstigmətist, stigˈmahtist/ *n* a person marked with the stigmata of Christ

stigmat·ize, -ise /ˈstigmətiez/ *vt* **1** to describe or identify in disparaging terms **2** to mark with the stigmata of Christ – **stigmatization** /-ˈzaysh(ə)n/ *n*

stilboestrol, *NAm* **stilbestrol** /stilˈbeestrəl/ *n* a synthetic compound used as an oestrogenic drug [*stilbene* (an aromatic hydrocarbon) + *oestrus* + *-ol*]

[1]**stile** /stiel/ *n* **1** a step or set of steps for passing over a fence or wall **2** a turnstile [ME, fr OE *stigel*; akin to OE *stǣger* stair – more at STAIR]

[2]**stile** *n* any of the vertical members in a frame or panel into which the secondary members are fitted ☞ ARCHITECTURE [prob fr D *stijl* post]

stiletto /stiˈletoh/ *n, pl* **stilettos, stilettoes** **1** a slender rodlike dagger **2** a pointed instrument for piercing holes (e g for eyelets) in leather, cloth, etc **3** *Br* an extremely narrow tapering high heel on a woman's shoe [It, dim. of *stilo* stylus, dagger, fr L *stilus* stylus – more at STYLE]

[1]**still** /stil/ *adj* **1a** devoid of or abstaining from motion ⟨*~ water*⟩ **b** having no effervescence; not carbonated ⟨*~ orange*⟩ **c** of, being, or designed for taking a static photograph as contrasted with a moving picture **2a** uttering no sound; quiet **b** low in sound; subdued **3a** calm, tranquil **b** free from noise or turbulence [ME *stille*, fr OE; akin to OHG *stilli* still, OE *steall* stall] – **stillness** *n*

²still *vt* **1a** to allay, calm **b** to put an end to; settle **2** to arrest the motion or noise of; quiet ⟨~ *the wind*⟩ ~ *vi* to become motionless or silent; quiet *USE* chiefly poetic

³still *adv* **1** as before; even at this or that time ⟨*drink it while it's* ~ *hot*⟩ **2** in spite of that; nevertheless ⟨*very unpleasant;* ~, *we can't help it*⟩ **3a** EVEN 2b ⟨*a* ~ *more difficult problem*⟩ **b** YET 1a

⁴still *n* **1** a still photograph; *specif* a photograph of actors or of a scene from a film **2** quiet, silence – chiefly poetic

⁵still *n* an apparatus used in distillation, esp of spirits, consisting of either the chamber in which the vaporization is carried out or the entire equipment [ME *stillen* to distil, short for *distillen*]

stillage /ˈstilij/ *n* a stand or frame on which articles are kept off the floor (e g while drying or awaiting packing) [modif of D *stellage* scaffolding, fr MD, fr *stellen* to place]

ˈstill,birth /-,buhth/ *n* the birth of a dead infant

,stillˈborn /-ˈbawn/ *adj* **1** dead at birth **2** failing from the start; abortive – **stillborn** /ˈ-,-/ *n*

,still ˈlife *n, pl* **still lifes** a picture showing an arrangement of inanimate objects (e g fruit or flowers)

¹stilly /ˈstil·li/ *adv* in a calm manner [¹*still* + ²*-ly*]

²stilly /ˈstili/ *adj* still, quiet – poetic [⁴*still* + *-y*]

stilt /stilt/ *n pl* **stilts,** (*2*) **stilts,** *esp collectively* **stilt** **1a** either of 2 poles each with a rest or strap for the foot, that enable the user to walk along above the ground **b** any of a set of piles, posts, etc that support a building above ground or water level **2** any of various notably long-legged 3-toed wading birds related to the avocets [ME *stilte*; akin to OHG *stelza* stilt, OE *steall* position, stall – more at ¹STALL]

stilted /ˈstiltid/ *adj* stiffly formal and often pompous [fr pp of *stilt* (to raise on or as if on stilts)] – **stiltedly** *adv,* **stiltedness** *n*

Stilton /ˈstilt(ə)n/ *n* a cream-enriched white cheese that has a wrinkled rind and is often blue-veined [*Stilton,* village in Cambridgeshire, England, where it was orig sold]

stimulant /ˈstimyooələnt/ *n* **1** sthg (e g a drug) that produces a temporary increase in the functional activity or efficiency of (a part of) an organism **2** STIMULUS 1 – **stimulant** *adj*

stimulate /ˈstimyoo,layt/ *vt* **1** to excite to (greater) activity **2a** to function as a physiological stimulus to **b** to arouse or affect by the action of a stimulant (e g a drug) ~ *vi* to act as a stimulant or stimulus [L *stimulatus,* pp of *stimulare,* fr *stimulus* goad; akin to L *stilus* stake, stylus – more at STYLE] – **stimulator** *n,* **stimulative** /-lətiv/ *adj,* **stimulation** /-ˈlaysh(ə)n/ *n*

stimulus /ˈstimyooləs/ *n, pl* **stimuli** /-li, -lie/ **1** sthg that rouses or incites to activity; an incentive **2** sthg (e g light) that directly influences the activity of living organisms (e g by exciting a sensory organ or evoking muscular contraction or glandular secretion) [L]

¹sting /sting/ *vb* **stung** /stung/ *vt* **1a** to give an irritating or poisonous wound to, esp with a sting ⟨stung *by a bee*⟩ **b** to affect with sharp quick pain ⟨*hail* stung *their faces*⟩ **2** to cause to suffer acute mental pain ⟨stung *with remorse*⟩; *also* to incite or goad thus ⟨stung *into action*⟩ **3** to overcharge, cheat ⟨stung *by a street trader*⟩ – infml ~ *vi* **1** to use a sting; to have stings ⟨*nettles* ~⟩ **2** to feel a sharp burning pain [ME *stingen,* fr OE *stingan*; akin to ON *stinga* to sting, Gk *stachys* spike of grain, *stochos* target, aim] – **stingingly** *adv*

²sting *n* **1a** a stinging; *specif* the thrust of a sting into the flesh **b** a wound or pain caused (as if) by stinging **2** *also* **stinger** a sharp organ of a bee, scorpion, stingray, etc that is usu connected with a poison gland or otherwise adapted to wound by piercing and injecting a poisonous secretion **3** a stinging element, force, or quality ⟨*a joke with a* ~ *in the tail*⟩ – **stingless** *n*

stingo /ˈsting·goh/ *n, chiefly Br* a strong beer [irreg fr ²*sting*]

ˈsting,ray /-,ray/ *n* any of numerous rays with a whiplike tail having 1 or more large sharp spines capable of inflicting severe wounds

stingy /ˈstinji/ *adj* **1** mean or ungenerous in giving or spending **2** meanly scanty or small [prob fr (assumed) E dial. *stinge* (sting); akin to OE *stingan* to sting] – **stingily** *adv,* **stinginess** *n*

¹stink /stingk/ *vi* **stank** /stangk/, **stunk** /stungk/; **stunk** **1** to emit a strong offensive smell **2** to be offensive; *also* to be in bad repute or of bad quality **3** to possess sthg to an offensive degree – usu + *with* ⟨*he* ~s *with money*⟩ *USE* (*except 1*) infml [ME *stinken,* fr OE *stincan*; akin to OHG *stinkan* to emit a smell] – **stinky** *adj*

²stink *n* **1** a strong offensive smell; a stench **2** a public outcry against sthg offensive – infml

ˈstink-,bomb *n, Br* a small capsule which emits a foul smell when broken

stinker /ˈstingkə/ *n* **1** an offensive or contemptible person **2** sthg extremely difficult or unpleasant ⟨*the examination was a real* ~⟩ *USE* infml [¹STINK + ²-ER]

ˈstink,horn /-,hawn/ *n* a fungus noted for its foul smell

¹stinking /ˈstingking/ *adj* **1** severe and unpleasant ⟨*a* ~ *cold*⟩ – infml **2** offensively drunk – slang

²stinking *adv* to an extreme degree ⟨*got* ~ *drunk*⟩ – infml

stinking mayweed /ˈmay,weed/ *n* a foul-smelling Eurasian composite plant with white and yellow flowers [*mayweed* fr *may-* (fr ME *maythe,* a composite plant, fr OE *mægtha*) + *weed*]

stink out *vt* **1** to cause to stink or be filled with a stench ⟨*the leaking gas* stank *the house* out⟩ **2** to drive out (as if) by subjecting to an offensive or suffocating smell

ˈstink,weed /-,weed/ *n* any of various strong-scented or foetid plants

ˈstink,wood /-,wood/ *n* (the unpleasant-smelling wood of) a S African tree of the laurel family; *also* any of several similar trees

¹stint /stint/ *vt* to restrict to a small share or allowance; be frugal with ~ *vi* to be sparing or frugal [ME *stinten* to stop, fr OE *styntan* to blunt, dull; akin to ON *stuttr* scant, L *tundere* to beat, OE *stocc* stock] – **stinter** *n*

²stint *n* **1** restraint, limitation **2** a definite quantity or period of work assigned

³stint *n, pl* **stints,** *esp collectively* **stint** any of several small sandpipers [ME *stynte*]

stipe /stiep/ *n* a usu short plant stalk (e g supporting the cap of a fungus) [NL *stipes,* fr L, tree trunk; akin to L *stipare* to press together – more at STIFF] – **stiped** *adj*

stipend /ˈstiepend/ *n* a fixed sum of money paid periodically (e g to a clergyman) as a salary or to meet expenses [alter. of ME *stipendy*, fr L *stipendium*, fr *stip-*, *stips* gift + *pendere* to weigh, pay – more at PENDANT]

[1]**stipendiary** /stie'pendyəri, sti-/ *adj* of or receiving a stipend

[2]**stipendiary** *n* one who receives a stipend

stipendiary magistrate *n* a legally qualified paid magistrate

stipes /'stiepeez/ *n, pl* **stipites** /'stipi,teez/ a peduncle [NL *stipit-*, *stipes*, fr L, tree trunk – more at STIPE] – **stipitate** /'stipi,tayt/ *adj*

[1]**stipple** /'stipl/ *vt* **stippling** /'stipling, 'stipl·ing/ **1a** to paint, engrave, or draw in stipple **b** to apply (e g paint) in stipple **2** to speckle, fleck [D *stippelen* to spot, dot; akin to L *stipare* to press together] – **stippler** *n*

[2]**stipple** *n* (the effect produced by) a method of painting using small points, dots, or strokes to represent degrees of light and shade

stipulate /'stipyoo,layt/ *vt* **1** to specify as a condition or requirement of an agreement or offer ⟨~ *quality and quantity*⟩ **2** to give a guarantee of in making an agreement [L *stipulatus*, pp of *stipulari* to demand some term in an agreement] – **stipulator** *n* – **stipulate for** to demand as an express term in an agreement ⟨*we* stipulated for *marble*⟩

stipulation /,stipyoo'laysh(ə)n/ *n* sthg (e g a condition) stipulated [STIPULATE + -ION] – **stipulatory** /'stipyoolət(ə)ri/ *adj*

stipule /'stipyoohl/ *n* a small appendage at the base of the leaf in many plants [NL *stipula*, fr L, stalk; akin to L *stipes* tree trunk] – **stipular** *adj*, **stipulated, stipulate** /-lət, -,layt/ *adj*

[1]**stir** /stuh/ *vb* **-rr-** *vt* **1a** to cause a slight movement or change of position of ⟨*the breeze* ~red *the leaves*⟩ **b** to disturb the quiet of; agitate **2a** to disturb the relative position of the particles or parts of (a fluid or semifluid), esp by a continued circular movement in order to make the composition homogeneous ⟨~ *one's tea*⟩ **b** to mix (as if) by stirring ⟨~ *pigment into paint*⟩ **3** to bestir, exert ⟨*unable to* ~ *himself to wash the car*⟩ **4a** to rouse to activity; produce strong feelings in ⟨*the news* ~red *him to action*⟩ **b** to provoke – often + *up* ⟨~ *up trouble*⟩ ~ *vi* **1a** to make a slight movement **b** to begin to move (e g in waking) **2** to (begin to) be active or busy **3** to pass an implement through a substance with a circular movement [ME *stiren*, fr OE *styrian*; akin to MHG *stürn* to incite] – **stirrer** *n*

[2]**stir** *n* **1a** a state of disturbance, agitation, or brisk activity **b** widespread notice and discussion ⟨*caused quite a* ~ *in the neighbourhood*⟩ **2** a slight movement **3** a stirring movement

[3]**stir** *n* prison – slang [origin unknown]

'stir-,frying *n* a Chinese method of cooking in which small pieces of food are stirred together while being rapidly fried in hot oil – **stir-fry** *vt*

stirk /stuhk/ *n, Br* a young (1- to 2-year old) bull or cow [ME, fr OE *stirc*; akin to L *sterilis* sterile]

stirps /stuhps/ *n, pl* **stirpes** /'stuhpeez/ a race, variety, etc in the biological classification of living things [L, lit., stem, stock – more at TORPID]

stirring /'stuhring/ *adj* rousing, inspiring

stirrup /'stirəp/ *n* **1** STIRRUP IRON **2** the stapes ☞ NERVE **3** a short rope by which another rope is suspended from the yard of a sailing ship for seamen to walk along ☞ SHIP [ME *stirop*, fr OE *stigrāp*; akin to OHG *stegareif* stirrup; both fr a prehistoric NGmc-WGmc compound whose first element is akin to OHG *stīgan* to go up and whose second is represented by OE *rāp* rope – more at STAIR]

'stirrup ,cup *n* a farewell usu alcoholic drink; *specif* one taken on horseback

'stirrup ,iron *n* either of a pair of D-shaped metal frames that are attached by a strap to a saddle and in which the rider's feet are placed

'stirrup ,leather *n* the strap from which a stirrup iron is suspended

'stirrup ,pump *n* a portable hand pump held in position by a foot bracket and used esp in fire fighting

[1]**stitch** /stich/ *n* **1** a local sharp and sudden pain, esp in the side **2a** a single in-and-out movement of a threaded needle in sewing, embroidering, or suturing **b** a portion of thread left in the material after 1 stitch **3a** a single loop of thread or yarn round a stitching implement **b** such a loop after being worked to form 1 of a series of links in a fabric **4** a series of stitches that are formed in a particular manner or constitute a complete step or design **5** a method of stitching **6** the least scrap of clothing – usu neg ⟨*without a* ~ *on*⟩; infml [ME *stiche*, fr OE *stice*; akin to OE *stician* to stick] – **in stitches** in a state of uncontrollable laughter

[2]**stitch** *vt* **1** to fasten, join, or close (as if) with stitches; sew **2** to work on or decorate (as if) with stitches ~ *vi* to sew – **stitcher** *n*

'stitch,wort /-,wuht/ *n* any of several large chickweeds ☞ PLANT [ME *stichewort*, fr OE *sticwyrt* agrimony, fr *stice* stab, puncture, stitch in the side + *wyrt* herb – more at STITCH, WORT]

stithy /'stidhi/ *n* a smithy [ME, anvil, fr ON *stethi*; akin to OE *stede* stead]

stoat /stoht/ *n, pl* **stoats,** *esp collectively* **stoat** a European weasel with a long black-tipped tail [ME *stote*]

stochastic /stoh'kastik/ *adj* **1** random; *specif* involving a random variable ⟨*a* ~ *process*⟩ **2** involving chance or probability ⟨*a* ~ *model of radiation-induced mutation*⟩ [Gk *stochastikos* skilful in aiming, fr *stochazesthai* to aim at, guess at, fr *stochos* target, aim, guess – more at STING] – **stochastically** *adv*

[1]**stock** /stok/ *n* **1** a supporting framework or structure: e g **a** *pl* the frame or timbers holding a ship during construction **b** *pl* a wooden frame with holes for the feet (and hands) in which offenders are held for public punishment **c(1)** the part to which the barrel and firing mechanism of a gun are attached **(2)** the butt (e g of a whip or fishing rod) **d** the beam of a plough to which handles, cutting blades, and mouldboard are attached **2a** the main stem of a plant or tree **b(1)** a plant (part) consisting of roots and lower trunk onto which a scion is grafted **(2)** a plant from which cuttings are taken **3** the crosspiece of an anchor **4a** the original (e g a man, race, or language) from which others derive; a source **b(1)** the descendants of an individual; family, lineage **(2)** a compound organism **c** [3]RACE 2, 3a **d** a group of closely related languages **5a** *sing or pl in constr* livestock **b** a store or supply accumulated (e g of raw materials or finished goods) **6a** a debt or fund due (e g from a government) for money loaned at interest; *also, Br* capital or a debt or fund which continues to bear interest but is not usually redeemable as far as the original sum is concerned **b** (preference) shares –

often pl **7** any of a genus of plants of the mustard family with usu sweet-scented flowers **8** a wide band or scarf worn round the neck, esp by some clergymen **9a** the liquid in which meat, fish, or vegetables have been simmered that is used as a basis for soup, gravy, etc **b** raw material from which sthg is made **10a** an estimate or appraisal of sthg ⟨*take ~ of the situation*⟩ **b** the estimation in which sby or sthg is held ⟨*his ~ with the electorate remains high – Newsweek*⟩ **11** a type of brick [ME *stok*, fr OE *stocc* tree-trunk, stump, block of wood; akin to OHG *stoc* stick, MIr *tūag* bow] – **in stock** in the shop and ready for delivery; ON HAND – **out of stock** having no more on hand; sold out

²**stock** *vt* **1** to fit to or with a stock **2** to provide with (a) stock; supply ⟨*~ a stream with trout*⟩ **3** to procure or keep a stock of ⟨*we don't ~ that brand*⟩ *~ vi* to take in a stock – often + *up* ⟨*~ up on tinned food*⟩

³**stock** *adj* **1a** kept in stock regularly ⟨*clearance sale of ~ goods*⟩ **b** regularly and widely available or supplied ⟨*dresses in all the ~ sizes*⟩ **2** used for (breeding and rearing) livestock ⟨*a ~ farm*⟩ **3** commonly used or brought forward; standard – chiefly derog ⟨*the ~ answer*⟩

¹**stockade** /sto'kayd/ *n* **1** a line of stout posts set vertically to form a defence **2** an enclosure or pen made with posts and stakes [Sp *estacada*, fr *estaca* stake, pale, of Gmc origin; akin to OE *staca* stake]

²**stockade** *vt* to fortify or surround with a stockade

stockbreeder /'stok,breedə/ *n* one who breeds livestock – **stockbreeding** *n*

'**stock,broker** /-,brohkə/ *n* a broker who buys and sells securities – **stockbroking, stockbrokerage** *n*

'**stockbroker ,belt** *n* an area on the outskirts of a large town or city that is inhabited chiefly by wealthy middle-class people

'**stock ,car** *n* a racing car having the chassis of a commercially produced assembly-line model

'**stock ,dove** *n* a Eurasian dove that is smaller and darker than a woodpigeon [ME *stokdove*, fr *stok* stock + *dove* dove; prob fr its nesting in hollow tree-trunks]

'**stock ex,change** *n* (a building occupied by) an association of people organized to provide an auction market among themselves for the purchase and sale of securities

'**stock,fish** /-,fish/ *n* cod, haddock, etc dried in the open air without salt [ME *stokfish*, fr MD *stocvisch*, fr *stoc* stick + *visch* fish]

stockinet, stockinette /,stoki'net/ *n* a soft elastic usu cotton fabric used esp for bandages [alter. of earlier *stocking net*]

stocking /'stoking/ *n* **1** a usu knitted close-fitting often nylon covering for the foot and leg **2** an area of distinctive colour on the lower part of the leg of an animal [obs *stock* to cover with a stocking] – **stockinged** *adj*

'**stocking ,stitch** *n* a knitting stitch made by alternately knitting and purling rows of stitches to form a fabric with an even surface and uniform pattern

,**stock-in-'trade** *n* **1** the equipment necessary to or used in a trade or business **2** sthg like the standard equipment of a tradesman or business ⟨*the tact and charm that are the ~ of a successful society hostess*⟩

stockist /'stokist/ *n, Br* one (e g a retailer) who stocks goods, esp of a particular kind or brand

'**stock,jobber** /-,jobə/ *n* a stock-exchange member who deals only with brokers or other jobbers

'**stockman** /-mən/ *n, Austr & NAm* one who owns or takes care of livestock

'**stock ,market** *n* STOCK EXCHANGE; *also* transactions on it

¹'**stock,pile** /-,piel/ *n* an accumulated store; *esp* a reserve supply of sthg essential accumulated for use during a shortage

²**stockpile** *vt* **1** to place or store in or on a stockpile **2** to accumulate a stockpile of

'**stock,pot** /-,pot/ *n* a pot in which stock is prepared or kept

'**stock ,saddle** *n* a deep-seated saddle with a high pommel used orig by cattlemen

,**stock-'still** *adj* completely motionless ⟨*stood ~*⟩

'**stock,taking** /-,tayking/ *n* **1** the checking or taking of an inventory of goods or supplies on hand (e g in a shop) **2** estimating a situation at a given moment (e g by considering past progress and resources)

stocky /'stoki/ *adj* short, sturdy, and relatively thick in build – **stockily** *adv*, **stockiness** *n*

'**stock,yard** /-,yahd/ *n* a yard in which cattle, pigs, horses, etc are kept temporarily for slaughter, market, or shipping

stodge /stoj/ *n* **1** filling (starchy) food **2** turgid and unimaginative writing – infml [origin unknown]

stodgy /'stoji/ *adj* **1** *of food* heavy and filling **2** dull, boring ⟨*a ~ novel*⟩ – infml – **stodgily** *adv*, **stodginess** *n*

stoep /stoohp/ *n, SAfr* a raised veranda or open porch [Afrik, fr MD – more at ³STOOP]

stogie, stogy /'stohji/ *n, chiefly NAm* a (roughly made slender inexpensive) cigar [*Conestoga*, town in Pennsylvania, USA]

¹**stoic** /'stoh·ik/ *n* **1** *cap* a member of an ancient Greek or Roman school of philosophy equating happiness with knowledge and holding that wisdom consists in self-mastery and submission to natural law **2** sby apparently or professedly indifferent to pleasure or pain [ME, fr L *stoicus*, fr Gk *stōikos*, lit., of the portico, fr *Stoa* (*Poikilē*) the Painted Portico, portico at Athens where Zeno taught]

²**stoic, stoical** /-kl/ *adj* **1** *cap* (characteristic) of the Stoics or their doctrines **2** not affected by or showing passion or feeling; *esp* firmly restraining response to pain or distress ⟨*a ~ indifference to cold*⟩ – **stoically** *adv*

stoichiometry /,stoyki'omətri/ *n* (the determination of) the quantitative relationship between 2 or more chemically or physically reacting substances [Gk *stoicheion* element + E *-metry*] – **stoichiometric** /-ki·oh'metrik/ *adj*

stoicism /'stoh·i,siz(ə)m/ *n* **1** *cap* the philosophy of the Stoics **2a** indifference to pleasure or pain **b** repression of emotion

stoke /stohk/ *vt* **1** to poke or stir up (e g a fire); *also* to supply with fuel **2** to feed abundantly *~ vi* to stir up or tend a fire (e g in a furnace); supply a furnace with fuel [D *stoken*; akin to MD *stuken* to push]

'**stoke,hold** /-,hohld/ *n* a compartment containing a steamship's boilers and furnaces

'**stoke,hole** /-,hohl/ *n* the space in which stokers work when tending a ship's furnaces

stoker /'stohkə/ *n* one employed to tend a furnace,

esp on a ship, and supply it with fuel [STOKE + ²-ER]

¹**stole** /stohl/ *past of* STEAL

²**stole** *n* **1** an ecclesiastical vestment consisting of a long usu silk band worn traditionally over both shoulders and hanging down in front by bishops and priests, and over the left shoulder by deacons ☞ GARMENT **2** a long wide strip of material worn by women usu across the shoulders, esp with evening dress [ME, fr OE, fr L *stola*, fr Gk *stolē* equipment, robe, fr *stellein* to set up, make ready – more at ¹STALL]

stolen /'stohlən/ *past part of* STEAL

stolid /'stolid/ *adj* difficult to arouse emotionally or mentally; unemotional [L *stolidus* dull, stupid; akin to OHG *stal* place – more at ¹STALL] – **stolidly** *adv*, **stolidity** /sto'lidəti/ *n*

stolon /'stohlon/ *n* a horizontal branch from the base of a plant (e g the strawberry) that produces new plants [NL *stolon-*, *stolo*, fr L, branch, sucker; akin to Arm *ste Cn* branch, OHG *stal* place – more at ¹STALL] – **stolonate** *adj*, **stoloniferous** /,stohlə'nif(ə)rəs/ *adj*

stoma /'stohmə/ *n, pl* **stomata** /'stohmətə, stoh'-mahtə/ *also* **stomas** **1** any of various small simple bodily openings, esp in a lower animal **2** any of the minute openings in the epidermis of a plant organ (e g a leaf) through which gases pass **3** a permanent surgically made opening, esp in the abdominal wall [NL, fr Gk *stomat-*, *stoma* mouth] – **stomal** *adj*

¹**stomach** /'stumək/ *n* **1a** (a cavity in an invertebrate animal analogous to) a saclike organ formed by a widening of the alimentary canal of a vertebrate, that is between the oesophagus at the top and the duodenum at the bottom and in which the first stages of digestion occur ☞ DIGESTION **b** the part of the body that contains the stomach; belly, abdomen **2a** desire for food; appetite **b** inclination, desire – usu neg ⟨*had no ~ for an argument*⟩ [ME *stomak*, fr MF *estomac*, fr L *stomachus* gullet, oesophagus, stomach, fr Gk *stomachos*, fr *stoma* mouth; akin to MBret *staffu* mouth, Av *staman-*]

²**stomach** *vt* **1** to find palatable or digestible ⟨*can't ~ rich food*⟩ **2** to bear without protest or resentment ⟨*couldn't ~ her attitude*⟩ ***USE*** usu neg

stomacher /'stumәkə/ *n* a separate panel of richly embroidered or jewelled fabric ending in a point at or below the waist and worn on the centre front of a bodice in the 15th and 16th c

stomachic /stə'makik/ *adj* **1** of the stomach **2** stimulating the function of the stomach; improving digestion – **stomachic** *n*, **stomachically** *adv*

'**stomach ,pump** *n* a suction pump with a flexible tube for removing liquids from the stomach or injecting liquids into it

stomat- /stohmət-/, **stomato-** *comb form* mouth; stoma ⟨sto matitis⟩ ⟨stomata*l*⟩ [NL, fr Gk, fr *stomat-*, *stoma*]

stomatitis /,stohmə'tietis/ *n, pl* **stomatitides** /-tədeez/, **stomatitises** any of numerous inflammatory diseases of the mouth [NL]

stomatology /,stohmə'toləji/ *n* a branch of medicine dealing with the mouth and its disorders [ISV] – **stomatologist** *n*, **stomatological** /-tə'lojikl/ *adj*

¹**stomp** /stomp/ *vi* to walk or dance with a heavy step – infml [alter. of ¹*stamp*]

²**stomp** *n* a jazz dance characterized by heavy stamping

¹**stone** /stohn/ *n, pl* **stones,** (3) **stone** *also* **stones** **1** a concretion of earthy or mineral matter: **a(1)** a piece of this, esp one smaller than a boulder **(2)** rock **b** a piece of rock for a specified function: e g **(1)** a building or paving block **(2)** a gem **(3)** a sharpening stone **(4)** a smooth flat surface on which a printing forme is made up **c** CALCULUS 1a **2** the hard central portion of a fruit (e g a peach or date) **3** an imperial unit of weight equal to 14lb (about 6.35kg) ☞ UNIT [ME, fr OE *stān*; akin to OHG *stein* stone, Gk *stear* hard fat]

²**stone** *vt* **1** to hurl stones at; *esp* to kill by pelting with stones **2** to face, pave, or fortify with stones **3** to remove the stones or seeds of (a fruit) **4** to rub, scour, or polish with or on a stone

³**stone** *adj* (made) of stone

stone- *comb form* completely ⟨stone-*dead*⟩ ⟨stone-*cold*⟩

'**Stone ,Age** *n* the first known period of prehistoric human culture characterized by the use of stone tools and weapons

,**stone-'broke** *adj, chiefly NAm* stony-broke – infml

'**stone,chat** /-,chat/ *n* (any of various birds related to) a common small Eurasian bird, the male of which has a black head and chestnut underparts

'**stone,crop** /-,krop/ *n* any of several plants with usu fleshy leaves that grow esp on rocks and walls; *esp* an evergreen creeping plant with pungent leaves

stone curlew *n* a large Old World and tropical American wading bird with a large head and yellow eyes

stoned *adj* intoxicated by alcohol or a drug (e g marijuana) – infml [fr pp of ²*stone* (to make numb or insensible)]

'**stone ,fly** *n* an insect with an aquatic flesh-eating larva and an adult used by anglers for bait

'**stone ,fruit** *n* a fruit with a (large) stone; a drupe

,**stone-'ground** *adj* ground with millstones ⟨*~ flour*⟩

'**stone ,lily** *n* a fossil crinoid

'**stone's ,throw** *n* a short distance

,**stone'wall** /-'wawl/ *vi, chiefly Br* **1** to bat excessively defensively and cautiously in cricket; *broadly* to behave obstructively **2** to obstruct or delay parliamentary debate – **stonewaller** *n*

,**stone 'wall** *n* a wall-like resistance or obstruction (e g in politics or public affairs)

'**stone,ware** /-,weə/ *n* opaque ceramic ware that is fired at a high temperature and is nonporous – compare EARTHENWARE

'**stone,work** /-,wuhk/ *n* masonry – **stoneworker** *n*

'**stone,wort** /-,wuht/ *n* any of a family of freshwater green algae often encrusted with chalky deposits

stony *also* **stoney** /'stohni/ *adj* **1** containing many stones or having the nature of stone **2a** insensitive to pity or human feeling **b** showing no movement or reaction; dumb, expressionless ⟨*a ~ glance*⟩ **3** stony-broke – infml – **stonily** *adv*, **stoniness** *n*

,**stony-'broke** *adj, Br* completely without funds; broke – infml

,**stony'hearted** /-'hahtid/ *adj* unfeeling, cruel – **stonyheartedness** *n*

stood /stood/ *past of* STAND

¹**stooge** /stoohj/ *n* **1** one who usu speaks the feed lines in a comedy duo **2** one who plays a subordinate

or compliant role to another **3** *chiefly NAm* a nark; STOOL PIGEON *USE* (*2&3*) infml [origin unknown]

[2]**stooge** *vi* **1** to act as a stooge – usu + *for* **2** to move, esp fly, aimlessly to and fro or at leisure – usu + *around* or *about* *USE* infml

stook /stook/ *n, chiefly Br* [1]SHOCK [ME *stowke, stouk*; akin to MLG *stūke* tree stump, pile, sleeve, OE *stocu* sleeve, *stocc* stock] – **stook** *vt*

[1]**stool** /stoohl/ *n* **1a** a seat usu without back or arms supported by 3 or 4 legs or a central pedestal **b** a low bench or portable support for the feet or for kneeling on **2** a discharge of faecal matter **3** (a shoot or growth from) a tree stump or plant crown from which shoots grow out [ME, fr OE *stōl*; akin to OHG *stuol* chair, OSlav *stolŭ* seat, throne, OE *standan* to stand]

[2]**stool** *vi* to throw out shoots from a stump or crown

'stool,ball /-,bawl/ *n* a game resembling cricket that is played chiefly in S England, esp by women, and is characterized by underarm bowling

stoolie /'stoohli/ *n, NAm* a nark; STOOL PIGEON – infml [*stool (pigeon)* + *-ie*]

'stool ,pigeon *n, chiefly NAm* sby acting as a decoy; *esp* a police informer [prob fr the early practice of fastening the decoy bird to a stool]

[1]**stoop** /stoohp/ *vi* **1a** to bend the body forwards and downwards, sometimes simultaneously bending the knees **b** to stand or walk with a temporary or habitual forward inclination of the head, body, or shoulders **2a** to condescend ⟨*the gods* ~ *to intervene in the affairs of men*⟩ **b** to lower oneself morally ⟨~ed *to spying*⟩ **3** *of a bird* to fly or dive down swiftly, usu to attack prey ~ *vt* to bend (a part of the body) forwards and downwards [ME *stoupen*, fr OE *stūpian*; akin to OE *stēap* steep, deep – more at [1]STEEP]

[2]**stoop** *n* **1a** an act of bending the body forwards **b** a temporary or habitual forward bend of the back and shoulders **2** the descent of a bird, esp on its prey

[3]**stoop** *n, chiefly NAm* a porch, platform, entrance stairway, or small veranda at a house door [D *stoep*; akin to OE *stæpe* step – more at STEP]

[1]**stop** /stop/ *vb* **-pp-** *vt* **1a** to close by filling or obstructing **b** to hinder or prevent the passage of ⟨~ *the flow of blood*⟩ **2a** to close up or block off (an opening) **b** to make impassable; choke, obstruct **c** to cover over or fill in (a hole or crevice) **3a** to restrain, prevent **b** to withhold; CUT OFF ⟨~ped *his wages*⟩ **4a** to cause to cease; check, suppress **b** to discontinue ⟨~ *running*⟩ **5a** to deduct or withhold (a sum due) **b** to instruct one's bank not to honour or pay ⟨~ *a cheque*⟩ **6a** to arrest the progress or motion of; cause to halt ⟨~ped *the car*⟩ **b** to beat in a boxing match by a knockout **7** to change the pitch of **a** (e g a violin string) by pressing with the finger **b** (a woodwind instrument) by closing 1 or more finger holes **c** (a French horn) by putting the hand into the bell **d** (e g a trumpet) by putting a mute into the bell **8** to get in the way of, esp so as to be wounded or killed ⟨~ped *a bullet*⟩ – infml ~ *vi* **1a** to cease activity or operation **b** to come to an end, esp suddenly; close, finish **2a** to cease to move on; halt **b** to pause, hesitate **3a** to break one's journey – often + *off* ⟨~ped *off at Lisbon*⟩ **b** *chiefly Br* to remain ⟨~ *at home*⟩ **c** *chiefly NAm* to make a brief call; DROP IN – usu + *by* [ME *stoppen*, fr OE *-stoppian*; akin to OHG *stopfōn* to stop, stuff; both fr a prehistoric WGmc word borrowed fr (assumed) VL *stuppare* to stop with tow, fr L *stuppa* tow, fr Gk *styppē*] – **stoppable** *adj*

[2]**stop** *n* **1** a cessation, end ⟨*soon put a* ~ *to that*⟩ **2a** (a switch or handle operating) a graduated set of organ pipes of similar design and tone quality **b** a corresponding set of vibrators or reeds of a reed organ **3a** sthg that impedes, obstructs, or brings to a halt; an impediment, obstacle **b** (any of a series of markings, esp f-numbers, for setting the size of) the circular opening of an optical system (e g a camera lens) **c** STOPPER 2 **4** a device for arresting or limiting motion **5** stopping or being stopped **6a** a halt in a journey ⟨*made a brief* ~ *to refuel*⟩ **b** a stopping place ⟨*a bus* ~⟩ **7** a consonant in the articulation of which there is a stage (e g in the /p/ of *apt* or the /g/ of *tiger*) when the breath passage is completely closed – compare CONTINUANT **8** – used in telegrams and cables to indicate a full stop **9** *chiefly Br* any of several punctuation marks; *specif* FULL STOP

[3]**stop** *adj* serving or designed to stop ⟨~ *line*⟩ ⟨~ *signal*⟩

'stop ,bath *n* an acid bath used to stop photographic development of a negative or print

'stop,cock /-,kok/ *n* a cock for stopping or regulating flow (e g of fluid through a pipe)

stop down *vt* to reduce the effective aperture of (a lens) by means of a diaphragm

stope /stohp/ *n* a usu steplike underground excavation formed as ore is removed [prob fr LG *stope*, lit., step; akin to OE *stæpe* step – more at STEP]

stopgap /'stop,gap/ *n* sthg that serves as a temporary expedient; a makeshift

,stop-'go *adj* alternately active and inactive

'stop-,off *n* a stopover

'stop,over /-,ohvə/ *n* a stop at an intermediate point in a journey

stoppage /'stopij/ *n* **1** a deduction from pay **2** a concerted cessation of work by a group of employees that is usu more spontaneous and less serious than a strike [[1]STOP + -AGE]

[1]**stopper** /'stopə/ *n* **1** sby or sthg that brings to a halt or causes to stop operating or functioning; a check **2** sby or sthg that closes, shuts, or fills up; *specif* sthg (e g a bung or cork) used to plug an opening [[1]STOP + [2]-ER]

[2]**stopper** *vt* to close or secure (as if) with a stopper

stopping /'stoping/ *adj, of a train* that stops at most intermediate stations

,stop 'press *n* (space reserved for) late news added to a newspaper after printing has begun

'stop,watch /-,woch/ *n* a watch that can be started and stopped at will for exact timing

storage /'stawrij/ *n* **1a** (a) space for storing **b** MEMORY 4 **2a** storing or being stored (e g in a warehouse) **b** the price charged for keeping goods in storage

'storage ,battery *n* STORAGE CELL

'storage ,cell *n* one or a connected set of secondary cells; an accumulator

storax /'stawraks/ *n* **1** a fragrant balsam obtained from the bark of an Asiatic tree of the witch-hazel family and used in perfumery **2** (any of a genus of trees or shrubs that yield) benzoin [ME, fr LL, alter. of L *styrax*, fr Gk]

[1]**store** /staw/ *vt* **1** to supply; *esp* to provide with a store for the future ⟨~ *a ship with provisions*⟩ **2** to

collect as a reserve supply ⟨~ *vegetables for winter use*⟩ – often + *up* or *away* **3** to place or leave in a location (e g a warehouse, library, or computer memory) for preservation or later use or disposal **4** to provide storage room for; hold ⟨*boxes for* storing *the surplus*⟩ [ME *storen,* fr OF *estorer* to construct, restore, store, fr L *instaurare* to renew, restore, fr *in-* + *-staurare* (akin to Gk *stauros* stake)] – **storable** *adj*

[2]**store** *n* **1a** sthg stored or kept for future use **b** *pl* articles accumulated for some specific object and drawn on as needed ⟨*military* ~s⟩ **c** sthg accumulated **d** a source from which things may be drawn as needed; a reserve fund **2** storage – usu + *in* ⟨*furniture kept in* ~⟩ **3** a large quantity, supply, or number **4** a warehouse **5a** DEPARTMENT STORE **b** *chiefly NAm* SHOP 1 **6** *chiefly Br* MEMORY 4 – **in store** about to happen; imminent ⟨*there's a nasty surprise* in store *for you*⟩

[3]**store** *adj* of, kept in, or used for a store

'store,front /-,frunt/ *n, NAm* a shopfront

'store,house /-,hows/ *n* **1** a warehouse **2** an abundant supply or source

'store,keeper /-,keepə/ *n* **1** sby who keeps and records stock (e g in a warehouse) **2** *NAm* a shopkeeper

'storeman /-mən/ *n, Br* sby who is employed to organize and handle stored goods or parts, esp in industry

'storeroom /-roohm, -room/ *n* a place for the storing of goods or supplies

storey, *NAm chiefly* **story** /'stawri/ *n* (a set of rooms occupying) a horizontal division of a building [ME *storie,* fr ML *historia* picture, storey of a building, fr L, history, tale; prob fr pictures adorning the windows of medieval buildings]

storeyed, *NAm chiefly* **storied** /'stawrid/ *adj* having a specified number of storeys ⟨*a 2-*storeyed *house*⟩

storiated /'stawri,aytid/ *adj* ornamented with elaborate designs [ML *historiatus,* pp of *historiare* to tell a story in pictures, fr LL, to relate, fr L *historia* history]

storied /'stawrid/ *adj* celebrated in story or history

stork /stawk/ *n* any of various large mostly Old World wading birds that have long stout bills and are related to the ibises and herons [ME, fr OE *storc;* akin to OHG *storah* stork, OE *stearc* stiff – more at STARK]

storksbill /'stawks,bil/ *n* any of several plants of the geranium family with elongated pointed fruits

[1]**storm** /stawm/ *n* **1a** a violent disturbance of the weather marked by high winds, thunder and lightning, rain or snow, etc **b(1)** wind having a speed of 113 to 117km/h (64 to 72mph) **(2)** WHOLE GALE **2** a disturbed or agitated state; a sudden or violent commotion **3** a violent shower of objects (e g missiles) **4** a tumultuous outburst ⟨*a* ~ *of abuse*⟩ **5** a violent assault on a defended position [ME, fr OE; akin to OHG *sturm* storm, OE *styrian* to stir] – **by storm** (as if) by using a bold frontal movement to capture quickly

[2]**storm** *vi* **1a** *of wind* to blow with violence **b** to rain, hail, snow, or sleet ⟨*it was* ~ing *in the mountains*⟩ **2** to move in a sudden assault or attack ⟨~ed *ashore at zero hour*⟩ **3** to be in or to exhibit a violent passion; rage ⟨~ing *at the unusual delay*⟩ **4** to rush about or move impetuously, violently, or angrily ⟨*the mob* ~ed *through the streets*⟩ ~ *vt* to attack or take (e g a fortified place) by storm

'storm,bound /-,bownd/ *adj* confined or delayed by a storm or its effects

'storm ,cone *n, Br* a usu tarred canvas cone hoisted to determine the direction of an impending storm

'storm ,door *n, NAm* a door placed outside an ordinary external door for protection against severe weather

'storm ,lantern *n, chiefly Br* HURRICANE LAMP

'storm ,petrel *n* a small sooty black and white petrel frequenting the N Atlantic and Mediterranean

'storm ,trooper *n* **1** a member of a Nazi party militia **2** a member of a force of shock troops

'storm,water /-,wawtə/ *n* surface water produced by heavy rain ⟨*a* ~ *drainage system*⟩

stormy /'stawmi/ *adj* marked by turmoil or fury ⟨*a* ~ *life*⟩ ⟨*a* ~ *conference*⟩ ['STORM + [1]-Y] – **stormily** *adv,* **storminess** *n*

stormy petrel *n* **1** STORM PETREL **2** sby fond of strife

[1]**story** /'stawri/ *n* **1a** an account of incidents or events **b** a statement of the facts of a situation in question ⟨*according to their* ~⟩ **c** an anecdote; *esp* an amusing one **2a** a short fictional narrative **b** the plot of a literary work **3** a widely circulated rumour **4** a lie **5** a legend, romance **6** a news article or broadcast [ME *storie,* fr OF *estorie,* fr L *historia* history]

[2]**story** *n, chiefly NAm* a storey

'story,book /-,book/ *adj* fairy-tale

'story,teller /-,telə/ *n* **1** a relator of tales or anecdotes **2** a liar

stotinka /sto'tingkə, stoh-/ *n, pl* **stotinki** /-ki/ ☞ *Bulgaria* at NATIONALITY [Bulg]

stoup /stoohp/ *n* **1** a large drinking mug or glass **2** a basin for holy water at the entrance of a church [ME *stowp,* prob of Scand origin; akin to ON *staup* cup]

[1]**stout** /stowt/ *adj* **1** firm, resolute ⟨~ *resistance*⟩ **2** physically or materially strong: **a** sturdy, vigorous **b** staunch, enduring **c** solid, substantial **3** forceful ⟨*a* ~ *attack*⟩; *also* violent ⟨*a* ~ *wind*⟩ **4** corpulent, fat – chiefly euph [ME, fr OF *estout,* of Gmc origin; akin to OHG *stolz* proud] – **stoutish** *adj,* **stoutly** *adv,* **stoutness** *n*

[2]**stout** *n* a dark sweet heavy-bodied beer

,stout'hearted /-'hahtid/ *adj* courageous – **stoutheartedly** *adv*

[1]**stove** /stohv/ *n* **1a** an enclosed appliance that burns fuel or uses electricity to provide heat chiefly for domestic purposes **b** a cooker **2** *chiefly Br* a hothouse [ME, heated room, steam room, fr MD or MLG; akin to OHG *stuba* heated room, steam room; both fr a prehistoric WGmc-NGmc word borrowed fr (assumed) VL *extufa,* deriv of L *ex-* + Gk *typhein* to smoke]

[2]**stove** *past of* STAVE

'stove,pipe /-,piep/ *n* (metal) piping used as a stove chimney or to connect a stove with a flue

stow /stoh/ *vt* **1** to put away; store **2a** to pack away in an orderly fashion in an enclosed space **b** to fill (e g a ship's hold) with cargo **3** to cram in (e g food) – usu + *away* ⟨~ed *away a huge dinner*⟩; infml **4** to stop, desist – slang; esp in *stow it* [ME *stowen* to place, fr *stowe* place, fr OE *stōw;* akin to OFris *stō* place, Gk *stylos* pillar – more at [2]STEER]

stowage /'stowij/ *n* **1** goods in storage or to be

stowed **2a** storage capacity **b** a place for storage **3** the state of being stored [STOW + -AGE]

[1]**stowaway** /'stoh·a,way/ *n* sby who stows away

[2]**stowaway** *adj* designed to be dismantled or folded for storage ⟨~ *tables and chairs*⟩

stow away *vi* to hide oneself aboard a vehicle, esp a ship, as a means of travelling without payment or escaping from a place undetected

STP *n* a synthetic hallucinogenic drug chemically related to mescaline and amphetamine [fr *STP*, a trademark for a motor fuel additive]

strabismus /strə'bizməs/ *n* SQUINT 1 [NL, fr Gk *strabismos* condition of squinting, fr *strabizein* to squint, fr *strabos* squint-eyed; akin to Gk *strephein* to twist – more at STROPHE] – **strabismic** /-mik/ *adj*

straddle /'stradl/ *vb* **straddling** /'stradling, 'stradl·-ing/ *vi* to stand or esp sit with the legs wide apart ~ *vt* **1** to stand, sit, or be astride ⟨~ *a horse*⟩ **2** to bracket (a target) with missiles (e g shells or bombs) **3** to be on land on either side of ⟨*the village* ~s *the frontier*⟩ [irreg fr *stride*] – **straddle** *n*, **straddler** *n*

strafe /strahf, strayf/ *vt* to rake (e g ground troops) with fire at close range, esp with machine-gun fire from low-flying aircraft [G *Gott strafe England* God punish England, slogan of the Germans in WW I] – **strafe** *n*, **strafer** *n*

straggle /'stragl/ *vi* **straggling** /'stragling, 'stragl·-ing/ **1** to lag behind or stray away from the main body of sthg, esp from a line of march **2** to move or spread untidily away from the main body of sthg ⟨straggling *branches*⟩ [ME *straglen*] – **straggle** *n*, **straggler** *n*

straggly /'stragli/ *adj* loosely spread out or scattered irregularly ⟨*a* ~ *beard*⟩

[1]**straight** /strayt/ *adj* **1a** free from curves, bends, angles, or irregularities ⟨~ *hair*⟩ ⟨~ *timber*⟩ ⟨*a* ~ *stream*⟩ **b** generated by a point moving continuously in the same direction ⟨*a* ~ *line*⟩ **c** of, occupying, or passing through a fielding position in front of the batsman and near the line between the wickets or its extension behind the bowler ⟨*a* ~ *drive*⟩ **2** direct, uninterrupted: e g **a** holding to a direct or proper course or method ⟨*a* ~ *thinker*⟩ **b** candid, frank ⟨*gave me a* ~ *answer*⟩ ⟨~ *talking*⟩ **c** coming directly from a trustworthy source ⟨*a* ~ *tip on the horses*⟩ **d** consecutive ⟨*6* ~ *wins*⟩ **e** having the cylinders arranged in a single straight line ⟨*a* ~ *8-cylinder engine*⟩ **f** upright, vertical ⟨*the picture isn't quite* ~⟩ **3a** honest, fair ⟨~ *dealing*⟩ **b** properly ordered or arranged (e g with regard to finance) ⟨*be* ~ *after the end of the month*⟩ ⟨*set us* ~ *on that issue*⟩ **c** correct ⟨*get the facts* ~⟩ **4** unmixed ⟨~ *gin*⟩ **5a** not deviating from the general norm or prescribed pattern ⟨*preferred acting in* ~ *dramas to musicals or comedies*⟩ **b** accepted as usual, normal, or proper **6** *chiefly NAm* marked by no exceptions or deviations in support of a principle or party ⟨*a* ~ *ballot*⟩ **7a** conventional in opinions, habits, appearance etc **b** heterosexual *USE* (7) infml [ME *streght, straight*, fr pp of *strecchen* to stretch] – **straightish** *adj*, **straightness** *n*

[2]**straight** *adv* **1** in a straight manner **2** without delay or hesitation; immediately ⟨~ *after breakfast*⟩

[3]**straight** *n* **1** sthg straight: e g **a** a straight line or arrangement **b** a straight part of sthg; *esp* HOME STRAIGHT **2** a poker hand containing 5 cards in sequence but not of the same suit **3a** a conventional person **b** a heterosexual *USE* (*3*) infml

,straight and 'narrow *n the* way of life that is morally and legally irreproachable [prob alter. of *strait and narrow*; fr the admonition of Mt 7:14, 'strait is the gate and narrow is the way which leadeth unto life"]

,straighta'way /-ə'way/ *adv* without hesitation or delay; immediately

'straight,bred /-,bred/ *adj* produced from a single breed, strain, or type ⟨*a* ~ *Angus heifer*⟩ – compare CROSSBRED – **straightbred** *n*

straight chain *n* an open chain of atoms having no side chains

'straight,edge /-,ej/ *n* a piece of wood, metal, etc with an accurate straight edge for testing surfaces and (drawing) straight lines

straighten /'strayt(ə)n/ *vb* to make or become straight – usu + *up* or *out* – **straightener** *n*

,straight 'face *n* a face giving no evidence of emotion, esp amusement ⟨*keep a* ~⟩ – **straight-faced** *adj*

straight fight *n* a contest, esp an election contest, between 2 candidates only

,straight 'flush *n* a poker hand containing 5 cards of the same suit in sequence

,straight'forward /-'faw·wəd/ *adj* **1** free from evasiveness or ambiguity; direct, candid ⟨*a* ~ *account*⟩ **2** presenting no hidden difficulties ⟨*a perfectly* ~ *problem*⟩ **3** clear-cut, precise – **straightforwardly** *adv*, **straightforwardness** *n*

'straight,jacket /-jakit/ *n* a straitjacket

,straight'laced /-'layst/ *adj, chiefly NAm* straitlaced

,straight 'off *adv* immediately; AT ONCE

,straight-'out *adj, NAm* **1** forthright, blunt ⟨*gave him a* ~ *answer*⟩ **2** outright, thoroughgoing ⟨*a* ~ *Democrat*⟩

,straight 'up *adv, Br* truly, honestly – infml; used esp in asking or replying to a question ⟨*'This car's worth a good £1500."* 'Straight up?" 'Straight up."⟩

,straight'way /-'way/ *adv, archaic* immediately, forthwith ⟨~ *the clouds began to part*⟩

[1]**strain** /strayn/ *n* **1a** a lineage, ancestry **b** a group of plants, animals, microorganisms, etc at a level lower than a species ⟨*a high-yielding* ~ *of winter wheat*⟩ **c** a kind, sort ⟨*discussions of a lofty* ~⟩ **2** a trace, streak ⟨*a* ~ *of fanaticism*⟩ **3** a passage of verbal or musical expression – usu pl with sing. meaning **4** the tone or manner of an utterance or of a course of action or conduct ⟨*he continued in the same* ~⟩ [ME *streen* progeny, lineage, fr OE *strēon* gain, acquisition; akin to OHG *gistriuni* gain, L *struere* to heap up – more at STRUCTURE]

[2]**strain** *vt* **1a** to draw tight ⟨~ *the bandage over the wound*⟩ **b** to stretch to maximum extension and tautness ⟨~ *a canvas over a frame*⟩ **2a** to exert (e g oneself) to the utmost **b** to injure by overuse, misuse, or excessive pressure ⟨~ed *a muscle*⟩ **c** to cause a change of form or size in (a body) by application of external force **3** to squeeze or clasp tightly: e g **a** to hug **b** to compress painfully; constrict **4a** to cause to pass through a strainer; filter **b** to remove by straining ⟨~ *lumps out of the gravy*⟩ **5** to stretch beyond a proper limit ⟨*that story* ~s *my credulity*⟩ ~ *vi* **1a** to make (violent) efforts ⟨*has to* ~ *to reach the high notes*⟩ **b** to sustain a strain, wrench, or

distortion **c** to contract the muscles forcefully in physical exertion **2** to show great resistance; resist strongly **3** to show signs of strain; continue with considerable difficulty or effort ⟨~ing *under the pressure of work*⟩ [ME *strainen*, fr MF *estraindre*, fr L *stringere* to bind or draw tight, press together; akin to Gk *strang-*, *stranx* drop squeezed out, *strangalē* halter]

[3]**strain** *n* straining or being strained: e g **a** (a force, influence, or factor causing) physical or mental tension **b** excessive or difficult exertion or labour **c** a wrench, twist, or similar bodily injury resulting esp from excessive stretching of muscles or ligaments **d** the deformation of a body subjected to stress

strained *adj* **1** done or produced with excessive effort **2** subjected to considerable tension ⟨~ *relations*⟩

strainer /'straynə/ *n* **1** a device (e g a sieve) to retain solid pieces while a liquid passes through ⟨*tea* ~⟩ **2** any of various devices for stretching or tightening sthg [[2]STRAIN + [2]-ER]

'**strain** ,**gauge** *n* an extensometer

[1]**strait** /strayt/ *adj, archaic* narrow [ME, fr OF *estreit*, fr L *strictus* strait, strict – more at STRICT] – **straitly** *adv*, **straitness** *n*

[2]**strait** *n* **1** a narrow passageway connecting 2 large bodies of water – often pl with sing. meaning but sing. or pl in constr **2** a situation of perplexity or distress – usu pl with sing. meaning ⟨*in dire* ~s⟩

straiten /'strayt(ə)n/ *vt* **1** to subject to severely restricting difficulties, esp of a financial kind – often in *straightened circumstances* **2** *archaic* to restrict in range or scope [[1]STRAIT + [2]-EN]

'**strait,jacket, straightjacket** /-jakit/ *n* **1** a cover or outer garment of strong material used to bind the body and esp the arms closely, in restraining a violent prisoner or patient **2** sthg that restricts or confines like a straitjacket – **straitjacket** *vt*

,**strait'laced,** *NAm also* **straightlaced** /-'layst/ *adj* excessively strict in manners or morals

strake /strayk/ *n* (the width of) a continuous band of hull planking or plates running from stem to stern on a ship [ME; akin to OE *streccan* to stretch – more at STRETCH]

[1]**strand** /strand/ *n* a shore, beach [ME, fr OE; akin to ON *strönd* strand, L *sternere* to spread out – more at STREW]

[2]**strand** *vt* **1** to run, drive, or cause to drift onto a shore; run aground **2** to leave in a strange or unfavourable place, esp without funds or means to depart

[3]**strand** *n* **1a** any of the threads, strings, or wires twisted or laid parallel to make a cord, rope, or cable **b** sthg (e g a molecular chain) resembling a strand **2** an elongated or twisted and plaited body resembling a rope ⟨*a* ~ *of pearls*⟩ **3** any of the elements interwoven in a complex whole ⟨*follow the* ~s *of the story*⟩ [ME *strond*] – **stranded** *adj*

[4]**strand** *vt* to break a strand of (a rope) accidentally

strange /straynj/ *adj* **1** not native to or naturally belonging in a place; of external origin, kind, or character **2a** not known, heard, or seen before **b** exciting wonder or surprise **3** lacking experience or acquaintance; unaccustomed *to* [ME, fr OF *estrange*, fr L *extraneus*, lit., external, fr *extra* outside – more at EXTRA-] – **strangely** *adv*

'**strangeness** /-nis/ *n* the quantum property that explains the unexpectedly long lifetime possessed by certain elementary particles (e g kaons) [STRANGE + -NESS]

strange particle *n* an elementary particle (e g a kaon) with a strangeness quantum number different from zero

stranger /'straynjə/ *n* **1a** a foreigner, alien **b** sby who is unknown or with whom one is unacquainted **2** one ignorant of or unacquainted with sby or sthg ⟨*a* ~ *to books*⟩ [ME, fr MF *estrangier* foreign, foreigner, fr *estrange*]

strangle /strangl/ *vb* **strangling** /'strang·gling, 'strang·gl·ing/ *vt* **1** to choke (to death) by compressing the throat; throttle **2** to suppress or hinder the rise, expression, or growth of ~ *vi* to die (as if) from being strangled [ME *stranglen*, fr MF *estrangler*, fr L *strangulare*, fr Gk *strangalan*, fr *strangalē* halter – more at [2]STRAIN] – **strangler** *n*

'**strangle,hold** /-,hohld/ *n* a force or influence that prevents free movement or expression

strangles /'stranglz/ *n pl but sing or pl in constr* a contagious feverish disease of horses marked by nasal discharge, inflammation, and abscesses between the jawbones [pl of obs *strangle* (act of strangling)]

strangulate /'strang·gyoo,layt/ *vt* **1** to strangle **2** to constrict or compress (a blood vessel, loop of intestine, etc) in a way that interrupts the ability to act as a passage ⟨*a* ~d *hernia*⟩ ~ *vi* to become strangulated [L *strangulatus*, pp of *strangulare*] – **strangulation** /-'laysh(ə)n/ *n*

strangury /'strangyoori/ *n* slow and painful urination [ME, fr L *stranguria*, fr Gk *strangouria*, fr *strang-*, *stranx* drop squeezed out + *ourein* to urinate, fr *ouron* urine – more at [2]STRAIN, URINE]

[1]**strap** /strap/ *n* **1** a strip of metal or a flexible material, esp leather, for holding objects together or in position **2** (*the* use of, or punishment with) a strip of leather for flogging ⟨*gave him the* ~⟩ [alter. of *strop*, fr ME, band or loop of leather or rope, fr OE, thong for securing an oar; akin to MHG *strupfe* strap; all fr a prehistoric WGmc word borrowed fr L *struppus* band, strap, fr Gk *strophos* twisted band; akin to Gk *strephein* to twist – more at STROPHE] – **strapping** *n*

[2]**strap** *vt* **-pp- 1a** to secure with or attach by means of a strap **b** to support (e g a sprained joint) with adhesive plaster **2** to beat with a strap

'**strap,hanger** /-,hang·ə/ *n* a passenger in a train, bus, etc who has to hold a strap or handle for support while standing – **straphanging** *n*

strappado /stra'pahdoh, -'pay-/ *n, pl* **strappadoes, strappados** (an instrument to inflict) a former torture consisting of hoisting the victim by a rope and letting him/her fall almost to the ground [modif of It *strappata*, lit., sharp pull]

strapping /'straping/ *adj* big, strong, and sturdy in build

strass /stras/ *n* PASTE 3 [F *stras, strass*]

strata /'strahtə/ *pl of* STRATUM

stratagem /'stratəjəm/ *n* **1** an artifice or trick for deceiving and outwitting the enemy **2** a cleverly contrived trick or scheme [It *stratagemma*, fr L *strategema*, fr Gk *stratēgēma*, fr *stratēgein* to be a general, manoeuvre, fr *stratēgos* general, fr *stratos* army (akin to L *stratus*, pp of *sternere* to spread out) + *agein* to lead – more at STREW, AGENT]

strategic /strə'teejik/, **strategical** /-kl/ *adj* **1** of, marked by, or important in strategy ⟨*a* ~ *retreat*⟩ –

compare TACTICAL **2a** required for the conduct of war ⟨~ *materials*⟩ **b** of great importance within an integrated whole or to a planned effect **3** designed or trained to strike an enemy at the sources of its power ⟨*a* ~ *bomber*⟩ – **strategically** *adv*

strategist /ˈstratijist/ *n* one skilled in strategy

strategy /ˈstratiji/ *n* **1a(1)** the science and art of employing all the resources of a (group of) nation(s) to carry out agreed policies in peace or war **(2)** the science and art of military command exercised to meet the enemy in combat under advantageous conditions – compare TACTICS **b** a variety of or instance of the use of strategy **2a** a clever plan or method **b** the art of employing plans towards achieving a goal [Gk *stratēgia* generalship, fr *stratēgos*]

strath /strath/ *n* a flat wide river valley, esp in Scotland [ScGael *srath*]

strathspey /ˌstrathˈspay/ *n* (the music for) a Scottish dance that is similar to a reel and marked by gliding steps [*Strath Spey*, district of Scotland]

strati- /strati-/ *comb form* stratum ⟨strati*form*⟩ [NL *stratum*]

straticulate /straˈtikyoolət, -ˌlayt/ *adj* having thin parallel strata [(assumed) NL *straticulum*, dim. of *stratum*]

stratify /ˈstratifie/ *vt* to form, deposit, or arrange in strata ~ *vi* to become arranged in strata [NL *stratificare*, fr *stratum* + L *-ificare* -ify] – **stratification** /-ˈkaysh(ə)n/ *n*

stratigraphy /strəˈtigrəfi/ *n* (geology that deals with) the origin, distribution, and succession of strata [ISV] – **stratigraphic** /ˌstratiˈgrafik/ *adj*

strato- *comb form* stratus and ⟨strato*cumulus*⟩ [NL *stratus*]

stratocracy /strəˈtokrəsi/ *n* a military government [Gk *stratos* army – more at STRATAGEM]

stratocumulus /ˌstrahtohˈkyoohmyooləs, ˌstraytoh-/ *n* stratified cumulus consisting of large dark clouds often covering the whole sky, esp in winter ☞ WEATHER [NL]

stratosphere /ˈstratəˌsfiə/ *n* the upper part of the atmosphere above about 11km (7mi) in which the temperature changes little and clouds are rare [F *stratosphère*, fr NL *stratum* + *-o-* + F *sphère* sphere, fr L *sphaera*] – **stratospheric** /ˌstratəˈsferik/ *adj*

stratum /ˈstrahtəm, ˈstraytəm/ *n, pl* **strata** /-tə/ **1** a horizontal layer or series of layers of any homogeneous material: e g **a** a sheetlike mass of rock or earth deposited between beds of other rock **b** a layer of the sea or atmosphere **c** a layer of tissue **d** a layer in which archaeological remains are found on excavation **2** a socioeconomic level of society – often pl with sing. meaning ⟨*this* strata *of society*⟩ [NL, fr L, spread, bed, fr neut of *stratus*, pp of *sternere* to spread out – more at STREW]

stratus /ˈstrahtəs, ˈstraytəs/ *n, pl* **strati** /-tie/ a massive broad uniformly thick low cloud formation [NL, fr L, pp of *sternere*]

[1]**straw** /straw/ *n* **1** (a single stem of) dry stalky plant residue, specif stalks of grain after threshing, used for bedding, thatching, fodder, making hats, etc **2** a dry coarse stem, esp of a cereal grass **3a** sthg of small value or importance ⟨*she doesn't care a* ~⟩ **b** sthg too insubstantial to provide support or help ⟨*clutching at* ~s⟩ **4** a tube of paper, plastic, etc for sucking up a drink **5** pale yellow [ME, fr OE *strēaw*; akin to OHG *strō* straw, OE *strewian* to strew] – **strawy** *adj* – **straw in the wind** a hint or apparently insignificant fact that is an indication of a coming event

[2]**straw** *adj* of or resembling (the colour of) straw

[3]**straw** *vt* to cover (as if) with straw

strawberry /ˈstrawb(ə)ri/ *n* (the juicy edible usu red fruit of) any of several white-flowered creeping plants of the rose family [prob fr the straw-like appearance of the achenes on the surface]

strawberry blonde *n* (a woman with hair of) a reddish blonde colour

strawberry mark *n* a usu red and elevated birthmark composed of small blood vessels

strawberry roan *n* a roan horse with a light red ground colour

strawberry tree *n* a European evergreen tree of the heath family with clustered white flowers and fruits like strawberries

ˈstrawˌboard /-ˌbawd/ *n* coarse cardboard made of straw pulp and used usu for boxes and book covers

straw poll *n* an assessment made by an unofficial vote [prob fr the phrase *a straw in the wind* – more at [1]STRAW]

straw vote *n, NAm* STRAW POLL

[1]**stray** /stray/ *vi* **1** to wander from a proper place, course, or line of conduct or argument **2** to roam about without fixed direction or purpose [ME *straien*, fr MF *estraier*, fr (assumed) VL *extragare*, fr L *extra-* outside + *vagari* to wander – more at EXTRA-, VAGARY]

[2]**stray** *n* **1** a domestic animal wandering at large or lost **2** a person or animal that strays [ME, fr OF *estraié*, pp of *estraier*]

[3]**stray** *adj* **1** having strayed; wandering, lost **2** occurring at random or sporadically ⟨*a few* ~ *hairs*⟩ **3** not serving any useful purpose; unwanted ⟨~ *light*⟩

[1]**streak** /streek/ *n* **1** a line or band of a different colour from the background **2** a sample containing microorganisms (e g bacteria) implanted in a line on a solid culture medium (e g agar jelly) for growth **3a** an inherent quality; *esp* one which is only occasionally manifested ⟨*had a mean* ~ *in him*⟩ **b** a consecutive series ⟨*on a winning* ~⟩ [ME *streke*, fr OE *strica*; akin to OHG *strich* line, L *striga* furrow, row – more at STRIKE]

[2]**streak** *vt* to make streaks on or in ~ *vi* **1** to move swiftly ⟨*a jet* ~ing *across the sky*⟩ **2** to run through a public place while naked – infml – **streaker** *n*

streaked *adj* marked with stripes or linear discolorations

streaky /ˈstreeki/ *adj* **1** marked with streaks **2** *of meat, esp bacon* having lines of fat and lean ☞ MEAT **3** *of a shot in cricket* hit off the edge of the bat – **streakily** *adv*, **streakiness** *n*

[1]**stream** /streem/ *n* **1a** a body of running water, esp one smaller than a river, flowing in a channel on the earth **b** a body of flowing liquid or gas **2a** a steady succession of words, events, etc **b** a continuous moving procession **3** an unbroken flow (e g of gas or particles of matter) **4** a prevailing attitude or direction of opinion – esp in *go against/with the stream* **5** *Br* a group of pupils of the same general academic ability ⟨*the A* ~⟩ – compare SET 17 [ME *streme*, fr OE *strēam*; akin to OHG *stroum* stream, Gk *rhein* to flow, Skt *sarati* it flows – more at SERUM]

[2]**stream** *vi* **1** to flow (as if) in a stream **2** to run with a fluid ⟨*her eyes* ~ing *with the cold*⟩ ⟨*walls* ~ing *with condensation*⟩ **3** to trail out at full length ⟨*hair*

~ing *in the wind*⟩ **4** to pour in large numbers in the same direction **5** *Br* to practise the division of pupils into streams ~*vt* **1** to emit freely or in a stream **2** *Br* to divide (a school or an age-group of pupils) into streams

streamer /'streemə/ *n* **1a** a pennant **b** a strip of coloured paper used as a party decoration **c** BANNER 2 **2** a long extension of the sun's corona visible only during a total eclipse [[2]STREAM + [2]-ER]

[1]**'stream,line** /-,lien/ *n* **1** the path of a fluid (e g air or water) relative to a solid body past which the fluid is moving smoothly without turbulence **2** a contour given to a car, aeroplane, etc so as to minimize resistance to motion through a fluid (e g air)

[2]**streamline** *vt* **1** to design or construct with a streamline **2** to make simpler, more efficient, or better integrated

streamlined /'streem,liend/ *adj* **1a** having a streamline contour **b** effectively integrated; organized **2** having flowing lines

stream of consciousness *n* (a literary technique used to express) individual conscious experience considered as a continuous flow of reactions and experiences

street /street/ *n* **1** a thoroughfare, esp in a town or village, with buildings on either side ⟨*lives in a fashionable* ~⟩ **2** the part of a street reserved for vehicles [ME *strete*, fr OE *strǣt*; akin to OHG *strāza* street; both fr a prehistoric WGmc word borrowed fr LL *strata* paved road, fr L, fem of *stratus*, pp of *sternere* to spread out – more at STREW] – **on the street** idle, homeless, or out of a job – **on the streets** earning a living as a prostitute – **up/down one's street** suited to one's abilities or tastes

street arab *n, often cap A* ARAB 2a

'street,car /-,kah/ *n, NAm* a tram

streets /streets/ *adv, chiefly Br* FAR AND AWAY ⟨~ *ahead of the other girls*⟩

street theatre *n* drama dealing with contemporary social and political issues and often performed out of doors

'street,walker /-,wawkə/ *n* a prostitute who solicits in the streets – compare CALL GIRL – **streetwalking** *n*

'street,wise *adj* familiar with the (disreputable or criminal) life of city streets; *broadly* resourceful at surviving and prospering in modern urban life

strength /streng(k)th/ *n* **1** the quality of being strong; capacity for exertion or endurance **2** solidity, toughness **3a** legal, logical, or moral force **b** a strong quality or inherent asset ⟨*his* ~s *and weaknesses*⟩ **4a** degree of potency of effect or of concentration **b** intensity of light, colour, sound, or smell **5** force as measured in members ⟨*an army at full* ~⟩ **6** firmness of, or a rising tendency in, prices ⟨*stock markets were displaying remarkable drive and* ~ – *Financial Times*⟩ **7** a basis – chiefly in *on the strength of* [ME *strengthe*, fr OE *strengthu*; akin to OHG *strengi* strong – more at STRONG] – **strengthless** *adj* – **from strength to strength** with continuing success and progress

strengthen /'streng(k)thən/ *vb* to make or become stronger – **strengthener** *n*

strenuous /'strenyoo·əs/ *adj* **1** vigorously active **2** requiring effort or stamina [L *strenuus* – more at STARE] – **strenuously** *adv*, **strenuousness, strenuosity** /,strenyoo'osəti/ *n*

strep /strep/ *n* a streptococcus – infml – **strep** *adj*

strepto- *comb form* twisted; twisted chain ⟨streptococcus⟩ [NL, fr Gk, fr *streptos* twisted, fr *strephein* to twist – more at STROPHE]

streptococcus /,streptə'kokəs/ *n, pl* **streptococci** /-'kok(s)ie/ any of a genus of chiefly parasitic bacteria that occur in pairs or chains and include some that cause diseases in human beings and domestic animals [NL, genus name] – **streptococcal, streptococcic** /-'kok(s)ik/ *adj*

,strepto'kinase /-'kienayz, -nays/ *n* an enzyme produced by some streptococcal bacteria that breaks down blood clots [*strepto-* + *kinase* (an enzyme), fr *kineric*]

,strepto'mycin /-'miesin/ *n* an antibiotic obtained from a soil bacterium and used esp in the treatment of tuberculosis [NL *Streptomyces*, genus name of bacteria, fr *strepto-* + Gk *mykēs* fungus]

[1]**stress** /stres/ *n* **1a** the force per unit area producing or tending to produce deformation of a body; *also* the state of a body under such stress **b** (a physical or emotional factor that causes) bodily or mental tension **c** strain, pressure **2** emphasis, weight **3a** intensity of utterance given to a speech sound, syllable, or word so as to produce relative loudness **b** relative force or prominence given to a syllable in verse **c** ACCENT 2b [ME *stresse* stress, distress, fr *destresse* – more at DISTRESS] – **stressful** *adj*, **stressfully** *adv*, **stressless** *adj*

[2]**stress** *vt* **1** to subject to phonetic stress; accent **2** to subject to physical or mental stress **3** to lay stress on; emphasize – **stressor** *n*

[1]**stretch** /strech/ *vt* **1** to extend in a reclining position – often + *out* ⟨~ed *himself out on the carpet*⟩ **2** to extend to full length **3** to extend (oneself or one's limbs), esp so as to relieve muscular stiffness **4** to pull taut ⟨*canvas was* ~ed *on a frame*⟩ **5a** to enlarge or distend, esp by force **b** to strain ⟨~ed *his already thin patience*⟩ **6** to cause to reach (e g from one point to another or across a space) **7** to enlarge or extend beyond natural or proper limits ⟨~ *the rules*⟩ **8** to fell (as if) with a blow – often + *out*; infml ~*vi* **1a** to extend in space; reach ⟨*broad plains* ~ing *to the sea*⟩ **b** to extend over a period of time **2** to become extended without breaking **3a** to extend one's body or limbs **b** to lie down at full length [ME *strecchen*, fr OE *streccan*; akin to OHG *strecchan* to stretch, OE *starian* to stare] – **stretchable** *adj*, **stretchy** *adj* – **stretch a point** to go beyond what is strictly warranted in making a claim or concession – **stretch one's legs** to take a walk in order to relieve stiffness caused by prolonged sitting

[2]**stretch** *n* **1** an exercise of the understanding, imagination, etc beyond ordinary or normal limits **2** the extent to which sthg may be stretched ⟨*at full* ~⟩ **3** stretching or being stretched **4** a continuous expanse of time or space **5** the capacity for being stretched; elasticity **6** a term of imprisonment – infml

stretcher /'strechə/ *n* **1** a mechanism for stretching or expanding sthg **2a** a brick or stone laid with its length parallel to the face of the wall – compare HEADER ☞ BUILDING **b** a timber or rod used, esp when horizontal, as a tie (e g a tie-beam) in a load-bearing frame (e g for a building) **3** a device, consisting of a sheet of canvas or other material stretched between 2 poles, for carrying a sick, injured, or dead person **4** a rod or bar extending between 2 legs of a chair or table [[1]STRETCH + [2]-ER]

strew /strooh/ *vt* **strewed, strewn** /stroohn/ **1** to spread by scattering **2** to cover (as if) with sthg scattered **3** to become dispersed over [ME *strewen, strowen,* fr OE *strewian, strēowian*; akin to OHG *strewen* to strew, L *sternere* to spread out, Gk *stornynai*]

strewth /stroohth/ *interj* struth

stria /'strie·ə/ *n, pl* **striae** /'strie·i/ **1** a minute groove on the surface of a rock, crystal, etc **2** a narrow groove, ridge, line of colours, etc, esp when one of a parallel series [L, furrow, channel – more at STRIKE] – **striate** /'strie·ayt/ *vt,* **striate** /'strie·ət/, **striated** /strie'aytid/ *adj*

striated muscle *n* muscle that is marked by alternate light and dark bands, is made up of long fibres, and comprises the voluntary muscle of vertebrates – compare SMOOTH MUSCLE

striation /strie'aysh(ə)n/ *n* **1a** being striated **b** an arrangement of striae **2** a stria

stricken /'strikən/ *adj* afflicted or overwhelmed (as if) by disease, misfortune, or sorrow [fr pp of *strike*]

[1]**strickle** /'strikl/ *n* **1** an instrument for levelling off measures of grain **2** a tool for sharpening scythes [ME *strikell*; akin to OE *strīcan* to stroke – more at STRIKE]

[2]**strickle** *vt* to smooth or form with a strickle

strict /strikt/ *adj* **1a** stringent in requirement or control ⟨*under* ~ *orders*⟩ **b** severe in discipline ⟨*a* ~ *teacher*⟩ **2a** inflexibly maintained or kept to; complete ⟨~ *secrecy*⟩ **b** rigorously conforming to rules or standards **3** exact, precise ⟨*in the* ~ *sense of the word*⟩ [L *strictus,* fr pp of *stringere* to bind tight – more at [2]STRAIN] – **strictly** *adv,* **strictness** *n*

stricture /'strikchə/ *n* **1** an abnormal narrowing of a bodily passage **2** sthg that closely restrains or limits; a restriction **3** an unfavourable criticism; a censure *USE* (*2&3*) usu pl with sing. meaning [ME, fr LL *strictura,* fr L *strictus,* pp of *stringere* to bind tight]

[1]**stride** /stried/ *vb* **strode** /strohd/; **stridden** /'stridən/ *vi* to walk (as if) with long steps ~*vt* to move over or along (as if) with long steps [ME *striden,* fr OE *strīdan*; akin to MLG *striden* to straddle, OE *starian* to stare] – **strider** *n*

[2]**stride** *n* **1** a long step **2** an advance – often pl with sing. meaning ⟨*technology has made great* ~s⟩ **3a** (the distance covered in) an act of movement completed when the feet regain the initial relative positions **b** a state of maximum competence or capability ⟨*get into one's* ~⟩ **4** a striding gait ⟨*her loose-limbed* ~⟩ – **in one's stride** without becoming upset ⟨*took the dangers* in her stride⟩

strident /'stried(ə)nt/ *adj* characterized by harsh and discordant sound; *also* loud and obtrusive ⟨~ *slogans*⟩ [L *strident-, stridens,* prp of *stridere, stridēre* to make a harsh noise; akin to Gk & L *strix* owl] – **stridence, stridency** *n,* **stridently** *adv*

stride piano *n* a style of jazz piano playing in which the right hand plays the melody while the left hand alternates between a single note and a chord played an octave or more higher [fr the repeated strides taken by the left hand]

stridulate /'stridyoolayt/ *vi, esp of crickets, grasshoppers, etc* to make a shrill creaking noise by rubbing together special bodily structures [back-formation fr *stridulation,* fr F, fr L *stridulus* shrill, squeaky, fr *stridere, stridēre*] – **stridulatory** *adj,* **stridulation** /-'laysh(ə)n/ *n*

strife /strief/ *n* bitter conflict or dissension [ME *strif,* fr OF *estrif,* prob fr *estriver* to contend – more at STRIVE] – **strifeless** *adj*

strigose /'striegohs/ *adj* **1** having bristles or scales lying against a surface ⟨*a* ~ *leaf*⟩ **2** marked with fine grooves ⟨*the* ~ *wing cases of a beetle*⟩ [NL *strigosus,* fr *striga* bristle, fr L, furrow]

[1]**strike** /striek/ *vb* **struck** /struk/; **struck** *also* **stricken** /'strikən/ *vt* **1a** to strike at; hit **b** to make an attack on **c** to inflict ⟨~ *a blow*⟩ **2a** to haul down ⟨~ *a flag*⟩ **b** to dismantle (e g a stage set) **c** to take down the tents of (a camp) **3** to afflict suddenly ⟨stricken *by a heart attack*⟩ **4** to delete, cancel ⟨~ *a name from a list*⟩ **5a** to send down or out ⟨*trees* struck *roots deep into the soil*⟩ **b** to penetrate painfully ⟨*the news* struck *him to the heart*⟩ **6** to indicate by sounding ⟨*the clock* struck *7*⟩ **7a** *of light* to fall on **b** *of a sound* to become audible to **8** to cause suddenly to become ⟨struck *him dead*⟩ **9** to produce by stamping ⟨~ *a medal*⟩ **10a** to produce (fire) by striking **b** to cause (a match) to ignite **11a** to make a mental impact on ⟨*they were* struck *by its speed*⟩ ⟨*how does that* ~ *you?*⟩ **b** to occur suddenly to **12** to make and ratify (a bargain) **13** to produce (as if) by playing an instrument ⟨~ *a chord*⟩ ⟨~ *a gloomy note*⟩ **14a** to hook (a fish) by a sharp pull on the line **b** *of a fish* to snatch at (bait) **15** to arrive at (a balance) by computation **16** COME ACROSS ⟨~ *gold*⟩ **17** to assume (a pose) **18a** to place (a plant cutting) in a medium for growth and rooting **b** to propagate (a plant) in this manner **19** to cause (an arc) to form (e g between electrodes of an arc lamp) **20** to play or produce on keys or strings **21** *NAm* to engage in a strike against (an employer) ~*vi* **1** to take a course ⟨struck *off across the field*⟩ **2a** to aim a blow **b** to make an attack **3** to collide forcefully **4a** *of the time* to become indicated by a clock, bell, or chime ⟨*the hour had just* struck⟩ **b** to make known the time by sounding ⟨*the clock* struck⟩ **5** *of a fish* to seize bait or a lure **6** *of a plant cutting* to take root **7** to engage in a strike [ME *striken,* fr OE *strīcan* to stroke, go; akin to OHG *strīhhan* to stroke, L *stringere* to touch lightly, *striga, stria* furrow] – **strike oil** to achieve financial success

[2]**strike** *n* **1** STRICKLE 1 **2** an act of striking **3** a work stoppage by a body of workers, made as a protest or to force an employer to comply with demands **4** the direction of a horizontal line formed at the angle of intersection of an upward-sloping stratum and a horizontal plane **5** a pull on a line by a fish in striking **6** a success in finding or hitting sthg; *esp* a discovery of a valuable mineral deposit ⟨*a lucky oil* ~⟩ **7** a pitched ball in baseball that is either missed by the batter or hit outside the foul lines and that counts against him **8** the knocking down of all 10 pins with the first bowl in a frame in tenpin bowling **9** the opportunity to receive the bowling by virtue of being the batsman at the wicket towards which the bowling is being directed **10** an (air) attack on a target

'strike,bound /-,bownd/ *adj* subjected to a strike

'strike,breaker /-,braykə/ *n* one hired to replace a striking worker

'strike,breaking /-,brayking/ *n* action designed to break up a strike

strike down *vt* **1** to afflict suddenly; lay low ⟨struck down *by malaria*⟩ **2** to cause to die suddenly ⟨*a young poet* struck down *in his prime*⟩

strike off *vt* **1** to sever with a stroke **2** to forbid (sby) to continue in professional practice usu because of misconduct or incompetence ⟨struck *the doctor* off *for malpractice*⟩

strike out *vt* to delete ~*vi* to set out vigorously ⟨struck out *towards the coast*⟩

'strike ,pay *n* an allowance paid by a trade union to its members on strike

striker /'striekə/ *n* **1** a games player who strikes; *esp* a soccer player whose main duty is to score goals ☞ SPORT **2** a worker on strike [¹STRIKE + ²-ER]

strike up *vi* to begin to sing or play ~*vt* **1** to cause to begin singing or playing **2** to cause to begin ⟨strike up *a conversation*⟩

striking /'strieking/ *adj* attracting attention, esp because of unusual or impressive qualities – **strikingly** *adv*

Strine /strien/ *n, sometimes not cap* Australian English – chiefly humor [alter. of *Australian*]

¹string /string/ *n* **1** a narrow cord used to bind, fasten, or tie **2** a plant fibre (e g a leaf vein) **3a** the gut or wire cord of a musical instrument **b** a stringed instrument of an orchestra – usu pl **4a** a group of objects threaded on a string ⟨*a* ~ *of beads*⟩ **b** a set of things arranged (as if) in a sequence **c** a group of usu scattered business concerns ⟨*a* ~ *of shops*⟩ **d** the animals, esp horses, belonging to or used by sby **5** one who is selected (e g for a sports team) for the specified rank; *also, sing or pl in constr* a group of players so selected ⟨*usually plays for the first* ~⟩ ⟨*a second-string player*⟩ **6** a succession, sequence **7a** either of the inclined sides of a stair supporting the treads and risers ☞ ARCHITECTURE **b** STRING COURSE **8** *pl* conditions or obligations attached to sthg [ME, fr OE *streng*; akin to L *stringere* to bind tight – more at ²STRAIN] – **stringed** *adj*, **stringless** *adj*

²string *vt* **strung** /strung/ **1** to equip with strings **2a** to thread (as if) on a string **b** to tie, hang, or fasten with string **3** to remove the strings of ⟨~ *beans*⟩ **4** to extend or stretch like a string

³string *adj* made with wide meshes and usu of string ⟨~ *vest*⟩ ⟨~ *bag*⟩

string along *vi* **1** to accompany sby, esp reluctantly ⟨string along *with the crowd*⟩ **2** to agree; GO ALONG – usu + *with* ~*vt* to deceive, fool ⟨string *him* along *with false promises*⟩ *USE* infml

string bean *n* a French bean or runner bean with stringy fibres on the lines of separation of the pods

string course *n* a horizontal ornamental band (e g of bricks) in a building

stringent /'strinj(ə)nt/ *adj* **1** rigorous or strict, esp with regard to rules or standards **2** marked by money scarcity and credit strictness [L *stringent-, stringens*, prp of *stringere* to bind tight] – **stringency** *n*, **stringently** *adv*

stringer /'string·ə/ *n* **1** a horizontal structural support **2** a longitudinal structural part (e g in an aircraft fuselage or wing) to reinforce the skin **3** a correspondent working esp part-time for a publication or news agency [²STRING + ²-ER]

'string,halt /-,hawlt/ *n* lameness in the hind legs of a horse caused by muscular spasms [¹*string* (sinew, tendon) + ¹*halt*] – **stringhalted** *adj*

'string,piece /-,pees/ *n* the heavy squared timber lying along the top of the piles forming a dock front or timber pier

string tie *n* a narrow tie

string up *vt* to hang; *specif* to kill by hanging ⟨*they* strung *him* up *from the nearest tree*⟩

stringy /'string·i/ *adj* **1a** containing or resembling fibrous matter or string ⟨~ *hair*⟩ **b** sinewy, wiry **2** capable of being drawn out to form a string – **stringiness** *n*

'stringy,bark /-,bahk/ *n* (the thick fibrous bark of) any of several Australian eucalyptuses

¹strip /strip/ *vb* **-pp-** *vt* **1a** to remove clothing, covering, or surface or extraneous matter from **b** to deprive of possessions, privileges, or rank **2** to remove furniture, equipment, or accessories from **3** to press the last available milk from the teats of (esp a cow) **4a** to remove cured leaves from the stalks of (tobacco) **b** to remove the midrib from (tobacco leaves) **5** to damage the thread or teeth of (a screw, cog, etc) ~*vi* **1** to undress **2** to perform a striptease [ME *strippen*, fr OE *-strīpan*; akin to OHG *stroufen* to strip]

²strip *n* **1a** a long narrow piece of material **b** a long narrow area of land or water **2** LANDING STRIP **3** *Br* clothes worn by a rugby or soccer team [perh fr MLG *strippe* strap]

strip cartoon *n* a series of drawings (e g in a magazine) in narrative sequence

'strip ,club *n* a club which features striptease artists

'strip-,cropping *n* the growing of a cultivated crop (e g maize) in alternate strips with a turf-forming crop (e g hay) to minimize erosion of the land – **strip-crop** *vb*

stripe /striep/ *n* **1** a line or narrow band differing in colour or texture from the adjoining parts **2** a bar, chevron, etc of braid or embroidery worn usu on the sleeve of a uniform to indicate rank or length of service **3** *chiefly NAm* a distinct variety or sort; a type ⟨*men of the same political* ~⟩ [prob fr MD; akin to OE *strica* streak – more at STREAK] – **striped** *adj*, **stripeless** *adj*

'strip ,farming *n* **1** the growing of crops in separate strips of land allotted to individual farmers so that good and bad land is fairly distributed **2** strip-cropping

strip in *vt* to insert (typeset material) into a prepared space in a photocomposed sheet

'strip ,light *n* a fluorescent lamp

strip lighting *n* lighting provided by 1 or more strip lights

stripling /'stripling/ *n* an adolescent boy [ME]

strip mine *n, chiefly NAm* an opencast mine – **strip-mine** *vt*, **strip miner** *n*

stripper /'stripə/ *n* **1** sby who performs a striptease **2** a tool or solvent for removing sthg, esp paint [¹STRIP + ²-ER]

strip poker *n* a poker game in which a player pays his/her losses by removing articles of clothing

,strip'tease /-'teez/ *n* an act or entertainment in which a performer, esp a woman, undresses gradually in view of the audience – **stripteaser** *n*

stripy /'striepi/ *adj* striped

strive /striev/ *vi* **strove** /strohv/ *also* **strived; striven** /striv(ə)n/, **strived** **1** to struggle in opposition; contend 2 to endeavour; try hard [ME *striven*, fr OF *estriver*, of Gmc origin; akin to MHG *streben* to endeavour, OE *strīdan* to stride] – **striver** *n*

strobe /strohb/ *n* a stroboscope [by shortening & alter.]

strobila /stroh'bielə/ *n, pl* **strobilae** /-li, -lay/ a line of similar joined animal structures (e g the segmented body of a tapeworm) produced by budding [NL, fr Gk *strobilē* plug of lint shaped like a pinecone, fr *strobilos* pinecone] – **strobilar** *adj*

strobilation /ˌstrohbi'laysh(ə)n/ *n* the production of strobilae by asexual reproduction [NL *strobila*]

strobile /'strohbiel/ *n* CONE 1 [NL *strobilus*]

strobilus /stroh'bieləs/ *n, pl* **strobili** /-lie/ CONE 1 [NL, fr LL, pinecone, fr Gk *strobilos* twisted object, top, pinecone, fr *strobos* action of whirling – more at STROPHE]

stroboscope /'strohbəˌskohp/ *n* an instrument for measuring or observing motion, esp rotation or vibration, by allowing successive views of very short duration so that the motion appears slowed or stopped: e g **a** a lamp that flashes intermittently at varying frequencies **b** a disc with marks to be viewed under intermittent light, used to set up the speed of a record player turntable [Gk *strobos* whirling + ISV *-scope*] – **stroboscopic** /ˌstrohbə'skopik, ˌstro-/ *adj*, **stroboscopically** *adv*

strode /strohd/ *past of* STRIDE

stroganoff /'strogənof/ *n, often cap* a rich dish of strips of meat (e g beef) cooked in a sour-cream sauce [Count Paul *Stroganoff*, 19th-c Russ diplomat]

[1]**stroke** /strohk/ *vt* to pass the hand over gently in 1 direction [ME *stroken*, fr OE *strācian*; akin to OHG *strīhhan* to stroke – more at STRIKE] – **stroker** *n*

[2]**stroke** *n* **1** the act of striking; *esp* a blow with a weapon or implement **2** a single unbroken movement; *esp* one that is repeated **3** a striking of the ball in a game (e g cricket or tennis); *specif* an (attempted) striking of the ball that constitutes the scoring unit in golf **4a** an action by which sthg is done, produced, or achieved ⟨*a ~ of genius*⟩ **b** an unexpected occurrence ⟨*a ~ of luck*⟩ **5** (an attack of) sudden usu complete loss of consciousness, sensation, and voluntary motion caused by rupture, thrombosis, etc of a brain artery **6a** (the technique or mode used for) a propelling beat or movement against a resisting medium ⟨*what ~ does she swim?*⟩ ⟨*rowed a fast ~*⟩ **b** an oarsman who sits at the stern of a racing rowing boat and sets the pace for the rest of the crew **7** a vigorous or energetic effort ⟨*never does a ~*⟩ **8** (the distance of) the movement in either direction of a reciprocating mechanical part (e g a piston rod) **9** the sound of a striking clock ⟨*at the ~ of 12*⟩ **10** an act of stroking or caressing **11a** a mark or dash made by a single movement of an implement **b** *Br* a solidus [ME; akin to OE *strīcan* to stroke – more at STRIKE] – **at a stroke** by a single action – **off one's stroke** in a situation where one performs below a usual standard ⟨*it put him* off his stroke⟩

[3]**stroke** *vt* **1** to set the stroke for (a rowing crew) or for the crew of (a rowing boat) **2** to hit (a ball) with a controlled swinging blow ~ *vi* to row at a specified number of strokes a minute

stroke play *n* a golf competition scored by total number of strokes – compare MATCH PLAY

stroll /strohl/ *vi* to walk in a leisurely or idle manner [prob fr G dial. *strollen*] – **stroll** *n*

stroller /'strohlə/ *n, NAm* a pushchair [STROLL + [2]-ER]

strolling /'strohling/ *adj* going from place to place, esp in search of work ⟨*~ players*⟩

stroma /'strohmə/ *n, pl* **stromata** /-mətə/ **1** the supporting framework of an animal organ or of some cells **2a** a compact mass of fungal hyphae producing a fruiting body **b** the colourless matrix of a chloroplast in which the chlorophyll-containing layers are embedded [NL *stromat-*, *stroma*, fr L, bed covering, fr Gk *strōmat-*, *strōma*, fr *stornynai* to spread out – more at STREW] – **stromal, stromatal, stromatic** /stroh'matik/ *adj*

strong /strong/ *adj* **1** having or marked by great physical power **2** having moral or intellectual power **3** having great resources of wealth, talent, etc ⟨*a film with a ~ cast*⟩ **4** of a specified number ⟨*an army ten thousand ~*⟩ **5a** striking or superior of its kind ⟨*a ~ resemblance*⟩ **b** effective or efficient, esp in a specified area ⟨*~ on logic*⟩ **6** forceful, cogent ⟨*~ evidence*⟩ **7a** rich in some active agent (e g a flavour or extract) ⟨*~ tea*⟩ **b** *of a colour* intense **c** *of an acid or base* ionizing to a great extent in solution **d** magnifying by refracting greatly ⟨*a ~ lens*⟩ **8** moving with vigour or force ⟨*a ~ wind*⟩ **9** ardent, zealous ⟨*a ~ supporter*⟩ **10** well established; firm ⟨*~ beliefs*⟩ **11** not easily upset or nauseated ⟨*a ~ stomach*⟩ **12** having a pungent or offensive smell or flavour **13** tending to steady or higher prices ⟨*a ~ market*⟩ **14** of or being a verb that forms inflections by internal vowel change (e g *drink, drank, drunk*) – compare WEAK 7 [ME, fr OE *strang*; akin to OHG *strengi* strong, L *stringere* to bind tight – more at [2]STRAIN] – **strongish** *adj*, **strongly** *adv*

'strongˌarm /-ˌahm/ *adj* using or involving undue force ⟨*~ tactics*⟩

'strongˌbox /-ˌboks/ *n* a strongly made chest for money or valuables

strong breeze *n* wind having a speed of 39 to 49km/h (25 to 31mph)

strong drink *n* intoxicating liquor

strong gale *n* wind having a speed of 75 to 88km/h (47 to 54mph)

'strongˌhold /-ˌhohld/ *n* **1** a fortified place **2a** a place of refuge or safety **b** a place dominated by a specified group ⟨*a Tory ~*⟩

strong interaction *n* an interaction between elementary particles that is more powerful than any other known force and is responsible for the forces that bind protons and neutrons in atomic nuclei – compare WEAK INTERACTION

strong language *n* offensive language; *esp* swearing

'strong ˌman *n* **1** a man who performs feats of muscular strength **2** an autocratic leader – infml

ˌstrong-'minded *adj* marked by firmness and independence of judgment – **strong-mindedly** *adv*, **strong-mindedness** *n*

'strongˌpoint /-ˌpoynt/ *n* a small fortified defensive position

'strong ˌpoint *n* sthg in which one excels

'strong ˌroom *n* a (fireproof and burglarproof) room for money and valuables

strong suit *n* **1** a suit in a hand containing playing cards of high value **2** STRONG POINT

strontia /'strontyə/ *n* strontium oxide [NL, fr obs E *strontian*, fr *Strontian*, village in Scotland]

strontium /'strontyəm/ *n* a soft bivalent metallic

element of the alkaline-earth group chemically similar to calcium ☞ PERIODIC TABLE [NL, fr *strontia*]

ˌ**strontium '90** /ˈnienti/ *n* a radioactive isotope of strontium present in the fallout from nuclear explosions and hazardous because it can replace calcium in bone

[1]**strop** /strop/ *n* sthg, esp a leather band, for sharpening a razor [ME – more at STRAP]

[2]**strop** *vt* **-pp-** to sharpen on a strop

strophanthin /strohˈfanthin/ *n* any of several glycosides (e g ouabain) or mixtures of glycosides obtained from African plants of the periwinkle family [ISV, fr NL *Strophanthus*, genus of tropical trees or vines]

strophe /ˈstrohfi/ *n* **1** (the part of a chorale ode sung to accompany) a turning movement made by the classical Greek chorus **2** a rhythmic system composed of 2 or more lines repeated as a unit [Gk *strophē*, lit., act of turning, fr *strephein* to turn, twist; akin to Gk *strobos* action of whirling]

strophic /ˈstrofik, ˈstroh-/ *adj* **1** of, containing, or consisting of strophes **2** using the same music for successive stanzas of a song

stroppy /ˈstropi/ *adj, Br* quarrelsome, obstreperous – infml [perh by shortening & alter. fr *obstreperous*]

strove /strohv/ *past of* STRIVE

structural /ˈstrukch(ə)rəl/ *adj* **1a** of or affecting structure **b** used in or suitable for building structures ⟨~ *steel*⟩ **c** involved in or caused by structure, esp of the economy ⟨~ *unemployment*⟩ **2** of the physical make-up of a plant or animal body – **structurally** *adv*

structural formula *n* a chemical formula showing the arrangement of atoms and bonds in the molecule

structuralism /ˈstrukch(ə)rəˌliz(ə)m/ *n* a method or approach used in anthropology, literary criticism, linguistics, etc that seeks to analyse data in terms of the significance of underlying relationships and patterns of organization – **structuralist** *n or adj*

[1]**structure** /ˈstrukchə/ *n* **1a** sthg (e g a building) that is constructed **b** sthg organized in a definite pattern **2** manner of construction **3a** the arrangement of particles or parts in a substance or body ⟨*soil* ~⟩ ⟨*molecular* ~⟩ **b** arrangement or interrelation of elements ⟨*economic* ~⟩ [ME, fr L *structura*, fr *structus*, pp of *struere* to heap up, build; akin to L *sternere* to spread out – more at STREW] – **structureless** *adj*

[2]**structure** *vt* to form into a structure

strudel /ˈstroohdl/ *n* a pastry made from a thin sheet of dough rolled up with filling and baked ⟨*apple* ~⟩ [G, lit., whirlpool]

[1]**struggle** /ˈstrugl/ *vi* **struggling** /ˈstrugling, ˈstrugl·ing/ **1** to make violent or strenuous efforts against opposition **2** to proceed with difficulty or great effort [ME *struglen*] – **struggler** *n*

[2]**struggle** *n* **1** a violent effort; a determined attempt in adverse circumstances **2** a hard-fought contest

struggle for existence *n* the competition for food, space, etc that tends to eliminate less efficient individuals of a population, thereby increasing the chance of inherited traits being passed on from the more efficient survivors – compare NATURAL SELECTION

strum /strum/ *vb* **-mm-** *vt* **1** to brush the fingers lightly over the strings of (a musical instrument) in playing ⟨~ *a guitar*⟩; *also* to thrum **2** to play (music) on a guitar ⟨~ *a tune*⟩ ~ *vi* to strum a stringed instrument [imit] – **strummer** *n*

struma /ˈstroohmə/ *n, pl* **strumae** /-mi/, **strumas** **1** goitre **2** a swelling at the base of the capsule in many mosses **3** *archaic* scrofula [(1, 3) L – more at STRUT; (2) NL, fr L] – **strumose** /ˈstroohmohs/ *adj*

strumpet /ˈstrumpit/ *n* a prostitute [ME]

strung /strung/ *past of* STRING

ˌ**strung-ˈup** *adj* extremely nervous or tense

[1]**strut** /strut/ *vi* **-tt-** **1** to walk with a proud or erect gait **2** to walk with a pompous air; swagger [ME *strouten* to swell, protrude stiffly, swagger, fr OE *strūtian* to exert oneself; akin to L *struma* goitre, OE *starian* to stare] – **strutter** *n*

[2]**strut** *n* **1** a structural piece designed to resist pressure in the direction of its length ☞ ARCHITECTURE **2** a pompous step or walk

[3]**strut** *vt* **-tt-** to provide or stiffen with a strut

struth, strewth /stroohth/ *interj, chiefly Br* – used to express surprise, alarm, etc [short for *God's truth*]

struthious /ˈstroohthyəs/ *adj* of or like the ostriches [LL *struthio* ostrich, irreg fr Gk *strouthos*]

strychnine /ˈstrikneen/ *n* a poisonous alkaloid obtained from nux vomica and related plants and used as a poison (e g for rodents) and medicinally as a stimulant to the central nervous system [F, fr NL *Strychnos*, genus name, fr L, nightshade, fr Gk]

Stuart /ˈstyoo·ət/ *adj* of the Scottish royal house that ruled Scotland from 1371 to 1603 and Britain from 1603 to 1649 and from 1660 to 1714 [Robert *Stewart* (Robert II of Scotland) †1390] – **Stuart** *n*

[1]**stub** /stub/ *n* **1** [1]STUMP 2 **2** a short blunt part of a pencil, cigarette, etc left after a larger part has been broken off or used up **3a** a small part of a leaf or page (e g of a chequebook) left on the spine as a record of the contents of the part torn away **b** the part of a ticket returned to the user after inspection [ME *stubb*, fr OE *stybb*; akin to Gk *stypos* stem, *typtein* to beat]

[2]**stub** *vt* **-bb-** **1a** to grub up by the roots **b** to clear (land) by uprooting stumps **2** to extinguish (e g a cigarette) by crushing – usu + *out* **3** to strike (one's foot or toe) against an object

stubble /ˈstubl/ *n* **1** the stalky remnants of plants, esp cereal grasses, which remain rooted in the soil after harvest **2** a rough growth (e g of beard) resembling stubble [ME *stuble*, fr OF *estuble*, fr L *stupula* stalk, straw, alter. of *stipula* – more at STIPULE] – **stubbly** *adj*

stubborn /ˈstubən/ *adj* **1** (unreasonably) unyielding or determined **2** refractory, intractable ⟨*a* ~ *cold*⟩ [ME *stuborn*] – **stubbornly** *adv*, **stubbornness** *n*

stubby /ˈstubi/ *adj* short and thick like a stub

[1]**stucco** /ˈstukoh/ *n, pl* **stuccos, stuccoes** a cement or fine plaster used in the covering and decoration of walls [It, of Gmc origin; akin to OHG *stucki* piece, crust, OE *stocc* stock]

[2]**stucco** *vt* **stuccoes, stuccos; stuccoing; stuccoed** to coat or decorate with stucco

stuck /stuk/ *past of* STICK

ˌ**stuck-ˈup** *adj* superciliously self-important or conceited – infml

[1]**stud** /stud/ *n* **1** *sing or pl in constr* a group of animals, esp horses, kept primarily for breeding **2a** a male animal, esp a stallion, kept for breeding **b** a

sexually active man – vulg [ME *stod*, fr OE *stōd*; akin to OE *standan* to stand] – **at stud** for breeding as a stud ⟨*retired racehorses standing* at stud⟩

[2]**stud** *n* **1** any of the smaller upright posts in the walls of a building to which panelling or laths are fastened **2a** a rivet or nail with a large head used for ornament or protection **b** a solid button with a shank or eye on the back inserted through an eyelet in a garment as a fastener or ornament **3a** a piece (e g a rod or pin) projecting from a machine and serving chiefly as a support or axis **b** a metal cleat inserted in a horseshoe or snow tyre to increase grip **4** *NAm* the height from floor to ceiling [ME *stode*, fr OE *studu*; akin to OE *stōw* place – more at STOW]

[3]**stud** *vt* **-dd- 1** to provide (e g a building or wall) with studs **2** to decorate, cover, or protect with studs **3** to set thickly with a number of prominent objects ⟨*sky* ~ded *with stars*⟩

'stud,book /-,book/ *n* an official record of the pedigree of purebred horses, dogs, etc

'studding ,sail /'studing/ *n* an additional light sail set at the side of a square sail in light winds [origin unknown]

student /'styood(ə)nt/ *n* **1** a scholar, learner; *esp* one who attends a college or university **2** an attentive and systematic observer ⟨*a* ~ *of human nature*⟩ [ME, fr L *student-, studens*, fr prp of *studēre* to study – more at STUDY]

'studentship /-ship/ *n, Br* a grant for university study

student's t distribution *n, often cap S* T DISTRIBUTION [*Student*, pen name of W S Gossett †1937 Brit statistician]

studhorse /'stud,haws/ *n* a stallion kept esp for breeding

studied /'studid/ *adj* **1** carefully considered or prepared **2** deliberate, premeditated ⟨~ *indifference*⟩ – **studiedly** *adv*

studio /'styoohdi·oh/ *n, pl* **studios 1a** the workroom of a painter, sculptor, or photographer **b** a place for the study of an art (e g dancing, singing, or acting) **2** a place where films are made; *also, sing or pl in constr* a film production company including its premises and employees **3** a room equipped for the production of radio or television programmes [It, lit., study, fr L *studium*]

studio couch *n* an upholstered usu backless couch that can be converted into a double bed by sliding from underneath it the frame of a single bed – compare BEDSETTEE

studio flat *n* a small flat consisting typically of a main room, kitchen, and bathroom

studious /'styoohdi·əs/ *adj* **1** of, concerned with, or given to study **2a** marked by or suggesting serious thoughtfulness or diligence; earnest ⟨*a* ~ *expression on his face*⟩ **b** STUDIED 2 – **studiously** *adv*, **studiousness** *n*

studwork /'stud,wuhk/ *n* work supported, strengthened, held together, or ornamented by studs

[1]**study** /'studi/ *n* **1** a state of deep thought or contemplation – esp in *a brown study* **2a** the application of the mind to acquiring (specific) knowledge ⟨*the* ~ *of Latin*⟩ **b** a careful examination or analysis of a subject **3** a room devoted to study **4** a branch of learning **5** a literary or artistic work intended as a preliminary or experimental interpretation **6** an étude [ME *studie*, fr OF *estudie*, fr L *studium*; akin to L *studēre* to study]

[2]**study** *vi* to engage in study ~ *vt* **1** to engage in the study of ⟨~ *medicine*⟩ **2** to consider attentively or in detail

[1]**stuff** /stuf/ *n* **1a** materials, supplies, or equipment used in various activities ⟨*the plumber brought his* ~⟩ **b** personal property; possessions **2** a finished textile suitable for clothing; *esp* wool or worsted material **3a** an unspecified material substance ⟨*sold tons of the* ~⟩ **b** a group of miscellaneous objects ⟨*pick that* ~ *up off the floor*⟩ **4** the essence of a usu abstract thing ⟨*the* ~ *of greatness*⟩ **5a** subject matter ⟨*a teacher who knows his* ~⟩ **b** a task involving special knowledge or skill ⟨*the firemen were called on to do their* ~⟩ **6** worthless ideas, opinion, or writing; rubbish *USE* (*5&6*) infml [ME, fr MF *estoffe*, fr OF, fr *estoffer* to equip, stock, prob fr MHG *stopfen* to stop up, stuff, fr OHG *stopfōn* – more at STOP]

[2]**stuff** *vt* **1a** to fill (as if) by packing things in; cram **b** to gorge (oneself) with food **c** to fill (e g meat or vegetables) with a stuffing **d** to fill with stuffing or padding **e** to fill out the skin of (an animal) for mounting **f** to stop up (a hole); plug **2** to choke or block *up* (the nasal passages) **3** to force into a limited space; thrust **4** *Br, of a male* to have sexual intercourse with – vulg – **stuffer** *n*

,stuffed 'shirt *n* a smug, pompous, and usu reactionary person

stuffing /'stufing/ *n* material used to stuff sthg; *esp* a seasoned mixture used to stuff meat, eggs, etc

stuffy /'stufi/ *adj* **1a** badly ventilated; close **b** stuffed up ⟨*a* ~ *nose*⟩ **2** stodgy, dull **3** prim, straitlaced – **stuffily** *adv*, **stuffiness** *n*

stultify /'stultifie/ *vt* to make futile or absurd [LL *stultificare* to make foolish, fr L *stultus* foolish; akin to L *stolidus* stolid] – **stultification** /,stultifi'kaysh(ə)n/ *n*

[1]**stumble** /'stumbl/ *vi* **stumbling** /'stumbling/ **1** to trip in walking or running **2a** to walk unsteadily or clumsily **b** to speak or act in a hesitant or faltering manner **3** to come unexpectedly or by chance – + *upon, on,* or *across* [ME *stumblen*, prob of Scand origin; akin to Norw dial. *stumle* to stumble; akin to OE *stamerian* to stammer] – **stumbler** *n*, **stumblingly** *adv*

[2]**stumble** *n* an act of stumbling

'stumbling ,block /'stumbling/ *n* an obstacle to progress or understanding

stumer /'styoohmə/ *n, Br* a sham, fraud; *esp* a worthless or forged coin, note, or cheque – slang [origin unknown]

[1]**stump** /stump/ *n* **1a** the part of an arm, leg, etc remaining attached to the trunk after the rest is removed **b** a rudimentary or vestigial bodily part **2** the part of a plant, esp a tree, remaining in the ground attached to the root after the stem is cut **3** a remaining part; a stub **4** any of the 3 upright wooden rods that together with the bails form the wicket in cricket ☞ SPORT [ME *stumpe*; akin to OHG *stumpf* stump, ME *stampen* to stamp]

[2]**stump** *vt* **1** *of a wicketkeeper* to dismiss (a batsman who is outside his popping crease but not attempting to run) by breaking the wicket with the ball before it has touched another fieldsman **2** *NAm* to travel over (a region) making political speeches or supporting a cause **3** to baffle, bewilder – infml ⟨*was* ~ed *by her question*⟩ ~ *vi* **1** to walk heavily or noisily **2**

chiefly NAm to travel about making political speeches

[3]**stump** *vt or n* (to treat with) a short thick roll of leather, paper, etc usu pointed at both ends and used to soften lines in a drawing [n F or Flem; F *estompe*, fr Flem *stomp*, lit., stub, fr MD; akin to OHG *stumpf* stump; vb fr n]

stumper /'stumpə/ *n* **1** a wicketkeeper **2** a puzzling question; a teaser [[2]STUMP + [2]-ER]

stump up *vb, chiefly Br* to pay (what is due), esp unwillingly – infml

stumpy /'stumpi/ *adj* short and thick; stubby

stun /stun/ *vt* **-nn- 1** to make dazed or dizzy (as if) by a blow **2** to overcome, esp with astonishment or disbelief [ME *stunen*, modif of OF *estoner* – more at ASTONISH]

stung /stung/ *past of* STING

stunk /stunk/ *past of* STINK

stunner /'stunə/ *n* an unusually beautiful or attractive person or thing – infml [STUN + [2]-ER]

stunning /'stuning/ *adj* strikingly beautiful or attractive – infml – **stunningly** *adv*

stunsail, stuns'l /'stuns(ə)l/ *n* STUDDING SAIL [by contr]

[1]**stunt** /stunt/ *vt* to hinder or arrest the growth or development of [E dial. *stunt* (stubborn, stunted, abrupt), prob of Scand origin; akin to ON *stuttr* scant – more at STINT] – **stuntedness** *n*

[2]**stunt** *n* an unusual or difficult feat performed to gain publicity [prob alter. of *stump* (challenge)]

'**stunt** ,**man,** *fem* '**stunt** ,**woman** *n* sby employed, esp as a substitute for an actor, to perform dangerous feats

stupa /'stoohpə/ *n* a Buddhist shrine in the form of an earthen or brick mound usu containing sacred relics [Skt *stūpa*]

stupe /styoohp/ *n* a hot wet (medicated) cloth applied externally (e g to stimulate circulation) [ME, fr L *stuppa* coarse part of flax, tow, fr Gk *styppē*]

stupefy /'st(y)oohpifie/ *vt* **1** to make groggy or insensible **2** to astonish [MF *stupefier*, modif of L *stupefacere*, fr *stupēre* to be astonished + *facere* to make, do – more at DO] – **stupefaction** /,st(y)oohpi'faksh(ə)n/ *n*

stupendous /styooh'pendəs/ *adj* of astonishing size or greatness; amazing, astounding [L *stupendus*, gerundive of *stupēre*] – **stupendously** *adv*, **stupendousness** *n*

stupid /'styoohpid/ *adj* **1** slow-witted, obtuse **2** dulled in feeling or perception; torpid **3** annoying, exasperating – infml ⟨*this ~ torch won't work*⟩ [MF *stupide*, fr L *stupidus*, fr *stupēre* to be benumbed, be astonished; akin to Gk *typtein* to beat – more at TYPE] – **stupidly** *adv*, **stupidness, stupidity** /styooh'pidəti/ *n*

stupor /'styoohpə/ *n* a state of extreme apathy, torpor, or reduced sense or feeling (e g resulting from shock or intoxication) [ME, fr L, fr *stupēre*] – **stuporous** *adj*

sturdy /'stuhdi/ *adj* **1** strongly built or constituted; stout, hardy **2a** having physical strength or vigour; robust **b** firm, resolute [ME, fierce, brave, stubborn, fr OF *estourdi* stunned, fr pp of *estourdir* to stun, fr (assumed) VL *exturdire* to be dizzy as a thrush that is drunk from eating grapes, fr L *ex-* + *turdus* thrush – more at THRUSH] – **sturdily** *adv*, **sturdiness** *n*

sturgeon /'stuhj(ə)n/ *n* any of various usu large edible fishes whose roe is made into caviar [ME, fr OF *estourjon*, of Gmc origin; akin to OE *styria* sturgeon]

Sturm und Drang /,stuhm ən 'drang, shtuhm/ *n* a late 18th-c German movement characterized by highly emotional literature, often dealing with the individual's revolt against society [G, fr *Sturm und Drang* (*Storm and Stress*), drama by Friedrich von Klinger †1831 G writer]

[1]**stutter** /'stutə/ *vi* to speak with involuntary disruption or blocking of speech (e g by spasmodic repetition or prolongation of vocal sounds) ~ *vt* to say, speak, or sound (as if) with a stutter – compare STAMMER [freq of E dial. *stut* to stutter, fr ME *stutten*; akin to D *stotteren* to stutter, L *tundere* to beat – more at STINT] – **stutterer** *n*

[2]**stutter** *n* (a speech disorder involving) stuttering

[1]**sty** /stie/ *n, pl* **sties** *also* **styes** a pigsty [ME, fr OE *stig*; akin to ON *-stī* sty]

[2]**sty, stye** /~/ *n, pl* **sties, styes** an inflamed swelling of a sebaceous gland at the margin of an eyelid [short for obs *styan*, fr (assumed) ME, alter. of OE *stīgend*, fr *stīgan* to go up, rise – more at STAIR]

stygian /'stiji·ən/ *adj, often cap* extremely dark or gloomy – fml [L *stygius*, fr Gk *stygios*, fr *Styg-*, *Styx* Styx, mythical river of the underworld]

[1]**styl-, stylo-** *comb form* pillar ⟨stylo*bate*⟩ [L, fr Gk, fr *stylos* – more at [2]STEER]

[2]**styl-, styli-, stylo-** *comb form* style; styloid structure ⟨styl *ate*⟩ ⟨styli*form*⟩ ⟨stylo*graphic*⟩ [L *stilus* stake, stalk – more at STYLE]

-stylar /-'stielə, -'stielah/ *comb form* (→ *adj*) having (such or so many) pillars ⟨*amphi*stylar⟩ [Gk *stylos* pillar – more at [2]STEER]

[1]**style** /stiel/ *n* **1a** a stylus **b** a prolongation of a plant ovary bearing a stigma at the top ☞ PLANT **c** a slender elongated part (e g a bristle) on an animal **2a** a manner of expressing thought in language, esp when characteristic of an individual, period, etc **b** the custom or plan followed in spelling, capitalization, punctuation, and typographic arrangement and display **3** mode of address; a title **4a** a distinctive or characteristic manner of doing sthg **b** a fashionable or elegant life-style ⟨*lived in ~*⟩ **c** excellence or distinction in social behaviour, manners, or appearance [ME *stile, style*, fr L *stilus* stake, stylus, style of writing; akin to OE *stician* to stick] – **stylar** *adj*, **styleless** *adj*

[2]**style** *vt* **1** to designate by an identifying term; name **2** to fashion according to a particular mode – **styler** *n*

[3]**style** *n* a stile

[1]**-style** /-stiel/ *comb form* (→ *adj*) resembling ⟨*leather*-style *briefcase*⟩

[2]**-style** *comb form* (→ *adv*) in the style or manner of ⟨*seated on the floor Indian*-style⟩

stylet /'stielit/ *n* **1a** a slender surgical probe **b** a thin wire inserted into a catheter to maintain rigidity or into a hollow needle to keep it clear of obstruction **2** a relatively rigid elongated organ or part (e g a piercing mouthpart) of an animal **3** a stiletto [F, fr MF *stilet* stiletto, fr OIt *stiletto*]

stylish /'stielish/ *adj* fashionably elegant [[1]STYLE + -ISH] – **stylishly** *adv*, **stylishness** *n*

stylist /'stielist/ *n* **1** a writer who cultivates a fine literary style **2** one who develops, designs, or advises on styles

stylistic /stie'listik/ *adj* of esp literary or artistic style – **stylistically** *adv*

stylistics /stie'listiks/ *n pl but sing or pl in constr* the study of style, esp in literature

styl·ize, -ise /'stieliez/ *vt* to make (e g a work of art) conform to a conventional style rather than to nature – **stylization** /-'zaysh(ə)n/ *n*

stylo- – see [1] [2]STYL-

stylograph /'stielə,grahf, -,graf/ *n* a type of fountain pen that has a fine point fitted with a needle

styloid /'stieloyd/ *adj, esp of slender pointed skeletal parts* style-shaped

-stylous /-stieləs/ *comb form* (→ *adj*) having (such or so many) styles in the floral structure ⟨*mono*stylous⟩ [[1]*style*]

stylus /'stieləs/ *n, pl* **styli** /-lie/, **styluses** an instrument for writing, marking, incising, or following a groove: e g **a** an instrument used by the ancients for writing on clay or waxed tablets **b** a tiny piece of material (e g diamond) with a rounded tip used in a gramophone to follow the groove on a record [modif of L *stilus* stake, stylus – more at STYLE]

[1]**stymie** /'stiemi/ *n* a condition on a golf green where a ball nearer the hole lies in the line of play of another ball [perh fr Sc *stymie* person with poor eyesight]

[2]**stymie** *vt* to present an obstacle to; thwart

styptic /'stiptik/ *adj* tending to contract, bind, or check bleeding; astringent [ME *stiptik*, fr L *stypticus*, fr Gk *styptikos*, fr *styphein* to contract] – **styptic** *n*

styrax /'stie·əraks/ *n* STORAX 2 [L, fr Gk]

styrene /'stie·əreen/ *n* a liquid unsaturated hydrocarbon used chiefly in making rubber, plastics, etc [ISV, fr L *styrax*]

suable /'s(y)ooh·əbl/ *adj* liable to be sued – **suability** /,s(y)oohə'biləti/ *n*

suave /swahv/ *adj* smoothly though often superficially affable and polite [MF, pleasant, sweet, fr L *suavis* – more at SWEET] – **suavely** *adv*, **suavity** *n*

[1]**sub** /sub/ *n* a substitute – infml

[2]**sub** *vb* **-bb-** *vi* to act as a substitute ~ *vt* **1** to subedit **2** to subcontract *USE* infml

[3]**sub** *n* a submarine – infml

[4]**sub** *n, Br* **1** a small loan or advance **2** SUBSCRIPTION 2b *USE* infml [(1) short for *subsistence*]

[5]**sub** *n* a subeditor – infml

sub- /sub-/ *prefix* **1** under; beneath; below ⟨sub *soil*⟩ ⟨sub*marine*⟩ ⟨sub*abdominal*⟩ **2a** subordinate; secondary; next in rank below ⟨sub*editor*⟩ **b** subordinate portion of; subdivision of ⟨sub*committee*⟩ ⟨sub*family*⟩ ⟨sub*genus*⟩ ⟨sub*phylum*⟩ ⟨ sub*order*⟩ ⟨sub*kingdom*⟩ **c** repeated or further instance of (a specified action or process) ⟨sub*contract*⟩ ⟨sub*let*⟩ **3** bearing an incomplete, partial, or inferior resemblance to; approximately ⟨sub*dominant*⟩ ⟨sub-*Victorian*⟩ ⟨sub*literature*⟩ **4a** almost; nearly ⟨sub*erect*⟩ **b** adjacent to; bordering on ⟨sub*arctic*⟩ [ME, fr L, under, below, secretly, from below, up, near, fr *sub* under, close to – more at UP]

,sub'alpine /-'alpien/ *adj* **1** of the lower slopes of the Alps **2** *cap* of or growing on high upland slopes

[1]**subaltern** /'subəlt(ə)n/ *adj* low in rank or status; subordinate [LL *subalternus*, fr L *sub-* + *alternus* alternate, fr *alter* other (of two) – more at ALTER]

[2]**subaltern** *n* sby holding a subordinate position; *specif, Br* a commissioned Army officer ranking below captain

,suban'tarctic /-an'tahktik/ *adj* (characteristic) of or being a region just outside the antarctic circle [ISV] – **subantarctic** *n*

,sub-'aqua *adj* of underwater recreations (e g skin diving with an aqualung)

,suba'quatic /-ə'kwotik, -ə'kwa-/ *adj* subaqueous [ISV]

,sub'aqueous /-'akwi·əs/ *adj* existing, formed, or taking place in or under water

,sub'arctic /-'ahktik/ *adj* (characteristic) of or being a region just outside the arctic circle [ISV] – **subarctic** *n*

'subas,sembly /-ə,sembli/ *n* an assembled unit designed to be incorporated with other units in a finished product

,suba'tomic /-ə'tomik/ *adj* of the inside of an atom or of particles smaller than atoms

,subau'dition /-aw'dish(ə)n/ *n* the understanding or supplying of sthg not expressed – fml [LL *subaudition-, subauditio*, fr *subauditus*, pp of *subaudire* to understand, fr L *sub-* + *audire* to hear – more at AUDIBLE]

'sub,basement /-,baysmənt/ *n* a basement below the true basement

,sub'calibre /-'kalibə/ *adj* of smaller calibre than the barrel used for firing

,sub'cellular /-'selyoolə/ *adj* occurring inside cells; *also* derived from the artificial disruption of cells ⟨~ *particles*⟩

'sub,class /-,klahs/ *n* **1** a category in the biological classification of living things below a class and above an order **2** a subset

,sub'clavian /-'klayvyən/ *adj* (of or being an artery, nerve, etc) situated under the clavicle [NL *subclavius*, fr *sub-* + *clavicula* clavicle] – **subclavian** *n*

,sub'clinical /-'klinikl/ *adj* having (practically) undetectable symptoms ⟨*a* ~ *infection*⟩ – **subclinically** *adv*

'subcom,mittee /-kə,miti/ *n* a subdivision of a committee usu organized for a specific purpose

,sub'compact /-'kompakt/ *n, NAm* a small motor car

[1]**,sub'conscious** /-'konshəs/ *adj* **1** existing in the mind but not immediately available to consciousness ⟨*his* ~ *motive*⟩ **2** imperfectly or incompletely conscious ⟨*a* ~ *state*⟩ – **subconsciously** *adv*, **subconsciousness** *n*

[2]**,sub'conscious** *n* the mental activities below the threshold of consciousness

,sub'continent /-'kontinənt/ *n* **1** a landmass (e g Greenland) of great size but smaller than any of the generally recognized continents **2** a vast subdivision of a continent; *specif, often cap the* Indian subcontinent – **subcontinental** /-konti'nentl/ *adj*

[1]**,subcon'tract** /-kən'trakt/ *vt* **1** to engage a third party to perform under a subcontract all or part of (work included in an original contract) **2** to undertake (work) under a subcontract ~ *vi* to let out or undertake work under a subcontract – **subcontractor** *n*

[2]**,sub'contract** /-'kontrakt/ *n* a contract between a party to an original contract and a third party; *esp* one to provide all or a specified part of the work or materials required in the original contract

,sub'critical /-'kritikl/ *adj* of insufficient size to sustain a chain reaction ⟨*a* ~ *mass of fissile material*⟩

subculture /'sub,kulchə, ,-'--/ *n* **1** a culture (e g of bacteria) derived from another culture **2** (a group having) a shared pattern of behaviour and values distinguishable from the surrounding culture – **subculture** *vb*, **subcultural** /,sub'kulch(ə)rəl/ *adj*

,subcu'taneous /-kyooh'taynyəs, -ni·əs/ *adj* being, living, used, or made under the skin ⟨~ *fat*⟩ [LL *subcutaneus*, fr L *sub-* + *cutis* skin – more at [4]HIDE] – **subcutaneously** *adv*

,sub'deacon /-'deekən/ *n* a cleric ranking below a deacon [ME *subdecon*, fr LL *subdiaconus*, fr L *sub-* + LL *diaconus* deacon]

,subdi'aconate /-die'akənit, -nayt/ *n* the office or rank of a subdeacon

subdivide /,subdi'vied, '--,-/ *vt* to divide the parts of into more parts ~ *vi* to separate or become separated into subdivisions [ME *subdividen*, fr LL *subdividere*, fr L *sub-* + *dividere* to divide] – **subdivision** /,subdi'vizh(ə)n, '--,--/ *n*

,sub'dominant /-'dominənt/ *n* the fourth note of a diatonic scale – **subdominant** *adj*

subdue /səb'dyooh/ *vt* **1** to conquer and bring into subjection **2** to bring under control; curb ⟨~d *her fears*⟩ **3** to bring under cultivation **4** to reduce the intensity or degree of (e g colour) [ME *sodewen, subduen* (influenced in form and meaning by L *subdere* to subject), fr MF *soduire* to seduce (influenced in meaning by L *seducere* to seduce), fr L *subducere* to withdraw] – **subduer** *n*

sub'dued *adj* **1** brought under control (as if) by military conquest **2** reduced or lacking in force, intensity, or strength – **subduedly** *adv*

,sub'editor /-'editə/ *n* **1** an assistant editor **2** *chiefly Br* one who edits sthg (e g newspaper copy) in preparation for printing – **subedit** *vt*, **subeditorial** /-edi'tawri·əl/ *adj*

suberin /'syoohbərin/ *n* a complex waxy substance that is the basis of cork [F *subérine*, fr L *suber* cork tree, cork]

suber·ization, -isation /,syoohbərie'zaysh(ə)n/ *n* conversion of plant cell walls into corky tissue by impregnation with suberin – **suberized** /'syoohbəriezd/ *adj*

subfusc /'subfusk/ *n* formal academic dress for members of a university, esp Oxford University [L *subfuscus* brownish, dusky, fr *sub-* + *fuscus* dark brown – more at DUSK]

'sub,head /-,hed/, **'sub,heading** /-,heding/ *n* a subordinate caption, title, heading, or headline

,sub'human /-'hyoohmən/ *adj* less than human: e g **a** below the level expected of or suited to normal human beings **b** of animals lower than humans; *esp* anthropoid

,sub'jacent /-'jays(ə)nt/ *adj* **1** situated under or below **2** underlying ⟨~ *causes*⟩ *USE* fml [L *subjacent-, subjacens*, prp of *subjacēre* to lie under, fr *sub-* + *jacēre* to lie – more at ADJACENT] – **subjacency** *n*

[1]**subject** /'subjikt/ *n* **1a** a vassal **b(1)** sby subject to a ruler and governed by his/her law **(2)** sby who enjoys the protection of and owes allegiance to a sovereign power or state **2a** that of which a quality, attribute, or relation may be stated **b** the entity (e g the mind or ego) that sustains or assumes the form of thought or consciousness **3a** a department of knowledge or learning **b(1)** an individual whose reactions are studied **(2)** a dead body for anatomical study and dissection **c(1)** sthg concerning which sthg is said or done ⟨*a* ~ *of dispute*⟩ **(2)** sby or sthg represented in a work of art **d(1)** the term of a logical proposition denoting that of which sthg is stated, denied, or predicated **(2)** the word or phrase in a sentence or clause denoting that of which sthg is predicated or asserted **e** the principal melodic phrase on which a musical composition or movement is based [ME, fr MF, fr L *subjectus* one under authority & *subjectum* subject of a proposition, fr masc & neut of *subjectus*, pp of *subicere* to subject, lit., to throw under, fr *sub-* + *jacere* to throw – more at [2]JET] – **subjectless** *adj*

[2]**subject** *adj* **1** owing obedience or allegiance to another ⟨~ *nations*⟩ ⟨~ *to higher authority*⟩ **2a** liable or exposed to **b** having a tendency or inclination; prone to ⟨~ *to colds*⟩ **3** dependent or conditional on sthg ⟨*the plan is* ~ *to approval*⟩ *USE* usu + *to*

[3]**subject** /səb'jekt/ *vt* **1** to bring under control or rule **2** to make liable; expose **3** to cause to undergo sthg *USE* usu + *to* – **subjection** /-'jeksh(ə)n/ *n*

subjective /səb'jektiv/ *adj* **1** of or being a grammatical subject **2a** relating to, determined by, or arising from the mind or self ⟨~ *reality*⟩ **b** characteristic of or belonging to reality as perceived rather than as independent of mind; phenomenal **3a** peculiar to a particular individual; personal **b** arising from conditions within the brain or sense organs and not directly caused by external stimuli ⟨~ *sensations*⟩ **c** lacking in reality or substance; illusory – **subjectively** *adv*, **subjectivize** *vt*, **subjectivity** /,subjek'tivəti/ *n*

subjectivism /səb'jekti,viz(ə)m/ *n* **1** a theory that limits knowledge to conscious states and elements **2** a doctrine that individual feelings or reactions form the basis of moral or aesthetic judgments – **subjectivist** *n*

'subject ,matter *n* matter presented for consideration in speech, writing, or artistic form

'subject to *prep* depending on; conditionally upon ⟨~ *your approval, I will go*⟩

subjoin /,sub'joyn/ *vt* to annex, append – fml [MF *subjoindre*, fr L *subjungere* to join beneath, add, fr *sub-* + *jungere* to join – more at YOKE]

,sub 'judice /'joohdisi/ *adv* before a court; not yet judicially decided [L]

subjugate /'subjoogayt/ *vt* to conquer and hold in subjection [ME *subjugaten*, fr L *subjugatus*, pp of *subjugare*, lit., to bring under the yoke, fr *sub-* + *jugum* yoke – more at YOKE] – **subjugator** *n*, **subjugation** /-'gaysh(ə)n/ *n*

[1]**subjunctive** /səb'jungktiv/ *adj* of or being a grammatical mood that represents the denoted act or state not as fact but as contingent or possible or viewed emotionally (e g with doubt or desire) [LL *subjunctivus*, fr L *subjunctus*, pp of *subjungere* to join beneath, subordinate]

[2]**subjunctive** *n* (a verb form expressing) the subjunctive mood

[1]**sublease** /'sub,lees/ *n* a lease to a subtenant

[2]**,sub'lease** *vt* to make or obtain a sublease of

[1]**,sub'let** /-'let/ *vb* **-tt-; sublet** to lease or rent (all or part of a property) to a subtenant

[2]**'sub,let** *n* property for subletting

,sublieu'tenant /-lef'tenənt; *NAm* -looh'tenənt/ *n* ☞ RANK

sublimate /'sublimayt/ *vt* **1** SUBLIME 1 **2** to divert the expression of (an instinctual desire or impulse) from a primitive form to a socially or culturally acceptable one [ML *sublimatus*, pp of *sublimare*] – **sublimation** /-'maysh(ə)n/ *n*

[1]**sublime** /sə'bliem/ *vt* **1** to cause to pass from the solid to the vapour state (and recondense to the solid form) **2** to make finer or of higher worth ~ *vi* to pass directly from the solid to the vapour state [ME *sublimen*, fr MF *sublimer*, fr ML *sublimare* to refine, sublime, fr L, to elevate, fr *sublimis*]

[2]**sublime** *adj* **1** lofty, noble, or exalted in thought, expression, or manner **2** tending to inspire awe, usu because of elevated quality **3** outstanding as such ⟨~ *indifference*⟩ [L *sublimis*, lit., to or in a high position, fr *sub* under, up to + *limen* threshold, lintel – more at UP, [1]LIMB] – **sublimely** *adv*, **sublimity** /su'bliməti/ *n*

subliminal /,sub'liminl/ *adj* **1** *of a stimulus* inadequate to produce a sensation or perception **2** existing, functioning, or having effects below the level of conscious awareness ⟨*the ~ mind*⟩ ⟨*~ advertising*⟩ [*sub-* + L *limin-*, *limen* threshold] – **subliminally** *adv*

,sub'littoral /-'litərəl/ *n* the region in the sea between the lowest point exposed by a very low tide and the margin of the continental shelf – **sublittoral** *adj*

,sub'lunary /-'loohnəri/ *also* **sublunar** /-'loohnə/ *adj* mundane, terrestrial – chiefly poetic [modif of LL *sublunaris*, fr L *sub-* + *luna* moon – more at LUNAR]

,subma'chine ,gun /,submə'sheen/ *n* an automatic or semiautomatic portable rapid-firing firearm of limited range using pistol-type ammunition

[1]**,subma'rine** /-mə'reen/ *adj* being, acting, or growing under water, esp in the sea ⟨*~ plants*⟩

[2]**submarine** /'submə,reen, ,--'-/ *n* a vessel designed for undersea operations; *esp* a submarine warship that is typically armed with torpedoes or missiles and uses electric, diesel, or nuclear propulsion

submariner /'submə,reenə, sub'marinə/ *n* a crewman of a submarine

,submax'illa /-mak'silə/ *n, pl* **submaxillae** /-li/ *also* **submaxillas** (the bone of) the lower jaw, specif in humans [NL] – **submaxillary** /-mak'siləri/ *adj or n*

,sub'mediant /-'meedi·ənt/ *n* the sixth note of a diatonic scale

submerge /səb'muhj/ *vt* **1** to put under water **2** to cover (as if) with water; inundate ~ *vi* to go under water [L *submergere*, fr *sub-* + *mergere* to plunge – more at MERGE] – **submergence** *n*

submerged *adj* submersed

submersed /səb'muhst/ *adj* **1** covered with water **2** (adapted for) growing under water ⟨*~ plants*⟩ [fr pp of *submerse* (to submerge), fr L *submersus*, pp of *submergere*] – **submersion** /səb'muhsh(ə)n/ *n*

[1]**submersible** /səb'muhsəbl/ *adj* capable of going under water

[2]**submersible** *n* sthg submersible; *esp* a vessel used for undersea exploration and construction work that is either navigable or attached to a surface ship by cable

submicroscopic /,submiekrə'skopik/ *adj* too small to be seen in an ordinary light microscope [ISV] – **submicroscopically** *adv*

submission /səb'mish(ə)n/ *n* **1** an act of submitting sthg for consideration, inspection, etc **2** the state of being submissive, humble, or compliant **3** an act of submitting to the authority or control of another [ME, fr MF, fr L *submission-*, *submissio* act of lowering, fr *submissus*, pp of *submittere*]

submissive /səb'misiv/ *adj* willing to submit to others – **submissively** *adv*, **submissiveness** *n*

submit /səb'mit/ *vb* **-tt-** *vt* **1a** to yield to the authority or will of another **b** to subject to a process or practice **2a** to send or commit to another for consideration, inspection, etc **b** to put forward as an opinion; suggest ⟨*we ~ that the charge is not proved*⟩ ~ *vi* **1** to yield oneself to the authority or will of another **2** to allow oneself to be subjected to sthg [ME *submitten*, fr L *submittere* to lower, submit, fr *sub-* + *mittere* to send]

submucosa /,submyooh'kohzə/ *n* a supporting layer of loose connective tissue directly under a mucous membrane [NL] – **submucosal** *adj*

,sub'multiple /-'multipl/ *n* an exact divisor of a number ⟨*8 is a ~ of 72*⟩

,sub'normal /-'nawməl/ *adj* **1** lower or smaller than normal **2** having less of sthg, esp intelligence, than is normal [ISV] – **subnormally** *adj*, **subnormality** /-naw'maləti/ *n*

,sub'orbital /-'awbitl/ *adj* **1** situated beneath the orbit of the eye **2** being or involving less than 1 complete orbit ⟨*a spacecraft's ~ flight*⟩; *also* intended for suborbital flight ⟨*a ~ rocket*⟩

[1]**subordinate** /sə'bawd(ə)nət/ *adj* **1** occupying a lower class or rank; inferior **2** subject to or controlled by authority **3** *of a clause* functioning as a noun, adjective, or adverb in a complex sentence (e g the clause 'when he heard" in 'he laughed when he heard") [ME *subordinat*, fr ML *subordinatus*, pp of *subordinare* to subordinate, fr L *sub-* + *ordinare* to order – more at ORDAIN] – **subordinate** *n*, **subordinately** *adv*

[2]**subordinate** /sə'bawd(ə)nayt/ *vt* **1** to place in a lower order or class **2** to make subject or subservient; subdue – **subordinative** /sə'bawd(ə)nətiv/ *adj*, **subordination** /sə,bawdi'naysh(ə)n/ *n*

suborn /sə'bawn/ *vt* to induce to commit perjury or another illegal act [MF *suborner*, fr L *subornare*, fr *sub-* secretly + *ornare* to furnish, equip – more at ORNATE] – **suborner** *n*

suboxide /,sub'oksied/ *n* an oxide containing a relatively small proportion of oxygen [ISV]

'sub,plot /-,plot/ *n* a subordinate plot in fiction or drama

[1]**subpoena** /sə(b)'peenə/ *n* a writ commanding sby to appear in court [ME *suppena*, fr L *sub poena* under penalty (the first words of the writ)]

[2]**subpoena** *vt* **subpoenaing; subpoenaed** to serve with a subpoena

,sub'polar /,sub'pohlə/ *adj* subantarctic or subarctic

'sub,region /-,reej(ə)n/ *n* any of the divisions of a (biogeographic) region [ISV] – **subregional** /,-'---/ *adj*

,sub 'rosa /'rohzə/ *adv* in strict confidence; secretly [NL, lit., under the rose; fr the ancient custom of hanging a rose over the council table to indicate that all present were sworn to secrecy]

'subrou,tine /-rooh,teen/ *n* a subordinate routine; *esp* a sequence of computer instructions that can be used repeatedly [ISV]

subscribe /səb'skrieb/ *vt* **1** to write (one's name) underneath **2a** to sign with one's own hand **b** to give a written pledge to contribute ~ *vi* **1a** to give consent or approval to sthg written by signing **b** to give money (e g to charity) **c** to pay regularly in order to receive a periodical or service **2** to agree to purchase and pay for securities, esp of a new issue ⟨~d *for 1000 shares*⟩ **3** to feel favourably disposed *to* ***USE*** (*vi 1*) usu + *to* [ME *subscriben*, fr L *subscribere*, lit., to write beneath, fr *sub-* + *scribere* to write – more at [1]SCRIBE]

subscriber /səb'skriebə/ *n* sby who subscribes; *specif* the owner of a telephone who pays rental and call charges

subscriber trunk dialling *n* the system by which a telephone user can dial direct to any telephone within the system without being connected by an operator

subscript /'sub,skript/ *n* a distinguishing symbol written or printed below another character [L *subscriptus*, pp of *subscribere*] – **subscript** *adj*

subscription /səb'skripsh(ə)n/ *n* **1** a sum subscribed **2a** a purchase by prepayment for a certain number of issues (e g of a periodical) **b** *Br* membership fees paid regularly **3** a signature – fml [ME *subscripcioun* signature, fr L *subscription-, subscriptio*, fr *subscriptus*, pp of *subscribere*]

subsection /'sub,seksh(ə)n/ *n* a subdivision of a section

subsequent /'subsikwənt/ *adj* following in time or order; succeeding [ME, fr L *subsequent-, subsequens*, prp of *subsequi* to follow closely, fr *sub-* near + *sequi* to follow – more at SUB-, SUE] – **subsequently** *adv*

subserve /səb'suhv/ *vt* to serve as a means of furthering (e g a purpose or action) – fml [L *subservire* to serve, be subservient, fr *sub-* + *servire* to serve]

subservience /səb'suhvi·əns/ *n* obsequious servility

subservient /səb'suhvi·ənt/ *adj* **1** useful in an inferior capacity; subordinate **2** obsequiously submissive [L *subservient-, subserviens*, prp of *subservire*] – **subserviently** *adv*

subset /'sub,set/ *n* a set each of whose elements is an element of a larger set

'sub,shrub /-,shrub/ *n* an undershrub – **subshrubby** *adj*

subside /səb'sied/ *vi* **1** to sink or fall to the bottom; settle **2a** to descend; *esp* to sink so as to form a depression **b** *of ground* to cave in; collapse **3** to sink down; settle ⟨~d *into a chair*⟩ **4** to become quiet; abate [L *subsidere*, fr *sub-* + *sidere* to sit down, sink; akin to L *sedēre* to sit – more at SIT] – **subsidence** /səb'sied(ə)ns, 'subsid(ə)ns/ *n*

[1]**subsidiary** /səb'sidyəri, -'sij(ə)ri/ *adj* **1** serving to assist or supplement; auxiliary **2** of secondary importance [L *subsidiarius*, fr *subsidium* reserve troops]

[2]**subsidiary** *n* sby or sthg subsidiary; *esp* a company wholly controlled by another – compare HOLDING COMPANY, INVESTMENT COMPANY

subsid·ize, -ise /'subsi,diez/ *vt* to provide with a subsidy: e g **a** to purchase the assistance of by payment of a subsidy **b** to aid or promote (e g a private enterprise) with public money – **subsidizer** *n*, **subsidization** /,subsidie'zaysh(ə)n/ *n*

subsidy /'subsidi/ *n* a grant or gift of money (e g by a government to a person or organization, to assist an enterprise deemed advantageous to the public) [ME, fr L *subsidium* reserve troops, support, assistance, fr *sub-* near + *sedēre* to sit – more at SUB-, SIT]

subsist /səb'sist/ *vi* **1** to have or continue in existence **2** to have the bare necessities of life; be kept alive [LL *subsistere* to exist, fr L, to come to a halt, remain, fr *sub-* + *sistere* to come to a stand; akin to L *stare* to stand – more at STAND]

subsistence /səb'sist(ə)ns/ *n* **1** the state of subsisting **2** the minimum (e g of food and shelter) necessary to support life [ME, fr LL *subsistentia*, fr *subsistent-, subsistens*, prp of *subsistere*] – **subsistent** *adj*

subsistence farming *n* (a system of) farming that provides (almost) all the goods required by the farm household, usu without significant surplus for sale

subsoil /'sub,soyl/ *n* the layer of weathered material that underlies the surface soil

,sub'sonic /-'sonik/ *adj* **1** of, being, moving at, or using air currents moving at, a speed less than that of sound in air **2** infrasonic [ISV] – **subsonically** *adv*

'sub,space /-,spays/ *n* a subset of a space; *esp* one that has the properties (e g those of a vector space) of the including space

sub specie aeternitatis /,sub ,speki·ay ietuhni'tahtis/ *adv* seen in its essential or universal form [NL, lit., under the aspect of eternity]

subspecies /'sub,speeshiz/ *n* a category in the biological classification of living things that ranks (immediately) below a species [NL] – **subspecific** /,subspi'sifik/ *adj*

substance /'substəns/ *n* **1a** a fundamental or essential part or import ⟨*the* ~ *of his argument*⟩ **b** correspondence with reality ⟨*the allegations were without* ~⟩ **2** ultimate underlying reality **3a** (a) physical material from which sthg is made ⟨*an oily* ~⟩ **b** matter of particular or definite chemical constitution **4** material possessions; property ⟨*a man of* ~⟩ [ME, fr OF, fr L *substantia*, fr *substant-, substans*, prp of *substare* to stand under, fr *sub-* + *stare* to stand – more at STAND] – **in substance** in respect to essentials

,sub'standard /-'standəd/ *adj* deviating from or falling short of a standard or norm: e g **a** of a quality lower than that prescribed **b** in widespread use but not accepted as linguistically correct by some – compare NONSTANDARD

substantial /səb'stansh(ə)l/ *adj* **1a** having material existence; real **b** important, essential **2** ample to satisfy and nourish ⟨*a* ~ *meal*⟩ **3a** well-to-do, prosperous **b** considerable in quantity; significantly large **4** firmly constructed; solid **5** being largely but not wholly the specified thing ⟨*a* ~ *lie*⟩ [ME, fr OF or LL; OF *substantiel*, fr LL *substantialis*, fr L *substantia*] – **substantial** *n*, **substantially** *adv*, **substantialize** /-shə,liez/ *vb*, **substantiality** /səb,stanshi'aləti/ *n*

substantiate /səb'stanshi·ayt/ *vt* to establish (e g a statement or claim) by proof or evidence; verify – **substantiative** /-shi·ətiv/ *adj*, **substantiation** /-,stanshi'aysh(ə)n/ *n*

[1]**substantive** /'substəntiv/ *n* a noun; *broadly* a word or phrase functioning syntactically as a noun [ME *substantif*, fr MF, fr *substantif*, adj, having or expressing substance, fr LL *substantivus*] – **substantivize** /-ti,viez/ *vt*, **substantival** /-'tievl/ *adj*

[2]**substantive** /'substəntiv, səb'stantiv (*usu* səb'stantiv *when applied to position, rank, etc*)/ *adj* **1** being a totally independent entity; not inferred or derived

2a indicating or expressing existence ⟨*the* ~ *verb* to be⟩ **b** not requiring or involving a mordant ⟨*a* ~ *dyeing process*⟩ **3** relating to or functioning as a noun **4** defining rights and duties ⟨~ *law*⟩ **5** permanent and definite rather than temporary or acting ⟨~ *rank of colonel*⟩ [ME, fr LL *substantivus* having substance, fr L *substantia*] – **substantively** *adv*

substation /ˈsubˌstaysh(ə)n/ *n* a subsidiary station in which (the voltage of an) electric current is transformed for use

substituent /subˈstityoo·ənt/ *n* an atom or group that replaces another atom or group in a molecule [L *substituent-*, *substituens*, prp of *substituere*] – **substituent** *adj*

[1]**substitute** /ˈsubstityooht/ *n* sby or sthg that takes the place of another [ME, fr L *substitutus*, pp of *substituere* to put in place of, fr *sub-* + *statuere* to set up, place – more at STATUTE] – **substitute** *adj*, **substitutive** /-ˌtyoohtiv/ *adj*

[2]**substitute** *vt* **1a** to exchange for another **b** to introduce (an atom or group) as a substituent; *also* to alter (e g a compound) by introduction of a substituent ⟨*a* ~d *benzene ring*⟩ **2** to take the place of; *also* to introduce a substitute for ⟨~d *their centre forward in the second half*⟩ ~ *vi* to serve as a substitute – **substitutable** /ˌsubstiˈtyoohtəbl/ *adj*, **substitution** /ˌsubstiˈtyoohsh(ə)n/ *n*, **substitutional**, **substitutionary** *adj*

substrate /ˈsubstrayt/ *n* **1** a substratum **2** the base on which an organism lives ⟨*limpets live on a rocky* ~⟩ **3** a substance acted on (e g by an enzyme) [ML *substratum*]

ˌ**subˈstratum** /-ˈstrahtəm, -ˈstraytəm/ *n*, *pl* **substrata** /-tə/ an underlying support; a foundation: e g **a** matter considered as the enduring basis for all the qualities that can be perceived by the senses (e g colour) **b** a foundation, basis ⟨*his argument has a* ~ *of truth*⟩ **c** the subsoil [ML, fr L, neut of *substratus*, pp of *substernere* to spread under, fr *sub-* + *sternere* to spread out – more at STREW]

ˈ**subˌstructure** /-ˌstrukchə/ *n* the foundation or groundwork [*sub-* + *structure*] – **substructural** /subˈstrukch(ə)rəl/ *adj*

subsume /səbˈsyoohm/ *vt* to include as a member of a group or type [NL *subsumere*, fr L *sub-* + *sumere* to take up – more at CONSUME] – **subsumption** /-ˈsumpsh(ə)n, -ˈsumsh(ə)n/ *n*

subtenant /ˈsubˌtenənt/ *n* sby who rents from a tenant

subtend /səbˈtend/ *vt* **1a** to define in a given context by extending from one side to the other of ⟨*a hypotenuse* ~s *a right angle*⟩ ⟨*an arc* ~ed *by a chord*⟩ **b** to fix the angular extent of with respect to a fixed point ⟨*the angle* ~ed *at the eye by an object*⟩ **2** to be lower than, esp so as to embrace or enclose ⟨*a bract that* ~s *a flower*⟩ [L *subtendere* to stretch beneath, fr *sub-* + *tendere* to stretch – more at THIN]

subterfuge /ˈsubtəˌfyoohj/ *n* **1** deception or trickery used as a means of concealment or evasion **2** a trick or ruse [LL *subterfugium*, fr L *subterfugere* to escape, evade, fr *subter-* secretly (fr *subter* underneath; akin to L *sub* under) + *fugere* to flee – more at UP, FUGITIVE]

subterminal /ˌsubˈtuhminl/ *adj* situated or occurring near an end ⟨*a* ~ *band of colour*⟩ ⟨*a* ~ *collapse*⟩

ˌ**subterˈranean** /-təˈraynyən, -ni·ən/, **subterraneous** /-nyəs, -ni·əs/ *adj* **1** being or operating under the surface of the earth **2** hidden or out of sight [L *subterraneus*, fr *sub* under + *terra* earth – more at UP, TERRACE] – **subterraneanly** *adv*

subtitle /ˌsubˈtietl/ *n* **1** a secondary or explanatory title **2** a printed explanation (e g a fragment of dialogue or a translation) that appears on the screen during a film – **subtitle** *vt*

subtle /ˈsutl/ *adj* **1a** delicate, elusive ⟨*a* ~ *fragrance*⟩ **b** difficult to understand or distinguish **2** showing keen insight and perception **3** cleverly contrived; ingenious **4** artful, cunning [ME *sutil, sotil*, fr OF *soutil*, fr L *subtilis*, lit., finely woven, fr *sub-* + *tela* web; akin to L *texere* to weave – more at TECHNICAL] – **subtleness** *n*, **subtly** *adv*

subtlety /ˈsutl·ti/ *n* **1** the quality of being subtle **2** sthg subtle; *esp* a fine distinction [ME *sutilte*, fr OF *sutilté*, fr L *subtilitat-*, *subtilitas*, fr *subtilis*]

[1]**subtotal** /ˌsubˈtohtl/ *n* the sum of part of a series of figures

[2]**subtotal** *vb* to determine a subtotal (for)

subtract /səbˈtrakt/ *vt* to take away by subtraction ⟨~ *5 from 9*⟩ ~ *vi* to perform a subtraction [L *subtractus*, pp of *subtrahere* to draw from beneath, withdraw, fr *sub-* + *trahere* to draw – more at DRAW] – **subtracter** *n*

subtraction /səbˈtraksh(ə)n/ *n* the operation of finding for 2 given numbers a third number which when added to the first yields the second [SUBTRACT + -ION]

subtractive /səbˈtraktiv/ *adj* **1** tending to subtract **2** constituting or involving subtraction

subtrahend /ˌsubtrəˈhend/ *n* a number that is to be subtracted from another [L *subtrahendus*, gerundive of *subtrahere*]

subtropical /ˌsubˈtropikl/ *also* **subtropic** *adj* of or being the regions bordering on the tropical zone [ISV] – **subtropics** *n pl*

subulate /ˈsyoohbyoolət, -ˌlayt/ *adj* narrow and tapering to a fine point ⟨*a* ~ *leaf*⟩ ☞ PLANT [NL *subulatus*, fr L *subula* awl; akin to OHG *siula* awl, L *suere* to sew – more at SEW]

subunit /ˈsubˌyoohnit/ *n* a unit that forms a discrete part of a larger unit ⟨~s *of a protein*⟩

suburb /ˈsubuhb/ *n* **1** an outlying part of a city or large town **2** *pl* the residential area on the outskirts of a city or large town [ME, fr L *suburbium*, fr *sub-* near + *urbs* city – more at SUB-] – **suburban** /səˈbuhbən/ *adj or n*, **suburbanize** /səˈbuhbəˌniez/ *vt*, **suburbanization** /səˌbuhbənieˈzaysh(ə)n/ *n*

suburbanite /səˈbuhbəˌniet/ *n* a person who lives in the suburbs

suburbia /səˈbuhbyə/ *n* (the inhabitants of) the suburbs of a city [NL, fr E *suburb* + L *-ia* -y]

subvention /səbˈvensh(ə)n/ *n* the provision of assistance or financial support: e g **a** an endowment **b** a subsidy [LL *subvention-*, *subventio* assistance, fr L *subventus*, pp of *subvenire* to come up, come to the rescue, fr *sub-* up + *venire* to come – more at SUB-, COME] – **subventionary** *adj*

subversion /səbˈvuhsh(ə)n/ *n* a systematic attempt to overthrow or undermine a government by people working secretly within the country [ME, fr MF, fr LL *subversion-*, *subversio*, fr L *subversus*, pp of *subvertere*] – **subversionary** *adj*, **subversive** /-siv/ *adj or n*, **subversively** *adv*, **subversiveness** *n*

subvert /səbˈvuht/ *vt* to overthrow or undermine the power of [ME *subverten*, fr MF *subvertir*, fr L *subvertere*, lit., to turn from beneath, fr *sub-* + *vertere* to turn – more at [1]WORTH] – **subverter** *n*

subway /'sub,way/ *n* an underground way: e g **a** a passage under a street (e g for pedestrians, power cables, or water or gas mains) **b** *chiefly NAm* the underground

succeed /sək'seed/ *vi* **1a** to inherit sthg, esp sovereignty, rank, or title **b** to follow after another in order **2a** to have a favourable result; turn out well **b** to achieve a desired object or end ~ *vt* **1** to follow (immediately) in sequence **2** to come after as heir or successor [ME *succeden*, fr L *succedere* to go up, follow after, succeed, fr *sub-* near + *cedere* to go – more at SUB-, CEDE] – **succeeder** *n*

success /sək'ses/ *n* **1** a favourable outcome to an undertaking **2** the attainment of wealth or fame **3** sby or sthg that succeeds ⟨*he was an overnight* ~⟩ [L *successus* outcome, fr *successus*, pp of *succedere*]

suc'cessful /-f(ə)l/ *adj* **1** resulting in success ⟨*a* ~ *experiment*⟩ **2** having gained success ⟨*a* ~ *banker*⟩ – **successfully** *adv*, **successfulness** *n*

succession /sək'sesh(ə)n/ *n* **1a** the order or right of succeeding to a property, title, or throne **b** the line having such a right **2a** the act of following in order; a sequence **b** the act or process of becoming entitled to a deceased person's property or title **c** the change in the composition of an ecological system as the competing organisms respond to and modify the environment **3** *sing or pl in constr* a number of people or things that follow each other in sequence [ME, fr MF or L; MF, fr L *succession-*, *successio*, fr *successus*, pp] – **successional** *adj*, **successionally** *adv*

succession state *n* any of a number of states that succeed a former state in sovereignty over a territory

successive /sək'sesiv/ *adj* following one after the other in succession – **successively** *adv*, **successiveness** *n*

successor /sək'sesə/ *n* sby or sthg that follows another; *esp* a person who succeeds to throne, title, or office [ME *successour*, fr OF, fr L *successor*, fr *successus*, pp]

succinct /sək'singkt/ *adj* clearly expressed in few words; concise [ME, fr L *succinctus*, pp of *succingere* to gird from below, tuck up, fr *sub-* + *cingere* to gird – more at CINCTURE] – **succinctly** *adv*, **succinctness** *n*

suc,cinic 'acid /sək'sinik/ *n* a carboxylic acid found widely in nature and active in the Krebs cycle [F *succinique*, fr L *succinum* amber]

succory /'suk(ə)ri/ *n* the chicory plant [alter. of ME *cicoree*]

succotash /'sukətash/ *n* a dish of beans and green maize cooked together [of Algonquian origin; akin to Narraganset *msəkwataš* succotash]

[1]**succour,** *NAm chiefly* **succor** /'sukə/ *n* relief; *also* aid, help [ME *succur*, fr earlier *sucurs* (taken as pl), fr OF *sucors*, fr ML *succursus*, fr L *succursus*, pp of *succurrere* to run up, run to help, fr *sub-* up + *currere* to run – more at SUB-, CAR]

[2]**succour,** *NAm chiefly* **succor** *vt* to go to the aid of (sby in need or distress)

succubus /'sukyoobəs/ *n, pl* **succubi** /-,bie/ a female demon believed to have sexual intercourse with men in their sleep – compare INCUBUS 1 [ME, fr ML, alter. of LL *succuba* prostitute, fr L *succubare* to lie under, fr *sub-* + *cubare* to lie, recline – more at [2]HIP]

[1]**succulent** /'sukyoolənt/ *adj* **1** full of juice; juicy **2** *of a plant* having juicy fleshy tissues [L *suculentus*, fr *sucus* juice, sap; akin to L *sugere* to suck – more at SUCK] – **succulence** *n*, **succulently** *adv*

[2]**succulent** *n* a succulent plant (e g a cactus) ☞ PLANT

succumb /sə'kum/ *vi* **1** to yield or give in *to* **2** to die [F & L; F *succomber*, fr L *succumbere*, fr *sub-* + *-cumbere* to lie down; akin to L *cubare* to lie]

[1]**such** /such; *also (occasional weak form)* səch/ *adj or adv* **1a** of the kind, quality, or extent ⟨*his habits are* ~ *that we rarely meet*⟩ – used before *as* to introduce an example or comparison ⟨~ *trees as oak or pine*⟩ **b** of the same sort ⟨*there's no* ~ *place*⟩ **2** of so extreme a degree or extraordinary a nature ⟨*ever* ~ *a lot of people*⟩ ⟨*in* ~ *a hurry*⟩ – used before *as* to suggest that a name is unmerited ⟨*we forced down the soup,* ~ *as it was*⟩ [ME, fr OE *swilc*; akin to OHG *sulīh* such; both fr a prehistoric Gmc compound whose constituents are respectively represented by OE *swā* so & by OE *gelīc* like – more at SO, [3]LIKE]

[2]**such** *pron, pl* **such** **1** *pl* such people; those ⟨~ *as wish to leave may do so*⟩ **2** that thing, fact, or action ⟨~ *was the result*⟩ **3** *pl* similar people or things ⟨*tin and glass and* ~⟩ – **as such** intrinsically considered; in him-/herself, itself, or themselves ⟨as such *the gift was worth little*⟩

'such and ,such *adj* not named or specified – infml

[1]**'such,like** /-,liek/ *adj* of like kind; similar

[2]**suchlike** *pron, pl* **suchlike** a similar person or thing

[1]**suck** /suk/ *vt* **1a** to draw (e g liquid) into the mouth by the suction of the contracted lips and tongue **b** to eat by means of sucking movements of the lips and tongue **c** to take into the mouth as if sucking out a liquid ⟨~ed *his finger*⟩ **2** to draw in or up (as if) by suction ⟨*plants* ~ing *moisture from the soil*⟩ ~ *vi* **1** to draw sthg in (as if) by suction; *esp* to draw milk from a breast or udder with the mouth **2** to make a sound associated with suction ⟨~ed *at his pipe*⟩ **3** to act in an obsequious manner – infml ⟨~ing *up to his boss*⟩ [ME *souken*, fr OE *sūcan*; akin to OHG *sūgan* to suck, L *sugere*, Gk *hyein* to rain]

[2]**suck** *n* **1** the act of sucking **2** a sucking movement

[1]**sucker** /'sukə/ *n* **1a** a human infant or young animal that sucks, esp at a breast or udder; a suckling **b** a device for creating or regulating suction (e g a piston or valve in a pump) **c** a pipe or tube through which sthg is drawn by suction **d** a mouth (e g of a leech) or other animal organ adapted for sucking or sticking **e** a device, esp of rubber, that can cling to a surface by suction **2** a shoot from the roots or lower part of the stem of a plant **3** any of numerous freshwater fishes closely related to the carps and usu having thick soft lips **4a** a gullible person – infml **b** a person irresistibly attracted by sthg specified ⟨*a* ~ *for chocolate*⟩ – infml [[1]SUCK + [2]-ER]

[2]**sucker** *vt* to remove suckers from ⟨~ *tobacco*⟩ ~ *vi* to send out suckers

sucking /'suking/ *adj* not yet weaned; *broadly* very young

suckle /'sukl/ *vt* **suckling** /'sukling, 'sukl·ing/ **1** to give milk to from the breast or udder ⟨*a mother* suckling *her child*⟩ **2** to draw milk from the breast or udder of ⟨*lambs* suckling *the ewes*⟩ [prob back-formation fr *suckling*]

suckling /ˈsukling/ *n* a young unweaned animal

sucre /ˈsoohkray/ *n* ☞ *Ecuador* at NATIONALITY [Sp, fr Antonio José de *Sucre* †1830 S American liberator]

sucrose /ˈs(y)oohkrohs, -krohz/ *n* the disaccharide sugar obtained from sugarcane and sugar beet and occurring in most plants [ISV, fr F *sucre* sugar]

suction /ˈsuksh(ə)n/ *n* **1** the act of sucking **2** the action of exerting a force on a solid, liquid, or gaseous body by means of reduced air pressure over part of its surface [LL *suction-, suctio,* fr L *suctus,* pp of *sugere* to suck – more at SUCK] – **suctional** *adj*

ˈsuction ˌpump *n* a pump in which liquid is raised by suction under a retreating piston

suctorial /sukˈtawri·əl/ *adj* adapted for sucking up fluids or sticking by suction ⟨*a* ~ *mouth*⟩ [NL *suctorius,* fr L *suctus,* pp]

Sudanese /ˌsoohd(ə)nˈeez, ˈ--ˌ-/ *n or adj, pl* **Sudanese** (a native or inhabitant) of Sudan or the Sudan [*Sudan,* country in NE Africa; the *Sudan,* region in N Africa]

sudd /sud/ *n* floating vegetable matter that forms obstructive masses in the upper White Nile [Ar, lit., obstruction]

¹sudden /ˈsud(ə)n/ *adj* **1a** happening or coming unexpectedly ⟨*a* ~ *shower*⟩ **b** abrupt, steep **2** marked by or showing haste [ME *sodain,* fr MF, fr L *subitaneus,* fr *subitus* sudden, fr pp of *subire* to come up, fr *sub-* up + *ire* to go – more at SUB-, ISSUE] – **suddenly** *adv,* **suddenness** *n*

²sudden *n* – **all of a sudden** sooner than was expected; suddenly

sudden death *n* an extra period of play to break a tie (e g in golf) that ends the moment one side gains the lead

sudoriferous /ˌsoohdəˈrif(ə)rəs, ˌsyooh-/ *adj* producing or conveying sweat ⟨~ *glands*⟩ [LL *sudorifer,* fr L *sudor* sweat + *-ifer* -iferous – more at SWEAT]

sudorific /ˌs(y)oohdəˈrifik/ *adj* diaphoretic [NL *sudorificus,* fr L *sudor*] – **sudorific** *n*

Sudra /ˈs(y)oohdrə/ *n* a Hindu of the lowest caste, traditionally restricted to menial occupations [Skt *śūdra*] – **Sudra** *adj*

suds /sudz/ *n pl but sing or pl in constr* (the lather on) soapy water [prob fr MD *sudse* marsh; akin to OE *sēothan* to seethe – more at SEETHE] – **sudsless** *adj*

sudsy /ˈsudzi/ *adj* frothy, foamy

sue /s(y)ooh/ *vt* to bring a legal action against ~ *vi* **1** to make a request or application – usu + *for* or *to* **2** to take legal proceedings in court [ME *suen* to follow, make legal claim to, bring legal action against, fr OF *suivre,* fr (assumed) VL *sequere,* fr L *sequi* to follow, come or go after; akin to Gk *hepesthai* to follow] – **suer** *n*

suede, suède /swayd/ *n* leather with a napped surface [F *(gants de) Suède* Swedish (gloves)]

suet /ˈs(y)ooh·it/ *n* the hard fat round the kidneys and loins in beef and mutton, that yields tallow and is used in cooking [ME *sewet,* fr (assumed) AF, dim. of AF *sue,* fr L *sebum* tallow, suet – more at SOAP]

suffer /ˈsufə/ *vt* **1** to submit to or be forced to endure **2** to undergo, experience **3** to allow, permit ⟨~ *the little children to come unto me*⟩ ~ *vi* **1** to endure pain, distress, or death **2** to sustain loss or damage **3** to be handicapped or at a disadvantage [ME *suffren,* fr OF *souffrir,* fr (assumed) VL *sufferire,* fr L *sufferre,* fr *sub-* up + *ferre* to bear – more at SUB-, ²BEAR] – **sufferable** *adj,* **sufferably** *adv,* **sufferer** *n*

sufferance /ˈsuf(ə)rəns/ *n* tacit permission; tolerance implied by a lack of interference or objection ⟨*he was only there on* ~⟩

suffering /ˈsuf(ə)ring/ *n* the state of one who suffers

suffice /səˈfies/ *vi* to meet a need; be enough ⟨*a brief note will* ~⟩ ⟨~ *it to say he has resigned*⟩ ~ *vt* to be enough for [ME *sufficen,* fr MF *suffis-,* stem of *suffire,* fr L *sufficere,* lit., to put under, fr *sub-* + *facere* to make, do – more at DO]

sufficiency /səˈfish(ə)nsi/ *n* **1** sufficient means to meet one's needs **2** the quality of being sufficient; adequacy

sufficient /səˈfish(ə)nt/ *adj* enough to meet the needs of a situation [ME, fr L *sufficient-, sufficiens,* fr prp of *sufficere*] – **sufficiently** *adv*

¹suffix /ˈsufiks/ *n* an affix (e g *-ness* in *happiness*) appearing at the end of a word or phrase or following a root – compare INFIX, PREFIX [NL *suffixum,* fr L, neut of *suffixus,* pp of *suffigere* to fasten underneath, fr *sub-* + *figere* to fasten – more at DYKE] – **suffixal** *adj*

²suffix *vt* to attach as a suffix – **suffixation** /ˌsufikˈsaysh(ə)n/ *n*

suffocate /ˈsufəˌkayt/ *vt* **1** to stop the breathing of (e g by asphyxiation) **2** to deprive of oxygen **3** to make uncomfortable by want of cool fresh air ~ *vi* to become suffocated: **a** to die from being unable to breathe **b** to be uncomfortable through lack of air [L *suffocatus,* pp of *suffocare* to choke, stifle, fr *sub-* + *fauces* throat] – **suffocatingly** *adv,* **suffocative** /-tiv/ *adj,* **suffocation** /ˌsufəˈkaysh(ə)n/ *n*

Suffolk /ˈsufək/ *n* **1** any of an English breed of black-faced hornless sheep **2 Suffolk punch, Suffolk** any of an English breed of chestnut-coloured draught horses [*Suffolk,* county of England; (2) *punch* (a short stocky person or animal), prob short for *Punchinello*]

suffragan /ˈsufrəgən/ *adj or n* (of or being) **1** a diocesan bishop subordinate to a metropolitan **2** an Anglican bishop assisting a diocesan bishop and having no right of succession [n ME, fr MF, fr ML *suffraganeus,* fr *suffragium* support, prayer; adj fr n]

suffrage /ˈsufrij/ *n* **1** a vote given in favour of a question or in the choice of sby for an office **2** the right of voting [L *suffragium* vote, political support]

suffragette /ˌsufrəˈjet/ *n* a woman who advocates suffrage for her sex

suffragist /ˈsufrəjist/ *n* one who advocates extension of suffrage, esp to women

suffuse /səˈfyoohz/ *vt* to spread over or through, esp with a liquid or colour; permeate [L *suffusus,* pp of *suffundere,* lit., to pour beneath, fr *sub-* + *fundere* to pour – more at ⁴FOUND] – **suffusion** /-zh(ə)n/ *n,* **suffusive** /-siv/ *adj*

Sufi /ˈsoohfi/ *n* a Muslim mystic [Ar *ṣūfīy,* lit., (man) of wool] – **Sufi** *adj,* **Sufism** *n,* **Sufic** /-fik/ *adj*

[1]**sugar** /'shoogə/ *n* **1a** a sweet crystallizable material that consists (essentially) of sucrose, is colourless or white when pure tending to brown when less refined, is obtained commercially esp from sugarcane or sugar beet, and is important as a source of dietary carbohydrate and as a sweetener and preservative of other foods **b** any of a class of water-soluble carbohydrate compounds containing many hydroxyl groups that are of varying sweetness and include glucose, ribose, and sucrose **2** DEAR 1b [ME *sucre*, fr MF, fr ML *zuccarum*, fr OIt *zucchero*, fr Ar *sukkar*, fr Per *shakar*, fr Skt *śarkarā*; akin to Skt *śarkara* pebble]

[2]**sugar** *vt* **1** to make palatable or attractive **2** to sprinkle or mix with sugar

'sugar ,beet *n* a white-rooted beet grown for the sugar in its root

'sugar,cane *n* a stout tall grass widely grown in warm regions as a source of sugar

sugar-coated *adj* **1** covered with a hard coat of sugar **2** having its unpleasantness concealed

'sugar ,daddy *n* a usu elderly man who lavishes gifts and money on a young woman in return for sex or companionship – infml

sugar maple *n* a N American maple with a sweet sap that is the chief source of maple syrup and maple sugar

'sugar,plum /-,plum/ *n* a small round sweet usu of flavoured and coloured boiled sugar

sugary /'shoog(ə)ri/ *adj* **1** containing, resembling, or tasting of sugar **2** exaggeratedly or cloyingly sweet

suggest /sə'jest/ *vt* **1** to put forward as a possibility or for consideration **2a** to call to mind by thought or association; evoke **b** to indicate the presence of ⟨*her look* ~ed *irritation*⟩ [L *suggestus*, pp of *suggerere* to put under, furnish, suggest, fr *sub-* + *gerere* to carry – more at CAST] – **suggester** *n*

suggestible /sə'jestəbl/ *adj* easily influenced by suggestion – **suggestibility** /-jestə'biləti/ *n*

suggestion /sə'jesch(ə)n/ *n* **1a** the act of suggesting **b** sthg suggested; a proposal **2a** indirect means (e g the natural association of ideas) to evoke ideas or feeling **b** the impressing of an idea, attitude, desired action, etc on the mind of another **3** a slight indication; a trace

suggestive /sə'jestiv/ *adj* **1a** conveying a suggestion; indicative **b** conjuring up mental associations; evocative **2** suggesting sthg improper or indecent; risqué – **suggestively** *adv*, **suggestiveness** *n*

suicidal /,s(y)ooh·i'siedl/ *adj* **1** relating to or of the nature of suicide **2** marked by an impulse to commit suicide **3a** dangerous, esp to life **b** harmful to one's own interests – **suicidally** *adv*

suicide /'s(y)ooh·i,sied/ *n* **1a** (an) act of taking one's own life intentionally **b** ruin of one's own interests ⟨*political* ~⟩ **2** one who commits or attempts suicide [L *sui* (gen) of oneself + E *-cide*; akin to OE & OHG *sīn* his, L *suus* one's own, Skt *sva* oneself, one's own]

sui generis /,sooh·i 'jenəris/ *adj* unique [L, of its own kind]

[1]**suit** /s(y)ooht/ *n* **1** a legal action **2** a petition or appeal; *specif* courtship **3** a group of things forming a unit or constituting a collection – used chiefly with reference to armour, sails, and counters in games **4a** an outer costume of 2 or more matching pieces that are designed to be worn together ☞ GARMENT **b** a costume to be worn for a specified purpose or under particular conditions **5a** all the playing cards in a pack bearing the same symbol (i e hearts, clubs, diamonds, or spades) **b** all the cards in a particular suit held by 1 player ⟨*a 5-card* ~⟩ **c** the suit led ⟨*follow* ~⟩ [ME *siute* act of following, retinue, sequence, set, fr OF, act of following, retinue, fr (assumed) VL *sequita*, fr fem of *sequitus*, pp of *sequere* to follow – more at SUE]

[2]**suit** *vi* **1** to be appropriate or satisfactory ⟨*these prices don't* ~⟩ **2** to put on specially required clothing (e g a uniform or protective garb) – usu + *up* ~ *vt* **1** to accommodate, adapt **2a** to be good for the health or well-being of **b** to be becoming to; look right with **3** to satisfy, please ⟨~s *me fine*⟩ – **suit someone down to the ground** to suit sby extremely well

suitable /'s(y)oohtəbl/ *adj* appropriate, fitting – **suitableness** *n*, **suitably** *adv*, **suitability** /-tə'biləti/ *n*

suitcase /-,kays/ *n* a rectangular usu rigid case with a hinged lid and a handle, used for carrying articles (e g clothes)

suite /sweet/ *n* **1** *sing or pl in constr* a retinue; *esp* the personal staff accompanying an official or dignitary on business **2a** a group of rooms occupied as a unit **b(1)** a 17th- and 18th-c instrumental musical form consisting of a series of dances **(2)** a modern instrumental composition in several movements of different character **(3)** an orchestral concert arrangement in suite form of material drawn from a longer work (e g a ballet) **c** a set of matching furniture (e g a settee and 2 armchairs) for a room ⟨*a 3-piece* ~⟩ [F, alter. of OF *siute* – more at SUIT]

suiting /'s(y)oohting/ *n* fabric suitable for suits

suitor /'s(y)oohtə/ *n* one who courts a woman with a view to marriage [ME, follower, pleader, fr AF, fr L *secutor* follower, fr *secutus*, pp of *sequi* to follow – more at SUE]

sukiyaki /,soohki'yaki, -'yahki/ *n* a Japanese dish of thin slices of meat, soya-bean curd, and vegetables cooked in soy sauce, sake, and sugar [Jap]

sulcate /'sulkayt/ *adj* scored with (longitudinal) furrows ⟨*a* ~ *seedpod*⟩ [L *sulcatus*, pp of *sulcare* to furrow, fr *sulcus*]

sulcus /'sulkəs/ *n, pl* **sulci** /'sulsie/ a (shallow) furrow, esp on the surface of the brain between convolutions [L; akin to OE *sulh* plough, Gk *holkos* furrow, *helkein* to pull]

sulf-, sulfo- *comb form, NAm* sulph-, sulpho-

sulfur /'sulfə/ *n, NAm* sulphur – **sulfurous** *adj*

[1]**sulk** /sulk/ *vi* to be moodily silent [back-formation fr *sulky*]

[2]**sulk** *n* a fit of sulking – usu pl with sing. meaning

[1]**sulky** /'sulki/ *adj* sulking or given to fits of sulking [prob alter. of obs *sulke* (sluggish)] – **sulkily** *adv*, **sulkiness** *n*

[2]**sulky** *n* a light 2-wheeled 1-horse vehicle for 1 person used esp in trotting races [prob fr [1]*sulky*; fr its holding a solitary person]

sullage /'sulij/ *n* **1** refuse, sewage **2** silt [prob fr MF *soiller, souiller* to soil – more at [1]SOIL]

sullen /'sulən/ *adj* **1** silently gloomy or resentful; ill-humoured and unsociable **2** dismal, gloomy [ME *solain* sullen, solitary, prob fr (assumed) MF, fr L *solus* alone] – **sullenly** *adv*, **sullenness** *n*

sully /'suli/ *vt* to mar the purity of; tarnish [prob fr MF *soiller* to soil]

sulph-, sulpho-, *NAm* **sulf-, sulfo-** *comb form* sulphur; containing sulphur in the molecular structure ⟨sulph*anilamide*⟩ [F *sulf-, sulfo-*, fr L *sulphur, sulfur*]

'sulpha ,drug /'sulfə/ *n* any of various synthetic drugs chemically related to sulphanilamide that are used to kill or inhibit the growth of bacteria [*sulpha* short for *sulphanilamide*]

sulphanilamide /,sulfə'niləmied/ *n* a sulphonamide that is the parent compound of most of the sulpha drugs [*sulphanilic* (fr ISV *sulph-* + *aniline* + *-ic*) + *amide*]

sulphate /'sulfayt/ *n* **1** a salt or ester of sulphuric acid **2** the bivalent group or ion SO_4^{2+} characteristic of sulphuric acid and sulphates [modif of F *sulfate*, fr L *sulphur, sulfur*]

sulphide /'sulfied/ *n* a binary compound of sulphur, usu with a more electropositive element

sulphite /'sulfiet/ *n* a salt or ester of sulphurous acid [modif of F *sulfite*, alter. of *sulfate* sulphate]

sulphon- /sulfon-/ *comb form* sulphonic ⟨sulphona*mide*⟩

sulphonamide /sul'fonəmied/ *n* an amide (e g sulphanilamide) of a sulphonic acid; *also* SULPHA DRUG

sulphonate /'sulfənayt/ *n* a salt or ester of a sulphonic acid

sulphonic /sul'fonik, -'fohnik/ *n* of, being, or derived from the univalent acid group SO_3H ⟨~ *acid*⟩ [*sulphone* (fr ISV *sulph-* + *-one*) + *-ic*]

sulphonyl /'sulfənil, -niel/ *n* the bivalent group SO_2

sulphonylurea /,sulfənilyoo(ə)'ree·ə, -'yooəri·ə, -niel-/ *n* any of several synthetic compounds (e g chlorpropamide) given orally to lower the concentration of glucose in the blood in the treatment of diabetes mellitus [NL, fr ISV *sulphonyl* + NL *urea*]

¹sulphur /'sulfə/ *n* **1** a nonmetallic element chemically resembling oxygen that occurs esp as yellow crystals and is used esp in rubber vulcanization and in medicine for treating skin diseases ☞ PERIODIC TABLE **2** pale greenish yellow [ME *sulphur* brimstone, fr L *sulpur, sulphur, sulfur*]

²sulphur *vt* to treat with (a compound of) sulphur

sulphurate /'sulfyoo,rayt/ *vt* to sulphur – **sulphurator** *n*, **sulphuration** /-'raysh(ə)n/ *n*

sulphur bottom whale *n* BLUE WHALE [fr the yellowish splotches on its belly]

,sulphur di'oxide *n* a pungent toxic gas that is a major air pollutant and is used in making sulphuric acid, in bleaching, and as a food preservative

sulphuret /,sulfyoo'ret/ *vt* **-tt-** (*NAm* **-t-, -tt-**) to combine or impregnate with sulphur [NL *sulfuretum* sulphide, fr L *sulfur*]

sulphuric /sul'fyooərik/ *adj* of or containing (high valency) sulphur

sul,phuric 'acid *n* a corrosive oily strong acid that is a vigorous oxidizing and dehydrating agent

sulphur·ize, -ise /'sulfəriez/ *vt* to sulphur – **sulphurization** /-'zaysh(ə)n/ *n*

sulphurous /'sulf(ə)rəs, sul'fyooərəs/ *adj* **1** of or containing (low valency) sulphur **2** resembling or coming from (burning) sulphur

sul,phurous 'acid /sul'fyooərəs/ *n* a weak unstable acid used as a reducing and bleaching agent

sulphydryl /,sulf'hiedril/ *n* the highly reactive univalent group SH that is present in many biologically active compounds (e g coenzymes and enzyme inhibitors) [ISV *sulph-* + *hydr-* + *-yl*]

sultan /'sult(ə)n/ *n* a sovereign of a Muslim state [MF, fr Ar *sulṭān*] – **sultanate** /-ət/ *n*

sultana /səl'tahnə/ *n* **1** a female member of a sultan's family; *esp* a sultan's wife **2** (the raisin of) a pale yellow seedless grape [It, fem of *sultano* sultan, fr Ar *sulṭān*]

sultry /'sultri/ *adj* **1** oppressively hot and humid **2** (capable of) exciting strong sexual desire; sensual [obs *sulter* (to swelter), alter. of *swelter*] – **sultrily** *adv*, **sultriness** *n*

¹sum /sum/ *n* **1** a (specified) amount of money **2** the whole amount; the total **3** *the* gist – esp in *the sum and substance* **4a(1)** the result of adding numbers ⟨~ *of 5 and 7 is 12*⟩ **(2)** the limit of the sum of the first *n* terms of an infinite series as *n* increases indefinitely ☞ SYMBOL **b** numbers to be added; *broadly* a problem in arithmetic **c** UNION 3 [ME *summe*, fr OF, fr L *summa*, fr fem of *summus* highest; akin to L *super* over – more at ¹OVER] – **in sum** briefly

²sum *vt* **-mm-** to calculate the sum of – compare SUM UP ☞ SYMBOL

sumach, sumac /'s(h)oohmak/ *n* (the dried powdered leaves and flowers, used in tanning and dyeing, of) any of a genus of trees, shrubs, and climbing plants (e g poison ivy) with feathery leaves turning to brilliant colours in the autumn and red or whitish berries [ME *sumac*, fr MF, fr Ar *summāq*]

Sumerian /sooh'miəri·ən, -'meəri·ən/ *n* **1** a native or inhabitant of Sumer **2** the language of the Sumerians that has no known linguistic affinities [*Sumer*, ancient region of Babylonia] – **Sumerian** *adj*

summar·ize, -ise /'suməriez/ *vt* to express as or reduce to a summary – **summarizer** *n*, **summarization** /-'zaysh(ə)n/ *n*

¹summary /'sumәri/ *adj* **1** concise but comprehensive **2a** done quickly without delay or formality **b** of or using a summary proceeding; *specif* tried or triable in a magistrates' court ⟨*a* ~ *offence*⟩ ☞ LAW [ME, fr ML *summarius*, fr L *summa* sum] – **summarily** *adv*

²summary *n* a brief account covering the main points of sthg

summat /'sumət/ *pron, dial N Eng* something [alter. of *somewhat*, pron (something)]

summate /su'mayt/ *vt* SUM UP [back-formation fr *summation*]

summation /su'maysh(ə)n/ *n* **1** the act or process of forming a sum **2** a total **3** cumulative action or effect **4** (a) summing up of an argument – **summational** *adj*

¹summer /'sumə/ *n* **1** the season between spring and autumn comprising in the northern hemisphere the months of June, July, and August **2** a period of maturity **3** a year ⟨*a girl of 17* ~*s*⟩ – chiefly poetic [ME *sumer*, fr OE *sumor*; akin to OHG & ON *sumer* summer, Skt *samā* year, season]

²summer *adj* sown in the spring and harvested in the same year as sown ⟨~ *wheat*⟩ – compare WINTER

³summer *vi* to pass the summer ~ *vt* to provide (e g cattle or sheep) with pasture during the summer

⁴summer *n* a large horizontal beam or stone used esp in building [ME, packhorse, beam, fr MF *somier*, fr (assumed) VL *sagmarius*, fr LL *sagma* packsaddle, fr Gk]

'summer,house /-,hows/ *n* a small building in a

garden designed to provide a shady place in summer

'summer ,school *n* a course of teaching held during the summer vacation, esp on university premises

'summer,time /-,tiem/ *n* the summer season

summery /'sum(ə)ri/ *adj* of, suggesting, or suitable for summer

,summing-'up /'suming/ *n* **1** a concluding summary **2** a survey of evidence given by a judge to the jury before it considers its verdict

summit /'sumit/ *n* **1** a top; *esp* the highest point or peak ☞ GEOGRAPHY **2** the topmost level attainable; the pinnacle **3** a conference of highest-level officials [ME *somete*, fr MF, fr OF, dim. of *sum* top, fr L *summum*, neut of *summus* highest – more at SUM]

summon /'sumən/ *vt* **1** to convene, convoke **2** to command by a summons to appear in court **3** to call upon to come; SEND FOR ⟨~ *a doctor*⟩ **4** to call up or muster ⟨~ed *up his courage*⟩ [ME *somonen*, fr OF *somondre*, fr (assumed) VL *summonere*, alter. of L *summonēre* to remind secretly, fr *sub-* secretly + *monēre* to warn – more at SUB-, MIND] – **summoner** *n*

[1]**summons** /'sumənz/ *n, pl* **summonses** **1** a call or order by authority to appear at a particular place or to attend to sthg **2** a written notification warning sby to appear in court [ME *somouns*, fr OF *somonse*, fr pp of *somondre*]

[2]**summons** *vt* SUMMON 2

sumo /'s(y)oohmoh/ *n* Japanese wrestling in which a contestant loses if he is forced out of the contest area or thrown off his feet [Jap *sumō*]

sump /sump/ *n* **1** a pit or reservoir serving as a drain or receptacle for esp waste liquids: e g **a** a cesspool **b** *chiefly Br* the lower section of the crankcase used as a lubricating-oil reservoir in an internal-combustion engine ☞ CAR **2** the lowest part of a mine shaft, into which water drains [(1) ME *sompe* swamp; (2) G *sumpf*, lit., marsh, fr MHG – more at SWAMP]

sumptuary /'sum(p)choo·əri, -tyoo-/ *adj* designed to regulate personal expenditures and habits ⟨~ *laws*⟩ [L *sumptuarius*, fr *sumptus* expense, fr *sumptus*, pp of *sumere* to take, spend – more at CONSUME]

sumptuous /'sum(p)choo·əs, -tyoo-/ *adj* lavishly rich, costly, or luxurious [MF *sumptueux*, fr L *sumptuosus*, fr *sumptus*] – **sumptuously** *adv*, **sumptuousness** *n*

,sum 'total *n* a total arrived at through the counting of sums

sum up *vt* **1** to summarize **2** to form or express a rapid appraisal of ~ *vi* to present a summary

[1]**sun** /sun/ *n* **1a** the star nearest to the earth, round which the earth and other planets revolve ☞ ENERGY, SYMBOL **b** a star or other celestial body that emits its own light **2** the heat or light radiated from the sun *USE* (*1*) ASTRONOMY [ME *sunne*, fr OE; akin to OHG *sunna* sun, L *sol* – more at [1]SOLAR] – **sunless** *adj* – **under the sun** in the world; ON EARTH ⟨*he was the last person* under the sun *I expected to see*⟩

[2]**sun** *vb* **-nn-** to expose (e g oneself) to the rays of the sun

'sun,baked /-,baykt/ *adj* baked hard by exposure to sunshine

'sun,bathe /-,baydh/ *vi* to expose the body to the rays of the sun or a sunlamp – **sunbathe** *n*

'sun,beam /-,beem/ *n* a ray of light from the sun

'sun,bird /-,buhd/ *n* any of numerous small brilliantly coloured tropical Old World birds

'sun,blind /-,bliend/ *n, chiefly Br* an awning or a shade on a window (e g a venetian blind) that gives protection from the sun's rays

'sun,bonnet /-,bonit/ *n* a bonnet with a wide brim framing the face and usu having a ruffle at the back to protect the neck from the sun

'sun,bow /-,boh/ *n* an arch resembling a rainbow made by the sun shining through vapour or mist

[1]**'sun,burn** /-,buhn/ *vb* **sunburnt** /-,buhnt/, **sunburned** to burn or tan by exposure to sunlight [back-formation fr *sunburnt*, fr *sun* + *burnt*]

[2]**sunburn** *n* inflammation of the skin caused by overexposure to sunlight

'sun,burst /-buhst/ *n* an ornament or jewelled brooch representing a sun surrounded by rays

sundae /'sunday/ *n* an ice cream served with a topping of fruit, nuts, syrup, etc [prob alter. of *Sunday*]

'sun ,dance *n* a N American Indian religious ceremony held in honour of the sun

[1]**Sunday** /'sunday, -di/ *n* **1** the day of the week falling between Saturday and Monday, observed by Christians as a day of worship ☞ SYMBOL **2** a newspaper published on Sundays ⟨*further scandal in the* ~s⟩ [ME, fr OE *sunnandæg*; akin to OHG *sunnūntag* Sunday; both fr a prehistoric WGmc-NGmc compound whose components are represented by OE *sunne* sun & by OE *dæg* day] – **Sundays** *adv*

[2]**Sunday** *adj* **1** of or associated with Sunday **2** amateur ⟨~ *painters*⟩ – derog

,Sunday 'best *n sing or pl in constr* one's best clothes – infml

'Sunday ,school *n* a class usu of religious instruction held, esp for children, on Sundays

sunder /'sundə/ *vt* to break apart or in two; sever [ME *sunderen*, fr OE ge*sundrian, syndrian*; akin to OHG *suntarōn* to sunder, L *sine* without]

sundew /'sun,dyooh/ *n* any of a genus of bog plants with long glistening hairs on the leaves that attract and trap insects

'sun,dial /-,die·əl/ *n* an instrument to show the time of day by the shadow of a pointer on a graduated plate or cylindrical surface

'sun ,dog *n* **1** a parhelion **2** a small nearly round halo on the parhelic circle

'sun,down /-,down/ *n* sunset

'sun,drenched /-,drencht/ *adj* exposed to much hot sunshine

[1]**sundry** /'sundri/ *adj* miscellaneous, various ⟨~ *articles*⟩ [ME, different for each, fr OE *syndrig*; akin to OHG *suntarīg* sundry, OE *syndrian* to sunder, L *sine* without]

[2]**sundry** *pron pl in constr* an indeterminate number – chiefly in *all and sundry*

[3]**sundry** *n* **1** *pl* miscellaneous small articles or items **2** *Austr* EXTRA C

'sun,fish /-,fish/ *n* a large marine bony fish with a nearly oval body, a length of up to 3m (about 10ft), and a weight of 2 tonnes (about 2 tons)

'sun,flower /-,flowə/ *n* any of a genus of composite plants with large yellow-rayed flower heads bearing edible seeds that are often used as animal feed and yield an edible oil

sung /sung/ *past of* SING

'sun,glasses /-,glahsiz/ *n pl* glasses to protect the eyes from the sun

,sung 'mass *n* a mass in which prescribed parts are sung by the celebrant and congregation

'sun,hat /-,hat/ *n* an often large-brimmed hat worn to protect the head and face from the sun

sunk /sungk/ *past of* SINK

sunken /'sungkən/ *adj* **1** submerged; *esp* lying at the bottom of a body of water **2a** hollow, recessed **b** lying or constructed below the surrounding or normal level ⟨*a* ~ *bath*⟩ [fr obs pp of *sink*]

sunk fence *n* a ditch with a retaining wall or fence used to divide lands without defacing a landscape

sunlamp /'sun,lamp/ *n* an electric lamp that emits esp ultraviolet light and is used esp for tanning the skin

'sun,light /-,liet/ *n* sunshine

'sun,lit /-,lit/ *adj* lit (as if) by the sun

'sun,lounge /-,lownj/ *n, Br* a room having a large glazed area placed to admit much sunlight

sunn /sun/, **sunn hemp** *n* (the hemplike fibre from the bark of) an E Indian leguminous plant with slender branches and yellow flowers [Hindi *san,* fr Skt *śaṇa*]

sunna /'soonə, 'sunə/ *n, often cap* the body of Islamic custom and practice based on Muhammad's words and deeds [Ar *sunnah*]

Sunni /'sooni/ *n* **1** the Muslims of the branch of Islam that keeps to the orthodox tradition and acknowledges the first 4 caliphs as rightful successors of Muhammad – compare SHIA **2** a Sunnite [Ar *sunnīy,* fr *sunnah*] – **Sunni** *adj*

Sunnism /'soo,niz(ə)m/ *n* Islam as taught by the Sunni

Sunnite /'sooniet/ *n or adj* (an adherent) of Sunnism

sunny /'suni/ *adj* **1** bright with sunshine **2** cheerful, optimistic ⟨*a* ~ *disposition*⟩ **3** exposed to or warmed by the sun – **sunnily** *adv,* **sunniness** *n*

sunray pleats /'sunray/ *n pl* a series of very narrow overlapping knife pleats that are usu produced in fabric commercially

'sun,rise /-,riez/ *n* (the time of) the rising of the topmost part of the sun above the horizon as a result of the rotation of the earth

'sun,roof /-,roohf/ *n* a motor-car roof having an opening or removable panel

sunset /'sunsit, -,set/ *n* (the time of) the descent of the topmost part of the sun below the horizon as a result of the rotation of the earth

'sun,shade /-,shayd/ *n* sthg used as a protection from the sun's rays: e g **a** a parasol **b** an awning

'sun,shine /-,shien/ *n* **1** the sun's light or direct rays **2** a place or surface receiving the warmth and light of the sun ⟨*sat in the* ~⟩ – **sunshiny** *adj*

'sun,spot /-,spot/ *n* a transient dark marking on the visible surface of the sun caused by a relatively cooler area

'sun,stroke /-,strohk/ *n* heatstroke caused by direct exposure to the sun

'sun,tan /-,tan/ *n* a browning of the skin from exposure to the sun

'sun,trap /-,trap/ *n* a sheltered place that receives a large amount of sunshine

'sun,up /-,up/ *n* sunrise – infml

'sun,wise /-,wiez/ *adv* clockwise

Suomi /'sooh·əmi/ *n pl in constr* the Finnish people [Finn]

[1]sup /sup/ *vb* **-pp-** *chiefly dial* to drink (liquid) in small mouthfuls [ME *suppen,* fr OE *sūpan, suppan;* akin to OHG *sūfan* to drink, sip, OE *sūcan* to suck – more at SUCK]

[2]sup *n, chiefly dial* a mouthful, esp of liquid; a sip

[3]sup *vi* **-pp-** **1** to eat the evening meal **2** to make one's supper – + *on* or *off* [ME *soupen, suppen,* fr OF *souper,* fr *soupe* sop, soup – more at SOUP]

[1]super /'s(y)oohpə/ *n* **1** a superfine grade or extra large size **2** a police or other superintendent – infml [(1) [2]*super,* (2) short for *superintendent*]

[2]super *adj* – used as a general term of approval; infml ⟨*a* ~ *time*⟩ ⟨*it was just* ~⟩ [short for *superfine*]

super- /s(y)oohpə-/ *prefix* **1a(1)** higher in quantity, quality, or degree than; more than ⟨super*human*⟩ **(2)** in addition; extra ⟨super*tax*⟩ **b(1)** exceeding or so as to exceed a norm ⟨super*heat*⟩ ⟨super*saturate*⟩ **(2)** to an excessive degree ⟨super*subtle*⟩ ⟨super*sensitive*⟩ **c** surpassing all or most others of its kind (e g in size or power) ⟨super*tanker*⟩ **2** situated or placed above, on, or at the top of ⟨super*lunary*⟩ ⟨super*script*⟩ **3** having (the specified atom or radical) present in an unusually large proportion ⟨super*phosphate*⟩ **4** constituting a more inclusive category of ⟨super*family*⟩ **5** superior in status, title, or position ⟨super*power*⟩ [L, over, above, in addition, fr *super* over, above, on top of – more at [1]OVER]

superabundant /,soohpərə'bund(ə)nt, ,syooh-/ *adj* more than ample; excessive [ME, fr LL *superabundant-, superabundans,* fr prp of *superabundare* to exist in more than ample quantities] – **superabundance** *n,* **superabundantly** *adv*

,super'add /-'ad/ *vt* to add over and above sthg – fml [ME *superadden,* fr L *superaddere,* fr *super-* + *addere* to add] – **superaddition** /-ə'dish(ə)n/ *n*

,super'annuable /-'anyoo·əbl/ *adj* affording a pension on retirement ⟨*a* ~ *post*⟩ [*superannu*ation + *-able*]

,super'annuate /-'anyooayt/ *vt* **1** to make or declare obsolete or out-of-date **2** to retire on a pension, esp because of age or infirmity [back-formation fr *superannuated*] – **superannuation** /-anyoo 'aysh(ə)n/ *n*

,super'annuated *adj* incapacitated or disqualified for work, use, or continuance by advanced age: e g **a** obsolete **b** retired on a pension [ML *superannuatus,* pp of *superannuari* to be too old, fr L *super-* + *annus* year – more at ANNUAL]

superb /s(y)ooh'puhb/ *adj* **1** marked by grandeur or magnificence **2** of excellent quality ⟨*the meal was* ~⟩ [L *superbus* excellent, proud, fr *super* above + *-bus* (akin to OE *bēon* to be) – more at [1]OVER, BE] – **superbly** *adv,* **superbness** *n*

,super'calender /-'kaləndə/ *vt or n* (to process in) a stack of highly polished rolls used to give a very smooth finish to paper

'super,cargo /-,kahgoh/ *n* an officer in a merchant ship in charge of the commercial concerns of the voyage [Sp *sobrecargo,* fr *sobre-* over (fr L *super-*) + *cargo*]

'super,charge /-,chahj/ *vt* **1** to charge greatly or excessively (e g with energy or tension) ⟨~d *rhetoric*⟩ **2** to supply a charge to (e g an engine) at a pressure higher than that of the surrounding atmosphere – **supercharge** *n*

ˈsuperˌcharger *n* a device supplying fuel or air to an internal-combustion engine at a pressure higher than normal for greater efficiency

ˌsuperˈcilious /-ˈsili·əs/ *adj* coolly disdainful [L *superciliosus*, fr *supercilium* eyebrow, haughtiness, fr *super-* + *cilium* eyelid (akin to *celare* to hide) – more at HELL] – **superciliously** *adv*, **superciliousness** *n*

ˌsuperˌconducˈtivity /-ˌkondukˈtivəti/ *n* a complete disappearance of electrical resistance in various metals and alloys at temperatures near absolute zero – **superconducting** /-kənˈdukting/ *adj*, **superconductive** /-kənˈduktiv/ *adj*, **superconductor** /-kənˈduktə/ *n*

ˌsuperˈcool /-ˈkoohl/ *vb* to cool below the freezing point without solidification or crystallization

ˌsuperˈcritical /-ˈkritikl/ *adj, of an aerofoil, esp a wing* having supersonic airflow while travelling at subsonic speeds and therefore offering increased lift and speed

ˈsuperˌego /-ˌeegoh/ *n* the one of the 3 divisions of the mind in psychoanalytic theory that is only partly conscious, reflects social rules, and functions as a conscience to reward and punish – compare EGO, ID

ˌsuperˌeleˈvation /-ˌeliˈvaysh(ə)n/ *n* the vertical difference between the heights of the inner and outer edges of a highway, pavement, or railway track

ˌsupereˈrogatory /-iˈrogət(ə)ri/ *adj* **1** performed to an extent beyond that needed or required **2** superfluous, nonessential *USE* fml [ML *supererogatorius*, fr *supererogatus*, pp of *supererogare* to perform beyond the call of duty, fr LL, to expend in addition, fr L *super-* + *erogare* to expend public funds with the people's consent, fr *e-* + *rogare* to ask] – **supererogation** /-ˌerəˈgaysh(ə)n/ *n*

ˌsuperfeˈtation /-feeˈtaysh(ə)n/ *n* successive fertilization of 2 or more ova of different ovulations resulting in the presence of embryos of unlike ages in the same uterus [ML *superfetation-*, *superfetatio*, fr L *superfetatus*, pp of *superfetare* to conceive while already pregnant, fr *super-* + *fetus* act of bearing young, offspring – more at FOETUS]

ˌsuperˈficial /-ˈfish(ə)l/ *adj* **1a** of a surface **b** not penetrating below the surface ⟨~ *wounds*⟩ **2a** not thorough or profound; shallow **b** apparent rather than real ⟨~ *differences*⟩ [ME, fr LL *superficialis*, fr L *superficies*] – **superficially** *adv*, **superficialness** *n*, **superficiality** /-ˌfishiˈaləti/ *n*

ˌsuperˈficies /-ˈfisheez/ *n, pl* **superficies** **1** a surface **2** the external aspect or appearance of a thing *USE* fml [L, surface, fr *super-* + *facies* face, aspect – more at FACE]

ˈsuperˌfine /-ˌfien/ *adj* **1** of extremely fine size or texture ⟨~ *toothbrush bristles*⟩ **2** *esp of merchandise* of high quality or grade

ˌsuperˈfluity /-ˈflooh·əti/ *n* **1** an excess; a supply exceeding what is required **2** sthg unnecessary or superfluous [ME *superfluitee*, fr MF *superfluité*, fr LL *superfluitat-*, *superfluitas*, fr L *superfluus*]

superfluous /s(y)oohˈpuhfloo·əs/ *adj* exceeding what is sufficient or necessary [ME, fr L *superfluus*, lit., running over, fr *superfluere* to overflow, fr *super-* + *fluere* to flow – more at FLUID]

ˈsuperˌgiant /-ˌjie·ənt/ *n* a star of very great intrinsic luminosity, enormous size, and low density

ˌsuperˈheat /-ˈheet/ *vt* **1** to heat (a liquid) above the boiling point without conversion into vapour **2** to heat (a vapour) so as to cause to remain a gas without condensation ⟨~ed *steam*⟩ – **superheat** *n*, **superheater** *n*

¹ˌsuperˈheteroˌdyne /-ˈhetərəˌdien/ *adj* of or using a form of radio or television reception in which the radio frequency signal is heterodyned with a wave of a frequency such that the resultant is a signal superimposed on an intermediate frequency carrier [*super*sonic + *heterodyne*]

²ˌsuperˈheterodyne *n* a superheterodyne receiver

ˈsuperˌhighway /-ˌhieway/ *n, NAm* a motorway

ˌsuperˈhuman /-ˈhyoohmən/ *adj* **1** being above the human; divine ⟨~ *beings*⟩ **2** exceeding normal human power, size, or capability ⟨*a* ~ *effort*⟩ – **superhumanly** *adv*, **superhumanness, superhumanity** /-hyooh ˈmanəti/ *n*

ˌsuperimˈpose /-imˈpohz/ *vt* to place or lay over or above sthg – **superimposable** *adj*, **superimposition** /-ˌimpəˈzish(ə)n/ *n*

ˌsuperinˈcumbent /-inˈkumbənt/ *adj* lying and usu exerting pressure on sthg else [L *superincumbent-*, *superincumbens*, prp of *superincumbere* to lie on top of, fr *super-* + *incumbere* to lie down on – more at INCUMBENT] – **superincumbently** *adv*

ˌsuperinˈtend /-inˈtend/ *vt* to be in charge of; direct [LL *superintendere*, fr L *super-* + *intendere* to intend, attend, direct attention to – more at INTEND]

ˌsuperinˈtendence /-inˈtend(ə)ns/ *n* supervision, overseeing

ˌsuperinˈtendency /-inˈtend(ə)nsi/ *n* **1** the office or jurisdiction of a superintendent **2** superintendence

ˌsuperinˈtendent /-inˈtend(ə)nt/ *n* **1** one who supervises or manages sthg **2** a British police officer ranking next above a chief inspector [ML *superintendent-*, *superintendens*, fr LL, prp of *superintendere*] – **superintendent** *adj*

¹superior /s(y)oohˈpiəri·ə/ *adj* **1** situated higher up; upper **2** of higher rank or status **3** indifferent or unyielding to pain, temptation, etc **4a** greater in quality, amount, or worth **b** excellent of its kind **5a** *of an animal or plant part* situated above or at the top of another (corresponding) part **b(1)** *of a calyx* attached to and apparently arising from the ovary **(2)** *of an ovary* free from and above a floral envelope (e g the calyx) **6** *of a planet* further from the sun than the earth is **7** thinking oneself better than others; supercilious [ME, fr MF *superieur*, fr L *superior*, compar of *superus* upper, fr *super* over, above – more at ¹OVER] – **superiority** /-riˈorəti/ *n*

²superior *n* **1** a person who is above another in rank or office; *esp* the head of a religious house or order **2** sby or sthg that surpasses another in quality or merit

superior conjunction *n* a conjunction in which a lesser or secondary celestial body passes farther from the observer than the primary body round which it revolves ⟨~ *of Saturn*⟩

superiˈority ˌcomplex *n* an exaggeratedly high opinion of oneself – compare MEGALOMANIA 2

superiorly /s(y)oohˈpiəri·əli/ *adv* **1** in or to a higher position or direction **2** in a higher or better manner or degree; *also* in a haughty or condescending manner

superjacent /ˌsoohpəˈjays(ə)nt, ˌsyooh-/ *adj* lying above or on sthg – fml [L *superjacent-*, *superjacens*, prp of *superjacēre* to lie over or upon, fr *super-* + *jacēre* to lie; akin to L *jacere* to throw – more at ²JET]

[1]**superlative** /s(y)ooh'puhlətiv/ *adj* **1** of or constituting the degree of grammatical comparison expressing an extreme or unsurpassed level or extent **2** surpassing all others; of the highest degree ⟨*he spoke with ~ ease*⟩ [ME *superlatif*, fr MF, fr LL *superlativus*, fr L *superlatus* (pp of *superferre* to carry over, raise high), fr *super-* + *latus*, pp of *ferre* to carry – more at TOLERATE, [2]BEAR] – **superlatively** *adv*, **superlativeness** *n*

[2]**superlative** *n* **1** the superlative degree or form in a language **2** an exaggerated expression, esp of praise ⟨*talked in ~*s⟩

superlunary /,s(y)oohpə'loohnəri/ *also* **,super'lunar** /-'loohnə/ *adj* beyond the moon; celestial [L *super-* + *luna* moon – more at LUNAR]

'superman /-man/ *n* a person of extraordinary power or achievements – infml [trans of G *übermensch*]

'super,market /-,mahkit/ *n* a usu large self-service retail shop selling foods and household merchandise

,super'natant /-'nayt(ə)nt/ *n or adj* (a substance) floating on the surface [adj L *supernatant-, supernatans*, prp of *supernatare* to float, fr *super-* + *natare* to swim; n fr adj]

,super'natural /-'nach(ə)rəl/ *adj* **1** of an order of existence or an agency (e g a god or spirit) not bound by normal laws of cause and effect **2a** departing from what is usual or normal, esp in nature **b** attributed to an invisible agent (e g a ghost or spirit) [ML *supernaturalis*, fr L *super-* + *natura* nature] – **supernatural** *n*, **supernaturalism** *n*, **supernaturally** *adv*, **supernaturalness** *n*

,super'normal /-'nawml/ *adj* exceeding the normal or average – **supernormally** *adv*, **supernormality** /-naw'maləti/ *n*

,super'nova /-'nohvə/ *n* any of the rarely observed nova outbursts in which the luminosity reaches 100 million times that of the sun [NL]

[1]**,super'numerary** /-'nyoohmrəri/ *adj* exceeding the usual or stated number ⟨*a ~ tooth*⟩ [LL *supernumerarius*, fr L *super-* + *numerus* number – more at NIMBLE]

[2]**supernumerary** *n* **1** a person employed as an extra assistant or substitute **2** an actor employed to play a walk-on

,super'ordinate /-'awdinət/ *adj* superior in rank, class, or status [*super-* + *-ordinate* (as in *subordinate*)]

,super,ovu'lation /-,ovyoo'laysh(ə)n/ *n* production of exceptional numbers of eggs at one time

,super'phosphate /-'fosfayt/ *n* a fertilizer made from insoluble mineral phosphates by treatment with sulphuric acid

,super'pose /-'pohz/ *vt* **1** to lay (e g a geometric figure) on another so as to make all like parts coincide **2** to place or lay over or above – fml [prob fr F *superposer*, back-formation fr *superposition*, fr LL *superposition-, superpositio*, fr L *superpositus*, pp of *superponere* to superpose, fr *super-* + *ponere* to place – more at POSITION] – **superposable** *adj*, **superposition** /-pə'zish(ə)n/ *n*

'super,power /-,powə/ *n* an extremely powerful nation; *specif* any of a very few dominant states in the world

,super'saturate /-'sachoorayt/ *vt* to add to beyond the point of saturation – **supersaturation** /-,sachoo'raysh(ə)n/ *n*

,super'scribe /-'skrieb/ *vt* **1** to write on the top or outside **2** to write sthg (e g an address) on the outside or cover of [L *superscribere*, fr *super-* + *scribere* to write – more at [1]SCRIBE]

'super,script /-,skript/ *n* a distinguishing symbol written or printed above another character [L *superscriptus*, pp of *superscribere*] – **superscript** *adj*

,super'scription /-'skripsh(ə)n/ *n* words written on the surface of, outside, or above sthg else; an inscription [ME, fr MF, fr LL *superscription-, superscriptio*, fr L *superscriptus*]

,super'sede /-'seed/ *vt* **1** to take the place of (esp sthg inferior or outmoded) ⟨*buses ~d trams*⟩ **2** to displace in favour of another; supplant [MF *superseder* to refrain from, fr L *supersedēre* to be superior to, refrain from, fr *super-* + *sedēre* to sit – more at SIT] – **superseder** *n*, **supersedure** /-'seejə/ *n*, **supersession** /-'sesh(ə)n/ *n*

,super'sonic /-'sonik/ *adj* **1** (using, produced by, or relating to waves or vibrations) having a frequency above the upper threshold of human hearing of about 20,000Hz **2** of, being, or using speeds from 1 to 5 times the speed of sound in air **3** of supersonic aircraft or missiles ⟨*the ~ age*⟩ [L *super-* + *sonus* sound – more at [1]SOUND] – **supersonically** *adv*

,super'stition /-'stish(ə)n/ *n* **1** a belief or practice resulting from ignorance, fear of the unknown, trust in magic or chance, or a false conception of causation **2** an irrational abject attitude of mind towards the supernatural, nature, or God resulting from superstition [ME *supersticion*, fr MF, fr L *superstition-, superstitio*, fr *superstit-, superstes* standing over (as witness or survivor), fr *super-* + *stare* to stand – more at STAND] – **superstitious** /-'stishəs/ *adj*, **superstitiously** *adv*

'super,store /-,staw/ *n* a large supermarket

'super,stratum *n* an overlying stratum [*super-* + *-stratum* (as in *substratum*)]

'super,structure /-,strukchə/ *n* **1a** the part of a building above the ground **b** the structural part of a ship above the main deck **2** an entity or complex based on a more fundamental one – **superstructural** /-'strukchərəl/ *adj*

'super,tanker /-,tangkə/ *n* a very large tanker

'super,tax /-,taks/ *n* a tax paid in addition to normal tax by people with high incomes

,super'tonic /-'tonik/ *n* the second note of a diatonic scale

,super'vene /-'veen/ *vi* to happen in a way that interrupts some plan or process – fml [L *supervenire*, fr *super-* + *venire* to come – more at COME] – **supervenience** /-'veenyəns/ *n*, **supervenient** *adj*, **supervention** /-'vensh(ə)n/ *n*

supervise /'s(y)oohpə,viez/ *vt* to superintend, oversee [ML *supervisus*, pp of *supervidēre*, fr L *super-* + *vidēre* to see – more at WIT] – **supervisor** *n*, **supervisory** *adj*

,super'vision /-'vizh(ə)n/ *n* a critical watching and directing (e g of activities or an operation) [SUPERVISE + -ION]

supinate /'s(y)oohpi,nayt/ *vt* to rotate (the hand and forearm) so that the palm faces forwards or upwards [L *supinatus*, pp of *supinare* to lay backwards or on the back, fr *supinus*] – **supination** /-'naysh(ə)n/ *n*

[1]**supine** /'s(y)ooh,pien, ,-'-/ *adj* **1a** lying on the back or with the face upwards – compare PRONE 2 **b** marked by supination **2** mentally or morally lazy;

lethargic [L *supinus*; akin to L *sub* under, up to – more at UP] – **supinely** *adv*, **supineness** *n*

[2]**supine** *n* a Latin verbal noun formed from the stem of the past participle [ME *supyn*, fr LL *supinum*, fr L, neut of *supinus*, adj]

supper /'supə/ *n* **1** (the food for) a usu light evening meal or snack **2** a (fund-raising) social affair featuring a supper [ME, fr OF *souper*, fr *souper* to sup – more at [3]SUP]

supplant /sə'plahnt/ *vt* to take the place of (another), esp by force or treachery [ME *supplanten*, fr MF *supplanter*, fr L *supplantare* to overthrow by tripping up, fr *sub-* + *planta* sole of the foot – more at PLACE] – **supplanter** *n*, **supplantation** /,suplahn'taysh(ə)n/ *n*

[1]**supple** /'supl/ *adj* **1** compliant, often to the point of obsequiousness **2a** capable of easily being bent or folded; pliant **b** able to perform bending or twisting movements with ease and grace; lithe [ME *souple*, fr OF, fr L *supplic-*, *supplex* submissive, suppliant, lit., bending under, fr *sub-* + *plic-* (akin to *plicare* to fold) – more at [1]PLY] – **suppleness** *n*, **supplely** /'supl·i/, **supply** /'supli/ *adv*

[2]**supple** *vb* to make or become flexible or pliant

[1]**supplement** /'suplimənt/ *n* **1** sthg that completes, adds, or makes good a deficiency, or makes an addition ⟨*dietary* ~s⟩ **2** a part issued to update or extend a book or periodical **3** an angle or arc that when added to a given angle or arc equals 180° [ME, fr L *supplementum*, fr *supplēre* to fill up, complete – more at SUPPLY]

[2]**supplement** /'supliment/ *vt* to add a supplement to – **supplementer** *n*, **supplementation** /,suplimen'taysh(ə)n/ *n*

supplemental /,supli'mentl/ *adj* serving to supplement – **supplemental** *n*

supplementary /,supli'ment(ə)ri/ *adj* **1** additional **2** being or relating to a supplement or an angle that is a supplement

supplementary benefit *n* British social-security benefit paid to those who do not qualify for unemployment benefit

suppletion /sə'pleesh(ə)n/ *n* the recurrence of unrelated forms (e g *went, better*) of a word (e g *go, good*) [ML *suppletion-*, *suppletio* act of supplementing, fr L *suppletus*, pp] – **suppletive** /sə'pleetiv/ *adj*

suppletory /'suplit(ə)ri/ *adj* supplementary [L *suppletus*, pp of *supplēre*]

suppliant /'supli·ənt/ *adj* humbly imploring or entreating [MF, prp of *supplier* to supplicate, fr L *supplicare*] – **suppliant** *n*, **suppliantly** *adv*

supplicant /'suplikənt/ *n or adj* (a) suppliant – **supplicantly** *adv*

supplicate /'suplikayt/ *vi* to beg humbly; *esp* to pray to God ~ *vt* to ask humbly and earnestly of or for [ME *supplicaten*, fr L *supplicatus*, pp of *supplicare*, fr *supplic-*, *supplex* suppliant – more at SUPPLE] – **supplicatory** /-kət(ə)ri/ *adj*, **supplication** /-'kaysh(ə)n/ *n*

[1]**supply** /sə'plie/ *vt* **1** to provide for; satisfy ⟨supplies *a long-felt need*⟩ **2** to provide, furnish [ME *supplien*, fr MF *soupleier*, fr L *supplēre* to fill up, supplement, supply, fr *sub-* up + *plēre* to fill – more at SUB-, [1]FULL] – **supplier** *n*

[2]**supply** *n* **1a** the quantity or amount needed or available ⟨*in short* ~⟩ **b** provisions, stores – usu pl with sing. meaning **2** the act of filling a want or need ⟨~ *and demand*⟩ **3** the quantities of goods and services offered for sale at a particular time or at one price – compare DEMAND **4 supply, supply teacher** *Br* a teacher who fills a temporary vacancy

[3]**supply** *adj* of or for the raising of government revenue ⟨*a* ~ *bill*⟩

[1]**support** /sə'pawt/ *vt* **1** to bear, tolerate ⟨*could not* ~ *such behaviour*⟩ **2a(1)** to promote the interests of; encourage **(2)** to defend as valid or right **(3)** to argue or vote for ⟨~s *the Labour Party*⟩ **b(1)** to assist, help **(2)** to act with (a principal actor or actress) **c** to substantiate, corroborate **3a** to pay the costs of **b** to provide livelihood or subsistence for **4a** to hold up or serve as a foundation or prop for ⟨*steel girders* ~ *the building*⟩ **b** to maintain (a price) at a desired level by purchases or loans; *also* to maintain the price of by purchases or loans [ME *supporten*, fr MF *supporter*, fr LL *supportare*, fr L, to carry, fr *sub-* + *portare* to carry – more at [1]FARE] – **supportable** *adj*, **supportably** *adv*

[2]**support** *n* **1** supporting or being supported **2** maintenance, sustenance ⟨*without visible means of* ~⟩ **3** a device that supports sthg **4** *sing or pl in constr* a body of supporters

supporter /sə'pawtə/ *n* **1** an adherent or advocate ⟨*a Chelsea* ~⟩ **2** either of 2 figures (e g of men or animals) placed one on each side of a heraldic shield as if holding or guarding it [[1]SUPPORT + [2]-ER]

supporting /sə'pawting/ *adj* **1** that supports ⟨*a* ~ *wall*⟩ **2** of or being a film other than the main feature on a cinema programme

supportive /sə'pawtiv/ *adj* providing support; *esp* sustaining morale

suppose /sə'pohz/ *vt* **1a** to lay down tentatively as a hypothesis, assumption, or proposal ⟨~ *a fire broke out*⟩ ⟨~ *we wait a bit*⟩ **b(1)** to hold as an opinion; believe **(2)** to think probable or in keeping with the facts **(3)** to conjecture, think ⟨*when do you* ~ *he'll arrive?*⟩ **2** to devise for a purpose; intend ⟨*it's* ~d *to cure acne*⟩ **3** to presuppose **4** to allow, permit – used negatively ⟨*you're not* ~d *to go in there*⟩ **5** to expect because of moral, legal, or other obligations ⟨*drivers are* ~d *to wear seat belts*⟩ *USE* (*2, 4, & 5*) chiefly in *be supposed to* [ME *supposen*, fr MF *supposer*, fr ML *supponere* (perf indic *supposui*), fr L, to put under, substitute, fr *sub-* + *ponere* to put – more at POSITION] – **supposable** *adj*

sup'posed *adj* believed or imagined to be such ⟨*her* ~ *wealth*⟩ – **supposedly** /-zidli/ *adv*

supposing /sə'pohzing/ *conj* by way of hypothesis – compare SUPPOSE 1a

supposition /,supə'zish(ə)n/ *n* a hypothesis [ME, fr LL *supposition-*, *suppositio*, fr L, act of placing beneath, fr *suppositus*, pp of *supponere*] – **suppositional** *adj*, **suppositionaly** *adv*, **suppositive** /sə'pozətiv/ *adj*, **suppositively** *adv*

supposititious /sə,pozi'tishəs/ **suppositious** /,supə'zishəs/ *adj* **1a** fraudulently substituted **b** *of a child* illegitimate **2** hypothetical, assumed [L *suppositicius*, fr *suppositus*, pp of *supponere* to substitute; (2) influenced in meaning by *supposition*] – **supposititiously** *adv*, **supposititiousness** *n*

suppository /sə'pozət(ə)ri/ *n* a readily meltable cone or cylinder of medicated material for insertion into a bodily passage or cavity (e g the rectum) [ML *suppositorium*, fr LL, neut of *suppositorius* placed beneath, fr L *suppositus*, pp of *supponere* to put under]

suppress /sə'pres/ *vt* **1** to put down by authority or force **2** to stop the publication or revelation of **3a** to (deliberately) exclude a thought, feeling, etc from consciousness – compare REPRESS 2b **b** to hold back, check ⟨~ed *his impulse to laugh*⟩ **4** to inhibit the growth or development of [ME *suppressen*, fr L *suppressus*, pp of *supprimere*, fr *sub-* + *premere* to press – more at [2]PRESS] – **suppressible** *adj*, **suppression** /-sh(ə)n/ *n*, **suppressive** /-siv/ *adj*, **suppressively** *adv*, **suppressibility** /-,presə 'biləti/ *n*

suppressor /sə'presə/ *n* an electrical component (e g a capacitor) added to a circuit to suppress oscillations that would otherwise cause radio interference [SUPPRESS + [1]-OR]

suppurate /'supyoo,rayt/ *vi* to form or discharge pus [L *suppuratus*, pp of *suppurare*, fr *sub-* + *pur-*, *pus* pus – more at FOUL] – **suppurative** /-rətiv/ *adj*, **suppuration** /-'raysh(ə)n/ *n*

supra /'s(y)oohprə, -prah/ *adv* earlier in this writing; above [L]

supra- /s(y)oohprə-/ *prefix* **1** SUPER- 2 ⟨supra*orbital*⟩ **2** transcending ⟨supra*national*⟩ [L, fr *supra* above, beyond, earlier; akin to L *super* over – more at [1]OVER]

,supra'national /-'nash(ə)nl/ *adj* transcending national boundaries or interests – **supranationalism** *n*, **supranationalist** *n*

,supra'orbital /-'awbitl/ *adj* situated above the orbit of the eye [NL *supraorbitalis*, fr L *supra-* + ML *orbita* orbit]

suprarenal /-'reenl/ *adj* adrenal ⟨~ *gland*⟩ [NL *suprarenalis*, fr L *supra-* + *renes* kidneys]

su'premacy /s(y)ooh'preməsi/ *n* the state of being supreme; supreme authority, power, or position [*supreme* + *-acy* (as in *primacy*)]

supreme /s(y)ooh'preem/ *adj* **1** highest in rank or authority ⟨*the* ~ *commander*⟩ **2** highest in degree or quality [L *supremus*, superl of *superus* upper – more at SUPERIOR] – **supremely** *adv*

Supreme Court *n* the highest judicial tribunal in a nation or state

Supreme Soviet *n* the highest legislative body of the Soviet Union

supremo /s(y)ooh'preemoh/ *n, pl* **supremos** *chiefly Br* a ruler or director with unlimited powers ⟨*England's soccer* ~⟩ – infml [Sp & It, fr *supremo*, adj, supreme, fr L *supremus*]

sur- /suh-, sə-/ *prefix* above; over; beyond ⟨sur*tax*⟩ ⟨sur*real*⟩ ⟨sur*face*⟩ [ME, fr OF, fr L *super-*]

sura /'soorə/ *n* a chapter of the Koran [Ar *sūrah*, lit., row]

[1]**surcharge** /'suh,chahj/ *vt* **1** to subject to an additional or excessive charge **2** to overprint or mark with a new denomination or surcharge [ME *surchargen*, fr MF *surchargier*, fr *sur-* + *chargier* to charge]

[2]**surcharge** *n* **1a** an additional tax or cost **b** an extra fare **2** surcharging or being surcharged **3** an overprint; *esp* one on a stamp that alters the denomination

surcingle /'suh,sing·gl/ *n* a band passing round a horse's body usu to bind a saddle, rug, or pack fast to its back [ME *sursengle*, fr MF *surcengle*, fr *sur-* + *cengle* girdle, fr L *cingulum*, fr *cingere* to gird – more at CINCTURE]

surcoat /'suh,koht/ *n* an outer coat or cloak; *specif* a loose tunic worn over armour [ME *surcote*, fr MF, fr *sur-* + *cote* coat]

[1]**surd** /suhd/ *adj, of a speech sound* voiceless [L *surdus* deaf, silent, stupid; akin to L *susurrus* hum – more at [1]SWARM]

[2]**surd** *n* **1** an irrational root (e g $\sqrt{2}$); *also* an algebraic expression containing irrational roots ⟨$\sqrt{2} + 5i$ *is a* ~⟩ – compare IRRATIONAL NUMBER, RATIONAL NUMBER **2** a surd speech sound

[1]**sure** /shooə, shaw/ *adj* **1** firm, secure **2** reliable, trustworthy **3** assured, confident ⟨*felt* ~ *it was right*⟩ **4** bound, certain ⟨*it's* ~ *to rain*⟩ [ME, fr MF *sur*, fr L *securus* secure] – **sureness** *n* – **for sure** as a certainty – **to be sure** it must be acknowledged; admittedly

[2]**sure** *adv, chiefly NAm* surely, certainly – infml ⟨*I* ~ *am tired*⟩

,sure e'nough *adv* as one might confidently expect

,sure'fire /-'fie·ə/ *adj* certain to succeed – infml

,sure'footed /-'footid/ *adj* not liable to stumble or fall – **surefootedly** *adv*, **surefootedness** *n*

'surely /-li/ *adv* **1a** without danger; safely ⟨*slowly but* ~⟩ **b** without doubt; certainly **2** it is to be believed, hoped, or expected that ⟨~ *you like beer*⟩ [[1]SURE + [2]-LY]

surety /'shooəriti/ *n* **1** a guarantee **2** sby who assumes legal liability for the debt, default, or failure in duty (e g appearance in court) of another [ME *surte*, fr MF *surté*, fr L *securitat-*, *securitas* security, fr *securus*] – **suretyship** *n*

surf /suhf/ *n* the foam and swell of waves breaking on the shore [origin unknown]

[1]**surface** /'suhfis/ *n* **1** the external or upper boundary or layer of an object or body **2** (a portion of) the boundary of a three-dimensional object ⟨~ *of a sphere*⟩ **3** the external or superficial aspect of sthg [F, fr *sur-* + *face*] – **on the surface** to all outward appearances; superficially

[2]**surface** *vt* to apply the surface layer to ⟨~ *a road*⟩ ~ *vi* **1** to come to the surface; emerge **2** to wake up; *also* GET UP 1a – infml ⟨*he never* ~s *before 10*⟩ – **surfacer** *n*

[3]**surface** *adj* **1** situated or employed on the surface, esp of the earth or sea **2** lacking depth; superficial

,surface-'active *adj* capable of lowering the surface tension at the surface of contact between (gas and liquid) phases ⟨*soaps are typical* ~ *substances*⟩

'surface ,mail *n* mail sent by any means other than airmail

'surface ,structure *n* (the structure specified by) a formal representation of the phonetic form of a sentence

'surface ,tension *n* a property of liquids that produces an effect such that the surface of the liquid in contact with air or another gas tends to have the smallest possible area

surfactant /suh'fakt(ə)nt/ *n* a surface-active substance (e g a detergent) [*surf*ace-*act*ive + *-ant*] – **surfactant** *adj*

surfboard /'suhf,bawd/ *n* a usu long narrow buoyant board used in surfing – **surfboard** *vi*, **surfboarder** *n*

'surf,boat /-,boht/ *n* a boat for use in heavy surf

[1]**surfeit** /'suhfit/ *n* **1** an excessive amount **2** excessive indulgence in food, drink, etc [ME *surfait*, fr MF, fr *surfaire* to overdo, fr *sur-* + *faire* to do, fr L *facere* – more at DO]

[2]**surfeit** *vt* to fill to excess; satiate – **surfeiter** *n*

surficial /suh'fish(ə)l/ *adj* of a surface [*surf*ace + *-icial* (as in *superficial*)]

surfing /'suhfing/ *n* the activity or sport of planing on the front part of a wave, esp while standing or lying on a surfboard – **surfer** *n*

[1]**surge** /suhj/ *vi* **1** to rise and move (as if) in waves or billows ⟨*the crowd* ~d *past her*⟩ ⟨*felt the blood* surging *to her cheeks*⟩ **2** *esp of current or voltage* to rise suddenly to an excessive or abnormal value [MF *sourge-*, stem of *sourdre* to rise, surge, fr L *surgere* to go straight up, rise, fr *sub-* up + *regere* to lead straight – more at SUB-, [1]RIGHT]

[2]**surge** *n* **1** the motion of swelling, rolling, or sweeping forwards like a wave **2** a large rolling wave or succession of waves **3** a short-lived sudden rise of current or voltage in an electrical circuit

surgeon /'suhj(ə)n/ *n* a medical specialist who practises surgery [ME *surgien*, fr AF, fr OF *cirurgien*, fr *cirurgie* surgery]

'surgeon ,fish *n* any of various tropical fishes with 1 or more sharp movable spines near the base of the tail [fr the spines suggesting a surgeon's instruments]

surgeon's knot *n* a reef knot with a double turn in the first loop

surgery /'suhj(ə)ri/ *n* **1** medicine that deals with diseases and conditions requiring or amenable to operative or manual procedures **2a** the work done by a surgeon **b** OPERATION 3 **3** *Br* (the hours of opening of) a doctor's, dentist's, etc room where patients are advised or treated **4** *Br* a session at which a member of a profession (e g a lawyer) or esp an elected representative (e g an MP) is available for usu informal consultation [ME *surgerie*, fr OF *cirurgie, surgerie*, fr L *chirurgia*, fr Gk *cheirourgia*, fr *cheirourgos* surgeon, fr *cheirourgos* working with the hand, fr *cheir* hand + *ergon* work – more at CHIR-, [1]WORK]

surgical /'suhjikl/ *adj* **1a** of surgeons or surgery **b** used in (connection with) surgery ⟨*a* ~ *stocking*⟩ **2** following or resulting from surgery [*surgeon* + *-ical*] – **surgically** *adv*

surgical spirit *n, Br* a mixture consisting mainly of methylated spirits and used esp as a skin disinfectant

surly /'suhli/ *adj* irritably sullen and churlish [alter. of ME *sirly* lordly, imperious, fr *sir*] – **surlily** *adv*, **surliness** *n*

[1]**surmise** /suh'miez/ *vt* to infer on scanty evidence; guess [ME *surmisen* to accuse, fr MF *surmis*, pp of *surmetre*, fr L *supermittere* to throw on, fr *super-* + *mittere* to send – more at SMITE] – **surmiser** *n*

[2]**surmise** /suh'miez, 'suhmiez/ *n* a conjecture or guess – fml

surmount /suh'mownt/ *vt* **1** to overcome, conquer ⟨~ *an obstacle*⟩ **2** to get over or above **3** to stand or lie on the top of [ME *surmounten*, fr MF *surmonter*, fr *sur-* + *monter* to mount] – **surmountable** *adj*

surname /'suhnaym/ *n* the name shared in common by members of a family – **surname** *vt*

surpass /suh'pahs/ *vt* **1** to go beyond in quality, degree, or performance; exceed **2** to transcend the reach, capacity, or powers of ⟨*her beauty* ~es *description*⟩ [MF *surpasser*, fr *sur-* + *passer* to pass] – **surpassable** *adj*

surpassing /suh'pahsing/ *adj* greatly exceeding others – **surpassingly** *adv*

surplice /'suhplis/ *n* a loose white outer ecclesiastical vestment usu of knee length with large open sleeves [ME *surplis*, fr OF *surpliz*, fr ML *superpellicium*, fr *super-* + *pellicium* coat of skins, fr L, neut of *pellicius* made of skins, fr *pellis* skin]

surplus /'suhpləs/ *n* **1a** the amount in excess of what is used or needed **b** an excess of receipts over disbursements **2** the excess of a company's net worth over the par or stated value of its capital stock [ME, fr MF, fr ML *superplus*, fr L *super-* + *plus* more – more at PLUS] – **surplus** *adj*

surplus value *n* the difference in Marxist theory between the value of work done or of commodities produced and the wages paid

[1]**surprise** /sə'priez/ *n* **1** an act of taking unawares **2** sthg unexpected or surprising **3** the feeling caused by an unexpected event; astonishment [ME, fr MF, fr fem of *surpris*, pp of *surprendre* to take over, surprise, fr *sur-* + *prendre* to take – more at [4]PRIZE]

[2]**surprise** *vt* **1** to attack unexpectedly; *also* to capture by such action **2** to take unawares ⟨*to* ~ *someone in the act*⟩ **3** to fill with wonder or amazement – **surpriser** *n*

surprising /sə'priezing/ *adj* causing surprise; unexpected – **surprisingly** *adv*

surra /'sooərə/ *n* a severe Old World feverish disease of domestic animals that is caused by a trypanosome [Marathi *sūra* wheezing sound]

surreal /sə'riəl/ *adj* **1** having a dreamlike irrational quality **2** SURREALISTIC 1 [back-formation fr *surrealism*]

surrealism /sə'riə,liz(ə)m/ *n, often cap* a 20th-c movement in art and literature seeking to use the incongruous images formed by the unconscious to transcend reality as perceived by the conscious mind; *also* surrealistic practices or atmosphere [F *surréalisme*, fr *sur-* + *réalisme* realism] – **surrealist** *n or adj*

surrealistic /sə,riə'listik/ *adj* **1** of surrealism **2** SURREAL 1 – **surrealistically** *adv*

surrejoinder /,suhri'joyndə/ *n* a plaintiff's reply to a defendant's rejoinder

[1]**surrender** /sə'rendə/ *vt* **1a** to hand over to the power, control, or possession of another, esp under compulsion **b** to relinquish; GIVE UP **2** to abandon (oneself) to sthg unrestrainedly ~ *vi* to give oneself up into the power of another; yield [ME *surrenderen*, fr MF *surrendre*, fr *sur-* + *rendre* to give back, yield – more at RENDER]

[2]**surrender** *n* **1** the act or an instance of surrendering oneself or sthg **2** the voluntary cancellation of an insurance policy by the party insured in return for a payment

surreptitious /,surəp'tishəs/ *adj* done, made, or acquired by stealth; clandestine [ME, fr L *surrepticius*, fr *surreptus*, pp of *surripere* to snatch secretly, fr *sub-* + *rapere* to seize – more at RAPID] – **surreptitiously** *adv*, **surreptitiousness** *n*

surrey /'suri/ *n, NAm* a 4-wheeled 2-seat horse-drawn carriage [*Surrey*, county of England]

surrogate /'surəgət/ *n* **1a** a deputy **b** a local judicial officer in the USA who has jurisdiction over probate and the appointment of guardians **2** sthg that serves as a substitute [L *surrogatus*, pp of *surrogare* to choose in place of another, substitute, fr *sub-* + *rogare* to ask – more at [1]RIGHT]

[1]**surround** /sə'rownd/ *vt* **1a** to enclose on all sides **b** to be part of the environment of; be present round ⟨~ed *by luxury*⟩ **c** to form a ring round; encircle **2** to cause to be encircled or enclosed by sthg [ME

surrounden to overflow, fr MF *suronder*, fr LL *superundare*, fr L *super-* + *unda* wave; influenced in meaning by [6]*round* – more at WATER]

[2]**surround** *n* a border or edging

surroundings /sə'rowndingz/ *n pl* the circumstances, conditions, or objects by which one is surrounded

surtax /'suhtaks/ *n* a graduated income tax formerly imposed in the UK in addition to the normal income tax if one's net income exceeded a specified sum

surveillance /suh'vayləns, sə-/ *n* close watch kept over sby or sthg [F, fr *surveiller* to watch over, fr *sur-* + *veiller* to watch, fr L *vigilare*, fr *vigil* watchful – more at VIGIL] – **surveillant** *n*

[1]**survey** /suh'vay, '--/ *vt* **1a** to look over and examine closely **b** to examine the condition of and often give a value for (a building) **2** to determine and portray the form, extent, and position of (e g a tract of land) **3** to view as a whole or from a height ⟨~ed *the panorama below him*⟩ [ME *surveyen*, fr MF *surveeir* to look over, fr *sur-* + *veeir* to see – more at VIEW]

[2]**survey** /'suhvay/ *n* a surveying or being surveyed; *also* sthg surveyed

surveyor /sə'vay·ə/ *n* sby whose occupation is surveying land [[1]SURVEY + [1]-OR]

survival /sə'vievl/ *n* **1a** the condition of living or continuing ⟨*the* ~ *of the soul after death*⟩ **b** the continuation of life or existence ⟨*problems of* ~ *in arctic conditions*⟩ **2** sby or sthg that survives, esp after others of its kind have disappeared

survival of the fittest *n* NATURAL SELECTION

survive /sə'viev/ *vi* to remain alive or in existence; live on ⟨*managed to* ~ *on bread and water*⟩ ~ *vt* **1** to remain alive or in being after the death of ⟨*his son* ~d *him*⟩ **2** to continue to exist or live after ⟨~d *the earthquake*⟩ [ME *surviven*, fr MF *survivre* to outlive, fr L *supervivere*, fr *super-* + *vivere* to live – more at [1]QUICK] – **survivable** *adj*, **survivor** *n*, **survivability** /-və'biləti/ *n*

sus /sus/ *n* suspicion of loitering with intent to commit a crime ⟨~ *laws*⟩ – not used technically [short for *suspicion*]

susceptibility /sə,septə'biləti/ *n* **1** being susceptible **2** *pl* feelings, sensibilities **3** the ratio of the magnetization in a substance to the corresponding magnetizing force

susceptible /sə'septəbl/ *adj* **1** capable of submitting to an action, process, or operation **2** open, subject, or unresistant to some stimulus, influence, or agency **3** easily moved or emotionally affected; impressionable [LL *susceptibilis*, fr L *susceptus*, pp of *suscipere* to take up, admit, fr *sub-*, *sus-* up + *capere* to take – more at SUB-, HEAVE] – **susceptibleness** *n*, **susceptibly** *adv*

susceptive /sə'septiv/ *adj* **1** receptive **2** susceptible – **susceptiveness**, **susceptivity** /,susep'tivəti/ *n*

suslik /'suslik/ *n* any of several rather large short-tailed E European and Asian burrowing rodents [Russ]

[1]**suspect** /'suspekt/ *adj* (deserving to be) regarded with suspicion [ME, fr MF, fr L *suspectus*, fr pp of *suspicere*]

[2]**suspect** *n* sby who is suspected

[3]**suspect** /sə'spekt/ *vt* **1** to be suspicious of; distrust **2** to believe to be guilty without conclusive proof **3** to imagine to be true, likely, or probable [ME *suspecten*, fr L *suspectare*, fr *suspectus*, pp of *suspicere* to look up at, regard with awe, suspect, fr *sub-*, *sus-* up, secretly + *specere* to look at – more at SUB-, SPY]

suspend /sə'spend/ *vt* **1** to debar temporarily from a privilege, office, membership, or employment **2** to make temporarily inoperative ⟨~ *the rules*⟩ **3** to defer till later on certain conditions ⟨*a* ~ed *sentence*⟩ **4** to withhold ⟨~ *judgment*⟩ **5a** to hang, esp so as to be free on all sides **b** to hold immobile in a liquid or air ⟨*dust* ~ed *in the air*⟩ [ME *suspenden*, fr OF *suspendre* to hang up, interrupt, fr L *suspendere*, fr *sub-*, *sus-* up + *pendere* to cause to hang, weigh – more at SUB-, PENDANT]

su,spended ani'mation /sə'spendid/ *n* temporary suspension of the vital functions (e g in people nearly drowned)

suspender /sə'spendə/ *n* **1** an elasticated band with a fastening device for holding up a sock **2** *Br* any of the fastening devices on a suspender belt **3** *NAm* BRACE 4c – usu pl with sing. meaning [SUSPEND + [2]-ER]

su'spender ,belt *n*, *Br* a garment consisting of 2 pairs of short straps hanging from a belt or girdle to which are attached fastening devices for holding up a woman's stockings

suspense /sə'spens/ *n* a state of uncertain expectation as to a decision or outcome [ME, fr MF, fr *suspendre*] – **suspenseful** *adj*

suspension /sə'spensh(ə)n/ *n* **1a** temporary removal from office or privileges **b** temporary withholding or postponement **c** temporary abolishing of a law or rule **d** (the sustaining of) 1 or more notes of a chord held over into the following chord producing a momentary discord **2a** hanging or being hung **b** (the state of or a system consisting of) a solid that is dispersed, but not dissolved, in a solid, liquid, or gas, usu in particles of larger than colloidal size **3** the system of devices supporting the upper part of a vehicle on the axles [LL *suspension-*, *suspensio*, fr L *suspensus*, pp of *suspendere*]

su'spension ,bridge *n* a type of bridge that has its roadway suspended from 2 or more cables

suspensive /sə'spensiv/ *adj* characterized by suspense or having the power to suspend – **suspensively** *adv*

suspensory /sə'spens(ə)ri/ *adj* held in suspension; serving to suspend

suspensory ligament *n* a membrane that holds the lens of the eye in position

suspicion /sə'spish(ə)n/ *n* **1a** suspecting or being suspected ⟨*arrested on* ~ *of spying*⟩ **b** a feeling of doubt or mistrust **2** a slight touch or trace ⟨*just a* ~ *of garlic*⟩ [ME, fr L *suspicion-*, *suspicio*, fr *suspicere* to suspect – more at [3]SUSPECT]

suspicious /sə'spishəs/ *adj* **1** tending to arouse suspicion; dubious **2** inclined to suspect; distrustful ⟨~ *of strangers*⟩ **3** expressing or indicating suspicion – **suspiciously** *adv*, **suspiciousness** *n*

suss /sus/ *vt*, *Br* to uncover the truth about; detect ⟨*soon* ~ed *that he was lying*⟩ – slang [by shortening & alter. fr *suspect*]

Sussex spaniel /'susiks/ *n* any of a British breed of golden-haired spaniels with a short neck and legs and a long body [*Sussex*, county of England]

suss out *vt*, *Br* to reconnoitre – slang

sustain /sə'stayn/ *vt* **1** to give support or relief to **2** to provide with sustenance **3** to cause to continue; prolong **4** to support the weight of **5** to buoy up the spirits of **6a** to bear up under; endure **b** to suffer, undergo **7** to allow as valid ⟨*the court* ~ed *the motion*⟩ [ME *sustenen*, fr OF *sustenir*, fr L *sustinēre* to hold up, sustain, fr *sub-*, *sus-* up + *tenēre* to hold – more at SUB-, THIN] – **sustainable** *adj*, **sustainer** *n*

sustenance /'sustinəns/ *n* **1a** means of support, maintenance, or subsistence **b** food, provisions; *also* nourishment **2** sustaining [ME, fr OF, fr *sustenir*]

sustentation /,susten'taysh(ə)n/ *n* maintenance, upkeep – fml [ME, fr MF, fr L *sustentation-*, *sustentatio* act of holding up, fr *sustentatus*, pp of *sustentare* to hold up, fr *sustentus*, pp of *sustinēre*] – **sustentative** /su'stentətiv/ *adj*

susurration /,syoohsə'raysh(ə)n/ *n* a whispering or rustling sound – fml [ME, fr LL *susurration-*, *susurratio*, fr L *susurratus*, pp of *susurrare* to whisper, fr *susurrus* whisper, hum – more at [1]SWARM]

sutler /'sutlə/ *n* sby who sold provisions to an army in former times [obs D *soeteler*, fr LG *suteler* sloppy worker, camp cook; akin to OE be*sūtian* to dirty, Gk *hyein* to rain – more at SUCK]

sutra /'soohtrə/ *n* **1** a Hindu, esp Vedic, precept; *also* a collection of these precepts **2** a discourse of the Buddha [Skt *sūtra* thread, string of precepts, sutra; akin to L *suere* to sew – more at SEW]

suttee /,su'tee, '-,-/ *n* the custom of a Hindu widow willingly being cremated on the funeral pile of her husband; *also* such a widow [Skt *satī* wife who performs suttee, lit., good woman, fr fem of *sat* true, good; akin to OE *sōth* true – more at SOOTHE]

[1]**suture** /'soohchə/ *n* **1a** (a strand or fibre used in) the sewing together of parts of the living body **b** a stitch made with a suture **2a** the solid join between 2 bones (e g of the skull) **b** a furrow at the junction of animal or plant parts [MF & L; MF, fr L *sutura* seam, suture, fr *sutus*, pp of *suere* to sew] – **sutural** *adj*, **suturally** *adv*

[2]**suture** *vt* to unite, close, or secure with sutures ⟨~ *a wound*⟩

suzerain /'soohz(ə)rayn/ *n* **1** a feudal overlord **2** a dominant state controlling the foreign relations of an internally autonomous vassal state [F, fr (assumed) MF *suserain*, fr MF *sus* up (fr L *sursum*, fr *sub-* up + *versum* -wards, fr neut of *versus*, pp of *vertere* to turn) + *-erain* (as in *soverain* sovereign) – more at SUB-, [1]WORTH] – **suzerainty** /-rənti/ *n*

svedberg /'sfedbuhg, sved-/ *n* a unit of time equal to 10^{-13}s that is used to measure the speed with which particles in dispersion form a precipitate in an ultracentrifuge [The *Svedberg* †1971 Sw chemist]

svelte /sfelt, svelt/ *adj* slender, lithe [F, fr It *svelto*, fr pp of *svellere* to pluck out, modif of L *evellere*, fr *e-* + *vellere* to pluck – more at VULNERABLE] – **svelteness** *n*

Svengali /sfen'gahli, sven-/ *n* one who attempts, sometimes with sinister motives, to influence or mould another [*Svengali*, sinister hypnotist in the novel *Trilby* by George Du Maurier †1896 E artist & writer]

[1]**swab** /swob/ *n* **1** a wad of absorbent material used for applying medication, cleaning wounds, taking bacterial specimens, etc **2** a specimen taken with a swab [prob fr obs D *swabbe*; akin to LG *swabber* mop]

[2]**swab** *vt* **-bb- 1** to clean (a wound) with a swab **2** to clean (a surface, esp a deck) by washing (e g with a mop) – often + *down* [back-formation fr *swabber* mop; akin to LG *swabber* mop, ME *swabben* to sway] – **swabber** *n*

swaddle /'swodl/ *vt* **swaddling** /'swodling/ **1** to wrap (an infant) in swaddling clothes **2** to swathe, envelop [ME *swadelen*, *swathelen*, prob alter. of *swedelen*, *swethelen*, fr *swethel* swaddling band, fr OE; akin to OE *swathian* to swathe]

'**swaddling ,clothes** /'swodling/ *n pl* narrow strips of cloth wrapped round an infant to restrict movement

[1]**swag** /swag/ *vt* **-gg-** to hang (e g tapestries or curtains) in heavy folds [prob of Scand origin; akin to ON *sveggja* to cause to sway; akin to OHG *swingan* to swing]

[2]**swag** *n* **1a** sthg (e g a moulded decoration) hanging in a curve between 2 points **b** a suspended cluster (e g of flowers) **c** an arrangement of fabric hanging in a heavy curve or fold **2** *chiefly Austr* a pack or roll of personal belongings **3** goods acquired, esp by unlawful means; loot – infml

[1]**swage** /swayj/ *n* a tool for shaping metal by hammering [ME, ornamental border, fr MF *souage*]

[2]**swage** *vt* to shape (as if) by means of a swage

'**swage ,block** *n* a perforated cast-iron or steel block with a variety of grooved sides that is used in shaping metal (e g into bolts)

[1]**swagger** /'swagə/ *vi* to behave in an arrogant or pompous manner; *esp* to walk with an air of overbearing self-confidence or self-satisfaction [prob fr [1]*swag* + *-er* (as in *chatter*)] – **swaggerer** *n*, **swaggeringly** *adv*

[2]**swagger** *n* **1** an act or instance of swaggering **2** arrogant or conceitedly self-assured behaviour

'**swagger ,stick** *n* a short light usu leather-covered stick

swaggie /'swagi/ *n*, *Austr & NZ* a swagman

'**swag,man** /-,man/ *n*, *chiefly Austr* a tramp; *esp* one who carries a swag

Swahili /swah'heeli/ *n*, *pl* **Swahilis**, *esp collectively* **Swahili 1** a member of a Bantu-speaking people of Zanzibar and the adjacent coast **2** a Bantu language used in trade and government in E Africa and the Congo region ☞ LANGUAGE [Ar *sawāḥil*, pl of *sāḥil* coast]

swain /swayn/ *n* **1** a male admirer or suitor **2** a peasant; *specif* a shepherd – chiefly poetic [ME *swein* boy, servant, fr ON *sveinn*; akin to OE *swān* swain, L *suus* one's own – more at SUICIDE]

[1]**swallow** /'swoloh/ *n* any of numerous small long-winged migratory birds noted for their graceful flight, that have a short bill, a forked tail, and feed on insects caught while flying [ME *swalowe*, fr OE *swealwe*; akin to OHG *swalawa* swallow, Russ *solovei̮* nightingale]

[2]**swallow** *vt* **1** to take through the mouth and oesophagus into the stomach **2** to envelop, engulf ⟨~ed *up by the shadows*⟩ **3** to accept without question or protest; *also* to believe naively **4** to refrain from expressing or showing **5** to utter indistinctly ~ *vi* **1** to receive sthg into the body through the mouth and oesophagus **2** to perform the action of swallowing sthg, esp under emotional stress [ME *swalowen*, fr OE *swelgan*; akin to OHG *swelgan* to swallow] – **swallowable** *adj*, **swallower** *n*

[3]**swallow** *n* **1** an act of swallowing **2** an amount that can be swallowed at one time

'**swallow ,dive** *n*, *Br* a forward dive executed with the back arched and arms spread sideways

'swallow ,hole *n* SINK HOLE 2

'swallow,tail /-,tayl/ *n* **1** a deeply forked and tapering tail (e g of a swallow) **2** a tailcoat **3** any of various large butterflies with the hind wing lengthened to resemble a tail ☞ LIFE CYCLE – **swallow-tailed** *adj*

'swallow,wort /-,wuht/ *n* **1** CELANDINE 1 **2** any of several plants of the milkweed family [fr the shape of the pods]

swam /swam/ *past of* SWIM

swami /'swahmi/ *n* a Hindu ascetic or religious teacher – used as a title [Hindi *svāmī*, fr Skt *svāmin* owner, lord, fr *sva* one's own – more at SUICIDE]

[1]**swamp** /swomp/ *n* (an area of) wet spongy land sometimes covered with water [alter. of ME *sompe*, fr MD *somp* morass; akin to MHG *sumpf* marsh, Gk *somphos* spongy] – **swamp** *adj*, **swampy** *adj*, **swampiness** *n*

[2]**swamp** *vt* **1** to inundate, submerge **2** to overwhelm by an excess of work, difficulties, etc

[1]**swan** /swon/ *n* any of various heavy-bodied long-necked mostly pure white aquatic birds that are larger than geese and are graceful swimmers [ME, fr OE; akin to MHG *swan*, L *sonus* sound – more at [3]SOUND]

[2]**swan** *vi* **-nn-** to wander or travel aimlessly – infml

'swan ,dive *n*, *NAm* SWALLOW DIVE

'swan,herd /-,huhd/ *n* sby who tends swans

[1]**swank** /swangk/ *vi* to swagger; SHOW OFF – infml [perh fr MHG *swanken* to sway; akin to MD *swanc* supple]

[2]**swank** *n* (one given to) pretentiousness or swagger – infml

swanky /'swangki/ *adj* **1** showy, ostentatious **2** fashionably elegant; smart ***USE*** infml

swannery /'swon(ə)ri/ *n* a place where swans are bred or kept

swansdown /'swonz,down/ *n* **1** the soft downy feathers of the swan used esp as trimming on articles of dress **2** a heavy cotton flannel that has a thick nap on the face

'swan ,song *n* **1** a song said to be sung by a dying swan **2** a farewell appearance or final work or pronouncement

,swan-'upping /-'uping/ *n* the annual inspection and marking of royal swans on the River Thames [*upping* fr gerund of [3]*up* (to drive up & catch)]

[1]**swap** /swop/ *vb* **-pp-** *vt* to give in exchange; barter ~ *vi* to make an exchange ⟨~ *over to a metric system*⟩ [ME *swappen* to strike; fr the practice of striking hands in closing a business deal] – **swapper** *n*

[2]**swap** *n* **1** the act of exchanging one thing for another **2** sthg exchanged for another

swaraj /swə'rahj/ *n* Indian self-government [Skt *svarāj* self-ruling, fr *sva* one's self + *rājya* rule – more at SUICIDE, RAJ] – **swarajist** *n*

sward /swawd/ *n* (a piece of ground covered with) a surface of short grass [ME, fr OE *sweard*, *swearth* skin, rind; akin to MHG *swart* skin, hide, L *operire* to cover – more at WEIR] – **swarded** *adj*

swarf /swahf, swawf/ *n* material (e g metallic particles and abrasive fragments) removed by a cutting or grinding tool [of Scand origin; akin to ON *svarf* file dust; akin to OE *sweorfan* to file away – more at SWERVE]

[1]**swarm** /swawm/ *n* **1a** a colony of honeybees, esp when emigrating from a hive with a queen bee to start a new colony elsewhere **b** a cluster of free-floating or free-swimming zoospores or other single-celled organisms **2** *sing or pl in constr* a group of animate or inanimate things, esp when massing together ⟨~s *of sightseers*⟩ [ME, fr OE *swearm*; akin to OHG *swaram* swarm, & prob to L *susurrus* hum]

[2]**swarm** *vi* **1** to collect together and depart from a hive **2** to move or assemble in a crowd **3** to contain a swarm; teem ⟨*streets* ~ing *with cars*⟩ – **swarmer** *n*

[3]**swarm** *vi* to climb, esp with the hands and feet – usu + *up* ⟨~ *up a tree*⟩ [origin unknown]

'swarm ,spore *n* a zoospore or other minute mobile spore

swarthy /'swawdhi/ *adj* of a dark colour, complexion, or cast [alter. of obs *swarty*, fr *swart* (dark), fr ME, fr OE *sweart*; akin to OHG *swarz* black, L *sordes* dirt] – **swarthiness** *n*

swash /swosh/ *adj*, *of a typographical letter* having strokes ending in a flourish [obs *swash* (slanting)]

'swash,buckler /-,buklə/ *n* a swaggering adventurer or daredevil [*swash* (to bluster, swagger, move violently & noisily; prob of imit origin) + *buckler*]

'swash,buckling /-,bukling/ *adj* characteristic of or behaving like a swashbuckler [*swashbuckler*]

swastika /'swostikə/ *n* an ancient symbol in the shape of a cross with the ends of the arms extended at right angles in a clockwise or anticlockwise direction [Skt *svastika*, fr *svasti* welfare, fr *su-* well + *asti* he is; akin to OE *is*; fr its being regarded as a good luck symbol]

[1]**swat** /swot/ *vt* **-tt-** to hit with a sharp slapping blow; *esp* to kill (an insect) with such a blow [E dial., to squat, alter. of E *squat*]

[2]**swat** *n* **1** a quick crushing blow **2** a swatter

swatch /swoch/ *n* a sample piece (e g of fabric) [origin unknown]

swath /swawth/ *n* **1a** a row of cut grain or grass left by a scythe or mowing machine **b** the path cut in 1 passage (e g of a mower) **2** a long broad strip **3** a space cleared as if by a scythe [ME, fr OE *swæth* footstep, trace; akin to MHG *swade* swath]

[1]**swathe** /swaydh/ *vt* **1** to bind or wrap (as if) with a bandage **2** to envelop [ME *swathen*, fr OE *swathian*; akin to ON *svatha* to swathe, Lith *svaigti* to become dizzy] – **swather** *n*

[2]**swathe** *n* a swath

swatter /'swotə/ *n* a flyswatter

[1]**sway** /sway/ *vi* **1a(1)** to swing slowly and rhythmically back and forth **(2)** to walk in a swaying manner **b** to move gently from an upright to a leaning position **2** to fluctuate or alternate between one attitude or position and another ~ *vt* **1** to cause to swing, rock, or oscillate **2a** to exert a controlling influence on **b** to change the opinions of, esp by eloquence or argument **3** to hoist in place ⟨~ *up a mast*⟩ [alter. of earlier *swey* (to fall, swoon), fr ME *sweyen*, prob of Scand origin; akin to ON *sveigja* to sway; akin to OE *swathian* to swathe] – **swayer** *n*

[2]**sway** *n* **1** swaying or being swayed **2a** controlling influence or power ⟨*the Church held* ~⟩ **b** rule, dominion

'sway,back /-,bak/ *n* (the abnormal condition, esp in horses, of having) a sagging back – **swaybacked** *adj*

swear /sweə/ *vb* **swore** /swaw/; **sworn** /swawn/ *vt* **1** to utter or take (an oath) solemnly **2a** to assert as true or promise under oath ⟨*a* sworn *affidavit*⟩ **b** to promise emphatically or earnestly ⟨*she* swore *not to be late*⟩ **3a** to administer an oath to **b** to bind by an oath ⟨swore *him to secrecy*⟩ ~ *vi* **1** to take an oath **2** to use profane or obscene language [ME *sweren*, fr OE *swerian*; akin to OHG *swerien* to swear, Russ *svara* altercation] – **swearer** *n* – **swear by** to place great confidence in – **swear to** to have any positive conviction of ⟨*couldn't* swear to *his being the same man*⟩

swear in *vt* to induct into office by administration of an oath

swear out *vt, NAm* to procure (a warrant for arrest) by making a sworn accusation

[1]**sweat** /swet/ *vb* **sweated,** *NAm chiefly* **sweat** *vi* **1** to excrete sweat in visible quantities **2a** to emit or exude moisture ⟨*cheese* ~s *in ripening*⟩ **b** to gather surface moisture as a result of condensation **c** *esp of tobacco* FERMENT 1 **3** to undergo anxiety or tension ~ *vt* **1** to (seem to) emit from pores; exude **2** to get rid of (as if) by sweating ⟨~ *out a fever*⟩ **3a** to cause (e g a patient) to sweat **b** to exact work from under sweatshop conditions **4** to cause to exude or lose moisture: e g **a** to subject (esp tobacco) to fermentation **b** to cook (e g vegetables) gently in melted fat until the juices run out **5** to heat (e g solder) so as to melt and cause to run, esp between surfaces to unite them; *also* to unite by such means ⟨~ *a pipe joint*⟩ [ME *sweten*, fr OE *swǣtan*, fr *swāt* sweat; akin to OHG *sweiz* sweat, L *sudor* sweat, *sudare* to sweat] – **sweat blood** to work or worry intensely

[2]**sweat** *n* **1** the fluid excreted from the sweat glands of the skin; perspiration **2** moisture gathering in drops on a surface **3a** the state of one sweating ⟨*in a cold* ~⟩ **b** a spell of sweating **4** hard work; drudgery **5** a state of anxiety or impatience *USE* (*4&5*) infml – **no sweat** not a problem or difficulty – infml ⟨*I can do that all right,* no sweat⟩

'**sweat,band** /-,band/ *n* a band of material worn round the head or wrist or inserted in a hat or cap to absorb sweat

'**sweated** *adj* of or produced under a sweatshop system ⟨~ *labour*⟩ ⟨~ *goods*⟩

sweater /'swetə/ *n* [2]JUMPER 1 ☞ GARMENT [[1]SWEAT + [2]-ER]

'**sweat ,gland** *n* a tubular gland in the skin that secretes sweat through a minute pore on the surface of the skin ☞ NERVE

'**sweating ,sickness** *n* an epidemic fever characterized by profuse sweating and rapid death that appeared in Britain in the 15th and 16th c

sweatlet /'swetlit/ *n* a band of towelling worn round the wrist, esp in tennis, to absorb perspiration

sweat out *vt* to endure or wait through the course of

'**sweat ,shirt** *n* a loose collarless pullover of heavy cotton jersey

'**sweat,shop** /-,shop/ *n* a place of work in which workers are employed for long hours at low wages and under unhealthy conditions

sweaty /'sweti/ *adj* **1** covered with or smelling of sweat **2** causing sweat – **sweatily** *adv*, **sweatiness** *n*

swede /sweed/ *n* **1** *cap* a native or inhabitant of Sweden **2** a large type of turnip with edible yellow flesh [LG or obs D; (2) fr its having been introduced into Scotland from Sweden]

Swedish /'sweedish/ *n* **1** the N Germanic language spoken in Sweden and part of Finland ☞ LANGUAGE **2** *pl in constr* the people of Sweden [*Sweden*, country of NW Europe] – **Swedish** *adj*

[1]**sweep** /sweep/ *vb* **swept** /swept/ *vt* **1a** to remove or clean (as if) by brushing **b** to destroy completely; WIPE OUT – usu + *away* **c** to remove or take with a single forceful action ⟨swept *the books off the desk*⟩ **d** to drive or carry along with irresistible force **2** to move through or along with overwhelming speed or violence ⟨*a new craze* ~ing *the country*⟩ **3** to move lightly over with a rapid continuous movement **4** to cover the entire range of ⟨*his eyes* swept *the horizon*⟩ **5** to play a sweep in cricket at ~ *vi* **1a** to clean a surface (as if) by brushing **b** to move swiftly, forcefully, or devastatingly **2** to go with stately or sweeping movements ⟨*she* swept *out of the room*⟩ **3** to move or extend in a wide curve ⟨*the hills* ~ *down to the sea*⟩ **4** to play a sweep in cricket [ME *swepen*; akin to OE *swāpan* to sweep – more at SWOOP] – **sweep someone off his/her feet** to gain immediate and unquestioning support, approval, or acceptance by sby; *esp* to cause sby to fall in love with one – **sweep the board** to win convincingly; win everything (e g in a contest)

[2]**sweep** *n* **1a** a long oar **b** a windmill sail **2** a clearing out or away (as if) with a broom **3** a military reconnaissance or attack ranging over a particular area **4a** a curving course or line **b** the compass of a sweeping movement **c** a broad extent ⟨*unbroken* ~ *of woodland*⟩ **5** a sweepstake **6** obliquity with respect to a reference line **7** an attacking stroke in cricket played on one knee with a horizontal bat and designed to send the ball behind the batsman on the leg side

'**sweep,back** /-,bak/ *n* the backward slant of an aircraft wing in which the outer portion of the wing is behind the inner portion

sweeper /'sweepə/ *n* a defensive player in soccer who plays behind the backs as a last line of defence before the goalkeeper ☞ SPORT [[1]SWEEP + [2]-ER]

sweeping /'sweeping/ *adj* **1** extending in a wide curve or over a wide area **2a** extensive, wide-ranging ⟨~ *reforms*⟩ **b** marked by wholesale and indiscriminate inclusion – **sweepingly** *adv*, **sweepingness** *n*

'**sweepings** *n pl* refuse, rubbish, etc collected by sweeping

sweep-second hand *n* a watch or clock hand marking seconds that is mounted with the other hands and read on the same dial

'**sweep,stake** /-,stayk/ *n* **1** a race or contest in which the entire prize is awarded to the winner **2** a lottery *USE* often pl with sing. meaning but sing. or pl in constr [ME *swepestake* one who wins all the stakes in a game, fr *swepen* to sweep + *stake*]

[1]**sweet** /sweet/ *adj* **1a** being or inducing the one of the 4 basic taste sensations that is typically induced by sucrose – compare BITTER, SALT, SOUR **b** *of a beverage* containing a sweetening ingredient; not dry **2a** delightful, charming **b** marked by gentle good humour or kindliness **c** fragrant **d** pleasing to the ear or eye **3** much loved **4a** not sour, rancid, decaying, or stale **b** not salt or salted; fresh ⟨~ *butter*⟩ ⟨~ *water*⟩ **c** free from noxious gases and smells **d** free from excess of acid, sulphur, or corrosive salts ⟨~ *petroleum*⟩ [ME *swete*, fr OE *swēte*; akin to OHG *suozi* sweet, L *suavis*, Gk *hēdys*] – **sweetish** *adj*, **sweetly** *adv*, **sweetness** *n*

[2]**sweet** *n* **1** a darling or sweetheart **2** *Br* **a** dessert **b** a toffee, truffle, or other small piece of confectionery prepared with (flavoured or filled) chocolate or sugar; *esp* one made chiefly of (boiled and crystallized) sugar

ˌ**sweet-and-ˈsour** *adj* seasoned with a sauce containing sugar and vinegar or lemon juice ⟨~ *pork*⟩

sweet basil *n* a common basil with white flowers tinged with purple and leaves used as a herb in cooking

sweet bay *n* LAUREL 1

ˈ**sweetˌbread** /-ˌbred/ *n* the pancreas or thymus of a young animal (e g a calf) used for food

ˈ**sweetˌbrier** /-ˌbrie·ə/ *n* an Old World rose with stout prickles and white to deep rosy pink flowers

sweet cherry *n* (the large sweet fruit of) a white-flowered Eurasian cherry that is a cultivated variety of gean

sweet chestnut *n* SPANISH CHESTNUT

sweet cicely *n* a European plant of the carrot family with a strong aniseed smell [*cicely* by folk etymology fr *seseli* (a genus of perennial herbs), fr NL, fr L *seselis,* fr Gk]

ˈ**sweet ˌcorn** *n* (the young kernels of) a maize with kernels that contain a high percentage of sugar and are eaten as a vegetable when young and milky

sweeten /ˈsweet(ə)n/ *vt* **1** to make (more) sweet **2** to soften the mood or attitude of **3** to make less painful or trying **4** to free from sthg undesirable; *esp* to remove sulphur compounds from ⟨~ *natural gas*⟩ ~ *vi* to become sweet – **sweetener** *n*

ˈ**sweetˌheart** /-ˌhaht/ *n* a darling, lover

sweetie /ˈsweeti/ *n* **1** SWEET 1 **2** *Br* SWEET 2b *USE* infml

ˈ**sweetie ˌpie** *n* SWEET 1 – infml

sweeting /ˈsweeting/ *n* a sweet apple [ME *sweting,* fr *swete* sweet + *-ing* of (such) a kind, fr OE *-ing, -ung*]

ˈ**sweetˌmeat** /-ˌmeet/ *n* a crystallized fruit, sugar-coated nut, or other sweet or delicacy rich in sugar

sweet pea *n* a leguminous garden plant with slender climbing stems and large fragrant flowers

sweet pepper *n* (a pepper plant bearing) a large mild thick-walled capsicum fruit

sweet potato *n* (the large sweet edible tuberous root of) a tropical climbing plant of the bindweed family with purplish flowers

ˈ**sweet-ˌtalk** *vt, chiefly NAm* to blandish, coax – infml

sweet talk *n, chiefly NAm* flattery – infml

sweet tooth *n* a craving or fondness for sweet food

sweet william *n, often cap W* a widely cultivated Eurasian pink with small (mottled or striped) white to deep red or purple flowers [fr the name *William*]

[1]**swell** /swel/ *vb* **swollen** /ˈswohlən/, **swelled** *vi* **1a** to expand gradually beyond a normal or original limit **b** to be distended or puffed up ⟨*her ankle is badly* swollen⟩ **c** to curve outwards or upwards; bulge **2** to become charged with emotion ~ *vt* **1** to affect with a powerful emotion **2** to increase the size, number, or intensity of [ME *swellen,* fr OE *swellan*; akin to OHG *swellan* to swell]

[2]**swell** *n* **1** a rounded protuberance or bulge **2** a (massive) surge of water, often continuing beyond or after its cause (e g a gale) **3a** swelling **b(1)** a gradual increase and decrease of the loudness of a musical sound **(2)** a device used in an organ for governing loudness **(3)** *also* **swell organ** a division of an organ in which the pipes are enclosed in a box with shutters that open or shut to regulate the volume of sound **4** a person of fashion or high social position – infml

[3]**swell** *adj, chiefly NAm* excellent

swelling /ˈsweling/ *n* **1** sthg swollen; *specif* an abnormal bodily protuberance or enlargement **2** being swollen

[1]**swelter** /ˈsweltə/ *vi* to suffer, sweat, or be faint from heat [ME *sweltren,* freq of *swelten* to die, be overcome by heat, fr OE *sweltan* to die; akin to OHG *swelzan* to burn up, & prob to OE *swelan* to burn]

[2]**swelter** *n* a state of oppressive heat

sweltering /ˈswelt(ə)ring/ *adj* oppressively hot – **swelteringly** *adv*

ˌ**swept-ˈback** /swept/ *adj* possessing sweepback

ˌ**swept-ˈwing** *adj* having swept-back wings

swerve /swuhv/ *vb* to (cause to) turn aside abruptly from a straight line or course [ME *swerven,* fr OE *sweorfan* to wipe, file away; akin to OHG *swerban* to wipe off, Gk *syrein* to drag] – **swerve** *n*

[1]**swift** /swift/ *adj* **1** (capable of) moving at great speed **2** occurring suddenly or within a very short time **3** quick to respond; ready [ME, fr OE; akin to OE *swifan* to revolve – more at SWIVEL] – **swift** *adv,* **swiftly** *adv,* **swiftness** *n*

[2]**swift** *n* **1** any of several lizards that run swiftly **2** any of numerous dark-coloured birds noted for their fast darting flight in pursuit of insects, that superficially resemble swallows but are related to the hummingbirds and nightjars

[1]**swig** /swig/ *n* a quantity drunk in 1 draught – infml [origin unknown]

[2]**swig** *vb* **-gg-** to drink (sthg) in long draughts – infml – **swigger** *n*

[1]**swill** /swil/ *vt* **1** to wash, esp by flushing with water **2** to drink greedily ~ *vi* to drink or eat freely or greedily [ME *swilen,* fr OE *swillan*] – **swiller** *n*

[2]**swill** *n* **1** a semiliquid food for animals (e g pigs) composed of edible refuse mixed with water or skimmed or sour milk **2** RUBBISH 1

[1]**swim** /swim/ *vb* **-mm-; swam** /swam/; **swum** /swum/ *vi* **1** to propel oneself in water by bodily movements (e g of the limbs, fins, or tail) **2** to surmount difficulties; not go under ⟨*sink or* ~⟩ **3** to become immersed (as if) in a liquid ⟨*liver* ~ming *in gravy*⟩ **4** to have a floating or dizzy effect or sensation ~ *vt* **1a** to cross by swimming **b** to use (a stroke) in swimming **2** to cause to swim or float [ME *swimmen,* fr OE *swimman*; akin to OHG *swimman* to swim] – **swimmer** *n* – **swim against the tide** to move counter to the prevailing or popular trend

[2]**swim** *n* **1** an act or period of swimming **2a** an area frequented by fish **b** the main current of events ⟨*be in the* ~⟩

ˈ**swim ˌbladder** *n* the air bladder of a fish

swimmable /ˈswiməbl/ *adj* capable of being swum

swimmeret /ˈswimərеt/ *n* any of a series of small unspecialized appendages under the abdomen of many crustaceans that are used for swimming or carrying eggs

swimming /ˈswiming/ *adj* capable of, adapted to, or used in or for swimming

ˈ**swimming ˌbath** *n, Br* a usu indoor swimming pool

– often pl with sing. meaning but sing. or pl in constr

'swimming ,costume *n, chiefly Br* a close-fitting usu woman's garment for swimming

'swimmingly /-li/ *adv* very well; splendidly – infml ⟨*everything went* ~⟩

'swimming ,pool *n* an artificial pool made for people to swim in

'swim,suit /-,s(y)ooht/ *n* SWIMMING COSTUME

[1]**swindle** /'swindl/ *vb* **swindling** /'swindling/ to obtain property or take property from by fraud [back-formation fr *swindler*, fr G *schwindler* giddy person, fr *schwindeln* to be dizzy, fr OHG *swintilōn*, freq of *swintan* to diminish, vanish; akin to OE *swindan* to vanish, OIr *a-sennad* finally] – **swindler** *n*

[2]**swindle** *n* a fraud, deceit

swine /swien/ *n, pl* **swine** **1** PIG 1a – used esp technically or in literature **2** a contemptible person **3** sthg unpleasant ⟨*a* ~ *of a job*⟩ *USE* (*2 & 3*) infml [ME, fr OE *swin*; akin to OHG *swin* swine, L *sus* – more at [1]sow] – **swinish** *adj*

'swine ,fever *n* a highly infectious often fatal virus disease of pigs

'swine,herd /-,huhd/ *n* sby who tends pigs

[1]**swing** /swing/ *vb* **swung** /swung/ *vt* **1a** to cause to move vigorously through a wide arc or circle **b(1)** to cause to pivot or rotate **(2)** to cause to face or move in another direction ⟨~ *the car into a side road*⟩ **c** to make (a delivery of a cricket ball) swing **2** to suspend so as to allow to sway ⟨*to* ~ *a hammock*⟩ **3** to play or sing (e g a melody) in the style of swing music **4a** to influence decisively ⟨~ *a lot of votes*⟩ **b** to manage; BRING ABOUT ⟨*wasn't able to* ~ *that trip to Vienna*⟩ ~*vi* **1a** to move freely to and fro, esp when hanging from an overhead support **b** *of a bowled ball* to deviate from a straight path while travelling through the air before reaching the batsman **2** to die by hanging **3a** to turn (as if) on a hinge or pivot ⟨*she* swung *on her heel*⟩ **b** to convey oneself by grasping a fixed support **4** to play or sing with a lively compelling rhythm; *specif* to play swing music **5** to shift or fluctuate between 2 moods, opinions, etc **6a** to move along rhythmically ⟨~ing *down the street*⟩ **b** to start up in a smooth rapid manner ⟨*ready to* ~ *into action*⟩ **7** to engage freely in sex, specif wife-swapping – slang *USE* (*vt 4; vi 2*) infml [ME *swingen* to beat, fling, hurl, rush, fr OE *swingan* to beat, fling oneself, rush; akin to OHG *swingan* to fling, rush] – **swingable** *adj*, **swinger** *n*

[2]**swing** *n* **1a(1)** a stroke or blow delivered with a sweeping arm movement **(2)** a sweeping or rhythmic movement of the body or a bodily part **b** the regular movement of a freely suspended object to and fro along an arc **c** a steady vigorous rhythm or action ⟨*soon got into the* ~ *of it*⟩ **d(1)** a trend towards a high or low point in a fluctuating cycle (e g of business activity) **(2)** a shift from one condition, form, position, or object of attention or favour to another **2** the progression of an activity; course ⟨*the work is in full* ~⟩ **3** the arc or range through which sthg swings ⟨*a* ~ *of 10% to Labour*⟩ **4** a suspended seat on which one may swing to and fro **5** jazz played usu by a large dance band and characterized by a steady lively rhythm, simple harmony, and a basic melody often submerged in improvisation – **swing** *adj*

,swing 'door *n* a door that can be pushed open from either side and that swings closed when released

swingeing, swinging /'swinjing/ *adj, chiefly Br* severe, drastic ⟨~ *cuts in public expenditure*⟩ [fr prp of *swinge* (to beat, scourge), fr ME *swengen* to shake, fr OE *swengan*; akin to OE *swingan*]

swinging /'swing·ing/ *adj* lively and up-to-date – infml [fr prp of [1]*swing*]

swingletree /'swing·gl,tree/ *n* the pivoted swinging bar to which the traces of a harness are attached and by which a vehicle or implement (e g a plough) is drawn [*swingle* (cudgel; fr ME *swingel*, fr MD *swinghel*) + *tree*]

swingometer /,swing'omitə/ *n* a device for representing statistical movements, esp in the electoral support of a party, on a dial – infml

,swing-'wing *adj* of or being an aircraft having movable wings giving the best angles of sweepback for both low and high speeds

[1]**swipe** /swiep/ *n* a strong sweeping blow – infml [prob alter. of *sweep*]

[2]**swipe** *vi* to strike or hit out with a sweeping motion ~*vt* **1** to strike or wipe with a sweeping motion **2** to steal, pilfer *USE* infml

[1]**swirl** /swuhl/ *n* **1** a whirling mass or motion **2** a twisting shape, mark, or pattern [ME (Sc)] – **swirly** *adj*

[2]**swirl** *vi* to move in eddies or whirls – **swirlingly** *adv*

[1]**swish** /swish/ *vb* to move with (the sound of) a swish ⟨*windscreen wipers* ~ing⟩ ⟨*a cow* ~ing *its tail*⟩ [imit] – **swisher** *n*, **swishingly** *adv*

[2]**swish** *n* **1a** a sound as of a whip cutting the air **b** a light sweeping or brushing sound **2** a swishing movement – **swishy** *adj*

[3]**swish** *adj* smart, fashionable – infml [origin unknown]

[1]**Swiss** /swis/ *n, pl* **Swiss** a native or inhabitant of Switzerland [MF *Suisse*, fr MHG *Swizer*, fr *Swiz* Switzerland, country in central Europe]

[2]**Swiss** *adj* (characteristic) of Switzerland

,Swiss 'chard *n* chard

,Swiss 'roll *n* a thin sheet of sponge cake spread with jam and rolled up

[1]**switch** /swich/ *n* **1** a slender flexible twig or rod **2** a shift or change from one to another **3** a tuft of long hairs at the end of the tail of an animal (e g a cow) **4** a device for making, breaking, or changing the connections in an electrical circuit **5** a tress of hair attached to augment a hairstyle **6** *NAm* railway points [perh fr MD *swijch* twig]

[2]**switch** *vt* **1** to strike or beat (as if) with a switch **2** to whisk, lash **3** to shift, change **4a** to shift to another electrical circuit by means of a switch **b** to operate an electrical switch so as to turn *off* or *on* **5** *chiefly NAm* to turn from one railway track to another ~*vi* **1** to lash from side to side **2** to change, shift – **switchable** *adj*, **switcher** *n*

'switch,back /-,bak/ *n* **1** a zigzag road or railway in a mountainous region **2** *chiefly Br* any of various amusement rides; *esp* ROLLER COASTER

'switch,blade /-,blayd/ *n, NAm* a flick-knife

'switch,board /-,bawd/ *n* an apparatus consisting of a panel or frame on which switching devices are mounted; *specif* an arrangement for the manual switching of telephone calls

,switched-'on *adj* alive to experience; *also* swinging – infml

'switch,gear /-,giə/ *n* equipment used for the switching of esp large electrical currents

'switchman /-mən/ *n* sby who works a switch (e g on a railway)

'switch,over /-,ohvə/ *n* a conversion to a different system or method

'switch,yard /-,yahd/ *n, NAm* MARSHALLING YARD

[1]**swivel** /'swivl/ *n* a device joining 2 parts so that the moving part can pivot freely [ME; akin to OE *swīfan* to revolve, ON *sveigja* to sway – more at SWAY]

[2]**swivel** *vb* **-ll-** (*NAm* **-l-**, **-ll-**), /'swivl·ing/ to turn (as if) on a swivel

swivel chair *n* a chair that swivels on its base

swiz /swiz/ *n, pl* **-zz-** *Br* sthg that does not live up to one's hopes or expectations – infml [prob short for *swizzle* (cheat), alter. of *swindle*]

'swizzle ,stick /'swizl/ *n* a thin rod used to stir mixed drinks [*swizzle* prob fr obs *swizzle* (to tipple), perh fr *swig* + *guzzle*]

swob /swob/ *vt or n* **-bb-** (to) swab

swollen /'swohlən/ *past part of* SWELL

[1]**swoon** /swoohn/ *vi* to faint [ME *swounen*] – **swooningly** *adv*

[2]**swoon** *n* a partial or total loss of consciousness

[1]**swoop** /swoohp/ *vi* to make a sudden attack or downward sweep ~ *vt* to carry off abruptly; snatch [alter. of ME *swopen* to sweep, fr OE *swāpan*; akin to ON *svatha* to swathe – more at SWATHE]

[2]**swoop** *n* an act of swooping ⟨*arrested in a drug-squad* ~⟩

swoosh /swoosh, swoohsh/ *vi or n* (to make or move with) a rushing sound [imit]

swop /swop/ *vb or n* **-pp-** (to) swap

sword /sawd/ *n* **1** a cutting or thrusting weapon having a long usu sharp-pointed and sharp-edged blade **2** the use of force ⟨*the pen is mightier than the* ~ – E G Bulwer-Lytton⟩ **3** death caused (as if) by a sword – usu + *the* **4** sthg (e g the beak of a swordfish) that resembles a sword [ME, fr OE *sweord*; akin to OHG *swert* sword, Av *xvara* wound] – **swordlike** *adj*

'sword ,cane *n* a swordstick

'sword ,dance *n* a dance performed over, round, or brandishing swords; *esp* a Scottish-Highland solo dance usu performed in the angles formed by 2 swords crossed on the ground – **sword dancer** *n*

'sword,fish /-,fish/ *n* a very large oceanic food fish that has a long swordlike beak formed by the bones of the upper jaw

'sword ,grass *n* any of various grasses or sedges having leaves with a sharp or toothed edge

'sword ,knot *n* an ornamental cord or tassel tied to the hilt of a sword

,sword of 'Damocles /'daməkleez/ *n, often cap S* an impending disaster [fr the legend of the sword suspended by a single hair over the head of Damocles, a courtier of ancient Syracuse, as a reminder of the insecurity of a tyrant's happiness]

'sword,play /-,play/ *n* the art, skill, or practice of wielding a sword – **swordplayer** *n*

swordsman /'sawdzmən/ *n* one skilled in swordplay

'swordsman,ship /-ship/ *n* swordplay

'sword,stick /-,stik/ *n* a walking stick in which a sword blade is concealed

'sword-,swallower *n* a performer (e g at a circus) who causes or allows sword-blades to pass down his/her throat

'sword,tail /-,tayl/ *n* a small brightly marked Central American topminnow often kept in tropical aquariums

swore /swaw/ *past of* SWEAR

sworn /swawn/ *past part of* SWEAR

[1]**swot** /swot/ *n, Br* one who studies hard or excessively – infml [alter. of *sweat*]

[2]**swot** *vb* **-tt-** *Br vi* to study hard ~ *vt* to study (a subject) intensively – usu + *up* *USE* infml

swum /swum/ *past part of* SWIM

swung /swung/ *past of* SWING

,swung 'dash *n* a character ~ used esp to represent part or all of a previously spelt-out word

sybarite /'sibəriet/ *n, often cap* a voluptuary, sensualist [fr the notorious luxury of the people of the ancient city of Sybaris in Italy] – **sybaritism** /-,rietiz(ə)m/ *n*, **sybaritic** /-'ritik/ *adj*

sycamine /'sikəmien/ *n* the mulberry [L *sycaminus*, fr Gk *sykaminos*, of Sem origin; akin to Heb *shiqmāh* mulberry tree, sycamore]

sycamore /'sikə,maw/ *n* **1** a tree of Egypt and Asia Minor that is the sycamore of Scripture and has a sweet edible fruit **2** a Eurasian maple widely planted as a shade tree **3** *NAm* [2]PLANE [ME *sicamour*, fr MF *sicamor*, fr L *sycomorus*, fr Gk *sykomoros*, prob modif of a Sem word akin to Heb *shiqmāh* sycamore]

syce /sies/ *n* a groom, esp in India [Hindi *sā'is*, fr Ar]

syconium /sie'kohnyəm, -ni·əm/ *n, pl* **syconia** /-nyə, -ni·ə/ a multiple fleshy fruit (e g a fig) in which the ovaries are borne within an enlarged succulent receptacle [NL, fr Gk *sykon* fig + NL *-ium*]

sycophant /'sikə,fant/ *n* a self-seeking flatterer; a toady [L *sycophanta* informer, swindler, sycophant, fr Gk *sykophantēs* informer, fr *sykon* + *phainein* to show] – **sycophancy** /-si/ *n*, **sycophant** *adj*, **sycophantic** /-'fantik/ *adj*

sycosis /sie'kohsis/ *n* an inflammatory disorder of the hair follicles marked by raised spots [NL, fr Gk *sykōsis*, fr *sykon*]

syenite /'sie·i,niet/ *n* an igneous rock composed chiefly of feldspar [L *Syenites* (*lapis*) stone of Syene, fr *Syene*, ancient city in Egypt] – **syenitic** /-'nitik/ *adj*

syli /'sili/ *n* ☞ *Guinea* at NATIONALITY [native name in Guinea]

[1]**syllabic** /si'labik/ *adj* **1** constituting (the nucleus of) a syllable **2** enunciated with separation of syllables **3** of or constituting a type of verse (e g some French poetry) in which the metre is based on a count of syllables [LL *syllabicus*, fr Gk *syllabikos*, fr *syllabē* syllable] – **syllabically** *adv*

[2]**syllabic** *n* a syllabic character or sound

syllabify /si'labifie/ *vt* to form or divide into syllables [L *syllaba* syllable] – **syllabification** /-fi'kaysh(ə)n/ *n*

syllable /'siləbl/ *n* (a letter or symbol representing) an uninterruptible unit of spoken language that usu consists of 1 vowel sound either alone or with a consonant sound preceding or following ☞ ALPHABET [ME, fr MF *sillabe*, fr L *syllaba*, fr Gk *syllabē*, fr *syllambanein* to gather together, fr *syn-* + *lambanein* to take – more at LATCH] – **syllabled** *adj*

syllabub, sillabub /'siləbub/ *n* a cold dessert usu

made by curdling sweetened cream or milk with wine, cider, or other acidic liquid [origin unknown]

syllabus /'siləbəs/ *n, pl* **syllabi** /-bie/, **syllabuses** a summary of a course of study or of examination requirements [LL, alter. of L *sillybus* label for a book, fr Gk *sillybos*]

syllepsis /si'lepsis/ *n, pl* **syllepses** /-seez/ **1** the use of a word to modify or govern syntactically 2 or more words with only 1 of which it formally agrees (e g in 'neither he nor I knows") **2** the use of a word in the same grammatical relation to 2 adjacent words but in different senses (e g in 'departed in tears and a taxi") [L, fr Gk *syllēpsis*, fr *syllambanein*] – **sylleptic** /si'leptik/ *adj*

syllogism /'silə,jiz(ə)m/ *n* a pattern of deductive reasoning consisting of 2 premises and a conclusion (e g 'all men are mortal; Socrates is a man; therefore Socrates is mortal') [ME *silogisme*, fr MF, fr L *syllogismus*, fr Gk *syllogismos*, fr *syllogizesthai* to syllogize, fr *syn-* + *logizesthai* to calculate, fr *logos* reckoning, word – more at LEGEND] – **syllogistic** /-'jistik/ *adj*

syllog·ize, -ise /'siləjiez/ *vi* to reason by using syllogisms [ME *sylogysen*, fr LL *syllogizare*, fr Gk *syllogizesthai*]

sylph /silf/ *n* a slender graceful woman or girl [NL *sylphus*] – **sylphlike** *adj*

sylvan, silvan /'silvən/ *adj* **1** of, located in, or characteristic of the woods or forest **2** full of woods or trees [ML *silvanus, sylvanus*, fr L *silva, sylva* wood]

sym- – see SYN-

symbiont /'simbi,ont/ *n* an organism living in symbiosis [prob fr G, modif of Gk *symbiount-, symbiōn*, prp of *symbioun*] – **symbiontic** /-'ontik/ *adj*

symbiosis /,simbi'ohsis, -bie-/ *n, pl* **symbioses** /-seez/ the living together of 2 dissimilar organisms in intimate association (to their mutual benefit) [NL, fr G *symbiose*, fr Gk *symbiōsis* state of living together, fr *symbioun* to live together, fr *symbios* living together, fr *sym-* + *bios* life – more at [1]QUICK] – **symbiotic** /-'otik/ *adj*

symbiote /'simbi,oht, -bie-/ *n* a symbiont [F, fr Gk *symbiōtēs* companion, fr *symbioun* to live together]

symbol /'simbl/ *n* **1** sthg that stands for or suggests sthg else by reason of association, convention, etc **2** a sign used in writing or printing to represent operations, quantities, elements, relations, or qualities in a particular field (e g chemistry or music) ALPHABET [L *symbolum* token, sign, symbol, fr Gk *symbolon*, lit., token of identity verified by comparing its other half, fr *symballein* to throw together, compare, fr *syn-* + *ballein* to throw – more at DEVIL] – **symbology** /sim'boləji/ *n*

symbolic /sim'bolik/, **symbolical** /-kl/ *adj* of, using, constituting, or exhibiting a symbol or symbols – **symbolically** *adv*

symbolic logic *n* a method of developing and representing logical principles using a formalized system of symbols

symbolism /'simbə,liz(ə)m/ *n* **1** the literary and artistic mode of expression of the symbolists **2** a system of symbols – **symbolistic** /-'listik/ *adj*

symbolist /'simbəlist/ *n* **1** one who employs symbols or symbolism **2** any of a group of esp 19th-c French writers and artists who used symbols to convey a subjective view of reality and esp immaterial or intangible states or truths (e g by exploiting the nonliteral figurative resources of language) – **symbolist** *adj*

symbol·ize, -ise /'simbə,liez/ *vt* **1** to serve as a symbol of **2** to represent, express, or identify by a symbol – **symbolization** /-'zaysh(ə)n/ *n*

symmetrical /si'metrikl/, **symmetric** /si'metrik/ *adj* **1a** having the same proportions, design, shape, etc on both sides; *specif* capable of division by a longitudinal plane into similar halves **b** *of a flower* having the same number of members in each whorl of floral leaves **2** *of a chemical compound* having symmetry in the molecular structure [SYMMETRY + -ICAL] – **symmetrically** *adv*

symmetry /'simitri/ *n* **1** (beauty of form arising from) balanced proportions **2** the property of being symmetrical; *esp* correspondence in size, shape, and relative position of parts on opposite sides of a dividing line or median plane or about a centre or axis – compare BILATERAL SYMMETRY, RADIAL SYMMETRY [L *symmetria*, fr Gk, fr *symmetros* symmetrical, fr *syn-* + *metron* measure – more at MEASURE] – **symmetrize** /-triez/ *vt*

sympathetic /,simpə'thetik/ *adj* **1** existing or operating through an affinity, interdependence, or mutual association **2** appropriate to one's mood or temperament; congenial **3** given to or arising from compassion and sensitivity to others' feelings ⟨*a ~ gesture*⟩ **4** favourably inclined ⟨*not ~ to the idea*⟩ **5** of, being, mediated by, or acting on (the nerves of) the sympathetic nervous system **6** relating to musical sounds produced, or strings sounded, by sympathetic vibration [NL *sympatheticus*, fr L *sympathia* sympathy] – **sympathetically** *adv*

sympathetic nervous system *n* the part of the autonomic nervous system that contains nerve fibres in which the chief neurotransmitter is noradrenalin and whose activity tends to relax smooth muscle and cause the contraction of blood vessels – compare PARASYMPATHETIC NERVOUS SYSTEM

sympathetic vibration *n* a vibration produced in one body by vibrations of the same period in another

sympath·ize, -ise /'simpəthiez/ *vi* **1** to react or respond in sympathy **2** to share in distress or suffering; commiserate – **sympathizer** *n*

sympathomimetic /,simpəthohmi'metik/ *adj* simulating sympathetic nervous action in physiological effect ⟨~ *drugs*⟩ [ISV *sympath*etic + *-o-* + *mimetic*] – **sympathomimetic** *n*

sympathy /'simpəthi/ *n* **1a** relationship between people or things in which each is simultaneously affected in a similar way **b** unity or harmony in action or effect **2a** inclination to think or feel alike **b** tendency to favour or support – often pl with sing. meaning ⟨*Tory* sympathies⟩ **3** (the expression of) pity or compassion [L *sympathia*, fr Gk *sympatheia*, fr *sympathēs* having common feelings, sympathetic, fr *syn-* + *pathos* feelings, emotion, experience – more at PATHOS]

sympetalous /sim'petələs/ *adj* gamopetalous

symphonic /sim'fonik/ *adj* relating to or having the form or character of a symphony ⟨~ *music*⟩ – **symphonically** *adv*

symphonic poem *n* an extended orchestral composition, based on a legend, tale, etc and usu freer in form than a symphony

symphonist /'simfənist/ *n* a composer of symphonies

symphony /'simfəni/ *n* **1a** a usu long and complex sonata for symphony orchestra **b** a composition of similar proportions **2** sthg of great harmonious complexity or variety ⟨*the room was a ~ in blue*⟩ **3** *chiefly NAm* SYMPHONY ORCHESTRA [ME *symphonie* harmony, fr OF, fr L *symphonia*, fr Gk *symphōnia*, fr *symphōnos* concordant in sound, fr *syn-* + *phōnē* voice, sound – more at [1]BAN]

symphony orchestra *n* a large orchestra of wind instruments, strings, and percussion that plays symphonic works

symphysis /'simfisis/ *n, pl* **symphyses** /-seez/ an (almost) immovable joint between bones, esp where the surfaces are connected by fibrous cartilage without a joint membrane [NL, fr Gk, state of growing together, fr *symphyesthai* to grow together, fr *syn-* + *phyein* to make grow, bring forth – more at BE] – **symphyseal** /simfə'zee·əl/, **symphysial** /sim'fizi·əl/ *adj*

sympodial /sim'pohdi·əl/ *adj* having or involving the formation of an apparent main axis (e g of an inflorescence) from successive secondary axes [NL *sympodium* apparent main axis formed from secondary axes, fr Gk *syn-* + *podion* base – more at -PODIUM]

symposium /sim'pohzyəm, -zi·əm/ *n, pl* **symposia** /-zyə, -zi·ə/, **symposiums** **1** a party (e g after a banquet in ancient Greece) with music and conversation **2a** a formal meeting at which several specialists deliver short addresses on a topic – compare COLLOQUIUM **b** a published collection of opinions on a subject [L, fr Gk *symposion*, fr *sympinein* to drink together, fr *syn-* + *pinein* to drink – more at POTABLE]

symptom /'simptəm/ *n* **1** sthg giving (subjective) evidence or indication of disease or physical disturbance **2** sthg that indicates the existence of sthg else [LL *symptomat-*, *symptoma*, fr Gk *symptōmat-*, *symptōma* happening, attribute, symptom, fr *sympiptein* to happen, fr *syn-* + *piptein* to fall – more at FEATHER] – **symptomless** *adj*, **symptomatology** /-mə'toləji/ *n*

symptomatic /,simptə'matik/ *adj* **1** being a symptom of a disease **2** concerned with, affecting, or acting on symptoms ⟨*~ treatment for influenza*⟩ **3** characteristic, indicative – **symptomatically** *adv*

syn-, sym- *prefix* **1** with; along with; together ⟨sym*pathy*⟩ ⟨syn*thesis*⟩ **2** at the same time ⟨syn*aesthesia*⟩ [ME, fr OF, fr L, fr Gk, fr *syn* with, together with]

synaesthesia /,sinees'theez(h)yə/ *n* a subjective sensation or image (e g of colour) appropriate to a sense other than the one (e g hearing) being stimulated [NL, fr *syn-* + *-aesthesia* (as in *anaesthesia*)] – **synaesthetic** /-'thetik/ *adj*

synagogue /'sinəgog/ *n* (the house of worship and communal centre of) a Jewish congregation [ME *synagoge*, fr OF, fr LL *synagoga*, fr Gk *synagōgē* assembly, synagogue, fr *synagein* to bring together, fr *syn-* + *agein* to lead – more at AGENT] – **synagogal** /-'gogl/ *adj*

synapse /'sienaps/ *n* the point (between 2 nerves) across which a nervous impulse is transmitted [NL *synapsis*, fr Gk, juncture, fr *synaptein* to fasten together, fr *syn-* + *haptein* to fasten] – **synaptic** /si'naptik/ *adj*

synapsis /si'napsis/ *n, pl* **synapses** /-seez/ the joining of homologous chromosomes that occurs in meiotic cell division [NL, fr Gk, juncture] – **synaptic** *adj*

synarthrosis /,sinah'throhsis/ *n, pl* **synarthroses** /-seez/ an immovable joint between bones united by fibrous tissue [Gk *synarthrōsis*, fr *syn-* + *arthrōsis* arthrosis]

[1]**sync** *also* **synch** /singk/ *n* synchronization, synchronism ⟨*out of ~*⟩ – infml

[2]**sync** *also* **synch** *vt* to match film and magnetic track so that they run exactly in synchronization ⟨*are these rushes for ~ing?*⟩ – often + *up*; infml

syncarpous /sin'kahpəs/ *adj, of a flower, fruit, etc* having the carpels united in a compound ovary – **syncarpy** /'sin,kahpi/ *n*

synchro- *comb form* synchronized; synchronous ⟨synchro*mesh*⟩ [*synchronized* & *synchronous*]

synchromesh /'singkrə,mesh/ *adj* designed for effecting synchronized gear changing – **synchromesh** *n*

synchronic /sing'kronik/ *adj* of or dealing with phenomena, esp of language, at 1 point in time, ignoring historical antecedents – compare DIACHRONIC – **synchronically** *adv*

synchronism /'singkrə,niz(ə)m/ *n* **1** the quality of being synchronous; simultaneousness **2** (a table showing) chronological arrangement of historical events so as to indicate coincidence or coexistence – **synchronistic** /-'nistik/ *adj*

synchron·ize, -ise /'singkrə,niez/ *vi* to happen at the same time ~ *vt* **1** to arrange so as to indicate coincidence or coexistence **2** to make synchronous in operation ⟨*~ watches*⟩ **3** to make (sound) exactly simultaneous with the action in a film or a television programme – **synchronizer** *n*, **synchronization** /-'zaysh(ə)n/ *n*

synchronized swimming *n* swimming in which the movements of 1 or more swimmers are synchronized with a musical accompaniment so as to form changing patterns

synchronous /'singkrənəs/ *adj* **1** happening or arising at precisely the same time **2a** going on or operating together at exactly the same rate **b** recurring together **3** involving or indicating synchronism **4** geostationary [LL *synchronos*, fr Gk, fr *syn-* + *chronos* time] – **synchronously** *adv*

synchronous motor *n* an electric motor having a speed strictly proportional to the frequency of the operating current

synchrony /'singkrəni/ *n* synchronistic occurrence, arrangement, or treatment

synchrotron /'singkrətron/ *n* an apparatus that imparts very high speeds to charged particles by combining a high-frequency electric field and a low-frequency magnetic field

syncline /'singklien/ *n* a trough of stratified rock in which the layers dip towards each other from either side – compare ANTICLINE ☞ GEOGRAPHY [back-formation fr *synclinal*, fr Gk *syn-* + *klinein* to lean – more at [1]LEAN] – **synclinal** /-'klienl/ *adj*

syncopate /'singkə,payt/ *vt* to modify or affect (musical rhythm) by syncopation [ML *syncopatus*, pp of *syncopare*, fr LL *syncope*] – **syncopator** *n*

syncopation /,singkə'paysh(ə)n/ *n* (a rhythm or passage characterized by) a temporary displacement of the regular metrical accent in music caused typi-

Sign
A mark with a conventional meaning, used to replace or supplement words

Symbol
A sign used in writing or printing to represent operations, quantities, elements, relations, or qualities in a particular field

Accents and diacritics

ˊ	(é)	acute accent
ˋ	(è)	grave accent
^	(ô)	or ˆ or ˜ circumflex
~	(ñ)	tilde
—	(ō)	macron
˘	(ŭ)	breve
ˇ	(č)	haček
··	(oö)	diaeresis
¸	(ç)	cedilla
:	(i:)	colon

Airport signs

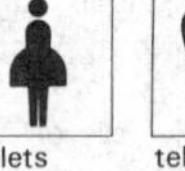

toilets men · toilets women · telephone

first aid · no smoking · bus

post · luggage · restaurant

Astronomy

☉	the sun, Sunday
◐ ☾ or ☽	the moon, Monday
●	new moon
☽ ◑ ◗ ◗	first quarter
○ or ⊛	full moon
☾ ◐ ☾ ◖	last quarter
☿	Mercury, Wednesday
♀	Venus, Friday
⊕ ⊖ or ♁	the earth
♂	Mars, Tuesday
♃	Jupiter, Thursday
♄	Saturn, Saturday
♅	Uranus
♆	Neptune
♇	Pluto
☄	comet
✳	fixed star
☌	conjunction – of bodies having the same longitude, or right ascension
□	quadrature – a difference of 90° in longitude, or right ascension
△	trine – a difference of 120° in longitude, or right ascension
☍	opposition – a difference of 180° in longitude, or right ascension
☊	ascending node
☋	descending node

Biology

♀ ○	female
♂ ♁ □	male
☿	neuter
⚥	neuter hermaphrodite
×	crossed with, hybrid
+	wild type
F_1	offspring of the first generation
F_2	offspring of the second generation

Business

@	at, each
c/o	care of
%	per cent
©	copyright
®	trademark

Computer flowcharts

▭	process
▽	merge
▱	input/output
◯	magnetic tape
◖	on-line storage
◇	decision
△	extract
▭	document
▭	punched tape
▽	off-line storage
⏢	manual operation
⧗	collate
◇	sort
▭	punched card
⛁	magnetic disk

Crosses

Latin · patriarchal · papal

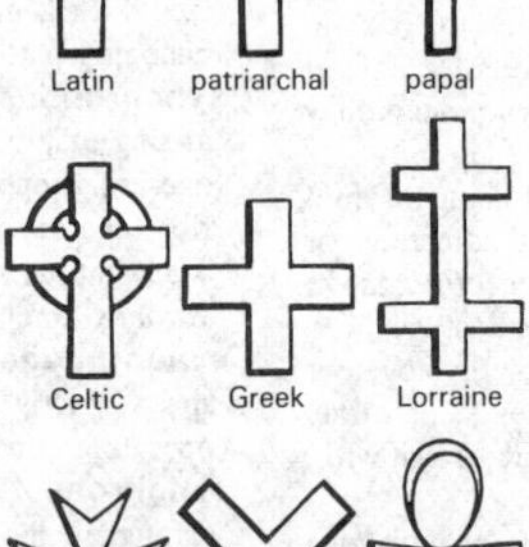

Celtic · Greek · Lorraine

Maltese · Saint Andrew's · ankh

Goods handling

1 fragile
2 keep dry
3 keep upright
4 handle with care
5 use no hooks
6 protect from heat

explosive · radioactive

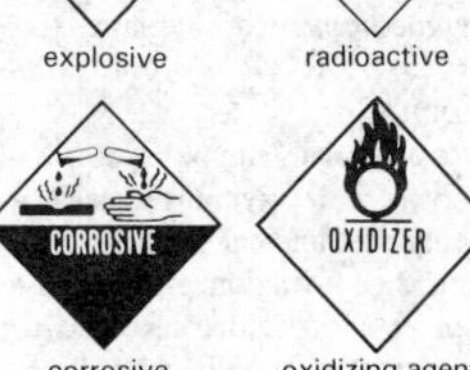

corrosive · oxidizing agent

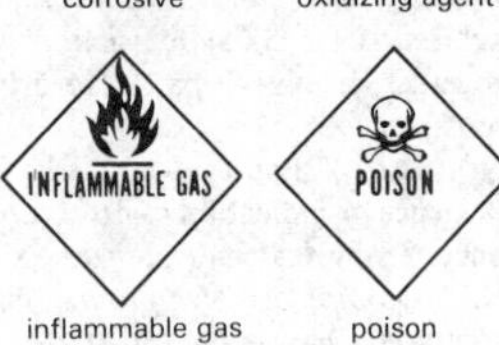

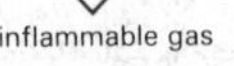

inflammable gas · poison

Mathematics

+	plus
−	minus
±	plus or minus
× or .	multiplied by
÷ : or /	divided by
=	equals
≠	is not equal to
>	is greater than
≫	is much greater than
<	is less than
≪	is much less than
≧ or ≥	is greater than or equal to
≦ or ≤	is less than or equal to
≯	is not greater than
≮	is not less than
≈	is approximately equal to
≡	is identical to
~	equivalent, similar
≅	is congruent to

☞ ALPHABET, NUMBER, PERIODIC TABLE, PHYSICS

∝	varies directly as, is proportional to
:	is to, the ratio of
∴	therefore
∞	infinity
∠	angle, the angle
∟	right angle
‖	parallel, is parallel to
√ *or* √	root – used without a figure to indicate a square root ⟨as in $\sqrt{4}=2$⟩ or with an index above the sign to indicate another degree ⟨as in $\sqrt[3]{3}$, $\sqrt[5]{7}$⟩
δ	δx, the increment or variation of x
∫	indefinite integral ⟨$\int 2x dx = x^2 + C$⟩
$\int_b^a$	the integral taken between the values a and b of the variable
σ	standard deviation of a population
Σ	sum, summation
μ	arithmetic mean of a population
χ^2	chi square
π	pi, the number 3.14159265 +, the ratio of the circumference of a circle to its diameter
!	factorial ⟨$4! = 4 \times 3 \times 2 \times 1$⟩
e *or* ∈	(1) the number 2.7182818 +, the base of the natural system of logarithms (2) the eccentricity of a conic section
°	degree ⟨60°⟩
′	minute; foot ⟨30′⟩ – used also to distinguish between values of the same variable or between different variables (as a', a'', a''', usu read *a* prime, *a* double prime, *a* triple prime)
″	second, inch ⟨30″⟩
x^2, x^3, etc	– used as exponents placed above and at the right of an expression to indicate that it is raised to a power whose degree is indicated by the figure ⟨a^2, the square of a⟩
x^{-2}, x^{-3}, etc	– used as exponents placed above and at the right of an expression to indicate that the reciprocal of the expression is raised to the power whose degree is indicated by the figure ⟨a^{-2} equals $1/a^2$⟩
$\sin^{-1}x$	arc sine of x
$\cos^{-1}x$	arc cosine of x
$\tan^{-1}x$	arc tangent of x
$\cot^{-1}x$	arc cotangent of x
$\sec^{-1}x$	arc secant of x
$\mathrm{cosec}^{-1}x$	arc cosecant of x
$\lvert z \rvert$	the absolute value of z
∪	union of two sets
∩	intersection of two sets
⊂	is included in, is a subset of
⊃	contains as a subset
∈ *or* ε	is an element of
∉	is not an element of
∅ *or* { }	empty set, null set

Road signs

Warning

Roundabout Slippery road Road works

Restriction

Maximum speed limit No entry Width limit

Information

One-way street No through road Entrance to controlled parking zone

Reference marks

*	asterisk *or* star
†	dagger
‡	double dagger
§	section *or* numbered clause
‖	parallel
¶ *or* ⁋	paragraph

Washing symbols

washable hand wash dry-cleanable

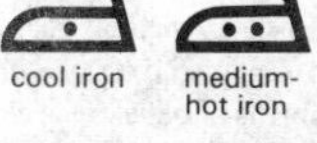

cool iron medium-hot iron hot iron

do not wash do not iron do not bleach

Miscellaneous

&	and
/	solidus *or* diagonal *or* slant; used to mean "or" (as in and/or), "and/or" (as in dead/wounded), "per" (as in feet/second), indicates end of a line of verse; separates the figures of a date (4/4/73)
<	derived from } used in etymologies
>	whence derived } used in etymologies
+	and } used in etymologies
*	assumed } used in etymologies
†	died – used esp in genealogies
✡	Star of David
℣	versicle
℟	response
☮	peace
♡	Kite mark. British Standards Institution

Signs of the Zodiac

cally by stressing the weak beat – **syncopative** /-,paytiv/ *adj*

syncope /'singkəpi/ *n* **1** temporary loss of consciousness; fainting **2** the dropping of 1 or more sounds or letters in a word (e g in *fo'c'sle* for *forecastle*) [LL, fr Gk *synkopē*, lit., cutting short, fr *synkoptein* to cut short, fr *syn-* + *koptein* to cut – more at CAPON] – **syncopal** /'singkəpl/ *adj*

syncretism /'singkri,tiz(ə)m/ *n* **1** the combination of different forms of belief or practice; *esp* eclecticism **2** the fusion of 2 or more orig different inflectional forms [NL *syncretismus*, fr Gk *synkrētismos* federation of Cretan cities, fr *syn-* + *Krēt-*, *Krēs* Cretan] – **syncretist** *n or adj*, **syncretistic** /-'tistik/ *adj*, **syncretic** /sing'kretik/ *adj*

syncytium /sin'siti·əm/ *n*, *pl* **syncytia** /-ti·ə/ (an organism consisting of) a mass of living material with many nuclei resulting from fusion of cells or repeated division of nuclei [NL, fr *syn-* + *cyt-*] – **syncytial** /-'sish(y)əl/ *adj*

syndactyly /sin'daktili/, **syndactylism** /-,liz(ə)m/ *n* a union of 2 or more digits that occurs normally (e g in many birds) and occas as an inherited abnormality in human beings [NL *syndactylia*, fr *syn-* + Gk *daktylos* finger]

syndic /'sindik/ *n* an agent who transacts business for a university or corporation [F, fr LL *syndicus* representative of a corporation, fr Gk *syndikos* assistant at law, advocate, representative of a state, fr *syn-* + *dikē* judgment, case at law – more at DICTION]

syndicalism /'sindikl,iz(ə)m/ *n* **1** a revolutionary doctrine according to which workers should seize control of the economy and the government by direct means (e g a general strike) **2** a system of economic organization in which industries are owned and managed by the workers [F *syndicalisme*, fr *chambre syndicale* trade union] – **syndical** *adj*, **syndicalist** *adj or n*

[1]**syndicate** /'sindikət/ *n* **1a** the office of a syndic **b** *sing or pl in constr* a council or body of syndics **2** *sing or pl in constr* a group of people or concerns who combine to carry out a particular transaction (e g buying or renting property) or to promote some common interest **3** a business concern that supplies material for simultaneous publication in many newspapers or periodicals [F *syndicat*, fr *syndic*]

[2]**syndicate** /'sindi,kayt/ *vt* **1** to form into or manage as a syndicate **2** to sell (e g a cartoon) to a syndicate for simultaneous publication in many newspapers or periodicals – **syndicator** *n*, **syndication** /-'kaysh(ə)n/ *n*

syndrome /'sindrohm/ *n* **1** a group of signs and symptoms that occur together and characterize a particular (medical) abnormality **2** a set of concurrent emotions, actions, etc that usu form an identifiable pattern [NL, fr Gk *syndromē* combination, syndrome, fr *syn-* + *dramein* to run – more at DROMEDARY]

[1]**syne** /sien; *often* zien/ *adv*, *chiefly Scot* since then; ago [ME (northern), prob fr ON *sīthan*; akin to OE *siththan* since – more at SINCE]

[2]**syne** *conj or prep*, *Scot* since

synecdoche /si'nekdəki/ *n* a figure of speech in which a part is used to mean the whole (e g *50 sail* instead of *50 ships*) or the whole to mean a part (e g in 'Leeds defeated Stoke") [L, fr Gk *synekdochē*, fr *syn-* + *ekdochē* sense, interpretation, fr *ekdechesthai* to receive, understand, fr *ex* from + *dechesthai* to receive; akin to Gk *dokein* to seem good – more at EX-, DECENT]

synecology /,sini'koləji/ *n* ecology that deals with the structure and development of ecological communities [G *synökologie*, fr *syn-* + *ökologie* ecology]

synergic /si'nuhjik/ *adj* working together; cooperating [NL *synergicus*, fr *synergia*] – **synergically** *adv*

synergism /'sinə,jiz(ə)m, si'nuh-/, **synergy** /-ji/ *n* cooperative action between 2 or more agencies (e g drugs or muscles) whose combined effect is greater than the sum of their separate effects [NL *synergismus* & *synergia*, fr Gk *synergos* working together, fr *syn-* + *ergon* work – more at WORK] – **synergistic** /-'jistik/ *adj*

synergist /'sinəjist, 'sinuh-/ *n* any of the agencies that together produce synergism

syngamy /'sing·gəmi/ *n* sexual reproduction by union of gametes [ISV]

synod /'sinəd, 'sinod/ *n* **1** a formal meeting to decide ecclesiastical matters **2** a church governing or advisory council **3** the ecclesiastical district governed by a synod [LL *synodus*, fr LGk *synodos*, fr Gk, meeting, assembly, fr *syn-* + *hodos* way, journey – more at CEDE] – **synodal** /'sinədl, 'si,nodl/ *adj*

synodic /si'nodik/ *also* **synodical** /-kl/ *adj* of a conjunction or the period between 2 successive conjunctions of the same celestial bodies [Gk *synodikos*, fr *synodos* meeting, conjunction]

synonym /'sinənim/ *n* any of 2 or more words or expressions in a language that are used with (nearly) the same meaning [ME *sinonyme*, fr L *synonymum*, fr Gk *synōnymon*, fr neut of *synōnymos* synonymous, fr *syn-* + *onyma* name – more at NAME] – **synonymic** /-'nimik/, **synonymical** *adj*, **synonymity** /,sinə'nimәti/ *n*

synonymous /si'nonimәs/ *adj* alike in meaning – **synonymously** *adv*

synonymy /si'nonimi/ *n* **1a** the study or distinguishing of synonyms **b** a list or collection of synonyms **2** being synonymous

synopsis /si'nopsis/ *n*, *pl* **synopses** /-seez/ a condensed statement or outline (e g of a narrative) [LL, fr Gk, lit., comprehensive view, fr *synopsesthai* to be going to see together, fr *syn-* + *opsesthai* to be going to see – more at OPTIC]

synoptic /si'noptik/ *also* **synoptical** /-kl/ *adj* **1** affording a comprehensive view of a whole **2** *often cap* of or being the first 3 Gospels of the New Testament **3** relating to or displaying meteorological conditions existing simultaneously over a broad area [Gk *synoptikos*, fr *synopsesthai*] – **synoptically** *adv*

synovia /si'nohvi·ə, sie-/ *n* a transparent viscous lubricating fluid secreted by a joint or tendon membrane ☞ ANATOMY [NL] – **synovial** *adj*

synovitis /,sienə'vietəs/ *n* inflammation of a synovial membrane [NL]

syntactic /sin'taktik/, **syntactical** /-kl/ *adj* of or conforming to the rules of syntax or syntactics [NL *syntacticus*, fr Gk *syntaktikos* arranging together, fr *syntassein*] – **syntactically** *adv*

syn'tactics *n pl but sing or pl in constr* a branch of semiotics dealing with the formal relations between signs or expressions; *also* syntax

syntax /'sintaks/ *n* (the part of grammar dealing

with) the way in which words are put together to form phrases, clauses, or sentences [F or LL; F *syntaxe,* fr LL *syntaxis,* fr Gk, fr *syntassein* to arrange together, fr *syn-* + *tassein* to arrange – more at TACTICS]

synthesis /'sinthəsis/ *n, pl* **syntheses** /-seez/ **1a** the composition or combination of separate or diverse elements into a coherent whole **b** the artificial production of a substance by chemical reaction **2** the third and final stage of a reasoned argument, based on the thesis and antithesis [Gk, fr *syntithenai* to put together, fr *syn-* + *tithenai* to put, place – more at DO] – **synthesist** *n,* **synthesize** *vt*

synthes·izer, -iser /'sinthə,siezə/ *n* an extremely versatile electronic musical instrument that produces a sound that can be altered in many ways (e g to mimic other instruments) and is usu played by means of a keyboard [SYNTHESIZE + [2]-ER]

[1]**synthetic** /sin'thetik/ *also* **synthetical** /-kl/ *adj* **1** asserting of a subject a predicate that is not part of the meaning of that subject – compare ANALYTIC **2** characterized by inflection rather than analysis ⟨~ *languages*⟩ **3** produced artificially; man-made ⟨~ *dyes*⟩ ⟨~ *drugs*⟩ ⟨~ *silk*⟩ [Gk *synthetikos* of composition, component, fr *syntithenai*] – **synthetically** *adv*

[2]**synthetic** *n* a product of (chemical) synthesis

syphilis /'sifəlis/ *n* a contagious usu venereal and often congenital disease caused by a spirochaetal bacterium – compare PRIMARY SYPHILIS, SECONDARY SYPHILIS, TERTIARY SYPHILIS [NL, fr *Syphilus,* hero of the poem *Syphilis sive Morbus Gallicus* (*Syphilis or the French disease*) by Girolamo Fracastoro †1553 It physician & poet] – **syphilitic** /-'litik/ *adj or n*

syphon /'siefən/ *vb or n* to siphon

Syriac /'siriak/ *n* a literary and liturgical language based on Aramaic, esp used by eastern Christian churches [L *syriacus* Syrian, fr Gk *syriakos,* fr *Syria,* ancient country in Asia] – **Syriac** *adj*

[1]**syringe** /sə'rinj/ *n* a device used to inject fluids into or withdraw them from sthg (e g the body or its cavities); *esp* one that consists of a hollow barrel fitted with a plunger and a hollow needle [ME *syring,* fr ML *syringa,* fr LL, injection, fr Gk *syring-, syrinx* panpipe, tube; akin to Gk *sōlēn* pipe, Skt *tūṇava* flute]

[2]**syringe** *vt* to irrigate or spray (as if) with a syringe

syrinx /'siringks/ *n, pl* **syringes** /si'rinjeez/, **syrinxes** the vocal organ of birds that is a modification of the lower trachea, bronchi, or both [NL, fr Gk, panpipe]

syrup /'sirəp/ *n* **1a** a thick sticky solution of (flavoured, medicated, etc) sugar and water **b** the concentrated juice of a fruit or plant (e g the sugar maple); *esp* the raw sugar juice obtained from crushed sugarcane after evaporation and before crystallization in sugar manufacture **2** cloying sweetness or sentimentality [ME *sirup,* fr MF *sirop,* fr ML *syrupus,* fr Ar *sharāb*] – **syrupy** *adj*

systaltic /si'staltik, si'stawltik/ *adj* alternately and regularly contracting and dilating; pulsating [Gk *systaltos,* (assumed) verbal of *systellein* to contract – more at SYSTOLE]

system /'sistəm/ *n* **1a** a group of body organs that together perform 1 or more usu specified functions ⟨*the digestive* ~⟩ **b** the body considered as a functional unit **c** a group of interrelated and interdependent objects or units **d** a group of devices or an organization that serves a common purpose ⟨*a telephone* ~⟩ ⟨*a heating* ~⟩ ⟨*a highway* ~⟩ ⟨*a data processing* ~⟩ **e** a major division of rocks including those formed during a period or era **f** a form of social, economic, or political organization ⟨*the capitalist* ~⟩ **2** an organized set of doctrines or principles usu intended to explain the arrangement or working of a systematic whole ⟨*the Newtonian* ~ *of mechanics*⟩ **3a** an organized or established procedure ⟨*the touch* ~ *of typing*⟩ **b** a manner of classifying, symbolizing, or formalizing ⟨*a taxonomic* ~⟩ ⟨*the decimal* ~⟩ **4** orderly methods **5** ESTABLISHMENT 2 – + *the* [LL *systemat-, systema,* fr Gk *systēmat-, systēma,* fr *synistanai* to combine, fr *syn-* + *histanai* to cause to stand – more at STAND] – **systemless** *adj*

systematic /,sistə'matik/ *also* **systematical** /-kl/ *adj* **1** relating to, consisting of, or presented as a system **2** methodical in procedure or plan; thorough ⟨~ *investigation*⟩ **3** of or concerned with classification; *specif* taxonomic [LL *systematicus,* fr Gk *systēmatikos,* fr *systēmat-, systēma*] – **systematically** *adv*

,syste'matics *n pl but sing in constr* (a system of) classification or taxonomy

systematist /'sistəmətist, si'stemətist, si'stee-/ *n* **1** a maker or follower of a system **2** a taxonomist

systemat·ize, -ise /'sistəmətiez/ *vt* to arrange according to a set method; order systematically – **systematizer** *n,* **systematization** /-'zaysh(ə)n/ *n*

systemic /si'steemik, si'stemik/ *adj* **1** affecting the body generally **2** *of an insecticide, pesticide, etc* making the organism, esp a plant, toxic to a pest by entering the tissues [SYSTEM + [1]-IC] – **systemically** *adv*

systemic circulation *n* the part of the blood circulation concerned with the distribution of blood to the tissues through the aorta rather than to the lungs through the pulmonary artery

system·ize, -ise /'sistəmiez/ *vt* to systematize – **systemization** /-'zaysh(ə)n/ *n*

systems analysis *n* the analysis of an activity (e g a procedure, a business, or a physiological function) typically by mathematical means in order to define its goals or purposes and to discover ways of accomplishing them efficiently – **systems analyst** *n*

systole /'sistəli/ *n* the recurrent contraction of the heart by which blood is forced on and the circulation kept up – compare DIASTOLE [Gk *systolē,* fr *systellein* to contract, fr *syn-* + *stellein* to send – more at [1]STALL] – **systolic** /si'stolik/ *adj*

syzygy /'siziji/ *n* a configuration in which 3 celestial bodies (e g the sun, moon, and earth) lie in a straight line [LL *syzygia* conjunction, fr Gk, fr *syzygos* yoked together, fr *syn-* + *zygon* yoke – more at YOKE] – **syzygial** /si'ziji·əl/ *adj*

T

t /tee/ *n, pl* **t's, ts** *often cap* (a graphic representation of or device for reproducing) the 20th letter of the English alphabet – **to a T** to perfection; exactly [short for *to a tittle*]

t' *definite article, NEng dial* the

't *pron* it

ta /tah/ *n, Br* thanks – infml [baby talk]

Taal /tahl/ *n* Afrikaans – usu + *the* [Afrik, fr D, language; akin to OE *talu* talk – more at TALE]

[1]**tab** /tab/ *n* **1a** a flap, loop, etc fixed to or projecting from sthg and used for gripping or suspending or to aid identification **b** a small auxiliary aerofoil hinged to a control surface (e g an aileron) **2** close surveillance; watch – usu pl with sing. meaning ⟨*the police are keeping* ~s *on him*⟩ **3** a tabulator **4** *Br* [1]TAG 2 **5** *chiefly NAm* a statement of money owed; a bill – infml ⟨*the company will pick up the* ~⟩ [perh akin to *tag*; (2, 5) partly short for [1]*table*; (3) by shortening]

[2]**tab** *vt* **-bb-** to provide or decorate with tabs

tabard /'tabəd/ *n* a short loosely fitting sleeveless or short-sleeved coat or cape: e g **a** an emblazoned tunic worn by a knight over his armour **b** a herald's official cape or coat emblazoned with his lord's arms **c** a straight-hanging sleeveless outer garment; *esp* one with slits at the sides for part or all of its length, worn by women [ME, fr OF *tabart*]

Tabasco /tə'baskoh/ *trademark* – used for a pungent condiment sauce made from hot peppers

tabby /'tabi/, **'tabby ,cat** *n* **1** a domestic cat with a usu buff and black striped and mottled coat **2** a female domestic cat [*tabby*, adj (striped & mottled), fr *tabby* (striped silk taffeta), fr F *tabis*, fr ML *attabi*, fr Ar *'attābī*, fr Al-*'Attābīya*, quarter in Baghdad where it was manufactured]

tabernacle /'tabə,nakl/ *n* **1** *often cap* a tent sanctuary used by the Israelites during the Exodus **2** a receptacle for the consecrated bread and wine used at Communion, often forming part of an altar **3** a support in which a mast is stepped and pivoted so that it can be lowered (e g to negotiate a bridge) [ME, fr OF, fr LL *tabernaculum*, fr L, tent, dim. of *taberna* hut – more at TAVERN] – **tabernacular** /,tabə'nakyoolə/ *adj*

tabes /'taybeez/ *n, pl* **tabes** wasting accompanying a chronic disease [L – more at THAW] – **tabetic** /tə'betik/ *adj or n*

tabes dorsalis /daw'sahlis/ *n* LOCOMOTOR ATAXIA [NL, dorsal tabes]

tabla /'tahblə/ *n* a pair of small hand drums of different sizes used esp in Indian classical music [Hindi *tabla*, fr Ar *ṭabla*]

tablature /'tabləchə/ *n* an instrumental notation indicating the string, fret, keys, or fingering to be used instead of the note to be sounded [MF, fr ML *tabulatus* tablet, fr L *tabula*]

[1]**table** /'taybl/ *n* **1a** a piece of furniture consisting of a smooth flat slab (e g of wood) fixed on legs **b** the food served at a meal; fare ⟨*keeps a good* ~⟩ **2** either of the 2 leaves of a backgammon board or either half of a leaf **3** a systematic arrangement of data usu in rows and columns **4** the upper flat surface of a gem **5** sthg having a flat level surface [ME, fr OE *tabule* & OF *table*; both fr L *tabula* board, tablet, list] – **on the table** *chiefly Br* under or put forward for discussion ⟨*so far the management have put nothing on the table*⟩ – **under the table 1** into a stupor ⟨*can drink you under the table*⟩ **2** not aboveboard

table 2 *vt* **1** to enter in a table **2a** *Br* to place on the agenda **b** *NAm* to remove from consideration indefinitely

tableau /'tabloh/ *n, pl* **tableaux** *also* **tableaus** /'tabloh(z)/ **1** a graphic representation of a group or scene **2** a depiction of a scene usu presented on a stage by silent and motionless costumed participants [F, fr MF *tablel*, dim. of *table*; (2) short for *tableau vivant*, fr F, lit., living picture]

'table,cloth /-,kloth/ *n* an often decorative cloth spread over a dining table before the places are set

table d'hôte /,tahblə 'doht/ *n* a meal often of several prearranged courses served to all guests at a stated hour and fixed price – compare À LA CARTE [F, lit., host's table]

tableland /'taybl,land/ *n* a broad level area elevated on all sides

table linen *n* linen (e g tablecloths and napkins) for the table

'table,mat /-,mat/ *n* a small often decorative mat placed under a hot dish to protect the surface of a table from heat

table salt *n* fine-grained free-flowing salt suitable for use at the table and in cooking

'table,spoon /-,spoohn/ *n* **1** a large spoon used for serving **2** a tablespoonful

'table,spoonful /-,spoohnf(ə)l/ *n, pl* **tablespoonfuls** *also* **tablespoonsful** as much as a tablespoon can hold ☞ UNIT

tablet /'tablit/ *n* **1** a flat slab or plaque suitable for or bearing an inscription **2a** a compressed block of a solid material ⟨*a* ~ *of soap*⟩ **b** a small solid shaped mass or capsule of medicinal material [ME *tablett*, fr MF *tablete*, dim. of *table*]

table tennis *n* a game resembling lawn tennis that is played on a tabletop with bats and a small hollow plastic ball

'table,ware /-,weə/ *n* utensils (e g glasses, dishes, plates, and cutlery) for table use

table wine *n* an unfortified wine usu served with food

tabloid /'tabloyd/ *n* a newspaper of which 2 pages make up 1 printing plate and which contains much photographic matter – compare BROADSHEET [fr *Tabloid*, a trademark for a concentrated form of drugs and chemicals]

[1]**taboo** *also* **tabu** /tə'booh/ *adj* **1a** too sacred or evil to be touched, named, or used **b** set apart as unclean or accursed **2** forbidden, esp on grounds of morality, tradition, or social usage [Tongan *tabu*]

[2]**taboo** *also* **tabu** *n, pl* **taboos** *also* **tabus** **1** a prohibition against touching, saying, or doing sthg for fear of harm from a supernatural force **2** a prohibition imposed by social custom

[3]**taboo** *also* **tabu** *vt* **1** to set apart as taboo **2** to avoid or ban as taboo

tabor *also* **tabour** /'taybə/ *n* a small drum with 1 head of soft calfskin used to accompany a pipe or fife played by the same person [ME, fr OF]

tabular /'tabyoolə/ *adj* **1a** having a broad flat surface **b** laminar **c** *of a crystal* having 2 parallel flat faces **2a** of or arranged in a table **b** computed by means of a table [L *tabularis* of boards, fr *tabula* board, tablet] – **tabularly** *adv*

tabula rasa /,tabyoolə 'rahsə/ *n, pl* **tabulae rasae** /,tabyooli 'rahsi/ the mind conceived of as blank or empty before receiving outside impressions [L, smoothed or erased tablet]

tabulate /'tabyoolayt/ *vt* to arrange in tabular form [L *tabula* tablet] – **tabulation** /-'laysh(ə)n/ *n*

tabulator /'tabyoo,laytə/ *n* **1** a business machine that sorts and selects information from marked or perforated cards **2** an attachment to a typewriter that is used for arranging data in columns [TABULATE + [1]-OR]

tacamahac /'takəmə,hak/ *n* **1** any of several aromatic gum resins used esp for incense **2** BALSAM POPLAR [Sp *tacamahaca*, fr Nahuatl *tecamaca*]

tacet /'tayset/ – used in music to indicate that a particular instrument is not to play during a movement or long section [L, lit., (it) is silent, fr *tacēre* to be silent – more at TACIT]

tachism /'tashiz(ə)m/ *n, often cap* ACTION PAINTING [F *tachisme*, fr *tache* stain, spot, blob, fr MF *teche, tache*, of Gmc origin; akin to OS *tēkan* sign] – **tachist** *adj or n, often cap*

tachistoscope /tə'kistə,skohp/ *n* an apparatus for briefly exposing visual stimuli that is used in the study of learning, attention, and perception [Gk *tachistos* (superl of *tachys* swift) + ISV *-scope*] – **tachistoscopic** /-'skopik/ *adj*

tachograph /'takə,grahf, -,graf/ *n* a device for automatically recording the speed and time of travel of a vehicle, esp a lorry [Gk *tachos* speed + E *-graph*]

tachometer /ta'komitə/ *n* a device for indicating speed of rotation (e g of a vehicle engine) [Gk *tachos* speed + E *-meter*]

tachy- *comb form* rapid; accelerated ⟨tachy*cardia*⟩ ⟨tachy*graphy*⟩ [Gk, fr *tachys*]

tachycardia /,taki'kahdi·ə/ *n* normal or abnormal rapid heart action – compare BRADYCARDIA [NL]

tachygraphy /ta'kigrəfi/ *n* shorthand, esp as used by the ancient Greeks and Romans and in medieval Greek and Latin writing [Gk *tachygraphos* stenographer, fr *tachy-* + *graphein* to write – more at CARVE] – **tachygraphic** /,taki'grafik/ *also* **tachygraphical** *adj*

tachymeter /ta'kimitə/ *n* a surveying instrument for determining distance, bearings, etc quickly [ISV]

tacit /'tasit/ *adj* implied or understood but not actually expressed [F or L; F *tacite*, fr L *tacitus* silent, fr pp of *tacēre* to be silent; akin to OHG *dagēn* to be silent] – **tacitly** *adv*

taciturn /'tasi,tuhn/ *adj* not communicative or talkative [F or L; F *taciturne*, fr L *taciturnus*, fr *tacitus*] – **taciturnity** /-'tuhnəti/ *n*

[1]**tack** /tak/ *n* **1** a small short sharp-pointed nail, usu with a broad flat head **2** the lower forward corner of a fore-and-aft sail ☞ SHIP **3a** the direction of a sailing vessel with respect to the direction of the wind ⟨*starboard ~, with the wind to starboard*⟩ **b** the run of a sailing vessel on 1 tack **c** a change of course from one tack to another **d** a course of action ⟨*off on a new ~*⟩ **4** a long loose straight stitch usu used to hold 2 or more layers of fabric together temporarily **5** a sticky or adhesive quality **6** SADDLERY 2 [ME *tak* sthg that attaches; akin to MD *tac* sharp point]

[2]**tack** *vt* **1a** to fasten or attach with tacks **b** to sew with long loose stitches in order to join or hold in place temporarily before fine or machine sewing **2** to add as a supplement ⟨~ *a postscript on a letter*⟩ **3** to change the course of (a close-hauled sailing vessel) from one tack to the other by turning the bow to windward ~ *vi* **1a** to tack a sailing vessel **b** *of a sailing vessel* to undergo being tacked **2a** to follow a zigzag course **b** to change one's policy or attitude abruptly – **tacker** *n*

[1]**tackle** /'takl/ *n* **1** a set of equipment used in a particular activity ⟨*fishing ~*⟩ **2a** a ship's rigging **b** an assembly of ropes and pulleys arranged to gain mechanical advantage for hoisting and pulling **3** an act of tackling [ME *takel*; akin to MD *takel* ship's rigging]

[2]**tackle** *vb* **tackling** /'takling, 'takl·ing/ *vt* **1** to attach or secure with or as if with tackle – often + *up* **2a** to take hold of or grapple with, esp in an attempt to stop or restrain **b(1)** to (attempt to) take the ball from (an opposing player) in hockey or soccer **(2)** to seize and pull down or stop (an opposing player with the ball) in rugby or American football **3** to set about dealing with ⟨~ *the problem*⟩ ~ *vi* to tackle an opposing player – **tackler** *n*

[1]**tacky** /'taki/ *adj* slightly sticky to the touch ⟨~ *varnish*⟩ [[2]*tack*] – **tackiness** *n*

[2]**tacky** *adj, NAm* shabby, shoddy – slang [*tacky* (an inferior horse or person), of unknown origin] – **tackily** *adv*, **tackiness** *n*

tact /takt/ *n* a keen sense of how to handle people or affairs so as to avoid friction or giving offence [F, sense of touch, fr L *tactus*, fr *tactus*, pp of *tangere* to touch – more at [1]TANGENT] – **tactful** *adj*, **tactfully** *adv*, **tactfulness** *n*, **tactless** *adj*, **tactlessly** *adv*, **tactlessness** *n*

tactic /'taktik/ *n* **1** a method of employing forces in combat **2** a device for achieving an end [NL *tactica*, fr Gk *taktikē*, fr fem of *taktikos*]

tactical /'taktikl/ *adj* **1a** involving operations of local importance or brief duration **b** of or designed for air attack in close support of friendly ground forces **2a** of small-scale actions serving a wider aim – compare STRATEGIC **b** characterized by adroit planning or manoeuvring to accomplish an end – **tactically** *adv*

tactician /tak'tish(ə)n/ *n* sby skilled in tactics

tactics /'taktiks/ *n pl but sing or pl in constr* **1a** the science and art of disposing and manoeuvring forces in combat – compare STRATEGY **b** the art or skill of employing available means to accomplish an end **2** a system or mode of procedure [NL *tactica*, pl, fr Gk *taktika*, fr neut pl of *taktikos* of order, of tactics, fit for arranging, fr *tassein* to arrange, place in battle formation; akin to Lith pa*togus* comfortable]

tactile /'taktiel/ *adj* of or perceptible by (the sense of) touch [F or L; F, fr L *tactilis*, fr *tactus*, pp of *tangere* to touch – more at [1]TANGENT] – **tactilely** *adv*, **tactility** /-'tiləti/ *n*

tactual /'takchooəl, -chəl/ *adj* tactile [L *tactus* sense of touch – more at TACT] – **tactually** *adv*

tadpole /'tad,pohl/ *n* the larva of an amphibian; *specif* a frog or toad larva with a rounded body, a long tail, and external gills ☞ LIFE CYCLE [ME *taddepol*, fr *tode* toad + *polle* head – more at [1]POLL]

taenia /'teenyə, -ni·ə/ *n, pl* **taeniae** /-ni,ee/, **taenias** **1** a band of nervous tissue or muscle **2** any of numerous tapeworms [L, fr Gk *tainia*; akin to Gk *teinein* to stretch – more at THIN]

taffeta /'tafitə/ *n* a crisp plain-woven lustrous fabric of various fibres used esp for women's clothing [ME, fr MF *taffetas*, fr OIt *taffettà*, fr Turk *tafta*, fr Per *tāftah* woven]

taffrail /'taf,rayl, 'tafrəl/ *n* a rail round the stern of a ship [modif of D *tafereel*, fr MD, picture, fr OF *tablel*, dim. of *table*]

taffy /'tafi/ *n, NAm* a porous and light-coloured toffee [origin unknown]

Taffy *n, Br* a Welshman – chiefly derog [modif of W *Dafydd* David, a common Welsh forename]

[1]**tag** /tag/ *n* **1** a loose hanging piece of torn cloth **2** a rigid binding on an end of a shoelace **3** a piece of hanging or attached material; *specif* a flap on a garment that carries information (e g washing instructions) **4a** a trite quotation used for rhetorical effect **b** a recurrent or characteristic verbal expression **c** a final speech or line (e g in a play) usu serving to clarify a point or create a dramatic effect **5** a marker of plastic, metal, etc used for identification or classification [ME *tagge*, prob of Scand origin; akin to Sw *tagg* barb]

[2]**tag** *vb* **-gg-** *vt* **1a** to provide with an identifying marker **b** to label, brand ⟨*had him* ~ged *as a chauvinist from the start*⟩ **2** to attach, append **3** LABEL 2 ~ *vi* to follow closely ⟨~ging *along behind*⟩

[3]**tag** *n* a game in which one player chases others and tries to make one of them it by touching him/her [origin unknown]

[4]**tag** *vt* **-gg-** to touch (as if) in a game of tag

Tagalog /tə'gahləg/ *n, pl* **Tagalogs**, *esp collectively* **Tagalog** **1** a member of a people of central Luzon in the Philippines **2** an Austronesian language of the Tagalog people ☞ LANGUAGE

tag day *n, NAm* FLAG DAY

tagetes /'tajitəs/ *n, pl* **tagetes** the marigold [NL, genus name]

tagliatelle /,talyə'teli/ *n pl* narrow ribbons of egg-enriched pasta [It, pl of *tagliatella*, deriv of *tagliare* to cut, fr LL *taliare* – more at TAILOR]

tahini /tah'heeni/ *n* a thick oily paste made from sesame seeds [Ar *ṭaḥīna*]

Tahitian /tah'heesh(ə)n/ *n* **1** a native or inhabitant of Tahiti **2** the Polynesian language of the Tahitians ☞ LANGUAGE [*Tahiti*, island in the S Pacific] – **Tahitian** *adj*

tahr /tah/ *n* a thar

tahsildar /tah'seeldah/ *n* a collector of revenues in India [Hindi *taḥṣīldār*]

Tai /tie/ *n, pl* **Tai** a member of a group of peoples of SE Asia

taiga /'tiegə/ *n* moist coniferous forest that begins where the tundra ends and is dominated by spruces and firs ☞ PLANT [Russ *taĭga*]

[1]**tail** /tayl/ *n* **1** (an extension or prolongation of) the rear end of the body of an animal **2** sthg resembling an animal's tail in shape or position ⟨*the* ~ *of a comet*⟩ **3** *pl* a tailcoat; *broadly* formal evening dress for men including a tailcoat and a white bow tie **4** the last, rear, or lower part of sthg **5** the reverse of a coin – usu pl with sing. meaning ⟨~s, *you lose*⟩; compare HEAD 3 **6** *sing or pl in constr* the group of relatively inexpert batsmen who bat towards the end of a side's innings **7** the stabilizing assembly (e g fin, rudder, and tailplane) at the rear of an aircraft **8** sby who follows or keeps watch on sby – infml **9** the trail of a fugitive ⟨*had the police on her* ~⟩ – infml **10a** women as sexual objects – vulg **b** *NAm* the buttocks – slang [ME, fr OE *tægel*; akin to OHG *zagal* tail, OIr *dūal* lock of hair] – **tailed** *adj*, **tailless** *adj*, **taillike** *adj*

[2]**tail** *vt* **1** to connect at an end or end to end **2a** to remove the tail of (an animal) **b** to remove the stalk of (e g a gooseberry) – compare TOP 1b **3** to fasten an end of (a tile, brick, or timber) into a wall or other support **4** to follow for purposes of surveillance – infml ~ *vi* **1** to diminish gradually in strength, volume, quantity, etc – usu + *off* or *away* **2** to follow closely

[3]**tail** *adj* entailed [ME *taille*, fr AF *taylé*, fr OF *taillié*, pp of *taillier* to cut, limit – more at TAILOR]

[4]**tail** *n* ENTAIL 1 – often in *in tail*

'tail,back /-,bak/ *n* a long queue of motor vehicles, esp when caused by an obstruction that blocks the road

'tail,board /-,bawd/ *n* a hinged or removable board or gate at the rear of a vehicle

'tail,coat /-,koht/ *n* a coat with tails; *esp* a man's formal evening coat with 2 long tapering skirts at the back – **tailcoated** *adj*

tail end *n* **1** the back or rear end **2** the concluding period

'tail,ender /-,endə/ *n* a relatively inexpert batsman who bats towards the end of a side's innings

[1]**'tail,gate** /-,gayt/ *n* a tailboard

[2]**tailgate** *vi* to drive dangerously close behind another vehicle

tailing /'tayling/ *n* residue separated in the preparation of grain, ore, etc – usu pl with sing. meaning

[1]**tailor** /'taylə/, *fem* **tailoress** /,taylə'res, '--,-/ *n* sby whose occupation is making or altering esp men's garments [ME *taillour*, fr OF *tailleur*, fr *taillier* to cut, fr LL *taliare*, fr L *talea* twig, cutting; akin to Gk *tēlis* fenugreek]

[2]**tailor** *vi* to do the work of a tailor ~ *vt* **1a** to make or fashion as the work of a tailor; *specif* to cut and stitch (a garment) so that it will hang and fit well **b** to make or adapt to suit a special need or purpose **2** to style with trim straight lines and finished handwork

tailored /'tayləd/ *adj* **1** made by a tailor **2** fashioned or fitted to resemble a tailor's work; *specif* cut so as to fit the figure well

tailoring /'tayləring/ *n* **1** the business or occupation of a tailor **2** the work or workmanship of a tailor

,tailor-'made *adj* made or fitted for a particular use or purpose

'tail,piece /-,pees/ *n* **1** a piece added at the end; an appendage **2** a triangular piece from which the strings of a stringed instrument are stretched to the pegs **3** an ornament placed below the text on a page (e g at the end of a chapter)

'tail;pipe /-,piep/ *n* the part of a jet engine that carries the exhaust gases rearwards and discharges them through an outlet

'tail,plane /-,playn/ *n* the horizontal stabilizing surfaces of an aircraft's tail

'tail,spin /-,spin/ *n* SPIN 2

'tail,stock /-,stok/ *n* an adjustable part of a lathe that holds the fixed spindle

tail wind *n* a wind having the same general direction as the course of an aircraft or ship

Taino /'tienoh/ *n* (the language of) an extinct Arawakan people of the Antilles and Bahamas

[1]**taint** /taynt/ *vt* **1** to touch or affect slightly with sthg bad ⟨*people* ~ed *with prejudice*⟩ **2** to affect with putrefaction; spoil **3** to contaminate morally; corrupt ~ *vi* to become affected with putrefaction; spoil [ME *tainten* to colour & *taynten* to attaint; ME *tainten*, fr AF *teinter*, fr MF *teint*, pp of *teindre*, fr L *tingere*; ME *taynten*, fr MF *ataint*, pp of *ataindre* – more at TINGE, ATTAIN]

[2]**taint** *n* a contaminating mark or influence – **taintless** *adj*

taipan /'tiepan/ *n* an extremely venomous snake of N Australia and the Pacific islands [native name in Australia]

Taiping /tie'ping/ *n* a supporter of a rebellion (1848–65) against the Manchu dynasty [Chin (Pek) *t'ai*[4] *ping*[2] peaceful]

taka /'tahkə, 'tahkah/ *n* ☞ *Bangladesh* at NATIONALITY [Bengali *ṭākā* rupee, fr Skt *ṭaṅka*, a stamped coin]

takahe /'tahkə,hee/ *n* a rare flightless New Zealand bird related to the rails [Maori]

[1]**take** /tayk/ *vb* **took** /took/; **taken** /'taykən/ *vt* **1a** to seize or capture physically ⟨took *1500 prisoners*⟩ **b** to get possession of (e g fish or game) by killing or capturing **c(1)** to capture and remove from play ⟨took *my pawn*⟩ **(2)** to win in a card game ⟨*able to* ~ *12 tricks with that hand*⟩ **2** to grasp, grip ⟨took *his arm and led him across the road*⟩ **3a** to catch or attack through a sudden effect ⟨~n *ill*⟩ **b** to surprise; come upon suddenly ⟨*her death* took *us by surprise*⟩ **c** to attract, delight ⟨*was quite* ~n *with him*⟩ **4a** to receive into one's body, esp through the mouth ⟨~ *medicine*⟩ **b** to eat or drink habitually ⟨*I don't* ~ *milk in my tea*⟩ **5a** to bring or receive into a relationship or connection ⟨*Mr Burton* took *us for French*⟩ ⟨took *her as his wife*⟩ **b** to copulate with (a passive partner) **6a** to acquire, borrow, or use without authority or right ⟨took *someone's hat by mistake*⟩ **b(1)** to pay to have (e g by contract or subscription) ⟨~ *a cottage for the summer*⟩ **(2)** to buy ⟨*the salesman persuaded him to* ~ *the estate car*⟩ **7a** to assume ⟨~ *shape*⟩ ⟨took *the name of Phillips*⟩ **b** to perform or conduct (e g a lesson) as a duty, task, or job ⟨*Miss Jones* ~s *Physics*⟩ **c** to commit oneself to ⟨~ *a vow*⟩ ⟨~ *a decision*⟩ **d** to involve oneself in ⟨~ *the trouble to learn Chinese*⟩ **e** to consider or adopt as a point of view ⟨~ *a more lenient view*⟩ ⟨~ *Shakespeare, now*⟩ **f** to claim as rightfully one's own ⟨~ *the credit*⟩ ⟨~ *the liberty of refusing*⟩ **8** to obtain by competition ⟨took *third place*⟩ **9** to pick out; choose ⟨~ *any card*⟩ **10** to adopt or avail oneself of for use ⟨~ *an opportunity*⟩: e g **a** to have recourse to as an instrument for doing sthg ⟨~ *a scythe to the weeds*⟩ **b** to use as a means of transport or progression ⟨~ *a plane to Paris*⟩ ⟨~ *the third turning on the right*⟩ **c(1)** to turn to for safety or refuge ⟨~ *cover*⟩ **(2)** to proceed to occupy or hold ⟨~ *a seat*⟩ ⟨~ *office*⟩ **d(1)** to need, require ⟨~s *a long time to dry*⟩ ⟨*that* ~s *some believing*⟩ ⟨~s *a size 9*⟩ **(2)** to govern ⟨*transitive verbs* ~ *an object*⟩ **11a** to derive, draw ⟨~s *its title from the name of the hero*⟩ **b(1)** to obtain or ascertain by testing, measuring, etc ⟨~ *his temperature*⟩ **(2)** to record in writing; WRITE DOWN 1 ⟨~ *notes*⟩ **(3)** to get or record by photography ⟨~ *some slides*⟩ ⟨~ *the children in their party clothes*⟩ **(4)** to get by transference from one surface to another ⟨~ *fingerprints*⟩ **12** to receive or accept either willingly or reluctantly ⟨~ *a bribe*⟩ ⟨~ *a risk*⟩: e g **a** to receive when bestowed or tendered ⟨~ *a degree*⟩ **b(1)** to endure, undergo ⟨took *a terrible beating*⟩ ⟨*can't* ~ *it any longer*⟩ **(2)** to support, withstand ⟨*won't* ~ *my weight*⟩ ⟨*I can* ~ *a lot of Mozart*⟩ **c(1)** to accept as true; believe ⟨took *her word for it*⟩ ⟨~ *it from me*⟩ **(2)** to follow ⟨~ *my advice*⟩ **(3)** to respond to in a specified way ⟨~ *things as they come*⟩ ⟨~ *the news calmly*⟩ **d** to indulge in and enjoy ⟨~ *one's ease*⟩ ⟨~ *a holiday*⟩ **e** to accept in payment, compensation, or recompense ⟨*they won't* ~ *dollars*⟩ **13a** to accommodate ⟨*the suitcase wouldn't* ~ *another thing*⟩ **b** to be affected injuriously by (e g a disease) ⟨~ *cold*⟩ **14a** to apprehend, understand ⟨*slow to* ~ *his meaning*⟩ **b** to look upon; consider ⟨~ *it as settled*⟩ **c** to feel, experience ⟨~ *pleasure*⟩ **15a** to lead, carry, or remove with one to another place ⟨~ *her a cup of tea*⟩ **b** to require or cause to go ⟨*her ability will* ~ *her to the top*⟩ **16a** to obtain by removing ⟨~ *eggs from a nest*⟩ **b** to subtract ⟨~ *2 from 4*⟩ **17** to undertake and make, do, or perform ⟨~ *a walk*⟩ ⟨~ *legal action*⟩ ⟨~ *one's revenge*⟩ **18a** to deal with ⟨~ *the comments one at a time*⟩ **b** to consider or view in a specified relation ⟨~n *together, the details were significant*⟩ **c** to apply oneself to the study of or undergo examination in ⟨~ *music lessons*⟩ ⟨~ *6 subjects at O Level*⟩ **d** to succeed in passing or surmounting ⟨*the horse* took *the fence easily*⟩ **19** to cheat, swindle ⟨*was* ~n *for £5000 by a con man*⟩ **20** to remove by death – euph ⟨*was* ~n *in his prime*⟩ ~ *vi* **1a** to receive property in law **b** *of a fish* to receive a lure or bait **2a** to have the natural or intended effect or reaction ⟨*did your vaccination* ~*?*⟩ ⟨*glue that* ~s *well on cloth*⟩ **b** to begin to grow; strike root ⟨*have the seeds* ~n *yet?*⟩ **3a** to be adversely affected as specified ⟨took *ill*⟩ **b** to be capable of being moved in a specified way ⟨*the table* ~s *apart for packing*⟩ **c** to admit of being photographed **4** *chiefly dial* – used as an intensifier or redundantly with a following verb ⟨took *and ducked her in the pond*⟩ [ME *taken*, fr OE *tacan*, fr ON *taka*: akin to MD *taken* to take] – **taker** *n* – **take account of** TAKE INTO ACCOUNT – **take action 1** to begin to act **2** to begin legal proceedings – **take advantage of 1** to use to advantage; profit by **2** to impose upon; exploit – **take after** to resemble (an older relative) in appearance, character, or aptitudes – **take against** *chiefly Br* to take sides against; come to dislike – **take apart 1** to disassemble, dismantle **2** to analyse, dissect **3** to treat roughly or harshly – infml – **take as read** to accept as axiomatic – **take**

a toss to fall off a horse – **take care** to be careful; exercise caution or prudence; be watchful – **take care of** to attend to or provide for the needs, operation, or treatment of – **take charge** to assume care, custody, command, or control – **take effect** 1 to become operative 2 to produce a result – **take exception** to object, demur ⟨took exception *to his critic's remarks*⟩ – **take five** to take a brief intermission – infml – **take for** to suppose, esp mistakenly, to be – **take for a ride** to deceive wilfully; hoodwink – infml – **take for granted** 1 to assume as true, real, or certain to occur 2 to value too lightly – **take from** to detract from ⟨*irritations that* took from *their general satisfaction*⟩ – **take heart** to gain courage or confidence – **take hold** 1 to grasp, grip, seize 2 to become attached or established; TAKE EFFECT – **take in good part** to accept without offence – **take in hand** to embark on the control or reform of – **take into account** to make allowances for ⟨took *the boy's age* into account⟩ – **take into consideration** TAKE INTO ACCOUNT; *specif* to take account of (additional offences admitted by a defendant) so that the sentence to be imposed will preclude any chance of subsequent prosecution ⟨*Smith asked for 21 other offences to be* taken into consideration⟩ – **take into one's head** to conceive as a sudden notion or resolve – **take in vain** to use (a name) profanely or without proper respect – **take it upon oneself** to venture, presume – **take offence** to be offended – **take on board** *Br* to apprehend fully; grasp – infml – **take one all one's time** *Br* to be the utmost one can manage ⟨*it* takes me all my time *to afford shoes for them all*⟩ – **take one's leave** to bid farewell – often + *of* – **take one's time** to be leisurely about doing sthg – **take part** to join, participate, share – **take place** to happen; COME ABOUT – **take root** 1 to become rooted 2 to become fixed or established – **take silk** to become a Queen's or King's Counsel – **take someone at his/her word** to believe sby literally – **take someone out of him-/herself** to provide sby with needful diversion – **take someone to task** to rebuke or scold sby – **take stock** 1 to make an inventory 2 to make an assessment – **take the biscuit** *Br* to be the most astonishing or preposterous thing heard of or seen, esp concerning a particular issue – infml – **take the field** 1 to go onto the playing field 2 to enter on a military campaign – **take the floor** 1 to rise (e g in a meeting) to make a formal address 2 to begin dancing – **take the gilt off the gingerbread** to take away the part that makes the whole attractive – **take the law into one's own hands** to seek redress by force – **take the mickey** to behave disrespectfully; mock – infml – **take the wind out of someone's sails** to frustrate sby by anticipating or forestalling him/her – **take the words out of someone's mouth** to utter the exact words about to be used by sby – **take to** 1 to betake oneself to, esp for refuge ⟨take to *the woods*⟩ 2 to apply or devote oneself to (e g a practice, habit or occupation) ⟨take to *begging*⟩ 3 to adapt oneself to; respond to ⟨takes to *water like a duck*⟩ 4 to conceive a liking or affectionate concern for – **take to heart** to be deeply affected by – **take to one's heels** to run away; flee – **take to task** to call to account for a shortcoming – **take to the cleaners** *Br* 1 to rob, defraud – infml 2 to criticize harshly – infml – **take turns, take it in turns** to act by turns – **what it takes** the qualities or resources needed for success or for attainment of a goal

[2]**take** *n* **1a** the action of killing or catching sthg (e g game or fish) **b** the uninterrupted recording, filming, or televising of sthg (e g a gramophone record or film sequence); *also* the recording or scene produced **2a** proceeds, takings **b** a share, cut ⟨*wanted a bigger* ~⟩ **c** the number or quantity (e g of animals or fish) taken at 1 time

takeaway /ˈtaykə,way/ *n, Br* **1** a cooked meal that is eaten away from the premises from which it was bought ⟨*a Chinese* ~ *for supper*⟩ **2** a shop or restaurant that sells takeaways

take back *vt* to retract, withdraw

take down *vt* **1** to pull to pieces **2** WRITE DOWN **3** to lower without removing ⟨took down *his trousers*⟩

take-home pay *n* the part of gross salary or wages remaining after deductions (e g for income tax)

take in *vt* **1a** to furl **b** to make (a garment) smaller (e g by altering the positions of the seams or making tucks) – compare LET OUT **2** to offer accommodation or shelter to **3** to receive (paid work) into one's house ⟨take in *washing*⟩ **4** to include ⟨*the holiday* took in *Venice*⟩ **5** to perceive, understand **6** to deceive, trick – infml

taken /ˈtaykən/ *past part of* TAKE

ˈ**take,off** /-,of/ *n* **1** an imitation; *esp* a caricature **2** an act of leaving or a rise from a surface (e g in making a jump, dive, or flight or in the launching of a rocket) **3** a starting point; a point at which one takes off

take off *vt* **1** to remove ⟨take *your shoes* off⟩ **2a** to release ⟨take *the brake* off⟩ **b** to discontinue, withdraw ⟨took off *the morning train*⟩ **c** to deduct ⟨took *10 per cent* off⟩ **3** to take or spend (a period of time) as a holiday, rest, etc **4** to mimic ⟨*mannerisms that her critics delighted in* taking off⟩ ~ *vi* **1** to start off or away; SET OUT ⟨took off *without delay*⟩ **2** to begin a leap or spring **3** to leave the surface; begin flight

take on *vt* **1a** to agree to undertake ⟨took on *new responsibilities*⟩ **b** to contend with as an opponent ⟨took on *the neighbourhood bully*⟩ **2** to engage, hire **3** to assume or acquire (e g an appearance or quality) ⟨*the city* takes on *a carnival air*⟩ ~ *vi* to become emotional or distraught – infml

take out *vt* **1a** to extract ⟨took *the appendix* out⟩ **b** to give vent to – usu + *on* ⟨take out *their frustrations on one another*⟩ **2** to escort or accompany in public **3a** to obtain officially or formally ⟨take out *a warrant*⟩ **b** to acquire (insurance) by making the necessary payment **4** to overcall (a bridge partner) in a different suit – **take it out on** to vent anger, vexation, or frustration on – **take it out of** **1** TAKE IT OUT ON **2** to fatigue, exhaust

ˈ**take,over** /-,ohvə/ *n* the action or an act of taking over; *esp* an act of gaining control of a business company by buying a majority of the shares – **take-over** *adj*

take over *vb* to assume control or possession (of) or responsibility (for) ⟨*military leaders* took over *the government*⟩

take up *vt* **1** to remove by lifting or pulling up ⟨*the council's* taking *the old tramlines* up⟩ **2** to receive internally or on the surface and hold ⟨*plants* take up *nutrients*⟩ **3a** to begin to engage in or study ⟨took up *Greek*⟩ ⟨*when did he* take up *sailing?*⟩ **b** to raise (a matter) for consideration ⟨took *her case* up *with a lawyer*⟩ **4** to occupy (e g space or time) entirely or exclusively ⟨*outside activities* took up *too much of his time*⟩ **5** to shorten (e g a garment) ⟨*will have to* take *that dress* up⟩ **6** to respond favourably to a bet, challenge, or proposal made by ⟨*I'll* take *you* up *on that*⟩ **7** to begin again or take over from another ⟨*she* took up *the story where she left off*⟩ ~ *vi* to begin again; resume – **take up the cudgels** to engage vigorously in a defence – **take up with** to begin to associate with; consort with

taking /'tayking/ *adj* attractive, captivating

takings /'taykingz/ *n pl* receipts, esp of money

¹tala /'tahlə/ *n* any of the ancient traditional rhythmic patterns of Indian music [Skt *tāla*, lit., hand-clapping]

²tala *n* ☞ *Western Samoa* at NATIONALITY [Samoan, fr E *dollar*]

talc /talk/ *n* **1** a soft usu greenish or greyish mineral consisting of a magnesium silicate **2** TALCUM POWDER [MF *talc* mica, fr ML *talk*, fr Ar *ṭalq*] – **talcose** /'talkohs/ *adj*

'talcum ,powder /'talkəm/ *n* a powder for toilet use consisting of perfumed talc [ML *talcum* mica, alter. of earlier *talk*]

tale /tayl/ *n* **1** a series of events or facts told or presented; an account **2a** a usu fictitious narrative; a story **b** a lie, a falsehood **c** a malicious report or piece of gossip [ME, fr OE *talu*; akin to ON *tala* talk, & prob to L *dolus* guile, deceit, Gk *dolos*]

'tale,bearer /-,beərə/ *n* a telltale, gossip – **talebearing** *adj or n*

talent /'talənt/ *n* **1a** any of several ancient units of weight **b** a unit of money equal to the value of a talent of gold or silver **2a** a special often creative or artistic aptitude **b** general ability or intelligence **3** a person or people of talent in a field or activity **4** *sing or pl in constr* sexually attractive members of the opposite sex ⟨*sat eyeing up the local* ~⟩ – slang [ME, fr OE *talente*, fr L *talenta*, pl of *talentum* unit of weight or money, fr Gk *talanton*; akin to L *tollere* to lift up – more at TOLERATE; (2–4) fr the parable of the talents in Mt 25:14–30] – **talented** *adj*, **talentless** *adj*

'talent ,scout *n* a person engaged in discovering and recruiting people with talent in a specialized field of activity

'talent ,show *n* a show consisting of a series of individual performances by amateurs who may be selected for training or professional engagements if talented

taler /'tahlə/ *n* any of numerous silver coins issued by various German states from the 15th to the 19th c [G – more at DOLLAR]

talipes /'talipeez/ *n* clubfoot [NL, fr L *talus* ankle + *pes* foot – more at FOOT]

talipot /'talipot/ *n* a tall showy palm,found esp in India, which has huge fan-shaped leaves used as umbrellas, fans, etc [Bengali *tālipōt* palm leaf]

talisman /'talizmən/ *n, pl* **talismans** **1** an engraved object believed to act as a charm **2** sthg believed to produce magical or miraculous effects [F *talisman* or Sp *talismán* or It *talismano*, fr Ar *ṭilsam*, fr MGk *telesma*, fr Gk, consecration, fr *telein* to initiate into the mysteries, complete, fr *telos* end – more at WHEEL] – **talismanic** /-'manik/ *adj* **talismanically** *adv*

¹talk /tawk/ *vt* **1** to express in speech; utter ⟨~ *nonsense*⟩ **2** to make the subject of conversation; discuss ⟨~ *business*⟩ **3** to bring to a specified state by talking; *esp* to persuade by talking ⟨~ed *them into agreeing*⟩ **4** to use (a language) for conversing or communicating ⟨~ *French*⟩ ~ *vi* **1** to express or exchange ideas verbally or by other means ⟨~ed *till daybreak*⟩ ⟨*they* ~ed *by using sign language*⟩ **2** to use speech; speak **3** to imitate human speech ⟨*her budgie can* ~⟩ **4a** to gossip ⟨*you know how people* ~⟩ **b** to reveal secret or confidential information ⟨*we have ways of making you* ~⟩ **5** to give a talk or lecture [ME *talken*; akin to OE *talu* tale] – **talker** *n* – **talk shop** to talk about one's job, esp outside working hours – **talk through one's hat** to voice irrational, or erroneous ideas, esp in attempting to appear knowledgeable – **talk turkey** *chiefly NAm* to speak frankly or bluntly

²talk *n* **1** a verbal exchange of thoughts or opinions; a conversation **2** meaningless speech; verbiage ⟨*it's all* ~⟩ **3** a formal discussion or exchange of views – often pl with sing. meaning **4** (the topic of) interested comment or gossip ⟨*the* ~ *of the town*⟩ **5** an often informal address or lecture **6** communicative sounds or signs functioning as talk ⟨*baby* ~⟩

talkative /'tawkətiv/ *adj* given to talking – **talkatively** *adv*, **talkativeness** *n*

talk back *vi* to answer impertinently

talk down *vt* **1** to defeat or silence by argument or by loud talking **2** to radio instructions to (a pilot) to enable him/her to land when conditions are difficult ~ *vi* to speak in a condescending or oversimplified fashion *to*

talkie /'tawki/ *n* a film with a synchronized sound track [*talk* + *movie*]

talking picture /'tawking/ *n* a talkie

talking point *n* a subject of conversation or argument

talking shop *n* a place (e g a parliament) where matters are discussed, often with no useful outcome

'talking-,to *n* a reprimand, scolding

talk out *vt* to clarify or settle by discussion ⟨*tried to* talk out *their differences*⟩

talk over *vt* to review or consider in conversation

talk show *n* CHAT SHOW

tall /tawl/ *adj* **1a** of above average height ⟨*a* ~ *woman*⟩ ⟨~ *trees*⟩ **b** of a specified height ⟨*5 feet* ~⟩ **2** *of a plant* of a higher growing variety or species **3** unreasonably difficult to perform ⟨*a* ~ *order*⟩ **4** highly exaggerated; incredible ⟨*a* ~ *story*⟩ [ME, prob fr OE *getæl* quick, ready; akin to OHG *gizal* quick, OE *talu* tale] – **tall** *adv*, **tallish** *adj*, **tallness** *n*

tallboy /'tawl,boy/ *n* **1** a tall chest of drawers supported on a low legged base **2** a double chest of drawers usu with the upper section slightly smaller than the lower [*tall* + *boy*]

tallith /'talith, 'tahlith, -lis/ *n, pl* **tallithim** /,tahlə'seem, -'teem, -'theem/,**taleysim** /tə'laysim/ a shawl with fringed corners traditionally worn over the head or shoulders by Jewish men during morning prayers [Heb *ṭallīth* cover, cloak]

tallow /'taloh/ *n* the solid white rendered fat of cattle and sheep used chiefly in soap, candles, and lubricants [ME *talgh, talow*; akin to MD *talch* tallow] – **tallowy** *adj*

¹tally /'tali/ *n* **1** a device for visibly recording or accounting esp business transactions; *specif* a wooden rod notched with marks representing numbers and split lengthways through the notches so that each of 2 parties may have a record of a transaction **2a** a record or account (e g of items or charges) ⟨*keep a daily ~ of accidents*⟩ **b** a record of the score (e g in a game) **3** a part or person that corresponds to an opposite or companion object or member; a counterpart [ME *talye*, fr ML *talea, tallia*, fr L *talea* twig, cutting – more at TAILOR]

[2]**tally** *vb vt* **1a** to mark (as if) on a tally; tabulate **b** to list or check off (e g a cargo) by items **2** to make a count of ~ *vi* **1a** to make a tally (as if) by tabulating **b** to register a point in a contest **2** to correspond, match ⟨*their stories ~*⟩

tally-ho /ˌtali ˈhoh/ *n* a call of a huntsman at the sight of a fox [prob fr F *taïaut*, a cry used to urge hounds in deer hunting]

tallyman /ˈtalimən/ *n* **1** one who checks or keeps an account or record (e g of receipt of goods) **2** *Br* one who sells goods on credit; *also* one who calls to collect hire purchase payments

Talmud /ˈtalmood, ˈtahl-/ *n* the authoritative body of Jewish tradition comprising the Mishnah and Gemara [LHeb *talmūdh*, lit., instruction] – **talmudic** /-ˈmoohdik, -ˈmoodik, -ˈmudik/ *also* **talmudical** *adj, often cap*, **talmudism** *n, often cap*

Talmudist /ˈtalmoodist, ˈtahl-/ *n* a specialist in talmudic studies

talon /ˈtalən/ *n* a claw of an animal, esp a bird of prey [ME, fr MF, heel, spur, fr (assumed) VL *talon-, talo*, fr L *talus* ankle, anklebone] – **taloned** *adj*

[1]**talus** /ˈtayləs/ *n* a slope; *esp* one of rock debris at the base of a cliff [F, fr L *talutium* slope indicating presence of gold under the soil]

[2]**talus** *n, pl* **tali** /-lie/ **1** the astragalus of a vertebrate, esp a human being; the anklebone **2** the ankle joint formed from the talus, tibia, and fibula [NL, fr L]

tamandua /ˌtamənˈdooə, təˈmandoo·ə/ *n* a tree-dwelling anteater of central and S America [Pg *tamanduá*, fr Tupi]

tamarack /ˈtamərak/ *n* (the wood of) any of several N American larches [origin unknown]

tamarin /ˈtamərin/ *n* any of numerous small long-tailed S American marmosets with silky fur [F, fr Galibi]

tamarind /ˈtamərind/ *n* (a tropical leguminous tree with) a fruit with an acid pulp used for preserves or in a cooling laxative drink [Sp & Pg *tamarindo*, fr Ar *tamr hindī*, lit., Indian date]

tamarisk /ˈtamərisk/ *n* any of a genus of chiefly tropical or Mediterranean shrubs and trees having tiny narrow leaves and masses of minute flowers [ME *tamarisc*, fr LL *tamariscus*, fr L *tamaric-, tamarix*]

tambala /tahmˈbahlə/ *n, pl* **tambala, tambalas** ☞ *Malawi* at NATIONALITY [native name in Malawi, lit., cockerel]

[1]**tambour** /ˈtambooə/ *n* **1** [1]DRUM 1 **2** (embroidery made on) a frame consisting of a set of 2 interlocking hoops between which cloth is stretched before stitching **3** a rolling top or front (e g of a rolltop desk) consisting of narrow strips of wood glued on canvas [F, drum, fr Ar *ṭanbūr*, modif of Per *tabīr*]

[2]**tambour** *vt* to embroider (e g cloth) using a tambour – **tambourer** *n*

tamboura, tambura /tamˈbooərə/ *n* an Asian stringed musical instrument used to produce a drone accompaniment to singing [Per *ṭambūra*]

tambourine /ˌtambəˈreen/ *n* a shallow one-headed drum with loose metallic discs at the sides that is held in the hand and played by shaking, striking with the hand, or rubbing with the thumb [MF *tambourin*, dim. of *tambour*]

[1]**tame** /taym/ *adj* **1** changed from a state of native wildness, esp so as to be trainable and useful to human beings **2** made docile and submissive **3** lacking spirit, zest, or interest [ME, fr OE *tam*; akin to OHG *zam* tame, L *domare* to tame, Gk *damnanai*] – **tamely** *adv*, **tameness** *n*

[2]**tame** *vt* **1a** to make tame; domesticate **b** to subject to cultivation **2** to deprive of spirit; subdue – **tamable, tameable** *adj*, **tamer** *n*

Tamil /ˈtamil/ *n* **1** a language of S India and Sri Lanka ☞ LANGUAGE **2** a Tamil-speaking person

tamis /ˈtami, ˈtamis/ *n* a cloth sieve [F]

Tammany /ˈtaməni/ *adj, chiefly NAm* of or constituting a group exercising municipal political power by corruption and autocratic control [*Tammany Hall*, headquarters of the Tammany Society, political organization in New York City, USA] – **Tammanyism** *n*

tammy /ˈtami/ *n* a tam-o'-shanter [by shortening & alter.]

tam-o'-shanter /ˌtam ə ˈshantə/ *n* a round flat woollen or cloth cap of Scottish origin, with a tight headband, a full crown, and usu a pom-pom on top ☞ GARMENT [*Tam o' Shanter*, hero of the poem of that name by Robert Burns †1796 Sc poet]

tamp /tamp/ *vt* **1** to fill up (a drill hole above a blasting charge) with material (e g clay) to confine the force of the explosion **2** to drive in or down by a succession of light or medium blows – often + *down* [prob back-formation fr obs *tampion, tampin* (plug), fr ME, fr MF *tapon, tampon*, fr (assumed) OF *taper* to plug, of Gmc origin; akin to OE *tæppa* tap] – **tamper** *n*

tamper /ˈtampə/ *vi* **1** to carry on underhand or improper negotiations (e g by bribery) **2** to interfere or meddle without permission ⟨*the car lock had been ~ed with*⟩ *USE* usu + *with* [prob fr MF *temprer* to temper, mix, meddle – more at TEMPER] – **tamperer** *n*, **tamperproof** /-ˌproohf/ *adj*

tampion /ˈtampi·ən/ *n* a plug or cover for the muzzle of a gun [obs *tampion, tampin* (plug)]

tampon /ˈtampon/ *vt or n* (to plug with) an absorbent plug put into a cavity (e g the vagina) to absorb secretions, arrest bleeding, etc [n F, lit., plug – more at TAMP; vb fr n]

tam-tam /ˈtam ˌtam/ *n* a gong [Hindi *ṭamṭam*]

[1]**tan** /tan/ *vb* **-nn-** *vt* **1** to convert (hide) into leather, esp by treatment with an infusion of tannin-rich bark **2** to make (skin) tan-coloured, esp by exposure to the sun **3** to thrash, beat – infml ~ *vi* to get or become tanned [ME *tannen*, fr MF *tanner*, fr ML *tannare*, fr *tanum, tannum* tanbark] – **tan someone's hide** *or* **tan the hide off someone** to beat sby severely; THRASH 2a –infml

[2]**tan** *n* **1** a brown colour given to the skin by exposure to sun or wind **2** (a) light yellowish brown [F, tanbark, fr OF, fr ML *tanum*] – **tannish** *adj*

[3]**tan** *adj* of the colour tan

tanager /ˈtanəjə/ *n* any of numerous chiefly woodland American birds of which the males are brightly coloured [NL *tanagra*, fr Pg *tangará*, fr Tupi]

tanbark /'tan,bahk/ *n* a bark (e g of an oak) rich in tannin, bruised or cut into small pieces, and used in tanning

¹tandem /'tandəm/ *n* **1** (a 2-seat carriage drawn by) horses harnessed one before the other **2** a bicycle or tricycle having 2 or more seats one behind the other [L, at last, at length (taken to mean 'lengthwise'), fr *tam* so; akin to OE *thæt* that] – **in tandem 1** in a tandem arrangement **2** in partnership or conjunction

²tandem *adv* one behind the other ⟨*ride* ~⟩

tandoori /tan'dawri/ *n* (meat cooked, usu on a long spit, by) a N Indian method of cooking using a large clay oven [Hindi *tāndurī*, fr *tāndur* oven, fr Ar *tannūr*, fr Aram *tannūra*, fr Akkadian *tinūru*]

¹tang /tang/ *n* **1** a projecting shank or tongue (e g on a knife, file, or sword) that connects with and is enclosed by a handle **2a** a sharp distinctive flavour **b** a pungent or distinctive smell **3** a faint suggestion; a trace [ME, of Scand origin; akin to ON *tangi* point of land, tang] – **tanged** *adj*, **tangy** *adj*

²tang *n* any of various large coarse seaweeds [of Scand origin; akin to Dan & Norw *tang* seaweed]

Tang *n* a Chinese dynasty (AD 618 to 907) under which printing developed and poetry and art flourished [Chin (Pek) *t'ang²*]

tangelo /'tanjiloh/ *n, pl* **tangelos** (the fruit of) a cross between a tangerine or mandarin orange tree and a grapefruit tree [blend of *tangerine* and *pomelo* (grapefruit; deriv of D *pompelmoes* shaddock)]

¹tangent /'tangənt/ *adj* **1** touching a curve or surface at only 1 point ⟨*straight line* ~ *to a curve*⟩ **2** having a common tangent at a point ⟨~ *curves*⟩ [L *tangent-, tangens*, prp of *tangere* to touch; akin to OE *thaccian* to touch gently, stroke]

²tangent *n* **1** the trigonometric function that for an acute angle in a right-angled triangle is the ratio between the shorter sides opposite and adjacent to the angle **2** a straight line tangent to a curve **3** an upright flat-ended metal pin at the inner end of a clavichord key that strikes the string to produce the note ***USE*** *(1&2)* ☞ MATHEMATICS [NL *tangent-, tangens*, fr *linea tangens* tangent line] – **fly/go off at/on a tangent** to change suddenly from one subject, course of action, etc, to another

tangential /tan'jensh(ə)l/ *adj* **1** of (the nature of) a tangent **2** acting along or lying in a tangent ⟨~ *forces*⟩ **3a** divergent, digressive **b** incidental, peripheral – **tangentially** *adv*

tangerine /tanjə'reen/ *n* **1** (a tree that produces) any of various mandarin oranges with deep orange skin and pulp; *broadly* MANDARIN 3 **2** (a) bright reddish orange [F *Tanger* Tangier, city & port in Morocco]

tangible /'tanjəbl/ *adj* **1a** capable of being perceived, esp by the sense of touch **b** substantially real; material **2** capable of being appraised at an actual or approximate value ⟨~ *assets*⟩ [LL *tangibilis*, fr L *tangere* to touch] – **tangibleness** *n*, **tangibly** *adv*, **tangibility** /-'biləti/ *n*

¹tangle /'tang·gl/ *vb* **tangling** /'tang·gling, 'tang·gl·-ing/ *vt* **1** to involve so as to be trapped or hampered **2** to bring together or intertwine in disordered confusion ~ *vi* **1** to become tangled **2** to engage in conflict or argument – usu + *with*; infml [ME *tangilen*, prob of Scand origin; akin to Sw dial. *taggla* to tangle]

²tangle *n* **1** a confused twisted mass **2** a complicated or confused state

tango /'tang·goh/ *n, pl* **tangos** (the music for) a ballroom dance of Latin-American origin in 4/4 time, characterized by long pauses and stylized body positions [AmerSp] – **tango** *vi*

Tango – a communications code word for the letter *t*

tangram /'tang·grəm, -,gram/ *n* a Chinese puzzle made by cutting a square into 5 triangles, a square, and a rhomboid which can be recombined in many different figures [perh fr Chin (Pek) *t'ang²* Chinese + E *-gram*]

¹tank /tangk/ *n* **1** a large receptacle for holding, transporting, or storing liquids or gas **2** an enclosed heavily armed and armoured combat vehicle that moves on caterpillar tracks [Pg *tanque*, alter. of *estanque*, fr *estancar* to stanch, fr (assumed) VL *stanticare* – more at STANCH] – **tankful** *n*

²tank *vt* to place, store, or treat in a tank

tanka /'tangkə/ *n* (a poem in) an unrhymed Japanese verse form of 5 lines containing 5, 7, 5, 7, and 7 syllables respectively – compare HAIKU [Jap]

tankage /'tangkij/ *n* **1** the capacity or contents of a tank **2** (fees charged for) storage in tanks

tankard /'tangkəd/ *n* a tall one-handled drinking vessel; *esp* a silver or pewter mug with a lid [ME]

,tanked-'up *adj* DRUNK 1 – infml

tank engine *n* a steam locomotive that carries its own water and coal and does not have a tender

tanker /'tangkə/ *n* a ship, aircraft, or road or rail vehicle designed to carry fluid, esp liquid, in bulk (e g an aircraft used for transporting fuel and usu capable of refuelling other aircraft in flight)

'tank ,top *n* a sleeveless pullover with a U-shaped neckline, usu worn over a shirt or jumper

tanner /'tanə/ *n, Br* a coin worth 6 old pence – infml [origin unknown]

tannery /'tanəri/ *n* a place where tanning is carried out

tannic /'tanik/ *adj* of, resembling, or derived from tan or a tannin [F *tannique*, fr *tannin*]

,tannic 'acid *n* tannin

tannin /'tanin/ *n* any of various soluble astringent complex phenolic substances of plant origin used esp in tanning, dyeing, and making ink [F, fr *tanner* to tan]

tanning /'taning/ *n* a beating, thrashing – infml [¹TAN + ²-ING]

Tannoy /'tanoy/ *trademark* – used for a loudspeaker apparatus that broadcasts to the public, esp throughout a large building

tansy /'tanzi/ *n* an aromatic composite plant with finely divided leaves that is a common weed [ME *tanesey*, fr OF *tanesie*, fr ML *athanasia*, fr Gk, immortality, fr *athanatos* immortal, fr *a-* + *thanatos* death – more at THANATOS]

tantalite /'tantə,liet/ *n* a heavy dark lustrous mineral consisting mainly of iron and tantalum oxide [Sw *tantalit*, fr NL *tantalum*]

tantal·ize, -ise /'tantəliez/ *vt* to tease or frustrate by presenting sthg desirable that is just out of reach [*Tantalus*, mythical King of Phrygia condemned in Hades to stand up to his chin in water that receded whenever he stooped to drink and under branches of fruit that receded whenever he tried to eat, fr L, fr Gk *Tantalos*] – **tantalizer** *n*, **tantalizing** *adj*

tantalum /'tantələm/ *n* a hard acid-resistant metallic element of the vanadium family ☞ PERIODIC TABLE [NL, fr L *Tantalus*; fr its inability to absorb acid]

tantamount /ˈtantə,mownt/ *adj* equivalent in value, significance, or effect *to* [obs *tantamount*, n (equivalent), fr AF *tant amunter* to amount to as much]

tantara /ˈtantərə, tanˈtahrə/ *n* the blare of a trumpet or horn [L *taratantara*, of imit origin]

tantra /ˈtantrə, ˈtuntrə/ *n, often cap* **1** any of a body of later Hindu and Buddhist scriptures marked by mysticism and magic **2** the doctrine and cult deriving from the tantras, including the practice of Shaktism [Skt, lit., warp, fr *tanoti* he stretches, weaves; akin to Gk *teinein* to stretch – more at THIN] – **tantric** *adj, often cap*, **Tantrism** *n*, **Tantrist** *n*

tantrum /ˈtantrəm/ *n* a fit of childish bad temper [origin unknown]

tanyard /ˈtanyahd/ *n* the part of a tannery which houses tanning vats

Tao /tow/ *n* **1** the principle of creative harmony which the Taoists believe orders the universe **2** *often not cap* the path of virtuous conduct of Confucian doctrine [Chin (Pek) *tao*[4], lit., way]

Taoism /ˈtowiz(ə)m/ *n* a Chinese philosophy traditionally founded by Lao-tzu in the 6th c BC that teaches action in conformity with nature rather than striving against it; *also* a religion developed from this philosophy together with folk and Buddhist religion and concerned with obtaining long life and good fortune often by magical means [*Tao*] – **Taoist** *adj or n*, **Taoistic** /-ˈistik/ *adj*

[1]**tap** /tap/ *n* **1a** a plug designed to fit an opening, esp in a barrel **b** a device consisting of a spout and valve attached to a pipe, bowl, etc to control the flow of a fluid **2** a removal of fluid from a body cavity **3** a tool for forming an internal screw thread **4** the act or an instance of tapping a telephone, telegraph, etc; *also* an electronic listening device used to do this **5** a small piece of metal attached to the sole or heel of tap-dancing shoes [ME *tappe*, fr OE *tæppa*; akin to OHG *zapho* tap] – **on tap 1** *of beer* on draught **2** readily available

[2]**tap** *vt* **-pp- 1** to let out or cause to flow by piercing or by drawing a plug from the containing vessel **2a** to pierce so as to let out or draw off a fluid (e g from a body cavity) **b** to draw from or upon ⟨~ *new sources of revenue*⟩ **c** to connect an electronic listening device to (e g a telegraph or telephone wire), esp in order to acquire secret information **3** to form an internal screw thread in (e g a nut) by means of a special tool **4** to get money from as a loan or gift – infml – **tapper** *n*

[3]**tap** *vb* **-pp-** *vt* **1a** to strike lightly, esp with a slight sound **b** to produce by striking in this manner – often + *out* ⟨~ped *out a tune*⟩ **2** to give a light blow with ⟨~ *a pencil on the table*⟩ ~ *vi* to strike a light audible blow; rap [ME *tappen*, fr MF *taper* to strike with the flat of the hand, of Gmc origin; akin to MHG *tāpe* paw, blow dealt with the paw] – **tapper** *n*

[4]**tap** *n* **1** (the sound of) a light blow **2** any of several usu rapid drumbeats on a snare drum

tapa /ˈtahpə/ *n* the bark of the paper mulberry [Marquesan & Tahitian]

ˈ**tap ˌdance** *n* a step dance tapped out audibly by means of shoes with hard soles or soles and heels to which taps have been added – **tap-dance** *vi*, **tap dancer** *n*, **tap dancing** *n*

[1]**tape** /tayp/ *n* **1** a narrow band of woven fabric **2** *the* string stretched above the finishing line of a race **3** a narrow flexible strip or band; *esp* MAGNETIC TAPE **4** a tape recording [ME, fr OE *tæppe*]

[2]**tape** *vt* **1** to fasten, tie, or bind with tape **2** to record on tape, esp magnetic tape ⟨~ *an interview*⟩ ~ *vi* to record sthg on esp magnetic tape – **have someone/something taped** to have fully understood or learnt how to deal with sby or sthg – infml

ˈ**tape ˌdeck** *n* a mechanism or self-contained unit that causes magnetic tape to move past the heads of a magnetic recording device in order to generate electrical signals or to make a recording

ˈ**tape ˌmeasure** *n* a narrow strip (e g of a limp cloth or steel tape) marked off in units (e g inches or centimetres) for measuring

[1]**taper** /ˈtaypə/ *n* **1a** a slender candle **b** a long waxed wick used esp for lighting candles, fires, etc **2** gradual diminution of thickness, diameter, or width [ME, fr OE *tapor, taper*]

[2]**taper** *vb vi* **1** to decrease gradually in thickness, diameter, or width towards one end **2** to diminish gradually ⟨*his voice* ~ed *off*⟩ ~ *vt* to cause to taper

ˈ**tape-reˌcord** /riˌkawd/ *vt* to make a tape recording of [back-formation fr *tape recording*]

tape recorder *n* a device for recording signals, esp sounds, on magnetic tape and for subsequently reproducing them

tape recording *n* (a) recording on magnetic tape

tapestry /ˈtapəstri/ *n* **1** a heavy handwoven textile used for hangings, curtains, and upholstery, characterized by complicated pictorial designs **2** a machine-made imitation of tapestry used chiefly for upholstery [ME *tapistry*, modif of MF *tapisserie*, fr *tapisser* to carpet, cover with tapestry, fr OF *tapis* carpet, fr Gk *tapēs* rug, carpet] – **tapestried** /-strid/ *adj*

tapeworm /ˈtaypˌwuhm/ *n* any of numerous cestode worms, which when adult are parasitic in the intestine of human beings or other vertebrates [fr its shape]

tapioca /ˌtapiˈohkə/ *n* (a milk pudding made with) a usu granular preparation of cassava starch used esp in puddings and as a thickening in liquid food [Sp & Pg, fr Tupi *typyóca*]

tapir /ˈtaypə/ *n, pl* **tapirs**, *esp collectively* **tapir** any of several large chiefly nocturnal hoofed mammals with long snouts found in tropical America and Asia that are related to the horses and rhinoceroses [Tupi *tapiíra*]

tappet /ˈtapit/ *n* a lever or projection moved by or moving some other piece (e g a cam) [irreg fr [3]*tap*]

taproom /ˈtapˌroohm, -room/ *n* a barroom

ˈ**tapˌroot** /-ˌrooht/ *n* a main root of a plant that grows vertically downwards and gives off small side roots [[1]*tap*]

taps /taps/ *n pl but sing or pl in constr, chiefly NAm* the last bugle call at night, blown as a signal that lights are to be put out; *also* a similar call blown at military funerals and memorial services [prob alter. of earlier *taptoo* tattoo – more at [1]TATTOO]

tapster /ˈtapstə/ *n* sby employed to serve drinks in a bar

tapu /ˈtahpooh, -ˈ-/ *n or adj, NZ* (a) taboo [Maori]

[1]**tar** /tah/ *n* **1a** a dark bituminous usu strong-smelling

viscous liquid obtained by heating and distilling wood, coal, peat, etc **b** a residue present in smoke from burning tobacco that contains resins, acids, phenols, etc **2** a sailor – infml [ME *terr, tarr*, fr OE *teoru*; akin to OE *trēow* tree – more at TREE; (2) short for *tarpaulin*]

[2]**tar** *vt* **-rr-** to smear with tar – **tar and feather** to smear (a person) with tar and cover with feathers as a punishment or humiliation – **tarred with the same brush** having the same faults

taramasalata /ˌtarəməsəˈlahtə/ *n* a pinkish paste made from fish roe (e g grey mullet or smoked cod), olive oil, and seasoning, usu eaten as a starter [NGk *taramosalata*]

tarantella /ˌtarənˈtelə/ *n* (music suitable for) a vivacious folk dance of southern Italy in $\frac{6}{8}$ time [It, fr *Taranto*, city & port in Italy]

tarantism /ˈtarənˌtiz(ə)m/ *n* a nervous disease causing dancelike body movements which was prevalent in medieval Italy and popularly attributed to the bite of the tarantula [NL *tarantismus*, fr *Taranto*]

tarantula /təˈranchoolə/ *n, pl* **tarantulas** *also* **tarantulae** /-li/ **1** a European wolf spider formerly held to be the cause of tarantism **2** any of various large hairy spiders that can bite sharply but are not significantly poisonous to human beings [ML, fr OIt *tarantola*, fr *Taranto*]

tarboosh *also* **tarbush** /tahˈboohsh/ *n* a usu red hat similar to the fez worn esp by Muslim men [Ar *ṭarbūsh*]

tardigrade /ˈtahdiˌgrayd/ *n or adj* (any) of a division of microscopic arthropods that live usu in water or damp moss [deriv of L *tardigradus* slow-moving, fr *tardus* slow + *gradi* to step, go – more at GRADE]

tardy /ˈtahdi/ *adj* **1** moving or progressing slowly; sluggish **2** delayed beyond the expected time; late [alter. of earlier *tardif*, fr MF, fr (assumed) VL *tardivus*, fr L *tardus*] – **tardily** *adv*, **tardiness** *n*

[1]**tare** /teə/ *n* **1** any of several vetches **2** *pl* a weed found in cornfields which is usu held to be darnel – used in the Bible [ME]

[2]**tare** *n* **1a** the weight of the wrapping material or container in which goods are packed **b** a deduction from the gross weight of a substance and its container made in allowance for the weight of the container **2** the weight of an unloaded goods vehicle **3** a container used as a counterweight in calculating the net weight of goods [ME, fr MF, fr OIt *tara*, fr Ar *ṭarḥa*, lit., that which is removed]

[3]**tare** *vt* to weigh in order to determine the tare

target /ˈtahgit/ *n* **1** a small round shield **2a** an object to fire at in practice or competition; *esp* one consisting of a series of concentric circles with a bull's-eye at the centre **b** sthg (e g an aircraft or installation) fired at or attacked **3a** an object of ridicule, criticism, etc **b** a goal, objective **4** a body, surface, or material bombarded with nuclear particles or electrons, esp to produce X rays [ME, fr MF *targette*, dim. of *targe* light shield, of Gmc origin; akin to ON *targa* shield]

target practice *n* the act of shooting at a target to improve one's aim

[1]**tariff** /ˈtarif/ *n* **1** a duty or schedule of duties imposed by a government on imported or in some countries exported goods **2** a schedule of rates or prices [It *tariffa*, fr Ar *taʻrīf* notification]

[2]**tariff** *vt* to subject to a tariff

tarlatan /ˈtahlətən/ *n* a sheer cotton fabric in open plain weave usu heavily sized for stiffness [F *tarlatane*]

[1]**tarmac** /ˈtahmak/ *n* **1** tarmacadam **2** a runway, apron, or road made of tarmac

[2]**tarmac** *vt* to apply tarmac to

tarmacadam /ˌtahməˈkadəm/ *n* a mixture of tar and aggregates used for surfacing roads

tarn /tahn/ *n* a small mountain lake ☞ GEOGRAPHY [ME *tarne*, of Scand origin; akin to ON *tjörn* small lake; akin to OE *teran* to tear]

[1]**tarnish** /ˈtahnish/ *vt* **1** to dull the lustre of (as if) by dirt, air, etc **2a** to mar, spoil **b** to bring discredit on ~ *vi* to become tarnished [MF *terniss-*, stem of *ternir*] – **tarnishable** *adj*

[2]**tarnish** *n* a film of chemically altered material on the surface of a metal (e g silver)

taro /ˈtahroh/ *n, pl* **taros** (the edible starchy tuberous rootstock of) a tropical plant of the arum family [Tahitian & Maori]

tarot /ˈtaroh/ *n* any of a set of 78 pictorial playing cards, including 22 trumps, used esp for fortune-telling [MF, fr It *tarocchi* (pl)]

tarpan /ˈtahpan/ *n* an extinct wild brown horse of Central Asia [Russ]

tarpaulin /tahˈpawlin/ *n* (a piece of) heavy waterproof usu tarred canvas material used for protecting objects or ground exposed to the elements [prob fr [1]*tar* + *-palling, -pauling* (fr *pall*)]

tarragon /ˈtarəgən/ *n* (a small European wormwood with) pungent aromatic leaves used as a flavouring (e g in chicken dishes and vinegar) [MF *targon*, fr ML *tarchon*, fr Ar *ṭarkhūn*]

tarry /ˈtari/ *vi* **1** to delay or be slow in acting or doing **2** to stay in or at a place [ME *tarien*]

tarseal /ˈtahseel/ *n, NZ* tarmac – **tarsealed** *adj*

tarsia /ˈtahsi·ə/ *n* intarsia [It, fr Ar *tarṣīʻ*]

tarsier /ˈtahsi·ə/ *n* any of several small nocturnal tree-dwelling E Indian mammals related to the lemurs [F, fr *tarse* tarsus, fr NL *tarsus*]

tarsometatarsus /ˌtahsohˌmetəˈtahsis/ *n* (the limb segment supported by) the large compound bone of the tarsus of a bird [NL, fr *tarsus* + *-o-* + *metatarsus*]

tarsus /ˈtahsəs/ *n, pl* **tarsi** /-sie/ **1** (the small bones that support) the back part of the foot of a vertebrate that includes the ankle and heel ☞ ANATOMY **2** the part of the limb of an arthropod furthest from the body ☞ ANATOMY **3** the plate of dense connective tissue that stiffens the eyelid [NL, fr Gk *tarsos* wickerwork mat, flat of the foot, ankle, edge of the eyelid; akin to Gk *tersesthai* to become dry – more at THIRST] – **tarsal** *adj or n*

[1]**tart** /taht/ *adj* **1** agreeably sharp or acid to the taste **2** caustic, cutting ⟨*a ~ rejoinder*⟩ [ME, fr OE *teart* sharp, severe; akin to MHG *traz* spite] – **tartish** *adj*, **tartishly** *adv*, **tartly** *adv*, **tartness** *n*

[2]**tart** *n* **1** a pastry shell or shallow pie containing a usu sweet filling (e g jam or fruit) **2** a prostitute; *broadly* a sexually promiscuous girl or woman – infml [ME *tarte*, fr MF] – **tarty** *adj*, **tartiness** *n*, **tartlet** *n*

tartan /ˈtaht(ə)n/ *n* (a usu twilled woollen fabric with) a plaid textile design of Scottish origin consisting of checks of varying width and colour usu patterned to designate a distinctive clan [prob fr MF *tiretaine* linsey-woolsey]

[1]**tartar** /ˈtahtə/ *n* **1** a substance consisting essentially of cream of tartar that is derived from the juice of grapes and deposited in wine casks as a reddish crust

or sediment **2** an incrustation on the teeth consisting esp of calcium salts – compare PLAQUE [ME, fr ML *tartarum*]

[2]**tartar** *n* **1** *cap, NAm chiefly* **Tatar** a member of a group of people found mainly in the Tartar Republic of the USSR, the north Caucasus, Crimea, and parts of Siberia **2** *cap, NAm chiefly* **Tatar** the language of the Tartars **3** an irritable, formidable, or exacting person [ME *Tartre*, fr MF *Tartare*, prob fr ML *Tartarus*, modif of Per *Tātār*, of Turkic origin; akin to Turk *Tatar*] – **Tartar** *adj*, **Tartarian** /tah'tari·ən, -'teəri·ən/ *adj*

tartar emetic *n* a complex tartrate of antimony and potassium used in dyeing as a mordant and in medicine, esp in the treatment of schistosomiasis

tartaric acid /tah'tarik/ *n* a strong carboxylic acid from plants that is usu obtained from tartar, and is used esp in food and medicines

tartar sauce /'tahtə/, **tartare sauce** /~, 'tah,tah/ *n* mayonnaise with chopped pickles, olives, capers, and parsley [F *sauce tartare*]

tart up *vt, chiefly Br* to dress up, esp cheaply or gaudily – infml

Tarzan /'tahz(ə)n, 'tahzan/ *n* a strong, well-built, and agile man [*Tarzan*, hero of adventure stories by Edgar Rice Burroughs †1950 US author]

tash /tash/ *n, Br* a moustache – infml [by shortening & alter.]

task /tahsk/ *n* **1** an assigned piece of work; a duty **2** sthg hard or unpleasant that has to be done; a chore [ME *taske*, fr ONF *tasque*, fr ML *tasca* tax or service imposed by a feudal superior, fr *taxare* to tax]

'task ,force *n* a temporary grouping under 1 leader for the purpose of accomplishing a definite objective

'task,master /-,mahstə/ *n* one who assigns tasks ⟨*a hard* ~⟩

Tasmanian devil /taz'maynyən, -ni·ən/ *n* a powerful flesh-eating burrowing Tasmanian marsupial that is about the size of a badger and has a black coat marked with white [*Tasmania*, island off SE Australia]

Tasmanian wolf *n* a flesh-eating Tasmanian marsupial that somewhat resembles a dog

[1]**tassel** /'tasl/ *n* **1** a dangling ornament (e g for a curtain or bedspread) consisting of a bunch of cords or threads usu of even length fastened at 1 end **2** the tassel-like flower clusters of some plants, esp maize [ME, clasp, tassel, fr OF, fr (assumed) VL *tassellus*, fr L *taxillus* small die; akin to L *talus* anklebone, die]

[2]**tassel** *vb* **-ll-** (*NAm* **-l-**, **-ll-**), **tasselling** /'tasl·ing/ *vt* to decorate with tassels ~ *vi* to form tassel flower clusters

[1]**taste** /tayst/ *vt* **1** to experience, undergo ⟨*has* ~d *defeat*⟩ **2** to test the flavour of by taking a little into the mouth **3** to eat or drink, esp in small quantities ⟨*the first food she has* ~d *in 2 days*⟩ **4** to perceive or recognize (as if) by the sense of taste ⟨*could* ~ *the salt on his lips*⟩ ~ *vi* **1** to test the flavour of sthg by taking a little into the mouth **2** to have perception, experience, or enjoyment – usu + *of* **3** to have a specified flavour – often + *of* ⟨*the milk* ~s *sour*⟩ ⟨*this drink* ~s *of aniseed*⟩ [ME *tasten* to touch, test, taste, fr OF *taster*, fr (assumed) VL *taxitare*, freq of L *taxare* to touch – more at TAX]

[2]**taste** *n* **1a** the act of tasting **b** a small amount tasted **c** a first acquaintance or experience of sthg ⟨*her first* ~ *of success*⟩ **2** (the quality of a dissolved substance as perceived by) the 1 of the 5 basic physical senses by which the qualities of dissolved substances in contact with taste buds on the tongue are interpreted by the brain as 1 or a combination of the 4 basic taste sensations sweet, bitter, sour, or salt **3** individual preference; inclination **4** (a manner or quality indicative of) critical judgment or discernment esp in aesthetic or social matters ⟨*a remark in bad* ~⟩ ⟨*his choice in furnishing showed* ~⟩

'taste ,bud *n* any of the small organs, esp on the surface of the tongue, that receive and transmit the sensation of taste

'tasteful /-f(ə)l/ *adj* showing or conforming to good taste – **tastefully** *adv*, **tastefulness** *n*

'tasteless /-lis/ *adj* **1** having no taste; insipid **2** showing poor taste – disapproved of by some speakers – **tastelessly** *adv*, **tastelessness** *n*

taster /'taystə/ *n* sby who tests food or drink by tasting, esp in order to assess quality [[1]TASTE + [2]-ER]

tastevin /'tayst,vanh/ *n* a shallow metal cup used in testing wine [F *tâte-vin, taste-vin*, fr MF *taste vin* drunkard, cup for testing wine, fr *taster* to test, taste + *vin* wine, fr L *vinum*]

tasty /'taysti/ *adj* **1** having an appetizing flavour **2** arousing interest ⟨*a* ~ *bit of gossip*⟩ – infml – **tastily** *adv*, **tastiness** *n*

[1]**tat** /tat/ *vb* **-tt-** *vi* to work at tatting ~ *vt* to make by tatting [back-formation fr *tatting*]

[2]**tat** *n, Br* low quality material or goods – infml [back-formation fr *tatty*]

ta-ta /'tah ,tah/ *interj, chiefly Br* goodbye – infml [baby talk]

Tatar /'tahtə/ *n* (a) Tartar [Per *Tātār*, of Turkic origin; akin to Turk *Tatar*]

tatter /'tatə/ *n* **1** an irregular torn shred, esp of material **2** *pl* tattered clothing; rags [ME, of Scand origin; akin to ON *töturr* tatter; akin to OHG *zotta* matted hair, tuft] – **in tatters 1** torn in pieces; ragged **2** in disarray; useless

tattered /'tatəd/ *adj* (dressed in clothes which are) old and torn

tattie /'tati/ *n, dial* a potato [by shortening & alter.]

tatting /'tating/ *n* (the act or art of making) a delicate handmade lace formed usu by making loops and knots using a single cotton thread and a small shuttle [origin unknown]

[1]**tattle** /'tatl/ *vb* **tattling** /'tatling, 'tatl·ing/ *vi* to chatter, gossip ~ *vt* to disclose (e g secrets) by gossiping [MD *tatelen*; akin to ME *tateren* to tattle] – **tattler** *n*

[2]**tattle** *n* chatter, gossip

[1]**tattoo** /ta'tooh/ *n, pl* **tattoos 1a** an evening drum or bugle call sounded as notice to soldiers to return to quarters **b** an outdoor military display given by troops as a usu evening entertainment **2** a rapid rhythmic beating or rapping [alter. of earlier *taptoo*, fr D *taptoe*, fr the phrase *tap toe!* taps shut!]

[2]**tattoo** *n, pl* **tattoos** (an indelible mark made by) tattooing [Tahitian *tatau*]

[3]**tattoo** *vt* **1** to mark (the body) by inserting pigments under the skin **2** to mark (a design) on the body by tattooing – **tattooer** *n*, **tattooist** *n*

tatty /'tati/ *adj* shabby, dilapidated – infml [perh akin to OE *tætteca* rag, ON *töturr* tatter – more at TATTER]

tau /taw, tow/ *n* the 19th letter of the Greek alphabet [Gk, of Sem origin; akin to Heb *tāw*, 23rd letter of the Heb alphabet]

taught /tawt/ *past & past part of* TEACH

[1]**taunt** /tawnt/ *vt* to provoke in a mocking way; jeer at [perh fr MF *tenter* to try, tempt – more at TEMPT] – **taunter** *n*, **tauntingly** *adv*

[2]**taunt** *n* a sarcastic provocation or insult

taupe /tohp/ *n or adj* brownish grey [n F, lit., mole, fr L *talpa*; adj fr n]

taurine /'tawrien/ *adj* of or resembling a bull [L *taurinus*, fr *taurus* bull; akin to Gk *tauros* bull, MIr *tarb*]

Taurus /'tawrəs/ *n* (sby born under) the 2nd sign of the zodiac in astrology which is pictured as a bull ☞ SYMBOL [ME, fr L, lit., bull] – **Taurean** *adj or n*

taut /tawt/ *adj* **1a** tightly drawn; tensely stretched **b** showing anxiety; tense **2** kept in good order ⟨*a ~ ship*⟩ [ME *tought*] – **tautly** *adv*, **tautness** *n*

taut-, tauto- *comb form* same ⟨tauto*merism*⟩ ⟨tauto*nym*⟩ [LL, fr Gk, fr *tauto* the same, contr of *to auto*]

tauten /'tawt(ə)n/ *vb* to make or become taut

tautog /'tawtog/ *n* a N American food fish of the wrasse family [Narraganset *tautauog*, pl]

tautology /taw'toləji/ *n* **1** (an instance of) needless repetition of an idea, statement, or word **2** a statement that is true by virtue of its logical form; an analytic proposition [LL *tautologia*, fr Gk, fr *tautologos* tautologous, fr *taut-* + *legein* to say – more at LEGEND] – **tautological** /,tawtə'lojikl/, **tautologous** /taw'toləgəs/ *adj*, **tautologically**, **tautologously** /-gəsli/ *adv*

tautomer /'tawtəmə/ *n* any of the forms of a tautomeric compound [ISV, fr *tautomeric*]

tautomerism /taw'toməriz(ə)m/ *n* isomerism in which the isomers change into one another with great ease so that they ordinarily exist together in equilibrium – **tautomeric** /,tawtə'merik/ *adj*

tavern /'tavən/ *n* INN 1a, b [ME *taverne*, fr OF, fr L *taberna*, lit., shed, hut, shop, fr *trabs* beam]

[1]**taw** /taw/ *vt* to dress (skins), usu by a dry process (e g with alum or salt) [ME *tawen* to prepare for use, fr OE *tawian*; akin to L *bonus* good]

[2]**taw** *n* the line from which players shoot at marbles [origin unknown]

tawdry /'tawdri/ *adj* cheap and tastelessly showy in appearance [obs *tawdry lace* (necklace), alter. of *St Audrey's Lace*, fr *St Audrey* (Etheldreda) †679 Queen of Northumbria; fr its being orig sold at a fair commemorating St Audrey] – **tawdrily** *adv*, **tawdriness** *n*

tawny /'tawni/ *adj* of a warm sandy or brownish orange colour like that of well-tanned skin [ME, fr MF *tanné*, pp of *tanner* to tan] – **tawniness** *n*

tawny owl *n* a common brown European owl

tawse /tawz/ *n, chiefly Scot* a leather strap slit into strips at the end, used for beating children [prob fr *taws*, pl of obs *taw* (tawed leather)]

[1]**tax** /taks/ *vt* **1** to assess (legal costs) **2** to levy a tax on **3** to charge, accuse *with* **4** to make strenuous demands on [ME *taxen* to estimate, assess, tax, fr MF *taxer*, fr ML *taxare*, fr L, to feel, estimate, censure, freq of *tangere* to touch – more at [1]TANGENT] – **taxable** *adj*, **taxingly** *adv*, **taxer** *n*

[2]**tax** *n* **1** a charge, usu of money, imposed by a government on individuals, organizations, or property, esp to raise revenue **2** a heavy demand or strain – **after tax** net – **before tax** gross

tax-, taxo- *also* **taxi-** *comb form* arrangement ⟨taxeme⟩ ⟨taxi*dermy*⟩ [Gk *taxi-*, fr *taxis*]

taxa /'taksə/ *pl of* TAXON

taxation /tak'saysh(ə)n/ *n* **1** the action of taxing; *esp* the imposition of taxes **2** revenue obtained from taxes **3** the amount assessed as a tax

,tax-'free *adj* exempted from tax

'tax ,haven *n* a country with a relatively low level of taxation, esp on incomes

[1]**taxi** /'taksi/ *n, pl* **taxis** *also* **taxies** a taxicab

[2]**taxi** *vb* **taxis, taxies; taxiing, taxying; taxied** *vi* **1** to ride in a taxi **2** *of an aircraft* to go at low speed along the surface of the ground or water ~ *vt* **1** to transport by taxi **2** to cause (an aircraft) to taxi

'taxi,cab /-,kab/ *n* a motor car that may be hired, together with its driver, to carry passengers, the fare usu being calculated by a taximeter [*taxi*meter *cab*]

taxidermy /'taksi,duhmi/ *n* the art of preparing, stuffing, and mounting the skins of animals [*tax-* + *derm-* + *-y*] – **taxidermist** *n*, **taxidermic** /-'duhmik/ *adj*

taximeter /'taksi,meetə/ *n* a meter fitted in a taxi to calculate the charge for each journey, usu determined by the distance travelled [F *taximètre*, modif of G *taxameter*, fr ML *taxa* tax, charge (fr *taxare* to tax) + *-meter*]

taxis /'taksis/ *n, pl* **taxes** /-seez/ **1** the manual restoration of a displaced body part, esp a hernia, by pressure **2** (a reflex reaction involving) movement by a freely motile usu simple organism (e g a bacterium) towards or away from a source of stimulation (e g a light, or a temperature or chemical gradient) – compare TROPISM [Gk, lit., arrangement, order, fr *tassein* to arrange – more at TACTICS]

-taxis *comb form*, (→ *n*), *pl* **-taxes** **1** arrangement; order ⟨*homo*taxis⟩ ⟨*para*taxis⟩ **2** orientation or movement towards or in relation to (a specified force or agent) ⟨*chemo*taxis⟩ [NL, fr Gk, fr *taxis*] – **tactic** *comb form* (→ *adj*)

taxman /'taks,man/ *n* **1** an official who collects taxes **2** *Br the* Inland Revenue personified – infml

taxo- – see TAX-

taxon /'takson/ *n, pl* **taxa** /'taksə/ *also* **taxons** (the name of) a taxonomic group or entity [NL, back-formation fr ISV *taxonomy*]

taxonomy /tak'sonəmi/ *n* (the study of the principles of) classification, specif of plants and animals according to their presumed natural relationships [F *taxonomie*, fr *tax-* + *-nomie* -nomy] – **taxonomist** *n*, **taxonomic** /,taksə'nomik/ *adj*, **taxonomically** *adv*

'tax,payer /-,payə/ *n* one who pays or is liable for a tax

'tax,paying /-,paying/ *adj* of or subject to the paying of a tax

,tax re,turn *n* a formal statement, made to the Inland Revenue, of one's income and allowable deductions for tax purposes

TB *n* tuberculosis [*TB* (abbr for *tubercle bacillus*)]

'T-,bar *adj* having or being 2 straps that fasten a shoe so that 1 lies along the length of the upper foot and 1 circles the ankle to form the shape of a T ☞ GARMENT

'T-,bone, T-bone steak *n* a thick steak from the thin

end of a beef sirloin containing a T-shaped bone ☞ MEAT

TCP *trademark* – used for an aqueous antiseptic solution

t distribution *n* a probability density function that is used esp in testing hypotheses concerning means of normal distributions whose standard deviations are unknown

tea /tee/ *n* **1a** a shrub cultivated esp in China, Japan, and the E Indies **b** the leaves of the tea plant prepared for the market, classed according to method of manufacture (e g green tea or oolong), and graded according to leaf size (e g pekoe) **2** an aromatic beverage prepared from tea leaves by infusion with boiling water **3** any of various plants somewhat resembling tea in appearance or properties; *also* an infusion of their leaves used medicinally or as a beverage ⟨*chamomile* ~⟩ **4a** refreshments including tea with sandwiches, cakes, etc served in the late afternoon **b** a late-afternoon or early-evening meal that is usu less substantial than the midday meal – compare HIGH TEA [Chin (Amoy) *t'e*]

'tea ,bag *n* a cloth or filter paper bag holding enough tea for an individual serving when infused

tea ball *n* a perforated metal ball-shaped container that holds tea leaves and is used in brewing tea, esp in a cup

tea bread *n* any of various light often sweet breads or plain cakes

tea cake *n* a round yeast-leavened (sweet) bread bun that often contains currants and is usu eaten toasted with butter

teach /teech/ *vb* **taught** /tawt/ *vt* **1** to cause to know (how), esp by showing or instructing ⟨*is* ~ing *me to drive*⟩ **2** to guide the studies of **3** to impart the knowledge of ⟨~ *algebra*⟩ **4** to instruct by precept, example, or experience **5** to cause to suffer the usu disagreeable consequences of sthg – infml ⟨*I'll* ~ *you to come home late*⟩ ~ *vi* to provide instruction [ME *techen* to show, instruct, fr OE *tǣcan*; akin to OE *tācn* sign – more at TOKEN]

teachable /'teechəbl/ *adj* **1** capable of being taught **2** apt and willing to learn – **teachableness** *n*, **teachably** *adv*, **teachability** /-'biləti/ *n*

teacher /'teechə/ *n* sby whose occupation is teaching [TEACH + [2]-ER]

,teacher's 'pet *n* sby who ingratiates him/herself with an authority, esp a teacher

tea chest *n* a large square box used for exporting tea ⟨*stored her books in a* ~⟩

'teach-,in *n* **1** an informally structured conference on a usu topical issue **2** an extended meeting for lectures, demonstrations, and discussions on a topic [*teach* + *-in* (as in *sit-in*)]

teaching /'teeching/ *n* **1** the profession of a teacher **2** sthg taught; *esp* a doctrine ⟨*the* ~s *of Confucius*⟩

teaching aid *n* a device (e g a record player, map, or picture) used in teaching

teaching hospital *n* a hospital that is affiliated to a medical school and provides medical students with the opportunity of gaining practical experience under supervision

teaching machine *n* any of various mechanical devices for presenting instructional material

'tea ,cloth *n* **1** a small cloth for a table or trolley on which tea is to be served **2** TEA TOWEL

'tea,house /-,hows/ *n* a restaurant, esp in China or Japan, where tea and light refreshments are served

teak /teek/ *n* (a tall E Indian tree of the vervain family with) hard yellowish brown wood used for furniture and shipbuilding [Pg *teca*, fr Malayalam *tēkka*]

teal /teel/ *n, pl* **teals,** *esp collectively* **teal** (any of several ducks related to) a small Old World dabbling duck the male of which has a distinctive green and chestnut head [ME *tele*; akin to MD *teling* teal]

[1]team /teem/ *n* **1a** two or more draught animals harnessed together **b** one or more draught animals together with harness and vehicle **2** *sing or pl in constr* a group formed for work or activity: e g **a** a group on 1 side (e g in a sporting contest or debate) **b** a crew, gang [ME *teme*, fr OE *tēam* offspring, lineage, group of draught animals; akin to OE *tēon* to draw, pull]

[2]team *vt* **1** to yoke or join in a team **2** to combine so as to form a harmonizing arrangement ⟨~ *the shoes with the dress*⟩ ~ *vi* **1** to come together (as if) in a team – often + *up* ⟨*let's* ~ *up with them for a night out*⟩ **2** to form a harmonizing combination

team handball *n* a game played indoors between 2 teams of 7 players each, whose aim is to put the ball into a goal by throwing, catching, and dribbling it with the hands

team spirit *n* willingness to subordinate personal aims to group objectives

teamster /'teemstə/ *n* **1** sby who drives a team of horses **2** *NAm* a lorry driver

team teaching *n* a system whereby a group of teachers with various qualifications work with a large group of pupils

'team,work /-,wuhk/ *n* mutual cooperation in a group enterprise

teapot /'tee,pot/ *n* a usu round pot with a lid, spout, and handle in which tea is brewed and from which it is served

teapoy /'tee,poy/ *n* a 3-legged ornamental stand or table [Hindi *tipāī*]

[1]tear /tiə/ *n* **1** a drop of clear salty fluid secreted by the lachrymal gland that lubricates the eye and eyelids and is often shed as a result of grief or other emotion **2** a transparent drop of (hardened) fluid (e g resin) [ME, fr OE *tæhher, tēar*; akin to OHG *zahar* tear, L *dacruma, lacrima*, Gk *dakry*] – **tearless** *adj* – **in tears** crying, weeping

[2]tear /teə/ *vb* **tore** /taw/; **torn** /tawn/ *vt* **1a** to pull apart by force **b** to wound by tearing; lacerate **2** to cause division or distress to ⟨*a mind* torn *with doubts*⟩ **3** to remove by force ⟨tore *the child from him*⟩ **4** to make or effect (as if) by tearing ⟨~ *a hole in the paper*⟩ ~ *vi* **1** to separate on being pulled ⟨*this cloth* ~s *easily*⟩ **2** to move or act with violence, haste, or force ⟨*went* ~ing *down the street*⟩ [ME *teren*, fr OE *teran*; akin to OHG *zeran* to destroy, Gk *derein* to skin] – **tearer** *n* – **tear a strip off** to rebuke angrily – infml – **tear at** to cause distress or pain to ⟨tore at *my heartstrings to see her go*⟩ – **tear into** to attack physically or verbally without restraint or caution – **tear one's hair** to experience or express grief, rage, desperation, or anxiety

[3]tear /teə/ *n* **1** damage from being torn – chiefly in *wear and tear* **2** a hole or flaw made by tearing

tearaway /'teərə,way/ *n, Br* an unruly and reckless young person – infml

tear away *vt* to remove (oneself or another) reluctantly ⟨*she could hardly* tear *herself* away *from the book*⟩

tear down *vt* to pull down, esp violently; demolish

teardrop /ˈtiə,drop/ *n* [1]TEAR 1

ˈ**tearful** /-f(ə)l/ *adj* **1** flowing with or accompanied by tears ⟨~ *entreaties*⟩ **2** causing tears **3** inclined or about to cry ⟨*was feeling a bit* ~⟩ – **tearfully** *adv*, **tearfulness** *n*

tear gas /tiə/ *n* a solid, liquid, or gaseous substance that on dispersion in the atmosphere blinds the eyes with tears and is used chiefly in dispelling crowds

tearing /ˈteəring/ *adj* violent, precipitate ⟨*in a* ~ *hurry*⟩ – infml

tearjerker /ˈtiə,juhkə/ *n* an excessively sentimental play, film, etc designed to provoke tears – infml – **tear-jerking** *adj*

tearoom /ˈtee,roohm/ *n* a restaurant where light refreshments are served

tea rose *n* any of numerous hybrid garden roses with abundant large usu tea-scented blossoms

tear up /teə/ *vt* **1** to tear into pieces **2** to cancel or annul, usu unilaterally ⟨tore up *the treaty*⟩

[1]**tease** /teez/ *vt* **1** to disentangle and straighten by combing or carding ⟨~ *wool*⟩ **2a** to (attempt to) disturb or annoy by persistently irritating or provoking **b** to persuade to acquiesce, esp by persistent small efforts; coax; *also* to obtain by repeated coaxing ⟨~d *the money out of her father*⟩ ~ *vi* to tease sby or sthg [ME *tesen*, fr OE *tǣsan*; akin to OHG *zeisan* to tease] – **teasingly** *adv*

[2]**tease** *n* sby or sthg that teases

[1]**teasel, teazel, teazle** /ˈteezl/ *n* **1** (a flower head of) a tall Old World plant of the scabious family with flower heads that are covered with stiff hooked bracts and were formerly used, when dried to raise a nap on woollen cloth **2** a wire substitute for the teasel [ME *tesel*, fr OE *tǣsel*; akin to OE *tǣsan* to tease]

[2]**teasel** *vt* **-ll-** (*NAm*, **-l-**, **-ll-**), /ˈteezl·ing/ to nap (cloth) with teasels

teaser /ˈteezə/ *n* **1** a frustratingly difficult problem **2** sby who derives malicious pleasure from teasing [[1]TEASE + [2]-ER]

Teasmade /ˈteezmayd/ *trademark* – used for an electrical appliance that can be set to make a pot of tea at a specified time and sounds an alarm when the tea is ready

teaspoon /ˈtee,spoohn/ *n* **1** a small spoon used esp for eating soft foods and stirring beverages **2** a teaspoonful

ˈ**tea,spoonful** /-f(ə)l/ *n, pl* **teaspoonfuls** *also* **teaspoonsful** as much as a teaspoon will hold ☞ UNIT

teat /teet/ *n* **1** NIPPLE 1 **2** a small projection or a nib (e g on a mechanical part); *specif* a rubber mouthpiece with usu 2 or more holes in it, attached to the top of a baby's feeding bottle [ME *tete*, fr OF, of Gmc origin; akin to OE *tit* teat, MHG *zitze*] – **teated** *adj*

teatime /ˈtee,tiem/ *n* the customary time for tea; late afternoon or early evening

ˈ**tea ,towel** *n* a cloth for drying the dishes

ˈ**tea ,tray** *n* a tray on which a tea service is carried

ˈ**tea ,trolley** *n, chiefly Br* a small trolley used in serving tea or light refreshments

teazel, teazle /ˈteezl/ *n* a teasel

tec /tek/ *n* a detective – infml [by shortening]

tech /tek/ *n, Br* a technical school or college – infml

technetium /tekˈneesh(y)əm/ *n* an artificially produced metallic element ☞ PERIODIC TABLE [NL, fr Gk *technētos* artificial, fr *technasthai* to devise by art, fr *technē*]

technical /ˈteknikl/ *adj* **1a** having special and usu practical knowledge, esp of a mechanical or scientific subject **b** marked by or characteristic of specialization **2** of a particular subject; *esp* of a practical subject organized on scientific principles **3** in the strict legal interpretation **4** of technique **5** of or produced by ordinary commercial processes without being subjected to special purification [Gk *technikos* of art, skilful, fr *technē* art, craft, skill; akin to Gk *tektōn* builder, carpenter, L *texere* to weave, OHG *dahs* badger] – **technically** *adv*, **technicalness** *n*

technical college *n* any of a number of British regional institutions offering courses at a less advanced level than a polytechnic and with a bias towards the vocational

technicality /,tekniˈkaləti/ *n* sthg technical; *esp* a detail meaningful only to a specialist ⟨*a legal* ~⟩

technical knockout /ˈnok,owt/ *n* the termination of a boxing match when a boxer is declared by the referee to be unable (e g because of injuries) to continue the fight

technical school *n* a secondary school providing education with a technical or commercial bias for children from age 11 to 16 or 18

technical sergeant *n* ☞ RANK

technician /tekˈnish(ə)n/ *n* **1** a specialist in the technical details of a subject or occupation ⟨*a medical* ~⟩ **2** sby who has acquired the technique of an area of specialization (e g an art) ⟨*a superb* ~ *and an artist of ingenuity*⟩

Technicolor /ˈtekni,kulə/ *trademark* – used for a process of colour photography in the cinema in which the 3 primary colours are recorded on separate films and then combined in a single print

technicolour /ˈtekni,kulə/ *n* vivid and often garish colour – **technicoloured** *adj*

technique /tekˈneek/ *n* **1** the manner in which an artist, performer, or athlete displays or manages the formal aspect of his/her skill **2a** a body of technical methods (e g in a craft or in scientific research) **b** a method of accomplishing a desired aim [F, fr *technique* technical, fr Gk *technikos*]

techno- *comb form* technical; technological ⟨*technocracy*⟩ [Gk, fr *technē*]

technocracy /tekˈnokrəsi/ *n* (management of society by) a body of technical experts; *also* a society so managed – chiefly derog – **technocrat** /ˈteknəkrat/ *n*, **technocratic** /,teknəˈkratik/ *adj*

technology /tekˈnoləji/ *n* **1** (the theory and practice of) applied science **2** the totality of the means and knowledge used to provide objects necessary for human sustenance and comfort [Gk *technologia* systematic treatment of an art, fr *techno-* + *-logia* -logy] – **technologist** *n*, **technological** /,teknəˈlojikl/ *adj*, **technologically** *adv*

techy /ˈtechi/ *adj* tetchy

tectonic /tekˈtonik/ *adj* of tectonics: e g **a** architectural **b** of the (forces involved in or structures resulting from) deformation of the earth's crust [LL *tectonicus*, fr Gk *tektonikos* of a builder, fr *tektōn* builder – more at TECHNICAL] – **tectonically** *adv*

tec'tonics *n pl but sing or pl in constr* **1** the science or art of construction (e g of a building) **2** (a branch of geology concerned with) structural features, esp those connected with folding and faulting.

ted /ted/ *vt* **-dd-** to turn over and spread (e g new-mown grass) for drying [(assumed) ME *tedden*; akin to OHG *zetten* to spread, ON *tethja* to spread manure, Gk *daiesthai* to divide, distribute – more at TIDE] – **tedder** *n*

Ted *n* TEDDY BOY – infml

teddy /'tedi/ *n* TEDDY BEAR – used esp by or to children

'teddy ,bear *n* a stuffed toy bear [*Teddy*, nickname of *Theodore* Roosevelt †1919 US president; fr a cartoon depicting the president sparing the life of a bear cub while hunting]

'teddy ,boy *n* any of a cult of (British) youths, esp in the 1950s, adopting the dress of the early 20th c and often having a reputation for unruly behaviour [*Teddy*, nickname for *Edward*, i e King Edward VII †1910]

Te Deum /,tay 'dayəm, ,tee 'dee-/ *n, pl* **Te Deums** a liturgical Christian hymn of praise to God [ME, fr LL *te deum laudamus* thee, God, we praise; fr the opening words of the hymn]

tedious /'teedi·əs/ *adj* tiresome because of length or dullness [ME, fr LL *taediosus*, fr L *taedium*] – **tediously** *adv*, **tediousness** *n*

tedium /'teedi·əm/ *n* tediousness; *also* boredom [L *taedium* disgust, irksomeness, fr *taedēre* to disgust, weary]

[1]**tee** /tee/ *n* **1** sthg shaped like a capital T **2** a mark aimed at in various games (e g curling) [ME]

[2]**tee** *n* **1** a peg or a small mound used to raise a golf ball into position for striking at the beginning of play on a hole **2** the area from which a golf ball is struck at the beginning of play on a hole [back-formation fr obs *teaz* (taken as pl); perh akin to Icel *tjā* to show, mark]

[3]**tee** *vt* to place (a ball) on a tee – often + *up*

tee-hee /,tee 'hee/ *interj* – used to express amusement or derision [ME *te he*, of imit origin]

[1]**teem** /teem/ *vi* **1** to abound ⟨*lakes that ~ with fish*⟩ **2** to be present in large quantities [ME *temen*, fr OE *tīman*, *tǣman*; akin to OE *tēam* offspring – more at TEAM]

[2]**teem** *vi, Br* to rain hard [ME *temen* to empty, pour out, fr ON *tœma*; akin to OE *tōm* empty]

teen /teen/ *adj* teenage – infml

teenage /'teenayj/, **teenaged** /'teenayjd/ *adj* of or being people in their teens – **teenager** *n*

teens /teenz/ *n pl* the numbers 13 to 19 inclusive; *specif* the years 13 to 19 in a lifetime [*-teen* (as in *thirteen*)]

teensy /'teenzi, 'teensi/, **teensy-weensy** /,teenzi 'weenzi, ,teensi 'weensi/ *adj* tiny – infml [baby-talk alter. of *teeny (-weeny)*]

teeny /'teeni/, **teeny-weeny** /,teeni 'weeni/ *adj* tiny – infml [*teeny* by alter. (influenced by *weeny*)]

teenybopper /'teeni ,bopə/ *n* a young teenage girl who zealously follows the latest trends in clothes, pop music, etc [*teen* + [4]*-y* + *bopper*]

tee off /tee/ *vi* to drive a golf ball from a tee

teepee /'tee,pee/ *n* a tepee

'tee ,shirt *n* a T-shirt

teeter /'teetə/ *vi* to move unsteadily; wobble, waver [ME *titeren* to totter, reel; akin to OHG *zittarōn* to shiver, Gk *dramein* to run, Skt *drāti* he runs]

teeth /teeth/ *pl of* TOOTH

teethe /teedh/ *vi* to cut one's teeth; grow teeth [back-formation fr *teething*] – **teething** *n*

'teething ,ring /'teedhing/ *n* a usu plastic ring for a teething infant to bite on

'teething ,troubles *n pl* temporary problems occurring with new machinery or during the initial stages of an activity

teetotal /tee'tohtl/ *adj* practising complete abstinence from alcoholic drinks [*total* + *total* (abstinence)] – **teetotalism** *n*

teetotaller /tee'tohtl·ə/, *NAm chiefly* **teetotaler** *n* sby teetotal

teetotum /,tee'tohtəm/ *n* a small top, usu inscribed with letters and used in games of chance; *broadly* any small top spun with the fingers ['*tee* + L *totum* all, fr neut of *totus* whole; fr the letter *T* inscribed on one side as an abbr of *totum* (take) all]

teff /tef/ *n* an African cereal grass grown for its grain which yields a white flour [Amharic *ṭēf*]

Teflon /'teflon/ *trademark* – used for polytetrafluoroethylene

teg /teg/ *n, chiefly Br* a sheep in its second year [(assumed) ME *tegge* (in place-names), fr (assumed) OE *tegga*; akin to OSw *takka* ewe]

tegument /'tegyoomənt/ *n* an integument [ME, fr L *tegumentum*, fr *tegere* to cover] – **tegumental** /-'mentl/ *adj*, **tegumentary** /-'ment(ə)ri/ *adj*

tektite /'tektiet/ *n* a rounded glassy body, prob of meteoritic origin [ISV, fr Gk *tēktos* molten, fr *tēkein* to melt – more at THAW] – **tektitic** /-'titik/ *adj*

tel-, telo- *comb form* end ⟨telophase⟩ [ISV, fr Gk *telos* – more at WHEEL]

telaesthesia /,teləs'theezyə, -zh(y)ə/ *n* perception (e g of an object) at a distance without the use of the sense organs [NL, fr *tele-* + *aesthesia*]

tele-, tel- *comb form* **1** distant; at a distance; over a distance ⟨tele*gram*⟩ ⟨tele*pathy*⟩ **2a** telegraph ⟨tele*printer*⟩ **b** television ⟨tele*cast*⟩ ⟨tele*camera*⟩ [NL, fr Gk *tēle-*, *tēl-*, fr *tēle* far off – more at PALAE-]

telecast /'telikahst/ *vb* to televise [*tele-* + broad*cast*] – **telecast** *n*, **telecaster** *n*

telecine /'teli,sini/ *n, chiefly Br* the conversion of filmed material into signals suitable for television broadcasting [*tele-* + *cine*matograph]

telecommunication /,telikə,myoohni'kaysh(ə)n/ *n* **1** communication at a distance (e g by telegraph) **2** a science that deals with telecommunication – usu pl with sing. meaning [ISV]

teledu /'telədooh/ *n* a flesh-eating mammal of Java and Sumatra that is related to the skunk, resembles the badger, and secretes an offensive-smelling liquid [Malay *tĕledu*]

telegram /'teligram/ *n* a message sent by telegraph and delivered as a written or typed note

[1]**telegraph** /'teligrahf, -graf/ *n* an apparatus or system for communicating at a distance, esp by making and breaking an electric circuit [F *télégraphe*, fr *télé-* tele- (fr Gk *tēle-*) + *-graphe* -graph]

[2]**telegraph** *vt* **1** to send or communicate (as if) by telegraph **2** to make known by signs, esp unknowingly and in advance ⟨*~ a punch*⟩ – **telegrapher** /tə'legrəfə/ *n*, **telegraphist** /tə'legrəfist/ *n*

telegraphese /,teligrah'feez, -gra-/ *n* the terse and abbreviated language characteristic of telegrams

telegraphic /,teli'grafik/ *adj* **1** of the telegraph **2** concise, terse – **telegraphically** *adv*

telegraphic address *n* a registered abbreviated direction for the delivery of telegrams

telegraphy /tə'legrəfi/ *n* the use or operation of a telegraphic apparatus or system

telekinesis /ˌteliki'neesis/ *n* psychokinesis carried out at an appreciable distance [NL, fr Gk *tēle-* + *kinēsis* motion – more at -KINESIS] – **telekinetic** /-'netik/ *adj*

telemark /'telimahk/ *n, often cap* a turn in skiing in which the outside ski is advanced ahead of the other ski and then turned inwards at a steadily widening angle [Norw, fr *Telemark*, region in Norway]

telemeter /'teliˌmeetə, tə'lemitə/ *n* an electrical apparatus for measuring a quantity (e g pressure or temperature) and transmitting the result to a distant point [ISV] – **telemeter** *n*, **telemetric** /ˌteli'metrik/ *adj*, **telemetry** /tə'lemətri/ *n*

telencephalon /ˌtelən'sefəlon/ *n* the front subdivision of the brain comprising the cerebral hemispheres and associated structures [NL, fr *tel-* + *encephalon*] – **telencephalic** /ˌtelensi'falik/ *adj*

teleology /ˌteli'oləji, ˌtee-/ *n* **1** a doctrine explaining phenomena by reference to goals or purposes **2** the character attributed to nature or natural processes of being directed towards an end or designed according to a purpose [NL *teleologia*, fr Gk *tele-*, *telos* end, purpose + *-logia* -logy – more at WHEEL] – **teleologist** *n*, **teleological** /ˌteli·ə'lojikl, ˌtee-/ *adj*

teleost /'teliˌost, 'tee-/ *n* BONY FISH [deriv of Gk *teleios* complete, perfect (fr *telos* end) + *osteon* bone – more at OSSEOUS] – **teleostean** /ˌteli'osti·ən, ˌtee-/ *adj or n*

telepathy /tə'lepəthi/ *n* communication directly from one mind to another without use of the known senses – **telepathist** *n*, **telepathic** /ˌteli'pathik/ *adj*

[1]**telephone** /'telifohn/ *n* **1** a device for reproducing sounds at a distance; *specif* one for converting sounds into electrical impulses for transmission, usu by wire, to a particular receiver ☞ TELECOMMUNICATION **2** the system of communications that uses telephones ⟨*get in touch by* ~⟩ [*tele-* + *-phone*] – **telephonic** /ˌteli'fonik/ *adj*, **telephony** /tə'lefəni/ *n*

[2]**telephone** *vi* to make a telephone call ~ *vt* **1** to send by telephone ⟨~ *a message*⟩ **2** to (attempt to) speak to by telephone – **telephoner** *n*

'telephone ˌbox *n, Br* a booth containing a public telephone

'telephone diˌrectory *n* a book giving the telephone numbers of subscribers

telephonist /tə'lefənist/ *n, Br* a telephone switchboard operator

telephoto /'teliˌfohtoh/ *adj* **1** of telephotography **2** being a camera lens system designed to give a large image of a distant object [short for *telephotographic*]

telephotography /ˌtelifə'tografi/ *n* the photography of distant objects (e g by a camera provided with a telephoto lens) [ISV] – **telephotographic** /ˌteliˌfohtə'grafik/ *adj*

teleport /'telipawt/ *vi* to transport oneself from one place to another using only the power of one's mind [*tele-* + *-port* (as in *transport*)] – **teleportation** *n*

teleprinter /'teliˌprintə/ *n* a typewriter keyboard that transmits telegraphic signals, a typewriting device activated by telegraphic signals, or a machine that combines both these functions ☞ TELECOMMUNICATION

TelePrompTer /'teliˌpromptə/ *trademark* – used for a device for unrolling a magnified script in front of a speaker on television

[1]**telescope** /'teliskohp/ *n* **1** a usu tubular optical instrument for viewing distant objects by means of the refraction of light rays through a lens or the reflection of light rays by a concave mirror **2** RADIO TELESCOPE [NL *telescopium*, fr Gk *tēleskopos* farseeing, fr *tēle-* tele- + *skopos* watcher; akin to Gk *skopein* to look – more at SPY]

[2]**telescope** *vi* **1** to slide one part within another like the cylindrical sections of a hand telescope **2** to become compressed under impact **3** to become condensed or shortened ~ *vt* **1** to cause to telescope **2** to condense, shorten

telescopic /ˌteli'skopik/ *adj* **1a** of or performed with a telescope **b** suitable for seeing or magnifying distant objects **2** able to discern objects at a distance **3** having parts that telescope – **telescopically** *adv*

'teleˌtex /-ˌteks/ *n* an advanced form of telex in which documents are scanned and then reproduced by the receiver ☞ TELECOMMUNICATION [prob blend of *telex* and *text*]

'teleˌtext /-ˌtekst/ *n* an information service provided by a television network broadcasting special pages of news, sports results, etc at the same time as ordinary programmes ☞ TELEVISION [*tele-* + *text*]

Teletype /'teliˌtiep/ *trademark* – used for a teleprinter

teletypewriter /ˌteli'tiepˌrietə/ *n, chiefly NAm* a teleprinter

televise /'teliviez/ *vt* to broadcast (an event or film) by television [back-formation fr *television*]

television /'telivizh(ə)n, --'--/ *n* **1** an electronic system of transmitting changing images together with sound along a wire or through space by converting the images and sounds into electrical signals **2** a television receiving set **3a(1)** the television broadcasting industry **(2)** a television broadcasting organization or station ⟨*Tyne-Tees* Television⟩ **b** the medium of television communication [F *télévision*, fr *télé-* tele- (fr Gk *tēle-*) + *vision*]

televisual /ˌteli'vizhyooəl/ *adj, chiefly Br* of or suitable for broadcast by television

telex /'teleks/ *n* a communications service involving teleprinters connected by wire through automatic exchanges; *also* a message by telex ☞ TELECOMMUNICATION [*tele*printer + *ex*change] – **telex** *vb*

tell /tel/ *vb* **told** /tohld/ *vt* **1** to count, enumerate ⟨*all* told *there were 27 present*⟩ **2a** to relate in detail; narrate ⟨~ *me a story*⟩ **b** to give utterance to; express in words **3** to make known; divulge **4a** to report to; inform **b** to assure emphatically ⟨*he did not do it, I* ~ *you*⟩ **5** to order ⟨told *her to wait*⟩ **6a** to ascertain by observing ⟨*can never* ~ *whether he's lying or not*⟩ **b** to distinguish, discriminate ⟨*can't* ~ *Bach from the Beatles*⟩ ~ *vi* **1** to give an account **2** to make a positive assertion; decide definitely ⟨*you can never* ~ *for certain*⟩ **3** to act as an informer – often + *on* **4** to take effect ⟨*the worry began to* ~ *on her nerves*⟩ **5** to serve as evidence or indication ⟨*will* ~ *against you in court*⟩ [ME *tellen*, fr OE *tellan*; akin to OHG *zellen* to count, tell, OE *talu* tale]

teller /'telə/ *n* **1** sby who relates or communicates ⟨*a* ~ *of stories*⟩ **2** sby who counts: e g **a** sby appointed to count votes **b** a member of a bank's staff concerned with the direct handling of money received or paid out

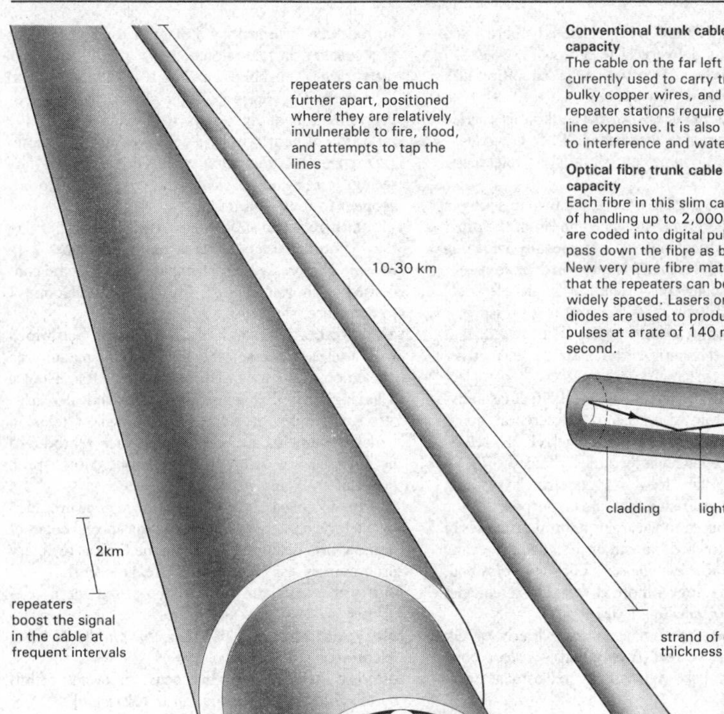
repeaters can be much further apart, positioned where they are relatively invulnerable to fire, flood, and attempts to tap the lines
10-30 km
2km
repeaters boost the signal in the cable at frequent intervals
cladding
light ray
core
strand of glass of similar thickness to human hair
copper core coaxial cable

Conventional trunk cable 10,000 call capacity
The cable on the far left is of the kind currently used to carry trunk calls. The bulky copper wires, and the regular repeater stations required, make the line expensive. It is also vulnerable to interference and water damage.

Optical fibre trunk cable 10,000 call capacity
Each fibre in this slim cable is capable of handling up to 2,000 calls. Calls are coded into digital pulses which pass down the fibre as bursts of light. New very pure fibre material means that the repeaters can be much more widely spaced. Lasers or light-emitting diodes are used to produce the light pulses at a rate of 140 million per second.

Digital sound
Sound takes the form of waves which travel through air, water and some solid objects. When sound is converted into an electrical signal by a microphone, it follows a waveform analogous to the sound. The electrical analogue waves are, by their nature, subject to distortion – for example when passing through the wires in a telephone system. This distortion can largely be avoided by digital transmission.

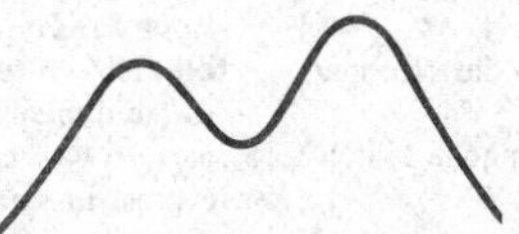

This representation of an analogue signal shows the varying height (amplitude) of the waveform.

A digital encoder "samples" the amplitude and assigns a numerical value for each height.

☞ TELEVISION, VIDEO

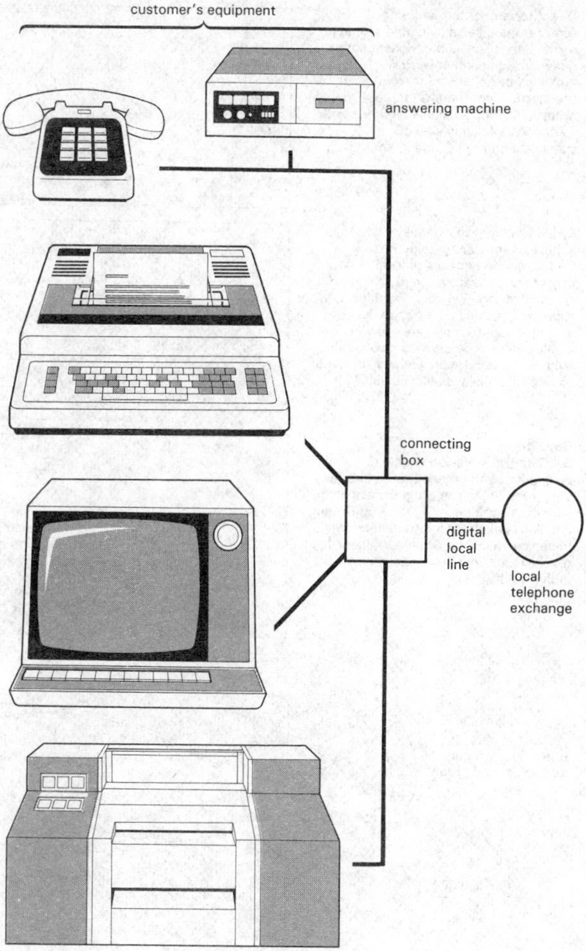

customer's equipment

answering machine

Telephone/Viewphone
The telephone can be used not only for transmitting speech but also for communicating computer data and visual images. Computers can 'talk' to each other in this way. When optical fibres are introduced, the viewphone could also become practicable because of the wide signal bandwidth they offer.

Teletex/Telex
Telex is a teleprinter system in which messages typed on the keyboard by the sender are reproduced on the receiver's teleprinter. Teletex is an advanced form of Telex with wider typographic facility – it can also be used to link up word processors in different locations.

connecting box

digital local line

local telephone exchange

Viewdata/data terminal
The Prestel service (British Telecom) enables subscribers to dial a computer and call up pages of information which are displayed on a special television set. Messages can also be written and transmitted.

Facsimile
This piece of equipment scans original documents and transmits the information through to the receiver, where the documents are reproduced.

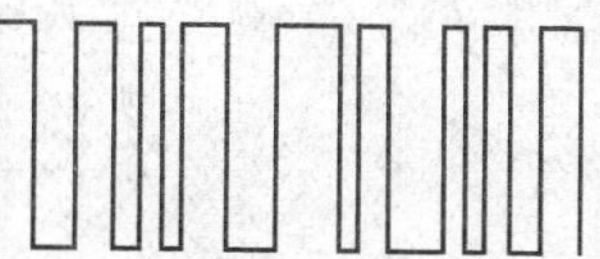

Each value is then put into code, rather like letters in Morse code, which can be transmitted in pulses.

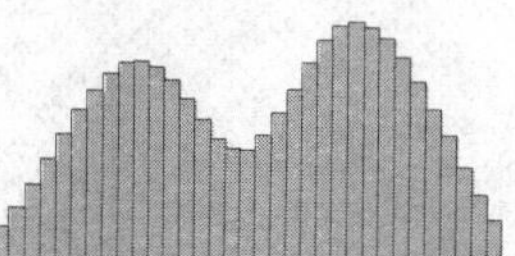

A digital decoder reconstructs the analogue waveform from the coded message. Even if some values are lost, the original waveform is still retrievable.

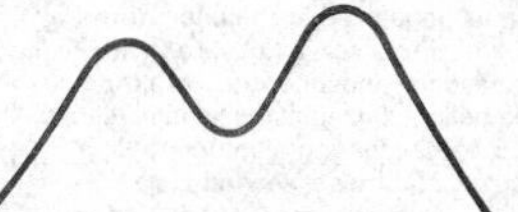

The final recreated wave form is in theory identical to the original.

Direct terrestrial transmission
Direct transmission is limited to line of sight – that is, the broadcast cannot pass through solid objects like hills or buildings or go around the curvature of the earth. Also, there is increasing pressure on the available airspace and frequencies for this kind of transmission are becoming limited.

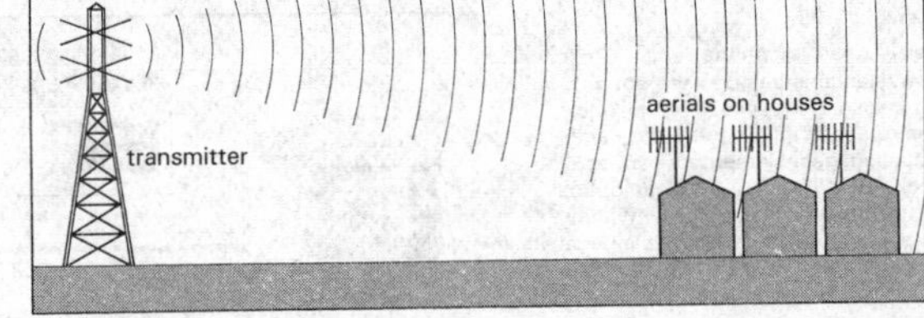

Cable or communal aerial
Where direct transmission is impracticable because of intervening objects, waves from the main transmitter are picked up by a local receiver (perhaps on a hilltop, as here) and retransmitted by cable to viewers. Cable can also be used as a subscriber system, in which viewers pay for films or news services.

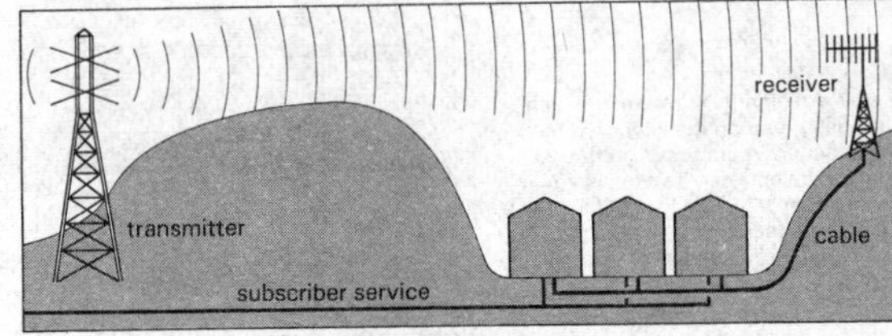

Satellite
Satellite transmission enables programmes to be distributed over a very wide area. The programmes are sent on a tight beam directly up to the satellite, which then retransmits on a wider beam over a whole continent to receivers serving groups of houses or individual houses.

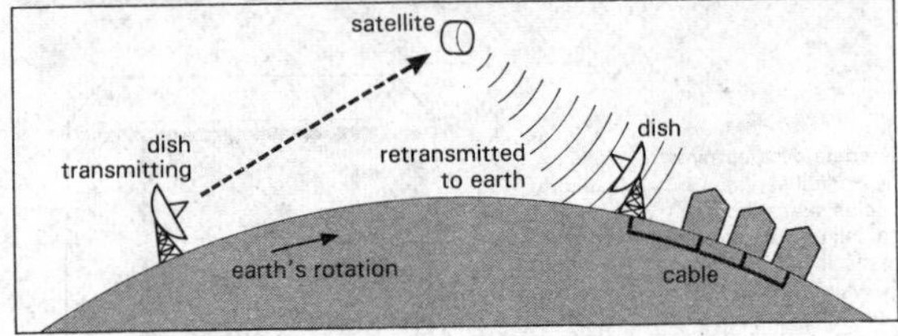

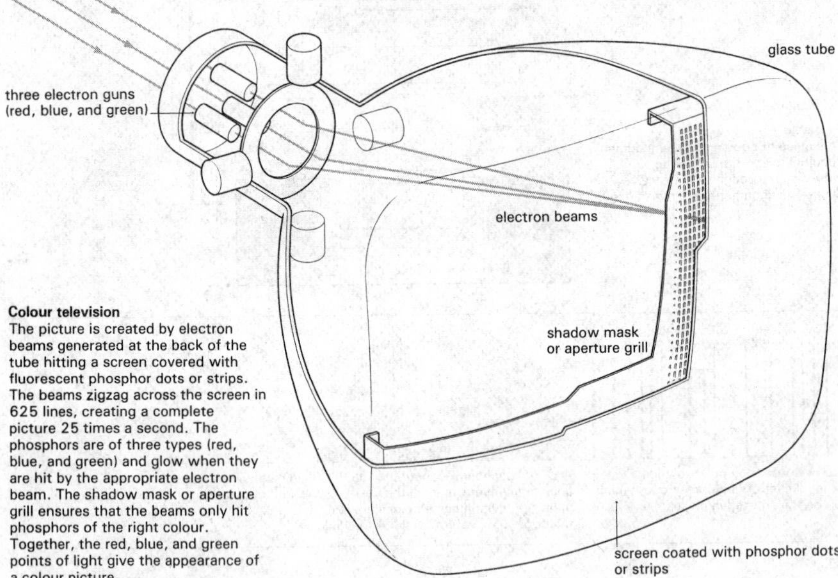

Colour television
The picture is created by electron beams generated at the back of the tube hitting a screen covered with fluorescent phosphor dots or strips. The beams zigzag across the screen in 625 lines, creating a complete picture 25 times a second. The phosphors are of three types (red, blue, and green) and glow when they are hit by the appropriate electron beam. The shadow mask or aperture grill ensures that the beams only hit phosphors of the right colour. Together, the red, blue, and green points of light give the appearance of a colour picture.

☞ TELECOMMUNICATION, VIDEO

Videodisc player
Prerecorded films and programmes on disc are 'read' by the player and displayed on the TV screen. Picture quality of discs is high but it is not possible to record on them in the home. When linked with a home computer there is great potential for educational purposes.

Teletext
In Britain Ceefax (BBC) and Oracle (ITV). Special TV sets receive and display 'pages' of information transmitted at the same time as ordinary broadcasts. These services are free.

Videocassette recorder
Television programmes can be recorded and replayed. Commercially recorded films, magazines, and educational programmes are available.

Viewdata
In Britain Prestel (British Telecom). This is a subscriber system available by telephone. 'Pages' of information can be dialled using a push-button control.

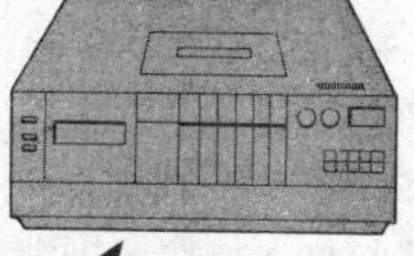

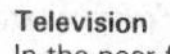

Television
In the near future the home television set will act as a central display screen for many service and entertainment media.

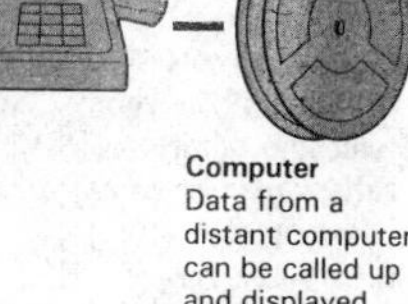

Computer
Data from a distant computer can be called up and displayed through the telephone network.

Satellite, cable, and subscription or pay TV
These services will gradually become available. Cable TV enables viewers to participate in programmes, for example by voting in talent contests.

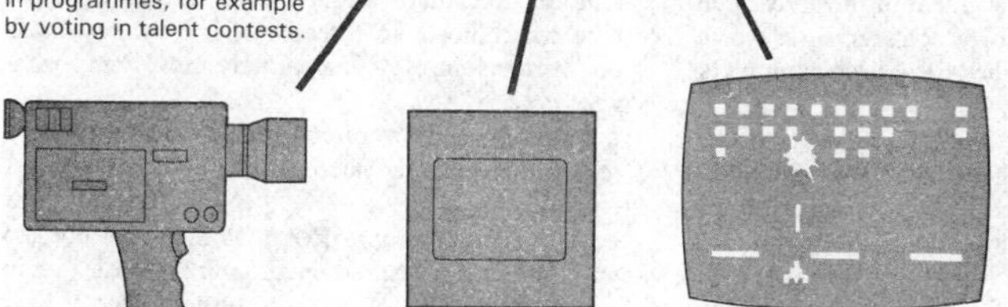

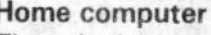

Camera
Home movies recorded with a camera connected to or incorporating a videocassette recorder can be shown on the television screen.

Slides and films
Slide and film projectors can be linked to the television screen.

Games
A wide range of TV games is available.

Home computer
The television screen can be used as a visual display unit for a microprocessor. Some home computers can be used to create TV games, depending on their graphic capability. ☞ COMPUTER

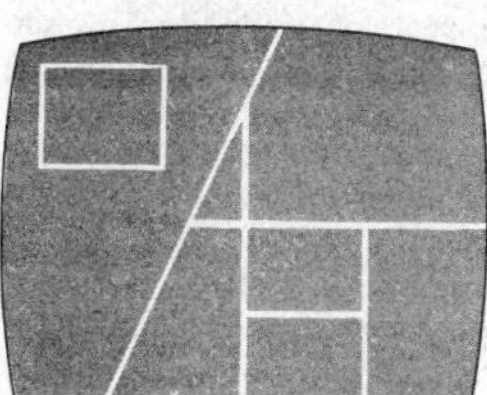

Display screen/ picture on picture
Developments in TV technology may eventually result in much larger screens. A split screen display enables the viewer to monitor other channels.

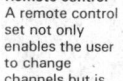

Remote control
A remote control set not only enables the user to change channels but is essential for dialling Teletext pages.

telling /ˈteling/ *adj* carrying great weight and producing a marked effect ⟨*the most* ~ *evidence against him*⟩ – **tellingly** *adv*

ˌtelling-ˈoff *n* a harsh or severe reprimand

tell off *vt* **1** to number and set apart; *esp* to assign to a special duty ⟨told off *a detail and put them to digging a trench*⟩ **2** to give a telling-off to

telltale /ˈtel,tayl/ *n* **1** sby who spreads gossip or rumours; *esp* an informer **2** a device for indicating or recording sthg (e g the position of a vessel's rudder) – **telltale** *adj*

tellur-, telluro- *comb form* **1** earth ⟨tellur*ian*⟩ **2** tellurium ⟨tellur*ide*⟩ [L *tellur-, tellus*; (2) NL *tellurium*]

tellurian /təˈl(y)ooəri·ən/ *n or adj* (an inhabitant) of the earth – fml

telluric /təˈl(y)ooərik/ *adj* **1** of or containing (high valency) tellurium **2** of the earth

telluride /ˈtelyooried/ *n* a binary compound of tellurium, usu with a more electropositive element or radical [ISV]

tellurium /təˈl(y)ooəri·əm/ *n* a semimetallic element chemically related to selenium and sulphur ☞ PERIODIC TABLE [NL, fr L *tellur-, tellus* earth]

tellurous /ˈtelyooərəs/ *adj* of or containing (low valency) tellurium [ISV]

telly /ˈteli/ *n, chiefly Br* (a) television – infml [by shortening & alter.]

telo- – see TEL-

telophase /ˈteləfayz, ˈtee-/ *n* the final stage of cell division in which the mitotic spindle disappears and 2 new nuclei appear, each with a set of chromosomes [ISV]

telson /ˈtelsən/ *n* the last segment of the body of an arthropod, esp a crustacean, or of a segmented worm [NL, fr Gk, end of a ploughed field; prob akin to Gk *telos* end]

Telugu /ˈteləgooh/ *n, pl* **Telugus**, *esp collectively* **Telugu** **1** a member of the predominant people of Andhra Pradesh in India **2** the language of the Telugu people ☞ LANGUAGE

temerity /təˈmerəti/ *n* unreasonable disregard for danger or opposition; *broadly* cheek, nerve [ME *temeryte*, fr L *temeritas*, fr *temere* at random, rashly, lit., in the dark; akin to OHG *demar* darkness, L *tenebrae*, Skt *tamas*]

[1]temp /temp/ *n* sby (e g a typist or secretary) employed temporarily – infml [short for *temporary*]

[2]temp *vi* to work as a temp – infml

[1]temper /ˈtempə/ *vt* **1** to moderate (sthg harsh) *with* the addition of sthg less severe ⟨~ *justice with mercy*⟩ **2** to bring to a suitable state, esp by mixing in or adding a liquid ingredient; *esp* to mix (clay) with water or a modifier and knead to a uniform texture **3** to bring (esp steel) to the right degree of hardness by reheating (and quenching) after cooling **4** to strengthen the character of through hardship ⟨*troops* ~ed *in battle*⟩ **5** to adjust the pitch of (a note, chord, or instrument) to a temperament [ME *temperen*, fr OE & OF; OE *temprian* & OF *temprer*, fr L *temperare* to moderate, mix, temper; prob akin to L *tempor-, tempus* time – more at TEMPORAL] – **temperable** *adj*, **temperer** *n*

[2]temper *n* **1** characteristic tone ⟨*the* ~ *of the times*⟩ **2** the state of a substance with respect to certain desired qualities (e g the degree of hardness or resilience given to steel by tempering) **3a** a characteristic cast of mind or state of feeling **b** composure, equanimity **c** (proneness to displays of) an uncontrolled and often disproportionate rage ⟨*he has/is in a terrible* ~⟩

tempera /ˈtempərə/ *n* (a work produced by) a method of painting using pigment ground and mixed with an emulsion (e g of egg yolk and water) [It, lit., temper, fr *temperare* to temper, fr L]

temperament /ˈtemprəmənt/ *n* **1a** a person's peculiar or distinguishing mental or physical character (which according to medieval physiology was determined by the relative proportions of the humours) **b** excessive sensitiveness or irritability **2** the modification of the musical intervals of the pure scale to produce a set of 12 fixed notes to the octave which enables a keyboard instrument to play in more than 1 key [ME, fr L *temperamentum*, fr *temperare* to mix, temper]

temperamental /ˌtemprəˈmentl/ *adj* **1** of or arising from individual character or constitution ⟨~ *peculiarities*⟩ **2a** easily upset or irritated; liable to sudden changes of mood **b** unpredictable in behaviour or performance – **temperamentally** *adv*

temperance /ˈtempərəns/ *n* **1** moderation, self-restraint **2** habitual moderation in the indulgence of the appetites; *specif* moderation in or abstinence from the use of alcoholic drink [ME, fr L *temperantia*, fr *temperant-, temperans*, prp of *temperare* to moderate, be moderate]

temperate /ˈtempərət/ *adj* **1** moderate: e g **a** not extreme or excessive ⟨*a* ~ *climate*⟩ ⟨*a* ~ *speech*⟩ **b** moderate in indulgence of appetite or desire; *esp* abstemious in the consumption of alcohol **2a** having a moderate climate **b** found in or associated with a temperate climate [ME *temperat*, fr L *temperatus*, fr pp of *temperare*] – **temperately** *adv*, **temperateness** *n*

temperate zone *n, often cap T&Z* either of the 2 regions between a polar circle and the nearest tropic

temperature /ˈtemprəchə/ *n* **1a** degree of hotness or coldness as measured on an arbitrary scale (e g in degrees Celsius) ☞ PHYSICS **b** the degree of heat natural to the body of a living being **2** an abnormally high body heat [L *temperatura* mixture, moderation, fr *temperatus*, pp of *temperare*]

tempered /ˈtempəd/ *adj* **1a** having the elements mixed in satisfying proportions **b** qualified or diluted by the mixture or influence of an additional ingredient **2** having a specified temper – in combination ⟨*short*-tempered⟩

tempest /ˈtempist/ *n* **1** a violent storm **2** a tumult, uproar [ME, fr OF *tempeste*, fr (assumed) VL *tempesta*, alter. of L *tempestas* season, weather, storm, fr *tempus* time – more at TEMPORAL]

tempestuous /temˈpeschoo·əs/ *adj* turbulent, stormy ⟨~ *weather*⟩ ⟨*a* ~ *debate*⟩ [LL *tempestuosus*, fr OL *tempestus* season, weather, storm, fr *tempus*] – **tempestuously** *adv*, **tempestuousness** *n*

Templar /ˈtemplə/ *n* a knight of a religious military order founded in Jerusalem in the early 12th c for the protection of pilgrims and suppressed in the 14th c [ME *templer*, fr OF *templier*, fr ML *templarius*, fr L *templum* temple]

template /ˈtemplayt/, **templet** /ˈtemplit/ *n* **1** a short piece or block placed horizontally in a wall under a beam to distribute its weight or pressure (e g over a door) **2a** a gauge, pattern, or mould used as a guide to the form of a piece being made **b** a molecule (e g of RNA) in a biological system that carries the genetic code for protein or other macromolecules **c** an overlay [*template* alter. (influenced by *plate*) of *templet*, prob fr F *templet*, dim. of *temple* temple of a loom]

[1]**temple** /'templ/ *n* **1a** a building dedicated to worship among any of various ancient civilizations (e g the Egyptians, the Greeks, and the Romans) and present-day non-Christian religions (e g Hinduism and Buddhism) **b** *often cap* any of 3 successive national sanctuaries in ancient Jerusalem **2** a place devoted or dedicated to a specified purpose **3** *chiefly NAm* a Reform or Conservative synagogue [ME, fr OE & OF; OE *tempel* & OF *temple*, fr L *templum* space marked out for observation of auguries, temple; prob akin to L *tempus* time]

[2]**temple** *n* the flattened space on either side of the forehead of some mammals (e g human beings) [ME, fr MF, fr (assumed) VL *tempula*, alter. of L *tempora* (pl) temples; prob akin to L *tempor-, tempus* time]

[3]**temple** *n* a device in a loom for keeping the cloth stretched [ME *tempylle*, fr MF *temple*, prob fr L *templum* temple (sanctuary), small timber]

tempo /'tempoh/ *n, pl* **tempi** /-pi/, **tempos** **1** the speed of a musical piece or passage indicated by any of a series of directions and often by an exact metronome marking **2** rate of motion or activity [It, lit., time, fr L *tempus*]

temporal /'temp(ə)rəl/ *adj* **1a** of time as opposed to eternity or space; *esp* transitory **b** of earthly life **c** of lay or secular concerns **2** of grammatical tense or a distinction of time ⟨when *is a* ~ *conjunction*⟩ [ME, fr L *temporalis*, fr *tempor-, tempus* time; akin to Lith *tempti* to stretch, & prob to L *tendere* to stretch – more at THIN] – **temporally** *adv*

temporality /,tempə'raləti/ *n* **1** civil or political power as distinguished from spiritual or ecclesiastical authority **2** an ecclesiastical property or revenue – often pl [TEMPORAL + -ITY]

temporal lobe *n* a large lobe at the side of each cerebral hemisphere that contains a sensory area associated with hearing and speech [*temporal* fr MF, fr LL *temporalis*, fr L *tempora* temples (of the head)]

[1]**temporary** /'temp(ə)rəri, 'tempə,reri/ *adj* lasting for a limited time [L *temporarius*, fr *tempor-, tempus* time] – **temporarily** /'temprərəli, tempə'rerəli/ *adv*, **temporariness** /'temp(ə)rərinis, 'tempə,rerinis/ *n*

[2]**temporary** *n* a temp

tempor·ize, -ise /'tempəriez/ *vi* **1** to comply temporarily with the demands of the time or occasion **2** to draw out negotiations so as to gain time [MF *temporiser*, fr ML *temporizare* to pass the time, fr L *tempor-, tempus*] – **temporizer** *n*, **temporization** /-'zaysh(ə)n/ *n*

tempt /tempt/ *vt* **1** to entice, esp to evil, by promise of pleasure or gain **2** to risk provoking the disfavour of ⟨*shouldn't* ~ *fate*⟩ **3a** to induce to do sthg **b** to cause to be strongly inclined ⟨*he was* ~ed *to call it quits*⟩ **c** to appeal to; entice ⟨*the idea* ~s *me*⟩ [ME *tempten*, fr OF *tempter, tenter*, fr L *temptare, tentare* to feel, try, tempt; akin to L *tendere* to stretch – more at THIN] – **temptable** *adj*, **tempter, temptress** *n*

temptation /temp'taysh(ə)n/ *n* **1** tempting or being tempted, esp to evil **2** sthg tempting

tempting /'tempting/ *adj* enticing – **temptingly** *adv*

tempura /tem'pooərə, 'tempərə/ *n* a Japanese dish of seafood or vegetables dipped in batter and fried [Jap *tenpura*]

ten /ten/ *n* **1** ☞ NUMBER **2** the tenth in a set or series ⟨*the* ~ *of diamonds*⟩ **3** sthg having 10 parts or members or a denomination of 10 **4** the number occupying the position 2 to the left of the decimal point in the Arabic notation; *also, pl* this position [ME, fr OE *tīene*, fr *tīen*, adj, ten; akin to OHG *zehan* ten, L *decem*, Gk *deka*, Skt *daśa*] – **ten** *adj or pron*, **tenfold** /-,fohld/ *adj or adv*, **tenth** /tenth/ *adj or n*

tenable /'tenəbl/ *adj* capable of being held, maintained, or defended [F, fr OF, fr *tenir* to hold, fr L *tenēre* – more at THIN] – **tenableness** *n*, **tenably** *adv*, **tenability** /-'biləti/ *n*

tenacious /tə'nayshəs/ *adj* **1** tending to stick or cling, esp to another substance **2a** persistent in maintaining or keeping to sthg valued as habitual **b** retentive ⟨*a* ~ *memory*⟩ [L *tenac-, tenax* tending to hold fast, fr *tenēre* to hold] – **tenaciously** *adv*, **tenaciousness** *n*, **tenacity** /tə'nasəti/ *n*

tenaculum /tə'nakyooləm/ *n, pl* **tenacula** /-lə/, **tenaculums** a slender sharp-pointed hook used mainly in surgery for seizing and holding parts (e g arteries) [NL, fr LL, instrument for holding, fr L *tenēre*]

[1]**tenant** /'tenənt/ *n* **1a** a holder of real estate by any kind of right **b** an occupant of lands or property of another; *specif* sby who rents or leases a house or flat from a landlord **2** an occupant, dweller [ME, fr MF, fr prp of *tenir* to hold] – **tenantless** *adj*, **tenancy** /-si/ *n*

[2]**tenant** *vt* to hold or inhabit as a tenant – **tenantable** *adj*

,tenant 'farmer *n* a farmer who works land owned by another and pays rent

tenantry /'tenəntri/ *n sing or pl in constr* tenants collectively

tench /tench/ *n, pl* **tench, tenches** a Eurasian freshwater fish related to the dace and noted for its ability to survive outside water [ME, fr MF *tenche*, fr LL *tinca*]

,Ten Com'mandments *n pl* the commandments given by God to Moses on Mt Sinai, recorded in Ex 20:1–17

[1]**tend** /tend/ *vt* to have charge of; take care of [ME *tenden*, short for *attenden* to attend]

[2]**tend** *vi* **1** to move, direct, or develop one's course in a specified direction **2** to show an inclination or tendency – + *to, towards*, or *to* and an infinitive [ME *tenden*, fr MF *tendre* to stretch, fr L *tendere* – more at THIN]

tendency /'tendənsi/ *n* **1a** a general trend or movement ⟨*the growing* ~ *for prices to rise faster than wages*⟩ **b** an inclination or predisposition to some particular end, or towards a particular kind of thought or action ⟨*his books show a* ~ *to drop into sentimentality*⟩ **2** the purposeful trend of sthg written or said [ML *tendentia*, fr L *tendent-, tendens*, prp of *tendere*]

tendentious *also* **tendencious** /ten'denshəs/ *adj* marked by a tendency in favour of a particular point of view – chiefly derog – **tendentiously** *adv*, **tendentiousness** *n*

[1]**tender** /'tendə/ *adj* **1a** having a soft or yielding

texture; easily broken, cut, or damaged **b** easily chewed **2a** physically weak **b** immature, young ⟨*children of ~ years*⟩ **3** fond, loving ⟨*a ~ lover*⟩ **4a** showing care ⟨*~ regard*⟩ **b** highly susceptible to impressions or emotions ⟨*a ~ conscience*⟩ **5a** gentle, mild ⟨*~ breeding*⟩ ⟨*~ irony*⟩ **b** delicate or soft in quality or tone **6a** sensitive to touch ⟨*~ skin*⟩ **b** sensitive to injury or insult ⟨*~ pride*⟩ **c** demanding careful and sensitive handling ⟨*a ~ situation*⟩ [ME, fr OF *tendre*, fr L *tener*; prob akin to Gk *terēn* soft, *teru* weak, delicate, Skt *taruṇa* tender, young] – **tenderly** *adv*, **tenderness** *n*

[2]**tender** *n* **1a** a ship employed to attend other ships (e g to supply provisions) **b** a boat or small steamer for communication between shore and a larger ship **2** a vehicle attached to a locomotive for carrying a supply of fuel and water [[1]TEND + [2]-ER]

[3]**tender** *vt* **1** to make a tender of **2** to present for acceptance ⟨*~ed his resignation*⟩ ~ *vi* to make a bid ⟨*the company ~s for and builds dams*⟩ [MF *tendre* to stretch, stretch out, offer – more at [2]TEND] – **tenderer** *n*

[4]**tender** *n* **1** an unconditional offer in satisfaction of a debt or obligation, made to avoid a penalty for nonpayment or nonperformance **2** an offer, proposal: e g **a** a formal esp written offer or bid for a contract **b** a public expression of willingness to buy not less than a specified number of shares at a fixed price from shareholders **3** sthg that may be offered in payment; *specif* money

'tender,foot /-,foot/ *n, pl* **tenderfeet** /-,feet/ *also* **tenderfoots** an inexperienced beginner [[1]*tender* + *foot*; orig sense, sby not hardened to frontier or outdoor life]

,tender'hearted /-'hahtid/ *adj* easily moved to love, pity, or sorrow – **tenderheartedly** *adv*

tender·ize, -ise /'tendəriez/ *vt* to make (meat or meat products) tender by beating or adding an enzyme that breaks down fibrous tissue – **tenderizer** *n*, **tenderization** /-'zaysh(ə)n/ *n*

tenderloin /'tendə,loyn/ *n* a pork or beef fillet ☞ MEAT

tendon /'tendən/ *n* a tough cord or band of dense white fibrous connective tissue that connects a muscle with a bone or other part and transmits the force exerted by the muscle ☞ ANATOMY [ML *tendon-, tendo*, fr L *tendere* to stretch – more at THIN] – **tendinous** /'tendənəs/ *adj*

tendril /'tendrəl/ *n* a slender spirally coiling sensitive organ that attaches a plant to its support [perh modif of MF *tendron*, alter. of *tendon*, lit., tendon, fr ML *tendon-, tendo*] – **tendriled, tendrilled** *adj*

[1]**-tene** /-teen/ *comb form* (→ *adj*) having (such or so many) chromosomal filaments ⟨*poly*tene⟩ [L *taenia* ribbon, band – more at TAENIA]

[2]**-tene** *comb form* (→ *n*) stage of meiotic prophase characterized by (such) chromosomal filaments ⟨*diplo*tene⟩ ⟨*pachy*tene⟩

tenement /'tenəmənt/ *n* **1** land or other property held by one person from another **2** (a flat in) a large building; *esp* one meeting minimum standards and typically found in the poorer parts of a large city [ME, fr MF, fr ML *tenementum*, fr L *tenēre* to hold – more at THIN]

tenesmus /tə'nezməs/ *n* an ineffectual urge to defecate or urinate [L, fr Gk *teinesmos*, fr *teinein* to stretch, strain – more at THIN]

tenet /'tenət/ *n* a principle, belief, or doctrine; *esp* one held in common by members of an organization or group [L, he holds, fr *tenēre* to hold]

,ten-gallon 'hat *n* COWBOY HAT [fr its great size]

,ten 'minute ,rule *n* a rule under which an MP may briefly introduce a private member's bill

tenner /'tenə/ *n, Br* a £10 note; *also* the sum of £10 – infml

tennis /'tenis/ *n* **1** REAL TENNIS **2** a singles or doubles game that is played with rackets and a light elastic ball on a flat court divided by a low net ☞ SPORT [ME *tenetz, tenys*, prob fr AF *tenetz* take, receive, imper of *tenir* to hold, take (called by server to opponent)]

tennis elbow *n* inflammation and pain of the elbow, usu resulting from excessive twisting movements of the hand

[1]**tenon** /'tenən/ *n* a projecting part of a piece of material (e g wood) for insertion into a mortise [ME, fr OF, fr *tenir* to hold – more at TENABLE]

[2]**tenon** *vt* **1** to unite by a tenon **2** to cut or fit for insertion in a mortise

'tenon ,saw *n* a woodworking saw that has a reinforced blade and is used for making fine cuts

tenor /'tenə/ *n* **1** the course of thought of sthg spoken or written **2a** the next to the lowest part in 4-part harmony **b** (sby with) the highest natural adult male singing voice **c** a member of a family of instruments having a range next lower than that of the alto **3** a continuance in a course or activity [ME, fr OF, fr L *tenor* uninterrupted course, fr *tenēre* to hold; (2) fr the fact that the *tenor* (continuous part, melodic line) in medieval polyphony was assigned to this voice] – **tenor** *adj*

tenor clef *n* a C clef placed so as to designate the fourth line of the staff as middle C ☞ MUSIC

tenpin /'ten,pin/ *n* a bottle-shaped pin used in tenpin bowling [back-formation fr *tenpins* (tenpin bowling), fr *ten pins*]

,tenpin 'bowling *n* an indoor bowling game using 10 pins and a large ball in which each player is allowed to bowl 2 balls in each of 10 frames

tenrec /'ten,rek/ *n* any of numerous small often spiny insect-eating mammals of Madagascar [F, fr Malagasy *tàndraka*]

[1]**tense** /tens/ *n* (a member of) a set of inflectional forms of a verb that express distinctions of time [ME *tens* time, tense, fr MF, fr L *tempus* – more at TEMPORAL]

[2]**tense** *adj* **1** stretched tight; made taut **2a** feeling or showing nervous tension **b** marked by strain or suspense **3** articulated with relatively tense muscles – used e g of the vowel /ee/ in contrast with the vowel /i/ [L *tensus*, fr pp of *tendere* to stretch – more at THIN] – **tensely** *adv*, **tenseness** *n*

[3]**tense** *vb* to make or become tense – often + *up*

tensile /'tensiel/ *adj* **1** ductile **2** of or involving tension – **tensility** /ten'siləti/ *n*

tensile strength *n* the greatest tension a substance can bear without breaking

tensimeter /ten'simitə/ *n* an instrument for measuring differences of vapour pressure [*tension* + *-meter*]

[1]**tension** /'tenshən/ *n* **1a** stretching or being stretched to stiffness **b** STRESS 1a **2a** either of 2 balancing forces causing or tending to cause extension **b** the stress resulting from the elongation of an elastic body **c** gas pressure; *esp* PARTIAL PRESSURE **3a** inner striving, unrest, or imbalance, often with

physiological indication of emotion **b** latent hostility **c** a balance maintained in an artistic work between opposing forces or elements **4** electrical potential ⟨*high* ~⟩ [MF or L; MF, fr L *tension-, tensio,* fr *tensus,* pp] – **tensional** *adj,* **tensionless** *adj*

[2]tension *vt* to tighten to a desired or appropriate degree – **tensioner** *n*

tensor /'tensə, -,saw/ *n* **1** a muscle that stretches a body part **2** a mathematical quantity that represents a mapping between 2 vector spaces [NL, fr L *tensus,* pp]

[1]tent /tent/ *n* **1** a collapsible shelter (e g of canvas) stretched and supported by poles **2** a canopy or enclosure placed over the head and shoulders to retain vapours or oxygen during medical treatment [ME *tente,* fr OF, fr L *tenta,* fem of *tentus,* pp of *tendere* to stretch – more at THIN] – **tented** *adj,* **tentless** *adj*

[2]tent *vi* to live in a tent ~*vt* to cover (as if) with a tent

tentacle /'tentəkl/ *n* **1** any of various elongated flexible animal parts, chiefly on the head or about the mouth, used for feeling, grasping, etc **2a** sthg like a tentacle (e g in grasping or feeling out) **b** a sensitive hair on a plant (e g the sundew) [NL *tentaculum,* fr L *tentare* to feel, touch, try – more at TEMPT] – **tentacled** *adj,* **tentacular** /ten'takyoolə/ *adj*

tentative /'tentətiv/ *adj* **1** not fully worked out or developed **2** hesitant, uncertain ⟨*a* ~ *smile*⟩ [ML *tentativus,* fr L *tentatus,* pp of *tentare*] – **tentative** *n,* **tentatively** *adv*

tenter /'tentə/ *n* an apparatus used for drying and stretching cloth [ME *teyntur, tentowre,* prob modif (influenced by MF *teindre* to dye) of ML *tentura,* fr L *tentus,* pp]

'tenter,hook /-,hook/ *n* a sharp hooked nail used esp for fastening cloth on a tenter **– on tenterhooks** in a state of uneasiness, strain, or suspense

,tenth-'rate /tenth/ *adj* of the lowest character or quality

'tent ,stitch *n* a short diagonal stitch used in embroidery and canvas work to form a solid background of even lines of parallel stitches

tenuous /'tenyoo·əs/ *adj* **1** not dense in consistency ⟨*a* ~ *fluid*⟩ **2** not thick ⟨*a* ~ *rope*⟩ **3** having little substance or strength ⟨*a* ~ *hold on reality*⟩ [L *tenuis* thin, slight, tenuous – more at THIN] – **tenuously** *adv,* **tenuousness** *n,* **tenuity** /tə'nyooh·əti/ *n*

tenure /'tenyə/ *n* **1a** the holding of property, an office, etc **b** *chiefly NAm* freedom from summary dismissal, esp from a teaching post **2** grasp, hold – fml [ME, fr OF *teneüre, tenure,* fr ML *tenitura,* fr (assumed) VL *tenitus,* pp of L *tenēre* to hold – more at THIN] – **tenured** *adj,* **tenurial** /tə'nyooəri·əl/ *adj*

tenuto /te'nyoohtoh/ *adv or adj* in a manner so as to hold a note or chord to its full value – used in music [It, fr pp of *tenere* to hold, fr L *tenēre*]

tepee /'tee,pee/ *n* a N American Indian conical tent, usu made of skins [Dakota *tipi,* fr *ti* to dwell + *pi* to use for]

tephigram /'tefigram/ *n* a chart showing vertical variations of atmospheric conditions [*T,* symbol for temperature + *phi,* name of former symbol for entropy + *-gram*]

tepid /'tepid/ *adj* **1** moderately warm ⟨*a* ~ *bath*⟩ **2** not enthusiastic ⟨*a* ~ *interest*⟩ [L *tepidus,* fr *tepēre* to be moderately warm; akin to Skt *tapati* it gives out heat, OIr *tess* heat] – **tepidly** *adv,* **tepidness** *n,* **tepidity** /te'pidəti/ *n*

tequila /tə'keelə/ *n* **1** a Mexican agave plant cultivated as a source of mescal **2** a Mexican spirit made by redistilling mescal [Sp, fr *Tequila,* district of Mexico]

ter- *comb form* 3 times; threefold; three ⟨ter*centenary*⟩ [L, fr *ter;* akin to Gk & Skt *tris* three times, L *tres* three – more at THREE]

tera- *comb form* billion (10^{12}) ⟨tera*ton*⟩ ⟨tera*hertz*⟩ ☞ PHYSICS [ISV, fr Gk *terat-, teras* marvel, monster; akin to Lith *keras* enchantment]

terat-, terato- *comb form* monster; monstrosity ⟨terato*logy*⟩ [Gk, fr *terat-, teras*]

teratogen /tə'ratəjən/ *n* sthg that causes developmental malformations in foetuses – **teratogenesis** /,terətə'jenəsis/ *n,* **teratogenic** /-'jenik/ *adj,* **teratogenicity** /-jə'nisəti/ *n*

teratology /,terə'toləji/ *n* the study of malformations in foetuses [Gk *terat-, teras* + ISV *-logy*] – **teratologist** *n,* **teratological** /,terətə'lojikl/ *adj*

teratoma /,terə'tohmə/ *n* a tumour derived from embryonic tissues and made up of a mixture of several types of tissue [NL, fr Gk *terat-, teras*] – **teratomatous** /-mətəs/ *adj*

terbium /'tuhbi·əm/ *n* a usu trivalent metallic element of the rare-earth group ☞ PERIODIC TABLE [NL, fr *Ytterby,* town in Sweden]

terce /tuhs/ *n, often cap* the third of the canonical hours observed at 9 am [ME, third, terce – more at TIERCE]

tercel /'tuhsl/ *n* a male of any of various hawks (e g the peregrine falcon), esp when used in falconry [ME *tercel,* fr MF, fr (assumed) VL *tertiolus,* fr dim. of L *tertius* third; perh fr the belief that the third egg of a clutch produced a male bird]

tercentenary /,tuhsen'teenəri, -'tenəri/ *n* a 300th anniversary or its celebration – **tercentenary** *adj*

tercentennial /,tuhsen'teni·əl/ *n* a tercentenary – **tercentennial** *adj*

tercet /'tuhsit/ *n* a unit or group of 3 lines of verse [It *terzetto,* fr dim. of *terzo* third, fr L *tertius* – more at THIRD]

terebene /'terəbeen/ *n* a mixture of terpenes from oil of turpentine [F *térébène,* fr *térébinthe* terebinth]

terebinth /'terəbinth/ *n* a small European tree of the sumach family yielding turpentine [ME *terebynt,* fr MF *terebinthe,* fr L *terebinthus* – more at TURPENTINE]

terebinthine /,terə'binthien/ *adj* consisting of or resembling turpentine [L *terebinthinus* of the terebinth]

teredo /tə'raydoh/ *n, pl* **teredos, teredines** /tə'redineez/ a shipworm [L *teredin-, teredo,* fr Gk *terēdōn;* akin to Gk *tetrainein* to bore – more at THROW]

terete /tə'reet/ *adj, of a plant or animal part* approximately cylindrical with a smooth surface [L *teret-, teres* well turned, rounded; akin to L *terere* to rub – more at THROW]

tergiversate /'tuhjivə,sayt, -giv-/ *vi* **1** to become a renegade **2** to act evasively or equivocally *USE* fml [L *tergiversatus,* pp of *tergiversari* to turn the back, shuffle, fr *tergum* back + *versare* to turn, fr *versus,* pp of *vertere* to turn – more at [1]WORTH] – **tergiversator** *n,* **tergiversation** /-'saysh(ə)n/ *n*

tergum /'tuhgəm/ *n, pl* **terga** /-gə/ the plate forming the back surface of a segment of an arthropod [NL, fr L, back] – **tergal** *adj*

[1]**term** /tuhm/ *n* **1a** an end, termination; *also* a time assigned for sthg (e g payment) **b** the time at which a pregnancy of normal length ends ⟨*had her baby at full* ~⟩ **2a** a limited or definite extent of time; *esp* the time for which sthg lasts ⟨*medium*-term *credit*⟩ **b** an estate or interest held for a term **c** any one of the periods of the year during which the courts are in session **3** any of the usu 3 periods of instruction into which an academic year is divided **4a** a mathematical expression connected to another by a plus or minus sign **b** an expression that forms part of a fraction or proportion or of a series or sequence **5** a concept, word, or phrase appearing as subject or predicate in a logical proposition **6a** a word or expression with a precise meaning; *esp* one peculiar to a restricted field ⟨*legal* ~s⟩ **b** *pl* diction of a specified kind ⟨*spoke in flattering* ~s⟩ **7** *pl* provisions relating to an agreement ⟨~s *of sale*⟩; *also* agreement on such provisions **8** *pl* mutual relationship ⟨*on good* ~s *with him*⟩ [ME *terme* boundary, end, fr OF, fr L *terminus*; akin to Gk *termōn* boundary, end, Skt *tarati* he crosses over – more at THROUGH] – **in terms** expressly, explicitly – **in terms of** in relation to; concerning

[2]**term** *vt* to apply a term to; call ⟨*wouldn't* ~ *it difficult*⟩

termagant /'tuhməgənt/ *n* **1** *cap* a violent character in English miracle plays representing an Islamic deity **2** an overbearing or nagging woman [ME]

terminable /'tuhminəbl/ *adj* capable of being terminated [ME, fr *terminen* to terminate, fr OF *terminer*, fr L *terminare*] – **terminableness** *n*

[1]**terminal** /'tuhminl/ *adj* **1a** of or being an end, extremity, boundary, or terminus **b** growing at the end of a branch or stem ⟨*a* ~ *bud*⟩ **2a** of or occurring in a term or each term **b** occurring at or causing the end of life ⟨~ *cancer*⟩ **3** occurring at or being the end of a period or series [L *terminalis*, fr *terminus*] – **terminally** *adv*

[2]**terminal** *n* **1** a device attached to the end of a wire or cable or to an electrical apparatus for convenience in making connections **2** the end of a carrier line (e g shipping line or airline) with its associated buildings and facilities ⟨*the West London air* ~⟩ **3** a device (e g a teleprinter) through which a user can communicate with a computer

terminate /'tuhminayt/ *vt* **1a** to bring to an end **b** to form the conclusion of **2** to serve as an ending, limit, or boundary of ~ *vi* **1** to extend only to a limit (e g a point or line); *esp* to reach a terminus ⟨*this train* ~s *at Glasgow*⟩ **2** to come to an end in time – often + *in* or *with* ⟨*the coalition* ~d *with the election*⟩ **3** to form an ending or outcome – often + *in* or *with* ⟨*the match* ~d *with the champion winning*⟩ [L *terminatus*, pp of *terminare*, fr *terminus*] – **termination** /-'naysh(ə)n/ *n*

terminator /'tuhmi,naytə/ *n* the dividing line between the illuminated and the unilluminated part of the moon or other celestial body [TERMINATE + [1]-OR]

terminology /,tuhmi'noləji/ *n* the technical terms used in a particular subject [ML *terminus* term, expression (fr L, boundary, limit) + E *-o-* + *-logy*] – **terminological** /-nə'lojikl/ *adj*, **terminologically** *adv*

'term in,surance *n* insurance for a specified period; *specif, chiefly Br* life insurance under which payment is made only if the insured dies within a specified period

terminus /'tuhminəs/ *n, pl* **termini** /-nie/, **terminuses** **1** a finishing point; an end **2** a post or stone marking a boundary **3** (the station, town, or city at) the end of a transport line or travel route **4** an extreme point or element [L, boundary, end – more at TERM]

termitarium /,tuhmi'teəri·əm, -mie-/ *n, pl* **termitaria** /-ri·ə/ a termites' nest [NL]

termite /'tuh,miet/ *n* any of numerous often destructive pale-coloured soft-bodied insects that live in colonies and feed on wood [NL *Termit-, Termes*, genus of termites, fr LL, a worm that eats wood, alter. of L *tarmit-, tarmes*; akin to Gk *tetrainein* to bore – more at THROW]

termless /'tuhmlis/ *adj* **1** having no term or end; boundless, unending **2** unconditioned, unconditional

,terms of 'reference *n pl* the precise delineation of competence (e g of a committee)

tern /tuhn/ *n* any of numerous water birds that are smaller than the related gulls and have a black cap, a white body, and often forked tails [of Scand origin; akin to Dan *terne* tern]

ternary /'tuhnəri/ *adj* **1a** of or proceeding by threes **b** threefold **c** ternate **2** using 3 as the base ⟨*a* ~ *logarithm*⟩ **3** third in order or rank [ME, fr L *ternarius*, fr *terni* three each; akin to L *tres* three – more at THREE]

ternate /'tuhnayt/ *adj* **1** arranged in threes ⟨~ *leaves*⟩ **2** composed of 3 leaflets or subdivisions ☞ PLANT [NL *ternatus*, fr ML, pp of *ternare* to treble, fr L *terni*] – **ternately** *adv*

terne /tuhn/ *n* terneplate

'terne,plate /-,playt/ *n* sheet iron or steel plated with an inferior alloy of about 4 parts lead to 1 part tin [prob fr F *terne* dull (fr MF, fr *ternir* to tarnish) + E *plate*]

terotechnology /,terohtek'noləji/ *n* a branch of technology that deals with the efficient installation and operation of equipment [Gk *tērein* to watch over + E *-o-* + *technology*]

terpene /'tuh,peen/ *n* any of various hydrocarbons present in essential oils (e g from conifers) and used esp as solvents and in organic synthesis [ISV *terp-* (fr G *terpentin* turpentine, fr ML *terbentina*) + *-ene* – more at TURPENTINE] – **terpenic** /tuh'peenik, -'pe-/ *adj*, **terpenoid** /'tuhpənoyd, tuh'peenoyd/ *adj or n*

terpsichorean /,tuhpsikə'ree·ən, ,tuhpsi'kawri·ən/ *adj* of dancing [*Terpsichore*, the muse of dancing and choral song, fr L, fr Gk *Terpsichorē*]

terra alba /,terə 'albə/ *n* any of several earthy white mineral substances (e g gypsum or kaolin) [NL, lit., white earth]

[1]**terrace** /'teris/ *n* **1** a relatively level paved or planted area adjoining a building **2** a raised embankment with a level top **3** a level usu narrow and steep-fronted area bordering a river, sea, etc **4a** a row of houses or flats on raised ground or a sloping site **b** a row of similar houses joined into 1 building by common walls **c** a street [MF, pile of earth, platform, terrace, fr OProv *terrassa*, fr *terra* earth, fr L, earth, land; akin to L *torrēre* to parch – more at THIRST]

[2]**terrace** *vt* to make into a terrace

'terraced *adj* being any of a continuous row of

dwellings connected by common sidewalls and forming a continuous row ⟨~ *houses*⟩

terracotta /,terə'kotə/ *n* **1** an unglazed brownish red fired clay used esp for statuettes and vases and as a building material **2** brownish orange [It *terra cotta*, lit., baked earth]

,terra 'firma /'fuhmə/ *n* dry land; solid ground [NL, lit., solid land]

terrain /tə'rayn/ *n* **1** (the physical features of) an area of land **2** an environment, milieu [F, land, ground, fr L *terrenum*, fr neut of *terrenus* of earth, fr *terra*]

terra incognita /,terə inkog'neetə, in'kognitə/ *n, pl* **terrae incognitae** /,teri inkog'neeti, in'kogniti/ an unexplored country or field of knowledge [L]

terrapin /'terəpin/ *n* any of several small edible freshwater reptiles of the same order as, and similar to, tortoises but adapted for swimming [of Algonquian origin; akin to Delaware *torope* turtle]

terrarium /tə'reəri·əm/ *n, pl* **terraria** /-ri·ə/, **terrariums** a vivarium for land-dwelling animals [NL, fr L *terra* + *-arium*]

terrazzo /te'rahtsoh/ *n* a mosaic flooring made by embedding and polishing small pieces of marble or granite in mortar [It, lit., terrace, perh fr OProv *terrassa*]

terreplein /'teə,playn/ *n* the level space behind a parapet of a rampart where guns are mounted [MF, fr OIt *terrapieno*, fr ML *terraplenum*, fr *terra plenus* filled with earth]

terrestrial /tə'restri·əl/ *adj* **1a** of the earth or its inhabitants **b** mundane, prosaic **2a** of land as distinct from air or water **b** *of organisms* living on or in land or soil **3** *of a planet* like the earth in density, composition, etc [ME, fr L *terrestris*, fr *terra* earth – more at TERRACE] – **terrestrial** *n*, **terrestrially** *adv*

terrible /'terəbl/ *adj* **1a** exciting intense fear; terrifying **b** formidable in nature ⟨*a ~ responsibility*⟩ **c** requiring great fortitude ⟨*a ~ order*⟩; *also* severe ⟨*a ~ winter*⟩ **2** extreme, great ⟨*a ~ amount of trouble arranging all this*⟩ **3** of very poor quality; awful ⟨*a ~ performance*⟩; *also* highly unpleasant ***USE*** *(2&3)* infml [ME, fr MF, fr L *terribilis*, fr *terrēre* to frighten – more at TERROR] – **terribleness** *n*

terribly /'terəbli/ *adv* very ⟨~ *lucky*⟩ – infml

terricolous /te'rikələs, tə-/ *adj* living on or in the ground [L *terricola* earth-dweller, fr *terra* earth + *colere* to inhabit – more at WHEEL]

terrier /'teri·ə/ *n* **1** (a member of) any of various breeds of usu small dogs, orig used by hunters to drive out small furred game from underground **2** *usu cap, Br* a territorial [(1) F (*chien*) *terrier*, lit., earth dog, fr *terrier* of earth, fr ML *terrarius*, fr L *terra*; (2) by shortening & alter.]

terrific /tə'rifik/ *adj* **1** exciting fear or awe **2** extraordinarily great or intense **3** unusually fine ***USE*** *(2&3)* infml [L *terrificus*, fr *terrēre* to frighten] – **terrifically** *adv*

terrify /'terifie/ *vt* **1** to fill with terror or apprehension **2** to drive or impel by menacing; scare, deter [L *terrificare*, fr *terrificus*] – **terrifyingly** *adv*

terrigenous /tə'rijənəs/ *adj* being or relating to sediment on the sea floor derived directly from erosion of the land surface [L *terrigena* earthborn, fr *terra* earth + *gignere* to beget – more at KIN]

terrine /tə'reen/ *n* **1** an earthenware baking dish **2** a food, esp pâté, cooked in a terrine [F – more at TUREEN]

¹territorial /,teri'tawri·əl/ *adj* **1a** of territory or land **b** of private property ⟨~ *magnates*⟩ **2a** of or restricted to a particular area or district **b** exhibiting territoriality ⟨~ *birds*⟩ – **territorially** *adv*

²territorial *n* a member of a territorial army, esp the Territorial Army and Volunteer Reserve

,terri,torial 'army *n* a voluntary force organized by a locality to provide a trained army reserve that can be mobilized in an emergency

Territorial Army and Volunteer Reserve *n* the present-day British territorial army

territoriality /,teri,tawri'aləti/ *n* (the pattern of behaviour associated with) the defence of a territory [¹TERRITORIAL + -ITY]

,terri,torial 'waters *n pl* the waters under the sovereign jurisdiction of a nation

territory /'terit(ə)ri/ *n* **1a** a geographical area under the jurisdiction of a government **b** an administrative subdivision of a country **c** a part of the USA not included within any state but with a separate legislature **2a** an indeterminate geographical area **b** a field of knowledge or interest **c** a geographical area having a specified characteristic ⟨*in Rolls Royce ~ – Annabel*⟩ **3a** an assigned area; *esp* one in which an agent or distributor operates **b** an area, often including a nesting site or den, occupied and defended by an animal or group of animals [ME, fr L *territorium*, lit., land round a town, prob fr *terra* land + *-torium* (as in *praetorium*) – more at TERRACE]

terror /'terə/ *n* **1** a state of intense fear **2** sby or sthg that inspires fear **3** REIGN OF TERROR **4** revolutionary violence (e g the planting of bombs) **5** an appalling person or thing; *esp* a brat – infml [ME, fr MF *terreur*, fr L *terror*, fr *terrēre* to frighten; akin to Gk *trein* to be afraid, flee, *tremein* to tremble – more at TREMBLE]

terrorism /'terə,riz(ə)m/ *n* the systematic use of terror, esp as a means of coercion – **terrorist** *adj or n*, **terroristic** /-'ristik/ *adj*

terror·ize, -ise /'terə,riez/ *vt* **1** to fill with terror or anxiety **2** to coerce by threat or violence – **terrorization** /-'zaysh(ə)n/ *n*

'terror-,stricken *adj* overcome with an uncontrollable terror

'terror-,struck *adj* terror-stricken

terry /'teri/ *n* an absorbent fabric with uncut loops on both faces [perh modif of F *tiré*, pp of *tirer* to draw – more at TIRADE] – **terry** *adj*

terse /tuhs/ *adj* concise; *also* brusque, curt [L *tersus* clean, neat, fr pp of *tergēre* to wipe off; akin to Gk *trōgein* to gnaw, L *terere* to rub – more at THROW] – **tersely** *adv*, **terseness** *n*

tertian /'tuhsh(ə)n/ *adj, of malarial symptoms* recurring at approximately 48-hour intervals [ME *tercian*, fr L *tertianus*, lit., of the third, fr *tertius* third – more at THIRD]

¹tertiary /'tuhshəri/ *n* **1** sby belonging to a monastic third order **2** *cap* the Tertiary period or system of rocks

²tertiary *adj* **1a** of third rank, importance, or value **b** of higher education **c** of or being a service industry – compare PRIMARY, SECONDARY **2** *cap* of or being the first period of the Cainozoic era or the corresponding system of rocks ☞ EVOLUTION **3** occurring in or being a third stage [L *tertiarius* of or containing a third, fr *tertius* third]

tertiary consumer *n* a carnivore that eats another carnivore – compare PRIMARY CONSUMER, SECONDARY CONSUMER ☞ FOOD

ˌtertiary ˈsyphilis *n* the third stage of syphilis marked by ulcers and tumours of the skin and usu skeletal, cardiovascular, and nervous disorders (e g locomotor ataxia)

tertium quid /ˌtuhshi·əm ˈkwid, ˌtuhti·əm/ *n* a middle course or intermediate element [LL, lit., third something]

tervalent /tuhˈvaylənt/ *adj* trivalent

Terylene /ˈterəleen, -lin/ *trademark* – used for a synthetic polyester textile fibre

terza rima /ˌtuhtsə ˈreemə/ *n* a verse form consisting of tercets, usu in iambic pentameter [It, lit., third rhyme]

tesla /ˈteslə/ *n* the SI unit of magnetic flux density ☞ PHYSICS [Nikola *Tesla* †1943 US electrician & inventor]

tessellate /ˈtesəlayt/ *vt* to make into or decorate with mosaic [LL *tessellatus*, pp of *tessellare* to pave with tesserae, fr L *tessella*, dim. of *tessera*] – **tessellation** /-ˈlaysh(ə)n/ *n*

tessellated /ˈtesəˌlaytid/ *adj* chequered

tessera /ˈtesərə/ *n, pl* **tesserae** /-ri/ a small piece of marble, glass, etc used in mosaic [L, prob deriv of Gk *tessares* four – more at FOUR; fr its having four corners]

tessitura /ˌtesəˈt(y)ooərə/ *n* the part of the register in which most of the notes of a melody or voice part lie or in which a voice or instrument naturally sounds its best [It, lit., texture, fr L *textura* – more at TEXTURE]

¹test /test/ *n* **1a** a critical examination, observation, or evaluation **b** a basis for evaluation **2** a means or instance of testing: e g **a** a procedure used to identify a substance ⟨*iodine ~ for the presence of starch*⟩ **b** a series of questions or exercises for measuring the knowledge, intelligence, etc of an individual or group **c** TEST MATCH **3** *chiefly Br* a cupel [ME, vessel in which metals were assayed, cupel, fr MF, fr L *testum* earthen vessel; akin to L *testa* earthen pot, shell, *texere* to weave – more at TECHNICAL]

²test *vt* to put to the test; try ⟨~*s my patience*⟩ ⟨*wet roads that ~ a car's tyres*⟩ ~ *vi* to apply a test as a means of analysis or diagnosis – often + *for* – **testable** *adj*, **tester** *n*

³test *n* an external hard or firm covering (e g a shell) of an invertebrate (e g a mollusc) [L *testa* shell]

testa /ˈtestə/ *n, pl* **testae** /ˈtesti/ the hard external coat of a seed [NL, fr L, shell]

testaceous /teˈstayshəs/ *adj* **1a** having a shell **b** consisting of shell, chalk, or other calcium-rich material **2** light brown [L *testaceus*, fr *testa* shell, earthen pot, brick]

testacy /ˈtestəsi/ *n* being testate

testament /ˈtestəmənt/ *n* **1** *cap* either of the 2 main divisions of the Bible **2** a tangible proof or tribute **3** a will **4** *archaic* a covenant between God and man [ME, fr LL & L; LL *testamentum* covenant with God, holy scripture, fr L, last will, fr *testari* to be a witness, call to witness, make a will, fr *testis* witness; akin to L *tres* three & to L *stare* to stand; fr the witness's standing by as a third party in a litigation – more at THREE, STAND] – **testamentary** /-ˈment(ə)ri/ *adj*

testate /ˈtestayt/ *adj* having made a valid will [ME, fr L *testatus*, pp of *testari* to make a will]

testator /teˈstaytə/, *fem* **testatrix** /teˈstaytriks/ *n* sby who leaves a will [ME *testatour*, fr AF, fr LL *testator*, fr L *testatus*, pp]

ˈtest ˌban *n* a self-imposed ban on the atmospheric testing of nuclear weapons

ˈtest-ˌbed *n* a piece of equipment for testing a component separately from its intended working environment

ˈtest ˌcard *n* a geometric pattern or fixed picture broadcast by a television transmitting station to facilitate the testing or adjustment of receivers

ˈtest ˌcase *n* a representative case whose outcome is likely to serve as a precedent

testcross /ˈtestˌkros/ *n* a genetic cross between a homozygous recessive individual and a corresponding suspected heterozygote to determine the genetic constitution of the latter – **testcross** /ˌ-ˈ-/ *vt*

ˈtest-ˌdrive *vt* **ˈtest-ˌdrove; ˈtest-ˌdriven** to drive (a motor vehicle) before buying in order to evaluate suitability

tested /ˈtestid/ *adj* subjected to or qualified through testing – often in combination ⟨*time-*tested *principles*⟩

tester /ˈtestə/ *n* the canopy over a bed, pulpit, or altar [ME, fr MF *testiere* headpiece, head covering, fr *teste* head, fr LL *testa* skull, fr L, shell – more at ¹TEST]

testicle /ˈtestikl/ *n* a testis, esp of a mammal and usu with its enclosing structures (e g the scrotum) ☞ REPRODUCTION [ME *testicule*, fr L *testiculus*, dim. of *testis*] – **testicular** /teˈstikyoolə/ *adj*

testify /ˈtestifie/ *vi* **1a** to make a statement based on personal knowledge or belief **b** to serve as evidence or proof **2** to make a solemn declaration under oath ~ *vt* **1a** to bear witness to **b** to serve as evidence of **2** to make known (a personal conviction) **3** to declare under oath [ME *testifien*, fr L *testificari*, fr *testis* witness] – **testifier** *n*

¹testimonial /ˌtestiˈmohnyəl, -ni·əl/ *adj* **1** of or constituting testimony **2** expressive of appreciation, gratitude, or esteem ⟨*a ~ dinner*⟩

²testimonial *n* **1** a letter of recommendation **2** an expression of appreciation or esteem (e g in the form of a gift)

testimony /ˈtestiməni/ *n* **1a** firsthand authentication of a fact **b** an outward sign; evidence ⟨*is ~ of his abilities*⟩ **c** a sworn statement by a witness **2** a public declaration of religious experience [ME, fr LL & L; LL *testimonium* Decalogue, fr L, evidence, witness, fr *testis* witness – more at TESTAMENT]

testis /ˈtestis/ *n, pl* **testes** /ˈtesteez/ a male reproductive gland ☞ REPRODUCTION [L, witness, testis; perh fr its being evidence of virility]

ˈtest ˌmatch *n* any of a series of international matches, esp cricket matches

testosterone /teˈstostərohn/ *n* a male steroid hormone, produced by the testes or made synthetically, that induces and maintains male secondary sex characters [*test*is + *-o-* + *ster*ol + *-one*]

ˈtest ˌpilot *n* a pilot who specializes in putting new or experimental aircraft through manoeuvres designed to test them by producing strains in excess of normal

ˈtest-ˌtube *adj, of a baby* conceived by artificial insemination, esp outside the mother's body

ˈtest ˌtube *n* a thin glass tube closed at 1 end and used in chemistry, biology, etc

testudo /teˈstyoohdoh/ *n, pl* **testudos** an overhead

cover of overlapping shields or a movable roofed shelter used by the ancient Romans to protect an attacking force [L *testudin-, testudo,* lit., tortoise, tortoise shell; akin to L *testa* shell – more at [1]TEST]

testy /'testi/ *adj* impatient, ill-humoured [ME *testif,* fr AF, headstrong, fr OF *teste* head – more at TESTER] – **testily** *adv,* **testiness** *n*

tetanic /te'tanik/ *adj* of, being, or tending to produce tetanus or tetany – **tetanically** *adv*

tetanus /'tet(ə)nəs/ *n* **1** (the bacterium, usu introduced through a wound, that causes) an infectious disease characterized by spasm of voluntary muscles, esp of the jaw **2** prolonged contraction of a muscle resulting from rapidly repeated motor impulses [ME, fr L, fr Gk *tetanos,* fr *tetanos* stretched, rigid; akin to Gk *teinein* to stretch – more at THIN] – **tetanize** /-iez/ *vt*

tetany /'tet(ə)ni/ *n* muscle spasm usu associated with deficient secretion of parathyroid hormones [ISV, fr L *tetanus*]

tetchy /'techi/ *adj* irritably or peevishly sensitive [perh fr obs *tetch* (habit, bad habit), prob fr ME *tecche, tache,* fr MF *teche, tache* stain, spot, fr OF] – **tetchily** *adv,* **tetchiness** *n*

[1]**tête-à-tête** /,tet ah 'tet, tayt ah atayt/ *adv or adj* (in) private [adv F, lit., head to head; adj fr adv]

[2]**tête-à-tête** *n* **1** a private conversation between 2 people **2** a seat (e g a sofa) designed for 2 people to sit facing each other

,tête-'bêche /besh/ *adj or adv* of a pair of stamps inverted in relation to one another [F, n, pair of inverted stamps, fr *tête* head + *-bêche,* alter. of MF *bechevet* head against foot]

[1]**tether** /'tedhə/ *n* **1** a rope, chain, etc by which an animal is fastened so that it can move only within a set radius **2** the limit of one's strength or resources – chiefly in *the end of one's tether* [ME *tethir,* prob of Scand origin; akin to ON *tjōthr* tether; akin to OHG *zeotar* pole of a wagon]

[2]**tether** *vt* to fasten or restrain (as if) by a tether

tetra-, tetr- *comb form* **1** four; having 4; having 4 parts ⟨tetra*gonal*⟩ **2** containing 4 atoms, groups, or chemical equivalents in the molecular structure ⟨tet*roxide*⟩ [ME, fr L, fr Gk; akin to Gk *tettares* four – more at FOUR]

tetrachord /'tetrə,kawd/ *n* a diatonic series of 4 notes with an interval of a perfect fourth between the first and last [Gk *tetrachordon,* fr neut of *tetrachordos* of four strings, fr *tetra-* + *chordē* string – more at YARN]

tetracycline /,tetrə'siekleen/ *n* any of several broad-spectrum antibiotics obtained esp from a soil bacterium [ISV *tetracyclic* + *-ine*]

tetrad /'tetrad/ *n* a group or arrangement of 4 cells, atoms, etc [Gk *tetrad-, tetras,* fr *tetra-*] – **tetradic** /te'tradik/ *adj*

tetraethyl lead /,tetrə,ethəl 'led/ *n* a poisonous liquid used as a petrol additive to prevent knocking in internal-combustion engines

tetragonal /te'tragənl/ *adj* (characteristic) of the tetragonal system [LL *tetragonalis* having four angles and four sides, fr *tetragonum* quadrangle, fr Gk *tetragōnon,* fr neut of *tetragōnos* tetragonal, fr *tetra-* + *gōnia* angle – more at -GON] – **tetragonally** *adv*

te'tragonal ,system *n* a crystal system characterized by 3 axes at right angles of which only 2 axes are equal

tetragrammaton /,tetrə'gramәton/ *n* the 4 Hebrew letters, usu transliterated YHWH or JHVH, used to refer to God in the Old Testament – compare YAHWEH [ME, fr Gk, fr neut of *tetragrammatos* having four letters, fr *tetra-* + *grammat-, gramma* letter – more at [2]GRAM]

tetrahedron /tetrə'heedrən/ *n, pl* **tetrahedrons, tetrahedra** /-drə/ a polyhedron of 4 faces ☞ MATHEMATICS [NL, fr LGk *tetraedron,* neut of *tetraedros* having four faces, fr Gk *tetra-* + *hedra* seat, face – more at SIT] – **tetrahedral** *adj*

tetrahydrocannabinol /,tetrə,hiedrəkə'nabinol/ *n* a hallucinogenic drug that is the main active constituent of marijuana [*tetrahydro-* (combined with four atoms of hydrogen) + *cannabin* + *-ol*]

tetralogy /te'traləji/ *n* a series of 4 connected works (e g novels) [Gk *tetralogia,* fr *tetra-* + *-logia* -logy]

tetramerous /te'tramərəs/ *adj* having or characterized by (sets or multiples of) 4 parts ⟨~ *flowers*⟩ [NL *tetramerus,* fr Gk *tetramerēs,* fr *tetra-* + *meros* part – more at MERIT]

tetrameter /te'tramitə/ *n* a line of verse consisting of 4 measures of 2 feet or of 4 metrical feet [Gk *tetrametron,* fr neut of *tetrametros* having four measures, fr *tetra-* + *metron* measure – more at MEASURE]

tetraploid /'tetrəployd/ *adj* having or being a chromosome number 4 times the haploid number [ISV] – **tetraploid** *n,* **tetraploidy** *n*

tetrapod /'tetrə,pod/ *n* a vertebrate animal with 2 pairs of limbs [NL *tetrapodus,* fr Gk *tetrapod-, tetrapous* four-footed, fr *tetra-* + *pod-, pous* foot – more at FOOT]

tetrarch /'tetrahk/ *n* a subordinate prince [ME, fr L *tetrarcha,* fr Gk *tetrarchēs,* fr *tetra-* + *-archēs* -arch] – **tetrarchic** /te'trahkik/ *adj*

tetratomic /,tetrə'tomik/ *adj* having 4 (replaceable) atoms (in the molecular structure) [ISV]

tetravalent /,tetrə'vaylənt/ *adj* having a valency of 4 [ISV]

tetter /'tetə/ *n* any of various pustular skin diseases (e g eczema or herpes) – not used technically [ME *teter,* fr OE; akin to OE *teran* to tear]

Teuton /'tyoohton/ *n* **1** a member of an ancient prob Germanic or Celtic people **2** a German [L *Teutoni,* pl] – **Teutonic** /tyooh'tonik/ *adj*

Teutonic /tyooh'tonik/ *n* Germanic

tex /teks/ *n* a unit of weight that is a measure of the fineness of textile yarns – compare DENIER [F, fr *textile* textile]

text /tekst/ *n* **1** (a work containing) the original written or printed words and form of a literary composition **2** the main body of printed or written matter, esp on a page or in a book **3a** a passage of Scripture chosen esp for the subject of a sermon or in authoritative support of a doctrine **b** a passage from an authoritative source providing a theme (e g for a speech) **4** a textbook **5** a theme, topic [ME, fr MF *texte,* fr ML *textus,* fr L, texture, context, fr *textus,* pp of *texere* to weave – more at TECHNICAL]

[1]**'text,book** /-,book/ *n* a book used in the study of a subject; *specif* one containing a presentation of the principles of a subject and used by students

[2]**textbook** *adj* conforming to the principles or

descriptions in textbooks: e g **a** ideal ⟨*tried hard to be a ~ Mum*⟩ **b** typical

textile /'tekstiel/ *n* **1** CLOTH 1; *esp* a woven or knitted cloth **2** a fibre, filament, or yarn used in making cloth [L, fr neut of *textilis* woven, fr *textus*, pp of *texere*]

textual /'tekstyooəl, 'tekschooəl/ *adj* of or based on a text [ME, fr ML *textus* text] – **textually** *adv*

,textual 'criticism *n* **1** the study of a literary work that aims to establish the original text **2** criticism of literature emphasizing a close reading and analysis of the text

[1]**texture** /'tekschə/ *n* **1** the structure formed by the threads of a fabric **2** identifying quality; character ⟨*the ~ of American culture*⟩ **3a** the size or organization of the constituent particles of a body or substance ⟨*a soil that is coarse in ~*⟩ **b** the visual or tactile surface characteristics of sthg, esp fabric ⟨*the ~ of an oil painting*⟩ ⟨*the roughish ~ of tweed*⟩ **4a** the distinctive or identifying part or quality ⟨*the rich ~ of his prose*⟩ **b** a pattern of musical sound created by notes or lines played or sung together [L *textura*, fr *textus*, pp of *texere* to weave – more at TECHNICAL] – **textural** *adj*, **textured** *adj*

[2]**texture** *vt* to give a particular texture to

textured vegetable protein *n* a vegetable substance made from high protein (soya) beans that is used as a meat substitute

[1]**-th** /-th/, **-eth** /-ith/ *suffix* (→ *adj*) – used in forming ordinal numbers ⟨*hundred*th⟩ ⟨*fortie*th⟩ [ME *-the*, *-te*, fr OE *-tha*, *-ta*; akin to OHG *-do* -th, L *-tus*, Gk *-tos*, Skt *-tha*]

[2]**-th, -eth** *suffix* (→ *n*) – used in forming fractions ⟨*a fortie*th⟩ ⟨*two hundred*ths *of an inch*⟩

[3]**-th** *suffix* (→ *n*) **1** act or process of ⟨*grow*th⟩ ⟨*bir*th⟩ **2** state or condition of ⟨*dear*th⟩ ⟨*fil*th⟩ [ME, fr OE; akin to OHG *-ida*, suffix forming abstract nouns, L *-ta*, Gk *-tē*, Skt *-tā*]

Thai /tie/ *n* **1** a native or inhabitant of Thailand **2** the language of Thailand ☞ LANGUAGE – **Thai** *adj*

thalamus /'thaləməs/ *n, pl* **thalami** /-mie/ the subdivision of the midbrain that forms a coordinating centre through which different nerve impulses are directed to appropriate parts of the brain cortex [NL, fr Gk *thalamos* inner chamber] – **thalamic** /thə'lamik/ *adj*

thalassaemia /,thalə'seemyə, -mi·ə/ *n* a hereditary anaemia common in Mediterranean regions and characterized esp by abnormally small red blood cells [NL, fr Gk *thalassa* sea + NL *-æmia*]

thalassic /thə'lasik/ *adj* **1** of deep seas ⟨*~ fishes*⟩ **2** of inland seas ⟨*~ civilizations*⟩ [F *thalassique*, fr Gk *thalassa*]

thaler /'tahlə/ *n* a taler

thalidomide /thə'lidəmied/ *adj or n* (of or affected by) a sedative and hypnotic drug found to cause malformation of infants born to mothers using it during pregnancy [n ph*thali*c acid + *-id-* (fr *imide*) + *-o-* + *imide*; adj fr n]

thall-, thallo- *comb form* thallium ⟨thall*ic*⟩ [NL]

thallium /'thali·əm/ *n* a poisonous metallic element chemically resembling lead ☞ PERIODIC TABLE [NL, deriv of Gk *thallos* green shoot; fr the bright green line in its spectrum] – **thallic** /'thalik/ *adj*, **thallous** *adj*

thallophyte /'thaləfiet/ *n* any of a primary group of living things with a plant body, typically a thallus, that includes the algae, fungi, and lichens ☞ PLANT [deriv of Gk *thallos* + *phyton* plant – more at PHYT-] – **thallophytic** /-'fitik/ *adj*

thallus /'thaləs/ *n, pl* **thalli** /-lie, -li/, **thalluses** a plant body (e g of an alga) that lacks differentiation into distinct tissues or parts (e g stem or leaves) [NL, fr Gk *thallos*, fr *thallein* to sprout; akin to Alb *dal* I come forth] – **thalloid** /'thaloyd/ *adj*

[1]**than** /dhən; *strong* dhan/ *conj* **1a** – used with comparatives to indicate the second member or the member taken as the point of departure in a comparison ⟨*older ~ I am*⟩ ⟨*easier said ~ done*⟩ **b** – used to indicate difference of kind, manner, or degree ⟨*would starve rather ~ beg*⟩ **2** rather than – usu only after *prefer, preferable* **3** other than; but ⟨*no alternative ~ to sack him*⟩ **4** *chiefly NAm* from – usu only after *different, differently* [ME *than, then* then, than – more at THEN]

[2]**than** *prep* in comparison with ⟨*older ~ me*⟩ ⟨*less ~ £1000*⟩

Thanatos /'thanətos/ *n* instinctual desire for death – compare EROS 1 [Gk, death; akin to Skt *adhvanīt* it vanished, L *fumus* smoke]

thane *also* **thegn** /thayn/ *n* **1** a free retainer of an Anglo-Saxon lord; *esp* one holding lands in exchange for military service **2** a Scottish feudal lord [ME *theyn*, fr OE *thegn*; akin to OHG *thegan* thane, Gk *tiktein* to bear, beget] – **thaneship** *n*

thank /thangk/ *vt* **1** to express gratitude to – used in *thank you*, usu without a subject, to express gratitude politely ⟨*~ you for the loan*⟩; used in such phrases as *thank God, thank heaven*, usu without a subject, to express the speaker's or writer's pleasure or satisfaction in sthg **2** to hold responsible ⟨*had only himself to ~ for his loss*⟩ [ME *thanken*, fr OE *thancian*; akin to OE *thanc* gratitude – more at THANKS] – **thanker** *n*

thankful /'thangkf(ə)l/ *adj* **1** conscious of benefit received; grateful **2** feeling or expressing thanks **3** well pleased; glad ⟨*he was ~ that the room was dark*⟩ – **thankfulness** *n*

thankfully /'thangkf(ə)li/ *adv* it is a matter for relief that ⟨*but ~ things have changed – Honey*⟩

thankless /'thangklis/ *adj* **1** not expressing or feeling gratitude **2** not likely to obtain thanks; unappreciated; *also* unprofitable, futile ⟨*it's a ~ job trying to grow tomatoes in England out of doors*⟩ – **thanklessly** *adv*, **thanklessness** *n*

thanks *n pl* **1** kindly or grateful thoughts; gratitude **2** an expression of gratitude ⟨*received with ~ the sum of £50*⟩ – often in an utterance containing no verb and serving as a courteous and somewhat informal expression of gratitude ⟨*many ~*⟩ [pl of ME *thank*, fr OE *thanc* thought, gratitude; akin to OHG *dank* gratitude, L *tongēre* to know] – **no thanks to** not as a result of any benefit conferred by ⟨*he feels better now,* no thanks to *you*⟩ – **thanks to 1** with the help of ⟨thanks to *modern medicine, man's life span is growing longer*⟩ **2** owing to ⟨*our arrival was delayed,* thanks to *the fog*⟩

thanksgiving /thangks'giving, '---/ *n* **1** an expression of gratefulness, esp to God **2** a prayer of gratitude

Thanksgiving Day *n* a day appointed for giving thanks for divine goodness: e g **a** the fourth Thursday in November observed as a public holiday in the USA **b** the second Monday in October observed as a public holiday in Canada

¹thank-ˌyou *n* a polite expression of one's gratitude [fr the phrase (*I*) *thank you,* used in expressing gratitude]

thar /thah/, **tahr** /tah/ *n* a Himalayan beardless wild goat [Nepali *thār*]

¹that /dhat/ *pron, pl* **those** /dhohz/ **1a** the thing or idea just mentioned ⟨*after* ~ *he went to bed*⟩ **b** a relatively distant person or thing introduced for observation or discussion ⟨*who is* ~*?*⟩ ⟨those *are chestnuts and these are elms*⟩ **c** the thing or state of affairs there ⟨*look at* ~*!*⟩ – sometimes used disparagingly of a person **d** the kind or thing specified as follows ⟨*the purest water is* ~ *produced by distillation*⟩ **e** what is understood from the context ⟨*take* ~*!*⟩ ⟨*how's* ~*?*⟩ **2** one of such a group; such ⟨~*'s life*⟩ **3** – used to indicate emphatic repetition of an idea previously presented ⟨*is he capable? He is* ~⟩ **4** *pl* the people; such ⟨those *who think the time has come*⟩ – compare ALL THAT, AND THAT, AT THAT, HOW'S THAT, LIKE THAT, THAT IS TO SAY [ME, fr OE *thæt,* neut demonstrative pron & definite article; akin to OHG *daz,* neut demonstrative pron & definite article, Gk *to,* L *istud,* neut demonstrative pron] – **that's a** THERE'S A – **that's that** that concludes the matter

²that *adj, pl* **those** **1** being the person, thing, or idea specified, mentioned, or understood ⟨~ *cake we bought*⟩ **2** the farther away or less immediately under observation ⟨*this chair or* ~ *one*⟩

³that /dhət; *strong* dhat/ *conj* **1a** – used to introduce a noun clause (1) as subject, object, or complement of a verb ⟨*said* ~ *he was afraid*⟩, (2) anticipated by *it* ⟨*it is unlikely* ~ *he'll be in*⟩, or (3) as complement to a noun or adjective ⟨*the fact* ~ *you're here*⟩ **b** – used to introduce a clause modifying an adverb or adverbial expression ⟨*will go anywhere* ~ *he's invited*⟩ **c** – used to introduce an emotional exclamation ⟨~ *it should come to this!*⟩ or express a wish ⟨*oh,* ~ *he would come!*⟩ **2** – used to introduce a subordinate clause expressing (1) purpose ⟨*worked harder* ~ *he might win esteem*⟩, (2) reason ⟨*glad* ~ *you are free of it*⟩, or (3) result ⟨*walked so fast* ~ *we couldn't keep up*⟩

⁴that /dhət; *strong* dhat/ *pron* **1** – used to introduce a usu restrictive relative clause in reference to a person, thing, or group as subject ⟨*it was George* ~ *told me*⟩ or as object of a verb or of a following preposition ⟨*the house* ~ *Jack built*⟩ **2a** at, in, on, by, with, for, or to which ⟨*the reason* ~ *he came*⟩ ⟨*the way* ~ *he spoke*⟩ **b** according to what; to the extent of what – used after a negative ⟨*has never been here* ~ *I know of*⟩

⁵that /dhat/ *adv* **1** to the extent indicated or understood ⟨*a nail about* ~ *long*⟩ **2** very, extremely – usu with the negative ⟨*not really* ~ *expensive*⟩ **3** *dial Br* to such an extreme degree ⟨*I'm* ~ *hungry I could eat a horse*⟩

thataway /ˈdhatəˌway/ *adv* in that direction or manner – infml [alter. of the phrase *that way*]

¹thatch /thach/ *vt* to cover (as if) with thatch [ME *thecchen,* fr OE *theccan* to cover; akin to OHG *decchen* to cover, L *tegere,* Gk *stegein* to cover, *stegos* roof, Skt *sthagati* he covers] – **thatcher** *n*

²thatch *n* **1** plant material (e g straw) used as a roof covering ☞ BUILDING **2** the hair of one's head – often humor; *broadly* anything resembling the thatch of a house

thaumaturgy /ˈthawməˌtuhji/ *n* the performance of miracles; *specif* magic [Gk *thaumatourgia,* fr *thaumatourgos* working miracles, fr *thaumat-, thauma* miracle + *ergon* work – more at THEATRE, ¹WORK] – **thaumaturgist** *n,* **thaumaturgic** /-ˈtuhjik/ *adj*

¹thaw /thaw/ *vt* to cause to thaw – often + *out* ~ *vi* **1a** to go from a frozen to a liquid state **b** to become free of the effect (e g stiffness, numbness, or hardness) of cold as a result of exposure to warmth – often + *out* **2** to be warm enough to melt ice and snow – + *it*; used in reference to the weather **3** to become less hostile ⟨*relations with E Germany have* ~ed⟩ **4** to become less aloof, cold, or reserved [ME *thawen,* fr OE *thawian*; akin to OHG *douwen* to thaw, Gk *tēkein* to melt, L *tabes* wasting disease]

²thaw *n* **1** the action, fact, or process of thawing ⟨*the* ~ *in relations with Western Europe*⟩ **2** a period of weather warm enough to thaw ice

THC *n* tetrahydrocannabinol [*tetrahydrocannabinol*]

¹the /*before consonants* dhə; *strong and before vowels* dhee/ *definite article* **1a** – used before nouns when the referent has been previously specified by context or circumstance ⟨*put* ~ *cat out*⟩ ⟨*ordered bread and cheese, but didn't eat* ~ *cheese*⟩ **b** – indicating that a following noun is unique or universally recognized ⟨~ *Pope*⟩ ⟨~ *south*⟩ ⟨~ *future*⟩ **c** – used before a noun denoting time to indicate the present or the period under consideration ⟨*book of* ~ *month*⟩ **d** – used before certain proper names ⟨~ *Mayflower*⟩ ⟨~ *Rhine*⟩ ⟨~ *Alhambra*⟩ ⟨~ *Alps*⟩ **e** – used before the name of a familiar accessory of daily life to indicate a service at hand ⟨*talked on* ~ *telephone*⟩ ⟨*turned off* ~ *gas*⟩ **f** – used before the names of certain diseases or conditions ⟨~ *jitters*⟩ ⟨~ *mumps*⟩ **g** – used before the names of parts of the body or of the clothing instead of a possessive adjective ⟨*inflammation of* ~ *bladder*⟩ ⟨*took him by* ~ *sleeve*⟩ **h** – used before the name of a branch of human endeavour or proficiency ⟨*play* ~ *piano*⟩ ⟨*study* ~ *arts*⟩ **i** – indicating an occupation or pursuit symbolically associated with a following noun ⟨~ *pulpit*⟩ ⟨~ *bottle*⟩ **J** – designating 1 of a class as the best or most worth singling out ⟨*this is* ~ *life*⟩ ⟨*you can't be* ~ *Elvis Presley!*⟩ **K** – used before the name of a Scottish clan to denote its chief ⟨~ *McTavish*⟩ **L** – used in prepositional phrases to indicate that the following noun serves as a basis for computation ⟨*sold by* ~ *dozen*⟩ **M** – used before the pl form of a number that is a multiple of 10 to denote a particular decade of a century or of a person's life ⟨*life in* ~ *twenties*⟩ **2a** which or who is – limiting the application of a modified noun to what is specified ⟨~ *right answer*⟩ ⟨*Peter* ~ *Great*⟩ **b** – used before a noun to limit its application to that specified by what follows ⟨~ *University of London*⟩ ⟨~ *man on my right*⟩ ⟨*didn't have* ~ *time to write*⟩ **3** – used before a singular noun to indicate generic use ⟨~ *dog is a mammal*⟩ ⟨*a history of* ~ *novel*⟩ **4a** that which is ⟨*nothing but* ~ *best*⟩ **b** those who are ⟨~ *élite*⟩ ⟨~ *British*⟩ **c** he or she who is ⟨~ *accused stands before you*⟩ **5** – used after *how, what, where, who,* and *why* to introduce various expletives ⟨*who* ~ *devil are you?*⟩ [ME, fr OE *thē,* masc demonstrative pron & definite article, alter. (influenced by oblique cases – e g *thæs,* gen – & neut, *thæt*) of *sē*; akin to Gk *ho,* masc demonstrative pron & definite article – more at THAT]

[2]**the** *adv* **1** than before; than otherwise – with comparatives ⟨*none ~ wiser for attending*⟩ ⟨*so much ~ worse*⟩ **2a** to what extent ⟨*~ sooner the better*⟩ **b** to that extent ⟨*the sooner ~ better*⟩ **3** beyond all others – with superlatives ⟨*likes this ~ best*⟩ ⟨*with ~ greatest difficulty*⟩ [ME, fr OE *thȳ* by that, instrumental of *thæt* that]

[3]**the** *prep* PER 2 [[1]*the*]

the-, theo- *comb form* god; God ⟨the*ism*⟩ ⟨theo*centric*⟩ [ME *theo-*, fr L, fr Gk *the-, theo-*, fr *theos*]

theatre, *NAm chiefly* **theater** /ˈthiətə/ *n* **1a** an outdoor structure for dramatic performances or spectacles in ancient Greece and Rome **b** a building for dramatic performances; *also* a cinema **2** a room with rising tiers of seats (e g for lectures) **3** a place of enactment of significant events or action ⟨*the ~ of public life*⟩ ⟨*the ~ of war*⟩ **4a** dramatic literature or performance **b** dramatic effectiveness ⟨*the effect is pure ~*⟩ **5** *the* theatrical world **6** *Br* OPERATING THEATRE [ME *theatre*, fr MF, fr L *theatrum*, fr Gk *theatron*, fr *theasthai* to see, view, fr *thea* act of seeing; akin to Gk *thauma* miracle]

ˌtheatre-in-the-ˈround *n* (a theatre arranged for) performance of a drama on a stage surrounded by an audience

ˌtheatre of the abˈsurd *n* theatre that seeks to represent the absurdity of human beings' existence in a meaningless universe by bizarre or fantastic means

theatrical /thiˈatrikl/ *adj* **1** of the theatre or the presentation of plays ⟨*a ~ costume*⟩ **2** marked by artificiality (e g of emotion) **3** marked by exhibitionism; histrionic ⟨*a ~ gesture*⟩ – **theatrically** *adv*, **theatricalism** *n*, **theatricality** /thiˌatriˈkaləti/ *n*

theˈatricals *n pl* the performance of plays ⟨*amateur ~*⟩

thebe /ˈtebay/ *n, pl* **thebe** ☞ *Botswana* at NATIONALITY [of Bantu origin]

theca /ˈtheekə/ *n, pl* **thecae** /ˈtheeˌsee, -ˌkee/ **1** an urn-shaped spore receptacle of a moss **2** an enveloping sheath or case of an animal (part) [NL, fr Gk *thēkē* case – more at [4]TICK] – **thecal, thecate** /-ˌkayt/ *adj*

thee /dhee/ *pron, archaic or dial* **1a** *objective case of* THOU **b** thou – used by Quakers, esp among themselves, in contexts where the subjective form would be expected ⟨*is ~ ready?*⟩ **2** thyself [ME, fr OE *thē* (acc & dat of *thū*) – more at THOU]

theft /theft/ *n* the act of stealing; *specif* dishonest appropriation of property with the intention of keeping it [ME *thiefthe*, fr OE *thīefth*; akin to OE *thēof* thief]

thegn /thayn/ *n* THANE 1

theine /ˈthee·in/ *n* caffeine [NL *theina*, fr *thea* tea, fr Chin (Amoy) *t'e*]

their /dhə; *strong* dheə/ *adj* **1** of them or themselves, esp as possessors ⟨*~ furniture*⟩, agents ⟨*~ verses*⟩, or objects of an action ⟨*~ being seen*⟩ **2** his or her; his, her, its ⟨*anyone in ~ senses* – W H Auden⟩ ***USE*** used attributively [ME, fr *their*, pron, fr ON *theirra*, gen pl demonstrative & personal pron; akin to OE *thæt* that]

theirs /dheəz/ *pron, pl* **theirs** **1** that which or the one who belongs to them – used without a following noun as a pronoun equivalent in meaning to the adjective *their* **2** his or hers; his, hers ⟨*I will do my part if everybody else will do ~*⟩

theism /ˈtheeˌiz(ə)m/ *n* belief in the existence of a creator god immanent in the universe but transcending it – **theist** *n or adj*, **theistic** /-ˈistik/, **theistical** *adj*

-theism /-thiˌiz(ə)m/ *comb form* (→ *n*) belief in (such) a god or (such or so many) gods ⟨*pan*theism⟩ ⟨*mono*theism⟩ [MF *-théisme*, fr Gk *theos* god] – **-theist** *comb form* (→ *n*)

[1]**them** /dhəm; *strong* dhem/ *pron, objective case of* THEY [ME; partly fr *tham*, fr OE *thǣm, thām*, dat pl demonstrative pron & definite article; partly fr *thelm*, fr ON, dat pl demonstrative & personal pron; akin to OE *thæt* – more at THAT]

[2]**them** /dhem/ *adj* those ⟨*~ blokes*⟩ – nonstandard

ˌthem-and-ˈus *adj* characterized by tension or resentment between those who exert authority and those over whom it is exerted

thematic /thiˈmatik/ *adj* **1a** of the stem of a word **b** *of a vowel* being the last part of a word stem before an inflectional ending **c** *of a verb form* containing a thematic vowel **2** of or constituting a theme [Gk *thematikos*, fr *themat-, thema* theme] – **thematically** *adv*

theme /theem/ *n* **1** a subject of artistic representation or a topic of discourse **2** STEM 4 **3** a melodic subject of a musical composition or movement **4** *NAm* a written exercise; a composition [ME *teme, theme*, fr OF & L; OF *teme*, fr L *thema*, fr Gk, lit., something laid down, fr *tithenai* to place – more at DO]

ˈtheme ˌsong *n* **1** a recurring melody in a musical play or in a film that characterizes the production or one of its characters **2** a signature tune

themselves /dhəmˈselvz/ *pron pl in constr* **1a** those identical people, creatures, or things that are they – used reflexively ⟨*nations that govern ~*⟩ or for emphasis ⟨*the team ~ were delighted*⟩ **b** himself or herself; himself, herself ⟨*hoped nobody would hurt ~*⟩ **2** their normal selves ⟨*soon be ~ again*⟩

[1]**then** /dhen/ *adv* **1** at that time **2a** soon after that; next in order (of time) ⟨*walked to the door, ~ turned*⟩ **b** besides; IN ADDITION ⟨*~ there is the interest to be paid*⟩ **3a** in that case ⟨*take it, ~, if you want it so much*⟩ **b** as may be inferred ⟨*your mind is made up, ~?*⟩ **c** accordingly, so – indicating casual connection in speech or writing ⟨*our hero, ~, was greatly relieved*⟩ **d** as a necessary consequence ⟨*if the angles are equal, ~ the complements are equal*⟩ **e** – used after *but* to offset a preceding statement ⟨*he lost the race, but ~ he never expected to win*⟩ [ME *than, then* then, than, fr OE *thonne, thænne*; akin to OHG *denne* then, than, OE *thæt* that]

[2]**then** *n* that time ⟨*since ~, he's been more cautious*⟩

[3]**then** *adj* existing or acting at that time ⟨*the ~ secretary of state*⟩

thenar /ˈtheenah, -nə/ *n* **1** the ball of the thumb **2** [2]PALM; *also* [1]SOLE 1a [NL, fr Gk – more at DEN] – **thenar** *adj*

thence /dhens/ *adv* **1** from there ⟨*fly to London and ~ to Paris*⟩ **2** from that preceding fact or premise ⟨*it ~ transpired*⟩ – chiefly fml [ME *thannes*, fr *thanne* from that place, fr OE *thanon*; akin to OHG *thanan* from that place, OE *thænne* then – more at THEN]

,thence'forth /-'fawth/ *adv* from that time or point on – chiefly fml

,thence'forward /-'faw·wood/ *adv* thenceforth

theo- – see THE-

theobromine /,thee·ə'brohmeen/ *n* an alkaloid that is closely related to caffeine, occurs esp in cacao beans and tea, and is used esp as a diuretic and heart stimulant [NL *Theobroma*, genus of trees, fr *the-* + Gk *brōma* food, fr *bibrōskein* to devour]

theocracy /thi'okrəsi/ *n* (a state having) government by immediate divine guidance or by officials regarded as divinely guided [Gk *theokratia*, fr *the-* + *-kratia* -cracy] – **theocrat** /'thee·ə,krat/ *n*, **theocratic** /-'kratik/ *also* **theocratical** *adj*

theodicy /thi'odəsi/ *n* a defence of the doctrines of God's goodness and omnipotence against arguments derived from the existence of evil [modif of F *théodicée*, fr *théo-* the- (fr L *theo-*) + Gk *dikē* judgment, right – more at DICTION]

theodolite /thi'od(ə)l,iet/ *n* a surveyor's instrument for measuring horizontal and usu also vertical angles [NL *theodelitus*] – **theodolitic** /-'itik/ *adj*

theogony /thi'ogəni/ *n* an account of the origin and genealogy of the gods [Gk *theogonia*, fr *the-* + *-gonia* -gony] – **theogonic** /,thee·ə'gonik/ *adj*

theologian /,thee·ə'lohjən/ *n* a specialist in theology

,theo'logical ,college /,theeə'lojikl/ *n* a college for the training of candidates for the clergy

theology /thi'oləji/ *n* **1** the study of God, esp by analysis of the origins and teachings of an organized religion **2** a theological theory, system, or body of opinion ⟨*Catholic* ~⟩ [ME *theologie*, fr L *theologia*, fr Gk, fr *the-* + *-logia* -logy] – **theological** /,thee·ə'lojikl/ *adj*

theophylline /thi'ofilin/ *n* an alkaloid similar to theobromine used esp to treat some types of heart failure and respiratory disorders [ISV *theo-* (fr NL *thea* tea) + *phyll-* + *-ine* – more at THEINE]

theorbo /thi'awboh/ *n, pl* **theorbos** a 17th-c musical instrument like a large lute but having an extra set of bass strings [modif of It *tiorba, teorba*]

theorem /'thiərəm, 'thee·ərəm/ *n* **1** a proposition in mathematics or logic deducible from other more basic propositions **2** an idea proposed as a demonstrable truth, often as a part of a general theory; a proposition [LL *theorema*, fr Gk *theōrēma*, fr *theōrein* to look at, fr *theōros* spectator, fr *thea* act of seeing – more at THEATRE] – **theorematic** /-'matik/ *adj*

theoretical /thiə'retikl, ,thee·ə-/ *also* **theoretic** /thiə'retik, ,thee·ə-/ *adj* **1a** relating to or having the character of theory; abstract **b** confined to theory or speculation; speculative ⟨~ *mechanics*⟩ **2** existing only in theory; hypothetical [LL *theoreticus*, fr Gk *theōrētikos*, fr *theōrein*] – **theoretically** *adv*

theoretician /,thiərə'tish(ə)n, ,thee·ə-/ *n* sby who specializes in the theoretical aspects of a subject

theorist /'thiərist, 'thee·ə-/ *n* a theoretician

theor·ize, -ise /'thiə,riez, 'thee·ə-/ *vi* to form a theory; speculate – **theorizer** *n*

theory /'thiəri, 'thee·ə-/ *n* **1a** a belief, policy, or procedure forming the basis for action ⟨*her method is based on the* ~ *that children want to learn*⟩ **b** an ideal or supposed set of facts, principles, or circumstances – often in *in theory* ⟨*in* ~, *we have always advocated freedom for all, but in practice B*⟩ **2** the general or abstract principles of a subject ⟨*music* ~⟩ **3** a scientifically acceptable body of principles offered to explain a phenomenon ⟨*wave* ~ *of light*⟩ **4a** a hypothesis assumed for the sake of argument or investigation **b** an unproved assumption; a conjecture **c** a body of theorems presenting a concise systematic view of a subject ⟨~ *of equations*⟩ [LL *theoria*, fr Gk *theōria*, fr *theōrein*]

,theory of 'games *n* GAME THEORY

,theory of 'numbers *n* NUMBER THEORY

theosophy /thi'osəfi/ *n* **1** teaching about God and the world stressing the validity of mystical insight **2** *often cap* the teachings of a modern movement originating in the USA in 1875 and following chiefly Buddhist and Brahmanic theories, esp of pantheistic evolution and reincarnation [ML *theosophia*, fr LGk, fr Gk *the-* + *sophia* wisdom – more at -SOPHY] – **theosophist** *n*, **theosophical** /,thee·ə'sofikl/ *adj*

therapeutic /therə'pyoohtik/ *adj* of the treatment of disease or disorders by remedial agents or methods [Gk *therapeutikos*, fr *therapeuein* to attend, treat, fr *theraps* attendant] – **therapeutically** *adv*

therapeutic index *n* a measure of the effectiveness of a drug which indicates how good the drug is at producing the desired therapeutic effects without causing toxic side effects

thera'peutics *n pl but sing or pl in constr* medicine dealing with the application of remedies to diseases

therapist /'therəpist/ *n* sby trained in methods of treatment and rehabilitation other than the use of drugs or surgery ⟨*a speech* ~⟩

therapy /'therəpi/ *n* therapeutic treatment of bodily, mental, or social disorders [NL *therapia*, fr Gk *therapeia*, fr *therapeuein*]

Theravada /,therə'vaydə/ *n* a conservative and nontheistic branch of Buddhism comprising sects chiefly in Sri Lanka and Indochina and viewing the original Pali scriptures alone as canonical – compare MAHAYANA [Pali *theravāda*, lit., doctrine of the elders]

[1]there /dheə/ *adv* **1** in or at that place ⟨*stand over* ~⟩ – often used to draw attention or to replace a name ⟨~ *goes John*⟩ ⟨*hello* ~*!*⟩ **2** thither ⟨*went* ~ *after church*⟩ **3a** now ⟨~ *goes the hooter*⟩ **b** at or in that point or particular ⟨~ *is where I disagree with you*⟩ **4** – used interjectionally to express satisfaction, approval, encouragement, or defiance ⟨~, *it's finished*⟩ ⟨*won't go, so* ~⟩ ⟨~, ~, *don't cry*⟩ [ME, fr OE *thǣr*; akin to OHG *dār* there, OE *thæt* that] – **there and back** for a round trip – **there it is** such is the unfortunate fact – **there's a** – used when urging a course of action ⟨*don't sulk,* there's a *dear!*⟩ – **there you are 1** HERE YOU ARE 1 **2** I told you so

[2]there *pron* – used to introduce a sentence or clause expressing the idea of existence ⟨*what is* ~ *to eat?*⟩ ⟨~ *shall come a time*⟩

[3]there *n* that place or point

[4]there *adj* **1** – used for emphasis, esp after a demonstrative ⟨*those men* ~ *can tell you*⟩ **2** – used for emphasis between a demonstrative and the following noun ⟨*that* ~ *cow*⟩; substandard

thereabouts /,dheərə'bowts/, *NAm also* **,therea'bout** *adv* **1** in that vicinity **2** near that time, number, degree, or quantity ⟨*a boy of 18 or* ~⟩

thereafter /dheə'rahftə/ *adv* after that

thereat /dheə'rat/ *adv* **1** at that place **2** at that occurrence *USE* fml

thereby /dheə'bie/ *adv* **1** by that means; resulting from which **2** in which connection ⟨*~ hangs a tale* – Shak⟩
there'd /dheəd/ there had; there would
therefor /,dheə'faw/ *adv* (in return) for that ⟨*ordered a change and gave his reasons ~*⟩ – fml
therefore /'-,-; *also* ,-'-/ *adv* **1** for that reason; to that end ⟨*We must go. I will ~ call a taxi*⟩ **2** by virtue of that; consequently ⟨*was tired and ~ irritable*⟩ **3** as this proves ⟨*I think, ~ I exist*⟩ ***USE*** (2&3) ☞ SYMBOL
therein /dheə'rin/ *adv* in that; *esp* in that respect ⟨*~ lies the problem*⟩ – fml
there'll /dheəl/ there will; there shall
thereof /dheə'rov/ *adv* **1** of that or it **2** from that or it ***USE*** fml
thereon /dheə'ron/ *adv* on or onto that or it ⟨*a text with a commentary ~*⟩ – fml
thereto /dheə'tooh/ *adv* to that matter or document ⟨*conditions attaching ~*⟩ – fml
theretofore /,dheətə'faw, -tooh-/ *adv* up to that time – fml
thereunder /dheə'rundə/ *adv* under that or it ⟨*the heading and the items listed ~*⟩ – fml
thereupon /,dheərə'pon/ *adv* **1** on that matter ⟨*if all are agreed ~*⟩ **2** immediately after that ***USE*** fml
therewith /dheə'widh/ *adv* **1** with that or it ⟨*a letter enclosed ~*⟩ – fml **2** *archaic* thereupon, forthwith
therm /thuhm/ *n* a quantity of heat equal to 100,000Btu (about 105,506MJ) [Gk *thermē* heat; akin to Gk *thermos* hot – more at WARM]
therm-, thermo- *comb form* heat ⟨therm*ion*⟩ ⟨thermo*stat*⟩ [Gk, fr *thermē*]
-therm /-thuhm/ *comb form* (→ *n*) animal having (such) a body temperature ⟨*ecto*therm⟩ [Gk *thermē*]
¹thermal /'thuhml/ *adj* **1 thermal, thermic** /'thuhmik/ of or caused by heat ⟨*~ stress*⟩ ⟨*~ insulation*⟩ **2** designed (e g with insulating air spaces) to prevent the dissipation of body heat ⟨*~ underwear*⟩ [Gk *thermē*] – **thermally** *adv*
²thermal *n* a rising body of warm air
Thermidor /'thuhmi,daw/ *n* the 11th month of the French Revolutionary calendar corresponding to 20 July–18 August [F, fr Gk *thermē* + *dōron* gift]
thermion /'thuhm,i·ən, -on/ *n* an electrically charged particle, specif an electron, emitted by an incandescent substance [ISV *therm-* + *ion*]
thermionic /,thuhmi'onik/ *adj* of or being (a device, esp a valve using) thermions
thermistor /'thuh,mistə/ *n* a semiconducting electrical resistor whose resistance varies significantly with temperature [*therm*al res*istor*]
Thermit /'thuhmiet, -mət/ *trademark* – used for thermite
thermite /'thuhmiet/ *n* a mixture of aluminium powder and iron oxide that produces a great deal of heat when ignited and is used in welding and in incendiary bombs [*therm-* + *-ite*]
thermochemistry /,thuhmoh'kemistri/ *n* chemistry dealing with the effects of heat on chemical reactions or on physical change of state – **thermochemical** /-'kemikl/ *adj*, **thermochemist** *n*
thermocline /'thuhmə,klien/ *n* a layer of water in a lake, sea, etc that separates an upper warmer zone from a lower colder zone; *specif* a stratum in which temperature declines at least 1°C with each metre increase in depth
thermocouple /'thuhmə,kupl, -moh-/ *n* a combination of 2 conductors for producing a thermoelectric effect used in measuring temperature differences
thermodynamics /,thuhmohdie'namiks, -di-/ *n pl but sing or pl in constr* (physics that deals with) the mechanical action of, or relations between, heat and other forms of energy – **thermodynamic** *adj*, **thermodynamically** *adv*, **thermodynamicist** /-die'naməsist/ *n*
,thermoe'lectric /-i'lektrik/ *adj* of or dependent on phenomena that involve relations between the temperature and the electrical properties of a metal or of 2 metals in contact – **thermoelectricity** *n*
thermoform /'thuhmə,fawm/ *vt* to give a final shape to (e g a plastic) with the aid of heat and usu pressure – **thermoformable** /-,fawməbl/ *adj*
'thermo,gram /-,gram/ *n* the record made by a thermograph
'thermo,graph /-,grahf, -graf/ *n* a self-registering thermometer [ISV]
thermography /thuh'mogrəfi/ *n* **1** a process of writing or printing involving heat **2** a technique for photographically recording variations in the heat emitted by various regions, esp of the body (e g for the detection of tumours) – **thermographic** /,thuhmə'grafik/ *adj*
thermolabile /,thuhmoh'laybiel/ *adj* unstable, specif losing characteristic properties, when heated above a moderate temperature [ISV] – **thermolability** /-lə'biləti/ *n*
thermoluminescence /,thuhmohloohmi'nes(ə)ns/ *n* phosphorescence developed in a previously excited substance that is then gently heated [ISV] – **thermoluminescent** *adj*
thermometer /thə'momitə/ *n* an instrument for determining temperature; *esp* a glass bulb attached to a fine graduated tube of glass and containing a liquid (e g mercury) that rises and falls with changes of temperature [F *thermomètre*, fr Gk *thermē* heat + F *-o-* + *-mètre* -meter – more at THERM] – **thermometry** /-tri/ *n*, **thermometric** /,thuh mə'metrik/ *adj*
thermonuclear /,thuhmoh'nyoohkli·ə/ *adj* of, using, or being (weapons using) transformations occurring in the nucleus of low atomic weight atoms (e g hydrogen) at very high temperatures ⟨*a ~ reaction*⟩ ⟨*~ bombs*⟩ [ISV]
thermophile /'thuhmə,fiel/ *n* a living organism thriving at relatively high temperatures – **thermophilic** /-'filik/ *adj*
thermopile /'thuhmə,piel/ *n* a device that consists of a number of thermoelectric units combined so as to multiply the effect (e g for determining intensities of radiation) [³*pile*]
thermoplastic /,thuhmə'plastik/ *adj* capable of softening or melting when heated and of hardening again when cooled ⟨*~ synthetic resins*⟩ – compare THERMOSETTING – **thermoplastic** *n*
thermoregulation /,thuhmohregyoo'laysh(ə)n/ *n* the natural maintenance of the living body at a constant temperature [ISV] – **thermoregulate** /-'regyoo,layt/ *vi*, **thermoregulatory** /-lət(ə)ri/ *adj*
thermos /'thuhmos, -məs/ *n* THERMOS FLASK
Thermos *trademark* – used for a Thermos flask
thermosetting /'thuhmoh,seting/ *adj* capable of

becoming permanently rigid when heated ⟨*a ~ plastic*⟩ – compare THERMOPLASTIC

[1]'Thermos ,flask *n, often not cap T* a cylindrical container with a vacuum between an inner and an outer wall used to keep material, esp liquids, either hot or cold for considerable periods

thermosphere /'thuhmə,sfiə/ *n* the part of the earth's atmosphere that begins at about 80km (50mi) above the earth's surface, extends to outer space, and is characterized by steadily increasing temperature with height [ISV]

thermostable /,thuhmoh'staybl/ *adj* stable, specif retaining characteristic properties, when heated above a moderate temperature – **thermostability** /-stə'biləti/ *n*

thermostat /'thuhmə,stat/ *n* an automatic device for regulating temperature – **thermostatic** /-'statik/ *adj*

thermotaxis /,thuhmə'taksis/ *n* the regulation of body temperature [NL] – **thermotactic** /-'taktik/ *adj*

thermotropism /thuh'motrə,piz(ə)m/ *n* a tropism in which a temperature gradient is the orienting factor [ISV] – **thermotropic** /,thuhmə'tropik/ *adj*

-thermy /-,thuhmi/ *comb form* (→ *n*) state of having (such) a body temperature ⟨*poikilo*thermy⟩ [NL *-thermia*, fr Gk *thermē* heat – more at THERM]

thesaurus /thi'sawrəs, 'thesərəs/ *n, pl* **thesauri** /-rie, -ri/, **thesauruses** a book of words or of information about a particular field or set of concepts; *esp* a book of words and their synonyms [NL, fr L, treasure, collection, fr Gk *thēsauros*]

these /dheez/ *pl of* THIS

thesis /'theesis/ *n, pl* **theses** /-,seez/ **1a** a proposition that a person offers to maintain by argument **b** a proposition to be proved or one advanced without proof; a hypothesis **2** the first stage of a reasoned argument presenting the case **3** a dissertation embodying the results of original research; *specif* one submitted for a doctorate in Britain **4** the unstressed part of a metrical foot [L, fr Gk, lit., act of laying down, fr *tithenai* to put, lay down – more at DO]

[1]thespian /'thespi·ən/ *adj, often cap* relating to the drama [*Thespis fl* 534 BC Gk poet, reputed founder of Gk drama]

[2]thespian *n* an actor – chiefly fml or humor

Thessalonians /,thesə'lohnyənz, -ni·ənz/ *n pl but sing in constr* either of 2 letters written by Paul to the Christians of Thessalonica and included as books in the New Testament

theta /'theetə, 'thaytə/ *n* the 8th letter of the Greek alphabet [Gk *thēta*, of Sem origin; akin to Heb *ṭēth*, 9th letter of the Heb alphabet]

theurgy /'thee,uhji/ *n* **1** the art or technique of evoking the aid of divine or kindly spirits **2** (the effects produced by) the intervention of a supernatural force in human affairs [LL *theurgia*, fr LGk *theourgia*, fr *theourgos* miracle worker, fr Gk *the-* + *ergon* work – more at [1]WORK] – **theurgist** *n*, **theurgic** /-'uhjik/, **theurgical** *adj*

thew /thyooh/ *n* **1** muscle, sinew – usu pl **2a** muscular power or development **b** strength, vitality ⟨*the naked ~ and sinew of the English language* – G M Hopkins⟩ [ME, personal quality, virtue, fr OE *thēaw*; akin to OHG kathau discipline]

they /dhay/ *pron pl in constr* **1a** those people, creatures, or things ⟨*~ taste better with sugar*⟩; *also, chiefly Br* that group ⟨*ask the committee whether ~ approve*⟩ **b** HE 2 ⟨*if anyone knows, ~ will tell you*⟩ **2a** PEOPLE 1 ⟨*~ say we'll have a hard winter*⟩ **b** the authorities ⟨*~ took my licence away*⟩ [ME, fr ON *their*, masc pl demonstrative & personal pron; akin to OE *thæt* that]

they'd /dhayd/ they had; they would

they'll /dhayl/ they will; they shall

they're /dheə/ they are

they've /dhayv/ they have

thi-, thio- *comb form* containing sulphur in the molecular structure ⟨thio*phosphate*⟩ ⟨thi*amine*⟩ [ISV, fr Gk *thei-, theio-* sulphur, fr *theion*]

thiamine *also* **thiamin** /'thie·əmin/ *n* a vitamin of the vitamin B complex that is essential to normal metabolism and nerve function and is widespread in plants and animals [*thiamine* alter. of *thiamin*, fr *thi-* + *-amin* (as in *vitamin*)]

thiazide /'thie·ə,zied/ *n* any of several synthetic drugs used as oral diuretics, esp in the treatment of high blood pressure and oedema [*thia-* + di*azine* + diox*ide*]

[1]thick /thik/ *adj* **1a** having or being of relatively great depth or extent between opposite surfaces ⟨*a ~ plank*⟩ **b** of comparatively large diameter in relation to length ⟨*a ~ rod*⟩ **2a** closely-packed; dense ⟨*the air was ~ with snow*⟩ ⟨*a ~ forest*⟩ **b** great in number **c** viscous in consistency ⟨*~ syrup*⟩ **d** foggy or misty ⟨*~ weather*⟩ **e** impenetrable to the eye ⟨*~ darkness*⟩ **3** measuring in thickness ⟨*12 centimetres ~*⟩ **4a** imperfectly articulated ⟨*~ speech*⟩ **b** plainly apparent; marked ⟨*a ~ French accent*⟩ **5a** sluggish, dull ⟨*my head feels ~ after too little sleep*⟩ **b** obtuse, stupid **6** on close terms; intimate ⟨*was quite ~ with his boss*⟩ **7** unreasonable, unfair ⟨*called it a bit ~ to be fired without warning*⟩ *USE* (*5b, 6, & 7*) infml [ME *thikke*, fr OE *thicce*; akin to OHG *dicki* thick, OIr *tiug*] – **thick** *adv*, **thicken** *vb*, **thickener** *n*, **thickish** *adj*, **thickly** *adv*

[2]thick *n* **1** the most crowded or active part ⟨*in the ~ of the battle*⟩ **2** the part of greatest thickness ⟨*the ~ of the thumb*⟩

,thick and 'thin *n* every difficulty and obstacle – esp in *through thick and thin*

thicket /'thikit/ *n* **1** a dense growth of shrubbery or small trees **2** sthg like a thicket in density or impenetrability [(assumed) ME *thikket*, fr OE *thiccet*, fr *thicce* thick]

thickhead /'thik,hed/ *n* a stupid person – infml – **thick-headed** /-'hedid/ *adj*

thickness /'thiknis/ *n* **1** the smallest of the 3 dimensions of a solid object **2** the thick part of sthg **3** a layer, ply ⟨*a single ~ of canvas*⟩ [[1]THICK + -NESS]

thickset /thik'set/ *adj* **1** closely placed; *also* growing thickly **2** heavily built; burly

,thick-'skinned *adj* callous, insensitive

,thick-'witted *adj* dull, stupid

thief /theef/ *n, pl* **thieves** /theevz/ sby who steals, esp secretly and without violence [ME *theef*, fr OE *thēof*; akin to OHG *diob* thief, Lith *tupėti* to crouch] – **thievery** /-əri/ *n*, **thievish** *adj*, **thievishness** *n*

thieve /theev/ *vb* to steal, rob [fr *thief*, by analogy to *grief* : *grieve*]

thigh /thie/ *n* the segment of the vertebrate hind limb nearest the body that extends from the hip to the knee and is supported by a single large bone [ME, fr OE *thēoh*; akin to OHG *dioh* thigh, L *tumēre* to swell – more at THUMB] – **thighed** /thied/ *adj*

thighbone /'thie,bohn/ *n* the femur ☞ ANATOMY

thimble /'thimbl/ *n* **1** a pitted metal or plastic cap or cover worn to protect the finger and to push the needle in sewing **2a** a thin metal grooved ring used to fit in a spliced loop in a rope as protection from chafing **b** a movable ring, tube, or lining in a hole [ME *thymbyl*, prob alter. of OE *thȳmel* thumbstall, fr *thūma* thumb]

'thimbleful /-f(ə)l/ *n* as much as a thimble will hold; *broadly* a very small quantity

'thimble,rig /-,rig/ *n* a swindling trick in which a small ball or pea is quickly shifted from under one to another of 3 small cups to fool the spectator guessing its location [*thimble* + [3]*rig* (to swindle)] – **thimblerig** *vi*, **thimblerigger** *n*

[1]thin /thin/ *adj* **-nn- 1a** having little depth between opposite surfaces 〈*a ~ book*〉 **b** measuring little in cross section 〈*~ rope*〉 **2** not dense or closely-packed 〈*~ hair*〉 **3** without much flesh; lean **4a** more rarefied than normal 〈*~ air*〉 **b** few in number **c** with few bids or offerings 〈*a ~ market*〉 **5** lacking substance or strength 〈*~ broth*〉 〈*a ~ plot*〉 **6** flimsy, unconvincing 〈*a ~ disguise*〉 **7** somewhat feeble and lacking in resonance 〈*a ~ voice*〉 **8** lacking in intensity or brilliance 〈*~ colour*〉 **9** lacking sufficient photographic contrast **10** disappointingly poor or hard – infml 〈*had a ~ time of it*〉 [ME *thinne*, fr OE *thynne*; akin to OHG *dunni* thin, L *tenuis* thin, *tenēre* to hold, *tendere* to stretch, Gk *teinein*] – **thin** *adv*, **thinly** *adv*, **thinness** *n*, **thinnish** *adj* – **thin end of the wedge** sthg apparently insignificant that is the forerunner of a more important development

[2]thin *vb* **-nn-** *vt* **1** to reduce in thickness or depth; attenuate **2** to reduce in strength or density **3** to reduce in number or bulk ~ *vi* **1** to become thin or thinner **2** to diminish in strength, density, or number

[1]thine /dhien/ *adj*, *archaic* thy – used esp before a vowel or *h* [ME *thin*, fr OE *thīn*]

[2]thine *pron*, *pl* **thine** *archaic or dial* that which belongs to thee – used without a following noun as a pronoun equivalent in meaning to the adjective *thy;* capitalized when addressing God; still surviving in the speech of Quakers, esp among themselves [ME *thin*, fr OE *thīn*, fr *thīn* thy – more at THY]

thing /thing/ *n* **1a** a matter, affair, concern 〈*~s are not improving*〉 **b** an event, circumstance 〈*that shooting was a terrible ~*〉 **2a(1)** a deed, act, achievement 〈*do great ~s*〉 **(2)** an activity, action 〈*abusive moralizing is about the least productive ~ to do – Nation Review (Melbourne)*〉 **b** a product of work or activity 〈*likes to make ~s*〉 **c** the aim of effort or activity 〈*the ~ is to get well*〉 **d** sthg necessary or desirable 〈*I've got just the ~ for you*〉 **3a** a separate and distinct object of thought (e g a quality, fact, idea, etc) **b** the concrete entity as distinguished from its appearances **c** an inanimate object as distinguished from a living being **d** *pl* imaginary objects or entities 〈*see ~s*〉 〈*hear ~s*〉 **4a** *pl* possessions, effects 〈*pack your ~s*〉 **b** an item of property – used in law **c** an article of clothing 〈*not a ~ to wear*〉 **d** *pl* equipment or utensils, esp for a particular purpose 〈*bring the tea ~s*〉 **5** an object or entity not (capable of being) precisely designated 〈*what's that ~ you're holding?*〉 **6a** a detail, point 〈*checks every little ~*〉 **b** a material or substance of a specified kind 〈*avoid starchy ~s*〉 **7a** a spoken or written observation or point 〈*there are some good ~s in his essay*〉 **b** an idea, motion 〈*says the first ~ he thinks of*〉 〈*for one ~*〉 **c** a piece of news or information 〈*couldn't get a ~ out of him*〉 **8** an individual, creature 〈*poor ~!*〉 **9** *the* proper or fashionable way of behaving, talking, or dressing 〈*it's the latest ~*〉 **10a** a preoccupation (e g a mild obsession or phobia) of a specified type 〈*has a ~ about driving*〉 – compare COMPLEX 2b **b** an intimate relationship; *esp* LOVE AFFAIR 1 〈*had a ~ going with her boss*〉 **c** sthg (e g an activity) that offers special interest and satisfaction to the individual – infml 〈*letting students do their own ~ – Newsweek*〉 *USE* (*10a, 10b, & 10c*) infml [ME, fr OE, thing, assembly; akin to OHG *ding* thing, assembly, Goth *theihs* time] – **of all things** – used to show surprise 〈*wants a xylophone* of all things〉

Thing *n* a legislative or deliberative assembly in a Scandinavian country [ON & Icel; Icel, assembly, parliament, fr ON]

thingamabob /'thing·əmə,bob/ *n* a thingamajig – infml [alter. of earlier *thingum*, fr *thing* + arbitrary suffix]

thingamajig, thingumajig /'thing·əmə,jig/ *n* sthg or sby that is hard to classify or whose name is unknown or forgotten – infml [alter. of earlier *thingum*]

thingie /'thing·i/ *n*, *Br* a thingamajig 〈*those pyramid-shaped ~s* -Punch〉 〈*old ~ who lives down the road*〉 – infml

thingummy /'thing·əmi/ *n* a thingamajig – infml [alter. of earlier *thingum*]

[1]think /thingk/ *vb* **thought** /thawt/ *vt* **1** to form or have in the mind **2** to have as an opinion; consider **3a** to reflect on – often + *over* 〈*~ the matter over*〉 **b** to determine by reflecting – often + *out* 〈*~ it out for yourself*〉 **4** to call to mind; remember 〈*I didn't ~ to ask his name*〉 **5** to devise by thinking – usu + *up* 〈thought *up a plan to escape*〉 **6** to have as an expectation 〈*we didn't ~ we'd have any trouble*〉 **7** to have one's mind full of 〈*talks and ~s business*〉 **8** to subject to the processes of logical thought – usu + *out* or *through* 〈*~ things out*〉 ~ *vi* **1a** to exercise the powers of judgment, conception, or inference **b** to have in mind or call to mind a thought or idea – usu + *of* **2** to have the mind engaged in reflection – usu + *of* or *about* **3** to hold a view or opinion – usu + *of* 〈*~s of himself as a poet*〉 **4** to have consideration – usu + *of* 〈*a man must ~ first of his family*〉 **5** to expect, suspect 〈*better than he ~s possible*〉 [ME *thenken*, fr OE *thencan*; akin to OHG *denken* to think, L *tongēre* to know – more at THANKS] – **thinkable** *adj*, **thinker** *n* – **think better of** to decide on reflection to abandon (a plan) – **think much of** to have at all a high opinion of 〈*didn't* think much of *the new car*〉

[2]think *n* an act of thinking 〈*if he thinks he can fool me, he's got another ~ coming*〉 – infml

[1]thinking /'thingking/ *n* **1** the action of using one's mind to produce thoughts **2** opinion that is characteristic (e g of a period, group, or individual) 〈*the current ~ on immigration*〉 – **put/have on one's thinking cap** to ponder or reflect on sthg

[2]thinking *adj* marked by use of the intellect

think over *vt* to ponder the advantages or disadvantages of; consider ⟨think *it* over⟩

'think ,tank *n sing or pl in constr* a group of people formed as a consultative body to evolve new ideas and offer expert advice

thin-layer chromatography *n* chromatography in which the absorbent medium is a thin layer (e g of kieselguhr) on a support (e g a glass plate) – **thin-layer chromatographic** *adj*

thinner /'thinə/ *n* liquid (e g turpentine) used esp to thin paint [[2]THIN + [2]-ER]

,thin-'skinned *adj* unduly susceptible to criticism or insult

thio- – see THI-

thiocarbamide /,thie·oh'kahbə,mied/ *n* thiourea [ISV]

thiol /'thie,ol, -,ohl/ *n* (the group SH characteristic of) a mercaptan [ISV *thi-* + [1]*-ol*] – **thiolic** /-'olik, -'ohlik/ *adj*

thiopental /,thie·oh'pental/ *n, NAm* thiopentone [*thio-* + *pento*barbit*al*]

thiopentone /,thie·oh'pentohn/ *n* a barbiturate used esp intravenously as a general anaesthetic and in psychotherapy [*thio-* + *pento*barbital + *-one*]

thiosulphate /,thie·oh'sulfayt/ *n* a salt or ester containing the group S_2O_3 [ISV]

thiourea /,thie·ohyoo(ə)'ree·ə, -'yooəri·ə/ *n* (a derivative of) a bitter compound used esp in photography and organic chemistry [NL, fr *thi-* + *urea*]

[1]third /thuhd/ *adj* **1a** next after the second in place or time ⟨*the ~ man in line*⟩ **b** ranking next to second in authority or precedence ⟨*~ mate*⟩ **c** being the forward gear or speed 1 higher than second in a motor vehicle **2a** being any of 3 equal parts into which sthg is divisible **b** being the last in each group of 3 in a series ⟨*take out every ~ card*⟩ [ME *thridde, thirde*, fr OE *thridda, thirdda*; akin to L *tertius* third, Gk *tritos, treis* three – more at THREE] – **third, thirdly** *adv*

[2]third *n* **1a** ☞ NUMBER **b** sthg or sby that is next after second in rank, position, authority, or precedence ⟨*the ~ in line*⟩ **c third, ,third 'class** *often cap* the third and usu lowest level of British honours degree **2** any of 3 equal parts of sthg **3a** (the combination of 2 notes at) a musical interval of 3 diatonic degrees **b** a mediant **4** the third forward gear or speed of a motor vehicle

,third-'class *adj* of a class or grade next below the second – **third-class** *adv*

third class *n* **1** the third group in a classification **2** the least expensive class of accommodation (e g on a ship)

,third de'gree *n* the subjection of a prisoner to torture to obtain information

,third-de,gree 'burn *n* a burn characterized by destruction of the skin and possibly the underlying tissues, loss of fluid, and sometimes shock – compare FIRST-DEGREE BURN, SECOND-DEGREE BURN

,third di'mension *n* (apparent) thickness or depth [fr its being the third dimension, in addition to length and breadth, of a solid body] – **third-dimensional** *adj*

,third'hand /-'hand/ *adj* **1** received from a second intermediary ⟨*~ information*⟩ **2** acquired after use by 2 previous owners – **thirdhand** *adv*

,third 'man *n* a fielding position in cricket lying near the boundary on the off side behind the slips ☞ SPORT

,third 'order *n, often cap T&O* an organization of lay people under a religious rule, directed by a religious order but living in secular society [trans of ML *tertius ordo*; fr the partial resemblance to an order of monks or nuns]

,third-'party *adj* of a third party; *specif* of insurance covering loss or damage sustained by sby other than the insured

,third 'party *n* **1** sby other than the principals ⟨*a ~ to a divorce proceeding*⟩ **2a** a major political party in addition to 2 others in a state normally characterized by a 2-party system **b** a political party whose electoral strength is so small that it can rarely gain control of a government

,third 'person *n* a set of linguistic forms (e g verb forms or pronouns) referring neither to the speaker or writer of the utterance in which they occur nor to the one to whom that utterance is addressed

,third 'rail *n* CONDUCTOR RAIL [fr its being third in addition to the 2 rails on which the wheels of a locomotive run]

,third-'rate *adj* third in quality or value; *broadly* of extremely poor quality – **third-rater** *n*

,third 'reading *n* the final stage of the consideration of a legislative bill before a vote ☞ LAW

,third 'world *n, often cap T&W, sing or pl in constr* **1** a group of nations, esp in Africa and Asia, that are not aligned with either the communist or the capitalist blocs **2** the underdeveloped nations of the world

[1]thirst /thuhst/ *n* **1** (the sensation of dryness in the mouth and throat associated with) a desire or need to drink **2** an ardent desire; a craving [ME, fr OE *thurst*; akin to OHG *durst* thirst, L *torrēre* to dry, parch, Gk *tersesthai* to become dry]

[2]thirst *vi* **1** to feel thirsty **2** to crave eagerly

thirsty /'thuhsti/ *adj* **1a** feeling thirst **b** deficient in moisture; parched ⟨*~ land*⟩ **2** having a strong desire; avid – **thirstily** *adv*, **thirstiness** *n*

thirteen /thuh'teen/ *n* ☞ NUMBER [ME *thrittene*, fr *thrittene*, adj, fr OE *thrēotīne*; akin to OE *tīen* ten – more at TEN] – **thirteen** *adj or pron*, **thirteenth** /-'teenth/ *adj or n*

thirty /'thuhti/ *n* **1** ☞ NUMBER **2** *pl* the numbers 30 to 39; *specif* a range of temperatures, ages, or dates in a century characterized by these numbers [ME *thritty*, fr *thritty*, adj, fr OE *thrītig*, fr *thrītig* group of 30, fr *thrīe* three + *-tig* group of ten – more at EIGHTY] – **thirtieth** /-ti·ith/ *adj or n*, **thirty** *adj or pron*, **thirtyfold** /-,fohld/ *adj or adv*

thirty-second note *n, NAm* a demisemiquaver

[1]this /dhis/ *pron, pl* **these** /dheez/ **1a** the thing or idea that has just been mentioned ⟨*who told you ~?*⟩ **b** what is to be shown or stated ⟨*do it like ~*⟩ **c** this time or place ⟨*expected to return before ~*⟩ **2a** a nearby person or thing introduced for observation or discussion ⟨*~ is iron and that is tin*⟩ ⟨*hello! ~ is Anne Fry speaking*⟩ **b** the thing or state of affairs here ⟨*please carry ~*⟩ ⟨*what's all ~?*⟩ [ME, pron & adj, fr OE *thes* (masc), *this* (neut); akin to OHG *dese* this; akin to OE *thæt* that]

[2]this *adj, pl* **these** **1a** being the person, thing, or idea that is present or near in time or thought ⟨*early ~ morning*⟩ ⟨*who's ~ Mrs Fogg anyway?*⟩ **b** the nearer at hand or more immediately under observation ⟨*~ country*⟩ ⟨*~ chair or that one*⟩ **c** constituting the immediate past or future period ⟨*have lived here these 10 years*⟩ **d** constituting what is to be shown or stated ⟨*have you heard ~ one?*⟩ **2** a certain ⟨*there was ~ Irishman — B*⟩

3**this** *adv* **1** to this extent ⟨*known her since she was ~ high*⟩ **2** to this extreme degree – usu + the negative ⟨*didn't expect to wait ~ long*⟩

thistle /'thisl/ *n* any of various prickly composite plants with (showy) heads of mostly tubular flowers [ME *thistel,* fr OE; akin to OHG *distill* thistle] – **thistly** /'thisli/ *adj*

thistledown /'thisl,down/ *n* the fluffy hairs from the ripe flower head of a thistle

'**thistle ,funnel** *n* a (glass) funnel with a globular top having a flaring mouth

thither /'dhidhə/ *adv* to or towards that place – chiefly fml [ME, fr OE *thider;* akin to ON *thathra* there, OE *thæt* that]

thixotropy /thik'sotrəpi/ *n* the property of various gels of becoming fluid when disturbed (e g by shaking) [ISV *thixo-* (fr Gk *thixis* act of touching, fr *thinganein* to touch) + *-tropy*] – **thixotropic** /,thiksə'trohpik, -'tropik/ *adj*

tho /dhoh/ *adv or conj* though – chiefly infml or poetic

thole /thohl/, **tholepin** /'thohl,pin/ *n* a peg, pin; *esp* either of a pair of wooden pegs serving as rowlocks on a boat [ME *tholle,* fr OE *thol;* akin to Gk *tylos* knob, callus, L *tumēre* to swell – more at THUMB]

Thomism /'toh,miz(ə)m/ *n* the scholastic, philosophical, and theological system of St Thomas Aquinas [prob fr (assumed) NL *thomismus,* fr St *Thomas* Aquinas †1274 It theologian] – **Thomist** *n or adj,* **Thomistic** /-'mistik/ *adj*

thong /thong/ *n* a narrow strip, esp of leather [ME, fr OE *thwong;* akin to ON *thvengr* thong, Av *thwązjaiti* he is distressed] – **thonged** *adj*

thorax /'thaw,raks/ *n, pl* **thoraxes, thoraces** /'thawrə,seez/ (a division of the body of an insect, spider, etc corresponding to) the part of the mammalian body between the neck and the abdomen; *also* its cavity in which the heart and lungs lie ☞ ANATOMY [ME, fr L *thorac-, thorax* breastplate, thorax, fr Gk *thōrak-, thōrax*] – **thoracic** /thaw'rasik, thə-/ *adj*

thoria /'thawri·ə, 'thoh-/ *n* a powdery white oxide of thorium used esp as a catalyst and in heat-resisting material and optical glass [NL, fr *thorium* + *-a*]

thorium /'thawri·əm, 'thoh-/ *n* a radioactive tetravalent metallic element ☞ PERIODIC TABLE [NL, fr ON *Thōrr* Thor, Norse god of thunder, weather, & crops]

thorn /thawn/ *n* **1** a woody plant (of the rose family) bearing sharp prickles of thorns **2** a short hard sharp-pointed plant part, specif a leafless branch **3** sby or sthg that causes irritation ⟨*he's been a ~ in my flesh for years*⟩ **4** an orig runic letter — used in Old and Middle English for either of the sounds /th/ or /dh/ – compare ETH [ME, fr OE; akin to OHG *dorn* thorn, Skt *tṛṇa* grass, blade of grass] – **thorned** *adj,* **thornless** *adj*

'**thorn ,apple** *n* a tall very poisonous coarse annual plant of the nightshade family with spherical prickly fruits

'**thorn,bush** /-,boosh/ *n* any of various thorny shrubs or small trees

thorny /'thawni/ *adj* **1** full of or covered in thorns **2** full of difficulties or controversial points ⟨*a ~ problem*⟩ – **thorniness** *n*

thoron /'thawron/ *n* a gaseous radioactive isotope of radon [NL, fr *thorium*]

1**thorough** /'thurə/ *prep or adv, archaic* through [ME *thorow,* fr OE *thurh, thuruh,* prep & adv]

2**thorough** *adj* **1** carried through to completion ⟨*a ~ search*⟩ **2a** marked by full detail ⟨*a ~ description*⟩ **b** painstaking ⟨*a ~ scholar*⟩ **c** complete in all respects ⟨*~ pleasure*⟩ **d** being fully and without qualification as specified ⟨*a ~ rogue*⟩ – **thoroughly** *adv,* **thoroughness** *n*

'**thorough,bass** /-,bays/ *n* a continuo

1'**thorough,bred** /-,bred/ *adj* **1** bred from the best blood through a long line; purebred **2a** *cap* of or being a Thoroughbred **b** having the characteristics associated with good breeding or pedigree

2**thoroughbred** *n* **1** *cap* any of an English breed of horses kept chiefly for racing that originated from crosses between English mares of uncertain ancestry and Arabian stallions **2** a purebred or pedigree animal **3** sby or sthg with the characteristics associated with good breeding

'**thorough,fare** /-,feə/ *n* **1** a public way (e g a road, street, or path); *esp* a main road **2** passage, transit ⟨*no ~*⟩

'**thorough,going** /-,goh·ing/ *adj* **1** extremely thorough or zealous **2** absolute, utter ⟨*a ~ villain*⟩

those /dhohz/ *pl of* 1 2THAT [ME, fr *those* these, fr OE *thās,* pl of *thes* this – more at THIS]

1**thou** /dhow/ *pron, archaic or dial* the one being addressed; you – capitalized when addressing God; sometimes used by Quakers as the universal form of address to 1 person [ME, fr OE *thū;* akin to OHG *dū* thou, L *tu,* Gk *sy*]

2**thou** /thow/ *n, pl* **thou, thous** **1** a thousand (of sthg, esp money) **2** a unit of length equal to $^1/_{1000}$in (about 25.4mm) [short for *thousand*]

1**though** *also* **tho** /dhoh/ *adv* however, nevertheless ⟨*it's hard work. I enjoy it ~*⟩ [ME, adv & conj, of Scand origin; akin to ON *thō* nevertheless; akin to OE *thēah* nevertheless, OHG *doh*]

2**though** *also* **tho** *conj* **1** in spite of the fact that; while ⟨*~ it's hard work, I enjoy it*⟩ **2** in spite of the possibility that; even if **3** and yet; but ⟨*it works, ~ not as well as we hoped*⟩

1**thought** /thawt/ *past of* THINK

2**thought** *n* **1a** thinking ⟨*lost in ~*⟩ **b** serious consideration ⟨*gave no ~ to the danger*⟩ **2** reasoning or conceptual power **3a** an idea, opinion, concept, or intention **b** the intellectual product or the organized views of a period, place, group, or individual **c** hope, expectation ⟨*gave up all ~ of winning*⟩ **4** a slight amount – in the adverbial phrase *a thought* ⟨*there's a ~ too much seasoning in the stew*⟩ [ME, fr OE *thōht;* akin to OE *thencan* to think – more at THINK]

'**thoughtful** /-f(ə)l/ *adj* **1a** having thoughts; absorbed in thought **b** showing careful reasoned thinking ⟨*a ~ analysis of the problem*⟩ **2** showing concern for others – **thoughtfully** *adv,* **thoughtfulness** *n*

'**thoughtless** /-lis/ *adj* **1** lacking forethought; rash **2** lacking concern for others [2THOUGHT + -LESS] – **thoughtlessly** *adv,* **thoughtlessness** *n*

thousand /'thowz(ə)nd/ *n, pl* **thousands, thousand** **1** ☞ NUMBER **2** the number occupying the position 4 to the left of the decimal point in the Arabic notation; *also, pl* this position **3** an indefinitely large number ⟨∼s *of ants*⟩ – often pl with sing. meaning [ME, fr OE *thūsend*; akin to OHG *dūsunt* thousand; both fr a prehistoric Gmc compound whose constituents are respectively akin to Russ *tys*yacha thousand, Skt *tavas* strong, L *tumēre* to swell, & to OE *hund* hundred] – **thousand** *adj*, **thousandth** *adj or n*

Thracian /ˈthraysh(y)ən/ *n* (the extinct language of) a native or inhabitant of Thrace [L *Thracius*, adj, fr Gk *Thraikios*, fr *Thraikē* Thrace, region of SE Europe] – **Thracian** *adj*

thrall /thrawl/ *n* **1a** a bondman **b** (sby in) a state of (moral) servitude **2** a state of complete absorption or enslavement ⟨*her beauty held him in* ∼⟩ [ME *thral*, fr OE *thrǣl*, fr ON *thrǣll*] – **thrall** *adj*, **thraldom** /-d(ə)m/, *NAm chiefly* **thralldom** *n*

[1]**thrash** /thrash/ *vt* **1** THRESH 1 **2a** to beat soundly (as if) with a stick or whip **b** to defeat heavily or decisively **3** to swing, beat, or strike wildly or violently ⟨∼ing *his arms*⟩ ∼ *vi* **1** THRESH 1 **2** to deal repeated blows (as if) with a flail or whip **3** to move or stir about violently; toss about – usu + *around* or *about* ⟨∼ *around in bed with a fever*⟩ [alter. of *thresh*] – **thrasher** *n*, **thrashing** *n*

[2]**thrash** *n* **1** an act of thrashing, esp in swimming **2** a wild party – infml

thrasher /ˈthrashə/ *n* any of numerous long-tailed American songbirds [prob alter. of *thrush*]

thrash out *vt* to discuss (e g a problem) exhaustively with a view to finding a solution; *also* to arrive at (e g a decision) in this way

thrawn /thrawn/ *adj, chiefly Scot* lacking in pleasing or attractive qualities: e g **a** perverse, recalcitrant **b** crooked, misshapen [ME (Sc) *thrawin*, fr pp of ME *thrawen* to twist] – **thrawnly** *adv*

[1]**thread** /thred/ *n* **1** a filament, group of filaments twisted together, or continuous strand formed by spinning and twisting together short textile fibres **2a** any of various natural filaments ⟨*the* ∼s *of a spider's web*⟩ **b** sthg (e g a thin stream of liquid) like a thread in length and narrowness **c** a projecting spiral ridge (e g on a bolt or pipe) by which parts can be screwed together **3** sthg continuous or drawn out: e g **a** a train of thought ⟨*I've lost the* ∼ *of this argument*⟩ **b** a pervasive recurring element ⟨*a* ∼ *of melancholy marked all his writing*⟩ **4** a precarious or weak support ⟨*to hang by a* ∼⟩ [ME *thred*, fr OE *thrǣd*; akin to OHG *drāt* wire, OE *thrāwan* to cause to twist or turn – more at THROW] – **threadless** *adj*, **threadlike** *adj*, **thready** *adj*

[2]**thread** *vt* **1a** to pass a thread through the eye of (a needle) **b** to arrange a thread, yarn, or lead-in piece in working position for use in (a machine) **2a(1)** to pass sthg through the entire length of ⟨∼ *a pipe with wire*⟩ **(2)** to pass (e g a tape or film) into or through sthg ⟨∼ed *elastic into the waistband*⟩ **b** to make one's way cautiously through or between ⟨∼ing *narrow alleys*⟩ **3** to string together (as if) on a thread ⟨∼ *beads*⟩ **4** to intermingle (as if) with threads ⟨*dark hair* ∼ed *with silver*⟩ **5** to form a screw thread on or in ∼ *vi* **1** to make one's way *through* **2** to form a thread when poured from a spoon – **threader** *n*

threadbare /ˈthred,beə/ *adj* **1** having the nap worn off so that the threads show; worn, shabby **2** hackneyed ⟨∼ *phrases*⟩ – **threadbareness** *n*

ˈ**thread ,mark** *n* a fine line of silk fibre put into a bank note to prevent counterfeiting

ˈ**thread,worm** /-,wuhm/ *n* any of various small usu parasitic nematode worms that infest the intestines, esp the caecum, of vertebrates

threat /thret/ *n* **1** an indication of sthg, usu unpleasant, to come **2** an expression of intention to inflict punishment, injury, or damage **3** sthg that is a source of imminent danger or harm; MENACE 2a [ME *thret* coercion, threat, fr OE *thrēat* coercion; akin to MHG *drōz* annoyance, L *trudere* to push, thrust]

threaten /ˈthret(ə)n/ *vt* **1** to utter threats against ⟨*he* ∼ed *his employees with the sack*⟩ **2a** to give ominous signs of ⟨*the clouds* ∼ *rain*⟩ **b** to be a source of harm or danger to **3** to announce as intended or possible ⟨*the workers* ∼ed *a strike*⟩ ∼ *vi* **1** to utter threats **2** to appear menacing ⟨*the sky* ∼ed⟩ – **threatener** *n*, **threateningly** *adv*

three /three/ *n* **1** ☞ NUMBER **2** the third in a set or series ⟨*the* ∼ *of hearts*⟩ **3** sthg having 3 parts or members or a denomination of 3 [ME, fr *three*, adj, fr OE *thrīe* (masc), *thrēo* (fem & neut); akin to OHG *drī* three, L *tres*, Gk *treis*] – **three** *adj or pron*, **threefold** /-,fohld/ *adj or adv*

,**three-ˈcolour** *adj* being or relating to a printing or photographic process in which 3 primary colours are used to reproduce all the colours of the subject

,**three-ˈD, 3-D** *n* three-dimensional form [*D*, abbr of *dimensional*]

three-day event *n* an equestrian contest involving dressage, cross-country, and showjumping and continuing over 3 days

,**three-ˈdecker** /ˈdekə/ *n* sthg with 3 tiers, layers, etc; *esp* a sandwich with 3 slices of bread and 2 fillings

,**three-diˈmensional** *adj* **1** having 3 dimensions **2** giving the illusion of depth – used of an image or pictorial representation, esp when this illusion is enhanced by stereoscopic means **3** describing or being described in great depth; *esp* lifelike ⟨*a story with* ∼ *characters*⟩ – **three-dimensionality** *n*

,**three-ˈhanded** *adj* played by 3 players ⟨∼ *bridge*⟩

three-legged race *n* a race between pairs in which each contestant has 1 leg tied to 1 of his/her partner's legs

three-line whip *n* an instruction from a party to its Members of Parliament that they must attend a debate and vote in the specified way – compare FREE VOTE, TWO-LINE WHIP [fr the triple underlining of words in the written instruction]

,**three of a ˈkind** *n* 3 cards of the same rank in 1 hand

,**three-ˈphase** *adj* of or operating by means of a combination of 3 circuits energized by alternating electromotive forces that differ in phase by one third of a cycle

,**three-point ˈlanding** *n* an aircraft landing in which the main wheels of the undercarriage touch the ground simultaneously with the tail wheel, skid, or nose wheel

,**three-point ˈturn** *n* a method of turning a vehicle round in a narrow road by first turning obliquely forwards, then reversing, and finally turning forwards again

,**three-ˈquarter** *adj* **1** consisting of 3 fourths of the whole **2** *esp of a view of a rectangular object* including 1 side and 1 end ⟨*a* ∼ *view of a vehicle*⟩

,**three-ˈquarter ,back** *n* a player in rugby, positioned between the halfbacks and the fullback ☞ SPORT – **three-quarter-back** *adj*

three-ring circus *n* **1** a circus with simultaneous performances in 3 rings **2** sthg confusing, engrossing, or spectacular

,three 'R's *n pl* *the* fundamentals taught in primary school; *esp* reading, writing, and arithmetic [fr the facetious phrase *reading, 'riting, and 'rithmetic*]

,three'score /-'skaw/ *n or adj* sixty

'threesome /-s(ə)m/ *n* a group of 3 people or things

three-spined stickleback *n* a stickleback of fresh and brackish waters that typically has 3 spines on its back

thremmatology /,thremə'toləji/ *n* the science of breeding animals and plants in domestication [Gk *thremmat-, thremma* nursling + E *-o-* + *-logy*; akin to Gk *trephein* to nourish – more at ATROPHY]

threnode /'threnohd, 'three-/ *n* a threnody – **threnodist** *n*, **threnodic** /thri'nodik/ *adj*

threnody /'threnədi, 'three-/ *n* a song of lamentation, esp for the dead [Gk *thrēnōidia*, fr *thrēnos* dirge (akin to Skt *dhraṇati* it sounds) + *aeidein* to sing – more at ODE]

threonine /'three·əneen, -nin/ *n* an amino acid found in most proteins and essential to normal nutrition [prob fr *threonic acid*]

thresh /thresh/ *vt* **1** to separate the seeds from (a harvested plant) by (mechanical) beating **2** to strike repeatedly ~ *vi* **1** to thresh grain **2** THRASH 2, 3 [ME *thresshen*, fr OE *threscan*; akin to OHG *dreskan* to thresh, L *terere* to rub – more at THROW]

thresher /'threshə/ *n* a large shark reputed to thresh the water to round up fish on which it feeds using the greatly elongated curved upper lobe of its tail [THRESH + [2]-ER]

threshold /'thresh,hohld, 'thresh·ohld/ *n* **1** the plank, stone, etc that lies under a door **2a** the doorway or entrance to a building **b** the point of entering or beginning ⟨*on the ~ of a new career*⟩ **3** the point at which a physiological or psychological effect begins to be produced by a stimulus of increasing strength **4** a level, point, or value above which sthg is true or will take place [ME *thresshold*, fr OE *threscwald*; akin to ON *threskjöldr* threshold, OE *threscan* to thresh]

threw /throoh/ *past of* THROW

thrice /thries/ *adv* **1** three times **2a** in a threefold manner or degree **b** to a high degree – usu in combination ⟨thrice-*blessed*⟩ [ME *thrie, thries*, fr OE *thriga*; akin to OFris *thria* three times, OE *thrīe* three]

thrift /thrift/ *n* **1** careful management, esp of money; frugality **2** any of a genus of tufted herbaceous plants; *esp* a sea-pink [ME, fr ON, prosperity, fr *thrīfask* to thrive] – **thriftless** *adj*, **thrifty** *adj*, **thriftily** *adv*, **thriftiness** /'thriftinis/ *n*

thrill /thril/ *vt* **1a** to cause to experience a sudden feeling of excitement **b** to cause to have a shivering or tingling sensation **2** to cause to vibrate or tremble perceptibly ~ *vi* **1** to experience a sudden tremor of excitement or emotion **2** to tingle, throb [ME *thirlen, thrillen* to pierce, fr OE *thyrlian*, fr *thyrel* hole, fr *thurh* through – more at THROUGH] – **thrill** *n*, **thrillingly** *adv*

thriller /'thrilə/ *n* a work of fiction or drama characterized by a high degree of intrigue or suspense [THRILL + [2]-ER]

thrips /thrips/ *n, pl* **thrips** any of an order of small sucking insects, most of which feed on and damage plants [L, woodworm, fr Gk]

thrive /thriev/ *vi* **throve** /throhv/, **thrived; thriven** /'thriv(ə)n/ *also* **thrived** **1** to grow vigorously **2** to gain in wealth or possessions [ME *thriven*, fr ON *thrīfask*, prob reflexive of *thrīfa* to grasp] – **thriver** /'thrievə/ *n*

thro /throoh/ *prep* through – now chiefly infml or poetic

throat /throht/ *n* **1a** the part of the neck in front of the spinal column **b** the passage through the neck to the stomach and lungs **2a** sthg throatlike, esp in being a constricted passageway **b** the opening of a tubular (plant) organ **3** the upper forward corner of a fore-and-aft 4-cornered sail ☞ SHIP [ME *throte*, fr OE; akin to OHG *drozza* throat] – **throated** *adj*

throaty /'throhti/ *adj* uttered or produced low in the throat; hoarse, guttural – **throatily** *adv*, **throatiness** *n*

[1]throb /throb/ *vi* **-bb-** **1** to pulsate with unusual force or rapidity **2** to (come in waves that seem to) beat or vibrate rhythmically ⟨*a* ~bing *pain*⟩ [ME *throbben*, prob of imit origin] – **throbber** *n*

[2]throb *n* a beat, pulse

throe /throh/ *n* **1** a pang or spasm – usu pl ⟨*death* ~s⟩ ⟨~s *of childbirth*⟩ **2** *pl* a hard or painful struggle ⟨*in the* ~s *of revolutionary change*⟩ [ME *thrawe, throwe, thrahe*, fr OE *thrag* time]

thromb-, thrombo- *comb form* blood clot; clotting of blood ⟨thromb*osis*⟩ [Gk *thrombos* clot]

thrombin /'thrombin/ *n* an enzyme formed from prothrombin that acts in the process of blood clotting by catalysing the conversion of fibrinogen to fibrin [ISV]

thrombocyte /'thrombəsiet/ *n* **1** a (nucleated) blood platelet **2** a cell of an invertebrate with the function of blood clotting similar to blood platelets [ISV] – **thrombocytic** /-'sitik/ *adj*

thrombosis /throm'bohsis/ *n, pl* **thromboses** /-seez/ the formation or presence of a blood clot within a blood vessel during life [NL, fr Gk *thrombōsis* clotting, deriv of *thrombos* clot] – **thrombotic** /-'botik/ *adj*

thrombus /'thrombəs/ *n, pl* **thrombi** /-bie/ a blood clot formed within a blood vessel and remaining attached to its place of origin – compare EMBOLUS [NL, fr Gk *thrombos*]

throne /throhn/ *n* **1** the chair of state of a sovereign or bishop **2** sovereignty [ME *trone, throne*, fr OF *trone*, fr L *thronus*, fr Gk *thronos* – more at [1]FIRM]

[1]throng /throng/ *n sing or pl in constr* **1** a multitude of assembled people, esp when crowded together **2** a large number [ME *thrang, throng*, fr OE *thrang, gethrang*; akin to OE *thringan* to press, crowd, OHG *dringan*, Lith *trenkti* to jolt]

[2]throng *vt* **1** to crowd upon (esp a person) **2** to crowd into ⟨*shoppers* ~ing *the streets*⟩ ~ *vi* to crowd together in great numbers

throstle /'throsl/ *n* SONG THRUSH [ME, fr OE – more at THRUSH]

[1]throttle /'throtl/ *vt* **throttling** /'throtling, 'throtl·ing/ **1a(1)** to compress the throat of; choke **(2)** to kill by such action **b** to prevent or check expression or activity of; suppress **2a** to control the flow of (e g steam or fuel to an engine) by means of a valve **b** to regulate, esp reduce the speed of (e g an engine), by such means – usu + *back* or *down* [ME *throtlen*, fr *throte* throat] – **throttler** *n*

[2]**throttle** *n* **1a** THROAT 1a **b** TRACHEA 1 **2** (the lever or pedal controlling) a valve for regulating the supply of a fluid (e g fuel) to an engine [perh alter. (influenced by [1]*throttle*) of E dial. *thropple* (throat), fr ME *throppill*]

[1]**through** *also* **thro,** *NAm also* **thru** /throoh/ *prep* **1a(1)** into at one side or point and out at the other ⟨*drove a nail* ~ *the board*⟩ ⟨*a path* ~ *the woods*⟩ (2) past ⟨*saw* ~ *the deception*⟩ **b** – used to indicate passage into and out of a treatment, handling, or process ⟨*flashed* ~ *my mind*⟩ ⟨*the matter has already passed* ~ *his hands*⟩ **2** – used to indicate means, agency, or intermediacy: e g **a** by means of; by the agency of **b** because of ⟨*failed* ~ *ignorance*⟩ **c** by common descent from or relationship with ⟨*related* ~ *their grandfather*⟩ **3a** over the whole surface or extent of ⟨*homes scattered* ~ *the valley*⟩ **b** – used to indicate movement within a large expanse ⟨*flew* ~ *the air*⟩ **c** among or between the parts or single members of ⟨*search* ~ *my papers*⟩ **d** – used to indicate exposure to a set of conditions ⟨*put her* ~ *hell*⟩ **4a** during the entire period of ⟨*all* ~ *her life*⟩ **b** against and in spite of (a noise) ⟨*heard his voice* ~ *the howling of the storm*⟩ **5a** – used to indicate completion, exhaustion, or accomplishment ⟨*got* ~ *the book*⟩ ⟨*went* ~ *a fortune in a year*⟩ **b** – used to indicate acceptance or approval, esp by an official body ⟨*got the bill* ~ *Parliament*⟩ **6** *chiefly NAm* up till and including ⟨*Monday* ~ *Friday*⟩ [ME *thurh, thruh, through*, fr OE *thurh*; akin to OHG *durh* through, L *trans* across, beyond, Skt *tarati* he crosses over]

[2]**through,** *NAm also* **thru** *adv* **1** from one end or side to the other ⟨*squeezed* ~⟩ **2a** all the way from beginning to end ⟨*read the letter* ~⟩ ⟨*train goes right* ~ *to London*⟩ **b** to a favourable or successful conclusion ⟨*see it* ~⟩ ⟨*I failed the exam, but he got* ~⟩ **3** to the core; completely ⟨*wet* ~⟩ **4** into the open; out ⟨*break* ~⟩ **5** *chiefly Br* in or into connection by telephone ⟨*put me* ~ *to him*⟩

[3]**through,** *NAm also* **thru** *adj* **1a** extending from one surface to the other ⟨*a* ~ *beam*⟩ **b** direct ⟨*a* ~ *road*⟩ **2a** allowing a continuous journey from point of origin to destination without change or further payment ⟨*a* ~ *train*⟩ ⟨*a* ~ *ticket*⟩ **b** starting at and destined for points outside a local zone ⟨~ *traffic*⟩ **3** arrived at completion, cessation, or dismissal; finished ⟨*you're* ~*: that was your last chance*⟩ ⟨*I'm* ~ *with women*⟩

,through and 'through *adv* thoroughly, completely

,through-com'posed *adj, of a song* having new music provided for each stanza [trans of G *durchkomponiert*]

[1]**,through'out** /-'owt/ *adv* **1** in or to every part; everywhere ⟨*of 1 colour* ~⟩ **2** during the whole time or action; from beginning to end ⟨*remained loyal* ~⟩

[2]**throughout** *prep* **1** in or to every part of; THROUGH 3a ⟨*cities* ~ *Europe*⟩ **2** during the entire period of; THROUGH 4a ⟨*troubled him* ~ *his life*⟩

'through,put /-,poot/ *n* the amount of material put through a process ⟨*the* ~ *of a computer*⟩

throve /throhv/ *past of* THRIVE

[1]**throw** /throh/ *vb* **threw** /throoh/; **thrown** /throhn/ *vt* **1** to propel through the air in some manner, esp by a forward motion of the hand and arm **2a** to cause to fall ⟨threw *his opponent*⟩ **b** UNSEAT 1 **3a** to fling (oneself) abruptly **b** to hurl violently ⟨*the ship was* ~n *against the rocks*⟩ **4a(1)** to put in a specified position or condition, esp suddenly ⟨*the news* threw *him into confusion*⟩ (2) to put *on* or *off* hastily or carelessly **b** to exert; BRING TO BEAR ⟨threw *all his weight behind the proposal*⟩ **c** to build, construct ⟨threw *a pontoon bridge over the river*⟩ **5** to shape by hand on a potter's wheel **6** to deliver (a punch) **7** to twist 2 or more filaments of (e g silk) into a thread or yarn **8** to make a cast of (dice or a specified number on dice) **9** to send forth; cast, direct ⟨*the setting sun* threw *long shadows*⟩ ⟨*he* threw *me a glance*⟩ **10** to commit (oneself) for help, support, or protection ⟨threw *himself on the mercy of the court*⟩ **11** to bring forth; produce ⟨threw *large litters*⟩ **12** to move (a lever or switch) so as to connect or disconnect parts of a mechanism **13** to project (the voice) **14** to give by way of entertainment ⟨~ *a party*⟩ **15** to disconcert; *also* THROW OFF 4 – infml ⟨*the problem didn't* ~ *her*⟩ **16** *chiefly NAm* to lose intentionally – infml ⟨~ *a game*⟩ ~ *vi* to cast, hurl [ME *thrawen, throwen* to cause to twist, throw, fr OE *thrāwan* to cause to twist or turn; akin to OHG *drāen* to turn, L *terere* to rub, Gk *tetrainein* to bore, pierce] – **thrower** *n* – **throw one's weight about/around** to exercise influence or authority, esp to an excessive degree or in an objectionable manner – infml – **throw together 1** KNOCK TOGETHER ⟨threw together *a delicious curry in no time*⟩ **2** to bring into casual association

[2]**throw** *n* **1a** an act of throwing **b** a method or instance of throwing an opponent in wrestling or judo **2** the distance sthg may be thrown ⟨*lived within a stone's* ~ *from school*⟩ **3** the amount of vertical displacement produced by a geological fault **4** (the distance of) the extent of movement of a cam, crank, or other pivoted or reciprocating piece

[1]**'throwa,way** /-ə,way/ *n* a line of dialogue (e g in a play) made to sound incidental by casual delivery

[2]**throwaway** *adj* **1** designed to be discarded after use; disposable ⟨~ *containers*⟩ **2** written or spoken (e g in a play) with deliberate casualness ⟨*a* ~ *remark*⟩

throw away *vt* **1** to get rid of as worthless or unnecessary **2a** to use in a foolish or wasteful manner **b** to fail to take advantage of **3** to make (e g a line in a play) unemphatic by casual delivery

'throw,back /-,bak/ *n* (an individual exhibiting) reversion to an earlier genetic type or phase

throw back *vt* **1** to delay the progress or advance of **2** to cause to rely; make dependent – + *on* or *upon*; usu pass ⟨thrown back *on his own resources*⟩ ~ *vi* to revert to an earlier genetic type or phase

throw down *vt* to demolish

'throw-,in *n* a throw made from the touchline in soccer to put the ball back in play after it has gone over the touchline

throw in *vt* **1** to add as a gratuity or supplement **2** to introduce or interject in the course of sthg ⟨threw in *a casual remark*⟩ **3** to cause (e g gears) to mesh ~ *vi* to enter into association or partnership *with* ⟨*agrees to* throw in *with a crooked ex-cop – Newsweek*⟩ **– throw in the sponge/towel** to abandon a struggle or contest; acknowledge defeat

throw off *vt* **1a** to cast off, often in an abrupt or vigorous manner ⟨throw off *the oppressors*⟩ ⟨throw *a cold* off⟩ **b** to divert, distract ⟨*dogs* thrown off *by a false scent*⟩ **2** to emit; GIVE OFF ⟨*stacks* throwing off *plumes of smoke*⟩ **3** to produce or execute in an offhand manner ⟨*a review* thrown off *in an odd half hour*⟩ **4** to cause to deviate or err ~ *vi* to begin hunting with a pack of hounds

throw out *vt* **1a** to remove from a place or from employment, usu in a sudden or unexpected manner **b** THROW AWAY 1 **2** to give expression to ⟨threw out *a remark that utterly foxed them*⟩ **3** to refuse to accept or consider ⟨*the assembly* threw out *the proposed legislation*⟩ **4** to give forth from within ⟨*in spring new shoots will be* thrown out *from the main stem*⟩ **5** to cause to extend from a main body ⟨throw out *a screen of cavalry*⟩ ⟨*rebuilt the house,* throwing out *a new wing to the west*⟩ **6** to confuse, disconcert ⟨*the question quite* threw *him* out⟩

throw over *vt* to forsake or abandon (esp a lover)

throwster /'throhstə/ *n* sby who throws textile filaments

throw up *vt* **1** to raise quickly ⟨threw up *his hands in horror*⟩ **2** GIVE UP 3b ⟨*the urge to* throw up *all intellectual work* – Norman Mailer⟩ **3** to build hurriedly **4** to bring forth ⟨*science will continue to* throw up *discoveries which threaten society* – *TLS*⟩ **5** to mention repeatedly by way of reproach **6** to vomit – infml ~ *vi* to vomit – infml **– throw up the sponge** THROW IN THE SPONGE/TOWEL

thru /throoh/ *prep, adv, or adj, NAm* through

thrum /thrum/ *vb* **-mm-** *vi* **1** to play or pluck a stringed instrument idly **2** to drum or tap idly **3** to sound with a monotonous hum ~ *vt* to play (e g a stringed instrument) in an idle or relaxed manner [imit]

1thrush /thrush/ *n* any of numerous small or medium-sized mostly drab-coloured birds many of which are excellent singers: e g **a** SONG THRUSH **b** MISTLE THRUSH [ME *thrusche,* fr OE *thrysce*; akin to OE *throstle* thrush, OHG *droscala,* L *turdus*]

2thrush *n* **1** a whitish intensely irritating fungal growth occurring on mucous membranes, esp in the mouth or vagina **2** a suppurative disorder of the feet in various animals, esp horses [prob of Scand origin; akin to Dan & Norw *trøske* thrush]

1thrust /thrust/ *vb* **thrust** *vt* **1** to push or drive with force **2** to push forth ⟨~ *out roots*⟩ **3** to stab, pierce **4** to put (an unwilling person) into a course of action or position ⟨*was* ~ *into power*⟩ **5** to press, force, or impose the acceptance of *on* or *upon* sby ~ *vi* **1** to force an entrance or passage – often + *into* or *through* **2** to make a thrust, stab, or lunge (as if) with a pointed weapon [ME *thrusten, thristen,* fr ON *thrȳsta*] – **thruster, thrustor** *n*

2thrust *n* **1a** a push or lunge with a pointed weapon **b(1)** a verbal attack **(2)** a concerted military attack **2a** a strong continued pressure **b** the sideways force of one part of a structure against another **c** the force exerted by a propeller, jet engine, etc to give forward motion **3a** a forward or upward push **b** a movement (e g by a group of people) in a specified direction

thrust stage *n* a stage that extends out into the auditorium [*thrust,* pp of 1*thrust*]

1thud /thud/ *vi* **-dd-** to move or strike with a thud [prob fr ME *thudden* to thrust, fr OE *thyddan*]

2thud *n* **1** 5BLOW 1 **2** a dull thump

thug /thug/ *n* **1** *often cap* a member of a former religious sect in India given to robbery and murder **2** a violent criminal [Hindi *ṭhag,* lit., thief, fr Skt *sthaga* rogue, fr *sthagati* he covers, conceals – more at THATCH] – **thuggish** *adj,* **thuggery** /'thugəri/ *n*

thuggee /thu'gee/ *n* murder and robbery as practised by the Thugs of India [Hindi *ṭhagī* robbery, fr *ṭhag*]

thulium /'thyoohli·əm/ *n* a trivalent metallic element of the rare-earth group ☞ PERIODIC TABLE [NL, fr L *Thule, Thyle* Thule, legendary land at the northernmost point of the world, fr Gk *Thoulē, Thylē*]

1thumb /thum/ *n* **1** the short thick digit of the human hand that is next to the forefinger and is opposable to the other fingers; *also* the corresponding digit in lower animals **2** the part of a glove or mitten that covers the thumb [ME *thoume, thoumbe,* fr OE *thūma*; akin to OHG *thūmo* thumb, L *tumēre* to swell, Gk *sōs* safe, whole] **– all thumbs** extremely awkward or clumsy ⟨*dropped everything he picked up and was* all thumbs⟩ **– under someone's thumb** under sby's control; in a state of subservience to sby ⟨*her father had her completely* under his thumb⟩

2thumb *vt* **1a** to leaf through (pages) with the thumb **b** to soil or wear (as if) by repeated thumbing **2** to request or obtain (a lift) in a passing vehicle ~ *vi* **1** to turn over pages **2** to travel by thumbing lifts; hitchhike

'thumb ,index *n* a series of notches cut in the unbound edge of a book for ease of reference – **thumb-index** /,- '--/ *vt*

'thumb,nail /-,nayl/ *adj* brief, concise ⟨*a* ~ *sketch*⟩

'thumb,print /-,print/ *n* an impression made by the thumb

'thumb,screw /-,skrooh/ *n* an instrument of torture for squeezing the thumb

,thumbs-'down *n* rejection, disapproval, or condemnation – infml

'thumb,stall /-,stawl/ *n* a protective covering or sheath for the thumb

,thumbs-'up *n* approval, affirmation – infml

'thumb,tack /-,tak/ *n, NAm* DRAWING PIN

1thump /thump/ *vt* **1** to strike or knock with a thump **2** to thrash; BEAT 1a **3** to produce (music) mechanically or in a mechanical manner ⟨~ed *out a tune on the piano*⟩ ~ *vi* **1** to inflict a thump **2** to produce a thumping sound ⟨*his heart* ~ed⟩ [imit] – **thumper** *n*

2thump *n* (a sound of) a blow or knock (as if) with sthg blunt or heavy

3thump *adv* with a thump

thumping /'thumping/ *adv, Br* VERY 1 – chiefly in *thumping great* and *thumping good*; infml [fr prp of 1*thump*]

1thunder /'thundə/ *n* **1** the low loud sound that follows a flash of lightning and is caused by sudden expansion of the air in the path of the electrical discharge **2** a loud reverberating noise ⟨*the* ~ *of big guns*⟩ [ME *thoner, thunder,* fr OE *thunor*; akin to OHG *thonar* thunder, L *tonare* to thunder] – **thunderous** /'thund(ə)rəs/ *adj,* **thunderously** *adv*

2thunder *vi* **1a** to give forth thunder – usu impersonally ⟨*it* ~ed⟩ **b** to make a sound like thunder ⟨*horses* ~ed *down the road*⟩ **2** to roar, shout ~ *vt* to utter in a loud threatening tone – **thunderer** *n*

'thunder,bolt /-,bohlt/ *n* **1a** a single discharge of lightning with the accompanying thunder **b** an imaginary bolt or missile cast to earth in a flash of lightning **2a** sthg like lightning in suddenness, effectiveness, or destructive power **b** a vehement threat or censure

ˈthunderˌclap /-ˌklap/ *n* (sthg loud or sudden like) a clap of thunder

ˈthunderˌcloud /-ˌklowd/ *n* a cloud charged with electricity and producing lightning and thunder

ˈthunderˌhead /-ˌhed/ *n* a rounded mass of cumulus cloud often appearing before a thunderstorm

thundering /ˈthund(ə)ring/ *adv, Br* very, thumping ⟨*a ~ great bore*⟩ – infml [fr prp of [2]*thunder*] – **thunderingly** *adv*

ˈthunderˌstorm /-ˌstawm/ *n* a storm accompanied by lightning and thunder

ˈthunderˌstruck /-ˌstruk/ *adj* dumbfounded, astonished

thundery /ˈthund(ə)ri/ *adj* producing or presaging thunder ⟨*a ~ sky*⟩

thurible /ˈthyooərəbl/ *n* a censer [ME *turrible*, fr MF *thurible*, fr L *thuribulum*, fr *thur-, thus* incense, fr Gk *thyos* incense, sacrifice, fr *thyein* to sacrifice – more at THYME]

Thuringian /thyooˈrinji·ən/ *n or adj* (a member) of an ancient Germanic people whose kingdom was overthrown by the Franks in the 6th c AD [L *Thuringi*, an ancient Gmc people living in Germany]

Thursday /ˈthuhzday, -di/ *n* the day of the week following Wednesday ☞ SYMBOL [ME, fr OE *thursdæg*, fr ON *thōrsdagr*; akin to OE *thunresdæg* Thursday, OHG *Donares tag*; all fr a prehistoric NGmc-WGmc compound whose components are represented by OHG *Donar*, Gmc god of the sky (fr *thonar, donar* thunder) and by OHG *tag* day – more at THUNDER, DAY] – **Thursdays** *adv*

thus /dhus/ *adv* **1** in the manner indicated; in this way **2** to this degree or extent; so ⟨*~ far*⟩ **3** because of this preceding fact or premise; consequently **4** as an example [ME, fr OE; akin to MD *dus* thus, OE *thæt*, neut demonstrative pron – more at THAT]

thwack /thwak/ *vb or n* (to) whack [imit]

[1]**thwart** /thwawt/ *vt* to defeat the hopes or aspirations of [ME *thwerten, thwarten*, fr *thwert, thwart* (adv) athwart, fr ON *thvert*, fr neut of *thverr* transverse, oblique; akin to OHG *dwerah* transverse, L *torquēre* to twist – more at TORTURE] – **thwarter** *n*

[2]**thwart** *n* a seat extending across a boat

thy /dhie/ *adj, archaic or dial* of thee or thyself – capitalized when addressing God; sometimes used by Quakers, esp among themselves; used attributively [ME *thin, thy*, fr OE *thīn*, gen of *thū* thou – more at [1]THOU]

thylacine /ˈthieləˌsien/ *n* TASMANIAN WOLF [NL *Thylacinus*, genus of marsupials, fr Gk *thylakos* sack, pouch]

thyme /tiem/ *n* any of a genus of plants of the mint family with small pungent aromatic leaves; *esp* a garden plant used in cooking as a seasoning and formerly in medicine [ME, fr MF *thym*, fr L *thymum*, fr Gk *thymon*, fr *thyein* to make a burnt offering, sacrifice; akin to L *fumus* smoke – more at FUME]

-thymia /-thiemyə, -mi·ə/ *comb form* (→ *n*) state of mental health ⟨*schizo*thymia⟩ [NL, fr Gk, fr *thymos* mind]

thymidine /ˈthiemədeen/ *n* a nucleoside containing thymine [*thymine* + *-idine*]

thymine /ˈthiemeen/ *n* a pyrimidine base that is 1 of the 4 bases whose order in the DNA chain codes genetic information – compare ADENINE, CYTOSINE, GUANINE, URACIL [G *thymin*, fr NL *thymus*]

thymol /ˈthieˌmol/ *n* an antiseptic phenol made esp from thyme oil and used chiefly as a fungicide [ISV, fr L *thymum*]

thymus /ˈthieməs/ *n* a gland in the lower neck region that functions in the development of the body's immune system and in humans tends to atrophy after sexual maturity ☞ DIGESTION [NL, fr Gk *thymos* warty excrescence, thymus] – **thymic** *adj*

thyr-, thyro- *comb form* thyroid ⟨thyro*toxicosis*⟩ ⟨thyr*oxine*⟩ [*thyroid*]

thyristor /thieˈristə/ *n* any of several semiconductor devices that act as switches or rectifiers [*thyr*atron (a gas-filled electron tube; fr *Thyratron*, a trademark) + tran*sistor*]

thyroglobulin /ˌthierohˈglobyoolin/ *n* an iodine-containing protein that is the form in which hormones of the thyroid gland are stored [ISV]

[1]**thyroid** /ˈthieroyd/ *also* **thyroidal** /thieˈroydl/ *adj* of or being (an artery, nerve, etc associated with) **a** the thyroid gland **b** the chief cartilage of the larynx [NL *thyroides*, fr Gk *thyreoeidēs* shield-shaped, thyroid, fr *thyreos* shield shaped like a door, fr *thyra* door – more at DOOR]

[2]**thyroid** *n* **1 thyroid, thyroid gland** a large endocrine gland that lies at the base of the neck and produces hormones (e g thyroxine) that increase the metabolic rate and influence growth and development ☞ DIGESTION **2** a preparation of mammalian thyroid gland containing thyroid hormones used in treating conditions in which the thyroid gland produces insufficient quantities of hormones – **thyroidectomy** /ˌthie roy'dektəmi/ *n*

thyroid-stimulating hormone *n* a hormone secreted by the front lobe of the pituitary gland that regulates the formation and secretion of thyroid hormones

thyrotoxicosis /ˌthierohˌtoksiˈkohsis/ *n* hyperthyroidism [NL]

thyrotrophin /ˌthierohˈtrohfin/, **thyrotropin** /-pin/ *n* THYROID-STIMULATING HORMONE [*thyrotroph*ic, *thyrotrop*ic + *-in*] – **thyrotrophic** /-ˈtrohfik/ *adj*

thyroxine /thieˈrokseen, -sin/, **thyroxin** /-ˈroksin/ *n* an io dine-containing amino acid that is the major hormone produced by the thyroid gland and is used to treat conditions in which the thyroid gland produces insufficient quantities of hormones [ISV]

thyrsus /ˈthuhsəs/ *n, pl* **thyrsi** /-sie/ **1** a staff, usu surmounted by a pine cone, that was carried by Bacchus and his followers **2** a flower cluster (e g in the lilac and horse chestnut) with a long main axis bearing short branches which in turn bear the flowers ☞ PLANT [(1) L, fr Gk *thyrsos*; (2) NL, fr L]

thyself /dhieˈself/ *pron, archaic or dial* that identical person that is thou; yourself – sometimes used by Quakers, esp among themselves

ti /tee/ *n* the 7th note of the diatonic scale in tonic sol-fa [alter. of *si*]

tiara /tiˈahrə/ *n* **1** the 3-tiered crown worn by the pope **2** a decorative usu jewelled band worn on the head by women on formal occasions [L, royal Persian headdress, fr Gk]

Tibetan /tiˈbet(ə)n/ *n* (the language of) a member of the indigenous Mongoloid people of Tibet ☞ LAN-

GUAGE [*Tibet*, country in central Asia] – **Tibetan** *adj*

tibia /ˈtibi·ə/ *n, pl* **tibiae** /ˈtibi,ee/ *also* **tibias** **1** the inner and usu larger of the 2 bones of the vertebrate hind limb between the knee and ankle; the shinbone – compare FIBULA ☞ ANATOMY **2** the 4th joint of the leg of an insect between the femur and tarsus ☞ ANATOMY [L] – **tibial** *adj*

tic /tik/ *n* **1** (a) local and habitual spasmodic motion of particular muscles, esp of the face; twitching **2** a persistent trait of character or behaviour ⟨*'you know" is a verbal ~ of many inexperienced speakers*⟩ [F]

tical /tiˈkahl, ˈtikl/ *n, pl* **ticals, tical** a baht [Thai, fr Malay *tikal*, a monetary unit]

tic douloureux /,tik ,doohləˈruh (*Fr* tik dulurø)/ *n* TRIGEMINAL NEURALGIA [F, painful twitch]

[1]**tick** /tik/ *n* **1** any of numerous related bloodsucking arachnids that feed on warm-blooded animals and often transmit infectious diseases **2** any of various usu wingless parasitic insects (e g the sheep ked) [ME *tyke, teke*; akin to MHG *zeche* tick, Arm *tiz*]

[2]**tick** *n* **1** a light rhythmic audible tap or beat; *also* a series of such sounds **2** a small spot or mark, typically ; *esp* one used to mark sthg as correct, to draw attention to sthg, to check an item on a list, or to represent a point on a scale – compare CROSS 5 **3** *Br* a moment, second – infml [ME *tek*; akin to MHG *zic* light push]

[3]**tick** *vi* **1** to make the sound of a tick **2** to function or behave characteristically ⟨*I'd like to know what makes him ~*⟩ ~ *vt* **1** to mark with a written tick **2** to mark or count (as if) by ticks ⟨*a meter ~ing off the cab fare*⟩

[4]**tick** *n* **1** a strong coarse fabric case of a mattress, pillow, or bolster **2** ticking [ME *tike*, prob fr MD; akin to OHG *ziahha* tick; both fr a prehistoric WGmc word borrowed fr L *theca* cover, fr Gk *thēkē* case; akin to Gk *tithenai* to place – more at DO]

[5]**tick** *n* credit, trust ⟨*bought it on ~*⟩ – infml [short for [1]*ticket*]

ˈ**tick,bird** /-,buhd/ *n* any of several African birds that perch on large mammals and feed on ticks

ticker /ˈtikə/ *n* sthg that produces a ticking sound: e g **a** a watch **b** HEART 1a – infml

ˈ**ticker ,tape** *n* a paper tape on which a certain type of telegraphic receiving instrument prints out its information

ticket /ˈtikit/ *n* **1a** a document that serves as a certificate, licence, or permit; *esp* a mariner's or pilot's certificate **b** a tag, label **2** an official notification issued to sby who has violated a traffic regulation **3** a usu printed card or piece of paper entitling its holder to the use of certain services (e g a library), showing that a fare or admission has been paid, etc **4** *Br* a certificate of discharge from the armed forces **5** *chiefly NAm* a list of candidates for nomination or election; *also* PLATFORM 1 **6** the correct, proper, or desirable thing – infml ⟨*hot sweet tea is just the ~* – Len Deighton⟩ [obs F *etiquet* (now *étiquette*) notice attached to sthg, fr MF *estiquet*, fr *estiquier* to attach, fr MD *steken* to stick; akin to OHG *sticken* to prick – more at [2]STICK]

ˈ**ticket ,agent** *n* **1** one who acts as an agent of a transport company to sell tickets for travel by train, boat, aircraft, or bus **2** a seller of theatre tickets

,**ticket-of-ˈleave** *n, pl* **tickets-of-leave** a former permit by which a convict who had served part of his sentence was released on certain conditions

ˈ**tick ,fever** *n* any of various diseases transmitted by the bites of ticks

ticking /ˈtiking/ *n* a strong linen or cotton fabric used esp for a case for a mattress or pillow [[4]*tick*]

[1]**tickle** /ˈtikl/ *vb* **tickling** /ˈtikling, ˈtikl·ing/ *vi* to have or cause a tingling or prickling sensation ~ *vt* **1a** to excite or stir up agreeably **b** to provoke to laughter **2** to touch (e g a body part) lightly and repeatedly so as to excite the surface nerves and cause uneasiness, laughter, or spasmodic movements [ME *tikelen*; akin to OE *tinclian* to tickle]

[2]**tickle** *n* **1** a tickling sensation **2** the act of tickling

ticklish /ˈtiklish/ *adj* **1** sensitive to tickling **2** easily upset **3** requiring delicate handling – **ticklishly** *adv*, **ticklishness** *n*

tick off *vt* to scold, rebuke ⟨*his father* ticked *him* off *for his impudence*⟩ [[3]*tick*]

tick over *vi* to operate at a normal or reduced rate of activity

ticktacktoe *also* **tic-tac-toe** /,tik,takˈtoh/ *n, NAm* NOUGHTS AND CROSSES [*tic-tac-toe* (former game in which players with eyes shut brought a pencil down on a slate marked with numbers and scored the number hit)]

ticktock /ˈtik,tok, ,-ˈ-/ *n* the rhythmic ticking of a clock [imit]

tic tac man /ˈtik ,tak ,man/ *n, Br* a bookmaker's assistant who signals changing odds at a race meeting by means of secret hand signals [*ticktack, tictac* (ticking or tapping sound), of imit origin]

tidal /ˈtiedl/ *adj* of, caused by, or having tides ☞ ENERGY – **tidally** *adv*

ˈ**tidal ,wave** *n* **1** an unusually high sea wave that sometimes follows an earthquake **2** an unexpected, intense, and often widespread reaction (e g a sweeping majority vote or an overwhelming impulse)

tidbit /ˈtid,bit/ *n, chiefly NAm* a titbit

tiddler /ˈtidlə/ *n, Br* sby or sthg small in comparison to others of the same kind; *esp* a minnow, stickleback, or other small fish [prob fr *tiddly*]

tiddly /ˈtidli/ *adj, Br* **1** very small ⟨*a ~ bit of food*⟩ **2** slightly drunk *USE* infml [alter. of *little*]

tiddlywinks /ˈtidli,wingks/ *n* a game whose object is to flick small discs from a flat surface into a small container [prob fr *tiddly*]

[1]**tide** /tied/ *n* **1a(1)** (a current of water resulting from) the periodic rise and fall of the surface of a body of water, specif the sea, that occurs twice a day and is caused by the gravitational attraction of the sun and moon **(2)** a periodic movement in the earth's crust caused by the same forces that produce ocean tides **(3)** a tidal distortion on one celestial body caused by the gravitational attraction of another **b** the level or position of water on a shore with respect to the tide; *also* the water at its highest level **2** sthg that fluctuates like the tides ⟨*the ~ of public opinion*⟩ **3** a flowing stream; a current [ME, time, fr OE *tīd*; akin to OHG *zīt* time, Gk *daiesthai* to divide] – **tideless** *adj*

[2]**tide** *vi* to drift with the tide, esp in navigating a ship into or out of an anchorage, harbour, or river

ˈ**tide,mark** /-,mahk/ *n* **1** a mark left by or indicating the (highest) position of the tide **2** a mark left on a bath that shows the level reached by the water; *also* a mark left on the body showing the limit of washing – chiefly infml

tide over *vt* to enable to surmount or withstand a difficulty [[2]*tide*]

tide table *n* a table of the height of the tide at various times of the day at 1 place

'tide,waiter /-,waytə/ *n* a customs inspector working on the docks or aboard ships

'tide,water /-,wawtə/ *n* **1a** water overflowing land at flood tide **b** water affected by the ebb and flow of the tide **2** low-lying coastal land

'tide,way /-,way/ *n* (a current in) a channel in which the tide runs

tiding /'tieding/ *n* a piece of news – usu pl with sing. meaning ⟨*good* ~s⟩ [ME, fr OE *tīdung*, fr *tīdan* to betide; akin to MD *tiden* to go, come, OE *tīd* time]

[1]tidy /'tiedi/ *adj* **1a** neat and orderly in appearance or habits; well ordered and cared for **b** methodical, precise ⟨*a* ~ *mind*⟩ **2** large, substantial – infml ⟨*a* ~ *profit*⟩ [ME, timely, in good condition, fr *tide* time] – **tidily** *adv*, **tidiness** *n*

[2]tidy *vb* to put (things) in order; make (things) neat or tidy – **tidier** *n*

[3]tidy *n* **1** a receptacle for odds and ends (e g sewing materials) **2** *chiefly NAm* a usu decorative cover used to protect the back, arms, or headrest of a chair or sofa from wear or dirt – compare ANTIMACASSAR

[1]tie /tie/ *n* **1a** a line, ribbon, or cord used for fastening or drawing sthg together **b** a structural element (e g a rod or angle iron) holding 2 pieces together **2** sthg that serves as a connecting link: e g **a** a moral or legal obligation to sby or sthg that restricts freedom of action **b** a bond of kinship or affection **3** a curved line that joins 2 musical notes of the same pitch to denote a single sustained note with the time value of the 2 ☞ MUSIC **4a** a match or game between 2 teams, players, etc ⟨*a cup* ~⟩ **b** (a contest that ends in) a draw or dead heat **5** a narrow length of material designed to be worn round the neck and tied in a knot in the front **6** *NAm* a railway sleeper [ME *teg, tye*, fr OE *tēag*; akin to ON *taug* rope, OE *tēon* to pull – more at [1]TOW] – **tieless** *adj*

[2]tie *vb* **tying, tieing** *vt* **1a** to fasten, attach, or close by knotting **b** to form a knot or bow in **c** to make by tying constituent elements ⟨~d *a wreath*⟩ ⟨~ *a fishing fly*⟩ **d** to make a bond or connection **2a** to unite in marriage **b** to unite (musical notes) by a tie **3** to restrain from independence or from freedom of action or choice; constrain (as if) by authority or obligation – often + *down* ⟨~d *down by his responsibilities*⟩ **4a** to even (the score) in a game or contest **b** to even the score of (a game) ~ *vi* to make a tie; *esp* to make an equal score ⟨*they* ~d *for first place*⟩

'tie-,beam *n* a beam joining the lower ends of opposite rafters ☞ ARCHITECTURE

'tie ,break, 'tie ,breaker *n* a contest or game used to select a winner from among contestants with tied scores at the end of a previous (phase of a) contest

'tie ,clip *n* a pin or clasp used to hold a tie in place

tied cottage /tied/ *n*, *Br* a house owned by an employer (e g a farmer) and reserved for occupancy by an employee

tied house *n* a public house in Britain that is bound to sell only the products of the brewery that owns or rents it out – compare FREE HOUSE

'tie-,dye *n* tie-dyeing

,tie-'dyeing *n* a hand method of producing patterns in textiles by tying portions of the fabric or yarn so that they will not absorb the dye – **tie-dyed** *adj*

'tie-,in *n* **1** sthg that ties in, relates, or connects **2** a book published to coincide with a film or television production to which it is related in some way; *also* the act of publishing such a book

tie in *vt* to bring into connection with sthg relevant; *esp* to coordinate so as to produce balance and unity ⟨*the illustrations were cleverly* tied in *with the text*⟩ ~ *vi* to be closely connected; *esp* to correspond ⟨*that* ties in *with what I know already*⟩

'tie,pin /-,pin/ *n* a decorative pin used to hold a tie in place

[1]tier /tiə/ *n* any of a series of levels (e g in an administration) ⟨*the top* ~ *of local government*⟩ [MF *tire* order, rank – more at ATTIRE]

[2]tier *vb* to place, arrange, or rise in tiers

tierce /tiəs/ *n* a sequence of 3 playing cards of the same suit [ME *terce, tierce* third part, fr MF, fr fem of *terz*, adj, third, fr L *tertius* – more at THIRD]

tiercel /'tiəsl/ *n* a tercel

'tie-,rod *n* a rod (e g of steel) used as a connecting member or brace

'tie-,up *n* a connection, association ⟨*a political* ~ *with gangsters*⟩

tie up *vt* **1** to attach, fasten, or bind securely; *also* to wrap up and fasten **2** to connect closely; link **3** to place or invest in such a manner as to make unavailable for other purposes ⟨*his money was* tied up *in stocks*⟩ **4** to keep busy ⟨*was* tied up *in conference all day*⟩ **5** *NAm* to restrain from operation or progress ⟨*traffic was* tied up *for miles*⟩ ~ *vi* **1** to dock **2** to assume a definite relationship ⟨*this* ties up *with what you were told before*⟩

tiff /tif/ *vi or n* (to have) a petty quarrel [origin unknown]

tiffany /'tifəni/ *n* a sheer silk gauze [prob fr obs F *tiphanie* Epiphany, fr LL *theophania*, fr LGk, deriv of Gk *theos* god + *phainein* to show]

tiffin /'tifin/ *n* a meal or snack taken at midday or in the middle of the morning, esp by the British in India [prob alter. of *tiffing*, gerund of obs *tiff* (to eat or drink between meals)]

tiger /'tiegə/, *fem* **tigress** /'tiegris/ *n, pl* **tigers,** (*1*) **tigers,** *esp collectively* **tiger** **1** a very large Asiatic cat having a tawny coat transversely striped with black **2** a fierce and often bloodthirsty person [ME *tigre*, fr OE *tiger* & OF *tigre*, both fr L *tigris*, fr Gk, of Iranian origin; akin to Av *tighra-* pointed; akin to Gk *stizein* to tattoo] – **tigerish** *adj*, **tigerishly** *adv*, **tigerishness** *n*, **tigerlike** *adj*

tiger beetle *n* any of numerous active flesh-eating beetles having larvae that tunnel in the soil

tiger cat *n* a serval, ocelot, or other wildcat of moderate size and variegated coloration

tiger lily *n* an Asiatic lily commonly grown for its drooping orange-coloured flowers densely spotted with black

tiger moth *n* any of a family of stout-bodied moths, usu with broad striped or spotted wings

'tiger's-,eye *also* **'tiger,eye** *n* a usu yellowish brown ornamental gemstone consisting mainly of silicates of sodium and iron

[1]tight /tiet/ *adj* **1** so close or solid in structure as to prevent passage (e g of a liquid or gas) ⟨*a ~ roof*⟩ – often in combination ⟨*an air*tight *compartment*⟩ **2a** fixed very firmly in place **b** firmly stretched, drawn, or set **c** fitting (too) closely **3** set close together ⟨*a ~ defensive formation in soccer*⟩ **4** difficult to get through or out of ⟨*in a ~ situation*⟩ ⟨*a ~ spot*⟩ **5** firm in control; *also* characterized by such firmness ⟨*ran a ~ ship*⟩ **6** evenly contested ⟨*a ~ match*⟩ **7** packed, compressed or condensed to (near) the limit ⟨*a ~ bale*⟩ ⟨*a ~ literary style*⟩ ⟨*~ schedule*⟩ **8** scarce in proportion to demand ⟨*~ money*⟩; *also* characterized by such a scarcity ⟨*a ~ labour market*⟩ **9** playing in unison ⟨*his three week old band was surprisingly ~ – The Age (Melbourne)*⟩ **10** stingy, miserly **11** intoxicated, drunk ***USE*** (*10&11*) infml [ME, alter. of *thight*, of Scand origin; akin to ON *thēttr* tight; akin to MHG *dīhte* thick, Skt *tanakti* it causes to coagulate] – **tightly** *adv*, **tightness** *n*

[2]**tight** *adv* **1** fast, tightly ⟨*the door was shut ~*⟩ **2** in a sound manner ⟨*sleep ~*⟩

tighten /'tiet(ə)n/ *vb* to make or become tight or tighter or more firm or severe – often + *up* – **tightener** *n*

tighten up *vi* to enforce regulations more stringently – usu + *on* ⟨*the government is* tightening up *on tax-dodgers*⟩

,tight'fisted /-'fistid/ *adj* reluctant to part with money

,tight-'lipped *adj* **1** having the lips compressed (e g in determination) **2** reluctant to speak; taciturn

'tight,rope /-,rohp/ *n* **1** a rope or wire stretched taut for acrobats to perform on **2** a dangerously precarious situation

tights /tiets/ *n pl* a skintight garment covering each leg (and foot) and reaching to the waist – **tight** *adj*

tigon /'tiegən/ *n* a hybrid produced by a mating between a tiger and a lioness [*tig*er + li*on*]

tigress /'tiegris/ *n* a female tiger; *also* a tigerish woman

tike /tiek/ *n* a tyke

tilde /'tildə/ *n* **1** a mark˜ placed esp over the letter *n* (e g in Spanish *señor*) to denote the sound /ny/ or over vowels (e g in Portuguese *irmã*) to indicate nasality **2** a swung dash, esp as used in mathematics to indicate similarity or equivalence ☞ SYMBOL [Sp, fr ML *titulus* tittle]

[1]**tile** /tiel/ *n* **1** a thin slab of fired clay, stone, or concrete shaped according to use: e g **a** a flat or curved slab for use on roofs **b** a flat and often ornamented slab for floors, walls, or surrounds **c** a tube-shaped or semicircular and open slab for constructing drains **2** a thin piece of resilient material (e g cork or linoleum) used esp for covering floors or walls [ME, fr OE *tigele*; akin to ON *tigl* tile; both fr a prehistoric WGmc-NGmc word borrowed fr L *tegula* tile; akin to L *tegere* to cover – more at THATCH] **–on the tiles** enjoying oneself socially, esp in an intemperate or wild manner ⟨*looks terrible this morning after a night out* on the tiles⟩

[2]**tile** *vt* to cover with tiles – **tiler** *n*, **tiling** *n*

[1]**till** /til, tl/ *prep* **1** until **2** *chiefly Scot* to [ME, fr OE *til*; akin to ON *til* to, till, OE *til* good]

[2]**till** *conj* until

[3]**till** /til/ *vt* to work (e g land) by ploughing, sowing, and raising crops [ME *tilien, tillen*, fr OE *tilian*; akin to OE *til* good, suitable, OHG *zil* goal] – **tillable** *adj*, **tillage** *n*, **tiller** *n*

[4]**till** *n* **1a** a receptacle (e g a drawer or tray) in which money is kept in a shop or bank **b** CASH REGISTER **2** the money contained in a till [AF *tylle*]

[5]**till** *n* glacial drift consisting of clay, sand, gravel, and boulders not deposited in distinct layers [origin unknown]

[1]**tiller** /'tilə/ *n* a lever used to turn the rudder of a boat from side to side [ME *tiler* stock of a crossbow, fr MF *telier*, lit., beam of a loom, fr ML *telarium*, fr L *tela* web – more at [3]TOIL]

[2]**tiller** *n* a sprout or stalk (from the base of a plant) [fr (assumed) ME, fr OE *telgor, telgra* twig, shoot; akin to OHG *zelga* twig, Gk *daidalos* ingeniously formed – more at CONDOLE]

[3]**tiller** *vi, of a plant* to put forth tillers

[1]**tilt** /tilt/ *vt* **1** to cause to slope ⟨*don't ~ the boat*⟩ **2** to point or thrust (as if) in a joust ⟨*~ a lance*⟩ *~ vi* **1** to shift so as to lean or incline **2a** to engage in combat with lances **b** to make an impetuous attack ⟨*~ at wrongs*⟩ [ME *tulten, tilten*; akin to Sw *tulta* to waddle] – **tiltable** *adj*, **tilter** *n*

[2]**tilt** *n* **1** a military exercise in which a mounted person charges at an opponent or mark **2** speed – in *at full tilt* **3** a written or verbal attack – + *at* **4a** tilting or being tilted **b** a sloping surface

[3]**tilt** *n* a canopy for a wagon, boat, lorry, or stall [ME *teld, telte* tent, canopy, fr OE *teld*; akin to OHG *zelt* tent]

tilth /tilth, tildh/ *n* the state of being tilled; *also* the condition of tilled land ⟨*land in good ~*⟩ [ME, fr OE, fr *tilian* to till]

tiltyard /'tilt,yahd/ *n* a yard or place for tilting contests

timbale /'timbayl/ *n* **1** (a creamy mixture of meat, vegetables, etc baked in) a cup-shaped mould **2** a small pastry shell filled with a cooked timbale mixture [F, lit., kettledrum, fr MF, alter. of *tamballe*, modif of OSp *atabal*, fr Ar *aṭ-ṭabl* the drum]

[1]**timber** /'timbə/ *n* **1a** growing trees or their wood **b** – used interjectionally to warn of a falling tree **2** wood suitable for carpentry or woodwork ☞ BUILDING **3** material, stuff; *esp* personal character or quality **4** *Br* wood or logs, esp when dressed for use [ME, fr OE, building, wood; akin to OHG *zimbar* wood, room, L *domus* house, Gk *demein* to build] – **timber** *adj*, **timberman** /-mən/ *n*

[2]**timber** *vt* to frame, cover, or support with timbers

timbered /'timbəd/ *adj* having walls framed by exposed timbers

timber hitch *n* a knot used to secure a line to a log or spar

timbering /'timb(ə)ring/ *n* a set or arrangement of timbers

'timber,line /-,lien/ *n* TREE LINE

timber wolf *n* a type of wolf formerly common over much of eastern N America

timbre /'tambə, 'timbə, 'tahmbə (*Fr* tɛ̃:br)/ *also* **timber** /'timbə/ *n* the quality given to a sound by its overtones: e g **a** the resonance by which the ear recognizes a voiced speech sound **b** the quality of tone distinctive of a particular singing voice or musical instrument [F, fr MF, bell struck by a hammer, fr OF, drum, fr MGk *tymbanon* kettledrum, fr Gk *tympanon* – more at TYMPANUM]

timbrel /'timbrəl/ *n* a small hand drum or tambourine [dim. of obs *timbre* (tambourine), fr ME, fr OF, drum]

[1]**time** /tiem/ *n* **1a** the measurable period during which an action, process, or condition exists or continues ☞ PHYSICS **b** a continuum in which events succeed one another ⟨*stand the test of* ~⟩ **c** leisure ⟨~ *for reading*⟩ **2a** the point or period when sthg occurs ⟨*at the* ~ *of writing*⟩ **b** the period required for an action ⟨*the winner's* ~ *was under 4 minutes*⟩ **3a** a period set aside or suitable for an activity or event ⟨*now is the* ~⟩ ⟨*a* ~ *for celebration*⟩ **b** an appointed, fixed, or customary moment for sthg to happen, begin, or end; *esp, Br* closing time in a public house as fixed by law ⟨*hurry up please, it's* ~ – T S Eliot⟩ **4a** a historical period – often pl with sing. meaning ⟨*modern* ~s⟩ **b** conditions or circumstances prevalent during a period – usu pl with sing. meaning ⟨~s *are hard*⟩ **c** *the* present time ⟨*issues of the* ~⟩ **d** the expected moment of giving birth or dying ⟨*her* ~ *is near*⟩ **e** the end or course of a future period ⟨*only* ~ *will tell*⟩ ⟨*will happen in* ~⟩ **5a** a period of apprenticeship **b** a term of imprisonment – infml **6** a season ⟨*very hot for this* ~ *of year*⟩ **7a** a tempo **b** the grouping of the beats of music; a rhythm, metre **8a** a moment, hour, day, or year as measured or indicated by a clock or calendar **b** any of various systems (e g sidereal or solar) of reckoning time **9a** any of a series of recurring instances or repeated actions ⟨*you've been told many* ~s⟩ **b** *pl* **(1)** multiplied instances ⟨*5* ~s *greater*⟩ **(2)** equal fractional parts of which a specified number equal a comparatively greater quantity ⟨*7* ~s *smaller*⟩ **10** a person's usu specified experience, esp on a particular occasion ⟨*a good* ~⟩ **11a** the hours or days occupied by one's work ⟨*make up* ~⟩ **b** an hourly rate of pay ⟨*on double* ~⟩ **12** the end of the playing time of a (section of a) game – often used as an interjection [ME, fr OE *tima*; akin to ON *tīmi* time, OE *tīd* – more at TIDE] – **at times** at intervals; occasionally – **behind the times** old-fashioned – **for the time being** for the present – **from time to time** at irregular intervals – **in time 1** sufficiently early **2** eventually **3** in correct tempo ⟨*learn to play* in time⟩ – **on time** at the appointed time – **time and (time) again** frequently, repeatedly

[2]**time** *vt* **1** to arrange or set the time of **2** to regulate the moment, speed, or duration of, esp to achieve the desired effect ⟨*an ill*-timed *remark*⟩ **3** to cause to keep time with sthg **4** to determine or record the time, duration, or speed of ⟨~ *a journey*⟩ ~ *vi* to keep or beat time – **timer** *n*

[3]**time** *adj* **1** of or recording time **2** (able to be) set to function at a specific moment ⟨*a* ~ *bomb*⟩ ⟨*a* ~ *switch*⟩

,time and a 'half *n* payment of a worker (e g for overtime) at 1½ times the regular wage rate

,time and 'motion *adj* of or concerned with studying the efficiency of working methods, esp in industry

'time ,capsule *n* a capsule that has contemporary articles sealed in it and is then buried (e g underneath a new building) with the intention that those who open it in future years may gain an impression of what life was like when it was buried

time clock *n* a clock that stamps an employee's starting and finishing times on a card

'time-con,suming *adj* using or taking up (too) much time ⟨~ *chores*⟩ ⟨~ *tactics*⟩

time exposure *n* (a photograph taken by) exposure of a photographic film for a relatively long time, usu more than 0.5s

'time-,honoured *adj* sanctioned by custom or tradition

time immemorial /imi'mawri·əl/ *n* time beyond living memory or historical record

'time,keeper /-,keepə/ *n* sby who records the time worked by employees, elapsed in a race, etc – **timekeeping** *n*

'time ,lag *n* an interval of time between 2 related phenomena

'time-,lapse *adj* of or constituting a method of cinema photography in which a slow action (e g the opening of a flower bud) is filmed in successive stages so as to appear speeded up on the screen

'timeless /-lis/ *adj* **1a** unending, eternal **b** not restricted to a particular time or date **2** not affected by time; ageless – **timelessly** *adv*, **timelessness** *n*

'timely /-li/ *adv or adj* at an appropriate time – **timeliness** *n*

,time-'out *n* a suspension of play in any of several sports (e g basketball); *broadly, NAm* a brief suspension of activity

,time out of 'mind *n* TIME IMMEMORIAL

'time,piece /-,pees/ *n* a clock, watch, etc that measures or shows progress of time; *esp* one that does not chime

times /tiemz/ *prep* multiplied by ⟨*2* ~ *2 is 4*⟩

'time,server /-,suhvə/ *n* sby who fits behaviour and ideas to prevailing opinions or to his/her superiors' views

'time-,sharing *n* **1** simultaneous access to a computer by many users **2** a method of sharing holiday accommodation whereby each of a number of people buys a share of a lease on a property, entitling him/her to spend a proportionate amount of time there each year

time signature *n* a sign placed on a musical staff being usu a fraction whose denominator indicates the kind of note taken as the time unit for the beat (e g 4 for a crotchet or 8 for a quaver) and whose numerator indicates the number of beats per bar ☞ MUSIC

[1]**'time,table** /-,taybl/ *n* **1** a table of departure and arrival times of public transport **2** a schedule showing a planned order or sequence of events, esp of classes (e g in a school)

[2]**timetable** *vt* to arrange or provide for in a timetable

'time,worn /-,wawn/ *adj* **1** worn or impaired by time **2** ancient, age-old

'time ,zone *n* a geographical region within which the same standard time is used

timid /'timid/ *adj* lacking in courage, boldness, or self-confidence [L *timidus*, fr *timēre* to fear] – **timidly** *adv*, **timidness, timidity** /ti'midəti/ *n*

timing /'tieming/ *n* selection for maximum effect of the precise moment for doing sthg [[2]TIME + [2]-ING]

timocracy /tie'mokrəsi/ *n* government in which **a** a certain amount of property is necessary for office **b** love of honour is the ruling principle [MF *tymocracie*, fr ML *timocratia*, fr Gk *timokratia*, fr *timē* price, value, honour + *-kratia* -cracy – more at PAIN] – **timocratic** /,tiemə'kratik/, **timocratical** *adj*

timorous /'tim(ə)rəs/ *adj* timid [ME, fr MF *timou-*

reus, fr ML *timorosus*, fr L *timor* fear, fr *timēre* to fear] – **timorously** *adv*, **timorousness** *n*

timothy /'timəthi/ *n* a European grass widely grown for hay [prob fr *Timothy* Hanson, 18th-c US farmer said to have introduced it from New England to the southern states of the USA]

Timothy *n* (either of 2 New Testament Pastoral Epistles addressed to) a disciple of the apostle Paul [L *Timotheus*, fr Gk *Timotheos*]

timpani /'timpəni/ *n pl but sing or pl in constr* a set of 2 or 3 kettledrums played by 1 performer (e g in an orchestra) [It, pl of *timpano* kettledrum, fr L *tympanum* drum – more at TYMPANUM] – **timpanist** *n*

[1]**tin** /tin/ *n* **1** a soft lustrous metallic element that is malleable and ductile at ordinary temperatures and is used as a protective coating, in tinfoil, and in soft solders and alloys ☞ PERIODIC TABLE **2** a box, can, pan, vessel, or sheet made of tinplate: e g **a** a hermetically sealed tinplate container for preserving foods **b** any of various usu tinplate or aluminium containers of different shapes and sizes in which food is cooked, esp in an oven ⟨*roasting* ~⟩ ⟨*loaf* ~⟩ **3** a strip of resonant material below the board on the front wall of a squash court ☞ SPORT [ME, fr OE; akin to OHG *zin* tin] – **tinful** *n*

[2]**tin** *vt* **-nn- 1** to cover or plate with tin or a tin alloy **2** *chiefly Br* [3]CAN 1a

tinctorial /tingk'tawri·əl/ *adj* of colours, dyeing, or staining [L *tinctorius*, fr *tinctus*, pp] – **tinctorially** *adv*

[1]**tincture** /'ting(k)chə/ *n* **1a** a substance that colours or stains **b** a colour, hue **2** a slight addition; a trace **3** a heraldic metal, colour, or fur **4** a solution of a substance in alcohol for medicinal use ⟨~ *of iodine*⟩ [ME, fr L *tinctura* act of dyeing, fr *tinctus*, pp of *tingere* to tinge]

[2]**tincture** *vt* to tint or stain with a colour

tinder /'tində/ *n* any combustible substance suitable for use as kindling [ME, fr OE *tynder*; akin to OHG *zuntra* tinder, OE *tendan* to kindle] – **tindery** *adj*

'tinder,box /-,boks/ *n* **1a** a metal box for holding tinder and usu a flint and steel for striking a spark **b** a highly inflammable object or place **2** a potentially unstable place, situation, or person

tine /tien/ *n* **1** a prong (e g of a fork) **2** a pointed branch of an antler [ME *tind*, fr OE; akin to OHG *zint* point, tine] – **tined** *adj*

tinea /'tini·ə/ *n* a fungous disease of the skin; *esp* ringworm [ME, fr ML, fr L, worm, moth] – **tineal** *adj*

tin fish *n* a torpedo – slang

tinfoil /,tin'foyl, '-,-/ *n* a thin metal sheeting of tin, aluminium, or a tin alloy

[1]**tinge** /tinj/ *vt* **tingeing, tinging 1** to colour with a slight shade **2** to impart a slight smell, taste, or other quality to [ME *tingen*, fr L *tingere* to dip, moisten, tinge; akin to OHG *dunkōn* to dip, Gk *tengein* to moisten]

[2]**tinge** *n* **1** a slight staining or suffusing colour **2** a slight modifying quality; a trace

tin glaze *n* an opaque ceramic glaze containing tin oxide – **tin glaze** *vt*

tingle /'ting·gl/ *vi or n* **tingling** /'ting·gling/ (to feel or cause) a stinging, prickling, or thrilling sensation [vb ME *tinglen*, alter. of *tinklen* to tinkle, tingle; n fr vb] – **tinglingly** *adv*, **tingly** *adj*

tin god *n* **1** a pompous and self-important person **2** sby unjustifiably esteemed or venerated *USE* infml

tin hat *n* a present-day military metal helmet – infml

[1]**tinker** /'tingkə/ *n* **1** a usu itinerant mender of household utensils **2** *chiefly Scot & Irish* a gipsy [ME *tinkere*]

[2]**tinker** *vi* to repair, adjust, or work with sthg in an unskilled or experimental manner – usu + *at* or *with* – **tinkerer** *n*

,tinker's 'cuss *n* DAMN 2 – chiefly in *not give a tinker's cuss* [prob fr the tinkers' reputation for swearing]

,tinker's 'damn, ,tinker's 'dam *n, NAm* TINKER'S CUSS

[1]**tinkle** /'tingkl/ *vb* **tinkling** /'tingkling, 'tingkl·ing/ *vi* to make (a sound suggestive of) a tinkle ~ *vt* **1** to sound or make known (the time) by a tinkle **2** to cause to (make a) tinkle [ME *tinklen*, freq of *tinken* to tinkle, of imit origin] – **tinkly** *adj*

[2]**tinkle** *n* **1** a series of short light ringing or clinking sounds **2** a jingling effect in verse or prose **3** *Br* a telephone call – infml **4** *Br* an act of urinating – euph

tinman /'tinmən/ *n* a tinsmith

tinner /'tinə/ *n* a tin miner or tinsmith

tinnitus /ti'nietəs/ *n* a subjective ringing or roaring sensation of noise [L, ringing, tinnitus, fr *tinnitus*, pp of *tinnire* to ring, of imit origin]

tinny /'tini/ *adj* **1** of, containing, or yielding tin **2a** having the taste, smell, or appearance of tin **b** not solid or durable; shoddy ⟨*a* ~ *car*⟩ **3** having a thin metallic sound – **tinnily** *adv*, **tinniness** *n*

,Tin Pan 'Alley *n* a district that is a centre for composers and publishers of popular music; *also, sing or pl in constr* the body of such composers and publishers

,tin'plate /-'playt/ *n* thin sheet iron or steel coated with tin – **tin-plate** *vt*

'tin-,pot *adj* paltry ⟨*a* ~ *little organization*⟩ – infml

[1]**tinsel** /'tins(ə)l/ *n* **1** a thread, strip, or sheet of metal, plastic, or paper used to produce a glittering and sparkling effect (e g in fabrics or decorations) **2** sthg superficial, showy, or glamorous ⟨*the* ~ *of stardom*⟩ [MF *estincelle, estancele, etincelle* spark, glitter, spangle – more at STENCIL] – **tinselled,** *NAm* **tinseled, tinselled** *adj*

[2]**tinsel** *adj* cheaply gaudy; tawdry

'tin,smith /-,smith/ *n* sby who works with sheet metal (e g tinplate)

'tin,stone /-,stohn/ *n* cassiterite

[1]**tint** /tint/ *n* **1a** a usu slight or pale coloration; a hue **b** any of various lighter or darker shades of a colour; *esp* one produced by adding white **2** a shaded effect in engraving produced by fine parallel lines close together **3** a panel of light colour serving as background for printing on [alter. of earlier *tinct*, fr L *tinctus* act of dyeing, fr *tinctus*, pp of *tingere* to tinge]

[2]**tint** *vt* to apply a tint to; colour – **tinter** *n*

tintinnabulation /,tinti,nabyoo'laysh(ə)n/ *n* **1** the ringing of bells **2** a sound as if of bells *USE* fml [L *tintinnabulum* bell, fr *tintinnare* to ring, jingle, of imit origin]

tiny /'tieni/ *adj* very small or diminutive ·[alter. of ME *tine*] – **tinily** *adv*, **tininess** *n*

[1]**tip** /tip/ *n* **1** the usu pointed end of sthg **2** a small

piece or part serving as an end, cap, or point ⟨*a filter*-tip *cigarette*⟩ [ME; akin to MHG *zipf* tip, OE *tæppa* tap – more at [1]TAP] – **tipped** *adj* – **on the tip of one's tongue** about to be uttered ⟨*it was* on the tip of my tongue *to tell him exactly what I thought*⟩

[2]**tip** *vt* **-pp-** **1a** to supply with a tip **b** to cover or adorn the tip of **2** to attach (an insert) in a book – usu + *in*

[3]**tip** *vb* **-pp-** *vt* **1** to overturn, upset – usu + *over* **2** to cant, tilt **3** *Br* to deposit or transfer by tilting ~ *vi* **1** to topple **2** to lean, slant [ME *tipen*] – **tip the scales 1** to register weight ⟨tips the scales *at 8 stone 4 ounces*⟩ **2** to shift the balance of power or influence ⟨*his greater experience* tipped the scales *in his favour*⟩

[4]**tip** *n* a place for tipping sthg (e g rubbish or coal); a dump

[5]**tip** *vt* **-pp-** to strike lightly [ME *tippe* (light blow, tap); akin to LG *tippen* to tap]

[6]**tip** *vb or n* **-pp-** (to give or present with) a sum of money in appreciation of a service performed [prob fr [5]*tip*]

[7]**tip** *n* **1** a piece of useful or expert information **2** a piece of inside information which, acted upon, may bring financial gain (e g by betting or investment) [prob fr [6]*tip*]

[8]**tip** *vt* **-pp-** to mention as a prospective winner, success, or profitable investment

'tip,off *n* a tip given usu as a warning

tip off *vt* to give a tip-off to ⟨*the police were* tipped off *about the raid*⟩

tipper /'tipə/ *n* a lorry, trailer, etc whose body can be tipped on its chassis to empty the contents [[3]TIP + [2]-ER]

tippet /'tipit/ *n* **1** a shoulder cape of fur or cloth often with hanging ends **2** a long black scarf worn over the surplice by Anglican clergymen during morning and evening prayer [ME *tipet*]

[1]**tipple** /'tipl/ *vb* **tippling** /'tipl·ing, 'tipling/ *vt* to drink (esp spirits), esp continuously in small amounts ~ *vi* DRINK 2 *USE* infml [back-formation fr obs *tippler* (seller of drink), fr ME *tipler, tipeler*] – **tippler** /'tiplə/ *n*

[2]**tipple** *n* DRINK 1b – infml

tipstaff /'tip,stahf/ *n, pl* **tipstaves** /-,stayvz/ an officer in certain lawcourts [obs *tipstaff* (staff tipped with metal)]

tipster /'tipstə/ *n* one who gives or sells tips, esp for gambling or speculation

tipsy /'tipsi/ *adj* **1** unsteady, staggering, or foolish from the effects of alcoholic drink **2** askew ⟨*a ~ angle*⟩ [[3]*tip* + *-sy* (as in *tricksy*)] – **tipsily** *adv*, **tipsiness** *n*

[1]**'tip,toe** /-,toh/ *n* the tip of a toe; *also* the ends of the toes ⟨*walk on ~*⟩

[2]**tiptoe** *adv* (as if) on tiptoe

[3]**tiptoe** *adj* **1** standing or walking (as if) on tiptoe **2** cautious, stealthy

[4]**tiptoe** *vi* **tiptoeing** **1** to stand, walk, or raise oneself on tiptoe **2** to walk silently or stealthily as if on tiptoe

,tip-'top *adj* excellent, first-rate ⟨*in ~ condition*⟩ – infml – **tip-top** *adv*

tirade /tie'rayd/ *n* a long vehement speech or denunciation [F, shot, tirade, fr MF, fr OIt *tirata*, fr *tirare* to draw, shoot; akin to Sp & Pg *tirar* to draw, shoot, OF *tirer*]

[1]**tire** /tie·ə/ *vi* to become tired ~ *vt* **1** to fatigue **2** to wear out the patience of [ME *tyren*, fr OE *tēorian, tȳrian*]

[2]**tire** *n* a woman's headband or hair ornament [ME, short for *attire*]

[3]**tire** *vt* to adorn (the hair) with an ornament

[4]**tire** *n, chiefly NAm* a tyre

tired /tie·əd/ *adj* **1** weary, fatigued **2** exasperated; FED UP ⟨~ *of listening to your complaints*⟩ **3a** trite, hackneyed ⟨*the same old ~ themes*⟩ **b** lacking freshness ⟨*a ~ skin*⟩ ⟨~, *overcooked asparagus*⟩ – **tiredly** *adv*, **tiredness** *n*

tireless /'tie·əlis/ *adj* indefatigable, untiring – **tirelessly** *adv*, **tirelessness** *n*

tiresome /'tie·əsəm/ *adj* wearisome, tedious – **tiresomely** *adv*, **tiresomeness** *n*

tiro /'tie,roh/ *n* a tyro

tisane /ti'zahn/ *n* an infusion (e g of dried herbs) used as a beverage or for medicinal effects [ME, fr MF, fr L *ptisana*, fr Gk *ptisanē*, lit., crushed barley]

tissue /'tishooh; *also* 'tisyooh/ *n* **1a** a fine gauzy often sheer fabric **b** a mesh, web ⟨*a ~ of lies*⟩ **2** a paper handkerchief **3** a cluster of cells, usu of a particular kind, together with their intercellular substance that form any of the structural materials of a plant or animal [ME *tissu*, a rich fabric, fr OF, fr pp of *tistre* to weave, fr L *texere* – more at TECHNICAL] – **tissuey** *adj*

tissue paper *n* a thin gauzy paper used esp for protecting sthg (e g by covering)

[1]**tit** /tit/ *n* **1** a teat or nipple **2** a woman's breast – infml [ME, fr OE – more at TEAT]

[2]**tit** *n* any of various small tree-dwelling insect-eating birds (e g a blue tit); *broadly* any of various small plump often long-tailed birds [short for *titmouse*]

titan /'tiet(ə)n/, *fem* **titaness** /,tiet(ə)n'es, '---/ *n* sby or sthg very large or strong; *also* sby notable for outstanding achievement [Gk, one of a family of mythical giants once ruling the earth]

titan-, titano- *comb form* titanium ⟨titan*ate*⟩ [NL *titanium*]

[1]**titanic** /tie'tanik/ *adj* colossal, gigantic [Gk *titanikos* of the Titans] – **titanically** *adv*

[2]**titanic** /ti'tanik, tie-/ *adj* of or containing titanium, esp when tetravalent [NL *titanium*]

titanium /titaynyəm, -ni·əm, tie-/ *n* a light strong metallic element used esp in alloys and combined in refractory materials and in coatings ☞ PERIODIC TABLE [NL, fr Gk *Titan*]

ti,tanium di'oxide *n* an oxide of titanium that is used esp as a pigment

titanous /ti'tanəs, tie-/ *adj* of or containing titanium, esp when trivalent [ISV]

titbit /'tit,bit/, *chiefly NAm* **tidbit** /'tid-/ *n* a choice or pleasing piece (e g of food or news) [perh fr *tit-* (as in *titmouse*) + *bit*]

titchy /'tichi/ *adj, Br* small, scant – infml [*tich, titch* (small person or thing), fr *Little Tich*, stage-name of Harry Ralph †1928 dwarfish E comedian]

titer /'tietə, 'teetə/ *n, chiefly NAm* a titre

titfer /'titfə/ *n, Br* a hat – infml [rhyming slang *tit for (tat)*]

,tit for 'tat /tat/ *n* an equivalent given in retaliation (e g for an injury) [alter. of earlier *tip for tap*, fr *tip* (blow) + *for* + *tap*]

[1]**tithe** /tiedh/ *vi* to pay a tithe or tithes ~ *vt* to levy a tithe on [ME *tithen*, fr OE *teogothian*, fr *teogotha* tenth] – **tithable** *adj*, **tither** *n*

[2]**tithe** *n* a tax or contribution of a 10th part of sthg (e g income) for the support of a religious establishment; *esp* such a tax formerly due in an English parish to support its church [ME, fr OE *teogotha* tenth; akin to MLG *tegede* tenth; both fr a prehistoric WGmc derivative of the word represented by OE *tīen* ten – more at TEN]

tithing /'tiedhing/ *n* a former small administrative division of England apparently orig consisting of 10 men with their families [ME, fr OE *tēothung*, fr *teogothian, tēothian* to tithe, take one tenth]

titi /'tee,tee/ *n* any of various small S American monkeys [Sp *tití*, fr Aymara *titi*, lit., little cat]

titian /'tish(ə)n/ *adj, often cap, esp of hair* reddish brown [*Titian* (Tiziano Vecelli) †1576 It painter]

titillate /'titi,layt/ *vt* to excite pleasurably; arouse by stimulation [L *titillatus*, pp of *titillare*] –**titillating** *adj*, **titillatingly** *adv*, **titillation** /-'laysh(ə)n/ *n*, **titillative** /-,laytiv/ *adj*

titivate, tittivate /'titivayt/ *vb* to smarten up (oneself or another) [perh fr [1]*tidy* + *-vate* (as in *renovate*)] – **titivation** /-'vaysh(ə)n/ *n*

[1]**title** /'tietl/ *n* **1** (a document giving proof of) legal ownership **2a** sthg that justifies or substantiates a claim **b** an alleged or recognized right **3a** a descriptive or general heading (e g of a chapter in a book) **b** the heading of a legal document or statute **c** a title page and the printed matter on it **d** written material introduced into a film or television programme to represent credits, dialogue, or fragments of narrative – usu pl with sing. meaning **4** the distinguishing name of a work of art (e g a book, picture or musical composition) **5** a descriptive name **6** a division of a legal document; *esp* one larger than a section or article **7** a literary work as distinguished from a particular copy ⟨*published 25 ~s last year*⟩ **8** designation as champion ⟨*the world heavyweight ~*⟩ **9** a hereditary or acquired appellation given to a person or family as a mark of rank, office, or attainment [ME, fr OF, fr L *titulus* inscription, title]

[2]**title** *vt* **1** to provide a title for **2** to designate or call by a title

titled *adj* having a title, esp of nobility

title deed *n* the deed constituting evidence of ownership

title page *n* a page of a book giving the title, author, publisher, and publication details

title role *n* the role in a production (e g a play) that has the same name as the title of the production

titmouse /'tit,mows/ *n, pl* **titmice** /-,mies/ [2]TIT [ME *titmose*, fr (assumed) ME *tit* any small object or creature + ME *mose* titmouse, fr OE *māse*; akin to OHG *meisa* titmouse]

Titoism /'teetoh,iz(ə)m/ *n* the policies associated with Tito; *specif* nationalist policies followed by a communist state independently of and often in opposition to the USSR [*Tito* (Josip Broz) †1980 President of Yugoslavia] – **Titoist** *n or adj*

titrate /'tietrayt/ *vb* to subject to or perform titration [*titre*] – **titratable** *adj*, **titrator** *n*

titration /tie'traysh(ə)n/ *n* a method or the process of determining the strength of, or the concentration of a substance in, a solution by finding the amount of test liquid needed to bring about a complete reaction with a liquid of known concentration

titre, *NAm chiefly* **titer** /'tietə, 'teetə/ *n* the strength of a solution or the concentration of a substance in solution as determined by titration [F *titre* title, proportion of gold or silver in a coin, fr OF *title* inscription, title]

titter /'titə/ *vi* to giggle, snigger [imit] – **titter** *n*

tittivate /'titivayt/ *vb* to titivate

tittle /'titl/ *n* **1** a point or small sign used as a diacritical mark in writing or printing **2** a very small part [ME *titel*, fr ML *titulus*, fr L, title]

[1]**tittle-,tattle** /'tatl/ *vi or n* (to) gossip, prattle [n redupl of [2]*tattle*; vb fr n]

titty /'titi/ *n* [1]TIT – infml

titular /'tityoolə/ *adj* **1** in title only; nominal ⟨*the ~ head of a political party*⟩ **2** of or constituting a title ⟨*the ~ hero of the play*⟩ [L *titulus* title] – **titularly** *adv*

tizzy /'tizi/ *n* a highly excited and confused state of mind – infml [origin unknown]

tmesis /tə'meesis/ *n* separation of parts of a grammatical compound by another word or words (e g in *every-bloody-where*) [LL, fr Gk *tmēsis* act of cutting, fr *temnein* to cut – more at TOME]

TNT *n* trinitrotoluene [*tri*ni*tro*toluene]

[1]**to** /,tooh; *unstressed preceeding vowels* too; *unstressed preceeding consonants* tə/ *prep* **1** – used to indicate a terminal point or destination: e g **a** a place where a physical movement or an action or condition suggestive of movement ends ⟨*drive ~ the city*⟩ ⟨*invited them ~ lunch*⟩ **b** a direction ⟨*the road ~ London*⟩ ⟨*turned his back ~ the door*⟩ **c** a terminal point in measuring or reckoning or in a statement of extent or limits ⟨*10 miles ~ the nearest town*⟩ ⟨*cost from £5 ~ £10*⟩ ⟨*wet ~ the skin*⟩ ⟨*not ~ my knowledge*⟩ ⟨*add salt ~ taste*⟩ **d** a point in time before which a period is reckoned ⟨*5 minutes ~ 5*⟩ ⟨*how long ~ dinner?*⟩ **e** a point of contact or proximity ⟨*pinned it ~ my coat*⟩ ⟨*applied polish ~ the table*⟩ **f** a purpose, intention, tendency, result, or end ⟨*a temple ~ Mars*⟩ ⟨*broken ~ pieces*⟩ ⟨*held them ~ ransom*⟩ ⟨*much ~ my surprise*⟩ **g** the one to or for which sthg exists or is done or directed ⟨*kind ~ animals*⟩ ⟨*my letter ~ John*⟩ **2** – used **a** to indicate addition, attachment, connection, belonging, or possession ⟨*add 17 ~ 20*⟩ ⟨*the key ~ the door*⟩ **b** to indicate accompaniment or response ⟨*danced ~ live music*⟩ ⟨*rose ~ the occasion*⟩ **3** – used to indicate relationship or conformity: e g **a** relative position ⟨*next door ~ me*⟩ **b** proportion or composition ⟨*400 ~ the box*⟩ ⟨*won by 17 points ~ 11*⟩ **c** correspondence to a standard ⟨*second ~ none*⟩ ⟨*compared him ~ a god*⟩ ⟨*true ~ type*⟩ **4a** – used to indicate that the following verb is an infinitive ⟨*wants ~ go*⟩ ⟨*got work ~ do*⟩; now often used with an intervening adverb ⟨*~ really understand*⟩ in spite of the disapproval of many; often used by itself at the end of a clause in place of an infinitive suggested by the preceding context ⟨*knows more than he seems ~*⟩ **b** for the purpose of ⟨*did it ~ annoy them*⟩ [ME, fr OE *tō*; akin to OHG *zuo* to, L *donec* as long as, until]

[2]**to** *adv* **1a** – used to indicate direction towards; chiefly in *to and fro* **b** close to the wind ⟨*the ship hove ~*⟩ **2** *of a door or window* into contact, esp with the frame ⟨*the door slammed ~*⟩ **3** – used to indicate application or attention; compare FALL TO, TURN TO **4** back into consciousness or awareness ⟨*brings her ~ with smelling salts*⟩ **5** AT HAND ⟨*saw her close ~*⟩

toad /tohd/ *n* **1** any of numerous tailless leaping amphibians that differ from the related frogs by living more on land and in having a shorter squatter body with a rough, dry, and warty skin **2** a loathsome and contemptible person or thing [ME *tode*, fr OE *tāde, tādige*]

'toad,flax /-,flaks/ *n* a common Eurasian perennial plant of the figwort family that has showy yellow and orange flowers

,toad-in-the-'hole *n* a dish of sausages baked in a thick Yorkshire-pudding batter

'toad,stool /-,stoohl/ *n* a (poisonous or inedible) umbrella-shaped fungus [ME *todestool, tadestool*, fr *tode, tade* toad + *stool*]

toady /'tohdi/ *vi or n* (to behave as) a sycophant [n fr earlier *toadeater* (mountebank's assistant who pretended to eat poisonous toads to prove the value of his master's antidote, servile dependant, sycophant); vb fr n] – **toadyism** *n*

,to-and-'fro *n or adj* (activity involving alternating movement) forwards and backwards

to and fro *adv* from one place to another; BACK AND FORTH

[1]toast /tohst/ *vt* **1** to make (e g bread) crisp, hot, and brown by heat **2** to warm thoroughly (e g at a fire) ~ *vi* to become toasted; *esp* to become thoroughly warm [ME *tosten*, fr MF *toster*, fr LL *tostare* to roast, fr L *tostus*, pp of *torrēre* to dry, parch – more at THIRST]

[2]toast *n* **1** sliced bread browned on both sides by heat **2a** sthg in honour of which people drink **b** a highly popular or admired person ⟨*she's the ~ of London*⟩ **3** an act of drinking in honour of sby or sthg [(2) fr the use of pieces of spiced toast to flavour drinks; (3) *[3]toast*]

[3]toast *vt* to drink to as a toast [*[2]toast*]

toaster /'tohstə/ *n* an electrical appliance for toasting esp bread [[1]TOAST + [2]-ER]

'toasting ,fork /'tohsting/ *n* a long-handled fork on which bread is held for toasting in front of or over a fire

'toast,master /-,mahstə/, *fem* **'toast,mistress** *n* sby who presides at a banquet, proposes toasts, and introduces after-dinner speakers

tobacco /tə'bakoh/ *n, pl* **tobaccos** **1** any of a genus of chiefly American plants of the nightshade family; *esp* a tall erect annual S American herb cultivated for its leaves **2** the leaves of cultivated tobacco prepared for use in smoking or chewing or as snuff; *also* cigars, cigarettes, or other manufactured products of tobacco [Sp *tabaco*, prob fr Taino, roll of tobacco leaves smoked by the Indians of the Antilles at the time of Columbus]

tobacco mosaic *n* any of several mosaic virus diseases of plants of the nightshade family, esp tobacco

tobacconist /tə'bakənist/ *n* a seller of tobacco, esp in a shop [irreg fr *tobacco* + *-ist*]

to-'be *adj* future – usu used after a noun; often in combination ⟨*a bride*-to-be⟩

toboggan /tə'bogən/ *vi or n* (to ride on) a long light sledge, usu curved up at the front and used esp for gliding downhill over snow or ice [n CanF *tobogan*, of Algonquian origin; akin to Micmac *tobâgun* sledge made of skin; vb fr n] – **tobogganist** *n*

toby /'tohbi/, **toby jug** *n* a small jug or mug generally used for beer and shaped somewhat like a stout man with a cocked hat for the brim [*Toby*, nickname for *Tobias*]

toccata /tə'kahtə/ *n* a musical composition in a free style and characterized by rapid runs, usu for organ or harpsichord [It, fr fem of *toccato*, pp of *toccare* to touch, fr (assumed) VL – more at TOUCH]

Toc H /'tok ,aych/ *n* a society of Christians for fellowship and charitable work, founded in Ypres in 1915 by Rev P T B Clayton [*toc* (signallers' former code word for the letter *t*) + *h*, initials of *T*albot *H*ouse, name of club from which the society developed]

Tocharian /to'kahri·ən/ *n* **1** a member of a people of supposed European origin inhabiting central Asia during the 1st millennium AD **2** an extinct language of central Asia [L *Tochari* (pl), fr Gk *Tocharoi*]

tocopherol /to'kofə,rol/ *n* a compound of high vitamin E potency obtained from germ oils or by synthesis [ISV, deriv of Gk *tokos* childbirth, offspring + *pherein* to carry, bear – more at [2]BEAR]

tocsin /'toksin/ *n* an alarm bell rung as a warning [MF *toquassen*, fr OProv *tocasenh*, fr *tocar* to touch, ring a bell (fr assumed VL *toccare*) + *senh* sign, bell, fr ML & L *signum*; ML, bell, fr LL, ringing of a bell, fr L, mark, sign – more at TOUCH, [1]SIGN]

[1]tod /tod/ *n, chiefly Scot & NEng* a fox [ME]

[2]tod *n, Br* [rhyming slang *Tod (Sloan)* own, alone, prob fr James Forman *(Tod) Sloan* †1933 US jockey] – **on one's tod** alone – slang

today /tə'day/ *adv or n* **1** (on) this day **2** (at) the present time or age [adv ME, fr OE *tōdæge, tōdæg*, fr *tō* to, at + *dæge*, dat of *dæg* day; n fr adv]

toddle /todl/ *vi* **toddling** /'todling, 'todl·ing/ **1** to walk haltingly in the manner of a young child **2a** to take a stroll; saunter **b** *Br* to depart ⟨*I'll just ~ off home*⟩ ***USE*** (*2*) infml [origin unknown] – **toddle** *n*

toddler /'todlə/ *n* a young child [TODDLE + [2]-ER]

toddy /'todi/ *n* a usu hot drink consisting of spirits mixed with water, sugar, and spices [Hindi *tāṛī* juice of the palmyra palm, fr *tāṛ* palmyra palm, fr Skt *tāla*]

to-'do *n, pl* **to-dos** bustle, fuss – infml

[1]toe /toh/ *n* **1a(1)** any of the digits at the end of a vertebrate's foot **(2)** the fore end of a foot or hoof **b** the front of sthg worn on the foot **2a** a part like a toe in position or form ⟨*the ~ of Italy*⟩ **b** the lowest part (e g of an embankment, dam, or cliff) [ME *to*, fr OE *tā*; akin to OHG *zēha* toe, L *digitus* finger, toe]

[2]toe *vt* **toeing** **1** to provide with a toe; *esp* to renew the toe of ⟨~ *a shoe*⟩ **2** to touch, reach, or drive with the toe – **toe the line** to conform rigorously to a rule or standard

toea /'toh·ə/ *n* ☞ *Papua New Guinea* at NATIONALITY [native name in Papua New Guinea]

'toe ,cap *n* a piece of material (e g steel or leather) attached to the toe of a shoe or boot to reinforce or decorate it

toed /tohd/ *adj* having a toe or toes, esp of a specified kind or number – usu in combination ⟨5-toed⟩ ⟨*round*-toed *shoes*⟩

'toe,hold /-,hohld/ *n* **1a** a hold or place of support for the toes (e g in climbing) **b** a slight footing ⟨*the firm had a ~ in the export market*⟩ **2** a wrestling hold in which the aggressor bends or twists his opponent's foot

'toe-,in *n* adjustment of the front wheels of a motor vehicle so that they are closer together at the front than at the back

toff /tof/ *n, chiefly Br* an upper-class usu

well-dressed person – infml [prob alter. of *tuft* (titled undergraduate)]

toffee, toffy /'tofi/ *n* a sweet with a texture ranging from chewy to brittle, made by boiling sugar, water, and often butter [alter. of *taffy*]

'toffee,apple *n* a toffee-covered apple held on a stick

'toffee,nosed *adj, Br* stuck-up – infml

toft /toft/ *n, Br* an entire holding comprising a homestead and additional land [ME, fr OE, fr ON *topt*]

tog /tog/ *vt* **-gg-** to dress, esp in fine clothing – usu + *up* or *out*; infml [*togs*]

toga /'tohgə/ *n* a loose outer garment worn in public by citizens of ancient Rome ☞ GARMENT [L; akin to L *tegere* to cover – more at THATCH] – **togaed** /'tohgəd/ *adj*

together /tə'gedhə/ *adv* **1a** in or into 1 place, mass, collection, or group ⟨*the men get ~ every Thursday for poker*⟩ **b** in joint agreement or cooperation; as a group ⟨*students and staff ~ presented the petition*⟩ **2a** in or into contact (e g connection, collision, or union) ⟨*mix these ingredients ~*⟩ ⟨*tie the ends ~*⟩ **b** in or into association, relationship, or harmony ⟨*colours that go well ~*⟩ **3a** at one time; simultaneously ⟨*everything happened ~*⟩ **b** in succession; without intermission ⟨*was depressed for days ~*⟩ **4** *of a single unit* in or into an integrated whole ⟨*pull yourself ~*⟩ **5a** to or with each other ⟨*eyes too close ~*⟩ – used as an intensive after certain verbs ⟨*add ~*⟩ ⟨*confer ~*⟩ **b** considered as a unit; collectively ⟨*these arguments taken ~ make a convincing case*⟩ [ME *togedere*, fr OE *togædere*, fr *tō* to + *gædere* together; akin to MHG *gater* together, OE *gaderian* to gather] – **together with** with the addition of

to'getherness /-nis/ *n* the feeling of belonging together

[1]toggle /'tog(ə)l/ *n* **1** a piece or device for holding or securing; *esp* a crosspiece attached to the end of or to a loop in a chain, rope, line, etc, usu to prevent slipping, to serve as a fastening, or as a grip for tightening **2** (a device having) a toggle joint [origin unknown]

[2]toggle *vt* **toggling** /'togl·ing/ to provide or fasten (as if) with a toggle

toggle joint *n* a device having 2 bars joined end to end so that when a force is exerted by a screw at the joint, a pressure is exerted along the 2 bars

togs /togz/ *n pl* clothes – infml [pl of slang *tog* (coat), short for obs *togeman, togman*]

[1]toil /toyl/ *n* long strenuous fatiguing labour [ME *toile*, fr AF *toyl*, fr OF *toeil* battle, confusion, fr *toeillier*] – **toilful** *adj*, **toilsome** /-s(ə)m/ *adj*

[2]toil *vi* **1** to work hard and long **2** to proceed with laborious effort ⟨*~ing wearily up the hill*⟩ [ME *toilen* to argue, struggle, fr AF *toiller*, fr OF *toeillier* to stir, disturb, dispute, fr L *tudiculare* to crush, grind, fr *tudicula* machine for crushing olives, dim. of *tudes* hammer; akin to L *tundere* to beat – more at 'STINT] – **toiler** *n*

[3]toil *n* sthg by or with which one is held fast or inextricably involved – usu pl with sing. meaning ⟨*caught in the ~s of the law*⟩ [MF *toile* cloth, net, fr L *tela* web, fr *texere* to weave, construct – more at TECHNICAL]

toile /twahl/ *n* **1** any of many plain or simple twill weave fabrics; *esp* linen **2** a muslin model of a garment [F, cloth, linen]

toilet /'toylit/ *n* **1** the act or process of dressing and grooming oneself **2a** a fixture or arrangement for receiving and disposing of faeces and urine **b** a room or compartment containing a toilet and sometimes a washbasin **3** cleansing in preparation for or in association with a medical or surgical procedure **4** formal or fashionable (style of) dress – fml [MF *toilette* cloth put over the shoulders while dressing the hair or shaving, dim. of *toile* cloth]

'toilet ,paper *n* a thin usu absorbent paper for sanitary use after defecation or urination

toiletry /'toylitri/ *n* an article or preparation (e g cologne) used in washing, grooming, etc – usu pl

toilette /toy'let, twah'let (*Fr* twalɛt)/ *n* TOILET 1, 4 [F, fr MF]

'toilet ,training *n* the process of training a child to control bladder and bowel movements and to use the toilet – **toilet train** *vt*

'toilet ,water *n* (a) liquid containing a high percentage of alcohol used esp as a light perfume

to-ing and fro-ing /,tooh·ing ənd 'froh·ing/ *n, pl* **to-ings and fro-ings** bustling unproductive activity [*to and fro*]

Tokay /'tohkay, toh'kie/ *n* a usu sweet dark gold wine made near Tokaj in Hungary

[1]token /'tohkən/ *n* **1** an outward sign or expression (e g of an emotion) **2a** a characteristic mark or feature ⟨*a white flag is a ~ of surrender*⟩ **b** an instance of a linguistic expression **3a** a souvenir, keepsake **b** sthg given or shown as a guarantee (e g of authority, right, or identity) **4** a coinlike piece issued **a** as money by anyone other than a government **b** for use in place of money (e g for a bus fare) **5** a certified statement redeemable for a usu specified form of merchandise to the amount stated thereon ⟨*a book ~*⟩ [ME, fr OE *tācen, tācn* sign, token; akin to OHG *zeihhan* sign, Gk *deiknynai* to show – more at DICTION] – **by the same token** furthermore and for the same reason

[2]token *adj* **1** done or given as a token, esp in partial fulfilment of an obligation or engagement ⟨*a ~ payment*⟩ **2** done or given merely for show ⟨*~ resistance*⟩

tokenism /'tohkə,niz(ə)m/ *n* the making of only a token effort

token money *n* **1** money of regular government issue having a greater face value than intrinsic value **2** a medium of exchange consisting of privately issued tokens

tol-, tolu- *comb form* toluene ⟨tolu*ic*⟩ [ISV, fr *tolu* balsam of Tolu (a balsam from a tropical Am tree), fr Sp *tolú*, fr Santiago de *Tolú*, town in Colombia]

tolbooth /'tol,boohth, 'tohl-/ *n, Scot* **1** TOWN HALL **2** a jail [ME *tolbothe, tollbothe* tollbooth, town hall, jail]

told /tohld/ *past of* TELL

Toledo /to'laydoh/ *n, pl* **Toledos** a finely tempered sword [*Toledo*, province & town in Spain]

tolerable /'tol(ə)rəbl/ *adj* **1** capable of being borne or endured ⟨*~ pain*⟩ **2** moderately good or agreeable ⟨*a ~ singing voice*⟩ – **tolerably** *adv*, **tolerability** /,tol(ə)rə'biləti/ *n*

tolerance /'tolərəns/ *n* **1** the ability to endure or adapt physiologically to the effects of a drug, virus, radiation, etc **2a** indulgence for beliefs or practices differing from one's own **b** the act of allowing sthg; toleration **3** an allowable variation from a standard dimension

tolerant /'tolərant/ *adj* inclined to tolerate; *esp* marked by forbearance or endurance – **tolerantly** *adv*

tolerate /'tolərayt/ *vt* **1** to endure or resist the action of (e g a drug) without grave or lasting injury **2** to allow to be (done) without prohibition, hindrance, or contradiction [L *toleratus*, pp of *tolerare* to endure, put up with; akin to OE *tholian* to bear, L *tollere* to lift up, *latus* carried (suppletive pp of *ferre*), Gk *tlēnai* to bear] – **tolerator** *n*, **tolerative** /-rətiv/ *adj*

toleration /tolə'raysh(ə)n/ *n* a government policy of permitting forms of religious belief and worship not officially established [TOLERATE + -ION]

¹toll /tol, tohl/ *n* **1** a fee paid for some right or privilege (e g of passing over a highway or bridge) or for services rendered **2** a grievous or ruinous price; *esp* cost in life or health [ME, fr OE; akin to ON *tollr* toll; both fr a prehistoric WGmc-NGmc word borrowed fr (assumed) VL *tolonium*, alter. of LL *telonium* customshouse, fr Gk *tolōnion*, fr *telōnēs* collector of tolls, fr *telos* tax, toll; akin to Gk *tlēnai* to bear]

²toll /tohl/ *vt* **1** to sound (a bell) by pulling the rope **2** to signal, announce, or summon (as if) by means of a tolled bell ~ *vi* to sound with slow measured strokes [ME *tollen*, perh fr *tollen* to attract, entice]

³toll /tohl/ *n* the sound of a tolling bell

tollbooth /'tolboohth, 'tohl-/ *n* a booth (e g on a bridge) where tolls are paid [ME *tolbothe, tollbothe* tollbooth, town hall, jail, fr *tol, toll* toll + *bothe* booth]

'toll ,bridge /tol, tohl/ *n* a bridge at which a toll is charged for crossing

tollgate /'tol,gayt, tohl-/ *n* a barrier across a road to prevent passage until a toll is paid

tollhouse /'tol,hows, tohl-/ *n* a house or booth where tolls are paid

tollie /'toli/ *n, SAfr* a castrated calf [Afrik, fr Zulu *iThole* calf]

tollroad /'tol,rohd, 'tohl-/ *n* a road maintained by collected tolls

Toltec /'toltek/ *n* a member of a Nahuatlan people of central and S Mexico [Sp *tolteca*, of AmerInd origin] – **Toltecan** *adj*

tolu- – see TOL-

toluene /'tolyoo,een/ *n* a toxic inflammable hydrocarbon that is used esp as a solvent and in organic synthesis [ISV]

tom /tom/ *n* the male of various animals; *esp* a tomcat [*Tom*, nickname for *Thomas*]

tomahawk /'tomə,hawk/ *n* a light axe used by N American Indians as a throwing or hand weapon [*tomahack* (in some Algonquian language of Virginia)]

tomato /tə'mahtoh/ *n, pl* **tomatoes** **1** any of a genus of S American plants of the nightshade family; *esp* one widely cultivated for its edible fruits **2** the usu large and rounded red, yellow, or green pulpy fruit of a tomato [alter. of earlier *tomate*, fr Sp, fr Nahuatl *tomatl*]

tomb /toohm/ *n* **1a** an excavation in which a corpse is buried **b** a chamber or vault for the dead, built either above or below ground and usu serving as a memorial **2** a tomblike structure; *esp* a large gloomy building [ME *tombe*, fr AF *tumbe*, fr LL *tumba* sepulchral mound, fr Gk *tymbos*; akin to L *tumēre* to be swollen – more at THUMB] – **tombless** *adj*

tombola /tom'bohlə/ *n* a lottery in which people buy tickets which may entitle them to a prize [It, fr *tombolare* to tumble, fr *tombare* to fall, fr (assumed) VL *tumbare* to tumble, fall, of imit origin]

tomboy /'tom,boy/ *n* a girl who behaves in a manner conventionally thought of as typical of a boy – **tomboyish** *adj*, **tomboyishly** *adv*, **tomboyishness** *n*

tombstone /'toohm,stohn/ *n* a gravestone

tomcat /'tom,kat/ *n* a male cat

Tom, Dick, and Harry /,tom ,dik ənd 'hari/ *n* people taken at random – often + *every* ⟨*not every ~ can join this club*⟩

tome /tohm/ *n* a (large scholarly) book [MF or L; MF, fr L *tomus*, fr Gk *tomos* section, roll of papyrus, tome, fr *temnein* to cut; akin to L *tondēre* to shear, Gk *tendein* to gnaw]

-tome /-'tohm/ *comb form* (→ *n*) cutting instrument ⟨*micro*tome⟩ [Gk *tomos*]

tomentum /tə'mentəm/ *n, pl* **tomenta** /-tə/ a covering of densely matted woolly hairs [NL, fr L, cushion stuffing; akin to L *tumēre* to be swollen – more at THUMB] – **tomentose** /-tohs/ *adj*

tomfool /,tom'foohl/ *n* an extremely foolish or stupid person

tomfoolery /,tom'foohləri/ *n* foolish trifling; nonsense

Tommy /'tomi/, **Tommy Atkins** /'atkinz/ *n* a British private soldier – infml [*Thomas* Atkins, name used as model in official army forms]

'tommy ,bar /'tomi/ *n, Br* a bar used to turn a box spanner [*Tommy*, nickname for *Thomas*]

tommyrot /'tomi,rot/ *n* utter foolishness or nonsense – infml [E dial. *tommy* (fool) + E *rot*]

tomography /tə'mogrəfi/ *n* a diagnostic technique using X-ray photographs in which the shadows of structures in front of and behind the section under scrutiny do not show [Gk *tomos* section + ISV *-graphy* – more at TOME] – **tomogram** /'tomə,gram/ *n*

tomorrow /tə'moroh/ *adv or n* **1** (on) the day after today **2** (in) the future ⟨*the world of ~*⟩ [ME *to morgen*, fr OE *tō morgen*, fr *tō* to + *morgen* morrow, morning – more at MORN]

tompion /'tompi·ən/ *n* a tampion

,Tom 'Thumb *n* a dwarf type, race, or individual [*Tom Thumb*, legendary E dwarf]

tomtit /'tom,tit/ *n* any of various small active birds; *esp* a blue tit [prob short for *tomtitmouse*, fr the name *Tom* + *titmouse*]

'tom-,tom /tom/ *n* a usu long and narrow small-headed drum commonly beaten with the hands [Hindi *ṭamṭam*]

-tomy /-təmi/ *comb form* (→ *n*) incision; cutting ⟨*laparo*tomy⟩ [NL *-tomia*, fr Gk, fr *-tomos* that cuts, fr *temnein* to cut – more at TOME]

¹ton /tun/ *n, pl* **tons** *also* **ton** **1a** LONG TON ☞ UNIT **b** SHORT TON ☞ UNIT **c** a tonne ☞ UNIT **2a** REGISTER TON **b** a unit approximately equal to the volume of 1 long ton of seawater, used in reckoning the displacement of ships, and equal to $0.991m^3$ ($35ft^3$) **3a** a great quantity – often pl with sing. meaning ⟨*~s of room on the back seat*⟩ **b** a great weight ⟨*this bag weighs a ~*⟩ **4** a group, score, or speed of 100 ***USE*** *(3&4)* infml [ME *tunne* unit of weight or capacity – more at TUN]

²ton /tonh (*Fr* tõ/ *n* **1** the prevailing fashion **2** the quality or state of being fashionable [F, lit., tone, fr L *tonus*]

tonal /'tohn(ə)l/ *adj* **1** of tone, tonality, or tonicity **2** having tonality – **tonally** *adv*

tonality /toh'naləti/ *n* **1** tonal quality **2a** KEY 7 **b** the organization of all the notes and chords of a piece of music in relation to a tonic

tondo /'tondoh/ *n, pl* **tondi** /-,dee/ a circular painting or relief [It, fr *tondo* round, short for *rotondo*, fr L *rotundus* – more at ROUND]

¹tone /tohn/ *n* **1** a vocal or musical sound; *esp* one of a specified quality ⟨*spoke in low* ~s⟩ **2a** a sound of a definite frequency with relatively weak overtones **b** WHOLE TONE **3** an accent or inflection of the voice expressive of a mood or emotion **4** (a change in) the pitch of a word often used to express differences of meaning **5** style or manner of verbal expression ⟨*seemed wise to adopt a conciliatory* ~⟩ **6a** colour quality or value **b** the colour that appreciably modifies a hue or white or black **7** the general effect of light, shade, and colour in a picture **8a** the state of (an organ or part of) a living body in which the functions are healthy and performed with due vigour **b** normal tension or responsiveness to stimuli **9a** prevailing character, quality, or trend (e g of morals) ⟨*lowered the* ~ *of the discussion*⟩ **b** distinction, style; ²TON **c** FRAME OF MIND **10** *chiefly NAm* NOTE 1a(1) [ME, fr L *tonus* tension, tone, fr Gk *tonos*, lit., act of stretching; akin to Gk *teinein* to stretch – more at THIN]

²tone *vt* **1** to impart tone to ⟨*medicine to* ~ *up the system*⟩ **2** to soften in colour, appearance, or sound ~ *vi* **1** to assume a pleasing colour quality or tint **2** to blend or harmonize in colour – **toner** *n*

tone arm *n* the movable arm of a record player or deck that carries the pickup and permits tracking

toned *adj* **1** having (a specified) tone; characterized or distinguished by a tone – often in combination ⟨*shrill*-toned⟩ **2** *of paper* having a slight tint

,tone-'deaf *adj* relatively insensitive to differences in musical pitch – **tone deafness** *n*

tone down *vt* to reduce in intensity, violence, or force ⟨*he was told to* tone down *his views*⟩

'tone ,group *n* a unit of speech consisting of a nucleus with or without other stressed and unstressed syllables

'tone ,language *n* a language (e g Chinese) in which variations in tone distinguish words of different meaning

toneless /'tohnlis/ *adj* lacking in expression [¹TONE + -LESS] – **tonelessly** *adv*, **tonelessness** *n*

toneme /'tohneem/ *n* an intonation phoneme in a tone language – **tonemic** /toh'neemik/ *adj*

tone poem *n* SYMPHONIC POEM – **tone poet** *n*

'tone-,row /roh/ *n* the 12 chromatic notes of the octave placed in a chosen fixed order that form the basis of the material of a twelve-tone musical composition

tonetic /toh'netik/ *adj* relating to linguistic tones, to tone languages, or to intonation – **tonetically** *adv*

tong /tong/ *n* a Chinese secret society or fraternal organization formerly notorious for gang warfare [Chin (Cant) *t'ong* hall]

Tongan /'tong·gən/ *adj or n* (of) an inhabitant, or the Polynesian language, of the Tonga islands ☞ LANGUAGE

tongs /tongz/ *n pl* any of various grasping devices consisting commonly of 2 pieces joined at 1 end by a pivot or hinged like scissors [ME *tonges*, pl of *tonge*, fr OE *tang*; akin to OHG *zanga* tongs, Gk *daknein* to bite]

¹tongue /tung/ *n* **1a** a fleshy muscular movable organ of the floor of the mouth in most vertebrates that bears sensory end organs and small glands and functions esp in tasting and swallowing food and in human beings as a speech organ ☞ NERVE **b** a part of various invertebrate animals that is analogous to the tongue of vertebrates **2** the tongue of an ox, sheep, etc used as food **3** the power of communication through speech **4a** a (spoken) language **b** manner or quality of utterance ⟨*a sharp* ~⟩ **c** ecstatic usu unintelligible utterance, esp in Christian worship – usu pl with sing. meaning ⟨*the gift of* ~s⟩ **d** the cry (as if) of a hound pursuing or in sight of game – esp in *give tongue* **5** a long narrow strip of land projecting into a body of water **6** sthg like an animal's tongue (e g elongated and fastened at 1 end only):e g **a** a movable pin in a buckle **b** a piece of metal suspended inside a bell so as to strike against the sides as the bell is swung **c** the pole of a (horse-drawn) vehicle **d** the flap under the lacing or buckles on the front of a shoe or boot **7** the rib on one edge of a board that fits into a corresponding groove in an edge of another board to make a flush joint **8** a tapering cone – in *tongue of flame/fire* [ME *tunge*, fr OE; akin to OHG *zunga* tongue, L *lingua*] – **tonguelike** *adj*

²tongue *vt* **1** to touch or lick (as if) with the tongue **2** to articulate (notes) by tonguing ~ *vi* to articulate notes on a wind instrument by successively interrupting the stream of wind with the action of the tongue

tongued /tungd/ *adj* having a tongue of a specified kind – often in combination ⟨*sharp*-tongued⟩

,tongue-in-'cheek *adj* characterized by irony or whimsical exaggeration – **tongue in cheek** *adv*

'tongueless /-lis/ *adj* lacking power of speech [¹TONGUE + -LESS]

'tongue-,tie *n* limited mobility of the tongue due to shortness of its fraenum

'tongue-,tied *adj* **1** affected with tongue-tie **2** unable to speak freely (e g because of shyness)

'tongue ,twister *n* a word or phrase difficult to articulate because of several similar consonantal sounds (e g 'she sells seashells on the seashore')

¹tonic /'tonik/ *adj* **1** marked by prolonged muscular contraction ⟨~ *convulsions*⟩ **2** increasing or restoring physical or mental tone **3** of or based on the first note of a scale **4** *of a syllable* bearing a principal stress or accent [Gk *tonikos*, fr *tonos* tension, tone] – **tonically** *adv*

²tonic *n* **1a** sthg (e g a drug) that increases body tone **b** sthg that invigorates, refreshes, or stimulates ⟨*a day in the country was a* ~ *for him*⟩ ⟨*a skin* ~⟩ **c** **tonic, tonic water** a carbonated drink flavoured with a small amount of quinine, lemon, and lime **2** the first note of a diatonic scale **3** an instance of tonic accent

tonic accent *n* relative phonetic prominence of a spoken syllable

tonicity /toh'nisəti/ *n* the property of possessing tone; *esp* healthy vigour of body or mind

,tonic 'sol-fa *n* a system of solmization that replaces the normal notation with sol-fa syllables

tonight /tə'niet/ *adv or n* (on) this night or the night following today [adv ME *to night, to niht*, fr OE *tō niht*, fr *tō* to, at + *niht* night; n fr adv]

'tonka ˌbean /'tongkə/ *n* (the coumarin-containing seed of) any of several leguminous trees [prob fr Tupi *tonka*]

tonky /'tongki/ *adj, NZ* socially pretentious – infml [perh blend of *tony* and *swanky*]

tonnage /'tunij/ *n* **1** a duty formerly levied on every cask of wine imported into England **2a** a duty or tax on vessels based on cargo capacity **b** a duty on goods per ton transported **3** ships considered in terms of the total number of tons registered or carried or of their carrying capacity **4** the carrying capacity of a merchant ship in units of 100ft^3 (about 2.83m^3) **5** total weight in tons shipped, carried, or produced [(1) ME, fr OF *tonne* tun – more at TUNNEL]

tonne /tun/ *n* a metric unit of weight equal to 1000kg ☞ UNIT [F, fr *tonne* tun, fr OF – more at TUNNEL]

tonneau /'tonoh/ *n, pl* **tonneaus** the (rear) seating compartment of a motor car [F, lit., tun, fr OF *tonel* – more at TUNNEL]

tonometer /toh'nomitə/ *n* an instrument (e g a tuning fork) for determining the exact pitch of tones [Gk *tonos* tone + E *-meter*] – **tonometry** *n*, **tonometric** /ˌtonə'metrik/ *adj*

tonoplast /'tohnəplast, 'to-/ *n* the membrane surrounding a vacuole in the cytoplasm of a plant cell [ISV *tono-* (fr Gk *tonos* tension) + *-plast* – more at TONE]

tonsil /'tons(ə)l/ *n* **1** either of a pair of prominent oval masses of spongy lymphoid tissue that lie 1 on each side of the throat at the back of the mouth ☞ NERVE **2** any of various masses of lymphoid tissue that are similar to tonsils [L *tonsillae*, pl, tonsils] – **tonsillar** *adj*

tonsill-, tonsillo- *comb form* tonsil ⟨tonsill*ectomy*⟩ ⟨tonsillo*tomy*⟩ [L *tonsillae*]

tonsillectomy /ˌtonsi'lektəmi/ *n* the surgical removal of the tonsils

tonsillitis /ˌtonsi'lietəs/ *n* inflammation of the tonsils [NL]

tonsorial /ton'sawri·əl/ *adj* of a barber or his work – usu humor [L *tonsorius*, fr *tonsus*, pp]

¹tonsure /'tonshə/ *n* **1** the Roman Catholic or Eastern rite of admission to the clerical state by the shaving of a portion of the head **2** the shaved patch on a monk's or other cleric's head [ME, fr ML *tonsura*, fr L, act of shearing, fr *tonsus*, pp of *tondēre* to shear – more at TOME]

²tonsure *vt* to shave the head of; *esp* to confer the tonsure on

tontine /'tonteen, -'-/ *n* a financial arrangement whereby a group of participants share various advantages on such terms that on the death or default of any member his/her advantages are distributed among the remaining members until 1 member remains or an agreed period has elapsed; *also* the share or right of each individual [F, fr Lorenzo *Tonti* †1695 It banker]

'ton-ˌup *adj, Br* of or being sby who has achieved a score, speed, etc of 100 ⟨*the local motorcycle ~ boys*⟩ ⟨*darts ~ boys are in record-breaking mood – The Sun*⟩ – infml

tony /'tohni/ *adj* marked by an aristocratic or fashionable manner or style [¹*tone* + ¹*-y*]

too /tooh/ *adv* **1** also; IN ADDITION ⟨*sell the house and furniture ~*⟩ **2a** to a regrettable degree; excessively ⟨*~ large a house for us*⟩ **b** to a higher degree than meets a standard ⟨*~ pretty for words*⟩ **3** indeed, so – used to counter a negative charge ⟨*'I didn't do it.' 'You did ~.'*⟩ [ME, fr OE *tō* to, too – more at TO]

took /took/ *past of* TAKE

¹tool /toohl/ *n* **1a** an implement that is used, esp by hand, to carry out work of a mechanical nature (e g cutting, levering, or digging) – not usu used with reference to kitchen utensils or cutlery **b** (the cutting or shaping part in) a machine tool **2** sthg (e g an instrument or apparatus) used in performing an operation, or necessary for the practice of a vocation or profession ⟨*books are the* ~s *of a scholar's trade*⟩ **3** sby who is used or manipulated by another **4** a penis – vulg [ME, fr OE *tōl*; akin to OE *tawian* to prepare for use – more at ¹TAW]

²tool *vt* **1** to work, shape, or finish with a tool; *esp* to letter or ornament (e g leather) by means of hand tools **2** to equip (e g a plant or industry) with tools, machines, and instruments for production – often + *up* ~ *vi* **1** to get tooled up for production – usu + *up* **2** to drive, ride ⟨~ed *round the neighbourhood in a small car*⟩ – infml

'toolˌbox /-ˌboks/ *n* a box for tools

'toolˌholder /-ˌhohldə/ *n* a device for holding a tool in a machine (e g a lathe)

'toolˌmaker /-ˌmaykə/ *n* a skilled worker who makes, repairs, maintains, and calibrates the tools and instruments of a machine shop – **toolmaking** *n*

'toolˌroom /-ˌroohm, -room/ *n* a room where tools are kept; *esp* a room in a machine shop in which tools are made, stored, and issued for use by workmen

'toolˌshed /-ˌshed/ *n* a shed for storing (garden) tools

toon /toohn/ *n* (the fragrant dark red wood of) an E Indian and Australian tree of the mahogany family [Hindi *tūn*, fr Skt *tunna*]

toot /tooht/ *vi* **1** to produce a short blast or similar sound ⟨*the horn* ~ed⟩ **2** to cause an instrument to toot ~ *vt* to cause to produce a short blast ⟨*~ a whistle*⟩ [prob imit] – **toot** *n*, **tooter** *n*

¹tooth /toohth/ *n, pl* **teeth** /teeth/ **1a** any of the hard bony structures that are borne esp on the jaws of vertebrates and serve esp for the seizing and chewing of food and as weapons ☞ DIGESTION **b** any of various usu hard and sharp projecting parts about the mouth of an invertebrate **2** a taste, liking ⟨*a sweet ~*⟩ **3a** a projection like the tooth of an animal (e g in shape, arrangement, or action) ⟨*a saw ~*⟩ **b** any of the regular projections on the rim of a cogwheel **4** *pl* effective means of enforcement [ME, fr OE *tōth*; akin to OHG *zand* tooth, L *dent-, dens*, Gk *odont-, odous*] – **toothlike** *adj*, **toothless** *adj* – **in the teeth of** in direct opposition to ⟨*rule had been imposed by conquest* in the teeth of *obstinate resistance* – A J Toynbee⟩

²tooth *vt* to provide with teeth, esp by cutting notches ⟨*~ a saw*⟩ ~ *vi*, *esp of cogwheels* to interlock

'toothˌache /-ˌayk/ *n* pain in or about a tooth

ˌtooth and 'nail *adv* with every available means

'toothˌbrush /-ˌbrush/ *n* a brush for cleaning the teeth

'toothˌcomb /-ˌkohm/ *n, Br* a comb with fine teeth

toothed *adj* having teeth, esp of a specified kind or number – often in combination ⟨*sharp*-toothed⟩

toothed whale *n* any of various whales with numerous simple conical teeth – compare WHALEBONE WHALE

'tooth,paste /-,payst/ *n* a paste for cleaning the teeth

'tooth,pick /-,pik/ *n* a pointed instrument for removing food particles lodged between the teeth

'tooth ,powder *n* a powder for cleaning the teeth

tooth shell *n* (the tapering tubular shell of) any of a class of marine molluscs

toothsome /'toohths(ə)m/ *adj* **1** delicious ⟨*crisp ~ fried chicken*⟩ **2** (sexually) attractive – **toothsomely** *adv*, **toothsomeness** *n*

'tooth,wort /-,wuht/ *n* a parasitic European plant of the broomrape family with a rootstock covered with tooth-shaped scales

toothy /'toohthi/ *adj* having or showing prominent teeth ⟨*a ~ grin*⟩ – **toothily** *adv*

tootle /'toohtl/ *vi* **tootling** /'toohtling/ **1** to toot gently or continuously **2** to drive or move along in a leisurely manner – infml [freq of *toot*] – **tootle** *n*, **tootler** *n*

tootsy *also* **tootsie** /'tootsi/ *n* FOOT 1 – used chiefly to children [baby-talk alter. of *foot*]

[1]**top** /top/ *n* **1a(1)** the highest point, level, or part of sthg **(2)** the (top of the) head – esp in *top to toe* **(3)** the head of a plant, esp one with edible roots ⟨*beet ~s*⟩ **(4)** a garment worn on the upper body **b(1)** the highest or uppermost region or part **(2)** the upper end, edge, or surface **2** a fitted or attached part serving as an upper piece, lid, or covering **3** a platform surrounding the head of a lower mast serving to spread the topmast rigging, or to mount guns ☞ SHIP **4** the highest degree or pitch conceivable or attained **5** the part nearest in space or time to the source or beginning **6** (sby or sthg in) the highest position (e g in rank or achievement) ⟨*~ of the class*⟩ **7** *Br* the transmission gear of a motor vehicle giving the highest ratio of propeller-shaft to engine-shaft speed and hence the highest speed of travel [ME, fr OE; akin to OHG *zopf* tip, tuft of hair] – **topped** *adj* – **off the top of one's head** in an impromptu manner ⟨*can't give the figures* off the top of my head⟩ – **on top of 1a** in control of ⟨*keep* on top of *my job*⟩ **b** informed about **2** in sudden and unexpected proximity to **3** in addition to ⟨*a bad idea to get chilled* on top of *getting wet* – Sylvia Townsend Warner⟩ – **on top of the world** in high spirits; in a state of exhilaration and well-being

[2]**top** *vt* **-pp- 1a** to cut the top off **b** to shorten or remove the top of (a plant); *also* to remove the calyx of (e g a strawberry) – compare TAIL 2b **2a** to cover with a top or on the top; provide, form, or serve as a top for **b** to supply with a decorative or protective finish or final touch **c** to complete the basic structure of (e g a high-rise building) by putting on a cap or uppermost section – usu + *out* or *off* **3a** to be or become higher than; overtop ⟨*~s the previous record*⟩ **b** to be superior to ⟨*~s everything of its kind in print*⟩ **c** to gain ascendancy over **4a** to rise to, reach, or be at the top of **b** to go over the top of; clear, surmount **5** to strike (a ball) above the centre, thereby imparting top spin

[3]**top** *adj* **1** of or at the top **2** foremost, leading ⟨*one of the world's ~ journalists*⟩ **3** of the highest quality, amount, or degree ⟨*~ form*⟩

[4]**top** *n* a child's toy that has a tapering point on which it is made to spin [ME, fr OE]

top-, topo- *comb form* place; locality ⟨topo*logy*⟩ ⟨topo*nymy*⟩ [ME, fr LL, fr Gk, fr *topos* – more at TOPIC]

topaz /'tohpaz/ *n* **1** a mineral that is predominantly a silicate of aluminium, usu occurs in variously coloured translucent or transparent crystals, and is used as a gem **2a** a yellow sapphire **b** a yellow quartz (e g cairngorm or citrine) [ME *topace*, fr OF, fr L *topazus*, fr Gk *topazos*]

top boot *n* a high boot often with light-coloured leather bands round the upper part

,top 'brass *n sing or pl in constr* BRASS HATS

'top,coat /-,koht/ *n* **1** a (lightweight) overcoat **2** a final coat of paint

,top 'dog *n* a person in a position of authority, esp through victory in a hard-fought competition – infml

,top 'drawer *n* the highest level, esp of society – esp in *out of the top drawer* – **top-drawer** *adj*

'top-,dress *vt* to scatter fertilizer over (land) without working it in [back-formation fr *topdressing*] – **top-dressing** *n*

[1]**tope** /tohp/ *vi* to drink alcoholic drink to excess [obs *tope* (interj used to wish good health before drinking)] – **toper** *n*

[2]**tope** *n* a small shark with a liver very rich in vitamin A [origin unknown]

topee, topi /'tohpi/ *n* a lightweight helmet-shaped sunhat made of pith or cork [Hindi *ṭopī*]

,top-'flight *adj* of the highest grade or quality; best

[1]**topgallant** /,top'galənt, tə'galənt/ *adj* of or being a part next above the topmast ⟨*~ sails*⟩ ⟨*the ~ mast*⟩ ☞ SHIP ['*top* + *gallant*, adj]

[2]**topgallant** *n* a topgallant mast or sail ☞ SHIP

top gear *n* a state of intense or maximum activity

'top-,hamper *n* the gear and fittings (e g spars and rigging) above a ship's upper deck

top hat *n* a man's tall-crowned hat usu of beaver or silk

,top-'heavy *adj* **1** having the top part too heavy for or disproportionate to the lower part **2** capitalized beyond what is prudent

,top-'hole *adj, chiefly Br* excellent – infml; not now in vogue

tophus /'tohfəs/ *n, pl* **tophi** /-fie/ a hard chalky deposit in tissues (e g cartilage) characteristic of gout [L, tufa]

topiary /'tohpyəri/ *adj or n* (of or being) the practice or art of training, cutting, and trimming trees or shrubs into odd or ornamental shapes; *also* (characterized by) such work [adj L *topiarius*, fr *topia* ornamental gardening, irreg fr Gk *topos* place; n fr adj]

topic /'topik/ *n* **1a** a heading in an outlined argument or exposition **b** the subject of a (section of a) discourse **2** a subject for discussion or consideration [L *Topica* Topics (work by Aristotle), fr Gk *Topika*, fr *topika*, neut pl of *topikos* of a place, of a rhetorical theme, fr *topos* place, rhetorical theme; akin to OE *thafian* to agree]

topical /'topikl/ *adj* **1a** of a place **b** designed for local application ⟨*a ~ remedy*⟩ **2a** of or arranged by topics ⟨*set down in ~ form*⟩ **b** referring to the topics of the day; of current interest – **topically** *adv*, **topicality** /,topi'kaləti/ *n*

'top,knot /-,not/ *n* **1** an ornament (e g of ribbons) worn as a headdress or as part of a hairstyle **2** an arrangement or growth of hair or feathers on top of the head

topless /'toplis/ *adj* **1** nude above the waist; *esp* having the breasts exposed **2** featuring topless waitresses or entertainers [[1]TOP + -LESS]

,top-'level *adj* very high in level of authority or importance ⟨~ *management*⟩

,top-'line *adj* top-level

topmast /'top,mahst/ *n* a mast that is next above the lowest mast

topminnow /'top,minoh/ *n* any of a family of numerous small viviparous fishes that feed on or near the surface of a body of water [[1]*top* + *minnow*; fr its swimming on the surface of the water]

topmost /'topmohst/ *adj* highest of all

,top-'notch *adj* of the highest quality – infml – **topnotcher** *n*

topo- – see TOP-

topographical /,topə'grafikl/, **topographic** *adj* **1** of or concerned with topography **2** of or concerned with the artistic representation of a particular locality ⟨*a* ~ *poem*⟩ ⟨~ *painting*⟩ – **topographically** *adv*

topography /to'pografi/ *n* **1** (the mapping or charting of) the configuration of a land surface, including its relief and the position of its natural and man-made features **2** the physical or natural features of an object or entity and their structural relationships [ME *topographie*, fr LL *topographia*, fr Gk, fr *topographein* to describe a place, fr *topos* place + *graphein* to write – more at CARVE] – **topographer** *n*

topology /to'poləji/ *n* **1** a branch of mathematics that deals with geometric properties which are unaltered by elastic deformation (e g stretching or twisting) **2** configuration ⟨~ *of a molecule*⟩ ⟨~ *of a magnetic field*⟩ [ISV] – **topological** /,topə'lojikl/ *adj*, **topologist** /to'poləjist/ *n*

toponym /'topə,nim, 'toh-/ *n* a place-name [ISV, back-formation fr *toponymy*]

toponymic /,topə'nimik/ *adj* of toponyms or toponymy – **toponymical** /-'nimikl/ *adj*

toponymy /to'ponəmi, 'toh-/ *n* the study of place-names [ISV, fr *top-* + Gk *onyma, onoma* name – more at NAME]

topper /'topə/ *n* **1** TOP HAT **2** sthg (e g a joke) that caps everything preceding – infml [[2]TOP + [2]-ER]

[1]topping /'toping/ *n* sthg that forms a top; *esp* a garnish or edible decoration on top of a food

[2]topping *adj, chiefly Br* excellent – not now in vogue

topple /'topl/ *vb* **toppling** /'topling, 'topl·ing/ *vi* **1** to fall (as if) from being top-heavy **2** to be or seem unsteady ~ *vt* **1** to cause to topple **2** to overthrow [freq of [2]*top*]

topsail /'top,sayl, 'topsl/ *also* **tops'l** /'topsl/ *n* **1** the sail next above the lowest sail on a mast in a square-rigged ship ☞ SHIP **2** the sail set above and sometimes on the gaff in a fore-and-aft rigged ship

top secret *adj* **1** demanding the greatest secrecy **2** containing information whose unauthorized disclosure could result in exceptionally grave danger to the nation – compare RESTRICTED, SECRET

[1]topside /'top,sied/ *n* **1** *pl* the sides of a ship above the waterline **2** a lean boneless cut of beef from the inner part of a round ☞ MEAT

[2]topside *adv or adj* on deck

topsoil /'top,soyl/ *n* surface soil, usu including the organic layer in which plants form roots and which is turned over in ploughing

top spin *n* a rotary motion imparted to a ball that causes it to rotate forwards in the direction of its travel [[1]*top*]

topsy-turvy /,topsi 'tuhvi/ *adj or adv* **1** UPSIDE DOWN **2** in utter confusion or disorder [prob deriv of *tops* (pl of [1]*top*) + obs *terve* (to turn upside down), fr ME *terven*] – **topsy-turvily** *adv*, **topsy-turvydom** *n*

top up *vt* **1** to make up to the full quantity, capacity, or amount **2** to increase (a money sum set aside for a specific purpose)

toque /tohk/ *n* a woman's small soft brimless hat [MF, soft hat with a narrow brim worn esp in the 16th c, fr OSp *toca* headdress]

tor /taw/ *n* a high rock or rocky mound [ME, fr OE *torr*]

Torah /'tawrə/ *n* **1** *the* Pentateuch; *broadly* Jewish Scripture and other sacred Jewish literature and oral tradition **2** a leather or parchment scroll of the Pentateuch used in a synagogue [Heb *tōrāh*]

torch /tawch/ *n* **1** a burning stick of resinous wood or twist of tow used to give light **2** sthg (e g wisdom or knowledge) that gives enlightenment or guidance **3** *Br* a small portable electric lamp powered by batteries [ME *torche*, fr OF, bundle of twisted straw or tow, torch, fr (assumed) VL *torca*; akin to L *torquēre* to twist – more at TORTURE]

'torch,bearer /-,beərə/ *n* sby in the forefront of a campaign or movement

tore /taw/ *past of* TEAR

toreador /'tori·ə,daw/ *n* a torero [Sp, fr *toreado*, pp of *torear* to fight bulls, fr *toro* bull, fr L *taurus* – more at TAURINE]

torero /to'reəroh/ *n, pl* **toreros** a matador, bullfighter [Sp, fr LL *taurarius*, fr L *taurus* bull]

toreutics /tə'roohtiks/ *n pl but sing in constr* the art of working in metal, esp by embossing or chasing [*toreutic*, adj, fr Gk *toreutikos*, fr *toreuein* to bore through, chase, fr *toreus* boring tool; akin to Gk *tetrainein* to bore – more at THROW] – **toreutic** *adj*

tori /'tawrie/ *pl of* TORUS

torii /'tawri,ee/ *n, pl* **torii** a Japanese gateway of light construction, commonly built at the approach to a Shinto shrine [Jap]

[1]torment /'tawment/ *n* **1** extreme pain or anguish of body or mind **2** a source of vexation or pain [ME, fr OF, fr L *tormentum* torture, fr *torquēre* to twist – more at TORTURE]

[2]torment /taw'ment/ *vt* to cause severe usu persistent distress of body or mind to – **tormentor** *also* **tormenter** *n*

tormentil /'tawməntil/ *n* a common yellow-flowered Eurasian plant of the rose family with a root used in tanning and dyeing [ME *turmentill*, fr ML *tormentilla*, prob fr L *tormentum*; prob fr its use in allaying pain]

torn /tawn/ *past part of* TEAR

tornado /taw'naydoh/ *n, pl* **tornadoes, tornados** a violent or destructive whirlwind, usu progressing in a narrow path over the land and accompanied by a funnel-shaped cloud [modif of Sp *tronada* thunderstorm, fr *tronar* to thunder, fr L *tonare* – more at THUNDER] – **tornadic** /taw'naydik, -'nadik/ *adj*

toroid /'tawroyd/ *n* (a body enclosed by) a surface generated by a plane closed curve (e g a circle) rotated about a line that lies in the same plane as the curve but does not intersect it [NL *torus*]

toroidal /taw'roydl/ *adj* of or shaped like a torus or toroid ⟨*a ~ resistance coil*⟩ – **toroidally** *adv*

[1]**torpedo** /taw'peedoh/ *n, pl* **torpedoes** **1** ELECTRIC RAY **2** a self-propelling cigar-shaped submarine explosive projectile used for attacking ships **3** *NAm* a charge of explosive in a container or case [L, lit., stiffness, numbness, fr *torpēre* to be stiff or numb; fr the paralysing effect of the electric ray's sting]

[2]**torpedo** *vt* **torpedoing; torpedoed** **1** to hit or destroy by torpedo **2** to destroy or nullify (e g a plan) – infml

torpedo boat *n* a small fast warship armed primarily with torpedoes

torpedo bomber *n* a military aeroplane designed to carry torpedoes

torpid /'tawpid/ *adj* **1a** having temporarily lost the power of movement or feeling (e g in hibernation) **b** sluggish in functioning or acting **2** lacking in energy or vigour [L *torpidus*, fr *torpēre* to be stiff or numb; akin to L *stirps* trunk, stock, lineage, OE *starian* to stare – more at STARE] – **torpidly** *adv*, **torpidity** /taw'pidəti/ *n*

torpor /'tawpə/ *n* **1a** a state of mental and motor inactivity with partial or total insensibility **b** extreme sluggishness of action or function **2** apathy [L, fr *torpēre*]

[1]**torque** /tawk/ *n* a twisted metal collar or neck chain worn by the ancient Gauls, Germans, and Britons [F, fr L *torques*, fr *torquēre* to twist – more at TORTURE]

[2]**torque** *n* **1** (a measure of the effectiveness of) a force that produces or tends to produce rotation or torsion ⟨*a car engine delivers ~ to the drive shaft*⟩ **2** a turning or twisting force [L *torquēre* to twist]

torque converter *n* a device for transmitting and amplifying torque, esp by hydraulic means

torr /taw/ *n, pl* **torr** a unit of pressure equal to 133.3Pa ☞ UNIT [Evangelista *Torricelli* †1647 It mathematician & physicist]

torrent /'torənt/ *n* **1** a violent stream of water, lava, etc **2** a raging tumultuous flow [F, fr L *torrent-*, *torrens*, fr *torrent-*, *torrens* burning, seething, rushing, fr prp of *torrēre* to parch, burn – more at THIRST]

torrential /tə'rensh(ə)l/ *adj* **1** resulting from the action of rapid streams **2** of, caused by, or resembling a torrent – **torrentially** *adv*

torrid /'torid/ *adj* **1a** parched with heat, esp of the sun **b** giving off intense heat **2** ardent, passionate ⟨*~ love letters*⟩ [L *torridus*, fr *torrēre*] – **torridly** *adv*, **torridness** *n*, **torridity** /tə'ridəti/ *n*

torrid zone *n* the belt of the earth between the tropics

torsion /'tawsh(ə)n/ *n* **1** the act or process of twisting or turning sthg, esp by forces exerted on one end while the other is fixed or twisted in the opposite direction **2** the state of being twisted **3** the twisting of a bodily organ on its own axis [LL *torsus*, pp of L *torquēre* to twist] – **torsional** *adj*

torsk /tawsk/ *n* a large edible marine fish related to the cod [of Scand origin; akin to Norw, Sw, & Dan *torsk* codfish, ON *thorskr*]

torso /'tawsoh/ *n, pl* **torsos, torsi** /'tawsi/ **1** (a sculptured representation of) the human trunk **2** sthg (e g a piece of writing) that is mutilated or left unfinished [It, lit., stalk, fr L *thyrsus* stalk, thyrsus]

tort /tawt/ *n* a wrongful act, other than breach of contract, for which a civil action for damages may be brought [ME, fr MF, fr ML *tortum*, fr L, neut of *tortus* twisted, fr pp of *torquēre*]

torte /'tawtə/ *n, pl* **torten** /'tawtən/, **tortes** /'tawtəz/ a gateau [G, prob fr It *torta*, fr LL, round loaf of bread]

tortfeasor /'tawt,feezə/ *n* one who commits a tort [F *tortfaiseur*, fr MF, fr *tort* + *faiseur* doer, maker, fr *faire* to make, do, fr L *facere* – more at DO]

torticollis /,tawti'kolis/ *n* a permanent twisting of the neck resulting in an abnormal carriage of the head [NL, fr L *tortus* twisted + *-i-* + *collum* neck – more at COLLAR]

tortilla /taw'teeyə/ *n* a round thin cake of unleavened maize bread, usu eaten hot with a topping or filling of minced meat or cheese [AmerSp, dim. of Sp *torta* cake, fr LL, round loaf of bread]

tortious /'tawchəs/ *adj* implying or involving a tort – **tortiously** *adv*

tortoise /'tawtəs, 'taw,toys/ *n* **1** any of an order of land and freshwater (and marine) reptiles with a toothless horny beak and a bony shell which encloses the trunk and into which the head, limbs, and tail may be withdrawn; *esp* a land tortoise commonly kept as a pet **2** sby or sthg slow or laggard [ME *tortu, tortuce*, fr MF *tortue* – more at TURTLE]

[1]**tortoiseshell** /'tawtəs,shel/ *n* **1** the mottled horny substance of the shell of some marine turtles used in inlaying and in making various ornamental articles **2** any of several butterflies with striking orange, yellow, brown, and black coloration

[2]**tortoiseshell** *adj* mottled black, brown, and yellow ⟨*~ cat*⟩

tortricid /'tawtrisid/ *n* any of a family of small stout-bodied moths many of whose larvae live in nests formed by rolling up plant leaves [NL *Tortricidae*, group name, fr *Tortric-*, *Tortrix*] – **tortricid** *adj*

tortrix /'tawtriks/ *n* a tortricid moth [NL *Tortric-*, *Tortrix*, genus of moths, fr L *tortus*, pp of *torquēre* to twist; fr its habit of twisting or rolling leaves to make a nest]

tortuous /'tawtyoo·əs/ *adj* **1** marked by repeated twists, bends, or turns **2a** marked by devious or indirect tactics **b** circuitous, involved [ME, fr MF *tortueux*, fr L *tortuosus*, fr *tortus* twist, fr *tortus*, pp of *torquēre*] – **tortuously** *adv*, **tortuousness** *n*, **tortuosity** /,tawtyoo'osəti/ *n*

[1]**torture** /'tawchə/ *n* **1** the infliction of intense physical or mental suffering as a means of punishment, coercion, or sadistic gratification **2** (sthg causing) anguish of body or mind [F, fr LL *tortura*, fr L *tortus*, pp of *torquēre* to twist; akin to OHG *drāhsil* turner, Gk *atraktos* spindle]

[2]**torture** *vt* **1** to subject to torture **2** to cause intense suffering to **3** to twist or wrench out of shape; *also* to pervert (e g the meaning of a word) – **torturer** *n*

torula /'toryoolə, 'tawrələ, 'tawyələ/ *n, pl* **torulae** /-li/ *also* **torulas** any of various fungi, esp yeasts, that lack sexual spores and do not produce alcoholic fermentations [NL, fr L *torus* protuberance]

torus /'tawrəs/ *n, pl* **tori** /-rie/ **1** a smooth rounded anatomical protuberance **2** RECEPTACLE 2 **3** a ring-shaped surface generated by a circle rotated about an axis in its plane that does not intersect the circle; *broadly* a toroid **4** a large convex semicircular moulding, esp on the base of a column, pedestal, etc ☞ ARCHITECTURE [NL, fr L, protuberance, bulge]

Tory /'tawri/ *n* **1a** a member of a major British political group of the 18th and early 19th c favouring at first the Stuarts and later royal authority and the established church and seeking to preserve the traditional political structure and defeat parliamentary reform – compare WHIG **b** CONSERVATIVE 1 **2** an American upholding the cause of the crown during the American Revolution [IrGael *tōraidhe* pursuer, robber, fr MIr *tōir* pursuit; orig applied to dispossessed Irish Royalists in the 17th c] – **Tory** *adj*, **Toryism** *n*

tosh /tosh/ *n* sheer nonsense – infml [origin unknown]

[1]**toss** /tos/ *vt* **1a** to fling or heave repeatedly about ⟨*a ship* ~ed *by waves*⟩ **b** BANDY 1 **2a** to throw with a quick, light, or careless motion ⟨~ *a ball around*⟩ **b** to throw up in the air ⟨~ed *by a bull*⟩ **c** to flip (a coin) to decide an issue **3** to lift with a sudden jerking motion ⟨~es *her head angrily*⟩ ~ *vi* **1** to move restlessly or turbulently; *esp* to twist and turn repeatedly ⟨~ed *sleeplessly all night*⟩ **2** to decide an issue by flipping a coin – often + *up* [prob of Scand origin; akin to Sw dial. *tossa* to spread, scatter] – **tosser** *n*

[2]**toss** *n* **1a** being tossed **b** a fall, esp from a horse – chiefly in *take a toss* **2** an act or instance of tossing: e g **a** an abrupt tilting or upward fling **b** an act or instance of deciding by chance, esp by tossing a coin **c** a throw **3** *Br* DAMN 2 – chiefly in *not give a toss*

toss off *vt* **1** to perform or write quickly and easily **2** to consume quickly; *esp* to drink in a single draught ~ *vi*, *Br* to masturbate – infml

tosspot /'tos,pot/ *n* a drunkard, sot

'toss-,up *n* **1** TOSS 2b **2** an even chance or choice – infml

tot /tot/ *n* **1** a small child; a toddler **2** a small amount or allowance of alcoholic drink ⟨*a* ~ *of rum*⟩ [origin unknown]

[1]**total** /'tohtl/ *adj* **1** comprising or constituting a whole; entire **2** complete ⟨*a* ~ *success*⟩ **3** concentrating all available personnel and resources on a single objective ⟨~ *war*⟩ [ME, fr MF, fr ML *totalis*, fr L *totus* whole, entire] – **totally** *adv*

[2]**total** *n* **1** a product of addition **2** an entire quantity

[3]**total** *vt* -ll- (*NAm* -l-, -ll-), /'tohtl·ing/ **1** to add up **2** to amount to

total eclipse *n* an eclipse in which one celestial body is completely obscured by another

total internal reflection *n* total reflection of a light ray from the more highly refractive of 2 adjacent media at their interface when the optical angle is exceeded

totalitarian /,tohtali'teəri·ən/ *adj* **1** authoritarian, dictatorial **2** of or constituting a political regime based on subordination of the individual to the state and strict control over all aspects of the life and productive capacity of the nation [*total* + *-itarian* (as in *authoritarian*)] – **totalitarianism** *n*

totality /toh'taləti/ *n* **1** an entire amount; a whole **2a** wholeness **b** a period during which one body is completely obscured by another during an eclipse

total·izator, -isator /'tohtl·ie,zaytə/ *n* a machine for registering bets and calculating winnings in pari-mutuel betting

total·ize, -ise /'tohtl,iez/ *vt* **1** to add up **2** to express as a whole; summarize – **totalizer** *n*

total utility *n* the degree of utility of an economic good (e g an article or service) considered as a whole

[1]**tote** /toht/ *vt* **1** to carry by hand or on the person **2** to transport, convey USE infml [origin unknown]

[2]**tote** *n* a totalizator

tote bag, tote *n* a large bag for carrying esp shopping or personal possessions

totem /'tohtəm/ *n* **1** a natural object serving as the emblem of a family or clan; *also* a carved or painted representation of this **2** sthg that serves as an emblem or revered symbol [Ojibwa *ototeman* his totem] – **totemic** /toh'temik/ *adj*

totemism /'tohtə,miz(ə)m/ *n* belief in a mystical relationship between a group or individual and a totem – **totemist** *n*

'totem ,pole *n* **1** a pole carved and painted with a series of totemic symbols erected before the houses of some N American Indian tribes **2** an order of rank; a hierarchy

tother, t'other /'tudhə/ *pron or adj, chiefly dial* the other [ME *tother*, alter. (by incorrect division of *thet other* the other, fr *thet* the – fr OE *thæt* – + *other*) of *other* – more at THAT]

[1]**totter** /'totə/ *vi* **1a** to tremble or rock as if about to fall **b** to become unstable; threaten to collapse **2** to move unsteadily; stagger [ME *toteren*]

[2]**totter** *n* an unsteady gait – **tottery** *adj*

totting /'toting/ *n*, *Br* the occupation of scavenging refuse for salable goods, esp illicitly [*tot* (bone, sthg salvaged from refuse), of unknown origin] – **totter** *n*

,totting-'up *n*, *Br* a legal procedure whereby a certain number of convictions for traffic offences disqualifies one from driving – infml

tot up *vt* to add together ⟨tot up *the score*⟩ ~ *vi* to increase by additions ⟨*the money soon* tots up⟩ [*tot* (to add up), short for [3]*total*]

Touareg /'twah,reg/ *n* a Tuareg

toucan /'tooh,kan/ *n* any of a family of fruit-eating birds of tropical America with brilliant colouring and a very large but light beak [F, fr Pg *tucano*, fr Tupi]

[1]**touch** /tuch/ *vt* **1** to bring a bodily part into contact with, esp so as to perceive through the sense of feeling; feel **2** to strike or push lightly, esp with the hand or foot or an implement **3** to lay hands on (sby afflicted with scrofula) with intent to heal **4a** to take into the hands or mouth ⟨*never* ~es *alcohol*⟩ **b** to put hands on in any way or degree ⟨*don't* ~ *anything before the police come*⟩; *esp* to commit violence against ⟨*swears he never* ~ed *the child*⟩ **5** to concern oneself with **6** to cause to be briefly in contact with sthg ⟨~ *a match to the wick*⟩ **7a(1)** to meet without overlapping or penetrating **(2)** to get to; reach ⟨*the speedometer needle* ~ed *80*⟩ **b** to be tangent to **8** to affect the interest of; concern **9a** to leave a mark or impression on ⟨*few reagents will* ~ *gold*⟩ **b** to harm slightly (as if) by contact; blemish ⟨*fruit* ~ed *by frost*⟩ **c** to give a delicate tint, line, or expression to ⟨*a smile* ~ed *her lips*⟩ **10** to draw or delineate with light strokes **11** to move to esp sympa-

thetic feeling ⟨~ed *by the loyalty of her friends*⟩ **12** to speak or tell of, esp in passing **13** RIVAL 3 **14** to induce to give or lend ⟨~ed *him for 10 quid*⟩ ~*vi* **1a** to feel sthg with a body part (e g the hand or foot) **b** to lay hands on sby to cure disease (e g scrofula) **2** to be in contact **3** to come close ⟨*his actions* ~ *on treason*⟩ **4** to have a bearing – + *on* or *upon* **5a** to make a brief or incidental stop on shore during a trip by water ⟨~ed *at several ports*⟩ **b** to treat a topic in a brief or casual manner – + *on* or *upon* *USE* (*vt 12*) fml; (*vt 13&14*) infml [ME *touchen*, fr OF *tuchier*, fr (assumed) VL *toccare* to knock, strike a bell, touch, of imit origin] – **touchable** *adj*, **toucher** *n* – **touch wood** **1** with a certain amount of luck ⟨*everything will be all right now,* touch wood⟩ **2** *Br* to touch a wooden surface as a gesture to bring luck

[2]**touch** *n* **1** a light stroke, tap, or push **2** the act or fact of touching **3** the sense of feeling, esp as exercised deliberately with the hands, feet, or lips **4** mental or moral sensitivity, responsiveness, or tact ⟨*has a wonderful* ~ *with children*⟩ **5** a specified sensation conveyed through the sense of touch ⟨*the velvety* ~ *of a fabric*⟩ **6** the testing of gold or silver on a touchstone **7** sthg slight of its kind: e g **a** a light attack ⟨*a* ~ *of fever*⟩ **b** a small amount; a trace ⟨*a* ~ *of spring in the air*⟩ **c** a bit, little – in the adverbial phrase *a touch* ⟨*aimed a* ~ *too low and missed*⟩ **8a** a manner or method of touching or striking esp the keys of a keyboard instrument **b** the relative resistance to pressure of the keys of a keyboard (e g of a piano or typewriter) **9** an effective and appropriate detail; *esp* one used in an artistic composition **10** a distinctive or characteristic manner, trait, or quality ⟨*a woman's* ~⟩ **11** the state or fact of being in contact or communication ⟨*out of* ~ *with modern times*⟩ **12** the area outside the touchlines in soccer or outside and including the touchlines in rugby **13a** an act of soliciting or receiving a gift or loan of money **b** sby who can be easily induced to part with money – chiefly in *a soft/easy touch* *USE* (*13*) slang

,touch and 'go *n* a highly uncertain or precarious situation

'touch,down /-,down/ *n* **1** the act of touching down a football **2** (the moment of) touching down (e g of an aeroplane or spacecraft)

touch down *vt* to place (the ball in rugby) by hand on the ground either positioned on or over an opponent's goal line in scoring a try, or behind one's own goal line as a defensive measure ~*vi* to reach the ground

touché /tooh'shay/ *interj* – used to acknowledge a hit in fencing or the success of an argument, accusation, or witty point [F, fr pp of *toucher* to touch, fr OF *tuchier*]

touched /tucht/ *adj* **1** emotionally moved (e g with gratitude) **2** slightly unbalanced mentally – infml

'touch,hole /-,hohl/ *n* the hole in early cannon or firearms through which the charge was ignited

[1]**touching** /'tuching/ *prep* in reference to; concerning – fml

[2]**touching** *adj* capable of arousing tenderness or compassion – **touchingly** *adv*

touch judge *n* a rugby linesman

'touch,line /-,lien/ *n* either of the lines that bound the sides of the field of play in rugby and soccer ☞ SPORT

'touch,mark /-,mahk/ *n* an identifying maker's mark impressed on pewter

touch off *vt* **1** to cause to explode (as if) by touching with a naked flame **2** to release with sudden intensity

'touch,paper /-,paypə/ *n* paper, impregnated with a substance (e g potassium nitrate), that burns slowly and is used esp for the ignition of fireworks

'touch,stone /-,stohn/ *n* **1** a black flintlike siliceous stone that when rubbed by gold or silver showed a streak of colour and was formerly used to test the purity of these metals **2** a test or criterion for determining the genuineness of sthg

'touch-,type *vi* to type without looking at the keyboard, using a system that assigns a particular finger to each key

touch up *vt* **1** to improve or perfect by small alterations; make good the minor defects of **2** to stimulate (as if) by a flick of a whip **3** to make often unwelcome physical advances to; touch with a view to arousing sexually – slang

'touch,wood /-,wood/ *n* wood so decayed as to be dry, crumbly, and useful for tinder

touchy /'tuchi/ *adj* **1** ready to take offence on slight provocation **2** calling for tact, care, or caution ⟨*sexism was a* ~ *subject with his wife*⟩ – **touchily** *adv*, **touchiness** *n*

[1]**tough** /tuf/ *adj* **1a** strong and flexible; not brittle or liable to cut, break, or tear **b** not easily chewed **2** severe or uncompromisingly determined ⟨*a* ~ *and inflexible foreign policy – New Statesman*⟩ **3** capable of enduring great hardship or exertion **4** very hard to influence **5** extremely difficult or testing ⟨*a* ~ *question to answer*⟩ **6** aggressive or threatening in behaviour **7** without softness or sentimentality **8** unfortunate, unpleasant – infml ⟨~ *luck*⟩ [ME, fr OE *tōh*; akin to OHG *zāhi* tough] – **toughly** *adv*, **toughness** *n*

[2]**tough** *n* a tough person; *esp* sby aggressively violent

[3]**tough** *adv* in a tough manner ⟨*talk* ~⟩

toughen /'tuf(ə)n/ *vb* to make or become tough

,tough-'minded *adj* unsentimental or realistic in disposition or outlook – **tough-mindedness** *n*

toupee /'tooh,pay/ *n* a wig or hairpiece worn to cover a bald spot [F *toupet* forelock, fr OF, dim. of *top, toup,* of Gmc origin; akin to OHG *zopf* tuft of hair – more at [1]TOP]

[1]**tour** /tooə/ *n* **1** a period during which an individual or unit is engaged on a specific duty, esp in 1 place ⟨*his regiment did a* ~ *in N Ireland*⟩ **2a** a journey (e g for business or pleasure) in which one returns to the starting point **b** a visit (e g to a historic site or factory) for pleasure or instruction ⟨*a guided* ~ *of the castle*⟩ **c** a series of professional engagements involving travel ⟨*a theatrical company on* ~⟩ [ME, fr MF, fr OF *tourn, tour* lathe, circuit, turn – more at [2]TURN]

[2]**tour** *vi* to make a tour ~*vt* **1** to make a tour of **2** to present (e g a theatrical production or concert) on a tour

touraco /'tooərə,koh/ *n, pl* **touracos** any of a family of African birds that have a long tail, a short stout beak, and red wing feathers [native name in W Africa]

tour de force /,tooə də 'faws (*Fr* tu:r də fɔrs)/ *n, pl* **tours de force** /~/ a feat of strength, skill, or ingenuity [F]

tourism /'tooə,riz(ə)m/ *n* **1** the practice of travelling for recreation **2** the organizing of tours for commercial purposes **3a** the promotion or encouragement of touring, esp at governmental level **b** the provision of services (e g accommodation) for tourists

tourist /'tooərist/ *n* **1** sby who makes a tour for recreation or culture **2** a member of a sports team that is visiting another country to play usu international matches – **tourist** *adj*

tourist class *n* the lowest class of accommodation (e g on a ship)

touristy /'tooəristi/ *adj* frequented by or appealing to tourists – chiefly derog

tourmaline /'tooəmə,leen/ *n* a variously coloured mineral consisting of a complex silicate and used as a gem when transparent [Sinhalese *toramalli* carnelian]

tournament /'tooənəmənt, 'taw-/ *n* **1** a contest between 2 parties of mounted knights armed with usu blunted lances or swords **2** a series of games or contests for a championship [ME *tornement,* fr OF *torneiement,* fr *torneier*]

tournedos /'tooənə,doh/ *n, pl* **tournedos** /-,doh(z)/ a small steak cut from the centre of a beef fillet and usu larded, tied, and held in shape with a skewer ☞ MEAT [F, fr *tourner* to turn (fr OF) + *dos* back, fr L *dorsum* – more at [1]TURN]

[1]**tourney** /'tooəni, 'tawni/ *vi* to take part in a tournament, esp in the Middle Ages [ME *tourneyen,* fr MF *torneier,* fr OF, fr *torn, tourn* lathe, circuit]

[2]**tourney** *n* a tournament, esp in the Middle Ages

tourniquet /'tooəni,kay, 'taw-/ *n* a bandage or other device for applying pressure to check bleeding or blood flow [F, turnstile, tourniquet, fr *tourner* to turn, fr OF – more at [1]TURN]

tousle /'towzl/ *vt* to dishevel, rumple [ME *touselen,* freq of *-tousen*; akin to OHG *zirzūsōn* to pull to pieces]

[1]**tout** /towt/ *vi* to solicit for customers ~ *vt* **1a** to solicit or peddle importunately **b** *Br* to sell (tickets in great demand) at exploitative prices **2a** *Br* to spy out information about (e g a racing stable or horse) **b** *NAm* to give a tip or solicit bets on (a racehorse) [ME *tuten* to peer; akin to OE *tōtian* to stick out, Norw *tyte*]

[2]**tout** *n* sby who touts: e g **a** sby who solicits custom, usu importunately **b** *Br* sby who offers tickets for a sold-out entertainment (e g a concert or football match) at vastly inflated prices

[3]**tout** *vt* to praise or publicize loudly or extravagantly ⟨~ed *as the most elaborate suburban shopping development – Wall Street Journal*⟩ [alter. of *toot*]

[1]**tow** /toh/ *vt* to draw or pull along behind, esp by a rope or chain [ME *towen,* fr OE *togian*; akin to OE *tēon* to draw, pull, OHG *ziohan,* L *ducere* to draw, lead]

[2]**tow** *n* **1** a rope or chain for towing **2** towing or being towed **3** sthg towed (e g a boat or car) – **in tow 1** being towed ⟨*a breakdown lorry with a car* in tow⟩ **2a** under guidance or protection ⟨*taken* in tow *by a friendly neighbour*⟩ **b** in the position of a dependent or devoted follower or admirer ⟨*a young man passed with a good-looking girl* in tow⟩

[3]**tow** *n* short or broken fibre (e g of flax or hemp) prepared for spinning [ME, fr OE *tow-* spinning; akin to ON *tō* tuft of wool for spinning, OE *tawian* to prepare for use – more at [1]TAW]

towage /'toh·ij/ *n* the price paid for towing [[1]TOW + -AGE]

[1]**toward** /tə'wawd/ *adj* happening at the moment; afoot [ME, fr OE *tōweard* facing, imminent, fr *tō* (prep) to + *-weard* -ward]

[2]**toward** *prep, NAm* towards

towards /tə'wawdz/ *prep* **1** moving or situated in the direction of ⟨*driving ~ town*⟩ **2a** along a course leading to ⟨*a long stride ~ disarmament*⟩ **b** in relation to ⟨*an attitude ~ life*⟩ **3** turned in the direction of ⟨*his back was ~ me*⟩ **4** not long before ⟨*~ the end of the afternoon*⟩ **5** for the partial financing of ⟨*will put it ~ a record*⟩ [ME *towardes,* fr OE *tōweardes,* alter. of *tōweard,* adj]

[1]**towel** /'towəl/ *n* **1** an absorbent cloth or paper for wiping or drying sthg (e g crockery or the body) after washing **2** SANITARY TOWEL [ME *towaille,* fr OF *toaille,* of Gmc origin; akin to OHG *dwahila* towel; akin to OHG *dwahan* to wash, OPruss *twaxtan* bath cloth]

[2]**towel** *vt* **-ll-** (*NAm* **-l-, -ll-**) to rub or dry (e g the body) with a towel

towelling, *NAm chiefly* **toweling** /'towəling/ *n* a cotton or linen fabric often used for making towels

[1]**tower** /'towə/ *n* **1** a building or structure typically higher than its diameter and high relative to its surroundings that may stand apart or be attached to a larger structure and that may be fully walled in or of skeleton framework ☞ CHURCH **2** a citadel, fortress **3 tower block, tower** a tall multi-storey building, often containing offices [ME *tour, tor,* fr OE *torr* & OF *tor, tur,* both fr L *turris,* fr Gk *tyrsis*] – **towered** *adj,* **towerlike** *adj*

[2]**tower** *vi* to reach or rise to a great height

towering /'towəring/ *adj* **1** impressively high or great ⟨*~ pines*⟩ **2** reaching a high point of intensity ⟨*a ~ rage*⟩ **3** going beyond proper bounds ⟨*~ ambitions*⟩ – **toweringly** *adv*

tower of strength *n* sby who can be relied on as a source of sympathy and support

towhead /'toh,hed/ *n* (sby with) a head of hair resembling tow, esp in being flaxen or tousled – **towheaded** /-'hedid/ *adj*

to wit /tə 'wit/ *adv* that is to say [arch *wit* (to know), fr ME *witen,* fr OE *witan* – more at WIT]

towline /'toh,lien/ *n* a towrope

town /town/ *n* **1a** a compactly settled area as distinguished from surrounding rural territory; *esp* one larger than a village but smaller than a city **b** a city **2** a neighbouring city, capital city, or metropolis ⟨*travels into ~ daily*⟩ **3** the city or urban life as contrasted with the country or rural life [ME, fr OE *tūn* enclosure, village, town; akin to OHG *zūn* enclosure, OIr *dūn* fortress] – **town** *adj* – **on the town** in usu carefree pursuit of entertainment or amusement (e g city nightlife)

town clerk *n* the chief official of a British town who until 1974 was appointed to administer municipal affairs and to act as secretary to the town council

town crier /'krie·ə/ *n* a town officer who makes public proclamations

townee /'towni, tow'nee/ *n* a townsman, esp as distinguished from a country dweller

town hall *n* the chief administrative building of a town

town house *n* **1** the city residence of sby having a

country seat **2** a terrace house typically of 3 storeys

town manager *n* an official employed to direct the administration of a town government

town planner *n* one who is professionally qualified to plan the control and development of the urban environment – **town planning** *n*

townscape /ˈtown,skayp/ *n* the overall visual aspect of a town

townsfolk /ˈtownz,fohk/ *n pl* townspeople

township /ˈtownship/ *n* **1** an ancient unit of administration in England identical in area with or being a division of a parish **2** an urban area inhabited by nonwhite citizens in S Africa

townsman /ˈtownzmən/, *fem* **ˈtowns,woman** *n* **1** a native or resident of a town or city **2** a fellow citizen of a town

ˈtowns,people /-,peepl/ *n pl* the inhabitants of a town or city

towrope /ˈtoh,rohp/ *n* a line used in towing a boat, car, etc

tox-, toxi-, toxo- *comb form* poison ⟨tox*aemia*⟩ [LL, fr L *toxicum* poison]

toxaemia /tokˈseemyə, -mi·ə/ *n* **1** an abnormal condition associated with the presence of toxic substances in the blood **2** pre-eclampsia [NL]

toxic /ˈtoksik/ *adj* **1** of or caused by a poison or toxin **2** poisonous [LL *toxicus*, fr L *toxicum* poison, fr Gk *toxikon* arrow poison, fr neut of *toxikos* of a bow, fr *toxon* bow, arrow] – **toxicity** /tokˈsisəti/ *n*

toxic-, toxico- *comb form* tox- ⟨toxico*logy*⟩ ⟨toxic*osis*⟩ [NL, fr L *toxicum*]

toxicological /,toksikəˈlojikl/, **toxicologic** *adj* of toxicology or toxins – **toxicologically** *adv*

toxicology /,toksiˈkoləji/ *n* a branch of biology that deals with poisons and their effects and with medical, industrial, legal, or other problems arising from them – **toxicologist** *n*

toxicosis /,toksiˈkohsis/ *n, pl* **toxicoses** /-seez/ a disorder caused by the action of a poison or toxin [NL]

toxigenic /,toksiˈjenik/ *adj* producing toxin ⟨~ *bacteria and fungi*⟩ – **toxigenicity** /-jəˈnisəti/ *n*

toxin /ˈtoksin/ *n* an often extremely poisonous protein produced by a living organism (e g a bacterium), esp in the body of a host [ISV]

toxophilite /tokˈsofiliet/ *n* a lover of or expert at archery – fml [Gk *toxon* bow, arrow + *philos* dear, loving] – **toxophilite** *adj*, **toxophily** /-fili/ *n*

toxoplasma /,toksəˈplazmə/ *n* any of a genus of parasitic protozoans that are typically serious pathogens of vertebrates including human beings [NL, genus name] – **toxoplasmic** /-ˈplazmik/ *adj*

toxoplasmosis /,toksohplazˈmohsis/ *n, pl* **toxoplasmoses** /-seez/ a disease, caused by toxoplasmas invading the tissues, that is often accompanied by damage to the central nervous system, esp of infants [NL]

¹toy /toy/ *n* **1** a trinket, bauble **2a** sthg for a child to play with **b** sthg designed for amusement or diversion rather than practical use ⟨*an executive* ~⟩ **3** sthg tiny; *esp* an animal of a breed or variety of exceptionally small size [ME *toye* dalliance, antic] – **toylike** *adj*

²toy *vi* **1** to act or deal *with* sthg without purpose or conviction **2** to amuse oneself as if with a toy – **toyer** *n*

³toy *adj* **1** designed or made for use as a toy ⟨*a ~ stove*⟩ **2** toylike, esp in being small

trabecula /trəˈbekyoolə/ *n, pl* **trabeculae** /-li/ *also* **trabeculas** **1** a small bar, rod, bundle of fibres, or dividing membrane in the framework of a body organ or part **2** a fold, ridge, or bar projecting into or extending from a plant part [NL, fr L, little beam, dim. of *trabs, trabes* beam] – **trabecular** *adj*, **trabeculate** /-lət/ *adj*

¹trace /trays/ *n* **1** a mark or line left by sthg that has passed; *also* a footprint **2** a vestige of some past thing; *specif* an engram **3** sthg traced or drawn (e g the graphic record made by a seismograph) **4** (the path taken by) the spot that moves across the screen of a cathode-ray tube **5** a minute and often barely detectable amount or indication, esp of a chemical ⟨*a ~ of a smile*⟩ [ME, fr MF, fr *tracier* to trace]

²trace *vt* **1a** to delineate, sketch **b** to write (e g letters or figures) painstakingly **c** to copy (e g a drawing) by following the lines or letters as seen through a semitransparent superimposed sheet **2a** to follow the trail of **b** to follow back or study in detail or step by step ⟨*~ the history of the labour movement*⟩ **c** to discover signs, evidence, or remains of ~ *vi* to be traceable historically [ME *tracen*, fr MF *tracier*, fr (assumed) VL *tractiare* to drag, draw, fr L *tractus*, pp of *trahere* to pull, draw – more at DRAW] – **traceable** *adj*

³trace *n* either of 2 straps, chains, or lines of a harness for attaching a vehicle to a horse [ME *trais*, pl, traces, fr MF, pl of *trait* pull, draught trace – more at TRAIT]

trace element *n* a chemical element present in minute quantities; *esp* one essential to a living organism for proper growth and development

tracer /ˈtraysə/ *n* **1** ammunition containing a chemical composition to mark the flight of projectiles by a trail of smoke or fire **2** a substance, esp a labelled element or atom, used to trace the course of a chemical or biological process [²TRACE + ²-ER]

tracery /ˈtraysəri/ *n* ornamental stone openwork in architecture, esp in the head of a Gothic window ☞ ARCHITECTURE, CHURCH – **traceried** *adj*

trache-, tracheo- *comb form* trachea ⟨trache*itis*⟩ ⟨tracheo*tomy*⟩ [NL, fr ML *trachea*]

trachea /trəˈkee·ə/ *n, pl* **tracheae** *also* **tracheas** **1** the main trunk of the system of tubes by which air passes to and from the lungs in vertebrates; the windpipe ☞ DIGESTION **2** VESSEL 3b **3** any of the small tubes carrying air in most insects and many other arthropods [ME, fr ML, fr LL *trachia*, fr Gk *tracheia* (*artēria*) rough (artery), fr fem of *trachys* rough; akin to Gk *thrassein* to trouble – more at DARK; (2, 3) NL, fr ML] – **tracheal** *adj*, **tracheate** /ˈtraki·ət, -ayt, ˈtray-/ *adj*

tracheotomy /,trakiˈotəmi/ *n* the surgical operation of cutting into the trachea, esp through the skin, usu to relieve suffocation by inhaled matter

trachoma /trəˈkohmə/ *n* a chronic contagious eye disease that is caused by a rickettsia and commonly causes blindness if left untreated [NL, fr Gk *trachōma*, fr *trachys* rough] – **trachomatous** /trəˈkomətəs, -ˈkoh-/ *adj*

trachyte /ˈtrakiet, ˈtray-/ *n* a usu light-coloured volcanic rock consisting chiefly of potash feldspar [F, fr Gk *trachys* rough]

trachytic /trəˈkitik/ *adj* of a texture of igneous rocks in which lath-shaped feldspar crystals are in almost parallel lines

tracing /ˈtraysing/ *n* sthg traced: e g **a** a copy (e g of a design or map) made on a superimposed semitransparent sheet **b** (a map of) the ground plan of a military installation

tracing paper *n* a semitransparent paper for tracing drawings

[1]**track** /trak/ *n* **1a** detectable evidence (e g a line of footprints or a wheel rut) that sthg has passed **b** a path beaten (as if) by feet **c** a specially laid-out course, esp for racing **d(1)** the parallel rails of a railway **(2)** a rail or length of railing along which sthg, esp a curtain, moves or is pulled **e(1)** any of a series of parallel elongated regions on a magnetic tape on which a recording is made ☞ VIDEO **(2)** a more or less independent sequence of recording (e g a single song) visible as a distinct band on a gramophone record **2** a recent or fossil footprint ⟨*the huge ~ of a dinosaur*⟩ **3a** the course along which sthg moves **b** the projection on the earth's surface of the path along which sthg (e g a missile) has flown **4** the condition of being aware of a fact or development ⟨*keep ~ of the costs*⟩ **5a** the width of a wheeled vehicle from wheel to wheel, usu from the outside of the rims **b** either of 2 endless usu metal belts on which a tracklaying vehicle travels [ME *trak*, fr MF *trac*, perh of Gmc origin; akin to MD *tracken, trecken* to pull, haul – more at TREK] – **trackless** *adj* – **in one's tracks** where one stands or is at the moment ⟨*was stopped* in his tracks⟩

[2]**track** *vt* **1** to follow the tracks or traces of **2** to observe or plot the course of (e g a spacecraft) instrumentally **3a** to make tracks on **b** *NAm* to carry on the feet and deposit ⟨*~ mud into the house*⟩ ~ *vi* **1a** *of a gramophone needle* to follow the groove of a record **b** *of a rear wheel of a vehicle* to follow accurately the corresponding fore wheel on a straight track **2** to move a film or television camera towards, beside, or away from a subject while shooting a scene **3** *NAm* to leave tracks (e g on a floor) – **tracker** *n*

track chargeman *n, Br* a worker employed to maintain a section of railway track

track down *vt* to search for until found ⟨track *a criminal* down⟩ ⟨track down *their new telephone number*⟩

track event *n* an athletic event that is a race – compare FIELD EVENT

ˈ**track,laying** /-ˌlaying/ *adj* of or being a vehicle that travels on 2 or more endless usu metal belts

track record *n* a record of past achievements, esp in public office

track suit *n* a warm loose-fitting suit worn by athletes when training

[1]**tract** /trakt/ *n* a short practical treatise; *esp* a pamphlet of religious propaganda [ME, modif of L *tractatus* treatise, fr *tractatus*, pp of *tractare* to draw out, handle, treat – more at TREAT]

[2]**tract** *n* **1** a region or area of land of indefinite extent **2** a system of body parts or organs that collectively serve some often specified purpose ⟨*the digestive ~*⟩ [L *tractus* action of drawing, extension, fr *tractus*, pp of *trahere* to pull, draw – more at DRAW]

tractable /ˈtraktəbl/ *adj* **1** easily taught or controlled ⟨*a ~ horse*⟩ **2** easily handled or wrought [L *tractabilis*, fr *tractare*] – **tractableness** *n*, **tractably** *adv*, **tractability** /ˌtraktəˈbiləti/ *n*

Tractarianism /trakˈteəri·əˌniz(ə)m/ *n* a system of High Church principles set forth in a series of tracts at Oxford (1833–41); the doctrines of the early Oxford Movement – **Tractarian** *adj*

traction /ˈtraksh(ə)n/ *n* **1** pulling or being pulled; *also* the force exerted in pulling **2** the drawing of a vehicle by motive power; *also* the motive power employed **3a** the adhesive friction of a body on a surface on which it moves ⟨*the ~ of a wheel on a rail*⟩ **b** a pulling force exerted on a skeletal structure (e g in treating a fracture) by means of a special device [ML *traction-, tractio*, fr L *tractus*, pp] – **tractional** *adj*, **tractive** /ˈtraktiv/ *adj*

traction engine *n* a large steam- or diesel-powered vehicle used to draw other vehicles or equipment over roads or fields and sometimes to provide power (e g for sawing or ploughing)

[1]**tractor** /ˈtraktə/ *n* **1** TRACTION ENGINE **2a** a 4-wheeled or tracklaying vehicle used esp for pulling or using farm machinery **b** a truck with a short chassis and no body except a driver's cab, used to haul a large trailer or trailers [NL, fr L *tractus*, pp]

[2]**tractor** *adj* pulling or pulled through the air with force exerted from the front ⟨*a ~ monoplane is pulled by its propeller*⟩

[1]**trad** /trad/ *adj, chiefly Br* traditional – infml

[2]**trad** *n* traditional jazz

[1]**trade** /trayd/ *n* **1a** the business or work in which one engages regularly **b** an occupation requiring manual or mechanical skill; a craft **c** the people engaged in an occupation, business, or industry **d** (the social group deriving its income from) commerce as opposed to the professions or landed property **2a** the business of buying and selling or bartering commodities **b** business, market ⟨*when ~ was brisk*⟩ ⟨*novelties for the tourist ~*⟩ **3** *sing or pl in constr* *the* people or group of firms engaged in a particular business or industry **4** TRADE WIND – usu pl **5** *chiefly NAm* a transaction; *also* an exchange of property usu without use of money [ME, course, way, track, fr MLG, track; akin to OHG *trata* track, course, OE *tredan* to tread]

[2]**trade** *vt* to give in exchange for another commodity; *also* to make an exchange of ⟨~d *secrets*⟩ ~ *vi* **1** to engage in the exchange, purchase, or sale of goods **2** to give one thing in exchange for another – **tradable** *also* **tradeable** *adj* – **trade on** to take often unscrupulous advantage of ⟨*they* traded on *her good nature*⟩

[3]**trade** *adj* **1** of or used in trade ⟨*a ~ agreement*⟩ **2** intended for or limited to people in a business or industry ⟨*a ~ publication*⟩ ⟨*~ discount*⟩

trade cycle *n* the regularly recurrent fluctuation in the level of economic activity

trade gap *n* the value by which a country's imports exceed its exports

ˈ**trade-,in** *n* an item of merchandise (e g a car or refrigerator) that is traded in

trade in *vt* to give as payment or part payment for a purchase or bill

ˈ**trade,mark** /-ˌmahk/ *n* **1** a name or distinctive symbol or device attached to goods produced by a particular firm or individual and legally reserved to the exclusive use of the owner of the mark as maker or seller ☞ SYMBOL **2** a distinguishing feature firmly associated with sby or sthg

trade name *n* **1a** the name used for an article by the trade **b** a name given by a manufacturer or seller to an article or service to distinguish it as his/hers **2** the name under which a concern does business

'trade-,off *n* a giving up of one thing in return for another, esp as a compromise

trader /'traydə/ *n* **1** a retail or wholesale dealer **2** a ship engaged in trade [[2]TRADE + [2]-ER]

tradescantia /,trayde'skanshi·ə/ *n* any of a genus of commonly grown houseplants with usu blue or violet flowers [NL, genus name, fr John *Tradescant* †1638 E traveller & gardener]

tradesman /'traydzmən/ *n* **1a** a shopkeeper **b** one who delivers goods to private houses **2** a workman in a skilled trade

trade union *also* **trades union** *n* an organization of workers formed for the purpose of advancing its members' interests – **trade unionism** *n*, **trade unionist** *n*

trade wind, trade *n* a wind blowing almost continually towards the equator from the NE in the belt between the N horse latitudes and the doldrums and from the SE in the belt between the S horse latitudes and the doldrums [obs *trade* (in a regular course or direction), fr [1]*trade* (course)]

trading estate /'trayding/ *n* INDUSTRIAL ESTATE

trading stamp *n* a printed stamp of a certain value given by a retailer to a customer, to be accumulated and redeemed in merchandise or cash

tradition /trə'dish(ə)n/ *n* **1** the handing down of information, beliefs, and customs by word of mouth or by example from one generation to another **2a** an inherited practice or opinion **b** conventions associated with a group or period ⟨*the title poem represents a complete break with 19th-c* ~ – F R Leavis⟩ **3** cultural continuity in attitudes and institutions [ME *tradicioun*, fr MF & L; MF *tradition*, fr L *tradition-, traditio* action of handing over, tradition – more at TREASON] – **traditionless** *adj*

traditional /trə'dish(ə)nl/ *adj* **1** of or handed down by tradition **2** of or being a style of jazz orig played in New Orleans in the early 1900s – **traditionally** *adv*

tra'ditionalism /-iz(ə)m/ *n* respect for tradition as opposed to modernism or liberalism – **traditionalist** *n or adj*, **traditionalistic** /-'istik/ *adj*

traduce /trə'dyoohs/ *vt* to (attempt to) damage the reputation or standing of, esp by misrepresentation – fml [L *traducere* to lead across, transfer, degrade, fr *tra-, trans-* trans- + *ducere* to lead – more at [1]TOW] – **traducement** *n*, **traducer** *n*

[1]traffic /'trafik/ *n* **1a** import and export trade **b** the business of bartering or buying and selling **c** illegal or disreputable trade ⟨*drug* ~⟩ **2** exchange ⟨*a lively* ~ *in ideas* – F L Allen⟩ **3a** the movement (e g of vehicles or pedestrians) through an area or along a route **b** the vehicles, pedestrians, ships, or aircraft moving along a route **c** the information or signals transmitted over a communications system **4a** the passengers or cargo carried by a transport system **b** the business of transporting passengers or freight **5** dealings between individuals or groups – fml [MF *trafique*, fr OIt *traffico*, fr *trafficare* to trade]

[2]traffic *vb* **-ck-** *vi* to carry on traffic ~ *vt* to trade, barter – **trafficker** *n*

trafficator /'trafi,kaytə/ *n*, *Br* INDICATOR 1c; *esp* a hinged retractable illuminated arm on the side of an old motor car [blend of *traffic* and *indicator*]

traffic circle *n*, *NAm* a roundabout

traffic cone *n* a conical marker used on a road or highway (e g for indicating roadworks)

traffic island *n* a paved or planted island in a road designed to guide the flow of traffic and provide refuge for pedestrians

traffic light *n* an automatically operated signal of coloured lights for controlling traffic – usu pl

traffic signal *n* a signal (e g traffic lights) for controlling traffic

tragacanth /'tragəkanth/ *n* a gum obtained from various Asiatic or E European leguminous plants, used in manufacturing (e g of books) and in pharmacy [MF *tragacanthe*, fr L *tragacantha*, fr Gk *tragakantha*, fr *tragos* goat + *akantha* thorn]

tragedian /trə'jeedi·ən/ *n* **1** a writer of tragedies **2** *fem* **tragedienne** an actor who plays tragic roles [*tragedienne* fr F *tragédienne*, fr MF, fr *tragedie*]

tragedy /'trajədi/ *n* **1** (a) serious drama in which destructive circumstances result in adversity for and usu the deaths of the main characters – compare COMEDY 1b **2** a disastrous event; a calamity **3** tragic quality or element [ME *tragedie*, fr MF, fr L *tragoedia*, fr Gk *tragōidia*, prob fr *tragos* goat + *aeidein* to sing – more at ODE]

tragic /'trajik/ *also* **tragical** /-kl/ *adj* **1** (expressive) of tragedy ⟨*the* ~ *significance of the atomic bomb* – H S Truman⟩ **2** of, appropriate to, dealing with, or treated in tragedy **3a** deplorable, lamentable ⟨*the* ~ *disparity between the actual and the ideal*⟩ **b** marked by a sense of tragedy [L *tragicus*, fr Gk *tragikos*, irreg fr *tragōidia*] – **tragically** *adv*

tragicomedy /,traji'komədi/ *n* a literary work in which tragic and comic elements are mixed in a usu ironic way; *also* a situation or event of such a character [MF *tragicomedie*, fr OIt *tragicomedia*, fr OSp, fr L *tragicomoedia*, fr *tragicus* + *comoedia* comedy] – **tragicomic** /-'komik/ *also* **tragicomical** *adj*

[1]trail /trayl/ *vi* **1a** to hang down so as to sweep the ground **b** *of a plant, branch, etc* to grow to such length as to droop over towards the ground **2a** to walk or proceed draggingly or wearily – usu + *along* **b** to lag behind; do poorly in relation to others **3** to move or extend slowly in thin streams ⟨*smoke* ~ing *from chimneys*⟩ **4a** to extend in an erratic course or line **b** to dwindle ⟨*voice* ~ing *off*⟩ **5** to follow a trail; track game ~ *vt* **1a** to drag loosely along a surface; allow to sweep the ground **b** to haul, tow **2a** to drag (e g a limb or the body) heavily or wearily **b** to carry or bring along as an addition **c** to draw along in one's wake ⟨~ing *clouds of glory do we come* – William Wordsworth⟩ **3a** TRACK 1a **b** to follow behind, esp in the footsteps of **c** to lag behind (e g a competitor) [ME *trailen*, fr MF *trailler* to tow, fr (assumed) VL *tragulare*, fr L *tragula* sledge, dragnet]

[2]trail *n* **1** the part of a gun carriage that rests on the ground when the piece is unlimbered **2a** sthg that follows as if being drawn behind **b** the streak of light produced by a meteor **3a** a trace or mark left by sby or sthg that has passed or is being followed ⟨*a* ~ *of blood*⟩ **b(1)** a track made by passage, esp through a wilderness **(2)** a marked path through a forest or mountainous region – **trailless** *adj*

'trail,blazer /-,blayzə/ *n* **1** a pathfinder **2** PIONEER 2 ⟨*a* ~ *in astrophysics*⟩ – **trailblazing** *adj*

trailer /'traylə/ *n* **1** a trailing plant **2** a wheeled vehicle designed to be towed (e g by a lorry or car);

specif, NAm CARAVAN 2 **3** a set of short excerpts from a film shown in advance for publicity purposes [[1]TRAIL + [2]-ER]

trailing edge *n* the rearmost edge of an aerofoil ☞ FLIGHT

[1]**train** /trayn/ *n* **1** a part of a gown that trails behind the wearer **2a** a retinue, suite **b** a moving file of people, vehicles, or animals **3** the vehicles, men, and sometimes animals that accompany an army with baggage, supplies, ammunition, or siege artillery **4** a connected series of ideas, actions, or events **5** a line of gunpowder laid to lead fire to a charge **6** a series of connected moving mechanical parts (e g gears) **7** a connected line of railway carriages or wagons with or without a locomotive [ME, fr MF, fr OF, fr *trainer* to draw, drag] – **trainful** *n*

[2]**train** *vt* **1** to direct the growth of (a plant), usu by bending, pruning, etc **2a** to form by instruction, discipline, or drill **b** to teach so as to make fit or proficient **3** to prepare (e g by exercise) for a test of skill **4** to aim at an object or objective ⟨~ed *his rifle on the target*⟩ ~ *vi* **1** to undergo training **2** to go by train [ME *trainen* to drag, allure, manipulate, fr MF *trainer*, fr OF, fr (assumed) VL *traginare*; akin to L *trahere* to draw – more at DRAW] – **trainable** *adj*

trainband /'trayn,band/ *n* a 17th- or 18th-c militia company in England or America [alter. of *trained band*]

'**train,bearer** /-,beərə/ *n* an attendant who holds the train of a robe or gown (e g on a ceremonial occasion)

trainee /,tray'nee/ *n* one who is being trained for a job

trainer /'traynə/ *n* an aircraft or piece of equipment for training the crew of an aircraft [[2]TRAIN + [2]-ER]

training /'trayning/ *n* **1** the bringing of a person or animal to a desired degree of proficiency in some activity or skill **2** the condition of being trained, esp for a contest ⟨*an athlete out of* ~⟩

training college *n, Br* a school offering specialized instruction ⟨*a* ~ *for traffic wardens*⟩

train oil *n* oil from a whale or other marine animal [obs *train* (train oil), fr ME *trane*, fr MD *trane* or MLG *trān*]

traipse /trayps/ *vi* to walk or trudge about, often to little purpose [origin unknown] – **traipse** *n*

trait /trayt, tray/ *n* a distinguishing (personal) quality or characteristic [MF, lit., act of drawing, fr L *tractus* – more at [2]TRACT]

traitor /'traytə/, *fem* **traitress** /'traytris/ *n* **1** sby who betrays another's trust **2** sby who commits treason [ME *traitre*, fr OF, fr L *traditor*, fr *traditus*, pp of *tradere* to hand over, deliver, betray, fr *trans-*, *tra-* trans- + *dare* to give – more at [2]DATE] – **traitorous** /'trayt(ə)rəs/ *adj*, **traitorously** *adv*

trajectory /trə'jektəri/ *n* **1** the curve that a planet, projectile, etc follows **2** a path, progression, or line of development like a physical trajectory [NL *trajectoria*, fr fem of *trajectorius* of passing, fr L *trajectus*, pp of *traicere* to cause to cross, cross, fr *trans-*, *tra-* trans- + *jacere* to throw – more at [2]JET]

tram /tram/ *n* any of various vehicles: e g **a** a boxlike wagon running on rails (e g in a mine) **b** *chiefly Br* a passenger vehicle running on rails and typically operating on urban streets [E dial., shaft of a wheelbarrow, prob fr LG *traam*, lit., beam]

'**tram,car** /-,kah/ *n* **1** TRAM a **2** *chiefly Br* TRAM b

'**tram,line** /-,lien/ *n, Br* **1** a track on which trams run **2** *pl* (the area between) either of the 2 pairs of sidelines on a tennis court that mark off the area used in doubles play ☞ SPORT

[1]**trammel** /'traml/ *n* **1** a net for catching birds or fish; *esp* one having 3 layers with the middle one finer-meshed and slack so that fish passing through carry some of the centre net through the coarser opposite net and are trapped **2** sthg that impedes freedom of action – usu pl with sing. meaning ⟨*the* ~s *of convention*⟩ **3a** an instrument for drawing ellipses **b** a compass for drawing large circles that consists of a beam with 2 sliding parts – usu pl with sing. meaning [ME *tramayle*, a kind of net, fr MF *tremail*, fr LL *tremaculum*, fr L *tres* three + *macula* mesh, spot – more at THREE]

[2]**trammel** *vt* **-ll-** (*NAm* **-l-**, **-ll-**), /'traml·ing/ **1** to enmesh **2** to impede the free play of

tramontane /trə'montayn/ *adj* **1** transalpine **2** lying on or coming from the other side of a mountain range [It *tramontano*, fr L *transmontanus*, fr *trans-* + *mont-*, *mons* mountain – more at [1]MOUNT]

[1]**tramp** /tramp/ *vi* **1** to walk or tread, esp heavily **2a** to travel about on foot **b** to journey as a tramp ~ *vt* **1** to trample **2** to travel or wander through on foot [ME *trampen*; akin to MLG *trampen* to stamp, OE *treppan* to tread – more at [1]TRAP] – **tramper** *n*

[2]**tramp** *n* **1** a wandering vagrant who survives by taking the occasional job or by begging or stealing money and food **2** a usu long and tiring walk **3** the heavy rhythmic tread of feet **4** an iron plate to protect the sole of a shoe **5** a merchant vessel that does not work a regular route but carries general cargo to any port as required **6** *chiefly NAm* a promiscuous woman

trample /'trampl/ *vb* **trampling** /'trampling/ *vi* **1** to tread heavily so as to bruise, crush, or injure **2** to treat destructively with ruthlessness or contempt – usu + *on, over*, or *upon* ⟨trampling *on the rights of others*⟩ ~ *vt* to press down, crush, or injure (as if) by treading [ME *tramplen*, freq of *trampen* to tramp] – **trample** *n*, **trampler** *n*

trampoline /,trampə'leen/ *n* a resilient sheet or web supported by springs in a frame and used as a springboard in tumbling [Sp *trampolín*, fr It *trampolino*, of Gmc origin; akin to MLG *trampen* to stamp] – **trampoliner** /-'leenə/ *n*, **trampolining** *n*

tramroad /'tram,rohd/ *n* a track for hauling trams in a mine

'**tram,way** /-,way/ *n, Br* a system of tracks (e g laid in the surface of urban streets) for trams

trance /trahns/ *n* **1** a state of semiconsciousness or unconsciousness with reduced or absent sensitivity to external stimulation **2** a usu self-induced state of altered consciousness or ecstasy in which religious or mystical visions may be experienced **3** a state of profound abstraction or absorption [ME, fr MF *transe*, fr *transir* to pass away, swoon, fr L *transire* to pass, pass away – more at TRANSIENT] – **trancelike** *adj*

tranche /trahnch (*Fr* trɑ̃ʃ)/ *n* a block of shares usu supplementary to an already existing issue [F, lit., slice, fr OF, fr *trenchier*, *trancher* to cut]

tranny /'trani/ *n, chiefly Br* TRANSISTOR RADIO – infml [*tran*sistor + *-y*]

tranquil /'trangkwil/ *adj* free from mental agitation

or from disturbance or commotion [L *tranquillus*] – **tranquilly** *adv*, **tranquillity** /trang'kwiləti/ *n*

tranquill·ize, -ise, *NAm chiefly* **tranquilize** /'trangkwiliez/ *vt* to make tranquil or calm; *esp* to relieve of mental tension and anxiety by drugs ~ *vi* to become tranquil

tranquill·izer, -iser, *NAm chiefly* **tranquilizer** /'trangkwi,liezə/ *n* a drug (e g diazepam) used to tranquillize [TRANQUILLIZE + ²-ER]

trans /tranz/ *adj* characterized by having identical atoms or groups on opposite sides of the molecule – usu ital; often in combination ⟨trans-*dichloroethylene*⟩; compare CIS [*trans*-]

trans- /tranz, trahnz/ *prefix* **1** on or to the other side of; across; beyond ⟨trans*atlantic*⟩ ⟨trans*continental*⟩ **2** beyond (a specified chemical element) in the periodic table ⟨trans*uranic*⟩ **3** through ⟨trans*cutaneous*⟩ ⟨trans-*sonic*⟩ **4** so or such as to change or transfer ⟨trans*literate*⟩ ⟨trans*location*⟩ ⟨trans*ship*⟩ [L *trans-, tra-* across, beyond, through, so as to change, fr *trans* across, beyond – more at THROUGH]

transact /tran'zakt/ *vt* to perform; CARRY OUT 1; *esp* to conduct ⟨*business to be* ~ed *by experts*⟩ [L *transactus*, pp of *transigere* to drive through, complete, transact, fr *trans-* + *agere* to drive, do – more at AGENT] – **transactor** *n*

transaction /tran'zaksh(ə)n, trahn-/ *n* **1** transacting **2a** sthg transacted; *esp* a business deal **b** *pl* the (published) record of the meeting of a society or association – **transactional** *adj*

transalpine /tran'zalpien, trahn-/ *adj* north of the Alps [L *transalpinus*, fr *trans-* + *Alpes* the Alps]

transatlantic /,tranzət'lantik, ,trahn-/ *adj* **1** crossing or extending across the Atlantic ocean ⟨*a* ~ *cable*⟩ **2** situated beyond the Atlantic ocean **3** (characteristic) of people or places situated beyond the Atlantic ocean; *specif, chiefly Br* American ⟨*a* ~ *accent*⟩

transceiver /tran'seevə, trahn-/ *n* a combined radio transmitter and receiver [*trans*mitter + *receiver*]

transcend /tran'send, trahn-/ *vt* **1a** to go beyond the limits of **b** to be or extend beyond and above (the universe or material existence) **2** to surpass, excel ~ *vi* to rise above or extend notably beyond ordinary limits [L *transcendere* to climb across, transcend, fr *trans-* + *scandere* to climb – more at SCAN]

transcendent /tran'send(ə)nt; *also* trahn-/ *adj* **1a** exceeding usual limits; surpassing **b** beyond the limits of ordinary experience **c** beyond the limits of possible experience and knowledge – used in Kantianism **2** transcending the universe or material existence – compare IMMANENT [L *transcendent-, transcendens*, prp of *transcendere*] – **transcendence, transcendency** *n*, **transcendently** *adv*

transcendental /,transen'dentl; *also* trahn-/ *adj* **1** of or employing the basic categories (e g space and time) presupposed by knowledge and experience ⟨*a* ~ *proof*⟩ **2** TRANSCENDENT 1a **3a** of or being a transcendental number **b** being, involving, or representing a function (e g sin *x*, log *x*, *e* Cx) that cannot be expressed by a finite number of algebraic operations ⟨~ *curves*⟩ **4a** TRANSCENDENT 1b **b** supernatural **c** abstruse, abstract **d** of transcendentalism – **transcendentally** *adv*

,transcen'dentalism /-,iz(ə)m/ *n* **1** a philosophy that emphasizes the basic categories of knowledge and experience, or asserts fundamental reality to be transcendent **2** a philosophy that asserts the primacy of the spiritual over the material – **transcendentalist** *adj or n*

transcendental number *n* a number (e g e or π) that cannot be the root of an algebraic equation with rational coefficients – compare ALGEBRAIC 2 ☞ NUMBER

transcontinental /,tranz,konti'nentl, trahnz-/ *adj* crossing or extending across a continent

transcribe /tran'skrieb; *also* trahn-/ *vt* **1a** to make a written copy or version of (e g sthg written or printed) **b** to write in a different medium; transliterate ⟨~ *a word in phonetics*⟩ ⟨~ *shorthand*⟩ **c** to write down, record **2** to transfer (data) from one recording form to another **3** to make a musical transcription of [L *transcribere*, fr *trans-* + *scribere* to write – more at ¹SCRIBE] – **transcriber** *n*

transcript /'transkript, 'trahn-/ *n* **1** a written, printed, or typed copy, esp of dictated or recorded material **2** an official written copy ⟨*a court reporter's* ~⟩ [ME, fr ML *transcriptum*, fr L, neut of *transcriptus*, pp of *transcribere*]

transcription /tran'skripsh(ə)n, trahn-/ *n* **1** transcribing **2** a copy, transcript: e g **a** an often free arrangement of a musical composition for some instrument or voice other than the original **b** a sound recording suitable for broadcasting and thus usu of high quality **3** the naturally occurring process of constructing a molecule of nucleic acid (e g messenger RNA) using a DNA molecule as a template, with resulting transfer of genetic information to the newly formed molecule – compare TRANSLATION 2 – **transcriptional** *adj*

transducer /tranz'dyoohsə, trahnz-/ *n* a device that transfers energy from one system to another; *esp* one that converts nonelectrical energy into electrical energy or vice versa [L *transducere* to lead across, fr *trans-* + *ducere* to lead – more at ¹TOW]

transect /tran'sekt/ *vt* to cut transversely [*trans-* + *-sect*] – **transection** /-'seksh(ə)n/ *n*

transept /'transept/ *n* (either of the projecting arms of) the part of a cross-shaped church that crosses the E end of the nave at right angles [NL *transeptum*, fr L *trans-* + *septum, saeptum* enclosure, wall – more at SEPTUM] – **transeptal** /-'septl/ *adj*

¹transfer /trans'fuh, trahns-/ *vb* **-rr-** *vt* **1a** to convey or cause to pass from one person, place, or situation to another **b** to move or send to another location ⟨~red *her business to the capital*⟩; *specif* to move (a professional soccer player) to another football club **2** to make over the possession or control of **3** to copy (e g a design) from one surface to another by contact ~ *vi* **1** to move to a different place, region, or situation **2** to change from one vehicle or transport system to another [ME *transferren*, fr L *transferre*, fr *trans-* + *ferre* to carry – more at ²BEAR] – **transferable, transferrable** /-'fuhrəbl/ *adj*, **transferral** /-'fuhrəl/ *n*, **transferor, transferrer** *n*, **transferee** /,transfuh'ree, trahns-/ *n*

²transfer /'transfuh, 'trahns-/ *n* **1** conveyance of right, title, or interest in property **2a** transferring **b** transference **3** sthg or sby that transfers or is transferred; *esp* a design or picture transferred by contact from one surface (e g specially prepared paper) to another **4** *NAm* a ticket entitling a passenger on a public conveyance to continue a journey on another route

transferable vote /trans'fuhrəbl/ *n* a vote which in

balloting by proportional representation may be transferred to a candidate other than the first choice

transferase /'transfərayz, -rays, 'trahns-/ *n* an enzyme that promotes transfer of a chemical group from one molecule to another

transference /'transf(ə)rəns, trans'fuhrəns, trahns-/ *n* the redirection of feelings and desires, esp those unconsciously retained from childhood, towards a new object (e g towards a psychoanalyst conducting therapy) [[1]TRANSFER + -ENCE] – **transferential** /,transfə'rensh(ə)l, ,trahns-/ *adj*

transfer paper /'transfuh, 'trahnsfuh/ *n* a paper with a special coating for transferring a design

transfer RNA *n* a relatively small RNA that transfers a particular amino acid to a growing polypeptide chain at the ribosome site for protein synthesis – compare MESSENGER RNA

transfiguration /,trans,figə'raysh(ə)n, ,trahns-/ *n* **1a** a change in form or appearance; a metamorphosis **b** an exalting, glorifying, or spiritual change **2** *cap* August 6 observed as a Christian festival in commemoration of the transfiguration of Christ as described in Mt 17:2 and Mk 9:2–3

transfigure /trans'figə, trahns-/ *vt* to give a new appearance to; transform outwardly and usu for the better [ME *transfiguren*, fr L *transfigurare*, fr *trans-* + *figurare* to shape, fashion, fr *figura* figure]

transfinite /trans'fieniet, trahns-/ *adj* **1** going beyond or surpassing any finite number, group, or magnitude **2** of or being a number that can be shown to be greater than the number of positive integers ⟨*the number of real numbers is a* ~ *quantity*⟩ [G *transfinit*, fr *trans-* (fr L) + *finit* finite, fr L *finitus*]

transfix /trans'fiks, trahns-/ *vt* **1** to pierce through (as if) with a pointed weapon **2** to hold motionless (as if) by piercing ⟨~ed *by horror*⟩ [L *transfixus*, pp of *transfigere*, fr *trans-* + *figere* to fasten, pierce – more at DYKE] – **transfixion** /-'fiksh(ə)n/ *n*

[1]**transform** /trans'fawm, trahns-/ *vt* **1** to change radically (e g in structure, appearance, or character) **2** to subject to mathematical transformation **3** to change (a current) in potential (e g from high voltage to low) or in type (e g from alternating to direct) **4** to cause (a cell) to undergo transformation ~ *vi* to become transformed [ME *transformen*, fr L *transformare*, fr *trans-* + *formare* to form, fr *forma* form] – **transformable** *adj*, **transformative** /-mətiv/ *adj*

[2]**transform** /'transfawm, 'trahns-/ *n* a mathematical element or linguistic structure producible by (a) transformation

transformation /,transfaw'maysh(ə)n, ,trahns-/ *n* **1** the operation of changing one configuration or expression into another in accordance with a mathematical rule **2** any of a set of rules for transforming the supposed underlying structures of (a) language into actual sentences **3** modification of plant or animal cell culture (e g by a cancer-producing virus) resulting in unlimited cell growth and division [[1]TRANSFORM + -ATION] – **transformational** *adj*

transformational grammar /-nl/ *n* a grammar that attempts to find a set of transformations for generating an infinite number of possible sentences

transformer /trans'fawmə, trahns-/ *n* an electrical device making use of the principle of mutual induction to convert variations of current in a primary circuit into variations of voltage and current in a secondary circuit [[1]TRANSFORM + [2]-ER]

transfuse /trans'fyoohz, trahns-/ *vt* **1** to diffuse into or through; *broadly* to spread across **2** to transfer (e g blood) into a vein [ME *transfusen*, fr L *transfusus*, pp of *transfundere*, fr *trans-* + *fundere* to pour – more at [4]FOUND] – **transfusible, transfusable** *adj*, **transfusion** /-'fyoohzh(ə)n/ *n*

transgress /trans'gres, trahns-/ *vt* **1** to go beyond limits set or prescribed by ⟨~ *the divine law*⟩ **2** to pass beyond or go over (a boundary) ~ *vi* to violate a command or law [F *transgresser*, fr L *transgressus*, pp of *transgredi* to step beyond or across, fr *trans-* + *gradi* to step – more at GRADE] – **transgressive** *adj*, **transgressor** *n*

transgression /trans'gresh(ə)n, trahns-/ *n* infringement or violation of a law, command, or duty [TRANSGRESS + -ION]

tranship /tranz'ship, trahnz-/ *vb* to transship

transhumance /trans'hyoohməns, trahns-/ *n* seasonal movement of livestock, esp sheep, between mountain and lowland pastures [F, fr *transhumer* to practise transhumance, fr Sp *trashumar*, fr *tras-* trans- (fr L *trans-*) + L *humus* earth – more at HUMBLE]

[1]**transient** /'tranzi·ənt/ *adj* **1** passing quickly away; transitory **2** making only a brief stay ⟨*a* ~ *summer migrant*⟩ [L *transeunt-*, *transiens*, prp of *transire* to go across, pass, fr *trans-* + *ire* to go] – **transience, transiency** *n*, **transiently** *adv*

[2]**transient** *n* **1** a transient guest or worker **2a** a temporary oscillation that occurs in a circuit because of a sudden change of voltage or load **b** a transient current or voltage

transilluminate /,tranzi'l(y)oohminayt, ,trahnz-/ *vt* to cause light to pass through; *esp* to pass light through (a body part) for medical examination – **transilluminator** *n*, **transillumination** /-'naysh(ə)n/ *n*

transistor /tran'zistə, trahn-/ *n* **1** any of several semiconductor devices that have usu 3 electrodes and make use of a small current to control a larger one **2** TRANSISTOR RADIO [[1]*trans*fer + re*sistor*; fr its transferring an electrical signal across a resistor]

tran'sistor·ize, -ise /-riez/ *vt* to construct (a device) using transistors – **transistorization** /-rie'zaysh(ə)n/ *n*

transistor radio *n* a radio using transistorized circuitry

[1]**transit** /'transit, -zit/ *n* **1a** passing or conveying through or over **b** a change, transition **2** passage of a smaller celestial body **a** across the disc of a larger one **b** over a meridian or through the field of a telescope **3** *NAm* conveyance of people or things from one place to another [L *transitus*, fr *transitus*, pp of *transire* to go across, pass] – **in transit** in passage ⟨*goods lost* in transit⟩

[2]**transit** *vi* to make a transit ~ *vt* to traverse

transit instrument *n* a telescope for observing the time of transit of a celestial body over a meridian

transition /tran'zish(ə)n, trahn-/ *n* **1a** passage from one state or stage to another **b** a movement, development, or evolution from one form, stage, or style to another ⟨*a* ~ *from the inorganic to the organic* – W R Inge⟩ **2a** a musical modulation **b** a musical passage leading from one section of a piece to another **3** an abrupt change in energy state or level (e g of an atomic nucleus or a molecule), usu accompanied by loss or gain of a single quantum of energy [L *transition-, transitio*, fr *transitus*, pp of *transire*] – **transitional** *adj*, **transitionally** *adv*

transition metal *n* any of various metallic elements (e g chromium, iron, or platinum) that have valency electrons in 2 shells instead of only 1

transitive /'transitiv, 'trahn-, -zitiv/ *adj* **1** having or containing a direct object ⟨*a ~ verb*⟩ ⟨*a ~ construction*⟩ **2** of or being a relation such that if the relation holds between a first element and a second and between the second element and a third, it holds between the first and third elements **3** of or characterized by transition [LL *transitivus*, fr L *transitus*, pp of *transire*] – **transitive** *n*, **transitively** *adv*, **transitiveness, transitivity** /transə'tivəti, trahn-, -zə-/ *n*

transitory /'transit(ə)ri, 'trahn-, -zi-/ *adj* **1** tending to pass away **2** of brief duration [ME *transitorie*, fr MF *transitoire*, fr LL *transitorius*, fr L, of or allowing passage, fr *transitus*, pp] – **transitorily** /'transit(ə)rəli, 'trahns-, -zi-, -'torəli/ *adv*, **transitoriness** *n*

translate /trans'layt, trahns-/ *vt* **1a** to bear, remove, or change from one place, state, form, or appearance to another ⟨*a country boy ~*d *to the city*⟩ ⟨*~ ideas into action*⟩ **b** to convey to heaven or to a nontemporal condition without death **c** to transfer (a bishop) from one see to another **2a** to turn into another language **b** to turn from one set of symbols into another **c** to express in different or more comprehensible terms **3** to subject (genetic information, esp messenger RNA) to translation ~ *vi* **1** to practise or make (a) translation **2** to undergo (a) translation [L *translatus* (pp of *transferre* to transfer, translate), fr *trans-* + *latus*, pp of *ferre* to carry – more at TOLERATE, [2]BEAR] – **translatable** *adj*, **translator** *n*

translation /trans'laysh(ə)n, trahns-/ *n* **1a** (a version produced by) a rendering from one language into another **b** a change to a different substance or form **c** uniform motion of a body in a straight line **2** the process of forming a protein molecule at a ribosome site of protein synthesis from information contained usu in messenger RNA – compare TRANSCRIPTION 3 [TRANSLATE + -ION] – **translational** *adj*

transliterate /tranz'litərayt, trahnz-, trans-, trahns-/ *vt* to represent or spell in the characters of another alphabet [*trans-* + L *littera* letter] – **transliteration** /-'raysh(ə)n/ *n*

translocation /,tranzloh'kaysh(ə)n, ,trahnz-/ *n* a change of location; *esp* the conduction of soluble material from one part of a plant to another – **translocate** /-loh'kayt/ *vb*

translucent /tranz'loohs(ə)nt, trahnz-/ *adj* permitting the passage of light: e g **a** transparent **b** transmitting and diffusing light so that objects beyond cannot be seen clearly ⟨*a ~ window of frosted glass*⟩ ⟨*~ porcelain*⟩ [L *translucent-, translucens*, prp of *translucēre* to shine through, fr *trans-* + *lucēre* to shine – more at [1]LIGHT] – **translucence, translucency** *n*, **translucently** *adv*

transmarine /,tranzmə'reen/ *adj* (coming from or extending) across the sea [L *transmarinus*, fr *trans-* + *mare* sea – more at MARINE]

transmigrate /,tranzmie'grayt, ,trahnz-/ *vi* **1** *of a soul* to pass at death from one body or being to another **2** to migrate [L *transmigratus*, pp of *transmigrare* to migrate to another place, fr *trans-* + *migrare* to migrate] – **transmigrator** *n*, **transmigration** /-mie'graysh(ə)n/ *n*, **transmigratory** /-'miegrət(ə)ri/ *adj*

transmission /trans'mish(ə)n, trahns-, tranz-, trahnz-/ *n* **1** transmitting ⟨*~ of a nerve impulse across a synapse*⟩; *esp* transmitting by radio waves or over a wire **2** the assembly by which the power is transmitted from a motor vehicle engine to the axle ☞ CAR **3** sthg transmitted [L *transmission-, transmissio*, fr *transmissus*, pp of *transmittere* to transmit] – **transmissive** /-'misiv/ *adj*

transmit /trans'mit, trahns-, tranz-, trahnz-/ *vb* **-tt-** *vt* **1a** to send or transfer from one person or place to another **b(1)** to convey (as if) by inheritance or heredity **(2)** to convey (infection) abroad or to another **2a(1)** to cause (e g light or force) to pass or be conveyed through a medium **(2)** to allow the passage of ⟨*glass ~*s *light*⟩ **b** to send out (a signal) either by radio waves or over a wire ~ *vi* to send out a signal by radio waves or over a wire [ME *transmitten*, fr L *transmittere*, fr *trans-* + *mittere* to send] – **transmissible** /-'misəbl/ *adj*, **transmittable** *adj*, **transmittal** *n*

trans'mitter /-tə/ *n* **1** the portion of a telegraphic or telephonic instrument that sends the signals **2** a radio or television transmitting station or set ☞ TELEVISION **3** a neurotransmitter [TRANSMIT + [2]-ER]

transmogrify /tranz'mogrifie/ *vt* to transform, often with grotesque or humorous effect [perh alter. of *transmigrate*] – **transmogrification** /-,mogrifi'kaysh(ə)n/ *n*

transmutation /,tranzmyooh'taysh(ə)n, ,trahnz-/ *n* **1** the conversion of base metals into gold or silver **2** the natural or artificial conversion of one element or nuclide into another [TRANSMUTE + -ATION] – **transmutative** /-'myoohtətiv/ *adj*

transmute /tranz'myooht, trahnz-/ *vt* **1** to change in form, substance, or characteristics **2** to subject (e g an element) to transmutation ~ *vi* to undergo transmutation [ME *transmuten*, fr L *transmutare*, fr *trans-* + *mutare* to change – more at [1]MISS] – **transmutable** *adj*

transnational /tranz'nash(ə)nl, trahnz-/ *adj* extending beyond national boundaries

transom /'transəm/ *n* a transverse piece in a structure: e g **a** a lintel **b** a horizontal crossbar in a window, over a door, or between a door and a window or fanlight above it ☞ ARCHITECTURE **c** any of several transverse timbers or beams secured to the sternpost of a boat [ME *traunsom*, prob fr L *transtrum*, fr *trans* across – more at THROUGH]

transonic /tran'sonik/ *also* **trans-sonic** /tranz 'sonik/ *adj* **1** of or being a speed near the speed of sound in air **2** (capable of) moving, or using air currents moving, at a transonic speed [*trans-* + *-sonic* (as in *supersonic*)]

transparency /tran'sparənsi, trahn-/ *n* **1** being transparent **2a** a picture or design on glass, film, etc viewed by a light shining through it from behind; *esp* SLIDE 5b **b** a framework covered with thin cloth or paper bearing a device for public display (e g for advertisement) and lit from within

transparent /tran'sparənt, trahn-/ *adj* **1a(1)** transmitting light without appreciable scattering so that bodies lying beyond are entirely visible – compare TRANSLUCENT 1b **(2)** penetrable by a specified form of radiation (e g X rays or ultraviolet) **b** fine or sheer enough to be seen through **2a** free from pretence or deceit ⟨~ *sincerity*⟩ **b** easily detected or seen through ⟨*a ~ lie*⟩ **c** readily understood ⟨*the meaning of this word is ~*⟩ [ME, fr ML *transparent-, transparens,* prp of *transparēre* to show through, fr L *trans-* + *parēre* to show oneself – more at APPEAR] – **transparence** *n,* **transparently** *adv,* **transparentness** *n*

transpire /tran'spie·ə, trahn-/ *vt* to pass off or give passage to (a gas or liquid) through pores or interstices; *esp* to excrete (e g water vapour) through a skin or other living membrane ~ *vi* **1** to give off a vapour; *specif* to give off or exude water vapour, esp from the surfaces of leaves **2** to pass in the form of a vapour, esp from a living body **3** to become known; come to light **4** to occur; TAKE PLACE – disapproved of by some speakers [MF *transpirer,* fr L *trans-* + *spirare* to breathe – more at SPIRIT]

[1]**transplant** /trans'plahnt, trahns-/ *vt* **1** to lift and reset (a plant) in another soil or place **2** to remove from one place and settle or introduce elsewhere **3** to transfer (an organ or tissue) from one part or individual to another [ME *transplaunten,* fr LL *transplantare,* fr L *trans-* + *plantare* to plant] – **transplantable** /-'plahntəbl/ *adj,* **transplanter** *n,* **transplantation** /-plahn'taysh(ə)n, -plan-/ *n*

[2]**transplant** /'trans,plahnt, 'trahns-/ *n* **1** transplanting **2** sthg transplanted

transpontine /tranz'pontien, trahnz-/ *adj* situated on the farther side of a bridge; *specif, Br* situated on the south side of the Thames [*trans-* + L *pont-, pons* bridge – more at FIND]

[1]**transport** /tran'spawt, trahn-/ *vt* **1** to transfer or convey from one place to another ⟨*mechanisms of ~ing ions across a living membrane*⟩ **2** to carry away with strong and often pleasurable emotion **3** to send to a penal colony overseas [ME *transporten,* fr MF or L; MF *transporter,* fr L *transportare,* fr *trans-* + *portare* to carry – more at [1]FARE] – **transportable** *adj*

[2]**transport** /'transpawt, 'trahn-/ *n* **1** the conveying of goods or people from one place to another **2** strong and often pleasurable emotion – often pl with sing. meaning ⟨*~s of joy*⟩ **3a** a ship or aircraft for carrying soldiers or military equipment **b** a lorry, aeroplane, etc used to transport people or goods **4** a mechanism for moving a tape, esp a magnetic tape, or disk past a sensing or recording head

transportation /,transpaw'taysh(ə)n, trahn-/ *n* **1** the act of transporting **2** banishment to a penal colony **3** *NAm* means of conveyance or travel from one place to another [[1]TRANSPORT + -ATION]

transport café *n, Br* an inexpensive roadside cafeteria catering mainly for long-distance lorry drivers

transporter /tran'spawtə, trahn-/ *n* a vehicle for transporting large or heavy loads ⟨*a tank ~*⟩ ⟨*a car ~*⟩ [[1]TRANSPORT + [2]-ER]

transport manager *n* a supervisor of the transport of a commercial or industrial organization

[1]**transpose** /tran'spohz, trahn-/ *vt* **1** to transfer from one place or period to another **2** to change the relative position of; alter the sequence of ⟨~ *letters to change the spelling*⟩ **3** to write or perform (music) in a different key **4** to bring (a term) from one side of an algebraic equation to the other with change of sign ~ *vi* to transpose music [ME *transposen,* fr MF *transposer,* fr L *transponere* (perf indic *transposui*) to change the position of, fr *trans-* + *ponere* to put, place – more at POSITION] – **transposable** *adj*

[2]**transpose** /'transpohz, 'trahn-/ *n* a matrix formed by interchanging the rows of a given matrix with its corresponding columns

transposition /,tranzpə'zish(ə)n, ,trahnz-/ *n* **1** transposing or being transposed **2a** the transfer of a term of an equation from one side to the other with a change of sign **b** a mathematical permutation that is the interchange of 2 elements [ML *transposition-, transpositio,* fr L *transpositus,* pp of *transponere*] – **transpositional** *adj*

transsexual /tranz'seksyoo(ə)l, -sh(ə)l, trahnz-/ *n* sby physically of one sex with an urge to belong to or resemble the opposite sex – **transsexual** *adj,* **transsexualism** *n*

transship, tranship /tranz'ship, trahnz-/ *vb* to transfer from one ship or conveyance to another for further transportation – **transshipment** *n*

transubstantiate /,tranz·səb'stanshiayt, ,trahnz-, -'stahn-/ *vb* to change into another substance [ML *transubstantiatus,* pp of *transubstantiare,* fr L *trans-* + *substantia* substance]

,transub,stanti'ation /-shi'aysh(ə)n/ *n* the miraculous change by which, according to Roman Catholic and Eastern Orthodox dogma, bread and wine used at communion become the body and blood of Christ when they are consecrated, although their appearance remains unchanged [TRANSUBSTANTIATE + -ION]

transude /tran'syoohd, trahn-/ *vi* to pass through a membrane or permeable substance ~ *vt* to permit passage of [NL *transudare,* fr L *trans-* + *sudare* to sweat – more at SWEAT] – **transudation** /-'daysh(ə)n/ *n*

transuranic /,tranzyoo'ranik/ *n or adj* (an element) having an atomic number greater than that of uranium

[1]**transversal** /tranz'vuhsl, trahnz-/ *adj* transverse ⟨~ *lines*⟩

[2]**transversal** *n* a line that intersects a system of lines

transverse /tranz'vuhs, trahnz-, '--/ *adj* lying or being across; set or made crosswise ☞ CAR [L *transversus,* fr pp of *transvertere* to turn across, fr *trans-* + *vertere* to turn – more at [1]WORTH] – **transversely** *adv*

transverse wave *n* a wave (e g a wave on a string or an electromagnetic wave in free space) in which the displacements of the medium or the vectors (e g of the electric and magnetic fields) describing the wave are perpendicular to the direction of propagation of the wave – compare LONGITUDINAL WAVE

transvestism /tranz'vestiz(ə)m, trahnz-/ *n* the adoption of the dress and often the behaviour of the opposite sex [G *transvestismus,* fr L *trans-* + *vestire* to clothe – more at [1]VEST] – **transvestite** /-'vestiet/ *adj or n*

[1]**trap** /trap/ *n* **1** a device for taking animals; *esp* one that holds by springing shut suddenly **2a** sthg designed to catch sby unawares; *also* PITFALL 1 **b** a situation from which it is impossible to escape ⟨*caught in a poverty ~*⟩; *also* a plan to trick a person into such a situation ⟨*police laid a ~ for the criminal*⟩ **3a** a trapdoor **b** a device from which a greyhound is released at the start of a race **4a** a device for hurling clay pigeons into the air **b** BUNKER 2b **5** a light usu 1-horse carriage with springs **6** any

of various devices for preventing passage of sthg often while allowing other matter to proceed; *esp* a device for drains or sewers consisting of a bend or partitioned chamber in which the liquid forms a seal to prevent the passage of sewer gas **7** *pl* a group of percussion instruments used esp in a dance or jazz band **8** the mouth – slang [ME, fr OE *treppe* & OF *trape* (of Gmc origin); akin to MD *trappe* trap, stair, OE *treppan* to tread, Skt *dravati* he runs]

[2]**trap** *vb* **-pp-** *vt* **1** to catch or take (as if) in a trap **2** to provide or set (a place) with traps **3** to stop, retain ⟨*these mountains ~ the rain*⟩ **4** to stop and control (the ball) in soccer, hockey, etc *~vi* to engage in trapping animals – **trapper** *n*

[3]**trap, 'trap,rock** *n* any of various dark-coloured fine-grained igneous rocks (e g basalt) used esp in road making [Sw *trapp*, fr *trappa* stair, fr MLG *trappe*; akin to MD *trappe* stair]

,trap'door /-'daw/ *n* a lifting or sliding door covering an opening in a floor, ceiling, etc

trap-door spider *n* any of various often large burrowing spiders that construct a nest topped with a hinged lid

trapeze /trə'peez/ *n* a gymnastic or acrobatic apparatus consisting of a short horizontal bar suspended by 2 parallel ropes [F *trapèze*, fr NL *trapezium*]

trapezium /trə'peezi·əm/ *n, pl* **trapeziums, trapezia** /-zi·ə/ *Br* a quadrilateral having only 2 sides parallel ☞ MATHEMATICS [NL, fr Gk *trapezion*, lit., small table, dim. of *trapeza* table, fr *tra-* four (akin to *tettares* four) + *peza* foot; akin to Gk *pod-, pous* foot – more at FOUR, FOOT]

trapezoid /'trapi,zoyd, trə'peezoyd/ *n, chiefly NAm* a trapezium [NL *trapezoïdes*, fr Gk *trapezoeidēs* trapezium-shaped, fr *trapeza*] – **trapezoidal** /-'zoydl/ *adj*

trappings /'trapingz/ *n pl* outward decoration or dress; *also* outward signs and accessories ⟨*all the ~ of power with none of the substance*⟩ [ME, fr gerund of *trappen* to clothe, adorn, fr *trappe* cloth, trap]

Trappist /'trapist/ *n* a member of a reformed branch of the Roman Catholic Cistercian Order established in 1664 at the monastery of La Trappe in Normandy and noted for its vow of silence [F *trappiste*, fr La *Trappe*] – **Trappist** *adj*

trapshooting /'trap,shoohting/ *n* shooting at clay pigeons sprung into the air from a trap so as to simulate the angles of flight of birds – **trapshooter** *n*

trash /trash/ *n* **1** sthg of little or no value: e g **a** junk, rubbish **b(1)** empty talk **(2)** inferior literary or artistic work **2** sthg in a crumbled or broken condition or mass **3** a worthless person; *also, sing or pl in constr* such people as a group – infml [of Scand origin; akin to Norw *trask* trash; akin to OE *teran* to tear]

'trash ,can *n, NAm* a dustbin

trashy /'trashi/ *adj* of inferior quality or worth ⟨*a ~ novel*⟩ [TRASH + [1]-Y] – **trashiness** *n*

trass /tras/ *n* a light-coloured tuff rock sometimes ground for use in a hydraulic cement [D, fr F *terrasse* pile of earth, terrace, fr MF – more at TERRACE]

trattoria /,tratə'ree·ə/ *n, pl* **trattorias, trattorie** /-'ree,ay/ an Italian restaurant [It, fr *trattore* innkeeper, restaurateur, fr F *traiteur*, fr *traiter* to treat, fr OF *traitier* – more at TREAT]

trauma /'trawmə/ *n, pl* **traumata** /-mətə/, **traumas** **1a** an injury (e g a wound) to living tissue caused by an outside agent **b** a disordered mental or behavioural state resulting from mental or emotional stress or shock **2** an agent, force, or mechanism that causes trauma [Gk *traumat-, trauma* wound] – **traumatic** /-'matik/ *adj*

traumatism /'trawmə,tiz(ə)m/ *n* (the development or occurrence of) trauma

[1]**travail** /'travayl, trə'vayl/ *n* **1** physical or mental exertion, esp of a painful or laborious nature **2** *archaic* labour pains [ME, fr OF, fr *travaillier* to torture, travail, fr (assumed) VL *tripaliare* to torture, fr *tripalium* instrument of torture, fr L *tripalis* having three stakes, fr *tri-* + *palus* stake – more at [1]POLE]

[2]**travail** *vi* **1** to labour hard – fml **2** *archaic* to suffer labour pains [ME *travailen*, fr OF *travaillier*]

[1]**travel** /'travl/ *vb* **-ll-** (*NAm* **-l-, -ll-**), /'travl·ing/ *vi* **1a** to go (as if) on a tour **b** to go as if by travelling ⟨*my mind ~led back to our last meeting*⟩ **c** to go from place to place as a sales representative ⟨*~s in cosmetics*⟩ **2a** to move or be transmitted from one place to another ⟨*wine ~s badly*⟩ **b** *esp of machinery* to move along a specified direction or path ⟨*the stylus ~s in a groove*⟩ **c** to move at high speed – infml ⟨*a car that can really ~*⟩ *~vt* **1a** to journey through or over ⟨*~ the world*⟩ **b** to follow (a course or path) as if by travelling **2** to traverse (a specified distance) **3** to cover (a place or region) as a sales representative [ME *travailen* to travail, journey, fr OF *travaillier* to travail] – **travel light** to travel with a minimum of equipment or baggage

[2]**travel** *n* **1** a journey, esp to a distant or unfamiliar place – often pl ⟨*set off on her ~s*⟩ **2a** movement, progression ⟨*the ~ of satellites round the earth*⟩ **b** the motion of a piece of machinery

'travel ,agent *n* sby engaged in selling and arranging personal transport, tours, or trips for travellers – **travel agency** *n*

'travelled, *NAm chiefly* **traveled** *adj* **1** experienced in travel ⟨*a widely ~ journalist*⟩ **2** used by travellers ⟨*a well-*travelled *route*⟩

traveller, *NAm chiefly* **traveler** /'travlə, 'travl·ə/ *n* **1** SALES REPRESENTATIVE **2** any of various devices for handling sthg that is being moved laterally **3** *dial Br* a gipsy [[1]TRAVEL + [2]-ER]

'traveller's ,cheque, *NAm* **traveler's check** *n* a cheque that is purchased from a bank, travel agency, etc, and that may be exchanged abroad for foreign currency

traveller's joy *n* a wild clematis of Europe and N Africa

travelling, *NAm chiefly* **traveling** /'travl·ing/ *adj* carried, used by, or accompanying a traveller ⟨*a ~ alarm clock*⟩ ⟨*a ~ companion*⟩ [fr gerund of [1]*travel*]

'travelling ,bag *n* a small bag carried by hand and designed to hold a traveller's clothing and personal articles

travelling fellowship *n* a fellowship enabling the holder to travel for study or research

travelling salesman *n* SALES REPRESENTATIVE

travelogue, *NAm also* **travelog** /'travə,log/ *n* **1** a film or illustrated talk or lecture on some usu exotic or remote place **2** a narrated documentary film about travel [*travel* + *-logue*]

[1]**traverse** /'travuhs, -'-/ *n* **1** sthg that crosses or lies

across **2** a transverse gallery in a large building (e g a church) **3** a route or way across or over: e g **a** a curving or zigzag way up a steep slope **b** the course followed in traversing **4** (a) traversing **5a** a lateral movement (e g of the saddle of a lathe carriage) **b** the lateral movement of a gun to change direction of fire **6** a survey consisting of a series of measured lines whose bearings are known [ME *travers*, fr MF *traverse*, fr *traverser* to cross, fr LL *transversare*, fr L *transversus*, pp of *transvertere* – more at TRANSVERSE]

[2]**traverse** /trəˈvuhs, ˈtravuhs/ *vt* **1** to pass or travel across, over, or through ⟨~ *a terrain*⟩ ⟨*light rays* traversing *a crystal*⟩ **2** to lie or extend across ⟨*the bridge* ~s *a brook*⟩ **3a** to move to and fro over or along **b** to ascend, descend, or cross (a slope or gap) at an angle **c** to move (a gun) to right or left ~ *vi* **1** to move back and forth or from side to side **2** to climb or ski across rather than straight up or down a hill – **traversable** /-ˈvuhsəbl/ *adj*, **traversal** *n*, **traverser** *n*

[3]**traverse** /ˈtravuhs, -ˈ-/ *adj* lying across

travertine /ˈtravətin/ *n* a mineral consisting of a calcium carbonate [F *travertin*, deriv of L *Tiburtinus* of Tibur, fr *Tibur*, region of ancient Italy]

[1]**travesty** /ˈtravəsti/ *n* **1** a crude or grotesque literary or artistic parody **2** a debased, distorted, or grossly inferior imitation ⟨*a* ~ *of justice*⟩ [obs *travesty* (disguised, parodied), fr F *travesti*, pp of *travestir* to disguise, fr It *travestire*, fr *tra-* across (fr L *trans-*) + *vestire* to dress, fr L – more at [1]VEST]

[2]**travesty** *vt* to make a travesty of

travois /trəˈvoy/ *n, pl* **travois** /-ˈvoyz/ *also* **travoises** a vehicle used by N American Plains Indians consisting of 2 trailing poles serving as shafts for a dog or horse and bearing a platform or net for the load [CanF *travois*, alter. of F *travail*, deriv of (assumed) VL *tripalium* instrument of torture – more at [1]TRAVAIL]

[1]**trawl** /trawl/ *vb* to fish (for or in) with a trawl [prob fr obs D *tragelen*]

[2]**trawl** *n* **1** a large conical net dragged along the sea bottom to catch fish **2** *NAm* a setline

trawler /ˈtrawlə/ *n* a boat used in trawling [[1]TRAWL + [2]-ER]

trawlerman /ˈtrawləmən/ *n* a fisherman who uses a trawl or mans a trawler

tray /tray/ *n* an open receptacle with a flat bottom and a low rim for holding, carrying, or exhibiting articles [ME, fr OE *trīg, trēg*; akin to OE *trēow* tree – more at TREE] – **trayful** *n*

treacherous /ˈtrech(ə)rəs/ *adj* **1** characterized by treachery; perfidious **2a** of uncertain reliability **b** providing insecure footing or support ⟨*a* ~ *surface of black ice*⟩ **c** marked by hidden dangers or hazards ⟨*the* ~ *waters round the coast*⟩ – **treacherously** *adv*, **treacherousness** *n*

treachery /ˈtrech(ə)ri/ *n* (an act of) violation of allegiance; (a) betrayal of trust [ME *trecherie*, fr OF, fr *trechier* to deceive]

treacle /ˈtreekl/ *n, chiefly Br* **1** any of the edible grades of molasses that are obtained in the early stages of sugar refining **2** GOLDEN SYRUP [ME *triacle* medicinal compound used as antidote to poison, fr MF, fr L *theriaca*, fr Gk *thēriakē* antidote against a poisonous bite, fr fem of *thēriakos* of a wild animal, fr *thērion* wild animal, dim. of *thēr* wild animal – more at FIERCE]

[1]**tread** /tred/ *vb* **trod** /trod/ *also* **treaded; trodden** /ˈtrod(ə)n/, **trod** *vt* **1a** to step or walk on or over **b** to walk along **2a** to beat or press with the feet **b** to subdue or repress as if by trampling **3** *of a male bird* to copulate with **4a** to form by treading ⟨~ *a path*⟩ **b** to execute by stepping or dancing ⟨~ *a measure*⟩ ~ *vi* **1** to move on foot **2a** to set foot **b** to put one's foot ⟨trod *on a stone*⟩ [ME *treden*, fr OE *tredan*; akin to OHG *tretan* to tread] – **treader** *n* – **tread on someone's toes/corns** to give offence or hurt sby's feelings, esp by encroaching on his/her rights – **tread water** to keep the body nearly upright in the water and the head above water by a treading motion of the feet, usu aided by the hands

[2]**tread** *n* **1** an imprint made (as if) by treading **2a** the action or an act of treading **b** the sound or manner of treading ⟨*the heavy* ~ *of feet*⟩ **3a** the part of a wheel or tyre that makes contact with a road or rail **b** the pattern of ridges or grooves made or cut in the face of a tyre ☞ CAR **4** (the width of) the upper horizontal part of a step ☞ ARCHITECTURE – **treadless** *adj*

[1]**treadle** /ˈtredl/ *n* a lever pressed by the foot to drive a machine (e g a sewing machine) [ME *tredel* step of a stair, fr OE, fr *tredan*]

[2]**treadle** *vi* to operate a treadle

treadmill /ˈtred,mil/ *n* **1a** a mill used formerly in prison punishment that was worked by people treading on steps inside a wide wheel with a horizontal axis **b** a mill worked by an animal treading an endless belt **2** a wearisome or monotonous routine

treason /ˈtreez(ə)n/ *n* **1** the betrayal of a trust **2** the offence of violating the duty of allegiance owed to one's crown or government [ME *tresoun*, fr OF *traison*, fr ML *tradition-*, *traditio*, fr L, act of handing over, fr *traditus*, pp of *tradere* to hand over, betray – more at TRAITOR] – **treasonous** *adj*

treasonable /ˈtreez(ə)nəbl/ *adj* of or being treason – **treasonably** *adv*

[1]**treasure** /ˈtrezhə/ *n* **1** wealth, esp in a form which can be accumulated or hoarded ⟨*buried* ~⟩ **2** sthg of great worth or value; *also* sby highly valued or prized [ME *tresor*, fr OF, fr L *thesaurus*, fr Gk *thēsauros*]

[2]**treasure** *vt* to hold or preserve as precious ⟨~d *those memories*⟩

ˈtreasure ˌhunt *n* a game in which each player or team tries to be first to find whatever has been hidden

treasurer /ˈtrezh(ə)rə/ *n* the financial officer of an organization (e g a society) – **treasurership** *n*

ˈtreasure ˌtrove /trohv/ *n* treasure that anyone finds; *specif* gold or silver money, plate, or bullion which is found hidden and whose ownership is not known [AF *tresor trové*, lit., found treasure]

treasury /ˈtrezh(ə)ri/ *n* **1a** a place in which stores of wealth are kept **b** the place where esp public funds that have been collected are deposited and disbursed **2** *often cap* (the building which houses) a government department in charge of finances, esp the collection, management, and expenditure of public revenues **3** a source or collection of treasures ⟨*a* ~ *of poems*⟩

ˈtreasury ˌbill *n* a bill issued by the treasury in return for money lent to the government

[1]**treat** /treet/ *vi* **1** to discuss terms of accommodation or settlement **2** to deal with a matter, esp in writing – usu + *of*; fml ⟨*a book* ~ing *of conservation*⟩ ~ *vt*

1 to deal with ⟨*food is plentiful and* ~ed *with imagination* – Cecil Beaton⟩ **2a** to behave oneself towards ⟨~ *a horse cruelly*⟩ **b** to regard and deal with in a specified manner – usu + *as* ⟨~ed *it as a serious matter*⟩ **3a** to provide with free food, drink, or entertainment – usu + *to* **b** to provide with enjoyment – usu + *to* **4** to care for or deal with medically or surgically ⟨~ *a disease*⟩ **5** to act on with some agent, esp so as to improve or alter **6** to deal with in speech or writing – fml [ME *treten,* fr OF *traitier,* fr L *tractare* to handle, deal with, fr *tractus,* pp of *trahere* to draw – more at DRAW] – **treatable** *adj,* **treater** *n*

[2]**treat** *n* **1** an entertainment given free of charge to those invited **2** a source of pleasure or amusement; *esp* an unexpected one ⟨*the cold beer on a hot day was a* ~⟩ – **a treat** very well or successfully ⟨*the speech went down* a treat⟩ – infml

treatise /'treetiz/ *n* a formal written exposition on a subject ⟨*a* ~ *on higher education*⟩ [ME *tretis,* fr AF *tretiz,* fr OF *traitier* to treat]

treatment /'treetmənt/ *n* **1a** treating sby or sthg **b** the actions customarily applied in a particular situation ⟨*the author got the standard* ~ *of cocktail parties and interviews*⟩ **2** a substance or technique used in treating

treaty /'treeti/ *n* **1** the action of treating, esp of negotiating – chiefly in *in treaty* **2** (a document setting down) an agreement or contract made by negotiation (e g between states) [ME *tretee,* fr MF *traité,* fr ML *tractatus,* fr L, handling, treatment, fr *tractatus,* pp of *tractare* to treat]

treaty port *n* any of numerous ports and inland cities in China, Japan, and Korea formerly open by treaty to foreign commerce

[1]**treble** /'trebl/ *n* **1a** the highest voice part in harmonic music; *also* sby, esp a boy, who performs this part **b** a member of a family of instruments having the highest range **c** a high-pitched voice or sound **d** the upper half of the whole vocal or instrumental tonal range **e** the higher part of the audio frequency range considered esp in relation to its electronic reproduction **2** sthg treble in construction, uses, amount, number, or value: e g **a** a type of bet in which the winnings and stake from a previous race are bet on the next of 3 races **b** (a throw landing on) the middle narrow ring on a dart board counting treble the stated score [ME, perh fr MF, trio, fr *treble,* adj]

[2]**treble** *adj* **1a** having 3 parts or uses **b** TRIPLE 2 **2a** relating to or having the range or part of a treble **b** high-pitched, shrill [ME, fr MF, fr L *triplus* – more at [3]TRIPLE] – **trebly** /'trebli/ *adv*

[3]**treble** *vb* to increase to 3 times the size, amount, or number

treble chance *n* a method of competing in football pools in which the chances of winning are based on the numbers of home wins, away wins, and draws

treble clef *n* a clef that places the note G above middle C on the second line of the staff ☞ MUSIC [fr its use for the notation of treble parts]

trebuchet /'trebyooshet/ *n* a medieval military engine for hurling missiles with great force [ME *trebochet,* fr MF *trebuchet*]

trecento /tray'chentoh/ *n* the 14th century, esp in Italian art [It, lit., three hundred, fr L *tres* three + *centum* hundred – more at THREE, HUNDRED]

[1]**tree** /tree/ *n* **1a** a tall woody perennial plant having a single usu long and erect main stem, generally with few or no branches on its lower part **b** a shrub or herbaceous plant having the form of a tree ⟨*rose* ~s⟩ ⟨*a banana* ~⟩ **2** a device for inserting in a boot or shoe to preserve its shape when not being worn **3a** a diagram or graph that branches, usu from a single stem ⟨*genealogical* ~⟩ **b** a much-branched system of channels, esp in an animal or plant body ⟨*the vascular* ~⟩ **4** *archaic* **a** *the* cross on which Jesus was crucified **b** *the* gallows [ME, fr OE *trēow;* akin to ON *trē* tree, Gk *drys,* Skt *dāru* wood] – **treeless** *adj,* **treelike** *adj*

[2]**tree** *vt* to drive to or up a tree ⟨~d *by a bull*⟩

'**tree,creeper** /-,kreepə/ *n* any of several small birds that have slender curved beaks and are usu seen climbing up tree trunks

tree fern *n* a treelike fern with a woody stem

tree frog *n* any of numerous tailless amphibians that frequent trees

tree line *n* the upper limit of tree growth in mountains or high latitudes

treenail *also* **trenail** /'tree,nayl, 'trenl/ *n* a hard wooden peg that swells in its hole when moistened

tree of heaven *n* a tropical Asian tree that is widely grown for shade and ornament

tree shrew *n* any of a family of tree-dwelling insect-eating mammals sometimes classified as true insectivores and sometimes as primitive ancestors of the primates

tree sparrow *n* a Eurasian sparrow that has a black spot behind the eye

tree surgeon *n* a specialist in treating diseased trees, esp for control of decay – **tree surgery** *n*

tree toad *n* TREE FROG

'**tree,top** /-,top/ *n* **1** the topmost part of a tree **2** *pl* the height or line marked by the tops of a group of trees

trefoil /'trefoyl, 'tree-/ *n* **1a** (a) clover; *broadly* any of several leguminous plants having leaves of 3 leaflets **b** a leaf consisting of 3 leaflets **2** a stylized figure or ornament in the form of a 3-lobed leaf or flower ☞ ARCHITECTURE [ME, fr MF *trefeuil,* fr L *trifolium,* fr *tri-* + *folium* leaf]

trehala /tri'hahlə/ *n* a sweet edible substance constituting the cocoon of an Asiatic beetle [prob fr F *tréhala,* fr Turk *tgala,* fr Per *tīghāl*]

trek /trek/ *vi or n* **-kk-** (to make) **1** a journey; *esp* an arduous one **2** *chiefly SAfr* a journey by ox wagon [n Afrik, fr MD *treck* pull, haul, fr *trecken* to pull, haul, migrate; akin to OHG *trechan* to pull; vb fr n]

[1]**trellis** /'trelis/ *n* a frame of latticework used as a screen or as a support for climbing plants [ME *trelis,* fr MF *treliz* fabric of coarse weave, trellis, fr (assumed) VL *trilicius* woven with triple thread, fr L *tri-* + *licium* thread] – **trellised** *adj*

[2]**trellis** *vt* to provide with a trellis; *esp* to train (e g a vine) on a trellis

'**trellis,work** /-,wuhk/ *n* latticework

trematode /'tremə,tohd, 'tree-/ *n* any of a class of parasitic flatworms including the flukes [deriv of Gk *trēmatōdēs* pierced with holes, fr *trēmat-, trēma* hole, fr *tetrainein* to bore – more at THROW] – **trematode** *adj*

[1]**tremble** /'trembl/ *vi* **trembling** /'trembling/ **1** to shake involuntarily (e g with fear or cold) **2** to be affected (as if) by a quivering motion ⟨*the building* ~d *from the blast*⟩ ⟨*his voice* ~d *with emotion*⟩ **3**

to be affected with fear or apprehension [ME *tremblen,* fr MF *trembler,* fr ML *tremulare,* fr L *tremulus* tremulous, fr *tremere* to tremble; akin to Gk *tremein* to tremble] – **trembler** *n*

[2]**tremble** *n* **1a** a fit or spell of involuntary shaking or quivering **b** a tremor or series of tremors **2** *pl but sing in constr* a severe disorder of livestock, esp cattle, characterized by muscular tremors, weakness, and constipation – **trembly** *adj*

tremendous /trəˈmendəs/ *adj* **1** such as to arouse awe or fear **2** of extraordinary size, degree, or excellence [L *tremendus,* fr gerundive of *tremere*] – **tremendously** *adv,* **tremendousness** *n*

tremolite /ˈtreməˌliet/ *n* a white or grey mineral consisting of a calcium magnesium silicate in the form of long slender crystals [F *trémolite,* fr *Tremola,* valley in Switzerland] – **tremolitic** /-ˈlitik/ *adj*

tremolo /ˈtreməloh/ *n, pl* **tremolos** **1a** the rapid reiteration of a musical note or of alternating notes to produce a tremulous effect **b** a perceptible rapid variation of pitch in the (singing) voice; vibrato **2** a mechanical device in an organ for causing a tremulous effect [It, fr *tremolo* tremulous, fr L *tremulus*]

tremor /ˈtremə/ *n* **1** a trembling or shaking, usu from physical weakness, emotional stress, or disease **2** a (slight) quivering or vibratory motion, esp of the earth **3** a thrill, quiver ⟨*experienced a sudden ~ of fear*⟩ [ME *tremour,* fr MF, fr L *tremor,* fr *tremere*]

tremulant /ˈtremyoolənt/ *n* a device to impart a vibration giving a sound a tremulous effect [G, fr It *tremolante,* fr *tremolante* tremulous, fr ML *tremulant-, tremulans,* prp of *tremulare* to tremble]

tremulous /ˈtremyooləs/ *adj* **1** characterized by or affected with trembling or tremors **2** uncertain, wavering [L *tremulus*] – **tremulously** *adv,* **tremulousness** *n*

trenail /ˈtree,nayl, ˈtrenl/ *n* a treenail

[1]**trench** /trench/ *n* **1** a deep narrow excavation (e g for the laying of underground pipes); *esp* one used for military defence **2** a long narrow usu steep-sided depression in the ocean floor [ME *trenche* track cut through a wood, fr MF, act of cutting, fr *trenchier* to cut]

[2]**trench** *vb* to dig a trench (in) – **trencher** *n*

trenchant /ˈtrenchənt/ *adj* **1** keen, sharp **2** vigorously effective and articulate **3a** incisive, penetrating **b** clear-cut, distinct [ME, fr MF, prp of *trenchier*] – **trenchancy** *n,* **trenchantly** *adv*

ˈtrench ˌcoat *n* **1** a waterproof overcoat with a removable lining, designed for wear in trenches **2** a double-breasted raincoat with deep pockets, a belt, and epaulettes

trencher /ˈtrenchə/ *n* a wooden platter for serving food [ME, fr MF *trencheoir,* fr *trenchier* to cut]

trencherman /ˈtrenchəmən/ *n* a hearty eater

trench fever *n* a disease marked by fever and pain in muscles, bones, and joints and transmitted by the body louse [fr its prevalence among soldiers serving in the trenches during WW I]

trench warfare *n* warfare conducted from a relatively permanent system of trenches

[1]**trend** /trend/ *vi* **1** to show a general tendency to move or extend in a specified direction **2** to deviate, shift ⟨*opinions ~ing towards conservatism*⟩ [ME *trenden* to turn, revolve, fr OE *trendan;* akin to MHG *trendel* disc, spinning top, OE *teran* to tear – more at [2]TEAR]

[2]**trend** *n* **1** a line of general direction **2a** a prevailing tendency or inclination **b** a general movement, esp in taste or fashion

ˈtrendˌsetter /-ˌsetə/ *n* sby who starts new trends, esp in fashion – **trendsetting** *n or adj*

[1]**trendy** /ˈtrendi/ *adj, chiefly Br* very fashionable; *also* characterized by uncritical adherence to the latest fashions or progressive ideas ⟨*his concern for good composition prevents the up-to-date from dwindling into the merely ~ – The Listener*⟩ – infml

[2]**trendy** *n, chiefly Br* sby trendy – chiefly derog ⟨*educational* trendies⟩

[1]**trepan** /triˈpan/ *n* **1** a primitive trephine **2** a heavy tool used in boring mine shafts [ME *trepane,* fr ML *trepanum,* fr Gk *trypanon* auger, fr *trypan* to bore, fr *trypa* hole; akin to Gk *tetrainein* to pierce – more at THROW]

[2]**trepan** *vt* **-nn-** to use a trephine on (the skull)

trepang /triˈpang/ *n* any of several large sea cucumbers that are used, esp in Chinese cookery, for making soup [Malay *tĕripang*]

trephine /triˈfeen/ *vt or n* (to operate on with, or extract by means of) a surgical instrument for cutting out circular sections, esp of bone or the cornea of the eye [n F *tréphine,* fr obs E *trefine, trafine,* fr L *tres fines* three ends, fr *tres* three + *fines,* pl of *finis* end; vb fr n]

trepidation /ˌtrepiˈdaysh(ə)n/ *n* nervous agitation or apprehension [L *trepidation-, trepidatio,* fr *trepidatus,* pp of *trepidare* to tremble, fr *trepidus* agitated; akin to OE *thrafian* to urge, push, Gk *trapein* to press grapes]

treponema /ˌtrepəˈneemə/ *n, pl* **treponemata** /-mətə/, **treponemas** any of a genus of spirochaetal bacteria that grow in human beings or other warm-blooded animals and include organisms causing syphilis and yaws [NL *Treponemat-, Treponema,* genus name, deriv of Gk *trepein* to turn + *nēma* thread, fr *nēn* to spin – more at TROPE, NEEDLE] – **treponemal, treponematous** *adj*

[1]**trespass** /ˈtrespəs/ *n* **1a** a violation of moral or social ethics; *esp* a sin **b** an unwarranted infringement **2** any unlawful act that causes harm to the person, property, or rights of another; *esp* wrongful entry on another's land [ME *trespas,* fr OF, crossing, trespass, fr *trespasser* to go across]

[2]**trespass** *vi* **1a** to err, sin **b** to make an unwarranted or uninvited intrusion *on* **2** to commit a trespass; *esp* to enter sby's property unlawfully [ME *trespassen,* fr MF *trespasser,* fr OF, lit., to go across, fr *tres* across (fr L *trans*) + *passer* to pass – more at THROUGH, [1]PASS] – **trespasser** *n*

tress /tres/ *n* **1** a plait of hair **2** a long lock of hair – usu pl [ME *tresse,* fr OF *trece*]

tressed /trest/ *adj* having tresses – usu in combination ⟨*golden*-tressed⟩

trestle /ˈtresl/ *n* **1** a (braced) frame serving as a support (e g for a table top) **2** a braced framework of timbers, piles, or girders for carrying a road or railway over a depression [ME *trestel,* fr MF, modif of (assumed) VL *transtellum,* fr L *transtillum,* dim. of *transtrum* transverse beam, transom – more at TRANSOM]

trestle table *n* a table consisting of a board or boards supported on trestles

ˈtrestleˌtree /-ˌtree/ *n* either of a pair of timber

crosspieces fixed fore and aft on the masthead to support the crosstrees and topmast ☞ SHIP

trevally /trə'vali/ *n* any of several marine spiny-finned Australian food fishes [origin unknown]

trews /troohz/ *n pl in constr, pl* **trews** trousers; *specif* tartan trousers [ScGael *triubhas*]

trey /tray/ *n* **1** the side of a dice or domino that has 3 spots **2** a playing card numbered 3 [ME *treye, treis,* fr MF *treie, treis,* fr L *tres* three]

tri- /trie-/ *comb form* **1** three ⟨tri*partite*⟩; having 3 elements or parts ⟨tri*graph*⟩ **2** into 3 ⟨tri*sect*⟩ **3a** thrice ⟨tri*weekly*⟩ **b** every third ⟨tri*monthly*⟩ [ME, fr L (fr *tri-, tres*) & Gk (fr *tri-, treis*) – more at THREE]

triable /'trie·əbl/ *adj* liable or subject to trial

triad /'trie,ad/ *n* **1** a union or group of 3 (closely) related or associated persons, beings, or things **2** a chord of 3 notes consisting of a root with its third and fifth and constituting the harmonic basis of tonal music **3** *often cap* any of various Chinese secret societies, esp engaging in drug trafficking [L *triad-, trias,* fr Gk, fr *treis* three] – **triadic** /-'adik/ *adj*

triage /tree'ahzh, '-,-/ *n* the sorting and treatment of patients or victims according to urgency [F, sorting, sifting, fr *trier* to sort, fr OF – more at TRY]

[1]**trial** /trie·əl/ *n* **1a** trying or testing **b** a preliminary contest or match (e g to evaluate players' skills) **2** the formal examination and determination by a competent tribunal of the matter at issue in a civil or criminal cause ☞ LAW **3** a test of faith, patience, or stamina by suffering or temptation; *broadly* a source of vexation or annoyance **4** an experiment to test quality, value, or usefulness **5** an attempt, effort **6a** a competition of vehicle-handling skills, usu over rough ground **b** a competition in which a working animal's skills are tested ⟨*a sheepdog* ~⟩ [AF, fr *trier* to try]

[2]**trial** *adj* **1** of a trial **2** made or done as, or used or tried out in, a test or experiment

,trial and 'error *n* a process of trying out many methods and discarding the least successful

trial court *n* the court before which issues of fact and law are first determined, as distinguished from a court of appeal

trialist /'trie·əlist/ *n* one who takes part in a sports trial (e g in motorcycling or cricket)

trial run *n* an exercise to test the performance of sthg (e g a vehicle or vessel); *also* EXPERIMENT 1

triangle /'trie,ang·gl/ *n* **1** a polygon of 3 sides and 3 angles ☞ MATHEMATICS **2** a percussion instrument consisting of a steel rod bent into the form of a triangle open at 1 angle and sounded by striking with a small metal rod **3** TRIAD 1 – compare ETERNAL TRIANGLE **4** *NAm* SET SQUARE [ME, fr L *triangulum,* fr neut of *triangulus* triangular, fr *tri-* + *angulus* angle]

triangular /trie'ang·gyoolə/ *adj* **1a** (having the form) of a triangle ⟨*a* ~ *plot of land*⟩ **b** having a triangular base or principal surface ⟨*a* ~ *table*⟩ ⟨*a* ~ *pyramid*⟩ **2** between or involving 3 elements, things, or people ⟨*a* ~ *love affair*⟩ [LL *triangularis,* fr L *triangulum*] – **triangularly** *adv,* **triangularity** /-,ang·gyoo'larəti/ *n*

triangulate /trie'ang·gyoolayt/ *vt* **1a** to divide into triangles **b** to give triangular form to **2** to survey, map, or determine by triangulation

triangulation /,trie,ang·gyoo'laysh(ə)n/ *n* the measurement of the angles and 1 side of a triangle to find an unknown position, distance, etc; *esp* the determination of the network of triangles into which any part of the earth's surface is divided in surveying, using this operation

Triassic /trie'asik/ *adj or n* (of or being) the earliest period of the Mesozoic era ☞ EVOLUTION [adj ISV, fr L *trias* triad; fr the three subdivisions of the European Triassic; n fr adj]

triatomic /,trie·ə'tomik/ *adj* **1** having 3 atoms in the molecule ⟨*ozone is* ~ *oxygen*⟩ **2** having 3 replaceable atoms or radicals [ISV]

triaxial /trie'aksi·əl/ *adj* having or involving 3 axes [ISV] – **triaxiality** /-,aksi'aləti/ *n*

tribal /'triebl/ *adj* (characteristic) of a tribe – **tribally** *adv*

tribalism /'triebl,iz(ə)m/ *n* **1** tribal consciousness and loyalty **2** strong loyalty or attachment to a group

tribasic /trie'baysik/ *adj* **1** *of an acid* having 3 replaceable hydrogen atoms **2** containing 3 atoms of a univalent metal **3** *of a (salt that is a) chemical base* having 3 hydroxyl groups in the molecular structure

tribe /trieb/ *n sing or pl in constr* **1a** a social group comprising numerous families, clans, or generations together with slaves, dependants, or adopted strangers **b** any of orig 3 political divisions of the ancient Roman people **2** a group of people having a common character or interest **3** a category in the classification of living things ranking above a genus and below a family; *also* a natural group irrespective of taxonomic rank ⟨*the cat* ~⟩ [ME, fr L *tribus,* a division of the Roman people, tribe]

tribesman /'triebzmən/, *fem* **tribeswoman** /-,woomən/ *n* a member of a tribe

tribo- *comb form* friction ⟨tribo*luminescence*⟩ [F, fr Gk *tribein* to rub; akin to L *terere* to rub – more at THROW]

triboelectricity /,triebohi,lek'trisəti, -,eelek-/ *n* a charge of electricity generated by friction (e g by rubbing glass with silk) – **triboelectric** /-i'lektrik/ *adj*

tribology /trie'boləji/ *n, Br* a science that deals with the design, friction, wear, and lubrication of interacting surfaces in relative motion (e g in bearings or gears) – **tribologist** *n, Br,* **tribological** /-bə'lojikl/ *adj, Br*

triboluminescence /,triebohloohmi'nes(ə)ns/ *n* luminescence due to friction [ISV] – **triboluminescent** *adj*

tribulation /tribyoo'laysh(ə)n/ *n* distress or suffering resulting from oppression [ME *tribulacion,* fr OF, fr L *tribulation-, tribulatio,* fr *tribulatus,* pp of *tribulare* to press, oppress, fr *tribulum* sledge used in threshing, fr *terere* to rub – more at THROW]

tribunal /trie'byoohnl/ *n* **1** a court of justice; *specif* a board appointed to decide disputes of a specified kind ⟨*rent* ~⟩ **2** sthg that arbitrates or determines ⟨*the* ~ *of public opinion*⟩ [L, platform for magistrates, fr *tribunus* tribune]

tribune /'tribyoohn/ *n* **1** an official of ancient Rome with the function of protecting the plebeian citizens from arbitrary action by the patrician magistrates **2** an unofficial defender of the rights of the individual [ME, fr L *tribunus,* fr *tribus* tribe] – **tribuneship** *n,* **tribunate** /'tribyoonayt, tri'byoohnət/ *n*

[1]**tributary** /'tribyoot(ə)ri/ *adj* **1** paying tribute to

another; subject **2** paid or owed as tribute **3** providing with material or supplies

[2]**tributary** *n* **1** a tributary ruler or state **2** a stream feeding a larger stream or a lake ☞ GEOGRAPHY

tribute /'tribyooht/ *n* **1** a payment by one ruler or nation to another in acknowledgment of submission or as the price of protection **2a** sthg (e g a gift or formal declaration) given or spoken as a testimonial of respect, gratitude, or affection **b** evidence of the worth or effectiveness of sthg specified – chiefly in *a tribute to* ⟨*the vote was a* ~ *to their good sense*⟩ [ME *tribut*, fr L *tributum*, fr neut of *tributus*, pp of *tribuere* to allot, bestow, grant, pay, fr *tribus* tribe]

tricarboxylic /,trie,kahbok'silik/ *adj* containing 3 carboxyl groups in the molecule

[1]**trice** /tries/ *vt* to haul up or in and lash or secure – usu + *up* [ME *trisen, tricen* to pull, trice, fr MD *trisen* to hoist]

[2]**trice** *n* a brief space of time – chiefly in *in a trice* [ME *trise*, lit., pull, fr *trisen*]

Tricel /'triesel/ *trademark* – used for a silky crease-resistant man-made fibre

triceps /'trie,seps/ *n, pl* **tricepses** /-seez/ *also* **triceps** a muscle with 3 points of attachment; *specif* the large muscle along the back of the upper arm that acts to straighten the arm at the elbow [NL *tricipit-, triceps*, fr L, three-headed, fr *tri-* + *capit-, caput* head – more at HEAD]

triceratops /trie'serə,tops/ *n* a large plant-eating Cretaceous dinosaur with 3 horns, a bony crest, and hoofed toes [NL, genus name, fr *tri-* + *cerat-* + Gk *ōps* face – more at EYE]

-trices /-triseez/ *pl of* -TRIX

trich-, tricho- *comb form* hair; filament ⟨trich*iasis*⟩ [NL, fr Gk, fr *trich-, thrix* hair; akin to MIr gairb*driuch* bristle]

trichiasis /tri'kie·əsis/ *n* a growing inwards of the hair, esp the eyelashes [LL, fr Gk, fr *trich* + *-iasis*]

trichina /tri'kienə/ *n, pl* **trichinae** /-ni/ *also* **trichinas** a small slender nematode worm that in the larval state is parasitic in the muscles of flesh-eating mammals (e g human beings and pigs) [NL, fr Gk *trichinos* made of hair, fr *trich-, thrix*] – **trichinal** *adj*

trichin·ized, -ised /'trikəniezd/ *adj, esp of meat* TRICHINOUS 1

trichinosis /,trikə'nohsis/ *n* infestation with or disease caused by trichinae and marked esp by muscular pain, fever, and oedema [NL]

trichinous /'trikinəs, tri'kienəs/ *adj* **1** infested with trichinae ⟨~ *meat*⟩ **2** of or involving trichinae or trichinosis ⟨~ *infection*⟩ [ISV]

trichloride /,trie'klawried/ *n* a compound of an element or radical with 3 atoms of chlorine [ISV]

trichocyst /'trikə,sist/ *n* any of the minute hairlike stinging or lassoing organs of some protozoans

trichology /tri'koləji/ *n* the study and treatment of disorders of hair growth, specif baldness [ISV] – **trichologist** *n*

trichome /'trie,kohm, 'tri-/ *n* a filamentous outgrowth; *esp* an epidermal hair structure on a plant [G *trichom*, fr Gk *trichōma* growth of hair, fr *trichoun* to cover with hair, fr *trich-, thrix* hair – more at TRICH-] – **trichomic** /-'kohmik/ *adj*

trichomonad /,trikə'mohnad/ *n* any of a genus of protozoans parasitic chiefly in the reproductive and urinary tracts of many animals including human beings [NL *Trichomonad-, Trichomonas*, genus name, fr *trich-* + LL *monad-, monas* monad] – **trichomonad, trichomonadal** /-'mohnədl/, **trichomonal** *adj*

trichomoniasis /,trikəmə'nie·əsis/ *n, pl* **trichomoniases** /-seez/ infection with or disease caused by trichomonads (e g a human vaginitis or urethritis or a bovine venereal disease) [NL, fr *Trichomonas* + *-iasis*]

trichopteran /tri'koptərən/ *n* any of an order of insects consisting of the caddis flies [deriv of Gk *trich-, thrix* hair + *pteron* wing – more at FEATHER] – **trichopteran** *adj*

trichotomy /tri'kotəmi/ *n* division into 3 parts, elements, or classes [prob fr (assumed) NL *trichotomia*, fr LGk *trichotomein* to trisect, fr Gk *tricha* threefold + *temnein* to cut] – **trichotomous** /-məs/ *adj*

trichromatic /,triekroh'matik/ *adj* **1** (consisting) of 3 colours **2a** of or being the theory that human colour vision involves 3 types of retinal sensory receptors **b** characterized by trichromatism ⟨~ *vision*⟩

trichromatism /,trie'krohmə,tiz(ə)m/ *n* vision in which all the fundamental colours are perceived, though not necessarily with equal facility

[1]**trick** /trik/ *n* **1a** a crafty practice or stratagem meant to deceive or defraud **b** a mischievous act ⟨*played a harmless* ~ *on me*⟩ **c** a deceptive, dexterous, or ingenious feat designed to puzzle or amuse ⟨*a conjurer's* ~s⟩ **2a** a habitual peculiarity of behaviour or manner ⟨*had a* ~ *of stammering slightly*⟩ **b** a deceptive appearance, esp when caused by art or sleight of hand ⟨*a mere* ~ *of the light*⟩ **3a** a quick or effective way of getting a result **b** a technical device or contrivance (e g of an art or craft) ⟨~s *of the trade*⟩ **4** the cards played in 1 round of a card game, often used as a scoring unit **5** a turn of duty at the helm [ME *trik*, fr ONF *trique*, fr *trikier* to deceive, cheat]

[2]**trick** *adj* **1** of or involving tricks or trickery ⟨*a* ~ *question*⟩ **2** skilled in or used for tricks ⟨*a* ~ *horse*⟩

[3]**trick** *vt* **1** to deceive by cunning or artifice – often + *into, out of* **2** to dress or embellish showily – usu + *out* or *up* ⟨~ed *out in a gaudy uniform*⟩

trickery /'trikəri/ *n* the use of crafty underhand ingenuity to deceive

[1]**trickle** /'trikl/ *vi* **trickling** /'trikling, 'trikl·ing/ **1** to flow in drops or a thin slow stream **2a** to move or go gradually or one by one ⟨*the audience* ~d *out of the hall*⟩ **b** to dissipate slowly ⟨*time* ~s *away*⟩ [ME *triklen*]

[2]**trickle** *n* a thin slow stream or movement

trickster /'trikstə/ *n* one who tricks: e g **a** a person who defrauds others by trickery **b** a person (e g a stage magician) skilled in the performance of tricks

tricksy /'triksi/ *adj* **1** full of tricks **2** difficult to follow or make out; *also* excessively elaborate ***USE*** infml – **tricksiness** *n*

tricky /'triki/ *adj* **1** inclined to or marked by trickery **2** containing concealed difficulties or hazards ⟨*a* ~ *path through the swamp*⟩ **3** requiring skill, adroitness, or caution (e g in doing or handling) ⟨~ *gadgets*⟩ – **trickily** *adv*, **trickiness** *n*

triclinic /trie'klinik/ *adj, esp of a crystal* having 3 unequal axes intersecting at oblique angles [ISV]

triclinium /trie'klini·əm/ *n, pl* **triclinia** /-ni·ə/ (a room furnished with) a couch used by ancient Romans for reclining at meals, extending round 3 sides of a table, and usu divided into 3 parts [L, fr Gk *triklinion*, fr *tri-* + *klinein* to lean, recline – more at [1]LEAN]

[1]**tricolour,** *NAm* **tricolor** /'trie,kulə/ *n* a flag of 3 colours [F *tricolore*, fr *tricolore* three-coloured, fr LL *tricolor*, fr L *tri-* + *color* colour]

[2]**tricolour, tricoloured,** *NAm* **tricolor, tricolored** *adj* having or using 3 colours

tricorn /'trie,kawn/ *adj* having 3 horns or corners [L *tricornis*]

tricorne, tricorn /'trie,kawn/ *n* COCKED HAT [F *tricorne*, fr *tricorne* three-cornered, fr L *tricornis*, fr *tri-* + *cornu* horn – more at HORN]

tricot /'trikoh (*Fr* triko)/ *n* a plain inelastic knitted fabric used esp in clothing (e g underwear) [F, fr *tricoter* to knit]

tricuspid /trie'kuspid/ *n or adj* (a tooth) having 3 cusps [adj L *tricuspid-, tricuspis*, fr *tri-* + *cuspid-, cuspis* point; n fr adj]

tricuspid valve *n* the heart valve of 3 flaps that stops blood flowing back from the right ventricle to the right atrium

tricycle /'triesikl/ *vi or n* (to ride or drive) a 3-wheeled pedal-driven vehicle [n F, fr *tri-* + Gk *kyklos* wheel – more at WHEEL; vb fr n] – **tricyclist** /-klist/ *n*

[1]**trident** /'tried(ə)nt/ *n* a 3-pronged (fish) spear **a** serving as the attribute of a sea god **b** used by ancient Roman gladiators [L *trident-, tridens*, fr *trident-, tridens* having three teeth, fr *tri-* + *dent-, dens* tooth – more at TOOTH]

[2]**trident** *adj* having 3 prongs or points [L *trident-, tridens*]

Tridentine /tri'dentien/ *adj* of a Roman Catholic council held in Trento from 1545 to 1563; *esp* promulgated by or based on the deliberations of this council ⟨*the ~ mass*⟩ [NL *Tridentinus*, fr L *Tridentum* Trento (Trent), town in NE Italy]

tried /tried/ *adj* **1** found to be good or trustworthy through experience or testing ⟨*a ~ recipe*⟩ **2** subjected to trials or severe provocation – often in combination ⟨*a sorely-*tried *father*⟩ [ME, fr pp of *trien* to try, test]

triennial /trie'enyəl, -ni·əl/ *adj* **1** consisting of or lasting for 3 years **2** occurring every 3 years – **triennial** *n*, **triennially** *adv*

triennium /trie'enyəm, -ni·əm/ *n, pl* **trienniums, triennia** /-nyə, -ni·ə/ a period of 3 years [L, fr *tri-* + *annus* year – more at ANNUAL]

trier /'trie·ə/ *n* **1** sby who makes an effort or perseveres **2** an implement (e g a tapered hollow tube) used in obtaining samples of bulk material, esp foodstuffs, for examination and testing [[1]TRY + [2]-ER]

trifid /'triefid/ *adj* deeply and narrowly cleft into 3 teeth, parts, or points [L *trifidus* split into three, fr *tri-* + *findere* to split – more at BITE]

[1]**trifle** /'triefl/ *n* **1** sthg of little value or importance; *esp* an insignificant amount (e g of money) **2** *chiefly Br* a dessert typically consisting of sponge cake soaked in wine (e g sherry), spread with jam or jelly, and topped with custard and whipped cream [ME *trufle, trifle*, fr OF *trufe, trufle* mockery] – **a trifle** to some small degree ⟨a trifle *annoyed at the delay*⟩

[2]**trifle** *vb* **trifling** /'triefling/ *vi* **1** to act heedlessly or frivolously – often + *with* ⟨*not a woman to be* ~d *with*⟩ **2** to handle sthg idly ~ *vt* to spend or waste in trifling or on trifles ⟨trifling *his time away*⟩ [ME *truflen, triflen*, fr OF *trufer, trufler* to mock, trick] – **trifler** *n*

trifling /'triefling/ *adj* lacking in significance or solid worth: e g **a** frivolous **b** trivial, insignificant

[1]**trifocal** /trie'fohkl/ *adj* having 3 focal lengths

[2]**trifocal** *n* a trifocal glass or lens

trifoliate /trie'fohli·ət, -ayt/ *adj* having (leaves with) 3 leaflets ⟨*a ~ leaf*⟩ ☞ PLANT

triforium /,trie'fawri·əm/ *n, pl* **triforia** /-ri·ə/ a gallery forming an upper storey to the aisle of a church and typically an arcaded storey between the nave arches and clerestory [ML]

triform /'trie,fawm/ *adj* having a triple form or nature [L *triformis*, fr *tri-* + *forma* form]

trifurcate /'triefuhkət, -kayt/ *adj* having 3 branches or forks [L *trifurcus*, fr *tri-* + *furca* fork] – **trifurcate** /-,kayt/ *vi*, **trifurcation** /-'kaysh(ə)n/ *n*

trig /trig/ *n* trigonometry – infml

trigeminal /,trie'jeminl/ *adj or n* (of) the trigeminal nerve [n NL *trigeminus*, fr L, threefold, fr *tri-* + *geminus* twin; adj fr n]

trigeminal nerve *n* either of a pair of cranial nerves that supply motor and sensory fibres mostly to the face

trigeminal neuralgia *n* an intense neuralgia involving 1 or more branches of the trigeminal nerve and characterized by intense pain in the face

[1]**trigger** /'trigə/ *n* **1** a device (e g a lever) connected with a catch as a means of release; *esp* the tongue of metal in a firearm which when pressed allows the gun to fire **2** a stimulus that initiates a reaction or signal in an electronic apparatus [alter. of earlier *tricker*, fr D *trekker*, fr MD *trecker* sthg that pulls, fr *trecken* to pull – more at TREK] – **trigger** *adj*, **triggered** *adj*

[2]**trigger** *vt* **1a** to release, activate, or fire by means of a trigger **b** to cause the explosion of ⟨*~ a missile with a proximity fuse*⟩ **2** to initiate or set off as if by pulling a trigger ⟨*an indiscreet remark that* ~ed *a fight*⟩ – often + *off* ~ *vi* to release a mechanical trigger

'**trigger-,happy** *adj* **1** irresponsible in the use of firearms **2a** aggressively belligerent **b** too prompt in one's response

trigonal /'trigənl/ *adj* of or being the division of the hexagonal crystal system characterized by a vertical axis of threefold symmetry [L *trigonalis* triangular, fr *trigonum* triangle, fr Gk *trigōnon*, fr neut of *trigōnos* triangular, fr *tri-* + *gōnia* angle – more at -GON] – **trigonally** *adv*

trigonometric function /,trigənə'metrik/ *n* **1** a function (specif the sine, cosine, tangent, cotangent, secant, or cosecant) of an arc or angle most simply expressed in terms of the ratios of pairs of sides of a right-angled triangle **2** the inverse (e g the arc sine) of a trigonometric function

trigonometry /,trigə'nomətri/ *n* the study of the properties of triangles and trigonometric functions and of their applications ☞ MATHEMATICS [NL *trigonometria*, fr Gk *trigōnon* + *-metria* -metry] – **trigonometric** /,trigənə'metrik/ *also* **trigonometrical** *adj*

trigraph /'trie,grahf, -,graf/ *n* three letters spelling a single speech sound (e g *eau* in *beau*) – **trigraphic** /-'grafik/ *adj*

trilateral /,trie'lat(ə)rəl/ *adj* having 3 sides ⟨*a triangle is* ~⟩ [L *trilaterus*, fr *tri-* + *later-*, *latus* side] – **trilaterally** *adv*

trilby /'trilbi/ *n, chiefly Br* a soft felt hat with an indented crown ☞ GARMENT [fr such a hat having been worn in the London stage version of *Trilby*, novel by George Du Maurier †1896 E artist & writer]

trilinear /,trie'lini·ə/ *adj* of or involving 3 lines

trilingual /,trie'ling·gwəl/ *adj* **1** of, containing, or expressed in 3 languages **2** using or able to use 3 languages, esp with the fluency of a native – **trilingually** *adv*

triliteral /,trie'lit(ə)rəl/ *n or adj* (a word or root) consisting of 3 letters, esp of 3 consonants [*tri-* + L *litera* letter] – **triliteralism** *n*

[1]**trill** /tril/ *n* **1** the alternation of 2 musical notes 2 semitones apart ☞ MUSIC **2** a sound resembling a musical trill **3** (a speech sound made by) the rapid vibration of the tip of the tongue against the ridge of flesh behind the front teeth, or of the uvula against the back of the tongue [It *trillo*, fr *trillare* to trill, prob fr D *trillen* to vibrate; akin to MD *trappe* step, trap]

[2]**trill** *vt* to utter as or with a trill ⟨~ *the* r⟩ ~ *vi* to play or sing with a trill – **triller** *n*

trillion /'trilyən/ *n* **1a** *Br* a million million millions (10^{18}) **b** *chiefly NAm* a million millions (10^{12}) **2** an indefinitely large number; a zillion – often pl with sing. meaning *USE* (*1*) ☞ NUMBER [F, fr *tri-* + *-illion* (as in *million*)] – **trillion** *adj*, **trillionth** /'trilyənth/ *adj or n*

trilobite /'trielə,biet/ *n* any of numerous extinct Palaeozoic marine arthropods that had a 3-lobed body ☞ EVOLUTION [deriv of Gk *trilobos* three-lobed, fr *tri-* + *lobos* lobe]

trilogy /'triləji/ *n* a group of 3 closely related works (e g novels) [Gk *trilogia*, fr *tri-* + *-logia* -logy]

[1]**trim** /trim/ *vb* **-mm-** *vt* **1** to decorate (e g clothes) with ribbons, lace, or ornaments; adorn **2** to make trim and neat, esp by cutting or clipping **3** to remove (as if) by cutting ⟨~ med *thousands from the running costs of the department*⟩ **4a** to cause (e g a ship, aircraft, or submarine) to assume a desired position by arrangement of ballast, cargo, passengers, etc **b** to adjust (e g a sail) to a desired position ~ *vi* to maintain a neutral attitude towards opposing parties or favour each equally [(assumed) ME *trimmen* to prepare, put in order, fr OE *trymian, trymman* to strengthen, arrange, fr *trum* strong, firm; akin to Skt *dāru* wood – more at TREE]

[2]**trim** *adj* **-mm-** appearing neat or in good order; compact or clean-cut in outline or structure ⟨~ *houses*⟩ ⟨*a* ~ *figure*⟩ – **trimly** *adv*, **trimness** *n*

[3]**trim** *n* **1** the readiness or fitness of a person or thing for action or use; *esp* physical fitness **2a** one's clothing or appearance **b** material used for decoration or trimming **c** the decorative accessories of a motor vehicle **3a** the position of a ship or boat, esp with reference to the horizontal **b** the inclination of an aircraft or spacecraft in flight with reference to a fixed point (e g the horizon), esp with the controls in some neutral position **4** (sthg removed by) trimming

trimaran /'triemə,ran/ *n* a sailing vessel used for cruising or racing that has 3 hulls side by side [*tri-* + *-maran* (as in *catamaran*)]

trimer /'triemə/ *n* a polymer formed from 3 molecules of a monomer [ISV *tri-* + *-mer* (as in *polymer*)] – **trimeric** /-'merik/ *adj*

trimester /tri'mestə, trie-/ *n* a period of (approximately) 3 months [F *trimestre*, fr L *trimestris* of 3 months, fr *tri-* + *mensis* month – more at MOON] – **trimestral** /-strəl/ *also* **trimestrial** /-stri·əl/ *adj*

trimeter /'trimitə/ *n* a line of verse consisting either of 3 measures of 2 feet or of 3 metrical feet [L *trimetrus*, fr Gk *trimetros* having 3 measures, fr *tri-* + *metron* measure – more at MEASURE]

trimmer /'trimə/ *n* **1** a short beam or rafter fitted at 1 side of an opening to support the free ends of floor joists, studs, or rafters **2** a person who modifies his/her policy, position, or opinions out of expediency [[1]TRIM + [2]-ER]

trimming /'triming/ *n* **1** *pl* pieces cut off in trimming sthg; scraps **2a** a decorative accessory or additional item (e g on the border of a garment) that serves to finish or complete **b** an additional garnish or accompaniment to a main item ⟨*turkey and all the* ~s⟩ – usu pl

trimorphic /trie'mawfik/, **trimorphous** /-fəs/ *adj* occurring in or having 3 distinct (crystalline) forms [Gk *trimorphos* having 3 forms, fr *tri-* + *-morphos* -morphous] – **trimorphism** *n*

trinary /'trienəri/ *adj* ternary [LL *trinarius*, fr L *trini* three each]

[1]**trine** /trien/ *adj* **1** triple **2** of or being an astrological trine [ME, fr MF *trin*, fr L *trinus*, back-formation fr *trini* three each; akin to L *tres* three – more at THREE]

[2]**trine** *n* **1** a triad **2** the astrological aspect of 2 celestial bodies 120 degrees apart ☞ SYMBOL – **trinal** *adj*

Trinitarian /trini'teəri·ən/ *n* an adherent of the doctrine of the Trinity – **Trinitarian** *adj*, **Trinitarianism** *n*

trinitrotoluene /,trie,nietroh'tolyoo,een/ *n* an inflammable derivative of toluene used as a high explosive and in chemical synthesis [ISV]

Trinity /'trinəti/ *n* **1** the unity of Father, Son, and Holy Spirit as 3 persons in 1 Godhead according to Christian theology **2** *not cap* TRIAD 1 **3** the Sunday after Whitsunday observed as a festival in honour of the Trinity [ME *trinite*, fr OF *trinité*, fr LL *trinitat-*, *trinitas* state of being threefold, fr L *trinus* trine]

,Trinity 'House *n* a British organization that licenses maritime pilots and maintains navigational markers (e g buoys and lighthouses) [*Trinity House*, 16th-c guild orig based at Deptford in Kent]

Trinity term *n* the university term beginning after Easter

trinket /'tringkit/ *n* a small (trifling) article; *esp* an ornament or piece of (cheap) jewellery [perh fr ME *trenket* small knife, fr ONF *trenquet*] – **trinketry** *n*

trinomial /trie'nohmyəl, -mi·əl/ *adj or n* (being) a polynomial of 3 terms [*tri-* + *-nomial* (as in *binomial*)]

trinucleotide /,trie'nyoohkli·ə,tied/ *n* a nucleotide consisting of 3 mononucleotides in combination; a codon

trio /'tree·oh/ *n, pl* **trios** **1a** (a musical composition for) 3 instruments, voices, or performers **b** the secondary or episodic division of a minuet, scherzo, etc

2 *sing or pl in constr* a group or set of 3 [F, fr It, fr *tri-* (fr L)]

triode /'trie,ohd/ *n* a thermionic valve with 3 electrodes used esp in amplification circuits

triolet /'trie·əlit, 'tree-/ *n* an 8-line poem or stanza in which the first and second lines are repeated [F, prob dim. of It *trio*]

¹trip /trip/ *vb* **-pp-** *vi* **1a** to dance, skip, or walk with light quick steps **b** to proceed smoothly, lightly, and easily; flow ⟨*words that* ~ *off the tongue*⟩ **2** to catch the foot against sthg so as to stumble **3** to make a mistake or false step (e g in morality or accuracy) **4** to stumble in articulation when speaking **5** to make a journey **6** to become operative or activated ⟨*the circuit breaker* ~s *when the voltage gets too high*⟩ **7** to get high on a psychedelic drug (e g LSD); TURN ON 2a – slang ~ *vt* **1a** to cause to stumble **b** to cause to fail **2** to detect in a fault or blunder; CATCH OUT – usu + *up* **3** to raise (an anchor) from the bottom so as to hang free **4** to release or operate (a device or mechanism), esp by releasing a catch or producing an electrical signal **5** to perform (e g a dance) lightly or nimbly – archaic except in *trip the light fantastic* ***USE*** (*vi 2, 3, & 4; vt 1*) often + *up* [ME *trippen*, fr MF *triper*, of Gmc origin; akin to OE *treppan* to tread – more at ¹TRAP]

²trip *n* **1a** a voyage, journey, or excursion **b** a single round or tour (e g on a business errand) **2** an error, mistake **3** a quick light step **4** a faltering step caused by stumbling **5** a device (e g a catch) for tripping a mechanism **6a** an intense, often visionary experience undergone by sby who has taken a psychedelic drug (e g LSD) **b** a highly charged emotional experience ⟨*his divorce was a really bad* ~⟩ **7** a self-indulgent or absorbing course of action, way of behaving, or frame of mind ⟨*on a nostalgia* ~⟩ ⟨*gave up the whole super-star* ~⟩ ***USE*** (*6&7*) infml

tripartite /trie'pahtiet/ *adj* **1** divided into or composed of 3 (corresponding) parts **2** made between or involving 3 parties ⟨*a* ~ *treaty*⟩ [ME, fr L *tripartitus*, fr *tri-* + *partitus* partite] – **tripartitely** *adv*, **tripartition** /-'tish(ə)n/ *n*

tripe /triep/ *n* **1** the stomach tissue of an ox, cow, etc for use as food **2** sthg inferior, worthless, or offensive – infml [ME, fr OF]

'trip-,hammer *n* a large hammer raised by machinery and then tripped to drop on work below

triphibious /trie'fibi·əs/ *adj* employing or involving land, naval, and air forces [*tri-* + *-phibious* (as in *amphibious*)]

triphosphate /trie'fosfayt/ *n* a compound that contains 3 phosphate groups

triphthong /'trifthong, 'trip-/ *n* **1** a vowel sound (e g /ie·ə/ in *fire*) composed of 3 elements **2** a trigraph [*tri-* + *-phthong* (as in *diphthong*)] – **triphthongal** /-'thong(ə)l/ *adj*

triplane /'trie,playn/ *n* an aeroplane with 3 main pairs of wings arranged one above the other

¹triple /'tripl/ *vb* **tripling** /'tripling, 'tripl·ing/ to make or become 3 times as great or as many [ME *triplen*, fr LL *triplare*, fr L *triplus*, adj]

²triple *n* **1** a triple sum, quantity, or number **2** a combination, group, or series of 3 [ME, fr L *triplus*, adj]

³triple *adj* **1** having 3 units or members **2** being 3 times as great or as many **3** marked by 3 beats per bar of music ⟨~ *metre*⟩ **4** having units of 3 components [MF or L; MF, fr L *triplus*, fr *tri-* + *-plus* multiplied by – more at DOUBLE] – **triply** *adv*

triple jump *n* an athletic field event consisting of a jump for distance combining a hop, a step, and a jump in succession

triple point *n* the condition of temperature and pressure under which the gaseous, liquid, and solid phases of a substance can exist in equilibrium

triplet /'triplit/ *n* **1** a unit of 3 lines of verse **2** a combination, set, or group of 3 **3** any of 3 children or animals born at 1 birth **4** a group of 3 musical notes performed in the time of 2 of the same value [²*triple* + *-et* (as in *doublet*)]

,triple-'tongue *vi* to use tongue movements to produce a very fast succession of detached notes on a wind instrument

triplex /'tripleks, 'trie-/ *adj* threefold, triple [L, fr *tri-* + *-plex* -fold – more at ¹SIMPLE]

¹triplicate /'triplikət/ *adj* **1** consisting of or existing in 3 corresponding or identical parts or examples ⟨~ *invoices*⟩ **2** being the third of 3 things exactly alike ⟨*file the* ~ *copy*⟩ [ME, fr L *triplicatus*, pp of *triplicare* to triple, fr *triplic-*, *triplex* threefold]

²triplicate /'triplikayt/ *vt* **1** to make triple **2** to prepare in triplicate – **triplication** /-'kaysh(ə)n/ *n*

³triplicate /'triplikət/ *n* **1** any of 3 things exactly alike; *specif* any of 3 identical copies **2** three copies all alike – + *in* ⟨*typed in* ~⟩

triplicity /tri'plisəti, trie-/ *n* **1** any of the 4 groups of 3 symmetrically placed signs into which the signs of the zodiac are divided **2** the quality or state of being triple [ME *triplicite*, fr LL *triplicitas* condition of being threefold, fr L *triplic-*, *triplex*]

tripod /'trie,pod/ *n* **1** a stool, table, or vessel (e g a cauldron) with 3 legs **2** a 3-legged stand (e g for a camera) [L *tripod-*, *tripus*, fr Gk *tripod-*, *tripous*, fr *tripod-*, *tripous* three-footed, fr *tri-* + *pod-*, *pous* foot – more at FOOT] – **tripodal** /'tripədl/ *adj*

tripos /'triepos/ *n* either part of the honours examination for the Cambridge BA degree [modif of L *tripus*; fr the three-legged stool formerly occupied by a participant in a disputation at the degree ceremonies]

tripper /'tripə/ *n, chiefly Br* one who goes on an outing or pleasure trip, esp one lasting only 1 day – often used disparagingly ⟨*in the summer the village pub is usually full of* ~s, *so we stay at home*⟩ [¹TRIP + ²-ER]

trippingly /'tripingli/ *adv* nimbly; *also* fluently

triptych /'trip,tik/ *n* a picture or carving on 3 panels side by side; *esp* an altarpiece consisting of a central panel hinged to 2 flanking panels that fold over it [Gk *triptychos* having 3 folds, fr *tri-* + *ptychē* fold]

'trip ,wire *n* a concealed wire placed near the ground that is used to trip up an intruder or to actuate an explosive or warning device when pulled

trireme /'trie,reem/ *n* a galley with 3 banks of oars [L *triremis*, fr *tri-* + *remus* oar – more at ¹ROW]

tris- *prefix* thrice; tripled – esp in complex chemical expressions [Gk *tris* – more at TER-]

trisect /trie'sekt, '--/ *vt* to divide into 3 (equal) parts – **trisection** /'trie,seksh(ə)n, -'--/ *n*, **trisector** /'trie,sektə, -'--/ *n*

trishaw /'trie,shaw/ *n* a passenger vehicle consisting of a tricycle with a rickshaw body over the rear wheels [*tri*cycle + rick*shaw*]

triskelion /tris'kelyn, trie-, -on/ *also* **triskele**

/'triskeel, trie-/ *n* a figure or symbol in the shape of 3 curved or bent branches radiating from a centre ⟨*the ~ of the Isle of Man*⟩ [*triskelion* fr NL, fr Gk *triskelēs* three-legged, fr *tri-* + *skelos* leg; *triskele* fr Gk *triskelēs*]

trismus /'trizməs/ *n* spasm of the muscles involved in chewing; lockjaw [NL, fr Gk *trismos* gnashing (of teeth), fr *trizein* to squeak, gnash; akin to L *stridēre* to creak – more at STRIDENT]

trisyllable /'trie,siləbl/ *n* a word of 3 syllables – **trisyllabic** /-si'labik/ *adj*, **trisyllabically** *adv*

trite /triet/ *adj* hackneyed from much use [L *tritus*, fr pp of *terere* to rub, wear away – more at THROW] – **tritely** *adv*, **triteness** *n*

tritiated /'trishiaytid, 'triti-/ *adj, of a molecule* containing tritium in place of hydrogen, esp as a radioactive label

triticale /,tritə'kayli/ *n* a cereal grass that is a hybrid between wheat and rye and has a high yield and rich protein content [NL, blend of *Triticum*, genus of wheat + *Secale*, genus of rye]

tritium /'trishi·əm, 'triti·əm/ *n* a radioactive isotope of hydrogen with atoms of 3 times the mass of ordinary hydrogen atoms [NL, fr Gk *tritos* third – more at THIRD]

triton /'triet(ə)n/ *n* (any of various large marine gastropod molluscs with) a heavy elongated conical shell [NL, genus name, fr L *Triton*, mythical marine demigod, fr Gk *Tritōn*]

triturate /'trityoorayt/ *vt* **1** to crush, grind **2** to reduce to a fine powder by rubbing or grinding [LL *trituratus*, pp of *triturare* to thresh, fr L *tritura* act of rubbing, threshing, fr *tritus*, pp] – **triturator** *n*, **triturable** /-rəbl/ *adj*, **trituration** /-'raysh(ə)n/ *n*

[1]**triumph** /'trie,um(p)f/ *n* **1** a ceremony attending the entering of ancient Rome by a general who had won a decisive victory over a foreign enemy – compare OVATION **2** the joy or exultation of victory or success **3** (a) notable success, victory, or achievement [ME *triumphe*, fr MF, fr L *triumphus*] – **triumphal** /-'um(p)fl/ *adj*

[2]**triumph** *vi* **1** to celebrate victory or success boastfully or exultantly **2** to obtain victory – often + *over*

triumphant /trie'um(p)fənt/ *adj* **1** victorious, conquering **2** rejoicing in or celebrating victory – **triumphantly** *adv*

triumvir /trie'umvə, -viə/ *n, pl* **triumvirs** *also* **triumviri** /-vərie/ a member of a commission or ruling body of 3 [L, back-formation fr *triumviri*, pl, commission of 3 men, fr *trium virum* of 3 men] – **triumviral** /-vərəl/ *adj*

triumvirate /trie'umvirət/ *n* **1** the office of triumvirs **2** *sing or pl in constr* **a** a body of triumvirs **b** a group of 3

triune /'trie,yoohn/ *adj, often cap* three in one – used of the Trinity [*tri-* + L *unus* one – more at ONE]

trivalent /trie'vaylənt, 'trivələnt/ *adj* having a valency of 3 [ISV]

trivet /'trivit/ *n* **1** a three-legged (iron) stand for holding cooking vessels over or by a fire; *also* a bracket that hooks onto a grate for this purpose **2** a (metal) stand with 3 feet for holding a hot dish at table [ME *trevet*, fr OE *trefet*, prob modif of LL *triped-*, *tripes*, fr L, three-footed, fr *tri-* + *ped-*, *pes* foot – more at FOOT]

trivia /'trivi·ə/ *n pl but sing or pl in constr* unimportant matters or details [NL, fr pl of L *trivium* crossroads; influenced in meaning by E *trivial*]

trivial /'trivi·əl/ *adj* **1** commonplace, ordinary **2a** of little worth or importance; insignificant **b** of or being the mathematically simplest case ⟨*a ~ solution to an equation*⟩ [L *trivialis* found everywhere, commonplace, trivial, fr *trivium* crossroads, fr *tri-* + *via* way – more at VIA] – **trivialness** *n*, **trivially** *adv*, **trivialize** *vt*, **trivialization** /-'zaysh(ə)n/ *n*, **triviality** /,trivi'aləti/ *n*

'**trivial ,name** *n* **1** the second part of a 2 word Latin name of an animal, plant, etc, that follows the genus name and denotes the species **2** a common or vernacular name of an organism or chemical

trivium /'trivi·əm/ *n, pl* **trivia** /'trivi·ə́/ grammar, rhetoric, and logic, forming the lower division of the 7 liberal arts in medieval universities – compare QUADRIVIUM [ML, fr L, meeting of 3 ways, crossroads]

triweekly /,trie'weekli/ *adj or adv* **1** (occurring or appearing) 3 times a week **2** (occurring or appearing) every 3 weeks

-trix /-triks/ *suffix* (→ *n*), *pl* **-trices** /-triseez, -trieseez/, **-trixes** **1** female ⟨*avia*trix⟩ ⟨*execu*trix⟩ **2** geometric line, point, or surface ⟨*direc*trix⟩ [ME, fr L, fem of *-tor*, suffix denoting an agent, fr *-tus*, pp ending + *-or* – more at [1]-ED]

tRNA /,tee ahr en 'ay/ *n* TRANSFER RNA

trocar *also* **trochar** /'trohkah/ *n* a sharp-pointed instrument used esp to insert a fine tube into a body cavity as a drainage outlet [F *trocart*, fr *trois* three (fr L *tres*) + *carre* side of a sword blade, fr *carrer* to make square, fr L *quadrare* – more at THREE, QUADRATE]

trochal /'trohkl/ *adj* resembling a wheel [Gk *trochos* wheel]

trochanter /tro'kantə/ *n* **1** a rough prominence at the upper part of the femur of many vertebrates **2** the second segment of an insect's leg counting from the body [Gk *trochantēr*; akin to Gk *trechein* to run] – **trochanteric** /,trokən'terik/ *adj*

troche /trohsh/ *n* a usu circular soothing medicinal tablet or lozenge held in the mouth until dissolved, esp for the relief of a sore throat [alter. of earlier *trochisk*, fr LL *trochiscus*, fr Gk *trochiskos*, fr dim. of *trochos* wheel]

trochee /'troh,kee/ *n* a metrical foot consisting of 1 long or stressed syllable followed by 1 short or unstressed syllable (e g in *apple*) [F *trochée*, fr L *trochaeus*, fr Gk *trochaios*, fr *trochaios* running, fr *trochē* run, course, fr *trechein* to run; akin to Gk *trochos* wheel, OIr *droch*] – **trochaic** /troh'kayik/ *adj or n*

trochlea /'trokli·ə/ *n, pl* **trochleas, trochleae** /-li,ee/ an anatomical structure resembling a pulley; *esp* a surface of a bone over which a tendon passes [NL, fr L, block of pulleys, fr Gk *trochileia*; akin to Gk *trechein* to run] – **trochlear** *adj*

trochophore /'trokə,faw/ *n* a free-swimming cilia-bearing larva, esp of marine annelid worms [deriv of Gk *trochos* wheel + *pherein* to carry – more at [2]BEAR]

trod /trod/ *past of* TREAD

trodden /'trod(ə)n/ *past part of* TREAD

troglodyte /'trogləldiet/ *n* **1** CAVE DWELLER **2** a person resembling a troglodyte, esp in being solitary or unsocial or in having primitive or outmoded ideas **3** APE 1 [L *troglodytae*, pl, fr Gk *trōglodytai*, fr *trōglē* hole, cave + *dyein* to enter; akin to Gk *trōgein* to gnaw] – **troglodytic** /-'ditik/ *adj*

trogon /'trohgon/ *n* any of a family of tropical birds with brilliant lustrous plumage [NL, genus name, fr Gk *trōgōn*, prp of *trōgein* to gnaw]

troika /'troykə/ *n* **1** (a Russian vehicle drawn by) a team of 3 horses abreast **2** TRIAD 1; *esp* an administrative or ruling body of 3 people [Russ *troĭka*, fr *troe* three; akin to OE *thrie* three]

Trojan /'trohj(ə)n/ *n* **1** a native of Troy **2** one who shows qualities (e g pluck or endurance) attributed to the defenders of ancient Troy – chiefly in *work like a Trojan* [ME, fr L *trojanus* of Troy, fr *Troia, Troja* Troy, ancient city in Asia Minor, fr Gk *Trōïa*] – **Trojan** *adj*

,Trojan 'horse *n* sby or sthg intended to undermine or subvert from within [fr the legend of a large hollow wooden horse filled with Greek soldiers and brought within the walls of Troy by a trick during the Trojan War]

[1]**troll** /trohl, trol/ *vt* **1** to sing loudly **2** to fish for or in with a hook and line drawn through the water behind a moving boat ~ *vi* **1** to sing or play an instrument in a jovial manner **2** to fish, esp by drawing a hook through the water **3** to move about; stroll, saunter ⟨*travel writers* ~ing *around from free hotel to free hotel – The Bookseller*⟩ [ME *trollen* to move about, roll] – **troller** *n*

[2]**troll** *n* (a line with) a lure used in trolling

[3]**troll** *n* a dwarf or giant of Germanic folklore inhabiting caves or hills [Norw *troll* & Dan *trold*, fr ON *troll* giant, demon; akin to MHG *trolle* monster, OE *treppan* to tread – more at [1]TRAP]

trolley *also* **trolly** /'troli/ *n* **1** a device (e g a grooved wheel or skid) attached to a pole that collects current from an overhead electric wire for powering an electric vehicle **2** *chiefly Br* **a** a shelved stand mounted on castors used for conveying sthg (e g food or books) **b** a basket on wheels that is pushed or pulled by hand and used for carrying goods (e g purchases in a supermarket) **3** *Br* a small 4-wheeled wagon that runs on rails **4** *NAm* TRAM b [E dial. *trolley, troll* (cart, truck), prob fr [1]*troll*]

'trolley,bus /-,bus/ *n* an electrically propelled bus running on a road and drawing power from 2 overhead wires via a trolley

'trolley ,car *n, NAm* TRAM b

trollop /'troləp/ *n* a slovenly or immoral woman [prob irreg fr G dial. *trolle*, fr MHG *trulle* prostitute – more at TRULL] – **trollopy** *adj*

trombone /trom'bohn/ *n* a brass instrument consisting of a long cylindrical metal tube with a movable slide for varying the pitch and a usual range 1 octave lower than that of the trumpet [It, aug of *tromba* trumpet, of Gmc origin; akin to OHG *trumba, trumpa* trumpet] – **trombonist** *n*

trommel /'troməl/ *n* a usu cylindrical revolving sieve, esp for screening or sizing ore [G, drum, fr MHG *trummel*, dim. of *trumme* drum – more at [1]DRUM]

trompe l'oeil /,tromp 'luh·i (*Fr* trɔ̃p lœːj)/ *n* (the effect produced by) a style of painting or decorating in which objects are depicted with three-dimensional reality [F *trompe-l'oeil*, lit., deceive the eye]

-tron /-tron/ *suffix* (→ *n*) device for the manipulation of subatomic particles ⟨*cyclo*tron⟩ [Gk, suffix denoting an instrument; akin to OE *-thor*, suffix denoting an instrument, L *-trum*]

[1]**troop** /troohp/ *n* **1** *sing or pl in constr* **a** a military subunit (e g of cavalry) corresponding to an infantry platoon **b** a collection of people or things **c** a unit of scouts under a leader **2** *pl* the armed forces [MF *trope, troupe* company, herd, of Gmc origin; akin to OE *thorp, throp* village]

[2]**troop** *vi* to move in a group, esp in a way that suggests regimentation ⟨*everyone* ~ed *into the meeting*⟩

trooper /'troohpə/ *n* **1a** a cavalry soldier; *esp* a private soldier in a cavalry or armoured regiment **b** the horse of a cavalry soldier **2** *chiefly NAm & Austr* a mounted policeman

trop-, tropo- *comb form* **1** turn; turning; change ⟨tropo*sphere*⟩ **2** tropism ⟨trop*ic*⟩ [ISV, fr Gk *tropos*]

trope /trohp/ *n* a figurative use of a word or expression [L *tropus*, fr Gk *tropos* turn, way, manner, style, trope, fr *trepein* to turn; akin to L *trepit* he turns]

troph-, tropho- *comb form* nutritive ⟨tropho*plasm*⟩ [F, fr Gk, fr *trophē* nourishment]

trophic /'trofik, 'trohfik/ *adj* **1** of nutrition or growth ⟨~ *disorders of muscle*⟩ ⟨~ *level*⟩ ☞ FOOD **2** *of a hormone* influencing the activity of a gland [F *trophique*, fr Gk *trophikos*, fr *trophē* nourishment, fr *trephein* to nourish – more at ATROPHY] – **trophically** *adv*

-trophic /-'trohfik, -'trofik/ *comb form* (→ *adj*) **1** of or characterized by (a specified mode of feeding) ⟨*zoo*trophic⟩ **2** attracted to, acting upon, or esp stimulating (sthg specified) ⟨*cortico*trophic⟩ [NL *-trophia* nutrition, fr Gk, fr *-trophos* nourishing, fr *trephein*] – **-trophism, -trophy** *comb form* (→ *n*)

trophoblast /'trofə,blast, 'troh-/ *n* a layer of ectoderm on the outside of the blastula of many placental mammals that nourishes the embryo [ISV] – **trophoblastic** /-'blastik/ *adj*

trophy /'trohfi/ *n* **1a** a memorial of an ancient Greek or Roman victory raised on or near the field of battle **b** a representation of such a memorial (e g on a medal); *also* an architectural ornament representing a group of military weapons **2** sthg gained or awarded in victory or conquest, esp when preserved as a memorial [MF *trophee*, fr L *tropaeum, trophaeum*, fr Gk *tropaion*, fr neut of *tropaios* of a turning, of a rout, fr *tropē* turn, rout, fr *trepein* to turn – more at TROPE]

[1]**tropic** /'tropik/ *n* **1** either of the 2 small circles of the celestial sphere on each side of and parallel to the equator at a distance of 23½ degrees, which the sun reaches at its greatest declination N or S **2a(1)** TROPIC OF CANCER **(2)** TROPIC OF CAPRICORN **b** *pl, often cap* the region between the 2 terrestrial tropics [ME *tropik*, fr L *tropicus* of the solstice, fr Gk *tropikos*, fr *tropē* turn]

[2]**tropic** /'trohpik/ *adj* **1** of, being, or characteristic of (a) tropism **2** TROPHIC 2 [*trop-*]

-tropic /-'trohpik/ *comb form* (→ *adj*) **1** turning, changing, or tending to turn or change in (a specified manner) or in response to (a specified stimulus) ⟨*geo*tropic⟩ **2** -TROPHIC 2 [F *-tropique*, fr Gk *-tropos* -tropous] – **-tropism, -tropy** *comb form* (→ *n*)

tropical /'tropikl/ *adj* **1** *also* **tropic** of, occurring in, or characteristic of the tropics **2** *of a sign of the zodiac* beginning at either of the tropics – **tropically** *adv*

'tropic ,bird /'tropik/ *n* any of several web-footed birds related to the gannets

tropic of Cancer /,tropik əv 'kansə/ *n* the parallel of latitude that is 23½ degrees N of the equator [fr the sign of the zodiac which its celestial projection intersects]

tropic of Capricorn /,tropik əv 'kapri,kawn/ *n* the parallel of latitude that is 23½ degrees S of the equator [fr the sign of the zodiac which its celestial projection intersects]

tropism /'trohpiz(ə)m/ *n* (an) involuntary orientation by (a part of) an organism, esp a plant, that involves turning or curving in response to a source of stimulation (e g light) – compare TAXIS 2 [ISV *-tropism,* fr *trop-*]

tropo- – see TROP-

tropology /tro'poləji/ *n* the figurative use of words [LL *tropologia,* fr LGk, fr Gk *tropos* trope + *-logia* -logy] – **tropological** /,tropə'lojikl/ *also* **tropologic** *adj*

tropopause /'tropə,pawz/ *n* the region at the top of the troposphere [ISV *tropo*sphere + *pause*]

troposphere /'tropə,sfiə/ *n* the part of the atmosphere below the stratosphere, in which temperature decreases rapidly with altitude and clouds form [ISV] – **tropospheric** /-'sferik/ *adj*

-tropous /-trəpəs/ *comb form* (→ *adj*) -TROPIC 1 ⟨*ana*tropous⟩ [Gk *-tropos,* fr *trepein* to turn – more at TROPE]

troppo /'tropoh/ *adj, Austr* mentally deranged by the heat of the tropics – infml [^{1}*tro*pic + ^{1}*-o*]

^{1}**trot** /trot/ *n* **1** a moderately fast gait of a horse or other quadruped in which the legs move in diagonal pairs **2** an instance or the pace of trotting or proceeding briskly **3** *pl but sing or pl in constr* diarrhoea – usu + *the;* humor [ME, fr MF, fr *troter* to trot, of Gmc origin; akin to OHG *trottōn* to tread, OE *tredan*] – **on the trot** in succession – infml

^{2}**trot** *vb* **-tt-** *vi* **1** to ride, drive, or proceed at a trot **2** to proceed briskly ~ *vt* **1** to cause to go at a trot **2** to traverse at a trot

Trot *n* a Trotskyite; *broadly* any adherent of the extreme left – chiefly derog

troth /trohth/ *n, archaic* one's pledged word; *also* betrothal – chiefly in *plight one's troth* [ME *trouth,* fr OE *trēowth* – more at TRUTH]

trot out *vt* **1** to produce or bring forward (as if) for display or scrutiny **2** to produce or utter in a trite or predictable manner ⟨trotted out *all the old clichés*⟩

Trotskyism /'trotski,iz(ə)m/ *n* the political, economic, and social principles advocated by Trotsky; *esp* adherence to the concept of permanent worldwide revolution [Leon *Trotsky* †1940 Russ Communist leader] – **Trotskyist, Trotskyite** /-,iet/ *n or adj*

trotter /'trotə/ *n* **1** a horse trained for trotting races **2** the foot of an animal, esp a pig, used as food [^{2}TROT + ^{2}-ER]

trotting /'troting/ *n* the sport of racing horses moving at a fast trot and pulling light 2-wheeled vehicles carrying a driver

troubadour /'troohbədaw, -dooə/ *n* any of a class of lyric poets and poet-musicians, chiefly in France in the 11th to 13th c, whose major theme was courtly love [F, fr OProv *trobador,* fr *trobar* to compose, prob fr (assumed) VL *tropare,* fr L *tropus* trope]

^{1}**trouble** /'trubl/ *vb* **troubling** /'trubling/ *vt* **1a** to agitate mentally or spiritually; worry **b** to produce physical disorder or discomfort in ⟨~d *with deafness*⟩ **c** to put to exertion or inconvenience ⟨*could I* ~ *you to close the door?*⟩ **2** to make (e g the surface of water) turbulent ~ *vi* **1** to become mentally agitated ⟨*refused to* ~ *over trifles*⟩ **2** to make an effort; be at pains ⟨*don't* ~ *to come*⟩ [ME *troublen,* fr OF *tourbler, troubler,* fr (assumed) VL *turbulare,* alter. of L *turbidare,* fr *turbidus* turbid, troubled]

^{2}**trouble** *n* **1a** being troubled **b** an instance of distress, annoyance, or disturbance **2** a cause of disturbance, annoyance, or distress: e g **a** public unrest or demonstrations of dissatisfaction – often pl with sing. meaning **b** effort made; exertion **c(1)** a disease, ailment, or condition of physical distress ⟨*heart* ~⟩ **(2)** a malfunction ⟨*engine* ~⟩ **d** pregnancy out of wedlock – chiefly in *in/into trouble* **3** a problem, snag ⟨*that's the* ~ *with these newfangled ideas*⟩ – **troublous** /'trubləs/ *adj, archaic or poetic*

'trouble,maker /-,maykə/ *n* one who causes trouble

'trouble,shooter /-,shoohtə/ *n* **1** a skilled workman employed to locate faults and make repairs in machinery and technical equipment **2** one who specializes or is expert in resolving disputes – **troubleshooting** *n*

'troublesome /-s(ə)m/ *adj* giving trouble or anxiety; annoying or burdensome ⟨*a* ~ *cough*⟩ ⟨*a* ~ *neighbour*⟩ – **troublesomely** *adv,* **troublesomeness** *n*

trough /trof/ *n* **1a** a long shallow receptacle for the drinking water or feed of farm animals **b** a long narrow container used for domestic or industrial purposes **2a** a conduit, drain, or channel for water **b** a long narrow or shallow trench between waves, ridges, etc **3a** the (region round the) lowest point of a regularly recurring cycle of a varying quantity (e g a sine wave) **b** an elongated area of low atmospheric pressure **c** a low point (in a trade cycle) [ME, fr OE *trog;* akin to OE *trēow* tree, wood – more at TREE]

trounce /trowns/ *vt* **1** to thrash or punish severely **2** to defeat decisively [origin unknown]

troupe /troohp/ *n* a company or troop (of theatrical performers) [F, fr MF – more at TROOP]

trouper /'troohpə/ *n* **1** a member of a troupe **2** a loyal or dependable person

trousers /'trowzəz/ *n pl, pl* **trousers** a 2-legged outer garment extending from the waist to the ankle or sometimes only to the knee ☞ GARMENT [alter. of earlier *trouse,* fr ScGael *triubhas*] – **trouser** *adj*

'trouser ,suit *n* a woman's suit consisting of a jacket and trousers

trousseau /'troohsoh/ *n, pl* **trousseaux, trousseaus** /-sohz/ the personal outfit of a bride including clothes, accessories, etc [F, fr OF, dim. of *trousse* bundle, fr *trousser* to truss]

trout /trowt/ *n, pl* **trouts,** (*1*) **trout,** *esp for different types* **trouts 1** any of various food and sport fishes of the salmon family restricted to cool clear fresh waters; *esp* any of various Old World or New World fishes some of which ascend rivers from the sea to breed – compare RAINBOW TROUT **2** an ugly unpleasant old woman – slang [ME, fr OE *trūht,* fr LL *trocta, tructa,* a fish with sharp teeth, fr Gk *trōktēs,* lit., gnawer, fr *trōgein* to gnaw – more at TERSE]

trouvaille /trooh'vie (*Fr* truvaːj)/ *n* a chance or

unexpected find; *also* an interesting or original idea [F, fr OF *trover, trouver* to compose, find]

trouvère /trooh'veə (*Fr* truvɛːr)/ *n* any of a class of late medieval French narrative poets [F, fr OF *troveor, troverre,* fr *trover* to compose, find, fr (assumed) VL *tropare* – more at TROUBADOUR]

trove /trohv/ *n* TREASURE TROVE

trover /'trohvə/ *n* a common law action to recover the value of goods wrongfully taken or kept by another [MF *trover* to find]

trow /troh/ *vb, archaic* to think, believe [ME *trowen,* fr OE *trēowan*; akin to OE *trēowe* faithful, true – more at TRUE]

[1]**trowel** /'trowəl/ *n* any of various smooth-bladed hand tools used to apply, spread, shape, or smooth loose or soft material; *also* a scoop-shaped or flat-bladed garden tool for taking up and setting small plants ☞ BUILDING [ME *truel,* fr MF *truelle,* fr LL *truella,* fr L *trulla,* dim. of *trua* ladle; akin to L *turbare* to disturb – more at TURBID]

[2]**trowel** *vt* **-ll-** (*NAm* **-l-, -ll-**), /'trowəling/ to smooth, mix, or apply (as if) with a trowel

troy /troy/ *adj* expressed in troy weight [ME *troye,* fr *Troyes,* city in France]

'**troy ,weight** *n* the series of units of weight based on the pound of 12oz and the ounce of 20 pennyweights or 480 grains

truant /'trooh·ənt/ *n* one who shirks duty; *esp* one who stays away from school without permission [ME, vagabond, idler, fr OF, vagrant, of Celt origin; akin to ScGael *truaghan* wretch] – **truant** *adj,* **truanting** *n,* **truancy** *n*

truce /troohs/ *n* a (temporary) suspension of fighting by agreement of opposing forces [ME *trewes,* pl of *trewe* agreement, fr OE *trēow* fidelity; akin to OE *trēowe* faithful – more at TRUE]

[1]**truck** /truk/ *vt* to give in exchange; barter ~ *vi* **1** to trade, barter **2** to negotiate or traffic, esp in an underhand way [ME *trukken,* fr OF *troquer*]

[2]**truck** *n* **1** (commodities suitable for) barter or small trade **2** close association; dealings – chiefly in *have no truck with* **3** payment of wages in goods instead of cash **4** miscellaneous small articles; *also* rubbish – infml

[3]**truck** *n* **1** a small strong wheel **2** a small wooden cap at the top of a flagstaff or masthead, usu having holes for flag or signal halyards **3a** a usu 4- or 6-wheeled vehicle for moving heavy loads; a lorry **b** a usu 2- or 4-wheeled cart for carrying heavy articles (e g luggage at railway stations) **4** *Br* an open railway goods wagon [prob fr L *trochus* iron hoop, fr Gk *trochos* wheel – more at TROCHEE]

[4]**truck** *vt* to load or transport on a truck ~ *vi* , *NAm* to be employed as a lorry driver – **truckage** *n*

trucker /'trukə/ *n, NAm* **1** one whose business is transporting goods by lorry **2** a lorry driver

truckle /'trukl/ *vi* **truckling** /'trukling/ to act in a subservient or obsequious manner – usu + *to* [fr the lower position of the truckle bed] – **truckler** *n*

'**truckle ,bed** *n* a low bed, usu on castors, that can be slid under a higher bed [ME *trookel, trocle* pulley, small wheel, fr L *trochlea* block of pulleys – more at TROCHLEA]

truculent /'trukyoolənt/ *adj* aggressively self-assertive; belligerent [L *truculentus,* fr *truc-, trux* fierce] – **truculence, truculency** *n,* **truculently** *adv*

[1]**trudge** /truj/ *vb* to walk steadily and laboriously (along or over) [origin unknown] – **trudger** *n*

[2]**trudge** *n* a long tiring walk

[1]**true** /trooh/ *adj* **1** steadfast, loyal ⟨*a ~ friend*⟩ **2a** in accordance with fact or reality ⟨*a ~ story*⟩ **b** essential ⟨*the ~ nature of socialist economics*⟩ **c** being that which is the case rather than what is claimed or assumed ⟨*the ~ dimensions of the problem*⟩ **d** consistent, conforming ⟨*~ to expectations*⟩ ⟨*~ to type*⟩ **3a(1)** properly so called ⟨*the ~ faith*⟩ **(2)** genuine, real ⟨*~ love*⟩ **b(1)** possessing the basic characters of and belonging to the same natural group as ⟨*a whale is a ~ but not a typical mammal*⟩ **(2)** typical ⟨*the ~ cats*⟩ **4a** accurately fitted, adjusted, balanced, or formed **b** exact, accurate ⟨*a ~ voice*⟩ ⟨*a ~ copy*⟩ **5** determined with reference to the earth's axis rather than the magnetic poles ⟨*~ north*⟩ [ME *trewe,* fr OE *trēowe* faithful; akin to OHG *gitriuwi* faithful, Skt *dāruṇa* hard, *dāru* wood – more at TREE]

[2]**true** *n* the state of being accurate (e g in alignment or adjustment) – chiefly in *in/out of true*

[3]**true** *vt* to bring or restore to a desired mechanical accuracy or form – **truer** *n*

[4]**true** *adv* **1** TRULY 1 **2a** without deviation; straight **b** without variation from type ⟨*breed ~*⟩ [ME *trewe,* fr *trewe,* adj]

true bill *n* a bill of indictment in the USA endorsed by a grand jury as warranting prosecution

,**true-'blue** *adj* staunchly loyal; *specif, Br* being a staunch supporter of the Conservative party [fr a traditional association of blue with fidelity & its adoption as a party colour by various Br conservative groups since the 17th c] – **true-blue** *n*

'**true,love** /-,luv/ *n* a sweetheart – poetic

true lover's knot, truelove knot *n* a complicated ornamental knot not readily untied and symbolic of mutual love

truffle /'trufl/ *n* **1** (any of several European fungi with) a usu dark and wrinkled edible fruiting body that grows under the ground and is eaten as a delicacy **2** a rich soft creamy sweet made with chocolate [modif of MF *truffe,* fr OProv *trufa,* fr (assumed) VL *tufera,* alter. of L *tuber* – more at TUBER] – **truffled** *adj*

trug /trug/ *n, Br* a shallow rectangular wooden basket for carrying garden produce [origin unknown]

truism /'trooh,iz(ə)m/ *n* an undoubted or self-evident truth – **truistic** /-'istik/ *adj*

trull /trul/ *n, archaic* a prostitute, strumpet [obs G *trulle,* fr MHG; akin to ON *troll* giant, demon – more at [3]TROLL]

truly /'troohli/ *adv* **1** in accordance with fact or reality; truthfully **2** accurately, exactly **3a** indeed **b** genuinely, sincerely ⟨*he was ~ sorry*⟩ **4** properly, duly ⟨*well and ~ beaten*⟩

[1]**trump** /trump/ *n* a trumpet (call) – chiefly poetic [ME *trompe,* fr OF]

[2]**trump** *n* **1a** a card of a suit any of whose cards will win over a card that is not of this suit **b** *pl* the suit whose cards are trumps for a particular hand **2** a worthy and dependable person – infml [alter. of [1]*triumph*] – **come/turn up trumps** to prove unexpectedly helpful or generous

[3]**trump** *vb* to play a trump on (a card or trick) when another suit was led

'trump ,card *n* **1** [2]TRUMP 1a **2** a telling or decisive factor; a clincher – esp in *play one's trump card*

trumpery /'trumpəri/ *adj* **1** worthless, useless **2** cheap, tawdry [ME *tromperie* deceit, fr MF, fr *tromper* to deceive] – **trumpery** *n*

[1]**trumpet** /'trumpit/ *n* **1** a wind instrument consisting of a usu metal tube, a cup-shaped mouthpiece, and a flared bell; *specif* a valved brass instrument having a cylindrical tube and a usual range from F sharp below middle C upwards for 2½ octaves **2** sthg that resembles (the flared bell or loud penetrating sound of) a trumpet: e g **a** a megaphone **b** the loud cry of an elephant [ME *trompette*, fr MF, fr OF *trompe* trump] – **trumpetlike** *adj*

[2]**trumpet** *vi* **1** to blow a trumpet **2** to make a sound as of a trumpet ~ *vt* to sound or proclaim loudly (as if) on a trumpet

'trumpet ,creeper *n* a N American woody climbing plant with large red trumpet-shaped flowers

trumpeter /'trumpitə/ *n* **1** a trumpet player; *specif* one who gives (military) signals with a trumpet **2a** any of several long-legged long-necked S American birds related to the cranes **b** TRUMPETER SWAN **c** any of an Asiatic type of domestic pigeon with a rounded crest and heavily feathered feet

'trumpeter ,swan *n* a rare white N American wild swan noted for its sonorous voice

'trumpet ,flower *n* (any of various plants with) a trumpet-shaped flower

'trumpet ,shell *n* a triton

trump up *vt* to concoct, fabricate ⟨*charges* trumped up *by the police*⟩

[1]**truncate** /'trungkayt, -'-/ *vt* to shorten (as if) by cutting off a part [L *truncatus*, pp of *truncare*, fr *truncus* trunk] – **truncation** /-'kaysh(ə)n/ *n*

[2]**'truncate** *adj* having the end square or even ⟨*the ~ leaves of the tulip tree*⟩ ☞ PLANT

truncated /'trungkaytid, -'--/ *adj* having the apex replaced by a plane section, esp one parallel to the base ⟨~ *cone*⟩

truncheon /'trunchən/ *n* **1** a staff of office or authority **2** a short club carried esp by policemen [ME *tronchoun* broken spear, fr MF *tronchon*, fr (assumed) VL *truncion-*, *truncio*, fr L *truncus* trunk]

[1]**trundle** /'trundl/ *n* a small wheel or roller [alter. of earlier *trendle*, fr ME, circle, ring, wheel, fr OE *trendel*; akin to OE *trendan* to revolve – more at TREND]

[2]**trundle** *vb* **trundling** /'trundling/ to move heavily or pull along (as if) on wheels

'trundle ,bed *n* TRUCKLE BED

trunk /trungk/ *n* **1a** the main stem of a tree as distinguished from branches and roots **b** the human or animal body apart from the head and limbs **c** the main or central part of sthg (e g an artery, nerve, or column) **2** a large rigid box used usu for transporting clothing and personal articles **3** a proboscis; *esp* the long muscular proboscis of the elephant **4** *pl* men's usu close-fitting shorts worn chiefly for swimming or sports **5** a chute, shaft, or similar (major) supply channel **6** TRUNK LINE **7** *NAm* [3]BOOT 4 [ME *tronke* box, trunk, fr MF *tronc*, fr L *truncus* trunk, torso]

'trunk ,call *n* a telephone call made on a trunk line ☞ TELECOMMUNICATION

'trunk ,line *n* a major route of communication: e g **a** a main line of a railway system **b** a telephone line between towns

'trunk ,road *n* a road of primary importance, esp for long distance travel

trunnion /'trunyən/ *n* a pin or pivot on which sthg can be rotated or tilted; *esp* either of 2 opposite projections on which a gun barrel can be tilted vertically [F *trognon* core, stump]

[1]**truss** /trus/ *vt* **1a** to secure tightly; bind – often + *up* **b** to bind the wings or legs of (a fowl) closely in preparation for cooking **2** to support or stiffen (e g a bridge) with a truss [ME *trussen*, fr OF *trousser*]

[2]**truss** *n* **1a** a corbel; BRACKET 1 **b** a usu triangular assemblage of members (e g beams) forming a rigid framework (e g in a roof or bridge) **2** a device worn to reduce a hernia by pressure **3** a compact flower or fruit cluster (e g of tomatoes) – **trussing** *n*

[1]**trust** /trust/ *n* **1** confident belief in or reliance on (the ability, character, honesty, etc of) sby or sthg ⟨*take it on* ~⟩ **2** financial credit **3a** a property interest held by one person for the benefit of another **b** a combination of companies formed by a legal agreement **4a** a charge or duty imposed in faith or as a condition of some relationship **b** responsible charge or office ⟨*in a position of* ~⟩ **c** care, custody ⟨*child committed to his* ~⟩ [ME, prob of Scand origin; akin to ON *traust* trust; akin to OE *trēowe* faithful – more at TRUE] – **trustful** *adj*, **trustfully** *adv* – **in trust** in the care or possession of a trustee

[2]**trust** *vi* **1** to place confidence; depend ⟨~ *in God*⟩ **2** to be confident; hope ⟨*we'll see you soon, I* ~⟩ ~ *vt* **1a** to place in sby's care or keeping **b** to permit to do or be without fear or misgiving ⟨*won't* ~ *it out of his sight*⟩ **2a** to place confidence in; rely on – also used ironically ⟨~ *him to arrive late!*⟩ **b** to expect or hope, esp confidently ⟨*I* ~ *you are well?*⟩ **3** to extend credit to – **trustable** *adj*, **trusting** *adj*, **trustingly** *adv*

'trust ,company *n* a company that functions as a corporate and personal trustee and usu also engages in the normal activities of a commercial bank

trustee /tru'stee/ *n* **1** a country charged with the supervision of a trust territory **2a** a natural or legal person appointed to administer property in trust for a beneficiary **b** any of a body of people administering the affairs of a company or institution and occupying a position of trust – **trusteeship** *n*

'trust ,territory *n* a non-self-governing territory placed under an administrative authority by the United Nations

'trust,worthy /-,wuhdhi/ *adj* dependable, reliable – **trustworthily** *adv*, **trustworthiness** *n*

[1]**trusty** /'trusti/ *adj* trustworthy – **trustily** *adv*, **trustiness** *n*

[2]**trusty** *n* a trusted person; *specif* a convict considered trustworthy and allowed special privileges

truth /troohth/ *n, pl* **truths** /troohdhz, troohths/ **1** sincerity, honesty **2a(1)** the state or quality of being true or factual ⟨*there's* ~ *in what she says*⟩ **(2)** reality, actuality ⟨~ *is stranger than fiction*⟩ **(3)** *often cap* a transcendent (e g spiritual) reality **b** a judgment, proposition, idea, or body of statements that is (accepted as) true ⟨*scientific* ~s⟩ **3** conformity to an original or to a standard [ME *trouthe*, fr OE *trēowth* fidelity; akin to OE *trēowe* faithful – more at TRUE] – **truthful** *adj*, **truthfully** *adv*, **truthfulness** *n*

ˈ**truth ˌtable** *n* a table that shows whether a compound statement is true or false in formal logic for each combination of truth-values of its component statements

ˈ**truth-ˌvalue** *n* the truth or falsity of a (logical) statement

¹**try** /trie/ *vt* **1a** to investigate judicially **b** to conduct the trial of **2a(1)** to test by experiment or trial – often + *out* **(2)** to investigate the state, capabilities, or potential of, esp for a particular purpose ⟨~ *the shop next door*⟩ **b** to subject to sthg that tests the patience or endurance **3** to melt down and obtain in a pure state – usu + *out* ⟨~ *out whale oil from blubber*⟩ **4** to make an attempt at ~ *vi* to make an attempt [ME *trien*, fr AF *trier*, fr OF, to pick out, sift, prob fr LL *tritare* to rub to pieces, fr *tritus*, pp of *terere* to rub – more at THROW] – **try for size** to test for appropriateness or fittingness – **try one's hand** to make an attempt for the first time

²**try** *n* **1** an experimental trial; an attempt **2** a score in rugby that is made by touching down the ball behind the opponent's goal line and that entitles the scoring side to attempt a kick at the goal for additional points

trying /ˈtrie·ing/ *adj* irritating, annoying, or demanding – **tryingly** *adv*

try on *vt* **1** to put on (a garment) in order to examine the fit or appearance **2** *Br* to attempt to impose on sby ⟨*don't go* trying *anything* on *with me, mate*⟩ – infml – **try-on** /ˈ-ˌ-/ *n*

tryout /ˈtrieˌowt/ *n* an experimental performance or demonstration; *specif* a test of the ability of sby (e g an actor or athlete) or sthg to meet requirements

trypanosome /triˈpanəˌsohm, ˈtripanəˌsohm, trie-/ *n* any of a genus of parasitic protozoans that infest the blood of various vertebrates including human beings and some types of which cause sleeping sickness [NL *Trypanosoma*, genus name, fr Gk *trypanon* auger + NL *-soma* -some – more at TREPAN]

trypanosomiasis /ˌtripənəsəˈmie·əsis, triˌpanə-, trie-/ *n* infection with or disease caused by trypanosomes [NL]

trypsin /ˈtripsin/ *n* (any of several enzymes similar to) an enzyme from pancreatic juice that breaks down protein in an alkaline medium [Gk *tryein* to wear down + ISV *-psin* (as in *pepsin*); akin to L *terere* to rub – more at THROW] – **tryptic** /-tik/ *adj*

tryptamine /ˈtriptəˌmeen/ *n* (any of various hallucinogenic substances derived from) a derivative of tryptophan [*trypt*ophan + *amine*]

tryptophan /ˈtriptəˌfan/, **tryptophane** /-ˌfayn/ *n* an amino acid that is widely distributed in proteins and is essential to animal life [ISV *trypt*ic + *-o-* + *-phane*]

trysail /ˈtrieˌsayl, ˈtriesl/ *n* a small fore-and-aft sail used esp as a storm sail [obs *at try* (lying to)]

ˈ**try ˌsquare** /trie/ *n* an L-shaped instrument used for marking out right angles and testing whether work (e g brickwork or carpentry) is square

¹**tryst** /trist, triest/ *n* **1** an agreement, esp by lovers, to meet **2** an appointed meeting or meeting place *USE* poetic [ME, fr OF *triste* watch post, prob of Scand origin; akin to ON *traust* trust]

²**tryst** *vi, chiefly Scot* to make a tryst – poetic

tsar, czar, tzar /zah/ *n* **1** a male ruler of Russia before 1917 **2** one having great power or authority [Russ *tsar'*, fr Goth *kaisar*, fr Gk or L; Gk, fr L *Caesar* – more at CAESAR] – **tsarism** *n*, **tsarist** *n or adj*

tsarevitch, tsarevich /ˈzahrəvich/ *n* the (eldest) son of the Russian tsar [Russ *tsarevich*, fr *tsar'* + *-evich*, patronymic suffix]

tsarina /zahˈreenə/ *n* the wife of a tsar [prob modif of G *zarin*, fr *zar* tsar, fr Russ *tsar'*]

tsaritza /zahˈritsə/ *n* a tsarina [Russ *tsaritsa*, fem of *tsar'*]

tsetse /ˈtetsi, ˈtsetsi/, ˈ**tsetse ˌfly** *n, pl* **tsetse, tsetses** any of several two-winged flies that occur in Africa south of the Sahara desert and transmit diseases, esp sleeping sickness, by bites [Afrik, fr Tswana *tsêtsê*]

ˈ**T-ˌshirt** /tee/ *n* a collarless upper garment of light stretchy fabric for casual wear ☞ GARMENT [fr its being shaped like a T]

ˈ**T ˌsquare** *n* a ruler with a crosspiece or head at 1 end used in making parallel lines

tsunami /tsooˈnahmi/ *n* a great sea wave produced by underwater earth movement or volcanic eruption [Jap] – **tsunamic** *adj*

Tswana /chˈwahnə, ˈswahnə, ˈtswahnə/ *n, pl* **Tswanas,** *esp collectively* **Tswana** a member, or the Bantu language, of a group of peoples dwelling between the Orange and Zambezi rivers

Tuareg /ˈtwahreg/ *n, pl* **Tuaregs,** *esp collectively* **Tuareg** a member of a nomadic people chiefly inhabiting the central and W Sahara [Ar *Tawāriq*]

tuatara /ˌtooh·əˈtahrə/ *n* a large spiny reptile living on islands off the coast of New Zealand [Maori *tuatára*]

¹**tub** /tub/ *n* **1a** any of various wide low often round vessels typically made of wood, metal, or plastic, and used industrially or domestically (e g for washing clothes or holding soil for shrubs) **b** a small round (plastic) container in which cream, ice cream, etc may be bought **2** BATH 2b **3** an old or slow boat – infml [ME *tubbe*, fr MD; akin to MLG *tubbe* tub] – **tubful** *n*

²**tub** *vb* **-bb-** to wash or bath in a tub

tuba /ˈtyoohbə/ *n* a large brass instrument having valves, a conical tube, a cup-shaped mouthpiece, and a usual range an octave lower than that of the euphonium [It, fr L, trumpet]

tubal /ˈtyoohbl/ *adj* of or involving a (fallopian) tube

tubby /ˈtubi/ *adj* podgy, fat [*tub* + ¹*-y*] – **tubbiness** *n*

tube /tyoohb/ *n* **1a** a hollow elongated cylinder; *esp* one to convey fluids **b** a slender channel within a plant or animal body **2** any of various usu cylindrical structures or devices: e g **a** a small cylindrical container of soft metal or plastic sealed at one end, and fitted with a cap at the other, from which a paste is dispensed by squeezing **b** TEST TUBE **c** the basically cylindrical section between the mouthpiece and bell of a wind instrument **3** ELECTRON TUBE; *specif, chiefly NAm* a thermionic valve **4** *Br* (a train running in) an underground railway running through deep bored tunnels **5** *chiefly Austr* a can of beer – infml [F, fr L *tubus*; akin to L *tuba* trumpet] – **tubelike** *adj*

tube foot *n* any of the small flexible tubular parts of starfish and some other echinoderms that are used esp in locomotion and grasping

ˈ**tubeless** /-lis/ *adj* being a pneumatic tyre that does

not depend on an inner tube to be airtight [TUBE + -LESS]

tuber /'tyoohbə/ *n* (a root resembling) a short fleshy usu underground stem (e g a potato) that is potentially able to produce a new plant – compare BULB, CORM [L, lump, tuber, truffle; akin to L *tumēre* to swell – more at THUMB] – **tuberous** *adj*

tubercle /'tyoohb·ə,kl/ *n* **1** a small knobby prominence, esp on a plant or animal **2** a small abnormal lump in an organ or in the skin; *esp* one characteristic of tuberculosis [L *tuberculum*, dim. of *tuber*] – **tubercled** *adj*, **tuberculate** /tyooh'buhkyoolət, -layt/ *also* **tuberculated** /-,laytid/ *adj*

tubercle bacillus *n* the bacterium that causes tuberculosis

tubercular /tyoo'buhkyoolə/ *adj* **1** of, resembling, or being a tubercle **2** tuberculous – **tubercularly** *adv*

tuberculin /tyoo'buhkyoolin/ *n* a sterile liquid extracted from the tubercle bacillus and used in the diagnosis of tuberculosis, esp in humans and cattle [ISV]

tu'berculin ,test *n* a test for hypersensitivity to tuberculin as an indication of past or present tubercular infection

tuberculosis /tyoo,buhkyoo'lohsis, tə-/ *n* a serious infectious disease of human beings and other vertebrates caused by the tubercle bacillus and characterized by fever and the formation of abnormal lumps in the body [NL] – **tuberculoid** /-loyd/ *adj*

tuberculous /tyoo'buhkyooləs, tə-/ *adj* **1** of, being, or affected with tuberculosis ⟨*a* ~ *process*⟩ **2** caused by or resulting from the presence or products of the tubercle bacillus ⟨~ *peritonitis*⟩ – **tuberculously** *adv*

tuberose /'tyoohbərohs/ *n* a bulbous Mexican plant of the daffodil family cultivated for its spike of fragrant white single or double flowers [NL *tuberosa*, specific epithet, fr L, fem of *tuberosus* tuberous, fr *tuber*]

tubicolous /tyoo'bikələs/ *adj, of an annelid worm* living in a self-constructed tube-shaped case or cover [L *tubus* tube + E *-colous*]

tubifex /'tyoohbifeks/ *n, pl* **tubifex, tubifexes** any of a genus of slender reddish worms that live in self-constructed tube-shaped cases in fresh or brackish water and are widely used as food for aquarium fish [NL *Tubific-, Tubifex*, genus name, fr L *tubus* tube + *facere* to make – more at [1]DO]

tubing /'tyoohbing/ *n* **1** (a length of) material in the form of a tube **2** a series or system of tubes

tubocurarine /,tyoohbohkyoo'rahrin, -reen/ *n* an alkaloid that is obtained chiefly from the bark and stems of a S American climbing plant and constitutes the chief active constituent of curare [ISV *tubo-* (fr L *tubus* tube) + *curare* + *-ine*; fr its being shipped in sections of hollow bamboo]

tub-thumper /'tub ,thumpə/ *n* an impassioned or ranting public speaker – **tub-thumping** *n or adj*

tubular /'tyoohbyoolə/ *also* **tubulous** /-ləs/ *adj* **1** having the form of or consisting of a tube ⟨*a* ~ *calyx*⟩ **2** made of or fitted with tubes or tube-shaped pieces – **tubularly** *adv*, **tubularity** /-'larəti/ *n*

tubule /'tyoohbyoohl/ *n* a small tube; *esp* a slender tubular anatomical structure [L *tubulus*, dim. of *tubus*]

[1]**tuck** /tuk/ *vt* **1a** to draw into a fold or folded position **b** to make a tuck or series of tucks in **2** to place in a snug often concealed or isolated spot ⟨*cottage* ~ed *away in the hills*⟩ **3a** to push in the loose end or ends of so as to make secure or tidy **b** to cover snugly by tucking in bedclothes ⟨~ed *up in bed*⟩ **4** to eat – usu + *away* ~ *vi* to eat heartily – usu + *in* or *into* ***USE*** (*vt 4; vi*) infml [ME *tuken* to pull up sharply, scold, fr OE *tūcian* to ill-treat; akin to OE *togian* to pull – more at [1]TOW]

[2]**tuck** *n* **1** a (narrow) fold stitched into cloth to shorten, decorate, or reduce fullness **2** the part of a vessel where the ends of the lower planks meet under the stern **3** (an act of) tucking **4** a body position (e g in diving) in which the knees are bent, the thighs drawn tightly to the chest, and the hands clasped round the shins **5** *Br* food, esp chocolate, pastries, etc, as eaten by schoolchildren ⟨*a* ~ *shop*⟩ – infml

[1]**tucker** /'tukə/ *n, Austr & NZ* food ⟨*a* ~ *bag*⟩ – infml [[1]TUCK + [2]-ER]

[2]**tucker** *vt, chiefly NAm* to exhaust – often + *out* [obs *tuck* (to scold) + *-er* (as in [1]*batter*)]

tucket /'tukit/ *n, archaic* a fanfare on a trumpet [prob fr obs *tuk* (to beat the drum, sound the trumpet), fr ME *tukken*, fr ONF *toquer* to touch, strike, fr (assumed) VL *toccare* – more at TOUCH]

'tuck-,in *n, chiefly Br* a hearty meal – infml

-tude /-tyoohd, -choohd/ *suffix* (→ *n*) -ness ⟨*pleni*tude⟩ ⟨*alti*tude⟩ [MF or L; MF, fr L *-tudin-, -tudo*]

Tudor /'tyoohdə/ *adj* **1** of the English royal house that ruled from 1485 to 1603 **2** (characteristic) of the Tudor period [Henry *Tudor* (Henry VII of England) †1509] – **Tudor** *n*

Tuesday /'tyoohzday, -di/ *n* the day of the week following Monday ☞ SYMBOL [ME *tiwesday*, fr OE *tīwesdæg*; akin to OHG *zīostag* Tuesday; both fr a prehistoric WGmc-NGmc compound whose components are represented by OE *Tīw*, god of war & by OE *dæg* day – more at DEITY] – **Tuesdays** *adv*

tufa /'tyoohfə/ *n* a porous rock formed as a deposit by springs [It *tufo*, fr L *tophus*] – **tufaceous** /tyooh'fayshəs/ *adj*

tuff /tuf/ *n* a rock composed of volcanic ash (fused by heat) [MF *tuf*, fr OIt *tufo* tufa] – **tuffaceous** /tu'fayshəs/ *adj*

tuffet /'tufit/ *n* **1** TUFT 1a **2** a low seat [alter. of [1]*tuft*]

[1]**tuft** /tuft/ *n* **1a** a small cluster of long flexible hairs, feathers, grasses, etc attached or close together at the base **b** a bunch of soft fluffy threads cut off short and used for ornament **2** a clump, cluster [ME, modif of MF *tufe*] – **tufted** *adj*, **tufty** *adj*

[2]**tuft** *vt* **1** to adorn with a tuft or tufts **2** to make (e g a mattress) firm by stitching at intervals and sewing on tufts

[1]**tug** /tug/ *vb* **-gg-** to pull hard (at) [ME *tuggen*; akin to OE *togian* to pull – more at [1]TOW]

[2]**tug** *n* **1a** a hard pull or jerk **b** a strong pulling force ⟨*felt the* ~ *of the past*⟩ **2** a struggle between 2 people or opposite forces **3a tug, tugboat** a strongly built powerful boat used for towing or pushing large ships (e g in and out of dock) **b** an aircraft that tows a glider

,tug-of-'war *n, pl* **tugs-of-war** **1** a struggle for supremacy **2** a contest in which teams pulling at opposite ends of a rope attempt to pull each other across a line marked between them

tugrik, tugric /'toohgrik/ *n* ☞ *Mongolia* at

NATIONALITY [Mongolian *dughurik*, lit., round thing, wheel]

tuition /tyooh'ish(ə)n/ *n* teaching, instruction [ME *tuicioun* protection, fr OF *tuicion*, fr L *tuition-, tuitio*, fr *tuitus*, pp of *tueri* to look at, look after] – **tuitional** *adj*

tularaemia, *NAm* **tularemia** /ˌtoohlə'reemyə, -mi·ə/ *n* an infectious disease of rodents, human beings, and some domestic animals that is caused by a bacterium and is transmitted esp by the bites of insects [NL, fr *Tulare* County, district of California, USA, where it was first discovered] – **tularaemic** /-'reemik/ *adj*

tulip /'tyoohlip/ *n* (the flower of) any of a genus of Eurasian bulbous plants of the lily family widely grown for their showy flowers [NL *tulipa*, fr Turk *tülbend* turban, fr Per *dulband*]

'tulip ˌtree *n* a tall N American tree of the magnolia family with large tulip-shaped flowers and soft white wood used esp for cabinetwork and wooden utensils; *broadly* any of various trees with tulip-shaped flowers

'tulipˌwood /-ˌwood/ *n* the wood of the N American tulip tree; whitewood

tulle /t(y)oohl/ *n* a sheer, often silk, net used chiefly for veils and dresses [F, fr *Tulle*, city in France]

tum /tum/ *n* STOMACH 1b – infml [short for *tummy*]

¹tumble /'tumbl/ *vb* **tumbling** /'tumbling, 'tumbl·ing/ *vi* **1a** to perform gymnastic feats in tumbling **b** to turn end over end in falling or flight **2a** to fall suddenly and helplessly **b** to suffer a sudden overthrow or defeat **c** to decline suddenly and sharply ⟨*the stock market* ~d⟩ **3** to roll over and over, to and fro, or around **4** to move hurriedly and confusedly ⟨~d *into his clothes*⟩ **5** to realize suddenly – often + *to*; infml ~ *vt* **1** to cause to tumble (e g by pushing) **2** to rumple, disorder **3** to whirl in a tumbler (e g in drying clothes) [ME *tumblen*, freq of *tumben* to dance, fr OE *tumbian*; akin to OHG *tūmōn* to reel, ON *tumba* to tumble]

²tumble *n* **1** a confused heap **2** an act of tumbling; *specif* a fall ⟨*took a nasty* ~⟩

'tumbleˌdown /-ˌdown/ *adj* dilapidated, ramshackle

ˌtumble-'drier /'drie·ə/, **tumbler-drier** /'tumblə/ *n* a machine consisting of a rotating heated drum in which wet laundry is dried – **tumble-dry** *vb*

tumbler /'tumblə/ *n* **1a** an acrobat **b** any of various domestic pigeons that tumble or somersault backwards in flight or on the ground **2** a relatively large drinking glass without a foot, stem, or handle **3a** a movable obstruction (e g a lever, wheel, or pin) in a lock that must be adjusted to a particular position (e g by a key) before the bolt can be moved **b** a lever that when released by the trigger forces the hammer of a firearm forwards **4a** a tumble-drier **b** a revolving drum, often lined with abrasive material, in which gemstones, castings, etc are polished by friction [¹TUMBLE + ²-ER] – **tumblerful** *n*

tumbleweed /'tumblˌweed/ *n* a plant that breaks away from its roots in the autumn and is blown about by the wind

tumbling /'tumbling, 'tumbl·ing/ *n* the skill, practice, or sport of executing gymnastic feats without the use of apparatus

tumbrel, tumbril /'tumbrəl/ *n* **1** a farm cart that can be tipped to empty the contents **2** a vehicle used to carry condemned people to a place of execution during the French Revolution [ME *tombrel*, fr OF *tumberel* tipcart, fr *tomber* to tumble, of Gmc origin; akin to OHG *tūmōn* to reel – more at TUMBLE]

tumefaction /ˌtyoohmi'faksh(ə)n/ *n* **1** swelling or becoming tumorous **2** SWELLING 1 [MF, fr L *tumefactus*, pp of *tumefacere* to cause to swell, fr *tumēre* to swell + *facere* to make, do – more at THUMB, ¹DO]

tumescent /tyooh'mes(ə)nt/ *adj* somewhat swollen; *esp, of the penis or clitoris* engorged with blood in response to sexual stimulation [L *tumescent-, tumescens*, prp of *tumescere* to swell up, fr *tumēre*] – **tumescence** *n*

tumid /'tyoohmid/ *adj* **1** *esp of body parts* swollen, protuberant, or distended **2** bombastic, turgid [L *tumidus*, fr *tumēre*] – **tumidly** *adv*, **tumidity** /-'midəti/ *n*

tummy /'tumi/ *n* STOMACH 1b – infml [baby-talk]

tumour, *NAm chiefly* **tumor** /'tyoohmə/ *n* an abnormal mass of tissue that arises without obvious cause from cells of existing tissue and possesses no physiological function [L *tumor*, fr *tumēre*] – **tumorous** *adj*

tumult /'tyoohmult/ *n* **1a** commotion, uproar (e g of a crowd) **b** a turbulent uprising; a riot **2** violent mental or emotional agitation [ME *tumulte*, fr MF, fr L *tumultus*; akin to Skt *tumula* noisy, L *tumēre* to swell]

tumultuous /tyooh'multyoo·əs, -choo·əs/ *adj* **1** marked by commotion; riotous **2** marked by violent turbulence or upheaval ⟨~ *passions*⟩ – **tumultuously** *adv*, **tumultuousness** *n*

tumulus /'tyoohmyooləs/ *n, pl* **tumuli** /-lie/ an ancient grave; a barrow [L; akin to L *tumēre* to swell – more at THUMB]

tun /tun/ *n* **1** a large cask, esp for wine **2** any of various units of liquid capacity of about 954l [ME *tunne*, fr OE]

¹tuna /'tyoohnə/ *n* (the edible fruit of) any of various prickly pears [Sp, fr Taino]

²tuna *n, pl* **tuna,** *esp for different types* **tunas** **1** any of numerous large vigorous food and sport fishes related to the mackerels **2** **tuna, 'tuna ˌfish** the flesh of a tuna, often canned for use as food [AmerSp, alter. of Sp *atún*, modif of Ar *tūn*, fr L *thunnus*, fr Gk *thynnos*]

tundra /'tundrə/ *n* a level or undulating treeless plain with a permanently frozen subsoil that is characteristic of arctic and subarctic regions ☞ PLANT [Russ, of Finno-Ugric origin; akin to Lapp *tundar* hill]

¹tune /tyoohn/ *n* **1a** a pleasing succession of musical notes; a melody **b** *the* dominant tune in a musical composition **2** correct musical pitch (with another instrument, voice, etc) **3a** accord, harmony ⟨*in* ~ *with the times*⟩ **b** general attitude; approach ⟨*soon changed his* ~⟩ **4** amount, extent – chiefly in *to the tune of* *USE* (*2&3a*) chiefly in *in/out of tune* [ME, alter. of *tone*]

²tune *vi* **1** to bring a musical instrument or instruments into tune, esp with a standard pitch – usu + *up* **2** to become attuned **3** to adjust a receiver for the reception of a particular broadcast or station – + *in* or *to* ⟨~ *in again next week*⟩ ~ *vt* **1** to adjust the musical pitch of; *esp* to cause to be in tune **2a** to bring into harmony; attune **b** to adjust for optimum performance – often + *up* ⟨~d *up the engine*⟩ **3** to adjust (a radio or television receiver) to respond to signals of a particular frequency – often + *in* – **tunable, tuneable** *adj*, **tuner** *n*

ˌtuned-ˈin *adj* informed about and responsive to current trends, opinions, etc – infml

tuneful /ˈtyoohnf(ə)l/ *adj* melodious, musical – **tunefully** *adv*, **tunefulness** *n*

ˈtuneless /-lis/ *adj* without an intended or recognizable melody; not tuneful – **tunelessly** *adv*, **tunelessness** *n*

tune out *vt* to adjust a receiving set to avoid the reception of ⟨tuned out *the heterodyne whistle*⟩

tung /tung/, **ˈtung ˌtree** *n* a Chinese tree of the spurge family whose seeds yield an oil used in paints and varnishes [Chin (Pek) *t'ung*²]

tungst- *also* **tungsto-** *comb form* tungsten ⟨tungst*ate*⟩ ⟨tungst*ic*⟩ [ISV, fr *tungsten*]

tungsten /ˈtungstən/ *n* a hard polyvalent metallic element with a high melting point that is used esp for electrical purposes and in hard alloys (e g steel) ☞ PERIODIC TABLE [Sw, fr *tung* heavy + *sten* stone]

Tungus /ˈtoong·goohz, ˈtun-/ *n, pl* **Tunguses,** *esp collectively* **Tungus** a member, or the Tungusic languages, of a Mongoloid people of E Siberia ☞ LANGUAGE [Russ]

Tungusic /toongˈgoohzik, tun-/ *adj or n* (of) a subfamily of Altaic languages of Manchuria and E Siberia

tunic /ˈtyoohnik/ *n* **1** a simple (hip- or knee-length) slip-on garment usu belted or gathered at the waist **2** an enclosing or covering membrane or tissue ⟨*the ~ of a seed*⟩ **3** a close-fitting jacket with a high collar worn esp as part of a uniform ⟨*a soldier's ~*⟩ [L *tunica*, of Sem origin; akin to Heb *kuttōneth* coat]

¹tunicate /ˈtyoohnikət, -kayt/ *adj* **1a** having or covered with an enclosing or lining membrane **b** having, arranged in, or made up of concentric layers ⟨*a ~ bulb*⟩ **2** of the tunicates [L *tunicatus*, fr *tunica*]

²tunicate *n* any of a major group of marine chordate animals with a simple nervous system and a thick covering layer; SEA SQUIRT [NL *Tunicata*, group name, fr neut pl of L *tunicatus* tunicate]

tunicle /ˈtyoohnikl/ *n* a short vestment worn by a subdeacon over the alb during mass ☞ GARMENT [ME, fr L *tunicula*, dim. of *tunica*]

ˈtuning ˌfork /ˈtyoohning/ *n* a 2-pronged metal implement that gives a fixed tone when struck and is useful for tuning musical instruments and setting pitches for singing

¹tunnel /ˈtunl/ *n* **1** a hollow conduit or recess (e g for a propeller shaft) **2a** a man-made horizontal passageway through or under an obstruction **b** a subterranean passage (e g in a mine) [ME *tonel* tube-shaped net, fr MF, tun, fr OF, fr *tonne* tun, fr ML *tunna*, of Celt origin; akin to MIr *tonn* skin, hide; akin to L *tondēre* to shear – more at TOME]

²tunnel *vb* **-ll-** (*NAm* **-l-**, **-ll-**), /ˈtunl·ing/ *vt* **1** to make a passage through or under **2** to make (e g one's way) by excavating a tunnel ~ *vi* **1** to make or pass through a tunnel **2** to pass through an electric potential barrier ⟨*electrons* ~ling *through an insulator between semiconductors*⟩

tunnel vision *n* a condition in which the edges of the visual field are lost, leaving good vision only straight ahead

tunny /ˈtuni/ *n, pl* **tunnies,** *esp collectively* **tunny** ²TUNA [modif of MF *thon* or OIt *tonno*; both fr OProv *ton*, fr L *thunnus*, fr Gk *thynnos*]

¹tup /tup/ *n* **1** the heavy metal head of a steam hammer, pile driver, etc **2** *chiefly Br* RAM 1 [ME *tupe* ram]

²tup *vt* **-pp-** *chiefly Br, of a ram* to copulate with (a ewe)

tupelo /ˈtyoohpəloh/ *n, pl* **tupelos** (the pale soft wood of) any of a genus of mostly N American trees of the dogwood family [Creek *ito opilwa* swamp tree]

Tupi /toohˈpee/ *n, pl* **Tupis,** *esp collectively* **Tupi** (the language of) a member of a group of peoples inhabiting esp the Amazon valley ☞ LANGUAGE

Tupian /ˈtooh,pee·ən, -ˈ--/ *adj* **1** of or being the Tupi **2** Tupi-Guaranian

Tupi-Guaranian /ˌtoohpee ˌgwahrəˈnee·ən, toohˈ-pee/ *adj or n* (of) a language stock of tropical S America

tuppence /ˈtup(ə)ns/ *n* (a) twopence – **tuppenny** /ˈtup(ə)ni/ *adj*

Turanian /tyooˈraynyən, -ni·ən/ *n or adj* (a member of any) of the peoples of Ural-Altaic stock [Per *Tūrān* Turkestan, the region north of the Amu Darya (Oxus) River]

turban /ˈtuhbən/ *n* (a headdress, esp for a lady, resembling) a headdress worn esp by Muslims and Sikhs and made of a long cloth wound round a cap or directly round the head ☞ GARMENT [MF *turbant*, fr It *turbante*, fr Turk *tülbend*, fr Per *dulband*] – **turbaned, turbanned** *adj*

turbellarian /ˌtuhbiˈleəri·ən/ *adj or n* (of or being) any of a class of mostly aquatic and free-living flatworms [deriv of L *turbellae* (pl) bustle, stir, dim. of *turba* confusion, crowd; fr the tiny eddies created in water by the cilia]

turbid /ˈtuhbid/ *adj* **1a** opaque (as if) with disturbed sediment; cloudy **b** thick with smoke or mist **2** (mentally or emotionally) confused [L *turbidus* confused, turbid, fr *turba* confusion, crowd; akin to OHG *dweran* to stir, L *turbare* to throw into disorder, disturb, Gk *tyrbē* confusion] – **turbidly** *adv*, **turbidness, turbidity** /-ˈbitəti/ *n*

turbinate /ˈtuhbinət, -ˌnayt/ *adj* **1** shaped like a top or an inverted cone ⟨*a ~ seed capsule*⟩ **2** of or being any of several thin bony or cartilaginous plates on the walls of the nasal passages [L *turbinatus*, fr *turbin-*, *turbo*]

turbine /ˈtuhbien/ *n* a rotary engine whose central driving shaft is fitted with vanes whirled round by the pressure of water, steam, exhaust gases, etc ☞ CAR, ENERGY, FLIGHT [F, fr L *turbin-*, *turbo* top, whirlwind, whirl; akin to L *turbare* to disturb]

turbo- /tuhboh-/ *comb form* consisting of, incorporating, or driven by a turbine ⟨turbo*jet engine*⟩ ⟨turbo*charger*⟩ [*turbine*]

turbocharger /ˈtuhboh,chahjə/ *n* a supercharger, esp for a car engine, driven by exhaust gas turbines ☞ CAR – **turbocharge** *vt*

turbofan /ˈtuhboh,fan/ *n* (a jet engine with) an extra large fan in front of the main compressor ☞ FLIGHT

ˈturbo,jet /-jet/ *n* (an aircraft powered by) a turbojet engine

turbojet engine *n* a jet engine in which a compressor driven by power from a turbine supplies compressed air to the combustion chamber and in which thrust is derived from the rearward explosion of hot gases ☞ FLIGHT

'turbo,prop /-,prop/ *n* (an aircraft powered by) an engine that has a turbine-driven propeller for providing the main thrust

turbot /'tuhbət/ *n, pl* **turbot,** *esp for different types* **turbots** a large European flatfish that is a highly valued food fish [ME, fr OF *tourbot*]

turbulence /'tuhbyooləns/ *n* **1** wild commotion or agitation **2** irregular atmospheric motion, esp when characterized by strong currents of rising and falling air **3** the formation of disturbances that interfere with the smooth flow of a liquid or gas ☞ FLIGHT

turbulent /'tuhbyoolənt/ *adj* **1** causing unrest, violence, or disturbance ⟨*a* ~ *crowd*⟩ **2** agitated, stormy, or tempestuous ⟨~ *water*⟩ ⟨*a* ~ *childhood*⟩ **3** exhibiting physical turbulence [L *turbulentus,* fr *turba* confusion, crowd] – **turbulently** *adv*

turbulent flow *n* a fluid flow in which the velocity at a given point varies erratically in magnitude and direction – compare LAMINAR FLOW

Turco-, Turko- /tuhkoh-/ *comb form* **1** Turkic; Turk ⟨Turco*phile*⟩ **2** Turkish and ⟨Turco-*Greek*⟩ [*Turco-* fr ML *Turcus* Turk; *Turko-* fr *Turk*]

turd /tuhd/ *n* **1** a piece of excrement **2** a despicable person *USE* vulg [ME *tord, turd,* fr OE *tord*; akin to MD *tort* dung, OE *teran* to tear – more at [2]TEAR]

tureen /tyoo'reen, tə-/ *n* a deep (covered) dish from which a food, esp soup, is served at table [F *terrine,* fr MF, fr fem of *terrin* of earth, fr (assumed) VL *terrinus,* fr L *terra* earth – more at TERRACE]

[1]turf /tuhf/ *n, pl* **turfs, turves** /tuhvz/ **1** (a piece of or an artificial substitute for) the upper layer of soil bound by grass and plant roots into a thick mat **2** (a piece of dried) peat **3** *the* sport or business of horse racing or the course on which horse races are run [ME, fr OE; akin to OHG *zurba* turf, Skt *darbha* tuft of grass] – **turfy** *adj*

[2]turf *vt* to cover with turf

'turf ac,countant *n, Br* a bookmaker

'turfman /-mən/ *n, chiefly NAm* a devotee of horse racing; *esp* one who owns and races horses

turf out *vt, chiefly Br* to dismiss or throw out forcibly – infml

turgid /'tuhjid/ *adj* **1** distended, swollen; *esp* exhibiting excessive turgor **2** in a pompous inflated style; laboured [L *turgidus,* fr *turgēre* to be swollen] – **turgidly** *adv,* **turgidness** *n,* **turgescence** /tuh'jes(ə)ns/ *n,* **turgescent** *adj,* **turgidity** /tuh'jidəti/ *n*

turgor /'tuhgə/ *n* the normal state of firmness and tension in living (plant) cells [LL, turgidity, swelling, fr L *turgēre*]

Turk /tuhk/ *n* **1** a member of any of a group of central Asian peoples speaking Turkic languages **2** a native or inhabitant of Turkey **3** *archaic* a Muslim [ME, fr MF or Turk; MF *Turc,* fr ML or Turk; ML *Turcus,* fr Turk *Türk*]

turkey /'tuhki/ *n pl* **turkeys,** *esp collectively* **turkey** (the flesh of) a large orig American bird that is farmed for its meat in most parts of the world [*Turkey,* country in W Asia and SE Europe; fr confusion with the guinea fowl, supposed to be imported from Turkish territory]

'turkey ,buzzard *n* a N American vulture

Turkey red *n* alizarin [*Turkey*]

Turki /'tuhki/ *adj* **1** TURKIC 2 **2** of or being any of the central Asian Turkic languages [Per *turkī,* fr *Turk* Turk, fr Turk *Türk*] – **Turki** *n*

Turkic /'tuhkik/ *adj* **1** of a branch of the Altaic language family including Turkish **2** of the peoples who speak Turkic languages – **Turkic** *n*

[1]Turkish /'tuhkish/ *adj* **1** (characteristic) of Turkey or the Turks **2** TURKIC 1

[2]Turkish *n* **1** the Turkic language of the Republic of Turkey ☞ LANGUAGE **2 Turkish, Turkish tobacco** an aromatic tobacco grown chiefly in Turkey and Greece

,Turkish 'bath *n* a steam bath followed by a rub-down, massage, and cold shower – compare SAUNA

,Turkish 'coffee *n* a strong usu sweetened coffee made from very finely ground beans

,Turkish de'light *n* a jellylike confection, usu cut in cubes and dusted with sugar

Turkmen /'tuhk,men/ *n* a Turkic language of the area E of the Caspian Sea ☞ LANGUAGE [Per *Turkmēn, Turkmān* Turkoman]

Turkoman /'tuhkəmən/ *n, pl* **Turkomans 1** a member of any of a group of peoples chiefly inhabiting central Asia **2** Turkmen [ML *Turcomannus,* fr Per *Turkmān,* fr *turkmān* resembling a Turk, fr *Turk*]

,Turk's 'head *n* an ornamental turban-shaped knot

turmeric /'tuhmərik/ *n* **1** an E Indian plant of the ginger family **2** the cleaned, boiled, dried, and usu powdered underground stem of the turmeric plant used as a colouring agent or condiment [modif of MF *terre merite* saffron, fr ML *terra merita,* lit., deserving or deserved earth]

turmoil /'tuhmoyl/ *n* an extremely confused or agitated state [origin unknown]

[1]turn /tuhn/ *vt* **1a** to make rotate or revolve ⟨~ *a wheel*⟩ **b(1)** to cause to move through an arc of a circle ⟨~ *a key*⟩ **(2)** to alter the functioning of (as if) by turning a knob ⟨~ *the oven to a higher temperature*⟩ **c** to perform by rotating or revolving ⟨~ *cartwheels*⟩ **2a** to reverse the sides or surfaces of so as to expose another side ⟨~ *the page*⟩: e g **(1)** to dig or plough so as to bring the lower soil to the surface **(2)** to renew (e g a garment) by reversing the material and resewing ⟨~ *a collar*⟩ **b** to throw into disorder or confusion ⟨*everything* ~ed *topsy-turvy*⟩ **c** to disturb the mental balance of; unsettle ⟨*a mind* ~ed *by grief*⟩ – compare TURN SOMEONE'S HEAD **d** to cause to change or reverse direction ⟨~ed *his car in the street*⟩ ⟨~ed *his steps towards home*⟩ **3a** to bend or change the course or outcome of ⟨~ *the tide of history*⟩ **b** to go round or about ⟨~ed *the corner at full speed*⟩ **c** to reach or go beyond (e g an age or time) ⟨*he's just* ~ed *21*⟩ **4a** to direct, present, or point (e g the face) in a specified direction **b** to aim, train ⟨*cannon were* ~ed *on the troops*⟩ **c** to direct, induce, or influence in a specified direction, esp towards or away from sby or sthg ⟨~ed *his thoughts inwards*⟩ ⟨~ed *the boy against his parents*⟩ **d** to apply, devote ⟨~ed *his hand to plumbing*⟩ **e(1)** to drive, send ⟨~ing *hunters off his land*⟩ ⟨~ed *them out of their home*⟩ **(2)** to direct into or out of a receptacle (as if) by inverting ⟨~ *the meat into a pot*⟩ ⟨~ed *the contents of her handbag out*⟩ **5a** to make acid or sour **b** to cause to become by change; transform, convert ⟨*illness* ~ed *his hair white*⟩ ⟨~ *pounds into drachmas*⟩ **6a** to give a rounded form to ⟨~ *the heel of a sock*⟩ ⟨~ing *wood on a lathe*⟩ **b** to fashion elegantly or neatly ⟨*well* ~ed *ankles*⟩

⟨*a knack for* ~ing *a phrase*⟩ 7 to fold, bend ⟨~ *his collar up*⟩ **8** to gain in the course of business – esp in *turn an honest penny* ~ *vi* **1a** to (appear to) move round (as if) on an axis or through an arc of a circle ⟨*I tossed and* ~ed *all night*⟩ **b(1)** to become giddy or dizzy **(2)** *of the stomach* to feel nauseated **c** to centre or hinge on sthg ⟨*the argument* ~s *on this point*⟩ **2a** to direct one's course ⟨*didn't know which way to* ~⟩ **b(1)** to change or reverse direction ⟨*the main road* ~s *sharply to the right*⟩ ⟨*his luck* ~ed⟩ **(2)** to become reversed or inverted **3a** to change position so as to face another way ⟨*they* ~ed *to stare at him*⟩ ⟨*he* ~ed *away and refused to look*⟩ **b** to change one's attitude to one of hostility ⟨*the worm will* ~⟩ ⟨~ed *against his parents*⟩ **c** to make a sudden violent physical or verbal assault – usu + *on* or *upon* ⟨*she* ~ed *on him with ferocity*⟩ **4a** to direct one's attention, efforts, or interests to or away from sby or sthg ⟨~ed *to studying law*⟩ ⟨~ *to chapter 4*⟩ **b** to have recourse; resort ⟨~ed *to a friend for help*⟩ **5a** to become changed, altered, or transformed: e g **(1)** to change colour ⟨*the leaves have* ~ed⟩ **(2)** to become acid or sour ⟨*the milk had* ~ed⟩ **b** to become by change ⟨*water had* ~ed *to ice*⟩ ⟨~ *traitor*⟩ **6** to become folded or bent [ME *turnen*; partly fr OE *tyrnan, turnian* to turn, fr ML *tornare*, fr L, to turn on a lathe, fr *tornus* lathe, fr Gk *tornos*; partly fr OF *torner, tourner* to turn, fr ML *tornare*; akin to L *terere* to rub – more at THROW] – **turnable** *adj* – **turn a blind eye** to refuse to see; be oblivious – **turn a deaf ear** to refuse to listen – **turn a hair** to show any reaction (e g of surprise or alarm) ⟨*did not* turn a hair *when told of the savage murder* – *TLS*⟩ – **turn back the clock** to revert to an earlier or past state or condition – **turn colour** to change colour; *esp* to grow pale or red – **turn in one's grave** to be disturbed at goings-on that would have shocked one when alive – said of a dead person ⟨*Malthus would* turn in his grave *at your opinions*⟩ – **turn King's/Queen's evidence** *Br, of an accomplice* to testify for the prosecution in court – **turn one's back on** to reject, deny ⟨turned his back on *the past*⟩ – **turn one's hand** to apply oneself; SET TO WORK – **turn someone's head** to cause sby to become infatuated or to harbour extravagant notions of conceit ⟨*success had not* turned his head⟩ – **turn someone's stomach 1** to disgust sby completely ⟨*that sort of conduct* turns my stomach⟩ **2** to sicken, nauseate ⟨*the foul smell* turned his stomach⟩ – **turn tail** to run away; flee – **turn the other cheek** to respond to injury or unkindness with patience; forgo retaliation – **turn the scale/scales 1** to register a usu specified weight **2** to prove decisive ⟨*air support might just* turn the scale⟩ – **turn the tables** to bring about a reversal of the relative conditions or fortunes of 2 contending parties – **turn turtle** to capsize, overturn

[2]turn *n* **1a** a turning about a centre or axis; (a) rotation **b** any of various rotating or pivoting movements (in dancing) **2a** a change or reversal of direction, stance, position, or course ⟨*illegal left* ~s⟩ ⟨*an about* ~⟩ **b** a deflection, deviation ⟨*the twists and* ~s *of the story*⟩ **c** the place of a change in direction; a turning **3** a short trip out and back or round about ⟨*took a* ~ *through the park*⟩ **4** an act or deed of a specified kind ⟨*one good* ~ *deserves another*⟩ **5a** a place, time, or opportunity granted in succession or rotation ⟨*waiting his* ~ *in the queue*⟩ **b** a period of duty, action, or activity **c** (the performer who gives) a short act or performance (e g in a variety show) **6** a musical ornament played on the principal note and the notes next above and below ☞ MUSIC **7a** an alteration, change ⟨*an unusual* ~ *of events*⟩ ⟨*a* ~ *for the better*⟩ **b** a point of change in time ⟨*the* ~ *of the century*⟩ **8** a style of expression ⟨*an odd* ~ *of phrase*⟩ **9a** the state or manner of being coiled or twisted **b** a single coil (e g of rope wound round an object) **10** a bent, inclination ⟨*an optimistic* ~ *of mind*⟩ **11a** a spell or attack of illness, faintness, etc **b** a nervous start or shock ⟨*gave me quite a* ~⟩ [ME; partly fr OF *tourn, tour* lathe, circuit, turn (partly fr L *tornus* lathe; partly fr OF *torner, tourner* to turn); partly fr ME *turnen* to turn] – **at every turn** on every occasion; constantly, continually – **by turns** one after another in regular succession – **in turn** in due order of succession; alternately – **on the turn** at the point of turning ⟨*tide is* on the turn⟩ ⟨*milk is* on the turn⟩ – **out of turn 1** not in due order of succession ⟨*play* out of turn⟩ **2** at a wrong time or place ⟨*spoke* out of turn⟩ – **to a turn** to perfection ⟨*roasted* to a turn⟩ – **turn and turn about** BY TURNS

turnabout /ˈtuhnəˌbowt/ *n* a change or reversal of direction, trend, etc

turn away *vt* to refuse admittance or acceptance to

ˈturnˌbuckle /-ˌbukl/ *n* a device that connects and pulls together the ends of a wire, stay, etc to make it taut

ˈturnˌcoat /-ˌkoht/ *n* one who switches to an opposing side or party; a traitor

ˈturnˌdown /-ˌdown/ *adj* worn turned down ⟨~ *collar*⟩

turn down *vt* **1** to reduce the intensity, volume, etc of (as if) by turning a control ⟨turn *the radio* down⟩ **2** to decline to accept; reject

turner /ˈtuhnə/ *n* one who forms articles on a lathe [[1]TURN + [2]-ER] – **turnery** *n*

ˈTurner's ˌsyndrome /ˈtuhnəz/ *n* a genetically determined condition in women that is associated with the presence of only 1 X chromosome and no Y chromosome and that is characterized by a stocky physique with incomplete and infertile sex glands [Henry Hubert *Turner b* 1892 US physician]

turn in *vt* **1** to deliver, hand over; *esp* to deliver up to an authority **2** to give, execute ⟨turned in *a good performance*⟩ ~ *vi* to go to bed – infml

turning /ˈtuhning/ *n* **1** a place of turning, turning off, or turning back, esp on a road ⟨*take the third* ~ *on the right*⟩ **2a** a forming or being formed by use of a lathe **b** *pl* waste produced in turning sthg on a lathe **3** the width of cloth that is folded under for a seam or hem

ˈturning ˌpoint *n* a point at which a significant change occurs

turnip /ˈtuhnip/ *n* (a plant of the mustard family with) a thick white-fleshed root eaten as a vegetable or fed to stock [prob fr [1]*turn* + *neep*; fr the well-rounded root]

turnkey /ˈtuhnˌkee/ *n* a prison warden

ˈturnˌoff /-ˌof/ *n* **1** a turning off **2** a place where one turns off; *esp* a motorway junction

turn off *vt* **1** to stop the flow or operation of (as if) by turning a control ⟨turn *the radio* off⟩ **2** to cause to lose (sexual) interest – infml ~ *vi* to deviate from a straight course or from a main road ⟨turned off *into a side road*⟩

turn on *vt* **1** to cause to flow or operate (as if) by turning a control ⟨turn *the water* on *full*⟩ ⟨turned on *the charm*⟩ **2a** to cause to undergo an intense often visionary experience by taking a drug; *broadly* to cause to get high **b** to excite or interest pleasurably and esp sexually ~ *vi* to become turned on *USE* (*vt 2*) infml – **turn-on** /'--/ *n*

'turn,out /-,owt/ *n* **1** a turning out **2** people in attendance (e g at a meeting) ⟨*a good* ~ *tonight*⟩ **3** manner of dress; getup **4** quantity of produce yielded

turn out *vt* **1** to put (e g a horse) to pasture **2a** to turn inside out **b** to empty the contents of, esp for cleaning **3** to produce often rapidly or regularly (as if) by machine **4** to equip or dress in a specified way ⟨*he was nicely* turned out⟩ **5** to put out (esp a light) by turning a switch **6** to call (e g a guard) out from rest or shelter and into formation ~ *vi* **1** to leave one's home for a meeting, public event, etc ⟨*voters* turned out *in droves*⟩ **2** to prove to be ultimately ⟨*the play* turned out *to be a flop*⟩ **3** to get out of bed – infml

'turn,over /-,ohvə/ *n* **1** a small semicircular filled pastry made by folding half of the crust over the other half **2a** the total sales revenue of a business **b** the ratio of sales to average stock for a stated period **3** (the rate of) movement (e g of goods or people) into, through, and out of a place

turn over *vt* **1** to cause (an internal-combustion engine) to revolve and usu to fire **2** to think over; meditate on **3** to deliver, surrender **4a** to receive and dispose of (a stock of merchandise) **b** to do business to the amount of ⟨turning over *£1000 a week*⟩ ~ *vi* **1** *of an internal combustion engine* to revolve at low speed **2** *of merchandise* to be stocked and disposed of – **turn over a new leaf** to make a change for the better, esp in one's way of living

'turn,pike /-,piek/ *n* **1** *chiefly NAm* a road on which a toll is payable **2** *archaic* a tollgate [ME *turnepike* revolving frame bearing spikes and serving as a barrier, fr *turnen* to turn + *pike*]

'turn,round /-,rownd/ *n* (the time taken for) the arrival, unloading and loading, servicing, and departure of a ship, aircraft, etc

turn round *vt* to complete the processing of or work on ⟨*can* turn round *a batch of 50 inside 2 hours*⟩

turnsole /-,sohl/ *n* any of several plants whose flowers or stems are supposed to turn with the sun; *esp* a heliotrope [ME *turnesole*, fr MF *tournesol*, fr OIt *tornasole*, fr *tornare* to turn (fr ML) + *sole* sun, fr L *sol* – more at [1]SOLAR]

'turn,spit /-,spit/ *n* a small dog formerly used in a treadmill to turn a spit

'turn,stile /-,stiel/ *n* a gate with arms pivoted on the top that turns to admit 1 person at a time

'turn,stone /-,stohn/ *n* any of various migratory wading birds resembling and the related to plovers and sandpipers [fr a habit of turning over stones to find food]

'turn,table /-,taybl/ *n* **1** a circular platform for turning wheeled vehicles, esp railway engines **2** the platform on which a gramophone record is rotated while being played

turn to *vi* to apply oneself to work

'turn-,up *n* **1** *chiefly Br* a turned-up hem, esp on a pair of trousers **2** an unexpected or surprising event – esp in *turn-up for the book*; infml

turn up *vt* **1** to find, discover **2** to increase the intensity, volume, etc of (as if) by turning a control ⟨turn *the sound* up⟩ ~ *vi* **1** to come to light unexpectedly **2** to appear, arrive **3** to happen or occur unexpectedly **4** *of a sailing vessel* TACK 1b – **turn up one's nose** to show scorn or disdain

[1]turpentine /'tuhpən,tien/ *n* **1a** a yellow to brown semifluid oleoresin exuded from the terebinth tree **b** an oleoresin obtained from various conifers **2a** an essential oil obtained from turpentines by distillation and used esp as a solvent and paint thinner **b** WHITE SPIRIT [ME *terbentyne, turpentyne*, fr MF & ML; MF *terbentine, tourbentine*, fr ML *terbentina*, fr L *terebinthina*, fem of *terebinthinus* of terebinth, fr *terebinthus* terebinth, fr Gk *terebinthos*]

[2]turpentine *vt* to apply turpentine to

'turpentine ,tree *n* a terebinth or other tree that yields turpentine

turpitude /'tuhpityoohd/ *n* baseness, depravity ⟨*moral* ~⟩ [MF, fr L *turpitudo*, fr *turpis* vile, base]

turps /tuhps/ *n pl but sing in constr* turpentine [by shortening & alter.]

turquoise /'tuhkwoys, -kwoyz/ *n* **1** a sky blue to greenish mineral consisting of a hydrated copper aluminium phosphate and used as a gem **2** light greenish blue [ME *turkeis, turcas*, fr MF *turquoyse*, fr fem of *turquoys* Turkish, fr OF, fr *Turc* Turk]

turret /'turit/ *n* **1** a little tower, often at the corner of a larger building ☞ CHURCH **2** a rotatable holder (e g for a tool or die) in a lathe, milling machine, etc **3** a usu revolving armoured structure on warships, forts, tanks, aircraft, etc in which guns are mounted [ME *touret*, fr MF *torete, tourete*, fr OF, dim. of *tor, tur* tower – more at TOWER] – **turreted** *adj*

turtle /'tuhtl/ *n* any of several marine reptiles of the same order as and similar to tortoises but adapted for swimming; *broadly, NAm* any of the land, freshwater, and sea reptiles of this order [prob modif of F *tortue*, prob fr (assumed) VL *tartaruca*, fr LL *tartarucha*, fem of *tartaruchus* of Tartarus (the underworld), fr Gk *tartarouchos*, fr *Tartaros* Tartarus; fr an ancient notion that the turtle was an infernal creature]

'turtle,dove /-,duv/ *n* any of several small wild pigeons noted for plaintive cooing [ME *turtle, turtil*, fr OE *turtla*, fr L *turtur*, of imit origin]

'turtle,neck /-,nek/ *n* a high close-fitting neckline, esp of a sweater ☞ GARMENT

turves /tuhvz/ *pl of* TURF

[1]Tuscan /'tuskən/ *n* **1** a native or inhabitant or the Italian language of Tuscany **2** the standard literary dialect of Italian [ME, fr L *tuscanus*, adj, Etruscan, fr *Tusci* Etruscans]

[2]Tuscan *adj* **1** (characteristic) of Tuscany **2** of or being a Roman order of architecture that is a modification of the Greek Doric and is plain in style ☞ ARCHITECTURE

tush /tush/ *interj* – used to express disdain or reproach [ME *tussch*]

tusk /tusk/ *vt or n* (to dig up or gash with) a long greatly enlarged tooth of an elephant, boar, walrus, etc, that projects when the mouth is closed and serves for digging food or as a weapon [n ME, alter. of *tux*, fr OE *tūx*; akin to OE *tūsc* long pointed tooth; vb fr n] – **tusked** *adj*, **tusklike** *adj*

tusker /'tuskə/ *n* an animal with tusks; *esp* a male elephant with 2 large tusks

tussah /'tusə/, **tussore** /'tusaw/ *n* (silk or silk fabric made from a brownish silk filament produced by) any of several oriental silkworms that are larvae of saturniid moths [Hindi *tasar*]

tussive /'tusiv/ *adj* of or involved in coughing – used technically [L *tussis* cough]

[1]**tussle** /'tusl/ *vi* **tussling** /'tusling/ to struggle roughly; scuffle [ME *tussillen*, freq of ME *-tusen, -tousen* to tousle – more at TOUSLE]

[2]**tussle** *n* a (physical) contest or struggle

tussock /'tusək/ *n* a compact tuft of grass, sedge, etc [origin unknown] – **tussocky** *adj*

'**tussock ˌgrass** *n* any of various grasses or sedges that typically grow in tussocks

'**tussock ˌmoth** *n* any of numerous dull-coloured or white moths whose larvae have long tufts or brushes of hair

[1]**tut** /tut; *or clicked* t [ʇ]/, **tut-tut** *interj* – used to express disapproval or impatience [origin unknown]

[2]**tut, ˌtut-'tut** *vi* **-tt-** to express disapproval or impatience by uttering 'tut' or 'tut-tut'

tutelage /'tyoohtilij/ *n* **1** guardianship **2** the state or period of being under a guardian or tutor **3** instruction, esp of an individual [L *tutela* protection, guardian, fr *tutus*, pp of *tueri* to look at, guard]

tutelary /'tyoohtiləri/ *also* **tutelar** /-lə/ *adj* **1** having the guardianship of sby or sthg ⟨*a ~ deity*⟩ **2** of a guardian

[1]**tutor** /'tyoohtə/ *n* **1** a private teacher **2** a British university teacher who **a** gives instruction to students, esp individually **b** is in charge of the social and moral welfare of a group of students **3** *Br* an instruction book [ME, fr MF & L; MF *tuteur*, fr L *tutor*, fr *tutus*, pp of *tueri*] – **tutorship** *n*

[2]**tutor** *vt* to teach or guide usu individually; coach ~ *vi* to do the work of a tutor

[1]**tutorial** /tyooh'tawri·əl/ *adj* of or involving (individual tuition by) a tutor – **tutorially** *adv*

[2]**tutorial** *n* a class conducted by a tutor for 1 student or a small number of students

tutti /'toohti/ *n, adj, or adv* (a passage or section to be) performed by all the performers [It, masc pl of *tutto* all, fr (assumed) VL *tottus*, fr L *totus*]

tutti-frutti /ˌtoohti 'froohti/ *n* (a confection, esp an ice cream, containing) a mixture of chopped, dried, or candied fruits [It *tutti frutti*, lit., all fruits]

tutu /'tooh,tooh/ *n* a very short projecting stiff skirt worn by a ballerina [F, fr (baby talk) *cucu, tutu* backside, alter. of *cul*, fr L *culus*]

tu-whit tu-whoo /tə ˌwit tə 'wooh/ *n* the cry of a (tawny) owl [imit]

tuxedo /tuk'seedoh/ *n, pl* **tuxedos, tuxedoes** *NAm* DINNER JACKET [*Tuxedo* Park, resort in New York]

tuyere, tuyère /'tweeyeə (*Fr* tyijɛːr)/ *n* a nozzle through which a blast of air is delivered to a forge or furnace [F *tuyère*, fr MF, fr *tuyau* pipe]

TV /ˌtee 'vee/ *n* television [*t*ele*v*ision]

twa /twah/, **twae** /twaw/ *n, adj, or pron, Scot* two

twaddle /'twodl/ *vi or n* **twaddling** /'twodl·ing, 'twodling/ (to speak or write) rubbish or drivel [prob alter. of E dial. *twattle* (idle talk), perh alter. of *tattle*] – **twaddler** *n*

twain /twayn/ *n, adj, or pron, archaic* two [ME, fr OE *twēgen* – more at TWO]

[1]**twang** /twang/ *n* **1** a harsh quick ringing sound like that of a plucked bowstring **2** nasal speech or resonance [imit] – **twangy** /'twang·i/ *adj*

[2]**twang** *vi* to speak or sound with a twang ~ *vt* **1** to utter or cause to sound with a twang **2** to pluck the string of

twat /twot/ *n* **1** the female genitals **2** *Br* an unpleasant or despicable person ***USE*** vulg [origin unknown]

twayblade /'tway,blayd/ *n* any of several orchids having a single pair of opposite leaves on the stems [E dial. *tway* (two)]

tweak /tweek/ *vb* to pinch and pull with a sudden jerk and twist [ME *twikken*, fr OE *twiccian* to pluck – more at [1]TWITCH] – **tweak** *n*

twee /twee/ *adj* excessively sentimental, pretty, or coy [prob baby-talk alter. of *sweet*] – **tweeness** *n*

tweed /tweed/ *n* **1** a rough woollen fabric made usu in twill weaves and used esp for suits and coats **2** *pl* tweed clothing; *specif* a tweed suit [alter. of Sc *tweel* twill, fr ME *twyll*]

Tweedledum and Tweedledee /tweedl,dum ən tweedl'dee/ *n* 2 individuals or groups that are practically indistinguishable [*tweedle* (to chirp) + *dum* (imit of a low musical note) & *dee* (imit of a high musical note)]

tweedy /'tweedi/ *adj* **1** of or resembling tweed **2a** given to or associated with wearing tweeds **b** suggesting the outdoors in taste or habits; *esp* brisk and healthy in manner – **tweediness** *n*

tween /tween/ *prep* between – chiefly poetic [ME *twene*, short for *betwene*]

tweet /tweet/ *vi or n* (to) chirp [imit]

tweeter /'tweetə/ *n* a small loudspeaker that responds mainly to the higher frequencies – compare WOOFER

tweezers /'tweezəz/ *n pl, pl* **tweezers** a small metal instrument that is usu held between thumb and forefinger, is used for plucking, holding, or manipulating, and consists of 2 prongs joined at 1 end [obs *tweeze*, n (etui), short for obs *etweese*, fr pl of obs *etwee*, fr F *étui*]

twelfth /twel(f)th/ *n* **1** ☞ NUMBER **2** *often cap, Br the* twelfth of August on which the grouse-shooting season begins [ME *twelfte, twelfthe*, adj & n, fr OE *twelfta*, fr *twelf* twelve + *-ta* -th] – **twelfth** *adj or adv*, **twelfthly** *adj*

ˌtwelfth 'man *n* the reserve member of a cricket team

ˌTwelfth 'Night *n* the eve or evening of Epiphany [fr Epiphany being the 12th day after Christmas]

twelve /twelv/ *n* **1** ☞ NUMBER **2** the twelfth in a set or series **3** sthg having 12 parts or members or a denomination of 12 [ME, fr *twelve*, adj, fr OE *twelf*; akin to OHG *zwelif* twelve; both fr a prehistoric Gmc compound whose first element is represented by OE *twā* two, & whose second by OE *-leofan* (in *endleofan* eleven) – more at TWO, ELEVEN] – **twelve** *adj or pron*, **twelvefold** /-,fohld/ *adj or adv*

'**twelve,month** /-,munth/ *n* a year – archaic or poetic

ˌtwelve-'note *adj* twelve-tone

ˌtwelve-'tone *adj* of or being serial music based on a tone-row

twenty /'twenti/ *n* **1** ☞ NUMBER **2** *pl the* numbers 20 to 29; *specif* a range of temperature, ages, or dates in a century characterized by those numbers **3** sthg (e g a bank note) having a denomination of 20

[ME, fr *twenty*, adj, fr OE *twēntig*, n, group of 20, fr *twēn-* (akin to OE *twā* two) + *-tig* group of 10 – more at TWO, EIGHTY] – **twentieth** /-ith/ *adj or n*, **twenty** *adj or pron*, **twentyfold** /-,fohld/ *adj or adv*

,twenty-'one *n* **1** ☞ NUMBER **2** pontoon [(2) trans of F *vingt-et-un*] – **twenty-one** *adj or pron*

20/20 /,twenti 'twenti/ *adj, of a person's vision* normal [fr the assessment of normal vision as the ability to read characters at a distance of 20ft]

,twenty-'two *n* **1** ☞ NUMBER **2** either of 2 lines across a rugby pitch 22m from each goal; *also* the area between such a line and a goal line – **twenty-two** *adj or pron*

twerp *also* **twirp** /twuhp/ *n* a silly, insignificant, or contemptible person – infml [origin unknown]

Twi /ch'wee, twee, chee/ *n* a dialect of Akan; *also* a literary language based on this

twi- /twie-/ *prefix, archaic* two; double; doubly; twice ⟨twi- *headed*⟩ ⟨twi*bill*⟩ [ME, fr OE; akin to OHG *zwi-* twi-, L *bi-*, Gk *di-*, OE *twā* two]

twice /twies/ *adv* **1** on 2 occasions ⟨~ *a week*⟩ **2** two times;in doubled quantity or degree ⟨~ *2 is 4*⟩ ⟨~ *as much*⟩ [ME *twiges, twies*, fr OE *twiga*; akin to OE *twi-*]

,twice-'laid *adj, of a rope* made from strands of used rope

,twice-'told *adj* familiar, well-known – chiefly in *a twice-told tale*

[1]twiddle /'twidl/ *vb* **twiddling** /'twidling, 'twidl·ing/ *vi* to play negligently with sthg ~ *vt* to rotate lightly or idly ⟨~d *the knob on the radio*⟩ [prob imit]

[2]twiddle *n* a turn, twist

[1]twig /twig/ *n* a small woody shoot or branch, usu without its leaves [ME *twigge*, fr OE; akin to OHG *zwīg* twig, OE *twā* two] – **twigged** *adj*, **twiggy** *adj*

[2]twig *vb* **-gg-** to catch on (to); understand – infml [perh fr ScGael *twig* I understand]

twilight /'twie,liet/ *n* **1a** the light from the sky between full night and sunrise or esp between sunset and full night **b** the period between sunset and full night **2a** a shadowy indeterminate state **b** a period or state of decline ⟨*elderly ladies in their* ~ *years*⟩ [ME, fr *twi-* + *light*]

twilight sleep *n* a drug-induced state in which awareness and memory of pain is dulled or removed

'twilight ,zone *n* a decaying urban area

twilit /'twie,lit/ *adj* **1** lighted (as if) by twilight **2** shadowy, obscure [*twi*light + *lit*]

twill /twil/ *n* (a fabric with) a textile weave in which the weft threads pass over 1 and under 2 or more warp threads to give an appearance of diagonal lines – compare DOUBLE TWILL [ME *twyll*, fr OE *twilic* having a double thread, modif of L *bilic-, bilix*, fr *bi-* + *licium* thread] – **twilled** *adj*

[1]twin /twin/ *adj* **1** born with one other or as a pair at 1 birth ⟨~ *brother*⟩ ⟨~ *girls*⟩ **2a** having or made up of 2 similar, related, or identical units or parts **b** being one of a pair, esp of officially associated towns [ME, fr OE *twinn* twofold, two by two; akin to ON *tvinnr* two by two, OE *twā* two]

[2]twin *n* **1** either of 2 offspring produced at 1 birth **2** either of 2 people or things closely related to or resembling each other **3 twin, 'twin ,crystal** a compound crystal composed of 2 or more (parts of) related crystals grown together in an oriented manner – **twinship** *n*

[3]twin *vb* **-nn-** *vt* **1** to bring together in close association **2** to form into a twin crystal ~ *vi* **1** to become paired or closely associated **2** to give birth to twins **3** to grow as a twin crystal

,twin 'bed *n* either of 2 matching single beds

[1]twine /twien/ *n* **1** a strong string of 2 or more strands twisted together **2** a coil, twist **3** an act of twining or interlacing [ME *twin*, fr OE *twīn*; akin to MD *twijn* twine, OE *twā* two]

[2]twine *vt* **1a** to twist together **b** to form by twisting; weave **2** to twist or coil round sthg ~ *vi* to coil round a support – **twiner** *n*

'twin,flower /-,flowə/ *n, NAm* a low-growing shrub of the honeysuckle family with opposite leaves and pairs of fragrant usu pink flowers

twinge /twinj/ *vi or n* **twinging, twingeing** (to feel) **1** a sudden sharp stab of pain **2** an emotional pang ⟨*a* ~ *of conscience*⟩ [vb ME *twengen* to tweak, squeeze, fr OE *twengan*; n fr vb]

[1]twinkle /'twingkl/ *vb* **twinkling** /'twingkling, 'twingkl·ing/ *vi* **1** to shine with a flickering or sparkling light **2** to appear bright with gaiety or amusement ⟨*his eyes* ~d⟩ ~ *vt* to cause to shine (as if) with a flickering light [ME *twinklen*, fr OE *twinclian*; akin to MHG *zwinken* to blink] – **twinkler** *n*

[2]twinkle *n* **1** an instant, twinkling **2** an (intermittent) sparkle or gleam – **twinkly** /'twingkli/ *adj*

twinkling /'twingkling/ *n* a very short time; a moment

'twin ,set *n* a jumper and cardigan designed to be worn together, usu by a woman

[1]twirl /twuhl/ *vi* to revolve rapidly ~ *vt* **1** to cause to rotate rapidly; spin **2** TWINE 2 [perh of Scand origin; akin to Norw dial. *tvirla* to twirl; akin to OHG *dweran* to stir – more at TURBID]

[2]twirl *n* **1** an act of twirling **2** a coil, whorl – **twirly** *adj*

twirp /twuhp/ *n* a twerp

[1]twist /twist/ *vt* **1a** to join together by winding; *also* to mingle by interlacing **b** to make by twisting strands together **2** to wind or coil round sthg **3a** to wring or wrench so as to dislocate or distort ⟨~ed *my ankle*⟩ **b** to distort the meaning of; pervert **c** to contort ⟨~ed *his face into a grin*⟩ **d** to pull off, turn, or break by a turning force **e** to cause to move with a rotating motion **f** to form into a spiral **g** WARP 1b ⟨*a* ~ed *mind*⟩ ~ *vi* **1** to follow a winding course; snake **2a** to turn or change shape by a turning force **b** to take on a spiral shape **c** to dance the twist **3** *of a ball* to rotate while following a curving path **4** TURN 3a ⟨~ed *round to see behind him*⟩ [ME *twisten*, fr OE *-twist* rope; akin to MD *twist* quarrel, twine, OE *twā* two] – **twist someone's arm** to bring strong pressure to bear on sby ⟨*he decided to come with us, but we had to* twist his arm *a bit first*⟩

[2]twist *n* **1** sthg formed by twisting: e g **a** a thread, yarn, or cord formed by twisting 2 or more strands together **b** tobacco twisted into a thick roll **c** a screw of paper used as a container **d** a curled strip of citrus peel used to flavour a drink ⟨ *gin, ice, bitters and a* ~ *of lemon*⟩ **2a** a twisting or being twisted **b** a dance popular esp in the 1960s and performed with gyrations, esp of the hips **c** a spiral turn or curve **3a** torsional strain **b** the angle through or amount by which a thing is twisted **4a** a turning off a straight course; a bend **b** a (personal) eccentricity or idiosyncrasy **c** a distortion of meaning or sense **5** an unexpected turn or development ⟨*a strange* ~ *of fate*⟩ **6** a dive in which the diver twists the body sideways for 1 or more half or full turns before entering the water – **twisty** *adj*

'twist ,drill *n* a drill bit having deep spiral grooves extending from the cutting edges to the smooth portion of the shank

twister /'twistə/ *n* **1** *NAm* a tornado, waterspout, etc in which the rotatory ascending movement of a column of air is very apparent **2** a dishonest person; a swindler – infml [[1]TWIST + [2]-ER]

[1]**twit** /twit/ *vt* **-tt-** to tease, taunt [ME *atwiten* to reproach, fr OE *ætwītan*, fr *æt* at + *wītan* to reproach; akin to OHG *wīzan* to punish, OE *witan* to know]

[2]**twit** *n, Br* an absurd or silly person [prob alter. of *twat*]

[1]**twitch** /twich/ *vt* to move or pull with a sudden motion ~ *vi* **1** to pull, pluck ⟨~ed *at my sleeve*⟩ **2** to move jerkily or involuntarily [ME *twicchen*; akin to OE *twiccian* to pluck, OHG *gizwickan* to pinch] – **twitcher** *n*

[2]**twitch** *n* **1** a short sudden pull or jerk **2** a physical or mental pang **3** a loop of rope or a strap that is tightened over a horse's upper lip as a restraining device **4** (the recurrence of) a short spasmodic contraction or jerk; a tic – **twitchily** *adv*, **twitchy** *adj*

[3]**twitch** *n* COUCH GRASS [alter. of *quitch*]

twite /twiet/ *n* a finch of N Europe that resembles the linnet [imit]

[1]**twitter** /'twitə/ *vi* **1** to utter twitters **2** to talk in a nervous chattering fashion **3** to tremble with agitation; flutter ~ *vt* to utter (as if) in twitters [ME *twiteren*; akin to OHG *zwizzirōn* to twitter]

[2]**twitter** *n* **1** a nervous agitation – esp in *all of a twitter* **2** a small tremulous intermittent sound characteristic of birds – **twittery** *adj*

twixt /twikst/ *prep* between – chiefly poetic [ME *twix*, short for *betwix, betwixt*]

[1]**two** /tooh/ *pron, pl in constr* **1** two unspecified countable individuals ⟨*only* ~ *were found*⟩ **2** a small approximate number of indicated things ⟨*only a shot or* ~ *were fired*⟩ [ME *twa* (adj) two, fr OE *twā* (fem & neut); akin to OE *twēgen* two (masc), *tū* (neut), OHG *zwēne*, L *duo*, Gk *dyo*]

[2]**two** *n, pl* **twos** **1** ☞ NUMBER **2** the second in a set or series ⟨*the* ~ *of spades*⟩ **3** sthg having 2 parts or members or a denomination of 2 – **two** *adj*, **twofold** *adj or adv*

,two-'bit *adj, NAm* petty, small-time [[3]*bit* 1b(2)]

,two-di'mensional *adj* **1** having 2 dimensions **2** lacking depth of characterization

,two-'edged *adj* double-edged

,two-'faced *adj* double-dealing, hypocritical – **two-facedness** /'faystnis/ *n*

2,4,5-T *n* a compound used as a defoliant, esp in brush and weed control, that is thought to cause genetic defects [*2,4,5* (fr the substitution of chlorine atoms in positions 2,4,5 in phenoxyacetic acid) *t*richlorophenoxy acetic acid]

,two-'handed *adj* **1** used with both hands ⟨*a* ~ *sword*⟩ **2** requiring 2 people ⟨*a* ~ *saw*⟩ **3** ambidextrous

,two-line 'whip *n* an instruction from a party to its Members of Parliament that they should attend a debate and vote in the specified way – compare FREE VOTE, THREE-LINE WHIP [fr the double underlining of some words in the written instruction]

,two-'party *adj* characterized by 2 major political parties of comparable strength

twopence *also* **tuppence** /'tup(ə)ns/ *n* (a coin worth) 2 pence

twopenny *also* **tuppenny** /'tup(ə)ni/ *adj* costing or worth twopence

twopenny-halfpenny /,tup(ə)ni 'haypni/ *adj, chiefly Br* of little value or importance

'two-,piece *n or adj* (a suit of clothes, swimming costume, etc) consisting of 2 matching pieces

two-ply /,-'-, '-,-/ *adj* consisting of 2 strands, layers, or thicknesses ⟨~ *wool*⟩

twosome /'toohs(ə)m/ *n* **1** a group of 2 people or things **2** a golf single

'two-,step *n* (a piece of music for) a ballroom dance in either $\frac{2}{4}$ or $\frac{4}{4}$ time

'two-,stroke *adj or n* (of, being, or powered by) an internal-combustion engine with a cycle of 2 strokes comprising 1 up-and-down movement of a piston

,two-'time *vb* to be unfaithful to (a spouse or lover) by having a secret relationship with another – **two-timer** *n*

'two-,tone *adj* **1** *also* **two-toned** having 2 colours or shades **2** of or being popular music played by groups consisting of black, esp W Indian, and white musicians and including elements of reggae and new wave – **two-tone** *n*

.22 /,tooh 'tooh; *also* ,poynt ,tooh 'tooh/ *n* a small-bore rifle with a calibre of 0.22in (5.6mm)

,two-'up *n* a game in which players bet on the fall of tossed coins

,two-'way *adj* **1** moving or allowing movement or use in 2 (opposite) directions ⟨*a* ~ *road*⟩ ⟨~ *traffic*⟩ **2a** *of a radio, telephone, etc* designed for both sending and receiving messages **b** involving mutual responsibility or a reciprocal relationship **3** involving 2 participants **4** usable in either of 2 ways

,two-way 'mirror *n* a piece of glass that reflects an image from one side and can be seen through from the other

,two-way 'switch *n* either of 2 electrical switches (e g at the top and bottom of a stairway) controlling a single device, esp a light

,two-winged 'fly *n* any of a large order of insects including the housefly, mosquito, and gnat with functional front wings and greatly reduced rear wings used to control balance

[1]**-ty** /-ti/ *suffix* (→ *n*) – used in forming numbers of (so many) times 10 ⟨*twenty*⟩ ⟨*fifty*⟩ [ME, fr OE *-tig* group of 10; akin to OE *tīen* ten]

[2]**-ty** *suffix* (→ *n*) quality or condition of ⟨*puberty*⟩ ⟨*cruelty*⟩ [ME *-te*, fr OF *-té*, fr L *-tat-, -tas* – more at -ITY]

tycoon /tie'koohn/ *n* a businessman of exceptional wealth and power [Jap *taikun* shogun, fr Chin (Pek) *ta*[4] great + *chün*[1] ruler] – **tycoonery** /-nəri/ *n*

tying /'tie·ing/ *pres part of* TIE

tyke, tike /tiek/ *n* **1** a (mongrel) dog **2** *chiefly Br* a boorish churlish person **3** a small child **4** a native of Yorkshire *USE* (*3&4*) infml [ME *tyke* dog, cur, churl, fr ON *tīk* bitch]

tymbal /'timbl/ *n* the vibrating membrane in the shrilling organ of a cicada [alter. of *timbal* (kettledrum), fr F *timbale* – more at TIMBALE]

tympanic bone /tim'panik/ *n* a bone enclosing part of the middle ear and supporting the tympanic membrane

tympanic membrane *n* a thin membrane separating the outer ear from the middle ear that functions in the mechanical reception of sound waves and in their transmission to the site of sensory reception; the eardrum

tympanites /ˌtimpəˈnieteez/ *n* a distension of the abdomen caused by accumulation of gas in the intestinal tract or peritoneal cavity [ME, fr LL, fr Gk *tympanitēs*, fr *tympanon*] – **tympanitic** /-ˈnitik/ *adj*

tympanum /ˈtimpənəm/ *n, pl* **tympana** /-nə/, **tympanums 1a(1)** TYMPANIC MEMBRANE ☞ NERVE **(2)** MIDDLE EAR **b** a thin tense membrane covering the hearing-organ of an insect **2a** the recessed triangular face of a pediment **b** the space within an arch and above a lintel (e g in a medieval doorway) [ML & L; ML, eardrum, fr L, drum, architectural panel, fr Gk *tympanon* drum, kettledrum; akin to Gk *typtein* to beat] – **tympanic** /timˈpanik/ *adj*

Tynwald /ˈtinwəld, ˈtien-/ *n* the Manx Parliament [ON *thingvöllr* location of parliamentary meetings, fr *thing* assembly, parliament + *völlr* field]

[1]**type** /tiep/ *n* **1a** a person or thing (e g in the Old Testament) regarded as foreshadowing another (e g in the New Testament) **b** a model, exemplar, or characteristic specimen (possessing the distinguishable or essential qualities of a class) **c** a lower taxonomic category selected as reference for a higher category ⟨*a ~ genus*⟩ **2a** (any of) a collection of usu rectangular blocks or characters bearing a relief from which an inked print can be made **b** a typeface ⟨*italic ~*⟩ **c** printed letters **3a** a set of qualities common to a number of individuals that distinguish them as an identifiable class (e g the form common to all instances of a linguistic expression **b(1)** a member of a specified class or variety of people ⟨*sporting ~*s⟩ **(2)** a person of a specified nature ⟨*he's a peculiar ~*⟩ **c** a particular kind, class, or group with distinct characteristics **d** sthg distinguishable as a variety; a sort [LL *typus*, fr L & Gk; L *typus* image, fr Gk *typos* blow, impression, model, fr *typtein* to strike, beat; akin to L *stuprum* defilement] – **typal** *adj*

[2]**type** *vt* **1** to represent beforehand as a type; prefigure **2** to represent in terms of typical characteristics; typify **3** to write with a typewriter; *also* to keyboard **4a** to identify as belonging to a type **b** to determine the natural type of (e g a blood sample) ~ *vi* to use a typewriter

-type *comb form* (*n* → *adj*) of (such) a type; resembling ⟨*Cheddar-*type *cheese*⟩

ˈtypeˌcast /-ˌkahst/ *vt* **typecast** to cast (an actor) repeatedly in the same type of role; *broadly* to stereotype

ˈtypeˌface /-ˌfays/ *n* (the appearance of) a single design of printing type

ˈtypeˌfounder /-ˌfowndə/ *n* one engaged in the design and production of metal printing type for hand composition – **typefounding** *n*, **typefoundry** *n*

ˈtype ˌmetal *n* an alloy of lead, antimony, and tin, used in making printing type

ˈtypeˌscript /-ˌskript/ *n* a typewritten manuscript (e g for use as printer's copy) [*type* + manu*script*]

ˈtypeˌset /-ˌset/ *vt* **-tt-; typeset** to set in type; compose – **typesetter** *n*, **typesetting** *n*

ˈtypeˌwrite /-ˌriet/ *vb* **typewrote** /-ˌroht/; **typewritten** /-ˌritn/ to write with a typewriter [back-formation fr *typewriter*]

ˈtypeˌwriter /-ˌrietə/ *n* a machine with a keyboard for writing in characters resembling type

[1]**typhoid** /ˈtiefoyd/ *adj* **1** (suggestive) of typhus **2** of or being typhoid [NL *typhus*; (2) [2]*typhoid*]

[2]**typhoid, typhoid fever** *n* a serious communicable human disease caused by a bacterium and marked esp by fever, diarrhoea, headache, and intestinal inflammation

typhoon /tieˈfoohn/ *n* a tropical cyclone occurring in the Philippines or the China sea [alter. (influenced by Chin (Cant) *taaî fung* typhoon, fr *taaî* great + *fung* wind) of earlier *touffon*, fr Ar *ṭūfān* hurricane, fr Gk *typhōn* whirlwind; akin to Gk *typhein* to smoke]

typhus /ˈtiefəs/ *n* a serious human disease marked by high fever, stupor alternating with delirium, intense headache, and a dark red rash, caused by a rickettsia, and transmitted esp by body lice [NL, fr Gk *typhos* fever; akin to Gk *typhein* to smoke – more at DEAF]

typical /ˈtipikl/ *adj* **1** *also* **typic** being or having the nature of a type; symbolic, representative **2a** having or showing the essential characteristics of a type ⟨*~ suburban houses*⟩ **b** showing or according with the usual or expected (unfavourable) traits ⟨*just ~ of him to get so annoyed*⟩ – **typically** *adv*, **typicalness, typicality** /-ˈkaləti/ *n*

typify /ˈtipifie/ *vt* **1a** to represent in symbolic fashion (e g by an image or model) **b** to constitute a typical instance of **2** to embody the essential characteristics of – **typification** /-fiˈkaysh(ə)n/ *n*

typist /ˈtiepist/ *n* one who uses a typewriter, esp as an occupation

typo /ˈtiepoh/ *n, pl* **typos** a printing error – infml [short for *typographical* (*error*)]

typographer /tieˈpografə/ *n* **1** a compositor **2** a specialist in the design, choice, and arrangement of typographical matter

typography /tieˈpografi/ *n* the style, arrangement, or appearance of typeset matter [ML *typographia*, fr Gk *typos* impression, cast + *-graphia* -graphy – more at TYPE] – **typographic** /-pəˈgrafik/, **typographical** *adj*, **typographically** *adv*

typology /tieˈpoləji/ *n* the doctrine, study, or analysis and classification of (theological) types – **typologist** *n*, **typological** /-pəˈlojikl/ *adj*

tyramine /ˈtierəmin, ˈti-/ *n* an amine derived from tyrosine that has an action on the sympathetic nervous system similar to that of adrenalin [ISV *tyr*osine + *amine*]

tyrannical /tiˈranikl/ *also* **tyrannic** *adj* characteristic of a tyrant or tyranny; oppressive, despotic [L *tyrannicus*, fr Gk *tyrannikos*, fr *tyrannos* tyrant] – **tyrannically** *adv*

tyrannicide /tiˈranisied/ *n* the killing or killer of a tyrant [F, fr L *tyrannicida* & *tyrannicidium*, fr *tyrannus* + *-i-* + *-cida* & *-cidium* – more at -CIDE]

tyrann·ize, -ise /ˈtiraniez/ *vb* to exercise power (over) with unjust and oppressive cruelty

tyrannosaur /tiˈranəˌsaw/, **tyrannosaurus** /tiˌranəˈsawrəs/ *n* a very large flesh-eating dinosaur of the Cretaceous period having small forelegs and walking on its hind legs [NL *Tyrannosaurus*, genus name, deriv of Gk *tyrannos* tyrant + *sauros* lizard – more at SAURIAN]

tyranny /ˈtirəni/ *n* **1** a government in which absolute power is vested in a single ruler **2** oppressive power (exerted by a tyrant) **3** sthg severe, oppressive, or inexorable in effect [ME *tyrannie*, fr MF, fr ML *tyrannia*, fr L *tyrannus* tyrant] – **tyrannous** *adj*

tyrant /'tie(ə)rənt/ *n* **1** a ruler who exercises absolute power, esp oppressively or brutally **2** one who exercises authority harshly or unjustly [ME *tirant*, fr OF *tyran, tyrant*, fr L *tyrannus*, fr Gk *tyrannos*]

,tyrant 'flycatcher *n* any of various large American flycatchers

tyre, *NAm chiefly* **tire** /tie·ə/ *n* a continuous solid or inflated hollow rubber cushion set round a wheel to absorb shock ☞ CAR [ME *tire* metal hoop forming the tread of a wheel, prob fr [2]*tire*]

,Tyrian 'purple /'tiri·ən/ *n* a crimson or purple dye related to indigo, obtained by the ancient Greeks and Romans from gastropod molluscs, and now made synthetically [*Tyre*, maritime city in ancient Phoenicia]

tyro, tiro /'tie·əroh/ *n, pl* **tyros, tiros** a beginner, novice [ML, fr L *tiro* young soldier, novice]

Tyrolean /ti'rohli·ən, ,tirə'lee·ən/ *adj* of the Tyrol [*Tyrol, Tirol*, region of Europe in the Alps]

tyrosine /'tierəseen, 'ti-, -sin/ *n* an amino acid that occurs in most proteins and is the parent compound from which adrenalin and melanin are formed [ISV, irreg fr Gk *tyros* cheese]

tzaddik /'tsahdik/ *n, pl* **tzaddikim** /-kim/ a zaddik

tzar /zah/ *n* a tsar

tzigane /(t)si'gahn/ *n* a (Hungarian) gipsy [F, fr Hung *cigány*]

U

u /yooh/ *n, pl* **u's, us** *often cap* (a graphic representation of or device for reproducing) the 21st letter of the English alphabet

1U *adj, chiefly Br* upper-class [*u*pper-class]

2U *n or adj* (a film that is) certified in Britain as suitable for all age groups [*u*niversal]

ubiety /yooh'bie·əti/ *n* the state of being in a definite place [L *ubi* where + E *-ety* (as in *society*)]

ubiquitous /yooh'bikwitəs/ *adj* existing or being everywhere at the same time; omnipresent [*ubiquity* fr L *ubique* everywhere, fr *ubi* where + *-que*, enclitic generalizing particle; akin to L *quis* who – more at WHO] – **ubiquitously** *adv*, **ubiquitousness, ubiquity** *n*

'U-,boat *n* a German submarine [trans of G *u-boot*, short for *unterseeboot*, fr *unter* under + *see* sea + *boot* boat]

udder /'udə/ *n* a large pendulous organ consisting of 2 or more mammary glands enclosed in a common envelope and each having a single nipple [ME, fr OE *ūder*; akin to OHG *ūtar* udder, L *uber*, Gk *outhar*, Skt *ūdhar*]

UFO /'yoohfoh, ,yooh ef 'oh/ *n, pl* **UFO's, UFOs** an unidentified flying object; *esp* FLYING SAUCER [*u*nidentified *f*lying *o*bject]

ugh /ookh, uh/ *interj* – used to express disgust or horror

ugli /'ugli/, **'ugli ,fruit** *n* a large citrus fruit that is a cross between a grapefruit and a tangerine [prob alter. of *ugly*; fr its unattractive wrinkled skin]

ugly /'ugli/ *adj* **1** frightful, horrible ⟨*an ~ wound*⟩ **2** offensive or displeasing to any of the senses, esp to the sight **3** morally offensive or objectionable **4a** ominous, threatening ⟨*an ~ customer*⟩ ⟨*~ weather*⟩ **b** surly, quarrelsome ⟨*an ~ disposition*⟩ [ME, fr ON *uggligr*, fr *uggr* fear; akin to ON *ugga* to fear] – **uglily** *adv*, **ugliness** *n*, **uglify** /-,fie/ *vt*

,ugly 'duckling *n* sby who or sthg that appears unpromising but turns out successful [*The Ugly Duckling*, story by Hans Christian Andersen †1875 Dan writer, in which an ugly 'duckling' grows into a beautiful swan]

Ugrian /'yoohgri·ən, 'ooh-/ *n or adj* (a member) of the E division of the Finno-Ugric peoples [ORuss *Ugre* Hungarians]

Ugric /'yoohgrik, 'ooh-/ *adj* of the languages of the Ugrians

uh-huh /u 'hu/ *interj* – used to indicate affirmation or agreement

uhlan /'oohlahn, 'yoohlən/ *n* any of a body of Prussian light cavalry orig modelled on Tartar lancers [G, fr Pol *ulan*, fr Turk *oğlan* boy, servant]

Uitlander /'ayt,landə, owt-/ *n, SAfr* a foreigner; *esp* a British resident in the former republics of the Transvaal and Orange Free State [Afrik]

ukase /yooh'kayz/ *n* **1** a proclamation by a Russian emperor or government having the force of law **2** an edict [F & Russ; F, fr Russ *ukaz*, fr *ukazat'* to show, order; akin to OSlav *u-* away, L *au-*, Skt *ava-* & to OSlav *kazati* to show]

Ukrainian /yooh'kraynyən, -ni·ən/ *n* **1** a native or inhabitant of the Ukraine **2** the Slavonic language of the Ukrainians ☞ LANGUAGE [*Ukraine*, region of E Europe, now part of the USSR] – **Ukrainian** *adj*

ukulele /,yoohkə'layli/ *n* a small usu 4-stringed guitar of Portuguese origin [Hawaiian *'ukulele*, fr *'uku* small person, flea + *lele* jumping]

ulama /'oohləmah/ *n sing or pl in constr* the body of theologians and scholars who form the highest religious authority in Islam [Ar, Turk, & Per; Turk & Per *'ulemā*, fr Ar *'ulamā*]

-ular /-yoolə/ *suffix* (→ *adj*) of, relating to, or resembling ⟨*angu*lar⟩ [L *-ularis*, fr *-ulus, -ula, -ulum* -ule + *-aris* -ar]

ulcer /'ulsə/ *n* **1** a persistent open sore in skin or mucous membrane that often discharges pus **2** sthg that festers and corrupts [ME, fr L *ulcer-, ulcus*; akin to Gk *helkos* wound] – **ulcerous** *adj*

ulcerate /'ulsə,rayt/ *vb* to (cause to) become affected (as if) with an ulcer – **ulcerative** *adj*, **ulceration** /-'raysh(ə)n/ *n*

-ule /-yoohl, -yool/ *suffix* (→ *n*) a small kind of ⟨*gran*ule⟩ [F & L; F, fr L *-ulus, -ula, -ulum*, masc, fem, & neut dim. suffixes]

-ulent /-yoolənt/ *suffix* (→ *adj*) full of (a specified thing) ⟨*succ*ulent⟩ ⟨*corp*ulent⟩ [L *-ulentus*]

ullage /'ulij/ *n* the amount by which a container (e g a tank or bottle) is less than full [ME *ulage*, fr MF *eullage* act of filling a cask, fr *eullier* to fill a cask, fr OF *ouil* eye, bunghole, fr L *oculus* eye]

ulna /'ulnə/ *n* the bone of the human forearm on the little-finger side; *also* a corresponding part of the forelimb of vertebrates above fishes ☞ ANATOMY [NL, fr L, elbow] – **ulnar** *adj*

ulotrichous /yooh'lotrikəs/ *adj* having woolly or crisp hair [deriv of Gk *oulotrich-, oulothrix*, fr *oulos* curly (akin to Gk *eilyein* to roll) + *trich-, thrix* hair – more at VOLUBLE, TRICH-] – **ulotrichy** *n*

ulster /'ulstə/ *n* a long loose overcoat made of heavy material [*Ulster*, ancient kingdom & former province of Ireland (name now used also for its 2 divisions: **a** Northern Ireland **b** a province of Eire)]

'Ulsterman /-mən/, *fem* **'Ulster,woman** *n* a native or inhabitant of Ulster

ulterior /ul'tiəri·ə/ *adj* going beyond what is openly said or shown; intentionally concealed ⟨*~ motives*⟩ [L, farther, further, compar of (assumed) L *ulter* situated beyond, fr *uls* beyond; akin to L *ollus, ille* that one, OIr ind*oll* beyond] – **ulteriorly** *adv*

ultima /'ultimə/ *n* the last syllable of a word [L, fem of *ultimus* last]

1ultimate /'ultimət/ *adj* **1a** last in a progression or series ⟨*their ~ destination was Paris*⟩ **b** eventual **2a** fundamental, basic ⟨*~ reality*⟩ **b** incapable of further analysis, division, or separation **3** maximum, greatest ⟨*the ~ sacrifice*⟩ [ML *ultimatus* last, final, fr LL, pp of *ultimare* to come to an end, be last, fr L *ultimus* farthest, last, final, superl of (assumed) L *ulter* situated beyond] – **ultimateness** *n*

[2]**ultimate** *n* sthg ultimate; *the* highest point ⟨*the ~ in stupidity*⟩

'ultimately /-li/ *adv* finally; AT LAST

ultimatum /,ulti'maytəm/ *n, pl* **ultimatums, ultimata** /-tə/ a final proposition or demand; *esp* one whose rejection will end negotiations and cause a resort to direct action [NL, fr ML, neut of *ultimatus* final]

ultimo /'ultimoh/ *adj* of or occurring in the previous month – compare PROXIMO [L *ultimo mense* in the last month]

ultra /'ultrə/ *adj* going beyond others or beyond due limit [*ultra-*]

ultra- /,ultrə-/ *prefix* **1** beyond in space; on the other side of; trans- ⟨ultra*montane*⟩ ⟨ultra*planetary*⟩ **2** beyond the range or limits of; super- ⟨ultra*microscopic*⟩ ⟨ultra*sound*⟩ **3** excessively; extremely ⟨ultra *modern*⟩ ⟨ultra*conservative*⟩ [L, fr *ultra* beyond, adv & prep, fr (assumed) L *ulter* situated beyond]

ultracentrifuge /,ultrə'sentri,fyoohj, -,fyoohzh/ *n* a high-speed centrifuge able to sediment colloidal or other small particles – **ultracentrifugal** /-,sentri'fyoohg(ə)l, -sen'trifyoog(ə)l/ *adj*

ultrahigh frequency /,ultrə'hie/ *n* a radio frequency in the range between 300 megahertz and 3000 megahertz

ultraism /'ultrə,iz(ə)m/ *n* the advocacy of extreme measures – **ultraist** *adj or n,* **ultraistic** /-'istik/ *adj*

[1]**ultramarine** /,ultrəmə'reen/ *n* **1** a deep blue pigment **2** vivid deep blue [ML *ultramarinus* coming from beyond the sea]

[2]**ultramarine** *adj* situated across the sea [ML *ultramarinus,* fr L *ultra-* + *mare* sea – more at MARINE]

,ultra'microscope /-'miekrə,skohp/ *n* an apparatus for making visible by scattered light particles too small to be perceived by the ordinary microscope [back-formation fr *ultramicroscopic*]

,ultra,micro'scopic /-,miekrə'skopik/ *adj* **1** too small to be seen with an ordinary microscope **2** of an ultramicroscope [ISV] – **ultramicroscopically** *adv*

,ultramon'tane /-mon'tayn/ *adj* **1** of countries or peoples beyond the Alps or other mountains **2** favouring greater or absolute supremacy of papal over national or diocesan authority in the Roman Catholic church [ML *ultramontanus,* fr L *ultra-* + *mont-, mons* mountain – more at [1]MOUNT] – **ultramontane** *n, often cap,* **ultramontanism** /-'mon təniz(ə)m/ *n*

[1]**,ultra'sonic** /-'sonik/ *adj* supersonic: **a** *of waves and vibrations* having a frequency above about 20,000Hz **b** using, produced by, or relating to ultrasonic waves or vibrations ⟨*an ~ dog whistle*⟩ – **ultrasonically** *adv*

[2]**ultrasonic** *n* an ultrasonic wave or frequency

'ultra,sound /-,sownd/ *n* ultrasonic sound vibrations

'ultra,structure /-,strukchə/ *n* FINE STRUCTURE

[1]**,ultra'violet** /-'vie·ələt/ *n* electromagnetic radiation having a wavelength between the violet end of the visible spectrum and X rays ☞ PHYSICS

[2]**ultraviolet** *adj* relating to, producing, or employing ultraviolet ⟨*an ~ lamp*⟩

,ultra 'vires /'vie(ə)reez/ *adv or adj* beyond legal power or authority [NL, lit., beyond power]

ululate /'yoohyoo,layt/ *vi* to howl, wail [L *ululatus,* pp of *ululare,* of imit origin] – **ululant** *adj,* **ululation** /-'laysh(ə)n/ *n*

umbel /'umb(ə)l/ *n* an inflorescence typical of plants of the carrot family in which the axis is very much contracted so that the flower stalks spring from the same point to form a flat or rounded flower cluster ☞ PLANT [NL *umbella,* fr L, dim. of *umbra*] – **umbelled** *adj,* **umbellate** /'umbəlayt, um'belət/ *adj*

umbellifer /um'belifə/ *n* a plant of the carrot family [NL *Umbelliferae,* group name, fr fem pl of *umbellifer* bearing umbels] – **umbelliferous** /,umbə'lifərəs/ *adj*

[1]**umber** /'umbə/ *n* **1** a brown earth used as a pigment – compare BURNT UMBER, RAW UMBER **2** dark or yellowish brown [prob fr obs *umber* (shade, colour), fr ME *umbre* shade, shadow, fr MF, fr L *umbra* – more at UMBRAGE]

[2]**umber** *adj* of the colour of umber

[3]**umber** *vt* to darken (as if) with umber

umbilical /um'bilikl, ,umbi'liekl/ *adj* of or near the navel [NL *umbilicalis,* fr L *umbilicus*]

umbilical cord *n* **1** a cord arising from the navel that connects the foetus with the placenta ☞ REPRODUCTION **2** a cable conveying power to a rocket or spacecraft before takeoff; *also* a tethering or supply line (e g for an astronaut outside a spacecraft or a diver underwater)

umbilicate /um'bilikət, -,kayt/, **umbilicated** /-,kaytid/ *adj* **1** depressed like a navel **2** having an umbilicus – **umbilication** /-'kaysh(ə)n/ *n*

umbilicus /um'bilikəs, ,umbi'liekəs/ *n, pl* **umbilici** /-kie, -sie/, **umbilicuses** **1** a small depression in the embryonic abdominal wall at the point of attachment of the umbilical cord **2** any of several anatomical depressions comparable to an umbilicus; *esp* HILUM 1a [L – more at NAVEL]

umbles /'umb(ə)lz/ *n pl* the entrails of an animal, esp a deer, formerly used as food [ME, alter. of *nombles,* fr MF, pl of *nomble* fillet of beef, pork loin, modif of L *lumbulus,* dim. of *lumbus* loin – more at LOIN]

umbo /'umboh/ *n, pl* **umbones** /um'bohneez/, **umbos** **1** the boss of a shield **2** a rounded anatomical elevation [L; akin to L *umbilicus*] – **umbonal** /um'bohnl, 'umbənl/ *adj,* **umbonate** /um'bohnət, 'umbənayt/ *adj*

umbra /'umbrə/ *n, pl* **umbras, umbrae** /'umbri/ **1** a region of total shadow, esp in an eclipse **2** the central dark region of a sunspot [L] – **umbral** *adj*

umbrage /'umbrij/ *n* **1** a feeling of pique or resentment ⟨*took ~ at the chairman's comment*⟩ **2** *archaic* shady branches; foliage [ME, shade, shadow, fr MF, fr L *umbraticum,* neut of *umbraticus* of shade, fr *umbratus,* pp of *umbrare* to shade, fr *umbra* shade, shadow; akin to Lith *unksna* shadow]

umbrageous /um'brayjəs/ *adj, archaic* shadowy, shady – **umbrageously** *adv,* **umbrageousness** *n*

umbrella /um'brelə/ *n* **1** a collapsible shade for protection against weather, consisting of fabric stretched over hinged ribs radiating from a central pole **2** the bell-shaped or saucer-shaped largely gelatinous structure that forms the chief part of the body of most jellyfishes **3** sthg which provides protection ⟨*the American nuclear* ~⟩ **4** sthg that embraces a broad range of elements or factors ⟨*the Electricity Council:* ~ *of the area electricity boards – The Economist*⟩ [It *ombrella,* modif of L *umbella,* dim. of *umbra*]

um'brella ,tree *n* an American magnolia having large leaves clustered at the ends of the branches

Umbrian /'umbri·ən/ *n* **1a** a member of a people of ancient Umbria **b** a native or inhabitant of the Italian province of Umbria **2** the Italic language of ancient Umbria [*Umbria,* ancient province of Italy] – **Umbrian** *adj*

Umbundu /oom'boondooh/ *n* a Congo language of Angola

umiak /'oohmi,ak/ *n* an open Eskimo boat made of a wooden frame covered with hide [Esk]

umlaut /'umlowt, 'oomlowt/ *n* (a mark¨ placed over a letter in some Germanic languages to indicate) the change of a vowel caused by the influence of a following vowel or semivowel [G, fr *um-* round, transformation + *laut* sound]

[1]umpire /'umpie·ə/ *n* **1** one having authority to settle a controversy or question between parties **2** a referee in any of several sports (e g cricket, table tennis, badminton, and hockey) [ME *oumpere,* alter. (by incorrect division of *a noumpere*) of *noumpere,* fr MF *nomper* not equal, not paired, fr *non-* + *per* equal, fr L *par*]

[2]umpire *vb* to act as or supervise (e g a match) as umpire

umpteen /,ump'teen/ *adj* very many; indefinitely numerous – infml [blend of *umpty* (such and such) + *-teen* (as in *thirteen*)] – **umpteen** *n,* **umpteenth** *adj*

un /ən/ *pron, dial* one [by alter.]

[1]un- /un-/ *prefix* **1** not; in-, non- ⟨un*skilled*⟩ ⟨un*dressed*⟩ ⟨un*belief*⟩ **2** opposite of; contrary to ⟨un*grateful*⟩ ⟨un*thinking*⟩ ⟨un*rest*⟩ [ME, fr OE; akin to OHG *un-* un-, L *in-,* Gk *a-, an-,* OE *ne* not – more at NO]

[2]un- *prefix* **1** do the opposite of; reverse (a specified action); DE- 1a, DIS- 1a ⟨un*bend*⟩ ⟨un*dress*⟩ ⟨un*fold*⟩ **2a** deprive of; remove (sthg specified) from; remove ⟨un*frock*⟩ ⟨un*sex*⟩ ⟨un*nerve*⟩ **b** release from; free from ⟨un*hand*⟩ ⟨un*tie*⟩ **c(1)** remove from; extract from; take out of ⟨un*earth*⟩ ⟨un*sheathe*⟩ **(2)** dislodge from ⟨un*horse*⟩ ⟨un*seat*⟩ **d** cause to cease to be ⟨un*man*⟩ **3** completely ⟨un*loose*⟩ [ME, fr OE *un-, on-,* alter. of *and-* against – more at ANTE-]

unabashed *adj*

unabated *adj*

unable /un'ayb(ə)l/ *adj* not able; incapable: **a** unqualified, incompetent **b** impotent, helpless

unabridged *adj*

unaccented *adj*

unacceptable *adj*

unaccompanied *adj*

unaccountable /,unə'kowntəbl/ *adj* **1** inexplicable, strange **2** not to be called to account; not responsible [[1]UN- + ACCOUNTABLE] – **unaccountably** *adv,* **unaccountability** /-tə'biləti/ *n*

unaccounted /,unə'kowntid/ *adj* not explained – often + *for* [[1]UN + ACCOUNTED]

unaccustomed /,unə'kustəmd/ *adj* **1** not customary; not usual or common **2** not used *to* – **unaccustomedly** *adv*

una corda /,oohnə 'kawdə/ *adv or adj* with the soft pedal depressed – used in piano music [It, lit., one string; fr the fact that the soft pedal on a grand piano shifts the hammers so that they strike only 1 string for each note]

unadopted /,unə'doptid/ *adj, Br* not looked after by local authority ⟨*an* ~ *road*⟩ [[1]UN- + ADOPTED]

unadorned /,unə'dawnd/ *adj* not decorated; plain, simple

unadulterated /,unə'dultəraytid/ *adj* unmixed, esp with anything inferior; pure – **unadulteratedly** *adv*

unadventurous *adj*

unadvised /,unəd'viezd/ *adj* not prudent; indiscreet, rash – compare ILL-ADVISED – **unadvisedly** /-zidli/ *adv*

unaffected /,unə'fektid/ *adj* **1** not influenced or changed mentally, physically, or chemically **2** free from affectation; genuine – **unaffectedly** *adv,* **unaffectedness** *n*

unaging, unageing /un'ayjing/ *adj* ageless

unaided *adj*

unalienable /un'ayli·ənəbl, -'aylyənəbl/ *adj* inalienable

unaligned /,unə'liend/ *adj* nonaligned

unalterable *adj*

unaltered *adj*

unambiguous *adj*

,un-A'merican *adj* not consistent with US customs, principles, or traditions [[1]UN- + AMERICAN]

unanimous /yoo'nanimәs/ *adj* **1** being of one mind; agreeing **2** characterized by the agreement and consent of all ⟨*a* ~ *decision*⟩ [L *unanimus,* fr *unus* one + *animus* mind – more at ONE, ANIMATE] – **unanimously** *adv,* **unanimity** /,yoohnə'niməti/ *n*

unannounced *adj*

unanswerable /un'ahns(ə)rəbl/ *adj* not answerable; *esp* irrefutable – **unanswerably** *adv,* **unanswerabillty** /-rə'biləti/ *n*

unanswered *adj*

unanticipated *adj*

unappealing *adj*

unappet·izing, -ising /un'apətiezing/ *adj* not appetizing; insipid – **unappetizingly** *adv*

unapproachable /,unə'prohchəbl/ *adj* **1** physically inaccessible **2** reserved, unfriendly [[1]UN- + APPROACHABLE] – **unapproachably** *adv,* **unapproachability** /-chə'biləti/ *n*

unapt /,un'apt/ *adj* **1** unsuitable, inappropriate **2** not accustomed and not likely ⟨*a man* ~ *to tolerate carelessness*⟩ **3** dull, backward – **unaptly** *adv,* **unaptness** *n*

unarmed /,un'ahmd/ *adj* **1** not armed or armoured **2** having no spines, spurs, claws, etc

unashamed /,unə'shaymd/ *adj* without guilt, self-consciousness, or doubt [[1]UN- + ASHAMED] – **unashamedly** /-midli/ *adv*

unasked /,un'ahskt/ *adj* **1** not asked or invited **2** not sought or asked for ⟨~ *advice*⟩

unassailable /,unə'sayləbl/ *adj* not liable to doubt, attack, or question [[1]UN- + ASSAILABLE] – **unassailably** *adv,* **unassailability** /-lə'biləti/ *n*

unassisted *adj*

unassuming /,unə'syoohming/ *adj* not arrogant or presuming; modest [[1]UN- + ASSUMING] – **unassumingness** *n*

unattached /,unə'tacht/ *adj* **1** not assigned or committed; *esp* not married or engaged **2** not joined or united ⟨~ *polyps*⟩ ⟨~ *buildings*⟩

unattainable *adj*
unattractive *adj*
unauthorized *adj*
unavailable *adj*
unavailing /,unə'vayling/ *adj* futile, useless [¹UN- + AVAILING] – **unavailingly** *adv*, **unavailingness** *n*
unavoidable /,unə'voydəbl/ *adj* not avoidable; inevitable – **unavoidably** *adv*
unaware /,unə'weə/ *adj* ignorant or unconscious *of* what is happening around one; unperceptive [¹UN- + AWARE] – **unawareness** *n*
unawares /,unə'weəz/ *adv* **1** without noticing or intending **2** suddenly, unexpectedly [*un-* + *aware* + *-s*, adv suffix, fr ME, fr *-s*, gen sing. ending of nouns – more at ¹-s]
unbacked /,un'bakt/ *adj* lacking support or aid [¹UN- + BACKED]
unbalance /un'baləns/ *vt* to put out of balance; *esp* to derange mentally
un'balanced *adj* not balanced: e g **a** not in equilibrium **b** mentally disordered or deranged **c** not adjusted so as to make credits equal to debts ⟨*an ~ account*⟩
unbar /,un'bah/ *vt* **-rr-** to remove a bar from; unlock, open
unbearable /un'beərəbl/ *adj* not endurable; intolerable – **unbearably** *adv*
unbeatable /un'beetəbl/ *adj* **1** not able to be defeated **2** outstandingly good of its kind – **unbeatably** *adv*
unbeaten /un'beet(ə)n/ *adj* not defeated ⟨*an ~ record*⟩ [¹UN- + BEATEN]
unbecoming /,unbi'kuming/ *adj* not attractive or showing to advantage; *esp* improper, unseemly ⟨*~ conduct*⟩ [¹UN- + BECOMING] – **unbecomingly** *adv*, **unbecomingness** *n*
unbeknown /,unbi'nohn/ *adj* happening without one's knowledge – usu + *to* [¹*un-* + obs *beknown* (known)]
unbeknownst /,unbi'nohnst/ *adj* unbeknown [irreg fr *unbeknown*]
unbelief /,unbi'leef/ *n* incredulity or scepticism, esp in matters of religious faith
unbelievable /,unbi'leevəbl/ *adj* too improbable for belief; incredible – **unbelievably** *adv*
unbeliever /,unbi'leevə/ *n* one who does not believe, esp in a particular religion
unbelieving /,unbi'leeving/ *adj* marked by unbelief; sceptical – **unbelievingly** *adv*
unbend /,un'bend/ *vb* **unbent** /,un'bent/ *vt* **1** to put into or allow to return to a straight position **2a** to unfasten (e g a sail) from a spar or stay **b** to cast loose or untie (e g a rope) ~ *vi* **1** to become more relaxed, informal, or outgoing in manner **2** to become straight
unbending /un'bending/ *adj* **1** unyielding, inflexible ⟨*an ~ will*⟩ **2** aloof or unsociable in manner [¹UN- + BENDING]
unbiased /un'bie·əst/ *adj* free from all prejudice and partiality [¹UN- + BIASED] – **unbiasedness** *n*
unbidden /un'bidn/ *adj* unasked, uninvited
unbind /un'biend/ *vt* **unbound** /un'bownd/ **1** to untie, unfasten **2** to set free; release
unblemished *adj*
unblinking /,un'blingking/ *adj* showing no signs of emotion [¹UN- + BLINKING] – **unblinkingly** *adv*
unblushing /,un'blushing/ *adj* shameless, unabashed [¹UN- + BLUSHING] – **unblushingly** *adv*
unbolt /un'bohlt/ *vt* to open or unfasten by withdrawing a bolt
unborn /,un'bawn/ *adj* **1** not yet born **2** still to appear; future ⟨*~ ages*⟩
unbosom /un'boozəm/ *vt* to disclose the thoughts or feelings of (oneself) [²*un-* + *bosom*]
unbound /un'bownd/ *adj* not fastened or confined [¹UN- + ⁴BOUND]
unbounded /un'bowndid/ *adj* having no limits or constraints – **unboundedness** *n*
unbowed /un'bowd/ *adj* not bowed down; *esp* not subdued
unbrace /un'brays/ *vt* to free or relax (as if) by untying or removing a brace or bond
unbreakable *adj*
unbridle /un'briedl/ *vt* to set free or loose (from a bridle)
un'bridled *adj* **1** not confined by a bridle **2** unrestrained, ungoverned
unbroken /un'brohkən/ *adj* **1** whole, intact **2** not beaten or improved on ⟨*an ~ record*⟩ **3** not subdued or tamed; *esp* not trained for service or use ⟨*~ colts*⟩ **4** uninterrupted ⟨*miles of ~ forest*⟩ **5** not disorganized or in disarray ⟨*advanced in ~ ranks*⟩ [¹UN- + BROKEN]
unbuckle /un'bukl/ *vt* to loose the buckle of; unfasten
unburden /un'buhd(ə)n/ *vt* to free or relieve from anxiety, cares, etc [²UN- + ²BURDEN]
unbusinesslike *adj*
unbutton /un'but(ə)n/ *vt* **1** to undo the buttons of **2** to free from constraint, tension, etc – **unbuttoned** *adj*
uncage /un'kayj/ *vt* to free from restraint [²UN- + ²CAGE]
uncalled-for /un'kawld faw/ *adj* **1** unnecessary **2** offered without provocation or justification; gratuitous ⟨*an ~ display of temper*⟩
uncanny /un'kani/ *adj* **1** eerie, mysterious **2** beyond what is normal or expected ⟨*an ~ sense of direction*⟩ – **uncannily** *adv*, **uncanniness** *n*
uncaring *adj*
unceasing *adj*
unceremonious /,unserə'mohnyəs, -ni·əs/ *adj* **1** not ceremonious; informal **2** abrupt, rude ⟨*an ~ dismissal*⟩ – **unceremoniously** *adv*, **unceremoniousness** *n*
uncertain /un'suhtn/ *adj* **1** not reliable or trustworthy **2a** not definitely known; undecided, unpredictable ⟨*the outcome is ~*⟩ **b** not confident or sure; doubtful ⟨*~ of the truth*⟩ **3** variable, changeable ⟨*~ weather*⟩ [¹UN- + ¹CERTAIN] – **uncertainly** *adv*, **uncertainness** *n*
uncertainty /un'suht(ə)nti/ *n* the state of being uncertain; doubt
un'certainty ,principle *n* a principle in quantum mechanics:it is impossible to determine both the momentum and position of a tiny particle (e g a photon)
unchain /un'chayn/ *vt* to free (as if) by removing a chain; set loose
unchallenged *adj*
unchangeable *adj*
unchanged *adj*
unchanging *adj*
uncharacteristic *adj*
uncharitable /un'charitəbl/ *adj* severe in judging

others; harsh [[1]UN- + CHARITABLE] – **uncharitableness** *n*, **uncharitably** *adv*

unchecked *adj*

unchivalrous *adj*

unchristian /un'kristi·ən/ *adj* **1** contrary to the Christian spirit or character **2** barbarous, uncivilized [[1]UN- + [2]CHRISTIAN]

[1]**uncial** /'unsi·əl/ *adj* written in the style or size of uncials [L *uncialis* inch-high, fr *uncia* twelfth part, ounce, inch] – **uncially** *adv*

[2]**uncial** *n* (a letter in) a style of handwriting formed of somewhat large rounded usu separated letters and used esp in early medieval Greek and Latin manuscripts

unciform /'unsi,fawm/ *adj* hook-shaped [NL *unciformis*, fr L *uncus* hook + *-formis* -form – more at [3]ANGLE]

uncinate /'unsi,nayt/ *adj, of a plant or animal part* having a hook-shaped tip [L *uncinatus*, fr *uncinus* hook]

uncircumcised /,un'suhkəm,siezd/ *adj* **1** not circumcised **2** spiritually impure; heathen – **uncircumcision** /-,suhkəm'sizh(ə)n/ *n*

uncivil /un'sivl/ *adj* ill-mannered, impolite [[1]UN- + CIVIL] – **uncivilly** *adv*

uncivilized /un'sivl·iezd/ *adj* **1** not civilized; barbarous **2** remote from settled areas; wild

unclaimed *adj*

unclasp /un'klahsp/ *vt* **1** to open the clasp of **2** to open or cause (e g a clenched hand) to be opened

unclassified /un'klasified/ *adj* **1** not divided into classes or placed in a class **2** not subject to a security classification

uncle /'ungkl/ *n* **1a** the brother of one's father or mother **b** the husband of one's aunt **2** a man who is a very close friend of a young child or its parents [ME, fr OF, fr L *avunculus* mother's brother; akin to OE *ēam* uncle, OIr *aue* grandson, L *avus* grandfather]

unclean /un'kleen/ *adj* **1** morally or spiritually impure **2a** ritually prohibited as food **b** ceremonially unfit or defiled **3** dirty, filthy – **uncleanness** *n*

unclear *adj*

,Uncle 'Sam /sam/ *n* the American nation, people, or government [prob jocular expansion of *US*, abbr of *United States*]

,Uncle 'Tom /tom/ *n* a black American eager to win the approval of white people and willing to cooperate with them – chiefly derog [*Uncle Tom*, faithful black slave in the novel *Uncle Tom's Cabin* by Harriet Beecher Stowe †1896 US author]

unclothe /un'klohdh/ *vt* to strip of clothes

[1]**unco** /'ungkoh/ *adj, chiefly Scot* **1** strange, unknown **2** extraordinary, remarkable [ME (Sc) *unkow*, alter. of ME *uncouth*]

[2]**unco** *adv, chiefly Scot* extremely, remarkably

uncoil /un'koyl/ *vb* to (cause to) unwind

uncoined /un'koynd/ *adj* not minted ⟨~ *metal*⟩

uncomfortable /un'kumftəbl/ *adj* **1** causing discomfort **2** feeling discomfort; ill at ease – **uncomfortably** *adv*

uncommercial /,unkə'muhsh(ə)l/ *adj* **1** not engaged in or related to commerce **2** not based on commercial principles **3** not commercially viable

uncommitted /,unkə'mitid/ *adj* not pledged to a particular belief, allegiance, or course of action [[1]UN- + COMMITTED]

uncommon /un'komən/ *adj* **1** not normally encountered; unusual **2** remarkable, exceptional – **uncommonly** *adv*, **uncommonness** *n*

uncommunicative /,unkə'myoohnikətiv/ *adj* not forthcoming; reserved

uncomplicated /un'komplikaytid/ *adj* not complex; straightforward [[1]UN- + COMPLICATED]

uncomprehending *adj*

uncompromising /un'komprəmiezing/ *adj* not making or accepting a compromise; unyielding – **uncompromisingly** *adv*

unconcealed *adj*

unconcern /,unkən'suhn/ *n* **1** lack of interest; indifference **2** freedom from anxiety

unconcerned /,unkən'suhnd/ *adj* **1** not involved or interested **2** not anxious or worried – **unconcernedly** /-nidli/ *adv*, **unconcernedness** /-kən'suhndnis, -nidnis/ *n*

unconditional /,unkən'dish(ə)nl/ *adj* absolute, unqualified – **unconditionally** *adv*

unconditioned /,unkən'dish(ə)nd/ *adj* not dependent on conditioning or learning [[1]UN- + CONDITIONED]

unconfined *adj*

unconformable /,unkən'fawməbl/ *adj* not conforming – **unconformably** *adv*

unconformity /,unkən'fawməti/ *n* (the junction between rocks corresponding to) discontinuity in the sequence of deposited rock strata, caused by a period of erosion or no deposition [[1]UN- + CONFORMITY]

uncongenial /,unkən'jeenyəl, -ni·əl/ *adj* **1** not sympathetic or compatible ⟨~ *roommates*⟩ **2** disagreeable, unpleasant ⟨*an* ~ *task*⟩ – **uncongeniality** /-kən,jeeni'aləti/ *n*

unconquerable /un'kongk(ə)rəbl/ *adj* **1** indomitable, unyielding **2** incapable of being surmounted – **unconquerably** *adv*

unconquered *adj*

unconscionable /un'konsh(ə)nəbl/ *adj* **1** unscrupulous, unprincipled **2** excessive, unreasonable – **unconscionably** *adv*

[1]**unconscious** /un'konshəs/ *adj* **1** not knowing or perceiving **2a** not possessing mind or having lost consciousness ⟨~ *matter*⟩ ⟨~ *for 3 days*⟩ **b** not marked by or resulting from conscious thought, sensation, or feeling ⟨~ *motivation*⟩ **3** not intentional or deliberate ⟨~ *bias*⟩ – **unconsciously** *adv*, **unconsciousness** *n*

[2]**unconscious** *n* the part of the mind that does not ordinarily enter a person's awareness but nevertheless influences behaviour and may be manifested in dreams or slips of the tongue

unconsidered /,unkən'sidəd/ *adj* **1** disregarded, unnoticed **2** not carefully thought out ⟨~ *opinions*⟩

unconstitutional /,unkonsti'tyoohsh(ə)nl/ *adj* not consistent with the political constitution – **unconstitutionally** *adv*, **unconstitutionality** /-'aləti/ *n*

uncontrollable *adj*

uncontroversial *adj*

unconventional /,unkən'vensh(ə)nl/ *adj* not bound by convention; out of the ordinary – **unconventionally** *adv*, **unconventionality** /-'aləti/ *n*

unconvincing *adj*

uncooperative *adj*

uncork /,un'kawk/ *vt* **1** to draw a cork from **2** to release from a pent-up state; unleash

uncounted /un'kowntid/ *adj* **1** not counted **2** innumerable

uncouple /ˌun'kupl/ *vt* **1** to release (dogs) from a couple **2** to detach, disconnect – **uncoupler** *n*

uncouth /un'koohth/ *adj* awkward and uncultivated in speech or manner; boorish [ME, fr OE *uncūth*, fr *un-* + *cūth* familiar, known; akin to OHG *kund* known, OE *can* know – more at [1]CAN] – **uncouthly** *adv*, **uncouthness** *n*

uncover /un'kuvə/ *vt* **1** to disclose, reveal **2a** to remove the cover from **b** to remove the hat from (one's head)

un'covered *adj* **1** not supplied with a covering **2** not covered by insurance or social security [[1]UN- + COVERED]

uncritical /un'kritikl/ *adj* lacking in discrimination or critical analysis – **uncritically** *adv*

uncrowned /un'krownd/ *adj* **1** not having yet been crowned **2** having a specified status in fact but not in name ⟨*the* ~ *champion*⟩

unction /'ungksh(ə)n/ *n* the act of anointing as a rite of consecration or healing [ME *unctioun*, fr L *unction-, unctio*, fr *unctus*, pp of *unguere* to anoint – more at OINTMENT]

unctuous /'ungktyoo·əs/ *adj* **1** fatty, oily, or greasy in texture or appearance **2** marked by ingratiating smoothness and false sincerity [ME, fr MF or ML; MF *unctueux*, fr ML *unctuosus*, irreg fr L *unctum* ointment, fr neut of *unctus*, pp] – **unctuously** *adv*, **unctuousness** *n*

uncultivated *adj*

uncurl /un'kuhl/ *vb* to (cause to) become straightened out from a curled or coiled position

uncut /un'kut/ *adj* **1** not cut down or into **2** not shaped by cutting ⟨*an* ~ *diamond*⟩ **3** *of a book* not having the folds of the leaves trimmed off **4** not abridged or curtailed

undamaged *adj*

undated *adj*

undaunted /un'dawntid/ *adj* not discouraged by danger or difficulty – **undauntedly** *adv*

undec- *comb form* eleven ⟨undec*illion*⟩ [L *undecim*, fr *unus* one + *decem* ten – more at ONE, TEN]

undeceive /ˌundi'seev/ *vt* to free from deception, illusion, or error

undecided /ˌundi'siedid/ *adj* **1** in doubt **2** without a result ⟨*the match was left* ~⟩ [[1]UN- + DECIDED] – **undecidedly** *adv*, **undecidedness** *n*

undemanding *adj*

undemocratic *adj*

undemonstrative /ˌundi'monstrətiv/ *adj* not showing one's feelings; reserved – **undemonstratively** *adv*, **undemonstrativeness** *n*

undeniable /ˌundi'nie·əbl/ *adj* **1** plainly true; incontestable ⟨~ *evidence*⟩ **2** unquestionably excellent or genuine – **undeniably** *adv*

[1]**under** /'undə/ *adv* **1** in or to a position below or beneath sthg **2a** in or to a lower rank or number ⟨*£10 or* ~⟩ **b** to a subnormal degree; deficiently – often in combination ⟨under-*staffed*⟩ **3** in or into a condition of subjection, subordination, or unconsciousness **4** so as to be covered, buried, or sheltered **5** BELOW 3 [ME, adv & prep, fr OE; akin to OHG *untar* under, L *inferus* situated beneath, lower, *infra* below, Skt *adha*]

[2]**under** *prep* **1a** below or beneath so as to be overhung, surmounted, covered, protected, or hidden ⟨~ *cover of darkness*⟩ **b** using as a pseudonym or alias ⟨*wrote* ~ *the name 'George Eliot'*⟩ **2a(1)** subject to the authority, control, guidance, or instruction of ⟨*served* ~ *the general*⟩ **(2)** during the rule or control of ⟨*India* ~ *the Raj*⟩ **b** receiving or undergoing the action or effect of ⟨~ *pressure*⟩ ⟨*courage* ~ *fire*⟩ ⟨~ *ether*⟩ ⟨~ *discussion*⟩ ⟨~ *sail*⟩ **3** within the group or designation of ⟨~ *this heading*⟩ **4** less than or inferior to ⟨~ *an hour*⟩; *esp* falling short of (a standard or required degree)

[3]**under** *adj* **1a** lying or placed below, beneath, or on the lower side **b** facing or pointing downwards **2** lower in rank or authority; subordinate **3** lower than usual, proper, or desired in amount or degree ***USE*** often in combination

underachiever /ˌundərə'cheevə/ *n* one who fails to achieve his/her scholastic potential

ˌunder'act /-'akt/ *vt* **1** to perform (a dramatic part) without adequate force or skill **2** to perform with restraint for greater dramatic impact or personal force ~ *vi* to perform feebly or with restraint

ˌunder'age /-'ayj/ *adj* below the legal age

[1]**'underˌarm** /-ˌahm/ *adj* **1** under or on the underside of the arm ⟨~ *seams*⟩ **2** made with the hand brought forwards and up from below shoulder level

[2]**underarm** *vt or adv* (to throw) with an underarm motion ⟨*bowl* ~⟩

[3]**underarm** *n* the part of a garment that covers the underside of the arm

'underˌbelly /-ˌbeli/ *n* **1** the underside of an animal, object, etc **2** a vulnerable area ⟨*the soft* ~ *of capitalism*⟩

ˌunder'bid /-'bid/ *vb* **-dd-; underbid** *vt* **1** to bid less than (a competing bidder) **2** to bid (a hand of cards) at less than the strength of the hand warrants ~ *vi* to bid too low – **underbidder** /'--ˌ--/ *n*

'underˌbody /-ˌbodi/ *n* **1** the lower part of an animal's body **2** the under surface of the body of a vehicle

ˌunder'bred /-'bred/ *adj* of inferior or mixed breed ⟨*an* ~ *dog*⟩

'underˌbrush /-ˌbrush/ *n, NAm* undergrowth in a wood or forest

ˌunder'capital·ized, -ised /-'kapitl·iezd/ *adj* having too little capital for efficient operation

'underˌcarriage /-ˌkarij/ *n* **1** a supporting framework (e g of a motor vehicle) **2** the part of an aircraft's structure that supports its weight, when in contact with the land or water ☞ FLIGHT

ˌunder'charge /-'chahj/ *vb* to charge (e g a person) too little – **undercharge** /'--ˌ-/ *n*

'underˌclothes /-ˌklohdhz/ *n pl* underwear

'underˌclothing /-ˌklohdhing/ *n* underwear

'underˌcoat /-ˌkoht/ *n* **1** a growth of short hair or fur partly concealed by a longer growth ⟨*a dog's* ~⟩ **2** a coat (e g of paint) applied as a base for another coat

'underˌcover /-ˌkuvə/ *adj* acting or done in secret; *specif* engaged in spying

'underˌcroft /-ˌkroft/ *n* a crypt [ME, fr *under* + *crofte* crypt, fr MD, fr ML *crupta*, fr L *crypta*]

'underˌcurrent /-ˌkurənt/ *n* **1** a current below the upper currents or surface **2** a hidden opinion, feeling, or tendency

[1]**ˌunder'cut** /-'kut/ *vt* **-tt-; undercut** **1** to cut away the underpart of ⟨~ *a vein of ore*⟩ **2** to cut away material from the underside of so as to leave a portion overhanging **3** to offer sthg at lower prices than or work for lower wages than (a competitor)

[2]**'underˌcut** *n* **1** the action or result of undercutting

2 *Br* the underside of sirloin; a beef tenderloin 3 *NAm* a notch cut in a tree to determine the direction of falling during felling

,underde'veloped /-di'veləpt/ *adj* 1 not normally or adequately developed ⟨~ *muscles*⟩ ⟨*an* ~ *film*⟩ 2 failing to realize a potential economic level – **underdevelopment** *n*

'under,dog /-,dog/ *n* 1 an (expected) loser in a contest 2 a victim of injustice or persecution

,under'done /-'dun/ *adj* not thoroughly cooked

,under'dress /-'dres/ *vi* to dress less formally than is appropriate – **underdressed** *adj*

,underem'ployment /-im'ploymənt/ *n* 1 less than full employment of the work force in an economy 2 employment at less than full time; partial or inadequate employment – **underemployed** *adj*

,under'estimate /-'estimayt/ *vt* 1 to estimate as being less than the actual size, quantity, etc 2 to place too low a value on; underrate – **underestimate** /'undər,estimət/ *n*, **underestimation** /,undər ,esti'maysh(ə)n/ *n*

,underex'pose /-ik'spohz/ *vt* to expose insufficiently – **underexposure** /-ik'spohzhə/ *n*

,under'feed /-'feed/ *vt* **underfed** /-'fed/ to feed with too little food

'under,felt /-,felt/ *n* a thick felt underlay placed under a carpet

,under'foot /-'foot/ *adv* 1 under the feet, esp against the ground ⟨*trampled* ~⟩ 2 in the way ⟨*children always getting* ~⟩

'under,garment /-,gahmənt/ *n* a garment to be worn under another

,under'go /-'goh/ *vt* **underwent** /-'went/; **undergone** /-'gon/ to be subjected to; experience

'under,grad /-,grad/ *n* an undergraduate – infml

'under,graduate /-,gradyoo-ət/ *n* a college or university student who has not taken a first degree

[1],under'ground /-'grownd/ *adv* 1 beneath the surface of the earth 2 in or into hiding or secret operation

[2]underground *adj* 1 growing, operating, or situated below the surface of the ground 2a conducted in hiding or in secret b existing or operated outside the establishment, esp by the avant-garde

[3]'under,ground *n* 1 *sing or pl in constr* a a secret movement or group esp in an occupied country, for concerted resistive action b a conspiratorial organization set up for disruption of a civil order c a usu avant-garde group or movement that functions outside the establishment 2 *Br* a usu electric underground urban railway; *also* a train running in an underground

'under,growth /-,grohth/ *n* shrub, bushes, saplings, etc growing under larger trees in a wood or forest

[1]underhand /,undə'hand; *sense 2* '--,-/ *adv* 1 in an underhand manner; secretly 2 underarm

[2]underhand *adj* 1 not honest and aboveboard; sly 2 UNDERARM 2

,under'hung /-'hung/ *adj* 1 *of a lower jaw* projecting beyond the upper jaw – compare PROGNATHOUS 2 having an underhung jaw

,underin'sured /-in'shooəd, -in'shawd/ *adj* not sufficiently insured

,under'laid /-'layd/ *adj* 1 placed underneath 2 having sthg laid or lying underneath

[1],under'lay /-'lay/ *vt* **,under'laid** /-'layd/ 1 to cover or line the bottom of; give support to on the underside or below 2 to raise by sthg laid under

[2]'under,lay *n* sthg that is (designed to be) laid under sthg else ⟨*a carpet with foam* ~⟩

,under'lie /-'lie/ *vt* **underlying** /-'lie·ing/; **underlay** /-'lay/; **underlain** /-'layn/ 1 to lie or be situated under 2 to form the basis or foundation of 3 to be concealed beneath the exterior of ⟨underlying *hostility*⟩

,under'line /-'lien/ *vt* 1 to mark (a word or passage) with a line underneath 2 to emphasize, stress – **underline** /'--,-/ *n*

'underling /-ling/ *n* a subordinate or inferior

'under,lip /-,lip/ *n* the lower lip

,under'manned /-'mand/ *adj* inadequately staffed

'under,mentioned /-,mensh(ə)nd/ *adj, Br* referred to at a later point in a text

,under'mine /-'mien/ *vt* 1 to form a mine under; sap 2 to weaken or destroy gradually or insidiously

[1]underneath /,undə'neeth/ *prep* directly below; close under [ME *undernethe*, prep & adv, fr OE *underneothan*, fr *under* + *neothan* below – more at BENEATH]

[2]underneath *adv* 1 under or below an object or a surface; beneath 2 on the lower side

[3]underneath *n* the bottom part or surface ⟨*the* ~ *of the bowl*⟩

,under'nourished /-'nurisht/ *adj* supplied with less than the minimum amount of the foods essential for sound health and growth – **undernourishment** *n*

,under'paid /-'payd/ *adj* receiving less than adequate or normal pay

'under,pants /-,pants/ *n pl* men's pants

'under,part /-,paht/ *n* a part lying on the lower side, esp of a bird or mammal

'under,pass /-,pahs/ *n* a tunnel or passage taking a road and pavement under another road or a railway

'under,pin /-,pin/ *vt* **-nn-** to form part of, strengthen, or replace the foundation of ⟨~ *a sagging building*⟩

'under,pinning /-,pining/ *n* 1 the material and construction (e g a foundation) used for support of a structure 2 a basis, support – often pl with sing. meaning

,under'play /-'play/ *vt* 1 to underact (a role) 2 to play down the importance of

'under,plot /-,plot/ *n* a subplot

,under'price /-'pries/ *vt* to price too low

,under'privileged /-'priv(i)lijd/ *adj* deprived of some of the fundamental social or economic rights of a civilized society ⟨~ *children*⟩

,underpro'duction /-prə'duksh(ə)n/ *n* the production of less than enough or of less than the usual supply – **underproductive** /-'duktiv/ *adj*

,under'proof /-'proohf/ *adj* containing less alcohol than proof spirit

,under'quote /-'kwoht/ *vt* 1 to quote a lower price than (another person) 2 to quote a price for (e g goods or services) that is lower than another's offer or the market price

,under'rate /-'rayt/ *vt* to rate too low; undervalue

,under'score /-'skaw/ *vt* to underline – **underscore** /'--,-/ *n*

[1],under'sea /-'see/ *adj* 1 being or carried on under the sea or under the surface of the sea ⟨~ *oil deposits*⟩ ⟨~ *warfare*⟩ 2 designed for use under the surface of the sea

[2]undersea, underseas *adv* beneath (the surface of) the sea

'under,seal /-,seel/ *n* a protective corrosion-proof substance (e g bitumen) used esp to coat vehicle undersurfaces – **underseal** /,--'-, '--,-/ *vt*

'under,secretary /-,sekrətri, -,teri/ *n* a secretary immediately subordinate to a principal secretary

,under'sell /-'sel/ *vt* **,under'sold** /-'sohld/ **1** to be sold cheaper than ⟨*imported cars that ~ domestic ones*⟩ **2** to make little of the merits of ⟨*he* undersold *himself*⟩; *esp* to promote or publicize in a (deliberately) low-key manner

,under'sexed /-'sekst/ *adj* deficient in sexual drive or interest

,under'shoot /-'shooht/ *vt* **undershot** /-'shot/ **1** to shoot short of or below (a target) **2** *of an aircraft* to land short of (a runway)

,under'shot /-'shot/ *adj* **1** underhung **2** moved by water passing beneath ⟨*an ~ wheel*⟩

'under,shrub /-,shrub/ *n* a small low-growing shrub

'under,side /-,sied/ *n* the side or surface lying underneath

'under,signed /-,siend/ *n, pl* **undersigned** *the* one who signs his/her name at the end of a document

,under'sized /-'siezd/ *also* **'under,size** *adj* of less than average size

'under,slung /-,slung/ *adj, of a vehicle frame* suspended below the axles

'under,spin /-,spin/ *n* backspin

,under'staffed /-'stahft/ *adj* undermanned

understand /,undə'stand/ *vb* **understood** /-'stood/ *vt* **1a** to grasp the meaning of; comprehend **b** to have a thorough knowledge of or expertise in ⟨*~ finance*⟩ **2** to assume, suppose ⟨*we ~ that he is abroad*⟩ **3** to interpret in one of a number of possible ways ⟨*as I ~ it*⟩ **4** to supply mentally (sthg implied though not expressed) *~ vi* **1** to have a grasp or understanding of sthg **2** to believe or infer sthg to be the case **3** to show a sympathetic or tolerant attitude ⟨*if he loves her he'll ~*⟩ [ME *understanden*, fr OE *understandan*, fr *under* + *standan* to stand] – **understandable** *adj*, **understandably** *adv*, **understandability** /-də 'biləti/ *n*

[1]**,under'standing** /-'standing/ *n* **1** a mental grasp; comprehension **2** the power of comprehending; intelligence; *esp* the power to make experience intelligible by applying concepts **3a** a friendly or harmonious relationship **b** an informal mutual agreement

[2]**understanding** *adj* tolerant, sympathetic – **understandingly** *adv*

,under'state /-'stayt/ *vt* **1** to state as being less than is the case **2** to present with restraint, esp for greater effect – **understatement** /'--,--/ *n*

'under,steer /-,stiə/ *n* the tendency of a motor vehicle to turn less sharply than the driver intends – **understeer** /,--'-/ *vi*

,under'strength /-'streng(k)th/ *adj* deficient in strength; *esp* lacking the sufficient or prescribed number of staff ⟨*a firm 500 ~*⟩

[1]**understudy** /,undə'studi, '--,--/ *vi* to study another actor's part in order to take it over in an emergency *~ vt* to prepare (e g a part) as understudy; *also* to prepare a part as understudy to

[2]**'under,study** *n* one who is prepared to act another's part or take over another's duties

'under,surface /-,suhfəs/ *n* the underside

,under'take /-'tayk/ *vt* **,under'took** /-'took/; **,under'taken** /-'taykən/ **1** to take upon oneself as a task **2** to put oneself under obligation to do; contract **3** to guarantee, promise

'under,taker /-,taykə/ *n* sby whose business is preparing the dead for burial and arranging and managing funerals [UNDERTAKE + [2]-ER]

'under,taking /-,tayking/ *n* **1** the business of an undertaker **2** an enterprise **3** a pledge, guarantee

'under,tenant /-,tenənt/ *n* a subtenant

,under-the-'counter *adj* surreptitious and usu illicit – infml [fr the hiding of illicit wares under the counter of shops where they are sold]

'under,things /-,thingz/ *n pl* underwear – infml

'under,tone /-,tohn/ *n* **1** a subdued utterance **2** an underlying quality (e g of emotion) **3** a subdued colour; *specif* one seen through and modifying another colour

'under,tow /-,toh/ *n* **1** an undercurrent that flows in a different direction from the surface current, esp out to sea **2** a hidden tendency often contrary to the one that is publicly apparent

,under'value /-'valyooh/ *vt* **1** to value, rate, or estimate below the real worth ⟨*~ stock*⟩ **2** to assign an insufficient value to ⟨*was ~d as a poet*⟩ – **undervaluation** /-,valyoo'aysh(ə)n/ *n*

,under'water /-'wawtə/ *adj* **1** situated, used, or designed to operate below the surface of the water **2** being below the waterline of a ship – **underwater** *adv*

,under 'way *adv* **1** in or into motion **2** in progress; afoot [prob fr D *onderweg*, fr MD *onderwegen*, lit., under or among the ways]

'under,wear /-,weə/ *n* clothing worn next to the skin and under other clothing ☞ GARMENT

underweight /,undə'wayt; *noun* '--,-/ *adj or n* (of a) weight below average or normal

[1]**'under,wing** /-,wing/ *n* any of various moths that have the hind wings banded with contrasting colours

[2]**'under,wing** *adj* placed or growing underneath the wing ⟨*a bird's ~ coverts*⟩

'under,world /-,wuhld/ *n* **1** the place of departed souls; Hades **2** the world of organized crime

,under'write /-'riet/ *vb* **underwrote** /-'roht/; **underwritten** /-'ritn/ *vt* **1** to write under or at the end of sthg else **2** to set one's signature to (an insurance policy) thereby assuming liability in case of specified loss or damage; *also* to assume (a sum or risk) by way of insurance **3** to subscribe to; agree to **4a** to agree to purchase (a security issue) usu on a fixed date at a fixed price with a view to public distribution **b** to guarantee financial support of *~ vi* to carry on the business of an underwriter

'under,writer /-,rietə/ *n* **1** one who underwrites sthg, esp an insurance policy **2** one who selects risks to be solicited or rates the acceptability of risks solicited

undescended /,undi'sendid/ *adj, of a testis* retained within the abdomen rather than descending into the scrotum at the normal age [[1]UN + DESCENDED]

undeserved *adj* – **undeservedly** *adj*

undeserving *adj*

undesirable /,undi'zie·ərəbl/ *n or adj* (sby or sthg) unwanted or objectionable ⟨*~ elements in society*⟩ – **undesirably** *adv*, **undesirability** /-rə'biləti/ *n*

undetectable *adj*

undetected *adj*

undeterred *adj*

undeveloped *adj*

undies /'undiz/ *n pl* underwear; *esp* women's underwear – infml [by shortening & alter.]
undignified *adj*
undiminished *adj*
undisclosed *adj*
undisguised *adj*
undistinguished *adj*
undisturbed *adj*
undivided *adj*
undo /un'dooh/ *vb* **undid** /un'did/; **undone** /un'dun/ *vt* **1** to open or loosen by releasing a fastening **2** to reverse or cancel out the effects of **3** to destroy the standing, reputation, hopes, etc of ~ *vi* to come open or apart – **undoer** *n*
undock /un'dok/ *vi* **1** to move away from a dock (e g at sailing time) **2** to become undocked ~ *vt* to separate (e g 2 spacecraft) mechanically while in space
undoing /un'dooh·ing/ *n* (a cause of) ruin or downfall
1**undone** /un'dun/ *past part of* UNDO
2**undone** *adj* not performed or finished [1UN- + DONE]
undoubted /un'dowtid/ *adj* not disputed; genuine [1UN- + DOUBTED] – **undoubtedly** *adv*
undreamed /un'dreemd, un'dremt/ *also* **undreamt** /un'dremt/ *adj* not conceived of; unimagined – usu + *of* [1UN- + DREAMED]
1**undress** /un'dres/ *vt* to remove the clothes or covering of ~ *vi* to take off one's clothes
2**undress** *n* **1** ordinary dress – compare FULL DRESS **2** a state of having little or no clothing on
un'dressed *adj* **1** partially or completely unclothed **2** not fully processed or finished ⟨~ *hides*⟩ **3** not cared for or tended ⟨*an* ~ *wound*⟩ [1UN- + DRESSED]
undrinkable *adj*
undue /un'dyooh/ *adj* **1** not yet due **2** excessive, immoderate
undulant fever /'undyoolənt/ *n* a persistent human brucellosis
1**undulate** /'undyoo,layt/, **undulated** /-,laytid/ *adj* having a wavy surface, edge, or markings ⟨*the* ~ *margin of a leaf*⟩ ☞ PLANT [L *undulatus*, fr (assumed) L *undula*, dim. of L *unda* wave – more at WATER]
2**undulate** *vi* **1** to rise and fall in waves; fluctuate **2** to have a wavy form or appearance [LL *undula* small wave, fr (assumed) L]
undulation /,undyoo'laysh(ə)n/ *n* **1a** a gentle rising and falling (as if) in waves **b** a wavelike motion; *also* a single wave or gentle rise **2** a wavy appearance, outline, or form
undulatory /'undyoolət(ə)ri/ *adj* undulating, wavy
unduly /un'dyoohli/ *adv* excessively
undying /un'die·ing/ *adj* eternal, perpetual
unearned /un'uhnd, un'uhnt/ *adj* not gained by work, service, or skill ⟨~ *income*⟩
unearned increment *n* an increase in the value of property (e g land) due to increased demand rather than the owner's labour or investment
unearth /un'uhth/ *vt* **1** to dig up out of the ground **2** to make known or public
unearthly /un'uhthli/ *adj* **1** not terrestrial ⟨~ *radio sources*⟩ **2** exceeding what is normal or natural; supernatural ⟨*an* ~ *light*⟩ **3** weird, eerie **4** unreasonable, preposterous ⟨*getting up at an* ~ *hour*⟩ – compare UNGODLY 2 – **unearthliness** *n*
unease /un'eez/ *n* a feeling of disquiet or awkwardness
uneasy /un'eezi/ *adj* **1** marked by lack of physical or mental ease; uncomfortable, awkward **2** apprehensive, worried **3** precarious, unstable ⟨*an* ~ *truce*⟩ [1UN- + EASY] – **uneasily** *adv*, **uneasiness** *n*
uneatable *adj* inedible
uneconomic /,unekə'nomik, -eekə-/ *also* **uneconomical** /-kl/ *adj* not economically practicable
unedifying *adj*
uneducated *adj*
unemployable /,unim'ployəbl/ *adj* not acceptable for employment
unemployed /,unim'ployd/ *adj* **1** not engaged in a job **2** not invested [1UN- + EMPLOYED] – **unemployed** *n pl in constr*
unemployment /,unim'ploymənt/ *n* the state of being unemployed; lack of available employment
,unem'ployment ,benefit *n* a sum of money paid (e g by the state) at regular intervals to an unemployed worker
unending *adj*
unendurable *adj*
unenforceable *adj*
unenterprising *adj*
unenthusiastic *adj*
unenviable *adj*
unequal /un'eekwəl/ *adj* **1a** not of the same measurement, quantity, or number as another **b** not like in quality, nature, or status **c** not the same for every member of a group, class, or society ⟨~ *rights*⟩ **2** badly balanced or matched **3** not uniform **4** incapable of meeting the requirements of sthg – + *to* – **unequally** *adv*
un'equalled *adj* not equalled; unparalleled
unequivocal /,uni'kwivəkl/ *adj* clear, unambiguous – **unequivocally** *adv*
unerring /un'uhring/ *adj* faultless, unfailing ⟨~ *judgment*⟩ – **unerringly** *adv*
unethical *adj*
uneven /un'eev(ə)n/ *adj* **1a** not level, smooth, or uniform **b** varying from the straight or parallel **c** irregular, inconsistent **d** varying in quality ⟨*an* ~ *performance*⟩ **2** UNEQUAL 2 ⟨*an* ~ *contest*⟩ – **unevenly** *adv*, **unevenness** *n*
uneventful /,uni'ventf(ə)l/ *adj* without any noteworthy or untoward incidents – **uneventfully** *adv*
unexceptionable /,unik'sepsh(ə)nəbl/ *adj* beyond reproach or criticism; unimpeachable [*un-* + obs *exception* (to take exception, object)] – **unexceptionableness** *n*, **unexceptionably** *adv*
unexceptional /,unik'sepsh(ə)nl/ *adj* commonplace, ordinary
unexpected /,unik'spektid/ *adj* not expected or foreseen – **unexpectedly** *adv*, **unexpectedness** *n*
unexplained *adj*
unexploded *adj*
unexplored *adj*
unexpurgated *adj*
unfailing /un'fayling/ *adj* that can be relied on; constant ⟨*a subject of* ~ *interest*⟩ [1UN- + FAILING] – **unfailingly** *adv*, **unfailingness** *n*
unfair /un'feə/ *adj* **1** unjust, dishonest **2** not equitable, esp in business dealings ⟨~ *competition*⟩ – **unfairly** *adv*, **unfairness** *n*

unfaithful /un'faythf(ə)l/ *adj* **1** disloyal, faithless **2** not faithful to a marriage partner, lover, etc, esp in having sexual relations with another person [[1]UN- + FAITHFUL] – **unfaithfully** *adv*, **unfaithfulness** *n*

unfaltering /un'fawltəring/ *adj* not wavering or hesitating; firm – **unfalteringly** *adv*

unfamiliar /,unfə'mili·ə, -yə/ *adj* **1** not well-known; strange ⟨*an ~ place*⟩ **2** not well acquainted ⟨*~ with the subject*⟩ [[1]UN- + FAMILIAR] – **unfamiliarly** *adv*, **unfamiliarity** /,unfəmili'arəti/ *n*

unfasten /un'fahs(ə)n/ *vt* **1** to loosen, undo **2** to untie, detach

unfavourable /un'fayv(ə)rəbl/ *adj* **1** expressing disapproval; negative **2** disadvantageous, adverse ⟨*an ~ economic climate*⟩ – **unfavourably** *adv*

unfeeling /un'feeling/ *adj* not kind or sympathetic; hardhearted [[1]UN- + FEELING] – **unfeelingly** *adv*, **unfeelingness** *n*

unfetter /un'fetə/ *vt* **1** to release from fetters ⟨*~ a prisoner*⟩ **2** to free from restraint; liberate

unfilled *adj*

unfinished /un'finisht/ *adj* **1** not brought to the desired final state; incomplete **2** subjected to no other processes after coming from the loom [[1]UN- + FINISHED]

[1]**unfit** /un'fit/ *adj* **1** unsuitable, inappropriate **2** incapable, incompetent ⟨*~ for duty*⟩ **3** physically or mentally unsound [[1]UN- + [3]FIT] – **unfitness** *n*

[2]**unfit** *vt* **-tt-** to make unfit; disqualify ⟨*~ted by temperament for the scholastic life*⟩

unflagging /un'flaging/ *adj* never flagging; tireless – **unflaggingly** *adv*

unflappable /un'flapəbl/ *adj* remaining calm and composed; imperturbable [[1]*un-* + *flap* (state of excitement) + *-able*] – **unflappability** /-pə'biləti/ *n*

unflattering /un'flatəring/ *adj* not flattering; *esp* unfavourable ⟨*~ comments*⟩ – **unflatteringly** *adv*

unfledged /un'flejd/ *adj* **1** not feathered; not ready for flight **2** not fully developed; immature

unflinching /un'flinching/ *adj* not flinching or shrinking; steadfast – **unflinchingly** *adv*

unfold /un'fohld/ *vt* **1** to open the folds of; spread or straighten out **2** to disclose gradually ~ *vi* **1** to open from a folded state **2** to open out gradually to the mind or eye

unforeseeable *adj*

unforeseen *adj*

unforgettable /,unfə'getəbl/ *adj* incapable of being forgotten; memorable – **unforgettably** *adv*

unforgivable *adj*

unformed /un'fawmd/ *adj* not shaped; *esp* immature, undeveloped

[1]**unfortunate** /un'fawch(ə)nət/ *adj* **1a** unsuccessful, unlucky **b** accompanied by or resulting in misfortune ⟨*an ~ decision*⟩ **2** unsuitable, inappropriate ⟨*an ~ choice of words*⟩

[2]**unfortunate** *n* an unfortunate person

un'fortunately /-li/ *adv* **1** in an unfortunate manner **2** as is unfortunate ⟨*~ the matter is not so simple*⟩

unfounded /un'fowndid/ *adj* lacking a sound basis; groundless

unfreeze /un'freez/ *vb* **unfroze** /-'frohz/; **unfrozen** /-'frohz(ə)n/ to (cause to) thaw

unfrequented /,unfri'kwentid, -'freekwəntid/ *adj* not often visited or travelled over

unfriendly *adj*

unfrock /un'frok/ *vt* to deprive (esp a priest) of the right to exercise the functions of office

unfulfilled *adj*

unfurl /un'fuhl/ *vb* to (cause to) open out from a furled state; unroll

unfurnished *adj*

ungainly /un'gaynli/ *adj* lacking in grace or dexterity; clumsy [[1]*un-* + *gainly* (suitable, graceful), fr *gain* (direct, handy), fr ME *gayn*, fr OE *gēn*, fr ON *gegn*] – **ungainliness** *n*

ungenerous /un'jen(ə)rəs/ *adj* **1** petty, uncharitable **2** stingy, mean [[1]UN- + GENEROUS] – **ungenerously** *adv*

ungentlemanly *adj*

ungodly /un'godli/ *adj* **1a** denying God or disobedient to him; heathen **b** sinful, wicked **2** indecent, outrageous ⟨*gets up at an ~ hour*⟩ – compare UNEARTHLY 4 – **ungodliness** *n*

ungovernable /un'guv(ə)nəbl/ *adj* not capable of being controlled or restrained

ungraceful *adj*

ungracious /un'grayshəs/ *adj* rude, impolite [[1]UN- + GRACIOUS] – **ungraciously** *adv*, **ungraciousness** *n*

ungrateful /un'graytf(ə)l/ *adj* **1** showing no gratitude **2** disagreeable, unpleasant – **ungratefully** *adv*, **ungratefulness** *n*

ungrudging /un'grujing/ *adj* generous, wholehearted ⟨*~ praise*⟩ – **ungrudgingly** *adv*

unguarded /un'gahdid/ *adj* **1** vulnerable to attack **2** showing lack of forethought or calculation; imprudent – **unguardedly** *adv*, **unguardedness** *n*

unguent /'ung·gwənt/ *n* a soothing or healing salve; ointment [ME, fr L *unguentum* – more at OINTMENT]

unguis /'ung·gwis/ *n, pl* **ungues** /-gweez/ **1** a nail, claw, or hoof, esp on a digit of a vertebrate **2** a narrow pointed base of a petal [L]

[1]**ungulate** /'ungyoolət, -,layt/ *adj* **1** having hoofs **2** of or belonging to the ungulates [LL *ungulatus*, fr L *ungula* hoof, fr *unguis* nail, hoof]

[2]**ungulate** *n* any of the group consisting of the hoofed mammals [NL *Ungulata*, group name, fr neut pl of LL *ungulatus*]

unhampered *adj*

unhand /un'hand/ *vt* to remove the hands from; let go

unhappily /un'hapəli/ *adv* **1** in an unhappy manner **2** UNFORTUNATELY 2

unhappy /un'hapi/ *adj* **1** not fortunate; unlucky **2** sad, miserable **3** unsuitable, inappropriate ⟨*an ~ remark*⟩ – **unhappiness** *n*

unharmed *adj*

unhealthy /un'helthi/ *adj* **1** not in or conducive to good health **2** unnatural; *esp* morbid ⟨*an ~ interest in death*⟩ – **unhealthily** *adv*, **unhealthiness** *n*

unheard /un'huhd/ *adj* **1** not perceived by the ear **2** not given a hearing

un'heard-of *adj* previously unknown; unprecedented

unheeded *adj*

unhelpful *adj*

unheralded *adj*

unhinge /un'hinj/ *vt* **1** to remove (e g a door) from hinges **2** to make unstable; unsettle ⟨*her mind was ~d by grief*⟩

unholy /un'hohli/ *adj* **1** wicked, reprehensible ⟨*an ~ alliance*⟩ **2** terrible, awful – infml ⟨*making an ~ racket*⟩ – **unholiness** *n*

unhook /un'hook/ *vt* **1** to remove from a hook **2** to unfasten the hooks of

unhorse /un'haws/ *vt* to dislodge (as if) from a horse

unhurried /un'hurid/ *adj* not hurried; leisurely – **unhurriedly** *adv*

unhurt *adj*

unhygienic *adj*

uni- /yoohni-/ *prefix* one; single ⟨uni*cellular*⟩ [ME, fr MF, fr L, fr *unus* – more at ONE]

uniaxial /,yoohni'aksi·əl/ *adj* of or having only 1 axis – **uniaxially** *adv*

uni'cameral /-'kamərəl/ *adj* of or having a single legislative chamber [*uni-* + *cameral* (as in *bicameral*)] – **unicamerally** *adv*

uni'cellular /-'selyoolə/ *adj* having or consisting of a single cell – **unicellularity** /-,selyoo'larəti/ *n*

unicorn /'yoohni,kawn/ *n* a mythical animal usu depicted as a white horse with a single horn in the middle of the forehead [ME *unicorne,* fr OF, fr LL *unicornis,* fr L, having one horn, fr *uni-* + *cornu* horn – more at HORN]

'uni,cycle /-,siekl/ *n* any of various vehicles that have a single wheel and are propelled usu by pedals [*uni* + *-cycle* (as in *tricycle*)] – **unicyclist** /-,sieklist/ *n*

unidentified *adj*

,unidi'rectional /-di'reksh(ə)nl, -die-/ *adj* involving, functioning in, or moving in a single direction – **unidirectionally** *adv*

Unification church *n* the church of the Moonies

¹uniform /'yoohni,fawm/ *adj* **1** not varying in character, appearance, quantity, etc ⟨*a ~ speed*⟩ **2** conforming to a rule, pattern, or practice; consonant [MF *uniforme,* fr L *uniformis,* fr *uni-* + *-formis* -form] – **uniformly** *adv,* **uniformness** *n*

²uniform *vt* to clothe in a uniform ⟨*a ~ed officer*⟩

³uniform *n* dress of a distinctive design or fashion worn by members of a particular group and serving as a means of identification

Uniform – a communications code word for the letter *u*

uniformitarian /,yoohni,fawmi'teəri·ən/ *n or adj* (an adherent) of uniformitarianism

uniformitarianism /,yoohni,fawmi'teəri·ə,niz(ə)m/ *n* the theory that all geological changes can be accounted for by processes (e g faulting) existing and acting as at present

uniformity /,yoohni'fawməti/ *n* **1a** lack of variation or diversity; *esp* sameness, monotony **b** an instance of uniformity **2** consistency in conduct or opinion, esp in religion [¹UNIFORM + -ITY]

unify /'yoohni,fie/ *vt* to make into a unit or a coherent whole; unite [LL *unificare,* fr L *uni-* + *-ficare* -fy] – **unifier** *n,* **unifiable** *adj,* **unification** /-fi'kaysh(ə)n/ *n*

,uni'lateral /-'lat(ə)rəl/ *adj* **1a** done or undertaken by 1 person or party ⟨*~ disarmament*⟩ **b** of or affecting 1 side **2** produced or arranged on or directed towards 1 side ⟨*a stem bearing ~ flowers*⟩ **3** having only 1 side – **unilaterally** *adv*

,uni'locular /-'lokyoolə/ *adj* containing a single cavity ⟨*~ anthers*⟩

unimaginative *adj*

unimpaired *adj*

unimpeachable /,unim'peechəbl/ *adj* **1** not to be doubted; beyond question **2** irreproachable, blameless [¹UN- + IMPEACHABLE] – **unimpeachably** *adv*

unimportant *adj*

unimpressed *adj*

unimproved /,unim'proohvd/ *adj* **1** not improved for use (e g by being cultivated) ⟨*~ land*⟩ **2** not used or employed advantageously

uninhabited *adj*

uninhibited /,unin'hibitid/ *adj* acting spontaneously without constraint or regard for what others might think [¹UN- + INHIBITED] – **uninhibitedly** *adv,* **uninhibitedness** *n*

uninitiated *adj*

uninspiring *adj*

unintelligible *adj*

unintentional *adj*

uninterested *adj*

uninteresting *adj*

uninterrupted *adj*

uninucleate /,yoohni'nyoohkliayt, -ət/ *adj* having a single nucleus

uninvited *adj*

¹union /'yoohnyən/ *n* **1a(1)** the formation of a single political unit from 2 or more separate and independent units **(2)** a uniting in marriage; *also* SEXUAL INTERCOURSE **b** combination, junction **2a(1)** an association of independent individuals (e g nations) for some common purpose **(2)** a political unit made up from previously independent units **b** TRADE UNION **3** the set of all elements belonging to 1 or more of a given collection of 2 or more sets ☞ SYMBOL **4** a coupling for pipes (and fittings) [ME, fr MF, fr LL *union-, unio* oneness, union, fr L *unus* one – more at ONE]

²union *adj* of, dealing with, or constituting a union

'union ,card *n* a card certifying personal membership of a trade union

union cloth *n* any of various cloths having warp and weft threads of different fibres

Union Flag *n* UNION JACK

unionism /'yoohnyə,niz(ə)m/ *n* **1** adherence to the principles of trade unions **2** *cap* adherence to the policy of union between the states of the USA, esp during the Civil War **3** *cap* the principles and policies of the Unionist party

unionist /'yoohnyənist/ *n* an advocate or supporter of union or unionism

Unionist *adj* of or constituting a political party of N Ireland that supports the union with Britain and draws support generally from the Protestant community

union·ize, -ise /'yoohnyə,niez/ *vt* to cause to become a member of or subject to the rules of a trade union; form into a trade union – **unionization** /-'zaysh(ə)n/

,Union 'Jack /jak/ *n* the national flag of the UK combining crosses representing England, Scotland, and N Ireland [¹*jack* (small national flag flown by a ship)]

'union ,suit *n, NAm* COMBINATIONS 3

uniparous /yoo'nipərəs/ *adj* producing only 1 egg or offspring at a time; *also* having produced 1 offspring

unipolar /,yoohni'pohlə/ *adj* having, produced by, or acting by a single magnetic or electrical pole – **unipolarity** /-pə'larəti/ *n*

unique /yooh'neek, yoo-/ *adj* **1a** sole, only ⟨*his ~ concern*⟩ **b** producing only 1 result ⟨*the ~ factorization of a number into prime factors*⟩ **2** without a like or equal; unequalled **3** very rare or unusual –

disapproved of by some speakers [F, fr L *unicus*, fr *unus* one – more at ONE] – **uniquely** *adv*, **uniqueness** *n*

unisex /ˈyoohni,seks/ *adj* **1** able to be worn by both sexes ⟨*a ~ hair style*⟩ **2** dealing in unisex products or styles ⟨*a ~ barber's*⟩

,uniˈsexual /-ˈseksyooəl, -ˈseksh(ə)l/ *adj* of or restricted to 1 sex: **a** male or female but not both **b** dioecious ⟨*a ~ flower*⟩ – **unisexually** *adv*, **unisexuality** /-,seksyooˈaləti, -shooˈaləti/ *n*

unison /ˈyoohnis(ə)n, -z(ə)n/ *n* **1a** (the state of) identity in musical pitch; the interval between 2 notes of the same pitch **b** the writing, playing, or singing of parts in a musical passage at the same pitch or in octaves **2** harmonious agreement or union [MF, fr ML *unisonus* having the same sound, fr L *uni-* + *sonus* sound – more at [3]SOUND] – **unison** *adj*

unit /ˈyoohnit/ *n* **1a(1)** the first and lowest natural number; one **(2)** a single quantity regarded as a whole in calculation **b** the number occupying the position immediately to the left of the decimal point in the Arabic notation; *also, pl* this position **2** a determinate quantity (e g of length, time, heat, value, or housing) adopted as a standard of measurement 👁 **3a** a single thing, person, or group that is a constituent of a whole **b** a part of a military establishment that has a prescribed organization (e g of personnel and supplies) **c** a piece of apparatus serving to perform 1 particular function [back-formation fr *unity*] – **unit** *adj*, **unitive** *adj*, **unitize** *vt*

unitarian /,yoohniˈteəri·ən/ *n* **1** *often cap* a person who rejects the doctrine of the Trinity and believes in one god who is a single being **2** *cap* a member of a Christian denomination that stresses individual freedom of belief, the free use of reason in religion, a united world community, and liberal social action [NL *unitarius*, fr L *unitas* unity] – **unitarian** *adj, often cap*, **unitarianism** *n, often cap*

unitary /ˈyoohnit(ə)ri/ *adj* **1a** of or relating to a unit **b** based on or characterized by unity or units **2** undivided, whole – **unitarily** /ˈyoohnit(ə)rəli, ,yoohniˈterəli/ *adv*

unit character *n* a natural character inherited either as a whole or not at all; *esp* one dependent on the presence or absence of a single gene

unite /yooˈniet, yooh-/ *vt* **1** to join together to form a single unit **2** to link by a legal or moral bond ⟨~d *by marriage*⟩ ~ *vi* **1** to become (as if) 1 unit **2** to act in concert [ME *uniten*, fr LL *unitus*, pp of *unire*, fr L *unus* one – more at ONE] – **uniter** *n*

uˈnited *adj* **1** combined, joined **2** relating to or produced by joint action ⟨*a ~ effort*⟩ **3** in agreement; harmonious – **unitedly** *adv*

U,nited Reˈformed *adj* of the United Reformed Church formed in 1972 by the union of the Presbyterian Church of England and the Congregational Church of England and Wales

unit membrane *n* a 3-layered semipermeable membrane structure consisting of a lipid layer 2 molecules thick that contains protein molecules [fr its being the basic structural unit of the cell]

unit trust *n* an investment company that minimizes the risk to investors by collective purchase of shares in many different enterprises – compare INVESTMENT TRUST

unity /ˈyoohnəti/ *n* **1a** the state of being 1 or united ⟨*strength lies in ~*⟩ **b(1)** a definite amount taken as 1 or for which 1 is made to stand in calculation ⟨*in a table of natural sines the radius of the circle is regarded as ~*⟩ **(2)** a number by which any element of an arithmetical or mathematical system can be multiplied without change in the resultant value **2a** concord, harmony **b** continuity and agreement in aims and interests ⟨*~ of purpose*⟩ **3** singleness of effect or symmetry in a literary or artistic work **4** a whole made up of related parts [ME *unite*, fr OF *unité*, fr L *unitat-, unitas*, fr *unus* one]

[1]**univalent** /,yoohniˈvayl ənt/ *adj* **1** having a valency of 1 **2** *of a chromosome* not pairing with another chromosome at meiotic cell division [ISV]

[2]**univalent** *n* a univalent chromosome

ˈ**uni,valve** /-,valv/ *adj* having or consisting of 1 valve

[1]**universal** /,yoohniˈvuhs(ə)l/ *adj* **1** including or covering all or a whole without limit or exception **2** present or occurring everywhere or under all conditions **3** including a major part or the greatest portion (e g of mankind) ⟨*~ practices*⟩ **4** affirming or denying sthg of, or denoting, every member of a class ⟨*'no man knows everything' is a ~ negative*⟩ [ME, fr MF, fr L *universalis*, fr *universum* universe] – **universalize** *vt*, **universally** *adv*, **universalness** *n*, **universality** /-ˈsaləti/ *n*

[2]**universal** *n* **1** a universal proposition in logic **2** a general concept or term

universal coupling *n* UNIVERSAL JOINT

,uniˈversal,ism /-,iz(ə)m/ *n* **1** *often cap* a theological doctrine that everyone will eventually be saved **2** universality – **universalist** /,yoohniˈvuhs(ə)l·ist/ *n or adj, often cap*

universal joint *n* a shaft coupling capable of transmitting rotation from one shaft to another at an angle ☞ CAR

universe /ˈyoohni,vuhs/ *n* **1a(1)** all things that exist; the cosmos **(2)** a galaxy **b** the whole world; everyone **2** POPULATION 5 [L *universum*, fr neut of *universus* entire, whole, fr *uni-* + *versus* turned towards, fr pp of *vertere* to turn – more at [1]WORTH]

university /,yoohniˈvuhsəti/ *n* (the premises of) an institution of higher learning that provides facilities for full-time teaching and research, is authorized to grant academic degrees, and in Britain receives a Treasury grant ⟨*she's at ~*⟩ [ME *universite*, fr OF *université*, fr ML *universitat-, universitas*, fr L *universus*]

university extension *n* a system by which a university provides public lectures and courses

univocal /yoohˈnivəkl/ *adj* having 1 meaning only [LL *univocus*, fr L *uni-* + *voc-, vox* voice – more at VOICE] – **univocally** *adv*

unjust /unˈjust/ *adj* characterized by injustice; unfair – **unjustly** *adv*, **unjustness** *n*

unjustifiable *adj*

unjustified *adj*

unkempt /unˈkempt/ *adj* **1** not combed; dishevelled ⟨*~ hair*⟩ **2** not neat or tidy [[1]*un-* + *kempt* (combed, neat), fr ME, pp of *kemben* to comb, fr OE *cemban*]

unkind /unˈkiend/ *adj* **1** not pleasing or mild ⟨*an ~ climate*⟩ **2** lacking in kindness or sympathy; harsh – **unkindly** *adv*, **unkindness** *n*

unknowable /unˈnoh·əbl/ *adj* not knowable; *esp* lying beyond the limits of human experience or understanding

Measures and weights

The measures and weights shown on these pages are provided as a quick guide to common conversion factors. For comprehensive details see the following pages.

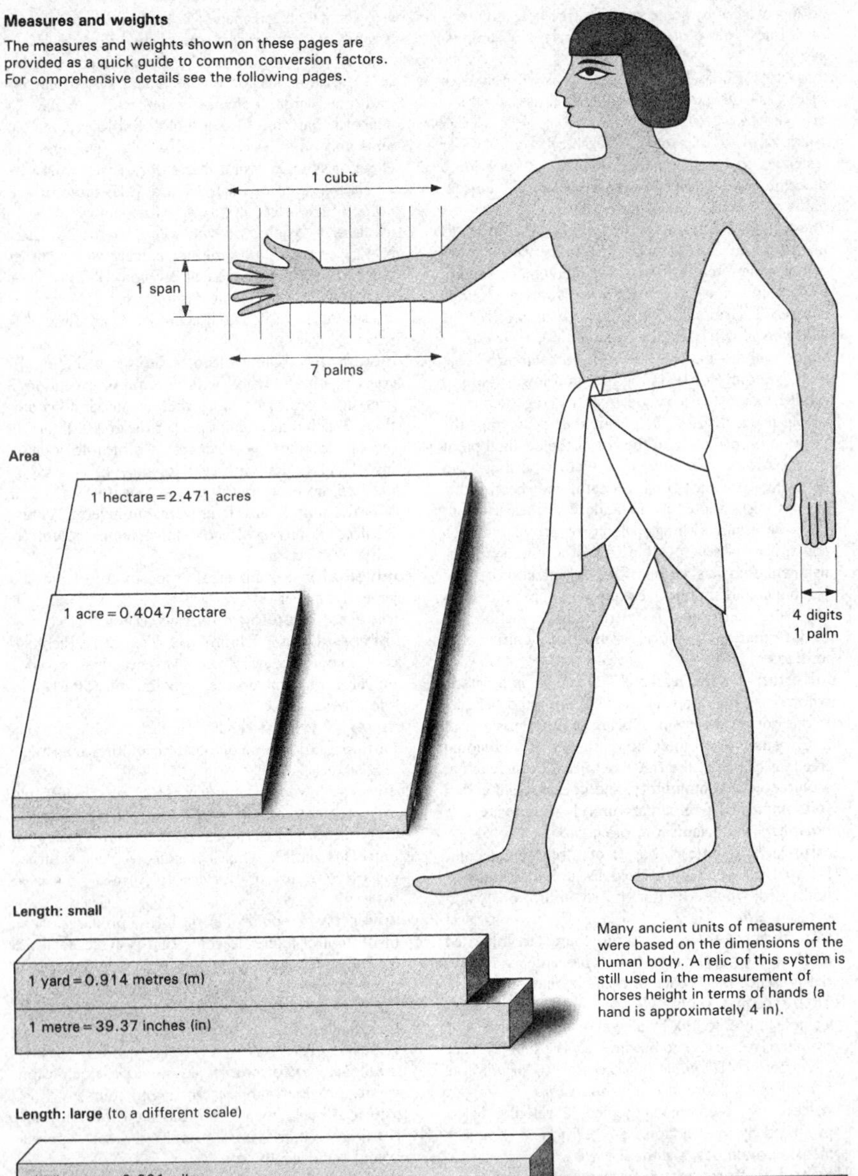

Many ancient units of measurement were based on the dimensions of the human body. A relic of this system is still used in the measurement of horses height in terms of hands (a hand is approximately 4 in).

Weight

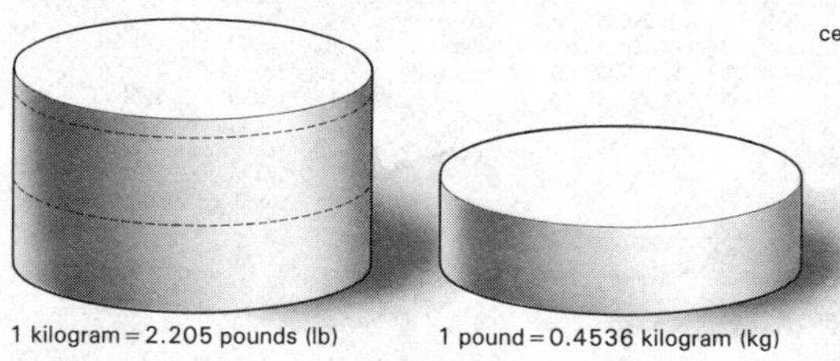

1 kilogram = 2.205 pounds (lb) 1 pound = 0.4536 kilogram (kg)

Liquid capacity

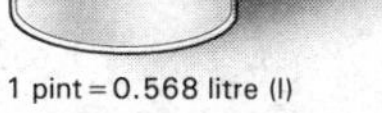

1 litre = 1.76 pints 1 pint = 0.568 litre (l)

Conversions

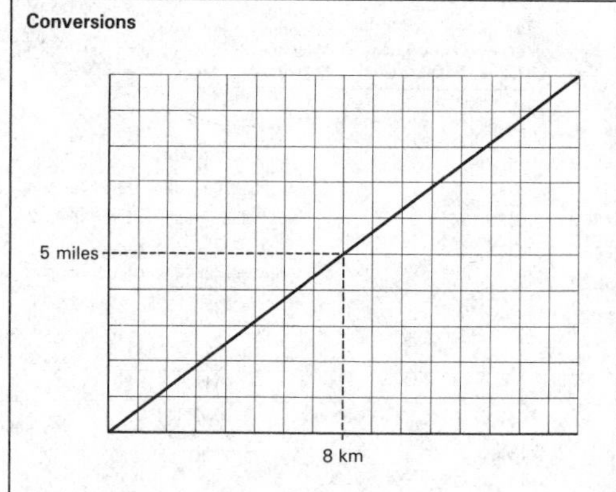

Conversion graphs can be made for any pair of units. Joining the origin of the graph to a known point where the units are equal will enable you to obtain the conversion immediately

Temperature

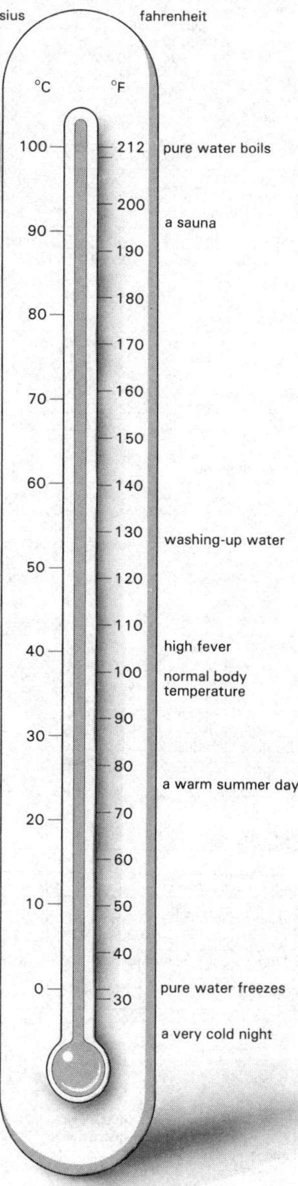

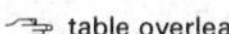 table overleaf

Length

	m	cm	in	ft	yd
1 metre	1	100	39.3701	3.28084	1.09361
1 centimetre	0.01	1	0.393701	0.0328084	0.0109361
1 inch	0.0254	2.54	1	0.0833333	0.0277778
1 foot	0.3048	30.48	12	1	0.3333333
1 yard	0.9144	91.44	36	3	1

1 kilometre = 100m
1 mile = 1760yd

	km	mi	n.mi
1 kilometre	1	0.621371	0.539957
1 mile	1.60934	1	0.868976
1 nautical mile	1.85200	1.15078	1

1 light year = 9.46070×10^{15} metres = 5.87848×10^{12} miles
1 Astronomical Unit = 1.495×10^{11} metres
1 parsec = 3.0857×10^{16} metres = 3.2616 light years

1 digit	=	1.9 cm	$\frac{3}{4}$ in
1 hand	=	10 cm	4 in
1 palm (length)	=	approx 20 cm	8 in
(breadth)	=	or 10 cm	4 in
1 span	=	approx 23 cm	9 in
1 cubit	=	approx 46 cm	18 in
1 pace	=	approx 75 cm	30 in
1 link	=	20.1 cm	$7\frac{11}{12}$ in
1 ell	=	1.14 m	45 in
1 fathom	=	1.83 m	6 ft
1 rod, pole, or perch	=	5.03 m	$5\frac{1}{2}$ yd
1 chain	=	20.1 m	22 yd
1 furlong	=	201 m	220 yd
1 league (variable)	=	5 km	3 mi

Area

1 are	=	100 m^2	119.6 yd^2
1 hectare	=	100 are	2.471 acres
1 km^2	=	100 hectares	0.387 mi^2
1 acre	=	0.4047 hectare	4840 yd^2
1 rood	=	1011.7 m^2	$\frac{1}{4}$ acre
1 mi^2	=	2.59 km^2	640 acres

Cubic measure

		1 cubic inch	=	16.4 cm^3
1728 cu in	=	1 cubic foot	=	0.0283 m^3
27 cu ft	=	1 cubic yard	=	0.765 m^3
		1 cu centimetre	=	0.061 in^3
1000 cu cm	=	1 cu decimetre	=	0.035 ft^3
1000 cu dm	=	1 cu metre	=	1.308 yd^3

Capacity measure

		1 fluid ounce	=	28.4 ml
5 fl oz	=	1 gill	=	0.142 l
4 gill	=	1 pint	=	0.568 l
2 pt	=	1 quart	=	1.136 l
4 qt	=	1 gallon	=	4.546 l
		1 millilitre	=	0.002 pt
10 ml	=	1 centilitre	=	0.018 pt
10 cl	=	1 decilitre	=	0.176 pt
10 dl	=	1 litre	=	1.76 pt

Weight

		1 grain	=	64.8 mg
		1 dram	=	1.772 g
16 drams	=	1 ounce	=	28.35 g
16 oz	=	1 pound	=	0.4536 kg
14 pounds	=	1 stone	=	6.35 kg
2 stones	=	1 quarter	=	12.7 kg
4 quarters	=	1 hundredweight	=	50.8 kg
20 cwt	=	1 (long) ton	=	1.016 tonnes
		1 milligram	=	0.015 grain
10 mg	=	1 centigram	=	0.154 grain
10 cg	=	1 decigram	=	1.543 grain
10 dg	=	1 gram	=	15.43 grain = 0.035 oz
1000 g	=	1 kilogram	=	2.205 lb
1000 kg	=	1 tonne (metric ton)	=	0.984 (long) ton
1 slug	=	14.5939 kg	=	32.174 lb

Troy weight

		1 grain	=	0.0648 g
24 grains	=	1 pennyweight (dwt)	=	1.555 g
20 dwt (480 grains)	=	1 ounce	=	31.1035 g
12 oz (5760 grains)	=	1 pound	=	373.27 g

Velocity

	m/sec	km/hr	mi/hr	ft/sec
1 metre per second	1	3.6	2.23694	3.28084
1 kilometre per hour	0.277778	1	0.621371	0.911346
1 mile per hour	0.44704	1.609344	1	1.46667
1 foot per second	0.3048	1.09728	0.681817	1

1 knot = 1 nautical mile per hour = 0.514444 metre per second

Temperature

°Fahrenheit = $(\frac{9}{5} \times \chi°C) + 32$

°Centigrade = $\frac{5}{9} \times (\chi°F - 32)$

where χ is the temperature needing converting

Pressure

	N/m^2(Pa)	kg/cm^2	lb/in^2	atmos
1 newton per square metre (pascal)	1	1.01972×10^{-5}	1.45038×10^{-4}	9.86923×10^{-6}
1 kilogram per square centimetre	980.665×10^2	1	14.2234	0.967841
1 pound per square inch	6.89476×10^3	0.0703068	1	0.068046
1 atmosphere	1.01325×10^5	1.03323	14.6959	1

1 pascal = 1 newton per square metre = 10 dynes per square centimetre
1 bar = 10^5 newtons per square metre = 0.986923 atmosphere
1 torr = 133.322 newtons per square metre = 1/760 atmosphere
1 atmosphere = 760 mm Hg = 29.92 in Hg = 33.90 ft water (all at 0°C.)

Work and energy

	J	cal	kWhr	btu
1 joule	1	0.238846	2.77778×10^{-7}	9.47813×10^{-4}
1 calorie	4.1868	1	1.16300×10^{-6}	3.96831×10^{-3}
1 kilowatt hour	3.6×10^{6}	8.59845×10^{5}	1	3412.14
1 British Thermal Unit	1055.06	251.997	2.93071×10^{-4}	1

1 joule = 1 newton metre = 1 watt second = 10^7 ergs = 0.737561 ft lb
1 electron volt = $1.602\ 10 \times 10^{-19}$ joule

Force

	N	kg	dyne	poundal	lb
1 newton	1	0.101972	10^5	7.23300	0.224809
1 kilogram force	9.80665	1	9.80665×10^5	70.9316	2.20462
1 dyne	10^{-5}	1.01972×10^{-6}	1	7.23300×10^{-5}	2.24809×10^{-6}
1 poundal	0.138255	1.40981×10^{-2}	1.38255×10^4	1	0.031081
1 pound force	4.44822	0.453592	4.44823×10^5	32.174	1

Apothecaries weight

		1 grain	=	0.0648 g
20 grains	=	1 scruple	=	1.296 g
3 scruples (60 grains)	=	1 drachm	=	3.888 g
8 drachms (480 grains)	=	1 ounce	=	31.1035 g

Apothecaries capacity measure

		1 minim	=	0.059 ml
60 minims	=	1 fluid drachm	=	3.55 ml
8 fl drachm	=	1 fluid ounce	=	28.4 ml
20 fl oz	=	1 pint	=	0.568 l
8 pt	=	1 gallon	=	4.546 l

UK cookery measures

1 teaspoonful	=	6 ml
1 dessertspoonful	=	12 ml
1 tablespoonful	=	18 ml
1 cupful	=	284 ml

US cookery measures

1 teaspoonful	=	5 ml
1 tablespoonful	=	15 ml
1 cupful	=	237 ml

US measures

Capacity measure

		1 minim	=	0.059 ml
60 minims	=	1 fluid dram	=	3.6966 ml
8 fl drams	=	1 fluid ounce	=	0.296 dl
16 fl oz	=	1 pint	=	0.473 l
2 pt	=	1 quart	=	0.946 l
4 qt	=	1 gallon	=	3.785 l

Dry measure

		1 pint	=	0.551 l
2 pt	=	1 quart	=	1.101 l
8 qt	=	1 peck	=	8.809 l
4 pecks	=	1 bushel	=	35.238 l

Weight

25 lb	=	1 US quarter = 12.7 kg
4 quarters (100 lb)	=	1 US hundredweight (cwt) = 45.36 kg
20 cwt (2000 lb)	=	1 US (short) ton = 907.19 kg

Clothing

Women's clothes

British and American sizes with average cm/in equivalents

British	8	10	12	14	16	18	20
bust	76 cm	81 cm	86 cm	91 cm	97 cm	102 cm	107 cm
hips	81 cm	86 cm	91 cm	97 cm	102 cm	107 cm	112 cm
waist	58 cm	58 cm	61 cm	66 cm	71 cm	76 cm	81 cm
American	**6**	**8**	**10**	**12**	**14**	**16**	**18**
bust	30 in	32 in	34 in	36 in	38 in	40 in	42 in
hips	32 in	34 in	36 in	38 in	40 in	42 in	44 in
waist	23 in	23 in	24 in	26 in	28 in	30 in	32 in

Women's shoes

British	3	3½	4	4½	5	5½	6	6½	7	7½
American	4½	5	5½	6	6½	7	7½	8	8½	9
Continental	35½	36	36½	37	37½	38	38½	39	39½	40

Men's shirts

British	14	14½	15	15½	16	16½	17
American	14	14½	15	15½	16	16½	17
Continental	36	37	38	39	41	42	43

Men's shoes

British	7	7½	8	8½	9	9½	10	10½	11	11½
American	8½	9	9½	10	10½	11	11½	12	12½	13
Continental	40	40½	41	41½	42	42½	43	43½	44	44½

unknowing /un'noh·ing/ *adj* not knowing – **unknowingly** *adv*

1**unknown** /un'nohn/ *adj* not known; *also* having an unknown value ⟨*an ~ quantity*⟩

2**unknown** *n* **1** a person who is little known (e g to the public) **2** a symbol in a mathematical equation representing an unknown quantity

,**Unknown 'Soldier** *n* an unidentified soldier whose body is entombed in a national memorial as a representative of all of the same nation who died in a war, esp either of the world wars

unlace /un'lays/ *vt* to undo the lacing of

unlatch /un'lach/ *vt* to open or loose by lifting a latch ~ *vi* to become unlatched

unlawful /un'lawf(ə)l/ *adj* **1** illegal **2** not morally right or conventional – **unlawfully** *adv*, **unlawfulness** *n*

unlay /un'lay/ *vt* **unlaid** /-'layd/ to untwist the strands of (e g a rope)

unlearn /un'luhn/ *vt* to put out of one's knowledge or memory

unlearned /un'luhnd, -'luhnt/ *adj* **1** not educated **2** ignorant **3** not gained by study or training

unleash /un'leesh/ *vt* to free (as if) from a leash; loose from restraint or control

unleavened *adj*

unless /ən'les/ *conj* **1** except on the condition that ⟨*won't work ~ you put in some money*⟩ **2** without the necessary accompaniment that; except when ⟨*we swim ~ it's very cold*⟩ [ME *unlesse*, alter. of *onlesse*, fr *on* + *lesse* less]

unlettered /un'letəd/ *adj* illiterate [1UN- + LETTERED]

unlicensed *adj*

1**unlike** /,un'liek/ *prep* **1** different from **2** not characteristic of ⟨*~ him to be late*⟩ **3** in a different manner from [1UN- + 4LIKE]

2**unlike** *adj* **1** marked by dissimilarity; different **2** unequal – **unlikeness** *n*

un'likely /-li/ *adj* **1** having a low probability of being or occurring ⟨*an ~ possibility*⟩ **2** not believable; improbable ⟨*an ~ story*⟩ **3** likely to fail; unpromising **4** not foreseen ⟨*the ~ result*⟩ – **unlikelihood** *n*, **unlikeliness** *n*

unlimber /un'limbə/ *vt* to detach (a gun) from the limber and so make ready

unlimited /un'limited/ *adj* **1** lacking any controls or restrictions **2** boundless, infinite – **unlimitedly** *adv*

unlisted /un'listid/ *adj* **1** not appearing on a list **2** *chiefly NAm* ex-directory

unload /un'lohd/ *vt* **1a(1)** to take off or out **(2)** to take the cargo from **b** to give vent to; pour forth **2** to relieve of sthg burdensome **3** to draw the charge from **4** DUMP 2 ~ *vi* to perform the act of unloading – **unloader** *n*

unlock /un'lok/ *vt* **1** to unfasten the lock of **2** to open, release **3** to provide a key to; disclose ⟨*~ the secrets of nature*⟩ ~ *vi* to become unlocked

unlooked-for /un'lookt faw/ *adj* not foreseen or expected

unloose /un'loohs/ *vt* **1** to relax the strain of ⟨*~ a grip*⟩ **2** to release (as if) from restraints; set free **3** to loosen the ties of

unloosen /un'loohs(ə)n/ *vt* to unloose

unlovely /,un'luvli/ *adj* disagreeable, unpleasant – **unloveliness** *n*

unlucky /un'luki/ *adj* **1** marked by adversity or failure ⟨*an ~ year*⟩ **2** likely to bring misfortune ⟨*an ~ omen*⟩ **3** having or meeting with bad luck ⟨*~ people*⟩ – **unluckily** *adv*, **unluckiness** *n*

unmade /,un'mayd/ *adj*, *of a bed* not put in order ready for sleeping

unmake /,un'mayk/ *vt* **unmade** /-'mayd/ **1** to undo, destroy **2** to deprive of rank or office; depose **3** to change the nature of

unman /,un'man/ *vt* **-nn-** **1** to deprive of manly vigour, fortitude, etc **2** to castrate, emasculate

unmanageable *adj*

unmanly /un'manli/ *adj* **1** lacking in manly virtues; weak, cowardly **2** effeminate – **unmanliness** *n*

unmanned /,un'mand/ *adj* not manned ⟨*an ~ spaceflight*⟩

unmannerly /un'manəli/ *adj* discourteous, rude – **unmannerliness** *n*

unmarried *adj*

unmask /un'mahsk/ *vt* **1** to remove a mask from **2** to reveal the true nature of; expose

unmentionable /un'mensh(ə)nəbl/ *adj* not fit to be mentioned; unspeakable

un'mentionables *n pl* underwear – euph or humor

unmerited *adj*

unmindful /un'miendf(ə)l/ *adj* not taking into account; forgetful *of*

unmistakable /,unmi'staykəbl/ *adj* clear, obvious [1UN- + MISTAKABLE] – **unmistakably** *adv*

unmitigated /un'mitigaytid/ *adj* **1** not diminished in severity, intensity, etc **2** out-and-out, downright ⟨*the evening was an ~ disaster*⟩ ⟨*an ~ evil*⟩ – **unmitigatedly** *adv*

unmixed *adj*

unnamed *adj*

unnatural /un'nachərəl/ *adj* **1** not in accordance with nature or a normal course of events **2a** not in accordance with normal feelings or behaviour; perverse **b** artificial or contrived in manner – **unnaturally** *adv*, **unnaturalness** *n*

unnecessary /un'nesəs(ə)ri, -,seri/ *adj* not necessary – **unnecessarily** *adv*

unnerve /un'nuhv/ *vt* to deprive of nerve, courage, or the power to act – **unnervingly** *adv*

unnumbered /,un'numbəd/ *adj* **1** innumerable **2** without an identifying number ⟨*~ pages*⟩

unobserved *adj*

unobstructed *adj*

unobtainable *adj*

unobtrusive /,unəb'troohsiv, -ziv/ *adj* not too easily seen or noticed; inconspicuous – **unobtrusively** *adv*, **unobtrusiveness** *n*

unoccupied /un'okyoopied/ *adj* not occupied; *esp* not lived in; empty

unofficial *adj*

unopposed *adj*

unoriginal *adj*

unorthodox /un'awthədoks/ *adj* not conventional in behaviour, beliefs, doctrine, etc – **unorthodoxly** *adv*, **unorthodoxy** *n*

unpack /un'pak/ *vt* **1** to remove the contents of **2** to remove or undo from packing or a container ~ *vi* to set about unpacking sthg – **unpacker** *n*

unpaid *adj*

unpaired /,un'peəd/ *adj* not paired; *esp* not matched or mated

unpalatable /un'palətəbl/ *adj* **1** not pleasing to the taste **2** unpleasant, disagreeable – **unpalatability** /-tə'biləti/ *n*

unparalleled /un'parəleld/ *adj* having no equal or match; unique [¹UN- + PARALLELED]

unpardonable *adj*

unparliamentary /ˌunpahlə'mentəri; *also* -lyə-/ *adj* not in accordance with parliamentary practice

unpatriotic *adj*

unperson /un'puhs(ə)n/ *n, pl* **unpersons** a person who, usu for political or ideological reasons, is officially unrecognized

unperturbed *adj*

unpick /un'pik/ *vt* to undo (e g sewing) by taking out stitches

unpin /un'pin/ *vt* **-nn- 1** to remove a pin from **2** to loosen or unfasten by removing a pin

unplaced /un'playst/ *adj, chiefly Br* having failed to finish in a leading place in a competition, esp a horse race [¹UN- + PLACED]

unplanned *adj*

unplayable *adj*

unpleasant /un'plez(ə)nt/ *adj* not pleasant or agreeable; displeasing – **unpleasantly** *adv*

un'pleasantness /-nis/ *n* **1** the state of being unpleasant **2** an unpleasant situation, experience, etc

unplug /un'plug/ *vt* **-gg- 1a** to take a plug out of **b** to remove an obstruction from **2** to disconnect from an electric circuit by removing a plug ⟨~ *the refrigerator*⟩

unplumbed /un'plumd/ *adj* not thoroughly explored [¹UN- + PLUMBED]

unpolitical /ˌunpə'litikl/ *adj* not interested or engaged in politics

unpopular *adj* – **unpopularity** *n*

unprecedented /un'presidentid/ *adj* having no precedent; novel – **unprecedentedly** *adv*

unpredictable *adj*

unprejudiced /un'prejoodist, -jə-/ *adj* impartial, fair

unpremeditated *adj*

unprepared *adj*

unprepossessing *adj*

unpretentious /ˌunpri'tenshəs/ *adj* not seeking to impress others by means of wealth, standing, etc; not affected or ostentatious – **unpretentiously** *adv*, **unpretentiousness** *n*

unprincipled /un'prinsip(ə)ld/ *adj* without moral principles; unscrupulous – **unprincipledness** *n*

unprintable /un'printəbl/ *adj* unfit to be printed

unprofitable *adj*

unpromising *adj*

unpronounceable *adj*

unprotected *adj*

unprovoked *adj*

unputdownable /ˌunpoot'downəbl/ *adj, chiefly Br* compulsively readable – infml

unqualified /un'kwolified/ *adj* **1** not having the necessary qualifications **2** not modified or restricted by reservations ⟨~ *approval*⟩ – **unqualifiedly** /-fiedli, -ˌfie·idli/ *adv*

unquestionable /un'kwesch(ə)nəbl/ *adj* not able to be called in question; indisputable ⟨~ *evidence*⟩ – **unquestionably** *adv*

unquestioned *adj*

unquestioning /un'kwesch(ə)ning/ *adj* not expressing doubt or hesitation ⟨~ *obedience*⟩ – **unquestioningly** *adv*

unquiet /un'kwie·ət/ *adj* **1** agitated, turbulent **2** physically or mentally restless; uneasy – **unquietly** *adv*, **unquietness** *n*

unquote /ˌun'kwoht/ *n* – used orally to indicate the end of a direct quotation

unravel /un'ravl/ *vb* **-ll-** (*NAm* **-l-**, **-ll-**), /un'ravling, -'ravl·ing/ *vt* **1** to disentangle **2** to clear up or solve (sthg intricate or obscure) ~ *vi* to become unravelled

unread /un'red/ *adj* **1** not read **2** not familiar with or versed in a specified field

unreal *adj*

unrealistic *adj*

unreasonable /un'reez(ə)nəbl/ *adj* **1** not governed by or acting according to reason ⟨~ *people*⟩ **2** excessive, immoderate ⟨~ *demands*⟩ – **unreasonableness** *n*, **unreasonably** *adv*

unreasoning /un'reezəning/ *adj* not moderated or controlled by reason ⟨~ *fear*⟩ – **unreasoningly** *adv*

unreel /un'reel/ *vt* to unwind from a reel ~ *vi* to become unreeled

unrelated *adj*

unrelenting /ˌunri'lenting/ *adj* **1** not weakening in determination; stern **2** not letting up in vigour, pace, etc – **unrelentingly** *adv*

unreliable *adj*

unrelieved *adj*

unremitting /ˌunri'miting/ *adj* constant, incessant – **unremittingly** *adv*

unremunerative *adj*

unrepeatable *adj*

unrepresentative *adj*

unrequited *adj*

unreserved /ˌunri'zuhvd/ *adj* **1** entire, unqualified ⟨~ *enthusiasm*⟩ **2** frank and open in manner [¹UN- + RESERVED] – **unreservedly** /-vidli/ *adv*, **unreservedness** /-'zuhvdnis, -vidnis/ *n*

unresponsive *adj*

unrest /un'rest/ *n* agitation, turmoil

unrestrained /unri'straynd/ *adj* not held in check; uncontrolled [¹UN- + RESTRAINED] – **unrestrainedly** /-nidli/ *adv*, **unrestrainedness** /-nidnis/ *n*

unrestricted *adj*

unrewarding *adj*

unripe *adj*

unrivalled, *NAm chiefly* **unrivaled** /un'rievld/ *adj* unequalled, unparalleled [¹UN- + RIVALLED]

unroll /un'rohl/ *vt* to open out; uncoil ~ *vi* to be unrolled; unwind

unround /ˌun'rownd/ *vt* SPREAD 1c

unruffled /un'rufld/ *adj* **1** poised, serene **2** smooth, calm ⟨~ *water*⟩ [¹UN- + RUFFLED]

unruly /un'roohli/ *adj* difficult to discipline or manage [ME *unreuly*, fr *un-* + *reuly* disciplined, fr *reule* rule] – **unruliness** *n*

unsaddle /un'sadl/ *vt* **1** to take the saddle from **2** to throw from the saddle ~ *vi* to remove the saddle from a horse

unsafe *adj*

unsaid /un'sed/ *adj* not said or spoken

unsatisfactory *adj*

unsatisfying *adj*

unsaturated /un'sachooraytid/ *adj* not saturated: e g **a** capable of absorbing or dissolving more of sthg ⟨*an* ~ *solution*⟩ **b** able to form products by chemical addition; *esp* containing double or triple bonds between carbon atoms

unsavoury /un'sayvəri/ *adj* disagreeable, distasteful; *esp* morally offensive

unscathed /un'skaydhd/ *adj* entirely unharmed or uninjured

unschooled /un'skoohld/ *adj* untaught, untrained [[1]UN- + SCHOOLED]

unscientific /,unsie·ən'tifik/ *adj* **1** not in accordance with the principles and methods of science **2** without scientific knowledge – **unscientifically** *adv*

unscramble /,un'skrambl/ *vt* **1** to separate into original components **2** to restore (scrambled communication) to intelligible form – **unscrambler** *n*

unscrew /un'skrooh/ *vt* **1** to remove the screws from **2** to loosen or withdraw by turning ~ *vi* to become unscrewed

unscrupulous /un'skroohpyooləs/ *adj* without moral scruples; unprincipled – **unscrupulously** *adv*, **unscrupulousness** *n*

unseasonable /un'seez(ə)nəbl/ *adj* **1** untimely, inopportune **2** not normal for the season of the year ⟨~ *weather*⟩ – **unseasonableness** *n*, **unseasonably** *adv*

unseat /,un'seet/ *vt* **1** to dislodge from one's seat, esp on horseback **2** to remove from a (political) position

unseeing *adj*

unseemly /un'seemli/ *adj* not conforming to established standards of good behaviour or taste [[1]UN- + SEEMLY]

[1]**unseen** /,un'seen/ *adj* done without previous preparation ⟨*an* ~ *translation*⟩ [[1]UN- + SEEN]

[2]**unseen** *n, chiefly Br* a passage of unprepared translation ⟨*doing Latin* ~s⟩

unselfish /un'selfish/ *adj* not selfish; generous – **unselfishly** *adv*, **unselfishness** *n*

unsentimental *adj*

unserviceable *adj*

unsettle /un'setl/ *vt* **1** to move from a settled state or condition **2** to perturb or agitate ~ *vi* to become unsettled – **unsettlingly** *adv*

unsettled /un'setld/ *adj* **1a** not calm or tranquil; disturbed **b** variable, changeable ⟨~ *weather*⟩ **2** not resolved or worked out; undecided **3** not inhabited or populated ⟨~ *land*⟩ **4** not paid or discharged ⟨~ *debts*⟩ [[1]UN- + SETTLED] – **unsettledness** *n*

unsex /,un'seks/ *vt* to deprive of sexual power or the typical qualities of one's sex

unshackle /un'shakl/ *vt* to free from shackles

unshakable *adj*

unshaven *adj*

unsheathe /un'sheedh/ *vt* to draw (as if) from a sheath or scabbard

unship /,un'ship/ *vb* **-pp-** *vt* **1** to take out of a ship **2** to remove (e g an oar or tiller) from position ~ *vi* to become or be suitable for being detached or removed

unsight /,un'siet/ *vt* to prevent from seeing ⟨*the goalkeeper was* ~ed *and missed the ball*⟩

unsightly /un'sietli/ *adj* not pleasing to the eye; ugly

unsigned *adj*

unsinkable *adj*

unskilled /,un'skild/ *adj* **1** of, being, or requiring workers who are not skilled in any particular branch of work **2** showing a lack of skill

unsling /un'sling/ *vt* **unslung** /-'slung/ **1** to remove from being slung **2** to release from slings

unsociable /un'sohsh(i)əbl/ *adj* not liking social activity; reserved, solitary – **unsociableness** *n*, **unsociably** *adv*, **unsociability** /-sh(i)ə 'biləti/ *n*

unsocial /un'sohsh(ə)l/ *adj* **1** marked by or showing a dislike for social interaction **2** *Br* worked at a time that falls outside the normal working day and precludes participation in normal social activities ⟨~ *hours*⟩ – **unsocially** *adv*

unsold *adj*

unsolicited *adj*

unsophisticated /,unsə'fisti,kaytid/ *adj* **1** pure, unadulterated **2** not socially or culturally sophisticated **3** simple, straightforward – **unsophistication** /-'kaysh(ə)n/ *n*

unsound /,un'sownd/ *adj* **1** not healthy or whole **2** mentally abnormal ⟨*of* ~ *mind*⟩ **3** not firmly made, placed, or fixed **4** not valid or true; specious ⟨*an* ~ *premise*⟩ [[1]UN- + [1]SOUND] – **unsoundly** *adv*, **unsoundness** *n*

unsparing /,un'speəring/ *adj* **1** not merciful; hard, ruthless **2** liberal, generous – **unsparingly** *adv*

unspeakable /un'speekəbl/ *adj* **1** incapable of being expressed in words **2** too terrible or shocking to be expressed [[1]UN- + SPEAKABLE] – **unspeakably** *adv*

unspecified *adj*

unspoiled *adj*

unspoilt *adj*

unspoken *adj*

unsportsmanlike *adj*

unspotted /,un'spotid/ *adj* morally blameless [[1]UN- + SPOTTED]

unstable /un'staybl/ *adj* not stable; not firm or fixed; not constant: e g **a** apt to move, sway, or fall; unsteady ⟨*an* ~ *tower*⟩ **b** characterized by inability to control the emotions – **unstableness** *n*, **unstably** *adv*

[1]**unsteady** /un'stedi/ *vt* to make unsteady

[2]**unsteady** *adj* **1** not firm or stable; *also* walking in an erratic or staggering manner **2** changeable, fluctuating **3** not uniform or even; irregular [[1]UN- + [1]STEADY] – **unsteadily** *adv*, **unsteadiness** *n*

unstinting *adj*

unstop /,un'stop/ *vt* **-pp-** **1** to free from an obstruction **2** to remove a stopper from

unstoppable /un'stopəbl/ *adj* determined, forceful [[1]UN- + STOPPABLE] – **unstoppably** *adv*

unstreamed /,un'streemd/ *adj* not divided into educational streams

unstressed /un'strest/ *adj* **1** not bearing a stress or accent ⟨~ *syllables*⟩ **2** not subjected to stress ⟨~ *wires*⟩

unstring /un'string/ *vt* **unstrung** /-'strung/ **1** to loosen or remove the strings of **2** to make mentally disordered or unstable ⟨*was* unstrung *by the news*⟩

unstuck /un'stuk/ *adj* [[2]UN- + STUCK] – **come unstuck** to go wrong; be unsuccessful

unstudied /un'studid/ *adj* **1** not acquired by study **2** not done or planned for effect [[1]UN- + STUDIED]

unsubstantiated *adj*

unsuccessful *adj*

unsuitable /un's(y)oohtəbl/ *adj* not suitable or fitting; inappropriate – **unsuitably** *adv*, **unsuitability** /-tə'biləti/ *n*

unsuited *adj*

unsung /,un'sung/ *adj* not celebrated or praised (e g in song or verse) [[1]UN- + SUNG]

unsupported *adj*
unsure *adj*
unsurpassable *adj*
unsuspecting *adj*
unswerving /un'swuhving/ *adj* not deviating; constant ⟨~ *loyalty*⟩
unsympathetic *adj*
unsystematic *adj*
untangle /un'tang·gl/ *vt* to loose from tangles or entanglement; unravel
untapped /un'tapt/ *adj* **1** not yet tapped ⟨*an ~ keg*⟩ **2** not drawn on or exploited ⟨*as yet ~ markets*⟩
untarnished *adj*
untaught /,un'tawt/ *adj* **1** not educated; ignorant **2** not acquired by teaching; natural ⟨~ *kindness*⟩
untenable /un'tenəbl/ *adj* not able to be defended ⟨*an ~ opinion*⟩ – **untenability** /-nə'biləti/ *n*
unthinkable /un'thingkəbl/ *adj* contrary to what is acceptable or probable; out of the question – **unthinkably** *adv*, **unthinkability** /-kə'biləti/ *n*
unthinking /un'thingking/ *adj* not taking thought; heedless, unmindful – **unthinkingly** *adv*
unthought /,un'thawt/ *adj* not anticipated; unexpected – often + *of* or *on*
untidy /un'tiedi/ *adj* not neat; slovenly, disorderly – **untidily** *adv*, **untidiness** *n*
untie /un'tie/ *vt* **1** to free from sthg that fastens or restrains **2a** to separate out the knotted parts of **b** to disentangle, resolve ~ *vi* to become untied
[1]**until** /un'til, ən-/ *prep* **1** up to as late as ⟨*not available ~ tomorrow*⟩ **2** up to as far as ⟨*stay on the train ~ Birmingham*⟩ [ME, fr *un-* unto, until (akin to OE *oth* to, until, OHG *unt* unto, until, OE *ende* end) + *til*, *till* till]
[2]**until** *conj* up to the time that; until such time as
untimely /un'tiemli/ *adj* **1** occurring before the natural or proper time; premature ⟨~ *death*⟩ **2** inopportune, unseasonable ⟨*an ~ joke*⟩ ⟨~ *frost*⟩ – **untimeliness** *n*
untitled /un'tietld/ *adj* **1** not named ⟨*an ~ novel*⟩ **2** not called by a title ⟨~ *nobility*⟩
unto /'untoo, -tə/ *prep*, *archaic* TO 1, 2, 3 [ME, fr *un-* unto, until + *to*]
untold /un'tohld/ *adj* **1** incalculable, vast **2** not told or related
[1]**untouchable** /un'tuchəbl/ *adj* **1** that may not be touched **2** lying beyond reach ⟨~ *mineral resources buried deep within the earth*⟩ – **untouchability** /-chə'biləti/ *n*
[2]**untouchable** *n* sby or sthg untouchable; *specif*, *often cap* a member of a large formerly segregated hereditary group in India who in traditional Hindu belief can defile a member of a higher caste by contact or proximity
untouched *adj*
untoward /,untə'wawd/ *adj* not favourable; adverse, unfortunate – **untowardly** *adv*, **untowardness** *n*
untraceable *adj*
untried /un'tried/ *adj* not tested or proved by experience
untrod /un'trod/, **untrodden** /-d(ə)n/ *adj* not trod; unexplored
untroubled *adj*
untrue /un'trooh/ *adj* **1** not faithful; disloyal **2** not level or exact ⟨~ *doors and windows*⟩ **3** inaccurate, false – **untruly** *adv*
untrustworthy *adj*
untruth /,un'troohth/ *n* **1** lack of truthfulness **2** sthg untrue; a falsehood
untruthful /un'troohthf(ə)l/ *adj* not telling the truth; false, lying – **untruthfully** *adv*, **untruthfulness** *n*
untutored /un'tyoohtəd/ *adj* **1** having no formal learning or education **2** not produced by instruction; native ⟨*his ~ shrewdness*⟩
unusable *adj*
unused /un'yoohst; *senses 2a and 2b* -'yoohzd/ *adj* **1** unaccustomed – usu + *to* **2a** fresh, new **b** not used up ⟨~ *sick leave*⟩ [[1]UN- + USED]
unusual /un'yoohzhooəl, -zhəl/ *adj* **1** uncommon, rare **2** different, unique ⟨*an ~ painting*⟩ [[1]UN- + USUAL] – **unusually** *adv*, **unusualness** *n*
unutterable /un'ut(ə)rəbl/ *adj* **1** beyond the powers of description; inexpressible **2** out-and-out, downright ⟨*an ~ fool*⟩ – **unutterably** *adv*
unvarnished /,un'vahnisht/ *adj* not adorned or glossed; plain ⟨*told the ~ truth*⟩
unvarying *adj*
unveil /un'vayl/ *vt* **1** to remove a veil or covering from **2** to make public; divulge ~ *vi* to remove a veil or protective cloak
unvoiced /un'voyst/ *adj* **1** not expressed in words **2** voiceless
unwanted *adj*
unwarranted /un'worəntid/ *adj* not justified; (done) without good reason
unwary *adj*
unwashed /un'wosht/ *adj* not cleaned (as if) with soap and water
unwavering /un'wayv(ə)ring/ *adj* fixed, steadfast [[1]UN- + WAVERING] – **unwaveringly** *adv*
unwelcome *adj*
unwell /un'wel/ *adj* in poor health
unwieldy /un'weeldi/ *adj* difficult to move or handle; cumbersome [[1]*un-* + *wieldy* (capable of wielding, active), fr *wield* + [1]*-y*] – **unwieldily** *adv*, **unwieldiness** *n*
unwilling /un'wiling/ *adj* loath, reluctant ⟨*was ~ to learn*⟩ [[1]UN- + [1]WILLING] – **unwillingly** *adv*, **unwillingness** *n*
unwind /un'wiend/ *vb* **unwound** /-'wownd/ *vt* to cause to uncoil; unroll ~ *vi* **1** to become unwound **2** to become less tense; relax
unwise /un'wiez/ *adj* foolish, imprudent – **unwisely** *adv*, **unwisdom** /-'wizd(ə)m/ *n*
unwitting /un'witing/ *adj* **1** not intended; inadvertent ⟨*an ~ mistake*⟩ **2** ignorant, unaware ⟨*an ~ accomplice*⟩ [[1]*un-* + *witting*, prp of arch *wit* (to know), fr ME *witen*, fr OE *witan* – more at WIT] – **unwittingly** *adv*
unwonted /un'wohntid, -'won-/ *adj* out of the ordinary; unusual – **unwontedly** *adv*, **unwontedness** *n*
unworkable *adj*
unworldly /un'wuhldli/ *adj* **1** naive, unsophisticated **2** not swayed by material considerations (e g of wealth or personal gain) [[1]UN- + WORLDLY] – **unworldliness** *n*
unworn /,un'wawn/ *adj* **1** not impaired by use; not worn away **2** never worn; new
unworthy /un'wuhdhi/ *adj* **1a** lacking in excellence or quality; poor **b** base, dishonourable **2** not befitting one's position or condition of life ⟨*behaviour ~ of an ambassador*⟩ **3** not deserving ⟨~ *of attention*⟩ – **unworthily** *adv*, **unworthiness** *n*

unwrap /un'rap/ *vt* **-pp-** to remove the wrapping from ⟨~ *a package*⟩

unwritten /un'ritn/ *adj* **1** not (formally) written down **2** containing no writing; blank

unwritten constitution *n* a constitution not embodied in a single document but based chiefly on custom and precedent

unyielding /un'yeelding/ *adj* **1** lacking in softness or flexibility **2** firm, obdurate – **unyieldingly** *adv*

unyoke /un'yohk/ *vt* to free from a yoke or harness

unzip /un'zip/ *vb* **-pp-** to open (as if) by means of a zip

[1]up /up/ *adv* **1a** at or towards a relatively high level ⟨*live* ~ *in the mountains*⟩ **b** from beneath the ground or water to the surface **c** above the horizon **d** upstream **e** in or to a raised or upright position ⟨*hands* ~*!*⟩; *specif* out of bed ⟨*soon be* ~ *and about*⟩ **f** off or out of the ground or a surface ⟨*pull* ~ *a daisy*⟩ **g** UPWARDS 1b **h** to the top; *esp* so as to be full ⟨*top* ~ *the radiator*⟩ **2a** into a state of, or with, greater intensity or activity ⟨*speak* ~⟩ **b** into a faster pace or higher gear **3a** in or into a relatively high condition or status ⟨*family went* ~ *in the world*⟩ – sometimes used interjectionally as an expression of approval ⟨~ *BBC 2! – The Listener*⟩ **b** above a normal or former level ⟨*sales are* ~⟩: e g **(1)** UPWARDS 2b **(2)** higher in price **c** ahead of an opponent ⟨*we're 3 points* ~⟩ **4a(1)** in or into existence, evidence, prominence, or prevalence ⟨*new houses haven't been* ~ *long*⟩ **(2)** in or into operation or full power ⟨*get* ~ *steam*⟩ **b** under consideration or attention; *esp* before a court ⟨~ *for robbery*⟩ **5** so as to be together ⟨*add* ~ *the figures*⟩ **6a** entirely, completely ⟨*eat* ~ *your spinach*⟩ **b** so as to be firmly closed, joined, or fastened **c** so as to be fully inflated **7** in or into storage **8** in a direction conventionally the opposite of down: **a(1)** to windward **(2)** with rudder to leeward – used with reference to a ship's helm **b** in or towards the north **c** so as to arrive or approach ⟨*walked* ~ *to her*⟩ – compare TURN UP **d** to or at the rear of a theatrical stage **e** *chiefly Br* to or in the capital of a country or a university city ⟨~ *in London*⟩ **9** in or into parts ⟨*chop* ~⟩ **10** to a stop – usu + *draw, bring, fetch,* or *pull* [partly fr ME *up* upwards, fr OE *ūp*; partly fr ME *uppe* on high, fr OE; both akin to OHG *ūf* up, L *sub* under, Gk *hypo* under, *hyper* over – more at [1]OVER]

[2]up *adj* **1** moving, inclining, bound, or directed upwards or up **2** ready, prepared ⟨*dinner's* ~*!*⟩ **3** going on, taking place; *esp* being the matter ⟨*what's* ~*?*⟩ **4** at an end ⟨*time's* ~⟩; *esp* hopeless ⟨*it's all* ~ *with him now*⟩ **5a** well informed **b** ABREAST 2 ⟨~ *on her homework*⟩ **6** *of a road* being repaired; having a broken surface **7** ahead of an opponent ⟨*2 strokes* ~ *after 9 holes*⟩ **8** *of a ball in court games* having bounced only once on the ground or floor after being hit by one's opponent and therefore playable ⟨*not* ~⟩ **9** *Br, of a train* travelling towards a large town; *specif* travelling towards London – compare DOWN 5 – **up against** faced with; confronting – **up against it** in great difficulties

[3]up *vb* **-pp-** *vi* – used with *and* and another verb to indicate that the action of the following verb is either surprisingly or abruptly initiated ⟨*he* ~*ped and married*⟩ ~ *vt* **1** to increase ⟨*they* ~ped *the price of milk*⟩ **2** RAISE 8c

[4]up *prep* **1a** up along, round, through, towards, in, into, or on ⟨*walk* ~ *the hill*⟩ ⟨*water* ~ *my nose*⟩ **b** at the top of ⟨*the office is* ~ *those stairs*⟩ **2** *Br* (up) to ⟨*going* ~ *the West End*⟩ – nonstandard

[5]up *n* **1** (sthg in) a high position or an upward incline **2** a period or state of prosperity or success ⟨*has had some* ~s *and downs*⟩ **3** the part of a ball's trajectory in which it is still rising after having bounced ⟨*hit the ball on the* ~⟩

,up-and-'coming *adj* likely to advance or succeed

,up-and-'down *adj* **1** marked by alternate upward and downward movement **2** perpendicular **3** hilly

,up and 'down *adv* TO AND FRO

,up-and-'up *n, chiefly Br* a potentially or increasingly successful course – chiefly in *on the up-and-up*

Upanishad /ooh'panishad, ooh'pahnishahd/ *n* a collection of Vedic philosophical treatises forming the main body of Hindu scriptures [Skt *upaniṣad*] – **Upanishadic** /-'shadik, -'shahdik/ *adj*

upas /'yoohpəs/ *n* **1a** a tall Asiatic and E Indian tree of the fig family with a milky juice that contains poisonous glucosides used as an arrow poison **b** a shrub or tree of the same region yielding an arrow poison like strychnine **2** a poisonous concentrate of the juice or latex of a upas [Malay *pohon upas* poison tree]

[1]upbeat /'up,beet/ *n* an unaccented (e g the last) beat in a musical bar

[2]upbeat *adj, chiefly NAm* optimistic, cheerful – infml

up-bow /'up ,boh/ *n* a stroke in playing a bowed instrument (e g a violin) in which the bow is moved across the strings from the tip to the heel

upbraid /up'brayd/ *vt* to scold or reproach severely [ME *upbreyden,* fr OE *ūpbregdan*] – **upbraider** *n*

upbringing /'up,bring·ing/ *n* a particular way of bringing up a child ⟨*had a strict Calvinist* ~⟩

upcoming /'up,kuming/ *adj, NAm* about to happen; forthcoming

,up-'country *adj* **1** (characteristic) of an inland, upland, or outlying region **2** not socially or culturally sophisticated – **up-country** /'- ,--/ *n*, **up-country** /,- '--/ *adv*

[1]update /,up'dayt/ *vt* to bring up to date

[2]'up,date *n* an act of updating ⟨*a computer file* ~⟩

updraught /'up,drahft/ *n* an upward movement of air or other gas

upend /,up'end/ *vt* **1** to cause to stand on end **2** to knock down

upfield /,up'feeld/ *adv or adj* downfield

upgrade /,up'grayd/ *vt* to raise or improve the grade of; *esp* to advance to a job requiring a higher level of skill, esp as part of a training programme

upgrowth /'up,grohth/ *n* the process or result of growing upwards; development

upheaval /up'heevl/ *n* **1** an upheaving, esp of part of the earth's crust **2** (an instance of) extreme agitation or radical change

upheave /,up'heev/ *vt* to heave up; lift – **upheaver** *n*

[1]uphill /'up,hil/ *n* rising ground

[2],up'hill *adv* upwards on a hill or incline

[3],up'hill *adj* **1** situated on elevated ground **2** going up; ascending **3** difficult, laborious ⟨*an* ~ *struggle*⟩

uphold /up'hohld/ *vt* **upheld** /-'held/ **1** to give support to; maintain **2** to support against an opponent or challenge ⟨~ *the ruling of the lower court*⟩ – **upholder** *n*

upholster /up'hohlstə, -'hol-/ *vt* to provide with

upholstery [back-formation fr *upholstery*] – **upholsterer** *n*

up'holstery /-ri/ *n* materials (e g fabric, padding, and springs) used to make a soft covering, esp for a seat [ME *upholdester* dealer in small articles, upholsterer, fr *upholden* to uphold, fr *up* + *holden* to hold]

upkeep /'up,keep/ *n* (the cost of) maintaining or being maintained in good condition

upland /'uplənd/ *n* (an area of) high (inland) land – often pl with sing. meaning ☞ GEOGRAPHY – **upland** *adj*, **uplander** *n*

[1]**uplift** /up'lift/ *vt* **1** to raise, elevate **2** to improve the spiritual, social, or intellectual condition of – **uplifter** *n*

[2]**'up,lift** *n* **1** a moral or social improvement **2** influences intended to uplift

,up-'market *adj* being, producing, dealing in, or using goods designed to appeal to the more prosperous or higher-status section of a market – **up-market** *adv*

upon /ə'pon/ *prep* on – chiefly fml

[1]**upper** /'upə/ *adj* **1a** higher in physical position, rank, or order **b** farther inland ⟨*the* ~ *Thames*⟩ **2** being the branch of a legislature consisting of 2 houses that is usu more restricted in membership, is in many cases less powerful, and possesses greater traditional prestige than the lower house **3** *cap* being a later division of the specified geological period or series ⟨Upper *Carboniferous*⟩ [ME, fr *uppe* up + *-er* – more at UP]

[2]**upper** *n* the parts of a shoe or boot above the sole – **on one's uppers** at the end of one's means

[3]**upper** *n* a stimulant drug; *esp* amphetamine – infml [*up* + [2]*-er*]

,upper-'case *adj* CAPITAL 2 [fr the compositor's practice of keeping capital letters in the upper of a pair of type cases]

upper case *n* **1** a type case containing capitals and usu small capitals, fractions, symbols, and accents **2** capital letters ☞ ALPHABET

,upper 'class *n* the class occupying the highest position in a society; *esp* the wealthy or the aristocracy – **upper-class** *adj*

,upper 'crust *n sing or pl in constr* the highest social class – infml

uppercut /'upə,kut/ *n* a swinging blow directed upwards with a bent arm – **uppercut** *vb*

,upper 'hand *n* mastery, advantage – + *the*

uppermost /'upə,mohst/ *adv* in or into the highest or most prominent position – **uppermost** *adj*

upper partial *n* OVERTONE 1a

uppish /'upish/ *adj* **1** hit up and travelling far in the air **2** uppity – infml – **uppishly** *adv*, **uppishness** *n*

uppity /'upəti/ *adj* putting on airs of superiority; supercilious – infml [prob fr *up* + *-ity* (arbitrary suffix)] – **uppityness** *n*

uprate /,up'rayt/ *vt* to raise in rank, status, size, or power

[1]**upright** /'up,riet/ *adj* **1a** perpendicular, vertical **b** erect in carriage or posture **c** having the main part perpendicular ⟨*an* ~ *freezer*⟩ **2** marked by strong moral rectitude – **uprightly** *adv*, **uprightness** *n*

[2]**upright** *adv* in an upright or vertical position

[3]**upright** *n* **1** sthg that stands upright **2 upright, upright piano** a piano with vertical frame and strings

uprising /'up,riezing/ *n* a usu localized rebellion

upriver /,up'rivə/ *adv or adj* towards or at a point nearer the source of a river

uproar /'up,raw/ *n* a state of commotion or violent disturbance [by folk etymology fr D *oproer*, fr MD, fr *op* up + *roer* motion; akin to OE *up* up, & *hrēran* to stir]

uproarious /,up'rawri·əs/ *adj* **1** marked by noise and disorder **2** extremely funny ⟨*an* ~ *comedy*⟩ – **uproariously** *adv*, **uproariousness** *n*

uproot /,up'rooht/ *vt* **1** to remove by pulling up by the roots **2** to displace from a country or traditional habitat or environment – **uprooter** *n*

uprush /'up,rush/ *n* an upward rush (e g of gas or liquid)

upsadaisy /'upsə,dayzi/ *interj* upsydaisy

,ups and 'downs *n pl* alternating rises and falls, esp in fortune

[1]**upset** /up'set/ *vb* **-tt-; upset** *vt* **1** to thicken and shorten (e g a heated iron bar) by hammering on the end **2** to overturn, knock over **3a** to trouble mentally or emotionally **b** to throw into disorder **4** to make somewhat ill ~ *vi* to become overturned – **upsetter** *n*

[2]**'up,set** *n* **1** a minor physical disorder ⟨*a stomach* ~⟩ **2** an emotional disturbance **3** an unexpected defeat (e g in politics)

'upset ,price *n* the minimum price fixed for property offered at auction or public sale

upshot /'up,shot/ *n* the final result; the outcome – infml [[1]*up* + [1]*shot*; orig sense, the final shot in an archery contest]

,upside 'down /'up,sied/ *adv* **1** with the upper and the lower parts reversed **2** in or into great disorder or confusion [alter. of ME *up so doun*, fr *up* + *so* + *doun* down] – **upside-down** *adj*

'up,sides *adv, Br* so as to be even or equal – usu + *of* or *with*; infml

upsilon /'upsilon, -'sie-, 'yoohp-/ *n* the 20th letter of the Greek alphabet [MGk *y psilon*, lit., simple *y*; fr the desire to distinguish it from *oi*, which was pronounced the same in later Greek]

[1]**upstage** /,up'stayj/ *adv* at the rear of a theatrical stage; *also* away from the audience or film or television camera

[2]**upstage** *adj* **1** of or at the rear of a stage **2** haughty, aloof [(2) [4]*upstage*]

[3]**'up,stage** *n* the part of a stage that is farthest from the audience or camera

[4]**upstage** *vt* **1** to force (an actor) to face away from the audience by holding a dialogue with him/her from an upstage position **2** to steal attention from

[1]**upstairs** /,up'steəz/ *adv* **1** up the stairs; to or on a higher floor **2** to or at a higher position – compare KICK UPSTAIRS

[2]**upstairs** *adj* situated above the stairs, esp on an upper floor

[3]**upstairs** /'-,-, ,-'-/ *n pl but sing or pl in constr* the part of a building above the ground floor

upstanding /up'standing/ *adj* **1** erect, upright **2** marked by integrity; honest – **upstandingness** *n*

upstart /'up,staht/ *n* one who has risen suddenly (e g from a low position to wealth or power); *esp* one who claims more personal importance than he/she warrants [*upstart* (to rise suddenly), fr [1]*up* + [1]*start*] – **upstart** *adj*

upstate /'up,stayt/ *n* the chiefly northerly sections of a state of the USA – **upstate** *adv or adj*

upstream /ˌup'streem/ *adv or adj* in the direction opposite to the flow of a stream

upstroke /'upˌstrohk/ *n* an upward stroke

upsurge /'upˌsuhj/ *n* a rapid or sudden rise

upswept /'upˌswept/ *adj* swept or brushed upwards

upswing /'upˌswing/ *n* **1** an upward swing **2** a marked increase or rise

upsydaisy /'upsəˌdayzi/ *interj* – used to express comfort and reassurance (e g to a small child after a fall) [irreg fr [1]*up*]

uptake /'upˌtayk/ *n* **1** an absorbing and incorporating, esp into a living organism **2** understanding, comprehension ⟨*quick on the* ~⟩ – infml [Sc *uptake* to understand]

ˌup-'tempo /'tempoh/ *adj or n* (played at) a fast-moving tempo (e g in jazz)

upthrow /'upˌthrow/ *n* an upward displacement (e g of a rock stratum)

upthrust /'upˌthrust/ *n* an upward thrust; *esp* a geological upheaval – **upthrust** *vb*

uptight /ˌup'tiet/ *adj* **1** tense, nervous, or uneasy **2** angry, indignant *USE* infml – **uptightness** *n*

'up to *prep* **1** – used to indicate an upward limit or boundary ⟨*sank* ~ *his knees in mud*⟩ ⟨~ *50,000 copies a month*⟩ **2** as far as; until **3a** equal to ⟨*didn't feel* ~ *par*⟩ **b** good enough for ⟨*my German isn't* ~ *reading Schiller*⟩ **4** engaged in (a suspect activity) ⟨*what's he* ~*?*⟩ **5** being the responsibility of ⟨*it's* ~ *me*⟩

ˌup-to-'date *adj* **1** including the latest information **2** abreast of the times; modern – **up-to-dateness** *n*

ˌup-to-the-'minute *adj* **1** including the very latest information **2** completely up-to-date

ˌup'town *adv, adj, or n, chiefly NAm* (to, towards, or in) the upper part or residential district of a town or city

[1]**upturn** /ˌup'tuhn/ *vt* **1** to turn up or over **2** to direct upwards ~ *vi* to turn upwards

[2]**'upˌturn** *n* an upward turn, esp towards better conditions or higher prices

upward /'upwood/ *adj* moving or extending upwards; ascending ⟨*an* ~ *movement*⟩ – **upwardly** *adv*

upwards *adv* **1a** from a lower to a higher place, condition, or level; in the opposite direction from down **b** so as to expose a particular surface ⟨*held out his hand, palm* ~⟩ **2a** to an indefinitely greater amount, price, figure, age, or rank ⟨*from £5* ~⟩ **b** towards a higher number, degree, or rate ⟨*attendance figures have risen* ~⟩

'upwards of *adv* more than; IN EXCESS OF ⟨*they cost* ~ *£25*⟩

upwind /ˌup'wind/ *adv or adj* in the direction from which the wind is blowing

ˌup 'yours *interj, Br* – used to express contemptuous defiance and dismissal; slang; [short for *up your arse*]

ur /uh/ *interj* er

ur-, uro- *comb form* **1** urine ⟨*uric*⟩ **2** urinary tract ⟨uro*logy*⟩ **3** urinary and ⟨uro*genital*⟩ [NL, fr Gk *our-, ouro-*, fr *ouron* urine – more at URINE]

Ur- *prefix* original; primitive ⟨Ur-*form*⟩ [G, fr OHG *ir-, ur-* thoroughly (perfective prefix)]

uracil /'yooərəsil/ *n* a base that is one of the 4 bases whose order in the polynucleotide chain of RNA codes genetic information – compare ADENINE, CYTOSINE, GUANINE, THYMINE [ISV *ur-* + *acetic* + *-il* (substance relating to)]

uraemia /yoo'reemyə, -mi·ə/ *n* accumulation in the blood of toxic constituents normally eliminated by the kidneys [NL, fr *ur-* + *-aemia*]

Ural-Altaic /ˌyooərəl al'tayik/ *n* a postulated group comprising the Uralic and Altaic languages – **Ural-Altaic** *adj*

Uralic /yoo(ə)'ralik, -'ray-/ *n* a language family comprising the Finno-Ugric and Samoyed languages [*Ural* mountains, NW Asia] – **Uralic** *adj*, **Uralian** /-'raylyən/ *adj*

[1]**uran-, urano-** *comb form* sky; heaven ⟨urano*metry*⟩ [L, fr Gk *ouran-, ourano-*, fr *ouranos*]

[2]**uran-, urano-** *comb form* uranium ⟨uran*yl*⟩ [F, fr NL *uranium*]

uranic /yoo(ə)'ranik/ *adj* of or containing uranium, esp with a relatively high valency [ISV]

uranium /yoo(ə)'raynyəm, -ni·əm/ *n* a heavy radioactive polyvalent metallic element found in pitchblende ☞ ENERGY, PERIODIC TABLE [NL, fr *Uranus*]

uranium 235 *n* a light isotope of uranium of mass number 235 that when bombarded with slow neutrons undergoes rapid fission into smaller atoms with the release of neutrons and atomic energy ☞ ENERGY

uranium 238 *n* an isotope of uranium of mass number 238 that absorbs fast neutrons to form a uranium isotope of mass number 239 which then decays through neptunium to form plutonium of mass number 239 ☞ ENERGY

uranography /ˌyooərə'nogrəfi/ *n* the description and mapping of the heavens and celestial bodies [Gk *ouranographia* description of the heavens, fr *ouran-* uran- + *-graphia* -graphy] – **uranographic** /-noh'grafik, -nə-/, **uranographical** *adj*

uranometry /ˌyooərə'nomətri/ *n* (the making of) a map or catalogue of celestial bodies, esp stars [NL *uranometria*, fr *uran-* + *-metria* -metry]

uranous /'yooərənəs/ *adj* of or containing uranium, esp with a relatively low valency

Uranus /yoo(ə)'raynəs, 'yooərənəs/ *n* the planet 7th in order from the sun ☞ ASTRONOMY, SYMBOL [LL, fr Gk *Ouranos*, the sky personified as a god in Gk mythology, fr *ouranos* sky, heaven]

urate /'yooəˌrayt/ *n* a salt of uric acid [F, fr *urique* uric, fr E *uric*] – **uratic** /-'ratik/ *adj*

urban /'uhbən/ *adj* (characteristic) of or constituting a city or town [L *urbanus*, fr *urbs* city]

urbane /uh'bayn/ *adj* notably polite or smooth in manner; suave [L *urbanus* urban, urbane] – **urbanely** *adv*, **urbanity** /uh'banəti/ *n*

ˌurban guer'rilla *n* a terrorist who operates in towns

urbanist /'uhbənist/ *n, chiefly NAm* a specialist in town planning

urbanite /'uhbəˌniet/ *n, chiefly NAm* one living in a city

urban·ize, -ise /'uhbəˌniez/ *vt* **1** to cause to take on urban characteristics **2** to impart an urban way of life to – **urbanization** /-'zaysh(ə)n/ *n*

ˌurban re'newal *n* the planned replacement or rehabilitation of substandard urban buildings

urceolate /'uhsi·ələt, -ˌlayt/ *adj* shaped like an urn [NL *urceolatus*, fr L *urceolus*, dim. of *urceus* pitcher]

urchin /'uhchin/ *n* **1** a hedgehog **2** a mischievous and impudent young boy, esp one who is scruffy **3** SEA URCHIN [ME, fr MF *herichon*, fr L *ericius*, fr *er*; akin to Gk *chēr* hedgehog, L *horrēre* to bristle, tremble – more at HORROR]

Urdu /'ooədooh, 'uhdooh/ *n* an Indic language that is an official language of Pakistan, is written usu in Persian script, and is widely used in India, esp by Muslims ☞ LANGUAGE [Hindi *urdū-zabān*, lit., camp language]

-ure *suffix* (*vb* → *n*) **1** act or process of ⟨*exposure*⟩ ⟨*closure*⟩ **2** body performing (a specified function) ⟨*legislature*⟩ [ME, fr OF, fr L *-ura*]

urea /yoo(ə)'ree·ə, 'yooəri·ə/ *n* a nitrogen-containing compound that is present in urine and is a final product of protein decomposition [NL, fr F *urée*, fr *urine*]

ureter /yoo(ə)'reetə/ *n* a duct that carries away the urine from a kidney to the bladder or cloaca ☞ DIGESTION [NL, fr Gk *ourētēr*, fr *ourein* to urinate – more at URINE] – **ureteral, ureteric** /,yooərə'terik/ *adj*

urethane /'yooərə,thayn/, **urethan** /-thən/ *n* **1a** a compound that is the ethyl ester of carbamic acid and is used esp as a solvent **b** an ester of carbamic acid other than the ethyl ester **2** polyurethane [F *uréthane*, fr *ur-* + *éth-* eth- + *-ane*]

urethr-, urethro- *comb form* urethra ⟨urethr*itis*⟩ ⟨urethro*scope*⟩ [NL, fr LL *urethra*]

urethra /yoo(ə)'reethrə/ *n, pl* **urethras, urethrae** /-thri/ the canal that in most mammals carries off the urine from the bladder and in the male serves also as a spermatic duct ☞ DIGESTION [LL, fr Gk *ourēthra*, fr *ourein* to urinate] – **urethral** *adj*

urethritis /,yooəri'thrietəs/ *n* inflammation of the urethra [NL]

[1]**urge** /uhj/ *vt* **1** to advocate or demand earnestly or pressingly **2** to undertake the accomplishment of with energy or enthusiasm **3a** to try to persuade **b** to serve as a motive or reason for **4** to force or impel in a specified direction or to greater speed ~ *vi* to urge an argument, claim, etc [L *urgēre* – more at WREAK] – **urger** *n*

[2]**urge** *n* a force or impulse that urges

urgent /'uhjənt/ *adj* **1** calling for immediate attention; pressing ⟨~ *appeals*⟩ **2** conveying a sense of urgency [ME, fr MF, fr L *urgent-, urgens*, prp of *urgēre*] – **urgency** /-si/ *n*, **urgently** *adv*

-urgy /-uhji/ *comb form* (→ *n*) technology; art; technique ⟨*metallurgy*⟩ ⟨*dramaturgy*⟩ [NL *-urgia*, fr Gk *-ourgia*, fr *-ourgos* working, fr *-o-* + *ergon* work – more at [1]WORK]

-uria /-'yooəri·ə/ *comb form* (→ *n*) **1** usu pathological presence or excess of (a specified substance) in urine ⟨*albuminuria*⟩ ⟨*pyuria*⟩ **2** condition of producing (a specified amount of) urine ⟨*polyuria*⟩ [NL, fr Gk *-ouria*, fr *ouron* urine – more at URINE]

uric /'yooərik/ *adj* of or found in urine

,uric 'acid *n* a compound that is present in small quantities in mammalian urine and is the chief excretory product of birds and most reptiles

urin-, urino- *comb form* ur- ⟨urino*genital*⟩ ⟨urin*ary*⟩ [ME, fr OF, fr L, fr *urina* urine]

urinal /yoo(ə)'rienl/ *n* a fixture used for urinating into, esp by men; *also* a room, building, etc containing a urinal [ME, fr OF, fr LL, fr L *urina*]

urinalysis /,yooəri'naləsis/ *n* (diagnostic) chemical analysis of urine [NL, irreg fr *urin-* + *analysis*]

urinary /'yooərin(ə)ri/ *adj* **1** relating to (or occurring in or constituting the organs concerned with the formation and discharge of) urine **2** excreted as or in urine

urinate /'yooəri,nayt/ *vi* to discharge urine – **urination** /-'nay sh(ə)n/ *n*

urine /'yooərin/ *n* waste material that is secreted by the kidney in vertebrates and forms a clear amber and usu slightly acid fluid in mammals but is semisolid in birds and reptiles [ME, fr MF, fr L *urina*; akin to Gk *ouron* urine, *ourein* to urinate, OE *wæter* water] – **urinous** /-nəs/ *adj*

urinogenital /,yooərinoh'jenitl/ *adj* genitourinary

urn /uhn/ *n* **1** an ornamental vase on a pedestal used esp for preserving the ashes of the dead after cremation **2** a large closed container, usu with a tap at its base, in which large quantities of tea, coffee, etc may be heated or served [ME *urne*, fr L *urna*]

uro- – see UR-

urochord /'yooəroh,kawd/ *n* the notochord of a tunicate [deriv of Gk *oura* tail + NL *chorda* notochord, fr L, cord] – **urochordal** /-'kawdl/ *adj*

urodele /'yooərə,deel/ *n* any of an order of amphibians (e g newts) that have a tail throughout life [F *urodèle*, deriv of Gk *oura* tail + *dēlos* evident, showing – more at SQUIRREL] – **urodele** *adj*

urogenital /,yooəroh'jenitl/ *adj* genitourinary [ISV]

urology /yoo(ə)'roləji/ *n* a branch of medicine dealing with the genitourinary tract – **urologist** *n*, **urologic** /,yooərə'lojik/, **urological** *adj*

-uronic /-yoo(ə)'ronik/ *suffix* (→ *adj*) connected with urine – in names of certain organic acids derived from sugars or compounds of such acids ⟨*hyaluronic*⟩ [Gk *ouron* urine]

uropygial gland /,yooəroh'piji·əl/ *n* a large gland that opens at the base of the tail feathers in most birds and usu secretes an oily fluid which the bird uses in preening its feathers

uropygium /-'piji·əm/ *n* the prominence at the rear end of a bird's body that supports the tail feathers [NL, fr Gk *ouropygion*, fr *oura* tail + *pygē* rump – more at STEATOPYGIA] – **uropygial** *adj*

urostyle /'yooərə,stiel/ *n* a bony rod of fused vertebrae that forms the end part of the vertebral column of frogs and toads [ISV, deriv of Gk *oura* tail + *stylos* pillar – more at [2]STEER]

,Ursa 'Major /'uhsə/ *n* the most conspicuous of the N constellations that is situated near the N pole of the heavens and contains 7 stars pictured as a plough, 2 of which are in a line indicating the direction of the Pole Star [L, lit., greater bear]

,Ursa 'Minor *n* a constellation that includes the N pole of the heavens and 7 stars which resemble Ursa Major with the Pole Star at the tip of the handle [L, lit., lesser bear]

ursine /'uhsin, -sien/ *adj* of or resembling a bear or the bear family [L *ursinus*, fr *ursus* bear]

Ursprache /'ooə,shprahkhə/ *n* a parent language; *esp* one reconstructed from the evidence of later languages [G, fr *Ur-* Ur- + *sprache* language]

urticaria /uhti'keəri·ə/ *n* an allergic disorder marked by raised itching patches of skin and caused by contact with a specific factor (e g a food or drug) [NL, fr L *urtica* nettle] – **urticarial** *adj*

urticate /'uhti,kayt/ *vi* to produce weals or itching; *esp* to induce urticaria [ML *urticatus*, pp of *urticare* to sting, fr L *urtica*] – **urtication** /-'kaysh(ə)n/ *n*

urus /'yooərəs/ *n* an aurochs [L, of Gmc origin; akin to OHG *ūro* urus – more at AUROCHS]

us /əs; *strong* us/ *pron* **1** *objective case of* WE ⟨*please let ~ go*⟩ **2** *chiefly Br* me ⟨*give ~ a kiss*⟩ – nonstandard [ME, fr OE *ūs*; akin to OHG *uns* us, L *nos*]

usable *also* **useable** /'yoohzəbl/ *adj* **1** capable of being used **2** convenient for use – **usableness** *n*, **usably** *adv*, **usability** /-zə'biləti/ *n*

usage /'yoohsij, -zij/ *n* **1a** (an instance of) established and generally accepted practice or procedure **b** (an instance of) the way in which words and phrases are actually used in a language **2** the action, amount, or manner of using

usance /'yoohz(ə)ns/ *n* the time allowed by custom for payment of a bill of exchange in foreign commerce [[2]USE + -ANCE]

[1]**use** /yoohs/ *n* **1a** using or being used ⟨*in daily ~*⟩ ⟨*made good ~ of his time*⟩ **b** a way of using sthg ⟨*a machine with many different ~*s⟩ **2a** habitual or customary usage **b** a liturgical form or observance; *esp* a liturgy having modifications peculiar to a local church or religious order **3a** the right or benefit of using sthg ⟨*gave him the ~ of her car*⟩ **b** the ability or power to use sthg (e g a limb) **c** the legal enjoyment of property **4a** a purpose or end ⟨*put learning to practical ~*⟩ **b** practical worth or application ⟨*saving things that might be of ~*⟩ **5** a favourable attitude; a liking ⟨*had no ~ for modern art*⟩ [ME *us*, fr OF, fr L *usus*, fr *usus*, pp of *uti* to use]

[2]**use** /yoohz/ *vb* **used** / *vt* yoohzd; *vi* yoohst/ *vt* **1** to put into action or service **2** to consume or take (e g drugs) regularly **3** to carry out sthg by means of ⟨*~ tact*⟩ **4** to expend or consume **5** to treat in a specified manner ⟨*~*d *the prisoners cruelly*⟩ *~ vi* – used in the past with *to* to indicate a former fact or state ⟨*~*d *to dislike fish*⟩ ⟨*didn't ~*d *to be so pernickety*⟩ – **user** /'yoohzə/ *n*

used /*senses* [1] *and 2* yoohzd; *sense 3* yoohst/ *adj* **1** employed in accomplishing sthg **2** that has endured use; *specif* secondhand **3** accustomed ⟨*I'm not ~ to drinking – SEU S*⟩

useful /'yoohsf(ə)l/ *adj* **1** having utility, esp practical worth or applicability; *also* helpful **2** of highly satisfactory quality – **usefully** *adv*, **usefulness** *n*

useless /'yoohslis/ *adj* **1** having or being of no use **2** inept – infml – **uselessly** *adv*, **uselessness** *n*

user-friendly *adj* **1** *of a computer system* designed for easy operation by guiding users along a series of simple steps **2** easy to operate or understand – **user-friendliness** *n*

use up /yoohz/ *vt* **1** to consume completely **2** to deprive wholly of strength or useful properties; exhaust

[1]**usher** /'ushə/ *n* **1** an officer or servant who acts as a doorkeeper (e g in a court of law) **2** an officer who walks before a person of rank **3** *fem* **usherette** /-'ret/ one who shows people to their seats (e g in a theatre) [ME *ussher*, fr MF *ussier*, fr (assumed) VL *ustiarius* doorkeeper, fr L *ostium, ustium* door, mouth of a river; akin to L *or-, os* mouth – more at ORAL]

[2]**usher** *vt* **1** to conduct to a place **2** to precede as an usher **3** to inaugurate, introduce ⟨*~ in a new era*⟩

usquebaugh /'uskwi,baw/ *n, Irish & Scot* whisky [IrGael *uisce beathadh*]

usual /'yoohzhooəl, -zhəl/ *adj* **1** in accordance with usage, custom, or habit; normal **2** commonly or ordinarily used ⟨*followed his ~ route*⟩ [LL *usualis*, fr L *usus* use] – **usually** *adv*, **usualness** *n* – **as usual** in the accustomed or habitual way ⟨as usual *he was late*⟩

usufruct /'yoohz(y)oo,frukt, -s(y)oo-/ *n* the legal right of using and enjoying sthg belonging to another [L *ususfructus*, fr *usus et fructus* use and enjoyment]

usurer /'yoohzhərə/ *n* one who lends money, esp at an exorbitant rate [ME, fr AF, fr ML *usurarius*, fr L *usura*]

usurp /yooh'suhp, -'zuhp/ *vt* to seize and possess by force or without right ⟨*~ a throne*⟩ *~ vi* to seize possession wrongfully [ME *usurpen*, fr MF *usurper*, fr L *usurpare*, lit., to take possession of by use, fr *usu* (abl of *usus* use) + *rapere* to seize – more at RAPID] – **usurper** *n*, **usurpation** /-'paysh(ə)n/ *n*

usury /'yoohzyəri, -zhəri/ *n* **1** the lending of money at (exorbitant) interest **2** an exorbitant or illegal rate or amount of interest [ME, fr ML *usuria*, alter. of L *usura*, fr *usus*, pp of *uti* to use] – **usurious** /-'zyooəri·əs, -'zhooə-/ *adj*, **usuriously** *adv*

ut /ut, ooht/ *n* [3]DO [ME, fr ML – more at GAMUT]

utensil /yooh'tens(i)l/ *n* **1** an implement, vessel, or device used in the household, esp the kitchen **2** a useful tool or implement [ME, vessels for domestic use, fr MF *utensile*, fr L *utensilia*, fr neut pl of *utensilis* useful, fr *uti* to use]

uterine /'yoohtərin, -rien/ *adj* **1a** born of the same mother but by a different father **b** matrilineal **2** of or affecting the uterus [ME, fr LL *uterinus*, fr L *uterus*]

uterus /'yoohtərəs/ *n, pl* **uteri** /-,rie, -ri/ *also* **uteruses** **1** an organ of the female mammal for containing and usu for nourishing the young during development before birth ☞ REPRODUCTION **2** a structure in some lower animals analogous to the uterus in which eggs or young develop [L]

[1]**utilitarian** /yooh,tili'teəri·ən/ *n* an advocate of utilitarianism

[2]**utilitarian** *adj* **1** marked by utilitarian views or practices **2a** of or aiming at utility **b** made for or aiming at practical use rather than beautiful appearance

u,tili'tarianism /-niz(ə)m/ *n* **1** a doctrine that the criterion for correct conduct should be the usefulness of its consequences; *specif* a theory that the aim of action should be the greatest happiness of the greatest number **2** utilitarian character, spirit, or quality

[1]**utility** /yooh'tiləti/ *n* **1** fitness for some purpose; usefulness **2** sthg useful or designed for use **3** a business organization performing a public service [ME *utilite*, fr MF *utilité*, fr L *utilitat-, utilitas*, fr *utilis* useful, fr *uti* to use]

[2]**utility** *adj* **1** capable of serving as a substitute in various roles or positions ⟨*a ~ player*⟩ **2** serving primarily for utility rather than beauty; utilitarian ⟨*~ furniture*⟩ **3** designed or adapted for general use

util·ize, -ise /'yoohtiliez/ *vt* to make use of; turn to practical use or account [F *utiliser*, fr *utile* useful, fr L *utilis*] – **utilizable** *adj*, **utilizer** *n*, **utilization** /-'zaysh(ə)n/ *n*

[1]**utmost** /'ut,mohst/ *adj* **1** situated at the farthest or most distant point; extreme **2** of the greatest or

highest degree ⟨*a matter of ~ concern*⟩ [ME, alter. of *utmest,* fr OE *ūtmest,* superl adj, fr *ūt* out, adv – more at OUT]

[2]**utmost** *n* **1** the highest point or degree **2** the best of one's abilities, powers, etc ⟨*did his ~ to help*⟩

utopia /yooh'tohpi·ə/ *n* **1** *often cap* a place or state of ideal (political and social) perfection **2** an impractical scheme for social or political improvement [*Utopia,* imaginary ideal country in *Utopia* by Sir Thomas More †1535 E statesman & writer, fr Gk *ou* not, no + *topos* place]

[1]**utopian** /yooh'tohpi·ən/ *adj, often cap* **1** impossibly ideal, esp in social and political organization **2** proposing impractically ideal social and political schemes – **utopianism** *n*

[2]**utopian** *n* **1** a believer in human perfectibility **2** an advocate of utopian schemes

utricle /'yoohtrikl/ *n* a small pouched part of an animal or plant body; *esp* the larger chamber of the membranous labyrinth of the ear into which the semicircular canals open ☞ NERVE [L *utriculus,* dim. of *uter* leather bag] – **utricular** /-'trikyoolə/ *adj*

[1]**utter** /'utə/ *adj* absolute, total ⟨*~ desolation*⟩ [ME, remote, fr OE *ūtera* outer, compar adj fr *ūt* out, adv – more at OUT] – **utterly** *adv*

[2]**utter** *vt* **1a** to emit as a sound **b** to give (verbal) expression to **2** to put (e g currency) into circulation; *specif* to circulate (e g a counterfeit note) as if legal or genuine – used technically [ME *uttren,* fr *utter* outside, adv, fr OE *ūtor,* compar of *ūt* out] – **utterer** *n,* **utterable** /'ut(ə)rəbl/ *adj*

utterance /'ut(ə)rəns/ *n* **1** an oral or written statement **2** vocal expression; speech – esp in *give utterance to* [[2]UTTER + -ANCE]

uttermost /'utə,mohst/ *adj* extreme, utmost [ME, alter. of *uttermest,* fr [1]*utter* + *-mest* (as in *utmest* utmost)]

utu /'ooh,tooh/ *n, NZ* retribution [Maori]

'**U-,turn** /yooh/ *n* **1** a turn executed by a motor vehicle without reversing that takes it back along the direction from which it has come **2** a total reversal of policy ⟨*a ~ on wage controls – The Economist*⟩

uvula /'yoohvyoolə/ *n, pl* **uvulas, uvulae** /-li/ the fleshy lobe hanging in the middle of the back of the soft palate ☞ NERVE [ML, dim. of L *uva* grape, uvula; akin to OE *īw* yew]

uvular /'yoohvyoolə/ *adj* **1** of the uvula ⟨*~ glands*⟩ **2** produced with the aid of the uvula ⟨*a French ~ /r/*⟩ – **uvularly** *adv*

uxorious /uk'sawri·əs, ug'zaw-/ *adj* (excessively) fond of or submissive to one's wife – fml [L *uxorius,* fr *uxor* wife] – **uxoriously** *adv,* **uxoriousness** *n*

Uzbeg /'oozbeg, 'uzbeg/ *n* (an) Uzbek

Uzbek /'oozbek, 'uzbek/ *n* **1** a member of a Turkic people inhabiting central Asia **2** the Turkic language of the Uzbek people ☞ LANGUAGE

V

v /vee/ *n, pl* **v's** *or* **vs** *often cap* **1** (a graphic representation of or device for reproducing) the 22nd letter of the English alphabet **2** five ☞ NUMBER

V-1 /,vee 'wun/ *n* a flying bomb used by the Germans in WW II, esp against targets in England [G *vergeltungswaffe*, fr *vergeltung* reprisal + *waffe* weapon]

V-2 /,vee 'tooh/ *n* a long-range rocket used by the Germans in WW II, esp against targets in England ☞ SPACE

vac /vak/ *n, Br* a vacation, esp from college or university – infml

vacancy /'vaykənsi/ *n* **1** physical or mental inactivity; idleness **2** a vacant office, post, or room **3** an empty space **4** the state of being vacant

vacant /'vaykənt/ *adj* **1** not occupied by an incumbent or officer ⟨*a ~ office*⟩ **2** without an occupant ⟨*a ~ room*⟩ **3** free from activity or work ⟨*~ hours*⟩ **4a** stupid, foolish ⟨*a ~ mind*⟩ **b** expressionless ⟨*a ~ look*⟩ **5** not lived in ⟨*~ houses*⟩ [ME, fr OF, fr L *vacant-, vacans*, prp of *vacare* to be empty, be free] – **vacantly** *adv*, **vacantness** *n*

vacant possession *n* availability (e g of a house) for immediate occupation

vacate /vay'kayt/ *vt* **1** to annul legally **2** to give up the possession or occupancy of **3** to make vacant; leave empty ⟨*with instructions to ~ the cinema*⟩ [L *vacatus*, pp of *vacare*]

¹vacation /vay'kash(ə)n, və-/ *n* **1** a scheduled period during which activity (e g of a university) is suspended **2** an act of vacating **3** *chiefly NAm* a holiday ⟨*had a restful ~ at the beach*⟩ [ME *vacacioun*, fr MF *vacation*, fr L *vacation-, vacatio* freedom, exemption, fr *vacatus*]

²vacation *vi, chiefly NAm* to take or spend a holiday – **vacationer** *n*

vaccinate /'vaksinayt/ *vt* **1** to inoculate with cowpox virus in order to produce immunity to smallpox **2** to administer a vaccine to, usu by injection ~ *vi* to perform or practise the administration of vaccine – **vaccinator** *n*, **vaccination** /-'naysh(ə)n/ *n*

¹vaccine /'vak,seen, -sin/ *adj* of cowpox or vaccination ⟨*a ~ pustule*⟩ [L *vaccinus* of or from cows, fr *vacca* cow; akin to Skt *vaśa* cow]

²vaccine *n* material (e g a preparation of killed or modified virus or bacteria) used in vaccinating – **vaccinal** /'vaksin(ə)l/ *adj*

vaccinia /vak'sini·ə/ *n* cowpox [NL, fr *vaccinus*] – **vaccinial** *adj*

vacillate /'vasə,layt/ *vi* **1a** to sway through imperfect balance **b** to fluctuate, oscillate **2** to hesitate or waver in choosing between opinions or courses of action [L *vacillatus*, pp of *vacillare* to sway, waver – more at PREVARICATE] – **vacillatingly** *adv*, **vacillator** *n*, **vacillation** /-'laysh(ə)n/ *n*

vacuity /və'kyooh·əti/ *n* **1** an empty space **2** vacuousness, meaninglessness **3** sthg (e g an idea) that is stupid or inane [L *vacuitas*, fr *vacuus* empty]

vacuolate /'vakyoo(ə),layt, -lət/, **vacuolated** /-,laytid/ *adj* containing 1 or more vacuoles

vacuolation /,vakyooə'laysh(ə)n/ *n* the development or formation of vacuoles

vacuole /'vakyoo,ohl/ *n* a small cavity or space containing air or fluid in the tissues of an organism or in the protoplasm of an individual cell [F, lit., small vacuum, fr L *vacuum*] – **vacuolar** /'vakyooələ, -'ohlə/ *adj*

vacuous /'vakyoo·əs/ *adj* **1** empty **2** stupid, inane ⟨*a ~ expression*⟩ **3** idle, aimless [L *vacuus*] – **vacuously** *adv*, **vacuousness** *n*

¹vacuum /'vakyoohm, 'vakyooəm, 'vakyoom/ *n, pl* **vacuums, vacua** /'vakyooh·ə/ **1a** a space absolutely devoid of matter **b** a space from which as much air or other substance as possible has been removed (e g by an air pump) **c** an air pressure below atmospheric pressure **2a** a vacant space; a void **b** a state of isolation from outside influences **3** VACUUM CLEANER [L, fr neut of *vacuus* empty; akin to L *vacare* to be empty]

²vacuum *adj* of, containing, producing, or using a partial vacuum

³vacuum /'vakyoohm, 'vakyoom/ *vb* to clean using a vacuum cleaner

'vacuum ,brake *n* a continuous brake system worked by vacuum and used esp on trains

'vacuum ,cleaner *n* an (electrical) appliance for removing dust and dirt (e g from carpets or upholstery) by suction – **vacuum-clean** *vb*

'vacuum ,flask *n, chiefly Br* a cylindrical container with a vacuum between an inner and an outer wall used to keep material, esp liquids, either hot or cold for considerable periods

'vacuum-,packed *adj* packed in a wrapping from which most of the air has been removed ⟨*~ bacon*⟩

'vacuum ,pump *n* a pump for producing a vacuum

vade mecum /,vaydi 'meekəm, ,vahday 'maykəm/ *n, pl* **vade mecums** **1** a book for ready reference **2** sthg regularly carried about by a person [L, go with me]

vag-, vago- *comb form* vagus nerve ⟨vag*al*⟩ ⟨vago*tomy*⟩ [ISV, fr NL *vagus*]

¹vagabond /'vagə,bond/ *adj* **1** (characteristic) of a wanderer **2** leading an unsettled, irresponsible, or disreputable life [ME, fr MF, fr L *vagabundus*, fr *vagari* to wander] – **vagabondish** *adj*

²vagabond *n* a wanderer; *esp* a tramp – **vagabondage** *n*, **vagabondism** *n*

vagal /'vaygəl/ *adj* of, affected or controlled by, or being the vagus nerve [ISV] – **vagally** *adv*

vagary /'vaygəri/ *n* an erratic, unpredictable, or extravagant notion, action, etc [prob fr L *vagari* to wander; akin to L *vagus* wandering – more at PREVARICATE] – **vagarious** /və'geəri·əs/ *adj*

vagina /və'jienə/ *n, pl* **vaginae** /-ni/, **vaginas** **1** a canal in a female mammal that leads from the uterus to the external orifice of the genital canal ☞ REPRODUCTION **2** a sheath; *esp* a leaf base that forms a sheath, usu round the main stem [L, lit., sheath] – **vaginal** /və'jienl, 'vajinl/ *adj*

vaginismus /,vaji'nizməs/ *n* a painful spasmodic contraction of the vagina [NL, fr L *vagina*]

vaginitis /,vaji'nietəs/ *n* inflammation of the vagina or of a covering structure (e g a tendon sheath) [NL]

vago- – see VAG-

[1]**vagrant** /'vaygrənt/ *n* **1** one who has no established residence or lawful means of support **2** a wanderer, vagabond [ME *vagraunt*, prob modif of MF *waucrant, wacrant* wandering, fr OF, fr prp of *waucrer, wacrer* to roll, wander, of Gmc origin; akin to OE *wealcan* to roll – more at WALK]

[2]**vagrant** *adj* **1** wandering about from place to place, usu with no means of support **2** having no fixed course; random – **vagrancy** /-si/ *n*, **vagrantly** *adv*

vague /vayg/ *adj* **1a** not clearly defined, expressed, or understood; indistinct ⟨*a* ~ *idea*⟩ **b** not clearly felt or sensed ⟨*a* ~ *longing*⟩ **2** not thinking or expressing one's thoughts clearly ⟨~ *about dates and places*⟩ [MF, fr L *vagus*, lit., wandering] – **vaguely** *adv*, **vagueness** *n*

vagus /'vaygəs/ *n, pl* **vagi** /-ji/ either of a pair of cranial nerves that supply chiefly the heart and viscera [NL *vagus nervus*, lit., wandering nerve]

vain /vayn/ *adj* **1** idle, worthless **2** unsuccessful, ineffectual **3** having or showing excessive pride in one's appearance, ability, etc; conceited [ME, fr OF, fr L *vanus* empty, vain – more at WANE] – **vainly** *adv*, **vainness** *n* – **in vain** to no end; without success or result

vainglorious /,vayn'glawri·əs/ *adj* boastful – **vaingloriously** *adv*, **vaingloriousness** *n*

vainglory /,vayn'glawri/ *n* **1** excessive or ostentatious pride **2** vanity

Vaishnava /,viesh'nahvə/ *n* a member of a major Hindu sect devoted to the cult of Vishnu [Skt *vaiṣṇava* of Vishnu, fr *Viṣṇu* Vishnu, second of the 3 chief Hindu gods]

valance /'vayləns, 'va-/ *n* **1** a piece of drapery hung as a border, esp along the edge of a bed, canopy, or shelf **2** a pelmet [ME *vallance*, perh fr *Valence*, commune in France]

vale /vayl/ *n* VALLEY 1a – poetic or in place-names [ME, fr OF *val*, fr L *valles, vallis*; akin to L *volvere* to roll – more at VOLUBLE]

valediction /,valə'diksh(ə)n/ *n* **1** an act of bidding farewell **2** an address or statement of farewell or leave-taking *USE* fml [L *valedictus*, pp of *valedicere* to say farewell, fr *vale* farewell + *dicere* to say – more at DICTION]

[1]**valedictory** /,valə'dikt(ə)ri/ *adj* expressing or containing a farewell – fml [L *valedictus*]

[2]**valedictory** *n* VALEDICTION 2 – fml

valency /'vaylənsi/, *NAm chiefly* **valence** /'vayləns/ *n* **1** the degree of combining power of an element or radical as shown by the number of atomic weights of a univalent element (e g hydrogen) with which the atomic weight of the element will combine or for which it can be substituted or with which it can be compared **2** a unit of valency ⟨*the 4* valencies *of carbon*⟩ [LL *valentia* power, capacity, fr L *valent-, valens*, prp of *valēre* to be strong]

-valent /-'vaylənt/ *comb form* (→ *adj*) **1** having (such) a valency ⟨*bi*valent⟩ ⟨*multi*valent⟩ **2** having (so many) chromosomal strands or homologous chromosomes ⟨*uni*valent⟩ [ISV, fr L *valent-, valens*]

valentine /'valəntien/ *n* **1** a sweetheart chosen on St Valentine's Day **2** a gift or greeting card sent or given, esp to a sweetheart, on St Valentine's Day

valerate /'valərayt/ *n* a salt or ester of valeric acid

valerian /və'liəri·ən/ *n* any of several usu perennial plants, many of which possess medicinal properties [ME, fr MF or ML; MF *valeriane*, fr ML *valeriana*, prob fr fem of *valerianus* of Valeria, fr *Valeria*, Roman province in SE Europe]

va,leric 'acid /və'liərik, və'lerik/ *n* a liquid acid of disagreeable smell obtained from valerian or made synthetically and used esp in organic synthesis [*valerian*; fr its occurrence in the root of valerian]

valet /'valay/ *n* a gentleman's male servant who performs personal services (e g taking care of clothing); *also* an employee (e g of a hotel) who performs similar services for patrons [MF *vaslet, varlet, valet* young nobleman, page, domestic servant, fr (assumed) ML *vassellittus*, dim. of ML *vassus* servant – more at VASSAL]

valeta /və'leetə/ *n* a veleta

valetudinarian /,vali,tyoohdi'neəri·ən/ *n* a person of a weak or sickly constitution; *esp* a hypochondriac – fml [L *valetudinarius* sickly, infirm, fr *valetudin-, valetudo* state of health, sickness, fr *valēre* to be strong, be well] – **valetudinarian** *adj*, **valetudinarianism** *n*

valetudinary /,vali'tyoohdin(ə)ri/ *n or adj* (a) valetudinarian – fml [L *valetudinarius*]

valgus /'valgəs/ *n* the position of a bone or part that is turned outwards to an abnormal degree at its joint ⟨*the toe is in* ~⟩ – compare VARUS [NL, fr L, bowlegged – more at WALK]

valiant /'vali·ənt/ *adj* characterized by or showing valour; courageous [ME *valiaunt*, fr MF *vaillant*, fr OF, fr prp of *valoir* to be of worth, fr L *valēre* to be strong – more at WIELD] – **valiance** *n*, **valiant** *n*, **valiantly** *adv*, **valiantness** *n*

valid /'valid/ *adj* **1** having legal efficacy; *esp* executed according to the proper formalities ⟨*a* ~ *contract*⟩ **2a** well-grounded or justifiable; relevant and meaningful **b** logically sound [MF or ML; MF *valide*, fr ML *validus*, fr L, strong, fr *valēre*] – **validly** *adv*, **validness** *n*, **validity** /və'lidəti/ *n*

validate /'validayt/ *vt* **1** to make legally valid **2** to corroborate, authenticate ⟨*experiments to* ~ *his hypothesis*⟩ – **validation** /-'daysh(ə)n/ *n*

valine /'vay,leen, 'va-/ *n* an essential amino acid that occurs in most proteins [ISV, fr *valeric (acid)*]

Valium /'vali·əm/ *trademark* – used for diazepam

valley /'vali/ *n* **1a** an elongated depression of the earth's surface, usu between hills or mountains ☞ GEOGRAPHY **b** an area drained by a river and its tributaries **2a** a hollow, depression **b** the internal angle formed at the meeting of 2 roof surfaces [ME *valey*, fr OF *valee*, fr *val* valley – more at VALE]

Valois /'valwah (*Fr* valwa)/ *adj* of the French royal house that ruled from 1328 to 1589 [Philippe de *Valois* (Philip VI of France) †1350]

valonia /və'lohnyə, -ni·ə/ *n* dried acorn cups, esp from a Eurasian evergreen oak, used in tanning or dressing leather [It *vallonia*, fr MGk *balanidia*, pl of *balanidion*, dim. of Gk *balanos* acorn – more at [1]GLAND]

valor·ize, -ise /'valəriez/ *vt* to (try to) enhance the price, value, or status of by organized usu governmental action [Pg *valorizare*, fr *valor* value, price, fr ML] – **valorization** /-'zaysh(ə)n/ *n*

valorous /'valərəs/ *adj* valiant – **valorously** *adv*

valour, *NAm chiefly* **valor** /'valə/ *n* strength of mind or spirit that enables sby to encounter danger with firmness; personal bravery [ME, fr MF, fr ML *valor* value, valor, fr L *valēre* to be strong]

valse /vals/ *n* a (concert) waltz [F, fr G *walzer*]

[1]valuable /'valyoo(ə)bl/ *adj* **1** having (high) money value **2** of great use or worth ⟨~ *advice* ⟩ – **valuableness** *n*, **valuably** *adv*

[2]valuable *n* a usu personal possession of relatively great money value – usu pl

valuation /,valyoo'aysh(ə)n/ *n* **1** the act of valuing sthg, esp property **2** the estimated or determined value, esp market value, of a thing **3** judgment or appraisal of worth or character – **valuational** *adj*, **valuationally** *adv*

valuator /'valyoo,aytə/ *n* sby who judges the (money) value of sthg

[1]value /'valyooh/ *n* **1** a fair return or equivalent for sthg exchanged **2** the worth in money or commodities of sthg **3** relative worth, utility, or importance ⟨*had nothing of ~ to say*⟩ **4a** a numerical quantity assigned or computed **b** the magnitude of a physical quantity **5** the relative duration of a musical note **6a** relative lightness or darkness of a colour **b** the relation of one part in a picture to another with respect to lightness and darkness **7** sthg (e g a principle or quality) intrinsically valuable or desirable **8** DENOMINATION 3 [ME, fr MF, fr (assumed) VL *valuta*, fr fem of *valutus*, pp of L *valēre* to be worth, be strong]

[2]value *vt* **1a** to estimate the worth of in terms of money ⟨~ *a necklace*⟩ **b** to rate in terms of usefulness, importance, etc **2** to consider or rate highly; esteem ⟨*a* ~d *helper*⟩ – **valuer** *n*

,value-'added ,tax *n, often cap V, A, & T* a tax levied at each stage of the production and distribution of a commodity and passed on to the consumer as a form of purchase tax

'value ,judgment *n* a judgment attributing a value (e g good, evil, or desirable) to a particular action or thing, usu as contrasted with a tolerant, factual, or objective assessment

'valueless /-lis/ *adj* worthless – **valuelessness** *n*

valuta /və'l(y)oohtə/ *n* the agreed or exchange value of a currency [It, value, fr (assumed) VL *valuta*]

valve /valv/ *n* **1** a structure, esp in the heart or a vein, that closes temporarily to obstruct passage of material or permits movement of fluid in 1 direction only **2a** any of numerous mechanical devices by which the flow of liquid, gas, or loose material in bulk may be controlled, usu to allow movement in 1 direction only ☞ CAR **b** a device in a brass musical instrument for quickly varying the tube length in order to change the fundamental tone by a definite interval **3** any of the separate joined pieces that make up the shell of an (invertebrate) animal; *specif* either of the 2 halves of the shell of a bivalve mollusc **4** any of the segments or pieces into which a ripe seed capsule or pod separates **5** *chiefly Br* a vacuum- or gas-filled device for the regulation of electric current by the control of free electrons or ions [NL *valva*, fr L, a leaf of a folding door; akin to L *volvere* to roll – more at VOLUBLE] – **valved** *adj*, **valveless** *adj*

valvular /'valvyoolə/ *adj* **1** resembling or functioning as a valve; *also* opening by valves **2** of a valve, esp of the heart

vamoose /va'moohs/ *vi, chiefly NAm* to depart quickly – slang [Sp *vamos* let us go, suppletive 1st person pl imper (fr L *vadere* to go) of *ir* to go, fr L *ire* – more at WADE, ISSUE]

[1]vamp /vamp/ *n* **1** the part of a shoe or boot covering the front of the foot **2** a simple improvised musical accompaniment [ME *vampe* sock, fr OF *avantpié*, fr *avant-* fore- + *pié* foot, fr L *ped-*, *pes* – more at VANGUARD, FOOT; (2) [2]*vamp*]

[2]vamp *vt* **1** to provide (a shoe) with a new vamp **2** to patch (sthg old) with a new part ⟨~ *up old sermons*⟩ ~ *vi* to play a musical vamp – **vamper** *n*

[3]vamp *n* a woman who uses her charm to seduce and exploit men [short for *vampire*]

vampire /'vampie·ə/ *n* **1** a dead person believed to come from the grave at night and suck the blood of sleeping people **2** any of various S American bats that feed on blood and are dangerous to human beings and domestic animals, esp as transmitters of disease (e g rabies); *also* any of several other bats that do not feed on blood but are sometimes reputed to do so [F, fr G *vampir*, of Slav origin; akin to Serb *vampir* vampire]

vampirism /'vampiriz(ə)m/ *n* **1** belief in vampires **2** the actions of a vampire

[1]van /van/ *n, dial Eng* a winnowing device (e g a fan) [ME, fr MF, fr L *vannus* – more at WINNOW]

[2]van *n* the vanguard [by shortening]

[3]van *n* **1** an enclosed motor vehicle used for transport of goods, animals, furniture, etc **2** *chiefly Br* an enclosed railway goods wagon [short for *caravan*]

vanadic /və'naydik, -'na-/ *adj* of or containing vanadium, esp with a relatively high valency – **vanadate** /'vanə,dayt/ *n*

vanadium /və'naydi·əm/ *n* a malleable polyvalent metallic element found combined in minerals and used esp to form alloys ☞ PERIODIC TABLE [NL, fr ON *Vanadīs* Freya, Norse goddess of love & beauty]

va,nadium pen'toxide /pen'toksied/ *n* a compound used esp in making glass and as a catalyst

vanadous /'vanədəs/ *adj* of or containing vanadium, esp with a relatively low valency

Van Allen belt /van 'alən/ *n* a belt of intense ionizing radiation in the earth's outer atmosphere [James A *Van Allen b* 1914 US physicist]

vandal /'vandl/ *n* **1** *cap* a member of a Germanic people who overran Gaul, Spain, and N Africa in the 4th and 5th c AD and in 455 sacked Rome **2** one who wilfully or ignorantly destroys or defaces (public) property [L *Vandalii* (pl), of Gmc origin] – **vandal** *adj, often cap*, **Vandalic** /-'dalik/ *adj*

'vandal,ism /-,iz(ə)m/ *n* wilful destruction or defacement of property – **vandalize** *vt*, **vandalistic** /-'istik/ *adj*

Van de Graaff generator /,van də 'grahf/ *n* an electrostatic generator [Robert J *Van de Graaff* †1967 US physicist]

van der Waals forces /,van də 'wahlz, 'vahlz/ *n pl* the relatively weak attractive forces that are operative between neutral atoms and molecules and that arise because of differences in electric potential [Johannes *van der Waals* †1923 D physicist]

Vandyke /ˌvan'diek/ *n* **1a** a wide collar with a deeply indented edge **b** (any of) a series of V-shaped points forming a decorative edging **2** a trim pointed beard [Sir Anthony *Vandyke* (originally Van Dyck) †1641 Flem painter]

Vandyke brown *n* a dark brown pigment [fr its use by the painter Vandyke]

vane /vayn/ *n* **1** WEATHER VANE **2** a thin flat or curved object that is rotated about an axis by wind or water ⟨*the* ~s *of a windmill*⟩; *also* a device revolving in a similar manner and moving in water or air ⟨*the* ~s *of a propeller*⟩ **3** the flat expanded part of a feather ☞ ANATOMY **4a** the target of a levelling staff **b** any of the sights of a compass or quadrant [ME (southern), fr OE *fana* banner; akin to OHG *fano* cloth, L *pannus* cloth, rag] – **vaned** *adj*

vanguard /'vangahd/ *n* **1** *sing or pl in constr* the troops moving at the head of an army **2** the forefront of an action or movement [ME *vantgard*, fr MF *avant-garde*, fr OF, fr *avant-* fore- (fr *avant* before, fr L *abante*) + *garde* guard – more at ADVANCE]

vanilla /və'nilə/ *n* **1** any of a genus of tropical American climbing orchids whose long capsular fruits yield an important flavouring; *also* VANILLA POD **2** a commercially important extract of the vanilla pod that is used esp as a flavouring [NL, genus name, fr Sp *vainilla* vanilla (plant and fruit), dim. of *vaina* sheath, fr L *vagina* sheath, vagina]

vanilla pod *n* the fruit of a vanilla

vanillin /və'nilin/ *n* the chief fragrant component of vanilla

vanish /'vanish/ *vi* **1a** to pass quickly from sight; disappear **b** to cease to exist **2** to assume the value zero ~ *vt* to cause to disappear [ME *vanisshen*, fr MF *evaniss-*, stem of *evanir*, fr (assumed) VL *exvanire*, alter. of L *evanescere* to dissipate like vapour, vanish, fr *e-* + *vanescere* to vanish, fr *vanus* empty] – **vanisher** *n*

'vanishing ˌcream /'vanishing/ *n* a light cosmetic cream used chiefly as a foundation for face powder

vanishing point *n* **1** a point at which receding parallel lines seem to meet when represented in linear perspective **2** a point at which sthg disappears or ceases to exist

vanity /'vanəti/ *n* **1** sthg vain, empty, or worthless **2** the quality of being vain or futile; worthlessness **3** excessive pride in oneself; conceit [ME *vanite*, fr OF *vanité*, fr L *vanitat-*, *vanitas* quality of being empty or vain, fr *vanus* empty, vain – more at WANE]

'vanity ˌcase *n* a small bag used by women for carrying toilet articles and cosmetics

vanquish /'vangkwish, 'van-/ *vt* **1** to overcome, conquer ⟨*the* ~ed *foe*⟩ **2** to gain mastery over (an emotion, passion, etc) [ME *venquissen*, fr MF *venquis*, preterite of *veintre* to conquer, fr L *vincere* – more at VICTOR] – **vanquishable** *adj*, **vanquisher** *n*

vantage /'vahntij/ *n* **1** a position giving a strategic advantage or commanding perspective **2** *Br* ADVANTAGE 3 [ME, fr AF, fr MF *avantage* – more at ADVANTAGE]

vanward /'vanwood/ *adj* located in the vanguard; forward

vapid /'vapid/ *adj* lacking liveliness, interest, or force; insipid [L *vapidus* flat tasting; akin to L *vappa* vapid wine, & prob to L *vapor* steam] – **vapidly** *adv*, **vapidness** *n*, **vapidity** /va'pidəti/ *n*

vapor·ize, -ise /'vaypəˌriez/ *vt* **1** to convert (e g by the application of heat) into vapour **2** to destroy by conversion into vapour ~ *vi* to become vaporized – **vaporizable** *adj*, **vaporizer** *n*, **vaporization** /-'zaysh(ə)n/ *n*

vaporous /'vayp(ə)rəs/ *adj* **1** resembling, consisting of, or characteristic of vapour **2** producing vapours; volatile **3** containing or obscured by vapours; misty – **vaporously** *adv*, **vaporousness** *n*

^{1}**vapour,** *NAm chiefly* **vapor** /'vaypə/ *n* **1** smoke, fog, etc suspended floating in the air and impairing its transparency **2** a substance in the gaseous state; *esp* such a substance that is liquid under normal conditions **3** *pl, archaic* a depressed or hysterical condition [ME *vapour*, fr MF *vapeur*, fr L *vapor* steam, vapour]

^{2}**vapour,** *NAm chiefly* **vapor** *vi* **1** to rise or pass off in vapour **2** to emit vapour

vapourer moth /'vaypərə/ *n* a tussock moth the female of which has vestigial wings and cannot fly

vapouring /'vayp(ə)ring/ *n* an idle, extravagant, or high-flown expression or speech – usu pl [fr gerund of ^{2}*vapour* (to say foolish or boastful things)]

'vapour ˌpressure *n* the pressure exerted by a vapour that is in equilibrium with its solid or liquid form

'vapour ˌtrail *n* a contrail

vari-, vario- *comb form* varied; diverse ⟨vari*form*⟩ [L *varius* – more at VARIOUS]

^{1}**variable** /'veəri·əbl/ *adj* **1** subject to variation or changes ⟨~ *winds*⟩ **2** having the characteristics of a variable ⟨*a* ~ *number*⟩ **3** *of a biological group or character* not true to type; aberrant – **variableness** *n*, **variably** *adv*, **variability** /-ə'biləti/ *n*

^{2}**variable** *n* **1** sthg (e g a variable star) that is variable **2** (a symbol representing) a quantity that may assume any of a set of values – compare RANDOM VARIABLE

variable star *n* a star with a usu regularly varying brightness

variance /'veəri·əns/ *n* **1** a discrepancy **2** dissension, dispute – esp in *at variance* **3** the square of the standard deviation [VARY + -ANCE] – **at variance** not in harmony or agreement

^{1}**variant** /'veəri·ənt/ *adj* varying (slightly) from the standard form ⟨~ *readings*⟩

^{2}**variant** *n* any of 2 or more people or things displaying usu slight differences: e g **a** sthg that shows variation from a type or norm **b** any of 2 or more different spellings, pronunciations, or forms of the same word

variation /ˌveəri'aysh(ə)n/ *n* **1a** varying or being varied **b** an instance of varying **c** the extent to which or the range in which a thing varies **2** DECLINATION 3 **3** a change in the mean motion or orbit of a celestial body **4** the repetition of a musical theme with modifications in rhythm, tune, harmony, or key **5a** divergence in characteristics of an organism or genotype from those typical or usual of its group **b** an individual or group exhibiting variation **6** a solo dance in ballet – **variational** *adj*, **variationally** *adv*

varicella /ˌvari'sela/ *n* CHICKEN POX [NL, irreg dim. of *variola*]

varicocele /'varikohˌseel/ *n* a varicose enlargement of the veins of the spermatic cord [NL, fr L *varic-*, *varix* + *-o-* + *-cele*]

varicoloured /'veəri,kuləd/ *adj* having various colours

varicose /'varikəs, -kohs/ *also* **varicosed** *adj* abnormally swollen or dilated ⟨~ *veins*⟩ [L *varicosus* full of dilated veins, fr *varic-, varix* dilated vein] – **varicosity** /-'kosəti/ *n*

varied /'veərid/ *adj* **1** having numerous forms or types; diverse **2** variegated – **variedly** /'veəri·idli, -rid-/ *adv*

variegate /'veəri·ə,gayt, -ri,gayt/ *vt* to diversify in appearance, esp with patches of different colours; dapple [L *variegatus*, pp of *variegare*, fr *varius* various + *-egare* (akin to L *agere* to drive) – more at AGENT] – **variegator** *n*, **variegation** /-'gaysh(ə)n/ *n*

variety /və'rie·əti/ *n* **1** the state of having different forms or types; diversity **2** an assortment of different things, esp of a particular class **3a** sthg differing from others of the same general kind; a sort **b** any of various groups of plants or animals ranking below a species **4** theatrical entertainment consisting of separate performances (e g of songs, skits, acrobatics, etc) [MF or L; MF *varieté*, fr L *varietat-, varietas*, fr *varius* various]

variety meat *n, chiefly NAm* edible offal of a slaughtered animal

variform /'veəri,fawm/ *adj* varied in form

variola /və'rie·ələ/ *n* smallpox, cowpox, or any of various other virus diseases marked by a rash of pustular spots [NL, fr ML, pustule, pox, fr LL, pustule] – **variolous** *adj*

variorum /,veəri'awrəm, ,va-/ *n* an edition or text with notes by different people [L *variorum* of various persons (gen pl masc of *varius*), in the phrase *cum notis variorum* with the notes of various persons]

various /'veəri·əs/ *adj* **1a** of differing kinds; diverse ⟨~ *remedies*⟩ **b** dissimilar in nature or form; unlike **2** having a number of different aspects or characteristics ⟨~ *genius*⟩ **3** more than one; several ⟨*stop at* ~ *towns*⟩ [L *varius*; prob akin to L *varus* bent, crooked – more at PREVARICATE] – **variousness** *n*

'variously /-li/ *adv* in various ways; at various times

varix /'variks/ *n, pl* **varices** /'vari,seez/ **1** an abnormally dilated and lengthened vein, artery, or lymph vessel; *esp* a varicose vein **2** any of the prominent ridges across each whorl of a gastropod shell [L *varic-, varix*]

varlet /'vahlit/ *n* a base unprincipled person [ME, fr MF *vaslet, varlet* young nobleman, page – more at VALET]

varmint /'vahmint/ *n, dial or NAm* **1** an animal or bird considered a pest **2** a rascal [alter. of *vermin*]

¹varnish /'vahnish/ *n* **1** a liquid preparation that forms a hard shiny transparent coating on drying **2** outside show; VENEER 3 [ME *vernisch*, fr MF *vernis*, fr OIt or ML; OIt *vernice*, fr ML *veronic-, veronix* sandarac (resin)] – **varnishy** *adj*

²varnish *vt* **1** to apply varnish to **2** to cover (sthg unpleasant) with a fair appearance; gloss *over* – **varnisher** *n*

'varnish ,tree *n* any of various trees from which varnish or lacquer can be prepared

varsity /'vahsiti/ *n, Br* university – now chiefly humor [by shortening & alter.]

varus /'vayrəs/ *n* the position of a bone or part that is turned inwards at its joint to an abnormal degree ⟨*the toe is in* ~⟩ – compare VALGUS [NL, fr L, bent, knock-kneed]

varve /vahv/ *n* a band of sediment composed of 2 distinct layers of silt or clay believed to comprise an annual cycle of deposition in a body of still water [Sw *varv* turn, layer; akin to OE *hweorfan* to turn – more at WHARF] – **varved** *adj*

vary /'veəri/ *vt* **1** to make a (partial) change in **2** to ensure variety in; diversify ~ *vi* **1** to exhibit or undergo change **2** to deviate **3** to take on values ⟨*y* varies *inversely with x*⟩ **4** to exhibit biological variation [ME *varien*, fr MF or L; MF *varier*, fr L *variare*, fr *varius* various] – **varyingly** *adv*

vas-, vaso- *comb form* vessel (e g blood vessel) ⟨vaso*dilator*⟩ [NL, fr L *vas* vessel]

vascular /'vaskyoolə/ *adj* of or being a channel or system of channels conducting blood, sap, etc in a plant or animal; *also* supplied with or made up of such channels, esp blood vessels ⟨*a* ~ *tumour*⟩ [NL *vascularis*, fr L *vasculum* small vessel, dim. of *vas*] – **vascularity** /-'larəti/ *n*

vascular bundle *n* a single strand of the vascular system of a plant consisting usu of xylem and phloem together with parenchyma cells and fibres

vascular·ize, -ise /'vaskyoolə,riez/ *vb* to make or become vascular – **vascularization** /-'zaysh(ə)n/ *n*

vascular plant *n* a plant having a specialized liquid conducting system that includes xylem and phloem

vascular ray *n* any of several wedges of parenchymatous tissue formed from cambium that connect xylem and phloem in a vascular plant

vasculum /'vaskyooləm/ *n, pl* **vascula** /-lə/ a usu metal and commonly cylindrical box used in collecting plants [NL, fr L, small vessel]

vas deferens /,vaz 'defərenz, vas/ *n, pl* **vasa deferentia** /,vaysə defə'renshi·ə, -si·ə, -shə, ,vayzə/ a duct, esp of a higher vertebrate animal, that carries sperm from the testis towards the penis [NL, lit., deferent vessel]

vase /vahz/ *n* an ornamental vessel usu of greater depth than width, used esp for holding flowers [F, fr L *vas* vessel; akin to Umbrian *vasor* vessels] – **vaselike** /'-,-/ *adj*

vasectomy /və'sektəmi, va-/ *n* surgical cutting out of a section of the vas deferens, usu to induce permanent sterility [ISV] – **vasectomize** *vt*

Vaseline /,vas(ə)l'een/ *trademark* – used for petroleum jelly

vasiform /'vasi,fawm/ *adj* having the form of a hollow tube [NL *vasiformis*, fr L *vas* + *-iformis* -iform]

vaso- – see VAS-

vasoactive /,vasoh'aktiv, ,vayzoh-/ *adj* affecting, esp in relaxing or contracting, the blood vessels – **vasoactivity** /-ak'tivəti/ *n*

'vasocon,striction *n* narrowing of the diameter of blood vessels [ISV] – **vasoconstrictive** /'---,--/ *adj*

'vasocon,strictor /-kən,striktə/ *n* a sympathetic nerve fibre, drug, etc that induces or initiates vasoconstriction

,vasodi'lation /-die'laysh(ə)n/ *n* widening of the blood vessels, esp as a result of nerve action [ISV]

'vasodi,lator /-die,laytə/ *n* a parasympathetic nerve fibre, drug, etc that induces or initiates vasodilation

,vaso'motor /-'mohtə/ *adj* of or being nerves or centres controlling the size of blood vessels [ISV]

ˌ**vaso'pressin** /-'presin/ *n* a polypeptide pituitary hormone that increases blood pressure and decreases urine flow [fr *Vasopressin,* a trademark]

ˌ**vaso'pressor** /-'presə/ *adj* causing a rise in blood pressure by constricting the blood vessels – **vasopressor** *n*

vassal /'vas(ə)l/ *n* **1** sby under the protection of another who is his/her feudal lord **2** sby in a subservient or subordinate position [ME, fr MF, fr ML *vassallus,* fr *vassus* servant, vassal, of Celt origin; akin to W *gwas* boy, servant] – **vassal** *adj*

vast /vahst/ *adj* very great in amount, degree, intensity, or esp in extent or range [L *vastus;* akin to OIr *fot* length] – **vastly** *adv,* **vastness** *n*

[1]**vat** /vat/ *n* **1** a tub, barrel, or other large vessel, esp for holding liquids undergoing chemical change or preparations for dyeing or tanning **2** a liquid containing a dye in a soluble form, that, on textile material being steeped in the liquor and then exposed to the air, is converted to the original insoluble dye by oxidation and is precipitated in the fibre [ME *fat, vat,* fr OE *fæt;* akin to OHG *vaz* vessel, Lith *puodas* pot]

[2]**vat** *vt* **-tt-** to put into or treat in a vat

[3]**vat** *n, often cap, Br* VALUE-ADDED TAX

vat dye *n* a water-insoluble generally fast dye used in the form of a vat liquor

Vatican /'vatikən/ *n* the official residence of the Pope and the administrative centre of Roman Catholicism [L *Vaticanus* Vatican Hill (in Rome)] – **Vatican** *adj*

vaticinate /və'tisiˌnayt, va-/ *vb* to prophesy, predict – fml [L *vaticinatus,* pp of *vaticinari,* fr *vates* prophet + *-cinari* (akin to L *canere* to sing) – more at CHANT] – **vaticinator** *n,* **vaticination** /-'naysh(ə)n/ *n*

vaudeville /'vawdəˌvil/ *n* **1** a light often comic theatrical piece frequently combining pantomime, dialogue, dancing, and song **2** *NAm* VARIETY 4 [F, fr MF, popular satirical song, alter. of *vaudevire,* fr *vau-de-Vire* valley of Vire, fr *vau, val* valley + *de* from, of (fr L) + *Vire,* town in NW France where such songs were composed – more at VALE, DE-]

[1]**vault** /vawlt, volt/ *n* **1a** an arched structure of masonry, usu forming a ceiling or roof ☞ CHURCH **b** sthg (e g the sky) resembling a vault **2a** an underground passage, room, or storage compartment **b** a room or compartment for the safekeeping of valuables **3a** a burial chamber, esp beneath a church or in a cemetery **b** a prefabricated container, usu of metal or concrete, into which a coffin is placed at burial [ME *voute,* fr MF, fr (assumed) VL *volvita* turn, vault, prob fr *volvitare*] – **vaulted** *adj,* **vaulty** *adj*

[2]**vault** *vt* to form or cover (as if) with a vault

[3]**vault** *vb* to bound vigorously (over); *esp* to execute a leap (over) using the hands or a pole [MF *volter,* fr OIt *voltare,* fr (assumed) VL *volvitare* to turn, leap, freq of L *volvere* to roll – more at VOLUBLE] – **vaulter** *n*

[4]**vault** *n* an act of vaulting

[1]**vaulting** /'vawlting, 'volting/ *n* vaulted construction

[2]**vaulting** *adj* **1** reaching for the heights ⟨~ *ambition*⟩ **2** designed for use in vaulting

'**vaulting** ˌ**horse** *n* an apparatus like a pommel horse without pommels that is used for vaulting in gymnastics

vaunt /vawnt/ *vt* to call attention to, proudly and often boastfully [ME *vaunten,* fr MF *vanter,* fr LL *vanitare,* fr L *vanitas* vanity] – **vaunter** *n,* **vauntingly** *adv*

vavasour /'vavəˌsooə/ *n* a feudal tenant ranking directly below a baron [ME, fr OF *vavassor,* prob fr ML *vassus vassorum* vassal of vassals]

VD /ˌvee 'dee/ *n* VENEREAL DISEASE

VDU /ˌvee dee 'yooh/ *n* a device for the visual display of information (e g from a computer) typically in the form of text presented on a cathode-ray tube [*v*isual *d*isplay *u*nit]

've /v/ *vb* have ⟨*we've been there*⟩ [by contr]

veal /veel/ *n* the flesh of a young calf used as food ☞ MEAT [ME *veel,* fr MF, fr L *vitellus* small calf, dim. of *vitulus* calf – more at WETHER] – **vealy** *adj*

[1]**vector** /'vektə/ *n* **1a** a quantity (e g velocity or force) that has magnitude and direction and that is commonly represented by a directed line segment whose length represents the magnitude and whose orientation in space represents the direction **b** a course or compass direction, esp of an aircraft **2** an organism (e g an insect) that transmits a disease-causing agent [NL, fr L, carrier, fr *vectus,* pp of *vehere* to carry – more at WAY] – **vectorial** /-'tawri·əl/ *adj*

[2]**vector** *vt* to change the direction of (the thrust of a jet engine) for steering

vector product *n* a vector *c* whose length is the product of the lengths of 2 vectors *a* and *b* and the sine of their included angle, whose direction is perpendicular to their plane, and whose sense for the vector product *ab* is that of a right-handed screw with axis *c* when *a* is rotated into *b*

vector space *n* a set whose elements are generalized vectors and which is a commutative group under addition that is also closed under an operation of multiplication by elements of a given field

vector sum *n* the sum of vectors that for 2 vectors is geometrically represented by the diagonal of a parallelogram whose sides represent the 2 vectors being added

Veda /'veedə, 'vay-/ *n* any of 4 canonical collections of hymns, prayers, and liturgical formulas that comprise the earliest Hindu sacred writings [Skt, lit., knowledge; akin to Gk *eidenai* to know – more at WIT]

Vedanta /və'dahntə, -'dan-/ *n* an orthodox system of Hindu philosophy developing the speculations of the Upanishads on ultimate reality and the liberation of the soul [Skt *Vedānta,* lit., end of the Veda, fr *Veda* + *anta* end; akin to OE *ende* end] – **Vedantism** *n,* **Vedantist** *n*

Vedantic /və'dantik/ *adj* **1** of the Vedanta philosophy **2** Vedic

Vedda, Veddah /'vedə/ *n* a member of an aboriginal people of Sri Lanka [Sinhalese *vedda* hunter]

vedette /vi'det/ *n* a mounted sentinel stationed in advance of pickets [F, fr It *vedetta,* alter. of *veletta,* prob fr Sp *vela* watch, fr *velar* to keep watch, fr L *vigilare* to wake, watch, fr *vigil* awake]

Vedic /'veedik, 'vay-/ *adj* of the Vedas, the language in which they are written, or Hindu history and culture between 1500 BC and 500 BC

[1]**veer** /viə/ *vt* to let or pay out (e g a rope) [ME *veren,* of LG or D origin; akin to MD *vieren* to slacken, MLG *vīren*]

[2]**veer** /viə/ *vi* **1** to change direction, position, or inclination **2** *of the wind* to shift in a clockwise

direction – compare BACK 2 3 to wear ship ~ *vt* to direct to a different course; *specif* WEAR 7 [MF *virer*, prob of Celt origin; akin to OIr *fiar* oblique; akin to OE *wīr* wire] – **veeringly** *adv*

[3]**veer** *n* a change in direction, position, or inclination

veg /vej/ *n, pl* **veg** *Br* a vegetable ⟨*meat and two* ~⟩ – infml

vegan /'veegən, vaygən/ *n* a strict vegetarian who avoids food or other products derived from animals [by contr fr *vegetarian*] – **vegan** *adj*, **veganism** *n*

[1]**vegetable** /'vej(i)təbl/ *adj* **1a** of, constituting, or growing like plants **b** consisting of plants **2** made or obtained from plants or plant products [ME, fr ML *vegetabilis* vegetative, fr *vegetare* to grow, fr L, to animate, fr *vegetus* lively, fr *vegēre* to rouse, excite – more at [1]WAKE] – **vegetably** *adv*

[2]**vegetable** *n* **1** PLANT 1b **2** a usu herbaceous plant (e g the cabbage, bean, or potato) grown for an edible part which is usu eaten with the principal course of a meal; *also* this part of the plant **3a** a person with a dull undemanding existence **b** a person whose physical and esp mental capacities are severely impaired by illness or injury

vegetable ivory *n* the hard white opaque endosperm of the seed of a S American palm that is used as a substitute for ivory

,vegetable 'marrow *n* (any of various large smooth-skinned elongated fruits, used as a vegetable, of) a cultivated variety of a climbing plant of the cucumber family

'vegetable ,oil *n* an oil of plant origin

vegetal /'vejitl/ *adj* **1** vegetable **2** vegetative [ML *vegetare* to grow]

[1]**vegetarian** /,veji'teəri·ən/ *n* one who practises vegetarianism [[2]*vegetable* + *-arian*]

[2]**vegetarian** *adj* **1** of vegetarians or vegetarianism **2** consisting wholly of vegetables ⟨*a* ~ *diet*⟩

,vege'taria,nism /-,niz(ə)m/ *n* the often ethically based theory or practice of living on a diet that excludes the flesh of animals and often other animal products and that is made up of vegetables, fruits, cereals, and nuts – compare LACTO-VEGETARIANISM

vegetate /'veji,tayt/ *vi* **1a** to grow in the manner of a plant **b** to produce vegetation **2** to lead a passive monotonous existence [ML *vegetatus*, pp of *vegetare* to grow]

vegetation /,veji'taysh(ə)n/ *n* **1** plant life or total plant cover (e g of an area) **2** an abnormal outgrowth on a body part (e g a heart valve) [VEGETATE + -ION] – **vegetational** *adj*, **vegetationally** *adv*

vegetative /'vejitətiv/ *adj* **1a** of or functioning in nutrition and growth as contrasted with reproductive functions ⟨*a* ~ *nucleus*⟩ **b** of or involving propagation by nonsexual processes or methods **2** relating to, composed of, or suggesting vegetation ⟨~ *cover*⟩ **3** affecting, arising from, or relating to involuntary bodily functions – **vegetatively** *adv*, **vegetativeness** *n*

vehement /'vee·əmənt/ *adj* **1** intensely felt; impassioned **2** forcibly expressed [MF, fr L *vehement-*, *vehemens*; akin to L *vehere* to carry] – **vehemently** *adv*, **vehemence** *n*

vehicle /'vee·ək(ə)l/ *n* **1** any of various usu liquid media acting esp as solvents, carriers, or binders for active ingredients (e g drugs) or pigments **2** a means of transmission; a carrier **3** a medium through which sthg is expressed or communicated **4** MOTOR VEHICLE **5** a work created to display the talents of a particular performer [F *véhicule*, fr L *vehiculum* carriage, conveyance, fr *vehere* to carry – more at WAY]

vehicular /vee'ikyoolə/ *adj* of or designed for vehicles, esp motor vehicles

[1]**veil** /vayl/ *n* **1a** a length of cloth worn by women as a covering for the head and shoulders and often, esp in eastern countries, the face; *specif* the outer covering of a nun's headdress **b** a piece of sheer fabric attached for protection or ornament to a hat or headdress **c** any of various liturgical cloths; *esp* one used to cover the chalice **2** *the* cloistered life of a nun **3** a concealing curtain or cover of cloth **4a** sthg that hides or obscures like a veil **b** a disguise, pretext ⟨*under the* ~ *of national defence preparations for war began*⟩ **5** a velum [ME *veile*, fr ONF, fr L *vela*, pl of *velum* veil]

[2]**veil** *vt* to cover, provide, or conceal (as if) with a veil ~ *vi* to put on or wear a veil

veiled /vayld/ *adj* **1** indistinct, muffled **2** disguised ⟨~ *threats*⟩

veiling /'vayling/ *n* **1** a veil **2** any of various light sheer fabrics

[1]**vein** /vayn/ *n* **1** a deposit of ore, coal, etc, esp in a rock fissure **2a** BLOOD VESSEL – not used technically **b** any of the tubular converging vessels that carry blood from the capillaries towards the heart – compare ARTERY ☞ ANATOMY **3a** any of the vascular bundles forming the framework of a leaf **b** any of the thickened cuticular ribs that serve to stiffen the wings of an insect **4** a streak or marking suggesting a vein (e g in marble) **5** a distinctive element or quality; a strain **6** a frame of mind; a mood [ME *veine*, fr OF, fr L *vena*] – **veinal** *adj*, **veinlet** /-lit/ *n*, **veiny** *adj*

[2]**vein** *vt* to pattern (as if) with veins

veining /'vayning/ *n* a pattern of veins

velar /'veelə/ *adj* **1** of or forming a velum, esp the soft palate **2** formed with the back of the tongue touching or near the soft palate ⟨*the* ~ /k/ *of* cool⟩ [NL *velaris*, fr *velum*] – **velar** *n*, **velarize** *vt*

Velcro /'velkroh/ *trademark* – used for a fastening device consisting of 2 pieces, esp strips, of fabric that stick to each other by means of very small hooks that cling to loops

veld, veldt /velt, felt/ *n* a (shrubby or thinly forested) grassland, esp in southern Africa ☞ PLANT [Afrik *veld*, fr MD, field; akin to OE *feld* field]

veleta, valeta /və'leetə/ *n* a ballroom dance of English origin in waltz time [Sp *veleta* weather vane, fr *vela* cloth, veil, fr L *vela*, pl of *velum* veil]

velleity /və'lee·əti/ *n* a slight wish or inclination – fml [NL *velleitas*, fr L *velle* to wish, will – more at WILL]

vellum /'veləm/ *n* **1** a fine-grained skin (e g calf) prepared esp for writing on or binding books **2** a strong cream-coloured paper [ME *velim*, fr MF *veelin*, fr *veelin*, adj, of a calf, fr *veel* calf – more at VEAL]

velocipede /və'losipeed/ *n* **1** an early type of bicycle propelled by the rider's feet in contact with the ground **2** *NAm* a child's tricycle [F *vélocipède*, fr L *veloc-*, *velox* + *ped-*, *pes* foot – more at FOOT]

velocity /və'losəti/ *n* **1** speed, esp of inanimate things **2** speed in a given direction [MF *velocité*, fr L *velocitat-*, *velocitas*, fr *veloc-*, *velox* quick; akin to L *vehere* to carry – more at WAY]

velour, velours /və'looə/ *n, pl* **velours** /-z/ **1** any of various fabrics with a pile or napped surface resembling velvet **2** a fur felt finished with a long velvety nap, used esp for hats [F *velours* velvet, velour, fr MF *velours, velour,* fr OF *velous,* fr L *villosus* shaggy, fr *villus* shaggy hair]

velouté /və'loohtay/ *n* a basic white sauce made with a roux and chicken, veal, or fish stock – compare BÉCHAMEL [F, lit., velvety, fr MF, fr *velours* velvet]

velskoen /'velskoohn, 'fel-/ *n, SAfr* a strong heavy shoe, esp of rawhide [Afrik, fr *vel* skin + *skoen* shoe]

velum /'veeləm/ *n, pl* **vela** /-lə/ a curtainlike membrane or anatomical partition; *esp* SOFT PALATE [NL, fr L, curtain, veil]

velutinous /və'loohtinəs/ *adj* covered with fine silky hairs [NL *velutinus,* fr ML *velutum* velvet, prob fr OIt *velluto* shaggy, fr (assumed) VL *villutus*]

velvet /'velvit/ *n* **1** a fabric (e g of silk, rayon, or cotton) characterized by a short soft dense pile **2** sthg suggesting velvet in softness, smoothness, etc **3** the soft skin that envelops and nourishes the developing antlers of deer [ME *veluet, velvet,* fr MF *velu* shaggy, fr (assumed) VL *villutus,* fr L *villus* shaggy hair; akin to L *vellus* fleece – more at WOOL]

velveteen /'velvi,teen/ *n* a fabric made with a short close weft pile in imitation of velvet

,velvet 'glove *n* outward affability concealing ruthless inflexibility

velvety /'velviti/ *adj* soft and smooth like velvet

ven-, veni-, veno- *comb form* vein ⟨venation⟩ ⟨veni*puncture*⟩ [L *vena*]

vena cava /,veenə 'kayvə/ *n, pl* **venae cavae** /,veeni 'kayvi/ either of the 2 large veins by which, in air-breathing vertebrates, the blood is returned to the right atrium of the heart ☞ ANATOMY [NL, lit., hollow vein] – **vena caval** *adj*

venal /'veenl/ *adj* open to corrupt influence, esp bribery [L *venalis,* fr *venum* (acc) sale; akin to Gk *ōneisthai* to buy, Skt *vasna* price] – **venally** *adv,* **venality** /vee'naləti/ *n*

venation /vee'naysh(ə)n/ *n* an arrangement or system of veins in a leaf, insect wing, etc [L *vena* vein] – **venational** *adj*

vend /vend/ *vi* to sell ~ *vt* **1** to sell, esp in a small way **2** to sell by means of a vending machine [L *vendere* to sell, vt, contr of *venum dare* to give for sale] – **vendable** /'vendəbl/ *adj,* **vendee** /,ven'dee/ *n,* **vendible** /'vendəbl/ *adj*

Venda /'vendə/ *n* a Bantu language of the N Transvaal

vendace /'vendəs/ *n, pl* **vendace** *also* **vendaces** a whitefish of various European lakes [NL *vandesius,* fr MF *vandoise*]

vendetta /ven'detə/ *n* **1** a blood feud arising from the murder or injury of a member of one family by a member of another **2** a prolonged bitter feud [It, lit., revenge, fr L *vindicta* – more at VINDICTIVE]

'vending ma,chine /'vending/ *n* a coin-operated machine for selling merchandise – compare SLOT MACHINE

vendor, vender /'vendə/ *n* **1** a seller; *specif, Br* the seller of a house **2** VENDING MACHINE [VEND + [1]-OR, [2]-ER]

[1]**veneer** /və'niə/ *n* **1** a thin layer of wood of superior appearance or hardness used esp to give a decorative finish (e g to joinery) **2** a protective or ornamental facing (e g of brick or stone) **3** a superficial or deceptively attractive appearance [G *furnier,* fr *furnieren* to veneer, fr F *fournir* to complete, equip – more at FURNISH]

[2]**veneer** *vt* **1** to overlay (e g a common wood) with veneer; *broadly* to face with a material giving a superior surface **2** to conceal under a superficial and deceptive attractiveness – **veneerer** *n*

veneering /və'niəring/ *n* **1** material used as veneer **2** a veneered surface

venepuncture *also* **venipuncture** /'veni,pungkchə/ *n* surgical puncture of a vein, esp for the withdrawl of blood or for intravenous medication

venerable /'ven(ə)rəbl/ *adj* **1** – used as a title for an Anglican archdeacon, or for a Roman Catholic who has been accorded the lowest of 3 degrees of recognition for sanctity **2** made sacred, esp by religious or historical association **3a** commanding respect through age, character, and attainments **b** impressive by reason of age ⟨*under ~ pines*⟩ [VENERATE + -ABLE] – **venerableness** *n,* **venerably** *adv,* **venerability** /-rə'biləti/ *n*

venerate /'venərayt/ *vt* to regard with reverence or admiring deference [L *veneratus,* pp of *venerari,* fr *vener-, venus* love, charm – more at WIN] – **venerator** *n*

veneration /,venə'raysh(ə)n/ *n* **1** reverential respect, deference, or honour **2** the state of being venerated [VENERATE + -ION]

venereal /və'niəri·əl/ *adj* **1** of sexual desire or sexual intercourse **2a** resulting from or contracted during sexual intercourse ⟨*~ infections*⟩ **b** of or affected with venereal disease ⟨*a high ~ rate*⟩ [ME *venerealle,* fr L *venereus,* fr *vener-, venus* love, sexual desire]

ve'nereal di,sease *n* a contagious disease (e g gonorrhoea or syphilis) that is typically acquired during sexual intercourse

venereology /və,niəri'oləji/ *n* medicine dealing with venereal diseases [ISV *venereal* + *-o-* + *-logy*] – **venereologist** *n,* **venereological** /-ri·ə'lojikl/ *adj*

[1]**venery** /'venəri/ *n* the art, act, or practice of hunting [ME *venerie,* fr MF, fr *vener* to hunt, fr L *venari* – more at VENISON]

[2]**venery** *n* the pursuit of sexual pleasure [ME *venerie,* fr ML *veneria,* fr L *vener-, venus* sexual desire]

venesection *also* **venisection** /'veni,seksh(ə)n/ *n* the operation of opening a vein for letting blood [NL *venae section-, venae sectio,* lit., cutting of a vein]

ve,netian 'blind /və'neesh(ə)n/ *n* a blind (e g for a window) made of horizontal slats that may be adjusted so as to vary the amount of light admitted [*Venetian* of Venice, city in Italy]

Ve,netian 'glass *n* coloured and elaborately decorated glassware made at Murano near Venice

Ve,netian 'red *n* an earthy haematite used as a pigment; *also* a synthetic iron oxide pigment

vengeance /'venj(ə)ns/ *n* punishment inflicted in retaliation for injury or offence [ME, fr OF, fr *vengier* to avenge, fr L *vindicare* to lay claim to, avenge – more at VINDICATE] – **with a vengeance 1** with great force or vehemence **2** to an extreme or excessive degree

vengeful /'venjf(ə)l/ *adj* revengeful, vindictive [obs *venge* (revenge)] – **vengefully** *adv,* **vengefulness** *n*

venial /'veenyəl, -ni·əl/ *adj* forgivable, pardonable [ME, fr OF, fr LL *venialis,* fr L *venia* favour, indulgence, pardon; akin to L *venus* love, charm – more at WIN] – **venially** *adv,* **venialness** *n*

ˌ**venial 'sin** *n* a sin that does not deprive the soul of divine grace – compare MORTAL SIN

venin /'venin/ *n* any of various toxic substances in snake venom [*ven*om + *-in*]

venipuncture /'veni,pungkchə/ *n* venepuncture

venire facias /ve,nie·əri 'fayshi,as/ *n* a writ directing a US sheriff to summon jurors [ME, fr ML, you should cause to come]

venisection /'veni,seksh(ə)n/ *n* venesection

venison /'venis(ə)n/ *n* the flesh of a deer as food [ME, flesh of a wild animal taken by hunting, fr OF *veneison* hunting, game, fr L *venation-, venatio,* fr *venatus,* pp of *venari* to hunt, pursue; akin to OE *winnan* to struggle – more at WIN]

Venite /vi'nieti/ *n* a liturgical chant composed of parts of Psalms 95 and 96 [L, O come, fr *venire* to come; fr the opening word of Ps 95:1]

Venn diagram /ven/ *n* a graph that uses plane shapes (e g circles) to represent logical relations between and operations on sets and the terms of propositions by the inclusion, exclusion, or intersection of the shapes [John *Venn* †1923 E logician]

venom /'venəm/ *n* **1** poisonous matter normally secreted by snakes, scorpions, bees, etc and transmitted chiefly by biting or stinging **2** ill will, malevolence [ME *venim, venom,* fr OF *venim,* fr (assumed) VL *venimen,* alter. of L *venenum* magic charm, drug, poison; akin to L *venus* love, charm]

venomous /'venəməs/ *adj* **1a** poisonous **b** spiteful, malevolent ⟨~ *criticism*⟩ **2** able to inflict a poisoned wound [VENOM + -OUS] – **venomously** *adv,* **venomousness** *n*

venous /'veenəs/ *adj* **1** having or consisting of veins ⟨*a* ~ *system*⟩ **2** *of blood* containing carbon dioxide rather than oxygen [L *venosus,* fr *vena* vein] – **venously** *adv,* **venosity** /vi'nosəti/ *n*

[1]**vent** /vent/ *vt* **1** to provide with a vent **2** to give (vigorous) expression to [ME *venten,* prob fr MF *esventer* to expose to the air, fr *es-* ex- (fr L *ex-*) + *vent* wind, fr L *ventus* – more at [1]WIND]

[2]**vent** *n* **1** a means of escape or release; an outlet – chiefly in *give vent to* **2a** the anus, esp of the cloaca of a bird or reptile **b** an outlet of a volcano; a fumarole ☞ GEOGRAPHY **c** a hole at the breech of a gun through which the powder is ignited – **ventless** *adj*

[3]**vent** *n* a slit in a garment; *specif* an opening in the lower part of a seam (e g of a jacket or skirt) [ME *vente,* alter. of *fente,* fr MF, slit, fissure, fr *fendre* to split, fr L *findere* – more at BITE]

ventage /'ventij/ *n* a small hole (e g a flute stop)

ventail /'ventayl/ *n* the lower movable front of a medieval helmet [ME, fr MF *ventaille,* fr *vent* wind]

ventifact /'ventifakt/ *n* a stone shaped or polished by wind-blown sand [L *ventus* wind + E *-i-* + *-fact* (as in *artifact*)]

ventilate /'ventilayt/ *vt* **1** to examine freely and openly; expose publicly **2** to expose to (a current of fresh) air; oxygenate **3a** *of a current of air* to pass or circulate through so as to freshen **b** to cause fresh air to circulate through [LL *ventilatus,* pp of *ventilare,* fr L, to fan, winnow, fr *ventulus,* dim. of *ventus* wind – more at WIND] – **ventilative** /-,laytiv/ *adj*

ventilation /,venti'laysh(ə)n/ *n* **1** the act or process of ventilating **2** a system or means of providing fresh air

ventilator /'venti,laytə/ *n* an apparatus or aperture for introducing fresh air or expelling stagnant air [VENTILATE + [1]-OR]

ventr-, ventro- *comb form* ventral and ⟨ventro*lateral*⟩ [L *ventr-, venter* belly; akin to OHG *wanast* paunch, L *vesica* bladder]

ventral /'ventrəl/ *adj* **1a** abdominal **b** relating to or situated near or on the front or lower surface of an animal or aircraft opposite the back – compare DORSAL **2** being or located on the lower or inner surface of a plant structure [F, fr L *ventralis,* fr *ventr-, venter*] – **ventrally** *adv*

ventricle /'ventrikl/ *n* a cavity of a bodily part or organ: e g **a** a chamber of the heart which receives blood from a corresponding atrium and from which blood is pumped into the arteries ☞ ANATOMY **b** any of the system of communicating cavities in the brain that are continuous with the central canal of the spinal cord [ME, fr L *ventriculus,* fr dim. of *ventr-, venter*] – **ventricular** /ven'trikyoolə/ *adj*

ventriloquism /ven'trilə,kwiz(ə)m/ *n* the production of the voice in such a manner that the sound appears to come from a source other than the vocal organs of the speaker and esp from a dummy manipulated by the producer of the sound [LL *ventriloquus* ventriloquist, fr L *ventr-, venter* + *loqui* to speak; fr the belief that the voice is produced from the ventriloquist's stomach] – **ventriloquist** *n,* **ventriloquial** /,ventri 'lohkwi·əl/ *adj*

[1]**venture** /'venchə/ *vt* **1** to expose to hazard; risk, gamble **2** to face the risks and dangers of; brave **3** to offer at the risk of opposition or censure ⟨~ *an opinion*⟩ ~ *vi* to proceed despite danger; dare to go or do [ME *venteren,* by shortening & alter. fr *aventuren,* fr *aventure* adventure]

[2]**venture** *n* **1** an undertaking involving chance, risk, or danger, esp in business **2** sthg (e g money or property) at risk in a speculative venture

'**venture ,capital** *n* capital (available to be) invested in a new or fresh enterprise

'**venture ,scout** *n* a senior member of the British Scout movement aged from 16 to 20

'**venturesome** /-s(ə)m/ *adj* **1** ready to take risks; daring **2** involving risk; hazardous – **venturesomely** *adv,* **venturesomeness** *n*

venturi /ven'tyooəri/ *n* a short tube that is inserted in a wider pipeline and is used for measuring flow rate of a fluid or for providing suction [G B *Venturi* †1822 It physicist]

venturous /'venchərəs/ *adj* venturesome – **venturously** *adv,* **venturousness** *n*

venue /'venyooh/ *n* **1** the place in which a legal case is to be tried and from which the jury is drawn **2** the place where a gathering takes place [ME *venyw* action of coming, fr MF *venue,* fr *venir* to come, fr L *venire* – more at COME]

venule /'venyoohl/ *n* a small vein (connecting the capillary network with the larger systemic veins) ☞ ANATOMY [L *venula,* dim. of *vena* vein]

Venus /'veenəs/ *n* the planet second in order from the sun ☞ ASTRONOMY, SYMBOL [ME, fr L *Vener-, Venus,* Roman goddess of love & beauty, fr *vener-, venus* sexual desire]

ˌ**Venus'-'flytrap, Venus's-flytrap** *n* an insect-eating plant of the sundew family

Venusian /vi'nyoohzh(ə)n/ *adj* of or coming from the planet Venus – **Venusian** *n*

veracious /və'rayshəs/ *adj* **1** reliable in testimony; truthful **2** true, accurate [L *verac-, verax* – more at

VERY] – **veraciously** *adv*, **veraciousness** *n*, **veracity** /və'rasəti/ *n*

veranda, verandah /və'randə/ *n* a usu roofed open gallery or portico attached to the outside of a building [Hindi *varaṇḍā*]

veratrine /'verə,treen/ *n* a poisonous mixture of alkaloids obtained from sabadilla seed and used esp to reduce inflammation and as an insecticide [NL *veratrina*, fr *Veratrum*, genus of herbs]

verb /vuhb/ *n* any of a class of words that characteristically are the grammatical centre of a predicate and express an act, occurrence, or mode of being [ME *verbe*, fr MF, fr L *verbum* word, verb – more at WORD]

[1]**verbal** /'vuhbl/ *adj* **1** of, involving, or expressed in words **2** of or formed from a verb **3** spoken rather than written; oral ⟨*a ~ contract*⟩ **4** verbatim, word-for-word [MF or LL; MF, fr LL *verbalis*, fr L *verbum*] – **verbally** *adv*

[2]**verbal** *n* **1** a word that combines characteristics of a verb with those of a noun or adjective **2** *Br* a spoken statement; *esp* one made to the police admitting or implying guilt and used in evidence

verbalism /'vuhbl,iz(ə)m/ *n* **1** a verbal expression **2** an excessive emphasis on words as opposed to the ideas or realities they represent

verbal·ize, -ise /'vuhbl,iez/ *vi* **1** to speak or write verbosely **2** to express sthg in words *~vt* **1** to convert into a verb **2** to name or describe in words – **verbalizer** *n*, **verbalization** /-'zaysh(ə)n/ *n*

,verbal 'noun *n* a noun derived from, and having some of the constructions of, a verb; *esp* a gerund

verbatim /vuh'baytim/ *adv or adj* in the exact words [ME, fr ML, fr L *verbum* word]

verbena /vuh'beenə/ *n* vervain; *esp* a cultivated one grown for its showy spikes of flowers [NL, genus of herbs or subshrubs, fr L, sing. of *verbenae* sacred boughs, certain medicinal plants – more at VERVAIN]

verbiage /'vuhbi·ij/ *n* wordiness, verbosity [F, fr MF *verbier* to chatter, fr *verbe* speech, fr L *verbum* word]

verbose /vuh'bohs/ *adj* **1** containing more words than necessary **2** given to wordiness – **verbosely** *adv*, **verboseness** *n*, **verbosity** /-'bosəti/ *n*

verboten /feə'bohtn, vuh-/ *adj* prohibited, esp by authority – chiefly humor [G, fr pp of *verbieten* to forbid]

verdant /'vuhd(ə)nt/ *adj* **1a** green in tint or colour ⟨*~ grass*⟩ **b** green with growing plants ⟨*~ fields*⟩ **2** immature, unsophisticated [modif of MF *verdoyant*, fr prp of *verdoyer* to be green, fr OF *verdoier*, fr *verd*, *vert* green, fr L *viridis*, fr *virēre* to be green] – **verdancy** /-si/ *n*, **verdantly** *adv*

verd antique, verde antique /,vuhd an'teek/ *n* **1** a decorative green mottled or veined serpentine **2** a dark green porphyry [It *verde antico*, lit., ancient green]

verderer, verderor /'vuhdərə/ *n* a former English judicial officer of the royal forests [AF, fr OF *verdier*, fr *verd* green]

verdict /'vuhdikt/ *n* **1** the decision of a jury on the matter submitted to them **2** an opinion, judgment [alter. of ME *verdit*, fr AF, fr OF *ver* true (fr L *verus*) + *dit* saying, dictum, fr L *dictum* – more at VERY]

verdigris /'vuhdigris; *also* -,gree/ *n* **1a** a green or greenish blue poisonous pigment resulting from the action of acetic acid on copper **b** normal copper acetate **2** a green or bluish deposit formed on copper, brass, or bronze surfaces [ME *vertegrez*, fr OF *vert de Grice*, lit., green of Greece]

verdure /'vuhdyə, -jə/ *n* **1** (the greenness of) growing vegetation **2** a condition of health, freshness, and vigour [ME, fr MF, fr *verd* green] – **verdureless** *adj*, **verdurous** *adj*, **verdurousness** *n*

[1]**verge** /vuhj/ *n* **1** a rod or staff carried as an emblem of authority or symbol of office **2** sthg that borders, limits, or bounds: e g **a** an outer margin of an object or structural part **b** the edge of a roof projecting over the gable **3** the brink, threshold **4** *Br* a surfaced or planted strip of land at the side of a road [ME, penis, rod, fr MF, fr L *virga* rod, stripe – more at WHISK; (2-4) fr the obs phrase *within the verge* within the area subject to the authority of a verge-bearer]

[2]**verge** *vi* – **verge on** to be near to; border on

[3]**verge** *vi* **1** *of the sun* to incline towards the horizon; sink **2** to move or extend *towards* a specified condition [L *vergere* to bend, incline – more at WRENCH]

verger /'vuhjə/ *n* **1** a church official who keeps order during services or serves as an usher or sacristan **2** *chiefly Br* an attendant who carries a verge (e g before a bishop or justice)

veridical /vi'ridikl/ *adj* **1** truthful, veracious **2** not illusory; genuine [L *veridicus*, fr *verus* true + *dicere* to say – more at VERY, DICTION] – **veridically** *adv*, **veridicality** /-'kaləti/ *n*

verification /,verifi'kaysh(ə)n/ *n* verifying or being verified

verify /'verifie/ *vt* **1** to substantiate in law, esp formally or on oath **2** to ascertain the truth, accuracy, or reality of **3** to bear out, fulfil ⟨*my fears were* verified⟩ [ME *verifien*, fr MF *verifier*, fr ML *verificare*, fr L *verus* true – more at VERY] – **verifier** *n*, **verifiable** /'-----, ,--'---/ *adj*

verily /'verəli/ *adv*, *archaic* **1** indeed, certainly **2** truly, confidently [ME *verraily*, fr *verray* very]

verisimilitude /,verisi'milityoohd/ *n* **1** the quality or state of appearing to be true **2** a statement that has the appearance of truth *USE* fml [L *verisimilitudo*, fr *verisimilis* appearing to be true, fr *veri similis* like the truth] – **verisimilitudinous** /-'tyoohdinəs/ *adj*

veritable /'veritəbl/ *adj* being in fact the thing named and not false or imaginary – often used to stress the aptness of a metaphor ⟨*a ~ mountain of references*⟩ – **veritableness** *n*, **veritably** *adv*

verity /'veriti/ *n* **1** the quality or state of being true or real **2** sthg (e g a statement) that is true; *esp* a permanently true value or principle [ME *verite*, fr MF *verité*, fr L *veritat-*, *veritas*, fr *verus* true]

verjuice /'vuh,joohs/ *n* the sour juice of crab apples or unripe fruit formerly used in cooking [ME *verjus*, fr MF, fr *vert jus*, lit., green juice]

verkramp /fiə'krump/ *adj*, *SAfr* (characteristic) of a verkrampte [prob modif of Afrik *bekrompe* narrow-minded, fr D *bekrimpen* to shrink, restrict]

verkrampte /fiə'krumptə/ *n*, *SAfr* a person holding ultraconservative or bigoted views, esp on social, political, or religious matters – compare KRAGDADIGE, VERLIGTE [Afrik, fr *verkramp* + *-te*, noun suffix]

verlig /fiə'likh/ *adj*, *SAfr* LIBERAL 4 [Afrik, enlightened, fr D *verlichten* to light, enlighten]

[1]**verligte** /fiə'likhtə/ *adj*, *SAfr* LIBERAL 4 ⟨*significant ~ moves in the race relations field – The Star*

(*Johannesburg*)⟩ [Afrik, fr *verlig* + *-te*, noun suffix]

²**verligte** *n, SAfr* an advocate of liberal policies – compare KRAGDADIGE, VERKRAMPTE

vermeil /'vuhmayl/ *n* gilded silver, bronze, or copper [MF, fr *vermeil*, adj – more at VERMILION] – **vermeil** *adj*

vermi- *comb form* worm ⟨vermi*form*⟩ [NL, fr LL, fr L *vermis* – more at WORM]

vermian /'vuhmyən, -mi·ən/ *adj* of or resembling worms [ISV]

vermicelli /,vuhmi'cheli/ *n* **1** pasta in the form of long thin solid threads smaller in diameter than spaghetti **2** small thin sugar strands that are used as a decoration (e g on iced cakes) [It, fr pl of *vermicello*, dim. of *verme* worm, fr L *vermis*]

vermicular /vuh'mikyoolə/ *adj* **1a** resembling a worm in form or motion **b** vermiculate **2** of or caused by worms [NL *vermicularis*, fr L *vermiculus*, dim. of *vermis*]

vermiculate /vuh'mikyoolət/, **vermiculated** /-,laytid/ *adj* **1** marked with irregular or wavy lines ⟨*a ~ nut*⟩ **2** full of worms; worm-eaten **3** tortuous, intricate – fml [L *vermiculatus*, fr *vermiculus*] – **vermiculation** /-'laysh(ə)n/ *n*

vermiculite /vuh'mikyooliet/ *n* any of various minerals of hydrous silicates derived from mica that expand on heating to form a lightweight highly water-absorbent material [L *vermiculus* little worm]

vermiform /'vuhmi,fawm/ *adj* resembling a worm in shape [NL *vermiformis*, fr *vermi-* + *-formis* -form]

,**vermiform ap'pendix** *n* a narrow short blind tube that extends from the caecum in the lower right-hand part of the abdomen ☞ DIGESTION

vermilion, vermillion /və'milyən/ *adj or n* (of the brilliant red colour of) mercuric sulphide used as a pigment [ME *vermilioun*, fr OF *vermeillon*, fr *vermeil*, adj, bright red, vermilion, fr LL *vermiculus* kermes, fr L, little worm; adj fr n]

vermin /'vuhmin/ *n, pl* **vermin** **1** *pl* **a** lice, rats, or other common harmful or objectionable animals **b** birds and mammals that prey on game **2** an offensive person [ME, fr MF, fr (assumed) L *vermin-*, *vermen* worm; akin to L *vermis* worm – more at WORM] – **verminous** *adj*, **verminously** *adv*

vermouth /'vuhməth/ *n* a dry or sweet alcoholic drink that has a white wine base and is flavoured with aromatic herbs [F *vermout*, fr G *wermut* wormwood, fr OHG *wermuota* – more at WORMWOOD]

¹**vernacular** /və'nakyoolə/ *adj* **1a** expressed or written in a language or dialect native to a region or country rather than a literary, learned, or foreign language **b** of or being the normal spoken form of a language **2** of or being the common building style of a period or place [L *vernaculus* native, fr *verna* slave born in his master's house, native] – **vernacularly** *adv*

²**vernacular** *n* **1** the local vernacular language **2** the mode of expression of a group or class – **vernacularism** *n*

vernal /'vuhnl/ *adj* **1** of or occurring in the spring ⟨*~ equinox*⟩ **2** fresh, youthful [L *vernalis*, alter. of *vernus*, fr *ver* spring; akin to Gk *ear* spring] – **vernally** *adv*

vernal·ize, -ise /'vuhnl,iez/ *vt* to hasten the flowering and fruiting of (plants), esp by chilling seeds, bulbs, or seedlings – **vernalization** /-'zaysh(ə)n/ *n*

vernation /vuh'naysh(ə)n/ *n* the arrangement of foliage leaves within the bud – compare AESTIVATION [NL *vernation-*, *vernatio*, fr L *vernatus*, pp of *vernare* to behave as in spring, fr *vernus* vernal]

¹**vernier** /'vuhnyə, -ni·ə/ *n* **1** a short specially graduated scale that slides along another graduated scale allowing fine measurements of parts of graduations to be made **2a** a small auxiliary device used with a main device to obtain fine adjustment **b** any of 2 or more small supplementary rocket engines or gas nozzles on a rocket vehicle for making fine adjustments in the velocity or attitude [Pierre *Vernier* †1637 F mathematician]

²**vernier** *adj* having or comprising a vernier

Veronal /və'rohnl/ *trademark* – used for barbitone

veronica /və'ronikə/ *n* speedwell [NL, genus of herbs]

verruca /və'roohkə/ *n, pl* **verrucas** also **verruccae** /-ki/ **1** a wart or warty skin growth **2** a warty prominence on a plant or animal [L – more at WART] – **verrucose** /'verookohs/ *adj*

versant /'vuhsənt/ *n* **1** the slope of a mountain (chain) **2** the general slope of land [F, fr MF, fr prp of *verser* to turn, pour, fr L *versare* to turn; fr its shedding of water]

versatile /'vuhsətiel/ *adj* **1** embracing a variety of subjects, fields, or skills; *also* turning with ease from one thing to another **2** capable of moving easily forwards or backwards, or esp up and down ⟨*~ antennae*⟩ ⟨*~ anther*⟩ **3** having many uses or applications ⟨*~ building material*⟩ [F or L; F, fr L *versatilis* turning easily, fr *versatus*, pp of *versare* to turn, fr *versus*, pp of *vertere*] – **versatilely** *adv*, **versatileness** *n*, **versatility** /-'tiləti/ *n*

verse /vuhs/ *n* **1** a line of metrical writing **2a** (an example of) metrical language or writing, distinguished from poetry esp by its lower level of intensity **b** POETRY 2 **c** a body of metrical writing (e g of a period or country) ⟨*Elizabethan ~*⟩ **3** a stanza **4** any of the short divisions into which a chapter of the Bible is traditionally divided [ME *vers*, fr OF, fr L *versus*, lit., turning, fr *versus*, pp of *vertere* to turn – more at ¹WORTH]

versed *adj* possessing a thorough knowledge (of) or skill *in* – chiefly in *well versed in* [L *versatus*, pp of *versari* to be active, be occupied (in), passive of *versare* to turn, fr *versus*, pp]

versicle /'vuhsikl/ *n* a short verse or sentence (e g from a psalm) said or sung by a leader in public worship and followed by a response from the congregation ☞ SYMBOL [ME, fr L *versiculus*, dim. of *versus* verse]

versicolour /'vuhsi,kulə/, **'versi,coloured** *adj* **1** having various colours; variegated **2** changeable in colour; iridescent ⟨*~ silk*⟩ [L *versicolor*, fr *versus*, pp of *vertere* to turn, change + *color* colour]

versify /'vuhsifie/ *vi* to compose verses *~ vt* to turn into verse – **versifier** *n*, **versification** /-fi'kaysh(ə)n/ *n*

version /'vuhsh(ə)n, -zh(ə)n/ *n* **1** a translation from another language; *esp, often cap* a translation of (part of) the Bible **2a** an account or description from a particular point of view, esp as contrasted with another account **b** an adaptation of a work of art into another medium ⟨*the film ~ of the novel*⟩ **c** an arrangement of a musical composition **3** a form or variant of a type or original ⟨*an experimental* ~ *of the plane*⟩ **4** manual turning of a foetus in the uterus to aid delivery [MF, fr ML *version-, versio* act of turning, fr L *versus*, pp of *vertere*] – **versional** *adj*

vers libre /,veə 'leebrə/ *n, pl* **vers libres** /~/ FREE VERSE [F] – **vers-librist** *n*

verso /'vuhsoh/ *n, pl* **versos** a left-hand page – contrasted with *recto* [NL *verso* (*folio*) the page being turned]

versus /'vuhsəs/ *prep* **1** against **2** in contrast to or as the alternative of ⟨*free trade* ~ *protection*⟩ [ML, towards, against, fr L, adv, so as to face, fr pp of *vertere* to turn]

vert /vuht/ *n* **1** green forest vegetation **2** green – used in heraldry [ME *verte*, fr MF *vert*, fr *vert* green – more at VERDANT]

vertebra /'vuhtibrə/ *n, pl* **vertebrae** /-bri/, **vertebras** any of the bony or cartilaginous segments composing the spinal column ☞ ANATOMY [L, joint, vertebra, fr *vertere* to turn – more at [1]WORTH] – **vertebral** *adj*

[1]**vertebrate** /'vuhtibrət, -brayt/ *adj* **1** having a spinal column **2** of the vertebrates [NL *vertebratus*, fr L, jointed, fr *vertebra*]

[2]**vertebrate** *n* any of a large group of animals (e g mammals, birds, reptiles, amphibians, and fishes) with a segmented backbone, together with a few primitive forms in which the backbone is represented by a notochord [deriv of NL *vertebratus*]

vertex /'vuhteks/ *n, pl* **vertices** /'vuhtiseez/ *also* **vertexes** **1a(1)** the point opposite to and farthest from the base in a figure **(2)** the termination or intersection of lines or curves ⟨*the* ~ *of an angle*⟩ **(3)** a point where an axis of an ellipse, parabola, or hyperbola intersects the curve **b** ZENITH 1 **2** the top of the head **3** the highest point; the summit ***USE*** (*1a*) ☞ MATHEMATICS [L *vertic-, vertex, vortic-, vortex* whirl, whirlpool, top of the head, summit, fr *vertere* to turn]

vertical /'vuhtikl/ *adj* **1** situated at the highest point; directly overhead or in the zenith **2** perpendicular to the plane of the horizon or to a primary axis **3** of, involving, or integrating discrete elements (e g from lowest to highest) ⟨*a* ~ *business organization*⟩ ⟨*the* ~ *arrangement of society*⟩ **4** of or concerning the relationships between people of different rank in a hierarchy – compare HORIZONTAL 2 [MF or LL; MF, fr LL *verticalis*, fr L *vertic-, vertex*] – **vertical** *n*, **vertically** *adv*, **verticalness** *n*, **verticality** /-'kaləti/ *n*

verticil /'vuhtisil/ *n* WHORL 1 [NL *verticillus*, dim. of L *vertex* whirl]

verticillate /vuh'tisilət, -layt, ,vuhti'silayt/ *adj* whorled; *esp* arranged in a transverse whorl like the spokes of a wheel ⟨*a* ~ *shell*⟩

vertiginous /vuh'tijinəs/ *adj* **1** characterized by or suffering from vertigo **2** inclined to frequent and often pointless change; inconstant **3** causing or tending to cause dizziness ⟨*the* ~ *heights*⟩ **4** marked by turning; rotary [L *vertiginosus*, fr *vertigin-, vertigo*] – **vertiginously** *adv*

vertigo /'vuhtigoh/ *n* a disordered state in which the individual loses balance and the surroundings seem to whirl dizzily [L *vertigin-, vertigo*, fr *vertere* to turn]

vervain /'vuhvayn/ *n* any of a genus of plants that bear often showy flowers in heads or spikes; *esp* one with spikes of small lilac flowers [ME *verveine*, fr MF, fr L *verbena*, sing. of *verbenae* sacred boughs, certain medicinal plants; akin to L *verber* rod, Gk *rhabdos*]

verve /vuhv/ *n* **1** the spirit and enthusiasm animating artistic work **2** energy, vitality [F, fantasy, caprice, animation, fr L *verba*, pl of *verbum* word – more at WORD]

'vervet ,monkey /'vuhvit/ *n* a S and E African tree-dwelling monkey [F *vervet*]

[1]**very** /'veri/ *adj* **1** properly so called; actual, genuine ⟨*the* ~ *man you met*⟩ **2** absolute ⟨*the* ~ *thing for the purpose*⟩ ⟨*the* veriest *fool alive* – John Milton⟩ **3** being no more than; mere ⟨*the* ~ *thought terrified me*⟩ ***USE*** used attributively [ME *verray, verry*, fr OF *verai*, fr (assumed) VL *veracus*, alter. of L *verac-, verax* truthful, fr *verus* true; akin to OE *wǣr* true, OHG *wāra* trust, care, Gk *ēra* (acc) favour]

[2]**very** *adv* **1** to a high degree; exceedingly **2** – used as an intensive to emphasize *same, own*, or the superlative degree ⟨*the* ~ *best shop in town*⟩

,very ,high 'frequency *n* a radio frequency in the range between 30MHz and 300MHz

Very light /'viəri, 'veri/ *n* a white or coloured ball of fire that is projected from a Very pistol and that is used as a signal flare [Edward W *Very* †1910 US naval officer]

Very pistol *n* a pistol for firing Very lights

,very 'well /veri/ *adv* **1** – used to express often reluctant consent or agreement ⟨~, *we'll go tomorrow*⟩ **2** with certainty; unquestionably ⟨*you know* ~ *what you should do*⟩

vesica /'vesikə/ *n, pl* **vesicae** /-,see/ an internal sac or tube of an insect phallus [NL, fr L, bladder – more at VENTR-]

vesical /'vesikl/ *adj* of a bladder, esp the urinary bladder [L *vesica* bladder]

vesicant /'vesikənt/ *n* a drug, war gas, etc that induces blistering [L *vesica* bladder, blister] – **vesicant** *adj*

vesicate /'vesikayt/ *vb* to blister [L *vesica* blister] – **vesication** /-'kaysh(ə)n/ *n*

vesicle /'vesikl/ *n* **1a** a membranous usu fluid-filled pouch (e g a cyst, vacuole, or cell) in a plant or animal **b** a blister **c** a pocket of embryonic tissue that is the beginning of an organ **2** a small cavity in a mineral or rock [MF *vesicule*, fr L *vesicula* small bladder, blister, fr dim. of *vesica*] – **vesicular** /ve'sikyoolə/ *adj*, **vesiculate** /-lət, -layt/ *adj*, **vesicularity** /ve,sikyoo'larəti/ *n*

[1]**vesper** /'vespə/ *n* **1** *cap* EVENING STAR **2** *archaic* evening, eventide [ME, fr L, evening, evening star – more at WEST]

[2]**vesper** *adj* of vespers or the evening

vespers /'vespəz/ *n pl but sing or pl in constr, often cap* **1** the sixth of the canonical hours that is said or sung in the late afternoon **2** a service of evening worship [F *vespres*, fr ML *vesperae*, fr L, pl of *vespera* evening; akin to L *vesper* evening star]

vespertilian /,vespə'tilyən/ *adj* of bats [L *vespertilio* bat, fr *vesper*]

vespertine /'vespətien/ *adj* **1** active or flourishing in the evening: e g **a** *of an animal* feeding or flying in early evening **b** *of a flower* opening in the evening **2** of or occurring in the evening ⟨~ *shadows*⟩ – fml [L *vespertinus*, fr *vesper*]

vespiary /'vespi·əri/ *n* a nest of a social wasp [L *vespa* + E *-iary* (as in *apiary*)]

vespine /'vespien/ *adj* of or resembling wasps, esp wasps that live in colonies [L *vespa* wasp]

vessel /'vesl/ *n* **1a** a hollow utensil (e g a jug, cup, or bowl) for holding esp liquid **b** sby into whom some quality (e g grace) is infused **2** a large hollow structure designed to float on and move through water carrying a crew, passengers, or cargo **3a** a tube or canal (e g an artery) in which a body fluid is contained and conveyed or circulated **b** a conducting tube in a plant [ME, fr OF *vaissel*, fr LL *vascellum*, dim. of L *vas* vase, vessel – more at VASE]

[1]**vest** /vest/ *vt* **1a** to give (e g property or power) into the possession or discretion of another **b** to clothe with a particular authority, right, or property **2** to clothe (as if) with a garment; *esp* to robe in ecclesiastical vestments ~ *vi* to become legally vested [ME *vesten*, fr MF *vestir* to clothe, invest, fr L *vestire* to clothe, fr *vestis* clothing, garment – more at WEAR]

[2]**vest** *n* **1** *chiefly Br* a usu sleeveless undergarment for the upper body **2** *chiefly NAm* a waistcoat [F *veste*, fr It, fr L *vestis* garment] – **vested** *adj*, **vestlike** *adj*

[1]**vestal** /'vestl/ *adj* **1** of a vestal virgin **2** chaste; *esp* virgin [ME *vestalle*, fr L *vestalis*, fr *Vesta*, Roman goddess of the hearth & household] – **vestally** *adv*

[2]**vestal, ,vestal 'virgin** *n* a priestess of the Roman goddess Vesta, responsible for tending the sacred fire perpetually kept burning on her altar

,vested 'interest /'vestid/ *n* **1a** an interest carrying a legal right **b** an interest (e g in an existing political or social arrangement) in which the holder has a strong personal commitment **2** sby or sthg having a vested interest in sthg; *specif* a group enjoying benefits from an existing privilege

vestiary /'vesti·əri, 'vestyəri/ *n* a room where clothing is kept; a vestry [ME *vestiarie*, fr OF, vestry – more at VESTRY]

vestibule /'vestibyoohl/ *n* **1** a lobby or chamber between the outer door and the interior of a building **2** any of various bodily cavities, esp when serving as or resembling an entrance to some other cavity or space: e g **a** the central cavity of the bony labyrinth of the ear **b** the part of the mouth cavity outside the teeth and gums [L *vestibulum*] – **vestibuled** *adj*, **vestibular** /ve'stibyoolə/ *adj*

vestige /'vestij/ *n* **1a** a trace or visible sign left by sthg vanished or lost **b** a minute remaining amount **2** a small or imperfectly formed body part or organ that remains from one more fully developed in an earlier stage of the individual, in a past generation, or in closely related forms [F, fr L *vestigium* footstep, footprint, track] – **vestigial** /ve'stij(y)əl/ *adj*, **vestigially** *adv*

vestment /'vestmənt/ *n* **1** an outer garment; *esp* a robe of ceremony or office **2** any of the ceremonial garments and insignia worn by ecclesiastical officiants and assistants as appropriate to their rank and to the rite being celebrated [ME *vestement*, fr OF, fr L *vestimentum*, fr *vestire* to clothe] – **vestmental** /-'mentl/ *adj*

,vest-'pocket *adj*, *NAm* adapted to fit into the waistcoat pocket ⟨*a ~ edition of a book*⟩; *broadly* very small

vestry /'vestri/ *n* **1a** a sacristy **b** a room used for church meetings and classes **2a** the business meeting of an English parish **b** an elective administrative body in an Episcopal parish in the USA [ME *vestrie*, prob modif of MF *vestiarie*, fr ML *vestiarium*, fr L *vestire*; fr its use as a robing room for the clergy]

vesture /'veschə/ *n* clothing, apparel – fml [ME, fr MF, fr *vestir* to clothe – more at VEST]

Vesuvian /vi's(y)oohvi·ən/ *adj* of or resembling the volcano Vesuvius [*Vesuvius*, volcano near Naples in Italy]

[1]**vet** /vet/ *n* sby qualified and authorized to treat diseases and injuries of animals [short for *veterinary (surgeon)*]

[2]**vet** *vt* **-tt-** **1** to subject (a person or animal) to a physical examination or checkup **2** *chiefly Br* to subject to careful and thorough appraisal ⟨~ *your application*⟩

[3]**vet** *adj or n*, *NAm* (a) veteran

vetch /vech/ *n* any of a genus of climbing or twining leguminous plants including valuable fodder and soil-improving plants [ME *vecche*, fr ONF *veche*, fr L *vicia*; akin to OE *wicga* insect, L *vincire* to bind, OE *wīr* wire]

vetchling /'vechling/ *n* any of various small leguminous plants

veteran /'vet(ə)rən/ *n* **1** sby who has had long experience of an occupation, skill, or (military) service **2** **veteran, veteran car** *Br* an old motor car; *specif* one built before 1916 **3** *NAm* a former serviceman [L *veteranus*, fr *veteranus* old, of long experience, fr *veter-*, *vetus* old – more at WETHER] – **veteran** *adj*

'Veterans ,Day *n* a day set aside in the USA and Canada in commemoration of the end of hostilities in 1918 and 1945; *esp* November 11 observed as a public holiday in Canada and some states of the USA – compare REMEMBRANCE SUNDAY

veterinarian /,vet(ə)ri'neəri·ən/ *n*, *chiefly NAm* [1]VET

[1]**veterinary** /'vet(ə)rinəri/ *adj* of or being the medical care of animals, esp domestic animals [L *veterinarius* of beasts of burden, fr *veterinae* beasts of burden, fr fem pl of *veterinus* of beasts of burden; akin to L *veter-*, *vetus* old]

[2]**veterinary,** *Br chiefly* **'veterinary ,surgeon** *n* [1]VET

[1]**veto** /'veetoh/ *n*, *pl* **vetoes** **1** an authoritative prohibition **2** a right to declare inoperative decisions made by others; *esp* a power vested in a chief executive to prevent permanently or temporarily the enactment of measures passed by a legislature [L, I forbid, fr *vetare* to forbid]

[2]**veto** *vt* **vetoing; vetoed** to subject to a veto – **vetoer** *n*

vex /veks/ *vt* **vexed** *also* **vext** **1a** to bring distress, discomfort, or agitation to **b** to irritate or annoy by petty provocations; harass **2** to puzzle, baffle [ME *vexen*, fr MF *vexer*, fr L *vexare* to agitate, trouble]

vexation /vek'saysh(ə)n/ *n* a cause of trouble; an affliction [VEX + -ATION]

vexatious /vek'sayshəs/ *adj* **1** causing vexation; distressing **2** intended to harass – **vexatiously** *adv*, **vexatiousness** *n*

,vexed 'question /vekst/ *n* a question that has been discussed at length, usu without a satisfactory solution being reached

vexillum /vek'siləm/ *n*, *pl* **vexilla** /-lə/ a square flag of the ancient Roman cavalry [L] – **vexillary** /-ləri/ *adj*

via /'vie·ə/ *prep* **1** passing through or calling at (a place) on the way **2** through the medium of; *also* by means of [L, abl of *via* way; akin to Gk *hiesthai* to hurry – more at VIM]

viable /ˈvie·əbl/ *adj* **1** (born alive and developed enough to be) capable of living **2** capable of growing or developing ⟨~ *seeds*⟩ ⟨~ *eggs*⟩ **3** capable of working; practicable ⟨~ *alternatives*⟩ [F, fr MF, fr *vie* life, fr L *vita* – more at VITAL] – **viably** *adv*, **viability** /-əˈbiləti/ *n*

viaduct /ˈvie·ə,dukt/ *n* a usu long bridge, esp on a series of arches, that carries a road, railway, canal, etc over a deep valley [L *via* way, road + E *-duct* (as in *aqueduct*)]

vial /ˈvie·əl, viel/ *n* a phial [ME *fiole, viole*, fr MF *fiole*, fr OProv *fiola*, fr L *phiala* – more at PHIAL]

via media /,vie·ə ˈmeedi·ə/ *n* a middle way; a compromise [L]

viand /ˈvie·ənd/ *n* **1** a (choice or tasty) item of food **2** *pl* provisions, food ***USE*** fml [ME, fr MF *viande*, fr ML *vivanda* food, alter. of L *vivenda*, neut pl of *vivendus*, gerundive of *vivere* to live – more at QUICK]

viaticum /vieˈatikəm/ *n, pl* **viaticums, viatica** /-kə/ **1** an allowance (e g of food or travelling expenses) for a journey **2** the Christian Eucharist given to a person in danger of death [L – more at VOYAGE]

vibes /viebz/ *n pl* **1** *sing or pl in constr* a vibraphone **2** VIBRATIONS 3 ***USE*** infml [by shortening & alter.] – **vibist** *n*

vibrant /ˈviebrənt/ *adj* **1a** oscillating or pulsating rapidly **b** pulsating with life, vigour, or activity ⟨*a* ~ *personality*⟩ **2** sounding as a result of vibration; resonant ⟨*a* ~ *voice*⟩ – **vibrantly** *adv*

vibraphone /ˈviebrə,fohn/ *n* a percussion instrument resembling the xylophone but having metal bars and motor-driven resonators for sustaining its sound and producing a vibrato [L *vibrare* + ISV *-phone*] – **vibraphonist** /-,fohnist/ *n*

vibrate /vieˈbrayt/ *vt* **1** to cause to swing or move to and fro; cause to oscillate **2** to emit (e g sound) (as if) with a vibratory motion **3** to mark or measure by oscillation ⟨*a pendulum* vibrating *seconds*⟩ **4** to set in vibration ~ *vi* **1** to move to and fro; oscillate **2** to have an effect as of vibration; throb ⟨*music* vibrating *in the memory*⟩ **3** to be in a state of vibration; quiver [L *vibratus*, pp of *vibrare* to shake, vibrate – more at WIPE] – **vibrative** /vieˈbrətiv/ *adj*, **vibratory** /-t(ə)ri/ *adj*

vibratile /ˈviebrətiel/ *adj* **1** characterized by vibration **2** used in vibratory motion ⟨*the* ~ *organs of insects*⟩ – **vibratility** /-ˈtiləti/ *n*

vibration /vieˈbraysh(ə)n/ *n* **1a** a periodic motion of the particles of an elastic body or medium in alternately opposite directions from a position of equilibrium **b** an oscillation or quivering **2** an instance of vibrating **3a** a characteristic aura or spirit felt to emanate from sby or sthg and instinctively sensed or experienced **b** a distinctive usu emotional atmosphere capable of being sensed – usu pl with sing. meaning – **vibrational** *adj*, **vibrationless** *adj*

vibrato /viˈbrahtoh/ *n, pl* **vibratos** a slightly tremulous effect imparted to musical tone to add expressiveness, by slight and rapid variations in pitch [It, fr pp of *vibrare* to vibrate, fr L]

vibrator /vieˈbraytə/ *n* a vibrating electrical apparatus used in massage, esp to provide sexual stimulation [VIBRATE + [1]-OR]

vibrissa /vieˈbrisə/ *n, pl* **vibrissae** /-si/ any of the stiff hairs on a mammal's face (e g round the nostrils) that are often organs of touch [L; akin to L *vibrare*]

viburnum /vieˈbuhnəm, vi-/ *n* a guelder rose or related shrub or tree of the honeysuckle family with white or pink flowers [NL, genus name, fr L, wayfaring tree]

vicar /ˈvikə/ *n* **1** a Church of England incumbent receiving a stipend but formerly not the tithes of a parish **2** a clergyman exercising a broad pastoral responsibility as the representative of a prelate [ME, fr L *vicarius* substitute, deputy, fr *vicarius* vicarious] – **vicarship** *n*

vicarage /ˈvikərij/ *n* the benefice or house of a vicar

,vicar apoˈstolic /,apəˈstolik/ *n, pl* **vicars apostolic** a Roman Catholic titular bishop who governs a territory not organized as a diocese

,vicar-ˈgeneral *n, pl* **vicars-general** an administrative deputy of a Roman Catholic or Anglican bishop or of the head of a religious order

vicarial /vieˈkeəri·əl, vi-/ *adj* **1** VICARIOUS 1 **2** of a vicar [L *vicarius*]

vicariate /vieˈkeəri·ət, vi-/ *n* the office, jurisdiction, or tenure of a vicar [ML *vicariatus*, fr L *vicarius* vicar]

vicarious /vieˈkeəri·əs, vi-/ *adj* **1a** serving instead of another **b** delegated ⟨~ *authority*⟩ **2** performed or suffered by one person as a substitute for, or to the benefit of, another ⟨*a* ~ *sacrifice*⟩ **3** experienced through imaginative participation in the experience of another ⟨~ *pleasure*⟩ [L *vicarius*, fr *vicis* change, alternation, stead – more at WEEK] – **vicariously** *adv*, **vicariousness** *n*

,Vicar of ˈChrist *n* the Roman Catholic pope

[1]vice /vies/ *n* **1a** moral depravity or corruption; wickedness **b** a grave moral fault **c** a habitual and usu minor fault or shortcoming **2** habitual abnormal behaviour in a domestic animal detrimental to its health or usefulness **3** sexual immorality; *esp* prostitution [ME, fr OF, fr L *vitium* fault, vice]

[2]vice, *NAm chiefly* **vise** /vies/ *n* any of various tools, usu attached to a workbench, that have 2 jaws that close for holding work by operation of a screw, lever, or cam [ME *vis, vice* screw, fr MF *vis, viz* something winding, fr L *vitis* vine – more at WITHY] – **vicelike** /ˈ-,-/ *adj*

[3]vice, *NAm chiefly* **vise** *vt* to hold, force, or squeeze (as if) with a vice

[4]vice *prep* in the place of; succeeding [L, abl of *vicis* change, alternation, stead – more at WEEK]

vice- /vies-/ *prefix* **1** person next in rank below or qualified to act in place of; deputy ⟨*vice-president*⟩ ⟨*viceroy*⟩ **2** office next in rank below ⟨*vice-admiralty*⟩ [ME *vis-, vice-*, fr MF, fr LL *vice-*, fr L *vice*, abl of *vicis*]

vice admiral *n* ☞ RANK [MF *visamiral*, fr *vis-* vice- + *amiral* admiral]

,vice-ˈchancellor *n* an officer ranking next below a chancellor; *esp* the administrative head of a British university [ME *vichauncellor*, fr MF *vischancelier*, fr *vis-* + *chancelier* chancellor]

vicennial /viˈsenyəl, -ni·əl/ *adj* occurring once every 20 years [LL *vicennium* period of 20 years, fr L *vicies* 20 times + *annus* year; akin to L *viginti* twenty – more at VIGESIMAL, ANNUAL]

viceregal /,viesˈreegl/ *adj* of a viceroy – **viceregally** *adv*

vicereine /ˈvies,rayn/ *n* **1** the wife of a viceroy **2** a woman viceroy [F, fr *vice-* + *reine* queen, fr L *regina*, fem of *reg-*, *rex* king – more at ROYAL]

viceroy /ˈviesroy/ *n* the governor of a country or province who rules as the representative of his sovereign [MF *vice-roi*, fr *vice-* + *roi* king, fr L *reg-*, *rex*] – **viceroyalty** /viesˈroyəlti/ *n*, **viceroyship** /ˈviesroyship/ *n*

ˈ**vice** ˌ**squad** *n sing or pl in constr* a police department enforcing laws concerning gambling, pornography, and prostitution

vice versa /ˌviesi ˈvuhsə, ˌviesə, ˌvies/ *adv* with the order changed and relations reversed; conversely ⟨*Ann hates Jane and* ~⟩ [L]

vichyssoise /ˌvishiˈswahz/ *n* a thick soup made of pureed leeks and potatoes, cream, and chicken stock and usu served cold [F, fr fem of *vichyssois* of Vichy, fr *Vichy*, town in France]

Vichy water /ˈveeshi/ *n* a natural sparkling mineral water from Vichy in France

vicinage /ˈvisinij/ *n* vicinity [ME *vesinage*, fr MF, fr *vesin* neighbouring, fr L *vicinus*]

vicinal /ˈvisinl/ *adj* **1** of a limited district; local **2** adjacent, neighbouring *USE* fml [L *vicinalis*, fr *vicinus* neighbour, fr *vicinus* neighbouring]

vicinity /viˈsinəti/ *n* **1** a surrounding area or district **2** NEIGHBOURHOOD 3b **3** being near; proximity – fml [MF *vicinité*, fr L *vicinitat-*, *vicinitas*, fr *vicinus* neighbouring, fr *vicus* row of houses, village; akin to Goth *weihs* village, Gk *oikos*, *oikia* house]

vicious /ˈvishəs/ *adj* **1** having the nature or quality of vice; depraved ⟨~ *habits*⟩ **2** *esp of language or reasoning* defective, faulty **3a** dangerous, refractory ⟨*a* ~ *horse*⟩ **b** unpleasantly fierce, malignant, or severe ⟨*a* ~ *form of flu*⟩ **4** malicious, spiteful ⟨~ *gossip*⟩ **5** worsened by internal causes that reciprocally augment each other ⟨*a* ~ *wage-price spiral*⟩ [ME, fr MF *vicieus*, fr L *vitiosus* full of faults, corrupt, fr *vitium* blemish, vice] – **viciously** *adv*, **viciousness** *n*

ˌ**vicious** ˈ**circle** *n* **1** a chain of events in which the apparent solution of 1 difficulty creates a new problem that makes the original difficulty worse **2** the logical fallacy of using 1 argument or definition to prove or define a second on which the first depends

vicissitude /viˈsisityoohd/ *n* **1** a change or alteration (e g in nature or human affairs) **2** an accident of fortune – usu pl ⟨*the* ~s *of daily life*⟩ **3** the quality of being changeable; mutability – fml [MF, fr L *vicissitudo*, fr *vicissim* in turn, fr *vicis* change, alternation – more at WEEK] – **vicissitudinous** /-ˈtyoohdinəs/ *adj*

victim /ˈviktim/ *n* **1** a living animal offered as a sacrifice in a religious rite **2** sby or sthg that is adversely affected by a force or agent: e g **a** one who or that which is injured, destroyed, or subjected to oppression or mistreatment ⟨*a* ~ *of cancer*⟩ ⟨*a* ~ *of the car crash*⟩ ⟨*a* ~ *of frequent political attacks*⟩ **b** a dupe, prey [L *victima*; akin to OHG *wīh* holy, Skt *vinakti* he sets apart]

victim·ize, -ise /ˈviktimiez/ *vt* **1** to make a victim of **2** to punish selectively (e g by unfair dismissal) – **victimizer** *n*, **victimization** /-ˈzaysh(ə)n/ *n*

victor /ˈviktə/ *n* a person, country, etc that defeats an enemy or opponent; a winner [ME, fr L, fr *victus*, pp of *vincere* to conquer, win; akin to OE *wīgan* to fight, OSlav *věkŭ* strength] – **victor** *adj*

Victor – a communications code word for the letter *v*

victoria /vikˈtawri·ə/ *n* **1** a low 4-wheeled carriage for 2 with a folding hood **2** any of a genus of S American water lilies with large spreading leaves and immense bright white flowers **3** a large red sweet type of plum [*Victoria* †1901 Queen of England]

Vicˌ**toria** ˈ**Cross** *n* a bronze Maltese cross that is the highest British military decoration [Queen *Victoria*]

[1]**Victorian** /vikˈtawri·ən/ *adj* **1** (characteristic) of the reign of Queen Victoria or the art, letters, or taste of her time **2** typical of the moral standards or conduct of the age of Queen Victoria, esp in being prudish or hypocritical **3** of a place called Victoria (e g the State in Australia or the capital of British Columbia)

[2]**Victorian** *n* sby living during Queen Victoria's reign

Victoriana /vikˌtawriˈahnə/ *n* articles, esp ornaments, from the Victorian period [NL, neut pl of *Victorianus* Victorian]

victorious /vikˈtawri·əs/ *adj* **1a** having won a victory **b** (characteristic) of victory **2** successful, triumphant – **victoriously** *adv*, **victoriousness** *n*

victory /ˈvikt(ə)ri/ *n* **1** the overcoming of an enemy or antagonist ⟨~ *was ours*⟩ **2** achievement of mastery or success in a struggle or endeavour [ME, fr MF *victorie*, fr L *victoria*, fr fem of (assumed) L *victorius* of winning or conquest, fr L *victus*, pp of *vincere*]

[1]**victual** /ˈvitl/ *n* **1** food usable by human beings **2** *pl* supplies of food; provisions [alter. of ME *vitaille*, fr MF, fr LL *victualia*, pl, provisions, victuals, fr neut pl of *victualis* of nourishment, fr L *victus* nourishment, fr *victus*, pp of *vivere* to live – more at QUICK]

[2]**victual** *vb* **-ll-** (*NAm* **-l-**, **-ll-**), /ˈvitl·ing/ *vb* to supply with or lay in food

victualler, *NAm also* **victualer** /ˈvitl·ə/ *n* **1** PUBLICAN 2 **2** sby who or sthg that provisions an army, a navy, or a ship with food **3** a provisioning ship

vicuña, vicuna /viˈkyoohnə/ *n* **1** (the wool from the fine undercoat of) a wild ruminant mammal of the Andes related to the domesticated llama and alpaca **2** a fabric made of vicuña wool; *also* a sheep's wool imitation of this [Sp *vicuña*, fr Quechua *wikúña*]

vide /ˈviedi/ *vb imper* see – used to direct a reader to another item [L, fr *vidēre* to see – more at WIT]

videlicet /viˈdeliˌset/ *adv* that is to say; namely – used to introduce 1 or more examples [ME, fr L, fr *vidēre* to see + *licet* it is permitted, fr *licēre* to be permitted – more at LICENCE]

[1]**video** /ˈvidioh/ *adj* **1** of television; *specif* of reproduction of a television image or used in its transmission or reception ⟨*a* ~ *signal*⟩ – compare AUDIO **2** of a form of magnetic recording for reproduction on a television screen [L *vidēre* to see + E *-o* (as in *audio*)]

[2]**video** *n* **1** **video,** ˈ**videore**ˌ**corder,** ˌ**videocas**ˈ**sette re**ˌ**corder** a machine for videotaping ☞ TELEVISION **2** *chiefly NAm* television

ˈ**video**ˌ**disc** /-disk/ *n* a disc, similar to a gramophone record, on which information is stored in digital form and is used to play back prerecorded video material on a television screen, as a computer memory unit, etc ☞ TELEVISION, VIDEO

video nasty *n* a video film of (allegedly) sensational

nature, usu including scenes of explicit sex, violence, and horror

videotape /'vidioh,tayp/ *vt* to make a recording of (e g sthg that is televised) on magnetic tape ☞ VIDEO [*video tape*] – **videotape** *n*

vie /vie/ *vi* **vying; vied** to strive for superiority; contend ⟨~d *with each other for the prize*⟩ [modif of MF *envier* to invite, challenge, wager, fr L *invitare* to invite] – **vier** *n*

Vietcong /,vee·et'kong/ *n, pl* **Vietcong** an adherent of the Vietnamese communist movement supported by N Vietnam and engaged in warfare against the S Vietnamese regime during the Vietnam War [Vietnamese *Viêt Nam công-san* Vietnam communists]

Vietnamese /,vee·itnə'meez/ *n, pl* **Vietnamese** (the official Austroasiatic language of) a native or inhabitant of Vietnam ☞ LANGUAGE [*Vietnam*, country in SE Asia] – **Vietnamese** *adj*

vieux jeu /,vyuh 'zhuh/ *adj* out-of-date; OLD HAT [F, lit., old game]

[1]**view** /vyooh/ *n* **1** the act of seeing or examining; inspection; *also* a survey ⟨*a* ~ *of English literature*⟩ **2** a way of regarding sthg; an opinion ⟨*in my* ~ *the conference has no chance of success*⟩ **3** a scene, prospect ⟨*the lovely* ~ *from the balcony*⟩; *also* an aspect ⟨*the rear* ~ *of the house*⟩ **4** extent or range of vision; sight ⟨*tried to keep the ship in* ~⟩ **5** an intention, object ⟨*bought a gun with a* ~ *to murdering his mother*⟩ **6** the foreseeable future ⟨*no hope in* ~⟩ **7** a pictorial representation [ME *vewe*, fr MF *veue, vue*, fr OF, fr *veeir, voir* to see, fr L *vidēre* – more at WIT] – **in view of 1** taking the specified feature into consideration ⟨in view of *his age, the police have decided not to prosecute*⟩ **2** able to be seen by or from ⟨in *full* view of *interested spectators*⟩ – **on view** open to public inspection

[2]**view** *vt* **1a** to see, watch **b** to look on in a specified way; regard ⟨*doesn't* ~ *himself as a rebel*⟩ **2** to look at attentively; inspect ⟨~ed *the house but decided not to buy it*⟩ **3** to survey or examine mentally; consider ⟨~ *all sides of a question*⟩ **4** to see (a hunted animal) break cover ~*vi* to watch television – **viewable** *adj*

viewdata /'vyooh,dahtə, -,daytə/ *n* information held in a computer and accessible to users via a television set ☞ TELECOMMUNICATION, TELEVISION

viewer /'vyooh·ə/ *n* **1** an optical device used in viewing **2** sby who watches television [[2]VIEW + [2]-ER]

viewfinder /'vyooh,fiendə/ *n* a device on a camera for showing what will be included in the picture ☞ CAMERA

,**view hal'loo** /ha'looh/ *n, pl* **view halloos** a shout given by a hunter on seeing a fox break cover

'**viewless** /-lis/ *adj* **1** affording no view **2** holding no opinions – **viewlessly** *adv*

'**view,phone** /-,fohn/ *n* a telephone allowing its user to see the person with whom he/she is in contact on a small screen ☞ TELECOMMUNICATION

'**view,point** /-,poynt/ *n* a standpoint; POINT OF VIEW

vigesimal /vie'jesiməl/ *adj* based on the number 20 [L *vicesimus, vigesimus* twentieth; akin to L *viginti* twenty, Gk *eikosi*]

vigil /'vijil/ *n* **1a** a devotional watch formerly kept on the night before a religious festival **b** the day before a religious festival, observed as a day of spiritual preparation **2** the act of keeping awake at times when sleep is customary; *also* a period of wakefulness **3** an act or period of watching or surveillance; a watch [ME *vigile*, fr OF, fr LL & L; LL *vigilia* watch on the eve of a feast, fr L, wakefulness, watch, fr *vigil* awake, watchful; akin to L *vigēre* to be vigorous, *vegēre* to be active, rouse – more at WAKE]

'**vigilance com,mittee** /'vijiləns/ *n sing or pl in constr, NAm* an unauthorized self-appointed committee of citizens organized to suppress and punish crime or immorality without recourse to the established legal processes (e g when the processes of law appear inadequate)

vigilant /'vijilənt/ *adj* alert and watchful, esp to avoid danger [ME, fr MF, fr L *vigilant-, vigilans*, fr prp of *vigilare* to keep watch, stay awake, fr *vigil* awake] – **vigilance** /-ləns/ *n*, **vigilantly** *adv*

vigilante /,viji'lanti/ *n, NAm* a member of a vigilance committee [Sp, watchman, guard, fr *vigilante* vigilant, fr L *vigilant-, vigilans*]

'**vigil ,light** *n* a candle lighted devotionally (e g in a Roman Catholic church) before a shrine or image

vignette /vi'nyet, vee-/ *n* **1** a decorative design (e g of vine leaves, tendrils, and grapes) on a title page or at the beginning or end of a chapter **2** a picture (e g an engraving or photograph) that shades off gradually into the surrounding background **3a** a short descriptive literary sketch **b** a brief incident or scene (e g in a play or film) [F, fr MF *vignete*, fr dim. of *vigne* vine – more at VINE] – **vignettist** *n*

vigorous /'vigərəs/ *adj* **1** possessing or showing vigour; full of active strength **2** done with vigour; carried out forcefully and energetically ⟨~ *exercises*⟩ [ME, fr MF, fr OF, fr *vigor*] – **vigorously** *adv*, **vigorousness** *n*

vigour, *NAm* **vigor** /'vigə/ *n* **1** active physical or mental strength or force **2** active healthy well-balanced growth, esp of plants **3** intensity of action or effect; force [ME, fr MF *vigor*, fr L, fr *vigēre* to flourish]

Viking /'vieking/ *n* **1** a Norse trader and warrior of the 8th to 10th c **2** a Scandinavian [ON *vīkingr*]

vile /viel/ *adj* **1a** morally despicable or abhorrent **b** physically repulsive; foul **2** tending to degrade ⟨~ *employments*⟩ **3** disgustingly or utterly bad; contemptible ⟨*in a* ~ *temper*⟩ [ME, base, common, worthless, fr OF *vil*, fr L *vilis* of small worth] – **vilely** *adv*, **vileness** *n*

vilify /'vilifie/ *vt* to utter slanderous and abusive statements against; defame [ME *vilifien* to make less valuable, fr LL *vilificare*, fr L *vilis* + *facere* to make, do] – **vilifier** *n*, **vilification** *n*

villa /'vilə/ *n* **1** a country mansion **2** an ancient Roman mansion and the surrounding agricultural estate **3** *Br* a detached or semidetached suburban house, usu having a garden and built before WW I [It, fr L; akin to L *vicus* row of houses – more at VICINITY]

village /'vilij/ *n* **1** a group of dwellings in the country, larger than a hamlet and smaller than a town **2** *sing or pl in constr* the residents of a village **3** sthg (e g a group of burrows or nests) suggesting a village [ME, fr MF, fr OF, fr *ville* farm, village, fr L *villa* country estate]

villager /'vilijə/ *n* **1** an inhabitant of a village **2** a rustic

villain /'vilən/ *n* **1** a scoundrel, rascal; *also* a criminal **2** a character in a story or play whose evil

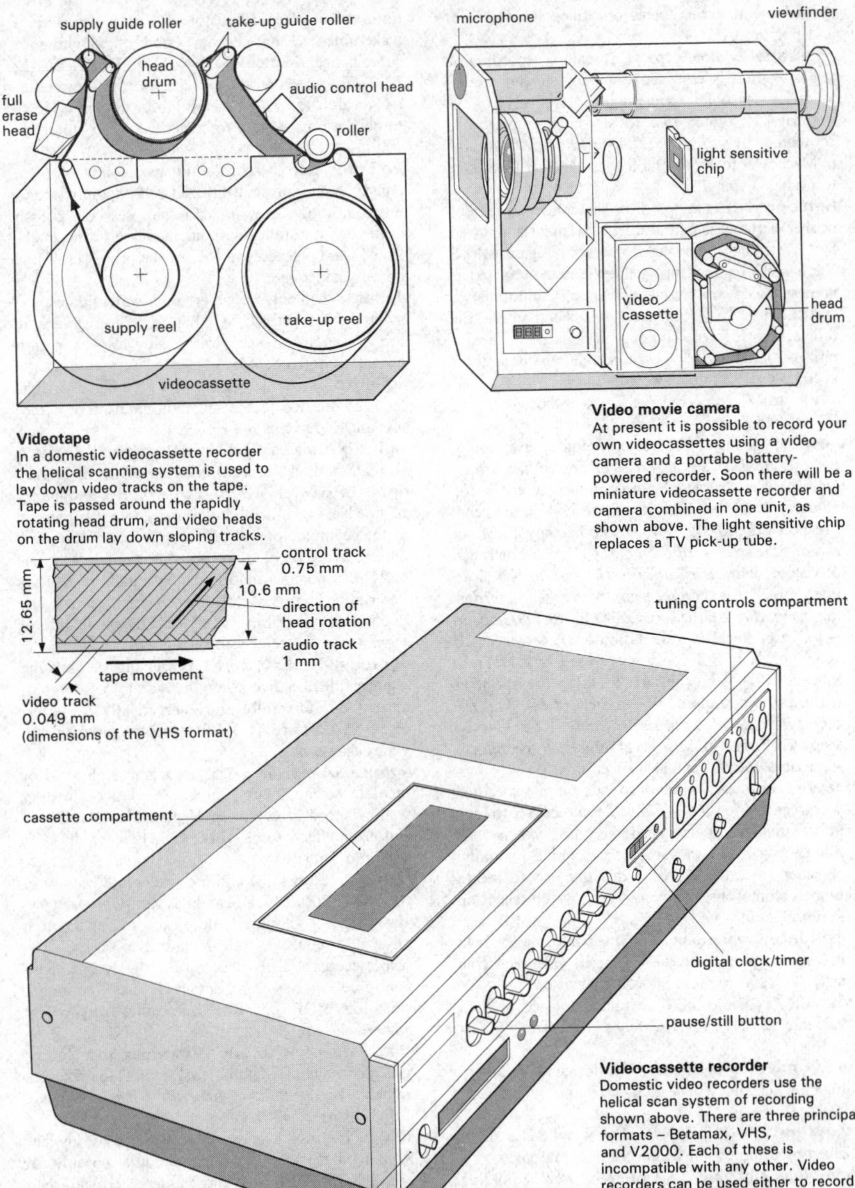

Videotape
In a domestic videocassette recorder the helical scanning system is used to lay down video tracks on the tape. Tape is passed around the rapidly rotating head drum, and video heads on the drum lay down sloping tracks.

Video movie camera
At present it is possible to record your own videocassettes using a video camera and a portable battery-powered recorder. Soon there will be a miniature videocassette recorder and camera combined in one unit, as shown above. The light sensitive chip replaces a TV pick-up tube.

Videocassette recorder
Domestic video recorders use the helical scan system of recording shown above. There are three principal formats – Betamax, VHS, and V2000. Each of these is incompatible with any other. Video recorders can be used either to record television programmes or to play back commercially prerecorded cassettes (feature films or home education).

☞ TELECOMMUNICATION, TELEVISION

Signal detection systems

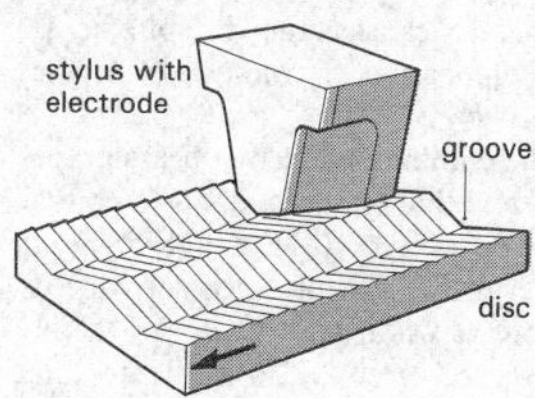

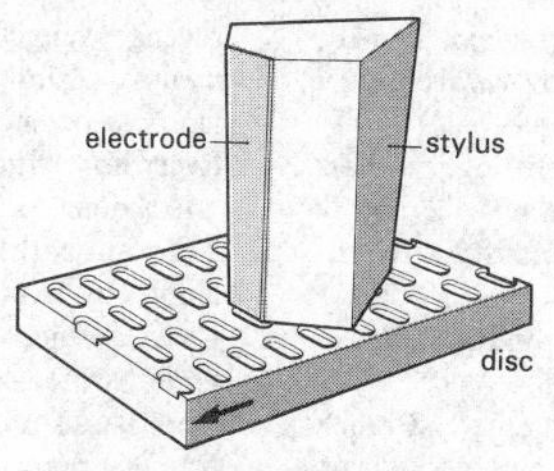

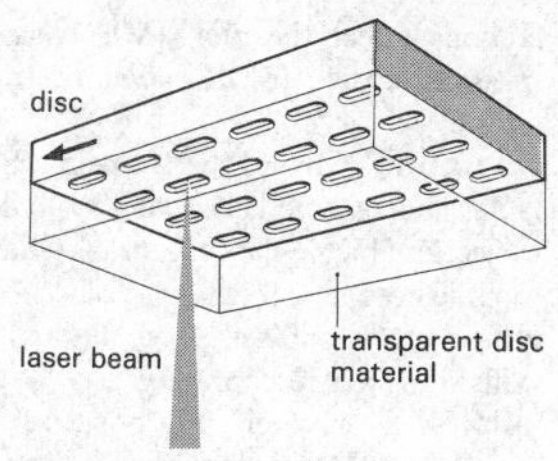

Grooved capacitance
In this videodisc system the stylus/electrode moves along grooves in a disc of electrically conductive material, picking up the picture and sound information stored there as pits. The disc must be protected by a special sleeve when it is not being played.

Grooveless capacitance
A stylus/electrode moves over the surface of the conductive disc picking up information encoded in the pits of one track and guided by tracking signals between the lines of pits. The disc must be protected by a special sleeve.

Optical
A laser beam is focussed onto pits in the underside of a rapidly spinning disc. The pits are lined by a reflective layer and covered by a plastic coating. Dust and dirt on the disc surface are thus out of focus and have little effect.

Videodisc
Videodiscs are prerecorded and offer better picture quality than videocassettes. They have a particularly high potential as an educational medium since information can quickly be found. Some machines are able to advance a sequence frame by frame for analysis, and it will be possible to link some videodisc players to home computers.

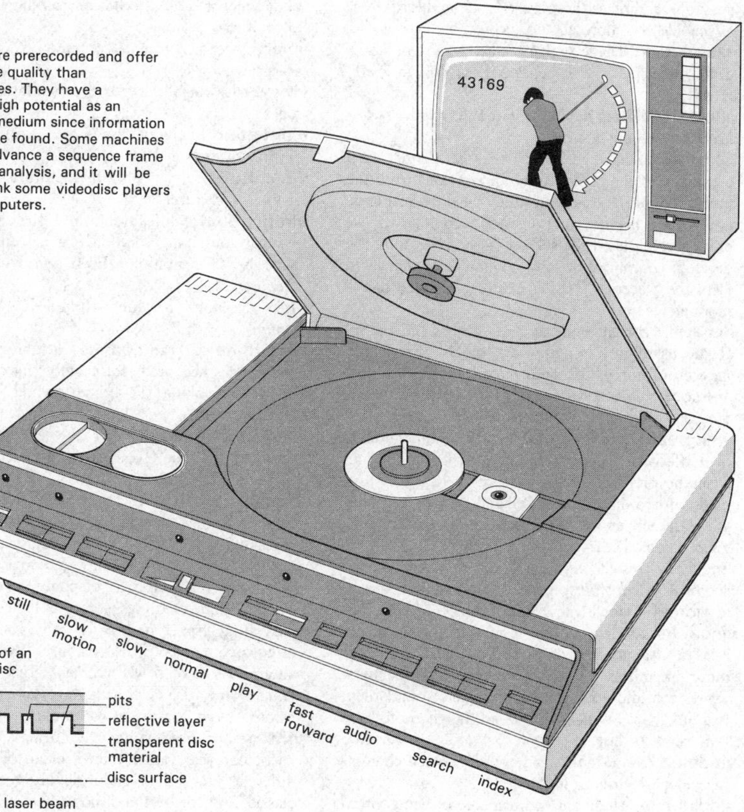

43169

still
slow motion
slow
normal
play
fast forward
audio
search
index

cross section of an optical videodisc

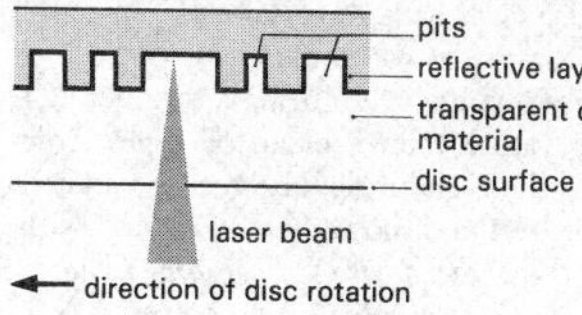

pits
reflective layer
transparent disc material
disc surface
laser beam
direction of disc rotation

actions affect the plot [ME *vilain, vilein,* fr MF, peasant, churl, fr ML *villanus,* fr L *villa* country estate]

villainous /'vilənəs/ *adj* **1** being, befitting, or characteristic of a villain; evil ⟨*a ~ attack*⟩ **2** highly objectionable ⟨*~ weather*⟩ – **villainously** *adv,* **villainousness** *n*

villainy /'viləni/ *n* **1** villainous conduct; *also* a villainous act **2** depravity

villanelle /,vilə'nel/ *n* (a poem in) a chiefly French verse form consisting of 5 tercets and a quatrain using 2 rhymes [F, fr It *villanella,* fr *villano* peasant, fr ML *villanus*]

-ville /-,vil/ *suffix* (*adj, n* → *n*) place or thing of (such) a nature ⟨*dulls*ville⟩ – infml [*-ville,* suffix occurring in names of towns, fr F, fr OF, fr *ville* village]

villein /'vilən/ *n* **1** a free village peasant **2** an unfree peasant standing as the slave of his feudal lord [ME *vilain, vilein* – more at VILLAIN]

villeinage, villenage /'vilənij/ *n* the tenure or status of a villein [ME *vilenage,* fr MF, fr OF, fr *vilein, vilain*]

villous /'viləs/ *adj* having villi or soft long hairs ⟨*~ leaves*⟩ – **villously** *adv*

villus /'viləs/ *n, pl* **villi** /'vilie/ a small slender part: e g **a** any of the many minute projections from the membrane of the small intestine that provide a large area for the absorption of digested food **b** any of the branching parts on the surface of the chorion of the developing embryo of most mammals that help to form the placenta [NL, fr L, tuft of shaggy hair – more at VELVET]

vim /vim/ *n* robust energy and enthusiasm – infml [L, accus of *vis* strength; akin to Gk *is* strength, *hiesthai* to hurry, OE *wāth* pursuit]

vinaceous /vie'nayshəs/ *adj* of the colour wine [L *vinaceus* of wine, fr *vinum* wine – more at WINE]

vinaigrette /,vinə'gret/ *n* **1** a small ornamental box or bottle with a perforated top used for holding an aromatic preparation (e g smelling salts) **2** (a dish made with) a sharp sauce of oil and vinegar flavoured with salt, pepper, mustard, herbs, etc and used esp on green salads [F, fr *vinaigre* vinegar]

vincible /'vinsəbl/ *adj* capable of being overcome or subdued [L *vincibilis,* fr *vincere* to conquer – more at VICTOR] – **vincibleness** *n,* **vincibility** /-'biləti/ *n*

vinculum /'vingkyooləm/ *n pl* **vinculums, vincula** /-lə/ a straight horizontal mark placed over 2 or more members of a compound mathematical expression and equivalent to brackets round them (e g in a–b–c=a–[b–c]) [L, bond, fr *vincire* to bind – more at VETCH]

vindaloo /,vində'looh/ *n* a hot curry, specif containing vinegar [origin unknown]

vindicable /'vindikəbl/ *adj* capable of being vindicated – **vindicability** /-'biləti/ *n*

vindicate /'vindikayt/ *vt* **1a** to exonerate, absolve **b** to provide justification for; justify **2** to maintain the existence of; uphold ⟨*~ his honour*⟩ [L *vindicatus,* pp of *vindicare* to lay claim to, avenge, fr *vindic-, vindex* claimant, avenger] – **vindicator** *n*

vindication /,vindi'kaysh(ə)n/ *n* justification against denial or censure; defence [VINDICATE + -ION]

vindicatory /'vindi,kaytəri, -kət(ə)ri/ *adj* **1** providing vindication; justificatory **2** punitive, retributive

vindictive /vin'diktiv/ *adj* **1a** disposed to seek revenge; vengeful **b** intended as revenge ⟨*~ punishments*⟩ **2** intended to cause anguish; spiteful [L *vindicta* revenge, vindication, fr *vindicare*] – **vindictively** *adv,* **vindictiveness** *n*

vine /vien/ *n* **1** the climbing plant that bears grapes **2** (a plant with) a stem that requires support and that climbs by tendrils or twining [ME, fr OF *vigne,* fr L *vinea* vine, vineyard, fr fem of *vineus* of wine, fr *vinum* wine – more at WINE] – **viny** *adj*

'vine,dresser /-,dresə/ *n* sby who cultivates and prunes grapevines, esp as an occupation

vinegar /'vinigə/ *n* a sour liquid obtained esp by acetic fermentation of wine, cider, etc and used as a condiment or preservative [ME *vinegre,* fr OF *vinaigre,* fr *vin* wine (fr L *vinum*) + *aigre* keen, sour – more at EAGER]

vinegarish /'vinigərish/ *adj* VINEGARY 2

vinegary /'vinig(ə)ri/ *adj* **1** containing or resembling vinegar; sour **2** bitter or irascible in character or manner

vinery /'vienəri/ *n* an area or building in which vines are grown

vineyard /'vinyahd, -yəd/ *n* a plantation of grapevines

vingt-et-un /,vant ay 'uhn (*Fr* vε̃t e œ̃)/ *n* pontoon [F, lit., twenty-one]

viniculture /'vini,kulchə/ *n* viticulture [L *vinum* + ISV *-i-* + *culture*]

vinification /,vinifi'kaysh(ə)n/ *n* the conversion of a sugar-containing solution (e g a fruit juice) into wine by fermentation [F, fr *vin* wine + *-i-* + *-fication*]

vino /'veenoh/ *n* wine – infml [It & Sp, fr L *vinum*]

vin ordinaire /van awdi'neə/ *n* table wine that is undistinguished and sufficiently inexpensive for everyday drinking [F, ordinary wine]

vinous /'vienəs/ *adj* **1** of or made with wine ⟨*~ medications*⟩ **2** (showing the effects of being) addicted to wine [L *vinosus,* fr *vinum* wine] – **vinously** *adv,* **vinosity** /vie'nosəti/ *n*

¹vintage /'vintij/ *n* **1a(1)** a season's yield of grapes or wine from a vineyard **(2)** wine, specif one of a particular type, region, and year and usu of superior quality that is dated and allowed to mature **b** *sing or pl in constr* a collection of contemporaneous and similar people or things; a crop **2** the act or time of harvesting grapes or making wine **3** a period of origin or manufacture ⟨*a piano of 1845 ~*⟩ [ME, alter. of *vendage,* fr MF *vendenge,* fr L *vindemia,* fr *vinum* wine, grapes + *demere* to take off, fr *de-* + *emere* to take – more at WINE, REDEEM]

²vintage *adj* **1** of a vintage; *esp* being a product of 1 particular year rather than a blend of wines from different years **2** of enduring interest or quality; classic **3** of the best and most characteristic – with a proper noun ⟨*~ Shaw: a wise and winning comedy – Time*⟩ **4** *Br, of a motor vehicle* built between 1917 and 1930 ⟨*a ~ Rolls*⟩

vintager /'vintijə/ *n* sby concerned with the production of grapes and wine

vintner /'vintnə/ *n* WINE MERCHANT [ME *vineter,* fr OF *vinetier,* fr ML *vinetarius,* fr L *vinetum* vineyard, fr *vinum* wine]

vinyl /'vienl/ *n* (a plastic that is a polymer of a derivative of) a univalent radical $CH_2{=}CH$ derived from ethylene by removal of 1 hydrogen atom [ISV, fr L *vinum* wine] – **vinylic** /-'nilik/ *adj*

viol /ˈvie·əl/ *n* any of a family of bowed stringed instruments chiefly of the 16th and 17th c with usu 6 strings and a fretted fingerboard, played resting on or between the player's knees [MF *viole* viol, viola, fr OProv *viola* viol]

[1]**viola** /viˈohlə/ *n* a musical instrument of the violin family that is intermediate in size and range between the violin and cello and is tuned a 5th below the violin [It & Sp, viol, viola, fr OProv, viol] – **violist** *n*

[2]**viola** /ˈvie·ələ, vieˈohlə/ *n* VIOLET 1; *esp* any of various cultivated violets with (variegated) flowers resembling but smaller than those of pansies [L]

violaceous /ˌvie·əˈlayshəs/ *adj* of the colour violet [L *violaceus*, fr *viola* violet] – **violaceously** *adv*

viola da braccio /viˌohlə də ˈbrachioh/ *n, pl* **viole da braccio** /viˌohlay/ a member of the early violin family; *esp* a viola [It, arm viol]

viˌola da ˈgamba /ˈgambə/ *n, pl* **viole da gamba** a bass member of the viol family having a range like that of the cello [It, leg viol]

viˌola dáˈmore /daˈmawri/ *n, pl* **viole d'amore** a bowed stringed instrument which is related to the viol family but has no frets and is played under the chin [It, viol of love]

violate /ˈvie·əlayt/ *vt* **1** to fail to comply with; infringe ⟨~ *the law*⟩ **2** to do harm to; *specif* to rape **3** to fail to respect; desecrate ⟨~ *a shrine*⟩ **4** to interrupt, disturb ⟨~ *your privacy*⟩ [ME *violaten*, fr L *violatus*, pp of *violare*; akin to L *vis* strength – more at VIM] – **violator** *n*, **violable** /ˈvie·ələbl/ *adj*, **violative** /-tiv/ *adj*, **violation** /-ˈlaysh(ə)n/ *n*

violence /ˈvie·ələns/ *n* **1** (an instance of) exertion of physical force so as to injure or abuse **2** unjust or unwarranted distortion; outrage ⟨*did* ~ *to her feelings*⟩ **3a** intense or turbulent action or force ⟨*the* ~ *of the storm*⟩ **b** (an instance of) vehement feeling or expression; fervour **4** distortion or misinterpretation of meaning ⟨*editor did* ~ *to the text*⟩

violent /ˈvie·ələnt/ *adj* **1** marked by extreme force or sudden intense activity ⟨*a* ~ *attack*⟩ **2a** notably furious or vehement ⟨*a* ~ *denunciation*⟩; *also* excited or mentally disordered to the point of loss of self-control ⟨*the patient became* ~ *and had to be restrained*⟩ **b** extreme, intense ⟨~ *pain*⟩ **3** caused by force; not natural ⟨*a* ~ *death*⟩ [ME, fr MF, fr L *violentus*; akin to L *violare* to violate] – **violently** *adv*

violet /ˈvie·ələt/ *n* **1** any of a genus of plants with often sweet-scented flowers, usu of all 1 colour, esp as distinguished from the usu larger-flowered violas and pansies **2** bluish purple [ME, fr MF *violete*, dim. of *viole* violet, fr L *viola*]

violin /ˌvie·əˈlin/ *n* a bowed stringed instrument having a fingerboard with no frets, 4 strings, and a usual range from G below middle C upwards for more than 4½ octaves [It *violino*, dim. of *viola*] – **violinist** *n*

violoncello /ˌvie·ələnˈcheloh/ *n, pl* **violoncellos** a cello [It, dim. of *violone*, aug of *viola*] – **violoncellist** *n*

VIP *n, pl* **VIPs** a person of great influence or prestige ⟨*a* ~ *lounge*⟩ [*v*ery *i*mportant *p*erson]

viper /ˈviepə/ *n* **1a** (any of various Old World snakes related to) the adder **b** PIT VIPER **2** a malignant or treacherous person [MF *vipere*, fr L *vipera*]

viperish /ˈviepərish/ *adj* spitefully abusive; venomous

viperous /ˈviep(ə)rəs/ *adj* **1 viperous, viperine** of or like a viper; venomous **2** viperish – **viperously** *adv*

ˌviper's ˈbugloss *n* a coarse bristly Old World plant of the borage family with showy blue tubular flowers

virago /viˈrahgoh/ *n, pl* **viragoes, viragos 1** a loud overbearing woman; a termagant **2** *archaic* a woman of great stature, strength, and courage [L *viragin-*, *virago*, fr *vir* man – more at VIRILE] – **viraginous** /viˈrajinəs/ *adj*

vireo /ˈvirioh/ *n, pl* **vireos** any of various small insect-eating American birds [L, a small bird, fr *virēre* to be green]

virescence /viˈres(ə)ns/ *n* the state of becoming green, esp of plant organs (e g petals) that are not normally green [*virescent* fr L *virescent-*, *virescens*, prp of *virescere* to become green, incho of *virēre*] – **virescent** *adj*

[1]**virgin** /ˈvuhjin/ *n* **1** an unmarried girl or woman **2** *often cap* (a statue or picture of) *the* Virgin Mary **3** a person, esp a girl, who has not had sexual intercourse **4** a female animal that has never copulated [ME, fr OF *virgine*, fr L *virgin-*, *virgo* young woman, virgin] – **virginity** /vəˈjinəti/ *n*

[2]**virgin** *adj* **1** free of impurity or stain; unsullied **2** being a virgin **3** characteristic of or befitting a virgin; modest **4** untouched, unexploited; *specif* not altered by human activity ⟨*a* ~ *forest*⟩ **5** *of metal* produced directly from ore; not scrap

[1]**virginal** /ˈvuhjinl/ *adj* **1** (characteristic) of a virgin or virginity; *esp* pure, chaste **2** fresh, untouched, uncorrupted – **virginally** *adv*

[2]**virginal** *n* a small rectangular harpsichord popular in the 16th and 17th c – often pl with sing. meaning [prob fr L *virginalis* of a virgin, fr *virgin-*, *virgo*]

ˌvirgin ˈbirth *n* **1** birth from a virgin **2** *often cap V&B* the doctrine that Jesus was born of a virgin mother

Virginia /vəˈjinyə, -ni·ə/ *n* a usu mild-flavoured flue-cured tobacco grown orig in N America and used esp in cigarettes [*Virginia*, state of the USA]

Virˌginia ˈcreeper *n* a climbing plant of the grape family with reddish leaves composed of 5 leaflets and bluish black berries

Virˌginia ˈreel *n* an American country dance

Virˌginia ˈstock *n* an annual plant of the mustard family with small pink, white, red, or lilac flowers

ˌVirgin ˈMary /ˈmeəri/ *n* *the* mother of Jesus

virgin wool *n* new wool not yet processed

Virgo /ˈvuhgoh/ *n* (sby born under) the 6th sign of the zodiac in astrology, which is pictured as a woman holding an ear of corn ☞ SYMBOL [L, lit., virgin] – **Virgoan** /ˈ---, -ˈ--/ *adj or n*

virgo intacta /ˌvuhgoh inˈtaktə/ *n* a virgin human female with an unbroken hymen [L, untouched virgin]

viridescent /ˌviriˈdes(ə)nt/ *adj* slightly green [L *viridis* green – more at VERDANT]

viridian /viˈridi·ən/ *n* (a chrome oxide pigment having) a strong bluish green colour [L *viridis*]

virile /ˈviriel/ *adj* **1** having the nature, properties, or qualities (often thought of as typical) of a man; *specif* capable of functioning as a male in copulation **2** vigorous, forceful **3** characteristic of or associated with adult males; masculine [MF or L; MF *viril*, fr L *virilis*, fr *vir* man, male; akin to OE & OHG *wer* man, Skt *vīra*]

virilism /'viri,liz(ə)m/ *n* the abnormal appearance of male secondary sex characters **a** precociously in the male **b** in the female

virility /və'riləti/ *n* **1** power to procreate **2** manly vigour; masculinity [VIRILE + -ITY]

virology /vie·ə'roləji/ *n* a branch of science that deals with viruses [NL *virus* + ISV *-logy*] – **virologic** /-rə'lojik/, **virological** *adj*, **virologically** *adv*, **virologist** /-'roləjist/ *n*

virtual /'vuhchooəl/ *adj* **1** that is such in essence or effect though not formally recognized or admitted ⟨*a ~ dictator*⟩ **2** formed by the apparent convergence of light rays ⟨*a ~ image*⟩ – compare REAL 2d [ME, possessed of certain physical virtues, fr ML *virtualis*, fr L *virtus* strength, virtue]

virtually /'vuhchəli, -chooəli/ *adv* almost entirely; for all practical purposes

virtue /'vuhtyooh, -chooh/ *n* **1a** conformity to a standard of right; morality **b** a particular moral excellence ⟨*truthfulness is a ~*⟩ **2** a beneficial or commendable quality ⟨*has the ~ of being easily assembled*⟩ **3** a capacity to act; potency **4** chastity, esp in a woman [ME *virtu*, fr OF, fr L *virtut-*, *virtus* strength, manliness, virtue, fr *vir* man – more at VIRILE] – **virtueless** *adj* – **by virtue of 1** through the force of; having as a right **2** as a result of; because of

virtuosity /,vuhtyooh'osəti/ *n* great technical skill, esp in the practice of a fine art

[1]**virtuoso** /,vuhtyooh'ohsoh, -zoh/ *n, pl* **virtuosos, virtuosi** /-si, -zi/ **1** one skilled in or having a taste for the fine arts **2** one who excels in the technique of an art, esp in musical performance [It, fr *virtuoso*, adj, virtuous, skilled, fr LL *virtuosus* virtuous, fr L *virtus*] – **virtuosic** /-'ohzik, -'ohsik/ *adj*

[2]**virtuoso** *adj* (characteristic) of a virtuoso; having the manner or style of a virtuoso

virtuous /'vuhchoo·əs/ *adj* **1** having or exhibiting virtue; *esp* morally excellent; righteous **2** chaste – **virtuously** *adv*, **virtuousness** *n*

virulence /'viryooləns, -rə-/, **virulency** /-si/ *n* **1** extreme bitterness or malignity of temper; rancour **2** malignancy, venomousness **3** the relative capacity of a pathogen to overcome body defences

virulent /'viryoolənt, -rə-/ *adj* **1a** *of a disease* severe and developing rapidly **b** able to overcome bodily defensive mechanisms ⟨*a ~ strain of bacterium*⟩ **2** extremely poisonous or venomous **3** full of malice; malignant **4** objectionably harsh or strong ⟨*a ~ purple*⟩ [ME, fr L *virulentus*, fr *virus* poison] – **virulently** *adv*

virus /'vie·ərəs/ *n* **1a** the causative agent of any infectious disease – not now used technically **b** (a disease caused by) any of a large group of submicroscopic often disease-causing agents that typically consist of a protein coat surrounding an RNA or DNA core and that multiply only in living cells **2** sthg that poisons the mind or soul ⟨*the ~ of racism*⟩ [NL, fr L, slimy liquid, poison, stench; akin to OE *wāse* marsh, Gk *ios* poison, Skt *viṣa*] – **viral** *adj*, **viricide** /'vie·ərə,sied/ *n*, **viricidal** /-'siedl/ *adj*, **viricidally** *adv*

[1]**visa** /'veezə/ *n* an endorsement made on a passport by the proper authorities (e g of a country at entrance or exit) denoting that the bearer may proceed [F, fr L, neut pl of *visus*, pp]

[2]**visa** *vt* **visaing; visaed** to provide (a passport) with a visa

visage /'vizij/ *n* **1** a face, countenance **2** an aspect, appearance ⟨*grimy ~ of a mining town*⟩ *USE* fml or poetic [ME, fr OF, fr *vis* face, fr L *visus* sight, fr *visus*, pp of *vidēre* to see – more at WIT] – **visaged** *adj*

vis-à-vis /,vee zah 'vee/ *prep* **1** face to face with; opposite **2** in relation to [F, lit., face to face]

viscacha /vis'kachə/, **vizcacha** /viz-/ *n* any of several S American burrowing rodents related to the chinchilla [Sp *vizcacha*, fr Quechua *wiskácha*]

viscera /'visərə/ *n pl* the internal body organs collectively

visceral /'visərəl/ *adj* **1** deeply or intensely felt ⟨*~ sensation*⟩ **2** of or located on or among the viscera **3** instinctive, unreasoning ⟨*a ~ conviction*⟩ – fml – **viscerally** *adv*

viscid /'visid/ *adj* **1a** adhesive, sticky **b** glutinous, viscous **2** covered with a sticky layer ⟨*~ leaves*⟩ [LL *viscidus*, fr L *viscum* birdlime – more at VISCOUS] – **viscidly** *adv*, **viscidity** /vi'sidəti/ *n*

viscometer /vis'komitə/ *n* an instrument for measuring viscosity [*visco*sity + *-meter*] – **viscometry** /-tri/ *n*, **viscometric** /,viskə'metrik/ *adj*

viscose /'viskohs, -kohz/ *n* **1** a viscous solution made by treating cellulose with caustic alkali solution and carbon disulphide and used in making rayon and cellulose films **2** viscose rayon [obs *viscose*, adj (viscous)] – **viscose** *adj*

viscosimeter /,viskoh'simitə/ *n* a viscometer [ISV *viscos*ity + *-meter*] – **viscosimetric** /,vis,kosi'metrik/ *adj*

viscosity /vis'kosəti/ *n* **1** being viscous **2** (a measure of the force needed to overcome) the property of a liquid, gas, or semifluid that enables it to offer resistance to flow

viscount /'viekownt/ *n* a member of the peerage in Britain ranking below an earl and above a baron [ME *viscounte*, fr MF *viscomte*, fr ML *vicecomit-*, *vicecomes*, fr LL *vice-* + *comit-*, *comes* count – more at [3]COUNT] – **viscountcy** /-si/ *n*, **viscounty** /-ti/ *n*

viscountess /,viekown'tes, 'viekowntis/ *n* **1** the wife or widow of a viscount **2** a woman having the rank of a viscount

viscous /'viskəs/ *adj* **1** viscid **2** having or characterized by (high) viscosity ⟨*~ flow*⟩ [ME *viscouse*, fr LL *viscosus* full of birdlime, viscous, fr L *viscum* mistletoe, birdlime; akin to OHG *wīhsila* cherry, Gk *ixos* mistletoe] – **viscously** *adv*, **viscousness** *n*

viscus /'viskəs/ *n, pl* **viscera** /'visərə/ the heart, liver, intestines, or other internal body organ located esp in the great cavity of the trunk [L (pl *viscera*)]

vise /vies/ *vt or n, chiefly NAm* (to hold with) a mechanical vice

Vishnu /'vishnooh/ *n* the preserver god of the Hindu sacred triad – compare BRAHMA, SIVA [Skt *Viṣṇu*]

visibility /,vizə'biləti/ *n* **1** being visible **2** the clearness of the atmosphere as revealed by the greatest distance at which prominent objects can be identified visually with the naked eye

visible /'vizəbl/ *adj* **1** capable of being seen ⟨*stars ~ to the naked eye*⟩ ⟨*~ light*⟩ **2a** exposed to view ⟨*the ~ horizon*⟩ **b** in the public eye; prominent ⟨*a panel of highly ~ people*⟩ **3** capable of being perceived; noticeable ⟨*her ~ impatience*⟩ **4** tangibly or implicitly present **5** of or being trade in goods rather than services ⟨*~ exports*⟩ – compare INVISIBLE [ME, fr

MF or L; MF, fr L *visibilis*, fr *visus*, pp] – **visibleness** *n*, **visibly** *adv*

,visible ho'rizon *n* HORIZON 1a

Visigoth /'vizi,goth/ *n* a member of the western division of the Goths [LL *Visigothi*, pl] – **Visigothic** /-'gothik/ *adj*

vision /'vizh(ə)n/ *n* **1a** sthg (revelatory) seen in a dream, trance, or ecstasy **b** a mental image of sthg immaterial ⟨*had* ~s *of missing the train*⟩ **2a** the power of imagination; *also* the manner of perceiving mental images ⟨*an artist's* ~⟩ **b** discernment, foresight ⟨*a man of* ~⟩ **c** a supernatural apparition **3a** the act or power of seeing; SIGHT 3a **b** the sense by which the qualities of an object (e g colour, luminosity, shape, and size) constituting its appearance are perceived and which acts through the eye **4a** sthg seen **b** a lovely or charming sight [ME, fr OF, fr L *vision-*, *visio*, fr *visus*, pp of *vidēre* to see – more at WIT] – **visional** *adj*, **visionally** *adv*, **visionless** *adj*

[1]**visionary** /'vizh(ə)nri, -əri/ *adj* **1a** able or likely to see visions **b** disposed to daydreaming or imagining; dreamy **2a** of the nature of a vision; illusory **b** impracticable, utopian ⟨*a* ~ *scheme*⟩ **3** of or characterized by visions or the power of vision – **visionariness** *n*

[2]**visionary** *n* **1** one who sees visions; a seer **2** one whose ideas or projects are impractical; a dreamer

[1]**visit** /'vizit/ *vt* **1a** *archaic, of God* to comfort ⟨~ *us with Thy salvation* – Charles Wesley⟩ **b** to afflict ⟨*a city frequently* ~ed *by the plague*⟩ **c** to inflict punishment for ⟨~ed *the sins of the fathers upon the children*⟩ **2a** to pay a call on for reasons of kindness, friendship, ceremony, or business ⟨~ing *the sick*⟩ **b** to reside with temporarily as a guest **c** to go or come to look at or stay at (e g for business or sightseeing) **d** to go or come officially to inspect or oversee ⟨*a bishop* ~ing *the parish*⟩ ~ *vi* to make a visit or visits [ME *visiten*, fr OF *visiter*, fr L *visitare*, freq of *visere* to go to see, fr *vidēre* to see] – **visitable** *adj*

[2]**visit** *n* **1a** an act of visiting; a call **b** a temporary residence as a guest **c** an extended but temporary stay ⟨*his annual* ~s *abroad*⟩ **2** an official or professional call; a visitation

visitant /'vizit(ə)nt/ *n* **1** a (supernatural) visitor **2** VISITOR 2 – **visitant** *adj*

visitation /,vizi'taysh(ə)n/ *n* **1** the act or an instance of visiting; *esp* an official visit (e g for inspection) **2a** a special dispensation of divine favour or wrath **b** a severe trial; an affliction **3** *cap the* visit of the Virgin Mary to Elizabeth recounted in Luke 1:39–56 and celebrated on July 2 by a Christian festival – **visitational** *adj*

visitatorial /,vizitə'tawri·əl/ *adj* of visitation or an official visitor

'visiting ,card /'viziting/ *n* a small card of introduction bearing the name and sometimes the address and profession of the owner

,visiting pro'fessor *n* a professor invited to join an academic staff for a limited time

visitor /'vizitə/ *n* **1** sby who or sthg that makes (formal) visits **2** a migratory bird that visits a locality for a short time at regular intervals

'visitors' ,book *n* a book in which visitors (e g to a place of interest or hotel) write their names and addresses and sometimes comments

visor, vizor /'viezə/ *n* **1** the (movable) part of a helmet that covers the face **2** a usu movable flat sunshade attached at the top of a vehicle windscreen **3** *chiefly NAm* a peak on a cap [ME *viser*, fr AF, fr OF *visiere*, fr *vis* face – more at VISAGE] – **visored** *adj*, **visorless** *adj*

vista /'vistə/ *n* **1** a distant view esp through or along an avenue or opening; a prospect **2** an extensive mental view (e g over a stretch of time or a series of events) [It, sight, fr *visto*, pp of *vedere* to see, fr L *vidēre* – more at WIT] – **vistaless** *adj*

visual /'viz(h)yooəl/ *adj* **1** of, used in, or produced by vision ⟨~ *organs*⟩ ⟨~ *impressions*⟩ **2** visible ⟨*a* ~ *equivalent for his feelings*⟩ **3** producing mental images; vivid **4** done or executed by sight only ⟨~ *navigation*⟩ [ME, fr LL *visualis*, fr L *visus* sight, fr *visus*, pp of *vidēre* to see] – **visually** *adv*

,visual 'aid *n* an instructional device (e g a chart or film) that appeals chiefly to vision

,visual di'splay ,unit *n* a device that has a cathode ray tube on which information (held in a computer) may be displayed or updated; a VDU ☞ COMPUTER, TELEVISION

,visual 'field *n* the entire expanse of space visible at a given instant without moving the eyes

visual·ize, -ise /'vizhooə,liez/ *vt* **1** to make visible **2** to see or form a mental image of – **visualization** /-'zaysh(ə)n/ *n*

,visual 'purple *n* a light-sensitive red or purple pigment in the retinal rods of various vertebrates; *specif* rhodopsin

vital /'vietl/ *adj* **1** concerned with or necessary to the maintenance of life ⟨~ *organs*⟩ **2** full of life and vigour; animated **3** concerned with, affecting, or being a manifestation of life or living beings **4a** tending to renew or refresh the living; invigorating **b** of the utmost importance; essential to continued worth or well-being [ME, fr MF, fr L *vitalis* of life, fr *vita* life; akin to L *vivere* to live – more at QUICK] – **vitally** *adv*

,vital ca'pacity *n* the breathing capacity of the lungs expressed as the maximum volume of air that can be forcibly exhaled

vitalism /'vietl,iz(ə)m/ *n* a doctrine that the functions of a living organism are due to a vital principle and are not wholly explicable by the laws of physics and chemistry – **vitalist** *n or adj*, **vitalistic** /-'istik/ *adj*

vitality /vie'taləti/ *n* **1a** the quality which distinguishes the living from the dead or inanimate **b** capacity to live and develop; *also* physical or mental liveliness **2** power of enduring ⟨*the* ~ *of an idiom*⟩

vital·ize, -ise /'vietl,iez/ *vt* to endow with vitality; animate – **vitalization** /-'zaysh(ə)n/ *n*

vitals /'vietlz/ *n pl* **1** the vital organs (e g the heart, liver, or brain) **2** essential parts

,vital sta'tistics *n pl* **1** statistics relating to births, deaths, health, etc **2** facts considered to be interesting or important; *specif* a woman's bust, waist, and hip measurements

vitamin /'vitəmin, 'vie-/ *n* any of various organic compounds that are essential in minute quantities to the nutrition of most animals and act esp as (precursors of) coenzymes in the regulation of metabolic processes [L *vita* life + ISV *amine*]

,vitamin 'A *n* any of several fat-soluble vitamins found in egg yolk, milk, cod-liver oil, etc that are converted into retinal in the animal body and whose lack results in night blindness

ˌvitamin ˈB *n* **1** VITAMIN B COMPLEX **2** VITAMIN B_1 **3** VITAMIN B_2 **4** VITAMIN B_6 **5** VITAMIN B_{12}

vitamin B_1 /ˌbee ˈwun/ *n* thiamine

vitamin B_2 /ˌbee ˈtooh/ *n* riboflavin

vitamin B_6 /ˌbee ˈsiks/ *n* (a vitamin B chemically related to) pyridoxine

vitamin B_{12} /ˌbee ˈtwelv/ *n* a cobalt-containing water-soluble vitamin B that occurs esp in liver, is essential for normal blood formation and nerve function, and whose lack or malabsorption results in pernicious anaemia

ˌvitamin ˈB ˌcomplex *n* a group of water-soluble vitamins that are found in most foods and include biotin, choline, folic acid, nicotinic acid, and pantothenic acid

ˌvitamin ˈC *n* a water-soluble vitamin found in (citrus) fruits, spinach, cabbage, or other plant parts that is used as an antioxidant for preserving foods and whose lack results in scurvy

ˌvitamin ˈD *n* any of several fat-soluble vitamins chemically related to the steroids and found esp in animal products (e g fish liver oils, or milk) that are essential for normal bone and tooth structure: e g **a** VITAMIN D_2 **b** VITAMIN D_3

vitamin D_2 /ˌdee ˈtooh/ *n* a synthetic vitamin D used to treat rickets and as a rat poison

vitamin D_3 /ˌdee ˈthree/ *n* the main naturally occurring vitamin D, found in most fish liver oils and formed in the skin of human being on exposure to sunlight

ˌvitamin ˈE *n* any of several fat-soluble compounds found esp in leaves and oils made from seeds whose lack leads to infertility and the degeneration of muscle in many vertebrates animals; *esp* tocopherol

vitamin·ize, -ise /ˈvitəmiˌniez, ˈvie-/ *vt* to provide or supplement with vitamins – **vitaminization** /-ˈzaysh(ə)n/ *n*

ˌvitamin ˈK *n* any of several chemically related naturally occurring or synthetic fat-soluble vitamins essential for the clotting of blood [Dan *k*oagulation coagulation]

vitellin /viˈtelin/ *n* a phosphorus-containing protein in egg yolk [*vitellus*]

vitelline membrane /viˈtelin, -lien/ *n* the membrane that encloses the developing embryo in an egg and that in many invertebrates acts to prevent other spermatozoa from entering

vitellus /viˈteləs/ *n* YOLK 2 [L, lit., small calf – more at VEAL] – **vitelline** /-lin, -lien/ *adj*

vitiate /ˈvishiayt/ *vt* **1** to make faulty or defective; debase ⟨*a spirit* ~d *by luxury*⟩ **2** to invalidate [L *vitiatus*, pp of *vitiare*, fr *vitium* fault, vice] – **vitiator** *n*

viticulture /ˈvitiˌkulchə/ *n* (the science of) the cultivation of grapevines [L *vitis* vine + E *culture* – more at WITHY] – **viticultural** /-ˈkulchərəl/ *adj*, **viticulturist** /-ˈkulchərist/ *n*

vitreous /ˈvitri·əs/ *adj* **1a** resembling glass in colour, composition, brittleness, etc ⟨~ *rocks*⟩ **b** characterized by low porosity and usu translucence ⟨~ *china*⟩ **2** of or being the vitreous humour [L *vitreus*, fr *vitrum* glass – more at WOAD] – **vitreously** *adv*, **vitreousness** *n*

ˌvitreous ˈhumour *n* the colourless transparent jelly that fills the eyeball behind the lens ☞ NERVE

vitrify /ˈvitrifie/ *vb* to convert into or become glass or a glassy substance (by heat and fusion) [F *vitrifier*, fr MF, fr L *vitrum* glass] – **vitrifiable** /ˈ-----, ˌ--ˈ---/ *adj* **vitrification** /-fiˈkaysh(ə)n/ *n*

vitriol /ˈvitri·əl/ *n* **1a** a (hydrated) sulphate of iron, copper, zinc, etc **b** concentrated sulphuric acid **2** virulent speech, expression, feeling, etc [ME, fr MF, fr ML *vitriolum*, alter. of LL *vitreolum*, neut of *vitreolus* glassy, fr L *vitreus* vitreous] – **vitriolic** /-ˈolik/ *adj*

vitta /ˈvitə/ *n, pl* **vittae** /ˈviti/ a stripe, streak [NL, fr L, fillet; akin to L *viēre* to plait – more at WIRE]

vittles /ˈvitlz/ *n pl* food [alter. of *victuals*]

vituperate /viˈtyoohpərayt/ *vt* to subject to severe or abusive censure; berate ~ *vi* to use harsh condemnatory language [L *vituperatus*, pp of *vituperare*, fr *vitium* fault + *parare* to make, prepare – more at PARE] – **vituperator** *n*, **vituperative** /-rətiv/ *adj*, **vituperation** /-ˈraysh(ə)n/ *n*

viva /ˈvievə, ˈveevə/ *n chiefly Br* VIVA VOCE

vivacious /viˈvayshəs/ *adj* lively in temper or conduct; sprightly [L *vivac-, vivax*, lit., long-lived, fr *vivere* to live – more at QUICK] – **vivaciously** *adv*, **vivaciousness** *n*, **vivacity** /viˈvasəti/ *n*

vivandière /viˌvonˈdyeə (*Fr* vivɑ̃djɛːr)/ *n* a woman who in former times accompanied European, esp French, regiments to sell food and drink [F, fem of MF *vivandier*, fr ML *vivanda* food – more at VIAND]

vivarium /vieˈveəri·əm/ *n, pl* **vivaria** /-ri·ə/, **vivariums** an enclosure for keeping and observing plants or esp terrestrial animals indoors [L, park, preserve, fr *vivus* alive – more at QUICK]

viva voce /ˌvievə ˈvohsi, ˌveevə, ˈvohchi/ *n, adj, or adv* (an examination conducted) by word of mouth [adv L, with the living voice; adj & n fr adv]

viverrid /vieˈverid/ *n* a civet, genet, mongoose, or related slender weasel-like flesh-eating mammal with usu retractable claws [NL *Viverridae*, group name, fr *Viverra*, type genus, fr L *viverra* ferret] – **viverrid** *adj*

vivid /ˈvivid/ *adj* **1** full of vigorous life or freshness; lively ⟨~ *personality*⟩ **2** *of a colour* very intense **3** producing a strong or clear impression on the senses; *specif* producing distinct mental images ⟨*a* ~ *description*⟩ [L *vividus*, fr *vivere* to live – more at QUICK] – **vividly** *adv*, **vividness** *n*

vivify /ˈvivifie/ *vt* **1** to give (renewed) life to; animate **2** to impart vitality or vividness to [MF *vivifier*, fr LL *vivificare*, fr L *vivificus* enlivening, fr *vivus* alive] – **vivifier** *n*, **vivification** /-fiˈkaysh(ə)n/ *n*

viviparous /viˈvipərəs/ *adj* **1** producing living young, instead of eggs, from within the body in the manner of nearly all mammals, many reptiles, and a few fishes ☞ LIFE CYCLE **2** germinating while still attached to the parent plant ⟨*the* ~ *seed of the mangrove*⟩ [L *viviparus*, fr *vivus* + *-parus* -parous] – **viviparously** *adv*, **viviparousness** *n*, **viviparity** /ˌviviˈparəti/ *n*

vivisect /ˈvivisekt, --ˈ-/ *vb* to perform vivisection (on) [back-formation fr *vivisection*] – **vivisector** /ˈ----/ *n*

vivisection /viviˈseksh(ə)n/ *n* operation or (distressful) experimentation on a living animal, usu in the course of medical or physiological research [L *vivus* + E *section*] – **vivisectional** *adj*, **vivisectionally** *adv*, **vivisectionist** *n*

vixen /ˈviks(ə)n/ *n* **1** a female fox **2** a scolding ill-tempered woman [(assumed) ME (southern) *vixen*, alter. of ME *fixen*, fr OE *fyxe*, fem of *fox*] – **vixenish** *adj*, **vixenishly** *adv*

vizard /'vizəd/ *n* a mask for disguise or protection [alter. of ME *viser* mask, visor]

vizcacha /viz'kachə/ *n* a viscacha

vizier /vi'ziə/ *n* a high executive officer of various Muslim countries, esp of the former Ottoman Empire [Turk *vezir*, fr Ar *wazīr*] – **vizierate** /-rət, -rayt/ *n*, **vizierial** /-ri·əl/ *adj*, **viziership** *n*

vizor /'viezə/ *n* a visor

vlei /flie/ *n, pl* **vleis** *SAfr* a marshy depression [Afrik *vlei* meadow, valley, fr MD *valeye* valley, field, fr OF *valee* – more at VALLEY]

V neck /vee/ *n* (a garment with) a V-shaped neck ☞ GARMENT

vocable /'vohkəbl/ *n* a word considered as a combination of sounds or letters without regard to its meaning [MF, word, name, fr L *vocabulum*, fr *vocare* to call – more at VOICE]

vocabulary /voh'kabyooləri, və-/ *n* **1** a list of words, and sometimes phrases, usu arranged alphabetically and defined or translated ⟨*a ~ at the back of the book*⟩ **2a** the words employed by a language, group, or individual or in a field of work or knowledge ⟨*her limited ~*⟩ **b** a list or collection of terms or codes available for use (e g in an indexing system) **3** a supply of expressive techniques or devices (e g of an art form) [MF *vocabulaire*, prob fr ML *vocabularium*, fr neut of *vocabularius* verbal, fr L *vocabulum*]

¹**vocal** /'vohkl/ *adj* **1** uttered by the voice; oral **2** of, composed or arranged for, or sung by the human voice **3a** having or exercising the power of producing voice, speech, or sound **b** given to strident or insistent expression; outspoken [ME, fr L *vocalis*, fr *voc-*, *vox* voice – more at VOICE] – **vocally** *adv*, **vocality** /-'kaləti/ *n*

²**vocal** *n* **1** a vocal sound **2** a usu accompanied musical composition or passage for the voice

vocal cords *n pl* either of 2 pairs of mucous membrane folds in the cavity of the larynx whose free edges vibrate to produce sound

vocalic /voh'kalik/ *adj* containing, consisting of, being, functioning as, or associated with a vowel or voiced speech segment [L *vocalis* vowel, fr *vocalis* vocal] – **vocalically** *adv*

vocalism /'vohkl,iz(ə)m/ *n* vocal art or technique in singing

vocalist /'vohkl·ist/ *n* a singer

vocal·ize, -ise /'vohkl,iez/ *vt* to give voice to; utter; *specif* to sing ~ *vi* **1** to utter vocal sounds **2** to sing (without words) – **vocalizer** *n*, **vocalization** /-'zaysh(ə)n/ *n*

vocation /voh'kaysh(ə)n, və-/ *n* **1a** a summons or strong inclination to a particular state or course of action; *esp* a divine call to the religious life **b** an entry into the priesthood or a religious order **2** the work in which a person is regularly employed; a career **3** the special function of an individual or group [ME *vocacioun*, fr L *vocation-*, *vocatio* summons, fr *vocatus*, pp of *vocare* to call – more at VOICE]

vocational /voh'kaysh(ə)nl, və-/ *adj* of or being training in a skill or trade to be pursued as a career ⟨~ *courses*⟩ [VOCATION + ¹-AL] – **vocationally** *adv*

vocative /'vokətiv/ *n* (a form in) a grammatical case expressing the one addressed [ME *vocatif*, adj, fr MF, fr L *vocativus*, fr *vocatus*] – **vocative** *adj*, **vocatively** *adv*

vociferate /voh'sifərayt, və-/ *vb* to cry out or utter loudly; clamour, shout [L *vociferatus*, pp of *vociferari*, fr *voc-*, *vox* voice + *ferre* to bear – more at VOICE, ²BEAR] – **vociferant** *n*, **vociferator** *n*, **vociferation** /-'raysh(ə)n/ *n*

vociferous /voh'sif(ə)rəs, və-/ *adj* marked by or given to vehement insistent outcry – **vociferously** *adv*, **vociferousness** *n*

vocoder /'voh,kohdə/ *n* an electronic mechanism that reduces speech signals to low-frequency signals which can be transmitted over a communications system of limited bandwidth [*voice coder*]

vodka /'vodkə/ *n* a colourless and unaged neutral spirit distilled from a mash (e g of rye or wheat) [Russ, fr *voda* water; akin to OE *wæter* water]

voe /voh/ *n* an inlet or narrow bay of the Orkney or Shetland islands [of Scand origin; akin to Norw *vaag* bay, inlet, ON *vāgr* creek, bay]

vogue /vohg/ *n* **1** the prevailing, esp temporary, fashion ⟨*long skirts were in ~*⟩ **2** popular acceptance or favour; popularity ⟨*book enjoyed a great ~ about 1960*⟩ [MF, action of rowing, course, fashion, fr OIt *voga*, fr *vogare* to row; akin to OSp *bogar* to row] – **vogue** *adj*

¹**voice** /voys/ *n* **1a** sound produced by humans, birds, etc by forcing air from the lungs through the larynx in mammals or syrinx in birds **b(1)** (the use, esp in singing or acting, of) musical sound produced by the vocal cords and resonated by the cavities of the head, throat, lungs, etc **(2)** the power or ability to sing **(3)** any of the melodic parts in a vocal or instrumental composition **(4)** condition of the vocal organs with respect to singing ⟨*be in good ~*⟩ **c** expiration of air with the vocal cords drawn close so as to vibrate audibly (e g in uttering vowels or consonant sounds such as /v/ or /z/) **d** the faculty of utterance; speech **2** a sound suggesting vocal utterance ⟨*the ~ of a foghorn*⟩ **3** an instrument or medium of expression ⟨*the party became the ~ of the workers*⟩ **4a** the expressed wish or opinion ⟨*claimed to follow the ~ of the people*⟩ **b** right of expression; say ⟨*I have no ~ in this matter*⟩ **c** expression – chiefly in *give voice to* **5** distinction of form or a particular system of inflections of a verb to indicate whether it is the subject of the verb that acts ⟨*the passive ~*⟩ [ME, fr OF *vois*, fr L *voc-*, *vox*; akin to OHG *giwahanen* to mention, L *vocare* to call, Gk *epos* word, speech]

²**voice** *vt* **1** to express (a feeling or opinion) in words; utter **2** to adjust (e g an organ pipe) in manufacture, for producing the proper musical sounds **3** to pronounce with voice

'voice ,box *n* the larynx

voiced *adj* **1** having a usu specified type of voice ⟨*soft-*voiced⟩ **2** uttered with vocal cord vibration (e g in /b/) – **voicedness** *n*

'voiceless /-lis/ *adj* not voiced (e g in /p/) [¹VOICE + -LESS] – **voicelessly** *adv*, **voicelessness** *n*

'voice-,over *n* the voice of an unseen narrator in a film or television programme; *also* the voice of a visible character indicating his thoughts

'voice,print /-,print/ *n* a pattern of sound frequencies and amplitudes in the voice that is hypothetically distinctive for each person [*voice* + *-print* (as in *fingerprint*)]

¹**void** /voyd/ *adj* **1** containing nothing; unoccupied

2a devoid ⟨*a nature* ~ *of all malice*⟩ **b** having no members or examples; *specif, of a suit* having no cards represented in a particular hand **3** vain, useless **4** of no legal effect **5** having no holder or occupant; vacant ⟨*a* ~ *bishopric*⟩ – fml [ME *voide*, fr OF, fr (assumed) VL *vocitus*, deriv of L *vacuus* – more at VACUUM] – **voidness** *n*

[2]**void** *n* **1a** empty space; vacuum **b** an opening, gap **2** a feeling of lack, want, or emptiness

[3]**void** *vt* **1** to make empty or vacant; clear **2** to discharge or emit ⟨~ *excrement*⟩ **3** to nullify, annul ⟨~ *a contract*⟩ [ME *voiden*, fr MF *vuidier*, fr (assumed) VL *vocitare*, fr *vocitus*] – **voidable** *adj*, **voider** *n*

voile /voyl/ *n* a fine soft sheer fabric used esp for women's summer clothing or curtains [F, veil, fr L *vela*, neut pl of *velum*]

volant /'vohlənt/ *adj* (capable of) flying [MF, fr L *volant-*, *volans*, prp of *volare* to fly]

volar /'vohlə/ *adj* of the palm of the hand or the sole of the foot [L *vola* palm of the hand, sole of the foot]

[1]**volatile** /'volə,tiel/ *n* a volatile substance [ME *volatil* winged creature, fr OF, fr *volatilie* group of birds, fr ML *volatilia*, fr L, neut pl of *volatilis* winged, volatile]

[2]**volatile** *adj* **1** capable of being readily vaporized at a relatively low temperature ⟨*alcohol is a* ~ *liquid*⟩ **2a** lighthearted, lively **b** dangerously unstable; explosive ⟨*a* ~ *social situation*⟩ **3a** frivolously changeable; fickle **b** characterized by rapid change **4** evanescent, transitory [F, fr L *volatilis* winged, flying, fr *volatus*, pp of *volare* to fly] – **volatility** /-'tiləti/ *n*

volatil·ize, -ise /və'lati,liez/ *vb* to (cause to) evaporate as vapour – **volatilizable** *adj*, **volatilization** /-'zaysh(ə)n/ *n*

vol-au-vent /,vol oh 'vonh, '- - ,-/ *n* a round case of puff pastry filled with a mixture of meat, poultry, or fish in a thick sauce [F, lit., flight in the wind]

volcanic /vol'kanik/ *adj* **1a** of or produced by a volcano **b** characterized by volcanoes **2** explosively violent; volatile ⟨~ *emotions*⟩ – **volcanically** *adv*

volcanic glass *n* natural glass produced by the rapid cooling of molten lava

volcanicity /,volkə'nisəti/, **volcanism** /'volkə,niz(ə)m/ *n* volcanic power or action

volcano /vol'kaynoh/ *n, pl* **volcanoes, volcanos** **1** (a hill or mountain surrounding) an outlet in a planet's crust from which molten or hot rock and steam issue ☞ GEOGRAPHY **2** a dynamic or violently creative person; *also* a situation liable to become violent [It *vulcano*, fr L *Volcanus, Vulcanus* Vulcan, Roman god of fire & metalworking] – **volcanology** /,volkə'noləji/ *n*, **volcanologist** *n*

vole /vohl/ *n* any of various small plant-eating rodents usu with a stout body, blunt nose, and short ears [earlier *vole-mouse*, fr *vole-* (of Scand origin; akin to ON *völlr* field) + *mouse*]

volition /və'lish(ə)n/ *n* **1** (an act of making) a free choice or decision **2** the power of choosing or determining; will [F, fr ML *volition-*, *volitio*, fr L *vol-* (stem of *velle* to will, wish) + *-ition-*, *-itio* (as in L *position-*, *positio* position) – more at WILL] – **volitional** *adj*

volitive /'volətiv/ *adj* of the will – fml

[1]**volley** /'voli/ *n* **1a** a flight of arrows, bullets, or other missiles **b** simultaneous discharge of a number of missile weapons **c(1)** (the course of) the flight of the ball, shuttle, etc before striking the ground; *also* a return or succession of returns made by hitting the ball, shuttle, etc before it touches the ground **(2)** a kick of the ball in soccer before it touches the ground **2** a burst or emission of many things at once or in rapid succession ⟨*a* ~ *of oaths*⟩ [MF *volee* flight, fr *voler* to fly, fr L *volare*]

[2]**volley** *vb* **volleying; volleyed** *vt* **1** to discharge (as if) in a volley **2** to propel (an object that has not yet hit the ground), esp with an implement or the hand or foot ~ *vi* **1** to be discharged (as if) in a volley **2** to make a volley – **volleyer** *n*

'**volley,ball** /-,bawl/ *n* a game between 2 teams of usu 6 players who volley a ball over a high net in the centre of a court

volt /vohlt, volt/ *n* the derived SI unit of electrical potential difference and electromotive force equal to the difference of potential between 2 points in a conducting wire carrying a constant current of 1 ampere when the power dissipated between these 2 points is equal to 1 watt ☞ PHYSICS [Alessandro *Volta* †1827 It physicist]

voltage /'vohltij, 'voltij/ *n* an electric potential difference; electromotive force

voltaic /vol'tayik/ *adj* galvanic [Alessandro *Volta*]

voltameter /vohl'tamitə, vol-/ *n* an apparatus for measuring the quantity of electricity passed through a conductor by the amount of electrolysis produced [ISV *volta*ic + *-meter*] – **voltametric** /,voltə'metrik/ *adj*

volte-face /,volt 'fahs, fas/ *n* a sudden reversal of attitude or policy; an about-face [F, fr It *voltafaccia*, fr *voltare* to turn (fr (assumed) VL *volvitare*, freq of L *volvere* to roll) + *faccia* face, fr (assumed) VL *facia*]

voltmeter /'volt,meetə, 'vohlt-/ *n* an instrument for measuring in volts the differences of potential between different points of an electrical circuit [ISV]

voluble /'volyoobl/ *adj* characterized by ready or rapid speech; talkative [MF or L; MF, variable, rotating, fr L *volubilis*, fr *volvere* to roll; akin to OE *wealwian* to roll, Gk *eilyein* to roll, wrap] – **volubleness** *n*, **volubly** *adv*, **volubility** /-'biləti/ *n*

volume /'volyoohm, 'volyoom/ *n* **1a** a series of printed sheets bound typically in book form; a book **b** a series of issues of a periodical **2** space occupied as measured in cubic units (e g litres); cubic capacity **3a** an amount; *also* a bulk, mass **b** the amount of a substance occupying a particular volume **c** (the representation of) mass in art or architecture **d** a considerable quantity; a great deal – often pl with sing. meaning; esp in *speak volumes for* **4** the degree of loudness or the intensity of a sound [ME, fr MF, fr L *volumen* roll, scroll, fr *volvere* to roll] – **volumed** *adj*

volumetric /,volyoo'metrik/ *adj* **1** of or involving the measurement of volume **2** of or for (or being chemical analysis using known volumes of) solutions of chemical compounds of standard concentration – **volumetrically** *adv*

volume unit *n* the difference in decibels between the power level in an audio circuit and a power level of 1mW in a 500ohm circuit

voluminous /və'lyoohminəs/ *adj* **1** having or containing a large volume; *specif, of a garment* very full

2a consisting of or (capable of) filling a large volume or several volumes ⟨*a ~ correspondence*⟩ **b** writing much or at great length [LL *voluminosus,* fr L *volumin-, volumen*] – **voluminously** *adv,* **voluminousness** *n,* **voluminosity** /və,lyoohmi'nosəti/ *n*

voluntarism /'voləntə,riz(ə)m/ *n* the principle of relying on voluntary action rather than compulsion – **voluntarist** *n,* **voluntaristic** /-'ristik/ *adj*

[1]**voluntary** /'volənt(ə)ri/ *adj* **1** proceeding from free choice or consent **2** acting without compulsion and without payment ⟨*~ workers*⟩ **3** intentional ⟨*~ manslaughter*⟩ **4** of, subject to, or regulated by the will ⟨*~ behaviour*⟩ **5** having power of free choice ⟨*man is a ~ agent*⟩ **6** provided or supported by voluntary action ⟨*a ~ hospital*⟩ [ME, fr L *voluntarius,* fr *voluntas* will, fr *velle* to will, wish – more at WILL] – **voluntarily** /'volənt(ə)rəli, ,volən'terəli/ *adv,* **voluntariness** *n*

[2]**voluntary** *n* an organ piece played before or after a religious service

'**voluntaryism** /-,iz(ə)m/ *n* voluntarism – **voluntaryist** *n*

'**voluntary ,muscle** *n* muscle (e g most striated muscle) under voluntary control

voluntary school *n* a school built by an independent usu religious body but maintained by a British local education authority

[1]**volunteer** /,volən'tiə/ *n* one who undertakes a service of his/her own free will; *esp* sby who enters into military service voluntarily [obs F *voluntaire* (now *volontaire*), fr *voluntaire,* adj, voluntary, fr L *voluntarius*]

[2]**volunteer** *adj* being, consisting of, or engaged in by volunteers ⟨*a ~ army*⟩

[3]**volunteer** *vt* **1** to offer or bestow voluntarily ⟨*~ one's services*⟩ **2** to communicate voluntarily; say ~ *vi* to offer oneself as a volunteer

voluptuary /və'luptyoo(ə)ri/ *n* one whose chief interest is luxury and sensual pleasure – **voluptuary** *adj*

voluptuous /və'luptyoo·əs/ *adj* **1** causing delight or pleasure to the senses; conducive to, occupied with, or arising from sensual gratification ⟨*a ~ dance*⟩ **2** suggestive of sensual pleasure ⟨*a ~ mouth*⟩; *broadly* sexually attractive, esp owing to shapeliness [ME, fr L *voluptuosus,* fr *voluptas* pleasure; akin to Gk *elpis* hope, L *velle* to wish – more at WILL] – **voluptuously** *adv,* **voluptuousness** *n*

volute /və'lyooht/ *n* **1** a form that is shaped like a spiral or curled over on itself like a scroll **2** an ornament characteristic of classical architecture that is shaped like a roll of material or a scroll ☞ ARCHITECTURE **3** (the short-spined thick shell of) any of numerous marine gastropod molluscs [L *voluta,* fr fem of *volutus,* pp of *volvere* to roll] – **volute, voluted** *adj*

volution /və'lyoohsh(ə)n, -'looh-/ *n* **1** a rolling or revolving motion **2** a spiral turn; a twist ☞ ARCHITECTURE [L *volutus,* pp]

volva /'volvə/ *n* a thin membrane round the base of the stem supporting the cap of a fungus [NL, fr L *volva, vulva* integument – more at VULVA]

volvox /'volvoks/ *n* any of a genus of green single-celled microorganisms that exist combined together in spherical colonies [NL, genus name, fr L *volvere* to roll – more at VOLUBLE]

volvulus /'volvyooləs/ *n* twisting of the intestine upon itself, causing obstruction and pain [NL, fr L *volvere*]

vomer /'vohmə/ *n* a bone of the skull of most vertebrate animals that in human beings forms part of the division between the nostrils [NL, fr L, ploughshare] – **vomerine** /-rien, -rin/ *adj*

[1]**vomit** /'vomit/ *n* **1** a vomiting; *also* the vomited matter **2** an emetic [ME, fr MF, fr L *vomitus,* fr *vomitus,* pp of *vomere* to vomit; akin to ON *vāma* nausea, Gk *emein* to vomit]

[2]**vomit** *vb* **1** to disgorge (the contents of the stomach) through the mouth **2** to eject (sthg) violently or abundantly; spew – **vomiter** *n*

vomitory /'vomit(ə)ri/ *n* an entrance piercing the banks of seats of a theatre, amphitheatre, or stadium [LL *vomitorium,* fr L *vomitus,* pp; fr its disgorging the spectators]

[1]**voodoo** /'voohdooh/ *n, pl* **voodoos 1** a set of magical beliefs and practices, mainly of W African origin, practised chiefly in Haiti and characterized by communication by trance with deities **2a** one skilled in (voodoo) spells and necromancy **b** a voodoo spell [LaF *voudou,* of African origin; akin to Ewe *vo*[1] *du*[3] tutelary deity, demon] – **voodoo** *adj,* **voodooism** *n*

[2]**voodoo** *vt* **voodoos; voodooing; voodooed** to bewitch (as if) by means of voodoo

Voortrekker /'faw,trekə, 'fooə-/ *n* a S African pioneer of Dutch descent who moved north from the Cape of Good Hope in 1838 to evade British rule [Afrik, fr *voor* before, in front + *trekker* emigrant, fr *trek* to pull, move, emigrate]

voracious /və'rayshəs/ *adj* **1** having a huge appetite; ravenous **2** excessively eager; insatiable ⟨*a ~ reader*⟩ [L *vorac-, vorax,* fr *vorare* to devour; akin to OHG *querdar* bait, L *gurges* whirlpool] – **voraciously** *adv,* **voraciousness** *n,* **voracity** /və'rasəti/ *n*

-vorous /-v(ə)rəs/ *comb form* (→ *adj*) eating; feeding on ⟨*herbi*vorous⟩ [L *-vorus,* fr *vorare* to devour]

vortex /'vawteks/ *n, pl* **vortices** /'vawtiseez/ *also* **vortexes 1a** a mass of whirling water, air, etc that tends to form a cavity or vacuum in the centre of the circle into which material is drawn; *esp* a whirlpool or whirlwind **b** a region within a body of fluid in which the fluid is rotating **2** sthg that resembles a whirlpool in violent activity or in engulfing or overwhelming [NL *vortic-, vortex,* fr L *vertex, vortex* whirlpool – more at VERTEX] – **vortical** *adj,* **vorticity** /vaw'tisəti/ *n*

vorticella /,vawti'selə/ *n, pl* **vorticellae** /-li/, **vorticellas** any of a genus of bell-shaped cilia-bearing protozoans [NL, genus name, fr L *vortic-, vortex*]

vorticism /'vawti,siz(ə)m/ *n* an English art movement active from about 1912 and related to cubism and futurism [L *vortic-, vortex*] – **vorticist** *n or adj*

vorticose /'vawtikohs, -kohz/ *adj* vortical

votary /'vohtəri/, **votarist** /-rist/ *n* a staunch admirer, worshipper, or advocate; a devotee [L *votum* vow]

[1]**vote** /voht/ *n* **1a** a (formal) expression of opinion or will in response to a proposed decision **b** BALLOT 1 **2** the collective verdict of a body of people expressed by voting **3** *the* franchise **4** a definable group of voters ⟨*getting the Labour ~ to the polls*⟩ **5** a sum of money voted for a special use [ME (Sc), fr L *votum* vow, wish – more at VOW]

[2]**vote** *vi* **1** to cast one's vote; *esp* to exercise a political

franchise **2** to express an opinion ~ *vt* **1** to choose, decide, or authorize by vote **2a** to judge by general agreement; declare ⟨*concert was* ~d *a flop*⟩ **b** to offer as a suggestion; propose ⟨*I* ~ *we all go home*⟩ – infml – **voter** *n*

'voteless /-lis/ *adj* denied the political franchise [[1]VOTE + -LESS]

'voting ma,chine /'vohting/ *n* a mechanical device for recording votes

votive /'vohtiv/ *adj* **1** offered or performed in fulfilment of a vow and often in gratitude or devotion **2** consisting of or expressing a religious vow, wish, or desire [L *votivus*, fr *votum* vow] – **votively** *adv*, **votiveness** *n*

vouch /vowch/ *vi* **1** to give or act as a guarantee *for* **2** to supply supporting evidence or personal assurance *for* [ME *vochen, vouchen* to assert, call to witness, fr MF *vocher*, fr L *vocare* to call, summon, fr *voc-, vox* voice – more at VOICE]

voucher /'vowchə/ *n* **1a** a documentary record of a business transaction **b** a written certificate or authorization **2** *Br* a ticket that can be exchanged for specific goods or services [MF *vocher, voucher* to vouch]

vouchsafe /vowch'sayf/ *vt* **1** to grant as a special privilege or in a gracious or condescending manner **2** to condescend, deign *to* do sthg – **vouchsafement** *n*

voussoir /vooh'swah/ *n* any of the wedge-shaped blocks forming an arch or vault ☞ ARCHITECTURE [F, fr (assumed) VL *volsorium*, fr *volsus*, pp of L *volvere* to roll – more at VOLUBLE]

[1]vow /vow/ *n* a solemn and often religiously binding promise or assertion; *specif* one by which a person binds him-/herself to an act, service, or condition [ME *vowe*, fr OF *vou*, fr L *votum*, fr neut of *votus*, pp of *vovēre* to vow; akin to Gk *euchesthai* to pray, vow]

[2]vow *vt* **1** to promise solemnly; swear **2** to dedicate or consecrate by a vow **3** to resolve to bring about ⟨~ *revenge*⟩ ~ *vi* to make a vow – **vower** *n*

[3]vow *vt* to avow, declare [ME *vowen*, short for *avowen*]

vowel /vowl/ *n* (a letter, in English usu *a, e, i, o, u*, and sometimes *y*, representing) any of a class of speech sounds (e g /ee/ or /i/) characterized by lack of closure in the breath channel or lack of audible friction ☞ ALPHABET [ME, fr MF *vouel*, fr L *vocalis* – more at VOCALIC]

vox populi /,voks 'popyoolie, -li/ *n* the opinion of the general public [L, voice of the people]

[1]voyage /'voyij/ *n* a considerable course or period of travelling by other than land routes; *broadly* a journey [ME, fr OF *voiage*, fr LL *viaticum*, fr L, travelling money, fr neut of *viaticus* of a journey, fr *via* way – more at VIA]

[2]voyage *vb* to make a voyage (across) – **voyager** *n*

voyeur /vwah'yuh/ *n* **1** one who obtains sexual gratification by visual means, specif by looking at sexual organs and sexual acts **2** a prying observer who is usu seeking the sordid or the scandalous [F, lit., one who sees, fr MF, fr *voir* to see, fr L *vidēre* – more at WIT] – **voyeurism** *n*, **voyeuristic** /-'ristik/ *adj*, **voyeuristically** *adv*

vroom /vroom, vroohm/ *n* a noise of an engine revving up or of a high-speed vehicle [imit]

'V ,sign /vee/ *n* a gesture made by raising the index and middle fingers in a V **a** with the palm outwards signifying victory **b** with the palm inwards signifying insult or contempt

vug, vugg, vugh /vug/ *n* a small (crystal-lined) cavity in an ore seam or in rock [Corn dial. *vooga* underground chamber, fr L *fovea* small pit] – **vuggy** *adj*

vulcan·ization, -isation /,vulkənie'zaysh(ə)n/ *n* the process of chemically treating rubber or similar material to give it elasticity, strength, stability, etc [L *Vulcanus* Vulcan – more at VOLCANO] – **vulcanize** *vb*

vulcanology /,vulkə'noləji/ *n* volcanology [ISV] – **vulcanologist** *n*

vulgar /'vulgə/ *adj* **1** generally used, applied, or accepted **2a** of or being the common people; plebeian **b** generally current; public ⟨~ *opinion*⟩ **3a** lacking in cultivation, breeding, or taste; coarse **b** ostentatious or excessive in expenditure or display; pretentious **4** lewdly or profanely indecent; obscene [ME, fr L *vulgaris* of the mob, vulgar, fr *volgus, vulgus* mob, common people; akin to Skt *varga* group] – **vulgarly** *adv*, **vulgarity** /vul'garəti/ *n*

,vulgar 'fraction *n* a fraction in which both the denominator and numerator are explicitly present and are separated by a horizontal or slanted line

vulgarian /vul'geəri·ən/ *n* a vulgar and esp rich person

vulgarism /'vulgə,riz(ə)m/ *n* **1** a word or expression originated or used chiefly by illiterate people **2** vulgarity

vulgar·ize, -ise /'vulgəriez/ *vt* **1** to diffuse generally; popularize **2** to make vulgar; coarsen – **vulgarizer** *n*, **vulgarization** /-'zaysh(ə)n/ *n*

,Vulgar 'Latin *n* the informal Latin of ancient Rome, established as the chief source of the Romance languages

vulgate /'vulgayt, -gət/ *n* **1** *cap the* Latin version of the Bible authorized and used by the Roman Catholic church **2** a commonly accepted text or reading [ML *vulgata*, fr LL *vulgata editio* edition in general circulation]

vulnerable /'vuln(ə)rəbl/ *adj* **1** capable of being physically or mentally wounded **2** open to attack or damage; assailable [LL *vulnerabilis*, fr L *vulnerare* to wound, fr *vulner-, vulnus* wound; akin to Goth *wilwan* to rob, L *vellere* to pluck, Gk *oulē* wound] – **vulnerableness** *n*, **vulnerably** *adv*, **vulnerability** /-rə'biləti/ *n*

vulnerary /'vulnərəri/ *n or adj* (a remedy) used for or useful in healing wounds [adj L *vulnerarius*, fr *vulner-, vulnus*; n fr adj]

vulpine /'vulpien/ *adj* **1** of or resembling a fox **2** foxy, crafty [L *vulpinus*, fr *vulpes* fox; akin to Gk *alōpēx* fox]

vulture /'vulchə/ *n* **1** any of various large usu bald-headed birds of prey that are related to the hawks, eagles, and falcons and feed on carrion ☞ FOOD **2** a rapacious or predatory person [ME, fr L *vultur*] – **vulturous** *adj*, **vulturine** /-rien/ *adj*

vulva /'vulvə/ *n, pl* **vulvas, vulvae** /-vi/ the (opening between the projecting) external parts of the female genital organs [NL, fr L *volva, vulva* integument, womb; akin to Skt *ulva* womb, L *volvere* to roll – more at VOLUBLE] – **vulval, vulvar** *adj*

vying /'vie·ing/ *pres part of* VIE

W

w /ˈdubl,yooh/ *n, pl* **w's, ws** *often cap* (a graphic representation of, or device for reproducing,) the 23rd letter of the English alphabet

Waac /wak/ *n* a member of the Women's Army Auxiliary Corps in WW I [*W*omen's *A*rmy *A*uxiliary *C*orps]

Waaf /waf/ *n* a member of the Women's Auxiliary Air Force in and immediately after WW II [*W*omen's *A*uxiliary *A*ir *F*orce]

Wac /wak/ *n* a member of the Women's Army Corps established in the USA during WW II [*W*omen's *A*rmy *C*orps]

wack /wak/ *n, N Eng* – used as a familiar form of address [short for *wacker,* perh fr *whacker* (heavy blow, anything large), fr *whack*]

wacky /ˈwaki/ *adj, chiefly NAm* absurdly or amusingly eccentric or irrational; crazy – infml [perh fr E dial. *whacky* (fool)] – **wackily** *adv,* **wackiness** *n*

[1]**wad** /wod/ *n* **1a** a soft mass, esp of a loose fibrous material, variously used (e g to stop an aperture or pad a garment) **b(1)** a soft plug used to retain a powder charge, esp in a muzzle-loading cannon or gun **(2)** a felt or paper disc that separates the components of a shotgun cartridge **2** a roll of paper money **3** *chiefly NAm* a considerable amount – infml; often pl with sing. meaning ⟨*getting* ~s *of publicity*⟩ [origin unknown]

[2]**wad** *vt* **-dd- 1** to form into a wad or wadding **2a** to insert a wad into ⟨~ *a gun*⟩ **b** to hold in by a wad ⟨~ *a bullet in a gun*⟩ **3** to stuff, pad, or line with some soft substance **4** *chiefly NAm* to roll or crush tightly ⟨~ *his shirt up into a ball*⟩ – **wadder** *n*

wadding /ˈwoding/ *n* stuffing or padding in the form of a soft mass or sheet of short loose fibres

[1]**waddle** /ˈwodl/ *vi* **waddling** /ˈwadl·ing, ˈwodling/ **1** to walk with short steps swinging the forepart of the body from side to side **2** to move clumsily in a manner suggesting a waddle ⟨*car* ~d *out of the drift* – Len Deighton⟩ [freq of *wade*] – **waddler** *n*

[2]**waddle** *n* an awkward clumsy swaying gait

[1]**waddy** /ˈwodi/ *n, Austr* CLUB 1a [native name in Australia]

[2]**waddy** *vt, Austr* to attack or beat with a club

[1]**wade** /wayd/ *vi* **1** to walk through a medium (e g water) offering more resistance than air **2** to proceed with difficulty or effort ⟨~ *through a dull book*⟩ **3** to attack with determination or vigour – + *in* or *into* ⟨~ *into a task*⟩ ~ *vt* to cross by wading [ME *waden,* fr OE *wadan*; akin to OHG *watan* to go, wade, L *vadere* to go] – **wadable** *adj*

[2]**wade** *n* an act of wading ⟨*a* ~ *in the brook*⟩

wader /ˈwaydə/ *n* **1** *pl* high waterproof boots used for wading **2** any of many long-legged birds (e g sandpipers and snipes) that wade in water in search of food [[1]WADE + [2]-ER]

wadge /woj/ *n, Br* a thick bundle; a wad – infml [alter. of *wedge*]

wadi /ˈwodi/ *n* the bed of a stream in regions of SW Asia and N Africa that is dry except during the rainy season [Ar *wādiy*]

ˈ**wading ˌbird** /ˈwayding/ *n* WADER 2

Waf /waf/ *n* a member of the women's component of the US Air Force formed after WW II [*W*omen in the *A*ir *F*orce]

wafer /ˈwayfə/ *n* **1a** a thin crisp biscuit; *also* a biscuit consisting of layers of wafer sometimes sandwiched with a filling **b** a round piece of thin unleavened bread used in the celebration of the Eucharist **2** an adhesive disc of dried paste used, esp formerly, as a seal [ME, fr ONF *waufre,* of Gmc origin; akin to MD *wafel, wafer* waffle]

waff /wof, waf/ *n, chiefly Scot* **1** a waving motion **2** a puff, gust [E dial. *waff* (to wave), fr ME (northern) *waffen,* alter. of ME *waven*]

[1]**waffle** /ˈwofl/ *n* a cake of batter that is baked in a waffle iron and has a crisp dimpled surface [D *wafel,* fr MD *wafel, wafer*; akin to OE *wefan* to weave]

[2]**waffle** *vi* **waffling** /ˈwofl·ing, ˈwofling/ *chiefly Br* to talk or write foolishly, inconsequentially, and usu at length; blather – infml ⟨*can* ~ *tiresomely off the point* – *TLS*⟩ [freq of obs *woff* (to yelp), of imit origin] – **waffler** *n*

[3]**waffle** *n, chiefly Br* empty or pretentious words – infml – **waffly** *adj*

ˈ**waffle ˌiron** *n* a cooking utensil with 2 hinged metal parts that shut on each other and impress surface projections on the waffle being cooked

[1]**waft** /woft/ *vb* to convey or be conveyed lightly (as if) by the impulse of wind or waves [(assumed) ME *waughten* to guard, convoy, fr MD or MLG *wachten* to watch, guard; akin to OE *wæccan* to watch – more at WAKE] – **wafter** *n*

[2]**waft** *n* **1** sthg (e g a smell) that is wafted; a whiff **2** a slight breeze; a puff

[1]**wag** /wag/ *vb* **-gg-** *vi* **1** to move to and fro, esp with quick jerky motions **2** to move in chatter or gossip ⟨*tongues* ~ged⟩ ~ *vt* **1** to cause to swing to and fro, esp with quick jerky motions; *esp* to nod (the head) or shake (a finger) in assent or mild reproof – often + *at* **2** to move (e g the tongue) animatedly in conversation [ME *waggen*; akin to MHG *wacken* to totter, OE *wegan* to move – more at WAY] – **wagger** *n*

[2]**wag** *n* an act of wagging; a shake

[3]**wag** *n* a wit, joker [prob short for obs *waghalter* (gallows bird), fr [1]*wag* + *halter*]

[1]**wage** /wayj/ *vt* to engage in or carry on (a war, conflict, etc) [ME *wagen* to pledge, give as security, fr ONF *wagier,* fr *wage*]

[2]**wage** *n* **1a** a payment for services, esp of a manual kind, usu according to contract and on an hourly, daily, weekly, or piecework basis – usu pl with sing. meaning; compare SALARY **b** *pl* the share of the national product attributable to labour as a factor in

production 2 a recompense, reward – usu pl with sing. meaning but sing. or pl in constr ⟨*the* ~s *of sin is death* – Rom 6:23 (RSV)⟩ [ME, pledge, wage, fr ONF, of Gmc origin; akin to Goth *wadi* pledge – more at WED] – **wageless** *adj*

[1]**wager** /ˈwayjə/ *n* **1** sthg (e g a sum of money) risked on an uncertain event **2** sthg on which bets are laid ⟨*do a stunt as a* ~⟩ [ME, pledge, bet, fr AF *wageure*, fr ONF *wagier* to pledge]

[2]**wager** *vb* to lay as or make a bet – **wagerer** *n*

ˈ**wage ˌslave** *n* a person dependent on wages or a salary for his/her livelihood

waggery /ˈwagəri/ *n* **1** mischievous merriment **2** a jest; *esp* PRACTICAL JOKE

waggish /ˈwagish/ *adj* befitting or characteristic of a wag; humorous ⟨*a* ~ *disposition*⟩ – **waggishly** *adv*, **waggishness** *n*

waggle /ˈwagl/ *vb* **waggling** /ˈwagling, ˈwagl·ing/ to (cause to) sway or move repeatedly from side to side; wag [freq of [1]*wag*] – **waggle** *n*, **waggly** *adj*

Wagnerian /vahgˈniəri·ən/ *adj* (suggestive) of the music of Wagner, esp in grandiose scale or dramatic intensity [Richard *Wagner* †1883 G composer]

wagon, *chiefly Br* **waggon** /ˈwagən/ *n* **1** a usu 4-wheeled vehicle for transporting bulky or heavy loads, often having a removable canopy, and drawn orig by animals **2** TROLLEY 2a; *esp* one used in a dining room or for serving light refreshments (e g afternoon tea) **3** *Br* a railway goods vehicle [D *wagen*, fr MD – more at WAIN] – **on/off the wagon** abstaining/no longer abstaining from alcoholic drinks – infml

wagoner /ˈwagənə/ *n* the driver of a wagon

wagonette /wagəˈnet/ *n* a light horse-drawn wagon with 2 inward-facing seats along the sides behind a forward-facing front seat

wagon-lit /ˌvagonh ˈlee/ *n*, *pl* **wagons-lits**, **wagon-lits** /lee(z)/ a sleeping car on a continental train [F, fr *wagon* railway car + *lit* bed]

wagtail /ˈwagˌtayl/ *n* any of numerous chiefly Old World birds with trim slender bodies and very long tails that they habitually jerk up and down

Wahhabi, Wahabi /wahˈhahbi, wə-/ *n* a member of a strict Muslim sect founded in Arabia in the 18th c by Muhammad ibn-Abdul Wahhab and revived by ibn-Saud in the 20th c [Ar *wahhābiy*, fr Muḥammad b ʼAbd al-*Wahhāb* (Abdul-Wahhab) †1787 Arab religious reformer] – **Wahhabism** *n*, **Wahhabite** /-ˌbiet/ *adj or n*

wahine /wahˈheeni, -nay/ *n* a Polynesian woman [Maori & Hawaiian]

ˈ**wah-wah ˌpedal** /ˈwah ˌwah/ *n* WA-WA PEDAL

waif /wayf/ *n* **1** a piece of property found but unclaimed **2** a stray helpless person or animal; *esp* a homeless child [ME, fr ONF, adj, lost, unclaimed, prob of Scand origin]

[1]**wail** /wayl/ *vi* **1** to express sorrow by uttering mournful cries; lament **2** to make a sound suggestive of a mournful cry **3** to express dissatisfaction plaintively; complain [ME *wailen*, of Scand origin; akin to ON *væla*, *vāla* to wail; akin to ON *vei* woe – more at WOE] – **wailer** *n*

[2]**wail** *n* **1** a usu loud prolonged high-pitched cry expressing grief or pain **2** a sound suggestive of wailing ⟨*the* ~ *of an air-raid siren*⟩

ˈ**wailful** /-f(ə)l/ *adj* sorrowful, mournful – usu poetic – **wailfully** *adv*

wain /wayn/ *n* **1** a usu large and heavy wagon for farm use **2** *cap* URSA MAJOR [ME, wagon, chariot, fr OE *wægn*; akin to MD *wagen* wagon, OE *wegan* to move – more at WAY]

[1]**wainscot** /ˈwaynskət/ *n* **1a** a usu panelled wooden lining of an interior wall **b** the lower part of an interior wall when finished differently from the remainder of the wall **2** *Br* a fine grade of oak imported for woodwork [ME, fr MD *wagenschot*]

[2]**wainscot** *vt* **-t-**, **-tt-** to line (as if) with boards or panelling

wainscoting, wainscotting /ˈwaynskəting, ˈwaynzˌkoting/ *n* (material used for) a wainscot

wainwright /ˈwaynˌriet/ *n* sby who makes and repairs wagons

waist /wayst/ *n* **1a** the (narrow) part of the body between the chest and hips **b** the greatly constricted part of the abdomen of a wasp, fly, etc **2** the part of sthg corresponding to or resembling the human waist: e g **a(1)** the part of a ship's deck between the poop and forecastle **(2)** the middle part of a sailing ship between foremast and mainmast ☞ SHIP **b** the middle section of the fuselage of an aircraft **3** the part of a garment covering the body at the waist or waistline [ME *wast*; akin to OE *weaxan* to grow – more at [3]WAX]

ˈ**waistˌband** /-ˌband/ *n* a band (e g on trousers or a skirt) fitting round the waist

ˈ**waistˌcoat** /-ˌkoht/ *n*, *chiefly Br* a sleeveless upper garment that fastens down the centre front and usu has a V-neck; *esp* such a garment worn under a jacket as part of a man's suit – **waistcoated** *adj*

ˌ**waist-ˈdeep** *adj or adv* waist-high

waisted /ˈwaystid/ *adj* having a waist, esp of a specified kind – often in combination ⟨*high*-waisted⟩

ˌ**waist-ˈhigh** *adj or adv* up to the waist

ˈ**waistˌline** /-ˌlien/ *n* **1** an imaginary line encircling the narrowest part of the waist; *also* the part of a garment corresponding to this line or to the place where fashion dictates this should be **2** body circumference at the waist

[1]**wait** /wayt/ *vt* **1a** to stay in place in expectation of; await ⟨~ *your turn*⟩ **b** to delay in hope of a favourable change in ⟨~ *out a storm*⟩ **2** to delay serving (a meal), esp in expectation of further arrivals – infml ~ *vi* **1a** to remain stationary in readiness or expectation ⟨~ *for a train*⟩ **b** to pause for another to catch up **2a** to look forward expectantly ⟨*just* ~ing *to see his rival lose*⟩ **b** to hold back expectantly ⟨*have to* ~ *till Thursday*⟩ **3** to serve at meals – usu in *wait at table* or NAm *wait on table* **4** to be ready and available ⟨*slippers* ~ing *by the bed*⟩ [ME *waiten*, fr ONF *waitier* to watch, of Gmc origin; akin to OHG *wahta* watch, OE *wæccan* to watch – more at WAKE] – **wait on/upon 1** to act as an attendant to; serve **2** to await **3** *archaic* to make a formal call on

[2]**wait** *n* **1** any of a group who serenade for gratuities, esp at the Christmas season **2** an act or period of waiting ⟨*a long* ~ *for the bus*⟩ [ME *waite* watchman, public musician, wait, fr ONF, watchman, watch, of Gmc origin; akin to OHG *wahta* watch]

waiter /ˈwaytə/ *n* **1** *fem* **waitress** one who waits at table (e g in a restaurant), esp as a regular job **2** a salver, tray [[1]WAIT + [2]-ER]

ˈ**waiting ˌgame** /ˈwayting/ *n* a postponement of action in the hope of a more favourable opportunity later

'waiting ,list *n* a list of those waiting (e g for a vacancy or for sthg to become available), arranged usu in order of application

'waiting ,room *n* a room for the use of people who are waiting (e g for a train or to see a doctor)

waive /wayv/ *vt* **1** to refrain from demanding or enforcing; relinquish, forgo **2** to put off from immediate consideration; postpone [ME *weiven*, fr ONF *weyver*, fr *waif* lost, unclaimed]

waiver /'wayvə/ *n* (a document giving proof of) the relinquishing of a right [AF *weyver*, fr ONF *weyver* to abandon, waive]

[1]**wake** /wayk/ *vb* **waked, woke** /wohk/; **waked, woken** /'wohkən/, **woke** *vi* **1** to be or remain awake ⟨*her* waking *hours*⟩ **2** to awake – often + *up* ~ *vt* **1** to rouse (as if) from sleep; awake – often + *up* **2** to arouse, evoke ⟨~ *memories*⟩ **3** to arouse conscious interest in; alert – usu + *to* ⟨~ *him to the fact of her existence*⟩ [partly fr ME *waken* (past *wook*, pp *waken*), fr OE *wacan* to awake (past *wōc*, pp *wacen*), and partly fr ME *wakien, waken* (past & pp *waked*), fr OE *wacian* to be awake (past *wacode*, pp *wacod*); akin to OE *wæccan* to watch, L *vegēre* to rouse, excite] – **waker** *n*

[2]**wake** *n* **1a** an annual English parish festival formerly held in commemoration of the church's patron saint **b** VIGIL 1a **2** a watch held over the body of a dead person prior to burial and sometimes accompanied by festivity; *broadly* any festive leavetaking **3** *Br* an annual holiday in northern England – usu pl but sing. or pl in constr ⟨*we all go off to Blackpool during* ~s *week*⟩

[3]**wake** *n* the track left by a moving body (e g a ship) in a fluid (e g water) [of Scand origin; akin to ON *vök* hole in ice; akin to ON *vökr* damp – more at HUMOUR]

'wakeful /-f(ə)l/ *adj* **1** not sleeping or able to sleep **2** spent without sleep ⟨*a* ~ *night*⟩ – **wakefully** *adv*, **wakefulness** *n*

waken /'waykən/ *vi* to awake – often + *up* ~ *vt* to rouse out of sleep; wake [ME *waknen*, fr OE *wæcnian*; akin to ON *vakna* to awaken, OE *wæccan* to watch] – **wakener** *n*

'wake-,robin *n, Br* any of various arums; *esp* a cuckoopint

Waldenses /wol'denseez/ *n pl* a Christian reforming sect arising in S France in the 12th c, adopting Calvinist doctrines in the 16th c, and later living chiefly in Piedmont [ME *Waldensis*, fr ML *Waldenses, Valdenses*, fr Peter *Waldo* (or *Valdo*), 12th-c F heretic] – **Waldensian** /-si·ən/ *adj or n*

[1]**wale** /wayl/ *n* **1** a ridge or lump raised on the body by a heavy blow or slash (e g with a whip) **2** any of a number of extra thick and strong planks in the sides of a wooden ship **3** any of a series of even ribs in a fabric (e g corduroy) [ME, fr OE *walu*; akin to ON *valr* round, L *volvere* to roll – more at VOLUBLE]

[2]**wale** *n, dial Br* **1** an act of choosing; a choice **2** the best part; the pick [ME (Sc & northern) *wal*, fr ON *val*; akin to OHG *wala* choice, OE *wyllan* to wish – more at WILL]

waler /'waylə/ *n, often cap* a horse (formerly exported to India for use in the British Indian army) from New South Wales [New South *Wales*, state of Australia]

[1]**walk** /wawk/ *vi* **1** *of a spirit* to move about in visible form; appear **2a** to move along on foot; advance by steps, in such a way that at least 1 foot is always in contact with the ground **b** to go on foot for exercise or pleasure **c** to go at a walk **3** *of an inanimate object* to move in a manner suggestive of walking **4** *archaic* to pursue a course of action or way of life; conduct oneself ⟨~ *in darkness* – Jn 8:12 (AV)⟩ ~ *vt* **1** to pass on foot through, along, over, or on ⟨~ *the streets*⟩ ⟨~ *a tightrope*⟩ **2a** to cause (an animal) to go at a walk ⟨~ *a horse*⟩ **b** to take (an animal) for a walk ⟨~ing *a dog*⟩ **c** to cause (an inanimate object) to move in a manner suggestive of walking **3** to accompany on foot; walk with ⟨~ed *her home*⟩ **4** to bring to a specified condition by walking ⟨~ed *us off our feet*⟩ **5** to follow on foot for the purposes of examining, measuring, etc ⟨~ed *the horse before the jump-off*⟩ [partly fr ME *walken* (past *welk*, pp *walken*), fr OE *wealcan* to roll, toss (past *wēolc*, pp *wealcen*), and partly fr ME *walkien* (past *walked*, pp *walked*), fr OE *wealcian* to roll up, muffle up; akin to MD *walken* to knead, press, full, L *valgus* bowlegged] – **walk off with 1a** to steal and take away **b** to take away unintentionally **2** to win or gain, esp by outdoing one's competitors without difficulty ⟨walked off with *first prize*⟩ – **walk over** to treat contemptuously – **walk tall** to bear oneself proudly – **walk the plank** to be forced to walk, esp blindfold, along a board laid over the side of a ship until one falls into the sea

[2]**walk** *n* **1a** an act or instance of going on foot, esp for exercise or pleasure ⟨*go for a* ~⟩ **b** SPACE WALK **2** a route for walking ⟨*many delightful* ~s *in the neighbourhood*⟩ **3** a place designed for walking: e g **a** a path specially arranged or surfaced for walking; a footpath **b** a railed or colonnaded platform **c** a promenade **4** a place where animals (e g sheep) are kept with minimal restraint **5** distance to be walked ⟨*a quarter of a mile's* ~ *from here*⟩ **6a** the gait of a 2-legged animal in which the feet are lifted alternately with 1 foot always (partially) on the ground **b** the slow 4-beat gait of a quadruped, specif a horse, in which there are always at least 2 feet on the ground **c** a low rate of speed ⟨*the shortage of raw materials slowed production to a* ~⟩ **7** a route regularly traversed by a person (e g a postman or policeman) in the performance of a particular activity **8** a manner of walking ⟨*his* ~ *is just like his father's*⟩ **9** an occupation, calling – chiefly in *walk of life* **10** a journey undertaken on foot along a usu agreed route to earn money promised by sponsors for charity – esp in *sponsored walk, charity walk*

walkabout /'wawkə,bowt/ *n* **1** a short period of wandering bush life engaged in occasionally by an Australian aborigine for ceremonial reasons **2** an informal walk among the crowds by a public figure ⟨*the Queen on her Jubilee* ~⟩

walker /'wawkə/ *n* sthg used in walking; *specif* a framework designed to support a baby learning to walk or a cripple who cannot walk unaided [[1]WALK + [2]-ER]

walkies /'wawkiz/ *n pl* a walk – used esp to children or animals

walkie-talkie /,wawki 'tawki/ *n* a compact battery-operated transceiver

'walk-,in *adj* large enough for a person to enter and move around in ⟨*a* ~ *safe*⟩

[1]**walking** /'wawking/ *n* the condition of a surface as it will affect sby going on foot ⟨*the* ~ *is slippery*⟩ [[1]WALK + [2]-ING]

[2]**walking** *adj* **1a** animate; *esp* human ⟨*a* ~ *encyclo-*

pedia⟩ **b** able to walk; ambulatory **c** that moves in a manner suggestive of walking ⟨*a* ~ *toy*⟩ **d** guided or operated by a walker ⟨*a* ~ *plough*⟩ **2a** used for or in walking ⟨~ *shoes*⟩ **b** characterized by or consisting of walking ⟨*a* ~ *tour*⟩ [(1) fr prp of [1]*walk*; (2) fr gerund of [1]*walk*]

'walking ,papers *n pl, chiefly NAm* MARCHING ORDERS – infml

'walk-,on *n* (sby who has) a small usu nonspeaking part in a dramatic production

'walk,out /-,owt/ *n* **1** STRIKE 3 **2** the action of leaving a meeting or organization as an expression of protest

walk out *vi* **1** to go on strike **2** to depart suddenly, often as an expression of protest **3** *chiefly Br* COURT 1 – often + *with*; no longer in vogue – **walk out on** to leave in the lurch; abandon

'walk,over /-,ohvə/ *n* an easily won contest; *also* an advance from one round of a competition to the next without contest, due to the withdrawal or absence of other entrants

'walk-,through *n* a perfunctory performance of a play or acting part (e g in an early stage of rehearsal)

'walk,way /-,way/ *n* a passage or platform for walking

[1]**wall** /wawl/ *n* **1** a usu upright and solid structure, esp of masonry or concrete, having considerable height and length in relation to width and serving esp to divide, enclose, retain, or support: e g **a** a structure bounding a garden, park, or estate **b** any of the upright enclosing structures of a room or house **c** RETAINING WALL **d** the surface of a wall ⟨*the* ~ *is painted cream*⟩ **2** a material layer enclosing space ⟨*the* ~ *of a container*⟩ **3** sthg resembling a wall: e g **a** an almost vertical rock surface **b** sthg that acts as a barrier or defence ⟨*tariff* ~⟩ [ME, fr OE *weall*; akin to MHG *wall*; both fr a prehistoric WGmc word borrowed fr L *vallum* rampart, fr *vallus* stake, palisade; akin to ON *völr* round stick, L *volvere* to roll – more at VOLUBLE] – **walled** *adj*, **wall-less** *adj*, **wall-like** *adj* – **to the wall** into a hopeless position ⟨*small businesses being driven* to the wall *by government policy*⟩ – **up the wall** *Br* into a state of exasperation – infml

[2]**wall** *vt* **1a** to protect or surround (as if) with a wall ⟨*a lake* ~ed *in by mountains*⟩ **b** to separate or shut out (as if) by a wall ⟨~ed *off half the house*⟩ **2a** to immure **b** to close (an opening) (as if) with a wall *USE* (2) usu + *up* – **waller** *n*, **walling** *n*

wallaby /'woləbi/ *n, pl* **wallabies** *also esp collectively* **wallaby** any of various small or medium-sized and usu less dull-coloured kangaroos [*wolabā*, native name in New South Wales, Australia]

'Wallace's ,line /'wolisiz/ *n* a hypothetical boundary separating the characteristic Asiatic flora and fauna from that of Australasia [Alfred Russel *Wallace* †1913 Br naturalist]

wallah /'wolə/ *n* a person who does a specified type of work or performs a specified duty – usu in combination; infml ⟨*the book* ~ *was an itinerant peddler* – George Orwell⟩ [Hindi *-wālā* man, one in charge, fr Skt *pāla* protector; akin to Skt *pāti* he protects – more at FUR]

wallaroo /,wolə'rooh/ *n, pl* **wallaroos** a euro [*wolarū*, native name in New South Wales, Australia]

wallboard /'wawl,bawd/ *n* a structural boarding of any of various materials (e g wood pulp, gypsum, or plastic) used esp for sheathing interior walls and ceilings

wallet /'wolit/ *n* **1** a holder for paper money, usu with compartments for other items (e g credit cards and stamps) **2** a flat case or folder ⟨*a* ~ *of maps*⟩ [ME *walet* travelling bag]

walleye /'wawl,ie/ *n* **1** an eye with a whitish iris or opaque white (area in the) cornea **2** (a squint marked by) an eye that turns outwards [back-formation fr *walleyed*, by folk etymology fr ME *wawil-eghed*, part trans of ON *vagl-eygr*, fr *vagl* beam, roost + *eygr* eyed] – **walleyed** *adj*

'wall ,fern *n* a polypody

'wall,flower /-,flowə/ *n* **1** any of several Old World perennial plants of the mustard family; *esp* a hardy erect plant with showy fragrant flowers **2** sby who from shyness or unpopularity remains on the sidelines of a social activity; *esp* a woman who fails to get partners at a dance – infml

Walloon /wo'loohn/ *n* **1** a member of a chiefly Celtic French-speaking people of S Belgium and adjacent parts of France **2** the French dialect of the Walloons [MF *Wallon*, adj & n, of Gmc origin; prob akin to OHG *Walah* Celt, Roman, OE *Wealh* Celt, Welshman – more at WELSH] – **Walloon** *adj*

[1]**wallop** /'woləp/ *n* **1** a powerful body blow; [2]PUNCH 2 – sometimes used interjectionally; infml **2** emotional or psychological force; impact – infml **3** *Br* beer – slang [ME, gallop, fr ONF *walop*, fr *waloper* to gallop]

[2]**wallop** *vt* **1** to hit with force: thrash **2** to beat by a wide margin; trounce *USE* infml – **walloper** *n*, **walloping** *n*

walloping /'woləping/ *adj* large, whopping – infml

[1]**wallow** /'woloh/ *vi* **1** to roll or lie around lazily or luxuriously ⟨*pigs* ~ing *in mud*⟩ **2** to indulge oneself immoderately; revel *in* ⟨~ing *in sentiment*⟩ **3** *of a ship* to struggle laboriously in or through rough water; *broadly* to pitch ⟨*ship* ~ed *down the coast*⟩ [ME *walwen*, fr OE *wealwian* to roll – more at VOLUBLE] – **wallower** *n*

[2]**wallow** *n* **1** an act or instance of wallowing **2a** a muddy or dusty area used by animals for wallowing **b** a depression formed (as if) by the wallowing of animals

'wall ,painting *n* (a) representational or decorative painting directly on (some surface in immediate contact with) a wall (e g in encaustic, fresco, or tempera)

[1]**'wall,paper** /-,paypə/ *n* decorative paper for the walls of a room

[2]**wallpaper** *vb* to apply wallpaper to (the walls of a room)

'wall ,rock *n* rock through which a fault or vein runs

'wall ,rue *n* a small delicate spleenwort found esp on walls or cliffs

'Wall ,Street *n* the influential financial interests of the US economy [*Wall Street* in New York City, site of the New York Stock Exchange]

,wall-to-'wall *adj, of carpeting* covering the whole floor of a room

wally /'woli/ *adj or n, Br* (of or being) an ineffectual or foolish person – slang [perh fr E dial. *wally* pickled cucumber]

walnut /'wawl,nut/ *n* (an edible nut or the wood of)

any of a genus of trees with richly grained wood used for cabinetmaking and veneers [ME *walnot*, fr OE *wealhhnutu*, lit., foreign nut, fr *Wealh* Welshman, foreigner + *hnutu* nut – more at WELSH, NUT]

Wal'purgis ,Night /val'pooəgis/ *n* the eve of May Day on which, according to Germanic legend, witches gather in an annual ceremony [part trans of G *walpurgisnacht*, fr *Walpurgis* St Walburga †777 E saint whose feast day falls on May Day + G *nacht* night]

walrus /'wawlrəs/ *n, pl* **walruses,** *esp collectively* **walrus** either of 2 large sea mammals of northern seas, related to the seals, and hunted for their tough heavy hide, ivory tusks, and the oil yielded by the blubber [D, of Scand origin; akin to Dan & Norw *hvalros* walrus, ON *rosmhvalr*]

,walrus mou'stache *n* a thick moustache that droops down at each side

[1]waltz /wawlts/ *n* (music for or in the tempo of) a ballroom dance in $\frac{3}{4}$ time with strong accent on the first beat [G *walzer*, fr *walzen* to roll, dance, fr OHG *walzan* to turn, roll – more at WELTER]

[2]waltz *vi* **1** to dance a waltz **2** to move *along* in a lively or confident manner **3** to proceed easily or boldly; breeze ⟨~ed *through his finals*⟩ ~ *vt* **1** to dance a waltz with ⟨~ed *her round the room*⟩ **2** to grab and lead (e g a person) unceremoniously; march – usu + *off* ***USE*** (*vi 2&3; vt* 2) infml – **waltzer** *n*

wampum /'wompəm/ *n* beads of polished shells strung together and used by N American Indians as money and ornaments [short for *wampumpeag*, fr Narraganset *wampompeag*, fr *wampan* white + *api* string + *-ag*, pl suffix]

wan /won/ *adj* **-nn-** **1a** suggestive of poor health; pallid **b** lacking vitality; feeble **2** *of light* dim, faint [ME, fr OE, dark, livid] – **wanly** *adv*, **wanness** *n*

wand /wond/ *n* a slender rod **a** carried as a sign of office **b** used by conjurers and magicians [ME, slender stick, fr ON *vöndr*; akin to OE *windan* to wind, twist – more at [4]WIND]

wander /'wondə/ *vi* **1** to go or travel idly or aimlessly ⟨~ *across the room*⟩ **2** to follow or extend along a winding course; meander ⟨*road* ~s *across the plain*⟩ **3a** to deviate (as if) from a course; stray ⟨*eyes* ~ed *from the page*⟩ **b** to lose concentration; stray in thought ⟨*as the lecturer droned on, the student's mind began to* ~⟩ **c** to think or speak incoherently or illogically ⟨*as the fever worsened, the patient began to* ~⟩ ~ *vt* to roam over ⟨~ed *the hillside in search of shelter*⟩ [ME *wandren*, fr OE *wandrian*; akin to MHG *wandern* to wander, OE *windan* to wind, twist] – **wander** *n*, **wanderer** *n*

[1]wandering /'wondəring/ *n* **1** a going about from place to place **2** movement away from the proper or usual course or place ***USE*** often pl with sing. meaning

[2]wandering *adj* **1** winding, meandering ⟨*a* ~ *course*⟩ **2** not keeping a rational or sensible course ⟨~ *thoughts*⟩ **3** nomadic ⟨~ *tribes*⟩

,Wandering 'Jew *n* **1** a Jew of medieval legend condemned by Christ to wander over the earth till Christ's second coming **2** *not cap W* either of 2 trailing or creeping plants with showy often white-striped foliage

wanderlust /'wondə,lust/ *n* eager longing for or impulse towards travelling [G, fr *wandern* to wander + *lust* desire, pleasure]

wanderoo /,wondə'rooh/ *n, pl* **wanderoos** **1** a purple-faced langur of Sri Lanka **2** a macaque of the Indian subcontinent [Sinhalese *vanduru*, pl of *vandurā*, fr Skt *vānara* monkey, fr *vanar-*, *vana* forest; akin to Av *vana* forest]

[1]wane /wayn/ *vi* **1** to decrease in size or extent; dwindle: e g **a** *of the moon, satellites, etc* to diminish in phase or intensity **b** *of light or colour* to become less brilliant; dim **2** to fall gradually from power, prosperity, or influence; decline [ME *wanen*, fr OE *wanian*; akin to OHG *wanōn* to wane, OE *wan* wanting, deficient, L *vanus* empty, vain]

[2]wane *n* **1a** the act or process of waning **b** a time of waning; *specif* the period from full phase of the moon to the new moon **2** a defect in prepared timber characterized by bark or lack of wood at a corner or edge – **waney, wany** *adj* – **on the wane** in a state of decline; waning

wangle /'wang·gl/ *vt* **wangling** /'wang·gling/ **1** to adjust or manipulate for personal or fraudulent ends **2** to bring about or get by devious means ⟨~ *an invitation*⟩ ***USE*** infml [perh alter. of *waggle*] – **wangler** *n*

wank /wangk/ *vi, Br* to masturbate – vulg [origin unknown] – **wank** *n*

Wankel engine /'wangkl/ *n* a rotary internal-combustion engine that has an eccentrically mounted rounded triangular rotor functioning as a piston and rotating in a space in the engine, and that has only 2 major moving parts [Felix *Wankel b* 1902 G engineer]

wanker /'wangkə/ *n* **1** one who masturbates – vulg **2** a foolish or superficial fellow – slang

[1]want /wont/ *vt* **1** to fail to possess, esp in customary or required amount; lack ⟨*his answer* ~s *courtesy*⟩ **2a** to have a desire for ⟨*he* ~s *to go*⟩ **b** to have an inclination to; like ⟨*say what you* ~, *he is efficient*⟩ **3a** to have need of; require ⟨*the room* ~s *decorating*⟩ **b** to suffer from the lack of; need ⟨*thousands still* ~ *food and shelter*⟩ **4** to wish or demand the presence of ⟨*the boss* ~s *you*⟩ **5** ought – + *to* and infinitive ⟨*you* ~ *to see a doctor about that cold*⟩ ~ *vi* **1** to be deficient or short by a specified amount ⟨*it* ~s *3 minutes to 12*⟩ **2** to be needy or destitute **3** to have need; be lacking in the specified respect ⟨*never* ~s *for friends*⟩ **4** *chiefly NAm* to desire to come or go ⟨~s *out of the syndicate*⟩ [ME *wanten*, fr ON *vanta*; akin to OE *wan* deficient]

[2]want *n* **1a** the quality or state of lacking sthg required or usual ⟨*he suffers from a* ~ *of good sense*⟩ **b** extreme poverty **2** sthg wanted; a need ⟨*supply your* ~s⟩

wanting /'wonting/ *adj* **1** not present or in evidence; absent **2a** not up to the required standard or expectation ⟨*a candidate tested and found* ~⟩ **b** lacking in the specified ability or capacity; deficient ⟨~ *in gratitude*⟩

[1]wanton /'wont(ə)n/ *adj* **1** mischievous **2** sexually unbridled; promiscuous **3** having no just foundation or provocation; malicious ⟨~ *indifference to the needs of others*⟩ **4** uncontrolled, unbridled ⟨~ *inflation*⟩ **5** luxuriant, lavish – now chiefly poetic [ME, fr *wan-* deficient, wrong, mis- (fr OE, fr *wan* deficient) + *towen*, pp of *teen* to draw, train, discipline, fr OE *tēon* – more at TOW] – **wantonly** *adv*, **wantonness** *n*

[2]wanton *n* a wanton person; *esp* a lewd or lascivious woman

wapentake /'wopəntayk, 'wapən-/ *n* a former subdivision of some English shires corresponding to a hundred [ME, fr OE *wǣpentæc*, fr ON *vāpnatak* act of grasping weapons, fr *vāpn* weapon + *tak* act of grasping, fr *taka* to take; prob fr the brandishing of weapons as an expression of approval when the chief of the wapentake entered upon his office – more at WEAPON, TAKE]

wapiti /'wopiti/ *n, pl* **wapitis,** *esp collectively* **wapiti** an American deer similar to the European red deer but larger [of Algonquian origin; akin to Cree *wapitew* white, whitish; fr its white rump and tail]

[1]war /waw/ *n* **1** a state or period of usu open and declared armed hostile conflict between states or nations **2** a struggle between opposing forces or for a particular end ⟨*a ~ against disease*⟩ [ME *werre*, fr ONF, of Gmc origin; akin to OHG *werra* strife; akin to OHG *werran* to confuse, L *verrere* to sweep]

[2]war *vi* **-rr- 1** to engage in warfare **2a** to be in active or vigorous conflict **b** to be opposed or inconsistent ⟨*~ring principles*⟩

[1]warble /'wawbl/ *vb* **warbling** /'wawbling, 'wawbl·ing/ *vi* to sing or sound in a trilling manner or with many turns and variations ~ *vt* to render musically, esp in an ornamented or trilling manner [ONF *werbler*, fr *werble* tune, modulation, of Gmc origin; akin to MHG *wirbel* whirl, tuning peg, OHG *wirbil* whirlwind – more at WHIRL] – **warble** *n*

[2]warble *n* (a swelling under the hide of cattle, horses, etc caused by) the maggot of a warble fly [perh of Scand origin; akin to obs Sw *varbulde* boil, fr *var* pus + *bulde* swelling] – **warbled** *adj*

'warble ,fly *n* any of various 2-winged flies whose larvae live under the skin of various mammals and cause swellings

warbler /'wawblə/ *n* any of numerous small Old World birds (e g a whitethroat) which are related to the thrushes and many of which are noted songsters [[1]WARBLE + [2]-ER]

'war ,bride *n* a woman who marries a (foreign) serviceman met during a time of war

'war ,chest *n* a fund accumulated to finance a war

'war ,crime *n* a crime (e g genocide or maltreatment of prisoners) committed during or in connection with war – **war criminal** *n*

'war ,cry *n* **1** a cry used during charging or rallying by a body of fighters in war **2** a slogan used esp to rally people to a cause

ward /wawd/ *n* **1** the inner court of a castle or fortress **2** a division of a prison or hospital **3** a division of a city or town for electoral or administrative purposes **4** a projecting ridge of metal in a lock casing or keyhole allowing only a key with a corresponding notch to operate; *also* a corresponding notch on a key **5** a person under guard, protection, or surveillance; *esp* one under the care or control of a legal guardian ⟨*~ of court*⟩ [ME, fr OE *weard* act of watching or guarding; akin to OHG *warta* act of watching, OE *warian* to beware of, guard – more at [1]WARE] – **warded** *adj*

[1]-ward /-wood/ *also* **-wards** /-woodz/ *suffix* (→ *adj*) **1** facing or tending in (such) a direction ⟨*home*ward⟩ ⟨*north*ward⟩ **2** occurring or situated in (such) a direction ⟨*left*ward⟩ [*-ward* fr ME, fr OE *-weard*; akin to OHG *-wart, -wert* -ward, L *vertere* to turn; *-wards* fr *-wards*, adv suffix – more at WORTH]

[2]-ward *suffix* (→ *adv*), *chiefly NAm* -wards [ME, fr OE *-weard*, fr *-weard*, adj suffix]

'war ,dance *n* a dance performed esp by primitive peoples as preparation for battle or in celebration of victory

warden /'wawd(ə)n/ *n* **1** one having care or charge of sthg; a guardian **2** the governor of a town, district, or fortress **3** an official charged with special supervisory duties or with the enforcement of specified laws or regulations ⟨*game ~*⟩ ⟨*air-raid ~*⟩ ⟨*traffic ~*⟩ **4** any of various British college officials **5** *NAm* a prison governor [ME *wardein*, fr ONF, fr *warder* to guard, of Gmc origin; akin to OHG *wartēn* to watch] – **wardenship** *n*

[1]warder /'wawdə/, *fem* **wardress** /'wawdris/ *n* **1** *Br* a prison guard **2** *archaic* a watchman, guard [ME, one who guards a gate, fr AF *wardere*, fr *warde* act of guarding, of Gmc origin; akin to OHG *warta* act of watching] – **wardership** *n*

[2]warder *n* a staff formerly used by a king or commander in chief to signal orders [ME, perh fr *warden* to guard]

ward off *vt* to deflect, avert [*ward* (to guard), fr ME *warden*, fr OE *weardian*; akin to OHG *wartēn* to watch, ON *vartha* to guard, OE *weard* ward]

wardrobe /'waw,drohb/ *n* **1** a room or (movable) cupboard, esp fitted with shelves and a rail or pegs, where clothes are kept **2a** a collection of clothes (e g belonging to 1 person) **b** a collection of stage costumes and accessories **3** the department of a royal or noble household entrusted with the care of clothes, jewels, and personal articles [ME *warderobe*, fr ONF, fr *warder* to guard + *robe* robe]

wardroom /'wawdroohm, -room/ *n* the space in a warship allotted to the commissioned officers excepting the captain

-wards /-woodz/ *suffix* (→ *adv*) **1** in (such) a spatial or temporal direction ⟨*up*wards⟩ ⟨*after*wards⟩ **2** towards (such) a point, position, or place ⟨*earth*wards⟩ [ME, fr OE *-weardes*, gen sing. neut of *-weard*, adj suffix – more at [1]-WARD]

wardship /'wawdship/ *n* **1** care and protection of a ward; tutelage **2** being under a guardian

[1]ware /weə/ *vt* to beware of – used chiefly as a command to hunting animals [ME *waren*, fr OE *warian*; akin to OHG bi*warōn* to protect, OE *wær* aware]

[2]ware *n* **1a** manufactured articles or products of art or craft; goods – often in combination ⟨*tin*ware⟩ **b** *pl* goods for sale **2** articles of fired clay; *esp* a specified make of pottery or china ⟨*Parian ~*⟩ [ME, fr OE *waru*; akin to MHG *ware* ware, & prob to OE *wær* aware]

warehouse /'weə,hows/ *vt or n* (to deposit, store, or stock in) a structure or room for the storage of merchandise or commodities – **warehouser** /-zə/ *n*

'ware,houseman /-mən/ *n* one who controls or works in a warehouse

warfare /'waw,feə/ *n* **1** hostilities, war **2** struggle, conflict [ME, fr *werre, warre* war + *fare* journey, passage – more at [2]FARE]

warfarin /'wawfərin/ *n* a synthetic compound that is used in medicine to prevent the blood clotting (e g in the treatment of thrombosis) and is also used as a rodent poison [*W*isconsin *A*lumni *R*esearch *F*oundation (its patentee) + coum*arin*]

'war ,game *n* **1** an exercise or simulated battle to

test military ability **2** an enactment of a conflict in miniature using counters or models to represent the combatants – **wargaming** *n*

warhead /'waw,hed/ *n* the section of a missile containing the explosive, chemical, or incendiary charge

'war-,horse *n* **1** a powerful horse used in war **2** a veteran soldier or public figure **3** a work of art (e g a musical composition) that has become hackneyed from repetition in the standard repertoire

'war,like /-,liek/ *adj* **1** fond of war **2** of or useful in war **3** hostile

warlock /'wawlok/ *n* a man practising black magic; a sorcerer [ME *warloghe*, fr OE *wǣrloga* one who breaks faith, the Devil, fr *wǣr* faith, troth + *-loga* (fr *lēogan* to lie); akin to OE *wǣr* true – more at VERY, [3]LIE]

warlord /'waw,lawd/ *n* a supreme military leader

[1]warm /wawm/ *adj* **1a** having or giving out heat to a moderate or adequate degree ⟨*a ~ bath*⟩; *also* experiencing heat to this degree ⟨*are you ~ enough?*⟩ **b** serving to maintain or preserve heat, esp to a satisfactory degree ⟨*a ~ sweater*⟩ **c** feeling or causing sensations of heat brought about by strenuous exertion ⟨*a ~ climb*⟩ **2a** marked by enthusiasm; cordial ⟨*a ~ welcome*⟩ **b** marked by excitement, disagreement, or anger ⟨*a ~ debate*⟩ **3** affectionate and outgoing in temperament ⟨*a ~ personality*⟩ **4** dangerous, hostile **5** *of a trail, scent, etc* newly made; fresh **6** *of a colour* producing an impression of being warm; *specif* in the range yellow to red **7** near to a goal, object, or solution sought – chiefly in children's games [ME, fr OE *wearm*; akin to OHG *warm* warm, L *formus*, Gk *thermos* warm, hot] – **warmish** *adj*, **warmness** *n*, **warmly** *adv*

[2]warm *vt* **1** to make warm **2** to infuse with a feeling of love, friendship, well-being, or pleasure **3** to reheat (cooked food) for eating – often + *up* in Br or *over* in NAm ~ *vi* **1** to become warm **2** to become filled with interest, enthusiasm, or affection – + *to* or *towards* ⟨*did not ~ to the newcomer*⟩ ⟨*~ing to his theme*⟩ – **warm the cockles of one's heart** to make one happy; cheer, encourage

[3]warm *n* **1** an act of getting or making warm ⟨*come to the fire for a ~*⟩ **2** *Br* a warm place or state ⟨*sit here in the ~*⟩

,warm-'blooded *adj* **1** having a relatively high and constant body temperature more or less independent of the environment – compare COLD-BLOODED **2** fervent or ardent in spirit – **warm-bloodedness** *n*

,warm 'front *n* an advancing edge of a warm air mass

,warm'hearted /-'hahtid/ *adj* marked by ready affection, cordiality, generosity, or sympathy – **warmheartedly** *adv*, **warmheartedness** *n*

'warming ,pan /'wawming/ *n* a usu long-handled flat covered pan (e g of brass) filled with hot coals, formerly used to warm a bed

warmonger /'waw,mung·gə/ *n* one who attempts to stir up war – **warmongering** *n*

warmth /wawmth/ *n* the quality or state of being warm **a** in temperature **b** in feeling ⟨*a child needing human ~*⟩

'warm-,up *n* the act or an instance of warming up; *also* a procedure (e g a set of exercises) used in warming up

warm up *vi* **1** to engage in exercise or practice, esp before entering a game or contest; *broadly* to get ready **2** HOT UP ~ *vt* HOT UP; *esp* to put (an audience) into a receptive mood (e g before a show), esp by telling jokes, singing, etc

warn /wawn/ *vt* **1a** to give notice to beforehand, esp of danger or evil ⟨*~ them of the floods*⟩ **b** to give admonishing advice to; counsel ⟨*~ them not to open the door*⟩ **c** to notify, inform ⟨*~ them of my intentions*⟩ **2** to order to go or stay away – often + *off* or *away* ~ *vi* to give a warning [ME *warnen*, fr OE *warnian*; akin to OHG *warnōn* to take heed, OE *wær* careful, aware – more at WARY] – **warner** *n*

warning /'wawning/ *n* sthg that warns; *also* NOTICE 1b [WARN + [2]-ING] – **warning** *adj*, **warningly** *adv*

warning coloration *n* an animal's conspicuous colouring that warns off potential enemies

,war of at'trition *n* a war of little movement in which the side with the largest reserves (e g of men and supplies) gains the victory

'War ,Office *n* the former British Government department in charge of the army – now part of the Ministry of Defence

,war of 'nerves *n* (a conflict characterized by) the use of psychological tactics (e g bluff, threats, or intimidation) designed to destroy the enemy's morale

[1]warp /wawp/ *n* **1a** a series of yarns extended lengthways in a loom and crossed by the weft **b** the cords forming the carcass of a pneumatic tyre **2** a rope for warping a ship or boat **3** sediment deposited by (standing) water **4a** a twist or curve that has developed in sthg formerly flat or straight ⟨*a ~ in a door panel*⟩ **b** a mental twist or aberration [ME, fr OE *wearp*; akin to OHG *warf* warp, ON *verpa* to throw; (4) [2]*warp*] – **warpage** *n*

[2]warp *vt* **1a** to turn or twist (e g planks) out of shape, esp out of a plane **b** to cause to think or act wrongly; pervert **2** to arrange (yarns) so as to form a warp **3** to manoeuvre (e g a ship) by hauling on a line attached to a fixed object ~ *vi* **1** to become warped **2** to move a ship by warping [ME *warpen*, fr OE *weorpan* to throw; akin to ON *verpa* to throw, Gk *rhembein* to whirl; (vt 2) ME *warpen*, fr [1]*warp*; (vt 3) [1]*warp*] – **warper** *n*

'war ,paint *n* **1** paint put on the body by N American Indians as a sign of going to war **2** ceremonial dress; regalia **3** cosmetics *USE* (*2&3*) infml

'war ,party *n* a group of N American Indians going on a warlike expedition

warpath /'waw,pahth/ *n* the route taken by a war party of N American Indians – **on the warpath** pursuing an angry or hostile course; taking or starting to take action in a struggle or conflict

'warp ,beam *n* a roller on which the warp is wound for a loom

,warp-'knitted *adj* produced in machine knitting with the yarns running in a lengthways direction

warplane /'waw,playn/ *n* an (armed) military aircraft

[1]warrant /'worənt/ *n* **1a** a sanction, authorization; *also* evidence for or token of authorization **b** a guarantee, security **c** a ground, justification; *also* proof ⟨*his assertion was totally without ~*⟩ **2** a commission or document giving authority: e g **a** a document authorizing sby to receive money or other consideration ⟨*travel ~*⟩ **b** a document authorizing an officer to make an arrest, a search, etc **c** an official certificate of appointment issued to a noncommissioned officer **d(1)** a short-term obligation of a governmental body (e g a municipality) issued in anticipation of revenue (2) a document issued by a company giving to the holder the right to purchase the capital stock of the company at a stated price either prior to a stipulated date or at any future time [ME, protector, warrant, fr ONF *warant*, modif of a Gmc noun represented by OHG *werēnto* guarantor, fr prp of *werēn* to warrant; akin to OHG *wāra* trust, care – more at VERY] – **warrantless** *adj*

²**warrant** *vt* **1** to declare or maintain with certainty ⟨*I'll* ~ *he'll be here by noon*⟩ **2** to guarantee to be as represented **3** to give sanction to ⟨*the law* ~s *this procedure*⟩ **4a** to prove or declare the authenticity or truth of **b** to give assurance of the nature of or for the undertaking of; guarantee **5** to serve as or give adequate ground or reason for ⟨*the situation* ~s *dramatic action*⟩ [ME *warranten*, fr ONF *warantir*, fr *warant*] – **warrantable** *adj*, **warrantor** /-taw, -tə/, **warranter** *n*

warrantee /ˌworənˈtee/ *n* sby to whom a warranty is made

ˈ**warrant ˌofficer** *n* ☞ RANK

warrant officer first class *n* ☞ RANK

warrant officer second class *n* ☞ RANK

warranty /ˈworənti/ *n* **1** a collateral undertaking that a fact regarding the subject of a contract is or will be as declared **2** sthg that authorizes, supports, or justifies; a warrant **3** a usu written guarantee of the soundness of a product and of the maker's responsibility for repair or replacement [ME *warantie*, fr ONF, fr *warantir* to warrant]

warren /ˈworən/ *n* **1** an area of ground (or a structure) where rabbits breed **2a** a crowded tenement or district **b** a maze of narrow passageways or cubbies; *broadly* anything intricate or confused [ME *warenne* land reserved for breeding game (esp rabbits), fr ONF]

warrior /ˈwori·ə/ *n* a man engaged or experienced in warfare [ME *werriour*, fr ONF *werreieur*, fr *werreier* to make war, fr *werre* war]

warship /ˈwawˌship/ *n* an (armed) ship for use in warfare

wart /wawt/ *n* **1** a horny projection on the skin, usu of the hands or feet, caused by a virus; *also* a protuberance, esp on a plant, resembling this **2** an ugly or objectionable man or boy – chiefly Br schoolboy slang **3** a blemish – often in *warts and all* [ME, fr OE *wearte*; akin to OHG *warza* wart, L *verruca*] – **warty** *adj*

warthog /ˈwawtˌhog/ *n* any of a genus of African wild pigs with 2 pairs of rough warty lumps on the face and large protruding tusks

wartime /ˈwawˌtiem/ *n* a period during which a war is in progress

war-weary /ˈ-ˌ--, ˌ-ˈ--/ *adj* exhausted and dejected by prolonged war

wary /ˈweəri/ *adj* marked by caution and watchful prudence in detecting and escaping danger [arch *ware* (conscious, cautious), fr ME *war, ware*, fr OE *wær* careful, aware, wary; akin to OHG *giwar* aware, attentive, L *vereri* to fear, Gk *horan* to see] – **warily** *adv*, **wariness** *n*

was /wəz; *strong* woz/ *past 1 & 3 sing of* BE [ME, fr OE, 1 & 3 sing. past indic of *wesan* to be; akin to ON *vera* to be, *var* was, Skt *vasati* he lives, dwells]

¹**wash** /wosh/ *vt* **1a** to cleanse (as if) by the action of liquid (e g water) **b** to remove (e g dirt) by applying liquid **2** *of an animal* to cleanse (fur or a furry part) by licking or by rubbing with a paw moistened with saliva **3a** to flush or moisten (a body part or injury) with liquid **b** to suffuse with light **c** to pass water over or through, esp so as to carry off material from the surface or interior **4** to flow along, over, or against ⟨*waves* ~ing *the shore*⟩ **5** to move, carry, or deposit (as if) by the force of water in motion ⟨*houses* ~ed *away by the flood*⟩ **6a** to agitate (e g crushed ore) in water to separate valuable material; *also* to separate (particles) thus **b** to pass (e g a gas) through or over a liquid to carry off impurities or soluble components **7** to cover or daub lightly with a thin coating (e g of paint or varnish) **8** to cause to swirl ⟨~ing *coffee round in his cup*⟩ ~ *vi* **1a** to wash oneself or a part of one's body **b** to wash articles; do the washing ☞ SYMBOL **2** to bear washing without damage ⟨*does this dress* ~*?*⟩ **3** to drift along on water **4** to pour or flow in a stream or current **5** to gain acceptance; inspire belief ⟨*his story didn't* ~ *with me*⟩ ⟨*an interesting theory, but it just won't* ~⟩ – infml [ME *washen*, fr OE *wascan*; akin to OHG *waskan* to wash, OE *wæter* water] – **wash one's hands of** to disclaim interest in, responsibility for, or further connection with

²**wash** *n* **1a** (an instance of) washing or being washed **b** articles for washing **c** an area or structure equipped with facilities for washing a vehicle ⟨*a car* ~⟩ **2** the surging action of waves **3a** a piece of ground washed by the sea or river **b** a shallow body of water **4a** worthless esp liquid waste; *also* swill **b** vapid writing or speech **5a** a thin coat of paint (e g watercolour) **b** a thin liquid used for coating a surface (e g a wall) **6** a lotion **7** loose or eroded surface soil, rock debris, etc transported and deposited by running water **8a** BACKWASH 1 **b** a disturbance in the air produced by the passage of an aircraft

washable /ˈwoshəbl/ *adj* capable of being washed without damage ☞ SYMBOL – **washability** /-ˈbiləti/ *n*

ˈ**washˌbasin** /-ˌbays(ə)n/ *n* a basin or sink usu connected to a water supply for washing the hands and face

ˈ**washˌboard** /-ˌbawd/ *n* a corrugated board for scrubbing clothes on when washing

washbowl /-ˌbohl/ *n* a washbasin

ˈ**washˌcloth** /-ˌkloth/ *n, NAm* FLANNEL 3

wash down *vt* **1** to send downwards by action of a liquid; *esp* to facilitate the swallowing of (food) by taking gulps of liquid **2** to wash the whole surface of ⟨washed down *and scrubbed the front step*⟩

ˈ**wash ˌdrawing** *n* (a) watercolour painting done (mainly) in washes, esp in black, white, and grey tones only

ˌ**washed-ˈout** *adj* **1** faded in colour **2** listless, exhausted – infml

ˌ**washed-ˈup** *adj* no longer successful or useful; finished – infml ⟨*all* ~ *as a footballer at the age of 28*⟩

washer /ˈwoshə/ *n* **1** WASHING MACHINE **2** a thin flat ring (e g of metal or leather) used to ensure tightness or prevent friction in joints and assemblies [¹WASH + ²-ER]

ˌ**washer-ˈup** *n, chiefly Br* a person employed to wash up; a dishwasher – infml

ˈ**washerwoman** /-woomən/, *masc* ˈ**washerman** /-mən/ *n* a woman who takes in washing

Washeteria /,woshə'tiəri·ə/ *trademark* – used for a launderette

wash-hand basin *n, Br* a washbasin

'wash,house /-,hows/ *n* a building used or equipped for washing clothes

washing /'woshing/ *n* articles, esp clothes, that have been or are to be washed [[1]WASH + [2]-ING]

'washing ma,chine *n* a machine for washing esp clothes and household linen

'washing ,soda *n* a transparent crystalline hydrated sodium carbonate

,washing-'up *n, chiefly Br* the act or process of washing dishes and kitchen utensils; *also* the dishes and utensils to be washed

'wash-,leather *n* a soft leather similar to chamois

wash off *vb* to (cause to) disappear as the result of washing

'wash,out /-,owt/ *n* **1** the washing out or away of a road, railway line, etc by a large amount of water; *also* a place where this has occurred **2** a failure, fiasco

wash out *vt* **1a** to wash free of a usu unwanted substance (e g dirt) ⟨washed *the milk bottles* out *before putting them on the doorstep*⟩ **b** to remove (e g a stain) by washing ⟨washed *the tea stain* out *of the tablecloth*⟩ **2a** to cause to fade by laundering **b** to deplete the strength or vitality of ⟨*feeling very* washed out⟩ ~ *vi* to become depleted of colour or vitality; fade

'washroom /-,roohm, -room/ *n, NAm* TOILET 2b – euph

'wash,stand /-,stand/ *n* a piece of furniture used, esp formerly, to hold a basin, jug, etc needed for washing one's face and hands

'wash,tub /-,tub/ *n* a tub in which clothes are washed or soaked

wash up *vi* **1** *Br* to wash used dishes and kitchen utensils, esp after a meal **2** *NAm* to wash one's face and hands ~ *vt* **1** to bring into the shore ⟨*a dead whale was* washed up *on the sand*⟩ **2** *Br* to wash (the dishes and utensils) after a meal

'wash,woman /-,woomən/ *n, NAm* a washerwoman

washy /'woshi/ *adj* **1** weak, watery ⟨~ *tea*⟩ **2** deficient in colour; pallid **3** lacking in vigour, individuality, or definite form – **washiness** *n*

wasn't /'woznt/ was not

wasp /wosp/ *n* any of numerous largely flesh-eating slender narrow-waisted insects many of which have an extremely painful sting; *esp* a very common social wasp with black and yellow stripes ☞ DEFENCE [ME *waspe*, fr OE *wæps, wæsp*; akin to OHG *wafsa* wasp, L *vespa* wasp, OE *wefan* to weave – more at WEAVE] – **wasplike** *adj*

WASP, Wasp /wosp/ *n* an American of N European, esp British, stock and of Protestant background; *esp* one in North America considered to be a member of the dominant and most privileged class [*w*hite *A*nglo-*S*axon *P*rotestant] – **Waspish** *adj*, **Waspy** *adj*

waspish /'wospish/ *adj* resembling a wasp in behaviour; *esp* snappish – **waspishly** *adv*, **waspishness** *n*

wasp waist *n* a very slender waist – **wasp-waisted** *adj*

[1]wassail /'wosayl/ *n* **1** a toast to sby's health made in England in former times **2 wassail, wassail bowl, wassail cup** a liquor made of spiced ale or wine and often baked apples, and served in a large bowl, esp formerly, at Christmas and other festive occasions **3** *archaic* revelry, carousing [ME *wæs hæil*, fr ON *ves heill* be well, fr *ves* (imper sing. of *vera* to be) + *heill* healthy – more at WAS, WHOLE]

[2]wassail *vi* **1** to carouse **2** *dial Eng* to sing carols from house to house at Christmas – **wassailer** *n*

'Wassermann ,test /'vahsəmən, 'wahsəmən/ *n* a test for the presence of a specific antibody in blood serum used in the detection of syphilis [August von *Wassermann* †1925 G bacteriologist]

wast /wəst, wost/ *archaic past 2 sing of* BE

wastage /'waystij/ *n* **1a** loss, decrease, or destruction of sthg (e g by use, decay, or leakage); *esp* wasteful or avoidable loss of sthg valuable **b** waste, refuse **2** reduction or loss in numbers (e g of employees or students), usu caused by individuals leaving or retiring voluntarily – esp in *natural wastage*

[1]waste /wayst/ *n* **1a** a sparsely settled, barren, or devastated region; a desert **b** uncultivated land **c** a broad and empty expanse (e g of water) **2** wasting or being wasted **3** gradual loss or decrease by use, wear, or decay **4** damaged, defective, or superfluous material produced by a manufacturing process: e g **a** material rejected during a textile manufacturing process and used usu for wiping away dirt and oil **b** fluid (e g steam) allowed to escape without being used **5** human or animal refuse [ME *waste, wast*; (1) fr ONF *wast*, fr *wast*, adj, desolate, waste, fr L *vastus*; akin to OHG *wuosti* desolate, waste, L *vanus* empty; (2–5) fr ME *wasten* to waste]

[2]waste *vt* **1** to lay waste; devastate **2** to cause to be reduced in physical bulk or strength; enfeeble **3** to wear away gradually; consume **4** to spend or use carelessly or inefficiently; squander ~ *vi* **1** to lose weight, strength, or vitality – often + *away* **2** to become consumed gradually and esp wastefully [ME *wasten*, fr ONF *waster*, fr L *vastare*, fr *vastus* desolate, waste] – **waste one's breath** to accomplish nothing by speaking

[3]waste *adj* **1a** uninhabited, desolate **b** not cultivated or used; not productive ⟨~ *energy*⟩ ⟨~ *land*⟩ **2** ruined, devastated **3** discarded as refuse ⟨~ *material*⟩ **4** serving to conduct or hold refuse material; *specif* carrying off superfluous fluid ⟨~ *pipe*⟩ [ME *waste, wast*, fr ONF *wast*]

'waste,basket /-,bahskit/ *n* WASTEPAPER BASKET

'waste ,bin *n, Br* a container for refuse, esp from a kitchen; *also* WASTEPAPER BASKET

wasted /'waystid/ *adj* **1** laid waste; ravaged **2** impaired in strength or health; emaciated **3** unprofitably used, made, or expended ⟨~ *effort*⟩

'wasteful /-f(ə)l/ *adj* given to or marked by waste; prodigal – **wastefully** *adv*, **wastefulness** *n*

'wasteland /-lənd, -land/ *n* **1** (an area of) barren or uncultivated land ⟨*a desert* ~⟩ **2** a desolate or barely inhabitable place or area **3** sthg (e g a way of life) that is spiritually and emotionally dry or unsatisfying

,waste'paper /-'paypə/ *n* paper discarded as used or unwanted

,waste'paper ,basket *n* a receptacle for refuse, esp wastepaper

waste product *n* **1** debris resulting from a process (e g of manufacture) that is of no further use to the system producing it **2** material (e g faeces) discharged from, or stored in an inert form in, a living body as a by-product of metabolic processes

waster /ˈwaystə/ *n* **1** one who spends or consumes extravagantly without thought for the future **2** a good-for-nothing, idler [²WASTE + ²-ER]

wasting /ˈwaysting/ *adj* undergoing or causing decay or loss of strength ⟨~ *diseases such as tuberculosis*⟩ – **wastingly** *adv*

wastrel /ˈwaystrəl/ *n* **1** a vagabond, waif **2** a waster [irreg fr ²*waste*]

¹**watch** /woch/ *vi* **1** to remain awake during the night, esp in order to keep vigil ⟨~ *by his bedside*⟩ **2a** to be attentive or vigilant; wait *for* ⟨~ed *for a chance to get her revenge*⟩ **b** to keep guard ⟨~ *over their flocks*⟩ **3** to be closely observant of an event or action ~ *vt* **1** to keep under protective guard **2a** to observe closely, esp in order to check on action or change ⟨*being* ~ed *by the police*⟩ **b** to look at (an event or moving scene) ⟨~ *television*⟩ ⟨~ed *the train till it went out of sight*⟩ **3a** to take care of; tend ⟨~ *the baby*⟩ **b** to be careful of ⟨~es *his diet*⟩ **c** to take care that ⟨~ *you don't spill it*⟩ **4** to be on the alert for; bide ⟨~ed *his opportunity*⟩ [ME *wacchen*, fr OE *wæccan* – more at WAKE] – **watcher** *n* – **watch it** to be careful; LOOK OUT – **watch one's step** to proceed with extreme care; act or talk warily – **watch over** to have charge of; superintend

²**watch** *n* **1a** the act of keeping awake or alert to guard, protect, or attend ⟨*kept* ~ *by the patient's bedside*⟩ ⟨*kept a close* ~ *on his movements*⟩ **b** a state of alert and continuous attention; lookout **2** a wakeful interval during the night – usu pl ⟨*the silent* ~es *of the night*⟩ **3** a watchman; *also, sing or pl in constr* a body of watchmen, specif those formerly assigned to patrol the streets of a town at night **4a** a period of keeping guard **b(1)** a period of time during which a part of a ship's company is on duty while another part rests **(2)** *sing or pl in constr* the part of a ship's company on duty during a particular watch **5** a small portable timepiece powered esp by a spring or battery and usu worn on a wrist – **on the watch** on the alert

ˈ**watch-ˌcase** *n* the outside metal case covering the mechanism of a watch

ˈ**watch comˌmittee** *n* a British local government committee that formerly supervised police discipline and public order

ˈ**watchˌdog** /-ˌdog/ *n* **1** a dog kept to guard property **2** a person or group (e g a committee) that guards against inefficiency, undesirable practices, etc

ˈ**watchful** /-f(ə)l/ *adj* carefully observant or attentive; ON THE WATCH ⟨*kept a* ~ *eye on the proceedings*⟩ – **watchfully** *adv*, **watchfulness** *n*

ˈ**watchˌglass** /-ˌglahs/ *n* a transparent cover protecting the face of a watch

watching brief /ˈwoching/ *n* instructions to a barrister to follow a case on behalf of sby not directly involved; *broadly* observation of proceedings on behalf of another

ˈ**watchˌmaking** /-ˌmayking/ *n* the making or repairing of watches or clocks – **watchmaker** *n*

ˈ**watchman** /-mən/ *n, pl* **watchmen** sby who keeps watch; a guard ⟨*a night* ~⟩

ˈ**watch ˌnight,** ˈ**watch night ˌservice** *n* a devotional service lasting until after midnight, esp on New Year's Eve

watch out *vi* **1** to be on the lookout *for* **2** to be careful; take care – often imper

ˈ**watchˌtower** /-ˌtowə/ *n* a tower from which a lookout can keep watch

ˈ**watchˌword** /-ˌwuhd/ *n* **1** a word or phrase used as a sign of recognition among members of the same group – compare PASSWORD 1 **2** a motto that embodies a guiding principle

¹**water** /ˈwawtə/ *n* **1a** the colourless odourless liquid that descends from the clouds as rain, forms streams, lakes, and seas, is a major constituent of all living matter, and is an oxide of hydrogen which freezes at 0°C and boils at 100°C **b** a natural mineral water – usu pl with sing. meaning ⟨*went to Bath to take the* ~s⟩ **2a(1)** *pl* the water occupying or flowing in a particular bed ⟨*the* ~s *of the Nile*⟩ **(2)** *chiefly Br* a body of water (e g a river or lake) ⟨*Derwent* ~⟩ **b(1)** *pl* a stretch of sea surrounding and controlled by a country ⟨*territorial* ~s⟩ **(2)** the sea of a specified part of the earth – often pl with sing. meaning ⟨*in tropical* ~s⟩ **c** a water supply ⟨*threatened to turn off the* ~⟩ **3** travel or transport by water ⟨*we went by* ~⟩ **4a** the level of water at a specified state of the tide – compare HIGH WATER, LOW WATER **b** the surface of the water ⟨*swam under* ~⟩ **5** liquid containing or resembling water: e g **a** a pharmaceutical or cosmetic preparation (e g a toilet water) made with water **b** a watery solution of a gaseous or readily volatile substance ⟨*ammonia* ~⟩ **c** a watery fluid (e g tears, urine, or sap) formed or circulating in a living body **6** degree of excellence ⟨*a scholar of the first* ~⟩ **7** a wavy lustrous pattern (e g of a textile) [ME, fr OE *wæter*; akin to OHG *wazzar* water, Gk *hydōr*, L *unda* wave] – **waterless** *adj* – **water under the bridge** past events which it is futile to attempt to alter

²**water** *vt* **1** to moisten, sprinkle, or soak with water ⟨~ *the garden*⟩ **2a** to supply with water for drink ⟨~ *the horses*⟩ **b** to supply water to ⟨~ *a ship*⟩ **3** to be a source of water for ⟨*land* ~ed *by the Thames*⟩ **4** to impart a lustrous appearance and wavy pattern to (cloth) by calendering ⟨~ed *silk*⟩ **5a** to dilute (as if) by the addition of water ⟨~ *the programme to suit the Radicals – The Times*⟩ – often + *down* **b** to add to the total par value of (securities) without a corresponding addition to the assets represented by the securities ~ *vi* **1** to form or secrete water or watery matter (e g tears or saliva) **2a** to take on a supply of water **b** *of an animal* to drink water – **waterer** *n*

ˈ**water ˌbailiff** *n, Br* an official employed to enforce bylaws relating to (waters used for) angling

ˈ**water ˌbed** *n* a bed with a water-filled plastic or rubber mattress

ˈ**water ˌbiscuit** *n* an unsweetened biscuit made with flour and water

ˈ**water ˌblister** *n* a blister with a clear watery content that does not contain pus or blood

ˈ**water ˌbloom** *n* an accumulation of (blue-green) algae at or near the surface of a body of water

ˈ**water ˈboatman** *n* any of various aquatic bugs that swim on their backs

ˈ**waterˌborne** /-ˌbawn/ *adj* supported or carried by water ⟨~ *commerce*⟩ ⟨~ *infection*⟩

ˈ**waterˌbuck** /-ˌbuk/ *n, pl* **waterbucks,** *esp collectively* **waterbuck** any of various Old World antelopes that commonly frequent streams or wet areas

ˈ**water ˌbuffalo** *n* an often domesticated Asiatic buffalo

ˈ**water ˌcannon** *n* a device for shooting out a jet of water with great force (e g to disperse a crowd)

'water ˌcart *n* a cart or truck equipped with a tank or barrels for hauling or sprinkling water

'water ˌchestnut *n* **1** (any of a genus of aquatic plants with) an edible nutlike 4-pronged fruit **2** (the edible tuber of) any of several Asian sedges

'water ˌclock *n* an instrument designed to measure time by the fall or flow of water

'water ˌcloset *n* (a room or structure containing) a toilet with a bowl that can be flushed with water

'waterˌcolour /-ˌkulə/ *n* **1** a paint made from pigment mixed with water rather than oil **2** (a work produced by) the art of painting with watercolours

'water-ˌcool *vt* to cool by means of esp circulating water ⟨*a* ~ed *engine*⟩

'waterˌcourse /-ˌkaws/ *n* (a natural or man-made channel for) a stream of water

'waterˌcraft /-ˌkrahft/ *n, pl* **watercraft** **1** skill in handling boats, sailing, etc **2** a vessel for water transport

'waterˌcress /-ˌkres/ *n* any of several cresses of wet places widely grown for use in salads

'water-diˌviner *n, chiefly Br* one who searches for water using a divining rod; a dowser

ˌwatered-'down *adj* modified or reduced in force or effectiveness ⟨*a* ~ *version of the original*⟩

'waterˌfall /-ˌfawl/ *n* a vertical or steep descent of the water of a river or stream ☞ GEOGRAPHY

'water-ˌfinder *n, chiefly NAm* a water-diviner, dowser

'water ˌflea *n* any of various small active dark or brightly coloured aquatic crustaceans

'waterˌfowl /-ˌfowl/ *n, pl* **waterfowls,** *esp collectively* **waterfowl** **1** a bird, esp a duck, that frequents water **2** *pl* swimming game birds (e g duck) as distinguished from upland game birds (e g grouse)

'waterˌfront /-ˌfrunt/ *n* land or a section of a town fronting or bordering on a body of water

'water ˌgas *n* a poisonous inflammable gaseous mixture that consists chiefly of carbon monoxide and hydrogen, is usu made by blowing air and then steam over red-hot coke or coal, and is used esp as a fuel

'water ˌgate *n* **1** a gate giving access to a body of water **2** a floodgate

'water ˌgauge *n* an instrument that indicates the height of water, esp in a steam boiler; *also* pressure expressed in terms of the depth of water

'water ˌglass *n* **1** an open box or tube with a glass bottom used for examining objects under water **2** a solution of sodium or potassium silicate used esp as a cement, as a protective coating and fireproofing agent, and in preserving eggs

'water ˌhammer *n* a (sound of) concussion of moving water against the sides of a containing pipe or vessel

'water ˌhazard *n* an open watercourse (e g a pond or ditch) on a golf course

ˌwater 'hemlock *n* cowbane

'water ˌhen *n* any of various birds (e g a coot or moorhen) related to the rails

'water ˌhole *n* a natural hollow in which water collects, used esp by animals as a drinking place

ˌwater 'hyacinth *n* a showy S American floating aquatic plant that often clogs waterways in warm regions

'water ˌice *n* a frozen dessert of water, sugar, and flavouring

'watering ˌcan /'wawt(ə)ring/ *n* a vessel having a handle and a long spout often fitted with a rose, used for watering plants

'watering ˌplace *n* **1** a place where water may be obtained; *esp* one where animals, esp livestock, come to drink **2** a health or recreational resort featuring mineral springs or bathing; *esp* a spa

'water ˌjacket *n* an outer casing which holds water or through which water circulates, esp for cooling

'water ˌjump *n* an obstacle (e g in a steeplechase) consisting of a pool or ditch of water

'water ˌlevel *n* **1** the level reached by the surface of a body of water **2** WATER TABLE

'water ˌlily *n* any of a family of aquatic plants with floating leaves and usu showy colourful flowers

'waterˌline /-ˌlien/ *n* the level on the hull of a vessel to which the surface of the water comes when it is afloat; *also* any of several lines marked on the hull to correspond with this level

'waterˌlogged /-ˌlogd/ *adj* filled or soaked with water ⟨~ *soil*⟩; *specif, of a vessel* so filled with water as to be (almost) unable to float ['*water* + *log* (to cause to become like a log)] – **waterlog** *vt*

waterloo /ˌwawtə'looh/ *n, pl* **waterloos** *often cap* a decisive defeat [*Waterloo,* village in Belgium, scene of Napoleon's defeat by British & Prussian armies in 1815]

'water ˌmain *n* a major pipe for conveying water

'waterman /-mən/ *n* a man who works on or near water or who engages in water recreations; *esp* a boatman whose boat and services are available for hire

[1]**'waterˌmark** /-ˌmahk/ *n* **1** a mark indicating the height to which water has risen **2** (the design or the metal pattern producing) a marking in paper visible when the paper is held up to the light

[2]**watermark** *vt* to mark (paper) with a watermark

'water ˌmeadow *n* a meadow kept fertile by a regular influx of water (e g from the flooding of a bordering river)

'waterˌmelon /-ˌmelən/ *n* (an African climbing plant of the cucumber family that bears) a large oblong or roundish fruit with a hard green often striped or variegated rind, a sweet watery pink pulp, and many seeds

'water ˌmill *n* a mill whose machinery is moved by water ☞ ENERGY

water of crystallization *n* water of hydration present in many crystallized substances that is usu essential for maintenance of a particular crystal structure

ˌwater of hy'dration *n* water that is chemically combined with a substance to form a hydrate and can be expelled (e g by heating) without essentially altering the composition of the substance

'water ˌouzel *n* DIPPER 2

'water ˌparting *n, chiefly NAm* WATERSHED 1

'water ˌpepper *n* an annual plant of wet places with extremely acrid peppery juice

'water ˌpipe *n* **1** a pipe for conveying water **2** a large chiefly oriental smoking apparatus consisting of a bowl containing tobacco or other smoking material mounted on a vessel of water through which smoke is drawn and cooled before reaching the mouth

'water ˌpistol *n* a toy pistol designed to shoot a jet of liquid

ˌwater 'plantain *n* any of a genus of marsh or aquatic plants with acrid juice

'water ˌpolo *n* a game played in water by teams of

7 swimmers using a ball that is thrown or dribbled with the object of putting it into a goal

'water,power /-,powə/ *n* the power derived from movement of a body of water; *also* a fall of water suitable for such use

[1]**'water,proof** /-,proohf/ *adj* impervious to water; *esp* covered or treated with a material to prevent passage of water – **waterproofness** *n*

[2]**waterproof** *n* (a garment made of) waterproof fabric

[3]**waterproof** *vt* to make waterproof – **waterproofer** *n*, **waterproofing** *n*

'water ,rail *n* a Eurasian rail with olive brown upper parts, conspicuous black and white bars on the flanks, and a long red bill

'water ,rat *n* WATER VOLE

'water ,rate *n* the charge made to a British householder for the use of the public water supply

'water-re,pellent *adj* treated with a finish that is resistant but not impervious to penetration by water

'water-re,sistant *adj* water-repellent

'water ,scorpion *n* any of numerous aquatic bugs with the abdomen extended into a long breathing tube

'water,shed /-,shed/ *n* **1** a dividing ridge between 2 drainage areas ☞ GEOGRAPHY **2** a crucial turning point

'water,side /-,sied/ *n* the margin of a body of water

'water,sider /-,siedə/ *n, Austr & NZ* a docker

'water ,ski *n* a board used singly or in pairs for standing on and planing over water while being towed at speed – **water-ski** *vi*, **water-skier** *n*

'water-,skiing *n* the sport of planing and jumping on water skis

'water-,softener *n* a substance or device for softening hard water

'water ,spaniel *n* a rather large spaniel with a heavy curly coat, used esp for retrieving waterfowl

'water,spout /-,spowt/ *n* a funnel-shaped column of rotating wind usu extending from the underside of a cumulus or cumulonimbus cloud down to a cloud of spray torn up from the surface of a sea, lake, etc

'water sup,ply *n* the source, means, or process of supplying water (e g to a town or house), usu including reservoirs, tunnels, and pipelines

'water ,system *n* a river with its tributaries

'water ,table *n* the level below which the ground is wholly saturated with water

'water,tight /-,tiet/ *adj* **1** of such tight construction or fit as to be impermeable to water **2** *esp of an argument* impossible to disprove; without loopholes **3** isolated from other ideas, influences, etc; discrete ⟨*experiences cannot be divided into* ~ *compartments*⟩ – **watertightness** *n*

'water ,tower *n* **1** a tower supporting a raised water tank to provide the necessary steady pressure to distribute water **2** a fire fighting apparatus that can supply water at various heights and at great pressure

'water ,vapour *n* water in a vaporous form, esp when below boiling temperature and diffused (e g in the atmosphere)

'water ,vole *n* a common large vole of W Europe that inhabits river banks and often digs extensive tunnels

'water ,wagon *n, chiefly NAm* WATER CART

'water,way /-,way/ *n* **1** a navigable route or body of water **2** a groove at the edge of a ship's deck for draining the deck

'water,weed /-,weed/ *n* any of various aquatic plants (e g a pondweed) with inconspicuous flowers

'water,wheel /-,weel/ *n* **1** a wheel made to rotate by direct action of water, and used esp to drive machinery **2** a wheel for raising water

'water ,wings *n pl* a pair of usu air-filled floats worn to give support to the body of sby learning to swim

'water ,witch *n, NAm* a dowser – **water witching** *n*

'water,works /-,wuhks/ *n, pl* **waterworks** **1** the reservoirs, mains, building, and pumping and purifying equipment by which a water supply is obtained and distributed (e g to a city) – often pl with sing. meaning **2** *chiefly Br* the urinary system – euph or humor **3** (the shedding of) tears – infml ⟨*turns on the* ~ *whenever she wants her own way*⟩

'water,worn /-,wawn/ *adj* worn or smoothed by the action of water

watery /'wawt(ə)ri/ *adj* **1a** consisting of or filled with water **b** containing, sodden with, or yielding water or a thin liquid ⟨*a* ~ *solution*⟩ ⟨~ *vesicles*⟩ **c** containing too much water ⟨~ *soup*⟩ **d** secreting water, esp tears ⟨~ *eyes*⟩ **2a** pale, faint ⟨~ *sun*⟩ ⟨*a* ~ *smile*⟩ **b** vapid, wishy-washy ⟨*a* ~ *writing style*⟩ – **waterily** *adv*, **wateriness** *n*

Watson-Crick /,wots(ə)n 'krik/ *adj* of the double-helix structure of DNA ⟨*guanine involved in a* ~ *base pair – Nature*⟩ [J D *Watson b* 1928 US biologist and F H C *Crick b* 1916 E biologist]

watt /wot/ *n* the SI unit of power equal to the power that in 1s gives rise to an energy of 1J ☞ PHYSICS [James *Watt* †1819 Sc engineer]

wattage /'wotij/ *n* amount of power expressed in watts

[1]**wattle** /'wotl/ *n* **1** (material for) a framework of poles interwoven with slender branches or reeds and used, esp formerly, in building ☞ BUILDING **2a** a fleshy protuberance usu near or on the head or neck, esp of a bird **b** [2]BARBEL **3** *Austr* ACACIA 1 [ME *wattel*, fr OE *watel*; akin to OHG *wadal* bandage] – **wattled** *adj*

[2]**wattle** *vt* **wattling** /'wotling, 'wotl·ing/ **1** to form or build of or with wattle **2a** to interlace to form wattle **b** to unite or make solid by interweaving light flexible material

,wattle and 'daub /dawb/ *n* a framework of wattle covered and plastered with clay and used in building construction ☞ BUILDING

[1]**wave** /wayv/ *vi* **1** to flutter or sway to and fro ⟨*flags* waving *in the breeze*⟩ ⟨*corn* ~d *to and fro in the wind*⟩ **2** to give a signal or salute by moving (sthg held in) the hand ⟨~d *cheerily to them*⟩ **3** to be flourished to and fro ⟨*his sword* ~d *and flashed*⟩ **4** to follow a curving line or form; undulate ~ *vt* **1** to cause to swing to and fro **2** to direct by waving; signal ⟨~ *the car to a halt*⟩ **3a** to move (the hand or an object) to and fro in greeting, farewell, or homage **b** to convey by waving ⟨~d *farewell*⟩ **4** to brandish, flourish ⟨~d *a pistol menacingly*⟩ **5** to give a curving or undulating shape to ⟨~d *her hair*⟩ [ME *waven*, fr OE *wafian* to wave with the hands; akin to OE *wæfre* restless – more at WAVER] – **waver**

n – **wave aside** to dismiss or put out of mind; disregard

[2]**wave** *n* **1a** a moving ridge or swell on the surface of a liquid (e g the sea) ☞ ENERGY **b** open water – usu pl with sing. meaning; chiefly poetic **2a** a shape or outline having successive curves **b** a waviness of the hair **c** an undulating line or streak **3** sthg that swells and dies away: e g **a** a surge of sensation or emotion ⟨*a ~ of anger swept over her*⟩ **b** a movement involving large numbers of people in a common activity ⟨*~s of protest*⟩ **c** a sudden increase or wide occurrence of a specified activity ⟨*a ~ of house-buying*⟩ **4** a sweep of the hand or arm or of some object held in the hand, used as a signal or greeting **5** a rolling or undulatory movement or any of a series of such movements passing along a surface or through the air **6** a movement like that of an ocean wave: e g **a** a surging movement; an influx ⟨*a sudden ~ of new arrivals*⟩ **b** *sing or pl in constr* a line of attacking or advancing troops, aircraft, etc **7** (a complete cycle of) a periodic variation of pressure, electrical or magnetic intensity, electric potential, etc by which energy is transferred progressively from point to point without a corresponding transfer of a medium ⟨*light ~*⟩ ⟨*radio ~*⟩ ⟨*sound ~*⟩ **8** an undulating or jagged line constituting a graphic representation of an action ⟨*a sine ~*⟩ **9** a marked change in temperature; a period of hot or cold weather – compare HEAT WAVE, COLD WAVE – **wavelet** /-lit/ *n*, **wavelike** *adj*

'**wave ˌband** *n* a band of radio frequency waves

'**wave eˌquation** *n* a partial differential equation of the second order whose solutions describe wave phenomena

'**waveˌform** /-ˌfawm/ *n* (the graphic representation of) the variation of a quantity (e g voltage) with respect to some other factor (e g time or distance)

'**wave ˌfront** *n* a surface composed at any instant of all the points just reached by a wave in its propagation through a medium

'**wave ˌfunction** *n* a quantum mechanical function representing the probability of finding a specified elementary particle within a specified volume of space

'**waveˌguide** /-ˌgied/ *n* a metal tube of such dimensions that it will propagate electromagnetic waves, esp microwaves

'**waveˌlength** /-ˌleng(k)th/ *n* the distance in the line of advance of a wave from any 1 point to the next point of corresponding phase (e g from 1 peak to the next) ☞ PHYSICS – **be on somebody's/the same wavelength** to have the same outlook, views, etc as sby else

wave mechanics *n pl but sing or pl in constr* a theory of matter that gives a mathematical interpretation of the structure of matter based on the concept that elementary particles (e g electrons, protons, or neutrons) possess wave properties

'**wave ˌnumber** *n* the number of waves per unit distance of radiant energy; the reciprocal of the wavelength

waver /'wayvə/ *vi* **1** to vacillate between choices; fluctuate **2a** to sway unsteadily to and fro; reel **b** to quiver, flicker ⟨*~ing flames*⟩ **c** to hesitate as if about to give way; falter **3** to make a tremulous sound; quaver [ME *waveren*; akin to OE *wæfre* restless, *wefan* to weave – more at WEAVE] – **waverer** *n*, **waveringly** *adv*

'**wave ˌtheory** *n* the theory that light and other electromagnetic radiation consists of waves

'**wave ˌtrain** *n* a succession of similar waves at equal intervals

wavy /'wayvi/ *adj* **1** having waves ⟨*~ hair*⟩ **2** having a wavelike form or outline ⟨*~ line*⟩ – **wavily** *adv*, **waviness** *n*

'**wa-wa ˌpedal, wah-wah pedal** /'wah ˌwah/ *n* an electronic device, connected to an amplifier and operated by a foot pedal, that is used (e g with an electric guitar) to produce a fluctuating muted effect [imit]

[1]**wax** /waks/ *n* **1** beeswax **2a** any of numerous plant or animal substances that are harder, more brittle, and less greasy than fats **b** a solid substance (e g ozocerite or paraffin wax) of mineral origin consisting usu of higher hydrocarbons **c** a pliable or liquid composition used esp for sealing, taking impressions, or polishing **d** a resinous preparation used by shoemakers for rubbing thread **3** a waxy secretion; *esp* cerumen [ME, fr OE *weax*; akin to OHG *wahs* wax, Lith *vaškas*] – **waxlike** *adj*

[2]**wax** *vt* to treat or rub with wax

[3]**wax** *vi* **1** to increase in size and strength; *esp, of the moon, satellites, etc* to increase in phase or intensity **2** *archaic* to assume a specified quality or state; become ⟨*~ed lyrical*⟩ [ME *waxen*, fr OE *weaxan*; akin to OHG *wahsan* to increase, Gk *auxanein*, L *augēre*]

[4]**wax** *n* a fit of temper – infml [perh fr [3]*wax*]

'**waxˌbill** /-ˌbil/ *n* any of numerous Old World birds with white, pink, or reddish bills of a waxy appearance

ˌ**waxed 'paper, wax paper** *n* paper coated or impregnated with wax to make it resistant to water and grease, used esp as a wrapping for food

waxen /'waks(ə)n/ *adj* **1** made of or covered with wax **2** resembling wax, esp in being pliable, smooth, or pallid

'**wax ˌinsect** *n* a scale insect that secretes a wax from its body

'**wax ˌpalm** *n* an Andean palm whose stem yields a resinous wax used in candles

'**waxˌwing** /-ˌwing/ *n* a Eurasian bird with a pinkish-chestnut crest, crimson-tipped wings, and a short yellow-tipped tail

'**waxˌwork** /-ˌwuhk/ *n* **1** an effigy in wax, usu of a person **2** *pl but sing or pl in constr* an exhibition of wax effigies

waxy /'waksi/ *adj* **1** made of, full of, or covered with wax **2** resembling wax, esp in smooth whiteness or pliability – **waxiness** *n*

[1]**way** /way/ *n* **1a** a thoroughfare for travel or transport from place to place ⟨*lives across the ~*⟩ ⟨*the Pennine* Way⟩ **b** an opening for passage ⟨*this door is the only ~ out*⟩ **c** space or room, esp for forward movement ⟨*move that chair, please, it's in my ~*⟩ ⟨*get out of the ~!*⟩ **2** the course to be travelled from one place to another;a route ⟨*ask one's ~ to the station*⟩ ⟨*lost her ~*⟩ **3a** a course leading in a direction or towards an objective ⟨*took the easy ~ out*⟩ **b** the course of one's life ⟨*puts opportunities in her ~*⟩ **c** what one desires, or wants to do ⟨*always manages to get her own ~*⟩ **4a** the manner in which sthg is done or happens ⟨*the British ~ of life*⟩ ⟨*don't like the ~ he's breathing*⟩ **b** a method of doing or accomplishing; a means ⟨*the best ~ to make coffee*⟩ **c** a characteristic, regular, or habitual

manner or mode of being, behaving, or happening ⟨*knows nothing of the* ~s *of the world*⟩ ⟨*endearing little* ~s⟩ **d** a feature, respect ⟨*useful in more* ~s *than one*⟩ **5** a category, kind ⟨*porridge is all right in its* ~⟩ **6** the distance to be travelled in order to reach a place or point ⟨*a long* ~ *from home*⟩ ⟨*Christmas is still a long* ~ *off*⟩ **7** an advance accompanied by or achieved through a specific action ⟨*working her* ~ *through college*⟩ ⟨*hacked his* ~ *through the jungle*⟩ **8a** a direction – often in combination ⟨*come this* ~⟩ ⟨*split it 4* ~s⟩ ⟨*a one-*way *street*⟩ **b** (the direction of) the area in which one lives ⟨*do drop in if you're ever down our* ~⟩ **9** a state of affairs; a condition ⟨*that's the* ~ *things are*⟩ ⟨*my finances are in a bad* ~⟩ **10** *pl but sometimes sing in constr* an inclined structure on which a ship is built or supported in launching **11** motion or speed of a ship or boat through the water [ME, fr OE *weg*; akin to OHG *weg* way, OE *wegan* to move, L *vehere* to carry] – **by the way** incidentally – usu used to introduce or to comment on the introduction of a new subject – **by way of 1** to be considered as; as a sort of ⟨by way of *light relief*⟩ **2** by the route through; via **3** in the form of ⟨*money recovered* by way of *grants*⟩ – **in a way** from one point of view; to some extent – **in the way of** in the form of ⟨*what have we* in the way *of food?*⟩ – **no way** under no circumstances – infml – **on one's way** ON THE WAY 1 – **on the way 1** while moving along a course; in the course of travelling **2** coming, approaching; *specif* conceived but not yet born – **on the way out** about to disappear or die ⟨*many of these old customs are* on the way out⟩ – **out of the way 1** unusual, remarkable ⟨*didn't know he'd said anything* out of the way⟩ ⟨*the house wasn't anything* out of the way⟩ **2** in or to a secluded or remote place **3** done, completed ⟨*got his homework* out of the way⟩ – **under way** in progress; started

[2]**way** *adv* **1** AWAY 7 ⟨*is* ~ *ahead of the class*⟩ **2** *chiefly NAm* all the way ⟨*pull the switch* ~ *back*⟩ – **way back** long ago ⟨*friends from* way back⟩

'way,bill /-,bil/ *n* a document showing the number of passengers or parcels carried and the fares charged

'way,farer /-,feərə/ *n* a traveller, esp on foot [ME *weyfarere*, fr *wey, way* way + *-farere* traveller, fr *faren* to go – more at [1]FARE]

waylay /way'lay/ *vt* **waylaid** /way'layd/ **1** to attack from ambush **2** to accost ⟨waylaid *me after the lesson and asked where I'd been the week before*⟩

'way,leave /-,leev/ *n* a right-of-way over private property (e g as granted to an electricity company laying cables)

,way-'out *adj* far-out – infml [*way out* (adverbial phrase), fr [2]*way* + *out*]

ways /wayz/ *n pl but sing in constr, NAm* WAY 6 ⟨*a long* ~ *from home*⟩ [ME *wayes*, fr gen of [1]*way*]

-ways /-wayz/ *suffix* (→ *adv*) in (such) a way, direction, or manner ⟨*side*ways⟩ ⟨*length*ways⟩ [ME, fr *ways, wayes*, gen of *way*]

,ways and 'means *n pl* **1** methods and resources for accomplishing sthg, esp for paying expenses **2** *often cap W&M* methods and resources for raising revenue for the use of government

'way,side /-,sied/ *n* the side of or land adjacent to a road – **wayside** *adj*

'way ,station *n, NAm* an intermediate stopping place

[1]**wayward** /-wood/ *adj* **1** following one's own capricious or wanton inclinations; ungovernable **2** following no clear principle or law; unpredictable [ME, short for *awayward* turned away, fr *away*, adv + *-ward*] – **waywardly** *adv*, **waywardness** *n*

we /wi; *strong* wee/ *pron pl in constr* **1** I and the rest of a group; you and I; you and I and another or others; I and another or others not including you ⟨*may* ~ *go, sir?*⟩ – compare OUR, OURS, US, I **2** I – used, esp formerly, by sovereigns; used by writers to maintain an impersonal character **3** YOU 1 – used esp to children and the sick ⟨*how are* ~ *feeling today, Mr Jones?*⟩ [ME, fr OE *wē*; akin to OHG *wir* we, Skt *vayam*]

weak /week/ *adj* **1a** deficient in physical vigour; feeble **b** not able to sustain or exert much weight, pressure, or strain **c** not able to resist external force or withstand attack **2a** lacking determination or decisiveness; ineffectual **b** unable to withstand temptation or persuasion **3** not factually grounded or logically presented ⟨*a* ~ *argument*⟩ **4a** unable to function properly ⟨~ *eyes*⟩ **b** lacking skill or proficiency **c** wanting in vigour or strength **5a** deficient in a specified quality or ingredient ⟨~ *in trumps*⟩ **b** lacking normal intensity or potency ⟨~ *strain of virus*⟩ **c** mentally or intellectually deficient **d** deficient in strength or flavour; dilute ⟨~ *coffee*⟩ **6** not having or exerting authority or political power ⟨~ *government*⟩ **7** of or constituting a verb (conjugation) that in English forms inflections by adding the suffix *-ed* or *-d* or *-t* – compare STRONG 14 **8** UNSTRESSED 1 **9** characterized by falling prices ⟨*a* ~ *market*⟩ **10** ionizing only slightly in solution ⟨~ *acids and bases*⟩ [ME *weike*, fr ON *veikr*; akin to OE *wīcan* to yield, L *vicis* change – more at WEEK] – **weaken** *vb*, **weakish** *adj*, **weakly** *adv*

weak interaction *n* an interaction between elementary particles that is responsible for some particle decay processes, for nuclear beta decay, and for emission and absorption of neutrinos – compare STRONG INTERACTION

,weak-'kneed *adj* lacking in resolution; easily intimidated

weakling /'weekling/ *n* a person or animal weak in body, character, or mind

weakly /'weekli/ *adj* feeble, poorly – **weakliness** *n*

,weak-'minded *adj* **1** lacking willpower or resolution **2** feebleminded – **weak-mindedness** *n*

weakness /'weeknis/ *n* **1** a fault, defect **2** (an object of) a special desire or fondness ⟨*have a* ~ *for ice cream*⟩ [WEAK + -NESS]

weak sister *n, chiefly NAm* a member of a group who is weak and needs aid

weal, wheal /weel/ *n* WELT 3, [2]SCAR 1 [alter. of [1]*wale*]

Weald /weeld/ *n* *the* area of open grassland, once wooded, covering parts of Sussex, Kent, and Surrey [alter. of ME *Weeld*, fr OE *weald* forest]

wealth /welth/ *n* **1** the state of being rich **2** abundance of money and valuable material possessions **3** abundant supply; a profusion ⟨*a* ~ *of detail*⟩ [ME *welthe*, fr *wele* well-being, prosperity, fr OE *wela*; akin to OE *wel* well] – **wealthy** *adj*, **wealthily** *adv*, **wealthiness** *n*

wean /ween/ *vt* **1** to accustom (a child or other young mammal) to take food other than mother's milk **2** to cause to abandon a state of usu unwholesome dependence or preoccupation ⟨*to ~ your minds from hankering after false standards* – A T Quiller-Couch⟩ **3** to cause to become acquainted with an idea, writer, etc at an early age; bring up *on* [ME *wenen*, fr OE *wenian* to accustom, wean; akin to OE *wunian* to be used to – more at WONT]

weaner /ˈweenə/ *n* a young animal recently weaned [WEAN + ²-ER]

weanling /ˈweenling/ *n* a child or animal newly weaned

weapon /ˈwepən/ *n* **1** an instrument of offensive or defensive combat **2** a means used to further one's cause in conflict ⟨*his caustic wit was his best ~*⟩ [ME *wepen*, fr OE *wǣpen*; akin to ON *vāpn* weapon]

ˈweaponry /-ri/ *n* (the science of designing and making) weapons

¹wear /weə/ *vb* **wore** /waw/; **worn** /wawn/ *vt* **1a** to have or carry on the body as clothing or adornment ⟨wore *a coat*⟩ **b** to dress in (a particular manner, colour, or garment), esp habitually ⟨*~ green*⟩ **c** to have (hair) in a specified style **2** to hold the rank, dignity, or position signified by (an ornament) ⟨*~ the royal crown*⟩ **3a** to have or show on the face ⟨wore *a happy smile*⟩ **b** to show or fly (a flag or colours) on a ship **4** to impair, damage, or diminish by use or friction ⟨*letters on the stone* worn *away by weathering*⟩ **5** to produce gradually by friction or attrition ⟨*~ a hole in the rug*⟩ **6** to exhaust or lessen the strength of; weary **7** to cause (a ship, esp a square-rigged vessel) to go about with the stern presented to the wind **8** *chiefly Br* to find (a claim, proposal etc) acceptable; STAND FOR – infml ⟨*just won't ~ that feeble excuse*⟩ *~ vi* **1a** to endure use, esp to a specified degree; last ⟨*this material ~*s *well*⟩ **b** to retain vitality or young appearance to a specified degree ⟨*you've* worn *well*⟩ **2a** to diminish or decay through use **b** to go by slowly or tediously ⟨*the day ~*s *on*⟩ **c** to grow or become by attrition, use, or the passage of time ⟨*hair ~*ing *thin*⟩ **3** *of a ship, esp a square-rigged vessel* to change to an opposite tack by turning the stern to the wind – compare TACK, GYBE [ME *weren*, fr OE *werian*; akin to ON *verja* to clothe, invest, spend, L *vestis* clothing, garment, Gk *hennynai* to clothe] – **wearable** *adj*, **wearer** *n* – **wear the trousers** to have the controlling authority in a household – **wear thin 1** to become weak or ready to give way ⟨*his patience was* wearing thin⟩ **2** to become trite, unconvincing, or out-of-date ⟨*that argument's* wearing *a bit* thin⟩

²wear *n* **1** wearing or being worn ⟨*clothes for everyday ~*⟩ **2** clothing, usu of a specified kind ⟨*men's ~*⟩; *esp* clothing worn for a specified occasion – often in combination ⟨*swim*wear⟩ **3** capacity to withstand use; durability ⟨*plenty of ~ left in it*⟩ **4** minor damage or deterioration through use

ˌwear and ˈtear *n* the normal deterioration or depreciation which sthg suffers in the course of use

wear down *vt* to weary and overcome by persistent resistance or pressure

wearing /ˈweəring/ *adj* causing fatigue; tiring – **wearingly** *adv*

wearisome /ˈwiəris(ə)m/ *adj* causing weariness; tiresome – **wearisomely** *adv*, **wearisomeness** *n*

wear off *vi* to decrease gradually and finally end ⟨*the effect of the drug* wore off⟩

wear out *vt* **1** to make useless by long or excessive wear or use **2** to tire, exhaust *~ vi* to become useless from long or excessive wear or use

¹weary /ˈwiəri/ *adj* **1** exhausted, tired **2** expressing or characteristic of weariness ⟨*a ~ smile*⟩ **3** having one's patience, tolerance, or pleasure exhausted – + *of* **4** wearisome [ME *wery*, fr OE *wērig*; akin to OHG *wuorag* intoxicated, Gk *hōrakian* to faint] – **wearily** *adv*, **weariness** *n*

²weary *vb* to make or become weary

weasel /ˈweezl/ *n, pl* **weasels**, *esp collectively* **weasel** any of various small slender flesh-eating mammals with reddish brown fur which, in northern forms, turns white in winter [ME *wesele*, fr OE *weosule*; akin to OHG *wisula* weasel, L *virus* slimy liquid, stench – more at VIRUS]

¹weather /ˈwedhə/ *n* the prevailing (bad) atmospheric conditions, esp with regard to heat or cold, wetness or dryness, calm or storm, and clearness or cloudiness [ME *weder*, fr OE; akin to OHG *wetar* weather, OSlav *vetrŭ* wind] – **under the weather** mildly ill or depressed; not fully well – infml

²weather *adj* windward

³weather *vt* **1** to expose or subject to atmospheric conditions **2** to sail or pass to the windward of **3** to bear up against and come safely through ⟨*~ a storm*⟩ *~ vi* to undergo or be resistant to change by weathering ⟨*wood ~*s *better if creosoted*⟩

ˈweather-ˌbeaten *adj* **1** worn or damaged by exposure to weather **2** toughened or tanned by the weather

ˈweatherˌboard /-ˌbawd/ *n* **1** a board fixed horizontally and usu overlapping the board below to form a protective outdoor wall covering that will throw off water **2** a sloping board fixed to the bottom of a door for excluding rain, snow, etc

ˈweatherˌboarding /-ˌbawding/ *n* (a method of constructing the wall of a building using) weatherboards ☞ BUILDING

ˈweather-ˌbound *adj* unable to proceed or take place because of bad weather

ˈweatherˌcock /-ˌkok/ *n* WEATHER VANE; *esp* one in the figure of a cockerel

weathered /ˈwedhəd/ *adj* **1** seasoned by exposure to the weather **2** altered in form by weathering; *also* altered by artificial means, esp staining, to produce a similar effect ⟨*~ oak*⟩

weather eye *n* **1** an eye quick to observe coming changes in the weather **2** a constant and shrewd alertness

ˈweatherˌglass /-ˌglahs/ *n* a barometer

weathering /ˈwedhəring/ *n* **1** (the changes in colour, composition, form, etc resulting from) the action of the elements on exposed objects, esp rocks **2** a slope given to a surface so that it will shed water

weatherly /ˈwedhəli/ *adj, of a vessel* able to sail close to the wind with little leeway

ˈweatherˌman /-ˌman/ *n* sby, esp a meteorologist, who reports and forecasts the weather, usu on the radio or television

ˈweather ˌmap *n* a map or chart showing meteorological conditions at a given time and over an extended region

ˈweatherˌproof /-ˌproohf/ *adj* able to withstand exposure to weather without damage or loss of function – **weatherproof** *vt*, **weatherproofness** *n*

ˈweather ˌsatellite *n* a satellite put into orbit round

Weather monitoring and forecasting by satellite

A geostationary meteorological satellite orbits the earth at a height of 36,000 kilometres over the equator and remains more or less fixed in location relative to the earth. This enables it to relay data constantly over the same part of the world.

high resolution picture data
raw environmental data

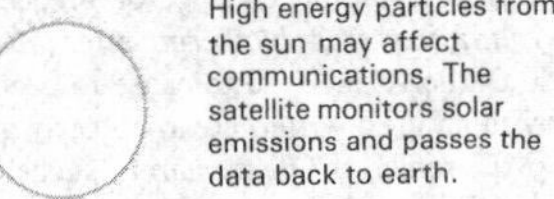

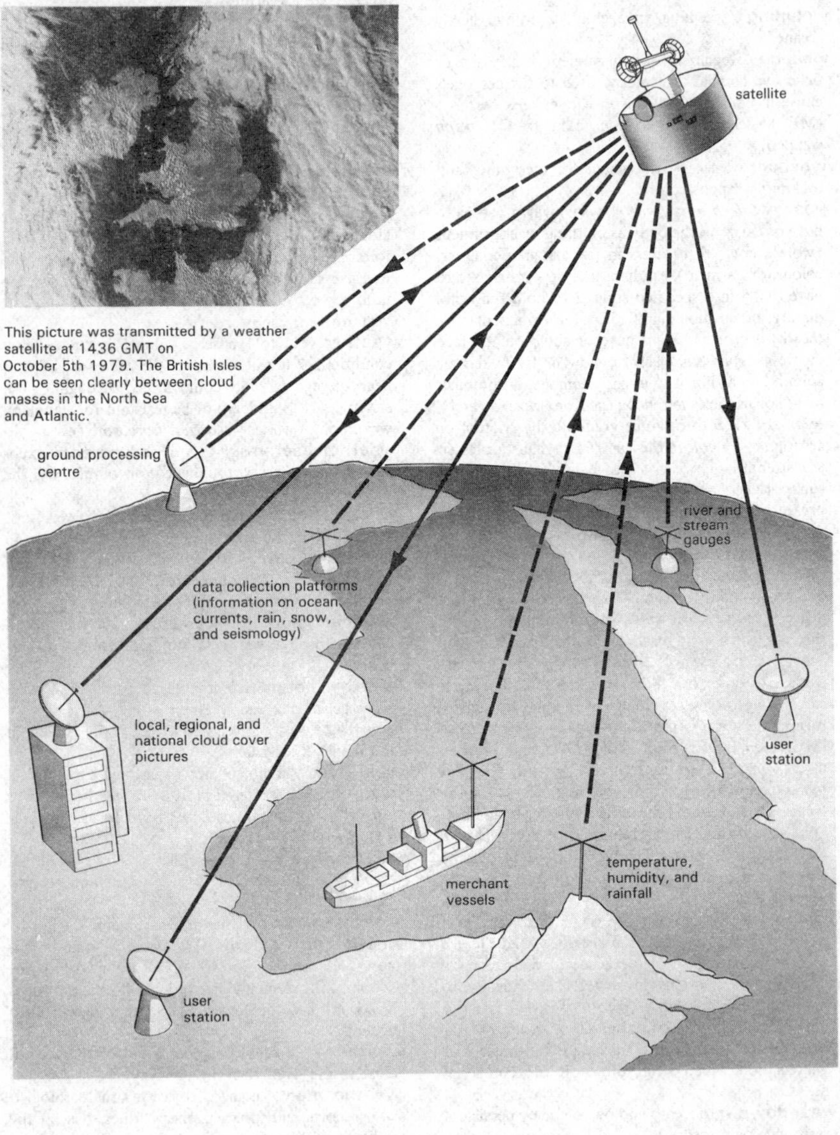

High energy particles from the sun may affect communications. The satellite monitors solar emissions and passes the data back to earth.

This picture was transmitted by a weather satellite at 1436 GMT on October 5th 1979. The British Isles can be seen clearly between cloud masses in the North Sea and Atlantic.

satellite

ground processing centre

river and stream gauges

data collection platforms (information on ocean currents, rain, snow, and seismology)

local, regional, and national cloud cover pictures

user station

merchant vessels

temperature, humidity, and rainfall

user station

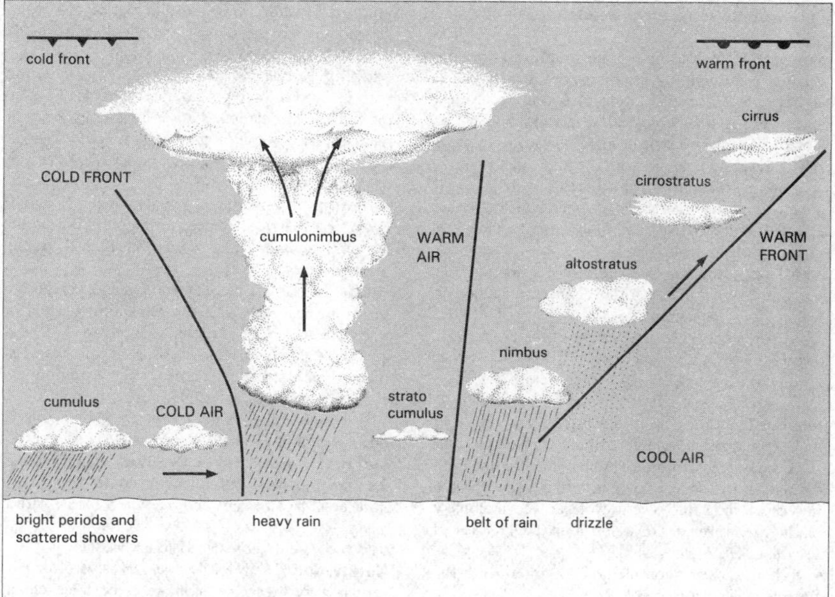

A depression, also known as a cyclone, is an area of low atmospheric pressure. Clouds form to give rainfall as warm tropical air meets and rises over cold polar air. In the northern hemisphere winds in a cyclone circulate in an anticlockwise direction — in the southern hemisphere they go clockwise.

cloud amount	wind	weather
⦶	◎ calm	═ mist
◔	○— 1-2 knots	≡ fog
◕	○⁄ 3-7 knots	, drizzle
◑		• rain
⊕		✳ snow
◕		△ hail
◑		rain shower
●	add 5 knots for each half feather	cold front
⊗ sky obscured		warm front

A weather map shows temperature, speed and direction of winds, atmospheric pressure (the curving lines, called isobars, link areas of equal pressure), fronts (areas where warm and cold air meet, usually producing rain), and local conditions.

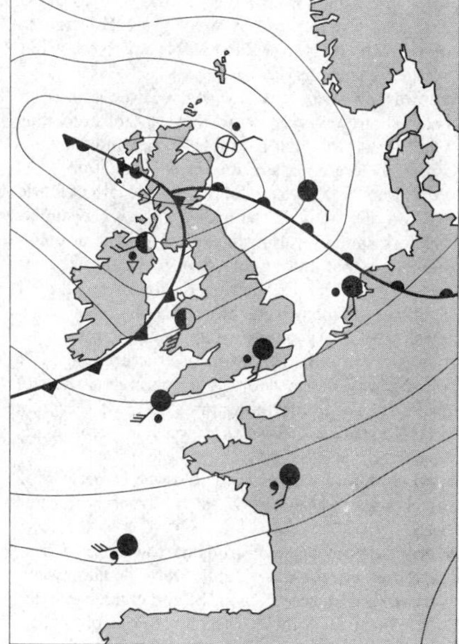

the earth to relay back meteorological observations

'weather ,ship *n* a ship that makes observations on weather conditions for use by meteorologists

'weather ,station *n* a station for taking, recording, and reporting meteorological observations

'weather ,strip *n* a strip of material used to exclude rain, snow, and cold air from the joints of a door or window ☞ ARCHITECTURE – **weather-strip** *vt*

'weather ,vane *n* a movable device attached to an elevated structure (e g a spire) in order to show the direction of the wind

'weather-,wise *adj* **1** skilful in forecasting the weather **2** skilful in forecasting changes in opinion or feeling ⟨*a ~ politician*⟩

'weather,worn /-,wawn/ *adj* WEATHER-BEATEN 1

[1]weave /weev/ *vb* **wove** /wove/, **weaved; woven** /'wohv(ə)n/, **weaved** *vt* **1a** to form (cloth) by interlacing strands (e g of yarn), esp on a loom **b** to interlace (e g threads) into a fabric, design, etc **c** to make (e g a basket) by intertwining **2** *of spiders and insects* SPIN 2 **3a** to produce by elaborately combining elements into a coherent whole **b** to introduce; work in – usu + *in* or *into* ~ *vi* to work at weaving; make cloth [ME *weven*, fr OE *wefan*; akin to OHG *weban* to weave, Gk *hyphos* web]

[2]weave *n* a pattern or method for interlacing the threads of woven fabrics

[3]weave *vb* **weaved** *vt* to direct (e g the body or one's way) in a winding or zigzag course, esp to avoid obstacles ~ *vi* to move by weaving [ME *weven* to move to and fro, wave; akin to ON *veifa* to wave, Skt *vepate* he trembles]

weaver /'weevə/ *n* **1** sby who weaves, esp as an occupation **2 weaver, weaverbird** any of numerous Old World birds that resemble finches and usu construct elaborate nests of interlaced vegetation

[1]web /web/ *n* **1** a woven fabric; *esp* a length of fabric still on the loom **2** SPIDER'S WEB; *also* a similar network spun by various insects **3** a tissue or membrane; *esp* that uniting fingers or toes either at their bases (e g in human beings) or for most of their length (e g in many water birds) **4** a thin metal sheet, plate, or strip (e g joining the upper and lower flanges of a girder or rail) **5** an intricate structure suggestive of sthg woven; a network **6** a continuous sheet of paper for use in a printing press [ME, fr OE; akin to ON *vefr* web, OE *wefan* to weave] – **webbed** *adj*, **webby** *adj*, **weblike** *adj*

[2]web *vb* **-bb-** *vt* **1** to cover with a web or network **2** to entangle, ensnare ~ *vi* to construct or form a web

webbing /'webing/ *n* a strong narrow closely woven tape used esp for straps, upholstery, or harnesses

weber /'vaybə, 'weebə/ *n* the SI unit of magnetic flux ☞ PHYSICS [Wilhelm *Weber* †1891 G physicist]

'web,foot /-,foot/ *n* a foot with webbed toes – **web-footed** /-'--/ *adj*

,web 'offset *n* offset printing by web press

web press *n* a press that prints a continuous roll of paper

wed /wed/ *vb* **-dd-; wedded** *also* **wed** *vt* **1** to marry **2** to unite as if by marriage ~ *vi* to enter into matrimony [ME *wedden*, fr OE *weddian*; akin to MHG *wetten* to pledge, OE *wedd* pledge, OHG *wetti*, Goth *wadi*, L *vad-*, *vas* bail, security]

we'd /wid; *strong* weed/ we had; we would; we should

wedded /'wedid/ *adj* **1** joined in marriage **2** conjugal, connubial ⟨~ *bliss*⟩ **3** strongly emotionally attached; committed *to*

wedding /'weding/ *n* **1** a marriage ceremony, usu with its accompanying festivities; nuptials **2** a joining in close association **3** a wedding anniversary or its celebration – usu in combination ⟨*golden* ~⟩

wedding breakfast *n* a celebratory meal that follows a marriage ceremony

'wedding ,ring *n* a ring usu of plain metal (e g gold) given by 1 marriage partner to the other during the wedding ceremony and worn thereafter to signify marital status

[1]wedge /wej/ *n* **1** a piece of wood, metal, etc tapered to a thin edge and used esp for splitting wood or raising heavy objects **2a** sthg wedge-shaped ⟨*a ~ of pie*⟩ **b** (a shoe with) a wedge-shaped sole raised at the heel and tapering towards the toe **c** an iron golf club with a broad face angled for maximum loft **3** sthg causing a breach or separation [ME *wegge*, fr OE *wecg*; akin to OHG *wecki* wedge, Lith *vagis*]

[2]wedge *vt* **1** to fasten or tighten by driving in a wedge **2** to force or press into a narrow space; cram – usu + *in* or *into* **3** to split or force apart (as if) with a wedge

wedged /wejd/ *adj* shaped like a wedge

Wedgwood /'wejwood/ *trademark* – used for pottery (e g earthenware, stoneware, or bone china) made by Josiah Wedgwood and his successors and typically decorated with a classical cameo-like design in white relief

,Wedgwood 'blue *adj or n* (of) a light greyish blue colour typically used in Wedgwood ware [Josiah *Wedgwood* †1795 E potter]

wedlock /'wedlok/ *n* the state of being married; marriage [ME *wedlok*, fr OE *wedlāc* marriage bond, fr *wedd* pledge + *-lāc*, suffix denoting activity] – **out of wedlock** with the natural parents not legally married to each other ⟨*born* out of wedlock⟩

Wednesday /'wenzday, -di, 'wednz-/ *n* the day of the week following Tuesday ☞ SYMBOL [ME, fr OE *wōdnesdæg*; akin to ON *ōthinsdagr* Wednesday; both fr a prehistoric WGmc-NGmc compound whose components are represented by OE *Wōden* Odin, the chief god in Gmc mythology, & by OE *dæg* day] – **Wednesdays** *adv*

[1]wee /wee/ *adj* very small; diminutive – often used to or by children or to convey an impression of Scottishness [ME *we*, fr *we*, n, little bit, fr OE *wǣge* weight; akin to OE *wegan* to move, weigh – more at WAY]

[2]wee *n* (an act of passing) urine – used esp by or to children [short for *wee-wee*] – **wee** *vi*

[1]weed /weed/ *n* **1** an unwanted wild plant which often overgrows or chokes out more desirable plants **2a** an obnoxious growth or thing **b** an animal, esp a horse, unfit to breed from **3** *Br* a weedy person – infml **4a** TOBACCO 2 – chiefly humor; usu + *the* **b** MARIJUANA 2 – slang; usu + *the* [ME, fr OE *wēod*; akin to OS *wiod* weed] – **weedless** *adj*

[2]weed *vi* to remove weeds or sthg harmful ~ *vt* **1** to clear of weeds ⟨~ *a garden*⟩ **2** to remove the undesirable parts of ⟨~ *the files*⟩ – **weeder** *n*

weed out *vt* to get rid of (sby or sthg harmful or unwanted); remove

weeds /weedz/ *n pl* MOURNING 2a [ME *wede* garment, fr OE *wǣd*, *gewǣde*; akin to ON *vāth* cloth, clothing, Lith *austi* to weave]

weedy /'weedi/ *adj* **1** covered with or consisting of weeds ⟨~ *pastures*⟩ **2** noticeably weak, thin, and ineffectual – infml – **weediness** *n*

week /week/ *n* **1a** any of several 7-day cycles used in various calendars **b** a week beginning with a specified day or containing a specified event ⟨*Easter* ~⟩ **2a** a period of 7 consecutive days **b** the working days during each 7-day period ⟨*stays in London during the* ~⟩ **c** a weekly period of work ⟨*works a 40-hour* ~⟩ **3** a time 7 days before or after a specified day ⟨*next Sunday* ~⟩ [ME *weke*, fr OE *wicu, wucu*; akin to OHG *wehha* week, L *vicis* change, alternation, OE *wīr* wire – more at WIRE] – **week in, week out** for an indefinite or seemingly endless number of weeks

'weekday /-day/ *n* any day of the week except (Saturday and) Sunday

[1]**weekend** /,week'end, '-,-/ *n* the end of the week; *specif* the period from Friday night to Sunday night

[2]**,week'end** *vi* to spend the weekend (e g at a place) – **weekender** *n*

[1]**weekly** /'weekli/ *adv* every week; once a week; by the week

[2]**weekly** *adj* **1** occurring, appearing, or done weekly **2** calculated by the week

[3]**weekly** *n* a weekly newspaper or periodical

'week,night /-,niet/ *n* a night of any day of the week except Saturday and Sunday

weeny /'weeni/ *also* **weensy** /'weenzi/ *adj* exceptionally small; tiny – infml [*wee* + t*iny*]

weenybopper /'weeni,bopə/ *n* an esp female preadolescent who pursues pop idols and follows the latest fashions [*weeny* + *-bopper* (as in *teenybopper*)]

[1]**weep** /weep/ *vb* **wept** /wept/ *vt* **1** to express deep sorrow for, usu by shedding tears; bewail **2** to pour forth (tears) from the eyes **3** to exude (a fluid) slowly; ooze **4** to bring to a specified condition by shedding tears ⟨wept *herself to sleep*⟩ ~ *vi* **1a** to express passion (e g grief) by shedding tears **b** to mourn *for* sby or sthg **2** to give off or leak fluid slowly; ooze [ME *wepen*, fr OE *wēpan*; akin to OHG *wuoffan* to weep, OSlav *vabiti* to call to]

[2]**weep** *n* a fit of weeping

weeper /'weepə/ *n* **1** a professional mourner **2** a small statue of a mourning figure on a funeral monument **3** sthg (e g a black veil or hatband) worn as a sign of mourning, esp in the 18th and 19th c – usu pl with sing. meaning [[1]WEEP + [2]-ER]

weepie /'weepi/ *n* a sad or sentimental film or play – infml

weeping /'weeping/ *adj, of a tree* (being a variety) having slender drooping branches ⟨~ *willow*⟩

weepy /'weepi/ *adj* inclined to weep; tearful

weever /'weevə/ *n* any of several edible marine fishes with a broad spiny head and venomous spines on the dorsal fin [ONF *wivre* viper, modif of L *vipera*]

weevil /'weevl/ *n* any of numerous usu small beetles with a long snout bearing jaws at the tip, many of which are injurious, esp as larvae, to grain, fruit, etc [ME *wevel*, fr OE *wifel*; akin to OHG *wibil* beetle, OE *wefan* to weave] – **weevily, weevilly** *adj*

wee-wee /'wee ,wee/ *vi or n* (to) wee [baby talk]

weft /weft/ *n* the thread or yarn that interlaces the warp in a fabric; the crosswise yarn in weaving [ME, fr OE; akin to ON *veptr* weft, OE *wefan* to weave – more at WEAVE]

,weft-'knitted *adj* produced in machine knitting with the yarns running crosswise or in a circle

Wehrmacht /'veəmakht/ *n* the German armed forces just before and during WW II [G, fr *wehr* defence + *macht* force, might]

weigh /way/ *vt* **1** to ascertain the weight of (as if) on a scale **2** to consider carefully; evaluate – often + *up* ⟨~ *the pros and cons*⟩ **3** to measure (a definite quantity) (as if) on a scale – often + *out* ~ *vi* **1a** to have weight or a specified weight **b** to register a weight (e g on a scale) – + *in* or *out*; compare WEIGH IN 1, WEIGH OUT **2** to merit consideration as important; count ⟨*evidence will* ~ *heavily against him*⟩ **3** to be a burden or cause of anxiety to – often + *on* or *upon* ⟨*her responsibilities* ~ed *upon her*⟩ [ME *weyen*, fr OE *wegan* to move, carry, weigh – more at WAY] – **weighable** *adj*, **weigher** *n* – **weigh anchor** to pull up an anchor preparatory to sailing

'weigh,bridge /-,brij/ *n* a large scale used for weighing vehicles which usu consists of a plate level with the surface of a road onto which the vehicles are driven

weigh down *vt* **1** to make heavy; weight **2** to oppress, burden

weigh in *vi* **1** to have oneself or one's possessions (e g luggage) weighed; *esp* to be weighed after a horse race or before a boxing or wrestling match **2** to make a contribution; join in ⟨*a bystander* weighed in *to stop the fight*⟩ – **weigh-in** /'-,-/ *n*

weigh out *vi* to be weighed after a boxing or wrestling match

[1]**weight** /wayt/ *n* **1a** the amount that a quantity or body weighs, esp as measured on a particular scale **b(1)** any of the classes into which contestants in certain sports (e g boxing and wrestling) are divided according to body weight **(2)** a horse carrying a usu specified weight in a handicap race ⟨*the top* ~ *won the race*⟩ **(3)** poundage required to be carried by a horse in a handicap race **2a** a quantity weighing a certain amount ⟨*equal* ~s *of flour and sugar*⟩ **b** a heavy object thrown or lifted as an athletic exercise or contest **3a** a system of units of weight ⟨*troy* ~⟩ **b** any of the units of weight used in such a system **c** a piece of material (e g metal) of known weight for use in weighing articles **4a** sthg heavy; a load **b** a heavy object to hold or press sthg down or to counterbalance ⟨*the* ~s *of the clock*⟩ **5a** a burden, pressure ⟨*took a* ~ *off my mind*⟩ **b** corpulence **6a** relative heaviness ⟨~ *is a quality of material substances*⟩ **b** the force with which a body is attracted towards a celestial body (e g the earth) by gravitation and which is equal to the product of the mass of the body and the local gravitational acceleration **7a** relative importance, authority, or influence ⟨*his views don't carry much* ~⟩ **b** *the* main force or strength ⟨*the* ~ *of the argument*⟩ **8** a numerical value assigned to an item to express its relative importance in a frequency distribution *USE* (*1a & 3a, b*) ☞ UNIT [ME *wight, weght*, fr OE *wiht*; akin to ON *vætt* weight, OE *wegan* to weigh]

[2]**weight** *vt* **1** to load or make heavy (as if) with a weight **2** to oppress with a burden ⟨~ed *down with cares*⟩ **3** to assign a statistical weight to **4** to arrange in such a way as to create a bias ⟨*a wage structure* ~ed *heavily in favour of employees with long service*⟩

weighting /'wayting/ *n, Br* an additional sum paid

on top of wages; *esp* one paid to offset the higher cost of living in a particular area ⟨*a London ~ of £500*⟩

ˈweightless /-lis/ *adj* having little weight; lacking apparent gravitational pull – **weightlessly** *adv*, **weightlessness** *n*

ˈweight-ˌlifter *n* one who lifts heavy weights, esp barbells, in competition or as an exercise – **weight-lifting** *n*

ˈweight ˌtraining *n* physical training involving the lifting of usu heavy weights, esp barbells

ˈweightˌwatcher *n* one who is dieting to lose weight – **weightwatching** *n*

weighty /ˈwayti/ *adj* **1** of much importance, influence, or consequence; momentous **2** heavy, esp in proportion to bulk ⟨*~ metal*⟩ **3** burdensome, onerous ⟨*the ~ cares of state*⟩ – **weightily** *adv*, **weightiness** *n*

weir /wiə/ *n* **1** a fence or enclosure set in a waterway for trapping fish **2** a dam in a stream to raise the water level or control its flow [ME *were*, fr OE *wer*; akin to ON *ver* fishing place, OHG *werien, werren* to defend, L aperire to open, operire to close, cover]

weird /wiəd/ *adj* **1** of or caused by witchcraft or the supernatural **2** of a strange or extraordinary character; odd – infml [ME (Sc) *werd* fateful, fr *werd* fate, destiny, fr OE *wyrd*; akin to ON *urthr* fate, OE *weorthan* to become – more at [1]WORTH] – **weirdly** *adv*, **weirdness** *n*

weirdie, weirdy /ˈwiədi/ *n* sby who is very strange or eccentric – infml

weirdo /ˈwiədoh/ *n, pl* **weirdos** a weirdie – infml

ˌWeird ˈSisters *n pl* *the* Fates

welch /welch/ *vi* to welsh – **welcher** *n*

Welch /welsh/ *adj* Welsh – now only in names ⟨*the Royal ~ Fusiliers*⟩

[1]welcome /ˈwelkəm/ *interj* – used to express a greeting to a guest or newcomer on his/her arrival [ME, alter. of *wilcume*, fr OE, fr *wilcuma* desirable guest; akin to OHG *willicomo* desirable guest; prob both fr a prehistoric WGmc compound whose constituents are represented by OE *willa, will* desire & by OE *cuma* guest; akin to OE *cuman* to come – more at [2]WILL, COME]

[2]welcome *vt* **1** to greet hospitably and with courtesy **2** to greet or receive in the specified, esp unpleasant, way ⟨*they ~d the intruder with a hail of bullets*⟩ **3** to receive or accept with pleasure ⟨*~s danger*⟩ ⟨*~d the appearance of his new book*⟩ – **welcomer** *n* – **welcome with open arms** to greet or accept with great cordiality or pleasure

[3]welcome *adj* **1** received gladly into one's presence or companionship ⟨*was always ~ in their home*⟩ **2** giving pleasure; received with gladness, esp because fulfilling a need ⟨*a ~ relief*⟩ **3** willingly permitted or given the right ⟨*you're ~ to read it*⟩ **4** – used in the phrase 'You're welcome" as a reply to an expression of thanks – **welcomely** *adv*, **welcomeness** *n*

[4]welcome *n* **1** a greeting or reception on arrival or first appearance **2** the hospitable treatment that a guest may expect ⟨*outstayed their ~*⟩

[1]weld /weld/ *vi* to become or be capable of being welded ~ *vt* **1a** to fuse (metallic parts) together by heating and allowing the metals to flow together or by hammering or compressing with or without previous heating **b** to unite (plastics) in a similar manner by heating or by using a chemical solvent **c** to repair, produce, or create (as if) by such a process **2** to unite closely or inseparably [alter. of obs *well* (to weld), fr ME *wellen* to boil, well, weld] – **weldable** *adj*, **welder** *n*, **weldability** /-ˈbiləti/ *n*

[2]weld *n* a welded joint

welfare /ˈwelfeə/ *n* **1** well-being ⟨*concerned for her child's ~*⟩ **2** WELFARE WORK **3** aid in the form of money or necessities for those not well able to provide for themselves (e g through poverty, age, or handicap) [ME, fr the phrase *wel faren* to fare well]

ˌwelfare ˈstate *n* (a country operating) a social system based on the assumption by the state of responsibility for the individual and social welfare of its citizens

ˈwelfare ˌwork *n* organized efforts to improve the living conditions of the poor, elderly, etc – **welfare worker** *n*

welkin /ˈwelkin/ *n* **1a** *the* sky, firmament **b** heaven **2** the upper atmosphere ***USE*** poetic [ME, lit., cloud, fr OE *wolcen*; akin to OHG *wolkan* cloud, OSlav *vlaga* moisture]

[1]well /wel/ *n* **1** (a pool fed by) a spring of water **2** a pit or hole sunk into the earth to reach a supply of water **3** an enclosure round the pumps of a ship **4** a shaft or hole sunk in the earth to reach a natural deposit (e g oil or gas) **5** an open space extending vertically through floors of a structure ⟨*a stair ~*⟩ **6** a vessel, space, or hole having a construction or shape suggesting a well for water ☞ CAR **7** a source from which sthg springs; a fountainhead **8** *Br* the open space in front of the judge in a law court [ME *welle*, fr OE (northern & Midland) *welle*; akin to OHG *wella* wave, OE *weallan* to bubble, boil]

[2]well *vi* **1** to rise to the surface and usu flow forth ⟨*tears ~ed from her eyes*⟩ **2** to rise to the surface like a flood of liquid ⟨*longing ~ed up in his breast*⟩ [ME *wellen*, fr OE (northern & Midland) *wellan* to cause to well; akin to MHG *wellen* to cause to well, OE *weallan* to bubble, boil, L *volvere* to roll – more at VOLUBLE]

[3]well *adv* **better** /ˈbetə/; **best** /best/ **1** in a good or proper manner; rightly **2** in a way appropriate to the circumstances: e g **a** satisfactorily, advantageously **b** with good appearance or effect ⟨*carried himself ~*⟩ **c** with skill or aptitude ⟨*~ caught!*⟩ **d** with prudence; sensibly ⟨*would do ~ to ask*⟩ ⟨*we may ~ wonder*⟩ **3** in a kind or friendly manner; favourably ⟨*spoke ~ of your idea*⟩ **4** in a prosperous manner ⟨*he lives ~*⟩ **5a** to an extent approaching completeness; thoroughly ⟨*after being ~ dried with a towel*⟩ **b** on a close personal level; intimately ⟨*knew her ~*⟩ **6a** easily, fully ⟨*~ worth the price*⟩ **b** much, considerably ⟨*~ over a million*⟩ **c** in all likelihood; indeed ⟨*may ~ be true*⟩ [ME *wel*, fr OE; akin to OHG *wela* well, OE *wyllan* to wish – more at WILL] – **as well 1** also; IN ADDITION ⟨*there were other features* as well⟩ ⟨*she's pretty* as well⟩ **2** to the same extent or degree ⟨*open* as well *to the poor as to the rich*⟩ **3** with equivalent or preferable effect ⟨*might just* as well *have stayed at home*⟩ ⟨*you may* as well *tell him*⟩ **4** [5]WELL 2, 4 – **as well as** [2]BESIDES 2 ⟨*skilful* as well as *strong*⟩ – **well and truly** totally, completely – **well away 1** making good progress **2** (almost) DRUNK 1 – infml – **well out of** lucky to be free from

[4]well *interj* **1** – used to express surprise, indignation, or resignation **2** – used to indicate a pause in talking or to introduce a remark

[5]**well** *adj* **1** satisfactory, pleasing ⟨*all's ~ that ends ~*⟩ **2** advisable, desirable ⟨*it's ~ to ask*⟩ **3** prosperous, well-off **4** HEALTHY 1 **5** being a cause for thankfulness; fortunate ⟨*it is ~ that this has happened*⟩ – **wellness** *n*

we'll /weel/ we will; we shall

,well-ad'vised *adj* **1** acting with wisdom; prudent **2** resulting from or showing wisdom ⟨*~ plans*⟩

,well-ap'pointed *adj* having good and complete facilities, furniture, etc ⟨*a ~ house*⟩

,well-be'haved *adj* showing proper manners or conduct

,well-'being *n* the state of being happy, healthy, or prosperous

,well'born /-'bawn/ *adj* born of a respected and esp noble family

,well-'bred *adj* **1** having or indicating good breeding; refined **2** of good pedigree

,well-'built *adj* broad and sturdy in physique

,well-con'nected *adj* having useful social or family contacts

,well-di'sposed *adj* having a favourable or sympathetic disposition ⟨*was ~ towards his workmates*⟩

,well-'done *adj* cooked thoroughly

,well-'favoured *adj* good-looking; handsome – not now in vogue

,well-'found *adj* properly equipped ⟨*a ~ ship*⟩

,well-'founded *adj* based on good grounds or reasoning ⟨*a ~ argument*⟩

,well-'groomed *adj* well dressed and scrupulously neat

,well-'grounded *adj* **1** having a good basic knowledge ⟨*~ in Latin and Greek*⟩ **2** well-founded

'well,head /,hed/ *n* **1** the source of a spring or stream **2** WELL 7 **3** the top of or a structure built over a well

,well-'heeled *adj* having a great deal of money; wealthy – infml

,well-'hung *adj* **1** having large breasts **2** having a large penis *USE* vulg

wellies /'weliz/ *n pl* WELLINGTON BOOTS – infml [by shortening & alter.]

,well-in'formed *adj* **1** having a good knowledge of a wide variety of subjects **2** having reliable information on a usu specified topic, event, etc

,wellington 'boot, wellington /'welingt(ə)n/ *n, chiefly Br* a waterproof rubber boot that usu reaches the knee [Arthur Wellesley, 1st Duke of *Wellington* †1852 Br general & statesman]

wellingtonia /,weling'tohnyə, -ni·ə/ *n* BIG TREE [NL, fr 1st Duke of *Wellington*]

,well-in'tentioned *adj* well-meaning

,well-'knit *adj* well constructed; *esp* having a compact usu muscular physique ⟨*a ~ athlete*⟩

,well-'known *adj* fully or widely known; *specif* famous

,well-'lined *adj* full of money – infml ⟨*~ pockets*⟩

,well-'meaning *adj* having or based on good intentions though often failing ⟨*~ but misguided idealists*⟩

,well-'meant *adj* based on good intentions

,well-'nigh *adv* almost, nearly

,well-'off *adj* **1** well-to-do, rich **2** in a favourable or fortunate situation ⟨*you don't know when you're ~*⟩ **3** well provided ⟨*not very ~ for sheets*⟩

,well-'oiled *adj, chiefly Br* DRUNK 1 – infml

,well-pre'served *adj* retaining a youthful appearance

,well-'read /red/ *adj* well-informed through much and varied reading

,well-'rounded *adj* **1** having a pleasantly curved or rounded shape ⟨*a ~ figure*⟩ **2** having or consisting of a background of broad experience or education ⟨*a ~ person*⟩ **3** agreeably complete and well-constructed

Wellsian /'welzi·ən/ *adj* (characteristic) of the writings of H G Wells, esp in describing or foretelling a possible future [H G *Wells* †1946 E writer]

,well-'spoken *adj* **1** speaking clearly, courteously, and usu with a refined accent **2** spoken in a pleasing or fitting manner ⟨*~ words*⟩

'well,spring /-,spring/ *n* **1** a source of continual supply **2** FOUNTAINHEAD 1

,well-'stacked *adj* having large breasts – slang

,well-'thought-of *adj* of good repute

,well-'timed *adj* said or done at an opportune moment; timely

,well-to-'do *adj* moderately rich; prosperous

,well-'tried *adj* thoroughly tested and found reliable

,well-'turned *adj* **1** pleasingly formed; shapely ⟨*a ~ ankle*⟩ **2** concisely and appropriately expressed ⟨*a ~ compliment*⟩

,well-up'holstered *adj, of a person* plump – humor

,well-'versed *adj* having a sound knowledge of a subject; conversant with sthg – + *in*

'well-,wisher *n* one who feels goodwill towards a person, cause, etc – **well-wishing** *adj or n*

,well-'worn *adj* **1** having been much used or worn ⟨*~ shoes*⟩ **2** made trite by overuse; hackneyed

wels /welz/ *n* a large freshwater catfish of central and E Europe [G, fr MHG]

welsh /welsh/ *vi* **1** to evade an obligation, esp payment of a debt **2** to break one's word *USE* usu + *on* [prob fr *Welsh*, adj] – **welsher** *n*

Welsh *n* **1** *pl in constr* the people of Wales **2** the Celtic language of the Welsh ☞ LANGUAGE [ME *Walsche, Welsse*, fr *walisch, welisch*, adj, Welsh, fr OE (northern & Midland) *wælisc, welisc* Celtic, Welsh, foreign, fr OE *Wealh* Celt, Welshman, foreigner, of Celtic origin; akin to the source of L *Volcae*, a Celtic people of SE Gaul] – **Welsh** *adj*, **Welshman** *n*

,Welsh 'dresser *n* [1]DRESSER 1; *specif* one having open shelves above a flat surface with drawers and small cupboards below

,Welsh 'poppy *n* a widely cultivated European poppy with large yellow flowers

,Welsh 'rabbit *n* WELSH RAREBIT

,Welsh 'rarebit /'reəbit/ *n* a snack of melted cheese (and ale) on toast [alter. of *Welsh rabbit*]

[1]**welt** /welt/ *n* **1** a strip, usu of leather, between a shoe sole and upper through which they are fastened together **2** a doubled edge, strip, insert, or seam (e g on a garment) for ornament or reinforcement **3** (a ridge or lump raised on the body usu by) a heavy blow [ME *welte*]

[2]**welt** *vt* **1** to provide with a welt **2a** to raise a welt on the body of **b** to hit hard

weltanschauung /'veltahn,showəng/ *n, pl* **weltanschauungs, weltanschauungen** /-əng·ən/ *often cap* a particular conception of the nature and purpose of the world; a philosophy of life [G, fr *welt* world + *anschauung* view]

[1]**welter** /ˈweltə/ *vi* **1** to writhe, toss; *also* to wallow **2** to become soaked, sunk, or involved *in* sthg [ME *welteren*; akin to MD *welteren* to roll, OHG *walzan*, L *volvere* – more at VOLUBLE]

[2]**welter** *n* **1** a state of wild disorder; a turmoil **2** a chaotic mass or jumble ⟨*a bewildering* ~ *of data*⟩

ˈ**welter,weight** /-ˌwayt/ *n* a boxer who weighs not more than 10st 7lb (66.7kg) if professional or above 63.5kg (about 10st) but not more than 67kg (about 10st 8lb) if amateur [prob fr [2]*welt*]

weltschmerz /ˈvelt,shmeəts/ *n, often cap* mental depression caused by contemplating the state of the world; *esp* sentimental pessimism [G, fr *welt* world + *schmerz* pain]

wen /wen/ *n* **1** a cyst formed by obstruction of a sebaceous gland and filled with fatty material **2** an abnormally large overcrowded city, esp London [ME *wenn*, fr OE; akin to MLG *wene* wen]

[1]**wench** /wench/ *n* **1** a female servant or rustic working girl **2** a young woman; a girl – now chiefly humor or dial [ME *wenche*, short for *wenchel* child, fr OE *wencel*; akin to OHG *winchan* to stagger – more at WINK]

[2]**wench** *vi, of a man* to have sexual relations habitually with women, esp prostitutes – **wencher** *n*

wend /wend/ *vt* to proceed on (one's way) [ME *wenden*, fr OE *wendan*; akin to OHG *wenten* to turn, OE *windan* to twist – more at [4]WIND]

Wend *n* a member of a Slavonic people of eastern Germany [G *Wende*, fr OHG *Winida*; akin to OE *Winedas*, pl, Wends] – **Wendish** *adj*

ˈ**wendy ˌhouse** /ˈwendi/ *n, often cap W, chiefly Br* a small toy house for children to play in [*Wendy*, character in *Peter Pan*, children's book by J M Barrie †1937 Sc writer]

Wensleydale /ˈwenzli,dayl/ *n* a crumbly mild-flavoured English cheese [*Wensleydale*, district in Yorkshire]

went /went/ *past of* GO [ME, past & pp of *wenden*]

wentletrap /ˈwentl,trap/ *n* (the usu white shell of) any of a family of marine snails [D *wenteltrap* winding stair, fr MD *wendeltrappe*, fr *wendel* turning + *trappe* stairs]

were /wə; *strong* wuh/ *past 2 sing, past pl, substandard past 1 & 3 sing, or past subjunctive of* BE [ME *were* (suppletive sing. past subj & 2 sing. past indic of *been* to be), *weren* (suppletive past pl of *been*), fr OE *wǣre* (sing. past subj & 2 sing. past indic of *wesan* to be), *wǣron* (past pl indic of *wesan*), *wǣren* (past pl subj of *wesan*) – more at WAS]

we're /wiə/ we are

weren't /wuhnt/ were not

werewolf /ˈweə,woolf, ˈwiə-/ *n, pl* **werewolves** /-woolvz/ a person transformed into a wolf or capable of assuming a wolf's form [ME, fr OE *werwulf*; akin to OHG *werwolf* werewolf; both fr a prehistoric WGmc compound whose constituents are represented by OE *wer* man & by OE *wulf* wolf – more at VIRILE, WOLF]

wert /wuht/ *archaic past 2 sing of* BE

Wesleyanism /ˈwezli·ə,niz(ə)m/ *n* Methodism [John *Wesley* †1791 E preacher] – **Wesleyan** *adj or n*

[1]**west** /west/ *adj or adv* towards, at, belonging to, or coming from the west [adv ME, fr OE; akin to OHG *westar* to the west, & prob to L *vesper* evening, Gk *hesperos*; adj fr adv]

[2]**west** *n* **1** (the compass point corresponding to) the direction 90° to the left of north that is the general direction of sunset **2** *often cap* regions or countries lying to the west of a specified or implied point of orientation: e g **a** the part of the USA to the west of the Mississippi **b** the non-Communist countries of Europe and America **3** European civilization in contrast with that of the Orient – **westward** /-wood/ *adv, adj, or n,* **westwards** /-woodz/ *adv*

ˈ**West ˌCountry** *n* *the* West of England

ˌ**West ˈEnd** *n* *the* western part of central London where the main shopping centres, theatres, etc are located – **West-End** *adj*

wester /ˈwestə/ *vi* to turn or decline westwards ⟨*the half moon* ~s *low* – A E Housman⟩ [ME *westren*, fr [1]*west*]

[1]**westerly** /ˈwestəli/ *adj or adv* west [obs *wester* (western)]

[2]**westerly** *n* a wind from the west

[1]**western** /ˈwestən/ *adj* **1** *often cap* (characteristic) of a region conventionally designated West: e g **a** of or stemming from European traditions in contrast with those of the Orient **b** of the non-Communist countries of Europe and America **c** of the American West **2** west **3** *cap* of the Roman Catholic or Protestant segment of Christianity [ME *westerne*, fr OE; akin to OHG *westrōni* western, OE *west*] – **westernmost** /-ˌmohst/ *adj*

[2]**western** *n, often cap* a novel, film, etc dealing with cowboys, frontier life, etc in the W USA, esp during the latter half of the 19th c

Westerner /ˈwestənə/ *n, chiefly NAm* a native or inhabitant of the West, esp the W USA

ˌ**western ˈhemisphere** *n* the half of the earth comprising N and S America and surrounding waters

western·ize, -ise /ˈwestəniez/ *vb* to imbue or be imbued with qualities associated with the West – **westernization** /-ˈzaysh(ə)n/ *n*

western saddle *n, often cap W* STOCK SADDLE

ˌ**West Gerˈmanic** *n* a group of the Germanic languages including English, Frisian, Dutch, and German

ˌ**West ˈIndian** *n* **1** a native or inhabitant of the W Indies **2** a descendant of W Indians [*West Indies* (formerly *West India*), group of islands round the Caribbean Sea] – **West Indian** *adj*

westing /ˈwesting/ *n* **1** distance due west in longitude from the preceding point of measurement **2** westerly progress

Westminster /ˈwest,minstə, -ˈ--/ *n* the British Parliament [*Westminster*, district of London in which the Houses of Parliament are situated]

ˌ**west-northˈwest** *n* a compass point midway between west and northwest

ˌ**west-southˈwest** *n* a compass point midway between west and southwest

[1]**wet** /wet/ *adj* **-tt- 1** consisting of, containing, or covered or soaked with liquid (e g water) **2** rainy **3** still moist enough to smudge or smear ⟨~ *paint*⟩ **4** involving the use or presence of liquid ⟨~ *processes*⟩ **5** *of an aircraft wing* containing fuel tanks **6** *chiefly Br* feebly ineffectual or dull – infml **7** *chiefly NAm* permitting the sale or consumption of alcoholic drink ⟨*a* ~ *State*⟩ – compare DRY 4 [ME, partly fr pp of *weten* to wet & partly fr OE *wǣt* wet; akin to ON

vātr wet, OE *wæter* water] – **wetly** *adv*, **wetness** *n*, **wettish** *adj* – **wet behind the ears** immature, inexperienced – infml

[2]**wet** *n* **1** moisture, wetness **2** rainy weather; rain **3** *chiefly Br* a wet person; a drip – infml

[3]**wet** *vt* **-tt-;** (2) **wet** **1** to make wet **2** to urinate in or on [ME *weten*, fr OE *wǣtan*, fr *wǣt*, adj] – **wettable** *adj*, **wettability** *n* – **wet one's whistle** to take an esp alcoholic drink – infml

weta /'waytə/ *n* any of various large wingless long-horned New Zealand insects that resemble grasshoppers [Maori]

,wet and 'dry *n* emery paper that can be used either moistened or dry

'wet,back /-,bak/ *n, NAm* a Mexican who enters the USA illegally [[1]*wet* + [1]*back*; fr a person having to swim or wade across the Rio Grande in order to cross from Mexico into Texas]

,wet 'blanket *n* one who quenches or dampens enthusiasm or pleasure

,wet 'dream *n* an erotic dream culminating in orgasm

'wet ,fish *n, Br* fresh uncooked fish ⟨*a ~ merchant*⟩

wether /'wedhə/ *n* a male sheep castrated before sexual maturity [ME, ram, fr OE; akin to OHG *widar* ram, L *vitulus* calf, *vetus* old, Gk *etos* year]

wetland /'wetlənd, -,land/ *n* land or areas (e g tidal flats or swamps) containing much soil moisture – usu pl with sing. meaning

'wet-,look *adj, of a material, esp plastic or leather, or sthg made from it* having a shiny rather wrinkled finish ⟨*~ shoes*⟩ – **wet look** *n*

wet-nurse /'-,-, ,-'-/ *vt* **1** to act as wet nurse to **2** to give constant and often excessive care to

'wet ,nurse *n* a woman who cares for and suckles another's children

wet rot *n* (decay in timber caused by) any of various fungi that attack wood that has a high moisture content

'wet ,suit *n* a close-fitting suit made of material, usu rubber, that admits water but retains body heat so as to insulate its wearer (e g a skin diver), esp in cold water

wetter /'wetə/ *n* **1** a worker who wets material in any of several manufacturing processes **2** WETTING AGENT [[3]WET + [2]-ER]

'wetting ,agent /'weting/ *n* a substance that prevents a surface from being repellent to a wetting liquid

we've /wiv; *strong* weev/ we have

[1]**whack** /wak/ *vt* **1** to strike with a smart or resounding blow **2** *chiefly Br* to get the better of; defeat ***USE*** infml [prob imit] – **whacker** *n*

[2]**whack** *n* **1** (the sound of) a smart resounding blow **2** a portion, share **3** an attempt, go ⟨*have a ~ at it*⟩ ***USE*** infml

whacked /wakt/ *adj, chiefly Br* completely exhausted; DONE IN – infml

[1]**whacking** /'waking/ *adj* extremely big; whopping – infml

[2]**whacking** *adv* very, extremely – infml ⟨*a ~ great oil tanker*⟩

whacko /,wak'oh/ *interj, Br* – used to express delight; infml

whacky /'waki/ *adj* wacky

[1]**whale** /wayl/ *n, pl* **whales,** *esp collectively* **whale** any of an order of often enormous aquatic mammals that superficially resemble large fish, have tails modified as paddles, and are frequently hunted for oil, flesh, or whalebone [ME, fr OE *hwæl*; akin to OHG *hwal* whale] – **whale of a time** an exceptionally enjoyable time

[2]**whale** *vi* to engage in whale fishing and processing

[3]**whale** *vt, NAm* to hit or defeat soundly – infml [origin unknown]

'whale,back /-,bak/ *n* sthg shaped like the back of a whale

'whale,boat /-,boht/ *n* a long narrow rowing boat with pointed ends, formerly used for hunting whales

'whale,bone /-,bohn/ *n* a horny substance found in 2 rows of plates up to 4m (about 12ft) long attached along the upper jaw of whalebone whales and used for stiffening things

'whalebone ,whale *n* any of various usu large whales that have whalebone instead of teeth, which they use to filter krill from large volumes of sea water – compare TOOTHED WHALE

'whale ,oil *n* TRAIN OIL

whaler /'waylə/ *n* a person or ship engaged in whaling

whaling /'wayling/ *n* the occupation of catching and processing whales for oil, food, etc

[1]**wham** /wam/ *n* (the sound made by) a forceful blow – infml [imit]

[2]**wham** *interj* – used to express the noise of a forceful blow or impact; infml

[3]**wham** *vb* **-mm-** *vt* to throw or strike with a loud impact ~ *vi* to crash or explode with a loud impact ***USE*** infml

[1]**whang** /wang/ *vt* to throw, strike, or work at with force – infml [*whang* (thong, lash), alter. of ME *thong, thwang*]

[2]**whang** *n* a loud sharp vibrant sound – infml [imit]

whangee /wang'ee/ *n* **1** any of several Chinese bamboos **2** a walking stick or riding crop of whangee [prob fr Chin (Pek) *huang*[2] *li*[2], fr *huang*[2] yellow + *li*[2] bamboo cane]

whare /'wori/ *n* **1** a Maori house of traditional design **2** *NZ* a hut or shack [Maori]

wharf /wawf/ *n, pl* **wharves** /wawvz/ *also* **wharfs** a structure built along or out from the shore of navigable water so that ships may load and unload [ME, fr OE *hwearf* embankment, wharf; akin to OE *hweorfan* to turn, OHG *hwerban*, Gk *karpos* wrist]

wharfage /'wawfij/ *n* **1** (the charge for) the use of a wharf **2** a system of wharves

wharfinger /'waw,finjə/ *n* the owner or manager of a commercial wharf [irreg fr *wharfage*]

[1]**what** /wot/ *pron, pl* **what** **1a(1)** – used as an interrogative expressing inquiry about the identity, nature, purpose, or value of sthg or the character, nature, occupation, position, or role of sby ⟨*~ is this?*⟩ **(2)** – used to ask for repetition of sthg not properly heard or understood ⟨*he bought ~?*⟩ **b** – used as an exclamation expressing surprise or excitement and frequently introducing a question ⟨*~, no breakfast?*⟩ **c** – used to direct attention to a statement that the speaker is about to make ⟨*guess ~*⟩ ⟨*you know ~*⟩ **d** *chiefly Br* – used in demanding assent ⟨*a clever play, ~?*⟩; not now in vogue **2** [4]THAT 1, WHICH 3, WHO 2 ⟨*gilded rat-holes ~ pass for public hostelries – Punch*⟩ – substandard **3** that

which; the one that ⟨*no income but* ~ *he gets from his writing*⟩ **4a** WHATEVER 1a ⟨*say* ~ *you will*⟩ **b** how much – used in exclamations ⟨~ *it must cost!*⟩ [ME, fr OE *hwæt*, neut of *hwa* who – more at WHO] **– or what** – used at the end of a question to express inquiry about additional possibilities ⟨*is it raining, or snowing,* or what?⟩ **– what about 1** what news or plans have you concerning **2** *also* **what do you say to, what's wrong with** let's; HOW ABOUT **– what for 1** for what purpose or reason; why – usu used with the other words of a question between *what* and *for* ⟨what *did you do that* for?⟩ except when used alone **2** punishment, esp by blows or by a sharp reprimand ⟨*gave him* what for *in violent Spanish* – *New Yorker*⟩ **– what have you** any of various other things that might also be mentioned ⟨*paper clips, pins, and* what have you⟩ **– what if 1** what will or would be the result if **2** what does it matter if **– what it takes** the qualities or resources needed for success or for attainment of a usu specified goal ⟨*she's really got* what it takes *to get to the top*⟩ **– what not** WHAT HAVE YOU **– what of 1** what is the situation with respect to **2** what importance can be assigned to **– what of it** what does it matter **– what's what** the true state of things ⟨*knows* what's what *when it comes to fashion*⟩

²**what** *adv* in what respect?; how much? ⟨~ *does he care?*⟩ [ME, fr OE *hwæt*, fr *hwæt*, pron]

³**what** *adj* **1a** – used with a following noun as an adjective equivalent in meaning to the interrogative pronoun *what* ⟨~ *minerals do we export?*⟩ **b** WHICH 1 ⟨~ *size do you take?*⟩ **c** how remarkable or striking – used esp in exclamatory utterances and dependent clauses ⟨~ *a suggestion!*⟩ **2** the that; as much or as many as ⟨*told him* ~ *little I knew*⟩ ['*what*]

¹**whatever** /wot'evə/ *pron* **1a** anything or everything that ⟨*take* ~ *you want*⟩ **b** no matter what **2** what in the world? – infml ⟨~ *do you mean?*⟩ **– or whatever** or anything else at all – infml ⟨*buffalo or rhinoceros* or whatever – Alan Moorehead⟩

²**whatever** *adj* **1a** any that; all that ⟨*buy peace on* ~ *terms could be obtained* – C S Forester⟩ **b** no matter what **2** of any kind at all – used after a noun with *any* or with a negative ⟨*of any shape* ~⟩ ⟨*no food* ~⟩

whatnot /'wot,not/ *n* **1** a lightweight open set of shelves for bric-a-brac **2** other usu related goods, objects, etc ⟨*carrying all his bags and* ~⟩ **3** a whatsit *USE* (*2&3*) infml [*what not?*]

'what's his ,name, *fem* **'what's her ,name** *n* sby whose name is not known or has been forgotten – infml

whatsit /'wotsit/ *n* sby or sthg that is of unspecified, nondescript, or unknown character, or whose name has been forgotten – infml [*what's it?*]

whatsoever /,wotsoh'evə/ *pron or adj* whatever

'what with *prep* having as a contributory circumstance or circumstances ⟨*very busy* what with *all these guests to feed*⟩

whaup /wawp/ *n, pl* **whaup** *also* **whaups** *chiefly Scot* a curlew [imit]

wheal /weel/ *n* a weal

wheat /weet/ *n* (any of various grasses cultivated in most temperate areas for) a cereal grain that yields a fine white flour and is used for making bread and pasta, and in animal feeds [ME *whete*, fr OE *hwǣte*; akin to OHG *weizzi* wheat, *hwīz, wīz* white – more at WHITE]

'wheat,ear /-,iə/ *n* any of several small usu white-rumped Old World Eurasian birds related to the thrushes [back-formation fr earlier *wheatears*, prob by folk etymology or euphemism fr *white* + *arse*]

wheaten /'weet(ə)n/ *adj* made of (the grain, meal, or flour of) wheat

'wheat ,germ *n* the embryo of the wheat kernel separated in milling and used esp as a source of vitamins

whee /wee/ *interj* – used to express delight or exuberance

wheedle /'weedl/ *vb* **wheedling** /'weedling, 'weedl·ing/ *vt* **1** to influence or entice by soft words or flattery **2** to cause to part with sthg by wheedling – + *out of* ⟨~ *her out of her last £5*⟩ ~ *vi* to use soft words of flattery [origin unknown]

¹**wheel** /weel/ *n* **1** a circular frame of hard material that may be (partly) solid or spoked and that is capable of turning on an axle **2** a contrivance or apparatus having as its principal part a wheel: e g **a** a chiefly medieval instrument of torture to which the victim was tied while his/her limbs were broken by a metal bar **b** any of various revolving discs or drums that produce an arbitrary value on which to gamble, usu by stopping at a particular number ⟨*roulette* ~⟩ **3** sthg resembling a wheel in shape or motion; *esp* CATHERINE WHEEL **4a** a curving or circular movement **b** a rotation or turn, usu about an axis or centre; *specif* a turning movement of troops or ships in line in which the units preserve alignment and relative positions **5a** *pl* the workings or controlling forces of sthg ⟨*the* ~*s of government*⟩ **b** *chiefly NAm* a person of importance, esp in an organization ⟨*a big* ~⟩ **6** *pl* a motor vehicle, esp a motor car *USE* (*5b&6*) infml [ME, fr OE *hweogol, hwēol*; akin to ON *hvēl* wheel, Gk *kyklos* circle, wheel, Skt *cakra*, L *colere* to cultivate, inhabit, Gk *telos* end] – **wheelless** *adj*

²**wheel** *vi* **1** to turn (as if) on an axis; revolve **2** to change direction as if revolving on a pivot ⟨~*ed round and walked away*⟩ **3** to move or extend in a circle or curve ⟨*birds in* ~ing *flight*⟩ **4** to alter or reverse one's opinion – often + *about* or *round* ~ *vt* **1** to cause to turn (as if) on an axis; rotate **2** to convey or move (as if) on wheels; *esp* to push (a wheeled vehicle or its occupant) ⟨~ *the baby into the shade*⟩ **3** to cause to change direction as if revolving on a pivot **4** to make or perform in a circle or curve **– wheel and deal** to pursue one's own usu commercial interests, esp in a shrewd or unscrupulous manner

,wheel and 'axle *n* a simple machine consisting of a grooved wheel turned by a cord or chain with a rigidly attached axle (e g for winding up a weight) together with the supporting standards

'wheel ,animal *n* a rotifer

'wheel,barrow /-,baroh/ *n* a load-carrying device that consists of a shallow box supported at 1 end by usu 1 wheel and at the other by a stand when at rest or by handles when being pushed

'wheel,base /-,bays/ *n* the distance between the front and rear axles of a vehicle

'wheel,chair /-,cheə/ *n* an invalid's chair mounted on wheels

wheeled /weeld/ *adj* equipped with or moving on

wheels ⟨~ *vehicles*⟩ – often in combination ⟨*2*-wheeled⟩

wheeler /'weelə/ *n* **1** a maker of wheels **2** a draught animal (e g a horse) pulling in the position nearest the front wheels of a wagon **3** sthg (e g a vehicle or ship) that has wheels – esp in combination ⟨*side*-wheeler⟩ [[2]WHEEL + [2]-ER]

,wheeler-'dealer *n, chiefly NAm* a shrewd operator, esp in business or politics [fr the vb phrase *wheel and deal*] – **wheeler-dealing** *n*

'wheel,horse /-,haws/ *n* WHEELER 2

'wheel,house /-,hows/ *n* a deckhouse for a vessel's helmsman

wheelie /'weeli/ *n* a manoeuvre in which a motorcycle, motor car, etc is momentarily balanced on its rear wheel or wheels

'wheel ,lock *n* (a gun having) a gunlock in which sparks are struck from a flint or a piece of iron pyrites by a revolving wheel

wheelsman /'weelzmən/ *n, NAm* a helmsman

'wheel,wright /-,riet/ *n* sby who makes or repairs wheels, esp wooden ones for carts

[1]ween /ween/ *adj, Scot & NEng* FEW 2 [ME (Sc) *quheyne*, fr OE *hwǣne, hwēne*, adv, somewhat, fr *hwōn* little, few]

[2]ween *n, Scot & NEng* a considerable number or amount

[1]wheeze /weez/ *vi* **1** to breathe with difficulty, usu with a whistling sound **2** to make a sound like that of wheezing ~ *vt* to utter wheezily [ME *whesen*, prob of Scand origin; akin to ON *hvæsa* to hiss; akin to OE *hwǣst* action of blowing, L *queri* to complain]

[2]wheeze *n* **1** a sound of wheezing **2** a cunning trick or expedient – infml – **wheezy** *adj*, **wheezily** *adv*, **wheeziness** *n*

[1]whelk /welk/ *n* any of numerous large marine snails; *esp* one much used as food in Europe [ME *welke*, fr OE *weoloc*; akin to L *volvere* to turn – more at VOLUBLE]

[2]whelk *n* a pustule, pimple [ME *whelke*, fr OE *hwylca*, fr *hwelian* to suppurate]

[1]whelp /welp/ *n* **1** any of the young of various flesh-eating mammals, esp a dog **2** a disagreeable or impudent child or youth [ME, fr OE *hwelp*; akin to OHG *hwelf* whelp]

[2]whelp *vt* to give birth to (esp a puppy) ~ *vi*, *esp of a bitch* to bring forth young

[1]when /wen/ *adv* **1** at what time? **2a** at or during which time ⟨*the day ~ we met*⟩ **b** and then; WHEREUPON 1 [ME, fr OE *hwanne, hwenne*; akin to OHG *hwanne* when, OE *hwā* who – more at WHO]

[2]when *conj* **1a** at or during the time that ⟨*went fishing ~ he was a boy*⟩ **b** as soon as ⟨*will look nice ~ finished*⟩ **c** whenever ⟨*~ he listens to music, he falls asleep*⟩ **2** in the event that; if **3a** considering that ⟨*why smoke ~ you know it's bad for you?*⟩ **b** in spite of the fact that; although ⟨*gave up politics ~ he might have done well*⟩ [ME, fr OE *hwanne, hwenne*, fr *hwanne, hwenne*, adv]

[3]when *pron* what or which time ⟨*since ~ have you known that?*⟩

[4]when *n* a date, time ⟨*worried about the wheres and ~s*⟩

whence /wens/ *adv or conj* **1a** from where?; from which place, source, or cause? **b** from which place, source, or cause **2** to the place from which ⟨*returned ~ they came*⟩ ***USE*** chiefly fml [adv ME *whennes*, fr *whenne* whence (fr OE *hwanon*) + *-s*, adv suffix; akin to OHG *hwanān* whence, OE *hwā* who]

whencesoever /,wens·soh'evə/ *conj, archaic* from whatever place or source

[1]whenever /wen'evə/ *conj* **1** at every or whatever time ⟨*roof leaks ~ it rains*⟩ ⟨*can go ~ he likes*⟩ **2** in any circumstance ⟨*~ possible, he tries to help*⟩ – **or whenever** or at any similar time – infml ⟨*in 1922* or whenever⟩

[2]whenever *adv* when in the world? – infml ⟨*~ did you find the time?*⟩

[1]whensoever /,wensoh'evə/ *conj* whenever

[2]whensoever *adv, obs* at any time whatever

[1]where /weə/ *adv* **1a** at, in, or to what place? ⟨*~ is the house?*⟩ **b** at, in, or to what situation, direction, circumstances, or respect? ⟨*~ does this plan lead?*⟩ **2** at, in, or to which (place) ⟨*has reached the size ~ traffic is a problem*⟩ ⟨*the town ~ she lives*⟩ [ME, fr OE *hwǣr*; akin to OHG *hwār* where, OE *hwā* who – more at WHO]

[2]where *conj* **1a** at, in, or to the place at which ⟨*stay ~ you are*⟩ **b** [2]WHEREVER ⟨*goes ~ he likes*⟩ **c** in a case, situation, or respect in which ⟨*outstanding ~ endurance is called for*⟩ **2** whereas, while ⟨*he wants a house, ~ I would prefer a flat*⟩ – **where it's at** the real scene of the action – slang

[3]where *n* **1** what place or point? ⟨*~ are you from?*⟩ **2** a place, point ⟨*bought from any old ~*⟩ – infml

[1]whereabouts /,weərə'bowts/ *also* **whereabout** *adv or conj* in what vicinity ⟨*do you know ~ he lives?*⟩ [ME *wheraboutes* (fr *wher aboute* + *-s*, adv suffix) & *wher aboute*, fr *where, wher* where + *about, aboute* about]

[2]whereabouts /'weərə,bowts/ *n pl but sing or pl in constr* the place or general locality where a person or thing is ⟨*his present ~ are a secret*⟩

whereas /weə'raz/ *conj* **1** in view of the fact that; since – used, esp formally, to introduce a preamble **2** while on the contrary; although [ME *where as*, fr *where + as*]

whereat /weə'rat/ *conj, archaic* **1** at or towards which **2** in consequence of which; whereupon

whereby /weə'bie/ *conj* **1** in accordance with which ⟨*a law ~ children receive cheap milk*⟩ **2** by which means – chiefly fml

where'er /weə'reə/ *adv or conj* wherever – poetic

[1]wherefore /'weəfaw, ,-'-/ *adv* **1** for what reason; why **2** for that reason; therefore ***USE*** chiefly fml [ME *wherfor, wherfore*, fr *where, wher* + *for, fore* for]

[2]'where,fore *n* a reason, cause – chiefly in *the whys and wherefores* ⟨*wants to know all the whys and ~s*⟩

wherefrom /weə'from/ *conj* from which – chiefly fml

[1]wherein /weə'rin/ *adv* in what; how ⟨*showed him ~ he was wrong*⟩ – chiefly fml

[2]wherein *conj* in which; where ⟨*the city ~ he lived*⟩ – chiefly fml

whereinto /weə'rintooh/ *conj, archaic* into which

whereof /weə'rov/ *conj, pron, or adv, archaic* of what, which, or whom

whereon /weə'ron/ *adv or conj, archaic* on which or what ⟨*the base ~ it rests*⟩

wherethrough /weə'throoh/ *conj, archaic* through which

whereto /weə'tooh/ *adv or conj* to which or what; whither ⟨*~ tends all this* – Shak⟩ – chiefly fml

whereunto /weə'runtooh/ *adv or conj, archaic* whereto

whereupon /,weərə'pon/ *adv or conj* **1** closely following and in consequence of which ⟨*he saw me coming,* ~ *he offered me his seat*⟩ **2** on which; whereon – chiefly fml

[1]**wherever** /weə'revə/ *adv* where in the world? – chiefly infml ⟨~ *have you been?*⟩ **– or wherever** or anywhere else at all – chiefly infml ⟨*go to China* or wherever⟩

[2]**wherever** *conj* at, in, or to every or whatever place ⟨*he can sleep* ~ *he likes*⟩

wherewith /weə'widh/ *conj* with or by means of which – chiefly fml

wherewithal /'weəwi,dhawl/ *n* means, resources; *specif* money ⟨*didn't have the* ~ *for an expensive dinner*⟩

wherry /'weri/ *n* **1** a long light rowing boat used to transport passengers on rivers and about harbours **2** a large light barge, lighter, or fishing boat used in Britain [ME *whery*]

[1]**whet** /wet/ *vt* **-tt- 1** to sharpen by rubbing on or with sthg (e g a stone) **2** to make keen or more acute; stimulate ⟨~ *the appetite*⟩ [ME *whetten*, fr OE *hwettan*; akin to OHG *wezzen* to whet, *waz* sharp] – **whetter** *n*

[2]**whet** *n* **1** a goad, incitement **2** an appetizer

whether /'wedhə/ *conj* – used usu with correlative *or* or with *or whether* to indicate **a** an indirect question involving alternatives ⟨*decide* ~ *he should agree or protest*⟩ or a choice between 2 alternatives ⟨*I wonder* ~ *he heard*⟩ **b** indifference between alternatives ⟨*seated him next to her* ~ *by accident or design*⟩ [ME, fr OE *hwæther, hwether*, fr *hwæther, hwether*, pron, which of two; akin to OHG *hwedar* which of two, L *uter*, Gk *poteros*, OE *hwā* who]

whetstone /'wet,stohn/ *n* **1** a stone for sharpening an edge (e g of a chisel⟩ **2** sthg that stimulates or makes keen

whew /fyooh/ *n* a half-formed whistle uttered as an exclamation expressing amazement, discomfort, or relief [imit]

whey /way/ *n* the watery part of milk separated from the curd, esp in cheese-making, and rich in lactose, minerals, and vitamins [ME, fr OE *hwæg*; akin to MD *wey* whey] – **wheyey** *adj*

,**whey-'faced** *adj* having a pale face (e g from fear)

[1]**which** /wich/ *adj* **1** being what one or ones out of a known or limited group? ⟨~ *tie should I wear?*⟩ **2** whichever ⟨*it will not fit, turn it* ~ *way you like*⟩ **3** – used to introduce a nonrestrictive relative clause by modifying the noun which refers either to a preceding word or phrase or to a whole previous clause ⟨*he may come, in* ~ *case I'll ask him*⟩ [ME, of what kind, which, fr OE *hwilc*; akin to OHG *wilīh* of what kind, which; both fr a prehistoric Gmc compound whose first constituent is akin to OE *hwā* who & whose second is represented by OE *-lic* -ly – more at WHO, -LY]

[2]**which** *pron, pl* **which 1** what one out of a known or specified group? ⟨~ *of those houses do you live in?*⟩ **2** whichever ⟨*take* ~ *you like*⟩ **3** – used to introduce a relative or esp a nonrestrictive relative clause; used in any grammatical relation except that of a possessive; used esp in reference to an animal, thing, or idea ⟨*the office in* ~ *I work*⟩ ⟨*a large dog,* ~ *bit me*⟩, or to a human group, esp when a singular verb follows ⟨*this tribe,* ~ *has aroused much interest among anthropologists*⟩; often used in reference to a whole previous clause or even to a preceding sentence ⟨*can sing,* ~ *is an advantage*⟩ ⟨*can be overcome by basing these programs on need not race.* Which *is fine* – *Nation Review* (*Melbourne*)⟩

[1]**whichever** /wi'chevə/ *pron, pl* **whichever 1** whatever one out of a group ⟨*take 2 of the 4 optional papers,* ~ *you prefer*⟩ **2** no matter which **3** which in the world? – chiefly infml ⟨~ *did you choose?*⟩

[2]**whichever** *adj* being whatever one or ones out of a group; no matter which ⟨*its soothing effect will be the same* ~ *way you take it* – *Punch*⟩

whichsoever /,wichsoh'evə/ *pron or adj, archaic* whichever

whidah /'widə/ *n* a whydah

[1]**whiff** /wif/ *n* **1** a quick puff, slight gust, or inhalation, esp of air, a smell, smoke, or gas **2** a slight trace ⟨*a* ~ *of scandal*⟩ [imit]

[2]**whiff** *vi* **1** to emit whiffs; puff **2** to inhale an odour; sniff **3** to smell unpleasant

whiffle /'wifl/ *vi* **whiffling** /'wifling/ **1** to blow with or emit a light whistling sound ⟨*the wind* ~d *in the leaves*⟩ **2** to be undecided; vacillate ⟨*do stop* whiffling!⟩ [prob freq of [2]*whiff*] – **whiffler** *n*

'**whiffle,tree** /-,tree/ *n, NAm* a swingletree [alter. of *whippletree*]

Whig /wig/ *n or adj* **1** (a member) of a major British political group of the 18th and early 19th c seeking to limit royal authority and increase parliamentary power – compare TORY 1 **2** *NAm* (a member) of an American political party formed about 1834 and succeeded about 1854 by the Republican party [n short for *Whiggamore* (member of a Scottish group that marched to Edinburgh in 1648 to oppose the court party); adj fr n] – **Whiggery, Whiggism** *n*, **Whiggish** *adj*

[1]**while** /wiel/ *n* **1** a period of time, esp when short and marked by the occurrence of an action or condition; a time ⟨*stay here for a* ~⟩ **2** the time and effort used; trouble ⟨*it's worth your* ~⟩ [ME, fr OE *hwīl*; akin to OHG *hwīla* time, L *quies* rest, quiet]

[2]**while** *conj* **1a** during the time that **b** providing that; as long as ⟨~ *there's life there's hope*⟩ **2a** when on the other hand; whereas **b** in spite of the fact that; although ⟨~ *respected, he is not liked*⟩

[3]**while** *prep, archaic or dial* until

while away *vt* to pass (time) in a leisurely, often pleasant, manner ⟨while away *the afternoon*⟩

whiles /wielz/ *adv, chiefly Scot* sometimes [ME (Sc) *quhilis* sometimes, formerly, fr ME (Sc) *quhile*, ME *while*, fr OE *hwīle* formerly]

whilst /wielst/ *conj, chiefly Br* while [ME *whilest*, alter. of *whiles*, fr *while* + *-s*, adv suffix]

whim /wim/ *n* **1** a sudden, capricious, or eccentric idea or impulse; a fancy **2** a large capstan formerly used in mines for raising ore or water [short for *whim-wham* (trifle, trinket), of unknown origin]

whimbrel /'wimbrəl/ *n* a small Eurasian curlew [perh imit]

whimper /'wimpə/ *vi or n* **1** (to make) a low plaintive whining sound **2** (to make) a petulant complaint or protest [imit]

whimsical /'wimzikl/ *adj* **1** full of whims; capricious **2** resulting from or suggesting whimsy; *esp* quizzical, playful ⟨*a* ~ *smile*⟩ [*whimsy*] – **whimsically** *adv*, **whimsicalness, whimsicality** /-'kaləti/ *n*

whimsy, whimsey /'wimzi/ *n* **1** a whim, caprice **2** an affected or fanciful device, creation, or style, esp in writing or art [irreg fr *whim-wham*]

whin /win/ *n* furze [ME *whynne*, of Scand origin; akin to Norw *kvein* bent grass]

whinchat /'winchat/ *n* a small brown and buff Old World bird [*whin* + [2]*chat*]

[1]**whine** /wien/ *vi* to utter or make a whine ~ *vt* to utter or express (as if) with a whine [ME *whinen*, fr OE *hwīnan* to whiz; akin to ON *hvīna* to whiz] – **whiner** *n*, **whiningly** *adv*

[2]**whine** *n* **1** (a sound like) a prolonged high-pitched cry, usu expressive of distress or pain **2** a querulous or peevish complaint – **whiny, whiney** *adj*

whinge, winge /winj/ *vi, chiefly Austr & dial Br* to complain, moan [(assumed) ME *whingen*, fr OE *hwinsian*] – **whinger** *n*

whinny /'wini/ *vb or n* (to make or utter with or as if with) a low gentle neigh or similar sound [prob imit]

whinstone /'win,stohn/ *n* any of various dark fine-grained igneous rocks (e g basalt) [*whin* (very hard rock), fr ME (northern) *quin*]

[1]**whip** /wip/ *vb* **-pp-** *vt* **1** to take, pull, jerk, or move very quickly ⟨~ped *out a gun*⟩ **2a** to strike with a whip or similar slender flexible implement, esp as a punishment; *also* to spank **b** to drive or urge on (as if) by using a whip **c** to strike as a whip does ⟨*rain* ~ping *the pavement*⟩ **3a** to bind or wrap (e g a rope or rod) with cord for protection and strength **b** to wind or wrap (e g cord) round sthg **4** to oversew (an edge, hem, or seam) using a whipstitch; *also* to hem or join (e g ribbon or lace) by whipping **5** to beat (e g eggs or cream) into a froth with a whisk, fork, etc **6** to overcome decisively; defeat – infml **7** to snatch suddenly; *esp* STEAL 1 – slang ~ *vi* to move, go, or come quickly or violently ⟨~ped *out of the turning at top speed*⟩ [ME *wippen, whippen*; akin to MD *wippen* to move up and down, sway, OE *wīpian* to wipe] – **whipper** *n* – **whip into shape** to bring (sby or sthg) into a desired state, esp by hard work or practice

[2]**whip** *n* **1** an instrument consisting usu of a lash attached to a handle, used for driving and controlling animals and for punishment **2** a dessert made by whipping some of the ingredients ⟨*prune* ~⟩ **3** a light hoisting apparatus consisting of a single pulley, a block, and a rope **4** one who handles a whip: e g **a** a driver of horses; a coachman **b** a whipper-in **5a** a member of Parliament or other legislative body appointed by a political party to enforce discipline and to secure the attendance and votes of party members **b** *often cap* an instruction (e g a three-line whip or a two-line whip) to each member of a political party in Parliament to be in attendance for voting **c** (the privileges and duties of) membership of the official parliamentary representation of a political party ⟨*was deprived of the Labour* ~⟩ **6** a whipping or thrashing motion **7** the quality of resembling a whip, esp in being flexible – **whiplike** *adj*

'whip,cord /-,kawd/ *n* **1** a thin tough cord made of tightly braided or twisted hemp or catgut **2** a usu cotton or worsted cloth with fine diagonal cords or ribs [fr its use in making whips]

,whip 'hand *n* a controlling position; *the* advantage

whip in *vt* to keep (hounds in a pack) from scattering by use of a whip

'whip,lash /-,lash/ *n* **1** the lash of a whip **2 whiplash, whiplash injury** injury to the neck resulting from a sudden sharp whipping movement of the neck and head (e g in a car collision)

,whipper-'in /'wipə/ *n, pl* **whippers-in** a huntsman's assistant who whips in the hounds

whippersnapper /'wipə,snapə/ *n* an insignificant but impudent person, esp a child [prob alter. of earlier *snippersnapper*, prob fr *snip* + *snap*]

whippet /'wipit/ *n* (any of) a breed of small swift slender dogs related to greyhounds [prob fr [1]*whip*]

whipping /'wiping/ *n* **1** a severe beating or chastisement **2a** stitching with or stitches made using whipstitch **b** material used to whip or bind [[1]WHIP + [2]-ING]

'whipping ,boy *n* **1** a boy formerly educated with a prince and punished in his stead **2** a scapegoat

whippletree /'wipl,tree/ *n* a swingletree [perh irreg fr *whip* + *tree*]

whippoorwill /'wipə,wil/ *n* a N American nightjar [imit]

whippy /'wipi/ *adj* unusually resilient; springy ⟨*a* ~ *fishing rod*⟩ [[2]WHIP + [1]-Y]

'whip-,round *n, chiefly Br* a collection of money made usu for a benevolent purpose – infml ⟨*had a* ~ *to buy him a leaving present*⟩

whipsaw /'wip,saw/ *n* any of various types of saw with a long flexible blade [[2]*whip*]

whip scorpion *n* any of an order of arachnids with a long slender tail but no sting

whipstitch /'wip,stich/ *n* a very small overcasting stitch

whipstock /'wip,stok/ *n* the handle of a whip

whip up *vt* **1** to stir up; stimulate ⟨whipped up *the emotions of the crowd*⟩ **2** to produce in a hurry ⟨*I'll* whip *a meal* up *in no time*⟩

[1]**whirl** /wuhl/ *vi* **1** to move along a curving or circling course, esp with force or speed ⟨*planets* ~ing *in their orbits*⟩ **2** to turn abruptly or rapidly round (and round) on an axis; rotate, wheel ⟨*he* ~ed *round to face me*⟩ **3** to pass, move, or go quickly ⟨*she* ~ed *down the hallway*⟩ **4** to become giddy or dizzy; reel ⟨*my head's* ~ing⟩ ~ *vt* **1** to convey rapidly; whisk ⟨*the ambulance* ~ed *him away*⟩ **2** to cause to turn usu rapidly round (and round) on an axis; rotate [ME *whirlen*, prob of Scand origin; akin to ON *hvirfla* to whirl; akin to OHG *wirbil* whirlwind, OE *hweorfan* to turn – more at WHARF] – **whirler** *n*, **whirly** *adj*

[2]**whirl** *n* **1** (sthg undergoing or having a form suggestive of) a rapid rotating or circling movement **2a** a confused tumult; a bustle ⟨*the social* ~⟩ **b** a confused or disturbed mental state; a turmoil ⟨*my mind is in a* ~ *all the time* – Arnold Bennett⟩ **3** an experimental or brief attempt; a try – infml ⟨*I'll give it a* ~⟩

whirligig /'wuhli,gig/ *n* **1** a child's toy (e g a top) that whirls **2a** sthg that continuously whirls, moves, or changes **b** a whirling or circling course (e g of events) [ME *whirlegigg*, fr *whirlen* to whirl + *gigg* top – more at [1]GIG]

'whirligig ,beetle *n* any of numerous beetles that live mostly on the surface of water where they move swiftly about in curves

whirlpool /'wuhl,poohl/ *n* **1** (sthg resembling, esp

in attracting or engulfing power) a circular eddy of rapidly moving water with a central depression into which floating objects may be drawn **2** WHIRL 2a

ˈwhirl,wind /-ˌwind/ *n* **1** a small rapidly rotating windstorm of limited extent marked by an inward and upward spiral motion of the lower air round a core of low pressure **2** a confused rush; a whirl

whirlybird /ˈwuhli,buhd/ *n* a helicopter – infml; not now in vogue

whirr, whir /wuh/ *vi or n* **-rr-** (to make or revolve or move with) a continuous buzzing or vibrating sound made by sthg in rapid motion [vb ME (Sc) *quirren*, prob of Scand origin; akin to Dan *hvirre* to whirl, whirr; akin to OE *hweorfan* to turn; n fr vb]

whish /wish/ *vi or n* (to) swish [imit]

whisht /wist, wisht/ *vi, dial Br* [1]WHIST [imit]

[1]**whisk** /wisk/ *n* **1** a quick light brushing or whipping motion **2a** any of various small usu hand-held kitchen utensils used for whisking food **b** a small bunch of flexible strands (e g twigs, feathers, or straw) attached to a handle for use as a brush [ME *wisk*, prob of Scand origin; akin to ON *visk* wisp; akin to OE *wiscian* to plait, L *virga* branch, rod]

[2]**whisk** *vi* to move lightly and swiftly ~ *vt* **1** to convey briskly ⟨~ed *the children off to bed*⟩ **2** to mix or fluff up (as if) by beating with a whisk **3** to brush or wipe off (e g crumbs) lightly **4** to brandish lightly; flick ⟨~ed *its tail*⟩

whisker /ˈwiskə/ *n* **1a** a hair of the beard or sideboards **b** a hair's breadth ⟨*lost the race by a* ~⟩ **2** any of the long projecting hairs or bristles growing near the mouth of an animal (e g a cat) **3** a thin hairlike crystal (e g of sapphire or a metal) of exceptional mechanical strength [back-formation fr *whiskers* (moustache), fr [2]*whisk* + [2]*-er* + *-s*] – **whiskered** *adj*, **whiskery** *adj*, **whiskeriness** *n*

whiskey /ˈwiski/ *n* whisky produced in Ireland or the USA

Whiskey – used as a communications code word for the letter *w*

whisky /ˈwiski/ *n* a spirit distilled from fermented mash of rye, corn, wheat, or esp barley [IrGael *uisce beathadh* & ScGael *uisge beatha*, lit., water of life]

[1]**whisper** /ˈwispə/ *vi* **1** to speak softly with little or no vibration of the vocal cords **2** to make a hissing or rustling sound like whispered speech ~ *vt* **1** to address or order in a whisper **2** to utter in a whisper **3** to report or suggest confidentially ⟨*it is* ~ed *that he will soon resign*⟩ [ME *whisperen*, fr OE *hwisprian*; akin to OHG *hwispalōn* to whisper, ON *hvísla* – more at WHISTLE] – **whisperer** *n*

[2]**whisper** *n* **1a** whispering; *esp* speech without vibration of the vocal cords **b** a hissing or rustling sound like whispered speech **2** sthg communicated (as if) by whispering: e g **a** a rumour ⟨~s *of scandal*⟩ **b** a hint, trace

[1]**whist** /wist/ *vi, dial Br* to be silent; hush – often used as an interjection to call for silence [imit]

[2]**whist** *n* (any of various card games similar to) a card game for 4 players in 2 partnerships in which each trick made in excess of 6 tricks scores 1 point [alter. of earlier *whisk*, prob fr [2]*whisk*; fr whisking up the tricks]

ˈwhist ˌdrive *n, Br* an evening of whist playing with a periodic change of partners, usu with prizes at the finish

[1]**whistle** /ˈwisl/ *n* **1** a device (e g a small wind instrument) in which the forcible passage of air, steam, the breath, etc through a slit or against a thin edge in a short tube produces a loud sound ⟨*a police* ~⟩ ⟨*a factory* ~⟩ **2** (a sound like) a shrill clear sound produced by whistling or by a whistle ⟨*the* ~ *of the wind*⟩ [ME, fr OE *hwistle*; akin to ON *hvīsla* to whisper, *hvīna* to whiz – more at WHINE]

[2]**whistle** *vb* **whistling** /ˈwisling/ *vi* **1** to utter a (sound like a) whistle (by blowing or drawing air through the puckered lips) **2** to make a whistle by rapid movement; *also* to move rapidly (as if) with such a sound ⟨*the train* ~d *by*⟩ **3** to blow or sound a whistle ~ *vt* **1** to send, bring, call, or signal to (as if) by whistling **2** to produce, utter, or express by whistling ⟨~ *a tune*⟩ – **whistleable** *adj*, **whistler** *n* – **whistle for** to demand or request in vain ⟨*did a sloppy job so he can* whistle for *his money*⟩

ˈwhistle-ˌstop *n* **1** *NAm* **a** a small station at which trains stop only on signal **b** a small community **2** *chiefly NAm* a brief personal appearance (to give an election speech) by a politician during a tour – **whistle-stop** *adj*

whit /wit/ *n* the smallest part imaginable; a bit ⟨*not a* ~ *abashed*⟩ [alter. of ME *wiht, wight* creature, thing, bit, fr OE *wiht*; akin to OHG *wiht* creature, thing, ON *vættr* creature]

Whit *n* Whitsuntide

[1]**white** /wiet/ *adj* **1a** free from colour **b** of the colour white **c** light or pallid in colour ⟨*lips* ~ *with fear*⟩ **d** *of wine* light yellow or amber in colour **e** *Br, of coffee* served with milk or cream **2a** of a group or race characterized by reduced pigmentation **b** of or for white people ⟨~ *schools*⟩ **3** free from spot or blemish: e g **a(1)** free from moral impurity; innocent **(2)** *of a wedding* in which the woman wears white clothes as a symbol of purity **b** not intended to cause harm ⟨*a* ~ *lie*⟩ **4a** dressed in white **b** accompanied by snow ⟨*a* ~ *Christmas*⟩ **5** notably ardent; passionate ⟨*in a* ~ *rage*⟩ **6** reactionary, counterrevolutionary – compare RED 5a **7** *of light, sound, electromagnetic radiation, etc* consisting of a wide range of frequencies simultaneously ⟨~ *noise*⟩ [ME, fr OE *hwīt*; akin to OHG *hwīz* white, Skt *śveta*] – **whitely** *adv*, **whitish** *adj*, **whiteness** *n*

[2]**white** *n* **1** the achromatic and lightest colour that belongs to objects that reflect diffusely nearly all incident light **2** a white or light-coloured part of sthg: e g **a** the mass of albumin-containing material surrounding the yolk of an egg **b** the white part of the ball of the eye **c** (the player playing) the light-coloured pieces in a two-handed board game **3** sby or sthg that is or approaches the colour white: e g **a** *pl* white (sports) clothing ⟨*tennis* ~s⟩ **b** a white animal (e g a butterfly or pig) **4** *pl* leucorrhoea **5** sby belonging to a light-skinned race

ˌwhite ˈant *n* a termite

whitebait /ˈwiet,bayt/ *n* (any of various small food fishes similar to) the young of any of several European herrings (e g the common herring or the sprat) eaten whole [[1]*white* + [2]*bait*]

ˈwhite,beam /-ˌbeem/ *n* a European tree of the rose family with leaves covered in fine white hairs on the undersurface, white flowers, and scarlet berries

ˈwhite,beard /-ˌbiəd/ *n* an old man; a greybeard

white blood cell, white cell *n* any of the white or colourless blood cells that have nuclei, do not contain haemoglobin, and are primarily concerned with body

[ME *welden* to control, fr OE *wieldan*; akin to OHG *waltan* to rule, L *valēre* to be strong, be worth] – **wielder** *n*

wiener /'weenə/ *n, NAm* a frankfurter [short for *wienerwurst*, fr G, fr *wiener* of Vienna + *wurst* sausage]

Wiener schnitzel /'veenə ,shnitsəl/ *n* a thin breadcrumbed fried veal escalope [G, fr *wiener* + *schnitzel* cutlet]

wife /wief/ *n, pl* **wives** /wievz/ **1** a woman acting in a specified capacity – in combination ⟨*fish*wife⟩ **2** a married woman, esp in relation to her husband ⟨*John's* ~⟩ **3** *dial* a woman [ME *wif*, fr OE *wīf*; akin to OHG *wīb* wife] – **wifehood** *n*, **wifeless** *adj*

'wifelike /-liek/ *adj* wifely

'wifely /-li/ *adj* of or befitting a good wife – **wifeliness** *n*

'wife-,swapping *n* the temporary exchange of sexual partners by 2 or more married couples

wig /wig/ *n* a manufactured covering of natural or synthetic hair for the (bald part of a) head [short for *periwig*] – **wigged** *adj*, **wigless** *adj*

wigeon /'wijin/ *n, pl* **wigeons,** *esp collectively* **wigeon** a widgeon

wigging /'wiging/ *n* a severe scolding – infml [*wig* (rebuke), perh fr *bigwig*]

¹wiggle /'wigl/ *vb* **wiggling** /'wigling, 'wigl·ing/ to (cause to) move with quick jerky or turning motions or smoothly from side to side ⟨*his toes* ~d⟩ [ME *wiglen*, fr or akin to MD or MLG *wiggelen* to totter; akin to OE *wegan* to move – more at WAY] – **wiggler** *n*

²wiggle *n* **1** a wiggling movement **2** a wavy line; a squiggle – **wiggly** *adj*

wigwag /'wig,wag/ *vb* **-gg-** *vi* to send a signal (as if) by waving a flag or light according to a code ~ *vt* **1** to signal by wigwagging **2** to cause to wigwag [E dial. *wig* to move + E *wag*] – **wigwag** *n*

wigwam /'wig,wam/ *n* a N American Indian hut having a framework of poles covered with bark, rush mats, or hides [Abnaki & Massachuset *wīkwâm*]

wilco /'wilkoh/ *interj* – used esp in radio and signalling to indicate that a message received will be complied with [*will* comply]

¹wild /wield/ *adj* **1a** (of organisms) living in a natural state and not (ordinarily) tame, domesticated, or cultivated **b(1)** growing or produced without the aid and care of humans ⟨~ *honey*⟩ **(2)** related to or resembling a corresponding cultivated or domesticated organism ⟨~ *strawberries*⟩ **2** not (amenable to being) inhabited or cultivated **3a(1)** free from restraint or regulation; uncontrolled **(2)** emotionally overcome ⟨~ *with grief*⟩; *also* passionately eager or enthusiastic ⟨*was* ~ *about jazz*⟩ **(3)** very angry; infuriated ⟨*drove me* ~ *with his whining*⟩ **b** marked by great agitation ⟨~ *frenzy*⟩; *also* stormy ⟨*a* ~ *night*⟩ **c** going beyond reasonable or conventional bounds; fantastic ⟨*beyond my* ~est *dreams*⟩ **d** indicative of strong passion or emotion ⟨*a* ~ *gleam in his eyes*⟩ **4** uncivilized, barbaric **5a** deviating from the intended or regular course ⟨*the throw was* ~⟩ **b** having no logical basis; random ⟨*a* ~ *guess*⟩ **6** *of a playing card* able to represent any card designated by the holder [ME *wilde*, fr OE; akin to OHG *wildi* wild, W *gwyllt*] – **wildish** *adj*, **wildly** *adv*, **wildness** *n*

²wild *n* **1** WILDERNESS 1a **2** a wild, free, or natural state or existence ⟨*living in the* ~⟩

³wild *adv* in a wild manner: e g **a** without regulation or control ⟨*rhododendrons growing* ~⟩ **b** off an intended or expected course

,wild and 'woolly *adj* **1** lacking refinement; uncivilized ⟨*a* ~ *town*⟩ **2** impractical, visionary ⟨*a* ~ *idealist*⟩

,wild 'boar *n* an Old World wild pig from which most domestic pigs have derived

¹'wild,cat /-,kat/ *n, pl* **wildcats,** (*1b*) **wildcats,** *esp collectively* **wildcat** **1a** either of 2 cats that resemble but are heavier in build than the domestic cat and are usu held to be among its ancestors **b** any of various small or medium-sized cats (e g the lynx or ocelot) **2** a savage quick-tempered person **3** a wildcat oil or gas well

²wildcat *adj* **1** operating, produced, or carried on outside the bounds of standard or legitimate business practices ⟨*a* ~ *insurance scheme*⟩ **2** of or being an oil or gas well drilled in territory not known to be productive **3** initiated by a group of workers without formal union approval or in violation of a contract ⟨*a* ~ *strike*⟩

³wildcat *vi* **-tt-** to prospect and drill an experimental oil or gas well – **wildcatter** *n*

wildebeest /'wildə,beest, 'vil-/ *n, pl* **wildebeests,** *esp collectively* **wildebeest** a gnu [Afrik *wildebees* (pl *wildebeeste*), fr *wilde* wild + *bees* ox, beast]

wilderness /'wildənis/ *n* **1a** a (barren) region or area that is (essentially) uncultivated and uninhabited by human beings **b** an empty or pathless area or region ⟨*the remote* ~es *of space*⟩ **c** a part of a garden or nature reserve devoted to wild growth **2** a confusing multitude or mass **3** *the* state of exclusion from office or power [ME, fr *wildern* wild, fr OE *wilddēoren* of wild beasts]

,wild-'eyed *adj* **1** glaring wildly **2** excessively idealistic; impracticable ⟨~ *schemes*⟩

'wild,fire /-,fie·ə/ *n* **1** sthg that spreads very rapidly – usu in *like wildfire* **2** a phosphorescent glow (e g will-o'-the-wisp)

'wild,fowl /-,fowl/ *n* a wild duck, goose, or other game bird, esp a waterfowl – **wildfowler** *n*, **wildfowling** *n*

,wild-'goose ,chase *n* a hopeless pursuit after sthg unattainable

,wild 'horse *n* a horse of the Russian Steppes that is the sole surviving wild ancestor of the domestic horse

,wild 'hyacinth *n* a common European spring-flowering woodland plant of the lily family with spikes of blue drooping flowers; a bluebell

wilding /'wielding/ *n* (the fruit of) a plant, esp a wild apple or crab apple, growing uncultivated [¹*wild* + *-ing* one belonging to or descended from such a kind, fr ME, fr OE]

'wild,life /-,lief/ *n* wild animals

,wild 'man *n* **1** a savage **2** a radical extremist

,wild 'oat *n* **1** a wild grass common as a weed in meadows ☞ PLANT **2** *pl* offences and indiscretions of youth; *esp* premarital promiscuity – usu in *sow one's wild oats*

,wild 'silk *n* silk, produced by wild silkworms, that is coarser and stronger than cultivated silk

,wild 'thyme *n* a low-growing thyme with clusters of pink flowers

'wild ,type *n* the typical form of an organism as ordinarily encountered in contrast to atypical mutant individuals ☞ SYMBOL – **wild-type** *adj*

ˌwild ˈWest *n* the W USA in its frontier period

[1]**wile** /wiel/ *n* a deceitful or beguiling trick or stratagem – usu pl [ME *wil*, fr (assumed) ONF, prob of Gmc origin; akin to OE *wigle* divination – more at WITCH]

[2]**wile** *vt* **1** to lure; entice **2** to while [(2) by alter.]

wilful, *NAm chiefly* **willful** /ˈwilf(ə)l/ *adj* **1** obstinately and often perversely self-willed **2** done deliberately; intentional – **wilfully** *adv*, **wilfulness** *n*

[1]**will** /wil/ *vb, pres sing & pl* **will;** *pres neg* **won't** /wohnt/; *past* **would** /wəd; *strong* **wood/** *va* **1** – used to express choice, willingness, or consent or in negative constructions refusal ⟨*can find no one who ~ take the job*⟩ ⟨*if we ~ all do our best*⟩; used in the question form with the force of a request ⟨*~ you please stop talking*⟩ or of an offer or suggestion ⟨*~ you have some tea?*⟩ **2** – used to express custom or inevitable tendency ⟨*accidents ~ happen*⟩; used with emphatic stress to express exasperation ⟨*he ~ call the record player the 'gramophone"* – John Fowles⟩ **3** – used to express futurity ⟨*tomorrow morning I ~ wake up in this first-class hotel suite* – Tennessee Williams⟩ **4** can ⟨*the back seat ~ hold 3 passengers*⟩ **5** – used to express logical probability ⟨*that ~ be the milkman*⟩ **6** – used to express determination or to command or urge ⟨*I have made up my mind to go, and go I ~*⟩ ⟨*you ~ do as I say, at once*⟩ *~ vi* **1** to wish, desire ⟨*whether we ~ or no*⟩ **2** *archaic* to be about to go ⟨*thither ~ I then* – Sir Walter Scott⟩ [ME (1 & 3 sing. pres indic), fr OE *wille* (infinitive *wyllan*); akin to OHG *wili* (3 sing. pres indic) wills, L *velle* to wish, will]

[2]**will** *n* **1** a desire, wish: e g **a** a resolute intention ⟨*where there's a ~ there's a way*⟩ **b** an inclination ⟨*I did it against my ~*⟩ **c** a choice, wish ⟨*the ~ of the people*⟩ **2** what is wished or ordained by the specified agent ⟨*God's ~ be done*⟩ **3a** a mental power by which one (apparently) controls one's wishes, intentions, etc ⟨*has a ~ of her own*⟩ **b** an inclination to act according to principles or ends ⟨*the ~ to believe*⟩ **c** a specified attitude towards others ⟨*bear him no ill ~*⟩ **4** willpower, self-control ⟨*a man of iron ~*⟩ **5** a (written) legal declaration of the manner in which sby would have his/her property disposed of after his/her death [ME, fr OE *willa* will, desire; akin to OE *wille*] – **will-less** *adj* – **at will** as one wishes; as or when it pleases or suits oneself

[3]**will** *vt* **1** to bequeath **2a** to determine deliberately; purpose **b** to decree, ordain ⟨*Providence ~s it*⟩ **c** to (attempt to) cause by exercise of the will ⟨*~ed her to go away*⟩ *~ vi* to exercise the will – **willer** *n*

willie /ˈwili/ *n, Br* a penis – euph [*Willie*, nickname for *William*]

willies /ˈwiliz/ *n pl* nervousness, jitters – + *the*; infml [origin unknown]

[1]**willing** /ˈwiling/ *adj* **1** inclined or favourably disposed in mind; ready ⟨*~ to work*⟩ **2** prompt to act or respond ⟨*a ~ horse*⟩ **3** done, borne, or given without reluctance ⟨*~ help*⟩ – **willingly** *adv*, **willingness** *n*

[2]**willing** *n* cheerful alacrity – in *show willing*

will-o'-the-wisp /ˌwil ə dhə ˈwisp/ *n* **1** a phosphorescent light sometimes seen over marshy ground and often caused by the combustion of gas from decomposed organic matter **2** an enticing but elusive goal **3** an unreliable or elusive person [*Will* (nickname for *William*) + *of* + *the* + *wisp*]

willow /ˈwiloh/ *n* **1** any of a genus of trees and shrubs bearing catkins of petal-less flowers **2** an object made of willow wood; *esp* a cricket bat – infml [ME *wilghe, wilowe*, fr OE *welig*; akin to MHG *wilge* willow, Gk *helikē*] – **willowlike** *adj*

ˈ**willow,herb** /-ˌhuhb/ *n* any of a genus of plants of the evening-primrose family; *esp* ROSEBAY WILLOWHERB

ˈ**willow ˌpattern** *n* china tableware decorated with a usu blue-and-white story-telling design of oriental style [fr the large willow tree in the design]

ˈ**willow ˌwarbler** *n* a small greenish Old World warbler

willowy /ˈwiloh·i/ *adj* **1** full of willows **2a** supple, pliant **b** gracefully tall and slender

ˈ**willˌpower** /-ˌpowə/ *n* self-control, resoluteness

willy-nilly /ˌwili ˈnili/ *adv or adj* **1** by compulsion; without choice **2** (carried out or occurring) in a haphazard or random manner ⟨*distributed the gifts ~ among the crowd*⟩ [alter. of *will I nill I* or *will ye nill ye* or *will he nill he*; arch *nill* (to be unwilling) fr ME *nilen*, fr OE *nyllan*, fr *ne* not + *wyllan* to wish]

willy-willy /ˈwili ˌwili/ *n, Austr* a whirlwind [prob fr native name in Australia]

ˈ**Wilson's diˌsease** /ˈwils(ə)nz/ *n* a congenital disease, caused by an inability of the body to deal with copper in the diet, in which the liver degenerates and there is often severe mental disorder [Samuel *Wilson* †1937 E neurologist]

[1]**wilt** /wilt/ *archaic pres 2 sing of* [1]WILL

[2]**wilt** *vi* **1** *of a plant* to lose freshness and become flaccid; droop **2** to grow weak or faint; languish *~ vt* to cause to wilt [alter. of earlier *welk*, fr ME *welken*, prob fr MD; akin to OHG er*welkēn* to wilt]

[3]**wilt** *n* a disease of plants marked by wilting

Wilton /ˈwilt(ə)n/ *n* (a carpet woven in) a weave in which the threads of the cut or uncut pile form an integral part of the carpet structure – compare AXMINSTER [*Wilton*, town in Wiltshire, England]

wily /ˈwieli/ *adj* full of wiles; crafty – **wilily** *adv*, **wiliness** *n*

wimp /wimp/ *n* an ineffectual or foolish person – slang [perh fr *weak* + *limp*]

wimple /ˈwimpl/ *vt or n* **wimpling** /ˈwimpl·ing/ (to cover with or as if with) a cloth covering worn over the head and round the neck and chin, esp by women in the late medieval period and by some nuns [n ME *wimpel*, fr OE; akin to OE *wīpian* to wipe; vb fr n]

Wimpy /ˈwimpi/ *trademark* – used for a fried hamburger served in a plain bread bun

[1]**win** /win/ *vb* **-nn-; won** /wun/ *vi* **1a** to gain the victory in a contest; succeed ⟨*always ~s at chess*⟩ **b** to be right in an argument, dispute, etc; *also* to have one's way ⟨*OK, you ~, we'll go to the theatre*⟩ **2** to succeed in arriving at a place or a state – esp in *to win free ~ vt* **1a** to get possession of by qualities or fortune ⟨*~ their approval*⟩ ⟨won *£10*⟩ **b** to obtain by effort; earn ⟨*striving to ~ a living from the soil*⟩ **2a** to gain (as if) in battle or contest ⟨*~ the victory*⟩ **b** to be the victor in ⟨won *the war*⟩ **3a** to solicit and gain the favour of; *also* to persuade – usu + *over* or *round* **b** to induce (a woman) to accept oneself in marriage **4** to obtain (e g ore, coal, or clay) by mining **5** to reach by expenditure of effort ⟨*~ the summit*⟩ [ME *winnen*, fr OE *winnan* to struggle;

akin to OHG *winnan* to struggle, L *venus* love, charm] – **winnable** *adj*

²**win** *n* **1** a victory or success, esp in a game or sporting contest **2** first place at the finish, esp of a horse race

wince /wins/ *vi* to shrink back involuntarily (e g from pain); flinch [ME *wenchen* to be impatient, dart about, fr (assumed) ONF *wenchier*, of Gmc origin; akin to OHG *wankōn* to totter, OE *wincian* to wink] – **wince** *n*

wincey /'winsi/ *n* a plain or twilled fabric, usu with a cotton or linen warp and wool weft, used esp for shirts and nightclothes [alter. of *linsey* (linsey-woolsey)]

winceyette /,winsi'et/ *n* a lightweight usu cotton fabric napped on 1 or both sides

¹**winch** /winch/ *n* **1** any of various machines or instruments for hoisting or pulling; a windlass **2** a crank or handle for giving motion to a machine (e g a grindstone) [ME *winche* roller, reel, fr OE *wince*; akin to OE *wincian* to wink]

²**winch** *vt* to hoist (as if) with a winch – often + *up* – **wincher** *n*

¹**wind** /wind/ *n* **1** a (natural) movement of air, esp horizontally ☞ ENERGY **2** a force or agency that carries along or influences; a trend ⟨*the* ~*s of change*⟩ **3a** BREATH 4 ⟨*the fall knocked the* ~ *out of him*⟩ **b** BREATH 2a ⟨*soon recovered his* ~⟩ **c** the pit of the stomach **4** gas generated in the stomach or the intestines **5** mere talk; idle words **6** air carrying a scent (e g of a hunter or game) **7a** musical wind instruments collectively, esp as distinguished from stringed and percussion instruments **b** *sing or pl in constr* the group of players of such instruments **8** (a compass point corresponding to) a direction from which the wind may blow [ME, fr OE; akin to OHG *wint* wind, L *ventus*, Gk *aēnai* to blow, Skt *vāti* it blows] – **windless** *adj*, **windlessly** *adv*, **windlessness** *n* – **before the wind** in the same direction as the main force of the wind – **close to the wind 1** as nearly as possible against the main force of the wind **2** close to a point of danger; near the permissible limit – **have the wind up** to be scared or frightened – **in the wind** about to happen; astir, afoot – **off the wind** away from the direction from which the wind is blowing – **on the wind** towards the direction from which the wind is blowing – **put the wind up** to scare, frighten – **under the wind 1** to leeward **2** in a place protected from the wind; under the lee

²**wind** /wind/ *vt* **1** to detect or follow by scent **2** to make short of breath **3** to rest (e g a horse) in order to allow the breath to be recovered

³**wind** /wiend/ *vt* **winded, wound** /wownd/ to sound (e g a call or note) on a horn [¹*wind*]

⁴**wind** /wiend/ *vb* **wound** /wownd/ *also* **winded** *vi* **1** to bend or warp **2** to have a curving course; extend or proceed in curves ⟨*path* ~*s down the hill*⟩ **3** to coil, twine **4** to turn when lying at anchor **5** to undergo winding ⟨*car window won't* ~⟩ ~ *vt* **1a** to surround or wrap with sthg pliable ⟨~ *the baby in a shawl*⟩ **b** to turn completely or repeatedly, esp about an object; coil ⟨~ *wool into a ball*⟩ **c(1)** to hoist or haul by means of a rope or chain and a windlass **(2)** to move (a ship) by hauling on a capstan **d(1)** to tighten the spring of ⟨~ *the clock*⟩ **(2)** to put into the specified state or position by winding ⟨~ *the speedometer back*⟩ **e** to raise to a high level (e g of excitement or tension) – usu + *up* ⟨wound *himself up into a frenzy*⟩ **2** to make (one's way or course) (as if) by a curving route [ME *winden*, fr OE *windan* to twist, move with speed or force, brandish; akin to OHG *wintan* to wind, Umbrian oha*vendu* let him turn aside] – **winder** /'wiendə/ *n*

⁵**wind** /wiend/ *n* a coil, turn

windage /'windij/ *n* **1** the difference between the diameter of the bore of a gun and that of the projectile cylinder **2** the amount of sight deflection necessary to compensate for wind displacement in aiming a gun [¹*wind*]

windbag /'wind,bag/ *n* an excessively talkative person – infml

windblown /'wind,blohn/ *adj* blown by the wind; *esp* shaped or deformed by the prevailing winds ⟨~ *trees*⟩

windbreak /'wind,brayk/ *n* sthg (e g a growth of trees or a fence) that breaks the force of the wind

'**wind-,broken** /wind/ *adj, of a horse* broken-winded

'**wind,burn** /-,buhn/ *n* irritation caused by wind on the skin – **windburned, windburnt** *adj*

'**wind,cheater** /-,cheetə/ *n, chiefly Br* a weatherproof or windproof coat or jacket; an anorak

'**wind,chill** /-,chil/ *n* the still-air temperature with the same cooling effect on exposed human flesh as a given combination of temperature and wind speed

'**wind-,cone** /wind/ *n* a wind-sock

wind down /wiend/ *vi* to become gradually more relaxed; unwind ~ *vt* to bring to an end gradually; cause to cease ⟨*are* winding down *their operations in France*⟩

windfall /'wind,fawl/ *n* **1** sthg, esp a fruit, blown down by the wind **2** an unexpected gain or advantage; *esp* a legacy

'**wind,flower** /-,flowə/ *n* ANEMONE 1; *esp* WOOD ANEMONE

'**wind,gall** /-,gawl/ *n* a soft tumour or swelling on a horse's leg in the region of the fetlock joint – **windgalled** *adj*

'**wind,hover** /-,hovə/ *n, Br* a kestrel

winding /'wiending/ *n* **1** material (e g wire) wound or coiled about an object (e g an armature); *also* a single turn of the wound material **2** the manner of winding sthg **3** a curved course, line, or progress ⟨*the* ~*s of the path*⟩ [⁴WIND + ²-ING] – **windingly** *adv*

'**winding-,sheet** /'wiending/ *n* a sheet in which a corpse is wrapped for burial

'**wind ,instrument** /wind/ *n* a musical instrument (e g a trumpet, clarinet, or organ) sounded by wind; *esp* a musical instrument sounded by the player's breath

windjammer /'wind,jamə/ *n* **1** a large fast square-rigged sailing vessel **2** *Br* a windcheater

¹**windlass** /'windləs/ *n* any of various machines for hoisting or hauling: e g **a** a horizontal drum supported on vertical posts and turned by a crank so that the hoisting rope is wound round the drum **b** a steam, electric, etc winch with a horizontal or vertical shaft and 2 drums, used to raise a ship's anchor [ME *wyndlas*, alter. of *wyndas*, fr ON *vindāss*, fr *vinda* to wind + *āss* pole; akin to OHG *wintan* to wind]

²**windlass** *vt* to hoist or haul with a windlass

windlestraw /'windl,straw/ *n, Scot & N Eng* a dry thin stalk of grass [(assumed) ME, fr OE *windel-*

strēaw, fr *windel* basket (fr *windan* to wind) + *strēaw* straw]

[1]**windmill** /'wind,mil/ *n* **1** a mill operated by vanes that are turned by the wind ☞ ENERGY **2** a toy consisting of lightweight vanes that revolve at the end of a stick

[2]**windmill** *vb* to (cause to) move like a windmill

wind off /wiend/ *vt* to remove by unwinding

window /'windoh/ *n* **1** an opening, esp in the wall of a building, for admission of light and air that is usu fitted with a frame containing glass and capable of being opened and shut ☞ ARCHITECTURE **2** a pane (e g of glass) in a window **3** sthg (e g a shutter, opening, or valve) suggestive of or functioning like a window **4** a transparent panel in an envelope, through which the address on the enclosure is visible **5** a range of wavelengths in the electromagnetic spectrum that can pass through a planet's atmosphere **6** an interval of time within which a rocket or spacecraft must be launched to accomplish a particular mission **7** an area at the limits of the earth's atmosphere through which a spacecraft must pass for successful reentry [ME *windowe*, fr ON *vindauga*, fr *vindr* wind + *auga* eye; akin to OE *wind* & to OE *ēage* eye – more at EYE] – **windowless** *adj*

'**window ,box** *n* a box for growing plants on the (outside) sill of a window

'**window-,dress** *vt* to make appear more attractive or favourable by distortion or skilful presentation [back-formation fr *window dressing*]

'**window ,dressing** *n* **1** the display of merchandise in a shop window **2** the means by which sthg is made superficially more attractive or favourable – **window dresser** *n*

'**window-,shop** *vi* to look at the displays in shop windows for amusement or to assess goods, prices, etc – **window-shopper** *n*

windpipe /'wind,piep/ *n* the trachea – not used technically ☞ DIGESTION

'**wind ,rose** /wind/ *n* a diagram showing for a given place the relative frequency and usu strength of winds from different directions [G *windrose* compass card]

windrow /'windroh/ *n* a row of hay, grain, etc raked up to dry

windscreen /'wind,skreen/ *n, Br* a transparent screen, esp of glass, at the front of a (motor) vehicle

windshield /'wind,sheeld/ *n, NAm* a windscreen

'**wind-,sleeve** /wind/ *n* a wind-sock

'**wind-,sock** /wind/ *n* a truncated cloth cone that is open at both ends and mounted on a pole and is used to indicate the direction of the wind, esp at airfields

,**Windsor 'chair** /'winzə, 'windzə/ *n* a wooden chair with a spindle back, legs that slant outwards, and usu a slightly concave seat [*Windsor*, town in England]

'**wind-,surfing** /wind/ *n* the sport of sailing with sailboards

windswept /'wind,swept/ *adj* **1** swept by wind ⟨*a ~ beach*⟩ **2** dishevelled (as if) from being exposed to the wind ⟨*a ~ appearance*⟩

'**wind ,tunnel** /wind/ *n* a tunnel-like apparatus through which air is blown at a known velocity to determine the effects of wind pressure on an object placed in the apparatus

wind up /wiend/ *vt* **1** to bring to a conclusion; *specif* to bring (a business) to an end by liquidation **2** to put in order; settle **3** WIND 1d(1) **4** *Br* to deceive playfully; pull (someone's) leg – slang ~ *vi* **1a** to come to a conclusion **b** to arrive in a place, situation, or condition at the end of or because of a course of action ⟨wound up *a millionaire*⟩ **2** to give a preliminary swing to the arms (e g before bowling)

windward /'windwood/ *adj, adv, or n* (in or facing) the direction from which the wind is blowing – compare LEEWARD

windy /'windi/ *adj* **1a** windswept **b** marked by strong or stormy wind **2** FLATULENT 1 **3** verbose, bombastic **4** *chiefly Br* frightened, nervous – infml – **windily** *adv*, **windiness** *n*

[1]**wine** /wien/ *n* **1** fermented grape juice containing varying percentages of alcohol together with ethers and esters that give it bouquet and flavour **2** the usu fermented juice of a plant or fruit used as a drink ⟨*rice* ~⟩ **3** sthg that invigorates or intoxicates **4** the colour of red wine [ME *win*, fr OE *wīn*; akin to OHG *wīn* wine; both fr a prehistoric Gmc word borrowed fr L *vinum* wine, of non-IE origin; akin to the source of Gk *oinos* wine]

[2]**wine** *vb* to entertain with or drink wine – usu in *wine and dine*

'**wine ,bar** *n, Br* an establishment providing wine and usu food for consumption on the premises

'**wine ,cellar** *n* a room for storing wines; *also* a stock of wines

'**wine ,gallon** *n* a US unit of liquid capacity equal to 8 US pt (about 3.785l)

'**wine,glass** /-,glahs/ *n* any of several variously shaped and sized drinking glasses for wine, that usu have a rounded bowl and are mounted on a stem and foot

'**wine,grower** /-,groh·ə/ *n* a person who cultivates a vineyard and makes wine – **wine growing** *n*

'**wine ,merchant** *n, Br* a usu wholesale dealer in alcoholic drinks, esp wine

winery /'wienəri/ *n, chiefly NAm* a wine-making establishment

'**wine ,taster** *n* a person who evaluates wine by tasting

'**wine ,tasting** *n* a promotional occasion at which sellers of wine offer (potential) customers a chance to sample their products prior to purchase

winey /'wieni/ *adj* winy

[1]**wing** /wing/ *n* **1a** (a part of a nonflying bird or insect corresponding to) any of the movable feathered or membranous paired appendages by means of which a bird, bat, or insect flies ☞ ANATOMY **b** any of various body parts (e g of a flying fish or flying lemur) providing means of limited flight **2** an appendage or part resembling a wing in shape, appearance, or position: e g **a** any of various projecting anatomical parts **b** a sidepiece at the top of a high-backed armchair **c** a membranous, leaflike, or woody expansion of a plant, esp along a stem or on a seed pod **d** any of the aerofoils that develop a major part of the lift which supports a heavier-than-air aircraft **e** *Br* a mudguard, esp when forming an integral part of the body of a motor vehicle **3** a means of flight – usu pl with sing. meaning ⟨*fear lent me* ~s⟩ **4** a part of a building projecting from the main or central part **5a** any of the pieces of scenery at the side of a stage **b** *pl* the area at the side of the stage out of sight of the audience **6a** a left or right flank of an army or fleet

b(1) any of the attacking positions or players on either side of a centre position in certain team sports (2) the left or right section of a playing field that is near the sidelines 7 *sing or pl in constr* a group or faction holding distinct opinions or policies within an organized body (e g a political party) – compare LEFT WING, RIGHT WING 8 *pl* a pilot's badge, esp in the British armed forces 9 an operational and administrative unit of an air force; *specif* a unit of the Royal Air Force higher than a squadron and lower than a group [ME *winge*, of Scand origin; akin to Dan & Sw *vinge* wing; akin to Skt *vāti* it blows – more at [1]WIND] – **wingless** *adj*, **winglike** *adj*, **winglet** *n* – **in the wings** in the background; in readiness to act – **on the wing** in flight; flying – **under one's wing** under one's protection; in one's care

[2]**wing** *vt* **1a** to fit with wings **b** to enable to fly or move swiftly **2a** to wound in the wing **b** to wound (e g with a bullet) without killing ⟨~ed *by a sniper*⟩ **3a** to traverse (as if) with wings **b** to make (one's way) by flying ~*vi* to go (as if) with wings; fly

'wing ,case *n* an elytron

wing chair *n* an upholstered armchair with a high solid back and sidepieces that provide a rest for the head and protection from draughts

wing commander *n* ☞ RANK

wingding /'wing,ding/ *n, chiefly NAm* **1** a wild, lively, or lavish party **2** a pretended fit or illness *USE* infml [origin unknown]

winge /winj/ *vi* to whinge

winged /wingd/ *adj* **1** having or using wings – often in combination ⟨~ *seeds*⟩ ⟨*strong*-winged⟩ **2** swift, rapid

winger /'wing·ə/ *n, chiefly Br* a player (e g in soccer) in a wing position

,wing-'footed *adj* swift – poetic ⟨*a* ~ *messenger*⟩

'wing ,nut *n* a nut that has projecting wings or flanges so that it may be turned by finger and thumb

'wing,span /-,span/ *n* the distance from the tip of one of a pair of wings to that of the other

[1]**wink** /wingk/ *vi* **1** to shut 1 eye briefly as a signal or in teasing; *also, of an eye* to shut briefly **2** to avoid seeing or noting sthg – usu + *at* ⟨~ *at his absence*⟩ **3** to gleam or flash intermittently; twinkle ~*vt* to cause (one's eye) to wink [ME *winken*, fr OE *wincian*; akin to OHG *winchan* to stagger, wink, L *vacillare* to sway – more at PREVARICATE]

[2]**wink** *n* **1** a brief period of sleep; a nap ⟨*didn't get a* ~ *all night*⟩ **2** an act of winking **3** the time of a wink; an instant ⟨*quick as a* ~⟩ **4** a hint or sign given by winking – infml ⟨*the bloke tipped him the* ~ – Richard Llewellyn⟩

winkle /'wingkl/ *n* [2]PERIWINKLE

winkle out *vt* **winkling** /'wingkling, 'wingkl·ing/ *chiefly Br* to displace or extract from a position; *also* to discover or identify with difficulty ⟨winkling out *the facts about the country's stocks of coal – The Observer*⟩ [*winkle*; fr the process of extracting a winkle from its shell]

'winkle-,picker *n, chiefly Br* a (man's) shoe with a pointed toe ☞ GARMENT

winner /'winə/ *n* sthg (expected to be) successful ⟨*this new scheme is a real* ~⟩ – infml [[1]WIN + [2]-ER]

[1]**winning** /'wining/ *n* **1a** the act of sby or sthg that wins; victory **b** acquisition, gaining **2** *pl* money won by success in a game or competition

[2]**winning** *adj* tending to please or delight ⟨*a* ~ *smile*⟩ – **winningly** *adv*

winnow /'winoh/ *vt* **1a** to get rid of (sthg undesirable or unwanted); remove – often + *out* **b** to separate, sift ⟨~ *a mass of evidence*⟩ **2** to remove waste matter from (e g grain) by exposure to a current of air **3** to blow on; fan ⟨*the wind* ~ing *his thin white hair – Time*⟩ ~*vi* **1** to separate chaff from grain by exposure to a current of air **2** to separate desirable and undesirable elements [ME *winewen*, fr OE *windwian* to fan, winnow; akin to OHG *wintōn* to fan, L *vannus* winnowing fan, *ventus* wind – more at [1]WIND] – **winnower** *n*

wino /'wienoh/ *n, pl* **winos** *chiefly NAm* an alcoholic, esp one addicted to wine – infml

win out *vi* WIN THROUGH

winsome /'wins(ə)m/ *adj* pleasing and engaging, often because of a childlike charm and innocence [ME *winsum*, fr OE *wynsum*, fr *wynn* joy; akin to OHG *wunna* joy, L *venus* love – more at WIN] – **winsomely** *adv*, **winsomeness** *n*

[1]**winter** /'wintə/ *n* **1** the season between autumn and spring comprising in the N hemisphere the months December, January, and February **2** the colder part of the year **3** a year – usu pl ⟨*happened many* ~s *ago*⟩ **4** a period of inactivity or decay [ME, fr OE; akin to OHG *wintar* winter] – **winterless** *adj*, **winterlike** *adj*

[2]**winter** *adj* **1** of, during, or suitable for winter ⟨*a* ~ *holiday*⟩ **2** sown in autumn and harvested the following spring or summer ⟨~ *wheat*⟩ – compare SUMMER

[3]**winter** *vi* to pass or survive the winter ~*vt* to keep or feed (e g livestock) during the winter

winter aconite *n* a small Old World plant of the buttercup family with bright yellow flowers that often bloom through snow

winter garden *n* a garden, either outside or in a conservatory, containing plants that flourish in winter

'winter,green /-,green/ *n* **1** any of several perennial evergreen plants related to the heaths **2** (the flavour of) an essential oil from a wintergreen

winter·ize, -ise /'wintəriez/ *vt* to make ready for or proof against winter weather – **winterization** /-'zaysh(ə)n/ *n*

winter quarters *n pl but sing or pl in constr* a winter residence or station of a military unit, circus, etc

,winter 'sport *n* a usu open-air sport on snow or ice (e g skiing or tobogganing)

win through *vi* to reach a desired or satisfactory end, esp after overcoming difficulties

wintry, wintery /'wint(ə)ri/ *adj* **1** characteristic of winter; cold, stormy **2a** weathered (as if) by winter; aged, hoary **b** chilling, cheerless ⟨*a bitter* ~ *smile*⟩ – **wintrily** *adv*, **wintriness** *n*

winy, winey /'wieni/ *adj* having the taste or qualities of wine

[1]**wipe** /wiep/ *vt* **1a** to clean or dry by rubbing, esp with or on sthg soft ⟨~ *the dishes*⟩ **b** to draw or pass for rubbing or cleaning ⟨~d *a cloth over the table*⟩ **c** to put into the specified state by rubbing ⟨~ *your hands dry*⟩ **2a** to remove (as if) by rubbing ⟨~ *that smile off your face*⟩ **b** to erase completely; obliterate ⟨~ *the scene from his memory*⟩ **3** to spread (as if) by wiping ⟨~ *grease on my skates*⟩ [ME *wipen*, fr OE *wīpian*; akin to OHG *wīfan* to wind round, L

vibrare to vibrate] – **wipe the floor with** to defeat decisively

[2]**wipe** *n* **1** an act or instance of wiping **2** power or capacity to wipe

'**wipe-,clean** *adj* that can be cleaned merely with a wipe

'**wipe,out** /-,owt/ *n* a fall from a surfboard caused usu by loss of control

wipe out *vt* **1** to clean the inside of (sthg hollow) by wiping **2** to destroy completely; annihilate **3** to obliterate, cancel

wiper /'wiepə/ *n* **1a** sthg (e g a towel or sponge) used for wiping **b** a mechanically operated rubber strip for cleaning windscreens **2** a cam; *also* a tappet [[1]WIPE + [2]-ER]

[1]**wire** /wie·ə/ *n* **1** metal in the form of a usu very flexible thread or slender rod **2a** a line of wire for conducting electrical current **b** a telephone or telegraph wire or system **c** a telegram, cablegram **3** a barrier or fence of usu barbed wire **4** *pl, chiefly NAm* strings ⟨*that woman behind the president pulling the* ~s⟩ [ME, fr OE *wīr*; akin to OHG *wiara* fine gold, L *viēre* to plait, Gk *iris* rainbow] – **wirelike** *adj*

[2]**wire** *vt* **1** to provide or connect with wire or wiring **2** to send or send word to by telegraph ~ *vi* to send a telegraphic message – **wirable** *adj*, **wirer** *n*

wired /wie·əd/ *adj* **1** reinforced or bound with wire **2** provided with wires (e g for electric connections) **3** fenced with wire **4** *chiefly NAm* addicted (to a drug) ⟨~ *on heroin*⟩ – slang

'**wire,draw** /-,draw/ *vt* **wiredrew** /-,drooh/; **wiredrawn** /-,drawn/ to spin out to excessive subtlety; attenuate ⟨~n *comparisons*⟩

'**wire ,gauge** *n* a gauge for measuring the diameter of wire

,**wire 'gauze** *n* a thin fabric of fine wire mesh

,**wire'haired** /-'heəd/ *adj, esp of a dog* having a stiff wiry coat of hair

[1]**wireless** /'wie·əlis/ *adj, chiefly Br* of radiotelegraphy, radiotelephony, or radio [[1]WIRE + -LESS]

[2]**wireless** *n* **1** WIRELESS TELEGRAPHY **2** *chiefly Br* RADIO 1, 2, 3d

[3]**wireless** *vt, chiefly Br* to radio

,**wireless te'legraphy** *n* the wireless transmission and reception of signals, usu voice communications, by means of electromagnetic waves

'**wireman** /-mən/ *n, pl* **wiremen** /~/ a maker of or worker with wire; *esp* one who wires electric or electronic circuitry

,**wire 'netting** *n* a network of coarse woven wire

,**wire 'rope** *n* a rope formed wholly or chiefly of wires

'**wire,tap** /-,tap/ *n* an electrical connection for wiretapping

'**wire,tapping** /-,taping/ *n* the act or an instance of tapping a telephone or telegraph wire

,**wire 'wool** *n* an abrasive material consisting of fine wire strands woven into a mass and used for scouring esp kitchen utensils (e g pans)

'**wire,worm** /-,wuhm/ *n* the slender hard-coated larva of various click beetles, destructive esp to plant roots

wiring /'wie·əring/ *n* a system of wires; *esp* an arrangement of wires that carries electric currents

wirra /'wirə/ *interj, Irish* – used to express lament, grief, or concern [*oh wirra*, fr IrGael *a Muire*, lit., O Mary]

wiry /'wie·əri/ *adj* **1** resembling wire, esp in form and flexibility **2** lean and vigorous; sinewy – **wirily** *adv*, **wiriness** *n*

wisdom /'wizd(ə)m/ *n* **1a** accumulated learning; knowledge **b** the thoughtful application of learning; insight **c** good sense; judgment ⟨*had the* ~ *to refuse*⟩ **2** the teachings of the ancient wise men [ME, fr OE *wīsdōm*, fr *wīs* wise]

,**Wisdom of 'Solomon** /'soləmən/ *n* a didactic book included in the Protestant Apocrypha

'**wisdom ,tooth** *n* any of the 4 molar teeth in humans which are the last to erupt on each side at the back of each jaw [fr its being cut usu at an age when one may have acquired some wisdom]

[1]**wise** /wiez/ *n* manner, way ⟨*in any* ~⟩ [ME, fr OE *wīse*; akin to OHG *wīsa* manner, Gk *eidos* form, *idein* to see – more at WIT]

[2]**wise** *adj* **1a** characterized by or showing wisdom; marked by understanding, discernment, and a capacity for sound judgment **b** judicious, prudent ⟨*not* ~ *to eat oysters*⟩ **2** well-informed ⟨*I'm none the* ~r⟩ **3** possessing inside knowledge; shrewdly cognizant – often + *to* ⟨*was* ~ *to what was happening*⟩ **4** *archaic* skilled in magic or divination [ME *wis*, fr OE *wīs*; akin to OHG *wīs* wise, OE *witan* to know – more at WIT] – **wisely** *adv*, **wiseness** *n*

-**wise** /-,wiez/ *comb form* (*n* → *adv*) **1a** in the manner of ⟨*entered the room crab*wise⟩ **b** in the position or direction of ⟨*a clock*wise *movement*⟩ ⟨*laid it out length*wise⟩ **2** with regard to; in respect of ⟨*career*wise *it's a good idea*⟩ [ME, fr OE *-wīsan*, fr *wīse* manner]

wiseacre /'wiezaykə/ *n* one who pretends to be clever or knowledgeable; SMART ALEC [MD *wijssegger* soothsayer, modif of OHG *wīzzago*; akin to OE *witega* soothsayer, *witan* to know]

wisecrack /'wiez,krak/ *vi or n* (to make) a sophisticated or knowing witticism – infml – **wisecracker** *n*

'**wise ,guy** *n* a conceited and self-assertive person; *esp* a know-it-all – infml ⟨*OK* ~, *you try and fix it*⟩

wisent /'vee,zent/ *n* the European bison [G, fr OHG *wisant, wisunt* – more at BISON]

wise up *vb* to (cause to) become informed or aware – infml

[1]**wish** /wish/ *vt* **1** to express the hope that sby will have or attain (sthg) ⟨*I* ~ *them success*⟩; *esp* to bid ⟨~ *him good night*⟩ **2a** to give form to (a wish) **b** to feel or express a wish for; want ⟨*I* ~ *to be alone*⟩ **c** to request in the form of a wish; order ⟨*he* ~es *us to leave*⟩ ~ *vi* **1** to have a desire – usu + *for* **2** to make a wish ⟨~ *on a star*⟩ [ME *wisshen*, fr OE *wȳscan*; akin to OHG *wunsken* to wish, L *venus* love, charm – more at WIN] – **wisher** *n* – **wish on/upon 1** to hope or will that (sby else) should have to suffer (a difficult person or situation) **2** to confer or foist (sthg unwanted) on (sby)

[2]**wish** *n* **1a** an act or instance of wishing or desire; a want ⟨*his* ~ *to become a doctor*⟩ **b** an object of desire; a goal ⟨*you got your* ~⟩ **2a** an expressed will or desire ⟨*obeyed their* ~es⟩ **b** an expressed greeting – usu pl ⟨*send my best* ~es⟩ **3** a ritual act of wishing ⟨*made a* ~⟩

'**wish,bone** /-,bohn/ *n* a forked bone in front of the breastbone of a bird consisting chiefly of the 2 clavicles fused at their lower ends [fr the superstition that when 2 people pull it apart the one getting the longer piece will have a wish granted]

'**wishful** /-f(ə)l/ *adj* **1a** expressive of a wish **b** having a wish; desirous **2** according with wishes rather than reality ⟨~ *thinking*⟩ – **wishfully** *adv*, **wishfulness** *n*

wishy-washy /'wishi ˌwoshi/ *adj* **1** lacking in strength or flavour **2** lacking in character or determination; ineffectual *USE* infml [redupl of *washy*]

wisp /wisp/ *n* **1** a small handful; *esp, chiefly Br* a pad of hay or straw for grooming an animal **2a** a thin separate streak or piece ⟨*a* ~ *of smoke*⟩ **b** sthg frail, slight, or fleeting ⟨*a* ~ *of a girl*⟩ **3** a flock of birds (e g snipe) [ME] – **wispish** *adj*, **wispily** *adv*, **wisplike** *adj*, **wispy** *adj*

wisteria /wi'stiəri·ə, -'steə-/, **wistaria** /wi'steəri·ə/ *n* any of a genus of chiefly Asiatic climbing plants with showy blue, white, purple, or rose flowers like those of the pea [NL, genus name, fr Caspar *Wistar* †1818 US physician]

wistful /'wistf(ə)l/ *adj* **1** full of unfulfilled desire; yearning **2** musingly sad; pensive [blend of *wishful* and obs *wistly* (intently), prob fr [1]*whist* + *-ly*] – **wistfully** *adv*, **wistfulness** *n*

wit /wit/ *n* **1** reasoning power; intelligence ⟨*past the* ~ *of man to understand*⟩ ⟨*slow* ~s⟩ **2a** mental soundness; sanity ⟨*frightened her out of her* ~s⟩ **b** mental resourcefulness; ingenuity ⟨*was at my* ~s *end*⟩ **3a** the ability to relate seemingly disparate things so as to illuminate or amuse **b(1)** a talent for banter or raillery **(2)** repartee, satire **4** a witty individual **5** *archaic* a person of superior intellect; a thinker **6** *archaic* SENSE 2 – usu pl ⟨*alone and warming his five* ~s, *the white owl in the belfry sits* – Alfred Tennyson⟩ *USE* (*1&2*) often pl with sing. meaning [ME, fr OE; akin to OHG *wizzi* knowledge, OE *witan* to know, L *vidēre* to see, Gk *eidenai* to know, *idein* to see]

witch /wich/ *n* **1** one who is credited with supernatural powers; *esp* a woman practising witchcraft **2** an ugly old woman; a hag **3** a charming or alluring woman – no longer in vogue [ME *wicche*, fr OE *wicca*, masc, wizard & *wicce*, fem, witch; akin to MHG *wicken* to bewitch, OE *wigle* divination, OHG *wīh* holy – more at VICTIM] – **witchlike** *adj*, **witchy** *adj*

'**witch,craft** /-ˌkrahft/ *n* (the use of) sorcery or magic

'**witch ,doctor** *n* a professional sorcerer, esp in a primitive tribal society

witchery /'wichəri/ *n* witchcraft

ˌ**witches'-'broom** *n* an abnormal tufted growth of small branches on a tree or shrub caused esp by fungi or viruses

witchetty, witchetty grub, witchety /'wichəti/ *n* any of various large white grubs regarded by Australian Aborigines as a delicacy [native name in Australia]

'**witch ,hazel** *n* (a soothing mildly astringent lotion made from the bark of) any of a genus of shrubs with slender-petalled yellow flowers borne in late autumn or early spring [*witch, wych* (a tree with pliant branches), fr ME *wyche*, fr OE *wice, wic*]

'**witch-,hunt** *n* the searching out and harassment of those with unpopular views – **witch-hunter** *n*, **witch-hunting** *n or adj*

witching /'wiching/ *adj* of or suitable for witchcraft ⟨*the very* ~ *time of night* – Shak⟩

witenagemot, witenagemote /ˌwitinəgə'mot, '----ˌ-/ *n* an Anglo-Saxon council convened from time to time to advise the king [OE *witena gemōt*, fr *witena* (gen pl of *wita* sage, adviser) + *gemōt* assembly, fr *ge-* (perfective prefix) + *mōt* assembly]

with /widh/ *prep* **1a** in opposition to; against ⟨*had a fight* ~ *his brother*⟩ **b** so as to be separated or detached from ⟨*I disagree* ~ *you*⟩ **2a** in relation to ⟨*the Italian frontier* ~ *Yugoslavia*⟩ **b** – used to indicate the object of attention, behaviour, or feeling ⟨*in love* ~ *her*⟩ **c** in respect to; so far as concerns ⟨*the trouble* ~ *this machine*⟩ – sometimes used redundantly ⟨*get it finished* ~⟩ **d** – used to indicate the object of an adverbial expression of imperative force ⟨*off* ~ *his head*⟩ **3a** – used to indicate accompaniment or association ⟨*live* ~ *the gipsies*⟩ **b** – used to indicate one to whom a usu reciprocal communication is made ⟨*talking* ~ *a friend*⟩ **c** – used to express agreement or sympathy ⟨*must conclude,* ~ *him, that the painting is a forgery*⟩ **d** able to follow the reasoning of ⟨*are you* ~ *me?*⟩ **4a** on the side of; for ⟨*vote* ~ *the government*⟩ **b** employed by ⟨*he's a salesman* ~ *ICI*⟩ **5a** – used to indicate the object of a statement of comparison, equality, or harmony ⟨*level* ~ *the street*⟩ ⟨*dress doesn't go* ~ *her shoes*⟩ **b** as well as ⟨*can ride* ~ *the best of them*⟩ **c** in addition to – used to indicate combination ⟨*his money,* ~ *his wife's, comes to a million*⟩ **d** inclusive of ⟨*costs £5* ~ *tax*⟩ **6a** by means of; using **b** through the effect of ⟨*pale* ~ *anger*⟩ **7a** – used to indicate manner of action ⟨*ran* ~ *effort*⟩ **b** – used to indicate an attendant or contributory circumstance ⟨*stood there* ~ *his hat on*⟩ **c** in possession of; having, bearing ⟨*came* ~ *good news*⟩ **d** in the possession or care of ⟨*the decision rests* ~ *you*⟩ **e** so as to have or receive ⟨*got off* ~ *a light sentence*⟩ **8a** – used to indicate a close association in time ⟨~ *the outbreak of war they went home*⟩ **b** in proportion to ⟨*the pressure varies* ~ *the depth*⟩ **9a** notwithstanding; IN SPITE OF ⟨*love her* ~ *all her faults*⟩ **b** EXCEPT FOR 2 ⟨*very similar,* ~ *1 important difference*⟩ **10** in the direction of ⟨~ *the wind*⟩ [ME, against, from, with, fr OE; akin to OE *wither* against, OHG *widar* against, back, Skt *vi* apart]

withal /wi'dhawl/ *adv* **1** together with this; besides **2** on the other hand; nevertheless [ME, fr *with* + *all, al* all]

withdraw /widh'draw/ *vb* **withdrew** /-'drooh/; **withdrawn** /-'drawn/ *vt* **1a** to draw back, away, or aside; remove ⟨~ *one's hand*⟩ **b** to remove (money) from a place of deposit **2** to take back; retract ⟨~ *my offer*⟩ ~ *vi* **1a** to go back or away; retire from participation **b** to retreat **2** to become socially or emotionally detached ⟨*had* ~n *into himself*⟩ **3** to retract a statement [ME, fr *with* from + *drawen* to draw] – **withdrawable** *adj*

withdrawal /widh'drawəl/ *n* **1a** the act or an instance of withdrawing **b(1)** social or emotional detachment **(2)** a pathological retreat from objective reality (e g in some schizophrenic states) **2a** removal of money or other assets from a place of deposit or investment **b** the discontinuance of use of a drug, often accompanied by unpleasant side effects

with'drawing ,room /widh'drawing/ *n, archaic* DRAWING ROOM

withdrawn /widh'drawn/ *adj* **1** secluded, isolated **2** socially detached and unresponsive; *also* shy – **withdrawnness** *n*

withe /with/ *n* a slender flexible branch or twig used esp for binding things together [ME, fr OE *withthe*; akin to OE *wīthig* withy]

wither /ˈwidhə/ *vi* **1** to become dry and shrivel (as if) from loss of bodily moisture **2** to lose vitality, force, or freshness ~ *vt* **1** to cause to wither **2** to make speechless or incapable of action; stun ⟨~ed *him with a look* – Dorothy Sayers⟩ [ME *widren*; prob akin to ME *weder* weather] – **withering** *adj*, **witheringly** *adv*

withers /ˈwidhəz/ *n pl* the ridge between the shoulder bones of a horse or other quadruped ☞ ANATOMY [prob fr obs *wither-* (against), fr ME, fr OE, fr *wither* against; fr the withers being the parts which resist the pull in drawing a load]

withershins /ˈwidhə,shinz/ *adv* widdershins [by alter.]

withhold /widhˈhohld/ *vt* **withheld** /-ˈheld/ **1** to hold back from action; check **2** to refrain from granting or giving ⟨~ *permission*⟩ [ME *withholden*, fr *with* from + *holden* to hold – more at WITH] – **withholder** *n*

^{1}**within** /wiˈdhin/ *adv* **1** in or into the interior; inside ⟨*enquire* ~⟩ **2** in one's inner thought, mood, or character [ME *withinne*, fr OE *withinnan*, fr *with* + *innan* inwardly, within, fr *in*]

^{2}**within** *prep* **1** inside – used to indicate enclosure or containment, esp in sthg large ⟨~ *the castle walls*⟩ **2** – used to indicate situation or circumstance in the limits or compass of: e g **a(1)** before the end of ⟨*gone* ~ *a week*⟩ **(2)** since the beginning of ⟨*been there* ~ *the last week*⟩ **b(1)** not beyond the quantity, degree, or limitations of ⟨*lives* ~ *his income*⟩ **(2)** in or into the scope or sphere of ⟨~ *his rights*⟩ **(3)** in or into the range of ⟨~ *reach*⟩ **(4)** – used to indicate a specific difference or margin ⟨~ *a mile of the town*⟩ **3** to the inside of; into

^{3}**within** *n* an inner place or area ⟨*revolt from* ~⟩

ˈ**with-it** *adj* up-to-date, fashionable – infml; no longer in vogue

^{1}**without** /wiˈdhowt/ *prep* **1** – used to indicate the absence or lack of or freedom from sthg ⟨*go* ~ *sleep*⟩ ⟨*did it* ~ *difficulty*⟩ **2** outside – now chiefly poetic [ME *withoute*, fr OE *withūtan*, fr *with* + *ūtan* outside, fr *ūt* out]

^{2}**without** *adv* **1** with sthg lacking or absent ⟨*has learned to do* ~⟩ **2** on or to the exterior; outside – now chiefly poetic

^{3}**without** *conj, chiefly dial* unless ⟨~ *you have a stunt, what is there?* – *Punch*⟩

^{4}**without** *n* an outer place or area ⟨*seen from* ~⟩

withstand /widhˈstand/ *vt* **withstood** /-ˈstood/ **1** to resist with determination; *esp* to stand up against successfully **2** to be proof against ⟨*boots won't* ~ *the wet*⟩ [ME *withstanden*, fr OE *withstandan*, fr *with* against + *standan* to stand – more at WITH]

withy /ˈwidhi/ *n* **1** OSIER 1 **2** a withe of osier [ME, fr OE *wīthig*; akin to OHG *wīda* willow, L *vitis* vine, *viēre* to plait – more at WIRE]

witless /ˈwitlis/ *adj* **1** lacking wit or understanding; foolish **2** CRAZY 1

witling /ˈwitling/ *n* a would-be wit

^{1}**witness** /ˈwitnis/ *n* **1** testimony **2** sby who gives evidence, specif before a tribunal **3** sby asked to be present at a transaction so as to be able to testify to its having taken place **4** sby who personally sees or hears an event take place **5a** sthg serving as evidence; a sign ⟨*these low marks are* ~ *to their lack of application*⟩ **b** public affirmation by word or example of usu religious faith or conviction **6** *cap* a member of the Jehovah's Witnesses [ME *witnesse*, fr OE *witnes* knowledge, testimony, witness, fr *wit*]

^{2}**witness** *vt* **1** to testify to **2** to act as legal witness of (e g by signing one's name) **3** to give proof of; betoken ⟨*his appearance* ~es *what he has suffered*⟩ – often in the subjunctive ⟨*has suffered badly, as* ~ *his appearance*⟩ **4** to observe personally or directly; see for oneself ⟨~ed *the historic event*⟩ **5** to be the scene or time of ⟨*structures which this striking Dorset hilltop once* ~ed – *TLS*⟩ ~ *vi* **1** to bear witness **2** to bear witness to one's religious convictions ⟨*opportunity to* ~ *for Christ* – Billy Graham⟩

ˈ**witness-,box** *n, chiefly Br* an enclosure in which a witness testifies in court

ˈ**witness ,stand** *n, NAm* a witness-box

-witted /-ˈwitid/ *comb form* (*adj* → *adj*) having wit or understanding of the specified kind ⟨*dull*-witted⟩

witticism /ˈwiti,siz(ə)m/ *n* a witty and often ironic remark [*witty* + *-cism* (as in *criticism*)]

witty /ˈwiti/ *adj* **1** amusingly or ingeniously clever in conception or execution ⟨*a* ~ *musical theme*⟩ **2** having or showing wit ⟨*a* ~ *speaker*⟩ **3** quick to see or express illuminating or amusing relationships or insights – **wittily** *adv*, **wittiness** *n*

wives /wievz/ *pl of* WIFE

wiz /wiz/ *n* WIZARD 2 – infml

^{1}**wizard** /ˈwizəd/ *n* **1** a man skilled in magic **2** one who is very clever or skilful, esp in a specified field ⟨*a* ~ *at maths*⟩ – infml [ME *wysard* wise man, fr *wis, wys* wise]

^{2}**wizard** *adj, chiefly Br* great, excellent – infml

wizardry /ˈwizədri/ *n* the art or practices of a wizard; sorcery

wizen /ˈwiz(ə)n/ *vb* to (cause to) become dry, shrunken, and wrinkled, often as a result of aging – usu in past [ME *wisenen*, fr OE *wisnian*; akin to OHG *wesanēn* to wither, L *viēre* to twist together, plait – more at WIRE]

wo /woh/ *interj* whoa

woad /wohd/ *n* (a European plant of the mustard family formerly grown for) the blue dyestuff yielded by its leaves [ME *wod*, fr OE *wād*; akin to OHG *weit* woad, L *vitrum* woad, glass]

^{1}**wobble** /ˈwobl/ *vb* **wobbling** /ˈwobl·ing, ˈwobling/ *vi* **1a** to proceed with an irregular swerving or staggering motion ⟨~d *down the road on his bicycle*⟩ **b** to rock unsteadily from side to side **c** to tremble, quaver **2** to waver, vacillate ~ *vt* to cause to wobble [prob fr LG *wabbeln*; akin to OE *wǣfre* restless – more at WAVER] – **wobbler** *n*, **wobbliness** *n*, **wobbly** *adj*

^{2}**wobble** *n* **1** an unequal rocking motion **2** an act or instance of vacillating or fluctuating

Wodehousian /ˈwood,howsi·ən, -zi-, ,-ˈ---/ *adj* of or suggesting the writings of P G Wodehouse, esp in depicting upper-class foolishness [P G *Wodehouse* †1979 E comic novelist]

wodge /woj/ *n, Br* a usu bulky mass or chunk – infml ⟨*a* ~ *of papers*⟩ [prob alter. of *wedge*]

^{1}**woe** /woh/ *interj* – used to express grief, regret, or distress [ME *wa, wo*, fr OE *wā*; akin to ON *vei*, interj, woe, L *vae*]

^{2}**woe** *n* **1** great sorrow or suffering caused by misfortune, grief, etc **2** a calamity, affliction – usu pl ⟨*economic* ~s⟩ [ME *wo*, fr *wo*, interj]

woebegone /'wohbi,gon/ *adj* expressive of great sorrow or misery ⟨*a* ~ *look*⟩ [ME *wo begon*, fr *wo*, n + *begon*, pp of *begon* to go about, beset, fr OE *begān*, fr *be-* + *gān* to go – more at GO]

woeful *also* **woful** /'wohf(ə)l/ *adj* **1** feeling or expressing woe ⟨~ *prophecies*⟩ **2** inspiring woe; grievous ⟨*it was* ~ *to see him spoiling it* – Henry James⟩ – **woefully** *adv*, **woefulness** *n*

wog /wog/ *n*, *chiefly Br* a nonwhite person; *broadly* any dark-skinned foreigner – derog [prob short for *golliwog*]

woggle /'wogl/ *n*, *chiefly Br* a usu leather band used to secure a scout's neckerchief at the throat [origin unknown]

wok /wawk, wok/ *n* a bowl-shaped cooking utensil used esp for stir-frying Chinese food [Chin (Cant) *wôk*]

woke /wohk/ *past of* WAKE

woken /'wohkən/ *past part of* WAKE

wold /wohld/ *n* **1** an upland area of open country **2** *pl*, *cap* a hilly or rolling region – in names of various English geographical areas ⟨*the Yorkshire* Wolds⟩ [ME *wald*, *wold*, fr OE *weald*, *wald* forest; akin to OHG *wald* forest]

[1]**wolf** /woolf/ *n*, *pl* **wolves** /woolvz/, (*1*) **wolves**, *esp collectively* **wolf** **1** (the fur of) any of various large predatory flesh-eating mammals that resemble the related dogs, prey on livestock, and usu hunt in packs – compare COYOTE, JACKAL **2** a fiercely rapacious person **3a** dissonance in some chords produced on instruments with fixed notes tuned by unequal temperament (e g organs and pianos) **b** a harshness due to faulty vibration in various notes in a bowed instrument **4** a man who pursues women in an aggressive way – infml [ME, fr OE *wulf*; akin to OHG *wolf*, L *lupus*, Gk *lykos*; (3) G, fr the howling sound] – **wolflike** *adj* – **keep the wolf from the door** to avoid or prevent starvation or want – **wolf in sheep's clothing** one who cloaks a hostile intention with a friendly manner

[2]**wolf** *vt* to eat greedily; devour – often + *down*

'wolf ˌcub *n*, *Br* CUB SCOUT – no longer used technically

'wolf ˌdog *n* **1** any of various large dogs formerly kept for hunting wolves **2** the offspring of a wolf and a domestic dog

'wolfˌfish /-ˌfish/ *n* any of several large ferocious sea blennies with strong teeth

'wolfˌhound /-ˌhownd/ *n* any of several large dogs used, esp formerly, in hunting large animals (e g wolves)

wolfish /'woolfish/ *adj* befitting or suggestive of a wolf (e g in savage appearance, fierceness, or greed) – **wolfishly** *adv*, **wolfishness** *n*

wolfram /'woolfrəm/ *n* **1** tungsten **2** wolframite [G]

wolframite /'woolfrəˌmiet/ *n* a brownish-black mineral containing tungsten, iron, and manganese [G *wolframit*, fr *wolfram*]

wolfsbane /'woolfsˌbayn/ *n* a (yellow-flowered Eurasian) aconite

'wolf ˌspider *n* any of various active wandering ground spiders

'wolf ˌwhistle *n* a distinctive whistle sounded by a man to express sexual admiration for a woman – **wolf-whistle** *vi*

Wolof /'wohlof/ *n* a Niger-Congo language of Senegambia ☞ LANGUAGE

wolverine /'woolvəreen/ *n*, *pl* **wolverines**, *esp collectively* **wolverine** (the blackish fur of) a strong ferocious flesh-eating mammal of northern forests and tundra [prob irreg fr *wolv-* (as in *wolves*)]

woman /'woomən/ *n*, *pl* **women** /'wimin/ **1a** an adult female human as distinguished from a man or child **b** a woman belonging to a particular category (e g by birth, residence, membership, or occupation) – usu in combination ⟨*council*woman⟩ **2** womankind **3** distinctively feminine nature; womanliness ⟨*there's something of the* ~ *in him*⟩ **4a** a charwoman ⟨*the daily* ~⟩ **b** a personal maid, esp in former times **5a** a female sexual partner; *esp* a mistress **b** GIRLFRIEND 1 – chiefly derog [ME, fr OE *wīfman*, fr *wīf* woman, wife + *man* human being, man] – **womanless** *adj*

'womanhood /-hood/ *n* **1a** the condition of being an adult female as distinguished from a child or male **b** the distinguishing character or qualities of a woman or of womankind **2** women, womankind

womanish /'woomənish/ *adj* unsuitable to a man or to a strong character of either sex; effeminate ⟨~ *fears*⟩ [WOMAN + -ISH] – **womanishly** *adv*, **womanishness** *n*

womanˑize, -ise /'woomәniez/ *vi* to associate with many women habitually, esp for sexual relations – **womanizer** *n*

ˌwoman'kind /-'kiend/ *n sing or pl in constr* female human beings; women as a whole, esp as distinguished from men

[1]**'womanˌlike** /-ˌliek/ *adj* womanly

[2]**womanlike** *adv* in the manner of a woman

'womanly /-li/ *adj* having or exhibiting the good qualities befitting a woman – **womanliness** *n*

womb /woohm/ *n* **1** the uterus ☞ REPRODUCTION **2a** a hollow enveloping cavity or space **b** a place where sthg is generated [ME *wamb*, *womb*, fr OE; akin to OHG *wamba* belly] – **wombed** /woohmd/ *adj*

wombat /'wombat/ *n* any of several stocky Australian marsupial mammals resembling small bears [native name in New South Wales, Australia]

womble /'wombl/ *n* any of a group of public-spirited furry fictional creatures that live on Wimbledon Common where they collect litter [the *Wombles*, creatures in children's books by Elisabeth Beresford *fl* 1970 E writer]

womenfolk /'wiminˌfohk/ *also* **womenfolks** *n pl* **1** women in general **2** the women of a family or community

ˌwomen'kind /-'kiend/ *n* womankind

ˌWomen's 'Institute *n* a British organization of women who meet regularly and engage in various social and cultural activities

ˌwomen's 'lib /lib/ *n*, *often cap W&L* WOMEN'S LIBERATION

ˌWomen's Libe'ration *n* a modern feminist movement stressing the social and psychological emancipation of women as well as the improvement of their civil and legal status

ˌwomen's 'rights *n pl* legal, political, and social rights for women equal to those of men

[1]**won** /wun/ *past of* WIN

[2]**won** /won/ *n*, *pl* **won** ☞ *Korea (North)*, & *Korea (South)* at NATIONALITY [Korean *wŏn*]

[1]**wonder** /'wundə/ *n* **1a** a cause of astonishment or

admiration; a marvel ⟨*it's a ~ he wasn't killed*⟩ **b** a miracle **2** rapt attention or astonishment at sthg unexpected, strange, new to one's experience, etc ⟨*gazed in ~ at the snow*⟩ [ME, fr OE *wundor*; akin to OHG *wuntar* wonder]

[2]**wonder** *adj* noted for outstanding success or achievement ⟨*~ drugs*⟩

[3]**wonder** *vi* **1a** to be in a state of wonder; marvel *at* **b** to feel surprise ⟨*I shouldn't ~ if he's late*⟩ **2** to feel curiosity or doubt; speculate ⟨*~ about his motives*⟩ ~ *vt* to be curious or in doubt about – with a clause ⟨*~ who she is*⟩ – **wonderer** *n*

'**wonderful** /-f(ə)l/ *adj* **1** exciting wonder; astonishing ⟨*a sight ~ to behold*⟩ **2** unusually good; admirable – **wonderfully** *adv*, **wonderfulness** *n*

'**wonder,land** /-,land/ *n* **1** a fairylike imaginary place **2** a place that excites admiration or wonder

'**wonderment** /-mənt/ *n* **1** astonishment, marvelling **2** a cause of or occasion for wonder **3** curiosity

'**wonder,struck** /-,struk/ *adj* overcome with wonder; astonished

'**wonder-,worker** *n* a performer of wonders – **wonder-working** *adj*

wondrous /'wundrəs/ *adj* wonderful – poetic [alter. of ME *wonders*, fr gen of [1]*wonder*] – **wondrous** *adv*, *archaic*, **wondrously** *adv*, **wondrousness** *n*

wonky /'wongki/ *adj*, *Br* awry, crooked; *also* shaky, unsteady ⟨*he's still a bit ~ after the flu*⟩ – infml [alter. of E dial. *wankle*, fr ME *wankel*, fr OE *wancol*]

[1]**wont** /wohnt/ *adj* **1** accustomed, used ⟨*places where people are ~ to meet*⟩ **2** inclined, apt ⟨*her letters are ~ to be tedious*⟩ *USE* + *to* and infin; fml [ME *woned, wont*, fr pp of *wonen* to dwell, be used to, fr OE *wunian*; akin to OHG *wonēn* to dwell, be used to, L *venus* love, charm – more at WIN]

[2]**wont** *n* customary practice – fml ⟨*according to my ~*⟩

won't /wohnt/ will not

wonted /'wohntid/ *adj* customary, habitual – used attributively; fml ⟨*spoke with his ~ slowness*⟩ – **wontedly** *adv*, **wontedness** *n*

woo /wooh/ *vt* **1** to try to win the affection of and a commitment of marriage from (a woman); court **2** to solicit or entreat, esp with importunity ~ *vi* to court a woman [ME *wowen*, fr OE *wōgian*] – **wooer** *n*

[1]**wood** /wood/ *n* **1** a dense growth of trees, usu greater in extent than a copse and smaller than a forest – often pl with sing. meaning **2a** a hard fibrous plant tissue that is basically xylem and makes up the greater part of the stems and branches of trees or shrubs beneath the bark **b** wood suitable or prepared for some use (e g burning or building) ☞ ENERGY **3** sthg typically made of wood: e g **a** a golf club with a wooden head **b** a wooden cask ⟨*wine from the ~*⟩ **c** [2]BOWL 1 [ME *wode*, fr OE *widu, wudu*; akin to OHG *witu* wood, OIr *fid* tree] – **not see the wood for the trees** to be unable to see broad outlines because of a mass of detail – **out of the wood** *Br* escaped from peril or difficulty

[2]**wood** *adj* **1** WOODEN 1 **2** suitable for cutting, storing, or carrying wood ⟨*a ~ saw*⟩

wood alcohol *n* methanol

'**wood a,nemone** *n* a common Eurasian anemone that grows esp in woodland and has white or pinkish flowers

woodbine /'wood,bien/ *n* **1** honeysuckle **2** VIRGINIA CREEPER [ME *wodebinde*, fr OE *wudubinde*, fr *wudu* wood + *bindan* to tie, bind; fr its winding round trees]

[1]'**wood,block** /-,blok/ *n* a woodcut – **wood-block** *adj*

[2]**woodblock** *adj*, *of a floor* made of parquet

'**wood,chuck** /-,chuk/ *n* a thickset N American marmot [by folk etymology fr Ojibwa *otchig* fisher, marten, or Cree *otcheck*]

'**wood ,coal** *n* lignite

'**wood,cock** /-,kok/ *n*, *pl* **woodcocks**, *esp collectively* **woodcock** an Old World long-billed wading bird of wooded regions that is related to the sandpipers and shot as game

'**wood,craft** /-,krahft/ *n* **1** skill and practice in anything relating to woods or forests, esp in surviving, travelling, and hunting **2** skill in shaping or making things from wood

'**wood,cut** /-,kut/ *n* (a print taken from) a relief-printing surface consisting of a wooden block with a design cut esp in the direction of the grain – compare WOOD ENGRAVING

'**wood,cutter** /-,kutə/ *n* one who chops down trees

'**wood,cutting** /-,kuting/ *n* the action or occupation of cutting wood or timber

wooded /'woodid/ *adj* covered with growing trees

wooden /'wood(ə)n/ *adj* **1** made or consisting of or derived from wood **2** lacking ease or flexibility; awkwardly stiff – **woodenly** *adv*, **woodenness** *n*

'**wood en,graving** *n* (a print taken from) a relief-printing surface consisting of a wooden block with a design cut esp against the grain – compare WOODCUT

'**wooden,head** /-,hed/ *n* a blockhead

,**wooden'headed** /-'hedid/ *adj* dense, stupid

,**wooden 'spoon** *n* a consolation or booby prize

wood hyacinth *n*, *NAm* WILD HYACINTH

'**wood ,ibis** *n* a large American wading bird that frequents wooded swamps

'**woodland** /-lənd/ *n* land covered with trees, scrub, etc – often pl with sing. meaning – **woodland** *adj*, **woodlander** *n*

'**wood,lark** /-,lahk/ *n* a small European lark with a melodious song usu delivered during flight

'**wood,louse** /-,lows/ *n*, *pl* **woodlice** /-,lies/ a small ground-living crustacean with a flattened elliptical body often capable of rolling into a ball in defence

'**woodman** /-mən/ *n* a woodsman; *specif* a forester or woodcutter

'**wood,pecker** /-,pekə/ *n* any of numerous usu multicoloured birds with very hard bills used to drill holes in the bark or wood of trees to find insect food or to dig out nesting cavities

'**wood,pigeon** /-,pijin/ *n* a large European wild pigeon

'**wood,pile** /-,piel/ *n* a pile of wood (e g firewood) – **in the woodpile** doing or responsible for secret mischief ⟨*the No 1 villain* in the woodpile – Howard Whitman⟩

'**wood ,pulp** *n* pulp from wood used in making cellulose derivatives (e g paper or rayon)

woodruff /'wood,ruf/ *n* any of several plants of the madder family; *esp* a small European sweet-scented plant used in perfumery and for flavouring wine [ME *woderove*, fr OE *wudurofe*, fr *wudu* wood +

-rofe (perh akin to OHG *rāba* turnip) – more at [1]RAPE]

'wood ,screw *n* a pointed screw that has an external screw thread and a slotted head to receive the blade of a screwdriver

'wood,shed /-,shed/ *n* a shed for storing wood, esp firewood

woodsman /'woodzmən/ *n* one who lives in, frequents, or works in the woods

wood sorrel *n* any of a genus of plants with acid sap; *esp* a stemless plant of shady places with leaves made up of 3 leaflets that is sometimes held to be the original shamrock

'wood ,spirit *n* methanol

'wood ,wasp *n* any of various wasplike insects with larvae that burrow in woody plants

'wood,wind /-,wind/ *n* **1** any of a group of wind instruments (e g a clarinet, flute, or saxophone) that is characterized by a cylindrical or conical tube of wood or metal, usu with finger holes or keys, that produces notes by the vibration of a single or double reed or by the passing of air over a mouth hole **2** *sing or pl in constr* the woodwind section of a band or orchestra – often pl with sing. meaning

'wood,work /-,wuhk/ *n* **1** work made of wood; *esp* wooden interior fittings (e g mouldings or stairways) **2** the craft of constructing things from wood – **woodworker** *n*, **woodworking** *adj*

'wood,worm /-,wuhm/ *n* an insect larva, esp that of the furniture beetle, that bores in dead wood; *also* an infestation of woodworm

woody /'woodi/ *adj* **1** overgrown with or having many woods **2a** of or containing (much) wood, wood fibres, or xylem ⟨~ *plants*⟩ **b** *of a plant stem* tough and fibrous **3** characteristic of or suggestive of wood ⟨*wine with a ~ flavour*⟩ – **woodiness** *n*

,woody 'nightshade *n* bittersweet

[1]**woof** /woohf/ *n* **1** the weft **2** a basic or essential element or material [alter. of ME *oof*, fr OE *ōwef*, fr *ō-* (fr *on*) + *wefan* to weave – more at WEAVE]

[2]**woof** /woof/ *vi or n* (to make) the low gruff sound characteristic of a dog [imit]

woofer /'woohfə/ *n* a loudspeaker that responds mainly to low frequencies – compare TWEETER

wool /wool/ *n* **1** the soft wavy coat of various hairy mammals, esp the sheep, that is made up of keratin fibres covered with minute scales **2** sthg, esp a garment or fabric, made of wool ⟨*I always wear ~ in the winter*⟩ **3a** a dense felted hairy covering, esp on a plant **b** a wiry or fibrous mass (e g of steel or glass) – usu in combination [ME *wolle*, fr OE *wull*; akin to OHG *wolla* wool, L *vellus* fleece, *lana* wool, *lanugo* down] – **woolled, wooled** *adj*

'wool,gathering /-,gadh(ə)ring/ *n* indulging in idle daydreaming – **woolgather** *vi*, **woolgatherer** *n*

[1]**woollen,** *NAm chiefly* **woolen** /'woolən/ *adj* **1** made of wool **2** of or for the manufacture or sale of woollen products ⟨~ *mills*⟩ ⟨*the ~ industry*⟩

[2]**woollen,** *NAm chiefly* **woolen** *n* **1** a fabric made of wool **2** *pl* garments of woollen fabric

[1]**woolly,** *NAm also* **wooly** /'wooli/ *adj* **1** (made) of or resembling wool; *also* bearing (sthg like) wool **2a** lacking in clearness or sharpness of outline ⟨*a ~ TV picture*⟩ **b** marked by mental vagueness or confusion ⟨*~ thinking*⟩ **3** boisterously rough – chiefly in *wild and woolly* – **woollily** *adv*, **woolliness** *n*

[2]**woolly, woolie,** *NAm also* **wooly** *n, chiefly Br* a woollen jumper or cardigan

,woolly 'bear *n* any of various rather large very hairy caterpillars of (tiger) moths

woolpack /'wool,pak/ *n* **1** a bale of wool **2** a rounded cumulus cloud rising from a horizontal base

'wool,sack /-,sak/ *n* *the* official seat of the Lord Chancellor in the House of Lords

'wool,sorter's di,sease /'wool,sawtəz/ *n* lung anthrax resulting esp from inhalation of bacterial spores from contaminated wool or hair

'wool ,stapler *n* sby who grades raw wool before selling it to a manufacturer

woomera /'woomərə/ *n* a wooden rod that has a hooked end and is used by Australian aborigines for throwing a spear [native name in Australia]

woosh /woosh, woohsh/ *vi or n* (to make) a swishing sound [imit]

woozy /'woohzi/ *adj* **1** mentally unclear or hazy **2** dizzy or slightly nauseous ***USE*** infml [perh fr *woolly* + dizzy] – **woozily** *adv*, **wooziness** *n*

wop /wop/ *n, often cap* an Italian – chiefly derog [It dial. *guappo* blusterer, swaggerer, bully]

,Worcester 'sauce /'woostə/ *n* a pungent sauce containing soy sauce, vinegar, and spices [*Worcester, Worcestershire,* former county of England (now *Hereford and Worcester*) where it was orig made]

,Worcestershire 'sauce /'woostəshiə, -shə/ *n* WORCESTER SAUCE

[1]**word** /wuhd/ *n* **1a** sthg that is said **b** *pl* **(1)** talk, discourse ⟨*putting one's feelings into ~s*⟩ **(2)** the text of a vocal musical composition **c** a short remark, statement, or conversation ⟨*would like to have a ~ with you*⟩ **2a** a meaningful unit of spoken language that can stand alone as an utterance and is not divisible into similar units; *also* a written or printed representation of a spoken word that is usu set off by spaces on either side ⟨*the number of ~s to a line*⟩ 👁 ☞ ALPHABET **b** a string of adjacent binary digits that is typically longer than a byte and is processed by a computer as a unit ⟨*a 16-bit ~*⟩ **3** an order, command ⟨*don't move till I give the ~*⟩ **4** *often cap* **a** *the* divine wisdom manifest in the creation and redemption of the world, and identified in Christian thought with the second person of the Trinity **b** GOSPEL 1 **c** the expressed or manifested mind and will of God **5a** news, information ⟨*sent ~ that he would be late*⟩ **b** rumour ⟨*~ has it that they're leaving*⟩ **6** the act of speaking or of making verbal communication ⟨*in ~ and deed*⟩ **7** a promise ⟨*kept her ~*⟩ **8** *pl* a quarrelsome utterance or conversation ⟨*been having ~s with my wife*⟩ **9** a verbal signal; a password **10** *the* most appropriate description ⟨*'hot" wasn't the ~ for it*⟩ [ME, fr OE; akin to OHG *wort* word, L *verbum*, Gk *eirein* to say, speak] – **wordless** *adj* – **from the word go** from the beginning – **in a word** IN SHORT – **in so many words** in exactly those terms ⟨*implied that such actions were criminal but did not say so* in so many words⟩ – **my word** – used to express surprise or astonishment – **of one's word** that can be relied on to keep a promise – used only after *man* or *woman* ⟨*a man of* his word⟩

[2]**word** *vt* to express in words; phrase

'word-,blindness *n* **1** alexia **2** dyslexia

,word-for-'word *adj, of a report or translation* in or following the exact words; verbatim – **word for word** *adv*

Words with J, Q, X and Z

J

basenji
bijou(x)
djinn
donjon
hadj
hadji
*hajj
*hajji
hejira
jabot
jacinth
jadeite
jaeger
jalap
jamb
jargoon
jarl
jean
*jejune
*jejunum
jess
jetsam
jewfish
jihad
jinn
jinni
**jinx
joinder
joule
*juju
junta
jural
juror
jussive
moujik
raj
raja(h)
sapajou
sjambok
swaraj

Q

aliquot
aqueous
barque
bisque
cirque
claque
clique
cliqu(e)y
coquina
cumquat
kumquat
maquis
quadrat
quadric
quag
quagga
quaich
quaigh
quanta
quantum
quartan
quean
quern
**quetzal
quietus
quinone
quinsy
quint
quintal
quirt
quoin
quondam
roquet
rorqual
sequela
sequent
siliqua
silique
squab
squama(e)
squill
squilla
squinch
torque

X

ataxia
ataxic
axial
axil
axilla(e)
axolotl
axon
bauxite
beaux
calyx
calx(es)
codex
coccyx
crux(es)
dexter
dextral
dioxide
duplex
efflux
flax(en)
flexion
flexor
flexure
foxtail
hallux
hexad
hexane
hexose
hexyl
hyrax
ibex
ilex
infix
lexical
lux
luxate
maxilla
maximal
maxwell
meninx
moxie
murex
nix
nixie
onyx
oryx
oxbow
oxeye
oxlip
oxymora
oxyntic
pax
phalanx
phlox
plexus
pollex
praxis
prolix
pyrexia
pyrexic
pyx
pyxis
radix(es)
reflux
salpinx
sax
saxhorn
scolex
sexism
sext
simplex
spadix
storax
syrinx
toxin
triplex
tuxedo
varix
xanthic
xebec
xenon
*xerox
xiphoid
xylem
xylene

Z

adz(e)
azimuth
azo
azoic
azurite
azygous
bazaar
bazooka
benzine
benzoic
benzoin
benzol
bezant
bezel
bezique
bonze
borzoi
braze
colza
coryza
cozy
crozier
diazo
dozen(th)
elegize
evzone
faze
fez
*frizz
fuze
fuzee
gazebo
izard
kazoo
lazar
lazaret
mazer
mestiza
*mezuzah
*mezzo
mitzvah
*mizzen
*mizzle
*muezzin
muzhik
ouzel
oyez
panzer
podzol
pretzel
raze
rhizome
seizure
sizar
syzygy
teazel
tzigane
vizard
vizier
wizen
zaddik
zaffre
zany
zareba
zebu
zein
zenana
zener
zeolite
zeta
zeugma
zibet
zincate
zinced
zincic
zincked
zincous
zing(y)
zinnia
zircon
*zizz
zloty
zombi(e)
zonate
zonked
zooid(al)
zoril
zorilla
zygoma
zygote
zymase
zymogen
zymotic
zymurgy

*double JQX or Z

**combination of J, Q, X, Z

Words for word games

Scrabble®, and many nonproprietary paper games, depend on making the best use of a set of jumbled letters. Here are some useful shorter words containing 'difficult' letters or letter combinations. They are all defined at their own places in the dictionary.

2-letter words

ad
ae
ah
ai
am
an
as
at
ax
ay
be
bo
by
da
do
ee
eh
el
em
en
er
ex
fa
go
ha
he
hi
ho
id
if
in
is
it
jo
ka
ky
la
lo
ma
me
mi
mo
mu
my
na
no
nu
od
of
oh
on
or
ow
ox
oy
pa
pi
po
re
sh
si
so
ta
ti
to
un
up
ur
us
ut
we
wo
xi
xu
ye

Words with no vowels

crypt
cwm
cyst
glyph
gym
gyp
gypsy
hymn
lymph
lynch
lynx
myrrh
myth
nymph
pygmy
pyx
rhythm
shyly
spry
sylph
sync(h)
syzygy
tryst
wynd
wynn

Words with many vowels

adieu
aerie
audio
cooee
eerie
queue

Words with repeated letters

bobby
coccyx
daddy
lolly
mummy
ninny
fluff
poppy
potto
sissy
tatty
titty
zizz

Common anagrams

abets – baste – bates – beast – beats
acres – cares – races – scare
amen – mane – mean – name
aster – rates – stare – tares – tears
capers – crapes – pacers – recaps – scrape – spacer
capes – paces – scape – space
caret – cater – crate – trace
coins – icons – scion – sonic
dale – deal – lade – lead
danger – gander – garden – ranged
drapes – parsed – spared – spread
east – eats – sate – seat – seta
emit – item – mite – time
emits – items – mites – smite – times
glare – lager – large – regal
hares – hears – share – shear
inert – inter – nitre – trine
inks – kins – sink – skin
laves – salve – slave – vales
leap – pale – peal – plea
least – slate – stale – steal – tales
limes – miles – slime – smile
mate – meat – tame – team
notes – onset – stone – tones
pares – pears – rapes – reaps – spare
pastel – plates – pleats – staple
parts – sprat – strap – traps
paste – pates – spate – tapes
pores – poser – prose – ropes – spore
priest – ripest – sprite – stripe – tripes
serve – sever – veers – verse
skate – stake – steak – takes – teaks

wording /'wuhding/ *n* the act or manner of expressing in words ⟨*the exact* ~ *of the will*⟩

ˌword of 'mouth *n* oral communication

ˌword-'perfect *adj* having memorized sthg perfectly

'word ˌpicture *n* a graphic verbal description

'wordˌplay /-ˌplay/ *n* verbal wit

word processor *n* a machine for producing typewritten text that uses a microprocessor and data storage device to carry out certain typing tasks automatically – **word processing** *n*

'word ˌsquare *n* a series of words of equal length arranged in a square pattern to read the same horizontally and vertically

wordy /'wuhdi/ *adj* using or containing (too) many words – **wordily** *adv*, **wordiness** *n*

wore /waw/ *past of* WEAR

¹work /wuhk/ *n* **1** activity in which one exerts strength or faculties to do or produce sthg: **a** sustained physical or mental effort to achieve a result **b** the activities that afford one's accustomed means of livelihood **c** a specific task, duty, function, or assignment **2a** the (result of) expenditure of energy by natural phenomena **b** the transference of energy that is produced by the motion of the point of application of a force and is measured by the product of the force and the distance moved along the line of action ☞ PHYSICS **3a** (the result of) a specified method of working ⟨*the* ~ *of many hands*⟩ – often in combination ⟨*can't do needle*work⟩ ⟨*clever camera* ~⟩ **b** sthg made from a specified material – often in combination ⟨*iron*work⟩ ⟨*porcelain* ~⟩ **4a** a fortified structure (e g a fort, earthen barricade, or trench) **b** *pl* structures in engineering (e g docks, bridges, or embankments) or mining (e g shafts or tunnels) **5** *pl but sing or pl in constr* a place where industrial activity is carried out; a factory – often in combination ⟨*a water*works⟩ ⟨*a tile*works⟩ **6** *pl* the working or moving parts of a mechanism ⟨*the* ~s *of a clock*⟩ **7** an artistic production or creation **8** *pl* performance of moral or religious acts ⟨*salvation by* ~s⟩ **9a** effective operation; an effect, result ⟨*wait for time to do its healing* ~⟩ **b** activity, behaviour, or experience of the specified kind ⟨*dancing reels is thirsty* ~⟩ **10** a workpiece **11** *pl* **a** everything possessed, available, or belonging – infml; + *the* **b** subjection to all possible abuse – infml; usu + *get* ⟨*get the* ~s⟩ or *give* ⟨*gave him the* ~s⟩ [ME *werk, work,* fr OE *werc, weorc*; akin to OHG *werc,* Gk *ergon*] – **workless** *adj* – **at work 1** engaged in working; busy; *esp* engaged in one's regular occupation **2** at one's place of work – **in the works** in process of preparation, development, or completion – **one's work cut out** as much as one can do – **out of work** without regular employment; unemployed

²work *adj* **1** suitable for wear while working ⟨~ *clothes*⟩ **2** used for work ⟨~ *elephant*⟩

³work *vb* **worked, wrought** /rawt/ *vt* **1** to bring to pass; effect ⟨~ *miracles*⟩ **2a** to fashion or create sthg by expending labour on; forge, shape ⟨~ *flint into tools*⟩ **b** to make or decorate with needlework; embroider ⟨~ *a sampler*⟩ **3** to prepare or form into a desired state for use by kneading, hammering, etc **4** to operate ⟨*a pump* ~ed *by hand*⟩ ⟨*switches are* ~ed *from a central tower*⟩ **5** to solve (a problem) by reasoning or calculation – usu + *out* **6** to cause to labour ⟨~ed *his horses nearly to death*⟩ **7** to carry on an operation in (a place or area) ⟨*the salesman* ~ed *both sides of the street*⟩ **8** to finance by working ⟨~ed *his way through college*⟩ **9a** to manoeuvre (oneself or an object) gradually or with difficulty into or out of a specified condition or position ⟨*the screw* ~ed *itself loose*⟩ **b** to contrive, arrange ⟨*we can* ~ *it so that you can take your holiday early*⟩ **10** to excite, provoke ⟨~ed *himself into a rage*⟩ ~ *vi* **1a** to exert oneself, esp in sustained, purposeful, or necessary effort ⟨~ed *all day over a hot stove*⟩ ⟨~ing *for the cause*⟩ **b** to perform work or fulfil duties regularly for wages or a salary **2** to operate, function ⟨*the lifts don't* ~ *at night*⟩ **3** to exert an influence or have a tendency ⟨*events have* ~ed *in our favour*⟩ **4** to produce a desired effect; succeed ⟨*hope your plan will* ~⟩ **5a** to make one's way slowly and with difficulty; move or progress laboriously ⟨*just* ~ing *through her own teenage rebellion thing – Annabel*⟩ **b** to sail to windward **6** to produce artefacts by shaping or fashioning a specified material ⟨*she* ~s *in copper*⟩ **7a** to be in agitation or restless motion ⟨*her mouth* ~ed *nervously*⟩ **b** FERMENT 1 **c** to move slightly in relation to another part **d** to get into a specified condition by slow or imperceptible movements ⟨*the knot* ~ed *loose*⟩ [ME *werken, worken,* fr OE *wyrcan*; akin to OE *weorc*] – **work on** to strive to influence or persuade; affect – **work to rule** to obey the rules of one's work precisely and so reduce efficiency, esp as a form of industrial action

workable /'wuhkəbl/ *adj* **1** capable of being worked ⟨~ *vein of coal*⟩ **2** practicable, feasible – **workableness** *n*, **workability** /-kə'biləti/ *n*

workaday /'wuhkəday/ *adj* **1** of or suited for working days **2** prosaic, ordinary [alter. of earlier *workyday,* fr obs *workyday,* n (workday)]

workbag /'wuhkˌbag/ *n* a bag for implements or materials for work, esp needlework

'workˌbasket /-ˌbahskit/ *n* a basket for needlework implements and materials

'workˌbench /-ˌbench/ *n* a bench on which work, esp of mechanics or carpenters, is performed

'workˌbook /-ˌbook/ *n* an exercise book of problems to be solved directly on the pages

'workˌbox /-ˌboks/ *n* a box for work instruments and materials

worked /wuhkt/ *adj* that has been subjected to work; *esp* embroidered

ˌworked 'up *adj* emotionally aroused; excited

worker /'wuhkə/ *n* **1a** one who works, esp at manual or industrial work or with a particular material – often in combination **b** a member of the working class **2** any of the sexually underdeveloped usu sterile members of a colony of ants, bees, etc that perform most of the labour and protective duties of the colony

'worker-ˌpriest *n* a Roman Catholic priest who for missionary purposes spends part of each weekday as a worker in a secular job

workforce /'wuhkˌfaws/ *n sing or pl in constr* the workers engaged in a specific activity or potentially available ⟨*the factory's* ~⟩

'work-ˌharden *vt* to harden and strengthen (metal) by hammering, rolling, etc

'workˌhouse /-ˌhows/ *n* **1** *Br* an institution formerly maintained at public expense to house paupers **2** *NAm* a house of correction for minor offenders

'work-ˌin *n* a continuous occupation of a place of employment by employees continuing to work normally as a protest, usu against the threat of factory closure

work in *vt* **1** to cause to penetrate by persistent effort ⟨work *the ointment thoroughly* in⟩ **2** to insinuate unobtrusively ⟨worked in *a few topical jokes*⟩; *also* to find room for

[1]**working** /ˈwuhking/ *adj* **1a** that functions or performs labour ⟨*a ~ model*⟩ **b** *of a domestic animal* trained or bred for useful work ⟨*a ~ dog*⟩ **2** adequate to permit effective work to be done ⟨*a ~ majority*⟩ **3** serving as a basis for further work ⟨*~ draft*⟩ **4** during which one works ⟨*~ hours*⟩; *also* during which one discusses business or policy ⟨*a ~ lunch*⟩ [(1) fr prp of [1]*work*; (2–4) fr gerund of [1]*work*]

[2]**working** *n* **1** (a part of) a mine, quarry, or similar excavation **2** the fact or manner of functioning or operating – usu pl with sing. meaning ⟨*the ~s of his mind*⟩

working capital *n* capital actively turned over in or available for use in the course of business activity

ˌworking ˈclass *n sing or pl in constr* the class of people who work (manually) for wages – often pl with sing. meaning; compare PROLETARIAT – **working-class** *adj*

ˌworking ˈday *n* **1** a day on which work is done as distinguished from Sunday or a holiday **2** the period of time in a day during which work is performed

ˈworking ˌdrawing *n* a scale drawing of an object to be made or a structure to be built that is used as a guide by the workman

ˈworkingˌman /-ˌman/ *n* one who works for wages, esp in a manual job

ˈworking ˌparty *n, chiefly Br* a committee set up (e g by a government) to investigate and report on a particular problem

ˈwork ˌload *n* the amount of work or of working time expected from or assigned to an employee

ˈworkman /-mən/, *fem* **ˈworkˌwoman** *n* an artisan

ˈworkmanˌlike /-ˌliek/ *also* **workmanly** /-li/ *adj* worthy of a good workman: **a** skilful **b** efficient in appearance

ˈworkmanˌship /-ˌship/ *n* the relative art or skill of a workman; craftsmanship; *also* the quality or finish exhibited by a thing ⟨*a vase of exquisite ~*⟩

ˈworkˌmate /-ˌmayt/ *n, chiefly Br* a companion at work

ˌwork of ˈart *n* **1** a product of any of the fine arts, esp when of high artistic quality **2** a human creation that gives high aesthetic satisfaction ⟨*the wedding cake was a ~*⟩

work off *vt* to dispose of or get rid of by work or activity ⟨work off *a debt*⟩ ⟨work off *one's anger*⟩

ˈworkˌout /-ˌowt/ *n* a practice or exercise to test or improve fitness, ability, or performance, esp for sporting competition

work out *vt* **1a** to find out by calculation ⟨*couldn't* work out *how the prices stayed so low – Cosmopolitan*⟩ **b** to devise by resolving difficulties ⟨work out *an agreement*⟩ **c** to elaborate in detail ⟨work out *a scheme*⟩ **2** to discharge (e g a debt) by labour **3** to exhaust (e g a mine) by working ~ *vi* **1a** to prove effective, practicable, or suitable ⟨*their marriage didn't* work out⟩ **b** to amount to a total or calculated figure – often + *at* or *to* ⟨works out *at £17.50*⟩ ⟨*gas heating might* work out *expensive*⟩ **c** *of a sum* to yield a result **2** to engage in a workout

work over *vt* **1** to subject to thorough examination, study, or treatment **2** to beat up thoroughly; manhandle – infml

ˈworkˌpeople /-ˌpeepl/ *n pl, chiefly Br* workers, employees

ˈworkˌpiece /-ˌpees/ *n* sthg being worked on

ˈworkroom /-roohm, -room/ *n* a room used for esp manual work

works /wuhks/ *adj* of a place of industrial labour ⟨*~ council*⟩ ⟨*~ doctor*⟩

ˈworkˌshop /-ˌshop/ *n* **1** a room or place (e g in a factory) in which manufacture or repair work is carried out **2** a brief intensive educational programme for a relatively small group of people in a given field that emphasizes participation

ˈworkˌshy /-ˌshie/ *adj* disliking work; lazy

ˈworkˌtable /-ˌtaybl/ *n* a table often with drawers for holding working materials and implements; *esp* one used for sewing

ˈworkˌtop /-ˌtop/ *n* a flat surface (e g of Formica) on a piece of esp kitchen furniture (e g a cupboard or dresser) suitable for working on

ˌwork-to-ˈrule *n* an instance of industrial action designed to reduce output by deliberately keeping very rigidly to rules and regulations – compare WORK TO RULE

work up *vt* **1** to stir up; rouse ⟨*can't* work up *much interest*⟩ **2** to produce by mental or physical work ⟨worked up *a comedy act*⟩ ⟨worked up *a sweat in the gymnasium*⟩ **3** to improve, esp by mental work ⟨work up *your French*⟩ ~ *vi* to rise gradually in intensity or emotional tone ⟨work up *to a climax*⟩

[1]**world** /wuhld/ *n* **1** the earth with its inhabitants and all things on it ⟨*travel round the ~*⟩ **2** the course of human affairs ⟨*knowledge of the ~*⟩ **3** the human race **4** the concerns of earthly existence or secular affairs as distinguished from heaven and the life to come or religious and ecclesiastical matters **5** the system of created things; the universe **6a** a division, section, or generation of the inhabitants of the earth distinguished by living together at the same place or at the same time ⟨*the medieval ~*⟩ **b** a distinctive class of people or their sphere of interest ⟨*the academic ~*⟩ ⟨*woman's ~*⟩ **7a** human society as a whole ⟨*all the ~ knows*⟩ ⟨*withdraw from the ~*⟩; *also* the public ⟨*announced his discovery to the ~*⟩ **b** fashionable or respectable people; public opinion **8** a part or section of the earth that is a separate independent unit ⟨*the third ~*⟩ **9a** one's personal environment in the sphere of one's life or work ⟨*the external ~*⟩ ⟨*the ~ of Van Gogh*⟩ **b** a particular aspect of one's life ⟨*the ~ of dreams*⟩ **10** an indefinite multitude or a great quantity or amount ⟨*makes a ~ of difference*⟩ **11** KINGDOM 4 ⟨*the animal ~*⟩ **12** a planet; *esp* one that is inhabited *USE* (*except 10 & 12*) + *the* [ME, fr OE *woruld* human existence, this world, age; akin to OHG *weralt* age, world; both fr a prehistoric WGmc-NGmc compound whose first constituent is represented by OE *wer* man & whose second is akin to OE *eald* old – more at VIRILE, OLD] **– best of both worlds** the benefit of the advantages of 2 alternatives, esp without their disadvantages **– for all the world** in every way; exactly ⟨*copies which look* for all the world *like the original*⟩ **–for the world** in any circumstances; for anything ⟨*wouldn't hurt her feelings* for the world⟩ **– in the world** among innumerable possibilities; ever ⟨*what* in the world *is it?*⟩ **– out of this world** of extraordinary excellence; superb

[2]**world** *adj* **1** of the whole world ⟨*a ~ championship*⟩ **2** extending or found throughout the world; worldwide ⟨*a ~ state*⟩ ⟨*brought about ~ peace*⟩

ˌ**world-ˈclass** *adj* of the highest quality in the world, esp in playing a sport or game ⟨*a ~ polo player*⟩

ˌ**world ˈfair** *n* an international exhibition featuring exhibits and participants from all over the world

worldling /ˈwuhldling/ *n* a worldly person; one who is not interested in spiritual affairs

worldly /ˈwuhldli/ *adj* of or devoted to this world and its pursuits rather than to religion or spiritual affairs ⟨*my ~ goods*⟩ – **worldliness** *n*

ˌ**worldly-ˈminded** *adj* devoted to or engrossed in worldly interests – **worldly-mindedness** *n*

ˌ**worldly-ˈwise** *adj* possessing a practical and often shrewd and materialistic understanding of human affairs; sophisticated

ˌ**world ˈseries** *n* a series of baseball games played each year between the winners of the major US leagues to decide the championship of the USA

ˈ**world-ˌshaking** *adj* earthshaking

ˌ**world ˈview** *n* a weltanschauung

ˌ**world ˈwar** *n* a war engaged in by (most of) the principal nations of the world; *esp, cap both Ws* either of 2 such wars of the first half of the 20th c

ˌ**world-ˈweary** *adj* bored with the life of the world and its material pleasures – **world-weariness** *n*

ˌ**worldˈwide** /-ˈwied/ *adj* extended throughout or involving the entire world – **worldwide** *adv*

[1]**worm** /wuhm/ *n* **1a** an annelid worm; *esp* an earthworm **b** any of numerous relatively small elongated soft-bodied invertebrate animals: e g **(1)** a (destructive) caterpillar, maggot, or other insect larva **(2)** a shipworm **(3)** a blindworm **2** a human being who is an object of contempt, loathing, or pity; a wretch **3** infestation with or disease caused by parasitic worms – usu pl with sing. meaning but sing. or pl in constr **4a** the thread of a screw **b** a short revolving screw whose threads engage with a worm wheel or a rack **c** a spiral condensing tube used in distilling [ME, fr OE *wyrm* serpent, worm; akin to OHG *wurm* serpent, worm, L *vermis* worm] – **wormlike** *adj*

[2]**worm** *vi* to proceed windingly or insidiously ~ *vt* **1** to free (e g a dog) from worms **2a** to cause to move or proceed (as if) in the manner of a worm **b** to insinuate or introduce (oneself) by devious or subtle means **c** to make (one's way) insidiously or deviously ⟨*tried to ~ her way out of the situation*⟩ **3** to obtain or extract by artful or insidious questioning or by pleading, asking, or persuading – usu + *out of* ⟨*~ed the secret out of her*⟩ – **wormer** *n*

ˈ**wormˌcast** /-ˌkahst/ *n* a small heap of earth excreted by an earthworm on the soil surface

ˈ**worm-ˌeaten** *adj* **1** eaten or burrowed into (as if) by worms ⟨*~ timber*⟩ **2** worn-out, antiquated ⟨*~ regulations*⟩

ˈ**worm ˌgear** *n* **1** WORM WHEEL **2** a gear consisting of a worm and a worm wheel working together

ˈ**wormˌhole** /-ˌhohl/ *n* a hole or passage burrowed by a worm

ˌ**worm's-ˌeye ˈview** *n* a view from a humble position – usu humor

ˈ**worm ˌwheel** *n* a toothed wheel gearing with the thread of a worm

ˈ**wormwood** /-wood/ *n* **1** a European composite plant yielding a bitter slightly aromatic dark green oil used in absinthe **2** sthg bitter or mortifying; bitterness [ME *wormwode*, alter. of *wermode*, fr OE *wermōd*; akin to OHG *wermuota* wormwood]

wormy /ˈwuhmi/ *adj* containing, infested with, having, or damaged by (many) worms

worn /wawn/ *past part of* WEAR

ˌ**worn-ˈout** *adj* exhausted or used up (as if) by wear

worriment /ˈwurimənt/ *n* worrying; *also* trouble, anxiety – infml

worrisome /ˈwuris(ə)m/ *adj* **1** causing distress or worry **2** inclined to worry or fret – **worrisomely** *adv*, **worrisomeness** *n*

[1]**worry** /ˈwuri/ *vt* **1a** to harass by tearing, biting, etc, esp at the throat ⟨*a dog ~*ing *sheep*⟩ **b** to shake or pull at with the teeth ⟨*a terrier ~*ing *a rat*⟩ **c** to touch or disturb repeatedly **2** to subject to persistent or nagging attention or effort **3** to afflict with mental distress or agitation; make anxious ~ *vi* **1** to work at sthg difficult ⟨*he* worried *away at the problem till he found a solution*⟩ **2** to feel or experience concern or anxiety; fret [ME *worien* to seize by the throat, choke, fr OE *wyrgan* to strangle; akin to OHG *wurgen* to strangle, Lith *veržti* to constrict] – **worriedly** *adv*, **worrier** *n* – **not to worry** *Br* do not worry; do not feel anxious, dispirited, or troubled – infml

[2]**worry** *n* **1** mental distress or agitation resulting from concern, usu for sthg impending or anticipated; anxiety **2** a cause of worry; a trouble, difficulty

ˈ**worry ˌbeads** *n pl* a string of beads fingered so as to calm oneself and keep one's hands occupied

[1]**worse** /wuhs/ *adj, comparative of* BAD *or* ILL **1** of lower quality **2** in poorer health [ME *werse, worse*, fr OE *wiersa, wyrsa*; akin to OHG *wirsiro* worse] – **worsen** /ˈwuhs(ə)n/ *vb* – **the worse for** harmed by ⟨*none* the worse for *his fall*⟩

[2]**worse** *n, pl* **worse** sthg worse

[3]**worse** *adv, comparative of* BAD, BADLY, *or* ILL in a worse manner; to a worse extent or degree ⟨*raining ~ than ever*⟩

ˌ**worse-ˈoff** *adj* in poorer economic circumstances

[1]**worship** /ˈwuhship/ *n* **1** (an act of) reverence offered to a divine being or supernatural power **2** a form of religious practice with its creed and ritual **3** extravagant admiration for or devotion to an object of esteem ⟨*~ of the dollar*⟩ **4** *chiefly Br* a person of importance – used as a title for various officials (e g magistrates and some mayors) [ME *worshipe* worthiness, repute, respect, reverence paid to a divine being, fr OE *weorthscipe* worthiness, repute, respect, fr *weorth* worthy, worth + *-scipe* -ship]

[2]**worship** *vb* **-pp-** (*NAm* **-p-**, **-pp-**) *vt* **1** to honour or reverence as a divine being or supernatural power **2** to regard with great, even extravagant respect, honour, or devotion ~ *vi* to perform or take part in (an act of) worship – **worshipper** *n*

ˈ**worshipful** /-f(ə)l/ *adj* **1** rendering worship or veneration **2** *chiefly Br* – used as a title for various people or groups of rank or distinction – **worshipfully** *adv*, **worshipfulness** *n*

[1]**worst** /wuhst/ *adj, superlative of* BAD *or* ILL **1** most productive of evil ⟨*the ~ thing you could have done*⟩ **2** most wanting in quality ⟨*the ~ student*⟩ [ME *werste, worste*, fr OE *wierresta, wyrsta*, superl of the root of OE *wiersa* worse]

[2]**worst** *n, pl* **worst** **1** the worst state or part ⟨*always at my ~ before breakfast*⟩ **2** sby or sthg that is worst **3** the utmost harm of which one is capable ⟨*do your*

~⟩ **– at worst, at the worst** under the worst circumstances; seen in the worst light **– if the worst comes to the worst** if the very worst thing happens

[3]**worst** *adv, superlative of* BAD, BADLY, *or* ILL in the worst manner; to the worst extent or degree ⟨*the* worst-*dressed woman*⟩

[4]**worst** *vt* to get the better of; defeat

worsted /'woostid/ *n* **1** a smooth compact yarn from long wool fibres used esp for firm napless fabrics, carpeting, or knitting **2** a fabric made from worsted yarns [ME, fr *Worsted* (now *Worstead*), village in Norfolk, England] – **worsted** *adj*

[1]**wort** /wuht/ *n* a (herbaceous) plant – now used only in combination ⟨*stink*wort⟩ [ME, fr OE *wyrt* root, herb, plant – more at [1]ROOT]

[2]**wort** *n* a dilute solution containing sugars obtained typically from malt by infusion and fermented to form beer [ME, fr OE *wyrt*; akin to MHG *würze* brewer's wort, OE *wyrt* root, herb]

[1]**worth** /wuhth/ *vi, archaic* [ME *worthen* to become, fr OE *weorthan*; akin to OHG *werdan* to become, L *vertere* to turn] **– woe worth** cursed be

[2]**worth** *prep* **1a** equal in value to **b** having property equal to ⟨*he's ~ £1,000,000*⟩ **2** deserving of ⟨*well ~ the effort*⟩ [ME, fr OE *weorth* (adj) worthy, of (a specified) value; akin to OHG *werd* worthy, worth] **– worth it** worthwhile

[3]**worth** *n* **1a** (money) value **b** the equivalent of a specified amount or figure ⟨*3 quids*worth *of petrol*⟩ **2** moral or personal merit, esp high merit ⟨*proved his ~*⟩

'**worthless** /-lis/ *adj* **1a** lacking worth; valueless ⟨*~ currency*⟩ **b** useless ⟨*~ to continue searching*⟩ **2** contemptible, despicable – **worthlessly** *adv*, **worthlessness** *n*

,**worth'while** /-'wiel/ *adj* worth the time or effort spent

[1]**worthy** /'wuhdhi/ *adj* **1a** having moral worth or value ⟨*a ~ cause*⟩ **b** honourable, meritorious ⟨*they were all honoured and ~ men*⟩ **2** important enough; deserving ⟨*a deed ~ to be remembered*⟩ ⟨*a ~ opponent*⟩ – **worthily** *adv*, **worthiness** *n*

[2]**worthy** *n* a worthy or prominent person – often humor

-worthy /-,wuhdhi/ *comb form* (*n* → *adj*) **1** fit or safe for ⟨*a sea*worthy *vessel*⟩ **2** deserving of ⟨*praise*worthy⟩ ⟨*note*worthy⟩

wossname /'wos,naym/ *n, Br* – used to replace a momentarily forgotten noun; slang ⟨*look a gift horse in the ~ – Punch*⟩ [alter. of *what's its name*]

wotcher /'wochə/ *interj, Br* – used as a greeting; slang [alter. of *what cheer*]

would /wəd; *strong* wood/ *past of* WILL **1a** to desire, wish ⟨*as ye ~ that men should do to you* – Lk 6:31 (AV)⟩ **b** – used in auxiliary function with *rather* or *soon, sooner* to express preference ⟨*~ sooner die than face them*⟩ **2a** – used in auxiliary function to express wish, desire, or intent ⟨*those who ~ forbid gambling*⟩ or, in negative constructions, reluctance ⟨*~ not hurt a fly*⟩; used in the question form with the force of a polite request ⟨*~ you please help me?*⟩ or of an offer or suggestion ⟨*~ you like some tea?*⟩ **b** – used in auxiliary function in reported speech or writing to represent *shall* or *will* ⟨*said he ~ come*⟩ ⟨*knew I ~ enjoy the trip*⟩ **3a** used to ⟨*we ~ meet often for lunch*⟩ – used with emphatic stress to express exasperation ⟨*she ~ keep complaining*⟩ **b** – used in auxiliary function with emphatic stress as a comment on the annoyingly typical ⟨*you ~ say that*⟩ **4** – used in auxiliary function to introduce a contingent fact, possibility, or presumption (1) in the main clause of a conditional sentence ⟨*it ~ break if you dropped it*⟩ ⟨*he ~ have won if he hadn't tripped*⟩ (2) after a verb expressing desire, request, or advice ⟨*wish he ~ go*⟩ **5** could ⟨*door would*n't *open*⟩ **6** – used in auxiliary function to soften direct statement ⟨*~ be glad to know*⟩ ⟨*that ~ be the milkman*⟩ [ME *wolde*, fr OE; akin to OHG *wolta* wished, desired]

'**would-be** *adj* desiring or intended to be ⟨*a ~ rapist – Daily Mirror*⟩

wouldn't /'woodnt/ would not

wouldst /woodst/, **wouldest** /'woodist/ *archaic past 2 sing of* WILL

[1]**wound** /woohnd/ *n* **1** an injury to the body or to a plant (e g from violence or accident) that involves tearing or breaking of a membrane (e g the skin) and usu damage to underlying tissues **2** a mental or emotional hurt or blow [ME, fr OE *wund*; akin to OHG *wunta* wound]

[2]**wound** *vt* to cause a wound to or in ~ *vi* to inflict a wound

[3]**wound** /wownd/ *past of* WIND

wounded /'woohndid/ *adj* injured, hurt by, or suffering from a wound ⟨*a ~ soldier*⟩ ⟨*~ pride*⟩

woundwort /'woohnd,wuht/ *n* any of various plants, esp of the mint family, with soft downy leaves (formerly) used in dressing wounds

[1]**wove** /wohv/ *past of* WEAVE

[2]**wove** *n* paper made in such a way that no fine lines run across the grain – compare LAID

woven /'wohv(ə)n/ *past part of* WEAVE

[1]**wow** /wow/ *interj* – used to express strong feeling (e g pleasure or surprise); slang

[2]**wow** *n* a striking success; a hit – slang [[1]*wow*]

[3]**wow** *vt* to excite to enthusiastic admiration or approval – slang

[4]**wow** *n* a distortion in reproduced sound that is heard as a slow rise and fall in the pitch of the sound and is caused by variations in the speed of the reproducing system – compare FLUTTER 3 [imit]

wowzer /'wowzə/ *n, Austr & NZ* an oppressively puritanical person; a killjoy – slang [origin unknown]

WPB *n* WASTEPAPER BASKET – infml [*waste*paper *b*asket]

[1]**wrack** /rak/ *n* **1** destruction ⟨*~ and ruin*⟩ **2** (a remnant of) sthg destroyed [ME, fr OE *wræc* misery, punishment, sthg driven by the sea; akin to OE *wrecan* to drive, punish – more at WREAK]

[2]**wrack** *n* (dried) marine vegetation; *esp* kelp [ME *wrak* wreck, wreckage, fr MD or MLG; akin to OE *wræc* sthg driven by the sea]

[3]**wrack** *vt* [4]RACK

[4]**wrack** *n* [1]RACK

wraith /rayth/ *n, pl* **wraiths** /rayths; *also* raydhz/ an apparition of a living person in his/her exact likeness seen before or after death [perh alter. of obs Sc *warth* (guardian angel), fr ON *vörthr* guardian]

[1]**wrangle** /'rang·gl/ *vb* **wrangling** /'rang·gling/ *vi* to dispute angrily or peevishly; bicker ~ *vt*, *NAm* to herd and care for (livestock, esp horses) on the range [ME *wranglen*; akin to OHG *ringan* to struggle – more at WRING]

[2]**wrangle** *n* an angry, noisy, or prolonged dispute or quarrel

wrangler /ˈrang·glə/ *n* **1** a bickering disputant **2** the holder of a Cambridge first in mathematics – **wranglership** *n*

[1]**wrap** /rap/ *vb* **-pp-** *vt* **1a** to envelop, pack, or enfold in sthg flexible **b** to fold round sthg specified ⟨~ *a blanket round her*⟩ **2a** to obscure or surround with the specified covering ⟨~ped *in mist*⟩ ⟨*the affair was* ~ped *in scandal*⟩ **b** to involve completely; engross – usu + *up* ⟨~ped *up in his daughter*⟩ ~ *vi* to curl round sthg; be a wraparound ⟨*skirt that* ~s *over*⟩ [ME *wrappen*]

[2]**wrap** *n* **1** a wrapping; *specif* a waterproof wrapping placed round food to be frozen, esp in a domestic freezer **2** an article of clothing that may be wrapped round a person; *esp* an outer garment (e g a shawl) – **under wraps** secret

[1]**wraparound** /ˈrapə,rownd/ *adj* **1** made to be wrapped round the body ⟨*a* ~ *skirt*⟩ **2** shaped to follow a contour; *esp* made to curve from the front round to the side ⟨*a* ~ *windscreen*⟩

[2]**wraparound** *n* an object or garment that encircles or esp curves and laps over

wrapper /ˈrapə/ *n* that in which sthg is wrapped: e g **a** a fine quality tobacco leaf used for the covering of a cigar **b** DUST JACKET [[1]WRAP + [2]-ER]

wrapping /ˈraping/ *n* material used to wrap an object

wrap up *vt* to bring to a usu successful conclusion; end – infml ~ *vi* **1** to protect oneself with outer garments ⟨wrap up *warm*⟩ **2** *Br* to stop talking; SHUT UP – slang

wrasse /ras/ *n* any of numerous usu brilliantly coloured marine spiny-finned (food) fishes [Corn *gwragh, wragh*]

wrath /roth/ *n* **1** strong vengeful anger or indignation **2** retributory, esp divine, chastisement [ME, fr OE *wrǣththu*, fr *wrāth* wroth – more at WROTH] – **wrathful** *adj*

wreak /reek/ *vt* **1** to give free play to (malevolent feeling); inflict ⟨~ed *his wrath on her*⟩ ⟨~ed *her revenge*⟩ **2** to cause or create (havoc or destruction) [ME *wreken*, fr OE *wrecan* to drive, punish, avenge; akin to OHG *rehhan* to avenge, L *urgēre* to drive on, urge]

wreath /reeth/ *n, pl* **wreaths** /reedhz/ **1** sthg intertwined into a circular shape; *esp* a garland ⟨*lay a* ~ *on the coffin*⟩ **2** a representation of a wreath (e g in heraldry) **3** a drifting and coiling whorl ⟨~s *of smoke*⟩ [ME *wrethe*, fr OE *writha*; akin to OE *wrīthan* to twist – more at WRITHE]

wreathe /reedh/ *vt* **1** to cause (the face) to take on a happy joyful expression – usu pass ⟨*face* ~d *in smiles*⟩ **2a** to shape (e g flowers) into a wreath **b** to coil about sthg **3** to encircle (as if) with a wreath ⟨*bust* ~d *with laurel*⟩ ~ *vi* to twist or move in coils; writhe ⟨*smoke* ~d *from the chimney*⟩ [*wreath*]

[1]**wreck** /rek/ *n* **1** sthg cast up on the land by the sea, esp after a shipwreck **2a** (a) shipwreck **b** wrecking or being wrecked; destruction ⟨*after the* ~ *of our hopes*⟩ **3a** the broken remains of sthg (e g a building or vehicle) wrecked or ruined **b** a person or animal of broken constitution, health, or spirits ⟨*a mere* ~ *of his former self*⟩ [ME *wrek*, fr AF, of Scand origin; akin to ON *rek* wreck; akin to OE *wrecan* to drive]

[2]**wreck** *vt* **1** to cast ashore **2a** to reduce to a ruinous state by violence ⟨~ *a train*⟩ **b** to cause (a vessel) to be shipwrecked **c** to involve in disaster or ruin ⟨~ *one's marriage*⟩ ~ *vi* to become wrecked

wreckage /ˈrekij/ *n* **1** wrecking or being wrecked **2** broken and disordered parts or material from a wrecked structure

wrecker /ˈrekə/ *n* **1a** sby who wrecks ships (e g by false lights) for plunder **b** sby whose work is the demolition of buildings **2a** sby who searches for or works on the wrecks of ships (e g for rescue or plunder) **b** *NAm* a breakdown lorry **c** *NAm* a dealer in scrap, esp scrapped motor vehicles [[2]WRECK + [2]-ER]

wren /ren/ *n* a very small European bird that has a short erect tail and is noted for its loud song [ME *wrenne*, fr OE *wrenna*; akin to OHG *rentilo* wren]

Wren *n* a woman serving in the Women's Royal Naval Service [*W*omen's *R*oyal *N*aval Service]

[1]**wrench** /rench/ *vi* to pull or strain at sthg with violent twisting ⟨*he* ~ed *at the handle*⟩ ~ *vt* **1** to pull or twist violently ⟨~ *the door open*⟩ **2** to injure or disable by a violent twisting or straining **3** to distort, pervert ⟨~ *language*⟩ **4** to snatch forcibly; wrest ⟨~ *the knife from her hand*⟩ [ME *wrenchen*, fr OE *wrencan*; akin to OHG *renken* to wrench, L *vergere* to bend, incline]

[2]**wrench** *n* **1a** a violent twisting or a sideways pull **b** (a sharp twist or sudden jerk causing) a strain to a muscle, ligament, etc (e g of a joint) **c** (sthg causing) acute emotional distress or violent mental change **2a** a spanner with jaws adjustable for holding nuts of different sizes **b** *NAm* a spanner

wrest /rest/ *vt* **1** to obtain or take away by violent wringing or twisting **2** to obtain with difficulty by force or determined labour ⟨~ *a living from the stony soil*⟩ **3** WRENCH 3 [ME *wrasten, wresten*, fr OE *wrǣstan*; akin to OE *wrīthan* to twist – more at WRITHE]

[1]**wrestle** /ˈresl/ *vb* **wrestling** /ˈresling, ˈresl·ing/ *vi* **1** to contend with an opponent in wrestling **2** to engage in a violent or determined struggle; grapple ⟨wrestling *with cumbersome luggage*⟩ ⟨~ *with a problem*⟩ ~ *vt* **1** to wrestle with **2** to push, pull, or manhandle by force [ME *wrastlen, wrestlen*, fr OE *wrǣstlian*, freq of *wrǣstan*] – **wrestler** /ˈreslə/ *n*

[2]**wrestle** *n* the action or an instance of wrestling; *esp* a wrestling bout

wrestling /ˈresling/ *n* a sport or contest in which 2 unarmed individuals struggle hand to hand with each attempting to subdue or unbalance his opponent

wretch /rech/ *n* **1** a profoundly unhappy or unfortunate person **2** a base, despicable, or vile person or animal [ME *wrecche*, fr OE *wrecca* outcast, exile; akin to OE *wrecan* to drive, drive out – more at WREAK]

wretched /ˈrechid/ *adj* **1** deeply afflicted, dejected, or unfortunate **2** deplorably bad ⟨*was in* ~ *health*⟩ ⟨~ *workmanship*⟩ **3** (appearing) mean, squalid, or contemptible ⟨*dressed in* ~ *old clothes*⟩ **4** causing annoyance; damned – used as a general expression of annoyance ⟨*lost my* ~ *socks*⟩ [irreg fr *wretch*] – **wretchedly** *adv*, **wretchedness** *n*

wrick /rik/ *vt, chiefly Br* [3]RICK

[1]**wriggle** /ˈrigl/ *vb* **wriggling** /ˈrigling, ˈrigl·ing/ *vi* **1** to move the body or a bodily part to and fro with short writhing motions; squirm **2** to move or advance by twisting and turning **3** to extricate or insinuate oneself by manoeuvring, equivocation, eva-

sion, or ingratiation ⟨*managed to* ~ *out of a difficult question*⟩ ~ *vt* **1** to cause to move in short quick contortions ⟨*she* ~d *her hips*⟩ **2** to manoeuvre into a state or place by wriggling **3** to make (one's way) by wriggling [ME *wrigglen*, fr or akin to MLG *wriggeln* to wriggle; akin to OE *wrigian* to turn – more at WRY] – **wriggler** *n*, **wriggly** *adj*

[2]**wriggle** *n* a short or quick writhing motion or contortion

wright /riet/ *n* a craftsman – usu in combination ⟨*ship* wright⟩ ⟨*play*wright⟩ [ME, fr OE *wyrhta*, *wryhta* worker, maker; akin to OE *weorc* work]

wring /ring/ *vt* **wrung** /rung/ **1** to twist or compress, esp so as to extract liquid ⟨~ *the towel dry*⟩ **2a** to expel or obtain (as if) by twisting and compressing ⟨~ *the water from the towel*⟩ **b** to exact or extort by coercion or with difficulty ⟨~ *a confession from the suspect*⟩ **3a** to twist so as to strain, sprain, or break ⟨~ *a chicken's neck*⟩ **b** to twist together (one's clasped hands) as a sign of anguish **4** to distress, torment ⟨*a tragedy that* ~s *the heart*⟩ **5** to shake (sby's hand) vigorously in greeting [ME *wringen*, fr OE *wringan*; akin to OHG *ringan* to struggle, OE *wyrgan* to strangle – more at WORRY] – **wring** *n*

wringer /ˈring·ə/ *n* a mangle [WRING + [2]-ER]

[1]**wrinkle** /ˈringkl/ *n* **1** a small ridge, crease, or furrow formed esp in the skin due to aging or stress or on a previously smooth surface (e g by shrinkage or contraction) **2** a valuable trick or dodge for effecting a result – infml [ME, back-formation fr *wrinkled* twisted, winding, prob fr OE *gewrinclod*, pp of *gewrinclian* to wind, fr *ge-*, perfective prefix + *-wrinclian* (akin to *wrencan* to wrench)] – **wrinkly** *adj*

[2]**wrinkle** *vb* **wrinkling** /ˈringkling, ˈringkl·ing/ *vi* to become marked with or contracted into wrinkles ~ *vt* to contract into wrinkles

wrist /rist/ *n* **1** (a part of a lower animal corresponding to) the (region of the) joint between the human hand and the arm **2** the part of a garment or glove covering the wrist [ME, fr OE; akin to OE *wrǣstan* to twist, wrest – more at WREST]

ˈwrist,band /-ˌband/ *n* a band (e g on the sleeve of a garment) encircling the wrist

ˈwrist ˌpin *n* a stud or pin that forms a bearing for a connecting rod

ˈwrist,watch /-ˌwoch/ *n* a small watch attached to a bracelet or strap and worn round the wrist

wristy /ˈristi/ *adj* characterized by or tending to use a lot of wrist movement (e g in hitting a ball with a bat or club) – **wristily** *adv*

writ /rit/ *n* **1a** an order in writing issued under seal in the name of the sovereign or of a court or judicial officer commanding or forbidding an act specified in it ⟨~ *of habeas corpus*⟩ **b** a written order constituting a symbol of the power and authority of the issuer ⟨*over the border where the king's* ~ *did not run*⟩ **2** *archaic* sthg written; writing – esp in *holy writ*, *sacred writ* [ME, fr OE; akin to OE *writan* to write]

write /riet/ *vb* **wrote** /roht/; **written** /ˈritn/ *also* **writ** /rit/ *vt* **1a** to form (legible characters, symbols, or words) on a surface, esp with an instrument ⟨~ *an inscription*⟩ ⟨~ *'I love you'*⟩ **b** to spell in writing ⟨*words* written *alike but pronounced differently*⟩ **c** to cover, fill, or fill in by writing ⟨wrote *ten pages*⟩ ⟨~ *a cheque*⟩ **2** to set down in writing: e g **a** to be the author of; compose ⟨~s *poems and essays*⟩ ⟨~ *a string quartet*⟩ **b** to use (a specific script or language) in writing ⟨~ *a clear hand*⟩ ⟨~ *shorthand*⟩ ⟨~ *Braille*⟩ ⟨~ *French*⟩ **3** to express, record, or reveal (as if) in writing ⟨*it is* written⟩ ⟨written *on my heart*⟩ **4** to make (a quality or condition) evident – usu pass ⟨*guilt was* written *all over his face*⟩ **5** to introduce or remove by writing ⟨~ *a clause into a contract*⟩ ⟨~ *a character out of a serial*⟩ **6** to introduce or transfer (information) into or from a computer memory **7** *chiefly NAm* to communicate with in writing ⟨wrote *them on his arrival*⟩ ~ *vi* **1** to make significant written characters, inscriptions, words, or sentences ⟨*learning to* ~⟩ ⟨~ *in ink*⟩; *also* to be adapted to writing ⟨*pen* ~s *badly*⟩ **2** to compose, communicate by, or send a letter ⟨~ *back*⟩ ⟨~ *for information*⟩ **3** to produce or compose a written work, esp professionally, for publication or performance ⟨~ *for 'The Times'*⟩ ⟨~ *for woodwind*⟩ ⟨*his wife* ~s⟩ [ME *writen*, fr OE *writan* to scratch, draw, inscribe; akin to OHG *rīzan* to tear, Gk *rhinē* file, rasp] – **writable** /ˈrietəbl/ *adj*

ˈwrite-ˌdown *n* a deliberate reduction in the book value of an asset (e g to reflect the effect of obsolescence or deflation)

write down *vt* **1** to record in written form **2** to disparage, injure, or minimize by writing ~ *vi* to write so as to appeal to a lower level of taste, comprehension, or intelligence – usu + *to*

ˈwrite-ˌoff *n* sthg written off as a total loss ⟨*he survived, but the car was a* ~⟩

write off *vt* **1** to cancel ⟨write off *a bad debt*⟩ **2** to concede to be irreparably lost, useless, or dead ⟨*this two square miles isn't being* written off *as a ghetto* – Colin MacInnes⟩ ~ *vi* to write and send a letter

write out *vt* to put in writing; *esp* to put into a full and complete written form

writer /ˈrietə/ *n* **1** one who writes as an occupation; an author **2** *Scot* WRITER TO THE SIGNET [WRITE + [2]-ER]

ˌwriter's ˈcramp *n* a painful spasmodic cramp of the hand or finger muscles brought on by excessive writing

ˌWriter to the ˈSignet *n* a Scottish solicitor

ˈwrite-ˌup *n* a written, esp flattering, account

write up *vt* **1a** to write an account of; describe ⟨wrote up *the fire*⟩ **b** to put into finished written form ⟨write up *my notes*⟩ **2** to bring up to date the writing of (e g a diary) **3** to praise or maximize in writing

writhe /riedh/ *vt* to twist (the body or a bodily part) in pain ~ *vi* **1** to proceed with twists and turns **2** to twist (as if) from pain or struggling **3** to suffer keenly ⟨~ *under an insult*⟩ [ME *writhen*, fr OE *writhan* to twist; akin to ON *ritha* to twist, OE *wrigian* to turn – more at WRY] – **writhe** *n*

writing /ˈrieting/ *n* **1** the act, practice, or occupation of literary composition **2a** written letters or words; *esp* handwriting ⟨*put it in* ~⟩ ⟨*I can't read your* ~⟩ ☞ ALPHABET **b** a written composition ⟨*the* ~s *of Marx*⟩ **c** a written or printed letter, notice, document, or inscription [WRITE + [2]-ING] – **writing on the wall** an omen of one's unpleasant fate

ˈwriting ˌdesk *n* a desk often with a sloping top for writing on

-graphy] – **xylographer** *n*, **xylograph** /ˈzielə,grahf, -,graf/ *n*, **xylographic** /-ˈgrafik/ *adj*, **xylographical** *adj*

xylophone /ˈzielə,fohn/ *n* a percussion instrument that has a series of wooden bars graduated in length and sounded by striking with 2 small wooden hammers – **xylophonist** /-,fohnist, zieˈlofənist/ *n*

Y

y /wie/ *n, pl* **y's, ys** *often cap* **1** (a graphic representation of or device for reproducing) the 25th letter of the English alphabet **2** one designated *y*, esp as the 2nd in a series that includes *x, y,* and sometimes *z*

¹-y *also* **-ey** /-i/ *suffix (n, vb → adj)* **1a** covered with; full of ⟨*blossomy*⟩ ⟨*dirty*⟩ ⟨*hairy*⟩ **b** having the quality of ⟨*waxy*⟩ ⟨*weary*⟩ ⟨*merry*⟩ **c** addicted to; enthusiastic about ⟨*horsy*⟩ **d** like; like that of ⟨*wintry*⟩ – often derog ⟨*stagy*⟩ **2** tending or inclined to ⟨*sleepy*⟩ ⟨*sticky*⟩ ⟨*curly*⟩ **3** slightly; rather; -ish ⟨*chilly*⟩ [ME, fr OE *-ig*; akin to OHG *-ig, -y*, L *-icus*, Gk *-ikos*, Skt *-ika*]

²-y *suffix* (→ *n*) **1** state, condition, or quality of ⟨*beggary*⟩ ⟨*courtesy*⟩ **2** whole body or group sharing (a specified class or state) ⟨*soldiery*⟩ ⟨*company*⟩ [ME *-ie*, fr OF, fr L *-ia*, fr Gk *-ia, -eia*]

³-y *suffix* (*n* → *n*) instance of (a specified action) ⟨*entreaty*⟩ ⟨*inquiry*⟩ [ME *-ie*, fr AF, fr L *-ium*]

⁴-y *suffix* (→ *n*) little; dear ⟨*doggy*⟩ ⟨*granny*⟩ – used esp in pet names by or to children [ME]

yabby, yabbie /'yabi/ *n* a small Australian freshwater crayfish, often used as bait [native name in Australia]

¹yacht /yot/ *n* any of various relatively small sailing or powered vessels that characteristically have a sharp prow and graceful lines and are used for pleasure cruising or racing [obs D *jaght*, fr MLG *jacht*, short for *jachtschiff*, lit., hunting ship]

²yacht *vi* to race or cruise in a yacht – **yachting** *n*

'yacht ˌclub *n* a club organized to promote and regulate yachting and boating

yachtsman /'yotsmən/ *n* sby who owns or sails a yacht

yack /yak/ *n or vi* ² ³YAK – slang

yackety-yack /ˌyakəti 'yak/ *n or vi* ² ³YAK – slang [redupl of *yak*]

YAG *n* synthetic yttrium aluminium garnet used esp as a gemstone and in lasers [*y*ttrium *a*luminium *g*arnet]

yah /yah/ *interj* – used to express disgust, defiance, or derision [prob imit of the sound of retching]

yahoo /'yah·hooh, 'yay-/ *n, pl* **yahoos** an uncouth, rowdy, or degraded person [*Yahoo*, one of a race of human brutes in *Gulliver's Travels* by Jonathan Swift †1745 Ir satirist]

Yahweh /'yahway/, **Yahveh** /'yahvay/ *n* the God of the Hebrews – compare TETRAGRAMMATON [Heb *Yahweh*]

Yahwism /'yahwiz(ə)m, -viz(ə)m/ *n* the worship of Yahweh among the ancient Hebrews

Yahwistic /yah'wistik, -'vis-/ *adj* **1** characterized by the use of *Yahweh* as the name of God **2** of Yahwism

¹yak /yak/ *n, pl* **yaks,** *esp collectively* **yak** a large long-haired wild or domesticated ox of Tibet and nearby mountainous regions [Tibetan *gyak*]

²yak, yack /yak/ *n* persistent or voluble talk – slang [prob imit]

³yak, yack *vi* **-kk-** to talk persistently; chatter – slang

Yale /yayl/ *trademark* – used for a type of lock that has a revolving barrel which is prevented from turning by a set of pins until the correct key is inserted

yam /yam/ *n* **1** (any of various related plants with) an edible starchy tuberous root used as a staple food in tropical areas **2** *NAm* a moist-fleshed usu orange sweet potato [earlier *iname*, fr Pg *inhame* & Sp *ñame*]

yammer /'yamə/ *vi* **1** to wail, whimper **2** to complain, grumble ⟨~ing *at the umpire*⟩ **3** to talk volubly; clamour ~ *vt* to say in voluble complaint *USE* infml [alter. of ME *yomeren* to murmur, be sad, fr OE *gēomrian*; akin to OHG *jāmaron* to be sad] – **yammer** *n*

yang /yang/ *n* the masculine active principle in nature that in Chinese thought eternally interacts with its opposite and complementary principle, yin [Chin (Pek) *yang*²]

yank /yangk/ *vb* to pull or extract (sthg) with a quick vigorous movement ⟨~ *a tooth out*⟩ – infml [origin unknown] – **yank** *n*

¹Yankee /'yangki/ *n* a native or inhabitant of **a** *chiefly Br* the USA **b** *chiefly NAm* the N USA **c** *NAm* New England [perh fr the D names *Jantje* or *Jan Kees*, allegedly used as nicknames by early Dutch settlers in America] – **Yankee** *adj*

²Yankee – a communications code word for the letter *y*

¹yap /yap/ *vi* **-pp-** **1** to bark snappishly; yelp **2** to talk in a shrill insistent querulous way; scold – infml [imit] – **yapper** *n*

²yap *n* **1** a quick sharp bark; a yelp **2** (foolish) chatter – infml

yapock, yapok /yə'pok/ *n* a grey and white S American aquatic opossum with webbed hind feet [*Oyapock, Oyapok*, river in S America]

'yapp ˌbinding /yap/ *n, Br* bookbinding (e g for Bibles) having rounded outer corners and limp overhanging leather covers [*Yapp fl* 1860 E bookseller]

Yarborough /'yahb(ə)rə/ *n* a hand in bridge or whist containing no card higher than a 9 [Charles Anderson Worsley, 2nd Earl of *Yarborough* †1897 E nobleman who allegedly bet 1000 to 1 against the dealing of such a hand]

¹yard /yahd/ *n* **1a** a unit of length equal to 3ft (about 0.914m) ☞ UNIT **b** a unit of volume equal to 1yd³ (about 0.765m³) **2** a long spar tapered towards the ends to support and spread a sail ☞ SHIP [ME *yarde* twig, stick, rod, unit of length, fr OE *gierd*; akin to OHG *gart* stick, L *hasta* spear]

²yard *n* **1a** a small usu walled and often paved area open to the sky and adjacent to a building; a courtyard **b** the grounds of a specified building or group of buildings – in combination ⟨*a farm*yard⟩ ⟨*a church*yard⟩ **2a** an area with its buildings and facilities set aside for a specified business or activity – often in combination ⟨*a brick*yard⟩ **b** a system of tracks for the storage and maintenance of railway carriages and wagons and the making up of trains **3** *cap, Br* SCOTLAND YARD – + *the* **4** *NAm* a garden of a house [ME, fr OE *geard* enclosure, yard; akin to OHG *gart* enclosure, L *hortus* garden]

[3]**yard** *vt* to drive into or confine in a restricted area; herd, pen

[1]**yardage** /'yahdij/ *n* (the charge for) the use of a livestock enclosure at a railway station [[2]*yard*]

[2]**yardage** *n* the length, extent, or volume of sthg as measured in yards [[1]*yard*]

yardarm /'yahd,ahm/ *n* either end of the yard of a square-rigged ship ☞ SHIP

yardman /'yahdmən, -man/ *n* sby who works **a** in a timber yard **b** in a railway yard

'yard,master /-,mahstə/ *n* the man in charge of operations in a railway yard

,yard of 'ale *n* (the amount contained in) a slender horn-shaped glass about 1m (3ft) tall that holds 1 or 2l (2 or 3pt)

'yard,stick /-,stik/ *n* **1** a graduated measuring stick 1yd long **2** a standard basis of calculation or judgment; a criterion

yarmulke, yarmelke, yarmulka /'yahmulkə/ *n* a skullcap worn by esp Orthodox and Conservative Jewish males, in the synagogue and the home ☞ GARMENT [Yiddish, fr Ukrainian & Pol *jarmu* a skullcap]

[1]**yarn** /yahn/ *n* **1a** THREAD 1; *esp* a spun thread (e g of wood, cotton, or hemp) as prepared and used for weaving, knitting, and rope-making **b** a similar strand of metal, glass, asbestos, paper, or plastic **2a** a narrative of adventures; *esp* a tall tale **b** a conversation, chat ***USE*** (*2*) infml [ME, fr OE *gearn*; akin to OHG *garn* yarn, Gk *chordē* string, L *hernia* rupture]

[2]**yarn** *vi* to tell a yarn; *also* to chat garrulously – infml

'yarn-,dye *vt* to dye before weaving or knitting

yarrow /'yaroh/ *n* a strong-scented Eurasian composite plant with dense heads of small usu white flowers ☞ PLANT [ME *yarowe*, fr OE *gearwe*; akin to OHG *garwa* yarrow]

yashmak /'yashmak/ *also* **yasmak** /~, 'yas-/ *n* a veil worn over the face by Muslim women, so that only the eyes remain exposed [Turk *yaşmak*]

yataghan /'yatə,gan, 'yatəgən/ *n* a sword without a guard used formerly by Muslims and typically having a long blade with a double curved edge [Turk *yatağan*]

yatter /'yatə/ *vi* to chatter, prattle – infml [perh blend of *yap* and *chatter*]

[1]**yaw** /yaw/ *n* the action of yawing; *esp* a side-to-side movement [origin unknown]

[2]**yaw** *vi* **1** to deviate erratically from a course **2** *of an aircraft, spacecraft, or projectile* to deviate from a straight course by esp side-to-side movement

yawl /yawl/ *n* **1** a small boat carried on a ship **2** a fore-and-aft rigged sailing vessel with sails set from a mainmast and a mizzenmast that is situated aft of the rudder [LG *jolle*]

[1]**yawn** /yawn/ *vi* **1** to open wide; gape ⟨*a* ~*ing chasm*⟩ **2** to open the mouth wide and inhale, usu in reaction to fatigue or boredom ~ *vt* to utter with a yawn [ME *yenen, yanen*, fr OE *ginian*; akin to OHG *ginēn* to yawn, L *hiare*, Gk *chainein*] – **yawner** *n*, **yawningly** *adv*

[2]**yawn** *n* **1** a deep usu involuntary intake of breath through the wide open mouth **2** a boring thing or person – slang ⟨*thought the cathedral a big* ~ – Kenneth Tynan⟩

yawp, yaup /yawp/ *vi, chiefly NAm* **1** to make a raucous noise; squawk **2** to clamour, complain ***USE*** infml [ME *yolpen*] – **yawp** *n*, **yawper** *n*

yaws /yawz/ *n pl but sing or pl in constr* an infectious tropical disease caused by a spirochaetal bacterium and marked by ulcerating sores [of Cariban origin; akin to Calinago *yáya* yaws]

'y-,axis /wie/ *n* **1** the axis that intersects the x-axis in a plane Cartesian coordinate system **2** that 1 of the 3 axes in a 3-dimensional rectangular coordinate system that is not the x- or z-axis

'Y ,chromosome *n* a sex chromosome that in humans occurs paired with an X chromosome in each male cell and does not occur in female cells

[1]**ye** /yee/ *pron, archaic or dial* the ones being addressed; you – used orig only as a nominative pl pron [ME, fr OE *gē*; akin to OHG *ir* you – more at YOU]

[2]**ye** /dhee, yee/ *definite article, archaic* the ⟨*Ye Olde Gifte Shoppe*⟩ [alter. of OE —*ē* the; fr the use by early printers of the letter *y* to represent — (*th*) of manuscripts]

[1]**yea** /yay/ *adv* **1** more than this; indeed ⟨*boys,* ~ *and girls too*⟩ **2** *archaic* yes [ME *ye, ya*, fr OE *gēa*; akin to OHG *jā* yes]

[2]**yea** *n* **1** affirmation, assent **2** *chiefly NAm* (a person casting) an affirmative vote

yeah /yeə/ *adv* yes – used in writing to represent a casual pronunciation [by alter.]

year /yiə/ *n* **1a** the period of about 365¼ solar days required for 1 revolution of the earth round the sun **b** the time required for the apparent sun to return to an arbitrary fixed or moving reference point in the sky **2a** a cycle in the Gregorian calendar of 365 or 366 days divided into 12 months beginning with January and ending with December **b** a period of time equal to 1 year of the Gregorian calendar but beginning at a different time **3** a calendar year specified usu by a number **4** *pl* age ⟨*a man in* ~s *but a child in understanding*⟩; *also* old age ⟨*beginning to show his* ~s⟩ **5** a period of time (e g that in which a school is in session) other than a calendar year **6** *sing or pl in constr* the body of students who enter a school, university, etc in 1 academic year [ME *yere*, fr OE *gēar*; akin to OHG *jār* year, Gk *hōros* year, *hōra* season, hour, L *ire* to go – more at ISSUE] – **year in, year out** for an indefinite or seemingly endless number of successive years

'year,book /-,book/ *n* a book published yearly as a report or summary of statistics or facts

,year 'dot *n* – **from/since the year dot** for a very long time

,year-'end *n* the end of the (fiscal) year – **year-end** *adj*

yearling /'yiəling/ *n* sby or sthg 1 year old: e g **a** an animal 1 year old or in its second year **b** a racehorse between January 1st of the year following its birth and the next January 1st – **yearling** *adj*

yearly /'yiəli/ *adj* **1** reckoned by the year **2** done or occurring once every year; annual – **yearly** *adv*

,**Yearly 'Meeting** *n* an organization uniting several Quarterly Meetings of the Quakers

yearn /yuhn/ *vi* **1** to long persistently, wistfully, or sadly ⟨~ *for home*⟩ ⟨~ *to travel*⟩ **2** to feel tenderness or compassion ⟨*her heart* ~ed *towards the child*⟩ [ME *yernen,* fr OE *giernan;* akin to OHG *gerōn* to desire, L *hortari* to urge, encourage, Gk *chairein* to rejoice] – **yearner** *n,* **yearningly** *adv*

,**year of 'grace** *n* a year of the Christian era ⟨*the* ~ *1982*⟩

,**year-'round** *adj* effective, employed, or operating for the full year; not seasonal ⟨*a* ~ *resort*⟩

yeast /yeest/ *n* **1** a (commercial preparation of) yellowish surface froth or sediment that consists largely of fungal cells, occurs esp in sweet liquids in which it promotes alcoholic fermentation, and is used esp in making alcoholic drinks and as a leaven in baking **2** a minute fungus that is present and functionally active in yeast, usu has little or no mycelium, and reproduces by budding [ME *yest,* fr OE *gist;* akin to MHG *jest* foam, Gk *zein* to boil]

yeasty /'yeesti/ *adj* **1** of or resembling yeast **2a** churning with growth and change; turbulent **b** trivial, frivolous – **yeastily** *adv,* **yeastiness** *n*

yegg /yeg, yayg/ *n, chiefly NAm* a safecracker, burglar – slang [origin unknown]

¹yell /yel/ *vi* to utter a sharp loud cry, scream, or shout ⟨~ *for help*⟩ ⟨~ *with laughter*⟩ ~ *vt* to utter or declare (as if) with a scream; shout ⟨~ *curses*⟩ [ME *yellen,* fr OE *giellan;* akin to OHG *gellan* to yell, OE *galan* to sing] – **yeller** *n*

²yell *n* a scream, shout

¹yellow /'yeloh/ *adj* **1a** of the colour yellow **b** yellowish through age, disease, or discoloration; sallow **c** having a yellow or light brown complexion or skin **2a** featuring sensational or scandalous items or ordinary news sensationally distorted ⟨~ *journalism*⟩ **b** dishonourable, cowardly – infml ⟨*too* ~ *to fight*⟩ [ME *yelwe, yelow,* fr OE *geolu;* akin to OHG *gelo* yellow, L *helvus* light bay, Gk *chlōros* greenish yellow, Skt *hari* yellowish] – **yellowish** *adj,* **yellowy** *adj*

²yellow *vb* to make or become yellow

³yellow *n* **1** a colour whose hue resembles that of ripe lemons or dandelions and lies between green and orange in the spectrum **2** sthg yellow: e g **a** sby with yellow or light brown skin **b** the yolk of an egg **c** a yellow ball (e g in snooker) **3** *pl but sing in constr* any of several plant diseases caused esp by viruses and marked by yellowing of the foliage and stunting

,**yellow 'bile** *n* the one of the 4 humours in medieval physiology believed to be secreted by the liver and to cause irascibility

,**yellow 'fever** *n* an often fatal infectious disease of warm regions caused by a mosquito-transmitted virus and marked by fever, jaundice, and often bleeding

,**yellow 'flag** *n* a yellow Eurasian iris that grows in damp places

'**yellow,hammer** /-,hamə/ *n* a common Eurasian bunting, the male of which is largely yellow with a reddish-brown back [alter. of earlier *yelambre,* fr (assumed) ME *yelwambre,* fr ME *yelwe* yellow + (assumed) ME *ambre* yellowhammer, fr OE *amore;* akin to OHG *amaro* yellowhammer, *amari* emmer]

yellow jack *n* **1** YELLOW FEVER **2** a flag raised on ships in quarantine

,**yellow 'ochre** *adj or n* (of) an orange-yellow colour

,**Yellow 'Pages** *n pl* a telephone directory that lists organizations and services alphabetically within sections classified according to the nature of their business

,**yellow 'peril** *n, often cap Y&P* a danger to Western civilization held to arise from expansion of the power and influence of Oriental peoples

,**yellow 'pimpernel** *n* a common European pimpernel with nearly prostrate stems and bright yellow flowers

yelp /yelp/ *vi or n* (to utter) a sharp quick shrill cry ⟨*dogs* ~⟩ [vb ME *yelpen* to boast, cry out, fr OE *gielpan* to boast, exult; akin to OHG *gelph* outcry, Lith *gulbinti* to praise; n fr vb] – **yelper** *n*

¹yen /yen/ *n, pl* **yen** ☞ *Japan* at NATIONALITY [Jap *en*]

²yen *n* a strong desire or propensity; a longing – infml [obs E slang *yen-yen* (craving for opium), fr Chin (Cant) *in-yăn,* fr *in* opium + *yăn* craving]

³yen *vi* **-nn-** to yearn

yeoman /'yohmən/ *n, pl* **yeomen** **1** a petty officer who **a** carries out visual signalling in the British navy **b** carries out clerical duties in the US navy **2** a small farmer who cultivates his own land [ME *yoman* attendant in a noble household, freeholder, prob contr of *yong man* young man]

'**yeomanly** /-li/ *adj* becoming or suitable to a yeoman; sturdy, loyal – **yeomanly** *adv*

,**yeoman of the 'guard** *n* a member of a military corps attached to the British Royal Household who serve as ceremonial attendants of the sovereign and as warders of the Tower of London

'**yeomanry** /-ri/ *n sing or pl in constr* **1** the body of small landed proprietors **2** a British volunteer cavalry force created from yeomen in 1761 as a home defence force and reorganized in 1907 as part of the territorial force

yep /yep/ *adv* yes – used in writing to represent a casual or American pronunciation [by alter.]

yer /yə/ your – used in writing to represent a nonstandard pronunciation [by alter.]

-yer – see ²-ER

yerba maté /,yuhbə 'mahtay, ,yeəbə/ *n* maté [AmerSp *yerba mate,* fr *yerba* herb + *mate* maté]

¹yes /yes/ *adv* **1** – used in answers expressing affirmation, agreement, or willingness; contrasted with *no* ⟨*are you ready?* Yes, *I am*⟩ **2** – used in answers correcting or contradicting a negative assertion or direction ⟨*don't say that!* Yes, *I will*⟩ **3** YEA 1 **4** – indicating uncertainty or polite interest or attentiveness ⟨Yes? *What do you want?*⟩ [ME, fr OE *gēse*]

²yes *n* an affirmative reply or vote; an aye

yeshiva, yeshivah /yə'sheevə/ *n, pl* **yeshivas, yeshivoth** /-,voht, -,vohth/ **1** a school for Talmudic study **2** an orthodox Jewish rabbinic seminary **3** a Jewish day school providing secular and religious instruction [LHeb *yĕshībhāh*]

'**yes-,man** *n* one who endorses or supports everything said to him, esp by a superior; a sycophant – infml

¹yesterday /'yestəday, -di/ *adv* on the day before

today ⟨*saw him* ~⟩ [ME *yisterday*, fr OE *giestran dæg*, fr *giestran* yesterday + *dæg* day; akin to OHG *gestaron* yesterday, L *heri*, Gk *chthes*]

[2]**yesterday** *n* **1** the day before today **2** recent time; time not long past

yesteryear /'yestə,yiə/ *n* **1** last year **2** the recent past ***USE*** poetic [*yester*day + *year*] – **yesteryear** *adv*

[1]**yet** /yet/ *adv* **1a** again; IN ADDITION ⟨*gives* ~ *another reason*⟩ **b** EVEN 2b ⟨*a* ~ *higher speed*⟩ **2a** up to this or that time; so far – not in affirmative statements ⟨*hasn't had breakfast* ~⟩ **b** STILL 1, 2 ⟨*have* ~ *to learn the truth*⟩ **c** at some future time and despite present appearances ⟨*we may win* ~⟩ **3** nevertheless ⟨*strange and* ~ *true*⟩ [ME, fr OE *gīet*; akin to OFris *ieta* yet] – **yet again** still 1 more time

[2]**yet** *conj* but nevertheless

yeti /'yeti/ *n* ABOMINABLE SNOWMAN [Tibetan]

yew /yooh/ *n* (the wood of) any of a genus of evergreen coniferous trees and shrubs with stiff straight leaves and red fruits [ME *ew*, fr OE *īw*; akin to OHG *īwa* yew, OIr *ēo*]

'**Y-fronts** /wie/ *n pl in constr, pl* **Y-fronts** men's closely fitting underpants in which the front seams take the form of an inverted Y

YHWH *n* Yahweh – compare TETRAGRAMMATON

yid /yid/ *n, often cap* a Jew – chiefly derog [Yiddish, fr MHG *Jude, Jüde*, fr OHG *Judo, Judeo*, fr L *Judaeus* – more at JEW]

Yiddish /'yidish/ *n* a High German language containing elements of Hebrew and Slavonic that is usu written in Hebrew characters and is spoken by Jews chiefly in or from E Europe [Yiddish *yidish*, short for *yidish daytsh*, lit., Jewish German] – **Yiddish** *adj*

Yiddisher /'yidishə/ *adj* **1** Yiddish **2** Jewish [Yiddish *Yidisher*]

[1]**yield** /yeeld/ *vt* **1** to give or render as fitting, rightfully owed, or required ⟨~ed *allegiance to his master*⟩ **2** to give up possession of on claim or demand: e g **a** to surrender or submit (oneself) to another **b** to give (oneself) up to an inclination, temptation, or habit **c** to relinquish (e g a position of advantage or point of superiority) ⟨~ *precedence*⟩ **3a** to bear or bring forth as a natural product ⟨*the tree* ~s *good fruit*⟩ **b** to give as a return or in result of expended effort ⟨*properly handled this soil should* ~ *good crops*⟩ **c** to produce as revenue ⟨*the tax is expected to* ~ *millions*⟩ ⟨*a bond that* ~s *12 per cent*⟩ ~ *vi* **1** to be fruitful or productive **2** to give up and cease resistance or contention; submit, succumb **3** to give way to pressure or influence; submit to urging, persuasion, or entreaty **4** to give way under physical force (e g bending, stretching, or breaking) **5** to give place or precedence; acknowledge the superiority of another [ME *yielden*, fr OE *gieldan*; akin to OHG *geltan* to pay] – **yielder** *n*

[2]**yield** *n* **1** (the amount of) sthg yielded or produced ⟨~ *of wheat per acre*⟩ **2** the capacity of yielding produce ⟨*high* ~ *strain of wheat*⟩

yielding /'yeelding/ *adj* lacking rigidity or stiffness; flexible

yin /yin/ *n* the feminine passive principle in nature that in Chinese thought eternally interacts with its opposite and complementary principle, yang [Chin (Pek) *yin*[1]]

yip /yip/ *vi or n* **-pp-** *chiefly NAm* (to utter) a short sharp cry [imit]

yippee /yi'pee/ *interj* – used to express exuberant delight or triumph

-yl *comb form* (→ *n*) chemical radical ⟨*eth*yl⟩ ⟨*carbon*yl⟩ ⟨*phen*yl⟩ [Gk *hylē* matter, material, lit., wood]

ylang-ylang, ilang-ilang /,eelang 'eelang/ *n* (a perfume distilled from the fragrant yellow flowers of) a Malayan tree of the custard-apple family [Tag]

yob /yob/ *n, Br* a loutish youth; *esp* a hooligan – slang [back slang for *boy*]

yobbo /'yoboh/ *n, Br* a yob – slang

[1]**yodel** /'yohdl/ *vb* **-ll-** (*NAm* **-l-, -ll-**), /'yohdling, 'yohdl·ing/ to sing, shout, or call (a tune) by suddenly changing from a natural voice to a falsetto and back [G *jodeln*] – **yodeller** *n*

[2]**yodel** *n* a yodelled song, shout, or cry

yoga /'yohgə/ *n* **1** *cap* a Hindu philosophy teaching the suppression of all activity of body, mind, and will so that the self may attain liberation from them **2** a system of exercises for attaining bodily or mental control and well-being [Skt, lit., yoking, fr *yunakti* he yokes; akin to L *jungere* to join – more at YOKE] – **yogic** *adj, often cap*

yogh /yohk, yohg, yohkh/ *n* a letter ʒ which in Old and Middle English represented a velar or palatal fricative and of which traces remain in the modern spelling *gh* [ME *yogh, ʒogh*]

yoghourt, yoghurt, yogurt /'yogət/ *n* a slightly acid semisolid food made of milk fermented by bacteria [Turk *yoğurt*]

yogi /'yohgi/ *n* **1** sby who practises or is a master of yoga **2** *cap* an adherent of Yoga philosophy [Skt *yogin*, fr *yoga*]

yoicks /yoyks/ *interj, archaic* – used as a cry of encouragement to foxhounds

[1]**yoke** /yohk/ *n* **1a** a bar or frame by which 2 draught animals (e g oxen) are joined at the heads or necks for working together **b** an arched device formerly laid on the neck of a defeated person **c** a frame fitted to sby's shoulders to carry a load in 2 equal portions **d** a crosspiece on a rudder to which steering lines are attached **2** *sing or pl in constr* 2 animals yoked or worked together **3a** an oppressive agency **b** a tie, link; *esp* marriage **4** a fitted or shaped piece at the top of a garment from which the rest hangs [ME *yok*, fr OE *geoc*; akin to OHG *joh* yoke, L *jugum*, Gk *zygon*, L *jungere* to join]

[2]**yoke** *vt* **1** to attach (a draught animal) to (sthg) **2** to join (as if) by a yoke

yokel /'yohkl/ *n* a naive or gullible rustic; a country bumpkin [perh fr E dial. *yokel* (green woodpecker), of imit origin]

yolk *also* **yoke** /yohk/ *n* **1** the usu yellow spheroidal mass of stored food that forms the inner portion of the egg of a bird or reptile and is surrounded by the white **2** a mass of protein, lecithin, cholesterol, etc that is stored in an ovum as food for the developing embryo [ME *yolke*, fr OE *geoloca*, fr *geolu* yellow – more at YELLOW] – **yolked** *adj*, **yolky** *adj*

'**yolk ,sac** *n* a membranous sac, nearly vestigial in placental mammals, attached to an embryo and containing the yolk ☞ LIFE CYCLE

Yom Kippur /,yom ki'pooə, 'kipə/ *n* a Jewish holiday observed with fasting and prayer on the 10th day of the Jewish year [Heb *yōm kippūr*, fr *yōm* day + *kippūr* atonement]

yon /yon/ *adj or adv, archaic or dial* yonder [adj ME, fr OE *geon*; akin to OHG *ienēr*, adj, that, Gk *enē* day after tomorrow; adv fr adj]

yonder /'yondə/ *adj or adv* over there [adv ME, fr *yond* (fr OE *geond*) + *-er* (as in *hither*); adj fr adv]

yoni /'yohni/ *n* a stylized representation of the female genitals used in Hindu temples to symbolize the feminine cosmic principle – compare LINGA [Skt, vulva]

yonks /yongks/ *n, Br* a long time; ages – infml [origin unknown]

yoo-hoo /'yooh ˌhooh/ *interj* – used to attract attention or as a call to people – **yoo-hoo** /ˌ-'-/ *vi*

yore /yaw/ *n* time (long) past – usu in *of yore* [ME, fr *yore*, adv, long ago, fr OE *geāra*, fr *gēar* year]

york /yawk/ *vt* to bowl (a batsman) out with a yorker [back-formation fr *yorker*]

yorker /'yawkə/ *n* a ball bowled in cricket that is aimed to bounce on the popping crease and so pass under the bat [prob fr *Yorkshire*, where it was allegedly introduced]

Yorkist /'yawkist/ *adj* of the English royal house of York that ruled from 1461 to 1485 [Edward, Duke of *York* (Edward IV of England) †1483] – **Yorkist** *n*

ˌYorkshire 'fog /'yawkshiə, -shə/ *n* a perennial grass with a velvety stem [*Yorkshire*, county in N England]

Yorkshireman /'yorkshiəmən, -shə-/, *fem* **'Yorkshireˌwoman** *n* a native of Yorkshire

ˌYorkshire 'pudding *n* a savoury baked pudding made from a batter and usu eaten before or with roast beef

ˌYorkshire 'terrier *n* a compact toy terrier with long straight silky hair mostly bluish grey but tan on the head and chest

Yoruba /'yoroobə/ *n, pl* **Yorubas,** *esp collectively* **Yoruba 1** a member of a Negro people of the coast of W Africa, esp SW Nigeria **2** the Kwa language of the Yoruba ☞ LANGUAGE

you /yoo; *strong* yooh/ *pron, pl* **you 1** the one being addressed – used as subject or object ⟨*can I pour ~ a cup of tea?*⟩; sometimes used as an exclamation with vocatives ⟨*~ angel*⟩ ⟨*~ scoundrels*⟩ **2** a person; one ⟨*funny, when ~ come to think of it*⟩ [ME, fr OE *ēow*, dat & accus of *gē* you (pl); akin to OHG *iu*, dat of *ir* you, Skt *yūyam* you] – **you get** there is or are ⟨*within the Chinese language* you get *quite different sounds – SEU S*⟩

you-'all *pron, chiefly S US* you – usu used in addressing 2 or more people or sometimes 1 person as representing also another or others

you'd /yoohd/ you had; you would

ˌyou-know-'where *n* a place understood but unspecified

ˌyou-know-'who *n* sby understood but unspecified

you'll /yoohl/ you will; you shall

¹young /yung/ *adj* **younger** /'yung·gə/; **youngest** /'yung·gist/ **1a** in the first or an early stage of life, growth, or development **b** JUNIOR 1 **c** of an early or tender age for eating or drinking ⟨*fresh ~ lamb*⟩ **2** recently come into being; new ⟨*a ~ industry*⟩ ⟨*the night is ~*⟩ **3** of or having the characteristics (e g vigour or gaiety) of young people ⟨*a ~ style of dress*⟩ **4** tending towards the size of ⟨*the chapel was a ~ cathedral*⟩ [ME *yong*, fr OE *geong*; akin to OHG *jung* young, L *juvenis*] – **youngish** /'yung·gish/ *adj*, **youngness** *n*

²young *n pl* **1** young people; youth **2** immature offspring, esp of an animal – **with young** *of a female animal* pregnant

younger /'yung·gə/ *adj* inferior in age; junior – used before or after sby's name to distinguish him/her from his/her father or mother ⟨*William Pitt the* Younger⟩

youngling /'yungling/ *n* a young person or animal – **youngling** *adj*

ˌyoung 'person *n* sby between the ages of 14 and 17 – used in English law; compare CHILD 2c (2)

youngster /'yungstə/ *n* **1** a young person or creature **2** a child, baby

ˌYoung 'Turk /tuhk/ *n* a radical member of a political party [*Young Turks*, a 20th-c revolutionary party in Turkey]

your /yə; *strong* yaw/ *adj* **1** of you or yourself or yourselves, esp as possessor or possessors ⟨*~ bodies*⟩, agent or agents ⟨*~ contributions*⟩, or object or objects of an action ⟨*~ injury*⟩ –used with certain titles in the vocative ⟨*~ Eminence*⟩ **2** of one or oneself ⟨*when you face north, east is on ~ right*⟩ **3** – used for indicating sthg well-known and characteristic; infml ⟨*~ typical commuter*⟩ ***USE*** used attributively [ME, fr OE *ēower*, gen of *gē* you (pl)]

you're /yaw, yooə/ you are

yours /yawz/ *pron, pl* **yours** that which or the one who belongs to you – used without a following noun as a pronoun equivalent in meaning to the adjective *your*; often used in the complimentary close of a letter ⟨*~ truly*⟩ [ME, fr *your* + *-s* -'s] – **yours truly 1** I, me, myself ⟨*I can take care of* yours truly⟩ **2** your letter ⟨yours truly *of the 19th*⟩

yourself /yə'self, yaw'self/ *pron, pl* **yourselves** /-'selvz/ **1a** that identical person or creature that is you – used reflexively ⟨*enjoy* yourselves, *everyone*⟩, for emphasis ⟨*carry it ~*⟩, or in absolute constructions **b** your normal self ⟨*soon be ~ again*⟩ **2** oneself

youth /yoohth/ *n, pl* **youths** /yoohdhz/ **1** the time of life when one is young; *esp* adolescence ⟨*lived there in his ~*⟩ **2a** a young male adolescent **b** young people – often pl in constr ⟨*modern ~*⟩ **3** the quality of being youthful ⟨*preserved her ~*⟩ [ME *youthe*, fr OE *geoguth*; akin to OE *geong* young – more at YOUNG]

'youthful /-f(ə)l/ *adj* **1** (characteristic) of youth ⟨*~ complexion*⟩ ⟨*~ optimism*⟩ **2** not yet mature or old; young ⟨*~ dancers*⟩ – **youthfully** *adv*, **youthfulness** *n*

'youth ˌhostel *n* a lodging typically providing inexpensive bed and breakfast accommodation for members of the YHA, esp young travellers or hikers – **youth-hosteller** *n*, **youth-hostelling** *n*

you've /yoohv/ you have

yow /yow/ *n* a yell of pain – often used interjectionally [imit]

yowl /yowl/ *vi or n* (to utter) the loud long wail of a cat or dog in pain or distress [vb ME *yowlen*, prob of imit origin; n fr vb]

yo-yo /'yoh ˌyoh/ *n, pl* **yo-yos** a toy that consists of 2 discs separated by a deep groove in which a string is attached and wound and that is made to fall and rise when held by the string [native name in Philippines]

ytterbium /i'tuhbi·əm/ *n* a bivalent or trivalent metallic element of the rare-earth group that resembles and occurs with yttrium ☞ PERIODIC TABLE [NL, fr *Ytterby*, town in Sweden]

yttrium /'itri·əm/ *n* a trivalent metallic rare-earth element ☞ PERIODIC TABLE [NL, fr *yttria* (yttrium oxide), irreg fr *Ytterby*]

yuan /'yooh·ən, yooh'ahn/ *n, pl* **yuan** ☞ *China* at NATIONALITY [Chin (Pek) *yüan*[2]]

yucca /'yukə/ *n* any of a genus of sometimes treelike plants of the lily family with long often rigid leaves and a large cluster of white flowers [NL, genus name, fr Sp *yuca*]

yule /yoohl/ *n, often cap, archaic* Christmas [ME *yol*, fr OE *geōl*; akin to ON *jōl* winter feast, Christmas]

'Yule ,log *n* a large log formerly put on the hearth on Christmas Eve as the foundation of the fire

yummy /'yumi/ *adj* highly attractive or pleasing, esp to the palate; delicious – infml [*yum-yum*]

yum-yum /,yum 'yum/ *interj* – used to express pleasurable satisfaction, esp in the taste of food [imit of the sound of smacking the lips]

Yurak /yoo'rak, 'yooərak/ *n* a Uralic language of N Russia and Siberia

yurt /yooət/ *n* a collapsible domed tent of skins or felt used by Mongol nomads of Central Asia [Russ *yurta*, of Turkic origin; akin to Turk *yurt* dwelling]

Z

z /zed/ *n, pl* **z's, zs** *often cap* **1** (a graphic representation of or device for reproducing) the 26th letter of the English alphabet **2** one designated *z*, esp as the 3rd in a series that includes *x, y,* and *z*

zabaglione /,zabə'lyohni/ *n* a thick creamy dessert made by whipping eggs, sugar, and (Marsala) wine over hot water [It]

zaddik, tzaddik /'tsahdik/ *n, pl* **zaddikim** /tsah'dikim/ an exceptionally righteous and saintly person by Jewish religious standards, often credited with supernatural powers [Heb *ṣaddīq* just, righteous]

zaffre /'zafə/ *n* an impure oxide of cobalt used esp as a blue ceramic colouring [It *zaffera*]

zaire /zah'iə/ *n, pl* **zaire** ☞ *Zaire* at NATIONALITY [F *zaïre*, fr *Zaïre* (Congo), river in central Africa]

[1]**zany** /'zayni/ *n* one who acts the buffoon to amuse others [It *zanni,* a traditional masked clown, fr It (dial.) *Zanni,* nickname for *Giovanni* John]

[2]**zany** *adj* fantastically or absurdly ludicrous – **zanily** *adv,* **zaniness** *n*

[1]**zap** /zap/ *interj* – used to indicate a sudden or instantaneous occurrence; infml [imit]

[2]**zap** *vb* **-pp-** *vt* **1** to overwhelm, overcome **2** to propel vigorously **3** *chiefly NAm* to destroy, kill ~ *vi* to move with speed or force *USE* slang

zapateado /,zahpətay'ahdoh/ *n* a Latin American dance marked by rhythmic stamping or tapping of the feet [Sp, fr *zapatear* to strike or tap with the shoe, fr *zapato* shoe]

zappy /'zapi/ *adj* **1** energetic, dynamic ⟨*the ~ presentation of a TV commercial*⟩ **2** fast-moving ⟨*a ~ little car*⟩ *USE* infml

zareba, zariba /zə'reebə/ *n* an improvised stockade constructed, esp of thorny bushes, in parts of Africa [Ar *zarībah* enclosure]

zarzuela /zah'zwaylə/ *n* a traditional Spanish comic opera [Sp]

'z-,axis /zed/ *n* that 1 of the 3 axes in a 3-dimensional rectangular coordinate system that is not the x- or y-axis

zeal /zeel/ *n* eagerness and ardent interest in pursuit of sthg; keenness [ME *zele,* fr LL *zelus,* fr Gk *zēlos*]

zealot /'zelət/ *n* a zealous person; *esp* a fanatical partisan [LL *zelotes,* fr Gk *zēlōtēs,* fr *zēlos*] – **zealot** *adj,* **zealotry** /-tri/ *n*

zealous /'zeləs/ *adj* filled with or characterized by zeal ⟨~ *missionaries*⟩ – **zealously** *adv,* **zealousness** *n*

zebra /'zebrə, 'zeebrə/ *n, pl* **zebras,** *esp collectively* **zebra** any of several black and white striped fast-running African mammals related to the horse ☞ DEFENCE, FOOD [It, fr Sp *cebra*] – **zebrine** /-brien/ *adj,* **zebroid** /-broyd/ *adj*

,zebra 'crossing *n* a crossing in Britain marked by a series of broad white stripes to indicate that pedestrians have the right of way across a road

'zebra ,finch *n* a small largely grey and white Australian weaver bird

zebu /'zeeb(y)ooh/ *n* an ox of any of several breeds of domesticated Asiatic oxen with a large fleshy hump over the shoulders [F *zébu*]

Zechariah /,zekə'rie·ə/ *n* (a prophetic book of the Old Testament attributed to) a Hebrew prophet of the 6th c BC [Heb *Zĕkharyāh*]

zed /zed/ *n, chiefly Br* the letter *z* [ME, fr MF *zede,* fr LL *zeta* zeta, fr Gk *zēta*]

zee /zee/ *n, NAm* zed

zein /'zee·in/ *n* a protein in maize used esp in making textile fibres, printing inks, coatings, etc [NL *Zea,* genus of grasses including Indian corn, fr Gk, wheat; akin to Skt *yava* barley]

zeitgeist /'tsiet,giest/ *n* the general intellectual and moral character or cultural climate of an era [G, fr *zeit* time + *geist* spirit]

Zen /zen/ *n* a Japanese sect of Mahayana Buddhism that aims at enlightenment by direct intuition through meditation (e g on paradoxes) [Jap, religious meditation, fr Chin (Pek) *ch'an*^{2}, fr Pali *jhāna,* fr Skt *dhyāna,* fr *dhyāyati* he thinks – more at SEMANTIC]

zenana /ze'nahnə/ *n* the women's quarters in an eastern, esp Muslim, house [Hindi *zanāna,* fr Per, fr *zan* woman]

Zend-Avesta /,zend ə'vestə/ *n* the Avesta [F, fr MPer *Avastāk va Zand* Avesta and commentary]

zener diode /'zeenə/ *n, often cap Z* a silicon semiconductor device that is used to provide a stable voltage for reference or voltage regulation [Clarence *Zener b*1905 US physicist]

zenith /'zenith/ *n* **1** the point of the celestial sphere that is directly opposite the nadir and vertically above the observer **2** the highest point reached in the heavens by a celestial body **3** the culminating point or stage ⟨*at the ~ of his powers* – John Buchan⟩ [ME *senith,* fr MF *cenith,* fr ML, fr OSp *zenit,* modif of Ar *samt* (*ar-ra's*) path (above the head)]

zenithal /'zenithəl/ *adj* **1** of or located at or near the zenith **2** showing correct directions from the centre ⟨*a ~ map*⟩

zeolite /'zee·ə,liet/ *n* (a synthetic silicate resembling) any of various minerals that are hydrous aluminium silicates analogous in composition to the feldspars and can act as ion-exchangers (e g in water softening) [Sw *zeolit,* fr Gk *zein* to boil + *-o-* + Sw *-lit* -lite, fr F *-lite* – more at YEAST] – **zeolitic** /-'litik/ *adj*

Zephaniah /,zefə'nie·ə/ *n* (an apocalyptic book of the Old Testament attributed to) a Hebrew prophet of the 7th c BC [Heb *Sĕphanyāh*]

zephyr /'zefə/ *n* **1** a gentle breeze, esp from the west **2** any of various lightweight fabrics or articles of clothing [ME *Zephirus,* west wind (personified), fr

L *Zephyrus, zephyrus* (god of the) west wind, zephyr, fr Gk *Zephyros, zephyros*]

zeppelin /ˈzep(ə)lin/ *n, often cap* a large rigid cigar-shaped airship of a type built in Germany in the early 20th c; *broadly* an airship [Count Ferdinand von *Zeppelin* †1917 G general & aeronaut]

[1]zero /ˈziəroh/ *n, pl* **zeros** *also* **zeroes** **1** the arithmetical symbol 0 or denoting the absence of all magnitude or quantity **2** ☞ NUMBER **3** the point of departure in reckoning; *specif* the point from which the graduation of a scale begins **4a** nothing ⟨*slow down to ~ in the traffic*⟩ **b** the lowest point ⟨*his spirits fell to ~*⟩ [F or It; F *zéro*, fr It *zero*, fr ML *zephirum*, fr Ar *ṣifr*]

[2]zero *adj* **1** having no magnitude or quantity ⟨*~ growth*⟩ **2a** *of a cloud ceiling* limiting vision to 15m (about 50ft) or less **b** *of horizontal visibility* limited to 50m (about 165ft) or less

[3]zero *vt* to adjust the sights of (e g a rifle) *~ vi* **1** to concentrate firepower on a specified target **2** to move near to or focus attention as if on a target; close ⟨*reporters* ~ed *in on Miss World*⟩ *USE* (*vi*) usu + *in on*

ˈzero ˌhour *n* the time at which an event is scheduled to take place [fr its being marked by the count of zero in a countdown]

zest /zest/ *n* **1** the outer peel of a citrus fruit used as flavouring **2** piquancy, spice ⟨*danger added ~ to the proceedings*⟩ **3** keen enjoyment; gusto ⟨*her ~ for living*⟩ [obs F (now *zeste*)] – **zestful** *adj*, **zesty** *adj*

zeta /ˈzeetə/ *n* the 6th letter of the Greek alphabet [Gk *zēta*]

zeugma /ˈzyoohgmə/ *n* the use of a word to modify or govern 2 or more words, usu in such a manner that it applies to each in a different sense (e g in 'opened the door and her heart to the homeless boy') [L, fr Gk, lit., joining, fr *zeugnynai* to join; akin to L *jungere* to join – more at YOKE]

zibet /ˈzibit/ *n* a common Asian civet [It *zibetto* & ML *zibethum*, fr Ar *zabād* civet perfume]

ziggurat /ˈzigərat/ *n* a temple tower of ancient Mesopotamia in the form of a stepped pyramid [Akkadian *ziqqurratu* pinnacle]

[1]zigzag /ˈzigˌzag/ *n* a line, course, or pattern consisting of a series of sharp alternate turns or angles ⟨*a blue shirt with red ~*s⟩ [F]

[2]zigzag *adj* forming or going in a zigzag; consisting of zigzags ⟨*a ~ path up the hill*⟩ – **zigzag** *adv*

[3]zigzag *vb* **-gg-** *vt* to form into a zigzag *~ vi* to proceed along or consist of a zigzag course

zilch /zilch/ *adj or n, chiefly NAm* zero – slang [by alter.]

zillion /ˈzilyən/ *n* an indefinitely large number – often pl with sing. meaning; infml ⟨~s *of mosquitoes*⟩ [z + *-illion* (as in *million*)]

[1]zinc /zingk/ *n* a bluish white bivalent metallic element that occurs abundantly in minerals and is used esp as a protective coating for iron and steel ☞ PERIODIC TABLE [G *zink*] – **zincic** *adj*, **zincous** *adj*

[2]zinc *vt* **-c-**, **-ck-** to treat or coat with zinc

zincate /ˈzingkayt/ *n* a compound formed by reaction of zinc oxide or zinc with alkaline solutions

ˌzinc ˈoxide *n* a white solid used esp as a pigment and in medicinal and cosmetic preparations

ˌzinc ˈwhite *n* zinc oxide used as a pigment

[1]zing /zing/ *n* energy, vim – infml [*zing* (a shrill humming noise), of imit origin]

[2]zing *vi* to move briskly or with a humming sound – infml

zingy /ˈzing·i/ *adj* strikingly exciting or attractive ⟨*a ~ musical*⟩ ⟨*a ~ new outfit*⟩ – infml [[1]*zing*]

zinnia /ˈzinyə, ˈzini·ə/ *n* any of a small genus of tropical American composite plants with showy flower heads and long-lasting ray flowers [NL, genus name, fr Johann *Zinn* †1759 G botanist]

Zion /ˈzieˌon, ˈzie·ən/ *n* **1a** the Jewish people **b** the Jewish homeland **2** heaven [*Zion*, citadel in Palestine which was the nucleus of Jerusalem, fr ME *Sion*, fr OE, fr LL, fr Heb *Ṣīyōn*]

Zionism /ˈzie·əˌniz(ə)m/ *n* a movement for setting up a Jewish homeland in Palestine – **Zionist** *adj or n*

[1]zip /zip/ *vb* **-pp-** *vi* **1** to move with speed and vigour ⟨*waitresses* ~ped *by*⟩ **2** to become open, closed, or attached by means of a zip **3** to travel with a sharp hissing or humming sound *~ vt* **1a** to close or open (as if) with a zip **b** to enclose by means of a zip ⟨*~ him into his wet suit*⟩ **c** to cause (a zip) to open or shut **2** to add zest or life to – often + *up* [imit of the sound of a speeding object; (vi 2, vt 1) [2]*zip* 3]

[2]zip *n* **1** a light sharp hissing sound **2** energy, liveliness **3** *chiefly Br* a fastener that joins 2 edges of fabric by means of 2 flexible spirals or rows of teeth brought together by a sliding clip – **zippy** *adj*, **zippily** *adv*

[3]zip *adj* zip-up ⟨*a ~ jacket*⟩

ˈzip ˌcode *n, often cap Z&I&P* a 5-digit number that is used in the postal address of a place in the USA to assist sorting – compare POSTCODE [*zone improvement plan*]

ˌzip ˈfastener /ˈfahs(ə)nə/ *n, chiefly Br* ZIP 3

zipped /zipt/ *adj* zip-up

zipper /ˈzipə/ *n, chiefly NAm* ZIP 3

ˈzip-ˌup *adj* fastened by means of a zip

zircon /ˈzuhkon/ *n* a variously coloured mineral consisting of a zirconium silicate and used as a gem when transparent [G, modif of F *jargon* jargoon, zircon, fr It *giargone*]

zirconium /zuhˈkohnyəm, -ni·əm/ *n* a steel-grey ductile chiefly tetravalent metallic element that occurs widely in combined form (e g in zircon) and is used esp in alloys and in heat-resisting ceramic materials ☞ PERIODIC TABLE [NL, fr ISV *zircon*]

zither /ˈzidhə/ *n* a stringed instrument having usu 30 to 40 strings over a shallow horizontal soundboard and played with plectrum and fingers [G, fr L *cithara* lyre, fr Gk *kithara*] – **zitherist** *n*

zizz /ziz/ *vi or n, Br* (to) nap, doze – infml [imit of the sound of a sleeper's breathing]

zloty /ˈzloti/ *n, pl* **zlotys** /ˈzloteez/ *also* **zloty** ☞ *Poland* at NATIONALITY [Pol z ty]

zo-, **zoo-** *comb form* animal; animal kingdom ⟨*zoo*id⟩ ⟨*zoo*logy⟩ [Gk *zōi-*, *zōio-*, fr *zōion*; akin to Gk *zōē* life – more at QUICK]

-zoa /-ˈzoh·ə/ *comb form* (→ *n pl*) animals – in taxa ⟨*Metazoa*⟩ [NL, fr Gk *zōia*, pl of *zōion*]

zodiac /ˈzohdiak/ *n* an imaginary belt in the heavens that encompasses the apparent paths of all the principal planets except Pluto, has the ecliptic as its central line, and is divided into 12 constellations or signs each taken for astrological purposes to extend 30 degrees of longitude ☞ SYMBOL [ME, fr MF *zodiaque*, fr L *zodiacus*, fr Gk *zōidiakos*, fr *zōidia-*

kos, adj, of carved figures, of the zodiac, fr *zōidion* carved figure, sign of the zodiac, fr dim. of *zōion* living being, figure; akin to Gk *zōē* life – more at QUICK] – **zodiacal** /zoh'die·əkl, zə-/ *adj*

zo,diacal 'light /zoh'die·əkl, zə-/ *n* a diffuse glow seen in the west after twilight and in the east before dawn

[1]**-zoic** /-'zoh·ik/ *comb form* (→ *adj*) being an animal that has (such) a mode of existence ⟨*holo*zoic⟩ ⟨*sapro*zoic⟩ [Gk *zōikos* of animals, fr *zōion* animal – more at ZO-]

[2]**-zoic** *comb form* (→ *adj*) of or being (such) a geological era ⟨*Archaeo*zoic⟩ ⟨*Meso*zoic⟩ [Gk *zōē* life]

zombie, *NAm also* **zombi** /'zombi/ *n* **1** a human in the W Indies capable only of automatic movement who is held, esp in Haitian voodooism, to have died and been reanimated **2** a person resembling the walking dead; *esp* a shambling automaton [of Niger-Congo origin; akin to Kongo *nzambi* god] – **zombielike** *adj*

[1]**zone** /zohn/ *n* **1a** any of 5 great divisions of the earth's surface with respect to latitude and temperature **b** a portion of the surface of a sphere included between 2 parallel planes **2a** a subdivision of a biogeographic region that supports a similar fauna and flora throughout its extent **b** a distinctive layer of rock or other earth materials **3** an area distinct from adjoining parts ⟨*an erogenous* ~⟩ **4** any of the sections into which an area is divided for a particular purpose ⟨*a smokeless* ~⟩ [L *zona* belt, zone, fr Gk *zōnē*; akin to Lith *juosti* to gird] – **zonal** *adj*, **zonate, zonated** *adj*

[2]**zone** *vt* **1** to arrange in, mark off, or partition into zones **2** to assign to a zone ⟨*neighbourhood has been* ~d *as residential*⟩ – **zoner** *n*

'zone ,melting *n* the purification of a crystalline material, esp a metal, by passing a molten part of itself through it to pick up impurities

zone refine *vt* to produce or refine by zone melting

zonked /zongkt/ *adj* **1** highly intoxicated by alcohol, LSD, etc – often + *out* **2** completely exhausted *USE* slang [origin unknown]

zoo /zooh/ *n, pl* **zoos** a zoological garden or collection of living animals usu open to the public [short for *zoological (garden)*]

zoo- – see ZO-

zoogeography /,zoh·əji'ogrəfi/ *n* zoology dealing with the geographical distribution of animals [ISV] – **zoogeographer** *n*, **zoogeographic** /,zoh·əjee·ə'grafik/ *also* **zoogeographical** *adj*

zooid /'zoh·oyd/ *n* an entity that resembles but is not wholly the same as a separate individual organism; *esp* a more or less independent animal produced by fission, proliferation, or other methods that do not directly involve sex – **zooidal** /zoh'oydl/ *adj*

,zoo,logical 'garden /,zooh·ə'lojikl, ,zoh·ə-/ *n* a garden or park where wild animals are kept for exhibition – often pl with sing. meaning

zoology /zooh'oləji, zoh-/ *n* (biology that deals with) animals and animal life, usu excluding human beings [NL *zoologia*, fr *zo-* + *-logia* -logy] – **zoologist** *n*, **zoological** /-ə'lojikl/ *also* **zoologic** *adj*, **zoologically** *adv*

[1]**zoom** /zoohm/ *vi* **1** to move with a loud low hum or buzz **2** to rise sharply ⟨*retail sales* ~ed⟩ ~ *vt* to operate the zoom lens of (e g a camera) [imit]

[2]**zoom** *n* **1** an act or process of zooming **2** ZOOM LENS

zoom lens *n* a lens (e g in a camera) in which the image size can be varied continuously so that the image remains in focus at all times

zoomorphic /,zoh·ə'mawfik/ *adj* resembling the form of (part of) an animal ⟨*a* ~ *orchid*⟩ ⟨*a* ~ *deity*⟩ [ISV]

-zoon /-'zoh·ən/ *comb form* (→ *n*), *pl* **-zoa** animal; zooid ⟨*haematozoon*⟩ ⟨*spermatozoon*⟩ [NL, fr Gk *zōion*]

zoonosis /zoh'onəsis, ,zoh·ə'nohsis/ *n, pl* **zoonoses** /-seez/ any disease (e g rabies or anthrax) communicable from lower animals to human beings [NL, fr *zo-* + Gk *nosos* disease] – **zoonotic** /,zoh·ə'notik/ *adj*

zoophilous /zoh'ofiləs/ *adj* having an attraction to or preference for animals: e g **a** adapted for pollination by animals other than insects – compare ENTOMOPHILOUS **b** *of a blood-sucking insect* preferring lower animals to human beings as a source of food

zoophyte /'zoh·ə,fiet/ *n* a coral, sponge, or other (branching or treelike) invertebrate animal resembling a plant [Gk *zōophyton*, fr *zōi-, zō-* zo- + *phyton* plant – more at PHYT-] – **zoophytic** /-'fitik/ *adj*

zooplankton /,zoh·ə'plangktən, -ton/ *n* planktonic animal life – compare PHYTOPLANKTON – **zooplanktonic** /-plangk'tonik/ *adj*

zoospore /'zoh·ə,spaw/ *n* a spore capable of independent movement [ISV]

'zoot ,suit /zooht/ *n* a flamboyant suit typically consisting of a thigh-length jacket with wide padded shoulders and trousers tapering to narrow cuffs [*zoot* prob arbitrary rhyme on *suit*]

zoril /'zoril/ *n* a zorilla

zorilla /zo'rilə/ *n* a S African animal that resembles the weasel [F *zorille*, fr Sp *zorilla, zorillo*, dim. of *zorra, zorro* fox]

Zoroastrianism /,zoroh'astri·əniz(ə)m/ *n* a Persian dualistic religion founded in the 6th c BC by the prophet Zoroaster, promulgated in the Avesta, and characterized by worship of a supreme god Ahura Mazda who is engaged in a constant cosmic struggle against the evil spirit Ahriman – **Zoroastrian** *adj or n*

Zouave /zooh'ahv, zwahv/ *n* a member of a French infantry unit, orig composed of Algerians, wearing a brilliant uniform [F, fr Berber *Zwāwa*, an Algerian tribe]

zucchetto /tsooh'ketoh, sooh-, zooh-/ *n, pl* **zucchettos** a skullcap worn by Roman Catholic ecclesiastics, coloured according to the rank of the wearer [It, fr *zucca* gourd, head, fr LL *cucutia* gourd]

zucchini /zooh'keeni, tsooh-/ *n, pl* **zucchini, zucchinis** *chiefly NAm* a courgette [It, pl of *zucchino*, dim. of *zucca* gourd]

[1]**Zulu** /'zoohlooh/ *n* **1** a member of a Bantu-speaking people of Natal **2** a Bantu language of the Zulus – **Zulu** *adj*

[2]**Zulu** – a communications code word for the letter *z*

Zuni, Zuñi /'zoohn(y)ee/ *n, pl* **Zunis, Zuñis,** *esp collectively* **Zuni, Zuñi** a member, or the language, of an American Indian people of NE Arizona [Amer Sp] – **Zunian, Zuñian** *adj*

zwieback /'swee,bak, 'zwee-/ *n* a usu sweetened rich

bread that is baked and then sliced and toasted until dry and crisp [G, lit., twice baked, fr *zwie-* twice (fr OHG *zwi-*) + *backen* to bake, fr OHG *bahhan* – more at TWI-, BAKE]

Zwinglian /ˈzwing·gli·ən, ˈtsving-/ *adj* of (the teachings of) Ulrich Zwingli, esp the doctrine that Christ's presence in the Eucharist is symbolic [Ulrich *Zwingli* †1531 Swiss theologian] – **Zwinglian** *n*

zwitterion /ˈtsvitə,rie·ən/ *n* an ion with both a positive and a negative charge [G, fr *zwitter* hybrid + *ion*] – **zwitterionic** /-rieˈonik/ *adj*

zyg-, zygo- *comb form* pair ⟨zygo*dactyl*⟩ [NL, fr Gk, fr *zygon* yoke – more at YOKE]

zygodactyl /,ziegəˈdaktil/ *adj, of a bird* having 2 toes pointing forwards and 2 backwards [ISV *zyg-* + Gk *daktylos* toe] – **zygodactyl** *n*, **zygodactylous** *adj*

zygoma /zieˈgohmə, zi-/ *n, pl* **zygomata** /-mətə/ *also* **zygomas** ZYGOMATIC ARCH [NL *zygomat-, zygoma*, fr Gk *zygōma*, fr *zygoun* to join together, fr *zygon*] – **zygomatic** /-ˈmatik/ *adj*

,zygo,matic ˈarch /,ziegəˈmatik, zi-/ *n* the arch of bone that extends along the front or side of the skull beneath the eye socket

zygomorphic /,ziegohˈmawfik, ,zi-, -gə-/ *adj* symmetrical about only 1 longitudinal plane ⟨*the ~ flowers of the toadflax*⟩ – **zygomorphism, zygomorphy** /ˈ--,--/ *n*

zygospore /ˈziegoh,spaw, ˈzi-, -gə-/ *n* a plant spore (e g in some algae), formed by union of 2 similar sexual cells, that grows to produce the phase of the plant that produces asexual spores – compare OOSPORE [ISV]

zygote /ˈziegoht, ˈzigoht/ *n* (the developing individual produced from) a cell formed by the union of 2 gametes [Gk *zygōtos* yoked, fr *zygoun*] – **zygotic** /-ˈgotik/ *adj*

zygotene /ˈziegə,teen/ *n* the stage in meiotic cell division in which homologous chromosomes pair intimately [ISV]

-zygous /-zigəs/ *comb form* (→ *adj*) having (such) a zygotic constitution ⟨*hetero*zygous⟩ [Gk *-zygos* yoked, fr *zygon*]

zym-, zymo- *comb form* **1** fermentation ⟨zym*urgy*⟩ **2** enzyme ⟨zymo*gen*⟩ [NL, fr Gk, leaven, fr *zymē*]

zymase /ˈziemayz, -mays/ *n* an enzyme or complex of enzymes that promotes the breakdown of glucose [ISV]

zymogen /ˈziemәjen, -jən/ *n* an inactive protein secreted by living cells and activated by catalysis to form an enzyme [ISV]

zymogenic /,ziemәˈjenik/ *adj* **1** producing fermentation **2** of a zymogen

zymology /zieˈmoləji/ *n* the science of fermentation [NL *zymologia*, fr *zym-* + *-logia* -logy]

zymotic /zieˈmotik/ *adj* **1** of, causing, or caused by fermentation **2** relating to, being, or causing an infectious or contagious disease [Gk *zymōtikos*, fr *zymōtos* fermented, fr *zymoun* to ferment, fr *zymē*] – **zymotically** *adv*

zymurgy /ˈziemuhji/ *n* chemistry that deals with fermentation processes

zzz /z *esp prolonged*/ *interj* – used as a visual representation of sleep or snoring, esp in cartoons [imit of snoring]

Foreign Phrases

Pronunciation of Foreign Phrases

All foreign phrases are given an anglicized pronunciation which the English speaker will easily be able to say. In addition, the International Phonetic Alphabet symbols are given where appropriate to help those people who are interested in the way the word or phrase is pronounced in its own language.

Pronunciation of Latin phrases is very variable. We have tried as far as possible to use the modern system of Latin pronunciation, with the exception that for reasons of economy all written *v*s are shown only as /v/, although the pronunciation /w/ is equally acceptable.

A

absit omen ˌabsit 'ohmen/ perish the thought! [L, lit., let the omen be absent]

ab urbe condita /ab ˌooəbay 'konditah/ from the founding of the city (Rome, founded 753 BC) – used by the Romans in reckoning dates [L]

à coup sûr /ah ˌkooh 'sooə (*Fr* a ku syr)/ surely, definitely [F, lit., with sure stroke]

ad arbitrium /ad ah'bitri·əm/ at will, arbitrarily [L]

ad/in utrumque paratus /ad ˌoohtrəmkway pə'rahtəs, in/ prepared for either (event) [L]

ad majorem Dei gloriam /ad maˌyawrem ˌdayee 'glawriam/ to the greater glory of God – motto of the Society of Jesus [L]

ad patres /ad 'pahtrayz/ deceased [L, lit., to the fathers]

à droite /ah 'drwaht (*Fr* a drwat)/ to or on the right [F]

ad vivum /ad 'veevəm/ to the life [L]

aequo animo /ˌiekwoh 'animoh/ calmly [L, lit., with even or equal mind]

à gauche /ah 'gohsh (*Fr* a goːʃ)/ to or on the left [F]

age quod agis /ˌagay kwod 'agis/ to the business in hand [L, lit., do what you are doing]

à huis clos /ah 'wee ˌkloh (*Fr* a ɥi klo)/ in private [F, lit., with closed doors]

aide-toi, le ciel t'aidera /ed 'twah lə ˌsyel tedə'rah (*Fr* ɛd twa lə sjɛl tɛdəra)/ heaven helps those who help themselves [F, lit., help yourself, heaven will help you]

à la belle étoile /ah lah ˌbel ay'twahl (*Fr* a la bɛːl etwal)/ under the stars; in the open air at night [F, lit., at or by the light of the beautiful star]

à la française /ah lah fron'sez (*Fr* a la frɑ̃sɛːz)/ in the French style [F]

à l'anglaise /ah long'glez (*Fr* a lɑ̃glɛːz)/ in the English style [F]

alea jacta est/jacta alea est /ˌalayə ˌyaktə est/ the die is cast [L, attributed to Julius Caesar on crossing the Rubicon]

alter idem /ˌaltə(r) 'idem, ˌalteə/ a second self [L]

amor patriae /ˌamaw 'patriˌie/ love of one's country [L]

amor vincit omnia /ˌamaw ˌvinkit 'omni·ə/ love conquers all things [L]

anno aetatis suae /ˌanoh ieˌtahtis 'sooh·ie/ in the (specified) year of his/her age [L]

anno mundi /ˌanoh 'moondi/ in the year of the world – used in reckoning dates from the supposed time of the creation of the world [L]

anno urbis conditae /ˌanoh ˌooəbis 'konditie/ in the year of the founding of the city (Rome, founded 753 BC) [L]

à peu près /ah ˌpuh 'pray (*Fr* a pø prɛ)/ nearly, approximately [F]

à pied /ˌah 'pyay (*Fr* a pje)/ on foot [F]

après moi le déluge /apray 'mwah lə dayˌloohzh (*Fr* aprɛ mwa lə delyːʒ)/ after me the deluge [F, alter. of *après nous le déluge* after us the deluge, attributed to Mme de Pompadour, but orig a French proverb]

arrivederci /ˌarivə'deəchi/ goodbye [It]

ars est celare artem /ˌahz est keˌlahray 'ahtem/ true art is to conceal art [L]

ars longa, vita brevis /ˌahz 'long·gə ˌveetə 'brevis/ art is long, life is short [L, Seneca, *De Brevitate Vitae*]

au contraire /ˌoh kon'treə (*Fr* o kɔ̃trɛːr)/ on the contrary [F]

audentes fortuna juvat /owˌdentayz ˌfawtoonə 'yoohvat, faw'toohnə/ fortune favours the bold [L, Vergil, *Aeneid*]

au pays des aveugles, les borgnes sont rois /oh ˌpay dayz a'vuhglə lay bawnyə sonh 'rwah (*Fr* o pei dez avøgl le bɔrɲ sɔ̃ rwa)/ in the country of the blind the one-eyed are kings [F]

aurea mediocritas /ˌowrayə medi'okritas/ the golden mean; the happy medium [L]

au reste /oh 'rest (*Fr* o rɛst)/ for the rest; besides [F]

auspicium melioris aevi /owˌspiki·əm meliˌawris 'ievi/ an omen of a better age – motto of the Order of St Michael and St George [L]

aussitôt dit, aussitôt fait /ositoh ˌdee ositoh 'fay (*Fr* osito di osito fɛ)/ no sooner said than done [F]

aut Caesar aut nihil/nullus /owt ˌkiesah owt 'nihil, 'seezə, 'nooləs/ all or nothing [L, lit., either Caesar or nothing/no one]

autres temps, autre moeurs /ohtrə ˌtom ohtrə 'muh (*Fr* oːtrə tɑ̃ oːtrə mœːr)/ other times other customs [F]

aux armes! /ohz 'ahm (*Fr* oz arm)/ to arms! [F]

aut vincere, aut mori /owt ˌvinkəray owt 'mori/ to conquer or die (L)

ave atque vale /ˌahvay atkway ˈvahlay/ hail and farewell [L]
à votre santé /ah ˌvotrə sonˈtay (*Fr* a voːtr sɑ̃te)/ to your health – used when drinking a toast [F]

B

bien entendu /ˌbyan ontonˈdooh (*Fr* bjɛ̃ ɑ̃tɑ̃dy)/ of course; naturally [F, lit., well understood]
bonjour /bonhˈzhooə (*Fr* bɔ̃ʒuːr)/ good morning; good afternoon [F]
bonsoir /bonhˈswah (*Fr* bɔ̃swaːr)/ good evening; good night [F]

C

cadit quaestio /ˌkadit ˈkwiestioh/ the argument collapses [L, lit., the question drops]
ça ne fait rien /ˌsa nə ˌfay reeˈanh (*Fr* sa nə fɛ rjɛ̃)/ it doesn't matter [F]
carpe diem /ˌkahpay ˈdee·em/ enjoy the present [L, Horace, *Odes*]
cave canem /ˌkavay ˈkanem/ beware of the dog [L]
cedant arma togae /kaydant ˌahmə ˈtohgie/ let military power give way to civil power [L, lit., let arms yield to the toga – Cicero, *De Officiis*]
cela va sans dire /səˌlah vah sonh ˈdiə (*Fr* səla va sɑ̃ diːr)/ that goes without saying [F]
ce n'est que le premier pas qui coûte /sə ˌnay kə lə ˌprəmyay ˌpah kee ˈkooht (*Fr* sə ne kə lə prəmje pa ki kut)/ it is only the first step that counts [F]
c'est-à-dire /ˌset ah ˈdiə (*Fr* sɛtadiːr)/ that is to say; namely [F]
c'est autre chose /set ˌohtrə ˈshohz (*Fr* sɛt oːtrə ʃoːz)/ that's another matter [F]
c'est magnifique, mais ce n'est pas la guerre /say ˌmanyiˈfeek may sə nay ˌpah lah ˈgeə (*Fr* sɛ maɲifik mɛ sə nɛ pa la gɛːr)/ it's magnificent, but it isn't war [F, attributed to a French general watching the charge of the Light Brigade at the battle of Balaclava]
c'est plus qu'un crime, c'est une faute /say ˌplooh kən ˈkreem ˌset oohn ˈfoht (*Fr* sɛ ply kœ krim sɛt yn foːt)/ it's worse than a crime, it's a blunder [F]
cetera desunt /ˌketərə ˈdaysoont/ the rest is missing [L]
chacun à son goût /shaˌkuhn ah sonh ˈgooh (*Fr* ʃakœ̃ a sɔ̃ gu)/ everyone to his/her own taste [F]
cherchez la femme /ˌsheəshay lɑh ˈfɑm *Fr* ʃɛrʃe la fam)/ there's a woman at the bottom of it [F, lit., look for the woman – attributed to Dumas *père*]
che sarà sarà /kay səˌrah səˈrah/ what will be, will be [It]
civis Romanus sum /ˌkivis rohˈmahnəs soom/ I am a Roman citizen [L, Cicero, *In Verrem*]
cogito, ergo sum /ˌkogitoh eəgoh ˈsoom, ˈkojitoh, uhgoh/ I think therefore I exist [L, Descartes, *Discours de la méthode*]
compte rendu /ˌkomt ronˈdooh (*Fr* kɔ̃t rɑ̃dy)/ a report, account (e g of proceedings in an investigation [F]
corruptio optimi pessima /koˌrooptioh ˌoptimi ˈpesimə/ the corruption of the best is the worst of all [L]
coup de foudre /ˌkooh də ˈfoohdrə (*Fr* ku də fudr)/ love at first sight [F, lit., thunderbolt]
coup de maître /ˌkooh də ˈmetrə (*Fr* ku də mɛːtr)/ a masterstroke [F]
coup d'essai /ˌkooh deˈsay (*Fr* ku desɛ)/ an experiment, trial [F]
coûte que coûte /ˌkooht kə ˈkooht (*Fr* kut kə kut)/ whatever the cost [F]
credo quia absurdum /ˌkraydoh ˌkwee·ə abˈsuhdəm/ I believe it because it is absurd [L]
custos morum /ˌkoostohs ˈmawrəm/ a guardian of morals; a censor [L]

D

d'accord /daˈkaw (*Fr* dakɔːr)/ in agreement [F]
de bonne grâce /də ˌbon ˈgrahs (*Fr* də bɔn grɑːs)/ with a good grace; willingly [F]
de gustibus non est disputandum /day ˌgoostibəs nohn est ˌdispoohˈtandəm/ there is no disputing about tastes [L]
Dei gratia /ˌdayee ˈgrahtiah/ by the grace of God [L]
de integro /ˌday inˈtegroh/ anew, afresh [L]
delenda est Carthago /dayˌlendə est kahˈtahgoh/ Carthage must be destroyed [L, attributed to Cato the Elder]
delineavit /dayˌliniˈahvit/ he/she drew this [L]
de mal en pis /də ˌmal om ˈpee (*Fr* də ˌmal ɑ̃ pi)/ from bad to worse [F]
de minimis non curat lex /day ˌminimees nohn ˌkooərat ˈleks/ the law does not concern itself with trifles [L, Bacon. *Letters*]
de mortuis nil nisi bonum /day ˌmawtooh·ees nil nisi ˈbonəm/ (speak) nothing but good of the dead [L]
Deo favente /ˌdayoh faˈventay/ with God's favour [L]
Deo gratias /ˌdayoh ˈgrahtiahs/ thanks be to God [L]
de profundis /day proˈfoondees/ out of the depths [L, *Psalm 130*]
Deus vult /ˌdayəs ˈvoolt/ God wills it – the rallying cry of the First Crusade [L]
dies faustus /ˌdee·ayz ˈfowstəs/ lucky day [L]
dies infaustus /ˌdee·ayz inˈfowstəs/ unlucky day [L]
dies irae /ˌdee·ayz ˈiərie/ the day of wrath – used of the Judgment Day [L]
Dieu avec nous /ˌdyuh avek ˈnooh (*Fr* djø avɛk nu)/ God (be) with us [F]
Dieu et mon droit /ˌdyuh ay monh ˈdrwah (*Fr* djø e mɔ̃ drwa)/ God and my right – the motto on the royal arms of Britain [F]
Dieu vous garde /ˌdyuh vooh ˈgahd (*Fr* djø vu gard)/ God keep you [F]
dis aliter visum /ˌdees ˌaliteə ˈveesəm/ the gods decreed otherwise [L, Vergil, *Aeneid*]
divide et impera /diˌveeday et ˈimperə/ divide and rule [L, attributed to Machiavelli]
Domine, dirige nos /ˌdominay diˈrigay ˌnohs/ Lord, direct us – motto of the City of London [L]
dominus vobiscum /ˌdominəs vohˈbiskəm/ the Lord be with you [L]
dulce et decorum est pro patria mori /ˌdoolkay et deˌkawrəm ˈest proh ˌpatriah ˈmori/ it is a sweet and glorious thing to die for one's country [L, Horace, *Odes*]
dum spiro, spero /doom ˌspiəroh ˈsperoh/ where there's life, there's hope [L, lit., while I breathe, I hope]

E

ecce signum /ˌekay 'signəm/ look at the proof [L, lit., behold the sign]
embarras de richesses /ˌombahˌrah də ree'shes (*Fr* ɑ̃bara də riʃɛs)/ confusing abundance [F, lit., embarrassment of riches]
embarras du choix /ˌombahˌrah dooh 'shwah (*Fr* ɑ̃bara dy ʃwa)/ too many things to choose from [F, lit., embarrassment of choice]
en ami /ˌon a'mee (*Fr* ɑ̃n ami)/ as a friend [F]
en effet /ˌon ay'fay (*Fr* ɑ̃n efɛ)/ in fact, indeed [F]
en famille /ˌon fa'mee (*Fr* ɑ̃ famiːj)/ among the family; at home; informally [F]
enfant gâté /ˌonfonh 'gahtay (*Fr* ɑ̃fɑ̃ gɑte)/ a spoilt child [F]
enfin /on'fanh (*Fr* ɑ̃fɛ̃)/ in conclusion; in a word; finally [F]
en pantoufles /ˌom pon'toohflə (*Fr* ɑ̃ pɑ̃tufl)/ free and easy; informal [F, lit., in slippers]
en plein air /om ˌplen 'eə (*Fr* ɑ̃ plɛn ɛːr)/ in the open air [F]
en plein jour /om ˌplanh 'zhooə (*Fr* ɑ̃ plɛ̃ ʒuːr)/ in broad daylight [F]
en règle /ˌonh 'reglə (*Fr* ɑ̃ rɛgl)/ in order [F]
épater les bourgeois /ˌaypaˌtay lay booə'zhwah (*Fr* epate le burʒwa)/ to shock the middle classes [F]
e pluribus unum /ay ˌplooəribəs 'oohnəm/ one out of the many – former motto of the USA [L]
esprit de l'escalier/d'escalier /eˌspree də le'skalyay, de'skalyay (*Fr* ɛspri də lɛskalje, dɛskalje)/ a witty retort that occurs to one too late [F, lit., staircase wit]
esse quam videri /ˌesay kwam vi'deəri/ to be rather than to seem [L]
est modus in rebus /est ˌmodəs in 'raybəs/ there is a proper measure in all things; always observe the golden mean [L, Horace, *Saturnalia*]
et in Arcadia ego /ˌet in ahˌkahdi·ə 'egoh/ I, too, lived in Arcadia [L]
et tu, Brute /et 'tooh ˌbroohtay/ you too, Brutus [L, attributed to Caesar on seeing his friend, Brutus, among his assassins]
ex animo /eks 'animoh/ from the heart; sincerely [L]
exceptis excipiendis /ekˌskeptees ekˌskipi'endees/ with the proper or necessary exceptions [L]
exceptio probat regulam de rebus non exceptis /ekˌskeptioh prohbat 'regoolam day ˌraybas nohn ek'skeptees/ the exception proves the rule [L]
ex libris /eks 'librees/ from the books of – used on bookplates [L]
ex nihilo nihil fit /eks ˌnihiloh ˌnihil 'fit/ nothing is created from nothing [L]

F

facile princeps /ˌfakilay 'prinkeps/ (one who is) easily first; the acknowledged leader [L]
femme de chambre /ˌfam də 'shombrə (*Fr* fam də ʃɑ̃br)/ a chambermaid, lady's maid [F]
festina lente /feˌsteenə 'lentay/ make haste slowly; more haste less speed [L]
fiat justitia, ruat caelum /ˌfee·at 'yoohstiti·ə ˌrooh·at 'kieləm/ let justice be done, though the heavens should fall [L]
fiat lux /ˌfee·at 'looks/ let there be light [L]
Fidei Defensor /fiˌday·i di'fensaw/ Defender of the Faith – used as a title of the sovereigns of Britain [L]
fidus Achates /ˌfidəs ə'kahtayz, ə'kahteez/ a faithful friend [L, lit., faithful Achates – Vergil, *Aeneid*]
fille de joie /ˌfee də zhwah (*Fr* fiːj də ʒwa)/ a prostitute [F, lit., girl of joy]
fils /fees (*Fr* fis)/ son, junior – used after French surnames to distinguish a son from his father [F]
fluctuat nec mergitur /ˌflooktooat nek 'meəgitooə/ it is tossed by the waves but does not sink – the motto of Paris [L]
fortes fortuna adjuvat /ˌfawtayz fawˌtoohnə ad'yoohvat/ fortune favours the brave [L, Terence, *Phormio*]
fuit Ilium /ˌfooh·it 'ili·əm/ Troy is no more [L, Vergil, *Aeneid*]
furor loquendi /ˌfooraw lo'kwendi/ a mania for speaking [L]
furor poeticus /ˌfooraw poh'etikəs/ a poetic frenzy [L]
furor scribendi /ˌfooraw skri'bendi/ a mania for writing [L]

G

gaudeamus igitur /ˌgowdayˌahmus 'igitooə/ let us then rejoice [L]
gnothi seauton /ˌgnohthi say'owton/ know thyself [Gk]
grand monde /ˌgrom 'mond (*Fr* grɑ̃ mɔ̃ːd)/ high society [F]
guerre à outrance /ˌgeər ah ooh'tronhs (*Fr* gɛːr a utrɑ̃ːs)/ war to the bitter end [F]

H

hic et ubique /ˌhik et 'oobikway/ here and everywhere [L]
hic jacet /ˌhik 'yaket/ here lies – used on tombstones [L]
hoc age /ˌhok 'agay/ apply yourself to the task in hand [L, lit., do this]
homme d'affaires /ˌom da'feə (*Fr* ɔm dafɛːr)/ a businessman [F]
homo sum: humani nil a me alienum puto /ˌhomoh 'soom hoohˌmahni nil ah may ˌali'aynəm ˌpoohtoh/ I am a man; I regard nothing that concerns man as foreign to my interests [L, Terence, *Heauton Timorumenos*]
honi soit qui mal y pense /ˌoni swah kee ˌmal ee 'ponhs (*Fr* ɔni swa ki mal i pɑ̃s)/ shame on the one who thinks ill of it – motto of the Order of the Garter [F]
humanum est errare/errare humanum est /hoohˌmanhnəm est e'rahray/ to err is human [L]

I

ich dien /ˌikh 'deen (*Ger* iç diːn)/ I serve – motto of the Prince of Wales [G]
ici on parle français /eeˌsee om ˌpahl 'fronsay (*Fr* isi ɔ̃ parl frɑ̃sɛ)/ French is spoken here [F]
id est /ˌid 'est/ that is [L]
ignorantia juris neminem excusat /ignawˌranti·ə ˌyooəris ˌneminem eks'koohzat/ ignorance of the law excuses no one [L]

il faut cultiver notre jardin /eel ˌfoh ˌkooltivay notrə zhah'danh (*Fr* il foː kultive nɔtr ʒardɛ̃)/ we must mind our own affairs [F, lit., we must tend our garden – Voltaire, *Candide*]
in aeternum /ˌin ie'tuhnəm/ forever [L]
in futuro /in fooh'tooəroh/ in the future [L]
in limine /in 'leeminay/ on the threshold; at the beginning [L]
in saecula saeculorum /in ˌsiekoolə ˌsiekoo-'lawrəm/ for ever and ever [L]
in statu pupillari /in ˌstatooh ˌpoohpi'lahri/ in a state of wardship; as a pupil or ward [L]
inter nos /ˌinte 'nohs/ between ourselves [L]
intra muros /ˌintrə 'mooərohs/ within the walls [L]
invenit /in'venit/ he/she devised this [L]
in vino veritas /in ˌveenoh 'veritas/ there is truth in wine [L]

J

j'adoube /zha'doohb (*Fr* ʒadub)/ I adjust – used in chess when touching a piece without intending to move it [F]
jeu de mots /ˌzhuh də 'moh (*Fr* ʒø də mo)/ a pun [F, lit., game of words]
jus divinum /ˌyoos di'veenəm/ divine law [L]
j'y suis, j'y reste /zhee ˌswee zhee 'rest (*Fr* ʒi sɥi ʒi rɛst)/ here I am, here I stay [F, attributed to Marshal MacMahon during the attack on the Malakoff in the Crimea]

K

ktema es aei /kˌtaymah es ah'ay/ possession forever – applied to a work of art or literature of enduring significance [Gk]

L

laborare est orare /labawˌrahray est o'rahray/ to work is to pray [L]
lacrimae rerum /ˌlakrimie 'reərəm/ **1** pity for misfortune **2** the tragedy of life [L, lit., (1) tears for things (2) tears in things, Vergil, *Aeneid*]
laisser-aller/laissez aller /ˌlesay 'alay (*Fr* lese ale)/ a lack of restraint; letting go [F]
lapsus calami /ˌlapsəs 'kaləmi/ a slip of the pen [L]
lasciate ogni speranza, voi ch'entrate /lashahte 'onyee speˌranzə voy kenˌtrate/ abandon all hope, you who enter [It, Dante, *Inferno*]
le cœur a ses raisons que la raison ne connaît point /lə ˌkuhr ah say re'zonh kə lah reˌzonh nə ˌkonay 'pwanh (*Fr* lə kœːr a se rɛsɔ̃ kə la rɛzɔ̃ nə kɔnɛpwɛ̃)/ the heart has reasons of its own of which reason knows nothing [F, Pascal, *Pensées*]
le style, c'est l'homme /lə ˌsteel say 'lom (*Fr* lə stil se lɔm)/ the style is the man himself [F, Buffon]
le roi est mort, vive le roi /lə ˌrwah ay 'maw ˌveev lə 'rwah (*Fr* lə rwa e mɔːr viːv lə rwa)/ the king is dead, long live the king [F]
l'état, c'est moi /layˌtah say 'mwah (*Fr* leta se mwa)/ I am the state [F, attributed to Louis XIV]
loco citato /ˌlokoh ki'tahtoh/ in the passage already quoted [L]
lusu naturae /ˌloohsəs na'tooərie/ a freak [L, lit., a sport of nature]

M

ma foi! /ˌmah 'fwah (*Fr* ma fwa)/ indeed! [F, lit., my faith]
man spricht Deutsch /man ˌshprikht 'doych (*Ger* man ʃpriçt dɔɪtʃ)/ German spoken [G]
mariage de convenance /marˌiahzh də ˌkonvə'nonhs (*Fr* marjaːʒ də kɔ̃vənɑ̃ːs)/ a marriage of convenience [F]
mauvais quart d'heure /ˌmohvay ˌkah 'duh (*Fr* movɛ kaːr dœːr)/ a brief but unpleasant experience [F, lit., bad quarter of an hour]
meden agan /ˌmayden 'agan/ nothing in excess; moderation in all things [Gk]
me judice /ˌmay 'yoohdikay/ in my opinion [L, lit., I being judge]
mens sana in corpore sano /menz ˌsahnə in ˌkawpəray 'sahnoh/ a sound mind in a sound body [L, Juvenal, *Satires*]
meum et tuum /ˌmayəm et 'tooh·əm/ mine and yours – used to express rights of private property [L]
mirabile dictu /miˌrahbilay 'diktooh/ astonishing to relate [L]
mirabile visu /miˌrahbilay 'veesooh/ wonderful to behold [L]
morituri te salutamus /ˌmoritooəri tay ˌsalooh'tahməs/ we, who are about to die, salute you – a greeting spoken by gladiators to their Emperor before a combat [L]
multum in parvo /ˌmooltəm in 'pahvoh/ a great deal in a small space [L, lit., much in little]
mutatis mutandis /moohˌtahtees mooh'tandees/ when all the necessary changes have been made [L]

N

natura non facit saltum /naˌtooərə ˌnohn fakit 'saltəm/ nature does not make a leap [L]
nemo me impune lacessit /ˌnaymoh may imˌpoohnay la'kesit/ no one attacks me with impunity – motto of Scotland and of the Order of the Thistle [L]
ne quid nimis /ˌnay kwid 'nimis/ nothing in excess [L]
n'est-ce pas? /ˌnes 'pah (*Fr* nɛs pa)/ isn't that so? [F]
nicht wahr? /ˌnikht 'vah (*Ger* niçt vaːr)/ isn't that so? [G]
nil desperandum /ˌnil despə'randəm/ never give up hope [L]
nolens volens /ˌnolenz 'volenz/ willy-nilly [L]
nosce te ipsum /ˌnoskay tay 'ipsəm/ know thyself – compare GNOTHI SEAUTON [L]
nostalgie de la boue /ˌnostalˌzhee də lah 'booh (*Fr* nɔstalʒi də la bu)/ hankering for a life of physical degradation and squalor [F, lit., nostalgia for the mud]
nuit blanche /ˌnweeh 'blonhsh (*Fr* nɥi blɑ̃ʃ)/ a sleepless night [F, lit., white night]

O

omne ignotum pro magnifico /ˌomnay igˌnohtəm proh mag'nifikoh/ the unknown tends to be exaggerated in importance or difficulty [L, lit., everything unknown (is taken) as grand – Tacitus, *Agricola*]

omnia mutantur, nos et mutamur in illis /ˌomni·ə mooh'tantooə nohs et mooh'tahmooə(r) in ˌilees/ all things are changing, and we are changing with them [L]
onus probandi /ˌo(h)nəs pro'bandi/ the burden of proof [L]
opere citato /ˌopəray ki'tahtoh/ in the work already quoted [L]
ora pro nobis /ˌawrə proh 'nohbis/ pray for us [L]
o tempora! o mores! /oh ˌtempərə oh 'mawrayz/ oh the times! oh the customs! [L, Cicero, *In Catilinam*]
où sont les neiges d'antan? /ˌooh son lay ˌnezh don'tonh (*Fr* u sɔ̃ le nɛːʒ dɑ̃tɑ̃)/ where are the snows of yesteryear? [F, Villon]

P

panem et circenses /ˌpa(h)nem et kiə'kensayz/ bread and circuses [L, Juvenal, *Satires*]
par avion /ˌpahr a'vyonh (*Fr* par avjɔ̃)/ by aeroplane – used on airmail [F]
par exemple /ˌpahr eg'zompl (*Fr* par ɛgzɑ̃ːpl)/ for example [F]
parturiunt montes, nascetur ridiculus mus /pahˌtooəri·ənt 'montayz naˌskaytooə ri'dikooləs moos/ the mountains are in labour and a ridiculous mouse will be brought forth [L, Horace, *Ars Poetica*]
pater patriae /ˌpateə 'patri·ie/ a father of his country [L]
pax vobiscum /ˌpaks voh'biskəm/ peace be with you [L]
peccavi /pe'kahvi/ I have sinned [L]
peine forte et dure /pen ˌfawt ay 'dooə (*Fr* pɛn fɔrt e dyːr)/ torture [F, lit., severe and hard punishment]
per ardua ad astra /peə(r) ˌahdwə ad 'astrə/ through danger to the stars – motto of the Royal Air Force [L]
père /peə (*Fr* pɛːr)/ father, senior – used after French surnames to distinguish a father from his son [F]
perfide Albion /peəˌfeed al'byonh (*Fr* pɛrfid albjɔ̃)/ perfidious Albion; England [F]
pinxit /'pingksit/ he/she painted this [L]
pleno jure /ˌplaynoh 'yooəray/ with full right or authority [L]
plus ça change, plus c'est la même chose /ˌploohs sah 'shonzh ˌploohs say lah ˌmem 'shohz (*Fr* plys sa ʃɑ̃ʒ plys se la mɛm ʃoz)/ the essential nature of a thing does not change [F, lit., the more something changes, the more it is the same thing]
plus royalist que le roi /ˌplooh royahˌleest kə lə 'rwah (*Fr* ply rwajalist kə lə rwa)/ more royalist than the king [F]
poeta nascitur, non fit /pohˌaytə 'naskitooə ˌnohn 'fit/ a poet is born, not made [L]
post obitum /ˌpohst 'obitəm/ after death [L]
pour encourager les autres /pooər ˌongkooəruhˌzhay layz 'ohtrə (*Fr* puːr ɑ̃kuraʒe lez oːtrə)/ in order to encourage the others [F, Voltaire, *Candide*]
pro aris et focis /proh ˌahrees et 'fokees/ for faith and home [L, lit., for altars and firesides]
pro bono publico /proh ˌbo(h)noh 'pooblikoh/ for the public good [L]
pro patria /proh 'patriah/ for one's country [L]

Q

quand même /kom 'mem (*Fr* kɑ̃ mɛːm)/ all the same [F]
quantum sufficit /ˌkwantəm 'soofikit/ a sufficient quantity – formerly used in medical prescriptions [L]
quis custodiet ipsos custodes? /kwis kooˌstodi·et ˌipsos 'koostodayz/ who will guard the guards themselves? [L, Juvenal, *Satires*]
qui s'excuse s'accuse /kee sekˌskoohz sa'koohz (*Fr* ki sɛkskyz sakyz)/ whoever excuses him-/herself accuses him-/herself [F]
qui va là? /ˌkee vah 'lah (*Fr* ki va la)/ who goes there? [F]
quo vadis? /ˌkwoh 'vahdis/ where are you going? [L]
quoad hoc /ˌkwoh·ad 'hok/ to this extent [L, lit., as far as this]
quod erat demonstrandum /ˌkwod eˌrat demən'strandəm/ which was to be proved [L]
quod erat faciendum /ˌkwod eˌrat faki'endəm/ which was to be done [L]
quod vide /ˌkwod 'veeday/ which see – used to draw a reader's attention to a cross-reference [L]
quos deus vult perdere prius dementat /kwohs ˌdayəs voolt ˌpeədəray ˌpree·əs day'mentat/ those whom a god wishes to destroy he first drives insane [L]
quot homines, tot sententiae /kwot ˌhominayz tot sen'tenti·ie/ there are as many opinions as there are men [L, Terence, *Phormio*]

R

raison d'état /ˌrezonh day'tah (*Fr* rɛzɔ̃ deta)/ for the good of the country as a whole [F, lit., reason of state]
répondez s'il vous plaît /rayˌponday sil vooh 'play (*Fr* repɔ̃de sil vu plɛ)/ please reply [F]
requiescat in pace /rekwiˌeskat in 'pahkay/ (may he/she) rest in peace – used on tombstones [L]
respice finem /reˌspikay 'feenem/ consider the outcome [L, lit., look to the end]
resurgam /re'sooəgam/ I shall rise again [L]
revenons à nos moutons /rəvəˌnonh ah noh mooh'tonh (*Fr* rəvnɔ̃ a no mutɔ̃)/ let's get back to the subject [F, lit., let us return to our sheep]
rus in urbe /ˌroos in ooəbay/ the country in the city [L, Martial, *Epigrammata*]

S

sal Atticum /ˌsal 'atikəm/ Attic salt; wit [L]
salus populi suprema lex esto /ˌsaləs 'popooli sooˌpraymə 'leks ˌestoh/ let the welfare of the people be the supreme law [L, Cicero, *De Legibus*]
san gêne /sonh 'zhen (*Fr* sɑ̃ ʒɛn)/ without embarrassment or constraint [F]
sans peur et sans reproche /sonh 'puhr ay ˌsonh rə'prosh (*Fr* sɑ̃ pœːr e sɑ̃ rəprɔʃ)/ without fear and without reproach [F]
sans souci /ˌsonh sooh'see (*Fr* sɑ̃ susi)/ carefree [F, lit., without worry]
sauve qui peut /ˌsohv kee 'puh (*Fr* sov ki pø)/ every man for himself [F, lit., let whoever can save him-/herself]
scripsit /'skripsit/ he/she wrote his [L]

sculpsit /ˈskoolpsit/ he/she carved this [L]

se defendendo /ˌsay dayfenˈdendoh/ in self-defence [L]

semper eadem /ˌsempeə(r) ayˈahdem/ always the same (fem) – motto of Queen Elizabeth I [L]

semper fidelis /ˌsempeə fiˈdaylis/ always faithful [L]

semper idem /ˌsempeə(r) ˈidem/ always the same (masc) [L]

semper paratus /ˌsempeə pəˈrahtəs/ always prepared [L]

se habla español /se ˌabla espaˈnyol/ Spanish spoken [Sp]

Senatus Populusque Romanus /seˌnahtəs popooˌlooskway rohˈmahnəs/ the senate and people of Rome [L]

se non è vero è ben trovato /say ˌnon ay ˈveroh ay ben troˈvahtoh/ even if it is not true, it is well conceived [It]

sic transit gloria mundi /sik ˌtransit ˌglawri·ə ˈmoondi/ thus earthly glory passes away [L, Thomas à Kempis, *The Imitation of Christ*]

si jeunesse savait, si vieillesse pouvait! /see zhuhˌnes ˈsavay see vyayˌes ˈpoohvay (*Fr* si ʒønɛs savɛ si vjɛjɛs puvɛ)/ if youth only knew, if old age only could! [F]

s'il vous plaît /ˌsil vooh ˈplay (*Fr* sil vu plɛ)/ please [F]

si monumentum requiris, circumspice /see monooˌmentəm reˈkwiəris ˌkiəkəmˈspikay/ if you seek his monument, look around you – epitaph of Sir Christopher Wren in St Paul's Cathedral, of which he was architect [L]

si parla italiano /see ˌpahlah itaˈlyahnoh/ Italian spoken [It]

siste viator /ˌsistay viˈahtaw/ stop, traveller – used on Roman roadside tombs [L]

si vis pacem, para bellum /see vis ˌpahkem parə ˈbeləm/ if you want peace, prepare for war [L]

status in quo /ˌsta(h)təs in ˈkwoh/ the existing state of affairs [L, lit., the state in which]

sub verbo/sub voce /soob ˈveəboh, ˈvokay/ – used to introduce a cross-reference in a dictionary or index [L, lit., under the word]

suo jure /ˌsooh·oh ˈyooəray/ in his/her own right [L]

suo loco /ˌsooh·oh ˈlokoh/ in its proper place [L]

suum cuique /ˌsooh·əm ˈkooh·ikway/ to each his/her own [L]

T

tant mieux! /ˌtom ˈmyuh (*Fr* tɑ̃ mjœ)/ so much the better! [F]

tant pis! /ˌtom ˈpee (*Fr* tɑ̃ pi)/ too bad! [F, lit., so much the worse]

tempora mutantur, nos et mutamur in illis /ˌtempawrə moohˈtantooə ˌnohs et moohˈtahmooə in ˈilees/ the times are changing, and we are changing with them [L]

tempus edax rerum /ˌtempəs ˌedaks ˈreərəm/ time, that devours all things [L, Ovid, *Metamorphoses*]

tempus fugit /ˌtempəs ˈfoo(h)git/ time flies [L]

timeo Danaos, et dona ferentes /ˌtimayoh ˌdanah·ohs et ˌdonə feˈrentayz/ I fear the Greeks, even when they bring gifts [L, Vergil, *Aeneid*]

tout à fait /ˌtooht ah ˈfay (*Fr* tut a fɛ)/ altogether, absolutely [F]

tout comprendre c'est tout pardonner /ˌtooh komˈprondrə say ˌtooh pahdoˈnay (*Fr* tu kɔ̃prɑ̃dr se tu pardɔne)/ to understand all is to forgive all [F]

tout court /ˌtooh ˈkooə (*Fr* tu kur)/ simply [F]

tout de même /ˌtooh də ˈmem (*Fr* tu də mɛm)/ all the same; nevertheless [F]

tout de suite /ˌtooht ˈsweet (*Fr* tu də sɥit)/ at once; immediately [F]

tout ensemble /ˌtooht onˈsombl (*Fr* tut ɑ̃sɑ̃bl)/ all together [F]

tout est perdu fors l'honneur /ˌtooht ay peəˌdooh faw loˈnuh (*Fr* tut e pɛrdy fɔr lɔnœːr)/ all is lost save honour [F, attributed to François I after the battle of Pavia]

tout le monde /ˌtoohl ˈmond (*Fr* tu lə mɔ̃d)/ everybody (F, lit., all the world]

trahison des clercs /ˌtrah·eeˈzonh day ˈkleə (*Fr* traizɔ̃ de klɛːr)/ betrayal of standards by the intellectuals [F]

tranche de vie /ˌtronhsh də ˈvee (*Fr* trɑ̃ːʃ də vi)/ a slice of life [F]

tria juncta in uno /ˌtree·ə ˌyoongktə in ˈoohnoh/ three joined in one – motto of the Order of the Bath [L]

U

Übermensch /ˈoohbəmensh (*Ger* yːbərmɛnʃ)/ superman [G]

und so weiter /ˌoont zoh ˈvietə (*Ger* unt zoː vaɪtər)/ and so on; et cetera [G]

uno animo /ˌoohnoh ˈanimoh/ unanimously [L, lit., with one mind]

urbi et orbi /ˌooəbi et ˈawbi/ to the city (Rome) and to the world [L]

ut infra /oot ˈinfrə/ as below [L]

ut supra /oot ˈsoohprə/ as above [L]

V

vade retro me, Satana /ˌvahday ˈretroh may saˈtahnə/ get thee behind me, Satan [L, *Vulgate, Mt 16:23, Mk 8:33, Luke 4:8*]

vario lectio /ˌvahri·ə ˈlektioh/ a variant reading [L]

vedi Napoli e poi mori /vaydi ˈnapoli ay ˌpoy ˈmori/ see Naples and die [It]

veni, vidi, vici /ˌvayni ˌvidi ˌveeki/ I came, I saw, I conquered [L, attributed to Julius Caesar after his victory over Pharnaces]

verbatim ac litteratim /veəˌbahtim ak liteˈrahtim/ word for word and letter for letter [L]

verbum sapienti sat est /ˌveəbəm sapiˌenti ˈsat est/ a word to the wise is enough [L]

vive le roi! /ˌveev lə ˈrwah (*Fr* viv lə rwa)/ long live the king! [F]

vogue la galère /ˌvohg lah gaˈleə (*Fr* vɔg la galɛːr)/ keep going, whatever happens [F, lit., let the galley keep rowing]

voilà tout /ˌvwahlah ˈtooh (*Fr* vwala tu)/ that's all [F]

vox populi, vox Dei /voks ˌpopooli voks ˌdayee/ the voice of the people is the voice of God [L, Alcuin, *Epistles*]

Abbreviations

A

a 1 acceleration 2 acre 3 answer 4 are – a metric unit of area 5 area 6 atto-
A 1 ampere 2 Associate
AA 1 Alcoholics Anonymous 2 antiaircraft 3 Automobile Association
AAA 1 Amateur Athletic Association 2 American Automobile Association
AAM air-to-air missile
A and M ancient and modern – used of hymns
AB 1 able seaman; able-bodied seaman 2 *NAm* bachelor of arts [NL *artium baccalaureus*]
ABA Amateur Boxing Association
ABC 1 American Broadcasting Company 2 Australian Broadcasting Commission
abl ablative
ABM antiballistic missile
Abp archbishop
abr abridged; abridgment
ABRO Animal Breeding Research Organization
abs absolute
ABS Association of Broadcasting Staff
ABTA /'abtə, ˌay bee tee 'ay/ Association of British Travel Agents
AC 1 alternating current 2 appellation contrôlée 3 athletic club
a/c account
ACA Associate of the Institute of Chartered Accountants
acad academic; academy
ACAS /'aykas, ˌay see ˌay 'es/ Advisory Conciliation and Arbitration Service
acc 1 according to 2 account 3 accusative
ACCA Association of Certified and Corporate Accountants
acct account; accountant
ACCT Association of Cinematograph and Television Technicians
accus accusative
ACGB Arts Council of Great Britain
ACIS Associate of the Chartered Institute of Secretaries
ack acknowledge; acknowledgment
ACP African, Caribbean, and Pacific
acpt acceptance
act active
ACT Australian Capital Territory
actg acting
ACTU Australian Council of Trade Unions
ACV air-cushion vehicle
ACW aircraftwoman
AD anno domini
ADAS /'aydas/ Agricultural Development and Advisory Service
ADC 1 aide-de-camp 2 amateur dramatic club
addn addition
ADH antidiuretic hormone
ad inf ad infinitum
adj 1 adjective 2 adjustment – used in banking 3 adjutant
Adm admiral
adv 1 adverb; adverbial 2 against [L *adversus*]
ad val ad valorem
advt advertisement
AEA Atomic Energy Authority
AEB Associated Examining Board
AEC Atomic Energy Commission – a US organization
AEI Associated Electrical Industries
AERE Atomic Energy Research Establishment
aet, aetat of the specified age; aged [L *aetatis*]
AEU Amalgamated Engineering Union – now AUEW
AEW airborne early warning
AF 1 Anglo-French 2 audio frequency
AFA Amateur Football Association
AFAM Ancient Free and Accepted Masons
AFC 1 Air Force Cross 2 Association Football Club 3 automatic frequency control
AFL-CIO American Federation of Labor and Congress of Industrial Organizations
AFM Air Force Medal
Afr Africa; African
AFV armoured fighting vehicle
AG 1 adjutant general 2 attorney general 3 joint-stock company [G *Aktiengesellschaft*]
AGC automatic gain control
agcy agency
AGM *chiefly Br* annual general meeting
AGR advanced gas-cooled reactor
agric agricultural; agriculture
agt agent
AH anno hegirae
AHA Area Health Authority
AI artificial insemination
AIA Associate of the Institute of Actuaries
AIB Associate of the Institute of Bankers
AID 1 Agency for International Development – a US agency 2 artificial insemination by donor
AIH artificial insemination by husband
AJC Australian Jockey Club
AK Alaska
AKA also known as
Ala Alabama
ALA Associate of the Library Association
ald alderman
alg algebra
ALS autograph letter signed
alt 1 alternate 2 altitude 3 alto
Alta Alberta
am ante meridiem
Am 1 America; American 2 Amos – used for the book of the Bible
AM 1 Albert Medal 2 amplitude modulation 3 associate member 4 *NAm* master of arts [NL *artium magister*]
AMA 1 American Medical Association 2 Australian Medical Association
AMDEA Association of Manufacturers of Domestic Electrical Appliances

AMDG to the greater glory of God [L *ad majorem Dei gloriam*]
amdt amendment
Amer America; American
amt amount
AMU atomic mass unit
an in the year [L *anno*]
anal 1 analogous; analogy 2 analysis; analytic
anat anatomical; anatomy
Angl Anglican
ann 1 annals 2 annual 3 annuity
anon anonymous
ant antonym
Ant Antrim
anthrop anthropological; anthropology
A/O account of
aob any other business
AOC Air Officer Commanding
AP Associated Press
APB *chiefly NAm* all points bulletin
APEX /'aypeks, ˌay pee ee 'eks/ Association of Professional, Executive, Clerical, and Computer Staff
APO army post office
Apoc 1 Apocalypse 2 Apocrypha; apocryphal
Apocr Apocrypha
app 1 apparent; apparently 2 appendix 3 appointed
appl applied
appro /'aproh/ approval
approx /ə'proks/ approximate; approximately
Apr April
apt apartment
APT Advanced Passenger Train
ar 1 arrival; arrive 2 in the year of the reign [L *anno regni*]
AR 1 annual return 2 Arkansas 3 autonomous republic
ARA Associate of the Royal Academy
ARAM Associate of the Royal Academy of Music
ARC Agricultural Research Council
ARCA Associate of the Royal College of Art
arch 1 archaic 2 architect; architectural; architecture
Arch archbishop
archaeol archaeological; archaeology
ARCM Associate of the Royal College of Music
ARCS Associate of the Royal College of Science
ARIBA Associate of the Royal Institute of British Architects
arith arithmetic; arithmetical
Ariz Arizona
Ark Arkansas
Arm Armagh
ARP air-raid precautions
arr 1 arranged by – used in music 2 arrival; arrives
art 1 article 2 artificial 3 artillery
arty artillery
AS 1 airspeed 2 Anglo-Saxon 3 antisubmarine
ASA 1 Advertising Standards Authority 2 American Standards Association 3 Amateur Swimming Association
asap as soon as possible
ASE Amalgamated Society of Engineers
ASEAN /'asian/ Association of South-East Asian Nations
ASH /ash/ Action on Smoking and Health
ASLEF /'azlef/ Associated Society of Locomotive Engineers and Firemen
ASSET /'aset/ Association of Supervisory Staffs, Executives and Technicians
assoc association
ASSR Autonomous Soviet Socialist Republic
asst assistant
asstd assorted
ASTMS /'astemz, ˌay es ˌtee em 'es/ Association of Scientific, Technical, and Managerial Staffs
astr astronomer; astronomy
astrol astrologer; astrology
astron astronomer; astronomy
at atomic
ATC 1 air traffic control 2 Air Training Corps
atm atmosphere; atmospheric
at no atomic number
att attorney
attn for the attention of
attrib /ə'trib/ attributive; attributively
atty attorney
ATV Associated Television
at wt atomic weight
AU 1 angstrom unit 2 astronomical unit
AUEW Amalgamated Union of Engineering Workers
aug augmentative – used in grammar
Aug August
AUT Association of University Teachers
auth authorized
auto /'awtoh/ automatic
aux auxiliary
av 1 average 2 avoirdupois
Av avenue
AV 1 ad valorem 2 audiovisual 3 Authorized Version (of the Bible)
avdp avoirdupois
Ave avenue
AVM Air Vice Marshal
avn aviation
az azimuth

B

b 1 born 2 bowled by – used in cricket 3 breadth 4 bye – used in cricket
B 1 bachelor 2 bel 3 bishop – used in chess 4 black – used esp on lead pencils 5 British
BA 1 Bachelor of Arts 2 British Academy 3 British Airways 4 British Association
BAA British Airports Authority
BAC /ˌbee ay 'see; *also* bak/ 1 British Agricultural Council 2 British Aircraft Corporation
BAFTA /'baftə/ British Academy of Film and Television Arts
bal balance – used in book-keeping
BALPA /'balpə/ British Airline Pilots' Association
b and b, *often cap B & B, Br* bed and breakfast
b and w black and white
BAOR British Army of the Rhine
Bap Baptist
bap baptize; baptized
BAPS /ˌbee ay pee 'es, baps/ British Association of Plastic Surgeons
Bapt Baptist
bar barometer; barometric
Bar 1 barrister 2 Baruch – used for the book of the Apocrypha
BArch Bachelor of Architecture
Bart baronet
BB 1 Boys' Brigade 2 double black – used on lead pencils
BBBC British Boxing Board of Control
BBC /bee bee 'see; *humor* beeb/ British Broadcasting Corporation
BBFC British Board of Film Censors
BC 1 before Christ 2 British Columbia 3 British Council
BCD binary-coded decimal
BCh Bachelor of Surgery [ML *baccalaureus chirurgiae*]
BCom Bachelor of Commerce
BCS British Computer Society
bd 1 bond 2 bound
BD 1 Bachelor of Divinity 2 bank draft 3 barrels per day 4 brought down
BDA British Dental Association
bdc bottom dead centre
BDS Bachelor of Dental Surgery

BE bill of exchange
BEA British European Airways – now BA
BEd Bachelor of Education
Beds Bedfordshire
BEF British Expeditionary Force
BEM British Empire Medal
BEng Bachelor of Engineering
Berks /bahks, buhks/ Berkshire
bet between
BeV billion electron volts
bf bloody fool
b/f brought forward
BFPO British Forces Post Office
BG brigadier general
BGC British Gas Council
BH Brinell hardness
B'ham /*often* brum/ Birmingham
bhp brake horsepower
BHS British Home Stores
Bib Bible; biblical
bibliog bibliographical; bibliography
BIM British Institute of Management
biog biographical; biography
biol biological; biology
BIR Board of Inland Revenue
BIS Bank for International Settlements
bk book
bkg banking
BL **1** Bachelor of Law **2** bill of lading **3** British Legion **4** British Leyland **5** British Library
bldg building
BLitt Bachelor of Letters [ML *baccalaureus litterarum*]
blvd boulevard
BM **1** Bachelor of Medicine **2** bench mark **3** British Medal **4** British Museum
BMA British Medical Association
BMC British Medical Council
BMJ British Medical Journal
BMR basal metabolic rate
BMTA British Motor Trade Association
BMus Bachelor of Music
bn billion
BNOC British National Oil Corporation
BO body odour – euph
BOAC British Overseas Airways Corporation – now BA
BOC British Oxygen Company
BOD biochemical oxygen demand; biological oxygen demand
bor borough
BOSS /bos/ Bureau of State Security – a SAfr organization
bot **1** botanical; botany; botanist **2** bottle
BOT Board of Trade
BOTB British Overseas Trade Board
Bp bishop
BP **1** boiling point **2** British Petroleum **3** British Pharmacopoeia
B/P bill payable
BPAS British Pregnancy Advisory Service
BPC British Pharmaceutical Codex
BPD barrels per day
BPharm Bachelor of Pharmacy
BPhil /ˌbee 'fil/ Bachelor of Philosophy
bpi bits per inch; bytes per inch
bps bits per second
Bq becquerel
br branch
Br **1** British **2** brother
BR British Rail
B/R bill receivable
BRCS British Red Cross Society
Brig brigade; brigadier
Brig-Gen brigadier-general
Brit /brit/ Britain; British
bro /broh/ brother
bros, Bros brothers
BRS British Road Services
BS **1** Bachelor of Surgery **2** balance sheet **3** bill of sale **4** British Standard **5** *NAm* Bachelor of Science
BSA Building Societies Association
BSc /ˌbee es 'see/ Bachelor of Science
BSC **1** British Steel Corporation **2** British Sugar Corporation
BSI **1** British Standards Institution **2** Building Societies Institute
BSJA British Show Jumping Association
BSocSc, BSSc Bachelor of Social Science
BST British Standard Time; British Summer Time
Bt Baronet
BTA British Tourist Authority
BTh Bachelor of Theology
Btu British thermal unit
Bucks /buks/ Buckinghamshire
bull bulletin
BUPA /'byoohpə, 'boohpə/ British United Provident Association
bus business
BV Blessed Virgin
BVM Blessed Virgin Mary
BVMS, BVM & S Bachelor of Veterinary Medicine and Surgery
bvt brevet
BW bacteriological warfare; biological warfare
BYOB bring your own booze; bring your own bottle

C

c **1** canine – used in dentistry **2** carat **3** caught by – used in cricket **4** centi- **5** century **6** chapter **7** circa **8** cloudy **9** cold **10** college **11** colt **12** copyright **13** cubic
C **1** calorie **2** castle – used in chess **3** Catholic **4** Celsius **5** centigrade **6** *Br* Conservative **7** corps **8** coulomb
ca circa
CA **1** California **2** chartered accountant **3** chief accountant **4** Consumers' Association **5** current account
CAA Civil Aviation Authority
CAB Citizens' Advice Bureau
cal **1** calibre **2** (small) calorie
Cal **1** California **2** (large) calorie
Calif California
Cambs Cambridgeshire
CAMRA /'kamrə/ Campaign for Real Ale
can canto
Can Canada; Canadian
c and b caught and bowled by – used in cricket
C and G City and Guilds
C and W country and western
Cant Canticles – used for the book of the Bible
Cantab /'kantab/ of Cambridge – used with academic awards <MA ~ > [L *Cantabrigiensis*]
Cantuar of Canterbury – used chiefly in the signature of the Archbishop of Canterbury [L *Cantuariensis*]
cap **1** capital **2** capitalize; capitalized
CAP Common Agricultural Policy
caps /(1) *sometimes* kaps/ **1** capital letters **2** capsule
Capt captain
Car Carlow
Card cardinal
CARD /kahd, ˌsee ay ah 'dee/ Campaign Against Racial Discrimination
CAT **1** College of Advanced Technology **2** computerized axial tomography
cath **1** cathedral **2** catholic
cav cavalry
CB **1** Citizens' Band **2** Companion of the (Order of the) Bath
CBC Canadian Broadcasting Corporation
CBD Cash before delivery
CBE Commander of the (Order of the) British Empire
CBI Confederation of British Industry

CBS Columbia Broadcasting System
cc 1 carbon copy **2** chapters **3** cubic centimetre
CC 1 Chamber of Commerce **2** County Council **3** Cricket Club
CCF Combined Cadet Force
cd candela
c/d carried down
CD 1 civil defence **2** diplomatic corps [F *corps diplomatique*]
Cdr Commander
Cdre Commodore
CE 1 Church of England **2** civil engineer **3** Council of Europe
CEGB Central Electricity Generating Board
cemy cemetery
CEng Chartered Engineer
CENTO /sentoh/ Central Treaty Organization
CERN /suhn/ European Organization for Nuclear Research [F *Conseil Européen pour la Recherche Nucléaire*]
cert certificate; certified; certify
CET Central European Time
cf compare [L *confer*, imper of *conferre* to compare – more at CONFER]
CF Chaplain to the Forces
c/f carried forward
CFE College of Further Education
cfi cost, freight, and insurance
CG 1 centre of gravity **2** coast guard **3** consul general
CGM Conspicuous Gallantry Medal
cgs centimetre-gram-second (system)
CGS Chief of General Staff
CGT General Confederation of Labour [F *Confédération Générale du Travail*]
ch 1 chain – a unit of length **2** central heating **3** chapter **4** check – used in chess **5** child; children **6** church
CH 1 clubhouse **2** Companion of Honour
chap 1 chaplain **2** chapter
ChB Bachelor of Surgery [ML *baccalaureus Chirurgiae*]
CHE Campaign for Homosexual Equality
chem chemical; chemist; chemistry
Ches Cheshire
chk check – used in chess
chm 1 chairman **2** checkmate – used in chess
ChM Master of Surgery [ML *Chirurgiae Magister*]
chron, chronol chronological; chronology
Chron Chronicles – used for the books of the Bible
Ci curie
CI Channel Islands
CIA Central Intelligence Agency
cia company [Sp *compañía*]
CID Criminal Investigation Department
cie company [F *compagnie*]
CIE 1 Companion of the (Order of the) Indian Empire **2** Transport Organization of Ireland [IrGael *Coras Iompair Eireann*]
cif cost, insurance, and freight
CIGS Chief of the Imperial General Staff
CII Chartered Insurance Institute
C in C Commander in Chief
circ 1 circa **2** *often cap* circus
CIS Chartered Institute of Secretaries
cit citation; cited
civ civil; civilian
CJ chief justice
cl 1 centilitre **2** clerk
clin clinical
CLit Companion of Literature
Cllr *Br* councillor
Clo close – used in street names
cm centimetre
cmd command
cmdg commanding
Cmdr Commander
Cmdre Commodore
CMG Companion of (the Order of) St Michael and St George
cml commercial
CMS Church Missionary Society
CNAA Council for National Academic Awards
CND Campaign for Nuclear Disarmament
CNS central nervous system
co /(1) *often pronounced* koh *in the phrase* sby and co *eg* Jones and Co/ **1** company **2** county
CO 1 commanding officer **2** Commonwealth Office **3** conscientious objector
c/o 1 care of **2** carried over
COD 1 cash on delivery **2** Concise Oxford Dictionary
C of C Chamber of Commerce
C of E 1 Church of England **2** Council of Europe
C of S Church of Scotland
cog cognate
COHSE /'kohzi/ Confederation of Health Service Employees
COI Central Office of Information
col 1 colour; coloured **2** column
Col 1 Colonel **2** Colorado **3** Colossians – used for the book of the Bible
coll 1 college **2** colloquial
colloq colloquial; colloquially
Colo Colorado
com, comm 1 commerce; commercial **2** commission **3** committee
Com, Comm 1 Commander **2** Commodore **3** Commonwealth **4** Communist
comb combination; combined; combining
comdg commanding
Comdr Commander
Comdt Commandant
comp 1 comparative; compare **2** compiled; compiler **3** composition **4** comprehensive
compar comparative; comparison
con 1 consolidated **2** consul
Con, Cons Conservative
conc concentrate; concentrated; concentration
conf conference
conj 1 conjugation **2** conjunction; conjunctive
Conn Connecticut
cons 1 consecrated **2** consigned; consignment **3** consolidated **4** consonant **5** consulting
const constant
constr construction
cont 1 containing **2** contents **3** continent; continental **4** continued
contd continued
contr contralto
contrib contribution; contributor
Copt Coptic
Cor 1 Corinthians – used for the books of the Bible **2** coroner
CORE /kaw/ Congress of Racial Equality – a US organization
Corp 1 Corporal **2** corporation
cos /koz/ cosine
COS chief of staff
cosec cosecant
cosech hyperbolic cosecant
cosh hyperbolic cosine
cot cotangent
coth hyperbolic cotangent
Coun councillor
coy company – used esp for a military company
cp 1 candlepower **2** compare
CP 1 Communist Party **2** Country Party – an Australian political party
CPAG Child Poverty Action Group
cpd compound
Cpl Corporal
CPO 1 Chief Petty Officer **2** *Br* compulsory purchase order
CPR Canadian Pacific Railway
CPRE Council for the Preservation of Rural England

cps 1 characters per second 2 cycles per second
CPSA Civil and Public Services Association
CPSU Communist Party of the Soviet Union
CPU central processing unit
cr credit; creditor
Cr councillor
CR conditioned reflex; conditioned response
CRAC Careers Research and Advisory Centre
CRC Cancer Research Campaign
cresc, cres 1 crescendo 2 *often cap* crescent – used esp in street names
crit critical; criticism
CRO 1 cathode ray oscilloscope 2 Criminal Records Office
CRT cathode-ray tube
cs case; cases
CS 1 chartered surveyor 2 Civil Service 3 Court of Session – the supreme civil court of Scotland
CSC 1 Civil Service Commission 2 Conspicuous Service Cross
CSD Civil Service Department
CSE Certificate of Secondary Education
CSI Companion of the (Order of the) Star of India
CSIRO Commonwealth Scientific and Industrial Research Organization – an Australian organization
CSM Company Sergeant Major
CSO 1 Central Statistical Office 2 Community Service Order
ct 1 carat 2 *often cap* court
CT Connecticut
CTC Cyclists' Touring Club
ctr centre
cu cubic
Cumb Cumbria
CV curriculum vitae
CVO Commander of the (Royal) Victorian Order
CW chemical warfare
Cwlth Commonwealth
CWS Cooperative Wholesale Society
cwt hundredweight

D

d 1 date 2 daughter 3 day 4 deca- 5 deci- 6 delete 7 penny; pence – used before introduction of decimal currency [L *denarius, denarii*] 8 density 9 departs 10 diameter 11 died 12 dose 13 drizzle
D 1 dimensional 2 Duke
da deca-
DA 1 deposit account 2 *NAm* district attorney
Dak Dakota
Dan Daniel – used for the book of the Bible
D & C dilatation and curettage
dat dative
dB /ˌdee 'bee/ decibel
DBE Dame Commander of the (Order of the) British Empire
dbl double
DC 1 from the beginning [It *da capo*] 2 Detective Constable 3 direct current 4 District of Columbia 5 District Commissioner
DCB Dame Commander of the (Order of the) Bath
DCh Doctor of Surgery [ML *Chirurgiae Doctor*]
DCL 1 Distillers Company Limited 2 Doctor of Civil Law
DCM Distinguished Conduct Medal
DCMG Dame Commander of (the Order of) St Michael and St George
DCVO Dame Commander of the (Royal) Victorian Order
DD 1 direct debit 2 Doctor of Divinity
DDS Doctor of Dental Surgery
DE 1 Delaware 2 Department of Employment
deb debenture
dec 1 deceased 2 declared – used esp in cricket 3 declension 4 declination 5 decrease 6 decrescendo
Dec December
def 1 defendant 2 defence 3 deferred – used esp for deferred shares 4 definite 5 definition
deg degree
del delegate; delegation
Del Delaware
Dem Democrat; Democratic
DEng /ˌdee 'enj/ Doctor of Engineering
dent dental; dentist; dentistry
dep 1 departs; departure 2 deposed 3 deposit 4 depot 5 deputy
dept department
der, deriv derivation; derivative; derived
DES Department of Education and Science
det detached; detachment
Det Detective
Deut Deuteronomy – used for the book of the Bible
DF Defender of the Faith [ML *defensor fidei*]
DFC Distinguished Flying Cross
DFM Distinguished Flying Medal
DG 1 by the grace of God [LL *Dei gratia*] 2 director general
DHSS Department of Health and Social Security
DI Detective Inspector
diag diagram
dial dialect
diam diameter
dict 1 dictator 2 dictionary
diff difference; different
dim 1 dimension 2 diminuendo 3 diminutive
DIN /din/ German Industrial Standards [G *Deutsche Industrie-Norm*]
Dip Diploma
Dip AD Diploma in Art and Design
Dip Ed /ˌdip 'ed/ Diploma in Education
Dip HE Diploma in Higher Education
dir director
dis disused
dist 1 distance 2 distilled 3 district
div 1 divergence 2 divide; divided 3 dividend 4 division 5 divorced
DIY do-it-yourself
dk dark
dl decilitre
DLitt /ˌdee 'lit/ Doctor of Letters [L *doctor litterarum*]
DLT Development Land Tax
dm decimetre
DM Doctor of Medicine
DMus Doctor of Music
do ditto
DOA dead on arrival – used chiefly in hospitals
dob date of birth
doc document
DOC Denominaziòne d'Origine Contròllata
DOD Department of Defense – a US government department
DOE Department of the Environment
dom domestic
DOM to God, the best and greatest [ML *Deo optimo maximo*]
Don Donegal
DoT Department of Trade
doz /*sometimes* duz/ dozen
DP 1 data processing 2 displaced person
dpc damp proof course
DPH Diploma in Public Health
DPhil /ˌdee 'fil/ Doctor of Philosophy
DPM Diploma in Psychological Medicine

DPP Director of Public Prosecutions
dpt department
dr 1 debtor **2** drachma **3** dram **4** drawer
Dr 1 doctor **2** Drive – used in street names
Dri drive
DS 1 from the sign [It *dal segno*] **2** Detective Sergeant
DSc doctor of science
DSC Distinguished Service Cross
DSM Distinguished Service Medal
DSO Distinguished Service Order
dsp 1 died without issue [L *decessit sine prole*] **2** dessertspoon; dessertspoonful
DST daylight saving time
Dt Deuteronomy
DTh, D Theol doctor of theology
dup duplicate
DV God willing [L *Deo volente*]
DVLC Driver and Vehicle Licensing Centre
dz dozen

E

E 1 Earl **2** earth – used esp on electrical plugs **3** East; Easterly; Eastern **4** energy **5** English **6** exa-
ea each
E and OE errors and omissions excepted
EAW Electrical Association for Women
EBU European Broadcasting Union
EC East Central – a London postal district
eccl ecclesiastic; ecclesiastical
Eccles, Ec Ecclesiastes – used for the book of the Bible
Ecclus Ecclesiasticus – used for the book of the Apocrypha
ECG electrocardiogram; electrocardiograph
ecol ecological; ecology
econ economics; economist; economy
ECS European Communication Satellite
ECSC European Coal and Steel Community
ECT electroconvulsive therapy
ECU European Currency Unit
ed, edit edited; edition; editor
Ed 1 editor **2** education
EDP electronic data processing
educ education; educational
EE Early English
EEC European Economic Community
EEG electroencephalogram; electroencephalograph
EFTA /'eftə/ European Free Trade Association
EFL English as a foreign language
e g for example [L *exempli gratia*]
EHF extremely high frequency
EHT extremely high tension
elec, elect electric; electrical; electricity
ELF extremely low frequency
Eliz Elizabethan
ELT English language teaching
em electromagnetic
EMA European Monetary Agreement
embryol embryology
emer emeritus
emf electromotive force
EMI Electrical and Musical Industries
Emp Emperor; Empress
emu electromagnetic unit
enc, encl enclosed; enclosure
ency, encyc, encycl encyclopedia
ENE east-northeast
ENEA European Nuclear Energy Agency
eng 1 engine; engineer; engineering **2** engraved; engraver; engraving
Eng England; English
ENO English National Opera
ENON English National Opera North
Ens ensign
ENSA /'ensə/ Entertainments National Service Association
ENT ear, nose, and throat
entom entomological; entomology
env envelope
EO Executive Officer
EOC Equal Opportunities Commission
ep en passant
Ep epistle
EP electroplate
EPA Environmental Protection Agency
Eph, Ephes Ephesians – used for the book of the Bible
Episc Episcopal; Episcopalian
EPNS electroplated nickel silver
eq equal
equiv equivalent
ER 1 Eastern Region **2** King Edward [NL *Edwardus Rex*] **3** Queen Elizabeth [NL *Elizabetha Regina*]
ESA European Space Agency
Esd Esdras – used for the books of the Apocrypha
ESE east-southeast
ESL English as a second language
ESN educationally subnormal
esp /esp/ especially
Esq *also* **Esqr** esquire
est 1 established **2** estate **3** estimate; estimated
EST 1 Eastern Standard Time **2** electro-shock treatment
Esth Esther – used for the book of the Bible
esu electrostatic unit
ETA estimated time of arrival
ETD estimated time of departure
ethnol ethnologist; ethnology
et seq 1 and the following one [L *et sequens*] **2** and the following ones [L *et sequentes* (masc & fem pl), or *et sequentia* (neut pl)]
ETU Electrical Trades Union
ety, etym, etymol etymological; etymologist; etymology
EUA European Unit of Account
euph euphemistic
eV electron volt
EVA extravehicular activity
evap evaporate; evaporated
ex 1 examined **2** example **3** except **4** exchange
Ex, Exod Exodus – used for the book of the Bible
exc except
Exc excellency
ex div without dividend
exec executive
ex lib from the books (of) – used on bookplates [L *ex libris*]
exor executor
exp 1 experimental **2** export; exported **3** exponential **4** express
expt experiment
exptl experimental
exrx executrix
ext 1 extension **2** exterior **3** external; externally **4** extinct
Ez, Ezr Ezra – used for the book of the Bible
Ezek Ezekiel – used for the book of the Bible

F

f 1 fathom **2** female **3** femto- **4** force **5** forte **6** frequency **7** focal length **8** folio **9** following (e g page) **10** foot
F 1 Fahrenheit **2** false **3** farad **4** Fellow **5** filial generation **6** fine – used esp on lead pencils **7** forward **8** French
FA Football Association
FAA 1 Fleet Air Arm **2** Federal Aviation Agency – a US government agency

fac facsimile
Fahr Fahrenheit
FAI International Aeronautical Federation [F *Fédération aéronautique internationale*]
F and F fixtures and fittings
FANY /'fani, ˌef ay en 'wie/ First Aid Nursing Yeomanry
FAO Food and Agriculture Organization (of the United Nations)
fas free alongside ship
fath fathom
FBA Fellow of the British Academy
FBI Federal Bureau of Investigation
FBR fast breeder reactor
FC 1 Football Club 2 Forestry Commission
FCA Fellow of the (Institute of) Chartered Accountants
FCC Federal Communications Commission – a US government organization
FCII Fellow of the Chartered Insurance Institute
FCIS Fellow of the Chartered Institute of Secretaries
FCO Foreign and Commonwealth Office
fcp foolscap
FCS Fellow of the Chemical Society
FD Defender of the Faith [L *Fidei Defensor*]
FDA Food and Drug Administration – a US government organization
Feb February
fec he/she made it [L *fecit*]
fed federal; federation
fem 1 female 2 feminine – used in grammar
Ferm Fermanagh
FET field-effect transistor
ff 1 folios 2 following (e g pages) 3 fortissimo
FH fire hydrant
FIDE World Chess Federation [F *Fédération Internationale des Échecs*]
FIFA /'feefə/ International Football Federation [F *Fédération Internationale de Football Association*]
fig 1 figurative; figuratively 2 figure
fin 1 finance; financial 2 finish
fl 1 floor 2 flourished – used to indicate a period of renown of sby whose dates of birth and death are unknown [L *floruit*] 3 fluid
FL 1 Florida 2 focal length
Fla Florida
fl oz fluid ounce
Flt Lt Flight Lieutenant
Flt Off Flight Officer
Flt Sgt Flight Sergeant
fm fathom
FM Field Marshal
fml formal
fo, fol folio
FO 1 Field Officer 2 Flying Officer 3 Foreign Office
fob free on board
foc free of charge
FOC Father of the Chapel (in a Trade Union)
FOE Friends of the Earth
for 1 free on rail 2 foreign 3 forest; forestry
fp 1 forte-piano 2 freezing point
FPA 1 Family Planning Association 2 Foreign Press Association
fpm feet per minute
fps 1 feet per second 2 foot-pound-second
fr from
Fr 1 Father 2 French 3 Friar
FRCM Fellow of the Royal College of Music
FRCOG Fellow of the Royal College of Obstetricians and Gynaecologists
FRCP Fellow of the Royal College of Physicians
FRCS Fellow of the Royal College of Surgeons
FRCVS Fellow of the Royal College of Veterinary Surgeons
freq frequency; frequent; frequentative; frequently
Fri Friday
FRIBA Fellow of the Royal Institute of British Architects
FRIC Fellow of the Royal Institute of Chemistry
FRICS Fellow of the Royal Institution of Chartered Surveyors
front frontispiece
FRPS Fellow of the Royal Photographic Society
FRS Fellow of the Royal Society
frt freight
FSA Fellow of the Society of Actuaries
FSH follicle-stimulating hormone
ft 1 feet; foot 2 fort
FT Financial Times
ftd fitted
fth, fthm fathom
ft lb foot-pound
fur furlong
fwd 1 foreword 2 forward; forwards
FWD 1 four-wheel drive 2 front-wheel drive

G

g 1 gauge 2 giga 3 good 4 gram
G 1 gauss 2 German 3 gigagauss 4 acceleration due to gravity 5 gulf
Ga 1 gate 2 Georgia (USA)
GA 1 General Assembly 2 Gamblers Anonymous
gal, gall /*sometimes* gal/ gallon
Gal Galatians – used for the book of the Bible
galv galvanized
gar garage
GATT /gat/ General Agreement on Tariffs and Trade
gaz gazette; gazetteer
GB Great Britain
GBE Knight/Dame Grand Cross of the (Order of the) British Empire
GBH *Br* grievous bodily harm
GC George Cross
GCB Knight/Dame Grand Cross of the (Order of the) Bath
GCE General Certificate of Education
GCHQ Government Communications Headquarters
GCMG Knight/Dame Grand Cross of (the Order of) St Michael and St George
GCVO Knight/Dame Grand Cross of the (Royal) Victorian Order
gd good
Gdns Gardens – used esp in street names
GDP gross domestic product
GDR German Democratic Republic
GEC General Electric Company
gen 1 genitive 2 genus
Gen Genesis – used for the book of the Bible
geog geographic; geographical; geography
geol geologic; geological; geology
geom geometric; geometrical; geometry
ger gerund
GHQ general headquarters
gi gill
GI gastrointestinal
Gib Gibraltar
Gk Greek
Glam Glamorgan
GLC 1 Greater London Council 2 gas-liquid chromatography
Glos Gloucestershire
GLS General Lighting Service
gm gram
GM 1 general manager 2 George Medal 3 guided missile

GMC 1 General Medical Council 2 general management committee
GMT Greenwich Mean Time
GMWU General and Municipal Workers Union
GNB Good News Bible
GNP gross national product
Gnr gunner
GOC General Officer Commanding
gov 1 government 2 governor
govt government
GP 1 general practitioner 2 Grand Prix
Gp Capt Group Captain
GPDST Girls' Public Day School Trust
GPI general paralysis of the insane
GPO general post office
GQ general quarters
gr 1 grade 2 grain 3 gram 4 gravity 5 gross
Gr Greek
GR King George [L *Georgius Rex*]
grad graduate; graduated
gram grammar; grammatical
gro gross
Gro Grove – used in street names
gr wt gross weight
Gs gauss
GS General Staff
GSO general staff officer
gt great
GT grand tourer
gtd guaranteed
GTT glucose tolerance test
gyn, gynaecol gynaecology

H

h 1 hect-; hecto 2 height 3 high 4 hot 5 hour 6 husband
H 1 harbour 2 hard – used esp on lead pencils 3 hardness 4 henry – used in physics 5 hospital
ha hectare
Hab Habakkuk – used for the book of the Bible
Hag Haggai – used for the book of the Bible
h and c hot and cold (water)
Hants /hants/ Hampshire [OE *Hantescire*, var of *Hamtunscir*]
HB hard black – used on lead pencils
HBM His/Her Britannic Majesty
HC 1 Holy Communion 2 House of Commons
HCF highest common factor
hdbk handbook
HDip higher diploma
hdqrs headquarters
HE 1 high explosive 2 His Eminence 3 His/Her Excellency
Heb Hebrews – used for the book of the Bible
HEC Health Education Council
HEO Higher Executive Officer
her heraldry
Here, Heref Herefordshire
Herts Hertfordshire
HEW Department of Health, Education, and Welfare – a US government department
hf half
HF high frequency
hg 1 hectogram 2 haemoglobin
HG 1 His/Her Grace 2 Home Guard
HGV *Br* heavy goods vehicle
HH 1 double hard – used on lead pencils 2 His/Her Highness 3 His Holiness
HI Hawaii
HIH His/Her Imperial Highness
HIM His/Her Imperial Majesty
hist historian; historical; history
hl hectolitre
HL House of Lords
hm hectometre
HM 1 headmaster 2 headmistress 3 His/Her Majesty
HMAS His/Her Majesty's Australian Ship
HMCS His/Her Majesty's Canadian Ship
HMF His/Her Majesty's Forces
HMG His/Her Majesty's Government
HMI His/Her Majesty's Inspector (of Schools)
HMNZS His/Her Majesty's New Zealand Ship
HMS His/Her Majesty's Ship
HMSO His/Her Majesty's Stationery Office
HMV His Master's Voice
HNC Higher National Certificate
HND Higher National Diploma
ho house
HO Home Office
hon honour; honourable; honorary
Hon (the) Honourable
Hons *Br* honours
Hon Sec *Br* Honorary Secretary
hort, hortic horticultural; horticulture
Hos Hosea – used for the book of the Bible
hos, hosp hospital
HP 1 high pressure 2 hire purchase 3 horsepower 4 Houses of Parliament
HPF highest possible frequency
HPLC high performance liquid chromatography
HQ headquarters
hr hour
HR 1 holiday route 2 House of Representatives
HRH His/Her Royal Highness
hrt hormone replacement therapy
HRW heated rear window
HSH His/Her Serene Highness
HSO Higher Scientific Officer
HST high speed train
ht height
HT 1 high-tension 2 under this title [L *hoc titulo*]
HTR high-temperature reactor
HUD head-up display
humor humorous; humorously
Hung Hungarian; Hungary
HV 1 high velocity 2 high-voltage
HW 1 high water 2 hot water
HWM high-water mark
hwy highway
hy henry – used in physics
Hz hertz

I

i intransitive
I 1 inductance 2 island; isle
Ia, IA Iowa
IA Institute of Actuaries
IAA indoleacetic acid
IAAF International Amateur Athletic Federation
IABA International Amateur Boxing Association
IAEA International Atomic Energy Agency
IALC instrument approach and landing chart
IAM Institute of Advanced Motorists
IARU International Amateur Radio Union
IAS indicated airspeed
IATA /ie'ahtə/ International Air Transport Association
ib ibidem
IB Institute of Bankers
IBA Independent Broadcasting Authority
ibid ibidem
IBM International Business Machines
IBRD International Bank for Reconstruction and Development
i/c in charge
IC integrated circuit
ICA Institute of Contemporary Arts
ICAO International Civil Aviation Organization
ICBM intercontinental ballistic missile

ICC International Cricket Conference
ICE 1 Institution of Civil Engineers **2** internal-combustion engine
ICFC Industrial and Commercial Finance Corporation
ICFTU International Confederation of Free Trade Unions
IChemE Institute of Chemical Engineers
ICI Imperial Chemical Industries
ICJ International Court of Justice
ICL International Computers Limited
ICRF Imperial Cancer Research Fund
ICS Indian Civil Service
id idem
ID 1 Idaho **2** (proof of) identification **3** inner diameter **4** intelligence department
IDA International Development Association
IDB *chiefly SAfr* illicit diamond buying
i e that is [L *id est*]
IEE Institution of Electrical Engineers
IF intermediate frequency
IFC International Finance Corporation
IG inspector general
IHS Jesus [taken as abbr of L *Iesus hominum salvator*; orig, part transliteration of Gk ΙΗΣ, short for ΙΗΣΟΥΣ *Iēsous* Jesus]
IL Illinois
ILEA /ie el ee 'ay, 'ili·ə/ Inner London Education Authority
ill, illus, illust illustrated; illustration
Ill Illinois
ILO 1 International Labour Organization **2** International Labour Office
ILP Independent Labour Party
ILS instrument landing system
IM intramuscular
IMechE Institution of Mechanical Engineers
IMF International Monetary Fund
imit imitative; imitation
imp 1 Emperor; Empress [L *Imperator, Imperatrix*] **2** imperative **3** imperfect **4** imperial
imper imperative
in inch
IN Indiana
inc /(2) *often* ingk/ **1** increase **2** *chiefly NAm* incorporated
incl included; including; inclusive
ind 1 independent **2** indicative **3** industrial; industry
Ind Indiana
indic indicative
inf 1 below [L *infra*] **2** infantry **3** infinitive
infin infinitive
infml informal
in loc cit in the place cited [L *in loco citato*]
INP International News Photo
INRI Jesus of Nazareth, King of the Jews [L *Iesus Nazarenus Rex Iudaeorum*]
ins insurance
INS 1 inertial navigation system **2** International News Service
insp inspector
inst 1 instant **2** institute; institution
int 1 integral **2** interior **3** intermediate **4** internal **5** international **6** interpreter **7** intransitive
inter intermediate
interj interjection
interrog interrogation; interrogative; interrogatively
intl international
in trans in transit [L *in transitu*]
intro introduction
I/O input/output
IOC International Olympic Committee
IOF Independent Order of Foresters
IOM Isle of Man
IOOF Independent Order of Odd Fellows
IOW Isle of Wight
IPA International Phonetic Alphabet
IPC International Publishing Corporation
IPM 1 inches per minute **2** Institute of Personnel Management
IPPF International Planned Parenthood Federation
IPS inches per second
IQS Institute of Quantity Surveyors
Ir Irish
IR 1 information retrieval **2** infrared **3** Inland Revenue
IRA Irish Republican Army
IRBM intermediate range ballistic missile
IRN Independent Radio News
IRO 1 Inland Revenue Office **2** International Refugee Organization
is island; isle
IS International Socialist
Isa, Is Isaiah – used for the book of the Bible
ISBN International Standard Book Number
ISD international subscriber dialling
isl island
ISO 1 Imperial Service Order **2** International Standardization Organization
ISTC Iron and Steel Trades Confederation
IStructE Institution of Structural Engineers
ISV International Scientific Vocabulary
IT Information Technology
ita initial teaching alphabet
ITA Independent Television Authority – now IBA
ital italic; italicized
Ital, It Italian
ITB Industry Training Board
ITN Independent Television News
ITO International Trade Organization
ITT International Telephone and Telegraph (Corporation)
ITU International Telecommunications Union
ITV Independent Television
IU international unit
IUD intrauterine device
IV intravenous; intravenously
IVR International Vehicle Registration
IW 1 inside width **2** isotopic weight
IWC International Whaling Commission
IWW Industrial Workers of the World
IYHF International Youth Hostels Federation

J

J 1 joule **2** Judge **3** Justice
JA Judge Advocate
JA, J/A joint account
JAG judge advocate general
Jan January
Jas James – used for the book of the Bible
JC 1 Jesus Christ **2** Julius Caesar
JCD 1 Doctor of Canon Law [NL *juris canonici doctor*] **2** Doctor of Civil Law [NL *juris civilis doctor*]
JCL Job Control Language
JCR Junior Common Room
jct junction
Jer Jeremiah – used for the book of the Bible
JJ Justices
jnr junior

Jo Joel – used for the book of the Bible
Jon Jonah – used for the book of the Bible
Josh Joshua – used for the book of the Bible
journ journalistic
JP Justice of the Peace
Jr junior
jt, jnt joint
Jud Judith – used for the book of the Apocrypha
JUD Doctor of both Civil and Canon Law [L *juris utriusque doctor*]
Judg Judges – used for the books of the Bible
Jul July
Jun June

K

k 1 carat 2 kilo- 3 kitchen 4 knot 5 kosher
K 1 kelvin 2 king – used in chess 3 knit
KANU /'kahnooh/ Kenya African National Union
KB 1 King's Bench 2 Knight Bachelor
KBE Knight (Commander of the Order of the) British Empire
kc kilocycle
KC 1 Kennel Club 2 King's Counsel
kcal /'kay ˌkal/ kilocalorie
KCB Knight Commander of the (Order of the) Bath
KCIE Knight Commander of the (Order of the) Indian Empire
KCMG Knight Commander of (the Order of) St Michael and St George
KCSI Knight Commander of the (Order of the) Star of India
kc/s kilocycles per second
KCVO Knight Commander of the (Royal) Victorian Order
KD knocked down
KE kinetic energy
Ker Kerry
KeV kilo-electron volt
kg 1 keg 2 kilogram
KG Knight of the (Order of the) Garter
KGB (Soviet) State Security Committee [Russ *Komitet Gosudarstvennoye Bezopastnosti*]
Kgs Kings – used for the books of the Bible
kHz kilohertz
Kild Kildare
Kilk Kilkenny
kit kitchen
kJ kilajoule
KKK Ku Klux Klan
kl kilolitre
km kilometre
kn knot
KP Knight of (the Order of) St Patrick
kph kilometres per hour
KS Kansas
KStJ Knight of (the Order of) St John
kt karat
KT 1 knight – used in chess 2 Knight Templar 3 Knight of the (Order of the) Thistle
kV kilovolt
kW kilowatt
kWh, kwh kilowatt-hour
KWIC keyword in context
KWOC keyword out of context
Ky, KY Kentucky

L

l 1 Lady 2 lake 3 large 4 left 5 length 6 Liberal 7 pound [L *libra*] 8 lightning 9 line 10 litre 11 little 12 long 13 last 14 lower 15 lumen
L 1 Latin 2 live – used esp on electrical plugs 3 *Br* learner (driver)
La 1 lane – used esp in street names 2 Louisiana
LA 1 law agent 2 Library Association 3 *Br* local authority 4 Los Angeles 5 Louisiana
Lab /(*1*) lab *in the phrase* Lib/Lab pact/ 1 Labour 2 Labrador
LAC Leading Aircraftman
LACW Leading Aircraftwoman
Lam Lamentations – used for the book of the Bible
Lancs /langks/ Lancashire
lang language
lat latitude
Lat 1 Latin 2 Latvia
lb 1 pound [L *libra*] 2 leg bye
LBC London Broadcasting Company
lbf pound-force
lbw leg before wicket
lc 1 letter of credit 2 in the place cited [L *loco citato*] 3 lowercase
LC 1 left centre 2 Library of Congress 3 Lord Chamberlain 4 Lord Chancellor
LCC London County Council
lcd 1 liquid crystal display 2 lowest (*or* least) common denominator
LCJ Lord Chief Justice
LCM lowest (*or* least) common multiple
LCpl lance corporal
ld load
Ld Lord
LD lethal dose – often used with a numerical subscript to indicate the percent of a test group of organisms killed by the dose <LD_{50}>
Ldg Leading – used chiefly in titles
LDS Licentiate in Dental Surgery
LEA Local Education Authority
led light emitting diode
leg legato
Leics Leicestershire
Leit Leitrim
LEM lunar excursion module
Lev, Levit Leviticus
lf 1 light face 2 low frequency
LF low frequency
lge lounge
lh left hand
LH luteinizing hormone
LHA Local Health Authority
LHD Doctor of Letters; Doctor of Humanities [L *litterarum humaniorum doctor*]
Ll 1 Light Infantry 2 librarian; library
Lib /lib *in the phrase* Lib/Lab pact/ Liberal
Lieut Lieutenant
LIFO last in, first out
Lim Limerick
Lincs /lingks/ Lincolnshire
ling linguistics
Linn Linnaean; Linnaeus
lit 1 litre 2 literature
Litt D doctor of letters; doctor of literature [ML *litterarum doctor*]
LJ Lord Justice
Lk Luke – used for the book of the Bible
ll lines
LL Lord Lieutenant
LLB Bachelor of Laws [NL *legum baccalaureus*]
LLD Doctor of Laws [NL *legum doctor*]
LLM Master of Laws [NL *legum magister*]
lm lumen
LMG light machine gun
LNG liquefied natural gas
LOB Location of Offices Bureau
loc cit in the place cited [L *loco citato*]
Lond Londonderry
long longitude
Long Longford
loq he/she speaks [L *loquitur*]
Lou Louth
LP low pressure
LPG liquefied petroleum gas
LPO London Philharmonic Orchestra
LPS Lord Privy Seal
LRAM Licentiate of the Royal Academy of Music

LS 1 left side 2 Linnaean Society
LSE London School of Economics
LSI large-scale integration
LSO London Symphony Orchestra
lt light
LT 1 lieutenant 2 low-tension
LTA Lawn Tennis Association
Lt Cdr Lieutenant Commander
Lt Col Lieutenant Colonel
Ltd limited
Lt Gen Lieutenant General
LV 1 low velocity 2 low voltage 3 *Br* luncheon voucher
LVT 1 landing vehicle, tracked 2 landing vehicle (tank)
LW 1 long wave 2 low water
LWB long wheelbase
LWM low-water mark
LWR light water reactor
LWT London Weekend Television
lx lux

M

m 1 maiden (over) – used in cricket 2 male 3 married 4 masculine 5 mass 6 metre 7 middle 8 mile 9 thousand [L *mille*] 10 milli- 11 million 12 minute – used for the unit of time 13 molar 14 month
M 1 Mach 2 Master 3 mega- 4 Member 5 Monsieur 6 motorway
mA milliampere
MA 1 Massachusetts 2 Master of Arts [ML *magister artium*] 3 Middle Ages 4 Military Academy
MAA Motor Agents' Association
Mac, Macc Maccabees – used for the book of the Apocrypha
mach machine; machinery; machinist
MAFF Ministry of Agriculture, Fisheries, and Food
mag 1 magnesium 2 magnetic; magnetism 3 magnitude
Maj Major
Maj Gen Major General
Mal Malachi – used for the book of the Bible
man manual
Man Manitoba
M & S Marks and Spencer
manuf manufacture; manufacturing
mar maritime
Mar March
MArch Master of Architecture
Marq Marquess; Marquis
masc masculine – used in grammar
MASH /mash/ *NAm* mobile army surgical hospital
Mass Massachusetts
Matt Matthew – used for the book of the Bible
max /maks/ maximum
mb millibar
MB Bachelor of Medicine [NL *medicinae baccalaureus*]
MBA Master of Business Administration
MBE Member of the (Order of the) British Empire
MBSc Master of Business Science
mc 1 megacycle 2 millicurie
MC 1 Master of Ceremonies 2 Member of Congress 3 Military Cross
MCA Monetary Compensatory Amount
MCC Marylebone Cricket Club
mcg microgram
MCh, MChir Master of Surgery [NL *magister chirurgiae*]
MCom Master of Commerce
Mc/s megacycles per second
Md Maryland
MD 1 Managing Director 2 Doctor of Medicine [NL *medicinae doctor*] 3 right hand – used in music [It *mano destra*]
MDS Master of Dental Surgery
Me Maine
ME Middle English
Mea Meath
meas measure
mech mechanic; mechanical; mechanics
MEcon Master of Economics
med /(*1*) med/ 1 medical; medicine 2 medieval 3 medium
MEd /ˌem 'ed/ Master of Education
meg megohm
MEng Master of Engineering
MEP Member of the European Parliament
mer meridian
met /(*1*) met *in the phrase* met office/ 1 meteorological; meteorology 2 metropolitan
metal, metall metallurgical; metallurgy
meteor, meteorol meteorological; meteorology
MeV mega-electron-volts
mf 1 medium frequency 2 mezzo forte 3 millifarad
mfd manufactured
mfg manufacturing
MFH Master of Foxhounds
MFI Manufacture of Furniture Institute
mg milligram
MG machine gun
Mgr 1 Monseigneur 2 Monsignor
mh millihenry
MHD magnetohydrodynamics
MHR Member of the House of Representatives
MHz megahertz
mi mile; mileage
MI 1 Michigan 2 military intelligence
Mic Micah – used for the book of the Bible
Mich Michigan
MICR magnetic ink character recognition
mid middle
Middx Middlesex
mil, milit military
min 1 minimum 2 minor 3 minute – used for the unit of time
Min Minister; Ministry
Minn Minnesota
MIO minimum identifiable odour
misc miscellaneous; miscellany
Miss Mississippi
MIT Massachusetts Institute of Technology
mixt mixture
Mk Mark
MKS metre-kilogram-second
ml /(*2*) *sometimes* mil/ 1 mile 2 millilitre
mL millilambert
MLA Member of the Legislative Assembly
MLC 1 Member of the Legislative Council 2 Meat and Livestock Commission
MLD minimum lethal dose
MLitt /ˌem 'lit/ Master of Letters [L *magister litterarum*]
Mlle mademoiselle [F]
MLR minimum lending rate
MLS microwave landing system
mm millimetre
MM 1 Maelzel's metronome 2 messieurs [F] 3 Military Medal
MMB Milk Marketing Board
Mme madame [F]
Mmes mesdames [F]
mmf magnetomotive force
MN 1 Merchant Navy 2 Minnesota
mo *NAm* month
MO 1 Medical Officer 2 Missouri 3 modus operandi 4 money order
MoC Mother of the Chapel (in a Trade Union)
mod 1 moderate 2 moderato 3 modern 4 modulus
MoD /ˌem oh 'dee, mod/ Ministry of Defence
MOH Medical Officer of Health
mol 1 molecular; molecule 2 mole

mol wt molecular weight
mon monetary
Mon 1 Monaghan 2 Monday
Mont Montana
morph morphological; morphology
mp mezzo piano
MP 1 Member of Parliament 2 Metropolitan Police 3 Military Police; Military Policeman
mpg miles per gallon
mph miles per hour
MPhil /ˌem 'fil/ Master of Philosophy
mpm metres per minute
mps metres per second
mr milliroentgen
Mr *see entry in main text*
MR 1 map reference 2 Master of the Rolls
MRA Moral Re-Armament
MRC Medical Research Council
MRCA multi-role combat aircraft
MRCOG Member of the Royal College of Obstetricians and Gynaecologists
MRCP Member of the Royal College of Physicians
MRCS Member of the Royal College of Surgeons
MRCVS Member of the Royal College of Veterinary Surgeons
mRNA /ˌem ahr en 'ay/ messenger RNA
Mrs *see entry in main text*
ms millisecond
Ms *see entry in main text*
MS 1 left hand – used in music [It *mano sinistra*] 2 manuscript 3 Mississippi 4 multiple sclerosis
MSC 1 Manpower Services Commission 2 Metropolitan Special Constabulary
MSc /ˌem es 'see/ Master of Science
msec millisecond
MSG monosodium glutamate
Msgr *chiefly NAm* Monseigneur; Monsignor
MSI medium-scale integration
msl mean sea level
MSS manuscripts
Mt 1 Matthew 2 Mount
MT Montana
MTB motor torpedo-boat
MTech /ˌem 'tek/ Master of Technology
mth month
mun municipal
mus 1 museum 2 music; musical; musician
mv millivolt
MV 1 mezza voce 2 motor vessel
MVO Member of the (Royal) Victorian Order
MW 1 medium wave 2 megawatt
mW milliwatt
Mx maxwell
myth, mythol mythological; mythology

N

n 1 name 2 nano- 3 born [L *natus*] 4 net 5 new 6 neuter 7 nominative 8 noon 9 noun 10 numerical aperture
N 1 knight – used in chess 2 newton 3 North; Northerly; Northern 4 neutral – used esp on electric plugs
n/a no account – used in banking
NA 1 North America 2 not applicable
NAAFI /'nafi/ Navy, Army, and Air Force Institutes
NAD 1 no appreciable disease 2 nothing abnormal detected
Nah Nahum – used for the book of the Bible
NALGO /'nalgoh/ National and Local Government Officers Association
NAm North America; North American
NASA /'nasə/ National Aeronautics and Space Administration – a US government organization
nat national; nationalist
natl national
NATO /'naytoh/ North Atlantic Treaty Organization
NATSOPA /nat'sohpə/ National Society of Operative Printers, Graphical and Media Personnel
naut nautical
nav navigable; navigation
nb no ball – used in cricket
NB 1 Nebraska 2 New Brunswick 3 note well [L *nota bene*]
NBC National Broadcasting Company – a US company
nbg *Br* no bloody good – infml
NC 1 no charge 2 North Carolina
NCB National Coal Board
NCC Nature Conservancy Council
NCCL National Council for Civil Liberties
NCH National Children's Home
NCO non-commissioned officer
NCP National Car Parks
NCR National Cash Register (Company)
NCT National Childbirth Trust
ncv no commercial value
nd no date
ND, NDak North Dakota
NE 1 modern English [*New English*] 2 New England 3 Northeast; Northeastern
NEB 1 National Enterprise Board 2 New English Bible
Nebr, Neb Nebraska
NEC National Executive Committee
NEDC National Economic Development Council
neg negative
Neh Nehemiah – used for the book of the Bible
NEI not elsewhere included
NERC Natural Environment Research Council
neut neuter
Nev Nevada
NF 1 National Front 2 Newfoundland 3 no funds
Nfld Newfoundland
NFS not for sale
NFU National Farmers' Union
NFWI National Federation of Women's Institutes
ng no good
NGA National Graphical Association
NH New Hampshire
NHS National Health Service
NI 1 National Insurance 2 Northern Ireland
NJ New Jersey
NL 1 New Latin 2 it is not permitted [L *non licet*]
NLC National Liberal Club
NLF National Liberation Front
nm 1 nanometre 2 nautical mile
NM, N Mex New Mexico
NMR nuclear magnetic resonance
NNE north-northeast
NNW north-northwest
no 1 not out – used in cricket 2 number [L *numero*, abl of *numerus*] 3 *NAm* north
nom nominative
NOP National Opinion Poll
Nor, Norm Norman
Norf Norfolk
norm normal
Northants /naw'thants, nawth'hants/ Northamptonshire
Northumb Northumberland
nos numbers
Notts /nots/ Nottinghamshire
Nov November
np new paragraph
NP Notary Public
NPL National Physical Laboratory
NPN negative-positive-negative
nr near
NR Northern Region
NRA National Rifle Association
NS 1 not specified 2 Nova Scotia 3 *NAm* nuclear ship
NSB National Savings Bank
nsec *also* **ns** nanosecond
NSF not sufficient funds

NSPCC National Society for the Prevention of Cruelty to Children
NSU nonspecific urethritis
NSW New South Wales
NT 1 National Trust 2 New Testament 3 no trumps
NTP normal temperature and pressure
NTS National Trust for Scotland
nt wt net weight
NUBE /'nyoohbi/ National Union of Bank Employees
NUGMW National Union of General and Municipal Workers
NUJ National Union of Journalists
num numeral
Num, Numb Numbers – used for the book of the Bible
NUM National Union of Mineworkers
NUPE /'nyoohpi/ National Union of Public Employees
NUR National Union of Railwaymen
NUS 1 National Union of Seamen 2 National Union of Students
NUT National Union of Teachers
NUTGW National Union of Tailors and Garment Workers
NV Nevada
NW Northwest; Northwestern
NWT Northwest Territories (of Canada)
NY New York
NYC New York City
NYO National Youth Orchestra
NZ New Zealand

O

o 1 ohm 2 old
O Ohio
o- ortho-
O & M organization and methods
OAP *Br* old-age pensioner
OAS 1 Organization of American States 2 Organisation de l'Armée Secrète – used for an organization dedicated to retaining French rule in Algeria
OAU Organization of African Unity
ob he/she died [L *obiit*]
Ob, Obad Obadiah – used for the book of the Bible
OB 1 outside broadcast 2 *Br* old boy
OBE Officer of the (Order of the) British Empire
obj object; objective – used esp in grammar
obs 1 obsolete 2 obstetrical; obstetrics
o/c overcharge
OC *Br* Officer Commanding
occas occasionally
OCR optical character reader; optical character recognition
oct octavo
Oct October
OCTU Officer Cadets Training Unit
OD, (*2, 5, & 6*) **O/D** 1 officer of the day 2 on demand 3 ordnance datum 4 outer diameter 5 overdraft 6 overdrawn
OE Old English
Oe oersted
OECD Organization for Economic Cooperation and Development
OED Oxford English Dictionary
off office; officer; official
OFM Order of Friars Minor
OFS Orange Free State
OFT Office of Fair Trading
OG *Br* old girl
OH Ohio
ohc overhead camshaft
OHMS On His/Her Majesty's Service
ohv overhead value
OK, Okla Oklahoma
OM Order of Merit
ONC Ordinary National Certificate
OND Ordinary National Diploma
ono or near offer – used with prices of goods for sale
Ont Ontario
op opus
OP 1 observation post 2 opposite prompt – used to designate part of the theatrical stage 3 out of print
op cit in the work cited [L *opere citato*]
OPEC /'ohpek/ Organization of Petroleum Exporting Countries
opp opposite
ops operations
opt 1 optative – used in grammar 2 optical; optician; optics 3 optional
OR 1 operational research 2 Oregon 3 other ranks 4 owner's risk
orch 1 orchestra; orchestral 2 orchestrated by
ord 1 order 2 ordinary 3 ordnance
Oreg, Ore Oregon
org 1 organic 2 organization; organized
orig original; originally; originator
Ork Orkney
ornith ornithology
OS 1 ordinary seaman 2 Ordnance Survey 3 out of stock 4 outsize
O/S outstanding
OSA Order of St Augustine
OSB Order of St Benedict
OSF Order of St Francis
OT 1 occupational therapy; Occupational Therapist 2 Old Testament; 3 overtime
OTC Officers' Training Corps
OU Open University
OUDS Oxford University Dramatic Society
OXFAM /'oksfam/ Oxford Committee for Famine Relief
Oxon /'okson/ 1 Oxfordshire [L *Oxonia*] 2 of Oxford – used chiefly with academic awards <*MA* ~> [L *Oxoniensis*]
oz ounce; ounces [It *onza*]

P

p 1 page 2 participle 3 past 4 pence; penny 5 per 6 piano – used as an instruction in music 7 pico- 8 pint 9 power 10 premolar 11 pressure
P 1 parental generation 2 parking 3 pawn – used in chess 4 peta-poise 5 poise 6 Prince 7 purl
pa per annum
Pa 1 Pennsylvania 2 pascal
PA 1 Pennsylvania 2 personal assistant 3 press agent 4 public address (system) 5 purchasing agent
PABX *Br* private automatic branch (telephone) exchange
Pac Pacific
PAL /,pee ay 'el, pal/ phase alternation line – a system of transmitting colour television programmes
palaeont palaeontology
P & L profit and loss
P & O Peninsular and Oriental (Steamship Company)
p & p *Br* postage and packing
par 1 paragraph 2 parallel 3 parish
part participial; participle
PAS 1 para-aminosalicyclic acid 2 Pregnancy Advisory Service
pass passive
pat patent; patented
path, pathol pathological; pathology
PAX /paks/ *Br* private automatic (telephone) exchange
PAYE pay as you earn
PBAB please bring a bottle
PBX private branch (telephone) exchange

pc 1 per cent 2 postcard
PC 1 police constable 2 Privy Councillor
pcm pulse code modulation
pct *chiefly NAm* per cent
pd paid
PD 1 per diem 2 potential difference 3 *NAm* police department
Pde parade – used in street names
pdl poundal
PDSA People's Dispensary for Sick Animals
PDT Pacific daylight time
PE physical education
ped pedal
PEI Prince Edward Island
pen peninsula
Penn, Penna Pennsylvania
PEP *Br* Political and Economic Planning
PER Professional Employment Register
perf 1 perforated 2 performance
perh perhaps
perm permanent
perp *often cap* perpendicular
per pro /ˌpuh 'proh/ by the agency (of) [L *per procurationem*]
pers person; personal
PERT /puht/ programme evaluation and review technique
Pet Peter – used for the book of the Bible
pF picofarad
PF Procurator Fiscal
PFA Professional Footballers' Association
PFLP Popular Front for the Liberation of Palestine
PG 1 paying guest 2 postgraduate
PGA Professional Golfers' Association
PH public health
phar, pharm pharmaceutical; pharmacist; pharmacy
PhB /ˌpee aych 'bee/ Bachelor of Philosophy [L *philosophiae baccalaureus*]
PhD /ˌpee aych 'dee/ Doctor of Philosophy [L *philosophiae doctor*]
phil philosophy
Phil 1 Philippians – used for the book of the Bible 2 Philharmonic
Philem Philemon – used for the book of the Bible
phon phonetics
phr phrase
phys 1 physical 2 physics
physiol physiology
PI petrol injection
pizz pizzicato
pk 1 *often cap* park – used esp in street names 2 peck
pkg package
pkt packet
pl 1 *often cap* place – used esp in street names 2 platoon 3 plural
PL Poet Laureate
PLA Port of London Authority
plc public limited company
PLO Palestine Liberation Organization
PLP Parliamentary Labour Party
PLR Public Lending Right
plup pluperfect
pm 1 post meridiem 2 premium
PM 1 postmortem 2 Prime Minister 3 Provost Marshal
PMB Potato Marketing Board
PMG 1 Paymaster General 2 Postmaster General
PMH production per man-hour
PMS pre-menstrual syndrome
PMT pre-menstrual tension
pn 1 promissory note 2 pronoun
PNdB perceived noise decibel
PNP positive-negative-positive
PO 1 Petty Officer 2 Pilot Officer 3 postal order 4 Post Office
POB Post Office box
POD pay on delivery
POE 1 port of embarkation 2 port of entry
pol, polit political; politics
pop population
POP *Br* Post Office Preferred
por 1 pay on receipt 2 pay on return
pos positive
poss 1 possessive – used in grammar 2 possible
pot 1 potential 2 potentiometer
POUNC Post Office Users' National Council
POW prisoner of war
pp 1 pages 2 past participle 3 by proxy [L *per procurationem*] 4 pianissimo
PP 1 parcel post 2 parish priest
ppd, PP 1 postpaid 2 prepaid
PPE Philosophy, Politics, and Economics
ppm parts per million
PPS 1 Parliamentary Private Secretary 2 further postscript [L *post-postscriptum*]
ppt precipitate
pptn precipitation
PQ Province of Quebec
pr 1 pair 2 present 3 price 4 pronoun
Pr 1 Priest 2 Prince
PR 1 proportional representation 2 public relations 3 Puerto Rico
PRAM /pram/ programmable random access memory
PRB Pre-Raphaelite Brotherhood
Preb Prebendary
prec preceding
pred predicate
pref 1 preface 2 preferred 3 prefix
prelim preliminary
prem premium
prep 1 preparation; preparatory 2 preposition
pres present
Pres President
Presb Presbyterian
prev previous; previously
Prin Principal
PRO 1 Public Records Office 2 public relations officer
prob probable; probably
proc proceedings
prod production
Prof Professor
prom promontory
PROM /prom/ programmable read-only memory
pron 1 pronoun 2 pronounced, pronunciation
prop 1 proposition 2 proprietor
PROP /prop/ Preservation of the Rights of Prisoners
pros prosody
Prot 1 Protectorate 2 Protestant
prov 1 province; provincial 2 provisional
Prov 1 Proverbs – used for the book of the Bible 2 Provost
prox proximo
PRT petroleum revenue tax
Ps Psalms – used for the book of the Bible
PS 1 Police Sergeant 2 postscript [L *postscriptum*] 3 Private Secretary 4 prompt side – used to designate part of the theatrical stage
PSA Property Services Agency
PSBR Public Sector Borrowing Requirement
pseud pseudonym; pseudonymous
psf pounds per square foot
psi pounds per square inch
PST Pacific Standard Time
PSV *Br* public service vehicle
psychol, psych psychology
pt 1 part 2 pint 3 point 4 port
PT 1 Pacific time 2 physical training
PTA Parent-Teacher Association
Pte Private
PTE Passenger Transport Executive
PTFE polytetrafluoroethylene
ptg printing
PTO please turn over
Pty *chiefly Austr, NZ, & SAfr* Proprietary
pu per unit
pub, pub 1 public 2 published; publisher; publishing

PVA polyvinyl acetate
PVC polyvinyl chloride
Pvt *chiefly NAm* Private
pw per week
PW *Br* policewoman
pwr power
PWR pressurized water reactor
pwt pennyweight
PX post exchange

Q

q 1 quarto **2** quintal **3** quire
Q queen – used in chess
QB Queen's Bench
QC Queen's Counsel
QED which was to be demonstrated [L *quod erat demonstrandum*]
QEH Queen Elizabeth Hall (London)
QF quick-firing
QM quartermaster
QMG Quartermaster General
QMS Quartermaster Sergeant
QPM Queen's Police Medal
QPR Queen's Park Rangers
qqv which (*pl*) see [L *quae vide*]
qr 1 quarter **2** quire
QS quarter sessions
QSO quasi-stellar object
qt quart
qto quarto
qty quantity
qu, ques question
Que Quebec
quot quotation
qv which see [L *quod vide*]

R

r 1 radius **2** railway **3** recto **4** resistance **5** right **6** runs – used in cricket
R 1 rabbi **2** radical – used in chemistry **3** rain **4** Réaumur **5** rector **6** queen [L *regina*] **7** registered (as a trademark) **8** king [L *rex*] **9** ring road **10** river **11** röntgen **12** rook – used in chess **13** Royal
RA 1 Rear Admiral **2** Royal Academician; Royal Academy **3** Royal Artillery
RAA Royal Academy of Arts
RAAF Royal Australian Air Force
Rabb Rabbinic
RAC 1 Royal Armoured Corps **2** Royal Automobile Club
rad 1 radian **2** radius
RADA /'rahdə/ Royal Academy of Dramatic Art
RAF /ˌahr ay 'ef, raf/ Royal Air Force
RAFVR Royal Air Force Volunteer Reserve
RAH Royal Albert Hall (London)
rall rallentando
RAM /(*1*) ram, ˌahr ay 'em/ **1** random access memory **2** Royal Academy of Music
RAMC Royal Army Medical Corps
RAN Royal Australian Navy
R and A Royal and Ancient – used as the title of St Andrews Golf Club
R & B rhythm and blues
R and D research and development
RAOC Royal Army Ordnance Corps
RAS Royal Astronomical Society
RB Rifle Brigade
RBA Royal (Society of) British Artists
RBC red blood cells; red blood count
RBS Royal (Society of) British Sculptors
RC 1 Red Cross **2** reinforced concrete **3** Roman Catholic
RCA Royal College of Art
RCAF Royal Canadian Air Force
RCGP Royal College of General Practitioners
RCM Royal College of Music
RCMP Royal Canadian Mounted Police
RCN 1 Royal Canadian Navy **2** Royal College of Nursing
RCO Royal College of Organists
RCOG Royal College of Obstetricians and Gynaecologists
RCP Royal College of Physicians
RCS 1 Royal College of Science **2** Royal College of Surgeons **3** Royal Corps of Signals
RCT Royal Corps of Transport
RCVS Royal College of Veterinary Surgeons
rd *often cap R* road
RDC Rural District Council
RE 1 religious education **2** Royal Engineers
rec 1 receipt **2** recommended **3** recreation
recd received
ref 1 reference **2** referred
refl reflex; reflexive
reg 1 regiment **2** register; registered **3** registrar; registry **4** regulation **5** regulo
regd registered
Reg Prof Regius Professor
regt regiment
rel relating; relation; relative
REM /rem/ röntgen equivalent man
REME /'reemi/ Royal Electrical and Mechanical Engineers
Rep 1 republic **2** Republican
repr reprint; reprinted
req 1 require; required **2** requisition
reqd required
res 1 reserve **2** residence; resides
resp respective; respectively
ret 1 retired **2** return; returned
retd 1 retired **2** returned
rev 1 revenue **2** reverse **3** review; reviewed **4** revised; revision
Rev /(*2*) rev/ **1** Revelation – used for the book of the Bible **2** Reverend
REV reentry vehicle
Revd Reverend
RF 1 radio frequency **2** Rugby Football
RFC 1 Royal Flying Corps **2** Rugby Football Club
RFH Royal Festival Hall (London)
RFU Rugby Football Union
RGS Royal Geographical Society
rh 1 relative humidity **2** right hand
RH Royal Highness
RHA 1 Road Haulage Association **2** Royal Horse Artillery
rhet rhetoric
RHG Royal Horse Guards
rhs right hand side
RHS 1 Royal Historical Society **2** Royal Horticultural Society **3** Royal Humane Society
RI 1 refractive index **2** religious instruction **3** Rhode Island
RIBA Royal Institute of British Architects
RIC Royal Institute of Chemistry
RICS Royal Institution of Chartered Surveyors
RIP 1 may he rest in peace [L *requiescat in pace*] **2** may they rest in peace [L *requiescant in pace*]
rit /rit/ ritardando
RK religious knowledge
RL Rugby League
rm 1 ream **2** room
RM 1 Royal Mail **2** Royal Marines
RMA Royal Military Academy (Sandhurst)
rms root-mean-square
RN Royal Navy
RNAS Royal Naval Air Service
RNIB Royal National Institute for the Blind

RNLI Royal National Lifeboat Institution
RNR Royal Naval Reserve
RNVR Royal Naval Volunteer Reserve
RNZAF Royal New Zealand Air Force
RNZN Royal New Zealand Navy
ROC Royal Observer Corps
rom roman (type)
Rom Romans – used for the book of the Bible
ROM /rom/ read only memory
Ros, Rosc Roscommon
RoSPA /'rospə/ Royal Society for the Prevention of Accidents
RP 1 Received Pronunciation 2 Regius Professor
RPC Royal Pioneer Corps
RPI *Br* retail price index
rpm 1 *Br, often cap* retail price maintenance 2 revolutions per minute
RPO Royal Philharmonic Orchestra
rps revolutions per second
RPS Royal Photographic Society
rpt 1 repeat 2 report
RQ respiratory quotient
RRB Race Relations Board
RS 1 right side 2 Royal Society
RSA 1 Royal Scottish Academician; Royal Scottish Academy 2 Royal Society of Arts
RSC Royal Shakespeare Company
RSE Royal Society of Edinburgh
RSFSR Russian Soviet Federated Socialist Republic [Russ *Rossiĭskaya Sovetskaya Federativnaya Sotsialisticheskaya Respublika*]
RSG rate support grant
RSL Royal Society of Literature
RSM 1 Regimental Sergeant Major 2 Royal Society of Medicine
RSPB Royal Society for the Protection of Birds
RSPCA Royal Society for the Prevention of Cruelty to Animals
RSSPCC Royal Scottish Society for the Prevention of Cruelty to Children
RSV Revised Standard Version (of the Bible)
RSVP please answer [F *répondez s'il vous plaît*]
rt right
RT 1 radiotelephone; radiotelephony 2 room temperature
RTE Irish Radio and Television [IrGael *Radio Telefis Éireann*]
Rt Hon Right Honourable
Rt Rev, Rt Revd Right Reverend
RU Rugby Union
RUC Royal Ulster Constabulary
RV Revised Version (of the Bible)
RW 1 Right Worshipful 2 Right Worthy
ry, rwy railway
RYA Royal Yachting Association

S

s 1 school 2 scruple 3 second 4 shilling 5 singular 6 sire 7 small 8 snow 9 son 10 succeeded
S 1 saint 2 sea 3 siemens 4 Signor 5 society 6 South; Southerly; Southern 7 sun
SA 1 Salvation Army 2 sex appeal 3 small arms 4 limited liability company; Ltd [F *société anonyme*] 5 Society of Actuaries 6 South Africa 7 South America
SABC South African Broadcasting Corporation
sae stamped addressed envelope
SALT /sawlt/ Strategic Arms Limitation Talks
Sam, Saml Samuel – used for the books of the Bible
SAM /sam/ surface-to-air missile
SANROC /'sanrok/ South African Non-Racial Olympics Committee
SAS Special Air Service
Sask Saskatchewan
Sat Saturday
SATB soprano, alto, tenor, bass
SAYE save-as-you-earn
sb substantive
SBN Standard Book Number
sc 1 scene 2 scilicet 3 small capitals
s/c self-contained
Sc Scots
SC 1 South Carolina 2 special constable
ScD /ˌes see 'dee/ Doctor of Science [ML *Scientiae Doctor*]
SCE Scottish Certificate of Education
SCF Save the Children Fund
sch school
sci science; scientific
SCM 1 State Certified Midwife 2 Student Christian Movement
Scot Scotland; Scottish
SCR 1 senior common room 2 script 3 scripture
SCS Society of Civil Servants
SD 1 sine die 2 Social Democrat 3 South Dakota 4 standard deviation
SDA 1 Scottish Development Agency 2 Sex Discrimination Act
S Dak South Dakota
SDLP Social Democratic and Labour Party
SDP Social Democratic Party
SE southeast; southeastern
SEATO /'seetoh/ Southeast Asia Treaty Organization
sec 1 second; secondary 2 secretary 3 section 4 according to [L *secundum*] 5 secant
SECAM /'seekam/ sequence by colour-memory – a system of transmitting colour television programmes [F *séquentiel couleur à mémoire*]
sect section; sectional
secy secretary
sem seminary
Sem Semitic
SEM scanning electron microscope
sen 1 Senate; Senator 2 Senior
SEN State Enrolled Nurse
Sep, Sept September
seq the following [L *sequens, sequentes, sequentia*]
seqq the following [L *sequentes, sequentia*]
Serg, Sergt Sergeant
SET Selective Employment Tax
sf sforzando
SF science fiction
SFA Scottish Football Association
SG 1 Solicitor General 2 *often not cap* specific gravity
sgd signed
SGHWR steam-generating heavy water reactor
Sgt Sergeant
Sgt Maj Sergeant Major
Shak Shakespeare
SHAPE /shayp/ Supreme Headquarters Allied Powers Europe
SHO senior house officer
SI International System of Units [F *Système International d'Unités*]
sig signature
Sig Signor
sin sine
sing singular
SIS Secret Intelligence Service
sit situated; situation
SJ Society of Jesus
SLADE /slayd/ Society of Lithographic Artists, Designers and Etchers
Slo Sligo
SLP Scottish Labour Party
SLR single lens reflex
sm small

SM Sergeant Major
SNCF the French National Railways [F *Société nationale des chemins de fer français*]
SNP Scottish National Party
snr senior
So south
SO 1 Scientific Officer 2 Stationery Office
soc /*sometimes* sok/ society
sociol sociological; sociologist; sociology
SOGAT /'sohgat/ Society of Graphical and Allied Trades
sol 1 solicitor 2 soluble 3 solution
Som Somerset
sop soprano
sp 1 species 2 specific 3 spelling 4 spell out
SP 1 without issue [L *sine prole*] 2 starting price
SPCK Society for Promoting Christian Knowledge
SPD 1 supplementary petroleum duty 2 the W German Social Democratic Party [G *Sozialdemokratische Partei Deutschlands*]
specif specific; specifically
SPG Special Patrol Group
sp gr specific gravity
SPL sound pressure level
spp species (pl)
SPQR the Senate and the people of Rome [L *senatus populusque Romanus*]
SPR Society for Psychical Research
SPRC Society for the Prevention and Relief of Cancer
SPUC Society for the Protection of the Unborn Child
sq square
Sqn Ldr Squadron Leader
sr steradian
Sr 1 senior 2 Señor 3 Sir 4 Sister
SR 1 Senior Registrar 2 Southern Region
SRC Science Research Council
SRN State Registered Nurse
SRO 1 standing room only 2 Statutory Rules and Orders
SRV space rescue vehicle
SS 1 saints 2 steamship 3 Sunday school
SSC Solicitor in the Supreme Court – a Scottish legal officer
SSE south-southeast
SSgt staff sergeant
SSM surface-to-surface missile
SSR Soviet Socialist Republic
SSRC Social Science Research Council
SST supersonic transport
SSW south-southwest
st 1 stanza 2 stitch 3 stone 4 stumped by
St 1 Saint 2 street
sta station; stationary
Staffs /stafs/ Staffordshire
stbd starboard
std standard
STD 1 doctor of sacred theology [L *sacrae theologiae doctor*] 2 subscriber trunk dialling
Ste saint (female) [F *sainte*]
stg sterling
sth south
STOL /stol/ short takeoff and landing
STP standard temperature and pressure
str 1 strait 2 stroke – used in rowing
STUC Scottish Trades Union Congress
STV Scottish Television
subj 1 subject 2 subjunctive
suff suffix
Sun Sunday
sup 1 superior 2 superlative 3 supplement; supplementary 4 supra
superl superlative
supp, suppl supplement; supplementary
supt superintendent
surg surgeon; surgery; surgical
surv survey; surveying; surveyor
Sus Susanna – used for the book of the Apocrypha
SW 1 shortwave 2 southwest; southwestern
SWALK /swalk/ sealed with a loving kiss
SWAPO /'swahpoh/ South-West Africa People's Organization
SWG standard wire guage
Sx Sussex
SYHA Scottish Youth Hostels Association
syl, syll syllable
sym symmetrical
syn synonym; synonymous; synonymy
syst system

T

t 1 time 2 ton; tonne 3 transitive
T 1 temperature 2 tera- 3 tesla 4 true
TA Territorial Army
TAB /tab, ˌtee ay 'bee/ typhoid-paratyphoid A and B (vaccine)
TAM television audience measurement
T & AVR Territorial and Army Volunteer Reserve
tan /tan/ tangent
TASS /tas/ the official news agency of the Soviet Union [Russ *Telegrafnoye agentsvo Sovietskovo Soyuza*]
TB tubercle bacillus
tbs, tbsp tablespoon; tablespoonful
TC technical college
TCCB Test and County Cricket Board
Tce *Br* terrace – used esp in street names
tech 1 technical; technically; technician 2 technological; technology
technol technological; technology
TEFL /ˌtee ee ef 'el, 'tefl/ teaching English as a foreign language
tel 1 telegram 2 telegraph; telegraphic 3 telephone
temp 1 temperature 2 temporary 3 in the time of [L *tempore*]
ten tenuto
Tenn Tennessee
Terr, Terr 1 terrace – used esp in street names 2 territory
TES Times Educational Supplement
TESL /ˌtee ee es 'el, 'tesl/ teaching English as a second language
Test Testament
Tex Texas
TG transformational grammar
TGIF thank God it's Friday
TGWU Transport and General Workers' Union
Th Thursday
TH town hall
ThB /ˌtee aych 'bee/ bachelor of theology [NL *theologiae baccalaureus*]
ThD /ˌtee aych 'dee/ doctor of theology [NL *theologiae doctor*]
theol theologian; theological; theology
THES /ˌtee aych ee 'es, thes/ Times Higher Educational Supplement
Thess Thessalonians – used for the books of the Bible
ThM /ˌtee aych 'em/ master of theology [NL *theologiae magister*]
Tho, Thos /*sometimes* thos/ Thomas
Thur, Thurs Thursday
Tim Timothy – used for the books of the Bible
tinct tincture
Tip Tipperary
TIR International Road Transport [F *Transport International Routiers*]
Tit Titus – used for the book of the Bible
TKO technical knock-out
TLS Times Literary Supplement

TM 1 trademark 2 transcendental meditation
TN Tennessee
TO telegraph office
Tob Tobit – used for the book of the Apocrypha
topog topography
TOPS /tops/ Training Opportunities Scheme
tot total
TPI Town Planning Institute
Tpr Trooper
tr 1 transitive 2 translated; translation; translator 3 transpose 4 trill 5 trustee
trans 1 transitive 2 translated; translation; translator
transf transfer; transferred
transl translated; translation
treas treasurer; treasury
trib tributary
trop tropic; tropical
trs transpose
TSB Trustee Savings Bank
TSH thyroid-stimulating hormone
tsp teaspoon; teaspoonful
TT 1 teetotal; teetotaller 2 Tourist Trophy 3 tuberculin tested
TTL transistor transistor logic
Tue, Tues Tuesday
TU trade union
TUC Trades Union Congress
TV television
TVP textured vegetable protein
TWA Trans-World Airlines
TX Texas
typ, typog typographer; typography
Tyr Tyrone

U

u 1 unit 2 upper
U 1 uncle 2 Unionist 3 university
UAE United Arab Emirates
UAR United Arab Republic
UAU Universities Athletic Union
uc upper case
UC University College
UCATT Union of Construction, Allied Trades, and Technicians
UCCA /'ukə/ Universities Central Council on Admissions
UCL University College, London
UDA Ulster Defence Association
UDI unilateral declaration of independence
UDR Ulster Defence Regiment
UEFA /'yoohfə, yooh'ayfə/ Union of European Football Associations
UGC University Grants Committee
UHF ultrahigh frequency
UHT ultrahigh temperature
UJ universal joint
UK United Kingdom
UKAEA United Kingdom Atomic Energy Authority
ult 1 ultimate 2 ultimo
UMIST /yoohmist/ University of Manchester Institute of Science and Technology
UN United Nations
UNA United Nations Association
unan unanimous
UNCTAD /'ungktad/ United Nations Commission for Trade and Development
UNESCO /yooh'neskoh/ United Nations Educational, Scientific, and Cultural Organization
UNICEF /'yoohnisef/ United Nations Children's Fund [*United Nations Children's Emergency Fund*, its former name]
Unit Unitarian
univ 1 universal 2 university
UNO /'yoohnoh/ United Nations Organization
UNRWA /'unrə/ United Nations Relief and Works Agency
UP Uttar Pradesh
UPI United Press International
UPOW Union of Post Office Workers
UPU Universal Postal Union
URC United Reformed Church
US United States
USA 1 United States Army 2 United States of America
USAF United States Air Force
USDAW /'uzdaw/ Union of Shop, Distributive, and Allied Workers
USN United States Navy
USS United States ship
USSR Union of Soviet Socialist Republics
usu usual; usually
UT 1 Universal time 2 Utah
UU Ulster Unionist
UV ultraviolet
UVF Ulster Volunteer Force

V

v 1 vector 2 verb 3 verse 4 versus 5 very 6 verso 7 vice 8 vide 9 von – used in German personal names
V 1 velocity 2 volt; voltage 3 volume
va verbal auxiliary
Va Virginia
VA 1 Veterans Administration – a US organization 2 Vicar Apostolic 3 Vice-Admiral 4 (Order of) Victoria and Albert 5 Virginia 6 volt-ampere
vac vacant
V & A Victoria and Albert Museum
var 1 variable 2 variant 3 variation 4 variety 5 various
Vat Vatican
VAT /vat, ˌvee ay 'tee/ value-added tax
vb verb; verbal
VC 1 Vice Chairman 2 Vice Chancellor 3 Vice Consul 4 Victoria Cross
VCR video cassette recorder
VD venereal disease
VDQS vin délimité de qualité supérieure
VDU visual display unit
VE Victory in Europe
VED Vehicle Excise Duty
vel velocity
Ven Venerable
ver verse
vert vertical
Vet MB Bachelor of Veterinary Medicine
VG 1 very good 2 Vicar General
VHF very high frequency
vi 1 verb intransitive 2 see below [L *vide infra*]
VI Virgin Islands
Vic 1 vicar 2 Victoria
Vis, Visc Viscount; Viscountess
viz videlicet
VLF very low frequency
voc vocative
vocab /*sometimes* 'vohkab/ vocabulary
vol 1 volume 2 volunteer
VP Vice-President
VR 1 Queen Victoria [NL *Victoria Regina*] 2 Volunteer Reserve
VS 1 verse 2 veterinary surgeon
VSO Voluntary Service Overseas
VSOP Very Special Old Pale – a type of brandy
vt verb transitive
Vt Vermont
VTOL /'veetol/ vertical takeoff and landing
VTR video tape recorder
vulg vulgar; vulgarly
Vulg Vulgate
vv 1 verses 2 vice versa 3 volumes

W

w 1 week 2 weight 3 white 4 wicket 5 wide 6 width 7 wife 8 with
W 1 Watt 2 West; Westerly; Western

WAAC /wak, ˌdubl yooh ˌay ay ˈsee/ **1** Women's Army Auxiliary Corps – the women's component of the British army from 1914 to 1918 **2** Women's Army Auxiliary Corps – the women's component of the US army from 1942 to 1948
WAAF /waf, ˌdubl yooh ˌay ay ˈef/ Women's Auxiliary Air Force – the women's component of the RAF
WAC /wak, ˌdubl yooh ay ˈsee/ Women's Army Corps – the women's component of the US army
WAF /waf, ˌdubl yooh ay ˈef/ Women in the Air Force – the women's component of the USAF
War, Warw Warwickshire
WAR Women Against Rape
Wash Washington
Wat Waterford
Wb weber
WBA World Boxing Association
WBC 1 white blood cells; white blood count **2** World Boxing Council
WC 1 water closet **2** West Central – a London postal district
WCC World Council of Churches
WCdr Wing Commander
WCT World Championship Tennis
WD 1 War Department **2** Works Department
WEA Workers' Education Association
Wed, Weds Wednesday
wef with effect from
Westm Westmeath
WEU Western European Union
Wex Wexford
wf wrong fount
WFTU World Federation of Trade Unions
Wg Cdr Wing Commander
wh watt-hour
WHO World Health Organization
WI 1 West Indies **2** Wisconsin **3** Women's Institute
Wick Wicklow
Wilts /wilts/ Wiltshire
WIPO World Intellectual Property Organization – a branch of the United Nations
Wis, Wisc Wisconsin
Wisd, Wis Wisdom – used for the book of the Apochrypha
wk 1 week **2** work
wkly weekly
wkt wicket
Wlk walk – used in street names
Wm William
WMO World Meteorological Organization
WNP Welsh National Party
WNW west-northwest
w/o without
WO Warrant Officer
Worcs Worcestershire
WOW War on Want
wpb wastepaper basket
WPC Woman Police Constable
wpm words per minute
WPS Woman Police Sergeant
WR Western Region
WRAC /rak, ˌdubl yooh ˌahr ay ˈsee/ Women's Royal Army Corps
WRAF Women's Royal Air Force
WRNS /renz, ˈdubl yooh ˌahr en ˈes/ Women's Royal Naval Service
WRP Workers' Revolutionary Party
WRVS Women's Royal Voluntary Service
WS Writer to the Signet – a Scottish solicitor
WSW west-southwest
wt weight
W Va, WV West Virginia
WW World War
WWF World Wildlife Fund
Wyo, Wy Wyoming

X

x 1 ex **2** extra
X Christ [Gk *X* (chi), initial letter of *Christos* Christ]
XL extra large
XT Christ (Gk *X* (chi), initial letter of *Christos* Christ]

Y

y year
yd yard
yeo yeomanry
YHA Youth Hostels Association
YMCA Young Men's Christian Association
YMHA Young Men's Hebrew Association
Yorks /yawks/ Yorkshire
yr 1 year **2** younger **3** your
YWCA Young Women's Christian Association
YWHA Young Women's Hebrew Association

Z

Zach Zachariah – used for the book of the Bible
ZANU /ˈzahnooh/ Zimbabwe African National Union
ZAPU /ˈzahpooh/ Zimbabwe African People's Union
Zech Zechariah – used for the book of the Bible
Zeph Zephaniah – used for the book of the Bible
zoo, zool zoological; zoology
ZPG zero population growth

Abbreviations used in this Dictionary

A

A ampere
ab about
abbr abbreviation
abl ablative
acc accusative
AD Anno Domini
adj adjective
adv adverb
AF Anglo-French
Afrik Afrikaans
Alb Albanian
alter. alteration
am ante meridiem
AmerF American French
AmerInd American Indian
AmerSp American Spanish
amt amount
apprec appreciative
approx approximate, approximately
Ar Arabic
Arab Arabian
Aram Aramaic
arch archaic
Arm Armenian
Assyr Assyrian
attrib attributive
aug augmentative
Austr Australian
Av Avestan
AV Authorized Version

B

b born
Bab Babylonian
BC before Christ
Beng Bengali
Br British
Bret Breton
Btu British thermal unit
Bulg Bulgarian

C

c centi-
c century
C Celsius, centigrade
C coulomb
Can Canadian
CanF Canadian French
Cant Cantonese
cap capital, capitalized
Catal Catalan
Celt Celtic
cgs centimetre-gram-second
Chin Chinese
cm centimetre
comb combining
compar comparative
conj conjunction
constr construction
contr contraction
Copt Coptic
Corn Cornish
cti central
cwt hundredweight

D

D Dutch
Dan Daniel
Dan Danish
dat dative
deriv derivative
derog derogatory
dial. dialect
dim. diminutive
dr dram

E

E East, Eastern
E English
e g for example
Egypt Egyptian
Eng English, England
Esk Eskimo
esp especially
etc etcetera
euph euphemistic

F

f femto-
F Fahrenheit
F Farad
F French [1601–]
fem feminine
Finn Finnish
fl floruit (flourished)
fl oz fluid ounce
Flem Flemish
fml formal
fr from
Fr French
freq frequentative
Fris Frisian
ft foot

G

G German
Gael Gaelic
gall gallon
gen genitive
Gen Genesis
Ger German
Gk Greek [to 200 AD]
Gmc Germanic
Goth Gothic

H

h hour
ha hectare
Heb Hebrew
Hitt Hittite
hp horsepower
humor humorous
Hung Hungarian
Hz hertz

I

Icel Icelandic
i e that is
IE Indo-European
imit imitative
imper imperative
in inch
incho inchoative
Ind Indian
indef indefinite
indic indicative
infin infinitive
infml informal
interj interjection
interrog interrogative
IrGael Irish Gaelic
irreg irregular, irregularly
Isa Isaiah
ISV International Scientific Vocabulary
It Italian

J

J joule
Jap Japanese
Jav Javanese
Jer Jeremiah
journ journalistic

K

k kilo-
kg kilogram
km kilometre

L

l litre
L Latin [to 200 AD]
LaF Louisiana French
lat latitude
lb pound
Lat Latin
LG Low German
LGk Late Greek [201–600]
LHeb Late Hebrew
lit. literally
Lith Lithuanian
Lk Luke
LL Late Latin [201–600]
long longitude

M

m metre
m milli-

M mega-
masc masculine
MBret Middle Breton
MD Middle Dutch [1100–1500]
ME Middle English [1151–1500]
MexSp Mexican Spanish
MF Middle French [1301–1600]
MFlem Middle Flemish [1301–1600]
MGk Middle Greek [601–1500]
MHeb Middle Hebrew
MHG Middle High German [1100–1500]
MHz megahertz
mi mile
Mid Eng Midlands
Mid US Mid United States
mil military
min minute
MIr Middle Irish [1001–1500]
ML Medieval Latin [601–1500]
ml millilitre
MLG Middle Low German [1100–1500]
mm millimetre
modif modification
MPer Middle Persian
mph miles per hour
Mt Matthew
Mt Mount
MW Middle Welsh [1151–1500]

N

n nano-
n noun
N North, Northern
N Newton
NAm North American
naut nautical
NE Eng North East England
neg negative
N Eng North England
neut neuter
New Eng US New England, United States
NGk New Greek [1501–]
NHeb New Hebrew [19th–20th century]
NL New Latin [1501–]
nom nominative
Norw Norwegian
NW Eng North West England
NW US North West United States
NZ New Zealand

O

obs obsolete
occas occasionally
OCatal Old Catalan
OE Old English [–1150]
OF Old French [–1300]
OFris Old Frisian [–1500]
OHG Old High German [–1100]
OIr Old Irish [601–1100]
OIt Old Italian
OL Old Latin
ON Old Norse [–*ab* 1350]
ONF Old North French
OPer Old Persian
OPg Old Portuguese
OProv Old Provençal
OPruss Old Prussian
orig original, originally
ORuss Old Russian [1101–1500]
OS Old Saxon [–12th century]
OSlav Old Slavonic
OSp Old Spanish
OSw Old Swedish
OW Old Welsh [–*ab* 1150]
oz ounce

P

p pence
p pico-
Pa pascal
PaG Pennsylvania German
part participle
pass passive
Pek Pekingese
Per Persian
perf perfect
perh perhaps
pers person
Pg Portuguese
phr(s) phrase(s)
pl plural
pm post meridiem
Pol Polish
pp past participle
prep preposition
pres present
prob probably
pron pronoun
pron pronunciation
Prov Provençal
prp present participle

Q

qr quarter
qt quart

R

RC Roman Catholic
redupl reduplication
refl reflexive
rel relative
Rom Roman
RSV Revised Standard Version
Russ Russian
RV Revised Version

S

s second
S South, Southern
SAfr South Africa, South African
sby somebody
Sc Scots
Scand Scandinavian
ScGael Scottish Gaelic
Scot Scotland, Scottish
Sem Semitic
Serb Serbian
SEU S Survey of English Usage (Spoken)
SEU W Survey of English Usage (Written)
Shak Shakespeare
SI Système International d'Unités
sing. singular
Skt Sanskrit
Slav Slavonic
Sp Spanish
specif specifically
st stone
St Saint
Ste Sainte
sthg something
subj subjunctive
substand substandard
superl superlative
S US Southern United States
Sw Swedish
SW Eng South Western England
SW US South Western United States
Syr Syriac

T

Tag Tagalog
tech technical
TES Times Educational Supplement
THES Times Higher Educational Supplement
TLS Times Literary Supplement
trans translation
Turk Turkish

U

UK United Kingdom
US United States
USA United States of America
usu usually

V

V volt
va verbal auxiliary
var variant
vb verb
vi verb intransitive
VL Vulgar Latin (used only for assumed forms)
voc vocative
vt verb transitive
vulg vulgar

W

W watt
W Welsh
W West, Western
WI West Indian
W US Western United States
WWI World War 1
WWII World War 2

Y

yd yard

Pronunciation symbols used in this Dictionary

Vowels

a	as in bad, fat	oh	as in note, Joan		
ah	,, father, oompah	oo	,, put, cook		
aw	,, saw, awful	ooh	,, boot, lute		
ay	,, make, hay	ooə	,, jury, cure		
e	,, bed, head	ow	,, now, bough		
ee	,, sheep, key	owə	,, our, power		
eə	,, there, hair	oy	,, boy, loiter		
i	,, ship, lick	oyə	,, lawyer, sawyer		
ie	,, bite, lied	u	,, cut, luck		
ie·ə	,, fire, liar	uh	,, bird, absurd		
iə	,, here, fear	ə	,, mother, about		
o	,, pot, crop				

Consonants

b	as in bad	ng	as in sung
ch	,, cheer	nh	,, restaurant
d	,, day	p	,, pot
dh	,, they	r	,, red
f	,, few	s	,, soon
g	,, gay	sh	,, fish
h	,, hot	t	,, tea
j	,, jump	th	,, thing
k	,, king	v	,, view
kh	,, loch	w	,, wet
l	,, led	y	,, yet
m	,, man	z	,, zero
n	,, sun	zh	,, pleasure